The Complete Works of Shakespeare

The Complete Works of Shakespeare

Updated Fourth Edition

Edited by

David Bevington
The University of Chicago

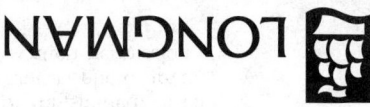 LONGMAN

An imprint of Addison Wesley Longman, Inc.

New York • Reading, Massachusetts • Menlo Park, California • Harlow, England
Don Mills, Ontario • Sydney • Mexico City • Madrid • Amsterdam

Acquisitions Editor: Lisa Moore
Project Coordination: Ruttle, Shaw & Wetherill, Inc.
Cover Designer: Paul Lacy
Page i Photo: National Portrait Gallery, London.
The Chandos Portrait of Shakespeare by an unknown artist.
Photo Researcher: Sandy Schneider
Production Manager: Angel Gonzalez Jr.
Manufacturing Manager: Willie Lane
Compositor: The Clarinda Company
Printer and Binder: RR Donnelley & Sons Company
Cover Printer: The Lehigh Press, Inc.

ABOUT THE COVER: A detail from J.C. Visscher's panoramic view of London, done in 1616 or slightly before that. What is labelled as "The Globe," shown here enlarged, appears in the center of Visscher's large illustration near its lower edge, located on the south side of the Thames River across from the city of London and St. Paul's Church (i.e. Cathedral). The viewer looks north toward the city from Southwark, where the Globe and other theatres were located. Actually, the theatre building labelled as "The Globe" may in fact be the Rose Theatre, and in any event the first Globe Theatre, in which so many of Shakespeare's plays were acted after its construction in 1599, burned to the ground in 1613, so that it could not have appeared in Visscher's illustration.

This drawing shows us, in any event, an Elizabethan theatre, polygonal in shape, with superstructures over the stage and a flag flown when a play was in performance. The people gathered around the theatre are not drawn to scale; the building could hold at least 2,000 spectators. Evidently it featured more bays than are shown in Visscher's drawing, so that it was essentially cylindrical. For a contemporary drawing of the inside of an Elizabethan public theatre (the Swan, c. 1596) and for further details about the stage, see pp. xliv–xlv in the General Introduction to this present volume.

Library of Congress Cataloging-in-Publication Data

Shakespeare, William, 1564–1616.
 [Works. 1997]
 The complete works of Shakespeare / edited by David Bevington.—
Update 4th ed.
 p.   cm.
 Includes bibliographical references and index.
 ISBN 0-673-99996-3
 I. Bevington, David M.   II. Title.
PR2754.B4   IN PROCESS
822.3'3—dc20   96-6733
                                    CIP

Copyright © 1997 by Addison-Wesley Educational Publishers Inc.

ISBN 0-321-01254-2

678910 – DOW – 03 02 01

Contents

Preface

This is the updated fourth edition of *The Complete Works of Shakespeare*. The original edition was edited by Hardin Craig, whom I never knew personally but whose work I admired. In early 1968 I was asked by Scott, Foresman to undertake a new edition of his work, focusing on new and more critically oriented introductions and on a thorough review of the editing of the original texts; that second edition appeared in 1973 with both our names, leading in some quarters to the erroneous impression that my name was Craig Bevington. In 1980 Scott, Foresman published a third edition with my name alone as editor, since that edition had been completely reset with extensive reconsideration of introductions, notes, stage directions, the text itself, the organization of the volume by genres, and still more. Members of an editorial advisory board, whose names are listed in the front of that volume, carefully reviewed every aspect of the project.

This fourth edition, published by HarperCollins, made use of the computer tapes used to print the text of the third edition in order to reduce to a minimum the opportunity for introduction of any new errors, but has also made possible a careful reconsideration of every aspect of the book, including the Bantam Shakespeare text. I have been given permission to use all the work done on the Bantam Shakespeare, issued in twenty-nine paperback volumes in 1988, with David Kastan, James Hammersmith, and Robert Kean Turner serving as associate editors. I am happy to acknowledge their contribution both to the Bantam Shakespeare (which, in its turn, made use of materials from the third edition published by Scott, Foresman) and to the fourth edition undertaking, which incorporates virtually all that we did in the Bantam project, along with a thorough reexamination of what that Bantam edition managed to achieve. A new editorial advisory board, consisting of some new consultants and some who participated in the third edition, has thoughtfully gone over everything in this fourth edition; their names appear in the front of this volume. What we have, then, is an edition that has (I devoutly hope) profited from a succession of reworkings, each attempting to save what was best in the past along with the insights of new editors and consultants. There is no end to the process of finding the right phrase for a gloss, and the past decade has been a revolutionary one in terms of textual theory and of critical interpretation, so that the attempt to keep an edition like this as up to date as possible is, to say the least, a challenging one. I have been amazed at the extent to which the printer's copy has been heavily marked with corrections and revisions at every stage of the process.

Organization of the Volume

As in this third edition, the arrangement here is by genres: comedies, histories, tragedies, romances, and nondramatic poems. This arrangement is close to that of Shakespeare's First Folio of 1623, though that volume did not include the poems and did not attempt (as does this present edition) to arrange the plays within each genre in the approximate order in which they were written.

The claim to being a "Complete Works" is necessarily an approximate claim. No edition of Shakespeare today can hope, or even desire, to include all the plays and poems that have been attributed to him in whole or in part. The second printing of the Shakespeare Third Folio of 1664 included, along with *Pericles*, the following: *The London Prodigal, The History of Thomas Lord Cromwell, Sir John Oldcastle, The Puritan or the Widow of Watling Street, A Yorkshire Tragedy*, and *The Tragedy of Locrine*. None of these attributions has much credibility, other than that of *Pericles*. Nor are editors inclined to include a group of plays attributed to Shakespeare in a seventeenth-century collection found in the library of King Charles II, including *Fair Em, Mucedorus*, and *The Merry Devil of Edmonton*. Still other attributions that are generally disregarded include *The Birth of Merlin* and *Arden of Feversham*.

More serious is the claim of *Edward III*, an English history play first published in 1596, attributed to Shakespeare in a booksell-er's leaflet in 1654, and actually included by Edward Capell in his Shakespeare edition of 1760. Stronger still as a contender is the material added as a revision to a manuscript play called *The Book of Sir Thomas More* (c. 1595) written in a hand that many scholars view as compatible with the surviving Shakespeare signatures. Most important of all, the tragicomedy called *The Two Noble Kinsmen*, attributed in the Stationers' Register and on the 1634 title page to John Fletcher and William Shakespeare, appears to be a collaboration in 1613 between these two men as Shakespeare was on the verge of his retirement. These last two works certainly merit a place in a "Complete Works." The only justification that can be offered here for excluding *The Book of Sir Thomas More* is that Shakespeare's contribution to it is fragmentary; he was evidently called in to supply a new scene for a play written by another playwright who had run into trouble with the censor. *The Two Noble Kinsmen*, written collaboratively by Shakespeare and John Fletcher, is included in this present updating (in 1996) of our fourth edition originally published in 1992. Since Shakespeare probably collaborated elsewhere, in *Pericles*, for example (which the Folio editors excluded from their edition along with *The Two Noble Kinsmen*), it would be arbitrary to include one and not the other. This edition does not include, however, *The Passionate Pilgrim*, a little volume of 1599 attributed to Shakespeare by its unscrupulous publisher but containing no new poems that are convincingly his. Nor does this present edition include various poems, including "Shall I die? Shall I fly" questionably attributed to Shakespeare. This edition does include *Venus and Adonis* and *The Rape of Lucrece*, which are unquestionably his, "The Phoenix and Turtle," "A Lover's Complaint," which was published with the Sonnets in 1609, and "A Funeral Elegy for Master William Peter" by "W.S.," 1612.

Text

I and various members of the editorial advisory board have tried to review in detail all the issues of textual scholarship that have been debated in the last decade or so. I have decided against printing two texts of *King Lear* (Folio and Quarto) for reasons I argue at length in a review of the Oxford Shakespeare (*Shakespeare Quarterly*, 30, 1987, 501–119). Basically, my reasons are that we cannot be at all sure that the revisions incorporated in the Folio version are not theatrical cuts and changes motivated by considerations of performance more than by authorial design. Just as importantly, two texts of *King Lear* add considerably to the cost and bulk of a one-volume Shakespeare, and perhaps ask the student reader to deal with complex textual issues before that reader has had a chance to become acquainted with the play. For similar reasons, the revised passages in *Hamlet* and other two-text plays are included in a single text rather than being relegated to appendixes. Although I subscribe entirely to the view that we have texts for many of Shakespeare's major plays rather than a single text, I regard this as a matter of stage history and of changing critical interpretation rather than as a matter to be put before the reader in a text designed primarily for classroom use. This edition takes seriously the idea of a ''Complete Works'' by hesitating to exclude passages indisputably written by Shakespeare until it can be shown that Shakespeare really wanted them left out. The practice of inclusion does produce, in the case of *King Lear* and *Hamlet*, for example, plays too long to have been performed in the Elizabethan theater in their entirety, but the alternative of presenting theatrically cut versions does omit Shakespearean material and may come no closer than a conflated text to representing what Shakespeare might have wanted us to read. Since we cannot know what he intended in any event, it's best to give the reader substantially all that he wrote. (This should not include, to be sure, clear instances of false starts that Shakespeare simply abandoned.)

Many textual studies in the last decade have produced what seem to me clear advances in clarity and modernization of Shakespeare's language. This edition expands and normalizes speech prefixes, uses modern forms of capitalization and spelling and punctuation, and generally tries to make Shakespeare's language as available as possible to today's reader without altering the essential nature of that language. *Porpentine* sounds like a colorful Shakespearean word, but historical dictionaries (especially the *Oxford English Dictionary*) indicate that the word is essentially an Elizabethan variation of *porcupine*. The same is true of *mushrumps* for *mushrooms*, *apricocks* for *apricots*, *swound* and *sound* for *swoon*, *god-den* and *good-en* for *good e'en*, *wrack* for *wreck*, *vtmost* for *utmost*, *handkercher* for *handkerchief*, *bankrout* for *bankrupt*, *housewom'er* for *housew'er*, *accompt* for *account*, and many more. Characters do sometimes speak idiosyncratically or in dialect, of course, and one must take care to distinguish between *lanthorn* as a perfectly normal Elizabethan spelling (hence modernized in this edition) and instances in which the word is pointedly spelled this way to make a pun on *horn* (as in *A Midsummer Night's Dream*, Act 5). Sometimes the distinction is a hard one to make: is *Moth*, for example, meant to indicate a winged insect, or a *mote*, that is, tiny speck of dust? The spelling *moth* is unquestionably used to mean the latter in Elizabethan spelling, as in ''A moth it is to trouble the mindes eye'' (Q2 of *Hamlet*, 1.1.116). What then of the characters named *Moth* in *A Midsummer Night's Dream* and *Love's Labor's Lost*? This edition chooses the modernized spelling *Mote*, though both meanings may hover about the word.

Conversely, this edition chooses the older form of *Ancient* instead of the modern *Ensign* (as in *Ancient Iago*), since the word appears to include the meaning of ''old and trustworthy.'' This edition prints *huswife* instead of *housewife* to avoid the modern connotations of *home-maker* and to include the suggestion of *hussy*, as when Shakespeare refers to the bitch goddess Fortune as ''the false huswife Fortune'' (*Antony and Cleopatra*, 4.15.46). The older spelling *persever* is necessary for scansion in lieu of the modern spelling *persevere*, since the older form makes clear the stress on the second syllable. So too with *conster* (accented on the first syllable) for *construe*. *Beholding* is obviously related to *beholden*, but has its own history as a word. Strong verbal forms like *holp* for *helped* and *drave* for *drove* are essential to the structure of Shakespeare's language and need to be retained. Unfamiliar forms of prefixes, as in *unauspicious*, *uncertain*,

uncurable, and the like, cannot be changed without altering Shakespeare's language.

Proper names pose a problem, since we allow inconsistencies and anachronisms; this edition uses standard forms like *Bolingbroke* and *Calpurnia*, while respecting Shakespeare's tendency to anglicize foreign proper names like *Biron* and *Rousillon*. Place names like *Bristol* and *Rouen* are more easily recognized than in their usual Elizabethan forms *Bristow* and *Roan*.

In general, this edition has tried to modernize vigorously and to avoid older spellings like *strook* (*struck*), *fift* (*fifth*), *murther* (*murder*), and *Bullingbrook* (*Bolingbroke*) that do give some flavor of Elizabethan pronunciation but contribute to inconsistency and archaism in an edition that cannot preserve all indications of pronunciation as an old-spelling edition would. This edition adopts modern distinctions between *beside* (next to) and *besides* (in addition), *sometime* (former) and *sometimes* (occasionally), *mean* (of low birth) and *means* (resources available), *it* and *its*, and so on, even when Elizabethan usage is inconsistent in such matters. *More* replaces the Elizabethan *mo*, since the original distinction between *mo* and *more* is inconsistently applied in early texts; *enough* replaces *enow*. Hyphenation in this edition generally follows the practice of the ninth edition of *Webster's New Collegiate Dictionary*.

This fourth edition goes further than did the third edition in the modernizing of contractions. Forms like *lov'd* and *help'd* are now expanded to *loved* and *helped*, correspondingly, final *-ed* forms that require an extra syllable in the scansion are printed as *closed*, *amazed*, *finished*, and the like. Contractions are sometimes required for scansion in words like *fall'n*, *med'cine*, and *heav'n* as a means of indicating an abbreviated pronunciation, but such contractions are inconsistently applied in the early texts and there are many instances in which the contraction can be expanded and the metrical scansion of the verse left up to the reader; *flower* and *flow'r*, or *preposterous* and *prepost'rous*, for example, are often nearly indistinguishable today, and the scansion often allows for extra syllables in any case. Contractions like *whe'er*, *to 't*, *let's*, *th' ignorant*, *o' th' people*, *that's*, *e'en*, and *on 't* remain necessary. On the other hand, apostrophes in forms like *'twixt* and *'Zounds* are increasingly unnecessary today; this edition follows *Webster's* ninth edition in rendering these words as *twixt* and *Zounds*. Forms like *th' art* and *y' are* can, I think, be modernized to *thou'rt* and *you're* without significant loss of meaning, especially since the varying forms of such contractions in the original texts are likely to be the work of compositors.

Like most recent editions, this one takes care to preserve grammatical forms in Shakespeare that seem incorrect today but were evidently allowable in his day. Such forms as ''I drunk him to his bed,'' ''He was contract to Lady Lucy,'' ''You have swam,'' and ''I did not see him since'' are all legitimate. Singular forms of verbs can be paired with plural nouns, as in ''here comes the lords,'' or ''My old bones aches.'' This edition makes no attempt, as did some nineteenth-century editions, to regularize Shakespeare's use of *my* and *mine*, *showed* and *shown*, *further* and *farther*, *towards* and *toward*. On the other hand, this edition does not preserve forms like *mo* (for *more*) or *mean* (for *means*) that are inconsistently employed in Shakespeare's text and may be spelling variants of compositors or scribes. The expression ''for sport sake'' is regarded in this edition as a spelling variant of the more recognizable ''for sport's sake''; similarly, ''for God's sake'' is the normal form in Shakespeare's text and is an allowable modernization for the occasional ''for God sake'' that may well be only a compositor's variant form.

Indications of place for each scene are provided in the interpretive notes at the foot of the column. The consultants have helped me rethink these indications in theatrical terms, and to avoid overly specific or nontheatrical assertions based on sources or editorial tradition. Where the scene is fluid, continuous, or ambiguous, or where the implied location shifts in mid scene, I have tried to indicate as much in the notes. Providing indication of place is potentially restrictive and misleading; for "the forest of Arden" invites the reader to imagine a real forest rather than a stage, and for this reason some modern editions prefer to avoid indications of place entirely. My experience, however, is that many readers can be helped by knowing that the scene in much of *King Lear* moves between Albany's palace in the north of Great Britain to Gloucester's house in the southwest, and eventually to Dover. References in mid scene to "Hames Castle" or "the Tower" can be clarified for the reader by knowing the location that Shakespeare invites us to have in mind. Perhaps our concept of place should be guided by Shakespeare's own suggestions, in which he makes use of the theater to invite us on an imaginative journey to battlefields, distant lands, ships at sea, palaces, and banqueting halls. His scene is both fluid and imaginatively particular.

A similar problem concerns act and scene division. The indications in the First Folio are boldly visible. This edition chooses, like other recent editions, to make the act and scene markings less intrusive in order to promote a sense of fluidity from scene to scene. The act and scene numbers are in boldface to make them visible, since being able to find one's place is essential for classroom use or play rehearsal, but they are set to one side of the column. A printer's asterisk between scenes indicates a bare stage; absence of such a printer's device indicates that the action is continuous, even though a new scene is marked in accord with editorial tradition. These divisions do not appear in most Quarto texts, are probably not Shakespearean, at times do not reflect even a plausible structuring of the play into five acts (the length of acts in *Love's Labor's Lost*, for example, is very uneven), and at times interrupts the flow from one continuous scene to another (as in *Romeo and Juliet*, Act 2, scenes 1 and 2). The scene divisions are often simply those of editorial tradition. Until some international Shakespeare congress legislates a new standard, however, the traditional scene division of the Globe text represents a standard for reference, and I have retained it as the most universal available. I have tried in the notes and through the system of printer's asterisks to indicate when the conventional system is theatrically misleading, and I have provided through line numbers (TLN) at the top of each page to give the reader a more reliable and truly universal key, though not yet widely in use except by textual scholars. These through line numbers, inclusive for each column of text, are keyed to Charlton Hinman's facsimile edition of the First Folio (New York, Norton, 1968). Where the text is based on a Quarto edition, the equivalent line numbers in the First Folio are provided, with parenthetical additions where the Quarto text provides material not included in the Folio version.

With the help of the editorial advisory board, I have made an effort to provide helpful and consistent stage directions. All editorially added stage directions are in square brackets so that the reader can know at all times when the language is from the original text and when it has been provided subsequently. Because the early texts tend to be sparse in their provision of stage directions, many of the directions here are in fact added. I have tried to avoid the manifold dangers of intruding on the text, such as insulting the reader with stage directions that spell out the obvious, or speculating about matters that can't be reliably determined (such as when a character rises after having kneeled), or specifying an action for which the actor has various options. When Antony says "The nobleness of life / is to do thus," for example (*Antony and Cleopatra*, 1.1.38-39), does he kiss Cleopatra or indicate more broadly, with a sweep of his arm, an entire Egyptian way of life that he is embracing? Conversely, however, the omission of any mention of stage action leaves some readers in the dark and promotes the view that these texts are not intended for the theater.

One matter in which I have found the "received" editorial tradition to be excessively timid is in the handling of short lines of verse. In the early texts, both Folio and Quarto, short lines of verse are almost universally printed from the left-hand margin, following the speech prefix. Although Shakespeare clearly conceived many such short lines as linked together into verse (usually iambic pentameter); the decision to arrange short lines in verse patterns by the use of indentation is essentially an editorial decision. My view is that editors, even today, are too willing to link short lines when the case for linkage is metrically unconvincing. I do not suggest printing all such short lines from the left-hand margin, since many linkings are entirely plausible and occur in passages plainly written as verse. I do, however, opt not to link short lines when the result is metrically erratic, realizing of course that this calls for an aesthetic judgment—but then so does the decision to link. I resist producing large numbers of hexameter or tetrameter or trimeter lines this way, granting that Shakespeare does occasionally use these forms. And, like the editors of the Oxford Shakespeare, I resist linking when either the first two or the last two of three short lines might be linked to produce a good pentameter line; rather than choose arbitrarily between two equally suitable choices, I prefer not to link at all. The result, in my opinion, increases our sense of Shakespeare's flexibility as a writer of verse and avoids a straightjacket he did not have to worry about.

Line numbers in the text indicate that a gloss is to be found at the foot of the column for some word or phrase in the line thus indicated. In my opinion, this system of citation (used also by the Pelican Shakespeare) is less disfiguring than bubbles or footnote numbers next to the word or phrase in question, which would be numerous. At the same time, this system offers more guidance than one in which no indication is provided that a gloss is available to the reader.

The textual notes at the back of this book alert the reader to all substantive changes from the chosen copy text for each play or poem. This system is, I think, less disfiguring than the text than the square brackets I used in the third edition to indicate passages that were added from some authority other than the copy text.

Introductions and other supportive materials

I have carefully gone over all introductory material with the assistance of the editorial advisory board, attempting especially to raise issues that have been brought forward in the critical debate of the last twelve years or so, such as race and colonialism in *The Tempest*, conflict between the sexes in *Othello* and *The Taming of the Shrew* (among many others), issues of power and subversion in the history plays, and the like. My hope has been to conduct a forum on matters of critical concern, and to make room for new and controversial perspectives as well as more traditional ones. Introductions should open up as many topics as time and space permit, rather than providing dogmatic interpretations from a particular bias. I have extensively revised and updated the bibliographies (*Suggestions for Reading and Research*) in order to reflect as much as possible the extraordinary developments in Shakespeare criticism in recent times. I have worked hard on the commentary notes, both in the Bantam edition and in this present edition, incorporating here whatever I have been able to learn from the endless and wonderful task of contemplating the richness and ambiguity of Shakespeare's language. In all of this I've been helped more than I can say by the editorial board members, by my colleagues at the University of Chicago and elsewhere, by my wife Peggy, and by the editorial staff of Longman.

To complement this edition, and to provide the kind of visual experience necessary for fuller appreciation of Shakespeare as a dramatist, the updated fourth edition of *The Complete Works of Shakespeare* is accompanied by a full array of high-quality videos of Shakespeare's plays in production, including all of the BBC Television productions of Shakespeare's plays. In addition, this Longman video collection offers a number of plays in more than one production (including, for example, Franco Zeffirelli's *Romeo and Juliet*, 1968), to make possible a comparison of contrasting interpretations. Some interpretations available in this way depart from the Shakespeare text in ways that provide unusually challenging and imaginative insights; Akira Kurosawa's *Ran* (1986), for example, transforms *King Lear* into the tragic story of a Japanese warlord and his three sons, while his *Throne of Blood* (1957) is an equally bold translation of *Macbeth* in terms of Japanese history and folklore. For more information on how to qualify for any or all of these videos, instructors are invited to contact their Longman representative or the publisher.

Updated Fourth Edition

To the fourth edition, described above, I have added some corrections and additions. They are not extensive enough to need the name "fifth edition," and indeed I hope the volume justifies itself more or less as it stands. I have, however, done the following:

I have brought the section on "Shakespeare Criticism" in the General Introduction up to date by discussing the critical scene in the early and mid 1990s.

Most important, this updated edition includes *The Two Noble Kinsmen*, by Shakespeare and John Fletcher, with introduction, commentary notes, and (in the back of the book, under "Textual Notes") a set of collations indicating all departures from the original quarto text. This play should

have been included earlier in *The Complete Works*, because it contains a substantial amount of significant dramatic writing by Shakespeare. Our earlier decision not to include it was based on considerations of cost and physical size of a one-volume Shakespeare. It certainly needs to be included now.

A number of errors scattered through the book, some of them pointed out to me by sharp-eyed colleagues and friends who use this edition in their teaching, are now corrected.

I have worked through the complex textual situation of *Troilus and Cressida* once again and have incorporated here what I hope are more consistent applications of textual theory about this two-text play. In the main, this has meant giving increasing weight to the authority of the Folio text.

"A Funeral Elegy for Master William Peter," by "W.S.," 1612, recently argued by Donald Foster and Richard Abrams to be a Shakespearean composition, seems sufficiently worth study in terms of the complex authorship question that it is now included in this edition, with an introduction and detailed set of commentary notes.

"A Lover's Complaint," too often neglected by readers of Shakespeare, has a new introduction that reflects the complexity of the critical issues it raises.

Appendix 1 ("Canon, Dates, and Early Texts") now includes an account of the date and early publishing history of *The Two Noble Kinsmen*. Appendix II ("Sources") gives an account of the play's use of Chaucer's "The Knight's Tale" and other materials.

I have attempted to bring the bibliography up to date with the addition of a good number of items.

The index reflects the changes noted above.

I wish especially to thank Donald Foster, Richard Abrams, and Lars Engle for help on "A Funeral Elegy for Master William Peter." As before, I am deeply grateful to anyone who would like to call to my attention errors or deficiencies in this edition as it now stands. Corrections can be added whenever new printings are called for.

David Bevington

General Introduction

Life in Shakespeare's England

England during Shakespeare's lifetime (1564–1616) was a proud nation with a strong sense of national identity, but it was also a small nation by modern standards. Probably not more than five million people lived in the whole of England, considerably fewer than now live in London. England's territories in France were no longer extensive, as they had been during the fourteenth century and earlier; in fact, by the end of Queen Elizabeth's reign (1558–1603), England had virtually retired from the territories she had previously controlled on the Continent, especially in France. Wales was a conquered principality. England's overseas empire in America had scarcely begun, with the Virginia settlement in the 1580s. Scotland was not yet a part of Great Britain; union with Scotland would not take place until 1707, despite the fact that King James VI of Scotland assumed the English throne in 1603 as James I of England. Ireland, although declared a kingdom under English rule in 1541, was more a source of trouble than of economic strength. The last years of Elizabeth's reign, especially from 1597 to 1601, were plagued by the rebellion of the Irish under Hugh O'Neill, Earl of Tyrone. Thus, England of the sixteenth and early seventeenth centuries was both small and isolated.

The Social and Economic Background

By and large, England was a rural land. Much of the kingdom was still wooded, though timber was being used increasingly in manufacturing and shipbuilding. The area of the midlands, today heavily industrialized, was still at that time a region of great trees, green fields, and clear streams. England's chief means of livelihood was agriculture. This part of the economy was generally in a bad way, however,

"Enclosure" was a problem throughout the sixteenth century in England. Crop lands were converted into pasturage. The livelihood of the ploughman was threatened by the pasturing of sheep and the growing production of wool.

and people who lived off the land did not share in the prosperity of many Londoners. A problem throughout the sixteenth century was that of "enclosure": the conversion by rich landowners of croplands into pasturage. Farmers and peasants complained bitterly that they were being dispossessed and starved for the benefit of livestock. Rural uprisings and food riots were common, to the dismay of the authorities. Some Oxfordshire peasants arose in 1596, threatening to massacre the gentry and march on London; other riots had occurred in 1586 and 1591. There were thirteen riots in Kent alone during Elizabeth's reign. Unrest continued into the reign of James I, notably the midlands' rising of 1607. Although the government did what it could to inhibit enclosure, the economic forces at work were too massive and too inadequately understood to be curbed by governmental fiat. Pasture used large areas with greater efficiency than crop farming, and required far less labor. The wool produced by the pasturing of sheep was needed in ever increasing amounts for the manufacture of cloth.

The wool industry also experienced occasional economic difficulties, to be sure; overexpansion in the early years of the sixteenth century created a glutted market that collapsed disastrously in 1551, producing widespread unemployment. Despite such fluctuations and reversals, however, the wool industry at least provided handsome profits for some landowners and middlemen. Mining and manufacture in coal, iron, tin, copper, and lead, although insignificant by modern standards, were also expanding at a significant rate. Trading companies exploited the rich new resources of the Americas, as well as of Eastern Europe and the Orient. Queen Elizabeth aided economic development by keeping England out of war with her continental enemies as long as possible, despite provocations from those powers and despite the eagerness of some of her advisers to retaliate. Certainly England's economic condition was better than the economic condition of the rest of the Continent; an Italian called England "the land of comforts." Yet although some prosperity did exist, it was not evenly distributed. Especially during Shakespeare's first years in London, in the late 1580s and the 1590s, the gap between rich and poor grew more and more extreme. Elizabeth's efforts at peacemaking were no longer able to prevent years of war with the Catholic powers of the Continent. Taxation grew heavier, and inflation proceeded at an unusually rapid rate during this period. A succession of bad harvests compounded the miseries of those who dwelled on the land. When the hostilities on the Continent ceased for a time in about 1597, a wave of returning veterans added to unemployment and crime. The rising prosperity experienced by Shakespeare and other fortunate Londoners was undeniably real, but it was not universal. Nowhere was the contrast between rich and poor more visible than in London.

London

Sixteenth-century London was at once more attractive and less attractive than twentieth-century London. It was full of trees and gardens; meadows and cultivated lands reached in some places to its very walls. Today we can perhaps imagine the way in which it bordered clear streams and green fields, when we approach from a distance some noncommercial provincial city such as Lincoln, York, or Hereford. Partly surrounded by its ancient wall, London was by no means a large metropolis. With 190,000–200,000 inhabitants in the city proper and its suburbs, it was nonetheless the largest city of Europe, and its dominance among English cities was even more striking; in 1543–1544, London paid thirty times the subsidy of Norwich, then the second largest city in the kingdom (15,000 inhabitants). Although London's population had expanded into the surrounding area in all directions, the city proper stretched along the north bank of the Thames River from the old Tower of London on the east to St. Paul's Cathedral and the Fleet Ditch on the west—a distance of little more than a mile. Visitors approaching London from the south bank of the Thames (the Bankside) and crossing London Bridge could see virtually all of this exciting city lying before them. London Bridge itself was one of the major attractions of the city, lined with shops and richly decorated on occasion for the triumphal entry of a king or queen.

Yet London had its grim and ugly side as well. On London Bridge could sometimes be seen the heads of executed traitors. The city's houses were generally small and

Sixteenth-century London was a city teeming with activity. Pedestrians were often forced to make way for the livestock being driven through the streets.

crowded; its streets were often narrow and filthy. In the absence of sewers, open ditches in the streets served to collect and carry off refuse. Frequent epidemics of the bubonic plague were the inevitable result of unsanitary conditions and medical ignorance. Lighting of the streets at night was generally nonexistent, and the constabulary was notoriously unreliable. Shakespeare gives us unforgettable satires of night watchmen and bumbling police officials in *Much Ado About Nothing* (Dogberry and the night watch) and *Measure for Measure* (Constable Elbow). Prostitution thrived in the suburbs, conveniently located, although beyond the reach of the London authorities. Again, we are indebted to Shakespeare for a memorable portrayal in *Measure for Measure* of just such a demimonde (Mistress Overdone the bawd, Pompey her pimp, and various customers). Houses of prostitution were often to be found in the vicinity of the public theaters, since the theaters also took advantage of suburban locations to escape the stringent regulations imposed by London's Lord Mayor and Council of Aldermen. The famous Globe Theatre, for example, was on the south bank of the Thames, a short distance west of London Bridge. Another theatrical building (called simply "The Theatre"), used earlier by Shakespeare and the Lord Chamberlain's players, was located in Finsbury Fields, a short distance across Moorfields from London's northeast

London Bridge, lined with shops, houses, and severed heads on poles, provided a colorful route for those traveling between the north and south banks of the Thames. A number of Elizabethan theaters, including the Globe, were located on the south bank.

corner. The suburbs also housed various con games and illegal operations, some of them brilliantly illustrated (and no doubt exaggerated) in Ben Jonson's *The Alchemist* (1610).

Roughly half of London's total population, perhaps one hundred thousand people, lived within its walls, and as many more in the suburbs. The royal palace of Whitehall, Westminster Abbey (then known as the Abbey Church of St. Peter), the Parliament House, and Westminster Hall were well outside London, two miles or so to the west on the Thames River. They remain today in the same location, in Westminster, although the metropolis of London has long since surrounded these official buildings.

Travel

Travel was still extremely painful and slow because of the poor condition of the roads. Highway robbers were a constant threat. (The celebrated highway robbery in Shakespeare's *1 Henry IV* takes place at Gads Hill, on the main road between London and Canterbury.) English inns seem to have been good, however, and certainly much better than the inns of the Continent. Travel on horseback was the most common method of transportation, and probably the most comfortable, since coach building was a new and imperfect art. Coaches of state, some of which we see in prints and pictures of the era, were lumbering affairs, no doubt handsome enough in processions, but springless, unwieldly, and hard to transport. Carts and wagons were used for carrying merchandise, but packsaddles were safer and quicker. Under such difficulties, no metropolitan area such as London could possibly have thrived in the interior. London depended for its commercial greatness upon the Thames River and its access to the North Sea.

Commerce

When Elizabeth came to the English throne in 1558, England's chief foreign trade was with Antwerp, Bruges, and other Belgian cities. Antwerp was an especially important market for England's export of wool cloth. This market was seriously threatened, however, since the Low Countries were under the domination of the Catholic King of Spain, Philip II. When Philip undertook to punish his Protestant subjects in the Low Countries for their religious heresy, many of Elizabeth's counselors and subjects urged her to come to the defense of England's Protestant neighbors and trading allies. Elizabeth held back. Philip's armies attacked Antwerp in 1576 and again in 1585, putting to an end the commercial ascendancy of that great northern European metropolis. Perhaps as many as one-third of Antwerp's merchants and artisans settled in London, bringing with them their expert knowledge of commerce and manufacture. The influx of so many skilled workers and merchants into London produced problems of unemployment and overcrowding but contributed nevertheless to London's emergence as a leading port of trade.

English ships assumed a dominant position in Mediterranean trade, formerly carried on mainly by the Venetians. In the Baltic Sea, England captured trade that had previously been controlled by the Hanseatic League. Bristol thrived on commerce with Ireland and subsequently on trade with the Western Hemisphere. Boston and Hull increased their business with Scandinavian ports. The Russia Company was founded in 1555; the Levant Company became the famous East India Company in 1600; and the Virginia Company opened up trade with the New World in the Western Hemisphere. Fisheries were developed in the North Sea, in the waters north of Ireland, and off the banks of Newfoundland. Elizabeth and her ministers encouraged this commercial expansion.

The Poor Laws and Apprenticeship

Despite the new prosperity experienced by many Elizabethans, especially in London, unemployment remained a serious problem. The suppression of the monasteries in 1536–1539, as part of Henry VIII's reformation of the Catholic Church, had dispossessed a large class of persons who were not easily reemployed. Other causes of unemployment, such as the periodic collapse of the wool trade, dispossession of farm workers by enclosure of land, the sudden influx of skilled artisans from Antwerp, and the return of army veterans, have already been mentioned. Elizabethan Parliaments attempted to cope with the problem of unemployment but did so in ways that seem unduly harsh today. Several laws were passed between 1531, when the distinction between those needing charity and those unwilling to work first became law, and 1597–1598. The harshest of the laws was that of 1547, providing that vagabonds be branded and enslaved for two years; escape was punishable by death or life enslavement. This act was repealed in 1549, but subsequent acts of 1572 and 1576 designated ten classes of vagrants and required municipal authorities to provide work for the healthy unemployed of each town or parish. This localization of responsibility laid the basis for what has been known historically as the "poor rate" (a local tax levied for the support of the poor) and for that sinister

The taverns of Cheapside in London were popular and occasionally rowdy.

institution, the workhouse. The provisions of this act remained in force for centuries. The most comprehensive laws were those of the Parliament of 1597–1598, which repeated many provisions of earlier acts and added harsh, punitive penalties intended to send vagabonds back to the parishes in which they had been born or had last worked. After 1597, no begging was permitted; the poor were supposed to be provided for by the "poor rate" already established.

Regulations for apprentices were no less strict. An act of Parliament of 1563, known as the Statute of Artificers, gave the craft trades of England—still organized as medieval guilds—virtually complete authority over the young per-sons apprenticed to a trade. The law severely limited access to apprenticeship to sons of families with estates worth at least forty shillings of income. Apprenticeship usually began between the ages of fourteen and seventeen, and lasted for a period of not less than seven years. During this time, the young worker lived with the family of the employer. Without such an extensive apprenticeship, entry into the skilled crafts was virtually impossible. Apprenticeships were not open, however, in all guilds, and the law courts subsequently ruled that apprenticeship rules did not apply to crafts developed after 1563, so that exceptions did exist. All able-bodied workers not bound to crafts were supposed to work in agriculture. Acting companies, such as the com-pany Shakespeare joined, were not technically organized as guilds, though the boys who played women's parts did serve out an apprenticeship. We do not know whether Shakespeare actually served such an indenture before becoming a full member of his acting company.

Although some Elizabethans rose to great wealth, poverty and unemployment were widespread.

Social Change

The opportunities for rapid economic advance in Elizabe-than England, though limited almost entirely to those who were already prosperous, did produce social change and a quality of restlessness in English society. "New men" at court were an increasing phenomenon under the Tudor monarchs, especially Henry VII and Henry VIII, who tended to rely on loyal counselors of humble origin rather than on the once-too-powerful nobility. Cardinal Wolsey, for exam-ple, rose from obscurity to become the most mighty subject of Henry VIII's realm, with a newly built residence (Hamp-ton Court) rivaling the splendor of the King's own palaces. He was detested as an upstart by old aristocrats, such as the Duke of Norfolk, and his sudden fall was as spectacular as had been his rise to power. The Earl of Leicester, Queen Elizabeth's first favorite, was a descendant of the Edmund Dudley who had risen from unpretentious beginnings to great eminence under Henry VII, Queen Elizabeth's grand-father. Although Queen Elizabeth did not contribute sub-stantially to the new aristocracy—she created only three peers from 1573 onward—new and influential families were numerous throughout the century. Conversely, the ancient families discovered that they were no longer entrusted with positions of highest authority. To be sure, the aristocracy remained at the apex of England's social struc-ture. New aspirants to power emulated the aristocracy by purchasing land and building splendid residences, rather than defining themselves as a rich new "middle class." Bourgeois status was something the new men put behind them as quickly as they could. Moreover, social mobility could work in both directions: upward and downward. Many men were quickly ruined by the costly and competi-tive business of seeking favor at the Tudor court. The poor, in a vast majority, enjoyed virtually no rights at all.

Nonetheless, the Elizabethan era was one of greater oppor-tunity for rapid social and economic advancement among persons of wealth than England had heretofore known. Increased economic contacts with the outside world inevitably led to the importation of new styles of living. Such new fashions, together with the rapid changes now possible in social position, produced a reaction of dismay from those who feared the destruction of traditional English values. Attitudes toward Italy veered erratically between condem-nation and admiration: on the one hand, Italy was the home of the Catholic Church and originator of many supposedly decadent fashions, whereas, on the other hand, Italy was the cradle of humanism and the country famed for Venice's experiment in republican government. To many conserva-tive Englishmen, the word *Italianate* connoted a whole range of villainous practices, including diabolical methods of torture and revenge: poisoned books of devotion that would kill the unsuspecting victims who kissed them, ingeniously contrived chairs that would close upon the person who sat in them, and the like. The revenge plays of

Shakespeare's contemporaries, such as *Antonio's Revenge* by John Marston, *The Revenger's Tragedy* perhaps by Cyril Tourneur or Thomas Middleton, and *The White Devil* by John Webster, offer spectacular caricatures of the so-called Italianate style in murder. The name of Italy was also associated with licentiousness, immorality, and outlandish fashions in clothes. France, too, was accused of encouraging such extravagances in dress as ornamented headdresses, stiffly pleated ruffs, padded doublets, puffed or double sleeves, and richly decorated hose. Rapid changes in fashion added to the costliness of being up to date and thereby increased the outcry against vanity in dress. Fencing, dicing, the use of cosmetics, the smoking of tobacco, the drinking of imported wines, and almost every vice known to humanity were attributed by angry moralists to the corrupting influence from abroad.

Not all Englishmen deplored continental fashion, of course. Persons of advanced taste saw the importation of European styles as a culturally liberating process. Fashion thus became a subject of debate between moral traditionalists and those who welcomed the new styles. The controversy was a bitter one, with religious overtones, in which the reformers' angry accusations became increasingly extreme. This attack on changing fashion was, in fact, an integral part of the Puritan movement. It therefore stressed the sinfulness, not only of extravagance in clothing, but also of the costliness in building great houses and other such worldly pursuits. Those whose sympathies were Puritan became more and more disaffected with the cultural values represented by the court, and thus English society drifted further and further toward irreconcilable conflict.

Shakespeare's personal views on this controversy are hard to determine and do not bear importantly on his achievement as an artist. Generally, however, we can observe that his many references to changes in fashion cater neither to the avant-garde nor to reactionary traditionalists. Shakespeare's audience was, after all, a broadly national

one. It included many well-informed Londoners who viewed "Italianate" fashion neither with enthusiasm nor with alarm, but with satiric laughter. Such spectators would certainly have seen the point, for example, in Mercutio's witty diatribe at the expense of the new French style in fencing. The object of his scorn is Tybalt, who, according to Mercutio, "fights as you sing prick-song" and fancies himself to be "the very butcher of a silk button." "Is not this a lamentable thing," asks Mercutio rhetorically, "that we should be thus afflicted with these strange flies, these fashionmongers, these pardon-me's, who stand so much on the new form that they cannot sit at ease on the old bench?" (*Romeo and Juliet*, 2.4.20–35). In a similar vein, Shakespeare's audience would have appreciated the joking in *The Merchant of Venice* about England's servile imitation of continental styles in clothes. "What say you, then, to Falconbridge, the young baron of England?" asks Nerissa of her mistress Portia concerning one of Portia's many suitors. Portia replies, "How oddly he is suited! I think he bought his doublet in Italy, his round hose in France, his bonnet in Germany, and his behavior everywhere" (1.2.64–74). Court butterflies in Shakespeare's plays who bow and scrape and fondle their plumed headgear, like Le Beau in *As You Like It* and Osric in *Hamlet*, are the objects of ridicule. Hotspur in *1 Henry IV*, proud northern aristocrat that he is, has nothing but contempt for an effeminate courtier, "perfumèd like a milliner," who has come from King Henry to discuss the question of prisoners (1.3.36). Throughout Shakespeare's plays, the use of cosmetics generally has the negative connotation of artificial beauty used to conceal inward corruption, as in Claudius' reference to "the harlot's cheek, beautied with plastering art" (*Hamlet*, 3.1.52). Yet Shakespeare's treatment of newness in fashion is never shrill in tone. Nor does he fail in his dramas to give an honorable place to the ceremonial use of wealth and splendid costuming. His plays thus avoid both extremes in the controversy over changing fashions, though they give

This brothel scene, featuring gambling or dicing, illustrates some of the vices that were attributed to the corrupting influence from abroad.

plentiful evidence as to the liveliness and currency of the topic.

Shakespeare also reflects a contemporary interest in the problem of usury, especially in *The Merchant of Venice*. Although usury was becoming more and more of a necessity, emotional attitudes toward it changed only slowly. The traditional moral view condemned usury as forbidden by Christian teaching; on the other hand, European governments of the sixteenth century found themselves increasingly obliged to borrow large sums of money. The laws against usury were alternatively relaxed and enforced, according to the economic exigencies of the moment. Shakespeare's plays capture the Elizabethan ambivalence of attitude toward this feared but necessary practice (see Introduction to *The Merchant of Venice*). Similarly, most Englishmen had contradictory attitudes toward what we today would call the law of supply and demand in the marketplace. Conservative moralists complained bitterly when merchants exploited the scarcity of some commodity by forcing up prices; the practice was denounced as excessive profit taking and declared to be sinful, like usury. In economic policy, then, as in matters of changing fashion or increased social mobility, many Englishmen were ambivalent about the perennial conflict between the old order and the new.

Elizabethan Houses

Those fortunate Englishmen who grew wealthy in the reign of Elizabeth took special pleasure in building themselves fine new houses with furnishings to match. Chimneys were increasingly common, so that smoke no longer had to escape through a hole in the roof. Pewter, or even silver dishes, took the place of the wooden spoon and trencher. Beds, and even pillows, became common. Carpets were replacing rushes as covering for the floors; wainscoting, tapestries or hangings, and pictures appeared on the walls; and glass began to be used extensively for windows.

Despite the warnings of those moralists who preached against the vanity of worldly acquisition, domestic comfort made considerable progress in Elizabethan England. Many splendid Tudor mansions stand today, testifying to the important social changes that had taken place between the strife-torn fifteenth century and the era of relative peace under Elizabeth. The battlement, the moat, the fortified gate, and the narrow window used for archery or firearms generally disappeared in favor of handsome gardens and terraces. At the lower end of the social scale, the agricultural laborers who constituted the great mass of the English population were generally poor, malnourished, and uneducated, but they seem to have enjoyed greater physical

Tudor mansions were often splendid, with impressive gardens and terraces. Shown here is Old Moreton Hall, in Cheshire, built in 1559.

security than did their ancestors in the fifteenth century, and no longer needed to bring their cows, pigs, and poultry into their dwellings at night in order to protect them from thieves. City houses, of which many exist today, were often large and imposing structures, three or four stories in height, and framed usually of strong oak with the walls filled in with brick and plaster. Although the frontage on the streets of London was usually narrow, many houses had trees and handsome gardens at the rear. Of course London also had its plentiful share of tenements for the urban poor.

With the finer houses owned by the fortunate elite came features of privacy that had been virtually unknown to previous generations. Life in the household of a medieval lord had generally focused on the great hall, which could serve variously as the kitchen, dining hall, and sitting room for the entire family and its retainers. The men drank in the hall in the evenings and slept there at night. The new dwellings of prosperous Elizabethans, on the other hand, featured private chambers into which the family and the chief guests could retire.

The Elizabethans built well. Not only do we still admire their houses, but also we can see from their oriel windows and stained glass, their broad staircases, their jewels, and their costumes that they treasured the new beauty of their lives made possible by the culture of the Renaissance. Although the graphic and plastic arts did not thrive in England to the same extent as in Italy, France, and the Low Countries, England made lasting achievements in architecture, as well as in music, drama, and all forms of literature.

The Political and Religious Background

England under the Tudors suffered from almost unceasing religious conflict. The battle over religion affected every aspect of life and none more so than politics. At the very beginning of the Tudor reign, to be sure, England's problem was not religious but dynastic. Henry VII, the first of the Tudor kings, brought an end to the devastating civil wars of the fifteenth century by his overthrow of Richard III at the battle of Bosworth Field in 1485. The civil wars thus ended were the so-called Wars of the Roses, between the Lancastrian House of Henry VI (symbolized by the red rose) and the Yorkist House of Edward IV (symbolized by the white rose). Shakespeare chose these eventful struggles as the subject for his first series of English history plays, from *Henry VI* in three parts to *Richard III*. The House of Lancaster drew its title from John of Gaunt, Duke of Lancaster, father of Henry IV and great-grandfather of Henry VI; the House of York drew its title from Edmund Langley, Duke of York, great-grandfather of Edward IV and Richard III. Because John of Gaunt and Edmund Langley had been brothers, virtually all the noble contestants in this War of the Roses were cousins of one another, caught in a remorseless dynastic struggle for

control of the English crown. Many of them lost their lives in the fighting. By 1485, England was exhausted from civil conflict. Although Henry VII's own dynastic claim to the throne was weak, he managed to suppress factional opposition and to give England the respite from war so desperately needed. His son, Henry VIII, inherited a throne in 1509 that was more secure than it had been in nearly a century.

Henry VIII's notorious marital difficulties, however, soon brought an end to dynastic security and civil accord. Moreover, religious conflict within the Catholic Church was growing to the extent that a break with Rome appeared inevitable. Henry's marriage troubles precipitated that momentous event. Because he divorced his first wife, Katharine of Aragon, in 1530 without the consent of Rome, he was excommunicated by the Pope. His response in 1534 was to have himself proclaimed "Protector and only Supreme Head of the Church and Clergy of England." This decisive act signaled the beginning of the Reformation in England, not many years after Martin Luther's momentous break with the Papacy in 1517 and the consequent beginning of Lutheran Protestantism on the Continent. In England, Henry's act of defiance split the Church and the nation. Many persons chose Sir Thomas More's path of martyrdom rather than submit to Henry's new title as supreme head of the English church. Henry's later years did witness a period of retrenchment in religion, after the downfall of Thomas Cromwell in 1540, and indeed Henry's break with Rome had had its origin in political and marital strife rather than in matters of dogma and liturgy. Nevertheless, the establishment of an Anglican church was now an accomplished fact. The accession of Henry's ten-year-old son Edward VI in 1547 gave reformers an opportunity to bring about rapid changes in English Protestantism. Archbishop Cranmer's forty-two articles of religion (1551) and his prayer book laid the basis for the Anglican Church of the sixteenth century.

The death of the sickly Edward VI in 1553 brought with it an intense crisis in religious politics and a temporary reversal of England's religious orientation. The Duke of Northumberland, Protector and virtual ruler of England in Edward's last years, attempted to secure a Protestant succession and his own power by marrying his son to Lady Jane Grey, a granddaughter of Henry VII, whom Edward had named heir to the throne, but the proclamation of Lady Jane as queen ended in failure. She was executed, as were her husband and father-in-law. For five years, England returned to Catholicism under the rule of Edward's elder sister Mary, daughter of the Catholic Queen Katharine of Aragon. The crisis accompanying such changes of government during this midcentury period was greatly exacerbated by the fact that all three of Henry VIII's living children were considered illegitimate by one faction or another of the English people. In Protestant eyes, Mary was the daughter of the divorced Queen Katharine, whose marriage to Henry had never been valid because she had previously been the spouse of Henry individual conscience; she drew the line, however, where matters of conscience tended to "exceed their bounds and grow to be matter of faction." In practice, this meant that she did not tolerate avowed Catholics on the religious right or Brownists and Unitarians (who denied the doctrine of the Trinity) on the religious left. The foundation for this so-called Elizabethan compromise was the thirty-nine articles, adopted in 1563 and based in many respects upon Cranmer's forty-two articles of 1551. The compromise did not please everyone, of course, but it did achieve a remarkable degree of consensus during Elizabeth's long reign.

Queen Elizabeth and Tudor Absolutism

Elizabeth had to cope with a religiously divided nation and with extremists of both right and left who wished her downfall. She was a woman, in an age openly skeptical of women's ability or right to rule. Her success in dealing with such formidable odds was in large measure the result of her personal style as a monarch. Her combination of imperious will and femininity and her brilliant handling of her many contending male admirers have become legendary. She remained unmarried throughout her life, in part, at least, because marriage would have upset the delicate balance she maintained among rival groups, both foreign and domestic. Marriage would have committed her irretrievably

VIII's older brother Arthur. This Arthur had died at a young age, in 1502, shortly after his state marriage to the Spanish princess. If, as the Protestants insisted, Arthur had consummated the marriage, then Katharine's subsequent union with her deceased husband's brother was invalid, and Henry was free, instead, to marry Anne Boleyn—the mother-to-be of Elizabeth. In Catholic eyes, however, both Elizabeth and her brother Edward VI (son of Jane Seymour, Henry VIII's third wife) were the bastard issue of Henry's bigamous marriages; Henry's one and only true marriage in the Catholic faith was that to Katharine of Aragon. Edward and Elizabeth were regarded by many Catholics, at home and abroad, not only as illegitimate children, but also as illegitimate rulers, to be disobeyed and even overthrown by force. Thus, dynastic and marital conflicts became matters of grave political consequence.

Because of these struggles, Elizabeth's accession to the throne in 1558 remained an uncertainty until the last moment. Once she actually became ruler, England returned once more to the Protestant faith. Even then, tact and moderation were required to prevent open religious war. Elizabeth's genius at compromise prompted her to seek a middle position for her church, one that combined an episcopal form of church government (owing no allegiance to the Pope) with an essentially traditional form of liturgy and dogma. As much as was practicable, she left matters up to

The Knights of the Garter belonged to the highest order of knighthood; many were influential courtiers and favorites of Queen Elizabeth. A masterful politician, Elizabeth remained unmarried throughout her life. A marriage would have upset the political balance and would have committed her to one foreign nation or to one constituency at home.

to either one foreign nation or to one constituency at home. She chose instead to bestow her favor on certain courtiers, notably Robert Dudley (whom she elevated to be the Earl of Leicester) and, after Leicester's death in 1588, Robert Devereux, second Earl of Essex. Her relationship with these men, despite her partiality to them, was marked by her outbursts of tempestuous jealousy. In addition, she relied on the staid counsel of her hard-working ministers: Lord Burghley, Sir Francis Walsingham, Burghley's son Robert Cecil, and a few others.

In her personal style as monarch, Elizabeth availed herself of the theory of absolute supremacy. Under all the Tudors, England was nominally at least an absolute monarchy in an age when many of England's greatest rivals—France, Spain, the Holy Roman Empire—were also under absolutist rule. The rise of absolutism throughout Renaissance Europe was the result of an increase of centralized national power and a corresponding decrease in autonomous baronial influence. Henry VII's strong assertion of his royal authority at the expense of the feudal lords corresponded roughly in time with the ascendancy of Francis I of France (1515) and Charles V of the Holy Roman Empire (1519). Yet England had long enjoyed a tradition of rule by consensus. When Elizabeth came to the throne, England was already in some ways a "limited" monarchy. Parliament, and especially the members of the House of Commons, claimed prerogatives

of their own and were steadily gaining in both experience and power. In the mid-1560s, for example, the Commons made repeated attempts to use parliamentary tax-levying authority as a means of obliging Elizabeth to name a Protestant successor to the throne. The attempt, despite its failure to achieve its immediate goal, was significant; the Commons had shown that they were a force to be reckoned with. Even though Elizabeth made skillful rhetorical use of the theory of absolutism, portraying herself as God's appointed deputy on earth, her idea of absolutism should not be confused with despotism. To be sure, Elizabeth learned to avoid Parliamentary interference in her affairs whenever possible; there were only thirteen sessions of Parliament in her forty-five years of rule. Still, Parliament claimed the right to establish law and to levy taxes on which the monarchy had to depend. Elizabeth needed all her considerable diplomatic skills in dealing with her Parliaments and with the English people, who were self-reliant and proud of their reputation for independence. Elizabeth had more direct authority over her Privy Council, since she could appoint its members herself, yet even here she consulted faithfully with them on virtually everything she did. Nor were her closest advisers reluctant to offer her advice. Many vocal leaders in her government, including Walsingham and Leicester, urged the Queen during the 1570s and 1580s to undertake a more active military role on the Continent against the

Catholic powers. So did her later favorite, the Earl of Essex. With remarkable tact, she managed to retain the loyalty of her militant and sometimes exasperated counselors, and yet to keep England out of war with Spain until that country actually launched an invasion attempt in 1588 (the Great Armada).

Catholic Opposition

During her early years, Elizabeth sought through her religious compromise to ease the divisions of her kingdom and attempted to placate her enemies abroad (notably Philip of Spain) rather than involve England in a costly war. For about twelve years, while England's economy gained much-needed strength, this policy of temporizing succeeded. Yet Elizabeth's more extreme Catholic opponents at home and abroad could never be reconciled to the daughter of that Protestant "whore," Anne Boleyn. England's period of relative accommodation came to an end in 1569 and 1570, with Catholic uprisings in the north and with Papal excommunication of the English Queen. As a declared heretic, Elizabeth's very life was in danger; her Catholic subjects were encouraged by Rome to disobey her and to seek means for her violent overthrow.

Conspirators did, in fact, make attempts on the Queen's life, notably in the so-called Babington conspiracy of 1586. This plot, brought to light by Secretary of State Walsingham, sought to place Mary Queen of Scots on the English throne in Elizabeth's stead. Mary was Elizabeth's kinswoman; Mary's grandmother, sister to Henry VIII, had been married to James IV of Scotland. So long as Elizabeth remained childless, Mary was a prominent heir to the English throne. Catholics pinned their hopes on her succession, by force if necessary; Protestant leaders urged Elizabeth to marry and give birth to a Protestant heir or at least to name a Protestant successor. Mary had abdicated the Scottish throne in 1567 after the sensational murder of her Catholic counselor David Rizzio, the murder of Mary's husband, the Earl of Darnley (in which Mary was widely suspected to have taken part), and her subsequent marriage to Darnley's slayer, the Earl of Bothwell. Taking refuge in England, Mary remained a political prisoner and the inevitable focus of Catholic plotting against Elizabeth for approximately two decades. She, in fact, assented in writing to Babington's plot against Elizabeth. All that long while Elizabeth resisted demands from her Protestant advisers that she execute her kinswoman and thereby end a constant threat to the throne; Elizabeth was reluctant to kill a fellow monarch and agreed fully with

Along with the defeat of the Spanish Armada in 1588, the 1587 beheading of Mary, Queen of Scots, shown holding a crucifix and surrounded by official witnesses in this contemporary illustration, virtually ended any serious Catholic challenge to Elizabeth's throne.

Mary's son James that "anointing by God cannot be defiled by man." Nonetheless, Mary's clear involvement in the Babington conspiracy led to the so-called Bond of Associa-tion, in which thousands of Englishmen pledged to prevent the succession of any person plotting Elizabeth's death, and then at last to Mary's execution in 1587. By that time, Spain was mounting an invasion against England, the Great Armada of 1588, and Elizabeth's temporizing tactics were no longer feasible. The long years of peace had done their work, however, and England was considerably stronger and more resolute than thirty years before. With Elizabeth's tacit approval, Sir Francis Drake and other naval commanders carried the fighting to Spain's very shore and to her American colonies. The war with Spain continued from 1588 until about 1597.

Elizabeth's great compromise dealt not only with the political dangers of opposition but also with the more central religious issues. England was sorely divided, as was much of Europe, on such matters as whether Christ's body was transsubstantially present in the Mass, as Catholic faith maintained; whether good works were efficacious in salva-tion or whether people could be saved by God's grace alone, as the Reformers insisted; whether a portion of humankind was predeterminately damned, as the Calvinists believed; and the like. During the turbulent years of the Reformation, many people died for their faith. In general, the Elizabethan compromise insisted on allegiance to the English throne, church, and ecclesiastical hierarchy but allowed some latitude in matters of faith. The degree of elaboration in vestments and ritual was also an explosive issue on which the English church attempted to steer a central and pragmatic course, although conflicts inevitably arose within the church itself.

Protestant Opposition

The threat from the religious left was no less worrisome than that from the right. Protestant reformers had experienced their first taste of power at the time of Henry VIII's break with Rome in 1534. Under Thomas Cromwell, Cardinal Wol-sey's successor as the King's chief minister, the monasteries were suppressed and William Tyndale's English Bible was authorized. The execution of Cromwell introduced a period of conservative retrenchment, but the accession of Edward VI in 1547 brought reform once more into prominence. Thereafter, Mary's Catholic reign drove most of the reform-ers into exile on the Continent. When they returned after 1558, many had been made more radical by their continen-tal experience.

To be sure, reform covered a wide spectrum, from moderation to radicalism. Some preferred to work within the existing hierarchical structure of church and state, whereas others were religious separatists. Only the more radical groups, such as the Brownists and Anabaptists,

endorsed ideas of equality and communal living. The abusive epithet "Puritan," applied indiscriminately to all reformers, tended to obscure the wide range of difference in the reform movement. The reformers were, to some extent, united by a dislike for formal ritual and ecclesiastical garments, by a preference for a simple and pious manner of living, and by a belief in the literal word of the Bible rather than the patristic teachings of the church. They stressed personal responsibility in religion and were Calvinist in their emphasis on human depravity and the need for grace through election. Yet at first only the more radical were involved in a movement to establish an entirely separate church.

The radicals on the religious left, even if they represented at first only a minority of the reformers, posed a serious threat to Elizabeth's government. Their program bore an ironic resemblance to that of the Catholic opposition on the religious right. In their theoretical writings, the extreme reformers justified overthrow of what they considered to be tyrannical rule, just as Catholic spokesmen had absolved Elizabeth's subjects of obedience to her on the grounds that she was illegitimate. Both extremes appealed to disobedi-ence in the name of a higher religious law. Among the reforming theoreticians was John Ponet, whose Short Trea-tise of Politic Power (1556) argued that a monarch is subject to a social contract and must rule according to laws that are equally subscribed to by Parliament, the clergy, and the people.

The Doctrine of Passive Obedience

Elizabeth's government countered such assaults on its authority, from both the right and the left, with many arguments, of which perhaps the most central was that of passive obedience. This doctrine condemned rebellion under virtually all circumstances. Its basic assumption was that the king or queen is God's appointed deputy on earth. To depose such a monarch must therefore be an act of disobedience against God's will. Since God is all-wise and all-powerful, his placing of an evil ruler in power must proceed from some divine intention, such as the punish-ment of a wayward people. Rebellion against God's "scourge" merely displays further disobedience to God's will. A people suffering under a tyrant must wait patiently for God to remove the burden, which he will surely do when the proper time arrives.

This doctrine was included in the official book of homilies of the Church of England and was read from the pulpit at regular intervals. The best-known such homily, entitled Against Disobedience and Willful Rebellion, had been preceded by such tracts as William Tyndale's Obedience of a Christian Man (1528); a book of homilies, published in 1547, including an "Exhortation Concerning Good Order and Obedience"; Thomas Cranmer's Notes for a Sermon on the *Rebellion* of 1549; and Hugh Latimer's *Sermon on the Lord's Prayer* (1552). Shakespeare heard such homilies often, and he expresses their ideas through several of his characters, such as John of Gaunt and the Bishop of Carlisle in *Richard II* (1.2.37–41, 4.1.115–150). This is not to say that he endorses such ideas, for he sets them in dramatic opposition to other and more heterodox concepts. We can say, nevertheless, that Shakespeare's audience would have recognized in Gaunt's speeches a clear expression of a familiar and officially correct position.

The Political Ideas of Machiavelli

The orthodoxies of the Elizabethan establishment were under attack, not only from the Catholic right and the Protestant left, but also from a new and revolutionary point of view that set aside all criteria of religious morality. Tudor defense of order was based, as we have seen, on the assumption that the monarch rules in accord with a divine plan, a higher Law of Nature to which every just ruler is attuned. Political morality must be at one with religious morality. Catholic and Protestant critiques of the Tudor establishment made similar assumptions, even though they appealed to revolution in the name of that religious morality. To Niccolò Machiavelli, on the other hand, politics was a manipulative science best governed by the dictates of social expediency. His philosophy did not, as many accusingly charged, lead necessarily to the cynical promotion of mere self-interest, he did argue, in his *Discourses* and *The Prince*, that survival and political stability are the first obligations of any ruler. Machiavelli regarded religion as a tool of the enlightened ruler rather than as a morally absolute guide. He extolled in his ideal leader the quality of *virtù*—a mixture of cunning and forcefulness. He saw history as a subject offering practical lessons in the kind of pragmatic statecraft he proposed.

Machiavelli was a hated name in England, and most of his works were never available in an English printed edition during Shakespeare's lifetime. (*The Florentine History* was translated in 1595.) Nevertheless, his writings were available in Italian, French, and Latin editions, and in manuscript English translations. His ideas certainly had a profound impact on the England of the 1590s. Marlowe caricatures the Italian writer in his *The Jew of Malta*, but he clearly was fascinated by what Machiavelli had to say. Shakespeare, too, reveals a complex awareness. However much he may lampoon the Machiavellian type of conscienceless villain in *Richard III*, he shows us more plausible pragmatists in *Richard II* and *1 Henry IV*. Conservative theories of the divine right of kings are set in debate with the more heterodox ambitions of Henry Bolingbroke (who then adopts the most orthodox of political vocabularies once he is king). Bolingbroke is not a very attractive figure, but he does succeed politically where Richard has failed.

Shakespeare reveals himself thus as less a defender of the established order than as a great dramatist able to give sympathetic expression to the aspirations of all sides in a tense political struggle. His history plays have been variously interpreted as defenses of monarchy and as subtle pleas for rebellion, but the consensus today is that the plays use political conflict as a way of probing the motivations of social behavior. To be sure, the plays do stress the painful consequences of disorder and present, on the whole, an admiring view of monarchy (especially in *Henry V*), despite the manifest limitations of that institution. Certainly, we can sense that Shakespeare's history plays were written for a generation of Englishmen who had experienced political crisis and who could perceive issues of statecraft in Shakespeare's plays that were relevant to England's struggles in the 1580s and the 1590s. The play of *King John*, for example, deals with a king whose uncertain claim to the throne is challenged by France and the Papacy in the name of John's nephew, Arthur; Elizabeth faced a similar situation in her dilemma over her kinswoman, Mary Queen of Scots. Elizabeth also bitterly acknowledged the cogency of a popular analogy comparing her reign with that of King Richard II, and, when Shakespeare's play about Henry IV's overthrow of Richard was apparently revived for political purposes shortly before the Earl of Essex's abortive rebellion against Elizabeth in 1601, Shakespeare's acting company had some explaining to do to the authorities (see Introduction to *Richard II*). Nevertheless, Shakespeare's attitudes toward the issues of his own day are ultimately unknowable and unimportant, since his main concern seems to have been with the dramatization of political conflict, rather than with the urging of a controversial position.

Shakespeare on Religion

Our impressions of Shakespeare's personal sympathies in religion are similarly obscured by his refusal to use his art for polemical purposes. Although various attempts have been made to prove him a Catholic sympathizer or a loyal moderate Anglican, we see in his plays a spectrum of religious attitudes portrayed with an extraordinary range of insight. In matters of doctrine, his characters are at various times acquainted with Catholic theology (like the Ghost of Hamlet's father) or with the controversy concerning salvation by faith or good works (see *Measure for Measure*, 1.2.24–25), but a consistent polemical bias is absent. Some Catholic prelates are schemers, like Pandulph in *King John*. Ordinarily, however, Shakespeare's satirical digs at ecclesiastical pomposity and hypocrisy have little to do with the Catholic question. Cardinal Beaufort in *1 Henry VI* is a political maneuverer, but so are many of his secular rivals. Cardinal Wolsey in *Henry VIII* is motivated by personal ambition, rather than by any sinister conspiracy of the international church. Many of Shakespeare's nominally

Catholic clerics, such as Friar Laurence in *Romeo and Juliet* or Friar Francis in *Much Ado About Nothing,* are gentle and well-intentioned people, even if occasionally bumbling. We can certainly say that Shakespeare consistently avoids the chauvinistic anti-Catholic baiting so often found in the plays of his contemporaries.

The same avoidance of extremes can be seen in his portrayal of Protestant reformers, though the instances in this case are few. Malvolio in *Twelfth Night* is fleetingly compared with a "Puritan" (2.3.139–146), although Shakespeare insists that no extensive analogy can be made. Angelo in *Measure for Measure* is sometimes thought to be a critical portrait of the Puritan temperament. Even if this were so, Shakespeare's satire is extremely indirect compared with the lampoons written by his contemporaries Ben Jonson and Thomas Dekker.

Stuart Absolutism

Queen Elizabeth's successor, James I of the Scottish house of Stuarts, reigned from 1603 to 1625. Like Elizabeth, he was a strong believer in the divine right of kings. The English people did not take to this northerner, with his eccentric personal habits, however, in part because of long-standing enmities between England and Scotland. As a result, James was less successful in dealing with the heterogeneous and antagonistic forces that Elizabeth had kept in precarious balance. At the Hampton Court Conference of 1604, relations quickly broke down between James and the Puritan wing of the Church, so that even its more moderate adherents joined forces with the separatists. James had similar difficulties with an increasingly radical group in the House of Commons. In the widening rift between the absolutists and those who defended the supremacy of Parliament, James' court moved toward the right. Catholic sympathies at court became common. Civil war was still a long way off and by no means inevitable; the beheading of King Charles I (James' son) would not occur until 1649. Still, throughout James' reign, the estrangement between the right and the left was becoming more and more uncomfortable. The infamous Gunpowder Plot of 1605, in which Guy Fawkes and other Catholic conspirators were accused of having plotted to blow up the houses of Parliament, raised hysteria to a new intensity. Penal laws against papists were harshly enforced. The Parliament of 1614 included in its membership John Pym, Thomas Wentworth, and John Eliot—men who were to become turbulent spokesmen against taxes imposed without Parliamentary grant, imprisonment without the stating of specific criminal charges, and other purported abuses of royal power. The polarization of English society naturally affected the London theaters. Popular London audiences (often Puritan in sympathy) eventually grew disaffected with the stage, while even the popular acting companies came under the increasing domination of the court. Shakespeare's late plays reflect the increasing influence of a courtly audience.

The Intellectual Background

Renaissance Cosmology

In learning, as in politics and religion, Shakespeare's England was a time of conflict and excitement. Medieval ideas of a hierarchical and ordered creation were under attack but were still widely prevalent, and were used to justify a hierarchical order in society itself. According to the so-called Ptolemaic system of the universe, formulated by Ptolemy of Alexandria in the second century A.D., the earth stood at the center of creation. Around it moved, in nine concentric spheres, the heavenly bodies of the visible universe, in order as follows (from the earth outward): the moon, Mercury, Venus, the sun, Mars, Jupiter, Saturn, the fixed stars on a single plane, and lastly the *primum mobile,* imparting motion to the whole system. (See the accompanying illustration.) Some commentators proposed alternate arrangements or speculated as to the existence of one or two additional spheres, in particular a "crystalline sphere" between the fixed stars and the *primum mobile.* These additional spheres were needed to cope with matters not adequately explained in Ptolemaic astronomy, such as the precession of the equinoxes. More troublesomely, the seemingly erratic retrograde motion of the planets—that is, the refusal of Mars and other planets to move around the earth in steady orbit—called forth increasingly ingenious theories, such as Tycho Brahe's scheme of epicycles. Still, the conservative appeal of the earth-centered cosmos remained very strong. How could one suppose that the earth was not at the center of the universe?

The *primum mobile* was thought to turn the entire universe around the earth once every twenty-four hours. Simultaneously, the individual heavenly bodies moved more slowly around the earth on their individual spheres, constantly changing position with respect to the fixed stars. The moon, being the only heavenly body that seemed subject to change in its monthly waxing and waning, was thought to represent the boundary between the unchanging universe and the incessantly changing world. Beneath the moon, in the "sublunary" sphere, all creation was subject to death as a result of Adam's fall from grace; beyond the moon lay perfection. Hell was imagined to exist deep within the earth, as in Dante's *Inferno,* or else outside the *primum mobile* and far below the created universe in the realm of chaos, as in Milton's *Paradise Lost.*

Heaven or the Empyrean stood, according to most Ptolemaic systems, at the top of the universe. Between heaven and earth dwelled the nine angelic orders, each associated with one of the nine concentric spheres. According to a work attributed to Dionysius the Areopagite, *On the*

Heavenly Hierarchy (fifth century A.D.), the nine angelic orders consisted of three hierarchies. Closest to God were the contemplative orders of Seraphim, Cherubim, and Thrones; next, the intermediate orders of Dominions, Powers, and Virtues; and finally the active orders of Principalities, Archangels, and Angels. These last served as God's messengers and intervened from time to time in the affairs of mortals. Ordered life among humans, although manifestly imperfect when compared with the eternal bliss of the angelic orders, still modeled itself on that platonic idea of perfect harmony. Thus the state, the church, and the family all resembled one another because they resembled (however distantly) the kingdom of God. An eloquent expression of the order of creation is to be found in Richard Hooker's *Of the Laws of Ecclesiastical Polity* (1594–1597).

The devils of hell were fallen angels, with Satan as their leader. Such evil spirits might assume any number of shapes, such as demons, goblins, wizards, or witches. Believers in evil spirits generally made no distinction between orthodox Christian explanations of evil and the more primitive folklore of witchcraft. Belief in witchcraft was widespread indeed; King James I took the matter very seriously. So did Reginald Scot's *The Discovery of Witch-craft* (1584), though its author also attempted to confute what he regarded as ignorant superstition and charlatanism. Throughout Shakespeare's lifetime, belief and skepticism about such matters existed side by side.

A similar ambiguity pertained to belief in the Ptolemaic universe itself. All major poets of the Renaissance, including Shakespeare, Spenser, and Milton (who completed *Para-dise Lost* after 1660), represented the universe in cosmic terms as described by Ptolemy. Yet Nicolaus Copernicus' revolutionary theory of a sun-centered solar system (*De revolutionibus orbium coelestium*, published on the Continent in 1543) and the discovery of a new star in Cassiopeia in 1572 stimulated much new thought. Galileo Galilei, born in the same year as Shakespeare (1564), published in 1610 the results of his telescopic examinations of the moon, thereby further confirming Copernicus' hypothesis. Although the news of Galileo's astounding discovery came too late to affect any but the latest of Shakespeare's plays, a sense of excitement and dislocation was apparent throughout most of the years of his writing career. Thomas Nashe, in 1595, referred familiarly to Copernicus as the author "who held that the sun remains immobile in the center of the world, and that the earth is moved about the sun" (Nashe, *Works*, ed. R. B. McKerrow, 1904–1910, 3.94). John Donne lamented in 1611–1612 that the "new philosophy" (i.e., the new science) "calls all in doubt." Skeptical uncertainty about the cosmos was on the rise. The poetic affirmations in Renaissance art of traditional ideas of the cosmos can best be understood as a response to uncertainty—a statement of faith in an age of increasing doubt.

Ptolemy's earth-centered system of the universe (top) was challenged by the sun-centered system of Copernicus (bottom) with the publishing of De revolutionibus orbium coelestium in 1543. Shakespeare, like other major poets of the English Renaissance, poetically represents the universe in cosmic terms as described by Ptolemy, but also reflects uncertainties generated by the new cosmology.

Alchemy and Medicine

In all areas of Renaissance learning, the new and the old science were confusedly juxtaposed. Alchemy, for example, made important contributions to learning, despite its superstitious character. Its chief goal was the transformation of base metals into gold, on the assumption that all metals were ranked on a hierarchical scale and could be raised from lower to higher positions on that scale by means of certain alchemical techniques. Other aims of alchemy included the discovery of a universal cure for diseases and of a means for preserving life indefinitely. Such aims encouraged quackery and prompted various exposés, such as Chaucer's "The Canon's Yeoman's Tale" (late fourteenth century) and Jonson's The Alchemist (1610). Yet many of the procedures used in alchemy were essentially chemical procedures, and the science of chemistry received a valuable impetus from constant experimentation. Queen Elizabeth was seriously interested in alchemy throughout her life.

In physics, medicine, and psychology, as well, older concepts vied with new. Traditional learning apportioned all physical matter into four elements: earth, air, fire, and water. Each of these was thought to be a different combination of the four "qualities" of the universe: hot, cold, moist, and dry. Earth combined cold and dry; air, hot and moist; fire, hot and dry; and water, cold and moist. Earth and water were the baser or lower elements, confined to the physical world; fire and air were aspiring elements, tending upward. Humans, as a microcosm of the larger universe, contained in themselves the four elements. The individual's temperament, or "humor," or "complexion," depended on which "humor" predominated in that person. The four humors in humans corresponded to the four elements of physical matter. The blood was hot and moist, like air; yellow bile or choler was hot and dry, like fire; phlegm was cold and moist, like water; and black bile was cold and dry, like earth. A predominance of blood in an individual created a sanguine or cheerful temperament, yellow bile (or humor) produced a choleric or irascible temperament, phlegm produced a phlegmatic or stolid temperament, and black bile produced a melancholic temperament. Diet could affect the balance among these humors, since an excess of a particular food would stimulate overproduction of one humor. The stomach and the liver, which converted food into humors, were regarded as the seat of human passions. The spleen was thought to be the seat of laughter, sudden impulse, or caprice, and also melancholy. (Hotspur, in 1 Henry IV, is said to be "governed by a spleen," 5.2.19.) Strong emotional reactions could be explained in terms of the physiology of the humors: in anger, the blood rushed to the head and thereby produced a flush of red color and staring eyes; in fear, the blood migrated to the heart and thus left the face and liver pale, and so on. Sighs supposedly cost the heart a drop of blood, while wine could refortify it (as Falstaff insists in 2 Henry IV, 4.3.90–123). The signs of youth were warmth and moisture, as in Desdemona's "hot and moist" hand (Othello, 3.4.39); those of age were "a moist eye, a dry hand, a yellow cheek, a white beard, a decreasing leg, an increasing belly" (2 Henry IV, 1.2.179–181). A common remedy for illness was to let blood and thereby purge the body of unwanted humors.

The name traditionally associated with such theories was that of Galen, the most celebrated of ancient writers on medicine (c. 130 A.D.). A more revolutionary name was that of Paracelsus, a famous German physician (c. 1493–1541) who attacked the Aristotelianism of his time and urged a more unfettered pragmatic research into pharmacy and medicine. Such experimentalism bore fruit in the anatomical research of Vesalius and in William Harvey's investigations of the circulation of the blood (c. 1616). Nevertheless, the practice of medicine in Renaissance times remained under the influence of the "humors" theory until quite late, and its ideas are to be found throughout Shakespeare's writings.

Gedruckt zu Frankfurt am Mayn/durch Johan Scratthenber. 1598.

Alchemists employed relatively sophisticated equipment in their futile search for the "philosopher's stone," a reputed substance supposed to possess the property of changing other metals into gold and silver.

Learning

In learning generally, and in theories of education, new ideas conflicted with old. The curriculum of schools and colleges in the Renaissance was inherited largely from the Middle Ages and displayed many traditional characteristics. The curriculum consisted of the seven Liberal Arts: a lower division, called the trivium, comprised of grammar, rhetoric, and logic; and an upper division, called the quadrivium, comprised of arithmetic, geometry, astronomy, and music. In addition, there were the philosophical studies associated chiefly with Aristotle: natural philosophy, ethics, and metaphysics.

Aristotle's name had a towering influence in medieval times and remained important to the Renaissance as well.

The four humors of black bile, blood, yellow bile or choler, and phlegm, as shown in this illustration from an illuminated manuscript, were believed to govern the human personality by producing a disposition toward melancholic, sanguine, choleric, or phlegmatic temperaments.

Even among his Renaissance admirers, however, Aristotle proved more compelling in practical matters than in the abstract scholastic reasoning associated with his name in the Middle Ages. The Italian Aristotelians whose work made its way into England were interested primarily in the science of human behavior. Aristotelian ethics was for them a practical subject, telling people how to live usefully and well and how to govern themselves politically. Rhetoric was the science of persuasion, enabling people to use eloquence for socially useful goals. Poetry was a kind of rhetoric, a language of persuasion which dramatists, too, might use for morally pragmatic ends.

At the same time, new thinkers were daring to attack Aristotle by name as a symbol of traditional medieval thought. The attack was not always fair to Aristotle himself, whose work had been bent to the *a priori* purposes of much medieval scholasticism. Nevertheless, his name had assumed such symbolic importance that he had to be confronted directly. The Huguenot logician Petrus Ramus (1515–1572), defiantly proclaiming that "everything that Aristotle taught is false," argued for rules of logic as derived from observation. He urged, for example, that his students learn about rhetoric from observing in detail Cicero's effect on his listeners, rather than by the rote practice of syllogism. Actually, Ramus' thought was less revolutionary in its concepts of logic than in the tremendous ferment of opinion caused by his iconoclastic teaching.

A basic issue at stake in the anti-Aristotelian movement was that of traditional authority versus independent observation. How do people best acquire true knowledge—through the teachings of their predecessors or through their own discovery? The issue had profound implications for religious truth as well: should individuals heed the collective wisdom of the earthly church or read the Bible with their individual perceptions as their guide? Is "reason" an accretive wisdom handed down by authority or a quality of the individual soul? Obviously, a middle ground exists between the two extremes, and no new thinker of the Renaissance professed to abandon entirely the use of ancient authority. For men like Henricus Agrippa (1486–1535) and Sir Francis Bacon (1561–1626), however, scholastic tradition had exerted its oppressive influence far too long. Authority needed to be examined critically and scientifically. Bacon, in his *The Advancement of Learning* (1605), fought against the blind acceptance of ancient wisdom and argued that "knowledge derived from Aristotle, and exempted from liberty of examination, will not rise again higher than the knowledge of Aristotle." Sir Walter Ralegh and others joined in the excited new search for what human "reason" could discover when set free from scholastic restraint. Such belief in the perfectibility of human reason owed some of its inspiration to Italian Neoplatonic humanists like Giovanni Pico della Mirandola (1463–1494), who, in his *Oration on the Dignity of Man*, celebrated a human race "constrained by no limits" in accordance with the potential of its own free will. The new learning did not seem to trouble these men in their religious faith, although a tension between scientific observation and faith in miracles was to become plentifully evident in the seventeenth century.

The Nature of Humankind

Medieval thought generally assigned to humankind a uniquely superior place in the order of creation on earth. That assumption of superiority rested on biblical and patristic teachings about the hierarchy of creation, in which humanity stood at the apex of physical creation nearest God and the angels. Humankind was thus supreme on earth in the so-called chain of being. Human reason, though subject to error because of sinfulness, enabled humans to aspire toward divinity. Humans were, in the view of medieval philosophers, the great amphibians, as well as the microcosm of the universe, part bestial and part immortal,

This guide, graphically setting forth the ideals to which every English gentlewoman and gentleman should aspire, illustrates the Renaissance concept that outward deportment and accomplishments should correctly and invariably mirror a person's inner nature.

doomed by Adam's fall to misery and death in this life but promised eternal salvation through Christ's atonement. Right reason, properly employed, could lead to the truths of revealed Christianity and thus give humankind a glimpse of the heavenly perfection one day to be ours. Renaissance Neoplatonism, as expounded, for example, in Castiglione's *The Courtier* (translated by Sir Thomas Hoby, 1561), offered humanity a vision of a platonic ladder, extending from the perception of a woman's beauty to the experiencing of God's transcendent love.

Protestant thought of the Renaissance did not wholly disagree with this formulation, but it did place a major new emphasis on human reprobation. The idea was not new, for Saint Augustine (354–430) had insisted on human depravity and our total dependence on God's inscrutable grace, but, in the years of the Reformation, this theology took on a new urgency. Martin Luther (1483–1540), by rejecting venera-tion of the Virgin Mary and the saints, and by taking away the sacraments of confession and penance, by which individual Christians could seek the institutional comforts of the Catholic Church, exposed the individual sinner to agonies of conscience that could result in a sense of

alienation and loss. The rewards were great for those who found new faith in God's infinite goodness, but the hazards of predestinate damnation were fearsome to those who were less sure of their spiritual welfare. Luther's God was inscrutable, majestic, and infallible. Luther's God decreed salvation for the elect and damnation for all others, and his will could not be challenged or questioned. The individual was to blame for sin, even though God hardened the hearts of the reprobate. John Calvin (1509–1564) placed even greater stress on predestinate good and evil and insisted that the grace of salvation was founded on God's freely given mercy that humans could not possibly deserve. Salvation was God's to give or withhold as he wished; humans might not repine that in his incomprehensible wisdom God has "barred the door of life to those whom he has given over to damnation." Faced with such a view of human spiritual destiny, the individual Christian's lot was one of potential tragedy. The human soul was a battleground of good and evil.

Michel de Montaigne (1533–1592), Shakespeare's great French contemporary, provided a very different and hetero-dox way of thinking about human imperfection. In his

"Apology for Raymond Sebond" and other of his essays, Montaigne questioned the assumption of humanity's superiority to the animal kingdom, and in doing so gave Shakespeare a fundamentally different way to consider the nature of humankind—a way that reflects itself, for example, in Hamlet's observations on humans as "quintessence of dust." Montaigne stressed humans' arrogance, vanity, and frailty. He was unconvinced of humanity's purported moral superiority to the animals and argued that animals are no less endowed with a soul. Montaigne undermined, in other words, the hierarchy in which the human race was the unquestioned master of the physical world, just as Copernican science overturned the earth-centered cosmos and Machiavelli's political system dismissed as an improbable fiction the divinely constituted hierarchy of the state. Montaigne's very choice of the essay as his favorite literary form bespeaks his commitment to attempts and explorations, rather than to definite solutions. Montaigne was not alone in his skepticism about human nature; his ideas had much in common with Bernardino Telesio's *De Rerum Natura* and with the writings of the Italian Giordano Bruno. Montaigne was followed in the seventeenth century by that overpowering iconoclast, Thomas Hobbes, who extended the concept of mechanical laws governing human society and human psychology. Hobbes postdates Shakespeare, to be sure, but one has only to consider Iago's philosophy of the assertive individual will (in *Othello*) or Edmund's contempt for his father Gloucester's astrological pieties (in *King Lear*) to see the enormous impact on Shakespeare of the new heterodoxies of his age. Shakespeare makes us aware that skeptical thought can be used by dangerous men like Iago, Edmund, and Richard III to promote their own villainies in a world no longer held together by the certitudes of traditional faith, but he also shows us the gullibility of some traditionalists and the abuses of power that can be perpetrated in the name of ancient and divine privilege by a king like Richard II. Above all, Shakespeare delights in the play of mind among competing ideas, inviting us to wonder, for example, if Caliban in *The Tempest* is not invested with natural qualities that Prospero, his Christian colonizer, does not sufficiently understand, and whether some of the other supposedly civilized Europeans who come to Caliban's island do not have a great deal to learn from its uncivilized beauty.

The Drama Before Shakespeare

When William Shakespeare made his first acquaintance with the professions of acting and playwriting in the late 1580s, the English theater was already a flourishing institution with a long and complex history. In order to understand what opportunities it offered Shakespeare, we need to look briefly at that history.

The Liturgical Drama

The sixth-century Catholic Church had been largely responsible for closing down the late Roman theater, with its bloody gladiatorial contests and its pervasive moral decadence. Thereafter, for about four centuries the theater officially did not exist in Western Europe. Paradoxically, it was the Church in the tenth century that sponsored the beginnings of a new dramatic form within the liturgy (the prescribed form of worship) of the Church itself. This dramatic activity perhaps began as an insertion into the regular service of a "trope" or musical composition designed to be sung antiphonally by members of a monastic community. The earliest of these may have been composed for Easter morning, at the supremely important moment of Christ's resurrection. The Mass itself had long displayed semidramatic characteristics, and the first Easter expansions must not have seemed particularly revolutionary to anyone involved. The simplest of the early tropes (though perhaps not the first), composed at St. Gall in Switzerland some time early in the tenth century, consists merely of a chanted interrogation, "*Quem quaeritis in sepulchro, Christicolae?*" ("Whom do you seek in the sepulcher, O followers of Christ?"), and a chanted response, "*Jesum Nazarenum crucifixum, o caelicolae*" ("Jesus of Nazareth who was crucified, O heaven-dwellers"), followed by an announcement that Christ is risen as he had predicted. From other early texts of this sort, we can guess that this simple antiphon was accompanied by some stylized semidramatic assignment of roles to members of the religious community as the three Marys visiting Christ's tomb and as the angels guarding the tomb. At any rate, tenth-century tropes of Easter soon included use of simple costume, physical movement toward the tomb, and appropriate gestures.

Other actions were appropriate to such a dramatic representation of the Resurrection: the visit of the disciples to the sepulchre, the appearance of Christ as a gardener to Mary Magdalene, and his appearance to the disciples on the road to Emmaus. Moreover, other seasons of the year afforded similar opportunities, especially Christmas; the crèche was already a venerable custom, and Christmas tropes may have originated as early as Easter tropes or possibly even earlier.

In any event, Christmas liturgical dramatic activity grew apace, perhaps more rapidly than at Easter because of the sacred inhibitions associated with the Resurrection. By the twelfth century, Christmas liturgical drama had become lengthy and complex, including not only the visit of the shepherds and the Magi but also the slaughter of the innocents and the flight into Egypt. Simultaneously, liturgical plays were developed for other festivals in the liturgical calendar. Some were in the vernacular: by the end of the twelfth century, an Anglo-Norman poet had written a play of Adam featuring the creation of humankind, the expulsion from the garden of Eden, the slaughter of Abel by Cain, and

Corpus Christi plays were often performed either in procession on moving pageant wagons or in arena theaters with scaffolds located around the acting area. This illustration shows a procession around a square in Brussels in 1615, using staging methods perhaps not unlike those in use in England during the fifteenth and sixteenth centuries.

a lengthy procession of prophets announcing the advent of Christ. Such early vernacular plays may well have influenced the development of Latin liturgical drama. The twelfth century also saw a play about Daniel in the lions' den, various Saint Nicholas plays in which that popular saint performed miracles, a play at Tegernsee about the Antichrist, a play about the conversion of Saint Paul, and many others. In other words, by 1200 or thereabouts, the liturgical drama had produced plays of considerable length and complexity for numerous religious festivals throughout the year. Montecassino in Italy had a complex Passion play by this date. The late twelfth or early thirteenth century saw the performance at Benediktbeuren in Germany of the impressive "Carmina Burana" plays for Easter and Christmas.

The Corpus Christi Play

Although one might suppose that these liturgical plays would be gathered together into larger cycles of the divine

history of the world, compilations of this sort do not seem generally to have taken place. Liturgical plays continued to be performed individually at appropriate times in the Church calendar. Most religious communities owned and produced one or two such plays year after year, but no communities owned or produced very many such plays. The plays were numerous but scattered throughout Western Europe.

What appears to have happened instead of the forming of liturgical plays into a cycle is that the various craft guilds of certain towns, especially in England, banded together with the ecclesiastical authorities to produce a summer festival that would be both civic and religious in nature. One impetus was the institution of the feast of Corpus Christi in the early fourteenth century. The feast was designed to honor the Eucharist (the sacrament of the Lord's Supper) in a joyous mood, uninhibited by the somber reflections on Christ's crucifixion that are appropriate to Passion Week. The date chosen, the Thursday after Trinity Sunday, came during a slack period in the liturgical calendar in very late spring. In May or June the days of the year are longest, and the English weather is generally cooperative. The cycles that thus originated were performed on other festivals of the early summer season besides Corpus Christi day, but that festival has given its name to the genre.

The feast of Corpus Christi regularly featured elaborate processions through town, and, indeed, these processions may have preceded the plays themselves. Various guilds were usually assigned events in the divine history of the world for which they undertook to present dramatized renditions. The plays written for such guilds had to be numerous in most towns, since there were many guilds: the York cycle, for example, had forty-eight plays; the Towneley cycle (probably) acted at Wakefield), thirty-two; the so-called N-Town or *Ludus Coventriae* cycle (perhaps acted in the vicinity of Lincoln), forty-three. The texts were evidently not translations from the Latin liturgical drama but were English compositions often based on medieval narrative accounts of the divine history of the world. Such versions contained much patristic and legendary material, as well as straightforward biblical narrative; for example, the account of Christ's harrowing of hell, based on the apocryphal Gospel of Saint Thomas rather than on the Bible itself, had become an accepted part of the story. More noncanonical still are accounts of Mary's childhood and of her marriage to Joseph. The cycles varied somewhat as to content, but they tended to choose many of the same traditional stories embodied in Church liturgy. The main figures in these favorite stories—Abel, Noah, Abraham, and Isaac—were often seen as "typological," that is, prefiguring by their piety and suffering the advent of Christ himself.

The common core of most cycles included the following: the creation, the fall of Adam and expulsion from Paradise, Cain's slaying of Abel, Noah's flood, Abraham and Isaac, Moses, the prophets, the annunciation, the visit of the shepherds and the Magi, the flight into Egypt, the slaughter of the innocents, the baptism, the temptation in the wilderness, the raising of Lazarus, the entry into Jerusalem and the entire Passion sequence, the burial, the harrowing of hell, the Resurrection, Christ's appearances to the disciples, his Ascension, and the day of doom. Other subjects were often added, such as the story of Pentecost, the assumption of the blessed Virgin Mary, and the coming of Antichrist.

Sometimes these medieval "pageants" were acted by individual craft guilds on pageant wagons before a series of audiences gathered at fixed locales throughout the town. Recent investigations have shown, however, the formidable difficulties involved in performing a complete cycle of plays in narrow streets, with each pageant having to wait in line until the preceding pageant had finished. Street processions have remained common but may, in some cases, have involved

displays in *tableau vivant* rather than a full performance of each play. Certainly, in some towns the plays themselves were acted, not on pageant wagons, but in the round, in arena theaters with several scaffolds on the periphery or even in the center of the acting area. Scaffolds variously represented Heaven and hell, Pilate's judgment hall, the house of the Last Supper, and the like. In the marketplace or in the cathedral close, the pageants may have been ranged in order about the open space so that the spectators themselves could move from scene to scene. Multiple-place staging certainly existed in London and in the south of England, and was the regular form of the mystery-play stage on the Continent. (The Corpus Christi plays are sometimes called "mystery" plays, since they were acted by the "mystery" or trade guilds.)

As many as twenty full-scope plays, mostly of the Corpus Christi type, may have existed at one time in England, though the complete texts of only four have been preserved. The York, Towneley, and N-Town cycles have already been mentioned; a fourth extant cycle was acted at Chester. In addition, two fragments exist of a cycle acted at Coventry, one each from Norwich and Newcastle-on-Tyne, and several other single scenes from places not located. A Cornish cycle, written in Celtic, presents some Old Testament episodes and a Passion sequence more like certain continental religious dramas than the English plays we have been discussing.

Shakespeare probably saw Corpus Christi plays in his youth, before they were suppressed by Protestant authorities, and he appears to recollect them at times in his plays. When Hamlet says disparagingly of bombastic acting that "it out-herods Herod" (*Hamlet*, 3.2.14), he is thinking of the stage bully of the slaughter of the innocents who, in the Coventry version, "ragis in the pagond [pageant] and in the strete also." Herod was indeed legendary for his rant. The Porter in *Macbeth* is surely alluding to Christ's harrowing of hell when he complains, "But this place is too cold for hell. / I'll devil-porter it no further" (2.3.16–17). The medieval heritage adds a remarkable dimension to this scene: Macbeth's castle becomes a kind of hell, as the Porter jokingly observes, and Macduff's arrival takes on an aspect of deliverance through which Macbeth and his "fiend-like queen" (5.8.70) will be brought to account. Henry V has Herod in mind again in his speech to the beleaguered citizens of Harfleur, when he bids them surrender lest they see their naked infants "spitted upon pikes" and the children's mothers howling in grief "as did the wives of Jewry" At Herod's bloody-hunting slaughtermen" (3.3.38–41). More broadly, the cosmic structure of the cycle plays, bound together in their many episodes by an overarching narrative of divine history, offered a model of construction that Shakespeare would apply in modified form to his writing of English history plays.

Saints' Plays and Morality Plays

Saints' plays were also widely current in England, although few examples survive today. These dramas resembled the Corpus Christi cycles in their staging and their panoramic religious spectacle, but they differed from the cycles in that they told about the lives and miracles of individual saints and martyrs rather than, as in the cycles, telling the entire divine history of the human race as incorporated chiefly in the Old and New Testaments. Some particular cases, to be sure, incorporated features of both saints' lives and Corpus Christi drama. The story of Mary Magdalene, for example, was derived in part from the biblical accounts of her meetings with Christ, but the narrative had been enormously expanded to include legendary reports of her travels and miraculous deeds as a saint. St. Paul was another biblical figure whose sudden conversion and subsequent travels gave to his story the characteristics of a typical saint's life. As a group, however, saints' plays offered more emphasis on miraculous conversion from sin to grace and on the wondrous intervention of saints in the lives of ordinary people than did the Corpus Christi cycles.

Shakespeare's debt to saints' plays is indirect and hard to demonstrate. Some of his history plays reveal a pattern of conversion followed by glorious acts, as in the saga of Henry V, but this story was inherent in the myth of Henry V that Shakespeare inherited. Comedies of repentance, such as *Measure for Measure* and *The Winter's Tale*, show us a pattern of redemptive sorrow and renewal in which the protagonist is given an almost miraculous second chance. Shakespeare's late romances are especially illuminated by this tradition of conversion narratives. We cannot be sure, however, that he encountered such stories through saints' plays (which were suppressed by the English Reformation),

Four allegorical characters in the morality play Hickescorner *were Contemplation, Perseverance, Imagination, and Free Will.*

since nondramatic sources, such as the *Legenda Aurea* or Golden Legend of the lives of the saints, were more immediately available to him.

Shakespeare's awareness of the morality play is easier to prove. Indeed, this genre had survived well enough into the late sixteenth century to make a significant impact on the plays of Shakespeare, Ben Jonson, and others. The morality play chose as its distinctive mode the allegorical rendition of humanity's spiritual journey through life to an eventual preparation for death and judgment before God. Allegory was not unknown in the cycles or in the saints' plays, but it became the staple of the morality play. The earliest texts, from the sixteenth century, include *The Castle of Perseverance, Mankind,* and *Everyman.* Although the last of these focuses atypically on the moment of death, more typical early morality plays tell a story of spiritual struggle and eventual triumph over sin. This simple plot had an advantage over the cycles and saints' plays in that it could be adapted to the religious and social controversies of the era. The Corpus Christi cycles and saints' plays were, after all, tied to biblical or legendary events; when Reformation authorities sought to suppress the "idolatrous" representation of God on stage or banned worship of the Virgin Mary and the saints, the cycles and saints' plays were doomed. Even though they were occasionally staged late enough in the sixteenth century for Shakespeare to have seen performances, they belonged chiefly to an earlier, pre-Reformation era. The morality play, on the other hand, thrived on controversy. Its plot of soul struggle between the forces of good and evil for the allegiance of Mankind or Everyman, and his wavering progress toward eventual salvation, could and did frequently serve as a vehicle for portraying many social phenomena of the sixteenth century.

In John Skelton's political morality play called *Magnificence* (1515–1518), for example, the protagonist is a representative king figure who must choose between evil counselors urging fiscal extravagance on the one hand and wise counselors urging fiscal prudence on the other hand. The plot, telling of the king's temptation and his choosing of the wrong path before he is finally awakened to his folly, is essentially that of nonpolitical morality plays, such as *Hickescorner* or *Youth* (c. 1513–1520), in which the human protagonist inevitably succumbs to temptation but is eventually rescued through divine guidance. The issues in Skelton's play have embraced secular as well as spiritual concerns, while the simple story line and the dramatic structure have remained virtually unchanged. The study of a "historical" type, in this case a king, enables a play to comment on contemporary history and yet appeal simultaneously to a universal moral pattern. Skelton's play may allude indirectly to the fiscal recklessness of Henry VIII under Cardinal Wolsey's persuasive tutelage, but it discusses fiscal responsibility in general terms that also apply to any king—or to any human. Shakespeare's English history plays, especially the early plays about Henry VI and Richard III, owe an important debt to the tradition of the political morality, as exemplified by *Magnificence*.

Shakespeare's history play *King John* studies a king who had actually been the protagonist of the first play to represent an English monarch, *King Johan*, by John Bale (1538, later revised). Although Shakespeare may not have consulted Bale's play directly, Bale still had made an impressive contribution to the English history play by demonstrating how the morality structure could be used in the analysis of political crises. His play is an avowedly Protestant tract in the guise of a morality play, depicting its historical protagonist as a victim of Catholic duplicity and hence an example of what sixteenth-century England had to fear from its Catholic enemies. Later popular plays, combining a morality structure with a passionate interest in history and contemporary political theory, include Thomas Preston's *Cambises* (1560–1561) and John Pickering's *Horestes* (1567).

During the Reformation, the morality play was used polemically by both the Protestants and the Catholics. Dramatists were often commissioned by governmental authorities to write plays for public performance by touring actors as weapons of ideological persuasion. In Protestant plays, such as *Lusty Juventus* (c. 1547–1553) or *New Custom* (c. 1570), the villainous Vices were depicted as Catholic tempters; in Catholic plays, such as *Respublica* (1553), during the reign of Queen Mary), the Vices were Protestant. The protean flexibility of the morality formula enabled it to adapt itself to many different situations in this way. Polemical drama put ideology ahead of artistic concern, to be sure, but constant experimentation with new forms provided the popular drama of midcentury England with much-needed practical experience. One permutation

of the Reformation morality play, for example, proved of considerable importance to the development of English tragedy. In some Protestant morality plays that Calvinistically stress humankind's innate depravity, such as William Wager's *Enough Is as Good as a Feast* (c. 1559–1570) and Nathaniel Woodes' *The Conflict of Conscience* (1570–1581), spiritual struggle ends in failure rather than in triumph for the human protagonist. Among the great English tragedies of the late sixteenth century, Christopher Marlowe's *Doctor Faustus* (c. 1588) is most obviously indebted to such dramatic renditions of spiritual despair, but Shakespeare's *Macbeth* and other plays may also have learned something from a native homiletic tradition in tragedy.

In staging and acting, as well, the morality play served as an important transition from late medieval religious drama to the drama of the late sixteenth century. In its origins, as seen, for example, in *The Castle of Perseverance* (early fifteenth century), the morality play had been staged like many of the cycles or saints' plays, such as *Mary Magdalene*, in the round, with an open acting area surrounded by acting scaffolds on the periphery. The morality play developed great flexibility in its staging, however, just as it had developed flexibility in its approach to contemporary political or social issues. *Mankind* (c. 1471) required only an

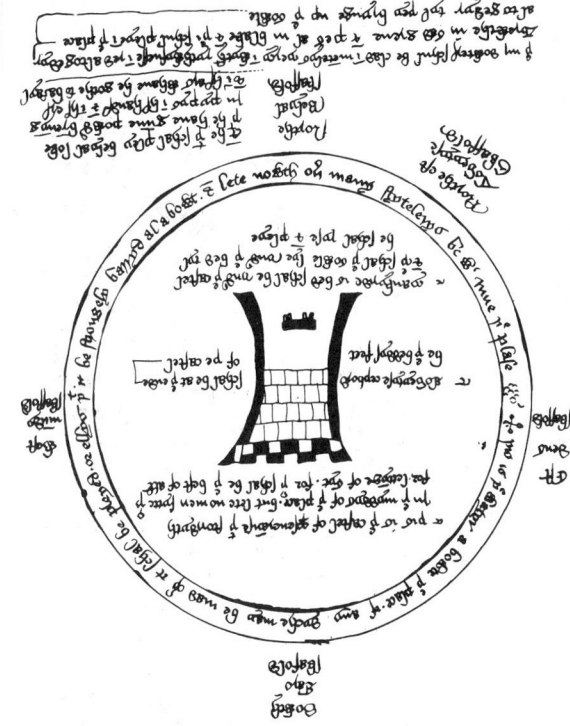

A fifteenth-century diagram for the presentation of The Castle of Perseverance shows the scaffolds surrounding the open acting area with the castle in the center.

This so-called Flower Portrait of Shakespeare is based on the Droeshout engraving.

This seventeenth-century painting by an unknown artist shows London as a thriving metropolis. The many boats on the Thames are evidence of the vital role the river played in the city's emergence as a center for international as well as national trade.

A seventeenth-century watercolor based on Claes Janszoon de Visscher's View of London *shows the Globe theater on the south bank of the Thames, a short distance west of London Bridge. In the vicinity were the competing Rose and Swan, making this area the leading theater district of London.*

Social classes and fashions in Shakespeare's England were clearly defined. People were required by law to dress according to their station. Shown here are an artisan, carrying a tool; a gaudily dressed woman, attired beyond her appointed station; and a "gentleman," privileged to wear his apparel.

This picture of the life of Sir Henry Unton (1557?-1596), probably commissioned by his widow, shows the important events of his life: his birth (we see him in his mother's arms, lower right); his life as a student at Oxford (above right); his travels to Europe and his expedition to the Netherlands under the command of the Earl of Leicester (top center); various scenes in Wadley House, his residence, including a feast with masquers in festive dress led in procession by Diana and Mercury; and finally his death and burial (lower left).

Few monarchs have ever influenced an age so pervasively and left their stamp on it so permanently as did Elizabeth I during her reign from 1558 to 1603. Elizabeth is celebrated in this portrait that commemorates the defeat of the Spanish Armada in 1588.

James I, who reigned in England from 1603 until 1625, gave his name to one of the most creative periods in the history of all theater—Jacobean drama. The word "Jacobean" is derived from Jacobus, the Latin word for James.

Chief dramatic rival for public acclaim during Shakespeare's later years was Ben Jonson, poet, playwright, critic, and literary high priest. The First Folio of 1623 contains a poetic eulogy of Shakespeare written by Jonson.

Edward Alleyn was a leading Elizabethan actor who was famous in the roles of Tamburlaine and Faustus. A rival of Shakespeare, he was active in the Admiral's men and Lord Strange's men. Alleyn was also the founder of Dulwich College.

Shakespeare presumably studied at Stratford grammar school, though the records have not survived. The school is shown here with the Pedagogue's House on the right.

The many conceptions of A Midsummer Night's Dream *through the years attest to the play's continual popularity. William Blake, the famous Romantic poet and artist, catches the fanciful and dreamlike flavor of the play in his engraving of the meeting of Oberon, Titania, Puck, and attendant fairies.*

In Peter Brook's famous production of A Midsummer Night's Dream, *the fairy queen Titania, under the spell of a love potion, embraces the weaver, Bottom, whom Puck has mischievously given an ass's ears and a clown's nose. This British production reflects a distinctly contemporary interpretation of the play.*

The English history play owed much to the excitement of the Armada Era. The English defeat of the Spanish Armada in 1588 came about two years before Shakespeare began writing his Henry VI plays. The Henry VI plays helped to establish the vogue of the English history play, which was to flourish throughout the decade to follow. Shakespeare dramatized the historic struggles of the Plantagenet, Lancastrian, and Yorkish families and showed the eventual triumph of the Tudors.

Certainly one of the greatest characters in Shakespeare's history plays is Sir John Falstaff. The nineteenth-century painting by Sir John Gilbert shows Falstaff reviewing his ragged troops from Act III of 2 Henry IV.

Elizabeth I was so taken by the comic character of Falstaff that she is believed to have ordered to see him in love. Falstaff is hidden in a clothes basket by Mrs. Ford and Mrs. Page in The Merry Wives of Windsor, *a comedy written for the Queen.*

Olivia Hussey and Leonard Whiting portrayed the star-crossed lovers Romeo and Juliet in Franco Zeffirelli's 1968 film. This very popular film production was the object of serious critical attention.

The faithful Earl of Kent (Colin Blakely), disguised as Caius, apprehensively watches over the mad King Lear (Laurence Olivier) during the storm in Granada Television's King Lear *(1983).*

Hamlet (Mel Gibson) turns on Ophelia (Helena Bonham-Carter) in Act 3 of Franco Zeffirelli's film version of Hamlet *(1990).*

Shylock (Dustin Hoffman) defiantly holds aloft the bond that entitles him to cut a pound of flesh nearest the heart of the merchant Antonio (Leigh Lawson) and brandishes the knife he intends to use. Peter Hall's production of The Merchant of Venice played on Broadway in January and February 1990, after having opened in London the previous season.

Henry V (Kenneth Branagh), exhausted yet triumphant after his victory over the French at the Battle of Agincourt, surveys the carnage of war amid his devoted followers in Act 4 of Branagh's film version of Henry V (1989).

Kate (Tracey Ullman) responds tempestuously to the broncobusting tactics of her wooer, Petruchio (Morgan Freeman), in A. J. Antoon's Central Park production for the New York Shakespeare Festival of The Taming of the Shrew as set in the American wild West of the late nineteenth century (1990).

Caius Marcius (Ian McKellen), about to be glorified with the surname "Coriolanus" for his triumph over the army of Aufidius at Corioles, is hoisted aloft by his triumphant soldiers in Act 1 of Peter Hall's Coriolanus at the National Theatre, London, in 1985.

acting platform, raised probably on trestles to a height of four or five feet, and a curtain backdrop through which the actors could enter and exit. A stage of this simplicity could be carried anywhere in England and set up at a moment's notice—on a village green, in a town hall, or in the banqueting hall of a lord's manor. The troupe acting *Mankind* was vastly more efficient and transportable than the company of twenty-two or more actors required for *The Castle of Perseverance; Mankind* required only six actors.

Troupes of four or five men and one boy apprentice (for women's roles) were quite standard in early Tudor England. Similar or even smaller troupes enacted folk plays and miracle plays, the texts of which are regrettably not as extensively preserved as those of morality plays. Such troupes traveled the length and breadth of the country, and dominated the field of popular entertainment from the late fifteenth century until Shakespeare's day. They were, in fact, the professional ancestors of the Shakespearean acting company. Under the direction of their leading player, who often acted the part of Vice since it was usually the choice role of the morality play, the actors were organized as repertory companies able to perform a number of plays on short notice and to present a remarkably large number of roles by the doubling of parts. They grew slowly in size as they prospered, but they retained their traditional organization. The best of the troupes gravitated to London, where, in 1576, a troupe of perhaps six or eight men and two boys founded England's first permanent theater. Shakespeare's company, the Lord Chamberlain's men (later the King's men), was only slightly larger than this, with perhaps ten actors who were partners or "sharers" in the company, two or more boys, and a few hired hands. Shakespeare's early plays, moreover, were sometimes structured for presentation by just such a company, much as earlier popular plays had been structured, with considerable doubling of parts and with a multiplicity of episodes allowing for the sequential presentation of numerous minor roles. The early history plays about Henry VI and Richard III are especially illustrative of this structural tradition.

Shakespeare's references to morality drama suggest a real familiarity. Prince Hal jestingly caricatures Falstaff as "that roasted Manningtree ox with the pudding in his belly, that reverend Vice, that grey iniquity, that father ruffian, that vanity in years . . . that old whitebearded Satan" (*1 Henry IV,* 2.4.447–458). Manningtree in Essex appears to have been renowned for its annual fair at which plays were acted and great-sized oxen were roasted; the Vice, as we have seen, was the chief comic tempter of most morality plays. Falstaff himself refers to the Vice's traditional dagger of lath in his contemptuous remarks about Justice Shallow: "And now is this Vice's dagger become a squire" (*2 Henry IV,* 3.2.317–318). Feste, in *Twelfth Night,* exits at one point with a promise to the audience that he will return soon "Like to the old Vice" with his "dagger of lath" and "his rage and his wrath" (4.2.120–131). Kent, in *King Lear,* speaks of

Goneril as having taken "Vanity the puppet's part against the royalty of her father" (2.2.36–37), as though she were a personified representation of pride in a morality play. The evocation of that genre strengthens our perception that good and evil are indeed battling over Lear's destiny on a cosmic scale. Richard III explicitly compares himself to "the formal Vice, Iniquity" in his use of sinister double entendres and his boasting to the audience of his cleverness (3.1.82–83).

Shakespeare's specific references to late medieval drama are less important, however, than his larger indebtedness to it. His use of a structural tradition of episodic multiplicity and of alternation between seriousness and comedy is especially evident in the early history plays. Of equal significance is his indebtedness to the Vice, the comic tempter of the morality play whose sinister but fascinating techniques of evil persuasion had become an enduring part of Tudor popular drama. The Vice's boastful and chortling brand of villainy is still clearly recognizable, though transmuted into superb poetry, in the insinuations of Richard III, Aaron the Moor (in *Titus Andronicus*), Iago (in *Othello*), and Edmund (in *King Lear*). As Bernard Spivack has argued, in his *Shakespeare and the Allegory of Evil,* Shakespeare's poetic vision of the contest between good and evil for human souls owes much to the morality tradition and to other forms of medieval drama.

Early Tudor Humanist Drama

The development of the morality play and of other medieval drama, briefly sketched in the preceding sections, tells only one part of the story of sixteenth-century drama. The trend we have observed in morality drama, toward the depiction of contemporary English life, manifested itself also in other kinds of plays that were not so plainly derived from the religious drama of the Middle Ages. A relatively new influence was that of classical and neoclassical drama, from the ancient classical world and from Renaissance Europe. Important, too, were the secular kinds of dramatic entertainment that had flourished in the English court even before the advent of neoclassicism. Early Tudor drama for courtly and well-educated audiences was heterogeneous because it reflected so many diverse impulses: the intensified renewal of classical learning that had come about through the activities of the new humanists, the ferment of ideologies introduced by the Reformation, the increase in social mobility in the Tudor court, and the like. In varying proportions, the courtly and intellectual drama of the period borrowed from the English morality play, from courtly pastimes such as the "disguising" (a kind of masque) and the dialogue or *débat,* from secular farce and romance, from classical and neoclassical literature, and even from the Corpus Christi cycles and saints' plays. The mixture, experimental and often uneven, was nonetheless stimulating, because it attempted to fuse English culture with that of neoclassical Europe.

The dramatists who associated themselves with the great humanist Sir Thomas More and with his patron Cardinal Morton shared many humanist ideals that can be seen in their plays. Henry Medwall, chaplain to Cardinal Morton, wrote a morality play called *Nature* (c. 1490–1501) that reveals an interest in Aristotelian ethics, as well as in traditional Christian ideas of salvation. Medwall also wrote *Fulgens and Lucrece* (c. 1490–1500), the earliest extant play in England to use an ancient Roman setting and a secular romantic love plot. The heroine, Lucrece, chooses the love of a virtuous but untitled "new" man at court in preference to a haughty and degenerate aristocrat. This *débat* was derived from *De Vera Nobilitate* by Buonaccorso of Pistoia, an ardent Italian humanist. Despite its ancient setting and romantic plot, it is also unmistakably relevant to the struggle between "new" men and old aristocrats in the court of Henry VII. Both of Medwall's plays were printed by John Rastell, another humanist in the service of Cardinal Morton. Rastell, who married More's sister, wrote a humanist interlude called *The Nature of the Four Elements* (c. 1517–1518), in which he excitedly discussed the latest scientific theories concerning the roundness of the world and other such new ideas. He is probably the author of *Of Gentleness and Nobility* (c. 1527–1530) as well, a play that iconoclastically asks whether monarchy and the inheritance of property are not social evils that ideally ought to be abolished. The influence of Thomas More's *Utopia* on this play is unmistakable.

John Heywood, son-in-law of John Rastell, was the most important and versatile dramatist of the humanist group. All his plays, except *Witty and Witless,* which has been preserved in manuscript, were printed by John Rastell or his son, William Rastell. Heywood's plays fall into two groups: the courtly disputations, such as *The Play of Love, The Play of the Weather,* and *Witty and Witless* (c. 1525–1533), and the more popular farces that may have been intended for popular audiences as well, such as *The Pardoner and the Friar, The Four PP,* and *John John the Husband* (c. 1513–1533). In the first group, *Weather* reveals a characteristic attention to humanist and courtly themes. In an obvious analogy to the Tudor concept of an absolutist yet benevolent monarchy, the various petitioners of the play complain to Jupiter about the weather but are finally persuaded to be grateful for the mixed weather that is provided them. Heywood is suggesting, in other words, that the English monarchy must bestow its favors impartially on all classes of persons and that all subjects ought to recognize the essential soundness of the social order as it presently exists. Heywood's second group of plays, on the other hand, eschews such courtly and political themes for a broader slapstick comedy in the vein of Chaucerian fabliau and French farce.

In addition to these humanist plays written by members of the Sir Thomas More circle, the learned drama of early Tudor England included many plays written for schoolboys or for the choristers attached to royal and noble households. The plays written under such auspices tended to reveal a much stronger interest in classical and neoclassical drama than did the plays written for popular audiences. Schoolmasters wrote dramatic texts derived from the classics for educational purposes; at court, sophisticated audiences were interested in the latest dramatic fashions from Italy or France. Ancient Greek drama did not receive nearly so much attention, however, as the Latin drama of Terence, Plautus, and Seneca. These Latin authors had long been used as schoolboys' texts, though they were frequently expurgated or allegorized into the terms of Christian morality in order to render them suitable for schoolboys' sensibilities. This academic tradition, on the Continent and in England, produced a number of imitative plays that could be acted by boys as part of their training in classical languages. Some plays, such as John Palsgrave's *Acolastus* (1540), were intended to be read rather than acted. Many others were Latin biblical plays in classical guise, such as Thomas Watson's *Absalom* (c. 1535–1544) and George Buchanan's *Jephthes* (1540–1545).

At court and in noble households, choristers were becoming noted for their acting ability. They performed chiefly during seasons of revels, such as in the Christmas season. They did not appear commercially before public audiences during the early Tudor period, as did the players of moralities and popular interludes. The Children of the Royal Chapel are known to have presented plays as early as 1506. The boys of St. Paul's School acted before King Henry VIII in 1528. Later, in the 1570s and 1580s, these children's groups were organized into professional acting companies. Children's plays were generally written by schoolmasters or choirmasters. The plays were heavily influenced by continental traditions and often depicted themes, such as that of the Prodigal Son, that were congenial to boys of school age. *Nice Wanton* (1547–1553) offers an instance of this sort. Biblical themes were common and were sometimes used to urge a political lesson in the presence of a courtly audience. *Godly Queen Hester* (1525–1529), for example, seems to defend the cause of Katharine of Aragon and to denounce the machinations of Cardinal Wolsey. *Jacob and Esau* (1547–1553) draws an unflattering comparison between the unregenerate Esau and those who refuse to abandon the Catholic faith. Classical subjects were, of course, much in demand as a way of educating youth, as in *Appius and Virginia* (1559–1567) and in Richard Edwards' *Damon and Pythias* (c. 1565).

Early Comedy

Schoolboys' drama was also vitally important in the development of classical or "regular" comedy on the English stage. Native morality drama was often highly comic, to be sure, especially in its depiction of the resourceful and scheming Vice; but English drama still had much to learn

Early Tudor drama employed the talents of boy actors on stage such as this company, the Children of the Royal Chapel.

from classical example about play construction and about the presentation of various types of characters. Perhaps the two best-known early English "regular" comedies were *Ralph Roister Doister* and *Gammer Gurton's Needle.*

Ralph Roister Doister, by Nicholas Udall, at one time headmaster of Eton, was acted probably between 1552 and 1554 by boy actors. Its staging is essentially that of Latin comedy, with two houses facing onto a street. The play employs a classical five-act structure and preserves the unities of time and place. (According to classical and neoclassical theory, a play's action should be limited to one location—a city, for example—and to a single day.) Stock comic types include the *miles gloriosus,* or braggart soldier, and the parasite. At the same time, Udall has transformed his heroine, usually a courtesan in Plautus' racy comedies, into a winsomely pious Englishwoman named Christian Custance. Ralph Roister Doister, the braggardly type for whom the play is named, is foiled in his mean-spirited determination to win Christian Custance away from her true love, Gawin Goodluck. Almost all the characters virtuously conspire to expose Ralph for his effrontery and pretended bravery; even Matthew Merrygreek, the fun-loving parasite, proves ultimately to be on the side of decency and fair play. Throughout, Udall has adapted Roman comedy to English customs and mores.

Gammer Gurton's Needle, written by William Stevenson, fellow of Christ's College, Cambridge, at about the same time as *Roister Doister,* is similarly designed for student acting. Stock Roman characters are transformed into hearty English types. Diccon the Bedlam, who engineers the farcical action of the lost needle, resembles not only the Roman parasite but also the English natural fool or zany. To some extent, he also reminds us of the mischievous and inventive Vice of the morality play. Other characters are even less purely Roman in their origin: Hodge, the clownish servant; Dame Chat, the shrewish neighbor; and Dr. Rat, the impoverished and ill-trained clergyman who spends most of his time drinking and complaining about his wretched lot. The play is an educated college man's

indulgent laugh at his country neighbors. Yet the play is, like *Ralph Roister Doister,* classically structured into five acts, with a single stage setting that preserves the unities of time and place.

In 1566, the members of Gray's Inn saw a production of George Gascoigne's *Supposes,* translated from the Italian of Ariosto (1509). Because it was a translation and not an English adaptation, this play preserves essentially in their original form the stock character types of neoclassical comedy: the parasite, the pantaloon or miserly aged rival in love, the overly watchful father, the clever servant, the bawdy nurse, and so on. The heroine, though no longer a Roman courtesan, as in Plautus, is nonetheless a self-possessed and sophisticated young woman who conducts a secret affair for some time without being detected by her father. The mores of this continental play must have seemed challengingly cosmopolitan to its fashionable courtly and intellectual audience. Just as importantly, the play offered graceful prose language as its medium, rather than the homely English verse of *Ralph Roister Doister* and *Gammer Gurton's Needle. Supposes* provided a new model for neoclassical comedy and was to become (with some of its continental morality anglicized) a source for Shakespeare's *The Taming of the Shrew.* Indeed, Shakespeare learned much about play construction, dialogue, and characterization from neoclassical comedies of this sort; perhaps his earliest comedy, *The Comedy of Errors,* owes a great deal to Plautus and to neoclassical imitators of that Latin comic writer. Another early Italian comedy in English, *The Bugbears,* was adapted from Grazzini's *La Spiritata* and acted in about 1563–1565 by boy actors.

Early Tragedy

In early English tragedy, as in early comedy, native and neoclassical traditions coalesced and sometimes clashed. Native conceptions of tragedy had partly originated in two great medieval commonplaces: the "wheel of fortune" and the "fall of princes." Both were incorporated in Chaucer's

"The Monk's Tale" and its source, Boccaccio's *De Casibus Virorum Illustrium*, which presented moral examples from the lives of famous men. Chaucer had defined "tragedy" as the story of a great person "that stood in greet prosperitee, / And is yfallen out of heigh degree / Into myserie, and endeth wrecchedly." His examples, taken from Boccaccio, included Lucifer, Adam, Samson, Hercules, Julius Caesar, and others. These were men or evil beings who had either fallen through sinful pride or had been brought low through the inevitable turn of fortune's wheel. Both types of tragedy illustrated to the medieval mind the folly of trusting to worldly expectations. The "fall of princes" tradition was extended into Elizabethan times through John Lydgate's Chaucerian imitation, *The Fall of Princes,* and its Tudor sequel *A Mirror for Magistrates* (1559, with many subsequent revisions and enlargements). The morality play contributed a pattern similar to that of Satan's tragic fall through pride; and, although the mankind figure of early morality plays invariably was recovered to God's grace by the end of the play, some early Elizabethan Calvinistic moralities (such as *Enough Is as Good as a Feast* or *The Longer Thou Livest the More Fool Thou Art*) featured human protagonists who were eternally damned. As we have already seen, Elizabethan moralities of this sort anticipated the tragic pattern of Marlowe's *Doctor Faustus.*

Native traditions of tragedy evolved quite independent of classical tragic drama and were, in some ways, strikingly different from it. Christian morality often served as a major explanation of the cause of tragic fall in medieval tragedy. Moreover, the focus was broad and cosmic, as in *Doctor Faustus.* Scenes of comic depravity alternated with scenes of tragic seriousness, especially in the morality plays. Classical tragedy, on the other hand, usually focused on a moment of crisis in the protagonist's life and presented this crisis in its full, tragic intensity without the undercutting of comic effect. In classical tragedy generally, narrative interest was subordinated to dramatic or lyrical interest. Unity of action, as understood by Renaissance theorists of drama, necessarily included unity of time and place. Thus, the gap between native and classical tragedy was potentially vast.

Perhaps the earliest classical tragedy in England was Thomas Norton and Thomas Sackville's *Gorboduc,* presented before Queen Elizabeth at Whitehall on January 18, 1562. The play attempted to offer Queen Elizabeth political advice on the need for naming a Protestant successor, by way of cautionary example in the fratricidal strife between Gorboduc's two sons. Although Sir Philip Sidney later complained about the play's violation of the unities in the fifth act, he praised it otherwise as "an exact model of all tragedies." To be sure, native concepts of tragedy are observable in *Gorboduc,* especially in its use of an ancient British setting and in its moral and Christian explanations of the causes of tragedy. Nevertheless, the classical element predominates.

This classical element is basically Senecan. Ancient Greek tragedy was relatively unknown to Elizabethan England except through Seneca's Roman adaptations. Seneca's ten plays were all translated into English by 1581 and had long been read in the schools as models of rhetoric (just as Terence and Plautus were also read). Seneca's plays were, in fact, closet dramas, intended to be recited rather than acted. Seneca provided *Gorboduc* with a model for its long declamatory speeches, its occasional passages of stichomythia (rapid one-line exchange of dialogue), its five-act structure punctuated by dumb shows, and its supernatural agents prognosticating doom. Moreover, *Gorboduc*'s blank verse, created to approximate the Latin meters of Seneca, set a style for blank verse tragedy that dominated the English stage throughout Shakespeare's career. (Blank verse had been used shortly before *Gorboduc* by the Earl of Surrey in his translations from Virgil's *Aeneid,* but never before in drama.) *Gorboduc* also made an important contribution to the English history play by its use of chronicle materials in a tragic setting.

Other Senecan plays followed, written at first for gentlemanly audiences of the universities and the Inns of Court, rather than for the popular stage. One such was George Gascoigne's *Jocasta* (1566). In 1588, eight gentlemen of Gray's Inn, including Thomas Hughes and Francis Bacon, presented before the Queen a drama similar in form to *Gorboduc,* called *The Misfortunes of Arthur.* This tragedy borrows from Seneca not only chorus, messengers, and machinery but also ideas, sentiments, and words. Like *Gorboduc, The Misfortunes of Arthur* is somewhat free with the classical unities. Also, it is based upon the chronicle history of Britain, which was to become one of the chief sources of subject matter for English tragedy.

Another principal source for tragic writers was the Italian short story, which, because it was also impassioned and serious, offered to writers of tragedy many themes. *Gismond of Salerne* dramatizes a well-known Italian tale and, like *Gorboduc* and *The Misfortunes of Arthur,* is Senecan in form and nature. It was acted before the Queen in 1566 or 1568. In the same storehouse of narrative, Shakespeare was later to find his sources for *Romeo and Juliet* and *Othello,* as well as for such comedies as *The Merchant of Venice* and *Measure for Measure.*

Sir Philip Sidney as Dramatic Critic

The kind of tragedy that Shakespeare and other popular dramatists wrote in the late sixteenth and early seventeenth centuries is not rigorously classical. It preserves many of the elements of English tragedy already enumerated: a broad narrative focus, frequent violations or total ignoring of the classical unities of time and place, the inclusion of comedy, and the like. Tragedy of this sort might never have developed in England to so high a point or might never have been accepted as the prevailing form of tragedy but for two things: in the first place, few Elizabethan dramatists learned their craft by studying the classical rules; in the second place, the Elizabethan audience, with a taste for native English drama, demanded new, varied, and sensational plots, accompanied by vaudeville clownery and songs. Such popular drama was often condemned by those critics who were familiar with classical literature, but to have made English tragedy conform with classical rules would have meant changing its nature. In France, where in Shakespeare's time the drama came under the control of the court and the learned classes, tragedy developed according to classical rules into the drama of Corneille and Racine; in England, on the other hand, Shakespeare and his contemporaries created a kind of tragedy particularly their own.

The most famous classical critic of the age, Sir Philip Sidney, took vigorous exception to the kind of tragedy in vogue during the 1580s. His views are set forth in *The Defence of Poesy,* written in 1581 or slightly later:

> Our tragedies and comedies not without cause cried out against, observing rules neither of honest civility nor skillful poetry, excepting *Gorboduc*—again I say of those that I have seen. Which notwithstanding as it is full of stately speeches and well-sounding phrases, climbing to the height of Seneca his style, and as full of notable morality, which it doth most delightfully teach, and so obtain the very end of poesy, yet in truth it is very defective in the circumstances, which grieves me, because it might not remain as an exact model of all tragedies. For it is faulty both in place and time, the two necessary companions of all corporal actions. For where the stage should alway represent but one place, and the uttermost time presupposed in it should be, both by Aristotle's precept and common reason, but one day, there is both many days and many places inartificially imagined.
>
> But if it be so in *Gorboduc,* how much more in all the rest? where you shall have Asia of the one side and Afric of the other, and so many other under-kingdoms, that the player, when he comes in, must ever begin with telling where he is, or else the tale will not be conceived. Now you shall have three ladies walk to gather flowers, and then we must believe the stage to be a garden. By and by we hear news of shipwreck in the same place; then we are to blame if we accept it not for a rock. Upon the back of that comes out a hideous monster with fire and smoke, and then the miserable beholders are bound to take it for a cave. While in the meantime two armies fly in, represented with four swords and bucklers, and then what hard heart will not receive it for a pitched field?
>
> Now of time they are much more liberal. For ordinary it is that two young princes fall in love; after many traverses she is got with child, delivered of a fair boy; he is lost, groweth a man, falleth in love, and is ready to get another child,—and all this in two hours space; which how absurd it is in sense even sense may imagine, and art hath taught, and all ancient examples justified, and at this day the ordinary players in Italy will not err in. . . .

Later he tells us that English plays are "neither right tragedies nor right comedies"; instead, they mingle clowns and kings with "neither decency nor discretion."

To be sure, Sidney's criticism is never narrowly classical; in the essay as a whole, he affirms the power of the artist to range freely in the world of wit and imagination and to create artifacts that are more universally "true" than either philosophy or history. At the same time, his strictures against the contemporary English stage do invoke classical ideals of unity that many dramatists and audiences ignored. Popular audiences of the time seem to have had no more difficulty imagining the lapse of twenty years than the lapse of two hours. Nor were they troubled by scenic shifts from one continent to another, or by shifts in tone from the comic to the pathetic, the grotesque, or the tragic. Because native English drama had never paid much attention to classical precept, it worked out its own sense of cohesion according to different criteria of multiplicity, alternating effects, sudden juxtapositions, typological recurrence, and the like.

John Lyly, George Peele, and Robert Greene

In facing the problem of understanding just what Elizabethan drama was and how it became what it was, we must recognize that the classification of drama into comedy and tragedy by the ancients does not tell the whole story. Even when we add the history or chronicle play to these two divisions of drama, we have, at best, a rough classification that leaves out a great deal and implies that these three forms were sharply discriminated. In fact, Elizabethan drama is, generally speaking, a blend of many elements. Nearly all Elizabethan tragedies have in them comic scenes and by-plots; most comedies have in them serious issues that might conceivably result in disaster; and history plays are often capable of being classified as comedies or as tragedies. To appreciate further this protean quality of genre in early Elizabethan drama, we might consider the varied works of a number of dramatists whose practice was successful on the stage and who influenced Shakespeare and his immediate contemporaries. Of these, John Lyly is one of the most important.

John Lyly (1554?–1606), grandson of the grammarian William Lyly or Lilly, educated at Oxford and Cambridge, first acquired fame not as a dramatist, but as a writer of prose. His *Euphues, The Anatomy of Wit,* published in 1578, and its sequel, *Euphues and His England* (1580), stand as the most sensational and brilliant effort in the struggle of English Renaissance prose to acquire a conscious artistic manner. The style is, to a remarkable extent, composed of rhetorical devices: antithesis, personification, rhetorical question, metaphor, simile, and, above all, balance reinforced by alliteration. Recondite tidbits and fanciful legends about natural history are garnered from Plutarch, Pliny, and many other writers. The overall result is a kind of handbook for the courtier, the lover, the traveler, and the statesman. Lyly's deliberately outrageous style was imitated by dozens of other writers, including Robert Greene and Thomas Lodge, and seems to have set a new fashion of smart speech in the court of Queen Elizabeth. "Euphuism" itself had a vast influence on the style of the drama and other literature, both in poetry and in prose. Shakespeare is one of those who imitated and also ridiculed euphuistic speech. (For amusing examples of Shakespeare's parodying of the euphuistic style, see Falstaff's speech in *1 Henry IV*, 2.4.397 ff., beginning "for though the camomile, the more it is trodden on the faster it grows, yet youth, the more it is wasted the sooner it wears," or Don Armado's love letter in *Love's Labor's Lost*, 4.1.61 ff.: "Shall I command thy love? I may. Shall I enforce thy love? I could. Shall I entreat thy love? I will," and so on.)

Lyly was also the author of at least eight comedies, written to suit the taste of the court and possibly all acted before the Queen by the children of the Chapel Royal or of St. Paul's School. The plays are often courtly debates in the tradition of Medwall's *Fulgens and Lucrece*, with much combat of wits and philosophical argument. These comedies are also sufficiently modeled on Plautus or Terence to indicate that the characteristic features of Latin comedy by this time (1580–1590) had become naturalized on the English stage. *Mother Bombie*, for example, is an adaptation of Latin comedy, containing such stock figures as the pedant, the rascally servant, the duped parent, the parasite, and the aged lover, although, as usual, in Lyly the clownery has an English flavor as well.

Indeed, however much Lyly may recall classical Latin comedy, he is most important as the inventor of a gay and fanciful type of love comedy to which Shakespeare was significantly indebted in several of his plays. Lyly's *Sappho and Phao, Endymion*, and *Midas* have romantic plots derived from Ovidian mythology. *Gallathea* uses a pastoral setting for its love story and male disguises for the heroines, as in *As You Like It*. *Love's Metamorphosis* and *The Woman in the Moon* are also pastoral comedies. *Campaspe*, like *The Merchant of Venice*, portrays conflicts of love and friendship. Lyly's flattery of Queen Elizabeth through topical allegory and his appeal to a courtly clientele are, to be sure, modes that Shakespeare does not generally adopt. On the other hand, Shakespeare learned a good deal from Lyly's sensitive portrayal of the psychology of love. The depiction is often wryly comic: Lyly's men abase themselves before women, vacillate between idealization and misogyny, and not infrequently fail as wooers—much as the young lords do in Shakespeare's most Lylyan play, *Love's Labor's Lost*. Shakespeare's lovers generally work toward a more successful and realistic completion of romantic expectations, but Shakespeare's interest in love comedy began, in part, with what Lyly had achieved.

George Peele (1558?–1597) was also active as a dramatist around the time that Shakespeare first came to London. Peele's *The Arraignment of Paris* (1581) offers a quality of blank verse not previously seen in comedy and shows how classical legend could be adapted to a thoroughly English celebration of the nation and its Queen. *The Old Wives' Tale* (c. 1588–1594) is a seemingly naive but actually skillful medley of folk legends in the spirit of popular romance. *David and Bethsabe* (c. 1581–1594) dramatizes a familar biblical narrative in terms of erotic love and kingly power. Peele also contributed importantly to the new and burgeoning genre of the English history play with his *Edward I* (1590–1593); it is, like other history plays of the Armada era, jingoistically anti-Spanish and features a popular folk-hero king who understands and respects the proud local customs of his people. *The Battle of Alcazar* (1588–1589), another play of the Armada era, revels in the exotic world of Africa and the Middle East, in the vaunting heroic vein of Christopher Marlowe's *Tamburlaine*. Peele also devised two London civic pageants.

Robert Greene (1558–1592), more than any other dramatist, opened up for Shakespeare the world of Greek romance—the kind of fiction ultimately derived from Heliodorus, Achilles Tatius, and other protonovelists of the Mediterranean world in the second through fourth centuries. The Greeks of that era were the merchants, traders, sailors, and schoolmasters of the Roman Empire, and the early form of prose romance they created was a reflection of the adventurous life they lived. This romantic fiction reveled in strange and improbable encounters, piracies, the exposure of infant children to the elements and their eventual restoration as grown-ups to their aging parents, the separation and reunion of indistinguishable twins, and many other plot devices rendered familiar to us in the writings of Renaissance authors for whom this kind of sensationalism was every bit as interesting and worthy of imitation as the classics of Virgil and Ovid. Stories of the Greek kind, translated into various languages and ultimately into English, were to serve as models for a number of Shakespeare's late romances, especially *Pericles, The Winter's Tale*, and *Cymbeline*. Indeed, the plot of *The Winter's Tale* came to Shakespeare by way of Greene's prose romance, *Pandosto*.

From Greek romantic fiction, and also, no doubt, from his own experience in life, Greene devised a type of plucky romantic heroine for his plays and novels that Shakespeare was to develop further in his comedies. The society depicted by Greek romance gave women great liberty, and, like them, Greene's heroines are independent, witty, and resourceful, though at the same time feminine. Greene's dramas are almost the first modern productions in which woman is in any degree represented as assuming a relatively dignified station in a mutually supportive love relationship with a man.

Greene also borrowed from Greek romantic fiction, and from other sources, an important element of pastoral. His plays, particularly *James IV* and *Friar Bacon and Friar Bungay* (c. 1589–1592), give us that blend of the pastoral and the romantic which the world has enjoyed in *As You Like It* and *Love's Labor's Lost*. *Friar Bacon* is particularly noteworthy for its multiple plot, its resourceful heroine, and its embracing of serious issues in a comic world. Greene must be regarded as the first great master of plot in English comedy.

Greene may also have written *George a Greene, the Pinner of Wakefield* (1587–1593), a play that exalts the virtues of England's yeoman class in defiance of the aristocracy and all foreign foes. The hero, George, is a patriot, a scorner of hereditary titles, and a representative of the common people against vested interests. As a new breed of English folk hero, he is so invincible that even Robin Hood must yield to his authority. The appeal of this dream of power to the artisans and yeomen in Greene's popular audiences must have been heady indeed.

Shortly before he fell victim to the notorious debaucheries of his bohemian existence (he was reported to have died from a surfeit of pickled herring and Rhenish wine), Greene wrote many pamphlets, some about London roguery, some about his own hard usage at the hands of the world. In one of the latter, *Groats-worth of Wit Bought with a Million of Repentance* (1592), he gave us our first personal reference to Shakespeare. (See "The Only Shake-scene in a Country" in the biographical account of Shakespeare's life and work, below.) Shakespeare was, of course, not the only dramatist to be influenced by Greene; Anthony Munday, Thomas Dekker, and most of the popular dramatists of the next decade were similarly indebted to Greene's example.

Thomas Kyd and Christopher Marlowe

While romantic comedy was being shaped and developed in the hands of Lyly, Peele, and Greene, the Senecan tradition was also finding its proponents on the English stage. The greatest genius in adapting Senecan action to the English theater was Thomas Kyd (1558–1594). His influence on his contemporaries and on later dramatists was immense; *The Spanish Tragedy* (c. 1583–1587) was probably acted more times during the sixteenth century than any other English play and became a pattern for subsequent revenge drama. Although Senecan tradition by no means accounts for all of the play's successful qualities, it remains a central part. Kyd catches the unabashed brutality and horror of the Senecan story and reveals it openly. Instead of having the action reported as taking place off the stage, as in Seneca and in most classical tragedy, he presents it directly. For tales of Greek mythology, he substitutes a modern story of love, conspiracy, murder, and political intrigue. He retains the Senecan ghost, the revenge motive, the spirit of stoicism, and a modified form of the chorus. The play deals both seriously and sensationally with the conflicting codes of revenge and Christian faith in God's providence. The protagonist Hieronimo, confronted with his son's murder and seemingly unable to obtain justice through the state, finds his pleas to the heavens unanswered and turns instead to a revenge that hardens his spirit and requires his own violent death as payment. The action is presided over by the spirit of Revenge, a choruslike figure whose aims share nothing in common with Christian views of justice and mercy. *The Spanish Tragedy* is also noteworthy for a style

The Spanish Tragedie:
OR,
Hieronimo is mad againe.

Containing the lamentable end of *Don Horatio*, and *Belimperia*; with the pittifull death of *Hieronimo*.

Newly corrected, amended, and enlarged with new Additions of the *Painters* part, and others, as it hath of late been diuers times acted.

LONDON,
Printed by W. White, for I. White and T. Langley, and are to be sold at their Shop ouer against the Sarazens head without New-gate. 1615.

BY PERMISSION OF THE FOLGER SHAKESPEARE LIBRARY

Thomas Kyd's The Spanish Tragedy *was perhaps the most popular play of the sixteenth century; it was performed more than any other English drama of the time.* The Spanish Tragedy *served as a pattern and influenced subsequent revenge drama—including Shakespeare's* Hamlet.

that is a tour de force of rhetorical figures, such as climax and oxymoron—an achievement both imitated and mocked by later dramatists. Probably Kyd is also the author of the first dramatic version of the story of Hamlet.

Kyd's work gave rise to a series of revenge plays, not only in his own time, but also later, in 1600 and the years following, when the revenge tragedy again became fashionable. Moreover, Kyd seems to have had a shaping influence on Greene and on Marlowe. For example, Marlowe's *The Jew of Malta* (c. 1589), in its extravagance and sensational intrigue, seems particularly indebted to *The Spanish Tragedy*.

Nevertheless, however much Kyd may have contributed in matters of style and form, Marlowe remains the leader in the great English type of Elizabethan tragedy. He shaped the genre that subsequently was perfected by Shakespeare. His achievement is all the more remarkable when we consider that he was born in the same year as Shakespeare (1564) and died in 1593, when Shakespeare had written no more than six or seven of his earliest plays. Marlowe's great contribution to English drama was a type of protagonist expressing something of the aspiration of the very Renaissance itself. Tamburlaine thirsts for world conquest; Dr. Faustus would go to the utmost bounds of knowledge and the power which knowledge gives; and Barabas in *The Jew of Malta* sets no limit to his longing for wealth.

Structurally, *Tamburlaine* (1587–1588) is a good deal closer to the English popular morality play than to classical drama. Each of the play's two parts consists of a linear sequence of conquests by the humbly born but seemingly invincible Tamburlaine, until at last death ends his glory. Because many characters appear in one episode only, the cast is large and yet within the capacities of an Elizabethan acting company. Doubling of parts, as in Shakespeare's early history plays, is both common and necessary. Structural unity is achieved through thematic repetition rather than through a narrowing of the narrative focus. At the same time, the language of *Tamburlaine* is rich and new in its vibrant appeal to limitless human aspiration. The Elizabethan playgoer is invited to forget moral considerations in evaluating the play's ruthless hero and to revel instead in the intoxicating spectacle of a baseborn shepherd "threat'ning the world with high astounding terms."

A profound ambivalence permeates all of Marlowe's plays and gives them a restless, brilliant energy that is characteristic of the times for which they were written. Tamburlaine is both a remorseless butcher of his enemies and a superhuman quester. He is fierce, mysterious, oriental, exotic, unknowable; as the projection of a universal human dream of aspiration, he is to be both admired and feared. Barabas in *The Jew of Malta* is at once colossally rich and colossally evil. Similarly, the protagonist of *Doctor Faustus* (c. 1588) is both a sinner who falls from grace and a noble but doomed Overreacher (as Harry Levin describes him), daring like Icarus to fly toward the sun. In medieval and Christian orthodox terms, Faustus is guilty of pride, the deadliest of the Deadly Sins; but in Renaissance terms he at least fleetingly resembles Prometheus, challenging the hierarchy of an oppressive and outmoded universe. In its free mixture of comedy and tragedy and its wholesale disregard of the classical unities, *Doctor Faustus* brilliantly demonstrates what the native and homiletic tradition of tragedy had to offer Shakespeare.

Edward II, perhaps Marlowe's last play (1591–1593), is ambivalent toward its paired central figures, Edward and Mortimer Junior. At first, the effeminate King seems chiefly in the wrong, while his baronial opponents lament England's decline. Toward the end of the play, however, the King becomes the sympathetic victim of a power-mad and Machiavellian Mortimer. Queen Isabella also changes radically from a long-suffering, neglected wife into a scheming adulteress. This shift in sympathy from the barons to King Edward is structurally much like that of Shakespeare's *Richard II*, and, unquestionably, Marlowe's history play had a profound effect on Shakespeare. Yet Marlowe's tone, as in his other plays, remains one of naturalistic amorality.

The Tragicall Hiſtory of the Life and Death
of Doctor FAVSTVS.

With new Additions.

Written by *Ch. Mar.*

Printed at London for *Iohn Wright*, and are to be ſold at his ſhop without Newgate, 1624.

The title page of the 1624 edition of Christopher Marlowe's Doctor Faustus *shows Faustus' conjuration of the devil. The play illustrates native rather than classical traditions of tragedy in its disregard of the unities and its free use of comedy.*

He wryly regards England's political struggles as one more manifestation of the restlessness and ambition afflicting all mortal endeavors. His world is one of constant turmoil in which persons of insatiable will must assert themselves and rise to the top, at whatever cost to themselves and to society. Shakespeare's world is basically different, even though he learned a great deal from Marlowe's tragic vision.

Marlowe first gave to English tragedy its realization of character and, still more, its dignity and seriousness. He endowed English drama with a spirit of aspiration. His enthusiasm for beauty of language, shared by Spenser, Greene, Peele, and others, provided a rich heritage for the young Shakespeare. Not the least among Marlowe's gifts to English drama was a new and more flexible blank-verse style. In the following prologue to *Tamburlaine the Great*, Part I, Marlowe does not treat each blank-verse line as a separate unit but runs the sense on from line to line in order to produce what might be described as a blank-verse paragraph, a thing most necessary to drama if it is to represent widely varying emotions, thoughts, and characters:

From jigging veins of rhyming mother wits,
And such conceits as clownage keeps in pay,

We'll lead you to the stately tent of war,
Where you shall hear the Scythian Tamburlaine
Threat'ning the world with high astounding terms,
And scourging kingdoms with his conquering sword.
View but his picture in this tragic glass,
And then applaud his fortunes as you please.

This is not only a manifesto of tragic seriousness; it is also, in spite of its elevated style, one of the first examples in English tragedy of vigorous, natural, straightforward expression. Tamburlaine in his utterances is a typical Renaissance poet on the themes of both love and war, as can be seen in the following evocation of the aspiring mind:

If all the pens that ever poets held
Had fed the feeling of their masters' thoughts,
And every sweetness that inspired their hearts,
Their minds, and muses on admired themes;
If all the heavenly quintessence they still
From their immortal flowers of poesy,
Wherein, as in a mirror, we perceive
The highest reaches of a human wit;
If these had made one poem's period,
And all combined in beauty's worthiness,
Yet should there hover in their restless heads
One thought, one grace, one wonder, at the least,
Which into words no virtue can digest.
—*Tamburlaine*, Pt. I, 5.2.98–110

Shakespeare's Dramatic Heritage

Shakespearean tragedy began, roughly speaking, with marked indebtedness to the tragic writing of Marlowe and Kyd: poetry, character, and style from Marlowe; motive, plot, and tragic intensity from Kyd. No evidence suggests that Shakespeare was ever particularly aware of, or influenced by, Aristotelian theories of tragedy. His wish was to hold "the mirror up to nature" and show "virtue her feature, scorn her own image, and the very age and body of the time his form and pressure" (*Hamlet*, 3.2.22–24). Sometimes he approximated Aristotelian ideals in his plays (most nearly, perhaps, in *Othello, Macbeth,* and *Coriolanus*), but not by conscious design. Nor was he a slavish borrower from Marlowe and Kyd, even in his early tragedies, such as *Titus Andronicus*. Greene and many others sought to imitate Marlowe in tragedy, with but indifferent success. Shakespeare, Marlowe's only successful imitator, soon outdistanced Marlowe in those very qualities for which he was indebted to him.

Similarly, the elements of Shakespearean comedy are, in part, derived from Lyly, Peele, and Greene. The contributions of Lyly and Peele were those of style, setting, and movement. Greene, primarily a writer of romance, an adapter of Greek romantic fiction, furnished the element of love and adventure which makes so many Elizabethan plays delightful merely as stories. He also put upon the stage the witty, independent-minded woman, usually in boy's clothes, who gives point and naturalness to love intrigue whether in serious drama or in comedy. Not only did

Shakespeare, who was a far greater genius than any of them, combine the elements of the comedies of these men and better the instruction, but, as his career went on, he realized on a broad scale the possibilities of the comic point of view in the representation of human life and character.

In the English history play, though he may have learned much from Marlowe, Peele, and others, Shakespeare was clearly an innovator as well. His early history plays on the reigns of Henry VI and Richard III were among the earliest such plays seen in London and were (at least some of them) enormous stage successes. Even here, however, we can see how much Shakespeare learned from such earlier plays as *Gorboduc* and *The Troublesome Reign of King John*.

London Theaters and Dramatic Companies

Throughout Shakespeare's life, the propriety of acting any plays at all was a matter of bitter controversy. Indeed, when one considers the power and earnestness of the opposition, one is surprised that such a wealth of dramatic excellence could come into being and that Shakespeare's plays should reflect so little the anger and hostility generated by this continuing conflict.

Religious and Moral Opposition to the Theater

From the 1570s onward, and even earlier, the city fathers of London revealed an ever increasing distrust of the public performance of plays. They fretted about the dangers of plague and of riotous assembly. They objected to the fact that apprentices idly wasted their time instead of working in their shops. And always the municipal authorities suspected immorality. Thus, by an order of the Common Council of London, dated December 6, 1574, the players were put under severe restrictions.

The order cites the reasons. The players, it was charged, had been acting in the innyards of the city, which in consequence were haunted by great multitudes of people, especially youths. These gatherings had been the occasions of frays and quarrels, "evil practices of incontinency in great inns"; the players published "uncomely and unshamefast speeches and doings," withdrew the Queen's subjects from divine service on Sundays and holidays, wasted the money of "poor and fond persons," gave opportunity to pick pockets, uttered "busy and seditious matters," and injured and maimed people by engines, by the falling of their scaffolds, and by weapons and powder used in plays. The order goes on to state the Common Council's fear that if the plays, which had been forbidden on account of the plague, should be resumed, God's wrath would manifest itself by an increase of the infection. Therefore, no innkeeper, tavern-keeper, or other person might cause or suffer to be openly played "any play, interlude, comedy, tragedy, matter, or show" which had not been first licensed by the Mayor and the Court of Aldermen.

The Mayor and aldermen did not always state their case plainly, because Queen Elizabeth was a patron of the players, and because the players had friends and patrons in the Privy Council and among the nobility; sometimes, however, they did so quite boldly. One sees the case against plays stated syllogistically in the following words of Thomas White, a preacher at Paul's Cross in 1577:

Look but upon the common plays of London, and see the multitude that flocketh to them and followeth them! Behold the sumptuous theater houses, a continual monument of London prodigality and folly! But I understand they are now forbidden because of the plague. I like the policy well if it hold still, for a disease is but botched and patched up that is not cured in the cause, and the cause of plagues is sin, if you look to it well, and the cause of sin are plays. Therefore the cause of plagues are plays. (From *A Sermon preached at Paul's Cross . . . in the Time of the Plague,* 1578.)

Moved, no doubt, by the prohibition of the Common Council, James Burbage, with a company of actors under the patronage of the Earl of Leicester, leased a site in Shoreditch, a London suburb in Middlesex, beyond the immediate jurisdiction of the official enemies in the Common Council, whose authority extended only to the city limits. By 1576, he had completed the Theatre. Perhaps he called it "the Theatre" because there was no other; Burbage erected what may have been England's first permanent commercial theatrical building. In general, the building combined features of the innyard and the animal-baiting house, having a central and probably paved courtyard open to the sky (like an innyard) and surrounding galleries on all sides (like an animal-baiting house). Burbage erected a stage at one side of the circular arena and put dressing rooms behind it to form the "tiring house" or backstage area for the actors; the facade of this "tiring house" served as a visible backdrop to the stage itself. Burbage's Theatre became the model for other public playhouses, such as the Curtain, the Swan, and the Globe, which were constructed later.

By building his playhouse in Shoreditch, Burbage gained immunity from the London authorities. The city fathers could not suppress plays or control them with perfect success if they were performed in Middlesex or (in the case of later playhouses) on the Bankside across the Thames in Surrey. In order to get at them in these suburban regions, the city authorities had to petition the Queen's Privy Council to give orders to the magistrates and officers of the law in these counties. The Queen's Privy Council, although always on the most polite terms with the Lord Mayor and his brethren of the city and always open to the argument that the assemblage of crowds caused the spread of the plague, was

The George Inn of Southwark, England, London's only surviving galleried inn, was destroyed by fire in 1676 but rebuilt the following year with two galleries instead of the original three. Despite these changes, the George Inn gives us the best picture we have of the kind of space in which traveling companies could mount their plays on bare platform stages.

to a much less degree in sympathy with the moral scruples of the city. Current arguments for the plays, derived from the works of scholars, poets, and playwrights, were numerous and often heard: namely, that classical antiquity gave precedent for dramatic spectacles; that by drawing a true picture of both the bad and the good in life, plays enabled people to choose the good; that people should have wholesome amusement; and that plays provided livelihood for loyal subjects of the Queen.

Of these arguments, to be sure, the Privy Council made little use, resting the case for plays instead on what was, no doubt, an unanswerable argument: that since the players were to appear before Her Majesty, the players needed practice in order to prepare themselves to please the royal taste. A good deal of politic fencing ensued, and, so far as orders, complaints, and denunciations were concerned, the reforming opposition had much the better of it. The preachers thundered against plays. Pamphleteers denounced all matters pertaining to the stage: Stephen Gosson in *The School of Abuse, Containing a Pleasant Invective Against Poets, Pipers, Players, Jesters and Suchlike*

Caterpillars of a Commonwealth (1579) and other works; Philip Stubbes in *The Anatomy of Abuses* (1583); and finally and most furiously of all, William Prynne in *Histrio-Mastix: The Players' Scourge or Actor's Tragedy* (1633). Gosson spoke of plays as "the inventions of the devil, the offerings of idolatry, the pomp of worldlings, the blossoms of vanity, the root of apostacy, food of iniquity, riot and adultery." "Detest them," he warned. "Players are masters of vice, teachers of wantonness, spurs to impurity, the sons of idleness."

At first, such diatribes represented an extreme reforming opinion obviously not shared by a majority of London viewers. They kept coming to plays, and the flourishing public theaters attracted the talents of the age's leading dramatists. An ominous note of polarization was sounded, however, early in the reign of James I (1603–1625) when the rift between the Puritans and the court broke into open antagonism. After about 1604, when James alienated the Puritans at the Hampton Court Conference, the split between popular audiences and the best drama of the age became increasingly evident. Shakespeare's company, now the King's men, moved, whether through choice or necessity, toward the precinct of the court. Although the public theater, with its capacity for large audiences, continued to serve as a lively center of theatrical activity, Puritan opposition to the stage gathered momentum. Many dramatists, in turn, grew more satirical of London customs and more attuned to courtly tastes. Eventually, in 1642, Puritan hostility forced the total closing of the theaters.

The Public Theaters

A year or more after Burbage built the Theatre in 1576, the Curtain was put up near it by Philip Henslowe, or possibly by Henry Laneman, or Lanman. About ten years later, Philip Henslowe built the Rose, the first playhouse on the Bankside (the southern bank of the Thames River). In 1599, James Burbage's sons Richard and Cuthbert dismantled the Theatre because of trouble about the lease of the land and rebuilt it as the Globe on the Bankside. This Globe playhouse burned on June 29, 1613, from the discharge of cannon backstage during a performance of *All Is True,* a play thought to be identical with Shakespeare's *Henry VIII.* The Globe was rebuilt, probably in its original polygonal form, that is, essentially round with a large number of sides. In 1600, Henslowe built the Fortune as a theater for the Lord Admiral's men, who were chief rivals to the Lord Chamberlain's men. The companies were differently organized, in that the Lord Chamberlain's men were joint sharers in their own enterprise and owners of their own theatrical building, whereas Henslowe owned the Fortune (and the Rose before it) and served as landlord to the Admiral's men—no doubt profiting handsomely from their activities.

Various records of these theatrical buildings have sur-

vived. One such record is the Fortune contract, preserved at Dulwich College among other invaluable papers of Edward Alleyn's father-in-law, Philip Henslowe. The contract for building the Fortune was let to the same contractor who had built the new Globe, and, since the specifications required that the Fortune should be like the Globe in all its main features, except that it was to be square instead of polygonal, we may gain from these specifications an idea of the Globe. A second documentary record is a drawing of the Swan, a Bankside theater, accompanying a description of the playhouse by Johannes De Witt, who visited London in 1596. The drawing, which was discovered in the University Library at Utrecht, is the work of one Van Buchell and may be based on drawings by De Witt himself. Besides the Fortune contract and the Swan drawing, we have two or three little pictures of the Elizabethan public stage on the title pages of published plays, the most important being that on the title page of William Alabaster's *Roxana* (1632). Just recently, in 1989, the discovery and excavation of the

This drawing of an Elizabethan public stage appeared on the title page of the published version of William Alabaster's play Roxana *(1632).*

foundations of the Rose playhouse, near the site of the Globe, have added invaluable archeological information about the dimensions of that acting arena.

The Public Stage

From these documents and pictures and from scattered references to the theaters, as well as from extended studies of stage directions and scenic conditions in plays themselves, we have a fairly clear idea of the public stage. Its features are these: a pit about seventy feet in diameter, usually circular and open to the sky; surrounding this, galleries in three tiers, containing the most expensive seats; and a rectangular stage, about forty-three by twenty-seven feet, wider than it was deep, raised about five and one-half feet above the surface of the yard, sometimes built on trestles so that it could be removed if the house was also customarily used for bearbaiting and bullbaiting. The flat, open stage usually contained one trapdoor. Part of the stage was afforded some protection from the weather by a brightly decorated wooden roof supported by posts, constituting the "heavens." Above this roof was a "hut," perhaps containing suspension gear for ascents and descents. (The Rose appears originally to have been generally smaller than what is described here, with a stage that tapered toward the front to

a width of only twenty-five feet or so. The building was somewhat expanded in 1592 but was still small compared with other theaters. The original building shows no certain evidence of a roof over the stage supported by pillars, but the later building appears to have had roof pillars at the front of the stage.)

At the back of the stage was a partition wall, the "tiring-house facade," with at least two doors in it connecting the stage with the actors' dressing rooms or "tiring house." In the Rose, the tiring-house facade seems to have curved with the polygonal shape of the theater building, but in the DeWitt drawing the Swan facade looks perfectly straight across. Some theaters appear to have had no more than two doors, left and right, as shown in the Swan drawing; other theaters may have had a third door in the center. The arrangement of the Globe playhouse in this important matter cannot be finally determined, although some particular scenes from Shakespeare's plays seem to demand a third door. In any case, the so-called inner stage, long supposed to have stood at the rear of the Elizabethan stage, almost certainly did not exist. A more modest "discovery space" could be provided at one of the curtained doors when needed, as for example in *The Tempest* when Ferdinand and Miranda are suddenly "discovered" at their game of chess by Prospero. Such scenes never called for

This diagram of the Swan Theatre (left) by Van Buchell (c. 1596), based on the observations of Johannes De Witt, shows features of the public playhouse shared by James Burbage's Theatre and the Globe. A modern sketch of the Swan Theatre (right) shows the open, encircling roof and a full view of the tiring house. Like the Globe and other open theaters, the design of the Swan seems to resemble the Elizabethan innyard with an added stage.

extensive action within the discovery space, however, and, indeed, the number of such discoveries in Elizabethan plays is very few. Well-to-do spectators who may have been seated in the gallery above the rear of the stage could not see into the discovery space. Accordingly, it was used sparingly for brief visual effects. Otherwise, the actors performed virtually all their scenes on the open stage. Sometimes curtains were hung over the tiring-house facade between the doors to facilitate scenes of concealment, as when Polonius and Claudius eavesdrop on Hamlet and Ophelia.

An upper station was sometimes used as an acting space, but not nearly so often as was once supposed. The gallery seats above the stage, sometimes known as the "Lord's room," were normally sold to well-to-do spectators. (We can see such spectators in the Swan drawing and in Alabaster's *Roxana*.) Occasionally, these box seats could be used by the actors, as when Juliet appears at her window (it is never called a balcony). In military sequences, as in the *Henry VI* plays, the tiring-house facade could represent the walls of a besieged city, with the city's defenders appearing "on the walls" (i.e., in the gallery above the stage) in order to parley with the besieging enemy standing below on the main stage. Such scenes were relatively infrequent, however, and usually required only a small number of persons to be aloft. A music room, when needed, could be located in one of the gallery boxes over the stage, but public theaters did not emulate the private stages with music rooms and entr'acte music until some time around 1609.

The use of scenery was almost wholly unknown on the Elizabethan public stage, although we do find occasional hints of the use of labels to designate a certain door or area as a fixed location (as, perhaps, in *The Comedy of Errors*). For the most part, the scene was unlimited and the concept of space was fluid. No proscenium arch or curtain stood between the actors and the audience, and so the action could not be easily interrupted. Only belatedly did the public companies adopt the private-theater practice of entr'acte music, as we have seen. Most popular Elizabethan plays were written to be performed nonstop. Five-act structure had little currency, especially at first, and the divisions in Shakespeare's text of this kind may be non-authorial. Acting tempo was brisk. The Prologue of *Romeo and Juliet* speaks of "the two hours' traffic of our stage." Plays were performed in the afternoons and had to be completed by dark in order to allow the audience to return safely to London. During the winter season, playing time was severely restricted. Outbreaks of plague often occasioned the closing of the theaters, especially in warm weather.

A capacity audience for the popular theaters came to about 2,000–3,000 persons. (The recently excavated Rose playhouse foundations suggest an audience there of around 2,000.) For the most part, the audience was affluent, consisting chiefly of the gentry and of London's substantial mercantile citizenry who paid two to three pence or more for gallery seats or the "Lord's room," but the ample pit or yard also provided room for small shopkeepers and artisans who stood for a penny. The spectators were lively, demanding, and intelligent. Although Shakespeare does allow Hamlet to refer disparagingly on one occasion to the "groundlings" who "for the most part are capable of nothing but inexplicable dumbshows and noise" (*Hamlet*, 3.2.11–12), Shakespeare appealed to the keenest understanding of his whole audience, thereby achieving a breadth of vision seldom found in continental courtly drama of the same period. The vitality and financial success of the Elizabethan public theater is without parallel in English history. The city of London itself had only about 100,000 inhabitants, yet throughout Shakespeare's career several companies were competing simultaneously for this audience and constantly producing new plays. Most new plays ran for only a few performances, so that the acting companies were always in rehearsal with new shows. The actors needed phenomenal memories and a gift of improvisation as well. Their acting seems to have been of a high caliber, despite the speed with

Elizabethan dancers, shown above, perform on a stage below a gallery of musicians. Imported stage designs from Italy made more use of perspective scenery than did the commercial theaters.

which they worked. Among other things, many of them were expert fencers and singers.

The London public stage inherited many of its practices from native and medieval traditions. The fluid, open stage, with spectators on four sides recalled the arena staging of many early Corpus Christi cycles, saints' plays, and morality plays. The adult professional companies were, as we have seen, descended from the itinerant troupes which had taken their portable booth stages to every part of England, setting up in innyards, street corners, noble houses, and palaces. The Elizabethan tiring-house facade and platform stage owed much to the simple curtained booth stage and trestle platform of the itinerant troupes, set up against one wall of an innyard or animal-baiting house. Yet when those same itinerant actors had set up their plays in noblemen's banqueting halls or at court, they encountered another space that had an important influence on their concept of a theater: the Tudor hall. We must next examine the significance of this indoor theatrical setting.

The Tudor Hall

The Tudor banqueting hall played a major part in the staging of much early Tudor drama. Medwall's *Fulgens and Lucrece,* one of the earliest such plays, was written to be performed during the intervals of a state banquet. The patrician guests were seated at tables, while servingmen bustled to and fro or stood crowded together at the doors in the hall "screen." This screen or partition traversed the lower end of the rectangular hall, providing a passageway to the kitchens and to the outside. Its doors—often two, sometimes three—were normally curtained to prevent drafts. This arrangement of the doors bears an interesting resemblance to that of many playhouses in late Elizabethan England, both public and private. Moreover, hall screens and passageways were normally surmounted by a gallery, where musicians could play—an architectural feature markedly resembling the upper galleries of late Elizabethan theaters. Could the Tudor hall screen provide a natural facade for dramatic action? Perhaps it did, although records from Shakespeare's era only rarely document an actual performance in front of the screen, whereas performances were common at the upper end of the hall in front of the dais or in the midst of the hall. The actors of *Fulgens and Lucrece* clearly made use of the doorways in the hall screen, sometimes joking with the servingmen as the actors pushed their way into the hall, but they probably acted in the center, among the spectators' tables. John Heywood's *Play of the Weather* calls for a similar *mise en scène.* Although this ready-made "stage" sufficed for most Tudor plays, the actors sometimes provided additional stage structures; *Weather,* for example, calls for a throne room into which Jupiter can retire without leaving the hall. Similar structures could represent a shop, an orchard, a mountain, or what have you.

Although both medieval and continental drama offered traditions of multiple staging, in which a series of simultaneously visible and adjacent structures would represent as fixed locations all the playing areas needed for the performance of a play, Tudor indoor staging seems to have made

The Tudor banqueting hall provided a place to "stage" much early Tudor drama. The actors performed on the floor among the tables of the guests. The Middle Temple Hall, shown here, later served as the location for a performance of Shakespeare's Twelfth Night *on February 2, 1602. The Middle Temple is one of the Inns of Court, where young men studied law and occasionally relaxed by staging dramatic entertainments.*

less use of this method than was once supposed. Nor did the various indoor theaters of Tudor England make extensive use of neoclassical staging from Italy, with its street scene in perspective created by means of lath-and-canvas stage "houses." Italian scenery of this sort came into use sooner in the court masque than in regular drama. Nevertheless, we do find in the Tudor indoor theater a neoclassical tendency toward a fixed locale, in preference to the unlimited open stage. *Gammer Gurton's Needle,* for example, acted probably in a university hall, seems to have used one stage structure, or possibly one door, to represent Gammer's house throughout the action, and another to represent Dame Chat's house. Shakespeare may have been influenced by this kind of fixed-locale staging in *The Comedy of Errors.*

The Private Stage

Despite such influences on the public stage, the most significant contribution of the Tudor hall and its hall screen was to the so-called private stage of the late Elizabethan period. In the 1570s, choir boys began performing professionally to courtly and intellectual audiences in London. The choir boys had long performed plays for the royal and noble households to which they were attached, but in the 1570s they were, in effect, organized into professional acting companies. Sebastian Westcote and the Children of Paul's may have originated this enterprise. Their theater was apparently some indoor hall in the vicinity of St. Paul's in London, outfitted much like the typical domestic Tudor hall to which the boys had grown accustomed. Comparable indoor "private" theaters soon followed at Blackfriars and Whitefriars.

At some point, a low stage was constructed in front of the hall screen, and seats were provided for all the spectators. Many of these seats were in the "pit," or what we would call the "orchestra," facing toward the stage at one end of the rectangular room. Other seats were in galleries along both sides of the room; these were quite elaborate in the so-called Second Blackfriars of 1596 and provided two or three tiers of seats. Elegant box seats stood at either side of the stage itself. The Second Blackfriars had a permanently built tiring house to the rear of the stage, with probably three doors. Above it was a gallery used variously as a lord's room, a music room, and an upper station for occasional acting.

The private theater flourished during the 1580s and again after 1598–1599, having been closed down during most of the 1590s because of its satirical activities. Although it was a commercial theater, it was "private" in its clientele, because its high price of admission (sixpence) excluded those who could stand in the yards of the "public" theaters for a penny (roughly the equivalent of an hour's wage for a skilled worker). Plays written for the more select audiences of the "private" theaters tended to be more satirical and

A reconstruction of the Second Blackfriars, featuring a rectangular stage, a tiring house with three doors, and a gallery.

oriented to courtly values than those written for the "public" theaters, although the distinction is not absolute.

London Private Theaters

The important private theaters of Shakespeare's London were two in the precinct, or "liberty," of Blackfriars, an early one in Whitefriars about which little is known, a later one there, and a theater at Paul's, the exact location and nature of which is not known. In the thirteenth century, the mother house of the Dominican friars, or Blackfriars, was established on the sloping ground between St. Paul's Cathedral and the river. It was a sizable institution, ultimately covering about five acres of ground. It stood on the very border of the city and, after the custom of the time, was made a liberty; that is to say, it had its own local government and was removed from the immediate jurisdiction of the city of London. After the suppression of the friary and the confiscation of its lands, the jealousy existing between the Privy Council, representing the crown, and the Mayor and aldermen, representing the city and probably also the rights of property holders, prevented the district of the Blackfriars from losing its political independence of the municipality. It was still a liberty and therefore attractive to players and other persons wishing to avoid the London authorities. At the same time, aristocrats residing in the area required protection, and the crown had certain rights still in its control.

From 1576 to 1584, the Children of the Queen's Chapel, one of the two most important companies of boy actors, had used a hall in the precinct of Blackfriars in which to act their plays. Here were acted at least some of John Lyly's plays. In 1596, James Burbage purchased property in this precinct and seems to have spent a good deal of money in its adaptation for use as an indoor theater (the so-called Second Blackfriars). He probably appreciated its advantages over Cripplegate or the Bankside of greater proximity to London and of protection against the elements, particularly for use in winter. But the aristocratic residents of the Blackfriars by petition to the Privy Council prevented him from making use of his theater. Plays within the city proper had only recently been finally and successfully prohibited, and the petitioners no doubt objected to their intrusion into Blackfriars on the grounds that the plays and their crowds were a nuisance.

Burbage's new indoor theater may have lain idle from the time of its preparation until 1600; but, in any case, in that year it became the scene of many plays. It was let by lease for the use of the Children of the Chapel, who in 1604 became the Children of the Queen's Revels. Their theater managers brought into their service a number of new dramatists—Ben Jonson, John Marston, George Chapman, and later John Webster. The vogue of the plays acted by the Children of the Chapel was so great as to damage the patronage of the established companies and to compel them to go on the road. Out of this rivalry between the children and the adult actors arose that open competition alluded to in *Hamlet* (2.2.328–362) and sometimes referred to today as the "War of the Theaters." In 1608, the Burbage interests secured the evacuation of the lease, so that the theater in Blackfriars became the winter playhouse of Shakespeare's company from that time forward.

System of Patronage

In 1572, common players of interludes, along with minstrels, bearwards, and fencers, were included within the hard terms of the act for the punishment of vagabonds, provided that such common players were not enrolled as the servants of a baron of the realm or of some honorable person of greater degree. The result was a system of patronage of theatrical companies in Elizabethan and Jacobean times, according to which players became the "servants" of some nobleman or of some member of the royal family.

By the time Shakespeare came to London in the late 1580s, more than a dozen of these companies were already in existence, some of which long antedated the passage of the act of 1572. Provincial records of the visits of players, to be sure, sometimes failed to distinguish actors from acrobats or other public performers who were similarly organized. Nonetheless, we have evidence that various companies of players performed in London and elsewhere in the late 1580s under the patronage of the Queen, the Earl of Worcester, the Earl of Leicester, the Earl of Oxford, the Earl of Sussex, the Lord Admiral, and Charles, Lord Howard of Effingham. These companies were eventually much reduced in number; usually only three adult companies acted at any given time in London during Shakespeare's prime. In

addition, the children's companies, privately controlled, acted intermittently but at times very successfully. The most important of these were the Children of the Chapel and Queen's Revels and the Children of Paul's, but there were also boy players of Windsor, Eton College, the Merchant Taylors, Westminster, and other schools.

Shakespeare and the London Theatrical Companies

We know that by 1592 Shakespeare had arrived in London and had achieved sufficient notice as a young playwright to arouse the resentment of a rival dramatist, Robert Greene. In that year, shortly before he died, Greene—or possibly his editor after Greene's death—lashed out at an "upstart crow, beautified with our feathers," who had had the audacity to fancy himself "the only Shake-scene in a country" (*Groatsworth of Wit*). This petulant outburst was plainly directed at Shakespeare, since Greene included in his remarks a parody of some lines from *3 Henry VI*. As a university man and an established dramatist, Greene seems to have resented the intrusion into his profession of a mere player who was not university trained. This "upstart crow" was achieving a very real success on the London stage. Shakespeare had probably already written *The Comedy of Errors, Love's Labor's Lost, The Two Gentlemen of Verona*, the *Henry VI* plays, and *Titus Andronicus*, and perhaps also *Richard III* and *The Taming of the Shrew*.

For which acting company or companies had he written these plays, however? By 1594, we know that Shakespeare was an established member of the Lord Chamberlain's company, important enough, in fact, to have been named, along with Will Kempe and Richard Burbage, as payee for court performances on December 26 and 28 of 1594. But when had he joined the Chamberlain's men, and for whom had he written and acted previously? These are the problems of the so-called dark years, during which Shakespeare came to London (perhaps around 1587) and got started on his career.

One prestigious acting company he could have joined was the Earl of Leicester's company, led by James Burbage, father of Shakespeare's later colleague, Richard Burbage. Leicester was a favorite minister of Queen Elizabeth until his death in 1588, and his company of actors received from the Queen in 1574 an extraordinary patent to perform plays anywhere in England, despite all local prohibitions, provided that the plays were approved beforehand by the master of the Queen's Revels. Since an act of 1572 had outlawed all unlicensed troupes, Leicester's men and a few similar companies attached to important noblemen were given a virtual monopoly over public acting. In 1576, Burbage built the Theatre for his company in the northeast suburbs of London. This group also toured the provinces. Conceivably, Shakespeare served an apprenticeship in this company, though no evidence exists to prove a connection.

Leicester's company had lost some of its prominence in 1583, when several of its best men joined the newly formed Queen's men, with Richard Tarlton as its most famous actor. The remaining members of Leicester's company disbanded in 1588 upon the death of the Earl, and many of its principal actors ultimately became part of Lord Strange's company. These probably included George Bryan, Will Kempe, and Thomas Pope, all of whom subsequently went on to become Lord Chamberlain's men.

Lord Strange's (The Earl of Derby's) Men

Besides Leicester's men and the Queen's men, other prominent companies of the 1580s and early 1590s included Lord Strange's men, the Lord Admiral's men, the Earl of Pembroke's men, and the Earl of Sussex's men. Scholars have long speculated that Shakespeare may have joined the company of Ferdinando Stanley, Lord Strange (who in 1593 became the Earl of Derby). The names of George Bryan, Will Kempe, and Thomas Pope appear on a roster of Strange's company in 1593, along with those of John Heminges and Augustine Phillips. All of these men later became part of the Lord Chamberlain's company, most of them when it was first formed in 1594. Shakespeare's name does not appear on the 1593 Lord Strange's list (which was a license for touring in the provinces), but he may possibly have stayed in London to attend to his writing while the company toured. Certainly, an important number of his later associates belonged to this group.

From about 1590 to 1594, Lord Strange's men formed an amalgamation with the Admiral's men, including the famous Edward Alleyn. This impressive combination of talents enjoyed a successful season in 1591–1592, with six performances at court. Alleyn's father-in-law, Philip Henslowe, recorded in his *Diary* the performances of the combined players in early 1592, probably at the Rose Theatre. Their repertory included a *Harey the vj* and a *Titus & Vespacia*. The latter play is, however, no longer thought to have any connection with Shakespeare's *Titus Andronicus;* and the *Harey the vj* may or may not have been Shakespeare's, since *3 Henry VI* was (according to its 1595 title page) acted by Pembroke's men, rather than Lord Strange's men. If Shakespeare was a member of the Strange-Admiral's combination in 1591–1592, we are at a loss to explain why Henslowe's 1592 list records so many performances of plays by Marlowe, Greene, Kyd, and others, and none that are certainly by Shakespeare. On the other hand, the *Harey the vj* may be his, and the title page of the 1594 Quarto of *Titus Andronicus* does list the Earl of Derby's men as performers of the play, in addition to the Earl of Pembroke's and the Earl of Sussex's men. (Lord Strange's men became officially known as the Earl of Derby's men when Lord Strange was made an earl in September of 1593.) At any rate, the company disbanded when the Earl died in

Clowns were enormously popular on the Elizabethan stage. Of the many Elizabethan clowns whose names are known to us, Richard Tarlton is one of the most famous. (Will Kempe, in Shakespeare's company, the Lord Chamberlain's men, is another; see p. lxix.) Tarlton is here shown inside an elaborate letter T, *dancing a jig with his pipe and tabor. Such jigs were often used at the conclusion of a play.*

April of 1594, leaving them without a patron. The connection with the Admiral's men was discontinued, with Alleyn returning to the Admiral's men and the rest of the group forming a new company under the patronage of Henry Carey, first Lord Hunsdon, the Lord Chamberlain.

The Earl of Pembroke's Men

The other company to which Shakespeare is most likely to have belonged prior to 1594 is the Earl of Pembroke's company. This group came to grief in 1593–1594, evidently as a result of virulent outbursts of the plague, which had kept the theaters closed during most of 1592 and 1593. Pembroke's men were forced to tour the provinces and then to sell a number of their best plays to the booksellers. Henslowe wrote to Alleyn in September of 1593 of the extreme financial plight of Pembroke's company: "As for my lord of Pembroke's [men], which you desire to know where they be, they are all at home and has been this five or six weeks, for they cannot save their charges [expenses] with travel, as I hear, and were fain to pawn their parell [apparel] for their charge." Soon thereafter this company disbanded.

Pembroke's men were associated with a significant number of Shakespeare's early plays. Among the playbooks they evidently sold in 1593–1594 were *The Taming of a*

Shrew and *The True Tragedy of Richard Duke of York.* The first of these was published in 1594 with the assertion that it had been "sundry times acted by the Right Honorable the Earle of Pembroke his Servants." Although the text of this quarto is not Shakespeare's play as we know it but, instead, an anonymous version, most scholars now feel certain that it was an imitation of Shakespeare's play and that the work performed by Pembroke's men was, in fact, Shakespeare's. The same conclusion pertains to a performance in 1594 of *"the Tamynge of a Shrowe"* at Newington Butts, a playhouse south of London Bridge. Henslowe's *Diary* informs us that the actors on this occasion were either the Lord Chamberlain's or the Lord Admiral's men. The probability, then, is that Shakespeare's *The Taming of the Shrew* passed from Pembroke's men to the Chamberlain's men when Pembroke's company collapsed in 1593–1594.

The True Tragedy of Richard Duke of York, published in 1595, was a "bad" quarto of Shakespeare's *3 Henry VI.* Its title page declared that it had been "sundry times acted by the Right Honorable the Earl of Pembroke his Servants." Probably they acted *2 Henry VI* as well, to which part three was a sequel. In addition, the 1594 Quarto of *Titus Andronicus* mentions on its title page the Earl of Pembroke's servants, although the Earl of Derby's and the Earl of Sussex's men are named there as well. Thus, Pembroke's men performed as many as four of Shakespeare's early plays—more than we can assign to any other known company. Nevertheless, their claim to Shakespeare remains uncertain. We simply do not know who acted several of Shakespeare's earliest plays, such as *The Comedy of Errors, Love's Labor's Lost,* and *The Two Gentlemen of Verona.* Lord Strange's (Derby's) men, as we have seen, did act something called *Harey the vj* and are named on the 1594 title page of *Titus Andronicus.* Sussex's men may conceivably have owned for a time some early Shakespearean plays that later went to the Lord Chamberlain's men, such as *Titus Andronicus.* The Queen's men, although associated with no known Shakespeare play, other than the old *King Lear*

(acted jointly with Sussex's men in 1593), were a leading company during the years in question. All we can say for sure is that the difficulties of 1592–1593 with the plague and the death of the Earl of Derby in 1594 led to a major reshuffling of the London acting companies. From this reshuffling emerged in 1594 the Lord Chamberlain's company, with Shakespeare and Richard Burbage (whose earlier history is also difficult to trace) as two of its earliest and most prominent members.

Shakespeare's Life and Work

The Early Years, 1564–c. 1594

Stratford-upon-Avon

About Shakespeare's place of birth, Stratford-upon-Avon, there is no doubt. He spent his childhood there and returned periodically throughout his life. During most or all of his long professional career in London, his wife and children lived in Stratford. He acquired property and took some interest in local affairs. He retired to Stratford and chose to be buried there. Its Warwickshire surroundings lived in his poetic imagination.

The Stratford of Shakespeare's day was a "handsome small market town" (as described by William Camden) of perhaps 1,500 inhabitants, with fairly broad streets and half-timbered houses roofed with thatch. It could boast of a long history and an attractive setting on the river Avon. A bridge of fourteen arches, built in 1496 by Sir Hugh Clopton, Lord Mayor of London, spanned the river. Beside the Avon stood Trinity Church, built on the site of a Saxon monastery. The chapel of the Guild of the Holy Trinity,

The earliest written reference to William Shakespeare is this record of his christening in the register of Holy Trinity Church at Stratford, April 26, 1564. The entry reads, "Gulielmus filius Johannes Shakspere."

The town of Stratford-upon-Avon as Shakespeare knew it. The house in which he is considered to have been born is on Henley Street; the larger house he purchased in 1597, New Place, is on Chapel Street.

dating from the thirteenth century, and an old King Edward VI grammar school were buildings of note. Stratford had maintained a grammar school at least since 1424 and probably long before that. It was a town without the domination of clergy, aristocracy, or great wealth. It lay in a rich agricultural region, in the county of Warwickshire. To the north of Stratford lay the Forest of Arden.

Shakespeare's Family

The family which bore the name of Shakespeare was well distributed throughout England, but was especially numerous in Warwickshire. A name "Saquespee," in various spellings, is found in Normandy at an early date. It means, according to J. Q. Adams, "to draw out the sword quickly." That name, in the form "Sakspee," with many variants, is found in England; also the name "Saksper," varying gradually to the form "Shakespeare." It may have been wrought into that form by the obvious military meaning of "one who shakes the spear."

Our first substantial records of the family begin with

Richard Shakespeare, who was, in all probability, Shakespeare's grandfather, a farmer living in the village of Snitterfield four miles from Stratford. He was a tenant on the property of Robert Arden of Wilmcote, a wealthy man with the social status of gentleman. Richard Shakespeare died about 1561, possessed of an estate valued at the very respectable sum of thirty-eight pounds and seventeen shillings.

His son John made a great step forward in the world by his marriage with Mary Arden, daughter of his father's landlord. John Shakespeare had some property of his own and through his wife acquired a good deal more. He moved from Snitterfield to Stratford at some date before 1552. He rose to great local importance in Stratford and bought several houses, among which was the one on Henley Street traditionally identified as Shakespeare's birthplace. William Shakespeare was born in 1564 and was baptized on April 26. The exact date of his birth is not known, but traditionally we celebrate it on April 23, the feast day of St. George, England's patron saint. (The date is at least plausible in view of the practice of baptizing infants shortly after birth.) The house in which Shakespeare was probably born, though almost entirely rebuilt and changed in various and unknown ways during the years that have intervened since Shakespeare's birth, still stands. It is of considerable size, having four rooms on the ground floor, and must, therefore, have been an important business house in the Stratford of those days. John Shakespeare's occupation seems to have been that of a tanner and glover; that is, he cured skins, made gloves and some other leather goods, and sold them in his shop. He was also a dealer in wool, grain, malt, and other farm produce.

The long story, beginning in 1552, of John Shakespeare's success and misfortunes in Stratford is attested to by many borough records. He held various city offices. He was ale taster (inspector of bread and malt), burgess (petty constable), affeeror (assessor of fines), city chamberlain (treasurer), alderman, and high bailiff of the town—the highest municipal office in Stratford. At some time around 1576, he applied to the Herald's office for the right to bear arms and style himself a gentleman. This petition was later to be renewed and successfully carried through to completion by his famous son. In 1577 or 1578, however, when William was as yet only thirteen or fourteen years old, John Shakespeare's fortunes began a sudden and mysterious decline. He absented himself from council meetings. He had to mortgage his wife's property and showed other signs of being in financial difficulty. He became involved in serious litigation and was assessed heavy fines. Although he kept his position on the corporation council until 1586 or 1587, he was finally replaced as alderman because of his failure to attend. Conceivably, John Shakespeare's sudden difficulties were the result of persecution for his Catholic faith, since John's wife's family had remained loyal to Catholicism, and the old faith was being attacked with new

SHAKESPEARE BIRTHPLACE TRUST

This house on Henley Street in Stratford is considered to have been the birthplace of Shakespeare. Its considerable size shows what must have been an important house of business. Shakespeare's father dealt chiefly in leather goods, though he also traded in wool, grain, and other farm produce.

vigor in the Warwickshire region in 1577 and afterwards. This hypothesis is unsubstantial, however, especially in view of the fact that some Catholics and Puritans seemed to have held posts of trust and to have remained prosperous in Stratford during this period. In the last analysis, we have little evidence as to John Shakespeare's religious faith or as to the reasons for his sudden reversal of fortune.

The family of Shakespeare's mother could trace its ancestry back to the time of William the Conqueror, and Shakespeare's father, in spite of his troubles, was a citizen of importance. John Shakespeare made his mark, instead of writing his name, but so did other men of the time who we know could read and write. His offices, particularly that of chamberlain, and the various public functions he discharged indicate that he must have had some education.

Shakespeare in School

Nicholas Rowe, who published in 1709 the first extensive biographical account of Shakespeare, reports the tradition that Shakespeare studied "for some time at a Free-School." Although the list of students who actually attended the King's New School at Stratford-upon-Avon in the late sixteenth century has not survived, we cannot doubt that Rowe is reporting accurately. Shakespeare's father, as a leading citizen of Stratford, would scarcely have spurned the

benefits of one of Stratford's most prized institutions. The town had had a free school since the thirteenth century, at first under the auspices of the Church. During the reign of King Edward VI (1547–1553), the Church lands were expropriated by the crown and the town of Stratford was granted a corporate charter. At this time, the school was reorganized as the King's New School, named in honor of the reigning monarch. It prospered. Its teachers, or "masters," regularly held degrees from Oxford during Shakespeare's childhood and received salaries that were superior to those of most comparable schools.

Much has been learned about the curriculum of such a school. A child would first learn the rudiments of reading and writing English by spending two or three years in a "petty" or elementary school. The child learned to read from a "hornbook," a single sheet of paper mounted on a board and protected by a thin transparent layer of horn, on which was usually printed the alphabet in small and capital letters and the Lord's Prayer. The child would also practice an ABC book with catechism. When the child had demonstrated the ability to read satisfactorily, the child was admitted, at about the age of seven, to the grammar school proper. Here the day was a rigorous one, usually extending from 6 A.M. in the summer or 7 A.M. in the winter until 5 P.M. Intervals for food or brief recreation came at midmorning, noon, and midafternoon. Holidays occurred at Christmas,

The hornbook pictured here—showing the alphabet and the Lord's Prayer—was part of a child's education in Shakespeare's time.

Easter, and Whitsuntide (usually late May and June), comprising perhaps forty days in all through the year. Discipline was strict, and physical punishment was common.

Latin formed the basis of the grammar school curriculum. The scholars studied grammar, read ancient writers, recited, and learned to write in Latin. A standard text was the *Grammatica Latina* by William Lilly or Lyly, grandfather of the later Elizabethan dramatist John Lyly. The scholars also became familiar with the *Disticha de Moribus* (moral proverbs) attributed to Cato, *Aesop's Fables,* the *Eclogues* of Baptista Spagnuoli Mantuanus or Mantuan (alluded to in

Love's Labor's Lost), the *Eclogues* and *Aeneid* of Virgil, the comedies of Plautus or Terence (sometimes performed in Latin by the children), Ovid's *Metamorphoses* and other of his works, and possibly some Horace and Seneca.

Shakespeare plentifully reveals in his dramatic writings an awareness of many of these authors, especially Plautus (in *The Comedy of Errors*), Ovid (in *A Midsummer Night's Dream* and elsewhere), and Seneca (in *Titus Andronicus*). Although he often consulted translations of these authors, he seems to have known the originals as well. He had, in Ben Jonson's learned estimation, "small Latin and less Greek"; the tone is condescending, but the statement does concede that Shakespeare had some of both. He would have acquired some Greek in the last years of his grammar schooling. By twentieth-century standards, Shakespeare had a fairly comprehensive amount of training in the ancient classics, certainly enough to account for the general, if unscholarly, references we find in the plays.

Shakespeare's Marriage

When Shakespeare was eighteen years old, he married Anne Hathaway, a woman eight years his senior. (The inscription on her grave states that she was sixty-seven when she died in August of 1623.) The bishop's register of Worcester, the central city of the diocese, shows for November 27, 1582, the issue of a bishop's license for the marriage of William Shakespeare and Anne "Whately"; the bond of sureties issued next day refers to her as "Hathaway." She has been identified with all reasonable probability as Agnes (or Anne) Hathaway, daughter of the then recently deceased Richard Hathaway of the hamlet of Shottery, a short distance from Stratford.

The obtaining of a license was not normally required for a marriage. William Shakespeare and Anne Hathaway seem to have applied for a license on this occasion because they wished to be married after only one reading of the banns rather than the usual three. (The reading of the banns, or announcement in church of a forthcoming marriage, usually on three successive Sundays, enabled any party to object to the marriage if he or she knew of any legal impediment.) Since the reading of all banns was suspended for long periods during Advent (before Christmas) and Lent (before Easter), a couple intending to marry shortly before Christmas might have had to wait until April before the banns could be read thrice. Accordingly, the bishop not uncommonly granted a license permitting couples to marry during the winter season with only one reading of the banns. To obtain such a license, two friends of the bride's family had to sign a bond obligating themselves to pay the bishop up to forty pounds, should any impediment to the marriage result in a legal action against the bishop for having issued the license.

The actual record of the marriage in a parish register has not survived, but presumably the couple were married

A schoolroom in Tudor England.

J. KOMENSKY: ORBIS SENSUALUM PICTUS, 1659

shortly after obtaining the license. They may have been married in Temple Grafton, where Anne had relatives. The couple took up residence in Stratford. Anne was already pregnant at the time of the marriage, for she gave birth to a daughter, Susanna, on May 26, 1583. The birth of a child six months after the wedding may explain the need for haste the previous November. These circumstances, and Anne's considerable seniority in age to William, have given rise to much speculation about matters that can never be satisfactorily resolved. We do know that a formal betrothal in the presence of witnesses could legally validate a binding relationship, enabling a couple to consummate their love without social stigma. We know also that Shakespeare dramatized the issue of premarital contract and pregnancy in *Measure for Measure*. Whether Shakespeare entered into such a formal relationship with Anne is, however, undiscoverable.

On February 2, 1585, Shakespeare's only other children, the twins Hamnet and Judith, were baptized in Stratford Church. The twins seem to have been named after Shakespeare's friends and neighbors, Hamnet Sadler, a baker, and his wife, Judith.

The Seven "Dark" Years

From 1585, the year in which his twins were baptized, until 1592, when he was first referred to as an actor and dramatist of growing importance in London, Shakespeare's activities are wholly unknown. Presumably, at some time during this period he made his way to London and entered its theatrical world, but otherwise we can only record traditions and guesses as to what he did between the ages of 21 and 28.

One of the oldest and most intriguing suggestions comes from John Aubrey, who, in collecting information in the late seventeenth century about actors and dramatists for his "Minutes of Lives," sought the help of one William Beeston.

John Dryden believed Beeston to be "the chronicle of the stage," and Aubrey seems also to have had a high opinion of Beeston's theatrical knowledge. In his manuscript, Aubrey made a note to himself: "W. Shakespeare—quaere [i.e., inquire of] Mr. Beeston, who knows most of him." Aubrey then cites Beeston as his authority for this tradition about Shakespeare:

Though, as Ben Jonson says of him, that he had but little Latin and less Greek, he understood Latin pretty well, for he had been in his younger years a schoolmaster in the country.

Beeston had been a theatrical manager all his life. He was the son of the actor Christopher Beeston, who had been a member of Shakespeare's company probably from 1596 until 1602 and who therefore had occasion to know Shakespeare well.

Shakespeare's own grammar school education would not have qualified him to be the master of a school, but he could have served as "usher" or assistant to the master. The idea that Shakespeare may have taught in this way is not unattractive. Although, as we have seen, he had some acquaintance with Plautus, Ovid, and other classical writers through his own grammar school reading, a stint as schoolmaster would have made these authors more familiar and readily accessible to him when he began writing his plays and nondramatic poems. His earliest works—*The Comedy of Errors, Love's Labor's Lost, Titus Andronicus, Venus and Adonis, The Rape of Lucrece*—show most steadily and directly the effect of his classical reading. Schoolteaching experience might have encouraged his ambitions to be a writer, like Marlowe or Greene, who went to London not to be actors but to try their hands at poetry and playwriting. All in all, however, it seems more probable that Shakespeare became a young actor rather than a schoolteacher.

Another tradition about the years from 1585 to 1592

asserts that Shakespeare served part of an apprenticeship in Stratford. This suggestion comes to us from one John Dowdall, who, traveling through Warwickshire in 1693, heard the story from an old parish clerk who was showing him around the town of Stratford. According to this parish clerk, Shakespeare had been bound as apprentice to a butcher but ran away from his master to London where he was received into a playhouse as "servitor." John Aubrey records a similar tradition: "When he [Shakespeare] was a boy he exercised his father's trade." Aubrey believed this trade to have been that of a butcher. Moreover, says Aubrey, "When he killed a calf, he would do it in a high style, and make a speech." No other evidence confirms, however, that Shakespeare was a runaway apprentice. The allusion to "killing a calf" may, instead, refer to an ancient rural amusement in which the slaughter of a calf was staged behind a curtain for the entertainment of visitors at county fairs. Conceivably, Shakespeare's participation in such a game during his youth may have given rise to the tradition that he had been a butcher's apprentice.

Another legend, that of Shakespeare's deer stealing, has enjoyed wide currency. We are indebted for this story to the Reverend Richard Davies, who, some time between 1688 and 1709, jotted down some gossipy interpolations in the manuscripts of the Reverend William Fulman. (Fulman himself was an antiquarian who had collected a number of notes about Shakespeare and Stratford.) According to Davies, Shakespeare was "much given to all unluckiness in stealing venison and rabbits, particularly from Sir ——— Lucy, who had him oft whipped and sometimes imprisoned and at last made him fly his native country, to his great advancement." This tradition has led to speculation by Nicholas Rowe that Justice Shallow of *2 Henry IV* and *The Merry Wives of Windsor* is a satirical portrait of Sir Thomas Lucy of Charlecote Hall and that Shakespeare even composed an irreverent ballad about Lucy that added to the urgency of Shakespeare's departure for London. In fact, however, there is no compelling reason to believe that Shallow is based on Lucy, on Justice William Gardiner of Surrey (as Leslie Hotson insists), or on any live Elizabethan. We don't know that Shakespeare ever drew contemporary portraits in his plays, as is sometimes alleged; is Polonius in *Hamlet* Lord Burghley, for example, or is he Shakespeare's original portrait of a minister of state who is also a busybody? Nor do we know if the deer-slaying incident took place at all. It makes interesting fiction but unreliable biography.

Shakespeare's Arrival in London

Because of the total absence of reliable information concerning the seven years from 1585 to 1592, we do not know how Shakespeare got his start in the theatrical world. He may have joined one of the touring companies that came to Stratford and then accompanied the players to London.

Edmund Malone offered the unsupported statement (in 1780) that Shakespeare's "first office in the theater was that of prompter's attendant." Presumably, a young man from the country would have had to begin at the bottom. Shakespeare's later work certainly reveals an intimate and practical acquaintance with technical matters of stagecraft. In any case, his rise to eminence as an actor and a writer seems to have been rapid. He was fortunate also in having at least one prosperous acquaintance in London, Richard Field, formerly of Stratford and the son of an associate of Shakespeare's father. Field was a printer, and in 1593 and 1594 he published two handsome editions of Shakespeare's first serious poems, *Venus and Adonis* and *The Rape of Lucrece*.

"The Only Shake-scene in a Country"

The first allusion to Shakespeare after his Stratford days is a vitriolic attack on him. It occurs in *Greene's Groats-worth of Wit Bought with a Million of Repentance*, written by Robert Greene during the last months of his wretched existence (he died in poverty in September of 1592). A famous passage in this work lashes out at the actors of the public theaters for having deserted Greene and for bestowing their favor instead on a certain upstart dramatist. The passage warns three fellow dramatists and University Wits, Christopher Marlowe, Thomas Nashe, and George Peele, to abandon the writing of plays before they fall prey to a similar ingratitude. The diatribe runs as follows:

. . . Base minded men all three of you, if by my misery you be not warned. For unto none of you (like me) sought those burs to cleave—those puppets, I mean, that spake from our mouths, those antics garnished in our colors. Is it not strange that I, to whom they all have been beholding, is it not like that you, to whom they all have been beholding, shall (were ye in that case as I am now) be both at once of them forsaken? Yes, trust them not. For there is an upstart crow, beautified with our feathers, that with his "Tiger's heart wrapped in a player's hide" supposes he is as well able to bombast out a blank verse as the best of you, and, being an absolute *Johannes Factotum*, is in his own conceit the only Shake-scene in a country.

The "burs" here referred to are the actors who have forsaken Greene in his poverty for the rival playwright "Shake-scene"—an obvious hit at Shakespeare. The sneer at a *"Johannes Factotum"* suggests another dig at Shakespeare for being a Jack-of-all-trades—actor, playwright, poet, and theatrical handyman in the directing and producing of plays. The most unmistakable reference to Shakespeare, however, is to be found in the burlesque line, "Tiger's heart wrapped in a player's hide," modeled after "O tiger's heart wrapped in a woman's hide!" from *3 Henry VI* (1.4.137). Shakespeare's success as a dramatist had led to an envious outburst from an older, disappointed rival. (Did Shakespeare possibly have this attack in mind some years later when he has Polonius object, in *Hamlet,* 2.2.111–112, " 'beautified' is a vile phrase"?)

Soon after Greene's death, Henry Chettle, who had seen the manuscript through the press (and who today is under suspicion of having written the attack himself), issued an apology in his *Kind-Heart's Dream*. The apology begins with a disclaimer of all personal responsibility for the incident and with Chettle's insistence that he has neither known nor wishes to know Marlowe (whom Greene's pamphlet had accused of atheism). Toward Shakespeare, on the other hand, Chettle expresses genuine concern and regret that Chettle had not done more to soften the acerbity of Greene's vitriol:

The other [i.e., Shakespeare], whom at that time I did not so much spare as since I wish I had, for that, as I have moderated the heat of living writers and might have used my own discretion (especially in such a case, the author being dead), that I did not I am as sorry as if the original fault had been my fault; because myself have seen his demeanor no less civil than he excellent in the quality he professes. Besides, divers of worship have reported his uprightness of dealing, which argues his honesty and his facetious grace in writing that approves his art.

This handsome apology reveals the young Shakespeare in a most attractive light. Chettle freely admits to having been impressed by Shakespeare's civility. He praises the young dramatists as "excellent in the quality he professes," that is, excellent as an actor. Chettle notes with approval that Shakespeare enjoys the favor of certain persons of importance, some of whom have borne witness to his uprightness in dealing. *Groats-worth of Wit*, then, with its rancorous attack on Shakespeare, has served paradoxically to reveal the fact that in 1592 Shakespeare was regarded as a man of pleasant demeanor, honest reputation, and acknowledged skill as an actor and writer.

Dramatic Apprenticeship

By the end of the year 1594, when after the long plague the theatrical companies were again permitted to act before London audiences, we find Shakespeare as a member of the Lord Chamberlain's company. Probably he had already written *The Comedy of Errors, Love's Labor's Lost, The Two Gentlemen of Verona*, the *Henry VI* plays, and *Titus Andronicus*. (A *Love's Labor's Won*, mentioned by Francis Meres in 1598, is possibly either a lost play or an alternate title for one of the extant comedies.) He may also have completed *The Taming of the Shrew, A Midsummer Night's Dream, Richard III, King John*, and *Romeo and Juliet*. Although a few scholars still question his authorship in part or all of *Titus* and the *Henry VI* plays, no one questions that they are from the period around 1590.

Shakespeare's early development is hard to follow because of difficulties in exact dating of the early plays and because some of the texts (such as *Love's Labor's Lost*) may have been later revised. As a learner making rapid progress in the skill of his art, Shakespeare was also subjected to outside influences which can only partly be determined.

Among these influences, we may be sure, were the plays of his contemporary dramatists. If we could define these influences and form an idea of the kinds of plays acceptable on the stage during Shakespeare's early period, we could better understand the milieu in which he began his work.

Fortunately, we know a fair amount concerning the dramatic repertory in London during Shakespeare's early years. Henslowe's *Diary*, for example, records the daily performances of plays by the Lord Strange's men, in conjunction with the Admiral's men, from February 19, 1592 to June 22, 1592. Many of their plays unfortunately are lost, but enough of them are preserved to indicate the sorts of drama then in vogue. The Strange-Admiral's repertory included Christopher Marlowe's *The Jew of Malta*, Robert Greene's *Orlando Furioso* and *Friar Bacon and Friar Bungay*, Robert Greene and Thomas Lodge's *A Looking Glass for London and England*, Thomas Kyd's *The Spanish Tragedy*, the anonymous *A Knack to Know a Knave*, and possibly George Peele's *The Battle of Alcazar* and Shakespeare's *1 Henry VI*. We find, in other words, a tragedy with a villain as hero, a romantic comedy masquerading as a heroic play, a love comedy featuring a lot of magic, a biblical moral, England's first great revenge tragedy, a popular satiric comedy aimed at dissolute courtiers and usurers, a history play about Portugal's African empire, and an English history play. The titles of other works now lost suggest a similar amalgam of widely differing genres.

Comparatively few plays may have been written during the period when plays were forbidden because of the long plague of 1592–1594. When the Lord Chamberlain's men and the Lord Admiral's men acted under Henslowe's management at the suburban theater of Newington Butts from June 3 to 13, 1594, their repertories seem to have consisted largely of old plays. In this brief period, they are thought to have acted *Titus Andronicus, Hamlet* (the pre-Shakespearean version), *The Taming of a Shrew* (quite possibly Shakespeare's version), *The Jew of Malta*, a lost play called *Hester and Ahasuerus*, and others.

The Lord Admiral's men probably moved soon afterwards in 1594 to the Rose on the Bankside, across the river Thames from the city of London, where they continued to play under Henslowe's management until 1603. During the years 1594–1597, Henslowe kept in his *Diary* a careful record of their plays and of the sums of money taken in. This circumstance enables us to know a great deal more about the repertory of Shakespeare's rival company than we can ever know about his own. When the Lord Admiral's men began again in 1594, they had five of Marlowe's plays. They seem also to have had Peele's *Edward I*, Kyd's *The Spanish Tragedy*, and a *Henry V* play. They may also have had plays by both Greene and Peele (Henslowe's chaotic spelling makes it hard to determine), although some of the principal dramas of these two authors had probably ceased to be acted.

We do not know as much about the repertory of the Lord Chamberlain's company as we do about that of the Lord Admiral's men. We know enough, however, to be sure that in 1594 both companies were acting the same sorts of plays that had been on the boards in 1592. We have, therefore, grounds for assuming that, in spite of the loss of many plays (some of which may have been important), the chief contemporary influences upon Shakespeare during his early period were those of Marlowe, Greene, Peele, and Kyd. As an actor possibly in Lord Strange's company or the Earl of Pembroke's company, he would have been familiar with their plays.

Shakespeare learned also from Lyly, though perhaps more from reading Lyly's plays than from actually seeing or performing in them. The boy actors for whom Lyly wrote were forced by the authorities to suspend acting in about 1591 because of their tendency toward controversial satire, and a number of Lyly's plays were printed at that time. As a theatrical figure, therefore, Lyly belonged really to the previous decade.

The Early Plays

Although Shakespeare's genius manifests itself in his early work, his indebtedness to contemporary dramatists and to classical writers is also more plainly evident than in his later writings. His first tragedy, *Titus Andronicus* (c. 1589–1592), is more laden with quotations and classical references than any other tragedy he wrote. Its genre owes much to the revenge play that had been made so popular by Thomas Kyd. Like Kyd, Shakespeare turns to Seneca but also reveals on stage a considerable amount of sensational violence in a manner that is distinctly not classical. For his first villain, Aaron the Moor, Shakespeare borrows some motifs from the morality play and its gleefully sinister tempter, the Vice. Shakespeare may also have had in mind the boastful antics of Marlowe's Vicelike Barabas, in *The Jew of Malta*. Certainly, Shakespeare reveals an extensive

debt in his early works to Ovid and to the vogue of Ovidian narrative poetry in the early 1590s, as, for example, in his repeated allusions to the story of Philomela and Tereus (in *Titus Andronicus*) and in his Ovidian poems, *Venus and Adonis* and *The Rape of Lucrece* (1593, 1594).

Shakespeare was still questing for a suitable mode in tragedy and was discovering that the English drama of the 1590s offered no single, clear model. His only other early tragedy, *Romeo and Juliet* (c. 1594–1596), proved to be as different a tragedy from *Titus Andronicus* as could be imagined. Revenge is still prominent in *Romeo and Juliet* but is ultimately far less compelling a theme than the brevity of love and the sacrifice the lovers make of themselves to one another. Shakespeare's source is not the revenge drama of Seneca or Kyd, but a romantic love narrative derived from the fiction of Renaissance Italy. Elements of comedy so predominate in the play's first half that one senses a closer affinity to *A Midsummer Night's Dream* than to *The Spanish Tragedy*.

Shakespeare discovered his true bent more quickly in comedy than in tragedy. Again, however, he experimented with a wide range of models and genres. *The Comedy of Errors* (c. 1589–1594) brings together elements of two plots from the Latin drama of Plautus. The character types and situations are partly derivative, but Shakespeare still reveals an impressive skill in plot construction. *Love's Labor's Lost* (c. 1588–1597) is Shakespeare's most Lylyan early comedy, with its witty debates and its amicable, if brittle, war between the sexes. The play also features an array of humorous characters, including a clownish bumpkin, a country slut, a fantastic courtier, a pedant, a country curate, and the like, whose mannerisms and wordplay add to the rich feast of language in a play that centers its attention on proper and improper styles. *The Two Gentlemen of Verona* (c. 1590–1594) and *The Taming of the Shrew* (c. 1590–1593) are derived from Italianate romantic fiction and comedy. In both, Shakespeare skillfully combines simultaneous plots that offer contrasting views on love and

A contemporary illustration of Titus Andronicus, *the earliest of Shakespeare's tragedies. Shakespeare's early plays demonstrated that he was more than a slavish imitator of predecessors such as Kyd and Marlowe.*

THE GREAT POND AT ELVETHAM
arranged for the Second Day's Entertainment.

A. Her Majestie's presence seate and traine.   B. Nereus and his followers.   C. The pinnace of Neæra and her musicke.   D. The Ship-ile.
E. A boate with musicke, attending on the pinnace of Neæra.   F. The Fort-mount.   G. The Snaile-mount.   H. The Roome of Estate.
I. Her Majestie's Court.   K. Her Majestie's Wardrop.   L. The place whence Silvanus and his companie issued.

An entertainment presented by the Earl of Hertford to Queen Elizabeth during her visit to Elvethan in 1591 is seemingly referred to by Shakespeare in A Midsummer Night's Dream, 2.1.157–164. *The scene shows an elaborate water pageant in honor of the Queen, who appears enthroned at the left of the picture.*

friendship. (*The Taming of the Shrew* makes effective use of a "frame" plot involving a group of characters who serve as audience for the rest of the play.) *A Midsummer Night's Dream* (c. 1595), with its four brilliantly interwoven actions involving court figures, lovers, fairies, and Athenian tradesmen, shows us Shakespeare already at the height of his powers in play construction, even though the comic emphasis on love's irrationality in this play is still in keeping with Shakespeare's early style. The early comedies do not ignore conflict and danger, as we see in the threatened execution of Egeon in *The Comedy of Errors* and the failure of courtships in *Love's Labor's Lost,* but these plays do not as yet fully explore the social dilemmas of *The Merchant of Venice,* the narrowly averted catastrophe of *Much Ado About Nothing,* or the melancholy vein of *As You Like It*

and *Twelfth Night.* On stage, early comedies such as *The Comedy of Errors* and *The Taming of the Shrew* are as hilariously funny as anything Shakespeare ever wrote.

Shakespeare's early history plays show a marked affinity with those of Marlowe, Peele, and Greene. Yet today Shakespeare is given more credit for pioneering in the genre of the English history play than he once was. If all the *Henry VI* plays (c. 1589–1592) are basically his, as scholars now often allow, he had more imitators in this genre than predecessors. He scored a huge early success with the heroic character of Lord Talbot in *1 Henry VI,* and by the time Richard Duke of Gloucester had emerged from the *Henry VI* plays to become King Richard III, Shakespeare's fame as a dramatist was assured. He had, of course, learned much from Marlowe's "mighty line" in *Tamburlaine*

(1587–1588) and perhaps from Peele's *The Battle of Alcazar* (1588–1589). The anonymous *Famous Victories of Henry V* (1583–1588) must have preceded and influenced his work. Even so, Shakespeare had done much more than simply "beautify" himself with the "feathers" of earlier dramatists, as Greene (or Chettle) enviously charged. Even in his earliest work, Shakespeare already displayed an extraordinary ability to transcend the models from which he learned.

The Anti-Stratfordian Movement

What we know of Shakespeare's life so far is really quite considerable. The information we have is just the kind one would expect. It hangs together and refers to one man and one career. Though lacking in the personal details we should like to have, it is both adequate and plausible. Yet the past hundred years or so have seen the growth of a tendency to doubt Shakespeare's authorship of the plays and poems ascribed to him. The phenomenon is sometimes called the "anti-Stratfordian" movement, since its attack is leveled at the literary credentials of the man who was born in Stratford and later became an actor in London. Although based on no reliable evidence, the movement has persisted long enough to become a kind of myth. It also has the appeal of a mystery thriller: who really wrote Shakespeare's plays? A brief account must be made here of the origins of the anti-Stratfordian movement.

Beginning in the late eighteenth century, and especially in the mid nineteenth century, a few admirers of Shakespeare began to be troubled by the scantiness of information about England's greatest author. As we have already seen, good reasons exist for the scarcity: the great London fire of 1666 that destroyed many records, the relatively low social esteem accorded to popular dramatists during the Elizabethan period, and the like. Also, we do actually know more about Shakespeare than about most of his contemporaries in the theater, despite the difficulties imposed by the passage of time. Still, some nineteenth-century readers saw only that they knew far less about Shakespeare than about many authors of more recent date.

Moreover, the impressions of the man did not seem to square with his unparalleled literary greatness. William Shakespeare had been brought up in a small country town; were his parents cultured folk or even literate? No record of his schooling has been preserved; was Shakespeare himself able to read and write, much less write immortal plays and poems? The anti-Stratfordians did not deny the existence of a man called Shakespeare from Stratford-upon-Avon, but they found it incredible that such a person should be connected with the works ascribed to him. Mark Twain, himself an anti-Stratfordian, was fond of joking that the plays were not by Shakespeare but by another person of the same name. Beneath the humor in this remark lies a deep-seated

mistrust: how could a country boy have written so knowledgeably and eloquently about the lives of kings and queens? Where could such a person have learned so much about the law, about medicine, about the art of war, about heraldry? The puzzle seemed a genuine one, even though no one until the late eighteenth century had thought to question Shakespeare's authorship of the plays—least of all his colleagues and friends, such as Ben Jonson, who admitted that Shakespeare's classical learning was "small" but insisted that Shakespeare was an incomparable genius.

The first candidate put forward in the anti-Stratfordian cause as the "real" author of the plays was Sir Francis Bacon, a reputable Elizabethan writer with connections at court and considerable cultural attainments. Yet the ascription of the plays to Bacon was based on no documentary evidence. It relied, instead, on the essentially snobbish argument that Bacon was better born and purportedly better educated than Shakespeare—an argument that appealed strongly to the nineteenth century in which a university education was becoming more and more a distinctive mark of the cultivated person. The assertion of Bacon's authorship was also based on a conspiratorial theory of history; that is, its believers had to assume the existence of a mammoth conspiracy in Elizabethan times in which Shakespeare would allow his name to be used by Bacon as a *nom de plume* and in which Shakespeare's friends, such as Ben Jonson, would take part. (Jonson knew Shakespeare too well, after all, to have been duped for a period of almost twenty years.) The motive for such an arrangement, presumably, was that Bacon did not deign to lend his dignified name to the writing of popular plays (since they were considered subliterary) and so chose a common actor named Shakespeare to serve as his alter ego. This theory of an elaborate hoax involving England's greatest literary giant has proved powerfully attractive to modern writers like Mark Twain, who sometimes refer to themselves as rebels against the cultural "Establishment" of their own times.

The claim that Bacon wrote Shakespeare's works was soon challenged in the name of other prominent Elizabethans: the Earl of Oxford, the Earl of Southampton, Anthony Bacon, the Earl of Rutland, the Earl of Devonshire, Christopher Marlowe, and others. Since documentary claims as to Bacon's authorship of the Shakespearen canon were nonexistent, other Elizabethans could be proposed to fill his role just as satisfactorily as Bacon himself. The anti-Stratfordian movement gained momentum and came to include several prominent persons, including Delia Bacon and Sigmund Freud, as well as Mark Twain. One of the appeals of the anti-Stratfordian movement in recent years has proved to be a kind of amateur sleuthing or scholarship, carried on by professional lawyers, doctors, and the like, who have explored Shakespeare's interest in law and medicine as a hobby and have convinced themselves that Shakespeare's wisdom in these subjects entitles him to claim a better birth than that of a glover's son from Stratford. Ingenious efforts at "deciphering" hidden meanings in the works have been adduced to prove one authorship claim or another. The academic "Establishments" of modern universities have been accused of perpetuating Shakespeare's name out of mere vested self-interest: Shakespeare scholarship is an industry, and its busy workers need to preserve their source of income.

We must ask in all seriousness, however, whether such assertions are not offering answers to nonexistent questions. Responsible scholarship has admirably dispelled the seeming mystery of Shakespeare's humble beginnings. T. W. Baldwin, for example, in *William Shakespeare's Petty School* (1943) and *William Shakspere's Small Latine and Lesse Greeke* (1944) has shown just what sort of classical training Shakespeare almost surely received in the free grammar school of Stratford. It is precisely the sort of training that would have enabled him to use classical authors as he does, with the familiarity of one who likes to read. His Latin and Greek were passable but not strong; he often consulted modern translations, as well as classical originals. Just as importantly, Shakespeare's social background was, in fact, typical of many of the greatest writers of the English Renaissance. He earned his living by his writing, and thus had one of the strongest of motives for success. So did his contemporaries Marlowe (who came from a shoemaker's family) and Jonson (whose stepfather was a brickmason). Greene, Peele, Nashe, and many others sold plays and other writings for a livelihood. Although a few wellborn persons, such as Bacon and Sir Philip Sidney, also made exceptional contributions to literature and although a number of courtiers emulated Henry VIII and Elizabeth as gifted amateurs in the arts, the court was not the direct or major source of England's literary greatness. Most courtiers were not, like Shakespeare, professional writers. A man like Bacon lacked Shakespeare's connection with a commercial acting company. Surely the theater was a more relevant "university" for Shakespeare than Oxford or Cambridge, where most of his studies would have been in ancient languages and in divinity.

Shakespeare in the Theater, c. 1594–1601

By the year 1594, Shakespeare had already achieved a considerable reputation as a poet and dramatist. We should not be surprised that many of his contemporaries thought of his nondramatic writing as his most significant literary achievement. Throughout his lifetime, in fact, his contemporary fame rested, to a remarkable degree, on his nondramatic poems, *Venus and Adonis*, *The Rape of Lucrece*, and the *Sonnets* (which were circulated in manuscript prior to their unauthorized publication in 1609). One of the

earliest tributes suggesting the importance of the poems is to be found in an anonymous commendatory verse prefixed to Henry Willobie's *Willobie His Avisa* (1594). It summarizes the plot and theme of *The Rape of Lucrece*:

> Though *Collatine* have dearly bought,
> To high renown, a lasting life,
> And found—that most in vain have sought—
> To have a fair and constant wife,
>   Yet Tarquin plucked his glittering grape,
>   And Shakespeare paints poor Lucrece' rape.

Richard Barnfield, in his *Poems in Divers Humors* (1598), praised the "honey-flowing vein" of Shakespeare's *Venus and Adonis* and *The Rape of Lucrece*. The poet Edmund Spenser may also have had Shakespeare's nondramatic poetry in mind when in *Colin Clout's Come Home Again* (in a passage probably composed in 1594–1595) he listed twelve contemporary poets, most of them by fictional names, and included that of Aetion, "though last not least." Aetion has been identified by many scholars as Shakespeare, though other candidates have been proposed as well. Spenser wrote of Aetion:

> A gentler shepherd may nowhere be found,
> Whose muse, full of high thought's invention,
> Doth like himself heroically sound.

Yet Shakespeare's plays were also highly regarded by his contemporaries, even if those plays were accorded a literary status below that given to the narrative and lyrical poems. Francis Meres insisted, in 1598, that Shakespeare deserved to be compared not only with Ovid for his verse but also with Plautus and Seneca for his comedies and tragedies:

> As the soul of Euphorbus was thought to live in Pythagoras, so the sweet, witty soul of Ovid lives in mellifluous and honey-tongued Shakespeare: witness his *Venus and Adonis*, his *Lucrece*, his sugared sonnets among his private friends, etc.
> As Plautus and Seneca are accounted the best for comedy and tragedy among the Latins, so Shakespeare among the English is the most excellent in both kinds for the stage: for comedy, witness his *Gentlemen of Verona*, his *Errors*, his *Love's Labor's Lost*, his *Love's Labor's Won*, his *Midsummer Night's Dream*, and his *Merchant of Venice*; for tragedy, his *Richard the II*, *Richard the III*, *Henry the IV*, *King John*, *Titus Andronicus*, and his *Romeo and Juliet*.

Comedy and tragedy were, after all, literary forms sanctioned by classical precept. By calling Shakespeare's English history plays "tragedies," Meres endowed them with the respectability of an ancient literary tradition, recognizing, too, that many of Shakespeare's historical plays culminate in the death of an English king.

John Weever, too, in his epigram *Ad Gulielmum Shakespeare* in *Epigrams in the Oldest Cut and Newest Fashion* (1599), mentioned not only the ever-popular narrative poems but also *Romeo and Juliet* and a history play about one of the Richards:

Honey-tongued Shakespeare! When I saw thine issue,
I swore Apollo got them and none other:
Their rosy-tainted features clothed in tissue,
Some heaven-born goddess said to be their mother;
Rose-cheeked Adonis, with his amber tresses,
Fair fire-hot Venus, charming him to love her;
Chaste Lucretia virgin-like her dresses,
Proud lust-stung Tarquin seeking still to prove her;
Romeo, Richard—more whose names I know not.
Their sugared tongues and power-attractive beauty
Say they are saints, although that saints they show not,
For thousands vows to them subjective duty;
They burn in love thy children. Shakespeare het them.
Go, woo thy muse more nymphish brood beget them.

Even Gabriel Harvey, an esteemed classical scholar and friend of Edmund Spenser, considered Shakespeare's play *Hamlet* to be worthy of no less praise than the best of the Ovidian poems. Harvey's comments are to be found in a marginal note to a copy of Speght's *Chaucer*, written down some time between 1598 and 1601:

The younger sort takes much delight in Shakespeare's *Venus and Adonis*, but his *Lucrece* and his tragedy of *Hamlet, Prince of Denmark* have it in them to please the wiser sort.

Shakespeare's growing fame was even such that his dramatic characters began to enter into the intellectual life of the time. The name of Falstaff became a byword almost as soon as he made his appearance on the stage. The references were not always friendly. A play written to be performed by the rival Admiral's company in answer to *1 Henry IV*, called *Sir John Oldcastle* (1599), took Falstaff to task for being a "pampered glutton" and an "aged counsellor to youthful sin." Evidently, the authors of this attack were offended by the fact that Falstaff had been named "Oldcastle" in an early version of *1 Henry IV*, thereby dishonoring the name of one whom many Puritans regarded as a martyr to their cause (see the Introduction to *1 Henry IV*). Generally, however, the references during this period to Falstaff and his cronies were fond. In a letter to a friend in London, for example, Sir Charles Percy fretted jocosely that his prolonged stay in the country among his rustic neighbors might cause him to "be taken for Justice Silence or Justice Shallow" (1600). In another letter, from the Countess of Southampton to her husband (written seemingly in 1599), Falstaff's name had become so familiar that it was used apparently as a privately understood substitute for the name of some real person in an item of court gossip:

All the news I can send you, that I think will make you merry, is that I read in a letter from London that Sir John Falstaff is by his Mistress Dame Pintpot made father of a godly miller's thumb, a boy that's all head and very little body; but this is a secret.

Shakespeare's immense popularity as a dramatist was bound to invite some resentment. One irreverent reaction is to be found in the so-called *Parnassus* trilogy (1598–1603). The three plays in this series consist of *The Pilgrimage to*

Falstaff and Mistress Quickly are shown here in a composite theatrical illustration of about 1662. The engraving, used as the frontispiece to Francis Kirkman's The Wits, or Sport upon Sport, *also shows other theatrical types. Visible are candelabras and footlights for stage lighting and a curtained area used perhaps for "discoveries." Spectators are visible in the gallery above, as they are also in the De Witt drawing of the Swan Theatre on p. xlvi and in Alabaster's* Roxana *on p. xlv.*

BETTMANN/HULTON

Henry Fuseli's nineteenth-century interpretation of Falstaff shows him in the tavern in Eastcheap with Doll Tearsheet on his lap while Prince Hal and Poins, disguised as tapsters, enter from behind. Falstaff is perhaps saying, "Peace, good Doll, do not speak like a death's-head" (2 Henry IV, 2.4.232–233).

Chaucer's, Gower's and Spenser's and Mr. Shakespeare's," which Gullio will then pass off as his own inspiration. When Ingenioso does so extempore, producing, among other things, a fine parody of *Venus and Adonis,* Gullio is as delighted as a child. Although he admires Spenser, Chaucer, and Gower, Gullio confesses that Shakespeare is his favorite; he longs to hang Shakespeare's portrait "in my study at the court" and vows he will sleep with *Venus and Adonis* under his pillow (*The Return from Parnassus,* Part I, 1009–1217). Later on (lines 1875–1880), some university graduates trying out as actors in Shakespeare's company are requested to recite a few famous lines from the beginning of *Richard III*—lines that, in the satirical context of this play, sound both stereotyped and bombastic. Shakespeare's fame made him an easy target for university "wits" who regarded the theater of London as lowbrow. Still, the portrait throughout is more satirical of those who plagiarize and idolize Shakespeare than of the dramatist's own work. In their backhanded tribute, the *Parnassus* authors make plain that Shakespeare was a household name even at the universities.

Shakespeare's Career and Private Life

During the years from 1594 to 1601, Shakespeare seems to have prospered as an actor and writer for the Lord Chamberlain's men. Whether he had previously belonged to Lord Strange's company or to the Earl of Pembroke's company, or possibly to some other group, is uncertain, but we know that he took part in 1594 in the general reorganization of the companies, out of which emerged the Lord Chamberlain's company. In 1595, his name appeared, for the first time, in the accounts of the Treasurer of the Royal Chamber as a member of the Chamberlain's company of players, which had presented two comedies before Queen Elizabeth at Greenwich in the Christmas season of 1594. This company usually performed at the Theatre, northeast of London, from 1594 until 1599, when they moved to the Globe playhouse south of the Thames. They seem to have been the victors in the intense economic rivalry between themselves and the Lord Admiral's company at the Rose playhouse under Philip Henslowe's management. Fortunately for all the adult companies, the boys' private theatrical companies were shut down during most of the 1590s. Shakespeare's company enjoyed a phenomenal success, and in short time it became the most successful theatrical organization in England.

The nucleus of the Chamberlain's company in 1594 was the family of Burbage. James Burbage, the father, was owner of the Theatre, Cuthbert Burbage was a manager, and Richard Burbage became the principal actor of the troupe. Together the Burbages owned five "shares" in the company, entitling them to half the profits. Shakespeare and four other principal actors—John Heminges, Thomas Pope, Augustine Phillips, and Will Kempe—owned one share each. Not

Parnassus and *The Return from Parnassus,* in two parts, all of which were acted by the students of St. John's College, Cambridge.

These *Parnassus* plays take a mordantly satirical view of English life around 1600, from the point of view of university graduates attempting to find gainful employment. The graduates discover, to their vocal dismay, that they must seek the patronage of fashion-mongering courtiers, complacent justices of the peace, professional acting companies who offer them pitifully small wages, and the like. One especially foolish patron, to whom the witty Ingenioso applies for a position, is a poetaster named Gullio. This courtly fop aspires to be a fashionable poet himself, and agrees to hire Ingenioso if the latter will help him with his verse writing. In fact, however, as Ingenioso scornfully observes in a series of asides, Gullio's verses are "nothing but pure Shakespeare and shreds of poetry that he hath gathered at the theaters." Most of all, Gullio loves to plagiarize from *Venus and Adonis* and *Romeo and Juliet.* With unparalleled presumption, he actually requests Ingenioso to compose poems "in two or three divers veins, in

First among the actors in Shakespeare's company was Richard Burbage (1567–1619). He played Hamlet, Othello, King Lear, and presumably other major roles including Macbeth, Antony, Coriolanus, and Prospero.

only was Shakespeare a full sharing actor, but also he was the principal playwright of the company. He was named as a chief actor in the 1616 edition of Ben Jonson's *Every Man in His Humor,* performed by the Chamberlain's company in 1598. Later tradition reports, with questionable reliability, that Shakespeare specialized in "kingly parts" or in the roles of older men, such as Adam in *As You Like It* and the Ghost in *Hamlet.* Shakespeare was more celebrated as a playwright than as an actor, and his acting responsibilities may well have diminished as his writing reputation grew. The last occasion on which he is known to have acted was in Jonson's *Sejanus* in 1603.

His prosperity appears in the first record of his residence in London. The tax returns, or Subsidy Rolls, of a Parliamentary subsidy granted to Queen Elizabeth for the year 1596 show that Shakespeare was a resident in the parish of St. Helen's, Bishopsgate, near the Theatre, and was assessed at

the respectable sum of five pounds. By the next year, Shakespeare had evidently moved to Southwark, near the Bear Garden, for the returns from Bishopsgate show his taxes delinquent. He was later located and the taxes paid.

In 1596, Shakespeare suffered a serious personal loss: the death of his only son Hamnet, at the age of eleven. Hamnet was buried at Stratford in August.

Shakespeare acquired property in Stratford during these years, as well as in London. In 1597 he purchased New Place, a house of importance and one of the two largest in the town. Shakespeare's family entered the house as residents shortly after the purchase and continued there until long after Shakespeare's death. The last of his family, his granddaughter, Lady Bernard, died in 1670, and New Place was sold.

Shakespeare was also interested in the purchase of land at Shottery in 1598. He was listed among the chief holders of corn and malt in Stratford that same year and sold a load of stone to the Stratford corporation in 1599.

No less suggestive of Shakespeare's rapid rise in the world is his acquisition of the right to bear arms, or, in other words, his establishment in the rank and title of gentleman. The Herald's College in London preserves two drafts of a grant of arms to Shakespeare's father, devised by one William Dethick and dated October 20, 1596. Although we may certainly believe that the application was put forward by William Shakespeare, John Shakespeare was still living, and the grant was drawn up in the father's name. The device for Shakespeare's coat-of-arms makes a somewhat easy use of the meaning of his name:

Gold on a bend sables, a spear of the first steeled argent. And for his crest of cognizance a falcon, his wings displayed argent,

This recreation of what New Place purportedly looked like during Shakespeare's ownership suggests that it must have indeed been an imposing structure. It was warmed by ten fireplaces and had surrounding grounds that included two gardens and two barns.

standing on a wreath of his colors, supporting a spear, gold steeled as aforesaid, set upon a helmet with mantles and tassels, as hath been accustomed and doth more plainly appear depicted on this margent.

According to one of the documents in the grant, John Shakespeare, at the height of his prosperity as a Stratford burgher, had applied twenty years before to the Herald's College for authority to bear arms. The family may not have been able to meet the expense of seeing the application through, however, until William Shakespeare had made his fortune. The grant of heraldic honors to John Shakespeare was confirmed in 1599.

A lawsuit during this period gives us a rather baffling glimpse into Shakespeare's life in the theater. From a writ discovered by Leslie Hotson (*Shakespeare Versus Shallow*, 1931) in the records of the Court of the Queen's Bench, Michaelmas term 1596, we learn that a person named William Wayte sought "for fear of death" to have William Shakespeare, Francis Langley, and two unknown women bound over to keep the peace. Earlier in the same term, moreover, Francis Langley had sworn out a similar writ against this same William Wayte and his stepfather William Gardiner, a justice of the peace in Surrey. Langley was owner of the Swan playhouse on the bankside, near the later-built Globe. His quarrel with Gardiner and Wayte appears to have jeopardized all the acting companies that performed plays south of the Thames, for William Gardiner's jurisdiction included the Bankside theater district. Gardiner and Wayte vengefully tried to drive the theaters out of the area. Possibly Shakespeare's company acted occasionally at the Swan in 1596. Hotson speculates that Shakespeare retaliated by immortalizing Gardiner and Wayte as Shallow and Slender in *The Merry Wives of Windsor*. The date of 1596 is too early for that play, and we do not know that Shakespeare drew contemporary portraits in his drama, but we can wonder if lawsuits of this sort gave him no very high opinion of the law's delay and the insolence of office.

During this period Shakespeare's plays began to appear occasionally in print. His name was becoming such a drawing card that it appeared on the title pages of the Second and Third Quartos of *Richard II* (1598), the Second Quarto of *Richard III* (1598), *Love's Labor's Lost* (1598), and the Second Quarto of *1 Henry IV* (1599).

In 1599, the printer William Jaggard sought to capitalize unscrupulously on Shakespeare's growing reputation by bringing out a slender volume of twenty or twenty-one poems called *The Passionate Pilgrim*, attributed to Shakespeare. In fact, only five of the poems were assuredly his, and none of them was newly composed for the occasion. Three came from *Love's Labor's Lost* (published in 1598) and two from Shakespeare's as yet unpublished sonnet sequence.

Contemporary Drama

Shakespeare was without doubt the leading dramatist of the period from 1594 to 1601, not only in our view, but also in that of his contemporaries. The earlier group of dramatists from whom he had learned so much—Lyly, Greene, Marlowe, Peele, Kyd, Nashe—were either dead or no longer writing plays. The group of dramatists who were to rival him in the 1600s and eventually surpass him in contemporary popularity had not yet become well known.

Ben Jonson's early career is obscure. He may have written an early version of his *A Tale of a Tub* in 1596 and *The Case Is Altered* in 1597, though both were later revised. Unquestionably, his first major play was *Every Man in His Humor* (1598), in which Shakespeare acted. This comedy did much to establish the new vogue of comedy of humors, a realistic and satirical kind of drama featuring "humors" characters whose personalities are dominated by some exaggerated trait. We are invited to laugh at the country simpleton, the jealous husband, the overly careful father, the cowardly braggart soldier, the poetaster, and the like. Shakespeare responded to the vogue of humors comedy in his *Henry IV* plays and *The Merry Wives*. Jonson followed his great success with *Every Man Out of His Humor* (1599), an even more biting vision of human folly. George Chapman also deserves important credit for the establishment of humors comedy, with his *The Blind Beggar of Alexandria* (1596) and *An Humorous Day's Mirth* (1597).

Despite the emergence of humors comedy, however, with its important anticipations of Jacobean and even Restoration comedy of manners, the prevailing comedy to be seen on the London stage between 1595 and 1601 was romantic comedy. William Haughton wrote *Englishmen for My Money* in 1598. Thomas Dekker's *Old Fortunatus*, the dramatization of a German folktale, appeared in 1599. Dekker's *Shoemakers' Holiday* (1599), despite its seemingly realistic touches of life among the apprentices of London, is a thoroughly romanticized saga of rags to riches. A young aristocrat disguises himself as a shoemaker to woo a mayor's daughter; love conquers social rank, and the King himself sentimentally blesses the union. Thomas Heywood wrote heroical romances and comedies, perhaps including *Godfrey of Boulogne* (1594), although most of his early works have disappeared. The boys' private theaters were closed during most of the 1590s, until 1598–1599, and thus the child actors could not perform the satirical comedies at which they were so adept.

Patriotic history drama also continued to flourish on the public stage during those years when Shakespeare wrote his best history plays. Heywood wrote the two parts of *Edward IV* between 1592 and 1599. The anonymous *Edward III* appeared in 1595 or earlier, enough in the vein of Shakeseare's histories that it is sometimes attributed (albeit on uncertain and impressionistic grounds) to him. *Sir*

Thomas More, by Munday, Dekker, Chettle, and perhaps Heywood, was written sometime in the later 1590s and very probably revised by Shakespeare himself. Chettle and Munday wrote a trilogy of plays about *Robert, Earl of Huntingdon*, or Robin Hood (1598–1599), on themes that remind us of Shakespeare's *As You Like It*. These plays were performed by the Admiral's men, who also produced the two parts of *Sir John Oldcastle* (1599–1600) by Drayton, Hathway, Munday, and others, in rivalry with Shakespeare's *Henry IV* plays.

Shakespeare's Work

Shakespeare thus wrote his greatest history plays for an audience that knew the genre well. The history play had first become popular just at the start of Shakespeare's career, during the patriotic aftermath of the defeat of the Spanish Armada (1588). Shakespeare himself did much to establish the genre. He wrote first his tetralogy, or four-play series, dealing with the Lancastrian wars of the fifteenth century, and then went backwards in historical time to King John's reign and to the famous reigns of Henry IV and Henry V.

His romantic comedies were also written for audiences that knew what to expect from the genre. From the comedies of Greene, Peele, Munday, and the rest, as well as Shakespeare himself, Elizabethan audiences were thoroughly familiar with such conventions as fairy charms, improbable adventures in forests, heroines disguised as young men, shipwrecks, love overcoming differences in social rank, and the like. Yet the conventions also demanded more than mere horseplay or foolish antics. Plays of this sort customarily affirmed "wholesome" moral values and appealed to generosity and decency. They were written, like the history plays, for a socially diversified, though generally intelligent and well-to-do, audience.

Several critical terms have been used to suggest the special quality of Shakespeare's comedies during this period of the later 1590s. "Romantic comedy" implies first of all a story in which the main action is about love, but it can also imply elements of the improbable and the miraculous. (The difference between the "romantic comedies" of the later 1590s and the "romances" of Shakespeare's last years, 1606–1613, is that, in part at least, romantic comedy seeks to "make wonder familiar," whereas the romances seek to make the familiar wonderful.) "Philosophical comedy" emphasizes the moral and sometimes Christian idealism underlying many of these comedies of the 1590s: the quest for deep and honest understanding between men and women in *Much Ado About Nothing*, the awareness of an eternal and spiritual dimension to love in *The Merchant of Venice*, and the theme of love as a mysterious force able to regenerate a corrupted social world from which it has been banished in *As You Like It*. "Love-game comedy" pays particular attention to the witty battle of the sexes that we find in several of these plays. "Festive comedy" urges the celebratory nature of comedy, especially in *Twelfth Night* and the *Henry IV* plays, in which Saturnalian revelry must contend against grim and disapproving forces of sobriety. "Comedy of forgiveness," although applicable to only a limited number of plays of this period (especially *Much Ado*), stresses the unexpected second chance that the world of comedy extends to even the most undeserving of heroes; Claudio is forgiven his ill treatment of Hero, although the play's villain, Don John, is not.

Shakespeare in the Theater, c.1601–1608

When the Globe, the most famous of the London public playhouses, was built in 1599, one-half interest in the property was assigned to the Burbage family, especially to the brothers Cuthbert and Richard Burbage. The other half was divided among five actor-sharers: Shakespeare, Will Kempe, Thomas Pope, Augustine Phillips, and John Heminges. Kempe left the company, however, in 1599 and subsequently became a member of the Earl of Worcester's men. His place as leading comic actor was taken by Robert Armin, an experienced man of the theater and occasional author, whose comic specialty was the role of the wise fool. We can observe in Shakespeare's plays the effects of Kempe's departure and of Armin's arrival. Kempe had apparently specialized in clownish and rustic parts, such as those of Dogberry in *Much Ado*, Lancelot Gobbo in *The Merchant of Venice*, and Bottom in *A Midsummer Night's Dream*. (We know that he played Dogberry because his name appears in the early Quarto, derived from the play manuscript; similar evidence links his name to the role of Peter in *Romeo and Juliet*.) For Armin, on the other hand, Shakespeare evidently created such roles as Touchstone in *As You Like It*, Feste in *Twelfth Night*, Lavatch in *All's Well That Ends Well*, and the Fool in *King Lear*.

Other shifts in personnel can sometimes be traced in Shakespeare's plays, especially changes in the number and ability of the boy actors (whose voices would suddenly start to crack at puberty). Shakespeare makes an amusing point about the relative size of two boy actors, for example, in *A Midsummer Night's Dream* and in *As You Like It*; this option may have been available to him only at certain times. On the other hand, not all changes in the company roster can be related meaningfully to Shakespeare's dramatic development. Augustine Phillips, who died in 1605, was a full actor-sharer of long standing in the company, but his "type" of role was probably not sharply differentiated from that of several of his associates. Shakespeare's plays, after all, involve many important supporting roles, and versatility in the undertaking of such parts must have been more common than specialization. (Phillips is remembered also

Among the members of Shakespeare's acting company were John Lowin, William Sly, and Nathaniel Field.

for his last will and testament: he left a bequest of "a thirty shillings piece in gold" to "my fellow, William Shakespeare," and similar bequests to other members of the troupe.)

With the reopening of the boys' acting companies in 1598–1599, a serious economic rivalry sprang up between them and the adult companies. The Children of the Chapel Royal occupied the theater in Blackfriars, and the Children of Paul's probably acted in their own singing school in St. Paul's churchyard. Their plays exploited a new vogue for satire. The satiric laughter was often directed at the city of London and its bourgeois inhabitants: socially ambitious tradesmen's wives, Puritan zealots, and the like. Other favorite targets included parvenu knights at court, would-be poets, and hysterical governmental officials. The price of admission at the private theaters was considerably higher than at the Globe or Rose, so the clientele tended to be more fashionable. Sophisticated authors like Ben Jonson, George Chapman, and John Marston tended to find writing for the boy actors more rewarding literarily than writing for the adult players.

One manifestation of the rivalry between public and private theaters was the so-called War of the Theaters, or Poetomachia. In part, this was a personal quarrel between Jonson on one side and Marston and Thomas Dekker on the other. Underlying this quarrel, however, was a serious hostility between a public theater and one that catered more to the elite. Dekker, with Marston's encouragement, attacked Jonson as a literary dictator and snob—one who subverted public decency. Jonson replied with a fervent defense of the artist's right to criticize everything that the artist sees wrong. The major plays in the exchange (1600–

1601) were Jonson's *Cynthia's Revels,* Dekker and Marston's *Satiromastix,* and Jonson's *The Poetaster.*

Shakespeare allows Hamlet to comment on the theatrical rivalry (2.2.330–362), with seeming regret for the fact that the boys have been overly successful and that many adult troupes have been obliged to tour the provinces. Most of all, though, Hamlet's remarks deplore the needless bitterness on both sides. The tone of kindly remonstrance makes it seem unlikely that Shakespeare took an active part in the fracas. To be sure, in the Cambridge play *2 Return from Parnassus* (1601–1603), the character called Will Kempe does assert that his fellow actor, Shakespeare, had put down the famous Ben Jonson:

Why, here's our fellow Shakespeare puts them all down, ay, and Ben Jonson, too. O, that Ben Jonson is a pestilent fellow! And he brought up Horace giving the poets a pill, but our fellow Shakespeare hath given him a purge that made him bewray his credit (lines 1809–1813).

Nevertheless, no play exists in which Shakespeare did put down Jonson, and the reference may be instead to *Satiromastix,* which was performed by Shakespeare's company. Or perhaps "put down" means simply "surpassed." In fact, Shakespeare and Jonson remained on cordial terms, despite their differences in artistic outlook.

Upon the death of Queen Elizabeth in 1603 and the accession to the throne of King James I, Shakespeare's company added an important new success to their already great prosperity. According to a document of instruction from King James to his Keeper of the Privy Seal, dated May 19, 1603, and endorsed as "The Players' Privilege," the acting company that had formerly been the Lord Chamberlain's men now became the King's company. The document

BY PERMISSION OF THE FOLGER SHAKESPEARE LIBRARY

BY PERMISSION OF THE HUNTINGTON LIBRARY, SAN MARINO, CALIFORNIA

Will Kempe (above), for whom Shakespeare created several clownish roles, was a member of the Lord Chamberlain's men and a noted Elizabethan comic. Kempe left the company in 1599 and was replaced by Robert Armin (right), an accomplished actor who specialized in fool's roles.

names Shakespeare, Richard Burbage, Augustine Phillips, John Heminges, Henry Condell, Will Sly, Robert Armin, Richard Cowley, and Lawrence Fletcher—the last, an actor who had played before the King and the Scottish court in 1599 and 1601. These players are accorded the usual privileges of exercising their art anywhere within the kingdom and are henceforth to be known as the King's company. The principal members of the troupe were also appointed to the honorary rank of Grooms of the Royal Chamber. We therefore find them duly recorded in the Accounts of the Master of the Wardrobe on March 15, 1604, as recipients of the customary grants of red cloth, so that they, dressed in the royal livery, might take part in the approaching coronation procession of King James. The same men are mentioned in these grants as in the Players' Privilege. Shakespeare's name stands second in the former document and first in the latter. In a somewhat similar manner, the King's players, as Grooms of the Royal Chamber, were called in attendance on the Spanish ambassador at Somerset House in August 1604.

The Revels Accounts of performances at court during the winter season of 1604–1605 contain an unusually full entry, listing several of Shakespeare's plays. The list includes *Othello, The Merry Wives of Windsor, Measure for Measure,* "The play of Errors," *Love's Labor's Lost, Henry V,* and *The Merchant of Venice.* The last play was "again commanded by the King's majesty," and so was performed a second time. This list also sporadically notes the names of "the poets which made the plays," ascribing three of these works to "Shaxberd." (Probably the final *d* is

an error for *e*, since the two characters are easily confused in Elizabethan handwriting; the word represents "Shaxbere" or "Shaxpere.") The entire entry was once called into question as a possible forgery but is now generally regarded as authentic.

A number of records during this period show us glimpses of Shakespeare as a man of property. On May 1, 1602, John and William Combe conveyed to Shakespeare one hundred and seven acres of arable land, plus twenty acres of pasture in the parish of Old Stratford, for the sizable payment of three hundred and twenty pounds. The deed was delivered to Shakespeare's brother Gilbert and not to the poet, who was probably at that time occupied in London. On September 28th of the same year, Shakespeare acquired the title to "one cottage and one garden by estimation a quarter of an acre," located opposite his home (New Place) in Stratford.

Shakespeare made still other real-estate investments in his home town. In 1605 he purchased an interest in the tithes of Stratford and adjacent villages from one Ralph Hubaud for the considerable sum of four hundred and forty pounds. The purchasing of tithes was a common financial transaction in Shakespeare's time, though unknown today. Tithes were originally intended for the support of the Church but had, in many cases, become privately owned and hence negotiable. The owners of tithes paid a fixed rental sum for the right to collect as many of these taxes as they could, up to the total amount due under the law. Shakespeare seems, on this occasion in 1605, to have bought from Ralph Hubaud a one-half interest, or "moiety," in certain tithes of Stratford and vicinity. Later, probably in 1609, Shakespeare was one of those who brought a bill of complaint before the Lord Chancellor, requesting that certain other titheholders be required to come into the High Court of Chancery and make answer to the complaints alleged, namely, that they had not paid their proportional part of an annual rental of twenty-seven pounds, thirteen shillings, and four pence on the whole property in the tithes to one Henry Barker. This Barker had the theoretical right to foreclose on the entire property if any one of the forty-two titheholders failed to contribute his share of the annual fee. The suit was, in effect, a friendly one, designed to ensure that all those who were supposed to contribute did so on an equitable and business-like basis.

We learn from the Stratford Registers of baptism, marriage, and burial of the changes in Shakespeare's family during this period. His father died in 1601, his brother Edmund in 1607, and his mother in 1608. On June 5, 1607, his daughter Susanna was married to Dr. John Hall in Holy Trinity Church, Stratford. Their first child, and Shakespeare's first grandchild, Elizabeth, was christened in the same church on February 21, 1608.

Shakespeare's Reputation, 1601–1608

Allusions to Shakespeare are frequent during this period of his life. One amusing reference is not literary but professes to tell about Shakespeare's prowess as a lover and rival of his good friend and theatrical colleague, Richard Burbage. Perhaps the joke was just a good bawdy story and should not be taken too seriously, but it is nonetheless one of the few anecdotes that date from Shakespeare's lifetime. Our informant is John Manningham, a young law student, who notes in his commonplace book in 1602 the following:

13 March 1601 [1602] . . . Upon a time, when Burbage played Richard III there was a citizen grew so far in liking with him that, before she went to the play, she appointed him to come that night unto her by the name of Richard the Third. Shakespeare, overhearing their conclusion, went before, and was entertained and at his game ere Burbage came. Then message being brought that Richard the Third was at the door, Shakespeare caused return to be made that William the Conqueror was before Richard the Third. Shakespeare's name William.

Other allusions of the time are more literary. Shakespeare's greatness is, by this time, taken for granted. Anthony Scoloker, for example, in his epistle prefatory to *Diaphantus, or the Passions of Love* (1604), attempts to describe an excellent literary work in this way:

It should be like the never-too-well read *Arcadia* . . . or to come home to the vulgar's element, like friendly Shakespeare's tragedies, where the comedian rides, when the tragedian stands on tip-toe. Faith, it should please all, like Prince Hamlet.

The antiquarian William Camden includes Shakespeare's name among his list of England's greatest writers in his *Remains of a Greater Work Concerning Britain* (1605):

These may suffice for some poetical descriptions of our ancient poets. If I would come to our time, what a world could I present to you out of Sir Philip Sidney, Edmund Spenser, Samuel Daniel, Hugh Holland, Ben Jonson, Thomas Campion, Michael Drayton, George Chapman, John Marston, William Shakespeare, and other most pregnant wits of these our times, whom succeeding ages may justly admire.

An attempt to use one of Shakespeare's plays for political purposes had some potentially serious repercussions. Two days before the abortive rebellion of the Earl of Essex on February 7, 1601, Shakespeare's company was commissioned to perform a well-known play in its repertory about King Richard II. This play must almost surely have been Shakespeare's. Evidently, the purpose of this extraordinary performance was to awaken public sympathy for Essex by suggesting that Queen Elizabeth was another Richard II, surrounded by corrupt favorites and deaf to the pleas of her subjects. Essex's avowed intention was to remove from positions of influence those men whom he considered his political enemies. Fortunately, Shakespeare's company was later exonerated of any blame in the affair (see the Introduction to *Richard II*).

Perhaps no other allusion to Shakespeare during this period can suggest so well as the following quotation the extent to which Shakespeare's plays had become familiar to English citizens everywhere. The quotation is taken from the notes of a certain Captain Keeling, commander of the East India Company's ship *Dragon*, off Sierra Leone, in the years 1607 and 1608:

1607, Sept. 5. I sent the interpreter, according to his desire, aboard the *Hector*, where he broke fast, and after came aboard me, where we gave the tragedy of *Hamlet*.
30. Captain Hawkins dined with me, where my companions acted *King Richard the Second*.
[March 31.] I invited Captain Hawkins to a fish dinner and had *Hamlet* acted aboard me, which I permit to keep my people from idleness and unlawful games or sleep.

Other Drama of the Period

Even without Shakespeare, the early Jacobean drama in England would rank as one of the most creative periods in the history of all theater. (The word *Jacobean* is derived from *Jacobus*, the Latin form of the name of King James I.) Shakespeare's earlier contemporaries—Lyly, Greene, Marlowe, Peele, Kyd—were dead or silent, but another generation of playwrights was at hand. George Chapman, John Marston, and Ben Jonson all began writing plays shortly before 1600. The names of Thomas Dekker and Thomas Heywood are perhaps to be associated with various lost plays as early as 1594, but these men are known today for the plays they wrote after 1599. Francis Beaumont, John Fletcher, Cyril Tourneur, and Thomas Middleton emerged into prominence in about 1606 or 1607. John Webster collaborated with Dekker and others in such plays as *Westward Ho* and *Sir Thomas Wyatt* around 1604, although he did not write his great tragedies until 1609–1614. Lesser talents, such as Henry Chettle, Anthony Munday, Henry Porter, John Day, and William Haughton, continued to pour forth an abundant supply of workmanlike plays. As Shakespeare's career developed, therefore, he enjoyed the fellowship and, no doubt, the rivalry of a remarkably gifted and diverse group of practicing dramatists.

Early Jacobean drama is, on the whole, characteristically different from the late Elizabethan drama that had preceded it. Other dramatists besides Shakespeare mirror his shift of focus from romantic comedies and patriotic histories to "problem" plays and tragedies. The boys' companies, reopening in 1598–1599 after virtually a decade of silence, did much to set the new tone. They avoided almost entirely the English history play, with its muscularly heroic style, so unsuited for the acting capabilities of boys. Besides, sophisticated audiences were sated with jingoistic fare, and even in the public theaters the genre had pretty well run its course. The fashion of the moment turned instead to revenge tragedy and satiric comedy.

The Jacobean revenge play owed much of its original inspiration to Thomas Kyd's *The Spanish Tragedy* (c. 1587), with its influential conventions: the intervention of supernatural forces, the feigned madness of the avenger, his difficulty in ascertaining the true facts of the murder, his morbid awareness of the conflict between human injustice and divine justice, his devising of a play within the play, and his invention of ingenious methods of slaughter in the play's gory ending. Kyd may also have written an early version of *Hamlet* featuring similar motifs. Shakespeare confronted cosmic issues of justice and human depravity in his revenge tragedy, *Hamlet* (c. 1599–1601), as indeed Kyd had done, but most followers of Kyd preferred to revel in the sensationalism of the genre. Some private-theater dramatists, such as Marston, subjected the conventions of the genre to caricature. Marston's revenge plays, written chiefly for Paul's boys and (after 1604) for the Children of the Queen's Revels, include *Antonio's Revenge* (1599–1601) and *The Malcontent* (1600–1604). These dramas are marked by flamboyantly overstated cynicism and are, in many ways, as close to satire as they are to tragedy. Marston had, in fact, made his first reputation as a nondramatic satirist, with *The Metamorphosis of Pygmalion's Image* and *The Scourge of Villainy* in 1598. His plays represent a continuation in dramatic form of the techniques of the Roman satirist. The typical Marstonian avenger, such as Malevole in *The Malcontent,* is an exaggeratedly unattractive authorial spokesman, pouring forth venomous hatred upon the loathsome and degenerate court in which he finds himself.

Similar in their exaggerated pursuit of the grotesque and the morbid are Cyril Tourneur's *The Atheist's Tragedy* (1607–1611) and a play often attributed to Tourneur, *The Revenger's Tragedy* (1606–1607). These plays are brilliant in the plotting of impossible situations and in the invention of cunning Italianate forms of torture and murder. Any

sympathetic identification with the characters of these plays is sacrificed in the interests of technical virtuosity. As a result, the plays are more ironic than cathartic in their effect; we are overwhelmed by life's dark absurdities rather than ennobled by a vision of humanity's tragic grandeur. *The Tragedy of Hoffman, or A Revenge for a Father* by Henry Chettle (Admiral's men, 1602) is similarly grotesque and lacking in sympathy for its revenger hero. To be sure, George Chapman's *Bussy D'Ambois* (1600–1604) and its sequel, *The Revenge of Bussy D'Ambois* (1607–1612), are thoughtful plays about human aspiration, in the vein of Marlowe's *Tamburlaine,* but even these plays employ a good deal of Senecan bloody melodrama.

The revenge play enjoyed a great popularity on the public stage and (in a caricatured form) on the private stage. The public theater did, however, cater also to its Puritan-leaning audiences with more pious and moral tragedy. *Arden of Feversham* (c. 1591) is a good early example of what has come to be called domestic or homiletic tragedy. In the studiously plain style of a broadside ballad, it sets forth the facts of an actual murder that had occurred in 1551 and had been reported in Holinshed's *Chronicles.* The play interprets those events earnestly and providentially. The most famous play in the genre of domestic tragedy is Thomas Heywood's *A Woman Killed with Kindness* (1603). It tells, not of a murder, but of an adultery, for which the goodhearted but offending wife must be perpetually banished by her grieving husband. The play succeeds in elevating the private sorrows of its ordinary characters to tragic stature. The moral stances appear to be unambiguous: adultery is a heinous offense but can be transcended by Christian forgiveness; dueling is evil. Still, a mix of sympathies is perhaps reflective of shifting public attitudes toward the role of women in marriage. Other plays in the vein of domestic tragedy include *A Yorkshire Tragedy* (1605–1608), *The Miseries of Enforced Marriage* (1605–1606), and *Two Lamentable Tragedies* (c. 1594–1598).

In comedy, the greatest writer of the period besides Shakespeare was Ben Jonson. His predilection was toward the private theater, though he continued to write occasionally for the public stage as well. To an ever-increasing extent, he fixed his satirical gaze on those values and institutions which Thomas Heywood cherished: the city of London, its bourgeois citizens, its traditional approach to morality, and its religious zeal. *Every Man Out of His Humor* (1599), written for the Chamberlain's men, features a foolish uxorious citizen, his socially aspiring wife, and her fashionmongering lover—humors types that were to appear again and again in the genre of satirical comedy known as "city comedy." (See Brian Gibbons, *Jacobean City Comedy,* 1968.) *Volpone* (1605–1606), though technically not a London city comedy, since it purportedly takes place in Venice, castigates greed among lawyers, businessmen, and other professional types. *The Alchemist* (1610) ridicules the affectations of petty shopkeepers, lawyers' clerks, Puritan divines, and others. *Bartholomew Fair* (1614) and *The Alchemist* give us Jonson's most memorable indictment of the Puritans.

Numerous other writers contributed to humors comedy and city comedy. George Chapman probably deserves more credit than he usually receives for having helped determine the shape of humors comedy in his *The Blind Beggar of Alexandria* (1596), *An Humorous Day's Mirth* (1597), *All Fools* (1599–1604), *May-Day* (1601–1609), *The Gentleman Usher* (1602–1604), and others. Francis Beaumont, assisted perhaps by John Fletcher, ridicules London grocers and apprentices for their naive tastes in romantic chivalry in *The Knight of the Burning Pestle* (1607–1610). Some satire in this vein, to be sure, is reasonably good-humored. *Eastward Ho* (1605), by Chapman, Jonson, and Marston, is genially sympathetic toward the life-style of the small shopkeeper, even though the play contains a good deal of satire directed at social climbing and sharp business practices. Thomas Dekker's collaboration with Thomas Middleton on *The Honest Whore* (Part I, 1604) gives us an amused and yet warm portrayal of a linen draper who succeeds in business by insisting that the customer is always right. Dekker often shows a wry but generous appreciation of bourgeois ethics, as in *The Shoemakers' Holiday* (1599). Yet even he turns against the Puritans in *If This Be Not a Good Play, the Devil Is in It* (1611–1612).

Marston shows his talent for city comedy in *The Dutch Courtesan* (1603–1605). Perhaps the most ingratiating and truly funny of the writers of city comedy, however, is Middleton. His *A Trick to Catch the Old One* (1604–1607) illustrates the tendency of Jacobean comedy to move away both from Shakespeare's romantic vein and Jonson's morally satirical vein toward a more lighthearted comedy of manners, anticipating the style of Restoration comedy. One of Middleton's most hilarious and philosophically unpretentious plays, though plotted with great ingenuity of situation, is *A Mad World, My Masters* (1604–1607). *Michaelmas Term*, written about the same time, exposes the sharp practices of usurers and lawyers. All these Middleton plays were written for Paul's boys.

Romantic comedy, though overshadowed by humors and city comedy during the 1600s, still held forth at the public theaters. A leading exponent was Thomas Heywood, in such plays as *The Fair Maid of the West*, or *A Girl Worth Gold* (1597–1610). Heywood also wrote English history plays designed to prove the sturdiness and historical importance of the London citizenry he so loved, as in *Edward IV* (1597–1599), *The Four Prentices of London* (c. 1600), and *If You Know Not Me You Know Nobody* (1605). Classical tragedy also continued to be written, despite the vogue of revenge tragedy. Ben Jonson rather dogmatically illustrated his classical theories of tragedy in *Sejanus* (1603) and *Catiline* (1611). Samuel Daniel wrote *Philotas* in 1604 and a revision of his *Cleopatra* in 1607. Heywood's *The Rape of Lucrece* appeared in 1606–1608. These are not, however, the immortal tragedies for which the Jacobean period is remembered.

Shakespeare's Work, 1601–1608

Shakespeare's plays of this period reveal many Jacobean characteristics. The comedies are few in number and lack the joyous affirmation we associate with *Twelfth Night* and earlier plays. *Measure for Measure*, for example, is not about young men and women happily in love, but about premarital sex and the insoluble problems that arise when vice-prone men attempt to legislate morality for their fellow mortals. Angelo, self-hating and out of emotional control, is a tragic hero providentially rescued from his own worst self. The Duke and Isabella must use ethically dubious means— the bed trick—to effect their virtuous aims. Comedy in the play deals darkly in terms of prostitution, slander, and police inefficiency.

All's Well That Ends Well, though less grim than *Measure for Measure* in its confrontation of human degeneracy, does apply a similar bed trick as its central plot device. Just as important, the obstacles to love are internal and psychological, rather than external; that is, the happy union of Bertram and Helena is delayed, not by parental objections or by accident (as in *Romeo and Juliet* and *A Midsummer Night's Dream*), but by Bertram's unreadiness for the demands of a mature marital relationship. *Troilus and Cressida* is a play in which love is paralyzed by a combination of external and internal forces. Troilus must hand Cressida over to the Greeks because his code of honor bids him put his country's cause before his own, and yet that code of "honor" is based on Paris' rape of Helen. Cressida simply gives herself up to Diomedes, knowing she is not strong enough to stand alone in a moral wilderness. The combatants in the greatest war in all history turn out to be petty bickerers, who play nasty games on one another and sulk when their reputations are impugned. The cause for which both sides fight is squalid and senseless.

In *Hamlet*, Shakespeare explores similar dilemmas posed by human carnality. Women are too often frail; men are too often importunate and brutal. How is a thoughtful person to justify his or her own existence? Should one struggle actively against injustice and personal wrong? How can one know what is really true or foresee the complex results of action? How, in *Othello*, can the protagonist resist temptation and inner weakness, prompting him to destroy the very thing on which his happiness depends? Is Macbeth tempted to sin by the weird sisters and his wife, or is the choice to murder Duncan ultimately his? To what extent is humanity responsible for its tragic fate? Most of all, in *King Lear*, are the heavens themselves indifferent to human bestiality? Must Cordelia die? Yet, despite these overwhelmingly pessimistic questions, and the tragic consequences they imply for all human life, Shakespeare's "great" tragedies affirm at least

Raphael Holinshed's Chronicles of England, Scotland, and Ireland, *which was published (1577, second edition in 1587) before Shakespeare's career began, served as principal historic source for many plays, including* Macbeth, King Lear, *and* Cymbeline, *as well as the history plays. Here, in a woodcut from the* Chronicles, *Macbeth and Banquo are shown encountering the three witches.*

the nobility of humanity's striving to know itself, and the redeeming fact that human goodness does exist (in Desdemona, Duncan, Cordelia), even if those who practice goodness are often slaughtered.

The Roman or classical tragedies are something apart from the "great" tragedies. They are more ironic in tone, more dispiriting, though they, too, affirm an essential nobility in humanity. Brutus misguidedly leads a revolution against Caesar but dies loyal to his great principles. Timon of Athens proves the appalling ingratitude of his fellow creature and resolutely cuts himself off from all human contact. Coriolanus proclaims himself an enemy of the Roman people and seeks to destroy them for their ingratitude, though he is compromised and destroyed at last by his promptings of human feeling. Antony, too, is pulled apart by an irreconcilable conflict. Yet, in this play at least, Shakespeare achieves, partly through the greatness of Cleopatra, a triumph over defeat that seems to offer a new resolution of humanity's tragic dilemma.

The Late Years: 1608–1616

In the summer of 1608, Shakespeare's acting company signed a twenty-one-year lease for the use of the Blackfriars playhouse, an indoor and rather intimate, artificially lighted theater inside the city of London, close to the site of St. Paul's cathedral. A private theater had existed on this spot since 1576, when the Children of the Chapel and then Paul's boys began acting their courtly plays for paying spectators in a building that had once belonged to the Dominicans, or Black Friars. James Burbage had begun construction in 1596 of the so-called Second Blackfriars theater in the same

building. Although James encountered opposition from the residents of the area and died before he could complete the work, James' son Richard did succeed in opening the new theater in 1600. At first, he leased it (for twenty-one years) to a children's company, but when that company was suppressed in 1608 for offending the French ambassador in a play by George Chapman, Burbage seized the opportunity to take back the unexpired lease and to set up Blackfriars as the winter playhouse for his adult company, the King's men. By this time, the adult troupes could plainly see that they needed to cater more directly to courtly audiences than they once had done. Their popular audiences were becoming increasingly disenchanted with the drama. Puritan fulminations against the stage gained in effect, especially when many playwrights refused to disguise their satirical hostility toward Puritans and the London bourgeoisie.

Several of Shakespeare's late plays may have been acted both at the Globe and at Blackfriars. The plays he wrote after 1608–1609—*Cymbeline, The Winter's Tale,* and *The Tempest*—all show the distinct influence of the dramaturgy of the private theaters. Also, we know that an increasing number of Shakespeare's plays were acted at the court of King James. *Othello, King Lear,* and *The Tempest* are named in court revels accounts, and *Macbeth* attentively flatters the Scottish royal ancestry of King James as though for a court performance. On the other hand, Shakespeare's plays certainly continued to be acted at the Globe to the very end of his career. The 1609 Quarto of *Pericles* advertises that it was acted "by his Majesty's Servants, at the Globe on the Bankside." The 1608 Quarto of *King Lear* mentions a performance at court and assigns the play to "his Majesty's servants playing usually at the Globe on the Bankside." Simon Forman saw *Macbeth, Cymbeline,* and *The Win-*

ter's Tale at the Globe. Finally, a performance of *Henry VIII* on June 29, 1613, resulted in the burning of the Globe to the ground, though afterwards it soon was rebuilt.

Shakespeare's last plays, written with a view to Blackfriars and the court, as well as to the Globe, are now usually called "romances" or "tragicomedies," or sometimes both. The term "romance" suggests a return to the kind of story Robert Greene had derived from Greek romance: tales of adventure, long separation, and tearful reunion, involving shipwreck, capture by pirates, riddling prophecies, children set adrift in boats or abandoned on foreign shores, the illusion of death and subsequent restoration to life, the revelation of the identity of long-lost children by birthmarks, and the like. The term "tragicomedy" suggests a play in which the protagonist commits a seemingly fatal error or crime, or (as in *Pericles*) suffers an extraordinarily adverse fortune to test his patience; in either event, he must experience agonies of contrition and bereavement until he is providentially delivered from his tribulations. The tone is deeply melancholic and resigned, although suffused also with a sense of gratitude for the harmonies that are mysteriously restored.

The appropriateness of such plays to the elegant atmosphere of Blackfriars and the court is subtle but real. Although one might suppose at first that old-fashioned naiveté would seem out of place in a sophisticated milieu, the naiveté is only superficial. Tragicomedy and pastoral romance were, in the period from 1606 to 1610, beginning to enjoy a fashionable courtly revival. The leading practitioners of the new genre were Beaumont and Fletcher, though Shakespeare made a highly significant contribution. Perhaps sophisticated audiences responded to pastoral and romantic drama as the nostalgic evocation of an idealized past, a chivalric "golden world" fleetingly recovered through an artistic journey back to naiveté and innocence. The evocation of such a world demands the kind of studied but informal artifice we find in many tragicomic plays of the period: the elaborate masques and allegorical shows, the descents of enthroned gods from the heavens (as in *Cymbeline*), the use of quaint Chorus figures like Old Gower or Time (in *Pericles* and *The Winter's Tale*), and the quasi-operatic blend of music and spectacle. At their best, such plays powerfully compel belief in the artistic world thus artificially created. The very improbability of the story becomes, paradoxically, part of the means by which an audience must "awake its faith" in a mysterious truth.

Shakespeare did not merely ape the new fashion in tragicomedy and romance. In fact, he may have done much to establish it. His *Pericles*, written seemingly in about 1606–1608 for the public stage before Shakespeare's company acquired Blackfriars, anticipated many important features, not only of Shakespeare's own later romances, but also of Beaumont and Fletcher's *The Maid's Tragedy* and *Philaster* (c. 1608–1611). Still, Shakespeare was on the verge of retirement, and the future belonged to Beaumont

This section of Wenceslaus Hollar's "Long View" of London dates from 1647, some years after Shakespeare's death, but gives nonetheless a fine view of two theater buildings on the south bank of the Thames River, across from the city. The two labels of "The Globe" and "Beere bayting" should in fact be reversed; the Globe (rebuilt in 1613) appears to the left and below the bearbaiting arena.

GUILDHALL LIBRARY, CITY OF LONDON

and Fletcher. Gradually, Shakespeare disengaged himself, spending more and more time in Stratford. His last-known stint as an actor was in Jonson's *Sejanus* in 1603. Some time in 1611 or 1612, he probably gave up his lodgings in London, though he still may have returned for such occasions as the opening performance of *Henry VIII* in 1613. He continued to be one of the proprietors of the newly rebuilt Globe, but his involvement in its day-to-day operations dwindled.

Shakespeare's Reputation, 1608–1616

Shakespeare's reputation among his contemporaries was undiminished in his late years, even though Beaumont and Fletcher were the new rage at the Globe and Blackfriars. Among those who apostrophized Shakespeare was John Davies of Hereford in *The Scourge of Folly* (entered in the Stationers' Register in 1610):

To our English Terence, Mr. Will Shakespeare.

Some say, good Will, which I, in sport, do sing:
Hadst thou not played some kingly parts in sport,

Thou hadst been a companion for a king,
And been a king among the meaner sort.
Some others rail. But, rail as they think fit,
Thou hast no railing, but a reigning, wit.
And honesty thou sow'st, which they do reap,
So to increase their stock which they do keep.

The following sonnet is from *Run and a Great Cast* (1614) by Thomas Freeman:

To Master W. Shakespeare.

Shakespeare, that nimble Mercury thy brain
Lulls many hundred Argus-eyes asleep,
So fit, for all thou fashionest thy vein,
At th' horse-foot fountain thou hast drunk full deep.
Virtue's or vice's theme to thee all one is.
Who loves chaste life, there's *Lucrece* for a lecher;
Who list read lust, there's *Venus and Adonis,*
True model of a most lascivious teacher.
Besides, in plays thy wit winds like Meander,
Whence needy new composers borrow more
Than Terence doth from Plautus or Menander.
But to praise thee aright, I want thy store.
Then let thine own works thine own worth upraise,
And help t' adorn thee with deservèd bays.

Ben Jonson took a more critical view, though he also admired Shakespeare greatly. In the Induction to his *Bartholomew Fair* (1631 edition), Jonson compared the imaginary world he presented in his play with the more improbable fantasies of romantic drama:

If there be never a servant-monster i' the fair, who can help it? He [the author, Jonson] says; nor a nest of antics? He is loath to make Nature afraid in his plays, like those that beget tales, Tempests, and suchlike drolleries to mix his head with other men's heels.

From this, one judges that Jonson had in mind not only *The Tempest* but also Shakespeare's other late romances. He similarly protested in the Prologue to his 1616 edition of *Every Man in His Humor* that his own playwriting was free of the usual romantic claptrap:

Where neither Chrous wafts you o'er the seas,
Nor creaking throne comes down the boys to please,
Nor nimble squib is seen to make afeard
The gentlewomen, nor rolled bullet heard
To say it thunders, nor tempestuous drum
Rumbles to tell you when the storm doth come.

Still, Shakespeare's reputation was assured. John Webster paid due homage, in his note To the Reader accompanying *The White Devil* (1612), to "the right happy and copious industry of M. *Shakespeare*, M. *Dekker*, & M. *Heywood*," along with Chapman, Jonson, Beaumont, and Fletcher.

Latest Records

Shakespeare's last recorded investment in real estate was the purchase of a house in Blackfriars, London, in 1613. There is no indication he lived there, for he had retired to Stratford.

He did not pay the full purchase price of one hundred and forty pounds, and the mortgage deed executed for the unpaid balance furnishes one of the six unquestioned examples of his signature.

John Combe, a wealthy bachelor of Stratford and Shakespeare's friend, left him a legacy of five pounds in his will at the time of Combe's death in 1613. At about the same time, John's kinsman William Combe began a controversial attempt to enclose Welcombe Common, that is, to convert narrow strips of arable land to pasture. Presumably, Combe was interested in a more efficient means of using the land. Enclosure was, however, an explosive issue, since many people feared they would lose the right to farm the land and would be evicted to make room for cattle and sheep. Combe attempted to guarantee Shakespeare and other titheholders that they would lose no money. He offered similar assurances to the Stratford Council, but the townspeople were adamantly opposed. Shakespeare was consulted by letter as a leading titheholder. The letter is lost, but, presumably, it set forth the Council's reasons for objecting to enclosure. Shakespeare's views on the controversy remain unknown. Eventually, the case went to the Privy Council, where Combe was ordered to restore the land to its original use.

One of the most interesting documents from these years consists of the records of a lawsuit entered into in 1612 by Stephen Belott against his father-in-law, Christopher Mountjoy, a Huguenot maker of women's ornamental headdresses who resided on Silver Street, St. Olave's parish, London. Belott sought to secure the payment of a dower promised him at the time of his marriage to Mountjoy's daughter. In this suit, Shakespeare was summoned as a witness and made deposition on five interrogatories. From this document we learn that Shakespeare was a lodger in Mountjoy's house at the time of the marriage in 1604 and probably for some time before that, since he states in his testimony that he had known Mountjoy for more than ten years. Shakespeare admitted that, at the solicitation of Mountjoy's wife, he had acted as an intermediary in the arrangement of the marriage between Belott and Mountjoy's daughter. Shakespeare declared himself unable, however, to recall the exact amount of the portion or the date on which it was to have been paid. Shakespeare's signature to his deposition is authentic and one of the best samples of his handwriting that we have.

In January of 1615 or 1616, Shakespeare drew up his last will and testament with the assistance of his lawyer Francis Collins, who had aided him earlier in some of his transactions in real estate. On March 25, 1616, Shakespeare revised his will in order to provide for the marriage of his daughter Judith and Thomas Quiney in that same year. Shakespeare's three quavering signatures, one on each page of this document, suggest that he was in failing health. The cause of his death on April 23 is not known. An intriguing bit of Stratford gossip is reported by John Ward, vicar of Holy

As with so many other things in his life, the curious terms of Shakespeare's will have led to endless and provocative conjecture.

Trinity in Stratford from 1662 to 1689, in his diary: "Shakespeare, Drayton, and Ben Jonson had a merry meeting, and it seems drank too hard, for Shakespeare died of a fever there contracted." The report comes fifty years after Shakespeare's death, however, and is hardly an expert medical opinion.

The will disposes of all the property of which Shakespeare is known to have died possessing, the greater share of it going to his daughter Susanna. His recently married daughter Judith received a dowry, a provision for any children that might be born of her marriage, and other gifts. Ten pounds went to the poor of Stratford; Shakespeare's sword went to Mr. Thomas Combe; twenty-six shillings and eight pence apiece went to Shakespeare's fellow actors Heminges, Burbage, and Condell to buy them mourning rings; and other small bequests went to various other friends and relatives.

An interlineation contains the bequest of Shakespeare's "second best bed with the furniture," that is, the hangings, to his wife. Anne's name appears nowhere else in the will. Some scholars, beginning with Edmund Malone, have taken this reference as proof of an unhappy marriage, confirming earlier indications, such as the hasty wedding to a woman who was William's senior by eight years and his prolonged residence in London for twenty years or more seemingly without his family. The evidence is inconclusive, however. Shakespeare certainly supported his family handsomely, acquired much property in Stratford, and retired there when he might have remained still in London. Although he showed no great solicitude for Anne's well-being in the will, her rights were protected by law; a third of her husband's estate went to her without having to be mentioned in the will. New Place was to be the home of Shakespeare's favorite daughter Susanna, wife of the distinguished Dr. John Hall. Anne Shakespeare would make her home with her daughter and, with her dower rights secured by law, would be quite as wealthy as she would need to be.

The date of Shakespeare's death (April 23, 1616) and his age (his fifty-third year) are inscribed on his monument. This elaborate structure, still standing in the chancel of Trinity Church, Stratford, was erected some time before 1623 by the London stonecutting firm of Gheerart Janssen and his sons. Janssen's shop was in Southwark, near the Globe, and may have been familiar to the actors. The bust of Shakespeare is a conventional sort of statuary for its time. Still, it is one of the only two contemporary likenesses we have. The other is the Droeshout engraving of Shakespeare in the Folio of 1623.

The epitaph on the monument reads as follows:

Iudicio Phylium, genio Socratem, arte Maronem;
Terra tegit, populus maeret, Olympus habet.
Stay passenger. Why goest thou by so fast?
Read, if thou canst, whom envious Death hath placed
Within this monument: Shakespeare, with whom
Quick Nature died, whose name doth deck this tomb
Far more than cost, sith all that he hath writ
Leaves living art but page to serve his wit.

Obiit anno domini 1616,
Aetatis 53, die 23 April.

These lines, of which the beginning Latin couplet compares Shakespeare with Nestor (King of Pylos) for wise judgment, Socrates for genius, and Virgil (Maro) for poetic art, and avers that the earth covers him, people grieve for him, and Mount Olympus (that is, heaven) has him, indicate the high reputation he enjoyed at the time of his death. More widely known, perhaps, are the four lines inscribed over Shakespeare's grave near the north wall of the chancel. A local tradition assigns them to Shakespeare himself and implies that he wrote them "to suit the capacity of clerks and sextons," whom he wished apparently to frighten out of the idea of opening the grave to make room for a new occupant:

Good friend, for Jesus' sake forbear
To dig the dust enclosèd here.
Blest be the man that spares these stones,
And curst be he that moves my bones.

Whether Shakespeare actually wrote these lines cannot, however, be determined.

Other Dramatists

The most significant new development in the drama of the period from about 1608 to 1616, apart from Shakespeare's new interest in romance and tragicomedy, was the emergence of the famous literary partners Francis Beaumont and John Fletcher. Beaumont, the son of a distinguished lawyer, studied for a while at Oxford and then at the Inner Temple before drifting into a literary career. In 1613, he married an heiress and retired almost completely from the theater. John Fletcher was the son of Richard Fletcher, Queen Elizabeth's chaplain and later Bishop of London. The young man probably studied at Cambridge. The father died in 1596 heavily in debt, leaving the young Fletcher to support a family of eight children. Fletcher became a professional writer, earning his living as chief dramatist for the King's men. He was Shakespeare's successor. Fletcher's cousins, Giles and Phineas Fletcher, gained some reputation as poets. Beaumont and Fletcher, who were close friends, regarded themselves also as poets and as members of the "tribe of Ben"—the disciples of the great Ben Jonson who often gathered together at the Mermaid Tavern for an evening of witty literary conversation.

What things have we seen
Done at the Mermaid! heard words that have been
So nimble, and so full of subtle flame,
As if that every one from whence they came
Had meant to put his whole wit in a jest,
And had resolved to live a fool the rest
Of his dull life!
(Master Francis Beaumont's Letter to Ben Jonson)

Beaumont and Fletcher actually collaborated on only about seven plays: *The Woman Hater,* a comedy (1606), *The* Maid's Tragedy, a tragedy (1608–1611), *Philaster,* a tragicomedy (1608–1610), *Cupid's Revenge,* a tragedy (c. 1607–1612), *The Coxcomb,* a comedy (1608–1610), *A King and No King,* a tragicomedy (1611), *The Scornful Lady,* a tragicomedy (1613–1616), and perhaps one or two others. They may have collaborated on *The Knight of the Burning Pestle* (c. 1607–1610), though it was chiefly Beaumont's. Beaumont also wrote *Mask of the Inner Temple and Gray's Inn* (1613). Fletcher unassisted wrote *The Faithful Shepherdess* (1608–1609), *The Night Walker* (c. 1611), *Bonduca* (1611–1614), *Valentinian* (1610–1614), and others. He also collaborated with several other writers, including Massinger, Middleton, Field, and Rowley. Importantly, he seems to have collaborated with Shakespeare on *The Two Noble Kinsmen* (1613–1616) and, conceivably, on *Henry VIII.* Eventually, most of these various dramatic enterprises were gathered together in 1647 as the works of Beaumont and Fletcher. They have remained known as such ever since, partly because the original collaboration of these two men did so much to set a new style in coterie drama.

The plays they wrote together, such as *The Maid's Tragedy* and *Philaster,* offer an interesting comparison with Shakespeare's contemporary writing in a similar genre. Beaumont and Fletcher often employ exotic settings, like Rhodes or Sicily. In such an environment, refined aristocratic characters are caught in dynastic struggles or in a rarified conflict between love and honor. They must cope with stereotyped villains, such as tyrants or shamelessly lustful courtiers. The sentiments are lofty, the rhetoric is mannered; elaborately contrived situations are offered with no pretense of verisimilitude. The characters live according to lofty chivalric codes and despise ill breeding above all else. In the plotting of the tragicomic reversal, the audience is sometimes deliberately deceived into believing something that is not true, so that the sudden happy outcome arrives as a theatrically contrived surprise. Disguising and masking are common motifs. The audience is deliberately made aware throughout of the play's theatrical artifice, statuesque scene building, and titillating sensationalism.

Although Shakespeare wrote no tragedies after *Coriolanus,* great tragedy did continue to appear on the Jacobean stage. John Webster wrote his two most splendid plays, *The White Devil* and *The Duchess of Malfi,* between 1609 and 1614. Both contain elements of the still-popular revenge tradition. They also manage to achieve a vision of triumphant human dignity in defeat that merits comparison with Shakespeare's greatest tragic achievement. Still to come were *The Changeling* (1622) by Thomas Middleton and William Rowley, *Women Beware Women* (c. 1620–1627) by Middleton, *'Tis Pity She's a Whore* (1629?–1633) by John Ford, and others. Although these tragedies are more concerned with the grotesque than are Shakespeare's great tragedies, and more obsessed with abnormal human psychology (incest, werewolfism, and the like), they are nonetheless sublime achievements in art. The genius of the age for tragedy did not die with Shakespeare. During Shakespeare's last years, George Chapman was also writing his best tragedies, including *Charles Duke of Byron* in 1608, *The Revenge of Bussy D'Ambois* in about 1610, and *Chabot, Admiral of France* between 1611 and 1622. Ben Jonson's *Catiline His Conspiracy,* a classical tragedy, appeared in 1611; Marston's *The Insatiate Countess,* in about 1610.

Shakespeare's Language: His Development as Poet and Dramatist

Language and Artistic Development

One indication of Shakespeare's greatness is his extraordinary development. As he worked through his writing career of more than twenty years, he constantly explored new themes, perfected genres and moved on to new ones, and saw ever more deeply into the human condition. Many of the works that have made him immortal were not written until he was nearly forty years old or more. The study of his development is, in itself, an interesting and complex subject. It is one that requires an accurate dating of his plays and poems.

The First Folio, published in 1623, gives no help in determining the order of composition of Shakespeare's plays. They are arranged in three groups—comedies, histories, and tragedies—without regard for dates of composition. The first comedy in the Folio is *The Tempest,* known to be one of Shakespeare's latest plays; the second is *The Two Gentlemen of Verona,* one of the earliest. The histories are arranged in order of the English kings whose reigns they treat, although Shakespeare clearly did not write them in that order. The tragedies show no discernible arrangement by date. We do have dating information, however, about eighteen of the thirty-six plays in the First Folio that had previously been published in single quarto volumes at various times and about *Pericles,* which was not included in the First Folio but existed as a quarto only until its inclusion in the Third Folio of 1663–1664. All the quarto editions, except *Romeo and Juliet* and *Love's Labor's Lost,* were entered in the Register of the Stationers' Company of London; two other plays, *As You Like It* (entered in the Stationers' Register in 1600) and *Antony and Cleopatra* (S.R. 1608), although not printed in quarto, were entered in the Stationers' Register possibly in order to forestall publication by printers who had no right to them. The date of entry of a play in the register indicates that, at least by that time, the play was in existence. The quarto editions have also certain information on their title pages regarding date, author, and publisher, and sometimes tell what theatrical company acted the play. Other kinds of external evidence of date include references to Shakespeare's plays in diaries, journals, or accounts of the period, and quotations from his plays in the literary works of Elizabethan and Jacobean writers. Allusions in Shakespeare's plays themselves to contemporary events, although difficult to prove beyond dispute, can sometimes be helpful. See Appendix I, at the end of this volume, for a detailed discussion on "Canon, Dates, and Early Texts" of each of Shakespeare's plays.

Once Shakespeare's plays have been arranged in approximate chronological order on the basis of the kinds of external evidence already described, we can perceive that his style underwent a continuous development from his earliest work to the end of his career as a dramatist. Matters of style are not easy to talk about precisely, and we can hardly expect to be able to date a particular passage as having been written in 1604, say, as distinguished from 1602. Overall, on the other hand, the early and late Shakespeare are strikingly distinguishable. Take, for example, the following two passages. One is from the Duke of Clarence's description of his dream in *Richard III* (1.4.21–

33), written in about 1591–1594, near the start of Shakespeare's career:

> O Lord, methought what pain it was to drown!
> What dreadful noise of water in my ears!
> What sights of ugly death within my eyes!
> Methoughts I saw a thousand fearful wracks;
> Ten thousand men that fishes gnawed upon;
> Wedges of gold, great anchors, heaps of pearl,
> Inestimable stones, unvalued jewels,
> All scattered in the bottom of the sea.
> Some lay in dead men's skulls, and in the holes
> Where eyes did once inhabit there were crept,
> As 'twere in scorn of eyes, reflecting gems,
> That wooed the slimy bottom of the deep
> And mocked the dead bones that lay scattered by.

The second is Prospero's description of his magic in *The Tempest* (5.1.33–50), from about 1610–1611 when Shakespeare was on the verge of retirement:

> Ye elves of hills, brooks, standing lakes, and groves,
> And ye that on the sands with printless foot
> Do chase the ebbing Neptune, and do fly him
> When he comes back; you demi-puppets that
> By moonshine do the green sour ringlets make,
> Whereof the ewe not bites; and you whose pastime
> Is to make midnight mushrooms, that rejoice
> To hear the solemn curfew; by whose aid,
> Weak masters though ye be, I have bedimmed
> The noontide sun, called forth the mutinous winds,
> And twixt the green sea and the azured vault
> Set roaring war; to the dread rattling thunder
> Have I given fire, and rifted Jove's stout oak
> With his own bolt; the strong-based promontory
> Have I made shake, and by the spurs plucked up
> The pine and cedar; graves at my command
> Have waked their sleepers, oped, and let 'em forth
> By my so potent art.

These two passages have been chosen for comparison, in part because they are both set speeches in blank verse, rich in formal characteristics. Put side by side, they reveal a stylistic shift that we can observe in other less formal poetry and even in prose. The shift is away from rhetorical balance toward a freedom from verse restraint, a deliberate syncopation of blank verse rhythms, and a complication of syntax.

Completely regular blank verse, invariably consisting of ten syllables to each unrhymed line, with an accent falling on every other syllable, soon becomes monotonous. The iambic pattern can, however, be varied by a number of subtle changes. Extra syllables, accented and unaccented, can be added to the line, or a line may occasionally be short by one or more syllables. The regular alternation of accented and unaccented syllables, producing the effect of five iambic "feet" in each line (each foot consisting of an accented and an unaccented syllable), can be interrupted by the occasional inversion of a foot. Pauses, or caesuras, may occur at several points in the line. Most importantly, the line can be "end-stopped"—with a strong pause at the end of the line—or "run on" without interruption into the next line. Variations of this sort can transform blank verse from a formal and rhetorical vehicle into one that is highly conversational and supple.

Shakespeare increasingly abandons formal end-stopped verse for a fluid and more conversational style. In the preceding two passages, the first introduces a grammatical stop at the end of every line, except the ninth, whereas the second passage tends to run on past the end of the line; it does so in all but the fifth and tenth lines. Similarly, the passage from *The Tempest* is more apt to introduce a grammatical pause in the middle of a verse line, whereas the passage from *Richard III* stops between clauses in midline only in line 9. Shakespeare's later style is freer in its use of so-called feminine ends at the ends of lines, that is, endings with an unstressed syllable added on to the final stress of the imabic pattern; "fly him," "pastime," and "thunder" are good examples of this. A corollary of Shakespeare's increased use of feminine line endings and nonstopped blank verse is that the lines of his later verse are more apt to end in conjunctions, prepositions, auxiliary verbs, possessive pronouns, and other lightly stressed words. The *Richard III* passage generally ends in strong verbs and nouns, such as "drown," "ears," "eyes," and so on, whereas the *Tempest* passage makes use of "that," "up," and "forth."

Stylistic traits such as these can be quantified to demonstrate a fairly steady course of progression from the early to later plays. Early plays have low percentages of run-on lines in relation to the total number of lines: *1 Henry VI* has 10.4 percent, *2 Henry VI* 11.4 percent, *3 Henry VI* 9.5 percent, *The Comedy of Errors* 12.9 percent, and *The Two Gentlement of Verona* 12.4 percent, whereas *Cymbeline* has 46.0 percent, *The Winter's Tale* 37.5 percent, *The Tempest* 41.5 percent, and *Henry VIII* 46.3 percent. Feminine or "double" endings run from a total of 9 in *Love's Labor's Lost* and 29 in *A Midsummer Night's Dream* to 708 in *Coriolanus*, 726 in *Cymbeline*, and 1,195 in *Henry VIII*. The actual number of light or weak endings increases from none in *The Comedy of Errors* and *The Two Gentlemen of Verona* to 104 in *Coriolanus*, 130 in *Cymbeline*, and 100 in *The Tempest*.

Other stylistic characteristics, though not discernible in the two examples form *Richard III* and *The Tempest*, spell out a similar development toward flexibility. For example, Shakespeare increasingly divides a verse line between two or more speakers. *The Comedy of Errors* and *1 Henry VI* do so hardly at all, whereas in *Cymbeline* the figures rise to a remarkable 85 percent of all instances in which one speaker stops speaking and another begins; *The Winter's Tale* does so in 87.6 percent of such instances, and *The Tempest*, in 84.5 percent.

Shakespeare's use of prose in his plays depends, to a significant extent, on genre, especially in his early work. At the start of his career, Shakespeare seldom uses prose, except in the speeches of clowns, servants, and rustics, whereas blank verse is his common vehicle of expression in speeches of heightened oratory or dramatic seriousness. *1*

Henry VI and *3 Henry VI, King John,* and *Richard II* are essentially written throughout in verse—usually blank verse. Prose is more common in the early comedies because of the presence of the Dromios, Christopher Sly, and Bottom the Weaver, but the love scenes are generally in verse. Poetry is important to the lyric plays of the mid-1590s, such as *The Merchant of Venice, A Midsummer Night's Dream,* and *Romeo and Juliet.* Prose assumes a major function, on the other hand, in plays of comic wit in the later 1590s, including *1 Henry IV* (45 percent), *2 Henry IV* (54 percent), *Much Ado About Nothing* (74 percent), and *The Merry Wives of Windsor* (81 percent), and here we see that comedy is used not for wisecracking servants so much as for Falstaff, Beatrice, and Benedick. Thereafter, prose is essential to Shakespeare's comic world. It also takes on a major function in *Hamlet* (31 percent), as, for instance, when Hamlet converses with his onetime friends Rosencrantz and Guildenstern, when he plagues Polonius with his satirical wit, or when he philosophizes with Horatio, though verse is, of course, appropriate for the soliloquies and the moments of confrontation with Claudius. In the other great tragedies as well, prose has become for Shakespeare an instrument of limitless flexibility. Although the mixture of prose and blank verse is thus hard to quantify in any steady progression of percentages, the pattern of increased versatility is undeniable. Many of the late plays make less use of prose because of their choice of subject, but all excel in prose comic scenes for Autolycus, Caliban, and many others.

In his use of rhyme, as well, Shakespeare's practice changes from the early to late plays. Early plays and those of the lyric period, such as *A Midsummer Night's Dream* and *Romeo and Juliet,* use a great deal of rhyme, whereas late plays, such as *The Tempest,* use practically none. The commonest form of rhyme is the iambic pentameter measure rhymed in couplet, as when Phoebe, quoting Marlowe's *Hero and Leander,* says in *As You Like It* (3.5.81–82):

> Dead shepherd, now I find thy saw of might,
> "Who ever loved that loved not at first sight?"

Shakespeare does not limit his use of rhyme to the couplet, however. *Romeo and Juliet* and *Love's Labor's Lost* each contains a number of complete sonnets, as well as rhymed sequences made up of a quatrain followed by a couplet, and a good deal of alternate rhyme. Doggerel lines of verse appear in some of the early plays.

One quite formal use of the rhymed couplet does not conform to the statistical pattern that we observe generally in the use of rhyme. Because the Elizabethan theater lacked a front curtain to mark a pause between scenes in a play, Elizabethan dramatists often gave emphasis to a scene ending by means of a rhymed couplet. Possibly the device served also as a cue to those actors backstage who were waiting to begin the next scene. At any rate, the use of scene-ending couplets is common in some plays that otherwise make little use of rhyme. For example, Act 1, scene 5 of *Hamlet* virtually ends with the following concluding statement by the protagonist:

> The time is out of joint. O cursèd spite,
> That ever I was born to set it right!

Apart from this convention, however, use of rhyme in Shakespeare is normally indicative of early style. His lovers in the early plays often speak in rhyme; later, they tend to use prose.

Impossible to quantify, but no less significant in any study of the evolution of Shakespeare's art, is his use of imagery. Images are key to his poetic imagination, and, in part, they can be appreciated out of chronological context, because Shakespeare's mind dwells incessantly on certain image clusters: the family as a metaphor for the state, the garden as an image of social order and disorder, images of medicine and healing applied to the ills of the individual and the commonwealth, images of sexual desire and activity, images of hunting and of other sports, biblical images (Eden, Cain and Abel, Christ's ministry, his Passion, the Last Judgment, etc.), mythological allusions (Danae, Actaeon, Phaethon, Noah, Niobe), and many others. Patterns of imagery have been well studied by Caroline Spurgeon in her *Shakespeare's Imagery and What It Tells Us* (1935), Maurice Charney in *The Function of Imagery in the Drama* (1961), and others. In addition, we can see throughout Shakespeare's career the evolution of an imagistic style, as convincingly demonstrated by Wolfgang Clemen in *The Development of Shakespeare's Imagery* (1951). The early Shakespeare uses figures of speech for decoration and amplification, and learns only gradually to integrate these figures into a presentation of theme, subject, and individual character. In Shakespeare's later work, simile is often transformed into metaphor and assumes an organic function in relation to the entire play. By the end of his career, virtually every aspect of his style has been transformed from one of formal and rhetorical regularity to one of vast flexibility and range.

Shakespeare's English

Pronunciation

How would Shakespeare's plays have sounded to our ears? The distance between Shakespearean and modern English is clearly not as great as in the case of Chaucer, and yet significant differences remain. Spoken English, especially in the pronunciation of vowel sounds, has undergone many striking changes since the early seventeenth century. We can assume that however much Shakespeare's own speech may have been colored by his Warwickshire boyhood, his acting company as a whole was most heavily influenced by London dialect. This form of English had

become notably more dominant than in Chaucer's day, though it also included an admixture of northern, eastern, and southern forms because of the cosmopolitan character of the city. Shakespeare often pokes fun at regional dialects in his plays, especially at Welsh, Scottish, and Irish, and at the accents of Frenchmen or other foreigners attempting to speak English (see, for example, *Henry V* and *The Merry Wives of Windsor*).

Here, in summary form, are some approximate suggestions for pronouncing words in Shakespeare that are not similarly pronounced today. These examples can be applied to similar words: for example, *way* and *say* have the same vowel sound as *day*; *night*, the same vowel sound as *wide*.

> *folk* (sound the *l*)
> *gnaw* (sound the *g*)
> *knife* (sound the *k*; *i* as in *wide*, below)
> *brush* (rhymes with *push*; *r* somewhat trilled)
> *dull* (rhymes with *pull*)
> *seam* (pronounced *same*, with open *a*)
> *old* (pronounced *auld*)
> *now* (pronounced *noo*)
> *house* (pronounced *hoos*)
> *soul* (pronounced *saul*)
> *know* (pronounced *knaw*, with sounded *k*)
> *own* (pronounced *awn*)
> *tune* (pronounced *tiwn*)
> *rule* (pronounced *riwl*; *r* somewhat trilled)
> *day* (pronounced *die*)
> *time* (pronounced *toime*)
> *wide* (pronounced *woide*)
> *join* (rhymes with *line*)
> *creeping* (pronounced *craypin*, with open *a*)
> *dissention* (in four syllables, without *sh* sound)
> *persuasion* (in four syllables, without *zh* sound)

A matter of more practical importance than phonetic changes is that of differences in Shakespeare's English and ours in the accentuation of syllables. Many cases of variable stress can be found in which he seems to have been at liberty to accent the word in two different ways; in other cases, words were customarily accented on a different syllable from that in current speech. For example, the following accentuations are either usual or frequent: *as-pect'*, *charac'ter*, *com'mendable*, *com'plete*, *con'-cealed*, *con'fessor*, *consort'* (as a noun), *contract'* (noun), *de'testable*, *dis'tinct*, *envy'*, *for'lorn*, *hu'mane*, *instinct'*, *ob'scure*, *persev'er*, *pi'oner*, *ple'beians*, *portents'*, *pur'-sue*, *record'* (noun), *reven'ue*, *se'cure*, *sinis'ter*, *wel-come'*.

Not only are *-tion* and *-sion* regularly pronounced as two syllables, but the same situation causes other words in which *e* or *i* stand before vowels to be uttered in Shakespeare's language with one more syllable than in ours; for example, *oce-an*, *courti-er*, *marri-age*. We may even have *cre-ature, tre-asure,* and *venge-ance.* Nasals and liquids are frequently pronounced as if an extra vowel were introduced between them and a preceding letter. Accordingly, we have *wrest(e)ler, Eng(e)land, assemb(e)ly,* and *ent(e)rance,* as well as *de-ar, you(e)r,* and *mo-re.* Final *-er* often has a greater syllabic importance than it has in later poetry. Final *-(e)s* in the genitive singular and the plural of nouns not ending in an *s-* sound may constitute a separate syllable; for example, "To show his teeth as white as whale's bone" (*Love's Labor's Lost,* 5.2.333).

The scanning of Shakespeare's verse requires knowing how many syllables he intended a given word to have, for, as compared to current English, (1) a Shakespearean word may have an additional syllable, or (2) it may have one fewer syllables, or (3) two adjoining syllables in different words may coalesce or elide. Spelling may not always indicate these differences to a modern reader.

1. The following lines give us extra-syllable words in *moon's, juggler, entrance,* and *complexion:*

> I do wander everywhere,
> Swifter than the *moon's* sphere.
> > (*A Midsummer Night's Dream,* 2.1.6–7)
>
> O me! You *juggler!* You cankerblossom!
> > (*A Midsummer Night's Dream,* 3.2.282)
>
> After the prompter, for our *entrance.*
> > (*Romeo and Juliet,* 1.4.8)
>
> Mislike me not for my *complexion.*
> > (*The Merchant of Venice,* 2.1.1)

Similarly, the words *captain, monstrous, esperance, this* (*this is*), *George* (*Richard III,* 5.5.9), *valiant, villain,* and *jealous* sometimes have extra syllables in pronunciation.

2. In the following line, *marry* is elided into one syllable:

> Good mother, do not *marry* me to yond fool.
> > (*The Merry Wives of Windsor,* 3.4.83)

Similarly, the words *lineal, journeying, carrion, celestial, herald, royal, malice, absolute, perjury, madame, needle, taken, heaven, spirit, devil, gentleman, unpeople, forward, gather, innocent, violet, Africa, eagle, listen,* and *venomous* have usually one fewer syllables than in current English.

3. The following examples are of elision between the syllables of adjoining words:

> Why should I joy in *an abortive* birth?
> > (*Love's Labor's Lost,* 1.1.104)
>
> The *lover, all* as frantic,
> > (*A Midsummer Night's Dream,* 5.1.10)
>
> Romans, *do me* right.   (*Titus Andronicus,* 1.1.204)

Differences in accentuation and lengthening or shortening of words thus have great importance in the reading and scanning of Shakespeare's verse. Shortening of words by elision or by slurring is common in Shakespeare, but at least

in this matter modern practice forms a good guide. Syllables ending in vowels are not infrequently elided before words beginning with a vowel, as in "How cáme / we ashóre" (*The Tempest,* 1.2.159) and "too hárd / a knót / for mé / t' untie" (*Twelfth Night,* 2.2.41). Syncopation, or the omission of a syllable, often occurs in words with *r,* as in "I wár-*rant* / it wíll" (*Hamlet,* 1.2.248); and in final *-er, -el,* and *-le,* as in "Trável you / far ón" (*The Taming of the Shrew,* 4.2.74). The following words and other similar ones may be treated as monosyllabic in Shakespeare's verse: *whether, ever, hither, other, father, evil, having.* Almost any unaccented syllable of a polysyllabic word (especially if it contains an *i*) may be softened and ignored. This syncopation is frequent in polysyllabic words and proper names: "Thoughts spécu / latíve" (*Macbeth,* 5.4.19) and "Did sláy / this Fórtinbras; / who bý / a seáled / compáct" (*Hamlet,* 1.1.90). Other occasions for slurring, as listed by Abbott in his *Shakespearian Grammar,* are light vowels preceded by heavy vowels, as in *power, dying,* and so on; plurals and possessives of nouns ending in an *s* sound, as in *empress'* and *Mars';* final *-ed* following *d* or *t,* as in "you háve / exceéded / all prómise" (*As You Like It,* 1.2.234); and the *-est* of superlatives (pronounced *-st*) after dentals and liquids, as "the stérn'st / good-níght" (*Macbeth,* 2.2.4) and "thy éldest / son's són" (*King John,* 2.1.177).

Grammar and Rhetoric

Shakespeare's grammar presents but few differences in forms from the grammar of current modern English. The *-eth* ending in the third person singular of the present tense, indicative mood, was very commonly used, especially in serious prose. Shakespeare frequently uses this older form, especially *hath, doth,* and *saith,* but seems to prefer the form in *-s* or *-es.* In a few cases, he also seems to use the old northern plural in *-s* or *-es* in the third person of the present indicative, as ". . . at those springs, On chaliced flowers that *lies*" (*Cymbeline,* 2.3.22–23). He does not always agree with modern usage in the forms of the past tenses and the perfect participles of the verbs that he employs. He retains some lost forms of the strong verbs, sometimes ignores distinctions we make between the past tense and the perfect participle, and treats some verbs as weak (or regular) which are now strong (or irregular). For example, he uses *arose* for *arisen, swam* for *swum, foughten* for *fought, gave* for *given, took* for *taken, sprung* for *sprang, writ* for *wrote, blowed* for *blew, weaved* for *wove,* and *shaked* for *shaken.* Forms like *degenerate* for *degenerated* and *exhaust* for *exhausted* are especially common. A few instances are to be found of the archaic *y-* with the past participle, as in *yclad.* For the possessive case of the neuter personal pronoun *it,* Shakespeare normally uses the regular form at that time, *his;* but he also uses the possessive form *it,* and in his plays first published in the First Folio in 1623 we find several occurrences of the new form *its.* Shakespeare uses the old form *moe,* as well as *more,* and *enow* as the plural of *enough,* though these forms have been modernized in this edition because they are used so inconsistently. He uses *near* and *next* along with *nearer* and *nearest,* as the comparative and superlative of *nigh.* These are the most obvious of the formal differences between Shakespeare's grammar and our own.

The functional differences are more considerable. Elizabethan language exercised an extraordinary freedom, even for English, in the use of one part of speech for another. Shakespeare uses verbs, adjectives, adverbs, and pronouns as nouns. He makes verbs out of nouns and adjectives and, of course, uses nouns as adjectives, for this is a distinguishing characteristic of English speech, but he also uses adverbs, verbs, and prepositional phrases as adjectives, as in "Looks he as freshly as he did . . . ?" (*As You Like It,* 3.2.227). Almost any adjective may be freely used as an adverb, as in "And in my house you shall be friendly lodged" (*The Taming of the Shrew,* 4.2.109). He makes active words—both adjectives and verbs—discharge a passive function, as in "the sightless [invisible] couriers of the air" (*Macbeth,* 1.7.23) and "this aspect of mine / Hath feared the valiant," that is, caused the valiant to be afraid (*The Merchant of Venice,* 2.1.8–9). He makes wider use of the infinitive as a verbal noun or as a gerundive participle than do we: "This to be true, I do engage my life" (*As You Like It,* 5.4.164–165), "My operant powers their functions leave to do" (*Hamlet,* 3.2.172), "Nor do I now make moan to be abridged" (*The Merchant of Venice,* 1.1.126), and "You might have saved me my pains, to have taken [by having taken] it away yourself" (*Twelfth Night,* 2.2.5–7). The functions of prepositions in Elizabethan English were so various that one can only refer the student to the notes to the text or to a dictionary.

In certain other features, however, as, for example, in the use of modal auxiliaries, Shakespeare's language is as restricted and conventional as ours is at formal levels, or even more so. *Shall* is regularly used in Shakespeare to express something inevitable in future time and is, therefore, the usual future tense for all persons. *Will,* which originally expressed intention, determination, or willingness, was, to be sure, beginning to encroach on *shall* for the expression of futurity in the second and third persons, but its use usually still retains in Shakespeare a consciousness of its original meaning. *Should* and *would* had their original senses of obligation and volition, respectively, and had other peculiarities, then as now, of considerable difficulty. The subjunctive mood was vital to Shakespeare as a means of expressing condition, doubt, concession, command, wish, or desire, and, in dependent clauses, indefinitiveness, purpose, or sometimes simple futurity. Note the following examples:

But if my father *had* not scanted me . . .
Yourself, renowned Prince, then *stood* as fair.
(*The Merchant of Venice,* 2.1.17, 20)

Live a thousand years,
I *shall* not find myself so apt to die.
(*Julius Caesar,* 3.1.161–162)
Lest your retirement *do amaze* your friends.
(*1 Henry IV,* 5.4.6)
'Twere best he speak no harm of Brutus here.
(*Julius Caesar,* 3.2.70)
Melt Egypt into Nile, and kindly creatures
Turn all to serpents! (*Antony and Cleopatra,* 2.5.79–80)
Yet were it true
To say this boy *were* like me.
(*The Winter's Tale,* 1.2.134–135)
And may direct his course as *please* himself.
(*Richard III,* 2.2.129)

Some other features of Shakespeare's grammar are as follows: he often omits the relative pronoun; he often uses the nominative case of the pronoun for the accusative case, and vice versa; he uses *him, her, me,* and *them* as true reflexives to mean *himself, herself, myself,* and *themselves;* he employs double negatives and double comparatives and superlatives; he shows a consciousness in the use of *thee* and *thou* of their application to intimates and inferiors and of their insulting quality when addressed to strangers (e.g., "If thou 'thou'-est him some thrice, it shall not be amiss," *Twelfth Night,* 3.2.43–44); he employs *which* to refer to both persons and things; and he does not discriminate closely between *ye,* nominative, and *you,* objective. He makes frequent use of the dative constructions, that is, the objective forms of the pronouns, *me, thee, you, him, her,* and so on, without prepositions where the meaning is "by me," "for me," "with me," "to me," "of me," and the like. For example:

I am appointed *him* [by him] to murder you.
(*The Winter's Tale,* 1.2.411)

She looks *us* [to us] like
A thing made more of malice than of duty.
(*Cymbeline,* 3.5.32–33)

One prominent feature of Shakespeare's grammar is his use of the ethical dative, a construction in which the pronoun is generally used to indicate the person interested in the statement. In *King John* (3.4.146), the phrase "John lays *you* plots," means something like "John lays plots which you may profit by." In the following, *me* means "to my detriment" or "to my disadvantage":

See how this river comes *me* cranking in
And cuts *me* from the best of all my land
A huge half-moon. (*1 Henry IV,* 3.1.95–97)

"Whip *me* such honest knaves" (*Othello,* 1.1.50) means "In my judgment such knaves should be whipped." In Quickly's description of Mistress Page, the dative *you* is equivalent to "mark you," "take notice":

. . . a civil modest wife, and one, I tell you, that will not miss *you* morning nor evening prayer, as any is in Windsor.
(*The Merry Wives of Windsor,* 2.2.92–94)

At times, however, the ethical dative is idiomatic and virtually without equivalent meaning in modern English; the sense of the passage is best obtained by omitting the pronoun.

Shakespeare, like other Renaissance poets, makes extensive use of the forms and figures of rhetoric. He is fond, for example, of using the abstract for the concrete, as in the words addressed by Surrey to Cardinal Wolsey: "Thou scarlet sin" (*Henry VIII*, 3.2.255). Transpositions are numerous, as are inversions, ellipses, and broken or confused constructions, as in the following examples:

> That thing you speak of,
> I took it for a man. (*Absolute construction*.)
> (*King Lear*, 4.6.77–78)

> Souls and bodies hath he divorced three. (*Transposition of adjective*.)
> (*Twelfth Night*, 3.4.238–239)

> A happy gentleman in blood and lineaments. (*Transposition of adjectival phrase*.)
> (*Richard II*, 3.1.9)

> Your state of fortune and your due of birth. (*Transposition of pronoun*.)
> (*Richard III*, 3.7.120)

> She calls me proud, and [says] that she could not love me. (*Ellipsis*.)
> (*As You Like It*, 4.3.17)

> Returning were as tedious as [to] go o'er. (*Ellipsis*.)
> (*Macbeth*, 3.4.139)

> They call him Doricles, and boasts himself
> To have a worthy feeding. (*Ellipsis of nominative*.)
> (*The Winter's Tale*, 4.4.168–169)

> Of all men else I have avoided thee. (*Confusion of two constructions*.)
> (*Macbeth*, 5.8.4)

> The venom of such looks, we fairly hope,
> Have lost their quality. (*Confusion of number arising from proximity*.)
> (*Henry V*, 5.2.18–19)

> Rather proclaim it, Westmorland, through my host
> That he which hath no stomach to this fight,
> Let him depart. (*Construction changed by change of thought*.)
> (*Henry V*, 4.3.34–36)

> For always I am Caesar. (*Inversion of adverb*.)
> (*Julius Caesar*, 1.2.212)

Shakespeare often uses rhetorical figures for symmetrical effects, especially in the early, ornamental style of *Richard III* and the nondramatic poems. Following are definitions of some of the most popular figures he uses, with illustrations from *Venus and Adonis*:

1. *Parison*. The symmetrical repetition of words in grammatically parallel phrases: "How love makes young men thrall, and old men dote" (line 837).
2. *Isocolon*. The symmetrical repetition of sounds and words in phrases of equal length, as in the previous example, and in this: "Or as the wolf doth grin before he barketh, / Or as the berry breaks before it staineth" (lines 459–460). Parison and isocolon are frequently combined.
3. *Anaphora*. The symmetrical repetition of a word at the beginning of a sequence of clauses or sentences, often at the beginning of lines. Anaphora is frequently combined with parison and isocolon, as in the second example already given, and in this: " 'Give me my hand,' saith he. 'Why dost thou feel it?' / 'Give me my heart,' saith she, 'and thou shalt have it' " (lines 373–374).
4. *Antimetabole*. The symmetrical repetition of words in inverted order: "She clepes him king of graves and grave for kings" (line 995).
5. *Anadiplosis*. The beginning of a phrase with the final words of the previous phrase: "O, thou didst kill me; kill me once again!" (line 499).
6. *Epanalepsis*. The symmetrical repetition of a word or words at the beginning and ending of a line: "He sees his love, and nothing else he sees" (line 287).
7. *Ploce*. The insistent repetition of a word within the same line or phrase: "Then why not lips on lips, since eyes in eyes?" (line 120).
8. *Epizeuxis*. An intensified form of ploce, repeating the word without another intervening word: " 'Ay me!' she cries, and twenty times, 'Woe, woe!' / And twenty echoes twenty times cry so" (lines 833–834).
9. *Antanaclasis*. The shifting of a repeated word from one meaning to another: "My love to love is love but to disgrace it," or " 'Where did I leave?' 'No matter where,' quoth he, / 'Leave me' " (lines 412, 715–716).

For other figures and illustrations, see Sister Miriam Joseph, *Shakespeare's Use of the Arts of Language* (1947) and Brian Vickers, "Shakespeare's Use of Rhetoric," in *A New Companion to Shakespeare Studies*, edited by Kenneth Muir and S. Schoenbaum (1971).

Vocabulary

Renaissance English was hospitable to foreign importation. Many words taken directly from Latin became a permanent part of the language, serving to enrich its power to express thought and its rhythmical capabilities; others were ultimately discarded. The principal borrowings were in the realm of learning and culture. Such words usually retained a vital sense of their original Latin meaning. Sometimes such words have not replaced native words of the same meaning, so that we have such pairs of synonyms as *acknowledge* and *confess*, just as Shakespeare had *wonder* and *admiration*. Because of this Latin heritage, even a slight knowledge of Latin is a great advantage in the correct understanding of Elizabethan writers, since many Latin borrowings have taken on since the sixteenth century a different shade of meaning from that in which they were borrowed. The Latin sense of *aggravate* ("to add weight to") still struggles for recognition; but *apparent* no longer means primarily "visible to sight," and "intention" does not convey the idea of "intentness." The *Oxford English Dictionary* (*OED*) provides a wealth of information about derivations and changes in meaning.

Latin words were often taken over in their Latin forms, as *objectum* and *subjectum*, *statua* and *aristocratia*, and later were made to conform to English spelling and stress, though a few, such as *decorum*, still have a Latin form. French continued to be drawn upon and sometimes caused a new Latin borrowing to be adopted in a French form, just as, on the other hand, such words as *adventure* were supplied with a *d* to make them conform to Latin spelling. This principle is illustrated in the pedantry of Holofernes when he objects (*Love's Labor's Lost*, 5.1.20) to "det" as the pronunciation of "debt." Spanish, Italian, and Dutch also supplied many terms. Spanish gave words having to do with commerce, religion, and the New World, such as *mosquito, alligator, ambuscado,* and *grandee.* From Italian came terms of art, learning, and dueling: *bandetto, portico, canto, stoccato.* The Dutch contributed many nautical and oriental words.

These foreign borrowings were a part of what might be called the linguistic ambition of the age, a desire for forcible expression. Language was in a plastic state, so that it had an unparalleled freedom in both vocabulary and form. With this freedom, to be sure, came some confusion, since the Elizabethan era saw few efforts at grammatical precision. Such efforts were later to be made by the age of Dryden and the Royal Society, and by learned men ever since, prompted by an awareness that English was too vague and irregular for use as a means of scientific expression. Still, we readily perceive that English profited from its Renaissance expansion and its subsequent absorption with Shakespeare and the English Bible. It gained, for example, an increased facility in making compounds. Shakespeare, with his *cloud-capped towers* and his *home-keeping wits,* was a genius at this. Also from Shakespeare's time came the English adaptability in the use of prefixes, such as *dis-, re-,* and *en-,* and of suffixes, such as *-ful, -less, -ness,* and *-hood.*

Editions
and Editors
of Shakespeare

The earliest complete edition of Shakespeare's plays was the so-called First Folio of 1623, sponsored by Shakespeare's theatrical colleagues, John Heminges and Henry Condell. (A "folio" book was one in which the printing sheets were folded only once, each producing two "leaves," or four rather large printed pages of about 13½ × 8¼ inches. In a "quarto" book, the sheets were folded twice, producing eight pages on four leaves half the folio size.) The First Folio brought together eighteen plays that had previously been published individually in quarto volumes and eighteen plays that had never before been published. It did not include Shakespeare's nondramatic poetry, of which *Venus and Adonis* and *The Rape of Lucrece* had been published in 1593–1594 and the sonnets in 1609. Nor did it include *Pericles* or *The Two Noble Kinsmen.*

The nature of the early printed texts, and their relationship to what Shakespeare actually wrote, is a complex subject requiring some understanding of the physical process by which Elizabethan plays were written, prepared for staging, licensed, and printed. What sorts of manuscripts lie behind the various printed early editions we have, and how were those manuscripts modified successively by scribes, governmental officials, theatrical producers, actors, editors, compositors, proofreaders, and editors of subsequent editions? The problem is amplified by the fact that none of Shakespeare's manuscripts survives today. Consequently, textual critics can only theorize about the kinds of printer's copy that appear to underlie the printed texts we have. The resulting theories are necessarily conjectural, and they appear increasingly so in an age when critical theory generally is wary of any attempts to construct an authorial presence in a literary work. What follows here is an attempt to set forth a widely adopted theory of textual origins, as devised by A. W. Pollard, R. B. McKerrow, W. W. Greg, Fredson Bowers, and others. Although, as we shall see, the various hypotheses about manuscript sources and types of quartos do not always account for the evidence, the theory itself still represents a once-prevailing set of assumptions against which the new textual scholarship offers its objections and qualifications, and hence needs to be laid out here. A good place to begin is with the hypothetical reconstruction of manuscripts.

Manuscripts: "Foul Papers"

Most often, it seems, Elizabethan dramatic companies obtained a play by commissioning a known professional dramatist to write a new play, to revise an old one, or to collaborate with another author. Usually, the company paid the dramatist a flat fee. Shakespeare, on the other hand, was a "sharer" in the Chamberlain's (later the King's) company; that is, he was part owner and took a share of the profits. He seems to have written plays, not for a fee, but as his chief contribution to the company's activities. Whatever the financial arrangement between author and company, in any case, the play became the property of the acting company, and the author gave up his individual right to sell it elsewhere. Moreover, he ordinarily wrote the play with a view not to publication, but to performance. Occasionally, a literary-minded author like Ben Jonson would see his plays through the press (and be scoffed at for his pretentiousness). Shakespeare, however, almost certainly did not do this. The quarto texts of his plays that appeared during his lifetime show no trace of having been prepared for the reader. They are playhouse documents.

When Shakespeare had finished writing a play, he presumably submitted a readable manuscript to his acting company. This draft in his handwriting, or any earlier draft, has been given the name of "foul papers," as distinguished from "fair copy," or a clean copy that might be prepared by the author or a playhouse scribe. (The term "foul papers" is Elizabethan, though whether these papers, in fact, found their way into printers' hands is a questionable theory largely attributable to R. B. McKerrow.) Actually, the foul papers need not have been especially messy, although a certain amount of deletion, interlineation, inconsistency, and illegibility was inevitable. These foul papers were usually preserved by the acting company and were often turned over to the printer (according to this theory) when the company decided to sell its rights in a play. The company presumably would prefer to hold on to its theatrical copy of the play and to dispose of the foul papers as of little further value if they chose to have a play printed. A manuscript of this sort naturally would pose some difficulties for the compositor.

Among the Shakespearean quarto texts thought by Greg and others to have been based on foul papers are the first quartos of *Titus Andronicus, Love's Labor's Lost, A Midsummer Night's Dream, Richard II, The Merchant of Venice, Much Ado About Nothing,* and *1* and *2 Henry IV,* and the second quartos of *Romeo and Juliet* and *Hamlet.* Three more first quartos—*Troilus and Cressida, Othello,* and *King Lear*—were also based presumably on foul papers, although each is an anomalous case. In addition, the First Folio contains several newly printed plays thought to be based on foul papers or a transcript thereof, including *The Comedy of Errors, The Taming of the Shrew, All's Well That Ends Well, Timon of Athens, Coriolanus,* and *Henry VIII.* Two more Folio plays are thought to be based on transcripts of foul papers by the scrivener Ralph Crane: *Measure for Measure* and *The Winter's Tale.* The text of *King John* seems to have been based on foul papers also, but with some reference to a playbook in the final two acts.

At their best, we might expect foul papers to be close to what Shakespeare wrote but also potentially laden with error. Some presumably foul-paper texts seem to preserve Shakespeare's work in an early state of composition: *Timon of Athens,* for example, seems never to have been finished by Shakespeare, since the text we have retains glaring inconsistencies and redundancies that he presumably would have straightened out in a final version. *Love's Labor's Lost* and *Romeo and Juliet* contain uncanceled duplicatory passages. On the other hand, *The Merchant of Venice, Richard II,* and the *Henry IV* plays are very good texts, and *Much Ado* is almost ready for stage production; the names of two actors appear among the speech prefixes, although other irregularities suggest that the manuscript was in the last stages of authorial revision. The hypothesis of "foul papers" therefore represents a whole spectrum of states from unrevised manuscript to a text that has been thoroughly worked over.

Unfortunately, no manuscript of a regular Shakespearean play has survived today. Moreover, the distinction between foul papers and a prompt copy used in the theater is not always as easily made as some scholars would like to assume; authors' papers were often used by the acting company without recopying and without extensive annotation. Existing play manuscripts from the Elizabethan period by dramatists other than Shakespeare do not, in fact, offer good examples of what Greg and others have termed foul papers. Nonetheless, in theoretical terms, an author's manuscript is thought to be identifiable behind the printed text through some of the following characteristics: vagueness in specifying the number of supernumeraries needed for a scene, lack of precision in the marking of entrances and especially exits, authorial stage directions that tend to describe stage business or the emotional states of the characters, speech prefixes that inconsistently refer to a character both by personal name and generic title, and so on. Thus, in *Love's Labor's Lost,* Navarre, Armado, and Holofernes are at times referred to as King, Braggart, and Pedant; Navarre is also called Ferdinand. See Appendix I at the end of this volume for a play-by-play summary of the kind of manuscript thought to lie behind each of Shakespeare's plays and poems.

Licensing for Performance

Before one of Shakespeare's plays could go into production, it had to be licensed by the Master of the Revels, an officer of the royal household responsible for supervising court entertainments. Since the beginning of Elizabeth's reign, and even earlier, dramatic performances throughout England had been made subject to governmental control. Elizabeth had authorized municipal and other local governments to scrutinize plays performed within their jurisdictions. In the vicinity of London, however, where municipal hostility toward the theater was particularly strong, she took the unusual step in 1581 of transferring licensing power to her own Master of the Revels. Since many public plays came to court, as we have seen, Elizabeth was inclined to protect the players against the city authorities in this way and to adopt the useful fiction that public performances were rehearsals of plays intended for her ultimate benefit.

The Master of the Revels did occasionally censor Shakespeare's plays. For example, the scene of Richard II's deposition, omitted from the three earliest quarto editions of the play, seems to have been disallowed for acting during Elizabeth's lifetime. (She was sensitive to a widespread and libelous analogy comparing her with Richard.) More often, one suspects, the mere threat of censorship was sufficient to keep the London dramatic companies in line. The Tudor establishment had no intention of tolerating openly seditious criticism in the drama. Generally, the Master of the Revels was more concerned with questions of religion and politics than with morals. Edmund Tilney served as Master of the Revels from 1579 to 1610, when he was succeeded by his

A CATALOGVE

of the feuerall Comedies, Histories, and Tragedies contained in this Volume.

John Heminges and Henry Condell, Shakespeare's fellow actors, organized the original table of contents for the First Folio, published in 1623. They collected thirty-six plays in the volume, omitting Pericles. Troilus and Cressida is included in the First Folio but not listed here in the contents.

deputy, Sir George Buc. In 1622, the office passed to Sir Henry Herbert.

The Playbook

The document on which the Master of the Revels affixed his seal of approval was the playbook, often referred to in recent scholarship as the "prompt-book" or "prompt-copy," that is, the version prepared by the acting company for use in actual production. Sometimes this version may have been a fair copy of the manuscript, readied for stage performance, that is, with the technical inconsistencies weeded out and with more businesslike stage directions added. One possibility is that the author's last draft might be converted into a playbook, if it was legible enough. Whatever manuscript was thus used, one might suppose that the playbook would undertake to normalize any inconsistent speech prefixes (such as those already noted in Love's Labor's Lost), in order to avoid confusion for actors and stage managers. Perhaps the prompter would add some stage directions, concentrating on such technical matters as entrances, exits, and occasional specific effects. In Julius Caesar, for example, we find such stage directions as "Enter Brutus in his orchard," "Thunder and lightning. Enter Julius Caesar in his nightgown," and "Brutus goes into the pulpit." We cannot be sure, however, that these are not authorial stage directions, and, indeed, recent evidence suggests that the acting company often did rather little to an authorial manuscript to ready it for production. Shakespeare was an acting member of his own company and must have known what his colleagues wanted, so that revision of his final draft need not have been extensive. Examination of existing playbooks by dramatists other than Shakespeare suggests that such playbooks were annotated in a variety of ways: sometimes with actors' names, sometimes with warnings for entrances and props, sometimes with calls for sound effects, and sometimes with stage directions repeated in more visible locations in the margins and highlighted with rules. Seldom does annotation follow a now-recoverable pattern within a manuscript or across various manuscripts. The category of "playbook" is not as certain today as it seemed to Greg and others.

Comparatively few of Shakespeare's printed texts are thought to be derived from playbooks, actually, since the playbook, bearing the official license of the Master of the Revels, was an invaluable document if the play was ever to be revived. Of the nineteen Shakespearean plays published in quarto prior to 1623, not one seems to have been printed from a playbook. The author's manuscript papers were far more expendable once the playbook had been prepared. Nevertheless, the First Folio does contain a few plays seemingly printed from playbooks or transcripts of playbooks, including As You Like It, Twelfth Night, Julius Caesar, and Macbeth (in a cut version). Two more plays—The Two Gentlemen of Verona and The Merry Wives of Windsor—were evidently printed from transcriptions by Ralph Crane of playbooks. Four additional plays seem to have been set from Shakespeare's drafts (or transcriptions of the drafts) that had already been annotated by the stage adapter, although not yet actually made into playbooks: 1 Henry VI, Antony and Cleopatra, perhaps Cymbeline, and The Tempest (in a transcription by Crane).

Playbooks are presumably not as likely to correspond with the author's intentions as his own papers, and indeed, some playbooks probably reflect changes occurring in the theater over a period of years. A playbook might be altered for the revival of an old favorite or might even represent a cut performance intended to be taken on tour—as perhaps in the case of Macbeth. Such a text might incorporate non-Shakespearean material; Macbeth seems to contain songs and lines attributed to Thomas Middleton.

Playbooks were presumably also used to copy out individual parts for each actor. Although such actors' "rolls," as they were called, could conceivably have been used to assemble a printed text, no Shakespearean play is known to have been printed in this fashion. A few plays, such as The Two Gentlemen of Verona and The Winter's Tale, were once thought to have been made up out of actors' rolls, since the texts of these plays generally omit stage directions and group characters' names at the head of each scene; however, these traits are now known to be the identifying characteristics of the professional scrivener named Ralph Crane. Apparently, Crane was employed to prepare copies (also including The Tempest, The Merry Wives of Windsor, and Measure for Measure) for the printers of the First Folio.

The So-called Bad Quartos

An acting company presumably had some concern as to how its plays would make their way into print. On occasion, a company might disband and sell its plays or experience financial difficulty and sell some older plays for ready money. According to Humphrey Moseley's "The Stationer to the Readers" in the Beaumont and Fletcher Folio (1646), actors sometimes sold patrons transcripts of what was acted. Still, an acting company had good reason to regard its plays as the very key to its economic prosperity and to be wary of premature publication. Popular plays that enjoyed long runs and could later be revived were especially valuable. Elizabethan acting companies regarded dramatic manuscripts as their property, to be withheld from publication as appropriate or to be sold for their benefit as opportunity arose.

By the same token, the temptation for booksellers to publish an edition of a popular play must have been considerable. Unfortunately, no copyright law protected the acting companies from piracy. If a bookseller could obtain a dramatic text in any way, all he had to do was to present his book at Stationers' Hall and enter it in the Stationers'

Register, or official record book of the London Company of Stationers (i.e., booksellers). By paying a fee, usually sixpence, he reserved the right to publish the work he had thus entered. Indeed, even if a book was printed without having been entered in the Stationers' Register, it evidently received the protection of copyright by the very act of printing. Copyright had considerable legal force. Although authors and acting companies could not copyright their plays, the stationers or booksellers enjoyed a tight monopoly. Their London Company of Stationers had a patent from the crown to restrict the number of presses operating in London, the number of books that could be printed, and so on. Legal safeguards were all on the side of the booksellers.

A. W. Pollard and other textual critics have argued that acting companies protected themselves by entering into agreements with cooperative booksellers. The acting companies, according to this theory, might allow a friendly bookseller or a printer to register a play for later publication. For example, on July 22, 1598, the printer James Roberts entered in the Stationers' Register "a booke of the Marchaunt of Venyce, or otherwise called the Jewe Of Venyce, Prouided, that yt bee not prynted by the said James Robertes or anye other whatsoeuer without lycence first had from the Right honorable the lord Chamberlen." This is what is generally known as a "staying entry," since Roberts agrees to "stay" or withhold publication pending further authorization from the acting company's patron. Similar entries occur in August of 1600 for *Much Ado About Nothing, As You Like It,* and *Henry V,* although an unauthorized Quarto of *Henry V* appeared in August of 1600. The argument that such staying entries were designed to forestall the piratical activities of less scrupulous publishers has been weakened, however, by Peter Blayney (*The Texts of King Lear and Their Origins,* Vol. I: *Nicholas Okes and the First Quarto,* 1982), who shows that a large proportion of books in the Stationers' Register was given only conditional entrance. Moreover, Blayney's research, indicating how small was the proportion of plays in the overall publication schedule of London publishers, calls into question the idea that stationers were so hungry for plays that they would resort to any means to get them. All in all, Pollard's theory that the printers of the so-called bad quartos were somehow unscrupulous has been thoroughly challenged.

Nonetheless, most textual scholars today agree that unauthorized quartos were not uncommon. Because the plays were publicly performed, a would-be pirate had easy access to repeated performances. Heminges and Condell, in their prefatory letter "To the great Variety of Readers" of the First Folio, complain about "divers stolen and surreptitious copies, maimed and deformed by the frauds and stealths of injurious imposters." Thomas Heywood similarly protests against pirated editions of his plays, which "have (unknown to me, and without any of my direction) accidentally come into the printer's hands, and therefore so corrupt and mangled (copied only by the ear) that I have been unable to know them" (Preface to *The Rape of Lucrece,* 1608).

How were such pirated texts obtained? Heywood says they were "copied only by the ear." Elsewhere, in *Pleasant Dialogues and Dramas* (1637), he complains about the pirating of one of his plays "by stenography." The stenographic hypothesis is not now widely accepted, however, chiefly because the systems of shorthand available in Shakespeare's day were inadequate and because attempts at shorthand reporting might well have been detected by an alert acting company. Besides, the pirated texts we have seem to rely heavily on the use of memory.

Most pirated texts, according to W. W. Greg, were put together by "memorial reconstruction." The usual culprits seem to have been one or more actors, in league with an unscrupulous printer. Most pirates were temporary actors hired to perform minor roles, rather than actor-sharers having a vested interest in the acting company and its stock of plays. Possibly, one or more such minor actors got together and slowly recited what they could remember of a play, while a scribe took down what they recited. The reporter or reporters of a pirated text can sometimes tentatively be identified by the relative accuracy of certain roles. For example, the actor who perhaps doubled the minor parts of Marcellus and Lucianus in *Hamlet* may have helped in the memorial reconstruction of the bad quarto of that play.

A quarto put together by memorial reconstruction reveals itself by certain characteristics, although the matter of identification is in some dispute. Such a text tends to give a fairly accurate rendition of the overall plot but garbles some speeches, transfers or misplaces lines of dialogue or even whole scenes, borrows scraps of phrases from other plays in which the actor-reporters may have acted, mislineates blank verse or crudely versifies passages of prose, ad-libs freely in half-remembered parts of the play, and so on. A memorially reported quarto is always shorter than the regular version. Visual impressions are often vivid, since the actor-reporters are remembering things they have seen on stage. The stage directions tend to be more frequent and more detailed than in either an author's manuscript or a playbook.

Approximately seven "bad" quartos have been identified in the Shakespeare canon, either as memorially reconstructed or pirated, or both. An unregistered and memorially reconstructed Quarto of *Romeo and Juliet,* published in 1597, was answered two years later by an authorized Second Quarto, "Newly corrected, augmented, and amended." (A similar phrase, "Newly corrected and augmented," appears in the title of the 1598 Quarto of *Love's Labor's Lost,* suggesting that a now-lost bad Quarto of that play had appeared prior to 1598.) The famous unauthorized Quarto of *Hamlet* appeared in 1603, perhaps memorially reconstructed and containing apparently some echoes of the lost pre-Shakespearean *Hamlet* known to have been in existence by 1589. Other memorially reported quartos include *Henry V* (1600), *The Merry Wives of Windsor* (1602), and *Pericles* (1609, the only substantive text we have of this play). In addition, the quartos published in 1594 and 1595 as *The First Part of the Contention betwixt the Two Famous Houses of York and Lancaster* and *The True Tragedy of Richard Duke of York* are now generally recognized to have been the memorially reconstructed and unauthorized quartos of *2* and *3 Henry VI.*

A few texts seem to have been put together by unusual circumstances that somewhat resemble memorial reconstruction, so that the number of quartos to be characterized as "bad" remains in dispute. *The Taming of the Shrew* was not printed until the Folio of 1623, but a Quarto did appear in 1594 of a very similar play, called *The Taming of a Shrew.* Its place names and characters' names are different from those of the Folio version, and the language differs throughout. Some scholars still regard the play as a source for Shakespeare. Nevertheless, the generally held view today is that *A Shrew* is a special kind of pirated text, one in which a rival dramatist has changed the language and the names of the characters to make the work seem his own. A different sort of anomaly is seen in *Richard III.* The 1597 Quarto shows many seemingly unmistakable signs of memorial reconstruction, and yet the text is much more accurate and full than in most bad quartos. Shakespeare's own company may have collaborated on this memorial reconstruction, perhaps while they were on tour and had no playbook with them. A somewhat similar circumstance occurs in the case of *King Lear*: the Quarto of 1608 seems to have been based on a draft to which Shakespeare's company somehow contributed. Overall, we can see that the category of "bad" quartos is problematic as to how many quartos belong in this group and how their various defects may have come about. Nonetheless, A. W. Pollard's distinction between "good" and "bad" continues to be embraced in some form by many textual critics today.

The "Good" Quartos

Despite their general unwillingness to see their plays in print, acting companies did sometimes sell texts to the printers for ready cash or to correct unauthorized quartos that had already appeared (as in the case of the good quartos of *Romeo and Juliet*, 1599, *Hamlet*, 1604–1605, and probably *Love's Labor's Lost*, 1598). The good quartos, according to Pollard's theory, were based generally on Shakespeare's own drafts or on transcripts of them. Good first quartos, as thus defined, include *Titus Andronicus* (1594), *Richard II* (1597), *1 Henry IV* (1598), *2 Henry IV* (1600), *A Midsummer Night's Dream* (1600), *The Merchant of Venice* (1600), *Much Ado About Nothing* (1600), *Troilus and Cressida* (1609, printed seemingly without permission of Shakespeare's company), and the late

First Quarto of *Othello* (1622). This is a short list and is sporadic in its time schedule; Shakespeare's company did not regularly dispose of its plays to the printers. Once a play had appeared in print, however, it was apt to be reprinted. *Richard II* went through five quartos before the Folio of 1623. At the other extreme, we have *2 Henry IV*, issued in only one quarto prior to 1623; possibly the printers ran off a large number of copies in anticipation of heavy sales, or perhaps, as Peter Blayney argues, the book-buying market may have been glutted with plays. Some quarto texts continued to appear after the Folio of 1623.

Licensing for Printing

Before a play could be printed, it had to be licensed. The licensing agency responsible for printed matter was a panel of London clergymen known as the "correctors of the press," operating under the authority of the Privy Council, the Bishop of London, the Archbishop of Canterbury, and the Lord Chamberlain. In 1606, Parliament passed a law forbidding references to the Deity in the texts of plays.

The Pavier Collection of 1619

A few years before the Shakespearean First Folio appeared in 1623, a bookseller named Thomas Pavier and a printer named William Jaggard made an apparent attempt to collect Shakespeare's plays. Pavier already owned the publishing rights to *Henry V*, for in August of 1600 he had received assignment of rights to the memorially reconstructed Quarto of the play published in that year. He brought out a Second Quarto of *Henry V* in 1602 and a Third (printed by Jaggard) in 1619 as part of his anthologizing project. In 1602, Pavier had also obtained the rights to *The First Part of the Contention* and *The True Tragedy of Richard Duke of York*, now generally regarded as the bad quartos of *2* and *3 Henry VI.* Pavier issued them in 1619 under the combined title *The Whole Contention between the Two Famous Houses, Lancaster and York*, printed by Jaggard. Pavier also included in his collection two pseudo-Shakespearean plays to which he owned the rights, *A Yorkshire Tragedy* and *Sir John Oldcastle*, and five Shakespearean plays to which he may have obtained rights or which he considered to be unowned: *A Midsummer Night's Dream, The Merchant of Venice, The Merry Wives of Windsor, King Lear,* and *Pericles.*

Pavier's evident intention was to publish these ten plays in a single volume, and, indeed, two such copies exist today—one in the Folger Library and one in the Lewis Collection at Texas Christian University. Pavier's scheme was frustrated, however, seemingly by the Lord Chamberlain at the instigation of Shakespeare's company. Pavier chose the expedient of publishing his plays separately, some with fraudulently early dates and names of publishers on their title pages in an apparent attempt to obscure the fact of new publication. Whether Pavier's texts contain any textual authority is a vexing question. They are, for the most part, copied from earlier quartos, and yet at times (in *Henry V, The Contention,* and *The True Tragedy*), they anticipate Folio readings in departing from their printed copy, and in the latter half of *King Lear,* the Pavier Quarto anticipates Folio line divisions. Possibly, this evidence points to an infusion of new manuscript source material into the Pavier quartos, but it may instead reflect a consultation of the Pavier quartos during the printing of the Folio.

Publishing Rights for the 1623 Folio

Pavier's dubious and abortive undertaking may possibly have given impetus to a more legitimate edition of Shakespeare's collected plays, some seven years after the author's death, although Shakespeare's company may already have been contemplating such an honor to its famous playwright. Ben Jonson's folio collection of plays in 1616 had established a major precedent for such a volume, despite the scorn of those who regarded all plays as subliterary. The large and tomelike folio format, normally reserved for edifying religious tracts, the ''works'' of classical authorities, and the like, might now be used also for a collection of plays.

The first task facing the supervisors of the Folio collection, Heminges and Condell, was the assembling of publishing rights to those eighteen Shakespearean plays that had already appeared in print. The most efficient means of doing so was to form a syndicate of publishers who already owned the rights to a large number of the plays. The colophon at the very end of the First Folio names those who took part: ''Printed at the charges of W. Jaggard, Ed. Blount, I. Smithweeke, and W. Aspley, 1623.'' William Jaggard had succeeded to the printing business of James Roberts in 1608. Despite Jaggard's part in the printing of the Pavier quartos of 1619, he evidently remained on good terms with Shakespeare's company and became (together with his son Isaac) the printer of the 1623 Folio. (William Jaggard died in November of 1623, but his son carried on the business.) Edward Blount had registered *Antony and Cleopatra* and *Pericles* in 1608, though he seems to have overlooked the fact, for *Antony* was reregistered in 1623, and *Pericles* never appeared in the Folio. John Smethwick had received from Nicholas Ling the rights to *Love's Labor's Lost, Romeo and Juliet,* and *Hamlet* in 1607. William Aspley owned the rights to *Much Ado About Nothing* and *2 Henry IV.* One other previously published play, *A Midsummer Night's Dream,* was ''derelict'' or no longer assigned to a publisher.

Some further negotiations must still have been necessary, with Richard Bonian and Henry Walley for *Troilus and Cressida,* with Nathaniel Butter for *King Lear,* with Thomas Pavier for *2* and *3 Henry VI, Titus Andronicus,* and *Henry V,* perhaps also with Edward White for *Titus Andronicus,*

Martin Droeshout's engraving on the title page of the First Folio is one of only two authentic likenesses of Shakespeare in existence.

with Matthew Law for *Richard III, Richard II,* and *1 Henry IV,* with Thomas Heyes for *The Merchant of Venice,* with Arthur Johnson for *The Merry Wives of Windsor,* and with Thomas Walkley for *Othello.* The last-minute inclusion of *Troilus and Cressida* between the histories and the tragedies with incomplete pagination may suggest that Bonian and Walley held out for a long time.

Eighteen plays had never before been printed. To secure rights to these plays, Messrs. Blount and Isaac Jaggard caused the following entry to be made in the Stationers' Register on November 8, 1623:

Mr. Blount, Isaac Jaggard: Entered for their copy under the hands of Mr. Dr. Worrall and Mr. Cole, Warden, Mr. William Shakespeare's Comedies, Histories, and Tragedies, so many of the said copies as are not formerly entered to other men, viz.: Comedies: *The Tempest, The Two Gentlemen of Verona, Measure for Measure, The Comedy of Errors, As You Like It, All's Well That Ends Well, Twelfth Night, The Winter's Tale.*

Histories: *The Third Part of Henry the Sixth, Henry the Eighth.*
Tragedies: *Coriolanus, Timon of Athens, Julius Caesar, Macbeth, Antony and Cleopatra, Cymbeline.*

The Stationers' Register list includes only sixteen names, since *The Taming of the Shrew* and *King John* were considered to have been published previously: *The Taming of a Shrew* and *The Troublesome Reign of King John,* now generally regarded as a pirated quarto and a source, respectively, had appeared in print in 1594 and 1591. Two plays on the list had actually been registered previously: *As You Like It* and *Antony and Cleopatra.* "The Third Part of Henry the Sixth" refers to *1 Henry VI,* since the other two *Henry VI* plays had already been published as bad quartos.

The Texts Used for the 1623 Folio

In addition to securing publishing rights, Heminges and Condell and their associates had the further task of selecting copy from which the printers were to set up their work. In the case of the eighteen as yet unpublished plays, the editors selected the best manuscripts they could find: the author's draft or perhaps a transcript of it for *All's Well,* the playbook for *As You Like It,* perhaps a scribal transcript for *Twelfth Night,* and so on. Perhaps the editors planned at first to give the printers clean new transcriptions of such plays, for the first four plays in the Folio—*The Tempest, The Two Gentlemen of Verona, The Merry Wives of Windsor,* and *Measure for Measure*—were all printed from copies made by the professional scribe Ralph Crane. If the editors had planned to continue this practice throughout the volume, however, they abandoned it after the fourth play and turned instead to a variety of sorts of copy. An alternative explanation is that the editors had these four clean copies on hand and chose to begin the volume with them simply because they were available and ready for the printer.

The complicated choices involved plays that had already been published. Printers, then as now, preferred to work from printed copy because of its legibility. Yet some published Shakespearean plays were unauthorized quartos, the "stolen and surreptitious copies" that Heminges and Condell had vowed to replace with more perfect copies. Although one might suppose that Heminges and Condell would have set aside bad quartos entirely, they did not always do so, perhaps because the manuscript alternatives were illegible or defective. In other cases, the editors had to make a more subtle choice between a "good" quarto and a still better manuscript. What the editors sometimes did in such cases was to use the inferior printed text but to annotate it by reference to a superior manuscript. This process of annotation might vary widely in its degree of thoroughness.

The use of unauthorized quartos as copy was, to be sure, unusual. The Folio text of *Henry V* seems to have been sporadically contaminated by the Third Quarto, which was derived from the pirated Quarto of 1600, but probably the Third Quarto did not, in fact, serve as printer's copy. On the other hand, the Folio text of *2 Henry VI* may actually have been set in part from pages of the Third Quarto, derived from the pirated First Quarto, and some editors argue that the same is basically true of *3 Henry VI.* Even in these questionable cases, an attempt seems to have been made to overcome the limitations of the bad quarto copy.

More often, one of the good quartos was corrected by checking it against a manuscript source. The Folio text of *Titus Andronicus,* for example, was evidently derived from a copy of the Third Quarto, but that copy may have been corrected by reference to some other copy, perhaps the playbook. In any case, a portion of Act 3 that is missing from all the early quartos must have been derived from some manuscript source. In some cases, later quartos supplied material missing from earlier ones, as in the case of the deposition scene from *Richard II.* In still other instances, as in *Richard III, Troilus and Cressida, Othello, King Lear, Hamlet,* and *2 Henry IV,* the relationship of Quarto text to the Folio text is extraordinarily complicated. See Appendix I for statements on the texts of each play.

The Printing of the 1623 Folio

The printing of the 1623 Folio continued from April of 1621 to December of 1623 in the printing shop of William and Isaac Jaggard. The compositors who actually set the type were, according to Charlton Hinman (*The Printing and Proof-Reading of the First Folio of Shakespeare,* 2 vols., 1963), five in number. For convenient reference, they are designated as compositors A through E. A and B were the principal workmen. E was evidently an inept apprentice, unfortunately brought into the project just in time to work on several of the tragedies. Still other compositors have been proposed since Hinman's time, namely, F, H, I, and J, at least some of which are problematic.

Compositors had to rely on their ability to memorize large segments of their copy—perhaps whole lines of verse—at a time, since they needed to look at the type they were setting manually. Hence, they were apt to make mistakes based on imperfect remembering. Less skillful compositors not infrequently introduced errors by transposing words in a line, substituting a new word for what was in the copy, or maiming the scansion of a line of verse by adding or subtracting syllables.

Compositors were largely responsible for the "pointing" or punctuation of the text. They also usually imposed their own spelling practices on their copy. No copy editor went over the materials first to normalize spelling, and the compositors were free to normalize as they chose. They occasionally used variant spellings to "justify" prose lines. Elizabethan spelling was, in any case, chaotic by our standards. The modern textual business of identifying compositors relies mainly on discovering the characteristic spelling habits of each.

Rather than setting their pages in numbered sequence right through an entire play, as we would assume, the compositors of the Folio used a system known as "casting off": that is, they estimated the amount of copy needed to fill a page of type and divided the whole text up into portions of the estimated correct length. They could then begin by setting pages six and seven, and would immediately start printing these two pages side by side on the same "forme" or side of a sheet. (When three large sheets are folded once and gathered together, the result is a "quire" of twelve pages, with pages one and twelve printed on the outer side or "forme" of the outermost sheet, pages two and eleven on the inner forme of that same sheet, pages three and ten on the outer forme of the middle sheet, and so on.) Since type was expensive and in limited supply in a printing shop, the type had to be redistributed into the type cases as soon as the requisite number of copies of any forme had been run off. Casting off enabled the printers to print and redistribute the type of pages six and seven without having to wait for all the intervening pages to be set up also. (The reappearance of distributed type is, in fact, one clue by which Hinman was able to discover that the Folio had been set up throughout by casting off rather than by printing in sequence.)

Despite the advantages of flexibility, casting off had its disadvantages. If a compositor discovered he had been given too little copy for a page of text, he had to stretch his material by heavy "leading" or spacing. If, on the other hand, he discovered he had been given too much copy for a page, he had to crowd his lines, print verse as prose, or even eliminate words and lines. Knowledge of this sort of printing information is useful to modern editors, since it enables them to determine when the compositors may have interfered with the text that Shakespeare wrote.

When a compositor had completed one entire forme, consisting of two pages of text to be printed on one side of a large printing sheet, the forme went into the press and the requisite number of copies was run off by hand. One side of the sheet, either the inner or outer forme, was printed at a time. Proofreading, or "press correction," may have been done in part by checking the "foul proof" before the press run began, but further proofreading took place while the printing continued. At first, a number of sides of the sheet would be printed in their uncorrected state, that is, entirely unproofread. When the press corrector found more errors, the presses would be stopped so that the errors might be corrected, after which printing would continue. Such interruptions might occur several times. Uncorrected or partially corrected sheets were not destroyed, however; paper was too costly for that. Later, when the stacks of sheets printed on one side were printed on the other side, errors would again be corrected as printing continued. Ultimately, when the sheets were gathered by three's into a quire of twelve pages and then sewn into a complete volume, no single copy of the Folio was apt to be exactly like another. In fact, the many copies of the First Folio extant today differ from one another

in their press variants. Even though we might regard this as evidence of carelessness, Jaggard's work on the First Folio seems to have been scrupulous when judged by the standards of the day.

At a guess, about 1,200 copies of the First Folio were printed and sold for twenty shillings. Approximately 230 copies survive today, of which seventy-nine bound folios, not all complete copies, plus some fragments, are to be found in the collection of the Folger Library, Washington, D.C.

The Later Folios

When after nine years the first edition of the Folio had been sold out, a second edition was printed in 1632 by Thomas Cotes. He had succeeded to the Jaggards' business after the death of Isaac in 1627. The Second Folio merely reprinted the text of the First Folio together with a considerable number of editorial emendations. These have no independent textual authority, although some of the more common-sense suggestions have since been adopted by modern editors. A third edition appeared in 1663, based on the second. A second issue of this same third edition in 1664 included seven new plays: *Pericles, The London Prodigal, Thomas Lord Cromwell, Sir John Oldcastle, The Puritan, A Yorkshire Tragedy,* and *Locrine.* Of these, only *Pericles* has gained general acceptance in the Shakespeare canon (see Appendix I and the Introduction to the play). A fourth edition of the Folio in 1685, based on the third, also included the seven new plays. Like the second and third editions, this fourth edition offered many emendations or new errors not based on any textual authority.

Later Editions

The first editor of Shakespeare in the modern sense of the term was Nicholas Rowe. His six-volume edition of 1709 (reedited in eight volumes in 1714) was based on the Fourth Folio, to which the publisher Jacob Tonson had acquired the rights. Rowe began many practices we now regard as standard for a reader's edition. He provided a complete list of *dramatis personae* for each play, whereas the earlier folios had done so only sporadically. Similarly, he extended the practice of announcing the locale at the beginning of a scene. He marked entrances and exits with more care than in the folios and provided more extensive division of the plays into acts and scenes. Although he did not consult Shakespeare's early texts, Rowe did offer a number of textual emendations. He also modernized spelling and punctuation.

Alexander Pope was Shakespeare's next editor. Pope's text, completed in 1725 in six volumes (second edition, 1728), was printed from a copy of Rowe's edition with Pope's annotations. Pope excluded *Pericles* and the spurious plays that had been added to the Third Folio, although a companion volume containing these plays appeared with the second edition of 1728, lacking Pope's name and perhaps not authorized by him. He completed Rowe's task of indicating locale for each of the scenes, and also completed the division of the text into acts and scenes. In fact, Pope used the "continental" system of marking a new scene whenever a major character comes on stage, so that his text contained many more scenes than did other editions. Most importantly, Pope regarded Shakespeare's text as something to be "improved," because it had been written in a barbaric age for irresponsible actors all too ready to take liberties with the text, and for ignorant spectators. Although he claimed to have consulted the early quartos, Pope excised parts of Shakespeare's text that he considered vulgar, regularized lines that struck him as defective, eliminated anachronisms he regarded as indecorous, and the like. Pope's edition reflected the "refined" eighteenth-century view of Shakespeare as a very rough diamond in need of polishing. Some of the "improvements" are convincing and have been adopted by more recent editors, but most are sophistications that, for a time, moved Shakespearean editing away from the purpose of recovering what Shakespeare had actually written.

A corrective was in order. Lewis Theobald took up the challenge, though he was to be rewarded for his pains by being crowned the King of Dullness in Pope's *The Dunciad* (1728 version). Theobald's edition appeared in 1733 and was later reissued several times. He was the first editor to consult the folios and quartos. He did not, however, wholly recognize the textual value of those quartos. He also failed to base his text directly on the earliest substantive texts; instead, he annotated a copy of Pope's edition, just as Pope had annotated Rowe and Rowe had annotated the Fourth Folio. Despite his consultation of the early texts and his occasional brilliance as an emender, therefore, Theobald inevitably perpetuated more errors than he eliminated from the Rowe-Pope tradition.

The convention of relying on one's predecessor's edition continued to afflict eighteenth-century editing of Shakespeare. Sir Thomas Hanmer (1743–1744) and William Warburton (1747) contributed some emendations that are used today but tended to follow their predecessors. (This Warburton is not, however, the John Warburton whose cook is said to have burned a number of now-lost early editions of plays by using them to line pie plates.) Even Dr. Johnson (1765), who set a standard of conservatism in admitting emendations to the Shakespearean text, based his edition on an annotated copy of Warburton's edition. Johnson's account of the text took an unfriendly view toward the interference of scribes, players, and printers; he shared Pope's dismay at the conditions under which Shakespeare wrote but mistrusted Pope's poetic "improvements" as too subjective.

Only with Edward Capell (1768) did an eighteenth-century editor finally base his text on the original Folio and quartos. Capell amassed an admirable collection of quartos

and was the first to recognize that they might sometimes be preferred as copy text to the Folio itself. Unlike his eighteenth-century predecessors, who generally dismissed the quartos as based on playbooks and hence contaminated by theatrical revision, Capell saw that they usually represented Shakespeare's own drafts. At the same time, Capell's principle of selection was too eclectic in that he was ready to choose any early printing, whether first printing or derivative, so long as it offered what he regarded as an improvement. Capell's work heavily influenced George Steevens' 1773 revision of Dr. Johnson's text.

Edmund Malone, at first a collaborator with Steevens and later his rival, issued a ten-volume edition in 1790. Malone reintroduced *Pericles*, which Pope and subsequent editors had eliminated along with the spurious plays of the Third Folio. Malone brought to his editing an extensive knowledge of Elizabethan documents, such as the Stationers' Register, Henslowe's *Diary*, and the records of the Master of the Revels. His most important contribution to theory of editing was to grant authority only to the earliest printing of any version of a play—a principle that he had trouble applying in some cases, however, because the false-dated Pavier quartos had yet to be sorted out. He left uncompleted a variorum edition recording all textual variants; this edition was finished in 1821 by James Boswell, son of Dr. Johnson's biographer, and became known as the Third Variorum because Isaac Reed's earlier editions (1803, 1813) had called themselves the First and Second Variorums. The so-called New Variorum Shakespeare continued this tradition under Henry Howard Furness, beginning in 1871.

Nineteenth-century editions were numerous. One of the most famous and influential was the "bowdlerized" or expurgated *Family Shakespeare* of the Rev. Thomas Bowdler, first appearing in 1804 and 1818 and soon extending throughout the English-speaking world. Other editions included those of S. W. Singer (1826, 1855–1856), John Payne Collier (1842–1844, 1853), Charles Knight (1838–1843), Alexander Dyce (1857, 1864–1867), Howard Staunton (1858–1860), Nikolaus Delius (1854–1860), H. N. Hudson (1851–1856), Thomas Keightley (1864), and Charles and Mary Cowden Clarke (1864–1868). Editors from this period were generally absorbed with reading different printed versions as if they represented different authorial versions and with an unresolved debate as to whether the "bad" quarto of *Hamlet*, among others, represented authorial versions or else derivative and corrupt versions of fuller texts.

The outstanding scholarly edition of the nineteenth century was the so-called Cambridge Shakespeare of William George Clark and William Aldis Wright (1863–1866), issued in 1864 in a single volume known as the Globe text. Although its choice of copy texts has been challenged in two or three instances by twentieth-century bibliographical research, the Globe text was soundly edited for its day and soon established itself as definitive. Its act and scene divisions and its line numbering became standards of reference for concordances, works of literary criticism, and the like.

Later nineteenth- and early twentieth-century editions included those of W. J. Rolfe (1871–1896), Appleton Morgan (1888), F. A. Marshall and others (The Henry Irving Shakespeare, 1888–1890), Sir Israel Gollancz (The Temple Shakespeare, 1894–1895), W. J. Craig (1891), C. H. Herford (1899), and Helen Porter and Charlotte Clarke (1903–1914). Influential American editions included those of W. A. Neilson (1906) and George Lyman Kittredge (1936).

The twentieth century has seen an enormous increase in the information available on bibliographical matters: memorial reconstruction of texts, printing-house procedures, the mechanics of book production, watermarks, printer's ornaments, Elizabethan handwriting, spelling, punctuation, and the like. Prominent among bibliographical studies are those that laid the basis for the standard "received" theories of editorial scholarship discussed above. These include A. W. Pollard's *Shakespeare's Folios and Quartos* (1909) and *Shakespeare's Hand in the Play of Sir Thomas More* (1923), R. B. McKerrow's *An Introduction to Bibliography for Literary Students* (1927) and *Prolegomena for the Oxford Shakespeare* (1939), W. W. Greg's *Principles of Emendation in Shakespeare* (1928) and *The Editorial Problem in Shakespeare* (third edition, 1954), and E. K. Chambers' *William Shakespeare: A Study of Facts and Problems* (1930). No less important are Alice Walker's *Textual Problems of the First Folio* (1953) and Fredson Bowers' *Bibliography and Textual Criticism* (1964). An updated survey of problems and methods is to be found in Philip Gaskell's *A New Introduction to Bibliography* (1972). Significant studies have also appeared on individual plays, such as that of Peter Alexander on the *Henry VI* plays and *Richard III*, Madeleine Doran also on *Henry VI*, J. Dover Wilson on *Hamlet*, George Williams on *Romeo and Juliet*, G. I. Duthie on *King Lear*, and Peter Blayney on *King Lear*.

During the twentieth century, bibliographical theories have, of course, continued to evolve. Sidney Lee, early in the century, still held by and large to Dr. Johnson's view that Heminges and Condell were right to denigrate the quartos because some of them offered such apparently deficient texts (a totalizing view of the quartos based on only a handful of them) and that the Folio was equally suspect because Heminges and Condell, though having denigrated the quartos, persisted in using some of them as printer's copy. Only in the 1930s and afterward did a consensus begin to develop as to how Shakespeare's play texts got transmitted into print. Pollard's distinction between good and bad quartos, although it relied too much on the notion that the printers of the bad quartos were unscrupulous and led to disagreement as to which quartos might, in fact, be

categorized as "bad," established the system of classification that continues, albeit with increasing reservations, to be used today.

Two main challenges face bibliographical scholars currently. The first asks whether the categories proposed by Pollard, Greg, and others, for all their being well established, are, in fact, viable. William B. Long and Paul Werstine have shown with disconcerting precision that many supposed "foul paper" characteristics are to be found in supposed playbooks, and the reverse, so that it is often virtually impossible to determine what was the nature of the copy underlying a printed text. (See, for example, William B. Long, "'A bed for woodstock': A Warning for the Unwary," *Medieval and Renaissance Drama in England*, 2, 1985, 91–118, and Paul Werstine, "'Foul Papers' and 'Prompt-books': Printer's Copy for Shakespeare's *Comedy of Errors*," *Studies in Bibliography*, 41, 1988, 232–246.) Empirical research, based in part on surviving manuscripts by dramatists other than Shakespeare, suggests that manuscripts annotated for use in the theater contain little of the normalization and regularization that Greg and McKerrow argued they would. Perhaps most decisively against Greg and McKerrow is the observation that neither the perfectly regularized and completely annotated playbook nor the first-and-final authorial draft called "foul papers" seems to be represented among extant manuscripts of Shakespeare's period. And, although theories of memorial reconstruction appear still to be useful, not even the theory of memorial reconstruction of a "bad" quarto by an actor or actors quite stands up as a complete explanation of the origin of such a quarto, because there are always discrepancies in the fit between the role(s) of the alleged reporter(s) and the quality of the reproduction of the play text. Steven Urkowitz and others challenge the category of "bad" quartos entirely by attempting to show how theatrical the readings in those quartos sometimes can be represented to be. (See, for example, Steven Urkowitz, "Five Woman Eleven Ways: Changing Images of Shakespearean Characters in the Earliest Texts," *Images of Shakespeare*, ed. Werner Habicht et al., 1988, pp. 292–304.)

The other challenge is the hypothesis of authorial revision, especially with regard to *King Lear, Hamlet, Troilus and Cressida, 2 Henry IV, The Contention, The True Tragedy, Richard III, Henry V, Othello*, and, to a lesser extent, *1 Henry IV* and *Richard II*. The case for Shakespeare as a conscious reviser is being made more and more strongly than ever before by Gary Taylor, Stanley Wells, Michael Warren, and others, and it is an argument that, of course, affects the issue of what text to edit. Is the Folio *King Lear* an authorial revision? If so, its claim to precedence over the Quarto version is strong. If, on the other hand, it represents theatrical revision, involving the acting company, then Shakespeare's role is less determinable. Does this uncertainty matter, or should we prefer the theatrically revised versions in any case? Were cuts made for reasons of length? Did actors have trouble with certain lines and wish to see them dropped or altered? Did actors' improvisations sometimes make their way into the text? In what ways did censorship contribute to revision? Were there other practical considerations at work, such as provincial touring, to which Shakespeare may have been asked to accede? Do we want a text that comes closest to what Shakespeare may have originally have written, or do we want the play in two states, both arguably authoritative. An edition can choose to print both, as in the new Oxford Shakespeare, but perhaps at the cost of making life unreasonably difficult for many readers and certainly at the cost of added paper. How is an editor to address the question of what is most useful for readers and students? The answer must depend in part on what any given edition is for and what audience it is addressing.

Textual controversies such as these have led to new twentieth-century editions of Shakespeare in which the textual method has been measurably advanced. Among the most significant are the New Cambridge Shakespeare of Sir Arthur Quiller-Couch and J. Dover Wilson, and the still-continuing Arden Shakespeare under a succession of general editors, including W. J. Craig, R. H. Case, Una Ellis-Fermor, Harold Jenkins, and Richard Proudfoot. Peter Alexander's edition of 1951 is often cited as a standard text. It was soon followed by C. J. Sisson's edition of 1954 and the London Shakespeare of John Munro, 1958. College editions reedited from original texts include the Pelican Shakespeare, under the general editorship of Alfred Harbage (1956–1969); the revision of Kittredge's edition by Irving Ribner (1971); the Signet Classic Shakespeare, under the general editorship of Sylvan Barnet (1972); the Riverside Shakespeare (1974), of which G. Blakemore Evans is the textual editor; this present edition; the still-continuing English New Penguin Shakespeare under the general editorship of T. J. B. Spencer and Stanley Wells; and the Bantam Shakespeare, edited by David Bevington (1988). Two major editorial undertakings of the 1980s are the controversial and impressive Oxford Shakespeare in several formats (a one-volume modern-spelling edition and a one-volume old-spelling edition, 1986; a Textual Companion, 1987; and individual editions of the plays and poems by various editors, still forthcoming, all under the general editorship of Stanley Wells and Gary Taylor), and the New Cambridge Shakespeare (in individual one-volume editions, still forthcoming, under the general editorship of Philip Brockbank, Brian Gibbons, and A. R. Braunmuller).

Norton has also issued its Norton Facsimile of The First Folio of Shakespeare, prepared by Charlton Hinman from the Folios of the Folger Library (1968). Older facsimiles of the First Folio are available in libraries, such as that prepared by Sidney Lee (1902) and J. Dover Wilson (in separate plays), but the Norton facsimile unquestionably sets a new standard of excellence. Facsimiles of the quartos are also available, including those prepared for the Oxford University Press by W. W. Greg and Charlton Hinman, and, most recently, a one-volume set edited by Kenneth Muir and Michael Allen, chiefly from the holdings of the Huntington Library. Xerox copies of early printed books, such as Shakespearean quartos, are to be found in many libraries through the S.T.C. (Short Title Catalogue) series of University Microfilms. Photographic copies of early texts are also frequently available on microfilm.

Shakespeare Criticism

In his own time, Shakespeare achieved a reputation for immortal greatness that is astonishing when we consider the low regard in which playwrights were then generally held. Francis Meres compared him to Ovid, Plautus, and Seneca, and proclaimed Shakespeare to be England's most excellent writer in both comedy and tragedy. John Weever spoke of "honey-tongued Shakespeare." The number of such praising allusions is high. Even Ben Jonson, a learned writer strongly influenced by the classical tradition, lauded Shakespeare as "a monument without a tomb," England's best poet, exceeding Chaucer, Spenser, Beaumont, Kyd, and Marlowe. In tragedy, Jonson compared Shakespeare with Aeschylus, Euripides, and Sophocles; in comedy, he insisted Shakespeare had no rival even in "insolent Greece or haughty Rome." This tribute appeared in Jonson's commendatory poem written for the Shakespeare First Folio of 1623.

To be sure, Jonson had more critical things to say about Shakespeare. Even in the Folio commendatory poem, Jonson could not resist a dig at Shakespeare's "small Latin, and less Greek." To William Drummond of Hawthornden, he objected that Shakespeare "wanted art" because in a play (The Winter's Tale) he "brought in a number of men saying they had suffered shipwreck in Bohemia, where there is no sea by some hundred miles." In Timber, or Discoveries, Jonson chided Shakespeare for his unrestrained facility in writing. "The players have often mentioned it as an honor to Shakespeare, that in his writing, whatsoever he penned he never blotted out [a] line. My answer hath been, would he had blotted a thousand." In a preface to his own play, Every Man in His Humor (1616 edition), Jonson satirized English history plays (such as Shakespeare's) that ''with three rusty swords, / And help of some few foot-and-half-foot words, / Fight over York and

Lancaster's long jars, / And in the tiring-house bring wounds to scars." He also jeered at plays lacking unity of time in which children grow to the age of sixty or older and at nonsensical romantic plays featuring fireworks, thunder, and a chorus that "wafts you o'er the seas."

These criticisms are all of a piece. As a classicist himself, Jonson held in high regard the classical unities. He deplored much English popular drama, including some of Shakespeare's plays, for their undisciplined mixture of comedy and tragedy. Measured against his cherished ideals of classical decorum and refinement of language, Shakespeare's histories and the late romances—*Pericles, Cymbeline, The Winter's Tale,* and *The Tempest*— seemed irritatingly naive and loose-jointed. Yet Jonson knew that Shakespeare had an incomparable genius, superior even to his own. Jonson's affection and respect for Shakespeare seem to have been quite unforced. In the midst of his critical remarks in *Timber,* he freely conceded that "I loved the man, and do honor his memory (on this side idolatry) as much as any. He was indeed honest, and of an open and free nature, had an excellent fantasy, brave notions, and gentle expressions."

The Age of Dryden and Pope

Jonson's attitude toward Shakespeare lived on into the Restoration period of the late seventeenth century. A commonplace of that age held it proper to "admire" Ben Jonson but to "love" Shakespeare. Jonson was the more correct poet, the better model for imitation. Shakespeare often had to be rewritten according to the sophisticated tastes of the Restoration (see Appendix III for an account of Restoration stage adaptations of Shakespeare), but he was also regarded as a natural genius. Dryden reflected this view in his *Essay of Dramatic Poesy* (1668) and his *Essay on the Dramatic Poetry of the Last Age* (1672). Dryden condemned *The Winter's Tale, Pericles,* and several other late romances for "the lameness of their plots" and for their "ridiculous incoherent story" which is usually "grounded on impossibilities." Not only Shakespeare, he charged, but several of his contemporaries "neither understood correct plotting nor that which they call *the decorum of the stage.*" Had Shakespeare lived in the Restoration, Dryden believed, he would doubtless have written "more correctly" under the influence of a language that had become more "courtly" and a wit that had grown more "refined." Shakespeare, he thought, had limitless "fancy" but sometimes lacked "judgment." Dryden regretted that Shakespeare had been forced to write in "ignorant" times and for audiences who "knew no better." Like Jonson, nevertheless, Dryden had the magnanimity to perceive that Shakespeare transcended his limitations. Shakespeare, said Dryden, was "the man who of all modern and perhaps ancient poets had the largest and most comprehensive soul." From a classical writer, this was high praise indeed.

Alexander Pope's edition of Shakespeare (1725) was based upon a similar estimate of Shakespeare as an untutored genius. Pope freely "improved" Shakespeare's language, rewriting lines and excising those parts he considered vulgar, in order to rescue Shakespeare from the barbaric circumstances of his Elizabethan milieu. Other critics of the Restoration and early eighteenth century who stressed Shakespeare's "natural" genius and imaginative powers were John Dennis, Joseph Addison, and the editors Nicholas Rowe and Lewis Theobald.

The Age of Johnson

Shakespeare was not without his detractors during the late seventeenth and early eighteenth centuries; after all, classical criticism tended to distrust imagination and fancy. Notable among the harsher critics of the Restoration period was Thomas Rymer, whose *Short View of Tragedy* (1692) included a famous attack on *Othello* for making too much out of Desdemona's handkerchief. In the eighteenth century, Voltaire spoke out sharply against Shakespeare's violation of the classical unities, though Voltaire also had some admiring things to say.

The most considered answer to such criticism in the later eighteenth century was that of Dr. Samuel Johnson, in his edition of Shakespeare's plays and its great preface (1765). Shakespeare, said Johnson, is the poet of nature who "holds up to his readers a faithful mirror of manners and of life. His characters are not modified by the customs of particular places, unpracticed by the rest of the world. . . . In the writings of other poets a character is too often an individual; in those of Shakespeare it is commonly a species." Johnson's attitudes were essentially classical in that he praised Shakespeare for being universal, for having provided a "just representation of general nature," and for having stood the test of time. Yet Johnson also magnanimously praised Shakespeare for having transcended the classical rules. Johnson triumphantly vindicated the mixture of comedy and tragedy in Shakespeare's plays and the supposed indecorum of his characters.

Of course, Johnson did not praise everything he saw. He objected to Shakespeare's loose construction of plot, careless huddling together of the ends of his plays, licentious humor, and, above all, the punning wordplay. He deplored Shakespeare's failure to satisfy the demands of poetic justice, especially in *King Lear,* and he regretted that Shakespeare seemed more anxious to please than to instruct. Still, Johnson did much to free Shakespeare from the constraint of an overly restrictive classical approach to criticism.

The Age of Coleridge

With the beginning of the Romantic period, in England and on the Continent, Shakespeare criticism increasingly turned away from classical precept in favor of a more spontaneous and enthusiastic approach to Shakespeare's creative genius.

The new Shakespeare became indeed a rallying cry for those who now deplored such "regular" dramatic poets as Racine and Corneille. Shakespeare became a seer, a bard with mystic powers of insight into the human condition. Goethe, in *Wilhelm Meister* (1796), conceived of Hamlet as the archetypal "Romantic" poet: melancholic, delicate, and unable to act.

Critical trends in England moved toward similar conclusions. Maurice Morgann, in his *Essay on the Dramatic Character of Sir John Falstaff* (1777), glorified Falstaff into a rare individual of courage, dignity, and—yes—honor. To do so, Morgann had to suppress much evidence as to Falstaff's overall function in the *Henry IV* plays. Dramatic structure, in fact, did not interest him; his passion was "character," and his study of Falstaff reflected a new Romantic preoccupation with character analysis. Like other character critics who followed him, Morgann tended to move away from the play itself and into a world where the dramatic personage being considered might lead an independent existence. What would it have been like to know Falstaff as a real person? How would he have behaved on occasions other than those reported by Shakespeare? Such questions fascinated Morgann and others because they led into grand speculations about human psychology and philosophy. Shakespeare's incomparably penetrating insights into character prompted further investigations of the human psyche.

Other late eighteenth-century works devoted to the study of character included Lord Kames' *Elements of Criticism* (1762), Thomas Whately's *Remarks on Some of the Characters of Shakespeare* (1785), William Richardson's *Philosophical Analysis and Illustration of Some of Shakespeare's Remarkable Characters* (1774), and William Jackson's *Thirty Letters on Various Subjects* (1782). Morgann spoke for this school of critics when he insisted, "It may be fit to consider them [Shakespeare's characters] rather as historic than dramatic beings; and, when occasion requires, to account for their conduct from the *whole* of character, from general principles, from latent motives, and from policies not avowed."

Samuel Taylor Coleridge, the greatest of the English Romantic critics, was profoundly influenced by character criticism, both English and continental. He himself made important contributions to the study of character. His conception of Hamlet, derived in part from Goethe and Hegel, as one who "vacillates from sensibility, and procrastinates from thought, and loses the power of action in the energy of resolve," was to dominate nineteenth-century interpretations of Hamlet. His insight into Iago's evil nature—"the motive-hunting of a motiveless malignity"—was also influential.

Nevertheless, Coleridge did not succumb to the temptation, as did so many character critics, of ignoring the unity of an entire play. Quite to the contrary, he affirmed in Shakespeare an "organic form" or "innate" sense of shape, developed from within, that gave new meaning to Shakespeare's fusion of comedy and tragedy, his seeming anachronisms, his improbable fictions, and his supposedly rambling plots. Coleridge heaped scorn on the eighteenth-century idea of Shakespeare as a "natural" but untaught genius. He praised Shakespeare not for having mirrored life, as Dr. Johnson had said, but for having created an imaginative world attuned to its own internal harmonies. He saw Shakespeare as an inspired but deliberate artist who fitted together the parts of his imaginative world with consummate skill. "The judgment of Shakespeare is commensurate with his genius."

In all this, Coleridge was remarkably close to his German contemporary and rival, August Wilhelm Schlegel, who insisted that Shakespeare was "a profound artist, and not a blind and wildly luxuriant genius." In Shakespeare's plays, said Schlegel, "The fancy lays claim to be considered as an independent mental power governed according to its own laws." Between them, Coleridge and Schlegel utterly inverted the critical values of the previous age, substituting "sublimity" and "imagination" for universality and trueness to nature.

Other Romantic critics included William Hazlitt (*Characters of Shakespear's Plays*, 1817), Charles Lamb (*On the Tragedies of Shakespeare*, 1811), and Thomas De Quincey (*On the Knocking at the Gate in Macbeth*, 1823). Hazlitt reveals a political liberalism characteristic of a number of Romantic writers in his skeptical view of Henry V's absolutism and his imperialist war against the French. John Keats has some penetrating things to say in his letters about Shakespeare's "negative capability," or his ability to see into characters' lives with an extraordinary self-effacing sympathy. As a whole, the Romantics were enthusiasts of Shakespeare, and sometimes even idolaters. Yet they consistently refused to recognize him as a man of the theater. Lamb wrote, "It may seem a paradox, but I cannot help being of opinion that the plays of Shakespeare are less calculated for performance on a stage than those of almost any other dramatist whatever." Hazlitt similarly observed: "We do not like to see our author's plays acted, and least of all, *Hamlet*. There is no play that suffers so much in being transferred to the stage." These hostile attitudes toward the theater reflected, in part, the condition of the stage in nineteenth-century England. In part, however, these attitudes were the inevitable result of character criticism, or what Lamb called the desire "to know the internal workings and movements of a great mind, of an Othello or a Hamlet for instance, the *when* and the *why* and the *how far* they should be moved." This fascination with character swept everything before it during the Romantic period.

A. C. Bradley and the Turn of the Century

The tendency of nineteenth-century criticism, then, was to exalt Shakespeare as a poet and a philosopher rather than as a playwright, and as a creator of immortal characters whose "lives" might be studied as though existing independent of a dramatic text. Not infrequently, this critical approach led to a biographical interpretation of Shakespeare through his plays, on the assumption that what he wrote was his own spiritual autobiography and a key to his own fascinating character. Perhaps the most famous critical study in this line was Edward Dowden's *Shakspere: A Critical Study of His Mind and Art* (1875), in which he traced a progression from Shakespeare's early exuberance and passionate involvement through brooding pessimism to a final philosophical calm.

At the same time, the nineteenth century also saw the rise of a more factual and methodological scholarship, especially in the German universities. Dowden, in fact, reflected this trend as well, for one of the achievements of philological study was to establish with some accuracy the dating of Shakespeare's plays and thus make possible an analysis of his artistic development. Hermann Ulrici's *Über Shakespeares dramatische Kunst* (1839) and Gottfried Gervinus' edition of 1849 were among the earliest studies to interest themselves in Shakespeare's chronological development.

The critic who best summed up the achievement of nineteenth-century Shakespeare criticism was A. C. Bradley, in his *Shakespearean Tragedy* (1904) and other studies. *Shakespearean Tragedy* dealt with the four "great" tragedies: *Hamlet, Othello, King Lear,* and *Macbeth.* Bradley revealed his Romantic tendencies in his focus on psychological analysis of character, but he also brought to his work a scholarly awareness of the text that had been missing in some earlier character critics. His work continues to have considerable influence today, despite modern tendencies to rebel against nineteenth-century idealism. To Bradley, Shakespeare's tragic world was ultimately explicable and profoundly moral. Despite the overwhelming impression of tragic waste in *King Lear,* he argued, we as audience experience a sense of compensation and completion that implies an ultimate pattern in human life. "Good, in the widest sense, seems thus to be the principle of life and health in the world; evil, at least in these worst forms, to be a poison. The world reacts against it violently, and, in the struggle to expel it, is driven to devastate itself." Humanity must suffer because of its fatal tendency to pursue some extreme passion, but humanity learns through suffering about itself and the nature of its world. We as audience are reconciled to our existence through purgative release; we smile through our tears. Cordelia is wantonly destroyed, but the fact of her transcendent goodness is eternal. Although in one sense she fails, said Bradley, she is "in another sense superior to the world in which [she] appears; is, in some way which we do not seek to define, untouched by the doom that overtakes [her]; and is rather set free from life than deprived of it."

Historical Criticism

The first major twentieth-century reaction against character criticism was that of the so-called historical critics. These critics insisted on a more hardheaded and skeptical appraisal of Shakespeare through better understanding of his historical milieu: his theater, his audience, and his political and social environment. In good part, this movement was the result of a new professionalism of Shakespearean studies in the twentieth century. Whereas earlier critics—Dryden, Pope, Johnson, and Coleridge—had generally been literary amateurs in the best sense, early twentieth-century criticism became increasingly the province of those who taught in universities. Historical research became a professional activity. Bradley himself was Professor of English Literature at Liverpool and Oxford, and did much to legitimize the incorporation of Shakespeare into the humanities curriculum. German scholarship produced the first regular periodical devoted to Shakespeare studies, *Shakespeare-Jahrbuch,* to be followed in due course in England and America by *Shakespeare Survey* (beginning in 1948), *Shakespeare Quarterly* (1950), and *Shakespeare Studies* (1965).

From the start, historical criticism took a new look at Shakespeare as a man of the theater. Sir Walter Raleigh (Professor of English Literature at Oxford, not to be confused with his Elizabethan namesake) rejected the Romantic absorption in psychology and turned his attention instead to the artistic methods by which plays affect theatergoing spectators. The poet Robert Bridges insisted that Shakespeare had often sacrificed consistency and logic for primitive theatrical effects designed to please his vulgar audience. Bridges' objections were often based on serious lack of information about Shakespeare's stage, but they had a healthy iconoclastic effect nonetheless on the scholarship of his time. In Germany, Levin Schücking pursued a similar line of reasoning in his *Character Problems in Shakespeare's Plays* (1917, translated into English in 1922). Schücking argued that Shakespeare had disregarded coherent structure and had striven instead for vivid dramatic effect ("episodic intensification") in his particular scenes. Schücking's *The Meaning of Hamlet* (1937) explained the strange contradictions of that play as resulting from primitive and brutal Germanic source materials which Shakespeare had not fully assimilated.

A keynote for historical critics of the early twentieth century was the concept of artifice or convention in the construction of a play. Perhaps the leading spokesman for this approach was E. E. Stoll, a student of G. L. Kittredge of Harvard University, himself a leading force in historical scholarship in America. Stoll vigorously insisted, in such works as *Othello: An Historical and Comparative Study* (1915), *Hamlet: An Historical and Comparative Study* (1919), and *Art and Artifice in Shakespeare* (1933), that a critic must never be sidetracked by moral, psychological, or biographical interpretations. A play, he argued, is an artifice arising out of its historical milieu. Its conventions are implicit agreements between playwright and spectator. They alter with time, and a modern reader who is ignorant of Elizabethan conventions is all too apt to be misled by his own post-Romantic preconceptions. For example, a calumniator like Iago in *Othello* is conventionally supposed to be believed by the other characters on stage. We do not need to speculate about the "realities" of Othello's being duped, and, in fact, we are likely to be led astray by such Romantic speculations. Stoll went so far as to affirm, in fact, that Shakespearean drama intentionally distorts reality through its theatrical conventions in order to fulfill its own existence as artifice. *Hamlet* is not a play about delay but a revenge story of a certain length, containing many conventional revenge motifs, such as the ghost and the "mousetrap" scheme used to test the villain, and deriving many of its circumstances from Shakespeare's sources; delay is a conventional device needed to continue the story to its conclusion.

Stoll's zeal led to excessive claims for historical criticism, as one might expect in the early years of a pioneering movement. At its extreme, historical criticism came close to implying that Shakespeare was a mere product of his environment. Indeed, the movement owed many of its evolutionist assumptions to the supposedly scientific "social Darwinism" of Thomas Huxley and other late nineteenth-century social philosophers. In more recent years, however, the crusading spirit has given way to a more moderate historical criticism that continues to be an important part of Shakespearean scholarship.

Alfred Harbage, for example, in *As They Liked It* (1947) and *Shakespeare and the Rival Traditions* (1952), has analyzed the audience for which Shakespeare wrote and the rivalry between popular and elite theaters in the London of his day. Harbage sees Shakespeare as a popular dramatist writing for a highly intelligent, enthusiastic, and socially diversified audience. More recently, in *The Privileged Playgoers of Shakespeare's London, 1576-1642* (1981), Ann Jennalie Cook has qualified Harbage's view, arguing that Shakespeare's audience was, for the most part, affluent and well connected. G. E. Bentley has amassed an invaluable storehouse of information about *The Jacobean and Caroline Stage* (1941–1968), just as E. K. Chambers earlier had collected documents and data on *The Elizabethan Stage* (1923). Other studies by these historical scholars include Chambers' *William Shakespeare: A Study of Facts and Problems* (1930), and Bentley's *Shakespeare and His Theatre* (1964) and *The Profession of Dramatist in Shakespeare's Time* (1971). T. W. Baldwin exemplifies the historical scholar who, like Stoll, claims too much for the method; nevertheless, much information on Shakespeare's schooling, reading, and professional theatrical life is avail-

able in such works as *William Shakspere's Small Latine and Lesse Greeke* (1944) and *The Organization and Personnel of the Shakespearean Company* (1927). Hardin Craig uses historical method in *An Interpretation of Shakespeare* (1948).

Historical criticism has contributed greatly to our knowledge of the staging of Shakespeare's plays. George Pierce Baker, in *The Development of Shakespeare as a Dramatist* (1907), continued the line of investigation begun by Walter Raleigh. Harley Granville-Barker brought to his *Prefaces to Shakespeare* (1930, 1946) a wealth of professional theatrical experience of his own. Ever since his time, the new theatrical method of interpreting Shakespeare has been based to an ever increasing extent on a genuine revival of interest in Shakespearean production. John Dover Wilson shows an awareness of the stage in *What Happens in Hamlet* (1935) and *The Fortunes of Falstaff* (1943). At its best, as in John Russell Brown's *Shakespeare's Plays in Performance* (1966), in John Styan's *Shakespeare's Stagecraft* (1967), in Michael Goldman's *Shakespeare and the Energies of Drama* (1972), and in Alan Dessen's *Elizabethan Drama and the Viewer's Eye* (1977), this critical method reveals many insights into the text that are hard to obtain without an awareness of theatrical technique.

Supporting this theatrical criticism, historical research has learned a great deal about the physical nature of Shakespeare's stage. J. C. Adams' well-known model of the Globe Playhouse, as presented in Irwin Smith's *Shakespeare's Globe Playhouse: A Modern Reconstruction* (1956), is now generally discredited in favor of a simpler building, as reconstructed by C. Walter Hodges (*The Globe Restored,* 1953, 2nd edition, 1968), Bernard Beckerman (*Shakespeare at the Globe,* 1962, 2nd edition, 1967), Richard Hosley ("The Playhouses and the Stage" in *A New Companion to Shakespeare Studies,* edited by K. Muir and S. Schoenbaum, 1971, and several other good essays), T. J. King (*Shakespearean Staging, 1599–1642,* 1971), and others. Information on the private theaters, such as the Blackfriars, where Shakespeare's plays were also performed, appears in William Armstrong, *The Elizabethan Private Theatres* (1958), Richard Hosley, "A Reconstruction of the Second Blackfriars" (*The Elizabethan Theatre,* 1969), Glynne Wickham, *Early English Stages* (1959–1972), and others. For further information on inn-yard theaters and on courtly or private theaters, see the contributions of Herbert Berry, D. F. Rowan, W. Reavley Gair, and others cited in the bibliography at the end of this volume.

A related pursuit of historical criticism has been the better understanding of Shakespeare through his dramatic predecessors and contemporaries. Willard Farnham, in *The Medieval Heritage of Elizabethan Tragedy* (1936), traces the evolution of native English tragedy through the morality plays of the early Tudor period. J. M. R. Margeson's *The Origins of English Tragedy* (1967) broadens the pattern to include still other sources for Elizabethan ideas on dramatic tragedy. Bernard Spivack, in *Shakespeare and the Allegory of Evil* (1958), sees Iago, Edmund, Richard III, and other boasting villains in Shakespeare as descendants of the morality Vice. In *Shakespeare and the Idea of the Play* (1962), Anne Righter traces the device of the play-within-the-play and the metaphor of the world as a stage back to medieval and classical ideas of dramatic illusion. Irving Ribner's *The English History Play in the Age of Shakespeare* (1959, revised 1965) examines Shakespeare's plays on English history in the context of the popular Elizabethan genre to which they belonged. Robert Weimann's *Shakespeare and the Popular Tradition in the Theatre* (translated from the German in 1978) is a Marxist study in the social dimension of dramatic form and function. Many other studies of this sort could be cited, including Glynne Wickham's *Shakespeare's Dramatic Heritage* (1969), Oscar J. Campbell's *Shakespeare's Satire* (1943), M. C. Bradbrook's *Themes and Conventions of Elizabethan Tragedy* (1935), and S. L. Bethell's *Shakespeare and the Popular Dramatic Tradition* (1944).

Another important concern of historical criticism has been the relationship between Shakespeare and the ideas of his age—cosmological, philosophical, and political. Among the first scholars to study Elizabethan cosmology were Hardin Craig in *The Enchanted Glass* (1936) and A. O. Lovejoy in *The Great Chain of Being* (1936). As their successor, E. M. W. Tillyard provided in *The Elizabethan World Picture* (1943) a definitive view of the conservative and hierarchical values which Elizabethans were supposed to have espoused. In *Shakespeare's History Plays* (1944), Tillyard extended his essentially conservative view of Shakespeare's philosophical outlook to the histories, arguing that they embody a "Tudor myth" and thereby lend support to the Tudor state. Increasingly, however, critics have disputed the extent to which Shakespeare in fact endorsed the "establishment" values of the Elizabethan world picture. Theodore Spencer, in *Shakespeare and the Nature of Man* (1942), discusses the impact on Shakespeare of radical new thinkers like Machiavelli, Montaigne, and Copernicus. In political matters, Henry A. Kelly's *Divine Providence in the England of Shakespeare's Histories* (1970) has challenged the existence of a single "Tudor myth" and has argued that Shakespeare's history plays reflect contrasting political philosophies set dramatically in conflict with one another. M. M. Reese's *The Cease of Majesty* (1961) also offers a graceful corrective to Tillyard's lucid but occasionally one-sided interpretations. Revisions in this direction continue in the work of the so-called new historicists and cultural materialists, to be discussed below.

Historical criticism has also yielded many profitable specialized studies, in which Shakespeare is illuminated by a better understanding of various sciences of his day. Lily Bess Campbell approaches Shakespearean tragedy through Renaissance psychology in *Shakespeare's Tragic Heroes:* *Slaves of Passion* (1930). Paul Jorgensen uses Elizabethan documents on the arts of war and generalship in his study *Shakespeare's Military World* (1956). Many similar studies examine Shakespeare in relation to law, medicine, and other professions. For a summary of historical scholarship having to do with Shakespeare's texts, see the earlier section entitled "Editions and Editors of Shakespeare."

"New" Criticism

As we have seen, historical criticism is still an important part of Shakespeare criticism; for better or worse, it is the stuff of many research-oriented universities and their Ph.D. programs. Since its beginning, however, historical criticism has had to face a critical reaction, generated, in part, by its own utilitarian and fact-gathering tendencies. The suggestions urged by Stoll and others that Shakespeare was the product of his cultural and theatrical environment tended to obscure his achievement as a poet. Amassing of information about Shakespeare's reading or his theatrical company often seemed to inhibit the scholar from responding to the power of words and images.

Such at any rate was the rallying cry of the *Scrutiny* group in England, centered on F. R. Leavis, L. C. Knights, and Derek Traversi, and the "new" critics in America, such as Cleanth Brooks. The new critics demanded close attention to the poetry without the encumbrance of historical research. Especially at first, the new critics were openly hostile to any criticism distracting readers from the text. The satirical force of the movement can perhaps best be savored in L. C. Knights' "How Many Children Had Lady Macbeth?" (1933), prompted by the learned appendices in Bradley's *Shakespearean Tragedy*: "When was the murder of Duncan first plotted? Did Lady Macbeth really faint? Duration of the action in *Macbeth*. Macbeth's age. 'He has no children.' "

In part, the new critical movement was (and still is) a pedagogical movement, a protest against the potential dryness of historical footnoting and an insistence that classroom study of Shakespeare ought to focus on a response to his language. Cleanth Brooks' "The Naked Babe and the Cloak of Manliness" (in *The Well Wrought Urn*, 1947) offers to the teacher a model of close reading that focuses on imagery and yet attempts to see a whole vision of the play through its language. G. Wilson Knight concentrates on imagery and verbal texture, sometimes to the exclusion of the play as a whole, in his *The Wheel of Fire* (1930), *The Imperial Theme* (1931), *The Shakespearian Tempest* (1932), *The Crown of Life* (1947), and others. William Empson is best known for his *Seven Types of Ambiguity* (1930) and *Some Versions of Pastoral* (1935). Derek Traversi's works include *An Approach to Shakespeare* (1938), *Shakespeare: The Last Phase* (1954), *Shakespeare: From Richard II to Henry V* (1957), and *Shakespeare: The Roman Plays* (1963). Perhaps the greatest critic of this school has been L. C. Knights, whose books include *Explorations* (1946), *Some Shakespearean Themes* (1959), *An Approach to Hamlet* (1960), and *Further Explorations* (1965). T. S. Eliot's perceptive and controversial observations have also had an important influence on critics of this school. Other studies making good use of the new critical method include Robert Heilman's *This Great Stage* (1948) and *Magic in the Web* (1956). Many of these critics are concerned not only with language but also with the larger moral and structural implications of Shakespeare's plays as discovered through a sensitive reading of the text.

More specialized studies of Shakespearean imagery and language include Caroline Spurgeon's *Shakespeare's Imagery and What It Tells Us* (1935). Its classifications are now recognized to be overly statistical and restricted in definition, but the work has nonetheless prompted valuable further study. Among later works are Sister Miriam Joseph's *Shakespeare's Use of the Arts of Language* (1947, partly reprinted in *Rhetoric in Shakespeare's Time*, 1962), Wolfgang Clemen's *The Development of Shakespeare's Imagery* (1951), and M. M. Mahood's *Shakespeare's Wordplay* (1957). The study of prose has not received as much attention as that of poetry, although Brian Vickers' *The Artistry of Shakespeare's Prose* (1968) and Milton Crane's *Shakespeare's Prose* (1951) make significant contributions. See also Edward Armstrong's *Shakespeare's Imagination* (1963) and Kirby Farrell's *Shakespeare's Creation: The Language of Magic and Play* (1975).

A more recent development in studies of Shakespeare's imagery has led to the examination of visual images in the theater as part of Shakespeare's art. Reginald Foakes ("Suggestions for a New Approach to Shakespeare's Imagery," *Shakespeare Survey*, 5, 1952, 81–92) and Maurice Charney (*Shakespeare's Roman Plays: The Function of Imagery in the Drama*, 1961) were among the first to notice that Caroline Spurgeon and other "new" critics usually excluded stage picture in their focus on verbal image patterns. Yet Shakespeare's extensive involvement with the practicalities of theatrical production might well lead one to suspect that he arranges his stage with care and that the plays are full of hints as to how he communicates through visual means. Costume, properties, the theater building, the blocking of actors in visual patterns onstage, expression, movement—all of these contribute to the play's artistic whole. Francis Fergusson analyzes the way in which the Elizabethan theatrical building provides *Hamlet* with an eloquently expressive idea of order and hierarchy, against which are ironically juxtaposed Claudius' acts of killing a king and marrying his widow (*The Idea of a Theater*, 1949). Other studies of stage imagery include Ann Pasternak Slater's *Shakespeare the Director* (1982) and David Bevington's *Action Is Eloquence: Shakespeare's Language of Gesture* (1984).

Another call for expansion of the occasionally narrow limits of "new" criticism comes from the so-called Chicago school of criticism, centered on R. S. Crane, Richard McKeon, Elder Olson, Bernard Weinberg, and others, who, in the 1950s and 1960s, espoused a formal or structural approach to criticism, using Aristotle as its point of departure. Crane was reacting to the new critics who, in his view, restricted the kinds of answers they could obtain by limiting themselves to one methodology. Critics hostile to the Chicago school have responded, to be sure, that Crane's own approach tends to produce its own dogmatism. Formalist analyses of Shakespeare plays are to be found, for example, in the work of W. R. Keast, Wayne Booth, and Norman Maclean; see *Critics and Criticism*, edited by R. S. Crane (1952) and the bibliography at the back of this book.

Psychological Criticism

In a sense, Freudian and other psychological criticism continues the "character" criticism of the nineteenth century. Freudian critics sometimes follow a character into a world outside the text, analyzing Hamlet (for instance) as though he were a real person whose childhood traumas can be inferred from the symptoms he displays. The most famous work in this vein is *Hamlet and Oedipus* (1910, revised 1949), by Freud's disciple, Ernest Jones. According to Jones, Hamlet's delay is caused by an oedipal trauma. Hamlet's uncle, Claudius, has done exactly what Hamlet himself incestuously and subconsciously wished to do: kill his father and marry his mother. Because he cannot articulate these forbidden impulses to himself, Hamlet is paralyzed into inactivity. Jones' critical analysis thus assumes, as did such Romantic critics as Coleridge, that the central problem of *Hamlet* is one of character and motivation: why does Hamlet delay? (Many modern critics would deny that this is a problem or would insist, at least, that by setting such a problem, Jones has limited the number of possible answers. Avi Erlich proposes an entirely different psychological reading of the play in *Hamlet's Absent Father*, 1977). Psychological criticism sometimes also reveals its affinities with nineteenth-century character criticism in its attempt to analyze Shakespeare's personality through his plays, as though the works constituted a spiritual autobiography. The terminology of psychological criticism is suspect to some readers because it is at least superficially anachronistic when dealing with a Renaissance writer. The terminology is also sometimes overburdened with technical jargon.

Nonetheless, psychological criticism has afforded many insights into Shakespeare not readily available through other modes of perception. Jones' book makes clear the intensity of Hamlet's revulsion toward women as a result of his mother's inconstancy. At a mythic level, Hamlet's story certainly resembles that of Oedipus, and Freudian criticism is often at its best when it shows us this universal aspect of the human psyche. Freudian terminology need not be anachronistic when it deals with timeless truths. Psychological criticism can reveal to us Shakespeare's preoccupation with certain types of women in his plays, such as the domineering and threatening masculine type (Joan of Arc, Margaret of Anjou) or, conversely, the long-suffering and patient heroine (Helena in *All's Well,* Hermione in *The Winter's Tale*). Psychological criticism is perhaps most useful in studying family relationships in Shakespeare. It also has much to say about the psychic or sexual connotations of symbol. Influential books include Norman O. Brown's *Life Against Death: The Psychoanalytical Meaning of History* (1959) and Norman Holland's *Psychoanalysis and Shakespeare* (1966) and *The Shakespearean Imagination* (1964).

Richard Wheeler's *Turn and Counter-Turn: Shakespeare's Development and the Problem Comedies* (1981) applies psychoanalytic method to a study of Shakespeare's development, in which, as Wheeler sees it, the sonnets and the problem plays are pivotal as Shakespeare turns from the safely contained worlds of romantic comedy (with nonthreatening heroines) and the English history play (in which women are generally denied anything more than a marginal role in state affairs) to the tragedies, in which sexual conflict is shown in all its potentially terrifying destructiveness. Wheeler's completion of C. L. Barber's *The Whole Journey: Shakespeare's Power of Development* (1986) continues the study of Shakespeare's development in the late plays. The dichotomies of gender and genre urged in these studies and continued by Linda Bamber (*Comic Women, Tragic Men: A Study of Gender and Genre in Shakespeare,* 1982), among others, have been challenged by Jonathan Goldberg in his essay, "Shakespearean Inscriptions: The Voicing of Power," in *Shakespeare and the Question of Theory* (edited by Patricia Parker and Geoffrey Hartman, 1985). A collection of essays under the editorship of Murray Schwartz and Coppélia Kahn, *Representing Shakespeare* (1980), affords a sample of recent work by Janet Adelman, David Willbern, Meredith Skura, David Sundelson, Madelon Gohlke Sprengnether, Joel Fineman, and others.

Much psychoanalytic criticism of the 1980s has sought to displace Freud's emphasis upon the relation of son and father in the oedipal triangle in favor of attention to the mother and child preoedipal relation; a model here is the work of Karen Horney (e.g., *Neurosis and Human Growth: The Struggle Toward Self-Realization* 1950). Jacques Lacan (*Écrits,* translated by Alan Sheridan, 1977) and Erik Erikson (*Childhood and Selfhood,* 1978) are also prominent theorists in the post-Freudian era. Despite such changes, the psychoanalytic critic still attempts to discover in the language of the play the means by which he or she can reconstruct an early stage in the development of one or more of the dramatic characters.

Mythological Criticism

Related to psychological criticism is the search for archetypal myth in literature, as an expression of the "collective unconscious" of the human race. Behind such an approach lie the anthropological and psychological assumptions of Jung and his followers. One of the earliest studies of this sort was Gilbert Murray's *Hamlet and Orestes* (1914), analyzing the archetype of revenge for a murdered father. Clearly this custom goes far back into tribal prehistory and emerges in varying but interrelated forms in many different societies. This anthropological universality enables us to look at *Hamlet* as the heightened manifestation of an incredibly basic story. *Hamlet* gives shape to urgings that are a part of our innermost social being. The struggle between the civilized and the primitive goes on in us as in the play *Hamlet.*

The vast interdisciplinary character of mythological criticism leaves it vulnerable to charges of speculativeness and glib theorizing. At its best, however, mythological criticism can illuminate the nature of our responses as audience to a work of art. Northrop Frye argues, in *A Natural Perspective* (1965), that we respond to mythic patterns by imagining ourselves participating in them communally. The Greek drama emerged, after all, from Dionysiac ritual. All drama celebrates in one form or another the primal myths of vegetation, from the death of the year to the renewal or resurrection of life. In his most influential book, *Anatomy of Criticism* (1957), Frye argues that mythic criticism presents a universal scheme for the investigation of all literature, or all art, since art is itself the ordering of our most primal stirrings. Frye sees in drama (as in other literature) a fourfold correspondence to the cyclical pattern of the year: comedy is associated with spring, romance with summer, tragedy with autumn, and satire with winter. Historically, civilization moves through a recurrent cycle from newness to decadence and decay; this cycle expresses itself culturally in a progression from epic and romance to tragedy, to social realism, and, finally, to irony and satire before the cycle renews itself. Thus, according to Frye, the genres of dramatic literature (and of other literary forms as well) have an absolute and timeless relationship to myth and cultural history. That is why we as audience respond so deeply to form and meaning as contained in genre. C. L. Barber, in *Shakespeare's Festive Comedy* (1959), makes a similar argument: our enjoyment of comedy arises from our intuitive appreciation of such "primitive" social customs as Saturnalian revels, May games, and fertility rites. John Holloway offers an anthropological study of Shakespeare's tragedies in *The Story of the Night* (1961).

Frye's critical system has not been without its detractors. For example, Frederick Crews (*Psychoanalysis and Literary Process,* 1970) argues that Frye's system is too self-contained in its ivory tower and too much an abstract artifact of the critical mind to be "relevant" to the social purposes of art. Nevertheless, Frye continues to be one of the most influential critics of the late twentieth century.

Typological Criticism

Another controversy of the later twentieth century has to do with the Christian interpretation of Shakespeare. Do the images and allusions of Shakespeare's plays show him to be deeply immersed in a Christian culture inherited from the Middle Ages? Does he reveal a typological cast of mind, so common in medieval literature, whereby a story can suggest through analogy a universal religious archetype? For example, does the mysterious Duke in Measure for Measure suggest to us a God figure, hovering unseen throughout the play to test human will and then to present humanity with an omniscient but merciful judgment? Is the wanton slaughter of the good Cordelia in King Lear reminiscent of the Passion of Christ? Can Portia in The Merchant of Venice be seen as an angelic figure descending from Belmont into the fallen human world of Venice? Often the operative question we must ask is: "How far should such analogy be pursued?" Richard II unquestionably likens himself to Christ betrayed by the disciples, and at times the play evokes images of Adam banished from Paradise, but do these allusions coalesce into a sustained analogy?

Among the most enthusiastic searchers after Christian meaning are J. A. Bryant, in Hippolyta's View (1961), Roy Battenhouse, in Shakespearean Tragedy: Its Art and Christian Premises (1969), and R. Chris Hassel, in Renaissance Drama and the English Church (1979) and Faith and Folly in Shakespeare: Romantic Comedies (1980). Their efforts have encountered stern opposition, however. One notable dissenter is Roland M. Frye, whose Shakespeare and Christian Doctrine (1963) argues that Shakespeare cannot be shown to have known much Renaissance theology and that, in any case, his plays are concerned with human drama rather than with otherworldly questions of damnation or salvation. Frye's argument stresses the incompatibility of Christianity and tragedy, as does also D. G. James' The Dream of Learning (1951) and Clifford Leech's Shakespeare's Tragedies and Other Studies in Seventeenth-Century Drama (1950). Virgil Whitaker's The Mirror Up to Nature (1965) sees religion as an essential element in Shakespeare's plays but argues that Shakespeare uses the religious knowledge of his audience as a shortcut to characterization and meaning, rather than as an ideological weapon. The controversy will doubtless long continue, even though the typological critics have had to assume a defensive posture.

Jan Kott and the Theater of the Absurd

At an opposite extreme from the Christian idealism of most typological critics is the iconoclasm of those who have been disillusioned by recent events in history. One who brilliantly epitomizes political disillusionment in the aftermath of World War II, especially in Eastern Europe, is Jan Kott. The evocative debunking of romantic idealism set forth in his Shakespeare Our Contemporary (1964, translated from the Polish) has enjoyed enormous influence since the 1960s, especially in the theater. Kott sees Shakespeare as a dramatist of the absurd and the grotesque. In this view, Shakespearean plays are often close to "black" comedy or comedy of the absurd, as defined by Antonin Artaud (The Theatre and Its Double, 1958) and Jerzy Grotowski (Towards a Poor Theatre, 1968). Indeed, Kott has inspired productions that expose traditional values to skepticism and ridicule. Portia and Bassanio in The Merchant of Venice become scheming adventurers; Henry V becomes a priggish warmonger. History is for Kott a nightmare associated with his country's experience in World War II, and Shakespeare's modernity can be seen in his sardonic portrayal of political opportunism and violence. Even A Midsummer Night's Dream is a play of disturbingly erotic brutality, Kott argues. Here is an interpretation of Shakespeare that was bound to have an enormous appeal in a world confronted by the assassinations of the Kennedys and Martin Luther King, Jr.; by incessant war in the Middle East, Southeast Asia, and much of the third world; by the threat of nuclear annihilation and ecological disaster; and by political leadership generally perceived as interested only in the public-relations techniques of self-preservation. An essentially ironic view of politics and, more broadly, of human nature has informed a good deal of criticism since Kott's day and has led to the dethronement of E. M. W. Tillyard and his essentially positive view of English patriotism and heroism in the history plays.

New Historicism and Cultural Materialism

A more recent way of investigating Shakespeare through the demystifying perspective of modern experience—the so-called new historicism— has focused on the themes of political self-fashioning and role playing in terms of power and subversion. This critical school has paid close attention to historians and cultural anthropolgists like Lawrence Stone (The Crisis of the Aristocracy, 1558–1641, 1965) and Clifford Geertz (Negara: The Theatre State in Nineteenth-Century Bali, 1980), who explore new ways of looking at the relationship between historical change and the myths generated to bring it about or to retain power. Geertz analyzes the way in which the ceremonies and myths of political rule can, in effect, become a self-fulfilling reality; kings and other leaders, acting out their roles in ceremonials designed to encapsulate the myth of their greatness and divine origin, essentially become what they have created in their impersonations of power. Such a view of political authority is an inherently skeptical one, seeing government as a process of manipulating illusions. When Shakespeare's English history plays—or indeed any plays dealing with conflicts of authority—are analyzed in these terms, subversion and containment become important issues. Do the plays of Shakespeare and other Renaissance dramatists celebrate the power of the Tudor monarchs, or do they question and undermine assumptions of hierarchy? Did Elizabethan drama serve to increase skepticism and pressure for change, or was it, conversely, a way of easing that pressure so that the power structure could remain in force?

The "new historicism" is a name applied to a kind of literary criticism practiced in America, prominently by Stephen Greenblatt. Especially influential have been his *Renaissance Self-Fashioning* (1980), *Shakespearean Negotiations* (1988), and his editing of the journal *Representations*. Those who pursue similar concerns, including Louis Montrose, Stephen Orgel, Richard Helgerson, Don E. Wayne, Frank Whigham, Richard Strier, Jonathan Goldberg, and Steven Mullaney, share Greenblatt's goals to a greater or lesser extent and think of themselves only with important reservations as "new historicists"; the term is misleadingly categorical, and Greenblatt, among others, is eager to enlarge the parameters of the method rather than to allow it to harden into an orthodoxy. (Greenblatt, in fact, prefers the term "poetics of culture" to "new historicism," even though the latter phrase remains better known.) Still, these critics do generally share a number of common concerns. Among the ways in which new historicists seek to separate themselves from earlier historical critics is by denying that the work of art is a unified and self-contained product of an independent creator in masterful control of the meaning of the work. Instead, the new historicists represent the work as shot through with the multiple and contradictory discourses of its time. New historicists also deny the notion that art merely "reflects" its historical milieu; instead, they argue that art is caught up in, and contributes to, the social practices of its time. Although the boundary between new and old historical criticism is often hard to draw, in general the new historicists are apt to be skeptical of the accepted canon of literary texts and are drawn to a markedly politicized reading of Renaissance plays. One finds everywhere in the new historicism a deep ambivalence toward political authority.

Mikhail Bakhtin's provocative ideas on carnival (*L'Oeuvre de François Rabelais et la Culture Populaire du Moyen Age*, 1970) have had an important influence in new historical circles, as reflected, for example, in the work of Michael Bristol (*Carnival and Theatre: Plebeian Culture and the Structure of Authority in Renaissance England*, 1985), Peter Stallybrass, Gail Paster, and others. Like new historicism, this critical approach looks at so-called high cultural entertainment, including Shakespeare, in relation to the practices of popular culture, thereby breaking down the distinction between "high" and "popular." Literary and nonliterary texts are subjected to the same kind of serious scrutiny. Popular origins of the theater receive new attention, as in Robert Weimann's *Shakespeare and the Popular Tradition in the Theater: Studies in the Social Dimension of Dramatic Form and Function* (published in German in 1967 and in English translation in 1978).

Cultural materialism, in Britain, takes an analogous approach to the dethroning of canonical texts and the emphasis on art as deeply implicated in the social practices of its time but differs from American new historicism on the issue of change. New historicism is sometimes criticized for its lack of a model for change and for its reluctant belief, instead (in Greenblatt's formulation especially), that all attempts at subversion through art are destined to be contained by power structures in society; art permits the expression of heterodox points of view, but only as a way of letting off steam, as it were, and thereby easing the presssures for actual radical change. British cultural materialism, in contrast, is more avowedly committed not only to radical political interpretation but also to rapid political change, partly in response to what are perceived to be more deeply roooted class differences than are found in America. Jonathan Dollimore's *Radical Tragedy* (1984) and *Political Shakespeare* (1985), edited by Dollimore and Alan Sinfield, enlist the dramatist on the side of class struggle. So do *Alternative Shakespeares*, edited by John Drakakis (1985), Malcolm Evans' *Signifying Nothing: Truth's True Content in Shakespeare's Text* (1986), and Terry Eagleton's *Shakespeare and Society* (1967) and *William Shakespeare* (1986). Raymond Williams, not himself a Shakespearean critic, is an acknowledged godfather of the movement.

Feminist Criticism

Feminist criticism is such an important and diverse field that it has necessarily and productively reached into a number of related disciplines, such as cultural anthropology and its wealth of information about family structures. In his *The Elementary Structures of Kinship* (1949, translated 1969) and other books, Claude Lévi-Strauss analyzes the way in which men, as fathers and as husbands, control the transfer of women from one family to another in an "exogamous" marital system designed to strengthen commercial and other ties among men. Recent feminist criticism has had a lot to say about patriarchal structures in the plays and poems of Shakespeare, some of it building upon Levi-Strauss' analysis of patriarchy; see, for example, Karen Newman, "Portia's Ring: Unruly Women and Structures of Exchange in *The Merchant of Venice*," *SQ*, 38 (1987), 10–33, and Lynda Boose, "The Father and the Bride in Shakespeare," *PMLA*, 97 (1982), 325–347. Coppélia Kahn has examined the ideology of rape in *The Rape of Lucrece*, showing how the raped woman is devalued by the shame that attaches to her husband, even though she is innocent (*Shakespeare Studies*, 9, 1976, 45–72).

Another important source of insight for feminist criticism is the anthropological work on rites of passage by Arnold Van Gennep (*The Rites of Passage*, translated by M. B. Vizedom and G. L. Caffee, 1960) and Victor Turner (*The Ritual Process*, 1969), among others. The focus here is on the dangers of transition at times of birth, puberty, marriage, death, and other turning points of human life. Feminist criticism, in dealing with such crises of transition, concerns itself not only with women's roles but also, more broadly, with gender relations, with family structures, and with the problems that males encounter in their quest for mature sexual identity. Coppélia Kahn's *Man's Estate; Masculine Identity in Shakespeare* (1981) looks particularly at the difficulty of the male in confronting the hazards of maturity. Robert Watson's *Shakespeare and the Hazards of Ambition* (1984) also looks at the male in the political context of career and self-fashioning. Marjorie Garber's *Coming of Age in Shakespeare* (1981) takes a broad look at maturation.

As these titles suggest, the models are often psychological, as well as anthropological. One focus of feminist criticism is the role of women in love and marriage. Feminist critics disagree among themselves as to whether the portrait painted by Shakespeare and other Elizabethan dramatists is a hopeful one, as argued, for example, by Juliet Dusinberre in *Shakespeare and the Nature of Women* (1975), or repressive, as argued by Lisa Jardine in *Still Harping on Daughters: Women and Drama in the Age of Shakespeare* (1983). Recent historians add an important perspective, especially Lawrence Stone in his *The Family, Sex, and Marriage in England, 1500–1800* (1977). Did the Protestant emphasis on marriage as a morally elevated and reciprocal relationship have the paradoxical effect of arousing in men an increased hostility and wariness toward women and a resulting increase in repression and violence? Or, as David Underdown suggests, should we look to economic explanations of hostility and wariness toward women in the Renaissance? His studies indicate that repression of women is greatest in regions of the country where their place in the economy offers the possibility of their having some control over family finances. (See *Revel, Riot, and Rebellion: Popular Culture in England, 1603–1660*, 1985, pp. 73–105, especially p. 99.)

Certainly, recent criticism has paid a lot of attention to male anxieties about women in Shakespeare's plays, as various male protagonists resolve to teach women a lesson (*The Taming of the Shrew*), succumb to dark fantasies of female unfaithfulness (*Much Ado About Nothing, Othello*), or are overwhelmed by misogynistic revulsion (*Hamlet, King Lear*). It is as though Shakespeare, in his plays and poems, works through the problems that men experience throughout their lives in their relationships with women, from the insecurities of courtship to the desire for possession and control in marriage, and from jealous fears of betrayal to the longing for escape into middle-age sexual adventure (as in *Antony and Cleopatra*). The late plays show us the preoccupation of the aging male with the marriage of his daughters (another form of betrayal) and with the approach of death.

Recently, feminist criticism has begun to increase its historical consciousness. Critics such as Gail Paster, Jean Howard, Lisa Jardine, and Karen Newman focus on the construction of gender in early modern England in terms of social and material conditions, abandoning the nonhistorical psychological model of earlier feminist criticism. See the bibliography at the end of this book for feminist studies by these and other feminist critics, including Catherine Belsey, Carol Neely, Peter Erickson, Meredith Skura, Margaret Loftis Ranald, and Marianne Novy.

Poststructuralism and Deconstruction

A major influence today in Shakespeare criticism, as in virtually all literary criticism of recent date, is the school of analysis known as poststructuralism or deconstruction; the terms, though not identical, significantly overlap. This school derives its inspiration originally from the work of certain French philosophers and critics, chief among whom are Ferdinand de Saussure, a specialist in linguistics, Michel Foucault, a historian of systems of discourse, and Jacques Derrida, perhaps the most highly visible exponent and practitioner of deconstruction. The ideas of these men were first introduced into American literary criticism by scholars at Yale such as Geoffrey Hartman, J. Hillis Miller, and Paul de Man. The ideas are controversial and difficult.

Poststructuralism and deconstruction begin with an insistence that language is a system of difference—one in which the signifiers (such as words and gestures) are essentially arbitrary to the extent that "meaning" and "authorial intention" are virtually impossible to fix precisely; that is, language enjoys a potentially infinite subjectivity. To an extent, this approach to the subjectivity of meaning in a work of art resembles "new" criticism in its mistrust of "message" in literature, but the new method goes further. It resists all attempts at paraphrase, for example, insisting that the words of a text cannot be translated into other words without altering something vital; indeed, there is no way of knowing if an author's words will strike any two readers or listeners in the same way. The very concept of an author has been challenged by Michel Foucault ("What Is an Author?" in *Language, Counter-Memory, Practice*, edited by Donald F. Bouchard, 1977). Deconstruction proclaims that there is no single identifiable author in the traditional sense; instead of a single text, we have a potentially infinite number of texts.

Both the theory and practice of deconstruction remain highly controversial. Although poststructuralism and deconstruction owe a debt to the general philosophical theory of signs and symbols known as semiotics, in which the function of linguistic signs is perceived to be artificially constructed, the new method also calls into question the very distinctions on which the discipline of semiotics is based. Derrida builds upon the work of Saussure and yet goes well beyond him in an insistence that words (signifiers) be left in play rather than attached to their alleged meaning (signifieds). Frank Lentricchia (*After the New Criticism*, 1980) takes the Yale school critics to task for interpreting Derrida in too formalist and apolitical a sense. Despite disagreements among theorists, nevertheless, the approach has deeply influenced Shakespeare criticism as a whole by urging critics to consider the suppleness with which signifiers (words) in the Shakespearean text are converted by listeners and readers into some approximation of meaning.

The ramifications of poststructuralism and deconstruction are increasingly felt in other forms of criticism, even those at least nominally at odds with poststructuralist assumptions. Some radical textual critics, for example, are fascinated by the unsettling prospects of the deconstructed text. What does one edit and how does one go about editing when words are to be left in play, to the infinite regress of meaning? The problems are acutely examined in a collection of essays called *The Division of the Kingdom*, edited by Gary Taylor and Michael Warren, on the two early and divergent texts of *King Lear* (1983). The method of linguistic analysis known as "speech-act theory," developed by the philosopher Warren Austin as a way of exploring how we perform certain linguistic acts when we swear oaths or make asseverations and the like, is sharply at variance with deconstruction in its premises about a correlation between speech and intended meaning, and yet it, too, can help us understand the instability of spoken or written language in Shakespeare. Joseph Porter's *The Drama of Speech Acts* (1979), for example, looks at ways in which Shakespeare's characters in the plays about Henry IV and Henry V reveal, through their language of oath making and oath breaking, asseveration, and the like, their linguistic adaptability or lack of adapability to historical change. Richard II resists historical change in the very way he speaks; Prince Hal embraces it. A third related field of analysis that is interested in the instability of meaning in Shakespeare's texts is metadramatic criticism, where the focus is on ways in which dramatic texts essentially talk about the drama itself, about artistic expression, and about the artist's quest for immortality in art. James Calderwood's *Shakespearean Metadrama* (1971) is an influential example.

At its extreme, then, deconstructive criticism comes close to undermining all kinds of "meaningfulness" in artistic utterance and to being thus at war with other methods of interpretation. Still, deconstruction continues to remain influential, because it also usefully challenges complacent formulations of meaning and because it promotes such a subtle view of linguistic complexity.

At its best, late twentieth-century criticism transcends the splintering effect of a heterogeneous critical tradition to achieve a synthesis that is at once unified and multiform in

its vision. The pluralistic approach aims at overall balance and a reinforcement of one critical approach through the methodology of another. Many of the works already cited in this introduction refuse to be constricted by methodological boundaries. The best historical criticism makes use of close explication of the text where appropriate; image patterns can certainly reinforce mythological patterns; typological interpretation, when sensibly applied, serves the cause of image study. Some fine books are so eclectic in their method that one hesitates to apply the label of any one critical school. Among such works are Maynard Mack's *King Lear in Our Time* (1965), David Young's *Something of Great Constancy: The Art of A Midsummer Night's Dream* (1966), R. G. Hunter's *Shakespeare and the Comedy of Forgiveness* (1965), Janet Adelman's *The Common Liar: An Essay on "Antony and Cleopatra"* (1973), Stanley Cavell's "The Avoidance of Love: A Reading of *King Lear*," in *Must We Mean What We Say?* (1969, reprinted in *Disowning Knowledge in Six Plays of Shakespeare*, 1987), and Paul Jorgensen's *Our Naked Frailties: Sensational Art and Meaning in Macbeth* (1971).

On the Verge of the Twenty-First Century

The sense of where we are in the late 1990s in Shakespeare criticism reflects the uncertainties and guardedly hopeful expectations of the academic profession as a whole. The period of the 1970s and 1980s, described previously, was one of extraordinary ferment, brought on by a host of developments: the Vietnam War and its aftermath, the assassinations of the Kennedys and Martin Luther King, the impact of French linguistic and philosophical thought on American intellectual writing, the frustrations of many academics with Reaganomics and their consequent fascination with British Marxism, emerging demands for minorities and for women, a revolution in social and sexual mores accompanied by a backlash in the name of "family values," and much more. The result was what must be regarded as a genuine revolution in methods of critical analysis and reading. The literary text became multivalent, ambiguous, deconstructed, dethroned as a unique artifact, and was seen, instead, as a product of and contributing to its social and intellectual environment. The author became a construction of criticism and of a new kind of literary history.

Shakespeare studies have taken a lead in all of this new exploration. Although one of the postmodern demands has been for a recanonizing of literature in favor of newer literature, works by women and minorities, and works from countries other than Britain and the United States instead of the traditional canon of dead white European males, Shakespeare not only has survived this recanonization but also has become more prominent than ever. Other Renaissance writers such as Ben Jonson, John Webster, Thomas

Dekker, Thomas Nashe, John Lyly, Edmund Spenser, and even Christopher Marlowe, John Milton, and John Donne have been the victims of declining enrollments in classes generally, but Shakespeare triumphs. Why?

One compelling answer is that Shakespeare is simply indispensable to postmodern critical inquiry. His texts are so extraordinarily responsive that new questions put to them—about the changing role of women, about cynicism in the political process, about the protean near-indeterminacy of meaning in language—evoke insights that are hard to duplicate in other literary texts. Shakespeare does not seem out of date. The very impulse of so much recent criticism to claim Shakespeare as "our contemporary," attuned to our own skepticisms and disillusionment and even despair (as in the writings of Jan Kott, for example), attests to his unparalleled engagement with the issues about which we care so deeply. Even those who argue that Shakespeare exhibits the male hangups of a patriarchal society and that he is a social snob who glorifies aristocracy and warfare do not see Shakespeare as a writer who is out of touch with the values of our contemporary society but, rather, as one who gives eloquent testimonial to structures that were alive in our cultural past and with which we sense a continuum today even if outward circumstances have changed. The best scholarship does not condemn Shakespeare for believing in kingship or for sometimes showing men as victorious in the battle of the sexes; instead, that criticism is interested in the whole process of the literary text's participation in the creation of culture. Even when recent scholarship is concerned with examining class and gender issues to clarify some of the systematic oppressiveness of early modern culture, it does so generally in an attempt to negotiate the relationship of the present to the past, rather than assuming a superiority in our modern world's approaches to issues of class, gender, and ethnicity.

To be sure, a number of Shakespeare's plays are in trouble today because they make us uncomfortable about these issues. *The Merchant of Venice* is, in the eyes of many, almost unproduceable, because the antisemitic emotions it explores are so distasteful. It is less often assigned now in classrooms than it once was, even though, when it is taught or produced onstage, it can lead to extraordinarily searching discussions of painful but real issues. The same is true of *The Taming of the Shrew*, which is being taken from the shelves of more than a few libraries because of its apparent flaunting of sexist behavior toward women. *Othello* offends some readers and viewers because of its racist language and, in the view of some, racial stereotypes. Yet, the power of Shakespeare's language continues to exert its spell despite, and in part because of, these troubling conflicts over the role of dramatic art in modern society.

The world of Shakespeare criticism today, after two decades or so of revolution, is seemingly one of consolidation. At a March 1995 meeting of the Shakespeare Association of America in Chicago, many conferees wondered:

Where is the profession going? What are the hot new issues? Who are the new critics that no one wants to miss? And, in fact, there seemed to be little dramatic excitement of this sort, little agreement as to any discernible new trend. To some, this is frustrating. Where does one turn for real creativity after a thoroughgoing revolution such as we have experienced?

To others, a time of stocktaking is potentially healthy. There seems to be relatively little interest in turning the clock back; postmodernism and indeterminacy have changed the critical landscape for better and for worse. Now that this new landscape begins to seem familiar, however, new members of the profession seem less anxious to resolve their own identity crises in terms of affiliating with some critical school or other. The critical challenges are there, not so stridently new as they were ten years ago, and adaptable to various uses.

The result is increasing variety in the kinds of critical work being done. Some of it is recognizably traditional, dealing with stage history and conditions of performance during Shakespeare's lifetime, as, for example, in T.J. King, *Casting Shakespeare's Plays: London Actors and Their Roles* (1992); William Ingram, *The Business of Playing: The Beginnings of the Adult Professional Theater in Elizabethan London* (1992); David Bradley, *From Text to Performance in the Elizabethan Theatre: Preparing the Play for the Stage* (1992); David Mann, *The Elizabethan Player: Contemporary Stage Representation* (1991); and John H. Astington, ed., *The Development of Shakespeare's Theater* (1992). Background and historical studies of the conditions that helped produce Shakespeare's theater can sometimes be informatively revisionist in the sense of toppling cherished older notions without at the same time being postmodern in approach. Examples here might include Richard Dutton, *Mastering the Revels: The Regulation and Censorship of English Renaissance Drama* (1991) and Leeds Barroll, *Politics, Plague, and Shakespeare's Theater: The Stuart Years* (1991).

Other studies are more openly revisionist in a postmodern vein, sometimes in dealing with hypotheses about bibliography and textual studies, as in Margreta de Grazia, *Shakespeare Verbatim: The Reproduction of Authenticity and the 1790 Apparatus* (1991) and Grace Ioppolo, *Revising Shakespeare* (1991). The New Folger Library Shakespeare, edited by Barbara Mowat and Paul Werstine (1992—), gives a more measured approach. Occasionally a conservative counterblast is heard, as in Brian Vickers's entertaining, learned, and feisty polemic, *Appropriating Shakespeare: Contemporary Critical Quarrels* (1993). A forum of essays edited by Ivo Kamps, called *Shakespeare Left and Right*, gives us a chance to weigh arguments from various sides.

What the contemporary critical scene does best is to free critics to be who they are and to write without paying dues to any particular affiliation. The results are refreshingly diverse. Among the books that show this spread of critical approaches are Karen Newman, *Fashioning Femininity and the English Renaissance Drama* (1991); Bruce R. Smith, *Homosexual Desire in Shakespeare's England* (1991); Janet Adelman, *Suffocating Mothers: Fantasies of Maternal Origin in Shakespeare's Plays, "Hamlet" to "The Tempest"* (1992); Alan Sinfield, *Faultlines: Cultural Materialism and the Politics of Dissident Reading* (1992); Valerie Traub, *Desire and Anxiety: Circulations of Sexuality in Shakespearean Drama* (1992); Richard Burt, *Licensed by Authority: Ben Jonson and the Discourses of Censorship* (1993); Linda Charnes, *Notorious Identity: Materializing the Subject in Shakespeare* (1993); Lars Engle, *Shakespearean Pragmatism: Market of His Time* (1993); Gail Kern Paster, *The Body Embarrassed: Drama and the Disciplines of Shame in Early Modern England* (1993); Meredith Anne Skura, *Shakespeare the Actor and the Purposes of Playing* (1993); Frances E. Dolan, *Dangerous Familiars: Representations of Domestic Crime in England, 1550–1700* (1994); Kim F. Hall, *Things of Darkness: Economies of Race and Gender in Early Modern England* (1994); Jean Howard, *The Stage and Social Struggle in Early Modern England* (1994); Robert Watson, *The Rest Is Silence: Death as Annihilation in the English Renaissance* (1994); and Katharine Eisaman Maus, *Inwardness and Theatre in the English Renaissance Drama* (1995), For other suggestions, see recent entries in the bibliography in Appendix A at the back of this volume.

The Comedies

The Comedy of Errors

Love's Labor's Lost

The Two Gentlemen of Verona

The Taming of the Shrew

A Midsummer Night's Dream

The Merchant of Venice

Much Ado About Nothing

The Merry Wives of Windsor

As You Like It

Twelfth Night; or, What You Will

All's Well that Ends Well

Measure for Measure

Troilus and Cressida

2

The
Comedy
of
Errors

The Comedy of Errors is a superb illustration of Shakespeare's "apprenticeship" in comedy. It is more imitative of classical comedy, especially of Plautus, than is Shakespeare's mature work. Its verbal humor, including the scatological jokes about breaking wind, the bawdy jests about cuckold's horns, and the overly ingenious banter (as in 2.2) is at times adolescent. The play abounds in the farcical humor of physical abuse, so endearing to children of all ages. It is perhaps the most uncomplicatedly funny of all Shakespeare's plays. Yet the softening touches of Shakespeare's maturity are unmistakably present as well. Shakespeare frames his farce of mistaken identity with old Egeon's tragicomic story of separation, threatened death, and eventual reunion. He adds characters to the Plautine original in order to enhance the love interest and to reconcile Plautus with English moral conventions. He touches upon themes of illusion, madness, and revelry that are to figure prominently in *A Midsummer Night's Dream* and in *Twelfth Night*, a later comedy of mistaken identity. In these respects, *The Comedy of Errors* is both a fascinating prelude to Shakespeare's later development and a rich achievement in its own right. On stage, it has not attracted the greatest Shakespearean actors, since it offers no complex or dominating roles, but it has seldom failed to delight audiences.

We cannot be sure precisely how early the play was written. A performance took place on December 28, 1594, at Gray's Inn, before an unruly assembly of lawyers, law students, and their guests. This was probably not the first performance, however. Topical allusions offer hints of an earlier date. When Dromio of Syracuse speaks of France as "armed and reverted, making war against her heir" (3.2.123–124), he clearly is referring to the Catholic League's opposition to Henry of Navarre, who was the apparent heir to the French throne until 1593, when he became king. Another allusion, to Spain's sending "whole armadas of carracks" (lines 135–136), would possibly have lost its comic point soon after the Invincible Armada of 1588. The play's style, characterization, and imitative con-

struction are all consistent with a date between 1589 and 1593.

Whatever the exact date, Shakespeare's youthful fascination with Plautus is manifest. Shakespeare's command of Latin, though sneered at by Ben Jonson, was undoubtedly good enough to have let him read Plautus with pleasure. He must have been drilled in Latin for years as a student in the town of Stratford-upon-Avon, and, if the seventeenth-century anecdotalist John Aubrey is right, he went on to teach Latin as a country schoolmaster before becoming an actor. Indeed, the influence of not only Plautus but also Ovid and Seneca (together with touches of Horace, Catullus, etc.) is a prominent feature of Shakespeare's early work, dramatic and nondramatic. Shakespeare may have consulted Plautus both in the original and in a contemporary translation, as was frequently his custom with non-English sources. From Renaissance Latin editions of Plautus, he apparently took the odd designation "Antipholis Sereptus" (i.e., "surreptus," snatched away), which appears in the Folio text in a stage direction at 2.1.0 to indicate the twin who was separated from his father. On the other hand, a translation by "W. W."(? William Warner), published in 1595, was registered in 1594 and might have been available earlier to Shakespeare in manuscript.

Plautus had much to offer Shakespeare and his fellow dramatists, especially in the way of tightly organized and complex plot construction. Native English drama of the sixteenth century tended to be episodic and panoramic in its design. Shakespeare's apprenticeship in neoclassical form can be seen in his precise observation of the unities of time and place—those unities which he openly disregarded in most of his later plays. At the play's beginning, Egeon is informed that he has until sundown to raise his ransom money, and the play then moves toward that point in time with periodic observations that it is now noon, now two o'clock, and so on. (At one point, time even seems to go backwards, but that is part of the illusion of madness.) The action is restricted to the city of Ephesus; events that have happened elsewhere, at an earlier time (such as the separation of the Antipholus family), are told to us by persons in the play, such as old Egeon. Although Shakespeare's company did not employ the sort of painted scenery drawn in perspective used by continental neoclassicists, with fixed locations for houses facing on a street, the original production of this play may nonetheless have used one stage "house" or door to represent the dwelling of Antipholus of Ephesus (the Phoenix) throughout the drama. The entire play can be staged as if all the action occurs in the vicinity of this single "house," with the Abbey near at hand. Never again does Shakespeare utilize such a neoclassical stage.

These unities of time and place are mechanical matters, but they do also harmonize with a more essential unity of action. The story moves, as though in perfect accord with neoclassical five-act theory, from exposition and complication to climax, anagnoresis (discovery), and peripeteia (reversal of fortune). The brilliance of the plotting is decidedly Plautine. Shakespeare pushes to its limit the interweaving of comic misunderstandings only to unravel all these seemingly tightly woven knots with ease. Yet the imitation of Plautus, even in matters of construction, is by no means slavish, for Shakespeare borrows both from Plautus' farce on the mistaken identity of twins *(The Menaechmi)* and from Plautus' best-known comedy *(Amphitruo),* in which a husband and his servant are excluded from their own house while a disguised visitor usurps the master's role within. Such ingenious adaptations and rearrangements were common among neoclassical dramatists like Ariosto, and, although Shakespeare seems not to have used any of the sixteenth-century analogues to this play, he does reveal an acquaintance with neoclassical comedy and an ability to compete with the best that Europe had to offer in this vein. Such versatility is noteworthy in a young dramatist who was to reveal himself in time as far less of a neoclassicist than a native English writer. Moreover, even if his self-imposed neoclassical training was only an apprenticeship, it was to prove invaluable to Shakespeare. Despite his later tendency toward "romantic" plotting—toward the depiction of multiple actions extending over widely separated spaces and extended periods of time—Shakespeare's greatest comedies continue to point toward the same gratifying resolution of dramatic conflict in a single and well-structured denouement.

For all its Plautine skill of design, however, *The Comedy of Errors* is quite far removed from *The Menaechmi* in tone and spirit. Gone are the cynicism, the satirical hardness, and the amoral tone of the Roman original. The characters, though still recognizable as types, are humanized. The familiar Plautine parasite is excluded entirely. The usual clever servant happily becomes the Dromio twins. Plautus' quack Doctor, Medicus, is hilariously transmuted into Dr. Pinch, a pedantic schoolmaster. The Courtesan's role is no longer prominent. Instead, Shakespeare creates Luciana, the virtuous sister of Adriana, who pleads the cause of forbearance in marriage and who eventually becomes the bride of Antipholus of Syracuse. *The Comedy of Errors* does not end, as do most of Shakespeare's later comedies, with a parade of couples to the altar, but the marriage of Antipholus and Luciana is at least one important step in that direction. Besides, we are told of yet another marriage still to come—that of Dromio of Ephesus to Luce, the kitchen wench. This belowstairs parody of wedded affection is thoroughly English in character and recalls a similar mirroring of courtship among the comic servants of Medwall's *Fulgens and Lucrece* (c. 1497). The motif is not sufficiently stressed to threaten the unity of the main plot, but the potentiality for double plotting is unmistakable.

An even more significant contrast to Plautine farce is to be found in the romantic saga of old Egeon and his long-lost wife, the Abbess. Their story is one not of mistaken identity (though that contributes to the denouement) but of painful separation, wandering, and reunion. Indeed, the note struck at the beginning of the play might seem tragic were we not already attuned to the conventional romantic expectation that separated members of a family are likely to be restored to one another again. Egeon, threatened with immediate execution, unfolds to us a narrative of wedded bliss interrupted by the malignancy of Fortune. In contrast to the tightly controlled unity of time of the farcical action, the romantic narrative extends (by recollection) over many years of error and suffering. Egeon's tragicomic story of testing and of patient endurance is very much like that of *Apollonius of Tyre,* a popular tale used by Shakespeare in his late romance *Pericles* (c. 1606–1608). The conventions of this sort of romance, ultimately Greek in origin, stress improbability: identical twins who can be told apart only by birthmarks, a storm at sea splitting a vessel in half and neatly dividing a family, and so on. The sea is emblematic of unpredictable Fortune, taking away with one hand and restoring with the other. The wife who is lost at sea, like her counterpart in *Apollonius* or *Pericles,* takes to a life of cloistered devotion, suggesting a pattern of symbolic death, healing, and ultimate rebirth. The ending of *The Comedy of Errors* has just a hint of death restored mysteriously to life: "After so long grief, such nativity!" (5.1.407).

Egeon's story of endurance counterpoints the farce in yet another way. His arraignment before the Duke of Ephesus introduces into the play a "tragic" world of law, punishment, and death. Egeon's date with the executioner is not illusory. His predicament is the result of the bitter "mortal and intestine jars" (1.1.11) between two cities caught in a frenzy of economic reprisals. The law cannot be merciful, even though the unfairness of Egeon's plight is manifest to everyone, including the Duke. These potentially tragic factors must not be overstressed, for the first scene is brief and we are reassured by the play's hilarious tone (and by our surmising that Egeon is father of the Antipholus twins) that all will be well. Still, Shakespeare's addition of this romance plot suggests his restlessness with pure farce. As in his later comedies, which are virtually all threatened by catastrophes, the denouement of *The Comedy of Errors* is deepened into something approaching miraculous recovery. Moreover, the backdrop of a near-tragic world of genuine suffering heightens our appreciation of comic unreality in the self-contained world of Plautine farce and stresses the illusory nature of the dilemmas arising out of purely mistaken identity. Such delusions are all the more comic because they are the delusions that supposedly sane people suffer: contentiousness and jealousy in marriage, concern for respectable appearances among one's neighbors, and the suspicion that one is always being cheated in money matters. These are the chimeras that, by being made to look so plausible and yet so patently insane, are farcically exploited in

Shakespeare's comic device: the inversion of madness and sanity, dreaming and waking, illusion and reality.

What happens when the behavior of one twin is mistaken for that of the other? The situation is, of course, amusing in itself, but it also serves as a test of the other characters, to discover what mad hypotheses they will construct. Adriana, faced with her husband's seeming refusal to come home to dinner, launches into a jealous tirade against husbands who neglect their wives for courtesans. The illusory situation, in other words, brings out her latent fears. We understand better now why she acts shrewishly: she fears rejection and the fading of her beauty, and she imagines that her fading beauty may be the cause of her husband's neglect. Actually, even as she speaks, her husband is busy making arrangements about a chain he means to give Adriana; but, when subsequently he is locked out of his own house and jumps to the conclusion that Adriana is being faithless, he resolves in his fury to bestow the chain on a courtesan in order to "spite my wife." He would actually do so were he not saved from this destructively revengeful impulse by the beneficently comic action of the farcical plot: through mistaken identity, the chain is delivered into the hands of his twin. Once again, illusion has prompted a character to assume the worst, to reveal his suspicions of a plot against him. And so it goes when Antipholus of Ephesus is arrested for nonpayment of the chain (he assumes that all merchants are thieves) or is denied his bail money by the servant he thinks he sent to fetch it (he assumes that all servants are thieves). We laugh at the endless capacity of the human mind for distortions of this self-punishing sort.

The metaphor used most often to convey this sense of bewilderment, even a confusion about one's own identity, is that of metamorphosis. All have drunk of Circe's cup (5.1.271) and have been transformed into animals—most of them into asses. All have hearkened to the mermaid's song and are enchanted. Ephesus, they conclude, must be haunted by sorcerers, witches, goblins, and spirits (4.3.11 ff.). Ephesus is, in fact, associated in the Bible with exorcism (Acts 19:13 ff.), and "Circe" suggests that Antipholus of Syracuse is a becalmed Odysseus. In such a mad world, the characters assume a license to embark on Saturnalian holiday. The experience of transformation thus leads to various forms of "release" from ordinary social behavior, but the experience is also disturbing and continually reminds the characters of exorcism, hell, and devils. The threat of incest hovers over the comic business of two brothers sharing a wife, and indeed there is a dark subtext to the twinning that is unavoidably present throughout the play: the twinned cities of Ephesus and Syracuse, the twinned brothers, the twinned servants, all of whom are trying to discover their identities amid the paradoxes of singleness and doubleness. The play's farcical action is never far from violence. Witches and fat kitchen wenches suggest a fascination with unruly women. The characters can explain their inverted world only by assuming that all men are lunatic, all honest women whores, and all true men thieves. "Do you know me, sir? . . . Am I myself?" "Am I in earth, or heaven, or in hell? / Sleeping or waking, mad or well advised?" (3.2.73–74, 2.2.211–212). Perhaps, as Barbara Freeman suggests, the whole play can be looked at as Egeon's dream. It is both reassuring and hilariously anticlimactic that these questionings can finally be dispelled by the most mundane of explanations: there are two Antipholuses and two Dromios.

Contained within this framework of madness and waking is a playful yet serious examination of the dynamics of courtship and marriage. The two most important women in the play are meaningfully paired and contrasted. Adriana, the shrewish wife, frets at social custom that allows her husband Antipholus to roam abroad while she is domestically confined. Her unmarried sister Luciana endorses the traditional view that husbands enjoy a precedence found everywhere in nature: males "are masters to their females, and their lords" (2.1.24). What Luciana calls obedience (line 29) her married sister calls "servitude" (line 26). Who is right? The debate, left unresolved, nonetheless raises skeptical questions about marital hierarchies. The plot also probes and tests through fantasies of inversion. A wife, believing herself rejected for having aged in her wifely obedience, locks her husband out of the house and dines with a stranger. Luciana meantime finds herself courted by what appears to be her own brother-in-law and thus must face a conflict between desire and loyalty to her sister. Of course, Adriana does not know that she is inverting authority by excluding her husband from his own hearth, but the plot of mistaken identities does allow her to act out her self-assertiveness without being, in fact, guilty of disloyalty. Her husband's role is to play the wandering male and to be eventually forgiven by his wife; presumably his exposure in Act 5 will make him a more tolerant husband, like Count Almaviva in Mozart's The Marriage of Figaro. The discovery of identities in Act 5 allows Luciana to marry the man she has learned to love, but without the guilt of her fantasy experience. Patriarchal values are restored by the play's conclusion, yet the partners in love and marriage have been, to some extent, liberated by their role playing in a plot of metamorphosis. These issues of domestic relations will be further explored in The Taming of the Shrew, Othello, and other plays.

The playfulness about illusion should not be overemphasized, for the play expends most of its energies in farce. The Dromios, with their incessant drubbings, are often the center of interest in performance, and rightly so. Shakespeare employs no behind-the-scenes manipulator of illusion, such as Puck in A Midsummer Night's Dream or the Duke in Measure for Measure. His interest in the metaphor of the world as a stage is discernible only as the foreshadowing of greatness to come. Nevertheless, Shakespeare's alterations of Plautus amply reveal the philosophic and idealistic direction that his subsequent comedy is to take.

The Comedy of Errors

[Dramatis Personae

SOLINUS, *Duke of Ephesus*
EGEON, *a merchant of Syracuse*
EMILIA, *Lady Abbess at Ephesus, and Egeon's wife*

ANTIPHOLUS OF EPHESUS, } *twin brothers,*
ANTIPHOLUS OF SYRACUSE, } *sons of Egeon*
} *and Emilia*
DROMIO OF EPHESUS, } *twin brothers,*
DROMIO OF SYRACUSE,} *bondsmen to the*
} *two Antipholuses*

ADRIANA, *wife of Antipholus of Ephesus*
LUCIANA, *her sister*
LUCE, *Adriana's kitchen maid (also known as* NELL*)*

BALTHASAR, *a merchant*
ANGELO, *a goldsmith*
FIRST MERCHANT, *friend to Antipholus of Syracuse*
SECOND MERCHANT, *to whom Angelo is a debtor*
DOCTOR PINCH, *a conjuring schoolmaster*
A COURTESAN
AN OFFICER
A MESSENGER

Jailer, Headsman, Officers, and other Attendants

SCENE: *Ephesus*]

1.1

Enter the Duke of Ephesus, with [Egeon] the merchant of Syracuse, Jailer, and other attendants.

EGEON
Proceed, Solinus, to procure my fall,
And by the doom of death end woes and all. 2
DUKE
Merchant of Syracusa, plead no more. 3
I am not partial to infringe our laws. 4
The enmity and discord which of late

Sprung from the rancorous outrage of your Duke 6
To merchants, our well-dealing countrymen,
Who, wanting guilders to redeem their lives, 8
Have sealed his rigorous statutes with their bloods, 9
Excludes all pity from our threatening looks.
For since the mortal and intestine jars 11
Twixt thy seditious countrymen and us,
It hath in solemn synods been decreed, 13
Both by the Syracusians and ourselves,
To admit no traffic to our adverse towns. 15
Nay, more, if any born at Ephesus 16
Be seen at any Syracusian marts and fairs; 17
Again, if any Syracusian born
Come to the bay of Ephesus, he dies,
His goods confiscate to the Duke's dispose, 20
Unless a thousand marks be levièd 21
To quit the penalty and to ransom him. 22
Thy substance, valued at the highest rate, 23
Cannot amount unto a hundred marks;
Therefore by law thou art condemned to die.
EGEON
Yet this my comfort: when your words are done,
My woes end likewise with the evening sun.
DUKE
Well, Syracusian, say in brief the cause
Why thou departedst from thy native home
And for what cause thou cam'st to Ephesus.
EGEON
A heavier task could not have been imposed
Than I to speak my griefs unspeakable. 32
Yet, that the world may witness that my end
Was wrought by nature, not by vile offense, 34
I'll utter what my sorrow gives me leave. 35
In Syracusa was I born, and wed
Unto a woman, happy but for me, 37
And by me, had not our hap been bad. 38
With her I lived in joy; our wealth increased
By prosperous voyages I often made
To Epidamnum, till my factor's death 41
And the great care of goods at random left 42
Drew me from kind embracements of my spouse;
From whom my absence was not six months old
Before herself, almost at fainting under
The pleasing punishment that women bear,

1.1. Location: Some editors argue that the play was staged according to classical practice with three visible doors backstage representing three "houses"—that of Antipholus of Ephesus (in the center), that of the Courtesan, and that of the Priory—with the stage itself representing a marketplace or open area. More probably, the stage may have been open and unlocalized. The present scene may be at the Duke's court.
2 doom judgment   **3 Syracusa** Syracuse, in Sicily   **4 partial** predisposed, biased

6 outrage violence   **8 wanting** lacking.   **guilders** money; the guilder was a Dutch coin worth about one shilling eight pence.   **redeem** ransom   **9 sealed** ratified.   **bloods** i.e., lives. (The grim analogy is to red sealing wax.)   **11 mortal** deadly.   **intestine** (The usual meaning, "civil" or "internal," may be used here with *mortal* as an intensifier.)   **jars** quarrels   **13 synods** assemblies   **15 To . . . towns** to allow no trade between our hostile towns   **16 Ephesus** a port on the Aegean coast of modern Turkey   **17 marts** markets   **20 confiscate** confiscated.   **dispose** disposal   **21 marks** money worth thirteen shillings four pence   **22 quit** pay   **23 Thy substance** the sum total of your wealth   **32 unspeakable** indescribable (but with a punning oxymoron on the literal sense: Egeon will speak that which cannot be spoken)   **34 by nature** i.e., by natural affection; here, a father's love   **35 gives me leave** allows me   **37–38 happy . . . bad** happy only in having me, and happy indeed through me if we had not suffered misfortune   **41 Epidamnum** (so spelled in Plautus' *The Menaechmi*): Epidamnus, a port on the coast of modern Albania.   **factor's** agent's   **42 care of** anxiety about

Had made provision for her following me,
And soon and safe arrivèd where I was.
There had she not been long but she became
A joyful mother of two goodly sons,
And, which was strange, the one so like the other
As could not be distinguished but by names.   52
That very hour and in the selfsame inn
A mean woman was deliverèd   54
Of such a burden male, twins both alike.
Those, for their parents were exceeding poor,
I bought and brought up to attend my sons.
My wife, not meanly proud of two such boys,   58
Made daily motions for our home return;   59
Unwilling I agreed. Alas, too soon
We came aboard.
A league from Epidamnum had we sailed   62
Before the always-wind-obeying deep
Gave any tragic instance of our harm.   64
But longer did we not retain much hope;
For what obscurèd light the heavens did grant
Did but convey unto our fearful minds
A doubtful warrant of immediate death,   68
Which, though myself would gladly have embraced,
Yet the incessant weepings of my wife—
Weeping before for what she saw must come—
And piteous plainings of the pretty babes,   72
That mourned for fashion, ignorant what to fear,   73
Forced me to seek delays for them and me.   74
And this it was, for other means was none:
The sailors sought for safety by our boat
And left the ship, then sinking-ripe, to us.   77
My wife, more careful for the latter-born,   78
Had fastened him unto a small spare mast
Such as seafaring men provide for storms;
To him one of the other twins was bound,
Whilst I had been like heedful of the other.
The children thus disposed, my wife and I,
Fixing our eyes on whom our care was fixed,   84
Fastened ourselves at either end the mast,
And, floating straight, obedient to the stream,   86
Was carried towards Corinth, as we thought.
At length the sun, gazing upon the earth,
Dispersed those vapors that offended us,   89
And by the benefit of his wishèd light
The seas waxed calm, and we discoverèd
Two ships from far, making amain to us,   92
Of Corinth that, of Epidaurus this.   93
But ere they came—O, let me say no more!
Gather the sequel by that went before.   95

DUKE
Nay, forward, old man. Do not break off so,
For we may pity, though not pardon thee.
EGEON
O, had the gods done so, I had not now   98
Worthily termed them merciless to us!   99
For, ere the ships could meet by twice five leagues,
We were encountered by a mighty rock,
Which being violently borne upon,
Our helpful ship was splitted in the midst,   103
So that in this unjust divorce of us
Fortune had left to both of us alike
What to delight in, what to sorrow for.   106
Her part, poor soul, seeming as burdenèd   107
With lesser weight, but not with lesser woe,
Was carried with more speed before the wind,
And in our sight they three were taken up
By fishermen of Corinth, as we thought.
At length, another ship had seized on us,
And, knowing whom it was their hap to save,
Gave healthful welcome to their shipwrecked guests, 114
And would have reft the fishers of their prey   115
Had not their bark been very slow of sail;   116
And therefore homeward did they bend their course.
Thus have you heard me severed from my bliss,
That by misfortunes was my life prolonged,
To tell sad stories of my own mishaps.
DUKE
And, for the sake of them thou sorrowest for,
Do me the favor to dilate at full   122
What have befall'n of them and thee till now.
EGEON
My youngest boy, and yet my eldest care,
At eighteen years became inquisitive
After his brother, and importuned me
That his attendant—so his case was like,   127
Reft of his brother, but retained his name—   128
Might bear him company in the quest of him,
Whom whilst I labored of a love to see,   130
I hazarded the loss of whom I loved.   131
Five summers have I spent in farthest Greece,
Roaming clean through the bounds of Asia,   133
And, coasting homeward, came to Ephesus—   134
Hopeless to find, yet loath to leave unsought   135
Or that or any place that harbors men.   136
But here must end the story of my life,
And happy were I in my timely death   138
Could all my travels warrant me they live.   139

---

52 As that they **54 mean** of low birth **58 not meanly** to no small
degree **59 motions** proposals, entreaties **62 league** a measure of
distance, about three miles **64 instance** proof, sign **68 doubtful**
dreadful **72 plainings** wailings **73 for fashion** in imitation **74 delays** i.e., delays from death **77 sinking-ripe** ready to sink **78 careful**
anxious. **latter-born** (Compare line 124, however, from which we
learn that the younger or "latter-born" was saved with the father.)
84 whom those on whom, or, him on whom **86 straight** at once
89 vapors clouds **92 making amain** proceeding at full speed
93 Epidaurus a Greek town southwest of Athens and Corinth; or possibly Dubrovnik, on the Adriatic coast **95 that** that which

98 had . . . so i.e., had the gods shown pity **99 Worthily** justly
103 helpful ship i.e., the mast **106 What** something **107 as** as if
114 healthful saving **115 reft** bereft **116 bark** sailing vessel
122 dilate at full relate at length **127 so . . . like** in a similar situation **128 Reft . . . name** (Evidently Egeon, presuming that the lost
son and servant are dead, has given their names to the surviving twin
brothers.) **130–131 Whom . . . loved** i.e., while I labored lovingly
to find the lost twin, I ran the risk of losing my younger son, whom I
loved no less **133 clean** entirely. **bounds** boundaries **134 coasting**
traveling along the coast **135 Hopeless** despairing **136 Or** either
138 timely speedy; opportune **139 travels** "travails," or hardships, as
well as travels. **warrant** assure

DUKE
Hapless Egeon, whom the fates have marked
To bear the extremity of dire mishap!   141
Now, trust me, were it not against our laws,
Against my crown, my oath, my dignity,   143
Which princes, would they, may not disannul,   144
My soul should sue as advocate for thee.
But though thou art adjudgèd to the death,   146
And passèd sentence may not be recalled   147
But to our honor's great disparagement,   148
Yet will I favor thee in what I can.
Therefore, merchant, I'll limit thee this day   150
To seek thy health by beneficial help.
Try all the friends thou hast in Ephesus;
Beg thou, or borrow, to make up the sum,
And live; if no, then thou art doomed to die.
Jailer, take him to thy custody.
JAILER   I will, my lord.
EGEON
Hopeless and helpless doth Egeon wend,
But to procrastinate his lifeless end.   *Exeunt.* 158

❖

1.2   *Enter Antipholus [of Syracuse], [First] Merchant,*
and Dromio [of Syracuse].

FIRST MERCHANT
Therefore give out you are of Epidamnum,   1
Lest that your goods too soon be confiscate.
This very day a Syracusian merchant
Is apprehended for arrival here
And, not being able to buy out his life,
According to the statute of the town
Dies ere the weary sun set in the west.
There is your money that I had to keep.   8
                                        [He gives money.]
S. ANTIPHOLUS *[giving the money to S. Dromio]*
Go bear it to the Centaur, where we host,   9
And stay there, Dromio, till I come to thee.
Within this hour it will be dinnertime.   11
Till that, I'll view the manners of the town,
Peruse the traders, gaze upon the buildings,
And then return and sleep within mine inn,
For with long travel I am stiff and weary.
Get thee away.
S. DROMIO
Many a man would take you at your word
And go indeed, having so good a means.   18
                          Exit Dromio [of Syracuse].
S. ANTIPHOLUS
A trusty villain, sir, that very oft,   19

When I am dull with care and melancholy,
Lightens my humor with his merry jests.   21
What, will you walk with me about the town
And then go to my inn and dine with me?
FIRST MERCHANT
I am invited, sir, to certain merchants,
Of whom I hope to make much benefit;
I crave your pardon. Soon at five o'clock,   26
Please you, I'll meet with you upon the mart
And afterward consort you till bedtime.   28
My present business calls me from you now.
S. ANTIPHOLUS
Farewell till then. I will go lose myself   30
And wander up and down to view the city.
FIRST MERCHANT
Sir, I commend you to your own content.   *Exit.*
S. ANTIPHOLUS
He that commends me to mine own content
Commends me to the thing I cannot get.
I to the world am like a drop of water   35
That in the ocean seeks another drop,
Who, falling there to find his fellow forth,   37
Unseen, inquisitive, confounds himself;   38
So I, to find a mother and a brother,
In quest of them, unhappy, lose myself.   40

Enter Dromio of Ephesus.

Here comes the almanac of my true date.—   41
What now? How chance thou art returned so soon?   42
E. DROMIO
Returned so soon? Rather approached too late:
The capon burns, the pig falls from the spit,
The clock hath strucken twelve upon the bell;
My mistress made it one upon my cheek.   46
She is so hot because the meat is cold;   47
The meat is cold because you come not home;
You come not home because you have no stomach;   49
You have no stomach, having broke your fast.
But we that know what 'tis to fast and pray
Are penitent for your default today.   52
S. ANTIPHOLUS
Stop in your wind, sir. Tell me this, I pray: 53
Where have you left the money that I gave you?
E. DROMIO
O—sixpence that I had o' Wednesday last
To pay the saddler for my mistress' crupper?   56
The saddler had it, sir; I kept it not.
S. ANTIPHOLUS
I am not in a sportive humor now.
Tell me, and dally not: where is the money?
We being strangers here, how dar'st thou trust

---

141 mishap (punning on *Hapless* in line 140)   **143 dignity** high office
144 would they even if they wished.   **disannul** annul, cancel
146 the death i.e., death by judicial sentence   **147 recalled** revoked
148 But except   **150 limit** allow, appoint   **158 procrastinate** postpone
1.2. Location: The street.
1 give out say   **8 keep** safeguard   **9 Centaur** the name of an inn,
identified by its sign over the door. In mythology, a centaur is half
horse, half man.   **host** lodge   **11 dinnertime** i.e., noon   **18 means**
(1) opportunity (2) money   **19 villain** servant. (Said good-humoredly.)

21 humor mood, disposition   **26 Soon at** about   **28 consort** accompany   **30 lose myself** roam freely   **35 to** in relation to   **37 forth** out
38 confounds himself mingles indistinguishably   **40 unhappy** unlucky
41 almanac . . . date (i.e., being born in the same hour, Dromio
serves as an almanac by which Antipholus can see his age)   **42 How
chance** how comes it   **46 made it one** i.e., struck (as a clock would
strike one o'clock)   **47 hot** angry   **49 stomach** appetite   **52 penitent**
doing penance (i.e., suffering hunger).   **default** fault   **53 wind** i.e.,
words   **56 crupper** leather strap on a saddle that is passed under the
horse's tail in order to keep the saddle from riding forward

So great a charge from thine own custody?   61
E. DROMIO
I pray you, jest, sir, as you sit at dinner.
I from my mistress come to you in post;   63
If I return, I shall be post indeed,   64
For she will scour your fault upon my pate.   65
Methinks your maw, like mine, should be your
  clock   66
And strike you home without a messenger.
S. ANTIPHOLUS
Come, Dromio, come, these jests are out of season;
Reserve them till a merrier hour than this.
Where is the gold I gave in charge to thee?
E. DROMIO
To me, sir? Why, you gave no gold to me.
S. ANTIPHOLUS
Come on, sir knave, have done your foolishness,
And tell me how thou hast disposed thy charge.   73
E. DROMIO
My charge was but to fetch you from the mart
Home to your house, the Phoenix, sir, to dinner;   75
My mistress and her sister stays for you.
S. ANTIPHOLUS
Now, as I am a Christian, answer me
In what safe place you have bestowed my money,   78
Or I shall break that merry sconce of yours   79
That stands on tricks when I am undisposed.   80
Where is the thousand marks thou hadst of me?
E. DROMIO
I have some marks of yours upon my pate,
Some of my mistress' marks upon my shoulders,
But not a thousand marks between you both.
If I should pay your worship those again,
Perchance you will not bear them patiently.
S. ANTIPHOLUS
Thy mistress' marks? What mistress, slave, hast
  thou?
E. DROMIO
Your worship's wife, my mistress at the Phoenix,
She that doth fast till you come home to dinner
And prays that you will hie you home to dinner.   90
S. ANTIPHOLUS
What, wilt thou flout me thus unto my face,
Being forbid? There, take you that, sir knave.
                    [He beats Dromio of Ephesus.]
E. DROMIO
What mean you, sir? For God's sake, hold your
  hands!
Nay, an you will not, sir, I'll take my heels.   94
                    Exit Dromio of Ephesus.
S. ANTIPHOLUS
Upon my life, by some device or other

The villain is o'erraught of all my money.   96
They say this town is full of cozenage,   97
As nimble jugglers that deceive the eye,
Dark-working sorcerers that change the mind,
Soul-killing witches that deform the body,
Disguisèd cheaters, prating mountebanks,   101
And many suchlike liberties of sin.   102
If it prove so, I will be gone the sooner.
I'll to the Centaur to go seek this slave.
I greatly fear my money is not safe.   Exit.

2.1   *Enter Adriana, wife to Antipholus [of Ephesus],
          with Luciana, her sister.*

ADRIANA
Neither my husband nor the slave returned
That in such haste I sent to seek his master?
Sure, Luciana, it is two o'clock.
LUCIANA
Perhaps some merchant hath invited him,
And from the mart he's somewhere gone to dinner.
Good sister, let us dine, and never fret.
A man is master of his liberty;
Time is their master, and when they see time   8
They'll go or come. If so, be patient, sister.
ADRIANA
Why should their liberty than ours be more?
LUCIANA
Because their business still lies out o' door.   11
ADRIANA
Look when I serve him so, he takes it ill.   12
LUCIANA
O, know he is the bridle of your will.
ADRIANA
There's none but asses will be bridled so.
LUCIANA
Why, headstrong liberty is lashed with woe.   15
There's nothing situate under heaven's eye
But hath his bound, in earth, in sea, in sky.   17
The beasts, the fishes, and the wingèd fowls
Are their males' subjects and at their controls.
Man, more divine, the master of all these,
Lord of the wide world and wild watery seas,
Endued with intellectual sense and souls,   22
Of more preeminence than fish and fowls,
Are masters to their females, and their lords.
Then let your will attend on their accords.   25
ADRIANA
This servitude makes you to keep unwed.

---

61 charge responsibility.   **from** out of   **63 post** haste   **64 post** door-
post of a tavern used for keeping reckonings   **65 scour** beat (with a
pun on the idea of keeping score)   **66 maw** stomach. (Applied usually to animals.)   **73 disposed** disposed of   **75 the Phoenix** the sign
of Antipholus of Ephesus' shop. (He lives and carries on his business
in the same dwelling.) In mythology, a phoenix is a fabulous bird that
periodically is regenerated from its own ashes.   **78 bestowed** deposited   **79 sconce** head   **80 stands on** insists on, engages in   **90 hie**
hasten   **94 an** if.   **take my heels** take to my heels

96 The . . . money the rascal has cheated me out of all my money
97 cozenage cheating   **101 mountebanks** charlatans   **102 liberties of
sin** persons allowed improper freedom to sin (with a suggestion of certain districts, as in the London area, that were exempt from civic jurisdiction and were, in a punning sense, places of ''license'')
2.1 Location: The house of Antipholus of Ephesus.
8 Time time alone.   **see time** see fit   **11 still** always   **12 Look when**
whenever   **15 lashed** scourged, castigated; also, bound   **17 his** its
22 intellectual sense reason   **25 accords** consent

LUCIANA
Not this, but troubles of the marriage bed.

ADRIANA
But, were you wedded, you would bear some sway.

LUCIANA
Ere I learn love, I'll practice to obey.

ADRIANA
How if your husband start some other where?   30

LUCIANA
Till he come home again, I would forbear.

ADRIANA
Patience unmoved! No marvel though she pause;
They can be meek that have no other cause.   33
A wretched soul, bruised with adversity,
We bid be quiet when we hear it cry;
But were we burdened with like weight of pain,
As much or more we should ourselves complain.
So thou, that hast no unkind mate to grieve thee,
With urging helpless patience would relieve me;   39
But if thou live to see like right bereft,   40
This fool-begged patience in thee will be left.   41

LUCIANA
Well, I will marry one day, but to try.   42
Here comes your man; now is your husband nigh.

Enter Dromio of Ephesus.

ADRIANA
Say, is your tardy master now at hand?

E. DROMIO   Nay, he's at two hands with me, and that   45
my two ears can witness.

ADRIANA
Say, didst thou speak with him? Know'st thou his
mind?

E. DROMIO
I? Ay, he told his mind upon mine ear.   48
Beshrew his hand, I scarce could understand it.   49

LUCIANA
Spake he so doubtfully thou couldst not feel his
meaning?   50

E. DROMIO   Nay, he struck so plainly I could too well
feel his blows, and withal so doubtfully that I could   52
scarce understand them.

ADRIANA
But say, I prithee, is he coming home?
It seems he hath great care to please his wife.

E. DROMIO
Why, mistress, sure my master is horn-mad.   56

ADRIANA
Horn-mad, thou villain?

E. DROMIO   I mean not cuckold-mad,
But sure he is stark mad.

When I desired him to come home to dinner,
He asked me for a thousand marks in gold.
" 'Tis dinnertime," quoth I. "My gold!" quoth he.
"Your meat doth burn," quoth I. "My gold!" quoth
he.
"Will you come home?" quoth I. "My gold!" quoth
he.
"Where is the thousand marks I gave thee, villain?"
"The pig," quoth I, "is burned." "My gold!" quoth
he.
"My mistress, sir—" quoth I. "Hang up thy mistress!   66
I know not thy mistress. Out on thy mistress!"

LUCIANA   Quoth who?

E. DROMIO   Quoth my master.
"I know," quoth he, "no house, no wife, no
mistress."
So that my errand, due unto my tongue,   71
I thank him, I bare home upon my shoulders;   72
For, in conclusion, he did beat me there.

ADRIANA
Go back again, thou slave, and fetch him home.

E. DROMIO
Go back again and be new beaten home?
For God's sake, send some other messenger.

ADRIANA
Back, slave, or I will break thy pate across.

E. DROMIO
And he will bless that cross with other beating.   78
Between you I shall have a holy head.   79

ADRIANA
Hence, prating peasant! Fetch thy master home.
[*She beats Dromio.*]

E. DROMIO
Am I so round with you as you with me,   81
That like a football you do spurn me thus?
You spurn me hence, and he will spurn me hither.
If I last in this service, you must case me in leather.
[*Exit.*]

LUCIANA
Fie, how impatience loureth in your face!   85

ADRIANA
His company must do his minions grace,   86
Whilst I at home starve for a merry look.
Hath homely age th' alluring beauty took
From my poor cheek? Then hath he wasted it.   89
Are my discourses dull? Barren my wit?   90
If voluble and sharp discourse be marred,   91
Unkindness blunts it more than marble hard.   92

30 **start . . . where** i.e., goes off elsewhere, after other women
33 **other cause** cause to be otherwise   39 **helpless** unavailing, unprofitable   40 **see . . . bereft** see your rights similarly taken away
41 **This . . . left** you will abandon this foolishly urged patience
42 **but to try** i.e., just to put it to the test   45 **at two hands** (alluding
to the beating he received at 1.2.92)   48 **told** (punning on "tolled")
49 **Beshrew** bad luck to.   **understand** (with pun on "stand under";
also in line 53)   50 **doubtfully** ambiguously   52 **doubtfully** dreadfully
56 **horn-mad** mad as a horned beast (with a quibble on the sense of
rage at being made a cuckold)

66 **Hang up** i.e., to hell with   71 **due . . . tongue** which I should
have delivered by my tongue   72 **I bare . . . shoulders** I took in the
form of a beating   78 **he . . . cross** i.e., he will add further devotion
in the form of a beating. (There is a pun on "to bless," to wound,
from the French *blesser. Cross* is a quibble on *across* in the previous
line.)   79 **holy** (punning on the sense "full of holes")   81 **round**
plainspoken (with pun on the sense of "spherical")   85 **loureth**
frowns, scowls   86 **minions** paramours, darlings.   **grace** honor, favor   89 **wasted** (1) squandered (2) laid waste to, ruined   90 **discourses** conversations   91 **voluble** fluent, agile   91–92 **sharp . . .
hard** (*Sharp discourse* is imagined as a knife that is blunted by his unkindness even more than it would be by hard marble.)

Do their gay vestments his affections bait?   93
That's not my fault; he's master of my state.   94
What ruins are in me that can be found
By him not ruined? Then is he the ground   96
Of my defeatures. My decayèd fair   97
A sunny look of his would soon repair.
But, too unruly deer, he breaks the pale   99
And feeds from home. Poor I am but his stale.   100

LUCIANA
Self-harming jealousy! Fie, beat it hence!

ADRIANA
Unfeeling fools can with such wrongs dispense.   102
I know his eye doth homage otherwhere,
Or else what lets it but he would be here?   104
Sister, you know he promised me a chain.
Would that alone o' love he would detain,   106
So he would keep fair quarter with his bed!   107
I see the jewel best enamelèd   108
Will lose his beauty; yet the gold bides still   109
That others touch, and often touching will   110
Wear gold; and no man that hath a name   111
By falsehood and corruption doth it shame.   112
Since that my beauty cannot please his eye,
I'll weep what's left away, and weeping die.

LUCIANA
How many fond fools serve mad jealousy!   115

Exeunt.

2.2   *Enter Antipholus of Syracuse.*

S. ANTIPHOLUS
The gold I gave to Dromio is laid up
Safe at the Centaur, and the heedful slave
Is wandered forth in care to seek me out
By computation and mine host's report.   4
I could not speak with Dromio since at first
I sent him from the mart. See, here he comes.

Enter Dromio of Syracuse.

How now, sir, is your merry humor altered?
As you love strokes, so jest with me again.   8
You know no Centaur? You received no gold?
Your mistress sent to have me home to dinner?

My house was at the Phoenix? Wast thou mad,
That thus so madly thou didst answer me?

S. DROMIO
What answer, sir? When spake I such a word?

S. ANTIPHOLUS
Even now, even here, not half an hour since.

S. DROMIO
I did not see you since you sent me hence
Home to the Centaur with the gold you gave me.

S. ANTIPHOLUS
Villain, thou didst deny the gold's receipt
And toldst me of a mistress and a dinner,
For which I hope thou felt'st I was displeased.

S. DROMIO
I am glad to see you in this merry vein.
What means this jest? I pray you, master, tell me.

S. ANTIPHOLUS
Yea, dost thou jeer and flout me in the teeth?   22
Think'st thou I jest? Hold, take thou that, and that.
Beats Dromio.

S. DROMIO
Hold, sir, for God's sake! Now your jest is earnest.   24
Upon what bargain do you give it me?

S. ANTIPHOLUS
Because that I familiarly sometimes
Do use you for my fool and chat with you,
Your sauciness will jest upon my love   28
And make a common of my serious hours.   29
When the sun shines let foolish gnats make sport,
But creep in crannies when he hides his beams.
If you will jest with me, know my aspect   32
And fashion your demeanor to my looks,
Or I will beat this method in your sconce.   34

S. DROMIO "Sconce" call you it? So you would leave battering, I had rather have it a head. An you use these 36
blows long, I must get a sconce for my head and in- 37
sconce it too, or else I shall seek my wit in my shoul- 38
ders. But I pray, sir, why am I beaten? 39

S. ANTIPHOLUS   Dost thou not know?

S. DROMIO   Nothing, sir, but that I am beaten.

S. ANTIPHOLUS   Shall I tell you why?

S. DROMIO   Ay, sir, and wherefore; for they say every
why hath a wherefore.

S. ANTIPHOLUS "Why," first—for flouting me; and then,
"wherefore"—for urging it the second time to me.

S. DROMIO
Was there ever any man thus beaten out of season, 47
When in the why and the wherefore is neither
  rhyme nor reason?
Well, sir, I thank you.

S. ANTIPHOLUS   Thank me, sir, for what?

93 affections passions. **bait** entice **94 state** outward estate, condition, i.e., clothes **96 ground** cause **97 defeatures** disfigurements.
decayèd fair impaired or perished beauty **99 pale** enclosure
100 from away from. **stale** rejected lover who has become a laughingstock (with a pun on *stale,* tiresomely lacking in freshness; she is
stale to him, he dear [*deer*] to her) **102 dispense** pardon, condone
by dispensation **104 lets** hinders **106 Would . . . detain** would
that he would withhold only that token of his affection (?) **107 So
. . . bed** provided he would remain faithful to his marriage bed
108–112 I see . . . shame (A difficult passage, evidently corrupt.
Adriana seemingly compares her beauty to that of a well-enameled
jewel that tarnishes in time through neglect, whereas some beauty,
like gold, is often touched and hence retains its luster through use;
this latter kind of beauty is not shamed through falsehood and corruption by men of *name* or reputation like Antipholus of Ephesus, as
Adriana feels she is being shamed.) **109 his** its **115 fond** doting
2.2 Location: The street before Antipholus of Ephesus' house.
4 computation estimation, reckoning **8 strokes** blows

22 in the teeth to my face **24 earnest** serious (with a pun on the financial sense: money paid as an installment to secure a bargain)
28 jest upon trifle with **29 common** public playground **32 aspect**
look, expression; also, astrological favor or disfavor of a planet
34 sconce head (with pun on the meaning "fort" in line 35 and "helmet" or "protective covering" in line 37; the *battering,* lines 35–36,
is both a beating and assault by a battering ram) **36 An** if **37–
38 insconce** shelter within a sconce or fortification **38–39 I shall
. . . shoulders** i.e., my head will be beaten into my shoulders
47 out of season inappropriately

S. DROMIO   Marry, sir, for this something that you gave 51
me for nothing.

S. ANTIPHOLUS   I'll make you amends next, to give you
nothing for something. But say, sir, is it dinnertime?

S. DROMIO   No, sir, I think the meat wants that I have. 55

S. ANTIPHOLUS   In good time, sir, what's that? 56

S. DROMIO   Basting. 57

S. ANTIPHOLUS   Well, sir, then 'twill be dry.

S. DROMIO   If it be, sir, I pray you, eat none of it.

S. ANTIPHOLUS   Your reason?

S. DROMIO   Lest it make you choleric and purchase me 61
another dry basting. 62

S. ANTIPHOLUS   Well, sir, learn to jest in good time.
There's a time for all things.

S. DROMIO   I durst have denied that before you were so
choleric.

S. ANTIPHOLUS   By what rule, sir?

S. DROMIO   Marry, sir, by a rule as plain as the plain
bald pate of Father Time himself.

S. ANTIPHOLUS   Let's hear it.

S. DROMIO   There's no time for a man to recover his
hair that grows bald by nature.

S. ANTIPHOLUS   May he not do it by fine and recovery? 73

S. DROMIO   Yes, to pay a fine for a periwig and recover
the lost hair of another man.

S. ANTIPHOLUS   Why is Time such a niggard of hair,
being, as it is, so plentiful an excrement? 77

S. DROMIO   Because it is a blessing that he bestows on
beasts, and what he hath scanted men in hair he hath
given them in wit.

S. ANTIPHOLUS   Why, but there's many a man hath
more hair than wit.

S. DROMIO   Not a man of those but he hath the wit to 83
lose his hair. 84

S. ANTIPHOLUS   Why, thou didst conclude hairy men
plain dealers without wit.

S. DROMIO   The plainer dealer, the sooner lost. Yet he 87
loseth it in a kind of jollity. 88

S. ANTIPHOLUS   For what reason?

S. DROMIO   For two, and sound ones too.

S. ANTIPHOLUS   Nay, not sound, I pray you. 91

S. DROMIO   Sure ones then.

S. ANTIPHOLUS   Nay, not sure, in a thing falsing. 93

S. DROMIO   Certain ones then.

S. ANTIPHOLUS   Name them.

S. DROMIO   The one, to save the money that he spends
in tiring; the other, that at dinner they should not drop 97
in his porridge.

S. ANTIPHOLUS   You would all this time have proved
there is no time for all things.

S. DROMIO   Marry, and did, sir; namely, e'en no time to
recover hair lost by nature.

S. ANTIPHOLUS   But your reason was not substantial
why there is no time to recover.

S. DROMIO   Thus I mend it: Time himself is bald and
therefore to the world's end will have bald followers.

S. ANTIPHOLUS   I knew 'twould be a bald conclusion. 107
But soft, who wafts us yonder? 108

Enter Adriana [beckoning them], and Luciana.

ADRIANA
Ay, ay, Antipholus, look strange and frown. 109
Some other mistress hath thy sweet aspects;
I am not Adriana, nor thy wife.
The time was once when thou unurged wouldst
    vow
That never words were music to thine ear,
That never object pleasing in thine eye,
That never touch well welcome to thy hand,
That never meat sweet-savored in thy taste,
Unless I spake, or looked, or touched, or carved to
    thee.
How comes it now, my husband, O, how comes it,
That thou art then estrangèd from thyself? 119
Thyself I call it, being strange to me
That, undividable, incorporate,
Am better than thy dear self's better part.
Ah, do not tear away thyself from me!
For know, my love, as easy mayst thou fall 124
A drop of water in the breaking gulf,
And take unmingled thence that drop again
Without addition or diminishing,
As take from me thyself and not me too. 128
How dearly would it touch thee to the quick, 129
Shouldst thou but hear I were licentious
And that this body, consecrate to thee, 131
By ruffian lust should be contaminate! 132
Wouldst thou not spit at me, and spurn at me,
And hurl the name of husband in my face,
And tear the stained skin off my harlot brow,
And from my false hand cut the wedding ring,
And break it with a deep-divorcing vow?
I know thou canst, and therefore see thou do it. 138
I am possessed with an adulterate blot;
My blood is mingled with the crime of lust.
For if we two be one, and thou play false,
I do digest the poison of thy flesh,
Being strumpeted by thy contagion. 143

---

51 Marry i.e., truly. (A shortened form of the oath "by the Virgin Mary.")   **55 wants that** lacks that which   **56 In good time** indeed   **57 Basting** (1) moistening with butter or drippings during cooking (2) beating   **61 choleric** (Hot or dry food was thought to produce or aggravate the choleric or irascible humor.)   **62 dry basting** hard beating   **73 fine and recovery** a legal procedure for converting an entailed estate, one in which the property is limited to specified heirs, into a fee simple, one in which the owner has unqualified ownership   **77 excrement** outgrowth (of hair)   **83–84 he . . . hair** (A reference to the venereal diseases in which loss of hair was a symptom.)   **87 dealer** i.e., dealer with women   **88 a kind of jollity** i.e., sexual pleasure   **91 not sound** invalid (with a pun on "venereally diseased")   **93 falsing** deceptive (continuing the joke on venereal disease)   **97 tiring** dressing the hair

107 bald i.e., senseless, stupid (continuing the joke about baldness)   **108 soft** gently, wait a minute.   **wafts** beckons   **109 strange** estranged, distant   **119 then** therefore.   **estrangèd from thyself** (1) behaving unlike yourself (2) estranged from me, your other half   **124 fall** let fall   **128 and not me too** i.e., even when we are separated we are indivisible   **129 the quick** the most sensitive or vulnerable part   **131 consecrate** consecrated   **132 contaminate** contaminated   **138 see thou do it** i.e., I imagine your doing it, or, go ahead (since you know you have the right) if you hear I am unfaithful   **143 strumpeted** made a strumpet

Keep then fair league and truce with thy true bed,   144
I live distained, thou undishonorèd.   145

S. ANTIPHOLUS
Plead you to me, fair dame? I know you not.
In Ephesus I am but two hours old,
As strange unto your town as to your talk,
Who, every word by all my wit being scanned,   149
Wants wit in all one word to understand.   150

LUCIANA
Fie, brother, how the world is changed with you!
When were you wont to use my sister thus?   152
She sent for you by Dromio home to dinner.

S. ANTIPHOLUS   By Dromio?

S. DROMIO   By me?

ADRIANA
By thee; and this thou didst return from him:
That he did buffet thee and in his blows
Denied my house for his, me for his wife.

S. ANTIPHOLUS
Did you converse, sir, with this gentlewoman?
What is the course and drift of your compact?   160

S. DROMIO
I, sir? I never saw her till this time.

S. ANTIPHOLUS
Villain, thou liest, for even her very words
Didst thou deliver to me on the mart.

S. DROMIO
I never spake with her in all my life.

S. ANTIPHOLUS
How can she thus then call us by our names,
Unless it be by inspiration?

ADRIANA
How ill agrees it with your gravity   167
To counterfeit thus grossly with your slave,   168
Abetting him to thwart me in my mood!   169
Be it my wrong you are from me exempt,   170
But wrong not that wrong with a more contempt.   171
Come, I will fasten on this sleeve of thine.
                              [She clings to him.]
Thou art an elm, my husband, I a vine,
Whose weakness, married to thy stronger state,
Makes me with thy strength to communicate.   175
If aught possess thee from me, it is dross,   176
Usurping ivy, brier, or idle moss,   177
Who, all for want of pruning, with intrusion   178
Infect thy sap and live on thy confusion.   179

S. ANTIPHOLUS [aside]
To me she speaks; she moves me for her theme.   180

What, was I married to her in my dream?
Or sleep I now and think I hear all this?
What error drives our eyes and ears amiss?
Until I know this sure uncertainty,   184
I'll entertain the offered fallacy.   185

LUCIANA
Dromio, go bid the servants spread for dinner.   186

S. DROMIO
O, for my beads! I cross me for a sinner.   187
                              [He crosses himself.]
This is the fairy land. O spite of spites,
We talk with goblins, elves, and sprites!   189
If we obey them not, this will ensue:
They'll suck our breath or pinch us black and blue.   191

LUCIANA
Why prat'st thou to thyself and answer'st not?   192
Dromio, thou drone, thou snail, thou slug, thou sot!   193

S. DROMIO
I am transformèd, master, am not I?

S. ANTIPHOLUS
I think thou art in mind, and so am I.

S. DROMIO
Nay, master, both in mind and in my shape.

S. ANTIPHOLUS
Thou hast thine own form.

S. DROMIO   No, I am an ape.   197

LUCIANA
If thou art changed to aught, 'tis to an ass.

S. DROMIO
'Tis true; she rides me and I long for grass.   199
'Tis so, I am an ass; else it could never be
But I should know her as well as she knows me.

ADRIANA
Come, come, no longer will I be a fool,
To put the finger in the eye and weep
Whilst man and master laughs my woes to scorn.
Come, sir, to dinner.—Dromio, keep the gate.—
Husband, I'll dine above with you today   206
And shrive you of a thousand idle pranks.—   207
Sirrah, if any ask you for your master,   208
Say he dines forth, and let no creature enter.—   209
Come, sister.—Dromio, play the porter well.

S. ANTIPHOLUS [aside]
Am I in earth, in heaven, or in hell?
Sleeping or waking, mad or well-advised?   212
Known unto these, and to myself disguised?
I'll say as they say, and persever so,
And in this mist at all adventures go.   215

---

144 Keep . . . truce i.e., if you keep faithful covenant   **145 distained** unstained (by contagion)   **149–150 Who . . . understand** i.e., and I, though listening intently to every word, cannot understand one word of what you've said   **152 use** treat   **160 compact** plot **167 gravity** social dignity   **168 grossly** obviously   **169 Abetting** helping.   **mood** anger   **170–171 Be it . . . contempt** even if we agree in blaming me that you are alienated from me, don't make that fault worse by subjecting it to greater contempt   **175 with . . . communicate** share in your strength   **176 If . . . dross** if anything usurps my possession of you, it is an impure substance   **177 idle** unprofitable   **178 Who** which.   **want** lack.   **intrusion** forced entry **179 confusion** ruin   **180 moves . . . theme** appeals to me as her subject of discourse

184 know . . . uncertainty can fathom the meaning of what is certainly a mystery. (Stated as an oxymoron.)   **185 entertain** accept. **fallacy** delusive notion, error   **186 spread** set the table   **187 beads** rosary beads   **189 sprites** spirits   **191 suck our breath** (This piece of folklore was perhaps connected with the old idea that the breath of a person was that person's soul. Fairies were famous for sucking and pinching.)   **192 prat'st thou** do you chatter   **193 sot** fool   **197 ape** i.e., counterfeit   **199 for grass** for freedom (as a horse put out to pasture)   **206 above** i.e., on the second floor, above Antipholus' shop **207 shrive** hear confession and give absolution   **208 Sirrah** (Customary form of address to servants.)   **209 forth** away from home **212 well-advised** in my right mind   **215 at all adventures** whatever may happen

S. DROMIO
    Master, shall I be porter at the gate?

ADRIANA
    Ay, and let none enter, lest I break your pate.

LUCIANA
    Come, come, Antipholus, we dine too late.
        [*Exeunt. Dromio of Syracuse remains as porter,
        visible to the audience but not to those approaching
        the door.*]

3.1   *Enter Antipholus of Ephesus, his man Dromio,*
        Angelo the goldsmith, and Balthasar the merchant.

E. ANTIPHOLUS
    Good Signor Angelo, you must excuse us all;
    My wife is shrewish when I keep not hours.   2
    Say that I lingered with you at your shop
    To see the making of her carcanet   4
    And that tomorrow you will bring it home.—
    But here's a villain that would face me down   6
    He met me on the mart, and that I beat him
    And charged him with a thousand marks in gold,   8
    And that I did deny my wife and house.   9
    Thou drunkard, thou, what didst thou mean by
        this?

E. DROMIO
    Say what you will, sir, but I know what I know.
    That you beat me at the mart, I have your hand to
        show.   12
    If the skin were parchment and the blows you gave
        were ink,
    Your own handwriting would tell you what I think.

E. ANTIPHOLUS
    I think thou art an ass.

E. DROMIO   Marry, so it doth appear
    By the wrongs I suffer and the blows I bear.
    I should kick, being kicked, and, being at that pass,   17
    You would keep from my heels and beware of
        an ass.

E. ANTIPHOLUS
    You're sad, Signor Balthasar. Pray God our cheer   19
    May answer my good will and your good welcome
        here.   20

BALTHASAR
    I hold your dainties cheap, sir, and your welcome
        dear.   21

E. ANTIPHOLUS
    O Signor Balthasar, either at flesh or fish,

A table full of welcome makes scarce one dainty
        dish.   23

BALTHASAR
    Good meat, sir, is common; that every churl affords.   24

E. ANTIPHOLUS
    And welcome more common, for that's nothing but
        words.

BALTHASAR
    Small cheer and great welcome makes a merry feast.

E. ANTIPHOLUS
    Ay, to a niggardly host and more sparing guest.   27
    But though my cates be mean, take them in good
        part;   28
    Better cheer may you have, but not with better
        heart.
        [*They approach the door of Antipholus of Ephesus'
        house.*]
    But soft! My door is locked. [*To Dromio.*] Go bid
        them let us in.

E. DROMIO [*calling*]
    Maud, Bridget, Marian, Cicely, Gillian, Ginn!

S. DROMIO [*speaking from the other side of the door*]
    Mome, malt-horse, capon, coxcomb, idiot, patch!   32
    Either get thee from the door or sit down at the
        hatch.   33
    Dost thou conjure for wenches, that thou call'st for
        such store   34
    When one is one too many? Go, get thee from the
        door.

E. DROMIO
    What patch is made our porter? My master stays in
        the street.   36

S. DROMIO
    Let him walk from whence he came, lest he catch
        cold on 's feet.   37

E. ANTIPHOLUS
    Who talks within there? Ho, open the door!

S. DROMIO
    Right, sir, I'll tell you when, an you'll tell me
        wherefore.   39

E. ANTIPHOLUS
    Wherefore? For my dinner. I have not dined today.

S. DROMIO
    Nor today here you must not. Come again when
        you may.

E. ANTIPHOLUS
    What art thou that keep'st me out from the house
        I owe?   42

**3.1 Location: Before the house of Antipholus of Ephesus. The scene
is continuous with the previous one.**
2 keep not hours am not punctual   **4 carcanet** necklace (the *chain* of
2.1.105 and line 115 below)   **6 face me down** maintain to my face
that   **8 charged** entrusted.   **with** i.e., with possession of   **9 deny** disown   **12 hand** i.e., handiwork on my body (with a pun on "handwriting")   **17 at that pass** in that situation   **19 sad** serious.   **cheer**
entertainment   **20 answer** agree with, match   **21 dainties** delicacies.
cheap of minor importance.   **dear** of primary importance

23 makes scarce scarcely equals   **24 churl** one of lower station
27 sparing frugal   **28 cates** provisions, dainties.   **mean** plain, simple
32 s.d. speaking . . . door (Dromio of Syracuse has remained onstage
since the end of the previous scene, visible to the audience but not to
those at the door. Alternatively, he could exit at the end of 2.2 and
speak now *within*, or enter at this point, but neither solution seems
satisfactory. Compare the entrances of Luce and Adriana at lines 47
and 60.)   **32 Mome** dolt, blockhead.   **malt-horse** brewer's horse;
stupid person.   **patch** fool, clown   **33 hatch** half-door that can be
kept closed while the upper half is opened   **34 conjure for** summon
by magic.   **store** quantity (of wenches)   **36 What . . . porter?** i.e.,
what clown is this who is acting as gatekeeper?   **stays** waits   **37 on's**
in his   **39 an** if.   **wherefore** why   **42 owe** own

S. DROMIO
The porter for this time, sir, and my name is
Dromio.   43

E. DROMIO
O villain! Thou hast stol'n both mine office and my
name.
The one ne'er got me credit, the other mickle blame. 45
If thou hadst been Dromio today in my place,
Thou wouldst have changed thy face for a name or
thy name for an ass.   47

*Enter Luce [above, concealed from Antipholus of
Ephesus and his companions].*

LUCE
What a coil is there, Dromio? Who are those at the
gate?   48

E. DROMIO
Let my master in, Luce.

LUCE   Faith, no, he comes too late,
And so tell your master.

E. DROMIO   O Lord, I must laugh!
Have at you with a proverb: Shall I set in my staff?   51

LUCE
Have at you with another: that's—When, can you
tell?   52

S. DROMIO
If thy name be called Luce, Luce, thou hast
answered him well.

E. ANTIPHOLUS *[to Luce]*
Do you hear, you minion? You'll let us in, I hope?   54

LUCE
I thought to have asked you.

S. DROMIO   And you said no.

E. DROMIO
So, come help. *[They beat the door.]* Well struck!
There was blow for blow.

E. ANTIPHOLUS *[to Luce]*
Thou baggage, let me in.

LUCE   Can you tell for whose sake? 57

E. DROMIO
Master, knock the door hard.

LUCE   Let him knock till it ache.

E. ANTIPHOLUS
You'll cry for this, minion, if I beat the door down.
[He knocks.]

LUCE
What needs all that, and a pair of stocks in the
town?   60

*Enter Adriana [above, concealed, like Luce and
Dromio of Syracuse, from those at the door].*

ADRIANA
Who is that at the door that keeps all this noise?   61

S. DROMIO
By my troth, your town is troubled with unruly
boys.

E. ANTIPHOLUS
Are you there, wife? You might have come before.

ADRIANA
Your wife, sir knave? Go get you from the door.
[Exit with Luce.]

E. DROMIO
If you went in pain, master, this "knave" would go
sore.   65

ANGELO
Here is neither cheer, sir, nor welcome. We would
fain have either.   66

BALTHASAR
In debating which was best, we shall part with
neither.   67

E. DROMIO
They stand at the door, master. Bid them welcome
hither.   68

E. ANTIPHOLUS
There is something in the wind, that we cannot
get in.   69

E. DROMIO
You would say so, master, if your garments were
thin.
Your cake is warm within; you stand here in the
cold.
It would make a man mad as a buck to be so bought
and sold.   72

E. ANTIPHOLUS
Go fetch me something. I'll break ope the gate.

S. DROMIO
Break any breaking here, and I'll break your knave's
pate.

E. DROMIO
A man may break a word with you, sir, and words
are but wind,   75
Ay, and break it in your face, so he break it not
behind.   76

---

43 for this time at this moment, for the time being   **45 The one . . .
blame** i.e., my name has never got me credit, my office has got me
much blame   **47 thy face for a name** i.e., to escape blame (?)
(Though perhaps this should read *thy pate for an aim,* i.e., for a blow,
as various editors have suggested.)   **s.d. Enter Luce [above]** (Here and
at line 60, Luce and then Adriana may enter above in such a way that
the audience understands them not to be visible to those who are
calling at the door.)   **48 coil** noise, disturbance   **51 Have . . . staff**
let me come at you with a proverb: Shall I take up my abode here?
(With a phallic joke.)   **52 When . . . tell** i.e., never. (Another proverbial expression, used derisively to turn aside a question.)   **54 minion** hussy.   **hope** (A line following with an answering rhyme may be
missing; perhaps it would have cleared up the present obscurity of
lines 55 and 56.)   **57 baggage** good-for-nothing

60 What . . . town i.e., why do we need to put up with this disturbance, when the town provides stocks for punishment?   **61 keeps**
keeps up   **65 If . . . sore** i.e., yourself and this "knave" she mentions are the same person.   **went** i.e., were   **66 fain** gladly   **67 debating** discussing.   **part** depart   **68 Bid them welcome** (Said ironically.)   **69 something . . . wind** something strange going on.
(Dromio of Ephesus in line 70, takes the phrase literally.)   **72 as a
buck** i.e., as a male deer in rutting season. (Compare *horn-mad,*
2.1.57.)   **bought and sold** i.e., betrayed, ill-treated   **75 break a word**
exchange words (punning on *break* in the previous lines)   **76 behind**
i.e., in farting

S. DROMIO
It seems thou want'st breaking. Out upon thee,
   hind!   77
E. DROMIO
Here's too much "Out upon thee!" I pray thee, let
   me in.
S. DROMIO
Ay, when fowls have no feathers and fish have no
   fin.   *[Exit.]* 79
E. ANTIPHOLUS
Well, I'll break in. Go borrow me a crow.   80
E. DROMIO
A crow without feather? Master, mean you so?
For a fish without a fin, there's a fowl without a
   feather.—
If a crow help us in, sirrah, we'll pluck a crow
   together.   83
E. ANTIPHOLUS
Go, get thee gone. Fetch me an iron crow.
BALTHASAR
Have patience, sir. O, let it not be so!
Herein you war against your reputation
And draw within the compass of suspect   87
Th' unviolated honor of your wife.
Once this: your long experience of her wisdom,   89
Her sober virtue, years, and modesty,   90
Plead on her part some cause to you unknown;
And doubt not, sir, but she will well excuse   92
Why at this time the doors are made against you.   93
Be ruled by me. Depart in patience,
And let us to the Tiger all to dinner,   95
And about evening come yourself alone
To know the reason of this strange restraint.
If by strong hand you offer to break in   98
Now in the stirring passage of the day,   99
A vulgar comment will be made of it,   100
And that supposèd by the common rout   101
Against your yet ungallèd estimation,   102
That may with foul intrusion enter in
And dwell upon your grave when you are dead;
For slander lives upon succession,   105
Forever housed where it gets possession.
E. ANTIPHOLUS
You have prevailed. I will depart in quiet,
And, in despite of mirth, mean to be merry.   108
I know a wench of excellent discourse,
Pretty and witty, wild and yet, too, gentle.
There will we dine. This woman that I mean,

My wife—but, I protest, without desert—   112
Hath oftentimes upbraided me withal.
To her will we to dinner. *[To Angelo.]* Get you home
And fetch the chain; by this I know 'tis made.   115
Bring it, I pray you, to the Porcupine,   116
For there's the house. That chain will I bestow—
Be it for nothing but to spite my wife—
Upon mine hostess there. Good sir, make haste.
Since mine own doors refuse to entertain me,
I'll knock elsewhere, to see if they'll disdain me.
ANGELO
I'll meet you at that place some hour hence.
E. ANTIPHOLUS
Do so. This jest shall cost me some expense. *Exeunt.*

3.2   *Enter Luciana with Antipholus of Syracuse.*

LUCIANA
And may it be that you have quite forgot   1
   A husband's office? Shall, Antipholus,   2
Even in the spring of love, thy love springs rot?   3
   Shall love, in building, grow so ruinous?
If you did wed my sister for her wealth,
   Then for her wealth's sake use her with more
     kindness;
Or if you like elsewhere, do it by stealth:
   Muffle your false love with some show of
     blindness.   8
Let not my sister read it in your eye;
   Be not thy tongue thy own shame's orator;
Look sweet, speak fair, become disloyalty;   11
   Apparel vice like virtue's harbinger.   12
Bear a fair presence, though your heart be tainted;
   Teach sin the carriage of a holy saint;   14
Be secret-false. What need she be acquainted?
   What simple thief brags of his own attaint?   16
'Tis double wrong to truant with your bed   17
   And let her read it in thy looks at board.   18
Shame hath a bastard fame, well managèd;   19
   Ill deeds is doubled with an evil word.
Alas, poor women! Make us but believe,
   Being compact of credit, that you love us.   22
Though others have the arm, show us the sleeve;
   We in your motion turn and you may move us.   24
Then, gentle brother, get you in again.
   Comfort my sister, cheer her, call her wife.

---

77 thou . . . breaking you need to be broken in by a beating. **hind** boor, menial **79 s.d. Exit** (If Dromio of Syracuse has been visible to the audience, he probably leaves at this point.) **80 crow** crowbar (introducing a quibble by Dromio of Ephesus) **83 pluck . . . together** pick a bone together, settle accounts **87 draw . . . suspect** bring under suspicion **89 Once this** to be brief, in short **90 virtue** merit, general excellence **92 excuse** justify **93 made** fastened **95 the Tiger** (Presumably an inn.) **98 offer** venture **99 stirring passage** bustle **100 vulgar** public **101 And . . . rout** and it will be presumed true by everyone **102 yet . . . estimation** still unsullied reputation **105 lives upon succession** passes from one generation to the next **108 in . . . mirth** despite my not feeling mirthful, or, in spite of the mockery

112 desert my deserving it **115 this** this time **116 Porcupine** (The name of the Courtesan's house.)
3.2 Location: Antipholus of Ephesus' house or in front of it, certainly so by line 163.
1 may can **2 office** duty **3 love springs** tender shoots of love **8 Muffle** hide. **show of blindness** deceptive appearance **11 fair** courteously. **become disloyalty** carry off your infidelity gracefully **12 harbinger** messenger, forerunner **14 carriage** demeanor **16 simple** simple-minded. **attaint** stain, dishonor; or possibly, conviction of crime **17 truant with** be faithless to **18 board** table **19 bastard fame** sham reputation **22 Being . . . credit** i.e., we who are made so that we are quick to believe **24 We . . . turn** we are governed by your motion, orbit (referring to the motion of the heavenly spheres)

'Tis holy sport to be a little vain   27
    When the sweet breath of flattery conquers strife.
S. ANTIPHOLUS
Sweet mistress—what your name is else, I know
    not,   29
    Nor by what wonder you do hit of mine—   30
Less in your knowledge and your grace you show
    not
    Than our earth's wonder, more than earth divine.   32
Teach me, dear creature, how to think and speak;
    Lay open to my earthy-gross conceit,   34
Smothered in errors, feeble, shallow, weak,
    The folded meaning of your words' deceit.   36
Against my soul's pure truth why labor you   37
    To make it wander in an unknown field?
Are you a god? Would you create me new?
    Transform me then, and to your power I'll yield.
But if that I am I, then well I know
    Your weeping sister is no wife of mine,
Nor to her bed no homage do I owe.
    Far more, far more to you do I decline.   44
O, train me not, sweet mermaid, with thy note,   45
    To drown me in thy sister's flood of tears!
Sing, siren, for thyself, and I will dote.
    Spread o'er the silver waves thy golden hairs,
And as a bed I'll take them and there lie,   49
    And in that glorious supposition think
He gains by death that hath such means to die.
    Let Love, being light, be drownèd if she sink!   52
LUCIANA
What, are you mad, that you do reason so?   53
S. ANTIPHOLUS
Not mad, but mated—how, I do not know.   54
LUCIANA
It is a fault that springeth from your eye.
S. ANTIPHOLUS
For gazing on your beams, fair sun, being by.   56
LUCIANA
Gaze where you should, and that will clear your
    sight.
S. ANTIPHOLUS
As good to wink, sweet love, as look on night.   58
LUCIANA
Why call you me "love"? Call my sister so.
S. ANTIPHOLUS
Thy sister's sister.
LUCIANA   That's my sister.
S. ANTIPHOLUS   No,
It is thyself, mine own self's better part,
Mine eye's clear eye, my dear heart's dearer heart,
My food, my fortune, and my sweet hope's aim,
My sole earth's heaven, and my heaven's claim.   64
LUCIANA
All this my sister is, or else should be.
S. ANTIPHOLUS
Call thyself sister, sweet, for I am thee.   66
Thee will I love and with thee lead my life;
Thou hast no husband yet, nor I no wife.
Give me thy hand.
LUCIANA   O, soft, sir! Hold you still.
I'll fetch my sister, to get her good will.   *Exit.* 70

Enter Dromio of Syracuse, [running].

S. ANTIPHOLUS   Why, how now, Dromio, where
runn'st thou so fast?
S. DROMIO   Do you know me, sir? Am I Dromio? Am I
your man? Am I myself?
S. ANTIPHOLUS   Thou art Dromio, thou art my man,
thou art thyself.
S. DROMIO   I am an ass, I am a woman's man, and be-   77
sides myself.   78
S. ANTIPHOLUS   What woman's man? And how besides   79
thyself?
S. DROMIO   Marry, sir, besides myself I am due to a
woman: one that claims me, one that haunts me, one
that will have me.
S. ANTIPHOLUS   What claim lays she to thee?
S. DROMIO   Marry, sir, such claim as you would lay to
your horse; and she would have me as a beast—not   86
that, I being a beast, she would have me, but that she,
being a very beastly creature, lays claim to me.
S. ANTIPHOLUS   What is she?
S. DROMIO   A very reverend body; ay, such a one as a
man may not speak of without he say "sir-reverence."   91
I have but lean luck in the match, and yet is she a   92
wondrous fat marriage.
S. ANTIPHOLUS   How dost thou mean, a fat marriage?
S. DROMIO   Marry, sir, she's the kitchen wench, and all
grease, and I know not what use to put her to but to   96
make a lamp of her and run from her by her own light.
I warrant her rags and the tallow in them will burn a   98
Poland winter. If she lives till doomsday, she'll burn a 99
week longer than the whole world.
S. ANTIPHOLUS   What complexion is she of?

---

27 **holy sport** virtuous jesting. (An oxymoron.)   **vain** false   **29 what
. . . else** what other name you may have   **30 wonder** miracle.   **hit
of** hit upon, guess   **32 earth's wonder** (Perhaps a reference to Queen
Elizabeth. Antipholus says, "You seem no less wise and graceful than
our divine queen, wonder of the earth.")   **34 earthy-gross conceit**
understanding gross as earth   **36 folded** concealed   **37 Against . . .
you** why are you working to oppose my soul's knowledge of the simple truth?   **44 decline** incline   **45 train** entice.   **mermaid** siren (in
classical myth, one of a group of nymphs who lured sailors to destruction with their sweet singing).   **note** song   **49 take** use   **52 light**
buoyant (with a pun on the sense of "wanton," perhaps carrying forward a common sexual pun in which *to die*, line 51, is to have sexual
climax. The idea in line 52 is that Love cannot possibly sink.)
53 reason talk, argue   **54 mated** amazed, confounded (with quibble
on the sense of "matched with a wife")   **56 by** near   **58 wink** close
the eyes

64 **My sole . . . claim** my sole heaven on earth and my claim on
heaven hereafter   **66 Call . . . thee** call yourself your own sister,
sweet one, because I am part of you, just as you think I should be
part of her   **70 good will** approval. (This is perhaps a mere excuse,
but it may be a sign she is attracted.)   **77–78 besides myself** also
myself (with a pun on the sense of "out of my mind")   **79 besides** (a
further quibble: "in addition to")   **86 a beast** (with a pun on
"abased," reflecting Elizabethan pronunciation of *beast* as "baste")
91 without unless.   **"sir-reverence"** i.e., save your reverence, an expression used in apology for the remark that follows it   **92 lean** poor,
meager   **96 grease** (with a pun on "grace," reflecting Elizabethan
pronunciation)   **98-99 a Poland winter** i.e., a long, cold winter

S. DROMIO   Swart like my shoe, but her face nothing 102
like so clean kept. For why? She sweats a man may go 103
over shoes in the grime of it. 104

S. ANTIPHOLUS   That's a fault that water will mend.

S. DROMIO   No, sir, 'tis in grain. Noah's flood could not 106
do it.

S. ANTIPHOLUS   What's her name?

S. DROMIO   Nell, sir; but her name and three quarters— 109
that's an ell and three quarters—will not measure her 110
from hip to hip.

S. ANTIPHOLUS   Then she bears some breadth?

S. DROMIO   No longer from head to foot than from hip
to hip. She is spherical, like a globe. I could find out
countries in her.

S. ANTIPHOLUS   In what part of her body stands Ireland?

S. DROMIO   Marry, sir, in her buttocks. I found it out by
the bogs.

S. ANTIPHOLUS   Where Scotland?

S. DROMIO   I found it by the barrenness, hard in the 120
palm of the hand.

S. ANTIPHOLUS   Where France?

S. DROMIO   In her forehead, armed and reverted, 123
making war against her heir. 124

S. ANTIPHOLUS   Where England?

S. DROMIO   I looked for the chalky cliffs, but I could 126
find no whiteness in them. But I guess it stood in her 127
chin, by the salt rheum that ran between France and it. 128

S. ANTIPHOLUS   Where Spain?

S. DROMIO   Faith, I saw it not, but I felt it hot in her
breath.

S. ANTIPHOLUS   Where America, the Indies?

S. DROMIO   O, sir, upon her nose, all o'er embellished
with rubies, carbuncles, sapphires, declining their rich 134
aspect to the hot breath of Spain, who sent whole ar- 135
madas of carracks to be ballast at her nose. 136

S. ANTIPHOLUS   Where stood Belgia, the Netherlands?

S. DROMIO   O, sir, I did not look so low. To conclude, 138
this drudge or diviner laid claim to me, called me 139
Dromio, swore I was assured to her, told me what 140
privy marks I had about me—as the mark of my shoul- 141
der, the mole in my neck, the great wart on my left
arm, that I amazed ran from her as a witch.

And, I think, if my breast had not been made of
faith and my heart of steel,
She had transformed me to a curtal dog and made
me turn i' the wheel. 145

S. ANTIPHOLUS
Go, hie thee presently; post to the road. 146
An if the wind blow any way from shore, 147
I will not harbor in this town tonight.
If any bark put forth, come to the mart, 149
Where I will walk till thou return to me.
If everyone knows us and we know none,
'Tis time, I think, to trudge, pack, and be gone. 152

S. DROMIO
As from a bear a man would run for life,
So fly I from her that would be my wife.   *Exit.*

S. ANTIPHOLUS
There's none but witches do inhabit here,
And therefore 'tis high time that I were hence.
She that doth call me husband, even my soul
Doth for a wife abhor. But her fair sister,
Possessed with such a gentle sovereign grace, 159
Of such enchanting presence and discourse,
Hath almost made me traitor to myself.
But, lest myself be guilty to self-wrong, 162
I'll stop mine ears against the mermaid's song.

Enter Angelo with the chain.

ANGELO
Master Antipholus—

S. ANTIPHOLUS   Ay, that's my name.

ANGELO
I know it well, sir. Lo, here's the chain.
I thought to have ta'en you at the Porcupine; 166
The chain unfinished made me stay thus long.
                         [*He presents the chain.*]

S. ANTIPHOLUS
What is your will that I shall do with this?

ANGELO
What please yourself, sir. I have made it for you. 169

S. ANTIPHOLUS
Made it for me, sir? I bespoke it not. 170

ANGELO
Not once, nor twice, but twenty times you have.
Go home with it and please your wife withal,
And soon at suppertime I'll visit you
And then receive my money for the chain.

S. ANTIPHOLUS
I pray you, sir, receive the money now,
For fear you ne'er see chain nor money more.

ANGELO
You are a merry man, sir. Fare you well.   *Exit.*

---

102 Swart swarthy, dark   **103 She sweats a man** she sweats so much
that a man   **104 over shoes** ankle-deep. (Her sweat makes mud of
her face's grime, so deep that a man would be ankle deep in it.)
106 in grain indelible, fast dyed   **109 Nell** (The maidservant appearing in 3.1 is named Luce; usually the two are assumed to be one person.)   **110 an ell** forty-five inches (with a pun on "a Nell")
120 barrenness callused hardness and dryness (perhaps with a pun on
"barren ness," a barren promontory)   **123 reverted** in rebellion. (See
the Introduction for an explanation of the reference to the French
war.)   **124 heir** (with a pun on "hair" and a joke about syphilis as
causing baldness)   **126 chalky cliffs** i.e., her teeth. (In his geographic
metaphor, Dromio of Syracuse identifies white teeth with the cliffs of
Dover.)   **127 them** i.e., her teeth   **128 salt rheum** nasal discharge.
(Here Dromio jokingly makes a comparison to the English Channel.)
134 carbuncles (1) precious stones (2) inflammations of the skin resembling large boils   **134–135 declining . . . aspect** looking or
bending downward   **135–136 armadas of carracks** fleets of galleons
136 ballast ballasted, loaded   **138 so low** (A joke about the female
genitalia. The Netherlands were known as the Low Countries.)
139 diviner sorceress   **140 assured** affianced   **141 privy** secret, personal

145 curtal dog dog with a docked tail (and hence not used in hunting).   **turn i' the wheel** run in a wheel to turn the spit   **146 hie** hasten.   **presently** at once.   **post** hasten.   **road** harbor, roadstead
147 An if if   **149 bark** ship   **152 pack** depart   **159 Possessed
with** having possession of   **162 to** of   **166 ta'en** overtaken,
met up with   **169 What please yourself** whatever you please
170 bespoke requested

S. ANTIPHOLUS
What I should think of this, I cannot tell.
But this I think: there's no man is so vain   179
That would refuse so fair an offered chain.
I see a man here needs not live by shifts,   181
When in the streets he meets such golden gifts.
I'll to the mart and there for Dromio stay;
If any ship put out, then straight away.   *Exit.* 184

❖

4.1   *Enter [Second] Merchant, [Angelo the] goldsmith,*
and an Officer.

SECOND MERCHANT [*to Angelo*]
You know since Pentecost the sum is due,   1
And since I have not much importuned you,   2
Nor now I had not, but that I am bound
To Persia and want guilders for my voyage.   4
Therefore make present satisfaction,   5
Or I'll attach you by this officer.   6

ANGELO
Even just the sum that I do owe to you   7
Is growing to me by Antipholus,   8
And in the instant that I met with you
He had of me a chain. At five o'clock
I shall receive the money for the same.
Pleaseth you walk with me down to his house,   12
I will discharge my bond and thank you too.

Enter Antipholus [and] Dromio
of Ephesus from the Courtesan's.

OFFICER
That labor may you save. See where he comes.

E. ANTIPHOLUS [*to Dromio of Ephesus*]
While I go to the goldsmith's house, go thou
And buy a rope's end; that will I bestow   16
Among my wife and her confederates
For locking me out of my doors by day.
But soft! I see the goldsmith. Get thee gone.   19
Buy thou a rope and bring it home to me.

E. DROMIO
I buy a thousand pound a year! I buy a rope!   21
                              Exit Dromio.

E. ANTIPHOLUS [*to Angelo*]
A man is well holp up that trusts to you!   22
I promisèd your presence and the chain,   23

But neither chain nor goldsmith came to me.
Belike you thought our love would last too long   25
If it were chained together, and therefore came not.

ANGELO [*showing a paper*]
Saving your merry humor, here's the note   27
How much your chain weighs to the utmost carat,
The fineness of the gold and chargeful fashion,   29
Which doth amount to three odd ducats more   30
Than I stand debted to this gentleman.
I pray you, see him presently discharged,
For he is bound to sea and stays but for it.

E. ANTIPHOLUS
I am not furnished with the present money;   34
Besides, I have some business in the town.
Good signor, take the stranger to my house,
And with you take the chain, and bid my wife
Disburse the sum on the receipt thereof.
Perchance I will be there as soon as you.

ANGELO
Then you will bring the chain to her yourself?

E. ANTIPHOLUS
No, bear it with you, lest I come not time enough.   41

ANGELO
Well, sir, I will. Have you the chain about you?

E. ANTIPHOLUS
An if I have not, sir, I hope you have,
Or else you may return without your money.

ANGELO
Nay, come, I pray you, sir, give me the chain.
Both wind and tide stays for this gentleman,
And I, too blame, have held him here too long.   47

E. ANTIPHOLUS
Good Lord! You use this dalliance to excuse   48
Your breach of promise to the Porcupine.
I should have chid you for not bringing it,   50
But, like a shrew, you first begin to brawl.

SECOND MERCHANT [*to Angelo*]
The hour steals on. I pray you, sir, dispatch.

ANGELO
You hear how he importunes me. The chain!   53

E. ANTIPHOLUS
Why, give it to my wife and fetch your money.

ANGELO
Come, come, you know I gave it you even now.
Either send the chain or send me by some token.   56

E. ANTIPHOLUS
Fie, now you run this humor out of breath.   57
Come, where's the chain? I pray you, let me see it.

SECOND MERCHANT
My business cannot brook this dalliance.   59
Good sir, say whe'er you'll answer me or no.   60
If not, I'll leave him to the officer.

---

179 **vain** foolish   181 **shifts** stratagems, tricks   184 **straight** at once
4.1. Location: The street.
1 Pentecost the commemoration of the descent of the Holy Ghost
upon the Apostles, celebrated on the seventh Sunday after Easter
2 since since then.   **importuned** harassed with demands, bothered
4 want lack   **5 present satisfaction** immediate payment   **6 attach** arrest, seize   **7 Even just** precisely   **8 growing** due, accruing
12 Pleaseth may it please   **16 a rope's end** a fragment of rope (to be
used as a whip).   **bestow** employ   **19 soft** i.e., wait a minute   **21 I**
. . . rope (An obscure line. Dromio may mean that in buying a rope
as he is bidden, he is purchasing for himself a thousand poundings or
beatings a year.)   **22 holp up** helped   **23 promisèd** was promised

25 **Belike** perhaps   27 **Saving** with respect for   29 **chargeful fashion**
expensive workmanship   30 **ducats** gold coins (of several European
countries)   34 **present** available   41 **time enough** in time   47 **too**
blame too blameworthy   48 **dalliance** idle delay   50 **chid** chided
53 **importunes** solicits urgently   56 **send me . . . token** send me with
some object of yours authorizing me to receive payment   57 **run . . .**
breath i.e., carry the joke too far   59 **brook** endure   60 **whe'er**
whether.   **answer** pay, give me satisfaction

E. ANTIPHOLUS
I answer you? What should I answer you?
ANGELO
The money that you owe me for the chain.
E. ANTIPHOLUS
I owe you none till I receive the chain.
ANGELO
You know I gave it you half an hour since.
E. ANTIPHOLUS
You gave me none. You wrong me much to say so.
ANGELO
You wrong me more, sir, in denying it.
Consider how it stands upon my credit.   68
SECOND MERCHANT
Well, officer, arrest him at my suit.   69
OFFICER [*to Angelo*]
I do, and charge you in the Duke's name to
    obey me.
ANGELO [*to Antipholus*]
This touches me in reputation.   71
Either consent to pay this sum for me,
Or I attach you by this officer.
E. ANTIPHOLUS
Consent to pay thee that I never had?
Arrest me, foolish fellow, if thou dar'st.
ANGELO
Here is thy fee. Arrest him, officer. [*He gives money.*]
I would not spare my brother in this case
If he should scorn me so apparently.   78
OFFICER [*to Antipholus*]
I do arrest you, sir. You hear the suit.
E. ANTIPHOLUS
I do obey thee till I give thee bail.—
But, sirrah, you shall buy this sport as dear
As all the metal in your shop will answer.
ANGELO
Sir, sir, I shall have law in Ephesus,
To your notorious shame, I doubt it not.   84

        Enter Dromio of Syracuse, from the bay.

S. DROMIO
Master, there's a bark of Epidamnum
That stays but till her owner comes aboard,
And then she bears away. Our freightage, sir,
I have conveyed aboard, and I have bought
The oil, the balsamum, and aqua vitae.   89
The ship is in her trim; the merry wind   90
Blows fair from land; they stay for naught at all
But for their owner, master, and yourself.
E. ANTIPHOLUS
How now? A madman? Why, thou peevish sheep,   93
What ship of Epidamnum stays for me?

S. DROMIO
A ship you sent me to, to hire waftage.   95
E. ANTIPHOLUS
Thou drunken slave, I sent thee for a rope
And told thee to what purpose and what end.
S. DROMIO
You sent me for a rope's end as soon.   98
You sent me to the bay, sir, for a bark.
E. ANTIPHOLUS
I will debate this matter at more leisure
And teach your ears to list me with more heed.   101
To Adriana, villain, hie thee straight. [*He gives a key.*]
Give her this key, and tell her, in the desk
That's covered o'er with Turkish tapestry
There is a purse of ducats; let her send it.
Tell her I am arrested in the street,
And that shall bail me. Hie thee, slave, begone!
On, officer, to prison till it come.
                    Exeunt [all but Dromio of Syracuse].
S. DROMIO
To Adriana! That is where we dined,
Where Dowsabel did claim me for her husband.   110
She is too big, I hope, for me to compass.   111
Thither I must, although against my will,
For servants must their masters' minds fulfill.   *Exit.*

4.2   *Enter Adriana and Luciana.*

ADRIANA
Ah, Luciana, did he tempt thee so?
    Mightst thou perceive austerely in his eye   2
That he did plead in earnest, yea or no?
    Looked he or red or pale, or sad or merrily?   4
What observation mad'st thou in this case
Of his heart's meteors tilting in his face?   6
LUCIANA
First he denied you had in him no right.   7
ADRIANA
He meant he did me none; the more my spite.   8
LUCIANA
Then swore he that he was a stranger here.
ADRIANA
And true he swore, though yet forsworn he were.   10
LUCIANA
Then pleaded I for you.
ADRIANA   And what said he?

95 **waftage** passage   98 **a rope's end** i.e., a whipping, or perhaps a
hangman's noose; see line 16 and note   101 **list** listen to
110 **Dowsabel** (Used ironically for Nell or Luce; derived from the
French *douce et belle*, "gentle and beautiful.")   111 **compass** achieve
(with added meaning of "put my arms around")
4.2. Location: The house of Antipholus of Ephesus.
2 **austerely** objectively, strictly   4 **or red** either red.   **or sad** either
sad   6 **meteors tilting** i.e., passions warring. (The next line begins a
passage of stichomythia, dialogue in which each speech consists of a
single line, much used in classical drama.)   7 **no** i.e., any   8 **spite**
vexation, grief   10 **true . . . were** i.e., though no foreigner, he spoke
true in the sense that he is a stranger to my heart and thus false to his
vows

68 **how . . . credit** how it affects my reputation for honesty   69 **at
my suit** on my petition   71 **touches** injures, affects   78 **apparently**
openly   84 **s.d. from the bay** i.e., presumably from a side entry
which we understand to represent the direction of the bay   89 **balsamum** balm.   **aqua vitae** strong liquor   90 **in her trim** rigged and
ready to sail   93 **peevish** silly.   **sheep** (with play on *ship* in next line)

LUCIANA
That love I begged for you he begged of me.

ADRIANA
With what persuasion did he tempt thy love?

LUCIANA
With words that in an honest suit might move.   14
First he did praise my beauty, then my speech.

ADRIANA
Didst speak him fair?

LUCIANA   Have patience, I beseech.   16

ADRIANA
I cannot, nor I will not, hold me still.
My tongue, though not my heart, shall have his
    will.   18
He is deformèd, crooked, old, and sere,   19
Ill faced, worse bodied, shapeless everywhere;   20
Vicious, ungentle, foolish, blunt, unkind,
Stigmatical in making, worse in mind.   22

LUCIANA
Who would be jealous then of such a one?
No evil lost is wailed when it is gone.

ADRIANA
Ah, but I think him better than I say,
    And yet would herein others' eyes were worse.   26
Far from her nest the lapwing cries away;   27
    My heart prays for him, though my tongue do
    curse.

Enter Dromio of Syracuse, [running, with the key].

S. DROMIO
Here, go—the desk, the purse! Sweet, now, make
    haste.   29

LUCIANA
How hast thou lost thy breath?

S. DROMIO   By running fast.

ADRIANA
Where is thy master, Dromio? Is he well?

S. DROMIO
No, he's in Tartar limbo, worse than hell.   32
A devil in an everlasting garment hath him,   33
One whose hard heart is buttoned up with steel;
A fiend, a fairy, pitiless and rough;   35
A wolf, nay, worse, a fellow all in buff;
A back friend, a shoulder clapper, one that
    countermands   37

The passages of alleys, creeks, and narrow lands;   38
A hound that runs counter and yet draws dryfoot
    well;   39
One that before the judgment carries poor souls to
    hell.   40

ADRIANA   Why, man, what is the matter?

S. DROMIO
I do not know the matter. He is 'rested on the case.   42

ADRIANA
What, is he arrested? Tell me at whose suit.

S. DROMIO
I know not at whose suit he is arrested well;
But is in a suit of buff which 'rested him, that can I
    tell.
Will you send him, mistress, redemption, the
    money in his desk?

ADRIANA
Go fetch it, sister. (*Exit Luciana.*) This I wonder at,
That he, unknown to me, should be in debt.
Tell me, was he arrested on a band?   49

S. DROMIO
Not on a band, but on a stronger thing:
A chain, a chain! Do you not hear it ring?

ADRIANA   What, the chain?

S. DROMIO
No, no, the bell. 'Tis time that I were gone.
It was two ere I left him, and now the clock
    strikes one.   54

ADRIANA
The hours come back! That did I never hear.

S. DROMIO
O, yes, if any hour meet a sergeant, 'a turns back
    for very fear.   56

ADRIANA
As if Time were in debt. How fondly dost thou
    reason!   57

S. DROMIO
Time is a very bankrupt and owes more than he's
    worth to season.   58
Nay, he's a thief too. Have you not heard men say
That Time comes stealing on by night and day?
If 'a be in debt and theft, and a sergeant in the way,   61
Hath he not reason to turn back an hour in a day?

Enter Luciana [with the purse].

14 honest honorable   **16 speak him fair** speak engagingly to him
18 his its   **19 sere** withered   **20 shapeless** misshapen   **22 Stigmatical
in making** deformed in body   **26 And . . . worse** i.e., and yet I wish
other women found him in a less favorable light   **27 lapwing** a bird
that flies away from its nest to divert attention from its young. (Proverbial.)   **29 Sweet** (An inoffensive term of endearment. Some editors
emend it to *Sweat.*)   **32 Tartar limbo** Tartarus or pagan hell, worse
than Christian hell   **33 everlasting garment** i.e., buff leather attire of
the police officer; everlasting both because of its durability and because of the joke about perpetual durance in limbo or jail. (*Everlasting* is itself the name of a coarse woolen fabric sometimes used for
the uniforms of petty officers of justice.)   **35 fairy** i.e., malevolent
spirit   **37 A back friend** i.e., a false friend; here the police officer
who comes up behind and claps his victim on the back to signify arrest.   **countermands** prohibits

38 passages movement of people.   **of** in.   **creeks** narrow or winding
passages.   **lands** glades, or stretches of land   **39 runs counter** follows
a trail in the direction opposite to that which the game has taken
(with a quibble on *counter,* a prison).   **draws dryfoot** follows game
by mere scent of the foot   **40 judgment** legal decision (with a pun on
"Judgment Day," continuing the joke about jail as Tartar limbo)
42 'rested on the case arrested in a lawsuit (with a pun on *case,*
meaning "the container," as distinguished from the *matter* contained
in it. Dromio means that his master has been arrested in his suit of
clothes.)   **49 band** bond. (But Dromio puns on the sense "neckband"
in the next line.)   **54 one** (*One* and *on* were pronounced very much
alike; the word here rhymes with *gone.*)   **56 hour** (with a pun on
"whore," similarly pronounced, or perhaps too on "ower," one who
owes).   **sergeant** arresting officer.   **'a** it, she, he   **57 fondly** foolishly
58 Time . . . season i.e., time has so worn itself out that it's more
trouble than it's worth to straighten matters out (?).   **to season** to
bring to fruition, make acceptable   **61 theft** i.e., a thief.   **in the way**
lying in wait to arrest

ADRIANA
Go, Dromio, there's the money. Bear it straight,   63
And bring thy master home immediately.
                                    [*Exit Dromio, with the purse.*]
Come, sister. I am pressed down with conceit—   65
Conceit, my comfort and my injury.   *Exeunt.*   66

♣

4.3   *Enter Antipholus of Syracuse, [wearing the chain].*

S. ANTIPHOLUS
There's not a man I meet but doth salute me
As if I were their well-acquainted friend,
And everyone doth call me by my name.
Some tender money to me; some invite me;   4
Some other give me thanks for kindnesses;   5
Some offer me commodities to buy.
Even now a tailor called me in his shop
And showed me silks that he had bought for me
And therewithal took measure of my body.
Sure, these are but imaginary wiles,   10
And Lapland sorcerers inhabit here.   11

Enter Dromio of Syracuse, [with the purse].

S. DROMIO   Master, here's the gold you sent me for.
What, have you got the picture of old Adam new-   13
appareled?   14
S. ANTIPHOLUS
What gold is this? What Adam dost thou mean?
S. DROMIO   Not that Adam that kept the Paradise, but   16
that Adam that keeps the prison; he that goes in the
calf's skin that was killed for the Prodigal; he that   18
came behind you, sir, like an evil angel, and bid you
forsake your liberty.
S. ANTIPHOLUS   I understand thee not.
S. DROMIO   No? Why, 'tis a plain case: he that went, like
a bass viol, in a case of leather; the man, sir, that,
when gentlemen are tired, gives them a sob and 'rests   24
them; he, sir, that takes pity on decayed men and gives   25
them suits of durance; he that sets up his rest to do   26

more exploits with his mace than a morris-pike.   27
S. ANTIPHOLUS   What, thou mean'st an officer?
S. DROMIO   Ay, sir, the sergeant of the band; he that   29
brings any man to answer it that breaks his band; one   30
that thinks a man always going to bed, and says, "God
give you good rest!"   32
S. ANTIPHOLUS   Well, sir, there rest in your foolery. Is
there any ships puts forth tonight? May we be gone?
S. DROMIO   Why, sir, I brought you word an hour since
that the bark *Expedition* put forth tonight, and then
were you hindered by the sergeant to tarry for the hoy   37
Delay. Here are the angels that you sent for to de-   38
liver you.   [*He gives the purse.*]
S. ANTIPHOLUS
The fellow is distract, and so am I,   40
And here we wander in illusions.
Some blessèd power deliver us from hence!

Enter a Courtesan.

COURTESAN
Well met, well met, Master Antipholus.
I see, sir, you have found the goldsmith now.
Is that the chain you promised me today?
S. ANTIPHOLUS
Satan, avoid! I charge thee, tempt me not.   46
S. DROMIO   Master, is this Mistress Satan?
S. ANTIPHOLUS   It is the devil.
S. DROMIO   Nay, she is worse, she is the devil's dam,   49
and here she comes in the habit of a light wench; and   50
thereof comes that the wenches say, "God damn me,"   51
that's as much to say, "God make me a light wench."
It is written they appear to men like angels of light;   53
light is an effect of fire, and fire will burn; ergo, light   54
wenches will burn. Come not near her.   55
COURTESAN
Your man and you are marvelous merry, sir.
Will you go with me? We'll mend our dinner here.   57
S. DROMIO   Master, if you do, expect spoon meat, or   58
bespeak a long spoon.   59
S. ANTIPHOLUS   Why, Dromio?
S. DROMIO   Marry, he must have a long spoon that must   61
eat with the devil.   62
S. ANTIPHOLUS   [*to the Courtesan*]
Avoid then, fiend! What tell'st thou me of supping?   63
Thou art, as you are all, a sorceress.
I conjure thee to leave me and be gone.
COURTESAN
Give me the ring of mine you had at dinner

---

63 straight straight away, immediately   **65 conceit** imaginings
66 Conceit . . . injury (Adriana is filled with imaginings, both of the
wrongs she has suffered and the comfort she can provide her wayward husband.)
4.3. Location: The street.
4 tender offer   **5 other** others   **10 imaginary wiles** tricks of the imagination   **11 Lapland sorcerers** (Lapland was said to surpass all nations
in the practice of witchcraft and sorcery.)   **13–14 have . . . appareled** (Dromio, noting the absence of the arresting officer, asks if his
master has gotten rid of that officer by arranging for him to have a
new apparel or "suit"—with a pun on "lawsuit." The officer is likened to old Adam in that his buff leather jerkin resembles Adam's garments of beasts' skins; see Genesis 3:21.)   **16 kept the Paradise** (This
sounds like an allusion to an inn of which the innkeeper was named
Adam.)   **18 calf's . . . Prodigal** (An allusion to the fatted calf killed
for the Prodigal Son's return; see Luke 15:23.)   **24 sob** (1) sobbing
cry (2) breathing space (followed by a pun on *'rests*, meaning "arrests" and "gives a rest to")   **25 decayed** financially ruined (with a
pun on the usual sense)   **26 durance** a kind of long-wearing cloth
like buff (with a pun on "imprisonment").   **sets . . . rest** stakes his
all (with a continuing pun on *'rest*; the metaphor of staking all one's
venture is from the game of primero)

27 mace staff of office carried by a constable.   **morris-pike** a
weapon, supposedly of Moorish origin   **29 band** troop   **30 band**
bond   **32 rest** (continuing the pun on *arrest*)   **37 hoy** a small coastal
vessel   **38 angels** gold coins worth about ten shillings   **40 distract**
deranged, distracted   **46 avoid** begone. (See Matthew 4:10.)
49 dam mother   **50 habit** demeanor, manner; also, dress.   **light**
wanton   **51 damn me** i.e., dam me, make me a mother   **53 angels
of light** (See 2 Corinthians 11:14, where Satan is referred to as transformed into an angel of light.)   **54 ergo** therefore   **55 will burn** i.e.,
will transmit venereal disease   **57 mend** supplement, complete
58 spoon meat food for infants, hence delicacies   **59 bespeak** order
61–62 he . . . devil (A proverbial idea.)   **63 What** why

Or, for my diamond, the chain you promised,
And I'll be gone, sir, and not trouble you.

S. DROMIO
Some devils ask but the parings of one's nail,
A rush, a hair, a drop of blood, a pin,
A nut, a cherrystone;
But she, more covetous, would have a chain.
Master, be wise. An if you give it her,   73
The devil will shake her chain and fright us with it.

COURTESAN
I pray you, sir, my ring, or else the chain!
I hope you do not mean to cheat me so?

S. ANTIPHOLUS
Avaunt, thou witch!—Come, Dromio, let us go.   77

S. DROMIO
"Fly pride," says the peacock. Mistress, that you
    know.   Exeunt [Antipholus and Dromio of Syracuse].   78

COURTESAN
Now, out of doubt Antipholus is mad,   79
Else would he never so demean himself.   80
A ring he hath of mine worth forty ducats,
And for the same he promised me a chain;
Both one and other he denies me now.
The reason that I gather he is mad,
Besides this present instance of his rage,   85
Is a mad tale he told today at dinner
Of his own doors being shut against his entrance.
Belike his wife, acquainted with his fits,   88
On purpose shut the doors against his way.
My way is now to hie home to his house   90
And tell his wife that, being lunatic,
He rushed into my house and took perforce   92
My ring away. This course I fittest choose,   93
For forty ducats is too much to lose.   [Exit.]

4.4   Enter Antipholus of Ephesus with a Jailer [or
          Officer].

E. ANTIPHOLUS
Fear me not, man, I will not break away.
I'll give thee ere I leave thee so much money
To warrant thee as I am 'rested for.   3
My wife is in a wayward mood today   4
And will not lightly trust the messenger.   5
That I should be attached in Ephesus,   6
I tell you, 'twill sound harshly in her ears.

          Enter Dromio of Ephesus with a rope's end.

Here comes my man. I think he brings the
    money.—
How now, sir? Have you that I sent you for?

E. DROMIO [giving the rope]
Here's that, I warrant you, will pay them all.

E. ANTIPHOLUS   But where's the money?

E. DROMIO
Why, sir, I gave the money for the rope.

E. ANTIPHOLUS
Five hundred ducats, villain, for a rope?

E. DROMIO
I'll serve you, sir, five hundred at the rate.   14

E. ANTIPHOLUS
To what end did I bid thee hie thee home?

E. DROMIO   To a rope's end, sir; and to that end am I
returned.

E. ANTIPHOLUS
And to that end, sir, I will welcome you.
                 [He starts to beat Dromio of Ephesus.]

OFFICER   Good sir, be patient.

E. DROMIO   Nay, 'tis for me to be patient. I am in adversity.

OFFICER   Good now, hold thy tongue.   22

E. DROMIO   Nay, rather persuade him to hold his hands.

E. ANTIPHOLUS   Thou whoreson, senseless villain!

E. DROMIO   I would I were senseless, sir, that I might
not feel your blows.

E. ANTIPHOLUS   Thou art sensible in nothing but blows,   27
and so is an ass.

E. DROMIO   I am an ass, indeed; you may prove it by
my long ears. I have served him from the hour of my   30
nativity to this instant and have nothing at his hands
for my service but blows. When I am cold, he heats
me with beating; when I am warm, he cools me with
beating. I am waked with it when I sleep, raised with
it when I sit, driven out of doors with it when I go
from home, welcomed home with it when I return.
Nay, I bear it on my shoulders, as a beggar wont her   37
brat, and I think when he hath lamed me I shall beg
with it from door to door.

          Enter Adriana, Luciana, Courtesan, and a
          schoolmaster called Pinch.

E. ANTIPHOLUS
Come, go along. My wife is coming yonder.

E. DROMIO [to Adriana]   Mistress, respice finem, respect   41
your end; or rather, to prophesy like the parrot,
"Beware the rope's end."

E. ANTIPHOLUS   Wilt thou still talk?   Beats Dromio.

COURTESAN [to Adriana]
How say you now? Is not your husband mad?

---

73 An if if   **77 Avaunt** begone   **78 Fly . . . peacock** i.e., the accusation of dishonesty coming from this woman, whom Dromio takes to
be dishonest, seems to him as out of place as a warning against pride
given by a peacock. *Pride* puns on the meaning "sexual desire."
79 out of doubt no doubt   **80 demean** conduct   **85 rage** madness
88 Belike presumably   **90 My way** my best course.   **hie home** hasten directly   **92 perforce** forcibly   **93 fittest** as most appropriate
4.4. Location: The street.
3 warrant thee guarantee your security   **4 wayward** perverse, ill-tempered   **5 lightly trust** easily believe   **6 attached** arrested

14 I'll . . . rate I'll supply you with five hundred ropes, sir, for that
amount   **22 Good now** pray you   **27 sensible in** sensitive to; also,
made sensible by   **30 ears** (with a pun on "years"; Dromio says he is
an ass for having served his master so long)   **37 wont** is accustomed
to (bear)   **41 respice finem** consider your end. (A pious sentiment on
the brevity of life and the approach of death; with a play on *respice
funem*, "consider the hangman's rope." A parrot might be taught to
say *respice finem*, or perhaps "rope.")

ADRIANA
His incivility confirms no less.—
Good Doctor Pinch, you are a conjurer;   47
Establish him in his true sense again,   48
And I will please you what you will demand.   49

LUCIANA
Alas, how fiery and how sharp he looks!   50

COURTESAN
Mark how he trembles in his ecstasy!   51

PINCH [to Antipholus]
Give me your hand, and let me feel your pulse.

E. ANTIPHOLUS [striking him]
There is my hand, and let it feel your ear.

PINCH
I charge thee, Satan, housed within this man,
To yield possession to my holy prayers
And to thy state of darkness hie thee straight!
I conjure thee by all the saints in heaven!

E. ANTIPHOLUS
Peace, doting wizard, peace! I am not mad.

ADRIANA
O, that thou wert not, poor distressèd soul!

E. ANTIPHOLUS
You minion, you, are these your customers?   60
Did this companion with the saffron face   61
Revel and feast it at my house today,
Whilst upon me the guilty doors were shut
And I denied to enter in my house?

ADRIANA
O husband, God doth know you dined at home,
Where would you had remained until this time,
Free from these slanders and this open shame!

E. ANTIPHOLUS
Dined at home? [To E. Dromio.] Thou villain, what
    sayest thou?

E. DROMIO
Sir, sooth to say, you did not dine at home.

E. ANTIPHOLUS
Were not my doors locked up and I shut out?

E. DROMIO
Pardie, your doors were locked and you shut out.   71

E. ANTIPHOLUS
And did not she herself revile me there?

E. DROMIO
Sans fable, she herself reviled you there.   73

E. ANTIPHOLUS
Did not her kitchen maid rail, taunt, and scorn me?

E. DROMIO
Certes, she did. The kitchen vestal scorned you.   75

E. ANTIPHOLUS
And did not I in rage depart from thence?

E. DROMIO
In verity you did. My bones bears witness,
That since have felt the vigor of his rage.

ADRIANA
Is 't good to soothe him in these contraries?   79

PINCH
It is no shame. The fellow finds his vein   80
And, yielding to him, humors well his frenzy.

E. ANTIPHOLUS [to Adriana]
Thou hast suborned the goldsmith to arrest me.   82

ADRIANA
Alas, I sent you money to redeem you
By Dromio here, who came in haste for it.

E. DROMIO
Money by me? Heart and good will you might,
But surely, master, not a rag of money.   86

E. ANTIPHOLUS
Went'st not thou to her for a purse of ducats?

ADRIANA
He came to me, and I delivered it.

LUCIANA
And I am witness with her that she did.

E. DROMIO
God and the rope maker bear me witness
That I was sent for nothing but a rope!

PINCH [to Adriana]
Mistress, both man and master is possessed;
I know it by their pale and deadly looks.   93
They must be bound and laid in some dark room.   94

E. ANTIPHOLUS [to Adriana]
Say wherefore didst thou lock me forth today?   95
[To E. Dromio.] And why dost thou deny the bag of
    gold?

ADRIANA
I did not, gentle husband, lock thee forth.

E. DROMIO
And, gentle master, I received no gold.
But I confess, sir, that we were locked out.

ADRIANA
Dissembling villain, thou speak'st false in both.

E. ANTIPHOLUS
Dissembling harlot, thou art false in all
And art confederate with a damnèd pack   102
To make a loathsome abject scorn of me!   103
But with these nails I'll pluck out those false eyes
That would behold in me this shameful sport.
            [He threatens Adriana.]

ADRIANA
O, bind him, bind him! Let him not come near me.   106

        Enter three or four, and offer to bind him. He
        strives.

PINCH
More company! The fiend is strong within him.

---

47 Doctor (An honorific term for any learned person. Pinch is not a
medical doctor.)   conjurer (Being able to speak Latin, Pinch could
conjure spirits.)   48 true sense right mind   49 please pay   50 sharp
angry   51 ecstasy fit, frenzy   60 minion hussy, i.e., Adriana
61 companion fellow, i.e., Pinch.   saffron yellow   71 Pardie (An
oath, from the French pardieu, "by God.")   73 Sans without
75 Certes certainly.   kitchen vestal (Ironically, her task was like that
of the vestal virgins of ancient Rome, to keep the fire burning.)

79 soothe encourage, humor.   contraries denials, lies   82 suborned
induced   86 rag scrap   93 deadly deathlike   94 bound . . . room
(The regular treatment for lunacy in Shakespeare's day.)   95 forth out
(also in line 97)   102 pack i.e., of conspirators   103 abject scorn
despicable object of contempt   106 s.d. offer attempt

LUCIANA
Ay me, poor man, how pale and wan he looks!

E. ANTIPHOLUS
What, will you murder me?—Thou jailer, thou,
I am thy prisoner. Will thou suffer them
To make a rescue?

OFFICER   Masters, let him go. 111
He is my prisoner, and you shall not have him.

PINCH
Go bind his man, for he is frantic too.
[They bind Dromio of Ephesus.]

ADRIANA
What wilt thou do, thou peevish officer? 114
Hast thou delight to see a wretched man
Do outrage and displeasure to himself? 116

OFFICER
He is my prisoner. If I let him go,
The debt he owes will be required of me.

ADRIANA
I will discharge thee ere I go from thee. 119
Bear me forthwith unto his creditor,
And, knowing how the debt grows, I will pay it. 121
Good Master Doctor, see him safe conveyed
Home to my house. O most unhappy day! 123

E. ANTIPHOLUS   O most unhappy strumpet!

E. DROMIO
Master, I am here entered in bond for you. 125

E. ANTIPHOLUS
Out on thee, villain! Wherefore dost thou mad me? 126

E. DROMIO   Will you be bound for nothing? Be mad,
good master; cry, "The devil!"

LUCIANA
God help, poor souls, how idly do they talk! 129

ADRIANA
Go bear him hence. Sister, go you with me. 130
Exeunt [Pinch and his assistants, carrying off
Antipholus and Dromio of Ephesus]. Manent Officer,
Adriana, Luciana, Courtesan.
Say now, whose suit is he arrested at?

OFFICER
One Angelo, a goldsmith. Do you know him?

ADRIANA
I know the man. What is the sum he owes?

OFFICER
Two hundred ducats.

ADRIANA   Say, how grows it due?

OFFICER
Due for a chain your husband had of him.

ADRIANA
He did bespeak a chain for me, but had it not. 136

COURTESAN
Whenas your husband all in rage today 137
Came to my house and took away my ring—

The ring I saw upon his finger now—
Straight after did I meet him with a chain.

ADRIANA
It may be so, but I did never see it.
Come, jailer, bring me where the goldsmith is.
I long to know the truth hereof at large. 143

Enter Antipholus and Dromio [of] Syracuse with
their rapiers drawn.

LUCIANA
God, for thy mercy! They are loose again. 145

ADRIANA
And come with naked swords. Let's call more help
To have them bound again.

OFFICER   Away! They'll kill us.
Run all out. Exeunt omnes, as fast as may be,
frighted. [Antipholus and Dromio of Syracuse
remain.]

S. ANTIPHOLUS
I see these witches are afraid of swords.

S. DROMIO
She that would be your wife now ran from you. 148

S. ANTIPHOLUS
Come to the Centaur. Fetch our stuff from thence. 149
I long that we were safe and sound aboard.

S. DROMIO
Faith, stay here this night. They will surely
do us no harm. You saw they speak us fair, give us 152
gold. Methinks they are such a gentle nation that,
for the mountain of mad flesh that claims marriage of
me, I could find in my heart to stay here still and turn 155
witch.

S. ANTIPHOLUS
I will not stay tonight for all the town.
Therefore, away, to get our stuff aboard.
Exeunt.

❖

5.1   Enter the [Second] Merchant and [Angelo] the
goldsmith.

ANGELO
I am sorry, sir, that I have hindered you; 1
But I protest he had the chain of me,
Though most dishonestly he doth deny it.

SECOND MERCHANT
How is the man esteemed here in the city?

ANGELO
Of very reverend reputation, sir,
Of credit infinite, highly beloved,
Second to none that lives here in the city.
His word might bear my wealth at any time. 8

SECOND MERCHANT
Speak softly. Yonder, as I think, he walks.

111 **make a rescue** take a prisoner by force from legal custody
114 **peevish** silly, senseless   116 **displeasure** injury, wrong   119 **discharge** pay, clear the debt   121 **knowing . . . grows** when I know
how the debt accrued   123 **unhappy** fatal, miserable   125 **entered in
bond** (1) pledged (2) tied   126 **mad** exasperate   129 **idly**
senselessly   130 s.d. **Manent** they remain onstage   136 **bespeak** order   137 **Whenas** when

1 **hindered** delayed   8 **might bear** is worth
5.1. Location: Before the priory and Antipholus of Ephesus' house.
143 **at large** in full, in detail   145 **naked** drawn   148 **would be**
claims to be   149 **stuff** goods, baggage   152 **speak us fair** speak
courteously to us   155 **still** always

Enter Antipholus and Dromio [of Syracuse] again,
[Antipholus wearing the chain].

ANGELO
'Tis so, and that self chain about his neck   10
Which he forswore most monstrously to have.   11
Good sir, draw near to me. I'll speak to him.—
Signor Antipholus, I wonder much
That you would put me to this shame and trouble
And, not without some scandal to yourself,
With circumstance and oaths so to deny   16
This chain which now you wear so openly.
Besides the charge, the shame, imprisonment,   18
You have done wrong to this my honest friend,   19
Who, but for staying on our controversy,   20
Had hoisted sail and put to sea today.
This chain you had of me. Can you deny it?

S. ANTIPHOLUS
I think I had. I never did deny it.

SECOND MERCHANT
Yes, that you did, sir, and forswore it too.

S. ANTIPHOLUS
Who heard me to deny it or forswear it?

SECOND MERCHANT
These ears of mine, thou know'st, did hear thee.
Fie on thee, wretch! 'Tis pity that thou liv'st
To walk where any honest men resort.

S. ANTIPHOLUS
Thou art a villain to impeach me thus.   29
I'll prove mine honor and mine honesty
Against thee presently, if thou dar'st stand.   31

SECOND MERCHANT
I dare, and do defy thee for a villain.   *They draw.* 32

Enter Adriana, Luciana, [the] Courtesan, and
others.

ADRIANA
Hold, hurt him not, for God's sake! He is mad.
Some get within him; take his sword away.   34
Bind Dromio too, and bear them to my house.

S. DROMIO
Run, master, run; for God's sake, take a house!   36
This is some priory. In, or we are spoiled!   37
                Exeunt [Antipholus and Dromio of Syracuse]
                                            to the priory.

Enter [Emilia, the] Lady Abbess.

ABBESS
Be quiet, people. Wherefore throng you hither?

ADRIANA
To fetch my poor distracted husband hence.
Let us come in, that we may bind him fast
And bear him home for his recovery.

ANGELO
I knew he was not in his perfect wits.

SECOND MERCHANT
I am sorry now that I did draw on him.

ABBESS
How long hath this possession held the man?

ADRIANA
This week he hath been heavy, sour, sad,   45
And much different from the man he was;
But till this afternoon his passion
Ne'er brake into extremity of rage.   48

ABBESS
Hath he not lost much wealth by wreck of sea?   49
Buried some dear friend? Hath not else his eye
Strayed his affection in unlawful love—   51
A sin prevailing much in youthful men,
Who give their eyes the liberty of gazing?
Which of these sorrows is he subject to?

ADRIANA
To none of these, except it be the last,
Namely, some love that drew him oft from home.

ABBESS
You should for that have reprehended him.   57

ADRIANA
Why, so I did.

ABBESS   Ay, but not rough enough.

ADRIANA
As roughly as my modesty would let me.

ABBESS
Haply in private.

ADRIANA   And in assemblies too.

ABBESS   Ay, but not enough.

ADRIANA
It was the copy of our conference.   62
In bed he slept not for my urging it;   63
At board he fed not for my urging it;
Alone, it was the subject of my theme;
In company I often glancèd it;   66
Still did I tell him it was vile and bad.   67

ABBESS
And thereof came it that the man was mad.
The venom clamors of a jealous woman   69
Poisons more deadly than a mad dog's tooth.
It seems his sleeps were hindered by thy railing,
And thereof comes it that his head is light.
Thou sayst his meat was sauced with thy
     upbraidings.
Unquiet meals make ill digestions;
Thereof the raging fire of fever bred,
And what's a fever but a fit of madness?
Thou sayst his sports were hindered by thy brawls.
Sweet recreation barred, what doth ensue
But moody and dull melancholy,
Kinsman to grim and comfortless despair,
And at her heels a huge infectious troop

---

10 **self** same 11 **forswore** denied under oath 16 **circumstance** details, particulars 18 **charge** cost 19 **honest** honorable 20 **on** as a
result of 29 **impeach** accuse 31 **presently** at once. **stand** take a
fighting stance, put yourself to the test 32 **defy** challenge. **villain**
base person 34 **within him** under his guard 36 **take** take refuge in
37 **spoiled** ruined, done for

45 **This week** all this week. **sad** melancholy 48 **brake** broke. **rage**
madness 49 **wreck of** shipwreck at 51 **Strayed** led astray 57 **reprehended** rebuked 62 **copy** topic, theme. **conference** conversation
63 **for** because of 66 **glancèd** alluded to 67 **Still** continually
69 **venom** venomous

Of pale distemperatures and foes to life?   82
In food, in sport, and life-preserving rest
To be disturbed would mad or man or beast.   84
The consequence is, then, thy jealous fits
Hath scared thy husband from the use of wits.

LUCIANA
She never reprehended him but mildly,
When he demeaned himself rough, rude, and
  wildly.   88
[*To Adriana.*] Why bear you these rebukes and
  answer not?

ADRIANA
She did betray me to my own reproof.—   90
Good people, enter and lay hold on him.

ABBESS
No, not a creature enters in my house.

ADRIANA
Then let your servants bring my husband forth.

ABBESS
Neither. He took this place for sanctuary,
And it shall privilege him from your hands
Till I have brought him to his wits again
Or lose my labor in assaying it.   97

ADRIANA
I will attend my husband, be his nurse,
Diet his sickness, for it is my office,   99
And will have no attorney but myself;   100
And therefore let me have him home with me.

ABBESS
Be patient, for I will not let him stir
Till I have used the approvèd means I have,   103
With wholesome syrups, drugs, and holy prayers,
To make of him a formal man again.   105
It is a branch and parcel of mine oath,   106
A charitable duty of my order.
Therefore depart and leave him here with me.

ADRIANA
I will not hence and leave my husband here;
And ill it doth beseem your holiness
To separate the husband and the wife.

ABBESS
Be quiet and depart. Thou shalt not have him. [*Exit.*]

LUCIANA [*to Adriana*]
Complain unto the Duke of this indignity.

ADRIANA
Come, go. I will fall prostrate at his feet
And never rise until my tears and prayers
Have won His Grace to come in person hither
And take perforce my husband from the Abbess.

SECOND MERCHANT
By this, I think, the dial points at five.
Anon, I'm sure, the Duke himself in person
Comes this way to the melancholy vale,
The place of death and sorry execution   121

Behind the ditches of the abbey here.   82

ANGELO   Upon what cause?

SECOND MERCHANT
To see a reverend Syracusian merchant,
Who put unluckily into this bay
Against the laws and statutes of this town,
Beheaded publicly for his offense.

ANGELO
See where they come. We will behold his death.

LUCIANA
Kneel to the Duke before he pass the abbey.

*Enter the Duke of Ephesus and [Egeon] the
merchant of Syracuse, barehead [and bound], with
the Headsman and other officers.*

DUKE
Yet once again proclaim it publicly,
If any friend will pay the sum for him,
He shall not die; so much we tender him.   132

ADRIANA [*kneeling*]
Justice, most sacred Duke, against the Abbess!

DUKE
She is a virtuous and a reverend lady.
It cannot be that she hath done thee wrong.

ADRIANA
May it please Your Grace, Antipholus my husband,
Who I made lord of me and all I had,
At your important letters, this ill day   138
A most outrageous fit of madness took him,
That desperately he hurried through the street—   140
With him his bondman, all as mad as he—   141
Doing displeasure to the citizens   142
By rushing in their houses, bearing thence
Rings, jewels, anything his rage did like.   144
Once did I get him bound and sent him home,
Whilst to take order for the wrongs I went   146
That here and there his fury had committed.
Anon, I wot not by what strong escape,   148
He broke from those that had the guard of him,
And with his mad attendant and himself,
Each one with ireful passion, with drawn swords,
Met us again and, madly bent on us,   152
Chased us away, till raising of more aid
We came again to bind them. Then they fled
Into this abbey, whither we pursued them;
And here the Abbess shuts the gates on us
And will not suffer us to fetch him out,
Nor send him forth that we may bear him hence.
Therefore, most gracious Duke, with thy command
Let him be brought forth and borne hence for help.   160

DUKE [*raising Adriana*]
Long since, thy husband served me in my wars,

---

82 **distemperatures** physical disorder, illness   84 **mad or** madden either 88 **demeaned** behaved, conducted 90 **She . . . reproof** i.e., she led me to see my own faults 97 **assaying** attempting 99 **office** duty 100 **attorney** agent, deputy 103 **approvèd** proved, tested 105 **formal** normal, made in proper form 106 **parcel** part, portion 121 **sorry** sad

132 **so . . . him** so much consideration we grant him (with suggestion also of "value" and "have pity on") 138 **important** importunate, pressing. **letters** (Adriana would seem to have been ward to the Duke and married at his urging.) 140 **That** so that. **desperately** recklessly 141 **all** totally 142 **displeasure** wrong, injury 144 **rage** madness, insanity 146 **take order** settle, make reparation 148 **wot** know. **strong** violent 152 **bent** turned 160 **help** cure

And I to thee engaged a prince's word,   162
When thou didst make him master of thy bed,
To do him all the grace and good I could.—
Go, some of you, knock at the abbey gate
And bid the Lady Abbess come to me.
I will determine this before I stir.   167

Enter a [Servant as] messenger.

SERVANT
O mistress, mistress, shift and save yourself!   168
My master and his man are both broke loose,
Beaten the maids a-row, and bound the doctor,   170
Whose beard they have singed off with brands of
  fire,
And ever as it blazed they threw on him
Great pails of puddled mire to quench the hair.   173
My master preaches patience to him, and the while
His man with scissors nicks him like a fool;   175
And sure, unless you send some present help,
Between them they will kill the conjurer.

ADRIANA
Peace, fool! Thy master and his man are here,
And that is false thou dost report to us.

SERVANT
Mistress, upon my life, I tell you true.
I have not breathed almost since I did see it.
He cries for you and vows, if he can take you,
To scorch your face and to disfigure you.   183

                                              Cry within.
Hark, hark! I hear him, mistress. Fly, begone!

DUKE
Come, stand by me. Fear nothing. Guard with
  halberds!   185

ADRIANA
Ay me, it is my husband! Witness you
That he is borne about invisible.
Even now we housed him in the abbey here,   188
And now he's there, past thought of human reason.

Enter Antipholus and Dromio of Ephesus.

E. ANTIPHOLUS
Justice, most gracious Duke, O, grant me justice!
Even for the service that long since I did thee,
When I bestrid thee in the wars and took   192
Deep scars to save thy life; even for the blood
That then I lost for thee, now grant me justice.

EGEON
Unless the fear of death doth make me dote,
I see my son Antipholus and Dromio.

E. ANTIPHOLUS
Justice, sweet prince, against that woman there!
She whom thou gav'st to me to be my wife,

That hath abused and dishonored me   199
Even in the strength and height of injury!
Beyond imagination is the wrong
That she this day hath shameless thrown on me.

DUKE
Discover how, and thou shalt find me just.   203

E. ANTIPHOLUS
This day, great Duke, she shut the doors upon me
While she with harlots feasted in my house.   205

DUKE
A grievous fault. Say, woman, didst thou so?

ADRIANA
No, my good lord. Myself, he, and my sister
Today did dine together. So befall my soul   208
As this is false he burdens me withal.   209

LUCIANA
Ne'er may I look on day nor sleep on night   210
But she tells to Your Highness simple truth.

ANGELO
O perjured woman! They are both forsworn.
In this the madman justly chargeth them.

E. ANTIPHOLUS
My liege, I am advisèd what I say,   214
Neither disturbèd with the effect of wine
Nor heady-rash provoked with raging ire,
Albeit my wrongs might make one wiser mad.
This woman locked me out this day from dinner.
That goldsmith there, were he not packed with her,   219
Could witness it, for he was with me then;
Who parted with me to go fetch a chain,   221
Promising to bring it to the Porcupine,
Where Balthasar and I did dine together.
Our dinner done, and he not coming thither,
I went to seek him. In the street I met him,
And in his company that gentleman.

                       [Indicating the Second Merchant.]
There did this perjured goldsmith swear me down   227
That I this day of him received the chain,
Which, God he knows, I saw not; for the which
He did arrest me with an officer.
I did obey, and sent my peasant home
For certain ducats. He with none returned.
Then fairly I bespoke the officer   233
To go in person with me to my house.
By the way we met
My wife, her sister, and a rabble more
Of vile confederates. Along with them
They brought one Pinch, a hungry, lean-faced
  villain,
A mere anatomy, a mountebank,   239
A threadbare juggler and a fortune-teller,   240
A needy, hollow-eyed, sharp-looking wretch,
A living dead man. This pernicious slave,

---

162 engaged pledged   **167 determine** settle   **168 shift** escape, depart
170 a-row one after another   **173 puddled** from filthy puddles
175 nicks . . . fool gives him a fantastic haircut in the short fashion of
the court fool   **183 scorch** (Compare the singeing of Pinch's beard at
line 171; also, score, slash.)   **185 halberds** long-handled spears with
blades   **188 housed him** i.e., drove him into   **192 bestrid** stood over
(to defend when fallen in battle)

199 abusèd maltreated   **203 Discover** reveal   **205 harlots** rascals,
vile companions   **208 So . . . soul** i.e., as I hope to be saved
209 he . . . withal he charges me with   **210 on** at   **214 am advisèd**
know very well   **219 packed** in conspiracy   **221 parted with** departed from   **227 swear me down** swear in the face of my denials
233 fairly civilly.   **bespoke** requested   **239 mere anatomy** absolute
skeleton.   **mountebank** quack, charlatan   **240 juggler** sorcerer

Forsooth, took on him as a conjurer 243
And, gazing in mine eyes, feeling my pulse,
And with no face, as 'twere, outfacing me, 245
Cries out I was possessed. Then all together 246
They fell upon me, bound me, bore me thence,
And in a dark and dankish vault at home
There left me and my man, both bound together,
Till, gnawing with my teeth my bonds in sunder,
I gained my freedom and immediately
Ran hither to Your Grace, whom I beseech
To give me ample satisfaction
For these deep shames and great indignities.

ANGELO
My lord, in truth, thus far I witness with him,
That he dined not at home but was locked out.

DUKE
But had he such a chain of thee, or no?

ANGELO
He had, my lord, and when he ran in here
These people saw the chain about his neck.

SECOND MERCHANT [to E. Antipholus]
Besides, I will be sworn these ears of mine
Heard you confess you had the chain of him
After you first forswore it on the mart,
And thereupon I drew my sword on you;
And then you fled into this abbey here,
From whence, I think, you are come by miracle.

E. ANTIPHOLUS
I never came within these abbey walls,
Nor ever didst thou draw thy sword on me.
I never saw the chain, so help me Heaven!
And this is false you burden me withal.

DUKE
Why, what an intricate impeach is this! 270
I think you all have drunk of Circe's cup. 271
If here you housed him, here he would have been.
If he were mad, he would not plead so coldly. 273
[To Adriana.] You say he dined at home; the
goldsmith here
Denies that saying. [To E. Dromio.] Sirrah, what say
you?

E. DROMIO
Sir, he dined with her there, at the Porcupine.

COURTESAN
He did, and from my finger snatched that ring.

E. ANTIPHOLUS
'Tis true, my liege. This ring I had of her.

DUKE [to the Courtesan]
Sawst thou him enter at the abbey here?

COURTESAN
As sure, my liege, as I do see Your Grace.

DUKE
Why, this is strange. Go call the Abbess hither.

I think you are all mated or stark mad. 282

Exit one to the Abbess.

EGEON
Most mighty Duke, vouchsafe me speak a word.
Haply I see a friend will save my life
And pay the sum that may deliver me.

DUKE
Speak freely, Syracusian, what thou wilt.

EGEON
Is not your name, sir, called Antipholus?
And is not that your bondman, Dromio?

E. DROMIO
Within this hour I was his bondman, sir,
But he, I thank him, gnawed in two my cords.
Now am I Dromio and his man, unbound.

EGEON
I am sure you both of you remember me.

E. DROMIO
Ourselves we do remember, sir, by you;
For lately we were bound, as you are now.
You are not Pinch's patient, are you, sir?

EGEON
Why look you strange on me? You know me well.

E. ANTIPHOLUS
I never saw you in my life till now.

EGEON
O, grief hath changed me since you saw me last,
And careful hours with Time's deformèd hand 299
Have written strange defeatures in my face. 300
But tell me yet, dost thou not know my voice?

E. ANTIPHOLUS Neither.

EGEON Dromio, nor thou?

E. DROMIO No, trust me, sir, nor I.

EGEON I am sure thou dost.

E. DROMIO Ay, sir, but I am sure I do not; and whatsoever a man denies, you are now bound to believe him.

EGEON
Not know my voice! O time's extremity,
Hast thou so cracked and splitted my poor tongue
In seven short years, that here my only son
Knows not my feeble key of untuned cares? 311
Though now this grainèd face of mine be hid 312
In sap-consuming winter's drizzled snow 313
And all the conduits of my blood froze up,
Yet hath my night of life some memory,
My wasting lamps some fading glimmer left, 316
My dull deaf ears a little use to hear.
All these old witnesses—I cannot err—
Tell me thou art my son Antipholus.

E. ANTIPHOLUS
I never saw my father in my life.

EGEON
But seven years since, in Syracusa, boy, 321

---

243 **took . . . as** pretended to be 245 **And . . . me** and, though he
seemed faceless (being so thin and scraggy), trying nonetheless to
stare me down 246 **possessed** mad 270 **intricate impeach** involved
accusation 271 **Circe's cup** the charmed cup, a draft of which
turned men into beasts (as told in Homer's *Odyssey*) 273 **coldly**
calmly, rationally

282 **mated** stupefied 299 **careful** full of care. **deformèd** deforming
(or perhaps referring to the withered hands of Father Time) 300 **defeatures** disfigurements, blemishes 311 **my . . . cares** my voice enfeebled by discordant cares 312 **grainèd** lined, furrowed 313 **In
. . . snow** i.e., by my white beard, sign of old age that dries up the
sap of youth 316 **wasting lamps** i.e., dimming eyes 321 **But** only

Thou know'st we parted. But perhaps, my son,
Thou sham'st to acknowledge me in misery.

E. ANTIPHOLUS
The Duke and all that know me in the city
Can witness with me that it is not so.
I ne'er saw Syracusa in my life.

DUKE
I tell thee, Syracusian, twenty years
Have I been patron to Antipholus,
During which time he ne'er saw Syracusa.
I see thy age and dangers make thee dote.

*Enter the Abbess, with Antipholus and Dromio of
Syracuse.*

ABBESS
Most mighty Duke, behold a man much wronged.
                              All gather to see them.

ADRIANA
I see two husbands, or mine eyes deceive me.

DUKE
One of these men is genius to the other;   333
And so of these, which is the natural man,
And which the spirit? Who deciphers them?   335

S. DROMIO
I, sir, am Dromio. Command him away.

E. DROMIO
I, sir, am Dromio. Pray, let me stay.

S. ANTIPHOLUS
Egeon art thou not? Or else his ghost?

S. DROMIO
O, my old master! Who hath bound him here?

ABBESS
Whoever bound him, I will loose his bonds
And gain a husband by his liberty.
Speak, old Egeon, if thou be'st the man
That hadst a wife once called Emilia
That bore thee at a burden two fair sons.   344
O, if thou be'st the same Egeon, speak,
And speak unto the same Emilia!

EGEON
If I dream not, thou art Emilia.
If thou art she, tell me where is that son
That floated with thee on the fatal raft?

ABBESS
By men of Epidamnum he and I
And the twin Dromio all were taken up;
But by and by rude fishermen of Corinth   352
By force took Dromio and my son from them,
And me they left with those of Epidamnum.
What then became of them I cannot tell;
I to this fortune that you see me in.

DUKE
Why, here begins his morning story right: 357
These two Antipholus', these two so like,
And these two Dromios, one in semblance—   359

Besides her urging of her wreck at sea—   360
These are the parents to these children,
Which accidentally are met together.
Antipholus, thou cam'st from Corinth first?

S. ANTIPHOLUS
No, sir, not I. I came from Syracuse.

DUKE
Stay, stand apart. I know not which is which.

E. ANTIPHOLUS
I came from Corinth, my most gracious lord—

E. DROMIO   And I with him.

E. ANTIPHOLUS
Brought to this town by that most famous warrior,
Duke Menaphon, your most renownèd uncle.

ADRIANA
Which of you two did dine with me today?

S. ANTIPHOLUS
I, gentle mistress.

ADRIANA   And are not you my husband?

E. ANTIPHOLUS   No, I say nay to that.

S. ANTIPHOLUS
And so do I. Yet did she call me so,
And this fair gentlewoman, her sister here,
Did call me brother. [*To Luciana.*] What I told you
    then
I hope I shall have leisure to make good,   376
If this be not a dream I see and hear.

ANGELO [*pointing to the chain Antipholus of Syracuse wears*]
That is the chain, sir, which you had of me.

S. ANTIPHOLUS
I think it be, sir. I deny it not.

E. ANTIPHOLUS [*to Angelo*]
And you, sir, for this chain arrested me.

ANGELO
I think I did, sir. I deny it not.

ADRIANA [*to Antipholus of Ephesus*]
I sent you money, sir, to be your bail,
By Dromio, but I think he brought it not.

E. DROMIO   No, none by me.

S. ANTIPHOLUS [*showing his purse to Adriana*]
This purse of ducats I received from you,
And Dromio my man did bring them me.
I see we still did meet each other's man,   387
And I was ta'en for him, and he for me,
And thereupon these errors are arose.

E. ANTIPHOLUS [*offering money*]
These ducats pawn I for my father here.

DUKE
It shall not need. Thy father hath his life.

COURTESAN
Sir, I must have that diamond from you.

E. ANTIPHOLUS [*giving the ring*]
There, take it, and much thanks for my good cheer.

ABBESS
Renownèd Duke, vouchsafe to take the pains   394

---

333 **genius** attendant spirit 335 **deciphers** distinguishes 344 **bur-den** birth 352 **rude** rough, simple 357 **his morning story** i.e., the history he related this morning 359 **semblance** appearance

360 **urging** urgent account 376 **leisure** opportunity 387 **still** continually 394 **vouchsafe** deign, agree

To go with us into the abbey here
And hear at large discoursèd all our fortunes,   396
And all that are assembled in this place,
That by this sympathizèd one day's error   398
Have suffered wrong. Go, keep us company,
And we shall make full satisfaction.
Thirty-three years have I but gone in travail
Of you, my sons, and till this present hour
My heavy burden ne'er deliverèd.
The Duke, my husband, and my children both,
And you the calendars of their nativity,   405
Go to a gossips' feast, and joy with me;   406
After so long grief, such nativity!
DUKE
With all my heart I'll gossip at this feast.   408
                    Exeunt omnes. Manent the two
                    Dromios and two brothers [Antipholus].
S. DROMIO [*to Antipholus of Ephesus*]
Master, shall I fetch your stuff from shipboard?
E. ANTIPHOLUS
Dromio, what stuff of mine hast thou embarked?
S. DROMIO
Your goods that lay at host, sir, in the Centaur.   411
S. ANTIPHOLUS
He speaks to me. —I am your master, Dromio.
Come, go with us. We'll look to that anon.
Embrace thy brother there; rejoice with him.
                    Exeunt [the two brothers Antipholus].
S. DROMIO
There is a fat friend at your master's house
That kitchened me for you today at dinner.   416
She now shall be my sister, not my wife.
E. DROMIO
Methinks you are my glass and not my brother.   418
I see by you I am a sweet-faced youth.
Will you walk in to see their gossiping?   420
S. DROMIO   Not I, sir; you are my elder.
E. DROMIO   That's a question. How shall we try it?
S. DROMIO   We'll draw cuts for the senior. Till then, lead 423
thou first.
E. DROMIO   Nay, then, thus:
We came into the world like brother and brother,
And now let's go hand in hand, not one before
    another.   *Exeunt.*

396 at large at length   **398 sympathizèd** shared in by all equally
405 calendars . . . nativity i.e., the Dromios, since the servants were
born at the same time as their masters   **406 gossips' feast** feast of the
godparents, christening feast   **408 gossip** i.e., be a hearty companion, take part   **411 lay at host** were put up at the inn   **416 kitchened** entertained in the kitchen   **418 glass** mirror   **420 gossiping**
merrymaking   **423 cuts** lots

Love's Labor's Lost

In much the same way that *The Comedy of Errors* is Shakespeare's apprenticeship to Plautus and neoclassical comedy, *Love's Labor's Lost* is his apprenticeship to John Lyly's courtly drama of the 1580s, to the court masque, and to conventions of Petrarchan lyric poetry. The play is word conscious and stylistically mannered to an extent that is unusual even for the pun-loving Shakespeare. The humor abounds in the pert repartee for which juvenile actors were especially fitted, and an extraordinarily high percentage of roles are assigned to boys: four women and a diminutive page (Mote) among seventeen named roles. The social setting is patrician and the entertainments aristocratic. In some ways, little seems to happen in *Love's Labor's Lost*. Fast-moving plot is replaced by a structure that includes a series of debates on courtly topics reminiscent of John Lyly: love versus honor, the flesh versus the spirit, pleasure versus instruction, art versus nature. The songs and sonnets composed by the courtiers for the ladies (4.3.23–116) gracefully caricature the excesses of the Petrarchan love convention (named for the influential Italian sonneteer, Francesco Petrarch): the lovers are "sick to death" with unrequited passion, they catalogue the charms of their proud mistresses, they express their exquisitely tortured emotions through elaborate poetical metaphors, and so on. Stage movements are often masquelike; characters group themselves and then pair off two by two, as in a formal dance. Actual masques and pageants, presented by the courtiers or devised for their amusement, are essential ingredients of the spectacle.

Yet beneath the brightly polished surfaces of this sophisticated comedy, we often catch glimpses of a candor and a simplicity that offset the tinsel and glitter. The wits ultimately disclaim (with some qualification) their wittiness, and the ladies confess they have tried too zealously to put down the men; both sides disavow the extreme postures they have striven so hard to maintain. The clowns, though deflated by mocking laughter for their naiveté and pomposity, deflate the courtiers, in turn, for lack of compassion. From this interplay among various forms of courtly wit, Petrarchism, pedantry, and rustic speech emerges a recommended style that is witty but not irresponsibly so, courtly yet sincere, polished and yet free of affectation or empty verbal ornament. This new harmony is aptly expressed by Berowne and Rosaline, whose witty quest for self-understanding in love foreshadows that of Benedick and Beatrice in *Much Ado About Nothing*. The perfect expression of the true style is found in the song at the end of the play; taking the form of a medieval literary debate between Spring and Winter, it beautifully fuses the natural and the artificial into a concordant vision transcending the mundane.

Like *The Comedy of Errors*, *Love's Labor's Lost* may either be a very early play or just an early play. It was published in quarto in 1598 "as it was presented before Her Highness this last Christmas" (1597). The text also purports to be "newly corrected and augmented," though we know of no earlier published version. Perhaps a play that was already several years old may have seemed in need of stylistic revision. Act 4 does, in fact, contain two long duplicatory passages, suggesting that a certain amount of rewriting did take place. The revisions alter the meaning only slightly, however, and give little support to the widely held notion that Shakespeare must have reworked the ending of his play. The unresolved ending, in which no marriages take place and in which the Princess's territorial claims to Aquitaine are left unsettled, should be regarded not as unfinished but as highly imaginative and indeed indispensable. The title, after all, assures us that "love's labors" will be lost, and the Princess affirms the principle of "form confounded."

Equally inconclusive are theories that the play was a topical satire written for a special audience or that it was a comparatively late play of Shakespeare's "lyric" period, 1594–1595. Topical hypotheses arise from the quest for Shakespeare's sources. Since the plot of *Love's Labor's Lost* is derived from no known literary source, may it have been drawn instead from the Elizabethan contemporary scene, poking fun at the pretentiousness of literary figures and intellectuals, such as John Florio, Thomas Nashe, Gabriel Harvey, Sir Walter Ralegh, and George Chapman? Or should we seek topical meaning in the undoubted currency of such names as Navarre (Henry of Navarre, King Henry IV of France), Berowne (Biron, Henry IV's general), Dumaine (De Mayenne, brother of the Catholic Guise), and others? From the point of view of dating the play, however, such names would have been distastefully controversial in a courtly comedy after 1589. That date saw the beginning in France of a bitter civil conflict between the Catholic Guise and Protestant Navarre, continuing until Henry abjured Protestantism in 1593 and assumed the French throne. In the 1580s, on the other hand, the tiny kingdom of Navarre would have seemed charmingly appropriate as a setting for Shakespeare's play. Such an early date, although by no means certain, would also help explain the Lylyan tone of the comedy and its early techniques of versification: the high percentage of rhymed lines in couplets and quatrains, the end-stopped blank verse, the use of various sonnet forms and of seven-stress (septenary) couplets, and the like. Possibly, then, the play was first written in about 1588–1589 for a boys' company and revised for Shakespeare's company in about 1596–1597.

The world of *Love's Labor's Lost* seems uneventful at first and remarkably unthreatened by danger or evil; only hintingly do reminders of mortality intrude upon the never-never-land of Navarre. There are, to be sure, occasional references to the Princess's "bedrid" father, to the plague, and to a "death's head," but the courtiers and we as audience are little prepared for the sudden appearance of Marcade in 5.2 and his announcement that the Princess's royal father is dead and that all lighthearted entertainments must now give way to mourning. Prior to this belated moment of reversal, the male characters are menaced by nothing worse than loss of dignity through breaking of their oaths. And although oath breaking was a matter of great seriousness to Elizabethan gentlemen, their doing so here is partly excused by the constancy of their devotion once they have fallen in love. In such an artificial world, the preservation of one's self-esteem assumes undue importance. Using the criteria of wit and self-awareness, Mote and Boyet, as manipulators and controllers of point of view, show us how to laugh at folly in love and pomposity in language. They present to us variations on a theme of courtly behavior, creating, in effect, a scale of manners ranging from the most aristocratic (the King and the Princess, Berowne and Rosaline) to the most absurdly pretentious (Armado, Holofernes). Nearly all the characters are mocked, but those at the lower end of the scale are especially vulnerable because they are grossly unself-aware and hence unteachable.

The King and his companions deserve to be mocked because of their transparent lack of self-knowledge, their affectation, and the futility of their vows against love. As Berowne concedes from the start, such defiance of love is at odds with a fundamental natural rhythm that ultimately cannot be thwarted—a rhythm that provides a counterpoint and corrective to the frequently artificial rhythms of courtly life. This natural rhythm asserts itself throughout the play until it becomes starkly insistent in the death of the Princess's royal father and in the resulting twelve-month delay of all marriages.

Hypocritical defiance of love is doomed to comic failure and satirical punishment. The basic devices used to expose this hypocrisy are misdirected love letters and overheard speech, both devices of unmasking. Appropriately, the young ladies administer their most amusing comeuppance to the men by seeing through their Muscovite masks. The code governing this merry conflict is one of "mock for mock" and "sport by sport o'erthrown" (5.2.140,153). In a prevailing legal metaphor, the young men are guilty of forswearing their written oaths, and must be punished for their perjury. Love is metaphorically a war, a siege, a battle of the sexes in which the women come off virtually unscathed. The language of love is that of parry and thrust (with occa-

sional bawdy overtones). The men naturally are chagrined to be put down by the ladies but are on their way to a cure: they laugh at their own pretentiousness and, even if hyperbolically, vow to cast aside all "affectation" and "maggot ostentation" in favor of "russet yeas and honest kersey noes" (lines 403–416). At the same time, Berowne's renunciation of artful language is cast in the form of a perfect fourteen-line sonnet; Shakespeare is having it both ways.

The clownish types are generally more victimized by their affectations. The fantastical Don Armado, as lover of Jaquenetta the country wench, apes the courtly conventions of the aristocrats to whose company he aspires. Enervated by base passion, penning wretched love letters, and worshiping a dairymaid as though she were an unapproachable goddess, he is a caricature of the Petrarchan lover. Generally, however, the affectations of the comic characters have to do with language rather than love. Armado himself is known as a phrasemaker, "a plume of feathers," a "weathercock": "Did you ever hear better?" (4.1.94–95). His letter to Jaquenetta, read aloud for the Princess's amusement, is an exquisite spoof of John Lyly's exaggeratedly mannered style, called Euphuism: "Shall I command thy love? I may. Shall I enforce thy love? I could. Shall I entreat thy love? I will. What shalt thou exchange for rags? Robes. For tittles? Titles. For thyself? Me" (lines 80–83). Here we see the repeated antitheses, the balanced structure (reflected also in the structure of the play), and the alliterative effects that so intoxicated literary sophisticates of the 1580s. In a similar spirit, other comic types are distinguished by their verbal habits: Constable Dull by his malapropisms (anticipating Dogberry and Elbow); Holofernes by his Latinisms, philological definitions, and varied epithets; Nathaniel by his deference to Holofernes as a fellow bookman; and Costard by his amiable but unlettered confusion over such grandiose terms as "remuneration" and "guerdon" (3.1.167–171). The word-conscious humor of the play gives us parodies of excruciatingly bad verse (as in Holofernes' "extemporal epitaph on the death of the deer," 4.2.49–61), teeth-grating puns (enfranchise, one Frances, 3.1.118–119), and the longest Latin word in existence (*honorificabilitudinitatibus*, 5.1.41).

A little of this sort of thing goes a long way, and occasional scenes of verbal sparring are as tedious as anything Shakespeare ever wrote. He tries to have it both ways, reveling in linguistic self-consciousness while laughing at its excesses. Yet the self-possessed characters do at least come to a realization that verbal overkill, like Petrarchan posturing, must be cast aside in favor of decorum and frankness in speech. There will always be "style," but it must be an appropriate style. The comic characters at their best help emphasize this same point. Costard especially is blessed with a pragmatic folk wisdom and simplicity that enable him to stand up unflinchingly to the ladies and gentlemen. He does not hesitate to tell the Princess that she is the "thickest and the tallest" of the ladies, for "truth is truth" (4.1.48). His forbearing description of Nathaniel as "a little o'erparted" (5.2.581) in the role of Alexander serves as a gentle rebuke to the wits, whose caustic observations on "The Nine Worthies" have gotten out of hand. Even Holofernes justly chides, before retiring in confusion as Judas Maccabaeus, that "This is not generous, not gentle, not humble" (line 626).

Even if the stylistic self-consciousness makes for labored reading at times, the play can be wonderfully funny in the theater. It provides numerous opportunities for sight gags, and it revels in comic character types who are funny even when their jokes are feeble. For all his indebtedness to Lyly's courtly drama in this play, Shakespeare has shaped it to the demands of a popular audience. Perhaps the greatest source of amusement is in Shakespeare's depiction of the war of the sexes. Nowhere else does he give us male characters who are so consistently baffled and tormented by women. The young women know from the start who they are and what men they are attracted to; we never see the women fall in love, for they have evidently made up their minds already. The men, conversely, flounder about absurdly from one inelegant posture to another, from futile asceticism to curiosity, infatuation, betrayal of their oaths, attempts to conceal their lovesickness from one another, and collapse of all pretenses when they are caught out. They have yet to come to terms with their own inner feelings and must be taught—and tortured—by the self-possessed young ladies. The men are at their most absurd when, having confessed to falling in love, they now rival one another in boasting of their respective mistresses and in striving to see who will succeed first. It never crosses their minds that they might be rejected now that they have deigned to come forward as suitors.

The masquing in Act 5 is thus a device by which the women can test and even humiliate the young men to show them how flighty and uncontrolled are their unfamiliar new emotions. The uncompleted ending of the play expresses an unfinished process: the young men must still apprentice themselves to mature self-reflection before they can be deemed worthy as husbands. Ironically, the young women consign the men to the very sort of celibate exercise in self-understanding that the men thought they were committing themselves to at the play's start. In these terms, too, we can see that some of the play's subplot characters are variations on a theme of male folly in love: Costard is the self-assured peasant, while Armado is the self-abnegating aristocrat. Armado exaggerates everything foolish that the aristocratic men have undergone and in Act 5 is fittingly the center of an absurd pageant, through which he becomes the comic scapegoat. Watching his performance in the pageant of "The Nine Worthies," the young aristocrats can laugh at the absurdities of male posturing and self-abasement that they are now slowly learning to control in themselves.

Above all, then, it is the play's unexpected ending that introduces an invaluable new insight on the courtiers' brittle war of wits. The death of the Princess's father brings everyone back to reality, to sober responsibility, to an awareness that marriage requires thoughtful decision. Devouring Time has entered the never-never-land of Navarre's park. The song at the end, appropriately cast in the form of a dialogue or debate, gives us the two voices of Spring and Winter, love and death, carnival and Lent, to remind us that human happiness and self-understanding are complex and perishable. And the song reminds us as well, in its "living art," of that subtle power of the imagination, which transforms time, love, and death into artistic creation.

Love's Labor's Lost

[*Dramatis Personae*

FERDINAND, *King of Navarre*
BEROWNE,
LONGAVILLE, } *lords attending the King*
DUMAINE,

THE PRINCESS OF FRANCE
ROSALINE,
MARIA, } *ladies attending the Princess*
KATHARINE,
BOYET, *a French lord attending the Princess*
MARCADE, *a French gentleman acting as messenger*
Two French LORDS

DON ADRIANO DE ARMADO, *a Spanish braggart*
MOTE, *his page*
NATHANIEL, *a curate*
HOLOFERNES, *a schoolmaster, called a pedant*
DULL, *a constable*
COSTARD, *a rustic, also referred to as a clown*
JAQUENETTA, *a dairymaid*
A FORESTER

*Lords and Attendants; Attendants disguised as
 blackamoors*

SCENE: *Navarre*]

1.1   *Enter Ferdinand, King of Navarre, Berowne,
           Longaville, and Dumaine.*

KING
Let fame, that all hunt after in their lives,
Live registered upon our brazen tombs,   2
And then grace us in the disgrace of death,   3
When, spite of cormorant devouring Time,   4
Th' endeavor of this present breath may buy   5
That honor which shall bate his scythe's keen edge   6
And make us heirs of all eternity.
Therefore, brave conquerors—for so you are,
That war against your own affections   9

And the huge army of the world's desires—
Our late edict shall strongly stand in force.   11
Navarre shall be the wonder of the world;
Our court shall be a little academe,   13
Still and contemplative in living art.   14
You three, Berowne, Dumaine, and Longaville,
Have sworn for three years' term to live with me
My fellow scholars and to keep those statutes
That are recorded in this schedule here.   18
                          [*He shows a document.*]
Your oaths are passed; and now subscribe your
    names,   19
That his own hand may strike his honor down   20
That violates the smallest branch herein.   21
If you are armed to do as sworn to do,   22
Subscribe to your deep oaths, and keep it, too.
LONGAVILLE [*signing*]
I am resolved. 'Tis but a three years' fast.
The mind shall banquet, though the body pine.   25
Fat paunches have lean pates, and dainty bits   26
Make rich the ribs but bankrupt quite the wits.
DUMAINE [*signing*]
My loving lord, Dumaine is mortified.   28
The grosser manner of these world's delights
He throws upon the gross world's baser slaves.   30
To love, to wealth, to pomp I pine and die,
With all these living in philosophy.   32
BEROWNE
I can but say their protestation over.   33
So much, dear liege, I have already sworn,   34
That is, to live and study here three years.
But there are other strict observances:
As, not to see a woman in that term,
Which I hope well is not enrollèd there;   38
And one day in a week to touch no food,   39
And but one meal on every day besides,   40
The which I hope is not enrollèd there;
And then to sleep but three hours in the night,
And not be seen to wink of all the day—   43
When I was wont to think no harm all night,   44
And make a dark night too of half the day—
Which I hope well is not enrollèd there.
O, these are barren tasks, too hard to keep,
Not to see ladies, study, fast, not sleep!

**1.1. Location: The King of Navarre's park. (The locale remains the
same throughout the play, sometimes immediately outside the gates
of Navarre's court.)**
2 registered recorded. **brazen** brass **3 grace** honor. **the disgrace
of death** (1) the taking away of the grace of life by death (2) the over-
throwing of death by proper fame **4 spite of** despite. **cormorant**
ravenous, rapacious. (The cormorant is a large, voracious seabird.)
5 breath breathing time, i.e., life itself; also, speech **6 bate** abate,
blunt **9 affections** emotions, passions

11 late recent **13 academe** academy. (From the name of the grove
near Athens where Plato and his followers gathered.) **14 Still** constant, calm. **living art** (1) the art of living (an idea probably derived
from the *ars vivendi* of the Roman Stoics) (2) infusing learning (*art*)
with vitality **18 schedule** document **19 passed** pledged **20 hand**
(1) armed hand of a warrior (2) handwriting **21 branch** i.e., clause
22 armed i.e., prepared (with a play on the military sense, as in *hand*,
line 20) **25 pine** languish, waste away **26 pates** heads. **dainty bits**
delicate morsels **28 mortified** i.e., dead to worldly desire
30 throws upon leaves to. **baser slaves** i.e., slaves to passion and
pleasure **32 With . . . philosophy** i.e., the pleasure afforded by
these (love, wealth, pomp) I find in philosophy (or, perhaps, living
with these companions in our commitment to philosophy) **33 over**
again **34 liege** lord **38 well** fervently. **enrollèd** written. **there**
i.e., on the document detailing the oaths **39 in a** of each **40 but**
only. **on** in **43 wink of all** close the eyes at any time during
44 wont accustomed. **think no harm** i.e., think it no harm to sleep
soundly

KING
Your oath is passed to pass away from these.
BEROWNE
Let me say no, my liege, an if you please.   50
I only swore to study with Your Grace
And stay here in your court for three years' space.   52
LONGAVILLE
You swore to that, Berowne, and to the rest.
BEROWNE
By yea and nay, sir, then I swore in jest.   54
What is the end of study, let me know?   55
KING
Why, that to know which else we should not know.
BEROWNE
Things hid and barred, you mean, from common
sense?   57
KING
Ay, that is study's godlike recompense.   58
BEROWNE
Come on, then, I will swear to study so   59
To know the thing I am forbid to know,
As thus: to study where I well may dine,
When I to feast expressly am forbid;
Or study where to meet some mistress fine,
When mistresses from common sense are hid;
Or, having sworn too-hard-a-keeping oath,   65
Study to break it and not break my troth.   66
If study's gain be thus, and this be so,   67
Study knows that which yet it doth not know.   68
Swear me to this, and I will ne'er say no.
KING
These be the stops that hinder study quite,   70
And train our intellects to vain delight.   71
BEROWNE
Why, all delights are vain, but that most vain
Which, with pain purchased, doth inherit pain: 73
As, painfully to pore upon a book   74
To seek the light of truth, while truth the while   75
Doth falsely blind the eyesight of his look.   76
Light seeking light doth light of light beguile;   77
So, ere you find where light in darkness lies,
Your light grows dark by losing of your eyes.   79
Study me how to please the eye indeed   80
By fixing it upon a fairer eye,   81

Who dazzling so, that eye shall be his heed   82
And give him light that it was blinded by.   83
Study is like the heaven's glorious sun,
That will not be deep searched with saucy looks.   85
Small have continual plodders ever won   86
Save base authority from others' books.   87
These earthly godfathers of heaven's lights,   88
That give a name to every fixèd star,
Have no more profit of their shining nights   90
Than those that walk and wot not what they are.   91
Too much to know is to know naught but fame;   92
And every godfather can give a name.   93
KING
How well he's read, to reason against reading!
DUMAINE
Proceeded well, to stop all good proceeding.   95
LONGAVILLE
He weeds the corn and still lets grow the weeding.   96
BEROWNE
The spring is near when green geese are a-breeding.   97
DUMAINE
How follows that?   Fit in his place and time.   98
BEROWNE
DUMAINE
In reason nothing.
BEROWNE   Something then in rhyme.   99
KING
Berowne is like an envious sneaping frost   100
That bites the firstborn infants of the spring.   101
BEROWNE
Well, say I am. Why should proud summer boast   102
Before the birds have any cause to sing?
Why should I joy in an abortive birth?   104
At Christmas I no more desire a rose
Than wish a snow in May's newfangled shows,   106
But like of each thing that in season grows.   107
So you to study, now it is too late,   108
Climb o'er the house to unlock the little gate.   109
KING
Well, sit you out. Go home, Berowne. Adieu.   110

50 an if if 52 space time 54 By . . . nay earnestly. (A meaning derived from Matthew 5:33–37; Berowne is using a pious equivocation frequently invoked by those not having a proper answer.) 55 end goal 57 common sense ordinary observation or intelligence 58 recompense compensation, payment 59 Come on (with a quibble on common, line 57) 65 too . . . oath an oath too hard to keep 66 troth faith 67–68 If . . . know if the true purpose of study should be as I've defined it—and indeed it is—then study as conventionally understood is quite oblivious to its own true function 70 stops obstacles 71 train lure, entice. vain (1) foolish (2) overly proud 73 pain labor, effort (with pun on "suffering"). purchased acquired. inherit take possession of 74 painfully laboriously. upon over 75 the while at that same time 76 falsely treacherously. his look its power to see; or, the looker's vision 77 Light . . . beguile i.e., searching for truth by excessive study paradoxically takes from the eyes their ability to see at all, just as staring at a bright light causes blindness 79 eyes sight 80 Study me let me study 81 fairer i.e., of a fair lady

82 Who dazzling so i.e., the man who has fixed his eye on a fair lady being thus dazzled. heed (1) protection, guard (2) object of attention 83 it i.e., his own eye 85 deep searched scrutinized. saucy presumptuous, insolent 86 Small little 87 Save except. base commonplace, lower 88 earthly godfathers astronomers (who name stars just as godparents pronounce the name of the child at a christening) 90 shining i.e., starlit 91 wot know 92 Too . . . fame the quest for superfluous knowledge leads only to an empty reputation for secondhand information 93 every . . . name i.e., anyone, acting as godparent, can do as much as astronomers 95 Proceeded advanced (in the academic sense of taking a degree) 96 He . . . weeding he pulls out the wheat and allows the weeds to grow 97 green geese i.e., young geese born the previous autumn and sold at green-goose fair, a season of merriment, held on Whitmonday; here, young simpletons 98 Fit in his appropriate to its 99 In reason nothing i.e., it doesn't follow at all logically. rhyme (Berowne, answering Dumaine, plays upon the proverbial phrase "neither rhyme nor reason.") 100 envious malignant, malicious. sneaping biting, nipping 101 infants buds 102 proud glorious 104 abortive monstrous, unnatural 106 May's . . . shows i.e., the display of spring flowers 107 like of approve of. season i.e., its proper season 108 too late i.e., too late in our lives to be students 109 Climb . . . gate i.e., you begin at the wrong end 110 sit you out don't take part

BEROWNE
No, my good lord, I have sworn to stay with you.
And though I have for barbarism spoke more   112
    Than for that angel knowledge you can say,
Yet, confident, I'll keep what I have sworn
    And bide the penance of each three years' day.   115
Give me the paper. Let me read the same,
And to the strictest decrees I'll write my name.
                                    [*He takes the paper.*]

KING
How well this yielding rescues thee from shame!

BEROWNE [*reads*]   "Item, That no woman shall come
within a mile of my court—" Hath this been
proclaimed?

LONGAVILLE   Four days ago.

BEROWNE   Let's see the penalty—"on pain of losing her
tongue." Who devised this penalty?

LONGAVILLE
Marry, that did I.

BEROWNE   Sweet lord, and why?   125

LONGAVILLE
To fright them hence with that dread penalty.

BEROWNE
A dangerous law against gentility!   127
[*He reads.*] "Item, If any man be seen to talk with a
woman within the term of three years, he shall endure
such public shame as the rest of the court can possibly
devise."
This article, my liege, yourself must break,
    For well you know here comes in embassy   133
The French King's daughter with yourself to
        speak—
    A maid of grace and complete majesty—   135
About surrender up of Aquitaine
    To her decrepit, sick, and bedrid father.   137
Therefore this article is made in vain,
    Or vainly comes th' admirèd Princess hither.

KING
What say you, lords? Why, this was quite forgot.

BEROWNE
So study evermore is overshot.   141
While it doth study to have what it would,   142
It doth forget to do the thing it should,
And when it hath the thing it hunteth most,
'Tis won as towns with fire—so won, so lost.   145

KING
We must of force dispense with this decree.   146
She must lie here, on mere necessity.   147

BEROWNE
Necessity will make us all forsworn   148

Three thousand times within this three years'
        space;
For every man with his affects is born,   150
    Not by might mastered, but by special grace.   151
If I break faith, this word shall speak for me: 152
I am forsworn on "mere necessity."
So to the laws at large I write my name.   [*He signs.*] 154
    And he that breaks them in the least degree
Stands in attainder of eternal shame.   156
    Suggestions are to other as to me;   157
But I believe, although I seem so loath,   158
I am the last that will last keep his oath.   159
But is there no quick recreation granted?   160

KING
Ay, that there is. Our court, you know, is haunted   161
    With a refinèd traveler of Spain,   162
A man in all the world's new fashion planted,   163
    That hath a mint of phrases in his brain;   164
One who the music of his own vain tongue   165
    Doth ravish like enchanting harmony;
A man of compliments, whom right and wrong   167
    Have chose as umpire of their mutiny.   168
This child of fancy, that Armado hight,   169
    For interim to our studies shall relate   170
In high-borne words the worth of many a knight   171
    From tawny Spain, lost in the world's debate.   172
How you delight, my lords, I know not, I,   173
But I protest I love to hear him lie,
And I will use him for my minstrelsy.   175

BEROWNE
Armado is a most illustrious wight,   176
A man of fire-new words, fashion's own knight.   177

LONGAVILLE
Costard the swain and he shall be our sport;   178
And so to study three years is but short.

    *Enter [Dull,] a constable, with Costard, with a
    letter.*

DULL   Which is the Duke's own person?   180
BEROWNE   This, fellow. What wouldst?   181

---

150 affects natural passions   **151 might** i.e., his own strength.   **special grace** divine intervention   **152 word** motto   **154 at large** as a whole, in general   **156 in attainder** under penalty, accused
157 Suggestions . . . me temptations affect me as much as they do any other   **158 loath** reluctant   **159 I . . . oath** I that speak last will be the last to break my oath (but with an equivocal meaning also of being the last person to keep his oath to the last)   **160 quick** lively
161–162 haunted With frequented by   **163 planted** established, involved   **164 mint** (1) place or source of invention (2) place where money is coined   **165 who** whom   **167 compliments** those formal manners that go to complete a gentleman (with a sense also of *complements*, the Quarto spelling, "something that fills up, completes, or makes perfect")   **168 mutiny** discord   **169 child of fancy** fantastic or grotesque creature.   **hight** is called. (An archaic, affected term.)
170 interim interlude   **171 high-borne** borne on high, elegantly lofty. (Or perhaps *highborn*, patrician, born of high rank.)   **172 tawny** sunburned.   **debate** warfare   **173 How you delight** what delights you   **175 for my minstrelsy** to act as my group of minstrels, as my court singer   **176 wight** person   **177 fire-new** newly coined   **178 Costard** (The name means a large apple; the term is frequently applied humorously or derisively to the head.)   **swain** rustic young fellow
180 Duke's i.e., King's   **181 fellow** (Customary form of address to a servant.)

112 for barbarism on the side of ignorance   **115 bide** endure.   **each . . . day** every day of the three years   **125 Marry** (A mild oath, derived from "by the Virgin Mary.")   **127 gentility** civilized custom   **133 in embassy** as an ambassador   **135 complete** perfect   **137 bedrid** bedridden   **141 overshot** wide of the mark by shooting over the target, mistaken   **142 would** desires   **145 with fire** by being burned down or bombarded by artillery (continuing the metaphor of siege in *overshot*, line 141)   **146 of force** necessarily   **147 lie** lodge.   **on mere** out of absolute   **148 forsworn** guilty of breaking an oath, perjured

DULL   I myself reprehend his own person, for I am His 182
Grace's farborough. But I would see his own person in 183
flesh and blood.
BEROWNE   This is he.
DULL   Señor Arm–Arm–commends you. There's vil- 186
lainy abroad. This letter will tell you more.

[He gives the letter to the King.]

COSTARD   Sir, the contempts thereof are as touching me. 188
KING   A letter from the magnificent Armado. 189
BEROWNE   How low soever the matter, I hope in God 190
for high words. 191
LONGAVILLE   A high hope for a low heaven. God grant 192
us patience!
BEROWNE   To hear, or forbear hearing?
LONGAVILLE   To hear meekly, sir, and to laugh moderately, or to forbear both.
BEROWNE   Well, sir, be it as the style shall give us cause 197
to climb in the merriness.
COSTARD   The matter is to me, sir, as concerning Jaque- 199
netta. The manner of it is, I was taken with the manner. 200
BEROWNE   In what manner?
COSTARD   In manner and form following, sir—all those 202
three. I was seen with her in the manor house, sitting 203
with her upon the form, and taken following her into 204
the park; which, put together, is "in manner and form
following." Now, sir, for the manner—it is the manner of a man to speak to a woman. For the form—in
some form.
BEROWNE   For the "following," sir?
COSTARD   As it shall follow in my correction; and God 210
defend the right! 211
KING   Will you hear this letter with attention?
BEROWNE   As we would hear an oracle.
COSTARD   Such is the sinplicity of man to hearken after 214
the flesh.
KING *[reads]*   "Great deputy, the welkin's vicegerent, 216
and sole dominator of Navarre, my soul's earth's god, 217
and body's fostering patron—" 218
COSTARD   Not a word of Costard yet.
KING *[reads]*   "So it is—"

COSTARD   It may be so, but if he say it is so, he is, in
telling true, but so. 222
KING   Peace!
COSTARD   Be to me and every man that dares not fight. 224
KING   No words!
COSTARD   Of other men's secrets, I beseech you. 226
KING *[reads]*   "So it is, besieged with sable-colored 227
melancholy, I did commend the black oppressing hu- 228
mor to the most wholesome physic of thy health- 229
giving air, and, as I am a gentleman, betook myself to
walk. The time when? About the sixth hour, when
beasts most graze, birds best peck, and men sit down
to that nourishment which is called supper. So much
for the time when. Now for the ground which—which,
I mean, I walked upon. It is yclept thy park. Then for 235
the place where—where, I mean, I did encounter that
obscene and most preposterous event that draweth 237
from my snow-white pen the ebon-colored ink which 238
here thou viewest, beholdest, surveyest, or seest. But
to the place where. It standeth north-northeast and by
east from the west corner of thy curious-knotted gar- 241
den. There did I see that low-spirited swain, that base 242
minnow of thy mirth—" 243
COSTARD   Me?
KING *[reads]*   "that unlettered, small-knowing soul—" 245
COSTARD   Me?
KING *[reads]*   "that shallow vassal—" 247
COSTARD   Still me?
KING *[reads]*   "which,   as   I   remember,   hight 249
Costard—"
COSTARD   O! Me.
KING *[reads]*   "sorted and consorted, contrary to thy 252
established   proclaimed   edict   and   continent   canon, 253
with, with—O, with—but with this I passion to say 254
wherewith—"
COSTARD   With a wench.
KING *[reads]*   "with a child of our grandmother Eve, a
female; or, for thy more sweet understanding, a
woman. Him I, as my ever-esteemed duty pricks me 259
on, have sent to thee, to receive the meed of punish- 260
ment, by thy sweet Grace's officer, Anthony Dull, a
man of good repute, carriage, bearing, and estima- 262
tion." 263
DULL   Me, an 't shall please you. I am Anthony Dull. 264

---

182 reprehend (Malapropism for "represent.")   **183 farborough** (Malapropism for "tharborough" or "third borough," a petty constable.)
186 commends you sends you his greetings   **188 contempts** (Malapropism for "contents.")   **189 magnificent Armado** boastful or grandiose Armado (with an allusion to the great Armada of Spain)
190 How low soever however debased   **191 high** lofty, exalted
192 low heaven i.e., small blessing   **197 be it** so be it.   **style** (with a
pun on "stile," giving point to *climb* in the next line)   **199 is to** applies to   **200 with the manner** with the stolen goods. (An Anglo-
French law term *mainoure*, from *manoeuvre*.)   **202 In manner and
form** (A familiar legal cliché of the time.)   **202–203 those three** i.e.,
manner and form following. (Costard proceeds to illustrate each term
as it applies to his case.)   **203 manor** (playing upon "manner")
204 form bench (playing upon *form* in line 202, as also with *following*)   **210 correction** punishment   **210–211 God defend the right**
(Prayer before mortal combat.)   **214 sinplicity** (This Quarto reading
may be a malapropism and has an ironic fitness, although it could
also be a simple misprint for "simplicity." Whether the joke is audible
in the theater is hard to say.)   **216 welkin's vicegerent** heaven's deputy. (A pompous phrase, as most in the letter are.)   **217 dominator**
ruler   **218 fostering** nurturing

222 but so i.e., not saying much   **224 Be to me** (Costard punningly
changes the King's "Peace"—i.e., "Be silent!"—to suit his own purposes; *Peace be to me* means "may I go undisturbed with the law's
blessing.")   **226 Of . . . secrets** (As in line 229, Costard changes the
King's meaning with witty wordplay: "Let's have no talk of other
men's secrets, which can get a person into trouble.")   **227 sable-colored** i.e., black   **228–229 black oppressing humor** black bile or
melancholy, oppressing with its black essence   **229 physic** medicine
235 yclept called. (Archaic usage.)   **237 obscene** disgusting
238 snow-white pen i.e., white goose quill.   **ebon-colored** i.e., black
(like ebony)   **241 curious-knotted** delicately or intricately designed
242 low-spirited ignoble   **243 minnow** contemptible little creature
245 unlettered illiterate   **247 vassal** slavish fellow   **249 hight** is
called. (Archaic usage.)   **252 sorted and consorted** associated
253 continent canon law enforcing restraint   **254 passion** grieve
259 pricks spurs   **260 meed** reward   **262–263 estimation** reputation
264 an 't if it

KING [reads]   "For Jaquenetta—so is the weaker vessel 265 called which I apprehended with the aforesaid swain —I keep her as a vessel of thy law's fury, and shall at 267 the least of thy sweet notice bring her to trial. Thine, 268 in all compliments of devoted and heartburning heat of duty,   Don Adriano de Armado."

BEROWNE   This is not so well as I looked for, but the best that ever I heard.

KING   Ay, the best for the worst. —But, sirrah, what say 273 you to this?

COSTARD   Sir, I confess the wench.

KING   Did you hear the proclamation?

COSTARD   I do confess much of the hearing it, but little of the marking of it.   278

KING   It was proclaimed a year's imprisonment to be taken with a wench.

COSTARD   I was taken with none, sir. I was taken with a damsel.

KING   Well, it was proclaimed "damsel."

COSTARD   This was no damsel neither, sir. She was a virgin.

KING   It is so varied too, for it was proclaimed "virgin." 286

COSTARD   If it were, I deny her virginity. I was taken with a maid.

KING   This "maid" will not serve your turn, sir.   289

COSTARD   This maid will serve my turn, sir.

KING   Sir, I will pronounce your sentence: you shall fast a week with bran and water.

COSTARD   I had rather pray a month with mutton and 293 porridge.   294

KING
And Don Armado shall be your keeper.
My Lord Berowne, see him delivered o'er.   296
And go we, lords, to put in practice that
Which each to other hath so strongly sworn.
[Exeunt the King, Longaville, and Dumaine.]

BEROWNE
I'll lay my head to any goodman's hat,   299
These oaths and laws will prove an idle scorn.   300
Sirrah, come on.

COSTARD   I suffer for the truth, sir; for true it is, I was taken with Jaquenetta, and Jaquenetta is a true girl; 303 and therefore, welcome the sour cup of prosperity! 304 Affliction may one day smile again, and till then, sit 305 thee down, sorrow!   Exeunt. 306

❖

265 **weaker vessel** i.e., woman. (See 1 Peter 3:7.) **267–268 at . . . notice** i.e., at your first hint   **268 bring her to trial** (with perhaps a bawdy double meaning of testing her mettle as a woman)   **273 best . . . worst** i.e., best example of the worst.   **sirrah** (Ordinary form of address to inferiors.)   **278 the marking of it** paying attention to it   **286 so varied** alternatively phrased (in typical legal jargon)   **289 serve your turn** i.e., get you out of your difficulty. (But Costard, in the next line, interprets the phrase in a ribald sense.)   **293– 294 mutton and porridge** mutton broth (with a pun on "mutton," whore)   **296 delivered o'er** handed over   **299 lay** wager.   **goodman's** i.e., yeoman's   **300 idle scorn** worthless object of mockery   **303 true** honest   **304 prosperity** (Malapropism for "adversity"?)   **305 Affliction** (Costard mixes this up with "prosperity.")   **305–306 sit thee down** i.e., stay, settle down with me

1.2   *Enter Armado and Mote, his page.*

ARMADO   Boy, what sign is it when a man of great spirit 1 grows melancholy?

MOTE   A great sign, sir, that he will look sad.

ARMADO   Why, sadness is one and the selfsame thing, dear imp.   5

MOTE   No, no, O Lord, sir, no.

ARMADO   How canst thou part sadness and melancholy, 7 my tender juvenal?   8

MOTE   By a familiar demonstration of the working, my 9 tough sēnor.   10

ARMADO   Why "tough sēnor"? Why "tough sēnor"?

MOTE   Why "tender juvenal"? Why "tender juvenal"?

ARMADO   I spoke it, tender juvenal, as a congruent epi- 13 theton appertaining to thy young days, which we may 14 nominate "tender."   15

MOTE   And I, tough sēnor, as an appertinent title to 16 your old time, which we may name "tough."

ARMADO   Pretty and apt.

MOTE   How mean you, sir? I pretty and my saying apt? Or I apt and my saying pretty?

ARMADO   Thou pretty, because little.   21

MOTE   Little pretty, because little. Wherefore apt?

ARMADO   And therefore apt, because quick.   23

MOTE   Speak you this in my praise, master?

ARMADO   In thy condign praise.   25

MOTE   I will praise an eel with the same praise.

ARMADO   What, that an eel is ingenious?

MOTE   That an eel is quick.   28

ARMADO   I do say thou art quick in answers. Thou 29 heat'st my blood.   30

MOTE   I am answered, sir.

ARMADO   I love not to be crossed.   32

MOTE [aside]   He speaks the mere contrary; crosses 33 love not him.

ARMADO   I have promised to study three years with the Duke.   36

MOTE   You may do it in an hour, sir.

ARMADO   Impossible.

MOTE   How many is one thrice told?   39

ARMADO   I am ill at reckoning; it fitteth the spirit of a 40 tapster.   41

1.2. Location: The same. Navarre's park.
s.d. Mote (The word in the First Quarto is *Moth*, pronounced identically with *mote* and meaning "dust speck." The sense of "moth" or tiny winged creature may also be present. There may possibly be a play also on *mot*, French for "word.")   **1 sign is it** is it a sign of   **5 imp** young shoot, child   **7 part** distinguish between   **8 juvenal** youth; satirist (after Juvenal, the Roman satirist)   **9 familiar** plain, easily understood.   **working** operation (of these emotions)   **10 sēnor** sir (with pun on "senior")   **13–14 congruent epitheton** appropriate epithet   **14 appertaining** belonging, suiting   **15 nominate** call   **16 appertinent** appropriate   **21 Thou . . . little** (Armado refers to the commonplace "little things are pretty.")   **23 quick** quick-witted   **25 condign** worthily deserved   **28 quick** full of life   **29–30 Thou . . . blood** you make me angry   **32 crossed** thwarted, opposed   **33 mere** absolute.   **crosses** coins. (So called because many of them were impressed with crosses.)   **36 Duke** i.e., King   **39 told** counted   **40 ill at reckoning** no good at arithmetic   **41 tapster** bartender

MOTE   You are a gentleman and a gamester, sir.   42

ARMADO   I confess both. They are both the varnish of a   43
complete man.   44

MOTE   Then I am sure you know how much the gross
sum of deuce-ace amounts to.   46

ARMADO   It doth amount to one more than two.

MOTE   Which the base vulgar do call three.   48

ARMADO   True.

MOTE   Why, sir, is this such a piece of study? Now here   50
is three studied ere ye'll thrice wink; and how easy it
is to put "years" to the word "three" and study three
years in two words, the dancing horse will tell you.   53

ARMADO   A most fine figure!   54

MOTE [aside]   To prove you a cipher.   55

ARMADO   I will hereupon confess I am in love; and as it
is base for a soldier to love, so am I in love with a base
wench. If drawing my sword against the humor of af-   58
fection would deliver me from the reprobate thought   59
of it, I would take Desire prisoner and ransom him to
any French courtier for a new-devised curtsy. I think   61
scorn to sigh; methinks I should outswear Cupid.   62
Comfort me, boy. What great men have been in love?

MOTE   Hercules, master.

ARMADO   Most sweet Hercules! More authority, dear
boy, name more; and, sweet my child, let them be
men of good repute and carriage.   67

MOTE   Samson, master; he was a man of good carriage,
great carriage, for he carried the town gates on his
back like a porter; and he was in love.

ARMADO   O well-knit Samson! Strong-jointed Samson!   71
I do excel thee in my rapier as much as thou didst me   72
in carrying gates. I am in love too. Who was Samson's
love, my dear Mote?

MOTE   A woman, master.

ARMADO   Of what complexion?   76

MOTE   Of all the four, or the three, or the two, or one of
the four.

ARMADO   Tell me precisely of what complexion.

MOTE   Of the sea-water green, sir.

ARMADO   Is that one of the four complexions?

MOTE   As I have read, sir; and the best of them, too.

ARMADO   Green indeed is the color of lovers; but to   83

have a love of that color, methinks Samson had small
reason for it. He surely affected her for her wit.   85

MOTE   It was so, sir, for she had a green wit.   86

ARMADO   My love is most immaculate white and red.

MOTE   Most maculate thoughts, master, are masked un-   88
der such colors.   89

ARMADO   Define, define, well-educated infant.   90

MOTE   My father's wit and my mother's tongue, assist me!

ARMADO   Sweet invocation of a child, most pretty and
pathetical!   94

MOTE
    If she be made of white and red,   95
        Her faults will ne'er be known,   96
    For blushing cheeks by faults are bred,   97
        And fears by pale white shown.   98
    Then if she fear, or be to blame,
        By this you shall not know,   100
    For still her cheeks possess the same   101
        Which native she doth owe.   102
A dangerous rhyme, master, against the reason of   103
white and red.   104

ARMADO   Is there not a ballad, boy, of the King and the   105
Beggar?   106

MOTE   The world was very guilty of such a ballad some
three ages since, but I think now 'tis not to be found;   108
or, if it were, it would neither serve for the writing nor   109
the tune.   110

ARMADO   I will have that subject newly writ o'er, that I
may example my digression by some mighty prece-   112
dent. Boy, I do love that country girl that I took in the
park with the rational hind Costard. She deserves   114
well.

MOTE [aside]   To be whipped; and yet a better love   116
than my master.

ARMADO   Sing, boy. My spirit grows heavy in love.

MOTE [aside] And that's great marvel, loving a light wench.   119

---

42 **gamester** gambler   43 **varnish** finish, ornament   44 **complete** accomplished   46 **deuce-ace** a throw of two and one in dice   48 **vulgar** common people   50 **piece** masterpiece   53 **dancing horse** (Probably a reference to a famous trained horse brought to London in
1591, named Morocco, that could count by tapping with its hoof.)
54 **figure** rhetorical flourish   55 **cipher** zero. (Mote takes Armado's
figure in line 54 to mean "numeral.")   58–59 **humor of affection** inclination to passion   59 **deliver me** save me.   **reprobate** depraved,
degrading   61 **new-devised curtsy** newfangled manner of bowing;
any new fashion   61–62 **think scorn** disdain   62 **outswear** overcome by swearing, or, swear to do without   67 **carriage** bearing
(with pun on "ability to carry" in the following speech; see Judges
16:3 for the account of Samson's deed)   71 **well-knit** well-proportioned   72 **in my rapier** in my swordsmanship. (The rapier replaced
the old-fashioned long sword in the 1590s.)   76 **complexion** skin
color; also temperament. (The four complexions were sanguine, choleric, phlegmatic, and melancholic, and were supposedly determined
by the relative proportions of the four humors.)   83 **Green** (A reference to lovers' "greensickness," an anemic condition of puberty.)

85 **affected** loved.   **wit** intelligence   86 **green** immature (with a punning reference perhaps to the seven green withes with which Samson
was bound, Judges 16:7–9)   88 **maculate** stained, polluted   89 **colors** (with a pun on "pretexts")   90 **Define** explain   94 **pathetical**
moving   95 **be made of** i.e., has a complexion that is. (With a play
on "maid." Mote also hints that the red and white are cosmetic.)
96 **Her . . . known** i.e., she will never be betrayed by blushes or pallor, since the red and white (perhaps cosmetic) will mask those effects
97 **by faults are bred** are caused by an awareness of being at fault
98 **fears** i.e., fears of detection   100 **this** i.e., her complexion or coloring (which is perhaps produced by cosmetics)   101–102 **For . . .
owe** i.e., for her cheeks are always (and therefore suspiciously) colored with the red and white of her natural coloration   103–104 **A
dangerous . . . red** i.e., a warning in rhyme against trusting in white
and red complexions. (The sentence plays on the contrast of *rhyme*
and *reason*.)   105–106 **ballad . . . Beggar** ballad of King Cophetua
and the beggar maid. (Compare 4.1.66–67.)   108 **since** ago
109–110 **it would . . . tune** i.e., both the lyrics and the tune would
seem out of date.   **serve** suffice   112 **example** give an example of.
digression lapse, waywardness   114 **rational** capable of reason. (Said
patronizingly.)   **hind** rustic or clown   116 **To . . . love** i.e., she deserves to be whipped, as prostitutes are whipped, and yet even at that
she deserves a better lover   119 **light** wanton (with a play on the opposite of *heavy*, line 118)

ARMADO I say, sing.
MOTE Forbear till this company be past.   121

*Enter [Costard the] clown, [Dull the] constable,
and [Jaquenetta, a] wench.*

DULL Sir, the Duke's pleasure is that you keep Costard
safe, and you must suffer him to take no delight nor   123
no penance, but 'a must fast three days a week. For   124
this damsel, I must keep her at the park. She is
allowed for the deywoman. Fare you well.   126
ARMADO[*aside*] I do betray myself with blushing.—Maid!
JAQUENETTA Man?
ARMADO I will visit thee at the lodge.
JAQUENETTA That's hereby.   130
ARMADO I know where it is situate.   131
JAQUENETTA Lord, how wise you are!
ARMADO I will tell thee wonders.
JAQUENETTA With that face?   134
ARMADO I love thee.
JAQUENETTA So I heard you say.
ARMADO And so, farewell.
JAQUENETTA Fair weather after you!
DULL Come, Jaquenetta, away!

Exeunt [Dull and Jaquenetta].

ARMADO Villain, thou shalt fast for thy offenses ere   140
thou be pardoned.
COSTARD Well, sir, I hope when I do it I shall do it on   142
a full stomach.   143
ARMADO Thou shalt be heavily punished.
COSTARD I am more bound to you than your fellows,   145
for they are but lightly rewarded.   146
ARMADO Take away this villain. Shut him up.
MOTE Come, you transgressing slave, away!
COSTARD Let me not be pent up, sir. I will fast, being
loose.
MOTE No, sir, that were fast and loose. Thou shalt to   151
prison.
COSTARD Well, if ever I do see the merry days of deso- 153
lation that I have seen, some shall see.   154
MOTE What shall some see?
COSTARD Nay, nothing, Master Mote, but what they
look upon. It is not for prisoners to be too silent in   157
their words, and therefore I will say nothing. I thank   158
God I have as little patience as another man, and   159
therefore I can be quiet.   *Exit [with Mote].*
ARMADO I do affect the very ground, which is base,   161
where her shoe, which is baser, guided by her foot,

which is basest, doth tread. I shall be forsworn, which 163
is a great argument of falsehood, if I love. And how   164
can that be true love which is falsely attempted? Love
is a familiar; Love is a devil. There is no evil angel but 166
Love. Yet was Samson so tempted, and he had an excellent strength; yet was Solomon so seduced, and he
had a very good wit. Cupid's butt shaft is too hard for 169
Hercules' club, and therefore too much odds for a   170
Spaniard's rapier. The first and second cause will not 171
serve my turn; the passado he respects not, the duello 172
he regards not. His disgrace is to be called boy, but his
glory is to subdue men. Adieu, valor! Rust, rapier! Be
still, drum! For your manager is in love; yea, he loveth. 175
Assist me, some extemporal god of rhyme, for I am   176
sure I shall turn sonnet. Devise, wit; write, pen; for I 177
am for whole volumes in folio.   *Exit.* 178

2.1 *Enter the Princess of France, with three attending
Ladies [Rosaline, Maria, Katharine] and three
Lords [one being Boyet].*

BOYET
Now, madam, summon up your dearest spirits.   1
Consider who the King your father sends,
To whom he sends, and what's his embassy: 3
Yourself, held precious in the world's esteem,
To parley with the sole inheritor   5
Of all perfections that a man may owe,   6
Matchless Navarre; the plea of no less weight   7
Than Aquitaine, a dowry for a queen.
Be now as prodigal of all dear grace
As Nature was in making graces dear   10
When she did starve the general world beside   11
And prodigally gave them all to you.   12
PRINCESS
Good Lord Boyet, my beauty, though but mean,   13
Needs not the painted flourish of your praise.   14
Beauty is bought by judgment of the eye,
Not uttered by base sale of chapmen's tongues.   16
I am less proud to hear you tell my worth   17
Than you much willing to be counted wise
In spending your wit in the praise of mine.

121 **Forbear** hold off 123 **suffer** allow 124 **penance** (Malapropism
for "pleasance," i.e., joy.) **'a** he. **For** as for 126 **allowed . . .
deywoman** approved or assigned to serve as dairymaid 130 **hereby**
close by 131 **situate** located 134 **With that face** i.e., you don't
mean it? (Slang, like most of Jaquenetta's expressions.) 140 **Villain**
(1) servant (2) rascal 142–143 **on . . . stomach** (with a pun on *full-
stomached*, with good courage) 145 **bound** obliged. **fellows** servants 146 **but lightly** only slightly 151 **fast and loose** A cheating
trick. **Thou shalt** you will go 153–154 **desolation** (Malapropism
for "consolation"?) 154 **some shall see** (Costard seems to imply that
some who have wronged him will see how he can revenge, although
he refuses to say so when Mote queries his meaning.) 157–158 **It
is . . . words** (This profound-sounding nonsense is characteristic of
Costard's speech.) 159 **patience** (Costard means the opposite of
what he says.) 161 **affect** love

163 **be forsworn** break my oath 164 **argument** proof 166 **familiar**
attendant evil spirit 169 **butt shaft** unbarbed arrow, used in archery
practice 170 **too much odds** at too great an advantage 171 **first
. . . cause** (An allusion to certain situations that necessitated a duel
according to the code of honor. Armado complains that Cupid will
not follow this code of honor.) 172 **passado** forward thrust with the
sword, one foot being advanced at the same time. **duello** established
code of duelists 175 **manager** skilled practitioner 176 **extemporal
. . . rhyme** god of impromptu poetry 177 **sonnet** i.e., sonneteer
178 **am for** am destined to produce. **folio** large format
2.1. Location: The same. Outside the gates of Navarre's court.
1 **dearest spirits** best wits 3 **embassy** message 5 **parley** meet, speak
6 **owe** own 7 **the plea of** that which is claimed is of 10 **dear** bearing a high price (playing on *dear*, "beloved," of the previous line)
11 **starve** i.e., withhold graces from. **beside** i.e., excepting yourself
12 **prodigally** extravagantly, too generously 13 **mean** average, moderate 14 **flourish** adornment 16 **uttered** (1) spoken (2) offered for
sale. **chapmen's** merchants' 17 **tell** (1) speak of (2) reckon

But now to task the tasker. Good Boyet,   20
You are not ignorant all-telling fame   21
Doth noise abroad Navarre hath made a vow: 22
Till painful study shall outwear three years,   23
No woman may approach his silent court.   24
Therefore to 's seemeth it a needful course,   25
Before we enter his forbidden gates,   26
To know his pleasure; and in that behalf,   27
Bold of your worthiness, we single you   28
As our best-moving fair solicitor.   29
Tell him the daughter of the King of France,
On serious business craving quick dispatch,
Importunes personal conference with His Grace.   32
Haste, signify so much, while we attend,   33
Like humble-visaged suitors, his high will.

BOYET
Proud of employment, willingly I go.

PRINCESS
All pride is willing pride, and yours is so.   36

Exit Boyet.

Who are the votaries, my loving lords,   37
That are vow-fellows with this virtuous duke?   38

A LORD
Lord Longaville is one.

PRINCESS   Know you the man?

MARIA
I know him, madam. At a marriage feast,
Between Lord Perigord and the beauteous heir   41
Of Jaques Falconbridge, solemnizèd
In Normandy, saw I this Longaville.
A man of sovereign parts he is esteemed,   44
Well fitted in arts, glorious in arms.   45
Nothing becomes him ill that he would well.   46
The only soil of his fair virtue's gloss—   47
If virtue's gloss will stain with any soil—   48
Is a sharp wit matched with too blunt a will,   49
Whose edge hath power to cut, whose will still wills   50
It should none spare that come within his power.   51

PRINCESS
Some merry mocking lord, belike. Is 't so?   52

MARIA
They say so most that most his humors know.

PRINCESS
Such short-lived wits do wither as they grow.
Who are the rest?

KATHARINE
The young Dumaine, a well-accomplished youth,
Of all that virtue love for virtue loved;   57
Most power to do most harm, least knowing ill,   58
For he hath wit to make an ill shape good   59
And shape to win grace though he had no wit.   60
I saw him at the Duke Alençon's once,
And much too little of that good I saw   62
Is my report to his great worthiness.   63

ROSALINE
Another of these students at that time
Was there with him, if I have heard a truth.
Berowne they call him; but a merrier man,   66
Within the limit of becoming mirth,   67
I never spent an hour's talk withal.   68
His eye begets occasion for his wit,   69
For every object that the one doth catch
The other turns to a mirth-moving jest,
Which his fair tongue, conceit's expositor,   72
Delivers in such apt and gracious words
That agèd ears play truant at his tales,   74
And younger hearings are quite ravishèd,
So sweet and voluble is his discourse.   76

PRINCESS
God bless my ladies! Are they all in love,
That every one her own hath garnishèd
With such bedecking ornaments of praise?

A LORD
Here comes Boyet.

Enter Boyet.

PRINCESS   Now, what admittance, lord?   80

BOYET
Navarre had notice of your fair approach,
And he and his competitors in oath   82
Were all addressed to meet you, gentle lady,   83
Before I came. Marry, thus much I have learned:
He rather means to lodge you in the field,
Like one that comes here to besiege his court,
Than seek a dispensation for his oath
To let you enter his unpeopled house.   88

Enter [the King of] Navarre, Longaville, Dumaine, and Berowne.

Here comes Navarre.

KING   Fair Princess, welcome to the court of Navarre.
PRINCESS   "Fair" I give you back again, and "welcome"

---

20 **task** (1) chastise (2) lay a task upon   21 **ignorant** unaware that. **fame** rumor   22 **noise** spread the news   23 **painful** strenuous   25 **to 's** to us. (The royal "we.")   **needful** necessary   27 **in that behalf** for that purpose   28 **Bold of** confident of.   **single** choose   29 **best-moving** most eloquent. **fair** just   32 **Importunes** requests   33 **Haste . . . attend** hurry, speak exactly this, while we await   36 **pride** (The Princess wittily interprets Boyet's *Proud* in line 35 as "vain" rather than, as he intended, "honored.")   37 **votaries** those who have taken vows   38 **vow-fellows** individuals bound by the same vow   41 **beauteous** beautiful   44 **sovereign parts** excellent qualities   45 **fitted** furnished. **in arts** with learning   46 **becomes him ill** is unbecoming in him. **would well** wants to do well   47 **soil . . . gloss** blot on the appearance of his general excellence   48 **gloss** fair appearance. **soil** blemish   49 **too . . . will** i.e., an insensitivity to the feelings of others   50 **Whose** i.e., the wit's. **still** continually   51 **his** its   52 **belike** most likely

57 **Of . . . loved** esteemed for his virtue by all who love virtue   58 **Most . . . ill** i.e., Dumaine, as a talented and graceful person, has the utmost power of doing the greatest harm by the ill employment of those qualities, yet he is ignorant of ill   59–60 **For . . . no wit** he has intelligence enough to compensate for a poor physique, if he had one, and conversely a physique shapely enough to compensate for lack of intelligence   62 **little** short, inadequate   63 **to** compared with   66 **Berowne** (The name suggests *brown* to Rosaline, as in the expression "brown study," the opposite of being merry.)   67 **becoming** suitable   68 **withal** with   69 **begets occasion** creates opportunities   72 **conceit's expositor** imagination's interpreter   74 **play truant** i.e., neglect important business   76 **voluble** fluent   80 **admittance** reception   82 **competitors** associates   83 **addressed** prepared   88 **unpeopled** inadequately staffed with servants

I have not yet. The roof of this court is too high to be   92
yours, and welcome to the wide fields too base to be
mine.

KING
You shall be welcome, madam, to my court.

PRINCESS
I will be welcome, then. Conduct me thither.

KING
Hear me, dear lady: I have sworn an oath.

PRINCESS
Our Lady help my lord! He'll be forsworn.

KING
Not for the world, fair madam, by my will.   99

PRINCESS
Why, will shall break it—will and nothing else.   100

KING
Your ladyship is ignorant what it is.

PRINCESS
Were my lord so, his ignorance were wise,
Where now his knowledge must prove ignorance.
I hear Your Grace hath sworn out housekeeping.   104
'Tis deadly sin to keep that oath, my lord,
And sin to break it.
But pardon me, I am too sudden-bold;
To teach a teacher ill beseemeth me.
Vouchsafe to read the purpose of my coming,   109
And suddenly resolve me in my suit.   110
                              [She gives him a paper.]

KING
Madam, I will, if suddenly I may.

PRINCESS
You will the sooner that I were away,   112
For you'll prove perjured if you make me stay.
                              [The King reads silently.]

BEROWNE [to Rosaline]
Did not I dance with you in Brabant once?   114

ROSALINE
Did not I dance with you in Brabant once?

BEROWNE
I know you did.

ROSALINE   How needless was it then
   To ask the question!

BEROWNE   You must not be so quick.   117

ROSALINE
'Tis long of you, that spur me with such questions.   118

BEROWNE
Your wit's too hot. It speeds too fast; 'twill tire.   119

ROSALINE
Not till it leave the rider in the mire.   120

BEROWNE
What time o' day?   121

ROSALINE
The hour that fools should ask.

BEROWNE
Now fair befall your mask!   123

ROSALINE
Fair fall the face it covers!   124

BEROWNE
And send you many lovers!

ROSALINE
Amen, so you be none.

BEROWNE
Nay, then will I be gone.   [He stands aside.]

KING [to the Princess]
Madam, your father here doth intimate   128
The payment of a hundred thousand crowns,   129
Being but the one half of an entire sum
Disbursèd by my father in his wars.   131
But say that he or we—as neither have—   132
Received that sum, yet there remains unpaid
A hundred thousand more, in surety of the which   134
One part of Aquitaine is bound to us,
Although not valued to the money's worth.   136
If then the King your father will restore
But that one half which is unsatisfied,
We will give up our right in Aquitaine
And hold fair friendship with His Majesty.
But that, it seems, he little purposeth,   141
For here he doth demand to have repaid   142
A hundred thousand crowns, and not demands,   143
On payment of a hundred thousand crowns,
To have his title live in Aquitaine—   145
Which we much rather had depart withal,   146
And have the money by our father lent,
Than Aquitaine, so gelded as it is.   148
Dear Princess, were not his requests so far
From reason's yielding, your fair self should make
A yielding 'gainst some reason in my breast   151
And go well satisfied to France again.

PRINCESS
You do the King my father too much wrong,
And wrong the reputation of your name,
In so unseeming to confess receipt   155
Of that which hath so faithfully been paid.

KING
I do protest I never heard of it;
And, if you prove it, I'll repay it back
Or yield up Aquitaine.

PRINCESS   We arrest your word.   159
Boyet, you can produce acquittances   160
For such a sum from special officers

---

92 **The roof of this court** i.e., the sky   99 **by my will** willingly. (A
common mild oath.)   100 **will** desire   104 **sworn out housekeeping**
renounced hospitality   109 **Vouchsafe** deign, agree   110 **suddenly
resolve** quickly answer   112 **that . . . away** to procure my departure
114 **Brabant** a province in central Belgium   117 **quick** sharp
118 **long of** on account of.   **spur** goad   119 **hot** ardent, eager
120 **mire** mud   121 **time o' day** time is it

123 **fair befall** good luck to   124 **fall** befall   128 **intimate** refer to,
discuss, imply   129 **The payment** i.e., that he has already paid
131 **his** i.e., the King of France's   132 **he** i.e., my father   134 **in
surety** as a guarantee   136 **valued** equal in value   141 **little purposeth** scarcely intends   142 **demand . . . repaid** insists he has already
repaid   143 **and not demands** i.e., instead of proposing or stipulating
145 **To have . . . Aquitaine** i.e., to regain his title to Aquitaine by
paying the 100,000 crowns that are owed to Navarre   146 **depart
withal** part with   148 **gelded** emasculated, weakened in value (with
one part cut away)   151 **A yielding . . . breast** i.e., a willingness on
my part to compromise, despite the fact that right is on my side
155 **unseeming** being apparently unwilling   159 **arrest** take as security   160 **acquittances** receipts for payment of a debt

Of Charles, his father.

KING   Satisfy me so.   162

BOYET
So please Your Grace, the packet is not come
Where that and other specialties are bound.   164
Tomorrow you shall have a sight of them.

KING
It shall suffice me, at which interview
All liberal reason I will yield unto.   167
Meantime, receive such welcome at my hand
As honor, without breach of honor, may
Make tender of to thy true worthiness.   170
You may not come, fair Princess, within my gates,
But here without you shall be so received   172
As you shall deem yourself lodged in my heart,   173
Though so denied fair harbor in my house.
Your own good thoughts excuse me, and farewell.
Tomorrow shall we visit you again.

PRINCESS
Sweet health and fair desires consort Your Grace!   177

KING
Thy own wish wish I thee in every place.
                              Exit [*with Longaville and Dumaine*].

BEROWNE [*to Rosaline*]   Lady, I will commend you to
mine own heart.

ROSALINE   Pray you, do my commendations. I would
be glad to see it.

BEROWNE   I would you heard it groan.

ROSALINE   Is the fool sick?   184

BEROWNE   Sick at the heart.

ROSALINE
Alack, let it blood.   186

BEROWNE
Would that do it good?

ROSALINE
My physic says "ay."   188

BEROWNE
Will you prick 't with your eye?   189

ROSALINE
Non point, with my knife.   190

BEROWNE
Now, God save thy life!

ROSALINE
And yours from long living!

BEROWNE
I cannot stay thanksgiving.   *Exit.* 193

            Enter Dumaine.

DUMAINE [*to Boyet*]
Sir, I pray you, a word. What lady is that same?

BOYET
The heir of Alençon, Katharine her name.

DUMAINE
A gallant lady. Monsieur, fare you well.   *Exit.*

       [*Enter Longaville.*]

LONGAVILLE [*to Boyet*]
I beseech you a word. What is she in the white?   197

BOYET
A woman sometimes, an you saw her in the light.   198

LONGAVILLE
Perchance light in the light. I desire her name.   199

BOYET
She hath but one for herself; to desire that were a
shame.

LONGAVILLE
Pray you, sir, whose daughter?

BOYET
Her mother's, I have heard.

LONGAVILLE
God's blessing on your beard!   203

BOYET
Good sir, be not offended.
She is an heir of Falconbridge.

LONGAVILLE
Nay, my choler is ended.   206
She is a most sweet lady.

BOYET
Not unlike, sir. That may be.   *Exit Longaville.* 208

       Enter Berowne.

BEROWNE
What's her name in the cap?

BOYET
Rosaline, by good hap.   210

BEROWNE
Is she wedded or no?

BOYET
To her will, sir, or so.   212

BEROWNE
O, you are welcome, sir. Adieu.

BOYET
Farewell to me, sir, and welcome to you.   214
                              Exit Berowne.

MARIA
That last is Berowne, the merry madcap lord.
Not a word with him but a jest.

BOYET   And every jest but a word. 216

PRINCESS
It was well done of you to take him at his word.   217

162 his father i.e., the King of Navarre's father (referred to in line 147). **Satisfy me so** prove to me that this is true **164 specialties** warrants, special documents **167 liberal** gentlemanlike **170 Make tender of** offer **172 without** outside **173 As** that **177 consort** attend **184 the fool** (A term of endearment or gentle raillery.) **186 let it blood** bleed it. (A reference to the medical practice of drawing blood.) **188 physic** medical knowledge **189 Will . . . eye** i.e., will you stab me through the heart with your glance, smiting me as with Cupid's arrow? (With wordplay on *eye* and *ay* in line 188.) **190 Non point** (1) not at all (2) it is dull **193 stay thanksgiving** stay long enough to thank you properly

197 What who **198 an** if **199 light in the light** wanton when her conduct is known or brought to light **203 God's . . . beard** (To insult or pluck a man's beard was a standard Elizabethan way to challenge someone to a duel.) **206 choler** anger **208 unlike** unlikely **210 hap** fortune **212 or so** or something of that kind **214 Farewell . . . you** you bid me "farewell" and I will say "you're welcome to go" **216 Not . . . jest** everything he says is a joke **217 take . . . word** i.e., vie with him in wordplay (with a pun on "take him literally")

BOYET
I was as willing to grapple as he was to board.   218
KATHARINE
Two hot sheeps, marry.
BOYET   And wherefore not ships?   219
No sheep, sweet lamb, unless we feed on your lips.
KATHARINE
You sheep, and I pasture. Shall that finish the jest?   221
BOYET
So you grant pasture for me.   [*Offering to kiss her.*]
KATHARINE   Not so, gentle beast.   222
My lips are no common, though several they be.   223
BOYET
Belonging to whom?
KATHARINE   To my fortunes and me.
PRINCESS
Good wits will be jangling; but, gentles, agree.   225
This civil war of wits were much better used
On Navarre and his bookmen, for here 'tis abused.   227
BOYET
If my observation, which very seldom lies,
By the heart's still rhetoric disclosèd with eyes,
Deceive me not now, Navarre is infected.   229
PRINCESS   With what?
BOYET
With that which we lovers entitle "affected."   232
PRINCESS   Your reason?
BOYET
Why, all his behaviors did make their retire   234
To the court of his eye, peeping thorough desire.   235
His heart, like an agate, with your print impressed,   236
Proud with his form, in his eye pride expressed.   237
His tongue, all impatient to speak and not see,   238
Did stumble with haste in his eyesight to be;   239
All senses to that sense did make their repair,   240
To feel only looking on fairest of fair.   241
Methought all his senses were locked in his eye,
As jewels in crystal for some prince to buy,   243
Who, tend'ring their own worth from where they
    were glassed,   244
Did point you to buy them, along as you passed.   245

His face's own margent did quote such amazes   246
That all eyes saw his eyes enchanted with gazes.
I'll give you Aquitaine and all that is his,   248
An you give him for my sake but one loving kiss.   249
PRINCESS
Come to our pavilion. Boyet is disposed.   250
BOYET
But to speak that in words which his eye hath disclosed.   251
I only have made a mouth of his eye,
By adding a tongue which I know will not lie.
ROSALINE
Thou art an old lovemonger and speakest skillfully.
MARIA
He is Cupid's grandfather, and learns news of him.
KATHARINE
Then was Venus like her mother, for her father is
    but grim.   256
BOYET
Do you hear, my mad wenches?
MARIA   No.
BOYET   What then, do you see?   257
KATHARINE
Ay, our way to be gone.
BOYET   You are too hard for me.   258
                                        Exeunt omnes.

❖

3.1   *Enter [Armado the] braggart and [Mote,]*
          his boy.

ARMADO   Warble, child. Make passionate my sense of   1
    hearing.
MOTE [*singing*]   Concolinel.   3
ARMADO   Sweet air! Go, tenderness of years. [*He gives a*   4
    key.] Take this key, give enlargement to the swain,   5
    bring him festinately hither. I must employ him in a   6
    letter to my love.
MOTE   Master, will you win your love with a French
    brawl?   9
ARMADO   How meanest thou? Brawling in French?   10
MOTE   No, my complete master, but to jig off a tune at   11
    the tongue's end, canary to it with your feet, humor it   12
    with turning up your eyelids, sigh a note and sing a

218 grapple, board (Tactics of sea warfare, here applied to wordplay, with bawdy overtones.)   **219 sheeps, ships** (Pronounced nearly alike by Elizabethans.)   **221 pasture** (with a play on "pastor," shepherd)   **222 So** provided   **223 common** common land for pasturing (with a bawdy suggestion of "available to all men").   **several** private enclosed land (with a pun on "more than one" and "parted")   **225 jangling** quarreling.   **gentles** gentlefolk   **227 bookmen** scholars.   **abused** misapplied   **229 still** silent   **232 affected** being in love   **234 behaviors** actions.   **make their retire** withdraw, retire. (Navarre was dumbstruck, unable to do anything except gaze at the Princess.)   **235 thorough** through   **236 agate** (An allusion to small figures cut in agate stones.)   **print impressed** image engraved   **237 Proud . . . expressed** proud of the form (of the Princess) imprinted on it, expressed that pride through the look in his eye   **238 to speak . . . see** at being able to speak only and not to see   **239 in his . . . be** to take part in his seeing   **240 that sense** i.e., the eyesight.   **make their repair** go   **241 To . . . looking** to express themselves solely through looking   **243 in crystal** enclosed within crystal glass   **244 Who, tend'ring** which, offering.   **glassed** encased in the glass (crystal) of his eyes   **245 point** appoint, direct, invite

246 His . . . amazes i.e., his expression of amazement offered such a visible commentary on what his eyes saw. (*Margents* or margins of books often bore commentary on the text proper.)   **248 I'll give you** i.e., I warrant you can have   **249 An** if   **250 disposed** inclined (to be merry)   **251 But** merely.   **his** i.e., the King's   **256 Then . . . grim** i.e., Boyet isn't nearly handsome enough to have given Venus her beauty   **257 Do you hear** i.e., won't you listen to me. (But the ladies parry Boyet's *hear* and *see* to their own witty purposes.)   **mad** high-spirited   **258 our . . . gone** the way out of here.   **hard** sharp, difficult to outwit   **s.d. omnes** all
3.1. Location: Navarre's park.
1 passionate impassioned, responsive   **3 Concolinel** (Unidentified; perhaps the name or refrain of a song.)   **4 air** song   **5 enlargement** release from confinement   **6 festinately** quickly   **9 brawl** a French dance figure   **10 Brawling** quarreling   **11 complete** accomplished.   **jig . . . tune** sing a jiglike tune   **12 canary** dance. (From the name of a lively dance; compare *jig*.)

note, sometimes through the throat as if you swallowed
love with singing love, sometimes through the nose as
if you snuffed up love by smelling love, with your hat
penthouse-like o'er the shop of your eyes, with your 17
arms crossed on your thin-belly doublet like a rabbit 18
on a spit, or your hands in your pocket like a man after 19
the old painting, and keep not too long in one tune, 20
but a snip and away. These are compliments, these are 21
humors; these betray nice wenches that would be 22
betrayed without these, and make them men of note— 23
do you note?—men that most are affected to these. 24
ARMADO   How hast thou purchased this experience?
MOTE   By my penny of observation.
ARMADO   But O, but O— 27
MOTE   "The hobbyhorse is forgot." 28
ARMADO   Call'st thou my love "hobbyhorse"?
MOTE   No, master; the hobbyhorse is but a colt, and 30
your love perhaps a hackney. But have you forgot 31
your love?
ARMADO   Almost I had.
MOTE   Negligent student, learn her by heart.
ARMADO   By heart and in heart, boy.
MOTE   And out of heart, master. All those three I will
prove. 37
ARMADO   What wilt thou prove?
MOTE   A man, if I live; and this, "by," "in," and
"without," upon the instant: "by" heart you love her
because your heart cannot come by her; "in" heart you 41
love her because your heart is in love with her; and
"out" of heart you love her, being out of heart that you 43
cannot enjoy her.
ARMADO   I am all these three.
MOTE   And three times as much more—[aside] and yet
nothing at all.
ARMADO   Fetch hither the swain. He must carry me a 48
letter.
MOTE [aside]   A message well sympathized—a horse 50
to be ambassador for an ass.
ARMADO   Ha, ha! What sayest thou?
MOTE   Marry, sir, you must send the ass upon the
horse, for he is very slow-gaited. But I go.
ARMADO   The way is but short. Away!

MOTE   As swift as lead, sir.
ARMADO   The meaning, pretty ingenious?
Is not lead a metal heavy, dull, and slow?
MOTE
Minime, honest master; or rather, master, no. 59
ARMADO
I say lead is slow.
MOTE   You are too swift, sir, to say so.
Is that lead slow which is fired from a gun?
ARMADO   Sweet smoke of rhetoric!
He reputes me a cannon, and the bullet, that's he.
I shoot thee at the swain.
MOTE   Thump, then, and I flee. 64
                                        [*Exit.*]
ARMADO
A most acute juvenal, voluble and free of grace! 65
By thy favor, sweet welkin, I must sigh in thy face. 66
Most rude melancholy, valor gives thee place. 67
My herald is returned.

Enter [Mote the] page and [Costard the] clown.

MOTE
A wonder, master! Here's a costard broken in a shin. 69
ARMADO
Some enigma, some riddle. Come, thy *l'envoi*; begin. 70
COSTARD   No egma, no riddle, no *l'envoi*, no salve in 71
the mail, sir. O, sir, plantain, a plain plantain. No 72
l'envoi, no *l'envoi*, no salve, sir, but a plantain.
ARMADO   By virtue, thou enforcest laughter; thy silly
thought, my spleen; the heaving of my lungs provokes 75
me to ridiculous smiling. O, pardon me, my stars! 76
Doth the inconsiderate take "salve" for *l'envoi*, and the 77
word *l'envoi* for a salve?
MOTE
Do the wise think them other? Is not *l'envoi* a salve?
ARMADO
No, page, it is an epilogue or discourse to make
plain
Some obscure precedence that hath tofore been sain. 81
I will example it: 82
The fox, the ape, and the humble-bee 83

---

17 penthouse-like like the projecting second story of a house built out
to shelter the shop on the ground floor   **18 arms crossed** (Betokening
melancholy; compare 4.3.131.)   **thin-belly doublet** (1) man's jacket
worn over his thin belly, thin because of lovesickness (2) a jacket thinly
padded in the waist   **19 after** in the style of   **20 old painting** (If Mote
refers here to a specific painting, it remains unidentified, but he may
merely mean "some old painting.")   **21 a snip and away** a snippet or
scrap of one song and then on to another.   **compliments** gentlemanly
accomplishments. (Or perhaps *complements*, those things that complete or make perfect.)   **22 humors** moods.   **nice** coy   **23 note** (1)
distinction (2) musical notation   **24 affected** inclined, drawn
27–28 But O . . . forgot (Probably the refrain of a popular song; it
turns up again in *Hamlet*, 3.2.133. The hobbyhorse was the figure of
a horse made of light material and fastened over the torso and head of
a morris dancer.)   **30–31 hobbyhorse, colt, hackney** (Slang terms for
prostitutes or wanton persons.)   **37 prove** demonstrate. (But Mote
then uses the word in line 39 also to mean "turn out to be.")
41 come by possess   **43 out of heart** discouraged, depressed   **48 me**
for me   **50 sympathized** matched

59 Minime not at all   **64 Thump** (Representing the sound of cannon.)
65 voluble quick-witted   **66 favor** good will, permission.   **welkin** sky
67 gives thee place gives way to you   **69 a costard . . . shin** an apple or a head with a bruised shin. (An *enigma*, as Armado points out,
since apples and heads don't have shins.)   **70 l'envoi** i.e., postscript
or commendatory statement to the reader attached to a composition;
here, an explanation   **71 egma** (Costard's attempt at *enigma*; he evidently mistakes this strange name, along with *riddle* and *l'envoi*, as a
kind of salve for his hurt shin.)   **salve** (With a play seemingly on
salve, meaning "hail!" Armado points out in his next speech that Costard has mistaken *salve*, a salutation, for *l'envoi*, a farewell.)   **72 mail**
pouch, bag (suggesting the bag of a mountebank or seller of cures).
plantain an old-fashioned herbal remedy (which Costard prefers to the
strange-sounding *egma*, etc.)   **75 spleen** i.e., laughter. (The *spleen*,
supposedly the seat of emotions and passions, was held to be the organ that controlled excessive mirth or anger.)   **76 ridiculous** scornful
(but with unintended meaning of "absurd")   **77 inconsiderate** mindless fellow.   **salve** (Here it is used in the Latin sense of "hail.")
81 precedence preceding discourse.   **tofore** previously.   **sain** said
82 example give an example of   **83 humble-bee** bumblebee

Were still at odds, being but three.   84
There's the moral. Now the *l'envoi*.   85
MOTE
I will add the *l'envoi*. Say the moral again.
ARMADO
The fox, the ape, and the humble-bee
Were still at odds, being but three.
MOTE
Until the goose came out of door,
And stayed the odds by adding four.   90
Now will I begin your moral, and do you follow with
my *l'envoi*.
The fox, the ape, and the humble-bee
Were still at odds, being but three.
ARMADO
Until the goose came out of door,
Staying the odds by adding four.
MOTE   A good *l'envoi*, ending in the goose. Would you   97
desire more?
COSTARD
The boy hath sold him a bargain—a goose, that's
flat.   99
Sir, your pennyworth is good, an your goose be fat.   100
To sell a bargain well is as cunning as fast and loose.   101
Let me see: a fat *l'envoi*—ay, that's a fat goose.
ARMADO
Come hither, come hither. How did this argument
begin?   103
MOTE
By saying that a costard was broken in a shin.   104
Then called you for the *l'envoi*.
COSTARD   True, and I for a plantain. Thus came your
argument in; then the boy's fat *l'envoi*, the goose that
you bought; and he ended the market.   108
ARMADO   But tell me, how was there a costard broken   109
in a shin?
MOTE   I will tell you sensibly.   111
COSTARD   Thou hast no feeling of it, Mote. I will speak
that *l'envoi*:
I Costard, running out, that was safely within,
Fell over the threshold and broke my shin.
ARMADO   We will talk no more of this matter.
COSTARD   Till there be more matter in the shin.   117
ARMADO   Sirrah Costard, I will enfranchise thee.   118
COSTARD   O, marry me to one Frances! I smell some
l'envoi, some goose, in this.   120

ARMADO   By my sweet soul, I mean setting thee at liberty, enfreedoming thy person. Thou wert immured, 122
restrained, captivated, bound.
COSTARD   True, true, and now you will be my purga- 124
tion and let me loose.   125
ARMADO   I give thee thy liberty, set thee from durance, 126
and in lieu thereof impose on thee nothing but this:
Bear this significant [*giving a letter*] to the country 128
maid Jaquenetta. There is remuneration. [*He gives* 129
money.] For the best ward of mine honor is rewarding 130
my dependents. Mote, follow.   [*Exit.*]
MOTE
Like the sequel, I. Seigneur Costard, adieu.   *Exit.* 132
COSTARD
My sweet ounce of man's flesh, my incony Jew!   133
Now will I look to his remuneration. [*He looks at his*
money.] Remuneration! O, that's the Latin word for
three farthings. Three farthings—remuneration. 136
"What's the price of this inkle?"—"One penny."— 137
"No, I'll give you a remuneration." Why, it carries it. 138
Remuneration! Why, it is a fairer name than French 139
crown. I will never buy and sell out of this word.   140

Enter Berowne.

BEROWNE   My good knave Costard, exceedingly well 141
met.   142
COSTARD   Pray you, sir, how much carnation ribbon 143
may a man buy for a remuneration?
BEROWNE   What is a remuneration?
COSTARD   Marry, sir, halfpenny farthing.   146
BEROWNE   Why, then, three farthing worth of silk.
COSTARD   I thank your worship. God be wi' you!
                                        [*He starts to leave.*]
BEROWNE   Stay, slave, I must employ thee.
As thou wilt win my favor, good my knave,
Do one thing for me that I shall entreat.
COSTARD   When would you have it done, sir?
BEROWNE   This afternoon.
COSTARD   Well, I will do it, sir. Fare you well.
BEROWNE   Thou knowest not what it is.
COSTARD   I shall know, sir, when I have done it.
BEROWNE   Why, villain, thou must know first.
COSTARD   I will come to your worship tomorrow morn-
ing.
BEROWNE   It must be done this afternoon. Hark, slave,
it is but this:
The Princess comes to hunt here in the park,
And in her train there is a gentle lady;

---

84 still continually.   **at odds** (1) at enmity (2) an odd number, i.e.,
three   **85 moral** riddle or allegory   **90 stayed the odds** (1) stopped
the enmity (2) changed odd to even.   **four** a fourth   **97 l'envoi . . .
goose** (Mote's joke is based on the fact that *l'envoi* ends with the
same sound as the French word for goose, *oie*. Armado made
himself the goose by playing Mote's game.)   **99 sold . . . goose** i.e.,
outwitted him.   **flat** certain   **100 your . . . good** i.e., you got your
money's worth.   **an** if   **101 fast and loose** a cheating trick. (See
1.2.151.)   **103 argument** discussion   **104 broken in a shin** with a cut
or bruised shin   **108 and . . . market** (Costard refers to the proverbial
expression "Three women and a goose make a market.")   **109 how**
in what sense   **111 sensibly** feelingly. (But Costard protests that Mote
cannot personally know what it *feels* like.)   **117 matter** pus (playing
on *matter*, business, in line 116)   **118 enfranchise** release from confinement. (Costard hears this as *en-Frances*, "provide with a
Frances.")   **120 goose** (Slang for "prostitute.")

122 immured imprisoned   **124–125 be my purgation** purge me of
guilt (with pun on the sense of giving a purgative so that Costard's
bowels will be *let loose*).   **126 set** release.   **durance** imprisonment
128 significant sign, token   **129 remuneration** payment   **130 ward**
guard   **132 the sequel** that which follows; *l'envoi*   **133 incony** fine,
rare, delicate.   **Jew** (Here it is a term of playful insult, possibly suggested by *juvenile*.)   **136 farthings** silver coins worth a quarter of a
penny   **137 inkle** a kind of linen tape   **138 carries it** wins the day
139–140 French crown (1) a coin (2) a bald head, the result of syphilis or "the French disease"   **140 out of** i.e., without using
141–142 exceedingly well met i.e., how fortunate to see you just
now   **143 carnation** flesh-colored   **146 halfpenny farthing** i.e., three
farthings (a *halfpenny*, worth two farthings, plus one farthing)

When tongues speak sweetly, then they name her
   name,
And Rosaline they call her. Ask for her,
And to her white hand see thou do commend   166
This sealed-up counsel. There's thy guerdon; go.   167
   [*Giving him a letter and a shilling.*]

COSTARD   Gardon, O sweet gardon! Better than remu-   168
neration, a 'levenpence farthing better. Most sweet   169
gardon! I will do it, sir, in print. Gardon! Remunera-   170
tion!   *Exit.*

BEROWNE
And I, forsooth, in love! I that have been Love's whip,
A very beadle to a humorous sigh,   173
A critic, nay, a night-watch constable,
A domineering pedant o'er the boy,   175
Than whom no mortal so magnificent!
This wimpled, whining, purblind, wayward boy,   177
This Senior Junior, giant dwarf, Dan Cupid,   178
Regent of love rhymes, lord of folded arms,   179
Th' anointed sovereign of sighs and groans,
Liege of all loiterers and malcontents,
Dread prince of plackets, king of codpieces,   182
Sole imperator and great general   183
Of trotting paritors—O my little heart!   184
And I to be a corporal of his field   185
And wear his colors like a tumbler's hoop!   186
What? I love, I sue, I seek a wife?
A woman, that is like a German clock,
Still a-repairing, ever out of frame,   189
And never going aright, being a watch,
But being watched that it may still go right?   191
Nay, to be perjured, which is worst of all;
And, among three, to love the worst of all—
A whitely wanton with a velvet brow,   194
With two pitch-balls stuck in her face for eyes;   195
Ay, and, by heaven, one that will do the deed   196
Though Argus were her eunuch and her guard.   197

And I to sigh for her, to watch for her,   198
To pray for her! Go to, it is a plague
That Cupid will impose for my neglect
Of his almighty dreadful little might.
Well, I will love, write, sigh, pray, sue, groan.
Some men must love milady, and some Joan. [*Exit.*] 203

❖

4.1   *Enter the Princess, a Forester, her Ladies, and her*
         Lords, [Boyet and others].

PRINCESS
Was that the King that spurred his horse so hard
Against the steep uprising of the hill?
BOYET
I know not, but I think it was not he.
PRINCESS
Whoe'er 'a was, 'a showed a mounting mind.   4
Well, lords, today we shall have our dispatch;   5
On Saturday we will return to France.
Then, Forester, my friend, where is the bush
That we must stand and play the murderer in?
FORESTER
Hereby, upon the edge of yonder coppice,   9
A stand where you may make the fairest shoot.   10
PRINCESS
I thank my beauty, I am fair that shoot,
And thereupon thou speak'st "the fairest shoot."
FORESTER
Pardon me, madam, for I meant not so.
PRINCESS
What, what? First praise me and again say no?   14
O short-lived pride! Not fair? Alack, for woe!
FORESTER
Yes, madam, fair.
PRINCESS   Nay, never paint me now. 16
Where fair is not, praise cannot mend the brow.   17
Here, good my glass, take this for telling true.   18
                        [*She gives him money.*]
Fair payment for foul words is more than due.
FORESTER
Nothing but fair is that which you inherit.   20
PRINCESS
See, see, my beauty will be saved by merit!   21

---

166 **commend** entrust   167 **counsel** private or secret communication.   **guerdon** reward.   **s.d. shilling** a silver coin worth twelve pence
168 **Gardon** (Costard anglicizes the French *guerdon*.)   168–169 **Better . . . better** (Costard delights that the shilling he has been given is
worth eleven pence and a farthing more than the three farthings he
had.)   170 **in print** i.e., most exactly   173 **beadle** parish officer responsible for whipping minor offenders.   **humorous** moody
175 **pedant** schoolmaster   177 **wimpled** blindfolded.   **purblind** quite
blind   178 **Dan** don, sir. (From the Latin *dominus*.)   179 **Regent**
ruler.   **folded arms** (Betokening melancholy; see 3.1.18.)
182 **plackets** slits in petticoats (referring bawdily to women).   **codpieces** flaps or pouches concealing the opening in the front of men's
breeches (referring bawdily to men)   183 **imperator** absolute ruler
184 **paritors** apparitors, summoners of ecclesiastical courts (who
could make a profit by spying out sexual offenders)   185 **corporal of
his field** Cupid's field officer   186 **tumbler's hoop** (Such hoops were
usually brightly decorated with silks and ribbons.)   189 **Still** always.
a-repairing needing repair.   **frame** order   191 **But being watched**
unless it is watched carefully (like a wandering wife)   194 **whitely**
pale of complexion (considered beautiful; but compare 4.3.250–273,
where the lords joke about the darkness of Rosaline's features).   **velvet** i.e., soft-skinned   195 **pitch-balls** balls made of pitch, a viscous
black substance created by distilling tar   196 **do the deed** engage in
sex   197 **Argus** a fabulous monster with a hundred eyes, some of
which were always awake. (Juno gave Argus custody over Io, of
whom Jove was enamored.)   **eunuch** i.e., guard in a seraglio

198 **watch** lose sleep, stay awake   203 **milady, Joan** (Opposite types
on the social scale—one a lady of quality and one a peasant
woman.)
4.1. Location: Navarre's park. A hunter's station at the edge of a
coppice.
4 **'a** he.   **mounting** (1) rising (2) aspiring   5 **dispatch** settlement
9 **coppice** grove of trees   10 **stand** hunter's station, toward which the
game is driven.   **fairest** most favorable. (The Princess chooses to play
on the word in a compliment to herself.)   14 **again** i.e., then
16 **paint** flatter   17 **fair** beauty.   **brow** forehead, i.e., face   18 **good
my glass** my true mirror (i.e., a counselor who will not flatter. The
Princess amuses herself with Renaissance commonplaces about the
value of honest counselors to a true prince, much to the discomfort of
the Forester.)   20 **inherit** possess   21 **my . . . merit** i.e., my beauty
is complimented again in return for my giving a gratuity. (To be *saved
by merit* was, however, a heresy according to orthodox Anglican doctrine, which taught salvation by faith rather than by merit or good
works.)

O heresy in fair, fit for these days!   22
A giving hand, though foul, shall have fair praise.
But come, the bow. [*She takes the bow.*] Now mercy
   goes to kill,   24
And shooting well is then accounted ill.   25
Thus will I save my credit in the shoot: 26
Not wounding, pity would not let me do 't;   27
If wounding, then it was to show my skill,
That more for praise than purpose meant to kill.   29
And, out of question, so it is sometimes,   30
Glory grows guilty of detested crimes,   31
When for fame's sake, for praise, an outward part,   32
We bend to that the working of the heart,   33
As I for praise alone now seek to spill
The poor deer's blood that my heart means no ill.   35

BOYET
Do not curst wives hold that self-sovereignty   36
Only for praise' sake when they strive to be
Lords o'er their lords?

PRINCESS
Only for praise, and praise we may afford
To any lady that subdues a lord.

Enter [Costard the] clown [with a letter].

BOYET
Here comes a member of the commonwealth.   41

COSTARD   God-i-good-e'en all! Pray you, which is the   42
head lady?

PRINCESS   Thou shalt know her, fellow, by the rest that
have no heads.

COSTARD   Which is the greatest lady, the highest?

PRINCESS   The thickest and the tallest.   47

COSTARD
The thickest and the tallest! It is so; truth is truth.
An your waist, mistress, were as slender as my wit,   49
One o' these maids' girdles for your waist should
   be fit.
Are not you the chief woman? You are the thickest
   here.

PRINCESS   What's your will, sir? What's your will?

COSTARD   I have a letter from Monsieur Berowne to one
Lady Rosaline.

PRINCESS
O, thy letter, thy letter! He's a good friend of mine.
Stand aside, good bearer. Boyet, you can carve;   56
Break up this capon.   [*The letter is given to Boyet.*]

BOYET   I am bound to serve.   57
This letter is mistook; it importeth none here.   58
It is writ to Jaquenetta.

PRINCESS   We will read it, I swear.
Break the neck of the wax, and everyone give ear.   60

BOYET (*reads*)   "By heaven, that thou art fair is most
infallible; true that thou art beauteous; truth itself that   62
thou art lovely. More fairer than fair, beautiful than
beauteous, truer than truth itself, have commiseration   64
on thy heroical vassal! The magnanimous and most   65
illustrate King Cophetua set eye upon the pernicious   66
and indubitate beggar Zenelophon; and he it was that   67
might rightly say, '*Veni, vidi, vici*'; which to annotha-   68
nize in the vulgar—O base and obscure vulgar!—vi-   69
delicet, 'He came, saw, and overcame.' He came, one;   70
saw, two; overcame, three. Who came? The King.
Why did he come? To see. Why did he see? To overcome. To whom came he? To the beggar. What saw
he? The beggar. Who overcame he? The beggar. The
conclusion is victory. On whose side? The King's. The
captive is enriched. On whose side? The beggar's. The
catastrophe is a nuptial. On whose side? The King's—   77
no, on both in one, or one in both. I am the King, for   78
so stands the comparison; thou the beggar, for so wit-   79
nesseth thy lowliness. Shall I command thy love? I   80
may. Shall I enforce thy love? I could. Shall I entreat
thy love? I will. What shalt thou exchange for rags?
Robes. For tittles? Titles. For thyself? Me. Thus, ex-   83
pecting thy reply, I profane my lips on thy foot, my   84
eyes on thy picture, and my heart on thy every part.
   Thine, in the dearest design of industry,   86
                  Don Adriano de Armado.
Thus dost thou hear the Nemean lion roar   88
   'Gainst thee, thou lamb, that standest as his prey.
Submissive fall his princely feet before,   90
   And he from forage will incline to play.   91
But if thou strive, poor soul, what art thou then?   92
Food for his rage, repasture for his den."   93

PRINCESS
What plume of feathers is he that indited this letter?   94
What vane? What weathercock? Did you ever hear
better?   95

---

22 in fair regarding beauty.   **these days** i.e., these times of religious controversy   **24 mercy** i.e., the Princess, who as a royal woman is an emblem of mercy   **25 then** i.e., when a merciful person like the Princess goes hunting   **26 credit** reputation   **27 Not . . . do 't** i.e., I can claim, if I miss, that pity restrained me   **29 That . . . kill** i.e., I shot to earn praise for my skill rather than for the sake of killing   **30 out of question** undoubtedly.   **sometimes** sometimes (that)   **31 Glory . . . crimes** i.e., an excessive desire for glory prompts us to commit detestable crimes   **32 an outward part** a superficial thing   **33 bend** force, adapt.   **that** i.e., fame   **35 The poor . . . ill** the blood of the poor deer that means me no harm   **36 curst** shrewish.   **hold** maintain   **41 commonwealth** ordinary citizenry   **42 God-i-good-e'en** God give you good evening   **47 The thickest and the tallest** (The Princess quips that *greatest* could be defined this way. Costard undiplomatically observes that the terms could indeed be applied to her.)   **49 An** if   **56 carve** (1) cut up, i.e., open (2) make courtly gestures

57 Break up cut up (a technical term in carving), i.e., open.   **capon** (Like the French *poulet, capon* designates figuratively a love letter.)   **bound** obliged   **58 mistook** mis-taken, misdirected.   **importeth** concerns   **60 wax** seal   **62 infallible** certain, incontrovertible   **64 commiseration** pity   **65 vassal** humble servant   **66 illustrate** illustrious.   **pernicious** (Armado may mean "penurious," or the text may be in error.)   **67 indubitate** undoubted.   **Zenelophon** Penelophon, the beggar maid in the ballad about King Cophetua. (See 1.2.105–106.)   **68 Veni, vidi, vici** I came, I saw, I overcame. (The words are Julius Caesar's terse account of his victory over King Pharnaces.)   **68– 69 annothanize** annotate (pseudo-Latin), or, anatomize, explain, interpret   **69 vulgar** vernacular   **69–70 videlicet** namely   **77 catastrophe** conclusion   **78–79 for . . . comparison** according to this analogy   **80 lowliness** low social standing   **83 tittles** insignificant specks or dots   **84 profane** desecrate   **86 dearest . . . industry** most excellent pattern of zealous gallantry   **88 Nemean lion** lion slain by Hercules in the first of his twelve labors   **90 Submissive fall** if you fall submissively   **91 forage** raging, ravening.   **incline** turn, shift   **92 strive** resist   **93 repasture** food   **94 What . . . feathers** what kind of bird, dandy.   **indited** wrote   **95 vane** weathervane (with play on "vain")

BOYET
I am much deceived but I remember the style.   96
PRINCESS
Else your memory is bad, going o'er it erewhile.   97
BOYET
This Armado is a Spaniard that keeps here in court,   98
A phantasime, a Monarcho, and one that makes
    sport   99
To the Prince and his bookmates.
PRINCESS   Thou fellow, a word.   100
Who gave thee this letter?
COSTARD   I told you—my lord.
PRINCESS
To whom shouldst thou give it?
COSTARD   From my lord to my lady.
PRINCESS
From which lord to which lady?
COSTARD
From my lord Berowne, a good master of mine,
To a lady of France that he called Rosaline.
PRINCESS
Thou hast mistaken his letter. Come, lords, away.   106
[To Rosaline.] Here, sweet, put up this; 'twill be thine
    another day.   [Exeunt Princess and attendants.]   107
BOYET
Who is the shooter? Who is the shooter?
ROSALINE   Shall I teach you to know?   108
BOYET
Ay, my continent of beauty.
ROSALINE   Why, she that bears the bow.   109
Finely put off!   110
BOYET
My lady goes to kill horns, but if thou marry,   111
Hang me by the neck if horns that year miscarry.   112
Finely put on!   113
ROSALINE
Well, then, I am the shooter.
BOYET   And who is your deer?   114
ROSALINE
If we choose by the horns, yourself come not near.   115
Finely put on, indeed!

MARIA
You still wrangle with her, Boyet, and she strikes at
    the brow.   117
BOYET
But she herself is hit lower. Have I hit her now?   118
ROSALINE   Shall I come upon thee with an old saying   119
that was a man when King Pépin of France was a little   120
boy, as touching the hit it?   121
BOYET   So I may answer thee with one as old, that was   122
a woman when Queen Guinevere of Britain was a little   123
wench, as touching the hit it.
ROSALINE
"Thou canst not hit it, hit it, hit it,
    Thou canst not hit it, my good man."
BOYET
"An I cannot, cannot, cannot,   127
    An I cannot, another can."
                                    Exit [Rosaline].
COSTARD
By my troth, most pleasant. How both did fit it!   129
MARIA
A mark marvelous well shot, for they both did
    hit it.   130
BOYET
A mark! O, mark but that mark! "A mark," says my
    lady!
Let the mark have a prick in 't to mete at, if it
    may be.   132
MARIA
Wide o' the bow hand! I' faith, your hand is out.   133
COSTARD
Indeed, 'a must shoot nearer, or he'll ne'er hit the
    clout.   134
BOYET [to Maria]
An if my hand be out, then belike your hand is in.   135
COSTARD
Then will she get the upshoot by cleaving the pin.   136
MARIA
Come, come, you talk greasily; your lips grow foul.   137

96 I . . . but I i.e., unless my memory fails me, I   97 Else otherwise.
going o'er it (1) reading it over (2) climbing over a stile, playing on
"style." erewhile just now   98 keeps lives, dwells   99 phantasime
one who entertains fantastic notions.   Monarcho (The nickname of
an eccentric Italian at the Elizabethan court who fancied himself the
emperor of the world; hence, anyone who displays absurd pretensions.)   100 To for.   bookmates fellow scholars   106 mistaken incorrectly delivered   107 up away.   'twill be thine i.e., it will be
your turn.   s.d. attendants (Perhaps the Forester exits here.)
108 shooter archer. (With a pun on "suitor." Boyet may be asking
who is to shoot, now that the Princess has left. Perhaps Rosaline has
been given the bow.)   109 continent of container of all   110 put off
answered evasively   111 horns i.e., deer   112 horns i.e., cuckold's
horns. (Boyet saucily suggests that, if Rosaline marries, cuckold's
horns will not be in short supply.)   miscarry do not appear   113 put
on urged, applied   114 deer (with pun on "dear"; Rosaline is the
natural target of all this double entendre about the huntress who is
hunting for a husband, since Berowne is known to have written her a
love letter)   115 If . . . near (Rosaline retorts to Boyet acerbically by
intimating that he couldn't possibly be her choice.)

117 she . . . brow i.e., she takes good aim at you (with pun on the
idea that she has also put Boyet down with a joke about cuckoldry)
118 hit lower i.e., in the heart, or, more bawdily, in the genital region.   hit her scored on her in this game of wit, described her situation aright   119 come upon thee answer or hit back (continuing the
metaphor of hunting and marksmanship)   120 was a man i.e., was
already old.   King Pépin Carolingian king (died 768)   121 as . . . hit
it concerning a catch or round, to be sung dancing. (The song itself is
obviously bawdy.)   122 So as long as, or similarly   123 Guinevere
King Arthur's unfaithful queen   127 An if   129 troth faith.   fit it fit
the lyrics to the tune. (Fit it often has a bawdy meaning as well.)
130 mark target   132 prick spot in the center of the target, the bull's-
eye (with sexual double meaning, as throughout this passage. Mark
here suggests "pudendum.")   mete at measure with the eye, aim at
133 Wide . . . hand wide of the mark on the left side, too far to the
left.   out inaccurate, out of practice   134 clout mark at the center of
the target (continuing the bawdry)   135 An if . . . is in i.e., if I'm out
of practice (sexually as well as at shooting), no doubt you're in practice.   belike most likely   136 upshoot leading or best shot.   cleaving
the pin splitting exactly the small nail holding the clout in place (with
sexual suggestion, as Maria observes in the next line)   137 greasily
indecently (referring to sexual double entendre in cleaving, hit it,
prick, your hand is in, etc.)

COSTARD
    She's too hard for you at pricks, sir. Challenge her to
        bowl.   138
BOYET
    I fear too much rubbing. Good night, my good owl.   139
                        [*Exeunt Boyet, Maria, and Katharine.*]
COSTARD
    By my soul, a swain, a most simple clown!   140
    Lord, Lord, how the ladies and I have put him
        down!
    O' my troth, most sweet jests, most incony
        vulgar wit!   142
    When it comes so smoothly off, so obscenely, as it
        were, so fit.   143
    Armado o' th' one side—O, a most dainty man!   144
    To see him walk before a lady and to bear her fan!
    To see him kiss his hand, and how most sweetly 'a
        will swear!
    And his page o' t'other side, that handful of wit!
    Ah, heavens, it is a most pathetical nit! *Shout within.* 148
    Sola, sola!   *Exit* [*Costard, running*]. 149

4.2   *Enter Dull, Holofernes the pedant, and Nathaniel.*

NATHANIEL   Very reverend sport, truly, and done in the   1
    testimony of a good conscience.   2
HOLOFERNES   The deer was, as you know, *sanguis,* in   3
    blood, ripe as the pomewater, who now hangeth like   4
    a jewel in the ear of *caelo,* the sky, the welkin, the 5
    heaven, and anon falleth like a crab on the face of *terra,* 6
    the soil, the land, the earth.
NATHANIEL   Truly, Master Holofernes, the epithets are
    sweetly varied, like a scholar at the least. But, sir, I 9
    assure ye, it was a buck of the first head.   10
HOLOFERNES   Sir Nathaniel, *haud credo.*   11
DULL   'Twas not a *haud credo,* 'twas a pricket.   12
HOLOFERNES   Most barbarous intimation! Yet a kind of   13
    insinuation, as it were, *in via,* in way, of explication; 14
    facere, as it were, replication, or rather, *ostentare,* to 15

show, as it were, his inclination, after his undressed,
unpolished, uneducated, unpruned, untrained, or
rather, unlettered, or, ratherest, unconfirmed fashion, 18
to insert again my *haud credo* for a deer.   19
DULL   I said the deer was not a *haud credo,* 'twas a
    pricket.
HOLOFERNES   Twice-sod simplicity, *bis coctus!*   22
    O thou monster Ignorance, how deformed dost
        thou look!
NATHANIEL
    Sir, he hath never fed of the dainties that are bred
        in a book.   24
    He hath not eat paper, as it were; he hath not drunk   25
    ink. His intellect is not replenished. He is only an ani-
    mal, only sensible in the duller parts;   27
    And such barren plants are set before us that we
        thankful should be—
    Which we of taste and feeling are—for those parts
        that do fructify in us more than he.   29
    For as it would ill become me to be vain, indiscreet,
        or a fool,
    So were there a patch set on learning, to see him in
        a school.   31
    But *omne bene,* say I, being of an old father's mind: 32
    "Many can brook the weather that love not the
        wind."   33
DULL
    You two are bookmen. Can you tell me by your wit
    What was a month old at Cain's birth that's not five
        weeks old as yet?
HOLOFERNES
    Dictynna, goodman Dull, Dictynna, goodman Dull.   36
DULL   What is Dictima?
NATHANIEL   A title to Phoebe, to Luna, to the moon.   38
HOLOFERNES
    The moon was a month old when Adam was no
        more,   39
    And raught not to five weeks when he came to
        fivescore.   40
    Th' allusion holds in the exchange.   41
DULL   'Tis true indeed. The collusion holds in the ex-   42
    exchange.

---

138 pricks informal or illegal archery (with sexual pun)   **139 rubbing**
grazing or striking together of the bowling balls (with sexual pun).
owl (Maria is so addressed because the owl is a bird of night and because to "take owl" is to take offense; also with a bawdy hint at *'ole,*
rhyming with *bowl.*)   **140 swain** peasant   **142 incony** fine, rare
143 obscenely (Perhaps a malapropism for "seemly," with unintended
appropriateness to the preceding passage.)   **fit** suitable   **144 dainty**
refined, elegant   **148 it** he.   **pathetical nit** i.e., touching little fellow.
(A *nit* is the egg of a small insect.)   **149 Sola** (A hunting cry.)
4.2. Location: Navarre's park.
1 reverend worthy of respect   **1–2 in the testimony** with the warrant
3–4 in blood in prime condition   **4 pomewater** a kind of apple.
who now which at one moment   **5 welkin** sky   **6 anon** at the next
moment.   **crab** crab apple   **9 at the least** to say the least   **10 of . . .
head** in its fifth year, hence with newly full antlers   **11 Sir** (Term of
address for ordinary clergymen.)   **haud credo** I cannot believe it
12 haud credo (Dull mistakes the Latin for something like "old gray
doe.")   **pricket** buck in its second year   **13 intimation** intrusion
14 insinuation hint, suggestion, beginning   **15 facere** to make.   **replication** explanation

18 unconfirmed inexperienced   **19 insert again** substitute, interpret.
(Holofernes' point is that Dull unwittingly makes sense by interpreting
haud credo as a doe rather than as a buck.)   **22 Twice-sod** twice sodden or cooked, boiled.   **bis coctus,** twice cooked. (Holofernes is incensed at Dull's twice insisting on his error.)   **24 of** on.   **dainties**
delicacies   **25 eat** eaten. (Pronounced "et.")   **27 sensible** capable of
perception   **29 Which we** we who.   **fructify** grow fruitful.   **he** in
him   **31 were . . . learning** (1) it would be setting a fool or dolt to
learn (2) it would be a disgrace to learning itself   **32 omne bene** all is
well.   **being . . . mind** agreeing as I do with one of the Church Fathers, one of the teachers of the early Christian Church   **33 Many
. . . wind** i.e., one must endure what one cannot change. (A proverb,
and hardly the wisdom of the Church Fathers.)   **brook** put up with
36, 38 Dictynna, Phoebe, Luna (Classical names for the moon. The
first is uncommon and is appropriate to the pedant. It occurs in Golding's translation of Ovid, a book that Shakespeare knew.)   **39 more**
older   **40 raught** reached, attained   **41 Th' allusion . . . exchange**
i.e., the riddle is still valid even if Cain's name (see line 35) is substituted for Adam's   **42 collusion** conspiracy. (Dull's error for
"allusion.")

HOLOFERNES   God comfort thy capacity! I say, th' allu- 44
sion holds in the exchange.

DULL   And I say the pollution holds in the exchange, for 46
the moon is never but a month old; and I say besides that 'twas a pricket that the Princess killed.

HOLOFERNES   Sir Nathaniel, will you hear an extemporal 49
epitaph on the death of the deer? And, to humor the
ignorant, call I the deer the Princess killed a pricket.

NATHANIEL   *Perge*, good Master Holofernes, *perge*, so it 52
shall please you to abrogate scurrility. 53

HOLOFERNES   I will something affect the letter, for it ar- 54
gues facility. 55
The preyful Princess pierced and pricked a pretty
pleasing pricket; 56
Some say a sore, but not a sore till now made sore
with shooting. 57
The dogs did yell. Put "l" to "sore," then sorel
jumps from thicket, 58
Or pricket sore, or else sorel. The people fall a-
hooting. 59
If sore be sore, then "l" to "sore" makes fifty sores
o' sorel. 60
Of one sore I an hundred make by adding but one
more "l."

NATHANIEL   A rare talent!

DULL   [*aside*]   If a talent be a claw, look how he claws 63
him with a talent.

HOLOFERNES   This is a gift that I have, simple, simple—
a foolish extravagant spirit, full of forms, figures,
shapes, objects, ideas, apprehensions, motions, revo- 67
lutions. These are begot in the ventricle of memory, 68
nourished in the womb of *pia mater*, and delivered 69
upon the mellowing of occasion. But the gift is good 70
in those in whom it is acute, and I am thankful for it.

NATHANIEL   Sir, I praise the Lord for you, and so may
my parishioners, for their sons are well tutored by you,
and their daughters profit very greatly under you. You 74
are a good member of the commonwealth.

HOLOFERNES   *Mehercle*, if their sons be ingenious, they 76
shall want no instruction; if their daughters be capa- 77
ble, I will put it to them. But *vir sapit qui pauca loqui-* 78

tur. A soul feminine saluteth us. 79

Enter Jaquenetta and [Costard] the clown.

JAQUENETTA   God give you good morrow, Master Person. 80

HOLOFERNES   Master Person, *quasi* pierce-one. And if 81
one should be pierced, which is the one? 82

COSTARD   Marry, Master Schoolmaster, he that is
likeliest to a hogshead. 84

HOLOFERNES   Of piercing a hogshead! A good luster of 85
conceit in a turf of earth; fire enough for a flint, pearl 86
enough for a swine. 'Tis pretty, it is well.

JAQUENETTA   Good Master Person, be so good as read
me this letter. It was given me by Costard and sent me
from Don Armado. I beseech you, read it.
[*She hands the letter to Nathaniel.*]

HOLOFERNES   "*Fauste, precor gelida quando pecus omne* 91
sub umbra ruminat," and so forth. Ah, good old Man- 92
tuan! I may speak of thee as the traveler doth of Venice:
Venezia, Venezia, 94
Chi non ti vede, chi non ti prezia. 95
Old Mantuan, old Mantuan! Who understandeth thee
not, loves thee not. [*He sings.*] Ut, re, sol, la, mi, fa. [*To* 97
Nathaniel, who is examining the letter.] Under pardon, 98
sir, what are the contents? Or rather, as Horace says in
his—What, my soul, verses?

NATHANIEL   Ay, sir, and very learned.

HOLOFERNES   Let me hear a staff, a stanza, a verse. *Lege,* 102
domine. 103

NATHANIEL   [*reads*]
"If love make me forsworn, how shall I swear to
love? 104
Ah, never faith could hold, if not to beauty vowed!
Though to myself forsworn, to thee I'll faithful prove;
Those thoughts to me were oaks, to thee like
osiers bowed. 107
Study his bias leaves and makes his book thine eyes, 108

---

44 comfort have pity on   **46 pollution** (Another error for "allusion,"
with perhaps unintended relevance to the linguistic *pollution* of
Holofernes' Latin.)   **49 extemporal** impromptu   **52 Perge** proceed
53 abrogate scurrility refrain from bawdry   **54 something . . . letter**
somewhat make use of alliteration   **54–55 argues** demonstrates
56 preyful intent upon prey   **57 sore** buck in its fourth year.   **made
sore** wounded   **58 Put "l" to "sore"** (The "l" is like a yelling noise
that alarms the buck.)   **sorel** buck in its third year   **59 Or** either
60 If sore be sore if it's a sore buck that is wounded.   **"l"** (As capital, L is Roman numeral fifty.)   **63 talent** i.e., talon.   **claws** (1)
scratches (2) flatters   **67 motions** impulses   **67–68 revolutions** turns
of thought   **68 ventricle of memory** one of the three sections of the
brain, believed to contain the memory   **69 pia mater** the membrane
surrounding the brain; the brain itself   **69–70 delivered . . . occasion** born when the moment is propitious   **74 under you** under your
instruction. (With unintended sexual double meaning.)   **76 Mehercle**
by Hercules.   **ingenious** clever   **77 want** lack   **77–78 capable** (1)
apt as pupils (2) able to bear children (an unconscious sexual pun that
goes back to *under you* in line 74)   **78 put it to them** (with unintended sexual meaning)

78–79 vir . . . loquitur he is a wise man who speaks little   **80 Person** (Normally pronounced "parson" in Elizabethan English, but here
pronounced "person," in rustic speech, thereby eliciting a pedantic
witticism from Holofernes.)   **81 quasi** that is, as if   **82 pierced** (Pronounced "persed"; playing on *pers-one*, "pierce one." This is sometimes taken as an allusion to Nashe's *Pierce Penniless, His Supplication to the Devil*, a fantastic satire in which the author, in the
character of Pierce, comments on the vices of the times; also to
Harvey's answer, *Pierce's Supererogation*, in which Pierce is referred
to as "the hogshead of wit"; compare line 85.)   **84 likeliest** most
like.   **hogshead** barrel (with a suggestion also of "fathead")
85 piercing a hogshead broaching a barrel, i.e., getting drunk   **85–
86 luster of conceit** spark of fancy   **91–92 Fauste . . . ruminat** (The
first line of the first eclogue of the Italian Renaissance poet Mantuan.
It was a well-known text in the schools. The passage means "Faustus,
I beg, while all the cattle chew their cud in the cool shade.")   **94–
95 Venezia . . . prezia** Venice, Venice, only he who sees you not
loves you not   **97 Ut** (Equivalent to the modern *do*. If Holofernes intends to sing the scale, *do, re, mi, fa, sol, la*, he displays his ignorance, but he may be singing a fragment of a melody.)   **98 Under
pardon** i.e., excuse me   **102 staff** stanza   **102–103 Lege, domine**
read, master   **104–117 If . . . tongue** (These lines were printed with
minor changes in *The Passionate Pilgrim*, 1599, a collection of poems
by various authors but attributed to Shakespeare. Two others of the
volume are from this play—that read by Longaville, 4.3.56–69, and
that by Dumaine, 4.3.97–116.)   **107 to me were** which seemed to
me as firm as.   **osiers** willows   **108 Study . . . leaves** i.e., the student leaves his studious inclination

Where all those pleasures live that art would
   comprehend.
If knowledge be the mark, to know thee shall
   suffice;   110
Well learnèd is that tongue that well can thee
   commend,
All ignorant that soul that sees thee without wonder;
   Which is to me some praise that I thy parts admire.
Thy eye Jove's lightning bears, thy voice his
   dreadful thunder,
Which, not to anger bent, is music and sweet fire.   115
Celestial as thou art, O, pardon love this wrong,   116
That sings heaven's praise with such an earthly
   tongue."   117
HOLOFERNES You find not the apostrophus, and so miss 118
the accent. Let me supervise the canzonet. [He takes the 119
letter.] Here are only numbers ratified, but, for the ele- 120
gancy, facility, and golden cadence of poesy—caret.   121
Ovidius Naso was the man. And why indeed "Naso"   122
but for smelling out the odoriferous flowers of fancy,   123
the jerks of invention? Imitari is nothing. So doth the   124
hound his master, the ape his keeper, the tired horse   125
his rider. But, damosella virgin, was this directed to   126
you?
JAQUENETTA   Ay, sir, from one Monsieur Berowne, one
of the strange queen's lords.   129
HOLOFERNES   I will overglance the superscript: "To the   130
snow-white hand of the most beauteous Lady Rosa-
line." I will look again on the intellect of the letter for   132
the nomination of the party writing to the person   133
written unto: "Your ladyship's in all desired employ-   134
ment, Berowne." Sir Nathaniel, this Berowne is one of   135
the votaries with the King, and here he hath framed a   136
letter to a sequent of the stranger queen's, which   137
accidentally, or by the way of progression, hath   138
miscarried.—Trip and go, my sweet; deliver this   139
paper into the royal hand of the King. It may concern   140
much. [He gives her the letter.] Stay not thy compliment.   141
I forgive thy duty. Adieu.   142
JAQUENETTA   Good Costard, go with me.—Sir, God save
your life!

COSTARD   Have with thee, my girl.   145
                              Exit [with Jaquenetta].
NATHANIEL   Sir, you have done this in the fear of God,
very religiously; and, as a certain Father saith—   147
HOLOFERNES   Sir, tell not me of the Father; I do fear col- 148
orable colors. But to return to the verses: did they   149
please you, Sir Nathaniel?
NATHANIEL   Marvelous well for the pen.   151
HOLOFERNES   I do dine today at the father's of a certain
pupil of mine, where, if before repast it shall please   153
you to gratify the table with a grace, I will, on my priv-   154
ilege I have with the parents of the foresaid child or
pupil, undertake your ben venuto; where I will prove   156
those verses to be very unlearned, neither savoring of
poetry, wit, nor invention. I beseech your society.   158
NATHANIEL   And thank you too; for society, saith the
text, is the happiness of life.
HOLOFERNES   And certes the text most infallibly con-   161
cludes it. [To Dull.] Sir, I do invite you too. You shall   162
not say me nay. Pauca verba. Away! The gentles are at   163
their game, and we will to our recreation.   Exeunt.   164

4.3   Enter Berowne, with a paper in his hand, alone.

BEROWNE   The King, he is hunting the deer; I am
coursing myself. They have pitched a toil; I am toiling   2
in a pitch—pitch that defiles. Defile! A foul word.   3
Well, set thee down, sorrow! For so they say the fool   4
said, and so say I—and I the fool. Well proved, wit! By
the Lord, this love is as mad as Ajax. It kills sheep; it   6
kills me, I a sheep. Well proved again o' my side! I will
not love; if I do, hang me. I' faith, I will not. O, but her
eye! By this light, but for her eye I would not love her.
Yes, for her two eyes. Well, I do nothing in the world
but lie, and lie in my throat. By heaven, I do love, and   11
it hath taught me to rhyme and to be melancholy; and
here is part of my rhyme, and here my melancholy.
Well, she hath one o' my sonnets already. The clown
bore it, the fool sent it, and the lady hath it—sweet
clown, sweeter fool, sweetest lady! By the world, I
would not care a pin, if the other three were in. Here   17

110 **mark** target   115 **bent** turned, directed   116 **pardon . . . wrong**
excuse this failure in my loving. (Or else, "O, pardon, love, this
wrong.")   118 **find** heed.   **apostrophus** apostrophes, marks of elision used to indicate omitted vowels and shortened pronunciation of
a word   119 **supervise** glance over, peruse.   **canzonet** i.e., poem
120 **only numbers ratified,** i.e., merely language made metrical
121 **caret** it is lacking   122 **Ovidius Naso** The Roman poet Ovid,
born in 43 B.C. (Naso, his surname, is derived from nasus, nose.)
123 **fancy** imagination   124 **jerks of invention** strokes of imagination.
Imitari to imitate   125 **tired** attired, harnessed, in full tackle   126 **damosella** i.e., damsel   129 **strange** foreign. (Jaquenetta seems mistakenly to believe that Berowne is attached to the Princess's retinue; or
this may be a matter on which Shakespeare changed his mind as he
revised.)   130 **superscript** address   132 **intellect** meaning, import,
contents   133 **nomination** name   134–135 **all desired employment**
any service you require of me   136 **votaries** those who have taken a
vow   137 **sequent** follower, attendant   138 **by . . . progression** in
process of delivery   139 **Trip and go** move nimbly and swiftly. (A
phrase from a popular song.)   140–141 **concern much** be of importance   141 **Stay . . . compliment** i.e., don't stand on ceremony
142 **forgive thy duty** set aside the requirement of a curtsy

145 **Have with thee** I'll go with you   147 **Father** Church Father
148–149 **colorable colors** plausible pretexts   151 **pen** penmanship,
or style   153 **repast** the meal   154 **gratify** (1) delight (2) grace.   **the
table** i.e., those at the table   156 **undertake your ben venuto** ensure
your welcome   158 **society** company   161–162 **certes . . . concludes it** certainly the biblical text you allude to (perhaps Ecclesiastes
4:8–12) infallibly demonstrates the point   163 **Pauca verba** few
words.   **gentles** gentlefolk   164 **game** i.e., hunting
4.3. Location: Navarre's park.
2 **coursing** pursuing.   **pitched a toil** set a snare   2–3 **toiling . . .
pitch** i.e., struggling in the toils of love. (Pitch means both "sticky
tar" and "a fixed opinion," with a quibbling reference to Rosaline's
eyes, which he has earlier, in 3.1.195, called two pitch-balls.)
3 **defiles** corrupts. (See Ecclesiasticus 13:1: "Whoso toucheth pitch
shall be defiled withal.")   4 **set thee down** i.e., stay, settle down
with me. (See 1.1.305–306.)   6 **mad as Ajax** (An allusion to the
story of Ajax, who, maddened by his failure in a contest for Achilles'
armor, attacked a flock of sheep, supposing them to be those who
had denied him the prize.)   11 **in my throat** i.e., utterly   17 **involved** (i.e., in love)

comes one with a paper. God give him grace to groan! 18
He stands aside.

The King entereth [with a paper].

KING Ay me!
BEROWNE [*aside*] Shot, by heaven! Proceed, sweet
Cupid. Thou hast thumped him with thy bird-bolt 21
under the left pap. In faith, secrets! 22
KING [*reads*]
"So sweet a kiss the golden sun gives not
   To those fresh morning drops upon the rose
As thy eyebeams, when their fresh rays have smote 25
   The night of dew that on my cheeks down flows. 26
Nor shines the silver moon one-half so bright
   Through the transparent bosom of the deep 28
As doth thy face, through tears of mine, give light;
   Thou shin'st in every tear that I do weep.
No drop but as a coach doth carry thee;
   So ridest thou triumphing in my woe.
Do but behold the tears that swell in me,
   And they thy glory through my grief will show.
But do not love thyself; then thou wilt keep
My tears for glasses, and still make me weep. 36
O queen of queens! How far dost thou excel,
No thought can think nor tongue of mortal tell."
How shall she know my griefs? I'll drop the paper.
Sweet leaves, shade folly. Who is he comes here? 40

*Enter Longaville [with papers]. The King steps
aside.*

What, Longaville, and reading! Listen, ear.
BEROWNE [*aside*]
   Now, in thy likeness, one more fool appear! 42
LONGAVILLE Ay me, I am forsworn!
BEROWNE [*aside*]
   Why, he comes in like a perjure, wearing papers. 44
KING [*aside*]
   In love, I hope. Sweet fellowship in shame!
BEROWNE [*aside*]
   One drunkard loves another of the name.
LONGAVILLE
   Am I the first that have been perjured so?
BEROWNE [*aside*]
   I could put thee in comfort: not by two that I know.
Thou makest the triumviry, the corner-cap of society, 49
The shape of Love's Tyburn, that hangs up
   simplicity. 50

LONGAVILLE
   I fear these stubborn lines lack power to move. 51
   [*Reading.*] "O sweet Maria, empress of my love!"—
   These numbers will I tear, and write in prose. 53
                          [*He tears the paper.*]
BEROWNE [*aside*]
   O, rhymes are guards on wanton Cupid's hose; 54
   Disfigure not his shop.
LONGAVILLE [*taking another paper*] This same shall go. 55
   (*He reads the sonnet.*)
"Did not the heavenly rhetoric of thine eye, 56
   'Gainst whom the world cannot hold argument, 57
Persuade my heart to this false perjury?
   Vows for thee broke deserve not punishment.
A woman I forswore, but I will prove,
   Thou being a goddess, I forswore not thee.
My vow was earthly, thou a heavenly love.
   Thy grace being gained cures all disgrace in me. 63
Vows are but breath, and breath a vapor is.
   Then thou, fair sun, which on my earth dost shine,
Exhal'st this vapor vow; in thee it is. 66
   If broken, then, it is no fault of mine.
If by me broke, what fool is not so wise
To lose an oath to win a paradise?" 69
BEROWNE [*aside*]
   This is the liver vein, which makes flesh a deity, 70
   A green goose a goddess. Pure, pure idolatry. 71
   God amend us, God amend! We are much out o'
      the way. 72

Enter Dumaine [with a paper].

LONGAVILLE
   By whom shall I send this?—Company! Stay.
                          [*He steps aside.*]
BEROWNE [*aside*]
   All hid, all hid—an old infant play. 74
   Like a demigod here sit I in the sky, 75
   And wretched fools' secrets heedfully o'ereye. 76
   More sacks to the mill! O heavens, I have my wish! 77
   Dumaine transformed! Four woodcocks in a dish! 78
DUMAINE O most divine Kate!
BEROWNE [*aside*] O most profane coxcomb!
DUMAINE
   By heaven, the wonder in a mortal eye! 81

---

18 **God . . . groan** i.e., may God grant that he be moved to groan for love. **s.d. He stands aside** (Possibly Berowne hides in a tree or some elevated place; see 4.3.75, 161.) **21 bird-bolt** blunt arrow for shooting birds **22 left pap** left breast (where the heart is located). **In faith, secrets** i.e., in truth, we will now hear a confession of love **25 smote** struck **26 night of dew,** i.e., tears that flow nightly **28 the deep** i.e., a body of water reflecting the moonlight **36 glasses** mirrors. **still** continually **40 shade** conceal **42 thy** i.e., the King's **44 perjure** perjurer. **wearing papers** (An allusion to the custom of attaching to a convicted perjurer's breast the papers involved in and setting forth his offense—in this case, the poem, which is an open indication of Longaville's having forsworn his oath of celibacy.) **49 triumviry** triumvirate. **corner-cap** three-cornered cap. **society** fellowship **50 Tyburn** a place of public execution in London (with reference here to the triangular structure of the gallows)

51 **stubborn** rough, harsh **53 numbers** verses **54 guards** trim, decorative embroideries. **hose** breeches **55 shop** (Possibly a bawdy reference to the place where love is physically produced, or possibly an error for *slop,* "breeches.") **56–69 Did . . . paradise** (See the note on 4.2.104–117.) **57 whom** i.e., which **63 grace** favor **66 Exhal'st** draws up. (It was thought that the sun drew up vapors from the earth, thereby producing meteors, will-o'-the-wisps, etc.) **69 To** as to **70 liver vein** i.e., the vein or style of a lover (since the liver was assumed to be the seat of the passions) **71 green goose** gosling, i.e., a young girl, a strumpet **72 amend** improve. **much . . . way** far gone **74 infant play** child's game of hide and seek (but with a suggestion also of a medieval religious play, in which God appears above) **75 in the sky** (Berowne speaks as though he were looking down on the others from some elevated position, possibly the gallery above the stage; see also 4.3.161.) **76 heedfully** attentively. **o'ereye** observe **77 More . . . mill** (A proverbial expression, "there's more to come.") **78 woodcocks** (Birds noted for their stupidity.) **81 mortal** human

BEROWNE [*aside*]
　By earth, she is not, Corporal. There you lie.　82
DUMAINE
　Her amber hairs for foul hath amber quoted.　83
BEROWNE [*aside*]
　An amber-colored raven was well noted.　84
DUMAINE
　As upright as the cedar.
BEROWNE [*aside*]　　　　　Stoop, I say!　85
　Her shoulder is with child.
DUMAINE　　　　　As fair as day.　86
BEROWNE [*aside*]
　Ay, as some days; but then no sun must shine.
DUMAINE
　O, that I had my wish!
LONGAVILLE [*aside*]　　　And I had mine!
KING [*aside*]
　And I mine too, good Lord!
BEROWNE [*aside*]
　Amen, so I had mine. Is not that a good word?　90
DUMAINE
　I would forget her, but a fever she　91
　Reigns in my blood and will remembered be.
BEROWNE [*aside*]
　A fever in your blood! Why, then incision　93
　Would let her out in saucers. Sweet misprision!　94
DUMAINE
　Once more I'll read the ode that I have writ.
BEROWNE [*aside*]
　Once more I'll mark how love can vary wit.　96
DUMAINE (*reads his sonnet*)
　　"On a day—alack the day!—　97
　　Love, whose month is ever May,
　　Spied a blossom passing fair　99
　　Playing in the wanton air.　100
　　Through the velvet leaves the wind,
　　All unseen, can passage find,　102
　　That the lover, sick to death,　103
　　Wished himself the heaven's breath.
　　'Air,' quoth he, 'thy cheeks may blow;
　　Air, would I might triumph so!
　　But, alack, my hand is sworn
　　Ne'er to pluck thee from thy thorn—
　　Vow, alack, for youth unmeet,　109
　　Youth so apt to pluck a sweet!
　　Do not call it sin in me
　　That I am forsworn for thee,

Thou for whom Jove would swear
Juno but an Ethiop were,　114
And deny himself for Jove,　115
Turning mortal for thy love.'"　116
This will I send, and something else more plain,
That shall express my true love's fasting pain.　118
O, would the King, Berowne, and Longaville
Were lovers too! Ill, to example ill,　120
Would from my forehead wipe a perjured note,　121
For none offend where all alike do dote.　122
LONGAVILLE [*advancing*]
　Dumaine, thy love is far from charity,　123
　That in love's grief desir'st society.　124
　You may look pale, but I should blush, I know,
　To be o'erheard and taken napping so.
KING [*advancing*]
　Come, sir, you blush! As his, your case is such;
　You chide at him, offending twice as much.
　You do not love Maria? Longaville
　Did never sonnet for her sake compile,
　Nor never lay his wreathèd arms athwart　131
　His loving bosom to keep down his heart?
　I have been closely shrouded in this bush
　And marked you both, and for you both did blush.
　I heard your guilty rhymes, observed your fashion,
　Saw sighs reek from you, noted well your passion.
　"Ay me!" says one. "O Jove!" the other cries;
　One, her hairs were gold, crystal the other's eyes.
　[*To Longaville.*] You would for paradise break faith
　　and troth;　139
　[*To Dumaine.*] And Jove, for your love, would
　　infringe an oath.　140
　What will Berowne say when that he shall hear　141
　Faith infringèd, which such zeal did swear?
　How will he scorn! How will he spend his wit!
　How will he triumph, leap, and laugh at it!
　For all the wealth that ever I did see
　I would not have him know so much by me.　146
BEROWNE [*advancing*]
　Now step I forth to whip hypocrisy.
　Ah, good my liege, I pray thee, pardon me.
　Good heart, what grace hast thou, thus to reprove　149
　These worms for loving, that art most in love?
　Your eyes do make no coaches; in your tears　151
　There is no certain princess that appears;　152
　You'll not be perjured, 'tis a hateful thing—
　Tush, none but minstrels like of sonneting!　154
　But are you not ashamed? Nay, are you not,

82 Corporal i.e., field officer for Cupid (see 3.1.185), with a play on "corporeal," fleshly　**83 quoted** designated. (Dumaine hyperbolically insists that her amber hair makes real amber seem foul, ugly, by comparison.)　**84 An . . . noted** i.e. (ironically), Dumaine has aptly described a black fowl (with pun on "foul") as amber-colored
85 Stoop (1) stooped, stunted (2) Dumaine should avoid such lofty comparisons　**86 is with child** i.e., is swollen, unshapely　**90 Is . . . word** (1) is that not kind of me? (2) is not *amen* known to be a good word?　**91 a** i.e., as a　**93 incision** letting blood　**94 in saucers** (1) by the bowlful (2) into bowls to catch the blood.　**misprision** (1) mistake (2) being released from confinement (of the veins)　**96 vary wit** inspire intellectual or artistic variety　**97–116 On . . . love** (See the note on 4.2.104–117.)　**99 passing** surpassingly　**100 wanton** frolicsome　**102 can** began to　**103 That** so that　**109 unmeet** inappropriate

114 Ethiop Ethiopian, black African. (Used here as an example of ugliness.)　**115 for Jove** to be Jove　**118 fasting** hungering　**120 example** serve as an example for　**121 note** mark, document. (See 4.3.44.)　**122 dote** love dotingly　**123 charity** Christian love　**124 That . . . society** you who, in your suffering from love, uncharitably desire others to suffer also. (Proverbial: "Misery loves company.")　**131 lay . . . athwart** i.e., fold his arms in the conventional sign of melancholy; compare 3.1.18　**139 troth** loyalty　**140 infringe** break　**141 when that** when　**146 by** about　**149 grace** dispensation, privilege.　**reprove** rebuke, condemn　**151 Your . . . coaches** (Alluding to the King's sonnet, 4.3.31–32.)　**152 certain** particular　**154 like** approve

All three of you, to be thus much o'ershot?   156
[*To Longaville.*] You found his mote; the King your
  mote did see;   157
But I a beam do find in each of three.   158
O, what a scene of foolery have I seen,
Of sighs, of groans, of sorrow, and of teen!   160
O me, with what strict patience have I sat,
To see a king transformèd to a gnat!   162
To see great Hercules whipping a gig,   163
And profound Solomon to tune a jig,   164
And Nestor play at pushpin with the boys,   165
And critic Timon laugh at idle toys!   166
Where lies thy grief, O, tell me, good Dumaine?
And, gentle Longaville, where lies thy pain?
And where my liege's? All about the breast.
A caudle, ho!

KING   Too bitter is thy jest.   170
Are we betrayed thus to thy overview?   171

BEROWNE
Not you to me, but I betrayed by you.
I, that am honest, I, that hold it sin
To break the vow I am engagèd in,   174
I am betrayed by keeping company
With men like you, men of inconstancy.
When shall you see me write a thing in rhyme?
Or groan for Joan? Or spend a minute's time
In pruning me? When shall you hear that I   179
Will praise a hand, a foot, a face, an eye,
A gait, a state, a brow, a breast, a waist,   181
A leg, a limb—   [*He starts to leave.*]

KING   Soft! Whither away so fast?
A true man or a thief, that gallops so?   183

BEROWNE
I post from love. Good lover, let me go.   184

*Enter Jaquenetta [with a letter], and [Costard the]
clown.*

JAQUENETTA
God bless the King!

KING   What present hast thou there?   185

COSTARD
Some certain treason.

KING   What makes treason here?   186

COSTARD
Nay, it makes nothing, sir.

KING   If it mar nothing neither,   187
The treason and you go in peace away together.

JAQUENETTA
I beseech Your Grace, let this letter be read.
Our parson misdoubts it; 'twas treason, he said.   190
             [*She gives the letter.*]

KING   Berowne, read it over.
           He [Berowne] reads the letter [silently].
[*To Jaquenetta.*] Where hadst thou it?

JAQUENETTA Of Costard.

KING [*to Costard*] Where hadst thou it?

COSTARD Of Dun Adramadio, Dun Adramadio.
             [*Berowne tears the letter.*]

KING
How now, what is in you? Why dost thou tear it?

BEROWNE
A toy, my liege, a toy. Your Grace needs not fear it.

LONGAVILLE
It did move him to passion, and therefore let's hear
  it.

DUMAINE [*gathering up the pieces*]
It is Berowne's writing, and here is his name.

BEROWNE [*to Costard*]
Ah, you whoreson loggerhead! You were born to do
  me shame.—   200
Guilty, my lord, guilty! I confess, I confess.

KING What?

BEROWNE
That you three fools lacked me fool to make up the
  mess.   203
He, he, and you—and you, my liege!—and I,
Are pickpurses in love, and we deserve to die.   205
O, dismiss this audience, and I shall tell you more.

DUMAINE
Now the number is even.

BEROWNE   True, true, we are four.
Will these turtles be gone?

KING   Hence, sirs. Away!   208

COSTARD
Walk aside the true folk, and let the traitors stay.   209
         [*Exeunt Costard and Jaquenetta.*]

BEROWNE
Sweet lords, sweet lovers, O, let us embrace!
  As true we are as flesh and blood can be.
The sea will ebb and flow, heaven show his face;
  Young blood doth not obey an old decree.
We cannot cross the cause why we were born;   214
Therefore of all hands must we be forsworn.   215

KING
What, did these rent lines show some love of thine?   216

BEROWNE
Did they, quoth you? Who sees the heavenly Rosaline,
That, like a rude and savage man of Ind   218
  At the first opening of the gorgeous east,   219

---

156 o'ershot wide of the mark, shooting beyond it; i.e., in error
157, 158 mote, beam i.e., small speck, large defect. (See Matthew
7:3–5, Luke 6:41–42.) **160 teen** affliction, grief **162 a gnat** i.e., a
tiny creature (with a play perhaps on *mote*) **163 whipping a gig** spinning a top **164 tune** play or sing **165 Nestor** wise old Greek
chieftain in the Trojan War. **pushpin** a child's game **166 critic** critical, censorious. **Timon** a fifth-century Athenian notorious for his
misanthropy. **laugh . . . toys** take delight in mindless entertainments
170 caudle warm drink given to sick people **171 overview** inspection **174 engagèd in** sworn to **179 pruning me** preening, i.e., trimming, dressing up myself **181 state** attitude, bearing **183 true** honest **184 post** hasten **185 present** i.e., writing **186 makes treason**
has treason to do **187 makes . . . mar** ("To make and mar" is a
proverbial phrase meaning to do and undo.)

190 misdoubts suspects **200 whoreson loggerhead** i.e., infernal
blockhead **203 mess** group of four at table **205 pickpurses** pick-
pockets (i.e., cheaters) **208 turtles** turtledoves, lovers. **sirs** (An acceptable form of address for both women and men.) **209 Walk . . .
folk** i.e., those who tell the truth are sent away for their efforts. (Costard's wry comment need not be offered as an aside.) **214 cross . . .
born** i.e., continue to defy love **215 of all hands** inevitably, in every
way, on every side **216 rent lines** torn verses **218 rude** ignorant.
Ind India **219 opening** i.e., dawning

Bows not his vassal head and, strucken blind,
    Kisses the base ground with obedient breast?
What peremptory eagle-sighted eye   222
    Dares look upon the heaven of her brow
That is not blinded by her majesty?

KING
    What zeal, what fury hath inspired thee now?
My love, her mistress, is a gracious moon,   226
    She an attending star, scarce seen a light.   227

BEROWNE
    My eyes are then no eyes, nor I Berowne.
    O, but for my love, day would turn to night!
Of all complexions the culled sovereignty   230
    Do meet as at a fair in her fair cheek,
Where several worthies make one dignity,   232
    Where nothing wants that want itself doth seek. 233
Lend me the flourish of all gentle tongues—   234
    Fie, painted rhetoric! O, she needs it not.   235
To things of sale a seller's praise belongs;   236
    She passes praise, then praise too short doth blot. 237
A withered hermit, fivescore winters worn,
    Might shake off fifty, looking in her eye.
Beauty doth varnish age, as if newborn,   240
    And gives the crutch the cradle's infancy.
O, 'tis the sun that maketh all things shine!

KING
    By heaven, thy love is black as ebony.

BEROWNE
    Is ebony like her? O word divine!
    A wife of such wood were felicity.   245
O, who can give an oath? Where is a book,   246
    That I may swear Beauty doth beauty lack
If that she learn not of her eye to look?   248
    No face is fair that is not full so black.

KING
    O paradox! Black is the badge of hell,
    The hue of dungeons and the school of night;   251
And beauty's crest becomes the heavens well.   252

BEROWNE
    Devils soonest tempt, resembling spirits of light. 253
    O, if in black my lady's brows be decked,   254
    It mourns that painting and usurping hair   255

Should ravish doters with a false aspect;   256
    And therefore is she born to make black fair.
Her favor turns the fashion of the days,   258
    For native blood is counted painting now;   259
And therefore red, that would avoid dispraise,   260
    Paints itself black to imitate her brow.

DUMAINE
    To look like her are chimney sweepers black.

LONGAVILLE
    And since her time are colliers counted bright. 263

KING
    And Ethiops of their sweet complexion crack.   264

DUMAINE
    Dark needs no candles now, for dark is light.

BEROWNE
    Your mistresses dare never come in rain,   266
    For fear their colors should be washed away.   267

KING
    'Twere good yours did; for, sir, to tell you plain,
    I'll find a fairer face not washed today.   269

BEROWNE
    I'll prove her fair, or talk till doomsday here.

KING
    No devil will fright thee then so much as she.   271

DUMAINE
    I never knew man hold vile stuff so dear.   272

LONGAVILLE [showing his shoe]
    Look, here's thy love; my foot and her face see.

BEROWNE
    O, if the streets were pavèd with thine eyes,   274
    Her feet were much too dainty for such tread!   275

DUMAINE
    O vile! Then, as she goes, what upward lies   276
    The street should see as she walked overhead.

KING
    But what of this? Are we not all in love?

BEROWNE
    Nothing so sure, and thereby all forsworn.

KING
    Then leave this chat, and, good Berowne, now prove
    Our loving lawful and our faith not torn.   281

DUMAINE
    Ay, marry, there, some flattery for this evil.   282

LONGAVILLE
    O, some authority how to proceed,
    Some tricks, some quillets, how to cheat the devil. 284

222 peremptory bold.   **eagle-sighted** (The eagle was believed to be the only bird able to look directly at the sun.)   **226 gracious** (1) exquisite (2) godly   **227 She** i.e., Rosaline.   **scarce . . . light** a light scarcely to be seen   **230 the culled sovereignty** those chosen as most worthy   **232 worthies** excellences.   **dignity** i.e., supreme example of beauty   **233 wants** is lacking.   **want** desire   **234 flourish** adornment, eloquence.   **gentle** noble   **235 painted** artificial   **236 of sale** for sale   **237 passes** surpasses.   **then praise . . . blot** i.e., any praise of her is inadequate and hence must detract   **240 varnish** embellish   **245 were** would be   **246 book** i.e., Bible   **248 If . . . look** unless Beauty herself learns from Rosaline's eyes how beauty should truly appear   **251 school** master, model (?)   **252 And . . . well** (ironically) and yet you assert that your dark-eyed beauty is suitable to adorn heaven. (Or, perhaps *beauty's crest* refers to the sun, and the line means ''and only the sun, i.e., a fair beauty, is suitable to grace the heavens.'')   **253 Devils . . . light** devils are all the more dangerous as tempters when they resemble angels. (Berowne suggests that Rosaline's dark beauty undercuts the traditional Neoplatonic association of light with beauty and virtue.)   **254 decked** adorned   **255 It mourns that** i.e., it is as though she is in mourning for the fact that.   **painting** cosmetics.   **usurping** i.e., false

256 false aspect misleading appearance   **258 favor** face.   **turns** alters, inverts   **259 native . . . now** i.e., a natural ruddy complexion is accounted cosmetic now (since rouge is so often used and so successfully deceptive)   **260 dispraise** disparagement, censure   **263 colliers** coal miners   **264 of . . . crack** boast to have attractive complexions   **266 come in** walk in, be exposed to   **267 colors** makeup   **269 I'll . . . today** i.e., many unwashed faces are cleaner and fairer than hers   **271 then** i.e., on doomsday   **272 hold . . . dear** value worthless things so highly   **274–275 O . . . tread** i.e., she walks so lightly that she would not even injure a street paved with your eyes   **276 what upward lies** (Dumaine bawdily suggests that a street paved with his eyes would be able to look up constantly under her dress.)   **281 torn** broken   **282 some . . . evil** i.e., give us some plausible way to put a good face on this difficulty   **284 quillets** verbal niceties, subtle distinctions

DUMAINE
  Some salve for perjury.
BEROWNE   O, 'tis more than need.
  Have at you, then, Affection's men-at-arms.   286
  Consider what you first did swear unto:
  To fast, to study, and to see no woman—
  Flat treason 'gainst the kingly state of youth.   289
  Say, can you fast? Your stomachs are too young,
  And abstinence engenders maladies.   291
  O, we have made a vow to study, lords,
  And in that vow we have forsworn our books.
  For when would you, my liege, or you, or you,
  In leaden contemplation have found out   295
  Such fiery numbers as the prompting eyes   296
  Of beauty's tutors have enriched you with?
  Other slow arts entirely keep the brain,   298
  And therefore, finding barren practicers,
  Scarce show a harvest of their heavy toil;
  But love, first learnèd in a lady's eyes,
  Lives not alone immurèd in the brain,   302
  But with the motion of all elements   303
  Courses as swift as thought in every power,   304
  And gives to every power a double power
  Above their functions and their offices.   306
  It adds a precious seeing to the eye:
  A lover's eyes will gaze an eagle blind.   308
  A lover's ear will hear the lowest sound,
  When the suspicious head of theft is stopped.   310
  Love's feeling is more soft and sensible   311
  Than are the tender horns of cockled snails.   312
  Love's tongue proves dainty Bacchus gross in taste.   313
  For valor, is not Love a Hercules,
  Still climbing trees in the Hesperides?   315
  Subtle as Sphinx, as sweet and musical   316
  As bright Apollo's lute strung with his hair.   317
  And when Love speaks, the voice of all the gods
  Make heaven drowsy with the harmony.
  Never durst poet touch a pen to write   320
  Until his ink were tempered with Love's sighs.   321
  O, then his lines would ravish savage ears
  And plant in tyrants mild humility.
  From women's eyes this doctrine I derive:
  They sparkle still the right Promethean fire;   325

  They are the books, the arts, the academes
  That show, contain, and nourish all the world;
  Else none at all in aught proves excellent.   328
  Then fools you were these women to forswear,   329
  Or, keeping what is sworn, you will prove fools.
  For wisdom's sake, a word that all men love,
  Or for love's sake, a word that loves all men,   332
  Or for men's sake, the authors of these women,
  Or women's sake, by whom we men are men,
  Let us once lose our oaths to find ourselves,   335
  Or else we lose ourselves to keep our oaths.
  It is religion to be thus forsworn,   337
  For charity itself fulfills the law,   338
  And who can sever love from charity?
KING
  Saint Cupid, then! And, soldiers, to the field!
BEROWNE
  Advance your standards, and upon them, lords;   341
  Pell-mell, down with them! But be first advised   342
  In conflict that you get the sun of them.   343
LONGAVILLE
  Now to plain dealing. Lay these glozes by.   344
  Shall we resolve to woo these girls of France?
KING
  And win them, too. Therefore let us devise
  Some entertainment for them in their tents.
BEROWNE
  First, from the park let us conduct them thither;
  Then homeward every man attach the hand   349
  Of his fair mistress. In the afternoon
  We will with some strange pastime solace them,   351
  Such as the shortness of the time can shape;
  For revels, dances, masques, and merry hours
  Forerun fair Love, strewing her way with flowers.   354
KING
  Away, away! No time shall be omitted
  That will betime and may by us be fitted.   356
BEROWNE
  Allons! Allons! Sowed cockle reaped no corn,   357
    And justice always whirls in equal measure.   358
  Light wenches may prove plagues to men forsworn;   359
  If so, our copper buys no better treasure. [Exeunt.]   360

286 Have at you I come at you, i.e., here it is. Affection's love's
289 state (1) condition (2) majesty 291 maladies (The Quarto here
supplies twenty-two lines that appear to be a first start for lines
292–339; seemingly they were meant to be canceled. See Textual
Notes.) 295 leaden sluggish, dull 296 numbers verses 298 arts
branches of knowledge. keep dwell within 302 immurèd walled
up, imprisoned 303 elements i.e., earth, air, fire, and water
304 Courses runs. power faculty, natural capacity 306 Above . . .
offices above and beyond their ordinary functions 308 gaze stare
310 When . . . stopped when even the most cautiously alert thief (or
one alert to the danger of being robbed) hears nothing 311 sensible
sensitive 312 cockled having a shell 313 Bacchus god of wine and
revelry 315 Hesperides where the golden apples grew (the gaining of
which was the eleventh of Hercules' twelve labors) 316 Sphinx a
mythological creature of ancient Thebes who destroyed all passersby
who could not solve her riddle 317 Apollo's lute (Apollo was the
Greek god of music, poetry, and prophecy.) 320 durst dares
321 tempered blended, modified 325 sparkle throw out, emit.
right true. Promethean fire divine fire. (From the legend that
Prometheus stole fire from heaven and gave it to mankind.)

328 Else otherwise. aught anything 329 forswear renounce
332 loves is lovable to, inspires with love 335 once for once, one
time. lose break 337 religion i.e., in keeping with the tenets of
our religion 338 For . . . law (From Romans 13:8: "for he that
loveth another hath fulfilled the law.") 341 Advance raise. standards flags serving as a military emblem. (The military metaphor is
not only amorous but bawdy.) 342 Pell-mell without keeping ranks,
in hand-to-hand combat. be first advised take care first of all
343 get . . . them i.e., take field position so that the sun is in their
eyes (with a play on the idea of "begetting a son") 344 glozes soph-
istries 349 attach seize 351 strange novel, fresh. solace entertain
354 Forerun come before, prepare the way for 356 betime happen.
fitted used. (The King resolves to take advantage of every minute.)
357 Allons come on, let's go. cockle a weed. corn wheat.
(Berowne says that without well-planned efforts there will be no results.) 358 measure proportion (again suggesting that reward comes
only from effort) 359 Light frivolous 360 copper coin of little
value. (Berowne's point is that, as beggars and forswearers, the men
cannot afford to be choosers.)

✤

5.1   *Enter [Holofernes] the pedant, [Nathaniel] the curate, and Dull [the constable].*

HOLOFERNES   *Satis quod sufficit.* 1

NATHANIEL   I praise God for you, sir. Your reasons at 2 dinner have been sharp and sententious, pleasant without scurrility, witty without affection, audacious 4 without impudency, learned without opinion, and 5 strange without heresy. I did converse this quondam 6 day with a companion of the King's who is intituled, 7 nominated, or called Don Adriano de Armado.

HOLOFERNES   *Novi hominem tanquam te.* His humor is 9 lofty, his discourse peremptory, his tongue filed, his 10 eye ambitious, his gait majestical, and his general behavior vain, ridiculous, and thrasonical. He is too 12 picked, too spruce, too affected, too odd, as it were, 13 too peregrinate, as I may call it. 14

NATHANIEL   A most singular and choice epithet. 15

[He] draw[s] out his table book.

HOLOFERNES   He draweth out the thread of his verbosity finer than the staple of his argument. I abhor such fa- 17 natical phantasimes, such insociable and point-devise 18 companions, such rackers of orthography, as to speak 19 "dout," fine, when he should say "doubt"; "det" 20 when he should pronounce "debt"—d, e, b, t, not d, e, t. He clepeth a calf "cauf," half "hauf"; neighbor 22 *vocatur* "nebor"; neigh abbreviated "ne." This is 23 abhominable—which he would call "abominable." 24 It insinuateth me of insanie. *Ne intelligis, domine?* To 25 make frantic, lunatic.

NATHANIEL   *Laus Deo, bone intelligo.* 27

HOLOFERNES   "Bone?" "Bone" for "bene?" Priscian a little 28 scratched; 'twill serve. 29

Enter [Armado the] braggart, [Mote, his] boy, [and Costard].

NATHANIEL   *Videsne quis venit?* 30

HOLOFERNES   *Video, et gaudeo.* 31

ARMADO *[to Mote]*   Chirrah! 32

HOLOFERNES   Quare "chirrah," not "sirrah"? 33

ARMADO   Men of peace, well encountered.

HOLOFERNES   Most military sir, salutation.

MOTE *[aside to Costard]*   They have been at a great feast of languages and stolen the scraps.

COSTARD *[to Mote]*   O, they have lived long on the alms basket of words. I marvel thy master hath not 39 eaten thee for a word, for thou art not so long by 40 the head as *honorificabilitudinitatibus.* Thou art easier 41 swallowed than a flapdragon. 42

MOTE *[to Costard]*   Peace! The peal begins. 43

ARMADO *[to Holofernes]*   Monsieur, are you not lettered? 45

MOTE   Yes, yes, he teaches boys the hornbook. What is 46 "a, b" spelled backward, with the horn on his head?

HOLOFERNES   Ba, *pueritia,* with a horn added. 48

MOTE   Ba, most silly sheep with a horn! You hear his learning.

HOLOFERNES   *Quis, quis,* thou consonant? 51

MOTE   The last of the five vowels, if you repeat them; or the fifth, if I.

HOLOFERNES   I will repeat them: a, e, i—

MOTE   The sheep. The other two concludes it—o, u. 55

ARMADO   Now, by the salt wave of the *Mediterraneum,* a sweet touch, a quick venue of wit! Snip, snap, quick 57 and home. It rejoiceth my intellect. True wit!

MOTE   Offered by a child to an old man—which is wit-old. 60

HOLOFERNES   What is the figure? What is the figure? 61

MOTE   Horns.

HOLOFERNES   Thou disputes like an infant. Go whip 63 thy gig. 64

MOTE   Lend me your horn to make one, and I will whip about your infamy *manu cita*—a gig of a cuckold's 66 horn.

5.1. Location: Navarre's park.
1 Satis quod sufficit enough is as good as a feast   **2 reasons** discussions, discourses   **4 affection** affectation   **5 opinion** arrogance, dogmatism   **6 strange** novel, new.   **this quondam** the other   **7 intituled** entitled, designated   **9 Novi . . . te** I know the man as well as I know you   **10 peremptory** positive, overbearing.   **filed** polished   **12 thrasonical** boastful. (From Thraso, a braggart soldier in Terence's play *Eunuchus.*)   **13 picked** fastidious.   **spruce** dapper, elegant   **14 peregrinate** having the manner of one who has traveled   **15 singular** unique.   **s.d. table book** notebook   **17 staple** fiber, thread.   **argument** subject matter   **18 phantasimes** persons who entertain fantastic notions.   **insociable** unsociable, unpleasant   **18–19 point-devise companions** extremely precise fellows   **19 rackers of orthography** torturers of spelling. (Holofernes' tirade reflects a conscious attempt of some Renaissance educators to bring the English spelling and pronunciation of certain borrowed words more nearly to their Latin originals.)   **20 fine** mincingly, too thinly. (Or perhaps an error for "*sine* b," "without b.")   **22 clepeth** calls   **23 vocatur** is called   **24 abhominable . . . abominable** (This is pedantic to the point of being simply wrong, since the supposed derivation of *abhominable* from *ab homine,* away from mankind, inhuman, is a false one, but it is a derivation that Shakespeare seems elsewhere to have accepted.)   **25 It . . . insanie** (1) to me it savors of insanity (2) it drives me mad.   **Ne intelligis, domine** do you understand me, sir   **27 Laus . . . intelligo** praise be to God, I understand well   **28 "Bone" for "bene"** i.e., the Latin should be *bene,* "well"   **28–29 Priscian . . . scratched** i.e., your Latin is a little faulty. (Priscian was a grammarian of the fifth or sixth century whose textbooks were considered standard.)

30 Videsne quis venit do you see who comes?   **31 Video, et gaudeo** I see and I rejoice. (This trivial Latin dialogue is after the manner of schoolboys' exercises.)   **32 Chirrah** (Possibly a corruption of the Greek *chaere,* "hail," or merely a dialectal pronunciation of *sirrah,* a term of address for a social inferior.)   **33 Quare** why   **39 alms basket** a basket used to gather scraps for the poor   **40 for a word** (Mote's name puns on the French *mot,* "word.")   **40–41 long . . . head** i.e., tall   **41 honorificabilitudinitatibus** (Once considered the longest word in existence. It is the dative or ablative plural of a Latin word meaning something like "honorableness.")   **42 flapdragon** the raisin or plum in burning brandy to be snapped with the mouth in the game of snapdragon   **43 peal** i.e., clatter of tongues, like a peal of bells   **45 lettered** i.e., educated. (Mote replies as though *lettered* meant "able to teach boys their letters.")   **46 hornbook** printed sheets of paper, covered by a protective thin layer of horn; used for teaching children their alphabet. (The *horn* sets up a joke on the sheep's or cuckold's horn.)   **48 pueritia** childishness, child   **51 Quis** who, what.   **consonant** i.e., nonentity, since the consonants cannot be sounded without also sounding the vowels   **55 The sheep** i.e., Holofernes, by saying "i," that is, "I," has labeled himself the sheep.   **concludes it** (1) completes the list of the five vowels (2) proves my point.   **o, u** i.e., O you   **57 venue** sally, thrust. (A fencing term, continued in *quick and home,* to the quick.)   **wit** intellect   **60 wit-old** mentally feeble (with a pun on "wittol," a contented cuckold)   **61 figure** metaphor, figure of speech   **63 Thou disputes** you reason   **63–64 whip thy gig** spin your spinning-top (as a child might do)   **66 manu cita** with a ready hand

COSTARD   An I had but one penny in the world, thou 68
shouldst have it to buy gingerbread. Hold, there is the
very remuneration I had of thy master, thou halfpenny 70
purse of wit, thou pigeon egg of discretion. [*He gives* 71
money.] O, an the heavens were so pleased that thou
wert but my bastard, what a joyful father wouldst thou
make me! Go to, thou hast it *ad dunghill*, at the fingers' ends, as they say.

HOLOFERNES   O, I smell false Latin! "Dunghill" for
"*unguem*."   77

ARMADO   Arts-man, *preambulate*. We will be singuled 78
from the barbarous. Do you not educate youth at the
charge-house on the top of the mountain?   80

HOLOFERNES   Or *mons*, the hill.

ARMADO   At your sweet pleasure, for the mountain.

HOLOFERNES   I do, sans question.   83

ARMADO   Sir, it is the King's most sweet pleasure and
affection to congratulate the Princess at her pavilion 85
in the posteriors of this day, which the rude multitude 86
call the afternoon.

HOLOFERNES   The posterior of the day, most generous 88
sir, is liable, congruent, and measurable for the after- 89
noon. The word is well culled, choice, sweet, and apt, 90
I do assure you, sir, I do assure.

ARMADO   Sir, the King is a noble gentleman, and my
familiar, I do assure ye, very good friend. For what is 93
inward between us, let it pass. I do beseech thee, re- 94
member thy courtesy. I beseech thee, apparel thy 95
head. And, among other importunate and most serious 96
designs, and of great import indeed, too—but let that
pass; for I must tell thee it will please His Grace, by
the world, sometimes to lean upon my poor shoulder
and with his royal finger thus dally with my excre- 100
ment, with my mustachio; but, sweetheart, let that 101
pass. By the world, I recount no fable! Some certain
special honors it pleaseth his greatness to impart to
Armado, a soldier, a man of travel, that hath seen the
world; but let that pass. The very all of all is—but, 105
sweetheart, I do implore secrecy—that the King
would have me present the Princess, sweet chuck, 107
with some delightful ostentation, or show, or pageant, 108
or antic, or firework. Now, understanding that the 109
curate and your sweet self are good at such eruptions
and sudden breaking out of mirth, as it were, I have
acquainted you withal, to the end to crave your assis- 112
ance.

HOLOFERNES   Sir, you shall present before her the Nine 114
Worthies. Sir Nathaniel, as concerning some enter- 115
tainment of time, some show in the posterior of this
day, to be rendered by our assistance, the King's command, and this most gallant, illustrate, and learned
gentleman, before the Princess—I say none so fit as to
present the Nine Worthies.   120

NATHANIEL   Where will you find men worthy enough
to present them?

HOLOFERNES   Joshua, yourself; myself; and this gallant 123
gentleman, Judas Maccabaeus; this swain, because of
his great limb or joint, shall pass Pompey the Great; 125
the page, Hercules—

ARMADO   Pardon, sir—error. He is not quantity enough
for that Worthy's thumb. He is not so big as the end of
his club.

HOLOFERNES   Shall I have audience? He shall present 130
Hercules in minority. His enter and exit shall be stran- 131
gling a snake; and I will have an apology for that pur- 132
pose.

MOTE   An excellent device! So, if any of the audience
hiss, you may cry, "Well done, Hercules! Now thou
crushest the snake!" That is the way to make an offense gracious, though few have the grace to do it.

ARMADO   For the rest of the Worthies?

HOLOFERNES   I will play three myself.

MOTE   Thrice-worthy gentleman!

ARMADO   Shall I tell you a thing?

HOLOFERNES   We attend.   142

ARMADO   We will have, if this fadge not, an antic. I be- 143
seech you, follow.

HOLOFERNES   *Via*, goodman Dull! Thou hast spoken no 145
word all this while.

DULL   Nor understood none neither, sir.

HOLOFERNES   *Allons!* We will employ thee.   148

DULL
I'll make one in a dance or so, or I will play   149
On the tabor to the Worthies, and let them dance
the hay.   150

HOLOFERNES
Most dull, honest Dull! To our sport, away!
                                                Exeunt.

---

68 An if   **70–71 halfpenny purse** a tiny purse, just large enough to
hold a halfpenny   **71 pigeon egg** i.e., tiny object   **77 unguem** *ad
unguem*, "to the fingernail," i.e., perfectly   **78 Arts-man** scholar.
preambulate walk (with me).   **singuled** set apart, distinguished
80 charge-house some kind of school   **83 sans** without   **85 congratulate** greet   **86 in the posteriors** at the end.   **rude** ignorant   **88 generous** cultivated, wellborn   **89 liable** apt.   **measurable** fitted
90 culled selected   **93 familiar** intimate acquaintance   **94 inward**
private.   **let it pass** never mind about that   **95 thy courtesy** i.e., that
you've removed your hat; or, that you should remove your hat in
courtesy (at which point, when Costard does so, Armado bids him put
it on again)   **96 importunate** urgent   **100–101 excrement**
outgrowth (of hair)   **101 sweetheart** (A term of endearment, here
spoken in friendship.)   **105 very all of all** sum of everything
107 chuck chick. (A term of endearment.)   **108 ostentation** display
109 antic a pageant or entertainment using fantastic costumes.
firework pyrotechnic display   **112 withal** with this

114–115 Nine Worthies (A conventional subject familiar to
Shakespeare's audience in poems, pageants, and tapestries. The nine
were three pagans, Hector of Troy, Alexander the Great, and Julius
Caesar; three Jews, Joshua, David, and Judas Maccabaeus; and three
Christians, Arthur, Charlemagne, and Godfrey of Boulogne. The list
varied, but Shakespeare makes an unusual departure when he introduces Pompey and Hercules.)   **120 present** represent   **123 myself**
(Holofernes does not here assign a part to himself (see, however, line
139), nor does he assign Nathaniel to Alexander or Armado to Hercules, as in the actual production. Perhaps changes occur later. This
present passage may represent an unrevised draft.)   **125 pass** represent   **130 audience** a hearing   **131 in minority** as a child.   **enter entrance**   **131–132 strangling a snake** (According to legend, Hercules
as an infant displayed his great strength by strangling two serpents
sent by the envious Juno to destroy him in his cradle.)   **132 apology**
explanatory prologue   **142 attend** listen   **143 if this fadge not** i.e.,
even if this fails.   **an antic** i.e., a show of some sort, perhaps of "The
Owl and the Cuckoo"   **145 Via** onward! (A cry of encouragement to
troops.)   **148 Allons** let's go   **149 make one** take part   **150 tabor**
small drum.   **hay** country dance

✢

5.2   *Enter the ladies* [*the Princess, Katharine, Rosaline, and Maria*].

PRINCESS
Sweethearts, we shall be rich ere we depart,
If fairings come thus plentifully in.   2
A lady walled about with diamonds!   3
Look you what I have from the loving King.
                                            [*She shows a jewel.*]
ROSALINE
Madam, came nothing else along with that?
PRINCESS
Nothing but this? Yes, as much love in rhyme
As would be crammed up in a sheet of paper,
Writ o' both sides the leaf, margent and all,   8
That he was fain to seal on Cupid's name.   9
ROSALINE
That was the way to make his godhead wax,   10
For he hath been five thousand years a boy.   11
KATHARINE
Ay, and a shrewd unhappy gallows, too.   12
ROSALINE
You'll ne'er be friends with him. 'A killed your sister. 13
KATHARINE
He made her melancholy, sad, and heavy,   14
And so she died. Had she been light, like you,   15
Of such a merry, nimble, stirring spirit,
She might ha' been a grandam ere she died.   17
And so may you, for a light heart lives long.
ROSALINE
What's your dark meaning, mouse, of this light
   word?   19
KATHARINE
A light condition in a beauty dark.   20
ROSALINE
We need more light to find your meaning out.
KATHARINE
You'll mar the light by taking it in snuff;   22
Therefore I'll darkly end the argument.   23
ROSALINE
Look what you do, you do it still i' the dark.   24

KATHARINE
So do not you, for you are a light wench.
ROSALINE
Indeed I weigh not you, and therefore light.   26
KATHARINE
You weigh me not? O, that's you care not for me.   27
ROSALINE
Great reason, for past cure is still past care.   28
PRINCESS
Well bandied both! A set of wit well played.   29
But, Rosaline, you have a favor too.   30
Who sent it? And what is it?
ROSALINE   I would you knew.   31
An if my face were but as fair as yours,   32
My favor were as great. Be witness this.   33
                            [*She shows a love token.*]
Nay, I have verses too, I thank Berowne;
The numbers true, and, were the numbering, too,   35
I were the fairest goddess on the ground.   36
I am compared to twenty thousand fairs.   37
O, he hath drawn my picture in his letter!
PRINCESS   Anything like?
ROSALINE
Much in the letters, nothing in the praise.   40
PRINCESS
Beauteous as ink—a good conclusion.   41
KATHARINE
Fair as a text B in a copybook.   42
ROSALINE
Ware pencils, ho! Let me not die your debtor,   43
My red dominical, my golden letter.   44
O, that your face were not so full of O's!   45
PRINCESS
A pox of that jest! And I beshrew all shrows.   46
But, Katharine, what was sent to you from fair
   Dumaine?
KATHARINE
Madam, this glove.   [*She shows a glove.*]
PRINCESS   Did he not send you twain?   48
KATHARINE
Yes, madam, and moreover

5.2. Location: Navarre's park. Near the ladies' tents.
2 fairings complimentary gifts   **3 A lady . . . diamonds** (The Princess has evidently received a brooch with a diamond-studded frame enclosing a portrait of a lady.)   **8 margent** margin   **9 That . . . name** so that he was obliged to append Cupid's name by sealing a slip of paper to the letter itself, or, for lack of room, place the seal on top of Cupid's name. (Probably the Princess shows her letter, as do the other ladies in turn when they show their love tokens.)   **10 godhead** divinity.   **wax** increase (with pun on the *wax* of the seal)   **11 he hath . . . boy** i.e., Cupid has remained young ever since the world began   **12 shrewd unhappy gallows** wicked, mischievous knave, deserving to be hanged   **13 'A killed your sister** (A mocking hint of a story, not developed here, of a young woman who died for love.)   **'A** he   **14 heavy** depressed   **15 light** (1) cheerful (2) unchaste   **17 grandam** grandmother   **19 dark** hidden.   **mouse** (A term of endearment.)   **light word** frivolous speech   **20 light condition** wanton temperament   **22 taking . . . snuff** (1) trimming the burning candlewick (2) taking offense   **23 darkly** obscurely   **24 Look what** whatever.   **do it . . . i' the dark** (with obvious sexual meaning)

26 weigh not you don't weigh as much as you   **27 weigh** regard seriously.   **that's** that means   **28 Great reason** with good reason.   **past cure . . . care** what can't be helped shouldn't be worried about. (Proverbial.) Rosaline implies that Katharine is incurable, and puns on *care,* "have fondness," in line 27.   **29 Well bandied both** i.e., both of you have wittily traded insults. (A tennis term, continued in *set*.)   **30 favor** love token   **31 would** wish   **32 An if**   **33 favor** personal appearance (playing on *favor,* "love token," in line 30).   **Be witness this** let this be witness   **35 numbers** meter.   **numbering** reckoning   **36 were** would be   **37 fairs** beautiful women   **40 letters** lettering.   **praise** i.e., contents, what he says of me   **41 ink** (Referring to Rosaline's dark complexion.)   **42 a text B** (Perhaps a heavily ornamented capital B, boldly dark like Rosaline's complexion.)   **43 Ware pencils** i.e., be wary of bringing painting into the argument, or be wary of this sketching of portraits. (*Pencils* are fine-tipped brushes.)   **Let . . . debtor** i.e., let me repay your insult   **44 red dominical** red lettering used in calendars to mark Sundays and holy days. (From *dies dominica,* "the Lord's day"; here, a jesting reference to Katharine's fair complexion.)   **45 O's** i.e., smallpox scars (to which the Princess replies in the next line with her curse, "A pox")   **46 of** on.   **beshrew all shrows** i.e., wish a plague on all shrews, scolds. (The Quarto/Folio spelling of *Shrowes* makes plain the rhyme with *O's* .)   **48 twain** two

Some thousand verses of a faithful lover,
A huge translation of hypocrisy,
Vilely compiled, profound simplicity.   52

MARIA [showing a letter and a pearl necklace]
This, and these pearls, to me sent Longaville.
The letter is too long by half a mile.

PRINCESS
I think no less. Dost thou not wish in heart
The chain were longer and the letter short?   55

MARIA
Ay, or I would these hands might never part.   57

PRINCESS
We are wise girls to mock our lovers so.

ROSALINE
They are worse fools to purchase mocking so.   59
That same Berowne I'll torture ere I go.
O, that I knew he were but in by th' week!   61
How I would make him fawn, and beg, and seek,
And wait the season, and observe the times,   63
And spend his prodigal wits in bootless rhymes,
And shape his service wholly to my hests,   65
And make him proud to make me proud that jests!   66
So pair-taunt-like would I o'ersway his state   67
That he should be my fool and I his fate.

PRINCESS
None are so surely caught when they are catched   69
As wit turned fool. Folly in wisdom hatched
Hath wisdom's warrant and the help of school,   71
And wit's own grace to grace a learnèd fool.

ROSALINE
The blood of youth burns not with such excess
As gravity's revolt to wantonness.   74

MARIA
Folly in fools bears not so strong a note   75
As fool'ry in the wise when wit doth dote,   76
Since all the power thereof it doth apply   77
To prove, by wit, worth in simplicity.   78

Enter Boyet.

PRINCESS
Here comes Boyet, and mirth is in his face.

BOYET
O, I am stabbed with laughter! Where's Her Grace?

PRINCESS
Thy news, Boyet?

BOYET   Prepare, madam, prepare!
Arm, wenches, arm! Encounters mounted are   82

51 translation communication, metaphor **52 simplicity** stupidity, silliness **55 in heart** truthfully **57 would** wish. (Perhaps Maria demonstrates what she means by wrapping the pearls around her hands, making them prisoner in her chain.) **59 purchase** earn, invite **61 in week** i.e., caught, trapped permanently **63 And wait . . . times** i.e., wait until it suits me, follow my schedule **64 bootless** fruitless **65 hests** behests **66 And . . . jests** i.e., and make him take satisfaction in glorifying me, the one who mocks him **67 pair-taunt-like** like one holding a winning hand (pair-taunt) in the card game of "post-and-pair" (with a pun on taunt) **69 surely** securely **71 warrant** guarantee **74 As gravity's revolt** as when a wise man turns **75 note** tee **76 dote** grow foolish **77 thereof** i.e., of wit stigma, notoriety **78 simplicity** foolishness **82 Encounters mounted are** skirmishes or assailants are readied, set in position

PRINCESS
Saint Denis to Saint Cupid! What are they   87
That charge their breath against us? Say, scout, say. 88

BOYET
Under the cool shade of a sycamore
I thought to close mine eyes some half an hour,
When, lo, to interrupt my purposed rest,   92
Toward that shade I might behold addressed
The King and his companions. Warily
I stole into a neighbor thicket by   95
And overheard what you shall overhear—
That, by and by, disguised they will be here.
Their herald is a pretty knavish page   98
That well by heart hath conned his embassage.
Action and accent did they teach him there: 99
"Thus must thou speak," and "thus thy body bear."
And ever and anon they made a doubt   101
Presence majestical would put him out;
"For," quoth the King, "an angel shalt thou see;   102
Yet fear not thou, but speak audaciously."   104
The boy replied, "An angel is not evil;
I should have feared her had she been a devil."
With that, all laughed and clapped him on the
   shoulder,
Making the bold wag by their praises bolder.   108
One rubbed his elbow thus, and fleered, and swore 109
A better speech was never spoke before.
Another, with his finger and his thumb,   111
Cried, "Via! We will do 't, come what will come."   112
The third he capered and cried, "All goes well!"   113
The fourth turned on the toe, and down he fell.   114
With that, they all did tumble on the ground
With such a zealous laughter, so profound,
That in this spleen ridiculous appears,   117
To check their folly, passion's solemn tears.

PRINCESS
But what, but what? Come they to visit us?

BOYET
They do, they do, and are appareled thus,   121
Like Muscovites or Russians, as I guess.
Their purpose is to parle, to court, and dance;   122
And everyone his love suit will advance.

84 surprised assaulted in a surprise attack **87 Saint Denis** patron saint of France. **to** against **88 charge their breath** aim their words. To charge is to attack at full gallop or to level, as in aiming a weapon. **92 might** could. **addressed** approaching **95 overhear** hear over again **98 conned** memorized. **embassage** message **99 Action** gesture **101 ever and anon** every now and then. **made a doubt** expressed a fear (that) **102 put him out** leave him confused and tongue-tied **104 audaciously** boldly **108 wag** young man **109 rubbed his elbow** (in a gesture of satisfaction, like rubbing the hands). **fleered** grinned **111 with . . . thumb** i.e., snapping his fingers. **112 Via** onward **113 capered** skipped, danced **114 turned on the toe** pirouetted **117 spleen ridiculous** ludicrous fit of laughter **121 Muscovites or Russians** (Costumes not uncommon in court masquerades.) **guess** (The unrhymed word suggests a missing line.) **122 parle** parley

Unto his several mistress, which they'll know   124
By favors several which they did bestow.
PRINCESS
And will they so? The gallants shall be tasked;   126
For, ladies, we will every one be masked,
And not a man of them shall have the grace,
Despite of suit, to see a lady's face.   129
Hold, Rosaline, this favor thou shalt wear,
And then the King will court thee for his dear.
Hold, take thou this, my sweet, and give me thine.   132
So shall Berowne take me for Rosaline.   133
            [*The Princess and Rosaline exchange favors.*]
And change you favors too. So shall your loves   134
Woo contrary, deceived by these removes.   135
            [*Katharine and Maria exchange favors.*]
ROSALINE
Come on, then, wear the favors most in sight.   136
KATHARINE
But in this changing what is your intent?
PRINCESS
The effect of my intent is to cross theirs.   138
They do it but in mockery merriment,   139
And mock for mock is only my intent.
Their several counsels they unbosom shall   141
To loves mistook, and so be mocked withal   142
Upon the next occasion that we meet,
With visages displayed, to talk and greet.   144
ROSALINE
But shall we dance, if they desire us to 't?
PRINCESS
No, to the death we will not move a foot,   146
Nor to their penned speech render we no grace,   147
But while 'tis spoke each turn away her face.
BOYET
Why, that contempt will kill the speaker's heart
And quite divorce his memory from his part.
PRINCESS
Therefore I do it; and I make no doubt
The rest will ne'er come in, if he be out.   152
There's no such sport as sport by sport o'erthrown,
To make theirs ours and ours none but our own.   154
So shall we stay, mocking intended game,
And they, well mocked, depart away with shame.
                            Sound trumpet [within].
BOYET
The trumpet sounds. Be masked; the maskers come.   157
                            [*The ladies mask.*]

Enter blackamoors with music; [Mote,] the boy,
with a speech, and [the King, Berowne, and] the

rest of the lords disguised [as Russians, and
visored].
MOTE
All hail, the richest beauties on the earth!
BEROWNE [*aside*]
Beauties no richer than rich taffeta.   159
MOTE
A holy parcel of the fairest dames   160
                The ladies turn their backs to him
That ever turned their—backs—to mortal views!
BEROWNE [*prompting Mote*]   "Their eyes," villain,
"their eyes."
MOTE
That ever turned their eyes to mortal views!
Out—
BOYET   True; out indeed.   166
MOTE
Out of your favors, heavenly spirits, vouchsafe   167
Not to behold—
BEROWNE [*to Mote*]   "Once to behold," rogue.
MOTE
Once to behold with your sun-beamèd eyes—
With your sun-beamèd eyes—
BOYET
They will not answer to that epithet.
You were best call it "daughter-beamèd eyes."   173
MOTE
They do not mark me, and that brings me out.   174
BEROWNE
Is this your perfectness? Begone, you rogue!   175
                            [*Exit Mote.*]
ROSALINE [*speaking as the Princess*]
What would these strangers? Know their minds,
Boyet.   176
If they do speak our language, 'tis our will
That some plain man recount their purposes.   178
Know what they would.
BOYET   What would you with the Princess?
BEROWNE
Nothing but peace and gentle visitation.   180
ROSALINE   What would they, say they?
BOYET
Nothing but peace and gentle visitation.
ROSALINE
Why, that they have, and bid them so be gone.
BOYET
She says you have it, and you may be gone.
KING
Say to her we have measured many miles   185
To tread a measure with her on this grass.   186

---

124 several respective, particular. **which** whom **126 tasked** tried, tested **129 suit** petition, entreaty (with a play on "suit of clothes") **132–133 Hold . . . Rosaline** (Possibly Shakespeare intended this couplet to replace lines 130–131.) **134 change** exchange **135 removes** exchanges **136 most in sight** conspicuously **138 cross** thwart **139 mockery** mocking **141 several counsels** various private intentions, secret purposes. **unbosom shall** will disclose **142 withal** with this **144 visages** faces **146 to the death** (as in "fight to the death") **147 penned speech** speech composed and written out with care. **grace** favor **152 out** confused, having forgotten his lines **154 theirs** i.e., their sport **157 s.d. blackamoors** i.e., attendants in blackface

159 taffeta i.e., their masks of taffeta cloth. (Their beauty is in their masks, says Berowne. Some editors assign the speech to Boyet.) **160 parcel** company **166 out** i.e., having forgotten his lines **167 vouchsafe** deign, agree **173 daughter-beamèd** (substituting *daughter* for *sun*, i.e., *son*) **174 mark** pay attention to **175 Is . . . perfectness** is this your idea of a perfectly memorized speech **176 What . . . minds** what do these strangers want? Learn their intentions. (Rosaline, masquerading as the Princess, presides.) **178 plain** plainspoken **180 visitation** visit **185 measured** traversed, paced **186 tread a measure** perform a dance

BOYET
They say that they have measured many a mile
To tread a measure with you on this grass.

ROSALINE
It is not so. Ask them how many inches
Is in one mile. If they have measured many,   190
The measure then of one is eas'ly told.

BOYET
If to come hither you have measured miles,
And many miles, the Princess bids you tell
How many inches doth fill up one mile.

BEROWNE
Tell her we measure them by weary steps.

BOYET
She hears herself.

ROSALINE   How many weary steps,
Of many weary miles you have o'ergone,
Are numbered in the travel of one mile?

BEROWNE
We number nothing that we spend for you.
Our duty is so rich, so infinite,
That we may do it still without account.   201
Vouchsafe to show the sunshine of your face,
That we, like savages, may worship it.

ROSALINE
My face is but a moon, and clouded too.   204

KING
Blessed are clouds, to do as such clouds do!
Vouchsafe, bright moon, and these thy stars, to
    shine,
Those clouds removed, upon our watery eyne.   207

ROSALINE
O vain petitioner! Beg a greater matter;
Thou now requests but moonshine in the water.   209

KING
Then in our measure do but vouchsafe one change.   210
Thou bidd'st me beg; this begging is not strange.   211

ROSALINE
Play, music, then! Nay, you must do it soon.
                              [*Music plays.*]
Not yet? No dance! Thus change I like the moon.

KING
Will you not dance? How come you thus estranged?   214

ROSALINE
You took the moon at full, but now she's changed.

KING
Yet still she is the moon, and I the man.   216
The music plays; vouchsafe some motion to it.   217

ROSALINE
Our ears vouchsafe it.

KING   But your legs should do it.   218

ROSALINE
Since you are strangers and come here by chance,   219
We'll not be nice. Take hands. We will not dance.   220
                              [*She offers her hand.*]

KING
Why take we hands, then?

ROSALINE   Only to part friends.
Curtsy, sweethearts, and so the measure ends.

KING
More measure of this measure! Be not nice.   223

ROSALINE
We can afford no more at such a price.

KING
Price you yourselves. What buys your company?   225

ROSALINE
Your absence only.

KING   That can never be.

ROSALINE
Then cannot we be bought. And so, adieu—
Twice to your visor, and half once to you.   228

KING
If you deny to dance, let's hold more chat.   229

ROSALINE
In private, then.

KING   I am best pleased with that.
                              [*They converse apart.*]

BEROWNE
Whitehanded mistress, one sweet word with thee.

PRINCESS [*speaking as Rosaline*]
Honey, and milk, and sugar—there is three.

BEROWNE
Nay then, two treys, an if you grow so nice—   233
Metheglin, wort, and malmsey. Well run, dice!   234
There's half a dozen sweets.

PRINCESS   Seventh sweet, adieu.
Since you can cog, I'll play no more with you.   236

BEROWNE
One word in secret.

PRINCESS   Let it not be sweet.

BEROWNE
Thou grievest my gall.

PRINCESS   Gall! Bitter.

BEROWNE   Therefore meet. 238
                              [*They converse apart.*]

190 measured (1) traversed (2) taken the measurement of   **201 account** reckoning   **204 a moon** (Earlier, at 4.3.226–227, the King described the Princess as a moon surrounded by her attending stars—as he does again at lines 206–207. But Rosaline, acting the part of the Princess, hints at changeability and reflected beauty more appropriate to Rosaline herself; see 3.1.194.)   **clouded** i.e., masked   **207 clouds** i.e., the mask.   **eyne** eyes   **209 moonshine . . . water** i.e., nothing at all. (Proverbial.)   **210 vouchsafe** permit.   **change** a round in dancing (with a play on the idea of the moon's changing)   **211 strange** odd (with a quibble on "foreign")   **214 How . . . estranged** why are you disaffected?   **216 man** i.e., man in the moon. (This unrhymed word suggests a missing line.)   **217 vouchsafe some motion** i.e., deign to dance

218 Our . . . it i.e., I deign to hear your *motion* or proposal. (Rosaline pretends not to understand an invitation to dance.)   **219 strangers** foreigners   **220 nice** coy   **223 More measure** i.e., (we wish) more quantity; we wish the kiss that should follow the curtsying   **225 Price you yourselves** set your own price on yourselves   **228 Twice . . . you** (Rosaline evidently curtsies—twice to the visor and the face behind it, then a perfunctory curtsy to her partner—but the line is obscure.)   **229 deny** refuse   **233 treys** threes.   **nice** subtle   **234 Metheglin** a spiced drink made from herbs and honey.   **wort** sweet unfermented beer.   **malmsey** a strong sweet wine   **236 cog** cheat   **238 Thou . . . gall** i.e., you cause me pain by irritating my sore. (Gall is bile, a bitter secretion of the liver. The Princess deliberately misinterprets Berowne's use of *gall*.)   **meet** fitting (with perhaps a play on "have a meeting")

DUMAINE
Will you vouchsafe with me to change a word?   239
MARIA [speaking as Katharine]
Name it.
DUMAINE   Fair lady—
MARIA   Say you so? Fair lord!   240
Take that for your "fair lady."
DUMAINE   Please it you,
As much in private, and I'll bid adieu.
                    [They converse apart.]
KATHARINE [speaking as Maria]
What, was your vizard made without a tongue?   243
LONGAVILLE
I know the reason, lady, why you ask.
KATHARINE
O, for your reason! Quickly, sir, I long.
LONGAVILLE
You have a double tongue within your mask   246
And would afford my speechless vizard half.   247
KATHARINE
"Veal," quoth the Dutchman. Is not "veal" a calf?   248
LONGAVILLE
A calf, fair lady!
KATHARINE   No, a fair lord calf.
LONGAVILLE
Let's part the word.
KATHARINE   No, I'll not be your half.   250
Take all and wean it; it may prove an ox.   251
LONGAVILLE
Look how you butt yourself in these sharp mocks!   252
Will you give horns, chaste lady? Do not so.
KATHARINE
Then die a calf, before your horns do grow.
LONGAVILLE
One word in private with you, ere I die.
KATHARINE
Bleat softly then. The butcher hears you cry.
                    [They converse apart.]
BOYET
The tongues of mocking wenches are as keen
    As is the razor's edge invisible,
Cutting a smaller hair than may be seen;
    Above the sense of sense, so sensible   260

Seemeth their conference. Their conceits have wings   261
Fleeter than arrows, bullets, wind, thought, swifter
    things.
ROSALINE
Not one word more, my maids. Break off, break off!
                    [The ladies break away from the gentlemen.]
BEROWNE
By heaven, all dry-beaten with pure scoff!   264
KING
Farewell, mad wenches. You have simple wits.
                    Exeunt [King, lords, and blackamoors. The ladies
                                        unmask.]
PRINCESS
Twenty adieus, my frozen Muscovits.
Are these the breed of wits so wondered at?
BOYET
Tapers they are, with your sweet breaths puffed
    out.   268
ROSALINE
Well-liking wits they have; gross, gross; fat, fat.   269
PRINCESS
O poverty in wit, kingly-poor flout!   270
Will they not, think you, hang themselves tonight?
Or ever but in vizards show their faces?
This pert Berowne was out of count'nance quite.   273
ROSALINE
They were all in lamentable cases!   274
The King was weeping-ripe for a good word.   275
PRINCESS
Berowne did swear himself out of all suit.   276
MARIA
Dumaine was at my service, and his sword.
    "Non point," quoth I. My servant straight was
    mute.   278
KATHARINE
Lord Longaville said I came o'er his heart;
    And trow you what he called me?
PRINCESS   Qualm, perhaps. 280
KATHARINE
Yes, in good faith.
PRINCESS   Go, sickness as thou art!
ROSALINE
Well, better wits have worn plain statute-caps.   282
But will you hear? The King is my love sworn.

239 vouchsafe . . . word deign to speak with me. (Change means "exchange.") 240 Say . . . lord (Maria mischievously takes Dumaine's request for a word literally and so cuts off his reply at "Fair lady.") 243 vizard mask. tongue (A leather projection held in the mouth to keep the mask on the face. Katharine asks Longaville why he is "holding his tongue," remaining silent.) 246 a double tongue i.e., (1) both the leather tongue of the mask and your own tongue (2) enough duplicity of speech for two 247 And . . . half i.e., you talk enough for the two of us 248 Veal i.e., as a Dutchman would pronounce "well" (with a possible pun on veil, mask, as well as veal, calf; also, in lines 245 and 248, Katharine punningly pronounces Longaville's name—long veal—and implies that he is a calf or dunce) 250 Let's part the word i.e., let's reach a compromise. (But Katharine wittily insists on the literal meaning; he must take all the word calf to himself.) your half (1) sharer with you of two halves (2) your partner in marriage 251 wean i.e., raise. ox (A type of stupidity.) 252 butt injure (with play on give horns in the next line, meaning both to butt with horns and to make a cuckold) 260 the sense of the reach of. sensible quick-witted

261 conference conversation. conceits fancies 264 dry-beaten beaten soundly without blood drawn. scoff mockery 268 Tapers candles. puffed out (1) blown out, extinguished (2) puffed up 269 Well-liking in good condition, plump (with a pun on liking, "like-king") 270 poverty in wit (The gibe applies to the young men and to Rosaline for her feeble witticism.) kingly-poor flout poor mockery of a king (with a possible play on kingly as the syllabically reversed form of liking, "ly-king") 273 out of count'nance flustered, embarrassed (with a play on the literal meaning, "without a face," i.e., masked) 274 cases (1) situations (2) masks 275 weeping-ripe ready to weep. good kind 276 out of all suit excessively and to no avail (with a play on the idea of "costume") 278 Non point not at all (quibbling also on the point of his sword. See the note on 2.1.190.) straight immediately 280 trow you would you believe. Qualm i.e., heartburn (with a play perhaps on came, line 279, as suggested by Elizabethan pronunciation) 282 better . . . statute-caps i.e., one could find better wits even among London apprentices (who were required by statute to wear identifiable caps)

PRINCESS
    And quick Berowne hath plighted faith to me.   284

KATHARINE
    And Longaville was for my service born.

MARIA
    Dumaine is mine, as sure as bark on tree.   286

BOYET
    Madam, and pretty mistresses, give ear: 287
    Immediately they will again be here
    In their own shapes, for it can never be   289
    They will digest this harsh indignity.   290

PRINCESS
    Will they return?

BOYET   They will, they will, God knows,
    And leap for joy, though they are lame with blows.
    Therefore change favors, and when they repair,   293
    Blow like sweet roses in this summer air.   294

PRINCESS
    How "blow"? How "blow"? Speak to be understood.

BOYET
    Fair ladies masked are roses in their bud;
    Dismasked, their damask sweet commixture shown,   297
    Are angels vailing clouds, or roses blown.   298

PRINCESS
    Avaunt, perplexity!—What shall we do   299
    If they return in their own shapes to woo?

ROSALINE
    Good madam, if by me you'll be advised,
    Let's mock them still, as well known as disguised.   302
    Let us complain to them what fools were here,
    Disguised like Muscovites in shapeless gear,   304
    And wonder what they were, and to what end
    Their shallow shows and prologue vilely penned,
    And their rough carriage so ridiculous,   307
    Should be presented at our tent to us.

BOYET
    Ladies, withdraw. The gallants are at hand.

PRINCESS
    Whip to our tents, as roes run o'er land.   310
        Exeunt [Princess, Rosaline, Katharine, and Maria].

        *Enter the King and the rest [Berowne, Longaville,
        and Dumaine, in their proper dress].*

KING
    Fair sir, God save you! Where's the Princess?

BOYET
    Gone to her tent. Please it Your Majesty
    Command me any service to her thither?   313

KING
    That she vouchsafe me audience for one word.

BOYET
    I will, and so will she, I know, my lord.   *Exit.*

BEROWNE
    This fellow pecks up wit as pigeons pease,
    And utters it again when God doth please.   317
    He is wit's peddler, and retails his wares
    At wakes and wassails, meetings, markets, fairs;   319
    And we that sell by gross, the Lord doth know,   320
    Have not the grace to grace it with such show.
    This gallant pins the wenches on his sleeve.   322
    Had he been Adam, he had tempted Eve.   323
    'A can carve too, and lisp. Why, this is he   324
    That kissed his hand away in courtesy.
    This is the ape of form, Monsieur the Nice,   326
    That, when he plays at tables, chides the dice   327
    In honorable terms. Nay, he can sing   328
    A mean most meanly; and in ushering   329
    Mend him who can. The ladies call him sweet.   330
    The stairs, as he treads on them, kiss his feet.
    This is the flower that smiles on everyone,
    To show his teeth as white as whale's bone;
    And consciences that will not die in debt
    Pay him the due of "honey-tongued Boyet."

KING
    A blister on his sweet tongue, with my heart,
    That put Armado's page out of his part!   337

        *Enter the ladies [wearing their original favors, with
        Boyet].*

BEROWNE
    See where it comes! Behavior, what wert thou   338
    Till this madman showed thee? And what art thou
        now?   339

KING
    All hail, sweet madam, and fair time of day!

PRINCESS
    "Fair" in "all hail" is foul, as I conceive.   341

KING
    Construe my speeches better, if you may.   342

PRINCESS
    Then wish me better. I will give you leave.   343

---

284 **plighted faith** pledged his love   286 **sure** firmly united
287 **give ear** listen   289 **In their own shapes** i.e., having put off their
disguises   290 **digest** stomach, put up with   293 **change favors** exchange love tokens (giving them back to their original owners). **repair** return   294 **Blow** bloom. (But the Princess wonders if *blow*
might mean to give *blows*, as in line 292.)   297 **damask** mingling red
and white. **commixture** mingling of complexion   298 **Are** i.e.,
they, the fair ladies, are. **vailing** letting fall, shedding. **blown**
blooming, fully opened   299 **Avaunt, perplexity** i.e., away, riddler
302 **as . . . disguised** i.e., in their familiar appearances just as previously
in their disguises   304 **shapeless gear** unshapely apparel   307 **rough
carriage** awkward bearing   310 **Whip** move quickly. **roes** roe deer
(with a pun on a *rose* sending out runners)   313 **Command . . .
thither** do you wish me to take any message to her there?

317 **utters** (1) speaks (2) sells.   **when . . . please** i.e., when the moment is propitious   319 **wakes and wassails** festivals and revels
320 **by gross** wholesale (i.e., as the source for the wit that Boyet re-
tails)   322 **pins . . . sleeve** i.e., flaunts his acquaintance with ladies
as one might wear a love token (?)   323 **had** would have   324 **'A** he.
carve i.e., woo with courtesy and affability. **lisp** (A courtly affectation.)   326 **ape of form** imitator of courtly manners. **Nice** fastidious
327 **tables** backgammon   328 **In honorable terms** in polite language
329 **mean** middle-ranged voice (alto or tenor). **meanly** moderately
well. **ushering** serving in the role of gentleman-usher   330 **Mend
. . . can** i.e., let anyone who can improve on him try to do so
337 **put . . . part** made Armado's page forget his lines   338 **it** i.e.,
Boyet. **Behavior** i.e., elegant manners   339 **madman** madcap.
showed thee i.e., showed just how elegant manners could be
341 **all hail** (The Princess deliberately misconstrues the King to have
referred to a hailstorm, foul weather.) **conceive** understand the
matter   342 **Construe** interpret   343 **Then . . . leave** i.e., in that
case you must greet me better. I will give you permission to try
again.

KING
　We came to visit you, and purpose now   344
　　To lead you to our court. Vouchsafe it, then.
PRINCESS
　This field shall hold me, and so hold your vow.   346
　　Nor God nor I delights in perjured men.   347
KING
　Rebuke me not for that which you provoke.
　　The virtue of your eye must break my oath.   349
PRINCESS
　You nickname virtue. "Vice," you should have
　　spoke,   350
　For virtue's office never breaks men's troth.   351
　Now by my maiden honor, yet as pure
　　As the unsullied lily, I protest,
　A world of torments though I should endure,
　　I would not yield to be your house's guest,
　So much I hate a breaking cause to be   356
　Of heavenly oaths, vowed with integrity.
KING
　O, you have lived in desolation here,
　　Unseen, unvisited, much to our shame.
PRINCESS
　Not so, my lord. It is not so, I swear.
　　We have had pastimes here and pleasant game:
　A mess of Russians left us but of late.   362
KING
　How, madam? Russians?
PRINCESS   Ay, in truth, my lord.
　Trim gallants, full of courtship and of state.   364
ROSALINE
　Madam, speak true.—It is not so, my lord.
　My lady, to the manner of the days,   366
　In courtesy gives undeserving praise.
　We four indeed confronted were with four
　In Russian habit. Here they stayed an hour
　And talked apace; and in that hour, my lord,   370
　They did not bless us with one happy word.   371
　I dare not call them fools; but this I think,
　When they are thirsty, fools would fain have drink.   373
BEROWNE
　This jest is dry to me. Gentle sweet,   374
　Your wit makes wise things foolish. When we greet,   375
　With eyes' best seeing, heaven's fiery eye,   376
　By light we lose light. Your capacity   377
　Is of that nature that to your huge store   378
　Wise things seem foolish and rich things but poor.

ROSALINE
　This proves you wise and rich, for in my eye—
BEROWNE
　I am a fool, and full of poverty.
ROSALINE
　But that you take what doth to you belong,   382
　It were a fault to snatch words from my tongue.   383
BEROWNE
　O, I am yours, and all that I possess!
ROSALINE
　All the fool mine?
BEROWNE   I cannot give you less.
ROSALINE
　Which of the vizards was it that you wore?   386
BEROWNE
　Where? When? What vizard? Why demand you this?   387
ROSALINE
　There, then, that vizard, that superfluous case   388
　That hid the worse and showed the better face.
KING [aside to his lords]
　We were descried. They'll mock us now downright.   390
DUMAINE [aside to the lords]
　Let us confess and turn it to a jest.
PRINCESS
　Amazed, my lord? Why looks Your Highness sad?   392
ROSALINE
　Help, hold his brows! He'll swoon! Why look you
　　pale?   393
　Seasick, I think, coming from Muscovy.
BEROWNE
　Thus pour the stars down plagues for perjury.
　　Can any face of brass hold longer out?   396
　Here stand I, lady. Dart thy skill at me.   397
　　Bruise me with scorn, confound me with a flout,   398
　Thrust thy sharp wit quite through my ignorance,
　　Cut me to pieces with thy keen conceit,
　And I will wish thee nevermore to dance,   401
　　Nor nevermore in Russian habit wait.   402
　O, never will I trust to speeches penned,
　　Nor to the motion of a schoolboy's tongue,
　Nor never come in vizard to my friend,   405
　　Nor woo in rhyme, like a blind harper's song!   406
　Taffeta phrases, silken terms precise,
　　Three-piled hyperboles, spruce affectation,   408
　Figures pedantical—these summer flies   409
　　Have blown me full of maggot ostentation.   410
　I do forswear them, and I here protest,
　　By this white glove—how white the hand, God
　　knows!—
　Henceforth my wooing mind shall be expressed

---

344 purpose intend   346 so hold so uphold   347 Nor neither
349 virtue power. (But the Princess, in the next line, insists on interpreting the word as "moral goodness," the opposite of "vice.")
350 nickname misname, mention in error   351 office action.   troth
faith   356 breaking cause i.e., cause of breaking   362 mess four-
some   364 Trim spruce, neatly got up.   courtship courtliness
366 to . . . days in the fashion of the time   370 talked apace spoke
rapidly, i.e., chattered   371 happy felicitous   373 When . . . drink
i.e., they are fools   374 dry stupid, dull (playing on thirsty in line
373)   375 foolish i.e., seem foolish by comparison.   greet regard,
look at   376 With . . . seeing with our eyes' sharpest acuity. (Or,
With eyes best seeing, "with our clear-seeing eyes.")   heaven's fiery
eye i.e., the sun   377 By . . . light i.e., the sun's powerful light
blinds us   378 to compared to

382–383 But . . . tongue i.e., you took the words right out of my
mouth   386 vizards masks   387 demand inquire   388 case covering,
mask   390 descried discovered   392 Amazed bewildered
393 brows forehead   396 face of brass brazen manner   397 Dart
thy skill shoot your verbal dexterity   398 confound destroy.   flout
jeer, insult   401 wish entreat   402 habit dress.   wait be in attendance   405 friend sweetheart   406 harper's minstrel's   408 Three-
piled deep-piled, as in costly velvet.   spruce fashionable   409 Figures figures of speech   410 blown filled with maggot eggs, made
foul.   ostentation pretension, vanity

In russet yeas and honest kersey noes. 414
And to begin, wench—so God help me, law!— 415
My love to thee is sound, sans crack or flaw. 416
ROSALINE
Sans "sans," I pray you.
BEROWNE   Yet I have a trick 417
Of the old rage. Bear with me, I am sick; 418
I'll leave it by degrees. Soft, let us see:
Write "Lord have mercy on us" on those three. 420
They are infected; in their hearts it lies;
They have the plague, and caught it of your eyes. 422
These lords are visited; you are not free, 423
For the Lord's tokens on you do I see. 424
PRINCESS
No, they are free that gave these tokens to us.
BEROWNE
Our states are forfeit. Seek not to undo us. 426
ROSALINE
It is not so, for how can this be true,
That you stand forfeit, being those that sue? 428
BEROWNE
Peace! For I will not have to do with you. 429
ROSALINE
Nor shall not, if I do as I intend.
BEROWNE [to the other lords]
Speak for yourselves. My wit is at an end.
KING
Teach us, sweet madam, for our rude transgression
Some fair excuse.
PRINCESS   The fairest is confession.
Were not you here but even now disguised? 434
KING
Madam, I was.
PRINCESS   And were you well advised? 435
KING
I was, fair madam.
PRINCESS   When you then were here,
What did you whisper in your lady's ear?
KING
That more than all the world I did respect her. 438
PRINCESS
When she shall challenge this, you will reject her. 439
KING
Upon mine honor, no.
PRINCESS   Peace, peace! Forbear.
Your oath once broke, you force not to forswear. 441

KING
Despise me when I break this oath of mine.
PRINCESS
I will, and therefore keep it. Rosaline,
What did the Russian whisper in your ear?
ROSALINE
Madam, he swore that he did hold me dear 445
As precious eyesight, and did value me
Above this world, adding thereto moreover
That he would wed me or else die my lover.
PRINCESS
God give thee joy of him! The noble lord
Most honorably doth uphold his word.
KING
What mean you, madam? By my life, my troth, 451
I never swore this lady such an oath.
ROSALINE
By heaven, you did. And to confirm it plain,
You gave me this. But take it, sir, again.
        [She offers him the Princess's favor.]
KING
My faith and this the Princess I did give.
I knew her by this jewel on her sleeve.
PRINCESS
Pardon me, sir, this jewel did she wear,
And Lord Berowne, I thank him, is my dear.
[To Berowne.] What, will you have me, or your pearl
    again?   [She offers Rosaline's favor.]
BEROWNE
Neither of either. I remit both twain. 460
I see the trick on 't: here was a consent, 461
Knowing aforehand of our merriment,
To dash it like a Christmas comedy. 463
Some carry-tale, some please-man, some slight zany, 464
Some mumble-news, some trencher-knight, some
    Dick, 465
That smiles his cheek in years and knows the trick 466
To make my lady laugh when she's disposed, 467
Told our intents before; which once disclosed,
The ladies did change favors, and then we,
Following the signs, wooed but the sign of she. 470
Now, to our perjury to add more terror,
We are again forsworn, in will and error.
Much upon this 'tis. [To Boyet.] And might not you 473
Forestall our sport, to make us thus untrue?
Do not you know my lady's foot by the squier, 475
    And laugh upon the apple of her eye? 476

414 russet simple homespun, russet brown in color. kersey plain woolen cloth 415 law la 416 sans without. (But, as Rosaline points out in the next line, he is still using French expressions.) 417 Yet still. trick trace 418 rage fever 420 Lord . . . us (Sign posted on houses containing the infectious plague within.) those three i.e., his companions 422 of from 423 visited infested by the plague. free free of infection. (But the Princess also quibbles on the meaning "generous with gifts.") 424 the Lord's tokens (1) plague sores as visible signs of infection (2) the love tokens given by the lords, the lords' tokens 426 states estates; status as bachelors. undo absolve us from forfeiture (of ourselves) by declaring us free (line 425) 428 being . . . sue being the plaintiffs, not the defendants. (How, Rosaline asks, can you bring legal action against yourselves?) 429 have have anything 434 but even now a short while ago 435 well advised in your right mind 438 respect value, regard 439 challenge lay claim to 441 force not have no hesitation

445 dear as valuable 451 troth faith 460 either the two. remit both twain give up both of them 461 on 't of it. consent agreement, plot 463 dash shatter 464 carry-tale gossipmonger, talebearer. please-man sycophant. slight zany insignificant clown 465 mumble-news prattler, gossip. trencher-knight i.e., parasite; one who feeds at his master's trencher or wooden dish. Dick (As in "Tom, Dick, and Harry.") 466 smiles . . . years i.e., smiles flatteringly so hard that he wrinkles his face 467 disposed i.e., disposed to be merry(?) 470 the sign of she the outward appearance of one's sweetheart 473 Much . . . 'tis i.e., it must have happened much this way 475 Do . . . squier i.e., don't you know how to suit her fancy. (Squier, rhyming with fire in line 477, means "square," carpenter's rule; Boyet should know the length of her foot.) 476 And . . . eye i.e., and know how to keep her eye amused, wittily catch her eye. (Apple means "pupil.")

And stand between her back, sir, and the fire,   477
  Holding a trencher, jesting merrily?   478
You put our page out. Go, you are allowed;   479
Die when you will, a smock shall be your shroud.   480
You leer upon me, do you? There's an eye
Wounds like a leaden sword.
BOYET   Full merrily   482
Hath this brave manage, this career, been run.   483
BEROWNE
Lo, he is tilting straight! Peace, I have done.   484

Enter [Costard the] clown.

Welcome, pure wit! Thou part'st a fair fray.   485
COSTARD
O Lord, sir, they would know
Whether the three Worthies shall come in or no.
BEROWNE
What, are there but three?
COSTARD   No, sir; but it is vara fine, 488
For every one pursents three.
BEROWNE   And three times thrice is nine.
COSTARD
Not so, sir, under correction, sir, I hope it is not so.   490
You cannot beg us, sir, I can assure you, sir; we
  know what we know.   491
I hope, sir, three times thrice, sir—
BEROWNE   Is not nine?
COSTARD   Under correction, sir, we know whereuntil it   493
doth amount.
BEROWNE   By Jove, I always took three threes for nine.
COSTARD   O Lord, sir, it were pity you should get your   496
living by reckoning, sir.   497
BEROWNE   How much is it?
COSTARD   O Lord, sir, the parties themselves, the actors,
sir, will show whereuntil it doth amount. For mine
own part, I am, as they say, but to parfect one man in   501
one poor man—Pompion the Great, sir.   502
BEROWNE   Art thou one of the Worthies?
COSTARD   It pleased them to think me worthy of
Pompey the Great. For mine own part, I know not the
degree of the Worthy, but I am to stand for him.   506
BEROWNE   Go bid them prepare.
COSTARD
We will turn it finely off, sir. We will take some care.
                                                    Exit.
KING
Berowne, they will shame us. Let them not approach.

BEROWNE
We are shame-proof, my lord; and 'tis some policy   510
To have one show worse than the King's and his
  company.
KING   I say they shall not come.
PRINCESS
Nay, my good lord, let me o'errule you now.
That sport best pleases that doth least know how,
Where zeal strives to content, and the contents   515
Dies in the zeal of that which it presents.   516
Their form confounded makes most form in mirth,   517
When great things laboring perish in their birth.   518
BEROWNE
A right description of our sport, my lord.   519

Enter [Armado the] braggart.

ARMADO [*to the King*]   Anointed, I implore so much   520
expense of thy royal sweet breath as will utter a
brace of words.   522
          [*He converses apart with the King and
                             delivers him a paper.*]
PRINCESS   Doth this man serve God?
BEROWNE   Why ask you?
PRINCESS   'A speaks not like a man of God his making.   525
ARMADO   That is all one, my fair, sweet, honey mon-
arch, for, I protest, the schoolmaster is exceeding fan-
tastical, too, too vain, too, too vain; but we will put it,
as they say, to *fortuna de la guerra.* I wish you the   529
peace of mind, most royal couplement!   *Exit.*   530
KING   Here is like to be a good presence of Worthies.   531
He presents Hector of Troy, the swain Pompey the
Great, the parish curate Alexander, Armado's page
Hercules, the pedant Judas Maccabaeus;
And if these four Worthies in their first show thrive,
These four will change habits and present the other
  five.
BEROWNE
There is five in the first show.
KING
You are deceived. 'Tis not so.
BEROWNE
The pedant, the braggart, the hedge-priest, the fool,
  and the boy.   539
Abate throw at novum, and the whole world again   540
Cannot pick out five such, take each one in his vein.   541
KING
The ship is under sail, and here she comes amain.   542

---

477 **And . . . fire** i.e., and shield her from too much heat   478 **trencher** wooden dish (with which to offer her refreshment)   479 **allowed**
treated like an allowed fool, allowed to make jests   480 **smock** woman's undergarment (since Boyet is constantly in women's company)
482 **a leaden sword** a mock weapon (no more threatening than Boyet's gaze)   483 **brave manage** fine maneuver on horseback. (Said sardonically.)   **career** gallop   484 **tilting straight** sparring with words
immediately   485 **Thou . . . fray** you interrupt a fine battle   488
vara very   490 **beg us** subject to   491 **beg us** prove us fools
493 **whereuntil** to what   496 **it were pity** it would be too bad if.
get make   497 **reckoning** arithmetic   501 **parfect** (He means "perform," "present.")   502 **Pompion** pumpkin. (Malapropism for *Pompey.*)   506 **degree** rank.   **stand for** represent, play

510 **some policy** a shrewd stratagem   515–516 **and the . . . presents**
and the (feeble) substance of what they perform is overwhelmed by
the zeal of the presentation   517 **Their . . . mirth** i.e., the artistic
chaos of their performance has its own reward in mirth   518 **laboring**
striving to be born   519 **right** apt.   **our sport** i.e., our appearance as
Muscovites   520 **Anointed** i.e., King   522 **brace** pair   525 **God his**
God's   529 **fortuna . . . guerra** the fortune of war   530 **couplement**
couple   531 **like** likely.   **presence** assembly   539 **hedge-priest** illiterate, rural priest   540 **Abate** barring, setting aside.   **throw at novum**
a lucky throw of the dice in a game of *novum* or nines, having five
and nine as its principal throws (joking on the business of offering
nine characters with just five actors)   541 **take . . . vein** i.e., each
one is such a fantastical type   542 **amain** suddenly

Enter [Costard, as] Pompey.

COSTARD
"I Pompey am—"

BEROWNE   You lie; you are not he.

COSTARD
"I Pompey am—"

BOYET   With leopard's head on knee.   544

BEROWNE
Well said, old mocker. I must needs be friends with
thee.   545

COSTARD
"I Pompey am, Pompey surnamed the Big—"

DUMAINE   "The Great."

COSTARD
It is "Great," sir.—"Pompey surnamed the Great,
That oft in field, with targe and shield, did make
my foe to sweat.   549
And traveling along this coast, I here am come by
chance,
And lay my arms before the legs of this sweet lass of
France."   *[He lays down his weapons.]*
If your ladyship would say "Thanks, Pompey," I had
done.

PRINCESS   Great thanks, great Pompey.

COSTARD   'Tis not so much worth; but I hope I was per-   555
fect. I made a little fault in "Great."   556

BEROWNE   My hat to a halfpenny Pompey proves the   557
best Worthy.   *[Costard stands aside.]*   558

Enter [Nathaniel the] curate, for Alexander.

NATHANIEL
"When in the world I lived, I was the world's
commander;
By east, west, north, and south, I spread my
conquering might.
My scutcheon plain declares that I am Alisander —"   561

BOYET
Your nose says, no, you are not; for it stands too
right.   562

BEROWNE *[to Boyet]*
Your nose smells "no" in this, most tender-smelling
knight.   563

PRINCESS
The conqueror is dismayed. Proceed, good Alexander.

NATHANIEL
"When in the world I lived, I was the world's
commander—"

BOYET
Most true; 'tis right. You were so, Alisander.

BEROWNE *[to Costard]*   Pompey the Great—

COSTARD   Your servant, and Costard.

BEROWNE   Take away the conqueror. Take away Alisander.

COSTARD *[to Nathaniel]*   O, sir, you have overthrown
Alisander the conqueror! You will be scraped out of   572
the painted cloth for this. Your lion, that holds his   573
poleax sitting on a closestool, will be given to Ajax;   574
he will be the ninth Worthy. A conqueror, and afeard
to speak? Run away for shame, Alisander. *[Exit
Nathaniel.]* There, an 't shall please you, a foolish mild   577
man, an honest man, look you, and soon dashed. He   578
is a marvelous good neighbor, faith, and a very good
bowler. But, for Alisander—alas, you see how 'tis—a,
little o'erparted. But there are Worthies a-   581
coming will speak their mind in some other sort.   582

PRINCESS   Stand aside, good Pompey.

                    [Costard stands aside.]

*Enter [Holofernes the] pedant, for Judas, and
[Mote] the boy, for Hercules.*

HOLOFERNES *[as presenter]*
"Great Hercules is presented by this imp,   584
Whose club killed Cerberus, that three-headed
canus;   585
And when he was a babe, a child, a shrimp,
Thus did he strangle serpents in his *manus*.   587
Quoniam he seemeth in minority,   588
Ergo I come with this apology."   589
[To Mote.] Keep some state in thy exit, and vanish.   590
                    Exit Boy.

[As Judas.] "Judas I am—"

DUMAINE   A Judas!   592

HOLOFERNES   Not Iscariot, sir.
"Judas I am, yclept Maccabaeus."   594

DUMAINE   Judas Maccabaeus clipped is plain Judas.   595

BEROWNE   A kissing traitor. How art thou proved Judas?   596

HOLOFERNES   "Judas I am—"

DUMAINE   The more shame for you, Judas.

HOLOFERNES   What mean you, sir?

BOYET   To make Judas hang himself.

572–573 You will . . . this (An allusion to the frequent representation of the Nine Worthies painted on an arras or tapestry.)
573–574 Your lion . . . closestool (A Renaissance memorial emblem
of Alexander described a lion sitting on a throne, holding a battle-ax.
A *closestool* is a seat in a privy.)   **574 Ajax** legendary Greek chieftain
at the Trojan War who coveted the slain Achilles' armor (with a pun
on *jakes*, "privy")   **577 an 't** if it   **578 dashed** rattled, daunted
581 o'erparted having a part too difficult   **582 sort** manner   **584 presented** played, represented.   **imp** child   **585 Cerberus** three-headed
dog at the entrance to Hades, the capturing of which was one of Hercules' twelve labors.   **canus** i.e., *canis*, "dog" (in Latin. *Canus* is
needed for the rhyme.)   **587 manus** hands   **588 Quoniam** since
589 Ergo therefore   **590 state** dignity   **592 A Judas** i.e., a traitor.
(The lords deliberately confuse the military hero Judas Maccabaeus
with Judas Iscariot, who betrayed Christ.)   **594 yclept** called
595 clipped (1) shortened (2) embraced (as Berowne uses it in line
596; with a play also on *yclept*)   **596 kissing** (A reference to Judas'
kiss of Jesus by which he betrayed his master; with a pun on *clipped*,
"embraced" or "kissed," in the preceding line.)

544 leopard's (referring to his coat of arms, customarily on the shield
rather than on the knee; perhaps Costard is holding his shield upside
down or awkwardly low)   **545 needs** necessarily   **549 targe** shield
555–556 perfect accurate in memorizing   **557 My hat to** I'll wager
my hat against   **558 s.d. for** as. (Also at 583 s.d.)   **561 scutcheon**
coat of arms   **562 right** straight. (Alexander was supposed to have
had a wry neck that twisted his head to one side.)   **563 Your . . .
this** i.e., your nose smells out the impostor because Nathaniel does
not smell as sweet as Alexander. (Berowne may be jibing again at
Boyet's fastidiousness, as in lines 464–482. Alexander was reputed to
have a bodily odor of "marvelous good savor" according to North's
translation of Plutarch.)   **tender-smelling** sensitive to smells

HOLOFERNES   Begin, sir. You are my elder.   601
BEROWNE   Well followed. Judas was hanged on an elder.
HOLOFERNES   I will not be put out of countenance.   603
BEROWNE   Because thou hast no face.
HOLOFERNES   [*pointing to his face*]   What is this?
BOYET   A citternhead.   606
DUMAINE   The head of a bodkin.   607
BEROWNE   A death's face in a ring.   608
LONGAVILLE   The face of an old Roman coin, scarce 609
seen.   610
BOYET   The pommel of Caesar's falchion.   611
DUMAINE   The carved-bone face on a flask.   612
BEROWNE   Saint George's half-cheek in a brooch.   613
DUMAINE   Ay, and in a brooch of lead.   614
BEROWNE   Ay, and worn in the cap of a tooth drawer. 615
And now forward, for we have put thee in counte- 616
nance.   617
HOLOFERNES   You have put me out of countenance.
BEROWNE   False. We have given thee faces.
HOLOFERNES   But you have outfaced them all.   620
BEROWNE
An thou wert a lion, we would do so.   621
BOYET
Therefore, as he is an ass, let him go.
And so adieu, sweet Jude! Nay, why dost thou stay?
DUMAINE   For the latter end of his name.
BEROWNE
For the ass to the Jude? Give it him. Jud-as, away!   625
HOLOFERNES
This is not generous, not gentle, not humble.   626
BOYET
A light for Monsieur Judas! It grows dark; he may
stumble.   [*Exit Holofernes.*]
PRINCESS
Alas, poor Maccabaeus, how hath he been baited!   628

Enter [Armado the] braggart [as Hector].

BEROWNE   Hide thy head, Achilles! Here comes Hector 629
in arms.
DUMAINE   Though my mocks come home by me, I will 631
now be merry.

601 You . . . elder i.e., you are my senior and so should take precedence. (But Berowne answers with a pun on *elder*, "elder tree," traditionally the tree on which Judas hanged himself.)   **603 put out of
countenance** disconcerted. (But Berowne in the next line takes *countenance* in its literal sense, "face.")   **606 citternhead** head of a cithern or guitar (often grotesquely carved)   **607 bodkin** a long, jeweled
pin for a lady's hair, or a small dagger (similarly carved)   **608 A
death's . . . ring** i.e., a death's-head ring worn as a *memento mori*
609–610 scarce seen i.e., worn almost smooth   **611 falchion**
curved sword. (The *pommel* or rounded knob on the hilt would be
carved.)   **612 flask** i.e., horn powder flask   **613 half-cheek** profile
614 of lead i.e., of inferior quality   **615 tooth drawer** (Tooth extrac-
tors were not highly regarded; a brooch worn by such people in the
cap might be of an inferior sort.)   **616–617 we . . . countenance**
i.e., we've drawn your portrait. (But Holofernes replies with a quibble
meaning "you have made me forget my lines.")   **620 outfaced** i.e.,
mocked them, put them down (playing on *faces* in line 619)   **621 An**
if.   **lion** (One of Aesop's fables tells of an ass that wears a lion's skin
until he is betrayed by his bray.)   **625 Jud-as** (Jude's *latter end* turns
out to be his *ass*.)   **626 gentle** courteous   **628 baited** set upon, attacked   **629 Achilles, Hector** (They were great antagonists in the Trojan War.)   **631 by me** to me, to my discomfiture (causing me to pay
for this later)

KING   Hector was but a Trojan in respect of this.   633
BOYET   But is this Hector?
KING   I think Hector was not so clean-timbered.   635
LONGAVILLE   His leg is too big for Hector's.
DUMAINE   More calf, certain.   637
BOYET   No, he is best endued in the small.   638
BEROWNE   This cannot be Hector.
DUMAINE   He's a god or a painter, for he makes faces.
ARMADO
"The armipotent Mars, of lances the almighty,   641
Gave Hector a gift—"
DUMAINE   A gilt nutmeg.   643
BEROWNE   A lemon.
LONGAVILLE   Stuck with cloves.
DUMAINE   No, cloven.   646
ARMADO   Peace!—
"The armipotent Mars, of lances the almighty,
Gave Hector a gift, the heir of Ilion;   649
A man so breathed that certain he would fight, yea 650
From morn till night, out of his pavilion.   651
I am that flower—"
DUMAINE   That mint.
LONGAVILLE   That columbine.
ARMADO   Sweet Lord Longaville, rein thy tongue.   655
LONGAVILLE   I must rather give it the rein, for it runs 656
against Hector.
DUMAINE   Ay, and Hector's a greyhound.   658
ARMADO   The sweet warman is dead and rotten. Sweet
chucks, beat not the bones of the buried. When he
breathed, he was a man. But I will forward with my 661
device. [*To the Princess.*] Sweet royalty, bestow on me 662
the sense of hearing.
                      Berowne steps forth [to whisper to Costard,
                                  and then resumes his place].
PRINCESS
Speak, brave Hector. We are much delighted.
ARMADO   I do adore thy sweet Grace's slipper.
BOYET   Loves her by the foot.
DUMAINE   He may not by the yard.   667
ARMADO
"This Hector far surmounted Hannibal—"
COSTARD   The party is gone. Fellow Hector, she is gone! 669
She is two months on her way.   670
ARMADO   What meanest thou?

633 a Trojan i.e., (1) a resident of Troy (2) a jolly companion, a roisterer.   **in respect of** in comparison with   **635 clean-timbered** clean-
limbed, well built   **637 calf** (1) lower part of leg (2) dolt   **638 best
. . . small** well endowed in the part of the leg below the calf
641 armipotent powerful in arms   **643 gilt** glazed with egg yolk,
saffron, etc.   **646 cloven** (Dumaine's witticism plays on the contrast
between a *lemon stuck with cloves* to serve as a confection in a drink
and a *leman* or lover who is *cloven* in the act of love.)   **649 Ilion**
Troy   **650 so breathed** i.e., in good condition, fit   **651 pavilion**
tent or camp to which the combatant retired when not engaged in
fight   **655 rein** restrain, control   **656 give it the rein** allow it to run
freely   **658 a greyhound** i.e., famed for his speed as a runner
661 forward go forward, continue   **662 device** dramatic contrivance
667 yard (Dumaine puns on the slang sense, "penis.")   **669 The
party is gone** i.e., Jaquenetta is ruined in reputation. (Costard may
have received this news from Berowne when Berowne whispers to
him. Or, if *The party is gone* is part of Armado's speech, as the
Quarto and the Folio seem to indicate, it may mean "The man is
dead.")   **670 on her way** i.e., pregnant

COSTARD   Faith, unless you play the honest Trojan, the 672
poor wench is cast away. She's quick; the child brags 673
in her belly already. 'Tis yours.

ARMADO   Dost thou infamonize me among potentates? 675
Thou shalt die.

COSTARD   Then shall Hector be whipped for Jaquenetta
that is quick by him and hanged for Pompey that is 678
dead by him. 679

DUMAINE   Most rare Pompey! 680

BOYET   Renowned Pompey!

BEROWNE   Greater than "Great"! Great, great, great
Pompey! Pompey the Huge!

DUMAINE   Hector trembles.

BEROWNE   Pompey is moved. More Ates, more Ates! 685
Stir them on, stir them on!

DUMAINE   Hector will challenge him.

BEROWNE   Ay, if 'a have no more man's blood in his
belly than will sup a flea. 689

ARMADO   By the North Pole, I do challenge thee.

COSTARD   I will not fight with a pole, like a northern 691
man. I'll slash; I'll do it by the sword. I bepray you, let 692
me borrow my arms again.

DUMAINE   Room for the incensed Worthies!

COSTARD   I'll do it in my shirt. [He takes off his doublet.]

DUMAINE   Most resolute Pompey!

MOTE   Master, let me take you a buttonhole lower. Do 697
you not see Pompey is uncasing for the combat? What 698
mean you? You will lose your reputation.

ARMADO   Gentlemen and soldiers, pardon me. I will not
combat in my shirt. 701

DUMAINE   You may not deny it. Pompey hath made the
challenge.

ARMADO   Sweet bloods, I both may and will. 704

BEROWNE   What reason have you for 't?

ARMADO   The naked truth of it is, I have no shirt. I go 706
woolward for penance. 707

BOYET   True, and it was enjoined him in Rome for want 708
of linen; since when, I'll be sworn, he wore none but 709
a dishclout of Jaquenetta's, and that 'a wears next his 710
heart for a favor. 711

Enter a messenger, Monsieur Marcade.

MARCADE   God save you, madam!

PRINCESS   Welcome, Marcade,
But that thou interruptest our merriment.

MARCADE   I am sorry, madam, for the news I bring

Is heavy in my tongue. The King your father—

PRINCESS   Dead, for my life!

MARCADE   Even so. My tale is told.

BEROWNE   Worthies, away! The scene begins to cloud.

ARMADO   For mine own part, I breathe free breath. I 719
have seen the day of wrong through the little hole of 720
discretion, and I will right myself like a soldier. 721

                    Exeunt [the] Worthies.

KING   How fares Your Majesty?

PRINCESS   Boyet, prepare. I will away tonight.

KING   Madam, not so. I do beseech you, stay.

PRINCESS   Prepare, I say. I thank you, gracious lords,
For all your fair endeavors, and entreat,
Out of a new-sad soul, that you vouchsafe
In your rich wisdom to excuse or hide 728
The liberal opposition of our spirits, 729
If overboldly we have borne ourselves
In the converse of breath; your gentleness 731
Was guilty of it. Farewell, worthy lord! 732
A heavy heart bears not a humble tongue. 733
Excuse me so, coming too short of thanks 734
For my great suit so easily obtained. 735

KING   The extreme parts of time extremely forms 736
All causes to the purpose of his speed, 737
And often at his very loose decides 738
That which long process could not arbitrate.
And though the mourning brow of progeny 740
Forbid the smiling courtesy of love 741
The holy suit which fain it would convince, 742
Yet since love's argument was first on foot,
Let not the cloud of sorrow jostle it
From what it purposed, since to wail friends lost
Is not by much so wholesome-profitable
As to rejoice at friends but newly found.

PRINCESS   I understand you not. My griefs are double. 748

BEROWNE   Honest plain words best pierce the ear of grief,
And by these badges understand the King. 750
For your fair sakes have we neglected time,
Played foul play with our oaths. Your beauty, ladies,

---

672 **the honest Trojan** i.e., the good-hearted fellow (as at line 633)
673 **quick** pregnant   675 **infamonize** slander   678–679 **that is
dead** i.e., whose hopes of having Jaquenetta having been killed
680 **rare** excellent   685 **Ates** i.e., incitements to mischief. (Ate was
the goddess of discord.)   689 **sup** feed   691–692 **a northern man** a
boorish ruffian from the north (for whom the stave or *pole* was a traditional weapon)   697 **take . . . lower** (1) help remove your doublet (2)
"take you down a peg," humiliate you   698 **uncasing** undressing
701 **combat** duel, fight   704 **bloods** men of mettle   706–707 **go
woolward for penance** i.e., with woolen clothing next to the skin and
no linen underwear. (Armado's lame excuse is that he does so to punish the flesh.)   708 **enjoined** required of   708–709 **want of linen**
lack of a clean shirt, etc. (Boyet sees through the excuse.)   710 **dishclout** dishcloth   711 **s.d. Marcade** (Perhaps the name suggests "Mar-
Arcadia.")

719–721 **I have . . . discretion** i.e., I now perceive my true situation, my wrong. (From the proverb "One may see day at a little
hole.")   721 **right myself** i.e., make honorable amends, do the right
thing   728 **hide** overlook   729 **liberal opposition** too-free antagonism   731 **converse of breath** conversation. **gentleness** courtesy
732 **guilty of** responsible for   733 **humble** i.e., suited to polite civilities   734 **so** therefore   735 **suit** i.e., the mission on which she came
(which the King evidently has granted)   736–737 **The . . . speed**
i.e., a few last moments demand quick decisions   737, 738 **his** i.e.,
time's   738 **loose** release, discharge. (An archery term.)   740 **progeny** i.e., the child of the dead king, the Princess   741 **Forbid** deny to
742 **The . . . convince** the love suit it would like to present.   **convince** give proof of   748 **double** i.e., because of my father's death,
and because I don't understand you   750 **badges** signs, i.e., my honest, plain words

Hath much deformed us, fashioning our humors
Even to the opposèd end of our intents,   754
And what in us hath seemed ridiculous—
As love is full of unbefitting strains,   756
All wanton as a child, skipping and vain,   757
Formed by the eye and therefore, like the eye,
Full of strange shapes, of habits, and of forms,
Varying in subjects as the eye doth roll
To every varied object in his glance;
Which parti-coated presence of loose love   762
Put on by us, if in your heavenly eyes
Have misbecomed our oaths and gravities,   764
Those heavenly eyes that look into these faults
Suggested us to make. Therefore, ladies,   766
Our love being yours, the error that love makes   767
Is likewise yours. We to ourselves prove false   768
By being once false forever to be true   769
To those that make us both—fair ladies, you.   770
And even that falsehood, in itself a sin,
Thus purifies itself and turns to grace.

PRINCESS
We have received your letters full of love,
Your favors, the ambassadors of love,
And in our maiden council rated them   775
At courtship, pleasant jest, and courtesy,   776
As bombast and as lining to the time.   777
But more devout than this in our respects   778
Have we not been, and therefore met your loves   779
In their own fashion, like a merriment.

DUMAINE
Our letters, madam, showed much more than jest.

LONGAVILLE
So did our looks.

ROSALINE   We did not quote them so.   782

KING
Now, at the latest minute of the hour,
Grant us your loves.

PRINCESS   A time, methinks, too short
To make a world-without-end bargain in.
No, no, my lord, Your Grace is perjured much,
Full of dear guiltiness, and therefore this: 787
If for my love—as there is no such cause—   788
You will do aught, this shall you do for me: 789
Your oath I will not trust, but go with speed
To some forlorn and naked hermitage,   791
Remote from all the pleasures of the world;

There stay until the twelve celestial signs   793
Have brought about the annual reckoning.
If this austere insociable life
Change not your offer made in heat of blood;
If frosts and fasts, hard lodging, and thin weeds   797
Nip not the gaudy blossoms of your love,
But that it bear this trial, and last love;   799
Then, at the expiration of the year,
Come challenge me, challenge me by these deserts,   801
And, by this virgin palm now kissing thine,
                              [giving him her hand]
I will be thine; and till that instance shut   803
My woeful self up in a mourning house,
Raining the tears of lamentation
For the remembrance of my father's death.
If this thou do deny, let our hands part,
Neither entitled in the other's heart.   808

KING
If this, or more than this, I would deny,
    To flatter up these powers of mine with rest,   810
The sudden hand of death close up mine eye!
    Hence, hermit, then. My heart is in thy breast.   812
                              [They converse apart.]

DUMAINE [to Katharine]
But what to me, my love? But what to me?
A wife?

KATHARINE   A beard, fair health, and honesty.
With threefold love I wish you all these three.

DUMAINE
O, shall I say, "I thank you, gentle wife"?

KATHARINE
Not so, my lord. A twelvemonth and a day
I'll mark no words that smooth-faced wooers say.
Come when the King doth to my lady come;
Then, if I have much love, I'll give you some.

DUMAINE
I'll serve thee true and faithfully till then.

KATHARINE
Yet swear not, lest ye be forsworn again.
                              [They converse apart.]

LONGAVILLE
What says Maria?

MARIA   At the twelvemonth's end
I'll change my black gown for a faithful friend.   824

LONGAVILLE
I'll stay with patience, but the time is long.   825

MARIA
The liker you. Few taller are so young.   826
                              [They converse apart.]

BEROWNE [to Rosaline]
Studies my lady? Mistress, look on me.   827
Behold the window of my heart, mine eye,

---

754 **opposèd** opposite   756 **strains** impulses   757 **wanton** frivolous.
vain foolish   762 **parti-coated presence** jesting or foolish appearance.
loose unrestrained   764 **misbecomed** been unbecoming to
766 **Suggested us to make** tempted us to commit all these follies of
love   767 **Our love being yours** i.e., since the love we offer you is
now yours   768–770 **We . . . you** i.e., we are false to our vows one
time, abandoning the studies we vowed to pursue, in order to be true
forever to you, fair ladies, who make us both false and true: false to
our former vow but true to you   775 **rated** evaluated   776 **At** as
merely   777 **bombast** (1) a loosely made fabric used for padding or
stuffing garments, for *lining* (2) puffed-up rhetoric, fit only to fill up
the time   778 **devout** serious.   **respects** considerations   779 **met** responded to   782 **quote** interpret   787 **dear** grievous and precious
788 **as . . . cause** i.e., though I can't see why it should inspire you in
that way   789 **aught** anything   791 **naked** austere

793 **twelve celestial signs** signs of the zodiac (encompassing one
year)   797 **hard lodging** uncomfortable accommodations.   **weeds**
garments   799 **last** remain, continue as   801 **challenge** claim.
deserts meritorious actions   803 **instance** instant   808 **entitled in**
having a claim to   810 **flatter up** pamper   812 **Hence, hermit then**
i.e., then off I go to be a hermit   824 **friend** sweetheart   825 **stay**
wait   826 **liker** more like. (Maria deliberately takes Longaville's *long*
in the sense of "tall.")   827 **Studies my lady** i.e., are you in a brown
study?

What humble suit attends thy answer there.   829
Impose some service on me for thy love.

ROSALINE
Oft have I heard of you, my Lord Berowne,
Before I saw you; and the world's large tongue   832
Proclaims you for a man replete with mocks,
Full of comparisons and wounding flouts,   834
Which you on all estates will execute   835
That lie within the mercy of your wit.
To weed this wormwood from your fruitful brain,   837
And therewithal to win me, if you please,
Without the which I am not to be won,
You shall this twelvemonth term from day to day
Visit the speechless sick and still converse   841
With groaning wretches, and your task shall be
With all the fierce endeavor of your wit
To enforce the painèd impotent to smile.   844

BEROWNE
To move wild laughter in the throat of death?
It cannot be. It is impossible.
Mirth cannot move a soul in agony.

ROSALINE
Why, that's the way to choke a gibing spirit,   848
Whose influence is begot of that loose grace   849
Which shallow laughing hearers give to fools.
A jest's prosperity lies in the ear
Of him that hears it, never in the tongue
Of him that makes it. Then if sickly ears,
Deafed with the clamors of their own dear groans,   854
Will hear your idle scorns, continue then,
And I will have you and that fault withal;   856
But if they will not, throw away that spirit,
And I shall find you empty of that fault,
Right joyful of your reformation.

BEROWNE
A twelvemonth? Well, befall what will befall,
I'll jest a twelvemonth in an hospital.

PRINCESS [to the King]
Ay, sweet my lord, and so I take my leave.

KING
No, madam, we will bring you on your way.   863

BEROWNE
Our wooing doth not end like an old play;
Jack hath not Jill. These ladies' courtesy
Might well have made our sport a comedy.

KING
Come, sir, it wants a twelvemonth and a day,   867
And then 'twill end.

BEROWNE   That's too long for a play.

Enter [Armado the] braggart.

ARMADO [to the King]   Sweet Majesty, vouchsafe me—
PRINCESS   Was not that Hector?
DUMAINE   The worthy knight of Troy.
ARMADO   I will kiss thy royal finger, and take leave. I
am a votary; I have vowed to Jaquenetta to hold the   873
plow for her sweet love three year. But, most es-   874
teemed greatness, will you hear the dialogue that the   875
two learned men have compiled in praise of the owl   876
and the cuckoo? It should have followed in the end of
our show.
KING   Call them forth quickly. We will do so.
ARMADO   Holla! Approach.

*Enter all [Holofernes, Nathaniel, Mote, Costard,
Jaquenetta, and others. They stand in two groups.]*

This side is Hiems, Winter, this Ver, the Spring; the
one maintained by the owl, th' other by the cuckoo.   882
Ver, begin.

The Song

SPRING [sings]

When daisies pied and violets blue,   884
     And lady-smocks all silver-white,   885
And cuckoo-buds of yellow hue   886
     Do paint the meadows with delight,
The cuckoo then on every tree
Mocks married men, for thus sings he:
                    Cuckoo!
Cuckoo, cuckoo! O word of fear,
Unpleasing to a married ear!   892

When shepherds pipe on oaten straws,
     And merry larks are plowmen's clocks,   894
When turtles tread, and rooks and daws,   895
     And maidens bleach their summer smocks,
The cuckoo then on every tree
Mocks married men, for thus sings he:
                    Cuckoo!
Cuckoo, cuckoo! O word of fear,
Unpleasing to a married ear!

WINTER [sings]

When icicles hang by the wall,
     And Dick the shepherd blows his nail,   903
And Tom bears logs into the hall,
     And milk comes frozen home in pail,
When blood is nipped, and ways be foul,   906
Then nightly sings the staring owl:
Tu-whit, tu-whoo! A merry note,

---

829 attends awaits   **832 the world's large tongue** i.e., universal report   **834 comparisons** sardonic similes.   **flouts** jeers, insults
835 all estates all classes of people   **837 weed** i.e., remove.   **wormwood** (A bitter-tasting herb, hence "bitterness.")   **841 still converse**
constantly associate   **844 the painèd impotent** helpless sufferers
848 gibing mocking, scornful   **849 loose grace** carelessly given approval. (Rosaline is saying that Berowne's mocking manner has been
nurtured by the fact that others have laughed shallowly and too easily
at his foolish raillery.)   **854 dear** heartfelt   **856 withal** in addition
863 bring accompany   **867 wants** lacks

873–874 hold the plow i.e., labor at farming   **875 dialogue** debate
875–876 the two learned men i.e., Holofernes and Nathaniel
882 maintained defended, championed   **884 pied** parti-colored
885 lady-smocks cuckooflowers   **886 cuckoo-buds of yellow** butter-
cups (?)   **892 Unpleasing** i.e., because the cuckoo suggests cuckoldry
894 clocks (i.e., because plowmen "rise with the lark")   **895 turtles
tread** turtledoves mate.   **rooks and daws** black birds related to the
crow   **903 blows his nail** blows on his fingernails (i.e., to keep
warm, and waiting patiently with nothing to do)   **906 nipped** chilled.
ways pathways

While greasy Joan doth keel the pot.   909

When all aloud the wind doth blow,
   And coughing drowns the parson's saw,   911
And birds sit brooding in the snow,
   And Marian's nose looks red and raw,
When roasted crabs hiss in the bowl,   914
Then nightly sings the staring owl:
Tu-whit, tu-whoo! A merry note,
While greasy Joan doth keel the pot.

ARMADO   The words of Mercury are harsh after the   918
  songs of Apollo. You that way; we this way.   919
                        Exeunt, [separately].

909 keel skim and stir; cool to prevent boiling   **911 saw** maxim,
moral observation   **914 crabs** crab apples   **918 Mercury** messenger
of the gods and associated with eloquence or sophistry, in antithesis
to Apollo, the god of music   **919 You . . . this way** (Armado may be
directing those who have presented Winter to exit in one direction
and those who have presented Spring, in another; he may also be referring to the audience.)

The Two Gentlemen of Verona

If by "romantic comedy" we mean a love story in which the lovers overcome parental obstacles, jealousies, separations, and dangers to be united at last in married bliss, then *The Two Gentlemen of Verona* is perhaps Shakespeare's first. Although *The Comedy of Errors* may be an earlier play, it is a farce of mistaken identity, with only a secondary interest in marriage, whereas *Love's Labor's Lost* is a courtly confection ending in the postponement of all marriages. No mention of *The Two Gentlemen of Verona* occurs until it is mentioned in Francis Meres' *Palladis Tamia: Wit's Treasury* of 1598, but the play is often dated around 1590–1594 on the basis of style: rhymed couplets, end-stopped verse, passages of excessive wit combat, and the like. *The Taming of the Shrew* (c. 1592–1594) is often dated a little later than *The Two Gentlemen of Verona*, although admittedly the two plays are much alike and perhaps ought to share the credit and the blame for Shakespeare's first experimentation with romantic comedy. In any event, this was to be the genre of Shakespeare's best-known "festive" comedies, from *A Midsummer Night's Dream* to *Twelfth Night*.

The Two Gentlemen of Verona, then, is Shakespeare's apprenticeship to the romantic fiction of Italy and other southern European countries, whence he later derived so many plots of threatened love. He locates his story in Italy and gives his characters Italian names. He uses the conventional plot devices of romantic fiction: inconstancy in love and in friendship, the disguise of the heroine as a page, the overhearing of false vows, banishment, elopement, capture by outlaws, and so on. Virtually all the characters have a recognizable ancestry, not only in continental fiction but in neoclassical drama as well: Lucetta is the usual female companion, Thurio is the rich but unwelcome rival wooer (the pantaloon), Antonio and the Duke are typically strong-willed fathers opposing the romantic marriages of their children, Speed and Lance are at least supposed to be the clever servants who deliver messages and arrange rendezvous, and the four young lovers are the romantic protagonists.

Even in this early apprenticeship, to be sure, Shakespeare departs from the neoclassical norm of his continental sources. The setting remains nominally Italian, but the tone is often heartily English, and Shakespeare's attitude toward his romantic models borders occasionally on the irreverent. Lucetta is a true friend of Julia and a virtuous counselor in love; the jest about her being a "broker" or a go-between (1.2.41) reminds us how unlike a bawdy duenna she really is. Thurio, Antonio, and the Duke are all portrayed with such amiable forbearance that they often seem inadequately motivated as the opponents of romantic happiness. Most of all, Speed and Lance have departed from their traditional roles as comic manipulators to become vaudeville jokesters.

Moreover, the very conventions of love and friendship are presented in such a way as to cast those conventions in an improbable light. What are we to make of the inconstant Proteus, who rejects his faithful Julia the moment he is away from her, tries instead to win the lady-fair of his dearest friend Valentine, informs the Duke of Valentine's plan to elope with Sylvia, and then attempts a violent assault on Sylvia's chastity? What sort of romantic hero is this, and why should he be rewarded by being forgiven and restored to his Julia? Most puzzling of all, is it credible that Valentine should respond to all this perfidy by offering to relinquish Sylvia to Proteus? By the same token, isn't it absurd that the outlaws in the forest near Mantua should turn out to be gentlemen in exile and that they should offer command of their group to Valentine, whom they have just captured? Isn't the Duke's forgiveness of his eloped daughter Sylvia rather sudden and unconvincing? These problems, which have troubled many readers of the play (though they generally seem less formidable to spectators of an actual production), can perhaps best be analyzed in two ways: as a result of Shakespeare's having combined two sources with conflicting conventions, thereby subjecting those conventions to a playfully ironic perspective, and as a result of Shakespeare's conscious interest in the theme of unexpected forgiveness for his erring protagonist.

Using a device of plotting that was to become customary in his romantic comedies, Shakespeare combines two fictional sources and thereby sets up a dramatic tension between the two. His chief source appears to have been *Diana*, a popular pastoral romance in Spanish by the Portuguese Jorge de Montemayor (1520–1561). Its heroine, Felismena (corresponding to Julia), is wooed by Don Felix (Proteus), whose father (Antonio) disapproves of the match and sends Don Felix away to court. Felismena, following after him disguised as a page, stops at an inn and is invited by the Host to listen to some music, whereupon she overhears Don Felix protesting his love to a new lady, Celia (Sylvia). At this point, the resemblance between *Diana* and Shakespeare's play breaks off. Even thus far, despite several striking resemblances, the story provides no counterpart for Valentine, Proteus' best friend and the faithful lover of Sylvia. Montemayor's romance is solely concerned with inconstancy in love.

For the motif of true friendship, Shakespeare may have turned to the story of Titus and Gisippus, as told by Sir Thomas Elyot in *The Governor* (1531). Here Gisippus, upon learning that his dear friend Titus has fallen in love with Gisippus' ladylove, not only relinquishes the lady to Titus but also actually smuggles him into bed with her, all unbeknownst to the lady. The point of this story, as of other well-known treatises on friendship, such as John Lyly's *Euphues* (1578) and *Endymion* (1588) or Richard Edwards' *Damon and Pythias* (1565), is that friendship is a higher form of human affection than erotic love, since it is disinterested, platonically pure, and capable of teaching selflessness to others. Such a tale of perfect friendship provides, however, no counterpart for Julia, the lady abandoned by Proteus. Shakespeare has neatly dovetailed the two stories, making a quartet of lovers out of two triangular situations. The false lover of the first story becomes also the false friend of the second—only to be overwhelmed at the end by the generosity of his true friend.

The dramatic problem created by combining these two stories is that they arouse different expectations. The one is dedicated to the virtue of constancy in love; the other, to friendship. Valentine's ultimate function is to demonstrate the triumph of selfless friendship over love, and yet his function in the plot of love rivalry is to demonstrate true loyalty to his Sylvia. His relinquishing of her to Proteus seems inconsistent with his vows as a lover. Conversely, Proteus' double perfidy, toward his lover Julia and his friend Valentine, seems to render him unworthy of the generous action Valentine bestows on him. Proteus' very name is synonymous with inconstancy; his namesake in the *Odyssey* was infamous for his ability to change shapes at will. (Valentine's name, on the other hand, betokens constancy in love.) The coupling of the two plots simultaneously intensifies Proteus' guilt and Valentine's magnanimity.

Yet Shakespeare makes a virtue out of the seeming lack of credibility. First, the very implausibility of Valentine's selflessness in love and of Proteus' sudden conversion to virtue allows Shakespeare to mock gently the literary commonplaces of his sources. At the same time, Shakespeare finds serious value in his conventional topics of love and friendship, through the device of paradox. The more unlikely Valentine's actions seem, the more transcendent and wondrous they are bound to appear. Shakespeare prepares for his climactic scene of forgiveness in several ways. First, he presents Proteus as an essentially noble person who has fallen through a single fault. Proteus is wellborn, accomplished, and handsome. The worthy Julia loves him for his good qualities, and he responds with sincerity and passion. He is equally ardent as a friend to Valentine. Only when he sees Sylvia does Proteus become helpless, "dazzlèd" (2.4.207). He cannot completely be blamed for being overwhelmed by passion, for the other lovers are no less obedient to love's command. According to the code of love

that infuses this play, love cannot choose its object. Proteus' unhappy fate is to love Sylvia. Yet he must also be held responsible for his actions and, indeed, blames himself for the desertion that he has consciously committed. His self-hatred increases as he turns flatterer, liar, betrayer, and finally would-be rapist. Like Angelo in *Measure for Measure,* Proteus is compulsively driven to abhorrent sin, but the choice is ultimately his. The psychological insight of that later dark comedy is lacking—the soliloquies do not create the suffocating atmosphere of a nightmare—but the pattern of a guilty fall is still manifest.

This pattern may, in turn, clarify Valentine's role as the selfless friend. He should not be taken too seriously as such; Shakespeare makes no attempt to conceal the absurd aspect of Valentine's self-righteous renunciation of the woman who has been unswervingly loyal to him and who has no wish to be traded from one lover to another as though she were the object of some kind of moralistic barter. Nonetheless, the very implausibility of Valentine's offer to relinquish Sylvia accentuates the noble intent behind the gesture. We are surprised, even comically surprised, because we don't expect such selflessness in human nature; but, if friendship is to be seen as a supreme achievement of the human spirit, it must transcend humanity's all-too-common penchant for rivalry and ingratitude. Valentine's generosity is not achieved without inner struggle. In the climactic scene of attempted rape, his first natural reaction is angry denunciation. What changes his mind is the depth and earnestness of Proteus' confession and desire for forgiveness: "If hearty sorrow / Be a sufficient ransom for offense, / I tender 't here" (5.4.74–76). Valentine responds in the name of mercy and at the prompting of divine example: "By penitence th' Eternal's wrath's appeased" (line 81). The more undeserved the pardon, the more selfless the act of him who pardons. Only by conquering his desire for Sylvia can Valentine teach his friend selflessness and thus reunite all four lovers in perfect joy. *The Two Gentlemen of Verona* is thus in part a comedy of forgiveness, anticipating later plays in which the romantic protagonist is equally culpable and yet equally forgiven: *Much Ado About Nothing, Measure for Measure, All's Well That Ends Well, Cymbeline,* and others (see R. G. Hunter's *Shakespeare and the Comedy of Forgiveness,* 1965.) *The Two Noble Kinsmen,* written very late (c. 1613) in collaboration with John Fletcher, is perhaps a troubled return to issues of friendship and sexual rivalry that are so prominent in *The Two Gentlemen of Verona.*

Forgiveness of Proteus must proceed no less from Julia than from Valentine. She, too, has much to pardon; as Proteus contritely observes, "O heaven! Were man / But constant, he were perfect" (5.4.110–111). Julia initiates a line of Shakespearean heroines, including Hero, Isabella, Helena, and Imogen in the plays already named, who must similarly cure inconstancy by their constancy. Like many Shakespearean heroines, Julia is plucky, resourceful, mod-

est but witty, patiently obedient in love and yet coyly flirta-
tious, a true friend, and long-suffering. Disguised as a page,
she overhears her lover's infidelity and yet never loses her
faith in him. She patiently delivers Proteus' messages to her
rival (like Viola in *Twelfth Night*) and gently acts as conscience to her erring master.

The repeated device of overhearing, as in later comedies,
provides a test for the protagonists' intentions. Thinking
themselves unobserved, they reveal their true natures for
better or for worse. In the ingeniously devised if improbable
climactic scene (5.4), Proteus as would-be ravisher is overheard by both his rejected mistress and his betrayed friend.
Conversely, Sylvia proves loyal and chaste whenever she is
silently observed by Julia (disguised as Sebastian) or by Valentine in the forest scenes. These overhearings suggest not
only that humanity's good and evil deeds are witnessed but
also that a beneficent providence will protect the virtuous.
Valentine's unseen presence assures that Sylvia will be
saved from rape and that Proteus will be prevented from
committing an actual crime of violence. As in later comedies of this sort, forgiveness is possible because the guilt remains one of intent only.

These slightly absurd but happy resolutions of conflict
take place in a forest near Mantua, the first of what Northrop
Frye calls Shakespeare's "green worlds" (*English Institute
Essays 1948*, pp. 58–73). Although sketchily presented,
this forest does anticipate the Forest of Arden and other sylvan restorative landscapes. Its inhabitants are banished men
protesting the injustice of society at court or fugitives from
unkind love. Valentine learns to prefer "unfrequented
woods" to "flourishing peopled towns." His "wild faction"
of outlaws desist from attacking "silly women or poor passengers" and appropriately swear "By the bare scalp of
Robin Hood's fat friar" (5.4.2–3; 4.1.36–37). They are
charmingly suited to their role of threatening and then re-
uniting the lovers, providentially capturing Sylvia just as she
is on her way to find Valentine. Their actions are highly improbable and poke fun at the very conventions they illustrate, but then the same can be said of Valentine's forgiveness of Proteus and the Duke's sudden reconciliation with
his prospective son-in-law, Valentine. Like Arden, this forest
is a strange place in which such changes of heart are expected to occur. The aura of improbability may also partly
explain the play's carelessness about social distinctions and
the realities of geography: the Duke is sometimes called the
Emperor, and at one point Valentine sets sail from Verona to
Milan (both located inland).

The buffoonish comedy of Lance and Speed performs
a function similar to that of romantic improbability by undercutting the artifice and melodrama of the love story. How
can we worry long over Valentine's banishment when
Lance bursts out, "Sir, there is a proclamation that you are
vanished" (3.1.217)? Or how can we fret about Proteus'
courtship of Sylvia when the love token he sends her is transformed into Lance's odoriferous dog? This sort of absurd anticlimax occurs at every turn. Lance's first soliloquy, about
the dog's refusal to mourn their departure from Verona (2.3),
is a brilliant example of what we would call vaudeville or
stand-up comic joking, but it also comments on the immediately preceding scene of Proteus' tearful farewell to Julia.
Lance's friendship for Speed, and especially his friendship
for the dog, delightfully blaspheme the play's serious interest
in true friendship. In one of Lance's funniest scenes (4.4.1–
38), he describes how he has selflessly taken on himself the
punishment meted out to the dog for urinating on Sylvia's
hooped petticoat. Similarly, the spectacle of Lance in love,
cataloguing his mistress's virtues and vices, insures us
against too deep an involvement in the hazards of Cupid.
The play continually reminds us of the folly of love without
denying its exquisite joys or its highest potential for selflessness.

The Two Gentlemen of Verona

The Names of All the Actors

DUKE [OF MILAN], *father to Sylvia*
VALENTINE }
PROTEUS, } *the two gentlemen*
ANTONIO, *father to Proteus*
THURIO, *a foolish rival to Valentine*
EGLAMOUR, *agent for Sylvia in her escape*
HOST [*of the inn*] *where Julia lodges*
OUTLAWS *with Valentine*
SPEED, *a clownish servant to Valentine*
LANCE, *the like to Proteus*
PANTHINO, *servant to Antonio*

JULIA, *beloved of Proteus*
SYLVIA, *beloved of Valentine*
LUCETTA, *waiting-woman to Julia*

[*Servants, Musicians*

SCENE: *Verona; Milan; the frontiers of Mantua*]

1.1   [*Enter*] *Valentine* [*and*] *Proteus.*

VALENTINE
Cease to persuade, my loving Proteus;
Home-keeping youth have ever homely wits.   2
Were 't not affection chains thy tender days   3
To the sweet glances of thy honored love,
I rather would entreat thy company
To see the wonders of the world abroad
Than, living dully sluggardized at home,
Wear out thy youth with shapeless idleness.   8
But since thou lov'st, love still, and thrive therein,   9
Even as I would when I to love begin.
PROTEUS
Wilt thou be gone? Sweet Valentine, adieu!
Think on thy Proteus when thou haply seest   12
Some rare noteworthy object in thy travel.
Wish me partaker in thy happiness
When thou dost meet good hap; and in thy danger,   15
If ever danger do environ thee,
Commend thy grievance to my holy prayers,   17

For I will be thy beadsman, Valentine.   18
VALENTINE
And on a love book pray for my success?   19
PROTEUS
Upon some book I love I'll pray for thee.
VALENTINE
That's on some shallow story of deep love,   21
How young Leander crossed the Hellespont.   22
PROTEUS
That's a deep story of a deeper love,
For he was more than over shoes in love.
VALENTINE
'Tis true; for you are over boots in love,
And yet you never swam the Hellespont.
PROTEUS
Over the boots? Nay, give me not the boots.   27
VALENTINE
No, I will not, for it boots thee not.   28
PROTEUS   What?
VALENTINE
To be in love, where scorn is bought with groans,
Coy looks with heartsore sighs, one fading moment's
   mirth
With twenty watchful, weary, tedious nights.   32
If haply won, perhaps a hapless gain;   33
If lost, why then a grievous labor won;
However, but a folly bought with wit,   35
Or else a wit by folly vanquishèd.
PROTEUS
So by your circumstance you call me fool.   37
VALENTINE
So by your circumstance I fear you'll prove.   38
PROTEUS
'Tis love you cavil at. I am not Love.   39
VALENTINE
Love is your master, for he masters you;
And he that is so yokèd by a fool
Methinks should not be chronicled for wise.   42
PROTEUS
Yet writers say, as in the sweetest bud
The eating canker dwells, so eating love   44
Inhabits in the finest wits of all.   45
VALENTINE
And writers say, as the most forward bud   46
Is eaten by the canker ere it blow,   47
Even so by love the young and tender wit
Is turned to folly, blasting in the bud,   49

1.1. Location: Verona. A street.
2 homely dull, simple   **3 affection** passion, love.   **tender** youthful
8 shapeless aimless   **9 still** always, constantly   **12 haply** by chance
15 hap fortune   **17 Commend thy grievance** commit your distress

18 beadsman one engaged to pray for others, using the beads of the rosary   **19 love book** manual of courtship or a love story (rather than a prayer book)   **21 shallow . . . deep** (playing on the oppositions of shallow and deep water, superficial and heartfelt love)   **22 Leander** famous lover of Greek legend who drowned as he swam the Hellespont to see his love Hero   **27 give . . . boots** i.e., don't make fun of me   **28 boots** profits, avails (with play on *boots* in line 27. This passage is full of punning, on *shallow* and *deep, over shoes, over boots,* etc.)   **32 watchful** wakeful   **33 hapless** unlucky   **35 However** either way.   **but** nothing but.   **wit** intellect (also in lines 36, 45, and 48)   **37 circumstance** detailed discourse   **38 circumstance** situation, condition   **39 cavil at** carp at, find fault with.   **Love** i.e., Cupid   **42 chronicled for wise** set down as being wise   **44 canker** cankerworm   **45 Inhabits** dwells   **46 forward** early   **47 blow** bloom   **49 blasting** withering

Losing his verdure even in the prime,   50
And all the fair effects of future hopes.   51
But wherefore waste I time to counsel thee   52
That art a votary to fond desire?   53
Once more adieu! My father at the road   54
Expects my coming, there to see me shipped.   55

PROTEUS
And thither will I bring thee, Valentine.   56

VALENTINE
Sweet Proteus, no. Now let us take our leave.
To Milan let me hear from thee by letters   58
Of thy success in love, and what news else
Betideth here in absence of thy friend;   60
And I likewise will visit thee with mine.   61

PROTEUS
All happiness bechance to thee in Milan!

VALENTINE
As much to you at home! And so, farewell.   *Exit.*

PROTEUS
He after honor hunts, I after love.
He leaves his friends to dignify them more;   65
I leave myself, my friends, and all, for love.   66
Thou, Julia, thou hast metamorphized me,
Made me neglect my studies, lose my time,   68
War with good counsel, set the world at naught;   69
Made wit with musing weak, heart sick with
    thought.   70

    [*Enter*] *Speed.*

SPEED
Sir Proteus, save you! Saw you my master?   71

PROTEUS
But now he parted hence to embark for Milan.   72

SPEED
Twenty to one, then, he is shipped already,   73
And I have played the sheep in losing him.   74

PROTEUS
Indeed, a sheep doth very often stray,
An if the shepherd be awhile away.   76

SPEED   You conclude that my master is a shepherd, then,
and I a sheep?

PROTEUS   I do.

SPEED   Why then, my horns are his horns, whether I   80
wake or sleep.

PROTEUS   A silly answer, and fitting well a sheep.

SPEED   This proves me still a sheep.

PROTEUS   True; and thy master a shepherd.

SPEED   Nay, that I can deny by a circumstance.   85

PROTEUS   It shall go hard but I'll prove it by another. 86

SPEED   The shepherd seeks the sheep, and not the sheep
the shepherd; but I seek my master, and my master
seeks not me. Therefore I am no sheep.

PROTEUS   The sheep for fodder follow the shepherd; the
shepherd for food follows not the sheep. Thou for
wages followest thy master; thy master for wages follows not thee. Therefore thou art a sheep.

SPEED   Such another proof will make me cry "Baa."   94

PROTEUS   But dost thou hear? Gav'st thou my letter to   95
Julia?

SPEED   Ay, sir. I, a lost mutton, gave your letter to her, 97
a laced mutton, and she, a laced mutton, gave me, a   98
lost mutton, nothing for my labor.

PROTEUS   Here's too small a pasture for such store of
muttons.

SPEED   If the ground be overcharged, you were best   102
stick her.   103

PROTEUS   Nay, in that you are astray. 'Twere best   104
pound you.   105

SPEED   Nay, sir, less than a pound shall serve me for 106
carrying your letter.

PROTEUS   You mistake. I mean the pound—a pinfold.   108

SPEED
From a pound to a pin? Fold it over and over,   109
'Tis threefold too little for carrying a letter to your
    lover.

PROTEUS   But what said she?

SPEED   [*first nodding*]   Ay.

PROTEUS   Nod—ay—why, that's "noddy."   113

SPEED   You mistook, sir. I say she did nod, and you ask
me if she did nod, and I say, "Ay."

PROTEUS   And that set together is "noddy."

SPEED   Now you have taken the pains to set it together,
take it for your pains.   118

PROTEUS   No, no, you shall have it for bearing the letter.

SPEED   Well, I perceive I must be fain to bear with you. 120

PROTEUS   Why, sir, how do you bear with me?

SPEED   Marry, sir, the letter, very orderly, having noth- 122
ing but the word "noddy" for my pains.

PROTEUS   Beshrew me, but you have a quick wit.   124

SPEED   And yet it cannot overtake your slow purse.

---

50 his verdure its flourishing vigor. **prime** spring **51 fair . . .
hopes** bright fulfillment of future happiness **52 wherefore** why
53 votary worshiper. **fond** foolish **54 road** roadstead, harbor
55 shipped aboard. (Shakespeare evidently assumes that Verona and
Milan are connected by water; Proteus also travels by ship, though
Julia later makes the journey by land.) **56 bring** accompany **58
To Milan** by letters sent to Milan **60 Betideth** occurs **61 visit** enrich with a similar benefit **65 friends** (including family). **dignify**
i.e., honor (by increasing his own fame). **66 leave** neglect **68 lose**
waste **69 War . . . counsel** reject good advice **70 thought** melancholy **71 save you** God save you **72 But now** just now. **parted**
departed **73, 74 shipped, sheep** (Elizabethan pronunciation doubtless
made the pun obvious.) **76 An if** if **80 my horns . . . horns** he
owns my horns; i.e., presumably my master is a cuckold. (Traditionally, husbands whose wives deceived them were supposed to grow
horns.)

85 circumstance process of reasoning **86 It . . . I'll** I'll be doing
pretty badly if I cannot **94 Baa** (with a pun on *bah*, as in "bah, hum-
bug") **95 dost thou hear** i.e., listen here **97 to her** (At 1.2.38 we
learn that Speed gave the letter to Lucetta.) **97, 98 lost, laced** (As
with *shipped*, *sheep*, above, the Elizabethan pronunciation of the two
words was similar.) **98 laced mutton** i.e., whore with tightly-laced
bodice or laced slashing in her dress **102 overcharged** overcrowded
103 stick stab (with bawdy suggestion of penetration) **104 astray** (1)
wandering like a lost sheep (2) going too far **105 pound** (1) im-
pound, shut up in an animal pen (2) beat **106 pound** (1) twenty shillings (2) a beating **108 pinfold** pen for stray animals **109 a pin**
i.e., an object worth very little. **Fold** (1) as in folding a letter (2)
multiply **113 noddy** a simpleton **118 take . . . pains** i.e., here's
your tip (playing on *taken the pains*, taken the trouble, in line 117)
120 fain content. **bear with** (1) put up with (2) carry for. (Speed sees
he is to get no tip.) **122 Marry** i.e., indeed. (Originally an oath,
"by the Virgin Mary.") **124 Beshrew me** (A mild oath.)

PROTEUS   Come, come, open the matter in brief. What 126
said she?
SPEED   Open your purse, that the money and the matter
may be both at once delivered.   129
PROTEUS [*giving him money*]   Well, sir, here is for your
pains. What said she?
SPEED   Truly, sir, I think you'll hardly win her.   132
PROTEUS   Why? Couldst thou perceive so much from her?
SPEED   Sir, I could perceive nothing at all from her, no, 134
not so much as a ducat for delivering your letter. And 135
being so hard to me that brought your mind, I fear 136
she'll prove as hard to you in telling your mind. Give 137
her no token but stones, for she's as hard as steel. 138
PROTEUS   What said she? Nothing?
SPEED   No, not so much as "Take this for thy pains." To
testify your bounty, I thank you, you have testerned 141
me; in requital whereof, henceforth carry your letters 142
yourself. And so, sir, I'll commend you to my master. 143
PROTEUS
Go, go, begone, to save your ship from wreck,
Which cannot perish having thee aboard,   145
Being destined to a drier death on shore.   146
                                        [*Exit Speed.*]
I must go send some better messenger.
I fear my Julia would not deign my lines,   148
Receiving them from such a worthless post.   *Exit.* 149

❖

1.2   *Enter Julia and Lucetta.*

JULIA
But say, Lucetta, now we are alone,
Wouldst thou then counsel me to fall in love?
LUCETTA
Ay, madam, so you stumble not unheedfully.   3
JULIA
Of all the fair resort of gentlemen   4
That every day with parle encounter me,   5
In thy opinion which is worthiest love?   6
LUCETTA
Please you repeat their names, I'll show my mind   7
According to my shallow simple skill.

JULIA
What think'st thou of the fair Sir Eglamour?   9
LUCETTA
As of a knight well-spoken, neat, and fine;
But, were I you, he never should be mine.
JULIA
What think'st thou of the rich Mercatio?
LUCETTA
Well of his wealth, but of himself, so-so.
JULIA
What think'st thou of the gentle Proteus?
LUCETTA
Lord, Lord, to see what folly reigns in us!
JULIA
How now? What means this passion at his name?   16
LUCETTA
Pardon, dear madam, 'tis a passing shame   17
That I, unworthy body as I am,
Should censure thus on lovely gentlemen.   19
JULIA
Why not on Proteus, as of all the rest?
LUCETTA
Then thus: of many good I think him best.
JULIA   Your reason?
LUCETTA
I have no other but a woman's reason:
I think him so because I think him so.
JULIA
And wouldst thou have me cast my love on him?
LUCETTA
Ay, if you thought your love not cast away.
JULIA
Why, he of all the rest hath never moved me.   27
LUCETTA
Yet he of all the rest I think best loves ye.
JULIA
His little speaking shows his love but small.
LUCETTA
Fire that's closest kept burns most of all.
JULIA
They do not love that do not show their love.
LUCETTA
O, they love least that let men know their love.
JULIA   I would I knew his mind.
LUCETTA [*giving a letter*]   Peruse this paper, madam.
JULIA   "To Julia." Say, from whom?
LUCETTA   That the contents will show.
JULIA   Say, say, who gave it thee?
LUCETTA
Sir Valentine's page; and sent, I think, from Proteus.
He would have given it you, but I, being in the way, 39
Did in your name receive it. Pardon the fault, I pray.
JULIA
Now, by my modesty, a goodly broker!   41

Dare you presume to harbor wanton lines?
To whisper, and conspire against my youth?
Now, trust me, 'tis an office of great worth,
And you an officer fit for the place.
There, take the paper. See it be returned,
Or else return no more into my sight.

[She gives the letter back.]

LUCETTA
To plead for love deserves more fee than hate.   48

JULIA
Will ye be gone?

LUCETTA   That you may ruminate.   *Exit.* 49

JULIA
And yet I would I had o'erlooked the letter.   50
It were a shame to call her back again
And pray her to a fault for which I chid her.   52
What 'fool is she, that knows I am a maid   53
And would not force the letter to my view!
Since maids, in modesty, say no to that
Which they would have the profferer construe ay.
Fie, fie, how wayward is this foolish love
That, like a testy babe, will scratch the nurse   58
And presently, all humbled, kiss the rod!   59
How churlishly I chid Lucetta hence,
When willingly I would have had her here!
How angerly I taught my brow to frown,   62
When inward joy enforced my heart to smile!
My penance is to call Lucetta back
And ask remission for my folly past.
What ho! Lucetta!

[Enter Lucetta.]

LUCETTA   What would your ladyship?

JULIA
Is 't near dinnertime?

LUCETTA   I would it were,
That you might kill your stomach on your meat   68
And not upon your maid.

[She drops the letter and stoops to pick it up.]

JULIA
What is 't that you took up so gingerly?

LUCETTA   Nothing.

JULIA   Why didst thou stoop, then?

LUCETTA
To take a paper up that I let fall.

JULIA   And is that paper nothing?

LUCETTA   Nothing concerning me.

JULIA
Then let it lie for those that it concerns.

LUCETTA
Madam, it will not lie where it concerns,   77

Unless it have a false interpreter.

JULIA
Some love of yours hath writ to you in rhyme.

LUCETTA
That I might sing it, madam, to a tune,   80
Give me a note. Your ladyship can set.   81

JULIA
As little by such toys as may be possible.   82
Best sing it to the tune of "Light o' Love."   83

LUCETTA
It is too heavy for so light a tune.   84

JULIA
Heavy! Belike it hath some burden then?   85

LUCETTA
Ay, and melodious were it, would you sing it.

JULIA
And why not you?

LUCETTA   I cannot reach so high.   87

JULIA
Let's see your song. How now, minion?   88

[She takes the letter.]

LUCETTA
Keep tune there still; so you will sing it out.   89
And yet methinks I do not like this tune.

JULIA   You do not?

LUCETTA   No, madam, 'tis too sharp.   92

JULIA   You, minion, are too saucy.

LUCETTA   Nay, now you are too flat,   94
And mar the concord with too harsh a descant.   95
There wanteth but a mean to fill your song.   96

JULIA
The mean is drowned with your unruly bass.   97

LUCETTA
Indeed, I bid the base for Proteus.   98

JULIA
This babble shall not henceforth trouble me.   99
Here is a coil with protestation!   100

[She tears the letter and drops the pieces.]

Go, get you gone, and let the papers lie.
You would be fing'ring them to anger me.

---

48 more fee better recompense   **49 That . . . ruminate** (I'm leaving) so that you can think carefully about this   **50 o'erlooked** read   **52 to a fault** to commit a fault   **53 'fool** a fool   **58 testy** fretful   **59 presently** immediately afterward.   **rod** spanking rod   **62 angerly** angrily **68 kill your stomach** (1) satisfy your appetite (2) appease your anger. **meat** (Pronounced "mate," with a pun on *maid* in the next line.) **77 lie where it concerns** tell falsehoods in matters of importance (punning on the meaning "be left for those whose business it is" in the preceding line)

80 That in order that   **81 note** (with a punning reference to Proteus' letter).   **set** (1) set to music (2) write a letter. (But Julia takes the word in the sense of setting store by something, regarding it of value.) **82 toys** trifles   **83 "Light o' Love"** (A familiar tune of the time.) **84 heavy** serious   **85 Belike** perhaps.   **burden** (1) bass accompaniment to a melody (2) heavy load (with an added sexual suggestion of the burden women must bear)   **87 reach so high** (1) sing so high (2) aspire to a person of Proteus' rank   **88 minion** hussy (with a pun on *minim*, half-note)   **89 tune** (1) pitch (2) temper, mood.   **so . . . out** (1) if you do so, you'll be able to sing the song completely (2) that way you'll get over your bad mood   **92 sharp** (1) high in pitch (2) saucy, bitter. (Perhaps Julia pinches or slaps Lucetta here and at line 94, or perhaps Lucetta is referring to her mistress' tone of voice.) **94 flat** (1) low in pitch (2) blunt   **95 descant** (1) soprano counterpoint sung above the melody (2) carping criticism   **96 wanteth but** is lacking only.   **mean** (1) middle or tenor voice between the *descant* and the *bass*, i.e., Proteus (2) opportunity   **97 unruly bass** (with pun on "base behavior")   **98 bid the base for** i.e., act in behalf of, intercede for (referring to the game of "prisoner's base," and with a pun on *base*, "bass, low")   **99 babble** i.e., idle chatter; or else *bauble*, foolish trifle—the letter   **100 coil with protestation** commotion or fuss about protestations of love (i.e., about Proteus' letter)

LUCETTA
  She makes it strange, but she would be best pleased   103
  To be so angered with another letter.   [*Exit.*]
JULIA
  Nay, would I were so angered with the same!   105
              [*She picks up some fragments.*]
  O hateful hands, to tear such loving words!
  Injurious wasps, to feed on such sweet honey   107
  And kill the bees that yield it with your stings!
  I'll kiss each several paper for amends.   109
  Look, here is writ "kind Julia." Unkind Julia!   110
  As in revenge of thy ingratitude,   111
  I throw thy name against the bruising stones,
  Trampling contemptuously on thy disdain.
              [*She throws down a fragment.*]
  And here is writ "love-wounded Proteus."
  Poor wounded name! My bosom as a bed
  Shall lodge thee till thy wound be throughly healed;   116
  And thus I search it with a sovereign kiss.   117
  But twice or thrice was "Proteus" written down.
  Be calm, good wind, blow not a word away
  Till I have found each letter in the letter,
  Except mine own name; that some whirlwind bear   121
  Unto a ragged, fearful, hanging rock
  And throw it thence into the raging sea!
  Lo, here in one line is his name twice writ,
  "Poor forlorn Proteus, passionate Proteus,
  To the sweet Julia." That I'll tear away;
  And yet I will not, sith so prettily   127
  He couples it to his complaining names.
  Thus will I fold them, one upon another.
  Now kiss, embrace, contend, do what you will.
          [*She puts some folded papers in her bosom.*]

          [*Enter Lucetta.*]

LUCETTA   Madam,
  Dinner is ready, and your father stays.   132
JULIA   Well, let us go.
LUCETTA
  What, shall these papers lie like telltales here?
JULIA
  If you respect them, best to take them up.   135
LUCETTA
  Nay, I was taken up for laying them down;   136
  Yet here they shall not lie, for catching cold.   137
              [*She gathers up the remaining fragments.*]
JULIA
  I see you have a month's mind to them.   138

LUCETTA
  Ay, madam, you may say what sights you see;
  I see things too, although you judge I wink.   140
JULIA   Come, come, will 't please you go?   *Exeunt.*

1.3   *Enter Antonio and Panthino.*

ANTONIO
  Tell me, Panthino, what sad talk was that   1
  Wherewith my brother held you in the cloister?   2
PANTHINO
  'Twas of his nephew Proteus, your son.
ANTONIO
  Why, what of him?
PANTHINO   He wondered that your lordship
  Would suffer him to spend his youth at home,   5
  While other men, of slender reputation,   6
  Put forth their sons to seek preferment out: 7
  Some to the wars, to try their fortune there,
  Some to discover islands far away,
  Some to the studious universities.
  For any or for all these exercises
  He said that Proteus your son was meet,   12
  And did request me to importune you   13
  To let him spend his time no more at home,
  Which would be great impeachment to his age   15
  In having known no travel in his youth.
ANTONIO
  Nor need'st thou much importune me to that
  Whereon this month I have been hammering.   18
  I have considered well his loss of time,
  And how he cannot be a perfect man,   20
  Not being tried and tutored in the world.   21
  Experience is by industry achieved
  And perfected by the swift course of time.
  Then tell me, whither were I best to send him?   24
PANTHINO
  I think your lordship is not ignorant
  How his companion, youthful Valentine,
  Attends the Emperor in his royal court.   27
ANTONIO   I know it well.
PANTHINO
  'Twere good, I think, your lordship sent him thither.
  There shall he practice tilts and tournaments,   30
  Hear sweet discourse, converse with noblemen,   31
  And be in eye of every exercise   32
  Worthy his youth and nobleness of birth.   33

103 makes it strange pretends indifference. (Lucetta says this speech for the audience's benefit, but it is a catty third-person reference to Julia rather than an aside, and Julia makes it clear in line 105 that she has heard it.) **105 Nay . . . same** i.e., indeed, I wish I had this same letter intact to pretend to be angry about **107 wasps** i.e., her fingers **109 several paper** separate scrap of paper **110 Unkind** unnatural, cruel **111 As** "as if," or, "thus" **116 throughly** thoroughly **117 search** probe, cleanse (as one would a wound). **sovereign** healing **121 that . . . bear** may some whirlwind bear *that*, my name **127 sith** since **132 stays** waits **135 respect** prize, esteem. **best to take** it were best you take **136 taken up** scolded (with a play on *take them up* in the preceding line) **137 for** for fear of **138 month's mind** inclination, liking

140 wink close the eyes
1.3. Location: Verona. Antonio's house.
1 sad serious **2 the cloister** any covered arcade attached to other buildings **5 suffer** allow **6 of slender reputation** i.e., of lower station than yourself **7 Put . . . out** send their sons away from home to seek advancement **12 meet** fitted **13 importune** urge **15 impeachment to his age** detriment or cause for reproach to him in his mature years **18 hammering** beating (an idea) into shape **20 perfect** i.e., educated, mature **21 tried** tested **24 were I best** would it be best for me **27 the Emperor** i.e., the Duke of Milan. (An apparent inconsistency.) **30 practice** perform, take part in **31 discourse** conversation. **converse** associate **32 in eye of** in a position to see **33 Worthy** worthy of

ANTONIO
I like thy counsel. Well hast thou advised,
And that thou mayst perceive how well I like it,
The execution of it shall make known.
Even with the speediest expedition   37
I will dispatch him to the Emperor's court.

PANTHINO
Tomorrow, may it please you, Don Alphonso,
With other gentlemen of good esteem,
Are journeying to salute the Emperor
And to commend their service to his will.   42

ANTONIO
Good company. With them shall Proteus go—

[Enter] Proteus, [reading a letter].

And in good time! Now will we break with him.   44

PROTEUS [to himself]
Sweet love, sweet lines, sweet life!
Here is her hand, the agent of her heart;
Here is her oath for love, her honor's pawn.   47
O, that our fathers would applaud our loves
To seal our happiness with their consents!   49
O heavenly Julia!

ANTONIO
How now? What letter are you reading there?

PROTEUS
May 't please your lordship, 'tis a word or two
Of commendations sent from Valentine,   53
Delivered by a friend that came from him.

ANTONIO
Lend me the letter. Let me see what news.

PROTEUS
There is no news, my lord, but that he writes
How happily he lives, how well beloved
And daily gracèd by the Emperor,   58
Wishing me with him, partner of his fortune.

ANTONIO
And how stand you affected to his wish?   60

PROTEUS
As one relying on your lordship's will,
And not depending on his friendly wish.

ANTONIO
My will is something sorted with his wish.   63
Muse not that I thus suddenly proceed,   64
For what I will, I will, and there an end.
I am resolved that thou shalt spend some time
With Valentinus in the Emperor's court.
What maintenance he from his friends receives,   68
Like exhibition thou shalt have from me.   69
Tomorrow be in readiness to go.
Excuse it not, for I am peremptory.   71

PROTEUS
My lord, I cannot be so soon provided.   72
Please you, deliberate a day or two.

ANTONIO
Look what thou want'st shall be sent after thee.   74
No more of stay. Tomorrow thou must go.—   75
Come on, Panthino. You shall be employed
To hasten on his expedition.

[Exeunt Antonio and Panthino.]

PROTEUS
Thus have I shunned the fire for fear of burning
And drenched me in the sea, where I am drowned.
I feared to show my father Julia's letter
Lest he should take exceptions to my love,
And with the vantage of mine own excuse
Hath he excepted most against my love.   83
O, how this spring of love resembleth
The uncertain glory of an April day,
Which now shows all the beauty of the sun,
And by and by a cloud takes all away!

[Enter Panthino.]

PANTHINO
Sir Proteus, your father calls for you.
He is in haste; therefore, I pray you, go.

PROTEUS
Why, this it is: my heart accords thereto,
And yet a thousand times it answers no.   Exeunt.

❖

2.1   Enter Valentine [and] Speed.

SPEED
Sir, your glove.   [Offering a glove.]
VALENTINE   Not mine. My gloves are on.
SPEED
Why, then, this may be yours, for this is but one.   2
VALENTINE
Ha! Let me see. Ay, give it me, it's mine.
Sweet ornament that decks a thing divine!
Ah, Sylvia, Sylvia!
SPEED [calling]   Madam Sylvia! Madam Sylvia!
VALENTINE   How now, sirrah?   7
SPEED   She is not within hearing, sir.
VALENTINE   Why, sir, who bade you call her?
SPEED   Your worship, sir, or else I mistook.
VALENTINE   Well, you'll still be too forward.   11
SPEED   And yet I was last chidden for being too slow.
VALENTINE   Go to, sir. Tell me, do you know Madam   13
Sylvia?
SPEED   She that your worship loves?

---

37 **expedition** swiftness   42 **commend** commit, dedicate   44 **in good time** i.e., just at the right time (here he comes).   **break with** reveal, disclose the plan to   47 **pawn** pledge   49 **seal** ratify   53 **commendations** greetings   58 **gracèd** favored   60 **stand you affected** are you disposed, inclined   63 **something sorted** rather in accordance   64 **Muse** wonder   68 **maintenance** allowance.   **friends** i.e., relatives   69 **exhibition** allowance of money   71 **Excuse it not** offer no excuses.   **peremptory** resolved

72 **provided** equipped   74 **Look what** whatever   75 **No more of stay** no more talk of delay   83 **excepted most against** most effectively hindered
2.1. Location: Milan. Perhaps at the Duke's palace, or in some unspecified location.
2 **one** (Pronounced like "on," thus providing a pun on the line above.)   7 **sirrah** fellow. (Form of address to inferiors.)   11 **still** always   13 **Go to** (An expression of remonstrance.)

VALENTINE   Why, how know you that I am in love?

SPEED   Marry, by these special marks: first, you have learned, like Sir Proteus, to wreathe your arms, like a malcontent; to relish a love song, like a robin redbreast; to walk alone, like one that had the pestilence; to sigh, like a schoolboy that had lost his A B C; to weep, like a young wench that had buried her grandam; to fast, like one that takes diet; to watch, like one that fears robbing; to speak puling, like a beggar at Hallowmas. You were wont, when you laughed, to crow like a cock; when you walked, to walk like one of the lions. When you fasted, it was presently after dinner; when you looked sadly, it was for want of money. And now you are metamorphized with a mistress, that when I look on you I can hardly think you my master.

VALENTINE   Are all these things perceived in me?

SPEED   They are all perceived without ye.

VALENTINE   Without me? They cannot.

SPEED   Without you? Nay, that's certain, for, without you were so simple, none else would. But you are so without these follies that these follies are within you, and shine through you like the water in an urinal, that not an eye that sees you but is a physician to comment on your malady.

VALENTINE   But tell me, dost thou know my lady Sylvia?

SPEED   She that you gaze on so as she sits at supper?

VALENTINE   Hast thou observed that? Even she I mean.

SPEED   Why, sir, I know her not.

VALENTINE   Dost thou know her by my gazing on her, and yet know'st her not?

SPEED   Is she not hard-favored, sir?

VALENTINE   Not so fair, boy, as well-favored.

SPEED   Sir, I know that well enough.

VALENTINE   What dost thou know?

SPEED   That she is not so fair as, of you, well-favored.

VALENTINE   I mean that her beauty is exquisite but her favor infinite.

SPEED   That's because the one is painted and the other out of all count.

VALENTINE   How painted? And how out of count?

SPEED   Marry, sir, so painted to make her fair that no man counts of her beauty.

VALENTINE   How esteem'st thou me? I account of her beauty.

SPEED   You never saw her since she was deformed.   60

VALENTINE   How long hath she been deformed?

SPEED   Ever since you loved her.

VALENTINE   I have loved her ever since I saw her, and still I see her beautiful.

SPEED   If you love her, you cannot see her.

VALENTINE   Why?

SPEED   Because Love is blind. O, that you had mine eyes, or your own eyes had the lights they were wont to have when you chid at Sir Proteus for going ungartered!

VALENTINE   What should I see then?

SPEED   Your own present folly and her passing deformity; for he, being in love, could not see to garter his hose, and you, being in love, cannot see to put on your hose.

VALENTINE   Belike, boy, then you are in love, for last morning you could not see to wipe my shoes.

SPEED   True, sir. I was in love with my bed. I thank you, you swinged me for my love, which makes me the bolder to chide you for yours.

VALENTINE   In conclusion, I stand affected to her.   81

SPEED   I would you were set; so your affection would cease.

VALENTINE   Last night she enjoined me to write some lines to one she loves.

SPEED   And have you?

VALENTINE   I have.

SPEED   Are they not lamely writ?

VALENTINE   No, boy, but as well as I can do them. Peace, here she comes.

[*Enter*] *Sylvia.*

SPEED [*aside*]   O excellent motion! O exceeding puppet! Now will he interpret to her.   92

VALENTINE   Madam and mistress, a thousand good-morrows.

SPEED [*aside*]   O, give ye good even! Here's a million of manners.   95

SYLVIA   Sir Valentine and servant, to you two thousand.   97

SPEED [*aside*]   He should give her interest, and she gives it him.   99

VALENTINE
As you enjoined me, I have writ your letter

Line numbers (right margin of left column): 18, 19, 21, 22, 23, 24, 25, 26, 27, 28, 29, 32, 33, 34, 35, 36, 37, 46, 47, 50, 52, 53, 54, 57, 58. Right column: 60, 67, 68, 69, 70, 72, 74, 75, 79, 81, 91, 92, 95, 97, 98, 99.

18 wreathe fold. (Folded arms were a conventional gesture of melancholy, such as love melancholy.)   **19 relish** sing, warble   **21 A B C** primer   **22–23 grandam** grandmother   **23 takes diet** diets for reasons of health.   **watch** lie awake, sit up at night   **24 puling** whiningly   **24–25 Hallowmas** All Saints' Day, November 1 (a day when beggars asked special alms)   **26–27 like one of the lions** i.e., proudly, manfully   **28 want** lack   **29 with** by.   **that** so that   **32 without ye** from your outside appearance   **33 Without me?** in my absence?   **34 without** unless   **35 would** i.e., would perceive them   **35–36 you are . . . follies** i.e., you so surround and encompass these follies   **37 urinal** glass container for medical examination of urine   **46 hard-favored** ugly   **47 fair** beautiful, blond-haired.   **well-favored** gracious, charming; also, good-looking. (But Speed takes the word in the sense of "looked upon with approval.")   **50 of** by   **52 favor** grace, charm   **53 painted** achieved by cosmetics   **54 out of all count** incalculable   **57 counts of** esteems   **58 How . . . me** i.e., are you impugning my judgment?   **account of** esteem

60 deformed i.e., transformed by the distorting perspective of Valentine's love for her   **67 Love** i.e., Cupid, traditionally represented as blind   **68 lights** sight   **69–70 going ungartered** i.e., neglecting appearance in dress, a traditional sign of love melancholy   **72 passing** surpassing, very great   **74–75 cannot . . . hose** i.e., you are in even worse shape than Proteus, and he was perfectly helpless   **79 swinged** thrashed   **81 I stand affected to** I am in love with. (But Speed quibbles on a bawdy sense of *stand*, suggesting Valentine would be better off if his desire were *set* or caused to subside and *cease. Set* also means "be seated," as contrasted with *stand* in the usual sense.)   **91 motion** puppet show.   **puppet** i.e., Sylvia   **92 interpret** i.e., supply dialogue or commentary, as for a puppet show   **95 give** i.e., God give.   **a million** i.e., an excessive amount   **97 servant** i.e., a man devoted to serving a lady in love   **98–99 He . . . him** i.e., he is the one who should be showing *interest* in her, as her *servant*, and yet she gives him *interest* by doubling what he has given her. (Playing on the financial meaning of *interest*.)

Unto the secret, nameless friend of yours,
Which I was much unwilling to proceed in
But for my duty to your ladyship.   [*Giving a letter.*] 103
SYLVIA
I thank you, gentle servant. 'Tis very clerkly done.   104
VALENTINE
Now trust me, madam, it came hardly off,   105
For, being ignorant to whom it goes,
I writ at random, very doubtfully.   107
SYLVIA
Perchance you think too much of so much pains?   108
VALENTINE
No, madam. So it stead you, I will write—   109
Please you command—a thousand times as much.
And yet—
SYLVIA
A pretty period! Well, I guess the sequel.   112
And yet I will not name it. And yet I care not.
And yet take this again. And yet I thank you,   114
Meaning henceforth to trouble you no more.
                    [*She offers him the letter.*]
SPEED [*aside*]
And yet you will, and yet another "yet."
VALENTINE
What means your ladyship? Do you not like it?
SYLVIA
Yes, yes. The lines are very quaintly writ,   118
But since unwillingly, take them again.
Nay, take them.   [*She gives back the letter.*]
VALENTINE   Madam, they are for you.
SYLVIA
Ay, ay. You writ them, sir, at my request,
But I will none of them. They are for you.
I would have had them writ more movingly.
VALENTINE
Please you, I'll write your ladyship another.
SYLVIA
And when it's writ, for my sake read it over.
And if it please you, so; if not, why, so.   127
VALENTINE
If it please me, madam? What then?
SYLVIA
Why, if it please you, take it for your labor.
And so good morrow, servant.   *Exit Sylvia.*
SPEED [*aside*]
O jest unseen, inscrutable, invisible
As a nose on a man's face, or a weathercock on a
    steeple!
My master sues to her, and she hath taught her
    suitor,
He being her pupil, to become her tutor.

O excellent device! Was there ever heard a better,
That my master, being scribe, to himself should
    write the letter?
VALENTINE   How now, sir? What, are you reasoning 137
with yourself?
SPEED   Nay, I was rhyming. 'Tis you that have the
reason.
VALENTINE   To do what?
SPEED   To be a spokesman from Madam Sylvia.
VALENTINE   To whom?
SPEED   To yourself. Why, she woos you by a figure.   144
VALENTINE   What figure?
SPEED   By a letter, I should say.
VALENTINE   Why, she hath not writ to me.
SPEED   What need she, when she hath made you write
to yourself? Why, do you not perceive the jest?
VALENTINE   No, believe me.
SPEED   No believing you, indeed, sir. But did you per- 151
ceive her earnest?   152
VALENTINE   She gave me none, except an angry word.
SPEED   Why, she hath given you a letter.
VALENTINE   That's the letter I writ to her friend.
SPEED   And that letter hath she delivered, and there an 156
end.   157
VALENTINE   I would it were no worse.
SPEED   I'll warrant you, 'tis as well.
For often have you writ to her, and she, in modesty,
Or else for want of idle time, could not again reply;
Or fearing else some messenger that might her mind
    discover,
Herself hath taught her love himself to write unto
    her lover.
All this I speak in print, for in print I found it. Why 164
muse you, sir? 'Tis dinnertime.
VALENTINE   I have dined.   166
SPEED   Ay, but hearken, sir: though the chameleon Love 167
can feed on the air, I am one that am nourished by my
victuals, and would fain have meat. O, be not like your 169
mistress; be moved, be moved!   *Exeunt.* 170

❖

2.2   *Enter Proteus [and] Julia.*

PROTEUS   Have patience, gentle Julia.
JULIA   I must, where is no remedy.   2

103 **duty** obedience, submission   104 **clerkly** in a scholarly manner (and perhaps with good penmanship)   105 **came hardly off** was done with difficulty   107 **doubtfully** uncertainly   108 **Perchance . . . pains** perhaps you think I have given you too much trouble   109 **So** so long as.   **stead** benefit   112 **A pretty period** a fine pause; i.e., to finish your eloquent protestation of devoted service with "And yet" is to spoil all that came before it   114 **again** back   118 **quaintly** ingeniously   127 **so** well and good

137 **reasoning** discussing   144 **figure** device   151 **No believing you** there's no believing anything you say (playing on *No, believe me* in the previous line)   152 **earnest** to be serious. (But Valentine takes the word as a noun meaning "money paid as an installment to secure a bargain.")   156–157 **there an end** there's nothing more to be said on that score   164 **speak . . . found it** i.e., speak precisely, as though having read the speech somewhere. (Speed claims that what he says is as infallible as if he had read it in a book.)   166 **dined** i.e., feasted on the sight of Sylvia   167 **chameleon** an animal popularly thought to be able to live on air.   **Love** (Love is also a chameleon because it is so changeable.)   169 **fain** gladly   170 **be moved** (1) be not hardhearted (2) be persuaded to go to dinner
2.2. Location: Verona. Julia's house.
2 where is where there is

PROTEUS
When possibly I can, I will return.

JULIA
If you turn not, you will return the sooner.   4
Keep this remembrance for thy Julia's sake.

[She gives him a ring.]

PROTEUS
Why, then, we'll make exchange. Here, take you
    this.   *[He gives her a ring.]*

JULIA
And seal the bargain with a holy kiss.   *[They kiss.]*

PROTEUS
Here is my hand for my true constancy;
And when that hour o'erslips me in the day   9
Wherein I sigh not, Julia, for thy sake,
The next ensuing hour some foul mischance
Torment me for my love's forgetfulness!
My father stays my coming. Answer not.   13
The tide is now—nay, not thy tide of tears;   14
That tide will stay me longer than I should.
Julia, farewell! *[Exit Julia.]* What, gone without a
    word?
Ay, so true love should do; it cannot speak,
For truth hath better deeds than words to grace it.   18

[Enter] Panthino.

PANTHINO
Sir Proteus, you are stayed for.

PROTEUS   Go. I come, I come.
Alas! This parting strikes poor lovers dumb.   *Exeunt.*

❖

2.3   *Enter Lance [with his dog, Crab].*

LANCE   Nay, 'twill be this hour ere I have done weeping. All the kind of the Lances have this very fault. I   2
have received my proportion, like the prodigious son,   3
and am going with Sir Proteus to the Imperial's court.   4
I think Crab, my dog, be the sourest-natured dog that
lives. My mother weeping, my father wailing, my sister crying, our maid howling, our cat wringing her
hands, and all our house in a great perplexity, yet did
not this cruel-hearted cur shed one tear. He is a stone,
a very pebblestone, and has no more pity in him than
a dog. A Jew would have wept to have seen our parting. Why, my grandam, having no eyes, look you,
wept herself blind at my parting. Nay, I'll show you
the manner of it. This shoe is my father. No, this left   14
shoe is my father. No, no, this left shoe is my mother.
Nay, that cannot be so neither. Yes, it is so, it is so—
it hath the worser sole. This shoe with the hole in it   17

is my mother, and this my father. A vengeance on 't!   18
There 'tis. Now, sir, this staff is my sister, for, look
you, she is as white as a lily and as small as a wand.   20
This hat is Nan, our maid. I am the dog. No, the dog is
himself, and I am the dog—O, the dog is me, and I
am myself. Ay, so, so. Now come I to my father: "Father, your blessing." Now should not the shoe speak
a word for weeping. Now should I kiss my father.
Well, he weeps on. Now come I to my mother. O, that
she could speak now like a wood woman! Well, I kiss   27
her. Why, there 'tis. Here's my mother's breath up and   28
down. Now come I to my sister; mark the moan she   29
makes. Now the dog all this while sheds not a tear nor
speaks a word; but see how I lay the dust with my
tears.

[Enter] Panthino.

PANTHINO   Lance, away, away, aboard! Thy master is
shipped, and thou art to post after with oars. What's   34
the matter? Why weep'st thou, man? Away, ass! You'll
lose the tide if you tarry any longer.

LANCE   It is no matter if the tied were lost, for it is the   37
unkindest tied that ever any man tied.

PANTHINO   What's the unkindest tide?

LANCE   Why, he that's tied here, Crab, my dog.

PANTHINO   Tut, man, I mean thou'lt lose the flood, and   41
in losing the flood, lose thy voyage, and in losing thy
voyage, lose thy master, and in losing thy master, lose
thy service, and in losing thy service—*[Lance puts his
hand over Panthino's mouth.]* Why dost thou stop my
mouth?

LANCE   For fear thou shouldst lose thy tongue.   47

PANTHINO   Where should I lose my tongue?

LANCE   In thy tale.

PANTHINO   In thy tail!

LANCE   Lose the tide, and the voyage, and the master,
and the service, and the tied? Why, man, if the river
were dry, I am able to fill it with my tears; if the wind
were down, I could drive the boat with my sighs.

PANTHINO   Come, come away, man. I was sent to call   55
thee.

LANCE   Sir, call me what thou dar'st.   57

PANTHINO   Wilt thou go?

LANCE   Well, I will go.   *Exeunt.*

❖

2.4   *Enter Valentine, Sylvia, Thurio, [and] Speed.*

SYLVIA   Servant!

VALENTINE   Mistress?

SPEED *[to Valentine]*   Master, Sir Thurio frowns on you.

---

4 turn not do not prove to be unfaithful   **9 o'erslips me** slips by me
unnoticed   **13 stays** awaits   **14 The tide** the high tide for departure
by sail   **18 grace** adorn
2.3. Location: Verona. A street.
2 kind kindred, race   **3 proportion** (A malapropism for "portion, allotment.")   **prodigious** (A malapropism for "prodigal.")   **4 Imperial's**
i.e., Emperor's   **14 This shoe** (Lance demonstrates.)   **17 sole** (with a
pun on "soul." Lance refers to a common debate as to whether a
woman's soul is inferior to a man's. *The hole in it* may also suggest a
bawdy joke about the feminine anatomy.)

18 A vengeance on 't (A mild curse, probably occasioned by the difficulty Lance has in pulling his shoe off. *There 'tis* in line 19 signals his
success in doing so.)   **20 small** slim   **27 wood** mad, distraught (with
punning allusion to a wooden shoe)   **28–29 up and down** i.e., exactly   **34 post** hasten.   **with oars** i.e., in a rowboat, in order to reach
the sailing vessel at anchor   **37 the tied** i.e., the dog that is tied
41 lose the flood miss the tide   **47 lose** (1) lose (2) loose   **55 call**
summon   **57 call me what** call me whatever names
2.4. Location: Milan. The Duke's palace.

VALENTINE   Ay, boy, it's for love.

SPEED   Not of you.

VALENTINE   Of my mistress, then.

SPEED   'Twere good you knocked him.   [*Exit.*] 7

SYLVIA [*to Valentine*]   Servant, you are sad.

VALENTINE   Indeed, madam, I seem so.

THURIO   Seem you that you are not?   10

VALENTINE   Haply I do.   11

THURIO   So do counterfeits.

VALENTINE   So do you.

THURIO   What seem I that I am not?

VALENTINE   Wise.

THURIO   What instance of the contrary?   16

VALENTINE   Your folly.

THURIO   And how quote you my folly?   18

VALENTINE   I quote it in your jerkin.   19

THURIO   My "jerkin" is a doublet.   20

VALENTINE   Well, then, I'll double your folly.

THURIO   How?   22

SYLVIA   What, angry, Sir Thurio? Do you change color?

VALENTINE   Give him leave, madam; he is a kind of chameleon.

THURIO   That hath more mind to feed on your blood   26
than live in your air.   27

VALENTINE   You have said, sir.   28

THURIO   Ay, sir, and done too, for this time.   29

VALENTINE   I know it well, sir; you always end ere you   30
begin.   31

SYLVIA   A fine volley of words, gentlemen, and quickly
shot off.

VALENTINE   'Tis indeed, madam, we thank the giver.

SYLVIA   Who is that, servant?

VALENTINE   Yourself, sweet lady, for you gave the fire.   36
Sir Thurio borrows his wit from your ladyship's looks,
and spends what he borrows kindly in your company.   38

THURIO   Sir, if you spend word for word with me, I shall
make your wit bankrupt.

VALENTINE   I know it well, sir; you have an exchequer   41
of words, and, I think, no other treasure to give your
followers, for it appears, by their bare liveries, that   43
they live by your bare words.   44

SYLVIA   No more, gentlemen, no more. Here comes my
father.

[*Enter the*] *Duke.*

DUKE
Now, daughter Sylvia, you are hard beset.   47
Sir Valentine, your father is in good health.
What say you to a letter from your friends
Of much good news?

VALENTINE   My lord, I will be thankful
To any happy messenger from thence.   51

DUKE
Know ye Don Antonio, your countryman?

VALENTINE
Ay, my good lord, I know the gentleman
To be of worth and worthy estimation,   54
And not without desert so well reputed.   55

DUKE   Hath he not a son?

VALENTINE
Ay, my good lord, a son that well deserves
The honor and regard of such a father.

DUKE   You know him well?

VALENTINE
I know him as myself, for from our infancy
We have conversed and spent our hours together.   61
And though myself have been an idle truant,
Omitting the sweet benefit of time   63
To clothe mine age with angel-like perfection,
Yet hath Sir Proteus—for that's his name—
Made use and fair advantage of his days;
His years but young, but his experience old;
His head unmellowed, but his judgment ripe.   68
And in a word—for far behind his worth
Comes all the praises that I now bestow—
He is complete in feature and in mind   71
With all good grace to grace a gentleman.

DUKE
Beshrew me, sir, but if he make this good,   73
He is as worthy for an empress' love
As meet to be an emperor's counselor.   75
Well, sir, this gentleman is come to me
With commendation from great potentates,
And here he means to spend his time awhile.
I think 'tis no unwelcome news to you.

VALENTINE
Should I have wished a thing, it had been he.

DUKE
Welcome him then according to his worth.
Sylvia, I speak to you, and you, Sir Thurio;
For Valentine, I need not cite him to it.   83
I will send him hither to you presently.   [*Exit.*]

VALENTINE
This is the gentleman I told your ladyship
Had come along with me, but that his mistress
Did hold his eyes locked in her crystal looks.

SYLVIA
Belike that now she hath enfranchised them   88

---

7 **'Twere . . . him** you'd better hit him   10 **that** what   11 **Haply**
perhaps   16 **instance** proof   18 **quote** notice, observe. (Pronounced
like *coat,* enabling Valentine to pun on that idea.)   19 **jerkin** close-
fitting jacket worn over, or in place of, the doublet   20 **My . . . doublet** i.e., what you ignorantly call my "jerkin" is in fact a doublet.
a doublet (with a play on *double* in the next line)   22 **How?** (An expression of annoyance or incredulity.)   26 **That** i.e., one who   27 **in
your air** (1) in the air you breathe, i.e., near you (2) listening to your
talk. (The phrase also plays on *chameleon* in the previous speech,
since chameleons were supposed to be able to live on air alone.)
28 **You have said** i.e., that's a lot of fine talk   29 **done** (1) acted, in
contrast to *said* (2) finished. (Thurio hints here that he's prepared to
duel with Valentine at some future date.)   30–31 **end . . . begin** i.e.,
stop before you come to actual blows   36 **fire** i.e., spark to set off
the volley   38 **kindly** fittingly, naturally, affectionately   41 **exchequer**
treasury   43 **bare** threadbare.   **liveries** uniforms worn by a gentleman's retainers   44 **bare** mere

47 **hard beset** strongly besieged (with two wooers at once)   51 **happy
messenger** bringer of good tidings   54 **worthy** worthy of   55 **without
desert** undeservedly   61 **conversed** (1) talked (2) associated
63 **Omitting** neglecting   68 **unmellowed** i.e., unmixed with gray hair
71 **complete in feature** perfect in shape of body and personal appearance   73 **Beshrew me** (A mild oath.)   **make this good** i.e., match
your description   75 **meet** suited   83 **cite** urge   88 **Belike that**
perhaps

Upon some other pawn for fealty.   89
VALENTINE
Nay, sure, I think she holds them prisoners still.
SYLVIA
Nay, then he should be blind, and being blind
How could he see his way to seek out you?
VALENTINE
Why, lady, Love hath twenty pair of eyes.
THURIO
They say that Love hath not an eye at all.
VALENTINE
To see such lovers, Thurio, as yourself.
Upon a homely object Love can wink.   96
SYLVIA
Have done, have done. Here comes the gentleman.

          [Enter] Proteus.

VALENTINE
Welcome, dear Proteus! Mistress, I beseech you,
Confirm his welcome with some special favor.
SYLVIA
His worth is warrant for his welcome hither,
If this be he you oft have wished to hear from.
VALENTINE
Mistress, it is. Sweet lady, entertain him   102
To be my fellow servant to your ladyship.
SYLVIA
Too low a mistress for so high a servant.
PROTEUS
Not so, sweet lady, but too mean a servant   105
To have a look of such a worthy mistress.   106
VALENTINE
Leave off discourse of disability.   107
Sweet lady, entertain him for your servant.
PROTEUS
My duty will I boast of, nothing else.   109
SYLVIA
And duty never yet did want his meed.   110
Servant, you are welcome to a worthless mistress.
PROTEUS
I'll die on him that says so but yourself.   112
SYLVIA
That you are welcome?
PROTEUS   That you are worthless.

          [Enter a Servant.]

SERVANT
Madam, my lord your father would speak with you.
SYLVIA
I wait upon his pleasure. [Exit Servant.] Come, Sir
Thurio,

Go with me. Once more, new servant, welcome.
I'll leave you to confer of home affairs.
When you have done, we look to hear from you.
PROTEUS
We'll both attend upon your ladyship.
                    [Exeunt Sylvia and Thurio.]
VALENTINE
Now tell me, how do all from whence you came?
PROTEUS
Your friends are well and have them much
    commended.   121
VALENTINE
And how do yours?
PROTEUS   I left them all in health.
VALENTINE
How does your lady, and how thrives your love?
PROTEUS
My tales of love were wont to weary you.
I know you joy not in a love discourse.
VALENTINE
Ay, Proteus, but that life is altered now.
I have done penance for contemning Love,   127
Whose high imperious thoughts have punished me
With bitter fasts, with penitential groans,
With nightly tears, and daily heartsore sighs;
For in revenge of my contempt of love
Love hath chased sleep from my enthrallèd eyes
And made them watchers of mine own heart's
    sorrow.   133
O gentle Proteus, Love's a mighty lord,
And hath so humbled me as I confess   135
There is no woe to his correction,   136
Nor to his service no such joy on earth.   137
Now, no discourse except it be of love.
Now can I break my fast, dine, sup, and sleep
Upon the very naked name of love.   140
PROTEUS
Enough. I read your fortune in your eye.
Was this the idol that you worship so?
VALENTINE
Even she. And is she not a heavenly saint?
PROTEUS
No, but she is an earthly paragon.
VALENTINE
Call her divine.
PROTEUS   I will not flatter her.
VALENTINE
O, flatter me, for love delights in praises.
PROTEUS
When I was sick, you gave me bitter pills,
And I must minister the like to you.
VALENTINE
Then speak the truth by her: if not divine,   148
Yet let her be a principality,   149

88–89 enfranchised . . . fealty set free his eyes in return for some
other pledge of fidelity, or, to pledge his fidelity somewhere else, or,
now that some other lover has pledged his service to her   96 homely
plain.   wink close the eyes   102 entertain take into service
105 mean lowly, unworthy   106 of from   107 Leave . . . disability
stop talking about your unworthiness   109 duty i.e., to Sylvia
110 want his meed lack its reward   112 die on die fighting with

121 them much commended i.e., sent warm greetings   127 contemning scorning   133 watchers of those who stay awake with
135 as that   136 to his correction compared to the woe of his punishment   137 to his service i.e., compared to serving Love   140 very
naked mere   148 by about   149 a principality a member of one of
the nine orders of angels

Sovereign to all the creatures on the earth.

PROTEUS
Except my mistress.

VALENTINE   Sweet, except not any,   151
Except thou wilt except against my love.   152

PROTEUS
Have I not reason to prefer mine own?   153

VALENTINE
And I will help thee to prefer her, too.   154
She shall be dignified with this high honor:
To bear my lady's train, lest the base earth
Should from her vesture chance to steal a kiss
And, of so great a favor growing proud,
Disdain to root the summer-swelling flower,   159
And make rough winter everlastingly.

PROTEUS
Why, Valentine, what braggartism is this?

VALENTINE
Pardon me, Proteus, all I can is nothing   162
To her whose worth makes other worthies nothing.   163
She is alone.

PROTEUS   Then let her alone.   164

VALENTINE
Not for the world. Why, man, she is mine own,
And I as rich in having such a jewel
As twenty seas, if all their sand were pearl,
The water nectar, and the rocks pure gold.
Forgive me that I do not dream on thee,   169
Because thou seest me dote upon my love.
My foolish rival, that her father likes
Only for his possessions are so huge,   172
Is gone with her along, and I must after;
For love, thou know'st, is full of jealousy.

PROTEUS   But she loves you?

VALENTINE
Ay, and we are betrothed. Nay, more, our marriage
    hour,
With all the cunning manner of our flight,
Determined of—how I must climb her window,   178
The ladder made of cords, and all the means
Plotted and 'greed on for my happiness.
Good Proteus, go with me to my chamber,
In these affairs to aid me with thy counsel.

PROTEUS
Go on before. I shall inquire you forth.   183
I must unto the road, to disembark   184
Some necessaries that I needs must use,
And then I'll presently attend you.

VALENTINE   Will you make haste?

PROTEUS   I will.   Exit [Valentine].
Even as one heat another heat expels,   189

Or as one nail by strength drives out another,
So the remembrance of my former love
Is by a newer object quite forgotten.
Is it mine eye, or Valentine's praise,
Her true perfection, or my false transgression
That makes me, reasonless, to reason thus?   195
She is fair; and so is Julia that I love—
That I did love, for now my love is thawed,
Which like a waxen image 'gainst a fire
Bears no impression of the thing it was.
Methinks my zeal to Valentine is cold,
And that I love him not as I was wont.
O, but I love his lady too, too much,
And that's the reason I love him so little.
How shall I dote on her with more advice,   204
That thus without advice begin to love her?   205
'Tis but her picture I have yet beheld,   206
And that hath dazzlèd my reason's light;
But when I look on her perfections,   208
There is no reason but I shall be blind.   209
If I can check my erring love, I will;   210
If not, to compass her I'll use my skill.   Exit. 211

❧

2.5   Enter, [meeting,] Speed and Lance [with his dog,
         Crab].

SPEED   Lance, by mine honesty, welcome to Milan!

LANCE   Forswear not thyself, sweet youth, for I am not
welcome. I reckon this always, that a man is never un-   3
done till he be hanged, nor never welcome to a place   4
till some certain shot be paid and the hostess say,   5
"Welcome!"

SPEED   Come on, you madcap, I'll to the alehouse with
you presently, where, for one shot of five pence, thou   8
shalt have five thousand welcomes. But sirrah, how
did thy master part with Madam Julia?

LANCE   Marry, after they closed in earnest they parted   11
very fairly in jest.   12

SPEED   But shall she marry him?

LANCE   No.

SPEED   How then? Shall he marry her?

LANCE   No, neither.

SPEED   What, are they broken?   17

LANCE   No, they are both as whole as a fish.   18

SPEED   Why, then, how stands the matter with them?

---

151 Sweet (A term of affection used with both men and women.)
152 Except . . . except unless you want to cast aspersions   **153 prefer** like better   **154 prefer** advance   **159 root** provide rooting for
162 can i.e., can say of her   **163 To her** compared to her   **164 is
alone** is peerless. (But Proteus plays on the sense of "let her be.")
169 that . . . thee i.e., that I seem neglectful of you   **172 for** because   **178 Determined of** is decided, arranged   **183 forth** out
184 road roadstead, harbor   **189 Even . . . expels** (It was a common
saying that the application of heat would relieve the pain of a burn.)

195 reasonless without justification, wrongly   **204 advice** deliberation, reflection   **205 without advice** unadvisedly (with a play on *with
advice* in the previous line)   **206 picture** i.e., outer appearance
208 perfections true qualities, not immediately apparent to view
209 no reason but no doubt but that   **210 check** restrain   **211 compass** obtain
2.5. Location: Milan. A street.
3–4 undone ruined   **5 shot** fee, tavern reckoning   **8 one . . . pence**
a fivepenny drink   **11 closed** (1) embraced (2) came to terms
12 fairly kindly, gently.   **jest** (Playing on the antithesis of *earnest* and
jest.)   **17 broken** no longer engaged. (But Lance plays on the word in
the sense of "smashed to pieces.")   **18 whole as a fish** (A proverbial
comparison.)

LANCE   Marry, thus: when it stands well with him, it 20 stands well with her.

SPEED   What an ass art thou! I understand thee not.

LANCE   What a block art thou, that thou canst not! My 23 staff understands me.

SPEED   What thou sayst?

LANCE   Ay, and what I do too. Look thee, I'll but lean, and my staff under-stands me.

SPEED   It stands under thee, indeed.

LANCE   Why, stand-under and under-stand is all one.

SPEED   But tell me true, will 't be a match?

LANCE   Ask my dog. If he say ay, it will; if he say no, it will; if he shake his tail and say nothing, it will.

SPEED   The conclusion is then that it will.

LANCE   Thou shalt never get such a secret from me but by a parable.   35

SPEED   'Tis well that I get it so. But Lance, how sayst 36 thou, that my master is become a notable lover?   37

LANCE   I never knew him otherwise.

SPEED   Than how?

LANCE   A notable lubber, as thou reportest him to be. 40

SPEED   Why, thou whoreson ass, thou mistak'st me.   41

LANCE   Why, fool, I meant not thee. I meant thy master.

SPEED   I tell thee my master is become a hot lover.

LANCE   Why, I tell thee I care not, though he burn 45 himself in love. If thou wilt, go with me to the 46 alehouse; if not, thou art an Hebrew, a Jew, and not worth the name of a Christian.

SPEED   Why?

LANCE   Because thou hast not so much charity in thee as to go to the ale with a Christian. Wilt thou go? 51

SPEED   At thy service.   *Exeunt.*

❧

2.6   *Enter Proteus solus.*

PROTEUS
To leave my Julia shall I be forsworn;
To love fair Sylvia shall I be forsworn;
To wrong my friend I shall be much forsworn.
And ev'n that power which gave me first my oath   4
Provokes me to this threefold perjury.   5
Love bade me swear, and Love bids me forswear.
O sweet-suggesting Love, if thou hast sinned,   7
Teach me, thy tempted subject, to excuse it!   8

At first I did adore a twinkling star,
But now I worship a celestial sun.
Unheedful vows may heedfully be broken,   11
And he wants wit that wants resolvèd will   12
To learn his wit t' exchange the bad for better.   13
Fie, fie, unreverent tongue, to call her bad
Whose sovereignty so oft thou hast preferred   15
With twenty thousand soul-confirming oaths!   16
I cannot leave to love, and yet I do;   17
But there I leave to love where I should love.
Julia I lose, and Valentine I lose.
If I keep them, I needs must lose myself.
If I lose them, thus find I by their loss
For Valentine, myself; for Julia, Sylvia.
I to myself am dearer than a friend,
For love is still most precious in itself,   24
And Sylvia—witness Heaven, that made her fair!—
Shows Julia but a swarthy Ethiop.   26
I will forget that Julia is alive,
Remembering that my love to her is dead;
And Valentine I'll hold an enemy,
Aiming at Sylvia as a sweeter friend.
I cannot now prove constant to myself
Without some treachery used to Valentine.
This night he meaneth with a corded ladder
To climb celestial Sylvia's chamber window,
Myself in counsel, his competitor.   35
Now presently I'll give her father notice
Of their disguising and pretended flight,   37
Who, all enraged, will banish Valentine;
For Thurio, he intends, shall wed his daughter.
But Valentine being gone, I'll quickly cross   40
By some sly trick blunt Thurio's dull proceeding.   41
Love, lend me wings to make my purpose swift,
As thou hast lent me wit to plot this drift!   *Exit.* 43

❧

2.7   *Enter Julia and Lucetta.*

JULIA
Counsel, Lucetta. Gentle girl, assist me;
And ev'n in kind love I do conjure thee,
Who art the table wherein all my thoughts   3
Are visibly charactered and engraved,   4
To lesson me and tell me some good means   5
How, with my honor, I may undertake
A journey to my loving Proteus.

LUCETTA
Alas, the way is wearisome and long!

---

20 stands well (with a bawdy pun about erection)   **23 block** block-head   **35 a parable** enigmatic talk   **36–37 how sayst thou** what do you say to this   **40 lubber** big, clumsy fellow (with obvious pun on "lover")   **41 whoreson** (A friendly term of abuse.)   **thou mistak'st me** you mistake my meaning. (But Lance replies to the sense of "you mistake me [Speed] for Valentine.")   **45–46 burn himself in love** (with a punning sense of "acquire venereal disease")   **51 go . . . Christian** i.e., go to a church-ale, a village festival used to raise money for the church

2.6. Location: Milan. The Duke's palace.
s.d. solus alone   **4 that power** i.e., Love   **5 Provokes** incites
7 sweet-suggesting sweetly seductive   **7–8 if thou . . . it** i.e., if even you, Love, have committed falsehoods or follies in love, teach frail me how to excuse myself by your example

11 Unheedful ill-considered.   **heedfully** after careful consideration **12 wants wit** lacks sense   **13 learn** teach   **15 preferred** recommended, urged   **16 soul-confirming** sworn on the soul   **17 leave** cease   **24 still** always   **26 Shows Julia but** reveals Julia to be by comparison no more than.   **Ethiop** i.e., dark-skinned, the antithesis of beauty to Elizabethans   **35 in counsel** taken into confidence. **competitor** associate, partner   **37 pretended** intended   **40 cross** thwart   **41 blunt** stupid   **43 drift** scheme
2.7. Location: Verona. Julia's house.
3 table tablet   **4 charactered** engraved, inscribed   **5 lesson** teach

JULIA
A true-devoted pilgrim is not weary
To measure kingdoms with his feeble steps; 10
Much less shall she that hath Love's wings to fly,
And when the flight is made to one so dear,
Of such divine perfection, as Sir Proteus.

LUCETTA
Better forbear till Proteus make return.

JULIA
O, know'st thou not his looks are my soul's food?
Pity the dearth that I have pinèd in 16
By longing for that food so long a time.
Didst thou but know the inly touch of love, 18
Thou wouldst as soon go kindle fire with snow
As seek to quench the fire of love with words.

LUCETTA
I do not seek to quench your love's hot fire,
But qualify the fire's extreme rage, 22
Lest it should burn above the bounds of reason.

JULIA
The more thou damm'st it up, the more it burns.
The current that with gentle murmur glides,
Thou know'st, being stopped, impatiently doth rage;
But when his fair course is not hinderèd,
He makes sweet music with th' enameled stones, 28
Giving a gentle kiss to every sedge 29
He overtaketh in his pilgrimage,
And so by many winding nooks he strays
With willing sport to the wild ocean. 32
Then let me go, and hinder not my course.
I'll be as patient as a gentle stream
And make a pastime of each weary step,
Till the last step have brought me to my love,
And there I'll rest, as after much turmoil
A blessèd soul doth in Elysium.

LUCETTA
But in what habit will you go along? 39

JULIA
Not like a woman, for I would prevent 40
The loose encounters of lascivious men.
Gentle Lucetta, fit me with such weeds 42
As may beseem some well-reputed page. 43

LUCETTA
Why, then, your ladyship must cut your hair.

JULIA
No, girl, I'll knit it up in silken strings
With twenty odd-conceited true-love knots. 46
To be fantastic may become a youth 47
Of greater time than I shall show to be. 48

LUCETTA
What fashion, madam, shall I make your breeches?

JULIA
That fits as well as "Tell me, good my lord,

What compass will you wear your farthingale?" 51
Why, ev'n what fashion thou best likes, Lucetta.

LUCETTA
You must needs have them with a codpiece, madam. 53

JULIA
Out, out, Lucetta! That will be ill-favored. 54

LUCETTA
A round hose, madam, now's not worth a pin, 55
Unless you have a codpiece to stick pins on. 56

JULIA
Lucetta, as thou lov'st me, let me have
What thou think'st meet and is most mannerly.
But tell me, wench, how will the world repute me
For undertaking so unstaid a journey? 60
I fear me it will make me scandalized.

LUCETTA
If you think so, then stay at home and go not.

JULIA Nay, that I will not.

LUCETTA
Then never dream on infamy, but go.
If Proteus like your journey when you come,
No matter who's displeased when you are gone.
I fear me he will scarce be pleased withal. 67

JULIA
That is the least, Lucetta, of my fear.
A thousand oaths, an ocean of his tears,
And instances of infinite of love 70
Warrant me welcome to my Proteus.

LUCETTA
All these are servants to deceitful men.

JULIA
Base men, that use them to so base effect!
But truer stars did govern Proteus' birth;
His words are bonds, his oaths are oracles, 75
His love sincere, his thoughts immaculate,
His tears pure messengers sent from his heart,
His heart as far from fraud as heaven from earth.

LUCETTA
Pray heav'n he prove so when you come to him!

JULIA
Now, as thou lov'st me, do him not that wrong
To bear a hard opinion of his truth. 81
Only deserve my love by loving him,
And presently go with me to my chamber
To take a note of what I stand in need of
To furnish me upon my longing journey. 85
All that is mine I leave at thy dispose, 86
My goods, my lands, my reputation;
Only, in lieu thereof, dispatch me hence.
Come, answer not, but to it presently.
I am impatient of my tarriance.   *Exeunt.* 90

---

51 **compass** circumference, fullness. **farthingale** hooped petticoat
53 **must needs** will have to. **codpiece** bagged appendage to the front
of close-fitting hose or breeches, often conspicuous and ornamented
54 **Out** (An expression of reproach or indignation.) **ill-favored** unsightly 55 **round hose** padded breeches 56 **stick pins on** (One
method used to decorate the codpiece.) 60 **unstaid** immodest, unconventional 67 **withal** with it 70 **infinite** infinity 75 **oracles** infallible indicators 81 **truth** faithfulness 85 **longing** prompted by longing 86 **at thy dispose** in your charge 90 **tarriance** delaying

10 **measure** traverse 16 **dearth** famine 18 **inly** inward 22 **qualify**
control, moderate 28 **enameled** having shiny, polished surfaces;
variegated 29 **sedge** grassy, rushlike plant 32 **wild** open 39 **habit**
apparel 40 **prevent** forestall 42 **weeds** garments 43 **beseem** suit
46 **odd-conceited** strangely devised 47 **fantastic** fanciful (in appearance) 48 **Of greater time** of more years

❖

3.1   *Enter [the] Duke, Thurio, [and] Proteus.*

DUKE
Sir Thurio, give us leave, I pray, awhile.   1
We have some secrets to confer about.   [*Exit Thurio.*]
Now, tell me, Proteus, what's your will with me?

PROTEUS
My gracious lord, that which I would discover   4
The law of friendship bids me to conceal;
But when I call to mind your gracious favors
Done to me, undeserving as I am,
My duty pricks me on to utter that   8
Which else no worldly good should draw from me.
Know, worthy prince, Sir Valentine, my friend,
This night intends to steal away your daughter.
Myself am one made privy to the plot.   12
I know you have determined to bestow her
On Thurio, whom your gentle daughter hates;
And should she thus be stol'n away from you,
It would be much vexation to your age.
Thus, for my duty's sake, I rather chose
To cross my friend in his intended drift   18
Than, by concealing it, heap on your head
A pack of sorrows which would press you down,
Being unprevented, to your timeless grave.   21

DUKE
Proteus, I thank thee for thine honest care,
Which to requite, command me while I live.   23
This love of theirs myself have often seen,
Haply when they have judged me fast asleep,
And oftentimes have purposed to forbid
Sir Valentine her company and my court.
But, fearing lest my jealous aim might err,   28
And so unworthily disgrace the man—
A rashness that I ever yet have shunned—
I gave him gentle looks, thereby to find
That which thyself hast now disclosed to me.
And, that thou mayst perceive my fear of this,
Knowing that tender youth is soon suggested,   34
I nightly lodge her in an upper tower,
The key whereof myself have ever kept;
And thence she cannot be conveyed away.

PROTEUS
Know, noble lord, they have devised a means
How he her chamber window will ascend
And with a corded ladder fetch her down;
For which the youthful lover now is gone,
And this way comes he with it presently,   42
Where, if it please you, you may intercept him.
But, good my lord, do it so cunningly
That my discovery be not aimèd at;   45
For, love of you, not hate unto my friend,   46

Hath made me publisher of this pretense.   47

DUKE
Upon mine honor, he shall never know
That I had any light from thee of this.

PROTEUS
Adieu, my lord. Sir Valentine is coming.   [*Exit.*]

*[Enter] Valentine, [hurrying elsewhere, concealing
a rope ladder beneath his cloak].*

DUKE
Sir Valentine, whither away so fast?

VALENTINE
Please it Your Grace, there is a messenger
That stays to bear my letters to my friends,
And I am going to deliver them.

DUKE   Be they of much import?

VALENTINE
The tenor of them doth but signify
My health and happy being at your court.

DUKE
Nay then, no matter. Stay with me awhile.
I am to break with thee of some affairs   59
That touch me near, wherein thou must be secret.   60
'Tis not unknown to thee that I have sought
To match my friend Sir Thurio to my daughter.

VALENTINE
I know it well, my lord, and sure the match
Were rich and honorable. Besides, the gentleman   64
Is full of virtue, bounty, worth, and qualities   65
Beseeming such a wife as your fair daughter.   66
Cannot Your Grace win her to fancy him?

DUKE
No, trust me. She is peevish, sullen, froward,   68
Proud, disobedient, stubborn, lacking duty,
Neither regarding that she is my child
Nor fearing me as if I were her father.
And, may I say to thee, this pride of hers,
Upon advice, hath drawn my love from her;   73
And, where I thought the remnant of mine age   74
Should have been cherished by her childlike duty,
I now am full resolved to take a wife,
And turn her out to who will take her in.   77
Then let her beauty be her wedding dower,
For me and my possessions she esteems not.

VALENTINE
What would Your Grace have me to do in this?

DUKE
There is a lady in Verona here   81
Whom I affect, but she is nice and coy   82
And naught esteems my agèd eloquence.
Now therefore would I have thee to my tutor—   84
For long agone I have forgot to court;   85

3.1. Location: Milan. The Duke's palace.
1 give us leave (A polite form of dismissal.)   4 discover reveal
8 pricks spurs   12 Myself . . . plot I am one who has been given private knowledge of the plot   18 cross thwart.   drift scheme   21 timeless untimely   23 command me ask any favor of me   28 jealous aim
suspicious conjecture   34 suggested tempted   42 presently now
45 discovery disclosure.   aimèd at guessed   46 For because

47 publisher proclaimer.   pretense intention   59 I am . . . thee of I
wish to disclose to you   60 touch me near are of vital concern to me
64 Were would be   65 virtue good accomplishments.   qualities attainments   66 Beseeming befitting   68 peevish willful.   froward perverse   73 Upon advice after some careful consideration   74 where
whereas   77 who whoever   81 Verona (An error for Milan, seemingly, but Verona fits the line metrically. Some editors emend "in Verona" to "of Verona.")   82 affect am fond of.   nice difficult to
please   84 to as, for   85 agone ago.   forgot forgotten how

Besides, the fashion of the time is changed—
How and which way I may bestow myself 87
To be regarded in her sun-bright eye.

VALENTINE
Win her with gifts if she respect not words. 89
Dumb jewels often in their silent kind 90
More than quick words do move a woman's mind. 91

DUKE
But she did scorn a present that I sent her.

VALENTINE
A woman sometimes scorns what best contents her.
Send her another. Never give her o'er,
For scorn at first makes after-love the more.
If she do frown, 'tis not in hate of you,
But rather to beget more love in you.
If she do chide, 'tis not to have you gone,
Forwhy the fools are mad if left alone. 99
Take no repulse, whatever she doth say;
For "Get you gone," she doth not mean "Away!" 101
Flatter and praise, commend, extol their graces;
Though ne'er so black, say they have angels' faces. 103
That man that hath a tongue, I say, is no man
If with his tongue he cannot win a woman.

DUKE
But she I mean is promised by her friends 106
Unto a youthful gentleman of worth,
And kept severely from resort of men,
That no man hath access by day to her. 109

VALENTINE
Why then I would resort to her by night.

DUKE
Ay, but the doors be locked and keys kept safe,
That no man hath recourse to her by night.

VALENTINE
What lets but one may enter at her window? 113

DUKE
Her chamber is aloft, far from the ground,
And built so shelving that one cannot climb it 115
Without apparent hazard of his life. 116

VALENTINE
Why then, a ladder quaintly made of cords 117
To cast up, with a pair of anchoring hooks,
Would serve to scale another Hero's tower, 119
So bold Leander would adventure it. 120

DUKE
Now, as thou art a gentleman of blood, 121
Advise me where I may have such a ladder.

VALENTINE
When would you use it? Pray, sir, tell me that.

DUKE
This very night; for Love is like a child
That longs for everything that he can come by.

VALENTINE
By seven o'clock I'll get you such a ladder.

DUKE
But hark thee, I will go to her alone.
How shall I best convey the ladder thither?

VALENTINE
It will be light, my lord, that you may bear it
Under a cloak that is of any length. 130

DUKE
A cloak as long as thine will serve the turn? 131

VALENTINE
Ay, my good lord.

DUKE   Then let me see thy cloak.
I'll get me one of such another length. 133

VALENTINE
Why, any cloak will serve the turn, my lord.

DUKE
How shall I fashion me to wear a cloak?
I pray thee, let me feel thy cloak upon me.
          [He pulls open Valentine's cloak.]
What letter is this same? What's here? "To Sylvia"?
And here an engine fit for my proceeding. 138
I'll be so bold to break the seal for once.   [He reads.]
"My thoughts do harbor with my Sylvia nightly, 140
    And slaves they are to me, that send them flying.
O, could their master come and go as lightly, 142
    Himself would lodge where, senseless, they are
        lying! 143
My herald thoughts in thy pure bosom rest them, 144
    While I, their king, that thither them importune, 145
Do curse the grace that with such grace hath blessed
        them, 146
    Because myself do want my servants' fortune. 147
I curse myself for they are sent by me, 148
That they should harbor where their lord should be."
What's here?
"Sylvia, this night I will enfranchise thee."
'Tis so; and here's the ladder for the purpose.
Why, Phaëthon, for thou art Merops' son, 153
Wilt thou aspire to guide the heavenly car,
And with thy daring folly burn the world?
Wilt thou reach stars because they shine on thee? 156
Go, base intruder, overweening slave! 157
Bestow thy fawning smiles on equal mates, 158
And think my patience, more than thy desert,
Is privilege for thy departure hence. 160
Thank me for this more than for all the favors
Which, all too much, I have bestowed on thee.

87 bestow behave, conduct   89 respect heed   90 kind nature
91 quick lively (as contrasted with Dumb, silent)   99 Forwhy because
101 For by   103 black dark of complexion   106 friends i.e.,
relatives   109 That so that. (Also in line 112.)   113 lets hinders
115 shelving projecting, overhanging   116 apparent plain, evident
117 quaintly skillfully   119, 120 Hero's, Leander (See the note to
1.1.22.)   120 So provided   121 blood good family

130 of any length tolerably long   131 turn purpose   133 such another the same   138 engine contrivance, i.e., the rope ladder
140 harbor reside   142 lightly easily, quickly   143 senseless insensible.   lying dwelling   144 them themselves   145 importune command   146 grace . . . grace good fortune, graciousness . . . charm,
favor   147 want lack   148 for since   153 Phaëthon, Merops (Phaëthon was the son of Helios, the sun god, and of Clymene, lawful wife
of Merops. Phaëthon aspired to guide the sun god's car [line 154] or
chariot and was slain by Zeus for his presumption after he had
scorched a large portion of the earth.)   for just because   156 reach
reach for   157 overweening presumptuous   158 equal mates i.e.,
women of your own social status   160 Is privilege for authorizes,
grants

But if thou linger in my territories
Longer than swiftest expedition   164
Will give thee time to leave our royal court,
By heaven, my wrath shall far exceed the love
I ever bore my daughter or thyself.
Begone! I will not hear thy vain excuse,
But, as thou lov'st thy life, make speed from hence.
                                                        [*Exit.*]

VALENTINE
And why not death rather than living torment?
To die is to be banished from myself,
And Sylvia is myself. Banished from her
Is self from self—a deadly banishment!
What light is light, if Sylvia be not seen?
What joy is joy, if Sylvia be not by?
Unless it be to think that she is by
And feed upon the shadow of perfection.   177
Except I be by Sylvia in the night,   178
There is no music in the nightingale;
Unless I look on Sylvia in the day,
There is no day for me to look upon.
She is my essence, and I leave to be   182
If I be not by her fair influence   183
Fostered, illumined, cherished, kept alive.
I fly not death, to fly his deadly doom;   185
Tarry I here, I but attend on death,   186
But, fly I hence, I fly away from life.

[*Enter Proteus and*] *Lance.*

PROTEUS   Run, boy, run, run, and seek him out.
LANCE   So-ho, so-ho!   189
PROTEUS   What seest thou?
LANCE   Him we go to find. There's not a hair on 's head   191
but 'tis a Valentine.   192
PROTEUS   Valentine?
VALENTINE   No.
PROTEUS   Who then? His spirit?
VALENTINE   Neither.
PROTEUS   What then?
VALENTINE   Nothing.
LANCE   Can nothing speak? Master, shall I strike?   199
PROTEUS   Who wouldst thou strike?
LANCE   Nothing.
PROTEUS   Villain, forbear.
LANCE   Why, sir, I'll strike nothing. I pray you—
PROTEUS   Sirrah, I say, forbear. Friend Valentine, a
word.
VALENTINE
My ears are stopped and cannot hear good news,
So much of bad already hath possessed them.

PROTEUS
Then in dumb silence will I bury mine,   208
For they are harsh, untunable, and bad.   209
VALENTINE   Is Sylvia dead?
PROTEUS   No, Valentine.
VALENTINE
No Valentine, indeed, for sacred Sylvia.   212
Hath she forsworn me?
PROTEUS   No, Valentine.
VALENTINE
No Valentine, if Sylvia have forsworn me.
What is your news?
LANCE   Sir, there is a proclamation that you are vanished.
PROTEUS
That thou art banished—O, that's the news!—
From hence, from Sylvia, and from me thy friend.
VALENTINE
O, I have fed upon this woe already,
And now excess of it will make me surfeit.
Doth Sylvia know that I am banished?
PROTEUS
Ay, ay; and she hath offered to the doom—   223
Which, unreversed, stands in effectual force—   224
A sea of melting pearl, which some call tears.
Those at her father's churlish feet she tendered;
With them, upon her knees, her humble self,
Wringing her hands, whose whiteness so became
   them
As if but now they waxèd pale for woe.
But neither bended knees, pure hands held up,
Sad sighs, deep groans, nor silver-shedding tears
Could penetrate her uncompassionate sire,
But Valentine, if he be ta'en, must die.   233
Besides, her intercession chafed him so,
When she for thy repeal was suppliant,   235
That to close prison he commanded her,   236
With many bitter threats of biding there.   237
VALENTINE
No more, unless the next word that thou speak'st
Have some malignant power upon my life;
If so, I pray thee, breathe it in mine ear,
As ending anthem of my endless dolor.   241
PROTEUS
Cease to lament for that thou canst not help,   242
And study help for that which thou lament'st.   243
Time is the nurse and breeder of all good.
Here if thou stay thou canst not see thy love;
Besides, thy staying will abridge thy life.
Hope is a lover's staff; walk hence with that
And manage it against despairing thoughts.   248
Thy letters may be here, though thou art hence,
Which, being writ to me, shall be delivered

---

164 expedition speed   **177 shadow** image   **178 Except** unless
182 leave cease   **183 influence** (An astrological term for the emana-
tions supposed to flow from the stars and to have power over the destinies of men.)   **185 I . . . doom** I shall not escape death by flying
from the Duke's sentence of death, or, from death's deadly sentence
186 Tarry I if I tarry.   **attend on** wait for   **189 So-ho** (Hunting cry
used when the game is sighted.)   **191 hair** (with pun on ''hare'')
192 Valentine (His name means ''token of true love.'')   **199 shall I
strike** (Lance wonders if he should strike at a *spirit,* line 195, to ward
off evil effects, as in *Hamlet,* 1.1.144.)

208 mine i.e., my news   **209 they** i.e., the news   **212 No Valentine**
(Valentine jests bitterly on the inappropriateness of his name and on
the loss of his very identity, playing on *No, Valentine* in the previous
line.)   **223 to the doom** i.e., to this news of the sentence
224 Which . . . force which, if not reversed, must certainly take effect   **233 But** but that   **235 repeal** recall from exile   **236 close**
tightly enclosed   **237 biding** permanently dwelling   **241 ending anthem** requiem   **242 that** what   **243 study** devise   **248 manage** wield

Even in the milk-white bosom of thy love.
The time now serves not to expostulate. 252
Come, I'll convey thee through the city gate,
And ere I part with thee confer at large 254
Of all that may concern thy love affairs.
As thou lov'st Sylvia, though not for thyself, 256
Regard thy danger, and along with me!

VALENTINE
I pray thee, Lance, an if thou seest my boy,
Bid him make haste and meet me at the north gate.

PROTEUS
Go, sirrah, find him out. Come, Valentine.

VALENTINE
O my dear Sylvia! Hapless Valentine!
    [*Exeunt Valentine and Proteus.*]

LANCE   I am but a fool, look you, and yet I have the
wit to think my master is a kind of a knave. But that's 263
all one, if he be but one knave. He lives not now that 264
knows me to be in love, yet I am in love. But a team of
horse shall not pluck that from me, nor who 'tis I love. 266
And yet 'tis a woman, but what woman, I will not tell
myself. And yet 'tis a milkmaid. Yet 'tis not a maid, for
she hath had gossips. Yet 'tis a maid, for she is her 269
master's maid, and serves for wages. She hath more
qualities than a water spaniel, which is much in a bare 271
Christian. [*Pulling out a paper.*] Here is the catalog of
her condition. "Imprimis: She can fetch and carry." 273
Why, a horse can do no more. Nay, a horse cannot 274
fetch, but only carry; therefore is she better than a 275
jade. "Item: She can milk." Look you, a sweet virtue in 276
a maid with clean hands.

    [*Enter*] Speed.

SPEED   How now, Signor Lance, what news with your
mastership?
LANCE   With my master's ship? Why, it is at sea. 280
SPEED   Well, your old vice still: mistake the word. What 281
news, then, in your paper?
LANCE   The black'st news that ever thou heardst.
SPEED   Why, man, how "black"?
LANCE   Why, as black as ink.
SPEED   Let me read them. 286
LANCE   Fie on thee, jolt-head! Thou canst not read. 287
SPEED   Thou liest. I can.
LANCE   I will try thee. Tell me this: who begot thee?
SPEED   Marry, the son of my grandfather.

LANCE   O illiterate loiterer! It was the son of thy grand- 291
mother. This proves that thou canst not read.
SPEED   Come, fool, come. Try me in thy paper.
LANCE   There. [*Giving him the paper.*] And Saint Nicho- 294
las be thy speed! 295
SPEED [*reads*]   "Imprimis: She can milk." 296
LANCE   Ay, that she can.
SPEED   "Item: She brews good ale."
LANCE   And thereof comes the proverb: "Blessing of
your heart, you brew good ale."
SPEED   "Item: She can sew."
LANCE   That's as much as to say, "Can she so?"
SPEED   "Item: She can knit."
LANCE   What need a man care for a stock with a wench, 304
when she can knit him a stock? 305
SPEED   "Item: She can wash and scour."
LANCE   A special virtue, for then she need not be
washed and scoured. 308
SPEED   "Item: She can spin."
LANCE   Then may I set the world on wheels, when she 310
can spin for her living. 311
SPEED   "Item: She hath many nameless virtues." 312
LANCE   That's as much as to say bastard virtues, that
indeed know not their fathers and therefore have no
names.
SPEED   Here follow her vices.
LANCE   Close at the heels of her virtues.
SPEED   "Item: She is not to be kissed fasting, in respect 318
of her breath." 319
LANCE   Well, that fault may be mended with a break-
fast. Read on.
SPEED   "Item: She hath a sweet mouth." 322
LANCE   That makes amends for her sour breath.
SPEED   "Item: She doth talk in her sleep."
LANCE   It's no matter for that, so she sleep not in her 325
talk.
SPEED   "Item: She is slow in words."
LANCE   O villain, that set this down among her vices!
To be slow in words is a woman's only virtue. I pray
thee, out with 't, and place it for her chief virtue.
SPEED   "Item: She is proud." 331
LANCE   Out with that too. It was Eve's legacy, and can-
not be ta'en from her.
SPEED   "Item: She hath no teeth."
LANCE   I care not for that neither, because I love crusts.
SPEED   "Item: She is curst." 336
LANCE   Well, the best is, she hath no teeth to bite.
SPEED   "Item: She will often praise her liquor." 338

252 expostulate discuss at length   **254 confer at large** discuss at length   **256 though not for thyself** even though not for your own sake   **263–264 that's . . . knave** i.e., it's all right so long as he's knavish in one thing only (that is, in love)   **264 He lives not now** there is no one alive   **266 horse** horses   **269 gossips** i.e., godparents to a child of hers.   **maid** (Lance quibbles on [1] maidservant [2] virgin. She is the first, even if no longer the second.)   **271 water spaniel** (A fawning, subservient kind of dog.)   **bare** (1) mere (2) naked, hairless   **273 condition** qualities.   **Imprimis** in the first place (to be followed, in a list, with each particular marked *Item*)   **274–275 cannot fetch** cannot be ordered to go and fetch something   **276 jade** (1) ill-conditioned mare (2) loose woman   **280 at sea** (1) on the high seas (2) adrift, at loose ends   **281 vice** (with added meaning of *Vice*, comic character in morality plays who speaks with double meaning)   **286 them** the news   **287 jolt-head** blockhead

291 loiterer idle person, lazy student   **294–295 Saint Nicholas** patron saint of scholars   **295 speed** protection (with a play on Speed's name)   **296 milk** (1) serve as a milkmaid (2) drain, bleed someone of money   **304 stock** dowry   **305 stock** stocking   **308 scoured** (1) scrubbed (2) beaten, drubbed. (*Washed* probably has a similar double meaning.)   **310 set . . . wheels** i.e., take life easy   **311 spin for her living** (Probably with a sexual double meaning, as in *Twelfth Night*, 1.3.100–102: "I hope to see a huswife take thee between her legs and spin it off.")   **312 nameless** inexpressible   **318–319 in respect of** on account of   **322 sweet mouth** sweet tooth (with a wanton sense)   **325 sleep** (with a pun on "slip"; pronunciation was similar)   **331 proud** (with additional meaning of "lascivious")   **336 curst** shrewish   **338 praise** appraise, taste

LANCE   If her liquor be good, she shall. If she will not,
I will, for good things should be praised.   340
SPEED   "Item: She is too liberal."   341
LANCE   Of her tongue she cannot, for that's writ down
she is slow of; of her purse she shall not, for that I'll
keep shut. Now, of another thing she may, and that 344
cannot I help. Well, proceed.
SPEED   "Item: She hath more hair than wit, and more
faults than hairs, and more wealth than faults."
LANCE   Stop there; I'll have her. She was mine and not
mine twice or thrice in that last article. Rehearse that 349
once more.
SPEED   "Item: She hath more hair than wit—"
LANCE   More hair than wit? It may be: I'll prove it. The
cover of the salt hides the salt, and therefore it is more 353
than the salt; the hair that covers the wit is more than
the wit, for the greater hides the less. What's next?
SPEED   "And more faults than hairs—"
LANCE   That's monstrous. O, that that were out!
SPEED   "And more wealth than faults."
LANCE   Why, that word makes the faults gracious. 359
Well, I'll have her; and if it be a match, as nothing is
impossible—
SPEED   What then?
LANCE   Why, then will I tell thee—that thy master
stays for thee at the north gate.   364
SPEED   For me?
LANCE   For thee? Ay, who art thou? He hath stayed for
a better man than thee.
SPEED   And must I go to him?
LANCE   Thou must run to him, for thou hast stayed so 369
long that going will scarce serve the turn.   370
SPEED   Why didst not tell me sooner? Pox of your love 371
letters!   [Exit.]
LANCE   Now will he be swinged for reading my 373
letter—an unmannerly slave, that will thrust himself
into secrets! I'll after, to rejoice in the boy's correction. 375
                                                  Exit.

❖

3.2   Enter [the] Duke [and] Thurio.

DUKE
Sir Thurio, fear not but that she will love you,
Now Valentine is banished from her sight.
THURIO
Since his exile she hath despised me most,
Forsworn my company, and railed at me,
That I am desperate of obtaining her.   5

DUKE
This weak impress of love is as a figure   6
Trenchèd in ice, which with an hour's heat   7
Dissolves to water and doth lose his form.   8
A little time will melt her frozen thoughts,
And worthless Valentine shall be forgot.

    [Enter] Proteus.

How now, Sir Proteus? Is your countryman,
According to our proclamation, gone?
PROTEUS   Gone, my good lord.
DUKE
My daughter takes his going grievously.
PROTEUS
A little time, my lord, will kill that grief.
DUKE
So I believe, but Thurio thinks not so.
Proteus, the good conceit I hold of thee—   17
For thou hast shown some sign of good desert—
Makes me the better to confer with thee.   19
PROTEUS
Longer than I prove loyal to Your Grace
Let me not live to look upon Your Grace.
DUKE
Thou know'st how willingly I would effect
The match between Sir Thurio and my daughter.
PROTEUS   I do, my lord.
DUKE
And also, I think, thou art not ignorant
How she opposes her against my will.   26
PROTEUS
She did, my lord, when Valentine was here.
DUKE
Ay, and perversely she persevers so.
What might we do to make the girl forget
The love of Valentine, and love Sir Thurio?
PROTEUS
The best way is to slander Valentine
With falsehood, cowardice, and poor descent,
Three things that women highly hold in hate.
DUKE
Ay, but she'll think that it is spoke in hate.
PROTEUS
Ay, if his enemy deliver it;   35
Therefore it must with circumstance be spoken   36
By one whom she esteemeth as his friend.
DUKE
Then you must undertake to slander him.
PROTEUS
And that, my lord, I shall be loath to do.
'Tis an ill office for a gentleman,
Especially against his very friend.   41
DUKE
Where your good word cannot advantage him   42
Your slander never can endamage him.

340 **praised** commended (with a play on the sense "appraise" in line
338)   341 **liberal** free   344 **another thing** (with bawdy suggestion,
playing on the idea of *her purse* which her husband is to *keep shut* to
strangers)   349 **Rehearse** repeat   353 **cover of the salt** lid of the salt
cellar.   **more** i.e., more visible or prominent, like hair on the head
359 **gracious** acceptable   364 **stays** waits   369 **run** i.e., not walk
(*go*, line 368) but run.   **stayed** tarried   370 **going** walking   371 **Pox**
i.e., a plague on   373 **swinged** thrashed   375 **correction** punishment
3.2. Location: Milan. The Duke's palace.
5 That so that

6 **impress** impression   7 **Trenchèd** cut   8 **his** its   17 **conceit** opinion
19 **the better** the rather, more willingly   26 **opposes her** contends
35 **deliver** speak   36 **circumstance** confirming detail   41 **very** true
42 **advantage** profit

Therefore the office is indifferent,   44
Being entreated to it by your friend.   45
PROTEUS
You have prevailed, my lord. If I can do it
By aught that I can speak in his dispraise,
She shall not long continue love to him.
But say this weed her love from Valentine,   49
It follows not that she will love Sir Thurio.
THURIO
Therefore, as you unwind her love from him,
Lest it should ravel and be good to none
You must provide to bottom it on me;   53
Which must be done by praising me as much
As you in worth dispraise Sir Valentine.
DUKE
And, Proteus, we dare trust you in this kind
Because we know, on Valentine's report,
You are already Love's firm votary
And cannot soon revolt and change your mind.
Upon this warrant shall you have access
Where you with Sylvia may confer at large;
For she is lumpish, heavy, melancholy,   62
And, for your friend's sake, will be glad of you,
Where you may temper her by your persuasion   64
To hate young Valentine and love my friend.
PROTEUS
As much as I can do, I will effect.
But you, Sir Thurio, are not sharp enough.
You must lay lime to tangle her desires   68
By wailful sonnets, whose composèd rhymes
Should be full-fraught with serviceable vows.   70
DUKE
Ay, much is the force of heaven-bred poesy.
PROTEUS
Say that upon the altar of her beauty
You sacrifice your tears, your sighs, your heart.
Write till your ink be dry, and with your tears
Moist it again, and frame some feeling line   75
That may discover such integrity.   76
For Orpheus' lute was strung with poets' sinews,   77
Whose golden touch could soften steel and stones,
Make tigers tame, and huge leviathans   79
Forsake unsounded deeps to dance on sands.
After your dire-lamenting elegies,
Visit by night your lady's chamber window
With some sweet consort. To their instruments   83
Tune a deploring dump. The night's dead silence   84
Will well become such sweet-complaining grievance.   85
This, or else nothing, will inherit her.   86

DUKE
This discipline shows thou hast been in love.   87
THURIO
And thy advice this night I'll put in practice.
Therefore, sweet Proteus, my direction-giver,
Let us into the city presently
To sort some gentlemen well skilled in music.   91
I have a sonnet that will serve the turn
To give the onset to thy good advice.   93
DUKE About it, gentlemen!
PROTEUS
We'll wait upon Your Grace till after supper,
And afterward determine our proceedings.
DUKE
Even now about it. I will pardon you.   *Exeunt.* 97

❧

4.1   *Enter certain Outlaws.*

FIRST OUTLAW
Fellows, stand fast. I see a passenger.   1
SECOND OUTLAW
If there be ten, shrink not, but down with 'em.

[Enter] Valentine [and] Speed.

THIRD OUTLAW
Stand, sir! And throw us that you have about ye.   3
If not, we'll make you sit, and rifle you.   4
SPEED *[to Valentine]*
Sir, we are undone. These are the villains
That all the travelers do fear so much.
VALENTINE   My friends—
FIRST OUTLAW
That's not so, sir. We are your enemies.
SECOND OUTLAW   Peace! We'll hear him.
THIRD OUTLAW
Ay, by my beard will we, for he is a proper man.   10
VALENTINE
Then know that I have little wealth to lose.
A man I am, crossed with adversity;   12
My riches are these poor habiliments,
Of which if you should here disfurnish me   14
You take the sum and substance that I have.
SECOND OUTLAW   Whither travel you?
VALENTINE   To Verona.
FIRST OUTLAW   Whence came you?
VALENTINE   From Milan.
THIRD OUTLAW   Have you long sojourned there?
VALENTINE
Some sixteen months, and longer might have stayed
If crooked fortune had not thwarted me.   22
FIRST OUTLAW   What, were you banished thence?

44 indifferent neither good nor bad   **45 your friend** i.e., the Duke
49 say . . . Valentine even supposing this should root out the love
she feels for Valentine   **53 bottom** wind, as a skein of thread
62 lumpish dull, spiritless   **64 temper** mould   **68 lime** birdlime, a
sticky substance smeared on twigs to ensnare small birds   **70 serviceable vows** vows of service   **75 frame** compose   **76 discover** reveal.
integrity true devotion   **77 Orpheus** legendary musician whose music had the power to move inanimate objects as well as animals.
sinews nerves   **79 leviathans** whales   **83 consort** company of musicians   **84 deploring** doleful.   **dump** mournful melody   **85 grievance**
grief   **86 inherit** put you in possession of

87 discipline teaching   **91 sort** choose   **93 To . . . to** to begin the
following of   **97 pardon you** i.e., excuse you your *waiting upon* or
attending upon me
4.1. Location: The frontiers of Mantua. A forest.
1 passenger traveler   **3 Stand** halt. (But the Third Outlaw puns on *sit,*
line 4, as the opposite of "stand up.")   **4 rifle** plunder   **10 proper**
good-looking   **12 crossed with** thwarted by   **14 disfurnish** deprive
22 crooked perverse, malignant

VALENTINE I was.
SECOND OUTLAW For what offense?
VALENTINE
For that which now torments me to rehearse:
I killed a man, whose death I much repent,   26
But yet I slew him manfully in fight
Without false vantage or base treachery.
FIRST OUTLAW
Why, ne'er repent it, if it were done so.
But were you banished for so small a fault?
VALENTINE
I was, and held me glad of such a doom.   32
SECOND OUTLAW Have you the tongues?   33
VALENTINE
My youthful travel therein made me happy,   34
Or else I had been often miserable.
THIRD OUTLAW
By the bare scalp of Robin Hood's fat friar,   36
This fellow were a king for our wild faction!   37
FIRST OUTLAW We'll have him. Sirs, a word.
    [The Outlaws confer in whispers.]
SPEED Master, be one of them;
    It's an honorable kind of thievery.
VALENTINE Peace, villain!   41
SECOND OUTLAW [returning to Valentine]
Tell us this: have you anything to take to?   42
VALENTINE Nothing but my fortune.
THIRD OUTLAW
Know, then, that some of us are gentlemen,
Such as the fury of ungoverned youth
Thrust from the company of awful men.   46
Myself was from Verona banished
For practicing to steal away a lady,   48
An heir, and near allied unto the Duke.
SECOND OUTLAW
And I from Mantua, for a gentleman
Who, in my mood, I stabbed unto the heart.   51
FIRST OUTLAW
And I for suchlike petty crimes as these.
But to the purpose—for we cite our faults
That they may hold excused our lawless lives;
And partly, seeing you are beautified
With goodly shape, and by your own report
A linguist, and a man of such perfection
As we do in our quality much want—   58
SECOND OUTLAW
Indeed, because you are a banished man,
Therefore, above the rest, we parley to you.   60
Are you content to be our general?
To make a virtue of necessity
And live, as we do, in this wilderness?

26 **rehearse** repeat 27 **I killed a man** (A lie, presumably intended to impress the outlaws.) 32 **held . . . doom** was pleased with such a light sentence 33 **the tongues** ability in foreign languages 34 **travel** (The Folio spelling, *trauaile*, may also suggest "laborious study.") 36 **friar** Friar Tuck 37 **were** would be suitable as. 41 **villain** i.e., you rogue 42 **anything to take to** any means of subsistence 46 **awful** law-abiding 48 **practicing** plotting 51 **mood** anger, displeasure 58 **quality** profession. **want** lack 60 **above the rest** for this reason chiefly. **parley to** confer with, negotiate with

THIRD OUTLAW
What sayst thou? Wilt thou be of our consort?   64
Say ay, and be the captain of us all.
We'll do thee homage and be ruled by thee,
Love thee as our commander and our king.
FIRST OUTLAW
But if thou scorn our courtesy, thou diest.
SECOND OUTLAW
Thou shalt not live to brag what we have offered.
VALENTINE
I take your offer and will live with you,
Provided that you do no outrages
On silly women or poor passengers.   72
THIRD OUTLAW
No, we detest such vile, base practices.
Come, go with us. We'll bring thee to our crews   74
And show thee all the treasure we have got.
Which, with ourselves, all rest at thy dispose. *Exeunt.*   76

❧

4.2   *Enter Proteus.*

PROTEUS
Already have I been false to Valentine,
And now I must be as unjust to Thurio.
Under the color of commending him   3
I have access my own love to prefer.   4
But Sylvia is too fair, too true, too holy
To be corrupted with my worthless gifts.
When I protest true loyalty to her,
She twits me with my falsehood to my friend.
When to her beauty I commend my vows,   9
She bids me think how I have been forsworn
In breaking faith with Julia, whom I loved.
And notwithstanding all her sudden quips,   12
The least whereof would quell a lover's hope,
Yet, spaniel-like, the more she spurns my love,
The more it grows and fawneth on her still.
But here comes Thurio. Now we must to her window
And give some evening music to her ear.

    [*Enter* Thurio [*and*] *musicians.*]

THURIO
How now, Sir Proteus, are you crept before us?
PROTEUS
Ay, gentle Thurio, for you know that love
Will creep in service where it cannot go.   20
THURIO
Ay, but I hope, sir, that you love not here.
PROTEUS
Sir, but I do, or else I would be hence.
THURIO   Who? Sylvia?

64 **consort** company 72 **silly** defenseless 74 **crews** bands 76 **dispose** disposal

4.2 Location: Milan. Outside the Duke's palace, under Sylvia's window.
3 **color** pretext 4 **prefer** urge 9 **commend** offer, direct 12 **quips** sharp, sarcastic remarks 20 **go** walk at an ordinary pace

PROTEUS   Ay, Sylvia—for your sake.

THURIO
I thank you for your own. Now, gentlemen,   24
Let's tune, and to it lustily awhile.   25

[Enter, at a distance, the] Host [of the inn, and]
Julia [disguised as a page. They talk apart.]

HOST   Now, my young guest, methinks you're ally-   26
cholly. I pray you, why is it?   27

JULIA   Marry, mine host, because I cannot be merry.

HOST   Come, we'll have you merry. I'll bring you where
you shall hear music and see the gentleman that you
asked for.   31

JULIA   But shall I hear him speak?

HOST   Ay, that you shall.

JULIA   That will be music.   *[Music plays.]*

HOST   Hark, hark!

JULIA   Is he among these?

HOST   Ay, but peace! Let's hear 'em.

Song

MUSICIAN
Who is Sylvia? What is she,
    That all our swains commend her?   39
Holy, fair, and wise is she;
    The heaven such grace did lend her,
That she might admirèd be.   42

Is she kind as she is fair?
    For beauty lives with kindness.   44
Love doth to her eyes repair   45
    To help him of his blindness,
And, being helped, inhabits there.

Then to Sylvia let us sing,
    That Sylvia is excelling.
She excels each mortal thing
    Upon the dull earth dwelling.
To her let us garlands bring.

HOST   How now? Are you sadder than you were before?
How do you, man? The music likes you not.   54

JULIA   You mistake. The musician likes me not.   55

HOST   Why, my pretty youth?

JULIA   He plays false, father.   57

HOST   How? Out of tune on the strings?

JULIA   Not so, but yet so false that he grieves my very
heartstrings.

HOST   You have a quick ear.

JULIA   Ay, I would I were deaf. It makes me have a slow   62
heart.

HOST   I perceive you delight not in music.

JULIA   Not a whit, when it jars so.   65

HOST   Hark, what fine change is in the music!   66

JULIA   Ay, that change is the spite.   67

HOST   You would have them always play but one thing?   68

JULIA   I would always have one play but one thing. But
Host, doth this Sir Proteus that we talk on often resort   70
unto this gentlewoman?

HOST   I tell you what Lance, his man, told me: he loved
her out of all nick.   73

JULIA   Where is Lance?

HOST   Gone to seek his dog, which tomorrow, by his
master's command, he must carry for a present to his
lady.

JULIA
Peace! Stand aside. The company parts.   78

[Julia and the Host stand aside.]

PROTEUS
Sir Thurio, fear not you. I will so plead
That you shall say my cunning drift excels.   80

THURIO
Where meet we?

PROTEUS   At Saint Gregory's well.

THURIO   Farewell.

[Exeunt Thurio and the musicians.]

[Enter] Sylvia [above, at her window].

PROTEUS
Madam, good even to your ladyship.

SYLVIA
I thank you for your music, gentlemen.
Who is that that spake?

PROTEUS
One, lady, if you knew his pure heart's truth,
You would quickly learn to know him by his voice.

SYLVIA   Sir Proteus, as I take it.

PROTEUS
Sir Proteus, gentle lady, and your servant.

SYLVIA
What's your will?

PROTEUS   That I may compass yours.   89

SYLVIA
You have your wish. My will is even this:
That presently you hie you home to bed.   91
Thou subtle, perjured, false, disloyal man!   92
Think'st thou I am so shallow, so conceitless,   93
To be seducèd by thy flattery,   94
That hast deceived so many with thy vows?

---

24 I thank . . . own i.e., it's just as well, for your own safety, that
you added that disclaimer   25 lustily heartily, with a will   26–
27 allycholly (A colloquial form of *melancholy*.)   31 asked for inquired about   39 swains youths, wooers   42 admirèd wondered at
44 beauty lives with kindness i.e., if she is kind also, her beauty will
be true beauty and not mere show   45 repair hasten, visit   54 likes
pleases   55 likes me not (1) displeases me with his music (2) does not
love me. (The first meaning is intended for the Host; the second is
hidden except from the audience.)   57 plays false (1) plays out of
tune (2) is unfaithful.   father (A form of address to an older man.)

62 deaf i.e., with an ear that is dead, not *quick* (line 61) in the sense
of "alive."   slow heavy (playing also on *slow* as the opposite of
quick)   65 jars is discordant   66 change modulation. (But Julia plays
on the sense of "fickleness.")   67 spite injury, annoyance   68 play
but one thing play only one musical piece. (But Julia plays on the
sense of "play only one role as lover"—probably with bawdy suggestion.)   70 talk on talk of   73 out of all nick i.e., beyond all reckoning   78 parts departs   80 drift scheme   89 will desire.   compass
yours (1) obtain your good will (2) perform your every wish   91 presently immediately.   hie hasten   92 subtle crafty   93 conceitless witless   94 To be as to be

Return, return, and make thy love amends.
For me, by this pale queen of night I swear,   97
I am so far from granting thy request
That I despise thee for thy wrongful suit,
And by and by intend to chide myself
Even for this time I spend in talking to thee.

PROTEUS
I grant, sweet love, that I did love a lady,
But she is dead.

JULIA [aside]   'Twere false, if I should speak it,   103
For I am sure she is not burièd.

SYLVIA
Say that she be, yet Valentine, thy friend,
Survives, to whom—thyself art witness—
I am betrothed. And art thou not ashamed
To wrong him with thy importunacy?   108

PROTEUS
I likewise hear that Valentine is dead.

SYLVIA
And so suppose am I, for in his grave,
Assure thyself, my love is burièd.

PROTEUS
Sweet lady, let me rake it from the earth.

SYLVIA
Go to thy lady's grave and call hers thence.
Or, at the least, in hers sepulcher thine.

JULIA [aside]   He heard not that.   115

PROTEUS
Madam, if your heart be so obdurate,
Vouchsafe me yet your picture for my love,
The picture that is hanging in your chamber.
To that I'll speak, to that I'll sigh and weep;
For since the substance of your perfect self
Is else devoted, I am but a shadow,   121
And to your shadow will I make true love.   122

JULIA [aside]
If 'twere a substance, you would, sure, deceive it   123
And make it but a shadow, as I am.   124

SYLVIA
I am very loath to be your idol, sir.
But since your falsehood shall become you well   126
To worship shadows and adore false shapes,
Send to me in the morning, and I'll send it.   128
And so, good rest.

PROTEUS   As wretches have o'ernight
That wait for execution in the morn.
                        [Exeunt Proteus and Sylvia separately.]

JULIA   Host, will you go?

HOST   By my halidom, I was fast asleep.   132

97 this pale . . . night i.e., the moon, Diana, goddess of chastity
103 if . . . it i.e., even if I should say such a thing in the sense that I
am slain in my heart by Proteus' faithlessness and thus transformed
into "Sebastian" **108 importunacy** importunity **115 He heard not
that** i.e., he will turn a deaf ear to such unwelcome talk **121 else**
elsewhere **121–122 I am . . . love** (Proteus plays on two meanings
of *shadow*: I am reduced to being nothing, but I will at least worship
your picture.) **123–124 If . . . I am** (Julia's rueful aside plays on the
antithesis of *substance* and *shadow*: If Sylvia's portrait were real like
her, you would be false to it and thus reduce it to emptiness, much as
I am driven to the use of disguise.) **126 since . . . well** i.e., since it
befits your false nature **128 Send** i.e., send a messenger **132 halidom** (Originally, a holy relic; here, a mild oath.)

JULIA   Pray you, where lies Sir Proteus?   133

HOST   Marry, at my house. Trust me, I think 'tis almost   134
day.

JULIA
Not so; but it hath been the longest night
That e'er I watched, and the most heaviest. [Exeunt.]   137

❧

4.3   Enter [Sir] Eglamour.

EGLAMOUR
This is the hour that Madam Sylvia
Entreated me to call and know her mind.
There's some great matter she'd employ me in.
Madam, madam!

        [Enter] Sylvia [above, at her window].

SYLVIA   Who calls?

EGLAMOUR   Your servant and your friend;
One that attends your ladyship's command.

SYLVIA
Sir Eglamour, a thousand times good morrow.

EGLAMOUR
As many, worthy lady, to yourself.
According to your ladyship's impose,   10
I am thus early come to know what service
It is your pleasure to command me in.

SYLVIA
O Eglamour, thou art a gentleman—
Think not I flatter, for I swear I do not—
Valiant, wise, remorseful, well accomplished.   15
Thou art not ignorant what dear good will   16
I bear unto the banished Valentine,
Nor how my father would enforce me marry
Vain Thurio, whom my very soul abhors.
Thyself hast loved, and I have heard thee say
No grief did ever come so near thy heart
As when thy lady and thy true love died,
Upon whose grave thou vowedst pure chastity.
Sir Eglamour, I would to Valentine,   24
To Mantua, where I hear he makes abode;
And, for the ways are dangerous to pass,   26
I do desire thy worthy company,
Upon whose faith and honor I repose.
Urge not my father's anger, Eglamour,
But think upon my grief, a lady's grief,
And on the justice of my flying hence
To keep me from a most unholy match,
Which heaven and fortune still rewards with
   plagues.   33
I do desire thee, even from a heart

133 lies lodges **134 Marry** indeed. (Originally, an oath, "by the Virgin Mary.") **house** inn. **Trust me** i.e., on my honor **137 watched**
stayed awake through
**4.3. Location: The same, early in the morning (and perhaps only a
short time after 4.2, which ends as it is "almost day," lines
134–135).**
10 impose command **15 remorseful** compassionate **16 dear** affectionate **24 would** wish to go **26 for** because **33 still** always. **rewards** reward

As full of sorrows as the sea of sands,
To bear me company and go with me;
If not, to hide what I have said to thee,
That I may venture to depart alone.

EGLAMOUR
Madam, I pity much your grievances,
Which, since I know they virtuously are placed,
I give consent to go along with you,
Recking as little what betideth me   42
As much I wish all good befortune you.   43
When will you go?

SYLVIA   This evening coming.

EGLAMOUR
Where shall I meet you?

SYLVIA   At Friar Patrick's cell,
Where I intend holy confession.

EGLAMOUR
I will not fail your ladyship.
Good morrow, gentle lady.

SYLVIA
Good morrow, kind Sir Eglamour.

                              Exeunt [separately].

❧

4.4   *Enter Lance [with his dog, Crab].*

LANCE   When a man's servant shall play the cur with
him, look you, it goes hard—one that I brought up of   2
a puppy, one that I saved from drowning when three
or four of his blind brothers and sisters went to it. I   4
have taught him, even as one would say precisely,
"Thus I would teach a dog." I was sent to deliver him
as a present to Mistress Sylvia from my master, and I
came no sooner into the dining chamber but he steps
me to her trencher and steals her capon's leg. O, 'tis a   9
foul thing when a cur cannot keep himself in all com-   10
panies! I would have, as one should say, one that takes   11
upon him to be a dog indeed, to be, as it were, a dog   12
at all things. If I had not had more wit than he, to take   13
a fault upon me that he did, I think verily he had been   14
hanged for 't; sure as I live, he had suffered for 't. You
shall judge. He thrusts me himself into the company
of three or four gentlemanlike dogs, under the Duke's
table. He had not been there—bless the mark!—a   18
pissing while but all the chamber smelt him. "Out   19
with the dog!" says one. "What cur is that?" says another. "Whip him out," says the third. "Hang him up,"
says the Duke. I, having been acquainted with the

smell before, knew it was Crab, and goes me to the   23
fellow that whips the dogs. "Friend," quoth I, "you
mean to whip the dog?" "Ay, marry do I," quoth he.
"You do him the more wrong," quoth I. " 'Twas I did
the thing you wot of." He makes me no more ado, but   27
whips me out of the chamber. How many masters
would do this for his servant? Nay, I'll be sworn I
have sat in the stocks for puddings he hath stolen, oth-   30
erwise he had been executed. I have stood on the pillory for geese he hath killed, otherwise he had suffered
for 't.—Thou think'st not of this now. Nay, I remember the trick you served me when I took my leave of
Madam Sylvia. Did not I bid thee still mark me and do
as I do? When didst thou see me heave up my leg and
make water against a gentlewoman's farthingale?   37
Didst thou ever see me do such a trick?

        [Enter] Proteus [and] Julia [disguised].

PROTEUS *[to Julia]*
Sebastian is thy name? I like thee well,
And will employ thee in some service presently.

JULIA
In what you please. I'll do what I can.

PROTEUS
I hope thou wilt. *[To Lance.]* How now, you
    whoreson peasant,   42
Where have you been these two days loitering?

LANCE   Marry, sir, I carried Mistress Sylvia the dog you
bade me.

PROTEUS   And what says she to my little jewel?   46

LANCE   Marry, she says your dog was a cur, and tells
you currish thanks is good enough for such a present.   48

PROTEUS   But she received my dog?

LANCE   No, indeed, did she not. Here have I brought
him back again.   *[He points to his dog.]*

PROTEUS   What, didst thou offer her this from me?

LANCE   Ay, sir, the other squirrel was stolen from me   53
by the hangman boys in the marketplace, and then   54
I offered her mine own, who is a dog as big as ten of
yours, and therefore the gift the greater.

PROTEUS
Go, get thee hence, and find my dog again,
Or ne'er return again into my sight.
Away, I say! Stayest thou to vex me here?
                              [Exit Lance with Crab.]
A slave, that still an end turns me to shame!—   60
Sebastian, I have entertainèd thee,   61
Partly that I have need of such a youth
That can with some discretion do my business—
For 'tis no trusting to yond foolish lout—
But chiefly for thy face and thy behavior,

---

42 Recking heeding, caring   **43 befortune** befall
4.4. Location: The same, some hours later.
2 of from   **4 blind** i.e., with eyes not yet opened.   **to it** i.e., to
drowning   **9 me** i.e., to my injury, to my detriment. (Compare lines
16, 23, and 27.)   **trencher** wooden dish or plate.   **capon's leg** leg
of a rooster, castrated to make the flesh succulent   **10 keep** restrain
11–12 one that takes upon him such a dog as undertakes   **12–13 a
dog at** adept at (but with literal meaning as well)   **13–14 to take
. . . did** to take the blame upon myself for the fault he did   **18 bless
the mark** (A phrase used to apologize for indecorous language.)
18–19 a pissing while a short while (but with literal meaning as well)

23 goes me i.e., I went   **27 wot of** know about.   **makes me** makes
30 puddings sausages made by stuffing animal entrails with spicy
minced meat, etc.   **37 farthingale** hooped petticoat   **42 whoreson
peasant** (A term of jocular familiarity.)   **46 jewel** (Proteus is thinking
of the small, elegant dog he intended as a present to Sylvia.)   **48 currish** i.e., mean-spirited (with a play on *cur*)   **53 squirrel** i.e., little
dog   **54 hangman** i.e., fit for the hangman   **60 still an end** continually.   **turns me to shame** brings shame upon me   **61 entertainèd**
taken into service

Which, if my augury deceive me not,
Witness good bringing up, fortune, and truth.   67
Therefore know thou, for this I entertain thee.
Go presently and take this ring with thee.
                                        [*He gives a ring.*]
Deliver it to Madam Sylvia.
She loved me well delivered it to me.   71

JULIA
It seems you loved not her, to leave her token.   72
She is dead, belike?

PROTEUS   Not so. I think she lives.   73

JULIA   Alas!

PROTEUS   Why dost thou cry "Alas"?

JULIA   I cannot choose but pity her.

PROTEUS   Wherefore shouldst thou pity her?

JULIA
Because methinks that she loved you as well
As you do love your lady Sylvia.
She dreams on him that has forgot her love;   80
You dote on her that cares not for your love.   81
'Tis pity love should be so contrary;
And thinking on it makes me cry "Alas!"

PROTEUS [*giving a letter*]
Well, give her that ring and therewithal   84
This letter. That's her chamber. Tell my lady
I claim the promise for her heavenly picture.
Your message done, hie home unto my chamber,
Where thou shalt find me, sad and solitary.   [*Exit.*]

JULIA
How many women would do such a message?
Alas, poor Proteus! Thou hast entertained
A fox to be the shepherd of thy lambs.
Alas, poor fool, why do I pity him   92
That with his very heart despiseth me?
Because he loves her, he despiseth me;
Because I love him, I must pity him.
This ring I gave him when he parted from me,
To bind him to remember my good will;
And now am I, unhappy messenger,
To plead for that which I would not obtain,
To carry that which I would have refused,
To praise his faith which I would have dispraised.   101
I am my master's true-confirmèd love,
But cannot be true servant to my master
Unless I prove false traitor to myself.
Yet will I woo for him, but yet so coldly
As, heaven it knows, I would not have him speed.   106

        [*Enter*] Sylvia [*attended*].

Gentlewoman, good day! I pray you, be my means
To bring me where to speak with Madam Sylvia.   108

SYLVIA
What would you with her, if that I be she?

67 **Witness** bear witness to   71 **delivered** who gave   72 **leave** part
with   73 **belike** perhaps   80 **him that** one who (i.e., Proteus)
81 **her** i.e., Sylvia   84 **therewithal** with it   92 **poor fool** i.e., Julia
herself   101 **would have** desire to have   106 **speed** succeed.   **s.d.
Enter Sylvia** (Perhaps the location of the scene has shifted by now to
inside the tower, near Sylvia's chamber [see line 85]. Earlier, at
4.2.81 s.d., she appeared at her window, above.)   108 **where to**
where I may

JULIA
If you be she, I do entreat your patience
To hear me speak the message I am sent on.

SYLVIA   From whom?

JULIA   From my master, Sir Proteus, madam.

SYLVIA   O, he sends you for a picture?

JULIA   Ay, madam.

SYLVIA   Ursula, bring my picture there.   116
                    [*A servant brings a picture.*]
Go, give your master this. Tell him from me,
One Julia, that his changing thoughts forget,
Would better fit his chamber than this shadow.

JULIA
Madam, please you peruse this letter.—
        [*She offers a letter but then withdraws it.*]
Pardon me, madam, I have unadvised   121
Delivered you a paper that I should not.
                    [*She gives another letter.*]
This is the letter to your ladyship.

SYLVIA
I pray thee, let me look on that again.

JULIA
It may not be. Good madam, pardon me.

SYLVIA   There, hold!
I will not look upon your master's lines.
I know they are stuffed with protestations
And full of newfound oaths, which he will break   129
As easily as I do tear his paper.   [*She tears the letter.*]

JULIA [*offering the ring*]
Madam, he sends your ladyship this ring.

SYLVIA
The more shame for him that he sends it me,
For I have heard him say a thousand times
His Julia gave it him at his departure.
Though his false finger have profaned the ring,
Mine shall not do his Julia so much wrong.

JULIA   She thanks you.

SYLVIA   What sayst thou?

JULIA
I thank you, madam, that you tender her.   139
Poor gentlewoman! My master wrongs her much.

SYLVIA   Dost thou know her?

JULIA
Almost as well as I do know myself.
To think upon her woes I do protest
That I have wept a hundred several times.   144

SYLVIA
Belike she thinks that Proteus hath forsook her?

JULIA
I think she doth, and that's her cause of sorrow.

SYLVIA   Is she not passing fair?   147

JULIA
She hath been fairer, madam, than she is.
When she did think my master loved her well,
She, in my judgment, was as fair as you;

116 **s.d. A servant . . . picture** (Perhaps the servant, anticipating its
need, has brought the picture onstage, since Sylvia promised at
4.2.128 to give it to a messenger from Proteus.)   121 **unadvised** inadvertently   129 **newfound** recently devised   139 **tender** feel sympathetically toward   144 **several** different   147 **passing** surpassingly

But since she did neglect her looking glass
And threw her sun-expelling mask away,   152
The air hath starved the roses in her cheeks
And pinched the lily tincture of her face,
That now she is become as black as I.   155

SYLVIA   How tall was she?

JULIA
About my stature; for at Pentecost,   157
When all our pageants of delight were played,   158
Our youth got me to play the woman's part,
And I was trimmed in Madam Julia's gown,   160
Which servèd me as fit, by all men's judgments,
As if the garment had been made for me.
Therefore I know she is about my height.
And at that time I made her weep agood,   164
For I did play a lamentable part:
Madam, 'twas Ariadne, passioning   166
For Theseus' perjury and unjust flight;
Which I so lively acted with my tears
That my poor mistress, movèd therewithal,
Wept bitterly; and would I might be dead
If I in thought felt not her very sorrow!

SYLVIA
She is beholding to thee, gentle youth.   172
Alas, poor lady, desolate and left!
I weep myself to think upon thy words.
Here, youth, there is my purse. [*She gives money.*] I
    give thee this
For thy sweet mistress' sake, because thou lov'st her.
Farewell.   [*Exit Sylvia, with attendants.*]

JULIA
And she shall thank you for 't, if e'er you know her—
A virtuous gentlewoman, mild and beautiful!
I hope my master's suit will be but cold,   180
Since she respects my mistress' love so much.   181
Alas, how love can trifle with itself!
Here is her picture. [*She looks at the picture.*] Let me
    see, I think
If I had such a tire, this face of mine   184
Were full as lovely as is this of hers;
And yet the painter flattered her a little,
Unless I flatter with myself too much.   187
Her hair is auburn, mine is perfect yellow;
If that be all the difference in his love,
I'll get me such a colored periwig.
Her eyes are gray as glass, and so are mine.
Ay, but her forehead's low, and mine's as high.   192

What should it be that he respects in her
But I can make respective in myself,   194
If this fond Love were not a blinded god?   195
Come, shadow, come, and take this shadow up,   196
For 'tis thy rival. [*She picks up the picture.*] O thou
    senseless form,   197
Thou shalt be worshiped, kissed, loved, and adored!
And, were there sense in his idolatry,   199
My substance should be statue in thy stead.   200
I'll use thee kindly for thy mistress' sake,
That used me so; or else, by Jove I vow,
I should have scratched out your unseeing eyes,
To make my master out of love with thee!   *Exit.*

❧

5.1   *Enter [Sir] Eglamour.*

EGLAMOUR
The sun begins to gild the western sky,
And now it is about the very hour
That Sylvia at Friar Patrick's cell should meet me.
She will not fail, for lovers break not hours
Unless it be to come before their time,
So much they spur their expedition.   6

        [*Enter*] *Sylvia.*

See where she comes.—Lady, a happy evening!

SYLVIA
Amen, amen! Go on, good Eglamour,
Out at the postern by the abbey wall.   9
I fear I am attended by some spies.   10

EGLAMOUR
Fear not. The forest is not three leagues off.
If we recover that, we are sure enough.   *Exeunt.* 12

❧

5.2   *Enter Thurio, Proteus, [and] Julia [disguised in
            page's attire].*

THURIO
Sir Proteus, what says Sylvia to my suit?

PROTEUS
O, sir, I find her milder than she was,
And yet she takes exceptions at your person.   3

THURIO   What, that my leg is too long?

PROTEUS   No, that it is too little.

THURIO
I'll wear a boot, to make it somewhat rounder.

---

152 sun-expelling mask mask to keep the complexion fair (considered more beautiful than a tan)   **155 black** of a dark complexion, tanned
157 Pentecost Whitsuntide (seven weeks after Easter)   **158 pageants of delight** delightful entertainments   **160 trimmed** dressed up
164 agood in earnest   **166 Ariadne** daughter of Minos, King of Crete. (Ariadne, having fallen in love with one of her father's captives, Theseus, gave him a clew of thread by which he was able to find his way out of the labyrinth. He fled with her but abandoned her on the island of Naxos.)   **passioning** sorrowing   **172 beholding** indebted, beholden
180 cold vain   **181 my mistress'** (Julia ironically refers thus to herself, as formerly beloved by her master, Proteus.)   **184 tire** headdress
187 flatter with myself (1) praise myself with flattery (2) flatter myself with deceiving hopes   **192 mine's as high** i.e., my forehead's no lower than hers. (High foreheads were much admired, as was yellow hair.)

194 But I can that I cannot.   **respective** worthy of regard (with a play on *respects*, line 193)   **195 fond** foolish   **196 shadow . . . shadow** i.e., the mere shadow of myself . . . the picture of Sylvia. (See also 4.2.120–124.)   **take . . . up** (1) pick up this picture (2) oppose, accept a challenge   **197 senseless** insensible   **199 sense** reason
200 My . . . stead i.e., my real person would be the object of his veneration, his idol, instead of Sylvia's mere picture
5.1. Location: Milan. An abbey.
6 expedition haste   **9 postern** small back or side door   **10 attended** followed (for hostile purposes)   **12 recover** reach.   **sure** safe
5.2. Location: Milan. The Duke's palace.
3 takes exceptions at finds fault with

JULIA [*aside*]
  But love will not be spurred to what it loathes.   7
THURIO   What says she to my face?
PROTEUS   She says it is a fair one.   9
THURIO
  Nay then, the wanton lies. My face is black.   10
PROTEUS
  But pearls are fair, and the old saying is,
  Black men are pearls in beauteous ladies' eyes.   12
JULIA [*aside*]
  'Tis true, such pearls as put out ladies' eyes,   13
  For I had rather wink than look on them.   14
THURIO   How likes she my discourse?
PROTEUS   Ill, when you talk of war.   16
THURIO
  But well, when I discourse of love and peace.
JULIA [*aside*]
  But better, indeed, when you hold your peace.   18
THURIO   What says she to my valor?
PROTEUS   O, sir, she makes no doubt of that.   20
JULIA [*aside*]
  She needs not, when she knows it cowardice.
THURIO   What says she to my birth?
PROTEUS   That you are well derived.   23
JULIA [*aside*]   True; from a gentleman to a fool.   24
THURIO   Considers she my possessions?
PROTEUS   O, ay, and pities them.   26
THURIO   Wherefore?
JULIA [*aside*]   That such an ass should owe them.   28
PROTEUS   That they are out by lease.   29

              [*Enter the*] *Duke.*

JULIA   Here comes the Duke.
DUKE
  How now, Sir Proteus? How now, Thurio?
  Which of you saw Eglamour of late?
THURIO   Not I.
PROTEUS   Nor I.
DUKE   Saw you my daughter?
PROTEUS   Neither.
DUKE   Why then,
  She's fled unto that peasant Valentine,   38
  And Eglamour is in her company.
  'Tis true, for Friar Laurence met them both
  As he in penance wandered through the forest.
  Him he knew well, and guessed that it was she,

But, being masked, he was not sure of it.   43
Besides, she did intend confession
At Patrick's cell this even, and there she was not.   45
These likelihoods confirm her flight from hence.
Therefore, I pray you, stand not to discourse,
But mount you presently and meet with me   48
Upon the rising of the mountain foot
That leads toward Mantua, whither they are fled.
Dispatch, sweet gentlemen, and follow me.   [*Exit.*] 51
THURIO
  Why, this it is to be a peevish girl,   52
  That flies her fortune when it follows her.   53
  I'll after, more to be revenged on Eglamour
  Than for the love of reckless Sylvia.   [*Exit.*] 55
PROTEUS
  And I will follow, more for Sylvia's love
  Than hate of Eglamour that goes with her.   [*Exit.*]
JULIA
  And I will follow, more to cross that love
  Than hate for Sylvia, that is gone for love.   *Exit.*

5.3   [*Enter*] *Sylvia,* [*led by*] *Outlaws.*

FIRST OUTLAW   Come, come,
  Be patient. We must bring you to our captain.
SYLVIA
  A thousand more mischances than this one   3
  Have learned me how to brook this patiently.   4
SECOND OUTLAW   Come, bring her away.
FIRST OUTLAW
  Where is the gentleman that was with her?   6
THIRD OUTLAW
  Being nimble-footed, he hath outrun us,
  But Moses and Valerius follow him.
  Go thou with her to the west end of the wood;
  There is our captain. We'll follow him that's fled.
  The thicket is beset; he cannot scape.   11
        [*Exeunt all but the First Outlaw and Sylvia.*]
FIRST OUTLAW
  Come, I must bring you to our captain's cave.
  Fear not. He bears an honorable mind
  And will not use a woman lawlessly.
SYLVIA
  O Valentine, this I endure for thee!   *Exeunt.*

5.4   *Enter Valentine.*

VALENTINE
  How use doth breed a habit in a man!   1

7 **spurred** incited (with a quibble on *boot*, i.e., "riding boot," in the preceding line)   9 **fair** i.e., pale. (Beneath the seeming compliment is a suggestion of effeminacy or fair-faced deception.)   10 **black** dark, tanned (as contrasted with *fair*, "light-skinned")   12 **pearls** i.e., rare and beautiful objects   13 **pearls** i.e., cataracts   14 **wink** close the eyes   16 **Ill . . . war** i.e., (1) you upset her with frightening talk of war (2) your absurd talk of war shows how ill-suited you are for manly pursuits   18 **hold your peace** are silent (with quibble on *peace* in previous line)   20 **makes . . . of** has no uncertainty about. (Another deliberately ambiguous reply.)   23 **derived** descended   24 **from . . . fool** (Julia plays on *derived* in another sense from that in line 23: "fallen away from, lowered.")   26 **pities** (1) shows concern for (2) despises   28 **owe** own   29 **out by lease** rented out. (If *possessions* in line 25 also suggests "possession by evil spirits," then Sylvia's contemptuous pity may be for the fact of their being *out by lease*, beyond Thurio's control.)   38 **peasant** i.e., base scoundrel

43 **being masked** i.e., since Sylvia was masked—perhaps with a *sun-expelling mask* (4.4.152) rather than a disguise   45 **even** evening   48 **presently** immediately   51 **Dispatch** make haste   52 **peevish** perverse   53 **flies her fortune** flees from her good fortune   55 **reckless** uncaring
5.3. Location: The frontiers of Mantua. The forest.
3 **more** greater   4 **learned** taught.   **brook** endure   6 **gentleman** i.e., Sir Eglamour   11 **beset** surrounded
5.4. Location: The forest.
1 **use** custom

This shadowy desert, unfrequented woods   2
I better brook than flourishing peopled towns.
Here can I sit alone, unseen of any,
And to the nightingale's complaining notes
Tune my distresses and record my woes.   6
O thou that dost inhabit in my breast,
Leave not the mansion so long tenantless,
Lest, growing ruinous, the building fall
And leave no memory of what it was!
Repair me with thy presence, Sylvia;
Thou gentle nymph, cherish thy forlorn swain!
                              [Shouting is heard within.]
What halloing and what stir is this today?
These are my mates, that make their wills their law,
Have some unhappy passenger in chase.   15
They love me well, yet I have much to do
To keep them from uncivil outrages.
Withdraw thee, Valentine. Who's this comes here?
                              [He stands aside.]

[Enter] Proteus, Sylvia, [and] Julia [disguised as
Sebastian].

PROTEUS
Madam, this service I have done for you—
Though you respect not aught your servant doth—   20
To hazard life and rescue you from him
That would have forced your honor and your love.
Vouchsafe me for my meed but one fair look;   23
A smaller boon than this I cannot beg,
And less than this, I am sure, you cannot give.
VALENTINE [aside]
How like a dream is this I see and hear!
Love, lend me patience to forbear awhile.
SYLVIA
O miserable, unhappy that I am!
PROTEUS
Unhappy were you, madam, ere I came;
But by my coming I have made you happy.
SYLVIA
By thy approach thou mak'st me most unhappy.   31
JULIA [aside]
And me, when he approacheth to your presence.
SYLVIA
Had I been seizèd by a hungry lion,
I would have been a breakfast to the beast
Rather than have false Proteus rescue me.
O, heaven be judge how I love Valentine,
Whose life's as tender to me as my soul!   37
And full as much—for more there cannot be—
I do detest false, perjured Proteus.
Therefore begone. Solicit me no more.
PROTEUS
What dangerous action, stood it next to death,
Would I not undergo for one calm look?   42
O, 'tis the curse in love, and still approved,   43
When women cannot love where they're beloved!

SYLVIA
When Proteus cannot love where he's beloved.
Read over Julia's heart, thy first, best love,
For whose dear sake thou didst then rend thy faith
Into a thousand oaths, and all those oaths
Descended into perjury, to love me.
Thou hast no faith left now, unless thou'dst two,
And that's far worse than none. Better have none
Than plural faith, which is too much by one.
Thou counterfeit to thy true friend!
PROTEUS   In love
Who respects friend?
SYLVIA   All men but Proteus.   54
PROTEUS
Nay, if the gentle spirit of moving words
Can no way change you to a milder form,
I'll woo you like a soldier, at arms' end,   57
And love you 'gainst the nature of love—force ye.
SYLVIA
O heaven!
PROTEUS [assailing her]   I'll force thee yield to my desire.
VALENTINE [coming forward]
Ruffian, let go that rude, uncivil touch,
Thou friend of an ill fashion!
PROTEUS   Valentine!   61
VALENTINE
Thou common friend, that's without faith or love!   62
For such is a friend now. Treacherous man,
Thou hast beguiled my hopes. Naught but mine eye
Could have persuaded me. Now I dare not say
I have one friend alive; thou wouldst disprove me.
Who should be trusted, when one's right hand
Is perjured to the bosom? Proteus,
I am sorry I must never trust thee more,
But count the world a stranger for thy sake.
The private wound is deepest. O time most accurst,
'Mongst all foes that a friend should be the worst!
PROTEUS
My shame and guilt confounds me.
Forgive me, Valentine. If hearty sorrow
Be a sufficient ransom for offense,
I tender 't here. I do as truly suffer   76
As e'er I did commit.
VALENTINE   Then I am paid,   77
And once again I do receive thee honest.   78
Who by repentance is not satisfied
Is nor of heaven nor earth. For these are pleased;   80
By penitence th' Eternal's wrath's appeased.
And, that my love may appear plain and free,
All that was mine in Sylvia I give thee.   82
JULIA   O me unhappy!   [She swoons.]
PROTEUS   Look to the boy.
VALENTINE   Why, boy! Why, wag! How now? What's   86
the matter? Look up. Speak.

---

2 desert deserted region   **6 record** sing   **15 Have** who have.   **unhappy passenger** unlucky traveler   **20 respect** heed   **23 meed** reward.   **fair** kind   **31 approach** amorous advances   **37 tender** dear   **42 undergo** undertake.   **calm** gentle, kind   **43 still approved** continually reaffirmed by experience

54 respects takes into consideration   **57 arms' end** sword's point (with bawdy suggestion)   **61 fashion** kind, sort   **62 common** ordinary, superficial   **76 tender** offer   **77 commit** sin   **78 receive** believe, acknowledge   **80 nor of** neither of.   **these** i.e., heaven and earth   **82 love** friendship   **86 wag** (A term of endearment for a youth.)

JULIA [*recovering*]   O good sir, my master charged me
to deliver a ring to Madam Sylvia, which, out of my
neglect, was never done.

PROTEUS
Where is that ring, boy?

JULIA [*giving her own ring*]   Here 'tis. This is it.

PROTEUS   How? Let me see.
Why, this is the ring I gave to Julia.

JULIA
O, cry you mercy, sir, I have mistook.   94
This is the ring you sent to Sylvia.
                              [*She offers another ring.*]

PROTEUS
But how cam'st thou by this ring? At my depart
I gave this unto Julia.

JULIA
And Julia herself did give it me;
And Julia herself hath brought it hither.
                              [*She reveals her identity.*]

PROTEUS   How? Julia?

JULIA
Behold her that gave aim to all thy oaths   101
And entertained 'em deeply in her heart.
How oft hast thou with perjury cleft the root!
O Proteus, let this habit make thee blush!   104
Be thou ashamed that I have took upon me
Such an immodest raiment, if shame live   106
In a disguise of love.   107
It is the lesser blot, modesty finds,
Women to change their shapes than men their
    minds.

PROTEUS
Than men their minds! 'Tis true. O heaven! Were man
But constant, he were perfect. That one error
Fills him with faults, makes him run through all th'
    sins;
Inconstancy falls off ere it begins.   113
What is in Sylvia's face but I may spy
More fresh in Julia's, with a constant eye?   115

VALENTINE
Come, come, a hand from either.
Let me be blest to make this happy close;   117
'Twere pity two such friends should be long foes.
                              [*Proteus and Julia join hands.*]

PROTEUS
Bear witness, heaven, I have my wish forever.

JULIA   And I mine.

          [*Enter the*] Duke [*and*] Thurio, [*led by*] Outlaws.

OUTLAWS   A prize, a prize, a prize!

VALENTINE
Forbear, forbear, I say! It is my lord the Duke.
                              [*The Duke and Thurio are released.*]

Your Grace is welcome to a man disgraced,
Banishèd Valentine.

DUKE   Sir Valentine!

THURIO [*advancing*]
Yonder is Sylvia, and Sylvia's mine.

VALENTINE [*drawing his sword*]
Thurio, give back, or else embrace thy death.   126
Come not within the measure of my wrath.   127
Do not name Sylvia thine; if once again,
Verona shall not hold thee. Here she stands.   129
Take but possession of her with a touch;
I dare thee but to breathe upon my love.

THURIO
Sir Valentine, I care not for her, I.
I hold him but a fool that will endanger
His body for a girl that loves him not.
I claim her not, and therefore she is thine.

DUKE
The more degenerate and base art thou,
To make such means for her as thou hast done   137
And leave her on such slight conditions.   138
Now, by the honor of my ancestry,
I do applaud thy spirit, Valentine,
And think thee worthy of an empress' love.
Know then I here forget all former griefs,   142
Cancel all grudge, repeal thee home again,   143
Plead a new state in thy unrivaled merit,   144
To which I thus subscribe: Sir Valentine,
Thou art a gentleman and well derived.
Take thou thy Sylvia, for thou hast deserved her.

VALENTINE
I thank Your Grace. The gift hath made me happy.
I now beseech you, for your daughter's sake,
To grant one boon that I shall ask of you.

DUKE
I grant it, for thine own, whate'er it be.

VALENTINE
These banished men, that I have kept withal,   152
Are men endued with worthy qualities.
Forgive them what they have committed here,
And let them be recalled from their exile.
They are reformèd, civil, full of good,
And fit for great employment, worthy lord.

DUKE
Thou hast prevailed. I pardon them and thee.
Dispose of them as thou know'st their deserts.
Come, let us go. We will include all jars   160
With triumphs, mirth, and rare solemnity.   161

VALENTINE
And, as we walk along, I dare be bold
With our discourse to make Your Grace to smile.
What think you of this page, my lord?

---

94 cry you mercy I beg your pardon   **101 gave aim to** was the object of   **104 habit** i.e., page's costume   **106–107 if shame . . . love** if a disguise undertaken for love can be thought shameful; or, if one who feigns love (such as Proteus) can feel shame   **113 Inconstancy . . . begins** i.e., inconstant love falls away from loving almost before it has even begun   **115 constant** steady, loyal   **117 close** union, conclusion

126 give back stand back   **127 measure** reach   **129 Verona** (Again, probably an error for *Milan*; see 3.1.81.)   **hold thee** keep you safe   **137 means** exertions   **138 on . . . conditions** on such easy terms   **142 griefs** grievances   **143 repeal** recall   **144 Plead . . . merit** i.e., I justify my abrupt reversal of my former judgment by arguing that there is a new state of affairs in your newly demonstrated superiority to Thurio   **152 kept withal** lived with   **160 include all jars** conclude all discords   **161 triumphs** festive celebrations.   **rare solemnity** marvelous festivity

DUKE
  I think the boy hath grace in him. He blushes.
VALENTINE
  I warrant you, my lord, more grace than boy.
DUKE   What mean you by that saying?
VALENTINE
  Please you, I'll tell you as we pass along,
  That you will wonder what hath fortunèd.   169
  Come, Proteus, 'tis your penance but to hear
  The story of your loves discoverèd.   171
  That done, our day of marriage shall be yours;
  One feast, one house, one mutual happiness.
                                                   Exeunt.

169 That so that. **wonder** marvel at. **fortunèd** happened **171 discoverèd** declared, disclosed

The Taming of the Shrew

Like his other early comedies, *The Taming of the Shrew* (c. 1592–1594) looks forward to Shakespeare's mature comic dramas in several ways. By skillfully juxtaposing two plots and an induction, or framing plot, it offers contrasting views on the battle of the sexes. This debate on the nature of the love relationship will continue through many later comedies. The play also adroitly manipulates the device of mistaken identity, as in *The Comedy of Errors,* inverting appearance and reality, dreaming and waking, and the master-servant relationship, in order to create a transformed Saturnalian world anticipating that of *A Midsummer Night's Dream* and *Twelfth Night.*

The induction sets up the theme of illusion, using an old motif known as "The Sleeper Awakened" (as found, for example, in *The Arabian Nights*). This device frames the main action of the play, giving to it an added perspective. *The Taming of the Shrew* purports, in fact, to be a play within a play, an entertainment devised by a witty nobleman as a practical joke on a drunken tinker, Christopher Sly. The jest is to convince Sly that he is not Sly at all, but an aristocrat suffering delusions. Outlandishly dressed in new finery, Sly is invited to witness a play from the gallery over the stage. In a rendition called *The Taming of a Shrew* (printed in 1594 and now generally thought to be taken from an earlier version of Shakespeare's play, employing a good deal of conscious originality along with some literary borrowing and even plagiarism), the framing plot concludes by actually putting Sly back out on the street in front of the alehouse where he was found. He awakes, recalls the play as a dream, and proposes to put the vision to good use by taming his own wife. Whether this ending reflects an epilogue now lost from the text of Shakespeare's play cannot be said, but it does reinforce the idea of the play as Sly's fantasy. Like Puck at the end of *A Midsummer Night's Dream,* urging us to dismiss what we have seen as the product of our own slumbering, Sly continually reminds us that the play is only an illusion or shadow.

With repeated daring, Shakespeare calls attention to the contrived nature of his artifact, the play. When, for example, Sly is finally convinced that he is, in fact, a noble lord recovering from madness and lustily proposes to hasten off to bed with his long-neglected wife, we are comically aware that the "wife" is an impostor, a young page in disguise. Yet this counterfeiting of roles is no more unreal than the employment of Elizabethan boy-actors for the parts of Katharina and Bianca in the "real" play. As we watch Sly watching a play, levels of meaning interplay in this evocative fashion. Again, the paintings offered to Sly by his new attendants call attention to art's ability to confound illusion and reality. In one painting, Cytherea is hidden by reeds "Which seem to move and wanton with her breath / Even as the waving sedges play wi' th' wind," and, in another painting, Io appears "As lively painted as the deed was done" (Induction, 2.50–56). Sly's function, then, is that of the naive observer who inverts illusion and reality in his mind, concluding that his whole previous life of tinkers and alehouses and Cicely Hackets has been unreal. As his attendants explain to him, "These fifteen years you have been in a dream; / Or when you waked, so waked as if you slept." We as audience laugh at Sly's naiveté, and yet we, too, are moved and even transformed by an artistic vision that we know to be illusory.

Like Sly, many characters in the main action of the play are persuaded, or nearly persuaded, to be what they are not. Lucentio and Tranio exchange roles of master and servant. Bianca's supposed tutors are, in fact, her wooers, using their lessons to disguise messages of love. Katharina is prevailed upon by her husband, Petruchio, to declare that the sun is the moon and that an old gentleman (Vincentio) is a fair young maiden. Vincentio is publicly informed that he is an impostor and that the "real" Vincentio (the Pedant) is at that very moment looking at him out of the window of his son Lucentio's house. This last ruse does not fool the real Vincentio, but it nearly succeeds in fooling everyone else. Baptista Minola is about to commit Vincentio to jail for the infamous slander of asserting that the supposed Lucentio is only a servant in disguise. Vincentio, as the newly arrived stranger, is able to see matters as they really are, but the dwellers of Padua have grown so accustomed to the mad and improbable fictions of their life that they are not easily awakened to reality.

Shakespeare multiplies these devices of illusion by combining two entirely distinct plots, each concerned, at least in part, with the comic inversion of appearance and reality: the shrew-taming plot involving Petruchio and Kate, and the more conventional romantic plot involving Lucentio and Bianca. The latter plot is derived from the *Supposes* of George Gascoigne, a play first presented at Gray's Inn in 1566, as translated from Ariosto's neoclassical comedy, *I Suppositi,* 1509. (Ariosto's work, in turn, was based upon Terence's *Eunuchus* and Plautus' *Captivi.*) The "Supposes" are mistaken identities or misunderstandings, the kind of hilarious farcical mix-ups with which Shakespeare had already experimented in *The Comedy of Errors.* Shakespeare has, as usual, both romanticized his source and moralized it in a characteristically English way. The heroine, who in the Roman comedy of Plautus and Terence would have been a courtesan, and who in *Supposes* is made pregnant by her clandestine lover, remains thoroughly chaste in Shakespeare's comedy. Consequently, she has no need for a pander, or go-between, such as the bawdy Duenna or Nurse of *Supposes.* The satire directed at the heroine's unwelcome old wooer is far less savage than in *Supposes,* where the "pantaloon," Dr. Cleander, is a villainously corrupt lawyer epitomizing the depravity of "respectable" society. Despite Shakespeare's modifications, however, the basic plot remains an effort to foil parental authority. The young lovers, choosing each other for romantic reasons, must fend off the materialistic calculations of their parents.

In a stock situation of this sort, the character types are also conventional. Gremio, the aged wealthy wooer, is actually labeled a "pantaloon" in the text (3.1.36−37) to stress his neoclassical ancestry. (Lean and foolish old wooers of this sort were customarily dressed in pantaloons, slippers, and spectacles on the Italian stage.) Gremio is typically "the graybeard," and Baptista Minola is "the narrow-prying father" (3.2.145−146). Even though Shakespeare renders these characters far less unattractive than in *Supposes,* their worldly behavior still invites reprisal from the young. Since Baptista Minola insists on selling his daughter Bianca to the highest bidder, it is fitting that her wealthiest suitor (the supposed Lucentio) should turn out in the end to be a penniless servant (Tranio) disguised as a man of affluence and position. In his traditional role as the clever servant of neoclassical comedy, Tranio skillfully apes the mannerisms of respectable society. He can deal in the mere surfaces—clothes or reputation—out of which a man's social importance is created, and can even furnish himself with a rich father. Gremio and Baptista deserve to be foiled, because they accept the illusion of respectability as real.

Even the romantic lovers of this borrowed plot are largely conventional. To be sure, Shakespeare emphasizes their virtuous qualities and their sincerity. He adds Hortensio (not in *Supposes*) to provide Lucentio with a genuine, if foolish, rival and Bianca with two wooers closer to her age than old Gremio. Lucentio and Bianca deserve their romantic triumph; they are self-possessed, witty, and steadfast to each other. Yet we know very little about them, nor have they seen deeply into each other. Lucentio's love talk is laden with conventional images in praise of Bianca's dark eyes and scarlet lips. At the play's end, he discovers, to his surprise, that she can be willful, even disobedient. Has her appearance of virtue concealed something from him and from us? Because the relationship between these lovers is superficial, they are appropriately destined to a superficial marriage as well. The passive Bianca becomes the proud and defiant wife.

By contrast, Petruchio and Kate are the more interesting lovers, whose courtship involves mutual self-discovery. Admittedly, we must not overstate the case. Especially at first,

these lovers are also stock types: the shrew tamer and his proverbially shrewish wife. Although Shakespeare seems not to have used any single source for this plot, he was well acquainted with crude, misogynistic stories demonstrating the need for putting women in their place. In a ballad called *A Merry Jest of a Shrewd and Curst Wife, Lapped in Morel's Skin* (printed c. 1550), for example, the husband tames his shrewish wife by flaying her bloody with birch rods and then wrapping her in the freshly salted skin of a plow horse named Morel. (This shrewish wife, like Kate, has an obedient and gentle younger sister who is their father's favorite.) Other features of Shakespeare's plot can be found in similar tales: the tailor scolded for devising a gown of outlandish fashion (Gerard Legh's *Accidence of Armory,* 1562), the wife obliged to agree with her husband's assertion of some patent falsehood (Don Juan Manuel's *El Conde Lucanor,* c. 1335), and the three husbands' wager on their wives' obedience (*The Book of the Knight of La Tour-Landry,* printed 1484). In the raw spirit of this sexist tradition, so unlike the refined Italianate sentiment of his other plot, Shakespeare introduces Petruchio as a man of reckless bravado who is ready to marry the ugliest or sharpest-tongued woman alive so long as she is rich. However much he may be later attracted by Kate's fiery spirit, his first attraction to her is crassly financial. Kate is, moreover, a thoroughly disagreeable young woman at first, described by those who know her as "intolerable curst / And shrewd and froward," and aggressive in her bullying of Bianca. She and Petruchio meet as grotesque comic counterparts.

At the play's end, the traditional pattern of male dominance and female acquiescence is still prominent. Kate achieves peace only by yielding to a socially ordained patriarchal framework in which a husband is the princely ruler of his wife. Kate is not like the young heroines of many other Shakespearean comedies (Portia in *The Merchant of Venice* and Rosalind in *As You Like It,* for example) who wittily guide their immature and overly romantic young men toward a pragmatic view of love and marriage; in this play, Kate is the one who must be taught by the self-assured male. Her shrewishness is an open threat to male control in the marital bond, and, accordingly, the play's comic finale celebrates containment of this threat in her, along with a sharp reminder of the torment to be endured by other husbands who have failed to tame their shrews.

Within this male-oriented frame of reference, however, Petruchio and Kate are surprisingly like Benedick and Beatrice of *Much Ado About Nothing.* Petruchio, for all his rant, is increasingly drawn to Kate by her spirit. As wit-combatants, they are worthy of one another's enmity—or love. No one else in the play is a fit match for either of them. Kate, too, is attracted to Petruchio, despite her war of words. Her guise of hostility is part defensive protection, part testing of his sincerity. If she is contemptuous of the wooers she has seen till now, she has good reason to be. We share her condescension toward the aged Gremio or the laughably inept Hortensio. She rightly fears that her father wishes to dispose of her so that he may auction off Bianca to the wealthiest competitor. Kate's jaded view of such marriage brokering is entirely defensible. Not surprisingly, she first views Petruchio, whose professed intentions are far from reassuring, as another mere adventurer in love. She is impressed by his "line" in wooing her but needs to test his constancy and sincerity. Possibly she is prepared to accept the prevailing Elizabethan view of marriage, with its dominant role for the husband, but only if she can choose a man deserving of her respect. She puts down most men with a shrewish manner that challenges their very masculinity; Petruchio is the first to be man enough to "board" her. Kate's rejection of men does not leave her very happy, however genuine her disdain is for most of those who come to woo. Petruchio's "schooling" is therefore curative. Having wooed and partly won her, he tests her with his late arrival at the marriage, his unconventional dress, and his crossing all her desires. In this display of willfulness, he shows her an ugly picture of what she herself is like. Most of all, however, he succeeds because he insists on what she, too, desires: a well-defined relationship, tempered by mutual respect and love. Kate is visibly a more contented person at the play's end. Her closing speech, with its fine blend of irony and self-conscious hyperbole, together with its seriousness of concern, expresses beautifully the way in which Kate's independence of spirit and her newfound acceptance of a domestic role are successfully fused.

The Taming of the Shrew

[Dramatis Personae

CHRISTOPHER SLY, *a tinker and beggar,*
HOSTESS *of an alehouse,*
A LORD,
A PAGE, SERVANTS, HUNTSMEN,
PLAYERS,

} *Persons in the Induction*

BAPTISTA, *a rich gentleman of Padua*
KATHARINA, *the shrew, also called Katharine and Kate, Baptista's elder daughter*
BIANCA, *Baptista's younger daughter*

PETRUCHIO, *a gentleman of Verona, suitor to Katharina*
GRUMIO, *Petruchio's servant*
CURTIS, NATHANIEL, PHILIP, JOSEPH, NICHOLAS, PETER, *and other servants of Petruchio*

GREMIO, *elderly suitor to Bianca*
HORTENSIO, *suitor to Bianca*
LUCENTIO, *son of Vincentio, in love with Bianca*
TRANIO, *Lucentio's servant*
BIONDELLO, *Lucentio's servant*
VINCENTIO, *a gentleman of Pisa*
A PEDANT (*or Merchant*) *of Mantua*
A WIDOW, *courted by Hortensio*

A TAILOR
A HABERDASHER
AN OFFICER
Other Servants of Baptista and Lucentio

SCENE: *Padua, and Petruchio's country house in Italy; the Induction is located in the countryside and at a Lord's house in England*]

Induction.1

Enter Beggar (Christopher Sly) and Hostess.

SLY   I'll feeze you, in faith.   1
HOSTESS   A pair of stocks, you rogue!   2
SLY   You're a baggage. The Slys are no rogues. Look in 3
the chronicles; we came in with Richard Conqueror. 4

Induction. 1. Location: Before an alehouse and, subsequently, before the Lord's house nearby. (See lines 75, 135.)
1 feeze you i.e., fix you, get even with you   **2 A . . . stocks** i.e., I'll have you put in the stocks   **3 baggage** contemptible woman or prostitute   **4 Richard** (Sly's mistake for "William.")

Therefore *paucas pallabris*, let the world slide. Sessa! 5

HOSTESS   You will not pay for the glasses you have
burst?

SLY   No, not a denier. Go by, Saint Jeronimy, go to thy 8
cold bed and warm thee. 9

HOSTESS   I know my remedy; I must go fetch the third- 10
borough.   *[Exit.]* 11

SLY   Third, or fourth, or fifth borough, I'll answer him 12
by law. I'll not budge an inch, boy. Let him come, and 13
kindly.   *Falls asleep.* 14

*Wind horns [within]. Enter a Lord from hunting,
with his train.*

LORD
Huntsman, I charge thee, tender well my hounds. 15
Breathe Merriman—the poor cur is embossed— 16
And couple Clowder with the deep-mouthed brach. 17
Sawst thou not, boy, how Silver made it good 18
At the hedge corner, in the coldest fault? 19
I would not lose the dog for twenty pound.

FIRST HUNTSMAN
Why, Bellman is as good as he, my lord.
He cried upon it at the merest loss, 22
And twice today picked out the dullest scent.
Trust me, I take him for the better dog.

LORD
Thou art a fool. If Echo were as fleet,
I would esteem him worth a dozen such.
But sup them well and look unto them all. 27
Tomorrow I intend to hunt again.

FIRST HUNTSMAN   I will, my lord.

LORD *[seeing Sly]*
What's here? One dead, or drunk? See, doth he
breathe?

SECOND HUNTSMAN *[examining Sly]*
He breathes, my lord. Were he not warmed with ale,
This were a bed but cold to sleep so soundly.

LORD
O monstrous beast, how like a swine he lies!
Grim death, how foul and loathsome is thine image! 34
Sirs, I will practice on this drunken man. 35
What think you, if he were conveyed to bed,
Wrapped in sweet clothes, rings put upon his
fingers,
37

A most delicious banquet by his bed, 38
And brave attendants near him when he wakes, 39
Would not the beggar then forget himself?

FIRST HUNTSMAN
Believe me, lord, I think he cannot choose. 41

SECOND HUNTSMAN
It would seem strange unto him when he waked.

LORD
Even as a flattering dream or worthless fancy. 43
Then take him up, and manage well the jest.
Carry him gently to my fairest chamber,
And hang it round with all my wanton pictures.
Balm his foul head in warm distillèd waters, 47
And burn sweet wood to make the lodging sweet.
Procure me music ready when he wakes,
To make a dulcet and a heavenly sound. 50
And if he chance to speak, be ready straight, 51
And with a low submissive reverence 52
Say, "What is it your honor will command?"
Let one attend him with a silver basin
Full of rosewater and bestrewed with flowers;
Another bear the ewer, the third a diaper, 56
And say, "Will 't please your lordship cool your
hands?"
Someone be ready with a costly suit,
And ask him what apparel he will wear;
Another tell him of his hounds and horse, 60
And that his lady mourns at his disease. 61
Persuade him that he hath been lunatic,
And when he says he is, say that he dreams, 63
For he is nothing but a mighty lord.
This do, and do it kindly, gentle sirs. 65
It will be pastime passing excellent, 66
If it be husbanded with modesty. 67

FIRST HUNTSMAN
My lord, I warrant you we will play our part
As he shall think by our true diligence 69
He is no less than what we say he is.

LORD
Take him up gently, and to bed with him,
And each one to his office when he wakes. 72
[Some bear out Sly.] Sound trumpets [within].
Sirrah, go see what trumpet 'tis that sounds. 73
[Exit a Servingman.]
Belike some noble gentleman that means, 74
Traveling some journey, to repose him here.

Enter [a] Servingman.

How now? Who is it?

SERVINGMAN   An 't please your honor, players 76
That offer service to your lordship.

---

5 paucas pallabris i.e., *pocas palabras,* "few words." (Spanish.)
Sessa (Of doubtful meaning; perhaps "be quiet," "cease," or "let it
go.")   **8 denier** French copper coin of little value.   **Go . . . Jeron-
imy** (Sly's variation of an often quoted line from Kyd's *The Spanish
Tragedy,* urging caution.)   **8–9 go . . . thee** (Perhaps a proverb; see
King Lear, 3.4.46–47.)   **10–11 thirdborough** constable   **12 Third**
(Sly shows his ignorance; the *third* in "thirdborough" derives from the
Old English word *frith,* "peace.")   **13 by law** in the law courts
14 kindly welcome. (Said ironically.)   **s.d. Wind** blow   **15 tender**
care for   **16 Breathe Merriman** give the dog Merriman time to recover its breath.   **embossed** foaming at the mouth from exhaustion
17 couple leash together.   **deep-mouthed brach** bitch hound with the
deep baying voice   **18 made it good** i.e., picked up the lost scent
19 in the coldest fault when the scent was lost by a *fault* or break in
the scent   **22 cried . . . loss** bayed to signal his recovery of the
scent after it had been completely lost   **27 sup them well** feed them a
good supper   **34 image** likeness (since sleep was regarded as a likeness of death)   **35 practice on** play a joke on   **37 sweet** perfumed

38 banquet light repast   **39 brave** finely arrayed   **41 cannot choose**
is bound to   **43 fancy** flight of imagination   **47 Balm** bathe, anoint
50 dulcet melodious   **51 straight** at once   **52 reverence** bow
56 ewer jug, pitcher.   **diaper** towel   **60 horse** horses   **61 disease**
i.e., mental derangement   **63 when . . . is** i.e., when he says he
must be mad indeed. (The *is* is stressed.)   **65 kindly** naturally (and
thus persuasively).   **gentle** kind   **66 passing** surpassingly   **67 husbanded with modesty** managed with decorum   **69 As** so that.   **by** as
a result of   **72 office** duty   **73 Sirrah** (Usual form of address to inferiors.)   **74 Belike** perhaps   **76 An 't** if it

Enter Players.

LORD
Bid them come near.—Now, fellows, you are welcome.
PLAYERS   We thank your honor.
LORD
Do you intend to stay with me tonight?
FIRST PLAYER
So please your lordship to accept our duty.   81
LORD
With all my heart. This fellow I remember
Since once he played a farmer's eldest son.—
'Twas where you wooed the gentlewoman so well.
I have forgot your name, but sure that part
Was aptly fitted and naturally performed.
SECOND PLAYER
I think 'twas Soto that your honor means.
LORD
'Tis very true. Thou didst it excellent.
Well, you are come to me in happy time,   89
The rather for I have some sport in hand   90
Wherein your cunning can assist me much.   91
There is a lord will hear you play tonight.
But I am doubtful of your modesties,   93
Lest, overeyeing of his odd behavior—   94
For yet his honor never heard a play—
You break into some merry passion   96
And so offend him; for I tell you, sirs,
If you should smile, he grows impatient.
FIRST PLAYER
Fear not, my lord, we can contain ourselves
Were he the veriest antic in the world.   100
LORD [*to a Servingman*]
Go, sirrah, take them to the buttery,   101
And give them friendly welcome every one.
Let them want nothing that my house affords.   103
                         Exit one with the Players.
Sirrah, go you to Barthol'mew my page,   104
And see him dressed in all suits like a lady.   105
That done, conduct him to the drunkard's chamber,
And call him "madam," do him obeisance.   107
Tell him from me, as he will win my love,   108
He bear himself with honorable action
Such as he hath observed in noble ladies
Unto their lords by them accomplishèd.   111
Such duty to the drunkard let him do
With soft low tongue and lowly courtesy,
And say, "What is 't your honor will command,
Wherein your lady and your humble wife
May show her duty and make known her love?"
And then with kind embracements, tempting kisses,

And with declining head into his bosom,   118
Bid him shed tears, as being overjoyed
To see her noble lord restored to health,
Who for this seven years hath esteemèd him   121
No better than a poor and loathsome beggar.
And if the boy have not a woman's gift
To rain a shower of commanded tears,
An onion will do well for such a shift,   125
Which in a napkin being close conveyed   126
Shall in despite enforce a watery eye.   127
See this dispatched with all the haste thou canst.
Anon I'll give thee more instructions.   129
                              Exit a Servingman.
I know the boy will well usurp the grace,   130
Voice, gait, and action of a gentlewoman.
I long to hear him call the drunkard husband,
And how my men will stay themselves from
   laughter   133
When they do homage to this simple peasant.
I'll in to counsel them. Haply my presence   135
May well abate the overmerry spleen   136
Which otherwise would grow into extremes.
                                       [*Exeunt.*]

✽

Induction.2

Enter aloft the drunkard [Sly], with attendants;
some with apparel, basin, and ewer and other
appurtenances; and Lord.

SLY   For God's sake, a pot of small ale.   1
FIRST SERVINGMAN
Will 't please your lordship drink a cup of sack?   2
SECOND SERVINGMAN
Will 't please your honor taste of these conserves?   3
THIRD SERVINGMAN
What raiment will your honor wear today?
SLY   I am Christophero Sly. Call not me "honor" nor
"lordship." I ne'er drank sack in my life; and if you
give me any conserves, give me conserves of beef. 7
Ne'er ask me what raiment I'll wear, for I have no
more doublets than backs, no more stockings than 9
legs, nor no more shoes than feet—nay, sometimes
more feet than shoes, or such shoes as my toes look 11
through the overleather.   12
LORD
Heaven cease this idle humor in your honor!   13

---

81 So please if it please. **duty** expression of respect **89 happy** opportune **90 The rather for** the more so since **91 cunning** professional skill **93 doubtful** apprehensive. **modesties** discretion, self-control **94 overeyeing of** witnessing **96 merry passion** outburst of laughter **100 veriest antic** oddest buffoon or eccentric **101 buttery** pantry, or a room for storing liquor (in butts) and other provisions **103 want** lack **104 Barthol'mew** (Pronounced "Bartlemy.") **105 in all suits** in every detail (with a pun on *suits* of clothes) **107 do him obeisance** show him dutiful respect **108 him** i.e., the page Bartholomew. **as he will** if he wishes to **111 by them accomplishèd** performed by the ladies

118 with . . . bosom bowing his head down onto his chest **121 him** himself **125 shift** purpose **126 napkin** handkerchief. **close** secretly **127 in despite** i.e., notwithstanding a natural inclination to laugh rather than cry **129 Anon** soon **130 usurp** assume **133 And how** i.e., and to see how **135 I'll in** I'll go in **136 spleen** mood. (The spleen was the supposed seat of laughter and anger.)
Induction. 2. Location: A bedchamber in the Lord's house.
s.d. aloft i.e., in the gallery over the rear facade of the stage **1 small** weak (and therefore cheap) **2 sack** sweet Spanish wine (suited for a gentleman to drink) **3 conserves** candied fruit **7 conserves of beef** preserved (salted) beef **9 doublets** men's jackets **11 as** that **12 overleather** upper leather of the shoe **13 idle** vain, foolish. **humor** whim, fancy

O, that a mighty man of such descent,
Of such possessions and so high esteem,
Should be infusèd with so foul a spirit!

SLY   What, would you make me mad? Am not I Chris-
topher Sly, old Sly's son of Burton-heath, by birth a 18
peddler, by education a cardmaker, by transmutation 19
a bearherd, and now by present profession a tinker? 20
Ask Marian Hacket, the fat alewife of Wincot, if she 21
know me not. If she say I am not fourteen pence on 22
the score for sheer ale, score me up for the lyingest 23
knave in Christendom. What, I am not bestraught: 24
here's—

THIRD SERVINGMAN
O, this it is that makes your lady mourn!

SECOND SERVINGMAN
O, this is it that makes your servants droop!

LORD
Hence comes it that your kindred shuns your house,
As beaten hence by your strange lunacy.   29
O noble lord, bethink thee of thy birth.
Call home thy ancient thoughts from banishment,   31
And banish hence these abject lowly dreams.
Look how thy servants do attend on thee,
Each in his office ready at thy beck.   34
Wilt thou have music? Hark, Apollo plays,   *Music.*   35
And twenty cagèd nightingales do sing.
Or wilt thou sleep? We'll have thee to a couch,
Softer and sweeter than the lustful bed
On purpose trimmed up for Semiramis.   39
Say thou wilt walk; we will bestrew the ground.   40
Or wilt thou ride? Thy horses shall be trapped,   41
Their harness studded all with gold and pearl.
Dost thou love hawking? Thou hast hawks will soar
Above the morning lark. Or wilt thou hunt?
Thy hounds shall make the welkin answer them   45
And fetch shrill echoes from the hollow earth.

FIRST SERVINGMAN
Say thou wilt course, thy greyhounds are as swift   47
As breathèd stags, ay, fleeter than the roe.   48

SECOND SERVINGMAN
Dost thou love pictures? We will fetch thee straight
Adonis painted by a running brook,   50
And Cytherea all in sedges hid,   51

Which seem to move and wanton with her breath,   52
Even as the waving sedges play wi' th' wind.

LORD
We'll show thee Io as she was a maid,   54
And how she was beguilèd and surprised,
As lively painted as the deed was done.   56

THIRD SERVINGMAN
Or Daphne roaming through a thorny wood,   57
Scratching her legs that one shall swear she bleeds,
And at that sight shall sad Apollo weep,
So workmanly the blood and tears are drawn.   60

LORD
Thou art a lord, and nothing but a lord.
Thou hast a lady far more beautiful
Than any woman in this waning age.   63

FIRST SERVINGMAN
And till the tears that she hath shed for thee
Like envious floods o'errun her lovely face,   65
She was the fairest creature in the world;
And yet she is inferior to none.   67

SLY
Am I a lord? And have I such a lady?
Or do I dream? Or have I dreamed till now?
I do not sleep: I see, I hear, I speak,
I smell sweet savors, and I feel soft things.
Upon my life, I am a lord indeed,
And not a tinker nor Christopher Sly.
Well, bring our lady hither to our sight,
And once again a pot o' the smallest ale.

SECOND SERVINGMAN
Will 't please your mightiness to wash your hands?
O, how we joy to see your wit restored!   77
O, that once more you knew but what you are!   78
These fifteen years you have been in a dream,
Or when you waked, so waked as if you slept.

SLY
These fifteen years! By my fay, a goodly nap.   81
But did I never speak of all that time?   82

FIRST SERVINGMAN
O, yes, my lord, but very idle words;
For though you lay here in this goodly chamber,
Yet would you say ye were beaten out of door,
And rail upon the hostess of the house,   86
And say you would present her at the leet   87
Because she brought stone jugs and no sealed
    quarts.   88
Sometimes you would call out for Cicely Hacket.

SLY
Ay, the woman's maid of the house.

THIRD SERVINGMAN
Why, sir, you know no house, nor no such maid,

---

18 Burton-heath (Perhaps Barton-on-the-Heath, about sixteen miles from Stratford, the home of Shakespeare's aunt.) **19 cardmaker** maker of cards or combs used to prepare wool for spinning **20 bearherd** keeper of a performing bear. **tinker** pot mender **21 alewife** woman who keeps an alehouse. **Wincot** small village about four miles from Stratford. (The parish register shows that there were Hackets living there in 1591.) **22–23 on the score** in debt (since such reckonings were originally notched or scored on a stick) **23 sheer** nothing but. **score me up for** reckon me to be **24 bestraught** distracted **29 As** as if **31 ancient** former **34 beck** nod **35 Apollo** i.e., as god of music **39 Semiramis** legendary queen of Assyria, famous for her voluptuousness **40 bestrew** i.e., scatter rushes on **41 trapped** adorned **45 welkin** sky, heavens **47 course** hunt the hare **48 breathed** in good physical condition, with good wind. **roe** small, swift deer **50 Adonis** a young huntsman with whom Venus is vainly in love. (See Ovid's *Metamorphoses,* Book X, and Shakespeare's poem, *Venus and Adonis.*) **51 Cytherea** one of the names for Venus (because of her association with the island of Cythera). **sedges** grassy marsh plants

52 wanton play seductively **54 Io** a woman who, according to Ovid, was seduced by Jove concealed in a mist and afterwards transformed into a heifer **56 as** as if **57 Daphne** a wood nymph beloved by Apollo, changed by Diana into a laurel tree to preserve her from Apollo's assault (*Metamorphoses,* Book I) **60 workmanly** skillfully **63 waning** degenerate **65 envious** spiteful **67 yet** even today **77 wit** mental faculties, senses **78 knew but** only knew **81 fay** faith **82 of** during **86 house** tavern **87 present** bring accusation against. **leet** manorial court **88 sealed quarts** quart containers officially stamped as a guarantee of that capacity

Nor no such men as you have reckoned up,
As Stephen Sly, and old John Naps of Greet,   93
And Peter Turf, and Henry Pimpernel,
And twenty more such names and men as these,
Which never were, nor no man ever saw.

SLY
Now Lord be thankèd for my good amends!   97

ALL
Amen.

Enter [the Page as a] lady, with Attendants.

SLY   I thank thee. Thou shalt not lose by it.

PAGE
How fares my noble lord?

SLY   Marry, I fare well,   99
For here is cheer enough. Where is my wife?

PAGE
Here, noble lord. What is thy will with her?

SLY
Are you my wife, and will not call me husband?
My men should call me "lord"; I am your goodman.   103

PAGE
My husband and my lord, my lord and husband,
I am your wife in all obedience.

SLY
I know it well.—What must I call her?

LORD   Madam.

SLY   Al'ce madam, or Joan madam?

LORD
Madam, and nothing else. So lords call ladies.

SLY
Madam wife, they say that I have dreamed
And slept above some fifteen year or more.

PAGE
Ay, and the time seems thirty unto me,
Being all this time abandoned from your bed.   112

SLY
'Tis much. Servants, leave me and her alone.
Madam, undress you and come now to bed.

PAGE
Thrice-noble lord, let me entreat of you
To pardon me yet for a night or two,
Or, if not so, until the sun be set.
For your physicians have expressly charged,
In peril to incur your former malady,
That I should yet absent me from your bed.
I hope this reason stands for my excuse.

SLY   Ay, it stands so that I may hardly tarry so long. But 122
I would be loath to fall into my dreams again. I will
therefore tarry in despite of the flesh and the blood.

Enter a [Servingman as] messenger.

SERVINGMAN
Your honor's players, hearing your amendment,
Are come to play a pleasant comedy,
For so your doctors hold it very meet,   127
Seeing too much sadness hath congealed your blood,
And melancholy is the nurse of frenzy.
Therefore they thought it good you hear a play
And frame your mind to mirth and merriment,
Which bars a thousand harms and lengthens life.

SLY   Marry, I will let them play it. Is not a comonty a   133
Christmas gambold or a tumbling-trick?   134

PAGE
No, my good lord, it is more pleasing stuff.

SLY   What, household stuff?   136

PAGE   It is a kind of history.   137

SLY   Well, we'll see 't. Come, madam wife, sit by my
side and let the world slip; we shall ne'er be younger.   139
                    [They sit over the stage.] Flourish.

1.1   *Enter Lucentio and his man, Tranio.*

LUCENTIO
Tranio, since for the great desire I had
To see fair Padua, nursery of arts,   2
I am arrived fore fruitful Lombardy,   3
The pleasant garden of great Italy,
And by my father's love and leave am armed
With his good will and thy good company,
My trusty servant, well approved in all,   7
Here let us breathe and haply institute   8
A course of learning and ingenious studies.   9
Pisa, renownèd for grave citizens,
Gave me my being, and my father first—   11
A merchant of great traffic through the world,   12
Vincentio, come of the Bentivolii.   13
Vincentio's son, brought up in Florence,   14
It shall become to serve all hopes conceived   15
To deck his fortune with his virtuous deeds.   16
And therefore, Tranio, for the time I study,   17
Virtue and that part of philosophy

---

93 **Stephen . . . Greet** (A Stephen Sly lived in Stratford during Shakespeare's day. *Greet* is a Gloucestershire hamlet not far from Stratford. The Folio reading, "Greece," is an easy misreading if Shakespeare wrote "Greete.")   97 **amends** recovery   99 **Marry** (A mild oath, derived from "by Mary.")   **fare well** (1) am fine (2) have plenty of good *cheer* (line 100), refreshment   103 **goodman** (A homely term for "husband.")   112 **abandoned** banished   122 **stands** is the case (with bawdy pun)

127 **meet** suitable   133 **Marry . . . play it** (Sly speaks now with imperial authority and condescension, unless the Folio punctuation should be amended to "Marry, I will. Let them play it.")   **133, 134 comonty, gambold** (Sly's words for *comedy* and *gambol*.)   136 **household stuff** i.e., domestic doings   137 **history** story   139 s.d. **They sit over the stage** (Possibly the Lord and some servingmen exeunt here or at line 113. At 1.1.249 ff., a servingman, the Page, and Sly speak, while the Lord is no longer heard from.)   **1.1. Location: Padua. A street before Baptista's house.**   2 **Padua . . . arts** (Padua's was one of the most renowned of universities during Shakespeare's time.)   3 **am arrived fore** have arrived at, or at the gates of, before. (Padua is not in Lombardy, but imprecise maps may have allowed Shakespeare to think of Lombardy as comprising all of northern Italy.)   7 **approved** tested and proved trustworthy   8 **breathe** pause, settle down.   **haply institute** perhaps begin   9 **ingenious** i.e., "ingenuous," liberal, befitting a wellborn person   11 **first** i.e., before me   12 **of great traffic** involved in extensive trade   13 **come of** descended from   14–16 **Vincentio's . . . deeds** it will befit Vincentio's son, brought up in Florence, to fulfill all the hopes entertained for him by his friends and relatives by adding virtuous deeds to what fortune has bestowed on him   17 **for the time** while

Will I apply that treats of happiness 19
By virtue specially to be achieved.
Tell me thy mind, for I have Pisa left
And am to Padua come as he that leaves
A shallow plash to plunge him in the deep, 23
And with satiety seeks to quench his thirst.

TRANIO
Mi perdonate, gentle master mine. 25
I am in all affected as yourself, 26
Glad that you thus continue your resolve
To suck the sweets of sweet philosophy.
Only, good master, while we do admire
This virtue and this moral discipline,
Let's be no stoics nor no stocks, I pray, 31
Or so devote to Aristotle's checks 32
As Ovid be an outcast quite abjured. 33
Balk logic with acquaintance that you have, 34
And practice rhetoric in your common talk; 35
Music and poesy use to quicken you; 36
The mathematics and the metaphysics,
Fall to them as you find your stomach serves you. 38
No profit grows where is no pleasure ta'en.
In brief, sir, study what you most affect. 40

LUCENTIO
Gramercies, Tranio, well dost thou advise. 41
If, Biondello, thou wert come ashore, 42
We could at once put us in readiness
And take a lodging fit to entertain
Such friends as time in Padua shall beget.
But stay awhile, what company is this?

TRANIO
Master, some show to welcome us to town. 47

*Enter Baptista with his two daughters, Katharina
and Bianca; Gremio, a pantaloon; [and] Hortensio,
suitor to Bianca. Lucentio [and] Tranio stand by.*

BAPTISTA
Gentlemen, importune me no farther,
For how I firmly am resolved you know:
That is, not to bestow my youngest daughter
Before I have a husband for the elder.
If either of you both love Katharina,
Because I know you well and love you well,
Leave shall you have to court her at your pleasure.

GREMIO
To cart her rather. She's too rough for me. 55
There, there, Hortensio, will you any wife?

KATHARINA [*to Baptista*]
I pray you, sir, is it your will
To make a stale of me amongst these mates? 58

HORTENSIO
"Mates," maid? How mean you that? No mates for
    you,
Unless you were of gentler, milder mold.

KATHARINA
I' faith, sir, you shall never need to fear;
Iwis it is not halfway to her heart. 62
But if it were, doubt not her care should be
To comb your noddle with a three-legged stool, 64
And paint your face, and use you like a fool. 65

HORTENSIO
From all such devils, good Lord deliver us!

GREMIO   And me too, good Lord!

TRANIO [*aside to Lucentio*]
Husht, master, here's some good pastime toward. 68
That wench is stark mad or wonderful froward. 69

LUCENTIO [*aside to Tranio*]
But in other's silence do I see
Maid's mild behavior and sobriety.
Peace, Tranio!

TRANIO [*aside to Lucentio*]
Well said, master. Mum, and gaze your fill.

BAPTISTA
Gentlemen, that I may soon make good
What I have said—Bianca, get you in.
And let it not displease thee, good Bianca,
For I will love thee ne'er the less, my girl.

KATHARINA   A pretty peat! It is best 78
Put finger in the eye, an she knew why. 79

BIANCA
Sister, content you in my discontent.—
Sir, to your pleasure humbly I subscribe. 81
My books and instruments shall be my company,
On them to look and practice by myself.

LUCENTIO [*aside to Tranio*]
Hark, Tranio, thou mayst hear Minerva speak. 84

HORTENSIO
Signor Baptista, will you be so strange? 85
Sorry am I that our good will effects 86
Bianca's grief.

GREMIO   Why will you mew her up, 87
Signor Baptista, for this fiend of hell,
And make her bear the penance of her tongue? 89

BAPTISTA
Gentlemen, content ye. I am resolved.
Go in, Bianca.   [*Exit Bianca.*]
And for I know she taketh most delight 92

19 apply study. **treats of** discusses, concerns **23 plash** pool **25 Mi perdonate** pardon me **26 affected** disposed **31 stocks** persons devoid of feeling, like wooden posts (with a play on *stoics*) **32 devote** devoted. **checks** restraints **33 As** so that. **Ovid** Latin love poet (used here to typify amorous light entertainment, as contrasted with the constraining philosophic study of Aristotle) **34 Balk logic** argue, bandy words. **acquaintance** acquaintances **35 common talk** ordinary conversation **36 quicken** refresh **38 stomach** inclination, appetite **40 affect** find pleasant **41 Gramercies** many thanks **42 Biondello** (Lucentio apostrophizes his absent servant.) **come ashore** (Padua, though inland, is given a harbor by Shakespeare, unless he is thinking of the canals that crossed northern Italy in the sixteenth century.) **47 s.d. pantaloon** foolish old man, a stock character in Italian comedy **55 cart** carry in a cart through the streets by way of punishment or public exposure (with a play on *court*)

58 stale laughingstock (with a play on the meaning "harlot," since a harlot might well be carted). **mates** rude fellows. (But Hortensio takes the word in the sense of "husband.") **62 Iwis** indeed. **it** i.e., marriage. **her** i.e., my, Kate's **64 comb your noddle** rake your head **65 paint** i.e., make red with scratches **68 toward** in prospect **69 wonderful froward** incredibly perverse **78 peat** darling, pet **79 Put . . . eye** i.e., weep. **an she knew why** if she could think of an excuse **81 pleasure** will. **subscribe** submit **84 Minerva** goddess of wisdom **85 strange** distant, estranged **86 effects** causes **87 mew** coop (as one would a falcon) **89 her . . . her** i.e., Bianca . . . Katharina's **92 for** because

In music, instruments, and poetry,
Schoolmasters will I keep within my house
Fit to instruct her youth. If you, Hortensio,
Or, Signor Gremio, you know any such,
Prefer them hither; for to cunning men   97
I will be very kind, and liberal
To mine own children in good bringing up.
And so farewell. —Katharina, you may stay,
For I have more to commune with Bianca.   *Exit.* 101

KATHARINA
Why, and I trust I may go too, may I not?
What, shall I be appointed hours,   103
As though, belike, I knew not what to take,   104
And what to leave? Ha!   *Exit.*

GREMIO   You may go to the devil's dam. Your gifts are 106
so good, here's none will hold you. —Their love is not 107
so great, Hortensio, but we may blow our nails to- 108
gether and fast it fairly out. Our cake's dough on both 109
sides. Farewell. Yet, for the love I bear my sweet 110
Bianca, if I can by any means light on a fit man to 111
teach her that wherein she delights, I will wish him to 112
her father.

HORTENSIO   So will I, Signor Gremio. But a word, I
pray. Though the nature of our quarrel yet never
brooked parle, know now, upon advice, it toucheth us 116
both, that we may yet again have access to our fair
mistress and be happy rivals in Bianca's love, to labor
and effect one thing specially.

GREMIO   What's that, I pray?

HORTENSIO   Marry, sir, to get a husband for her sister.

GREMIO   A husband? A devil.

HORTENSIO   I say a husband.

GREMIO   I say a devil. Think'st thou, Hortensio, though
her father be very rich, any man is so very a fool to be 125
married to hell?

HORTENSIO   Tush, Gremio, though it pass your patience 127
and mine to endure her loud alarums, why, man, 128
there be good fellows in the world, an a man could 129
light on them, would take her with all faults, and
money enough.

GREMIO   I cannot tell. But I had as lief take her dowry 132
with this condition: to be whipped at the high cross 133
every morning.

HORTENSIO   Faith, as you say, there's small choice in
rotten apples. But come, since this bar in law makes us 136
friends, it shall be so far forth friendly maintained till
by helping Baptista's eldest daughter to a husband

we set his youngest free for a husband, and then have 139
to 't afresh. Sweet Bianca! Happy man be his dole! He 140
that runs fastest gets the ring. How say you, Signor 141
Gremio?

GREMIO   I am agreed, and would I had given him the
best horse in Padua to begin his wooing that would
thoroughly woo her, wed her, and bed her and rid the
house of her! Come on.   *Exeunt ambo. Manent* 146
                                Tranio and Lucentio.

TRANIO
I pray, sir, tell me, is it possible
That love should of a sudden take such hold?

LUCENTIO
O Tranio, till I found it to be true,
I never thought it possible or likely.
But see, while idly I stood looking on,
I found the effect of love in idleness,   152
And now in plainness do confess to thee,
That art to me as secret and as dear   154
As Anna to the Queen of Carthage was,   155
Tranio, I burn, I pine, I perish, Tranio,
If I achieve not this young modest girl.
Counsel me, Tranio, for I know thou canst;
Assist me, Tranio, for I know thou wilt.

TRANIO
Master, it is no time to chide you now.
Affection is not rated from the heart.   161
If love have touched you, naught remains but so,
"Redime te captum quam queas minimo."   163

LUCENTIO
Gramercies, lad. Go forward. This contents;   164
The rest will comfort, for thy counsel's sound.

TRANIO
Master, you looked so longly on the maid,   166
Perhaps you marked not what's the pith of all.   167

LUCENTIO
O, yes, I saw sweet beauty in her face,
Such as the daughter of Agenor had,   169
That made great Jove to humble him to her hand,   170
When with his knees he kissed the Cretan strand.   171

TRANIO
Saw you no more? Marked you not how her sister
Began to scold and raise up such a storm
That mortal ears might hardly endure the din?

LUCENTIO
Tranio, I saw her coral lips to move,

139–140 have to 't renew combat **140 Happy . . . dole** i.e., may
happiness be the reward of him who wins. (Proverbial.) **141 the ring**
(An allusion to the sport of riding at the ring, with quibble on "wedding ring" and also sexual sense, "vulvar ring.") **146 s.d. ambo**
both. **Manent** they remain onstage **152 love in idleness** i.e., lust
bred by idleness, with a pun on *love-in-idleness*, the flower heartsease
or pansy, to which was attributed magical power in love. (See *A Midsummer Night's Dream*, 2.1.168.) **154 secret** trusted, intimate
155 Anna confidante of her sister Dido, Queen of Carthage, beloved
of Aeneas **161 rated** driven away by chiding **163 Redime . . . minimo** buy yourself out of bondage for as little as you can. (From Terence's *Eunuchus* as quoted in William Lilly's *Latin Grammar*.)
164 Gramercies thanks **166 so longly** for such a long time; perhaps,
also, so longingly **167 marked** noted. **pith** core, essence
169 daughter of Agenor Europa, beloved of Jove, who took the form
of a bull in order to abduct her **170 him** himself **171 kissed** i.e.,
knelt on

---

97 Prefer recommend. **cunning** skillful, learned **101 commune** discuss **103 appointed hours** given a timetable **104 belike** perhaps
106 dam mother. **gifts** endowments. (Said ironically.) **107 hold** detain. **Their love** i.e., the love of women **108–109 blow . . . together** i.e., twiddle our thumbs, wait patiently **109 fast . . . out** ab-
stain as best we can **109–110 Our cake's dough on both sides** i.e.,
we're both out of luck, getting nowhere **111 light on** come upon
112 wish commend **116 brooked parle** tolerated conference. **advice** reflection. **toucheth** concerns **125 very a** utterly a **127 pass**
exceed **128 alarums** i.e., loud, startling noises. (In military terms, a
call to arms.) **129 an** if **132 I cannot tell** i.e., I don't know about
that, don't know what to say. **had as lief** would as willingly
133 high cross cross set on a pedestal in a marketplace or center of a
town **136 bar in law** legal impediment, i.e., Baptista's refusal to receive suitors for Bianca

And with her breath she did perfume the air.
Sacred and sweet was all I saw in her.

TRANIO [*aside*]
Nay, then, 'tis time to stir him from his trance.—
I pray, awake, sir. If you love the maid,
Bend thoughts and wits to achieve her. Thus it
   stands:
Her elder sister is so curst and shrewd   181
That till the father rid his hands of her,
Master, your love must live a maid at home,
And therefore has he closely mewed her up,
Because she will not be annoyed with suitors.   185

LUCENTIO
Ah, Tranio, what a cruel father's he!
But art thou not advised he took some care   187
To get her cunning schoolmasters to instruct her?

TRANIO
Ay, marry, am I, sir; and now 'tis plotted.

LUCENTIO
I have it, Tranio.

TRANIO   Master, for my hand,   190
Both our inventions meet and jump in one.   191

LUCENTIO
Tell me thine first.

TRANIO   You will be schoolmaster
And undertake the teaching of the maid:
That's your device.

LUCENTIO   It is. May it be done?

TRANIO
Not possible; for who shall bear your part
And be in Padua here Vincentio's son,
Keep house and ply his book, welcome his friends,   197
Visit his countrymen, and banquet them?

LUCENTIO
Basta, content thee, for I have it full.   199
We have not yet been seen in any house,
Nor can we be distinguished by our faces
For man or master. Then it follows thus:
Thou shalt be master, Tranio, in my stead,
Keep house, and port, and servants, as I should.   204
I will some other be, some Florentine,
Some Neapolitan, or meaner man of Pisa.   206
'Tis hatched and shall be so. Tranio, at once
Uncase thee. Take my colored hat and cloak.   208
When Biondello comes, he waits on thee,
But I will charm him first to keep his tongue.   210

TRANIO   So had you need.
In brief, sir, sith it your pleasure is,
And I am tied to be obedient—   212
For so your father charged me at our parting,
"Be serviceable to my son," quoth he,
Although I think 'twas in another sense—

I am content to be Lucentio,
Because so well I love Lucentio.

               [*They exchange clothes.*]

LUCENTIO
Tranio, be so, because Lucentio loves.
And let me be a slave t' achieve that maid
Whose sudden sight hath thralled my wounded eye. 221

      Enter Biondello.

Here comes the rogue. —Sirrah, where have you
   been?

BIONDELLO
Where have I been? Nay, how now, where are you?
Master, has my fellow Tranio stol'n your clothes?
Or you stol'n his? Or both? Pray, what's the news?

LUCENTIO
Sirrah, come hither. 'Tis no time to jest,
And therefore frame your manners to the time.   227
Your fellow Tranio here, to save my life,
Puts my apparel and my countenance on,   229
And I for my escape have put on his;
For in a quarrel since I came ashore,
I killed a man, and fear I was descried.   232
Wait you on him, I charge you, as becomes,   233
While I make way from hence to save my life.
You understand me?

BIONDELLO   I, sir?—Ne'er a whit.   235

LUCENTIO
And not a jot of Tranio in your mouth.
Tranio is changed into Lucentio.

BIONDELLO
The better for him. Would I were so, too!

TRANIO
So could I, faith, boy, to have the next wish after,
That Lucentio indeed had Baptista's youngest
   daughter.
But, sirrah, not for my sake, but your master's, I
   advise
You use your manners discreetly in all kind of
   companies.
When I am alone, why, then I am Tranio,
But in all places else your master Lucentio.

LUCENTIO   Tranio, let's go.
One thing more rests, that thyself execute: 246
To make one among these wooers. If thou ask me
   why,
Sufficeth my reasons are both good and weighty.   248
                     Exeunt.

     The presenters above speak.

FIRST SERVINGMAN
My lord, you nod. You do not mind the play.   249

---

181 **curst** shrewish. **shrewd** ill-natured 185 **Because** so that. **annoyed with** troubled by 187 **advised** aware 190 **for my hand** for my part, i.e., it's my guess 191 **inventions** plans. **jump** tally, agree 197 **Keep house** entertain, receive guests. **ply his book** pursue his studies 199 **Basta** enough. **full** i.e., fully thought out 204 **port** state, style of living 206 **meaner** of a lower social class 208 **Uncase thee** remove your outer garments. **colored** (as opposed to blue generally worn by servants; see 4.1.81) 210 **charm** i.e., persuade 212 **sith** since

221 **Whose sudden sight** the sudden sight of whom 227 **frame** adapt, suit 229 **countenance** bearing, manner 232 **descried** observed 233 **as becomes** as is suitable 235 **I, sir** (Lucentio may hear this as "Ay, sir.") **Ne'er a whit** not in the least 246 **rests** remains to be done 248 **Sufficeth** it suffices that. **s.d. presenters** characters of the Induction, whose role it is to "present" the play proper 249 **mind** attend to

SLY   Yes, by Saint Anne, do I. A good matter, surely.
Comes there any more of it?
PAGE [as lady]   My lord, 'tis but begun.
SLY   'Tis a very excellent piece of work, madam lady.
Would 'twere done!   *They sit and mark.* 254

1.2   *Enter Petruchio and his man, Grumio.*

PETRUCHIO
Verona, for a while I take my leave
To see my friends in Padua, but of all   2
My best belovèd and approvèd friend,
Hortensio; and I trow this is his house.   4
Here, sirrah Grumio, knock, I say.
GRUMIO   Knock, sir? Whom should I knock? Is there any
man has rebused your worship?   7
PETRUCHIO   Villain, I say, knock me here soundly.   8
GRUMIO   Knock you here, sir? Why, sir, what am I, sir,
that I should knock you here, sir?
PETRUCHIO
Villain, I say, knock me at this gate,   11
And rap me well, or I'll knock your knave's pate.
GRUMIO
My master is grown quarrelsome. I should knock
you first,   13
And then I know after who comes by the worst.   14
PETRUCHIO   Will it not be?   15
Faith, sirrah, an you'll not knock, I'll ring it.   16
I'll try how you can *sol fa* and sing it.   17
                    He wrings him by the ears.
GRUMIO
Help, masters, help! My master is mad.   18
PETRUCHIO
Now knock when I bid you, sirrah villain.

                    Enter Hortensio.

HORTENSIO   How now, what's the matter? My old friend
Grumio and my good friend Petruchio? How do you   21
all at Verona?   22
PETRUCHIO
Signor Hortensio, come you to part the fray?
Con tutto il cuore ben trovato, may I say.   24
HORTENSIO
Alla nostra casa ben venuto,   25
Molto onorato signor mio Petruchio.—   26

Rise, Grumio, rise. We will compound this quarrel.   27
GRUMIO   Nay, 'tis no matter, sir, what he 'leges in Latin.   28
If this be not a lawful cause for me to leave his service!
Look you, sir: he bid me knock him and rap him
soundly, sir. Well, was it fit for a servant to use his
master so, being perhaps, for aught I see, two-and-   32
thirty, a pip out?   33
Whom would to God I had well knocked at first,
Then had not Grumio come by the worst.
PETRUCHIO
A senseless villain! Good Hortensio,
I bade the rascal knock upon your gate,
And could not get him for my heart to do it.   38
GRUMIO   Knock at the gate? O heavens! Spake you not
these words plain, "Sirrah, knock me here, rap me
here, knock me well, and knock me soundly"? And
come you now with "knocking at the gate"?   42
PETRUCHIO
Sirrah, begone, or talk not, I advise you.
HORTENSIO
Petruchio, patience. I am Grumio's pledge.   44
Why, this's a heavy chance twixt him and you,   45
Your ancient, trusty, pleasant servant Grumio.   46
And tell me now, sweet friend, what happy gale
Blows you to Padua here from old Verona?
PETRUCHIO
Such wind as scatters young men through the world
To seek their fortunes farther than at home,
Where small experience grows. But in a few,   51
Signor Hortensio, thus it stands with me:
Antonio, my father, is deceased,
And I have thrust myself into this maze,
Happily to wive and thrive as best I may.   55
Crowns in my purse I have, and goods at home,
And so am come abroad to see the world.
HORTENSIO
Petruchio, shall I then come roundly to thee   58
And wish thee to a shrewd, ill-favored wife?   59
Thou'dst thank me but a little for my counsel.
And yet I'll promise thee she shall be rich,
And very rich. But thou'rt too much my friend,
And I'll not wish thee to her.
PETRUCHIO
Signor Hortensio, twixt such friends as we
Few words suffice. And therefore, if thou know
One rich enough to be Petruchio's wife—
As wealth is burden of my wooing dance—   67

254 s.d. mark observe
1.2. Location: Padua. Before Hortensio's house.
2 of all above all   **4 trow** believe   **7 rebused** (A blunder for "abused.")   **8 Villain** i.e., wretch. (A term of abuse.)   **me** i.e., for me. (But Grumio, perhaps intentionally, misunderstands.)   **11 gate** door   **13–14 I should . . . worst** i.e., you're asking me to hit you—and I know who then will get the worst of it   **15 Will it not be?** i.e., aren't you going to do what I said?   **16 ring it** sound loudly, using a circular knocker or a bell (with a pun on *wring*)   **17 I'll . . . sing it** i.e., I'll make you cry out, howl. (To *sol fa* is to sing a scale.)
18 masters i.e., sirs. (Addressed to the audience.)   **21–22 How do you all** how are you and your family   **24 Con . . . trovato** with all my heart, well met   **25–26 Alla . . . Petruchio** welcome to our house, my much honored Petruchio. (Italian.)

27 compound settle   **28 'leges** alleges   **32–33 two . . . out** i.e., drunk, or not quite right in the head. (Derived from the card game called *one-and-thirty*.)   **33 pip** a spot on a playing card. (Hence, *a pip out* means "off by one," or "one in excess of thirty-one.")
38 for my heart i.e., for my life   **42 come you now with** do you now come along with   **44 pledge** surety   **45 this's** this is.   **heavy chance** sad occurrence   **46 ancient** long-standing.   **pleasant** merry   **51 in a few** in short   **55 Happily** with good luck. (*Happily* and *haply* were not always distinguished.)   **58 come roundly** speak plainly
59 shrewd shrewish.   **ill-favored** ill-natured (? Kate is not "ugly," the usual meaning of this term; see line 85.)   **67 burden** undersong, i.e., basis

Be she as foul as was Florentius' love,   68
As old as Sibyl, and as curst and shrewd   69
As Socrates' Xanthippe, or a worse,   70
She moves me not, or not removes, at least,   71
Affection's edge in me, were she as rough   72
As are the swelling Adriatic seas.
I come to wive it wealthily in Padua;
If wealthily, then happily in Padua.
GRUMIO   Nay, look you, sir, he tells you flatly what his
mind is. Why, give him gold enough and marry him   77
to a puppet or an aglet-baby, or an old trot with ne'er   78
a tooth in her head, though she have as many diseases
as two-and-fifty horses. Why, nothing comes amiss, so   80
money comes withal.   81
HORTENSIO
Petruchio, since we are stepped thus far in,
I will continue that I broached in jest.   83
I can, Petruchio, help thee to a wife
With wealth enough, and young and beauteous,
Brought up as best becomes a gentlewoman.
Her only fault, and that is faults enough,
Is that she is intolerable curst   88
And shrewd, and froward, so beyond all measure   89
That, were my state far worser than it is,   90
I would not wed her for a mine of gold.
PETRUCHIO
Hortensio, peace! Thou know'st not gold's effect.
Tell me her father's name and 'tis enough;
For I will board her, though she chide as loud   94
As thunder when the clouds in autumn crack.   95
HORTENSIO
Her father is Baptista Minola,
An affable and courteous gentleman.
Her name is Katharina Minola,
Renowned in Padua for her scolding tongue.
PETRUCHIO
I know her father, though I know not her,
And he knew my deceasèd father well.
I will not sleep, Hortensio, till I see her;
And therefore let me be thus bold with you
To give you over at this first encounter,   104
Unless you will accompany me thither.
GRUMIO   [to Hortensio]   I pray you, sir, let him go while
the humor lasts. O' my word, an she knew him as   107
well as I do, she would think scolding would do
little good upon him. She may perhaps call him half

a score knaves or so. Why, that's nothing; an he begin
once, he'll rail in his rope tricks. I'll tell you   111
what, sir: an she stand him but a little, he will throw   112
a figure in her face and so disfigure her with it that   113
she shall have no more eyes to see withal than a cat.
You know him not, sir.
HORTENSIO
Tarry, Petruchio, I must go with thee,
For in Baptista's keep my treasure is.   117
He hath the jewel of my life in hold,   118
His youngest daughter, beautiful Bianca,
And her withholds from me and other more,   120
Suitors to her and rivals in my love,
Supposing it a thing impossible,
For those defects I have before rehearsed,   123
That ever Katharina will be wooed.
Therefore this order hath Baptista ta'en,   125
That none shall have access unto Bianca
Till Katharine the curst have got a husband.
GRUMIO   Katharine the curst!
A title for a maid of all titles the worst.
HORTENSIO
Now shall my friend Petruchio do me grace,   130
And offer me disguised in sober robes
To old Baptista as a schoolmaster
Well seen in music, to instruct Bianca,   133
That so I may by this device at least
Have leave and leisure to make love to her,   135
And unsuspected court her by herself.

            Enter Gremio [with a paper], and Lucentio
            disguised [as a schoolmaster].

GRUMIO   Here's no knavery! See, to beguile the old   137
folks, how the young folks lay their heads together!
Master, master, look about you. Who goes there, ha?
HORTENSIO
Peace, Grumio, it is the rival of my love.
Petruchio, stand by awhile.   *[They stand aside.]*
GRUMIO   *[aside]*
A proper stripling and an amorous!   142
GREMIO   *[to Lucentio]*
O, very well, I have perused the note.   143
Hark you, sir, I'll have them very fairly bound—
All books of love, see that at any hand—   145
And see you read no other lectures to her.   146
You understand me. Over and besides
Signor Baptista's liberality,
I'll mend it with a largess. Take your paper too,   149
            [giving Lucentio the note]

68 **foul** ugly. **Florentius' love** (An allusion to John Gower's version
in *Confessio Amantis* of the fairy tale of the knight who promises to
marry an ugly old woman if she solves the riddle he must answer. After the fulfillment of all promises, she becomes young and beautiful.
Another version of this story is Chaucer's ''Tale of the Wife of Bath,''
from *The Canterbury Tales*.) 69 **Sibyl** prophetess of Cumae, to whom
Apollo gave as many years of life as she held grains of sand in her
hand 70 **Xanthippe** the philosopher's notoriously shrewish wife
71 **moves** affects, disturbs (setting up wordplay on *removes*) 72 **Affection's edge** the keen edge of desire 77 **mind** intention 78 **aglet-
baby** small figure carved on the tag of a lace. **trot** hag 80 **so** provided 81 **withal** with it 83 **that I broached** what I began
88 **intolerable** intolerably 89 **shrewd, and froward** ill-natured and
refractory 90 **state** estate 94 **board** accost, woo. (A metaphor from
naval warfare.) 95 **crack** make an explosive noise 104 **give you
over** leave you 107 **humor** whim. **O'** on. **an** if

111 **rope tricks** perhaps Grumio's version of ''rope-rhetorics,'' i.e.,
scolding in outrageous terms (?) or tricks worthy of hanging (?)
112 **stand** withstand 113 **figure** figure of speech 117 **keep** keeping
(with suggestion of ''fortified place,'' where one would store a treasure) 118 **hold** confinement (with a similar pun on ''stronghold'')
120 **other more** others besides me 123 **rehearsed** related, described
125 **this order** these measures 130 **grace** a favor 133 **seen** skilled
135 **make love to** woo 137 **Here's no knavery.** (Said sarcastically.)
142 **proper stripling** handsome young fellow. (Said ironically, in reference to Gremio.) 143 **note** (Evidently, a list of books for Bianca's
tutoring.) 145 **see** see to. **at any hand** in any case 146 **read . . .
lectures** teach no other lessons 149 **mend** improve, increase.
largess gift of money

And let me have them very well perfumed,
For she is sweeter than perfume itself
To whom they go to. What will you read to her?

LUCENTIO
Whate'er I read to her, I'll plead for you
As for my patron, stand you so assured,
As firmly as yourself were still in place—   155
Yea, and perhaps with more successful words
Than you, unless you were a scholar, sir.

GREMIO
O this learning, what a thing it is!

GRUMIO [aside]
O this woodcock, what an ass it is!   159

PETRUCHIO   Peace, sirrah!

HORTENSIO [coming forward]
Grumio, mum!—God save you, Signor Gremio.

GREMIO
And you are well met, Signor Hortensio.   162
Trow you whither I am going? To Baptista Minola.   163
I promised to inquire carefully
About a schoolmaster for the fair Bianca,
And by good fortune I have lighted well
On this young man, for learning and behavior
Fit for her turn, well read in poetry   168
And other books—good ones, I warrant ye.

HORTENSIO
'Tis well. And I have met a gentleman
Hath promised me to help me to another,   171
A fine musician to instruct our mistress.
So shall I no whit be behind in duty
To fair Bianca, so beloved of me.

GREMIO
Beloved of me, and that my deeds shall prove.

GRUMIO [aside]   And that his bags shall prove.   176

HORTENSIO
Gremio, 'tis now no time to vent our love.   177
Listen to me, and if you speak me fair,   178
I'll tell you news indifferent good for either.   179
Here is a gentleman whom by chance I met,
Upon agreement from us to his liking,   181
Will undertake to woo curst Katharine,
Yea, and to marry her, if her dowry please.

GREMIO   So said, so done, is well.   184
Hortensio, have you told him all her faults?

PETRUCHIO
I know she is an irksome brawling scold.
If that be all, masters, I hear no harm.

GREMIO
No, sayst me so, friend? What countryman?

PETRUCHIO   150
Born in Verona, old Antonio's son.
My father dead, his fortune lives for me,
And I do hope good days and long to see.

GREMIO
O sir, such a life with such a wife were strange.   192
But if you have a stomach, to 't, i' God's name.   193
You shall have me assisting you in all.
But will you woo this wildcat?

PETRUCHIO   Will I live?

GRUMIO
Will he woo her? Ay, or I'll hang her.

PETRUCHIO
Why came I hither but to that intent?
Think you a little din can daunt mine ears?
Have I not in my time heard lions roar?
Have I not heard the sea, puffed up with winds,
Rage like an angry boar chafèd with sweat?
Have I not heard great ordnance in the field,   202
And heaven's artillery thunder in the skies?
Have I not in a pitchèd battle heard
Loud 'larums, neighing steeds, and trumpets' clang?   205
And do you tell me of a woman's tongue,
That gives not half so great a blow to hear
As will a chestnut in a farmer's fire?
Tush, tush! Fear boys with bugs.

GRUMIO   For he fears none.   209

GREMIO   Hortensio, hark.
This gentleman is happily arrived,   211
My mind presumes, for his own good and ours.

HORTENSIO
I promised we would be contributors
And bear his charge of wooing, whatsoe'er.   214

GREMIO
And so we will, provided that he win her.

GRUMIO
I would I were as sure of a good dinner.   216

Enter Tranio, brave [as Lucentio], and Biondello.

TRANIO
Gentlemen, God save you. If I may be bold,
Tell me, I beseech you, which is the readiest way
To the house of Signor Baptista Minola?

BIONDELLO   He that has the two fair daughters, is 't he
you mean?

TRANIO   Even he, Biondello.   221

GREMIO
Hark you, sir, you mean not her to—

TRANIO
Perhaps him and her, sir. What have you to do?   224

PETRUCHIO
Not her that chides, sir, at any hand, I pray.   225

150 them i.e., the books   155 as as if.   still in place present all the
time   159 woodcock (A bird easily caught; proverbially stupid.)
162 you are well met i.e., how opportune to meet you just now
163 Trow know   168 Fit for her turn suited to her needs (something
that is true in more ways than Gremio realizes)   171 Hath who has.
help me to help me to obtain   176 bags moneybags   177 vent express   178 speak me fair deal with me civilly, courteously   179 indifferent equally   181 Upon . . . liking who, if we agree to terms
satisfactory to him. (In lines 213–214, we learn that Bianca's suitors
will bear his charge of wooing.)   184 So . . . is well i.e., that's all
very well, when his deeds match his words (which may not be soon)

192 were would be   193 a stomach an appetite, inclination
202 ordnance artillery.   field battlefield   205 'larums calls to arms
209 Fear . . . bugs frighten children with bugbears, bogeymen
211 happily fortunately, just when needed   214 charge expense
216 s.d. brave elegantly dressed   221 Even he yes, precisely, he
224 him and her i.e., both Baptista Minola and his daughter.   What
. . . do what's that to you?   225 at any hand on any account

TRANIO
  I love no chiders, sir. Biondello, let's away.

LUCENTIO [aside]
  Well begun, Tranio.

HORTENSIO   Sir, a word ere you go.
  Are you a suitor to the maid you talk of, yea or no?

TRANIO
  An if I be, sir, is it any offense?

GREMIO
  No, if without more words you will get you hence.

TRANIO
  Why, sir, I pray, are not the streets as free
  For me as for you?

GREMIO   But so is not she.

TRANIO
  For what reason, I beseech you?

GREMIO   For this reason, if you'll know,
  That she's the choice love of Signor Gremio.   234

HORTENSIO
  That she's the chosen of Signor Hortensio.

TRANIO
  Softly, my masters! If you be gentlemen,
  Do me this right: hear me with patience.
  Baptista is a noble gentleman,
  To whom my father is not all unknown;   239
  And were his daughter fairer than she is,
  She may more suitors have, and me for one.
  Fair Leda's daughter had a thousand wooers;   242
  Then well one more may fair Bianca have,
  And so she shall. Lucentio shall make one,
  Though Paris came in hope to speed alone.   245

GREMIO
  What, this gentleman will out-talk us all!

LUCENTIO
  Sir, give him head. I know he'll prove a jade.   247

PETRUCHIO
  Hortensio, to what end are all these words?

HORTENSIO [to Tranio]
  Sir, let me be so bold as ask you,   249
  Did you yet ever see Baptista's daughter?

TRANIO
  No, sir, but hear I do that he hath two,
  The one as famous for a scolding tongue
  As is the other for beauteous modesty.

PETRUCHIO
  Sir, sir, the first's for me. Let her go by.   254

GREMIO
  Yea, leave that labor to great Hercules,
  And let it be more than Alcides' twelve.   256

PETRUCHIO
  Sir, understand you this of me, in sooth: 257

The youngest daughter, whom you hearken for,   258
Her father keeps from all access of suitors,
And will not promise her to any man
Until the elder sister first be wed.
The younger then is free, and not before.

TRANIO
  If it be so, sir, that you are the man
  Must stead us all, and me amongst the rest;   264
  And if you break the ice and do this feat,
  Achieve the elder, set the younger free
  For our access, whose hap shall be to have her   267
  Will not so graceless be to be ingrate.   268

HORTENSIO
  Sir, you say well, and well you do conceive.   269
  And since you do profess to be a suitor,
  You must, as we do, gratify this gentleman,   271
  To whom we all rest generally beholding.   272

TRANIO
  Sir, I shall not be slack. In sign whereof,
  Please ye we may contrive this afternoon,   274
  And quaff carouses to our mistress' health,   275
  And do as adversaries do in law—   276
  Strive mightily, but eat and drink as friends.

GRUMIO, BIONDELLO
  O excellent motion! Fellows, let's be gone.   278

HORTENSIO
  The motion's good indeed, and be it so.
  Petruchio, I shall be your ben venuto.   Exeunt. 280

❖

2.1   Enter Katharina and Bianca [with her hands tied].

BIANCA
  Good sister, wrong me not, nor wrong yourself,
  To make a bondmaid and a slave of me.
  That I disdain. But for these other goods,   3
  Unbind my hands, I'll pull them off myself,   4
  Yea, all my raiment, to my petticoat,
  Or what you will command me will I do,
  So well I know my duty to my elders.

KATHARINA
  Of all thy suitors here I charge thee tell
  Whom thou lov'st best. See thou dissemble not.

BIANCA
  Believe me, sister, of all the men alive
  I never yet beheld that special face
  Which I could fancy more than any other.

KATHARINA
  Minion, thou liest. Is 't not Hortensio?   13

234 **choice** (1) chosen (2) excellent   239 **all** entirely   242 **Leda's daughter** Helen of Troy   245 **Though** even if.   **Paris** Trojan prince who abducted Helen from her husband, Menelaus.   **speed alone** succeed above all others   247 **prove a jade** tire like an ill-conditioned horse   249 **as ask** as to ask   254 **Let her go by** pass over her   256 **let . . . twelve** admit that it would exceed the twelve labors of Hercules (called *Alcides* because he was the reputed grandson of Alcaeus)   257 **of me** from me.   **sooth** truth

258 **hearken for** lie in wait for, seek to win   264 **Must stead** who must help   267 **whose hap** he whose good fortune   268 **to be ingrate** as to be ungrateful   269 **conceive** understand   271 **gratify** reward, requite   272 **beholding** beholden, indebted   274 **contrive** spend, pass (time)   275 **quaff carouses** drink toasts   276 **adversaries** opposing lawyers   278 **motion** suggestion   280 **ben venuto** welcome, i.e., host
2.1. Location: Padua. Baptista's house.
3 **goods** possessions   4 **Unbind** if you will unbind   13 **Minion** hussy

BIANCA
      If you affect him, sister, here I swear   14
      I'll plead for you myself but you shall have him.   15
KATHARINA
      O, then belike you fancy riches more: 16
      You will have Gremio to keep you fair.   17
BIANCA
      Is it for him you do envy me so?
      Nay, then, you jest, and now I well perceive
      You have but jested with me all this while.
      I prithee, sister Kate, untie my hands.
KATHARINA (strikes her)
      If that be jest, then all the rest was so.

               Enter Baptista.

BAPTISTA
      Why, how now, dame, whence grows this
           insolence?—
      Bianca, stand aside. Poor girl, she weeps.
      Go ply thy needle, meddle not with her.—   25
      For shame, thou hilding of a devilish spirit,   26
      Why dost thou wrong her that did ne'er wrong
           thee?
      When did she cross thee with a bitter word?   28
KATHARINA
      Her silence flouts me, and I'll be revenged.   29
                             [She] flies after Bianca.
BAPTISTA
      What, in my sight? Bianca, get thee in.
                                   Exit [Bianca].
KATHARINA
      What, will you not suffer me? Nay, now I see   31
      She is your treasure, she must have a husband;
      I must dance barefoot on her wedding day,   33
      And for your love to her lead apes in hell.   34
      Talk not to me. I will go sit and weep
      Till I can find occasion of revenge.   [Exit.]
BAPTISTA
      Was ever gentleman thus grieved as I?
      But who comes here?   38

               Enter Gremio, Lucentio [as a schoolmaster] in the
               habit of a mean man, Petruchio, with [Hortensio as
               a musician, and] Tranio [as Lucentio] with his boy
               [Biondello] bearing a lute and books.

GREMIO   Good morrow, neighbor Baptista.
BAPTISTA   Good morrow, neighbor Gremio. God save
      you, gentlemen.
PETRUCHIO
      And you, good sir. Pray, have you not a daughter
      Called Katharina, fair and virtuous?

BAPTISTA
      I have a daughter, sir, called Katharina.
GREMIO
      You are too blunt. Go to it orderly.   45
PETRUCHIO
      You wrong me, Signor Gremio; give me leave.—   46
      I am a gentleman of Verona, sir,
      That, hearing of her beauty and her wit,
      Her affability and bashful modesty,
      Her wondrous qualities and mild behavior,
      Am bold to show myself a forward guest
      Within your house, to make mine eye the witness
      Of that report which I so oft have heard.
      And, for an entrance to my entertainment,   54
      I do present you with a man of mine,
                             [presenting Hortensio]
      Cunning in music and the mathematics,   56
      To instruct her fully in those sciences,   57
      Whereof I know she is not ignorant.
      Accept of him, or else you do me wrong.   59
      His name is Litio, born in Mantua.
BAPTISTA
      You're welcome, sir, and he, for your good sake.
      But for my daughter Katharine, this I know,   62
      She is not for your turn, the more my grief.
PETRUCHIO
      I see you do not mean to part with her,
      Or else you like not of my company.   65
BAPTISTA
      Mistake me not, I speak but as I find.
      Whence are you, sir? What may I call your name?
PETRUCHIO
      Petruchio is my name, Antonio's son,
      A man well known throughout all Italy.
BAPTISTA
      I know him well. You are welcome for his sake.   70
GREMIO
      Saving your tale, Petruchio, I pray,   71
      Let us that are poor petitioners speak too.
      Bacare! You are marvelous forward.   73
PETRUCHIO
      O, pardon me, Signor Gremio, I would fain be
           doing.   74
GREMIO
      I doubt it not, sir, but you will curse your wooing.—
      Neighbors, this is a gift very grateful, I am sure of 76
      it. [To Baptista.] To express the like kindness, my-
      self, that have been more kindly beholding to you
      than any, freely give unto you this young scholar
      [presenting Lucentio], that hath been long studying
      at Rheims, as cunning in Greek, Latin, and other
      languages, as the other in music and mathemat-

---

14 **affect** love   15 **but you shall have him** if necessary for you to win
him   16 **belike** perhaps   17 **fair** resplendent with finery   25 **meddle
not with** have nothing to do with   26 **hilding** vicious (hence worthless) beast   28 **cross** contradict, thwart   29 **flouts** mocks, insults
31 **suffer me** let me have my own way   33, 34 **dance . . . day, lead
. . . hell** (Popularly supposed to be the fate of old maids.)   38 s.d.
habit dress.   **mean** of low social station. (Said here of a schoolmaster.)

45 **orderly** in a properly orderly manner   46 **give me leave** excuse
me   54 **entrance** entrance fee.   **entertainment** reception   56 **Cunning** skillful   57 **sciences** subjects, branches of knowledge   59 **Accept of** accept   62 **for** as for   65 **like not of** do not like   70 **know**
know of. (See also line 105.)   71 **Saving** with all due respect for
73 **Bacare** stand back   74 **fain** gladly.   **doing** getting on with the
business (with sexual suggestion)   76 **grateful** pleasing

ics. His name is Cambio. Pray, accept his service.   83

BAPTISTA   A thousand thanks, Signor Gremio. Welcome, good Cambio. [*To Tranio.*] But, gentle sir, methinks you walk like a stranger. May I be so bold to   86
know the cause of your coming?

TRANIO
Pardon me, sir, the boldness is mine own,
That, being a stranger in this city here,
Do make myself a suitor to your daughter,
Unto Bianca, fair and virtuous.
Nor is your firm resolve unknown to me
In the preferment of the eldest sister.   93
This liberty is all that I request,
That, upon knowledge of my parentage,   95
I may have welcome 'mongst the rest that woo,
And free access and favor as the rest.   97
And toward the education of your daughters
I here bestow a simple instrument,
And this small packet of Greek and Latin books.
If you accept them, then their worth is great.
           [*Biondello brings forward the lute and books.*]

BAPTISTA
Lucentio is your name? Of whence, I pray?   102

TRANIO
Of Pisa, sir, son to Vincentio.

BAPTISTA
A mighty man of Pisa. By report
I know him well. You are very welcome, sir.
[*To Hortensio.*] Take you the lute, [*to Lucentio*] and
    you the set of books;
You shall go see your pupils presently.   107
Holla, within!

          Enter a Servant.

            Sirrah, lead these gentlemen
To my daughters, and tell them both
These are their tutors. Bid them use them well.
        [*Exit Servant, with Lucentio and Hortensio.*]
We will go walk a little in the orchard,   111
And then to dinner. You are passing welcome,   112
And so I pray you all to think yourselves.

PETRUCHIO
Signor Baptista, my business asketh haste,
And every day I cannot come to woo.
You knew my father well, and in him me,
Left solely heir to all his lands and goods,
Which I have bettered rather than decreased.
Then tell me, if I get your daughter's love,
What dowry shall I have with her to wife?

BAPTISTA
After my death the one half of my lands,
And in possession twenty thousand crowns.   122

PETRUCHIO
And for that dowry I'll assure her of   123
Her widowhood, be it that she survive me,   124
In all my lands and leases whatsoever.
Let specialties be therefore drawn between us,   126
That covenants may be kept on either hand.

BAPTISTA
Ay, when the special thing is well obtained,
That is, her love; for that is all in all.

PETRUCHIO
Why, that is nothing, for I tell you, Father,   130
I am as peremptory as she proud-minded;
And where two raging fires meet together,
They do consume the thing that feeds their fury.
Though little fire grows great with little wind,
Yet extreme gusts will blow out fire and all.
So I to her, and so she yields to me,   136
For I am rough and woo not like a babe.

BAPTISTA
Well mayst thou woo, and happy be thy speed!   138
But be thou armed for some unhappy words.

PETRUCHIO
Ay, to the proof, as mountains are for winds,   140
That shakes not, though they blow perpetually.   141

     Enter Hortensio [as Litio], with his head broke.

BAPTISTA
How now, my friend, why dost thou look so pale?

HORTENSIO
For fear, I promise you, if I look pale.   143

BAPTISTA
What, will my daughter prove a good musician?

HORTENSIO
I think she'll sooner prove a soldier.   145
Iron may hold with her, but never lutes.   146

BAPTISTA
Why then, thou canst not break her to the lute?   147

HORTENSIO
Why, no, for she hath broke the lute to me.
I did but tell her she mistook her frets,   149
And bowed her hand to teach her fingering,
When, with a most impatient devilish spirit,
"Frets, call you these?" quoth she, "I'll fume with
    them."
And with that word she struck me on the head,
And through the instrument my pate made way;
And there I stood amazèd for a while,   155
As on a pillory, looking through the lute,   156

---

83 **Cambio** (In Italian, appropriately, the word means "change" or "exchange.")   86 **walk like a stranger** keep your distance, stand apart   93 **In the preferment of** in the precedence you give to   95 **upon knowledge of** when you know about   97 **favor** leave, permission   102 **Lucentio . . . name** (Baptista may have learned this information from a note accompanying the books and lute.)   107 **presently** immediately   111 **orchard** garden   112 **passing** exceedingly   122 **in possession** in immediate possession

123 **for** in exchange for   124 **widowhood** i.e., widow's share of the estate. **be it that she** if she should   126 **specialties** terms of contract   130 **Father** father-in-law   136 **So I** i.e., so I behave, like an extreme gust of wind   138 **happy be thy speed** may it turn out well for you   140 **to the proof** i.e., in armor, proof against her shrewishness   141 **shakes** shake. **s.d. broke** with a bleeding cut. (Hortensio usually appears on stage with his head emerging through a broken lute.)   143 **promise** assure   145 **prove a soldier** (1) turn out to be a good soldier (2) put a soldier to the test   146 **hold with** hold out against   147 **break** train (with pun in the next line)   149 **frets** ridges or bars on the fingerboard of the lute. (But Kate puns on the sense of "fume," "be indignant.")   155 **amazèd** bewildered   156 **As on a pillory** as if with my head in a wooden collar used as punishment

While she did call me rascal fiddler
And twangling Jack, with twenty such vile terms,   158
As had she studied to misuse me so.   159

PETRUCHIO
Now, by the world, it is a lusty wench!   160
I love her ten times more than e'er I did.
O, how I long to have some chat with her!

BAPTISTA [*to Hortensio*]
Well, go with me, and be not so discomfited.
Proceed in practice with my younger daughter;   164
She's apt to learn and thankful for good turns.—
Signor Petruchio, will you go with us,
Or shall I send my daughter Kate to you?

PETRUCHIO
I pray you, do.   *Exeunt. Manet Petruchio.*
                    I'll attend her here,   168
And woo her with some spirit when she comes.
Say that she rail, why then I'll tell her plain
She sings as sweetly as a nightingale.
Say that she frown, I'll say she looks as clear   172
As morning roses newly washed with dew.
Say she be mute and will not speak a word,
Then I'll commend her volubility
And say she uttereth piercing eloquence.   176
If she do bid me pack, I'll give her thanks,   177
As though she bid me stay by her a week.
If she deny to wed, I'll crave the day   179
When I shall ask the banns and when be married.   180
But here she comes; and now, Petruchio, speak.

                    Enter Katharina.

Good morrow, Kate, for that's your name, I hear.

KATHARINA
Well have you heard, but something hard of hearing.   183
They call me Katharine that do talk of me.

PETRUCHIO
You lie, in faith, for you are called plain Kate,
And bonny Kate, and sometimes Kate the curst;
But Kate, the prettiest Kate in Christendom,
Kate of Kate Hall, my superdainty Kate,
For dainties are all Kates, and therefore, Kate,   189
Take this of me, Kate of my consolation: 190
Hearing thy mildness praised in every town,
Thy virtues spoke of, and thy beauty sounded,   192
Yet not so deeply as to thee belongs,
Myself am moved to woo thee for my wife.   194

KATHARINA
Moved? In good time! Let him that moved you
hither   195

Remove you hence. I knew you at the first
You were a movable.

PETRUCHIO   Why, what's a movable?   197

KATHARINA
A joint stool.

PETRUCHIO   Thou hast hit it. Come, sit on me.   198

KATHARINA
Asses are made to bear, and so are you.   199

PETRUCHIO
Women are made to bear, and so are you.

KATHARINA
No such jade as you, if me you mean.   201

PETRUCHIO
Alas, good Kate, I will not burden thee,
For knowing thee to be but young and light.   203

KATHARINA
Too light for such a swain as you to catch,   204
And yet as heavy as my weight should be.

PETRUCHIO
Should be? Should—buzz!

KATHARINA   Well ta'en, and like a buzzard.   206

PETRUCHIO
O slow-winged turtle, shall a buzzard take thee?

KATHARINA
Ay, for a turtle, as he takes a buzzard.

PETRUCHIO
Come, come, you wasp, i' faith you are too angry.   209

KATHARINA
If I be waspish, best beware my sting.

PETRUCHIO
My remedy is then to pluck it out.

KATHARINA
Ay, if the fool could find it where it lies.

PETRUCHIO
Who knows not where a wasp does wear his sting?
In his tail.

KATHARINA   In his tongue.

PETRUCHIO   Whose tongue?

KATHARINA
Yours, if you talk of tales, and so farewell.   217

PETRUCHIO
What, with my tongue in your tail? Nay, come
again.
Good Kate, I am a gentleman—

KATHARINA   That I'll try.   *She strikes him.*

---

158 **Jack** knave   159 **As . . . so** as if she had planned how to abuse me so   160 **lusty** lively   164 **practice** instruction   168 **s.d. Manet** he remains onstage   172 **clear** serene   176 **piercing** moving   177 **pack** begone   179 **deny** refuse.   **crave the day** ask her to name the day   180 **ask the banns** have a reading of the required announcement in church of a forthcoming marriage   183 **heard, hard** (Pronounced nearly alike.)   189 **all Kates** (with a quibble on "cates," confections, delicacies)   190 **of me** from me.   **consolation** comfort   192 **sounded** proclaimed (with a quibble on "plumbed," as indicated by *deeply* in the next line)   194 **moved** impelled (followed by wordplay on the more literal meaning of *move* and *remove*)   195 **In good time** forsooth, indeed

197 **movable** (1) one easily changed or dissuaded (2) an article of furniture   198 **A joint stool** a well-fitted stool made by an expert craftsman   199 **bear** carry (with puns in the following lines suggesting "bear children" and "support a man during sexual intercourse")   201 **jade** an ill-conditioned horse   203 **For knowing** because I know. **light** (1) of delicate stature (2) lascivious (3) lacking a *burden* (see previous line) in the musical sense of lacking a bass undersong or accompaniment (4) elusive (in the following line)   204 **swain** young rustic in love   206 **Should . . . buzz** (Petruchio puns on *be* and "bee," and uses *buzz* in perhaps three senses: (1) an interjection of impatience or contempt (2) a bee's sound (3) rumor being buzzed about, to which, he implies, Kate had better listen.)   **buzzard** (1) figuratively, a fool (2) in the next line, an inferior kind of hawk, fit only to overtake a slow-winged *turtle* or turtledove, as Petruchio might overtake Kate (3) a buzzing insect, caught by a turtledove   209 **wasp** i.e., waspish, scolding woman (but suggested by *buzzard*, buzzing insect)   217 **talk of tales** i.e., idly tell stories (with pun on "tail")

PETRUCHIO
I swear I'll cuff you if you strike again.
KATHARINA   So may you lose your arms.
If you strike me, you are no gentleman,
And if no gentleman, why then no arms.   223
PETRUCHIO
A herald, Kate? O, put me in thy books!   224
KATHARINA   What is your crest, a coxcomb?   225
PETRUCHIO
A combless cock, so Kate will be my hen.   226
KATHARINA
No cock of mine. You crow too like a craven.   227
PETRUCHIO
Nay, come, Kate, come. You must not look so sour.
KATHARINA
It is my fashion when I see a crab.   229
PETRUCHIO
Why, here's no crab, and therefore look not sour.
KATHARINA   There is, there is.
PETRUCHIO
Then show it me.
KATHARINA   Had I a glass, I would.
PETRUCHIO   What, you mean my face?
KATHARINA   Well aimed of such a young one.   234
PETRUCHIO
Now, by Saint George, I am too young for you.
KATHARINA
Yet you are withered.
PETRUCHIO   'Tis with cares.
KATHARINA   I care not.
PETRUCHIO
Nay, hear you, Kate. In sooth, you scape not so.   237
KATHARINA
I chafe you if I tarry. Let me go.   238
PETRUCHIO
No, not a whit. I find you passing gentle.   239
'Twas told me you were rough, and coy, and sullen,   240
And now I find report a very liar,   241
For thou art pleasant, gamesome, passing courteous, 242
But slow in speech, yet sweet as springtime
    flowers.   243
Thou canst not frown, thou canst not look askance,   244
Nor bite the lip, as angry wenches will,
Nor hast thou pleasure to be cross in talk;   246
But thou with mildness entertain'st thy wooers,   247
With gentle conference, soft and affable.   248
Why does the world report that Kate doth limp?
O sland'rous world! Kate like the hazel twig

Is straight and slender, and as brown in hue
As hazelnuts, and sweeter than the kernels.
O, let me see thee walk. Thou dost not halt.   253
KATHARINA
Go, fool, and whom thou keep'st command.   254
PETRUCHIO
Did ever Dian so become a grove   255
As Kate this chamber with her princely gait?
O, be thou Dian, and let her be Kate,
And then let Kate be chaste and Dian sportful!   258
KATHARINA
Where did you study all this goodly speech?   259
PETRUCHIO
It is extempore, from my mother wit.   260
KATHARINA
A witty mother! Witless else her son.   261
PETRUCHIO   Am I not wise?   262
KATHARINA   Yes, keep you warm.   263
PETRUCHIO
Marry, so I mean, sweet Katharine, in thy bed.
And therefore, setting all this chat aside,
Thus in plain terms: your father hath consented
That you shall be my wife; your dowry 'greed on;
And will you, nill you, I will marry you.   268
Now, Kate, I am a husband for your turn,   269
For by this light, whereby I see thy beauty—
Thy beauty that doth make me like thee well—
Thou must be married to no man but me.

        Enter Baptista, Gremio, [and] Tranio [as
        Lucentio].

For I am he am born to tame you, Kate,
And bring you from a wild Kate to a Kate   274
Conformable as other household Kates.   275
Here comes your father. Never make denial;
I must and will have Katharine to my wife.
BAPTISTA
Now, Signor Petruchio, how speed you with my
    daughter?   278
PETRUCHIO
How but well, sir, how but well?
It were impossible I should speed amiss.
BAPTISTA
Why, how now, daughter Katharine, in your
    dumps?   281
KATHARINA
Call you me daughter? Now, I promise you,   282
You have showed a tender fatherly regard,
To wish me wed to one half-lunatic,
A madcap ruffian and a swearing Jack,   285

223 **no arms** no coat of arms (with pun on *arms* as limbs of the body)
224 **books** (1) books of heraldry, heraldic registers (2) grace, favor
225 **crest** (1) armorial device (2) a rooster's comb, setting up the joke
on *coxcomb,* the cap of the court fool   226 **A combless cock** i.e., a
gentle rooster (but with sexual suggestion).   **so** provided that   227 **a**
craven a cock that is not "game" or willing to fight   229 **crab** crab
apple   234 **aimed of** guessed for.   **young** i.e., inexperienced. (But
Petruchio picks up the word in the sense of "strong.")   237 **scape** escape   238 **chafe** annoy (but suggesting also "excite")   239 **passing**
very. (Also in line 242.)   240 **coy** disdainful   241 **a very** an utter
242 **pleasant** merry.   **gamesome** playful, spirited   243 **But slow**
never anything but slow   244 **askance** scornfully   246 **cross in talk**
always contradicting   247 **entertain'st** receive   248 **conference** conversation

253 **halt** limp   254 **whom thou keep'st command** i.e., order about
those whom you employ, your servants, not me   255 **Dian** Diana,
goddess of the hunt and of chastity.   **become** adorn   258 **sportful**
amorous   259 **study** memorize   260 **mother wit** native intelligence
261 **Witless . . . son** i.e., without the intelligence inherited from her,
he would have none at all   262–263 **wise . . . warm** (An allusion to
the proverbial phrase "enough wit to keep oneself warm.")   268 **will**
you, nill you whether you're willing or not   269 **for your turn** to suit
you   274 **wild Kate** (with a quibble on "wildcat")   275 **Conformable**
compliant   278 **speed** fare, get on   281 **in your dumps** in low spirits
282 **promise** assure   285 **Jack** ill-mannered fellow

That thinks with oaths to face the matter out. 286
PETRUCHIO
Father, 'tis thus: yourself and all the world
That talked of her have talked amiss of her.
If she be curst, it is for policy, 289
For she's not froward, but modest as the dove. 290
She is not hot, but temperate as the morn.
For patience she will prove a second Grissel, 292
And Roman Lucrece for her chastity. 293
And to conclude, we have 'greed so well together
That upon Sunday is the wedding day.
KATHARINA
I'll see thee hanged on Sunday first.
GREMIO Hark, Petruchio, she says she'll see thee
hanged first.
TRANIO
Is this your speeding? Nay then, good night our
part! 299
PETRUCHIO
Be patient, gentlemen. I choose her for myself.
If she and I be pleased, what's that to you?
'Tis bargained twixt us twain, being alone,
That she shall still be curst in company.
I tell you, 'tis incredible to believe
How much she loves me. O, the kindest Kate!
She hung about my neck, and kiss on kiss
She vied so fast, protesting oath on oath, 307
That in a twink she won me to her love.
O, you are novices! 'Tis a world to see 309
How tame, when men and women are alone,
A meacock wretch can make the curstest shrew.— 311
Give me thy hand, Kate. I will unto Venice
To buy apparel gainst the wedding day.— 313
Provide the feast, Father, and bid the guests.
I will be sure my Katharine shall be fine. 315
BAPTISTA
I know not what to say. But give me your hands.
God send you joy, Petruchio! 'Tis a match.
GREMIO, TRANIO
Amen, say we. We will be witnesses.
PETRUCHIO
Father, and wife, and gentlemen, adieu.
I will to Venice. Sunday comes apace.
We will have rings, and things, and fine array;
And kiss me, Kate. We will be married o' Sunday. 322
          Exeunt Petruchio and Katharine [separately].
GREMIO
Was ever match clapped up so suddenly? 323

BAPTISTA
Faith, gentlemen, now I play a merchant's part,
And venture madly on a desperate mart. 325
TRANIO
'Twas a commodity lay fretting by you; 326
'Twill bring you gain, or perish on the seas.
BAPTISTA
The gain I seek is quiet in the match.
GREMIO
No doubt but he hath got a quiet catch. 329
But now, Baptista, to your younger daughter.
Now is the day we long have lookèd for.
I am your neighbor, and was suitor first.
TRANIO
And I am one that love Bianca more
Than words can witness, or your thoughts can
  guess.
GREMIO
Youngling, thou canst not love so dear as I.
TRANIO
Graybeard, thy love doth freeze.
GREMIO   But thine doth fry.
Skipper, stand back. 'Tis age that nourisheth. 337
TRANIO
But youth in ladies' eyes that flourisheth.
BAPTISTA
Content you, gentlemen, I will compound this strife. 339
'Tis deeds must win the prize, and he of both 340
That can assure my daughter greatest dower 341
Shall have my Bianca's love.
Say, Signor Gremio, what can you assure her?
GREMIO
First, as you know, my house within the city
Is richly furnishèd with plate and gold, 345
Basins and ewers to lave her dainty hands; 346
My hangings all of Tyrian tapestry; 347
In ivory coffers I have stuffed my crowns; 348
In cypress chests my arras counterpoints, 349
Costly apparel, tents, and canopies, 350
Fine linen, Turkey cushions bossed with pearl, 351
Valance of Venice gold in needlework, 352
Pewter and brass, and all things that belongs
To house or housekeeping. Then at my farm
I have a hundred milch kine to the pail, 355
Sixscore fat oxen standing in my stalls,
And all things answerable to this portion. 357
Myself am struck in years, I must confess, 358

286 face brazen 289 policy cunning, ulterior motive 290 froward willful, perverse 292 Grissel patient Griselda, the epitome of wifely patience and devotion (whose story was told by Chaucer in "The Clerk's Tale" of The Canterbury Tales and earlier by Boccaccio and Petrarch) 293 Roman Lucrece Lucretia, a Roman lady who took her own life after her chastity had been violated by the Tarquin prince, Sextus. (Shakespeare tells the story in The Rape of Lucrece.) 299 speeding success. good night our part good-bye to what we hoped to get 307 vied went me one better, kiss for kiss 309 a world worth a whole world 311 meacock cowardly 313 gainst in anticipation of 315 fine elegantly dressed 322 kiss me (Petruchio probably kisses her.) 323 clapped up settled (by a shaking of hands)

325 desperate mart risky venture 326 lay fretting i.e., which lay in storage being destroyed by moths, weevils, or spoilage (with a pun on "chafing") 329 quiet catch (Said ironically; Gremio is sure that Kate will be anything but quiet.) 337 Skipper flighty fellow 339 compound settle 340 deeds (1) actions (2) legal deeds. he of both the one of you two 341 dower portion of a husband's estate settled on his wife in his will. (Also at line 387 and 4.4.45.) 345 plate silver utensils 346 lave wash 347 hangings draperies hung on beds and walls. Tyrian dark red or purple 348 crowns five-shilling coins 349 arras counterpoints counterpanes of tapestry 350 tents bed curtains 351 Turkey Turkish. bossed embossed 352 Valance fringes of drapery around the canopy or bed frame 355 milch kine to the pail dairy cattle 357 answerable to on the same scale as 358 struck advanced

And if I die tomorrow, this is hers,
If whilst I live she will be only mine.

TRANIO
That "only" came well in. Sir, list to me:
I am my father's heir and only son.
If I may have your daughter to my wife,
I'll leave her houses three or four as good,
Within rich Pisa walls, as any one
Old Signor Gremio has in Padua,
Besides two thousand ducats by the year   367
Of fruitful land, all which shall be her jointure.   368
What, have I pinched you, Signor Gremio?

GREMIO
Two thousand ducats by the year of land!
[Aside.] My land amounts not to so much in all.—
That she shall have, besides an argosy   372
That now is lying in Marseilles road.   373
[To Tranio.] What, have I choked you with an
    argosy?

TRANIO
Gremio, 'tis known my father hath no less
Than three great argosies, besides two galliases   376
And twelve tight galleys. These I will assure her,   377
And twice as much, whate'er thou off'rest next.

GREMIO
Nay, I have offered all. I have no more,
And she can have no more than all I have.
[To Baptista.] If you like me, she shall have me and
    mine.

TRANIO
Why then, the maid is mine from all the world,
By your firm promise. Gremio is outvied.   383

BAPTISTA
I must confess your offer is the best;
And, let your father make her the assurance,   385
She is your own; else, you must pardon me.
If you should die before him, where's her dower?

TRANIO
That's but a cavil. He is old, I young.   388

GREMIO
And may not young men die, as well as old?

BAPTISTA
Well, gentlemen, I am thus resolved:
On Sunday next, you know
My daughter Katharine is to be married.
Now, on the Sunday following shall Bianca
Be bride [to Tranio] to you, if you make this
    assurance;
If not, to Signor Gremio.
And so I take my leave, and thank you both.   Exit.

GREMIO
Adieu, good neighbor.—Now I fear thee not.
Sirrah, young gamester, your father were a fool
To give thee all, and in his waning age

Set foot under thy table. Tut, a toy!   400
An old Italian fox is not so kind, my boy.   Exit.

TRANIO
A vengeance on your crafty withered hide!
Yet I have faced it with a card of ten.   403
'Tis in my head to do my master good.
I see no reason but supposed Lucentio
Must get a father, called supposed Vincentio—
And that's a wonder. Fathers commonly
Do get their children; but in this case of wooing,   408
A child shall get a sire, if I fail not of my cunning.
                                               Exit.

❧

3.1   Enter Lucentio [as Cambio], Hortensio [as Litio],
         and Bianca.

LUCENTIO
Fiddler, forbear. You grow too forward, sir.
Have you so soon forgot the entertainment
Her sister Katharine welcomed you withal?

HORTENSIO
But, wrangling pedant, this is
The patroness of heavenly harmony.
Then give me leave to have prerogative,   6
And when in music we have spent an hour,
Your lecture shall have leisure for as much.   8

LUCENTIO
Preposterous ass, that never read so far   9
To know the cause why music was ordained!   10
Was it not to refresh the mind of man
After his studies or his usual pain?   12
Then give me leave to read philosophy,   13
And, while I pause, serve in your harmony.   14

HORTENSIO
Sirrah, I will not bear these braves of thine.   15

BIANCA
Why, gentlemen, you do me double wrong
To strive for that which resteth in my choice.
I am no breeching scholar in the schools;   18
I'll not be tied to hours nor 'pointed times,
But learn my lessons as I please myself.
And, to cut off all strife, here sit we down.
[To Hortensio.] Take you your instrument, play you
    the whiles;   22
His lecture will be done ere you have tuned.

HORTENSIO
You'll leave his lecture when I am in tune?

LUCENTIO
That will be never. Tune your instrument.

367 **ducats** gold coins   368 **Of** from.   **jointure** marriage settlement
372 **argosy** merchant vessel of the largest size   373 **road** roadstead,
harbor   376 **galliases** heavy, low-built vessels   377 **tight** watertight
383 **outvied** outbidden   385 **let** provided   388 **but a cavil** merely a
frivolous objection

400 **Set . . . table** i.e., become a dependent in your household.
a toy nonsense   403 **faced . . . ten** brazened it out with only a ten-
spot of cards   408 **get** beget (with a play on *get*, "obtain," in line
406)
3.1. Location: The same.
6 **prerogative** precedence   8 **lecture** lesson   9 **Preposterous** inverting
the natural order of things, unreasonable   10 **To know** as to know
12 **usual pain** regular labors   13 **read** teach   14 **serve in** present,
serve up   15 **braves** insults   18 **breeching scholar** i.e., schoolboy liable to be whipped   22 **the whiles** meantime

[Hortensio moves aside and tunes.]

BIANCA Where left we last?

LUCENTIO Here, madam. *[He reads.]*
  "Hic ibat Simois; hic est Sigeia tellus; 28
  Hic steterat Priami regia celsa senis." 29

BIANCA Conster them. 30

LUCENTIO *"Hic ibat,"* as I told you before, *"Simois,"* I
  am Lucentio, *"hic est,"* son unto Vincentio of Pisa,
  "Sigeia tellus," disguised thus to get your love; *"Hic
  steterat,"* and that Lucentio that comes a-wooing,
  "Priami," is my man Tranio, *"regia,"* bearing my port, 35
  "celsa senis," that we might beguile the old panta- 36
  loon. 37

HORTENSIO Madam, my instrument's in tune.

BIANCA Let's hear. *[He plays.]* O fie! The treble jars.

LUCENTIO Spit in the hole, man, and tune again. 40
          [Hortensio moves aside.]

BIANCA Now let me see if I can conster it: *"Hic ibat Simois,"* I know you not, *"hic est Sigeia tellus,"* I trust
  you not; *"Hic steterat Priami,"* take heed he hear us
  not, *"regia,"* presume not, *"celsa senis,"* despair not.

HORTENSIO
  Madam, 'tis now in tune.   *[He plays again.]*

LUCENTIO   All but the bass.

HORTENSIO
  The bass is right, 'tis the base knave that jars.
  [Aside.] How fiery and forward our pedant is!
  Now, for my life, the knave doth court my love.
  Pedascule, I'll watch you better yet. 49

BIANCA *[to Lucentio]*
  In time I may believe, yet I mistrust.

LUCENTIO
  Mistrust it not, for, sure, Aeacides 51
  Was Ajax, called so from his grandfather.

BIANCA
  I must believe my master; else, I promise you,
  I should be arguing still upon that doubt.
  But let it rest. —Now, Litio, to you:
  Good master, take it not unkindly, pray,
  That I have been thus pleasant with you both. 57

HORTENSIO *[to Lucentio]*
  You may go walk, and give me leave awhile.
  My lessons make no music in three parts.

LUCENTIO
  Are you so formal, sir? Well, I must wait. 60
  [Aside.] And watch withal; for, but I be deceived, 61
  Our fine musician groweth amorous.
          [He moves aside.]

HORTENSIO
  Madam, before you touch the instrument,
  To learn the order of my fingering, 64
  I must begin with rudiments of art,
  To teach you gamut in a briefer sort, 66
  More pleasant, pithy, and effectual
  Than hath been taught by any of my trade.
  And there it is in writing, fairly drawn. 69
          [He gives her a paper.]

BIANCA
  Why, I am past my gamut long ago.

HORTENSIO
  Yet read the gamut of Hortensio.

BIANCA *[reads]*
  "Gamut I am, the ground of all accord, 72
  A re, to plead Hortensio's passion;
  B mi, Bianca, take him for thy lord, 74
  C fa ut, that loves with all affection. 75
  D sol re, one clef, two notes have I; 76
  E la mi, show pity, or I die." 77
  Call you this gamut? Tut, I like it not.
  Old fashions please me best; I am not so nice 79
  To change true rules for odd inventions.

          Enter a [Servant as] messenger.

SERVANT
  Mistress, your father prays you leave your books
  And help to dress your sister's chamber up.
  You know tomorrow is the wedding day.

BIANCA
  Farewell, sweet masters both. I must be gone.

LUCENTIO
  Faith, mistress, then I have no cause to stay.
          [Exeunt Bianca, Servant, and Lucentio.]

HORTENSIO
  But I have cause to pry into this pedant.
  Methinks he looks as though he were in love.
  Yet if thy thoughts, Bianca, be so humble
  To cast thy wandering eyes on every stale, 89
  Seize thee that list. If once I find thee ranging, 90
  Hortensio will be quit with thee by changing. *Exit.* 91

          ❖

3.2 *Enter Baptista, Gremio, Tranio [as Lucentio],
        Katharine, Bianca, [Lucentio as Cambio], and
        others, attendants.*

28–29 **Hic . . . senis** here flowed the river Simois; here is the Sigeian land; here stood the lofty palace of old Priam. (Ovid, *Heroides*, I.33–34.) 30 **Conster** construe 35 **port** social position, style of living 36–37 **pantaloon** foolish old man, i.e., Gremio 40 **Spit in the hole** i.e., to make the peg stick 49 **Pedascule** (A word contemptuously coined by Hortensio, presumably the vocative of an invented Latinism, *pedasculus*, "little pedant.") 51 **Mistrust** (Lucentio plays upon Bianca's *mistrust* in line 50, in which she expresses skepticism about his secret wooing; his answer seeks to reassure her, while at the same time in "Litio's" hearing he seems to emphasize the truth of his instruction as he goes on with his lesson from the *Heroides*. Her reply is ambiguous in the same way.) **Aeacides** descendant of Aeacus, King of Aegina, father of Telamon and grandfather of Ajax 57 **pleasant** merry 60 **formal** precise 61 **but** unless

64 **order** method 66 **gamut** the scale, from the alphabet name (gamma) of the first note plus *ut*, its syllable name, now commonly called *do*. (The *gamut* of Hortensio begins on G instead of on C.) 69 **drawn** set out, copied 72 **ground** bass note, foundation. **accord** harmony 74 **B mi** (with a suggestion of "be my") 75 **fa ut** (The note C is the fourth note, or *fa*, of a scale based on G but is the first note, *ut*, or *do*, of the more universal major scale based on C. Similarly, D is the fifth note, or *sol*, in the G scale but is the second, or *re*, in the C scale; similarly, with E as sixth and third.) 76 **two notes** (hinting at Hortensio's disguise) 77 **E la mi** (suggesting "Ill am I") 79 **nice** capricious 89 **stale** decoy, bait 90 **Seize . . . list** let him who wants you have you. **ranging** inconstant. (The metaphor is that of a straying hawk.) 91 **be quit** get even. **changing** loving another **3.2. Location:** Padua. Before Baptista's house.

BAPTISTA [*to Tranio*]
Signor Lucentio, this is the 'pointed day
That Katharine and Petruchio should be married,
And yet we hear not of our son-in-law.
What will be said? What mockery will it be,
To want the bridegroom when the priest attends   5
To speak the ceremonial rites of marriage?
What says Lucentio to this shame of ours?

KATHARINA
No shame but mine. I must, forsooth, be forced
To give my hand opposed against my heart
Unto a mad-brain rudesby full of spleen,   10
Who wooed in haste and means to wed at leisure.
I told you, I, he was a frantic fool,   12
Hiding his bitter jests in blunt behavior.
And, to be noted for a merry man,   14
He'll woo a thousand, 'point the day of marriage,
Make friends, invite, and proclaim the banns,
Yet never means to wed where he hath wooed.
Now must the world point at poor Katharine
And say, "Lo, there is mad Petruchio's wife,
If it would please him come and marry her!"

TRANIO
Patience, good Katharine, and Baptista, too.
Upon my life, Petruchio means but well,
Whatever fortune stays him from his word.   23
Though he be blunt, I know him passing wise;
Though he be merry, yet withal he's honest.   25

KATHARINA
Would Katharine had never seen him though!
                                    Exit weeping.

BAPTISTA
Go, girl, I cannot blame thee now to weep,
For such an injury would vex a very saint,
Much more a shrew of thy impatient humor.

                    Enter Biondello.

BIONDELLO   Master, master! News, and such old news   30
as you never heard of!
BAPTISTA   Is it new and old too? How may that be?
BIONDELLO   Why, is it not news to hear of Petruchio's
coming?
BAPTISTA   Is he come?
BIONDELLO   Why, no, sir.
BAPTISTA   What, then?
BIONDELLO   He is coming.
BAPTISTA   When will he be here?
BIONDELLO   When he stands where I am and sees you
there.
TRANIO   But say, what to thine old news?   42
BIONDELLO   Why, Petruchio is coming in a new hat and
an old jerkin; a pair of old breeches thrice turned; a 44

pair of boots that have been candle-cases, one buck-   45
led, another laced; an old rusty sword ta'en out of the
town armory, with a broken hilt, and chapeless; with   47
two broken points; his horse hipped, with an old   48
mothy saddle and stirrups of no kindred; besides,
possessed with the glanders and like to mose in the   50
chine, troubled with the lampass, infected with the   51
fashions, full of windgalls, sped with spavins, rayed 52
with the yellows, past cure of the fives, stark spoiled 53
with the staggers, begnawn with the bots, swayed in   54
the back and shoulder-shotten; near-legged before,   55
and with a half-cheeked bit and a headstall of sheep's 56
leather which, being restrained to keep him from   57
stumbling, hath been often burst and now repaired
with knots; one girth six times pieced, and a woman's 59
crupper of velour, which hath two letters for her name 60
fairly set down in studs, and here and there pieced
with packthread.   62
BAPTISTA   Who comes with him?
BIONDELLO   O, sir, his lackey, for all the world capari- 64
soned like the horse; with a linen stock on one leg and 65
a kersey boot-hose on the other, gartered with a red   66
and blue list; an old hat, and the humor of forty fancies 67
pricked in 't for a feather—a monster, a very monster 68
in apparel, and not like a Christian footboy or a gentleman's lackey.

TRANIO
'Tis some odd humor pricks him to this fashion;   71
Yet oftentimes he goes but mean-appareled.

BAPTISTA   I am glad he's come, howsoe'er he comes.
BIONDELLO   Why, sir, he comes not.
BAPTISTA   Didst thou not say he comes?

---

5 want lack   **10 rudesby** unmannerly fellow.   **spleen** i.e., change-able temper   **12 frantic** violently insane   **14 to be noted for** in order to get a reputation as   **23 fortune . . . word** accident keeps him from fulfilling his promise   **25 merry** given to joking   **30 old** rare; or perhaps referring to Petruchio's old clothes   **42 to** about   **44 jerkin** man's jacket.   **turned** i.e., with the material reversed to get more wear

45 candle-cases i.e., discarded boots, used only as a receptacle for candle ends   **47 chapeless** without the chape, the metal plate or mounting of a scabbard, especially that which covers the point   **48 points** tagged laces for attaching hose to doublet.   **hipped** lamed in the hip. (Almost all the diseases here named are described in Gervase Markham's *How to Choose, Ride, Train, and Diet both Hunting Horses and Running Horses . . . Also a Discourse of Horsemanship,* probably first published in 1593.)   **50 glanders** contagious disease in horses causing swelling beneath the jaw and mucous discharge from the nostrils   **50–51 mose in the chine** suffer from glanders   **51 lampass** a thick, spongy flesh growing over a horse's upper teeth and hindering his eating   **52 fashions** i.e., farcins, or farcy, a disease like glanders.   **windgalls** soft tumors or swellings generally found on the fetlock joint, so called from having been supposed to contain air.   **sped** far gone.   **spavins** a disease of the hock, marked by a small bony enlargement inside the leg.   **rayed** defiled   **53 yellows** jaundice.   **fives** avives, a glandular disease causing swelling behind the ear   **53–54 stark spoiled with** completely destroyed by   **54 staggers** a disease causing palsylike staggering.   **bots** parasitic worms   **55 shoulder-shotten** with sprained or dislocated shoulder.   **near-legged before** with knock-kneed forelegs   **56 half-cheeked bit** one to which the bridle is attached halfway up the cheek or sidepiece and thus not giving sufficient control over the horse.   **headstall** part of the bridle over the head   **56–57 sheep's leather** (i.e., of inferior quality; pigskin was used for strongest harness)   **57 restrained** drawn back   **59 girth** saddle-strap passing under the horse's belly.   **pieced** mended   **60 crupper** leather loop passing under the horse's tail and fastened to the saddle.   **velour** velvet.   **two** her initials   **62 packthread** twine for securing parcels   **64 for all the world** in all respects   **64–65 caparisoned** outfitted   **65 stock** stocking   **66 kersey boot-hose** overstocking of coarse material for wearing under boots   **67 list** strip of cloth.   **the humor . . . fancies** i.e., with a caprice equal to some forty imaginings (?)   **68 pricked** pinned.   **for** in place of   **71 humor pricks** whim that spurs

BIONDELLO   Who? That Petruchio came?

BAPTISTA   Ay, that Petruchio came.

BIONDELLO   No, sir, I say his horse comes, with him on
his back.

BAPTISTA   Why, that's all one.   80

BIONDELLO
Nay, by Saint Jamy,
I hold you a penny,   82
A horse and a man
Is more than one,
And yet not many.

Enter Petruchio and Grumio.

PETRUCHIO
Come, where be these gallants? Who's at home?

BAPTISTA   You are welcome, sir.

PETRUCHIO   And yet I come not well.   88

BAPTISTA   And yet you halt not.   89

TRANIO
Not so well appareled as I wish you were.

PETRUCHIO
Were it better, I should rush in thus.   91
But where is Kate? Where is my lovely bride?
How does my father? Gentles, methinks you frown.
And wherefore gaze this goodly company,
As if they saw some wondrous monument,   95
Some comet, or unusual prodigy?   96

BAPTISTA
Why, sir, you know this is your wedding day.
First were we sad, fearing you would not come,
Now sadder that you come so unprovided.   99
Fie, doff this habit, shame to your estate,   100
An eyesore to our solemn festival!

TRANIO
And tell us, what occasion of import
Hath all so long detained you from your wife
And sent you hither so unlike yourself?

PETRUCHIO
Tedious it were to tell, and harsh to hear.
Sufficeth I am come to keep my word,   106
Though in some part enforcèd to digress,   107
Which at more leisure I will so excuse
As you shall well be satisfied withal.
But where is Kate? I stay too long from her.
The morning wears; 'tis time we were at church.

TRANIO
See not your bride in these unreverent robes.
Go to my chamber. Put on clothes of mine.

PETRUCHIO
Not I, believe me. Thus I'll visit her.

BAPTISTA
But thus, I trust, you will not marry her.

PETRUCHIO
Good sooth, even thus. Therefore ha' done with
words.   116
To me she's married, not unto my clothes.
Could I repair what she will wear in me   118
As I can change these poor accoutrements,
'Twere well for Kate and better for myself.
But what a fool am I to chat with you,
When I should bid good morrow to my bride
And seal the title with a lovely kiss!   *Exit.* 123

TRANIO
He hath some meaning in his mad attire.
We will persuade him, be it possible,
To put on better ere he go to church.

BAPTISTA
I'll after him, and see the event of this.   127
Exit [with all but Tranio and Lucentio].

TRANIO
But, sir, to love concerneth us to add   128
Her father's liking, which to bring to pass,
As I before imparted to your worship,
I am to get a man—whate'er he be
It skills not much, we'll fit him to our turn—   132
And he shall be Vincentio of Pisa
And make assurance here in Padua
Of greater sums than I have promisèd.
So shall you quietly enjoy your hope
And marry sweet Bianca with consent.

LUCENTIO
Were it not that my fellow schoolmaster
Doth watch Bianca's steps so narrowly,
'Twere good, methinks, to steal our marriage,   140
Which once performed, let all the world say no,
I'll keep mine own, despite of all the world.

TRANIO
That by degrees we mean to look into,
And watch our vantage in this business.   144
We'll overreach the graybeard, Gremio,
The narrow-prying father, Minola,   146
The quaint musician, amorous Litio,   147
All for my master's sake, Lucentio.

Enter Gremio.

Signor Gremio, came you from the church?

GREMIO
As willingly as e'er I came from school.

TRANIO
And is the bride and bridegroom coming home?

GREMIO
A bridegroom, say you? 'Tis a groom indeed,   152
A grumbling groom, and that the girl shall find.

---

80 **all one** the same thing   82 **hold** wager   88 **I come not well** i.e., I am not made to feel welcome; or, I come admittedly not well appareled   89 **halt** limp, move slowly   91 **Were it** even if it (my apparel) were.   **rush** come quickly (referring to *halt not* in line 89)   95 **monument** portent   96 **prodigy** omen   99 **unprovided** ill equipped   100 **habit** outfit.   **estate** position, station   106 **Sufficeth** it is enough that   107 **digress** i.e., deviate

116 **Good sooth** i.e., yes indeed   118 **Could . . . me** if I could amend in my character what she'll have to put up with   123 **lovely** loving   127 **event** outcome   128 **concerneth us** it concerns us, is in our best interest   132 **skills** matters   140 **steal our marriage** elope   144 **watch our vantage** look out for our best opportunity, advantage   146 **narrow-prying** suspicious, watchful   147 **quaint** skillful   152 **a groom indeed** a fine bridegroom he is. (Said ironically, with pun on the sense of "servant," "rough fellow.")

TRANIO

Curster than she? Why, 'tis impossible.

GREMIO

Why, he 's a devil, a devil, a very fiend.

TRANIO

Why, she's a devil, a devil, the devil's dam.   156

GREMIO

Tut, she's a lamb, a dove, a fool to him.   157
I'll tell you, Sir Lucentio. When the priest
Should ask if Katharine should be his wife,   159
"Ay, by Gog's wouns," quoth he, and swore so
    loud   160
That all amazed the priest let fall the book,
And as he stooped again to take it up,
This mad-brained bridegroom took him such a cuff   163
That down fell priest and book, and book and priest.
"Now take them up," quoth he, "if any list."   165

TRANIO

What said the wench when he rose again?

GREMIO

Trembled and shook, forwhy he stamped and swore   167
As if the vicar meant to cozen him.   168
But after many ceremonies done
He calls for wine. "A health!" quoth he, as if
He had been aboard, carousing to his mates   171
After a storm; quaffed off the muscatel
And threw the sops all in the sexton's face,   173
Having no other reason
But that his beard grew thin and hungerly   175
And seemed to ask him sops as he was drinking.   176
This done, he took the bride about the neck
And kissed her lips with such a clamorous smack
That at the parting all the church did echo.
And I seeing this came thence for very shame,
And after me, I know, the rout is coming.   181
Such a mad marriage never was before.   *Music plays.*
Hark, hark! I hear the minstrels play.

*Enter Petruchio, Kate, Bianca, Hortensio [as Litio],
Baptista, [with Grumio, and train].*

PETRUCHIO

Gentlemen and friends, I thank you for your pains.
I know you think to dine with me today,
And have prepared great store of wedding cheer;
But so it is my haste doth call me hence,
And therefore here I mean to take my leave.

BAPTISTA

Is 't possible you will away tonight?

PETRUCHIO

I must away today, before night come.

TRANIO

Make it no wonder. If you knew my business,   191
You would entreat me rather go than stay.
And, honest company, I thank you all   193
That have beheld me give away myself
To this most patient, sweet, and virtuous wife.
Dine with my father, drink a health to me,
For I must hence; and farewell to you all.

TRANIO

Let us entreat you stay till after dinner.

PETRUCHIO

It may not be.

GREMIO   Let me entreat you.

PETRUCHIO

It cannot be.

KATHARINA   Let me entreat you.

PETRUCHIO

I am content.

KATHARINA   Are you content to stay?

PETRUCHIO

I am content you shall entreat me stay;
But yet not stay, entreat me how you can.

KATHARINA

Now, if you love me, stay.

PETRUCHIO   Grumio, my horse.   204

GRUMIO   Ay, sir, they be ready. The oats have eaten the   205
horses.   206

KATHARINA   Nay, then,
Do what thou canst, I will not go today,
No, nor tomorrow—not till I please myself.
The door is open, sir, there lies your way.
You may be jogging whiles your boots are green.   211
For me, I'll not be gone till I please myself.
'Tis like you'll prove a jolly, surly groom,   213
That take it on you at the first so roundly.   214

PETRUCHIO

O Kate, content thee. Prithee, be not angry.

KATHARINA

I will be angry. What hast thou to do?—   216
Father, be quiet. He shall stay my leisure.   217

GREMIO

Ay, marry, sir, now it begins to work.   218

KATHARINA

Gentlemen, forward to the bridal dinner.
I see a woman may be made a fool
If she had not a spirit to resist.

PETRUCHIO

They shall go forward, Kate, at thy command.—
Obey the bride, you that attend on her.
Go to the feast, revel and domineer,   224

156 dam mother 157 a fool to i.e., a pitiable weak creature compared with 159 Should ask came to the point (in the service) where he is directed to ask 160 Gog's wouns God's (Christ's) wounds 163 took gave, struck 165 list choose 167 forwhy because 168 cozen cheat 171 aboard aboard ship 173 sops cakes or bread soaked in the wine 175 hungerly hungry looking, having a starved or famished look 176 ask him sops ask him for the sops 181 rout crowd, wedding party

191 Make it no wonder don't be amazed at it 193 honest worthy, kind 204 horse horses 205–206 oats . . . horses (A comic inversion.) 211 be . . . green (Proverbial for "getting an early start," with a sarcastic allusion to his unseemly attire.) green fresh, new 213 like likely. jolly arrogant, overbearing 214 take it on you i.e., throw your weight around. roundly unceremoniously 216 What . . . do what business is it of yours? 217 stay my leisure wait until I am ready 218 it . . . work i.e., things are starting to happen. (The metaphor is perhaps of liquor fermenting.) 224 domineer feast riotously

Carouse full measure to her maidenhead,
Be mad and merry, or go hang yourselves.
But for my bonny Kate, she must with me.   227
Nay, look not big, nor stamp, nor stare, nor fret;   228
I will be master of what is mine own.
She is my goods, my chattels; she is my house,
My household stuff, my field, my barn,
My horse, my ox, my ass, my anything;   232
And here she stands, touch her whoever dare.
I'll bring mine action on the proudest he   234
That stops my way in Padua.—Grumio,
Draw forth thy weapon. We are beset with thieves.   236
Rescue thy mistress, if thou be a man.—
Fear not, sweet wench, they shall not touch thee,
    Kate!
I'll buckler thee against a million.   239
            Exeunt Petruchio, Katharina, [and Grumio].
BAPTISTA
Nay, let them go—a couple of quiet ones!
GREMIO
Went they not quickly, I should die with laughing.
TRANIO
Of all mad matches never was the like.
LUCENTIO
Mistress, what's your opinion of your sister?
BIANCA
That, being mad herself, she's madly mated.
GREMIO
I warrant him, Petruchio is Kated.   245
BAPTISTA
Neighbors and friends, though bride and
    bridegroom wants   246
For to supply the places at the table,   247
You know there wants no junkets at the feast.   248
Lucentio, you shall supply the bridegroom's place,
And let Bianca take her sister's room.
TRANIO
Shall sweet Bianca practice how to bride it?   251
BAPTISTA
She shall, Lucentio. Come, gentlemen, let's go.
                                          Exeunt.

❖

4.1   *Enter Grumio.*

GRUMIO   Fie, fie on all tired jades, on all mad masters,   1
and all foul ways! Was ever man so beaten? Was ever   2
man so rayed? Was ever man so weary? I am sent be-   3
fore to make a fire, and they are coming after to warm

them. Now, were not I a little pot and soon hot, my   5
very lips might freeze to my teeth, my tongue to the
roof of my mouth, my heart in my belly, ere I should
come by a fire to thaw me. But I with blowing the   8
fire shall warm myself; for, considering the weather,
a taller man than I will take cold. Holla, ho! Curtis!   10

            Enter Curtis.

CURTIS   Who is that calls so coldly?
GRUMIO   A piece of ice. If thou doubt it, thou mayst
slide from my shoulder to my heel with no greater a
run but my head and my neck. A fire, good Curtis!   14
CURTIS   Is my master and his wife coming, Grumio?
GRUMIO   O, ay, Curtis, ay, and therefore fire, fire! Cast   16
on no water.   17
CURTIS   Is she so hot a shrew as she's reported?
GRUMIO   She was, good Curtis, before this frost. But,
thou know'st, winter tames man, woman, and beast;
for it hath tamed my old master and my new mistress
and myself, fellow Curtis.
CURTIS   Away, you three-inch fool! I am no beast.   23
GRUMIO   Am I but three inches? Why, thy horn is a foot,   24
and so long am I, at the least. But wilt thou make a
fire, or shall I complain on thee to our mistress, whose
hand—she being now at hand—thou shalt soon feel,
to thy cold comfort, for being slow in thy hot office?   28
CURTIS   I prithee, good Grumio, tell me, how goes the
world?
GRUMIO   A cold world, Curtis, in every office but thine,
and therefore fire. Do thy duty, and have thy duty, for   32
my master and mistress are almost frozen to death.
CURTIS   There's fire ready, and therefore, good Grumio,
the news.
GRUMIO   Why, "Jack boy, ho, boy!" and as much news   36
as wilt thou.
CURTIS   Come, you are so full of coney-catching.   38
GRUMIO   Why, therefore fire, for I have caught extreme
cold. Where's the cook? Is supper ready, the house
trimmed, rushes strewed, cobwebs swept, the serv-   41
ingmen in their new fustian, the white stockings, and   42
every officer his wedding garment on? Be the Jacks fair   43
within, the Jills fair without, the carpets laid, and   44
everything in order?

227 **for** as for   228 **big** threatening   232 **ox . . . anything** (This catalogue of a man's possessions is from the Tenth Commandment.)
234 **action** (1) lawsuit (2) attack   236 **Draw** (Perhaps Petruchio and
Grumio actually draw their swords.)   239 **buckler** shield, defend
245 **Kated** (Gremio's invention for "mated and matched with Kate.")
246 **wants** are lacking   246–247 **wants For to supply** are not present
to fill   248 **there wants no junkets** there is no lack of sweetmeats
251 **bride it** play the bride
4.1. Location: Petruchio's country house. A table is set out, with
seats.
1 **jades** ill-conditioned horses   2 **ways** roads   3 **rayed** dirtied

5 **a little . . . hot** (Proverbial expression for a person of small stature
soon angered.)   8 **come by** find   10 **taller** (with play on the meaning
"better," "finer")   14 **run** running start   16–17 **Cast . . . water** (Alludes to the round "Scotland's burning," in which the phrase "Fire,
fire!" is followed by "Pour on water, pour on water.")   23 **three-inch
fool** (Another reference to Grumio's size.)   **I am no beast** (Curtis protests being called *fellow* by Grumio, since Grumio in his previous
speech has paralleled himself with *beast*.)   24 **horn** i.e., cuckold's
horn. (Grumio retorts that he's not too small to cuckold Curtis.)
28 **hot office** i.e., duty of providing a fire   32 **have thy duty** receive
your reward   36 **Jack . . . boy** (The first line of another round or
catch.)   38 **coney-catching** cheating, trickery (with a play on *catch*,
"round," in the previous line)   41 **rushes** (Used to cover the floor.)
42 **fustian** coarse cloth of cotton and flax   43 **officer** household servant.   **Jacks** (1) servingmen (2) drinking vessels, usually of leather and
hence needing to be clean *within*   44 **Jills** (1) maidservants (2)
"gills," drinking vessels holding a quarter pint, often of metal and
hence in need of polishing *without*. (Grumio may joke that the maidservants cannot be expected to be clean *within*.)   **carpets** table
covers

CURTIS All ready; and therefore, I pray thee, news.

GRUMIO First, know my horse is tired, my master and mistress fallen out. 48

CURTIS How?

GRUMIO Out of their saddles into the dirt—and thereby hangs a tale. 50 51

CURTIS Let's ha 't, good Grumio. 52

GRUMIO Lend thine ear.

CURTIS Here.

GRUMIO There.   [He cuffs Curtis.]

CURTIS This 'tis to feel a tale, not to hear a tale.

GRUMIO And therefore 'tis called a sensible tale, and this cuff was but to knock at your ear and beseech listening. Now I begin: Imprimis, we came down a foul hill, my master riding behind my mistress— 57 59 60

CURTIS Both of one horse? 61

GRUMIO What's that to thee?

CURTIS Why, a horse.

GRUMIO Tell thou the tale. But hadst thou not crossed me, thou shouldst have heard how her horse fell and she under her horse; thou shouldst have heard in how miry a place, how she was bemoiled, how he left her with the horse upon her, how he beat me because her horse stumbled, how she waded through the dirt to pluck him off me, how he swore, how she prayed that never prayed before, how I cried, how the horses ran away, how her bridle was burst, how I lost my crupper, with many things of worthy memory, which now shall die in oblivion and thou return unexperienced to thy grave. 64 67 73

CURTIS By this reckoning he is more shrew than she.

GRUMIO Ay, and that thou and the proudest of you all shall find when he comes home. But what talk I of this? Call forth Nathaniel, Joseph, Nicholas, Philip, Walter, Sugarsop, and the rest. Let their heads be sleekly combed, their blue coats brushed, and their garters of an indifferent knit; let them curtsy with their left legs, and not presume to touch a hair of my master's horsetail till they kiss their hands. Are they all ready? 78 81 82

CURTIS They are.

GRUMIO Call them forth.

CURTIS [calling] Do you hear, ho? You must meet my master to countenance my mistress. 89

GRUMIO Why, she hath a face of her own.

CURTIS Who knows not that?

GRUMIO Thou, it seems, that calls for company to countenance her.

CURTIS I call them forth to credit her. 94

Enter four or five Servingmen.

GRUMIO Why, she comes to borrow nothing of them.

NATHANIEL Welcome home, Grumio!

PHILIP How now, Grumio?

JOSEPH What, Grumio!

NICHOLAS Fellow Grumio!

NATHANIEL How now, old lad?

GRUMIO Welcome, you; how now, you; what, you; fellow, you—and thus much for greeting. Now, my spruce companions, is all ready, and all things neat? 103

NATHANIEL All things is ready. How near is our master?

GRUMIO E'en at hand, alighted by this; and therefore be not—Cock's passion, silence! I hear my master. 107

Enter Petruchio and Kate.

PETRUCHIO
Where be these knaves? What, no man at door
To hold my stirrup nor to take my horse? 109
Where is Nathaniel, Gregory, Philip?

ALL SERVANTS Here, here, sir, here, sir.

PETRUCHIO
Here, sir! Here, sir! Here, sir! Here, sir!
You loggerheaded and unpolished grooms!
What, no attendance? No regard? No duty?
Where is the foolish knave I sent before? 115

GRUMIO
Here, sir, as foolish as I was before.

PETRUCHIO
You peasant swain, you whoreson, malt-horse drudge! 117
Did I not bid thee meet me in the park
And bring along these rascal knaves with thee?

GRUMIO
Nathaniel's coat, sir, was not fully made,
And Gabriel's pumps were all unpinked i' the heel. 121
There was no link to color Peter's hat, 122
And Walter's dagger was not come from sheathing. 123
There were none fine but Adam, Ralph, and Gregory; 124
The rest were ragged, old, and beggarly.
Yet, as they are, here are they come to meet you.

PETRUCHIO
Go, rascals, go and fetch my supper in.
                              Exeunt Servants.
[He sings.] "Where is the life that late I led? 128
Where are those—" Sit down, Kate, and welcome.— 129
                              [They sit at table.]
Soud, soud, soud, soud! 130

Enter Servants with supper.

---

48 **fallen out** quarreling (but with a pun on the literal sense in line 50) 50–51 **thereby hangs a tale** there's quite a story to tell about that (but with a risible suggestion of hanging by one's tail) 52 **ha 't** have it 57 **sensible** (1) capable of being felt (2) showing good sense 59 **Imprimis** in the first place 60 **foul** muddy 61 **of** on 64 **crossed** thwarted, interrupted 67 **bemoiled** befouled with mire 73 **of worthy** worthy of 78 **what** why 81 **blue coats** (Usual dress for servingmen.) 82 **indifferent** i.e., well matched and not flamboyant 89 **countenance** pay respects to (with a following pun on the meaning "face") 94 **credit** pay respects to (with another pun following, on "extend financial credit")

103 **spruce** lively, trim in appearance 107 **Cock's passion** by God's (Christ's) suffering 109 **hold my stirrup** i.e., help me dismount 115 **before** ahead (with pun in next line on "previously") 117 **swain** rustic. **whoreson . . . drudge** worthless plodding work animal, such as would be used on a treadmill to grind malt 121 **pumps** low-cut shoes. **unpinked** lacking in eyelets or in ornamental tracing in the leather 122 **link** blacking made from burnt "links" or torches 123 **sheathing** being fitted with a sheath 124 **fine** well clothed 128–129 **Where . . . those** (A fragment of a lost ballad, probably lamenting the man's loss of freedom in marriage.) 130 **Soud** (A nonsense song, or expression of impatience, or perhaps "food!")

Why, when, I say? —Nay, good sweet Kate, be
    merry.— 131
Off with my boots, you rogues! You villains, when?
    [*A Servant takes off Petruchio's boots.*]
[*He sings.*] "It was the friar of orders gray, 133
        As he forth walkèd on his way—" 134
Out, you rogue! You pluck my foot awry. 135
    [*He kicks the Servant.*]
Take that, and mend the plucking of the other. 136
Be merry, Kate.—Some water, here. What, ho!

    Enter one with water.

Where's my spaniel Troilus? Sirrah, get you hence,
And bid my cousin Ferdinand come hither—
    [*Exit Servant.*]
One, Kate, that you must kiss and be acquainted with.
Where are my slippers? Shall I have some water?
Come, Kate, and wash, and welcome heartily.
    [*A Servant offers water, but spills some.*]
You whoreson villain, will you let it fall?
    [*He strikes the Servant.*]

KATHARINA
Patience, I pray you, 'twas a fault unwilling. 144
PETRUCHIO
A whoreson, beetleheaded, flap-eared knave!— 145
Come, Kate, sit down. I know you have a stomach. 146
Will you give thanks, sweet Kate, or else shall I?— 147
What's this? Mutton?
FIRST SERVANT   Ay.
PETRUCHIO   Who brought it?
PETER   I.
PETRUCHIO
'Tis burnt, and so is all the meat.
What dogs are these? Where is the rascal cook?
How durst you, villains, bring it from the dresser 151
And serve it thus to me that love it not?
There, take it to you, trenchers, cups, and all. 153
    [*He throws the meat, etc., at them.*]
You heedless jolt-heads and unmannered slaves! 154
What, do you grumble? I'll be with you straight. 155
    [*They run out.*]
KATHARINA
I pray you, husband, be not so disquiet.
The meat was well, if you were so contented. 157
PETRUCHIO
I tell thee, Kate, 'twas burnt and dried away,
And I expressly am forbid to touch it;
For it engenders choler, planteth anger, 160
And better 'twere that both of us did fast,

Since, of ourselves, ourselves are choleric, 162
Than feed it with such overroasted flesh.
Be patient. Tomorrow 't shall be mended,
And for this night we'll fast for company. 165
Come, I will bring thee to thy bridal chamber. 166
    Exeunt.

    Enter Servants severally.

NATHANIEL   Peter, didst ever see the like?
PETER   He kills her in her own humor. 168

    Enter Curtis.

GRUMIO   Where is he?
CURTIS   In her chamber,
Making a sermon of continency to her, 171
And rails, and swears, and rates, that she, poor soul, 172
Knows not which way to stand, to look, to speak,
And sits as one new risen from a dream.
Away, away! For he is coming hither.   [*Exeunt.*]

    Enter Petruchio.

PETRUCHIO
Thus have I politicly begun my reign, 176
And 'tis my hope to end successfully.
My falcon now is sharp and passing empty, 178
And till she stoop she must not be full-gorged, 179
For then she never looks upon her lure.
Another way I have to man my haggard, 181
To make her come and know her keeper's call:
That is, to watch her, as we watch these kites 183
That bate and beat and will not be obedient. 184
She ate no meat today, nor none shall eat.
Last night she slept not, nor tonight she shall not.
As with the meat, some undeservèd fault
I'll find about the making of the bed,
And here I'll fling the pillow, there the bolster,
This way the coverlet, another way the sheets.
Ay, and amid this hurly I intend 191
That all is done in reverent care of her.
And in conclusion she shall watch all night, 193
And if she chance to nod I'll rail and brawl,
And with the clamor keep her still awake.
This is a way to kill a wife with kindness;
And thus I'll curb her mad and headstrong humor. 197
He that knows better how to tame a shrew,
Now let him speak. 'Tis charity to show.   *Exit.* 199

❧

131 When (An exclamation of impatience.)   **133–134 "It . . . way"** (A fragment of a lost ballad, probably bawdy.)   **135 Out** (Exclamation of anger or reproach.)   **136 mend the plucking of** do a better job of pulling off   **144 unwilling** not intentional   **145 beetleheaded** i.e., blockheaded (since a *beetle* is a pounding tool)   **146 stomach** appetite (with a suggestion also of "temper")   **147 give thanks** say grace   **151 dresser** one who "dresses" or prepares the food; or, possibly, sideboard   **153 trenchers** wooden dishes or plates   **154 jolt-heads** blockheads   **155 with you straight** after you at once (to get even for this)   **157 if . . . contented** if you had chosen to be pleased with it   **160 choler** the humor or bodily fluid, hot and dry in character, that supposedly produced ill temper and was thought to be aggravated by the eating of roast meat

162 of ourselves by our natures   **165 for company** as something to do together   **166 s.d. severally** separately   **168 kills . . . humor** i.e., uses anger to subdue anger in her   **171 sermon of continency** lecture on self-restraint   **172 rates** scolds. **that** so that   **176 politicly** with skillful calculation   **178 sharp** hungry. **passing** very   **179 stoop** fly down to the lure   **181 man** tame (with a pun on the sense of "assert masculine authority"). **haggard** wild female hawk; hence, an intractable woman   **183 watch her** keep her watching, i.e., awake. **kites** a kind of hawk (with a pun on *Kate*)   **184 bate and beat** beat the wings impatiently and flutter away from the hand or perch   **191 hurly** commotion. **intend** pretend   **193 watch** stay awake   **197 humor** disposition   **199 'Tis charity to show** this is to perform an act of Christian benevolence. (On the rhyme with *shrew*, see also the play's final lines.)

4.2   *Enter Tranio [as Lucentio] and Hortensio*
          [as Litio].

TRANIO
  Is 't possible, friend Litio, that Mistress Bianca
  Doth fancy any other but Lucentio?
  I tell you, sir, she bears me fair in hand.   3
HORTENSIO
  Sir, to satisfy you in what I have said,   4
  Stand by and mark the manner of his teaching.
                                    [*They stand aside.*]

        Enter Bianca [and Lucentio as Cambio].

LUCENTIO
  Now, mistress, profit you in what you read?   6
BIANCA
  What, master, read you? First resolve me that.   7
LUCENTIO
  I read that I profess, *The Art to Love.*   8
BIANCA
  And may you prove, sir, master of your art!
LUCENTIO
  While you, sweet dear, prove mistress of my heart!
              [*They move aside and court each other.*]
HORTENSIO [*to Tranio, coming forward*]
  Quick proceeders, marry! Now, tell me, I pray,   11
  You that durst swear that your mistress Bianca
  Loved none in the world so well as Lucentio.
TRANIO
  O despiteful love! Unconstant womankind!   14
  I tell thee, Litio, this is wonderful.   15
HORTENSIO
  Mistake no more. I am not Litio,
  Nor a musician, as I seem to be,
  But one that scorn to live in this disguise   18
  For such a one as leaves a gentleman   19
  And makes a god of such a cullion.   20
  Know, sir, that I am called Hortensio.
TRANIO
  Signor Hortensio, I have often heard
  Of your entire affection to Bianca;   23
  And since mine eyes are witness of her lightness,   24
  I will with you, if you be so contented,
  Forswear Bianca and her love forever.
HORTENSIO
  See how they kiss and court! Signor Lucentio,
  Here is my hand, and here I firmly vow
                                    [*giving his hand*]
  Never to woo her more, but do forswear her,
  As one unworthy all the former favors

That I have fondly flattered her withal.   31
TRANIO
  And here I take the like unfeignèd oath,
  Never to marry with her though she would entreat.
  Fie on her, see how beastly she doth court him!
HORTENSIO
  Would all the world but he had quite forsworn!   35
  For me, that I may surely keep mine oath,
  I will be married to a wealthy widow,
  Ere three days pass, which hath as long loved me
  As I have loved this proud disdainful haggard.   39
  And so farewell, Signor Lucentio.
  Kindness in women, not their beauteous looks,
  Shall win my love. And so I take my leave,
  In resolution as I swore before.   [*Exit.*]   43
TRANIO [*as Lucentio and Bianca come forward again*]
  Mistress Bianca, bless you with such grace
  As 'longeth to a lover's blessèd case!   45
  Nay, I have ta'en you napping, gentle love,   46
  And have forsworn you with Hortensio.
BIANCA
  Tranio, you jest. But have you both forsworn me?
TRANIO
  Mistress, we have.
LUCENTIO   Then we are rid of Litio.
TRANIO
  I' faith, he'll have a lusty widow now,   50
  That shall be wooed and wedded in a day.
BIANCA   God give him joy!
TRANIO   Ay, and he'll tame her.
BIANCA   He says so, Tranio?
TRANIO
  Faith, he is gone unto the taming-school.
BIANCA
  The taming-school! What, is there such a place?
TRANIO
  Ay, mistress, and Petruchio is the master,
  That teacheth tricks eleven-and-twenty long   58
  To tame a shrew and charm her chattering tongue.

              Enter Biondello.

BIONDELLO
  O master, master, I have watched so long
  That I am dog-weary, but at last I spied
  An ancient angel coming down the hill   62
  Will serve the turn.
TRANIO   What is he, Biondello?   63
BIONDELLO
  Master, a marcantant, or a pedant,   64

4.2. Location: Padua. Before Baptista's house.
3 bears . . . hand gives me encouragement, leads me on   **4 satisfy** convince   **6 read** (Evidently, both Bianca and "Cambio" carry books.)   **7 resolve** answer   **8 that I profess** what I practice.   **The Art to Love** Ovid's *Ars Amatoria*   **11 proceeders** (1) workers, doers (2) candidates for academic degrees (as suggested by the phrase *master of your art* in line 9)   **14 despiteful** cruel   **15 wonderful** cause for wonder   **18 scorn** scorns   **19 such a one** i.e., Bianca   **20 cullion** base fellow (referring to "Cambio"; literally the word means "testicle")   **23 entire** sincere   **24 lightness** wantonness

31 fondly foolishly   **35 Would . . . forsworn** i.e., may everyone in the world forsake her except the penniless "Cambio," and may she thus get what she deserves   **39 haggard** wild hawk   **43 In resolution** determined   **45 'longeth** belongs   **46 ta'en you napping** i.e., surprised you   **50 lusty** merry, lively   **58 eleven . . . long** i.e., right on the money. (Alluding to the card game called "one-and-thirty" referred to at 1.2.32–33.)   **62 ancient angel** i.e., fellow of the good old stamp. (Literally, an "angel" or gold coin bearing the stamp of the archangel Michael and thus distinguishable from more recent debased coinage.)   **63 Will . . . turn** who will serve our purposes   **64 marcantant** merchant.   **pedant** schoolmaster (though at lines 90–91 he speaks more like a merchant)

I know not what, but formal in apparel,
In gait and countenance surely like a father.
LUCENTIO   And what of him, Tranio?
TRANIO
If he be credulous and trust my tale,
I'll make him glad to seem Vincentio,
And give assurance to Baptista Minola
As if he were the right Vincentio.
Take in your love, and then let me alone.   72
                    [*Exeunt Lucentio and Bianca.*]

        Enter a Pedant.

PEDANT
God save you, sir!
TRANIO   And you sir! You are welcome.
Travel you far on, or are you at the farthest?
PEDANT
Sir, at the farthest for a week or two,
But then up farther, and as far as Rome,
And so to Tripoli, if God lend me life.
TRANIO
What countryman, I pray?
PEDANT   Of Mantua.
TRANIO
Of Mantua, sir? Marry, God forbid!
And come to Padua, careless of your life?
PEDANT
My life, sir? How, I pray? For that goes hard.   81
TRANIO
'Tis death for anyone in Mantua
To come to Padua. Know you not the cause?
Your ships are stayed at Venice, and the Duke,   84
For private quarrel twixt your Duke and him,
Hath published and proclaimed it openly.
'Tis marvel, but that you are but newly come,
You might have heard it else proclaimed about.
PEDANT
Alas, sir, it is worse for me than so,   89
For I have bills for money by exchange   90
From Florence, and must here deliver them.
TRANIO
Well, sir, to do you courtesy,
This will I do, and this I will advise you—
First, tell me, have you ever been at Pisa?
PEDANT
Ay, sir, in Pisa have I often been,
Pisa renownèd for grave citizens.
TRANIO
Among them know you one Vincentio?
PEDANT
I know him not, but I have heard of him;
A merchant of incomparable wealth.
TRANIO
He is my father, sir, and, sooth to say,
In count'nance somewhat doth resemble you.
BIONDELLO [*aside*]   As much as an apple doth an
oyster, and all one.   103

TRANIO
To save your life in this extremity,
This favor will I do you for his sake;
And think it not the worst of all your fortunes
That you are like to Sir Vincentio.
His name and credit shall you undertake,   108
And in my house you shall be friendly lodged.
Look that you take upon you as you should.   110
You understand me, sir. So shall you stay
Till you have done your business in the city.
If this be courtesy, sir, accept of it.
PEDANT
O sir, I do, and will repute you ever   114
The patron of my life and liberty.
TRANIO
Then go with me to make the matter good.   116
This, by the way, I let you understand:
My father is here looked for every day
To pass assurance of a dower in marriage   119
Twixt me and one Baptista's daughter here.
In all these circumstances I'll instruct you.
Go with me to clothe you as becomes you.
                                Exeunt.

                        ♣

4.3   *Enter Katharina and Grumio.*

GRUMIO
No, no, forsooth, I dare not for my life.
KATHARINA
The more my wrong, the more his spite appears.   2
What, did he marry me to famish me?
Beggars that come unto my father's door
Upon entreaty have a present alms;   5
If not, elsewhere they meet with charity.
But I, who never knew how to entreat,
Nor never needed that I should entreat,
Am starved for meat, giddy for lack of sleep,   9
With oaths kept waking, and with brawling fed.
And that which spites me more than all these wants,
He does it under name of perfect love,
As who should say, if I should sleep or eat   13
'Twere deadly sickness or else present death.
I prithee, go and get me some repast,
I care not what, so it be wholesome food.   16
GRUMIO   What say you to a neat's foot?   17
KATHARINA
'Tis passing good. I prithee, let me have it.   18
GRUMIO
I fear it is too choleric a meat.
How say you to a fat tripe finely broiled?
KATHARINA
I like it well. Good Grumio, fetch it me.

108 **credit** reputation   110 **take upon you** play your part   114 **repute you** regard you as   116 **make . . . good** carry out the plan   119 **pass assurance** convey a legal guarantee
4.3. Location: Petruchio's house. A table is set out, with seats.
2 **my wrong** the wrong done to me   5 **present** immediate (as in line 14)   9 **meat** food   13 **As who** as if one   16 **so** so long as   17 **neat's** ox's   18 **passing** extremely

72 **let me alone** i.e., count on me   81 **goes hard** is serious indeed
84 **stayed** detained   89 **than so** than that   90 **bills . . . exchange** promissory notes   103 **all one** no matter

GRUMIO
  I cannot tell. I fear 'tis choleric.
  What say you to a piece of beef and mustard?   22
KATHARINA
  A dish that I do love to feed upon.
GRUMIO
  Ay, but the mustard is too hot a little.
KATHARINA
  Why then, the beef, and let the mustard rest.   26
GRUMIO
  Nay then, I will not. You shall have the mustard,
  Or else you get no beef of Grumio.
KATHARINA
  Then both, or one, or anything thou wilt.
GRUMIO
  Why then, the mustard without the beef.
KATHARINA
  Go, get thee gone, thou false, deluding slave,
                                    [She] beats him.
  That feed'st me with the very name of meat!   32
  Sorrow on thee and all the pack of you,
  That triumph thus upon my misery!
  Go, get thee gone, I say.

      Enter Petruchio and Hortensio with meat.

PETRUCHIO
  How fares my Kate? What, sweeting, all amort?   36
HORTENSIO
  Mistress, what cheer?
KATHARINA   Faith, as cold as can be.
PETRUCHIO
  Pluck up thy spirits; look cheerfully upon me.
  Here, love, thou seest how diligent I am
  To dress thy meat myself and bring it thee.   40
  I am sure, sweet Kate, this kindness merits thanks.
  What, not a word? Nay, then thou lov'st it not,
  And all my pains is sorted to no proof.   43
  Here, take away this dish.
KATHARINA   I pray you, let it stand.
PETRUCHIO
  The poorest service is repaid with thanks,
  And so shall mine before you touch the meat.
KATHARINA   I thank you, sir.
HORTENSIO
  Signor Petruchio, fie, you are to blame.
  Come, Mistress Kate, I'll bear you company.
                                    [They sit at table.]
PETRUCHIO [aside to Hortensio]
  Eat it up all, Hortensio, if thou lovest me.—
  Much good do it unto thy gentle heart!
  Kate, eat apace. And now, my honey love,
  Will we return unto thy father's house
  And revel it as bravely as the best,   54
  With silken coats and caps and golden rings,
  With ruffs, and cuffs, and farthingales, and things,   56

With scarves, and fans, and double change of
    bravery,   57
  With amber bracelets, beads, and all this knavery.
  What, hast thou dined? The tailor stays thy leisure,   59
  To deck thy body with his ruffling treasure.   60

      Enter Tailor [with a gown].

  Come, tailor, let us see these ornaments.
  Lay forth the gown.

      Enter Haberdasher [with a cap].

                    What news with you, sir?
HABERDASHER
  Here is the cap your worship did bespeak.   63
PETRUCHIO
  Why, this was molded on a porringer—   64
  A velvet dish. Fie, fie, 'tis lewd and filthy.   65
  Why, 'tis a cockle or a walnut shell,   66
  A knack, a toy, a trick, a baby's cap.   67
  Away with it! Come, let me have a bigger.
KATHARINA
  I'll have no bigger. This doth fit the time,   69
  And gentlewomen wear such caps as these.
PETRUCHIO
  When you are gentle, you shall have one too,   71
  And not till then.
HORTENSIO [aside]   That will not be in haste.
KATHARINA
  Why, sir, I trust I may have leave to speak,
  And speak I will. I am no child, no babe.
  Your betters have endured me say my mind,   75
  And if you cannot, best you stop your ears.
  My tongue will tell the anger of my heart,
  Or else my heart, concealing it, will break.
  And rather than it shall, I will be free
  Even to the uttermost, as I please, in words.
PETRUCHIO
  Why, thou sayst true. It is a paltry cap,
  A custard-coffin, a bauble, a silken pie.   82
  I love thee well in that thou lik'st it not.
KATHARINA
  Love me or love me not, I like the cap,
  And it I will have, or I will have none.
                                    [Exit Haberdasher.]
PETRUCHIO
  Thy gown? Why, ay. Come, tailor, let us see 't.
  O, mercy, God, what masquing stuff is here?   87
  What's this, a sleeve? 'Tis like a demicannon.   88
  What, up and down carved like an apple tart?   89
  Here's snip, and nip, and cut, and slish and slash,

---

22 **I cannot tell** I don't know what to say   26 **let . . . rest** i.e., forget about the mustard   32 **the very name** the mere name   36 **all amort** dejected, dispirited   40 **dress** prepare   43 **sorted to no proof** proved to be to no purpose   54 **bravely** splendidly dressed   56 **farthingales** hooped petticoats

57 **bravery** finery   59 **stays** awaits   60 **ruffling treasure** finery trimmed with ruffles   63 **bespeak** order   64 **porringer** porridge bowl   65 **lewd** vile   66 **cockle** cockleshell   67 **trick** trifle   69 **fit the time** suit the current fashion   71 **gentle** mild. (Petruchio plays on Kate's *gentlewomen*, line 70, i.e., women of high social station.)   75 **endured me say** suffered me to say   82 **custard-coffin** pastry crust for a custard   87 **masquing** i.e., suited only for a masque   88 **demicannon** large cannon   89 **up and down** all over, exactly.   **like an apple tart** i.e., with slashing or slits like the slits on the crust of fruit tarts, here revealing the brighter fabric underneath

Like to a censer in a barber's shop. 91
Why, what i' devil's name, tailor, call'st thou this? 92

HORTENSIO [aside]
I see she's like to have neither cap nor gown.

TAILOR
You bid me make it orderly and well,
According to the fashion and the time.

PETRUCHIO
Marry, and did. But if you be remembered, 96
I did not bid you mar it to the time.
Go hop me over every kennel home, 98
For you shall hop without my custom, sir.
I'll none of it. Hence, make your best of it.

KATHARINA
I never saw a better fashioned gown,
More quaint, more pleasing, nor more
commendable. 102
Belike you mean to make a puppet of me. 103

PETRUCHIO
Why, true, he means to make a puppet of thee.

TAILOR
She says your worship means to make a puppet of
her.

PETRUCHIO
O, monstrous arrogance! Thou liest, thou thread,
thou thimble,
Thou yard, three-quarters, half-yard, quarter, nail! 107
Thou flea, thou nit, thou winter cricket, thou! 108
Braved in mine own house with a skein of thread? 109
Away, thou rag, thou quantity, thou remnant, 110
Or I shall so be-mete thee with thy yard 111
As thou shalt think on prating whilst thou liv'st! 112
I tell thee, I, that thou hast marred her gown.

TAILOR
Your worship is deceived. The gown is made
Just as my master had direction.
Grumio gave order how it should be done.

GRUMIO I gave him no order. I gave him the stuff. 117

TAILOR
But how did you desire it should be made?

GRUMIO Marry, sir, with needle and thread.

TAILOR
But did you not request to have it cut?

GRUMIO Thou hast faced many things. 121

TAILOR I have.

GRUMIO Face not me. Thou hast braved many men; 123
brave not me. I will neither be faced nor braved. I say 124
unto thee, I bid thy master cut out the gown, but I did
not bid him cut it to pieces. Ergo, thou liest. 126

TAILOR Why, here is the note of the fashion to testify.
[He displays his bill.]

PETRUCHIO Read it.

GRUMIO The note lies in 's throat if he say I said so. 129

TAILOR [reads] "Imprimis, a loose-bodied gown—" 130

GRUMIO Master, if ever I said loose-bodied gown, 131
sew me in the skirts of it and beat me to death with
a bottom of brown thread. I said a gown. 133

PETRUCHIO Proceed.

TAILOR [reads] "With a small compassed cape—" 135

GRUMIO I confess the cape.

TAILOR [reads] "With a trunk sleeve—" 137

GRUMIO I confess two sleeves.

TAILOR [reads] "The sleeves curiously cut." 139

PETRUCHIO Ay, there's the villainy.

GRUMIO Error i' the bill, sir, error i' the bill. I commanded the sleeves should be cut out and sewed up
again, and that I'll prove upon thee, though thy little 143
finger be armed in a thimble.

TAILOR This is true that I say. An I had thee in place 145
where, thou shouldst know it. 146

GRUMIO I am for thee straight. Take thou the bill, give 147
me thy mete-yard, and spare not me. 148

HORTENSIO God-a-mercy, Grumio, then he shall have 149
no odds. 150

PETRUCHIO Well, sir, in brief, the gown is not for me.

GRUMIO You are i' the right, sir, 'tis for my mistress.

PETRUCHIO Go, take it up unto thy master's use. 153

GRUMIO [to the Tailor] Villain, not for thy life! Take up
my mistress' gown for thy master's use!

PETRUCHIO Why sir, what's your conceit in that? 156

GRUMIO
O, sir, the conceit is deeper than you think for: 157
Take up my mistress' gown to his master's use!
O, fie, fie, fie!

PETRUCHIO [aside to Hortensio]
Hortensio, say thou wilt see the tailor paid.
[To Tailor.] Go, take it hence. Begone, and say no
more.

HORTENSIO [aside to the Tailor]
Tailor, I'll pay thee for thy gown tomorrow.
Take no unkindness of his hasty words.
Away, I say. Commend me to thy master.
Exit Tailor.

PETRUCHIO
Well, come, my Kate. We will unto your father's
Even in these honest, mean habiliments. 166
Our purses shall be proud, our garments poor,
For 'tis the mind that makes the body rich;

---

91 censer perfuming pan having an ornamental lid **92 i'** in (the)
96 Marry, and did indeed I did. **be remembered** recollect **98 hop
. . . home** hop on home over every street gutter **102 quaint** elegant
103 Belike perhaps **107 nail** a measure of length for cloth: 2¼
inches **108 nit** louse egg **109 Braved** defied. **with** by **110 quantity** fragment **111 be-mete** measure, i.e., thrash. **yard** yardstick
112 think on prating i.e., remember this thrashing and think twice before talking so again **117 stuff** material **121 faced** trimmed. (But
Grumio puns on the meaning "bullied.") **123 Face** bully. **braved**
dressed finely **124 brave** defy **126 Ergo** therefore

129 lies in 's throat i.e., lies utterly **130 Imprimis** first **131 loose-
bodied gown** (Grumio plays on *loose*, "wanton"; a gown fit for a
prostitute.) **133 bottom** i.e., ball or skein. (A weaver's term for '
bobbin.) **135 compassed** flared, cut on the bias so as to fall in a circle **137 trunk** full, wide **139 curiously** elaborately **143 prove
upon thee** prove by fighting you **145–146 in place where** in a suitable place **147 for thee straight** ready for you immediately. (Grumio
takes *place where* to refer to a place where they can fight, not a court
of law.) **bill** (1) the note ordering the gown (2) a weapon, a halberd
148 mete-yard measuring stick **149 God-a-mercy** God have mercy
150 odds advantage **153 take it up** take it away. (But Grumio
deliberately misinterprets both ex-
pressions in a bawdy sense.) **156 conceit** idea **157 deeper** more serious (but continuing the sexual idea of lifting up and using)
166 honest, mean habiliments respectable, plain clothes

And as the sun breaks through the darkest clouds,
So honor peereth in the meanest habit.   170
What, is the jay more precious than the lark
Because his feathers are more beautiful?
Or is the adder better than the eel
Because his painted skin contents the eye?   174
O, no, good Kate; neither art thou the worse
For this poor furniture and mean array.   176
If thou account'st it shame, lay it on me.
And therefore frolic; we will hence forthwith,
To feast and sport us at thy father's house.
[*To Grumio.*] Go call my men, and let us straight to
     him;
And bring our horses unto Long Lane end.
There will we mount, and thither walk on foot.
Let's see, I think 'tis now some seven o'clock,
And well we may come there by dinnertime.   184

KATHARINA
I dare assure you, sir, 'tis almost two,
And 'twill be suppertime ere you come there.

PETRUCHIO
It shall be seven ere I go to horse.
Look what I speak, or do, or think to do,   188
You are still crossing it.—Sirs, let 't alone.   189
I will not go today, and ere I do,
It shall be what o'clock I say it is.

HORTENSIO [*aside*]
Why, so this gallant will command the sun.   192

                                            [*Exeunt.*]

                      ❧

4.4 *Enter Tranio [as Lucentio], and the Pedant dressed
         like Vincentio [booted].*

TRANIO
Sir, this is the house. Please it you that I call?
PEDANT
Ay, what else? And but I be deceived,   2
Signor Baptista may remember me,   3
Near twenty years ago, in Genoa—
TRANIO
Where we were lodgers at the Pegasus.—   5
'Tis well; and hold your own in any case   6
With such austerity as 'longeth to a father.

          Enter Biondello.

PEDANT
I warrant you. But, sir, here comes your boy.
'Twere good he were schooled.   9

170 peereth in peeps through. **habit** attire **174 painted** patterned
176 furniture furnishings of attire **184 dinnertime** i.e., about noon
188 Look what whatever **189 still crossing** always contradicting or
defying **192 so** at this rate
4.4. Location: Padua. Before Baptista's house.
s.d. booted (signifying travel) **2 but** unless **3 may remember** (The
Pedant is rehearsing what he is to say.) **5 Where . . . Pegasus**
(Tranio is coaching the Pedant in further details of his story.) **the Pegasus** i.e., an inn, so named after the famous winged horse of classical myth **6 hold your own** play your part **9 schooled** i.e., rehearsed in his part

TRANIO
Fear you not him.—Sirrah Biondello,
Now do your duty throughly, I advise you.   11
Imagine 'twere the right Vincentio.   12
BIONDELLO Tut, fear not me.   13
TRANIO
But hast thou done thy errand to Baptista?
BIONDELLO
I told him that your father was at Venice
And that you looked for him this day in Padua.
TRANIO [*giving money*]
Thou'rt a tall fellow. Hold thee that to drink.   17
Here comes Baptista. Set your countenance, sir.   18

     *Enter Baptista, and Lucentio [as Cambio]. [The]
     Pedant [stands] bareheaded.*

Signor Baptista, you are happily met.   19
[*To the Pedant.*] Sir, this is the gentleman I told you
     of.
I pray you, stand good father to me now;
Give me Bianca for my patrimony.
PEDANT Soft, son!—   23
Sir, by your leave, having come to Padua
To gather in some debts, my son Lucentio
Made me acquainted with a weighty cause
Of love between your daughter and himself;
And, for the good report I hear of you   28
And for the love he beareth to your daughter
And she to him, to stay him not too long,   30
I am content, in a good father's care,
To have him matched. And if you please to like   32
No worse than I, upon some agreement
Me shall you find ready and willing
With one consent to have her so bestowed;   35
For curious I cannot be with you,   36
Signor Baptista, of whom I hear so well.
BAPTISTA
Sir, pardon me in what I have to say.
Your plainness and your shortness please me well.
Right true it is your son Lucentio here
Doth love my daughter, and she loveth him,
Or both dissemble deeply their affections.
And therefore, if you say no more than this,
That like a father you will deal with him
And pass my daughter a sufficient dower,   45
The match is made, and all is done.
Your son shall have my daughter with consent.
TRANIO
I thank you, sir. Where then do you know best   48
We be affied and such assurance ta'en   49
As shall with either part's agreement stand?   50

11 throughly thoroughly **12 right** real **13 fear not me** don't worry
about my doing my part **17 tall** fine. **Hold . . . drink** take that and
buy a drink **18 Set your countenance** i.e., put on the expression of
an austere father (line 7) **19 happily** fortunately **23 Soft** i.e., steady,
take it easy **28 for** because of **30 to stay him not** not to keep him
waiting **32 like** i.e., approve of the match **35 With one consent** in
unanimity **36 curious** overly particular **45 pass** settle on, give **48–
50 Where . . . stand** where in your view is the best place for us to be
betrothed and for legal assurances to be made that will confirm an
agreement satisfactory to both parties?

BAPTISTA
Not in my house, Lucentio, for you know
Pitchers have ears, and I have many servants.
Besides, old Gremio is hearkening still,   53
And happily we might be interrupted.   54

TRANIO
Then at my lodging, an it like you.   55
There doth my father lie, and there this night   56
We'll pass the business privately and well.   57
Send for your daughter by your servant here.
                    [He indicates Lucentio, and winks at him.]
My boy shall fetch the scrivener presently.   59
The worst is this, that at so slender warning
You are like to have a thin and slender pittance.   61

BAPTISTA
It likes me well. Cambio, hie you home,
And bid Bianca make her ready straight.
And if you will, tell what hath happened:
Lucentio's father is arrived in Padua,
And how she's like to be Lucentio's wife.
                    [Exit Lucentio.]

BIONDELLO
I pray the gods she may with all my heart!

TRANIO
Dally not with the gods, but get thee gone.
                    Exit [Biondello].
Signor Baptista, shall I lead the way?
Welcome! One mess is like to be your cheer.   70
Come, sir, we will better it in Pisa.

BAPTISTA   I follow you.   72
                    Exeunt [Tranio, Pedant, and Baptista].

        Enter Lucentio [as Cambio] and Biondello.

BIONDELLO   Cambio!
LUCENTIO   What sayst thou, Biondello?
BIONDELLO   You saw my master wink and laugh upon
you?
LUCENTIO   Biondello, what of that?
BIONDELLO   Faith, nothing; but he's left me here behind
to expound the meaning or moral of his signs and to-   79
kens.
LUCENTIO   I pray thee, moralize them.   81
BIONDELLO   Then thus. Baptista is safe, talking with the 82
deceiving father of a deceitful son.
LUCENTIO   And what of him?
BIONDELLO   His daughter is to be brought by you to the
supper.
LUCENTIO   And then?
BIONDELLO   The old priest at Saint Luke's church is at
your command at all hours.
LUCENTIO   And what of all this?

BIONDELLO   I cannot tell, except they are busied about a 91
counterfeit assurance. Take you assurance of her 92
cum privilegio ad imprimendum solum. To the 93
church take the priest, clerk, and some sufficient hon- 94
est witnesses.
If this be not that you look for, I have no more to
say,   96
But bid Bianca farewell forever and a day.
                    [Biondello starts to leave.]
LUCENTIO   Hear'st thou, Biondello?
BIONDELLO   I cannot tarry. I knew a wench married in
an afternoon as she went to the garden for parsley to
stuff a rabbit, and so may you, sir. And so, adieu, sir.
My master hath appointed me to go to Saint Luke's, to
bid the priest be ready to come against you come with 103
your appendix.   *Exit.* 104
LUCENTIO
I may, and will, if she be so contented.
She will be pleased; then wherefore should I doubt?
Hap what hap may, I'll roundly go about her.   107
It shall go hard if Cambio go without her.   *Exit.* 108

4.5   *Enter Petruchio, Kate, [and] Hortensio.*

PETRUCHIO
Come on, i' God's name, once more toward our
father's.   1
Good Lord, how bright and goodly shines the moon!

KATHARINA
The moon? The sun. It is not moonlight now.

PETRUCHIO
I say it is the moon that shines so bright.

KATHARINA
I know it is the sun that shines so bright.

PETRUCHIO
Now, by my mother's son, and that's myself,
It shall be moon, or star, or what I list   7
Or ere I journey to your father's house.—   8
Go on, and fetch our horses back again—
Evermore crossed and crossed, nothing but crossed!

HORTENSIO [to Katharina]
Say as he says, or we shall never go.

KATHARINA
Forward, I pray, since we have come so far,
And be it moon, or sun, or what you please;

53 **hearkening still** continually listening   54 **happily** haply, perhaps
55 **an it like** if it please   56 **lie** lodge   57 **pass** transact   59 **scrivener**
notary, one to draw up contracts.   **presently** at once   61 **like** likely.
slender pittance i.e., scanty banquet   70 **mess** dish.   **cheer** entertainment   72 **s.d. Exeunt** (Technically, the cleared stage may mark a
new scene, but the conversation of Lucentio and Biondello suggests
that they come creeping back on stage as the others leave rather than
doing the errands Baptista and Tranio bid them.)   79 **moral** hidden
meaning   81 **moralize** elucidate   82 **safe** i.e., safely out of the way

91 **except** unless   92 **counterfeit assurance** pretended betrothal
agreement.   **Take . . . of her** legalize your claim to her (by marriage)
93 **cum . . . solum** with exclusive printing rights. (A copyright formula often appearing on the title pages of books, here jokingly applied to the marriage and to procreation as an act of imprinting.)
94 **sufficient** meeting the legal requirement in number and social
standing   96 **that you look for** what you are looking for   103 **against
you come** in anticipation of your arrival   104 **appendix** something
appended, i.e., the bride (continuing the metaphor of printing)
107 **roundly . . . her** set about marrying her in no uncertain terms
108 **go hard** be unfortunate (with pun about erection)
4.5. Location: A road on the way to Padua.
1 **our father's** our father's house   7 **list** please   8 **Or ere** before

An if you please to call it a rush candle,   14
Henceforth I vow it shall be so for me.
PETRUCHIO
   I say it is the moon.
KATHARINA   I know it is the moon.
PETRUCHIO
   Nay, then you lie. It is the blessèd sun.
KATHARINA
   Then, God be blessed, it is the blessèd sun.
   But sun it is not, when you say it is not,
   And the moon changes even as your mind.
   What you will have it named, even that it is,
   And so it shall be so for Katharine.
HORTENSIO
   Petruchio, go thy ways. The field is won.   23
PETRUCHIO
   Well, forward, forward. Thus the bowl should run,
   And not unluckily against the bias.   25
   But soft! Company is coming here.

               Enter Vincentio.

   [*To Vincentio.*] Good morrow, gentle mistress. Where
      away?—   27
   Tell me, sweet Kate, and tell me truly too,
   Hast thou beheld a fresher gentlewoman?
   Such war of white and red within her cheeks!
   What stars do spangle heaven with such beauty
   As those two eyes become that heavenly face?—
   Fair lovely maid, once more good day to thee.—
   Sweet Kate, embrace her for her beauty's sake.
HORTENSIO [*aside*]
   'A will make the man mad, to make a woman of
      him.   35
KATHARINA [*embracing Vincentio*]
   Young budding virgin, fair, and fresh, and sweet,
   Whither away, or where is thy abode?
   Happy the parents of so fair a child!
   Happier the man whom favorable stars   39
   Allots thee for his lovely bedfellow!   40
PETRUCHIO
   Why, how now, Kate? I hope thou art not mad.
   This is a man, old, wrinkled, faded, withered,
   And not a maiden, as thou sayst he is.
KATHARINA
   Pardon, old father, my mistaking eyes,
   That have been so bedazzled with the sun
   That everything I look on seemeth green.   46
   Now I perceive thou art a reverend father.
   Pardon, I pray thee, for my mad mistaking.
PETRUCHIO
   Do, good old grandsire, and withal make known
   Which way thou travelest—if along with us,
   We shall be joyful of thy company.

VINCENTIO
   Fair sir, and you, my merry mistress,
   That with your strange encounter much amazed me,
   My name is called Vincentio, my dwelling Pisa,
   And bound I am to Padua, there to visit
   A son of mine, which long I have not seen.
PETRUCHIO
   What is his name?
VINCENTIO   Lucentio, gentle sir.
PETRUCHIO
   Happily met, the happier for thy son.
   And now by law as well as reverend age
   I may entitle thee my loving father.
   The sister to my wife, this gentlewoman,
   Thy son by this hath married. Wonder not,   62
   Nor be not grieved. She is of good esteem,   63
   Her dowry wealthy, and of worthy birth;
   Besides, so qualified as may beseem   65
   The spouse of any noble gentleman.
   Let me embrace with old Vincentio,
   And wander we to see thy honest son,   68
   Who will of thy arrival be full joyous.
                                        [*He embraces Vincentio.*]
VINCENTIO
   But is this true? Or is it else your pleasure,
   Like pleasant travelers, to break a jest   71
   Upon the company you overtake?
HORTENSIO
   I do assure thee, father, so it is.
PETRUCHIO
   Come, go along, and see the truth hereof,
   For our first merriment hath made thee jealous.   75
                                        Exeunt [*all but Hortensio*].
HORTENSIO
   Well, Petruchio, this has put me in heart.   76
   Have to my widow! And if she be froward,   77
   Then hast thou taught Hortensio to be untoward.   78
                                                                      Exit.

                              ❧

5.1   *Enter Biondello, Lucentio* [*no longer disguised*],
          and Bianca. Gremio is out before [*and stands
          aside*].

BIONDELLO   Softly and swiftly, sir, for the priest is
ready.
LUCENTIO   I fly, Biondello. But they may chance to need
thee at home; therefore leave us.
BIONDELLO   Nay, faith, I'll see the church a' your back,   5

---

62 by this by this time   **63 esteem** reputation   **65 so qualified** having
such qualities.   **beseem** befit   **68 wander** go (with a suggestion of
changing plans)   **71 pleasant** humorous, jocular.   **break a jest** play a
practical joke   **75 jealous** suspicious   **76 put me in heart** encouraged
me   **77 Have to** i.e., now for.   **froward** perverse   **78 untoward** unmannerly
5.1. Location: Padua. Before Lucentio's house.
s.d. out before i.e., onstage first. (Gremio does not see Biondello, Lucentio, and Bianca as they steal to church, or else he does not recognize Lucentio in his own person.)   **5 a' your back** at your back, behind you. (Biondello first wants to see them in church and safely
married.)

---

14 a rush candle a rush dipped into tallow; hence a very feeble light
23 go thy ways i.e., well done, carry on   **25 against the bias** off its
proper course. (The *bias* is an off-center weight in a bowling ball enabling the bowler to roll the ball in an oblique or curving path.)
27 Where away where are you going?   **35 'A** he   **39 whom** to whom
40 Allots allot   **46 green** young and fresh

and then come back to my master's as soon as I can.
[*Exeunt Lucentio, Bianca, and Biondello.*]

GREMIO
I marvel Cambio comes not all this while.

*Enter Petruchio, Kate, Vincentio, Grumio, with
attendants.*

PETRUCHIO
Sir, here's the door. This is Lucentio's house.
My father's bears more toward the marketplace;   9
Thither must I, and here I leave you, sir.

VINCENTIO
You shall not choose but drink before you go.   11
I think I shall command your welcome here,
And by all likelihood some cheer is toward.   *Knock.*   13

GREMIO [*advancing*]   They're busy within. You were
best knock louder.   15

Pedant looks out of the window.

PEDANT   What's he that knocks as he would beat down
the gate?

VINCENTIO   Is Signor Lucentio within, sir?

PEDANT   He's within, sir, but not to be spoken withal.   19

VINCENTIO   What if a man bring him a hundred pound
or two to make merry withal?

PEDANT   Keep your hundred pounds to yourself. He
shall need none, so long as I live.

PETRUCHIO [*to Vincentio*]   Nay, I told you your son
was well beloved in Padua.—Do you hear, sir? To
leave frivolous circumstances, I pray you, tell Signor   26
Lucentio that his father is come from Pisa and is
here at the door to speak with him.

PEDANT   Thou liest. His father is come from Padua and   29
here looking out at the window.

VINCENTIO   Art thou his father?

PEDANT   Ay, sir, so his mother says, if I may believe
her.

PETRUCHIO [*to Vincentio*]   Why, how now, gentleman!
Why, this is flat knavery, to take upon you another   35
man's name.

PEDANT   Lay hands on the villain. I believe 'a means to
cozen somebody in this city under my countenance.   38

Enter Biondello.

BIONDELLO [*aside*]   I have seen them in the church
together, God send 'em good shipping! But who is   40
here? Mine old master Vincentio! Now we are undone
and brought to nothing.

VINCENTIO [*seeing Biondello*]   Come hither, crackhemp.   43

BIONDELLO   I hope I may choose, sir.   44

VINCENTIO   Come hither, you rogue. What, have you
forgot me?

BIONDELLO   Forgot you? No, sir. I could not forget you,
for I never saw you before in all my life.

VINCENTIO   What, you notorious villain, didst thou
never see thy master's father, Vincentio?

BIONDELLO   What, my old worshipful old master? Yes,
marry, sir, see where he looks out of the window.

VINCENTIO   Is 't so, indeed?   *He beats Biondello.*

BIONDELLO   Help, help, help! Here's a madman will
murder me.   [*Exit.*]

PEDANT   Help, son! Help, Signor Baptista!
[*Exit from the window.*]

PETRUCHIO   Prithee, Kate, let's stand aside and see the
end of this controversy.   [*They stand aside.*]

*Enter [below] Pedant with servants, Baptista,
[and] Tranio [as Lucentio].*

TRANIO   Sir, what are you that offer to beat my servant?   59

VINCENTIO   What am I, sir? Nay, what are you, sir? O
immortal gods! O fine villain! A silken doublet, a velvet hose, a scarlet cloak, and a copintank hat! O, I am   62
undone, I am undone! While I play the good husband   63
at home, my son and my servant spend all at the university.

TRANIO   How now, what's the matter?

BAPTISTA   What, is the man lunatic?

TRANIO   Sir, you seem a sober ancient gentleman by
your habit, but your words show you a madman.   69
Why, sir, what 'cerns it you if I wear pearl and gold?   70
I thank my good father, I am able to maintain it.   71

VINCENTIO   Thy father! O villain, he is a sailmaker in
Bergamo.

BAPTISTA   You mistake, sir, you mistake, sir. Pray, what
do you think is his name?

VINCENTIO   His name! As if I knew not his name! I have
brought him up ever since he was three years old, and
his name is Tranio.

PEDANT   Away, away, mad ass! His name is Lucentio,
and he is mine only son, and heir to the lands of me,
Signor Vincentio.

VINCENTIO   Lucentio! O, he hath murdered his master!
Lay hold on him, I charge you, in the Duke's name.
O, my son, my son! Tell me, thou villain, where is my
son Lucentio?

TRANIO   Call forth an officer.

[*Enter an Officer.*]

Carry this mad knave to the jail. Father Baptista, I
charge you see that he be forthcoming.   88

VINCENTIO   Carry me to the jail?

GREMIO   Stay, officer, he shall not go to prison.

BAPTISTA   Talk not, Signor Gremio. I say he shall go to
prison.

---

9 father's i.e., father-in-law's, Baptista's.   **bears** lies. (A nautical
term.)   **11 You . . . but** i.e., I insist that   **13 cheer is toward** entertainment is in prospect   **15 s.d. window** i.e., probably the gallery to
the rear, over the stage   **19 withal** with   **26 circumstances** matters
29 from Padua i.e., from Padua, where we are right now. (Often
emended to "from Mantua," "from Pisa," "to Padua," etc.)   **35 flat**
downright   **38 cozen** cheat.   **under my countenance** by pretending
to be me   **40 good shipping** bon voyage, good fortune   **43 crackhemp** i.e., rogue likely to end up being hanged   **44 choose** do as I
choose

59 offer dare, presume   **62 copintank** high-crowned, sugar-loaf shape
63 good husband careful provider, manager   **69 habit** clothing
70 'cerns concerns   **71 maintain** afford   **88 forthcoming** ready to
stand trial when required

GREMIO Take heed, Signor Baptista, lest you be coney- 93
catched in this business. I dare swear this is the right 94
Vincentio.

PEDANT Swear, if thou dar'st.

GREMIO Nay, I dare not swear it.

TRANIO Then thou wert best say that I am not Lucentio. 98

GREMIO Yes, I know thee to be Signor Lucentio.

BAPTISTA Away with the dotard! To the jail with him!

Enter Biondello, Lucentio, and Bianca.

VINCENTIO Thus strangers may be haled and abused. 101
—O monstrous villain!

BIONDELLO O! We are spoiled and—yonder he is. 103
Deny him, forswear him, or else we are all undone.
Exeunt Biondello, Tranio, and Pedant,
as fast as may be. [Lucentio and Bianca] kneel.

LUCENTIO
Pardon, sweet Father.

VINCENTIO   Lives my sweet son?

BIANCA
Pardon, dear Father.

BAPTISTA   How hast thou offended?
Where is Lucentio?

LUCENTIO   Here's Lucentio,
Right son to the right Vincentio,
That have by marriage made thy daughter mine,
While counterfeit supposes bleared thine eyne. 110

GREMIO
Here's packing, with a witness, to deceive us all! 111

VINCENTIO
Where is that damnèd villain Tranio,
That faced and braved me in this matter so? 113

BAPTISTA
Why, tell me, is not this my Cambio?

BIANCA
Cambio is changed into Lucentio. 115

LUCENTIO
Love wrought these miracles. Bianca's love
Made me exchange my state with Tranio, 117
While he did bear my countenance in the town, 118
And happily I have arrivèd at the last
Unto the wishèd haven of my bliss.
What Tranio did, myself enforced him to;
Then pardon him, sweet Father, for my sake.

VINCENTIO I'll slit the villain's nose, that would have
sent me to the jail.

BAPTISTA *[to Lucentio]* But do you hear, sir? Have you
married my daughter without asking my good will?

VINCENTIO Fear not, Baptista, we will content you. Go 127

to. But I will in, to be revenged for this villainy. 128
Exit.

BAPTISTA And I, to sound the depth of this knavery.
Exit.

LUCENTIO Look not pale, Bianca. Thy father will not
frown.   *Exeunt [Lucentio and Bianca].*

GREMIO
My cake is dough, but I'll in among the rest, 132
Out of hope of all but my share of the feast. *[Exit.]* 133

KATHARINA Husband, let's follow, to see the end of
this ado.

PETRUCHIO First kiss me, Kate, and we will.

KATHARINA What, in the midst of the street?

PETRUCHIO What, art thou ashamed of me?

KATHARINA No, sir, God forbid, but ashamed to kiss.

PETRUCHIO
Why, then let's home again. *[To Grumio.]* Come,
sirrah, let's away.

KATHARINA
Nay, I will give thee a kiss. *[She kisses him.]* Now
pray thee, love, stay.

PETRUCHIO
Is not this well? Come, my sweet Kate.
Better once than never, for never too late. *Exeunt.* 143

❧

5.2 *Enter Baptista, Vincentio, Gremio, the Pedant,*
Lucentio, and Bianca; [Petruchio, Kate, Hortensio,]
Tranio, Biondello, Grumio, and [the] Widow; the
servingmen with Tranio bringing in a banquet.

LUCENTIO
At last, though long, our jarring notes agree, 1
And time it is, when raging war is done,
To smile at scapes and perils overblown. 3
My fair Bianca, bid my father welcome,
While I with selfsame kindness welcome thine.
Brother Petruchio, sister Katharina,
And thou, Hortensio, with thy loving widow,
Feast with the best, and welcome to my house. 8
My banquet is to close our stomachs up 9
After our great good cheer. Pray you, sit down, 10
For now we sit to chat as well as eat. *[They sit.]*

PETRUCHIO
Nothing but sit and sit, and eat and eat!

BAPTISTA
Padua affords this kindness, son Petruchio.

PETRUCHIO
Padua affords nothing but what is kind.

HORTENSIO
For both our sakes, I would that word were true.

93–94 **coney-catched** tricked 98 **wert best** might as well
101 **haled** hauled about, maltreated 103 **spoiled** ruined 110 **supposes** suppositions, false appearances (with an allusion to Gascoigne's
Supposes, an adaptation of *I Suppositi* by Ariosto, from which
Shakespeare took the Lucentio-Bianca plot of intrigue). **eyne** eyes
111 **packing** conspiracy. **with a witness** i.e., and no mistake, with a
vengeance 113 **faced and braved** stood up to and defied
115 **Cambio is changed** (A pun. *Cambio* in Italian means "change" or
"exchange.") 117 **state** social station 118 **countenance** appearance, identity 127–128 **Go to** i.e., don't worry. (An expression of
impatience or annoyance.)

132 **My . . . dough** i.e., I'm out of luck, I failed 133 **Out . . . but**
having hope for nothing other than 143 **once** at some time. (Compare with "better late than never.")
5.2. Location: Padua. Lucentio's house.
s.d. **banquet** i.e., dessert 1 **long** after long time 3 **scapes** escapes,
close calls 8 **with** upon 9 **stomachs** appetites (with pun on "quarrels") 10 **our . . . cheer** i.e., the wedding feast at Baptista's

PETRUCHIO
Now, for my life, Hortensio fears his widow.   16
WIDOW
Then never trust me if I be afeard.
PETRUCHIO
You are very sensible, and yet you miss my sense: 18
I mean Hortensio is afeard of you.   19
WIDOW
He that is giddy thinks the world turns round.
PETRUCHIO
Roundly replied.
KATHARINA   Mistress, how mean you that?   21
WIDOW   Thus I conceive by him.   22
PETRUCHIO
Conceives by me! How likes Hortensio that?
HORTENSIO
My widow says, thus she conceives her tale.   24
PETRUCHIO
Very well mended. Kiss him for that, good widow.
KATHARINA
"He that is giddy thinks the world turns round":
I pray you, tell me what you meant by that.
WIDOW
Your husband, being troubled with a shrew,
Measures my husband's sorrow by his woe.   29
And now you know my meaning.
KATHARINA
A very mean meaning.
WIDOW   Right, I mean you.   31
KATHARINA
And I am mean indeed, respecting you.   32
PETRUCHIO   To her, Kate!   33
HORTENSIO   To her, widow!
PETRUCHIO
A hundred marks, my Kate does put her down.   35
HORTENSIO   That's my office.
PETRUCHIO
Spoke like an officer. Ha' to thee, lad!   37
                              [He] drinks to Hortensio.
BAPTISTA
How likes Gremio these quick-witted folks?
GREMIO
Believe me, sir, they butt together well.   39
BIANCA
Head, and butt! An hasty-witted body   40

Would say your head and butt were head and horn.   41
VINCENTIO
Ay, mistress bride, hath that awakened you?
BIANCA
Ay, but not frighted me. Therefore I'll sleep again.
PETRUCHIO
Nay, that you shall not. Since you have begun,
Have at you for a bitter jest or two!   45
BIANCA
Am I your bird? I mean to shift my bush;   46
And then pursue me as you draw your bow.
You are welcome all.
          Exit Bianca [with Katharina and the Widow].
PETRUCHIO
She hath prevented me. Here, Signor Tranio,   49
This bird you aimed at, though you hit her not.   50
Therefore a health to all that shot and missed.   51
                              [He offers a toast.]
TRANIO
O, sir, Lucentio slipped me like his greyhound,   52
Which runs himself and catches for his master.
PETRUCHIO
A good swift simile, but something currish.   54
TRANIO
'Tis well, sir, that you hunted for yourself.
'Tis thought your deer does hold you at a bay.   56
BAPTISTA
O ho, Petruchio! Tranio hits you now.
LUCENTIO
I thank thee for that gird, good Tranio.   58
HORTENSIO
Confess, confess, hath he not hit you here?
PETRUCHIO
'A has a little galled me, I confess;   60
And as the jest did glance away from me,   61
'Tis ten to one it maimed you two outright.
BAPTISTA
Now, in good sadness, son Petruchio,   63
I think thou hast the veriest shrew of all.
PETRUCHIO
Well, I say no. And therefore for assurance   65
Let's each one send unto his wife;
And he whose wife is most obedient
To come at first when he doth send for her
Shall win the wager which we will propose.
HORTENSIO
Content. What's the wager?
LUCENTIO   Twenty crowns.

16 **for my life** upon my life.   **fears** is afraid of. (But the Widow takes the word in the sense of "frightens"; she protests she is not at all *afeard*, frightened, by Hortensio.)   18 **sensible** (1) sensitive (2) reasonable   19 **afeard** (Petruchio takes up the Widow's word and uses it in the sense of "suspicious," fearful she will be untrue.)   21 **Roundly** boldly   22 **Thus . . . him** i.e., that's what I think of him, Petruchio. (But Petruchio takes up *conceives* in the sense of "is made pregnant.")   24 **conceives** intends, interprets (with a possible pun on *tale* and "tail")   29 **Measures** judges.   **his** his own   31 **very mean** contemptible. (But the Widow takes up *mean* in the sense of "have in mind," and Kate replies in the sense of "moderate in shrewishness.")   32 **respecting** compared to   33 **To her** (A cry used to egg on fighting roosters.)   35 **marks** coins worth thirteen shillings four pence.   **put her down** overcome her. (But Hortensio takes up the phrase in a bawdy sense.)   37 **officer** (playing on Hortensio's speaking of his *office* or function). **Ha'** have, i.e., here's   39 **butt** butt heads   40 **butt** tail, bottom.   **An hasty-witted body** a quick-witted person

41 **head and horn** (alluding to the familiar joke about cuckold's horns)   45 **Have at you for** i.e., be on guard against.   **bitter** sharp   46 **Am . . . bush** i.e., if you mean to shoot your barbs at me, I intend to move out of the way, as a bird would fly to another bush (with a possible bawdy double meaning; *bush* can suggest pubic hair)   49 **prevented** forestalled   50 **This bird** i.e., Bianca, whom Tranio courted (*aimed at*) in his disguise as Lucentio   51 **a health** a toast   52 **slipped** unleashed   54 **swift** (1) quick-witted (2) concerning swiftness.   **currish** (1) ignoble (2) concerning dogs   56 **deer** (punning on "dear").   **does . . . bay** turns on you like a cornered animal and holds you at a distance   58 **gird** sharp, biting jest   60 **galled** scratched, chafed   61 **glance away from** ricochet off   63 **sadness** seriousness   65 **assurance** proof

PETRUCHIO   Twenty crowns!
   I'll venture so much of my hawk or hound,   72
   But twenty times so much upon my wife.
LUCENTIO   A hundred then.
HORTENSIO   Content.
PETRUCHIO   A match. 'Tis done.
HORTENSIO   Who shall begin?
LUCENTIO   That will I.
   Go, Biondello, bid your mistress come to me.
BIONDELLO   I go.   *Exit.*
BAPTISTA
   Son, I'll be your half Bianca comes.   81
LUCENTIO
   I'll have no halves; I'll bear it all myself.

      Enter Biondello.

   How now, what news?
BIONDELLO
   Sir, my mistress sends you word
   That she is busy and she cannot come.
PETRUCHIO
   How? She's busy and she cannot come?
   Is that an answer?
GREMIO   Ay, and a kind one too.
   Pray God, sir, your wife send you not a worse.
PETRUCHIO   I hope better.
HORTENSIO
   Sirrah Biondello, go and entreat my wife
   To come to me forthwith.   *Exit Biondello.*
PETRUCHIO   Oho, entreat her!
   Nay, then she must needs come.
HORTENSIO   I am afraid, sir,
   Do what you can, yours will not be entreated.

      Enter Biondello.

   Now, where's my wife?
BIONDELLO
   She says you have some goodly jest in hand.
   She will not come. She bids you come to her.
PETRUCHIO
   Worse and worse. She will not come!
   O, vile, intolerable, not to be endured!
   Sirrah Grumio, go to your mistress.
   Say I command her come to me.   *Exit [Grumio].*
HORTENSIO
   I know her answer.
PETRUCHIO   What?
HORTENSIO   She will not.
PETRUCHIO
   The fouler fortune mine, and there an end.   102

      Enter Katharina.

BAPTISTA
   Now, by my halidom, here comes Katharina!   103
KATHARINA
   What is your will, sir, that you send for me?

PETRUCHIO
   Where is your sister, and Hortensio's wife?
KATHARINA
   They sit conferring by the parlor fire.
PETRUCHIO
   Go fetch them hither. If they deny to come,
   Swinge me them soundly forth unto their husbands.   108
   Away, I say, and bring them hither straight.
                           [Exit Katharina.]
LUCENTIO
   Here is a wonder, if you talk of a wonder.
HORTENSIO
   And so it is. I wonder what it bodes.
PETRUCHIO
   Marry, peace it bodes, and love, and quiet life,
   An awful rule, and right supremacy,   113
   And, to be short, what not that's sweet and happy.
BAPTISTA
   Now, fair befall thee, good Petruchio!   115
   The wager thou hast won, and I will add
   Unto their losses twenty thousand crowns,
   Another dowry to another daughter,
   For she is changed, as she had never been.   119
PETRUCHIO
   Nay, I will win my wager better yet,
   And show more sign of her obedience,
   Her new-built virtue and obedience.

      Enter Kate, Bianca, and [the] Widow.

   See where she comes and brings your froward wives
   As prisoners to her womanly persuasion.—
   Katharine, that cap of yours becomes you not.
   Off with that bauble. Throw it underfoot.
                             [She obeys.]
WIDOW
   Lord, let me never have a cause to sigh
   Till I be brought to such a silly pass!   128
BIANCA
   Fie, what a foolish duty call you this?
LUCENTIO
   I would your duty were as foolish, too.
   The wisdom of your duty, fair Bianca,
   Hath cost me a hundred crowns since suppertime.
BIANCA
   The more fool you, for laying on my duty.   133
PETRUCHIO
   Katharine, I charge thee tell these headstrong women
   What duty they do owe their lords and husbands.
WIDOW
   Come, come, you're mocking. We will have no telling.
PETRUCHIO
   Come on, I say, and first begin with her.
WIDOW   She shall not.

---

72 of on   **81 be your half** take half your bet   **102 there an end** that's that   **103 by my halidom** (Originally an oath by the holy relics, but confused with an oath to the Virgin Mary.)

108 Swinge thrash.   **me** i.e., at my behest. (*Me* is used colloquially.) **113 awful rule** authority commanding awe or respect   **115 fair befall thee** good luck to you, and congratulations   **119 as . . . been** as if she had never existed, i.e., she is totally changed   **128 pass** state of affairs   **133 laying** wagering

PETRUCHIO

I say she shall—and first begin with her.

KATHARINA

Fie, fie! Unknit that threatening, unkind brow,
And dart not scornful glances from those eyes
To wound thy lord, thy king, thy governor.
It blots thy beauty as frosts do bite the meads,
Confounds thy fame as whirlwinds shake fair buds,   144
And in no sense is meet or amiable.
A woman moved is like a fountain troubled,   146
Muddy, ill-seeming, thick, bereft of beauty;
And while it is so, none so dry or thirsty   148
Will deign to sip or touch one drop of it.
Thy husband is thy lord, thy life, thy keeper,
Thy head, thy sovereign; one that cares for thee,
And for thy maintenance commits his body
To painful labor both by sea and land,   153
To watch the night in storms, the day in cold,   154
Whilst thou liest warm at home, secure and safe;
And craves no other tribute at thy hands
But love, fair looks, and true obedience—
Too little payment for so great a debt.
Such duty as the subject owes the prince,
Even such a woman oweth to her husband;
And when she is froward, peevish, sullen, sour,   161
And not obedient to his honest will,   162
What is she but a foul contending rebel
And graceless traitor to her loving lord?
I am ashamed that women are so simple   165
To offer war where they should kneel for peace,
Or seek for rule, supremacy, and sway,
When they are bound to serve, love, and obey.
Why are our bodies soft, and weak, and smooth,
Unapt to toil and trouble in the world,   170
But that our soft conditions and our hearts   171
Should well agree with our external parts?
Come, come, you froward and unable worms!   173
My mind hath been as big as one of yours,   174
My heart as great, my reason haply more,
To bandy word for word and frown for frown;
But now I see our lances are but straws,
Our strength as weak, our weakness past compare,   178
That seeming to be most which we indeed least are.   179
Then vail your stomachs, for it is no boot,   180
And place your hands below your husband's foot,
In token of which duty, if he please,
My hand is ready; may it do him ease.   183

PETRUCHIO

Why, there's a wench! Come on, and kiss me, Kate.
[They kiss.]

LUCENTIO

Well, go thy ways, old lad, for thou shalt ha 't.   185

VINCENTIO

'Tis a good hearing when children are toward.   186

LUCENTIO

But a harsh hearing when women are froward.

PETRUCHIO   Come, Kate, we'll to bed.
We three are married, but you two are sped.   189
[To Lucentio.] 'Twas I won the wager, though you hit
the white,   190
And, being a winner, God give you good night!   191
Exit Petruchio [and Katharina].

HORTENSIO

Now go thy ways. Thou hast tamed a curst shrew.   192

LUCENTIO

'Tis a wonder, by your leave, she will be tamed so.
[Exeunt.]

185 go thy ways well done. ha 't have it, the prize 186 'Tis . . .
toward i.e., one likes to hear when children are obedient 189 We
. . . sped i.e., all we three men have taken wives, but you two are
done for (sped) through disobedient wives 190 the white the center
of the target (with quibble on the name of Bianca, which in Italian
means "white") 191 being since I am 192 shrew pronounced
"shrow" (and thus spelled in the Folio). See also 4.1.198 and 5.2.28.

144 Confounds thy fame ruins your reputation 146 moved angry
148 none . . . thirsty there is no one so thirsty that he 153 painful
onerous 154 watch stay awake throughout 161 peevish obstinate
162 to his honest will (Kate may suggest that she will be obedient
when his will is decent and virtuous, not that his will is always so.)
165 simple foolish 170 Unapt to unfit for 171 conditions qualities
173 unable worms i.e., poor feeble creatures 174 big haughty
178 as weak i.e., as weak as straws 179 That seeming to be seeming to be that 180 vail your stomachs lower your pride. boot
profit, use 183 do him ease give him pleasure

A Midsummer Night's Dream

A Midsummer Night's Dream (c. 1594–1595) belongs to the period of transition from Shakespeare's experimental, imitative comedy to his mature, romantic, philosophical, festive vein. In its lighthearted presentation of love's tribulations, the play resembles Shakespeare's earlier comedies. The two sets of young lovers (Lysander and Hermia, Demetrius and Helena), scarcely distinguishable one from the other, are conventional figures. In them we find only a hint of the profound self-discovery experienced by Beatrice and Benedick (Much Ado About Nothing) or Rosalind and Orlando (As You Like It). At the same time, this play develops the motif of love as an imaginative journey from reality into a fantasy world created by the artist, ending in a return to a reality that has itself been partly transformed by the experience of the journey. (Shakespeare gives us an earlier hint of such an imaginary sylvan landscape in The Two Gentlemen of Verona.) This motif, with its contrasting worlds of social order and imaginative escape, remained an enduring vision for Shakespeare to the very last.

In construction, A Midsummer Night's Dream is a skillful interweaving of four plots involving four groups of characters: the court party of Theseus, the four young lovers, the fairies, and the "rude mechanicals" or would-be actors. Felix Mendelssohn's incidental music for the play evokes the contrasting textures of the various groups: Theseus' hunting horns and ceremonial wedding marches, the lovers' soaring and throbbing melodies, the fairies' pianissimo staccato, the tradesmen's clownish bassoon. Moreover, each plot is derived from its own set of source materials. The action involving Theseus and Hippolyta, for example, owes several details to Thomas North's translation (1579) of Plutarch's Lives of the Noble Grecians and Romans, to Chaucer's Knight's Tale and perhaps to his Legend of Good Women, and to Ovid's Metamorphoses (in the Latin text or in Arthur Golding's popular Elizabethan translation). The lovers' story, meanwhile, is Italianate and Ovidian in tone and also, in the broadest sense, follows the conventions of plot in Plautus' and Terence's Roman comedies, although no particular source is known. Shakespeare's rich fairy lore, by contrast, is part folk tradition and part learned. Although he certainly needed no books to tell him about mischievous spirits that could prevent churned milk from turning to butter, for instance, Shakespeare might have borrowed Oberon's name either from the French romance Huon of Bordeaux (translated into English by 1540), from Robert Greene's play James IV (c. 1591), or from Edmund Spenser's The Faerie Queene, II.i.8 (1590). Similarly, he may have taken Titania's name from the Metamorphoses, where it is used as an epithet for both Diana and Circe. Finally, for Bottom the weaver and company, Shakespeare's primary inspiration was doubtless his own theatrical experience, although even here he is indebted to Ovid for the story of Pyramus and Thisbe, and probably to Apuleius' Golden Ass (translated by William Adlington, 1566) for Bottom's transformation.

Each of the four main plots in A Midsummer Night's Dream contains one or more pairs of lovers whose happiness has been frustrated by misunderstanding or parental opposition. Theseus and Hippolyta, once enemies in battle, become husband and wife; their court marriage, constituting the overplot of the play, provides a framework for other dramatic actions that similarly oscillate between conflict and harmony. In fact, Theseus' actions are instrumental in setting in motion and finally resolving the tribulations of the other characters. In the beginning of the play, for example, the lovers flee from Theseus' Athenian law; at the end, they are awakened by him from their dream. The king and queen of fairies come to Athens to celebrate Theseus' wedding but quarrel with each other because Oberon has long been partial to Hippolyta and Titania, partial to Theseus. The Athenian tradesmen go off into the forest to rehearse their performance of "Pyramus and Thisbe" in anticipation of the wedding festivities.

The tragic love story of Pyramus and Thisbe, although it seems absurdly ill suited to a wedding, reminds us of the discord and potentially fatal misunderstandings that threaten even the best of relationships between men and women. For all his graceful bearing and princely authority, Theseus is a conquering male who freely admits that he has won the love of Hippolyta with his sword, doing her "injuries" (1.1.17). He never questions that the accord between them should now be stated in terms of male ascendancy over the female. The Amazonian Hippolyta may accept with good grace the marriage she previously resisted with all her might, like Kate in The Taming of the Shrew, and yet, in many recent stage productions, the actress playing Hippolyta has found it easy to cast doubt on the presumed tranquility of this forthcoming marriage by a display of feminist impatience at Theseus' urbanely patriarchal ways. The reconciliation of Oberon and Titania, meanwhile, reinforces the hierarchy of male over female in no uncertain terms. Having taught Titania a lesson for trying to keep a changeling boy from him, Oberon relents and eventually frees Titania from her debasing enchantment. She does not reproach him with so much as a word when she is awakened from her "vision." The four young lovers end up happily paired, but only after they have experienced rejection, rivalry, hatred, and the desire to kill. Thus, Theseus' wedding provides a ceremonial occasion of harmony and reconciliation but in such a way as to highlight the difficulties that have beset the drama's various couples.

Despite Theseus' cheerful preoccupation with marriage, his court embodies at first a stern attitude toward young love. As administrator of the law, Theseus must accede to the remorseless demands of Hermia's father, Egeus. The inflexible Athenian law sides with parentage, age, male dominance, wealth, and position against youth and romantic choice in love. The penalties are harsh: death or perpetual virginity—and virginity is presented in this comedy (despite the nobly chaste examples of Christ, St. Paul, and Queen Elizabeth) as a fate worse than death. Egeus is a familiar type, the interfering parent found in the Roman comedy of Plautus and Terence (and in Shakespeare's *Romeo and Juliet*). Indeed, the lovers' story is distantly derived from Roman comedy, which conventionally celebrated the triumph of young love over the machinations of age and wealth. Lysander reminds us that "the course of true love never did run smooth," and he sees its enemies as being chiefly external: the conflicting interests of parents or friends; mismating with respect to years and blood; war; death; or sickness (1.1.134–142). This description clearly applies to "Pyramus and Thisbe," and it is tested by the action of *A Midsummer Night's Dream* as a whole (as well as by other early Shakespearean plays, such as *Romeo and Juliet*). The archetypal story, whether ending happily or sadly, is an evocation of love's difficulties in the face of social hostility and indifference.

While Shakespeare uses several elements of Roman comedy in setting up the basic conflicts of his drama, he also introduces important modifications from the beginning. For example, he discards one conventional confrontation of classical and neoclassical comedy, in which the heroine must choose between an old, wealthy suitor supported by her family and the young but impecunious darling of her heart. Lysander is equal to his rival in social position, income, and attractiveness. Egeus' demand, therefore—that Hermia marry Demetrius rather than Lysander—seems simply arbitrary and unjust. Shakespeare emphasizes in this way the irrationality of Egeus' harsh insistence on being obeyed and of Theseus' rather complacent acceptance of the law's inequity. Spurned by an unfeeling social order, Lysander and Hermia are compelled to elope. To be sure, in the end Egeus proves to be no formidable threat; even he must admit the logic of permitting the lovers to couple as they ultimately desire. Thus, the obstacles to love are seen from the start as fundamentally superficial and indeed almost whimsical. Egeus is as heavy a villain as we are likely to find in this *jeu d'esprit*. Moreover, the very irrationality of his position prepares the way for an ultimate resolution of the conflict. Nevertheless, by the end of the first act, the supposedly rational world of conformity and duty, by its customary insensitivity to youthful happiness, has set in motion a temporary escape to a fantasy world where the law cannot reach.

In the forest, all the lovers—including Titania and Bottom—undergo a transforming experience engineered by the mischievous Puck. This experience demonstrates the universal power of love, which can overcome the queen of fairies as readily as the lowliest of humans. It also suggests the irrational nature of love and its affinity to enchantment, witchcraft, and even madness. Love is seen as an affliction taken in through the frail senses, particularly the eyes. When it strikes, the victim cannot choose but to embrace the object of his infatuation. By his amusing miscalculations, Puck shuffles the four lovers through various permutations with mathematical predictability. First, two gentlemen compete for one lady, leaving the second lady sadly unrequited in love; then everything is at cross-purposes, with each gentleman pursuing the lady who is in love with the other man; then the two gentlemen compete for the lady they both previously ignored. Finally, of course, Jack shall have his Jill—whom else should he have? The couples are properly united, as they evidently were at some time prior to the commencement of the play, when Demetrius had made love to Helena and Lysander and Hermia had courted each other.

Their experience in the forest is an unsettling one for the four young lovers. Although some of them seek out the forest as a place of refuge from the Athenian law, the place rapidly takes on the darker aspect of a nightmare. Hermia awakens from sleep to find Lysander gone and soon discovers that her dream of a serpent eating her heart away while Lysander watches smiling (2.2.155–156) is all too prophetically true. The forest is a place of testing of the lovers, and the test appears at first to show how they are all their own worst enemies. Helena, having been rejected by Demetrius, can only suppose that she is being mocked, with Lysander and Demetrius both paying court to her. Next, it occurs to her that Hermia must be part of their conspiracy, too. Even though Hermia and Helena recall to each other the selfless devotion they have known as young friends, they become hated rivals in their present mood of self-pity and injured self-regard. The threshold of sexual awakening, it would seem, confronts them with a hazardous rite of passage—one that is especially threatening to the nonsexual friendship of their adolescent years. The two young men respond to similar conflicts by turning on one another in characteristically aggressive male ways. Puck allows them to playact their intended mayhem in a way that cannot harm them and then brings all four lovers together where they can awaken from their nightmare of imagined persecution. When they thus awaken and return to the daylight world of Athens and the court, their renewed love and friendship are presumably deepened by their perception of how narrowly they have escaped from their own self-destructive imaginings. Their new happiness, they see, is better than what they deserve.

We sense that Puck is by no means unhappy about his knavish errors and manipulations: "Lord, what fools these mortals be!" Along with the other fairies in this play, Puck takes his being and his complex motivation from many denizens of the invisible world. As the agent of all-powerful love, Puck compares himself to Cupid. The love juice he administers comes from Cupid's flower, "love-in-idleness." Like Cupid, Puck acts at the behest of the gods, and yet he wields a power that the chiefest of the gods themselves cannot resist. Essentially, however, Puck is less a classical love deity than a prankish folk spirit, such as we find in every folklore: gremlin, leprechaun, hobgoblin, and the like. Titania's fairies recognize Puck as one who, for example, can deprive a beer barrel of its yeast so that it spoils rather than ferments. Puck characterizes himself as a practical joker, pulling stools out from under old ladies.

Folk wisdom imagines the inexplicable and unaccountable events in life to be caused by invisible spirits who laugh at mortals' discomfiture and mock them for mere sport. Puck is related to these mysterious spirits dwelling in nature, who must be placated with gifts and ceremonies. Although Shakespeare restricts Puck to a benign sportive role in dealing with the lovers or with Titania, the actual folk legends about Puck mentioned in this play are frequently disquieting. Puck is known to "mislead night wanderers, laughing at their harm"; indeed, he demonstrates as much with Demetrius and Lysander, engineering a confrontation that greatly oppresses the lovers, even though we perceive the sportful intent. At the play's end, Puck links himself and his fellows with the ghoulish apparitions of death and night: wolves howling at the moon, screech owls, shrouds, gaping graves. Associations of this sort go beyond mere sportiveness to the witchcraft and demonology involving spirits rising from the dead. Even Oberon's assurance that the fairies will bless all the marriages of this play, shielding their progeny against mole, harelip, or other birth defects, carries the implication that such misfortunes can be caused by offended spirits. The magic of this play is thus explicitly related to deep irrational powers and forces capable of doing great harm, although, of course, the spirit of comedy keeps such veiled threats safely at a distance in *A Midsummer Night's Dream*.

Oberon and Titania, in their view of the relationship between gods and humans, reflect yet another aspect of the fairies' spiritual ancestry—one more nearly related to the gods and goddesses of the world of Greek mythology. The king and queen of fairies assert that, because they are immortal, their regal quarrels in love must inevitably have dire consequences on earth, either in the love relationship of Theseus and Hippolyta or in the management of the weather. Floods, storms, diseases, and sterility abound, "And this same progeny of evils comes / From our debate, from our dissension. / We are their parents and original" (2.1.115–117). Even though this motif of the gods' quarreling over human affairs is Homeric or Virgilian in concep-

tion, the motif in this lighthearted play is more nearly mock-epic than truly epic. The consequences of the gods' anger are simply mirth-provoking, most of all in Titania's love affair with Bottom the weaver.

The story of Bottom and Titania is recognizably a metamorphosis in a playfully classical mode, a love affair between a god and an earthly creature, underscoring humans' dual nature. Bottom himself becomes half man and half beast, although he is ludicrously unlike the centaurs, mermaids, and other half-human beings of classical mythology. Whereas the head should be the aspiring part of him and his body the bestial part, Bottom wears an ass's head on his shoulders. His very name suggests the solid nature of his fleshly being (*bottom* is appropriately also a weaving term). He and Titania represent the opposites of flesh and spirit, miraculously yoked for a time in a twofold vision of man's absurd and ethereal nature.

A play bringing together fairies and mortals inevitably raises questions of illusion and reality. These questions reach their greatest intensity in the presentation of "Pyramus and Thisbe." This play within a play focuses our attention on the familiarly Shakespearean metaphor of art as illusion and of the world itself as a stage on which men and women are merely players. As Theseus observes, apologizing for the ineptness of the tradesmen's performance, "the best in this kind are but shadows" (5.1.210); that is, Shakespeare's own play is of the same order of reality as Bottom's play. Puck too, in his epilogue, invites any spectator offended by Shakespeare's play to dismiss it as a mere dream—as, indeed, the play's very title suggests. Theseus goes even further, linking dream to the essence of imaginative art, although he does so in a clearly critical and rather patronizing way. The artist, he says, is like the maniac or the lover in his or her frenzy of inspiration, giving "to airy nothing / A local habitation and a name" (5.1.16–17). Artistic achievements are too unsubstantial for Theseus; from his point of view they are the products of mere fantasy and irrationality, mere myths or fairy stories or old wives' tales. Behind this critical persona defending the "real" world of his court, however, we can hear Shakespeare's characteristically self-effacing defense of "dreaming."

"Pyramus and Thisbe," like the larger play surrounding it, attempts to body forth "the forms of things unknown." The play within the play gives us personified moonshine, a speaking wall, and an apologetic lion. Of course, it is an absurdly bad play, full of lame epithets, bombastic alliteration, and bathos. In part, Shakespeare here is satirizing the abuses of a theater he had helped reform. The players' chosen method of portraying imaginative matters is ridiculous and calls forth deliciously wry comments from the courtly spectators on stage: "Would you desire lime and hair to speak better?" (5.1.164–165). At the same time, those spectators on stage are actors in our play. Their sarcasms render them less sympathetic in our eyes; we see that their kind of sophistication is as restrictive as it is illuminating. Bottom and his friends have conceived moonshine and lion as they did because these simple men are so responsive to the terrifying power of art. A lion might frighten the ladies and get the men hanged. Theirs is a primitive faith, naive but strong, and in this sense it contrasts favorably with the jaded rationality of the court party. Theseus' valuable reminder that all art is only "illusion" is thus juxtaposed with Bottom's insistence that imaginative art has a reality of its own.

Theseus above all embodies the sophistication of the court in his description of art as a frenzy of seething brains. Genially scoffing at "These antique fables" and "these fairy toys" (5.1.3), he is unmoved by the lovers' account of their dreamlike experience. Limited by his own skepticism, Theseus has never experienced the enchantment of the forest. Even Bottom can claim more than that, for he has been the lover of the queen of fairies; and, although his language cannot adequately describe the experience, Bottom will see it made into a ballad called "Bottom's Dream." Shakespeare leaves the status of his fantasy world deliberately complex; Theseus' lofty denial of dreaming is too abrupt. Even if the Athenian forest world can be made only momentarily substantial in the artifact of Shakespeare's play, we as audience respond to its tantalizing vision. We emerge back into our lives wondering if the fairies were "real"; that is, we are puzzled by the relationship of these artistic symbols to the tangible concreteness of our daily existence. Unless our perceptions have been thus enlarged by sharing in the author's dream, we have not surrendered to the imaginative experience.

A Midsummer Night's Dream

[*Dramatis Personae*

THESEUS, *Duke of Athens*
HIPPOLYTA, *Queen of the Amazons, betrothed to Theseus*
PHILOSTRATE, *Master of the Revels*
EGEUS, *father of Hermia*

HERMIA, *daughter of Egeus, in love with Lysander*
LYSANDER, *in love with Hermia*
DEMETRIUS, *in love with Hermia and favored by Egeus*
HELENA, *in love with Demetrius*

OBERON, *King of the Fairies*
TITANIA, *Queen of the Fairies*
PUCK, *or* ROBIN GOODFELLOW
PEASEBLOSSOM,
COBWEB, *fairies attending*
MOTE, *Titania*
MUSTARDSEED,
Other FAIRIES *attending*

PETER QUINCE, *a carpenter,*	PROLOGUE
NICK BOTTOM, *a weaver,*	PYRAMUS
FRANCIS FLUTE, *a bellows mender,*	*repre-senting* THISBE
TOM SNOUT, *a tinker,*	WALL
SNUG, *a joiner,*	LION
ROBIN STARVELING, *a tailor,*	MOONSHINE

Lords and Attendants on Theseus and Hippolyta

SCENE: *Athens, and a wood near it*]

1.1   *Enter Theseus, Hippolyta, [and Philostrate,] with others.*

THESEUS
Now, fair Hippolyta, our nuptial hour
Draws on apace. Four happy days bring in
Another moon; but, O, methinks, how slow
This old moon wanes! She lingers my desires,   4
Like to a stepdame or a dowager   5
Long withering out a young man's revenue.   6

1.1. Location: Athens. Theseus' court.
4 lingers postpones, delays the fulfillment of   **5 stepdame** stepmother. **a dowager** i.e., a widow (whose right of inheritance from her dead husband is eating into her son's estate)   **6 withering out** causing to dwindle

HIPPOLYTA

Four days will quickly steep themselves in night;   7
Four nights will quickly dream away the time;
And then the moon, like to a silver bow
New bent in heaven, shall behold the night
Of our solemnities.

THESEUS   Go, Philostrate,   11
Stir up the Athenian youth to merriments.
Awake the pert and nimble spirit of mirth.
Turn melancholy forth to funerals;
The pale companion is not for our pomp.   15

               [*Exit Philostrate.*]

Hippolyta, I wooed thee with my sword   16
And won thy love doing thee injuries;
But I will wed thee in another key,
With pomp, with triumph, and with reveling.   19

     Enter Egeus and his daughter Hermia, and
     Lysander, and Demetrius.

EGEUS

Happy be Theseus, our renownèd duke!

THESEUS

Thanks, good Egeus. What's the news with thee?

EGEUS

Full of vexation come I, with complaint
Against my child, my daughter Hermia.—
Stand forth, Demetrius.—My noble lord,
This man hath my consent to marry her.—
Stand forth, Lysander.—And, my gracious Duke,
This man hath bewitched the bosom of my child.
Thou, thou Lysander, thou hast given her rhymes
And interchanged love tokens with my child.
Thou hast by moonlight at her window sung
With feigning voice verses of feigning love,   31
And stol'n the impression of her fantasy   32
With bracelets of thy hair, rings, gauds, conceits,   33
Knacks, trifles, nosegays, sweetmeats—messengers   34
Of strong prevailment in unhardened youth.   35
With cunning hast thou filched my daughter's heart,
Turned her obedience, which is due to me,
To stubborn harshness. And, my gracious Duke,
Be it so she will not here before Your Grace   39
Consent to marry with Demetrius,
I beg the ancient privilege of Athens:
As she is mine, I may dispose of her,
Which shall be either to this gentleman
Or to her death, according to our law
Immediately provided in that case.   45

THESEUS

What say you, Hermia? Be advised, fair maid.
To you your father should be as a god—

One that composed your beauties, yea, and one
To whom you are but as a form in wax
By him imprinted, and within his power
To leave the figure or disfigure it.   51
Demetrius is a worthy gentleman.

HERMIA

So is Lysander.

THESEUS   In himself he is;
But in this kind, wanting your father's voice,   54
The other must be held the worthier.

HERMIA

I would my father looked but with my eyes.

THESEUS

Rather your eyes must with his judgment look.

HERMIA

I do entreat Your Grace to pardon me.
I know not by what power I am made bold,
Nor how it may concern my modesty   60
In such a presence here to plead my thoughts;
But I beseech Your Grace that I may know
The worst that may befall me in this case
If I refuse to wed Demetrius.

THESEUS

Either to die the death or to abjure   65
Forever the society of men.
Therefore, fair Hermia, question your desires,
Know of your youth, examine well your blood,   68
Whether, if you yield not to your father's choice,
You can endure the livery of a nun,   70
For aye to be in shady cloister mewed,   71
To live a barren sister all your life,
Chanting faint hymns to the cold fruitless moon.
Thrice blessèd they that master so their blood
To undergo such maiden pilgrimage;
But earthlier happy is the rose distilled   76
Than that which, withering on the virgin thorn,
Grows, lives, and dies in single blessedness.

HERMIA

So will I grow, so live, so die, my lord,
Ere I will yield my virgin patent up   80
Unto his lordship, whose unwishèd yoke
My soul consents not to give sovereignty.

THESEUS

Take time to pause, and by the next new moon—
The sealing day betwixt my love and me
For everlasting bond of fellowship—
Upon that day either prepare to die
For disobedience to your father's will,
Or else to wed Demetrius, as he would,   88
Or on Diana's altar to protest   89
For aye austerity and single life.

DEMETRIUS

Relent, sweet Hermia, and, Lysander, yield

---

7 **steep themselves** saturate themselves, be absorbed in   11 **solemnities** festive ceremonies of marriage   15 **companion** fellow.   **pomp** ceremonial magnificence   16 **with my sword** i.e., in a military engagement against the Amazons, when Hippolyta was taken captive   19 **triumph** public festivity   31 **feigning** (1) counterfeiting (2) faining, desirous   32 **And . . . fantasy** and made her fall in love with you (imprinting your image on her imagination) by stealthy and dishonest means   33 **gauds** playthings.   **conceits** fanciful trifles   34 **Knacks** knickknacks   35 **prevailment in** influence on   39 **Be it so** if   45 **Immediately** directly, with nothing intervening

51 **leave** i.e., leave unaltered.   **disfigure** obliterate   54 **kind** respect.   **wanting** lacking.   **voice** approval   60 **concern** befit   65 **die the death** be executed by legal process   68 **blood** passions   70 **livery** habit, costume   71 **aye** ever.   **mewed** shut in. (Said of a hawk, poultry, etc.)   76 **earthlier happy** happier as respects this world.   **distilled** i.e., to make perfume   80 **patent** privilege   88 **Or** either   89 **protest** vow

Thy crazèd title to my certain right.　　92

LYSANDER
You have her father's love, Demetrius;
Let me have Hermia's. Do you marry him.

EGEUS
Scornful Lysander! True, he hath my love,
And what is mine my love shall render him.
And she is mine, and all my right of her
I do estate unto Demetrius.　　98

LYSANDER
I am, my lord, as well derived as he,　　99
As well possessed; my love is more than his;　　100
My fortunes every way as fairly ranked,　　101
If not with vantage, as Demetrius';　　102
And, which is more than all these boasts can be,
I am beloved of beauteous Hermia.
Why should not I then prosecute my right?
Demetrius, I'll avouch it to his head,　　106
Made love to Nedar's daughter, Helena,
And won her soul; and she, sweet lady, dotes,
Devoutly dotes, dotes in idolatry
Upon this spotted and inconstant man.　　110

THESEUS
I must confess that I have heard so much,
And with Demetrius thought to have spoke thereof;
But, being overfull of self-affairs,　　113
My mind did lose it. But, Demetrius, come,
And come, Egeus, you shall go with me;
I have some private schooling for you both.　　116
For you, fair Hermia, look you arm yourself　　117
To fit your fancies to your father's will,　　118
Or else the law of Athens yields you up—
Which by no means we may extenuate—　　120
To death or to a vow of single life.
Come, my Hippolyta. What cheer, my love?
Demetrius and Egeus, go along.　　123
I must employ you in some business
Against our nuptial, and confer with you　　125
Of something nearly that concerns yourselves.　　126

EGEUS
With duty and desire we follow you.
		Exeunt [all but Lysander and Hermia].

LYSANDER
How now, my love, why is your cheek so pale?
How chance the roses there do fade so fast?

HERMIA
Belike for want of rain, which I could well　　130
Beteem them from the tempest of my eyes.　　131

LYSANDER
Ay me! For aught that I could ever read,
Could ever hear by tale or history,

The course of true love never did run smooth;
But either it was different in blood—　　135

HERMIA
O cross! Too high to be enthralled to low.　　136

LYSANDER
Or else misgrafted in respect of years—　　137

HERMIA
O spite! Too old to be engaged to young.

LYSANDER
Or else it stood upon the choice of friends—　　139

HERMIA
O hell, to choose love by another's eyes!

LYSANDER
Or if there were a sympathy in choice,　　141
War, death, or sickness did lay siege to it,
Making it momentany as a sound,　　143
Swift as a shadow, short as any dream,
Brief as the lightning in the collied night　　145
That in a spleen unfolds both heaven and earth,　　146
And ere a man hath power to say "Behold!"
The jaws of darkness do devour it up.
So quick bright things come to confusion.　　149

HERMIA
If then true lovers have been ever crossed,　　150
It stands as an edict in destiny.
Then let us teach our trial patience,　　152
Because it is a customary cross,
As due to love as thoughts, and dreams, and sighs,
Wishes, and tears, poor fancy's followers.　　155

LYSANDER
A good persuasion. Therefore, hear me, Hermia:　　156
I have a widow aunt, a dowager
Of great revenue, and she hath no child.
From Athens is her house remote seven leagues;
And she respects me as her only son.　　160
There, gentle Hermia, may I marry thee,
And to that place the sharp Athenian law
Cannot pursue us. If thou lovest me, then,
Steal forth thy father's house tomorrow night;
And in the wood, a league without the town,　　165
Where I did meet thee once with Helena
To do observance to a morn of May,　　167
There will I stay for thee.

HERMIA　　　　　　　　My good Lysander!
I swear to thee, by Cupid's strongest bow,
By his best arrow with the golden head,　　170
By the simplicity of Venus' doves,　　171
By that which knitteth souls and prospers loves,

---

92 **crazèd** cracked, unsound　98 **estate unto** settle or bestow upon　99 **as well derived** as well born and descended　100 **possessed** endowed with wealth　101 **fairly** handsomely　102 **vantage** superiority　106 **head** i.e., face　110 **spotted** i.e., morally stained　113 **self-affairs** my own concerns　116 **schooling** admonition　117 **look you arm** take care you prepare　118 **fancies** likings, thoughts of love　120 **extenuate** mitigate, relax　123 **go** i.e., come　125 **Against** in preparation for　126 **nearly that** that closely　130 **Belike** very likely　131 **Beteem** grant, afford

135 **blood** hereditary station　136 **cross** vexation　137 **misgrafted** ill grafted, badly matched　139 **friends** relatives　141 **sympathy** agreement　143 **momentany** lasting but a moment　145 **collied** blackened (as with coal dust), darkened　146 **in a spleen** in a swift impulse, in a violent flash.　**unfolds** reveals　149 **quick** quickly; also, living, alive. **confusion** ruin　150 **ever crossed** always thwarted　152 **teach . . . patience** i.e., teach ourselves patience in this trial　155 **fancy's** amorous passion's　156 **persuasion** doctrine　160 **respects** regards　165 **without** outside　167 **do . . . May** perform the ceremonies of May Day　170 **best arrow** (Cupid's best gold-pointed arrows were supposed to induce love; his blunt leaden arrows, aversion.)　171 **simplicity** innocence.　**doves** i.e., those that drew Venus' chariot

And by that fire which burned the Carthage queen 173
When the false Trojan under sail was seen, 174
By all the vows that ever men have broke,
In number more than ever women spoke,
In that same place thou hast appointed me
Tomorrow truly will I meet with thee.

LYSANDER
Keep promise, love. Look, here comes Helena.

Enter Helena.

HERMIA
God speed, fair Helena! Whither away? 180

HELENA
Call you me fair? That "fair" again unsay.
Demetrius loves your fair. O happy fair! 182
Your eyes are lodestars, and your tongue's sweet air 183
More tunable than lark to shepherd's ear 184
When wheat is green, when hawthorn buds appear.
Sickness is catching. O, were favor so, 186
Yours would I catch, fair Hermia, ere I go;
My ear should catch your voice, my eye your eye,
My tongue should catch your tongue's sweet
    melody.
Were the world mine, Demetrius being bated, 190
The rest I'd give to be to you translated. 191
O, teach me how you look and with what art
You sway the motion of Demetrius' heart. 193

HERMIA
I frown upon him, yet he loves me still.

HELENA
O, that your frowns would teach my smiles such
    skill!

HERMIA
I give him curses, yet he gives me love.

HELENA
O, that my prayers could such affection move! 197

HERMIA
The more I hate, the more he follows me.

HELENA
The more I love, the more he hateth me.

HERMIA
His folly, Helena, is no fault of mine.

HELENA
None, but your beauty. Would that fault were mine!

HERMIA
Take comfort. He no more shall see my face.
Lysander and myself will fly this place.
Before the time I did Lysander see 204
Seemed Athens as a paradise to me. 205

O, then, what graces in my love do dwell,
That he hath turned a heaven unto a hell?

LYSANDER
Helen, to you our minds we will unfold.
Tomorrow night, when Phoebe doth behold 209
Her silver visage in the watery glass, 210
Decking with liquid pearl the bladed grass,
A time that lovers' flights doth still conceal, 212
Through Athens' gates have we devised to steal.

HERMIA
And in the wood, where often you and I
Upon faint primrose beds were wont to lie, 215
Emptying our bosoms of their counsel sweet, 216
There my Lysander and myself shall meet,
And thence from Athens turn away our eyes
To seek new friends and stranger companies. 219
Farewell, sweet playfellow. Pray thou for us,
And good luck grant thee thy Demetrius!
Keep word, Lysander. We must starve our sight
From lovers' food till morrow deep midnight.

LYSANDER
I will, my Hermia. (*Exit Hermia.*) Helena, adieu.
As you on him, Demetrius dote on you!

Exit Lysander.

HELENA
How happy some o'er other some can be! 226
Through Athens I am thought as fair as she.
But what of that? Demetrius thinks not so;
He will not know what all but he do know.
And as he errs, doting on Hermia's eyes,
So I, admiring of his qualities. 231
Things base and vile, holding no quantity, 232
Love can transpose to form and dignity.
Love looks not with the eyes, but with the mind,
And therefore is winged Cupid painted blind.
Nor hath Love's mind of any judgment taste; 236
Wings and no eyes figure unheedy haste. 237
And therefore is Love said to be a child,
Because in choice he is so oft beguiled. 239
As waggish boys in game themselves forswear, 240
So the boy Love is perjured everywhere.
For ere Demetrius looked on Hermia's eyne, 242
He hailed down oaths that he was only mine;
And when this hail some heat from Hermia felt,
So he dissolved, and showers of oaths did melt.
I will go tell him of fair Hermia's flight.
Then to the wood will he tomorrow night
Pursue her; and for this intelligence 248
If I have thanks, it is a dear expense. 249

173, 174 Carthage queen, false Trojan (Dido, Queen of Carthage, immolated herself on a funeral pyre after having been deserted by the Trojan hero Aeneas.) **180 fair** fair-complexioned (generally regarded by the Elizabethans as more beautiful than a dark complexion) **182 your fair** your beauty (even though Hermia is dark complexioned). **happy fair** lucky fair one **183 lodestars** guiding stars. **air** music **184 tunable** tuneful, melodious **186 favor** appearance, looks **190 bated** excepted **191 translated** transformed **193 sway** control. **motion** impulse **197 affection** passion. **move** arouse **204–205 Before . . . to me** (Hermia seemingly means that love has led to complications and jealousies, making Athens hell for her.)

209 Phoebe Diana, the moon **210 glass** mirror **212 still** always **215 faint** pale **216 counsel** secret thought **219 stranger companies** the company of strangers **226 o'er . . . can be** can be in comparison to some others **231 admiring of** wondering at **232 holding no quantity** i.e., unsubstantial, unshapely **236 Nor . . . taste** i.e., nor has Love, which dwells in the fancy or imagination, any *taste* or least bit of judgment or reason **237 figure** are a symbol of **239 in choice** in choosing. **beguiled** self-deluded, making unaccountable choices **240 waggish** playful, mischievous. **game** sport, jest **242 eyne** eyes. (Old form of plural.) **248 intelligence** information **249 a dear expense** i.e., a trouble worth taking on my part, or a begrudging effort on his part. **dear** costly

But herein mean I to enrich my pain,
To have his sight thither and back again.   *Exit.*

❖

1.2   *Enter Quince the carpenter, and Snug the joiner,*
and Bottom the weaver, and Flute the bellows
mender, and Snout the tinker, and Starveling the
tailor.

QUINCE   Is all our company here?

BOTTOM   You were best to call them generally, man by 2
man, according to the scrip.   3

QUINCE   Here is the scroll of every man's name which is
thought fit, through all Athens, to play in our interlude 5
before the Duke and the Duchess on his wedding day
at night.

BOTTOM   First, good Peter Quince, say what the play
treats on, then read the names of the actors, and so
grow to a point.   10

QUINCE   Marry, our play is "The most lamentable com- 11
edy and most cruel death of Pyramus and Thisbe."

BOTTOM   A very good piece of work, I assure you, and
a merry. Now, good Peter Quince, call forth your actors by the scroll. Masters, spread yourselves.

QUINCE   Answer as I call you. Nick Bottom, the weaver. 16

BOTTOM   Ready. Name what part I am for, and proceed.

QUINCE   You, Nick Bottom, are set down for Pyramus.

BOTTOM   What is Pyramus? A lover or a tyrant?

QUINCE   A lover, that kills himself most gallant for love.

BOTTOM   That will ask some tears in the true performing
of it. If I do it, let the audience look to their eyes. I will
move storms; I will condole in some measure. To the 23
rest—yet my chief humor is for a tyrant. I could play 24
Ercles rarely, or a part to tear a cat in, to make all split. 25
    "The raging rocks
    And shivering shocks
    Shall break the locks
     Of prison gates;
    And Phibbus' car   30
    Shall shine from far
    And make and mar
     The foolish Fates."
This was lofty! Now name the rest of the players. This is
Ercles' vein, a tyrant's vein. A lover is more condoling.

QUINCE   Francis Flute, the bellows mender.

FLUTE   Here, Peter Quince.

QUINCE   Flute, you must take Thisbe on you.

FLUTE   What is Thisbe? A wandering knight?

QUINCE   It is the lady that Pyramus must love.

FLUTE   Nay, faith, let not me play a woman. I have a
beard coming.

QUINCE   That's all one. You shall play it in a mask, and 43
you may speak as small as you will.   44

BOTTOM   An I may hide my face, let me play Thisbe too. 45
I'll speak in a monstrous little voice: "Thisne, Thisne!"
"Ah, Pyramus, my lover dear! Thy Thisbe dear, and
lady dear!"

QUINCE   No, no, you must play Pyramus, and Flute,
you Thisbe.

BOTTOM   Well, proceed.

QUINCE   Robin Starveling, the tailor.

STARVELING   Here, Peter Quince.

QUINCE   Robin Starveling, you must play Thisbe's
mother. Tom Snout, the tinker.

SNOUT   Here, Peter Quince.

QUINCE   You, Pyramus' father; myself, Thisbe's father;
Snug, the joiner, you, the lion's part; and I hope here
is a play fitted.

SNUG   Have you the lion's part written? Pray you, if it
be, give it me, for I am slow of study.

QUINCE   You may do it extempore, for it is nothing but
roaring.

BOTTOM   Let me play the lion too. I will roar that I will
do any man's heart good to hear me. I will roar that I
will make the Duke say, "Let him roar again, let him
roar again."

QUINCE   An you should do it too terribly, you would
fright the Duchess and the ladies, that they would
shriek; and that were enough to hang us all.

ALL   That would hang us, every mother's son.

BOTTOM   I grant you, friends, if you should fright the
ladies out of their wits, they would have no more discretion but to hang us; but I will aggravate my voice 74
so that I will roar you as gently as any sucking dove; I 75
will roar you an 'twere any nightingale.   76

QUINCE   You can play no part but Pyramus; for Pyramus
is a sweet-faced man, a proper man as one shall see in 78
a summer's day, a most lovely gentlemanlike man.
Therefore you must needs play Pyramus.

BOTTOM   Well, I will undertake it. What beard were I
best to play it in?

QUINCE   Why, what you will.

BOTTOM   I will discharge it in either your straw-color 84
beard, your orange-tawny beard, your purple-in-grain 85
beard, or your French-crown-color beard, your perfect 86
yellow.

QUINCE   Some of your French crowns have no hair at all, 88
and then you will play barefaced. But, masters, here
are your parts. [*He distributes parts.*] And I am to entreat you, request you, and desire you to con them by 91
tomorrow night, and meet me in the palace wood, a
mile without the town, by moonlight. There will we

1.2. Location: Athens.
2 generally (Bottom's blunder for "individually.")   **3 scrip** scrap. (Bottom's error for "script.")   **5 interlude** play   **10 grow to** come to
11 Marry (A mild oath; originally the name of the Virgin Mary.)
16 Bottom (As a weaver's term, a *bottom* was an object around which
thread was wound.)   **23 condole** lament, arouse pity   **24 humor** inclination, whim   **25 Ercles** Hercules. (The tradition of ranting came
from Seneca's *Hercules Furens*.)   **tear a cat** i.e., rant.   **make all split**
i.e., cause a stir, bring the house down   **30 Phibbus' car** Phoebus',
the sun god's, chariot

43 That's all one it makes no difference   **44 small** high-pitched
45 An if. (Also at line 68.)   **74 aggravate** (Bottom's blunder for
"moderate.")   **75 roar you** i.e., roar for you.   **sucking dove** (Bottom
conflates *sitting dove* and *sucking lamb*, two proverbial images of innocence.)   **76 an 'twere** as if it were   **78 proper** handsome   **84 discharge** perform.   **your** i.e., you know the kind I mean   **85 purple-in-
grain** dyed a very deep red. (From *grain*, the name applied to the
dried insect used to make the dye.)   **86 French-crown-color** i.e.,
color of a French crown, a gold coin   **88 crowns** heads bald from
syphilis, the "French disease"   **91 con** learn by heart

rehearse; for if we meet in the city, we shall be dogged with company, and our devices known. In the mean- 95 time I will draw a bill of properties, such as our play 96 wants. I pray you, fail me not.

BOTTOM   We will meet, and there we may rehearse most obscenely and courageously. Take pains, be perfect. 99 Adieu.

QUINCE   At the Duke's oak we meet.

BOTTOM   Enough. Hold, or cut bowstrings.   *Exeunt.* 102

♣

2.1   *Enter a Fairy at one door, and Robin Goodfellow [Puck] at another.*

PUCK
How now, spirit, whither wander you?

FAIRY
Over hill, over dale,
    Thorough bush, thorough brier,
Over park, over pale, 4
    Thorough flood, thorough fire,
I do wander everywhere,
Swifter than the moon's sphere; 7
And I serve the Fairy Queen,
To dew her orbs upon the green. 9
The cowslips tall her pensioners be. 10
In their gold coats spots you see;
Those be rubies, fairy favors; 12
In those freckles live their savors. 13
I must go seek some dewdrops here
And hang a pearl in every cowslip's ear.
Farewell, thou lob of spirits; I'll be gone. 16
Our Queen and all her elves come here anon. 17

PUCK
The King doth keep his revels here tonight.
Take heed the Queen come not within his sight.
For Oberon is passing fell and wrath, 20
Because that she as her attendant hath
A lovely boy, stolen from an Indian king;
She never had so sweet a changeling. 23
And jealous Oberon would have the child
Knight of his train, to trace the forests wild. 25
But she perforce withholds the lovèd boy, 26
Crowns him with flowers, and makes him all her joy.
And now they never meet in grove or green,

By fountain clear, or spangled starlight sheen, 29
But they do square, that all their elves for fear 30
Creep into acorn cups and hide them there.

FAIRY
Either I mistake your shape and making quite,
Or else you are that shrewd and knavish sprite 33
Called Robin Goodfellow. Are not you he
That frights the maidens of the villagery, 35
Skim milk, and sometimes labor in the quern, 36
And bootless make the breathless huswife churn, 37
And sometimes make the drink to bear no barm, 38
Mislead night wanderers, laughing at their harm? 39
Those that "Hobgoblin" call you, and "Sweet Puck," 40
You do their work, and they shall have good luck.
Are you not he?

PUCK   Thou speakest aright;
I am that merry wanderer of the night.
I jest to Oberon and make him smile
When I a fat and bean-fed horse beguile, 45
Neighing in likeness of a filly foal;
And sometimes lurk I in a gossip's bowl 47
In very likeness of a roasted crab, 48
And when she drinks, against her lips I bob
And on her withered dewlap pour the ale. 50
The wisest aunt, telling the saddest tale, 51
Sometimes for three-foot stool mistaketh me;
Then slip I from her bum, down topples she,
And "Tailor" cries, and falls into a cough; 54
And then the whole choir hold their hips and laugh, 55
And waxen in their mirth, and neeze, and swear 56
A merrier hour was never wasted there. 57
But, room, fairy! Here comes Oberon. 58

FAIRY
And here my mistress. Would that he were gone!

Enter [Oberon] the King of Fairies at one door, with his train, and [Titania] the Queen at another, with hers.

OBERON
Ill met by moonlight, proud Titania.

TITANIA
What, jealous Oberon? Fairies, skip hence.
I have forsworn his bed and company.

OBERON
Tarry, rash wanton. Am not I thy lord? 63

95 devices plans   **96 draw a bill** draw up a list   **99 obscenely** (An unintentionally funny blunder, whatever Bottom meant to say.)   **perfect** i.e., letter-perfect in memorizing your parts   **102 Hold . . . bowstrings** (An archers' expression, not definitely explained, but probably meaning here "keep your promises, or give up the play.")
2.1. Location: A wood near Athens.
3 Thorough through   **4 pale** enclosure   **7 sphere** orbit   **9 dew** sprinkle with dew.   **orbs** circles, i.e., fairy rings (circular bands of grass, darker than the surrounding area, caused by fungi enriching the soil)   **10 pensioners** retainers, members of the royal bodyguard   **12 favors** love tokens   **13 savors** sweet smells   **16 lob** country bumpkin   **17 anon** at once   **20 passing fell** exceedingly angry.   **wrath** wrathful   **23 changeling** child exchanged for another by the fairies   **25 trace** range through   **26 perforce** forcibly

29 fountain spring.   **starlight sheen** shining starlight   **30 square** quarrel   **33 shrewd** mischievous.   **sprite** spirit   **35 villagery** village population   **36 Skim milk** i.e., steal the cream.   **quern** hand mill (where Puck presumably hampers the grinding of grain)   **37 bootless** in vain. (Puck prevents the cream from turning to butter.)   **huswife** housewife   **38 barm** head on the ale. (Puck prevents the barm or yeast from producing fermentation.)   **39 Mislead night wanderers** i.e., mislead with false fire those who walk abroad at night (hence earning Puck his other names of Jack o' Lantern and Will o' the Wisp)   **40 Those . . . Puck** i.e., those who call you by the names you favor rather than those denoting the mischief you do   **45 bean-fed** well fed on field beans   **47 gossip's** old woman's   **48 crab** crab apple   **50 dewlap** loose skin on neck   **51 aunt** old woman.   **saddest** most serious   **54 Tailor** (possibly because she ends up sitting cross-legged on the floor, looking like a tailor, or else referring to the *tail* or buttocks)   **55 choir** company   **56 waxen** increase.   **neeze** sneeze   **57 wasted** spent   **58 room** stand aside, make room   **63 wanton** headstrong creature

TITANIA

Then I must be thy lady; but I know
When thou hast stolen away from Fairyland
And in the shape of Corin sat all day,   66
Playing on pipes of corn and versing love   67
To amorous Phillida. Why art thou here   68
Come from the farthest step of India,   69
But that, forsooth, the bouncing Amazon,
Your buskined mistress and your warrior love,   71
To Theseus must be wedded, and you come
To give their bed joy and prosperity.

OBERON

How canst thou thus for shame, Titania,
Glance at my credit with Hippolyta,   75
Knowing I know thy love to Theseus?
Didst not thou lead him through the glimmering
    night
From Perigenia, whom he ravishèd?   78
And make him with fair Aegles break his faith,   79
With Ariadne and Antiopa?   80

TITANIA

These are the forgeries of jealousy;
And never, since the middle summer's spring,   82
Met we on hill, in dale, forest, or mead,   83
By pavèd fountain or by rushy brook,   84
Or in the beachèd margent of the sea,   85
To dance our ringlets to the whistling wind,   86
But with thy brawls thou hast disturbed our sport.
Therefore the winds, piping to us in vain,
As in revenge, have sucked up from the sea
Contagious fogs which, falling in the land,   90
Hath every pelting river made so proud   91
That they have overborne their continents.   92
The ox hath therefore stretched his yoke in vain,   93
The plowman lost his sweat, and the green corn   94
Hath rotted ere his youth attained a beard;
The fold stands empty in the drownèd field,   96
And crows are fatted with the murrain flock;   97
The nine-men's morris is filled up with mud,   98

And the quaint mazes in the wanton green   99
For lack of tread are undistinguishable.
The human mortals want their winter here;   101
No night is now with hymn or carol blessed.
Therefore the moon, the governess of floods,   103
Pale in her anger, washes all the air,   104
That rheumatic diseases do abound.   105
And thorough this distemperature we see   106
The seasons alter: hoary-headed frosts
Fall in the fresh lap of the crimson rose,
And on old Hiems' thin and icy crown   109
An odorous chaplet of sweet summer buds
Is, as in mockery, set. The spring, the summer,
The childing autumn, angry winter, change   112
Their wonted liveries, and the mazèd world   113
By their increase now knows not which is which.   114
And this same progeny of evils comes
From our debate, from our dissension.   116
We are their parents and original.   117

OBERON

Do you amend it, then. It lies in you.
Why should Titania cross her Oberon?
I do but beg a little changeling boy
To be my henchman.

TITANIA   Set your heart at rest.   121
The fairy land buys not the child of me.
His mother was a vot'ress of my order,   123
And in the spicèd Indian air by night
Full often hath she gossiped by my side
And sat with me on Neptune's yellow sands,
Marking th' embarkèd traders on the flood,   127
When we have laughed to see the sails conceive
And grow big-bellied with the wanton wind;   129
Which she, with pretty and with swimming gait,   130
Following—her womb then rich with my young
    squire—
Would imitate, and sail upon the land
To fetch me trifles, and return again
As from a voyage, rich with merchandise.
But she, being mortal, of that boy did die;
And for her sake do I rear up her boy,
And for her sake I will not part with him.

OBERON

How long within this wood intend you stay?

TITANIA

Perchance till after Theseus' wedding day.
If you will patiently dance in our round   140

66, 68 Corin, Phillida (Conventional names of pastoral lovers.)
67 corn (Here, oat stalks.)   69 step farthest limit of travel, or, perhaps, steep, "mountain range"   71 buskined wearing half-boots
called buskins   75 Glance . . . Hippolyta make insinuations about
my favored relationship with Hippolyta   78 Perigenia i.e., Perigouna,
one of Theseus' conquests. (This and the following women are named
in Thomas North's translation of Plutarch's "Life of Theseus.")
79 Aegles i.e., Aegle, for whom Theseus deserted Ariadne according
to some accounts   80 Ariadne the daughter of Minos, King of Crete,
who helped Theseus to escape the labyrinth after killing the Minotaur;
later she was abandoned by Theseus.   Antiopa Queen of the Amazons and wife of Theseus; elsewhere identified with Hippolyta, but
here thought of as a separate woman   82 middle summer's spring beginning of midsummer   83 mead meadow   84 pavèd with pebbled
bottom.   rushy bordered with rushes   85 in on.   margent edge, border   86 ringlets dances in a ring. (See orbs in line 9.)   to to the
sound of   90 Contagious noxious   91 pelting paltry   92 continents
banks that contain them   93 stretched his yoke i.e., pulled at his
yoke in plowing   94 corn grain of any kind   96 fold pen for sheep or
cattle   97 murrain having died of the plague   98 nine-men's morris
i.e., portion of the village green marked out in a square for a game
played with nine pebbles or pegs

99 quaint mazes i.e., intricate paths marked out on the village green
to be followed rapidly on foot as a kind of contest.   wanton luxuriant
101 want lack.   winter i.e., regular winter season; or, proper observances of winter, such as the hymn or carol in the next line (?)
103 Therefore i.e., as a result of our quarrel   104 washes saturates
with moisture   105 rheumatic diseases colds, flu, and other respira-
tory infections   106 distemperature disturbance in nature   109 Hiems' the winter god's   112 childing fruitful, pregnant   113 wonted
liveries usual apparel.   mazèd bewildered   114 their increase their
yield, what they produce   116 debate quarrel   117 original origin
121 henchman attendant, page   123 was . . . order had taken a vow
to serve me   127 traders trading vessels.   flood flood tide
129 wanton (1) playful (2) amorous   130 swimming smooth, gliding
140 round circular dance

And see our moonlight revels, go with us;
If not, shun me, and I will spare your haunts.   142

OBERON
Give me that boy, and I will go with thee.

TITANIA
Not for thy fairy kingdom. Fairies, away!
We shall chide downright, if I longer stay.
Exeunt [Titania with her train].

OBERON
Well, go thy way. Thou shalt not from this grove   146
Till I torment thee for this injury.
My gentle Puck, come hither. Thou rememb'rest
Since once I sat upon a promontory,   149
And heard a mermaid on a dolphin's back
Uttering such dulcet and harmonious breath   151
That the rude sea grew civil at her song,   152
And certain stars shot madly from their spheres
To hear the sea-maid's music?

PUCK   I remember.

OBERON
That very time I saw, but thou couldst not,
Flying between the cold moon and the earth
Cupid, all armed. A certain aim he took   157
At a fair vestal thronèd by the west,   158
And loosed his love shaft smartly from his bow   159
As it should pierce a hundred thousand hearts;   160
But I might see young Cupid's fiery shaft   161
Quenched in the chaste beams of the watery moon,
And the imperial vot'ress passèd on,
In maiden meditation, fancy-free.   164
Yet marked I where the bolt of Cupid fell: 165
It fell upon a little western flower,
Before milk-white, now purple with love's wound,
And maidens call it love-in-idleness.   168
Fetch me that flower; the herb I showed thee once.
The juice of it on sleeping eyelids laid
Will make or man or woman madly dote   171
Upon the next live creature that it sees.
Fetch me this herb, and be thou here again
Ere the leviathan can swim a league.   174

PUCK
I'll put a girdle round about the earth
In forty minutes.   [*Exit.*]

OBERON   Having once this juice,   176
I'll watch Titania when she is asleep
And drop the liquor of it in her eyes.
The next thing then she waking looks upon,
Be it on lion, bear, or wolf, or bull,
On meddling monkey, or on busy ape,
She shall pursue it with the soul of love.

And ere I take this charm from off her sight,
As I can take it with another herb,
I'll make her render up her page to me.
But who comes here? I am invisible,
And I will overhear their conference.

Enter Demetrius, Helena following him.

DEMETRIUS
I love thee not; therefore pursue me not.
Where is Lysander and fair Hermia?
The one I'll slay; the other slayeth me.
Thou toldst me they were stol'n unto this wood;
And here am I, and wood within this wood   192
Because I cannot meet my Hermia.
Hence, get thee gone, and follow me no more.

HELENA
You draw me, you hardhearted adamant!   195
But yet you draw not iron, for my heart
Is true as steel. Leave you your power to draw,   197
And I shall have no power to follow you.

DEMETRIUS
Do I entice you? Do I speak you fair?   199
Or rather do I not in plainest truth
Tell you I do not nor I cannot love you?

HELENA
And even for that do I love you the more.
I am your spaniel; and, Demetrius,
The more you beat me I will fawn on you.
Use me but as your spaniel, spurn me, strike me,
Neglect me, lose me; only give me leave,
Unworthy as I am, to follow you.
What worser place can I beg in your love—
And yet a place of high respect with me—
Than to be usèd as you use your dog?

DEMETRIUS
Tempt not too much the hatred of my spirit,
For I am sick when I do look on thee.

HELENA
And I am sick when I look not on you.

DEMETRIUS
You do impeach your modesty too much   214
To leave the city and commit yourself   215
Into the hands of one that loves you not,
To trust the opportunity of night
And the ill counsel of a desert place   218
With the rich worth of your virginity.

HELENA
Your virtue is my privilege. For that   220
It is not night when I do see your face,
Therefore I think I am not in the night;
Nor doth this wood lack worlds of company,

---

142 spare shun   **146 from** go from   **149 Since** when   **151 dulcet**
sweet.   **breath** voice, song   **152 rude** rough   **157 all** fully.   **certain**
sure   **158 vestal** vestal virgin. (Contains a complimentary allusion to
Queen Elizabeth as a votaress of Diana and probably refers to an actual entertainment in her honor at Elvetham in 1591.)   **by** in the region of   **159 loosed** released   **160 As** as if   **161 might** could
164 fancy-free free of love's spell   **165 bolt** arrow   **168 love-in-idleness** pansy, heartsease   **171 or . . . or** either . . . or   **174 leviathan**
sea monster, whale   **176 forty** (Used indefinitely.)

192 and wood and mad, frantic (with an obvious wordplay on *wood*,
meaning ''woods'')   **195 adamant** lodestone, magnet (with pun on
hardhearted, since adamant was also thought to be the hardest of all
stones and was confused with the diamond)   **197 Leave you** give up
199 speak you fair speak courteously to you   **214 impeach** call into
question   **215 To leave** by leaving   **218 desert** deserted   **220 virtue**
goodness or power to attract.   **privilege** safeguard, warrant.   **For that**
because

For you, in my respect, are all the world.   224
Then how can it be said I am alone
When all the world is here to look on me?
DEMETRIUS
I'll run from thee and hide me in the brakes,   227
And leave thee to the mercy of wild beasts.
HELENA
The wildest hath not such a heart as you.
Run when you will. The story shall be changed:
Apollo flies and Daphne holds the chase,   231
The dove pursues the griffin, the mild hind   232
Makes speed to catch the tiger—bootless speed,   233
When cowardice pursues and valor flies!
DEMETRIUS
I will not stay thy questions. Let me go!   235
Or if thou follow me, do not believe
But I shall do thee mischief in the wood.
HELENA
Ay, in the temple, in the town, the field,
You do me mischief. Fie, Demetrius!
Your wrongs do set a scandal on my sex.   240
We cannot fight for love, as men may do;
We should be wooed and were not made to woo.
                                        [*Exit Demetrius.*]
I'll follow thee and make a heaven of hell,
To die upon the hand I love so well.   [*Exit.*] 244
OBERON
Fare thee well, nymph. Ere he do leave this grove
Thou shalt fly him, and he shall seek thy love.

                Enter Puck.

Hast thou the flower there? Welcome, wanderer.
PUCK
Ay, there it is.   [*He offers the flower.*]
OBERON   I pray thee, give it me.
I know a bank where the wild thyme blows,   249
Where oxlips and the nodding violet grows,   250
Quite overcanopied with luscious woodbine,   251
With sweet muskroses and with eglantine.   252
There sleeps Titania sometime of the night,   253
Lulled in these flowers with dances and delight;
And there the snake throws her enameled skin,   255
Weed wide enough to wrap a fairy in.   256
And with the juice of this I'll streak her eyes   257
And make her full of hateful fantasies.
Take thou some of it, and seek through this grove.
                        [*He gives some love juice.*]

A sweet Athenian lady is in love
With a disdainful youth. Anoint his eyes,
But do it when the next thing he espies
May be the lady. Thou shalt know the man
By the Athenian garments he hath on.
Effect it with some care, that he may prove
More fond on her than she upon her love;   266
And look thou meet me ere the first cock crow.
PUCK
Fear not, my lord, your servant shall do so.
                        Exeunt [separately].

                            ❧

2.2   *Enter Titania, Queen of Fairies, with her train.*

TITANIA
Come, now a roundel and a fairy song;   1
Then, for the third part of a minute, hence—   2
Some to kill cankers in the muskrose buds,   3
Some war with reremice for their leathern wings   4
To make my small elves coats, and some keep back
The clamorous owl, that nightly hoots and wonders
At our quaint spirits. Sing me now asleep.   7
Then to your offices, and let me rest.

        Fairies sing.

FIRST FAIRY
    You spotted snakes with double tongue,   9
        Thorny hedgehogs, be not seen;
    Newts and blindworms, do no wrong;   11
        Come not near our Fairy Queen.
CHORUS [*dancing*]
        Philomel, with melody   13
        Sing in our sweet lullaby;
    Lulla, lulla, lullaby, lulla, lulla, lullaby.
        Never harm
        Nor spell nor charm
    Come our lovely lady nigh.
    So good night, with lullaby.
FIRST FAIRY
    Weaving spiders, come not here;
        Hence, you long-legged spinners, hence!
    Beetles black, approach not near;
        Worm nor snail, do no offense.   23
CHORUS [*dancing*]
        Philomel, with melody
        Sing in our sweet lullaby;
    Lulla, lulla, lullaby, lulla, lulla, lullaby.
        Never harm
        Nor spell nor charm

224 in my respect as far as I am concerned, in my esteem
227 brakes thickets   **231 Apollo . . . chase** (In the ancient myth,
Daphne fled from Apollo and was saved from rape by being transformed into a laurel tree; here it is the female who *holds the chase,* or
pursues, instead of the male.)   **232 griffin** a fabulous monster with
the head and wings of an eagle and the body of a lion.   **hind** female
deer   **233 bootless** fruitless   **235 stay** wait for, put up with.   **questions** talk or argument   **240 Your . . . sex** i.e., the wrongs that you
do me cause me to act in a manner that disgraces my sex   **244 upon**
by   **249 blows** blooms   **250 oxlips** flowers resembling cowslip and
primrose   **251 woodbine** honeysuckle   **252 muskroses** a kind of
large, sweet-scented rose.   **eglantine** sweetbrier, another kind of rose
253 sometime of for part of   **255 throws** sloughs off, sheds
256 Weed garment   **257 streak** anoint, touch gently

266 fond on doting on
2.2. Location: The wood.
1 roundel dance in a ring   **2 the third . . . minute** (Indicative of the
fairies' quickness.)   **3 cankers** cankerworms (i.e., caterpillars or
grubs)   **4 reremice** bats   **7 quaint** dainty   **9 double** forked
11 Newts water lizards (considered poisonous, as were *blindworms*—
small snakes with tiny eyes—and spiders)   **13 Philomel** the nightingale. (Philomela, daughter of King Pandion, was transformed into a
nightingale, according to Ovid's *Metamorphoses* 6, after she had been
raped by her sister Procne's husband, Tereus.)   **23 offense** harm

Come our lovely lady nigh.
So good night, with lullaby.

[*Titania sleeps.*]

SECOND FAIRY
Hence, away! Now all is well.
One aloof stand sentinel.   32

[*Exeunt Fairies, leaving one sentinel.*]

Enter Oberon [and squeezes the flower on Titania's eyelids].

OBERON
What thou seest when thou dost wake,
Do it for thy true love take;
Love and languish for his sake.
Be it ounce, or cat, or bear,   36
Pard, or boar with bristled hair,   37
In thy eye that shall appear
When thou wak'st, it is thy dear.
Wake when some vile thing is near.   [*Exit.*]

Enter Lysander and Hermia.

LYSANDER
Fair love, you faint with wandering in the wood;
    And to speak truth, I have forgot our way.
We'll rest us, Hermia, if you think it good,
    And tarry for the comfort of the day.

HERMIA
Be it so, Lysander. Find you out a bed,
For I upon this bank will rest my head.

LYSANDER
One turf shall serve as pillow for us both;
One heart, one bed, two bosoms, and one troth.   48

HERMIA
Nay, good Lysander, for my sake, my dear,
Lie further off yet. Do not lie so near.

LYSANDER
O, take the sense, sweet, of my innocence!   51
Love takes the meaning in love's conference.   52
I mean that my heart unto yours is knit,
So that but one heart we can make of it;
Two bosoms interchainèd with an oath—
So then two bosoms and a single troth.
Then by your side no bed-room me deny,
For lying so, Hermia, I do not lie.   58

HERMIA
Lysander riddles very prettily.
Now much beshrew my manners and my pride   60
If Hermia meant to say Lysander lied.
But, gentle friend, for love and courtesy
Lie further off, in human modesty.   63
Such separation as may well be said
Becomes a virtuous bachelor and a maid,

So far be distant; and, good night, sweet friend.
Thy love ne'er alter till thy sweet life end!

LYSANDER
Amen, amen, to that fair prayer, say I,
And then end life when I end loyalty!
Here is my bed. Sleep give thee all his rest!

HERMIA
With half that wish the wisher's eyes be pressed!   71

[*They sleep, separated by a short distance.*]

Enter Puck.

PUCK
Through the forest have I gone,
But Athenian found I none
On whose eyes I might approve   74
This flower's force in stirring love.
Night and silence.—Who is here?
Weeds of Athens he doth wear.
This is he, my master said,
Despisèd the Athenian maid;
And here the maiden, sleeping sound,
On the dank and dirty ground.
Pretty soul, she durst not lie
Near this lack-love, this kill-courtesy.
Churl, upon thy eyes I throw
All the power this charm doth owe.   85

[*He applies the love juice.*]

When thou wak'st, let love forbid
Sleep his seat on thy eyelid.
So awake when I am gone,
For I must now to Oberon.   *Exit.*

Enter Demetrius and Helena, running.

HELENA
Stay, though thou kill me, sweet Demetrius!

DEMETRIUS
I charge thee, hence, and do not haunt me thus.

HELENA
O, wilt thou darkling leave me? Do not so.   92

DEMETRIUS
Stay, on thy peril! I alone will go.   [*Exit.*] 93

HELENA
O, I am out of breath in this fond chase!   94
The more my prayer, the lesser is my grace.   95
Happy is Hermia, wheresoe'er she lies,   96
For she hath blessèd and attractive eyes.
How came her eyes so bright? Not with salt tears;
If so, my eyes are oftener washed than hers.
No, no, I am as ugly as a bear,
For beasts that meet me run away for fear.
Therefore no marvel though Demetrius   102
Do, as a monster, fly my presence thus.   103
What wicked and dissembling glass of mine

---

32 sentinel (Presumably Oberon is able to outwit or intimidate this guard.) **36 ounce** lynx **37 Pard** leopard **48 troth** faith, trothplight **51 take . . . innocence** i.e., interpret my intention as innocent **52 Love . . . conference** i.e., when lovers confer, love teaches each lover to interpret the other's meaning lovingly **58 lie** tell a falsehood (with a riddling pun on *lie*, "recline") **60 beshrew** curse. (But mildly meant.) **63 human** courteous (and perhaps suggesting "humane," the Quarto spelling)

71 With . . . pressed i.e., may we share your wish, so that your eyes too are *pressed*, closed, in sleep **74 approve** test **85 owe** own **92 darkling** in the dark **93 on thy peril** i.e., on pain of danger to you if you don't obey me and stay **94 fond** doting **95 my grace** the favor I obtain **96 lies** dwells **102–103 no marvel . . . thus** i.e., no wonder that Demetrius flies from me as from a monster

Made me compare with Hermia's sphery eyne? 105
But who is here? Lysander, on the ground?
Dead, or asleep? I see no blood, no wound.
Lysander, if you live, good sir, awake.

LYSANDER [*awaking*]
And run through fire I will for thy sweet sake.
Transparent Helena! Nature shows art, 110
That through thy bosom makes me see thy heart.
Where is Demetrius? O, how fit a word
Is that vile name to perish on my sword!

HELENA
Do not say so, Lysander; say not so.
What though he love your Hermia? Lord, what
    though?
Yet Hermia still loves you. Then be content.

LYSANDER
Content with Hermia? No! I do repent
The tedious minutes I with her have spent.
Not Hermia but Helena I love.
Who will not change a raven for a dove?
The will of man is by his reason swayed, 121
And reason says you are the worthier maid.
Things growing are not ripe until their season;
So I, being young, till now ripe not to reason. 124
And, touching now the point of human skill, 125
Reason becomes the marshal to my will
And leads me to your eyes, where I o'erlook 127
Love's stories written in love's richest book.

HELENA
Wherefore was I to this keen mockery born? 129
When at your hands did I deserve this scorn?
Is 't not enough, is 't not enough, young man,
That I did never—no, nor never can—
Deserve a sweet look from Demetrius' eye,
But you must flout my insufficiency?
Good troth, you do me wrong, good sooth, you do, 135
In such disdainful manner me to woo.
But fare you well. Perforce I must confess
I thought you lord of more true gentleness. 138
O, that a lady, of one man refused, 139
Should of another therefore be abused! *Exit.* 140

LYSANDER
She sees not Hermia. Hermia, sleep thou there,
And never mayst thou come Lysander near!
For as a surfeit of the sweetest things
The deepest loathing to the stomach brings,
Or as the heresies that men do leave 145
Are hated most of those they did deceive, 146
So thou, my surfeit and my heresy,
Of all be hated, but the most of me! 148
And, all my powers, address your love and might 149

To honor Helen and to be her knight!   *Exit.*

HERMIA [*awaking*]
Help me, Lysander, help me! Do thy best
To pluck this crawling serpent from my breast!
Ay me, for pity! What a dream was here!
Lysander, look how I do quake with fear.
Methought a serpent ate my heart away,
And you sat smiling at his cruel prey. 156
Lysander! What, removed? Lysander! Lord!
What, out of hearing? Gone? No sound, no word?
Alack, where are you? Speak, an if you hear; 159
Speak, of all loves! I swoon almost with fear. 160
No? Then I well perceive you are not nigh.
Either death, or you, I'll find immediately.

                Exit. [*The sleeping Titania remains.*]

3.1
Enter the clowns [*Quince, Snug, Bottom, Flute, Snout, and Starveling*].

BOTTOM   Are we all met?

QUINCE   Pat, pat; and here's a marvelous convenient 2
place for our rehearsal. This green plot shall be our
stage, this hawthorn brake our tiring-house, and we 4
will do it in action as we will do it before the Duke.

BOTTOM   Peter Quince?

QUINCE   What sayest thou, bully Bottom? 7

BOTTOM   There are things in this comedy of Pyramus
and Thisbe that will never please. First, Pyramus must
draw a sword to kill himself, which the ladies cannot
abide. How answer you that?

SNOUT   By 'r lakin, a parlous fear. 12

STARVELING   I believe we must leave the killing out,
when all is done. 14

BOTTOM   Not a whit. I have a device to make all well.
Write me a prologue, and let the prologue seem to say, 16
we will do no harm with our swords, and that Pyramus
is not killed indeed; and for the more better assurance,
tell them that I, Pyramus, am not Pyramus but Bottom
the weaver. This will put them out of fear.

QUINCE   Well, we will have such a prologue, and it shall
be written in eight and six. 22

BOTTOM   No, make it two more: let it be written in eight
and eight.

SNOUT   Will not the ladies be afeard of the lion?

STARVELING   I fear it, I promise you.

BOTTOM   Masters, you ought to consider with yourself,
to bring in—God shield us!—a lion among la- 28
dies is a most dreadful thing. For there is not a more 29

---

105 compare vie.   **sphery eyne** eyes as bright as stars in their spheres
110 Transparent (1) radiant (2) able to be seen through, lacking in deceit.   **art** skill, magic power   **121 will** desire   **124 ripe not** (am) not ripened   **125 touching** reaching.   **point** summit.   **skill** judgment   **127 o'erlook** read   **129 Wherefore** why   **135 Good troth, good sooth** i.e., indeed, truly   **138 lord of** i.e., possessor of.   **gentleness** courtesy   **139 of** by   **140 abused** ill treated   **145–146 as . . . deceive** as renounced heresies are hated most by those persons who formerly were deceived by them.   **148 Of . . . of** by . . . by   **149 address** direct, apply

156 prey act of preying   **159 an if** if   **160 of all loves** for love's sake
3.1. Location: The action is continuous.
s.d. clowns rustics   **2 Pat** on the dot, punctually   **4 brake** thicket.
tiring-house attiring area, hence backstage   **7 bully** i.e., worthy, jolly, fine fellow   **12 By 'r lakin** by our ladykin, i.e., the Virgin Mary.
parlous perilous, alarming   **14 when all is done** i.e., when all is said and done   **16 Write me** i.e., write at my suggestion. (*Me* is used colloquially.)   **22 eight and six** alternate lines of eight and six syllables, a common ballad measure   **28–29 lion among ladies** (A contemporary pamphlet tells how, at the christening in 1594 of Prince Henry, eldest son of King James VI of Scotland, later James I of England, a "blackamoor" instead of a lion drew the triumphal chariot, since the lion's presence might have "brought some fear to the nearest.")

fearful wildfowl than your lion living, and we ought 30
to look to 't.

SNOUT   Therefore another prologue must tell he is not a
lion.

BOTTOM   Nay, you must name his name, and half his
face must be seen through the lion's neck, and he himself must speak through, saying thus or to the same
defect: "Ladies," or "Fair ladies, I would wish 37
you," or "I would request you," or "I would entreat
you, not to fear, not to tremble; my life for yours. If 39
you think I come hither as a lion, it were pity of my 40
life. No, I am no such thing; I am a man as other men 41
are." And there indeed let him name his name, and
tell them plainly he is Snug the joiner.

QUINCE   Well, it shall be so. But there is two hard things:
that is, to bring the moonlight into a chamber; for, you
know, Pyramus and Thisbe meet by moonlight.

SNOUT   Doth the moon shine that night we play our
play?

BOTTOM   A calendar, a calendar! Look in the almanac.
Find out moonshine, find out moonshine.

                    [They consult an almanac.]

QUINCE   Yes, it doth shine that night.

BOTTOM   Why then may you leave a casement of the
great chamber window where we play open, and the
moon may shine in at the casement.

QUINCE   Ay; or else one must come in with a bush of 55
thorns and a lantern and say he comes to disfigure, or 56
to present, the person of Moonshine. Then there is 57
another thing: we must have a wall in the great chamber; for Pyramus and Thisbe, says the story, did talk
through the chink of a wall.

SNOUT   You can never bring in a wall. What say you,
Bottom?

BOTTOM   Some man or other must present Wall. And let
him have some plaster, or some loam, or some rough- 64
cast about him, to signify wall; or let him hold his 65
fingers thus, and through that cranny shall Pyramus
and Thisbe whisper.

QUINCE   If that may be, then all is well. Come, sit down,
every mother's son, and rehearse your parts. Pyramus,
you begin. When you have spoken your speech, enter
into that brake, and so everyone according to his cue.

        Enter Robin [Puck].

PUCK [aside]
    What hempen homespuns have we swaggering here 72
    So near the cradle of the Fairy Queen? 73
    What, a play toward? I'll be an auditor; 74
    An actor, too, perhaps, if I see cause.

QUINCE   Speak, Pyramus. Thisbe, stand forth.

BOTTOM [as Pyramus]
    "Thisbe, the flowers of odious savors sweet—"

QUINCE   Odors, odors.

BOTTOM   "—Odors savors sweet;
    So hath thy breath, my dearest Thisbe dear.
    But hark, a voice! Stay thou but here awhile,
    And by and by I will to thee appear."   *Exit.*

PUCK
    A stranger Pyramus than e'er played here.   [Exit.] 83

FLUTE   Must I speak now?

QUINCE   Ay, marry, must you; for you must understand
he goes but to see a noise that he heard, and is to come
again.

FLUTE [as Thisbe]
    "Most radiant Pyramus, most lily-white of hue,
    Of color like the red rose on triumphant brier,   89
    Most brisky juvenal and eke most lovely Jew,   90
    As true as truest horse that yet would never tire.
    I'll meet thee, Pyramus, at Ninny's tomb."

QUINCE   "Ninus' tomb," man. Why, you must not 93
speak that yet. That you answer to Pyramus. You
speak all your part at once, cues and all. Pyramus, 95
enter. Your cue is past; it is "never tire."

FLUTE
    O—"As true as truest horse, that yet would never
    tire."   97

        [Enter Puck, and Bottom as Pyramus with the ass
        head.]

BOTTOM
    "If I were fair, Thisbe, I were only thine."   98

QUINCE   O, monstrous! O, strange! We are haunted.
Pray, masters! Fly, masters! Help!

        [Exeunt Quince, Snug, Flute,
                Snout, and Starveling.]

PUCK
    I'll follow you, I'll lead you about a round,   101
        Thorough bog, thorough bush, thorough brake,
        thorough brier.
    Sometimes a horse I'll be, sometimes a hound,
        A hog, a headless bear, sometimes a fire;   104
    And neigh, and bark, and grunt, and roar, and
        burn,
    Like horse, hound, hog, bear, fire, at every turn.   *Exit.*

BOTTOM   Why do they run away? This is a knavery of
them to make me afeard.

        Enter Snout.

---

30 **fearful** fear-inspiring   37 **defect** (Bottom's blunder for "effect.")
39 **my life for yours** i.e., I pledge my life to make your lives safe
40–41 **it were . . . life** i.e., I should be sorry, by my life; or, my life
would be endangered   55–56 **bush of thorns** bundle of thornbush
fagots (part of the accoutrements of the man in the moon, according
to the popular notions of the time, along with his lantern and his dog)
56 **disfigure** (Quince's blunder for "figure.")   57 **present** represent
64–65 **roughcast** a mixture of lime and gravel used to plaster the outside of buildings   72 **hempen homespuns** i.e., rustics dressed in
clothes woven of coarse, homespun fabric made from hemp   73 **cradle** i.e., Titania's bower   74 **toward** about to take place

83 **A stranger . . . here** (Either Puck refers to an earlier dramatic version played in the same theater, or he has conceived of a plan to
present a "stranger" Pyramus than ever seen before.)   89 **triumphant**
magnificent   90 **brisky juvenal** lively youth.   **eke** also.   **Jew** (An absurd repetition of the first syllable of *juvenal* and an indication of how
desperately Quince searches for his rhymes.)   93 **Ninus** mythical
founder of Nineveh (whose wife, Semiramis, was supposed to have
built the walls of Babylon where the story of Pyramus and Thisbe
takes place)   95 **part** (An actor's *part* was a script consisting only of
his speeches and their cues.)   97 s.d. **with the ass head** (This stage
direction, taken from the Folio, presumably refers to a standard stage
property.)   98 **fair** handsome.   **were** would be   101 **about a round**
roundabout   104 **fire** will-o'-the-wisp

SNOUT   O Bottom, thou art changed! What do I see on thee?

BOTTOM   What do you see? You see an ass head of your own, do you?   [Exit Snout.]

Enter Quince.

QUINCE   Bless thee, Bottom, bless thee! Thou art trans- 113
lated.   Exit. 114

BOTTOM   I see their knavery. This is to make an ass of me, to fright me, if they could. But I will not stir from this place, do what they can. I will walk up and down here, and will sing, that they shall hear I am not afraid.   [He sings.]
      The ouzel cock so black of hue,   120
         With orange-tawny bill,
      The throstle with his note so true,   122
         The wren with little quill—   123

TITANIA [awaking]
   What angel wakes me from my flowery bed?

BOTTOM [sings]
      The finch, the sparrow, and the lark,
         The plainsong cuckoo gray,   126
      Whose note full many a man doth mark,
         And dares not answer nay—   128
   For indeed, who would set his wit to so foolish a   129
   bird? Who would give a bird the lie, though he cry   130
   "cuckoo" never so?   131

TITANIA
   I pray thee, gentle mortal, sing again.
   Mine ear is much enamored of thy note;
   So is mine eye enthrallèd to thy shape;
   And thy fair virtue's force perforce doth move me   135
   On the first view to say, to swear, I love thee.

BOTTOM   Methinks, mistress, you should have little reason for that. And yet, to say the truth, reason and love
   keep little company together nowadays—the more the
   pity that some honest neighbors will not make them
   friends. Nay, I can gleek upon occasion.   141

TITANIA
   Thou art as wise as thou art beautiful.

BOTTOM   Not so, neither. But if I had wit enough to get
   out of this wood, I have enough to serve mine own   144
   turn.   145

TITANIA
   Out of this wood do not desire to go.
   Thou shalt remain here, whether thou wilt or no.
   I am a spirit of no common rate.   148
   The summer still doth tend upon my state,   149
   And I do love thee. Therefore, go with me.
   I'll give thee fairies to attend on thee,
   And they shall fetch thee jewels from the deep,
   And sing while thou on pressèd flowers dost sleep.

And I will purge thy mortal grossness so   154
That thou shalt like an airy spirit go.
Peaseblossom, Cobweb, Mote, and Mustardseed!   156

   Enter four Fairies [Peaseblossom, Cobweb, Mote,
   and Mustardseed].

PEASEBLOSSOM   Ready.
COBWEB   And I.
MOTE   And I.
MUSTARDSEED   And I.
ALL   Where shall we go?

TITANIA
   Be kind and courteous to this gentleman.
   Hop in his walks and gambol in his eyes;   160
   Feed him with apricots and dewberries,   161
   With purple grapes, green figs, and mulberries;
   The honey bags steal from the humble-bees,
   And for night tapers crop their waxen thighs
   And light them at the fiery glowworms' eyes,
   To have my love to bed and to arise;
   And pluck the wings from painted butterflies
   To fan the moonbeams from his sleeping eyes.
   Nod to him, elves, and do him courtesies.

PEASEBLOSSOM   Hail, mortal!
COBWEB   Hail!
MOTE   Hail!
MUSTARDSEED   Hail!

BOTTOM   I cry your worships mercy, heartily. I beseech   174
   your worship's name.

COBWEB   Cobweb.

BOTTOM   I shall desire you of more acquaintance, good   177
   Master Cobweb. If I cut my finger, I shall make bold   178
   with you.—Your name, honest gentleman?   179

PEASEBLOSSOM   Peaseblossom.

BOTTOM   I pray you, commend me to Mistress Squash,   181
   your mother, and to Master Peascod, your father.   182
   Good Master Peaseblossom, I shall desire you of more
   acquaintance too.—Your name, I beseech you, sir?

MUSTARDSEED   Mustardseed.

BOTTOM   Good Master Mustardseed, I know your pa-   186
   tience well. That same cowardly, giantlike ox-beef   187
   hath devoured many a gentleman of your house. I
   promise you, your kindred hath made my eyes water   189
   ere now. I desire you of more acquaintance, good
   Master Mustardseed.

TITANIA
   Come wait upon him; lead him to my bower.
      The moon methinks looks with a watery eye;
      And when she weeps, weeps every little flower,   194

113–114 translated transformed   120 ouzel cock male blackbird
122 throstle song thrush   123 quill (Literally, a reed pipe; hence, the bird's piping song.)   126 plainsong singing a melody without variations   128 dares . . . nay i.e., cannot deny that he is a cuckold
129 set his wit to employ his intelligence to answer   130 give . . .
lie call the bird a liar   131 never so ever so much   135 thy . . .
force the power of your unblemished excellence   141 gleek jest
144–145 serve . . . turn answer my purpose   148 rate rank, value
149 still . . . state always waits upon me as a part of my royal retinue

154 mortal grossness materiality (i.e., the corporal nature of a mortal
being)   156 Mote i.e., speck. (The two words moth and mote were
pronounced alike, and both meanings may be present.)   160 in his
eyes in his sight (i.e., before him)   161 dewberries blackberries
174 I cry . . . mercy I beg pardon of your worships (for presuming to
ask a question)   177 I . . . acquaintance I crave to be better acquainted with you   178–179 If . . . you (Cobwebs were used to
stanch bleeding.)   181 Squash unripe pea pod   182 Peascod ripe pea
pod   186–187 your patience what you have endured. (Mustard is
eaten with beef.)   189 water (1) weep for sympathy (2) smart, sting
194 she weeps i.e., she causes dew

Lamenting some enforcèd chastity.   195
Tie up my lover's tongue; bring him silently.   196

Exeunt.

❖

3.2   *Enter [Oberon,] King of Fairies.*

OBERON
I wonder if Titania be awaked;
Then, what it was that next came in her eye,
Which she must dote on in extremity.

[*Enter*] *Robin Goodfellow* [*Puck*].

Here comes my messenger. How now, mad spirit?
What night-rule now about this haunted grove?   5

PUCK
My mistress with a monster is in love.
Near to her close and consecrated bower,   7
While she was in her dull and sleeping hour,   8
A crew of patches, rude mechanicals,   9
That work for bread upon Athenian stalls,   10
Were met together to rehearse a play
Intended for great Theseus' nuptial day.
The shallowest thickskin of that barren sort,   13
Who Pyramus presented, in their sport   14
Forsook his scene and entered in a brake.   15
When I did him at this advantage take,
An ass's noll I fixèd on his head.   17
Anon his Thisbe must be answerèd,
And forth my mimic comes. When they him spy,   19
As wild geese that the creeping fowler eye,   20
Or russet-pated choughs, many in sort,   21
Rising and cawing at the gun's report,
Sever themselves and madly sweep the sky,   23
So, at his sight, away his fellows fly;
And, at our stamp, here o'er and o'er one falls;
He "Murder!" cries and help from Athens calls.
Their sense thus weak, lost with their fears thus
    strong,
Made senseless things begin to do them wrong,
For briers and thorns at their apparel snatch;
Some, sleeves—some, hats; from yielders all things
    catch.   30
I led them on in this distracted fear
And left sweet Pyramus translated there,
When in that moment, so it came to pass,
Titania waked and straightway loved an ass.

OBERON
This falls out better than I could devise.
But hast thou yet latched the Athenian's eyes   36
With the love juice, as I did bid thee do?

PUCK
I took him sleeping—that is finished too—
And the Athenian woman by his side,
That, when he waked, of force she must be eyed.   40

Enter Demetrius and Hermia.

OBERON
Stand close. This is the same Athenian.

PUCK
This is the woman, but not this the man.

[*They stand aside.*]

DEMETRIUS
O, why rebuke you him that loves you so?
Lay breath so bitter on your bitter foe.

HERMIA
Now I but chide; but I should use thee worse,
For thou, I fear, hast given me cause to curse.
If thou hast slain Lysander in his sleep,
Being o'er shoes in blood, plunge in the deep,   48
And kill me too.
The sun was not so true unto the day
As he to me. Would he have stolen away
From sleeping Hermia? I'll believe as soon
This whole earth may be bored, and that the moon   53
May through the center creep, and so displease
Her brother's noontide with th' Antipodes.   55
It cannot be but thou hast murdered him;
So should a murderer look, so dead, so grim.   57

DEMETRIUS
So should the murdered look, and so should I,
Pierced through the heart with your stern cruelty.
Yet you, the murderer, look as bright, as clear
As yonder Venus in her glimmering sphere.

HERMIA
What's this to my Lysander? Where is he?   62
Ah, good Demetrius, wilt thou give him me?

DEMETRIUS
I had rather give his carcass to my hounds.

HERMIA
Out, dog! Out, cur! Thou driv'st me past the bounds
Of maiden's patience. Hast thou slain him, then?
Henceforth be never numbered among men.
O, once tell true, tell true, even for my sake: 68
Durst thou have looked upon him being awake?
And hast thou killed him sleeping? O brave touch!   70
Could not a worm, an adder, do so much?   71
An adder did it; for with doubler tongue   72
Than thine, thou serpent, never adder stung.

---

195 enforcèd forced, violated; or, possibly, constrained (since Titania at this moment is hardly concerned about chastity)   **196 Tie . . . tongue** (Presumably Bottom is braying like an ass.)
3.2. Location: The wood.
5 night-rule diversion or misrule for the night.   **haunted** much frequented   **7 close** secret, private   **8 dull** drowsy   **9 patches** clowns, fools.   **rude mechanicals** ignorant artisans   **10 stalls** market booths   **13 barren sort** stupid company or crew   **14 presented** acted   **15 scene** playing area   **17 noll** noddle, head   **19 mimic** burlesque actor   **20 fowler** hunter of game birds   **21 russet-pated choughs** reddish brown or gray-headed jackdaws.   **in sort** in a flock   **23 Sever** i.e., scatter   **30 from . . . catch** i.e., everything preys on those who yield to fear

36 latched fastened, snared   **40 of force** perforce   **48 Being o'er shoes** having waded in so far   **53 whole** solid   **55 Her brother's** i.e., the sun's.   **th' Antipodes** the people on the opposite side of the earth (where the moon is imagined bringing night to noontime)   **57 dead** deadly, or deathly pale   **62 to** to do with   **68 once** once and for all   **70 brave touch!** fine stroke! (Said ironically.)   **71 worm** serpent   **72 doubler** (1) more forked (2) more deceitful

DEMETRIUS
You spend your passion on a misprised mood.   74
I am not guilty of Lysander's blood,
Nor is he dead, for aught that I can tell.

HERMIA
I pray thee, tell me then that he is well.

DEMETRIUS
And if I could, what should I get therefor?   78

HERMIA
A privilege never to see me more.
And from thy hated presence part I so.
See me no more, whether he be dead or no.   *Exit.*

DEMETRIUS
There is no following her in this fierce vein.
Here therefore for a while I will remain.
So sorrow's heaviness doth heavier grow   84
For debt that bankrupt sleep doth sorrow owe,   85
Which now in some slight measure it will pay,   86
If for his tender here I make some stay.   87
                    [*He*] lie[*s*] *down* [*and sleeps*].

OBERON
What hast thou done? Thou hast mistaken quite
And laid the love juice on some true love's sight.
Of thy misprision must perforce ensue   90
Some true love turned, and not a false turned true.

PUCK
Then fate o'errules, that, one man holding troth,   92
A million fail, confounding oath on oath.   93

OBERON
About the wood go swifter than the wind,
And Helena of Athens look thou find.   95
All fancy-sick she is and pale of cheer   96
With sighs of love, that cost the fresh blood dear. 97
By some illusion see thou bring her here.
I'll charm his eyes against she do appear.   99

PUCK
I go, I go, look how I go,
Swifter than arrow from the Tartar's bow.   [*Exit.*] 101

OBERON [*applying love juice to Demetrius' eyes*]
Flower of this purple dye,
Hit with Cupid's archery,
Sink in apple of his eye.   104
When his love he doth espy,
Let her shine as gloriously
As the Venus of the sky.
When thou wak'st, if she be by,
Beg of her for remedy.

74 **passion** violent feelings.   **misprised mood** anger based on misconception   78 **therefor** in return for that   84 **heavier** (1) harder to bear (2) more drowsy   85 **bankrupt** (Demetrius is saying that his sleepiness adds to the weariness caused by sorrow.)   86–87 **Which . . . stay** i.e., to a small extent, I will be able to "pay back" and hence find some relief from sorrow, if I pause here awhile (*make some stay*) while sleep "tenders" or offers itself by way of paying the debt owed to sorrow   90 **misprision** mistake   92 **that . . . troth** in that, for each man keeping true faith in love   93 **confounding . . . oath** i.e., breaking oath after oath   95 **look** i.e., be sure   96 **fancy-sick** lovesick. **cheer** face   97 **sighs . . . blood** (An allusion to the physiological theory that each sigh costs the heart a drop of blood.)   99 **against . . . appear** in anticipation of her coming   101 **Tartar's bow** (Tartars were famed for their skill with the bow.)   104 **apple** pupil

Enter Puck.

PUCK
Captain of our fairy band,
Helena is here at hand,
And the youth, mistook by me,
Pleading for a lover's fee.   113
Shall we their fond pageant see?   114
Lord, what fools these mortals be!

OBERON
Stand aside. The noise they make
Will cause Demetrius to awake.

PUCK
Then will two at once woo one;
That must needs be sport alone.   119
And those things do best please me
That befall preposterously.   121
                    [*They stand aside.*]

Enter Lysander and Helena.

LYSANDER
Why should you think that I should woo in scorn?
   Scorn and derision never come in tears.
Look when I vow, I weep; and vows so born,   124
   In their nativity all truth appears.   125
How can these things in me seem scorn to you,
Bearing the badge of faith to prove them true? 127

HELENA
You do advance your cunning more and more.   128
   When truth kills truth, O, devilish-holy fray! 129
These vows are Hermia's. Will you give her o'er?
   Weigh oath with oath, and you will nothing
   weigh.
Your vows to her and me, put in two scales,
Will even weigh, and both as light as tales.   133

LYSANDER
I had no judgment when to her I swore.

HELENA
Nor none, in my mind, now you give her o'er.

LYSANDER
Demetrius loves her, and he loves not you.

DEMETRIUS [*awaking*]
O Helen, goddess, nymph, perfect, divine!
To what, my love, shall I compare thine eyne?
Crystal is muddy. O, how ripe in show   139
Thy lips, those kissing cherries, tempting grow!
That pure congealèd white, high Taurus' snow,   141
Fanned with the eastern wind, turns to a crow   142
When thou hold'st up thy hand. O, let me kiss
This princess of pure white, this seal of bliss! 144

HELENA
O spite! O hell! I see you all are bent

113 **fee** privilege, reward   114 **fond pageant** foolish spectacle
119 **alone** unequaled   121 **preposterously** out of the natural order
124 **Look when** whenever   124–125 **vows . . . appears** i.e., vows made by one who is weeping give evidence thereby of their sincerity
127 **badge** identifying device such as that worn on servants' livery (here, his tears)   128 **advance** carry forward, display   129 **truth kills truth** i.e., one of Lysander's vows must invalidate the other
133 **tales** lies   139 **show** appearance   141 **Taurus** a lofty mountain range in Asia Minor   142 **turns to a crow** i.e., seems black by contrast   144 **seal** pledge

To set against me for your merriment.
If you were civil and knew courtesy,
You would not do me thus much injury.
Can you not hate me, as I know you do,
But you must join in souls to mock me too?   150
If you were men, as men you are in show,
You would not use a gentle lady so—
To vow, and swear, and superpraise my parts,   153
When I am sure you hate me with your hearts.
You both are rivals, and love Hermia,
And now both rivals to mock Helena.
A trim exploit, a manly enterprise,   157
To conjure tears up in a poor maid's eyes
With your derision! None of noble sort   159
Would so offend a virgin and extort   160
A poor soul's patience, all to make you sport.

LYSANDER
You are unkind, Demetrius. Be not so.
For you love Hermia; this you know I know.
And here, with all good will, with all my heart,
In Hermia's love I yield you up my part;
And yours of Helena to me bequeath,
Whom I do love, and will do till my death.

HELENA
Never did mockers waste more idle breath.

DEMETRIUS
Lysander, keep thy Hermia; I will none.   169
If e'er I loved her, all that love is gone.
My heart to her but as guestwise sojourned,   171
And now to Helen is it home returned,
There to remain.

LYSANDER   Helen, it is not so.

DEMETRIUS
Disparage not the faith thou dost not know,
Lest, to thy peril, thou aby it dear.   175
Look where thy love comes; yonder is thy dear.

Enter Hermia.

HERMIA
Dark night, that from the eye his function takes,   177
The ear more quick of apprehension makes;
Wherein it doth impair the seeing sense,
It pays the hearing double recompense.
Thou art not by mine eye, Lysander, found;
Mine ear, I thank it, brought me to thy sound.
But why unkindly didst thou leave me so?

LYSANDER
Why should he stay, whom love doth press to go?

HERMIA
What love could press Lysander from my side?

LYSANDER
Lysander's love, that would not let him bide—
Fair Helena, who more engilds the night   187

Than all yon fiery oes and eyes of light.   188
Why seek'st thou me? Could not this make thee
    know
The hate I bear thee made me leave thee so?

HERMIA
You speak not as you think. It cannot be.

HELENA
Lo, she is one of this confederacy!
Now I perceive they have conjoined all three
To fashion this false sport, in spite of me.   194
Injurious Hermia, most ungrateful maid!
Have you conspired, have you with these contrived   196
To bait me with this foul derision?   197
Is all the counsel that we two have shared—   198
The sisters' vows, the hours that we have spent
When we have chid the hasty-footed time
For parting us—O, is all forgot?
All schooldays' friendship, childhood innocence?
We, Hermia, like two artificial gods   203
Have with our needles created both one flower,
Both on one sampler, sitting on one cushion,
Both warbling of one song, both in one key,
As if our hands, our sides, voices, and minds
Had been incorporate. So we grew together,   208
Like to a double cherry, seeming parted,
But yet an union in partition,
Two lovely berries molded on one stem;   211
So, with two seeming bodies but one heart,
Two of the first, like coats in heraldry,   213
Due but to one and crownèd with one crest.   214
And will you rend our ancient love asunder,
To join with men in scorning your poor friend?
It is not friendly, 'tis not maidenly.
Our sex, as well as I, may chide you for it,
Though I alone do feel the injury.

HERMIA
I am amazèd at your passionate words.
I scorn you not. It seems that you scorn me.

HELENA
Have you not set Lysander, as in scorn,
To follow me and praise my eyes and face?
And made your other love, Demetrius,
Who even but now did spurn me with his foot,
To call me goddess, nymph, divine, and rare,
Precious, celestial? Wherefore speaks he this
To her he hates? And wherefore doth Lysander
Deny your love, so rich within his soul,
And tender me, forsooth, affection,   230
But by your setting on, by your consent?
What though I be not so in grace as you,   232
So hung upon with love, so fortunate,
But miserable most, to love unloved?
This you should pity rather than despise.

---

146 **set against** attack   150 **in souls** i.e., heart and soul   153 **super-praise** overpraise.   **parts** qualities   157 **trim** pretty, fine. (Said ironically.)   159 **sort** character, quality   160 **extort** twist, torture   169 **will none** i.e., want no part of her   171 **to . . . sojourned** only visited with her   175 **aby** pay for   177 **his** its   187 **engilds** gilds, brightens with a golden light

188 **oes** spangles (here, stars)   194 **in spite of me** to vex me   196 **contrived** plotted   197 **bait** torment, as one sets on dogs to bait a bear   198 **counsel** confidential talk   203 **artificial** skilled in art or creation   208 **incorporate** of one body   211 **lovely** loving   213–214 **Two . . . crest** i.e., we have two separate bodies, just as a coat of arms in heraldry can be represented twice on a shield but surmounted by a single crest   230 **tender** offer   232 **grace** favor

HERMIA
I understand not what you mean by this.
HELENA
Ay, do! Persever, counterfeit sad looks,   237
Make mouths upon me when I turn my back,   238
Wink each at other, hold the sweet jest up.   239
This sport, well carried, shall be chronicled.   240
If you have any pity, grace, or manners,
You would not make me such an argument.   242
But fare ye well. 'Tis partly my own fault,
Which death, or absence, soon shall remedy.
LYSANDER
Stay, gentle Helena; hear my excuse,
My love, my life, my soul, fair Helena!
HELENA
O excellent!
HERMIA [to Lysander] Sweet, do not scorn her so.
DEMETRIUS [to Lysander]
If she cannot entreat, I can compel.   248
LYSANDER
Thou canst compel no more than she entreat.
Thy threats have no more strength than her weak
    prayers.
Helen, I love thee, by my life, I do!
I swear by that which I will lose for thee,
To prove him false that says I love thee not.
DEMETRIUS [to Helena]
I say I love thee more than he can do.
LYSANDER
If thou say so, withdraw, and prove it too.   255
DEMETRIUS
Quick, come!
HERMIA   Lysander, whereto tends all this?
LYSANDER
Away, you Ethiope!
            [He tries to break away from Hermia.]
DEMETRIUS   No, no; he'll   257
Seem to break loose; take on as you would follow,   258
But yet come not. You are a tame man. Go!
LYSANDER [to Hermia]
Hang off, thou cat, thou burr! Vile thing, let loose,   260
Or I will shake thee from me like a serpent!
HERMIA
Why are you grown so rude? What change is this,
Sweet love?
LYSANDER   Thy love? Out, tawny Tartar, out!
Out, lothèd med'cine! O hated potion, hence!   264
HERMIA
Do you not jest?
HELENA   Yes, sooth, and so do you.   265
LYSANDER
Demetrius, I will keep my word with thee.

DEMETRIUS
I would I had your bond, for I perceive
A weak bond holds you. I'll not trust your word.   268
LYSANDER
What, should I hurt her, strike her, kill her dead?
Although I hate her, I'll not harm her so.
HERMIA
What, can you do me greater harm than hate?
Hate me? Wherefore? O me, what news, my love?   272
Am not I Hermia? Are not you Lysander?
I am as fair now as I was erewhile.   274
Since night you loved me; yet since night you left
    me.
Why, then you left me—O, the gods forbid!—
In earnest, shall I say?
LYSANDER   Ay, by my life!
And never did desire to see thee more.
Therefore be out of hope, of question, of doubt;
Be certain, nothing truer. 'Tis no jest
That I do hate thee and love Helena.
HERMIA [to Helena]
O me! You juggler! You cankerblossom!   282
You thief of love! What, have you come by night
And stol'n my love's heart from him?
HELENA   Fine, i' faith!
Have you no modesty, no maiden shame,
No touch of bashfulness? What, will you tear
Impatient answers from my gentle tongue?
Fie, fie! You counterfeit, you puppet, you!   288
HERMIA
"Puppet"? Why, so! Ay, that way goes the game.   289
Now I perceive that she hath made compare
Between our statures; she hath urged her height,
And with her personage, her tall personage,
Her height, forsooth, she hath prevailed with him.
And are you grown so high in his esteem
Because I am so dwarfish and so low?
How low am I, thou painted maypole? Speak!
How low am I? I am not yet so low
But that my nails can reach unto thine eyes.
            [She flails at Helena but is restrained.]
HELENA
I pray you, though you mock me, gentlemen,
Let her not hurt me. I was never curst;   300
I have no gift at all in shrewishness;
I am a right maid for my cowardice.   302
Let her not strike me. You perhaps may think,
Because she is something lower than myself,   304
That I can match her.
HERMIA   Lower? Hark, again!
HELENA
Good Hermia, do not be so bitter with me.
I evermore did love you, Hermia,

---

237 sad grave, serious   238 mouths i.e., mows, faces, grimaces.
upon at   239 hold . . . up keep up the joke   240 carried managed
242 argument subject for a jest   248 entreat i.e., succeed by entreaty
255 withdraw . . . too i.e., withdraw with me and prove your claim
in a duel. (The two gentlemen are armed.)   257 Ethiope (Referring to
Hermia's relatively dark hair and complexion; see also tawny Tartar
six lines later.)   258 take on as act as if, make a fuss as if   260 Hang
off let go   264 med'cine i.e., poison   265 sooth truly

268 weak bond i.e., Hermia's arm (with a pun on bond, "oath," in
the previous line)   272 what news what is the matter   274 erewhile
just now   282 cankerblossom worm that destroys the flower bud, or
wild rose   288 puppet (1) counterfeit (2) dwarfish woman (in reference to Hermia's smaller stature)   289 Why, so i.e., Oh, so that's
how it is   300 curst shrewish   302 right true   304 something
somewhat

Did ever keep your counsels, never wronged you,
Save that, in love unto Demetrius,
I told him of your stealth unto this wood. 310
He followed you; for love I followed him.
But he hath chid me hence and threatened me 312
To strike me, spurn me, nay, to kill me too.
And now, so you will let me quiet go, 314
To Athens will I bear my folly back
And follow you no further. Let me go.
You see how simple and how fond I am. 317

HERMIA
Why, get you gone. Who is 't that hinders you?

HELENA
A foolish heart, that I leave here behind.

HERMIA
What, with Lysander?

HELENA　　　　　　　With Demetrius.

LYSANDER
Be not afraid; she shall not harm thee, Helena.

DEMETRIUS
No, sir, she shall not, though you take her part.

HELENA
O, when she is angry, she is keen and shrewd. 323
She was a vixen when she went to school;
And though she be but little, she is fierce.

HERMIA
"Little" again? Nothing but "low" and "little"?
Why will you suffer her to flout me thus?
Let me come to her.

LYSANDER　　　　　　Get you gone, you dwarf!
You minimus, of hindering knotgrass made! 329
You bead, you acorn!

DEMETRIUS　　　　　You are too officious
In her behalf that scorns your services.
Let her alone. Speak not of Helena;
Take not her part. For, if thou dost intend 333
Never so little show of love to her,
Thou shalt aby it.

LYSANDER　　　　　Now she holds me not. 335
Now follow, if thou dar'st, to try whose right,
Of thine or mine, is most in Helena. [Exit.]

DEMETRIUS
Follow? Nay, I'll go with thee, cheek by jowl. 338
[Exit, following Lysander.]

HERMIA
You, mistress, all this coil is 'long of you. 339
Nay, go not back.

HELENA　　　　　I will not trust you, I, 340
Nor longer stay in your curst company.
Your hands than mine are quicker for a fray;
My legs are longer, though, to run away. [Exit.]

HERMIA
I am amazed and know not what to say. Exit.

310 **stealth** stealing away　312 **chid me hence** driven me away with his scolding　314 **so** if only　317 **fond** foolish　323 **keen** fierce, cruel. **shrewd** shrewish　329 **minimus** diminutive creature. **knotgrass** a weed, an infusion of which was thought to stunt the growth　333 **intend** give sign of　335 **aby** pay for　338 **cheek by jowl** i.e., side by side　339 **coil** turmoil, dissension. **'long of** on account of　340 **go not back** i.e., don't retreat. (Hermia is again proposing a fight.)

[Oberon and Puck come forward.]

OBERON
This is thy negligence. Still thou mistak'st,
Or else committ'st thy knaveries willfully.

PUCK
Believe me, king of shadows, I mistook.
Did not you tell me I should know the man
By the Athenian garments he had on?
And so far blameless proves my enterprise
That I have 'nointed an Athenian's eyes;
And so far am I glad it so did sort, 352
As this their jangling I esteem a sport. 353

OBERON
Thou seest these lovers seek a place to fight.
Hie therefore, Robin, overcast the night; 355
The starry welkin cover thou anon 356
With drooping fog as black as Acheron, 357
And lead these testy rivals so astray
As one come not within another's way. 359
Like to Lysander sometimes frame thy tongue,
Then stir Demetrius up with bitter wrong; 361
And sometimes rail thou like Demetrius.
And from each other look thou lead them thus,
Till o'er their brows death-counterfeiting sleep
With leaden legs and batty wings doth creep. 365
Then crush this herb into Lysander's eye, 366
[giving herb]
Whose liquor hath this virtuous property, 367
To take from thence all error with his might 368
And make his eyeballs roll with wonted sight. 369
When they next wake, all this derision 370
Shall seem a dream and fruitless vision,
And back to Athens shall the lovers wend
With league whose date till death shall never end. 373
Whiles I in this affair do thee employ,
I'll to my queen and beg her Indian boy;
And then I will her charmèd eye release
From monster's view, and all things shall be peace.

PUCK
My fairy lord, this must be done with haste,
For night's swift dragons cut the clouds full fast, 379
And yonder shines Aurora's harbinger, 380
At whose approach ghosts, wand'ring here and there,
Troop home to churchyards. Damnèd spirits all,
That in crossways and floods have burial, 383
Already to their wormy beds are gone.
For fear lest day should look their shames upon,

352 **so far** at least to this extent. **sort** turn out　353 **As** in that　355 **Hie** hasten　356 **welkin** sky　357 **Acheron** river of Hades (here representing Hades itself)　359 **As** that　361 **wrong** insults　365 **batty** batlike　366 **this herb** i.e., the antidote (mentioned in 2.1.184) to love-in-idleness　367 **virtuous** efficacious　368 **his** its　369 **wonted** accustomed　370 **derision** laughable business　373 **date** term of existence　379 **dragons** (Supposed by Shakespeare to be yoked to the car of the goddess of night or the moon.)　380 **Aurora's harbinger** the morning star, precursor of dawn　383 **crossways . . . burial** (Those who had committed suicide were buried at crossways, with a stake driven through them; those who intentionally or accidentally drowned (in *floods* or deep water) would be condemned to wander disconsolately for lack of burial rites.)

They willfully themselves exile from light
And must for aye consort with black-browed night.   387
OBERON
But we are spirits of another sort.
I with the Morning's love have oft made sport,   389
And, like a forester, the groves may tread   390
Even till the eastern gate, all fiery red,
Opening on Neptune with fair blessèd beams,
Turns into yellow gold his salt green streams.
But notwithstanding, haste, make no delay.
We may effect this business yet ere day.   [*Exit.*]
PUCK
    Up and down, up and down,
    I will lead them up and down.
    I am feared in field and town.
    Goblin, lead them up and down.   399
Here comes one.

    Enter Lysander.

LYSANDER
Where art thou, proud Demetrius? Speak thou now.
PUCK [*mimicking Demetrius*]
Here, villain, drawn and ready. Where art thou?   402
LYSANDER
I will be with thee straight.
PUCK   Follow me, then,   403
To plainer ground.
   [*Lysander wanders about, following the voice.*]

    Enter Demetrius.

DEMETRIUS   Lysander! Speak again!   404
Thou runaway, thou coward, art thou fled?
Speak! In some bush? Where dost thou hide thy
   head?
PUCK [*mimicking Lysander*]
Thou coward, art thou bragging to the stars,
Telling the bushes that thou look'st for wars,
And wilt not come? Come, recreant; come, thou
   child,   409
I'll whip thee with a rod. He is defiled
That draws a sword on thee.
DEMETRIUS   Yea, art thou there?
PUCK
Follow my voice. We'll try no manhood here.   412
               Exeunt.

    [*Lysander returns.*]

LYSANDER
He goes before me and still dares me on.
When I come where he calls, then he is gone.
The villain is much lighter-heeled than I.
I followed fast, but faster he did fly,

387 for aye forever **389 the Morning's love** Cephalus, a beautiful
youth beloved by Aurora; or perhaps the goddess of the dawn herself
390 forester keeper of a royal forest **399 Goblin** Hobgoblin. (Puck
refers to himself.) **402 drawn** with drawn sword **403 straight** immediately **404 plainer** more open. **s.d. Lysander wanders about**
(Lysander may exit here, but perhaps not; neither exit nor reentrance
is indicated in the early texts.) **409 recreant** cowardly wretch
412 try test

That fallen am I in dark uneven way,
And here will rest me. [*He lies down.*] Come, thou
   gentle day!
For if but once thou show me thy gray light,
I'll find Demetrius and revenge this spite. [*He sleeps.*]

    [*Enter*] Robin [*Puck*] *and Demetrius.*

PUCK
Ho, ho, ho! Coward, why com'st thou not?
DEMETRIUS
Abide me, if thou dar'st; for well I wot   422
Thou runn'st before me, shifting every place,
And dar'st not stand nor look me in the face.
Where art thou now?
PUCK   Come hither. I am here.
DEMETRIUS
Nay, then, thou mock'st me. Thou shalt buy this
   dear,   426
If ever I thy face by daylight see.
Now go thy way. Faintness constraineth me
To measure out my length on this cold bed.
By day's approach look to be visited.
          [*He lies down and sleeps.*]

    Enter Helena.

HELENA
O weary night, O long and tedious night,
  Abate thy hours! Shine comforts from the east,   432
That I may back to Athens by daylight
  From these that my poor company detest;
And sleep, that sometimes shuts up sorrow's eye,
Steal me awhile from mine own company.
        [*She lies down and*] sleep[*s*].
PUCK
    Yet but three? Come one more;
    Two of both kinds makes up four.
    Here she comes, curst and sad.   439
    Cupid is a knavish lad,
    Thus to make poor females mad.

    [*Enter Hermia.*]

HERMIA
Never so weary, never so in woe,
  Bedabbled with the dew and torn with briers,
I can no further crawl, no further go;
  My legs can keep no pace with my desires.
Here will I rest me till the break of day.
Heavens shield Lysander, if they mean a fray!
        [*She lies down and sleeps.*]
PUCK
    On the ground
    Sleep sound.
    I'll apply
    To your eye,
  Gentle lover, remedy.
    [*He squeezes the juice on Lysander's eyes.*]

422 Abide confront, face. **wot** know **426 buy** aby, pay for. **dear**
dearly **432 Abate** lessen, shorten **439 curst** ill-tempered

When thou wak'st,
Thou tak'st
True delight
In the sight
Of thy former lady's eye;
And the country proverb known,
That every man should take his own,
In your waking shall be shown:
  Jack shall have Jill;   461
  Naught shall go ill;
The man shall have his mare again, and all shall be
well.   [*Exit. The four sleeping lovers remain.*]

4.1 *Enter [Titania,] Queen of Fairies, and [Bottom the]
clown, and Fairies; and [Oberon,] the King, behind
them.*

TITANIA
Come, sit thee down upon this flowery bed,
  While I thy amiable cheeks do coy,   2
And stick muskroses in thy sleek smooth head,
  And kiss thy fair large ears, my gentle joy.
                           [*They recline.*]

BOTTOM   Where's Peaseblossom?
PEASEBLOSSOM   Ready.
BOTTOM   Scratch my head, Peaseblossom. Where's
Monsieur Cobweb?
COBWEB   Ready.
BOTTOM   Monsieur Cobweb, good monsieur, get you
your weapons in your hand, and kill me a red-hipped
humble-bee on the top of a thistle; and, good mon-
sieur, bring me the honey bag. Do not fret yourself
too much in the action, monsieur; and, good monsieur, have a care the honey bag break not. I would be
loath to have you overflown with a honey bag, sig-
nor. [*Exit Cobweb.*] Where's Monsieur Mustardseed?
MUSTARDSEED   Ready.
BOTTOM   Give me your neaf, Monsieur Mustardseed. 19
Pray you, leave your courtesy, good monsieur.   20
MUSTARDSEED   What's your will?
BOTTOM   Nothing, good monsieur, but to help Caval- 22
ery Cobweb to scratch. I must to the barber's, mon- 23
sieur, for methinks I am marvelous hairy about the
face; and I am such a tender ass, if my hair do but
tickle me I must scratch.
TITANIA
What, wilt thou hear some music, my sweet love?
BOTTOM   I have a reasonable good ear in music. Let's
have the tongs and the bones.   29

[Music: tongs, rural music.]
TITANIA
Or say, sweet love, what thou desirest to eat.
BOTTOM   Truly, a peck of provender. I could munch 31
your good dry oats. Methinks I have a great desire to
a bottle of hay. Good hay, sweet hay, hath no fellow. 33
TITANIA
I have a venturous fairy that shall seek
The squirrel's hoard, and fetch thee new nuts.
BOTTOM   I had rather have a handful or two of dried
peas. But, I pray you, let none of your people stir me. 37
I have an exposition of sleep come upon me.   38
TITANIA
Sleep thou, and I will wind thee in my arms.
Fairies, begone, and be all ways away.   40
                      [*Exeunt Fairies.*]
So doth the woodbine the sweet honeysuckle   41
Gently entwist; the female ivy so
Enrings the barky fingers of the elm.
O, how I love thee! How I dote on thee!
                      [*They sleep.*]

Enter Robin Goodfellow [Puck].

OBERON [*coming forward*]
Welcome, good Robin. Seest thou this sweet sight?
Her dotage now I do begin to pity.
For, meeting her of late behind the wood
Seeking sweet favors for this hateful fool,   48
I did upbraid her and fall out with her.
For she his hairy temples then had rounded
With coronet of fresh and fragrant flowers;
And that same dew, which sometime on the buds   52
Was wont to swell like round and orient pearls,   53
Stood now within the pretty flowerets' eyes
Like tears that did their own disgrace bewail.
When I had at my pleasure taunted her,
And she in mild terms begged my patience,
I then did ask of her her changeling child,
Which straight she gave me, and her fairy sent
To bear him to my bower in Fairyland.
And, now I have the boy, I will undo
This hateful imperfection of her eyes.
And, gentle Puck, take this transformèd scalp
From off the head of this Athenian swain,
That he, awaking when the other do,   65
May all to Athens back again repair,   66
And think no more of this night's accidents
But as the fierce vexation of a dream.
But first I will release the Fairy Queen.
           [*He squeezes an herb on her eyes.*]
  Be as thou wast wont to be;
  See as thou wast wont to see.

461 Jack shall have Jill (Proverbial for "boy gets girl.")
4.1. Location: The action is continuous. The four lovers are still
asleep onstage. (Compare with the Folio stage direction: "They sleep
all the act.")
2 amiable lovely.   **coy** caress   **19 neaf** fist   **20 leave your courtesy**
i.e., stop bowing, or put on your hat   **22–23 Cavalery** cavalier.
(Form of address for a gentleman.)   **23 Cobweb** (Seemingly an error,
since Cobweb has been sent to bring honey, while Peaseblossom has
been asked to scratch.)   **29 tongs . . . bones** instruments for rustic
music. (The tongs were played like a triangle, whereas the bones
were held between the fingers and used as clappers.)

s.d. Music . . . music (This stage direction is added from the Folio.)
31 peck of provender one-quarter bushel of grain   **33 bottle** bundle.
fellow equal   **37 stir** disturb   **38 exposition of** (Bottom's phrase for
"disposition to.")   **40 all ways** in all directions   **41 woodbine** bind-
weed, a climbing plant that twines in the opposite direction from that
of honeysuckle   **48 favors** i.e., gifts of flowers   **52 sometime** formerly   **53 orient pearls** i.e., the most beautiful of all pearls, those
coming from the Orient   **65 other** others   **66 repair** return

Dian's bud o'er Cupid's flower 72
Hath such force and blessèd power.
Now, my Titania, wake you, my sweet queen.

TITANIA [*awaking*]
My Oberon! What visions have I seen!
Methought I was enamored of an ass.

OBERON
There lies your love.

TITANIA　　　　　　　　　How came these things to pass?
O, how mine eyes do loathe his visage now!

OBERON
Silence awhile. Robin, take off this head.
Titania, music call, and strike more dead
Than common sleep of all these five the sense. 81

TITANIA
Music, ho! Music, such as charmeth sleep! [*Music.*] 82

PUCK [*removing the ass head*]
Now, when thou wak'st, with thine own fool's eyes
　peep.

OBERON
Sound, music! Come, my queen, take hands
　with me,
And rock the ground whereon these sleepers be.
　　　　　　　　　　　　　　[*They dance.*]
Now thou and I are new in amity,
And will tomorrow midnight solemnly 87
Dance in Duke Theseus' house triumphantly,
And bless it to all fair prosperity.
There shall the pairs of faithful lovers be
Wedded, with Theseus, all in jollity.

PUCK
　　　　Fairy King, attend, and mark:
　　　　I do hear the morning lark.

OBERON
　　　　Then, my queen, in silence sad, 94
　　　　Trip we after night's shade.
　　　　We the globe can compass soon,
　　　　Swifter than the wandering moon.

TITANIA
　　　　Come, my lord, and in our flight
　　　　Tell me how it came this night
　　　　That I sleeping here was found
　　　　With these mortals on the ground.
　　　　　　　　Exeunt [*Oberon, Titania, and Puck*].
　　　　　　　　　　　　Wind horn [*within*].

Enter Theseus and all his train; [*Hippolyta,
Egeus*].

THESEUS
Go, one of you, find out the forester,
For now our observation is performed; 103
And since we have the vaward of the day, 104
My love shall hear the music of my hounds.

Uncouple in the western valley; let them go. 106
Dispatch, I say, and find the forester.
　　　　　　　　　　　[*Exit an Attendant.*]
We will, fair queen, up to the mountain's top
And mark the musical confusion
Of hounds and echo in conjunction.

HIPPOLYTA
I was with Hercules and Cadmus once 111
When in a wood of Crete they bayed the bear 112
With hounds of Sparta. Never did I hear 113
Such gallant chiding; for, besides the groves, 114
The skies, the fountains, every region near
Seemed all one mutual cry. I never heard
So musical a discord, such sweet thunder.

THESEUS
My hounds are bred out of the Spartan kind, 118
So flewed, so sanded; and their heads are hung 119
With ears that sweep away the morning dew;
Crook-kneed, and dewlapped like Thessalian bulls; 121
Slow in pursuit, but matched in mouth like bells, 122
Each under each. A cry more tunable 123
Was never holloed to nor cheered with horn 124
In Crete, in Sparta, nor in Thessaly.
Judge when you hear. [*He sees the sleepers.*] But soft!
　What nymphs are these? 126

EGEUS
My lord, this is my daughter here asleep,
And this Lysander; this Demetrius is;
This Helena, old Nedar's Helena.
I wonder of their being here together. 130

THESEUS
No doubt they rose up early to observe
The rite of May, and hearing our intent,
Came here in grace of our solemnity. 133
But speak, Egeus. Is not this the day
That Hermia should give answer of her choice?

EGEUS　　It is, my lord.

THESEUS
Go bid the huntsmen wake them with their horns.
　　　　　　　　　　　[*Exit an Attendant.*]

Shout within. Wind horns. They all start up.

Good morrow, friends. Saint Valentine is past. 138
Begin these woodbirds but to couple now?

LYSANDER
Pardon, my lord.　　　　　　　　[*They kneel.*]

THESEUS　　　　I pray you all, stand up.
　　　　　　　　　　　[*They stand.*]

72 **Dian's bud** (Perhaps the flower of the *agnus castus* or chaste-tree, supposed to preserve chastity; or perhaps referring simply to Oberon's herb by which he can undo the effects of "Cupid's flower," the love-in-idleness of 2.1.166–168.) 81 **these five** i.e., the four lovers and Bottom 82 **charmeth** brings about, as though by a charm 87 **solemnly** ceremoniously 94 **sad** sober 103 **observation** i.e., observance to a morn of May (1.1.167) 104 **vaward** vanguard, i.e., earliest part

106 **Uncouple** set free for the hunt 111 **Cadmus** mythical founder of Thebes. (This story about him is unknown.) 112 **bayed** brought to bay 113 **hounds of Sparta** (A breed famous in antiquity for their hunting skill.) 114 **chiding** i.e., yelping 118 **kind** strain, breed 119 **So flewed** similarly having large hanging chaps or fleshy covering of the jaw. **sanded** of sandy color 121 **dewlapped** having pendulous folds of skin under the neck 122–123 **matched . . . each** i.e., harmoniously matched in their various cries like a set of bells, from treble down to bass 123 **cry** pack of hounds. **tunable** well tuned, melodious 124 **cheered** encouraged 126 **soft** i.e., gently, wait a minute 130 **wonder of** wonder at 133 **in . . . solemnity** in honor of our wedding ceremony 138 **Saint Valentine** (Birds were supposed to choose their mates on Saint Valentine's Day.)

I know you two are rival enemies;
How comes this gentle concord in the world,
That hatred is so far from jealousy   143
To sleep by hate and fear no enmity?

LYSANDER
My lord, I shall reply amazedly,
Half sleep, half waking; but as yet, I swear,
I cannot truly say how I came here.
But, as I think—for truly would I speak,
And now I do bethink me, so it is—
I came with Hermia hither. Our intent
Was to be gone from Athens, where we might,   151
Without the peril of the Athenian law—   152

EGEUS
Enough, enough, my lord; you have enough.
I beg the law, the law, upon his head.
They would have stol'n away; they would,
    Demetrius,
Thereby to have defeated you and me,   156
You of your wife and me of my consent,
Of my consent that she should be your wife.

DEMETRIUS
My lord, fair Helen told me of their stealth,
Of this their purpose hither to this wood,   160
And I in fury hither followed them,
Fair Helena in fancy following me.   162
But, my good lord, I wot not by what power—
But by some power it is—my love to Hermia,
Melted as the snow, seems to me now
As the remembrance of an idle gaud   166
Which in my childhood I did dote upon;
And all the faith, the virtue of my heart,
The object and the pleasure of mine eye,
Is only Helena. To her, my lord,
Was I betrothed ere I saw Hermia,
But like a sickness did I loathe this food;
But, as in health, come to my natural taste,
Now I do wish it, love it, long for it,
And will forevermore be true to it.

THESEUS
Fair lovers, you are fortunately met.
Of this discourse we more will hear anon.
Egeus, I will overbear your will;
For in the temple, by and by, with us
These couples shall eternally be knit.
And, for the morning now is something worn,   181
Our purposed hunting shall be set aside.
Away with us to Athens. Three and three,
We'll hold a feast in great solemnity.   184
Come, Hippolyta.
        [*Exeunt Theseus, Hippolyta, Egeus, and train.*]

DEMETRIUS
These things seem small and undistinguishable,
Like far-off mountains turnèd into clouds.

HERMIA
Methinks I see these things with parted eye,   188
When everything seems double.

HELENA   So methinks;
And I have found Demetrius like a jewel,   190
Mine own, and not mine own.

DEMETRIUS   Are you sure   191
That we are awake? It seems to me
That yet we sleep, we dream. Do not you think
The Duke was here, and bid us follow him?

HERMIA
Yea, and my father.

HELENA   And Hippolyta.

LYSANDER
And he did bid us follow to the temple.

DEMETRIUS
Why, then, we are awake. Let's follow him,
And by the way let us recount our dreams.
                            [*Exeunt the lovers.*]

BOTTOM [*awaking*]   When my cue comes, call me, and
I will answer. My next is "Most fair Pyramus." Heigh-
ho! Peter Quince! Flute, the bellows mender! Snout,
the tinker! Starveling! God's my life, stolen hence and 202
left me asleep! I have had a most rare vision. I have
had a dream, past the wit of man to say what dream it
was. Man is but an ass if he go about to expound this 205
dream. Methought I was—there is no man can tell
what. Methought I was—and methought I had—but
man is but a patched fool if he will offer to say what 208
methought I had. The eye of man hath not heard, the   209
ear of man hath not seen, man's hand is not able to   210
taste, his tongue to conceive, nor his heart to report, 211
what my dream was. I will get Peter Quince to write
a ballad of this dream. It shall be called "Bottom's   213
Dream," because it hath no bottom; and I will sing it   214
in the latter end of a play, before the Duke. Peradventure, to make it the more gracious, I shall sing it at her 216
death.   [*Exit.*]

❖

4.2   *Enter Quince, Flute, [Snout, and Starveling].*

QUINCE   Have you sent to Bottom's house? Is he come
home yet?

STARVELING   He cannot be heard of. Out of doubt he is
transported.   4

FLUTE   If he come not, then the play is marred. It goes
not forward. Doth it?

---

143 jealousy suspicion   **151 where** wherever; or, to where
152 Without outside of, beyond   **156 defeated** defrauded
160 hither in coming hither   **162 in fancy** driven by love   **166 idle
gaud** worthless trinket   **181 for** since. **something** somewhat   **184 in
great solemnity** with great ceremony

188 parted i.e., improperly focused   **190 – 191 like . . . mine own**
i.e., like a jewel that one finds by chance and therefore possesses but
cannot certainly consider one's own property   **202 God's** may God
save   **205 go about** attempt   **208 patched** wearing motley, i.e., a
dress of various colors. **offer** venture   **209–211 The eye . . . report**
(Bottom garbles the terms of 1 Corinthians 2:9.)   **213 ballad** (The
proper medium for relating sensational stories and preposterous
events.)   **214 hath no bottom** is unfathomable   **216 her** Thisbe's (?)
4.2. Location: Athens.
4 transported carried off by fairies; or, possibly, transformed

QUINCE   It is not possible. You have not a man in all
Athens able to discharge Pyramus but he.   8

FLUTE   No, he hath simply the best wit of any handi-   9
craft man in Athens.

QUINCE   Yea, and the best person too, and he is a very   11
paramour for a sweet voice.

FLUTE   You must say "paragon." A paramour is, God
bless us, a thing of naught.   14

Enter Snug the joiner.

SNUG   Masters, the Duke is coming from the temple,
and there is two or three lords and ladies more
married. If our sport had gone forward, we had all   17
been made men.   18

FLUTE   O sweet bully Bottom! Thus hath he lost six-   19
pence a day during his life; he could not have scaped   20
sixpence a day. An the Duke had not given him sixpence a day for playing Pyramus, I'll be hanged. He
would have deserved it. Sixpence a day in Pyramus, or
nothing.

Enter Bottom.

BOTTOM   Where are these lads? Where are these hearts?   25

QUINCE   Bottom! O most courageous day! O most
happy hour!

BOTTOM   Masters, I am to discourse wonders. But ask   28
me not what; for if I tell you, I am no true Athenian. I
will tell you everything, right as it fell out.

QUINCE   Let us hear, sweet Bottom.

BOTTOM   Not a word of me. All that I will tell you is that   32
the Duke hath dined. Get your apparel together,
good strings to your beards, new ribbons to your   34
pumps; meet presently at the palace; every man look   35
o'er his part; for the short and the long is, our play is
preferred. In any case, let Thisbe have clean linen; and   37
let not him that plays the lion pare his nails, for they
shall hang out for the lion's claws. And, most dear actors, eat no onions nor garlic, for we are to utter sweet
breath; and I do not doubt but to hear them say it is
a sweet comedy. No more words. Away! Go, away!
[*Exeunt.*]

❖

5.1   *Enter Theseus, Hippolyta, and Philostrate, [lords,
and attendants].*

HIPPOLYTA
'Tis strange, my Theseus, that these lovers speak of.   1

THESEUS
More strange than true. I never may believe   2

These antique fables nor these fairy toys.   3
Lovers and madmen have such seething brains,
Such shaping fantasies, that apprehend   5
More than cool reason ever comprehends.   6
The lunatic, the lover, and the poet   *same*
Are of imagination all compact.   8
One sees more devils than vast hell can hold;
That is the madman. The lover, all as frantic,
Sees Helen's beauty in a brow of Egypt.   11
The poet's eye, in a fine frenzy rolling,
Doth glance from heaven to earth, from earth to
heaven;
And as imagination bodies forth
The forms of things unknown, the poet's pen
Turns them to shapes and gives to airy nothing
A local habitation and a name.
Such tricks hath strong imagination   *dreams are temporary*
That, if it would but apprehend some joy,
It comprehends some bringer of that joy;   20
Or in the night, imagining some fear,   21
How easy is a bush supposed a bear!

HIPPOLYTA
But all the story of the night told over,
And all their minds transfigured so together,   *change is possible*
More witnesseth than fancy's images   25
And grows to something of great constancy;   26
But, howsoever, strange and admirable.   27

*Enter lovers: Lysander, Demetrius, Hermia, and
Helena.*

THESEUS
Here come the lovers, full of joy and mirth.
Joy, gentle friends! Joy and fresh days of love
Accompany your hearts!

LYSANDER   More than to us
Wait in your royal walks, your board, your bed!

THESEUS
Come now, what masques, what dances shall we
have,   32
To wear away this long age of three hours
Between our after-supper and bedtime?
Where is our usual manager of mirth?
What revels are in hand? Is there no play
To ease the anguish of a torturing hour?
Call Philostrate.

PHILOSTRATE   Here, mighty Theseus.

THESEUS
Say, what abridgment have you for this evening?   39
What masque? What music? How shall we beguile
The lazy time, if not with some delight?

---

8 discharge perform   **9 wit** intellect   **11 person** appearance   **14 a
. . . naught** a shameful thing   **17–18 we . . . men** i.e., we would
have had our fortunes made   **19–20 sixpence a day** i.e., as a royal
pension   **25 hearts** good fellows   **28 am . . . wonders** have wonders to relate   **32 of** out of   **34 strings** (to attach the beards)
35 pumps light shoes or slippers.   **presently** immediately   **37 preferred** selected for consideration
5.1. Location: Athens. The palace of Theseus.
1 that that which   **2 may** can

3 antique old-fashioned (punning, too, on *antic*, "strange," "grotesque").   **fairy toys** trifling stories about fairies   **5 fantasies** imaginations.   **apprehend** conceive, imagine   **6 comprehends** understands
8 compact formed, composed   **11 Helen's** i.e., of Helen of Troy, pattern of beauty.   **brow of Egypt** i.e., face of a gypsy   **20 bringer** i.e.,
source   **21 fear** object of fear   **25 More . . . images** testifies to
something more substantial than mere imaginings   **26 constancy** certainty   **27 howsoever** in any case.   **admirable** a source of wonder
32 masques courtly entertainments   **39 abridgment** pastime (to
abridge or shorten the evening)

PHILOSTRATE [*giving him a paper*]
  There is a brief how many sports are ripe.   42
  Make choice of which Your Highness will see first.

THESEUS [*reads*]
  "The battle with the Centaurs, to be sung   44
  By an Athenian eunuch to the harp"?
  We'll none of that. That have I told my love,
  In glory of my kinsman Hercules.   47
  [*He reads.*] "The riot of the tipsy Bacchanals,   48
  Tearing the Thracian singer in their rage"?   49
  That is an old device; and it was played   50
  When I from Thebes came last a conqueror.
  [*He reads.*] "The thrice three Muses mourning for the
    death   52
  Of Learning, late deceased in beggary"?   53
  That is some satire, keen and critical,
  Not sorting with a nuptial ceremony.   55
  [*He reads.*] "A tedious brief scene of young Pyramus
  And his love Thisbe; very tragical mirth"?
  Merry and tragical? Tedious and brief?
  That is, hot ice and wondrous strange snow.   59
  How shall we find the concord of this discord?

PHILOSTRATE
  A play there is, my lord, some ten words long,
  Which is as brief as I have known a play;
  But by ten words, my lord, it is too long,
  Which makes it tedious. For in all the play
  There is not one word apt, one player fitted.
  And tragical, my noble lord, it is,
  For Pyramus therein doth kill himself.
  Which, when I saw rehearsed, I must confess,
  Made mine eyes water; but more merry tears
  The passion of loud laughter never shed.

THESEUS   What are they that do play it?

PHILOSTRATE
  Hardhanded men that work in Athens here,
  Which never labored in their minds till now,
  And now have toiled their unbreathed memories   74
  With this same play, against your nuptial.   75

THESEUS
  And we will hear it.

PHILOSTRATE   No, my noble lord,
  It is not for you. I have heard it over,
  And it is nothing, nothing in the world;
  Unless you can find sport in their intents,
  Extremely stretched and conned with cruel pain   80

  To do you service.

THESEUS   I will hear that play;
  For never anything can be amiss
  When simpleness and duty tender it.   83
  Go, bring them in; and take your places, ladies.
    [*Philostrate goes to summon the players.*]

HIPPOLYTA
  I love not to see wretchedness o'ercharged,   85
  And duty in his service perishing.   86

THESEUS
  Why, gentle sweet, you shall see no such thing.

HIPPOLYTA
  He says they can do nothing in this kind.   88

THESEUS
  The kinder we, to give them thanks for nothing.
  Our sport shall be to take what they mistake;
  And what poor duty cannot do, noble respect   91
  Takes it in might, not merit.   92
  Where I have come, great clerks have purposèd   93
  To greet me with premeditated welcomes;
  Where I have seen them shiver and look pale,
  Make periods in the midst of sentences,
  Throttle their practiced accent in their fears,   97
  And in conclusion dumbly have broke off,
  Not paying me a welcome. Trust me, sweet,
  Out of this silence yet I picked a welcome;
  And in the modesty of fearful duty
  I read as much as from the rattling tongue
  Of saucy and audacious eloquence.
  Love, therefore, and tongue-tied simplicity
  In least speak most, to my capacity.   105

      [*Philostrate returns.*]

PHILOSTRATE
  So please Your Grace, the Prologue is addressed.   106

THESEUS   Let him approach.   [*A flourish of trumpets.*]

    Enter the Prologue [*Quince*].

PROLOGUE
  If we offend, it is with our good will.
    That you should think, we come not to offend,
  But with good will. To show our simple skill,
    That is the true beginning of our end.
  Consider, then, we come but in despite.
    We do not come, as minding to content you,   113
  Our true intent is. All for your delight
    We are not here. That you should here repent
    you,
  The actors are at hand; and, by their show,
  You shall know all that you are like to know.

---

42 **brief** short written statement, summary   44 **battle . . . Centaurs** (Probably refers to the battle of the Centaurs and the Lapithae, when the Centaurs attempted to carry off Hippodamia, bride of Theseus' friend Pirothous. The story is told in Ovid's *Metamorphoses* 12.) 47 **kinsman** (Plutarch's "Life of Theseus" states that Hercules and Theseus were near kinsmen. Theseus is referring to a version of the battle of the Centaurs in which Hercules was said to be present.) 48–49 **The riot . . . rage** (This was the story of the death of Orpheus, as told in *Metamorphoses* 11.)   50 **device** show, performance 52–53 **The thrice . . . beggary** (Possibly an allusion to Spenser's *Teares of the Muses,* 1591, though "satires" deploring the neglect of learning and the creative arts were commonplace.)   55 **sorting with** befitting   59 **strange** (Sometimes emended to an adjective that would contrast with *snow,* just as *hot* contrasts with *ice.*)   74 **toiled** taxed. **unbreathed** unexercised   75 **against** in preparation for   80 **stretched** strained. **conned** memorized

83 **simpleness** simplicity   85 **wretchedness o'ercharged** social or intellectual inferiors overburdened   86 **his service** its attempt to serve 88 **kind** kind of thing   91 **respect** evaluation, consideration 92 **Takes . . . merit** values it for the effort made rather than for the excellence achieved   93 **clerks** learned men   97 **practiced accent** i.e., rehearsed speech; or, usual way of speaking   105 **least** i.e., saying least. **to my capacity** in my judgment and understanding 106 **Prologue** speaker of the prologue. **addressed** ready   113 **minding** intending

THESEUS   This fellow doth not stand upon points. 118

LYSANDER   He hath rid his prologue like a rough colt; 119
he knows not the stop. A good moral, my lord: it is not 120
enough to speak, but to speak true.

HIPPOLYTA   Indeed, he hath played on his prologue like
a child on a recorder: a sound, but not in government. 123

THESEUS   His speech was like a tangled chain: nothing 124
impaired, but all disordered. Who is next?

*Enter Pyramus [Bottom], and Thisbe [Flute], and
Wall [Snout], and Moonshine [Starveling], and
Lion [Snug].*

PROLOGUE
Gentles, perchance you wonder at this show;
    But wonder on, till truth make all things plain.
This man is Pyramus, if you would know;
    This beauteous lady Thisbe is, certain.
This man with lime and roughcast doth present
    Wall, that vile wall which did these lovers sunder;
And through Wall's chink, poor souls, they are
        content
    To whisper. At the which let no man wonder.
This man, with lantern, dog, and bush of thorn,
    Presenteth Moonshine; for, if you will know,
By moonshine did these lovers think no scorn 136
    To meet at Ninus' tomb, there, there to woo.
This grisly beast, which Lion hight by name, 138
    The trusty Thisbe coming first by night
Did scare away, or rather did affright;
    And as she fled, her mantle she did fall, 141
    Which Lion vile with bloody mouth did stain.
Anon comes Pyramus, sweet youth and tall, 143
    And finds his trusty Thisbe's mantle slain;
Whereat, with blade, with bloody, blameful blade,
    He bravely broached his boiling bloody breast. 146
And Thisbe, tarrying in mulberry shade,
    His dagger drew, and died. For all the rest,
Let Lion, Moonshine, Wall, and lovers twain
At large discourse, while here they do remain. 150

Exeunt Lion, Thisbe, and Moonshine.

THESEUS   I wonder if the lion be to speak.

DEMETRIUS   No wonder, my lord. One lion may, when
many asses do.

WALL
In this same interlude it doth befall 154
That I, one Snout by name, present a wall;
And such a wall as I would have you think
That had in it a crannied hole or chink,
Through which the lovers, Pyramus and Thisbe,
Did whisper often, very secretly.
This loam, this roughcast, and this stone doth show

That I am that same wall; the truth is so.
And this the cranny is, right and sinister, 162
Through which the fearful lovers are to whisper.

THESEUS   Would you desire lime and hair to speak
better?

DEMETRIUS   It is the wittiest partition that ever I heard 166
discourse, my lord.

[Pyramus comes forward.]

THESEUS   Pyramus draws near the wall. Silence!

PYRAMUS
O grim-looked night! O night with hue so black! 169
    O night, which ever art when day is not!
O night, O night! Alack, alack, alack,
    I fear my Thisbe's promise is forgot.
And thou, O wall, O sweet, O lovely wall,
    That stand'st between her father's ground and
        mine,
Thou wall, O wall, O sweet and lovely wall,
    Show me thy chink, to blink through with mine
        eyne.   *[Wall makes a chink with his fingers.]*
Thanks, courteous wall. Jove shield thee well for
        this.
    But what see I? No Thisbe do I see.
O wicked wall, through whom I see no bliss!
    Cursed be thy stones for thus deceiving me!

THESEUS   The wall, methinks, being sensible, should 181
curse again. 182

PYRAMUS   No, in truth, sir, he should not. "Deceiving
me" is Thisbe's cue: she is to enter now, and I am to
spy her through the wall. You shall see, it will fall pat 185
as I told you. Yonder she comes.

Enter Thisbe.

THISBE
O wall, full often hast thou heard my moans
    For parting my fair Pyramus and me.
My cherry lips have often kissed thy stones,
    Thy stones with lime and hair knit up in thee.

PYRAMUS
I see a voice. Now will I to the chink,
    To spy an I can hear my Thisbe's face. 192
Thisbe!

THISBE   My love! Thou art my love, I think.

PYRAMUS
    Think what thou wilt, I am thy lover's grace, 194
    And like Limander am I trusty still. 195

THISBE
    And I like Helen, till the Fates me kill. 196

PYRAMUS
Not Shafalus to Procrus was so true. 197

THISBE
As Shafalus to Procrus, I to you.

---

118 **stand upon points** (1) heed niceties or small points (2) pay attention to punctuation in his reading. (The humor of Quince's speech is
in the blunders of its punctuation.)   119 **rid** ridden.   **rough** unbroken
120 **stop** (1) stopping of a colt by reining it in (2) punctuation mark
123 **recorder** wind instrument like a flute.   **government** control
124 **nothing** not at all   136 **think no scorn** think it no disgraceful
matter   138 **hight** is called   141 **fall** let fall   143 **tall** courageous
146 **broached** stabbed   150 **At large** in full, at length   154 **interlude**
play

162 **right and sinister** i.e., the right side of it and the left; or, running
from right to left, horizontally   166 **partition** (1) wall (2) section of a
learned treatise or oration   169 **grim-looked** grim-looking   181 **sensible** capable of feeling   182 **again** in return   185 **pat** exactly
192 **an** if   194 **lover's grace** i.e., gracious lover   195,
196 **Limander, Helen** (Blunders for "Leander" and "Hero.")
197 **Shafalus, Procrus** (Blunders for "Cephalus" and "Procris," also
famous lovers.)

PYRAMUS

O, kiss me through the hole of this vile wall!

THISBE

I kiss the wall's hole, not your lips at all.

PYRAMUS

Wilt thou at Ninny's tomb meet me straightway?

THISBE

'Tide life, 'tide death, I come without delay.   202

[Exeunt Pyramus and Thisbe.]

WALL

Thus have I, Wall, my part dischargèd so;

And, being done, thus Wall away doth go.   *[Exit.]*

THESEUS   Now is the mural down between the two neighbors.

DEMETRIUS   No remedy, my lord, when walls are so willful to hear without warning.   208

HIPPOLYTA   This is the silliest stuff that ever I heard.

THESEUS   The best in this kind are but shadows; and the worst are no worse, if imagination amend them.   210

HIPPOLYTA   It must be your imagination then, and not theirs.

THESEUS   If we imagine no worse of them than they of themselves, they may pass for excellent men. Here come two noble beasts in, a man and a lion.

Enter Lion and Moonshine.

LION

You, ladies, you, whose gentle hearts do fear

The smallest monstrous mouse that creeps on floor,

May now perchance both quake and tremble here,

When lion rough in wildest rage doth roar.

Then know that I, as Snug the joiner, am

A lion fell, nor else no lion's dam;   222

For, if I should as lion come in strife

Into this place, 'twere pity on my life.

THESEUS A very gentle beast, and of a good conscience.

DEMETRIUS   The very best at a beast, my lord, that e'er I saw.

LYSANDER   This lion is a very fox for his valor.   228

THESEUS   True; and a goose for his discretion.   229

DEMETRIUS   Not so, my lord, for his valor cannot carry his discretion, and the fox carries the goose.

THESEUS   His discretion, I am sure, cannot carry his valor; for the goose carries not the fox. It is well. Leave it to his discretion, and let us listen to the moon.

MOON

This lanthorn doth the hornèd moon present—   235

DEMETRIUS   He should have worn the horns on his head.   236   237

THESEUS   He is no crescent, and his horns are invisible   238
within the circumference.

MOON

This lanthorn doth the hornèd moon present;

Myself the man i' the moon do seem to be.

THESEUS   This is the greatest error of all the rest. The man should be put into the lanthorn. How is it else the man i' the moon?

DEMETRIUS   He dares not come there for the candle, for   245
you see it is already in snuff.   246

HIPPOLYTA   I am aweary of this moon. Would he would change!

THESEUS   It appears, by his small light of discretion, that he is in the wane; but yet, in courtesy, in all reason, we must stay the time.

LYSANDER   Proceed, Moon.

MOON   All that I have to say is to tell you that the lanthorn is the moon, I, the man i' the moon, this thornbush my thornbush, and this dog my dog.

DEMETRIUS   Why, all these should be in the lanthorn, for all these are in the moon. But silence! Here comes Thisbe.

Enter Thisbe.

THISBE

This is old Ninny's tomb. Where is my love?

LION *[roaring]*   O!

DEMETRIUS   Well roared, Lion.

[Thisbe runs off, dropping her mantle.]

THESEUS   Well run, Thisbe.

HIPPOLYTA   Well shone, Moon. Truly, the moon shines with a good grace.

[The Lion worries Thisbe's mantle.]

THESEUS   Well moused, Lion.   265

[Enter Pyramus; exit Lion.]

DEMETRIUS   And then came Pyramus.

LYSANDER   And so the lion vanished.

PYRAMUS

Sweet Moon, I thank thee for thy sunny beams;

I thank thee, Moon, for shining now so bright;

For, by thy gracious, golden, glittering gleams,

I trust to take of truest Thisbe sight.

But stay, O spite!

But mark, poor knight,

What dreadful dole is here?   274

Eyes, do you see?

How can it be?

O dainty duck! O dear!

Thy mantle good,

What, stained with blood?

Approach, ye Furies fell!   280

O Fates, come, come,   281

---

202 **'Tide** betide, come   208 **willful** willing. **without warning** i.e., without warning the parents. (Demetrius makes a joke on the proverb "Walls have ears.")   210 **in this kind** of this sort. **shadows** likenesses, representations   222 **lion fell** fierce lion (with a play on the idea of "lion skin")   228 **is . . . valor** i.e., his valor consists of craftiness and discretion   229 **a goose . . . discretion** i.e., as discreet as a goose, that is, more foolish than discreet   235 **lanthorn** (This original spelling, *lanthorn*, may suggest a play on the *horn* of which lanterns were made and also on a cuckold's horns; however, the spelling *lanthorn* is not used consistently for comic effect in this play or elsewhere. At 5.1.134, for example, the word is *lantern* in the original.)   236–237 **on his head** (as a sign of cuckoldry)

238 **crescent** a waxing moon   245 **for** because of, for fear of   246 **in snuff** (1) offended (2) in need of snuffing or trimming   265 **moused** shaken, torn, bitten   274 **dole** grievous event   280 **Furies** avenging goddesses of Greek myth. **fell** fierce   281 **Fates** the three goddesses (Clotho, Lachesis, Atropos) of Greek myth who spun, drew, and cut the thread of human life

Cut thread and thrum;   282
Quail, crush, conclude, and quell!   283
THESEUS   This passion, and the death of a dear friend,   284
would go near to make a man look sad.   285
HIPPOLYTA   Beshrew my heart, but I pity the man.
PYRAMUS
O, wherefore, Nature, didst thou lions frame?
Since lion vile hath here deflowered my dear,
Which is—no, no, which was—the fairest dame
That lived, that loved, that liked, that looked with
cheer.   290
    Come, tears, confound,
    Out, sword, and wound
The pap of Pyramus;   293
    Ay, that left pap,
    Where heart doth hop.   [He stabs himself.]
Thus die I, thus, thus, thus.
    Now am I dead,
    Now am I fled;
My soul is in the sky.
    Tongue, lose thy light;
    Moon, take thy flight.   [Exit Moonshine.]
Now die, die, die, die, die.   [Pyramus dies.]
DEMETRIUS   No die, but an ace, for him; for he is   303
but one.   304
LYSANDER   Less than an ace, man; for he is dead, he is
nothing.
THESEUS   With the help of a surgeon he might yet
recover, and yet prove an ass.   308
HIPPOLYTA   How chance Moonshine is gone before
Thisbe comes back and finds her lover?
THESEUS   She will find him by starlight.

[Enter Thisbe.]

Here she comes; and her passion ends the play.
HIPPOLYTA   Methinks she should not use a long one for
such a Pyramus. I hope she will be brief.
DEMETRIUS   A mote will turn the balance, which Pyra-   315
mus, which Thisbe, is the better: he for a man, God   316
warrant us; she for a woman, God bless us.
LYSANDER   She hath spied him already with those sweet
eyes.
DEMETRIUS   And thus she means, videlicet: 320
THISBE
    Asleep, my love?
    What, dead, my dove?
O Pyramus, arise!
    Speak, speak. Quite dumb?
    Dead, dead? A tomb

Must cover thy sweet eyes.
    These lily lips,
    This cherry nose,
These yellow cowslip cheeks,
    Are gone, are gone!
    Lovers, make moan.
His eyes were green as leeks.
    O Sisters Three,   333
    Come, come to me,
With hands as pale as milk;
    Lay them in gore,
    Since you have shore   337
With shears his thread of silk.
    Tongue, not a word.
    Come, trusty sword,
Come, blade, my breast imbrue!   341
                        [She stabs herself.]
    And farewell, friends.
    Thus Thisbe ends.
    Adieu, adieu, adieu.   [She dies.]
THESEUS   Moonshine and Lion are left to bury the dead.
DEMETRIUS   Ay, and Wall too.
BOTTOM [starting up, as Flute does also]   No, I assure
you, the wall is down that parted their fathers. Will it
please you to see the epilogue, or to hear a Bergomask   349
dance between two of our company?   350

[The other players enter.]

THESEUS   No epilogue, I pray you; for your play needs
no excuse. Never excuse; for when the players are all
dead, there need none to be blamed. Marry, if he that
writ it had played Pyramus and hanged himself in
Thisbe's garter, it would have been a fine tragedy; and
so it is, truly, and very notably discharged. But, come,
your Bergomask. Let your epilogue alone. [A dance.]
The iron tongue of midnight hath told twelve.   358
Lovers, to bed, 'tis almost fairy time.
I fear we shall outsleep the coming morn
As much as we this night have overwatched.   361
This palpable-gross play hath well beguiled   362
The heavy gait of night. Sweet friends, to bed.   363
A fortnight hold we this solemnity,
In nightly revels and new jollity.   Exeunt.

Enter Puck [carrying a broom].

PUCK
    Now the hungry lion roars,
    And the wolf behowls the moon,
    Whilst the heavy plowman snores,   368
        All with weary task fordone.   369
    Now the wasted brands do glow,   370
        Whilst the screech owl, screeching loud,

282 thread and thrum i.e., everything—the good and bad alike; literally, the warp in weaving and the loose end of the warp 283 Quail
overpower. quell kill, destroy 284–285 This . . . sad i.e., if one
had other reason to grieve, one might be sad, but not from this absurd
portrayal of passion 290 cheer countenance 293 pap breast
303 ace the side of the die featuring the single pip, or spot. (The pun
is on die as a singular of dice; Bottom's performance is not worth a
whole die but rather one single face of it, one small portion.)
304 one (1) an individual person (2) unique 308 ass (with a pun on
ace) 315 mote small particle 315–316 which . . . which whether
. . . or 320 means moans, laments (with a pun on the meaning,
"lodge a formal complaint"). videlicet to wit

333 Sisters Three the Fates 337 shore shorn 341 imbrue stain with
blood 349–350 Bergomask dance a rustic dance named from Bergamo, a province in the state of Venice 358 iron tongue i.e., of a
bell. told counted, struck ("tolled") 361 overwatched stayed up
too late 362 palpable-gross palpably gross, obviously crude
363 heavy drowsy, dull 368 heavy tired 369 fordone exhausted
370 wasted brands burned-out logs

Puts the wretch that lies in woe
   In remembrance of a shroud.
Now it is the time of night
   That the graves, all gaping wide,
Every one lets forth his sprite,   376
   In the church-way paths to glide.
And we fairies, that do run
   By the triple Hecate's team.   379
From the presence of the sun,
   Following darkness like a dream,
Now are frolic. Not a mouse   382
   Shall disturb this hallowed house.
I am sent with broom before,
To sweep the dust behind the door.   385

*Enter [Oberon and Titania,] King and Queen of
Fairies, with all their train.*

OBERON

Through the house give glimmering light,
   By the dead and drowsy fire;
Every elf and fairy sprite
   Hop as light as bird from brier;
And this ditty, after me,
Sing, and dance it trippingly.

TITANIA

First, rehearse your song by rote,   392
To each word a warbling note.
Hand in hand, with fairy grace,
Will we sing, and bless this place.
                    [Song and dance.]

OBERON

Now, until the break of day,
Through this house each fairy stray.
To the best bride-bed will we,
Which by us shall blessèd be;
And the issue there create   400
Ever shall be fortunate.
So shall all the couples three
Ever true in loving be;
And the blots of Nature's hand
Shall not in their issue stand;
Never mole, harelip, nor scar,
Nor mark prodigious, such as are   407
Despisèd in nativity,
Shall upon their children be.
With this field dew consecrate,   410
Every fairy take his gait,   411
And each several chamber bless,   412
Through this palace, with sweet peace;
And the owner of it blest
Ever shall in safety rest.

Trip away; make no stay;
Meet me all by break of day.
      Exeunt [Oberon, Titania, and train].

PUCK [*to the audience*]

If we shadows have offended,
Think but this, and all is mended,
That you have but slumbered here   420
While these visions did appear.
And this weak and idle theme,
No more yielding but a dream,   423
Gentles, do not reprehend.
If you pardon, we will mend.   425
And, as I am an honest Puck,
If we have unearnèd luck
Now to scape the serpent's tongue,   428
We will make amends ere long;
Else the Puck a liar call.
So, good night unto you all.
Give me your hands, if we be friends, 432
And Robin shall restore amends.   *[Exit.]* 433

420 **That . . . here** i.e., that it is a "midsummer night's dream"
423 **No . . . but** yielding no more than   425 **mend** improve
428 **serpent's tongue** i.e., hissing   432 **Give . . . hands** applaud
433 **restore amends** give satisfaction in return

376 **Every . . . sprite** every grave lets forth its ghost   379 **triple He-cate's** (Hecate ruled in three capacities: as Luna or Cynthia in heaven, as Diana on earth, and as Proserpina in hell.)   382 **frolic** merry   385 **behind** from behind, or else like sweeping the dirt under the carpet. (Robin Goodfellow was a household spirit who helped good housemaids and punished lazy ones, but he could, of course, be mischievous.)   392 **rehearse** recite   400 **create** created   407 **pro-digious** monstrous, unnatural   410 **consecrate** consecrated   411 **take his gait** go his way   412 **several** separate

The Merchant of Venice

Although Shylock is the most prominent character in *The Merchant of Venice,* he takes part in neither the beginning nor the ending of the play. And, although the play's title might seem to suggest that he is the "merchant" of Venice, Shylock is, strictly speaking, a moneylender whose usury is portrayed as the very opposite of true commerce. His vengeful struggle to obtain a pound of flesh from Antonio contrasts with the various romantic episodes woven together in this play: Bassanio's choosing of Portia by means of the caskets, Gratiano's wooing of Nerissa, Jessica's elopement with Lorenzo, Lancelot Gobbo's changing of masters, and the episode of the rings. In all these stories, friendship and love triumph over faithlessness and hatred. However much we may come to sympathize with Shylock's misfortunes and question the motives of his enemies, and however much we are made uncomfortable by the insularity of a Venetian ethic that has no genuine place for non-Christians or cultural outsiders, Shylock remains essentially the villain of a love comedy. His remorseless pursuit of Antonio darkens the mood of the play, and his overthrow signals the providential triumph of love and friendship, even though that triumph is not without its undercurrent of wry melancholy. Before we examine the painful issue of anti-Semitism more closely, we need to establish the structural context of this love comedy as a whole.

Like many of Shakespeare's philosophical and festive comedies, *The Merchant of Venice* presents two contrasting worlds—one idealized and the other marked by conflict and anxiety. To an extent, these contrasting worlds can be identified with the locations of Belmont and Venice. Belmont, to which the various happy lovers and their friends eventually retire, is a place of magic and love. As its name implies, it is on a mountain, and it is reached by a journey across water. It is pure, serene, ethereal. As often happens in fairy stories, on this mountain dwells a princess who must be won by means of a riddling contest. We usually see Belmont at night. Music surrounds it, and women preside over it. Even its caskets, houses, and rings are essentially feminine symbols. Venice, on the other hand, is a place of bustle and economic competition, seen most characteristically in the heat of the day. It lies low and flat, at a point where rivers reach the sea. Men preside over its contentious marketplace and its haggling law courts. Actually, the opposition of Venice and Belmont is not quite so clear-cut: Venice contains much compassionate friendship, whereas Belmont is subject to the arbitrary command of Portia's dead father. (Portia somewhat resembles Jessica in being imprisoned by her father's will.) Even though Portia descends to Venice in the angelic role of mercy giver, she also remains very human: sharp-tongued and even venomous in caricaturing her unwelcome wooers, crafty in her legal maneuvering, saucily prankish in her torturing of Bassanio about the rings. Nevertheless, the polarity of two contrasting localities and two groups of characters is vividly real in this play.

The play's opening scene, from which Shylock is excluded, sets forth the interrelated themes of friendship, romantic love, and risk or "hazard." The merchant who seemingly fulfills the title role, Antonio, is the victim of a mysterious melancholy. He is wealthy enough and surrounded by friends, but something is missing from his life. He assures his solicitous companions that he has no financial worries, for he has been too careful to trust all his cargoes to one sea vessel. Antonio, in fact, has no idea why he is so sad. The question is haunting. What is the matter? Perhaps the answer is to be found in a paradox: those who strive to prosper in the world's terms are doomed to frustration, not because prosperity will necessarily elude them, but because it will not satisfy the spirit. "You have too much respect upon the world," argues the carefree Gratiano. "They lose it that do buy it with much care" (1.1.74–75). Portia and Jessica, too, are at first afflicted by a melancholy that stems from the incompleteness of living isolated lives, with insufficient opportunities for love and sacrifice. They must learn, as Antonio learns with the help of his dear friend Bassanio, to seek happiness by daring to risk everything for friendship. Antonio's risk is most extreme: only when he has thrown away concern for his life can he discover what there is to live for.

At first, Bassanio's request for assistance seems just as materialistic as the worldliness from which Antonio suffers. Bassanio proposes to marry a rich young lady, Portia, in order to recoup his fortune lost through prodigality, and he needs money from Antonio so that he may woo Portia in proper fashion. She is "richly left," the heiress of a dead father, a golden fleece for whom this new Jason will make a quest. Bassanio's adventure is partly commercial. Yet his pilgrimage for Portia is magnanimous as well. The occasional modern practice of playing Bassanio and Portia as cynical antiheroes of a "black" comedy points up the problematic character of their materialism and calculation, but it gives only one aspect of the portrayal. Bassanio has lost his previous fortune through the amiable faults of reckless generosity and a lack of concern for financial prudence. The money he must now borrow, and the fortune he hopes to acquire, are to him no more than a means to carefree happiness. Although Portia's rich dowry is a strong consideration, he describes her also as "fair and, fairer than that word, / Of wondrous virtues" (1.1.162–163). Moreover, he enjoys the element of risk in wooing her. It is like shooting a second arrow in order to recover one that has been lost—double or nothing. This gamble, or "hazard," involves risk for Antonio as well as for Bassanio, and it ultimately brings a double reward to them both—spiritual as well as financial. Unless one recognizes these aspects of Bassanio's quest, as well as the clear fairy-tale quality with which Shakespeare deliberately invests this part of the plot, one cannot properly assess Bassanio's role in this romantic comedy.

Bassanio's quest for Portia can, in fact, never succeed until he disavows the very financial considerations that brought him to Belmont in the first place. This is the paradox of the riddle of the three caskets, an ancient parable stressing the need for choosing by true substance rather than by outward show. To choose "what many men desire," as the Prince of Morocco does, is to pin one's hopes on worldly wealth; to believe that one "deserves" good fortune, as the Prince of Aragon does, is to reveal a fatal pride in one's own merit. Bassanio perceives that, in order to win true love, he must "give and hazard all he hath" (2.7.9). He is not "deceived with ornament" (3.2.74). Just as Antonio must risk all for friendship, and just as Bassanio himself must later be willing to risk losing Portia for the sake of true friendship (in the episode of the rings), Bassanio must renounce worldly ambition and beauty before he can be rewarded with success. Paradoxically, only those who learn to subdue such worldly desires may then legitimately enjoy the world's pleasures. Only they have acknowledged the hierarchical subservience of the flesh to the spirit. These are the philosophical truisms of Renaissance Neoplatonism, depicting love as a chain or ladder from the basest carnality to the supreme love of God for humanity. On this ladder, perfect friendship and spiritual union are more sublimely Godlike than sexual fulfillment. This idealism may seem a strange doctrine for Bassanio the fortune hunter, but, actually, its conventional wisdom simply confirms his role as romantic hero. He and Portia are not denied worldly happiness or erotic pleasure; they are merely asked to give first thought to their Christian duty in marriage.

For Portia, marriage represents both a gain and a loss. She can choose only by her dead father's will; the patriarchal system, according to which a woman is given in marriage by her father to a younger man, is seemingly able to extend its control even beyond the grave. The prospect of marrying the Prince of Morocco or the Prince of Aragon dismays her, and yet she persists in her vow of obedience and is eventually rewarded by the man of her choice. It is as though the benign father knew how to set the terms of choice in such a way that the "lottery" of the caskets would turn out right for her. When she accepts Bassanio, too, she must make a dif-

ficult choice, for in legal terms she makes Bassanio master over everything she owns. Portia is at once spirited and submissive, able to straighten out Venice's legal tangles when all the men have failed and yet ready to call Bassanio her lord. Her teasing him about the ring is a sign that she will make demands of him in marriage, but it is a testing that cannot produce lasting disharmony so long as Bassanio is truly loyal. Portia is, from Bassanio's male point of view, the perfect woman: humanly attainable and yet never seriously threatening. Guided by her, Bassanio makes the potentially hazardous transition from the male-oriented friendships of Venice (especially with Antonio) to heterosexual union. Portia is more fortunate than Jessica, who must break with her faith and her father in order to find marital happiness. The two women are alike, however, in that they experience the play's central paradox of losing the world in order to gain the world. Through them, we see that this paradox illuminates the casket episode, the struggle for the pound of flesh, the elopement of Jessica, the ring episode, and even the comic foolery of Lancelot Gobbo.

Shylock, in his quest for the pound of flesh, represents a denial of all the paradoxical truths just described. As a usurer, he refuses to lend money interest-free in the name of friendship. Instead of taking risks, he insists on his bond. He spurns mercy and demands strict justice. By calculating all his chances too craftily, he appears to win at first but must eventually lose all. He has "too much respect upon the world" (1.1.74). His God is the Old Testament God of Moses, the God of wrath, the God of the Ten Commandments, with their forbidding emphasis on "Thou shalt not." (This oversimplified contrast between Judaism and Christianity was commonplace in Shakespeare's time.) Shylock abhors stealing but admires equivocation as a means of outmaneuvering a competitor; he approvingly cites Jacob's ruse to deprive Laban of his sheep (1.3.69–88). Any tactic is permissible so long as it falls within the realm of legality and contract.

Shylock's ethical outlook, then, justifies both usury and the old dispensation of the Jewish law. The two are philosophically combined, just as usury and Judaism had become equated in the popular imagination of Renaissance Europe. Even though lending at interest was becoming increasingly necessary and common, old prejudices against it still persisted. Angry moralists pointed out that the New Testament had condemned usury and that Aristotle had described money as barren. To breed money was therefore regarded as unnatural. Usury was considered sinful because it did not involve the usual risks of commerce; the lender was assured against loss of his principal by the posting of collateral and, at the same time, was sure to earn a handsome interest. The usurer seemed to be getting something for nothing. For these reasons, usury was sometimes declared illegal. Its practitioners were viewed as corrupt and grasping, hated as misers. In some European countries, Jews were permitted to practice this un-Christian living (and permitted to do very little else) and then, hypocritically, were detested for performing un-Christian deeds. Ironically, the moneylenders of England were Christians, and few Jews were to be found in any professions. Nominally excluded since Edward I's reign, the Jews had returned in small numbers to London but did not practice their Judaism openly. They attended Anglican services as required by law and then worshiped in private, relatively undisturbed by the authorities. Shylock may not be based on observation from London life. He is derived from continental tradition and reflects a widespread conviction that Jews and usurers were alike in being un-Christian and sinister.

Shylock is unquestionably sinister. On the Elizabethan stage, he apparently wore a red beard like Judas and had a hooked nose. He bears an "ancient grudge" against Antonio simply because Antonio is "a Christian." We recognize in Shylock the archetype of the supposed Jew who wishes to kill a Christian and obtain his flesh. In early medieval anti-Semitic legends of this sort, the flesh thus obtained was imagined to be eaten ritually during Passover. Because some Jews had once persecuted Christ, all were unfairly presumed to be implacable enemies of all Christians. These anti-Semitic superstitions were likely to erupt into hysteria at any time, as in 1594 when Dr. Roderigo Lopez, a Portuguese Jewish physician, was accused of having plotted against the life of Queen Elizabeth and of Don Antonio, pretender to the Portuguese throne. Christopher Marlowe's The Jew of Malta was revived for this occasion, enjoying an unusually successful run of fifteen performances, and scholars have often wondered if Shakespeare's play was not written under the same impetus. On this score, the evidence is inconclusive, and the play might have been written any time between 1594 and 1598 (when it is mentioned by Francis Meres), but, in any case, Shakespeare has made no attempt to avoid the anti-Semitic nature of his story.

To offset the portrayal of Jewish villainy, however, the play also dramatizes the possibility of conversion to Christianity, suggesting that Judaism is more a matter of benighted faith than of ethnic origin. Converted Jews were not new on the stage: they had appeared in medieval cycle drama, in the Croxton Play of the Sacrament (late fifteenth century), and more recently in The Jew of Malta, in which Barabas' daughter Abigail falls in love with a Christian and eventually becomes a nun. Shylock's daughter Jessica similarly embraces Christianity as Lorenzo's wife and is received into the happy comradeship of Belmont. Shylock is forced to accept Christianity, presumably for the benefit of his eternal soul (though today we find this deeply offensive, and it is sometimes cut from stage productions). Earlier in the play, Antonio repeatedly indicates his willingness to befriend Shylock if the latter will only give up usury, and he is even cautiously hopeful when Shylock offers him an interest-free loan: "The Hebrew will turn Christian; he grows kind" (1.3.177). To be sure, Antonio's denunciation of Shylock's usurious Judaism has been vehement and personal; we learn that he has spat on Shylock's gaberdine and kicked him as one would kick a dog. This violent disapproval offers no opportunity for the toleration of cultural and religious differences that we expect today from people of good will, but at least Antonio is prepared to accept Shylock if Shylock will embrace the Christian faith and its ethical responsibilities. Whether the play itself endorses Antonio's Christian point of view as normative or insists on a darker reading by making us uneasy with intolerance is a matter of unceasing critical debate. Quite possibly, the play's power to disturb emanates—at least in part—from the dramatic conflict of irreconcilable sets of values.

To Antonio, then, as well as to other Venetians, true Christianity is both an absolute good from which no deviation is possible without evil and a state of faith to which aliens may turn by abjuring the benighted creeds of their ancestors. By this token, the Prince of Morocco is condemned to failure in his quest for Portia, not so much because he is black as because he is an infidel, one who worships "blind fortune" and therefore chooses a worldly rather than a spiritual reward. Although Portia pertly dismisses him with "Let all of his complexion choose me so" (2.7.79), she professes earlier to find him handsome and agrees that he should not be judged by his complexion (2.1.13–22). Unless she is merely being hypocritical, she means by her later remark that black-skinned people are generally infidels, just as Jews are as a group un-Christian. Such pejorative thinking about persons as types is no doubt distressing and suggests—at least to a modern audience—the cultural limitation of Portia's view, but, in any case, it shows her to be no less well disposed toward black suitors than toward others who are also alien. She is glad not to be won by the Prince of Aragon because he, too, though nominally a Christian, is too self-satisfied and proud. All persons, therefore, may aspire to truly virtuous conduct, and those who choose virtue are equally blessed; however, the terms of defining that ideal in this play are essentially Christian. Jews and blacks may rise spiritually only by abandoning their pagan creeds for the new dispensation of charity and forgiveness.

The superiority of Christian teaching to the older Jewish dispensation was, of course, a widely accepted notion of Shakespeare's time. After all, these were the years when people fought and died to maintain their religious beliefs. Today, the notion of a single true church is less widely held, and we have difficulty understanding why anyone would wish to force conversion on Shylock. Modern productions find it tempting to portray Shylock as a victim of bigotry and to put great stress on his heartrending assertions of his humanity: "Hath not a Jew eyes? . . . If you prick us, do we not bleed?" (3.1.55–61). Shylock does indeed suffer from his enemies, and his sufferings add a tortured complexity to this play—even, one suspects, for an Elizabethan audience.

Those who profess Christianity must surely examine their own motives and conduct. Is it right to steal treasure from Shylock's house along with his eloped daughter? Is it considerate of Jessica and Lorenzo to squander Shylock's turquoise ring, the gift of his wife Leah, on a monkey? Does Shylock's vengeful insistence on law justify the quibbling countermeasures devised by Portia even as she piously declaims about mercy? Do Shylock's misfortunes deserve the mirthful parodies of Solanio ("My daughter! O my ducats!") or the hostile jeering of Gratiano at the conclusion of the trial? Because he stands outside Christian faith, Shylock can provide a perspective whereby we see the hypocrisies of those who profess a higher ethical code. Nevertheless, Shylock's compulsive desire for vengeance according to an Old Testament code of an eye for an eye cannot be justified by the wrongdoings of any particular Christian. In the play's control of an ethical point of view, such deeds condemn the doer rather than undermine the Christian standards of true virtue as ideally expressed. Shakespeare humanizes Shylock by portraying him as a believable and sensitive man, and he shows much that is to be regretted in Shylock's Christian antagonists, but he also allows Shylock to place himself in the wrong by his refusal to forgive his enemies.

Shylock thus loses everything through his effort to win everything on his own terms. His daughter, Jessica, by her elopement, follows an opposite course. She characterizes her father's home as "hell," and she resents being locked up behind closed windows. Shylock detests music and the sounds of merriment; Jessica's new life in Belmont is immersed in music. He is old, suspicious, miserly; she is young, loving, adventurous. Most important, she seems to be at least part Christian when we first see her. As Lancelot jests half in earnest, "If a Christian did not play the knave and get thee, I am much deceived" (2.3.11–12). Her removal from Shylock's house involves theft, and her running from Venice is, she confesses, an "unthrift love." Paradoxically, however, she sees this recklessness as of more blessed effect than her father's legalistic caution. As she says, "I shall be saved by my husband. He hath made me a Christian" (3.5.17–18).

Lancelot Gobbo's clowning offers a similarly paradoxical comment on the tragedy of Shylock. Lancelot debates whether or not to leave Shylock's service in terms of a soul struggle between his conscience and the devil (2.2.1–29). Conscience bids him stay, for service is a debt, a bond, an obligation, whereas abandonment of one's indenture is a kind of rebellion or stealing away. Yet Shylock's house is "hell" to Lancelot as it is to Jessica. Comparing his new master with his old, Lancelot observes to Bassanio, "You have the grace of God, sir, and he hath enough." Service with Bassanio involves imprudent risks, since Bassanio is a spendthrift. The miserly Shylock rejoices to see the ever hungry Lancelot, this "huge feeder," wasting the substance of a hated Christian. Once again, however, Shylock will lose ev-

erything in his grasping quest for security. Another spiritual renewal occurs when Lancelot encounters his old and nearly blind father (2.2). In a scene echoing the biblical stories of the Prodigal Son and of Jacob and Esau, Lancelot teases the old man with false rumors of Lancelot's own death in order to make their reunion seem all the more unexpected and precious. The illusion of loss gives way to joy: Lancelot is, in language adapted from the liturgy, "your boy that was, your son that is, your child that shall be."

In the episode of the rings, we encounter a final playful variation on the paradox of winning through losing. Portia and Nerissa cleverly present their new husbands with a cruel choice: disguised as a doctor of law and his clerk, who have just saved the life of Antonio from Shylock's wrath, the two wives ask nothing more for their services than the rings they see on the fingers of Bassanio and Gratiano. The two husbands, who have vowed never to part with these wedding rings, must therefore choose between love and friendship. Portia knows well enough that Bassanio's obedience to the Neoplatonic ideal of disinterested friendship is an essential part of his virtue. Just as he previously renounced beauty and riches before he could deserve Portia, he must now risk losing her for friendship's sake. The testing of the husbands' constancy does border at times on gratuitous harshness and exercise of power, for it deals with the oldest of masculine nightmares: cuckoldry. Wives are not without weapons in the struggle for control in marriage, and Portia and Nerissa enjoy trapping their new husbands in a no-win situation. Still, the threat is easily resolved by the dispelling of farcically mistaken identities. The young men have been tricked into bestowing their rings on their wives for a second time in the name of perfect friendship, thereby confirming a relationship that is both platonic and fleshly. As Gratiano bawdily points out in the play's last line, the ring is both a spiritual and a sexual symbol of marriage. The resolution of this illusory quarrel also brings to an end the merry battle of the sexes between wives and husbands. Having hinted at the sorts of misunderstandings that afflict even the best of human relationships and having proved themselves wittily able to torture and deceive their husbands, Portia and Nerissa submit at last to the patriarchal norms of their age and to the authority of Bassanio and Gratiano.

As defined by the accepted notions of gender relations in Shakespeare's time, then, all appears to be in harmony in Belmont. The disorders of Venice have been left far behind, however imperfectly they may have been resolved. Jessica and Lorenzo contrast their present happiness with the sufferings of less fortunate lovers of long ago: Troilus and Cressida, Pyramus and Thisbe, Aeneas and Dido, Jason and Medea. The tranquil joy found in Belmont is attuned to the music of the spheres, the singing of the "young-eyed cherubins" (5.1.62), although with a proper Christian humility the lovers also realize that the harmony of immortal souls is infinitely beyond their comprehension. Bound in by the grossness of the flesh, "this muddy vesture of decay" (5.1.64), they can only reach toward the bliss of eternity through music and the perfect friendship of true love. Even in their final joy, accordingly, the lovers find an incompleteness that lends a wistful and slightly melancholy reflective tone to the play's ending. That sense of imperfection is accentuated for us by our awareness that the play's serious problems of gender relations, friendship, and anti-Semitism have by no means been fully resolved; the final concord is one that arises out of discord. Even so, this concluding sense of the unavoidable incompleteness of all human life is of a very different order from that earlier melancholy of isolation and lack of commitment experienced by Portia, Jessica, Antonio, and others.

The Merchant of Venice

[*Dramatis Personae*

THE DUKE OF VENICE
ANTONIO, *a merchant of Venice*
BASSANIO, *his friend, suitor to Portia*
GRATIANO, *a follower of Bassanio, in love with Nerissa*
SOLANIO,
SALERIO,} *friends to Antonio and Bassanio*
LORENZO, *in love with Jessica*
LEONARDO, *servant to Bassanio*

PORTIA, *a rich heiress of Belmont*
NERISSA, *her waiting-gentlewoman*
BALTHASAR, *servant to Portia*
STEPHANO, *servant to Portia*
THE PRINCE OF MOROCCO, *suitor to Portia*
THE PRINCE OF ARAGON, *suitor to Portia*
A MESSENGER *to Portia*

SHYLOCK, *a rich Jew*
JESSICA, *his daughter*
TUBAL, *a Jew, Shylock's friend*
LANCELOT GOBBO, *a clown, servant to Shylock and then to Bassanio*
OLD GOBBO, *Lancelot's father*

Magnificoes of Venice, Officers of the Court of Justice, Jailor, Servants to Portia, and other Attendants

SCENE: *Partly at Venice and partly at Belmont, the seat of Portia*]

1.1   *Enter Antonio, Salerio, and Solanio.*

ANTONIO
In sooth, I know not why I am so sad.   1
It wearies me, you say it wearies you;
But how I caught it, found it, or came by it,
What stuff 'tis made of, whereof it is born,
I am to learn;   5
And such a want-wit sadness makes of me   6
That I have much ado to know myself.

1.1. Location: A street in Venice.
1 sad morose, dismal-looking   **5 am to learn** have yet to learn
6 such . . . of me sadness makes me so distracted, lacking in good sense

SALERIO
Your mind is tossing on the ocean,
There where your argosies with portly sail,   9
Like signors and rich burghers on the flood,   10
Or as it were the pageants of the sea,   11
Do overpeer the petty traffickers   12
That curtsy to them, do them reverence,   13
As they fly by them with their woven wings.

SOLANIO
Believe me, sir, had I such venture forth,   15
The better part of my affections would
Be with my hopes abroad. I should be still   17
Plucking the grass to know where sits the wind,
Peering in maps for ports and piers and roads;   19
And every object that might make me fear
Misfortune to my ventures, out of doubt
Would make me sad.

SALERIO   My wind cooling my broth
Would blow me to an ague when I thought   23
What harm a wind too great might do at sea.
I should not see the sandy hourglass run
But I should think of shallows and of flats,   26
And see my wealthy *Andrew* docked in sand,   27
Vailing her high-top lower than her ribs   28
To kiss her burial. Should I go to church   29
And see the holy edifice of stone
And not bethink me straight of dangerous rocks   31
Which, touching but my gentle vessel's side,
Would scatter all her spices on the stream,
Enrobe the roaring waters with my silks,
And, in a word, but even now worth this,   35
And now worth nothing? Shall I have the thought
To think on this, and shall I lack the thought
That such a thing bechanced would make me sad?   38
But tell not me. I know Antonio
Is sad to think upon his merchandise.

ANTONIO
Believe me, no. I thank my fortune for it,
My ventures are not in one bottom trusted,   42
Nor to one place; nor is my whole estate
Upon the fortune of this present year.   44
Therefore my merchandise makes me not sad.

SOLANIO
Why then, you are in love.

ANTONIO   Fie, fie!

SOLANIO
Not in love neither? Then let us say you are sad

Because you are not merry; and 'twere as easy
For you to laugh and leap, and say you are merry
Because you are not sad. Now, by two-headed
Janus,   50
Nature hath framed strange fellows in her time:
Some that will evermore peep through their eyes   52
And laugh like parrots at a bagpiper,   53
And other of such vinegar aspect   54
That they'll not show their teeth in way of smile
Though Nestor swear the jest be laughable.   56

Enter Bassanio, Lorenzo, and Gratiano.

Here comes Bassanio, your most noble kinsman,
Gratiano, and Lorenzo. Fare ye well.
We leave you now with better company.

SALERIO
I would have stayed till I had made you merry,
If worthier friends had not prevented me.   61

ANTONIO
Your worth is very dear in my regard.
I take it your own business calls on you,
And you embrace th' occasion to depart.   64

SALERIO   Good morrow, my good lords.

BASSANIO
Good signors both, when shall we laugh? Say,
when?   66
You grow exceeding strange. Must it be so?   67

SALERIO
We'll make our leisures to attend on yours.   68
           Exeunt Salerio and Solanio.

LORENZO
My lord Bassanio, since you have found Antonio,
We two will leave you, but at dinnertime,
I pray you, have in mind where we must meet.

BASSANIO   I will not fail you.

GRATIANO
You look not well, Signor Antonio.
You have too much respect upon the world.   74
They lose it that do buy it with much care.
Believe me, you are marvelously changed.

ANTONIO
I hold the world but as the world, Gratiano—
A stage where every man must play a part,
And mine a sad one.

GRATIANO   Let me play the fool.
With mirth and laughter let old wrinkles come,
And let my liver rather heat with wine   81
Than my heart cool with mortifying groans.   82

---

9 argosies large merchant ships. (So named from *Ragusa*, the modern city of Dubrovnik.)   **portly** majestic   **10 signors** gentlemen   **11 pageants** mobile stages used in plays or processions   **12 overpeer** look down upon   **13 curtsy** i.e., bob up and down, or lower topsails in token of respect (*reverence*)   **15 venture forth** investment risked   **17 still** continually   **19 roads** anchorages, open harbors   **23 blow . . . ague** i.e., start me shivering   **26 But** without it happening that. **flats** shoals   **27 Andrew** name of a ship (perhaps after the *St. Andrew*, a Spanish galleon captured at Cadiz in 1596)   **28 Vailing** lowering. (Usually as a sign of submission.)   **high-top** topmast   **29 burial** burial place.   **Should I** if I should   **31 bethink me straight** be put in mind immediately   **35 even now** a short while ago.   **this** i.e., the cargo of spices and silks   **38 bechanced** having happened   **42 bottom** ship's hold   **44 Upon . . . year** i.e., risked upon the chance of the present year

50 two-headed Janus a Roman god of all beginnings, represented by a figure with two faces   **52 peep . . . eyes** i.e., look with eyes narrowed by laughter   **53 at a bagpiper** i.e., even at a bagpiper, whose music was regarded as melancholic   **54 other** others. **vinegar aspect** sour, sullen looks   **56 Nestor** venerable senior officer in the *Iliad*, noted for gravity   **61 prevented** forestalled   **64 occasion** opportunity   **66 laugh** i.e., be merry together   **67 strange** distant.   **Must it be so** must you go? or, must you show reserve?   **68 attend on** wait upon, i.e., suit   **74 respect . . . world** concern for worldly affairs of business   **81 heat with wine** (The liver was regarded as the seat of the passions and wine as an agency for inflaming them.)   **82 mortifying** penitential and deadly. (Sighs were thought to cost the heart a drop of blood.)

Why should a man whose blood is warm within
Sit like his grandsire cut in alabaster?   84
Sleep when he wakes, and creep into the jaundice   85
By being peevish? I tell thee what, Antonio—
I love thee, and 'tis my love that speaks—
There are a sort of men whose visages
Do cream and mantle like a standing pond,   89
And do a willful stillness entertain   90
With purpose to be dressed in an opinion   91
Of wisdom, gravity, profound conceit,   92
As who should say, "I am Sir Oracle,   93
And when I ope my lips let no dog bark!"   94
O my Antonio, I do know of these
That therefore only are reputed wise
For saying nothing, when, I am very sure,
If they should speak, would almost damn those ears   98
Which, hearing them, would call their brothers
    fools.   99
I'll tell thee more of this another time.
But fish not with this melancholy bait   101
For this fool gudgeon, this opinion.—   102
Come, good Lorenzo.—Fare ye well awhile.
I'll end my exhortation after dinner.
LORENZO [to Antonio and Bassanio]
Well, we will leave you then till dinnertime.
I must be one of these same dumb wise men,   106
For Gratiano never lets me speak.
GRATIANO
Well, keep me company but two years more,   108
Thou shalt not know the sound of thine own
    tongue.
ANTONIO
Fare you well. I'll grow a talker for this gear.   110
GRATIANO
Thanks, i' faith, for silence is only commendable
In a neat's tongue dried and a maid not vendible.   112
              Exeunt [Gratiano and Lorenzo].
ANTONIO   Is that anything now?   113
BASSANIO   Gratiano speaks an infinite deal of nothing,
more than any man in all Venice. His reasons are as   115
two grains of wheat hid in two bushels of chaff; you
shall seek all day ere you find them, and when you
have them they are not worth the search.
ANTONIO
Well, tell me now what lady is the same   119

To whom you swore a secret pilgrimage,
That you today promised to tell me of.
BASSANIO
'Tis not unknown to you, Antonio,
How much I have disabled mine estate
By something showing a more swelling port   124
Than my faint means would grant continuance.   125
Nor do I now make moan to be abridged   126
From such a noble rate; but my chief care   127
Is to come fairly off from the great debts   128
Wherein my time, something too prodigal,   129
Hath left me gaged. To you, Antonio,   130
I owe the most, in money and in love,
And from your love I have a warranty   132
To unburden all my plots and purposes   133
How to get clear of all the debts I owe.
ANTONIO
I pray you, good Bassanio, let me know it;
And if it stand, as you yourself still do,   136
Within the eye of honor, be assured   137
My purse, my person, my extremest means
Lie all unlocked to your occasions.
BASSANIO
In my schooldays, when I had lost one shaft,   140
I shot his fellow of the selfsame flight   141
The selfsame way with more advisèd watch   142
To find the other forth, and by adventuring both   143
I oft found both. I urge this childhood proof
Because what follows is pure innocence.   145
I owe you much, and, like a willful youth,
That which I owe is lost; but if you please
To shoot another arrow that self way   148
Which you did shoot the first, I do not doubt,
As I will watch the aim, or to find both   150
Or bring your latter hazard back again   151
And thankfully rest debtor for the first.   152
ANTONIO
You know me well, and herein spend but time   153
To wind about my love with circumstance;   154
And out of doubt you do me now more wrong   155
In making question of my uttermost   156
Than if you had made waste of all I have.
Then do but say to me what I should do
That in your knowledge may by me be done,
And I am prest unto it. Therefore speak.   160
BASSANIO
In Belmont is a lady richly left;   161

84 in alabaster i.e., in a stone effigy upon a tomb   85 jaundice (Regarded as arising from the effects of too much choler or yellow bile, one of the four humors, in the blood.)   89 cream and mantle become covered with scum, i.e., acquire a lifeless, stiff expression.   standing stagnant   90 And . . . entertain and who maintain or assume a self-imposed, obstinate silence   91 opinion reputation   91–92 be . . . Of i.e., gain a reputation for   92 profound conceit deep thought   93 As . . . say as if to say   94 And . . . bark i.e., and I am worthy of great respect   98–99 would . . . fools i.e., would virtually condemn their hearers into calling them fools. (Compare Matthew 5:22, in which anyone calling another a fool is threatened with damnation.)   101–102 fish . . . opinion i.e., don't go fishing for a reputation of being wise, using your melancholy silence as the bait to fool people. (Gudgeon, a small fish, was thought of as a type of gullibility.)   106 dumb mute, speechless   108 keep if you keep   110 for this gear as a result of this business, i.e., your talk   112 neat's ox's.   vendible salable, i.e., in the marriage market   113 Is . . . now i.e., was all that talk about anything?   115 reasons reasonable ideas   119 the same i.e., the one

124 By . . . port by showing a somewhat more lavish style of living   125 grant continuance allow to continue   126–127 make . . . rate complain at being cut back from such a high style of living   128 to . . . off honorably to extricate myself   129 time youthful lifetime   130 gaged pledged, in pawn   132 warranty authorization   133 unburden disclose   136–137 if . . . honor if it looks honorable, as your conduct has always done   140 shaft arrow   141 his its.   selfsame flight same kind and range   142 advisèd careful   143 forth out.   adventuring risking   145 innocence ingenuousness, sincerity   148 self same   150 or either   151 hazard that which was risked   152 rest remain   153 spend but time only waste time   154 To . . . circumstance i.e., in not asking plainly what you want. (Circumstance here means "circumlocution.")   155 out of beyond   156 In . . . uttermost in showing any doubt of my intention to do all I can   160 prest ready   161 richly left left a large fortune (by her father's will)

And she is fair and, fairer than that word,
Of wondrous virtues. Sometime from her eyes   163
I did receive fair speechless messages.
Her name is Portia, nothing undervalued   165
To Cato's daughter, Brutus' Portia.   166
Nor is the wide world ignorant of her worth,
For the four winds blow in from every coast
Renownèd suitors, and her sunny locks
Hang on her temples like a golden fleece,
Which makes her seat of Belmont Colchis' strand,   171
And many Jasons come in quest of her.
O my Antonio, had I but the means
To hold a rival place with one of them,
I have a mind presages me such thrift   175
That I should questionless be fortunate.

ANTONIO
Thou know'st that all my fortunes are at sea;
Neither have I money nor commodity   178
To raise a present sum. Therefore go forth.   179
Try what my credit can in Venice do;
That shall be racked even to the uttermost   181
To furnish thee to Belmont, to fair Portia.
Go presently inquire, and so will I,   183
Where money is, and I no question make   184
To have it of my trust or for my sake.   *Exeunt.* 185

❧

1.2   *Enter Portia with her waiting woman, Nerissa.*

PORTIA   By my troth, Nerissa, my little body is aweary 1
of this great world.

NERISSA   You would be, sweet madam, if your miseries 3
were in the same abundance as your good fortunes
are; and yet, for aught I see, they are as sick that surfeit 5
with too much as they that starve with nothing. It is
no mean happiness, therefore, to be seated in the 7
mean. Superfluity comes sooner by white hairs, but 8
competency lives longer.   9

PORTIA   Good sentences, and well pronounced.   10

NERISSA   They would be better if well followed.

PORTIA   If to do were as easy as to know what were
good to do, chapels had been churches and poor
men's cottages princes' palaces. It is a good divine that 14
follows his own instructions. I can easier teach twenty
what were good to be done than to be one of the
twenty to follow mine own teaching. The brain may

devise laws for the blood, but a hot temper leaps o'er 18
a cold decree—such a hare is madness, the youth, to
skip o'er the meshes of good counsel, the cripple. But 20
this reasoning is not in the fashion to choose me a 21
husband. O me, the word "choose"! I may neither 22
choose who I would nor refuse who I dislike; so is the
will of a living daughter curbed by the will of a dead 24
father. Is it not hard, Nerissa, that I cannot choose one
nor refuse none?

NERISSA   Your father was ever virtuous, and holy men
at their death have good inspirations; therefore the
lottery that he hath devised in these three chests of
gold, silver, and lead, whereof who chooses his mean- 30
ing chooses you, will no doubt never be chosen by
any rightly but one who you shall rightly love. But 32
what warmth is there in your affection towards any of
these princely suitors that are already come?

PORTIA   I pray thee, overname them, and as thou nam- 35
est them I will describe them; and according to my
description level at my affection.   37

NERISSA   First, there is the Neapolitan prince.

PORTIA   Ay, that's a colt indeed, for he doth nothing but 39
talk of his horse, and he makes it a great appropriation 40
to his own good parts that he can shoe him him- 41
self. I am much afeard my lady his mother played false
with a smith.

NERISSA   Then is there the County Palatine.   44

PORTIA   He doth nothing but frown, as who should say, 45
"An you will not have me, choose." He hears merry 46
tales and smiles not. I fear he will prove the weeping 47
philosopher when he grows old, being so full of un- 48
mannerly sadness in his youth. I had rather be mar- 49
ried to a death's-head with a bone in his mouth than
to either of these. God defend me from these two!

NERISSA   How say you by the French lord, Monsieur 52
Le Bon?

PORTIA   God made him, and therefore let him pass for
a man. In truth, I know it is a sin to be a mocker, but
he! Why, he hath a horse better than the Neapolitan's,
a better bad habit of frowning than the Count Palatine;
he is every man in no man. If a throstle sing, he 58
falls straight a-capering. He will fence with his own 59
shadow. If I should marry him, I should marry twenty
husbands. If he would despise me, I would forgive
him, for if he love me to madness, I shall never re- 62
quite him.

163 Sometime once   **165–166 nothing undervalued To** of no less worth than   **166 Portia** (The same Portia as in Shakespeare's *Julius Caesar*.)   **171 Colchis'** (Jason adventured for the golden fleece in the land of Colchis, on the Black Sea.)   **strand** shore   **175 presages** i.e., which presages.   **thrift** profit and good fortune   **178 commodity** merchandise   **179 a present sum** ready money   **181 racked** stretched   **183 presently** immediately   **184 no question make** have no doubt   **185 of my trust** on the basis of my credit as a merchant.   **sake** i.e., personal sake
1.2. Location: Belmont. Portia's house.
1 troth faith   **3 would be** would have reason to be (weary)   **5 surfeit** overindulge   **7 mean** small (with a pun; see next note)   **7–8 in the mean** having neither too much nor too little   **8 comes sooner by** acquires sooner   **9 competency** modest means   **10 sentences** maxims.   **pronounced** delivered   **14 divine** clergyman

18 blood (Thought of as a chief agent of the passions, which in turn were regarded as the enemies of reason.)   **20 meshes** nets (used here for hunting hares).   **good counsel, the cripple** (Wisdom is portrayed as old and no longer agile.)   **20–22 But . . . husband** but this talk is not the way to help me choose a husband   **24 will . . . will** volition . . . testament   **30 who** whoever.   **his** i.e., the father's   **32 rightly . . . rightly** correctly . . . truly   **35 overname them** name them over   **37 level** aim, guess   **39 colt** i.e., wanton and foolish young man (with a punning appropriateness to his interest in horses)   **40 appropriation** addition   **41 good parts** accomplishments   **44 County** count.   **Palatine** one possessing royal privileges   **45 who should say** one might say   **46 An** if.   **choose** i.e., do as you please   **47–48 the weeping philosopher** i.e., Heraclitus of Ephesus, a melancholic and retiring philosopher of about 500 B.C., often contrasted with Democritus, the "laughing philosopher"   **49 sadness** melancholy   **52 by** about   **58 he is . . . no man** i.e., he borrows aspects from everyone but has no character of his own.   **throstle** thrush   **59 straight** at once   **62 if** even if

NERISSA What say you, then, to Falconbridge, the 64
young baron of England?

PORTIA You know I say nothing to him, for he understands not me, nor I him. He hath neither Latin,
French, nor Italian, and you will come into the court 68
and swear that I have a poor pennyworth in the Eng- 69
lish. He is a proper man's picture, but alas, who can 70
converse with a dumb show? How oddly he is suited! 71
I think he bought his doublet in Italy, his round hose 72
in France, his bonnet in Germany, and his behavior 73
everywhere.

NERISSA What think you of the Scottish lord, his
neighbor?

PORTIA That he hath a neighborly charity in him, for he
borrowed a box of the ear of the Englishman and swore 78
he would pay him again when he was able. I think the
Frenchman became his surety and sealed under for an- 80
other.   81

NERISSA How like you the young German, the Duke of
Saxony's nephew?

PORTIA Very vilely in the morning, when he is sober,
and most vilely in the afternoon, when he is drunk.
When he is best he is a little worse than a man, and
when he is worst he is little better than a beast. An 87
the worst fall that ever fell, I hope I shall make shift to 88
go without him.

NERISSA If he should offer to choose, and choose the 90
right casket, you should refuse to perform your father's
will if you should refuse to accept him.

PORTIA Therefore, for fear of the worst, I pray thee, set
a deep glass of Rhenish wine on the contrary casket, 94
for if the devil be within and that temptation without, 95
I know he will choose it. I will do anything, Nerissa,
ere I will be married to a sponge.

NERISSA You need not fear, lady, the having any of
these lords. They have acquainted me with their de-
terminations, which is indeed to return to their home
and to trouble you with no more suit, unless you may
be won by some other sort than your father's imposi- 102
tion depending on the caskets.   103

PORTIA If I live to be as old as Sibylla, I will die as chaste 104
as Diana, unless I be obtained by the manner of my 105
father's will. I am glad this parcel of wooers are so rea- 106
sonable, for there is not one among them but I dote on

his very absence, and I pray God grant them a fair
departure.

NERISSA Do you not remember, lady, in your father's
time, a Venetian, a scholar and a soldier, that came
hither in company of the Marquess of Montferrat?

PORTIA Yes, yes, it was Bassanio—as I think, so was
he called.

NERISSA True, madam. He, of all the men that ever my
foolish eyes looked upon was the best deserving a fair
lady.

PORTIA I remember him well, and I remember him
worthy of thy praise.

Enter a Servingman.

How now, what news?

SERVINGMAN The four strangers seek for you, madam, 121
to take their leave; and there is a forerunner come from 122
a fifth, the Prince of Morocco, who brings word the
Prince his master will be here tonight.

PORTIA If I could bid the fifth welcome with so good
heart as I can bid the other four farewell, I should be
glad of his approach. If he have the condition of a saint 127
and the complexion of a devil, I had rather he should 128
shrive me than wive me.   129
Come, Nerissa. [*To Servingman.*] Sirrah, go before. 130
Whiles we shut the gate upon one wooer, another
knocks at the door.   *Exeunt.*

1.3 *Enter Bassanio with Shylock the Jew.*

SHYLOCK Three thousand ducats, well.   1

BASSANIO Ay, sir, for three months.

SHYLOCK For three months, well.

BASSANIO For the which, as I told you, Antonio shall
be bound.

SHYLOCK Antonio shall become bound, well.

BASSANIO May you stead me? Will you pleasure me? 7
Shall I know your answer?

SHYLOCK Three thousand ducats for three months and
Antonio bound.

BASSANIO Your answer to that.

SHYLOCK Antonio is a good man.   12

BASSANIO Have you heard any imputation to the
contrary?

SHYLOCK Ho, no, no, no, no! My meaning in saying he
is a good man is to have you understand me that he is
sufficient. Yet his means are in supposition. He hath an 17
argosy bound to Tripolis, another to the Indies. I un-

---

64 **say you . . . to** do you say about. (But Portia wittily puns, in her
reply, on the literal sense of "speaking to.") 68–70 **come . . . English** i.e., bear witness that I can speak very little English 70 **He . . .
picture** i.e., he looks handsome 71 **dumb show** pantomime.
suited dressed 72 **doublet** upper garment corresponding to a jacket.
round hose short, puffed-out breeches 73 **bonnet** hat 78 **borrowed**
received. (But with a play on the idea of something that must be repaid.) 80–81 **became . . . another** guaranteed the Scot's payment
(of a box on the ear) and promised (literally, affixed his seal to a written promise) to give the Englishman yet another on his own behalf.
(An allusion to the age-old alliance of the French and the Scots
against the English.) 87 **An** if 88 **fall** befall. **make shift** manage
90 **offer** undertake 94 **Rhenish wine** a German white wine from the
Rhine Valley. **contrary** i.e., wrong 95 **if** even if 102 **sort** means
(with perhaps a suggestion too of "casting" or "drawing of lots")
102–103 **imposition** command, charge 104 **Sibylla** the Cumaean
Sibyl, to whom Apollo gave as many years as there were grains in her
handful of sand 105 **Diana** goddess of chastity and of the hunt
106 **parcel** assembly, group

121 **four** (Nerissa actually names six suitors; possibly a sign of revision or the author's early draft.) 122 **forerunner** herald 127 **condition** disposition, character 128 **complexion of a devil** (Devils were
thought to be black; but *complexion* can also mean "temperament,"
"disposition.") 129 **shrive me** act as my confessor and give absolution 130 **Sirrah** (Form of address to social inferior.)
1.3. Location: Venice. A public place.
1 **ducats** gold coins 7 **stead** supply, assist. **pleasure** oblige
12 **good** (Shylock means "solvent," a good credit risk; Bassanio interprets it in the moral sense.) 17 **sufficient** i.e., a good security. **in
supposition** doubtful, uncertain

derstand, moreover, upon the Rialto, he hath a 19
third at Mexico, a fourth for England, and other
ventures he hath squandered abroad. But ships are 21
but boards, sailors but men. There be land rats and
water rats, water thieves and land thieves—I mean
pirates—and then there is the peril of waters, winds,
and rocks. The man is, notwithstanding, sufficient.
Three thousand ducats. I think I may take his bond.

BASSANIO   Be assured you may.   27

SHYLOCK   I will be assured I may; and that I may be 28
assured, I will bethink me. May I speak with Antonio?

BASSANIO   If it please you to dine with us.

SHYLOCK   Yes, to smell pork, to eat of the habitation
which your prophet the Nazarite conjured the devil 32
into. I will buy with you, sell with you, talk with you,
walk with you, and so following, but I will not eat
with you, drink with you, nor pray with you. What
news on the Rialto? Who is he comes here?

Enter Antonio.

BASSANIO   This is Signor Antonio.

SHYLOCK [*aside*]
How like a fawning publican he looks!   38
I hate him for he is a Christian,   39
But more for that in low simplicity   40
He lends out money gratis and brings down   41
The rate of usance here with us in Venice.   42
If I can catch him once upon the hip,   43
I will feed fat the ancient grudge I bear him.   44
He hates our sacred nation, and he rails,   45
Even there where merchants most do congregate,
On me, my bargains, and my well-won thrift,   47
Which he calls interest. Cursèd be my tribe
If I forgive him!

BASSANIO   Shylock, do you hear?

SHYLOCK
I am debating of my present store,   50
And, by the near guess of my memory,
I cannot instantly raise up the gross   52
Of full three thousand ducats. What of that?
Tubal, a wealthy Hebrew of my tribe,
Will furnish me. But soft, how many months   55
Do you desire? [*To Antonio.*] Rest you fair, good
signor!
Your worship was the last man in our mouths.   57

ANTONIO
Shylock, albeit I neither lend nor borrow
By taking nor by giving of excess,   59
Yet, to supply the ripe wants of my friend,   60
I'll break a custom. [*To Bassanio.*] Is he yet possessed 61
How much ye would?   62

SHYLOCK   Ay, ay, three thousand ducats.

ANTONIO   And for three months.

SHYLOCK
I had forgot—three months, you told me so.
Well then, your bond. And let me see—but hear
you,
Methought you said you neither lend nor borrow
Upon advantage.

ANTONIO   I do never use it.   68

SHYLOCK
When Jacob grazed his uncle Laban's sheep—   69
This Jacob from our holy Abram was,   70
As his wise mother wrought in his behalf,
The third possessor; ay, he was the third—   72

ANTONIO
And what of him? Did he take interest?

SHYLOCK
No, not take interest, not as you would say
Directly interest. Mark what Jacob did.
When Laban and himself were compromised   76
That all the eanlings which were streaked and pied 77
Should fall as Jacob's hire, the ewes, being rank,   78
In end of autumn turnèd to the rams,
And when the work of generation was   80
Between these woolly breeders in the act,
The skillful shepherd peeled me certain wands,   82
And in the doing of the deed of kind   83
He stuck them up before the fulsome ewes,   84
Who then conceiving did in eaning time   85
Fall parti-colored lambs, and those were Jacob's.   86
This was a way to thrive, and he was blest;
And thrift is blessing, if men steal it not.   88

ANTONIO
This was a venture, sir, that Jacob served for,   89
A thing not in his power to bring to pass,
But swayed and fashioned by the hand of heaven.
Was this inserted to make interest good?   92
Or is your gold and silver ewes and rams?

SHYLOCK
I cannot tell. I make it breed as fast.   94
But note me, signor—

---

19 **the Rialto** the merchants' exchange in Venice and the center of
commercial activity   21 **squandered** scattered   27, 28 **assured** (Bassanio means that Shylock may trust Antonio, whereas Shylock means
that he will provide legal assurances.)   32 **Nazarite** Nazarene. (For
the reference to Christ's casting evil spirits into a herd of swine, see
Matthew 8:30–32, Mark 5:1–13, and Luke 8:32–33.)   38 **publican**
Roman tax gatherer (a term of opprobrium; see Luke 18:9–14); or,
innkeeper   39 **for** because   40 **low simplicity** humble foolishness
41 **gratis** without charging interest   42 **usance** usury, interest
43 **upon the hip** i.e., at my mercy. (A figure of speech from wrestling;
see Genesis 32:24–29.)   44 **fat** until fatted for the kill   45 **our sacred nation** i.e., the Hebrew people   47 **thrift** thriving   50 **I am . . .
store** I am considering my current supply of money (and that is why I
didn't answer you right away)   52 **gross** total   55 **soft** i.e., wait a
minute   57 **Your . . . mouths** i.e., we were just speaking of you. (But
with ominous connotation of devouring; compare line 44.)

59 **excess** interest   60 **ripe wants** pressing needs   61 **possessed** informed   62 **ye would** you want   68 **advantage** interest   69 **Jacob**
(See Genesis 27, 30:25–43.)   70 **Abram** Abraham   72 **third** i.e., after Abraham and Isaac.   **possessor** i.e., of the birthright of which,
with the help of Rebecca, he was able to cheat Esau, his elder brother
76 **compromised** agreed   77 **eanlings** young lambs or kids.   **pied**
spotted   78 **hire** wages, share.   **rank** in heat   80 **work of generation**
mating   82 **peeled . . . wands** i.e., partly stripped the bark of some
sticks. (*Me* is used colloquially.)   83 **deed of kind** i.e., copulation
84 **fulsome** lustful, well-fed   85 **eaning** lambing   86 **Fall** give birth
to   88 **thrift** thriving, profit   89 **venture . . . for** uncertain commercial venture on which Jacob risked his wages   92 **inserted . . .
good** brought in to justify the practice of usury   94 **I cannot tell** i.e., I
don't know about that

ANTONIO   Mark you this, Bassanio,
The devil can cite Scripture for his purpose.   96
An evil soul producing holy witness
Is like a villain with a smiling cheek,
A goodly apple rotten at the heart.
O, what a goodly outside falsehood hath!

SHYLOCK
Three thousand ducats. 'Tis a good round sum.
Three months from twelve, then let me see, the
    rate—

ANTONIO
Well, Shylock, shall we be beholding to you?   103

SHYLOCK
Signor Antonio, many a time and oft
In the Rialto you have rated me   105
About my moneys and my usances.
Still have I borne it with a patient shrug,
For sufferance is the badge of all our tribe.   108
You call me misbeliever, cutthroat dog,
And spit upon my Jewish gaberdine,   110
And all for use of that which is mine own.
Well then, it now appears you need my help.
Go to, then. You come to me and you say,   113
"Shylock, we would have moneys"—you say so,
You, that did void your rheum upon my beard   115
And foot me as you spurn a stranger cur   116
Over your threshold. Moneys is your suit.   117
What should I say to you? Should I not say,
"Hath a dog money? Is it possible
A cur can lend three thousand ducats?" Or
Shall I bend low, and in a bondman's key,   121
With bated breath and whispering humbleness,   122
Say this:
"Fair sir, you spit on me on Wednesday last,
You spurned me such a day, another time
You called me dog, and for these courtesies
I'll lend you thus much moneys"?

ANTONIO
I am as like to call thee so again,   128
To spit on thee again, to spurn thee too.
If thou wilt lend this money, lend it not
As to thy friends, for when did friendship take
A breed for barren metal of his friend?   132
But lend it rather to thine enemy,   133
Who, if he break, thou mayst with better face   134
Exact the penalty.

SHYLOCK   Why, look you how you storm!
I would be friends with you and have your love,
Forget the shames that you have stained me with,
Supply your present wants, and take no doit   138

Of usance for my moneys, and you'll not hear me.
This is kind I offer.   140
BASSANIO   This were kindness.   141
SHYLOCK   This kindness will I show.
Go with me to a notary, seal me there
Your single bond; and, in a merry sport,   144
If you repay me not on such a day,
In such a place, such sum or sums as are
Expressed in the condition, let the forfeit
Be nominated for an equal pound   148
Of your fair flesh, to be cut off and taken
In what part of your body pleaseth me.

ANTONIO
Content, in faith. I'll seal to such a bond
And say there is much kindness in the Jew.

BASSANIO
You shall not seal to such a bond for me!
I'll rather dwell in my necessity.   154

ANTONIO
Why, fear not, man, I will not forfeit it.
Within these two months—that's a month before
This bond expires—I do expect return
Of thrice three times the value of this bond.

SHYLOCK
O father Abram, what these Christians are,
Whose own hard dealings teaches them suspect
The thoughts of others! Pray you, tell me this:
If he should break his day, what should I gain
By the exaction of the forfeiture?
A pound of man's flesh taken from a man
Is not so estimable, profitable neither,   165
As flesh of muttons, beefs, or goats. I say
To buy his favor I extend this friendship.
If he will take it, so; if not, adieu.   168
And for my love, I pray you, wrong me not.   169

ANTONIO
Yes, Shylock, I will seal unto this bond.

SHYLOCK
Then meet me forthwith at the notary's.
Give him direction for this merry bond,
And I will go and purse the ducats straight,
See to my house, left in the fearful guard   174
Of an unthrifty knave, and presently
I'll be with you.   Exit.   176
ANTONIO   Hie thee, gentle Jew.
The Hebrew will turn Christian; he grows kind.

BASSANIO
I like not fair terms and a villain's mind.

ANTONIO
Come on. In this there can be no dismay;
My ships come home a month before the day.
                                                        Exeunt.

❧

96 devil . . . Scripture (See Matthew 4:6.) **103 beholding** beholden, indebted **105 rated** berated, rebuked **108 sufferance** endurance **110 gaberdine** loose outer garment like a cape or mantle **113 Go to** (An exclamation of impatience or annoyance.) **115 rheum** spittle **116 spurn** kick **117 suit** request **121 bondman's key** serf's tone of voice **122 bated** subdued **128 like** likely **132 A breed . . . metal** offspring from money, which cannot naturally breed. (One of the oldest arguments against usury was that it was thereby "unnatural.") **of** from **133 to** as if to **134 Who** from whom. **break** fail to pay on time **138 doit** a Dutch coin of very small value

140 kind kindly **141 were** would be (if seriously offered) **144 single bond** bond signed alone without other security; unconditional. (Shylock pretends the *condition*, line 147, is only a joke.) **148 nominated for** named, specified as. **equal** exact **154 dwell** remain **165 estimable** valuable **168 so** well and good **169 wrong me not** do not think evil of me **174 fearful** to be mistrusted **176 gentle** gracious, courteous (with a play on "gentile")

2.1   [*Flourish of cornets.*] *Enter* [*the Prince of*]
*Morocco, a tawny Moor all in white, and three or
four followers accordingly, with Portia, Nerissa,
and their train.*

MOROCCO
Mislike me not for my complexion,
The shadowed livery of the burnished sun,   2
To whom I am a neighbor and near bred.   3
Bring me the fairest creature northward born,
Where Phoebus' fire scarce thaws the icicles,   5
And let us make incision for your love
To prove whose blood is reddest, his or mine.   7
I tell thee, lady, this aspect of mine   8
Hath feared the valiant. By my love I swear,   9
The best-regarded virgins of our clime
Have loved it too. I would not change this hue,
Except to steal your thoughts, my gentle queen.

PORTIA
In terms of choice I am not solely led
By nice direction of a maiden's eyes;   14
Besides, the lott'ry of my destiny
Bars me the right of voluntary choosing.
But if my father had not scanted me,   17
And hedged me by his wit to yield myself   18
His wife who wins me by that means I told you,   19
Yourself, renownèd Prince, then stood as fair   20
As any comer I have looked on yet
For my affection.

MOROCCO   Even for that I thank you.   22
Therefore, I pray you, lead me to the caskets
To try my fortune. By this scimitar
That slew the Sophy and a Persian prince,   25
That won three fields of Sultan Solyman,   26
I would o'erstare the sternest eyes that look,   27
Outbrave the heart most daring on the earth,
Pluck the young sucking cubs from the she-bear,
Yea, mock the lion when 'a roars for prey,   30
To win thee, lady. But alas the while!
If Hercules and Lichas play at dice   32
Which is the better man, the greater throw
May turn by fortune from the weaker hand.
So is Alcides beaten by his page,
And so may I, blind Fortune leading me,
Miss that which one unworthier may attain,
And die with grieving.

PORTIA   You must take your chance,

And either not attempt to choose at all
Or swear before you choose, if you choose wrong
Never to speak to lady afterward
In way of marriage. Therefore be advised.   42

MOROCCO
Nor will not. Come, bring me unto my chance.   43

PORTIA
First, forward to the temple. After dinner   44
Your hazard shall be made.

MOROCCO   Good fortune then!
To make me blest or cursed'st among men.
    [*Cornets, and*] *exeunt.*

2.2   *Enter* [*Lancelot*] *the clown, alone.*

LANCELOT   Certainly my conscience will serve me to   1
run from this Jew my master. The fiend is at mine
elbow and tempts me, saying to me, "Gobbo, Lancelot
Gobbo, good Lancelot," or "Good Gobbo," or "Good
Lancelot Gobbo, use your legs, take the start, run
away." My conscience says, "No, take heed, honest
Lancelot, take heed, honest Gobbo," or, as aforesaid,
"Honest Lancelot Gobbo, do not run; scorn running
with thy heels." Well, the most courageous fiend bids   9
me pack. "Fia!" says the fiend. "Away!" says the fiend.   10
"For the heavens, rouse up a brave mind," says the   11
fiend, "and run." Well, my conscience, hanging about   12
the neck of my heart, says very wisely to me, "My hon-   13
est friend Lancelot, being an honest man's son," or
rather an honest woman's son—for indeed my father
did something smack, something grow to, he had a   16
kind of taste—well, my conscience says, "Lancelot,   17
budge not." "Budge," says the fiend. "Budge not," says
my conscience. "Conscience," say I, "you counsel
well." "Fiend," say I, "you counsel well." To be ruled by
my conscience, I should stay with the Jew my master,
who, God bless the mark, is a kind of devil; and to run   22
away from the Jew, I should be ruled by the fiend, who,
saving your reverence, is the devil himself. Certainly
the Jew is the very devil incarnation; and, in my con-   25
science, my conscience is but a kind of hard conscience
to offer to counsel me to stay with the Jew. The fiend
gives the more friendly counsel. I will run, fiend. My
heels are at your commandment. I will run.

Enter Old Gobbo, with a basket.

2.1. Location: Belmont. Portia's house.
s.d. accordingly similarly (i.e., dressed in white and dark-skinned like
Morocco)   **2 shadowed livery** i.e., dark complexion, worn as though
it were a costume of the sun's servants   **3 near bred** closely related
5 Phoebus' i.e., the sun's   **7 reddest** (Red blood was regarded as a
sign of courage.)   **8 aspect** visage   **9 feared** frightened   **14 nice direction** careful guidance   **17 scanted** limited   **18 wit** wisdom   **18–
19 yield . . . who** give myself to be the wife of him who   **20 then
. . . fair** would then have looked as attractive and stood as fair a
chance (with a play on "fair-skinned")   **22 For my** of gaining my
25 Sophy Shah of Persia   **26 fields** battles.   **Solyman** a Turkish sultan
ruling from 1520 to 1566   **27 o'erstare** outstare   **30 'a** he   **32 Lichas**
a page of Hercules (Alcides). See the note for 3.2.55.

42 be advised take warning, consider   **43 Nor will not** i.e., nor indeed will I violate the oath   **44 to the temple** i.e., in order to take
the oaths
2.2. Location: Venice. A street.
s.d. clown (1) country bumpkin (2) comic type in an Elizabethan acting company   **1 serve** permit   **9 with thy heels** i.e., emphatically
(with a pun on the literal sense)   **10 pack** begone.   **Fia** i.e., via,
away   **11 For the heavens** i.e., in heaven's name   **12–13 hanging
. . . heart** i.e., timidly   **16–17 something . . . taste** i.e., had a tendency to lechery   **22 God . . . mark** (An expression by way of apology for introducing something potentially offensive, as also in *saving
your reverence.*)   **25 incarnation** (Lancelot means "incarnate.")

GOBBO   Master young man, you, I pray you, which is 30
the way to master Jew's?

LANCELOT [*aside*] O heavens, this is my true-
begotten father, who, being more than sand-blind, 33
high-gravel-blind, knows me not. I will try confusions 34
with him.

GOBBO   Master young gentleman, I pray you, which is
the way to master Jew's?

LANCELOT Turn up on your right hand at the next
turning, but at the next turning of all on your left;
marry, at the very next turning, turn of no hand, but 40
turn down indirectly to the Jew's house.

GOBBO   By God's sonties, 'twill be a hard way to hit. 42
Can you tell me whether one Lancelot, that dwells
with him, dwell with him or no?

LANCELOT Talk you of young Master Lancelot? [*Aside.*]
Mark me now; now will I raise the waters.—Talk you 46
of young Master Lancelot?

GOBBO   No master, sir, but a poor man's son. His father, 48
though I say 't, is an honest exceeding poor man and,
God be thanked, well to live. 50

LANCELOT Well, let his father be what 'a will, we talk 51
of young Master Lancelot.

GOBBO   Your worship's friend, and Lancelot, sir. 53

LANCELOT But I pray you, ergo, old man, ergo, I be- 54
seech you, talk you of young Master Lancelot?

GOBBO   Of Lancelot, an 't please your mastership.

LANCELOT Ergo, Master Lancelot. Talk not of Master
Lancelot, Father, for the young gentleman, according 58
to Fates and Destinies and such odd sayings, the Sis- 59
ters Three and such branches of learning, is indeed 60
deceased, or, as you would say in plain terms, gone to
heaven.

GOBBO   Marry, God forbid! The boy was the very staff
of my age, my very prop.

LANCELOT Do I look like a cudgel or a hovel post, a 65
staff, or a prop? Do you know me, Father?

GOBBO   Alack the day, I know you not, young gentleman. But I pray you, tell me, is my boy, God rest his
soul, alive or dead?

LANCELOT Do you not know me, Father?

GOBBO   Alack, sir, I am sand-blind. I know you not.

LANCELOT Nay, indeed, if you had your eyes you
might fail of the knowing me; it is a wise father that 73
knows his own child. Well, old man, I will tell you 74
news of your son. [*He kneels.*] Give me your blessing.

Truth will come to light; murder cannot be hid long; a
man's son may, but in the end truth will out.

GOBBO   Pray you, sir, stand up. I am sure you are not
Lancelot, my boy.

LANCELOT Pray you, let's have no more fooling about
it, but give me your blessing. I am Lancelot, your 81
boy that was, your son that is, your child that shall be. 82

GOBBO   I cannot think you are my son.

LANCELOT I know not what I shall think of that; but I
am Lancelot, the Jew's man, and I am sure Margery
your wife is my mother.

GOBBO   Her name is Margery indeed. I'll be sworn, if
thou be Lancelot, thou art mine own flesh and blood.
Lord worshiped might he be, what a beard hast thou 89
got! Thou hast got more hair on thy chin than Dobbin
my fill horse has on his tail. 91

LANCELOT [*rising*] It should seem then that Dobbin's
tail grows backward. I am sure he had more hair of 93
his tail than I have of my face when I last saw him. 94

GOBBO   Lord, how art thou changed! How dost thou and
thy master agree? I have brought him a present. How
'gree you now?

LANCELOT Well, well; but for mine own part, as I have
set up my rest to run away, so I will not rest till 99
I have run some ground. My master's a very Jew. Give 100
him a present? Give him a halter! I am famished in his 101
service; you may tell every finger I have with my ribs. 102
Father, I am glad you are come. Give me your present 103
to one Master Bassanio, who indeed gives rare new
liveries. If I serve not him, I will run as far as God has 105
any ground. O rare fortune! Here comes the man. To
him, Father, for I am a Jew if I serve the Jew any longer. 107

*Enter Bassanio, with [Leonardo and] a follower
or two.*

BASSANIO You may do so, but let it be so hasted that 108
supper be ready at the farthest by five of the clock. See 109
these letters delivered, put the liveries to making, and
desire Gratiano to come anon to my lodging.
[*Exit a Servant.*]

LANCELOT To him, Father.

GOBBO   [*advancing*] God bless your worship!

BASSANIO Gramercy. Wouldst thou aught with me? 114

GOBBO   Here's my son, sir, a poor boy— 115

LANCELOT Not a poor boy, sir, but the rich Jew's man, 116

30 you (Gobbo uses the formal *you* but switches to the familiar *thou*,
line 88, when he accepts Lancelot as his son.) **33 sand-blind** dim-
sighted **34 high-gravel-blind** blinder than sand-blind. (A term seemingly invented by Lancelot.) **try confusions** (Lancelot's blunder for
"try conclusions," i.e., experiment, though his error is comically apt.)
40 marry i.e., by the Virgin Mary, indeed. (A mild interjection.)
42 sonties saints **46 raise the waters** i.e., start tears **48 master** (The
title was applied to gentlefolk only.) **50 well to live** enjoying a good
livelihood. (Perhaps Old Gobbo intends the phrase to mean "in good
health," since he protests that he is poor.) **51 'a** he **53 Your . . .
Lancelot** (Again, Old Gobbo denies that Lancelot is entitled to be
called "Master.") **54 ergo** therefore. (But Lancelot may use this Latin
word with no particular meaning in mind.) **58 Father** (1) old man (2)
Father **59–60 the Sisters Three** the three Fates **65 hovel post** support for a hovel or open shed **73–74 it is . . . child** (Reverses the
proverb "It is a wise child that knows his own father.")

81–82 your . . . shall be (Echoes the *Gloria* from the Book of Common Prayer: "As it was in the beginning, is now, and ever shall be.")
89 beard (Stage tradition has Old Gobbo mistaking Lancelot's long
hair for a beard.) **91 fill horse** cart horse **93 grows backward** (1)
grows inward, shorter (2) grows at the wrong end **94 of** in, on
99 set up my rest determined, risked all. (A metaphor from the card
game *primero*, in which a final wager is made, with a pun also on
rest as "place of residence.") **not rest** i.e., not stop running. (More
punning on *rest*.) **100 very** veritable. **Jew** (1) Hebrew (2) grasping
old usurer **101 halter** hangman's noose **102 tell** count. **tell . . .
ribs** (Comically reverses the usual saying of counting one's ribs with
one's fingers.) **103 Give me** give. (*Me* suggests "on my behalf.")
105 liveries uniforms or costumes for servants **107 a Jew** i.e., a villain (punning on the literal sense in *the Jew*. Compare with line 100.)
108 hasted hastened, hurried **109 farthest** latest **114 Gramercy**
many thanks. **aught** anything **115–116 poor . . . poor** unfortunate
. . . impoverished

that would, sir, as my father shall specify—

GOBBO   He hath a great infection, sir, as one would say, 118
to serve—

LANCELOT   Indeed, the short and the long is, I serve the
Jew, and have a desire, as my father shall specify—

GOBBO   His master and he, saving your worship's
reverence, are scarce cater-cousins— 123

LANCELOT   To be brief, the very truth is that the Jew,
having done me wrong, doth cause me, as my father,
being, I hope, an old man, shall frutify unto you— 126

GOBBO   I have here a dish of doves that I would bestow
upon your worship, and my suit is—

LANCELOT   In very brief, the suit is impertinent to 129
myself, as your worship shall know by this honest old
man, and, though I say it, though old man, yet poor
man, my father.

BASSANIO   One speak for both. What would you?

LANCELOT   Serve you, sir.

GOBBO   That is the very defect of the matter, sir. 135

BASSANIO
I know thee well; thou hast obtained thy suit.
Shylock thy master spoke with me this day,
And hath preferred thee, if it be preferment 138
To leave a rich Jew's service to become
The follower of so poor a gentleman.

LANCELOT   The old proverb is very well parted be- 141
tween my master Shylock and you, sir: you have the
grace of God, sir, and he hath enough.

BASSANIO
Thou speak'st it well. Go, father, with thy son.
Take leave of thy old master, and inquire
My lodging out. [To a Servant.] Give him a livery
More guarded than his fellows'. See it done. 147

LANCELOT   Father, in. I cannot get a service, no! I have
ne'er a tongue in my head, well! [He looks at his palm.]
If any man in Italy have a fairer table which doth offer 150
to swear upon a book, I shall have good fortune. Go 151
to, here's a simple line of life. Here's a small trifle of 152
wives! Alas, fifteen wives is nothing. Eleven widows
and nine maids is a simple coming-in for one man. 154
And then to scape drowning thrice, and to be in peril
of my life with the edge of a feather bed! Here are 156
simple scapes. Well, if Fortune be a woman, she's a 157
good wench for this gear. Father, come. I'll take my 158
leave of the Jew in the twinkling.

Exit clown [Lancelot, with Old Gobbo].

BASSANIO [giving Leonardo a list]
I pray thee, good Leonardo, think on this:
These things being bought and orderly bestowed, 161
Return in haste, for I do feast tonight 162
My best-esteemed acquaintance. Hie thee, go.

LEONARDO
My best endeavors shall be done herein.

[He starts to leave.]

Enter Gratiano.

GRATIANO [to Leonardo]
Where's your master?

LEONARDO   Yonder, sir, he walks.

Exit Leonardo.

GRATIANO   Signor Bassanio!

BASSANIO   Gratiano!

GRATIANO
I have a suit to you.

BASSANIO   You have obtained it.

GRATIANO   You must not deny me. I must go with you
to Belmont.

BASSANIO
Why, then you must. But hear thee, Gratiano;
Thou art too wild, too rude and bold of voice—
Parts that become thee happily enough, 173
And in such eyes as ours appear not faults,
But where thou art not known, why, there they
show
Something too liberal. Pray thee, take pain 176
To allay with some cold drops of modesty 177
Thy skipping spirit, lest through thy wild behavior
I be misconstered in the place I go to 179
And lose my hopes.

GRATIANO   Signor Bassanio, hear me:
If I do not put on a sober habit, 181
Talk with respect and swear but now and then,
Wear prayer books in my pocket, look demurely,
Nay more, while grace is saying, hood mine eyes 184
Thus with my hat, and sigh and say "amen,"
Use all the observance of civility,
Like one well studied in a sad ostent 187
To please his grandam, never trust me more. 188

BASSANIO   Well, we shall see your bearing.

GRATIANO
Nay, but I bar tonight. You shall not gauge me
By what we do tonight.

BASSANIO   No, that were pity.
I would entreat you rather to put on
Your boldest suit of mirth, for we have friends
That purpose merriment. But fare you well;
I have some business.

---

118 **infection** (Blunder for "affection" or "inclination.") 123 **cater-cousins** good friends 126 **frutify** (Lancelot may be trying to say "fructify," but he means "certify" or "notify.") 129 **impertinent** (Blunder for "pertinent.") 135 **defect** (Blunder for "effect," i.e., "purport.") 138 **preferred** recommended 141 **proverb** i.e., "He who has the grace of God has enough." **parted** divided 147 **guarded** trimmed with braided ornament 150 **table** palm of the hand. (Lancelot now reads the lines of his palm.) 151 **book** i.e., Bible. (The image is of a hand being laid on the Bible to take an oath.) 151–152 **Go to** (An expression of impatience.) 152 **simple** unremarkable. (Said ironically.) **line of life** curved line at the base of the thumb 154 **simple coming-in** modest beginning or income (with sexual suggestion) 156 **feather bed** (suggesting marriage bed or love bed; Lancelot sees sexual adventure and the dangers of marriage in his palm reading) 157 **scapes** (1) adventures (2) transgressions. **Fortune . . . woman** (Fortune was personified as a goddess.) 158 **gear** matter

161 **bestowed** i.e., stowed on board ship 162 **feast** give a feast for 173 **Parts** qualities 176 **liberal** free of manner (often with sexual connotation) 177 **allay** temper, moderate. **modesty** decorum 179 **misconstered** misconstrued 181 **habit** demeanor (with a suggestion of "clothes") 184 **saying** being said 187 **sad ostent** grave appearance 188 **grandam** grandmother

GRATIANO
  And I must to Lorenzo and the rest,
  But we will visit you at suppertime.   *Exeunt.*

2.3   *Enter Jessica and [Lancelot] the clown.*

JESSICA
  I am sorry thou wilt leave my father so.
  Our house is hell, and thou, a merry devil,
  Didst rob it of some taste of tediousness.
  But fare thee well. There is a ducat for thee.
                              [Giving money.]
  And, Lancelot, soon at supper shalt thou see
  Lorenzo, who is thy new master's guest.
  Give him this letter; do it secretly.   *[Giving a letter.]*
  And so farewell. I would not have my father
  See me in talk with thee.
LANCELOT   Adieu! Tears exhibit my tongue. Most 10
  beautiful pagan, most sweet Jew! If a Christian did not
  play the knave and get thee, I am much deceived. But, 12
  adieu! These foolish drops do something drown my
  manly spirit. Adieu!
JESSICA   Farewell, good Lancelot.   *[Exit Lancelot.]*
  Alack, what heinous sin is it in me
  To be ashamed to be my father's child!
  But though I am a daughter to his blood,
  I am not to his manners. O Lorenzo,
  If thou keep promise, I shall end this strife,
  Become a Christian and thy loving wife.   *Exit.*

❦

2.4   *Enter Gratiano, Lorenzo, Salerio, and Solanio.*

LORENZO
  Nay, we will slink away in suppertime,   1
  Disguise us at my lodging, and return
  All in an hour.
GRATIANO
  We have not made good preparation.
SALERIO
  We have not spoke us yet of torchbearers.   5
SOLANIO
  'Tis vile, unless it may be quaintly ordered,   6
  And better in my mind not undertook.
LORENZO
  'Tis now but four o'clock. We have two hours
  To furnish us.

        Enter Lancelot [with a letter].

         Friend Lancelot, what's the news?
LANCELOT   An it shall please you to break up this, it 10
  shall seem to signify.   *[Giving the letter.]*

LORENZO
  I know the hand. In faith, 'tis a fair hand,
  And whiter than the paper it writ on
  Is the fair hand that writ.
GRATIANO   Love news, in faith.
LANCELOT   By your leave, sir.   *[He starts to leave.]*
LORENZO   Whither goest thou?
LANCELOT   Marry, sir, to bid my old master the Jew to
  sup tonight with my new master the Christian.
LORENZO
  Hold here, take this. *[He gives money.]* Tell gentle
    Jessica
  I will not fail her. Speak it privately.
                  Exit clown [Lancelot].
  Go, gentlemen,
  Will you prepare you for this masque tonight?
  I am provided of a torchbearer.
SALERIO
  Ay, marry, I'll be gone about it straight.   24
SOLANIO
  And so will I.
LORENZO   Meet me and Gratiano.
  At Gratiano's lodging some hour hence.   26
SALERIO   'Tis good we do so.   *Exit [with Solanio].*
GRATIANO
  Was not that letter from fair Jessica?
LORENZO
  I must needs tell thee all. She hath directed   29
  How I shall take her from her father's house,
  What gold and jewels she is furnished with,
  What page's suit she hath in readiness.
  If e'er the Jew her father come to heaven,
  It will be for his gentle daughter's sake;   34
  And never dare misfortune cross her foot,   35
  Unless she do it under this excuse,   36
  That she is issue to a faithless Jew.   37
  Come, go with me. Peruse this as thou goest.
              [He gives Gratiano the letter.]
  Fair Jessica shall be my torchbearer.   *Exeunt.*

❦

2.5   *Enter [Shylock the] Jew and [Lancelot,] his man
      that was, the clown.*

SHYLOCK
  Well, thou shalt see, thy eyes shall be thy judge,
  The difference of old Shylock and Bassanio.—   2
  What, Jessica!—Thou shalt not gormandize,   3
  As thou hast done with me—What, Jessica!—
  And sleep and snore, and rend apparel out—   5
  Why, Jessica, I say!
LANCELOT   Why, Jessica!

2.3. Location: Venice. Shylock's house.
10 exhibit (Blunder for "inhibit," "restrain.") **12 get** beget
2.4. Location: Venice. A street.
1 in during **5 spoke . . . of** yet bespoken, ordered **6 quaintly ordered** skillfully and tastefully managed **10 An** if. **break up this** i.e.,
open the seal

24 straight at once **26 some hour** about an hour **29 must needs**
must **34 gentle** (with pun on "gentile"?) **35 foot** footpath **36 she**
i.e., Misfortune **37 she is issue** i.e., Jessica is daughter. **faithless**
pagan
2.5. Location: Venice. Before Shylock's house.
2 of between **3 gormandize** eat gluttonously **5 rend apparel out**
i.e., wear out your clothes

SHYLOCK
  Who bids thee call? I do not bid thee call.
LANCELOT   Your worship was wont to tell me I could
  do nothing without bidding.

        Enter Jessica.

JESSICA   Call you? What is your will?
SHYLOCK
  I am bid forth to supper, Jessica.
  There are my keys. But wherefore should I go?   13
  I am not bid for love—they flatter me—
  But yet I'll go in hate, to feed upon
  The prodigal Christian. Jessica, my girl,
  Look to my house. I am right loath to go.   17
  There is some ill a-brewing towards my rest,
  For I did dream of moneybags tonight.   19
LANCELOT   I beseech you, sir, go. My young master
  doth expect your reproach.   21
SHYLOCK   So do I his.
LANCELOT   And they have conspired together. I will
  not say you shall see a masque, but if you do, then it
  was not for nothing that my nose fell a-bleeding on
  Black Monday last at six o'clock i' the morning, falling   26
  out that year on Ash Wednesday was four year in th'
  afternoon.
SHYLOCK
  What, are there masques? Hear you me, Jessica:
  Lock up my doors, and when you hear the drum
  And the vile squealing of the wry-necked fife,   31
  Clamber not you up to the casements then,
  Nor thrust your head into the public street
  To gaze on Christian fools with varnished faces,   34
  But stop my house's ears—I mean my casements.
  Let not the sound of shallow foppery enter
  My sober house. By Jacob's staff I swear   37
  I have no mind of feasting forth tonight.
  But I will go.—Go you before me, sirrah.
  Say I will come.
LANCELOT   I will go before, sir. [*Aside to Jessica.*] Mis-
  tress, look out at window, for all this;
        There will come a Christian by,
        Will be worth a Jewess' eye.   [*Exit.*]
SHYLOCK
  What says that fool of Hagar's offspring, ha?   45
JESSICA
  His words were "Farewell, mistress," nothing else.
SHYLOCK
  The patch is kind enough, but a huge feeder,   47
  Snail-slow in profit, and he sleeps by day   48
  More than the wildcat. Drones hive not with me;
  Therefore I part with him, and part with him

To one that I would have him help to waste
His borrowed purse. Well, Jessica, go in.
Perhaps I will return immediately.
Do as I bid you. Shut doors after you.
Fast bind, fast find—   55
A proverb never stale in thrifty mind.   *Exit.*
JESSICA
  Farewell, and if my fortune be not crossed,
  I have a father, you a daughter, lost.   *Exit.*

❧

2.6   *Enter the masquers, Gratiano and Salerio.*

GRATIANO
  This is the penthouse under which Lorenzo   1
  Desired us to make stand.
SALERIO   His hour is almost past.
GRATIANO
  And it is marvel he outdwells his hour,   4
  For lovers ever run before the clock.
SALERIO
  O, ten times faster Venus' pigeons fly   6
  To seal love's bonds new-made than they are wont
  To keep obligèd faith unforfeited.   8
GRATIANO
  That ever holds. Who riseth from a feast   9
  With that keen appetite that he sits down?
  Where is the horse that doth untread again   11
  His tedious measures with the unbated fire   12
  That he did pace them first? All things that are
  Are with more spirit chasèd than enjoyed.
  How like a younger or a prodigal   15
  The scarfèd bark puts from her native bay,   16
  Hugged and embracèd by the strumpet wind!   17
  How like the prodigal doth she return,
  With overweathered ribs and ragged sails,   19
  Lean, rent, and beggared by the strumpet wind!   20

        Enter Lorenzo.

SALERIO
  Here comes Lorenzo. More of this hereafter.
LORENZO
  Sweet friends, your patience for my long abode;   22
  Not I, but my affairs, have made you wait.
  When you shall please to play the thieves for wives,
  I'll watch as long for you then. Approach;

---

13 **wherefore** why   17 **right loath** reluctant   19 **tonight** last night
21 **reproach** (Lancelot's blunder for "approach." Shylock takes it in
grim humor.)   26 **Black Monday** Easter Monday. (Lancelot's talk of
omens is perhaps intentional gibberish, a parody of Shylock's fears.)
31 **wry-necked** i.e., played with the musician's head awry   34 **varnished faces** i.e., painted masks   37 **Jacob's staff** (See Genesis 32:10
and Hebrews 11:21.)   45 **Hagar's offspring** (Hagar, a gentile and
Abraham's servant, gave birth to Ishmael; both mother and son were
cast out after the birth of Isaac.)   47 **patch** fool   48 **profit** profitable
labor

55 **Fast . . . find** i.e., something firmly secured or bound will always
be easily located
2.6. Location: Before Shylock's house, as in 2.5.
1 **penthouse** projecting roof or upper story of a house   4 **it . . . hour**
i.e., it is surprising that he is late   6 **Venus' pigeons** the doves that
drew Venus' chariot   8 **obligèd** bound by marriage or engagement.
unforfeited unbroken   9 **ever holds** always holds true   11 **untread**
retrace   12 **measures** paces   15 **younger** i.e., younger son, as in the
parable of the Prodigal Son (Luke 15). (Often emended to *younker*,
youth.)   16 **scarfèd** decorated with flags or streamers   17 **strumpet**
i.e., inconsistent, variable (likened metaphorically to the harlots with
whom the Prodigal Son wasted his fortune)   19 **overweathered ribs**
i.e., weather-beaten and leaking timbers   20 **rent** torn   22 **your patience** i.e., I beg your patience.   **abode** delay

Here dwells my father Jew. Ho! Who's within?   26

[Enter] Jessica, above [in boy's clothes].

JESSICA
Who are you? Tell me for more certainty,
Albeit I'll swear that I do know your tongue.
LORENZO   Lorenzo, and thy love.
JESSICA
Lorenzo, certain, and my love indeed,
For who love I so much? And now who knows
But you, Lorenzo, whether I am yours?
LORENZO
Heaven and thy thoughts are witness that thou art.
JESSICA *[throwing down a casket]*
Here, catch this casket. It is worth the pains.
I am glad 'tis night, you do not look on me,
For I am much ashamed of my exchange.   36
But love is blind, and lovers cannot see
The pretty follies that themselves commit,   38
For if they could, Cupid himself would blush
To see me thus transformèd to a boy.
LORENZO
Descend, for you must be my torchbearer.
JESSICA
What, must I hold a candle to my shames?   42
They in themselves, good sooth, are too too light. 43
Why, 'tis an office of discovery, love,   44
And I should be obscured.
LORENZO   So are you, sweet,
Even in the lovely garnish of a boy.   46
But come at once,
For the close night doth play the runaway,   48
And we are stayed for at Bassanio's feast.   49
JESSICA
I will make fast the doors, and gild myself   50
With some more ducats, and be with you straight.
                              [Exit above.]
GRATIANO
Now, by my hood, a gentle and no Jew.   52
LORENZO
Beshrew me but I love her heartily,   53
For she is wise, if I can judge of her,
And fair she is, if that mine eyes be true,
And true she is, as she hath proved herself;
And therefore, like herself, wise, fair, and true,
Shall she be placèd in my constant soul.

Enter Jessica [below].

What, art thou come? On, gentlemen, away!
Our masquing mates by this time for us stay.   60

---

26 **father** i.e., father-in-law   36 **exchange** change of clothes
38 **pretty** ingenious, artful   42 **hold a candle** i.e., stand by and witness (with a play on the idea of acting as torchbearer)   43 **light** immodest (with pun on literal meaning)   44 **'tis . . . discovery** i.e.,
torchbearing is intended to shed light on matters   46 **garnish** outfit,
trimmings   48 **close** dark, secretive.   **doth . . . runaway** i.e., is
quickly passing   49 **stayed** waited   50 **gild** adorn. (Literally, cover
with gold.)   52 **by my hood** (An asseveration.)   **gentle** gracious person (with pun on "gentile," as at 2.4.34)   53 **Beshrew** i.e., a mischief on. (A mild oath.)   60 **stay** wait. (Also in line 64.)

---

*Exit [with Jessica and Salerio;
Gratiano is about to follow them].*

Enter Antonio.

ANTONIO   Who's there?
GRATIANO   Signor Antonio?
ANTONIO
Fie, fie, Gratiano! Where are all the rest?
'Tis nine o'clock; our friends all stay for you.
No masque tonight. The wind is come about;
Bassanio presently will go aboard.
I have sent twenty out to seek for you.
GRATIANO
I am glad on 't. I desire no more delight
Than to be under sail and gone tonight.   *Exeunt.*

❦

2.7   *[Flourish of cornets.] Enter Portia, with [the
          Prince of] Morocco, and both their trains.*

PORTIA
Go, draw aside the curtains and discover   1
The several caskets to this noble prince.   2
Now make your choice.   *[The curtains are drawn.]*
MOROCCO
The first, of gold, who this inscription bears, 4
"Who chooseth me shall gain what many men
   desire";
The second, silver, which this promise carries,
"Who chooseth me shall get as much as he
   deserves";
This third, dull lead, with warning all as blunt, 8
"Who chooseth me must give and hazard all he
   hath."
How shall I know if I do choose the right?
PORTIA
The one of them contains my picture, Prince.
If you choose that, then I am yours withal.   12
MOROCCO
Some god direct my judgment! Let me see,
I will survey th' inscriptions back again.
What says this leaden casket?
"Who chooseth me must give and hazard all he
   hath."
Must give—for what? For lead? Hazard for lead?
This casket threatens. Men that hazard all
Do it in hope of fair advantages.
A golden mind stoops not to shows of dross.   20
I'll then nor give nor hazard aught for lead.   21
What says the silver with her virgin hue?
"Who chooseth me shall get as much as he
   deserves."
As much as he deserves! Pause there, Morocco,
And weigh thy value with an even hand.   25

2.7. Location: Belmont. Portia's house.
1 **discover** reveal   2 **several** different, various   4 **who** which   8 **dull**
(1) dull-colored (2) blunt.   **all as blunt** as blunt as lead   12 **withal**
with it   20 **dross** worthless matter. (Literally, the impurities cast off in
the melting down of metals.)   21 **nor give** neither give   25 **even**
impartial

If thou be'st rated by thy estimation,   26
Thou dost deserve enough; and yet enough
May not extend so far as to the lady;
And yet to be afeard of my deserving
Were but a weak disabling of myself.   30
As much as I deserve? Why, that's the lady.
I do in birth deserve her, and in fortunes,
In graces, and in qualities of breeding;
But more than these, in love I do deserve.
What if I strayed no farther, but chose here?
Let's see once more this saying graved in gold:
"Who chooseth me shall gain what many men
    desire."
Why, that's the lady; all the world desires her.
From the four corners of the earth they come
To kiss this shrine, this mortal breathing saint.   40
The Hyrcanian deserts and the vasty wilds   41
Of wide Arabia are as throughfares now
For princes to come view fair Portia.
The watery kingdom, whose ambitious head
Spits in the face of heaven, is no bar   45
To stop the foreign spirits, but they come,   46
As o'er a brook, to see fair Portia.
One of these three contains her heavenly picture.
Is 't like that lead contains her? 'Twere damnation   49
To think so base a thought; it were too gross   50
To rib her cerecloth in the obscure grave.   51
Or shall I think in silver she's immured,   52
Being ten times undervalued to tried gold?   53
O, sinful thought! Never so rich a gem
Was set in worse than gold. They have in England
A coin that bears the figure of an angel   56
Stamped in gold, but that's insculped upon;   57
But here an angel in a golden bed
Lies all within. Deliver me the key.
Here do I choose, and thrive I as I may!

PORTIA
There, take it, Prince; and if my form lie there,   61
Then I am yours.   [*He unlocks the golden casket.*]

MOROCCO   O hell! What have we here?
A carrion Death, within whose empty eye   63
There is a written scroll! I'll read the writing.
[*He reads.*]
        "All that glisters is not gold;
        Often have you heard that told.
        Many a man his life hath sold
        But my outside to behold.
        Gilded tombs do worms infold.

Had you been as wise as bold,
Young in limbs, in judgment old,
Your answer had not been inscrolled.   72
Fare you well; your suit is cold."
    Cold, indeed, and labor lost.
    Then, farewell, heat, and welcome, frost!
    Portia, adieu. I have too grieved a heart
    To take a tedious leave. Thus losers part.   77
                    Exit [with his train. Flourish of cornets.]

PORTIA
A gentle riddance. Draw the curtains, go.
Let all of his complexion choose me so.   79
        [*The curtains are closed, and*] *exeunt.*

❖

2.8   *Enter Salerio and Solanio.*

SALERIO
Why, man, I saw Bassanio under sail.
With him is Gratiano gone along,
And in their ship I am sure Lorenzo is not.

SOLANIO
The villain Jew with outcries raised the Duke,   4
Who went with him to search Bassanio's ship.

SALERIO
He came too late. The ship was under sail.
But there the Duke was given to understand
That in a gondola were seen together
Lorenzo and his amorous Jessica.
Besides, Antonio certified the Duke
They were not with Bassanio in his ship.

SOLANIO
I never heard a passion so confused,   12
So strange, outrageous, and so variable
As the dog Jew did utter in the streets:
"My daughter! O, my ducats! O, my daughter!
Fled with a Christian! O, my Christian ducats!
Justice! The law! My ducats, and my daughter!
A sealèd bag, two sealèd bags of ducats,
Of double ducats, stol'n from me by my daughter!
And jewels, two stones, two rich and precious
    stones,
Stol'n by my daughter! Justice! Find the girl!
She hath the stones upon her, and the ducats."

SALERIO
Why, all the boys in Venice follow him,
Crying his stones, his daughter, and his ducats.   24

SOLANIO
Let good Antonio look he keep his day,   25
Or he shall pay for this.

SALERIO   Marry, well remembered.
I reasoned with a Frenchman yesterday,   27

---

26 **estimation** valuation   30 **disabling** underrating   40 **mortal breathing** living   41 **Hyrcanian** (Hyrcania was the country south of the Caspian Sea celebrated for its wildness.)   **vasty** vast   45 **Spits** (The image is of huge waves breaking at sea.)   46 **spirits** i.e., men of
courage   49 **like** likely   50 **base** (1) ignoble (2) low in the natural
scale, as with lead, a *base* metal.   **it were** i.e., lead would be
51 **rib** i.e., enclose.   **cerecloth** wax cloth used in wrapping for
burial.   **grave** i.e., lead casket used for burial   52 **immured** enclosed, confined   53 **Being . . . to** which has only one tenth the
value of.   **tried** assayed, purified   56 **coin** i.e., the gold coin known
as the *angel*, which bore the device of the archangel Michael treading
on the dragon   57 **insculped upon** merely engraved upon the surface
61 **form** image   63 **carrion Death** death's-head

72 **inscrolled** i.e., written on this scroll   77 **part** depart   79 **complexion** temperament (not merely skin color)
2.8. Location: Venice. A street.
4 **raised** roused   12 **passion** passionate outburst   24 **stones** (In the
boys' jeering cry, the *two stones* suggest testicles; see line 20.)
25 **look . . . day** see to it that he repays his loan on time   27 **reasoned** talked

Who told me, in the narrow seas that part   28
The French and English, there miscarrièd
A vessel of our country richly fraught.   30
I thought upon Antonio when he told me,
And wished in silence that it were not his.

SOLANIO
You were best to tell Antonio what you hear.
Yet do not suddenly, for it may grieve him.

SALERIO
A kinder gentleman treads not the earth.
I saw Bassanio and Antonio part.
Bassanio told him he would make some speed
Of his return; he answered, "Do not so.
Slubber not business for my sake, Bassanio,   39
But stay the very riping of the time;   40
And for the Jew's bond which he hath of me,   41
Let it not enter in your mind of love.   42
Be merry, and employ your chiefest thoughts
To courtship and such fair ostents of love   44
As shall conveniently become you there."
And even there, his eye being big with tears,   46
Turning his face, he put his hand behind him,   47
And with affection wondrous sensible   48
He wrung Bassanio's hand; and so they parted.

SOLANIO
I think he only loves the world for him.
I pray thee, let us go and find him out   50
And quicken his embracèd heaviness   52
With some delight or other.

SALERIO   Do we so.   *Exeunt.*

2.9   *Enter Nerissa and a Servitor.*

NERISSA
Quick, quick, I pray thee, draw the curtain straight.   1
The Prince of Aragon hath ta'en his oath,
And comes to his election presently.   3

            [The curtains are drawn back.]

    *[Flourish of cornets.] Enter [the Prince of] Aragon,
    his train, and Portia.*

PORTIA
Behold, there stand the caskets, noble Prince.
If you choose that wherein I am contained,
Straight shall our nuptial rites be solemnized;
But if you fail, without more speech, my lord,
You must be gone from hence immediately.

28 **narrow seas** English Channel   30 **fraught** freighted   39 **Slubber
not business** don't do the business hastily and badly   40 **But . . .
time** i.e., pursue your business at Belmont until it is brought to completion   41 **for** as for   42 **of** preoccupied with   44 **ostents** expressions, shows   46 **there** thereupon, then   47 **behind him** (Antonio
turns away in tears while extending his hand back to Bassanio.)
48 **affection wondrous sensible** wondrously sensitive and keen emotion   50 **he . . . him** i.e., Bassanio is all he lives for   52 **quicken
. . . heaviness** lighten the sorrow he has embraced
2.9. Location: Belmont. Portia's house.
s.d. Servitor servant   1 **straight** at once   3 **election** choice.   **presently** immediately

ARAGON
I am enjoined by oath to observe three things:
First, never to unfold to anyone
Which casket 'twas I chose; next, if I fail
Of the right casket, never in my life
To woo a maid in way of marriage;
Lastly,
If I do fail in fortune of my choice,
Immediately to leave you and be gone.

PORTIA
To these injunctions everyone doth swear
That comes to hazard for my worthless self.

ARAGON
And so have I addressed me. Fortune now   19
To my heart's hope! Gold, silver, and base lead.
"Who chooseth me must give and hazard all he
    hath."
You shall look fairer ere I give or hazard.
What says the golden chest? Ha, let me see:
"Who chooseth me shall gain what many men
    desire."
What many men desire! That "many" may be meant   25
By the fool multitude, that choose by show,   26
Not learning more than the fond eye doth teach,   27
Which pries not to th' interior, but like the martlet   28
Builds in the weather on the outward wall,   29
Even in the force and road of casualty.   30
I will not choose what many men desire,
Because I will not jump with common spirits   32
And rank me with the barbarous multitudes.
Why then, to thee, thou silver treasure-house!
Tell me once more what title thou dost bear:
"Who chooseth me shall get as much as he
    deserves."
And well said too; for who shall go about
To cozen fortune, and be honorable   38
Without the stamp of merit? Let none presume   39
To wear an undeservèd dignity.
O, that estates, degrees, and offices   41
Were not derived corruptly, and that clear honor
Were purchased by the merit of the wearer!
How many then should cover that stand bare?   44
How many be commanded that command?   45
How much low peasantry would then be gleaned   46
From the true seed of honor, and how much honor   47
Picked from the chaff and ruin of the times
To be new-varnished? Well, but to my choice: 49
"Who chooseth me shall get as much as he
    deserves."
I will assume desert. Give me a key for this,
And instantly unlock my fortunes here.

                        [He opens the silver casket.]

19 **addressed me** prepared myself (by this swearing)   25–26 **meant
By** meant for   27 **fond** foolish   28 **martlet** swift   29 **in** exposed to
30 **force . . . casualty** power and path of mischance   32 **jump** agree
38 **cozen** cheat   39 **stamp** seal of approval   41 **estates, degrees** status, social rank   44 **cover . . . bare** i.e., wear hats (of authority) who
now stand bareheaded   45 **How . . . command** how many then
should be servants that are now masters   46 **gleaned** culled out
47 **the true seed of honor** i.e., persons of noble descent   49 **new-
varnished** i.e., having the luster of their true nobility restored to them

PORTIA
Too long a pause for that which you find there.

ARAGON
What's here? The portrait of a blinking idiot,
Presenting me a schedule! I will read it.   55
How much unlike art thou to Portia!
How much unlike my hopes and my deservings!
"Who chooseth me shall have as much as he
    deserves."
Did I deserve no more than a fool's head?
Is that my prize? Are my deserts no better?

PORTIA
To offend and judge are distinct offices   61
And of opposèd natures.

ARAGON   What is here?   62
[He reads.] "The fire seven times tried this;   63
    Seven times tried that judgment is
    That did never choose amiss.
    Some there be that shadows kiss;   66
    Such have but a shadow's bliss.
    There be fools alive, iwis,   68
    Silvered o'er, and so was this.   69
    Take what wife you will to bed,
    I will ever be your head.   71
    So begone; you are sped."   72

    Still more fool I shall appear   73
    By the time I linger here.   74
    With one fool's head I came to woo,
    But I go away with two.
    Sweet, adieu. I'll keep my oath,
    Patiently to bear my wroth.   78
                                    [Exeunt Aragon and train.]

PORTIA
Thus hath the candle singed the moth.
O, these deliberate fools! When they do choose,   80
They have the wisdom by their wit to lose.

NERISSA
The ancient saying is no heresy:
Hanging and wiving goes by destiny.

PORTIA   Come, draw the curtain, Nerissa.
                                    [The curtains are closed.]

        Enter Messenger.

MESSENGER
Where is my lady?

PORTIA   Here. What would my lord?   85

MESSENGER
Madam, there is alighted at your gate

A young Venetian, one that comes before
To signify th' approaching of his lord,
From whom he bringeth sensible regreets,   89
To wit, besides commends and courteous breath,   90
Gifts of rich value. Yet I have not seen   91
So likely an ambassador of love.   92
A day in April never came so sweet,
To show how costly summer was at hand,   94
As this fore-spurrer comes before his lord.   95

PORTIA
No more, I pray thee. I am half afeard
Thou wilt say anon he is some kin to thee,
Thou spend'st such high-day wit in praising him.   98
Come, come, Nerissa, for I long to see
Quick Cupid's post that comes so mannerly.   100

NERISSA
Bassanio, Lord Love, if thy will it be!   Exeunt.

                        ❧

3.1   [Enter] Solanio and Salerio.

SOLANIO   Now, what news on the Rialto?

SALERIO   Why, yet it lives there unchecked that Anto-   2
nio hath a ship of rich lading wrecked on the narrow   3
seas—the Goodwins, I think they call the place, a   4
very dangerous flat, and fatal, where the carcasses of   5
many a tall ship lie buried, as they say, if my gossip   6
Report be an honest woman of her word.   7

SOLANIO   I would she were as lying a gossip in that as
ever knapped ginger or made her neighbors believe   9
she wept for the death of a third husband. But it is
true, without any slips of prolixity or crossing the   11
plain highway of talk, that the good Antonio, the   12
honest Antonio—O, that I had a title good enough to
keep his name company!—

SALERIO   Come, the full stop.   15

SOLANIO   Ha, what sayest thou? Why, the end is, he
hath lost a ship.

SALERIO   I would it might prove the end of his losses.

SOLANIO   Let me say "amen" betimes, lest the devil   19
cross my prayer, for here he comes in the likeness of   20
a Jew.

        Enter Shylock.

How now, Shylock, what news among the merchants?

---

55 **schedule** written paper   **61–62 To offend . . . natures** i.e., you
have no right, having submitted your case to judgment, to attempt to
judge your own case; or, it is not for me to say, since I've been the
indirect cause of your discomfiture   **63 tried** tested, purified (?)   **this**
i.e., the wise sayings on the scroll (that have often been proved right
by hard experience); or, the silver   **66 shadows** illusions   **68 iwis**
certainly   **69 Silvered o'er** i.e., with silver hair and so apparently
wise   **71 I . . . head** i.e., you will always have a fool's head, be a
fool   **72 sped** done for   **73–74 Still . . . here** i.e., I shall seem all
the greater fool for wasting any more time here   **78 wroth** sorrow,
unhappy lot (a variant of *ruth*); or, anger   **80 deliberate** reasoning,
calculating   **85 my lord** (A jesting response to "my lady.")

89 **sensible regreets** tangible gifts, greetings   **90 commends** greetings.
breath speech   **91 Yet** heretofore   **92 likely** promising   **94 costly**
lavish, rich   **95 fore-spurrer** herald, harbinger   **98 high-day** holiday
(i.e., extravagant)   **100 post** messenger
3.1. Location: Venice. A street.
2 yet . . . unchecked i.e., a rumor is spreading undenied   **3–4 the
narrow seas** the English Channel, as at 2.8.28.   **4 Goodwins** Goodwin Sands, off the Kentish coast near the Thames estuary   **5 flat**
shoal, sandbank   **6 tall** gallant   **6–7 gossip Report** i.e., Dame Rumor   **9 knapped** nibbled   **11 slips of prolixity** lapses into long-wind-
edness; or, long-winded lies. *Slips* may be the cuttings or offshoots of
tediousness.   **11–12 crossing . . . talk** deviating from honest, plain
speech   **15 Come . . . stop** finish your sentence; rein in your tongue
as a horse is checked in its manage   **19 betimes** while there is yet
time   **20 cross** thwart; make the sign of the cross following

SHYLOCK   You knew, none so well, none so well as you, of my daughter's flight.

SALERIO   That's certain. I for my part knew the tailor that made the wings she flew withal. 26

SOLANIO   And Shylock for his own part knew the bird was fledge, and then it is the complexion of them all 28 to leave the dam. 29

SHYLOCK   She is damned for it.

SALERIO   That's certain, if the devil may be her judge.

SHYLOCK   My own flesh and blood to rebel!

SOLANIO   Out upon it, old carrion! Rebels it at these 33 years? 34

SHYLOCK   I say my daughter is my flesh and my blood.

SALERIO   There is more difference between thy flesh and hers than between jet and ivory, more between your 37 bloods than there is between red wine and Rhenish. 38 But tell us, do you hear whether Antonio have had any loss at sea or no?

SHYLOCK   There I have another bad match! A bankrupt, 41 a prodigal, who dare scarce show his head on the Rialto; a beggar, that was used to come so smug upon the mart! Let him look to his bond. He was wont to 44 call me usurer. Let him look to his bond. He was wont to lend money for a Christian courtesy. Let him look to his bond.

SALERIO   Why, I am sure, if he forfeit, thou wilt not take his flesh. What's that good for?

SHYLOCK   To bait fish withal. If it will feed nothing else, 50 it will feed my revenge. He hath disgraced me, and hindered me half a million, laughed at my losses, mocked at my gains, scorned my nation, thwarted my bargains, cooled my friends, heated mine enemies; and what's his reason? I am a Jew. Hath not a Jew eyes? Hath not a Jew hands, organs, dimensions, senses, affections, passions? Fed with the same food, hurt with the same weapons, subject to the same diseases, healed by the same means, warmed and cooled by the same winter and summer, as a Christian is? If you prick us, do we not bleed? If you tickle us, do we not laugh? If you poison us, do we not die? And if you wrong us, shall we not revenge? If we are like you in the rest, we will resemble you in that. If a Jew wrong a Christian, what is his humility? Revenge. If a 65 Christian wrong a Jew, what should his sufferance be 66 by Christian example? Why, revenge. The villainy you teach me I will execute, and it shall go hard but I will better the instruction.

Enter a Man from Antonio.

MAN   Gentlemen, my master Antonio is at his house and desires to speak with you both.

SALERIO   We have been up and down to seek him.

Enter Tubal.

SOLANIO   Here comes another of the tribe. A third cannot be matched, unless the devil himself turn Jew. 74
Exeunt gentlemen [Solanio, Salerio, with Man].

SHYLOCK   How now, Tubal, what news from Genoa? Hast thou found my daughter?

TUBAL   I often came where I did hear of her, but cannot find her.

SHYLOCK   Why, there, there, there, there! A diamond gone, cost me two thousand ducats in Frankfort! The 80 curse never fell upon our nation till now; I never felt it 81 till now. Two thousand ducats in that, and other precious, precious jewels. I would my daughter were dead at my foot, and the jewels in her ear! Would she were hearsed at my foot, and the ducats in her coffin! 85 No news of them? Why, so—and I know not what's spent in the search. Why, thou loss upon loss! The thief gone with so much, and so much to find the thief, and no satisfaction, no revenge! Nor no ill luck stirring but what lights o' my shoulders, no sighs but o' my breathing, no tears but o' my shedding.

TUBAL   Yes, other men have ill luck too. Antonio, as I heard in Genoa—

SHYLOCK   What, what, what? Ill luck, ill luck?

TUBAL   hath an argosy cast away, coming from Tripolis. 95

SHYLOCK   I thank God, I thank God. Is it true, is it true?

TUBAL   I spoke with some of the sailors that escaped the wreck.

SHYLOCK   I thank thee, good Tubal. Good news, good news! Ha, ha! Heard in Genoa?

TUBAL   Your daughter spent in Genoa, as I heard, one night fourscore ducats.

SHYLOCK   Thou stick'st a dagger in me. I shall never see my gold again. Fourscore ducats at a sitting? Fourscore ducats?

TUBAL   There came divers of Antonio's creditors in my company to Venice that swear he cannot choose but break. 108

SHYLOCK   I am very glad of it. I'll plague him, I'll torture him. I am glad of it.

TUBAL   One of them showed me a ring that he had of your daughter for a monkey.

SHYLOCK   Out upon her! Thou torturest me, Tubal. It was my turquoise; I had it of Leah when I was a 114 bachelor. I would not have given it for a wilderness of monkeys.

TUBAL   But Antonio is certainly undone.

SHYLOCK   Nay, that's true, that's very true. Go, Tubal, fee me an officer; bespeak him a fortnight before. I will 119 have the heart of him if he forfeit, for were he out of Venice I can make what merchandise I will. Go, Tubal, 121

26 the wings . . . withal i.e., the disguise she escaped in; with a play on *wings* or ornamented shoulder flaps sewn on garments   28 fledge ready to fly.   complexion natural disposition, as at 2.7.79   29 dam mother   33–34 Rebels . . . years (Solanio pretends to interpret Shylock's cry about the rebellion of his own flesh and blood as referring to his own carnal desires, his own erection.)   37 jet a black, hard mineral, here contrasted with the whiteness of ivory and Jessica's fair complexion   38 Rhenish i.e., a German white wine from the Rhine valley. Salerio seems to prefer the white wine as more refined than the red.   41 match bargain   44 mart marketplace, Rialto   50 To bait to act as bait for.   withal with   65 what is his humility? how does the Christian humble himself?   66 his sufferance the Jew's patient endurance

74 matched i.e., found to match them   80–81 The curse God's curse (such as the plagues visited upon Egypt in Exodus 7–12)   85 hearsed coffined   95 cast away shipwrecked   108 break go bankrupt   114 Leah Shylock's wife   119 fee hire.   officer bailiff.   bespeak engage   121 make . . . I will drive whatever bargains I please

and meet me at our synagogue. Go, good Tubal; at our synagogue, Tubal.   *Exeunt [separately].*

❧

3.2 *Enter Bassanio, Portia, Gratiano, [Nerissa,] and all their trains.*

PORTIA
I pray you, tarry. Pause a day or two
Before you hazard, for in choosing wrong   2
I lose your company. Therefore forbear awhile.
There's something tells me—but it is not love—
I would not lose you; and you know yourself
Hate counsels not in such a quality.   6
But lest you should not understand me well—
And yet a maiden hath no tongue but thought—
I would detain you here some month or two
Before you venture for me. I could teach you
How to choose right, but then I am forsworn.
So will I never be. So may you miss me.   12
But if you do, you'll make me wish a sin,
That I had been forsworn. Beshrew your eyes,
They have o'erlooked me and divided me!   15
One half of me is yours, the other half yours—
Mine own, I would say; but if mine, then yours,
And so all yours. O, these naughty times   18
Puts bars between the owners and their rights!   19
And so, though yours, not yours. Prove it so,   20
Let Fortune go to hell for it, not I.   21
I speak too long, but 'tis to peise the time,   22
To eke it and to draw it out in length,   23
To stay you from election.

BASSANIO   Let me choose,   24
For as I am, I live upon the rack.

PORTIA
Upon the rack, Bassanio? Then confess   26
What treason there is mingled with your love.   27

BASSANIO
None but that ugly treason of mistrust,   28
Which makes me fear th' enjoying of my love.   29
There may as well be amity and life
'Tween snow and fire, as treason and my love.

PORTIA
Ay, but I fear you speak upon the rack,
Where men enforcèd do speak anything.

BASSANIO
Promise me life, and I'll confess the truth.

PORTIA
Well then, confess and live.

BASSANIO   "Confess and love"
Had been the very sum of my confession.
O happy torment, when my torturer
Doth teach me answers for deliverance!
But let me to my fortune and the caskets.   39

PORTIA
Away, then! I am locked in one of them.
If you do love me, you will find me out.
Nerissa and the rest, stand all aloof.   42
Let music sound while he doth make his choice;
Then, if he lose, he makes a swanlike end,   44
Fading in music. That the comparison
May stand more proper, my eye shall be the stream
And watery deathbed for him. He may win;
And what is music then? Then music is
Even as the flourish when true subjects bow   49
To a new-crownèd monarch. Such it is
As are those dulcet sounds in break of day
That creep into the dreaming bridegroom's ear
And summon him to marriage. Now he goes,
With no less presence, but with much more love,   54
Than young Alcides when he did redeem   55
The virgin tribute paid by howling Troy   56
To the sea monster. I stand for sacrifice;   57
The rest aloof are the Dardanian wives,   58
With blearèd visages, come forth to view   59
The issue of th' exploit. Go, Hercules!   60
Live thou, I live. With much, much more dismay   61
I view the fight than thou that mak'st the fray.

A song, the whilst Bassanio comments on the caskets to himself.

Tell me where is fancy bred,   63
Or in the heart or in the head?   64
How begot, how nourishèd?
     Reply, reply.
It is engenderèd in the eyes,   67
With gazing fed, and fancy dies
In the cradle where it lies.   69
     Let us all ring fancy's knell.
     I'll begin it—Ding, dong, bell.
ALL   Ding, dong, bell.

BASSANIO
So may the outward shows be least themselves;   73
The world is still deceived with ornament.   74
In law, what plea so tainted and corrupt

3.2. Location: Belmont. Portia's house.

2 in choosing in your choosing. **6 quality** way, manner **12 So . . . So** that . . . therefore. **miss** i.e., fail to win **15 o'erlooked** bewitched **18 naughty** worthless, wicked **19 bars** barriers **20 though yours, not yours** (I am) yours by right but not by actual possession **20–21 Prove . . . not I** i.e., if it turn out thus (that you are cheated of what is justly yours, i.e., of me), let Fortune be blamed for it, not I, for I will not be forsworn **22 peise** retard (by hanging on of weights) **23 eke** eke out, augment **24 election** choice **26–27 confess What treason** (The rack was used to force traitors to confess.) **28 mistrust** misapprehension **29 fear** fearful about

39 fortune . . . caskets (Presumably the curtains are drawn at about this point, as in the previous "casket" scenes, revealing the three caskets.) **42 aloof** apart, at a distance **44 swanlike** (Swans were believed to sing when they came to die.) **49 flourish** sounding of trumpets **54 presence** noble bearing **55 Alcides** Hercules (called *Alcides*, as at 2.1.32–35, because he was the grandson of Alcaeus) rescued Hesione, daughter of the Trojan king Laomedon, from a monster to which, by command of Neptune, she was about to be sacrificed. Hercules was rewarded, however, not with the lady's love, but with a famous pair of horses. **56 howling** lamenting **57 stand for sacrifice** represent the sacrificial victim **58 Dardanian** Trojan **59 blearèd** tear-stained **60 issue** outcome **61 Live thou** if you live **63 fancy** love **64 Or** either **67 eyes** (Love entered the heart especially through the eyes.) **69 In the cradle** i.e., in its infancy, in the eyes **73 be least themselves** least represent the inner reality **74 still** ever

But, being seasoned with a gracious voice,
Obscures the show of evil? In religion,
What damnèd error but some sober brow
Will bless it and approve it with a text,   79
Hiding the grossness with fair ornament?
There is no vice so simple but assumes   81
Some mark of virtue on his outward parts.   82
How many cowards, whose hearts are all as false
As stairs of sand, wear yet upon their chins   84
The beards of Hercules and frowning Mars,
Who, inward searched, have livers white as milk?   86
And these assume but valor's excrement   87
To render them redoubted. Look on beauty,   88
And you shall see 'tis purchased by the weight,   89
Which therein works a miracle in nature,
Making them lightest that wear most of it.   91
So are those crispèd, snaky, golden locks,   92
Which maketh such wanton gambols with the wind
Upon supposèd fairness, often known   94
To be the dowry of a second head,   95
The skull that bred them in the sepulcher.   96
Thus ornament is but the guilèd shore   97
To a most dangerous sea, the beauteous scarf
Veiling an Indian beauty; in a word,   99
The seeming truth which cunning times put on
To entrap the wisest. Therefore, thou gaudy gold,
Hard food for Midas, I will none of thee;   102
Nor none of thee, thou pale and common drudge   103
'Tween man and man. But thou, thou meager lead,   104
Which rather threaten'st than dost promise aught,
Thy paleness moves me more than eloquence;
And here choose I. Joy be the consequence!
PORTIA [*aside*]
How all the other passions fleet to air,
As doubtful thoughts, and rash-embraced despair,   109
And shuddering fear, and green-eyed jealousy!
O love, be moderate, allay thy ecstasy,
In measure rain thy joy, scant this excess!   112
I feel too much thy blessing. Make it less,
For fear I surfeit.
BASSANIO [*opening the leaden casket*]
                    What find I here?
Fair Portia's counterfeit! What demigod   115
Hath come so near creation? Move these eyes?
Or whether, riding on the balls of mine,   117
Seem they in motion? Here are severed lips,

Parted with sugar breath; so sweet a bar   119
Should sunder such sweet friends. Here in her hairs 120
The painter plays the spider, and hath woven
A golden mesh t' entrap the hearts of men
Faster than gnats in cobwebs. But her eyes—   123
How could he see to do them? Having made one,
Methinks it should have power to steal both his
And leave itself unfurnished. Yet look how far   126
The substance of my praise doth wrong this shadow 127
In underprizing it, so far this shadow   128
Doth limp behind the substance. Here's the scroll,   129
The continent and summary of my fortune.   130
[*He reads.*] "You that choose not by the view
            Chance as fair, and choose as true.   132
            Since this fortune falls to you,
            Be content and seek no new.
            If you be well pleased with this,
            And hold your fortune for your bliss,
            Turn you where your lady is
            And claim her with a loving kiss."
A gentle scroll. Fair lady, by your leave,
I come by note, to give and to receive.   140
Like one of two contending in a prize,   141
That thinks he hath done well in people's eyes,
Hearing applause and universal shout,
Giddy in spirit, still gazing in a doubt
Whether those peals of praise be his or no,   145
So, thrice-fair lady, stand I, even so,
As doubtful whether what I see be true,
Until confirmed, signed, ratified by you.
PORTIA
You see me, Lord Bassanio, where I stand,
Such as I am. Though for myself alone
I would not be ambitious in my wish
To wish myself much better, yet for you
I would be trebled twenty times myself,
A thousand times more fair, ten thousand times
  more rich,
That only to stand high in your account   155
I might in virtues, beauties, livings, friends,   156
Exceed account. But the full sum of me   157
Is sum of something, which, to term in gross,   158
Is an unlessoned girl, unschooled, unpracticèd;
Happy in this, she is not yet so old
But she may learn; happier than this,
She is not bred so dull but she can learn;
Happiest of all is that her gentle spirit
Commits itself to yours to be directed

---

79 approve confirm **81 simple** unadulterated **82 his** its **84 stairs** steps **86 searched** surgically probed. **livers** (The liver was thought to be the seat of courage; for it to be deserted by the blood would be the condition of cowardice.) **87 excrement** outgrowth, such as a beard (as in this case) **88 redoubted** feared **89 purchased by the weight** bought (as cosmetics) at so much per ounce **91 lightest** most lascivious (with pun on the sense of "least heavy") **92 crispèd** curly **94 Upon supposèd fairness** i.e., on a woman supposed beautiful and fair-haired **95–96 To . . . sepulcher** i.e., to be a wig of hair taken from a woman now dead **97 guilèd** treacherous **99 Indian** i.e., swarthy, not fair **102 Midas** the Phrygian king whose touch turned everything to gold, including his food **103–104 pale . . . man** i.e., silver, used in commerce **109 As** such as **112 rain** rain down, or perhaps "rein." **scant** lessen **115 counterfeit** portrait. **demigod** i.e., the painter as creator **117 Or whether** or

119 so sweet a bar i.e., Portia's breath **120 sweet friends** i.e., her lips **123 Faster** more tightly **126 unfurnished** i.e., without a companion. **look how far** however far **127 shadow** painting, semblance **128 underprizing it** failing to do it justice. **so far** to a similar extent **129 the substance** the subject, i.e., Portia **130 continent** container **132 Chance as fair** hazard as fortunately **140 by note** by a bill of dues (i.e., the scroll). The commercial metaphor continues in *confirmed, signed, ratified* (line 148), *account* (155), *sum* (157), *term in gross* (158), etc. **141 prize** competition **145 his** for him **155 account** estimation **156 livings** possessions **157 account** calculation (playing on *account*, estimation, in line 155) **157–158 But . . . something** i.e., but the full sum of my worth can only be the sum of whatever I am **158 term in gross** denote in full

As from her lord, her governor, her king.
Myself and what is mine to you and yours
Is now converted. But now I was the lord   167
Of this fair mansion, master of my servants,
Queen o'er myself; and even now, but now,
This house, these servants, and this same myself
Are yours, my lord's. I give them with this ring,
Which when you part from, lose, or give away,
Let it presage the ruin of your love
And be my vantage to exclaim on you.   174
                          [*She puts a ring on his finger.*]

BASSANIO
Madam, you have bereft me of all words.
Only my blood speaks to you in my veins,
And there is such confusion in my powers   177
As, after some oration fairly spoke
By a belovèd prince, there doth appear
Among the buzzing pleasèd multitude,
Where every something being blent together   181
Turns to a wild of nothing save of joy   182
Expressed and not expressed. But when this ring   183
Parts from this finger, then parts life from hence.
O, then be bold to say Bassanio's dead!

NERISSA
My lord and lady, it is now our time,
That have stood by and seen our wishes prosper,   187
To cry, "good joy." Good joy, my lord and lady!

GRATIANO
My lord Bassanio and my gentle lady,
I wish you all the joy that you can wish—
For I am sure you can wish none from me.   191
And when your honors mean to solemnize
The bargain of your faith, I do beseech you
Even at that time I may be married too.

BASSANIO
With all my heart, so thou canst get a wife.   195

GRATIANO
I thank your lordship, you have got me one.
My eyes, my lord, can look as swift as yours.
You saw the mistrèss, I beheld the maid;   198
You loved, I loved; for intermission   199
No more pertains to me, my lord, than you.
Your fortune stood upon the caskets there,
And so did mine too, as the matter falls;   202
For wooing here until I sweat again,   203
And swearing till my very roof was dry   204
With oaths of love, at last, if promise last,   205
I got a promise of this fair one here

To have her love, provided that your fortune
Achieved her mistress.

PORTIA   Is this true, Nerissa?

NERISSA
Madam, it is, so you stand pleased withal.   209

BASSANIO
And do you, Gratiano, mean good faith?

GRATIANO   Yes, faith, my lord.

BASSANIO
Our feast shall be much honored in your marriage.

GRATIANO   We'll play with them the first boy for a thou- 213
sand ducats.

NERISSA   What, and stake down?   215

GRATIANO   No, we shall ne'er win at that sport, and
stake down.

        Enter Lorenzo, Jessica, and Salerio, a messenger
        from Venice.

But who comes here? Lorenzo and his infidel?
What, and my old Venetian friend Salerio?

BASSANIO
Lorenzo and Salerio, welcome hither,
If that the youth of my new interest here   221
Have power to bid you welcome.—By your leave,
I bid my very friends and countrymen,   223
Sweet Portia, welcome.

PORTIA   So do I, my lord.
They are entirely welcome.

LORENZO
I thank your honor. For my part, my lord,
My purpose was not to have seen you here,
But meeting with Salerio by the way,
He did intreat me, past all saying nay,
To come with him along.

SALERIO   I did, my lord,
And I have reason for it. Signor Antonio
Commends him to you.   [*He gives Bassanio a letter.*]

BASSANIO   Ere I ope his letter,   232
I pray you tell me how my good friend doth.

SALERIO
Not sick, my lord, unless it be in mind,
Nor well, unless in mind. His letter there
Will show you his estate.   [*Bassanio*] open[*s*] *the letter.* 236

GRATIANO [*indicating Jessica*]
Nerissa, cheer yond stranger, bid her welcome.   237
Your hand, Salerio. What's the news from Venice?
How doth that royal merchant, good Antonio?   239
I know he will be glad of our success.
We are the Jasons; we have won the fleece.   241

SALERIO
I would you had won the fleece that he hath lost.

PORTIA
There are some shrewd contents in yond same paper   243

---

167 But now a moment ago   **174 vantage to exclaim on** opportunity to reproach   **177 powers** faculties   **181–183 Where . . . expressed** i.e., in which every individual utterance, being blended and confused, turns into a hubbub of joy in which individual utterances cannot be distinguished   **187 That** we who   **191 For . . . me** i.e., I'm sure I can't wish you any more joy than you could wish for yourselves, or, I'm sure your wishes for happiness cannot take away from my happiness   **195 so** provided   **198 maid** (Nerissa is a lady-in-waiting, not a house servant.)   **199 intermission** delay (in loving) **202 falls** falls out, happens   **203 sweat again** sweated repeatedly **204 roof** roof of my mouth   **205 if promise last** i.e., if Nerissa's promise should last, hold out (with a play on *last* and at *last*, "finally")

209 so provided   **213 play** wager   **215 stake down** cash placed in advance. (But Gratiano, in his reply, turns the phrase into a bawdy joke; *stake down* to him suggests a non-erect phallus.)   **221 youth . . . interest** i.e., newness of my household authority   **223 very** true **232 Commends him** desires to be remembered   **236 estate** condition **237 stranger** alien   **239 royal merchant** i.e., chief among merchants **241 Jasons . . . fleece** (Compare with 1.1.170–172.)   **243 shrewd** cursed, grievous

That steals the color from Bassanio's cheek—
Some dear friend dead, else nothing in the world
Could turn so much the constitution
Of any constant man. What, worse and worse?   247
With leave, Bassanio; I am half yourself,
And I must freely have the half of anything
That this same paper brings you.
BASSANIO   O sweet Portia,
Here are a few of the unpleasant'st words
That ever blotted paper! Gentle lady,
When I did first impart my love to you,
I freely told you all the wealth I had
Ran in my veins, I was a gentleman;
And then I told you true. And yet, dear lady,
Rating myself at nothing, you shall see
How much I was a braggart. When I told you
My state was nothing, I should then have told you   259
That I was worse than nothing; for indeed
I have engaged myself to a dear friend,
Engaged my friend to his mere enemy,   262
To feed my means. Here is a letter, lady,
The paper as the body of my friend,
And every word in it a gaping wound
Issuing lifeblood. But is it true, Salerio?
Hath all his ventures failed? What, not one hit?   267
From Tripolis, from Mexico, and England,
From Lisbon, Barbary, and India,
And not one vessel scape the dreadful touch
Of merchant-marring rocks?
SALERIO   Not one, my lord.   271
Besides, it should appear that if he had
The present money to discharge the Jew   273
He would not take it. Never did I know   274
A creature that did bear the shape of man
So keen and greedy to confound a man.   276
He plies the Duke at morning and at night,
And doth impeach the freedom of the state   278
If they deny him justice. Twenty merchants,
The Duke himself, and the magnificoes   280
Of greatest port have all persuaded with him,   281
But none can drive him from the envious plea   282
Of forfeiture, of justice, and his bond.
JESSICA
When I was with him I have heard him swear
To Tubal and to Chus, his countrymen,   285
That he would rather have Antonio's flesh
Than twenty times the value of the sum
That he did owe him; and I know, my lord,
If law, authority, and power deny not,
It will go hard with poor Antonio.

PORTIA [to Bassanio]
Is it your dear friend that is thus in trouble?
BASSANIO
The dearest friend to me, the kindest man,
The best-conditioned and unwearied spirit   293
In doing courtesies, and one in whom
The ancient Roman honor more appears
Than any that draws breath in Italy.
PORTIA   What sum owes he the Jew?
BASSANIO
For me, three thousand ducats.
PORTIA   What, no more?
Pay him six thousand, and deface the bond;   299
Double six thousand, and then treble that,
Before a friend of this description
Shall lose a hair through Bassanio's fault.
First go with me to church and call me wife,
And then away to Venice to your friend;
For never shall you lie by Portia's side
With an unquiet soul. You shall have gold
To pay the petty debt twenty times over.
When it is paid, bring your true friend along.
My maid Nerissa and myself meantime
Will live as maids and widows. Come, away!
For you shall hence upon your wedding day.
Bid your friends welcome, show a merry cheer;   312
Since you are dear bought, I will love you dear.   313
But let me hear the letter of your friend.
BASSANIO [reads] "Sweet Bassanio, my ships have all
miscarried, my creditors grow cruel, my estate is
very low, my bond to the Jew is forfeit; and since in
paying it, it is impossible I should live, all debts are
cleared between you and I if I might but see you at
my death. Notwithstanding, use your pleasure. If
your love do not persuade you to come, let not my
letter."
PORTIA
O love, dispatch all business, and begone!
BASSANIO
Since I have your good leave to go away,
I will make haste; but till I come again
No bed shall e'er be guilty of my stay,
Nor rest be interposer twixt us twain.   *Exeunt.*

❧

3.3   *Enter [Shylock] the Jew and Solanio and Antonio
and the Jailer.*

SHYLOCK
Jailer, look to him. Tell not me of mercy.
This is the fool that lent out money gratis.
Jailer, look to him.
ANTONIO   Hear me yet, good Shylock.
SHYLOCK
I'll have my bond. Speak not against my bond.

247 **constant** settled, not swayed by passion   259 **state** estate
262 **mere** absolute   267 **hit** success   271 **merchant** merchant ship
273 **present** available.   **discharge** pay off   274 **He** i.e., Shylock
276 **keen** cruel.   **confound** destroy   278 **impeach . . . state** i.e., call
in question the ability of Venice to defend legally the freedom of
commerce of its citizens   280 **magnificoes** chief men of Venice
281 **port** dignity.   **persuaded** argued   282 **envious** malicious
285 **Chus** the Bishops' Bible spelling of *Cush*, son of Ham and grandson of Noah. *Tubal* was son of Japheth and grandson of Noah (Genesis 10:2, 6).

293 **best-conditioned** best natured   299 **deface** erase   312 **cheer**
countenance   313 **dear . . . dear** expensively . . . dearly
3.3. Location: Venice. A street.

I have sworn an oath that I will have my bond.
Thou calledst me dog before thou hadst a cause,
But since I am a dog, beware my fangs.
The Duke shall grant me justice. I do wonder,
Thou naughty jailer, that thou art so fond   9
To come abroad with him at his request.   10

ANTONIO   I pray thee, hear me speak.

SHYLOCK
I'll have my bond. I will not hear thee speak.
I'll have my bond, and therefore speak no more.
I'll not be made a soft and dull-eyed fool,   14
To shake the head, relent, and sigh, and yield
To Christian intercessors. Follow not.
I'll have no speaking. I will have my bond.   *Exit Jew.*

SOLANIO
It is the most impenetrable cur
That ever kept with men.

ANTONIO   Let him alone.   19
I'll follow him no more with bootless prayers.   20
He seeks my life. His reason well I know:
I oft delivered from his forfeitures
Many that have at times made moan to me;
Therefore he hates me.

SOLANIO   I am sure the Duke
Will never grant this forfeiture to hold.

ANTONIO
The Duke cannot deny the course of law;
For the commodity that strangers have   27
With us in Venice, if it be denied,
Will much impeach the justice of the state,
Since that the trade and profit of the city   30
Consisteth of all nations. Therefore go.
These griefs and losses have so bated me   32
That I shall hardly spare a pound of flesh
Tomorrow to my bloody creditor.
Well, jailer, on. Pray God Bassanio come
To see me pay his debt, and then I care not.   *Exeunt.*

❧

3.4   *Enter Portia, Nerissa, Lorenzo, Jessica, and
            [Balthasar,] a man of Portia's.*

LORENZO
Madam, although I speak it in your presence,
You have a noble and a true conceit   2
Of godlike amity, which appears most strongly
In bearing thus the absence of your lord.
But if you knew to whom you show this honor,
How true a gentleman you send relief,
How dear a lover of my lord your husband,   7
I know you would be prouder of the work
Than customary bounty can enforce you.   9

PORTIA
I never did repent for doing good,
Nor shall not now; for in companions
That do converse and waste the time together,   12
Whose souls do bear an equal yoke of love,
There must be needs a like proportion   14
Of lineaments, of manners, and of spirit;   15
Which makes me think that this Antonio,
Being the bosom lover of my lord,   17
Must needs be like my lord. If it be so,
How little is the cost I have bestowed
In purchasing the semblance of my soul   20
From out the state of hellish cruelty!   21
This comes too near the praising of myself;
Therefore no more of it. Hear other things:
Lorenzo, I commit into your hands
The husbandry and manage of my house   25
Until my lord's return. For mine own part,
I have toward heaven breathed a secret vow
To live in prayer and contemplation,
Only attended by Nerissa here,
Until her husband and my lord's return.
There is a monastery two miles off,
And there we will abide. I do desire you
Not to deny this imposition,   33
The which my love and some necessity
Now lays upon you.

LORENZO   Madam, with all my heart,
I shall obey you in all fair commands.

PORTIA
My people do already know my mind,
And will acknowledge you and Jessica
In place of Lord Bassanio and myself.
So fare you well till we shall meet again.

LORENZO
Fair thoughts and happy hours attend on you!

JESSICA
I wish your ladyship all heart's content.

PORTIA
I thank you for your wish and am well pleased
To wish it back on you. Fare you well, Jessica.
                        Exeunt [Jessica and Lorenzo].
Now, Balthasar,
As I have ever found thee honest-true,
So let me find thee still. Take this same letter,
                        [*giving a letter*]
And use thou all th' endeavor of a man
In speed to Padua. See thou render this
Into my cousin's hands, Doctor Bellario;
And look what notes and garments he doth give
    thee,   51
Bring them, I pray thee, with imagined speed   52
Unto the traject, to the common ferry   53

---

9 naughty worthless, wicked. **fond** foolish **10 abroad** outside
14 dull-eyed easily duped **19 kept** associated, dwelt **20 bootless**
unavailing **27 commodity** facilities or privileges for trading. **strangers** noncitizens, including Jews **30 Since that** since **32 bated** reduced
3.4. Location: Belmont. Portia's house.
2 conceit understanding **7 lover** friend **9 Than . . . you** than ordinary benevolence can make you

12 waste spend **14 must be needs** must be **15 lineaments** physical
features **17 bosom lover** dear friend **20 the semblance of my soul**
i.e., Antonio, so like my Bassanio **21 of hellish cruelty** to which
hellish cruelty has reduced him **25 husbandry and manage** care and
management **33 deny this imposition** refuse this charge imposed
51 look what whatever **52 imagined** all imaginable **53 traject** ferry.
(Italian *traghetto*.) **common** public

Which trades to Venice. Waste no time in words, 54
But get thee gone. I shall be there before thee.

BALTHASAR
Madam, I go with all convenient speed.   *[Exit.]* 56

PORTIA
Come on, Nerissa, I have work in hand
That you yet know not of. We'll see our husbands
Before they think of us.

NERISSA   Shall they see us?

PORTIA
They shall, Nerissa, but in such a habit 60
That they shall think we are accomplishèd 61
With that we lack. I'll hold thee any wager, 62
When we are both accoutred like young men
I'll prove the prettier fellow of the two,
And wear my dagger with the braver grace,
And speak between the change of man and boy
With a reed voice, and turn two mincing steps
Into a manly stride, and speak of frays
Like a fine bragging youth, and tell quaint lies, 69
How honorable ladies sought my love,
Which I denying, they fell sick and died—
I could not do withal! Then I'll repent, 72
And wish, for all that, that I had not killed them;
And twenty of these puny lies I'll tell, 74
That men shall swear I have discontinued school 75
Above a twelvemonth. I have within my mind 76
A thousand raw tricks of these bragging Jacks, 77
Which I will practice.

NERISSA   Why, shall we turn to men? 78

PORTIA   Fie, what a question's that,
If thou wert near a lewd interpreter!
But come, I'll tell thee all my whole device
When I am in my coach, which stays for us
At the park gate; and therefore haste away,
For we must measure twenty miles today.   *Exeunt.* 84

3.5   *Enter [Lancelot the] clown and Jessica.*

LANCELOT   Yes, truly, for look you, the sins of the father are to be laid upon the children; therefore, I promise you, I fear you. I was always plain with you, and 3
so now I speak my agitation of the matter. Therefore 4
be o' good cheer, for truly I think you are damned.
There is but one hope in it that can do you any good,
and that is but a kind of bastard hope, neither. 7

JESSICA   And what hope is that, I pray thee?

LANCELOT   Marry, you may partly hope that your fa-

ther got you not, that you are not the Jew's daughter. 10

JESSICA   That were a kind of bastard hope, indeed! So
the sins of my mother should be visited upon me.

LANCELOT   Truly, then, I fear you are damned both by
father and mother. Thus when I shun Scylla, your 14
father, I fall into Charybdis, your mother. Well, you 15
are gone both ways. 16

JESSICA   I shall be saved by my husband. He hath made 17
me a Christian.

LANCELOT   Truly, the more to blame he! We were 19
Christians enough before, e'en as many as could well 20
live one by another. This making of Christians will 21
raise the price of hogs. If we grow all to be pork eaters,
we shall not shortly have a rasher on the coals for 23
money. 24

        Enter Lorenzo.

JESSICA   I'll tell my husband, Lancelot, what you say.
Here he comes.

LORENZO   I shall grow jealous of you shortly, Lancelot,
if you thus get my wife into corners.

JESSICA   Nay, you need not fear us, Lorenzo. Lancelot
and I are out. He tells me flatly there's no mercy for me 30
in heaven because I am a Jew's daughter; and he says
you are no good member of the commonwealth, for in
converting Jews to Christians you raise the price of
pork.

LORENZO   I shall answer that better to the commonwealth than you can the getting up of the Negro's
belly. The Moor is with child by you, Lancelot. 37

LANCELOT   It is much that the Moor should be more 38
than reason; but if she be less than an honest woman, 39
she is indeed more than I took her for. 40

LORENZO   How every fool can play upon the word! I
think the best grace of wit will shortly turn into 42
silence, and discourse grow commendable in none
only but parrots. Go in, sirrah, bid them prepare for
dinner.

LANCELOT   That is done, sir. They have all stomachs. 46

LORENZO   Goodly Lord, what a wit-snapper are you!
Then bid them prepare dinner.

LANCELOT   That is done too, sir, only "cover" is the 49
word.

LORENZO   Will you cover then, sir? 51

---

54 **trades** plies back and forth   56 **convenient** due, proper   60 **habit** apparel, garb   61 **accomplishèd** supplied   62 **that** that which (with a bawdy suggestion)   69 **quaint** elaborate, clever   72 **do withal** help it   74 **puny** childish   75–76 **I . . . twelvemonth** i.e., that I am no mere schoolboy   76 **Above** more than   77 **Jacks** fellows   78 **turn to** turn into. (But Portia sees the occasion for a bawdy quibble on the idea of "turning toward, lying next to.")   84 **measure** traverse
3.5. Location: Belmont. Outside Portia's house.
3 **fear you** fear for you   4 **agitation** (A blunder for "cogitation"?)   7 **bastard** i.e., unfounded (but also anticipating the usual meaning in lines 9–10). **neither** i.e., to be sure

10 got begot   **14, 15 Scylla, Charybdis** twin dangers of the *Odyssey*, 12.255, a monster and a whirlpool guarding the straits presumably between Italy and Sicily. (*Fall into* plays on the idea of "whirlpool" as the female sexual anatomy.)   **16 gone** done for   **17 I . . . husband** (Compare 1 Corinthians 7:14: "the unbelieving wife is sanctified by the husband.")   **19–20 We . . . enough** there were enough of us Christians   **21 one by another** (1) as neighbors (2) off one another   **23 rasher** i.e., of bacon   **23–24 for money** even for ready money, at any price   **30 are out** have fallen out   **37 The Moor** (Lancelot has evidently impregnated some woman of the household, who, being of African heritage, is referred to as both "Negro" and "Moor.")
38–39 more than reason larger than is reasonable, than she should be (with wordplay on "Moor," "more," continued in line 40)
39–40 if she . . . for i.e., to describe her as something less than perfectly chaste would be to pay her a compliment, in my view   **42 best grace** highest quality   **46 stomachs** appetites   **49, 51 cover** spread the table for the meal. (But in line 52 Lancelot uses the word to mean "put on one's hat.")

LANCELOT   Not so, sir, neither. I know my duty.

LORENZO   Yet more quarreling with occasion! Wilt thou 53
show the whole wealth of thy wit in an instant? I pray
thee, understand a plain man in his plain meaning: go
to thy fellows, bid them cover the table, serve in the
meat, and we will come in to dinner.   57

LANCELOT   For the table, sir, it shall be served in; for the 58
meat, sir, it shall be covered; for your coming in to 59
dinner, sir, why, let it be as humors and conceits shall 60
govern.   *Exit [Lancelot the] clown.*

LORENZO
O dear discretion, how his words are suited!   62
The fool hath planted in his memory
An army of good words; and I do know
A many fools, that stand in better place,   65
Garnished like him, that for a tricksy word   66
Defy the matter. How cheer'st thou, Jessica?   67
And now, good sweet, say thy opinion:
How dost thou like the Lord Bassanio's wife?

JESSICA
Past all expressing. It is very meet   70
The Lord Bassanio live an upright life,
For, having such a blessing in his lady,
He finds the joys of heaven here on earth;
And if on earth he do not merit it,
In reason he should never come to heaven.   75
Why, if two gods should play some heavenly match
And on the wager lay two earthly women,   77
And Portia one, there must be something else   78
Pawned with the other, for the poor rude world   79
Hath not her fellow.

LORENZO   Even such a husband
Hast thou of me as she is for a wife.

JESSICA
Nay, but ask my opinion too of that!

LORENZO
I will anon. First let us go to dinner.

JESSICA
Nay, let me praise you while I have a stomach.   84

LORENZO
No, pray thee, let it serve for table talk;
Then, howsoe'er thou speak'st, 'mong other things
I shall digest it.

JESSICA   Well, I'll set you forth.   *Exeunt.* 87

❖

53 Yet . . . occasion i.e., still quibbling at every opportunity
57 meat food   **58 For** as for.   **table** (Here Lancelot quibblingly uses
the word to mean the food itself.)   **59 covered** (Here used in the
sense of providing a cover for each separate dish.)   **60 humors and
conceits** whims and fancies   **62 O dear discretion** O what precious
discrimination.   **suited** suited to the occasion   **65 A many** many.
better place higher social station   **66 Garnished** i.e., furnished with
words, or with garments   **66–67 that . . . matter** who for the sake of
ingenious wordplay disdain to speak sensibly   **67 How cheer'st thou**
i.e., what cheer, how are you doing   **70 meet** fitting   **75 In reason** it
stands to reason. (Jessica jokes that for Bassanio to receive unmerited
bliss on earth—unmerited because no person can earn bliss through
his or her own deserving—is to run the risk of eternal damnation.)
77 lay stake   **78 else** more   **79 Pawned** staked, wagered   **84 stomach** (1) appetite (2) inclination   **87 digest** (1) ponder, analyze (2)
"swallow," put up with (with a play also on the gastronomic sense).
set you forth (1) serve you up, as at a feast (2) set forth your praises

4.1   *Enter the Duke, the Magnificoes, Antonio,
Bassanio, [Salerio,] and Gratiano [with others. The
judges take their places.]*

DUKE   What, is Antonio here?

ANTONIO   Ready, so please Your Grace.

DUKE
I am sorry for thee. Thou art come to answer   3
A stony adversary, an inhuman wretch
Uncapable of pity, void and empty
From any dram of mercy.

ANTONIO   I have heard   6
Your Grace hath ta'en great pains to qualify   7
His rigorous course; but since he stands obdurate
And that no lawful means can carry me
Out of his envy's reach, I do oppose   10
My patience to his fury and am armed
To suffer with a quietness of spirit
The very tyranny and rage of his.   13

DUKE
Go one, and call the Jew into the court.

SALERIO
He is ready at the door. He comes, my lord.

Enter Shylock.

DUKE
Make room, and let him stand before our face.   16
Shylock, the world thinks, and I think so too,
That thou but leadest this fashion of thy malice   18
To the last hour of act, and then 'tis thought   19
Thou'lt show thy mercy and remorse more strange   20
Than is thy strange apparent cruelty;   21
And where thou now exacts the penalty,
Which is a pound of this poor merchant's flesh,
Thou wilt not only loose the forfeiture,   24
But, touched with human gentleness and love,
Forgive a moiety of the principal,   26
Glancing an eye of pity on his losses
That have of late so huddled on his back—
Enough to press a royal merchant down
And pluck commiseration of his state
From brassy bosoms and rough hearts of flint,   31
From stubborn Turks and Tartars never trained
To offices of tender courtesy.
We all expect a gentle answer, Jew.

SHYLOCK
I have possessed Your Grace of what I purpose,   35
And by our holy Sabbath have I sworn
To have the due and forfeit of my bond.

**4.1. Location: Venice. A court of justice. Benches, etc., are provided
for the justices.**
3 answer defend yourself against. (A legal term.)   **6 dram** sixty grains
apothecaries' weight, a tiny quantity   **7 qualify** moderate   **10 envy's**
malice's   **13 tyranny** cruelty   **16 our** (The royal plural.)   **18 thou
. . . fashion** you only maintain this pretense or form   **19 the last . . .
act** the brink of action   **20 remorse** pity.   **strange** remarkable
21 strange unnatural, foreign.   **apparent** (1) manifest, overt (2)
seeming   **24 loose** release, waive   **26 moiety** part, portion
31 brassy unfeeling, hard like brass   **35 possessed** informed

If you deny it, let the danger light 38
Upon your charter and your city's freedom! 39
You'll ask me why I rather choose to have
A weight of carrion flesh than to receive
Three thousand ducats. I'll not answer that,
But say it is my humor. Is it answered? 43
What if my house be troubled with a rat
And I be pleased to give ten thousand ducats
To have it baned? What, are you answered yet? 46
Some men there are love not a gaping pig, 47
Some that are mad if they behold a cat,
And others, when the bagpipe sings i' the nose,
Cannot contain their urine; for affection, 50
Mistress of passion, sways it to the mood
Of what it likes or loathes. Now, for your answer:
As there is no firm reason to be rendered
Why he cannot abide a gaping pig, 54
Why he a harmless necessary cat, 55
Why he a woolen bagpipe, but of force 56
Must yield to such inevitable shame
As to offend, himself being offended,
So can I give no reason, nor I will not,
More than a lodged hate and a certain loathing 60
I bear Antonio, that I follow thus
A losing suit against him. Are you answered? 62

BASSANIO
This is no answer, thou unfeeling man,
To excuse the current of thy cruelty. 64

SHYLOCK
I am not bound to please thee with my answers.

BASSANIO
Do all men kill the things they do not love?

SHYLOCK
Hates any man the thing he would not kill?

BASSANIO
Every offense is not a hate at first.

SHYLOCK
What, wouldst thou have a serpent sting thee twice?

ANTONIO
I pray you, think you question with the Jew. 70
You may as well go stand upon the beach
And bid the main flood bate his usual height; 72
You may as well use question with the wolf 73
Why he hath made the ewe bleat for the lamb;
You may as well forbid the mountain pines
To wag their high tops and to make no noise
When they are fretten with the gusts of heaven; 77
You may as well do anything most hard
As seek to soften that—than which what's
    harder?—
His Jewish heart. Therefore, I do beseech you,

Make no more offers, use no farther means,
But with all brief and plain conveniency 82
Let me have judgment, and the Jew his will.

BASSANIO [*to Shylock*]
For thy three thousand ducats here is six.

SHYLOCK
If every ducat in six thousand ducats
Were in six parts, and every part a ducat,
I would not draw them. I would have my bond. 87

DUKE
How shalt thou hope for mercy, rendering none?

SHYLOCK
What judgment shall I dread, doing no wrong?
You have among you many a purchased slave,
Which, like your asses and your dogs and mules,
You use in abject and in slavish parts, 92
Because you bought them. Shall I say to you,
"Let them be free, marry them to your heirs!
Why sweat they under burdens? Let their beds
Be made as soft as yours, and let their palates
Be seasoned with such viands"? You will answer 97
"The slaves are ours." So do I answer you:
The pound of flesh which I demand of him
Is dearly bought, is mine, and I will have it.
If you deny me, fie upon your law!
There is no force in the decrees of Venice.
I stand for judgment. Answer: shall I have it?

DUKE
Upon my power I may dismiss this court, 104
Unless Bellario, a learnèd doctor,
Whom I have sent for to determine this, 106
Come here today.

SALERIO   My lord, here stays without 107
A messenger with letters from the doctor,
New come from Padua.

DUKE
Bring us the letters. Call the messenger. [*Exit one.*]

BASSANIO
Good cheer, Antonio. What, man, courage yet!
The Jew shall have my flesh, blood, bones, and all,
Ere thou shalt lose for me one drop of blood.

ANTONIO
I am a tainted wether of the flock, 114
Meetest for death. The weakest kind of fruit 115
Drops earliest to the ground, and so let me.
You cannot better be employed, Bassanio,
Than to live still and write mine epitaph.

Enter Nerissa [*dressed like a lawyer's clerk*].

DUKE
Came you from Padua, from Bellario?

NERISSA
From both, my lord. Bellario greets Your Grace.
[*She presents a letter. Shylock whets his knife on his shoe.*]

BASSANIO
Why dost thou whet thy knife so earnestly?

38 **danger** injury   39 **Upon . . . freedom** (See 3.2.278.)   43 **humor** whim   46 **baned** killed, especially by poison or ratsbane   47 **love** who love.   **gaping pig** pig roasted whole with its mouth open   50 **affection** feeling, inclination   54, 55, 56 **he, he, he** one person, another, yet another   55 **necessary** i.e., useful for catching rats and mice   56 **woolen** i.e., with flannel-covered bag   60 **lodged** settled, steadfast.   **certain** unwavering, fixed   62 **losing** unprofitable   64 **current** flow, tendency   70 **think** bear in mind.   **question** argue   72 **main flood** sea at high tide.   **bate his** abate its   73 **use question with** interrogate   77 **fretten** fretted, i.e., disturbed, ruffled

82 **conveniency** propriety   87 **draw** receive   92 **parts** duties, capacities   97 **viands** food   104 **Upon** in accordance with   106 **determine this** resolve this legal dispute   107 **stays without** waits outside   114 **wether** ram, especially a castrated ram   115 **Meetest** fittest

SHYLOCK
To cut the forfeiture from that bankrupt there.
GRATIANO
Not on thy sole, but on thy soul, harsh Jew,
Thou mak'st thy knife keen; but no metal can,
No, not the hangman's ax, bear half the keenness   125
Of thy sharp envy. Can no prayers pierce thee?   126
SHYLOCK
No, none that thou hast wit enough to make.
GRATIANO
O, be thou damned, inexecrable dog,   128
And for thy life let justice be accused!   129
Thou almost mak'st me waver in my faith
To hold opinion with Pythagoras   131
That souls of animals infuse themselves
Into the trunks of men. Thy currish spirit
Governed a wolf who, hanged for human slaughter,   134
Even from the gallows did his fell soul fleet,   135
And, whilst thou layest in thy unhallowed dam,   136
Infused itself in thee; for thy desires
Are wolvish, bloody, starved, and ravenous.
SHYLOCK
Till thou canst rail the seal from off my bond,   139
Thou but offend'st thy lungs to speak so loud.   140
Repair thy wit, good youth, or it will fall
To cureless ruin. I stand here for law.   142
DUKE
This letter from Bellario doth commend
A young and learnèd doctor to our court.
Where is he?
NERISSA   He attendeth here hard by
To know your answer, whether you'll admit him.
DUKE
With all my heart. Some three or four of you
Go give him courteous conduct to this place.
    [Exeunt some.]
Meantime the court shall hear Bellario's letter.
[He reads.] "Your Grace shall understand that at the   150
receipt of your letter I am very sick; but in the instant
that your messenger came, in loving visitation was
with me a young doctor of Rome. His name is Balthasar. I acquainted him with the cause in controversy
between the Jew and Antonio the merchant. We
turned o'er many books together. He is furnished with
my opinion, which, bettered with his own learning,
the greatness whereof I cannot enough commend,
comes with him, at my importunity, to fill up Your   159
Grace's request in my stead. I beseech you, let his lack

of years be no impediment to let him lack a reverend   161
estimation, for I never knew so young a body with so
old a head. I leave him to your gracious acceptance,
whose trial shall better publish his commendation."   164
        Enter Portia for Balthasar [dressed like a doctor of
        laws, escorted].
You hear the learn'd Bellario, what he writes;
And here, I take it, is the doctor come.
Give me your hand. Come you from old Bellario?
PORTIA
I did, my lord.
DUKE   You are welcome. Take your place.
        [Portia takes her place.]
Are you acquainted with the difference   169
That holds this present question in the court?
PORTIA
I am informèd throughly of the cause.   171
Which is the merchant here, and which the Jew?
DUKE
Antonio and old Shylock, both stand forth.
        [Antonio and Shylock stand forth.]
PORTIA
Is your name Shylock?
SHYLOCK   Shylock is my name.
PORTIA
Of a strange nature is the suit you follow,
Yet in such rule that the Venetian law   176
Cannot impugn you as you do proceed.—   177
You stand within his danger, do you not?   178
ANTONIO
Ay, so he says.
PORTIA   Do you confess the bond?
ANTONIO
I do.
PORTIA   Then must the Jew be merciful.
SHYLOCK
On what compulsion must I? Tell me that.
PORTIA
The quality of mercy is not strained.   182
It droppeth as the gentle rain from heaven
Upon the place beneath. It is twice blest: 184
It blesseth him that gives and him that takes.
'Tis mightiest in the mightiest; it becomes
The thronèd monarch better than his crown.
His scepter shows the force of temporal power,
The attribute to awe and majesty,   189
Wherein doth sit the dread and fear of kings.
But mercy is above this sceptered sway;
It is enthronèd in the hearts of kings;
It is an attribute to God himself;
And earthly power doth then show likest God's
When mercy seasons justice. Therefore, Jew,
Though justice be thy plea, consider this,

125 hangman's executioner's. keenness (1) sharpness (2) savagery
126 envy malice 128 inexecrable that cannot be overly execrated or
detested 129 for thy life i.e., because you are allowed to live
131 Pythagoras ancient Greek philosopher who argued for the transmigration of souls 134 hanged for human slaughter (A possible allusion to the Elizabethan practice of trying and punishing animals for
various crimes.) 135 fell fierce, cruel. fleet flit, i.e., pass from the
body 136 dam mother. (Usually used of animals.) 139 rail revile,
use abusive language 140 offend'st injurest 142 cureless incurable
150 [He reads.] (In many modern editions, the reading of the letter is
assigned to a clerk, but the original text gives no such indication.)
159 comes with him i.e., my opinion is brought by him. importunity insistence

161 to let him lack such as would deprive him of 164 trial testing,
performance. publish make known. s.d. for i.e., disguised as
169 difference argument 171 throughly thoroughly. cause case
176 rule order 177 impugn find fault with 178 within his danger in
his power 182 strained forced, constrained 184 is twice blest
grants a double blessing 189 attribute to symbol of

That in the course of justice none of us
Should see salvation. We do pray for mercy,
And that same prayer doth teach us all to render
The deeds of mercy. I have spoke thus much
To mitigate the justice of thy plea,   201
Which if thou follow, this strict court of Venice
Must needs give sentence 'gainst the merchant
    there.

SHYLOCK
My deeds upon my head! I crave the law,   204
The penalty and forfeit of my bond.

PORTIA
Is he not able to discharge the money?

BASSANIO
Yes, here I tender it for him in the court,
Yea, twice the sum. If that will not suffice,
I will be bound to pay it ten times o'er,
On forfeit of my hands, my head, my heart.
If this will not suffice, it must appear
That malice bears down truth. And I beseech you,   212
Wrest once the law to your authority.   213
To do a great right, do a little wrong,
And curb this cruel devil of his will.

PORTIA
It must not be. There is no power in Venice
Can alter a decree establishèd.
'Twill be recorded for a precedent,
And many an error by the same example
Will rush into the state. It cannot be.

SHYLOCK
A Daniel come to judgment! Yea, a Daniel!   221
O wise young judge, how I do honor thee!

PORTIA
I pray you, let me look upon the bond.

SHYLOCK [giving the bond]
Here 'tis, most reverend doctor, here it is.

PORTIA
Shylock, there's thrice thy money offered thee.

SHYLOCK
An oath, an oath! I have an oath in heaven.
Shall I lay perjury upon my soul?
No, not for Venice.

PORTIA   Why, this bond is forfeit,
And lawfully by this the Jew may claim
A pound of flesh, to be by him cut off
Nearest the merchant's heart.—Be merciful.
Take thrice thy money; bid me tear the bond.

SHYLOCK
When it is paid according to the tenor.   233
It doth appear you are a worthy judge.
You know the law. Your exposition
Hath been most sound. I charge you by the law,
Whereof you are a well-deserving pillar,

Proceed to judgment. By my soul I swear
There is no power in the tongue of man
To alter me. I stay here on my bond.   240

ANTONIO
Most heartily I do beseech the court
To give the judgment.

PORTIA   Why then, thus it is:
You must prepare your bosom for his knife.

SHYLOCK
O noble judge! O excellent young man!

PORTIA
For the intent and purpose of the law
Hath full relation to the penalty   246
Which here appeareth due upon the bond.

SHYLOCK
'Tis very true. O wise and upright judge!
How much more elder art thou than thy looks!

PORTIA
Therefore lay bare your bosom.

SHYLOCK   Ay, his breast.
So says the bond, doth it not, noble judge?
"Nearest his heart," those are the very words.

PORTIA
It is so. Are there balance here   253
To weigh the flesh?

SHYLOCK   I have them ready.

PORTIA
Have by some surgeon, Shylock, on your charge,   255
To stop his wounds, lest he do bleed to death.

SHYLOCK
Is it so nominated in the bond?

PORTIA
It is not so expressed, but what of that?
'Twere good you do so much for charity.

SHYLOCK
I cannot find it. 'Tis not in the bond.

PORTIA
You, merchant, have you anything to say?

ANTONIO
But little. I am armed and well prepared.   262
Give me your hand, Bassanio; fare you well!
Grieve not that I am fall'n to this for you,
For herein Fortune shows herself more kind
Than is her custom. It is still her use   266
To let the wretched man outlive his wealth
To view with hollow eye and wrinkled brow
An age of poverty; from which ling'ring penance
Of such misery doth she cut me off.
Commend me to your honorable wife.
Tell her the process of Antonio's end,   272
Say how I loved you, speak me fair in death;   273
And, when the tale is told, bid her be judge
Whether Bassanio had not once a love.   275
Repent but you that you shall lose your friend,   276

201 To . . . plea i.e., to moderate your plea for strict justice   204 My
. . . head (Compare the cry of the crowd at Jesus' crucifixion: "His
blood be on us, and on our children," Matthew 27:25.)   212 bears
down truth overwhelms righteousness   213 Wrest once for once,
forcibly subject   221 Daniel (In the Apocrypha's story of Susannah
and the Elders, Daniel is the young man who rescues Susannah from
her false accusers.)   233 tenor conditions

240 stay here on remain committed to, insist upon   246 Hath . . . to
is fully in accord with   253 balance scales   255 on your charge at
your personal expense   262 armed i.e., fortified in spirit   266 still
her use i.e., commonly Fortune's practice   272 process story, manner   273 speak me fair speak well of me   275 a love a friend's love
276 Repent but you grieve only

And he repents not that he pays your debt.
For if the Jew do cut but deep enough,
I'll pay it instantly with all my heart.   279

BASSANIO
Antonio, I am married to a wife
Which is as dear to me as life itself;   281
But life itself, my wife, and all the world
Are not with me esteemed above thy life.
I would lose all, ay, sacrifice them all
Here to this devil, to deliver you.

PORTIA
Your wife would give you little thanks for that,
If she were by to hear you make the offer.   287

GRATIANO
I have a wife who, I protest, I love;
I would she were in heaven, so she could
Entreat some power to change this currish Jew.

NERISSA
'Tis well you offer it behind her back;
The wish would make else an unquiet house.

SHYLOCK
These be the Christian husbands. I have a daughter;
Would any of the stock of Barabbas   294
Had been her husband rather than a Christian!—
We trifle time. I pray thee, pursue sentence.   296

PORTIA
A pound of that same merchant's flesh is thine.
The court awards it, and the law doth give it.

SHYLOCK   Most rightful judge!

PORTIA
And you must cut this flesh from off his breast.
The law allows it, and the court awards it.

SHYLOCK
Most learnèd judge! A sentence! Come, prepare.

PORTIA
Tarry a little; there is something else.
This bond doth give thee here no jot of blood;
The words expressly are "a pound of flesh."
Take then thy bond, take thou thy pound of flesh,
But in the cutting it if thou dost shed
One drop of Christian blood, thy lands and goods
Are by the laws of Venice confiscate
Unto the state of Venice.

GRATIANO
O upright judge! Mark, Jew. O learnèd judge!

SHYLOCK
Is that the law?

PORTIA   Thyself shalt see the act;
For, as thou urgest justice, be assured
Thou shalt have justice, more than thou desir'st.

GRATIANO
O learnèd judge! Mark, Jew, a learnèd judge!

SHYLOCK
I take this offer, then. Pay the bond thrice
And let the Christian go.

BASSANIO   Here is the money.

PORTIA   Soft!   318
The Jew shall have all justice. Soft, no haste.   319
He shall have nothing but the penalty.

GRATIANO
O Jew! An upright judge, a learnèd judge!

PORTIA
Therefore prepare thee to cut off the flesh.
Shed thou no blood, nor cut thou less nor more
But just a pound of flesh. If thou tak'st more
Or less than a just pound, be it but so much
As makes it light or heavy in the substance   326
Or the division of the twentieth part   327
Of one poor scruple, nay, if the scale do turn   328
But in the estimation of a hair,
Thou diest, and all thy goods are confiscate.

GRATIANO
A second Daniel, a Daniel, Jew!
Now, infidel, I have you on the hip.   332

PORTIA
Why doth the Jew pause? Take thy forfeiture.

SHYLOCK
Give me my principal, and let me go.

BASSANIO
I have it ready for thee. Here it is.

PORTIA
He hath refused it in the open court.
He shall have merely justice and his bond.

GRATIANO
A Daniel, still say I, a second Daniel!
I thank thee, Jew, for teaching me that word.

SHYLOCK
Shall I not have barely my principal?

PORTIA
Thou shalt have nothing but the forfeiture,
To be so taken at thy peril, Jew.

SHYLOCK
Why, then the devil give him good of it!
I'll stay no longer question.   [He starts to go.]

PORTIA   Tarry, Jew!   344
The law hath yet another hold on you.
It is enacted in the laws of Venice,
If it be proved against an alien
That by direct or indirect attempts
He seek the life of any citizen,
The party 'gainst the which he doth contrive
Shall seize one half his goods; the other half
Comes to the privy coffer of the state,   352
And the offender's life lies in the mercy   353
Of the Duke only, 'gainst all other voice.   354
In which predicament, I say, thou stand'st;
For it appears, by manifest proceeding,
That indirectly and directly too

---

279 with . . . heart (1) wholeheartedly (2) literally, with my heart's
blood   **281 Which** who   **287 by** nearby   **294 Barabbas** a thief
whom Pontius Pilate set free instead of Christ in response to the people's demand (see Mark 15); also, the villainous protagonist of Marlowe's *The Jew of Malta*   **296 trifle** waste.   **pursue** proceed with

318 Soft i.e., not so fast   **319 all justice** precisely what the law provides   **326 substance** mass or gross weight   **327 division** fraction
328 scruple twenty grains apothecaries' weight, a small quantity
332 on the hip i.e., at a disadvantage. (A phrase from wrestling.)
344 I'll . . . question I'll stay no further pursuing of the case
352 privy coffer private treasury   **353 lies in** lies at   **354 'gainst . . .
voice** without appeal

Thou hast contrived against the very life
Of the defendant; and thou hast incurred
The danger formerly by me rehearsed.   360
Down therefore, and beg mercy of the Duke.

GRATIANO
Beg that thou mayst have leave to hang thyself!
And yet, thy wealth being forfeit to the state,
Thou hast not left the value of a cord;
Therefore thou must be hanged at the state's charge.   365

DUKE
That thou shalt see the difference of our spirit,
I pardon thee thy life before thou ask it.
For half thy wealth, it is Antonio's;   368
The other half comes to the general state,
Which humbleness may drive unto a fine.   370

PORTIA
Ay, for the state, not for Antonio.   371

SHYLOCK
Nay, take my life and all! Pardon not that!
You take my house when you do take the prop
That doth sustain my house. You take my life
When you do take the means whereby I live.

PORTIA
What mercy can you render him, Antonio?

GRATIANO
A halter gratis! Nothing else, for God's sake.   377

ANTONIO
So please my lord the Duke and all the court
To quit the fine for one half of his goods,   379
I am content, so he will let me have   380
The other half in use, to render it,   381
Upon his death, unto the gentleman
That lately stole his daughter.
Two things provided more: that for this favor
He presently become a Christian;   385
The other, that he do record a gift
Here in the court of all he dies possessed   387
Unto his son Lorenzo and his daughter.

DUKE
He shall do this, or else I do recant
The pardon that I late pronouncèd here.   389

PORTIA
Art thou contented, Jew? What dost thou say?

SHYLOCK
I am content.

PORTIA   Clerk, draw a deed of gift.

SHYLOCK
I pray you, give me leave to go from hence;
I am not well. Send the deed after me,
And I will sign it.

DUKE   Get thee gone, but do it.

GRATIANO
In christening shalt thou have two godfathers.
Had I been judge, thou shouldst have had ten more, 397
To bring thee to the gallows, not the font.
                                                                    Exit [Shylock].

DUKE [to Portia]
Sir, I entreat you home with me to dinner.

PORTIA
I humbly do desire Your Grace of pardon.
I must away this night toward Padua,
And it is meet I presently set forth.

DUKE
I am sorry that your leisure serves you not.
Antonio, gratify this gentleman,   404
For in my mind you are much bound to him.
                                                      Exeunt Duke and his train.

BASSANIO [to Portia]
Most worthy gentleman, I and my friend
Have by your wisdom been this day acquitted
Of grievous penalties, in lieu whereof,   408
Three thousand ducats due unto the Jew
We freely cope your courteous pains withal.   410
                                                                    [He offers money.]

ANTONIO
And stand indebted over and above
In love and service to you evermore.

PORTIA
He is well paid that is well satisfied,
And I, delivering you, am satisfied,
And therein do account myself well paid.
My mind was never yet more mercenary.
I pray you, know me when we meet again.   417
I wish you well, and so I take my leave.
                                                                    [She starts to leave.]

BASSANIO
Dear sir, of force I must attempt you further.   419
Take some remembrance of us as a tribute,
Not as fee. Grant me two things, I pray you:
Not to deny me, and to pardon me.   422

PORTIA
You press me far, and therefore I will yield.
Give me your gloves, I'll wear them for your sake.   424
And, for your love, I'll take this ring from you.   425
Do not draw back your hand; I'll take no more,
And you in love shall not deny me this.

BASSANIO
This ring, good sir? Alas, it is a trifle!
I will not shame myself to give you this.

---

360 **danger . . . rehearsed** penalty already cited by me   **365 charge** expense   **368 For** as for   **370 Which . . . fine** i.e., which penitence on your part may persuade me to reduce to a fine   **371 Ay . . . Antonio** i.e., yes, the state's half may be reduced to a fine, but not Antonio's half   **377 halter** hangman's noose   **379 quit** remit, relinquish, or perhaps settle for. (That is, Antonio may ask the court to forgive even the fine imposed in lieu of a heavier penalty.)   **380 so** provided that   **381 in use** in trust, or possibly, to be used as a source of income   **385 presently** at once   **387 of . . . possessed** i.e., what remains of the portion not placed under Antonio's trust (which will also go to Lorenzo and Jessica)   **389 late** lately

397 **ten more** i.e., to make up a jury of twelve. (Jurors were colloquially termed *godfathers*.)   **404 gratify** reward   **408 in lieu whereof** in return for which   **410 cope** requite   **417 know . . . again** i.e., consider our acquaintance well established. (But punning on *know* in the sense of "recognize" and "have sexual relations with"—meanings that are hidden from Bassanio by Portia's disguise.)   **419 of force** of necessity.   **attempt** urge   **422 pardon me** i.e., pardon my presumption in pressing the matter   **424 gloves** (Perhaps Bassanio removes his gloves, thereby revealing the ring that "Balthasar" asks of him.)   **425 for your love** i.e., for friendship's sake—a polite phrase, but with ironic double meaning as applied to husband and wife

PORTIA
I will have nothing else but only this;
And now, methinks, I have a mind to it.

BASSANIO
There's more depends on this than on the value.
The dearest ring in Venice will I give you,   433
And find it out by proclamation.
Only for this, I pray you, pardon me.

PORTIA
I see, sir, you are liberal in offers.   436
You taught me first to beg, and now, methinks,
You teach me how a beggar should be answered.

BASSANIO
Good sir, this ring was given me by my wife,
And when she put it on she made me vow
That I should neither sell nor give nor lose it.

PORTIA
That 'scuse serves many men to save their gifts.
An if your wife be not a madwoman,
And know how well I have deserved this ring,
She would not hold out enemy forever   445
For giving it to me. Well, peace be with you!
                Exeunt [*Portia and Nerissa*].

ANTONIO
My lord Bassanio, let him have the ring.
Let his deservings and my love withal
Be valued 'gainst your wife's commandement.   449

BASSANIO
Go, Gratiano, run and overtake him;
Give him the ring, and bring him, if thou canst,
Unto Antonio's house. Away, make haste!
              Exit Gratiano [*with the ring*].
Come, you and I will thither presently,
And in the morning early will we both
Fly toward Belmont. Come, Antonio.   *Exeunt.*

❖

4.2   *Enter* [*Portia and*] *Nerissa* [*still disguised*].

PORTIA [*giving a deed to Nerissa*]
Inquire the Jew's house out; give him this deed   1
And let him sign it. We'll away tonight
And be a day before our husbands home.
This deed will be well welcome to Lorenzo.

         Enter Gratiano.

GRATIANO   Fair sir, you are well o'erta'en.   5
My lord Bassanio upon more advice   6
Hath sent you here this ring and doth entreat
Your company at dinner.   [*He gives a ring.*]
PORTIA   That cannot be.
His ring I do accept most thankfully,
And so, I pray you, tell him. Furthermore,

I pray you, show my youth old Shylock's house.
GRATIANO
That will I do.
NERISSA   Sir, I would speak with you.
    [*Aside to Portia.*] I'll see if I can get my husband's
    ring,
Which I did make him swear to keep forever.
PORTIA [*aside to Nerissa*]
Thou mayst, I warrant. We shall have old swearing   15
That they did give the rings away to men;
But we'll outface them, and outswear them too.—   17
Away, make haste! Thou know'st where I will tarry.
NERISSA
Come, good sir, will you show me to this house?
      [*Exeunt, Portia separately from the others.*]

❖

5.1   *Enter Lorenzo and Jessica.*

LORENZO
The moon shines bright. In such a night as this,
When the sweet wind did gently kiss the trees
And they did make no noise, in such a night
Troilus methinks mounted the Trojan walls   4
And sighed his soul toward the Grecian tents
Where Cressid lay that night.
JESSICA   In such a night
Did Thisbe fearfully o'ertrip the dew,   7
And saw the lion's shadow ere himself,
And ran dismayed away.
LORENZO   In such a night
Stood Dido with a willow in her hand   10
Upon the wild sea banks, and waft her love   11
To come again to Carthage.
JESSICA   In such a night
Medea gathered the enchanted herbs   13
That did renew old Aeson.
LORENZO   In such a night
Did Jessica steal from the wealthy Jew   15
And with an unthrift love did run from Venice   16
As far as Belmont.
JESSICA   In such a night
Did young Lorenzo swear he loved her well,
Stealing her soul with many vows of faith,
And ne'er a true one.
LORENZO   In such a night
Did pretty Jessica, like a little shrew,
Slander her love, and he forgave it her.

433 dearest most expensive   **436 liberal** generous   **445 would . . .
out** i.e., would not remain   **449 commandement** (Pronounced in four
syllables.)
4.2. Location: Venice. A street.
1 this deed i.e., the deed of gift   **5 you . . . o'erta'en** I'm happy to
have caught up with you   **6 advice** consideration

15 old plenty of   **17 outface** boldly contradict
5.1. Location: Belmont. Outside Portia's house.
4 Troilus Trojan prince betrayed by his beloved, Cressida, after she
had been transferred to the Greek camp   **7 Thisbe** beloved of Pyramus who, arranging to meet him by night, was frightened by a lion
and fled; the tragic misunderstanding of her absence led to the suicides of both lovers. (See *A Midsummer Night's Dream*, Act 5.)
10 Dido Queen of Carthage, deserted by Aeneas.   **willow** (A symbol
of forsaken love.)   **11 waft** wafted, beckoned   **13 Medea** famous sorceress of Colchis who, after falling in love with Jason and helping him
to gain the Golden Fleece, used her magic to restore youth to Aeson,
Jason's father   **15 steal** (1) escape (2) rob   **16 unthrift** prodigal

JESSICA
I would out-night you, did nobody come.   23
But hark, I hear the footing of a man.   24

Enter [Stephano,] a messenger.

LORENZO
Who comes so fast in silence of the night?
STEPHANO   A friend.
LORENZO
A friend? What friend? Your name, I pray you,
friend?
STEPHANO
Stephano is my name, and I bring word
My mistress will before the break of day
Be here at Belmont. She doth stray about
By holy crosses, where she kneels and prays   31
For happy wedlock hours.
LORENZO   Who comes with her?
STEPHANO
None but a holy hermit and her maid.
I pray you, is my master yet returned?
LORENZO
He is not, nor we have not heard from him.
But go we in, I pray thee, Jessica,
And ceremoniously let us prepare
Some welcome for the mistress of the house.

Enter [Lancelot, the] clown.

LANCELOT   Sola, sola! Wo ha, ho! Sola, sola!   39
LORENZO   Who calls?
LANCELOT   Sola! Did you see Master Lorenzo? Master
Lorenzo, sola, sola!
LORENZO   Leave holloing, man! Here.
LANCELOT   Sola! Where, where?
LORENZO   Here.
LANCELOT   Tell him there's a post come from my mas-   46
ter, with his horn full of good news: my master will be   47
here ere morning.   [*Exit.*]
LORENZO
Sweet soul, let's in, and there expect their coming.   49
And yet no matter. Why should we go in?
My friend Stephano, signify, I pray you,   51
Within the house, your mistress is at hand,
And bring your music forth into the air.
                    [*Exit Stephano.*]
How sweet the moonlight sleeps upon this bank!
Here will we sit and let the sounds of music
Creep in our ears. Soft stillness and the night
Become the touches of sweet harmony.   57
Sit, Jessica. [*They sit.*] Look how the floor of heaven
Is thick inlaid with patens of bright gold.   59
There's not the smallest orb which thou behold'st
But in his motion like an angel sings,

Still choiring to the young-eyed cherubins.   62
Such harmony is in immortal souls,
But whilst this muddy vesture of decay   64
Doth grossly close it in, we cannot hear it.   65

[*Enter musicians.*]

Come, ho, and wake Diana with a hymn!   66
With sweetest touches pierce your mistress' ear
And draw her home with music.   *Play music.*
JESSICA
I am never merry when I hear sweet music.
LORENZO
The reason is, your spirits are attentive.   70
For do but note a wild and wanton herd,
Or race of youthful and unhandled colts,   72
Fetching mad bounds, bellowing and neighing loud,
Which is the hot condition of their blood;
If they but hear perchance a trumpet sound,
Or any air of music touch their ears,
You shall perceive them make a mutual stand,   77
Their savage eyes turned to a modest gaze
By the sweet power of music. Therefore the poet   79
Did feign that Orpheus drew trees, stones, and
floods,   80
Since naught so stockish, hard, and full of rage   81
But music for the time doth change his nature.
The man that hath no music in himself,
Nor is not moved with concord of sweet sounds,
Is fit for treasons, stratagems, and spoils;   85
The motions of his spirit are dull as night
And his affections dark as Erebus.   87
Let no such man be trusted. Mark the music.

Enter Portia and Nerissa.

PORTIA
That light we see is burning in my hall.
How far that little candle throws his beams!
So shines a good deed in a naughty world.   91
NERISSA
When the moon shone, we did not see the candle.
PORTIA
So doth the greater glory dim the less.
A substitute shines brightly as a king
Until a king be by, and then his state   95
Empties itself, as doth an inland brook
Into the main of waters. Music! Hark!   97
NERISSA
It is your music, madam, of the house.

---

62 Still choiring continually singing.   **young-eyed** eternally clear-
sighted. In Exekiel 10:12, the bodies and wings of cherubim are "full
of eyes round about."   **64 muddy . . . decay** i.e., mortal flesh
65 close it in i.e., enclose the soul.   **hear it** i.e., hear the music of
the spheres   **66 Diana** (Here, goddess of the moon; compare with
1.2.105.)   **70 spirits are attentive** (The spirits would be in motion
within the body in merriment, whereas in sadness they would be
drawn to the heart and, as it were, busy listening.)   **72 race** herd
77 mutual common or simultaneous   **79 poet** perhaps Ovid, with
whom the story of Orpheus was a favorite theme   **80 Orpheus** legendary musician.   **drew** attracted, charmed   **81 stockish** unfeeling
85 spoils acts of pillage   **87 Erebus** a place of primeval darkness on
the way to Hades   **91 naughty** wicked   **95 his** i.e., the substitute's
97 main of waters sea

---

23 out-night i.e., outdo in the verbal games we've been playing
24 footing footsteps   **31 holy crosses** wayside shrines   **39 Sola** (Imitation of a post horn.)   **46 post** courier   **47 horn** (Lancelot jestingly
compares the courier's post horn to a cornucopia.)   **49 expect** await
51 signify make known   **57 Become** suit.   **touches** strains, notes
(produced by the fingering of an instrument)   **59 patens** thin, circular
plates of metal

PORTIA

Nothing is good, I see, without respect.   99
Methinks it sounds much sweeter than by day.

NERISSA

Silence bestows that virtue on it, madam.

PORTIA

The crow doth sing as sweetly as the lark
When neither is attended; and I think   103
The nightingale, if she should sing by day,
When every goose is cackling, would be thought
No better a musician than the wren.
How many things by season seasoned are   107
To their right praise and true perfection!
Peace, ho! The moon sleeps with Endymion   109
And would not be awaked.   [*The music ceases.*]

LORENZO   That is the voice,
Or I am much deceived, of Portia.

PORTIA

He knows me as the blind man knows the cuckoo,
By the bad voice.

LORENZO   Dear lady, welcome home.

PORTIA

We have been praying for our husbands' welfare,
Which speed, we hope, the better for our words.   115
Are they returned?

LORENZO   Madam, they are not yet;
But there is come a messenger before,
To signify their coming.

PORTIA   Go in, Nerissa.
Give order to my servants that they take
No note at all of our being absent hence;
Nor you, Lorenzo; Jessica, nor you. [*A tucket sounds.*] 121

LORENZO

Your husband is at hand. I hear his trumpet.
We are no telltales, madam, fear you not.

PORTIA

This night, methinks, is but the daylight sick;
It looks a little paler. 'Tis a day
Such as the day is when the sun is hid.

*Enter Bassanio, Antonio, Gratiano, and their
followers.*

BASSANIO

We should hold day with the Antipodes,   127
If you would walk in absence of the sun.   128

PORTIA

Let me give light, but let me not be light;   129
For a light wife doth make a heavy husband,   130
And never be Bassanio so for me.

But God sort all! You are welcome home, my lord.   132

BASSANIO

I thank you, madam. Give welcome to my friend.
This is the man, this is Antonio,
To whom I am so infinitely bound.

PORTIA

You should in all sense be much bound to him,   136
For, as I hear, he was much bound for you.   137

ANTONIO

No more than I am well acquitted of.   138

PORTIA

Sir, you are very welcome to our house.
It must appear in other ways than words;
Therefore I scant this breathing courtesy.   141

GRATIANO [*to Nerissa*]

By yonder moon I swear you do me wrong!
In faith, I gave it to the judge's clerk.
Would he were gelt that had it, for my part,   144
Since you do take it, love, so much at heart.

PORTIA

A quarrel, ho, already? What's the matter?

GRATIANO

About a hoop of gold, a paltry ring
That she did give me, whose posy was   148
For all the world like cutler's poetry
Upon a knife, "Love me, and leave me not."

NERISSA

What talk you of the posy or the value?
You swore to me, when I did give it you,
That you would wear it till your hour of death
And that it should lie with you in your grave.
Though not for me, yet for your vehement oaths
You should have been respective and have kept it.   156
Gave it a judge's clerk! No, God's my judge,
The clerk will ne'er wear hair on 's face that had it.

GRATIANO

He will, an if he live to be a man.   159

NERISSA

Ay, if a woman live to be a man.

GRATIANO

Now, by this hand, I gave it to a youth,
A kind of boy, a little scrubbèd boy   162
No higher than thyself, the judge's clerk,
A prating boy, that begged it as a fee.   164
I could not for my heart deny it him.

PORTIA

You were to blame—I must be plain with you—
To part so slightly with your wife's first gift,
A thing stuck on with oaths upon your finger,
And so riveted with faith unto your flesh.
I gave my love a ring and made him swear
Never to part with it; and here he stands.
I dare be sworn for him he would not leave it,

---

99 respect comparison, context **103 neither is attended** i.e., either is alone **107 season** fit occasion (but playing on the idea of seasoning, spices) **109 Endymion** a shepherd loved by the moon goddess, who caused him to sleep a perennial sleep in a cave on Mount Latmos where she could visit him **115 speed** prosper (with a suggestion too of speedy return) **121 s.d. tucket** flourish on a trumpet **127–128 We . . . sun** i.e., if you, Portia, like a second sun, would always walk about during the sun's absence, we should never have night but would enjoy daylight even when the Antipodes, those who dwell on the opposite side of the globe, enjoy daylight **129 be light** be wanton, unchaste **130 heavy** sad (with wordplay on the antithesis of *light* and *heavy*)

132 sort decide, dispose **136 in all sense** in every way, with every reason **136–137 bound . . . bound** Portia plays on (1) obligated (2) indebted and imprisoned. **138 acquitted of** freed from **141 scant . . . courtesy** make brief these empty (i.e., merely verbal) compliments **144 gelt** gelded. **for my part** as far as I'm concerned **148 posy** a motto on a ring **156 respective** mindful, careful **159 an if** if **162 scrubbèd** stunted **164 prating** chattering

Nor pluck it from his finger, for the wealth
That the world masters. Now, in faith, Gratiano,   174
You give your wife too unkind a cause of grief.
An 'twere to me, I should be mad at it.   176

BASSANIO [*aside*]
Why, I were best to cut my left hand off
And swear I lost the ring defending it.

GRATIANO
My lord Bassanio gave his ring away
Unto the judge that begged it and indeed
Deserved it too; and then the boy, his clerk,
That took some pains in writing, he begged mine;
And neither man nor master would take aught   183
But the two rings.

PORTIA   What ring gave you, my lord?
Not that, I hope, which you received of me.

BASSANIO
If I could add a lie unto a fault,
I would deny it; but you see my finger
Hath not the ring upon it. It is gone.

PORTIA
Even so void is your false heart of truth.
By heaven, I will ne'er come in your bed
Until I see the ring!

NERISSA [*to Gratiano*]   Nor I in yours
Till I again see mine.

BASSANIO   Sweet Portia,
If you did know to whom I gave the ring,
If you did know for whom I gave the ring,
And would conceive for what I gave the ring,
And how unwillingly I left the ring,
When naught would be accepted but the ring,
You would abate the strength of your displeasure.

PORTIA
If you had known the virtue of the ring,   199
Or half her worthiness that gave the ring,
Or your own honor to contain the ring,   201
You would not then have parted with the ring.
What man is there so much unreasonable,
If you had pleased to have defended it
With any terms of zeal, wanted the modesty   205
To urge the thing held as a ceremony?   206
Nerissa teaches me what to believe:
I'll die for 't but some woman had the ring.

BASSANIO
No, by my honor, madam! By my soul,
No woman had it, but a civil doctor,   210
Which did refuse three thousand ducats of me
And begged the ring, the which I did deny him
And suffered him to go displeased away—
Even he that had held up the very life
Of my dear friend. What should I say, sweet lady?
I was enforced to send it after him.
I was beset with shame and courtesy.
My honor would not let ingratitude

So much besmear it. Pardon me, good lady!
For by these blessèd candles of the night,   220
Had you been there, I think you would have begged
The ring of me to give the worthy doctor.

PORTIA
Let not that doctor e'er come near my house.
Since he hath got the jewel that I loved,
And that which you did swear to keep for me,
I will become as liberal as you: 226
I'll not deny him anything I have,
No, not my body nor my husband's bed.
Know him I shall, I am well sure of it.   229
Lie not a night from home. Watch me like Argus;   230
If you do not, if I be left alone,
Now, by mine honor, which is yet mine own,
I'll have that doctor for my bedfellow.

NERISSA
And I his clerk; therefore be well advised   234
How you do leave me to mine own protection.

GRATIANO
Well, do you so. Let not me take him, then!   236
For if I do, I'll mar the young clerk's pen.   237

ANTONIO
I am th' unhappy subject of these quarrels.

PORTIA
Sir, grieve not you; you are welcome notwithstanding.

BASSANIO
Portia, forgive me this enforcèd wrong,
And in the hearing of these many friends
I swear to thee, even by thine own fair eyes
Wherein I see myself—

PORTIA   Mark you but that!
In both my eyes he doubly sees himself;
In each eye, one. Swear by your double self,   245
And there's an oath of credit.

BASSANIO   Nay, but hear me.   246
Pardon this fault, and by my soul I swear
I never more will break an oath with thee.

ANTONIO
I once did lend my body for his wealth,   249
Which, but for him that had your husband's ring,
Had quite miscarried. I dare be bound again,
My soul upon the forfeit, that your lord   252
Will nevermore break faith advisedly.   253

PORTIA
Then you shall be his surety. Give him this,   254
And bid him keep it better than the other.
[*She gives the ring to Antonio, who gives it to Bassanio.*]

ANTONIO
Here, Lord Bassanio. Swear to keep this ring.

BASSANIO
By heaven, it is the same I gave the doctor!

---

174 **masters** owns 176 **An** if. **mad** beside myself 183 **aught** anything 199 **virtue** power 201 **contain** retain 205 **wanted the modesty** who would have been so lacking in consideration as 206 **urge** insist upon receiving. **ceremony** something sacred 210 **civil doctor** i.e., doctor of civil law

220 **blessèd . . . night** i.e., stars 226 **liberal** generous (sexually as well as otherwise) 229 **Know** (with the suggestion of carnal knowledge) 230 **from** away from. **Argus** mythological monster with a hundred eyes 234 **be well advised** take care 236 **take** apprehend 237 **pen** (with sexual double meaning) 245 **double** i.e., deceitful 246 **of credit** worthy to be believed. (Said ironically.) 249 **wealth** welfare 252 **My . . . forfeit** at the risk of eternal damnation 253 **advisedly** intentionally 254 **surety** guarantor

PORTIA
I had it of him. Pardon me, Bassanio,
For by this ring the doctor lay with me.

NERISSA
And pardon me, my gentle Gratiano,
For that same scrubbèd boy, the doctor's clerk,
In lieu of this last night did lie with me.   262
                      [*Presenting her ring.*]

GRATIANO
Why, this is like the mending of highways
In summer, where the ways are fair enough.   264
What, are we cuckolds ere we have deserved it?   265

PORTIA
Speak not so grossly. You are all amazed.   266
Here is a letter; read it at your leisure.
                      [*She gives a letter.*]
It comes from Padua, from Bellario.
There you shall find that Portia was the doctor,
Nerissa there her clerk. Lorenzo here
Shall witness I set forth as soon as you,
And even but now returned; I have not yet
Entered my house. Antonio, you are welcome,
And I have better news in store for you
Than you expect. Unseal this letter soon.
                      [*She gives him a letter.*]
There you shall find three of your argosies
Are richly come to harbor suddenly.
You shall not know by what strange accident
I chancèd on this letter.

ANTONIO   I am dumb.   279

BASSANIO [*to Portia*]
Were you the doctor and I knew you not?

GRATIANO [*to Nerissa*]
Were you the clerk that is to make me cuckold?

NERISSA
Ay, but the clerk that never means to do it,
Unless he live until he be a man.

BASSANIO
Sweet doctor, you shall be my bedfellow.
When I am absent, then lie with my wife.

ANTONIO
Sweet lady, you have given me life and living;
For here I read for certain that my ships
Are safely come to road.

PORTIA   How now, Lorenzo?   288
My clerk hath some good comforts too for you.

NERISSA
Ay, and I'll give them him without a fee.
                      [*She gives a deed.*]
There do I give to you and Jessica,
From the rich Jew, a special deed of gift,
After his death, of all he dies possessed of.

LORENZO
Fair ladies, you drop manna in the way   294

Of starvèd people.

PORTIA   It is almost morning,
And yet I am sure you are not satisfied
Of these events at full. Let us go in;
And charge us there upon inter'gatories,   298
And we will answer all things faithfully.

GRATIANO
Let it be so. The first inter'gatory
That my Nerissa shall be sworn on is
Whether till the next night she had rather stay   302
Or go to bed now, being two hours to day.
But were the day come, I should wish it dark
Till I were couching with the doctor's clerk.
Well, while I live I'll fear no other thing
So sore as keeping safe Nerissa's ring.   *Exeunt.*   307

298 charge . . . inter'gatories require ourselves to answer all things under oath   **302 stay** wait   **307 ring** (with sexual suggestion)

262 In lieu of in return for   **264 In . . . enough** i.e., before repair is necessary   **265 cuckolds** husbands whose wives are unfaithful **266 grossly** stupidly, licentiously.   **amazed** bewildered   **279 dumb** at a loss for words   **288 road** anchorage   **294 manna** the food from heaven that was miraculously supplied to the Israelites in the wilderness (Exodus 16)

Much Ado About Nothing

Much Ado About Nothing belongs to a group of Shakespeare's most mature romantic comedies, linked by similar titles, that also includes *As You Like It* and *Twelfth Night*. All date from the period 1598 to 1600. These plays are the culmination of Shakespeare's exuberant, philosophical, and festive vein in comedy, with only an occasional anticipation of the darker problem comedies of the early 1600s. They also parallel the culmination of Shakespeare's writing of history plays, in *Henry IV* and *V.*

Much Ado excels in combative wit and in swift, colloquial prose. It differs, too, from several other comedies (including *A Midsummer Night's Dream* and *The Merchant of Venice*) in that it features no journey of the lovers, no heroine disguised as a man, no envious court or city contrasted with an idealized landscape of the artist's imagination. Instead, the prevailing motif is that of the mask. Prominent scenes include a masked ball (2.1), a charade offstage in which the villainous Borachio misrepresents himself as the lover of Hero (actually Margaret in disguise), and a marriage ceremony with the supposedly dead bride masking as her own cousin (5.3). The word *Nothing* in the play's title, pronounced rather like *noting* in Elizabethan English, suggests a pun on the idea of overhearing as well as of musical notation. Overhearings are constant and are essential to the process of both misunderstanding (as in the false rumor of Don Pedro's wooing Hero for himself) and clarification (as in the discovery by the night watch of the slander done to Hero's reputation, or in the revelation to Beatrice and Benedick of each other's true state of mind). The masks, or roles, that the characters incessantly assume are, for the most part, defensive and inimical to mutual understanding. How can they be dispelled? It is the search for candor and self-awareness in relationships with others, the quest for honesty and respect beneath conventional outward appearances, that provides the journey in this play.

Structurally, the play contrasts two pairs of lovers. The young ladies, Beatrice and Hero, are cousins and close friends. The gentlemen, Benedick and Claudio, Italian gentlemen and fellow officers under the command of Don Pedro, have returned from the war, in which they have fought bravely. These similarities chiefly serve, however, to accen-

tuate the differences between the two couples. Hero is modest, retiring, usually silent, and obedient to her father's will. Claudio appears ideally suited to her, since he is also respectful and decorous. They are conventional lovers in the roles of romantic hero and naive heroine. Beatrice and Benedick, on the other hand, are renowned for "a kind of merry war" between them. Although obviously destined to come together, they are seemingly too independent and skeptical of convention to be tolerant and accepting in love. They scoff so at romantic sentimentality that they cannot permit themselves to drop their satirical masks. Yet, paradoxically, their relationship is the more surefooted because it is relentlessly probing and candid.

As in some of his other comic double plots (*The Taming of the Shrew,* for example), Shakespeare has linked together two stories of diverse origins and contrasting tones in order to set off one against the other. The Hero-Claudio plot is Italianate in flavor and origin, sensational, melodramatic, and potentially tragic. In fact, the often told story of the maiden falsely slandered did frequently end in disaster—as, for example, in Edmund Spenser's *Faerie Queene,* 2.4 (1590). Spenser was apparently indebted to Ariosto's *Orlando Furioso* (translated into English by Sir John Harington, 1591), as were Peter Beverly in *The Historie of Ariodanto and Ieneura* (1566) and Richard Mulcaster in his play *Ariodante and Genevora* (1583). Shakespeare seems to have relied more on the Italian version by Matteo Bandello (Lucca, 1554) and its French translation by Belleforest, *Histoires Tragiques* (1569). Still other versions have been discovered, both nondramatic and dramatic, although it cannot be established that Shakespeare was reworking an old play. Various factual inconsistencies in Shakespeare's text (such as Leonato's wife Imogen and a "kinsman" who are named briefly in both Quarto and Folio but have no roles in the play) can perhaps be explained by Shakespeare's having worked quickly from more than one source.

Shakespeare's other plot, of Benedick and Beatrice, is much more English and his own. The battle of the sexes is a staple of English medieval humor (Chaucer's Wife of Bath, the Wakefield play of *Noah*) and of Shakespeare's own early comedy: Berowne and Rosaline in *Love's Labor's Lost,* Petruchio and Katharine in *The Taming of the Shrew.* The merry war of Benedick and Beatrice is Shakespeare's finest achievement in this vein and was to become a rich legacy in the later English comedy of William Congreve, Oscar Wilde, and Bernard Shaw. The tone is lighthearted, bantering, and reassuring, in contrast with the Italianate mood of vengeance and duplicity. No less English are the clownish antics of Dogberry and his crew, representing still another group of characters although not a separate plot. Like Constable Dull in *Love's Labor's Lost* or the tradesmen of *A Midsummer Night's Dream,* the buffoons of *Much Ado* function in a nominally Mediterranean setting but are nonetheless recognizable London types. Their preposterous antics not only puncture the ominous mood threatening our enjoyment of the main plot but also, absurdly enough, even help to abort a potential crime. When Dogberry comes, laughter cannot be far behind.

The two plots provide contrasting perspectives on the nature of love. Because it is sensational and melodramatic, the Claudio-Hero plot stresses situation at the expense of character. The conspiracy that nearly overwhelms the lovers is an engrossing story, but they themselves remain one-dimensional. They interest us more as conventional types, and hence as foils to Benedick and Beatrice, than as lovers in their own right. Benedick and Beatrice, on the other hand, are psychologically complex. Clearly, they are fascinated with each other. Beatrice's questions in the first scene, although abusive in tone, betray her concern for Benedick's welfare. Has he safely returned from the wars? How did he bear himself in battle? Who are his companions? She tests his moral character by high standards, suspecting that he will fail because she demands so much. We are not surprised when she lectures her docile cousin, Hero, on the folly of submitting to parental choice in marriage: "It is my cousin's duty to make curtsy and say, 'Father, as it please you.' But yet for all that, cousin, let him be a handsome fellow, or else make another curtsy and say, 'Father, as it please me'" (2.1.49–52). Beatrice remains single, not from love of spinsterhood, but from insistence on a nearly perfect mate. Paradoxically, she who is the inveterate scoffer is the true idealist. And we know from her unceasing fascination with Benedick that he, of all the men in her acquaintance, comes closest to her mark. The only fear preventing the revelation of her love—a not unnatural fear, in view of the insults she and Benedick exchange—is that he will prove faithless and jest at her weakness.

Benedick is similarly hemmed in by his posturing as "a professed tyrant to their sex." Despite his reputation as a perennial bachelor and his wry amusement at Claudio's newfound passion, Benedick confesses in soliloquy (2.3.7–33) that he could be won to affection by the ideal woman. Again, his criteria are chiefly those of temperament and moral character, although he by no means spurns wealth, beauty, and social position; the happiest couples are those well matched in fortune's gifts. "Rich she shall be, that's certain; wise, or I'll none; virtuous, or I'll never cheapen her; fair, or I'll never look on her; mild, or come not near me; noble, or not I for an angel; of good discourse, an excellent musician, and her hair shall be of what color it please God." This last self-mocking concession indicates that Benedick is aware of how impossibly much he is asking. Still, there is one woman, Beatrice, who may well possess all of these qualities except mildness. Even her sharp wit is part of her admirable intelligence. She is a match for Benedick, and he is a man who would never tolerate the submissive conventionality of someone like Hero. All that appears to be lacking, in fact, is any sign of fondness on Beatrice's part. For

him to make overtures would be to invite her withering scorn—not to mention the I-told-you-so mockery of his friends.

Benedick and Beatrice have been playing the game of verbal abuse for so long that they scarcely remember how it started—perhaps as a squaring-off between the only two intelligences worthy of contending with each other, perhaps as a more profoundly defensive reaction of two sensitive persons not willing to part lightly with their independence. They seem to have had a prior relationsip with each other that ended unhappily. They know that true involvement with others is a complex matter—one that can cause heartache. Yet the masks they wear with each other are scarcely satisfactory. At the masked ball (2.1), we see how hurtful the "merry war" has become. Benedick, attempting to pass himself off as a stranger in a mask, abuses Beatrice by telling her of her reputation for disdain; but she, perceiving who he is, retaliates by telling him as a purported stranger what she "really" thinks of Benedick. These devices cut deeply and confirm the worst fears of each. Ironically, these fears can be dispelled only by the virtuous deceptions practiced on them by their friends. Once Benedick is assured that Beatrice secretly loves him, masking her affection with scorn, he acquires the confidence he needs to make a commitment, and vice versa in her case. The beauty of the virtuous deceptions, moreover, is that they are so plausible—because, indeed, they are essentially true. Benedick overhears himself described as a person so satirical that Beatrice dare not reveal her affection, for fear of being repulsed (2.3). Beatrice learns that she is indeed called disdainful by her friends (3.1). Both lovers respond nobly to these revelations, accepting the accusations as richly deserved and placing no blame on the other. As Beatrice proclaims to herself, "Contempt, farewell, and maiden pride, adieu!" The relief afforded by this honesty is genuine and lasting.

Because Claudio knows so little about Hero and is content with superficial expectations, he is vulnerable to a far more ugly sort of deception. Claudio's first questions about Hero betray his romantically stereotyped attitudes and his willingness to let Don Pedro and Hero's father, Leonato, arrange a financially advantageous match. Claudio treasures Hero's outward reputation for modesty, an appearance easily besmirched. When a false rumor suggests that Don Pedro is wooing the lady for himself, Claudio's response is predictably cliché-ridden: all's fair in love and war, you can't trust friends in an affair of the heart, and so farewell Hero. The rumor has a superficial plausibility about it, especially when the villainous Don John steps into the situation. Motivated in part by pure malice and the sport of ruining others' happiness, Don John speaks to the masked Claudio at the ball (2.1) as though he were speaking to Benedick and, in this guise, pretends to reveal the secret "fact" of Don Pedro's duplicity in love. (The device is precisely that used by Beatrice to put down Benedick in the same scene.) With this specious confirmation, Claudio leaps to a wrong conclusion, thereby judging both his friend and mistress to be false. He gives them no chance to speak in their own defense. To be sure, Hero's father and uncle have also believed in the false report and have welcomed the prospect of the wealthy Don Pedro as Hero's husband. The lady herself raises no objection to marriage with the older man. Still, Claudio has revealed a lack of faith resulting from his slender knowledge of Hero and of himself.

The nearly tragic "demonstration" of Hero's infidelity follows the same course, because Claudio has not learned from his first experience. Once again, the villainous Don John first implants the insidious suggestion in Claudio's mind, then creates an illusion entirely plausible to the senses, and finally confirms it with Borachio's testimony. What Claudio and Don Pedro have actually seen is Margaret wooed at Hero's window, shrouded in the dark of night and seen from "afar off in the orchard." The power of suggestion is enough to do the rest. Don John's method, and his pleasure in evil, are much like those of his later counterparts, Iago in *Othello* and Edmund in *King Lear*. Indeed, John is compared with the devil, who has power over mortals' frail senses but must rely on their complicity and acquiescence in evil. Claudio is once again led to denounce faithlessly the virtuous woman whose loyalty he no longer deserves. Yet his fault is typically human and is shared by Don Pedro. Providence gives him a second chance, through the ludicrous and bumbling intervention of Dogberry's night watch. These men overhear the plot of Don John as soon as it is announced to us, so that we know justice will eventually prevail, even though it will also be farcically delayed. Once again, misunderstanding has become "much ado about nothing," an escalating of recriminations based on a purely chimerical assumption that must eventually be deflated. The painful experience is not without value, for it tests the characters' spiritual worth in a crisis. Beatrice, like Friar Francis, shows herself to be a person of unshakable faith in goodness. Benedick, though puzzled and torn in his loyalties, also passes the test and proves himself worthy of Beatrice. Claudio is found wanting, but Hero forgives and accepts him anyway. In her role as the granter of a merciful second chance, she foreshadows the beatifically symbolic nature of many of Shakespeare's later heroines.

Much Ado comes perhaps closer to potentially tragic action than Shakespeare's other festive comedies (though *The Merchant of Venice* is another). Claudio's failure is unnervingly like that of Othello. The fact that both men are too easily persuaded to reject and humiliate the innocent women they love suggests a deep inadequacy in each. The tempters (Don John, Iago) cannot alone be blamed; the male lovers themselves are too prone to believe the worst of women. In Claudio we can see a vulnerability in the very way he looks at courtship and marriage. As Benedick jests, Claudio talks almost as though he wants to buy Hero (1.1.172). Certainly his attitude is acquisitive and superficial; as the conquering hero returned from the wars, he is ready to settle down into married respectability, and he needs a socially eligible wife. He desires Hero for her beauty, for her wealth and family connections, and above all for her modesty and her reputation for virginal purity. These are attributes easily impugned by false apearances, and in his too-quick rejection of Hero we see in Claudio a deep cynicism about women. He fears the betrayal and loss of masculine self-esteem that a woman can bestow on him by sexual infidelity. To Claudio, Hero is a saint one moment and a whore the next.

Nor is he the only man to demean her (and women) thus. Don Pedro, his patron and older friend, is no less ready to believe Don John's lies, even though Don Pedro has been deceived by his brother before and should know better. Hero's father collapses in shame when he hears his daughter publicly accused of promiscuity, for Leonato's own reputation is on the line: as father in a patriarchal society, his responsibility is to guarantee the chastity of his daughter to the younger man who proposes to receive her. Leonato's first assumption is that she must be guilty if other men say so; even he is altogether ready to believe the worst of women. Virtually the whole male world of Messina is victimized by its own fear of womanly perfidy—a fear that seems to arise from male lack of self-assurance and a deep inner conviction of being unloved. Benedick is much to be commended for his skepticism about the slanderous attacks on Hero; in no way does he better prove his worthiness of being Beatrice's husband than in his defense of a traduced and innocent woman. Yet Benedick, too, suffers to such a degree from his own male insecurity that he nearly gives up Beatrice at the very end of the play, even as she is nearly ready to give up him. Despite their self-awareness, these lovers must be rescued from their autonomous self-defensiveness by one more intervention on the part of their friends. Benedick and Beatrice are not wholly unlike Claudio and Hero after all. Both pairs of lovers are saved from their own worst selves by a harmonizing force that works its will through strange and improbable means—even through Constable Dogberry and his watch.

Much Ado About Nothing

[Dramatis Personae

DON PEDRO, *Prince of Aragon*
LEONATO, *Governor of Messina*
ANTONIO, *his brother*

BENEDICK, *a young lord of Padua*
BEATRICE, *Leonato's niece*
CLAUDIO, *a young lord of Florence*
HERO, *Leonato's daughter*
MARGARET,}
URSULA,} *gentlewomen attending Hero*

DON JOHN, *Don Pedro's bastard brother*
BORACHIO,}
CONRADE,} *followers of Don John*

DOGBERRY, *Constable in charge of the Watch*
VERGES, *the Headborough, or parish constable,*
    Dogberry's partner
A SEXTON (FRANCIS SEACOAL)
FIRST WATCHMAN
SECOND WATCHMAN (GEORGE SEACOAL)

BALTHASAR, *a singer attending Don Pedro*
FRIAR FRANCIS
A BOY
MESSENGER *to Leonato*
Another MESSENGER

Attendants, Musicians, Members of the Watch,
    Antonio's Son and other Kinsmen

SCENE: *Messina*]

1.1   *Enter Leonato, Governor of Messina, Hero his*
    daughter, and Beatrice his niece, with a
    Messenger.

LEONATO [*holding a letter*]   I learn in this letter that
Don Pedro of Aragon comes this night to Messina.
MESSENGER   He is very near by this. He was not three
leagues off when I left him.   4
LEONATO   How many gentlemen have you lost in this
action?   6
MESSENGER   But few of any sort and none of name.   7

1.1. Location: Messina. Before Leonato's house.
4 leagues units of about three miles   **6 action** battle   **7 sort** rank.
name reputation, or noble name

LEONATO   A victory is twice itself when the achiever
brings home full numbers. I find here that Don Pedro
hath bestowed much honor on a young Florentine
called Claudio.
MESSENGER   Much deserved on his part and equally
remembered by Don Pedro. He hath borne himself 13
beyond the promise of his age, doing in the figure of
a lamb the feats of a lion. He hath indeed better
bettered expectation than you must expect of me to tell 16
you how.
LEONATO   He hath an uncle here in Messina will be 18
very much glad of it.
MESSENGER   I have already delivered him letters, and
there appears much joy in him, even so much that joy
could not show itself modest enough without a badge 22
of bitterness.   23
LEONATO   Did he break out into tears?
MESSENGER   In great measure.
LEONATO   A kind overflow of kindness. There are no 26
faces truer than those that are so washed. How much
better is it to weep at joy than to joy at weeping!
BEATRICE   I pray you, is Signor Mountanto returned 29
from the wars or no?
MESSENGER   I know none of that name, lady. There was
none such in the army of any sort.
LEONATO   What is he that you ask for, niece?
HERO   My cousin means Signor Benedick of Padua.
MESSENGER   O, he's returned, and as pleasant as ever 35
he was.
BEATRICE   He set up his bills here in Messina and chal- 37
lenged Cupid at the flight; and my uncle's fool, reading 38
the challenge, subscribed for Cupid and challenged 39
him at the bird-bolt. I pray you, how many hath he 40
killed and eaten in these wars? But how many hath he
killed? For indeed I promised to eat all of his killing.
LEONATO   Faith, niece, you tax Signor Benedick too 43
much, but he'll be meet with you, I doubt it not.   44
MESSENGER   He hath done good service, lady, in these
wars.
BEATRICE   You had musty victual, and he hath holp to 47
eat it. He is a very valiant trencherman; he hath an 48
excellent stomach.   49
MESSENGER   And a good soldier too, lady.
BEATRICE   And a good soldier to a lady, but what is he 51
to a lord?   52
MESSENGER   A lord to a lord, a man to a man, stuffed 53
with all honorable virtues.

13 remembered rewarded   **16 bettered** surpassed   **18 will** who will
22 modest moderate   **22–23 badge of bitterness** sign of sorrow, i.e.,
tears   **26 kind** natural   **29 Mountanto** montanto, an upward blow or
thrust in fencing   **35 pleasant** jocular   **37 bills** placards, advertise-
ments   **38 at the flight** to a long-distance archery contest. (Beatrice
mocks Benedick's pretentions as a lady killer.)   **my uncle's fool** (Perhaps a professional fool in her uncle's service.)   **39 subscribed for**
accepted on behalf of   **40 bird-bolt** a blunt-headed arrow used for
fowling (sometimes used by children because of its relative harmless-
ness and thus conventionally appropriate to Cupid)   **43 tax** disparage
44 meet even, quits   **47 musty victual** stale food.   **holp** helped
48 valiant trencherman great eater   **49 stomach** appetite (with a
mocking suggestion also of "courage")   **51 soldier to a lady** lady
killer (with a play on *to/too*)   **52 to** compared to   **53 stuffed** amply
supplied

BEATRICE   It is so, indeed, he is no less than a stuffed 55
man. But for the stuffing—well, we are all mortal.   56
LEONATO   You must not, sir, mistake my niece. There is
a kind of merry war betwixt Signor Benedick and her.
They never meet but there's a skirmish of wit between
them.
BEATRICE   Alas! He gets nothing by that. In our last
conflict, four of his five wits went halting off, and now 62
is the whole man governed with one; so that if he have
wit enough to keep himself warm, let him bear it for
a difference between himself and his horse, for it is all 65
the wealth that he hath left to be known a reasonable 66
creature. Who is his companion now? He hath every 67
month a new sworn brother.   68
MESSENGER   Is 't possible?
BEATRICE   Very easily possible. He wears his faith but 70
as the fashion of his hat; it ever changes with the next
block.   72
MESSENGER   I see, lady, the gentleman is not in your 73
books.   74
BEATRICE   No. An he were, I would burn my study. But 75
I pray you, who is his companion? Is there no young
squarer now that will make a voyage with him to the 77
devil?
MESSENGER   He is most in the company of the right
noble Claudio.
BEATRICE   O Lord, he will hang upon him like a 81
disease! He is sooner caught than the pestilence, and
the taker runs presently mad. God help the noble 83
Claudio! If he have caught the Benedick, it will cost 84
him a thousand pound ere 'a be cured.   85
MESSENGER   I will hold friends with you, lady.   86
BEATRICE   Do, good friend.
LEONATO   You will never run mad, niece.   88
BEATRICE   No, not till a hot January.   89
MESSENGER   Don Pedro is approached.

*Enter Don Pedro, Claudio, Benedick, Balthasar,
and [Don] John the Bastard.*

DON PEDRO   Good Signor Leonato, are you come to
meet your trouble? The fashion of the world is to avoid 92
cost, and you encounter it.   93
LEONATO   Never came trouble to my house in the
likeness of Your Grace. For trouble being gone,

comfort should remain; but when you depart from
me, sorrow abides and happiness takes his leave.
DON PEDRO   You embrace your charge too willingly.—I 98
think this is your daughter.
    [Presenting himself to Hero.]
LEONATO   Her mother hath many times told me so.
BENEDICK   Were you in doubt, sir, that you asked her?
LEONATO   Signor Benedick, no; for then were you a
child.
DON PEDRO   You have it full, Benedick. We may guess 104
by this what you are, being a man. Truly, the lady
fathers herself. Be happy, lady, for you are like an 106
honorable father.
BENEDICK   If Signor Leonato be her father, she would
not have his head on her shoulders for all Messina, as 109
like him as she is.   *[Don Pedro and Leonato talk aside.]*
BEATRICE   I wonder that you will still be talking, Signor
Benedick. Nobody marks you.
BENEDICK   What, my dear Lady Disdain! Are you yet
living?
BEATRICE   Is it possible disdain should die while she
hath such meet food to feed it as Signor Benedick? 116
Courtesy itself must convert to disdain, if you come in 117
her presence.
BENEDICK   Then is courtesy a turncoat. But it is certain
I am loved of all ladies, only you excepted; and I would
I could find in my heart that I had not a hard heart, for
truly I love none.
BEATRICE   A dear happiness to women! They would 123
else have been troubled with a pernicious suitor. I
thank God and my cold blood I am of your humor for 125
that. I had rather hear my dog bark at a crow than a 126
man swear he loves me.
BENEDICK   God keep your ladyship still in that mind! So
some gentleman or other shall scape a predestinate 129
scratched face.
BEATRICE   Scratching could not make it worse, an 'twere
such a face as yours were.   132
BENEDICK   Well, you are a rare parrot-teacher.   133
BEATRICE   A bird of my tongue is better than a beast of 134
yours.   135
BENEDICK   I would my horse had the speed of your
tongue and so good a continuer. But keep your way, 137
i' God's name; I have done.
BEATRICE   You always end with a jade's trick. I know 139
you of old.

55–56 a stuffed man i.e., a figure stuffed to resemble a man   **56 the stuffing** i.e., what he's truly made of.   **well . . . mortal** i.e., well, we all have our faults   **62 five wits** i.e., not the five senses, but the five faculties: memory, imagination, judgment, fantasy, common sense.   **halting** limping   **65 difference** heraldic feature distinguishing a junior member or branch of a family (with a play on the usual sense)   **65–67 it is . . . creature** i.e., his feeble wit is all he has left to identify him as rationally human   **68 sworn brother** brother in arms (*frater juratus*, an allusion to the ancient practice of swearing brotherhood)   **70 faith** allegiance, or fidelity   **72 block** mold for shaping hats   **73–74 in your books** in favor with you, in your good books   **75 An** if. (Also in line 131.)   **77 squarer** quarreler   **81 he** i.e., Benedick   **83 presently** immediately   **84 the Benedick** i.e., as if he were a disease   **85 'a** he   **86 hold friends** keep on friendly terms (so as not to earn your enmity)   **88 run mad** i.e., "catch the Benedick"   **89 not . . . January** i.e., not any time soon   **92 your trouble** i.e., the expense of entertaining me and my retinue   **93 encounter** go to meet

98 charge social responsibility and expense   **104 have it full** are well answered   **106 fathers herself** shows by appearance who her father is   **109 his head** i.e., with Leonato's white beard and signs of age   **116 meet** suitable (with a pun on "meat")   **117 convert** change   **123 dear happiness** precious piece of luck   **125–126 I am . . . that** I am of the same disposition in that matter, i.e., of loving no one   **129 scape** escape.   **predestinate** inevitable (for any man who should woo Beatrice)   **132 were** i.e., is   **133 rare** outstanding.   **parrot-teacher** i.e., one who would teach a parrot well, because you say the same things over and over   **134 of my tongue** taught to speak like me, i.e., incessantly   **134–135 of yours** taught to speak like you   **137 a continuer** i.e., in staying power   **139 a jade's trick** i.e., an ill-tempered horse's habit of slipping its head out of the collar or stopping suddenly (as Benedick does in this race of wits)

DON PEDRO   That is the sum of all, Leonato. Signor 141
Claudio and Signor Benedick, my dear friend Leonato
hath invited you all. I tell him we shall stay here at the
least a month, and he heartily prays some occasion
may detain us longer. I dare swear he is no hypocrite,
but prays from his heart.

LEONATO   If you swear, my lord, you shall not be
forsworn. [*To Don John.*] Let me bid you welcome, my
lord, being reconciled to the Prince your brother. I 149
owe you all duty.

DON JOHN   I thank you. I am not of many words, but I
thank you.

LEONATO   Please it Your Grace lead on?   153

DON PEDRO   Your hand, Leonato. We will go together. 154
Exeunt. Manent Benedick and Claudio.

CLAUDIO   Benedick, didst thou note the daughter of
Signor Leonato?

BENEDICK   I noted her not, but I looked on her.   157

CLAUDIO   Is she not a modest young lady?

BENEDICK   Do you question me as an honest man
should do, for my simple true judgment? Or would
you have me speak after my custom, as being a
professed tyrant to their sex?   162

CLAUDIO   No, I pray thee, speak in sober judgment.

BENEDICK   Why, i' faith, methinks she's too low for a 164
high praise, too brown for a fair praise, and too little
for a great praise. Only this commendation I can afford
her, that were she other than she is, she were unhandsome, and being no other but as she is, I do not
like her.

CLAUDIO   Thou thinkest I am in sport. I pray thee, tell
me truly how thou lik'st her.

BENEDICK   Would you buy her, that you inquire after
her?

CLAUDIO   Can the world buy such a jewel?

BENEDICK   Yea, and a case to put it into. But speak you 175
this with a sad brow? Or do you play the flouting Jack, 176
to tell us Cupid is a good hare-finder and Vulcan a rare 177
carpenter? Come, in what key shall a man take you, to 178
go in the song?   179

CLAUDIO   In mine eye she is the sweetest lady that ever
I looked on.

BENEDICK   I can see yet without spectacles, and I see no
such matter. There's her cousin, an she were not
possessed with a fury, exceeds her as much in beauty 184
as the first of May doth the last of December. But I
hope you have no intent to turn husband, have you?

CLAUDIO   I would scarce trust myself, though I had

sworn the contrary, if Hero would be my wife.

BENEDICK   Is 't come to this? In faith, hath not the world
one man but he will wear his cap with suspicion? Shall 190
I never see a bachelor of threescore again? Go to, 191
i' faith; an thou wilt needs thrust thy neck into a yoke,
wear the print of it and sigh away Sundays. Look, 193
Don Pedro is returned to seek you.

Enter Don Pedro.

DON PEDRO   What secret hath held you here, that you
followed not to Leonato's?

BENEDICK   I would Your Grace would constrain me to 197
tell.

DON PEDRO   I charge thee on thy allegiance.

BENEDICK   You hear, Count Claudio. I can be secret as
a dumb man—I would have you think so—but on
my allegiance, mark you this, on my allegiance! He is
in love. With who? Now that is Your Grace's part. 203
Mark how short his answer is: with Hero, Leonato's
short daughter.

CLAUDIO   If this were so, so were it uttered.   206

BENEDICK   Like the old tale, my lord: "It is not so, nor 207
'twas not so, but indeed, God forbid it should be so."

CLAUDIO   If my passion change not shortly, God forbid
it should be otherwise.

DON PEDRO   Amen, if you love her, for the lady is very
well worthy.

CLAUDIO   You speak this to fetch me in, my lord.   213

DON PEDRO   By my troth, I speak my thought.

CLAUDIO   And in faith, my lord, I spoke mine.

BENEDICK   And by my two faiths and troths, my lord, I 216
spoke mine.

CLAUDIO   That I love her, I feel.

DON PEDRO   That she is worthy, I know.

BENEDICK   That I neither feel how she should be loved
nor know how she should be worthy is the opinion
that fire cannot melt out of me. I will die in it at the
stake.

DON PEDRO   Thou wast ever an obstinate heretic in the
despite of beauty.   225

CLAUDIO   And never could maintain his part but in the 226
force of his will.   227

141 sum of all (Don Pedro and Leonato have been conversing apart
on other matters.)   **149 being** since you are   **153 Please it** may it
please   **154 go together** i.e., go arm in arm (thus avoiding the question of precedence in order of leaving).   **s.d. Manent** they remain onstage   **157 noted her not** gave her no special attention   **162 tyrant**
one cruel or pitiless in attitude   **164 low** short   **175 case** (1) jewel
case (2) clothing, outer garments. (There is also a bawdy play on the
meaning "female pudenda.")   **176 sad** serious.   **flouting Jack** i.e.,
mocking rascal   **177–178 to tell . . . carpenter** i.e., are you mocking us with nonsense? (Cupid was blind, not sharp-eyed like a hunter,
and Vulcan was a blacksmith, not a carpenter.)   **179 go in** join in,
harmonize with   **184 with a fury** by an avenging, infernal spirit

190 wear . . . suspicion i.e., marry and thus be suspected of wearing his cap to hide his cuckold's horns, signs of his wife's infidelity
191 Go to (An expression of impatience.)   **193 print** imprint (of the
matrimonial yoke).   **Sundays** i.e., when, owing to the domesticity of
the day, you cannot escape from your yokefellow   **197 constrain** order   **203 part** speaking part (i.e., to say, "With who?")   **206 If this
. . . uttered** i.e., if I really were in love with Hero and told
Benedick, he would blab the secret this way   **207 old tale** (In the English fairy tale known as "Mr. Fox," a murderous wooer, discovered
in his crimes by the lady he seeks to marry and victimize, repeatedly
disclaims her recital of what she has seen by the refrain here set in
quotations. The story is a variant of the theme known as "the Robber
Bridegroom." Benedick uses it mockingly here to characterize Claudio's reluctance to admit his "crime" of falling in love.)   **213 fetch
me in** get me to confess   **216 two faiths and troths** (Benedick jests
about his own duplicity in swearing allegiance to Don Pedro and
blood brotherhood to Claudio; those loyalties now clash.)   **225 despite** contempt   **226–227 in . . . will** by mere obstinacy (which, as
defined by the Schoolmen, was the state of the heretic)

BENEDICK   That a woman conceived me, I thank her; that
she brought me up, I likewise give her most humble
thanks. But that I will have a recheat winded in my 230
forehead or hang my bugle in an invisible baldrick, 231
all women shall pardon me. Because I will not do them 232
the wrong to mistrust any, I will do myself the right to
trust none; and the fine is, for the which I may go the 234
finer, I will live a bachelor. 235

DON PEDRO   I shall see thee, ere I die, look pale with
love.

BENEDICK   With anger, with sickness, or with hunger,
my lord, not with love. Prove that ever I lose more 239
blood with love than I will get again with drinking, 240
pick out mine eyes with a ballad-maker's pen and 241
hang me up at the door of a brothel house for the sign 242
of blind Cupid.

DON PEDRO   Well, if ever thou dost fall from this faith,
thou wilt prove a notable argument. 245

BENEDICK   If I do, hang me in a bottle like a cat and 246
shoot at me, and he that hits me, let him be clapped on
the shoulder and called Adam. 248

DON PEDRO   Well, as time shall try:
"In time the savage bull doth bear the yoke." 250

BENEDICK   The savage bull may; but if ever the sensible
Benedick bear it, pluck off the bull's horns and set
them in my forehead, and let me be vilely painted,
and in such great letters as they write, "Here is good
horse to hire," let them signify under my sign, "Here
you may see Benedick the married man."

CLAUDIO   If this should ever happen, thou wouldst be
horn-mad. 258

DON PEDRO   Nay, if Cupid have not spent all his quiver
in Venice, thou wilt quake for this shortly. 260

BENEDICK   I look for an earthquake too, then. 261

DON PEDRO   Well, you will temporize with the hours. 262
In the meantime, good Signor Benedick, repair to
Leonato's. Commend me to him, and tell him I will
not fail him at supper, for indeed he hath made great
preparation.

BENEDICK   I have almost matter enough in me for such 267
an embassage; and so I commit you— 268

CLAUDIO   To the tuition of God. From my house, if I 269
had it—

DON PEDRO   The sixth of July. Your loving friend, Benedick.

BENEDICK   Nay, mock not, mock not. The body of your
discourse is sometimes guarded with fragments, and 274
the guards are but slightly basted on neither. Ere you 275
flout old ends any further, examine your conscience. 276
And so I leave you.   *Exit.*

CLAUDIO
My liege, Your Highness now may do me good. 278

DON PEDRO
My love is thine to teach. Teach it but how,
And thou shalt see how apt it is to learn
Any hard lesson that may do thee good.

CLAUDIO
Hath Leonato any son, my lord?

DON PEDRO
No child but Hero; she's his only heir.
Dost thou affect her, Claudio?

CLAUDIO   O my lord, 284
When you went onward on this ended action, 285
I looked upon her with a soldier's eye,
That liked, but had a rougher task in hand
Than to drive liking to the name of love.
But now I am returned and that war thoughts 289
Have left their places vacant, in their rooms
Come thronging soft and delicate desires,
All prompting me how fair young Hero is,
Saying, I liked her ere I went to wars.

DON PEDRO
Thou wilt be like a lover presently
And tire the hearer with a book of words.
If thou dost love fair Hero, cherish it,
And I will break with her and with her father, 297
And thou shalt have her. Was 't not to this end
That thou began'st to twist so fine a story? 299

CLAUDIO
How sweetly you do minister to love,
That know love's grief by his complexion! 301
But lest my liking might too sudden seem,
I would have salved it with a longer treatise. 303

DON PEDRO
What need the bridge much broader than the flood? 304

230–232 But that . . . me i.e., women must pardon me for refusing to have my horn placed on my head (like a cuckold)   **230 recheat** hunting call sounded (*winded*) on a horn to assemble the hounds   **231 baldrick** strap that supports the horn (here invisible because the horn is the metaphorical one of cuckoldry)   **234 fine** end   **234–235 go the finer** be more finely dressed (since without a wife I will have more money to spend on clothing)   **239 Prove** if you can prove   **239–240 lose . . . drinking** (According to Elizabethan theory, each sigh cost the heart a drop of blood, whereas blood was replenished by wine.)   **241 ballad-maker's pen** i.e., such as would be used to write love ballads or satires   **242 sign** painted sign, such as hung over inns and shops   **245 notable argument** notorious subject for conversation, example   **246 bottle** wicker or leather basket (to hold the cat sometimes used as an archery target)   **248 Adam** (Probably refers to Adam Bell, archer outlaw of the ballads.)   **250 In . . . yoke** (Proverbial; also appearing in a varied form in Kyd's *The Spanish Tragedy,* 2.1.)   **258 horn-mad** stark mad. (From the fury of horned beasts; with allusion to cuckoldry.)   **260 Venice** (A city noted for licentiousness.)   **quake** (with a pun on *quiver* in the previous line)   **261 I . . . then** i.e., my falling in love will be at least as rare as an earthquake   **262 temporize . . . hours** come to terms, or become milder, in time (with perhaps a bawdy pun on *hours,* "whores," pronounced something like "hoors")

267 matter wit, intelligence   **268 embassage** mission.   **and so . . . you** (A conventional close, which Claudio and Don Pedro mockingly play with as though it were the complimentary close of a letter.)   **269 tuition** protection   **274 guarded** ornamented, trimmed   **275 guards . . . neither** trimmings are tenuously stitched on at best, have only the flimsiest connection   **276 flout old ends** quote or recite mockingly proverbial tags of wisdom (as well as fragments of cloth, or the *ends* of letters that Claudio and Don Pedro have been parodying).   **examine your conscience** look to your own behavior or speech   **278 do me good** do me some good, help me   **284 affect** love   **285 ended action** military action now ended   **289 now** now that   **297 break** open the subject (as also in line 314)   **299 twist** draw out the thread of   **301 his complexion** its outward appearance   **303 salved** i.e., accounted for, or, smoothed the way, as with an ointment   **304 What need** why need be.   **flood** river

The fairest grant is the necessity.   305
Look what will serve is fit. 'Tis once: thou lovest,   306
And I will fit thee with the remedy.
I know we shall have reveling tonight;
I will assume thy part in some disguise
And tell fair Hero I am Claudio,
And in her bosom I'll unclasp my heart   311
And take her hearing prisoner with the force   312
And strong encounter of my amorous tale.
Then after to her father will I break,
And the conclusion is, she shall be thine.
In practice let us put it presently.   *Exeunt.*

❖

1.2   *Enter Leonato and an old man [Antonio], brother to Leonato, [meeting].*

LEONATO   How now, brother, where is my cousin, 1
your son? Hath he provided this music?
ANTONIO   He is very busy about it. But brother, I can
tell you strange news that you yet dreamt not of.
LEONATO   Are they good?   5
ANTONIO   As the event stamps them, but they have a 6
good cover; they show well outward. The Prince and 7
Count Claudio, walking in a thick-pleached alley in 8
mine orchard, were thus much overheard by a man of 9
mine: the Prince discovered to Claudio that he loved 10
my niece your daughter and meant to acknowledge it
this night in a dance, and if he found her accordant, he 12
meant to take the present time by the top and instantly 13
break with you of it.
LEONATO   Hath the fellow any wit that told you this? 15
ANTONIO   A good sharp fellow. I will send for him, and
question him yourself.
LEONATO   No, no; we will hold it as a dream till it 18
appear itself. But I will acquaint my daughter withal, 19
that she may be the better prepared for an answer, if
peradventure this be true. Go you and tell her of it.
[Enter Antonio's Son, with a musician and others.] Cousins, you know what you have to do.—O, I cry you 23

mercy, friend; go you with me, and I will use your 24
skill.—Good cousin, have a care this busy time.   25
Exeunt.

❖

1.3   *Enter Sir [Don] John the Bastard and Conrade, his companion.*

CONRADE   What the goodyear, my lord! Why are you 1
thus out of measure sad?   2
DON JOHN   There is no measure in the occasion that
breeds; therefore the sadness is without limit.   4
CONRADE   You should hear reason.   5
DON JOHN   And when I have heard it, what blessing
brings it?
CONRADE   If not a present remedy, at least a patient
sufferance.   9
DON JOHN   I wonder that thou, being, as thou sayst
thou art, born under Saturn, goest about to apply a 11
moral medicine to a mortifying mischief. I cannot hide 12
what I am: I must be sad when I have cause and smile
at no man's jests, eat when I have stomach and wait 14
for no man's leisure, sleep when I am drowsy and
tend on no man's business, laugh when I am merry 16
and claw no man in his humor.   17
CONRADE   Yea, but you must not make the full show of
this till you may do it without controlment. You have 19
of late stood out against your brother, and he hath 20
ta'en you newly into his grace, where it is impossible 21
you should take true root but by the fair weather that
you make yourself. It is needful that you frame the 23
season for your own harvest.
DON JOHN   I had rather be a canker in a hedge than a 25
rose in his grace, and it better fits my blood to be 26
disdained of all than to fashion a carriage to rob love 27
from any. In this, though I cannot be said to be a
flattering honest man, it must not be denied but I am
a plain-dealing villain. I am trusted with a muzzle and 30
enfranchised with a clog; therefore I have decreed not 31
to sing in my cage. If I had my mouth, I would bite; if
I had my liberty, I would do my liking. In the
meantime let me be that I am, and seek not to alter me.
CONRADE   Can you make no use of your discontent?

---

305 The . . . necessity the best gift is one that is really needed
306 Look what whatever.   **'Tis once** in short, once and for all. (This
speech of Don Pedro's is overheard by a servant of Antonio's, as we
learn in the next scene.)   **311 in her bosom** i.e., in private with her
312 take . . . prisoner i.e., command her attention and assent
1.2. Location: Leonato's house.
1 cousin kinsman   **5 they** i.e., the news (often treated as a plural
noun, as at 2.1.167)   **6 event** outcome   **6–7 stamps . . . cover**
(The image is of news that is printed and bound in a book; Antonio
means that things look promising at the moment and will be good indeed if they turn out so.)   **8 thick-pleached alley** walk lined with
dense hedges of intertwined shrubs   **9 orchard** garden   **10 discovered** disclosed   **12 accordant** agreeing, consenting   **13 take
. . . top** i.e., seize the opportunity. (Proverbially, Occasion was
imagined bald in the back of the head but with a forelock of hair in
the front that opportunistically could be grabbed.)   **15 wit** sense, intelligence   **18–19 till . . . itself** till it manifests itself   **23–24 cry
you mercy** beg your pardon

24 friend (Addressed perhaps to the musician.)   **25 have . . . time**
i.e., take care of yourself
1.3. Location: Leonato's house.
1 What the goodyear i.e., what the deuce   **2 out of measure** immoderately   **4 breeds** causes (it)   **5 hear** listen to   **9 sufferance** endurance   **11 under Saturn** (hence, of a morose disposition)   **11–
12 goest . . . mischief** endeavor to cure with moral commonplaces a
deadly disease   **14 stomach** appetite   **16 tend on** attend to   **17 claw**
flatter.   **humor** whim   **19 controlment** restraint   **20 stood out** rebelled   **21 grace** favor   **23 frame** create   **25 canker** dog rose, one
that grows wild rather than being cultivated in formal gardens
26 blood mood, disposition   **27 fashion a carriage** counterfeit a behavior.   **rob love** gain undeserved affection   **30 trusted . . . muzzle**
i.e., trusted only as far as one trusts a muzzled animal   **31 enfranchised . . . clog** allowed freedom only to the extent of being hampered by a heavy wooden block.   **decreed** determined

DON JOHN   I make all use of it, for I use it only. Who ₃₆ comes here?

Enter Borachio.

What news, Borachio?

BORACHIO   I came yonder from a great supper. The Prince your brother is royally entertained by Leonato, and I can give you intelligence of an intended mar- ₄₁ riage.

DON JOHN   Will it serve for any model to build mischief ₄₃ on? What is he for a fool that betroths himself to ₄₄ unquietness?

BORACHIO   Marry, it is your brother's right hand.   ₄₆

DON JOHN   Who, the most exquisite Claudio?

BORACHIO   Even he.

DON JOHN   A proper squire! And who, and who? ₄₉ Which way looks he?

BORACHIO   Marry, one Hero, the daughter and heir of Leonato.

DON JOHN   A very forward March chick! How came you ₅₃ to this?

BORACHIO   Being entertained for a perfumer, as I was ₅₅ smoking a musty room, comes me the Prince and ₅₆ Claudio, hand in hand, in sad conference. I whipped ₅₇ me behind the arras, and there heard it agreed upon ₅₈ that the Prince should woo Hero for himself and, having obtained her, give her to Count Claudio.

DON JOHN   Come, come, let us thither. This may prove food to my displeasure. That young start-up hath all ₆₂ the glory of my overthrow. If I can cross him any way, ₆₃ I bless myself every way. You are both sure, and will ₆₄ assist me?

CONRADE   To the death, my lord.

DON JOHN   Let us to the great supper. Their cheer is the greater that I am subdued. Would the cook were o' my ₆₈ mind! Shall we go prove what's to be done? ₆₉

BORACHIO   We'll wait upon your lordship.   *Exeunt.*

✤

2.1   *Enter Leonato, his brother [Antonio], Hero his daughter, and Beatrice his niece [with Margaret and Ursula].*

LEONATO   Was not Count John here at supper?

ANTONIO   I saw him not.

BEATRICE   How tartly that gentleman looks! I never can ₃ see him but I am heartburned an hour after. ₄

HERO   He is of a very melancholy disposition.

BEATRICE   He were an excellent man that were made ₆ just in the midway between him and Benedick. The one is too like an image and says nothing, and the ₈ other too like my lady's eldest son, evermore tattling. ₉

LEONATO   Then half Signor Benedick's tongue in Count John's mouth, and half Count John's melancholy in Signor Benedick's face—

BEATRICE   With a good leg and a good foot, uncle, and money enough in his purse, such a man would win any woman in the world, if 'a could get her good will. ₁₅

LEONATO   By my troth, niece, thou wilt never get thee a husband if thou be so shrewd of thy tongue. ₁₇

ANTONIO   In faith, she's too curst. ₁₈

BEATRICE   Too curst is more than curst. I shall lessen God's sending that way; for it is said, "God sends a ₂₀ curst cow short horns," but to a cow too curst he sends ₂₁ none.

LEONATO   So, by being too curst, God will send you no horns.

BEATRICE   Just, if he send me no husband, for the which ₂₅ blessing I am at him upon my knees every morning and evening. Lord, I could not endure a husband with a beard on his face! I had rather lie in the woolen. ₂₈

LEONATO   You may light on a husband that hath no beard.

BEATRICE   What should I do with him? Dress him in my apparel and make him my waiting-gentlewoman? He that hath a beard is more than a youth, and he that hath no beard is less than a man; and he that is more than a youth is not for me, and he that is less than a man, I am not for him. Therefore I will even take sixpence in earnest of the bearward, and lead his apes ₃₇ into hell. ₃₈

LEONATO   Well, then, go you into hell?

BEATRICE   No, but to the gate; and there will the devil meet me, like an old cuckold, with horns on his head, and say, "Get you to heaven, Beatrice, get you to heaven, here's no place for you maids." So deliver I up my apes, and away to Saint Peter, for the heavens; he ₄₄ shows me where the bachelors sit, and there live we ₄₅ as merry as the day is long.

ANTONIO   [*to Hero*]   Well, niece, I trust you will be ruled by your father.

BEATRICE   Yes, faith, it is my cousin's duty to make curtsy and say, "Father, as it please you." But yet for all that, cousin, let him be a handsome fellow, or else make another curtsy and say, "Father, as it please me."

---

36 I . . . only it is my only resource, and I cultivate it alone   **41 intelligence** information   **43 model** design, ground plan   **44 What . . . fool** what kind of fool is he   **46 Marry** by the Virgin Mary, i.e., indeed   **49 proper squire** fine young man. (Said contemptuously.)   **53 forward March chick** precocious young thing (like a chick hatched early)   **55 entertained for** hired as   **56 smoking** sweetening the air of (with aromatic smoke).   **comes me** comes. (*Me* is used colloquially.)   **57 sad** serious   **58 arras** tapestry, hanging   **62 start-up** upstart   **63 cross** thwart (with allusion, in *bless myself*, to making the sign of the cross)   **64 sure** trustworthy   **68–69 o' my mind** i.e., of a mind to poison the food   **69 prove** try out
2.1. Location: Leonato's house.
3 tartly sour of disposition   **4 heartburned** afflicted with heartburn or indigestion

6 He were a man would be   **8 image** statue   **9 my . . . son** i.e., a spoiled child.   **tattling** chattering   **15 'a** he   **17 shrewd** sharp   **18 curst** shrewish   **20 that way** in that respect   **21 curst** i.e., savage, vicious. (God proverbially takes care that the vicious are limited in their ability to do harm.)   **25 Just** right, exactly so.   **no husband** If Beatrice has no husband, there can be no prospect of cuckold's horns. (She may also be jesting about a short penis here and in lines 20–22.)   **28 in the woolen** between blankets, without sheets   **37 in earnest** in token advance payment for.   **bearward** one who keeps and exhibits a bear (and sometimes apes)   **37–38 lead . . . hell** (An ancient proverb says, "Such as die maids do all lead apes in hell.")   **44 for the heavens** (A common interjection, like "Good heavens!" but here also carrying its literal meaning, i.e., bound for heaven.)   **45 bachelors** unmarried persons of either sex

LEONATO   Well, niece, I hope to see you one day fitted with a husband.

BEATRICE   Not till God make men of some other metal 55 than earth. Would it not grieve a woman to be overmastered with a piece of valiant dust? To make an account of her life to a clod of wayward marl? No, 58 uncle, I'll none. Adam's sons are my brethren, and truly I hold it a sin to match in my kindred. 60

LEONATO [to Hero]   Daughter, remember what I told you. If the Prince do solicit you in that kind, you 62 know your answer.

BEATRICE   The fault will be in the music, cousin, if you be not wooed in good time. If the Prince be too 65 important, tell him there is measure in everything, 66 and so dance out the answer. For, hear me, Hero: wooing, wedding, and repenting is as a Scotch jig, a 68 measure, and a cinquepace. The first suit is hot and 69 hasty, like a Scotch jig, and full as fantastical; the wedding, mannerly-modest, as a measure, full of state 71 and ancientry; and then comes Repentance, and with 72 his bad legs falls into the cinquepace faster and faster till he sink into his grave.

LEONATO   Cousin, you apprehend passing shrewdly. 75

BEATRICE   I have a good eye, uncle; I can see a church 76 by daylight. 77

LEONATO   The revelers are entering, brother. Make good room.   [The men put on their masks.]

Enter [as maskers] Prince [Don] Pedro, Claudio, and Benedick, and Balthasar, [Borachio,] and Don John.

DON PEDRO   Lady, will you walk a bout with your 80 friend?   [The couples pair off for the dance.] 81

HERO   So you walk softly and look sweetly and say nothing, I am yours for the walk, and especially when I walk away.

DON PEDRO   With me in your company?

HERO   I may say so, when I please.

DON PEDRO   And when please you to say so?

HERO   When I like your favor, for God defend the lute 88 should be like the case! 89

DON PEDRO   My visor is Philemon's roof; within the 90 house is Jove.

HERO   Why, then, your visor should be thatched. 92

DON PEDRO   Speak low, if you speak love. 93
    [They step aside.]

BALTHASAR   Well, I would you did like me. 94

MARGARET   So would not I for your own sake, for I have many ill qualities.

BALTHASAR   Which is one?

MARGARET   I say my prayers aloud.

BALTHASAR   I love you the better. The hearers may cry Amen.

MARGARET   God match me with a good dancer!

BALTHASAR   Amen.

MARGARET   And God keep him out of my sight when the dance is done! Answer, clerk. 104

BALTHASAR   No more words. The clerk is answered. 105
    [They step aside.]

URSULA   I know you well enough. You are Signor Antonio.

ANTONIO   At a word, I am not. 108

URSULA   I know you by the waggling of your head.

ANTONIO   To tell you true, I counterfeit him.

URSULA   You could never do him so ill-well unless you 111 were the very man. Here's his dry hand up and down. 112 You are he, you are he.

ANTONIO   At a word, I am not.

URSULA   Come, come, do you think I do not know you by your excellent wit? Can virtue hide itself? Go to, mum, you are he. Graces will appear, and there's an 117 end.   [They step aside.] 118

BEATRICE   Will you not tell me who told you so?

BENEDICK   No, you shall pardon me.

BEATRICE   Nor will you not tell me who you are?

BENEDICK   Not now.

BEATRICE   That I was disdainful and that I had my good wit out of the Hundred Merry Tales—well, this was 124 Signor Benedick that said so.

BENEDICK   What's he?

BEATRICE   I am sure you know him well enough.

BENEDICK   Not I, believe me.

BEATRICE   Did he never make you laugh?

BENEDICK   I pray you, what is he?

BEATRICE   Why, he is the Prince's jester, a very dull fool. Only his gift is in devising impossible slanders. None 132 but libertines delight in him, and the commendation 133 is not in his wit but in his villainy, for he both pleases 134

55 metal substance (with a play on "mettle")   58 marl clay, earth (such as was used by God to make Adam in Genesis 2)   60 match . . . kindred i.e., marry incestuously   62 in that kind to that effect (i.e., to marriage)   65 in good time (1) soon (2) in time to the music, rhythmically   66 important importunate, urgent.   measure (1) moderation (2) rhythm, dance   68–69 a measure a formal dance   69 cinquepace five-step lively dance, galliard. (The pun on "sink apace," as it was pronounced, is evident in lines 72–74: repentance will sink faster and faster, with a suggestion of detumescence.)   71–72 state and ancientry dignity and traditional stateliness   75 apprehend passing shrewdly understand with unusual perspicacity   76–77 see . . . daylight i.e., see something as plain as the nose on your face   80 walk a bout take a turn, join in a section of a dance (here probably a slow, stately pavane)   81 friend lover of either sex   88 favor face   88–89 God . . . case i.e., God forbid the face within should be as unhandsome as its cover, your visor   90 Philemon's roof i.e., the humble cottage in which the peasants Philemon and Baucis entertained Jove, or Jupiter, unawares. (See Ovid, Metamorphoses, 8.)

90–93 My . . . love (A fourteen-syllable rhymed couplet, the verse form of Arthur Golding's translation of the Metamorphoses, 1567.)   92 visor mask.   thatched i.e., whiskered, to resemble the thatch of a humble cottage   94–105 Balthasar (The speech prefixes in the Quarto text for Balthasar's lines read Bene. and Balth. Some editors speculate that Borachio is intended.)   104 clerk (So addressed because of Balthasar's repeatedly answering "Amen" like the parish clerk saying the responses.)   108 At a word in short   111 do . . . ill-well imitate his imperfections so perfectly   112 dry hand (A sign of age.)   up and down exactly   117 mum be silent   117–118 an end no more to be said   124 Hundred Merry Tales (A popular collection of anecdotes first published by John Rastell in 1526.)   132 Only his gift his only talent.   impossible incredible   133 libertines i.e., those who disregard conventional moral laws   134 villainy i.e., mocking, raillery; also, clownishness   134–135 pleases . . . angers them i.e., amuses some with his rudeness and angers others with his slanders

men and angers them, and then they laugh at him and 135
beat him. I am sure he is in the fleet. I would he had 136
boarded me.   137

BENEDICK   When I know the gentleman, I'll tell him 138
what you say.

BEATRICE   Do, do. He'll but break a comparison or two 140
on me, which peradventure not marked or not laughed 141
at strikes him into melancholy; and then there's a partridge wing saved, for the fool will eat no supper that
night. [*Music.*] We must follow the leaders.   144

BENEDICK   In every good thing.

BEATRICE   Nay, if they lead to any ill, I will leave them
at the next turning.   147

*Dance. Exeunt [all except Don John, Borachio, and
Claudio. Don John and Borachio are
unmasked.]*

DON JOHN [*to Borachio*]   Sure my brother is amorous 148
on Hero and hath withdrawn her father to break 149
with him about it. The ladies follow her, and but
one visor remains.

BORACHIO   And that is Claudio. I know him by his
bearing.

DON JOHN [*advancing to Claudio*]   Are not you Signor
Benedick?

CLAUDIO   You know me well. I am he.

DON JOHN   Signor, you are very near my brother in his 157
love. He is enamored on Hero. I pray you, dissuade 158
him from her; she is no equal for his birth. You may do
the part of an honest man in it.

CLAUDIO   How know you he loves her?

DON JOHN   I heard him swear his affection.

BORACHIO   So did I, too, and he swore he would marry
her tonight. Come, let us to the banquet.   165

Exeunt. Manet Claudio.

CLAUDIO
Thus answer I in name of Benedick,
But hear these ill news with the ears of Claudio.
'Tis certain so. The Prince woos for himself.
Friendship is constant in all other things
Save in the office and affairs of love;
Therefore all hearts in love use their own tongues. 171
Let every eye negotiate for itself
And trust no agent; for beauty is a witch
Against whose charms faith melteth into blood.   174
This is an accident of hourly proof,   175
Which I mistrusted not. Farewell therefore Hero!   176

Enter Benedick [unmasked].

BENEDICK   Count Claudio?

CLAUDIO   Yea, the same.

136 **fleet** i.e., crowd, company sailing past in the dance
137 **boarded** i.e., accosted (continuing the nautical metaphor begun
in *fleet*)   138 **know** become acquainted with   140 **break a comparison** i.e., make a scornful simile (as in a tilting or breaking of lances)
141 **peradventure** if it is   144 **leaders** i.e., of the dance   147 **turning** turning figure in the dance   148–149 **amorous on** i.e., courting
157–158 **near . . . love** close to my brother   165 **banquet** light repast of fruit, wine, and dessert.   **s.d. Manet** he remains onstage
171 **all** i.e., let all   174 **faith . . . blood** loyalty gives way to passion
175 **accident** occurrence   176 **mistrusted** suspected

BENEDICK   Come, will you go with me?

CLAUDIO   Whither?

BENEDICK   Even to the next willow, about your own 181
business, County. What fashion will you wear the gar- 182
land of? About your neck, like an usurer's chain? Or 183
under your arm, like a lieutenant's scarf? You must 184
wear it one way, for the Prince hath got your Hero. 185

CLAUDIO   I wish him joy of her.

BENEDICK   Why, that's spoken like an honest drover; so 187
they sell bullocks. But did you think the Prince would 188
have served you thus?

CLAUDIO   I pray you, leave me.

BENEDICK   Ho, now you strike like the blind man. 'Twas 191
the boy that stole your meat, and you'll beat the post. 192

CLAUDIO   If it will not be, I'll leave you.   *Exit.* 193

BENEDICK   Alas, poor hurt fowl! Now will he creep into 194
sedges. But that my Lady Beatrice should know me, 195
and not know me! The Prince's fool! Ha? It may be I go 196
under that title because I am merry. Yea, but so I am
apt to do myself wrong. I am not so reputed. It is the 198
base, though bitter, disposition of Beatrice that puts 199
the world into her person and so gives me out. Well, 200
I'll be revenged as I may.

*Enter the Prince [Don Pedro], Hero, Leonato. [All
are unmasked.]*

DON PEDRO   Now, signor, where's the Count? Did you
see him?

BENEDICK   Troth, my lord, I have played the part of Lady 204
Fame. I found him here as melancholy as a lodge in a 205
warren. I told him, and I think I told him true, that 206
Your Grace had got the good will of this young lady,
and I offered him my company to a willow tree, either 208
to make him a garland, as being forsaken, or to bind 209
him up a rod, as being worthy to be whipped.   210

DON PEDRO   To be whipped! What's his fault?

BENEDICK   The flat transgression of a schoolboy, who, 212
being overjoyed with finding a bird's nest, shows it
his companion, and he steals it.

DON PEDRO   Wilt thou make a trust a transgression? 215
The transgression is in the stealer.

BENEDICK   Yet it had not been amiss the rod had been

181 **willow** (An emblem of disappointed love.)   182 **County** count
182–183 **garland** i.e., of willow   183 **usurer's chain** heavy gold
chain, worn by rich men as if it were a badge of office   184 **lieutenant's scarf** sash worn as a badge of rank   185 **one way** one way or
the other   187 **drover** cattle dealer   188 **bullocks** oxen   191 **like
the blind man** (An unidentified allusion to some proverbial story.
Compare the romance *Lazarillo de Tormes*, in which the hero steals
his master's meat and revenges himself for the beating he receives by
causing the blind man to jump against a stone pillar.)   192 **post** (1)
pillar (2) bearer of news   193 **If . . . be** i.e., if you won't leave me
as I asked   194–195 **creep into sedges** i.e., hide himself away, as
wounded fowl creep into rushes along the river   196 **not know me**
i.e., misjudge me so harshly   198–200 **It is . . . out** it is Beatrice's
low and harsh disposition that causes her to attribute to the world her
own attitudes and to represent me accordingly   204 **Troth** by my
faith   204–205 **Lady Fame** Dame Rumor   205–206 **lodge in a warren** isolated gamekeeper's hut in a large game preserve   208 **offered . . . to** offered to accompany him to   209–210 **bind . . . rod**
tie several willow switches into a scourge for him   212 **flat** plain
215 **a trust** the act of trusting someone

made, and the garland too; for the garland he might
have worn himself, and the rod he might have bestowed on you, who, as I take it, have stolen his bird's
nest.

DON PEDRO   I will but teach them to sing and restore 222
them to the owner.

BENEDICK   If their singing answer your saying, by my 224
faith, you say honestly.

DON PEDRO   The Lady Beatrice hath a quarrel to you. 226
The gentleman that danced with her told her she is
much wronged by you.

BENEDICK   O, she misused me past the endurance of a 229
block! An oak but with one green leaf on it would have 230
answered her. My very visor began to assume life
and scold with her. She told me, not thinking I had
been myself, that I was the Prince's jester, that I was
duller than a great thaw; huddling jest upon jest with 234
such impossible conveyance upon me that I stood like 235
a man at a mark, with a whole army shooting at me. 236
She speaks poniards, and every word stabs. If her 237
breath were as terrible as her terminations, there were 238
no living near her; she would infect to the North Star. 239
I would not marry her, though she were endowed with
all that Adam had left him before he transgressed. She 241
would have made Hercules have turned spit, yea, and 242
have cleft his club to make the fire, too. Come, talk not 243
of her. You shall find her the infernal Ate in good ap- 244
parel. I would to God some scholar would conjure her, 245
for certainly, while she is here, a man may live as quiet 246
in hell as in a sanctuary, and people sin upon purpose
because they would go thither; so indeed all disquiet,
horror, and perturbation follows her.

Enter Claudio and Beatrice.

DON PEDRO   Look, here she comes.

BENEDICK   Will Your Grace command me any service to
the world's end? I will go on the slightest errand now
to the Antipodes that you can devise to send me on; I 253
will fetch you a toothpicker now from the furthest inch 254
of Asia, bring you the length of Prester John's foot, 255
fetch you a hair off the great Cham's beard, do you 256
any embassage to the Pygmies, rather than hold three 257

words' conference with this harpy. You have no em- 258
ployment for me?

DON PEDRO   None but to desire your good company.

BENEDICK   O God, sir, here's a dish I love not! I cannot
endure my Lady Tongue.   *Exit.*

DON PEDRO   Come, lady, come, you have lost the heart
of Signor Benedick.

BEATRICE   Indeed, my lord, he lent it me awhile, and I 265
gave him use for it, a double heart for his single one. 266
Marry, once before he won it of me with false dice; 267
therefore Your Grace may well say I have lost it.

DON PEDRO   You have put him down, lady, you have 269
put him down.

BEATRICE   So I would not he should do me, my lord, lest
I should prove the mother of fools. I have brought
Count Claudio, whom you sent me to seek.

DON PEDRO   Why, how now, Count? Wherefore are
you sad?

CLAUDIO   Not sad, my lord.

DON PEDRO   How then? Sick?

CLAUDIO   Neither, my lord.

BEATRICE   The Count is neither sad, nor sick, nor merry,
nor well; but civil count, civil as an orange, and some- 280
thing of that jealous complexion.   281

DON PEDRO   I' faith, lady, I think your blazon to be true, 282
though I'll be sworn, if he be so, his conceit is false. 283
Here, Claudio, I have wooed in thy name, and fair
Hero is won. I have broke with her father and his 285
good will obtained. Name the day of marriage, and
God give thee joy!

LEONATO   Count, take of me my daughter and with her
my fortunes. His Grace hath made the match, and all 289
grace say Amen to it.   290

BEATRICE   Speak, Count, 'tis your cue.

CLAUDIO   Silence is the perfectest herald of joy. I were
but little happy if I could say how much!—Lady, as
you are mine, I am yours. I give away myself for you
and dote upon the exchange.

BEATRICE   Speak, cousin, or if you cannot, stop his
mouth with a kiss, and let not him speak neither.
                                 [*Claudio and Hero kiss.*]

DON PEDRO   In faith, lady, you have a merry heart.

BEATRICE   Yea, my lord; I thank it, poor fool, it keeps on
the windy side of care. My cousin tells him in his ear 300
that he is in her heart.

CLAUDIO   And so she doth, cousin.

---

222 **them** i.e., the young birds in the nest   224 **answer your saying**
correspond to what you say   226 **to** with   229 **misused** abused
230 **block** (of wood)   234 **great thaw** i.e., time when roads are
muddy and impassable, obliging one to stay dully at home.   **huddling** piling, heaping up   235 **impossible conveyance** incredible dexterity   236 **at a mark** at the target, marking where the arrows hit
237 **poniards** daggers   238 **terminations** terms, expressions
239 **North Star** (Popularly supposed to be the most remote of stars.)
241 **all . . . him** i.e., Paradise before the fall of man   242 **Hercules . . . spit** (The Amazon Omphale forced the captive Hercules to
wear women's clothing and spin; turning the spit would be an even
more menial kitchen duty.)   243 **cleft** split   244 **Ate** goddess of discord   245 **scholar . . . conjure** (Scholars were supposed to be able
to conjure evil spirits back into hell by addressing them in Latin.)
246 **here** i.e., on earth. (As long as Beatrice is on earth, hell will
seem like a place of refuge.)   253 **Antipodes** people and region on
the opposite side of the earth   254 **toothpicker** toothpick
255 **Prester John** a legendary Christian king of the Far East   256 **great
Cham** the Khan of Tartary, ruler of the Mongols   257 **Pygmies** legendary small race thought to live in India

258 **harpy** legendary creature with a woman's face and body and a
bird's wings and claws   265 **he . . . awhile** (Beatrice refers seemingly to a previous love affair with Benedick in which she feels she
was won with false promises [*false dice*] but repaid him with deceit [a
double heart].)   266 **use** usury, interest. (She gave him double what
he gave her.)   267 **before** i.e., before the present   269 **put him
down** got the better of him. (But Beatrice plays with the phrase in its
literal and sexual sense.)   280 **civil** serious, grave (punning on *Seville*
for the city in Spain whence came bitter-tasting oranges)   280–
281 **something** somewhat   281 **jealous complexion** i.e., yellow, associated with melancholy and symbolic of jealousy   282 **blazon** description. (A heraldic term.)   283 **conceit** (1) notion, idea (2) heraldic
device (continuing the metaphor of *blazon*)   285 **broke** spoken
289–290 **all grace** i.e., the source of grace, God   300 **windy** windward, safe. (In sailing, the ship to windward has the advantage.)

BEATRICE   Good Lord, for alliance! Thus goes everyone 303
to the world but I, and I am sunburnt. I may sit in a 304
corner and cry, "Heigh-ho for a husband!"   305
DON PEDRO   Lady Beatrice, I will get you one.
BEATRICE   I would rather have one of your father's
getting. Hath Your Grace ne'er a brother like you? 308
Your father got excellent husbands, if a maid could
come by them.
DON PEDRO   Will you have me, lady?
BEATRICE   No, my lord, unless I might have another for
working days. Your Grace is too costly to wear every
day. But I beseech Your Grace, pardon me. I was born
to speak all mirth and no matter.   315
DON PEDRO   Your silence most offends me, and to be
merry best becomes you, for out o' question you were
born in a merry hour.
BEATRICE   No, sure, my lord, my mother cried; but then
there was a star danced, and under that was I born.
Cousins, God give you joy!
LEONATO   Niece, will you look to those things I told
you of?
BEATRICE   I cry you mercy, uncle. [*To Don Pedro.*] By 324
Your Grace's pardon.   *Exit Beatrice.* 325
DON PEDRO   By my troth, a pleasant-spirited lady.
LEONATO   There's little of the melancholy element in 327
her, my lord. She is never sad but when she sleeps,
and not ever sad then; for I have heard my daughter 329
say she hath often dreamt of unhappiness and waked 330
herself with laughing.
DON PEDRO   She cannot endure to hear tell of a husband.
LEONATO   O, by no means. She mocks all her wooers
out of suit.   334
DON PEDRO   She were an excellent wife for Benedick.
LEONATO   O Lord, my lord, if they were but a week
married they would talk themselves mad.
DON PEDRO   County Claudio, when mean you to go to
church?
CLAUDIO   Tomorrow, my lord. Time goes on crutches
till Love have all his rites.
LEONATO   Not till Monday, my dear son, which is hence
a just sevennight and a time too brief, too, to have all 343
things answer my mind.   344
DON PEDRO   Come, you shake the head at so long a
breathing, but I warrant thee, Claudio, the time shall 346
not go dully by us. I will in the interim undertake one
of Hercules' labors, which is to bring Signor Benedick
and the Lady Beatrice into a mountain of affection th'
one with th' other. I would fain have it a match, and I
doubt not but to fashion it, if you three will but

minister such assistance as I shall give you direction. 352
LEONATO   My lord, I am for you, though it cost me ten
nights' watchings.   354
CLAUDIO   And I, my lord.
DON PEDRO   And you too, gentle Hero?
HERO   I will do any modest office, my lord, to help my 357
cousin to a good husband.
DON PEDRO   And Benedick is not the unhopefullest hus- 359
band that I know. Thus far can I praise him: he is of a
noble strain, of approved valor and confirmed honesty. 361
I will teach you how to humor your cousin, that she
shall fall in love with Benedick; and I, with your two
helps, will so practice on Benedick that, in despite of
his quick wit and his queasy stomach, he shall fall in 365
love with Beatrice. If we can do this, Cupid is no
longer an archer; his glory shall be ours, for we are the
only love gods. Go in with me, and I will tell you my
drift.   *Exeunt.* 369

2.2   *Enter [Don] John and Borachio.*

DON JOHN   It is so. The Count Claudio shall marry the 1
daughter of Leonato.
BORACHIO   Yea, my lord, but I can cross it.   3
DON JOHN   Any bar, any cross, any impediment will be 4
medicinable to me. I am sick in displeasure to him, 5
and whatsoever comes athwart his affection ranges 6
evenly with mine. How canst thou cross this mar- 7
riage?
BORACHIO   Not honestly, my lord, but so covertly that
no dishonesty shall appear in me.
DON JOHN   Show me briefly how.
BORACHIO   I think I told your lordship, a year since, 12
how much I am in the favor of Margaret, the waiting
gentlewoman to Hero.
DON JOHN   I remember.
BORACHIO   I can, at any unseasonable instant of the 16
night, appoint her to look out at her lady's chamber
window.
DON JOHN   What life is in that, to be the death of this
marriage?
BORACHIO   The poison of that lies in you to temper. Go 21
you to the Prince your brother; spare not to tell him
that he hath wronged his honor in marrying the renowned Claudio—whose estimation do you mightily 24
hold up—to a contaminated stale, such a one as Hero. 25
DON JOHN   What proof shall I make of that?

---

303 alliance relationship by marriage. (Claudio has just called her
"cousin.") **303–304 goes . . . world** i.e., everyone gets married
304 sunburnt (The Renaissance considered dark complexions unattractive.) **305 Heigh-ho . . . husband** (The title of a ballad.)
308 getting begetting (playing on *get*, "procure," in the previous
speech) **315 matter** substance **324 cry you mercy** beg your pardon
(for not having obeyed earlier) **324–325 By . . . pardon** i.e., I beg
you to excuse my departure **327 melancholy element** i.e., earth, associated with the humor of melancholy in the old physiology
329 ever always **330 unhappiness** misfortune **334 out of suit** out of
being wooers to her **343 a just sevennight** exactly a week **344 answer my mind** suit my wishes **346 breathing** pause, interval

352 minister furnish, supply **354 watchings** staying awake
357 do . . . office play any seemly role **359 unhopefullest** most un-
promising **361 strain** ancestry. **approved** tested. **honesty** honor
365 queasy squeamish, delicate (about marriage) **369 drift** purpose
2.2. Location: Leonato's house.
1 shall is going to **3 cross** thwart. (Also in line 7.) **4 bar** obstacle
5 medicinable medicinal. **in displeasure to** with dislike of
6–7 whatsoever . . . mine whatever crosses his inclination runs parallel with mine **12 since** ago **16 unseasonable** unsuitable, unseemly
21 lies in rests with. **temper** mix, compound **24 estimation** worth,
reputation. **do you** you do **25 stale** prostitute

BORACHIO   Proof enough to misuse the Prince, to vex 27
Claudio, to undo Hero, and kill Leonato. Look you for
any other issue?

DON JOHN   Only to despite them I will endeavor any- 30
thing.

BORACHIO   Go, then, find me a meet hour to draw Don 32
Pedro and the Count Claudio alone. Tell them that you
know that Hero loves me. Intend a kind of zeal both to 34
the Prince and Claudio, as—in love of your brother's 35
honor, who hath made this match, and his friend's
reputation, who is thus like to be cozened with the 37
semblance of a maid—that you have discovered thus. 38
They will scarcely believe this without trial. Offer
them instances, which shall bear no less likelihood 40
than to see me at her chamber window, hear me call
Margaret Hero, hear Margaret term me Claudio; and 42
bring them to see this the very night before the
intended wedding—for in the meantime I will so
fashion the matter that Hero shall be absent—and
there shall appear such seeming truth of Hero's
disloyalty that jealousy shall be called assurance and 47
all the preparation overthrown. 48

DON JOHN   Grow this to what adverse issue it can, I will 49
put it in practice. Be cunning in the working this, and
thy fee is a thousand ducats. 51

BORACHIO   Be you constant in the accusation, and my
cunning shall not shame me.

DON JOHN   I will presently go learn their day of mar- 54
riage.   *Exit* [*with Borachio*].

❖

2.3   *Enter Benedick alone.*

BENEDICK   Boy!

[*Enter Boy.*]

BOY   Signor?

BENEDICK   In my chamber window lies a book. Bring it
hither to me in the orchard. 4

BOY   I am here already, sir. 5

BENEDICK   I know that, but I would have thee hence
and here again. *Exit* [*Boy*]. I do much wonder that one
man, seeing how much another man is a fool when he
dedicates his behaviors to love, will, after he hath
laughed at such shallow follies in others, become the

argument of his own scorn by falling in love; and such 11
a man is Claudio. I have known when there was no 12
music with him but the drum and the fife, and now 13
had he rather hear the tabor and the pipe. I have 14
known when he would have walked ten mile afoot to
see a good armor, and now will he lie ten nights 16
awake carving the fashion of a new doublet. He was 17
wont to speak plain and to the purpose, like an honest
man and a soldier, and now is he turned orthogra- 19
phy—his words are a very fantastical banquet, just so 20
many strange dishes. May I be so converted and see
with these eyes? I cannot tell; I think not. I will not be
sworn but Love may transform me to an oyster, but I'll
take my oath on it, till he have made an oyster of me,
he shall never make me such a fool. One woman is
fair, yet I am well; another is wise, yet I am well;
another virtuous, yet I am well; but till all graces be in
one woman, one woman shall not come in my grace.
Rich she shall be, that's certain; wise, or I'll none; 29
virtuous, or I'll never cheapen her; fair, or I'll never 30
look on her; mild, or come not near me; noble, or not 31
I for an angel; of good discourse, an excellent musi- 32
cian, and her hair shall be of what color it please God. 33
Ha! The Prince and Monsieur Love. I will hide me in
the arbor.   [*He hides.*]

Enter Prince [*Don Pedro*], *Leonato, Claudio.*

DON PEDRO   Come, shall we hear this music?
CLAUDIO
Yea, my good lord. How still the evening is,
As hushed on purpose to grace harmony! 38
DON PEDRO [*apart to them*]
See you where Benedick hath hid himself?
CLAUDIO [*apart in reply*]
O, very well, my lord. The music ended, 40
We'll fit the kid-fox with a pennyworth. 41

Enter Balthasar with music.

DON PEDRO
Come, Balthasar, we'll hear that song again.
BALTHASAR
O good my lord, tax not so bad a voice 43
To slander music any more than once.
DON PEDRO
It is the witness still of excellency 45

---

27 misuse abuse, deceive   **30 despite** torment, injure   **32 meet** suitable   **34 Intend** pretend   **35 as** i.e., saying as follows. (The words
between the dashes are to be understood as instructions to Don John
as to what he is to say.)   **37 like** likely.   **cozened** deceived, cheated
38 semblance semblance only, outward appearance.   **discovered** revealed   **40 instances** proofs   **42 hear . . . Claudio** (Many editors
read *Borachio* for *Claudio*. The present reading may be defended if
one imagines that, by arrangement with Margaret, Borachio is playing
the part of Claudio, but the reading may also be an inconsistency.)
47 jealousy suspicion.   **assurance** certainty   **48 preparation** i.e., for
marriage   **49 Grow . . . can** no matter what the adverse consequences may be   **51 ducats** gold coins   **54 presently** immediately
2.3. Location: Leonato's garden.
4 orchard garden   **5 I . . . already** i.e., I will be so quick as to use
no time at all. (But Benedick quibbles on the literal sense.)

11 argument subject   **12–13 there was . . . fife** i.e., his only commitment was to soldiering   **14 tabor . . . pipe** (Symbols of peaceful
merriment.)   **16 armor** suit of armor   **17 carving** planning.   **doublet**
jacket   **19–20 turned orthography** become fastidious and fashionable in his choice of language   **29 I'll none** I'll have none of her
30 cheapen make a bid for. (The idea of lessening her value by using
her may also be suggested, though historically it is a later meaning.)
31, 32 noble, angel (Each of these words involves a pun on the meaning "a coin," a noble being worth six shillings eightpence and an angel, ten shillings.)   **33 her hair . . . God** i.e., as long as she doesn't
dye it   **38 grace harmony** do honor to music   **40 The music ended**
when the music is over   **41 We'll . . . pennyworth** i.e., we'll give
our sly victim more than he bargained for. (Perhaps Benedick is called
kid-fox, a term from beast fable, because he is sly like a fox and is being duped in their game like a kid.)   **43 tax** task   **45–46 It . . . perfection** it is always characteristic of excellence to pretend not to know
its own skill

To put a strange face on his own perfection.   46
I pray thee, sing, and let me woo no more.   47
BALTHASAR
Because you talk of wooing, I will sing,   48
Since many a wooer doth commence his suit   49
To her he thinks not worthy, yet he woos,   50
Yet will he swear he loves.
DON PEDRO   Nay, pray thee, come,   51
Or if thou wilt hold longer argument,
Do it in notes.
BALTHASAR   Note this before my notes: 53
There's not a note of mine that's worth the noting.
DON PEDRO
Why, these are very crotchets that he speaks!   55
Note, notes, forsooth, and nothing.   [*Music.*] 56
BENEDICK [*aside*]   Now, divine air! Now is his soul rav-   57
ished! Is it not strange that sheeps' guts should hale   58
souls out of men's bodies? Well, a horn for my money,   59
when all's done.

The Song.

BALTHASAR
 Sigh no more, ladies, sigh no more.
  Men were deceivers ever,
 One foot in sea and one on shore,
  To one thing constant never.
 Then sigh not so, but let them go,
  And be you blithe and bonny,   66
 Converting all your sounds of woe
  Into Hey nonny, nonny.   68

 Sing no more ditties, sing no moe,   69
  Of dumps so dull and heavy;   70
 The fraud of men was ever so,
  Since summer first was leavy.   72
 Then sigh not so, but let them go,
  And be you blithe and bonny,
 Converting all your sounds of woe
  Into Hey nonny, nonny.

DON PEDRO   By my troth, a good song.
BALTHASAR   And an ill singer, my lord.
DON PEDRO   Ha, no, no, faith, thou sing'st well enough
for a shift.   80
BENEDICK [*aside*]   An he had been a dog that should   81
have howled thus, they would have hanged him,
and I pray God his bad voice bode no mischief. I

has as lief have heard the night raven, come what   84
plague could have come after it.
DON PEDRO   Yea, marry, dost thou hear, Balthasar? I   86
pray thee, get us some excellent music, for tomorrow
night we would have it at the Lady Hero's chamber
window.
BALTHASAR   The best I can, my lord.
DON PEDRO   Do so. Farewell. (*Exit Balthasar.*) Come
hither, Leonato. What was it you told me of today,
that your niece Beatrice was in love with Signor
Benedick?
CLAUDIO   O, ay! [*Apart to Pedro.*] Stalk on, stalk on; the   95
fowl sits.—I did never think that lady would have   96
loved any man.
LEONATO   No, nor I neither, but most wonderful that
she should so dote on Signor Benedick, whom she
hath in all outward behaviors seemed ever to abhor.
BENEDICK [*aside*]   Is 't possible? Sits the wind in that   101
corner?   102
LEONATO   By my troth, my lord, I cannot tell what to
think of it but that she loves him with an enraged   104
affection; it is past the infinite of thought.   105
DON PEDRO   Maybe she doth but counterfeit.
CLAUDIO   Faith, like enough.   107
LEONATO   O God, counterfeit? There was never counterfeit of passion came so near the life of passion as she
discovers it.   110
DON PEDRO   Why, what effects of passion shows she?
CLAUDIO [*apart to them*]   Bait the hook well; this fish
will bite.
LEONATO   What effects, my lord? She will sit you—you   114
heard my daughter tell you how.
CLAUDIO   She did indeed.
DON PEDRO   How, how, I pray you? You amaze me. I
would have thought her spirit had been invincible
against all assaults of affection.
LEONATO   I would have sworn it had, my lord—
especially against Benedick.
BENEDICK [*aside*]   I should think this a gull but that   122
the white-bearded fellow speaks it. Knavery cannot,
sure, hide himself in such reverence.
CLAUDIO [*apart to them*]   He hath ta'en th' infection.
Hold it up.   126
DON PEDRO   Hath she made her affection known to Benedick?
LEONATO   No, and swears she never will. That's her
torment.
CLAUDIO   'Tis true, indeed. So your daughter says.
"Shall I," says she, "that have so oft encountered him   132
with scorn, write to him that I love him?"

---

47 woo entreat   **48–51 Because . . . he loves** (Balthasar modestly claims to be unworthy of being *wooed*, i.e., entreated, but will comply, since he knows Don Pedro speaks with the hyperbole all wooers use in addressing women they actually consider unworthy.)   **53 notes** music   **55 crotchets** (1) whim, fancy (2) musical notes of brief duration   **56 nothing** (With a pun on *noting*; the two words were pronounced alike. Compare the same pun in the title of the play, where *Nothing* suggests "noting," or eavesdropping.)   **57 air** melody   **58 sheeps' guts** strings on musical instruments.   **hale** draw   **59 a horn** a hunting horn, a more masculine instrument than a lute. (But with a perhaps unconscious allusion to a cuckold's horns.)   **66 blithe and bonny** cheerful and joyful   **68 Hey nonny, nonny** (A nonsense refrain.)   **69 moe** more   **70 dumps** mournful songs; also, dances   **72 leavy** leafy   **80 for a shift** in a pinch   **81 An** if. (Also in line 161.)

84 lief willingly.   **night raven** some bird of night, portending disaster   **86 Yea, marry** (A continuation of Don Pedro's speech preceding Benedick's aside.)   **95–96 Stalk . . . sits** i.e., proceed stealthily; the hunted bird is hiding in the bush   **101–102 Sits . . . corner** is that the way the wind is blowing? (i.e., is that how things are?)   **104 enraged** maddened with passion   **105 infinite** farthest reach. (It's unbelievable but true.)   **107 like** likely   **110 discovers** betrays   **114 sit you** i.e., sit. (*You* is used idiomatically.)   **122 gull** trick, deception.   **but** except for the fact   **126 Hold it up** keep up the jest   **132 she** i.e., Beatrice

LEONATO   This says she now when she is beginning to write to him, for she'll be up twenty times a night, and there will she sit in her smock till she have writ a sheet 136 of paper. My daughter tells us all.

CLAUDIO   Now you talk of a sheet of paper, I remember a pretty jest your daughter told us of.

LEONATO   O, when she had writ it and was reading it over, she found "Benedick" and "Beatrice" between the sheet?

CLAUDIO   That.   143

LEONATO   O, she tore the letter into a thousand half- 144 pence; railed at herself, that she should be so immodest 145 to write to one that she knew would flout her. "I mea- 146 sure him," says she, "by my own spirit, for I should flout him if he writ to me. Yea, though I love him, I should."

CLAUDIO   Then down upon her knees she falls, weeps, sobs, beats her heart, tears her hair, prays, curses: "O sweet Benedick! God give me patience!"

LEONATO   She doth indeed; my daughter says so. And the ecstasy hath so much overborne her that my 154 daughter is sometimes afeard she will do a desperate outrage to herself. It is very true.

DON PEDRO   It were good that Benedick knew of it by some other, if she will not discover it.   158

CLAUDIO   To what end? He would make but a sport of it and torment the poor lady worse.

DON PEDRO   An he should, it were an alms to hang 161 him. She's an excellent sweet lady, and, out of all 162 suspicion, she is virtuous.

CLAUDIO   And she is exceeding wise.

DON PEDRO   In everything but in loving Benedick.

LEONATO   O my lord, wisdom and blood combating in 166 so tender a body, we have ten proofs to one that blood hath the victory. I am sorry for her, as I have just cause, being her uncle and her guardian.

DON PEDRO   I would she had bestowed this dotage on 170 me. I would have doffed all other respects and made 171 her half myself. I pray you, tell Benedick of it, and 172 hear what 'a will say.

LEONATO   Were it good, think you?

CLAUDIO   Hero thinks surely she will die; for she says she will die if he love her not, and she will die ere she make her love known, and she will die if he woo her, rather than she will bate one breath of her accustomed 178 crossness.   179

DON PEDRO   She doth well. If she should make tender of 180 her love, 'tis very possible he'll scorn it; for the man, as you know all, hath a contemptible spirit.   182

CLAUDIO   He is a very proper man.   183

DON PEDRO   He hath indeed a good outward happiness. 184

CLAUDIO   Before God, and in my mind, very wise.   185

DON PEDRO   He doth indeed show some sparks that are like wit.

CLAUDIO   And I take him to be valiant.

DON PEDRO   As Hector, I assure you; and in the man- 189 aging of quarrels you may say he is wise, for either he avoids them with great discretion or undertakes them with a most Christian-like fear.

LEONATO   If he do fear God, 'a must necessarily keep peace. If he break the peace, he ought to enter into a quarrel with fear and trembling.

DON PEDRO   And so will he do, for the man doth fear God, howsoever it seems not in him by some large 197 jests he will make. Well, I am sorry for your niece. Shall we go seek Benedick and tell him of her love?

CLAUDIO   Never tell him, my lord. Let her wear it out 200 with good counsel.   201

LEONATO   Nay, that's impossible. She may wear her heart out first.

DON PEDRO   Well, we will hear further of it by your daughter. Let it cool the while. I love Benedick well, and I could wish he would modestly examine himself, to see how much he is unworthy so good a lady.

LEONATO   My lord, will you walk? Dinner is ready.

[They walk aside.]

CLAUDIO   If he do not dote on her upon this, I will 209 never trust my expectation.

DON PEDRO   Let there be the same net spread for her; and that must your daughter and her gentlewomen carry. The sport will be when they hold one an 213 opinion of another's dotage, and no such matter; 214 that's the scene that I would see, which will be merely a dumb show. Let us send her to call him in to dinner. 216

[Exeunt Don Pedro, Claudio, and Leonato.]

BENEDICK [coming forward]   This can be no trick. The conference was sadly borne. They have the truth of 218 this from Hero. They seem to pity the lady. It seems her affections have their full bent. Love me? Why, it 220 must be requited. I hear how I am censured. They say I will bear myself proudly if I perceive the love come from her; they say too that she will rather die than give any sign of affection. I did never think to marry. I must not seem proud; happy are they that hear their detractions and can put them to mending. 226 They say the lady is fair; 'tis a truth, I can bear them witness; and virtuous; 'tis so, I cannot reprove it; 228 and wise but for loving me; by my troth, it is no addition to her wit, nor no great argument of her folly, for I will be horribly in love with her. I may

---

136 **smock** chemise   143 **That** i.e., that's it   144–145 **halfpence** i.e., small pieces   146 **flout** mock   154 **overborne** overwhelmed 158 **discover** reveal   161 **alms** good deed. (Hanging would be too good for him.)   162 **out of** beyond   166 **blood** natural feeling 170 **dotage** doting affection   171 **doffed** put or turned aside. **respects** considerations   172 **half myself** i.e., my wife   178 **bate** abate 179 **crossness** perversity, contrariety   180 **tender** offer   182 **contemptible** contemptuous   183 **proper** handsome   184 **outward happiness** fortune in his good looks

185 **Before God** i.e., by God, you're absolutely right   189 **Hector** the mightiest of the Trojans   197 **by** to judge by.   **large** broad, indelicate 200 **wear it out** eradicate it   201 **counsel** reflection, deliberation 209 **upon** as a result of, after   213 **carry** carry out   213–214 **they . . . dotage** each believes the other to be in love   214 **no such matter** the reality is quite otherwise   216 **dumb show** pantomime (lacking their usual banter)   218 **sadly borne** soberly conducted 220 **have . . . bent** i.e., are fully engaged. (The image is of a bow pulled taut.)   226 **their detractions** criticisms of themselves. **put . . . mending** undertake to remedy the defect   228 **reprove** refute

chance have some odd quirks and remnants of wit 232
broken on me, because I have railed so long against
marriage. But doth not the appetite alter? A man loves
the meat in his youth that he cannot endure in
his age. Shall quips and sentences and these paper 236
bullets of the brain awe a man from the career of his 237
humor? No, the world must be peopled. When I said 238
I would die a bachelor, I did not think I should live till
I were married. Here comes Beatrice. By this day,
she's a fair lady! I do spy some marks of love in her.

Enter Beatrice.

BEATRICE   Against my will I am sent to bid you come in
to dinner.
BENEDICK   Fair Beatrice, I thank you for your pains.
BEATRICE   I took no more pains for those thanks than
you take pains to thank me. If it had been painful I
would not have come.
BENEDICK   You take pleasure then in the message?
BEATRICE   Yea, just so much as you may take upon a 249
knife's point and choke a daw withal. You have no 250
stomach, signor. Fare you well.   *Exit.* 251
BENEDICK   Ha! "Against my will I am sent to bid you
come in to dinner." There's a double meaning in that.
"I took no more pains for those thanks than you took
pains to thank me." That's as much as to say, "Any
pains that I take for you is as easy as thanks." If I do
not take pity of her, I am a villain; if I do not love her,
I am a Jew. I will go get her picture.   *Exit.*

❧

3.1   *Enter Hero and two gentlewomen, Margaret and
Ursula.*

HERO
  Good Margaret, run thee to the parlor.
  There shalt thou find my cousin Beatrice
  Proposing with the Prince and Claudio.   3
  Whisper her ear and tell her I and Ursley   4
  Walk in the orchard, and our whole discourse
  Is all of her. Say that thou overheardst us,
  And bid her steal into the pleachèd bower,   7
  Where honeysuckles, ripened by the sun,
  Forbid the sun to enter, like favorites,
  Made proud by princes, that advance their pride   10
  Against that power that bred it. There will she hide
  her,   11
  To listen our propose. This is thy office.   12

Bear thee well in it and leave us alone.   13
MARGARET
  I'll make her come, I warrant you, presently.   [*Exit.*] 14
HERO
  Now, Ursula, when Beatrice doth come,
  As we do trace this alley up and down,   16
  Our talk must only be of Benedick.
  When I do name him, let it be thy part
  To praise him more than ever man did merit.
  My talk to thee must be how Benedick
  Is sick in love with Beatrice. Of this matter
  Is little Cupid's crafty arrow made,
  That only wounds by hearsay.

Enter Beatrice [behind].

                          Now begin,   23
  For look where Beatrice, like a lapwing, runs   24
  Close by the ground, to hear our conference.
URSULA [*to Hero*]
  The pleasant'st angling is to see the fish
  Cut with her golden oars the silver stream   27
  And greedily devour the treacherous bait.
  So angle we for Beatrice, who even now
  Is couchèd in the woodbine coverture.   30
  Fear you not my part of the dialogue.
HERO [*to Ursula*]
  Then go we near her, that her ear lose nothing
  Of the false sweet bait that we lay for it.
                          [*They approach the bower.*]
  No, truly, Ursula, she is too disdainful;
  I know her spirits are as coy and wild   35
  As haggards of the rock.
URSULA   But are you sure   36
  That Benedick loves Beatrice so entirely?
HERO
  So says the Prince and my new-trothèd lord.
URSULA
  And did they bid you tell her of it, madam?
HERO
  They did entreat me to acquaint her of it;
  But I persuaded them, if they loved Benedick,
  To wish him wrestle with affection
  And never to let Beatrice know of it.
URSULA
  Why did you so? Doth not the gentleman
  Deserve as full as fortunate a bed   45
  As ever Beatrice shall couch upon?   46
HERO
  O god of love! I know he doth deserve
  As much as may be yielded to a man;
  But Nature never framed a woman's heart
  Of prouder stuff than that of Beatrice.
  Disdain and scorn ride sparkling in her eyes,
  Misprizing what they look on, and her wit   52

---

232 quirks witty conceits or jokes   **236 sentences** saws, maxims
236–237 paper bullets i.e., words   **237–238 career of his humor**
pursuit of his inclination. (In horsemanship, a *career* is a short gallop.)
249–250 just . . . withal i.e., very little. (A daw or jackdaw is a
common blackbird, smaller than a crow.)   **251 stomach** appetite
3.1. Location: Leonato's garden.
3 Proposing conversing   **4 Ursley** (A nickname for *Ursula.*)
7 pleachèd formed by densely interwoven branches   **10–**
11 that . . . it i.e., who dare set themselves up against the very
princes who advanced them   **12 listen our propose** listen to our conversation.   **office** responsibility

13 leave us alone leave the rest to us   **14 presently** immediately
16 trace walk   **23 only . . . hearsay** wounds by mere report
24 lapwing bird of the plover family   **27 oars** i.e., fins   **30 woodbine**
coverture bower, or arbor, of honeysuckle   **35 coy** disdainful
36 haggards untamed female hawks.   **rock** i.e., mountainous terrain
45–46 as full . . . upon i.e., as good a wife as Beatrice   **52 Mis-**
prizing undervaluing, despising

Values itself so highly that to her
All matter else seems weak. She cannot love,   54
Nor take no shape nor project of affection,   55
She is so self-endearèd.
URSULA   Sure I think so,   56
And therefore certainly it were not good
She knew his love, lest she'll make sport at it.
HERO
Why, you speak truth. I never yet saw man,
How wise, how noble, young, how rarely featured, 60
But she would spell him backward. If fair-faced, 61
She would swear the gentleman should be her
  sister;
If black, why, Nature, drawing of an antic,   63
Made a foul blot; if tall, a lance ill-headed;
If low, an agate very vilely cut;   65
If speaking, why, a vane blown with all winds;
If silent, why, a block movèd with none.
So turns she every man the wrong side out
And never gives to truth and virtue that
Which simpleness and merit purchaseth.   70
URSULA
Sure, sure, such carping is not commendable.
HERO
No, not to be so odd and from all fashions   72
As Beatrice is cannot be commendable.
But who dare tell her so? If I should speak,
She would mock me into air; O, she would
  laugh me
Out of myself, press me to death with wit.   76
Therefore let Benedick, like covered fire,
Consume away in sighs, waste inwardly.   78
It were a better death than die with mocks,
Which is as bad as die with tickling.
URSULA
Yet tell her of it. Hear what she will say.
HERO
No, rather I will go to Benedick
And counsel him to fight against his passion.
And truly, I'll devise some honest slanders   84
To stain my cousin with. One doth not know
How much an ill word may empoison liking.
URSULA
O, do not do your cousin such a wrong!
She cannot be so much without true judgment—
Having so swift and excellent a wit
As she is prized to have—as to refuse   90
So rare a gentleman as Signor Benedick.

HERO
He is the only man of Italy,
Always excepted my dear Claudio.
URSULA
I pray you, be not angry with me, madam,
Speaking my fancy: Signor Benedick,
For shape, for bearing, argument, and valor,   96
Goes foremost in report through Italy.
HERO
Indeed, he hath an excellent good name.
URSULA
His excellence did earn it ere he had it.
When are you married, madam?
HERO
Why, every day, tomorrow. Come, go in.   101
I'll show thee some attires and have thy counsel
Which is the best to furnish me tomorrow.
                          [They walk away.]
URSULA [to Hero]
She's limed, I warrant you. We have caught her,
  madam.   104
HERO [to Ursula]
If it prove so, then loving goes by haps;   105
Some Cupid kills with arrows, some with traps.
                    [Exeunt Hero and Ursula.]
BEATRICE [coming forward]
What fire is in mine ears? Can this be true?   107
  Stand I condemned for pride and scorn so much?
Contempt, farewell, and maiden pride, adieu!
  No glory lives behind the back of such.   110
And Benedick, love on; I will requite thee,
  Taming my wild heart to thy loving hand.   112
If thou dost love, my kindness shall incite thee
  To bind our loves up in a holy band;   114
For others say thou dost deserve, and I
Believe it better than reportingly.   Exit. 116

                    ❧

3.2 *Enter Prince [Don Pedro], Claudio, Benedick, and
       Leonato.*

DON PEDRO I do but stay till your marriage be consum- 1
  mate, and then go I toward Aragon.   2
CLAUDIO I'll bring you thither, my lord, if you'll   3
  vouchsafe me.   4
DON PEDRO Nay, that would be as great a soil in the   5
  new gloss of your marriage as to show a child his new

54 **weak** unimportant 55 **project** conception, idea 56 **self-endearèd** full of self-love 60 **How** however. **rarely** excellently 61 **spell him backward** i.e., speak contrarily of him by characterizing his virtues as vices 63 **black** dark. **antic** buffoon, grotesque figure 65 **agate** i.e., diminutive person (alluding to the small figures cut in agate for rings) 70 **simpleness** integrity, plainness. **purchaseth** earn, deserve 72 **from** contrary to 76 **press me to death** (Pressing to death with weights was the usual punishment for those accused of crimes who refused to plead either guilty or not guilty.) 78 **Consume . . . sighs** (An allusion to the belief that each sigh cost the heart a drop of blood.) 84 **honest slanders** i.e., slanders that do not involve her virtue 90 **prized** esteemed

96 **argument** skill in discourse 101 **every day, tomorrow** tomorrow and every day thereafter 104 **limed** caught, like a bird in birdlime, a sticky substance spread on branches to trap the birds that perch on them 105 **by haps** by chance 107 **What . . . ears** (An allusion to the old saying that a person's ears burn when one is being discussed in one's absence.) 110 **No . . . such** nothing is gained by hiding behind such defenses 112 **Taming . . . hand** (A figure derived from the taming of the hawk by the hand of the falconer.) 114 **band** bond 116 **better than reportingly** on better evidence than mere report **3.2. Location: Leonato's house.**

1–2 **consummate** consummated 3 **bring** escort 4 **vouchsafe** allow 5 **soil** stain

coat and forbid him to wear it. I will only be bold with 7
Benedick for his company, for from the crown of his
head to the sole of his foot he is all mirth. He hath
twice or thrice cut Cupid's bowstring, and the little
hangman dare not shoot at him. He hath a heart as 11
sound as a bell, and his tongue is the clapper, for what
his heart thinks his tongue speaks.

BENEDICK   Gallants, I am not as I have been.

LEONATO   So say I. Methinks you are sadder. 15

CLAUDIO   I hope he be in love.

DON PEDRO   Hang him, truant! There's no true drop of 17
blood in him, to be truly touched with love. If he be
sad, he wants money. 19

BENEDICK   I have the toothache. 20

DON PEDRO   Draw it. 21

BENEDICK   Hang it! 22

CLAUDIO   You must hang it first and draw it afterwards.

DON PEDRO   What, sigh for the toothache?

LEONATO   Where is but a humor or a worm. 26

BENEDICK   Well, everyone can master a grief but he that 27
has it.

CLAUDIO   Yet say I, he is in love.

DON PEDRO   There is no appearance of fancy in him, 30
unless it be a fancy that he hath to strange disguises; 31
as, to be a Dutchman today, a Frenchman tomorrow,
or in the shape of two countries at once, as, a German
from the waist downward, all slops, and a Spaniard 34
from the hip upward, no doublet. Unless he have a 35
fancy to this foolery, as it appears he hath, he is no
fool for fancy, as you would have it appear he is. 37

CLAUDIO   If he be not in love with some woman, there
is no believing old signs. 'A brushes his hat o'
mornings. What should that bode?

DON PEDRO   Hath any man seen him at the barber's?

CLAUDIO   No, but the barber's man hath been seen
with him, and the old ornament of his cheek hath 43
already stuffed tennis balls. 44

LEONATO   Indeed he looks younger than he did by the
loss of a beard.

DON PEDRO   Nay, 'a rubs himself with civet. Can you 47
smell him out by that? 48

CLAUDIO   That's as much as to say the sweet youth's in
love.

DON PEDRO   The greatest note of it is his melancholy. 51

CLAUDIO   And when was he wont to wash his face? 52

DON PEDRO   Yea, or to paint himself? For the which I 53
hear what they say of him. 54

CLAUDIO   Nay, but his jesting spirit, which is now crept
into a lute string and now governed by stops. 56

DON PEDRO   Indeed, that tells a heavy tale for him.
Conclude, conclude he is in love.

CLAUDIO   Nay, but I know who loves him.

DON PEDRO   That would I know too. I warrant, one that
knows him not.

CLAUDIO   Yes, and his ill conditions; and, in despite of 62
all, dies for him.

DON PEDRO   She shall be buried with her face upwards. 64

BENEDICK   Yet is this no charm for the toothache. Old
signor, walk aside with me. I have studied eight or
nine wise words to speak to you, which these hobby- 67
horses must not hear.   [Exeunt Benedick and Leonato.] 68

DON PEDRO   For my life, to break with him about 69
Beatrice.

CLAUDIO   'Tis even so. Hero and Margaret have by this 71
played their parts with Beatrice, and then the two bears
will not bite one another when they meet.

Enter [Don] John the Bastard.

DON JOHN   My lord and brother, God save you!

DON PEDRO   Good e'en, brother. 75

DON JOHN   If your leisure served, I would speak with
you.

DON PEDRO   In private?

DON JOHN   If it please you. Yet Count Claudio may hear,
for what I would speak of concerns him.

DON PEDRO   What's the matter?

DON JOHN   [to Claudio]   Means your lordship to be
married tomorrow?

DON PEDRO   You know he does.

DON JOHN   I know not that, when he knows what I
know.

CLAUDIO   If there be any impediment, I pray you
discover it. 88

DON JOHN   You may think I love you not. Let that
appear hereafter, and aim better at me by that I now 90
will manifest. For my brother, I think he holds you 91
well and in dearness of heart hath help to effect your 92
ensuing marriage—surely suit ill spent and labor ill
bestowed.

DON PEDRO   Why, what's the matter?

DON JOHN   I came hither to tell you, and, circumstances 96

---

7 **be bold with** ask   11 **hangman** executioner; rogue. (Playfully applied to Cupid.)   15 **sadder** more serious   17 **truant** (i.e., from love)
19 **wants** lacks   20 **toothache** (Thought to be a common ailment of
lovers.)   21 **Draw** extract. (But Claudio jokes on the method of executing traitors, who were hanged first and then cut down alive and
drawn, i.e., disemboweled, and finally quartered.)   22 **Hang it** confound it   26 **Where** where there.   **humor or a worm** (A toothache
was ascribed to "humors," or unhealthy secretions, and to actual
worms in the teeth.)   27 **grief** pain.   **but** except   30–31 **fancy
. . . fancy** love . . . whim, liking   34 **slops** loose breeches   35 **no
doublet** i.e., with a hip-length cloak in place of, or covering, the
close-fitting doublet   37 **fool for fancy** i.e., lover   43–44 **the old
. . . tennis balls** i.e., Benedick's beard has gone to stuff tennis balls.
(He appears onstage beardless in this scene for the first time.)
47 **civet** perfume derived from the civet cat   48 **smell him out** (1) discern his secret (2) smell him coming   51 **note** mark

52 **wash** i.e., with cosmetics; similarly with *paint* in the next line
53–54 **For . . . him** that's what I hear people saying about him
56 **stops** (1) frets on the fingerboard (2) restraints   62 **ill conditions**
bad qualities   64 **buried . . . upwards** i.e., as the faithful, not as a
suicide, who were sometimes buried face downwards (?). (There is
also a sexual suggestion of her being smothered under Benedick, continuing the joke on *dies for him*, meaning to have an orgasm.)   67–
68 **hobbyhorses** i.e., buffoons. (Originally, figures in a morris dance
made to resemble a horse and rider.)   69 **For** upon.   **break** speak
71 **Margaret** (Ursula joined Hero in playing the trick on Beatrice, but
Margaret has been in on it.)   75 **e'en** evening, i.e., afternoon
88 **discover** reveal   90 **aim better at** judge better of.   **that** that which
91–92 **holds you well** thinks well of you   92 **holp** helped   96–
97 **circumstances shortened** without unnecessary details

shortened—for she has been too long a-talking of— 97
the lady is disloyal.   98

CLAUDIO   Who, Hero?

DON JOHN   Even she—Leonato's Hero, your Hero,
every man's Hero.

CLAUDIO   Disloyal?

DON JOHN   The word is too good to paint out her 103
wickedness. I could say she were worse; think you of
a worse title, and I will fit her to it. Wonder not till 105
further warrant. Go but with me tonight, you shall see 106
her chamber window entered, even the night before
her wedding day. If you love her then, tomorrow wed
her; but it would better fit your honor to change your
mind.

CLAUDIO   May this be so?

DON PEDRO   I will not think it.

DON JOHN   If you dare not trust that you see, confess not 113
that you know. If you will follow me, I will show you 114
enough; and when you have seen more and heard
more, proceed accordingly.

CLAUDIO   If I see anything tonight why I should not
marry her, tomorrow in the congregation, where I
should wed, there will I shame her.

DON PEDRO   And, as I wooed for thee to obtain her, I
will join with thee to disgrace her.

DON JOHN   I will disparage her no farther till you are
my witnesses. Bear it coldly but till midnight, and let 123
the issue show itself.

DON PEDRO   O day untowardly turned!   125

CLAUDIO   O mischief strangely thwarting!

DON JOHN   O plague right well prevented! So will you
say when you have seen the sequel.   [Exeunt.]

✤

3.3   *Enter Dogberry and his compartner [Verges] with
the Watch.*

DOGBERRY   Are you good men and true?

VERGES   Yea, or else it were pity but they should suffer
salvation, body and soul.   3

DOGBERRY   Nay, that were a punishment too good for
them, if they should have any allegiance in them, 5
being chosen for the Prince's watch.

VERGES   Well, give them their charge, neighbor Dog- 7
berry.

DOGBERRY   First, who think you the most desartless 9
man to be constable?

FIRST WATCH   Hugh Oatcake, sir, or George Seacoal,
for they can write and read.

DOGBERRY   Come hither, neighbor Seacoal. [*Seacoal, or
Second Watch, steps forward.*] God hath blessed you
with a good name. To be a well-favored man is the gift 15
of fortune, but to write and read comes by nature.

SEACOAL   Both which, Master Constable—

DOGBERRY   You have. I knew it would be your answer.
Well, for your favor, sir, why, give God thanks, and
make no boast of it; and for your writing and reading,
let that appear when there is no need of such vanity.
You are thought here to be the most senseless and fit 22
man for the constable of the watch; therefore bear you
the lantern. This is your charge: you shall comprehend 24
all vagrom men; you are to bid any man stand, in the 25
Prince's name.

SEACOAL   How if 'a will not stand?

DOGBERRY   Why, then, take no note of him, but let him
go, and presently call the rest of the watch together
and thank God you are rid of a knave.

VERGES   If he will not stand when he is bidden, he is
none of the Prince's subjects.

DOGBERRY   True, and they are to meddle with none but
the Prince's subjects. You shall also make no noise in
the streets; for, for the watch to babble and to talk is
most tolerable and not to be endured.   36

WATCH   We will rather sleep than talk. We know what 37
belongs to a watch.   38

DOGBERRY   Why, you speak like an ancient and most 39
quiet watchman, for I cannot see how sleeping should
offend. Only have a care that your bills be not stolen. 41
Well, you are to call at all the alehouses and bid those
that are drunk get them to bed.

WATCH   How if they will not?

DOGBERRY   Why, then, let them alone till they are
sober. If they make you not then the better answer,
you may say they are not the men you took them for.

WATCH   Well, sir.

DOGBERRY   If you meet a thief, you may suspect him,
by virtue of your office, to be no true man; and for 50
such kind of men, the less you meddle or make with 51
them, why, the more is for your honesty.   52

WATCH   If we know him to be a thief, shall we not lay
hands on him?

DOGBERRY   Truly, by your office you may, but I think
they that touch pitch will be defiled. The most 56
peaceable way for you, if you do take a thief, is to let
him show himself what he is and steal out of your
company.

VERGES   You have been always called a merciful man,
partner.

---

97 **a-talking of** under discussion (by us)   98 **disloyal** unfaithful
103 **paint out** portray in full   105–106 **till further warrant** till further
proof appears   113–114 **If . . . know** i.e., either trust your eyes or
admit that you're denying a certainty (or else shut up about it).   **that
. . . that** what . . . what   123 **coldly** calmly   125 **untowardly
turned** wretchedly altered
3.3. Location: A street.
3 **salvation** (A blunder for "damnation.")   5 **allegiance** (For "treachery.")   7 **charge** instructions   9 **desartless** (For "deserving.")

15 **a good name** (Sea coal was high-grade coal shipped from Newcas-
tle, not the charcoal usually sold by London colliers.)   **well-favored**
good-looking   22 **senseless** (For "sensible.")   24 **comprehend** (For
"apprehend.")   25 **vagrom** vagrant.   **stand** stand still, stop   36 **tolerable** (For "intolerable.")   37 **s.p. Watch** (Here and at lines 44, 48,
53, and 66 Shakespeare's text does not specify which watchman
speaks. These lines are sometimes assigned to the Second Watch,
Seacoal, but could be spoken by others of the watch.)   38 **belongs to**
are the duties of   39 **ancient** venerable, experienced   41 **bills** pikes,
with axes fixed to long poles   50 **true** honest   51 **meddle or make**
have to do   52 **is** it is   56 **they . . . defiled** (A commonplace, derived from Ecclesiasticus 13:1.)

DOGBERRY Truly, I would not hang a dog by my will, much more a man who hath any honesty in him.

VERGES If you hear a child cry in the night, you must call to the nurse and bid her still it.

WATCH How if the nurse be asleep and will not hear us?

DOGBERRY Why, then, depart in peace and let the child wake her with crying, for the ewe that will not hear her lamb when it baas will never answer a calf when he bleats.

VERGES 'Tis very true.

DOGBERRY This is the end of the charge: you, Constable, are to present the Prince's own person. If you 74 meet the Prince in the night, you may stay him.

VERGES Nay, by 'r Lady, that I think 'a cannot. 76

DOGBERRY Five shillings to one on 't, with any man that knows the statutes, he may stay him; marry, not without the Prince be willing, for indeed the watch ought to offend no man, and it is an offense to stay a man against his will.

VERGES By 'r Lady, I think it be so.

DOGBERRY Ha, ah ha! Well, masters, good night. An there be any matter of weight chances, call up me. Keep your fellows' counsels and your own, and good night. Come, neighbor. [He starts to leave with Verges.]

SEACOAL Well, masters, we hear our charge. Let us go sit here upon the church bench till two, and then all to bed.

DOGBERRY One word more, honest neighbors. I pray you, watch about Signor Leonato's door, for the wedding being there tomorrow, there is a great coil 92 tonight. Adieu. Be vigitant, I beseech you. 93

Exeunt [Dogberry and Verges].

Enter Borachio and Conrade.

BORACHIO What, Conrade!

SEACOAL [aside] Peace! Stir not.

BORACHIO Conrade, I say!

CONRADE Here, man. I am at thy elbow.

BORACHIO Mass, and my elbow itched; I thought there 98 would be a scab follow. 99

CONRADE I will owe thee an answer for that. And now, 100 forward with thy tale.

BORACHIO Stand thee close, then, under this pent- 102 house, for it drizzles rain, and I will, like a true 103 drunkard, utter all to thee. 104

SEACOAL [aside] Some treason, masters. Yet stand 105 close. 106

BORACHIO Therefore know I have earned of Don John a thousand ducats.

CONRADE Is it possible that any villainy should be so dear? 110

BORACHIO Thou shouldst rather ask if it were possible any villainy should be so rich; for when rich villains 112 have need of poor ones, poor ones may make what price they will.

CONRADE I wonder at it.

BORACHIO That shows thou art unconfirmed. Thou 116 knowest that the fashion of a doublet, or a hat, or a cloak, is nothing to a man. 118

CONRADE Yes, it is apparel.

BORACHIO I mean, the fashion. 120

CONRADE Yes, the fashion is the fashion.

BORACHIO Tush, I may as well say the fool's the fool. But seest thou not what a deformed thief this fashion 123 is?

SEACOAL [aside] I know that Deformed. 'A has been a vile thief this seven year; 'a goes up and down like a 126 gentleman. I remember his name.

BORACHIO Didst thou not hear somebody?

CONRADE No, 'twas the vane on the house.

BORACHIO Seest thou not, I say, what a deformed thief this fashion is, how giddily 'a turns about all the hot bloods between fourteen and five-and-thirty, sometimes fashioning them like Pharaoh's soldiers in the reechy painting, sometimes like god Bel's priests in 134 the old church-window, sometimes like the shaven 135 Hercules in the smirched worm-eaten tapestry, where 136 his codpiece seems as massy as his club? 137

CONRADE All this I see, and I see that the fashion wears 138 out more apparel than the man. But art not thou 139 thyself giddy with the fashion, too, that thou hast shifted out of thy tale into telling me of the fashion?

BORACHIO Not so, neither. But know that I have tonight wooed Margaret, the Lady Hero's gentlewoman, by the name of Hero. She leans me out at her mistress' 144 chamber window, bids me a thousand times good night—I tell this tale vilely; I should first tell thee how the Prince, Claudio, and my master, planted and placed and possessed by my master Don John, saw 148 afar off in the orchard this amiable encounter. 149

CONRADE And thought they Margaret was Hero?

BORACHIO Two of them did, the Prince and Claudio, but the devil my master knew she was Margaret; and

---

74 **present** represent 76 **by 'r Lady** i.e., by Our Lady. (A mild oath.) 92 **coil** to-do 93 **vigitant** (For "vigilant.") 98 **Mass** i.e., by the Mass. **my elbow itched** (Proverbially, a warning against questionable companions.) 99 **scab** i.e., scoundrel (with play on literal meaning) 100 **owe thee an answer** answer later 102–103 **penthouse** overhanging structure 103–104 **true drunkard** (Alludes to the commonplace that the drunkard tells all; Borachio's name in Spanish means "drunkard.") 105–106 **stand close** stay hidden 110 **dear** expensive

112 **villainy** i.e., instigator of villainy. **be so rich** pay so much 116 **unconfirmed** inexperienced 118 **is . . . man** does not make the man. (But Conrade plays on the phrase in the sense of "means nothing to a man.") 120 **I . . . fashion** i.e., my emphasis was on the mere fashion, not on the apparel itself. (But Conrade wittily refuses to allow the difference.) 123 **deformed thief** i.e., so called because fashion takes such varied and extreme shapes and because it impoverishes those who follow fashion 126 **up and down** about, here and there 134 **reechy** dirty, grimy. (Perhaps this painting is of the Israelites passing through the Red Sea.) **god Bel's priests** (Probably alludes to the story of Bel and the Dragon, from the apocryphal Book of Daniel, depicted in a stained-glass window.) 135–136 **shaven Hercules** (A reference either to young Hercules at the crossroads, choosing between virtue and vice, or in the service of Omphale—see 2.1.242, note—or, confusedly, to the story of Samson.) 137 **codpiece** decorative pouch at the front of a man's breeches (indelicately conspicuous in this tapestry) 138–139 **fashion . . . man** i.e., fashion prompts the discarding of clothes faster than honest use 144 **leans me** leans. (Me is an emphatic marker.) 148 **possessed** (misleadingly) informed; also, perhaps, possessed, as by the devil 149 **amiable** amorous

partly by his oaths, which first possessed them, partly
by the dark night, which did deceive them, but chiefly
by my villainy, which did confirm any slander that
Don John had made, away went Claudio enraged;
swore he would meet her, as he was appointed, next
morning at the temple, and there, before the whole
congregation, shame her with what he saw o'ernight
and send her home again without a husband.

SEACOAL   We charge you, in the Prince's name, stand!

FIRST WATCH   Call up the right Master Constable. We 162
have here recovered the most dangerous piece of 163
lechery that ever was known in the commonwealth. 164

SEACOAL   And one Deformed is one of them. I know
him; 'a wears a lock. 166

CONRADE   Masters, masters—

FIRST WATCH   You'll be made bring Deformed forth,
I warrant you.

CONRADE   Masters—

SEACOAL   Never speak, we charge you. Let us obey 171
you to go with us. 172

BORACHIO   We are like to prove a goodly commodity, 173
being taken up of these men's bills. 174

CONRADE   A commodity in question, I warrant you. 175
Come, we'll obey you.   *Exeunt.*

3.4   *Enter Hero, and Margaret and Ursula.*

HERO   Good Ursula, wake my cousin Beatrice, and
desire her to rise.

URSULA   I will, lady.

HERO   And bid her come hither.

URSULA   Well.   *[Exit.]* 5

MARGARET   Troth, I think your other rabato were better. 6

HERO   No, pray thee, good Meg, I'll wear this.

MARGARET   By my troth, 's not so good, and I warrant 8
your cousin will say so.

HERO   My cousin's a fool, and thou art another. I'll wear
none but this.

MARGARET   I like the new tire within excellently, if the 12
hair were a thought browner; and your gown's a most 13
rare fashion, i' faith. I saw the Duchess of Milan's
gown that they praise so.

HERO   O, that exceeds, they say. 16

MARGARET   By my troth, 's but a nightgown in respect 17
of yours: cloth o' gold, and cuts, and laced with silver, 18

set with pearls, down sleeves, side sleeves, and skirts, 19
round underborne with a bluish tinsel. But for a fine, 20
quaint, graceful, and excellent fashion, yours is worth 21
ten on 't. 22

HERO   God give me joy to wear it! For my heart is
exceeding heavy.

MARGARET   'Twill be heavier soon by the weight of
a man.

HERO   Fie upon thee! Art not ashamed?

MARGARET   Of what, lady? Of speaking honorably? Is
not marriage honorable in a beggar? Is not your lord 29
honorable without marriage? I think you would have
me say, "saving your reverence, a husband." An bad 31
thinking do not wrest true speaking, I'll offend 32
nobody. Is there any harm in "the heavier for a
husband"? None, I think, an it be the right husband
and the right wife; otherwise 'tis light, and not heavy. 35
Ask my Lady Beatrice else. Here she comes.

Enter Beatrice.

HERO   Good morrow, coz.

BEATRICE   Good morrow, sweet Hero.

HERO   Why, how now? Do you speak in the sick tune? 39

BEATRICE   I am out of all other tune, methinks.

MARGARET   Clap 's into "Light o' love." That goes 41
without a burden; do you sing it, and I'll dance it. 42

BEATRICE   Ye light o' love with your heels! Then, if your 43
husband have stables enough, you'll see he shall lack
no barns. 45

MARGARET   O illegitimate construction! I scorn that 46
with my heels. 47

BEATRICE   'Tis almost five o'clock, cousin; 'tis time you
were ready. By my troth, I am exceeding ill. Heigh-ho!

MARGARET   For a hawk, a horse, or a husband? 50

BEATRICE   For the letter that begins them all, H. 51

MARGARET   Well, an you be not turned Turk, there's no 52
more sailing by the star. 53

BEATRICE   What means the fool, trow? 54

MARGARET   Nothing I; but God send everyone their
heart's desire!

HERO   These gloves the Count sent me, they are an
excellent perfume. 58

162 right Master Constable (A comic title on the pattern of "Right
Worshipful," etc.)   **163 recovered** (For "discovered.")   **164 lechery**
(For "treachery.")   **166 lock** lock of hair hanging down on the left
shoulder; the lovelock   **171–172 Let . . . to** (A blunder for "obey
us and.")   **173 commodity** goods acquired   **174 taken up** (1) arrested (2) obtained on credit.   **bills** (1) pikes (2) bonds given as security   **175 in question** (1) subject to judicial examination (2) of doubtful value

3.4. Location: Leonato's house.

5 Well very well, as you wish   **6 rabato** tall collar supporting a ruff,
stiffened with wire or starch   **8 troth, 's** faith, it is   **12 tire within**
headdress in the inner room   **13 hair** hairpiece attached to the *tire*
(line 12)   **16 exceeds** i.e., exceeds comparison   **17 nightgown** dressing gown   **17–18 in respect of** compared to   **18 cuts** slashes in a
garment revealing the underlying fabric.   **laced** trimmed.   **silver** i.e.,
silver thread

19 down sleeves tight-fitting sleeves to the wrist.   **side sleeves** secondary ornamental sleeves hanging from the shoulder   **20 round underborne** with a lining around the edge of the skirt.   **tinsel** cloth,
usually silk, interwoven with threads of silver or gold   **21 quaint** elegant   **22 on 't** on it   **29 in** even in   **31 saving
. . . husband** (By this apologetic formula, Margaret suggests that Hero
is too prudish even to hear the word *husband* mentioned.)   **An bad** if
bawdy   **32 wrest** misinterpret   **35 light** (with a play on the meaning
"wanton")   **39 tune** i.e., mood   **41 Clap 's** let's shift.   **Light o' love**
(A popular song.)   **42 burden** bass accompaniment (with play on the
idea of "a weight of a man")   **43 Ye . . . heels** i.e., you're light-
heeled, wanton   **45 barns** (with pun on "bairns," children)   **46 illegitimate construction** false inference (but with a play on the idea of
bastard "bairns")   **47 with my heels** (A proverbial expression of
scorn.)   **50 For . . . husband** (*Heigh-ho* might be a cry of encouragement in the hunt or else "Heigh-ho for a husband!" as at
2.1.305.)   **51 H** (with a pun on "ache," pronounced "aitch." Beatrice complains of aching with a cold.)   **52 turned Turk** i.e., turned
apostate to the true faith (by violating your oath not to become a
lover)   **52–53 no . . . star** no more navigating by the North Star,
i.e., no certain truth in which to trust   **54 trow** I wonder   **58 perfume** (Gloves were often perfumed.)

BEATRICE   I am stuffed, cousin. I cannot smell.   59

MARGARET   A maid, and stuffed! There's goodly catching of cold.

BEATRICE   O, God help me, God help me! How long have you professed apprehension?   63

MARGARET   Ever since you left it. Doth not my wit   64 become me rarely?

BEATRICE   It is not seen enough; you should wear it in   66 your cap. By my troth, I am sick.   67

MARGARET   Get you some of this distilled *carduus bene-*   68 *dictus*, and lay it to your heart. It is the only thing for   69 a qualm.   70

HERO   There thou prick'st her with a thistle.

BEATRICE   *Benedictus!* Why *benedictus?* You have some moral in this *benedictus.*   73

MARGARET   Moral? No, by my troth, I have no moral meaning, I meant plain holy thistle. You may think   75 perchance that I think you are in love. Nay, by 'r Lady, I am not such a fool to think what I list, nor I list not to   77 think what I can, nor indeed I cannot think, if I would think my heart out of thinking, that you are in love or   79 that you will be in love or that you can be in love. Yet Benedick was such another, and now is he become a   81 man. He swore he would never marry, and yet now,   82 in despite of his heart, he eats his meat without grudg-   83 ing; and how you may be converted I know not, but   84 methinks you look with your eyes as other women do.

BEATRICE   What pace is this that thy tongue keeps?

MARGARET   Not a false gallop.   87

Enter Ursula.

URSULA   Madam, withdraw. The Prince, the Count, Signor Benedick, Don John, and all the gallants of the town are come to fetch you to church.

HERO   Help to dress me, good coz, good Meg, good Ursula.   [*Exeunt.*]

3.5   *Enter Leonato and the Constable [Dogberry] and the Headborough [Verges].*

LEONATO   What would you with me, honest neighbor?

DOGBERRY   Marry, sir, I would have some confidence   2 with you that decerns you nearly.   3

---

59 **stuffed** i.e., stuffed up with a cold. (But Margaret takes it in a bawdy sense.)   63 **professed apprehension** made claim to be witty   64 **left it** gave it up. (Margaret gibes at Beatrice's pretending not to know what the joking is all about.)   66–67 **wear . . . cap** i.e., wear it prominently visible, as a fool wears his coxcomb. (Beatrice jokes that Margaret's supposed wit is mere foolishness.)   68–69 **carduus benedictus** the blessed thistle, noted for medicinal properties (with a pun on "Benedick")   70 **a qualm** an attack of nausea (or misgiving)   73 **moral** hidden meaning   75 **holy thistle** the blessed thistle or *carduus benedictus* of 68–69   77 **list** please   79 **think . . . thinking** i.e., rack my brains   81 **such another** i.e., seemingly proof against love   81–82 **a man** i.e., like other men   83–84 **eats . . . grudging** i.e., is content to be like other men, to be in love   87 **Not . . . gallop** i.e., I'm not speaking at a false pace, at a canter; I speak the truth   **3.5. Location: Leonato's house.**   **s.d. Headborough** local constable   2 **confidence** (A blunder for "conference.")   3 **decerns** (For "concerns.")

LEONATO   Brief, I pray you, for you see it is a busy time with me.

DOGBERRY   Marry, this it is, sir.

VERGES   Yes, in truth it is, sir.

LEONATO   What is it, my good friends?

DOGBERRY   Goodman Verges, sir, speaks a little off the   9 matter—an old man, sir, and his wits are not so blunt   10 as, God help, I would desire they were, but, in faith, honest as the skin between his brows.   12

VERGES   Yes, I thank God I am as honest as any man living that is an old man and no honester than I.

DOGBERRY   Comparisons are odorous. *Palabras,* neigh-   15 bor Verges.

LEONATO   Neighbors, you are tedious.

DOGBERRY   It pleases your worship to say so, but we are the poor Duke's officers. But truly, for mine own   19 part, if I were as tedious as a king, I could find in my   20 heart to bestow it all of your worship.   21

LEONATO   All thy tediousness on me, ah?

DOGBERRY   Yea, an 'twere a thousand pound more than 'tis; for I hear as good exclamation on your   24 worship as of any man in the city, and though I be but a poor man, I am glad to hear it.

VERGES   And so am I.

LEONATO   I would fain know what you have to say.

VERGES   Marry, sir, our watch tonight, excepting your   29 worship's presence, ha' ta'en a couple of as arrant   30 knaves as any in Messina.

DOGBERRY   A good old man, sir; he will be talking. As they say, when the age is in, the wit is out. God help   33 us, it is a world to see! Well said, i' faith, neigh-   34 bor Verges. Well, God's a good man. An two men   35 ride of a horse, one must ride behind. An honest soul,   36 i' faith, sir, by my troth he is, as ever broke bread. But, God is to be worshiped, all men are not alike, alas, good neighbor!

LEONATO   Indeed, neighbor, he comes too short of you.

DOGBERRY   Gifts that God gives.

LEONATO   I must leave you.

DOGBERRY   One word, sir. Our watch, sir, have indeed comprehended two aspicious persons, and we would   44 have them this morning examined before your worship.

LEONATO   Take their examination yourself and bring it me. I am now in great haste, as it may appear unto you.

DOGBERRY   It shall be suffigance.   50

LEONATO   Drink some wine ere you go. Fare you well.

---

9 **Goodman** (Title of persons under the social rank of gentleman.)   10 **blunt** (He means "sharp.")   12 **honest . . . brows** (Proverbial expression of honesty.)   15 **odorous** (For "odious.")   **Palabras** (For *pocas palabras,* "few words" in Spanish.)   19 **poor Duke's officers** (For "Duke's poor officers.")   20 **tedious** (Dogberry evidently thinks *tedious* means "rich.")   21 **of** on   24 **exclamation** (Possibly for "acclamation.")   29 **tonight** last night.   **excepting** (For "respecting.")   30 **ha'** have   33 **when . . . out** (An adaptation of the proverb, "When ale is in, wit is out.")   34 **a world** i.e., wonderful. (Proverbial.)   35 **God's . . . man** i.e., God is good. (A proverbial saying.)   36 **of** on   44 **comprehended** (For "apprehended.")   **aspicious** (For "suspicious.")   50 **suffigance** (For "sufficient.")

[*Enter a Messenger.*]

MESSENGER My lord, they stay for you to give your
daughter to her husband.

LEONATO I'll wait upon them. I am ready.   54

[*Exeunt Leonato and Messenger.*]

DOGBERRY Go, good partner, go, get you to Francis Sea-   55
coal. Bid him bring his pen and inkhorn to the jail. We   56
are now to examination these men.   57

VERGES And we must do it wisely.

DOGBERRY We will spare for no wit, I warrant you.
Here's that shall drive some of them to a noncome.   60
Only get the learned writer to set down our excom-   61
munication, and meet me at the jail.   [*Exeunt.*]   62

❖

4.1 *Enter Prince [Don Pedro], [Don John the] Bastard,
Leonato, Friar [Francis], Claudio, Benedick, Hero,
and Beatrice [with attendants].*

LEONATO Come, Friar Francis, be brief—only to the
plain form of marriage, and you shall recount their
particular duties afterwards.

FRIAR You come hither, my lord, to marry this lady?

CLAUDIO No.

LEONATO To be married to her. Friar, you come to
marry her.

FRIAR Lady, you come hither to be married to this
Count?

HERO I do.

FRIAR If either of you know any inward impediment   11
why you should not be conjoined, I charge you on
your souls to utter it.

CLAUDIO Know you any, Hero?

HERO None, my lord.

FRIAR Know you any, Count?

LEONATO I dare make his answer: none.

CLAUDIO O, what men dare do! What men may do!
What men daily do, not knowing what they do!

BENEDICK How now? Interjections? Why, then, some   20
be of laughing, as, ah, ha, he!   21

CLAUDIO
Stand thee by, Friar. Father, by your leave,   22
Will you with free and unconstrainèd soul
Give me this maid, your daughter?

LEONATO
As freely, son, as God did give her me.

CLAUDIO
And what have I to give you back, whose worth
May counterpoise this rich and precious gift?   27

DON PEDRO
Nothing, unless you render her again.

CLAUDIO
Sweet Prince, you learn me noble thankfulness.   29

[*He hands Hero to Leonato.*]
There, Leonato, take her back again.
Give not this rotten orange to your friend;
She's but the sign and semblance of her honor.   32
Behold how like a maid she blushes here!
O, what authority and show of truth   34
Can cunning sin cover itself withal!
Comes not that blood as modest evidence   36
To witness simple virtue? Would you not swear,   37
All you that see her, that she were a maid,
By these exterior shows? But she is none:
She knows the heat of a luxurious bed.   40
Her blush is guiltiness, not modesty.

LEONATO
What do you mean, my lord?

CLAUDIO   Not to be married,   42
Not to knit my soul to an approvèd wanton.   43

LEONATO
Dear my lord, if you, in your own proof,   44
Have vanquished the resistance of her youth,
And made defeat of her virginity—

CLAUDIO
I know what you would say: if I have known her,   47
You will say she did embrace me as a husband,
And so extenuate the forehand sin.   49
No, Leonato,
I never tempted her with word too large,   51
But, as a brother to his sister, showed
Bashful sincerity and comely love.

HERO
And seemed I ever otherwise to you?

CLAUDIO
Out on thee, seeming! I will write against it.   55
You seem to me as Dian in her orb,   56
As chaste as is the bud ere it be blown;   57
But you are more intemperate in your blood
Than Venus, or those pampered animals
That rage in savage sensuality.

HERO
Is my lord well, that he doth speak so wide?   61

LEONATO
Sweet Prince, why speak not you?

DON PEDRO   What should I speak?
I stand dishonored, that have gone about   63
To link my dear friend to a common stale.   64

---

54 wait upon attend **55–56 Francis Seacoal** i.e., the Sexton of 4.2,
not George, the member of the watch in 3.3 **57 examination** (For
"examine.") **60 noncome** (Probably an unintended contraction for
non compos mentis, "not of sound mind," but Dogberry may have intended "nonplus.") **61–62 excommunication** (For "examination" or
"communication.")
4.1. Location: A church.
11 inward secret **20–21 some . . . he** (Benedick quotes from Lilly's
Latin grammar on the subject of interjections; according to Lilly, these
are to be classified as laughing interjections.) **22 Stand thee by** stand
aside **27 counterpoise** balance, be equivalent to

29 learn teach **32 sign and semblance** pretense and outward show
34 authority assurance **36 blood** i.e., blush. **modest evidence** evidence of modesty **37 witness** bear witness to **40 luxurious** lascivious, lustful **42 mean** imply, suggest. (But Claudio bitterly replies in
the sense of "intend.") **43 approvèd** proved **44 in . . . proof** in
making trial of her yourself **47 known her** i.e., known her sexually
49 extenuate excuse, lessen. **forehand sin** sin of anticipating (marriage) **51 large** broad, immodest **55 Out . . . seeming** i.e., shame
on you, a mere semblance of good **56 Dian . . . orb** i.e., Diana,
goddess of chastity, enthroned in the moon **57 be blown** open,
flower **61 wide** wide of the mark **63 gone about** undertaken
64 stale whore

LEONATO
  Are these things spoken, or do I but dream?
DON JOHN
  Sir, they are spoken, and these things are true.
BENEDICK   This looks not like a nuptial.
HERO   "True"! O God!   68
CLAUDIO   Leonato, stand I here?
  Is this the Prince? Is this the Prince's brother?
  Is this face Hero's? Are our eyes our own?
LEONATO
  All this is so. But what of this, my lord?
CLAUDIO
  Let me but move one question to your daughter,   73
  And by that fatherly and kindly power   74
  That you have in her, bid her answer truly.
LEONATO
  I charge thee do so, as thou art my child.
HERO
  O, God defend me, how am I beset!
  What kind of catechizing call you this?   78
CLAUDIO
  To make you answer truly to your name.
HERO
  Is it not Hero? Who can blot that name
  With any just reproach?
CLAUDIO   Marry, that can Hero!
  Hero itself can blot out Hero's virtue.   82
  What man was he talked with you yesternight
  Out at your window betwixt twelve and one?
  Now, if you are a maid, answer to this.
HERO
  I talked with no man at that hour, my lord.
DON PEDRO
  Why, then are you no maiden. Leonato,
  I am sorry you must hear. Upon mine honor,
  Myself, my brother, and this grievèd Count   89
  Did see her, hear her, at that hour last night
  Talk with a ruffian at her chamber window,
  Who hath indeed, most like a liberal villain,   92
  Confessed the vile encounters they have had
  A thousand times in secret.
DON JOHN
  Fie, fie, they are not to be named, my lord,
  Not to be spoke of!
  There is not chastity enough in language
  Without offense to utter them. Thus, pretty lady,
  I am sorry for thy much misgovernment.   99
CLAUDIO
  O Hero, what a Hero hadst thou been
  If half thy outward graces had been placed
  About thy thoughts and counsels of thy heart!
  But fare thee well, most foul, most fair! Farewell,

  Thou pure impiety and impious purity!
  For thee I'll lock up all the gates of love,   105
  And on my eyelids shall conjecture hang,   106
  To turn all beauty into thoughts of harm,
  And never shall it more be gracious.   108
LEONATO
  Hath no man's dagger here a point for me?
                                    [Hero swoons.]
BEATRICE
  Why, how now, cousin, wherefore sink you down?
DON JOHN
  Come, let us go. These things, come thus to light,
  Smother her spirits up.
            [Exeunt Don Pedro, Don John, and Claudio.]
BENEDICK
  How doth the lady?
BEATRICE   Dead, I think. Help, uncle!
  Hero, why, Hero! Uncle! Signor Benedick! Friar!
LEONATO
  O Fate, take not away thy heavy hand!
  Death is the fairest cover for her shame
  That may be wished for.
BEATRICE   How now, cousin Hero?
FRIAR   Have comfort, lady.
LEONATO
  Dost thou look up?
FRIAR   Yea, wherefore should she not? 119
LEONATO
  Wherefore? Why, doth not every earthly thing
  Cry shame upon her? Could she here deny
  The story that is printed in her blood?   122
  Do not live, Hero, do not ope thine eyes;
  For, did I think thou wouldst not quickly die,
  Thought I thy spirits were stronger than thy shames, 125
  Myself would, on the rearward of reproaches,   126
  Strike at thy life. Grieved I I had but one?
  Chid I for that at frugal nature's frame?   128
  O, one too much by thee! Why had I one?
  Why ever wast thou lovely in my eyes?
  Why had I not with charitable hand
  Took up a beggar's issue at my gates,   132
  Who, smirchèd thus and mired with infamy,
  I might have said, "No part of it is mine;
  This shame derives itself from unknown loins"?
  But mine, and mine I loved, and mine I praised,   136
  And mine that I was proud on, mine so much
  That I myself was to myself not mine,   138
  Valuing of her—why, she, O she, is fallen   139
  Into a pit of ink, that the wide sea   140
  Hath drops too few to wash her clean again
  And salt too little which may season give   142
  To her foul-tainted flesh!

68 **True** (A response to Don John's use of the term.)   **73 move** put
74 kindly natural   **78 catechizing** formal questioning used by the
Church to teach the principles of faith. The first question in the
Church of England's catechism is, "What is your name?"   **82 Hero it-**
self the name Hero (which in the story of Hero and Leander became a
name for a faithful lover)   **89 grievèd** (1) aggrieved, wronged (2)
struck with grief   **92 liberal** licentious   **99 much misgovernment**
great misconduct

105 **For thee** because of you   106 **conjecture** evil suspicion   108 **be**
gracious seem attractive, graceful   119 **wherefore** why   122 **blood**
i.e., blushes   125 **spirits** life-giving energies, vital powers   126 **on**
. . . reproaches following this public disgrace   128 **Chid** chided.
frame plan, order   132 **Took . . . issue** taken up a beggar's child
136 **mine** i.e., my own daughter   138–139 **That . . . her** i.e., that I
set no value on myself in caring so much for her   140 **that** such that
142 **season** preservative

BENEDICK   Sir, sir, be patient.
 For my part, I am so attired in wonder,
 I know not what to say.
BEATRICE
 O, on my soul, my cousin is belied!
BENEDICK
 Lady, were you her bedfellow last night?
BEATRICE
 No, truly, not; although, until last night,
 I have this twelvemonth been her bedfellow.
LEONATO
 Confirmed, confirmed! O, that is stronger made
 Which was before barred up with ribs of iron!   151
 Would the two princes lie and Claudio lie,
 Who loved her so that, speaking of her foulness,
 Washed it with tears? Hence from her! Let her die.
FRIAR Hear me a little;
 For I have only been silent so long
 And given way unto this course of fortune   157
 By noting of the lady. I have marked   158
 A thousand blushing apparitions
 To start into her face, a thousand innocent shames
 In angel whiteness beat away those blushes,
 And in her eye there hath appeared a fire
 To burn the errors that these princes hold   163
 Against her maiden truth. Call me a fool;
 Trust not my reading nor my observations,
 Which with experimental seal doth warrant 166
 The tenor of my book; trust not my age,   167
 My reverence, calling, nor divinity,
 If this sweet lady lie not guiltless here
 Under some biting error.
LEONATO   Friar, it cannot be.
 Thou seest that all the grace that she hath left
 Is that she will not add to her damnation
 A sin of perjury; she not denies it.
 Why seek'st thou then to cover with excuse
 That which appears in proper nakedness?   175
FRIAR
 Lady, what man is he you are accused of?
HERO
 They know that do accuse me; I know none.
 If I know more of any man alive
 Than that which maiden modesty doth warrant, 179
 Let all my sins lack mercy! O my father,
 Prove you that any man with me conversed   181
 At hours unmeet or that I yesternight   182
 Maintained the change of words with any creature, 183
 Refuse me, hate me, torture me to death!   184
FRIAR
 There is some strange misprision in the princes. 185

BENEDICK
 Two of them have the very bent of honor;   186
 And if their wisdoms be misled in this,
 The practice of it lives in John the Bastard, 188
 Whose spirits toil in frame of villainies.   189
LEONATO
 I know not. If they speak but truth of her,
 These hands shall tear her; if they wrong her honor,
 The proudest of them shall well hear of it.
 Time hath not yet so dried this blood of mine,
 Nor age so eat up my invention,   194
 Nor fortune made such havoc of my means,
 Nor my bad life reft me so much of friends, 196
 But they shall find, awaked in such a kind, 197
 Both strength of limb and policy of mind,   198
 Ability in means, and choice of friends,
 To quit me of them throughly.
FRIAR   Pause awhile, 200
 And let my counsel sway you in this case.
 Your daughter here the princes left for dead, 202
 Let her awhile be secretly kept in,   203
 And publish it that she is dead indeed.
 Maintain a mourning ostentation,   205
 And on your family's old monument   206
 Hang mournful epitaphs, and do all rites
 That appertain unto a burial.
LEONATO
 What shall become of this? What will this do? 209
FRIAR
 Marry, this, well carried, shall on her behalf 210
 Change slander to remorse. That is some good.
 But not for that dream I on this strange course, 212
 But on this travail look for greater birth. 213
 She—dying, as it must be so maintained,
 Upon the instant that she was accused—
 Shall be lamented, pitied, and excused
 Of every hearer; for it so falls out
 That what we have we prize not to the worth 218
 Whiles we enjoy it, but, being lacked and lost,
 Why then we rack the value, then we find 220
 The virtue that possession would not show us
 Whiles it was ours. So will it fare with Claudio.
 When he shall hear she died upon his words, 223
 Th' idea of her life shall sweetly creep
 Into his study of imagination,   225
 And every lovely organ of her life   226
 Shall come appareled in more precious habit, 227
 More moving-delicate, and full of life,

---

151 **before** already   157 **given . . . fortune** acceded to this turn of events   158 **By . . . lady** i.e., so that I might observe, or because I have been observing, Hero's reaction   163 **errors** (Personified as a heretic burned at the stake.)   166–167 **Which . . . book** i.e., by means of which observations and experience I have confirmed what I learned from books   175 **proper** true   179 **warrant** sanction, permit   181 **Prove you** if you prove   182 **unmeet** improper   183 **Maintained the change** held exchange   184 **Refuse** disown   185 **misprision** mistake, misunderstanding

186 **the very bent of** an absolute inclination of the mind toward   188 **practice** scheming   189 **frame** contriving   194 **eat** eaten. (Pronounced "et.")   **invention** power to plan (vengeance)   196 **reft** robbed   197 **kind** manner   198 **policy** shrewdness, contriving   200 **quit . . . throughly** settle accounts with them thoroughly   202 **the princes** whom the princes   203 **in** in hiding, at home   205 **Maintain . . . ostentation** perform all the outward signs of mourning   206 **monument** burial vault   209 **become of** result from   210 **carried** managed   212 **that** i.e., to "change slander to remorse"   213 **on this travail** (1) as a result of this effort (2) from this labor in childbirth   218 **to the worth** as fully as it deserves   220 **rack** stretch (as on a rack)   223 **upon** in consequence of   225 **study of imagination** musing, imaginative contemplation   226 **organ . . . life** aspect of her when she was alive   227 **habit** apparel

Into the eye and prospect of his soul, 229
Than when she lived indeed. Then shall he mourn,
If ever love had interest in his liver, 231
And wish he had not so accusèd her,
No, though he thought his accusation true.
Let this be so, and doubt not but success 234
Will fashion the event in better shape 235
Than I can lay it down in likelihood. 236
But if all aim but this be leveled false, 237
The supposition of the lady's death
Will quench the wonder of her infamy.
And if it sort not well, you may conceal her, 240
As best befits her wounded reputation,
In some reclusive and religious life, 242
Out of all eyes, tongues, minds, and injuries. 243

BENEDICK
Signor Leonato, let the Friar advise you.
And though you know my inwardness and love 245
Is very much unto the Prince and Claudio,
Yet, by mine honor, I will deal in this
As secretly and justly as your soul
Should with your body.

LEONATO   Being that I flow in grief, 249
The smallest twine may lead me.

FRIAR
'Tis well consented. Presently away; 251
For to strange sores strangely they strain the cure. 252
Come, lady, die to live. This wedding day
Perhaps is but prolonged. Have patience, and endure. 254
        Exit [with all but Benedick and Beatrice].

BENEDICK   Lady Beatrice, have you wept all this while?
BEATRICE   Yea, and I will weep a while longer.
BENEDICK   I will not desire that.
BEATRICE   You have no reason. I do it freely. 258
BENEDICK   Surely I do believe your fair cousin is wronged.
BEATRICE   Ah, how much might the man deserve of me that would right her!
BENEDICK   Is there any way to show such friendship?
BEATRICE   A very even way, but no such friend. 264
BENEDICK   May a man do it?
BEATRICE   It is a man's office, but not yours. 266
BENEDICK   I do love nothing in the world so well as you. Is not that strange?
BEATRICE   As strange as the thing I know not. It were as possible for me to say I loved nothing so well as you. But believe me not; and yet I lie not. I confess nothing,

nor I deny nothing. I am sorry for my cousin.
BENEDICK   By my sword, Beatrice, thou lovest me.
BEATRICE   Do not swear and eat it. 274
BENEDICK   I will swear by it that you love me, and I will make him eat it that says I love not you. 276
BEATRICE   Will you not eat your word?
BENEDICK   With no sauce that can be devised to it. I protest I love thee. 279
BEATRICE   Why, then, God forgive me!
BENEDICK   What offense, sweet Beatrice?
BEATRICE   You have stayed me in a happy hour. I was 282 about to protest I loved you.
BENEDICK   And do it with all thy heart.
BEATRICE   I love you with so much of my heart that none is left to protest. 286
BENEDICK   Come, bid me do anything for thee.
BEATRICE   Kill Claudio.
BENEDICK   Ha! Not for the wide world.
BEATRICE   You kill me to deny it. Farewell.   *[Going.]* 290
BENEDICK   Tarry, sweet Beatrice.
BEATRICE   I am gone, though I am here. There is no love 292 in you. Nay, I pray you, let me go.
BENEDICK   Beatrice—
BEATRICE   In faith, I will go.
BENEDICK   We'll be friends first.
BEATRICE   You dare easier be friends with me than fight with mine enemy.
BENEDICK   Is Claudio thine enemy?
BEATRICE   Is 'a not approved in the height a villain, that 300 hath slandered, scorned, dishonored my kinswoman? O, that I were a man! What, bear her in hand until 302 they come to take hands, and then, with public accusation, uncovered slander, unmitigated ran- 304 cor—O God, that I were a man! I would eat his heart in the marketplace.
BENEDICK   Hear me, Beatrice—
BEATRICE   Talk with a man out at a window! A proper 308 saying! 309
BENEDICK   Nay, but Beatrice—
BEATRICE   Sweet Hero! She is wronged, she is slandered, she is undone.
BENEDICK   Beat—
BEATRICE   Princes and counties! Surely, a princely testi- 314 mony, a goodly count, Count Comfect; a sweet gallant, 315 surely! O, that I were a man for his sake! Or that I had any friend would be a man for my sake! But manhood is melted into curtsies, valor into compliment, and men are only turned into tongue, and trim ones too. 319

---

229 prospect range of vision **231 interest in** claim upon. **liver** (The supposed seat of the passion of love.) **234 success** i.e., what succeeds or happens in time as my plan unfolds **235 event** outcome **236 lay . . . likelihood** anticipate its probable course **237 if . . . false** i.e., if every other aim miscarry **240 sort** turn out **242 reclusive** cloistered **243 injuries** insults **245 inwardness and love** close friendship **249 Being that** seeing that, since. **flow in** overflow with, or am afloat in **251 Presently** immediately **252 For . . . cure** strange diseases require strange and desperate cures **254 prolonged** deferred, put off **258 You . . . reason** (Beatrice twists Benedick's "I wish you weren't so unhappy," line 257, into "There's no need for you to bid me stop weeping.") **264 even** direct, straightforward **266 office** duty

274 eat it i.e., eat your words **276 eat it** i.e., eat my sword, be stabbed by it **279 protest** affirm. (Also in line 283.) **282 stayed** stopped. **in . . . hour** at an appropriate moment **286 protest** object (with a play on the sense of "affirm" in 279 and 283) **290 it** i.e., my request **292 gone** i.e., in spirit **300 approved in the height** proved in the highest degree **302 bear her in hand** delude her with false hopes **304 uncovered** open, unconcealed **308–309 proper saying** likely story **314 counties** counts **315 count** (1) the title (2) declaration of complaint in an indictment. **Comfect** candy or sweetmeat **319 are . . . tongue** have become mere (flattering) voices. **trim** nice, elegant, fine. (Used ironically.)

He is now as valiant as Hercules that only tells a lie 320
and swears it. I cannot be a man with wishing, there- 321
fore I will die a woman with grieving.

BENEDICK   Tarry, good Beatrice. By this hand, I love
thee.

BEATRICE   Use it for my love some other way than
swearing by it.

BENEDICK   Think you in your soul the Count Claudio
hath wronged Hero?

BEATRICE   Yea, as sure as I have a thought or a soul.

BENEDICK   Enough, I am engaged. I will challenge him. 330
I will kiss your hand, and so I leave you. By this hand,
Claudio shall render me a dear account. As you hear 332
of me, so think of me. Go comfort your cousin. I must
say she is dead. And so, farewell. [*Exeunt separately.*]

4.2   *Enter the Constables [Dogberry and Verges] and
the Town Clerk [Sexton] in gowns, Borachio,
[Conrade, and Watch].*

DOGBERRY   Is our whole dissembly appeared?   1

VERGES   O, a stool and a cushion for the sexton.
         [*Stool and cushion are brought. The Sexton sits.*]

SEXTON   Which be the malefactors?

DOGBERRY   Marry, that am I and my partner.   4

VERGES   Nay, that's certain; we have the exhibition to 5
examine.

SEXTON   But which are the offenders that are to be
examined? Let them come before Master Constable.

DOGBERRY   Yea, marry, let them come before me. [*The
prisoners are brought forward.*] What is your name,
friend?

BORACHIO   Borachio.

DOGBERRY   Pray, write down Borachio. Yours, sirrah? 13

CONRADE   I am a gentleman, sir, and my name is
Conrade.

DOGBERRY   Write down Master Gentleman Conrade.
Masters, do you serve God?

CONRADE, BORACHIO   Yea, sir, we hope.

DOGBERRY   Write down that they hope they serve God;
and write God first, for God defend but God should 20
go before such villains! Masters, it is proved already
that you are little better than false knaves, and it will
go near to be thought so shortly. How answer you for
yourselves?

CONRADE   Marry, sir, we say we are none.

DOGBERRY   A marvelous witty fellow, I assure you, but 26
I will go about with him. [*To Borachio.*] Come you 27

hither, sirrah. A word in your ear. Sir, I say to you, it
is thought you are false knaves.

BORACHIO   Sir, I say to you we are none.

DOGBERRY   Well, stand aside. 'Fore God, they are both
in a tale. Have you writ down that they are none?   32

SEXTON   Master Constable, you go not the way to
examine. You must call forth the watch that are their
accusers.

DOGBERRY   Yea, marry, that's the eftest way. Let the 36
watch come forth. Masters, I charge you in the
Prince's name accuse these men.

SEACOAL   This man said, sir, that Don John, the
Prince's brother, was a villain.

DOGBERRY   Write down Prince John a villain. Why, this
is flat perjury, to call a prince's brother villain.

BORACHIO   Master Constable—

DOGBERRY   Pray thee, fellow, peace. I do not like thy
look, I promise thee.

SEXTON   What heard you him say else?

FIRST WATCH   Marry, that he had received a thousand
ducats of Don John for accusing the Lady Hero
wrongfully.

DOGBERRY   Flat burglary as ever was committed.

VERGES   Yea, by mass, that it is.   51

SEXTON   What else, fellow?

SEACOAL   And that Count Claudio did mean, upon his
words, to disgrace Hero before the whole assembly,
and not marry her.

DOGBERRY   O villain! Thou wilt be condemned into
everlasting redemption for this.   57

SEXTON   What else?

WATCH   This is all.   59

SEXTON   And this is more, masters, than you can deny.
Prince John is this morning secretly stolen away. Hero
was in this manner accused, in this very manner
refused, and upon the grief of this suddenly died. Master Constable, let these men be bound and brought to
Leonato's. I will go before and show him their
examination.   [*Exit.*]

DOGBERRY   Come, let them be opinioned.   67

VERGES   Let them be in the hands—

CONRADE   Off, coxcomb!

DOGBERRY   God's my life, where's the sexton? Let him 70
write down the Prince's officer coxcomb. Come, bind
them. Thou naughty varlet!   72

CONRADE   Away! You are an ass, you are an ass.

DOGBERRY   Dost thou not suspect my place? Dost thou 74
not suspect my years? O, that he were here to write 75
me down an ass! But masters, remember that I am an
ass; though it be not written down, yet forget not that
I am an ass. No, thou villain, thou art full of piety, as 78
shall be proved upon thee by good witness. I am a wise

320–321 He . . . swears it a man need only tell lies and swear they
are true to gain a reputation for bravery nowadays   **330 I am engaged**
I pledge myself   **332 dear** costly
4.2. Location: The jail.
1 dissembly (A blunder for "assembly.")   **4 that am I** (Dogberry evidently understands *malefactors* to mean "factors," agents.)   **5 exhibition** (Possibly for "commission.")   **13 sirrah** (Used to address inferiors; Conrade objects.)   **20 defend** forbid   **26 witty** clever, cunning
27 go about with get the better of

32 in a tale in agreement   **36 eftest** (Some sort of invention for "easiest" or "deftest.")   **51 by mass** by the Mass   **57 redemption** (Dogberry means "damnation.")   **59 s.p. Watch** (Perhaps both Seacoal
and his partner speak.)   **67 opinioned** (For "pinioned.")   **70 God's**
may God save   **72 naughty** wicked   **74 suspect** (For "respect.")
75 my years (with an unconscious suggestion of "my ears," i.e., ass's
ears)   **78 piety** (For "impiety.")

fellow, and, which is more, an officer, and, which is
more, a householder, and, which is more, as pretty a
piece of flesh as any is in Messina, and one that knows
the law, go to, and a rich fellow enough, go to, and a
fellow that hath had losses, and one that hath two
gowns and everything handsome about him. Bring
him away. O, that I had been writ down an ass!

Exeunt.

❖

5.1   *Enter Leonato and his brother [Antonio].*

ANTONIO
  If you go on thus, you will kill yourself;
  And 'tis not wisdom thus to second grief   2
  Against yourself.
LEONATO   I pray thee, cease thy counsel,
  Which falls into mine ears as profitless
  As water in a sieve. Give not me counsel,
  Nor let no comforter delight mine ear
  But such a one whose wrongs do suit with mine.   7
  Bring me a father that so loved his child,
  Whose joy of her is overwhelmed like mine,
  And bid him speak of patience;
  Measure his woe the length and breadth of mine,   11
  And let it answer every strain for strain,   12
  As thus for thus, and such a grief for such,
  In every lineament, branch, shape, and form;
  If such a one will smile and stroke his beard,
  Bid sorrow wag, cry "hem!" when he should groan, 16
  Patch grief with proverbs, make misfortune drunk 17
  With candle wasters, bring him yet to me   18
  And I of him will gather patience.
  But there is no such man. For, brother, men
  Can counsel and speak comfort to that grief
  Which they themselves not feel; but tasting it,
  Their counsel turns to passion, which before
  Would give preceptial medicine to rage,   24
  Fetter strong madness in a silken thread,
  Charm ache with air and agony with words.   26
  No, no, 'tis all men's office to speak patience   27
  To those that wring under the load of sorrow,   28
  But no man's virtue nor sufficiency   29
  To be so moral when he shall endure   30
  The like himself. Therefore give me no counsel.
  My griefs cry louder than advertisement.   32
ANTONIO
  Therein do men from children nothing differ.

LEONATO
  I pray thee, peace. I will be flesh and blood;
  For there was never yet philosopher
  That could endure the toothache patiently,
  However they have writ the style of gods   37
  And made a push at chance and sufferance.   38
ANTONIO
  Yet bend not all the harm upon yourself.
  Make those that do offend you suffer, too.
LEONATO
  There thou speak'st reason. Nay, I will do so.
  My soul doth tell me Hero is belied,
  And that shall Claudio know; so shall the Prince
  And all of them that thus dishonor her.

Enter Prince [Don Pedro] and Claudio.

ANTONIO
  Here comes the Prince and Claudio hastily.
DON PEDRO
  Good e'en, good e'en.
CLAUDIO   Good day to both of you.
LEONATO
  Hear you, my lords—
DON PEDRO   We have some haste, Leonato.
LEONATO
  Some haste, my lord! Well, fare you well, my lord.
  Are you so hasty now? Well, all is one.   49
DON PEDRO
  Nay, do not quarrel with us, good old man.
ANTONIO
  If he could right himself with quarreling,
  Some of us would lie low.
CLAUDIO   Who wrongs him?   52
LEONATO
  Marry, thou dost wrong me, thou dissembler, thou! 53
  Nay, never lay thy hand upon thy sword;
  I fear thee not.
CLAUDIO   Marry, beshrew my hand   55
  If it should give your age such cause of fear.
  In faith, my hand meant nothing to my sword.   57
LEONATO
  Tush, tush, man, never fleer and jest at me.   58
  I speak not like a dotard nor a fool,
  As under privilege of age to brag
  What I have done being young or what would do
  Were I not old. Know, Claudio, to thy head,   62
  Thou hast so wronged mine innocent child and me
  That I am forced to lay my reverence by,   64
  And with gray hairs and bruise of many days
  Do challenge thee to trial of a man.   66
  I say thou hast belied mine innocent child.

5.1. Location: Near Leonato's house.
2 second assist, encourage   **7 suit with** match   **11 Measure his woe**
let his woe equal in scope   **12 answer . . . for strain** correspond,
pang for pang (with a musical sense also of echoing a refrain)
16 wag be off.   **cry "hem"** i.e., clear the throat as before some
wordy speech   **17 drunk** i.e., insensible to pain   **18 candle wasters**
those who waste candles by late study, bookworms, moral philosophers   **24 preceptial** consisting of precepts   **26 air** mere breath,
words   **27 office** duty   **28 wring** writhe   **29 sufficiency** ability,
power   **30 moral** prone to moralizing   **32 advertisement** advice,
counsel

37 writ the style of written in language worthy of   **38 made . . .
sufferance** scoffed at bad luck and suffering. (*Push* means "pish" or
else a defiant thrust.)   **sufferance** suffering   **49 all is one** it makes
no difference   **52 Some of us** i.e., Don Pedro and Claudio   **53 thou**
(Used contemptuously instead of the more polite *you*.)   **55 beshrew**
curse   **57 my . . . sword** I had no intention of using my sword
58 fleer sneer, jeer   **62 head** i.e., face   **64 my reverence** i.e., the
reverence due old age   **66 trial of a man** manly contest, i.e.,
duel

Thy slander hath gone through and through her
  heart,
And she lies buried with her ancestors—
O, in a tomb where never scandal slept,
Save this of hers, framed by thy villainy!   71

CLAUDIO
My villainy?

LEONATO   Thine, Claudio, thine, I say.

DON PEDRO
You say not right, old man.

LEONATO   My lord, my lord,
I'll prove it on his body if he dare,
Despite his nice fence and his active practice,   75
His May of youth and bloom of lustihood.   76

CLAUDIO
Away! I will not have to do with you.

LEONATO
Canst thou so daff me? Thou hast killed my child.   78
If thou kill'st me, boy, thou shalt kill a man.

ANTONIO
He shall kill two of us, and men indeed.
But that's no matter; let him kill one first.
Win me and wear me! Let him answer me.   82
Come follow me, boy. Come, sir boy, come
  follow me,
Sir boy, I'll whip you from your foining fence!   84
Nay, as I am a gentleman, I will.

LEONATO   Brother—

ANTONIO
Content yourself. God knows I loved my niece,   87
And she is dead, slandered to death by villains
That dare as well answer a man indeed
As I dare take a serpent by the tongue.
Boys, apes, braggarts, Jacks, milksops!

LEONATO   Brother Antony—

ANTONIO
Hold you content. What, man! I know them, yea,
And what they weigh, even to the utmost scruple—   94
Scambling, outfacing, fashionmonging boys,   95
That lie and cog and flout, deprave and slander,   96
Go anticly, show outward hideousness,   97
And speak off half a dozen dangerous words   98
How they might hurt their enemies, if they durst,
And this is all.

LEONATO
But brother Antony—

ANTONIO   Come, 'tis no matter.
Do not you meddle; let me deal in this.

DON PEDRO
Gentlemen both, we will not wake your patience.   103

My heart is sorry for your daughter's death;
But, on my honor, she was charged with nothing
But what was true and very full of proof.

LEONATO   My lord, my lord—

DON PEDRO   I will not hear you.

LEONATO
No? Come, brother, away! I will be heard.

ANTONIO
And shall, or some of us will smart for it.   110

         Exeunt ambo [*Leonato and Antonio*].

    Enter Benedick.

DON PEDRO
See, see, here comes the man we went to seek.

CLAUDIO   Now, signor, what news?

BENEDICK   Good day, my lord.

DON PEDRO   Welcome, signor. You are almost come to
part almost a fray.

CLAUDIO   We had like to have had our two noses 116
snapped off with two old men without teeth. 117

DON PEDRO   Leonato and his brother. What think'st
thou? Had we fought, I doubt we should have been 119
too young for them.

BENEDICK   In a false quarrel there is no true valor. I came
to seek you both.

CLAUDIO   We have been up and down to seek thee, for
we are high-proof melancholy and would fain have it 124
beaten away. Wilt thou use thy wit?

BENEDICK   It is in my scabbard. Shall I draw it?

DON PEDRO   Dost thou wear thy wit by thy side?

CLAUDIO   Never any did so, though very many have
been beside their wit. I will bid thee draw as we do the 129
minstrels, draw to pleasure us. 130

DON PEDRO   As I am an honest man, he looks pale. Art
thou sick, or angry?

CLAUDIO   What, courage, man! What though care killed
a cat, thou hast mettle enough in thee to kill care.

BENEDICK   Sir, I shall meet your wit in the career, an you 135
charge it against me. I pray you, choose another sub- 136
ject.

CLAUDIO   Nay, then, give him another staff. This last 138
was broke cross. 139

DON PEDRO   By this light, he changes more and more. I
think he be angry indeed.

CLAUDIO   If he be, he knows how to turn his girdle. 142

BENEDICK   Shall I speak a word in your ear?

CLAUDIO   God bless me from a challenge!

BENEDICK [*aside to Claudio*]   You are a villain. I jest not. I
will make it good how you dare, with what you dare,

---

71 framed devised **75 nice fence** dexterous swordsmanship. (Said contemptuously.) **76 lustihood** bodily vigor **78 daff** doff, brush aside **82 Win . . . me** (A proverbial expression, used as a challenge, meaning he'll have to overcome me before he can claim me as a prize.) **answer me** i.e., in a duel **84 foining** thrusting **87 Content yourself** i.e., don't try to stop me **94 scruple** small measure of weight **95 Scambling . . . boys** contentious, swaggering, dandified boys **96 cog** cheat. **deprave** defame, traduce **97 anticly** fantastically dressed. **hideousness** frightening appearance **98 dangerous** threatening, haughty **103 wake your patience** put your patience to any further test

110 s.d. ambo both **116 We had. . . had** we almost had **117 with** by **119 doubt** fear, suspect. (Said ironically.) **124 high-proof** to the highest degree. **fain** gladly **129 beside their wit** out of their wits (playing on *by thy side* in line 127) **130 draw** (1) draw your weapon (2) draw a bow across a musical instrument **135 career** short gallop at full speed (as in a tourney). **an if** **136 charge** level (as a weapon) **138 staff** spear shaft **139 broke cross** i.e., broken by clumsily allowing the spear to break crosswise against his opponent's shield. (In other words, Claudio accuses Benedick of having failed in his sally of wit.) **142 turn his girdle** i.e., turn his sword belt around so that he's ready to fight, or else weasle out of it. (A proverbial expression of uncertain meaning.)

and when you dare. Do me right, or I will protest 147
your cowardice. You have killed a sweet lady, and her
death shall fall heavy on you. Let me hear from you.

CLAUDIO   Well, I will meet you, so I may have good
cheer.   151

DON PEDRO   What, a feast, a feast?

CLAUDIO   I' faith, I thank him, he hath bid me to a calf's 153
head and a capon, the which if I do not carve most 154
curiously, say my knife's naught. Shall I not find a 155
woodcock too?   156

BENEDICK   Sir, your wit ambles well; it goes easily.   157

DON PEDRO   I'll tell thee how Beatrice praised thy wit
the other day. I said thou hadst a fine wit. "True," said
she, "a fine little one." "No," said I, "a great wit."
"Right," says she, "a great gross one." "Nay," said I,
"a good wit." "Just," said she, "it hurts nobody." 162
"Nay," said I, "the gentleman is wise." "Certain,"
said she, "a wise gentleman." "Nay," said I, "he hath 164
the tongues." "That I believe," said she, "for he swore 165
a thing to me on Monday night, which he forswore on
Tuesday morning. There's a double tongue; there's
two tongues." Thus did she, an hour together, trans- 168
shape thy particular virtues. Yet at last she concluded 169
with a sigh, thou wast the proper'st man in Italy. 170

CLAUDIO   For the which she wept heartily and said she
cared not.

DON PEDRO   Yea, that she did. But yet for all that, an if
she did not hate him deadly, she would love him
dearly. The old man's daughter told us all.   175

CLAUDIO   All, all. And, moreover, God saw him when 176
he was hid in the garden.   177

DON PEDRO   But when shall we set the savage bull's
horns on the sensible Benedick's head?

CLAUDIO   Yea, and text underneath, "Here dwells 180
Benedick, the married man"?

BENEDICK   Fare you well, boy. You know my mind. I
will leave you now to your gossiplike humor. You
break jests as braggarts do their blades, which, God 184
be thanked, hurt not.—My lord, for your many courtesies I thank you. I must discontinue your company.
Your brother the bastard is fled from Messina. You
have among you killed a sweet and innocent lady. For
my Lord Lackbeard there, he and I shall meet, and till
then peace be with him.   [Exit.]

DON PEDRO   He is in earnest.

CLAUDIO   In most profound earnest, and, I'll warrant
you, for the love of Beatrice.

DON PEDRO   And hath challenged thee?

CLAUDIO   Most sincerely.

DON PEDRO   What a pretty thing man is when he goes 196
in his doublet and hose and leaves off his wit!   197

CLAUDIO   He is then a giant to an ape; but then is an 198
ape a doctor to such a man.   199

DON PEDRO   But, soft you, let me be. Pluck up, my heart, 200
and be sad. Did he not say my brother was fled?   201

Enter Constables, [Dogberry and Verges, and the
Watch, with] Conrade and Borachio.

DOGBERRY   Come you, sir. If Justice cannot tame you,
she shall ne'er weigh more reasons in her balance. 203
Nay, an you be a cursing hypocrite once, you must be 204
looked to.

DON PEDRO   How now, two of my brother's men
bound? Borachio one!

CLAUDIO   Hearken after their offense, my lord.   208

DON PEDRO   Officers, what offense have these men
done?

DOGBERRY   Marry, sir, they have committed false report;
moreover, they have spoken untruths; secondarily,
they are slanders; sixth and lastly, they have belied a 213
lady; thirdly, they have verified unjust things; and to
conclude, they are lying knaves.

DON PEDRO   First, I ask thee what they have done;
thirdly, I ask thee what's their offense; sixth and lastly,
why they are committed; and to conclude, what you
lay to their charge.

CLAUDIO   Rightly reasoned, and in his own division; 220
and, by my troth, there's one meaning well suited.   221

DON PEDRO   Who have you offended, masters, that
you are thus bound to your answer? This learned con- 223
stable is too cunning to be understood. What's your
offense?

BORACHIO   Sweet Prince, let me go no farther to mine
answer. Do you hear me, and let this count kill me. I
have deceived even your very eyes. What your
wisdoms could not discover, these shallow fools have
brought to light, who in the night overheard me
confessing to this man how Don John your brother
incensed me to slander the Lady Hero, how you were 231
brought into the orchard and saw me court Margaret
in Hero's garments, how you disgraced her when you

---

147 Do me right give me satisfaction.   **protest** proclaim before
witnesses   **151 cheer** entertainment. (Claudio is ready to fight, he
says, for the pleasant diversion it should offer.)   **153–156 calf's
head, capon, woodcock** (In this feast of dueling, Claudio plans to
carve various dishes connoting foolishness, effeminate cowardice, and
stupidity.)   **155 curiously** daintily.   **naught** good for nothing
157 ambles i.e., minces along   **162 good** (1) keen (2) harmless.   **Just**
exactly   **164 a wise gentleman** i.e., an old fool   **164–165 hath the
tongues** masters several languages   **168–169 trans-shape** distort,
turn the wrong side out   **170 proper'st** handsomest   **175 old man's
daughter** i.e., Hero   **176–177 God . . . garden** (Alluding to the
trick played on Benedick to love Beatrice, and also to Genesis 3:8.)
180 text (In 1.1.251–256, Benedick vowed that, if he were ever to
fall in love, his friends might set a bull's horns on his head and label
him "Benedick the married man.")   **184 as . . . blades** i.e., as braggarts furtively damage their blades to make it appear they have been
fighting fiercely

196–197 goes . . . wit goes about fully dressed like a rational creature but forgets to equip himself with good sense   **198–199 He
. . . man** i.e., such a man looks like a hero in a fool's eyes, but
actually the fool is a wise man compared to him   **200–201 soft
. . . be sad** wait a minute, not so fast; let me think. Rouse yourself,
my heart, and be serious.   **201 s.d.** (The Quarto placement of this
stage direction after line 197 suggests that Dogberry is visible, strutting
and fussing with his prisoners, before he speaks.)   **203 ne'er
. . . balance** never again weigh arguments of reason in her scales.
(But the pronunciation of *reason* as "raisin" invokes the comic image
of a shopkeeper weighing produce.)   **204 an** if.   **cursing** accursed.
once in a word   **208 Hearken after** inquire into   **213 slanders** (For
"slanderers.")   **220 his** its.   **division** partition in a logical arrangement. (Said ironically.)   **221 well suited** nicely dressed up in the trappings of language   **223 bound** (playing on the meanings "pinioned"
and "headed for a destination").   **answer** trial, account   **231 incensed** incited

should marry her. My villainy they have upon record,
which I had rather seal with my death than repeat over
to my shame. The lady is dead upon mine and my 236
master's false accusation; and, briefly, I desire nothing
but the reward of a villain.

DON PEDRO [to Claudio]
Runs not this speech like iron through your blood?

CLAUDIO
I have drunk poison whiles he uttered it.

DON PEDRO [to Borachio]
But did my brother set thee on to this?

BORACHIO   Yea, and paid me richly for the practice of it. 242

DON PEDRO
He is composed and framed of treachery,
And fled he is upon this villainy.   244

CLAUDIO
Sweet Hero! Now thy image doth appear
In the rare semblance that I loved it first.   246

DOGBERRY   Come, bring away the plaintiffs. By this 247
time our sexton hath reformed Signor Leonato of the 248
matter. And masters, do not forget to specify, when 249
time and place shall serve, that I am an ass.

VERGES   Here, here comes Master Signor Leonato, and
the sexton, too.

*Enter Leonato, his brother [Antonio], and the
Sexton.*

LEONATO
Which is the villain? Let me see his eyes,
That when I note another man like him,
I may avoid him. Which of these is he?

BORACHIO
If you would know your wronger, look on me.

LEONATO
Art thou the slave that with thy breath hast killed
Mine innocent child?

BORACHIO   Yea, even I alone.

LEONATO
No, not so, villain, thou beliest thyself.
Here stand a pair of honorable men—   260
A third is fled—that had a hand in it.
I thank you, princes, for my daughter's death.
Record it with your high and worthy deeds.
'Twas bravely done, if you bethink you of it.

CLAUDIO
I know not how to pray your patience,
Yet I must speak. Choose your revenge yourself;
Impose me to what penance your invention   267
Can lay upon my sin. Yet sinned I not
But in mistaking.

DON PEDRO   By my soul, nor I.
And yet, to satisfy this good old man,
I would bend under any heavy weight
That he'll enjoin me to.

LEONATO
I cannot bid you bid my daughter live—
That were impossible—but, I pray you both,
Possess the people in Messina here   275
How innocent she died; and if your love
Can labor aught in sad invention,   277
Hang her an epitaph upon her tomb,
And sing it to her bones—sing it tonight.
Tomorrow morning come you to my house,
And since you could not be my son-in-law,
Be yet my nephew. My brother hath a daughter,
Almost the copy of my child that's dead,
And she alone is heir to both of us.   284
Give her the right you should have given her
   cousin,   285
And so dies my revenge.

CLAUDIO   O noble sir,
Your overkindness doth wring tears from me!
I do embrace your offer; and dispose   288
For henceforth of poor Claudio.   289

LEONATO
Tomorrow then I will expect your coming;
Tonight I take my leave. This naughty man   291
Shall face to face be brought to Margaret,
Who I believe was packed in all this wrong,   293
Hired to it by your brother.

BORACHIO   No, by my soul, she was not,
Nor knew not what she did when she spoke to me,
But always hath been just and virtuous
In anything that I do know by her.   298

DOGBERRY   Moreover, sir, which indeed is not under 299
white and black, this plaintiff here, the offender, did 300
call me ass. I beseech you, let it be remembered in his
punishment. And also the watch heard them talk of
one Deformed. They say he wears a key in his ear and 303
a lock hanging by it and borrows money in God's 304
name, the which he hath used so long and never paid 305
that now men grow hardhearted and will lend nothing for God's sake. Pray you, examine him upon that
point.

LEONATO   I thank thee for thy care and honest pains.

DOGBERRY   Your worship speaks like a most thankful
and reverend youth, and I praise God for you.

LEONATO   There's for thy pains.   [*He gives money.*]

DOGBERRY   God save the foundation!   313

LEONATO   Go, I discharge thee of thy prisoner, and I
thank thee.

DOGBERRY   I leave an arrant knave with your worship,
which I beseech your worship to correct yourself, for
the example of others. God keep your worship! I wish

---

236 upon in consequence of   **242 practice** cunning execution
244 upon i.e., having committed   **246 rare semblance** splendid likeness   **247 plaintiffs** (For "defendants.")   **248 reformed** (For "informed.")   **249 specify** (For "testify"?)   **260 honorable men** i.e.,
Don Pedro and Claudio, men of rank   **267 Impose me to** impose on
me

275 Possess inform   **277 aught** to any extent   **284 heir to both** (He
overlooks Antonio's son mentioned in 1.2.2.)   **285 right** equitable
treatment (quibbling on "rite," "ceremony")   **288 dispose** you may
dispose   **289 For henceforth** for the future   **291 naughty** wicked
293 packed involved as an accomplice   **298 by** concerning   **299–
300 under . . . black** written down in black and white   **303–
304 key . . . by it** (This is what Dogberry has made out of the lovelock mentioned in 3.3.166.)   **304–305 in God's name** (A phrase of
the professional beggar.)   **313 God . . . foundation** (A formula of
those who received alms at religious houses or charitable foundations.)

your worship well. God restore you to health! I humbly give you leave to depart; and if a merry meeting 320
may be wished, God prohibit it! Come, neighbor. 321
[Exeunt Dogberry and Verges.]

LEONATO
Until tomorrow morning, lords, farewell.

ANTONIO
Farewell, my lords. We look for you tomorrow.

DON PEDRO
We will not fail.

CLAUDIO   Tonight I'll mourn with Hero.

LEONATO *[to the Watch]*
Bring you these fellows on.— We'll talk with Margaret,
How her acquaintance grew with this lewd fellow. 326
Exeunt [separately].

❖

5.2 *Enter Benedick and Margaret, [meeting].*

BENEDICK   Pray thee, sweet Mistress Margaret, deserve well at my hands by helping me to the speech of 2
Beatrice.

MARGARET   Will you then write me a sonnet in praise of
my beauty?

BENEDICK   In so high a style, Margaret, that no man 6
living shall come over it, for in most comely truth thou 7
deservest it.

MARGARET   To have no man come over me! Why, shall
I always keep below stairs? 10

BENEDICK   Thy wit is as quick as the greyhound's
mouth; it catches.

MARGARET   And yours as blunt as the fencer's foils,
which hit but hurt not.

BENEDICK   A most manly wit, Margaret; it will not hurt
a woman. And so, I pray thee, call Beatrice. I give thee 16
the bucklers. 17

MARGARET   Give us the swords. We have bucklers of
our own.

BENEDICK   If you use them, Margaret, you must put in
the pikes with a vice, and they are dangerous weap- 21
ons for maids.

MARGARET   Well, I will call Beatrice to you, who I think
hath legs.   *Exit Margaret.*

BENEDICK   And therefore will come.

[He sings.] "The god of love,   26
        That sits above,
        And knows me, and knows me,
        How pitiful I deserve—" 29
I mean in singing; but in loving, Leander the good 30
swimmer, Troilus the first employer of panders, and a 31
whole bookful of these quondam carpetmongers, 32
whose names yet run smoothly in the even road of a
blank verse, why, they were never so truly turned
over and over as my poor self in love. Marry, I cannot 35
show it in rhyme. I have tried. I can find out no rhyme
to "lady" but "baby," an innocent rhyme; for "scorn," 37
"horn," a hard rhyme; for "school," "fool," a babbling 38
rhyme; very ominous endings. No, I was not born
under a rhyming planet, nor I cannot woo in festival 40
terms. 41

Enter Beatrice.

Sweet Beatrice, wouldst thou come when I called thee?

BEATRICE   Yea, signor, and depart when you bid me.

BENEDICK   O, stay but till then!

BEATRICE   "Then" is spoken; fare you well now. And
yet, ere I go, let me go with that I came, which is, with 46
knowing what hath passed between you and Claudio.

BENEDICK   Only foul words; and thereupon I will kiss
thee.

BEATRICE   Foul words is but foul wind, and foul wind is
but foul breath, and foul breath is noisome; therefore 51
I will depart unkissed.

BENEDICK   Thou hast frighted the word out of his right 53
sense, so forcible is thy wit. But I must tell thee
plainly, Claudio undergoes my challenge; and either I 55
must shortly hear from him, or I will subscribe him a 56
coward. And I pray thee now tell me, for which of my
bad parts didst thou first fall in love with me?

BEATRICE   For them all together, which maintained so
politic a state of evil that they will not admit any good 60
part to intermingle with them. But for which of my
good parts did you first suffer love for me? 62

BENEDICK   Suffer love! A good epithet. I do suffer love 63
indeed, for I love thee against my will.

BEATRICE   In spite of your heart, I think. Alas, poor
heart, if you spite it for my sake, I will spite it for
yours, for I will never love that which my friend hates.

BENEDICK   Thou and I are too wise to woo peaceably.

320 give you leave (For "ask your leave.")   **321 prohibit** (For "permit.")   **326 lewd** wicked, worthless
**5.2. Location: Leonato's garden (? At the scene's end, Leonato's
house is some distance away.)**
2 to the speech of i.e., to speak with   **6 style** (1) poetic style (2) stile,
stairs over a fence   **7 come over** (1) excel beyond (2) traverse, as one
would cross a stile (3) in Margaret's next speech, the phrase is taken
to mean "mount sexually."   **comely** good (with an allusion to Margaret's beauty)   **10 keep below stairs** dwell in the servants' quarters
16–17 I . . . bucklers i.e., I acknowledge myself beaten (in repartee). (Bucklers are shields with spikes [pikes] in their centers. Margaret
uses the word in a bawdy sense in her reply.)   **21 pikes** spikes in the
center of a shield.   **vice** screw. (Benedick's bawdy sense continues
Margaret's jest.)

26–29 The god . . . deserve (The beginning of an old song by
William Elderton.)   **29 How . . . deserve** how I deserve pity. (But
Benedick uses the phrase to mean "how little I deserve.")   **30 Leander** lover of Hero of Sestos; he swam the Hellespont nightly to see her
until he drowned   **31 Troilus** lover of Cressida, whose affair was assisted by her uncle Pandarus   **32 quondam** former, old-time.   **carpetmongers** (A scornful term for "ladies' men," derived from their
presence in the carpeted boudoirs of their lovers.)   **35 over and over**
i.e., head over heels   **37 innocent** childish   **38 hard** (1) exact (2) unpleasant, because of the association with cuckold's horns   **40–
41 festival terms** elevated language   **46 that I came** what I came for
51 noisome noxious   **53 his** its   **55 undergoes** bears   **56 subscribe**
formally proclaim in writing   **60 politic** prudently governed   **62 suffer** (1) experience (2) feel the pain of   **63 epithet** expression

BEATRICE   It appears not in this confession. There's not 69
one wise man among twenty that will praise himself.

BENEDICK   An old, an old instance, Beatrice, that lived 71
in the time of good neighbors. If a man do not erect in 72
this age his own tomb ere he dies, he shall live no 73
longer in monument than the bell rings and the 74
widow weeps.   75

BEATRICE   And how long is that, think you?

BENEDICK   Question: why, an hour in clamor and a 77
quarter in rheum. Therefore is it most expedient for 78
the wise, if Don Worm, his conscience, find no im- 79
pediment to the contrary, to be the trumpet of his own
virtues, as I am to myself. So much for praising myself,
who, I myself will bear witness, is praiseworthy. And
now tell me, how doth your cousin?

BEATRICE   Very ill.

BENEDICK   And how do you?

BEATRICE   Very ill too.

BENEDICK   Serve God, love me, and mend. There will I
leave you too, for here comes one in haste.

Enter Ursula.

URSULA   Madam, you must come to your uncle. Yonder's old coil at home. It is proved my lady Hero hath 90
been falsely accused, the Prince and Claudio mightily
abused, and Don John is the author of all, who is fled 92
and gone. Will you come presently?   93

BEATRICE   Will you go hear this news, signor?

BENEDICK   I will live in thy heart, die in thy lap, and be 95
buried in thy eyes; and moreover I will go with thee
to thy uncle's.   *Exeunt.*

❧

5.3   *Enter Claudio, Prince [Don Pedro, Balthasar], and
three or four with tapers.*

CLAUDIO   Is this the monument of Leonato?

A LORD   It is, my lord.

CLAUDIO   [*reading from a scroll*]

Epitaph.

"Done to death by slanderous tongues
    Was the Hero that here lies.
Death, in guerdon of her wrongs,   5
    Gives her fame which never dies.

So the life that died with shame
Lives in death with glorious fame."

Hang thou there upon the tomb,
Praising her when I am dumb.

                    [*He hangs up the scroll.*]

Now, music, sound, and sing your solemn hymn.

Song.

BALTHASAR

Pardon, goddess of the night,   12
Those that slew thy virgin knight;   13
For the which, with songs of woe,
Round about her tomb they go.
    Midnight, assist our moan;
    Help us to sigh and groan,
        Heavily, heavily.
    Graves, yawn and yield your dead,
    Till death be utterèd,   20
        Heavily, heavily.

CLAUDIO

Now, unto thy bones good night!
Yearly will I do this rite.

DON PEDRO

Good morrow, masters. Put your torches out.
    The wolves have preyed; and look, the gentle
        day,   25
Before the wheels of Phoebus, round about   26
    Dapples the drowsy east with spots of gray.
Thanks to you all, and leave us. Fare you well.

CLAUDIO

Good morrow, masters. Each his several way.   29

DON PEDRO

Come, let us hence, and put on other weeds,   30
    And then to Leonato's we will go.

CLAUDIO

And Hymen now with luckier issue speed 's   32
    Than this for whom we rendered up this woe.
                                          Exeunt.

❧

5.4   *Enter Leonato, Benedick, [Beatrice], Margaret,
Ursula, old man [Antonio], Friar [Francis], Hero.*

FRIAR

Did I not tell you she was innocent?

LEONATO

So are the Prince and Claudio, who accused her
Upon the error that you heard debated.
But Margaret was in some fault for this,   3
Although against her will, as it appears   5
In the true course of all the question.   6

69 It. . . confession i.e., you don't show your wisdom in praising
yourself for being wise   **71 instance** proverb (i.e., "He has ill neighbors that is fain to praise himself")   **72 time . . . neighbors** good
old times (when one's neighbors spoke well of one)   **73–75 he shall
. . . weeps** i.e., he will be memorialized only during the (brief) time
of the funeral service and the official mourning   **77 Question** i.e., an
easy question, which I will answer as follows.   **clamor** noise (of the
bell)   **78 rheum** tears (of the widow)   **79 Don . . . conscience** (The
action of the conscience was traditionally described as the gnawing of
a worm; compare with Mark 9:44–48.)   **90 old coil** great confusion
92 abused deceived   **93 presently** immediately   **95 die** (with the
common connotation of "experience sexual climax")
5.3. Location: A churchyard.
5 guerdon recompense

12 goddess of the night i.e., Diana, moon goddess, patroness of chastity   **13 knight** i.e., follower   **20 utterèd** fully expressed   **25 have
preyed** i.e., have ceased preying   **26 wheels of Phoebus** i.e., chariot
of the sun god   **29 several** separate   **30 weeds** garments   **32 Hymen**
god of marriage.   **speed 's** favor or speed us
5.4. Location: Leonato's house.
3 Upon because of   **5 against her will** unintentionally   **6 question**
investigation

ANTONIO

Well, I am glad that all things sorts so well.   7

BENEDICK

And so am I, being else by faith enforced   8
To call young Claudio to a reckoning for it.

LEONATO

Well, daughter, and you gentlewomen all,
Withdraw into a chamber by yourselves,
And when I send for you, come hither masked.
The Prince and Claudio promised by this hour
To visit me. You know your office, brother: 14
You must be father to your brother's daughter,
And give her to young Claudio.   *Exeunt ladies.*

ANTONIO

Which I will do with confirmed countenance.   17

BENEDICK

Friar, I must entreat your pains, I think.   18

FRIAR   To do what, signor?

BENEDICK

To bind me or undo me—one of them.   20
Signor Leonato, truth it is, good signor,
Your niece regards me with an eye of favor.

LEONATO

That eye my daughter lent her. 'Tis most true.   23

BENEDICK

And I do with an eye of love requite her.

LEONATO

The sight whereof I think you had from me,   25
From Claudio, and the Prince. But what's your will?   26

BENEDICK

Your answer, sir, is enigmatical.
But, for my will, my will is your good will   28
May stand with ours, this day to be conjoined
In the state of honorable marriage,
In which, good Friar, I shall desire your help.

LEONATO

My heart is with your liking.

FRIAR   And my help.
Here comes the Prince and Claudio.

*Enter Prince [Don Pedro] and Claudio, and two or
three other.*

DON PEDRO

Good morrow to this fair assembly.

LEONATO

Good morrow, Prince. Good morrow, Claudio.
We here attend you. Are you yet determined   35
Today to marry with my brother's daughter?

CLAUDIO

I'll hold my mind, were she an Ethiope.

LEONATO

Call her forth, brother. Here's the Friar ready.
                                        [*Exit Antonio.*]

DON PEDRO

Good morrow, Benedick. Why, what's the matter,
That you have such a February face,
So full of frost, of storm, and cloudiness?

CLAUDIO

I think he thinks upon the savage bull.   42
Tush, fear not, man! We'll tip thy horns with gold,
And all Europa shall rejoice at thee,   44
As once Europa did at lusty Jove   45
When he would play the noble beast in love.

BENEDICK

Bull Jove, sir, had an amiable low,
And some such strange bull leapt your father's cow
And got a calf in that same noble feat
Much like to you, for you have just his bleat.

*Enter [Leonato's] brother [Antonio], Hero,
Beatrice, Margaret, Ursula, [the ladies masked].*

CLAUDIO

For this I owe you. Here comes other reckonings.   51
Which is the lady I must seize upon?

ANTONIO

This same is she, and I do give you her.

CLAUDIO

Why then, she's mine. Sweet, let me see your face.

LEONATO

No, that you shall not, till you take her hand
Before this friar and swear to marry her.

CLAUDIO

Give me your hand before this holy friar.
I am your husband, if you like of me.   58

HERO [*unmasking*]

And when I lived, I was your other wife;
And when you loved, you were my other husband.

CLAUDIO

Another Hero!

HERO   Nothing certainer.
One Hero died defiled, but I do live,
And surely as I live, I am a maid.

DON PEDRO

The former Hero! Hero that is dead!

LEONATO

She died, my lord, but whiles her slander lived.   65

FRIAR

All this amazement can I qualify,   66
When, after that the holy rites are ended,
I'll tell you largely of fair Hero's death.   68
Meantime let wonder seem familiar,   69
And to the chapel let us presently.   70

BENEDICK

Soft and fair, Friar. Which is Beatrice?   71

---

7 sorts turn out   **8 being else** since otherwise I would be.   **by faith** i.e., by my promise to Beatrice   **14 office** duty   **17 confirmed countenance** straight face   **18 entreat your pains** i.e., impose on you   **20 undo** (1) ruin (2) untie, unbind   **23 That . . . her** (Alludes to Hero's role in tricking Beatrice into confessing her love for Benedick.)   **25–26 The sight . . . Prince** (Alludes to their role in tricking Benedick into confessing his love for Beatrice.)   **28 for** as for.   **is** is that   **35 yet** still

42 I . . . bull (A jocular reminiscence of the conversation in 1.1.250 ff.)   **44 Europa** Europe   **45 Europa** a princess whom Jove approached in the form of a white bull and bore on his back through the sea to Crete   **51 I owe you** i.e., I'll pay you back later (for calling me a calf and a bastard).   **other reckonings** i.e., other matters to be settled first   **58 like of** care for   **65 but whiles** only while   **66 qualify** moderate   **68 largely** at large, in full   **69 let . . . familiar** treat these marvels as ordinary matters   **70 let us presently** let us go at once   **71 Soft and fair** i.e., wait a minute

BEATRICE [*unmasking*]
I answer to that name. What is your will?
BENEDICK
Do not you love me?
BEATRICE   Why, no, no more than reason.
BENEDICK
Why, then your uncle and the Prince and Claudio
Have been deceived. They swore you did.
BEATRICE
Do not you love me?
BENEDICK   Troth, no, no more than reason.
BEATRICE
Why, then my cousin, Margaret, and Ursula   77
Are much deceived, for they did swear you did.
BENEDICK
They swore that you were almost sick for me.
BEATRICE
They swore that you were well-nigh dead for me.
BENEDICK
'Tis no such matter. Then you do not love me?
BEATRICE
No, truly, but in friendly recompense.
LEONATO
Come, cousin, I am sure you love the gentleman.   83
CLAUDIO
And I'll be sworn upon 't that he loves her;
For here's a paper written in his hand,
A halting sonnet of his own pure brain,   86
Fashioned to Beatrice.   [*He shows a paper.*]
HERO   And here's another
Writ in my cousin's hand, stol'n from her pocket,
Containing her affection unto Benedick.
                         [*She shows another paper.*]
BENEDICK   A miracle! Here's our own hands against 90
our hearts. Come, I will have thee, but by this light I 91
take thee for pity.
BEATRICE   I would not deny you, but by this good day,
I yield upon great persuasion, and partly to save your
life, for I was told you were in a consumption.   95
BENEDICK   Peace! I will stop your mouth. [*Kissing her.*]
DON PEDRO   How dost thou, Benedick, the married
man?
BENEDICK   I'll tell thee what, Prince: a college of wit- 99
crackers cannot flout me out of my humor. Dost thou
think I care for a satire or an epigram? No. If a man will 101
be beaten with brains, 'a shall wear nothing hand- 102
some about him. In brief, since I do purpose to marry, 103
I will think nothing to any purpose that the world can
say against it; and therefore never flout at me for what 105
I have said against it; for man is a giddy thing, and
this is my conclusion. For thy part, Claudio, I did
think to have beaten thee, but in that thou art like to 108
be my kinsman, live unbruised, and love my cousin.

---

77 my cousin i.e., Hero   **83 cousin** i.e., niece   **86 halting** limping.
his own pure purely his own   **90–91 against our hearts** i.e., to
prove our hearts guilty as charged   **95 in a consumption** i.e., wasting
away in sighs   **99 college** assembly   **101–103 If . . . him** i.e., if a
man allows himself to be cowed by ridicule, he'll never dare dress
handsomely or do anything conspicuous that will draw attention
105 flout mock   **108 in that** in view of the fact that.   **like** likely

---

CLAUDIO   I had well hoped thou wouldst have denied
Beatrice, that I might have cudgeled thee out of thy
single life, to make thee a double-dealer, which out of 112
question thou wilt be, if my cousin do not look 113
exceeding narrowly to thee.   114
BENEDICK   Come, come, we are friends. Let's have a
dance ere we are married, that we may lighten our
own hearts and our wives' heels.
LEONATO   We'll have dancing afterward.
BENEDICK   First, of my word! Therefore play, music. 119
Prince, thou art sad. Get thee a wife, get thee a wife.
There is no staff more reverend than one tipped with 121
horn.   122

          Enter Messenger.

MESSENGER
My lord, your brother John is ta'en in flight
And brought with armèd men back to Messina.
BENEDICK   Think not on him till tomorrow. I'll devise
thee brave punishments for him. Strike up, pipers. 126
                              Dance. [Exeunt.]

---

112 a double-dealer (1) a married man (2) a deceiver, adulterer
113–114 look . . . narrowly pay close attention   **119 of** on   **121–
122 tipped with horn** (Alludes to the usual joke about cuckolds, as at
line 43.)   **126 brave** fine

The Merry
Wives
of
Windsor

According to an early eighteenth-century tradition, Shakespeare composed *The Merry Wives of Windsor* at the behest of Queen Elizabeth. John Dennis, a critic and dramatist, asserted in 1702 that the Queen "was so eager to see it acted, that she commanded it to be finished in fourteen days." The editor Nicholas Rowe added in 1709 that the Queen, having been so pleased with Falstaff in the *Henry IV* plays, wished to see him in love. Such legends, emerging more than a century after the event, must be regarded with caution. Whether true or not, however, they do point to a passage of courtly flattery in the play that strongly suggests the presence of the court at some performance. The fairy blessing bestowed on Windsor Castle in Act 5 is unquestionably intended to celebrate the famous Order of the Garter. Mistress Quickly, disguised as leader of the fairies, orders her charges to sing nightly "Like to the Garter's compass, in a ring," to write *"Honi soit qui mal y pense,"* the motto of the Garter, and to tend carefully the "several chairs of order"—those decorated stalls in the Chapel of St. George belonging to the illustrious lords who made up the Order of the Garter. Every such "installment" receives her blessing, along with each knight's "coat," "crest," and "blazon" (5.5.36–75). The topical nature of this passage is stressed by its apparent lack of relevance to the plot.

Other extraneous bits of action may allude to courtly matters or to Windsor gossip. The business about the three German horse thieves and their Duke (4.3, 5), which makes little sense in the play as it stands, can perhaps be explained as an in-group joke on Frederick of Würtemburg, Count Mompelgard, a German nobleman obsessively intent on joining the Garter. He was the object of much anti-German scorn. His name, Mompelgard, is possibly scrambled into "garmombles" in the corrupt 1602 Quarto text, where the Folio text reads "cozen-germans" (4.5.74). Also, the geography of Windsor is rendered with loving and accurate attention to detail, as though for an audience familiar with its environs.

Such topical flourishes do not rob the drama of its general appeal; it has had great success, both as a stage play and in Verdi's and Nicolai's operatic versions, and was presumably popular with Shakespeare's London audience. Shakespeare never composed exclusively for special audiences, so far as we know, and indeed the blessing of Windsor Castle could have been added to a commercial play in order to render it particularly suitable for royal performance. The allusion to "the fat woman of Brentford," a notorious tavern keeper of Brentford (halfway between London and Windsor), would have been as meaningful to Shakespeare's London audience as to the court. The same may be true of the "luces" in the coat of arms of Justice Shallow (1.1.14), sometimes thought to ridicule Shakespeare's Stratford neighbor Sir Thomas Lucy, but believed by scholar critic Leslie Hotson to be a dig at William Gardiner, a Justice of the Peace in Surrey near London. The dig at the Brooke family, the lords of Cobham, in the disguise name (Brook) of the jealous Ford (as recorded in the bad quarto of 1602), must have amused knowledgeable Londoners; indeed, the satirical hit was evidently so offensive that the name had to be changed to "Broome" (as in the Folio text). Nevertheless, *The Merry Wives* could have been originally planned as entertainment to please Queen Elizabeth. A Feast of St. George in honor of the Garter was held at Westminster on April 23, 1597, in the Queen's presence. Among those elected to the Order was George Carey, Lord Hunsdon, the patron of Shakespeare's company and the new Lord Chamberlain. He was actually installed in the Order at Windsor in May. This date is early for a play that appears to borrow several comic figures from the *Henry IV* plays and perhaps from *Henry V* (usually dated 1599) as well. Recently, however, it has been argued persuasively that *The Merry Wives* may have been written while *2 Henry IV* was in the process of composition, making use of its comic types, but before they had actually appeared on the London stage. According to this theory, Nym was created first for *The Merry Wives* and was then reintroduced into *Henry V*. The dating and order of composition of these plays are still controversial, so that the dating of *The Merry Wives* must remain uncertain from 1597 to 1601.

Despite this uncertainty, Shakespeare's comic strategy in *The Merry Wives* seems reasonably clear: to translate highly popular comic figures, such as Falstaff, Bardolph, Pistol, and Slender, from the history plays into a ludicrously different kind of situation. Falstaff, the once resourceful and self-aware companion of Prince Hal, becomes the buffoonish wooer of two virtuously married women who thoroughly best him and subject him to a series of amusingly humiliating punishments. Prince Hal, too, of course, treats Falstaff as a scapegoat in the *Henry IV* plays and ultimately rejects him, but the farcical nature of the action in *The Merry Wives* exposes Falstaff to more openly satirical laughter and discomfiture than in the history plays. Some admirers of Falstaff have been dismayed by the falling off and dismiss the play as an insult to his greatness, but surely to view the play thus is to create false expectations and thereby miss the point of Shakespeare's comic intent. Falstaff and his companions should not be judged against their counterparts in the history plays, even though an awareness of their existence in that different context is an essential part of the jest. To see Falstaff in love—this tour de force required that Shakespeare devise a multiple plot as unlike that of the history plays as possible, in order to stress the comic discrepancy.

The result is a structurally complex comic plot that appropriately bears more resemblance to Shakespeare's other comedies than to the history plays. At the center of *The Merry Wives* is a familiar plot of romantic intrigue, featuring a young heroine (Anne Page) whose parents object to her attachment to young Fenton. They pester her with unwelcome rival wooers (Slender and Dr. Caius), obliging her finally to dupe her parents by a cleverly engineered elopement. This plot to outwit parents and rivals in the name of young love has an ancestry in the classical comedy of Plautus and in neoclassical comedy, though Shakespeare uses no particular recognizable source. To this plot he adds a second and parallel story of a lover (Falstaff) caught in the act of wooing two women. Italian *novelle* provide many situations of this sort, including that in which the husband is deceived by concealment of the lover in a clothes basket; see especially "Of Two Brethren and Their Wives" from *Riche His Farewell to Military Profession*, 1581, "Two Lovers of Pisa" from *Tarlton's News Out of Purgatory*, 1590, and the second story of the first day from Ser Giovanni Fiorentino's *Il Pecorone*, 1558. The effect of the combined plots is often farcelike, especially in the emphasis on swift, hilarious action and comic physical abuse at the expense of consistency in character. For example, we must accept as a given the preference of wise Master Page for Slender as his son-in-law and the inexplicable preference of Mistress Page for the suit of Dr. Caius. Reasons are stated, but symmetry of the design is paramount.

In addition, Shakespeare enriches these two plot situations with minor characters, such as the rival wooers, go-betweens, and informers, who inevitably come in conflict with one another and thereby reveal their "humors" or idiosyncrasies. Only tangentially connected with the plot, these characters are prized for their eccentricity. The Welsh Parson Evans and the French Dr. Caius nearly come to blows over Caius' courtship of Anne Page. They are safely kept apart by the genial Host of the Garter Inn and are reconciled to the extent of plotting against the Host for having deceived them both. (Perhaps they carry out their threat in the guise of the mysterious Germans who steal the Host's horses, though the text is murky on this point.) Justice Shallow, a humorous character in *2 Henry IV*, is given nominal justification in this play as cousin of Anne's second unwanted suitor, Slender, but Shallow's essential function is to quarrel with Falstaff about the latter's poaching and riotous behavior. This plot goes nowhere and indeed is little more than a means for the revelation of humorous characters. Shallow's is a cameo role, like many others, enabling him to assume the fatuous postures we also encounter in *2 Henry*

IV. Pistol and Nym, similarly requiring some pretext for being on hand, avenge their dismissal from Falstaff's service by informing the two husbands of Falstaff's designs on the two merry wives. Bardolph finds suitable employment as a bartender. Mistress Quickly's transformation is perhaps the most gloriously improbable of all: she becomes confidante of all three wooers of Anne Page (offering equal encouragement to each and receiving payment from each), as well as go-between for Falstaff and the two wives. She is no longer a married and then widowed hostess of a London tavern, but an unmarried housekeeper of Windsor. She triumphs over Falstaff in a way not possible in the history plays, joining the entire cast as they jeer at the discomfited horn-browed knight.

By providing occasion for the exhibition of idiosyncratic character for its own sake, side by side with his fast-moving farcical action, Shakespeare seems to have been responding to the newest dramatic genre of the late 1590s: the humors comedy. George Chapman's *The Blind Beggar of Alexandria* (1596) had done much to establish the new fashion. Ben Jonson's *Every Man in His Humor* (1598) either influenced Shakespeare or was influenced by him, depending upon the dates. Jonson's plot, like Shakespeare's, is chiefly a vehicle for displaying various humors or comically obsessed types: the overly watchful father, the jealous husband, the braggart soldier, the country simpleton intent on learning to quarrel like a gentleman, the waspishly impatient man. Similar types appear in *The Merry Wives*, although Shakespeare characteristically does not satirize affectation so much as cherish it.

Shakespeare's comic types endear themselves chiefly through their verbal traits: Nym with his use of the word "humor"; Pistol with his anachronistic terms, recondite allusions, stilted poetic inversions, and hyperboles ("O base Hungarian wight! Wilt thou the spigot wield?", 1.3.19–20); Mistress Quickly with her pungent homely metaphors (comparing a beard to "a glover's paring knife," 1.4.19–20) and her pat phrases ("But let that pass," line 14); Shallow with his legal jargon; and the French Caius and the Welsh Evans with their ability to "keep their limbs whole and hack our English" (3.1.73). Shakespeare also caricatures these humorous types by distinctive physical traits, such as Bardolph's "tinderbox" nose (1.3.23) or Slender's unappealing face and little yellow beard that so aptly suit his passion for bearbaiting and his idiotic deference to his superiors. We laugh at these deformities and yet see that no one is incorrigible. The characters amiably poke fun at one another, and every discomfiture leads ultimately to a reconciliation. Few escape laughter, even those we might regard as normative characters if this were a satire; the Host, for example, loses his horses, and Mistress Page is tricked at last by her daughter's elopement.

Nevertheless, the merry wives of the play's title come as close as any to representing the normative vision of the play, functioning as witty manipulators in a plot to expose hypocrisy and lechery. The devices they invent for Falstaff are rather like Maria's schemes for Malvolio in *Twelfth Night*, since all depend upon the complicity of the self-blinded victim. Falstaff is the dominant humors character of the play, obsessed both with lust and greed, amusing to us because the greed is predominant. His hypocritical reasons for wooing deserve comic reprisal, or "vengeance." His greed and his fatuous belief in his own charm overwhelm his natural sagacity and leave him vulnerable. He credulously accepts the bribes of the jealous Ford, disguised as Brook, and is deceived by the wives on no less than three occasions. For their part, the wives are delighted with their "sport," for they must devise increasingly clever schemes to offset Falstaff's growing suspicions. The more unlikely he is to return for more punishment, the greater must be their ingenuity in order to fool him once again. Mistress Ford enjoys the added pleasure of teaching her husband a lesson about jealousy. The wives' humorous plotting derives its sharpness from their potential to be faithless, if they choose, and hence from the power they enjoy over men like Ford and Falstaff, who are obsessed with groundless fantasies of betrayal or are compulsively in need of validating their masculinity through conquest of the female. The cleverness of their sport is justified by its moral intent, and, conversely, the moral point is deprived of any tedious didacticism by the good humor of the jest. In his final humiliation, plagued by virtually all the play's characters, reduced to an absurd belief in fairies, Falstaff becomes a scapegoat in the truest sense of that term: a horned figure who embodies the faults of an entire society and whose chastisement brings about purification. Yet, as Mistress Quickly observes, "nobody but has his fault" (1.4.13–14), and this comic rejection of Falstaff leads not to banishment but to a reconciling feast at the Pages' house. Without intending it, Falstaff has cured Ford's jealousy and has helped show that "Wives may be merry, and yet honest too." (4.2.97).

The Merry Wives is a remarkable play in terms of the relationship between comedy and history, the two genres most evident in Shakespeare's dramatic writing of the 1590s. The romantic plot of love's triumph, though nominally at the center of the plot, is decidedly secondary in importance. The more dominant motif of scapegoating and renewal concerns, not young lovers, but married women who claim the dominant position of wit. Falstaff's claim to wit and vitality in *1 Henry IV* and *2 Henry IV* gives place here to the ascendancy of domestic women; the comic principle shifts to them. Mistress Quickly, translated like Falstaff and his crew from the history plays into comedy, shares in this vindication of women's wit and virtue; no longer a tavern keeper or widow enduring Falstaff's broken promises or patiently supplying him with women, Quickly becomes a go-between in a comic plot of exposure of male philandering. Women are no longer on the periphery of a male-dominated world, as in the history plays, but in their element. At the same time, the women of this play embody married virtues for the most part, rather than the youthful companionship (Portia, Beatrice, Rosalind, Viola) of the romantic comedies. The location of the play in a part of England not far from where Shakespeare grew up, the inclusion of place names familiar from his youth, the fond portrait of a schoolboy's terror in coping with Latin paradigms, all suggest a kind of tribute to the world in which Shakespeare's own family affairs remained while he sought professional advancement in London. The mildly satiric celebration of bourgeois life, found nowhere else to such an extent in Shakespeare, gives a meaningful insight into an author who profited from the limited but increasing social mobility of his age.

The Merry Wives of Windsor

[Dramatis Personae

MISTRESS MARGARET PAGE, *a wife of Windsor*
MASTER GEORGE PAGE, *her husband*
ANNE PAGE, *their daughter*
WILLIAM PAGE, *a schoolboy, their son*

MISTRESS ALICE FORD, *a wife of Windsor*
MASTER FRANK FORD, *her husband*
JOHN, }
ROBERT, } *their servants*

SIR JOHN FALSTAFF
ROBIN, *his page*
BARDOLPH }
PISTOL, } *his followers*
NYM, }

SIR HUGH EVANS, *a Welsh parson*

DOCTOR CAIUS, *a French physician*
MISTRESS QUICKLY, *his housekeeper*
JOHN RUGBY, *his servant*

ROBERT SHALLOW, *a country justice of the peace*
ABRAHAM SLENDER, *his nephew*
PETER SIMPLE, *Slender's servant*

HOST *of the Garter Inn*
FENTON, *a gentleman in love with Anne Page*

Children of Windsor, disguised as fairies

SCENE: *Windsor, and the neighborhood*]

1.1 *Enter Justice Shallow, Slender, [and] Sir Hugh Evans.*

SHALLOW Sir Hugh, persuade me not. I will make a 1
Star Chamber matter of it. If he were twenty Sir John 2
Falstaffs, he shall not abuse Robert Shallow, Esquire.
SLENDER In the county of Gloucester, Justice of Peace
and Coram. 5

1.1. Location: Windsor. Before Master Page's house.
s.d. Sir courtesy title for a priest. **1 persuade** argue with **2 Star**
Chamber matter (The court of Star Chamber, composed chiefly of the
King's Privy Council, was the highest and most powerful court in the
realm.) **5 Coram** i.e., quorum, a title of certain justices whose presence was necessary to constitute a bench

SHALLOW Ay, cousin Slender, and Custalorum. 6
SLENDER Ay, and Ratolorum too. And a gentleman 7
born, Master Parson, who writes himself "Armigero" in 8
any bill, warrant, quittance, or obligation: "Armigero." 9
SHALLOW Ay, that I do, and have done any time these
three hundred years.
SLENDER All his successors gone before him hath
done 't, and all his ancestors that come after him may.
They may give the dozen white luces in their coat. 14
SHALLOW It is an old coat.
EVANS The dozen white louses do become an old coat
well. It agrees well, passant. It is a familiar beast to 17
man, and signifies love.
SHALLOW The luce is the fresh fish. The salt fish is an 19
old coat. 20
SLENDER I may quarter, coz. 21
SHALLOW You may, by marrying.
EVANS It is marring indeed, if he quarter it.
SHALLOW Not a whit.
EVANS Yes, py'r Lady. If he has a quarter of your coat, 25
there is but three skirts for yourself, in my simple 26
conjectures. But that is all one. If Sir John Falstaff have
committed disparagements unto you, I am of the
Church, and will be glad to do my benevolence to
make atonements and compromises between you. 30
SHALLOW The Council shall hear it. It is a riot. 31
EVANS It is not meet the Council hear a riot. There is no 32
fear of Got in a riot. The Council, look you, shall desire
to hear the fear of Got, and not to hear a riot. Take 34
your visaments in that. 35
SHALLOW Ha! O' my life, if I were young again, the
sword should end it.
EVANS It is petter that friends is the sword, and end it. 38
And there is also another device in my prain, which
peradventure prings goot discretions with it: there is
Anne Page, which is daughter to Master George Page,
which is pretty virginity.

6 cousin kinsman. **Custalorum** A corruption of Latin *custos rotulo-*
rum, "keeper of the rolls." **7 Ratolorum** (For *rotulorum*.) **8 Ar-**
migero Esquire, one entitled to bear arms. (A heraldic term.) **9 bill**
bill of financial exchange. **quittance** discharge from legal agreement.
obligation contract **14 give** display heraldically. **luces** pikes, freshwater fish. **coat** coat of arms **17 passant** (1) walking (in heraldic
language) (2) passing, exceeding. **familiar** (1) well known and part
of the family (2) overfamiliar (taking *louse* in the sense of a tiny biting
insect) **19–20 The luce . . . coat** (The meaning is unclear, though
Shallow is seemingly joking about Evans' pronunciation of *coat* as
"cod.") **21 quarter** combine the arms of two families by adding to
one's own coat the arms of another family in one quarter of the es-
cutcheon. **coz** cousin, kinsman **25 py'r Lady** by Our Lady. (Evans'
Welsh dialect often substitutes "p" for "b" at the start of words, as in
petter, prain, and *prings,* lines 38–40; substitutes "f" for "v" and "t"
for "d," as in *Fery goot,* line 133; leaves out initial "w," as in *'orld*
and *'oman,* lines 45, 210; etc.) **26 skirts** the tails of a long doublet
or coat. (Evans is still thinking of a literal coat that would be marred
by quartering, i.e., cutting into quarters.) **30 atonements** reconciliations. **compromises** i.e., settlement by arbitration **31 The Council**
. . . riot (The King's Privy Council, sitting in Star Chamber, frequently concerned itself with riots. Evans, however, understands
Council to refer to an ecclesiastical council.) **32 meet** fitting **34–**
35 Take . . . that take that into consideration. (*Visaments* means
"advisements.") **38 that friends is the sword** i.e., that the quarrel be
ended by friendly motions

SLENDER   Mistress Anne Page? She has brown hair and 43
speaks small like a woman? 44

EVANS   It is that fery person for all the 'orld, as just as 45
you will desire. And seven hundred pounds of
moneys, and gold, and silver, is her grandsire upon 47
his death's-bed—Got deliver to a joyful resurrec-
tions!—give, when she is able to overtake seventeen 49
years old. It were a goot motion if we leave our pribbles 50
and prabbles, and desire a marriage between 51
Master Abraham and Mistress Anne Page.

SLENDER   Did her grandsire leave her seven hundred
pound?

EVANS   Ay, and her father is make her a petter penny. 55

SHALLOW   I know the young gentlewoman. She has
good gifts. 57

EVANS   Seven hundred pounds and possibilities is goot 58
gifts.

SHALLOW   Well, let us see honest Master Page. Is Fal- 60
staff there?

EVANS   Shall I tell you a lie? I do despise a liar as I do
despise one that is false, or as I despise one that is not
true. The knight Sir John is there, and I beseech you
be ruled by your well-willers. I will peat the door for 65
Master Page. [He knocks.] What ho! Got pless your
house here!

PAGE [within]   Who's there?

EVANS   Here is Got's plessing, and your friend, and
Justice Shallow, and here young Master Slender, that
peradventures shall tell you another tale, if matters 71
grow to your likings.

[Enter] Master Page.

PAGE   I am glad to see your worships well. I thank you
for my venison, Master Shallow.

SHALLOW   Master Page, I am glad to see you. Much
good do it your good heart! I wished your venison
better; it was ill killed. How doth good Mistress 77
Page?—And I thank you always with my heart, la,
with my heart.

PAGE   Sir, I thank you.

SHALLOW   Sir, I thank you. By yea and no I do.

PAGE   I am glad to see you, good Master Slender.

SLENDER   How does your fallow greyhound, sir? I heard 83
say he was outrun on Cotswold. 84

PAGE   It could not be judged, sir. 85

SLENDER   You'll not confess, you'll not confess. 86

SHALLOW   That he will not. 'Tis your fault, 'tis your 87
fault. 'Tis a good dog.

PAGE   A cur, sir.

SHALLOW   Sir, he's a good dog, and a fair dog. Can
there be more said? He is good and fair. Is Sir John
Falstaff here?

PAGE   Sir, he is within; and I would I could do a good
office between you.

EVANS   It is spoke as a Christians ought to speak.

SHALLOW   He hath wronged me, Master Page.

PAGE   Sir, he doth in some sort confess it. 97

SHALLOW   If it be confessed, it is not redressed. Is not
that so, Master Page? He hath wronged me, indeed he
hath; at a word, he hath. Believe me, Robert Shallow, 100
Esquire, saith he is wronged.

[Enter Sir John] Falstaff, Bardolph, Nym, [and]
Pistol.

PAGE   Here comes Sir John.

FALSTAFF   Now, Master Shallow, you'll complain of me 103
to the King?

SHALLOW   Knight, you have beaten my men, killed my
deer, and broke open my lodge. 106

FALSTAFF   But not kissed your keeper's daughter?

SHALLOW   Tut, a pin! This shall be answered. 108

FALSTAFF   I will answer it straight: I have done all this. 109
That is now answered.

SHALLOW   The Council shall know this.

FALSTAFF   'Twere better for you if it were known in 112
counsel. You'll be laughed at. 113

EVANS   Pauca verba, Sir John, good worts. 114

FALSTAFF   Good worts? Good cabbage!—Slender, I 115
broke your head. What matter have you against me? 116

SLENDER   Marry, sir, I have matter in my head against 117
you, and against your coney-catching rascals, 118
Bardolph, Nym, and Pistol.

BARDOLPH   You Banbury cheese! 120

SLENDER   Ay, it is no matter.

PISTOL   How now, Mephistopheles? 122

SLENDER   Ay, it is no matter.

NYM   Slice, I say! Pauca, pauca. Slice, that's my humor. 124

SLENDER   Where's Simple, my man? Can you tell,
cousin?

EVANS   Peace, I pray you. Now let us understand. There
is three umpires in this matter, as I understand; that
is, Master Page, fidelicet Master Page; and there is my- 129
self, fidelicet myself; and the three party is, lastly and 130
finally, mine Host of the Garter. 131

---

97 in some sort to some extent   100 at a word in a word   103 of
about   106 lodge forest keeper's dwelling   108 pin trifle.   answered
accounted for. (But Falstaff plays on the meaning "replied to.")
109 straight (1) at once (2) straightforwardly   112–113 in counsel
secretly (playing on Council)   114 Pauca verba few words
115 worts vegetables, cabbages. (A quibble on Sir Hugh's pronunciation of words.)   116 broke your head made a slight bleeding wound
on your head   116, 117 matter (1) cause of complaint (2) matter of
consequence; pus   118 coney-catching cheating. (A coney is literally
a rabbit, a proverbially gullible animal.)   120 Banbury cheese (Banbury cheeses were noted for their thinness; a reference to Slender's
name and physique.)   122 Mephistopheles name of the devil in Marlowe's Doctor Faustus   124 Slice (1) speak briefly (2) I will slice with
my sword (3) a reference to Bardolph's calling Slender a cheese (?)
Pauca speak briefly.   humor mood   129 fidelicet i.e., videlicet,
namely   130 three third   131 Garter the name of an inn in Windsor

---

43 Mistress (Used of married or unmarried women.)   44 small with a
gentle, high voice   45 as just exactly   47–49 is . . . give has
. . . given (her)   50 motion plan   50–51 pribbles and prabbles
i.e., petty disputes   55 is make . . . penny will provide her a pretty
penny more   57 gifts natural endowments   58 possibilities pecuniary
prospects   60 honest worthy   65 well-willers well-wishers.   peat
beat, knock   71 tell . . . tale i.e., have something more to say to
you   77 ill i.e., illegally, by Falstaff. (See below, lines 105–106.)
83 fallow fawn-colored   84 on Cotswold i.e., in games held in the
Cotswold hills in Gloucestershire   85 judged fairly decided   86 confess admit (that your dog lost)   87 That . . . fault i.e., he (Page) certainly won't admit that. You (Slender) are in the wrong   87 fault (with
a suggestion of "loss of scent")

PAGE We three to hear it, and end it between them.

EVANS Fery goot. I will make a prief of it in my note- 133
book, and we will afterwards 'ork upon the cause with
as great discreetly as we can.

FALSTAFF Pistol!

PISTOL He hears with ears.

EVANS The tevil and his tam! What phrase is this, "He 138
hears with ear"? Why, it is affectations.

FALSTAFF Pistol, did you pick Master Slender's purse?

SLENDER Ay, by these gloves, did he—or I would I
might never come in mine own great chamber again 142
else—of seven groats in mill-sixpences, and two 143
Edward shovelboards, that cost me two shilling and 144
twopence apiece of Yed Miller, by these gloves. 145

FALSTAFF Is this true, Pistol?

EVANS No, it is false, if it is a pickpurse. 147

PISTOL
Ha, thou mountain-foreigner! Sir John and master
mine,   148
I combat challenge of this latten bilbo.   149
Word of denial in thy *labras* here!   150
Word of denial! Froth and scum, thou liest!

SLENDER [*indicating Nym*] By these gloves, then 'twas he.

NYM Be advised, sir, and pass good humors. I will say 153
"marry, trap with you" if you run the nuthook's 154
humor on me. That is the very note of it. 155

SLENDER By this hat, then, he in the red face had it. 156
For though I cannot remember what I did when you
made me drunk, yet I am not altogether an ass.

FALSTAFF [*to Bardolph*] What say you, Scarlet and John? 159

BARDOLPH Why, sir, for my part, I say the gentleman
had drunk himself out of his five sentences.

EVANS It is his five "senses." Fie, what the ignorance is!

BARDOLPH And being fap, sir, was, as they say, 163
cashiered. And so conclusions passed the careers. 164

SLENDER Ay, you spake in Latin then, too. But 'tis no
matter. I'll ne'er be drunk whilst I live again, but in
honest, civil, godly company, for this trick. If I be
drunk, I'll be drunk with those that have the fear of

God, and not with drunken knaves.

EVANS So Got 'udge me, that is a virtuous mind. 170

FALSTAFF You hear all these matters denied, gentlemen. You hear it.

[*Enter*] *Anne Page* [*with wine*]; *Mistress Ford*
[*and*] *Mistress Page* [*following*].

PAGE Nay, daughter, carry the wine in; we'll drink
within.   [*Exit Anne Page.*]

SLENDER O heaven! This is Mistress Anne Page.

PAGE How now, Mistress Ford?

FALSTAFF Mistress Ford, by my troth, you are very well
met. By your leave, good mistress.   [*He kisses her.*]

PAGE Wife, bid these gentlemen welcome.—Come,
we have a hot venison pasty to dinner. Come, gentle- 180
men, I hope we shall drink down all unkindness.
[*Exeunt all except Shallow, Slender, and Evans.*]

SLENDER I had rather than forty shillings I had my
book of songs and sonnets here. 183

[*Enter*] *Simple.*

How now, Simple, where have you been? I must wait
on myself, must I? You have not the book of riddles 185
about you, have you?

SIMPLE Book of riddles? Why, did you not lend it to
Alice Shortcake upon Allhallowmas last, a fortnight 188
afore Michaelmas? 189

SHALLOW Come, coz, come, coz, we stay for you. A 190
word with you, coz—marry, this, coz: there is as 191
'twere a tender, a kind of tender, made afar off by Sir 192
Hugh here. Do you understand me?

SLENDER Ay, sir, you shall find me reasonable. If it be
so, I shall do that that is reason.

SHALLOW Nay, but understand me.

SLENDER So I do, sir.

EVANS Give ear to his motions. Master Slender, I will 198
description the matter to you, if you be capacity of it. 199

SLENDER Nay, I will do as my cousin Shallow says. I
pray you, pardon me. He's a Justice of Peace in his
country, simple though I stand here. 202

EVANS But that is not the question. The question is
concerning your marriage.

SHALLOW Ay, there's the point, sir.

EVANS Marry, is it, the very point of it—to Mistress
Anne Page.

SLENDER Why, if it be so, I will marry her upon any
reasonable demands. 209

EVANS But can you affection the 'oman? Let us com-

133 **prief** brief, summary 138 **tam** dam, mother 142 **great chamber** hall 143 **groats** coins equal to four pence. **mill-sixpences** coins
stamped by means of the mill and press 144 **Edward shovelboards**
shillings coined in the reign of Edward VI (so called from their use in
the gambling game of shovelboard) 145 **Yed** Ed, Edward 147 **it is
false** i.e., Pistol is false, not *true* ("honest"). **if it** if he 148 **mountain-foreigner** i.e., Welshman 149 **combat challenge** challenge to
trial by combat. (A flowery way of issuing a challenge to a duel.)
latten mixed metal of yellow color, resembling brass. **bilbo** finely
tempered sword of Bilbao in Spain. (Here alludes to Slender's thinness.) 150 **labras** lips, i.e., face 153 **advised** on your guard. **pass
good humors** do nothing ill-natured 154 **marry, trap with you** (An
insulting phrase meaning something like "run off," "beat it.") 154–
155 **run . . . me** threaten me with a constable, or behave like one.
(A *nuthook* literally is a hooked stick used to pull nuts from trees; applied to a constable.) 155 **very note of it** truth of the matter
156 **he . . . face** i.e., Bardolph 159 **Scarlet and John** (Names of
Robin Hood's companions, Will Scarlet and Little John. *Scarlet* is humorously applied to Bardolph's color.) 163 **fap** drunk 164 **cashiered** deprived (of his senses; but perhaps suggesting, too, that he was
fleeced) 164 **conclusions . . . careers** i.e., his conclusions about
matters made a wild gallop, went wide of the mark; or, what happened to him got out of control. (*Careers* means "a short gallop at full
speed," "a feat of horsemanship.")

170 **'udge** (For "judge.") **mind** intent 180 **pasty to** meat pie for
183 **book of songs and sonnets** (Probably refers to Tottel's *Miscellany*,
published in 1557 and quite old-fashioned by the late 1590s.)
185 **book of riddles** (Such a book is mentioned as in the library of
Captain Cox in *Laneham's Letter*, 1575. No copy is extant earlier than
1629.) 188–189 **Allhallowmas . . . Michaelmas** (Simple's blunder.
Michaelmas occurs on September 29; Allhallowmas or All Saints'
Day, on November 1.) 190 **stay** wait 191 **marry** (A mild oath, originally "by the Virgin Mary.") 192 **tender** offer (of marriage). **afar
off** indirectly 198 **motions** proposals 199 **description** i.e., describe.
be . . . of it have the capacity to understand 202 **country** district.
simple though as sure as (but also suggesting "however humble I, his
kinsman, may appear to be") 209 **demands** requests

mand to know that of your mouth or of your lips; for
divers philosophers hold that the lips is parcel of the   212
mouth. Therefore, precisely, can you carry your good
will to the maid?

SHALLOW   Cousin Abraham Slender, can you love her?

SLENDER   I hope, sir, I will do as it shall become one
that would do reason.

EVANS   Nay, Got's lords and his ladies! You must speak
positable, if you can carry her your desires towards   219
her.

SHALLOW   That you must. Will you, upon good dowry,   221
marry her?

SLENDER   I will do a greater thing than that upon your
request, cousin, in any reason.

SHALLOW   Nay, conceive me, conceive me, sweet coz.   225
What I do is to pleasure you, coz. Can you love the   226
maid?

SLENDER   I will marry her, sir, at your request. But if
there be no great love in the beginning, yet heaven
may decrease it upon better acquaintance, when we   230
are married and have more occasion to know one another. I hope upon familiarity will grow more content.   232
But if you say, "Marry her," I will marry her. That I am
freely dissolved, and dissolutely.   234

EVANS   It is a fery discretion answer; save the faul is in   235
the 'ort "dissolutely." The 'ort is, according to our   236
meaning, "resolutely." His meaning is good.

SHALLOW   Ay, I think my cousin meant well.

SLENDER   Ay, or else I would I might be hanged, la!

[Enter Anne Page.]

SHALLOW   Here comes fair Mistress Anne.—Would I
were young for your sake, Mistress Anne!

ANNE   The dinner is on the table. My father desires your
worships' company.

SHALLOW   I will wait on him, fair Mistress Anne.   244

EVANS   'Od's plessed will! I will not be absence at the   245
grace.   *[Exeunt Shallow and Evans.]*

ANNE   Will 't please your worship to come in, sir?

SLENDER   No, I thank you, forsooth, heartily. I am very
well.

ANNE   The dinner attends you, sir.   250

SLENDER   I am not ahungry, I thank you, forsooth. *[To
Simple.]* Go, sirrah, for all you are my man, go wait   252
upon my cousin Shallow. *[Exit Simple.]* A Justice of   253
Peace sometimes may be beholding to his friend for a   254
man. I keep but three men and a boy yet, till my
mother be dead. But what though? Yet I live like a   256
poor gentleman born.

ANNE   I may not go in without your worship. They will
not sit till you come.

SLENDER   I' faith, I'll eat nothing. I thank you as much
as though I did.

ANNE   I pray you, sir, walk in.

SLENDER   I had rather walk here, I thank you. I bruised
my shin th' other day with playing at sword and
dagger with a master of fence—three veneys for a   265
dish of stewed prunes—and, by my troth, I cannot   266
abide the smell of hot meat since. Why do your dogs
bark so? Be there bears i' the town?

ANNE   I think there are, sir. I heard them talked of.

SLENDER   I love the sport well, but I shall as soon quarrel   270
at it as any man in England. You are afraid if you see
the bear loose, are you not?

ANNE   Ay, indeed, sir.

SLENDER   That's meat and drink to me, now. I have
seen Sackerson loose twenty times, and have taken   275
him by the chain. But, I warrant you, the women have
so cried and shrieked at it that it passed. But women,   277
indeed, cannot abide 'em—they are very ill-favored,   278
rough things.

[Enter Page.]

PAGE   Come, gentle Master Slender, come. We stay
for you.

SLENDER   I'll eat nothing, I thank you, sir.

PAGE   By Cock and pie, you shall not choose, sir.   283
Come, come.

SLENDER   Nay, pray you, lead the way.

PAGE   Come on, sir.

SLENDER   Mistress Anne, yourself shall go first.

ANNE   Not I, sir. Pray you, keep on.   288

SLENDER   Truly, I will not go first, truly, la! I will not do
you that wrong.

ANNE   I pray you, sir.

SLENDER   I'll rather be unmannerly than troublesome.
You do yourself wrong, indeed, la!   *Exeunt.*

1.2

Enter Evans and Simple [from dinner].

EVANS   Go your ways, and ask of Doctor Caius' house   1
which is the way. And there dwells one Mistress
Quickly, which is in the manner of his nurse, or his
dry nurse, or his cook, or his laundry, his washer, and   4
his wringer.

SIMPLE   Well, sir.

---

212 **parcel** part   219 **positable** (For "positively.")   221 **upon good dowry** on the strength of a prospect of a good dowry   225 **conceive** understand   226 **pleasure** please   230 **decrease** (For "increase." But with unintended comic meaning; the proverb "Marry first and love will after" contends with "Familiarity breeds contempt" in line 232.) 232 **hope** hope that.   **content** (Unwittingly suggesting "contempt," as in the proverb cited in line 230 above.)   234 **dissolved** (For "resolved.")   **dissolutely** (For "resolutely.")   235 **faul** i.e., fault 236 **'ort** word   244 **wait on him** keep him company   245 **'Od's** God's   250 **attends** waits for   252 **sirrah** Usual form of address to a social inferior.   **for all** even though   252–253 **wait upon** attend 254 **beholding** beholden   256 **what though** what of it

265 **fence** fencing.   **veneys** bouts in fencing   266 **stewed prunes** (A favorite dish at the "stews" or brothel houses; hence, an indelicate thing to say to Anne.)   270 **the sport** i.e., bearbaiting   275 **Sackerson** a famous bear at the Paris Garden near the theaters on the Bankside   277 **passed** i.e., surpassed description   278 **ill-favored** ugly 283 **Cock** (A perversion of *God*.)   **pie** service book of the pre-Reformation Church.   **shall not choose** must   288 **keep on** go ahead
1.2. Location: The same scene, a short time later, essentially continuous.
1 **ask of** inquire concerning   4 **dry nurse** i.e., attendant to an adult, not a child; a housekeeper.   **laundry** laundress

EVANS   Nay, it is petter yet. Give her this letter. [*He
gives a letter.*] For it is a 'oman that altogether's 8
acquaintance with Mistress Anne Page. And the letter 9
is to desire and require her to solicit your master's 10
desires to Mistress Anne Page. I pray you, begone. I
will make an end of my dinner; there's pippins and 12
cheese to come.   *Exeunt* [*separately*].

❖

1.3   *Enter Falstaff, Host, Bardolph, Nym, Pistol,* [*and
Robin, Falstaff's*] *Page.*

FALSTAFF   Mine Host of the Garter!

HOST   What says my bullyrook? Speak scholarly and 2
wisely.

FALSTAFF   Truly, mine Host, I must turn away some of
my followers.

HOST   Discard, bully Hercules, cashier. Let them wag; 6
trot, trot.

FALSTAFF   I sit at ten pounds a week. 8

HOST   Thou'rt an emperor—Caesar, Kaiser, and Phee- 9
zer. I will entertain Bardolph; he shall draw, he 10
shall tap. Said I well, bully Hector? 11

FALSTAFF   Do so, good mine Host.

HOST   I have spoke; let him follow. [*To Bardolph.*] Let me
see thee froth and lime. I am at a word. Follow. 14
[*Exit.*]

FALSTAFF   Bardolph, follow him. A tapster is a good
trade. An old cloak makes a new jerkin; a withered 16
servingman a fresh tapster. Go; adieu.

BARDOLPH   It is a life that I have desired. I will thrive.
[*Exit Bardolph.*]

PISTOL   O base Hungarian wight! Wilt thou the spigot 19
wield?

NYM   He was gotten in drink. Is not the humor con- 21
ceited? 22

FALSTAFF   I am glad I am so acquit of this tinderbox. 23
His thefts were too open. His filching was like an unskillful singer: he kept not time.

NYM   The good humor is to steal at a minute's rest. 26

PISTOL   "Convey," the wise it call. "Steal"? Foh! A fico 27
for the phrase!

FALSTAFF   Well, sirs, I am almost out at heels. 29

PISTOL   Why then, let kibes ensue. 30

FALSTAFF   There is no remedy; I must coney-catch, I 31
must shift. 32

PISTOL   Young ravens must have food.

FALSTAFF   Which of you know Ford of this town?

PISTOL   I ken the wight. He is of substance good. 35

FALSTAFF   My honest lads, I will tell you what I am 36
about. 37

PISTOL   Two yards, and more.

FALSTAFF   No quips now, Pistol. Indeed, I am in the
waist two yards about. But I am now about no waste;
I am about thrift. Briefly, I do mean to make love to
Ford's wife. I spy entertainment in her. She dis- 42
courses, she carves, she gives the leer of invitation. I 43
can construe the action of her familiar style; and the 44
hardest voice of her behavior, to be Englished rightly, 45
is, "I am Sir John Falstaff's."

PISTOL   [*to Nym*]   He hath studied her well and translated her will—out of honesty into English. 48

NYM   The anchor is deep. Will that humor pass? 49

FALSTAFF   Now, the report goes she has all the rule of
her husband's purse. He hath a legion of angels. 51

PISTOL   As many devils entertain; and "To her, boy!" 52
say I.

NYM   The humor rises; it is good. Humor me the an- 54
gels. 55

FALSTAFF   [*showing letters*]   I have writ me here a letter 56
to her; and here another to Page's wife, who even now 57
gave me good eyes too, examined my parts with most
judicious oeillades. Sometimes the beam of her view 59
gilded my foot, sometimes my portly belly.

PISTOL   [*to Nym*]   Then did the sun on dunghill shine.

NYM   [*to Pistol*]   I thank thee for that humor.

FALSTAFF   O, she did so course o'er my exteriors, with 63
such a greedy intention that the appetite of her eye did 64
seem to scorch me up like a burning glass! Here's 65

8–9 altogether's acquaintance is well acquainted   **10 solicit** plead
the case for   **12 pippins** a kind of apple
1.3. Location: The Garter Inn.
2 bullyrook fine fellow   **6 cashier** dismiss.   **wag** move on   **8 I sit at**
my expenses i.e.   **9 Kaiser** emperor   **9–10 Pheezer** i.e., Vizier (?) or,
one who beats or frightens, "does for" someone (?)   **10 entertain** employ.   **draw** draw liquor   **11 tap** serve as tapster.   **Hector** (The hero
of Troy, and a type of manliness, like *Hercules* in line 6.)   **14 froth**
draw liquor in such a way as to make it frothy, filling the glass with
less beer.   **lime** adulterate wine by putting lime into it to mask the
sour taste.   **at a word** a man of few words   **16 jerkin** jacket
19 Hungarian wight i.e., beggarly person   **21 gotten** begotten   **21–
22 conceited** ingenious   **23 acquit** rid.   **tinderbox** (alluding to Bardolph's fiery complexion)   **26 good humor** i.e., smart way to do it.
at a minute's rest i.e., within a minute's time. (Or possibly an error
for "minim rest," the shortest rest in music.)   **27 Convey . . . call**
i.e., those in the know use the cant phrase for stealing, "convey."
fico Italian for *fig*, an insulting phrase and obscene gesture of putting
the thumb between the second and third fingers

29 out at heels i.e., out of money. (Literally, with stockings or shoes
worn through at the heel.)   **30 kibes** chilblains. (Pistol interprets *out
at heels* literally.)   **31 coney-catch** catch rabbits, i.e., cheat victims in
a con game   **32 shift** devise a stratagem   **35 ken the wight** know the
person.   **of substance good** a person of means   **36–37 what I am
about** what I am up to. (But Pistol plays with the meaning "what I
measure round about the waist.")   **42 entertainment** (1) readiness to
receive me (2) a source of supply   **43 carves** shows courtesy and affability, or speaks affectedly.   **leer** come-hither glance   **44 construe** interpret (introducing an extended grammatical pun, continued in *style,
voice,* and *Englished*)   **45 hardest voice** (1) severest judgment (2)
most difficult construction.   **Englished** expressed in English   **48 will**
(1) intent (2) sexual desire (3) legal will.   **honesty** chastity   **49 The
. . . deep** i.e., the plan is fixed firmly, or is a deep one (?)   **Will
. . . pass** i.e., will my expression pass muster?   **51 angels** coins
stamped with the figure of the archangel Michael, worth about ten
shillings   **52 As . . . entertain** (Pistol, taking *legion of angels* in the
sense of "heavenly host," plays on the idea of a battle between them
and a legion of devils. Falstaff, with his devilish devices, is to take on
the angels and *entertain* them to his own use.)   **To her, boy** (A cry of
encouragement to a hunting hound.)   **54–55 Humor me the angels**
i.e., yes, take the money by this device. (Nym is seconding Pistol's
advice; the *humor* of the enterprise takes shape.)   **56 writ me** written.
(*Me* is used colloquially.)   **57 even now** just now   **59 oeillades** amorous glances   **63 course o'er** run her eyes over   **64 intention** intentness of gaze   **65 burning glass** magnifying glass to focus rays of the
sun

another letter to her. She bears the purse too; she is a
region in Guiana, all gold and bounty. I will be cheat- 67
ers to them both, and they shall be exchequers to me. 68
They shall be my East and West Indies, and I will trade
to them both. [*To Pistol.*] Go bear thou this letter to
Mistress Page. [*To Nym.*] And thou this to Mistress
Ford. We will thrive, lads, we will thrive.

PISTOL [*giving the letter back*]
Shall I Sir Pandarus of Troy become,   73
And by my side wear steel? Then Lucifer take all!   74

NYM   I will run no base humor. Here, take the humor-
letter. [*He gives the letter back.*] I will keep the havior of 76
reputation.   77

FALSTAFF [*to Robin*]
Hold, sirrah, bear you these letters tightly.   78
                              [*He gives the letters.*]
Sail like my pinnace to these golden shores.   79
Rogues, hence, avaunt! Vanish like hailstones, go!
Trudge, plod away o' the hoof! Seek shelter, pack!   81
Falstaff will learn the humor of the age: 82
French thrift, you rogues—myself and skirted page.   83
                              [*Exeunt Falstaff and Robin.*]
PISTOL
Let vultures gripe thy guts! For gourd and fullam
holds,   84
And high and low beguiles the rich and poor.   85
Tester I'll have in pouch when thou shalt lack,   86
Base Phrygian Turk!   87

NYM   I have operations which be humors of revenge.   88
PISTOL   Wilt thou revenge?
NYM   By welkin and her star!   90
PISTOL   With wit or steel?   91
NYM
With both the humors, I.   92
I will discuss the humor of this love to Page.   93
PISTOL
And I to Ford shall eke unfold   94
How Falstaff, varlet vile,
His dove will prove, his gold will hold,   96
And his soft couch defile.

NYM   My humor shall not cool. I will incense Page to

deal with poison; I will possess him with yellowness, 99
for the revolt of mine is dangerous. That is my true 100
humor.
PISTOL   Thou art the Mars of malcontents. I second 102
thee. Troop on.   *Exeunt.*

1.4   *Enter Mistress Quickly [and] Simple.*

QUICKLY [*calling*]   What, John Rugby!

[*Enter Rugby.*]

I pray thee, go to the casement and see if you can see
my master, Master Doctor Caius, coming. If he do, i'
faith, and find anybody in the house, here will be an
old abusing of God's patience and the King's English. 5
RUGBY   I'll go watch.
QUICKLY   Go; and we'll have a posset for 't soon at 7
night, in faith, at the latter end of a sea-coal fire. 8
[*Rugby goes to look out the window.*] An honest, will- 9
ing, kind fellow as ever servant shall come in house
withal, and, I warrant you, no telltale nor no breed- 11
bate. His worst fault is that he is given to prayer. He is 12
something peevish that way, but nobody but has his 13
fault. But let that pass. Peter Simple you say your
name is?
SIMPLE   Ay, for fault of a better.   16
QUICKLY   And Master Slender's your master?
SIMPLE   Ay, forsooth.
QUICKLY   Does he not wear a great round beard, like a
glover's paring knife?
SIMPLE   No, forsooth. He hath but a little whey face, 21
with a little yellow beard, a Cain-colored beard.   22
QUICKLY   A softly spirited man, is he not?   23
SIMPLE   Ay, forsooth. But he is as tall a man of his hands 24
as any is between this and his head. He hath fought 25
with a warrener.   26
QUICKLY   How say you? O, I should remember him. Does
he not hold up his head, as it were, and strut in his gait?
SIMPLE   Yes indeed does he.
QUICKLY   Well, heaven send Anne Page no worse

---

67 region in Guiana (A possible reference to Sir Walter Ralegh's *Discovery of the Large, Rich, and Beautiful Empire of Guiana,* published 1596.)   **67–68 cheaters** escheaters, officers appointed to look after the King's escheats, i.e., land reverted to the crown (with a quibble on the ordinary sense of "those who cheat")   **68 exchequers** treasuries   **73 Sir Pandarus** uncle of Cressida, and go-between in the story of Troilus and Cressida. (From his name originated the word *pander.*)   **74 And . . . steel** i.e., even though I am a soldier   **76–77 keep . . . reputation** behave reputably   **78 tightly** deftly, securely   **79 pinnace** a small, swift sailing vessel   **81 pack** be off   **82 humor** fashion   **83 French thrift** (Alludes to the current practice of economizing with one French page instead of a more numerous retinue.)   **skirted** wearing a doublet with long skirts or tails   **84 gourd and fullam** two kinds of false dice.   **holds** hold good, can still be used as a means of livelihood   **85 high and low** i.e., false dice weighted so as to produce high and low numbers   **86 Tester** sixpence.   **pouch** purse   **87 Phrygian Turk** (A term of opprobrium.)   **88 operations** plans   **90 welkin** sky   **91 wit or steel** i.e., cunning or violence   **92 both the humors** i.e., wit and sword   **93 discuss** declare   **94 eke** also   **96 prove** test

99 possess fill.   **yellowness** i.e., jealousy. (In the Folio text, Nym plans to incense *Ford* with jealousy, which seems more appropriate to Ford's jealous temperament, while in line 94 Pistol plans to speak to Page; however, in 2.1.104 ff., Nym speaks to Page, trying to make him jealous, and Pistol to Ford, and so it seems best to follow the Quarto assignments here in lines 93–94 and 98.)   **100 the revolt . . . dangerous** i.e., my turning against Falstaff will harm him   **102 the Mars** i.e., the most warlike and mighty   **1.4. Location: Doctor Caius' house.**   **5 old** plentiful, great   **7 a posset** a drink of hot milk curdled with ale or wine   **7–8 soon at night** as soon as night comes   **8 sea-coal** mineral coal brought by sea (as distinguished from charcoal)   **9 s.d. window** (Rugby perhaps looks offstage.)   **11 withal** with   **11–12 breedbate** mischief maker   **13 something peevish** somewhat foolish   **16 for fault of** in default of   **21 whey** i.e., pallid   **22 Cain-colored** (Cain is often pictured in old tapestries with a yellow or reddish beard.)   **23 softly spirited** gentle   **24 as tall . . . hands** as valiant a man, as stout of arms   **25 between . . . head** i.e., in these parts. (Proverbial.)   **26 warrener** gamekeeper fortune! Tell Master Parson Evans I will do what I can for your master. Anne is a good girl, and I wish—

[Rugby returns.]

RUGBY　Out, alas! Here comes my master.

QUICKLY　We shall all be shent. Run in here, good 34 young man; go into this closet. He will not stay long. 35 *[She shuts Simple in the closet.]* What, John Rugby! John! What, John, I say! Go, John, go inquire for my master. I doubt he be not well, that he comes not home. 38

[Exit Rugby.]
[Singing] "And down, down, adown-a," etc.

[Enter] Doctor Caius.

CAIUS　Vat is you sing? I do not like dese toys. Pray 40 you, go and vetch me in my closet *un boîtier vert*, a box, 41 a green-a box. Do intend vat I speak? A green-a box. 42

QUICKLY　Ay, forsooth, I'll fetch it you. *[Aside.]* I am glad he went not in himself. If he had found the young man, he would have been horn-mad. 45

[She goes to the door.]

CAIUS　*Fe, fe, fe, fe! Ma foi, il fait fort chaud. Je m'en vais à* 46 *la cour—la grande affaire.* 47

QUICKLY　Is it this, sir?　　　　*[She offers him a box.]*

CAIUS　*Oui; mets-le à ma* pocket. *Dépêche*, quickly! Vere is 49 dat knave Rugby?

QUICKLY　What, John Rugby! John!

[Enter Rugby.]

RUGBY　Here, sir.

CAIUS　You are John Rugby, and you are Jack Rugby. Come, take-a your rapier, and come after my heel to 54 the court.

RUGBY　'Tis ready, sir, here in the porch.

CAIUS　By my trot, I tarry too long. 'Od's me, *qu'ai-* 57 *j'oublié?* Dere is some simples in my closet dat I vill not 58 for the varld I shall leave behind.

QUICKLY　*[aside]*　Ay me, he'll find the young man there, and be mad!

CAIUS　*[going to the room]*　O *diable, diable!* Vat is in my 62 closet? Villainy! *Larron!* *[Pulling Simple out.]* Rugby, 63 my rapier!

QUICKLY　Good master, be content. 65

CAIUS　Wherefore shall I be content-a?

QUICKLY　The young man is an honest man.

CAIUS　What shall de honest man do in my closet? Dere is no honest man dat shall come in my closet.

QUICKLY　I beseech you, be not so phlegmatic. Hear the 70

truth of it: he came of an errand to me from Parson 71 Hugh.

CAIUS　Vell?

SIMPLE　Ay, forsooth, to desire her to—

QUICKLY　Peace, I pray you.

CAIUS　Peace-a your tongue.—Speak-a your tale.

SIMPLE　To desire this honest gentlewoman, your maid, to speak a good word to Mistress Anne Page for my master in the way of marriage.

QUICKLY　This is all, indeed, la! But I'll ne'er put my 80 finger in the fire, and need not. 81

CAIUS　Sir Hugh send-a you? Rugby, *baille* me some 82 paper. *[To Simple.]* Tarry you a little-a while. *[Rugby fetches paper, and Dr. Caius writes.]*

QUICKLY　*[aside to Simple]*　I am glad he is so quiet. If he had been throughly moved, you should have heard 85 him so loud and so melancholy. But notwithstanding, 86 man, I'll do you your master what good I can. And the 87 very yea and the no is, the French doctor, my master— 88 I may call him my master, look you, for I keep his house, and I wash, wring, brew, bake, scour, dress 90 meat and drink, make the beds, and do all myself— 91

SIMPLE　*[aside to Quickly]*　'Tis a great charge to come 92 under one body's hand.

QUICKLY　*[aside to Simple]*　Are you advised o' that? 94 You shall find it a great charge. And to be up early and down late. But notwithstanding—to tell you in your ear; I would have no words of it—my master 97 himself is in love with Mistress Anne Page. But notwithstanding that, I know Anne's mind: that's neither here nor there.

CAIUS　You jack'nape, give-a this letter to Sir Hugh. *[He* 101 *gives Simple the letter.]* By gar, it is a challenge. I will cut 102 his troat in de park, and I will teach a scurvy jackanape priest to meddle or make. You may be gone; it is not 104 good you tarry here. *[Exit Simple.]* By gar, I will cut all 105 his two stones. By gar, he shall not have a stone to 106 throw at his dog.

QUICKLY　Alas, he speaks but for his friend.

CAIUS　It is no matter-a ver dat. Do not you tell-a me dat 109 I shall have Anne Page for myself? By gar, I vill kill de jack priest; and I have appointed mine Host of de 111 Jarteer to measure our weapon. By gar, I will myself 112 have Anne Page.

QUICKLY　Sir, the maid loves you, and all shall be well. We must give folks leave to prate. What the goodyear! 115

---

34 shent blamed, disgraced　**35 closet** closet or private room　**38 doubt** fear　**40 toys** trifles, i.e., songs　**41 un boîtier vert** a green box　**42 Do intend** do you understand. (French *entendre*.)　**45 horn-mad** (1) enraged, like a horned beast (2) enraged like a jealous cuckold　**46–47 Ma foi . . . affaire** by my faith, it is very hot; I am going to court—the great affair　**49 Oui . . . Dépêche** yes, put it in my pocket; be quick　**54 your rapier** i.e., your master's rapier　**57 trot** truth, faith.　**'Od's me** God save me　**57–58 qu'ai-j'oublié** what have I forgotten?　**58 simples** medicinal herbs　**62 diable** devil　**63 Larron** robber　**65 content** calm　**70 phlegmatic** (Probably a blunder for "choleric," hot-tempered; phlegmatic is the very opposite in the physiology of humors.)

71 of an on an　**80–81 put . . . need not** i.e., meddle and risk hurting myself if I don't need to　**82 baille** fetch　**85 throughly moved** thoroughly angered　**86 melancholy** (Perhaps a blunder again, like *phlegmatic*, above.)　**87 you** for you, since you ask me　**87–88 the very yea and the no** the long and short of it　**90–91 dress meat** prepare food　**92 charge** responsibility　**94 Are . . . that** i.e., do you understand that? You can say that again　**97 I would . . . of it** I wouldn't want the word to get out　**101 jack'nape** ape, tame monkey; i.e., fop, worthless fellow　**102 gar** i.e., God　**104 meddle or make** meddle　**105–106 cut . . . stones** castrate him　**109 ver** for　**111 jack** (A contemptuous epithet.)　**112 Jarteer** Garter.　**measure our weapon** i.e., act as second or referee. (Literally, to make sure that the swords are of equal length.)　**115 What the goodyear** i.e., what the deuce (?)

CAIUS   Rugby, come to the court with me. [*To Mistress Quickly.*] By gar, if I have not Anne Page, I shall turn your head out of my door. Follow my heels, Rugby.
                                              [*Exeunt Caius and Rugby.*]

QUICKLY   You shall have An fool's head of your own. 119 No, I know Anne's mind for that. Never a woman in Windsor knows more of Anne's mind than I do, nor can do more than I do with her, I thank heaven.

FENTON [*within*]   Who's within there, ho?

QUICKLY   Who's there, I trow? Come near the house, I 124 pray you.

                    [*Enter*] Fenton.

FENTON   How now, good woman, how dost thou?

QUICKLY   The better that it pleases your good worship to ask.

FENTON   What news? How does pretty Mistress Anne?

QUICKLY   In truth, sir, and she is pretty, and honest, and 130 gentle, and one that is your friend, I can tell you that 131 by the way, I praise heaven for it.

FENTON   Shall I do any good, think'st thou? Shall I not lose my suit?

QUICKLY   Troth, sir, all is in His hands above. But notwithstanding, Master Fenton, I'll be sworn on a 136 book she loves you. Have not your worship a wart 137 above your eye?

FENTON   Yes, marry, have I. What of that?

QUICKLY   Well, thereby hangs a tale. Good faith, it is 140 such another Nan! But, I detest, an honest maid as 141 ever broke bread. We had an hour's talk of that wart. I shall never laugh but in that maid's company! But 143 indeed she is given too much to allicholy and musing. 144 But for you—well, go to.   145

FENTON   Well, I shall see her today. Hold, there's money for thee. [*He gives money.*] Let me have thy voice in my 147 behalf. If thou seest her before me, commend me.

QUICKLY   Will I? I' faith, that I will. And I will tell your worship more of the wart the next time we have confidence, and of other wooers.   151

FENTON   Well, farewell. I am in great haste now.

QUICKLY   Farewell to your worship.   [*Exit Fenton.*] Truly, an honest gentleman. But Anne loves him not, for I know Anne's mind as well as another does.— Out upon 't! What have I forgot?   *Exit.* 156

                              ❧

2.1   *Enter Mistress Page [with a letter].*

MRS. PAGE   What, have I scaped love letters in the holiday time of my beauty, and am I now a subject for them? Let me see.   [*She reads.*]
   "Ask me no reason why I love you, for though Love use Reason for his precisian, he admits him not for his 5 counselor. You are not young; no more am I. Go to 6 then, there's sympathy. You are merry; so am I. Ha, 7 ha! Then there's more sympathy. You love sack, and 8 so do I. Would you desire better sympathy? Let it suffice thee, Mistress Page—at the least, if the love of soldier can suffice—that I love thee. I will not say, "pity me"—'tis not a soldierlike phrase—but I say, "love me." By me,
            Thine own true knight,
            By day or night
            Or any kind of light,
            With all his might
            For thee to fight,
                              John Falstaff."
What a Herod of Jewry is this! O wicked, wicked world! 20 One that is well-nigh worn to pieces with age, to show himself a young gallant! What an unweighed behavior 22 hath this Flemish drunkard picked, i' the devil's 23 name, out of my conversation, that he dares in this 24 manner assay me? Why, he hath not been thrice in my 25 company. What should I say to him? I was then frugal 26 of my mirth. Heaven forgive me! Why, I'll exhibit a 27 bill in the Parliament for the putting down of men. 28 How shall I be revenged on him? For revenged I will be, as sure as his guts are made of puddings.   30

            [*Enter*] Mistress Ford.

MRS. FORD   Mistress Page! Trust me, I was going to 31 your house.

MRS. PAGE   And, trust me, I was coming to you. You look very ill.   34

MRS. FORD   Nay, I'll ne'er believe that. I have to show 35 to the contrary.

MRS. PAGE   Faith, but you do, in my mind.

MRS. FORD   Well, I do, then. Yet I say I could show you to the contrary. O Mistress Page, give me some counsel!

MRS. PAGE   What's the matter, woman?

MRS. FORD   O woman, if it were not for one trifling respect, I could come to such honor!   43

2.1. Location: Before Page's house.
5 precisian strict adviser   **6 counselor** practical guide   **7 sympathy** congeniality, agreement   **8 sack** a Spanish wine   **20 Herod of Jewry** bombastic ranter, like the comic villain of the Corpus Christi plays **22 unweighed** ill-considered   **23 Flemish drunkard** (The Flemish were proverbially heavy drinkers.)   **24 conversation** conduct   **25 assay** accost, address (with proposals of love)   **26 should I say** could I have said   **27 exhibit** introduce   **28 putting down** suppression (but with bawdy suggestion)   **30 puddings** mixture of meat, herbs, etc., stuffed into intestines of animals, as sausage   **31 Trust me** believe me   **34 ill** unhappy, out of sorts. (But Mistress Ford, in replying, plays on the sense of "ugly.")   **35 have** have something, i.e., the letter   **43 respect** matter, consideration

119 An (The Folio uses the same spelling, *An*, for *Anne*, in lines 120 and 121, suggesting a pun on *Anne Page;* Caius is to have a fool's head for wooing Anne.)   **124 trow** wonder.   **Come near** enter **130 honest** chaste   **131 gentle** well-bred.   **your friend** friendly disposed toward you   **136–137 a book** i.e., a Bible   **140–141 it . . . Nan** i.e., Anne is so remarkable a girl; so lively and merry   **141 detest** (For "protest.")   **143 but** except   **144 allicholy** (For "melancholy.")   **145 go to** i.e., enough; come, come   **147 voice** word of support   **151 confidence** (For "conference," blurred here with the notion of confiding.)   **156 Out upon 't** i.e., deuce take it

MRS. PAGE   Hang the trifle, woman, take the honor. What is it? Dispense with trifles. What is it?

MRS. FORD   If I would but go to hell for an eternal moment or so, I could be knighted.

MRS. PAGE   What? Thou liest! Sir Alice Ford? These knights will hack, and so thou shouldst not alter the 49 article of thy gentry. 50

MRS. FORD   We burn daylight. Here, read, read. Perceive 51 how I might be knighted. [*She gives a letter.*] I shall think the worse of fat men as long as I have an eye to make difference of men's liking. And yet he would not 54 swear, praised women's modesty, and gave such 55 orderly and well-behaved reproof to all uncomeliness 56 that I would have sworn his disposition would have gone to the truth of his words. But they do no more 58 adhere and keep place together than the Hundredth Psalm to the tune of "Greensleeves." What tempest, I 60 trow, threw this whale, with so many tuns of oil in his 61 belly, ashore at Windsor? How shall I be revenged on him? I think the best way were to entertain him with 63 hope, till the wicked fire of lust have melted him in his 64 own grease. Did you ever hear the like?

MRS. PAGE   Letter for letter, but that the name of Page and Ford differs! To thy great comfort in this mystery 67 of ill opinions, here's the twin brother of thy letter. 68 [*She shows her letter.*] But let thine inherit first, for I 69 protest mine never shall. I warrant he hath a thousand of these letters, writ with blank space for different names—sure, more—and these are of the second edition. He will print them, out of doubt; for he cares 73 not what he puts into the press, when he would put 74 us two. I had rather be a giantess and lie under Mount Pelion. Well, I will find you twenty lascivious turtles 76 ere one chaste man.

MRS. FORD [*comparing the letters*]   Why, this is the very same: the very hand, the very words. What doth he think of us?

MRS. PAGE   Nay, I know not. It makes me almost ready to wrangle with mine own honesty. I'll entertain my- 82 self like one that I am not acquainted withal; for, sure, 83 unless he know some strain in me that I know not 84

myself, he would never have boarded me in this fury. 85

MRS. FORD   "Boarding," call you it? I'll be sure to keep him above deck.

MRS. PAGE   So will I. If he come under my hatches, I'll never to sea again. Let's be revenged on him. Let's appoint him a meeting, give him a show of comfort in his suit, and lead him on with a fine-baited delay till 91 he hath pawned his horses to mine Host of the Garter.

MRS. FORD   Nay, I will consent to act any villainy 93 against him that may not sully the chariness of our 94 honesty. O, that my husband saw this letter! It would 95 give eternal food to his jealousy.

MRS. PAGE   Why, look where he comes, and my good- 97 man too. He's as far from jealousy as I am from giving 98 him cause, and that, I hope, is an unmeasurable distance.

MRS. FORD   You are the happier woman.

MRS. PAGE   Let's consult together against this greasy knight. Come hither.   [*They retire.*]

[*Enter*] *Master Page* [*with*] *Nym, Master Ford* [*with*] *Pistol.*

FORD   Well, I hope it be not so.

PISTOL
   Hope is a curtal dog in some affairs. 105
   Sir John affects thy wife. 106

FORD   Why, sir, my wife is not young.

PISTOL
   He woos both high and low, both rich and poor,
   Both young and old, one with another, Ford.
   He loves the gallimaufry. Ford, perpend. 110

FORD   Love my wife?

PISTOL
   With liver burning hot. Prevent, or go thou, 112
   Like Sir Actaeon, he, with Ringwood at thy heels.— 113
   O, odious is the name! 114

FORD   What name, sir?

PISTOL   The horn, I say. Farewell.
   Take heed, have open eye, for thieves do foot by night. 117
   Take heed, ere summer comes or cuckoo birds do sing. 118
   Away, Sir Corporal Nym! 119
   Believe it, Page, he speaks sense.   [*Exit.*]

FORD [*aside*]   I will be patient. I will find out this. 121

---

49 **hack** (Of uncertain meaning; perhaps "fight with swords," together with a play on the idea of sexual intercourse; see also *to hick and to hack*, 4.1.61. Mistress Page suggests that knights are likely to behave promiscuously.)   50 **article of thy gentry** character of your rank   51 **burn daylight** i.e., waste time   54 **make . . . liking** discriminate among men's looks and physiques   54–55 **would not swear** i.e., decorously avoided all profanity in my presence   56 **uncomeliness** unseemly behavior   58 **gone . . . of** supported, accorded with   60 **Greensleeves** (A popular tune, to which many sets of words have been sung, some of them erotic; compare 5.5.19.)   61 **trow** wonder. **tuns** (1) large casks (2) tons   63–64 **entertain . . . hope** lead him on   67–68 **mystery of ill opinions** i.e., situation in which Falstaff seems to have formed a low opinion of their virtue for no apparent reason   69 **inherit** come into possession, as of a legacy (since it is the "older" letter)   73 **out of** without   74 **into the press** (1) into the printing press (2) under his weight   76 **Pelion** mountain in Thessaly. (The giants, according to Greek mythology, heaped it on a neighboring mountain, Ossa, and Ossa on Olympus, in their attempts to overthrow the gods.)   **turtles** turtledoves, proverbially chaste, i.e., faithful to their mates   82 **wrangle** quarrel. **honesty** chastity. **entertain** treat   83 **withal** with   84 **strain** quality

85 **boarded** accosted, made advances to. (A term of naval warfare.)   91 **fine-baited** i.e., subtly alluring   93 **Nay** i.e., indeed, what's more   94 **chariness** scrupulous integrity   95 **that** if only   97–98 **goodman** husband   105 **curtal** having the tail docked. (A term of opprobrium or condescension.)   106 **affects** loves, aims at   110 **gallimaufry** a dish of miscellaneous ingredients; hence, the whole lot.   **perpend** consider   112 **liver burning hot** (Allusion to the liver as the seat of the passions.)   113 **Actaeon** huntsman who was changed into a stag by Diana as punishment for watching her and her nymphs at their bath and was torn to pieces by his own hounds. (Pistol urges Ford to avoid the fate of the horned beast: that of wearing a cuckold's horns.)   **Ringwood** one of Actaeon's hounds (mentioned in Golding's translation of Ovid)   114 **the name** i.e., the name of Actaeon or cuckold   117 **foot** walk   118 **cuckoo birds** (Associated with cuckoldry because of their call, "cuckoo," and because they lay eggs in other birds' nests.)   119 **Away** come away   121 **find out** make inquiry into

NYM [*to Page*]   And this is true. I like not the humor of
lying. He hath wronged me in some humors. I 123
should have borne the humored letter to her; but I 124
have a sword, and it shall bite upon my necessity. 125
He loves your wife; there's the short and the long.
My name is Corporal Nym. I speak and I avouch 'tis
true. My name is Nym, and Falstaff loves your wife.
Adieu. I love not the humor of bread and cheese, 129
and there's the humor of it. Adieu.

PAGE [*aside*]   "The humor of it," quoth 'a! Here's a 131
fellow frights English out of his wits.   132

FORD [*aside*]   I will seek out Falstaff.

PAGE [*aside*]   I never heard such a drawling, affecting 134
rogue.

FORD [*aside*]   If I do find it—well.   136

PAGE [*aside*]   I will not believe such a Cathayan, though 137
the priest o' the town commended him for a true man.

FORD [*aside*]   'Twas a good sensible fellow. Well.

[*Mistress Page and Mistress Ford come forward.*]

PAGE   How now, Meg?

MRS. PAGE   Whither go you, George? Hark you.
                              [*They converse apart.*]

MRS. FORD   How now, sweet Frank, why art thou
melancholy?

FORD   I melancholy? I am not melancholy. Get you
home, go.

MRS. FORD   Faith, thou hast some crotchets in thy head 146
now.—Will you go, Mistress Page?

MRS. PAGE Have with you. You'll come to dinner, George? 148

[*Enter Mistress*] Quickly.

[*Aside to Mistress Ford.*] Look who comes yonder. She
shall be our messenger to this paltry knight.

MRS. FORD [*aside to Mistress Page*]   Trust me, I thought
on her. She'll fit it.   152

MRS. PAGE [*to Mistress Quickly*]   You are come to see
my daughter Anne?

QUICKLY   Ay, forsooth; and, I pray, how does good Mistress Anne?

MRS. PAGE   Go in with us and see. We have an hour's
talk with you.
              [*Exeunt Mistress Page, Mistress Ford, and Mistress
                                        Quickly.*]

PAGE   How now, Master Ford?

FORD   You heard what this knave told me, did you not?

PAGE   Yes, and you heard what the other told me?

FORD   Do you think there is truth in them?

PAGE   Hang 'em, slaves! I do not think the knight would
offer it. But these that accuse him in his intent towards 164
our wives are a yoke of his discarded men—very 165
rogues, now they be out of service.

FORD   Were they his men?

PAGE   Marry, were they.

FORD   I like it never the better for that. Does he lie at the 169
Garter?

PAGE   Ay, marry, does he. If he should intend this 171
voyage toward my wife, I would turn her loose to him;
and what he gets more of her than sharp words, let it
lie on my head.   174

FORD   I do not misdoubt my wife, but I would be loath 175
to turn them together. A man may be too confident. I 176
would have nothing lie on my head. I cannot be thus
satisfied.

[*Enter*] Host.

PAGE   Look where my ranting Host of the Garter comes. 179
There is either liquor in his pate or money in his purse
when he looks so merrily.—How now, mine Host?

HOST   How now, bullyrook? Thou'rt a gentleman. [*He
turns and calls.*] Cavaleiro Justice, I say!   183

[*Enter*] Shallow.

SHALLOW   I follow, mine Host, I follow.—Good even 184
and twenty, good Master Page! Master Page, will you 185
go with us? We have sport in hand.

HOST   Tell him, cavaleiro justice. Tell him, bullyrook.

SHALLOW   Sir, there is a fray to be fought between Sir
Hugh the Welsh priest and Caius the French doctor.

FORD   Good mine Host o' the Garter, a word with you.

HOST   What sayst thou, my bullyrook?
                              [*They converse apart.*]

SHALLOW [*to Page*]   Will you go with us to behold it?
My merry Host hath had the measuring of their weap- 193
ons, and, I think, hath appointed them contrary 194
places; for, believe me, I hear the parson is no jester. 195
Hark, I will tell you what our sport shall be.
                              [*They converse apart.*]

HOST [*to Ford*]   Hast thou no suit against my knight,
my guest cavalier?

FORD   None, I protest. But I'll give you a pottle of burnt 199
sack to give me recourse to him and tell him my name 200
is Brook—only for a jest.   201

HOST   My hand, bully. Thou shalt have egress and
regress—said I well?—and thy name shall be Brook.
It is a merry knight.—Will you go, mynheers?   204

SHALLOW   Have with you, mine Host.   205

123–124 I . . . borne i.e., he wanted me to carry   125 upon my
necessity when I have need   129 humor . . . cheese (Alludes to the
scant rations Nym received as Falstaff's retainer.)   131 'a he   132 his
its   134 affecting affected   136 If . . . well if I find it's true, well,
I'll take steps   137 Cathayan person from Cathay, i.e., China; hence,
sharper, scoundrel   146 crotchets whims, fancies   148 Have with
you I'll go along with you   152 She'll fit it she is just the person for
the part   164 offer venture   165 yoke pair

169 lie lodge   171 intend propose making   174 lie on my head be
my responsibility. (But Ford, in his reply, sees a joke on cuckold's
horns.)   175 misdoubt mistrust   176 turn them together i.e., let
them loose together in the same pasture, as in line 172 above
179 ranting speaking in a high-flown, bombastic style   183 Cavaleiro Justice gallant justice. (Put here in the form of an honorific title.
A Spanish caballero is a gentleman trained in arms.)   184–185 Good
. . . twenty i.e., good afternoon, many times over   193–194 hath
had . . . weapons i.e., has been appointed referee   194–195 contrary places different meeting places   199 protest insist.   pottle two-
quart measure.   burnt heated   200 recourse access   201 Brook
(Ford's alias, usually spelled Brooke in the 1602 Quarto, was changed
to Broome—as it is spelled in the Folio—because Brooke was the
family name of Lord Cobham. See Introduction.)   204 mynheers gentlemen. (Dutch.)   205 Have with you I'll come with you. (Also in
line 215.)

PAGE I have heard the Frenchman hath good skill in his
rapier.

SHALLOW Tut, sir, I could have told you more. In these
times you stand on distance—your passes, stoccados, 209
and I know not what. 'Tis the heart, Master Page; 'tis 210
here, 'tis here. I have seen the time, with my long 211
sword I would have made you four tall fellows skip 212
like rats.

HOST Here, boys, here, here! Shall we wag?   214

PAGE Have with you. I had rather hear them scold than
fight.   *Exeunt* [*Host, Shallow, and Page*].

FORD Though Page be a secure fool, and stands so 217
firmly on his wife's frailty, yet I cannot put off my
opinion so easily. She was in his company at Page's 219
house, and what they made there I know not. Well, I 220
will look further into 't, and I have a disguise to sound 221
Falstaff. If I find her honest, I lose not my labor; if she
be otherwise, 'tis labor well bestowed.   [*Exit.*]

❖

2.2   *Enter Falstaff* [*and*] *Pistol.*

FALSTAFF I will not lend thee a penny.

PISTOL
Why, then the world's mine oyster,
Which I with sword will open.
I will retort the sum in equipage.   4

FALSTAFF Not a penny. I have been content, sir, you
should lay my countenance to pawn. I have grated 6
upon my good friends for three reprieves for you and 7
your coach-fellow Nym, or else you had looked 8
through the grate like a gemini of baboons. I am 9
damned in hell for swearing to gentlemen my friends 10
you were good soldiers and tall fellows. And when 11
Mistress Bridget lost the handle of her fan, I took 't 12
upon mine honor thou hadst it not.   13

PISTOL
Didst not thou share? Hadst thou not fifteen pence?

FALSTAFF Reason, you rogue, reason. Think'st thou I'll 15
endanger my soul gratis? At a word, hang no more
about me. I am no gibbet for you. Go. A short knife 17
and a throng! To your manor of Pickt-hatch, go. You'll 18

209 **you stand on distance** one relies on and attaches great importance to prescribed space between fencers. **passes** lunges. **stoccados** thrusts 210–211 **'Tis . . . 'tis here** i.e., real fencing, Master
Page, is a matter of the heart, not of this affected modern etiquette.
(Shallow perhaps taps his chest as he says, "'Tis here.")
211–212 **long sword** an old-fashioned, heavy weapon 212 **tall** valiant 214 **wag** go. (See 1.3.6.) 217 **secure** overconfident 219 **She**
i.e., Mistress Ford. **his** i.e., Falstaff's 220 **made** did 221 **sound**
plumb
2.2. Location: The Garter Inn.
4 **retort . . . equipage** i.e., pay back the whole amount in military
equipment 6 **lay . . . pawn** i.e., borrow money on the strength of
my patronage 6–7 **grated upon** i.e., persistently and irritatingly
begged 8 **coach-fellow** partner (like a fellow horse in harness)
9 **grate** i.e., of a debtors' prison window. **gemini** pair 10 **gentlemen my friends** my gentlemen friends 11 **tall** brave 12–13 **took 't
upon** swore by 15 **Reason** with good reason 17–18 **A short . . .
throng** i.e., with a short knife you might cut purses in a crowd
18 **Pickt-hatch** (A quarter in London, notorious in Elizabethan times
for criminal types and prostitutes, the houses having hatches, or half
doors, guarded with spikes.)

not bear a letter for me, you rogue? You stand upon
your honor? Why, thou unconfinable baseness, it is as 20
much as I can do to keep the terms of my honor 21
precise. Ay, ay, I myself sometimes, leaving the fear of 22
God on the left hand and hiding mine honor in my 23
necessity, am fain to shuffle, to hedge, and to lurch; 24
and yet you, you rogue, will ensconce your rags, your
cat-a-mountain looks, your red-lattice phrases, and 26
your bold-beating oaths, under the shelter of your 27
honor! You will not do it? You?

PISTOL
I do relent. What would thou more of man?

[*Enter*] *Robin.*

ROBIN Sir, here's a woman would speak with you.

FALSTAFF Let her approach.

[*Enter Mistress*] *Quickly.*

QUICKLY Give your worship good morrow.

FALSTAFF Good morrow, goodwife.

QUICKLY Not so, an 't please your worship.   34

FALSTAFF Good maid, then.

QUICKLY I'll be sworn: as my mother was, the first 36
hour I was born.   37

FALSTAFF I do believe the swearer. What with me?

QUICKLY Shall I vouchsafe your worship a word or two? 39

FALSTAFF Two thousand, fair woman, and I'll vouchsafe
thee the hearing.

QUICKLY There is one Mistress Ford, sir—I pray, come
a little nearer this ways. I myself dwell with Master
Doctor Caius—

FALSTAFF Well, on. Mistress Ford, you say—

QUICKLY Your worship says very true. I pray your
worship, come a little nearer this ways.

FALSTAFF I warrant thee, nobody hears. Mine own
people, mine own people.

QUICKLY Are they so? God bless them and make them
His servants!

FALSTAFF Well; Mistress Ford: what of her?

QUICKLY Why, sir, she's a good creature. Lord, Lord,
your worship's a wanton! Well, heaven forgive you
and all of us, I pray!

FALSTAFF Mistress Ford; come, Mistress Ford—

QUICKLY Marry, this is the short and the long of it: you
have brought her into such a canaries as 'tis wonder- 58
ful. The best courtier of them all, when the court lay at 59

20 **unconfinable** infinite 21 **terms** condition 22 **precise** pure. (A
term often associated with puritanism.) 22–23 **leaving . . . hand**
i.e., disregarding a proper fear of God 24 **fain . . . lurch** obliged to
practice trickery, to dodge, and to steal 26 **cat-a-mountain** cata-
mount, leopard or panther, wildcat. **red-lattice phrases** alehouse
talk. (Lattices painted red identified an alehouse.) 27 **bold-beating**
(Perhaps a conflation of "bold-faced" and "brow-beating.") 34 **Not
so** i.e., I am not a wife. **an 't** if it 36 **I'll be sworn** I'll swear to that
36–37 **as . . . born** (Mistress Quickly probably means "as much a
maid as when I was born, just like my mother before me," but what
she says is quite the opposite.) 39 **vouchsafe** deign to grant. (Used
with comical incorrectness here.) 58 **canaries** state of excitement.
(Confusing "quandary" with the dance called the canary?) 59 **lay**
resided

Windsor, could never have brought her to such a canary. Yet there has been knights, and lords, and gentlemen, with their coaches, I warrant you, coach after coach, letter after letter, gift after gift, smelling so sweetly, all musk, and so rushling, I warrant you, in 64 silk and gold, and in such alligant terms, and in such 65 wine and sugar of the best and the fairest, that would have won any woman's heart; and, I warrant you, they could never get an eye-wink of her. I had myself twenty angels given me this morning; but I defy all 69 angels, in any such sort, as they say, but in the way of 70 honesty; and, I warrant you, they could never get her so much as sip on a cup with the proudest of them all. And yet there has been earls, nay, which is more, pensioners, but I warrant you all is one with her.   74

FALSTAFF   But what says she to me? Be brief, my good she-Mercury.   76

QUICKLY   Marry, she hath received your letter, for the which she thanks you a thousand times, and she gives 78 you to notify that her husband will be absence from 79 his house between ten and eleven.

FALSTAFF   Ten and eleven?

QUICKLY   Ay, forsooth; and then you may come and see the picture, she says, that you wot of. Master Ford, her 83 husband, will be from home. Alas, the sweet woman leads an ill life with him. He's a very jealousy man. She leads a very frampold life with him, good heart.   86

FALSTAFF   Ten and eleven. Woman, commend me to her. I will not fail her.

QUICKLY   Why, you say well. But I have another mes- 89 senger to your worship. Mistress Page hath her hearty 90 commendations to you, too; and let me tell you in your ear, she's as fartuous a civil modest wife, and one, I 92 tell you, that will not miss you morning nor evening 93 prayer, as any is in Windsor, whoe'er be the other. And she bade me tell your worship that her husband is seldom from home, but she hopes there will come a time. I never knew a woman so dote upon a man. Surely I think you have charms, la! Yes, in truth.   98

FALSTAFF   Not I, I assure thee. Setting the attraction of my good parts aside, I have no other charms.   100

QUICKLY   Blessing on your heart for 't!

FALSTAFF   But, I pray thee, tell me this: has Ford's wife and Page's wife acquainted each other how they love me?

QUICKLY   That were a jest indeed! They have not so little grace, I hope. That were a trick indeed! But Mistress Page would desire you to send her your little page, of 107 all loves. Her husband has a marvelous infection to the 108 little page; and truly Master Page is an honest man.   109

Never a wife in Windsor leads a better life than she does. Do what she will, say what she will, take all, pay all, go to bed when she list, rise when she list—all is 112 as she will. And truly she deserves it, for if there be a kind woman in Windsor, she is one. You must send her your page, no remedy.   115

FALSTAFF   Why, I will.

QUICKLY   Nay, but do so, then. And, look you, he may come and go between you both. And in any case have a nayword, that you may know one another's mind, 119 and the boy never need to understand anything; for 'tis not good that children should know any wicked- ness. Old folks, you know, have discretion, as they say, and know the world.

FALSTAFF   Fare thee well. Commend me to them both. There's my purse; I am yet thy debtor. [*He gives money.*] Boy, go along with this woman. [*Exeunt Mistress Quickly and Robin.*] This news distracts me!   127

PISTOL [*aside*]
This punk is one of Cupid's carriers.   128
Clap on more sails! Pursue! Up with your fights!   129
Give fire! She is my prize, or ocean whelm them all!   130
                                          [*Exit.*]

FALSTAFF   Sayst thou so, old Jack? Go thy ways. I'll 131 make more of thy old body than I have done. Will they yet look after thee? Wilt thou, after the expense of so much money, be now a gainer? Good body, I thank thee. Let them say 'tis grossly done; so it be fairly 135 done, no matter.

[*Enter*] Bardolph [*with wine*].

BARDOLPH   Sir John, there's one Master Brook below would fain speak with you and be acquainted with you, and hath sent your worship a morning's draft of sack.

FALSTAFF   Brook is his name?

BARDOLPH   Ay, sir.

FALSTAFF   Call him in. Such Brooks are welcome to me, that o'erflows such liquor. [*Exit Bardolph.*] Aha! Mis- tress Ford and Mistress Page, have I encompassed 145 you? Go to. *Via!*   146

[*Enter Bardolph, with*] Ford [*disguised*].

FORD   Bless you, sir.

FALSTAFF   And you, sir. Would you speak with me?

FORD   I make bold to press with so little preparation 149 upon you.

FALSTAFF   You're welcome. What's your will? [*To Bar- dolph.*] Give us leave, drawer.   [*Exit Bardolph.*] 152

---

64 rushling i.e., rustling   **65 alligant** i.e., elegant, or eloquent (?)
69 twenty angels i.e., as a bribe to act as go-between. *Angels* are gold coins.   **defy** reject, spurn   **70 sort** manner   **74 pensioners** gen- tlemen bodyguards to a sovereign in the royal palace   **76 she-Mer- cury** woman messenger   **78–79 gives you to notify** bids you take no- tice   **79 absence** (For "absent.")   **83 wot** know   **86 frampold** disagreeable   **89–90 messenger** (For "message.")   **92 fartuous** (For "virtuous.")   **modest** decent, proper   **93 miss you** miss. (*You* is used colloquially.)   **98 have charms** use magic   **100 parts** qualities   **107– 108 of all loves** for love's sake   **108 infection to** (For "affection for.")
109 an honest a worthy

112 list wishes   **115 no remedy** no two ways about it   **119 nayword** watchword   **127 distracts** bewilders (with ecstasy)   **128 punk** whore.
carriers messengers   **129 Clap** put.   **fights** fighting sails, i.e., screens raised during naval engagements to conceal and protect the crew
130 prize booty.   **ocean whelm** let the ocean overwhelm. (Pistol evi- dently has designs on Mistress Quickly, though they do not material- ize in this play.)   **131 Sayst . . . ways** i.e., What do you think of that, Jack, my boy? Not bad.   **135 grossly** clumsily, badly (with pun on "corpulently").   **so** provided that.   **fairly** successfully, fortunately
145–146 encompassed you got round you, taken you in   **146 Go to** i.e., well, then!   **Via** go on. (A shout of encouragement.)   **149 prep- aration** advance notice   **152 Give us leave** i.e., leave us alone.
drawer tapster

FORD   Sir, I am a gentleman that have spent much. My name is Brook.

FALSTAFF   Good Master Brook, I desire more acquaintance of you.

FORD   Good Sir John, I sue for yours—not to charge 157 you, for I must let you understand I think myself in 158 better plight for a lender than you are, the which hath something emboldened me to this unseasoned intru- 160 sion; for they say if money go before, all ways do lie open.

FALSTAFF   Money is a good soldier, sir, and will on.

FORD   Troth, and I have a bag of money here troubles me. If you will help to bear it, Sir John, take all, or half, for easing me of the carriage. 166

FALSTAFF   Sir, I know not how I may deserve to be your porter.

FORD   I will tell you, sir, if you will give me the hearing.

FALSTAFF   Speak, good Master Brook. I shall be glad to be your servant.

FORD   Sir, I hear you are a scholar—I will be brief with you—and you have been a man long known to me, though I had never so good means as desire to make myself acquainted with you. I shall discover a thing to 175 you wherein I must very much lay open mine own imperfection. But, good Sir John, as you have one eye upon my follies, as you hear them unfolded, turn another into the register of your own, that I may pass 179 with a reproof the easier, sith you yourself know how 180 easy it is to be such an offender.

FALSTAFF   Very well, sir. Proceed.

FORD   There is a gentlewoman in this town; her husband's name is Ford.

FALSTAFF   Well, sir.

FORD   I have long loved her, and, I protest to you, bestowed much on her, followed her with a doting ob- 187 servance, engrossed opportunities to meet her, fee'd 188 every slight occasion that could but niggardly give me sight of her, not only bought many presents to give her but have given largely to many to know what she 191 would have given. Briefly, I have pursued her as love 192 hath pursued me, which hath been on the wing of all occasions. But whatsoever I have merited—either in my mind or in my means—meed I am sure I have 195 received none, unless experience be a jewel. That I have purchased at an infinite rate, and that hath taught me to say this:

"Love like a shadow flies when substance love pursues, 199
Pursuing that that flies, and flying what pursues." 200

FALSTAFF   Have you received no promise of satisfaction at her hands?

FORD   Never.

FALSTAFF   Have you importuned her to such a purpose?

FORD   Never.

FALSTAFF   Of what quality was your love, then?

FORD   Like a fair house built on another man's ground, so that I have lost my edifice by mistaking the place where I erected it.

FALSTAFF   To what purpose have you unfolded this to me?

FORD   When I have told you that, I have told you all. Some say that though she appear honest to me, yet in 213 other places she enlargeth her mirth so far that there is 214 shrewd construction made of her. Now, Sir John, here 215 is the heart of my purpose. You are a gentleman of excellent breeding, admirable discourse, of great ad- 217 mittance, authentic in your place and person, gener- 218 ally allowed for your many warlike, courtlike, and 219 learned preparations. 220

FALSTAFF   O, sir!

FORD   Believe it, for you know it. There is money. Spend it, spend it; spend more; spend all I have. [*He offers money.*] Only give me so much of your time in exchange of it as to lay an amiable siege to the honesty of 225 this Ford's wife. Use your art of wooing; win her to consent to you. If any man may, you may as soon as any.

FALSTAFF   Would it apply well to the vehemency of your affection that I should win what you would enjoy? Methinks you prescribe to yourself very preposterously.

FORD   O, understand my drift. She dwells so securely on the excellency of her honor that the folly of my soul dares not present itself; she is too bright to be looked against. Now, could I come to her with any detection 236 in my hand, my desires had instance and argument to 237 commend themselves. I could drive her then from the ward of her purity, her reputation, her marriage vow, 239 and a thousand other her defenses, which now are too 240 too strongly embattled against me. What say you to 't, Sir John?

FALSTAFF   Master Brook, I will first make bold with your money; next, give me your hand; and last, as I am a gentleman, you shall, if you will, enjoy Ford's wife.
[*He accepts the money and takes Ford's hand.*]

FORD   O, good sir!

FALSTAFF   I say you shall.

FORD   Want no money, Sir John, you shall want none. 248

FALSTAFF   Want no Mistress Ford, Master Brook, you shall want none. I shall be with her, I may tell you, by her own appointment. Even as you came in to me, her assistant or go-between parted from me. I say I shall be with her between ten and eleven, for at that time

157–158 charge you put you to expense   **160 something** somewhat. **unseasoned** unseasonable   **166 the carriage** the carrying of it **175 discover** reveal   **179 register** record   **180 sith** since   **187– 188 observance** attentiveness   **188 engrossed** seized. **fee'd** purchased   **191 largely** generously   **191–192 what . . . given** what she would like to have given to her   **195 meed** reward **199–200 Love . . . pursues** i.e., love runs away when pursued but pursues when run away from, just as a shadow seems to run away from a body (a *substance*) running in its direction but follows a body running the other way. (Proverbial.)

213 honest chaste   **214 enlargeth** gives free scope to   **215 shrewd construction** malicious interpretation   **217–218 of great admittance** i.e., widely received in society   **218 authentic** entitled to respect **219 allowed** acknowledged and approved   **220 preparations** accomplishments   **225 of it** for it.   **amiable** amorous   **236 against** directly toward (like looking at the sun)   **237 had instance** would have proof and precedent   **239 ward** defensive posture in fencing   **240 other her defenses** other defenses of hers   **248 Want** lack

the jealous rascally knave her husband will be forth. 254
Come you to me at night; you shall know how I
speed. 256

FORD   I am blest in your acquaintance. Do you know
Ford, sir?

FALSTAFF   Hang him, poor cuckoldly knave! I know him
not. Yet I wrong him to call him poor. They say the
jealous wittolly knave hath masses of money, for the 261
which his wife seems to me well-favored. I will use her 262
as the key of the cuckoldly rogue's coffer, and there's
my harvest home. 264

FORD   I would you knew Ford, sir, that you might avoid
him if you saw him.

FALSTAFF   Hang him, mechanical salt-butter rogue! I 267
will stare him out of his wits. I will awe him with my
cudgel; it shall hang like a meteor o'er the cuckold's 269
horns. Master Brook, thou shalt know I will predomi- 270
nate over the peasant, and thou shalt lie with his wife. 271
Come to me soon at night. Ford's a knave, and I will
aggravate his style: thou, Master Brook, shalt know 273
him for knave and cuckold. Come to me soon at night.
[Exit.]

FORD   What a damned Epicurean rascal is this! My heart 275
is ready to crack with impatience. Who says this is
improvident jealousy? My wife hath sent to him, the
hour is fixed, the match is made. Would any man
have thought this? See the hell of having a false
woman! My bed shall be abused, my coffers ransacked, my reputation gnawn at; and I shall not only
receive this villainous wrong but stand under the 282
adoption of abominable terms, and by him that does 283
me this wrong. Terms! Names! "Amaimon" sounds 284
well, "Lucifer" well, "Barbason" well, yet they are 285
devils' additions, the names of fiends. But "Cuckold!" 286
"Wittol!"—"Cuckold!" The devil himself hath not
such a name. Page is an ass, a secure ass. He will trust 288
his wife; he will not be jealous. I will rather trust a
Fleming with my butter, Parson Hugh the Welshman
with my cheese, an Irishman with my aqua vitae 291
bottle, or a thief to walk my ambling gelding, than my 292
wife with herself. Then she plots, then she ruminates,
then she devises; and what they think in their hearts
they may effect, they will break their hearts but they
will effect. Heaven be praised for my jealousy! Eleven
o'clock the hour. I will prevent this, detect my wife, be 297
revenged on Falstaff, and laugh at Page. I will about it;

better three hours too soon than a minute too late. Fie,
fie, fie! Cuckold, cuckold, cuckold!   *Exit.*

2.3   *Enter Caius [and] Rugby.*

CAIUS   Jack Rugby!
RUGBY   Sir?
CAIUS   Vat is de clock, Jack?
RUGBY   'Tis past the hour, sir, that Sir Hugh promised
to meet.
CAIUS   By gar, he has save his soul dat he is no come; he
has pray his Pible well dat he is no come. By gar, Jack
Rugby, he is dead already if he be come.
RUGBY   He is wise, sir. He knew your worship would
kill him if he came.
CAIUS   By gar, de herring is no dead so as I vill kill him. 11
Take your rapier, Jack. I vill tell you how I vill kill him.
RUGBY   Alas, sir, I cannot fence.
CAIUS   Villainy, take your rapier. 14
RUGBY   Forbear. Here's company.

[Enter] Page, Shallow, Slender, [and] Host.

HOST   Bless thee, bully Doctor!
SHALLOW   Save you, Master Doctor Caius! 17
PAGE   Now, good Master Doctor!
SLENDER   Give you good morrow, sir.
CAIUS   Vat be all you, one, two, tree, four, come for?
HOST   To see thee fight, to see thee foin, to see thee 21
traverse; to see thee here, to see thee there; to see thee 22
pass thy punto, thy stock, thy reverse, thy distance, 23
thy montant. Is he dead, my Ethiopian? Is he dead, 24
my Francisco? Ha, bully? What says my Aesculapius, 25
my Galen, my heart of elder, ha? Is he dead, bully 26
stale? Is he dead? 27
CAIUS   By gar, he is de coward jack priest of de vorld.
He is not show his face.
HOST   Thou art a Castilian King-Urinal. Hector of 30
Greece, my boy!
CAIUS   I pray you, bear witness that me have stay six or
seven, two, tree hours for him, and he is no come.

2.3. Location: A field near Windsor.
11 no dead so not so dead. (Compare with "dead as a herring.")
14 Villainy i.e., villain   **17 Save** God save   **21 foin** thrust
22 traverse march back and forth, or from side to side   **23–24 pass
. . . montant** employ your stroke or thrust with the point of the
sword, your stoccado or thrust, your backhand stroke, your keeping
of the prescribed distance between contestants, your upright thrust
24 Ethiopian i.e., one of dark complexion (?)   **25 Francisco** i.e.,
Frenchman.   **Aesculapius** i.e., doctor. (Literally, Greek god of medicine.)   **26 Galen** famous Greek physician.   **heart of elder** i.e., opposite of "heart of oak"; the elder has no heart (though Caius, with his
halting English, presumably is unaware of the insult)   **27 stale** i.e.,
Doctor. (Literally, "urine," which is used to make medical diagnosis;
see also *urinal* in Host's next speech, and *Mockwater*, lines 51–52. A
stale is also a dupe.)   **30 Castilian** i.e., Spanish. (An insulting term in
a time of war with Spain, though Caius, with his imperfect English,
is presumably oblivious of this. The term also suggests *Castalian* [Folio:
Castalion], relating to the sacred spring on Mount Parnassus.)   **Urinal**
(Comically appropriate to a doctor, who uses urine for diagnosis.)
Hector chief warrior of ancient Troy (not Greece)

---

254 **forth** away from home   256 **speed** succeed   261 **wittolly** willingly cuckolded   261–262 **for the which** for which reason
262 **well-favored** attractive   264 **harvest home** occasion for reaping a
profit   267 **mechanical** i.e., base. (Literally, one engaged in manual
occupation).   **salt-butter** butter preserved with salt, often old and of
inferior quality   269 **meteor** (An ominous sign.)   270–271 **predominate** be in the ascendancy. (An astrological term.)   273 **aggravate his
style** increase or add to his title (by adding *cuckold*)   275 **Epicurean**
pleasure-loving   282–283 **stand . . . terms** have to put up with being called names   284, 285 **Amaimon, Lucifer, Barbason** (Names of
devils; they occur in Scot's *Discovery of Witchcraft*, 1584.)   286 **additions** titles   288 **secure** overconfident   291 **aqua vitae** any strong
spirit like brandy. (Irish were known for their drinking, just as Welshmen for eating of cheese and Flemish for love of butter.)   292 **walk**
exercise   297 **prevent** come there before

SHALLOW   He is the wiser man, Master Doctor. He is a curer of souls, and you a curer of bodies. If you should fight, you go against the hair of your professions. Is it not true, Master Page? 36

PAGE   Master Shallow, you have yourself been a great fighter, though now a man of peace.

SHALLOW   Bodykins, Master Page, though I now be old 40 and of the peace, if I see a sword out, my finger itches to make one. Though we are justices and doctors and 42 churchmen, Master Page, we have some salt of our 43 youth in us. We are the sons of women, Master Page.

PAGE   'Tis true, Master Shallow.

SHALLOW   It will be found so, Master Page.—Master Doctor Caius, I am come to fetch you home. I am sworn of the peace. You have showed yourself a wise physician, and Sir Hugh hath shown himself a wise and patient churchman. You must go with me, Master Doctor.

HOST   Pardon, guest justice. A word, Monsieur Mock- 51 water. 52

CAIUS   Mockvater? Vat is dat?

HOST   "Mockwater," in our English tongue, is "valor," bully.

CAIUS   By gar, den, I have as mush mockvater as de Englishman. Scurvy jack-dog priest! By gar, me vill cut 57 his ears.

HOST   He will clapper-claw thee tightly, bully. 59

CAIUS   Clapper-de-claw? Vat is dat?

HOST   That is, he will make thee amends.

CAIUS   By gar, me do look he shall clapper-de-claw me, for, by gar, me vill have it.

HOST   And I will provoke him to 't, or let him wag. 64

CAIUS   Me tank you for dat.

HOST   And, moreover, bully—[aside to the others] but first, master guest and Master Page, and eke Cavaleiro Slender, go you through the town to Frogmore. 68

PAGE   Sir Hugh is there, is he?

HOST   He is there. See what humor he is in, and I will bring the Doctor about by the fields. Will it do well?

SHALLOW   We will do it.

PAGE, SHALLOW, AND SLENDER   Adieu, good Master Doctor.   [Exeunt Page, Shallow, and Slender.]

CAIUS [drawing his rapier]   By gar, me vill kill de priest, for he speak for a jackanape to Anne Page. 76

HOST   Let him die. But first, sheathe thy impatience; throw cold water on thy choler. Go about the fields with me through Frogmore. I will bring thee where Mistress Anne Page is, at a farmhouse a-feasting; and thou shalt woo her. Cried game? Said I well? 81

CAIUS [sheathing his rapier]   By gar, me dank you vor dat. By gar, I love you; and I shall procure-a you de good guest: de earl, de knight, de lords, de gentlemen, my patients.

HOST   For the which I will be thy adversary toward 86 Anne Page. Said I well?

CAIUS   By gar, 'tis good. Vell said.

HOST   Let us wag, then.

CAIUS   Come at my heels, Jack Rugby.   Exeunt.

3.1   *Enter Evans [and] Simple.*

EVANS   I pray you now, good Master Slender's serving-man, and friend Simple by your name, which way have you looked for Master Caius, that calls himself doctor of physic?

SIMPLE   Marry, sir, the Petty-ward, the Park-ward, 5 every way; Old Windsor way, and every way but the town way.

EVANS   I most fehemently desire you you will also look that way.

SIMPLE   I will, sir.   [Going aside.]

EVANS   Pless my soul, how full of cholers I am, and trempling of mind! I shall be glad if he have deceived me. How melancholies I am! I will knog his urinals 13 about his knave's costard when I have good opportu- 14 nities for the 'ork. Pless my soul!   [He sings.]
  "To shallow rivers, to whose falls 16
  Melodious birds sings madrigals;
  There will we make our peds of roses,
  And a thousand fragrant posies.
  To shallow—"
Mercy on me! I have a great dispositions to cry.
   [He sings.]
  "Melodious birds sing madrigals—
  Whenas I sat in Pabylon— 23
  And a thousand vagram posies. 24
  To shallow," etc.

   [Simple returns.]

SIMPLE   Yonder he is, coming this way, Sir Hugh.

EVANS   He's welcome.   [He sings.]
  "To shallow rivers, to whose falls—"
God prosper the right! What weapons is he?

SIMPLE   No weapons, sir. There comes my master, Master Shallow, and another gentleman, from Frogmore, over the stile, this way.

EVANS   Pray you, give me my gown; or else keep it in your arms.   [He reads in a book.]

   [Enter] Page, Shallow, [and] Slender.

SHALLOW   How now, Master Parson? Good morrow,

---

36 go . . . of i.e., act contrary to. (Literally, rub hair the wrong way.)   **40 Bodykins** i.e., by God's little body   **42 make one** join in   **43 salt** savor   **51 guest justice** i.e., a justice of the peace who is a paying guest in my inn. (Said to Shallow.)   **51–52 Mockwater** (See the note to line 27, above; said to Caius.)   **57 jack-dog** mongrel   **59 clapper-claw** thrash.   **tightly** soundly   **64 wag** go on his way, run for his life   **68 Frogmore** small village near Windsor   **76 for a jackanape** on behalf of an ape, i.e., Slender   **81 Cried game?** have I announced good sport? (A hunting cry.)

86 adversary (The Host again takes advantage of Caius' poor English; the expected word is "emissary" or "advocate.")
3.1. Location: A field near Frogmore.
5 the Petty-ward toward Windsor Petty (or Little) Park.   **the Park-ward** toward Windsor Great Park   **13 knog** knock   **14 costard** i.e., head. (Literally, apple.)   **16 To shallow rivers,** etc. (Lines from Marlowe's "Come live with me and be my love.")   **23 Whenas . . . Pabylon** (An insertion of a line from the metrical Psalms, number 137.)   **24 vagram** i.e., vagrant. (But Evans means "fragrant.")

good Sir Hugh. Keep a gamester from the dice and a 36
good student from his book, and it is wonderful. 37

SLENDER [aside]   Ah, sweet Anne Page!

PAGE   God save you, good Sir Hugh!

EVANS   God pless you from His mercy sake, all of you! 40

SHALLOW   What, the sword and the Word? Do you 41
study them both, Master Parson?

PAGE   And youthful still—in your doublet and hose 43
this raw rheumatic day?

EVANS   There is reasons and causes for it.

PAGE   We are come to you to do a good office, Master
Parson.

EVANS   Fery well. What is it?

PAGE   Yonder is a most reverend gentleman, who,
belike having received wrong by some person, is at 50
most odds with his own gravity and patience that ever
you saw.

SHALLOW   I have lived fourscore years and upward; I
never heard a man of his place, gravity, and learning
so wide of his own respect. 55

EVANS   What is he?

PAGE   I think you know him: Master Doctor Caius, the
renowned French physician.

EVANS   Got's will and His passion of my heart! I had as 59
lief you would tell me of a mess of porridge. 60

PAGE   Why?

EVANS   He has no more knowledge in Hibbocrates and 62
Galen—and he is a knave besides, a cowardly knave
as you would desires to be acquainted withal.

PAGE [to Shallow]   I warrant you, he's the man should 65
fight with him.

SLENDER [aside]   O sweet Anne Page!

SHALLOW   It appears so by his weapons. Keep them
asunder; here comes Doctor Caius. 69

[Enter] Host, Caius, [and] Rugby. [Evans and
Caius offer to fight.]

PAGE   Nay, good Master Parson, keep in your weapon.

SHALLOW   So do you, good Master Doctor.

HOST   Disarm them and let them question. Let them 72
keep their limbs whole and hack our English.

[Caius and Evans are disarmed.]

CAIUS [to Evans]   I pray you, let-a me speak a word
with your ear. Vherefore vill you not meet-a me?

EVANS [aside to Caius]   Pray you, use your patience.
[Aloud.] In good time.

CAIUS   By gar, you are de coward, de jack dog, john
ape.

EVANS [aside to Caius]   Pray you, let us not be
laughingstocks to other men's humors; I desire you
in friendship, and I will one way or other make you

amends. [Aloud.] I will knog your urinal about your
knave's cogscomb for missing your meetings and
appointments.

CAIUS   Diable! Jack Rugby—mine Host de Jarteer—
have I not stay for him to kill him? Have I not, at de 87
place I did appoint?

EVANS   As I am a Christians soul now, look you, this is
the place appointed. I'll be judgment by mine Host of 90
the Garter.

HOST   Peace, I say, Gallia and Gaul, French and Welsh, 92
soul curer and body curer!

CAIUS   Ay, dat is very good, excellent.

HOST   Peace, I say! Hear mine Host of the Garter. Am I
politic? Am I subtle? Am I a Machiavel? Shall I lose my 96
doctor? No, he gives me the potions and the motions. 97
Shall I lose my parson, my priest, my Sir Hugh? No,
he gives me the proverbs and the no-verbs. Give me 99
thy hand, terrestrial; so. Give me thy hand, celestial; 100
so. [He joins their hands.] Boys of art, I have deceived 101
you both; I have directed you to wrong places. Your
hearts are mighty, your skins are whole, and let burnt 103
sack be the issue. Come, lay their swords to pawn. 104
Follow me, lads of peace, follow, follow, follow.

SHALLOW   Trust me, a mad host. Follow, gentlemen, 106
follow.

SLENDER [aside]   O sweet Anne Page!

[Exeunt Shallow, Slender, Page, and Host.]

CAIUS   Ha, do I perceive dat? Have you make-a de sot 109
of us, ha, ha?

EVANS   This is well! He has made us his vloutingstog. I 111
desire you that we may be friends; and let us knog our
prains together to be revenge on this same scall, 113
scurvy, cogging companion, the Host of the Garter. 114

CAIUS   By gar, with all my heart. He promise to bring
me where is Anne Page. By gar, he deceive me too.

EVANS   Well, I will smite his noddles. Pray you, follow. 117

[Exeunt.]

✣

3.2   [Enter] Mistress Page [and] Robin.

MRS. PAGE   Nay, keep your way, little gallant. You were 1
wont to be a follower, but now you are a leader.
Whether had you rather, lead mine eyes or eye your 3
master's heels?

ROBIN   I had rather, forsooth, go before you like a man
than follow him like a dwarf.

36–37 Keep . . . wonderful i.e., it's as hard to keep a true student from his book as to keep a gamester from dice   40 from His mercy sake (The correct phrase is "for His mercy's sake.")   41 the Word i.e., the Bible   43 in . . . hose i.e., without a cloak, in close-fitting jacket and breeches   50 belike it would seem   55 wide . . . respect at variance with, or indifferent to, his own reputation   59–60 had as lief would just as soon   62 Hibbocrates Hippocrates, ancient Greek physician   65 he's i.e., Evans is.   should who is supposed to   69 s.d. offer make as if, prepare. (The stage direction is substantially from the Quarto.)   72 question talk, discuss

87 stay waited   90 judgment by ruled by the judgment of   92 Gallia and Gaul Wales and France   96 Machiavel Niccolò Machiavelli, an Italian political philosopher who symbolized crafty and ruthless ambition to Elizabethans; an intriguer   97 motions purges   99 proverbs . . . no-verbs i.e., wisdom and some Welsh colorful speech, or perhaps Thou-shalt-not's   100 terrestrial i.e., the Doctor, who treats the body   101 art learning   103–104 burnt sack heated and mulled wine, as at 2.1.199–200   104 issue outcome.   to pawn as a pledge or surety   106 Trust me believe me   109 sot fool   111 vloutingstog floutingstock, i.e., laughingstock   113 scall scald, i.e., scurvy   114 cogging companion cheating rascal   117 noddles head

3.2. Location: A street in Windsor.

1 keep your way keep on your way (in front of me)   3 Whether which of the two

MRS. PAGE   O, you are a flattering boy. Now I see you'll be a courtier.

[Enter] Ford.

FORD   Well met, Mistress Page. Whither go you?

MRS. PAGE   Truly, sir, to see your wife. Is she at home?

FORD   Ay, and as idle as she may hang together, for 11 want of company. I think if your husbands were dead 12 you two would marry.

MRS. PAGE   Be sure of that—two other husbands.

FORD   Where had you this pretty weathercock? 15

MRS. PAGE   I cannot tell what the dickens his name is my husband had him of.—What do you call your 17 knight's name, sirrah?

ROBIN   Sir John Falstaff.

FORD   Sir John Falstaff!

MRS. PAGE   He, he. I can never hit on 's name. There is such a league between my goodman and he! Is your 22 wife at home indeed?

FORD   Indeed she is.

MRS. PAGE   By your leave, sir. I am sick till I see her.

[Exeunt Mistress Page and Robin.]

FORD   Has Page any brains? Hath he any eyes? Hath he any thinking? Sure they sleep; he hath no use of them. Why, this boy will carry a letter twenty mile as easy as a cannon will shoot point-blank twelve score. He 29 pieces out his wife's inclination; he gives her folly 30 motion and advantage. And now she's going to my 31 wife, and Falstaff's boy with her. A man may hear this 32 shower sing in the wind. And Falstaff's boy with her! 33 Good plots! They are laid; and our revolted wives share damnation together. Well, I will take him, then torture 35 my wife, pluck the borrowed veil of modesty from the so-seeming Mistress Page, divulge Page himself for a 37 secure and willful Actaeon; and to these violent pro- 38 ceedings all my neighbors shall cry aim. [*A clock* 39 *strikes.*] The clock gives me my cue, and my assurance 40 bids me search. There I shall find Falstaff. I shall be rather praised for this than mocked, for it is as positive as the earth is firm that Falstaff is there. I will go.

[Enter] Page, Shallow, Slender, Host, Evans, Caius, [and Rugby].

SHALLOW, PAGE, ETC   Well met, Master Ford.

FORD [*aside*]   Trust me, a good knot. [*To them.*] I have 45 good cheer at home, and I pray you all go with me. 46

SHALLOW   I must excuse myself, Master Ford.

SLENDER   And so must I, sir. We have appointed to dine with Mistress Anne, and I would not break with her 49 for more money than I'll speak of.

SHALLOW   We have lingered about a match between Anne Page and my cousin Slender, and this day we shall have our answer.

SLENDER   I hope I have your good will, father Page.

PAGE   You have, Master Slender; I stand wholly for you. But my wife, Master Doctor, is for you altogether.

CAIUS   Ay, by gar, and de maid is love-a me. My nursh-a Quickly tell me so mush.

HOST   What say you to young Master Fenton? He capers, he dances, he has eyes of youth, he writes verses, he speaks holiday, he smells April and May. 61 He will carry 't, he will carry 't. 'Tis in his buttons he 62 will carry 't. 63

PAGE   Not by my consent, I promise you. The gentle-man is of no having. He kept company with the wild 65 Prince and Poins. He is of too high a region; he knows 66 too much. No, he shall not knit a knot in his fortunes 67 with the finger of my substance. If he take her, let him take her simply. The wealth I have waits on my 69 consent, and my consent goes not that way.

FORD   I beseech you heartily, some of you go home with me to dinner. Besides your cheer, you shall have sport: I will show you a monster. Master Doctor, you shall 73 go. So shall you, Master Page, and you, Sir Hugh.

SHALLOW   Well, fare you well. We shall have the freer 75 wooing at Master Page's. 76

[Exeunt Shallow and Slender.]

CAIUS   Go home, John Rugby. I come anon. 77

[Exit Rugby.]

HOST   Farewell, my hearts. I will to my honest knight Falstaff, and drink canary with him. [*Exit.*] 79

FORD [*aside*]   I think I shall drink in pipe-wine first 80 with him; I'll make him dance.—Will you go, gentles? 81

ALL   Have with you to see this monster. *Exeunt.* 82

❖

3.3   *Enter Mistress Ford [and] Mistress Page.*

MRS. FORD   What, John! What, Robert! 1

MRS. PAGE   Quickly, quickly! Is the buck basket— 2

---

11 as idle . . . together i.e., as idle as she can be without going to pieces; or, persons as idle as she (and you) are may keep company **12 want** lack **15 had you** did you find. **pretty weathercock** i.e., sprucely dressed little fellow. (A *weathercock* changes quickly, here in matters of fashion of dress. Robin may have a feather in his hat.) **17 had him of** got him from **22 league** friendship. **goodman** hus-band **29 point-blank** in a straight trajectory. **twelve score** i.e., 240 paces **30 pieces out** augments, encourages. **folly** wantonness **31 motion** motive, advancement. **advantage** opportunity **32–33 hear . . . wind** tell from the rising wind that a storm is com-ing up, i.e., that trouble is brewing **35 take him** take him by surprise **37 divulge** reveal **38 secure** overconfident. **Actaeon** i.e., horned man, cuckold. (See the note for 2.1.113.) **39 cry aim** applaud. (A term from archery.) **40 assurance** foreknowledge **45 knot** group, company **46 cheer** fare

49 break with break my promise to **61 holiday** in a fashion appropri-ate to a holiday, elegantly **62 carry 't** carry it off **62–63 'Tis . . . carry 't** i.e., he's sure to succeed **65 having** estate **65–66 wild . . . Poins** i.e., Prince Hal and Poins of *1 Henry IV* and *2 Henry IV* **66 region** social status **67 knit a knot in** mend **69 simply** i.e., by herself. **waits on** is subject to **73 monster** (As if Falstaff were a freak to be exhibited at a fair.) **75–76 We shall . . . Page's** i.e., the wooing of Anne will be less constrained if Caius, Evans, and Anne's father are not there **77 anon** at once **79 canary** a sweet wine from the Canaries. (But Ford plays on *canary* in the sense of "a lively dance" in his reply.) **80 pipe-wine** wine from the cask, or wood (with a pun on *pipe* as a musical instrument played for the *dance*, line 81. Ford means that he'll make Falstaff jump, make it hot for him.) **81 gentles** gentlemen **82 Have with you** we're coming **3.3. Location: Ford's house.** **1 What** i.e., move quickly **2 buck basket** basket for soiled clothes. (*Bucking* means "washing.")

MRS. FORD I warrant. What, Robert, I say!

[Enter] Servants [with a great basket].

MRS. PAGE Come, come, come.

MRS. FORD Here, set it down.

MRS. PAGE Give your men the charge. We must be brief. 6

MRS. FORD Marry, as I told you before, John and Robert, be ready here hard by in the brewhouse; and when I 8 suddenly call you, come forth, and without any pause or staggering take this basket on your shoulders. That done, trudge with it in all haste, and carry it among the whitsters in Datchet Mead, and there empty it in 12 the muddy ditch close by the Thames' side.

MRS. PAGE You will do it?

MRS. FORD I ha' told them over and over; they lack no direction.—Begone, and come when you are called.

[Exeunt Servants.]

MRS. PAGE Here comes little Robin.

[Enter] Robin.

MRS. FORD How now, my eyas musket, what news 18 with you?

ROBIN My master, Sir John, is come in at your back door, Mistress Ford, and requests your company.

MRS. PAGE You little Jack-a-Lent, have you been true 22 to us?

ROBIN Ay, I'll be sworn. My master knows not of your being here and hath threatened to put me into everlasting liberty if I tell you of it; for he swears he'll 26 turn me away. 27

MRS. PAGE Thou'rt a good boy. This secrecy of thine shall be a tailor to thee and shall make thee a new doublet and hose.—I'll go hide me.

MRS. FORD Do so.—Go tell thy master I am alone. [Exit Robin.] Mistress Page, remember you your cue.

MRS. PAGE I warrant thee. If I do not act it, hiss me.

[Exit.]

MRS. FORD Go to, then. We'll use this unwholesome humidity, this gross watery pumpkin. We'll teach him to know turtles from jays. 36

[Enter] Falstaff.

FALSTAFF "Have I caught thee, my heavenly jewel?" 37 Why, now let me die, for I have lived long enough. This is the period of my ambition. O, this blessed hour! 39

MRS. FORD O sweet Sir John!

FALSTAFF Mistress Ford, I cannot cog, I cannot prate, 41 Mistress Ford. Now shall I sin in my wish: I would thy husband were dead. I'll speak it before the best lord: I would make thee my lady.

MRS. FORD I your lady, Sir John? Alas, I should be a pitiful lady!

FALSTAFF Let the court of France show me such another. I see how thine eye would emulate the diamond. Thou hast the right arched beauty of the brow that becomes the ship-tire, the tire-valiant, or any tire of 50 Venetian admittance. 51

MRS. FORD A plain kerchief, Sir John. My brows be- 52 come nothing else, nor that well neither. 53

FALSTAFF By the Lord, thou art a tyrant to say so. Thou wouldst make an absolute courtier, and the firm 55 fixture of thy foot would give an excellent motion to 56 thy gait in a semicircled farthingale. I see what thou 57 wert, if Fortune thy foe were not, Nature thy friend. 58 Come, thou canst not hide it.

MRS. FORD Believe me, there's no such thing in me.

FALSTAFF What made me love thee? Let that persuade thee there's something extraordinary in thee. Come, I' cannot cog and say thou art this and that, like a many of these lisping hawthorn buds, that come like women 64 in men's apparel and smell like Bucklersbury in sim- 65 ple time. I cannot. But I love thee, none but thee; and 66 thou deserv'st it.

MRS. FORD Do not betray me, sir. I fear you love Mis- 68 tress Page.

FALSTAFF Thou mightst as well say I love to walk by the Counter gate, which is as hateful to me as the reek 71 of a limekiln.

MRS. FORD Well, heaven knows how I love you, and you shall one day find it.

FALSTAFF Keep in that mind. I'll deserve it.

MRS. FORD Nay, I must tell you, so you do, or else I could not be in that mind.

[Enter Robin.]

ROBIN Mistress Ford, Mistress Ford! Here's Mistress Page at the door, sweating and blowing and looking 79 wildly, and would needs speak with you presently. 80

FALSTAFF She shall not see me. I will ensconce me 81 behind the arras. 82

MRS. FORD Pray you, do so. She's a very tattling woman. [Falstaff hides himself behind the arras.]

[Enter Mistress Page.]

What's the matter? How now!

MRS. PAGE O Mistress Ford, what have you done? You're shamed, you're overthrown, you're undone 87 forever!

MRS. FORD What's the matter, good Mistress Page?

---

6 charge instructions 8 hard by close at hand 12 whitsters bleachers of linen. Datchet Mead a meadow along the Thames, near Windsor Park 18 eyas musket young male sparrow hawk 22 Jack-a-Lent figure of a man set up during Lent to be pelted by boys, a puppet 26 liberty i.e., unemployment 27 turn me away dismiss me 36 turtles turtledoves, models of constancy in love. jays i.e., loose women 37 Have . . . jewel (From Sir Philip Sidney's Astrophel and Stella.) 39 period goal 41 cog cheat, flatter. (Also in line 63.)

50 ship-tire woman's headdress resembling a ship. tire-valiant fanciful headdress 51 admittance fashion 52–53 become suit 55 absolute perfect 56 fixture setting, placing 57 semicircled farthingale petticoat with hoops at the sides and back but not extending in front 57–58 I see . . . friend i.e., I can imagine how impressive you would be at court if Fortune had not cast you in a lowly lot with only your natural beauty to assist you. ("Fortune My Foe" is the name of a popular ballad tune.) 64 hawthorn buds i.e., young fops 65 Bucklersbury a London street inhabited by herbalists 65–66 simple time midsummer, the time when apothecaries were supplied with simples or herbs 68 betray deceive 71 Counter gate gate of the Counter or debtors' prison in London 79 blowing puffing 80 presently at once 81 ensconce me hide myself 82 arras tapestry wall hanging 87 overthrown ruined

MRS. PAGE   O welladay, Mistress Ford, having an hon- 90
est man to your husband, to give him such cause of 91
suspicion!

MRS. FORD   What cause of suspicion?

MRS. PAGE   What cause of suspicion? Out upon you! 94
How am I mistook in you!

MRS. FORD   Why, alas, what's the matter?

MRS. PAGE   Your husband's coming hither, woman,
with all the officers in Windsor, to search for a
gentleman that he says is here now in the house, by
your consent, to take an ill advantage of his absence.
You are undone.

MRS. FORD   'Tis not so, I hope.

MRS. PAGE   Pray heaven it be not so, that you have
such a man here! But 'tis most certain your husband's
coming, with half Windsor at his heels, to search for
such a one. I come before to tell you. If you know
yourself clear, why, I am glad of it. But if you have a 107
friend here, convey, convey him out. Be not amazed! 108
Call all your senses to you; defend your reputation, or
bid farewell to your good life forever. 110

MRS. FORD   What shall I do? There is a gentleman, my
dear friend; and I fear not mine own shame so much
as his peril. I had rather than a thousand pound he
were out of the house.

MRS. PAGE   For shame! Never stand "you had rather" 115
and "you had rather." Your husband's here at hand!
Bethink you of some conveyance. In the house you 117
cannot hide him. O, how have you deceived me! Look,
here is a basket. If he be of any reasonable stature, he
may creep in here; and throw foul linen upon him, as
if it were going to bucking. Or—it is whiting time— 121
send him by your two men to Datchet Mead.

MRS. FORD   He's too big to go in there. What shall I do?

FALSTAFF [coming forward]   Let me see 't, let me see 't,
O, let me see 't! I'll in, I'll in. Follow your friend's
counsel. I'll in.

MRS. PAGE   What, Sir John Falstaff? [Aside to him.] Are
these your letters, knight?

FALSTAFF [aside to her]   I love thee. Help me away. Let
me creep in here. I'll never—

[He gets into the basket; they cover him with foul
linen.]

MRS. PAGE   Help to cover your master, boy.—Call your
men, Mistress Ford.—You dissembling knight!

MRS. FORD   What, John! Robert! John!

[Enter Servants.]

Go take up these clothes here quickly. Where's the
cowlstaff? Look how you drumble! Carry them to the 135
laundress in Datchet Mead. Quickly! Come.

[The Servants lift the basket and start to leave.]

[Enter] Ford, Page, Caius, [and] Evans.

FORD   Pray you, come near. If I suspect without cause,
why then make sport at me. Then let me be your jest;
I deserve it.—How now? Whither bear you this?

SERVANT   To the laundress, forsooth.

MRS. FORD   Why, what have you to do whither they
bear it? You were best meddle with buck washing. 142

FORD   Buck? I would I could wash myself of the buck!
Buck, buck, buck! Ay, buck! I warrant you, buck—
and of the season too, it shall appear. [Exeunt Servants 145
with the basket.] Gentlemen, I have dreamed tonight; 146
I'll tell you my dream. Here, here, here be my keys.
Ascend my chambers. Search, seek, find out. I'll
warrant we'll unkennel the fox. Let me stop this way 149
first. [He locks the door.] So, now uncape. 150

PAGE   Good Master Ford, be contented. You wrong 151
yourself too much. 152

FORD   True, Master Page. Up, gentlemen, you shall see 153
sport anon. Follow me, gentlemen.   [Exit.]

EVANS   This is fery fantastical humors and jealousies.

CAIUS   By gar, 'tis no the fashion of France. It is not
jealous in France.

PAGE   Nay, follow him, gentlemen. See the issue of his 158
search.   [Exeunt Page, Caius, and Evans.]

MRS. PAGE   Is there not a double excellency in this?

MRS. FORD   I know not which pleases me better, that
my husband is deceived, or Sir John.

MRS. PAGE   What a taking was he in when your hus- 163
band asked who was in the basket!

MRS. FORD   I am half afraid he will have need of 165
washing, so throwing him into the water will do him 166
a benefit.

MRS. PAGE   Hang him, dishonest rascal! I would all of
the same strain were in the same distress. 169

MRS. FORD   I think my husband hath some special
suspicion of Falstaff's being here, for I never saw him
so gross in his jealousy till now.

MRS. PAGE   I will lay a plot to try that, and we will yet 173
have more tricks with Falstaff. His dissolute disease
will scarce obey this medicine. 175

MRS. FORD   Shall we send that foolish carrion Mistress 176
Quickly to him, and excuse his throwing into the 177
water, and give him another hope, to betray him to
another punishment?

MRS. PAGE   We will do it. Let him be sent for tomorrow
eight o'clock, to have amends.

[Enter Ford, Page, Caius, and Evans.]

FORD   I cannot find him. Maybe the knave bragged of
that he could not compass. 183

---

90 **welladay** alas   91 **to your** as your   94 **Out upon you** i.e., for
shame   107 **clear** clear of blame   108 **friend** lover.   **amazed**
stunned, bewildered   110 **your good life** your respectability
115 **stand** lose time over   117 **conveyance** stratagem   121 **bucking**
washing.   **whiting time** bleaching time   135 **cowlstaff** pole on which
a "cowl" or basket is carried between two persons.   **drumble** are
sluggish

142 **buck washing** washing clothes. (But Ford puns on *buck* in the
sense of "horned male deer," resembling the cuckold, and also of
"copulating.")   145 **of the season** in the rutting season   146 **tonight**
last night   149 **unkennel** reveal, unearth   150 **uncape** i.e., unleash,
unloose (?)   151 **be contented** be calm   151–152 **wrong yourself**
put yourself in the wrong   153 **True** (Ford may mean that he is indeed too much wronged, or else placates Page by seeming to agree
with him.)   158 **issue** outcome   163 **taking** fright   165–166 **will
. . . washing** i.e., will have befouled himself in fright   169 **strain**
character, kind   173 **try** test   175 **obey this medicine** i.e., yield to
this first dose   176 **carrion** rotten old flesh, bawd (?)   177 **excuse**
make excuses for   183 **that** that which.   **compass** accomplish

MRS. PAGE [*aside to Mistress Ford*]   Heard you that?

MRS. FORD   You use me well, Master Ford, do you?

FORD   Ay, I do so.

MRS. FORD   Heaven make you better than your thoughts!

FORD   Amen!

MRS. PAGE   You do yourself mighty wrong, Master Ford.

FORD   Ay, ay, I must bear it.

EVANS   If there be anypody in the house, and in the chambers, and in the coffers, and in the presses, 192 heaven forgive my sins at the day of judgment!

CAIUS   By gar, nor I too. There is nobodies.

PAGE   Fie, fie, Master Ford, are you not ashamed? What spirit, what devil suggests this imagination? I would 196 not ha' your distemper in this kind for the wealth of 197 Windsor Castle.

FORD   'Tis my fault, Master Page. I suffer for it.

EVANS   You suffer for a pad conscience. Your wife is as honest a 'omans as I will desires among five thousand, and five hundred too.

CAIUS   By gar, I see 'tis an honest woman.

FORD   Well, I promised you a dinner. Come, come, walk in the park. I pray you, pardon me. I will 205 hereafter make known to you why I have done this.—Come, wife, come, Mistress Page, I pray you, pardon me. Pray, heartily, pardon me.

PAGE   Let's go in, gentlemen; but, trust me, we'll mock 209 him. I do invite you tomorrow morning to my house to breakfast. After, we'll a-birding together. I have a 211 fine hawk for the bush. Shall it be so? 212

FORD   Anything.

EVANS   If there is one, I shall make two in the company.

CAIUS   If there be one or two, I shall make-a the turd.

FORD   Pray you, go, Master Page.

[*Exeunt Ford and Page.*]

EVANS [*to Caius*]   I pray you now, remembrance 217 tomorrow on the lousy knave, mine Host. 218

CAIUS   Dat is good, by gar; with all my heart!

EVANS   A lousy knave, to have his gibes and his mockeries!   *Exeunt.*

❖

3.4   *Enter Fenton [and] Anne Page.*

FENTON
I see I cannot get thy father's love;   1
Therefore no more turn me to him, sweet Nan.   2

ANNE
Alas, how then?

FENTON   Why, thou must be thyself.   3

He doth object I am too great of birth,
And that, my state being galled with my expense,   5
I seek to heal it only by his wealth.
Besides these, other bars he lays before me—
My riots past, my wild societies;   8
And tells me 'tis a thing impossible
I should love thee but as a property.

ANNE   Maybe he tells you true.

FENTON
No, heaven so speed me in my time to come!   12
Albeit I will confess thy father's wealth   13
Was the first motive that I wooed thee, Anne,
Yet, wooing thee, I found thee of more value
Than stamps in gold or sums in sealèd bags;   16
And 'tis the very riches of thyself
That now I aim at.

ANNE   Gentle Master Fenton,
Yet seek my father's love; still seek it, sir.
If opportunity and humblest suit
Cannot attain it, why, then—hark you hither.

[*They converse apart.*]

[*Enter*] *Shallow, Slender, [and Mistress] Quickly.*

SHALLOW   Break their talk, Mistress Quickly. My kins- 22 man shall speak for himself.

SLENDER   I'll make a shaft or a bolt on 't. 'Slid, 'tis but 24 venturing.

SHALLOW   Be not dismayed.

SLENDER   No, she shall not dismay me. I care not for that, but that I am afeard. 28

QUICKLY [*to Anne*]   Hark ye, Master Slender would speak a word with you.

ANNE
I come to him. [*Aside.*] This is my father's choice.
O, what a world of vile ill-favored faults   32
Looks handsome in three hundred pounds a year!

QUICKLY   And how does good Master Fenton? Pray you, a word with you.   [*She draws him aside.*]

SHALLOW   She's coming. To her, coz! O boy, thou hadst 36 a father! 37

SLENDER   I had a father, Mistress Anne; my uncle can tell you good jests of him.— Pray you, uncle, tell Mistress Anne the jest how my father stole two geese out of a pen, good uncle.

SHALLOW   Mistress Anne, my cousin loves you. 42

SLENDER   Ay, that I do, as well as I love any woman in Gloucestershire.

SHALLOW   He will maintain you like a gentlewoman.

SLENDER   Ay, that I will, come cut and longtail, under 46 the degree of a squire. 47

---

192 presses cupboards, clothes presses   **196 suggests** incites, prompts you to.   **imagination** wild suspicion   **197 distemper** disorder of mind.   **in this kind** of this sort   **205 walk . . . park** i.e., stroll till dinnertime   **209 go in** i.e., go in to dinner at the proper time   **211 a-birding** go hunting small birds of the bush with a hawk and guns   **212 for the bush** for driving the small birds into the bush (where they can be shot)   **217–218 remembrance . . . Host** (A seeming allusion to the conversation at the end of 3.1 and to the plot carried out in 4.5.)
3.4. Location: Before Page's house.
1 love good will   **2 turn** direct   **3 be thyself** be your own mistress

5 state . . . expense estate being chafed away by my extravagance   **8 societies** companionships   **12 heaven . . . come** i.e., as I hope to be saved.   **speed** prosper   **13 Albeit** although   **16 stamps in gold** gold coins   **22 Break** interrupt   **24 I'll . . . on 't** i.e., I'll try it one way or another. (A *shaft* is a slender arrow; a *bolt*, a thick and blunt one.)   **'Slid** by his (God's) eyelid   **28 but . . . afeard** except that I am afraid. (Slender evidently doesn't understand what *dismayed* means.)   **32 ill-favored** ugly   **36–37 thou hadst a father** i.e., remember that your father wooed a woman; be like him. (But Slender misses the point.)   **42 cousin** i.e., kinsman   **46 come . . . longtail** i.e., come what may. (Literally, horses or dogs with docked and long tails, i.e., all sorts.)   **46–47 under the degree of** in the rank of

SHALLOW He will make you a hundred and fifty 48
pounds jointure. 49

ANNE Good Master Shallow, let him woo for himself.

SHALLOW Marry, I thank you for it; I thank you for that
good comfort. She calls you, coz. I'll leave you.
[He moves aside.]

ANNE Now, Master Slender—

SLENDER Now, good Mistress Anne—

ANNE What is your will?

SLENDER My will? 'Od's heartlings, that's a pretty jest 56
indeed! I ne'er made my will yet, I thank heaven; I am
not such a sickly creature, I give heaven praise.

ANNE I mean, Master Slender, what would you with
me?

SLENDER Truly, for mine own part, I would little or
nothing with you. Your father and my uncle hath
made motions. If it be my luck, so; if not, happy man 63
be his dole! They can tell you how things go better 64
than I can. You may ask your father. Here he comes.

[Enter] Page [and] Mistress Page.

PAGE
Now, Master Slender. Love him, daughter Anne.—
Why, how now? What does Master Fenton here?
You wrong me, sir, thus still to haunt my house.
I told you, sir, my daughter is disposed of.

FENTON
Nay, Master Page, be not impatient.

MRS. PAGE
Good Master Fenton, come not to my child.

PAGE She is no match for you.

FENTON Sir, will you hear me?

PAGE No, good Master Fenton.
Come, Master Shallow; come, son Slender, in.—
Knowing my mind, you wrong me, Master Fenton.
[Exeunt Page, Shallow, and Slender.]

QUICKLY *[to Fenton]* Speak to Mistress Page.

FENTON
Good Mistress Page, for that I love your daughter 78
In such a righteous fashion as I do,
Perforce, against all checks, rebukes, and manners 80
I must advance the colors of my love 81
And not retire. Let me have your good will.

ANNE Good Mother, do not marry me to yond fool.

MRS. PAGE I mean it not; I seek you a better husband. 84

QUICKLY *[aside to Anne]* That's my master, Master Doctor.

ANNE
Alas, I had rather be set quick i' the earth 86
And bowled to death with turnips! 87

MRS. PAGE
Come, trouble not yourself. Good Master Fenton,
I will not be your friend nor enemy.

My daughter will I question how she loves you,
And, as I find her, so am I affected.
Till then farewell, sir. She must needs go in; 91
Her father will be angry.

FENTON
Farewell, gentle mistress. Farewell, Nan.
[Exeunt Mistress Page and Anne.]

QUICKLY This is my doing, now. "Nay," said I, "will
you cast away your child on a fool, and a physician?
Look on Master Fenton." This is my doing.

FENTON
I thank thee; and I pray thee, once tonight 98
Give my sweet Nan this ring. There's for thy pains.
[He gives a ring and money.]

QUICKLY Now heaven send thee good fortune! *[Exit
Fenton.]* A kind heart he hath. A woman would run
through fire and water for such a kind heart. But yet I
would my master had Mistress Anne; or I would
Master Slender had her; or, in sooth, I would Master
Fenton had her. I will do what I can for them all three;
for so I have promised, and I'll be as good as my
word—but speciously for Master Fenton. Well, I must 107
of another errand to Sir John Falstaff from my two 108
mistresses. What a beast am I to slack it! *Exit.* 109

❧

3.5 *Enter Falstaff.*

FALSTAFF Bardolph, I say!

[Enter] Bardolph.

BARDOLPH Here, sir.

FALSTAFF Go fetch me a quart of sack; put a toast in 't. 3
[Exit Bardolph.] Have I lived to be carried in a basket,
like a barrow of butcher's offal, and to be thrown in 5
the Thames? Well, if I be served such another trick, I'll
have my brains ta'en out and buttered, and give them
to a dog for a New Year's gift. The rogues slighted me 8
into the river with as little remorse as they would have 9
drowned a blind bitch's puppies, fifteen i' the litter! 10
And you may know by my size that I have a kind of
alacrity in sinking; if the bottom were as deep as hell,
I should down. I had been drowned, but that the 13
shore was shelvy and shallow—a death that I abhor; 14
for the water swells a man, and what a thing should I
have been when I had been swelled! I should have
been a mountain of mummy. 17

[Enter Bardolph with sack.]

BARDOLPH Here's Mistress Quickly, sir, to speak with
you.

---

48 **make** give 49 **jointure** settlement in the marriage contract providing for the wife's widowhood 56 **'Od's heartlings** by God's little heart 63 **motions** offers. **so** well and good 63–64 **happy . . . dole** i.e., may whoever succeeds with you be happy. (Literally, may his lot in life be that of a happy man.) 78 **for that** because
80 **checks** reproofs. **manners** usage, (hostile) behavior 81 **advance the colors** raise high the standard (as in anticipation of battle)
84 **mean** intend 86 **quick** alive 87 **bowled** i.e., pelted with turnips as bowling balls

91 **affected** inclined 98 **once** sometime 107 **speciously** (For "specially.") 107–108 **must of** must undertake 109 **slack** be remiss about
3.5. Location: The Garter Inn.
3 **toast** piece of toast 5 **barrow** wheelbarrowful 8 **slighted me** dumped me heedlessly 9 **remorse** pity, compassion 10 **a blind bitch's puppies** a bitch's puppies, blind at birth 13 **down** sink
14 **shore** bottom near the edge. **shelvy** shelving, sloping
17 **mummy** dead flesh

FALSTAFF   Come, let me pour in some sack to the Thames water, for my belly's as cold as if I had swallowed snowballs for pills to cool the reins. [*He drinks.*] Call her in. 22

BARDOLPH   Come in, woman!

[*Enter Mistress*] *Quickly.*

QUICKLY   By your leave; I cry you mercy. Give your worship good morrow. 25

FALSTAFF   [*to Bardolph*] Take away these chalices. Go brew me a pottle of sack finely. 27 28

BARDOLPH   With eggs, sir?

FALSTAFF   Simple of itself. I'll no pullet sperm in my brewage. [*Exit Bardolph.*] How now? 30

QUICKLY   Marry, sir, I come to your worship from Mistress Ford.

FALSTAFF   Mistress Ford? I have had ford enough. I was thrown into the ford. I have my belly full of ford. 34

QUICKLY   Alas the day, good heart, that was not her fault. She does so take on with her men; they mistook their erection. 37 38

FALSTAFF   So did I mine, to build upon a foolish woman's promise.

QUICKLY   Well, she laments, sir, for it, that it would yearn your heart to see it. Her husband goes this morning a-birding. She desires you once more to come to her between eight and nine. I must carry her word quickly. She'll make you amends, I warrant you. 41 42

FALSTAFF   Well, I will visit her; tell her so. And bid her think what a man is. Let her consider his frailty, and then judge of my merit. 47

QUICKLY   I will tell her.

FALSTAFF   Do so. Between nine and ten, sayst thou?

QUICKLY   Eight and nine, sir.

FALSTAFF   Well, begone. I will not miss her. 52

QUICKLY   Peace be with you, sir.   [*Exit.*]

FALSTAFF   I marvel I hear not of Master Brook; he sent me word to stay within. I like his money well. O, here he comes.

[*Enter*] *Ford* [*disguised*].

FORD   Bless you, sir!

FALSTAFF   Now, Master Brook, you come to know what hath passed between me and Ford's wife?

FORD   That, indeed, Sir John, is my business.

FALSTAFF   Master Brook, I will not lie to you. I was at her house the hour she appointed me.

FORD   And sped you, sir? 63

FALSTAFF   Very ill-favoredly, Master Brook. 64

FORD   How so, sir? Did she change her determination? 65

FALSTAFF   No, Master Brook, but the peaking cornuto her husband, Master Brook, dwelling in a continual larum of jealousy, comes me in the instant of our encounter, after we had embraced, kissed, protested, and, as it were, spoke the prologue of our comedy; and at his heels a rabble of his companions, thither provoked and instigated by his distemper, and, forsooth, to search his house for his wife's love. 66 67 68 69 71

FORD   What, while you were there?

FALSTAFF   While I was there.

FORD   And did he search for you, and could not find you?

FALSTAFF   You shall hear. As good luck would have it, comes in one Mistress Page, gives intelligence of Ford's approach, and, in her invention and Ford's wife's distraction, they conveyed me into a buck basket.

FORD   A buck basket?

FALSTAFF   By the Lord, a buck basket! Rammed me in with foul shirts and smocks, socks, foul stockings, greasy napkins, that, Master Brook, there was the rankest compound of villainous smell that ever offended nostril. 84

FORD   And how long lay you there?

FALSTAFF   Nay, you shall hear, Master Brook, what I have suffered to bring this woman to evil for your good. Being thus crammed in the basket, a couple of Ford's knaves, his hinds, were called forth by their mistress to carry me in the name of foul clothes to Datchet Lane. They took me on their shoulders, met the jealous knave their master in the door, who asked them once or twice what they had in their basket. I quaked for fear lest the lunatic knave would have searched it; but fate, ordaining he should be a cuckold, held his hand. Well, on went he for a search, and away went I for foul clothes. But mark the sequel, Master Brook. I suffered the pangs of three several deaths: first, an intolerable fright to be detected with a jealous rotten bellwether; next, to be compassed, like a good bilbo, in the circumference of a peck, hilt to point, heel to head; and then, to be stopped in, like a strong distillation, with stinking clothes that fretted in their own grease. Think of that—a man of my kidney. Think of that—that am as subject to heat as butter; a man of continual dissolution and thaw. It was a miracle to scape suffocation. And in the height of this bath, when I was more than half stewed in grease, like a Dutch dish, to be thrown into the Thames and cooled, glowing hot, in that surge, like a horseshoe! Think of that—hissing hot—think of that, Master Brook! 91 100 101 102 103 104 105 106 108

---

22 **reins** kidneys   25 **cry you mercy** beg your pardon   27 **chalices** (A lofty name for drinking cups.)   28 **brew** prepare, concoct. **pottle** two-quart measure. **finely** tastefully   30 **Simple of itself** unadulterated. **I'll** I'll have   34 **ford** i.e., river, stream. (Literally, a shallow place in the river where one may cross.)   37 **take on with** berate, scold   38 **erection** (Blunder for "direction"; Falstaff plays bawdily on her malapropism.)   41 **that** so that   42 **yearn** grieve   47 **his** i.e., man's   52 **miss** fail   63 **sped you** did you succeed   64 **ill-favoredly** badly   65 **determination** decision

66 **peaking cornuto** sneaking horned person, i.e., cuckold   67 **dwelling** remaining, being   68 **larum** i.e., state of surprise and fear. **comes me** comes. (*Me* is used colloquially.)   69 **protested** i.e., solemnly swore our vows of love   71 **rabble** pack   84 **that** so that   91 **hinds** servants   100 **several** distinct   101 **with** by   102 **bellwether** castrated or old ram, leader of a flock (provided with a noisy bell and horned like a cuckold).   **compassed** (1) encompassed, surrounded (2) bent into a circle   103 **bilbo** finely tempered and flexible sword of Bilbao in Spain.   **peck** container holding a quarter of a bushel; i.e., a very small space.   **hilt to point** (Falstaff is bent over, head to toes, like a fine Spanish sword that could be bent thus without breaking.)   104 **stopped** shut, stoppered   105 **fretted** decayed   106 **kidney** temperament, constitution   108 **dissolution** liquefaction

FORD   In good sadness, sir, I am sorry that for my sake 114
you have suffered all this. My suit then is desperate;
you'll undertake her no more?

FALSTAFF   Master Brook, I will be thrown into Etna, as 117
I have been into Thames, ere I will leave her thus. Her
husband is this morning gone a-birding. I have
received from her another embassy of meeting. Twixt 120
eight and nine is the hour, Master Brook.

FORD   'Tis past eight already, sir.

FALSTAFF   Is it? I will then address me to my appoint- 123
ment. Come to me at your convenient leisure, and
you shall know how I speed; and the conclusion shall
be crowned with your enjoying her. Adieu. You shall
have her, Master Brook; Master Brook, you shall
cuckold Ford.   [Exit.]

FORD   Hum! Ha! Is this a vision? Is this a dream? Do I
sleep? Master Ford, awake! Awake, Master Ford!
There's a hole made in your best coat, Master Ford. 131
This 'tis to be married! This 'tis to have linen and
buck baskets! Well, I will proclaim myself what I am.
I will now take the lecher. He is at my house. He cannot scape me. 'Tis impossible he should. He cannot
creep into a halfpenny purse, nor into a pepperbox. 136
But, lest the devil that guides him should aid him, I
will search impossible places. Though what I am I cannot avoid, yet to be what I would not shall not make
me tame. If I have horns to make one mad, let the
proverb go with me: I'll be horn-mad.   Exit. 141

✤

4.1

*Enter Mistress Page, [Mistress] Quickly, [and]
William.*

MRS. PAGE   Is he at Master Ford's already, think'st thou?

QUICKLY   Sure he is by this, or will be presently. But
truly he is very courageous mad about his throwing 3
into the water. Mistress Ford desires you to come
suddenly.   5

MRS. PAGE   I'll be with her by and by. I'll but bring my
young man here to school.

[Enter Sir Hugh] Evans.

Look where his master comes. 'Tis a playing day, I 8
see.—How now, Sir Hugh, no school today?

EVANS   No. Master Slender is let the boys leave to play. 10

QUICKLY   Blessing of his heart!   11

MRS. PAGE   Sir Hugh, my husband says my son profits 12
nothing in the world at his book. I pray you, ask him 13
some questions in his accidence.   14

EVANS   Come hither, William. Hold up your head.
Come.

MRS. PAGE   Come on, sirrah, hold up your head.
Answer your master. Be not afraid.

EVANS   William, how many numbers is in nouns?   19

WILLIAM   Two.

QUICKLY   Truly, I thought there had been one number
more, because they say "'Od's nouns."   22

EVANS   Peace your tattlings!—What is "fair," William? 23

WILLIAM   *Pulcher.*

QUICKLY   Polecats? There are fairer things than pole- 25
cats, sure.

EVANS   You are a very simplicity 'oman. I pray you,
peace.—What is *lapis*, William?

WILLIAM   A stone.

EVANS   And what is "a stone," William?

WILLIAM   A pebble.

EVANS   No, it is *lapis*. I pray you, remember in your
prain.

WILLIAM   *Lapis.*

EVANS   That is a good William. What is he, William,
that does lend articles?

WILLIAM   Articles are borrowed of the pronoun, and be 37
thus declined, *singulariter, nominativo, hic, haec, hoc.* 38

EVANS   *Nominativo, hig, hag, hog.* Pray you, mark: *genitivo, huius.* Well, what is your accusative case?

WILLIAM   *Accusativo, hinc.*

EVANS   I pray you, have your remembrance, child.
Accusativo, hung, hang, hog.

QUICKLY   "Hang-hog" is Latin for bacon, I warrant 44
you.

EVANS   Leave your prabbles, 'oman.—What is the
focative case, William?

WILLIAM   O—*vocativo*, O.

EVANS   Remember, William, focative is *caret.*   49

QUICKLY   And that's a good root.

EVANS   'Oman, forbear.

MRS. PAGE   *[to Mistress Quickly]* Peace!

EVANS   What is your genitive case plural, William?

WILLIAM   Genitive case?

EVANS   Ay.

WILLIAM   *Genitivo—horum, harum, horum.*

QUICKLY   Vengeance of Jenny's case! Fie on her! Never 57
name her, child, if she be a whore.

EVANS   For shame, 'oman!

QUICKLY   You do ill to teach the child such words. He
teaches him to hick and to hack, which they'll do fast 61

114 **good sadness** all seriousness   117 **Etna** volcano in Sicily
120 **embassy** message   123 **address me to** prepare myself for, betake
myself to   131 **There's . . . coat** (A proverb suggesting that a reputation can easily be ruined.)   136 **halfpenny purse** small purse for small
coins   141 **horn-mad** frenzied like a horned animal in rutting season
(as at 1.4.45)

4.1. Location: A street in Windsor.
3 **courageous** (For "outrageously" or "ragingly"?)   5 **suddenly** at once
8 **playing day** holiday   10 **is let . . . play** i.e., has asked, as a visitor
of rank, that the boys be given a holiday   11 **of** on   12–13 **profits
. . . book** isn't making any progress in his studies   14 **accidence** rudiments of Latin grammar

19 **numbers** i.e., singular and plural   22 **'Od's nouns** by God's
wounds (confused with *odd* numbers, e.g., three)   23 **Peace your tattlings** cease your prattle   25 **Polecats** (Many of Quickly's misconstru-
ings are bawdy: *polecats*, "prostitutes"; *horum*, "whores"; *harum*,
"hare," "prostitute"; *Jenny's case*, "a whore's pudendum," or, "her
pregnancy"; etc.)   37 **Articles . . . pronoun** (William is reciting un-
comprehendingly from William Lilly's widely used Latin grammar,
which followed the ancient stoic grammarians in regarding demonstrative pronouns—*hic, haec, hoc*—as a sort of article, like *the*.)
38 **singulariter** in the singular.   **nominativo** in the nominative. (Similarly with *genitivo, accusativo*, and *vocativo*.)   44 **Hang-hog** (Bacon is
made by hanging up a hog.)   49 **caret** is lacking. (But Quickly interprets it as "carrot.")   57 **Vengeance of** i.e., a plague on   61 **to hick
and to hack** i.e., to drink and engage in sex; see 2.1.49

enough of themselves, and to call "whorum." Fie upon you!

EVANS 'Oman, art thou lunatics? Hast thou no understandings for thy cases and the numbers of the genders? Thou art as foolish Christian creatures as I would desires.

MRS. PAGE [to Mistress Quickly] Prithee, hold thy peace.

EVANS Show me now, William, some declensions of your pronouns.

WILLIAM Forsooth, I have forgot.

EVANS It is *qui, quae, quod.* If you forget your *qui's,* your *quae's,* and your *quod's,* you must be preeches. Go your ways and play, go.   74

MRS. PAGE He is a better scholar than I thought he was.

EVANS He is a good sprag memory. Farewell, Mistress 77 Page.

MRS. PAGE Adieu, good Sir Hugh. [*Exit Sir Hugh.*] Get you home, boy. [*Exit William.*] Come, we stay too long.   *Exeunt.*

❖

4.2 *Enter Falstaff [and] Mistress Ford.*

FALSTAFF Mistress Ford, your sorrow hath eaten up my sufferance. I see you are obsequious in your love, 2 and I profess requital to a hair's breadth, not only, Mistress Ford, in the simple office of love, but in all the accoutrement, complement, and ceremony of it. 5 But are you sure of your husband now?

MRS. FORD He's a-birding, sweet Sir John.

MRS. PAGE [*within*] What ho, gossip Ford! What ho! 8

MRS. FORD Step into the chamber, Sir John.
                    [*Exit Falstaff.*]

[*Enter*] *Mistress Page.*

MRS. PAGE How now, sweetheart, who's at home besides yourself?

MRS. FORD Why, none but mine own people.   12

MRS. PAGE Indeed?

MRS. FORD No, certainly. [*Aside to her.*] Speak louder.

MRS. PAGE Truly, I am so glad you have nobody here.

MRS. FORD Why?

MRS. PAGE Why, woman, your husband is in his old lines again. He so takes on yonder with my husband, 18 so rails against all married mankind, so curses all Eve's daughters, of what complexion soever, and so buffets himself on the forehead, crying, "Peer out, peer out!", 21 that any madness I ever yet beheld seemed but tameness, civility, and patience to this his distemper he is 23 in now. I am glad the fat knight is not here.

MRS. FORD Why, does he talk of him?

MRS. PAGE Of none but him, and swears he was carried out, the last time he searched for him, in a basket; protests to my husband he is now here, and hath drawn him and the rest of their company from their sport, to make another experiment of his suspi- 30 cion. But I am glad the knight is not here. Now he shall see his own foolery.

MRS. FORD How near is he, Mistress Page?

MRS. PAGE Hard by, at street end. He will be here anon.

MRS. FORD I am undone! The knight is here.

MRS. PAGE Why, then, you are utterly shamed, and he's but a dead man. What a woman are you! Away 37 with him, away with him! Better shame than murder.

MRS. FORD Which way should he go? How should I 39 bestow him? Shall I put him into the basket again?

[*Enter Falstaff.*]

FALSTAFF No, I'll come no more i' the basket. May I not go out ere he come?

MRS. PAGE Alas, three of Master Ford's brothers watch the door with pistols, that none shall issue out; otherwise you might slip away ere he came. But what make 45 you here?

FALSTAFF What shall I do? I'll creep up into the chimney.

MRS. FORD There they always use to discharge their 49 birding pieces.   50

MRS. PAGE Creep into the kilnhole.   51

FALSTAFF Where is it?

MRS. FORD He will seek there, on my word. Neither press, coffer, chest, trunk, well, vault, but he hath an 54 abstract for the remembrance of such places, and goes 55 to them by his note. There is no hiding you in the house.

FALSTAFF I'll go out, then.

MRS. PAGE If you go out in your own semblance, you die, Sir John—unless you go out disguised.

MRS. FORD How might we disguise him?

MRS. PAGE Alas the day, I know not! There is no woman's gown big enough for him; otherwise he might put on a hat, a muffler, and a kerchief, and so 64 escape.

FALSTAFF Good hearts, devise something. Any extremity rather than a mischief.   67

MRS. FORD My maid's aunt, the fat woman of Brent- 68 ford, has a gown above.   69

MRS. PAGE On my word, it will serve him; she's as big as he is. And there's her thrummed hat and her 71 muffler too. Run up, Sir John.

MRS. FORD Go, go, sweet Sir John. Mistress Page and I will look some linen for your head.   74

---

74 preeches breeched, i.e., whipped on the bare buttocks **77 sprag** sprack, lively, alert
4.2. Location: Ford's house.
2 sufferance suffering, pain. **obsequious** zealously devoted **5 complement** that which completes the whole, ceremoniousness **8 gossip** i.e., friend, neighbor. (Literally, fellow godparent.) **12 people** household servants **18 lines** vein, role. **takes on** is angry **21 Peer out** i.e., let my cuckold's horns come forth and be visible **23 to** compared to

30 experiment trial **37 What a** what kind of **39 should** can **45 make** do **49 use** make it a practice **50 birding pieces** guns for bird hunting **51 kilnhole** oven **54 press** clothes cupboard **55 abstract** inventory **64 muffler** kerchief or scarf worn by women over part of the face and neck **67 mischief** calamity **68–69 Brentford** a nearby village **69 above** upstairs **71 thrummed** made of or fringed with the unwoven ends of the warp threads **74 look** look for

MRS. PAGE   Quick, quick! We'll come dress you straight. 75
Put on the gown the while.   [*Exit Falstaff.*]

MRS. FORD   I would my husband would meet him in
this shape. He cannot abide the old woman of
Brentford. He swears she's a witch, forbade her my
house, and hath threatened to beat her.

MRS. PAGE   Heaven guide him to thy husband's cudgel, and the devil guide his cudgel afterwards!

MRS. FORD   But is my husband coming?

MRS. PAGE   Ay, in good sadness, is he, and talks of the 84
basket too, howsoever he hath had intelligence.

MRS. FORD   We'll try that; for I'll appoint my men to 86
carry the basket again, to meet him at the door with
it, as they did last time.

MRS. PAGE   Nay, but he'll be here presently. Let's go 89
dress him like the witch of Brentford.

MRS. FORD   I'll first direct my men what they shall do
with the basket. Go up. I'll bring linen for him
straight.   [*Exit.*]

MRS. PAGE   Hang him, dishonest varlet! We cannot 94
misuse him enough.
We'll leave a proof, by that which we will do,
Wives may be merry, and yet honest too.   97
We do not act that often jest and laugh;   98
'Tis old, but true, "Still swine eats all the draff." 99
                                            [*Exit.*]

[*Enter Mistress Ford with two*] Servants.

MRS. FORD   Go, sirs, take the basket again on your shoulders. Your master is hard at door. If he bid you set it 101
down, obey him. Quickly, dispatch!   [*Exit.*] 102

FIRST SERVANT   Come, come, take it up.

SECOND SERVANT   Pray heaven it be not full of knight
again.

FIRST SERVANT   I hope not. I had as lief bear so much
lead.   [*They take up the basket.*]

[*Enter*] Ford, Page, Caius, Evans, [*and*] Shallow.

FORD   Ay, but if it prove true, Master Page, have you
any way then to unfool me again?—Set down the bas- 109
ket, villain! Somebody call my wife. Youth in a basket!
O, you panderly rascals! There's a knot, a ging, a pack, 111
a conspiracy against me. Now shall the devil be 112
shamed.—What, wife, I say! Come, come forth! Be- 113
hold what honest clothes you send forth to bleaching!

PAGE   Why, this passes, Master Ford. You are not to go 115
loose any longer; you must be pinioned.

EVANS   Why, this is lunatics. This is mad as a mad dog.

SHALLOW   Indeed, Master Ford, this is not well, indeed.

FORD   So say I, too, sir.   119

[*Enter Mistress Ford.*]

Come hither, Mistress Ford—Mistress Ford, the honest woman, the modest wife, the virtuous creature,
that hath the jealous fool to her husband! I suspect
without cause, mistress, do I?

MRS. FORD   Heaven be my witness you do, if you
suspect me in any dishonesty.

FORD   Well said, brazenface! Hold it out.—Come forth, 126
sirrah!   [*He pulls clothes out of the basket.*]

PAGE   This passes!

MRS. FORD   Are you not ashamed? Let the clothes alone.

FORD   I shall find you anon.

EVANS   'Tis unreasonable. Will you take up your wife's 131
clothes? Come, away.

FORD   Empty the basket, I say!

MRS. FORD   Why, man, why?

FORD   Master Page, as I am a man, there was one
conveyed out of my house yesterday in this basket.
Why may not he be there again? In my house I am
sure he is. My intelligence is true; my jealousy is 138
reasonable. Pluck me out all the linen.   139

MRS. FORD   If you find a man there, he shall die a flea's
death.

PAGE   Here's no man.

SHALLOW   By my fidelity, this is not well, Master Ford. 143
This wrongs you.   144

EVANS   Master Ford, you must pray, and not follow the
imaginations of your own heart. This is jealousies.

FORD   Well, he's not here I seek for.

PAGE   No, nor nowhere else but in your brain.

FORD   Help to search my house this one time. If I find
not what I seek, show no color for my extremity; let 150
me forever be your table sport. Let them say of me, 151
"As jealous as Ford, that searched a hollow walnut for
his wife's leman." Satisfy me once more; once more 153
search with me.   [*Exeunt Servants with basket.*]

MRS. FORD [*calling upstairs*]   What ho, Mistress Page!
Come you and the old woman down. My husband
will come into the chamber.

FORD   Old woman? What old woman's that?

MRS. FORD   Why, it is my maid's aunt of Brentford.

FORD   A witch, a quean, an old, cozening quean! Have 160
I not forbid her my house? She comes of errands, does 161
she? We are simple men; we do not know what's
brought to pass under the profession of fortune-
telling. She works by charms, by spells, by the figure, 164
and such daubery as this is, beyond our element; we 165
know nothing.—Come down, you witch, you hag,
you! Come down, I say!

---

75 **straight** at once   84 **in good sadness** in all seriousness   86 **try** test
89 **presently** right away   94 **dishonest** lecherous   97 **honest** chaste
98 **act** i.e., act unchastely   99 **Still** quiet.   **draff** pigwash. (The proverb reinforces Mistress Page's point that merry talk does not ensure
wantonness; adulterous women are usually quiet about it.)   101 **hard
at door** right at the door   102 **dispatch** hurry   109 **unfool me** disbur-
den me of a reputation for folly   111 **a knot . . . pack** a company, a
gang, a confederacy   112–113 **Now . . . shamed** i.e., now truth will
out. (From the proverb "Tell the truth and shame the devil.")
115 **passes** surpasses, goes beyond all bounds   119 **So say I, too**
(Ford means that something is amiss, not, as Shallow intended to say,
that Ford's behavior is deplorable.)

126 **Hold it out** i.e., continue to maintain your falsehood   131 **take
up** pick up (but with unintended bawdy suggestion of lifting his wife's
dress)   138 **intelligence** information   139 **Pluck me out** pluck out for
me   143 **By my fidelity** upon my word   144 **wrongs you** does you
dishonor   150 **show . . . extremity** make no attempt to excuse my
extreme behavior   151 **your table sport** butt or laughingstock of the
company   153 **leman** lover   160 **quean** jade, hussy.   **cozening** deceiving   161 **of** on   164 **by the figure** i.e., by making wax figures
and sticking pins in them, or, by astrological charts   165 **daubery**
false show.   **beyond our element** beyond our comprehension, belonging to another world

MRS. FORD   Nay, good sweet husband!—Good gentlemen, let him not strike the old woman.

[*Enter Falstaff in woman's clothes, and Mistress Page.*]

MRS. PAGE   Come, Mother Prat, come, give me your hand.

FORD   I'll prat her. [*Beating him.*] Out of my door, you 172 witch, you rag, you baggage, you polecat, you 173 ronyon! Out, out! I'll conjure you, I'll fortune-tell you. 174
[*Exit Falstaff.*]

MRS. PAGE   Are you not ashamed? I think you have killed the poor woman.

MRS. FORD   Nay, he will do it.—'Tis a goodly credit for 177 you. 178

FORD   Hang her, witch!

EVANS   By Jeshu, I think the 'oman is a witch indeed. I like not when a 'oman has a great peard. I spy a great peard under his muffler.

FORD   Will you follow, gentlemen? I beseech you, follow. See but the issue of my jealousy. If I cry out 184 thus upon no trail, never trust me when I open again. 185

PAGE   Let's obey his humor a little further. Come, 186 gentlemen.
[*Exeunt Ford, Page, Shallow, Caius, and Evans.*]

MRS. PAGE   Trust me, he beat him most pitifully.

MRS. FORD   Nay, by the Mass, that he did not; he beat him most unpitifully, methought.

MRS. PAGE   I'll have the cudgel hallowed and hung o'er the altar. It hath done meritorious service.

MRS. FORD   What think you? May we, with the warrant of womanhood and the witness of a good conscience, pursue him with any further revenge?

MRS. PAGE   The spirit of wantonness is, sure, scared 196 out of him. If the devil have him not in fee simple, 197 with fine and recovery, he will never, I think, in the 198 way of waste, attempt us again. 199

MRS. FORD   Shall we tell our husbands how we have served him?

MRS. PAGE   Yes, by all means, if it be but to scrape the figures out of your husband's brains. If they can find 203 in their hearts the poor, unvirtuous, fat knight shall be any further afflicted, we two will still be the ministers. 205

MRS. FORD   I'll warrant they'll have him publicly shamed, and methinks there would be no period 207 to the jest, should he not be publicly shamed.

172 **prat** beat, teach a lesson, practice tricks on (?)   173 **rag** worthless person.   **baggage** hussy.   **polecat** whore   174 **ronyon** disreputable woman   177–178 **'Tis . . . you** it does you great credit. (Said ironically.)   184 **issue** conclusion   184–185 **cry . . . trail** bay like a hunting dog despite the absence of a scent   185 **open** give voice (like a hunting dog)   186 **obey his humor** humor him   196 **wantonness** lust   197 **fee simple** estate belonging to an owner and his heirs forever; hence, absolute possession   198 **fine and recovery** procedures by which an entailed estate was converted into fee simple. (Unless Falstaff already belongs to the devil outright, says Mistress Page, he won't try us again.)   199 **waste** spoliation, despoiling. (Another legal term.)   203 **figures** fantasies, conceits   205 **ministers** agents   207 **period** suitable conclusion

MRS. PAGE   Come, to the forge with it, then shape it. I 209 would not have things cool.   *Exeunt.*

4.3   *Enter Host and Bardolph.*

BARDOLPH   Sir, the Germans desire to have three of your horses. The Duke himself will be tomorrow at court, and they are going to meet him.

HOST   What duke should that be comes so secretly? I hear not of him in the court. Let me speak with the gentlemen. They speak English?

BARDOLPH   Ay, sir. I'll call them to you.

HOST   They shall have my horses, but I'll make them pay; I'll sauce them. They have had my house a week 9 at command. I have turned away my other guests. 10 They must come off. I'll sauce them. Come.   *Exeunt.* 11

4.4   *Enter Page, Ford, Mistress Page, Mistress Ford, and Evans.*

EVANS   'Tis one of the best discretions of a 'oman as 1 ever I did look upon.

PAGE   And did he send you both these letters at an 3 instant? 4

MRS. PAGE   Within a quarter of an hour.

FORD
Pardon me, wife. Henceforth do what thou wilt;
I rather will suspect the sun with cold 7
Than thee with wantonness. Now doth thy honor stand,
In him that was of late an heretic,
As firm as faith.

PAGE   'Tis well, 'tis well. No more.
Be not as extreme in submission as in offense.
But let our plot go forward. Let our wives
Yet once again, to make us public sport,
Appoint a meeting with this old fat fellow,
Where we may take him and disgrace him for it.

FORD
There is no better way than that they spoke of.

PAGE   How? To send him word they'll meet him in the park at midnight? Fie, fie, he'll never come.

EVANS   You say he has been thrown in the rivers and has been grievously peaten as an old 'oman. Methinks there should be terrors in him that he should not come. Methinks his flesh is punished; he shall have no desires.

PAGE   So think I too.

209 **Come . . . shape it** i.e., strike while the iron is hot
4.3. Location: The Garter Inn.
9 **sauce them** i.e., make them pay dearly   10 **at command** retained for their use upon their expected arrival   11 **come off** pay up
4.4. Location: Ford's house.
1 **'Tis** i.e., she is.   **best . . . 'oman** i.e., most discreet women
3–4 **at an instant** at the same time   7 **with** of

MRS. FORD
Devise but how you'll use him when he comes,   25
And let us two devise to bring him thither.

MRS. PAGE
There is an old tale goes that Herne the hunter,
Sometime a keeper here in Windsor Forest,   28
Doth all the wintertime, at still midnight,
Walk round about an oak, with great ragg'd horns;   30
And there he blasts the tree, and takes the cattle,   31
And makes milch kine yield blood, and shakes a
chain   32
In a most hideous and dreadful manner.
You have heard of such a spirit, and well you know
The superstitious idle-headed eld   35
Received and did deliver to our age
This tale of Herne the hunter for a truth.

PAGE
Why, yet there want not many that do fear   38
In deep of night to walk by this Herne's oak.
But what of this?

MRS. FORD   Marry, this is our device: 40
That Falstaff at that oak shall meet with us,
Disguised like Herne, with huge horns on his head.

PAGE
Well, let it not be doubted but he'll come.
And in this shape when you have brought him
thither,   44
What shall be done with him? What is your plot?

MRS. PAGE
That likewise have we thought upon, and thus:
Nan Page my daughter, and my little son,
And three or four more of their growth, we'll dress   48
Like urchins, aufs, and fairies, green and white,   49
With rounds of waxen tapers on their heads,   50
And rattles in their hands. Upon a sudden,
As Falstaff, she, and I are newly met,
Let them from forth a sawpit rush at once   53
With some diffusèd song. Upon their sight,   54
We two in great amazedness will fly.
Then let them all encircle him about,
And, fairylike, to pinch the unclean knight,
And ask him why, that hour of fairy revel,
In their so sacred paths he dares to tread
In shape profane.

MRS. FORD   And till he tell the truth,
Let the supposèd fairies pinch him sound   61
And burn him with their tapers.

MRS. PAGE   The truth being known,
We'll all present ourselves, dis-horn the spirit,
And mock him home to Windsor.

FORD   The children must
Be practiced well to this, or they'll ne'er do 't.

EVANS   I will teach the children their behaviors, and I
will be like a jackanapes also, to burn the knight with   67
my taber.   68

FORD
That will be excellent. I'll go buy them vizards.   69

MRS. PAGE
My Nan shall be the queen of all the fairies,
Finely attirèd in a robe of white.

PAGE
That silk will I go buy. [Aside.] And in that tire   72
Shall Master Slender steal my Nan away
And marry her at Eton. [To Mistress Page.] Go,
send to Falstaff straight.   74

FORD
Nay, I'll to him again in name of Brook.
He'll tell me all his purpose. Sure he'll come.

MRS. PAGE
Fear not you that. Go get us properties   77
And tricking for our fairies.   78

EVANS   Let us about it. It is admirable pleasures and
fery honest knaveries. [Exeunt Page, Ford, and Evans.]

MRS. PAGE   Go, Mistress Ford,
Send quickly to Sir John, to know his mind.
                                        [Exit Mistress Ford.]
I'll to the Doctor. He hath my good will,
And none but he, to marry with Nan Page.
That Slender, though well landed, is an idiot;   85
And he my husband best of all affects.   86
The Doctor is well moneyed, and his friends
Potent at court. He, none but he, shall have her,
Though twenty thousand worthier come to crave
her.   [Exit.]

♣

4.5   *Enter Host [and] Simple.*

HOST   What wouldst thou have, boor? What, thickskin?   1
Speak, breathe, discuss; brief, short, quick, snap.   2

SIMPLE   Marry, sir, I come to speak with Sir John
Falstaff from Master Slender.

HOST   There's his chamber, his house, his castle, his
standing bed and truckle bed. 'Tis painted about with   6
the story of the Prodigal, fresh and new. Go knock and   7
call. He'll speak like an Anthropophaginian unto thee.   8
Knock, I say.

SIMPLE   There's an old woman, a fat woman, gone up
into his chamber. I'll be so bold as stay, sir, till she
come down. I come to speak with her, indeed.

---

67 like a jackanapes disguised as an ape or monkey. (Evans actually
disguises himself as a satyr.)   **68 taber** taper, candle   **69 vizards** visors, masks   **72 tire** attire   **74 Eton** town across the Thames from
Windsor   **77 properties** theatrical props   **78 tricking** adornment, costumes   **85 well landed** rich in land   **86 he** i.e., him.   **affects** prefers
4.5. Location: The Garter Inn.
1 thickskin one slow or dull of feeling   **2 discuss** declare   **6 truckle
bed** trundle bed, low bed stored under the *standing bed* or regular
bed   **7 the Prodigal** (Compare *1 Henry IV*, 4.2.34 and *2 Henry IV*,
2.1.143, where this story from Luke 15:11–32 is again associated
with Falstaff.)   **8 Anthropophaginian** i.e., cannibal

---

25 use treat   **28 Sometime** formerly   **30 ragg'd** shaggy, pronged
31 blasts blights, or blasts with lightning.   **takes** bewitches
32 milch kine dairy cattle   **35 eld** old age, i.e., elders, an earlier
generation   **38 want** lack   **40 device** plan   **44 shape** disguise
48 growth size, age   **49 urchins, aufs** (Terms for goblins or elves.)
50 rounds circlets   **53 sawpit** a pit over which wood was sawed
54 diffusèd confused, disorderly   **61 sound** soundly

HOST   Ha, a fat woman? The knight may be robbed. I'll call.—Bully knight! Bully Sir John! Speak from thy lungs military. Art thou there? It is thine Host, thine Ephesian, calls.   16

FALSTAFF [within]   How now, mine Host?

HOST   Here's a Bohemian Tartar tarries the coming 18 down of thy fat woman. Let her descend, bully, let her descend. My chambers are honorable. Fie, privacy? Fie!

[Enter] Falstaff.

FALSTAFF   There was, mine Host, an old fat woman even now with me, but she's gone.

SIMPLE   Pray you, sir, was 't not the wise woman of 24 Brentford?

FALSTAFF   Ay, marry, was it, mussel shell. What would 26 you with her?

SIMPLE   My master, sir, my Master Slender, sent to her, seeing her go through the streets, to know, sir, whether one Nym, sir, that beguiled him of a chain, had the chain or no.

FALSTAFF   I spake with the old woman about it.

SIMPLE   And what says she, I pray, sir?

FALSTAFF   Marry, she says that the very same man that beguiled Master Slender of his chain cozened him of it.

SIMPLE   I would I could have spoken with the woman herself. I had other things to have spoken with her too from him.

FALSTAFF   What are they? Let us know.

HOST   Ay, come. Quick.

SIMPLE   I may not conceal them, sir.   41

HOST   Conceal them or thou diest.

SIMPLE   Why, sir, they were nothing but about Mistress Anne Page, to know if it were my master's fortune to have her or no.

FALSTAFF   'Tis, 'tis his fortune.

SIMPLE   What, sir?

FALSTAFF   To have her, or no. Go, say the woman told me so.

SIMPLE   May I be bold to say so, sir?

FALSTAFF   Ay, sir; like who more bold.   51

SIMPLE   I thank your worship. I shall make my master glad with these tidings.   [Exit.]

HOST   Thou art clerkly, thou art clerkly, Sir John. Was 54 there a wise woman with thee?

FALSTAFF   Ay, that there was, mine Host, one that hath taught me more wit than ever I learned before in my life. And I paid nothing for it, neither, but was paid for 58 my learning.

[Enter] Bardolph.

BARDOLPH   Out, alas, sir! Cozenage, mere cozenage!   60

HOST   Where be my horses? Speak well of them, 61 varletto.   62

BARDOLPH   Run away with the cozeners. For so soon as I came beyond Eton, they threw me off from behind one of them, in a slough of mire, and set spurs and away, like three German devils, three Doctor Faus- 66 tuses.   67

HOST   They are gone but to meet the Duke, villain. Do not say they be fled. Germans are honest men.

[Enter] Evans.

EVANS   Where is mine Host?

HOST   What is the matter, sir?

EVANS   Have a care of your entertainments. There is a 72 friend of mine come to town tells me there is three cozen-germans that has cozened all the hosts of 74 Reading, of Maidenhead, of Colnbrook, of horses and 75 money. I tell you for good will, look you. You are wise, and full of gibes and vloutingstocks, and 'tis not 77 convenient you should be cozened. Fare you well.   78
                    [Exit.]

[Enter] Caius.

CAIUS   Vere is mine Host de Jarteer?

HOST   Here, Master Doctor, in perplexity and doubtful 80 dilemma.

CAIUS   I cannot tell vat is dat. But it is tell-a me dat you make grand preparation for a duke de Jamany. By my 83 trot, dere is no duke that the court is know to come. I 84 tell you for good will. Adieu.   [Exit.]

HOST Hue and cry, villain, go!—Assist me, knight. I am 86 undone!—Fly, run, hue and cry, villain! I am undone!
                    [Exeunt Host and Bardolph.]

FALSTAFF   I would all the world might be cozened, for I have been cozened and beaten too. If it should come to the ear of the court how I have been transformed, and how my transformation hath been washed and cudgeled, they would melt me out of my fat drop by drop and liquor fishermen's boots with me. I warrant 93 they would whip me with their fine wits till I were as crestfallen as a dried pear. I never prospered since I 95 forswore myself at primero. Well, if my wind were but 96 long enough to say my prayers, I would repent.

[Enter Mistress] Quickly.

Now, whence come you?

QUICKLY   From the two parties, forsooth.

16 **Ephesian** i.e., boon companion   18 **Bohemian Tartar** i.e., barbarian, wild man.   **tarries** (who) awaits   24 **wise woman** i.e., fortune-teller   26 **mussel shell** i.e., one who gapes   41 **conceal** (For "reveal." The Host answers ironically with the same misused word.)   51 **like who more bold** as bold as the boldest   54 **clerkly** scholarly, wise   58 **was paid** (i.e., with a beating)   60 **Cozenage** double-dealing.   **mere** absolute

61 **Speak well of them** i.e., tell me good news of them   62 **varletto** varlet, rascal   66–67 **Doctor Faustuses** (Named for the German scholar-magician who practices devilish arts in Marlowe's play.)   72 **your entertainments** i.e., your guests   74 **cozen-germans** (1) cousins-german, close relatives (2) cozening or cheating Germans   75 **Reading** a town not far from Windsor. (Also true of *Maidenhead* and *Colnbrook*.)   77 **vloutingstocks** i.e., taunts   78 **convenient** fitting   80 **doubtful** full of doubts   83 **Jamany** Germany   84 **trot** troth.   **that . . . to come** whose arrival is known of at court   86 **Hue and cry, villain** (The Host bids Bardolph go raise the cry for pursuit of a felon.)   93 **liquor** saturate with oil to make waterproof   95 **crestfallen** i.e., shriveled   96 **forswore . . . primero** cheated in a gambling card game

FALSTAFF   The devil take one party and his dam the other! And so they shall be both bestowed. I have suffered more for their sakes, more than the villainous inconstancy of man's disposition is able to bear.

QUICKLY   And have not they suffered? Yes, I warrant, speciously one of them. Mistress Ford, good heart, is 105 beaten black and blue, that you cannot see a white spot about her.

FALSTAFF   What tell'st thou me of black and blue? I was beaten myself into all the colors of the rainbow, and I was like to be apprehended for the witch of Brentford. 110 But that my admirable dexterity of wit, my counterfeiting the action of an old woman, delivered me, the knave constable had set me i' the stocks, i' the common stocks, for a witch.

QUICKLY   Sir, let me speak with you in your chamber. You shall hear how things go, and, I warrant, to your content. Here is a letter will say somewhat. [*She gives a letter.*] Good hearts, what ado here is to bring you together! Sure, one of you does not serve heaven well, that you are so crossed.   120

FALSTAFF   Come up into my chamber.   *Exeunt.*

❖

4.6   *Enter Fenton [and] Host.*

HOST   Master Fenton, talk not to me. My mind is heavy. I will give over all.   2

FENTON
Yet hear me speak. Assist me in my purpose,
And, as I am a gentleman, I'll give thee
A hundred pound in gold more than your loss.

HOST   I will hear you, Master Fenton, and I will at the least keep your counsel.   7

FENTON
From time to time I have acquainted you
With the dear love I bear to fair Anne Page,
Who mutually hath answered my affection,
So far forth as herself might be her chooser,   11
Even to my wish. I have a letter from her   12
Of such contents as you will wonder at,
The mirth whereof so larded with my matter   14
That neither singly can be manifested
Without the show of both. Fat Falstaff
Hath a great scene; the image of the jest   17
I'll show you here at large. [*He shows a letter.*] Hark,
good mine Host.   18
Tonight at Herne's oak, just twixt twelve and one,
Must my sweet Nan present the Fairy Queen—   20
The purpose why is here—in which disguise,
While other jests are something rank on foot,   22

Her father hath commanded her to slip
Away with Slender, and with him at Eton
Immediately to marry. She hath consented.
Now, sir,
Her mother, even strong against that match   27
And firm for Doctor Caius, hath appointed
That he shall likewise shuffle her away,   29
While other sports are tasking of their minds,   30
And at the deanery, where a priest attends,
Straight marry her. To this her mother's plot
She, seemingly obedient, likewise hath
Made promise to the Doctor. Now, thus it rests: 34
Her father means she shall be all in white,
And in that habit, when Slender sees his time   36
To take her by the hand and bid her go,
She shall go with him. Her mother hath intended, 38
The better to denote her to the Doctor—
For they must all be masked and vizarded—
That quaint in green she shall be loose enrobed, 41
With ribbons pendent, flaring 'bout her head;
And when the Doctor spies his vantage ripe,
To pinch her by the hand, and on that token
The maid hath given consent to go with him.

HOST
Which means she to deceive, father or mother?

FENTON
Both, my good Host, to go along with me.
And here it rests: that you'll procure the vicar
To stay for me at church twixt twelve and one,
And, in the lawful name of marrying,
To give our hearts united ceremony.

HOST
Well, husband your device. I'll to the vicar.   52
Bring you the maid, you shall not lack a priest. 53

FENTON
So shall I evermore be bound to thee.
Besides, I'll make a present recompense.   *Exeunt.* 55

❖

5.1   *Enter Falstaff [and Mistress] Quickly.*

FALSTAFF   Prithee, no more prattling; go. I'll hold. This 1 is the third time; I hope good luck lies in odd numbers. Away, go. They say there is divinity in odd 3 numbers, either in nativity, chance, or death. Away!

QUICKLY   I'll provide you a chain, and I'll do what I can to get you a pair of horns.

FALSTAFF   Away, I say! Time wears. Hold up your 7 head, and mince.   [*Exit Mistress Quickly.*] 8

[*Enter*] Ford [*disguised*].

---

105 **speciously** (For "specially.")   110 **like** likely, about   120 **crossed** thwarted
4.6. Location: The Garter Inn, as before.
2 **give over** abandon   7 **keep your counsel** keep your secret   11 **So far forth** insofar   12 **to** according to   14 **larded . . . matter** intermingled with what concerns me   17 **image** form, idea   18 **at large** at length   20 **present** represent   22 **something rank** rather abundantly. **on foot** afoot, being devised

27 **even** equally   29 **shuffle** smuggle, steal   30 **tasking of** busily occupying   34 **it rests** matters stand   36 **habit** dress   38 **intended** arranged   41 **quaint** decorously   52 **husband** manage prudently
53 **Bring you** if you bring   55 **present** immediate
5.1. Location: The Garter Inn, as before.
1 **hold** persevere, keep the appointment   3 **divinity** mysterious power
7–8 **Hold up your head** i.e., keep up your spirits   8 **mince** trip off

How now, Master Brook? Master Brook, the matter will be known tonight or never. Be you in the park about midnight, at Herne's oak, and you shall see wonders.

FORD   Went you not to her yesterday, sir, as you told 13 me you had appointed?

FALSTAFF   I went to her, Master Brook, as you see, like a poor old man, but I came from her, Master Brook, like a poor old woman. That same knave Ford, her husband, hath the finest mad devil of jealousy in him, Master Brook, that ever governed frenzy. I will tell you: he beat me grievously, in the shape of a woman; for in the shape of man, Master Brook, I fear not Goliath 21 with a weaver's beam, because I know also life is a 22 shuttle. I am in haste. Go along with me; I'll tell you 23 all, Master Brook. Since I plucked geese, played 24 truant, and whipped top, I knew not what 'twas to be 25 beaten till lately. Follow me. I'll tell you strange things of this knave Ford, on whom tonight I will be revenged, and I will deliver his wife into your hand. Follow. Strange things in hand, Master Brook! Follow.
                                                   Exeunt.

5.2   *Enter Page, Shallow, [and] Slender.*

PAGE   Come, come. We'll couch i' the castle ditch till we 1 see the light of our fairies. Remember, son Slender, my daughter.

SLENDER   Ay, forsooth. I have spoke with her, and we have a nayword how to know one another. I come to 5 her in white and cry "mum," she cries "budget," and 6 by that we know one another.

SHALLOW   That's good too. But what needs either your 8 "mum" or her "budget"? The white will decipher her 9 well enough.—It hath struck ten o'clock.

PAGE   The night is dark; light and spirits will become it 11 well. Heaven prosper our sport! No man means evil but the devil, and we shall know him by his horns. Let's away. Follow me.
                                                   Exeunt.

5.3   *Enter Mistress Page, Mistress Ford, [and] Caius.*

MRS. PAGE   Master Doctor, my daughter is in green. When you see your time, take her by the hand, away with her to the deanery, and dispatch it quickly. Go 3 before into the park. We two must go together.

CAIUS   I know vat I have to do. Adieu.

MRS. PAGE   Fare you well, sir. [*Exit Caius.*] My husband will not rejoice so much at the abuse of Falstaff as he will chafe at the Doctor's marrying my daughter. But 'tis no matter. Better a little chiding than a great deal of heartbreak.

MRS. FORD   Where is Nan now, and her troop of fairies, and the Welsh devil Hugh?

MRS. PAGE   They are all couched in a pit hard by Herne's Oak, with obscured lights, which, at the very instant of Falstaff's and our meeting, they will at once display to the night.

MRS. FORD   That cannot choose but amaze him.   17

MRS. PAGE   If he be not amazed, he will be mocked. If 18 he be amazed, he will every way be mocked.   19

MRS. FORD   We'll betray him finely.

MRS. PAGE
Against such lewdsters and their lechery,
Those that betray them do no treachery.

MRS. FORD   The hour draws on. To the oak, to the oak!
                                                   Exeunt.

5.4   *Enter Evans [as a satyr] and [children disguised as] fairies.*

EVANS   Trib, trib, fairies. Come, and remember your 1 parts. Be pold, I pray you. Follow me into the pit, and when I give the watch'ords, do as I pid you. Come, come; trib, trib.
                                                   Exeunt.

*

5.5   *Enter Falstaff [disguised as Herne, wearing a buck's head].*

FALSTAFF   The Windsor bell hath struck twelve; the minute draws on. Now, the hot-blooded gods assist me! Remember, Jove, thou wast a bull for thy Europa; 3 love set on thy horns. O powerful Love, that in some respects makes a beast a man, in some other a man a beast! You were also, Jupiter, a swan for the love of 6 Leda. O omnipotent Love, how near the god drew to 7 the complexion of a goose! A fault done first in the form of a beast—O Jove, a beastly fault!—and then another fault in the semblance of a fowl; think on 't, Jove, a foul fault! When gods have hot backs, what shall poor men do? For me, I am here a Windsor stag, and the fattest, I think, i' the forest. Send me a cool rut-time, Jove, or who can blame me to piss my 14 tallow? Who comes here? My doe?   15

---

13 **yesterday** (Actually, the meeting appears to have been earlier this same day.)   21–22 **Goliath . . . beam** (See 1 Samuel 17:7: "The staff of his [Goliath's] spear was like a weaver's beam." See also 2 Samuel 21:19. A weaver's beam is a wooden cylinder in a loom.)
22–23 **life is a shuttle** (See Job 7:6: "My days are swifter than a weaver's shuttle.")   24–25 **plucked . . . top** i.e., committed various boyhood pranks. To whip a top is to set it spinning.
5.2. Location: Windsor Park.
1 **couch** hide   5 **nayword** password, watchword   6 **mum, budget** (*Mumbudget* connotes silence, as in a children's game by that name.)
8 **what needs** what need is there for   9 **decipher** identify   11 **become** suit

5.3. Location: Windsor Park, as before.
3 **dispatch** conclude

17 **cannot choose but amaze** is certain to astound and terrify   18–19 **mocked . . . mocked** deceived . . . ridiculed
5.4. Location: Windsor Park, as before.
1 **Trib** trip, move nimbly
5.5. Location: Windsor Park, as before.
3, 6–7 **bull . . . Europa, swan . . . Leda** (References to legends of Jupiter's animal disguises when engaged in various amours.)   14 **rut-time** mating season   14–15 **piss my tallow** i.e., sweat off and excrete excess fat during mating season, like a stag

[Enter] Mistress Page [and] Mistress Ford.

MRS. FORD Sir John? Art thou there, my deer, my male 16
deer?

FALSTAFF My doe with the black scut! Let the sky rain 18
potatoes; let it thunder to the tune of "Greensleeves," 19
hail kissing-comfits, and snow eringoes; let there 20
come a tempest of provocation, I will shelter me here. 21
[He embraces her.]

MRS. FORD Mistress Page is come with me, sweetheart.

FALSTAFF Divide me like a bribed buck, each a haunch. 23
I will keep my sides to myself, my shoulders for the
fellow of this walk, and my horns I bequeath your 25
husbands. Am I a woodman, ha? Speak I like Herne 26
the hunter? Why, now is Cupid a child of conscience; 27
he makes restitution. As I am a true spirit, welcome!
[A noise within.]

MRS. PAGE Alas, what noise?

MRS. FORD Heaven forgive our sins!

FALSTAFF What should this be?

MRS. FORD, MRS. PAGE Away, away! *[They run off.]*

FALSTAFF I think the devil will not have me damned,
lest the oil that's in me should set hell on fire. He
would never else cross me thus. 35

*[Enter] Evans, [disguised as a satyr, Mistress]
Quickly [as the Fairy Queen], Anne Page [and
children as] fairies, [with tapers, and] Pistol [as
Hobgoblin].*

QUICKLY *[as Fairy Queen]*
Fairies, black, gray, green, and white,
You moonshine revelers, and shades of night, 37
You orphan heirs of fixèd destiny, 38
Attend your office and your quality. 39
Crier Hobgoblin, make the fairy oyes. 40

PISTOL *[as Hobgoblin]*
Elves, list your names. Silence, you airy toys! 41
Cricket, to Windsor chimneys shalt thou leap.
Where fires thou find'st unraked and hearths
unswept, 43
There pinch the maids as blue as bilberry. 44
Our radiant Queen hates sluts and sluttery. 45

FALSTAFF
They are fairies. He that speaks to them shall die. 46
I'll wink and couch; no man their works must eye. 47
[He lies face downward.]

EVANS *[as a satyr]*
Where's Bead? Go you, and where you find a maid
That, ere she sleep, has thrice her prayers said,
Raise up the organs of her fantasy; 50
Sleep she as sound as careless infancy. 51
But those as sleep and think not on their sins, 52
Pinch them, arms, legs, backs, shoulders, sides, and
shins.

QUICKLY About, about! 54
Search Windsor Castle, elves, within and out.
Strew good luck, aufs, on every sacred room, 56
That it may stand till the perpetual doom 57
In state as wholesome as in state 'tis fit, 58
Worthy the owner, and the owner it.
The several chairs of order look you scour 60
With juice of balm and every precious flower.
Each fair installment, coat, and several crest 62
With loyal blazon evermore be blest! 63
And nightly, meadow fairies, look you sing,
Like to the Garter's compass, in a ring. 65
Th' expressure that it bears, green let it be, 66
More fertile-fresh than all the field to see;
And *"Honi soit qui mal y pense"* write 68
In em'rald tufts, flow'rs purple, blue, and white,
Like sapphire, pearl, and rich embroidery,
Buckled below fair knighthood's bending knee;
Fairies use flowers for their charactery. 72
Away, disperse! But till 'tis one o'clock,
Our dance of custom, round about the oak 74
Of Herne the hunter, let us not forget.

EVANS Pray you,
Lock hand in hand. Yourselves in order set;
And twenty glowworms shall our lanterns be
To guide our measure round about the tree. 79
But stay! I smell a man of middle-earth. 80

FALSTAFF Heavens defend me from that Welsh fairy,
lest he transform me to a piece of cheese! 82
[They discover Falstaff hiding.]

PISTOL
Vile worm, thou wast o'erlooked even in thy birth. 83

16 **deer** (with a pun on "dear") 18 **scut** tail, pudendum 19 **potatoes** i.e., sweet potatoes. (Regarded by Elizabethans as aphrodisiac.) **Greensleeves** (A popular tune; see the note for 2.1.60.) 20 **kissing-comfits** perfumed sweetmeats for sweetening the breath. **eringoes** candied root of a plant called sea holly. (Regarded as aphrodisiac.) 21 **provocation** i.e., sexual stimulation 23 **bribed** stolen (and then quickly cut up and divided by the poachers) 25 **fellow of this walk** i.e., keeper of this forest, perhaps Herne himself. (Falstaff punningly suggests he will "shoulder off" or repel the forester if he makes trouble.) 25–26 **my horns . . . husbands** (Falstaff will make the husbands wear cuckold's horns.) 26 **woodman** (1) hunter (2) woman chaser 27 **is Cupid . . . conscience** i.e., Cupid is keeping faith with me 35 **cross** thwart 37 **shades** spirits 38 **orphan** i.e., fatherless. (Fairies were thought to be the result of spontaneous birth.) **heirs . . . destiny** i.e., those endowed with power to fulfill destiny (?) 39 **Attend . . . quality** attend to your duties and particular functions 40 **oyes** hear ye. (The call of the public crier.) 41 **list** listen for. **toys** substanceless beings 43 **unraked** not raked together to last through the night 44 **bilberry** a kind of blueberry 45 **sluttery** sluttishness

46 **He . . . die** (A widespread tradition about fairies.) 47 **wink** close my eyes. **couch** lie hidden 50 **Raise . . . fantasy** i.e., give her elevating and pleasant dreams 51 **Sleep she** let her sleep. **careless** free of care 52 **as** who 54 **About** i.e., get to work 56 **aufs** elves 57 **perpetual doom** Day of Judgment 58 **In state . . . fit** i.e., as healthy in condition as it is fitting in dignity 60 **The several . . . order** i.e., the individual stalls of the Garter knights (in Saint George's chapel at Windsor) 62 **installment** stall, place or seat in which a knight is installed. **coat** coat of arms. **several crest** separate heraldic device 63 **loyal blazon** coat of arms, armorial bearings of a loyal knight. **blest** favored, fortunate 65 **compass** circle. (The garter was worn below the left knee by knights of the order.) 66 **expressure** image, picture 68 **Honi . . . pense** Evil to him who evil thinks. (The motto of the Order of the Garter.) 72 **charactery** writing 74 **dance of custom** customary dance 79 **measure** stately dance 80 **middle-earth** i.e., the earth, the center of the universe, conceived of as between the heavens and the underworld 82 **cheese** (The Welshman's favorite food; compare 2.2.290–291.) 83 **o'erlooked** bewitched, looked on with an evil eye

QUICKLY [to Fairies]
With trial-fire touch me his finger end.
If he be chaste, the flame will back descend
And turn him to no pain; but if he start,   86
It is the flesh of a corrupted heart.

PISTOL
A trial, come.

EVANS   Come, will this wood take fire?   88
          [They put the tapers to his fingers, and he starts.]

FALSTAFF   O, O, O!

QUICKLY
Corrupt, corrupt, and tainted in desire!
About him, fairies. Sing a scornful rhyme,
And, as you trip, still pinch him to your time.   92

                    The Song.

FAIRIES
     Fie on sinful fantasy!
     Fie on lust and luxury!   94
     Lust is but a bloody fire,   95
     Kindled with unchaste desire,
     Fed in heart, whose flames aspire,
     As thoughts do blow them, higher and higher.
     Pinch him, fairies, mutually!   99
     Pinch him for his villainy.
Pinch him, and burn him, and turn him about,
Till candles and starlight and moonshine be out.

     [During this song they pinch Falstaff. Doctor] Caius
     [enters one way, and steals away a fairy in
     green]; Slender, [another way, and takes off a
     fairy in white; and] Fenton [enters, and steals
     away Mistress Anne Page. A noise of hunting is
     heard within. Mistress Quickly, Evans, Pistol, and
     all the Fairies run away. Falstaff pulls off his
     buck's head, and rises.]

     [Enter] Page, Ford, [Mistress Page, and Mistress
     Ford].

PAGE
Nay, do not fly. I think we have watched you now.   103
Will none but Herne the hunter serve your turn?   104

MRS. PAGE
I pray you, come, hold up the jest no higher.   105
Now, good Sir John, how like you Windsor wives?
                    [She points to Falstaff's horns.]
See you these, husband? Do not these fair yokes   107
Become the forest better than the town?

FORD   Now, sir, who's a cuckold now? Master Brook,
Falstaff's a knave, a cuckoldly knave; here are his
horns, Master Brook. And, Master Brook, he hath
enjoyed nothing of Ford's but his buck basket, his
cudgel, and twenty pounds of money, which must be

paid to Master Brook. His horses are arrested for it,   114
Master Brook.

MRS. FORD   Sir John, we have had ill luck; we could
never meet. I will never take you for my love again,   117
but I will always count you my deer.   118

FALSTAFF   I do begin to perceive that I am made an ass.

FORD   Ay, and an ox too. Both the proofs are extant.   120

FALSTAFF   And these are not fairies? I was three or four
times in the thought they were not fairies; and yet the
guiltiness of my mind, the sudden surprise of my
powers, drove the grossness of the foppery into a   124
received belief, in despite of the teeth of all rhyme and   125
reason, that they were fairies. See now how wit may
be made a Jack-a-Lent when 'tis upon ill employment!   127

EVANS   Sir John Falstaff, serve Got, and leave your
desires, and fairies will not pinse you.

FORD   Well said, fairy Hugh.

EVANS   And leave you your jealousies too, I pray you.

FORD   I will never mistrust my wife again till thou art
able to woo her in good English.

FALSTAFF   Have I laid my brain in the sun and dried it,
that it wants matter to prevent so gross o'erreaching as   135
this? Am I ridden with a Welsh goat too? Shall I have   136
a coxcomb of frieze? 'Tis time I were choked with a   137
piece of toasted cheese.

EVANS   Seese is not good to give putter. Your belly is all
putter.

FALSTAFF   "Seese" and "putter"! Have I lived to stand
at the taunt of one that makes fritters of English? This
is enough to be the decay of lust and late walking   143
through the realm.

MRS. PAGE   Why, Sir John, do you think, though we
would have thrust virtue out of our hearts by the head
and shoulders, and have given ourselves without scruple to hell, that ever the devil could have made you
our delight?

FORD   What, a hodge pudding? A bag of flax?   150

MRS. PAGE   A puffed man?   151

PAGE   Old, cold, withered and of intolerable entrails?   152

FORD   And one that is as slanderous as Satan?

PAGE   And as poor as Job?   154

FORD   And as wicked as his wife?   155

EVANS   And given to fornications, and to taverns, and
sack, and wine, and metheglins, and to drinkings,   157
and swearings, and starings, pribbles and prabbles?   158

---

86 turn put   88 s.d. fingers fingertips. (The stage direction is from the Quarto.)   92 still continually   94 luxury lechery   95 bloody fire fire in the blood   99 mutually jointly, in unison   103 watched you caught you in the act   104 serve your turn satisfy you. (Addressed to Falstaff in the disguise of Herne or in mock reproof to Mistress Page— part of "the jest" of line 105.)   105 hold . . . higher maintain the jest no longer   107 these fair yokes i.e., the horns

114 arrested seized by warrant as a security for paying   117 meet (with a pun on "mate")   118 deer (with a pun on "dear")   120 ox i.e., fool (with reference to the ox's horns, the proofs that are extant, i.e., still in existence and also protuberant)   124 powers faculties. foppery deceit   125 received accepted.   in despite of the teeth of in the teeth of, in defiance of   127 Jack-a-Lent butt. (See the note for 3.3.22.)   135 wants matter lacks means   136 ridden with mastered by   137 coxcomb fool's cap.   frieze kind of coarse woolen cloth, common in Wales   143 decay ruin.   late walking keeping late hours (in pursuit of women)   150 hodge pudding large "pudding," or sausage, made with a medley of ingredients.   bag of flax i.e., a large, shapeless bag   151 puffed dropsied, corpulent   152 intolerable excessive   154 Job (See Job 1 for Job's sudden descent into poverty.)   155 his wife i.e., Job's wife, who advised him to curse God (Job 2:9)   157 metheglins spiced drink made from wort and honey, Welsh in origin   158 starings glaring, madly raving

FALSTAFF   Well, I am your theme. You have the start of 159
me. I am dejected. I am not able to answer the Welsh 160
flannel. Ignorance itself is a plummet o'er me. Use me 161
as you will.

FORD   Marry, sir, we'll bring you to Windsor, to one
Master Brook, that you have cozened of money, to
whom you should have been a pander. Over and 165
above that you have suffered, I think to repay that 166
money will be a biting affliction.

PAGE   Yet be cheerful, knight. Thou shalt eat a posset 168
tonight at my house, where I will desire thee to laugh
at my wife that now laughs at thee. Tell her Master
Slender hath married her daughter.

MRS. PAGE [aside]   Doctors doubt that. If Anne Page 172
be my daughter, she is, by this, Doctor Caius' wife. 173

[Enter Slender.]

SLENDER   Whoa, ho, ho, father Page!

PAGE   Son, how now? How now, son? Have you
dispatched?   176

SLENDER   Dispatched? I'll make the best in Gloucestershire know on 't. Would I were hanged, la, else! 178

PAGE   Of what, son?

SLENDER   I came yonder at Eton to marry Mistress Anne
Page, and she's a great lubberly boy. If it had not been
i' the church, I would have swinged him, or he should 182
have swinged me. If I did not think it had been Anne
Page, would I might never stir! And 'tis a postmas- 184
ter's boy.   185

PAGE   Upon my life, then, you took the wrong.

SLENDER   What need you tell me that? I think so, when
I took a boy for a girl. If I had been married to him,
for all he was in woman's apparel, I would not have
had him.

PAGE   Why, this is your own folly. Did not I tell you
how you should know my daughter by her garments?

SLENDER   I went to her in white and cried "mum," and
she cried "budget," as Anne and I had appointed.
And yet it was not Anne, but a postmaster's boy.

MRS. PAGE   Good George, be not angry. I knew of your
purpose, turned my daughter into green, and indeed
she is now with the Doctor at the deanery, and there
married.

[Enter Caius.]

CAIUS   Vere is Mistress Page? By gar, I am cozened! I
ha' married un garçon, a boy; un paysan, by gar, a boy. 201
It is not Anne Page. By gar, I am cozened.

MRS. PAGE   Why, did you take her in green?

CAIUS   Ay, by gar, and 'tis a boy. By gar, I'll raise all
Windsor.

FORD   This is strange. Who hath got the right Anne?

PAGE   My heart misgives me. Here comes Master
Fenton.

[Enter Fenton and Anne Page.]

How now, Master Fenton?

ANNE
Pardon, good Father! Good my Mother, pardon!

PAGE   Now, mistress, how chance you went not with
Master Slender?

MRS. PAGE
Why went you not with Master Doctor, maid?

FENTON
You do amaze her. Hear the truth of it.   214
You would have married her most shamefully,
Where there was no proportion held in love.   216
The truth is, she and I, long since contracted,   217
Are now so sure that nothing can dissolve us.   218
Th' offense is holy that she hath committed,
And this deceit loses the name of craft,
Of disobedience, or unduteous title,   221
Since therein she doth evitate and shun   222
A thousand irreligious cursèd hours
Which forcèd marriage would have brought upon
her.

FORD
Stand not amazed. Here is no remedy.
In love the heavens themselves do guide the state;
Money buys lands, and wives are sold by fate.   227

FALSTAFF   I am glad, though you have ta'en a special
stand to strike at me, that your arrow hath glanced. 229

PAGE
Well, what remedy? Fenton, heaven give thee joy!
What cannot be eschewed must be embraced.

FALSTAFF
When night dogs run, all sorts of deer are chased.

MRS. PAGE
Well, I will muse no further. Master Fenton,   233
Heaven give you many, many merry days!
Good husband, let us every one go home
And laugh this sport o'er by a country fire—
Sir John and all.

FORD   Let it be so. Sir John,
To Master Brook you yet shall hold your word,
For he tonight shall lie with Mistress Ford.   Exeunt.

---

159 theme i.e., subject of mirth.   start advantage   160 dejected (1)
overthrown (2) disheartened   161 flannel a Welsh cloth.   plummet
(A quibble on plumbet, a woolen fabric, suggested by flannel, and
plummet, "a line for fathoming." Falstaff laments that he has been
fathomed even by an ignorant Welshman.)   165 should have been
were to have been   166 above that above that which   168 eat im-
bibe.   posset curdled ale or wine   172 Doctors doubt that (Proverbial; i.e., the wise are skeptical. The saying particularly applies here
to Doctor Caius.)   173 this this time   176 dispatched finished the
business   178 on 't of it.   else if I don't   182 swinged thrashed
184–185 postmaster's boy boy of the master of the post-horses
201 paysan peasant, i.e., yokel

214 amaze bewilder   216 proportion equality   217 contracted betrothed   218 sure fast knit   221 unduteous title title of undutifulness
222 evitate avoid   227 Money . . . fate (A variant of the proverb
"Marriage and hanging go by destiny.")   229 stand concealed place
for shooting.   glanced (Falstaff takes comfort in the fact that, though
he was the main target of the plot of exposure, others have suffered
mild humiliation as well.)   233 muse grumble, complain

As You Like It

As You Like It represents, together with *Much Ado About Nothing* and *Twelfth Night,* the summation of Shakespeare's achievement in festive, happy comedy during the years 1598–1601. *As You Like It* contains several motifs found in other Shakespearean comedies: the journey from a jaded court into a transforming silvan environment and back to a revitalized court (as in *A Midsummer Night's Dream*); hence, a contrasting of two worlds in the play—one presided over by a virtuous but exiled older brother and the other, by a usurping younger brother (as in *The Tempest*); the heroine disguised as a man (as in *The Merchant of Venice, The Two Gentlemen of Verona, Cymbeline,* and *Twelfth Night*); and a structure of multiple plotting in which numerous groups of characters are thematically played off against one another (as in several of Shakespeare's comedies). What chiefly distinguishes this play from the others, however, is the nature and function of its pastoral setting— the Forest of Arden.

The Forest of Arden is seen in many perspectives. As a natural wilderness, it is probably most like the real forest Shakespeare knew near Stratford-upon-Avon in Warwickshire—a place capable of producing the vulgarity of an Audrey or the bumptuous clowning of a William. The forest bears the name of Shakespeare's mother, Mary Arden, the daughter of a prosperous Warwickshire farmer. Its name also owes something to the forest in Shakespeare's source, *Rosalynde,* based in turn on the forest of Ardennes in France. No less vividly, the place recalls for us Nottinghamshire and the Sherwood Forest of Robin Hood, where persons in retreat from a society seemingly beyond repair find refuge in a mythic folk world purged of social injustice. As the "golden world" (1.1.114), the forest evokes an even deeper longing for a mythological past age of innocence and plenty, when humans shared some attributes of the giants and the gods. This myth has its parallel in the biblical Garden of Eden, before the human race experienced "the penalty of Adam" (2.1.5). Finally, in another of its aspects, the forest is Arcadia, a pastoral landscape embodied in an ancient and sophisticated literary tradition and peopled by the likes of Corin, Silvius, and Phoebe.

All but the first of these Ardens, compared and contrasted with one another, involve some idealization, not only of nature and the natural landscape, but also of the human condition. These various Ardens place our real life in a complex perspective and force us to a fresh appraisal of our own ordinary existence. Duke Senior, for example, describes the forest environment as a corrective for the evils of society. He addresses his followers in the forest as "my co-mates and brothers in exile" (2.1.1), suggesting a kind of social equality that he could never know in the cramped formality of his previous official existence. The banished Duke Senior and his followers have had to leave behind their lands and revenues in the grip of the usurping Duke Frederick. No longer rich, though adequately provided with all of life's necessities, the Duke and his "merry men" live "like the old Robin Hood of England" and "fleet the time carelessly as they did in the golden world" (1.1.111–114). In this friendly society, a strong communal sense replaces the necessity for individual proprietorship. All comers are welcome, with food for all.

There are no luxuries in the forest, to be sure, but even this spare existence affords relief from the decadence of courtly life. "Sweet are the uses of adversity" (2.1.12), insists Duke Senior. He welcomes the cold of winter because it teaches him the true condition of humanity and of himself. The forest is serenely impartial: neither malicious nor compassionate. Death, and even killing for food, are an inevitable part of forest existence. The Duke concedes that his presence in the forest means the slaughter of deer, who were the original inhabitants; Orlando and Adam find that death through starvation in the forest is all too real a possibility. The forest is never guilty of the degrading perversity of humans at their worst, but it is also incapable of charity and forgiveness.

Shakespeare's sources reflect the complexity of his vision of Arden. The original of the Orlando story, which Shakespeare may not have used directly, is *The Cook's Tale of Gamelyn,* found in a number of manuscripts of *The Canterbury Tales* and wrongly attributed to Chaucer. This hearty English romance glorifies the rebellious and even violent spirit of its Robin Hood hero, the neglected youngest son Gamelyn, who, aided by faithful old Adam the Spencer, evades his wicked eldest brother in a cunning and bloody escape. As king of the outlaws in Sherwood Forest, Gamelyn eventually triumphs over his eldest brother (now the sheriff) and sees him hanged. Here, then, originates the motif of refuge from social injustice in Arden, even though most of the actual violence has been omitted from Shakespeare's version. (A series of Robin Hood plays on a similar theme, beginning in 1598 with Anthony Munday's *The Downfall of Robert Earl of Huntingdon After Called Robin Hood,* were being performed with great success by the Admiral's company, chief rivals of the Lord Chamberlain's company to which Shakespeare belonged.)

As You Like It is clearly indebted to Thomas Lodge's *Rosalynde: Euphues' Golden Legacy* (published in 1590), a prose narrative version of the Gamelyn story in the ornate Euphuistic style of the 1580s. (Lodge's Epistle to the Gentleman Readers, casually inviting them to be pleased with this story if they are so inclined—"*If you like it, so*"—probably gave Shakespeare a hint for the name of his own play.) Lodge accentuated the love story with its courtship in masquerade, provided some charming songs, and introduced the pastoral love motif involving Corin, Silvius, Phoebe, and Ganymede. Shakespeare's ordering of episode is generally close to that of Lodge. Pastoral literature, which had become a literary rage in the 1580s and early 1590s, owing particularly to Edmund Spenser's *Shepheardes Calendar* (1579) and Philip Sidney's *Arcadia* (1590), traced its ancestry through such Renaissance continental writers as Jorge de Montemayor, Jacopo Sannazaro, and Giovanni Battista Guarini to the so-called Greek romances, and finally back to the eclogues of Virgil, Theocritus, and Bion. A literary mode that had begun originally as a realistic evocation of difficult country life had become, in the Renaissance, an elegant vehicle for the loftiest and most patrician sentiments in love, for philosophic debate, and even for extensive political analysis and satire of the clergy.

Shakespeare's alterations and additions give us insight into his method of construction and his thematic focus. Whereas Lodge cheerfully accepts the pastoral conventions of his day, Shakespeare exposes those conventions to some criticism and considerable irony. Alongside the mannered and literary Silvius and Phoebe, he places William and Audrey, as peasantlike a couple as ever drew milk from a cow's teat. The juxtaposition holds up to critical perspective the rival claims of the literary and natural worlds by examining the defects of each in relation to the strengths of the other. William and Audrey are Shakespeare's own creation, based presumably on observation and also on the dramatic convention of the rustic clown and wench, as exemplified earlier in his Costard and Jaquenetta (*Love's Labor's Lost*).

Equally original, and essential to the many-sided debate concerning the virtues of the court versus those of the country, are Touchstone and Jaques. Touchstone is a professional court fool, dressed in motley, a new comic type in Shakespeare, created apparently in response to the recent addition to the Lord Chamberlain's company of the brilliant actor Robert Armin. Jaques is also a new type, the malcontent satirist, reflecting the very latest literary vogue in the nondramatic poetry and drama for the private theater of George Chapman, John Marston, and Ben Jonson. (The private theaters, featuring boy actors, reopened in 1598–1599 after nearly a decade of enforced silence and proceeded at once to specialize in satirical drama.) Touchstone and Jaques complement one another as critics and observers—one laughing at human folly with quizzical comic detachment and the other satirizing it with self-righteous scorn.

Once we have been exposed to this assortment of newly created characters, we can no longer view either pastoral life or pastoral love as simply as Lodge and other writers of the period portray them.

When *As You Like It* is compared with its chief source, Shakespeare can also be seen to have altered and considerably softened the characters of the wicked brothers Oliver and Frederick. Whereas Lodge's Saladyne is motivated by a greedy desire to seize his younger brother Rosader's property, Shakespeare's Oliver is envious of Orlando's natural goodness and popularity. As he confesses in soliloquy, Orlando is "so much in the heart of the world and especially of my own people . . . that I am altogether misprized" (1.1.159–161). In his warped way, Oliver desires to be more like Orlando, and in the enchanted forest of Arden he eventually becomes so. Duke Frederick, too, is plainly envious of goodness. Trying to persuade his daughter Celia of the need for banishing Rosalind, he argues, "thou wilt show more bright and seem more virtuous / When she is gone" (1.3.79–80). In spite of his obsession with the mere "seeming" of virtue, Duke Frederick acknowledges the power of a goodness that will eventually convert him along with the rest. Penitence and conciliation replace the vengeful conclusion of Lodge's novel, in which the nobles of France finally overthrow and execute the usurping king. Although Shakespeare's resolutions are sudden, like all miracles they attest to the inexplicable power of goodness.

The court of Duke Frederick is "the envious court," identified by this fixed epithet. In it, brothers turn unnaturally against brothers: the younger Frederick usurps his older brother's throne, whereas the older Oliver denies the younger Orlando his birthright of education. In still another parallel, both Rosalind and Orlando find themselves mistrusted as the children of Frederick's political enemies, Duke Senior and Sir Rowland de Boys. A daughter and a son are held to be guilty by association. "Thou art thy father's daughter. There's enough" (1.3.56), Frederick curtly retorts in explaining Rosalind's exile. And to Orlando, triumphant in wrestling with Charles, Frederick asserts, "I would thou hadst been son to some man else" (1.2.214). Here again, Frederick plaintively reveals his envy of goodness, even if at present any potential for goodness in him is thwarted by tyrannous whim. Many of Frederick's entourage might also be better persons if they only knew how to escape the insincerities of their courtly life. Charles the wrestler, for example, places himself at Oliver's service, and yet he would happily avoid breaking Orlando's neck if to do so were consistent with self-interest. Even Le Beau, the giddy fop so delighted at first with the cruel sport of wrestling, takes Orlando aside at some personal risk to warn him of Duke Frederick's foul humor. Ideally, Le Beau would prefer to be a companion of Orlando's "in a better world than this" (1.2.275). The vision of a regenerative Utopia secretly abides in the heart of this courtly creature.

It is easier to anatomize the defects of a social order than to propound solutions. As have other Utopian visionaries (including Thomas More), Shakespeare uses playful debate to elicit complicated responses on the part of his audience. Which is preferable, the court or the country? Jaques and Touchstone are adept gadflies, incessantly pointing out contradictions and ironies. Jaques, the malcontent railer derived from literary satire, takes delight in being out of step with everyone. Seemingly, his chief reason for having joined the others in the forest is to jibe at their motives for being there. To their song about the rejection of courtly ambition he mockingly supplies another verse, charging them with having left their wealth and ease out of mere willfulness (2.5.46–54). With ironic appropriateness, Jaques eventually decides to remain in the forest in the company of Frederick; Jaques cannot thrive on resolution and harmony. His humor is "melancholy," from which, as he observes, he draws consolation as a weasel sucks eggs (2.5.11–12). The others treat him as a sort of profane jester whose soured conceits add relish to their enjoyment of the forest life.

Despite his affectation, however, Jaques is serious and even excited in his defense of satire as a curative form of laughter (2.7.47–87). The appearance of Touchstone in the forest has reaffirmed in Jaques his profound commitment to a view of life as a meaningless process of decay governed by inexorable time. His function in such a life is to be mordant, unsparing. As literary satirist, he must be free to awaken people's minds to their own folly. To Duke Senior's protestation that the satirist is merely self-indulgent and licentious, Jaques counters with a thoughtful and classically Horatian defense of satire as an art form devoted not to libelous attacks on individuals but to exposing types of folly. Any observer who feels himself individually portrayed merely condemns himself by confessing his resemblance to the type. This particular debate between Duke Senior and Jaques ends, appropriately, in a draw. The Duke's point is well taken, for Jaques' famous "Seven Ages of Man" speech, so often read out of context, occurs in a scene that also witnesses the sacrifices and brave deeds that Orlando and Adam are prepared to undertake for each other. The feeling bond between the generations that they share refutes Jaques' cynical narrative of isolated self-interest. As though in answer to Jaques' acid depiction of covetous old age, we see old Adam's self-sacrifice and trust in Providence. Instead of "mere oblivion," we see charitable compassion prompting Duke Senior to aid Orlando and Orlando to aid Adam. Perhaps this vision seems of a higher spiritual order than that of Jaques. Nonetheless, without him the forest would lack a satirical perspective that continually requires us to reexamine our romantic assumptions about human happiness.

Touchstone's name suggests that he similarly offers a multiplicity of viewpoints. (A touchstone is a kind of stone used to test for gold and silver.) He shares with Jaques a skeptical view of life, but for Touchstone the inconsistency and ab-

surdity of life are occasions for wit and humor rather than melancholy and cynicism. As a professional fool, he observes that sane men are more foolish than he—as, for example, in their elaborate dueling code of the Retort Courteous and the Reply Churlish, leading finally to the Lie Circumstantial and the Lie Direct. He is fascinated by the games people make of their lives and is amused by their inability to be content with what they already have. Of the shepherd's life, he comments, "In respect that it is solitary, I like it very well; but in respect that it is private, it is a very vile life" (3.2.15–16). This paradox, though nonsensical, captures the restlessness of human striving for a life that can somehow combine the peaceful solitude of nature with the convenience and excitement of city life. Although Touchstone marries, even his marriage is a spoof of the institution rather than a serious attempt at commitment. Like all fools, who in Renaissance times were regarded as a breed apart, Touchstone exists outside the realm of ordinary human responses. There he can comment disinterestedly on human folly. He is prevented, however, from sharing fully in the human love and conciliation with which the play ends. He and Jaques are not touched by the play's regenerative magic; Jaques will remain in the forest, and Touchstone will remain forever a childlike entertainer.

The regenerative power of Arden, as we have seen, is not the forest's alone. What saves Orlando is the human charity practiced by him and by Duke Senior, who, for all his love of the forest, longs to rejoin that human society where he has "with holy bell been knolled to church" (2.7.120). Civilization at its best is no less necessary to the human spirit than is the natural order of the forest. In love, also, perception and wisdom must be combined with nature's gifts. Orlando, when we first see him, is a young man of the finest natural qualities but admittedly lacking experience in the nuances of complex human relationships. Nowhere does his lack of sophistication betray him more unhappily than in his first encounter with Rosalind, following the wrestling match. In response to her unmistakable hints of favor, he stands oxlike, tongue-tied. Later, however, in the forest, his first attempts at self-education in love lead him into an opposite danger: an excess of platitudinous manners parading in the guise of Petrarchism. (The Italian sonneteer Francis Petrarch has given to the language a name for the stereotypical literary mannerisms we associate with courtly love: the sighing and self-abasement of the young man, the chaste denial of love by the woman whom he worships, and the like.) Orlando's newfound self-abasement and idealization of his absent mistress are as unsatisfactory as his former naiveté. The sonnets he hangs on trees are too deserving of the delicious parody they get from Touchstone. Orlando must learn from Rosalind that a quest for true understanding in love avoids the extreme of pretentious mannerism as well as that of mere artlessness. Orlando as Petrarchan lover too much resembles Silvius, the lovesick young man, cowering before the imperious will of his coy mistress Phoebe. This stereotyped relationship, taken from the pages of fashionable pastoral romance, represents a posturing that Rosalind hopes to cure in Silvius and Phoebe even as she will also cure Orlando.

Rosalind is, above all, the realistic one, the plucky Shakespearean heroine showing her mettle in the world of men, emotionally more mature than her lover. Her concern is with a working and clear-sighted relationship in love, and to that end she daringly insists that Orlando learn something of woman's changeable mood. Above all, she must disabuse him of the dangerously misleading clichés of the Petrarchan love myth. When he protests he would die for love of Rosalind, she lectures him mockingly in her guise of Ganymede: "No, faith, die by attorney. The poor world is almost six thousand years old, and in all this time there was not any man died in his own person, videlicet, in a love cause." She debunks the legends of Troilus and Leander, youths supposed to have died for love who, if they had ever really existed, would no doubt have met with more prosaic ends. "But these are all lies. Men have died from time to time, and worms have eaten them, but not for love" (4.1.89–102). Rosalind wants Orlando to know that women are not goddesses but frail human beings who can be giddy, jealous, infatuated with novelty, irritatingly talkative, peremptory, and hysterical (4.1.142–149), though she is circumspect as to whether women can also be unfaithful. Orlando must be taught that love is a madness (3.2.390), and he must be cured, not of loving Rosalind, but of worshiping her with unrealistic expectations that can lead only to disillusionment. Rosalind teases him, as Portia does Bassanio in *The Merchant of Venice*, but she does not seriously threaten him with wantonness. Her disguise as Ganymede provides for her the perfect role in Orlando's approach to sexual manhood: he can learn to love "Ganymede" as a friend and then make the transition to heterosexual union in his blessed discovery that the friend is also the lover. Rosalind's own rite of passage is more easy; for all her reliance on her loving friendship with Celia, or "Aliena," she is ready to exclaim, "But what talk we of fathers, when there is such a man as Orlando?" (3.4.36–37). She is, like Portia, both spiritedly independent and ready to accept the conventional social pattern through which she is given by her father to a younger man. The forest is indeed a place where she can encounter her father "man to man," as it were, and be liberated from him while coming to terms with a patriarchal world. She is ready to give herself to Orlando, but she must educate him first. When Orlando has been sufficiently tested as to patience, loyalty, and understanding, she unmasks herself to him and simultaneously unravels the plot of ridiculous love we have come to associate with Silvius and Phoebe.

Rosalind's disguise name, Ganymede, taken from Jove's amorous cupbearer, has homoerotic connotations that are easily misinterpreted today. Shakespeare delicately acknowledges the suggestion, to be sure, both in Phoebe's pursuit of a young lady (but really a boy actor) in male attire, and in Orlando's courtship of "Ganymede" as though addressed to Rosalind. Yet this innocent titillation, found also in Shakespeare's source, is not meant to hint at homosexual attraction as we understand it. On the contrary, the point is that Orlando can speak frankly and personally to "Ganymede" as to a perfect friend, one to whom he can relate in platonically spiritual terms without the potentially distracting note of sexual interest. Posing as Ganymede, Rosalind can observe and test Orlando and thereby learn the truth about his capability for lifelong fidelity as only another man would have the opportunity to do. Once a disinterested love has grown strong between them, the unmasking of Rosalind's sexual identity makes possible a physical union between them to confirm and express the spiritual. In these terms, the play's happy ending affirms marriage as an institution, not simply as the expected denouement. The procession to the altar is synchronous with the return to civilization's other institutions, made whole again not solely by the forest but by the power of goodness embodied in Rosalind, Orlando, Duke Senior, and the others who persevere.

As You Like It

[*Dramatis Personae*

DUKE SENIOR, *a banished duke*
DUKE FREDERICK, *his usurping brother*
ROSALIND, *daughter of Duke Senior, later disguised as* GANYMEDE
CELIA, *daughter of Duke Frederick, later disguised as* ALIENA

OLIVER,
JAQUES, } *sons of Sir Rowland de Boys*
ORLANDO,

AMIENS }
JAQUES, } *lords attending Duke Senior*

LE BEAU, *a courtier attending Duke Frederick*
CHARLES, *a wrestler in the court of Duke Frederick*

ADAM, *an aged servant of Oliver and then Orlando*
DENNIS, *a servant of Oliver*

TOUCHSTONE, *the* CLOWN *or* FOOL

CORIN, *an old shepherd*
SILVIUS, *a young shepherd, in love with Phoebe*
PHOEBE, *a shepherdess*
WILLIAM, *a country youth, in love with Audrey*
AUDREY, *a country wench*
SIR OLIVER MAR-TEXT, *a country vicar*

HYMEN, *god of marriage*

Lords and Attendants waiting on Duke Frederick and Duke Senior

SCENE: *Oliver's house; Duke Frederick's court; and the Forest of Arden*]

1.1

Enter Orlando and Adam.

ORLANDO   As I remember, Adam, it was upon this fash- 1
ion bequeathed me by will but poor a thousand 2
crowns and, as thou sayst, charged my brother on his 3

blessing to breed me well; and there begins my 4
sadness. My brother Jaques he keeps at school, and 5
report speaks goldenly of his profit. For my part, he 6
keeps me rustically at home—or, to speak more
properly, stays me here at home unkept; for call you 8
that "keeping" for a gentleman of my birth, that
differs not from the stalling of an ox? His horses are
bred better, for besides that they are fair with their 11
feeding, they are taught their manage, and to that end 12
riders dearly hired. But I, his brother, gain nothing 13
under him but growth, for the which his animals on
his dunghills are as much bound to him as I. Besides
this nothing that he so plentifully gives me, the
something that nature gave me his countenance 17
seems to take from me. He lets me feed with his
hinds, bars me the place of a brother, and as much as 19
in him lies, mines my gentility with my education. 20
This is it, Adam, that grieves me; and the spirit of my
father, which I think is within me, begins to mutiny
against this servitude. I will no longer endure it,
though yet I know no wise remedy how to avoid it.

Enter Oliver.

ADAM   Yonder comes my master, your brother.
ORLANDO   Go apart, Adam, and thou shalt hear how 26
he will shake me up.   [*Adam stands aside.*] 27
OLIVER   Now, sir, what make you here? 28
ORLANDO   Nothing. I am not taught to make anything.
OLIVER   What mar you then, sir?
ORLANDO   Marry, sir, I am helping you to mar that 31
which God made, a poor unworthy brother of yours,
with idleness.
OLIVER   Marry, sir, be better employed, and be naught 34
awhile. 35
ORLANDO   Shall I keep your hogs and eat husks with 36
them? What prodigal portion have I spent, that I 37
should come to such penury? 38
OLIVER   Know you where you are, sir? 39
ORLANDO   O, sir, very well: here in your orchard. 40
OLIVER   Know you before whom, sir?
ORLANDO   Ay, better than him I am before knows me.
I know you are my eldest brother, and in the gentle 43
condition of blood you should so know me. The cour- 44
tesy of nations allows you my better, in that you are 45
the firstborn, but the same tradition takes not away

1.1. Location: The garden of Oliver's house.
1−3 it was . . . crowns it was in this way that I was left, by the terms of my father's will, a mere thousand crowns or £250   **3 crowns** coins worth five shillings.   **charged** it was charged, order was conveyed to   **3−4 on his blessing** as a condition of obtaining my father's blessing

4 breed educate   **5 keeps at school** maintains at the university
6 profit progress   **8 stays** detains.   **unkept** poorly supported   **11 fair** handsome   **12 manage** movements   **13 dearly** expensively
17 countenance lack of approval   **19 hinds** farm hands.   **bars me** excludes me from   **19−20 as in him lies** as he is able   **20 mines** undermines.   **education** i.e., lack of proper education   **26 Go apart** stand aside   **27 shake me up** abuse me   **28 make** do. (But Orlando takes it in the more usual sense.)   **31 Marry** i.e., indeed. (Originally an oath by the Virgin Mary.)   **34−35 be naught awhile** i.e., make yourself scarce   **36−38 Shall . . . penury** (Alluding to the story of the Prodigal Son, in Luke 15:11−32, who, having wasted his "portion" or inheritance, had to tend swine and eat with them.)   **39 where** in whose presence. (But Orlando sarcastically takes the more literal meaning.)   **40 orchard** garden   **43−44 in . . . blood** acknowledging the bond of our being of gentle birth   **44−45 courtesy of nations** recognized custom (of primogeniture, whereby the eldest son inherits all the land)

my blood, were there twenty brothers betwixt us. I have as much of my father in me as you, albeit I confess your coming before me is nearer to his reverence. 49

OLIVER What, boy!   *[He strikes Orlando.]*

ORLANDO Come, come, elder brother, you are too young in this.   *[He seizes Oliver by the throat.]* 52

OLIVER Wilt thou lay hands on me, villain? 53

ORLANDO I am no villain. I am the youngest son of Sir Rowland de Boys. He was my father, and he is thrice a villain that says such a father begot villains. Wert thou not my brother, I would not take this hand from thy throat till this other had pulled out thy tongue for saying so. Thou hast railed on thyself. 59

ADAM Sweet masters, be patient! For your father's 60 remembrance, be at accord. 61

OLIVER Let me go, I say.

ORLANDO I will not till I please. You shall hear me. My father charged you in his will to give me good education. You have trained me like a peasant, obscuring and hiding from me all gentlemanlike qualities. The 66 spirit of my father grows strong in me, and I will no longer endure it; therefore allow me such exercises as may become a gentleman, or give me the poor allottery 69 my father left me by testament. With that I will go buy my fortunes.   *[He releases Oliver.]*

OLIVER And what wilt thou do? Beg when that is spent? Well, sir, get you in. I will not long be troubled with you; you shall have some part of your will. I pray 74 you, leave me.

ORLANDO I will no further offend you than becomes me for my good.

OLIVER *[to Adam]* Get you with him, you old dog.

ADAM Is "old dog" my reward? Most true, I have lost my teeth in your service. God be with my old master! He would not have spoke such a word.

              Exeunt Orlando [and] Adam.

OLIVER Is it even so? Begin you to grow upon me? I will 82 physic your rankness and yet give no thousand 83 crowns neither.—Holla, Dennis!

    Enter Dennis.

DENNIS Calls your worship?

OLIVER Was not Charles, the Duke's wrestler, here to speak with me?

DENNIS So please you, he is here at the door and 88 importunes access to you.

OLIVER Call him in. *[Exit Dennis.]* 'Twill be a good way; and tomorrow the wrestling.

    Enter Charles.

CHARLES Good morrow to your worship. 92

OLIVER Good Monsieur Charles, what's the new news at the new court?

CHARLES There's no news at the court, sir, but the old news: that is, the old Duke is banished by his younger brother the new Duke, and three or four loving lords have put themselves into voluntary exile with him, whose lands and revenues enrich the new Duke; therefore he gives them good leave to wander. 100

OLIVER Can you tell if Rosalind, the Duke's daughter, be banished with her father?

CHARLES O, no; for the Duke's daughter, her cousin, so loves her, being ever from their cradles bred together, 104 that she would have followed her exile or have died to 105 stay behind her. She is at the court and no less be- 106 loved of her uncle than his own daughter, and never two ladies loved as they do.

OLIVER Where will the old Duke live?

CHARLES They say he is already in the Forest of Arden, and a many merry men with him; and there they live like the old Robin Hood of England. They say many young gentlemen flock to him every day and fleet the 113 time carelessly as they did in the golden world. 114

OLIVER What, you wrestle tomorrow before the new Duke?

CHARLES Marry, do I, sir; and I came to acquaint you with a matter. I am given, sir, secretly to understand that your younger brother Orlando hath a disposition to come in disguised against me to try a fall. Tomor- 120 row, sir, I wrestle for my credit, and he that escapes 121 me without some broken limb shall acquit him well. 122 Your brother is but young and tender, and for your love I would be loath to foil him, as I must for my 124 own honor if he come in. Therefore, out of my love to you, I came hither to acquaint you withal, that either 126 you might stay him from his intendment or brook 127 such disgrace well as he shall run into, in that it is a thing of his own search and altogether against my will. 129

OLIVER Charles, I thank thee for thy love to me, which thou shalt find I will most kindly requite. I had myself notice of my brother's purpose herein and have by underhand means labored to dissuade him from it, but 133 he is resolute. I'll tell thee, Charles, it is the stubbornest young fellow of France, full of ambition, an envious emulator of every man's good parts, a secret and 136 villainous contriver against me his natural brother. 137 Therefore use thy discretion. I had as lief thou didst 138 break his neck as his finger. And thou wert best look 139 to 't; for if thou dost him any slight disgrace, or if he 140

49 is nearer to his reverence places you closer to the respect that was due him **52 young** inexperienced (at fighting) **53 villain** i.e., wicked fellow. (But Orlando plays on the literal meaning of "bondman" or "serf," as well as Oliver's meaning.) **59 railed on thyself** insulted your own blood **60–61 your father's remembrance** the sake of your father's memory **66 qualities** accomplishments **69 allottery** portion **74 will** (1) desire (2) portion from your father's will **82 grow upon me** take liberties with me; grow too big for your breeches **83 physic** apply medicine to. **rankness** overgrowth, overweening **88 So please you** if you please

92 Good morrow good morning **100 good leave** full permission **104 being** they being **105–106 died to stay** died from being forced to stay **113 fleet** pass **114 carelessly** free from care. **golden world** the primal age of innocence and ease from which humankind was thought to have degenerated. (See Ovid, *Metamorphoses* 1.) **120 a fall** an overthrow **121 credit** reputation **122 shall** must **124 foil** defeat **126 withal** with this **127 stay** keep. **intendment** intent. **brook** endure **129 search** seeking **133 underhand** unobtrusive **136 emulator** rival. **parts** qualities **137 contriver** plotter. **natural** legitimate **138 lief** willingly **139–140 thou . . . to 't** you'd better beware

do not mightily grace himself on thee, he will practice 141
against thee by poison, entrap thee by some treacherous device, and never leave thee till he hath ta'en thy
life by some indirect means or other; for I assure thee,
and almost with tears I speak it, there is not one so
young and so villainous this day living. I speak but
brotherly of him, but should I anatomize him to thee as 147
he is, I must blush and weep, and thou must look pale
and wonder.

CHARLES   I am heartily glad I came hither to you. If he
come tomorrow, I'll give him his payment. If ever he
go alone again, I'll never wrestle for prize more. And 152
so God keep your worship!

OLIVER   Farewell, good Charles. *Exit [Charles].* Now
will I stir this gamester. I hope I shall see an end of 155
him; for my soul, yet I know not why, hates nothing
more than he. Yet he's gentle, never schooled and yet 157
learned, full of noble device, of all sorts enchantingly 158
beloved, and indeed so much in the heart of the world
and especially of my own people, who best know him,
that I am altogether misprized. But it shall not be so 161
long; this wrestler shall clear all. Nothing remains but 162
that I kindle the boy thither, which now I'll go about. 163
                                                    Exit.

❖

1.2   *Enter Rosalind and Celia.*

CELIA   I pray thee, Rosalind, sweet my coz, be merry. 1

ROSALIND   Dear Celia, I show more mirth than I am
mistress of, and would you yet I were merrier? Unless
you could teach me to forget a banished father, you
must not learn me how to remember any extraordi- 5
nary pleasure.

CELIA   Herein I see thou lov'st me not with the full
weight that I love thee. If my uncle, thy banished 8
father, had banished thy uncle, the Duke my father,
so thou hadst been still with me, I could have taught 10
my love to take thy father for mine. So wouldst thou,
if the truth of thy love to me were so righteously 12
tempered as mine is to thee. 13

ROSALIND   Well, I will forget the condition of my estate 14
to rejoice in yours.

CELIA   You know my father hath no child but I, nor
none is like to have. And truly, when he dies thou 17
shalt be his heir, for what he hath taken away from thy

father perforce I will render thee again in affection. By 19
mine honor, I will, and when I break that oath, let me
turn monster. Therefore, my sweet Rose, my dear
Rose, be merry.

ROSALIND   From henceforth I will, coz, and devise
sports. Let me see, what think you of falling in love? 24

CELIA   Marry, I prithee, do, to make sport withal. But
love no man in good earnest, nor no further in sport
neither than with safety of a pure blush thou mayst in 27
honor come off again. 28

ROSALIND   What shall be our sport, then?

CELIA   Let us sit and mock the good huswife Fortune 30
from her wheel, that her gifts may henceforth be bestowed equally.

ROSALIND   I would we could do so, for her benefits are
mightily misplaced, and the bountiful blind woman 34
doth most mistake in her gifts to women.

CELIA   'Tis true, for those that she makes fair she scarce 36
makes honest, and those that she makes honest she 37
makes very ill-favoredly. 38

ROSALIND   Nay, now thou goest from Fortune's office to
Nature's. Fortune reigns in gifts of the world, not in 40
the lineaments of Nature. 41

Enter [Touchstone the] Clown.

CELIA   No; when Nature hath made a fair creature, may
she not by Fortune fall into the fire? Though Nature
hath given us wit to flout at Fortune, hath not Fortune 44
sent in this fool to cut off the argument?

ROSALIND   Indeed, there is Fortune too hard for Nature,
when Fortune makes Nature's natural the cutter-off of 47
Nature's wit. 48

CELIA   Peradventure this is not Fortune's work neither 49
but Nature's, who perceiveth our natural wits too dull
to reason of such goddesses and hath sent this natural 51
for our whetstone; for always the dullness of the fool 52
is the whetstone of the wits.—How now, wit, whither 53
wander you? 54

TOUCHSTONE   Mistress, you must come away to your
father.

CELIA   Were you made the messenger?

TOUCHSTONE   No, by mine honor, but I was bid to
come for you.

ROSALIND   Where learned you that oath, Fool?

TOUCHSTONE   Of a certain knight that swore by his
honor they were good pancakes and swore by his 62
honor the mustard was naught. Now I'll stand to it the 63

---

distinguish himself at your expense.   **practice** plot   **147 brotherly** as
a brother should.   **anatomize** analyze   **152 go alone** walk unassisted
155 gamester sportsman. (Said sardonically.)   **157 gentle** gentlemanly
158 noble device lofty aspiration.   **sorts** classes of people.   **enchantingly** in an enchanting manner   **161 misprized** undervalued,
scorned   **162 clear all** solve everything   **163 kindle . . . thither** inflame the boy with desire to go to the wrestling match
1.2. Location: Duke Frederick's court. A place suitable for wrestling.
1 sweet my coz my sweet cousin   **5 learn** teach   **8 that** with which
10 so provided that   **12–13 righteously tempered** properly compounded   **14 condition of my estate** state of my fortunes   **17 like**
likely

19 perforce by force   **24 sports** pastimes   **27 pure** (1) mere (2) innocent   **28 come off** retire, leave   **30 huswife** one who manages
household affairs and operates the spinning wheel. (Shakespeare conflates this wheel with the commonplace wheel of Fortune.) *Huswife* is
used derogatorily here, with a suggestion of "hussy."   **34 bountiful
blind woman** i.e., Fortune   **36 scarce** rarely   **37 honest** chaste
38 ill-favoredly ugly   **40 gifts of the world** e.g., riches and power
41 lineaments characteristics.   **s.d. Touchstone** a stone used to test
for gold and silver   **44 flout** scoff   **47 natural** half-wit   **48 Nature's
wit** the intellect that Nature has given us   **49 Peradventure** perhaps
51 to reason of to discuss   **52 whetstone** sharpener   **53–54 whither
wander you** (An allusion to the expression "wandering wits.")
62 pancakes fritters (which might be made of meat and so require
mustard)   **63 naught** worthless.   **stand to it** maintain, argue

pancakes were naught and the mustard was good, and yet was not the knight forsworn. 65

CELIA   How prove you that in the great heap of your knowledge?

ROSALIND   Ay, marry, now unmuzzle your wisdom.

TOUCHSTONE   Stand you both forth now. Stroke your chins, and swear by your beards that I am a knave.

CELIA   By our beards, if we had them, thou art.

TOUCHSTONE   By my knavery, if I had it, then I were; but if you swear by that that is not, you are not forsworn. No more was this knight, swearing by his honor, for he never had any; or if he had, he had sworn it away before ever he saw those pancakes or that mustard.

CELIA   Prithee, who is 't that thou mean'st?

TOUCHSTONE   One that old Frederick, your father, loves.

CELIA   My father's love is enough to honor him enough. Speak no more of him; you'll be whipped for taxation 81 one of these days.

TOUCHSTONE   The more pity that fools may not speak wisely what wise men do foolishly.

CELIA   By my troth, thou sayest true; for since the little 85 wit that fools have was silenced, the little foolery that 86 wise men have makes a great show. Here comes Monsieur Le Beau.

Enter Le Beau.

ROSALIND   With his mouth full of news.

CELIA   Which he will put on us as pigeons feed their 90 young.

ROSALIND   Then shall we be news-crammed.

CELIA   All the better; we shall be the more mar- 93 ketable.—*Bonjour*, Monsieur Le Beau. What's the 94 news?

LE BEAU   Fair princess, you have lost much good sport.

CELIA   Sport? Of what color? 97

LE BEAU   What color, madam? How shall I answer you?

ROSALIND   As wit and fortune will.

TOUCHSTONE   Or as the Destinies decrees.

CELIA   Well said. That was laid on with a trowel. 101

TOUCHSTONE   Nay, if I keep not my rank— 102

ROSALIND   Thou losest thy old smell.

LE BEAU   You amaze me, ladies. I would have told you 104 of good wrestling, which you have lost the sight of.

ROSALIND   Yet tell us the manner of the wrestling.

LE BEAU   I will tell you the beginning, and if it please your ladyships you may see the end, for the best is yet 108 to do, and here, where you are, they are coming to 109 perform it.

CELIA   Well, the beginning, that is dead and buried.

LE BEAU   There comes an old man and his three sons—

CELIA   I could match this beginning with an old tale.

LE BEAU   Three proper young men, of excellent growth 114 and presence—

ROSALIND   With bills on their necks, "Be it known unto 116 all men by these presents." 117

LE BEAU   The eldest of the three wrestled with Charles, the Duke's wrestler, which Charles in a moment threw him and broke three of his ribs, that there is little hope of life in him. So he served the second, and so the 121 third. Yonder they lie, the poor old man their father making such pitiful dole over them that all the behold- 123 ers take his part with weeping.

ROSALIND   Alas!

TOUCHSTONE   But what is the sport, monsieur, that the ladies have lost?

LE BEAU   Why, this that I speak of.

TOUCHSTONE   Thus men may grow wiser every day. It is the first time that ever I heard breaking of ribs was sport for ladies.

CELIA   Or I, I promise thee. 132

ROSALIND   But is there any else longs to see this broken 133 music in his sides? Is there yet another dotes upon rib 134 breaking? Shall we see this wrestling, cousin?

LE BEAU   You must if you stay here, for here is the place appointed for the wrestling, and they are ready to perform it.

CELIA   Yonder, sure, they are coming. Let us now stay and see it.

Flourish. Enter Duke [Frederick], Lords, Orlando, Charles, and attendants.

DUKE FREDERICK   Come on. Since the youth will not be entreated, his own peril on his forwardness. 142

ROSALIND   Is yonder the man?

LE BEAU   Even he, madam.

CELIA   Alas, he is too young! Yet he looks successfully. 145

DUKE FREDERICK   How now, daughter and cousin? Are you crept hither to see the wrestling?

ROSALIND   Ay, my liege, so please you give us leave. 148

DUKE FREDERICK   You will take little delight in it, I can tell you, there is such odds in the man. In pity of the 150 challenger's youth I would fain dissuade him, but he 151 will not be entreated. Speak to him, ladies; see if you can move him.

CELIA   Call him hither, good Monsieur Le Beau.

DUKE FREDERICK   Do so. I'll not be by. [*He steps aside.*]

LE BEAU [*to Orlando*]   Monsieur the challenger, the princess calls for you.

ORLANDO [*approaching the ladies*]   I attend them with all respect and duty.

ROSALIND   Young man, have you challenged Charles the wrestler?

---

65 **forsworn** perjured   81 **taxation** censure, slander   **85–86 since . . . silenced** (Perhaps refers specifically to the Bishops' order of June 1599 banning satirical books.)   **90 put on** force upon   **93–94 marketable** i.e., like animals that have been crammed with food before being sent to market   **97 color** kind   **101 with a trowel** i.e., thick   **102 rank** i.e., status as a wit. (But Rosalind plays on the sense of "stench.")   **104 amaze** bewilder   **108–109 yet to do** still to come

114 **proper** handsome   116 **bills** proclamations   117 **these presents** the present document. (Rosalind uses this legal phrase to pun on *presence* in line 115.)   121 **So** similarly   123 **dole** lamentation   132 **promise** assure   133 **any else** anyone else who   **133–134 broken music** Literally, music arranged in parts for different instruments; here applied to the breaking of ribs.   134 **another** another who   **142 entreated . . . forwardness** i.e., entreated to desist, let the risk be blamed upon his own rashness   145 **successfully** i.e., as if he would be successful   **148 so . . . leave** if you will permit us   150 **odds** superiority.   **the man** i.e., Charles   151 **fain** willingly

ORLANDO   No, fair princess. He is the general challeng- 162
er. I come but in, as others do, to try with him the 163
strength of my youth.

CELIA   Young gentleman, your spirits are too bold for
your years. You have seen cruel proof of this man's
strength. If you saw yourself with your eyes or knew 167
yourself with your judgment, the fear of your adven- 168
ture would counsel you to a more equal enterprise. We 169
pray you, for your own sake, to embrace your own
safety and give over this attempt.

ROSALIND   Do, young sir. Your reputation shall not
therefore be misprized. We will make it our suit to the 173
Duke that the wrestling might not go forward.

ORLANDO   I beseech you, punish me not with your hard
thoughts, wherein I confess me much guilty to deny 176
so fair and excellent ladies anything. But let your fair
eyes and gentle wishes go with me to my trial,
wherein if I be foiled, there is but one shamed that was
never gracious, if killed, but one dead that is willing to 180
be so. I shall do my friends no wrong, for I have none
to lament me; the world no injury, for in it I have
nothing. Only in the world I fill up a place which may 183
be better supplied when I have made it empty.

ROSALIND   The little strength that I have, I would it
were with you.

CELIA   And mine, to eke out hers.

ROSALIND   Fare you well. Pray heaven I be deceived 188
in you!   189

CELIA   Your heart's desires be with you!

CHARLES   Come, where is this young gallant that is so
desirous to lie with his mother earth?

ORLANDO   Ready, sir, but his will hath in it a more
modest working.   194

DUKE FREDERICK   You shall try but one fall.

CHARLES   No, I warrant Your Grace, you shall not
entreat him to a second, that have so mightily
persuaded him from a first.

ORLANDO   You mean to mock me after; you should not
have mocked me before. But come your ways.   200

ROSALIND   Now Hercules be thy speed, young man! 201

CELIA   I would I were invisible, to catch the strong
fellow by the leg.   [Orlando and Charles] wrestle.

ROSALIND   O excellent young man!

CELIA   If I had a thunderbolt in mine eye, I can tell who
should down.   Shout. [Charles is thrown.] 206

DUKE FREDERICK   No more, no more.

ORLANDO   Yes, I beseech Your Grace. I am not yet well 208
breathed.   209

DUKE FREDERICK
How dost thou, Charles?

LE BEAU   He cannot speak, my lord.

DUKE FREDERICK
Bear him away. What is thy name, young man?
                                              [Charles is borne out.]

ORLANDO   Orlando, my liege, the youngest son of Sir
Rowland de Boys.

DUKE FREDERICK
I would thou hadst been son to some man else.
The world esteemed thy father honorable,
But I did find him still mine enemy.   216
Thou shouldst have better pleased me with this deed
Hadst thou descended from another house.
But fare thee well; thou art a gallant youth.
I would thou hadst told me of another father.
           Exit Duke [with train, and others. Rosalind and
                     Celia remain; Orlando stands apart from them.]

CELIA [to Rosalind]
Were I my father, coz, would I do this?

ORLANDO [to no one in particular]
I am more proud to be Sir Rowland's son,
His youngest son, and would not change that calling 223
To be adopted heir to Frederick.

ROSALIND [to Celia]
My father loved Sir Rowland as his soul,
And all the world was of my father's mind.
Had I before known this young man his son,
I should have given him tears unto entreaties   228
Ere he should thus have ventured.

CELIA [to Rosalind]   Gentle cousin,
Let us go thank him and encourage him.
My father's rough and envious disposition   231
Sticks me at heart.—Sir, you have well deserved. 232
If you do keep your promises in love
But justly as you have exceeded all promise,   234
Your mistress shall be happy.

ROSALIND [giving him a chain from her neck]   Gentleman, 235
Wear this for me, one out of suits with fortune,   236
That could give more, but that her hand lacks
   means.   237
[To Celia.] Shall we go, coz?

CELIA   Ay. Fare you well, fair gentleman.
                                  [Rosalind and Celia start to leave.]

ORLANDO [aside]
Can I not say, "I thank you"? My better parts
Are all thrown down, and that which here stands up
Is but a quintain, a mere lifeless block.   241

ROSALIND [to Celia]
He calls us back. My pride fell with my fortunes;
I'll ask him what he would.—Did you call, sir?   243
Sir, you have wrestled well and overthrown
More than your enemies.

CELIA   Will you go, coz?

ROSALIND   Have with you.—Fare you well.   247
                                                  Exit [with Celia].

162–163 the general challenger the one who is ready to take on all
comers. (Orlando is the challenger in a more limited sense.)
167–168 If . . . judgment if you saw yourself objectively 169 equal
i.e., where the odds are more equal   173 therefore on that account.
misprized despised, undervalued   176 wherein though.   to deny in
denying   180 gracious looked upon with favor   183 Only . . . I in
the world I merely   188–189 deceived in you i.e., mistaken in fearing you will lose   194 modest working decorous endeavor (than to
lie with one's mother earth—an endeavor, Orlando implies, with sexual overtones. Will also suggests sexual desire.)   200 come your
ways come on   201 Hercules be thy speed may Hercules help you
206 down fall   208–209 well breathed warmed up

216 still continually   223 calling position, name   228 unto in addition to   231 envious malicious   232 Sticks stabs   234 But justly exactly   235 s.d. chain (See 3.2.178, where Celia speaks of a chain
given to Orlando by Rosalind.)   236 out . . . fortune (1) whose petitions to Fortune are rejected (2) not wearing the livery of Fortune, not
in her service   237 could would   241 quintain wooden figure used
as a target in tilting   243 would wants   247 Have with you I'll go
with you

ORLANDO
What passion hangs these weights upon my
    tongue?
I cannot speak to her, yet she urged conference.   249
O poor Orlando, thou art overthrown!
Or Charles or something weaker masters thee.   251

          Enter Le Beau.

LE BEAU
Good sir, I do in friendship counsel you
To leave this place. Albeit you have deserved
High commendation, true applause, and love,
Yet such is now the Duke's condition   255
That he misconsters all that you have done.   256
The Duke is humorous. What he is indeed   257
More suits you to conceive than I to speak of.
ORLANDO
I thank you, sir. And, pray you, tell me this:
Which of the two was daughter of the Duke
That here was at the wrestling?
LE BEAU
Neither his daughter, if we judge by manners,
But yet indeed the taller is his daughter.   263
The other is daughter to the banished Duke,
And here detained by her usurping uncle
To keep his daughter company, whose loves
Are dearer than the natural bond of sisters.
But I can tell you that of late this Duke
Hath ta'en displeasure gainst his gentle niece,
Grounded upon no other argument   270
But that the people praise her for her virtues
And pity her for her good father's sake;
And, on my life, his malice gainst the lady
Will suddenly break forth. Sir, fare you well.   274
Hereafter, in a better world than this,   275
I shall desire more love and knowledge of you.
ORLANDO
I rest much bounden to you. Fare you well.   277
          [*Exit Le Beau.*]
Thus must I from the smoke into the smother,   278
From tyrant Duke unto a tyrant brother.
But heavenly Rosalind!   *Exit.*

          ✤

1.3   *Enter Celia and Rosalind.*

CELIA   Why, cousin, why, Rosalind! Cupid have mercy!
Not a word?
ROSALIND   Not one to throw at a dog.
CELIA   No, thy words are too precious to be cast away

upon curs. Throw some of them at me. Come, lame   5
me with reasons.   6
ROSALIND   Then there were two cousins laid up, when
the one should be lamed with reasons and the other
mad without any.
CELIA   But is all this for your father?
ROSALIND   No, some of it is for my child's father. O,   11
how full of briers is this working-day world!
CELIA   They are but burs, cousin, thrown upon thee in   13
holiday foolery. If we walk not in the trodden paths,   14
our very petticoats will catch them.
ROSALIND   I could shake them off my coat. These burs
are in my heart.
CELIA   Hem them away.   18
ROSALIND   I would try, if I could cry "hem" and have   19
him.
CELIA   Come, come, wrestle with thy affections.
ROSALIND   O, they take the part of a better wrestler than
myself.
CELIA   O, a good wish upon you! You will try in time,   24
in despite of a fall. But, turning these jests out of   25
service, let us talk in good earnest. Is it possible, on   26
such a sudden, you should fall into so strong a liking
with old Sir Rowland's youngest son?
ROSALIND   The Duke my father loved his father dearly.
CELIA   Doth it therefore ensue that you should love his
son dearly? By this kind of chase, I should hate him,   31
for my father hated his father dearly; yet I hate not   32
Orlando.
ROSALIND   No, faith, hate him not, for my sake.   34
CELIA   Why should I not? Doth he not deserve well?   35

          Enter Duke [*Frederick*], *with Lords.*

ROSALIND   Let me love him for that, and do you love
him because I do.—Look, here comes the Duke.
CELIA   With his eyes full of anger.
DUKE FREDERICK   [*to Rosalind*]
Mistress, dispatch you with your safest haste   39
And get you from our court.
ROSALIND   Me, uncle?
DUKE FREDERICK   You, cousin.   40
Within these ten days if that thou be'st found
So near our public court as twenty miles,
Thou diest for it.
ROSALIND   I do beseech Your Grace
Let me the knowledge of my fault bear with me.

249 urged conference invited conversation   **251 Or** either   **255 condition** disposition   **256 misconsters** misconstrues   **257 humorous** capricious   **263 taller** (Perhaps a textual error for *smaller* or *lesser*, or else an inconsistency on Shakespeare's part; at 1.3.113, Rosalind is shown to be the taller.)   **270 argument** reason   **274 suddenly** very soon   **275 world** state of affairs   **277 bounden** indebted   **278 from . . . smother** i.e., out of the frying pan into the fire. (*Smother* means "a dense suffocating smoke.")
1.3. Location: Duke Frederick's court.

5–6 lame . . . reasons throw some explanations (for your silence) at me   **11 my child's father** one who might father my children, i.e., Orlando   **13–14 They . . . foolery** i.e., these vexations you complain of aren't serious and are the result of your own fooling around. Burs stick where they are thrown.   **18 Hem** cough (since you say they are in the chest). A *bur* (lines 13–16) can be something that sticks in the throat.   **19 cry "hem"** clear away with a "hem" or a cough (with a play on the *hem* of a petticoat and also on *him*)   **24–25 O . . . fall** i.e., good luck to you; you'll undertake to wrestle with Orlando sooner or later, despite the danger of your being thrown down. (With sexual suggestion.)   **25–26 turning . . . service** i.e., dismissing this banter   **31 By . . . chase** to pursue this line of reasoning   **32 dearly** intensely   **34 faith** in truth   **35 deserve well** i.e., well deserve to be hated. (But Rosalind interprets it in the sense of "deserve favor." Conversely, line 35 may mean, "Why shouldn't I love him, since he deserves so well?")   **39 safest haste** speed necessary for your safety   **40 cousin** i.e., niece

If with myself I hold intelligence   45
Or have acquaintance with mine own desires,
If that I do not dream or be not frantic—   47
As I do trust I am not—then, dear uncle,
Never so much as in a thought unborn   49
Did I offend Your Highness.

DUKE FREDERICK   Thus do all traitors.
If their purgation did consist in words,   51
They are as innocent as grace itself.
Let it suffice thee that I trust thee not.

ROSALIND
Yet your mistrust cannot make me a traitor.
Tell me whereon the likelihood depends.

DUKE FREDERICK
Thou art thy father's daughter. There's enough.   56

ROSALIND
So was I when Your Highness took his dukedom;
So was I when Your Highness banished him.
Treason is not inherited, my lord;
Or, if we did derive it from our friends,   60
What's that to me? My father was no traitor.
Then, good my liege, mistake me not so much
To think my poverty is treacherous.   63

CELIA   Dear sovereign, hear me speak.

DUKE FREDERICK
Ay, Celia, we stayed her for your sake,   65
Else had she with her father ranged along.   66

CELIA
I did not then entreat to have her stay;
It was your pleasure and your own remorse.   68
I was too young that time to value her,   69
But now I know her. If she be a traitor,
Why, so am I. We still have slept together,   71
Rose at an instant, learned, played, eat together,   72
And wheresoe'er we went, like Juno's swans   73
Still we went coupled and inseparable.

DUKE FREDERICK
She is too subtle for thee; and her smoothness,
Her very silence, and her patience
Speak to the people, and they pity her.
Thou art a fool. She robs thee of thy name,   78
And thou wilt show more bright and seem more
     virtuous
When she is gone. Then open not thy lips.
Firm and irrevocable is my doom   81
Which I have passed upon her; she is banished.

CELIA
Pronounce that sentence then on me, my liege!
I cannot live out of her company.

DUKE FREDERICK
You are a fool. You, niece, provide yourself.   85

If you outstay the time, upon mine honor,
And in the greatness of my word, you die.   87
                         Exit Duke [with Lords].

CELIA
O my poor Rosalind, whither wilt thou go?
Wilt thou change fathers? I will give thee mine.   89
I charge thee, be not thou more grieved than I am.

ROSALIND
I have more cause.

CELIA   Thou hast not, cousin.
Prithee, be cheerful. Know'st thou not the Duke
Hath banished me, his daughter?

ROSALIND   That he hath not.

CELIA
No, hath not? Rosalind lacks then the love
Which teacheth thee that thou and I am one.
Shall we be sundered? Shall we part, sweet girl?
No, let my father seek another heir.
Therefore devise with me how we may fly,
Whither to go, and what to bear with us.
And do not seek to take your change upon you,   100
To bear your griefs yourself and leave me out;
For, by this heaven, now at our sorrows pale,   102
Say what thou canst, I'll go along with thee.

ROSALIND   Why, whither shall we go?

CELIA
To seek my uncle in the Forest of Arden.

ROSALIND
Alas, what danger will it be to us,
Maids as we are, to travel forth so far!
Beauty provoketh thieves sooner than gold.

CELIA
I'll put myself in poor and mean attire   109
And with a kind of umber smirch my face;   110
The like do you. So shall we pass along
And never stir assailants.

ROSALIND   Were it not better,
Because that I am more than common tall,
That I did suit me all points like a man?   114
A gallant curtal ax upon my thigh,   115
A boar spear in my hand, and—in my heart
Lie there what hidden woman's fear there will—
We'll have a swashing and a martial outside,   118
As many other mannish cowards have
That do outface it with their semblances.   120

CELIA
What shall I call thee when thou art a man?

ROSALIND
I'll have no worse a name than Jove's own page,
And therefore look you call me Ganymede.   123
But what will you be called?

---

45 **hold intelligence** am in communication 47 **If that** if.   **frantic** insane 49 **so much as** even 51 **purgation** clearing of guilt. (A medical, legal, and theological metaphor.) 56 **There's enough** that's enough 60 **friends** relatives 63 **To think** as to think 65 **stayed** kept 66 **ranged** roamed 68 **remorse** compassion 69 **that time** then 71 **still** continually 72 **at an instant** at the same time.   **eat** ate 73 **Juno's swans** i.e., yoked together (though according to Ovid it was Venus, not Juno, who used swans to draw her chariot) 78 **name** reputation 81 **doom** sentence 85 **provide yourself** get ready

87 **in . . . word** i.e., upon my authority as Duke 89 **change** exchange 100 **change** change of fortune 102 **pale** (Heaven is pale in sympathy with their plight.) 109 **mean** lowly 110 **umber** brown pigment (to give a tanned appearance appropriate to countrywomen) 114 **suit me all points** outfit myself in all ways 115 **curtal ax** broad cutting sword 118 **swashing** swaggering 120 **outface . . . semblances** bluff their way through with mere appearances 123 **Ganymede** Jupiter's cupbearer. (The name used for disguise also in Lodge's *Rosalynde*.)

CELIA
　Something that hath a reference to my state:
　No longer Celia, but Aliena.   126

ROSALIND
　But, cousin, what if we assayed to steal   127
　The clownish fool out of your father's court?
　Would he not be a comfort to our travel?   129

CELIA
　He'll go along o'er the wide world with me.
　Leave me alone to woo him. Let's away,   131
　And get our jewels and our wealth together,
　Devise the fittest time and safest way   133
　To hide us from pursuit that will be made
　After my flight. Now go we in content   135
　To liberty, and not to banishment.   *Exeunt.*

❖

2.1   *Enter Duke Senior, Amiens, and two or three*
　　　Lords, [dressed] like foresters.

DUKE SENIOR
　Now, my co-mates and brothers in exile,
　Hath not old custom made this life more sweet   2
　Than that of painted pomp? Are not these woods
　More free from peril than the envious court?   4
　Here feel we not the penalty of Adam,   5
　The seasons' difference, as the icy fang   6
　And churlish chiding of the winter's wind,   7
　Which when it bites and blows upon my body
　Even till I shrink with cold, I smile and say
　"This is no flattery; these are counselors
　That feelingly persuade me what I am."
　Sweet are the uses of adversity,   12
　Which, like the toad, ugly and venomous,   13
　Wears yet a precious jewel in his head;   14
　And this our life, exempt from public haunt,   15
　Finds tongues in trees, books in the running brooks,
　Sermons in stones, and good in everything.

AMIENS
　I would not change it. Happy is Your Grace
　That can translate the stubbornness of fortune
　Into so quiet and so sweet a style.

DUKE SENIOR
　Come, shall we go and kill us venison?
　And yet it irks me the poor dappled fools,   22
　Being native burghers of this desert city,   23
　Should in their own confines with forkèd heads   24
　Have their round haunches gored.

FIRST LORD   Indeed, my lord,
　The melancholy Jaques grieves at that,
　And in that kind swears you do more usurp   27
　Than doth your brother that hath banished you.
　Today my lord of Amiens and myself
　Did steal behind him as he lay along   30
　Under an oak whose antique root peeps out   31
　Upon the brook that brawls along this wood,   32
　To the which place a poor sequestered stag   33
　That from the hunter's aim had ta'en a hurt
　Did come to languish. And indeed, my lord,
　The wretched animal heaved forth such groans
　That their discharge did stretch his leathern coat
　Almost to bursting, and the big round tears
　Coursed one another down his innocent nose   39
　In piteous chase. And thus the hairy fool,
　Much markèd of the melancholy Jaques,   41
　Stood on th' extremest verge of the swift brook,   42
　Augmenting it with tears.

DUKE SENIOR   But what said Jaques?
　Did he not moralize this spectacle?   44

FIRST LORD
　O, yes, into a thousand similes.
　First, for his weeping into the needless stream: 46
　"Poor deer," quoth he, "thou mak'st a testament   47
　As worldings do, giving thy sum of more   48
　To that which had too much." Then, being there
　　alone,
　Left and abandoned of his velvet friends: 50
　"'Tis right," quoth he, "thus misery doth part   51
　The flux of company." Anon a careless herd,   52
　Full of the pasture, jumps along by him
　And never stays to greet him. "Ay," quoth Jaques,
　"Sweep on, you fat and greasy citizens;   55
　'Tis just the fashion. Wherefore do you look   56
　Upon that poor and broken bankrupt there?"   57
　Thus most invectively he pierceth through   58
　The body of the country, city, court,
　Yea, and of this our life, swearing that we
　Are mere usurpers, tyrants, and what's worse,   61
　To fright the animals and to kill them up   62
　In their assigned and native dwelling place.

DUKE SENIOR
　And did you leave him in this contemplation?

---

126 Aliena the estranged one　**127 assayed** tried　**129 travel** (1)
movement from place to place (2) labor, hardship (*travail*)　**131 woo**
persuade　**133 fittest** most appropriate　**135 content** contentment
2.1. Location: The Forest of Arden.
2 old custom long experience　**4 envious** malicious　**5–6 feel . . .
difference** we don't mind the consequences of Adam's original sin—
the hardship of the seasons. (*Not* is often emended to *but*.)　**6 as** such
as　**7 churlish** rough　**12 uses** profits　**13–14 like . . . head** (Alludes
to the widespread belief that the toad was a poisonous creature but
with a jewel embedded in its head that worked as an antidote.)
15 exempt cut off.　**haunt** society　**22 irks** grieves, vexes.　**fools** innocents　**23 burghers** citizens.　**desert city** uninhabited place
24 forkèd heads barbed hunting arrows, but also suggesting antlers

27 kind regard　**30 along** stretched out　**31 antique** (1) ancient or (2)
antic, "gnarled"　**32 brawls** noisily flows　**33 sequestered** separated
(from the herd)　**39 Coursed** followed　**41 markèd of** observed by
42 extremest verge very edge　**44 moralize** draw out the hidden
meaning of　**46 needless** having no need of more water. (Weeping
deer are common in literature.)　**47 testament** will　**48 worldings**
worldly men.　**sum of more** additional quantity　**50 of** by.　**velvet**
i.e., prosperous. (Velvet was an appropriately rich dress for a courtier;
the term also alludes here to the deers' velvety coat or to the covering
of their antlers during rapid growth.)　**51 'Tis right** i.e., that's how it
goes.　**part** depart from　**52 flux of company** stream of fellow creatures.　**Anon** soon.　**careless** carefree　**55 greasy** (1) fat and ready for
the kill (2) unctuously prosperous, like rich burghers or *citizens*
56 Wherefore do why should　**57 broken** (1) financially ruined (continuing the metaphor of *citizens*, line 55) (2) physically shattered
58 invectively vehemently　**61 what's worse** whatever is worse than
these　**62 up** off, utterly

SECOND LORD
We did, my lord, weeping and commenting
Upon the sobbing deer.
DUKE SENIOR   Show me the place.
I love to cope him in these sullen fits,   67
For then he's full of matter.   68
FIRST LORD   I'll bring you to him straight.   *Exeunt.*   69

❖

2.2   *Enter Duke [Frederick], with Lords.*

DUKE FREDERICK
Can it be possible that no man saw them?
It cannot be. Some villains of my court
Are of consent and sufferance in this.   3
FIRST LORD
I cannot hear of any that did see her.
The ladies, her attendants of her chamber,
Saw her abed, and in the morning early
They found the bed untreasured of their mistress.
SECOND LORD
My lord, the roynish clown, at whom so oft   8
Your Grace was wont to laugh, is also missing.
Hisperia, the princess' gentlewoman,
Confesses that she secretly o'erheard
Your daughter and her cousin much commend
The parts and graces of the wrestler   13
That did but lately foil the sinewy Charles,
And she believes wherever they are gone
That youth is surely in their company.
DUKE FREDERICK
Send to his brother. Fetch that gallant hither.   17
If he be absent, bring his brother to me;   18
I'll make him find him. Do this suddenly,   19
And let not search and inquisition quail   20
To bring again these foolish runaways.   *Exeunt.*   21

♣

2.3   *Enter Orlando and Adam, [meeting].*

ORLANDO   Who's there?
ADAM
What, my young master? O my gentle master,
O my sweet master, O you memory   3
Of old Sir Rowland! Why, what make you here?   4
Why are you virtuous? Why do people love you?
And wherefore are you gentle, strong, and valiant?   6
Why would you be so fond to overcome   7
The bonny prizer of the humorous Duke?   8

67 **cope** encounter   68 **matter** substance   69 **straight** at once
2.2. Location: Duke Frederick's court.
3 **Are . . . this** have conspired in and permitted this   8 **roynish**
coarse   13 **parts** good qualities   17 **Send . . . hither** i.e., send word
to Oliver. Bring Orlando here   18 **he** i.e., Orlando. **his brother** i.e.,
Oliver   19 **suddenly** speedily   20 **inquisition** inquiry. **quail** fail,
slacken   21 **again** back
2.3. Location: Before Oliver's house.
3 **memory** memorial   4 **what make you** what are you doing
6 **wherefore** why   7 **fond to** foolish as to   8 **bonny prizer** sturdy
prizefighter. **humorous** temperamental

Your praise is come too swiftly home before you.
Know you not, master, to some kind of men
Their graces serve them but as enemies?
No more do yours. Your virtues, gentle master,   12
Are sanctified and holy traitors to you.
O, what a world is this, when what is comely
Envenoms him that bears it!
ORLANDO
Why, what's the matter?
ADAM   O unhappy youth,
Come not within these doors! Within this roof
The enemy of all your graces lives.
Your brother—no, no brother; yet the son—
Yet not the son, I will not call him son
Of him I was about to call his father—
Hath heard your praises, and this night he means   22
To burn the lodging where you use to lie   23
And you within it. If he fail of that,
He will have other means to cut you off.
I overheard him and his practices.   26
This is no place, this house is but a butchery.   27
Abhor it, fear it, do not enter it.
ORLANDO
Why, whither, Adam, wouldst thou have me go?
ADAM
No matter whither, so you come not here.   30
ORLANDO
What, wouldst thou have me go and beg my food?
Or with a base and boist'rous sword enforce   32
A thievish living on the common road?
This I must do or know not what to do;
Yet this I will not do, do how I can.
I rather will subject me to the malice
Of a diverted blood and bloody brother.   37
ADAM
But do not so. I have five hundred crowns,
The thrifty hire I saved under your father,   39
Which I did store to be my foster nurse
When service should in my old limbs lie lame   41
And unregarded age in corners thrown.   42
Take that, and He that doth the ravens feed,   43
Yea, providently caters for the sparrow,   44
Be comfort to my age! Here is the gold; [*offering gold*]
All this I give you. Let me be your servant.
Though I look old, yet I am strong and lusty,   47
For in my youth I never did apply
Hot and rebellious liquors in my blood,
Nor did not with unbashful forehead woo   50
The means of weakness and debility;
Therefore my age is as a lusty winter,
Frosty but kindly. Let me go with you.
I'll do the service of a younger man

12 **No more** no better   22 **your praises** people's praise of you
23 **use** are accustomed   26 **practices** plots   27 **place** place for you.
butchery slaughterhouse   30 **so** provided that   32 **boist'rous** rough
37 **diverted blood** kinship diverted from the natural source   39 **thrifty
. . . saved** wages I thriftily saved   41 **lie lame** i.e., be performed only
lamely   42 **thrown** be thrown   43–44 **He . . . sparrow** (See Luke
12:6, 22–24, Psalms 147:9, etc.)   47 **lusty** vigorous   50 **unbashful
forehead** shameless countenance

In all your business and necessities.

ORLANDO
O good old man, how well in thee appears
The constant service of the antique world,   57
When service sweat for duty, not for meed!   58
Thou art not for the fashion of these times,
Where none will sweat but for promotion,
And having that do choke their service up   61
Even with the having. It is not so with thee.   62
But, poor old man, thou prun'st a rotten tree,
That cannot so much as a blossom yield
In lieu of all thy pains and husbandry.   65
But come thy ways. We'll go along together,
And ere we have thy youthful wages spent,
We'll light upon some settled low content.   68

ADAM
Master, go on, and I will follow thee
To the last gasp, with truth and loyalty.
From seventeen years till now almost fourscore
Here livèd I, but now live here no more.
At seventeen years many their fortunes seek,
But at fourscore it is too late a week;   74
Yet fortune cannot recompense me better
Than to die well and not my master's debtor.

Exeunt.

♣

2.4   *Enter Rosalind for Ganymede, Celia for Aliena,
and Clown, alias Touchstone.*

ROSALIND   O Jupiter, how weary are my spirits!
TOUCHSTONE   I care not for my spirits, if my legs were
not weary.
ROSALIND   I could find in my heart to disgrace my man's
apparel and to cry like a woman; but I must comfort   5
the weaker vessel, as doublet and hose ought to show   6
itself courageous to petticoat. Therefore courage, good
Aliena!
CELIA   I pray you, bear with me. I cannot go no further.
TOUCHSTONE   For my part, I had rather bear with you
than bear you; yet I should bear no cross if I did bear   11
you, for I think you have no money in your purse.
ROSALIND   Well, this is the Forest of Arden.
TOUCHSTONE   Ay, now am I in Arden; the more fool I.
When I was at home I was in a better place, but
travelers must be content.

Enter Corin and Silvius.

ROSALIND   Ay, be so, good Touchstone.—Look you
who comes here, a young man and an old in solemn
talk.   *[They stand aside and listen.]*

CORIN
That is the way to make her scorn you still.
SILVIUS
O Corin, that thou knew'st how I do love her!
CORIN
I partly guess, for I have loved ere now.
SILVIUS
No, Corin, being old, thou canst not guess,
Though in thy youth thou wast as true a lover
As ever sighed upon a midnight pillow.
But if thy love were ever like to mine—
As sure I think did never man love so—
How many actions most ridiculous
Hast thou been drawn to by thy fantasy?   29
CORIN
Into a thousand that I have forgotten.
SILVIUS
O, thou didst then never love so heartily!
If thou rememberest not the slightest folly
That ever love did make thee run into,
Thou hast not loved.
Or if thou hast not sat as I do now,
Wearing thy hearer in thy mistress' praise,   36
Thou hast not loved.
Or if thou hast not broke from company
Abruptly, as my passion now makes me,
Thou has not loved.
O Phoebe, Phoebe, Phoebe!   *Exit.*
ROSALIND
Alas, poor shepherd! Searching of thy wound,   42
I have by hard adventure found mine own.   43
TOUCHSTONE   And I mine. I remember, when I was in
love I broke my sword upon a stone and bid him take   45
that for coming a-night to Jane Smile; and I remember   46
the kissing of her batler and the cow's dugs that her   47
pretty chapped hands had milked; and I remember
the wooing of a peascod instead of her, from whom I   49
took two cods and, giving her them again, said with   50
weeping tears, "Wear these for my sake." We that are
true lovers run into strange capers; but as all is mortal   52
in nature, so is all nature in love mortal in folly.   53
ROSALIND   Thou speak'st wiser than thou art ware of.   54
TOUCHSTONE   Nay, I shall ne'er be ware of mine own   55
wit till I break my shins against it.   56
ROSALIND
Jove, Jove! This shepherd's passion
Is much upon my fashion.   58

---

57 **constant** faithful   58 **sweat** sweated.   **meed** reward   61–62 **do
choke . . . having** i.e., cease serving once they have gained promotion   65 **lieu of** return for   68 **low content** lowly contented state
74 **a week** in the week
2.4. Location: The Forest of Arden.
s.d. for i.e., disguised as   5–6 **comfort the weaker vessel** (Saint
Paul, in 1 Peter 3:7, bids husbands give honor to their wives "as unto
the weaker vessel.")   **doublet and hose** close-fitting jacket and
breeches; typical male attire   11 **cross** (1) burden (2) coin having on
it a figure of a cross

29 **fantasy** love imaginings   36 **Wearing** wearing out   42 **Searching
of** probing   43 **hard adventure** bad luck   45 **I broke . . . stone**
(Touchstone's parody of himself as a distraught lover imagines him attacking a stone as if it were his successful rival and bidding him
"Take that.")   46 **a-night** by night   47 **batler** club for beating clothes
in process of washing.   **dugs** udder   49 **peascod** pea pod. (Regarded
as a lucky gift by rustic lovers.)   **whom** i.e., which (referring to the
whole pea plant and symbolizing Jane Smile)   50 **her** i.e., the pea
plant, symbolizing Jane Smile   52 **mortal** subject to death   53 **mortal**
typically human, frail   54 **ware** aware. (But Touchstone plays upon
the meaning "wary.")   55–56 **Nay . . . against it** (Touchstone, as a
professional fool, laughs at the idea of stumbling on or discovering his
own capacity for saying something wise.)   58 **upon** after, according
to

TOUCHSTONE
And mine, but it grows something stale with me.   59
CELIA
I pray you, one of you question yond man
If he for gold will give us any food.
I faint almost to death.
TOUCHSTONE [*to Corin*]   Holla: you, clown!   62
ROSALIND
Peace, Fool! He's not thy kinsman.
CORIN   Who calls?
TOUCHSTONE
Your betters, sir.
CORIN   Else are they very wretched.
ROSALIND
Peace, I say.—Good even to you, friend.   65
CORIN
And to you, gentle sir, and to you all.
ROSALIND
I prithee, shepherd, if that love or gold
Can in this desert place buy entertainment,   68
Bring us where we may rest ourselves and feed.
Here's a young maid with travel much oppressed,
And faints for succor.
CORIN   Fair sir, I pity her   71
And wish, for her sake more than for mine own,
My fortunes were more able to relieve her;
But I am shepherd to another man
And do not shear the fleeces that I graze.   75
My master is of churlish disposition,   76
And little recks to find the way to heaven   77
By doing deeds of hospitality.
Besides, his cote, his flocks, and bounds of feed   79
Are now on sale, and at our sheepcote now,
By reason of his absence, there is nothing
That you will feed on. But what is, come see,
And in my voice most welcome shall you be.   83
ROSALIND
What is he that shall buy his flock and pasture?   84
CORIN
That young swain that you saw here but erewhile,   85
That little cares for buying anything.
ROSALIND
I pray thee, if it stand with honesty,   87
Buy thou the cottage, pasture, and the flock,
And thou shalt have to pay for it of us.   89
CELIA
And we will mend thy wages. I like this place   90
And willingly could waste my time in it.   91
CORIN
Assuredly the thing is to be sold.

Go with me. If you like upon report
The soil, the profit, and this kind of life,
I will your very faithful feeder be   95
And buy it with your gold right suddenly.   *Exeunt.* 96

❖

2.5   *Enter Amiens, Jaques, and others. [A table is set out.]*

Song.
AMIENS [*sings*]
Under the greenwood tree
Who loves to lie with me,   2
And turn his merry note   3
Unto the sweet bird's throat,   4
Come hither, come hither, come hither.
Here shall he see
No enemy
But winter and rough weather.

JAQUES   More, more, I prithee, more.
AMIENS   It will make you melancholy, Monsieur Jaques.
JAQUES   I thank it. More, I prithee, more. I can suck melancholy out of a song as a weasel sucks eggs. More, I prithee, more.
AMIENS   My voice is ragged. I know I cannot please you.   14
JAQUES   I do not desire you to please me, I do desire you to sing. Come, more, another stanzo. Call you   16
'em "stanzos"?
AMIENS   What you will, Monsieur Jaques.
JAQUES   Nay, I care not for their names; they owe me   19
nothing. Will you sing?   20
AMIENS   More at your request than to please myself.
JAQUES   Well then, if ever I thank any man, I'll thank you; but that they call "compliment" is like th'   23
encounter of two dog-apes, and when a man thanks   24
me heartily, methinks I have given him a penny and
he renders me the beggarly thanks. Come, sing; and   26
you that will not, hold your tongues.
AMIENS   Well, I'll end the song.—Sirs, cover the while;   28
the Duke will drink under this tree.—He hath been all
this day to look you.   [*Food and drink are set out.*]   30
JAQUES   And I have been all this day to avoid him. He
is too disputable for my company. I think of as many   32
matters as he, but I give heaven thanks and make no
boast of them. Come, warble, come.

---

59 **something** somewhat   62 **clown** yokel. (But Rosalind then alludes to the word as it applies to Touchstone in the more familiar sense.) 65 **even** evening, i.e., afternoon   68 **desert** uninhabited.   **entertainment** hospitality, provision   71 **for succor** for lack of food   75 **do . . . fleeces** i.e., do not obtain the profits from the flock   76 **churlish** miserly   77 **recks** reckons   79 **cote** cottage.   **bounds of feed** limits within which he has the right of pasturage   83 **in my voice** insofar as I have authority to speak   84 **What** who   85 **but erewhile** only a short time since   87 **stand** be consistent   89 **have to pay** have the money   90 **mend** improve   91 **waste** spend

95 **feeder** servant   96 **right suddenly** without delay
2.5. Location: The forest.
2 **Who** anyone who   3 **turn** attune, adapt.   **note** tune   4 **throat** voice   14 **ragged** hoarse   16 **stanzo** (Perhaps an affected or else unsophisticated pronunciation of "stanza.")   19–20 **they owe me nothing** (Jaques speaks of names as of something valuable only when written as signatures to a bond of indebtedness.)   23 **that** what. "compliment" courtesy   24 **dog-apes** dog-faced baboons   26 **beggarly** effusive, like the thanks of a beggar   28 **cover the while** set the table for a meal meanwhile   30 **to look** looking for   32 **disputable** inclined to dispute

Song.

AMIENS [*sings*]

 Who doth ambition shun
 And loves to live i' the sun,   36
 Seeking the food he eats
 And pleased with what he gets,
      All together here.
 Come hither, come hither, come hither.
  Here shall he see
  No enemy
 But winter and rough weather.

JAQUES I'll give you a verse to this note that I made 43
yesterday in despite of my invention. 44
AMIENS And I'll sing it.
JAQUES Thus it goes:

 If it do come to pass
 That any man turn ass,
 Leaving his wealth and ease,
 A stubborn will to please,
 Ducdame, ducdame, ducdame. 51
  Here shall he see
  Gross fools as he,
 An if he will come to me.

AMIENS What's that "ducdame"?
JAQUES 'Tis a Greek invocation, to call fools into a circle.
I'll go sleep, if I can; if I cannot, I'll rail against all the
firstborn of Egypt. 58
AMIENS And I'll go seek the Duke. His banquet is pre- 59
pared. *Exeunt* [*separately*].

2.6 *Enter Orlando and Adam.*

ADAM Dear master, I can go no further. O, I die for
food! Here lie I down and measure out my grave.
Farewell, kind master. [*He lies down.*]
ORLANDO Why, how now, Adam? No greater heart in
thee? Live a little, comfort a little, cheer thyself a little. 5
If this uncouth forest yield anything savage, I will 6
either be food for it or bring it for food to thee. Thy
conceit is nearer death than thy powers. For my sake 8

36 **live i' the sun** dwell in the open air, without the cares of the court
43 **note** tune 44 **in . . . invention** without even using my imagination 51 **Ducdame** (Unexplained. One possible suggestion is that it is
a corruption of the gypsy words *dukrā mē*, meaning "I foretell";
therefore, as the call of a gypsy fortune-teller at fairs, it is a "Greek"
[or sharper's] invocation. This also renders the allusion to Egypt intelligible, since "gypsy" is a corruption of "Egyptian." 58 **firstborn of
Egypt** (In Exodus 12:28–33, the firstborn of Egypt are slain by the
Lord to achieve the release of the Jews. Perhaps Jaques ironically
threatens to rail against the firstborn because of their role in the exile
of Moses and his followers into the wilderness, which seems similar
to the exile of Duke Senior and his men in the forest.) 59 **banquet**
wine and dessert after dinner. (This repast, now prepared on stage,
seemingly is to remain there during the short following scene.)
2.6. Location: The forest. The scene is continuous. By convention we
understand that Adam and Orlando are in a different part of the forest and do not "see" the table remaining onstage.
5 **comfort** comfort yourself 6 **uncouth** strange, wild 8 **conceit**
imagination

be comfortable; hold death awhile at the arm's end. I 9
will here be with thee presently, and if I bring thee not
something to eat, I will give thee leave to die; but if
thou diest before I come, thou art a mocker of my
labor. Well said! Thou look'st cheerly, and I'll be with 13
thee quickly. Yet thou liest in the bleak air. Come, I 14
will bear thee to some shelter; and thou shalt not die
for lack of a dinner, if there live anything in this desert.
[*He picks up Adam.*] Cheerly, good Adam! *Exeunt.*

2.7 *Enter Duke Senior and Lords, like outlaws.*

DUKE SENIOR

 I think he be transformed into a beast,
 For I can nowhere find him like a man.

FIRST LORD

 My lord, he is but even now gone hence.
 Here was he merry, hearing of a song.

DUKE SENIOR

 If he, compact of jars, grow musical, 5
 We shall have shortly discord in the spheres. 6
 Go seek him. Tell him I would speak with him.

   Enter Jaques.

FIRST LORD

 He saves my labor by his own approach.

DUKE SENIOR

 Why, how now, monsieur, what a life is this,
 That your poor friends must woo your company!
 What, you look merrily.

JAQUES

 A fool, a fool! I met a fool i' the forest,
 A motley fool. A miserable world! 13
 As I do live by food, I met a fool,
 Who laid him down and basked him in the sun,
 And railed on Lady Fortune in good terms,
 In good set terms, and yet a motley fool. 17
 "Good morrow, Fool," quoth I. "No, sir," quoth he,
 "Call me not fool till heaven hath sent me fortune." 19
 And then he drew a dial from his poke 20
 And, looking on it with lackluster eye,
 Says very wisely, "It is ten o'clock.
 Thus we may see," quoth he, "how the world wags. 23
 'Tis but an hour ago since it was nine,
 And after one hour more 'twill be eleven;
 And so from hour to hour we ripe and ripe,
 And then from hour to hour we rot and rot,
 And thereby hangs a tale." When I did hear
 The motley fool thus moral on the time, 29

9 **comfortable** comforted 13 **Well said** well done 14 **Yet** still
2.7. Location: The forest; the scene is continuous. (A light repast, set
out for the Duke in 2.5, has remained onstage during 2.6.)
5 **compact of jars** composed of discords 6 **the spheres** the concentric spheres of the old Ptolemaic solar system (which, by their movement, were thought to produce harmonious music) 13 **motley** wearing motley, the parti-colored dress of the professional jester 17 **set**
carefully composed 19 **Call . . . fortune** (An allusion to the proverb
"Fortune favors fools.") 20 **dial** portable sundial or watch. **poke**
pouch or pocket 23 **wags** goes 29 **moral** moralize

My lungs began to crow like Chanticleer,   30
That fools should be so deep-contemplative,
And I did laugh sans intermission   32
An hour by his dial. O noble fool!
A worthy fool! Motley's the only wear.   34

DUKE SENIOR   What fool is this?

JAQUES
O worthy fool! One that hath been a courtier,
And says, if ladies be but young and fair,
They have the gift to know it. And in his brain,
Which is as dry as the remainder biscuit   39
After a voyage, he hath strange places crammed   40
With observation, the which he vents   41
In mangled forms. O, that I were a fool!
I am ambitious for a motley coat.

DUKE SENIOR
Thou shalt have one.

JAQUES   It is my only suit,   44
Provided that you weed your better judgments
Of all opinion that grows rank in them   46
That I am wise. I must have liberty
Withal, as large a charter as the wind,   48
To blow on whom I please, for so fools have.
And they that are most gallèd with my folly,   50
They most must laugh. And why, sir, must they so?
The "why" is plain as way to parish church:
He that a fool doth very wisely hit   53
Doth very foolishly, although he smart,   54
Not to seem senseless of the bob. If not,   55
The wise man's folly is anatomized   56
Even by the squand'ring glances of the fool.   57
Invest me in my motley; give me leave   58
To speak my mind, and I will through and through
Cleanse the foul body of th' infected world,   60
If they will patiently receive my medicine.

DUKE SENIOR
Fie on thee! I can tell what thou wouldst do.

JAQUES
What, for a counter, would I do but good?   63

DUKE SENIOR
Most mischievous foul sin, in chiding sin.
For thou thyself hast been a libertine,
As sensual as the brutish sting itself;   66
And all th' embossèd sores and headed evils   67
That thou with license of free foot hast caught   68

Wouldst thou disgorge into the general world.   69

JAQUES   Why, who cries out on pride   70
That can therein tax any private party?   71
Doth it not flow as hugely as the sea,
Till that the weary very means do ebb?   73
What woman in the city do I name,
When that I say the city woman bears   75
The cost of princes on unworthy shoulders?   76
Who can come in and say that I mean her,   77
When such a one as she, such is her neighbor?
Or what is he of basest function   79
That says his bravery is not on my cost,   80
Thinking that I mean him, but therein suits   81
His folly to the mettle of my speech?   82
There then, how then? What then? Let me see
     wherein
My tongue hath wronged him. If it do him right,   84
Then he hath wronged himself. If he be free,   85
Why then my taxing like a wild goose flies,   86
Unclaimed of any man.—But who comes here?

Enter Orlando [with his sword drawn].

ORLANDO
Forbear, and eat no more!

JAQUES   Why, I have eat none yet.   88

ORLANDO
Nor shalt not, till necessity be served.

JAQUES
Of what kind should this cock come of?   90

DUKE SENIOR
Art thou thus boldened, man, by thy distress,
Or else a rude despiser of good manners,
That in civility thou seem'st so empty?

ORLANDO
You touched my vein at first. The thorny point   94
Of bare distress hath ta'en from me the show
Of smooth civility; yet am I inland bred   96
And know some nurture. But forbear, I say.   97
He dies that touches any of this fruit
Till I and my affairs are answerèd.   99

JAQUES
An you will not be answered with reason, I must
     die.   100

DUKE SENIOR
What would you have? Your gentleness shall force

---

30 crow i.e., laugh merrily.   **Chanticleer** a rooster   **32 sans** without   **34 only wear** only thing worth wearing   **39 dry** (According to Elizabethan physiology, a dry brain was marked by a strong memory but a slowness of apprehension.)   **remainder** remaining   **40 places** (1) nooks and corners (2) commonplaces, i.e., familiar ideas and quotations   **41 vents** utters   **44 suit** (1) request (2) suit of clothes   **46 rank** wild   **48 Withal** in addition.   **charter** license, privilege   **50 gallèd** rubbed sore   **53 He . . . hit** he whom a fool wittily attacks   **54 Doth** acts.   **smart** feels the sting   **55 senseless of the bob** insensible to the taunt. (It's prudent to appear calm and indifferent in the face of satire; otherwise, you are vulnerable.)   **If not** otherwise   **56 anatomized** dissected   **57 squand'ring glances** random hits   **58 Invest** dress   **60 Cleanse** purge. (A medical metaphor.)   **63 counter** (1) thing of no intrinsic value, a metal disk used in counting (2) parry   **66 brutish sting** carnal impulse   **67 embossèd** swollen.   **headed evils** sores that have come to a head   **68 license . . . foot** the licentious freedom of a libertine

69 disgorge vomit   **70 on pride** against extravagance in dress   **71 tax** blame.   **any private party** i.e., only some individual   **73 Till . . . ebb** until the ostentation finally subsides, having exhausted what fed it (?)   **75 the city woman** the typical citizen's wife   **76 The cost of princes** i.e., clothes rich enough to adorn a prince   **77 come in** i.e., come into court as a complainant   **79 what** who.   **basest function** lowest position in society   **80 That . . . cost** who says his finery is not bought at my expense (and is therefore none of my business)   **81 suits** (1) fits (2) dresses   **82 mettle** contents   **84 If . . . right** if I have described him accurately   **85 wronged himself** (by calling attention to the accuracy of my description).   **free** blameless   **86 taxing** criticism   **88 have eat** have eaten. (Pronounced "et.")   **90 Of . . . of** what sort of fighting cock is this?   **94 vein** condition, disposition.   **at first** i.e., in what you first suggested   **96 inland bred** i.e., raised in the center of civilization rather than on the outskirts   **97 nurture** education, training   **99 answerèd** satisfied   **100 An** if.   **reason** (A pun on "raisin" plays upon *fruit* in line 98.)

More than your force move us to gentleness.
ORLANDO
I almost die for food, and let me have it!
DUKE SENIOR
Sit down and feed, and welcome to our table.
ORLANDO
Speak you so gently? Pardon me, I pray you.
I thought that all things had been savage here,
And therefore put I on the countenance
Of stern commandment. But whate'er you are
That in this desert inaccessible,
Under the shade of melancholy boughs,   110
Lose and neglect the creeping hours of time;
If ever you have looked on better days,
If ever been where bells have knolled to church,   113
If ever sat at any good man's feast,
If ever from your eyelids wiped a tear
And know what 'tis to pity and be pitied,
Let gentleness my strong enforcement be,
In the which hope I blush and hide my sword.
           [He sheathes his sword.]
DUKE SENIOR
True is it that we have seen better days,
And have with holy bell been knolled to church,
And sat at good men's feasts, and wiped our eyes
Of drops that sacred pity hath engendered.
And therefore sit you down in gentleness,
And take upon command what help we have   124
That to your wanting may be ministered.   125
ORLANDO
Then but forbear your food a little while,
Whiles, like a doe, I go to find my fawn
And give it food. There is an old poor man
Who after me hath many a weary step
Limped in pure love. Till he be first sufficed,
Oppressed with two weak evils, age and hunger,   131
I will not touch a bit.
DUKE SENIOR   Go find him out,
And we will nothing waste till you return.   133
ORLANDO
I thank ye; and be blest for your good comfort!
           [Exit.]
DUKE SENIOR
Thou seest we are not all alone unhappy.
This wide and universal theater
Presents more woeful pageants than the scene
Wherein we play in.
JAQUES   All the world's a stage,
And all the men and women merely players.
They have their exits and their entrances,
And one man in his time plays many parts,
His acts being seven ages. At first the infant,
Mewling and puking in the nurse's arms.   143
Then the whining schoolboy, with his satchel
And shining morning face, creeping like snail

Unwillingly to school. And then the lover,
Sighing like furnace, with a woeful ballad
Made to his mistress' eyebrow. Then a soldier,
Full of strange oaths and bearded like the pard,   149
Jealous in honor, sudden, and quick in quarrel,   150
Seeking the bubble reputation
Even in the cannon's mouth. And then the justice,
In fair round belly with good capon lined,   153
With eyes severe and beard of formal cut,
Full of wise saws and modern instances;   155
And so he plays his part. The sixth age shifts
Into the lean and slippered pantaloon,   157
With spectacles on nose and pouch on side,
His youthful hose, well saved, a world too wide
For his shrunk shank; and his big manly voice,   160
Turning again toward childish treble, pipes
And whistles in his sound. Last scene of all,   162
That ends this strange, eventful history,
Is second childishness and mere oblivion,   164
Sans teeth, sans eyes, sans taste, sans everything.   165

Enter Orlando, with Adam.

DUKE SENIOR
Welcome. Set down your venerable burden
And let him feed.
ORLANDO   I thank you most for him.
           [He sets down Adam.]
ADAM   So had you need.
I scarce can speak to thank you for myself.
DUKE SENIOR
Welcome. Fall to. I will not trouble you
As yet to question you about your fortunes.—
Give us some music, and, good cousin, sing.   172
      [They eat, while Orlando and Duke Senior
               converse apart.]

Song.

AMIENS [*sings*]
Blow, blow, thou winter wind.
Thou art not so unkind
As man's ingratitude.
Thy tooth is not so keen,
Because thou art not seen,
Although thy breath be rude.   179
Heigh-ho, sing heigh-ho, unto the green holly.   180
Most friendship is feigning, most loving mere
folly.
Then heigh-ho, the holly!
This life is most jolly.

110 **melancholy** dark, shadowy   113 **knolled** knelled, rung
124 **upon command** for the asking   125 **wanting** need   131 **weak
evils** disabilities causing weakness   133 **waste** consume   143 **Mewling** crying with a catlike noise

149 **bearded . . . pard** having bristling mustaches like the leopard's
150 **Jealous in honor** quick to anger in matters of honor.   **sudden**
rash   153 **capon** rooster castrated to make the flesh more tender for
eating (and often presented to judges as a bribe)   155 **saws** sayings.
modern instances commonplace illustrations   157 **pantaloon** ridiculous, enfeebled old man. (A stock type in Italian comedy.)
160 **shank** calf   162 **his** its   164 **mere oblivion** total forgetfulness
165 **Sans** without   172 **cousin** (A term used by sovereigns to address
their nobility.)   179 **rude** rough   180 **holly** (An emblem of Christmas-
time and holiday cheer, as in "the holly and the ivy.")

Freeze, freeze, thou bitter sky,
That dost not bite so nigh   185
    As benefits forgot.
Though thou the waters warp,   187
Thy sting is not so sharp
    As friend remembered not.
Heigh-ho, sing heigh-ho, unto the green holly.
Most friendship is feigning, most loving mere
    folly.
        Then heigh-ho, the holly!
        This life is most jolly.

DUKE SENIOR [*to Orlando*]
If that you were the good Sir Rowland's son,
As you have whispered faithfully you were   195
And as mine eye doth his effigies witness   196
Most truly limned and living in your face,   197
Be truly welcome hither. I am the Duke
That loved your father. The residue of your fortune, 199
Go to my cave and tell me.—Good old man,
Thou art right welcome as thy master is.—
Support him by the arm. Give me your hand,
And let me all your fortunes understand.   *Exeunt.* 203

3.1   *Enter Duke [Frederick], Lords, and Oliver.*

DUKE FREDERICK
Not see him since? Sir, sir, that cannot be.   1
But were I not the better part made mercy,   2
I should not seek an absent argument   3
Of my revenge, thou present. But look to it: 4
Find out thy brother, wheresoe'er he is.
Seek him with candle. Bring him dead or living   6
Within this twelvemonth, or turn thou no more   7
To seek a living in our territory.
Thy lands and all things that thou dost call thine
Worth seizure do we seize into our hands,
Till thou canst quit thee by thy brother's mouth   11
Of what we think against thee.

OLIVER
O, that Your Highness knew my heart in this!
I never loved my brother in my life.

DUKE FREDERICK
More villain thou.—Well, push him out of doors,

And let my officers of such a nature   16
Make an extent upon his house and lands.   17
Do this expediently, and turn him going.   *Exeunt.* 18

3.2   *Enter Orlando [with a paper].*

ORLANDO
Hang there, my verse, in witness of my love;
    And thou, thrice-crownèd queen of night, survey   2
With thy chaste eye, from thy pale sphere above,
    Thy huntress' name that my full life doth sway.   4
O Rosalind! These trees shall be my books,
    And in their barks my thoughts I'll character,   6
That every eye which in this forest looks
    Shall see thy virtue witnessed everywhere.
Run, run, Orlando, carve on every tree
The fair, the chaste, and unexpressive she.   *Exit.* 10

Enter Corin and [Touchstone the] Clown.

CORIN   And how like you this shepherd's life, Master
Touchstone?

TOUCHSTONE   Truly, shepherd, in respect of itself, it is a   13
good life; but in respect that it is a shepherd's life, it is
naught. In respect that it is solitary, I like it very well;   15
but in respect that it is private, it is a very vile life.
Now in respect it is in the fields, it pleaseth me well;
but in respect it is not in the court, it is tedious. As it
is a spare life, look you, it fits my humor well; but as   19
there is no more plenty in it, it goes much against my
stomach. Hast any philosophy in thee, shepherd?

CORIN   No more but that I know the more one sickens
the worse at ease he is; and that he that wants money,   23
means, and content is without three good friends; that
the property of rain is to wet and fire to burn; that
good pasture makes fat sheep and that a great cause
of the night is lack of the sun; that he that hath learned
no wit by nature nor art may complain of good   28
breeding or comes of a very dull kindred.

TOUCHSTONE   Such a one is a natural philosopher.
Wast ever in court, shepherd?

CORIN   No, truly.

TOUCHSTONE   Then thou art damned.

CORIN   Nay, I hope.   34

TOUCHSTONE   Truly, thou art damned, like an ill-
roasted egg, all on one side.

---

185 nigh near (to the heart)   **187 warp** freeze so that the surface of
the ice cracks and forces up ridges   **195 faithfully** persuasively and
honestly   **196 effigies** likeness, portrait (often sculptured or painted in
memory of the dead)   **197 limned** painted   **199 The . . . fortune** the
rest of your adventure   **203 s.d. Exeunt** (The table must be removed
at this point.)

3.1. Location: Duke Frederick's court.
1 Not . . . since i.e., you mean to tell me you claim not to have seen
Orlando since I sent for him?   **2 better** greater.   **made** made of
3–4 I . . . present i.e., I would seek revenge not on the absent Orlando, but on you, who are right here   **6 Seek . . . candle** (See Luke
15:8.)   **7 turn** return   **11 quit thee** acquit yourself.   **by . . . mouth**
i.e., by direct testimony of Orlando (whom the Duke suspects to have
been murdered)

16 of such a nature who attend to such duties   **17 extent** writ of
seizure   **18 expediently** expeditiously.   **turn him going** send him
packing
3.2. Location: The forest.
2 thrice-crownèd queen i.e., Diana in the three aspects of her divinity: as Luna or Cynthia, goddess of the moon; as Diana, goddess on
earth; and as Hecate or Proserpina, goddess in the lower world
4 Thy huntress' i.e., Rosalind's, who is here thought of as accompanying Diana, patroness of the hunt and of chastity.   **sway** control
6 character inscribe   **10 unexpressive** inexpressible   **13 in respect of
itself** considered in and for itself   **15 naught** vile, of no social consequence   **19 spare** frugal.   **humor** temperament   **23 wants** lacks
28 wit wisdom.   **art** study.   **complain of** lament the lack of
34 hope i.e., hope not

CORIN   For not being at court? Your reason.

TOUCHSTONE   Why, if thou never wast at court, thou never sawst good manners; if thou never sawst good 39 manners, then thy manners must be wicked; and 40 wickedness is sin, and sin is damnation. Thou art in a parlous state, shepherd. 42

CORIN   Not a whit, Touchstone. Those that are good manners at the court are as ridiculous in the country as the behavior of the country is most mockable at the court. You told me you salute not at the court but you 46 kiss your hands; that courtesy would be uncleanly, if 47 courtiers were shepherds.

TOUCHSTONE   Instance, briefly; come, instance. 49

CORIN   Why, we are still handling our ewes, and their 50 fells you know are greasy. 51

TOUCHSTONE   Why, do not your courtier's hands sweat? And is not the grease of a mutton as wholesome as the 53 sweat of a man? Shallow, shallow. A better instance, I 54 say. Come.

CORIN   Besides, our hands are hard.

TOUCHSTONE   Your lips will feel them the sooner. Shallow again. A more sounder instance. Come.

CORIN   And they are often tarred over with the surgery 59 of our sheep; and would you have us kiss tar? The courtier's hands are perfumed with civet. 61

TOUCHSTONE   Most shallow man! Thou worms' meat, in 62 respect of a good piece of flesh indeed! Learn of the 63 wise, and perpend: civet is of a baser birth than tar, 64 the very uncleanly flux of a cat. Mend the instance, 65 shepherd.

CORIN   You have too courtly a wit for me. I'll rest.

TOUCHSTONE   Wilt thou rest damned? God help thee, shallow man! God make incision in thee! Thou art 69 raw. 70

CORIN   Sir, I am a true laborer: I earn that I eat, get that 71 I wear, owe no man hate, envy no man's happiness, glad of other men's good, content with my harm, and 73 the greatest of my pride is to see my ewes graze and my lambs suck.

TOUCHSTONE   That is another simple sin in you, to bring 76 the ewes and the rams together and to offer to get your 77 living by the copulation of cattle; to be bawd to a bell- 78 wether, and to betray a she-lamb of a twelvemonth to 79 a crooked-pated old cuckoldly ram, out of all reasonable 80

match. If thou beest not damned for this, the devil him- 81 self will have no shepherds; I cannot see else how thou 82 shouldst scape. 83

CORIN   Here comes young Master Ganymede, my new mistress's brother.

Enter Rosalind [with a paper, reading].

ROSALIND
"From the east to western Ind, 86
No jewel is like Rosalind.
Her worth, being mounted on the wind,
Through all the world bears Rosalind.
All the pictures fairest lined 90
Are but black to Rosalind. 91
Let no face be kept in mind
But the fair of Rosalind." 93

TOUCHSTONE   I'll rhyme you so eight years together, 94 dinners and suppers and sleeping hours excepted. It 95 is the right butter-women's rank to market. 96

ROSALIND   Out, fool! 97

TOUCHSTONE   For a taste:
If a hart do lack a hind, 99
Let him seek out Rosalind.
If the cat will after kind, 101
So, be sure, will Rosalind.
Wintered garments must be lined, 103
So must slender Rosalind.
They that reap must sheaf and bind; 105
Then to cart with Rosalind. 106
Sweetest nut hath sourest rind;
Such a nut is Rosalind.
He that sweetest rose will find
Must find love's prick and Rosalind. 110

This is the very false gallop of verses. Why do you 111 infect yourself with them?

ROSALIND   Peace, you dull fool! I found them on a tree.

TOUCHSTONE   Truly, the tree yields bad fruit.

ROSALIND   I'll graft it with you, and then I shall graft it 115 with a medlar. Then it will be the earliest fruit i' the 116 country; for you'll be rotten ere you be half ripe, and that's the right virtue of the medlar. 118

39, 40 manners (1) etiquette (2) morals   **42 parlous** perilous   **46–47 but you kiss** without kissing   **49 Instance** proof   **50 still** always   **51 fells** skins with the wool, or fleeces   **53–54 grease . . . sweat** (Human sweat was thought to be fat oozing from the pores.)   **59 tarred over** anointed with tar on their cuts and sores   **61 civet** a musky perfume derived from glands in the anal pouch of the civet cat (as Touchstone points out)   **62 worms' meat** food for worms, i.e., subject to decay of the flesh   **63 respect of** comparison with.   **piece of flesh** sample of humanity   **64 perpend** consider   **65 flux** secretion.   **Mend** improve   **69 incision** a cut, perhaps for the purpose of letting blood (here, to let out folly); or for seasoning as raw meat is scored and salted before cooking   **70 raw** inexperienced (with a play on "sore," requiring surgery)   **71 that** what.   **get** acquire by my labor   **73 content . . . harm** patient with my ill fortune   **76 simple sin** sin arising from simplicity   **77 offer** undertake   **78 cattle** livestock   **78–79 bellwether** the leading male sheep of a flock, wearing a bell   **80 crooked-pated** with crooked horns.   **cuckoldly** i.e., horned like a cuckold (husband of an unfaithful wife).   **out of** contrary to

81–82 If . . . shepherds i.e., your only possible escape from damnation would be if the devil should find shepherds too objectionable to have in hell under any circumstances   **83 scape** escape   **86 Ind** Indies   **90 lined** drawn   **91 black** dark-complexioned. (Thought to be ugly.)   **to** compared to   **93 fair** beauty   **94 together** without stop   **95–96 It is . . . market** i.e., the rhymes, all alike, follow each other precisely like a line of butter women or dairy women jogging along to market   **97 Out** (An exclamation here denoting comic indignation.)   **99 If . . . hind** if a male deer longs for a female deer. (Touchstone wryly suggests in his verses that Rosalind is the responsive object of male desire.)   **101 after kind** follow its natural instinct   **103 Wintered** used in winter.   **lined** (1) given a winter lining (2) stuffed. (The term was sometimes used for the copulating of dogs.)   **105 sheaf and bind** tie in a bundle. (Rewards entail obligations.)   **106 to cart** (1) onto the harvest cart (2) onto the cart used to carry prostitutes through the streets, exposing them to public ridicule   **110 prick** thorn. (With bawdy suggestion.)   **111 false gallop** canter   **115 you** (with a pun on "yew")   **116 medlar** a fruit like a small brown-skinned apple that is eaten when it starts to decay. (With a pun on "meddler.")   **118 right virtue** true quality

TOUCHSTONE   You have said; but whether wisely or no, let the forest judge.

Enter Celia, with a writing.

ROSALIND   Peace! Here comes my sister, reading. Stand aside.

CELIA [*reads*]

     "Why should this a desert be?
        For it is unpeopled? No.   124
     Tongues I'll hang on every tree,
        That shall civil sayings show: 126
     Some, how brief the life of man
        Runs his erring pilgrimage,   128
     That the stretching of a span   129
        Buckles in his sum of age;   130
     Some, of violated vows
        Twixt the souls of friend and friend;
     But upon the fairest boughs,
        Or at every sentence end,
     Will I 'Rosalinda' write,
        Teaching all that read to know
     The quintessence of every sprite   137
        Heaven would in little show.   138
     Therefore heaven Nature charged
        That one body should be filled
     With all graces wide-enlarged.   141
        Nature presently distilled
     Helen's cheek, but not her heart,   143
        Cleopatra's majesty,
     Atalanta's better part,   145
        Sad Lucretia's modesty.   146
     Thus Rosalind of many parts
        By heavenly synod was devised   148
     Of many faces, eyes, and hearts
        To have the touches dearest prized.   150
     Heaven would that she these gifts should have,
     And I to live and die her slave."

ROSALIND   O most gentle Jupiter, what tedious homily 153 of love have you wearied your parishioners withal, and never cried, "Have patience, good people!"

CELIA   How now? Back, friends. Shepherd, go off a 156 little. [*To Touchstone.*] Go with him, sirrah.   157

---

124 For because   **126 civil sayings** maxims of civilized life   **128 his erring** its wandering   **129–130 That . . . age** i.e., so that a very brief span encompasses his whole life. (A *span* is a handbreadth. See Psalm 39:5.)   **137 quintessence** highest perfection. (Literally, the fifth essence or element of the medieval alchemists, purer even than fire.) **sprite** spirit   **138 Heaven . . . show** that heaven wishes to show in one small person, Rosalind (who, in microcosm, embodies the supreme essence of the heavens, or macrocosm)   **141 wide-enlarged** widely distributed (i.e., that had been spread through the world but now are concentrated in Rosalind)   **143 Helen's . . . heart** i.e., the beauty of Helen of Troy but not her false heart   **145 Atalanta's better part** i.e., her beauty or her fleetness of foot, not her scornfulness and greed. (She refused to marry any man who was unable to defeat her in a foot race and, when challenged by Hippomenes, lost to him because Hippomenes dropped in her way three golden apples of the Hesperides.)   **146 Lucretia** An honorable Roman lady raped by Tarquin (whose story Shakespeare tells in *The Rape of Lucrece*).
148 synod assembly   **150 touches** traits   **153 Jupiter** (Often emended to "pulpiter.")   **156 Back** i.e., move back, away. (Addressed to Corin and Touchstone.)   **157 sirrah** A form of address to inferiors (here, Touchstone).

TOUCHSTONE   Come, shepherd, let us make an honorable retreat, though not with bag and baggage, yet 159 with scrip and scrippage.   *Exit* [*with Corin*]. 160

CELIA   Didst thou hear these verses?

ROSALIND   O, yes, I heard them all, and more, too, for some of them had in them more feet than the verses would bear.

CELIA   That's no matter. The feet might bear the verses.

ROSALIND   Ay, but the feet were lame and could not bear themselves without the verse and therefore stood 167 lamely in the verse.

CELIA   But didst thou hear without wondering how thy name should be hanged and carved upon these trees?

ROSALIND   I was seven of the nine days out of the 171 wonder before you came; for look here what I found 172 on a palm tree. I was never so berhymed since Pythagoras' time, that I was an Irish rat, which I can 174 hardly remember.

CELIA   Trow you who hath done this?   176

ROSALIND   Is it a man?

CELIA   And a chain that you once wore about his neck. 178 Change you color?

ROSALIND   I prithee, who?

CELIA   O Lord, Lord, it is a hard matter for friends to 181 meet; but mountains may be removed with earth- 182 quakes and so encounter.   183

ROSALIND   Nay, but who is it?

CELIA   Is it possible?   185

ROSALIND   Nay, I prithee now with most petitionary vehemence, tell me who it is.

CELIA   O wonderful, wonderful, and most wonderful wonderful! And yet again wonderful, and after that, out of all whooping!   190

ROSALIND   Good my complexion! Dost thou think, 191 though I am caparisoned like a man, I have a doublet 192 and hose in my disposition? One inch of delay more 193 is a South Sea of discovery. I prithee, tell me who is it 194 quickly, and speak apace. I would thou couldst stammer, that thou mightst pour this concealed man out of thy mouth as wine comes out of a narrow-mouthed bottle, either too much at once or none at all. I prithee, take the cork out of thy mouth that I may drink thy tidings.

CELIA   So you may put a man in your belly.   201

---

159 bag and baggage i.e., equipment appropriate to a retreating army **160 scrip and scrippage** shepherd's pouch and its contents **167 without** (1) without the help of (2) outside   **171–172 seven . . . wonder** (A reference to the common phrase "a nine days' wonder.") **174 Pythagoras** Greek philosopher credited with the doctrine of the transmigration of souls. **that** when.   **Irish rat** (Refers to a current belief that Irish enchanters could rhyme rats and other animals to death.) **which** a thing which   **176 Trow you** have you any idea   **178 And a chain** i.e., and with a chain   **181–183 friends . . . encounter** (A playful inversion of the proverb, "Friends may meet, but mountains never greet." Celia appears to be teasing Rosalind's eagerness to meet Orlando.)   **removed with** moved by   **185 possible** i.e., possible you don't know   **190 out . . . whooping** beyond all whooping, i.e., power to utter   **191 Good my complexion** O my (feminine) temperament, my woman's curiosity   **192 caparisoned** bedecked. (Usually said of a horse.)   **192–193 I have . . . disposition** i.e., that I have a man's patience   **194 a South Sea of discovery** i.e., as tedious as the long delays on exploratory voyages to the South Seas   **201 belly** (1) stomach (2) womb

ROSALIND   Is he of God's making? What manner of 202
man? Is his head worth a hat, or his chin worth a
beard?

CELIA   Nay, he hath but a little beard.

ROSALIND   Why, God will send more, if the man will be
thankful. Let me stay the growth of his beard, if thou 207
delay me not the knowledge of his chin.

CELIA   It is young Orlando, that tripped up the wrestler's heels and your heart both in an instant.

ROSALIND   Nay, but the devil take mocking. Speak sad 211
brow and true maid.   212

CELIA   I' faith, coz, 'tis he.

ROSALIND   Orlando?

CELIA   Orlando.

ROSALIND   Alas the day, what shall I do with my
doublet and hose? What did he when thou sawst him?
What said he? How looked he? Wherein went he? 218
What makes he here? Did he ask for me? Where 219
remains he? How parted he with thee? And when 220
shalt thou see him again? Answer me in one word.

CELIA   You must borrow me Gargantua's mouth first; 222
'tis a word too great for any mouth of this age's size.
To say ay and no to these particulars is more than to 224
answer in a catechism.   225

ROSALIND   But doth he know that I am in this forest
and in man's apparel? Looks he as freshly as he did
the day he wrestled?

CELIA   It is as easy to count atomies as to resolve the 229
propositions of a lover. But take a taste of my finding 230
him, and relish it with good observance. I found him 231
under a tree, like a dropped acorn.

ROSALIND   It may well be called Jove's tree, when it 233
drops forth such fruit.

CELIA   Give me audience, good madam.

ROSALIND   Proceed.

CELIA   There lay he, stretched along, like a wounded
knight.

ROSALIND   Though it be pity to see such a sight, it well
becomes the ground.   240

CELIA   Cry "holla" to thy tongue, I prithee; it curvets 241
unseasonably. He was furnished like a hunter.   242

ROSALIND   O, ominous! He comes to kill my heart.   243

CELIA   I would sing my song without a burden. Thou 244
bring'st me out of tune.   245

ROSALIND   Do you not know I am a woman? When I
think, I must speak. Sweet, say on.

Enter Orlando and Jaques.

CELIA   You bring me out.—Soft, comes he not here? 248

ROSALIND   'Tis he. Slink by, and note him.
                        [*They stand aside and listen.*]

JAQUES [*to Orlando*]   I thank you for your company,
but, good faith, I had as lief have been myself alone.

ORLANDO   And so had I; but yet, for fashion's sake, I
thank you too for your society.

JAQUES   God b' wi' you. Let's meet as little as we can. 254

ORLANDO   I do desire we may be better strangers.

JAQUES   I pray you, mar no more trees with writing
love songs in their barks.

ORLANDO   I pray you, mar no more of my verses with
reading them ill-favoredly.   259

JAQUES   Rosalind is your love's name?

ORLANDO   Yes, just.   261

JAQUES   I do not like her name.

ORLANDO   There was no thought of pleasing you when
she was christened.

JAQUES   What stature is she of?

ORLANDO   Just as high as my heart.

JAQUES   You are full of pretty answers. Have you not
been acquainted with goldsmiths' wives, and conned 268
them out of rings?   269

ORLANDO   Not so; but I answer you right painted cloth, 270
from whence you have studied your questions.

JAQUES   You have a nimble wit; I think 'twas made of
Atalanta's heels. Will you sit down with me? And we 273
two will rail against our mistress the world and all our
misery.

ORLANDO   I will chide no breather in the world but 276
myself, against whom I know most faults.

JAQUES   The worst fault you have is to be in love.

ORLANDO   'Tis a fault I will not change for your best
virtue. I am weary of you.

JAQUES   By my troth, I was seeking for a fool when I
found you.

ORLANDO   He is drowned in the brook. Look but in,
and you shall see him.

JAQUES   There I shall see mine own figure.

ORLANDO   Which I take to be either a fool or a cipher. 286

JAQUES   I'll tarry no longer with you. Farewell, good
Seigneur Love.

ORLANDO   I am glad of your departure. Adieu, good
Monsieur Melancholy.   [*Exit Jaques.*]

ROSALIND [*aside to Celia*]   I will speak to him like a
saucy lackey and under that habit play the knave 292
with him.—Do you hear, forester?

ORLANDO   Very well. What would you?

ROSALIND   I pray you, what is 't o'clock?

ORLANDO   You should ask me what time o' day.
There's no clock in the forest.

ROSALIND   Then there is no true lover in the forest, else

202 of God's making i.e., a real man, not of his tailor's making
207 stay wait for   **211–212 sad . . . maid** i.e., seriously and truthfully   **218 Wherein went he** in what clothes was he dressed
219 makes does   **220 remains** dwells   **222 Gargantua's mouth** (Gargantua is the giant of popular literature who, in Rabelais' novel, swallowed five pilgrims in a salad.)   **224–225 To . . . catechism** to give
even yes and no answers to these questions would take longer than to
go through the catechism (i.e., the formal questioning used in the
Church to teach the principles of faith)   **229 atomies** motes, specks
of dirt   **230 propositions** questions   **231 relish it** heighten its pleasant taste.   **observance** attention   **233 Jove's tree** the oak   **240 becomes** adorns   **241 holla** stop.   **curvets** prances   **242 furnished**
equipped, dressed   **243 heart** (with pun on "hart")   **244 burden** refrain, or bass part   **244–245 Thou bring'st** you put

248 Soft i.e., wait a minute, or, stop talking   **254 God b' wi' you**
God be with you, good-bye   **259 ill-favoredly** unsympathetically
261 just just so   **268 conned** memorized   **269 rings** (Verses or "posies" were often inscribed in rings.)   **270 right painted cloth** in the
true spirit of a painted cloth decorated with commonplace pictures
and cliché mottoes (frequently mythological or scriptural)   **273 Atalanta's heels** (See above, the note for line 145.)   **276 breather** living
being   **286 cipher** nonentity, zero   **292 habit** guise

sighing every minute and groaning every hour would detect the lazy foot of Time as well as a clock.   300

ORLANDO   And why not the swift foot of Time? Had not that been as proper?

ROSALIND   By no means, sir. Time travels in divers paces with divers persons. I'll tell you who Time ambles withal, who Time trots withal, who Time   305 gallops withal, and who he stands still withal.

ORLANDO   I prithee, who doth he trot withal?

ROSALIND   Marry, he trots hard with a young maid   308 between the contract of her marriage and the day it is solemnized. If the interim be but a se'nnight, Time's   310 pace is so hard that it seems the length of seven year.

ORLANDO   Who ambles Time withal?

ROSALIND   With a priest that lacks Latin and a rich man that hath not the gout, for the one sleeps easily because he cannot study and the other lives merrily because he feels no pain, the one lacking the burden of lean and wasteful learning, the other knowing no   317 burden of heavy tedious penury. These Time ambles withal.

ORLANDO   Who doth he gallop withal?

ROSALIND   With a thief to the gallows, for though he go   321 as softly as foot can fall, he thinks himself too soon   322 there.

ORLANDO   Who stays it still withal?

ROSALIND   With lawyers in the vacation; for they sleep between term and term, and then they perceive not   326 how Time moves.

ORLANDO   Where dwell you, pretty youth?

ROSALIND   With this shepherdess, my sister, here in the skirts of the forest, like fringe upon a petticoat.

ORLANDO   Are you native of this place?

ROSALIND   As the coney that you see dwell where she is   332 kindled.   333

ORLANDO   Your accent is something finer than you   334 could purchase in so removed a dwelling.   335

ROSALIND   I have been told so of many. But indeed an old religious uncle of mine taught me to speak, who   337 was in his youth an inland man, one that knew   338 courtship too well, for there he fell in love. I have   339 heard him read many lectures against it, and I thank God I am not a woman, to be touched with so many   341 giddy offences as he hath generally taxed their whole sex withal.

ORLANDO   Can you remember any of the principal evils that he laid to the charge of women?

ROSALIND   There were none principal; they were all like one another as halfpence are, every one fault seeming monstrous till his fellow fault came to match it.   348

ORLANDO   I prithee, recount some of them.

ROSALIND   No, I will not cast away my physic but on   350 those that are sick. There is a man haunts the forest that abuses our young plants with carving ''Rosalind'' on their barks, hangs odes upon hawthorns and elegies on brambles, all, forsooth, deifying the name of Rosalind. If I could meet that fancy-monger, I would   355 give him some good counsel, for he seems to have the quotidian of love upon him.   357

ORLANDO   I am he that is so love-shaked. I pray you, tell me your remedy.

ROSALIND   There is none of my uncle's marks upon you. He taught me how to know a man in love, in which cage of rushes I am sure you are not prisoner.   362

ORLANDO   What were his marks?

ROSALIND   A lean cheek, which you have not; a blue eye   364 and sunken, which you have not; an unquestionable   365 spirit, which you have not; a beard neglected, which you have not—but I pardon you for that, for simply   367 your having in beard is a younger brother's revenue.   368 Then your hose should be ungartered, your bonnet un-   369 banded, your sleeve unbuttoned, your shoe untied,   370 and everything about you demonstrating a careless desolation. But you are no such man. You are rather point-device in your accoutrements, as loving your-   373 self, than seeming the lover of any other.

ORLANDO   Fair youth, I would I could make thee believe I love.

ROSALIND   Me believe it? You may as soon make her that you love believe it, which I warrant she is apter to do than to confess she does. That is one of the points in the which women still give the lie to their con-   380 sciences. But in good sooth, are you he that hangs the   381 verses on the trees, wherein Rosalind is so admired?

ORLANDO   I swear to thee, youth, by the white hand of Rosalind, I am that he, that unfortunate he.

ROSALIND   But are you so much in love as your rhymes speak?

ORLANDO   Neither rhyme nor reason can express how much.

ROSALIND   Love is merely a madness and, I tell you,   390 deserves as well a dark house and a whip as madmen   391 do; and the reason why they are not so punished and cured is that the lunacy is so ordinary that the whippers are in love too. Yet I profess curing it by counsel.

ORLANDO   Did you ever cure any so?

ROSALIND   Yes, one, and in this manner. He was to imagine me his love, his mistress; and I set him every day to woo me. At which time would I, being but a

300 detect reveal   **305 withal** with   **308 hard** at an uncomfortable pace   **310 se'nnight** week   **317 lean** unremunerative.   **wasteful** making one waste away   **321–322 go as softly** walk as slowly   **326 term** court session   **332 coney** rabbit   **333 kindled** littered, born   **334 something** somewhat   **335 purchase** acquire.   **removed** remote   **337 religious** i.e., belonging to a religious order   **338 inland** from a center of civilization   **339 courtship** (1) wooing (2) knowledge of courtly manners   **341 touched** tainted   **348 his** its

350 physic medicine   **355 fancy-monger** dealer in love   **357 quotid-ian** fever recurring daily. (See *love-shaked*, line 358).   **362 cage of rushes** i.e., flimsy prison   **364 blue eye** i.e., having dark circles   **365 unquestionable** unwilling to be conversed with   **367–368 sim-ply . . . revenue** what beard you have is like a younger brother's in-heritance (i.e., small)   **369–370 bonnet unbanded** hat lacking a band around the crown   **373 point-device** faultless   **380 still** contin-ually   **381 good sooth** honest truth   **390 merely** utterly   **391 dark . . . whip** (The common treatment of lunatics.)

moonish youth, grieve, be effeminate, changeable, 399
longing and liking, proud, fantastical, apish, shallow,
inconstant, full of tears, full of smiles; for every passion
something and for no passion truly anything, as boys
and women are for the most part cattle of this color;
would now like him, now loathe him; then entertain 404
him, then forswear him; now weep for him, then spit
at him; that I drave my suitor from his mad humor of 406
love to a living humor of madness, which was to for- 407
swear the full stream of the world and to live in a nook
merely monastic. And thus I cured him; and this way 409
will I take upon me to wash your liver as clean as a 410
sound sheep's heart, that there shall not be one spot of
love in 't.

ORLANDO   I would not be cured, youth.

ROSALIND   I would cure you, if you would but call me
Rosalind and come every day to my cote and woo me. 415

ORLANDO   Now by the faith of my love, I will. Tell me
where it is.

ROSALIND   Go with me to it, and I'll show it you; and
by the way you shall tell me where in the forest you 419
live. Will you go?

ORLANDO   With all my heart, good youth.

ROSALIND   Nay, you must call me Rosalind.—Come,
sister, will you go?   *Exeunt.*

❖

3.3   Enter *[Touchstone the] Clown, Audrey; and Jaques
[apart].*

TOUCHSTONE   Come apace, good Audrey. I will fetch up 1
your goats, Audrey. And how, Audrey, am I the man 2
yet? Doth my simple feature content you?   3

AUDREY   Your features, Lord warrant us! What features? 4

TOUCHSTONE   I am here with thee and thy goats, as the
most capricious poet, honest Ovid, was among the 6
Goths.   7

JAQUES [*aside*]   O knowledge ill-inhabited, worse than 8
Jove in a thatched house!   9

TOUCHSTONE   When a man's verses cannot be under- 10
stood, nor a man's good wit seconded with the 11
forward child, understanding, it strikes a man more 12

dead than a great reckoning in a little room. Truly, I 13
would the gods had made thee poetical.

AUDREY   I do not know what "poetical" is. Is it honest
in deed and word? Is it a true thing?

TOUCHSTONE   No, truly; for the truest poetry is the most
feigning, and lovers are given to poetry, and what 18
they swear in poetry may be said as lovers they do 19
feign.   20

AUDREY   Do you wish then that the gods had made me
poetical?

TOUCHSTONE   I do, truly; for thou swear'st to me thou
art honest. Now, if thou wert a poet, I might have 24
some hope thou didst feign.   25

AUDREY   Would you not have me honest?

TOUCHSTONE   No, truly, unless thou wert hard- 27
favored; for honesty coupled to beauty is to have 28
honey a sauce to sugar.

JAQUES [*aside*]   A material fool!   30

AUDREY   Well, I am not fair, and therefore I pray the
gods make me honest.

TOUCHSTONE   Truly, and to cast away honesty upon a
foul slut were to put good meat into an unclean dish. 34

AUDREY   I am not a slut, though I thank the gods I am 35
foul.   36

TOUCHSTONE   Well, praised be the gods for thy foulness! Sluttishness may come hereafter. But be it as it
may be, I will marry thee, and to that end I have been
with Sir Oliver Mar-text, the vicar of the next village, 40
who hath promised to meet me in this place of the
forest and to couple us.

JAQUES [*aside*]   I would fain see this meeting.   43

AUDREY   Well, the gods give us joy!

TOUCHSTONE   Amen. A man may, if he were of a
fearful heart, stagger in this attempt; for here we have 46
no temple but the wood, no assembly but horn-beasts. 47
But what though? Courage! As horns are odious, they 48
are necessary. It is said, "Many a man knows no end 49
of his goods." Right! Many a man has good horns and 50
knows no end of them. Well, that is the dowry of his 51
wife; 'tis none of his own getting. Horns? Even so. 52
Poor men alone? No, no, the noblest deer hath them 53
as huge as the rascal. Is the single man therefore 54

---

399 **moonish** changeable   404 **entertain** receive cordially   **406 that**
with the result that.   **drave** drove   **406–407 mad . . . madness** mad
fancy of love to a real madness   **409 merely** utterly   **410 liver** (Supposed seat of the emotions, especially love.)   **415 cote** cottage
419 by on
3.3. Location: The forest.
1 apace quickly   **2 And how** i.e., what do you say   **3 simple feature**
plain appearance. (But Audrey, in her answer, may have her mind on
features as "parts of the body.")   **4 warrant** protect   **6 capricious**
witty, fanciful. (Derived from the Latin *caper*, "male goat"; hence,
"goatish, lascivious.")   **7 Goths** (with pun on "goats"; the two words
were pronounced alike)   **8 ill-inhabited** ill-lodged   **9 Jove . . . house**
(An allusion to Ovid's *Metamorphoses* 8, containing the story of Jupiter and Mercury lodging disguised in the humble cottage of Baucis
and Philemon.)   **10–11 verses . . . understood** (Ovid's verses were
misunderstood by the barbaric Goths, among whom he lived in exile,
just as Touchstone's wit is misunderstood by Audrey.)   **11 seconded
with** supported by   **12 forward** precocious

13 great . . . room exorbitant charge for refreshment or lodging in a
cramped tavern room. (Some scholars see in this passage an allusion
to the death of Christopher Marlowe, who was stabbed by Ingram
Frysar at an inn in Deptford in a quarrel over a tavern reckoning, May
30, 1593.)   **18 feigning** inventive, imaginative. (But Touchstone plays
on the sense of "false, lying.")   **19 may be said** i.e., it may be said
20 feign (with a further play on "desire")   **24 honest** chaste   **25 feign**
(1) pretend (2) desire   **27–28 hard-favored** ugly   **28 honesty** chastity
30 material full of sense   **34 foul** ugly   **35–36 I thank . . . foul** i.e.,
my looks are what God has given me   **40 Sir** (Courtesy title for a
clergyman.)   **43 fain** gladly   **46 stagger** hesitate   **47 horn-beasts** (Alludes to the joke about cuckolds having horns.)   **48 what though**
what though it be so.   **As though**   **49 necessary** unavoidable   **49–
50 knows . . . goods** i.e., is well off   **51 knows . . . them** i.e., is
endlessly supplied with cuckold's horns. (A sardonic interpretation of
the proverb in lines 49–50.)   **dowry** marriage gift   **52 getting** (1)
obtaining (2) begetting (since his wife's children will not be his).
Even so that's just how it is   **53 deer** (1) horned animal (2) dear husband   **54 rascal** (1) young deer that are lean and out of season (2)
poor ordinary husband

blessed? No. As a walled town is more worthier than
a village, so is the forehead of a married man more
honorable than the bare brow of a bachelor; and by
how much defense is better than no skill, by so much 58
is a horn more precious than to want.   59

Enter Sir Oliver Mar-text.

Here comes Sir Oliver. Sir Oliver Mar-text, you are
well met. Will you dispatch us here under this tree, or 61
shall we go with you to your chapel?

SIR OLIVER   Is there none here to give the woman?

TOUCHSTONE   I will not take her on gift of any man.

SIR OLIVER   Truly, she must be given, or the marriage is
not lawful.

JAQUES *[advancing]*   Proceed, proceed. I'll give her.

TOUCHSTONE   Good even, good Master What-ye-call-'t. 68
How do you, sir? You are very well met. God 'ild you 69
for your last company. I am very glad to see you. Even 70
a toy in hand here, sir.—Nay, pray be covered.   71

JAQUES   Will you be married, motley?

TOUCHSTONE   As the ox hath his bow, sir, the horse his 73
curb, and the falcon her bells, so man hath his desires; 74
and as pigeons bill, so wedlock would be nibbling.   75

JAQUES   And will you, being a man of your breeding,
be married under a bush like a beggar? Get you to 77
church, and have a good priest that can tell you what 78
marriage is. This fellow will but join you together as 79
they join wainscot; then one of you will prove a
shrunk panel and, like green timber, warp, warp.   81

TOUCHSTONE   I am not in the mind but I were better 82
to be married of him than of another, for he is not 83
like to marry me well; and not being well married, 84
it will be a good excuse for me hereafter to leave my
wife.

JAQUES   Go thou with me, and let me counsel thee.

TOUCHSTONE   Come, sweet Audrey. We must be mar- 88
ried, or we must live in bawdry. Farewell, good 89
Master Oliver; not

"O sweet Oliver,   91
O brave Oliver,   92
Leave me not behind thee";

but

"Wind away,   95
Begone, I say,
I will not to wedding with thee."   97
[Exeunt Jaques, Touchstone, and Audrey.]

SIR OLIVER   'Tis no matter. Ne'er a fantastical knave of 98
them all shall flout me out of my calling.   *Exit.*

3.4   *Enter Rosalind and Celia.*

ROSALIND   Never talk to me. I will weep.

CELIA   Do, I prithee, but yet have the grace to consider
that tears do not become a man.

ROSALIND   But have I not cause to weep?

CELIA   As good cause as one would desire; therefore
weep.

ROSALIND   His very hair is of the dissembling color.   7

CELIA   Something browner than Judas's. Marry, his 8
kisses are Judas's own children.   9

ROSALIND   I' faith, his hair is of a good color.

CELIA   An excellent color. Your chestnut was ever the 11
only color.   12

ROSALIND   And his kissing is as full of sanctity as the
touch of holy bread.   14

CELIA   He hath bought a pair of cast lips of Diana. A 15
nun of winter's sisterhood kisses not more religiously; 16
the very ice of chastity is in them.

ROSALIND   But why did he swear he would come this
morning, and comes not?

CELIA   Nay, certainly, there is no truth in him.

ROSALIND   Do you think so?

CELIA   Yes. I think he is not a pickpurse nor a horse-
stealer, but for his verity in love, I do think him as
concave as a covered goblet or a worm-eaten nut.   24

ROSALIND   Not true in love?

CELIA   Yes, when he is in, but I think he is not in.

ROSALIND   You have heard him swear downright he
was.

CELIA   "Was" is not "is." Besides, the oath of a lover is
no stronger than the word of a tapster; they are both
the confirmer of false reckonings. He attends here in 31
the forest on the Duke your father.

ROSALIND   I met the Duke yesterday and had much
question with him. He asked me of what parentage I 34

---

58 defense (1) fortifications (including a type known as "hornwork")
(2) the art of self-defense   **59 than to want** i.e., than to be without a
horn (recalling the "horn of plenty")   **61 dispatch us** finish off our
business   **68 What-ye-call-'t** (Probably joking on *Jakes* as "out-
house.")   **69 'ild you** yield you, reward you   **70 last** most recent—
i.e., present   **71 a toy in hand** a trifle to be attended to, or literally
by the hand.   **be covered** put on your hat, i.e., no need to show respect; or, cover up your bosom. (Said to Audrey, or perhaps to
Jaques, who may have removed his hat in sardonic deference to the
ceremony.)   **73 bow** yoke   **74 curb** chain or strap attached to the
horse's bit and used to control it.   **bells** (attached to a falcon's leg
during training)   **75 bill** stroke bill with bill   **77 under a bush** i.e., by
a "hedge-priest," an uneducated clergyman   **78–79 tell . . . is** expound the obligations of marriage   **81 warp** (1) shrivel and fit badly
together (2) stray from the true path   **82 I am . . . better** I do not
know but that it would be better for me. (Touchstone may be speak-
ing aside here.)   **83 of** by   **84 like** likely.   **well** (1) suitably (2) legally   **88–89 married** i.e., properly married, as Jaques suggests, not
by a hedge-priest. (Having been found out, Touchstone wryly defers
matters for the present.)   **91–97 O . . . thee** (Phrases from a current
ballad.)   **92 brave** worthy

95 Wind wend, go   **98 fantastical** affected
3.4. Location: The forest.
7 the dissembling color i.e., reddish, traditionally the color of Judas'
hair   **8 Something** somewhat   **9 Judas's own children** i.e., as false
and betraying as Judas' kiss   **11 Your chestnut** i.e., this chestnut
color that people talk about   **12 only** only fashionable   **14 holy
bread** ordinary leavened bread that was blessed after the Eucharist
and distributed to those who had not received communion   **15 cast**
(1) chaste, cold (2) molded, or (3) cast off.   **Diana** goddess of chastity
16 of winter's sisterhood i.e., devoted to barrenness and cold
24 concave hollow.   **a covered goblet** i.e., an empty goblet. (The
cover forms the top of the hollow sphere and is normally on only
when the goblet is empty.)   **31 false reckonings** (Tapsters, or barkeeps, were notorious for inflating bills.)   **34 question** conversation

was. I told him, of as good as he; so he laughed and let
me go. But what talk we of fathers, when there is such 36
a man as Orlando?

CELIA   O, that's a brave man! He writes brave verses, 38
speaks brave words, swears brave oaths, and breaks
them bravely, quite traverse, athwart the heart of his 40
lover, as a puny tilter, that spurs his horse but on 41
one side, breaks his staff like a noble goose. But all's 42
brave that youth mounts and folly guides. Who comes 43
here?

Enter Corin.

CORIN
Mistress and master, you have oft inquired
After the shepherd that complained of love,   46
Who you saw sitting by me on the turf,
Praising the proud disdainful shepherdess
That was his mistress.

CELIA   Well, and what of him?

CORIN
If you will see a pageant truly played
Between the pale complexion of true love   51
And the red glow of scorn and proud disdain,
Go hence a little, and I shall conduct you,
If you will mark it.

ROSALIND   O, come, let us remove!   54
The sight of lovers feedeth those in love.
Bring us to this sight, and you shall say
I'll prove a busy actor in their play.   *Exeunt.*

3.5   *Enter Silvius and Phoebe.*

SILVIUS
Sweet Phoebe, do not scorn me, do not, Phoebe!
Say that you love me not, but say not so
In bitterness. The common executioner,
Whose heart th' accustomed sight of death makes
    hard,
Falls not the ax upon the humbled neck   5
But first begs pardon. Will you sterner be   6
Than he that dies and lives by bloody drops?   7

Enter Rosalind, Celia, and Corin [behind].

PHOEBE
I would not be thy executioner;

I fly thee, for I would not injure thee.
Thou tell'st me there is murder in mine eye.
'Tis pretty, sure, and very probable,   11
That eyes, that are the frail'st and softest things,
Who shut their coward gates on atomies,   13
Should be called tyrants, butchers, murderers!
Now I do frown on thee with all my heart,
And if mine eyes can wound, now let them kill
    thee.
Now counterfeit to swoon; why, now fall down,
Or if thou canst not, O, for shame, for shame,
Lie not, to say mine eyes are murderers!   19
Now show the wound mine eye hath made in thee.
Scratch thee but with a pin, and there remains
Some scar of it; lean upon a rush,   22
The cicatrice and capable impressure   23
Thy palm some moment keeps; but now mine eyes,
Which I have darted at thee, hurt thee not,
Nor, I am sure, there is no force in eyes
That can do hurt.

SILVIUS   O dear Phoebe,
If ever—as that ever may be near—
You meet in some fresh cheek the power of fancy,   29
Then shall you know the wounds invisible
That love's keen arrows make.

PHOEBE   But till that time
Come not thou near me; and when that time comes,
Afflict me with thy mocks, pity me not,
As till that time I shall not pity thee.

ROSALIND [*advancing*]
And why, I pray you? Who might be your mother,   35
That you insult, exult, and all at once,   36
Over the wretched? What though you have no
    beauty—   37
As, by my faith, I see no more in you   38
Than without candle may go dark to bed—   39
Must you be therefore proud and pitiless?
Why, what means this? Why do you look on me?
I see no more in you than in the ordinary   42
Of nature's sale-work. 'Od's my little life,   43
I think she means to tangle my eyes too!   44
No, faith, proud mistress, hope not after it.
'Tis not your inky brows, your black silk hair,
Your bugle eyeballs, nor your cheek of cream   47
That can entame my spirits to your worship.   48
[*To Silvius.*]   You foolish shepherd, wherefore do
    you follow her,

---

36 **what** why   38 **brave** fine, excellent   40 **traverse** across, awry. (A
term from the medieval tournament, indicating a poorly aimed thrust.)
41 **puny** inexperienced. (Literally, junior.)   **but** only   42 **a noble
goose** i.e., a goose-headed young blade   42–43 **But . . . guides** but
everything is admirable that youth undertakes under the influence of
folly. (Said sardonically.)   46 **complained of** uttered a lament against
51 **pale complexion** (Sighing was believed to draw the blood from the
heart.)   54 **will mark** wish to see.   **remove** leave here and go
3.5. Location: The forest.
5 **Falls** lets fall   6 **But first begs pardon** without first begging pardon
(as executioners did in Elizabethan times)   7 **dies and lives** i.e.,
makes his living his life long

11 **sure** surely   13 **coward gates on atomies** i.e., sensitive eyelids to
protect against specks of dirt   19 **to say** by saying   22 **rush** a marsh
plant   23 **cicatrice** scarlike impression.   **capable impressure** perceptible impression   29 **fancy** love   35 **Who . . . mother** (1) what human mother could have produced so inhuman a daughter? (2) from
what sort of a mother did you learn such scorn?   36 **insult** exult
scornfully.   **all at once** i.e., all in a breath   37 **have no beauty** are
not particularly beautiful   38–39 **I see . . . bed** your looks are not
such as deserve to be seen in the candlelight at bedtime; they deserve
only to go to bed in the dark   42 **ordinary** common run   43 **sale-
work** ready-made products, i.e., not of the best quality, not distinctive.   **'Od's** may God save   44 **tangle** ensnare   47 **bugle** beadlike,
black and glassy   48 **to your worship** to the worship of you

Like foggy south, puffing with wind and rain?   50
You are a thousand times a properer man   51
Than she a woman. 'Tis such fools as you
That makes the world full of ill-favored children.   53
'Tis not her glass, but you, that flatters her,   54
And out of you she sees herself more proper   55
Than any of her lineaments can show her.—   56
But, mistress, know yourself. Down on your knees,
And thank heaven, fasting, for a good man's love!
For I must tell you friendly in your ear,
Sell when you can. You are not for all markets.
Cry the man mercy, love him, take his offer;   61
Foul is most foul, being foul to be a scoffer.—   62
So take her to thee, shepherd. Fare you well.

PHOEBE
Sweet youth, I pray you, chide a year together.   64
I had rather hear you chide than this man woo.

ROSALIND [to Phoebe]   He's fallen in love with your foulness, [to Silvius] and she'll fall in love with my
anger. If it be so, as fast as she answers thee with
frowning looks, I'll sauce her with bitter words. [To   69
Phoebe.] Why look you so upon me?

PHOEBE   For no ill will I bear you.

ROSALIND
I pray you, do not fall in love with me,
For I am falser than vows made in wine.   73
Besides, I like you not. [To Silvius.] If you will know
  my house,
'Tis at the tuft of olives here hard by.—
Will you go, sister?—Shepherd, ply her hard.—   76
Come, sister.—Shepherdess, look on him better,
And be not proud. Though all the world could see,   78
None could be so abused in sight as he.—   79
Come, to our flock.   Exit [with Celia and Corin].

PHOEBE
Dead shepherd, now I find thy saw of might,   81
"Who ever loved that loved not at first sight?"   82

SILVIUS
Sweet Phoebe—

PHOEBE   Ha, what sayst thou, Silvius?

SILVIUS   Sweet Phoebe, pity me.

PHOEBE
Why, I am sorry for thee, gentle Silvius.

SILVIUS
Wherever sorrow is, relief would be.   86
If you do sorrow at my grief in love,
By giving love, your sorrow and my grief
Were both extermined.   89

PHOEBE
Thou hast my love. Is not that neighborly?   90

SILVIUS
I would have you.

PHOEBE   Why, that were covetousness.   91
Silvius, the time was that I hated thee,
And yet it is not that I bear thee love;   93
But since that thou canst talk of love so well,   94
Thy company, which erst was irksome to me,   95
I will endure, and I'll employ thee too.
But do not look for further recompense
Than thine own gladness that thou art employed.

SILVIUS
So holy and so perfect is my love,
And I in such a poverty of grace,   100
That I shall think it a most plenteous crop
To glean the broken ears after the man
That the main harvest reaps. Loose now and then
A scattered smile, and that I'll live upon.   104

PHOEBE
Know'st thou the youth that spoke to me erewhile?   105

SILVIUS
Not very well, but I have met him oft,
And he hath bought the cottage and the bounds   107
That the old carlot once was master of.   108

PHOEBE
Think not I love him, though I ask for him.
'Tis but a peevish boy—yet he talks well—
But what care I for words? Yet words do well
When he that speaks them pleases those that hear.
It is a pretty youth—not very pretty—
But sure he's proud—and yet his pride becomes him.
He'll make a proper man. The best thing in him
Is his complexion; and faster than his tongue
Did make offense, his eye did heal it up.
He is not very tall—yet for his years he's tall.
His leg is but so-so—and yet 'tis well.
There was a pretty redness in his lip,
A little riper and more lusty red
Than that mixed in his cheek; 'twas just the
  difference
Betwixt the constant red and mingled damask.   123
There be some women, Silvius, had they marked
  him
In parcels as I did, would have gone near   125
To fall in love with him; but for my part,   126
I love him not nor hate him not; and yet
I have more cause to hate him than to love him.
For what had he to do to chide at me?   129
He said mine eyes were black and my hair black

50 **south** south wind (from which came fog and rain; i.e., Silvius'
sighs and tears)   51 **properer** better-looking (since handsome is as
handsome does)   53 **ill-favored** ugly   54 **glass** mirror   55 **out of you**
i.e., with you as her mirror   56 **lineaments** features   61 **Cry . . .**
mercy beg the man's pardon   62 **Foul . . . scoffer** i.e., ugliness is
most ugly when it is rough and abusive. (Plays on two meanings of
foul.)   64 **together** continuously   69 **sauce** rebuke   73 **in wine** while
drunk   76 **ply her hard** woo her energetically   78 **could see** could
look at you   79 **abused in sight** deceived through the eyes   81 **Dead**
shepherd i.e., Christopher Marlowe, who died in 1593.   **saw** saying.
of might forceful, convincing   82 **Who . . . sight** (From Marlowe's
Hero and Leander, Sestiad 1, 176, first published in 1598.)
86 **Wherever . . . be** sorrow cries out for relief   89 **Were both exter-**
mined would both be exterminated, ended

90 **Is . . . neighborly** i.e., I love you in the sense of loving one's
neighbor as oneself   91 **covetousness** (The tenth commandment forbids coveting anything that is one's neighbor's.)   93 **yet it is not** it
(the time) is not yet come   94 **since that** since   95 **erst** formerly
100 **poverty of grace** (i.e., love, my divinity, has been ungracious to
me)   104 **scattered** thrown negligently, as in the gleanings of the harvest   105 **erewhile** just now   107 **bounds** pastures   108 **carlot**
churl, countryman. (Perhaps a proper name.)   123 **mingled damask**
mingled red and white, i.e., the color of the damask rose   125 **In**
parcels piece by piece, in detail.   **gone near** come close   126 **fall**
falling   129 **what . . . do** what business had he

And, now I am remembered, scorned at me.   131
I marvel why I answered not again.   132
But that's all one; omittance is no quittance.   133
I'll write to him a very taunting letter,
And thou shalt bear it. Wilt thou, Silvius?

SILVIUS
Phoebe, with all my heart.

PHOEBE   I'll write it straight;   136
The matter 's in my head and in my heart.
I will be bitter with him and passing short.   138
Go with me, Silvius.   *Exeunt.*

❖

4.1   *Enter Rosalind and Celia, and Jaques.*

JAQUES   I prithee, pretty youth, let me be better acquainted with thee.

ROSALIND   They say you are a melancholy fellow.

JAQUES   I am so. I do love it better than laughing.

ROSALIND   Those that are in extremity of either are   5
abominable fellows and betray themselves to every
modern censure worse than drunkards.   7

JAQUES   Why, 'tis good to be sad and say nothing.

ROSALIND   Why then, 'tis good to be a post.

JAQUES   I have neither the scholar's melancholy, which
is emulation, nor the musician's, which is fantastical,   11
nor the courtier's, which is proud, nor the soldier's,
which is ambitious, nor the lawyer's, which is politic,   13
nor the lady's, which is nice, nor the lover's, which is 14
all these; but it is a melancholy of mine own, com-   15
pounded of many simples, extracted from many   16
objects, and indeed the sundry contemplation of my   17
travels, in which my often rumination wraps me in a   18
most humorous sadness.   19

ROSALIND   A traveler! By my faith, you have great
reason to be sad. I fear you have sold your own lands
to see other men's. Then to have seen much and to
have nothing is to have rich eyes and poor hands.

JAQUES   Yes, I have gained my experience.

Enter Orlando.

ROSALIND   And your experience makes you sad. I had
rather have a fool to make me merry than experience
to make me sad—and to travel for it too!   27

ORLANDO   Good day and happiness, dear Rosalind!

JAQUES   Nay, then, God b' wi' you, an you talk in blank   29
verse.

ROSALIND   Farewell, Monsieur Traveler. Look you lisp   31
and wear strange suits, disable all the benefits of your 32
own country, be out of love with your nativity, and   33
almost chide God for making you that countenance
you are, or I will scarce think you have swam in a   35
gondola. [*Exit Jaques.*] Why, how now, Orlando,   36
where have you been all this while? You a lover? An
you serve me such another trick, never come in my
sight more.

ORLANDO   My fair Rosalind, I come within an hour of
my promise.

ROSALIND   Break an hour's promise in love? He that will
divide a minute into a thousand parts and break but
a part of the thousandth part of a minute in the affairs
of love, it may be said of him that Cupid hath clapped   45
him o' the shoulder, but I'll warrant him heart-whole.   46

ORLANDO   Pardon me, dear Rosalind.

ROSALIND   Nay, an you be so tardy, come no more in
my sight. I had as lief be wooed of a snail.   49

ORLANDO   Of a snail?

ROSALIND   Ay, of a snail; for though he comes slowly,
he carries his house on his head—a better jointure, I   52
think, than you make a woman. Besides, he brings his   53
destiny with him.

ORLANDO   What's that?

ROSALIND   Why, horns, which such as you are fain to   56
be beholding to your wives for. But he comes armed in   57
his fortune and prevents the slander of his wife.   58

ORLANDO   Virtue is no horn-maker, and my Rosalind is
virtuous.

ROSALIND   And I am your Rosalind.

CELIA   It pleases him to call you so; but he hath a
Rosalind of a better leer than you.   63

ROSALIND   Come, woo me, woo me, for now I am in a
holiday humor and like enough to consent. What
would you say to me now, an I were your very, very
Rosalind?

ORLANDO   I would kiss before I spoke.

ROSALIND   Nay, you were better speak first, and when
you were graveled for lack of matter, you might take   70
occasion to kiss. Very good orators, when they are out, 71
they will spit; and for lovers lacking—God warrant   72
us!—matter, the cleanliest shift is to kiss.   73

ORLANDO   How if the kiss be denied?

---

131 am remembered remember   **132 again** back   **133 But . . . quittance** i.e., but just the same, my failure to answer him doesn't mean I won't do so later   **136 straight** immediately   **138 passing short** exceedingly curt
4.1. Location: The forest.
5 are . . . of go to extremes in   **7 modern censure** common judgment   **11 emulation** envy (of the fellow scholar).   **fantastical** extravagantly fanciful   **13 politic** grave and diplomatic, calculated   **14 nice** fastidious   **15–19 compounded . . . sadness** made up of many ingredients, extracted from the many objects of my observation and, indeed, from the diversified considerations of my travels, my frequent rumination upon which wraps me in a most whimsical and moody sadness   **27 travel** (meaning also "travail," labor)   **29 an** if

31 Look be sure. (Said ironically.)   **lisp** i.e., affect a foreign accent   **32 disable** disparage   **33 nativity** i.e., place of birth that determines nationality   **35 are** i.e., have   **35–36 swam . . . gondola** floated in a gondola, i.e., been in Venice, where almost all travelers go   **45–46 clapped . . . shoulder** i.e., accosted or arrested him. (Such a lover, Rosalind says, may be claimed by Cupid as a follower, but only superficially; his heart is still unbroken.)   **49 lief** willingly.   **of by**   **52 jointure** marriage settlement   **53 than . . . woman** than you, Orlando, are able to settle on your prospective wife   **56 horns** (1) snails' horns (2) cuckold's horns, signs of an unfaithful wife.   **fain** obliged   **57 beholding** beholden, indebted   **57–58 armed . . . fortune** i.e., with horns, which it was his fate to bear   **58 prevents** forestalls.   **slander** infamy. (The snail's horns, with which he is born, cannot betray his wife's infidelity, however certain it may be.)   **63 of . . . leer** better looking   **70 graveled** stuck. (Literally, run aground on a shoal.)   **71 out** at a loss through forgetfulness or confusion   **72 warrant** defend   **73 cleanliest shift** cleverest device

ROSALIND   Then she puts you to entreaty, and there begins new matter.

ORLANDO   Who could be out, being before his beloved mistress?

ROSALIND   Marry, that should you, if I were your mistress, or I should think my honesty ranker than 80 my wit.

ORLANDO   What, of my suit?   82

ROSALIND   Not out of your apparel, and yet out of your suit. Am not I your Rosalind?

ORLANDO   I take some joy to say you are, because I would be talking of her.

ORLANDO   Well, in her person I say I will not have you.

ORLANDO   Then in mine own person, I die.

ROSALIND   No, faith, die by attorney. The poor world is 89 almost six thousand years old, and in all this time 90 there was not any man died in his own person, 91 videlicet, in a love cause. Troilus had his brains 92 dashed out with a Grecian club, yet he did what he 93 could to die before, and he is one of the patterns of love. Leander, he would have lived many a fair year 95 though Hero had turned nun, if it had not been for a hot midsummer night; for, good youth, he went but forth to wash him in the Hellespont and being taken with the cramp was drowned; and the foolish chron- iclers of that age found it was—Hero of Sestos. But 100 these are all lies. Men have died from time to time, and worms have eaten them, but not for love.

ORLANDO   I would not have my right Rosalind of this 103 mind, for I protest her frown might kill me.

ROSALIND   By this hand, it will not kill a fly. But come, now I will be your Rosalind in a more coming-on 106 disposition; and ask me what you will, I will grant it.

ORLANDO   Then love me, Rosalind.

ROSALIND   Yes, faith, will I, Fridays and Saturdays and all.

ORLANDO   And wilt thou have me?

ROSALIND   Ay, and twenty such.

ORLANDO   What sayest thou?

ROSALIND   Are you not good?

ORLANDO   I hope so.

ROSALIND   Why then, can one desire too much of a good thing?—Come, sister, you shall be the priest and marry us.—Give me your hand, Orlando.— What do you say, sister?

ORLANDO   Pray thee, marry us.

CELIA   I cannot say the words.

ROSALIND   You must begin, "Will you, Orlando—"

CELIA   Go to. Will you, Orlando, have to wife this 123 Rosalind?

ORLANDO   I will.

ROSALIND   Ay, but when?

ORLANDO   Why now, as fast as she can marry us.

ROSALIND   Then you must say, "I take thee, Rosalind, for wife."

ORLANDO   I take thee, Rosalind, for wife.

ROSALIND   I might ask you for your commission; but I 131 do take thee, Orlando, for my husband. There's a girl goes before the priest, and certainly a woman's 133 thought runs before her actions.   134

ORLANDO   So do all thoughts; they are winged.

ROSALIND   Now tell me how long you would have her after you have possessed her.

ORLANDO   For ever and a day.

ROSALIND   Say "a day," without the "ever." No, no, Or- lando, men are April when they woo, December when they wed. Maids are May when they are maids, but the sky changes when they are wives. I will be more jealous of thee than a Barbary cock-pigeon over his 143 hen, more clamorous than a parrot against rain, more 144 newfangled than an ape, more giddy in my desires 145 than a monkey. I will weep for nothing, like Diana in 146 the fountain, and I will do that when you are disposed 147 to be merry; I will laugh like a hyena, and that when thou art inclined to sleep.

ORLANDO   But will my Rosalind do so?

ROSALIND   By my life, she will do as I do.

ORLANDO   O, but she is wise.

ROSALIND   Or else she could not have the wit to do this. The wiser, the waywarder. Make the doors upon a 154 woman's wit, and it will out at the casement; shut that, and 'twill out at the keyhole; stop that, 'twill fly with the smoke out at the chimney.

ORLANDO   A man that had a wife with such a wit, he might say, "Wit, whither wilt?"   159

ROSALIND   Nay, you might keep that check for it till 160 you met your wife's wit going to your neighbor's bed.

ORLANDO   And what wit could wit have to excuse that?

ROSALIND   Marry, to say she came to seek you there. You shall never take her without her answer unless you take her without her tongue. O, that woman that

80 honesty chastity.   **ranker** more corrupt. (Rosalind would rely on her wit to keep her lover off balance and since she herself has not yet con- sented) **133 goes . . . priest** who anticipates before the "priest" has even asked the question **134 runs . . . actions** i.e., goes flightily on, outstripping sane conduct **143 Barbary cock-pigeon** an ornamental pigeon actually from the orient, not the Barbary (north) coast of Af- rica. (Following Pliny, the cock-pigeon's jealousy was often contrasted with the mildness of the hen.) **144 against** in expectation of **145 newfangled** infatuated with novelty **146 for nothing** for no ap- parent reason **146–147 Diana in the fountain** (Diana frequently ap- peared as the centerpiece of fountains. Stow's *Survey of London* de- scribes the setting up of a fountain with a Diana in green marble in the year 1596.) **154 Make** make fast, shut **159 Wit, whither wilt** wit, where are you going? (A common Elizabethan expression imply- ing that one is talking fantastically, with a wildly wandering wit.) **160 check** retort

80 honesty chastity.   **ranker** more corrupt. (Rosalind would rely on her wit to keep her lover off balance and since they defend her chastity. She may use Orlando's *out*, line 77, in a sexual sense of not being admitted.) **82 of my suit** (Orlando means "out of my suit," at a loss for words in his wooing; but Rosalind puns on the meaning "suit of clothes"; to be out of apparel would be to be undressed.) **89 attor- ney** proxy **90 six . . . old** (A common figure in biblical calculation.) **91 died** who died **92 videlicet** namely.   **Troilus** hero of the story of Troilus and Cressida, in which he remains faithful to her, but she is faithless to him **92–93 had a . . . club** (Troilus was slain by Achilles with sword or spear in more traditional accounts. Rosalind's version is calculatedly unromantic.) **95 Leander** the hero of the story of Hero and Leander, who lost his life swimming the Hellespont to visit his sweetheart. (Rosalind's account of the cramp again undercuts roman- tic idealism.) **100 found it was** arrived at the verdict that the cause (of his death) was **103 right** real **106 coming-on** compliant

123 Go to (An exclamation of mild impatience.) **131 ask . . . com- mission** ask you what authority you have for taking her (since no one is here to give the bride away and since she herself has not yet con- sented)

cannot make her fault her husband's occasion, let her never nurse her child herself, for she will breed it like a fool! 166 167

ORLANDO   For these two hours, Rosalind, I will leave thee.

ROSALIND   Alas, dear love, I cannot lack thee two hours!

ORLANDO   I must attend the Duke at dinner. By two o'clock I will be with thee again.

ROSALIND   Ay, go your ways, go your ways. I knew what you would prove. My friends told me as much, and I thought no less. That flattering tongue of yours won me. 'Tis but one cast away, and so, come, death! Two o'clock is your hour? 177

ORLANDO   Ay, sweet Rosalind.

ROSALIND   By my troth, and in good earnest, and so God mend me, and by all pretty oaths that are not dangerous, if you break one jot of your promise or come one minute behind your hour, I will think you the most pathetical break-promise, and the most hollow lover, and the most unworthy of her you call Rosalind, that may be chosen out of the gross band of the unfaithful. Therefore beware my censure, and keep your promise. 184 186

ORLANDO   With no less religion than if thou wert indeed my Rosalind. So adieu. 189

ROSALIND   Well, Time is the old justice that examines all such offenders, and let Time try. Adieu. 192

Exit [Orlando].

CELIA   You have simply misused our sex in your love prate. We must have your doublet and hose plucked over your head and show the world what the bird hath done to her own nest. 193 194 195 196

ROSALIND   O coz, coz, coz, my pretty little coz, that thou didst know how many fathom deep I am in love! But it cannot be sounded; my affection hath an unknown bottom, like the Bay of Portugal. 199

CELIA   Or rather, bottomless, that as fast as you pour affection in, it runs out. 201

ROSALIND   No, that same wicked bastard of Venus, that was begot of thought, conceived of spleen, and born of madness, that blind rascally boy that abuses every-one's eyes because his own are out, let him be judge how deep I am in love. I'll tell thee, Aliena, I cannot be out of the sight of Orlando. I'll go find a shadow and sigh till he come. 203 204 205 208

CELIA   And I'll sleep.   *Exeunt.*

❖

4.2   *Enter Jaques and Lords [dressed as] foresters.*

JAQUES   Which is he that killed the deer?

FIRST LORD   Sir, it was I.

JAQUES   Let's present him to the Duke, like a Roman conqueror, and it would do well to set the deer's horns upon his head for a branch of victory. Have you no song, Forester, for this purpose? 5

SECOND LORD   Yes, sir.

JAQUES   Sing it. 'Tis no matter how it be in tune, so it make noise enough.   *Music.* 8

Song.

SECOND LORD   [*sings*]
    What shall he have that killed the deer?
    His leather skin and horns to wear.
    Then sing him home; the rest shall bear   12
        This burden.   13
    Take thou no scorn to wear the horn;   14
    It was a crest ere thou wast born.
        Thy father's father wore it,
        And thy father bore it.
    The horn, the horn, the lusty horn
    Is not a thing to laugh to scorn.   *Exeunt.*

❖

4.3   *Enter Rosalind and Celia.*

ROSALIND   How say you now? Is it not past two o'clock? And here much Orlando! 2

CELIA   I warrant you, with pure love and troubled brain he hath ta'en his bow and arrows and is gone forth—to sleep. 3

Enter Silvius [with a letter].

Look who comes here.

SILVIUS   [*to Rosalind*]
    My errand is to you, fair youth.
    My gentle Phoebe bid me give you this.
                               [*He gives the letter.*]
    I know not the contents, but as I guess
    By the stern brow and waspish action
    Which she did use as she was writing of it,
    It bears an angry tenor. Pardon me;
    I am but as a guiltless messenger.

ROSALIND   [*examining the letter*]
    Patience herself would startle at this letter
    And play the swaggerer. Bear this, bear all!   15
    She says I am not fair, that I lack manners;
    She calls me proud, and that she could not love me
    Were man as rare as phoenix. 'Od's my will!   18

---

166 **make . . . occasion** i.e., turn a defense of her own conduct into an accusation against her husband   167 **breed it** bring it up   177 **but one cast away** only one woman jilted   184 **pathetical** awful, miserable   186 **gross band** whole troop   189 **religion** strict fidelity   192 **try** determine, judge   193 **simply misused** absolutely slandered   194–196 **We . . . nest** i.e., we must expose you for what you are, a woman, and show everyone how a woman has defamed her own kind just as a foul bird proverbially fouls its own nest   199 **sounded** measured for depth   201 **that** so that   203 **bastard of Venus** i.e., Cupid, son of Venus and Mercury rather than Vulcan, Venus' husband   204 **thought** fancy.   **spleen** i.e., impulse   205 **abuses** deceives   208 **shadow** shady spot

4.2. Location: The forest.
5 **branch** wreath   8 **so** provided that   12–13 **bear This burden** (1) sing this refrain (2) wear the horns that all cuckolds must wear   14 **Take . . . scorn** be not ashamed. (Alludes to joke about cuckold's horns.)

4.3. Location: The forest.
2 **much** (Said ironically: A fat lot we see of Orlando!)   3 **warrant** assure   15 **play the swaggerer** (Patience herself would bluster and rant at such a letter.)   18 **phoenix** a fabulous bird of Arabia, the only one of its kind, which lived five hundred years, died in flames, and was reborn of its own ashes.   **'Od's my will** God's is my will

Her love is not the hare that I do hunt.
Why writes she so to me? Well, shepherd, well,
This is a letter of your own device.

SILVIUS
No, I protest, I know not the contents.
Phoebe did write it.

ROSALIND   Come, come, you are a fool,
And turned into the extremity of love.   24
I saw her hand; she has a leathern hand,   25
A freestone-colored hand. I verily did think   26
That her old gloves were on, but 'twas her hands;
She has a huswife's hand—but that's no matter.   28
I say she never did invent this letter;
This is a man's invention and his hand.

SILVIUS   Sure it is hers.

ROSALIND
Why, 'tis a boisterous and a cruel style,
A style for challengers. Why, she defies me,
Like Turk to Christian. Women's gentle brain
Could not drop forth such giant-rude invention,
Such Ethiop words, blacker in their effect   36
Than in their countenance. Will you hear the letter?   37

SILVIUS
So please you, for I never heard it yet;
Yet, heard too much of Phoebe's cruelty.

ROSALIND
She Phoebes me. Mark how the tyrant writes.   *Read.* 40
    "Art thou god to shepherd turned,
    That a maiden's heart hath burned?"
Can a woman rail thus?

SILVIUS   Call you this railing?

ROSALIND   *Read.*
    "Why, thy godhead laid apart,   45
    Warr'st thou with a woman's heart?"
Did you ever hear such railing?
    "Whiles the eye of man did woo me,
    That could do no vengeance to me."—   49
Meaning me a beast.   50
    "If the scorn of your bright eyne   51
    Have power to raise such love in mine,
    Alack, in me what strange effect
    Would they work in mild aspect!   54
    Whiles you chid me, I did love;   55
    How then might your prayers move!
    He that brings this love to thee
    Little knows this love in me;
    And by him seal up thy mind,   59
    Whether that thy youth and kind   60
    Will the faithful offer take
    Of me and all that I can make,   62

Or else by him my love deny,
And then I'll study how to die."

SILVIUS   Call you this chiding?

CELIA   Alas, poor shepherd!

ROSALIND   Do you pity him? No, he deserves no pity.—
Wilt thou love such a woman? What, to make thee an
instrument and play false strains upon thee? Not to be   69
endured! Well, go your way to her, for I see love hath
made thee a tame snake, and say this to her: that if she   71
love me, I charge her to love thee; if she will not, I will
never have her unless thou entreat for her. If you be a
true lover, hence, and not a word; for here comes
more company.   *Exit Silvius.*

    Enter Oliver.

OLIVER
Good morrow, fair ones. Pray you, if you know,
Where in the purlieus of this forest stands   77
A sheepcote fenced about with olive trees?

CELIA
West of this place, down in the neighbor bottom;   79
The rank of osiers by the murmuring stream   80
Left on your right hand brings you to the place.   81
But at this hour the house doth keep itself;
There's none within.

OLIVER
If that an eye may profit by a tongue,
Then should I know you by description,
Such garments and such years: "The boy is fair,
Of female favor, and bestows himself   87
Like a ripe sister; the woman, low   88
And browner than her brother." Are not you
The owner of the house I did inquire for?

CELIA
It is no boast, being asked, to say we are.

OLIVER
Orlando doth commend him to you both,   92
And to that youth he calls his Rosalind
He sends this bloody napkin. Are you he?   94
                    [*He produces a bloody handkerchief.*]

ROSALIND
I am. What must we understand by this?

OLIVER
Some of my shame, if you will know of me
What man I am, and how, and why, and where
This handkerchief was stained.

CELIA   I pray you, tell it.

OLIVER
When last the young Orlando parted from you
He left a promise to return again
Within an hour, and, pacing through the forest,
Chewing the food of sweet and bitter fancy,   102
Lo, what befell! He threw his eye aside,
And mark what object did present itself:

24 **turned** transformed 25 **leathern** leathery 26 **freestone-colored**
sandstone-colored, brownish-yellow 28 **hand** handwriting (with play
on "dishpan hands") 36 **Ethiop** i.e., black 36–37 **blacker . . .
countenance** even blacker in what they say than in their black appearance on the page 40 **Phoebes me** i.e., addresses me in her cruel
style 45 **thy . . . apart** having laid aside your godhead (for human
shape) 49 **vengeance** mischief, harm 50 **Meaning me** i.e., implying
that I am 51 **eyne** eyes 54 **in mild aspect** i.e., if they looked on me
mildly. (Suggests also astrological influence.) 55 **chid** chided 59 **by
. . . mind** i.e., send your thoughts in a letter via Silvius 60 **Whether
. . . kind** whether your youthful nature 62 **make** make offer of

69 **instrument** (1) tool (2) musical instrument 71 **tame snake** i.e., pathetic wretch 77 **purlieus** tracts of land on the border of a forest
79 **neighbor bottom** neighboring dell 80 **rank of osiers** row of willows 81 **Left** left behind, passed 87 **favor** features. **bestows** be-
haves 88 **ripe** mature or elder 92 **him** himself 94 **napkin** handkerchief 102 **fancy** love

Under an old oak, whose boughs were mossed with
   age
And high top bald with dry antiquity,
A wretched, ragged man, o'ergrown with hair,
Lay sleeping on his back. About his neck
A green and gilded snake had wreathed itself,
Who with her head, nimble in threats, approached
The opening of his mouth; but suddenly,
Seeing Orlando, it unlinked itself   112
And with indented glides did slip away   113
Into a bush, under which bush's shade
A lioness, with udders all drawn dry,   115
Lay couching, head on ground, with catlike watch,
When that the sleeping man should stir; for 'tis   117
The royal disposition of that beast
To prey on nothing that doth seem as dead.
This seen, Orlando did approach the man
And found it was his brother, his elder brother.

CELIA
O, I have heard him speak of that same brother,
And he did render him the most unnatural   123
That lived amongst men.

OLIVER   And well he might so do,
For well I know he was unnatural.

ROSALIND
But to Orlando: did he leave him there,
Food to the sucked and hungry lioness?

OLIVER
Twice did he turn his back and purposed so;
But kindness, nobler ever than revenge,
And nature, stronger than his just occasion,   130
Made him give battle to the lioness,
Who quickly fell before him; in which hurtling   132
From miserable slumber I awaked.

CELIA
Are you his brother?

ROSALIND   Was 't you he rescued?

CELIA
Was 't you that did so oft contrive to kill him?

OLIVER
'Twas I, but 'tis not I. I do not shame   136
To tell you what I was, since my conversion
So sweetly tastes, being the thing I am.

ROSALIND
But for the bloody napkin?

OLIVER   By and by.   139
When from the first to last betwixt us two
Tears our recountments had most kindly bathed,   141
As how I came into that desert place,
In brief, he led me to the gentle Duke,
Who gave me fresh array and entertainment,   144
Committing me unto my brother's love;
Who led me instantly unto his cave,

There stripped himself, and here upon his arm
The lioness had torn some flesh away,
Which all this while had bled; and now he fainted
And cried, in fainting, upon Rosalind.
Brief, I recovered him, bound up his wound,   151
And after some small space, being strong at heart,
He sent me hither, stranger as I am,
To tell this story, that you might excuse
His broken promise, and to give this napkin
Dyed in his blood unto the shepherd youth
That he in sport doth call his Rosalind.
          [Rosalind swoons.]

CELIA
Why, how now, Ganymede, sweet Ganymede!

OLIVER
Many will swoon when they do look on blood.

CELIA
There is more in it.—Cousin Ganymede!

OLIVER   Look, he recovers.

ROSALIND   I would I were at home.

CELIA   We'll lead you thither.—
I pray you, will you take him by the arm?
         [They help Rosalind up.]

OLIVER   Be of good cheer, youth. You a man? You lack
a man's heart.

ROSALIND   I do so, I confess it. Ah, sirrah, a body would   167
think this was well counterfeited. I pray you, tell your
brother how well I counterfeited. Heigh-ho!

OLIVER   This was not counterfeit. There is too great testimony in your complexion that it was a passion of   171
earnest.   172

ROSALIND   Counterfeit, I assure you.

OLIVER   Well then, take a good heart and counterfeit to
be a man.

ROSALIND   So I do; but, i' faith, I should have been a
woman by right.

CELIA   Come, you look paler and paler. Pray you, draw
homewards.—Good sir, go with us.

OLIVER
That will I, for I must bear answer back
How you excuse my brother, Rosalind.

ROSALIND   I shall devise something. But, I pray you,
commend my counterfeiting to him. Will you go?
         Exeunt.

         ❦

5.1   *Enter [Touchstone the] Clown and Audrey.*

TOUCHSTONE   We shall find a time, Audrey. Patience,
gentle Audrey.

AUDREY   Faith, the priest was good enough, for all the   3
old gentleman's saying.   4

TOUCHSTONE   A most wicked Sir Oliver, Audrey, a most
vile Mar-text. But Audrey, there is a youth here in the
forest lays claim to you.

---

112 unlinked uncoiled **113 indented** zigzag **115 udders . . . dry** (It
would therefore be fierce with hunger.) **117 When** for the moment
123 render him describe him as **130 just occasion** fair chance (of revenge) **132 hurtling** conflict, tumult **136 do not shame** am not
ashamed **139 for** as regards **141 recountments** relating of events
(to one another) **144 array** attire. **entertainment** hospitality,
provision

151 Brief in brief. **recovered** revived **167 a body** anybody
171–172 a passion of earnest a genuine swoon
5.1. Location: The forest.
3–4 the old gentleman's i.e., Jaques'

AUDREY   Ay, I know who 'tis. He hath no interest in me 8
in the world. Here comes the man you mean.

Enter William.

TOUCHSTONE   It is meat and drink to me to see a clown. 10
By my troth, we that have good wits have much to
answer for. We shall be flouting; we cannot hold. 12
WILLIAM   Good even, Audrey.
AUDREY   God gi' good even, William. 14
WILLIAM   And good even to you, sir.
[*He removes his hat.*]
TOUCHSTONE   Good even, gentle friend. Cover thy
head, cover thy head. Nay, prithee be covered. How
old are you, friend?
WILLIAM   Five-and-twenty, sir.
TOUCHSTONE   A ripe age. Is thy name William?
WILLIAM   William, sir.
TOUCHSTONE   A fair name. Wast born i' the forest here?
WILLIAM   Ay, sir, I thank God.
TOUCHSTONE   "Thank God"—a good answer. Art rich?
WILLIAM   Faith, sir, so-so.
TOUCHSTONE   "So-so" is good, very good, very excel-
lent good; and yet it is not, it is but so-so. Art thou
wise?
WILLIAM   Ay, sir, I have a pretty wit.
TOUCHSTONE   Why, thou sayst well. I do now remem-
ber a saying, "The fool doth think he is wise, but the
wise man knows himself to be a fool." The heathen 31
philosopher, when he had a desire to eat a grape, 32
would open his lips when he put it into his mouth, 33
meaning thereby that grapes were made to eat and 34
lips to open. You do love this maid? 35
WILLIAM   I do, sir.
TOUCHSTONE   Give me your hand. Art thou learned?
WILLIAM   No, sir.
TOUCHSTONE   Then learn this of me: to have is to have.
For it is a figure in rhetoric that drink, being poured 40
out of a cup into a glass, by filling the one doth empty 41
the other. For all your writers do consent that *ipse* is 42
he. Now, you are not *ipse,* for I am he.
WILLIAM   Which he, sir?
TOUCHSTONE   He, sir, that must marry this woman.
Therefore, you clown, abandon—which is in the
vulgar "leave"—the society—which in the boorish is
"company"—of this female—which in the common
is "woman"; which together is, abandon the society of
this female, or, clown, thou perishest; or, to thy better
understanding, diest; or, to wit, I kill thee, make thee
away, translate thy life into death, thy liberty into

bondage. I will deal in poison with thee, or in basti- 53
nado, or in steel; I will bandy with thee in faction, I 54
will o'errun thee with policy; I will kill thee a hundred 55
and fifty ways. Therefore tremble, and depart.
AUDREY   Do, good William.
WILLIAM   God rest you merry, sir.   *Exit.* 58

Enter Corin.

CORIN   Our master and mistress seeks you. Come,
away, away!
TOUCHSTONE   Trip, Audrey, trip, Audrey!—I attend, I 61
attend.   *Exeunt.*

5.2   *Enter Orlando [with his wounded arm in a sling]
and Oliver.*

ORLANDO   Is 't possible that on so little acquaintance
you should like her? That but seeing, you should love
her? And loving, woo? And, wooing, she should
grant? And will you persevere to enjoy her?
OLIVER   Neither call the giddiness of it in question, the 5
poverty of her, the small acquaintance, my sudden
wooing, nor her sudden consenting; but say with me,
"I love Aliena"; say with her that she loves me;
consent with both that we may enjoy each other. It
shall be to your good; for my father's house and all the
revenue that was old Sir Rowland's will I estate upon 11
you, and here live and die a shepherd.

Enter Rosalind.

ORLANDO   You have my consent. Let your wedding be
tomorrow. Thither will I invite the Duke and all 's 14
contented followers. Go you and prepare Aliena; for
look you, here comes my Rosalind.
ROSALIND   God save you, brother. 17
OLIVER   And you, fair sister.   [*Exit.*] 18
ROSALIND   O my dear Orlando, how it grieves me to
see thee wear thy heart in a scarf! 20
ORLANDO   It is my arm.
ROSALIND   I thought thy heart had been wounded with
the claws of a lion.
ORLANDO   Wounded it is, but with the eyes of a lady.
ROSALIND   Did your brother tell you how I counterfeited
to swoon when he showed me your handkerchief?
ORLANDO   Ay, and greater wonders than that.
ROSALIND   O I know where you are. Nay, 'tis true. 28
There was never anything so sudden but the fight of

8 interest in claim to   **10 clown** i.e., country yokel   **12 shall** must.
flouting scoffing, expressing contempt.   **hold** i.e., hold back, hold
our tongues   **14 God gi' good even** God give you good evening.
(Here, afternoon.)   **31–35 The heathen . . . open** (This is probably
Touchstone's way of telling William, whose mouth is no doubt gaping
like a rustic's, that the grape, i.e., Audrey, is not for his lips.)   **40–
42 drink . . . other** i.e., both Touchstone and William cannot possess
Audrey   **42 your writers** i.e., the authorities. (Touchstone's mock
learning in rhetoric draws upon Aristotle, Cicero, and Quintilian.)
consent agree.   **ipse** he himself. (In Latin, *"Ipse* he" means the man
of the hour, and especially the successful lover.)

53–54 bastinado beating with a cudgel   **54 bandy** contend.   **in faction** factiously   **55 o'errun . . . policy** overwhelm you with craft,
cunning   **58 God . . . merry** (Common salutation at parting.)
61 Trip go nimbly
5.2. Location: The forest.
5 giddiness sudden speed   **11 estate** settle as an estate, bestow
14 all 's all his   **17 brother** i.e., brother-in-law to be   **18 sister** (Rosalind is still dressed as a man, but Oliver evidently adopts the fiction
that "Ganymede" is Orlando's Rosalind. See 4.3.92 ff.)   **20 wear
. . . scarf** (Perhaps she suggests that Orlando has been wearing his
heart on his sleeve; literally, she refers to the scarf or bandage for his
wounded arm.)   **28 where you are** i.e., what you mean

two rams and Caesar's thrasonical brag of "I came, 30
saw, and overcame." For your brother and my sister
no sooner met but they looked, no sooner looked but
they loved, no sooner loved but they sighed, no
sooner sighed but they asked one another the reason,
no sooner knew the reason but they sought the
remedy; and in these degrees have they made a pair of 36
stairs to marriage which they will climb incontinent, or 37
else be incontinent before marriage. They are in the
very wrath of love, and they will together. Clubs 39
cannot part them.

ORLANDO   They shall be married tomorrow, and I will
bid the Duke to the nuptial. But O, how bitter a thing
it is to look into happiness through another man's
eyes! By so much the more shall I tomorrow be at the
height of heart-heaviness, by how much I shall think
my brother happy in having what he wishes for.

ROSALIND   Why, then, tomorrow I cannot serve your
turn for Rosalind?

ORLANDO   I can live no longer by thinking.

ROSALIND   I will weary you then no longer with idle
talking. Know of me then—for now I speak to some
purpose—that I know you are a gentleman of good con- 52
ceit. I speak not this that you should bear a good opin- 53
ion of my knowledge, insomuch I say I know you are; 54
neither do I labor for a greater esteem than may in 55
some little measure draw a belief from you to do 56
yourself good and not to grace me. Believe then, if you 57
please, that I can do strange things. I have, since I was
three years old, conversed with a magician, most 59
profound in his art and yet not damnable. If you do 60
love Rosalind so near the heart as your gesture cries it 61
out, when your brother marries Aliena shall you 62
marry her. I know into what straits of fortune she is
driven; and it is not impossible to me, if it appear not
inconvenient to you, to set her before your eyes 65
tomorrow, human as she is, and without any danger. 66

ORLANDO   Speak'st thou in sober meanings? 67

ROSALIND   By my life, I do, which I tender dearly, 68
though I say I am a magician. Therefore, put you in 69
your best array; bid your friends; for if you will be 70

married tomorrow, you shall, and to Rosalind, if you
will.

        Enter Silvius and Phoebe.

Look, here comes a lover of mine and a lover of hers.

PHOEBE [*to Rosalind*]
   Youth, you have done me much ungentleness,   74
   To show the letter that I writ to you.

ROSALIND
   I care not if I have. It is my study   76
   To seem despiteful and ungentle to you.
   You are there followed by a faithful shepherd.
   Look upon him; love him. He worships you.

PHOEBE [*to Silvius*]
   Good shepherd, tell this youth what 'tis to love.

SILVIUS
   It is to be all made of sighs and tears;
   And so am I for Phoebe.

PHOEBE   And I for Ganymede.

ORLANDO   And I for Rosalind.

ROSALIND   And I for no woman.

SILVIUS
   It is to be all made of faith and service;
   And so am I for Phoebe.

PHOEBE   And I for Ganymede.

ORLANDO   And I for Rosalind.

ROSALIND   And I for no woman.

SILVIUS
   It is to be all made of fantasy,   91
   All made of passion and all made of wishes,
   All adoration, duty, and observance,   93
   All humbleness, all patience and impatience,
   All purity, all trial, all observance;   95
   And so am I for Phoebe.

PHOEBE   And so am I for Ganymede.

ORLANDO   And so am I for Rosalind.

ROSALIND   And so am I for no woman.

PHOEBE [*to Rosalind*]
   If this be so, why blame you me to love you?   100

SILVIUS [*to Phoebe*]
   If this be so, why blame you me to love you?

ORLANDO
   If this be so, why blame you me to love you?

ROSALIND   Why do you speak too, "Why blame you me
to love you?"

ORLANDO   To her that is not here, nor doth not hear.

ROSALIND   Pray you, no more of this; 'tis like the
howling of Irish wolves against the moon. [*To Silvius.*]
I will help you, if I can. [*To Phoebe.*] I would love you, if
I could.—Tomorrow meet me all together. [*To Phoebe.*] I
will marry you, if ever I marry woman, and I'll be
married tomorrow. [*To Orlando.*] I will satisfy you, if
ever I satisfied man, and you shall be married
tomorrow. [*To Silvius.*] I will content you, if what
pleases you contents you, and you shall be married
tomorrow. [*To Orlando.*] As you love Rosalind, meet.

---

30 thrasonical boastful. (From Thraso, the boaster in Terence's *Eunuchus.*) **36 degrees** (Plays on the original meaning, "steps," and also on the rhetorical figure of climax illustrated by Rosalind's sentence as it moves from one step to the next by linked words, *looked, loved, sighed,* etc.) **pair** flight **37 incontinent** immediately (followed by a pun on the meaning "unchaste or sexually unrestrained") **39 wrath** impetuosity, ardor **52–53 conceit** intelligence, understanding **53 that** in order that **54 insomuch . . . are** from my saying I know you to be intelligent **55–57 neither . . . grace me** nor am I interested in winning approval except insofar as it may, by inspiring your confidence in my ability, prompt you to do something for your own benefit; it's not intended to bring favor on myself **59 conversed** associated **60 not damnable** not a practicer of forbidden or black magic, worthy of execution and damnation **61 gesture** bearing **61–62 cries it out** proclaims **65 inconvenient** inappropriate **66 human** i.e., the real Rosalind. **danger** i.e., the danger to the soul from one's involvement in magic or witchcraft **67 in sober meanings** seriously **68 tender dearly** value highly **69 though . . . magician** (According to Elizabethan antiwitchcraft statutes, some forms of witchcraft were punishable by death; Rosalind thus endangers her life by what she has said.) **70 bid** invite. **friends** family and friends

74 ungentleness discourtesy **76 study** conscious endeavor **91 fantasy** imagination **93 observance** devotion, respect **95 observance** (Perhaps a compositor's error, repeated from two lines previous; many editors emend it to *obedience.*) **100 to love you** for loving you

[*To Silvius.*] As you love Phoebe, meet. And as I love no woman, I'll meet. So fare you well. I have left you commands.
SILVIUS   I'll not fail, if I live.
PHOEBE   Nor I.
ORLANDO   Nor I.   *Exeunt [separately].*

❧

5.3   *Enter [Touchstone the] Clown and Audrey.*

TOUCHSTONE   Tomorrow is the joyful day, Audrey; tomorrow will we be married.
AUDREY   I do desire it with all my heart; and I hope it is no dishonest desire to desire to be a woman of the 4 world. Here come two of the banished Duke's pages. 5

Enter two Pages.

FIRST PAGE   Well met, honest gentleman.   6
TOUCHSTONE   By my troth, well met. Come, sit, sit, and a song.   [*They sit.*]
SECOND PAGE   We are for you. Sit i' the middle.   9
FIRST PAGE   Shall we clap into 't roundly, without hawk- 10 ing or spitting or saying we are hoarse, which are the 11 only prologues to a bad voice?   12
SECOND PAGE   I' faith, i' faith, and both in a tune, like 13 two gypsies on a horse.   14

Song.

BOTH PAGES
It was a lover and his lass,
  With a hey, and a ho, and a hey-nonny-no,
That o'er the green cornfield did pass   17
  In springtime, the only pretty ring time,   18
When birds do sing, hey ding a ding, ding,
Sweet lovers love the spring.

Between the acres of the rye,   21
  With a hey, and a ho, and a hey-nonny-no,
These pretty country folks would lie
  In springtime, the only pretty ring time,
When birds do sing, hey ding a ding, ding,
Sweet lovers love the spring.

This carol they began that hour,
  With a hey, and a ho, and hey-nonny-no,
How that a life was but a flower
  In springtime, the only pretty ring time,
When birds do sing, hey ding a ding, ding,
Sweet lovers love the spring.

And therefore take the present time,
  With a hey, and a ho, and a hey-nonny-no,
For love is crownèd with the prime   35
  In springtime, the only pretty ring time,
When birds do sing, hey ding a ding, ding,
Sweet lovers love the spring.

TOUCHSTONE   Truly, young gentlemen, though there was no great matter in the ditty, yet the note was very 40 untunable.   41
FIRST PAGE   You are deceived, sir. We kept time, we lost 42 not our time.
TOUCHSTONE   By my troth, yes; I count it but time lost to hear such a foolish song. God b' wi' you, and God mend your voices! Come, Audrey. *Exeunt [separately].*

❧

5.4   *Enter Duke Senior, Amiens, Jaques, Orlando, Oliver, [and] Celia.*

DUKE SENIOR
Dost thou believe, Orlando, that the boy
Can do all this that he hath promisèd?
ORLANDO
I sometimes do believe, and sometimes do not,
As those that fear they hope and know they fear.   4

Enter Rosalind, Silvius, and Phoebe.

ROSALIND
Patience once more, whiles our compact is urged.   5
[*To the Duke.*]   You say, if I bring in your Rosalind
You will bestow her on Orlando here?
DUKE SENIOR
That would I, had I kingdoms to give with her.
ROSALIND [*to Orlando*]
And you say you will have her when I bring her?
ORLANDO
That would I, were I of all kingdoms king.
ROSALIND [*to Phoebe*]
You say you'll marry me if I be willing?
PHOEBE
That will I, should I die the hour after.
ROSALIND
But if you do refuse to marry me
You'll give yourself to this most faithful shepherd?
PHOEBE   So is the bargain.
ROSALIND [*to Silvius*]
You say that you'll have Phoebe if she will?
SILVIUS
Though to have her and death were both one thing.
ROSALIND
I have promised to make all this matter even.   18
Keep you your word, O Duke, to give your daughter;

4 **dishonest** immodest   4–5 **woman of the world** married woman; also, one who advances herself socially   6 **honest** worthy   9 **We are for you** i.e., fine, we're ready   10 **clap . . . roundly** begin at once and with spirit   10–11 **hawking** clearing the throat   12 **only** customary   13 **in a tune** (1) in unison (2) keeping time   14 **on a** on one   17 **cornfield** field of grain   18 **ring time** time most apt for marriage   21 **Between the acres** i.e., on unplowed strips between the fields

5.3. Location: The forest.

35 **prime** (1) height of perfection (2) spring   40 **matter** sense, meaning. **note** music   41 **untunable** discordant   42 **deceived** mistaken
5.4. Location: The forest.
4 **they hope** i.e., that they merely hope   5 **urged** put forward
18 **make . . . even** set all this to rights, square accounts

You yours, Orlando, to receive his daughter;
Keep you your word, Phoebe, that you'll marry me,
Or else, refusing me, to wed this shepherd;
Keep your word, Silvius, that you'll marry her
If she refuse me; and from hence I go,
To make these doubts all even.

Exeunt Rosalind and Celia.

DUKE SENIOR
I do remember in this shepherd boy
Some lively touches of my daughter's favor.   27

ORLANDO
My lord, the first time that I ever saw him
Methought he was a brother to your daughter.
But, my good lord, this boy is forest-born
And hath been tutored in the rudiments
Of many desperate studies by his uncle,   32
Whom he reports to be a great magician,
Obscurèd in the circle of this forest.   34

Enter [Touchstone the] Clown and Audrey.

JAQUES   There is, sure, another flood toward, and these 35
couples are coming to the ark. Here comes a pair of 36
very strange beasts, which in all tongues are called
fools.

TOUCHSTONE   Salutation and greeting to you all!

JAQUES   Good my lord, bid him welcome. This is the
motley-minded gentleman that I have so often met in
the forest. He hath been a courtier, he swears.

TOUCHSTONE   If any man doubt that, let him put me to
my purgation. I have trod a measure; I have flattered a 44
lady; I have been politic with my friend, smooth with 45
mine enemy; I have undone three tailors; I have had 46
four quarrels and like to have fought one.   47

JAQUES   And how was that ta'en up?   48

TOUCHSTONE   Faith, we met and found the quarrel was
upon the seventh cause.

JAQUES   How seventh cause?—Good my lord, like this
fellow.

DUKE SENIOR   I like him very well.

TOUCHSTONE   God 'ild you, sir, I desire you of the like. 54
I press in here, sir, amongst the rest of the country
copulatives, to swear and to forswear, according as 56
marriage binds and blood breaks. A poor virgin, sir, 57
an ill-favored thing, sir, but mine own; a poor humor 58
of mine, sir, to take that that no man else will. Rich
honesty dwells like a miser, sir, in a poor house, as 60
your pearl in your foul oyster.   61

DUKE SENIOR   By my faith, he is very swift and senten- 62
tious.   63

TOUCHSTONE   According to the fool's bolt, sir, and such 64
dulcet diseases.   65

JAQUES   But for the seventh cause. How did you find
the quarrel on the seventh cause?

TOUCHSTONE   Upon a lie seven times removed—bear
your body more seeming, Audrey—as thus, sir. I did 69
dislike the cut of a certain courtier's beard. He sent me 70
word if I said his beard was not cut well, he was in
the mind it was: this is called the Retort Courteous. If I
sent him word again it was not well cut, he would
send me word he cut it to please himself: this is called
the Quip Modest. If again it was not well cut, he dis- 75
abled my judgment: this is called the Reply Churlish. If 76
again it was not well cut, he would answer I spake
not true: this is called the Reproof Valiant. If again it
was not well cut, he would say I lie: this is called the
Countercheck Quarrelsome. And so to the Lie Circum- 80
stantial and the Lie Direct.

JAQUES   And how oft did you say his beard was not
well cut?

TOUCHSTONE   I durst go no further than the Lie Circumstantial, nor he durst not give me the Lie Direct;
and so we measured swords and parted.   86

JAQUES   Can you nominate in order now the degrees of
the lie?

TOUCHSTONE   O sir, we quarrel in print, by the book, as 89
you have books for good manners. I will name you the
degrees. The first, the Retort Courteous; the second,
the Quip Modest; the third, the Reply Churlish; the
fourth, the Reproof Valiant; the fifth, the Countercheck Quarrelsome; the sixth, the Lie with Circumstance; the seventh, the Lie Direct. All these you may
avoid but the Lie Direct; and you may avoid that, too,
with an If. I knew when seven justices could not take 97
up a quarrel, but when the parties were met them- 98
selves, one of them thought but of an If, as, "If you
said so, then I said so"; and they shook hands and
swore brothers. Your If is the only peacemaker; much 101
virtue in If.

JAQUES   Is not this a rare fellow, my lord? He's as good
at anything and yet a fool.

DUKE SENIOR   He uses his folly like a stalking-horse, 105
and under the presentation of that he shoots his wit. 106

Enter Hymen, Rosalind, and Celia. Still music.
[Rosalind and Celia are no longer disguised.]

---

27 lively lifelike. **favor** appearance **32 desperate** dangerous
34 Obscurèd hidden (with a possible allusion to the magic circle that
protected the magician from the devil during incantation) **35 toward**
coming on **36 a pair** (In Genesis 7:2, God commands Noah to take
on board every "clean" beast by sevens, but those that are not clean,
by two.) **44 purgation** proof, trial. **measure** slow, stately dance
45 politic cunning, Machiavellian. **smooth** insinuating **46 undone**
bankrupted (by refusing to pay massive debts owed them) **47 like**
came close **48 ta'en up** settled, made up **54 'ild** yield, reward. **I
. . . like** I wish the same to you. (A polite phrase used to reply to a
compliment.) **56 copulatives** i.e., people about to copulate in
marriage **57 blood breaks** passion drives one to violate the marriage
vows **58 humor** whim **60 honesty** chastity **61 your pearl** i.e., the
pearl that one hears about

62 swift quick-witted **62–63 sententious** pithy **64 fool's bolt** (Alluding to the proverb "A fool's bolt [arrow] is soon shot.") **65 dulcet
diseases** pleasant afflictions, entertaining yet sharp. (Touchstone wryly
agrees with the Duke's assessment of the Fool as swift and sententious.) **69 seeming** seemly **70 dislike** express dislike of **75–76 disabled** disparaged **80 Countercheck** rebuff **86 measured swords**
(i.e., as in the mere preliminary to a duel) **89 in . . . book** in a precise way. (Touchstone is travestying books on the general subject of
honor and arms, which dealt with occasions and circumstances of the
duel.) **97–98 take up** settle **101 swore brothers** became sworn
brothers **105 stalking-horse** A real or artificial horse under cover of
which the hunter approached his game. **106 presentation** semblance. **s.d. Hymen** Roman god of faithful marriage. **Still** soft

HYMEN

> Then is there mirth in heaven, 107
> When earthly things made even 108
>> Atone together. 109
> Good Duke, receive thy daughter;
> Hymen from heaven brought her,
>> Yea, brought her hither,
> That thou mightst join her hand with his
> Whose heart within his bosom is. 114

ROSALIND [to the Duke]

> To you I give myself, for I am yours.
> [To Orlando.] To you I give myself, for I am yours.

DUKE SENIOR

> If there be truth in sight, you are my daughter.

ORLANDO

> If there be truth in sight, you are my Rosalind.

PHOEBE

> If sight and shape be true,
> Why then, my love adieu!

ROSALIND [to the Duke]

> I'll have no father, if you be not he.
> [To Orlando.] I'll have no husband, if you be not he.
> [To Phoebe.] Nor ne'er wed woman, if you be
>> not she.

HYMEN

> Peace, ho! I bar confusion.
> 'Tis I must make conclusion
>> Of these most strange events.
> Here's eight that must take hands
> To join in Hymen's bands,
>> If truth holds true contents. 129
> [To Orlando and Rosalind.]
>> You and you no cross shall part. 130
> [To Oliver and Celia.]
>> You and you are heart in heart.
> [To Phoebe.]
>> You to his love must accord 132
>> Or have a woman to your lord. 133
> [To Touchstone and Audrey.]
>> You and you are sure together, 134
>> As the winter to foul weather.
> [To All.]
>> Whiles a wedlock hymn we sing,
>> Feed yourselves with questioning, 137
>> That reason wonder may diminish 138
>> How thus we met, and these things finish.

Song.

> Wedding is great Juno's crown, 140
>> O blessèd bond of board and bed! 141

> 'Tis Hymen peoples every town;
>> High wedlock then be honorèd. 143
> Honor, high honor and renown
>> To Hymen, god of every town!

DUKE SENIOR [to Celia]

> O my dear niece, welcome thou art to me!
> Even daughter, welcome, in no less degree. 147

PHOEBE [to Silvius]

> I will not eat my word, now thou art mine;
> Thy faith my fancy to thee doth combine. 149

Enter Second Brother [Jaques de Boys].

JAQUES DE BOYS

> Let me have audience for a word or two.
> I am the second son of old Sir Rowland,
> That bring these tidings to this fair assembly.
> Duke Frederick, hearing how that every day
> Men of great worth resorted to this forest,
> Addressed a mighty power, which were on foot 155
> In his own conduct, purposely to take 156
> His brother here and put him to the sword;
> And to the skirts of this wild wood he came,
> Where, meeting with an old religious man,
> After some question with him, was converted 160
> Both from his enterprise and from the world,
> His crown bequeathing to his banished brother,
> And all their lands restored to them again
> That were with him exiled. This to be true
> I do engage my life.

DUKE SENIOR   Welcome, young man. 165

> Thou offer'st fairly to thy brothers' wedding: 166
> To one his lands withheld and to the other 167
> A land itself at large, a potent dukedom. 168
> First, in this forest let us do those ends 169
> That here were well begun and well begot; 170
> And after, every of this happy number 171
> That have endured shrewd days and nights with us 172
> Shall share the good of our returnèd fortune
> According to the measure of their states. 174
> Meantime, forget this new-fall'n dignity, 175
> And fall into our rustic revelry.
> Play, music! And you, brides and bridegrooms all,
> With measure heaped in joy, to th' measures fall. 178

JAQUES

> Sir, by your patience.—If I heard you rightly, 179
> The Duke hath put on a religious life
> And thrown into neglect the pompous court. 181

107 mirth joy   **108 made even** set straight   **109 Atone** are at one   **114 Whose** (Refers to Rosalind.)   **129 If . . . contents** if truth be true, i.e., if the newly revealed realities truly satisfy   **130 cross** vexation, mischance   **132 his** i.e., Silvius'.   **accord** agree   **133 to** for.   **lord** i.e., husband   **134 sure** closely united   **137 Feed** satisfy   **138 reason** understanding   **140 Juno's** (Juno was the Roman queen of the gods, presiding, in the Renaissance view, over faithful wedlock.)   **141 board and bed** sustenance and lodging; the household

143 High solemn   **147 Even . . . degree** i.e., you are as welcome as a daughter   **149 fancy** love.   **combine** unite   **155 Addressed** prepared.   **power** army   **156 In . . . conduct** under his own command   **160 question** conversation   **165 engage** pledge   **166 Thou offer'st fairly** you contribute handsomely   **167 the other** i.e., Orlando   **168 A land . . . large** i.e., an entire dukedom. (As husband of Rosalind, Orlando will eventually inherit as Duke.)   **169 do those ends** accomplish those purposes   **170 begot** conceived   **171 every** every one   **172 shrewd** hard, trying   **174 states** rank   **175 new-fall'n** newly acquired   **178 With . . . joy** with a full measure, overflowing with joy (with wordplay on *measure* and *measures*, "dances")   **179 by your patience** by your leave, i.e., let the music wait a moment   **181 pompous** ceremonious

JAQUES DE BOYS   He hath.

JAQUES
To him will I. Out of these convertites   183
There is much matter to be heard and learned.   184
[*To the Duke.*] You to your former honor I bequeath;
Your patience and your virtue well deserves it.
[*To Orlando.*] You to a love that your true faith doth
    merit;
[*To Oliver*] You to your land and love and great
    allies;   188
[*To Silvius*] You to a long and well-deservèd bed;
[*To Touchstone*] And you to wrangling, for thy
    loving voyage
Is but for two months victualed. So, to your
    pleasures.   191
I am for other than for dancing measures.

DUKE SENIOR   Stay, Jaques, stay.

JAQUES
To see no pastime I. What you would have
I'll stay to know at your abandoned cave.   *Exit.*

DUKE SENIOR
Proceed, proceed. We'll begin these rites,
As we do trust they'll end, in true delights.
                [*They dance.*] *Exeunt* [*all but Rosalind*].

[Epilogue]

ROSALIND   It is not the fashion to see the lady the epi-
    logue; but it is no more unhandsome than to see the 2
    lord the prologue. If it be true that good wine needs 3
    no bush, 'tis true that a good play needs no epilogue. 4
    Yet to good wine they do use good bushes, and good
    plays prove the better by the help of good epilogues.
    What a case am I in then, that am neither a good epi-
    logue nor cannot insinuate with you in the behalf of a 8
    good play! I am not furnished like a beggar; therefore 9
    to beg will not become me. My way is to conjure you, 10
    and I'll begin with the women. I charge you, O
    women, for the love you bear to men, to like as much
    of this play as please you; and I charge you, O men,
    for the love you bear to women—as I perceive by your
    simpering, none of you hates them—that between
    you and the women the play may please. If I were a 16
    woman I would kiss as many of you as had beards 17
    that pleased me, complexions that liked me, and 18
    breaths that I defied not; and I am sure as many as 19
    have good beards or good faces or sweet breaths will,
    for my kind offer, when I make curtsy, bid me fare- 21
    well.   *Exit.* 22

183 convertites converts   **184 matter** sound sense   **188 allies** kinfolk   **191 victualed** provisioned
Epilogue
2 unhandsome in bad taste   **3–4 good . . . bush** (A proverb derived
from the custom of displaying a piece of ivy or holly at the tavern
door to denote that wine was for sale there.)   **8 insinuate** ingratiate
myself   **9 furnished** equipped, decked out   **10 conjure** adjure, earnestly charge   **16–17 If . . . woman** (Women's parts on the Elizabethan stage were played by boys in feminine costume.)   **18 liked**
pleased   **19 defied** rejected, disdained   **21–22 bid me farewell** i.e.,
applaud me

Twelfth Night; or, What You Will

Twelfth Night is possibly the latest of the three festive comedies, including *Much Ado About Nothing* and *As You Like It,* with which Shakespeare climaxed his distinctively philosophical and joyous vein of comic writing. Performed on February 2, 1602, at the Middle Temple and written possibly as early as 1599, *Twelfth Night* is usually dated 1600 or 1601. This play is indeed the most festive of the lot. Its keynote is Saturnalian release and the carnival pursuit of love and mirth. Along with such familiar motifs (found, for example in *The Two Gentlemen of Verona, As You Like It,* and *The Merchant of Venice*) as the plucky heroine disguised as a man, *Twelfth Night* also returns to the more farcical routines of mistaken identity found in Shakespeare's early comedy. As a witness of the 1602 performance, John Manningham, observes, the play is "much like the *Comedy of Errors,* or *Menaechmi* in Plautus, but most like and near to that in Italian called *Inganni.*"

The carnival atmosphere is appropriate to the season designated in the play's title: the twelfth night of Christmas, January 6, the Feast of Epiphany. (The prologue to *Gl'Ingannati,* perhaps the Italian play referred to by Manningham, speaks of "La Notte di Beffania," Epiphany night.) Along with its primary Christian significance as the Feast of the Magi, Epiphany was also in Renaissance times the last day of the Christmas revels. Over a twelve-day period, from Christmas until January 6, noble households sponsored numerous performances of plays, masks, banquets, and every kind of festivity. (Leslie Hotson argues, in fact, that *Twelfth Night* was first performed on twelfth night in early 1601, in the presence of Queen Elizabeth.) Students left schools for vacations, celebrating release from study with plays and revels of their own. The stern rigors of a rule-bound society gave way temporarily to playful inversions of authority. The reign of the Boy Bishop and the Feast of Fools, for example, gave choristers and minor church functionaries the cherished opportunity to boss the hierarchy around, mock the liturgy with outrageous lampooning, and generally let off steam. Although such customs occasionally got

out of hand, the idea was to channel potentially destructive insubordination into playacting and thereby promote harmony. Behind these Elizabethan midwinter customs lies the Roman Saturnalia, with its pagan spirit of gift giving, sensual indulgence, and satirical hostility to those who would curb merriment. Shakespeare's play captures the medieval and Renaissance spirit of Epiphany by its often playful allusions to religious practice: Feste's disguise as "Sir Topas," the priest, Feste's joke about living by the church (3.1.3–7), Sir Toby's defense of "cakes and ale" and Feste's swearing by Saint Anne, mother of the Virgin Mary (2.3.115–116), Feste's joking about "clerestories" (4.2.38), and the like. Shakespeare lovingly evokes a tradition of festivals and ceremonies that incorporates self-mockery into its celebration of renewal at Christmas time.

Shakespeare's choice of sources for *Twelfth Night* underscores his commitment to mirth. Renaissance literature offered numerous instances of mistaken identity among twins and of the disguised heroine serving as page to her beloved. Among those in English were the anonymous play *Sir Clyomon and Sir Clamydes* (c. 1570–1583), Sir Philip Sidney's *Arcadia* (1590), and the prose romance *Parismus* by Emmanuel Forde (1598), featuring both a shipwreck and two characters with the names of Olivia and Violetta. Of particular significance, but largely for negative reasons, is Barnabe Riche's tale of "Apollonius and Silla" in *Riche His Farewell to Military Profession* (1581), which was based on François de Belleforest's 1571 French version of Matteo Bandello's *Novelle* (1554). Here we find most of the requisite plot elements: the shipwreck; Silla's disguise as a page in Duke Apollonius' court; her office as ambassador of love from Apollonius to the lady Julina, who thereupon falls in love with Silla; and the arrival of Silla's twin brother Silvio and his consequent success in winning Julina's affection. To Riche, however, this tale is merely a long warning against the enervating power of infatuation. Silvio gets Julina with child and disappears forthwith, making his belated reappearance almost too late to save the wrongly accused Silla. Riche's moralizing puts the blame on the gross and drunken appetite of carnal love. The total mismatching of affection with which the story begins, and the sudden realignments of desire based on mere outward resemblances, are seen as proofs of love's unreasonableness. Shakespeare, of course, retains and capitalizes on the irrational quality of love, as in *A Midsummer Night's Dream,* but in doing so he minimizes the harm done (Olivia is not made pregnant) and repudiates any negative moral judgments. The added subplot, with its rebuking of Malvolio's censoriousness, may have been conceived as a further answer to Riche, Fenton, and their sober school.

Shakespeare's festive spirit owes much, as Manningham observed, to Plautus and the neoclassical Italian comic writers. At least three Italian comedies called *Gl'Inganni* ("The Frauds") employ the motif of mistaken identity, and one of them, by Curzio Gonzaga (1592), supplies Viola's assumed name of "Cesare," or Cesario. Another play with the same title appeared in 1562. More useful is *Gl'Ingannati* ("The Deceived"), performed in 1531 and translated into French in 1543. Besides a plot line generally similar to *Twelfth Night* and the reference to La Notte di Beffania (Epiphany), this play offers the suggestive name *Malevolti,* "evil-faced," and *Fabio* (which resembles "Fabian"). It also contains possible hints for Malvolio, Sir Toby, and company, although the plot of the counterfeit letter is original with Shakespeare. Essentially, Shakespeare superimposes his own subplot on an Italianate novella plot, as he did in *The Taming of the Shrew* and *Much Ado About Nothing.* And it is in the Malvolio story that Shakespeare most pointedly defends merriment. Feste the professional fool, an original stage type for Shakespeare in *Twelfth Night* and in *As You Like It,* also reinforces the theme of seizing the moment of mirth.

This great lesson, of savoring life's pleasures while one is still young, is something that Orsino and Olivia have not yet learned when the play commences. Although suited to one another in rank, wealth, and attractiveness, they are unable to overcome their own willful posturing in the elaborate charade of courtship. Like Silvius in *As You Like It,* Orsino is the conventional wooer trapped in the courtly artifice of love's rules. He opens the play on a cloying note of self-pity. He is fascinated with his own degradation as a rejected suitor and bores his listeners with his changeable moods and fondness for poetical "conceits." He sees himself as a hart pursued by his desires "like fell and cruel hounds," reminding us that enervating lovesickness has, in fact, robbed him of his manly occupation, hunting. He sends ornately contrived messages to Olivia but has not seen her in so long that his passion has become unreal and fantastical, feeding on itself.

Olivia plays the opposite role of chaste, denying womanhood. She explains her retirement from the world as mourning for a dead brother (whose name we never learn), but this withdrawal from life is another unreal vision. Olivia's practice of mourning, whereby she will "water once a day her chamber round / With eye-offending brine" (1.1.28–29), is a lifeless ritual. As others view the matter, she is senselessly wasting her beauty and affection on the dead. "What a plague means my niece to take the death of her brother thus?" Sir Toby expostulates (1.3.1–2). Viola, though she, too, has seemingly lost a brother, is an important foil in this regard, for she continues to hope for her brother's safety, trusts his soul is in heaven if he is dead, and refuses to give up her commitment to life in any case. We suspect that Olivia takes a willful pleasure in self-denial not unlike Orsino's self-congratulatory suffering. She appears to derive satisfaction from the power she holds over Orsino, a power of refusal. And she must know that she looks stunning in black.

Olivia's household reflects, in part, her mood of self-denial. She keeps Malvolio as steward because he, too, dresses somberly, insists on quiet as befits a house in mourning, and maintains order. Yet Olivia also retains a fool, Feste, who is Malvolio's opposite in every way. Hard-pressed to defend his mirthful function in a household so given over to melancholy, Feste must find some way of persuading his mistress that her very gravity is itself the essence of folly. This is a paradox, because sobriety and order appeal to the conventional wisdom of the world. Malvolio, sensing that his devotion to propriety is being challenged by the fool's prating, chides Olivia for taking "delight in such a barren rascal" (1.5.80–81).

Feste must argue for an inversion of appearance and reality whereby many of the world's ordinary pursuits can be seen to be ridiculous. As he observes, in his habitually elliptical manner of speech, "*Cucullus non facit monachum* [the cowl doesn't make the monk]; that's as much to say as I wear not motley in my brain" (1.5.52–54). Feste wins his case by making Olivia laugh at her own illogic in grieving for a brother whose soul she assumes to be in heaven. By extension, Olivia has indeed been a fool for allowing herself to be deprived of happiness in love by her brother's death ("there is no true cuckold but calamity") and for failing to consider the brevity of youth ("beauty's a flower"). Yet, paradoxically, only one who professes to be a fool can point this out, enabled by his detachment and innocence to perceive simple but profound truths denied to supposedly rational persons. This vision of the fool as naturally wise, and of society as self-indulgently insane, fascinated Renaissance writers, from Erasmus' *In Praise of Folly* and Cervantes' *Don Quixote* to Shakespeare's *King Lear.*

Viola, although not dressed in motley, aligns herself with Feste's rejection of self-denial. Refreshingly, even comically, she challenges the staid artifice of Orsino's and Olivia's lives. She is an ocean traveler, like many of Shakespeare's later heroines (Marina in *Pericles,* Perdita in *The Winter's Tale),* arriving on Illyria's shore plucky and determined. On her first embassy to Olivia from Orsino, she exposes with disarming candor the willfully ritualistic quality of Olivia's existence. Viola discards the flowery set speech she had prepared and memorized at Orsino's behest; despite her charmingly conceited assertion that the speech has been "excellently well penned," she senses that its elegant but empty rhetoric is all too familiar to the disdainful Olivia. Instead, Viola departs from her text to urge seizing the moment of happiness. "You do usurp yourself," she lectures Olivia, "for what is yours to bestow is not yours to reserve" (1.5.183–184). Beauty is a gift of nature, and failure to use it is a sin against nature. Or, again, "Lady, you are the cruel'st she alive / If you will lead these graces [Olivia's beauty] to the grave / And leave the world no copy" (lines 236–238). An essential argument in favor of love, as in Shakespeare's sonnets, is the necessity of marriage and childbearing in order to perpetuate beauty. This approach is new to Olivia and catches her wholly by surprise. In part, she reacts, like Phoebe in *As You Like It,* with perverse logic, rejecting a too-willing wooer for one who is hard to get. Yet Olivia is also attracted by a new note of sincerity, prompting her to reenter life and accept maturely both the risks and rewards of romantic involvement. Her longing for "Cesario" is, of course, sexually misdirected, but the appearance of Viola's identical twin, Sebastian, soon puts all to rights.

The motifs of Olivia's attraction for another woman (both actors would have been boys) and of Orsino's deep fondness for a seeming young man ("Cesario"), which matures into sexual love, raise delicate suggestions of love between members of the same sex, as in *As You Like It.* Once again, however, we must approach the notion circumspectly, remembering that these situations are found in Shakespeare's sources and reflect a convention quite different from a modern psychological understanding of homosexuality. Like Rosalind, Viola uses her male attire to win Orsino's pure affection in a friendship devoid of sexual interest, since both seemingly are men. Friendship must come first; the Renaissance generally accorded a higher value to friendship than to erotic passion. Yet Shakespeare also insists, as did many of his contemporaries (including Montaigne), that friendship is not only possible between men and women but also that such a relationship, formalized in marriage, offers the best of all worlds; hence, the importance of Viola's male disguise. As "Cesario," she can teach Orsino about the conventions of love in relaxed and frank conversations that would not be possible if she were known to be a woman. She teaches him to avoid the beguiling but misleading myths of Petrarchan love (named after the Italian sonneteer Francis Petrarch, whose poems embody the idealization of courtly love) and so prepares him for the realities of marriage. Comparing men and women in love, she confides, "We men may say more, swear more, but indeed / Our shows are more than will; for still we prove / Much in our vows, but little in our love" (2.4.116–118). Once she and Orsino have achieved an instinctive rapport—all the more remarkable for their talking so often at cross-purposes—Viola's unmasking can make possible a physical communion as well. Orsino, no longer trapped in the futile worship of a seemingly unapproachable goddess, can come to terms with his sexuality as part of a unified and loving human relationship. The friendship of Sebastian and Antonio, meanwhile, sorely tested by the mix-ups of the mistaken identity plot, similarly places Sebastian in a love-and-friendship triangle like that involving Bassanio, Portia, and Antonio in *The Merchant of Venice.* The concern with betrayal in friendship surfaces repeatedly in Shakespeare, as for example in the Sonnets, in *Henry V* (2.3), and in *Timon of Athens.*

The below-stairs characters of the subplot, Sir Toby and the rest, share with Feste and Viola a commitment to joy. As Sir Toby proclaims in his first speech, "care's an enemy to life" (1.3.2–3). Even the simpleton Sir Andrew, although gulled by Sir Toby into spending his money on a hopeless pursuit of Olivia, seems none the worse for his treatment; he loves to drink in Sir Toby's company and can afford to pay for his entertainment. Sir Toby gives us some of the richly inventive humor of Falstaff, another lovable fat roguish knight. In this subplot, however, the confrontations between merriment and sobriety are more harshly drawn than in the main plot. Whereas the gracious Olivia is won away from her folly, the obdurate Malvolio can only be exposed to ridicule. He is chiefly to blame for the polarization of attitudes, for he insists on rebuking the mirth of others. His name (*Mal-volio,* the "ill-wisher") implies a self-satisfied determination to impose his rigid moral code on others. As Sir Toby taunts him, "Dost thou think, because thou art virtuous, there shall be no more cakes and ale?" (2.3.114–115). Malvolio's inflexible hostility provokes a desire for comic vengeance. The method is satiric: the clever manipulators, Maria and Sir Toby, invent a scheme to entrap Malvolio in his own self-deceit. The punishment fits the crime, for he has long dreamed of himself as "Count Malvolio," rich, powerful, and in a position to demolish Sir Toby and the rest. Without Malvolio's infatuated predisposition to believe that Olivia could actually love him and write such a letter as he finds, Maria's scheme would have no hope of success. He tortures the text to make it yield a suitable meaning, much in the style of Puritan theologizing. His conviction that Jove is with him (2.5.169) reminds us of the Puritan belief that prosperity of the "elect" is a sign of God's grace.

Indeed, Malvolio in some ways does resemble a Puritan, as Maria observes (2.3.139–147), even though she qualifies the assertion by saying that he is not a religious fanatic but a "time-pleaser." She directs her observation not at a religious group but at all who would be killjoys; if the Puritans are like that, she intimates, so much the worse for them. This uncharacteristic lack of charity gives a sharp tone to the vengeance practiced on Malvolio, evoking from Olivia a protestation that "he hath been most notoriously abused" (5.1.379). The belated attempt to make a reconciliation with him seems, however, doomed to failure, in light of his grim resolve to "be revenged on the whole pack of you." At the height of his discomfiture, he has been tricked into doing the two things he hates most: smiling affably and wearing sportive attire. The appearance of merriment is so grossly unsuited to him that he is declared mad and put into safekeeping. The apostle of sobriety in this play thus comes before us as a declared madman, while the fool Feste offers him sage comment in the guise of a priest. Wisdom and folly have changed places. The upside-down character of the play is epitomized in Malvolio's plaintive remark to Feste (no longer posing as the priest): "I am as well in my wits, Fool, as thou art" (4.2.88). Malvolio's comeuppance is richly deserved, but the severity of vengeance and counter-vengeance suggests that the triumph of festival will not last long. This brevity is, of course, inherent in the nature of such holiday release from responsibility. As Feste sings, "What's to come is still unsure. / In delay there lies no plenty."

Twelfth Night; or, What You Will

[*Dramatis Personae*

ORSINO, *Duke (or Count) of Illyria*
VALENTINE, *gentleman attending on Orsino*
CURIO, *gentleman attending on Orsino*

VIOLA, *a shipwrecked lady, later disguised as Cesario*
SEBASTIAN, *twin brother of Viola*
ANTONIO, *a sea captain, friend to Sebastian*
CAPTAIN *of the shipwrecked vessel*

OLIVIA, *a rich countess of Illyria*
MARIA, *gentlewoman in Olivia's household*
SIR TOBY BELCH, *Olivia's uncle*
SIR ANDREW AGUECHEEK, *a companion of Sir Toby*
MALVOLIO, *steward of Olivia's household*
FABIAN, *a member of Olivia's household*
FESTE, *a clown, also called* FOOL, *Olivia's jester*

A PRIEST
FIRST OFFICER
SECOND OFFICER

Lords, Sailors, Musicians, and other Attendants

SCENE: *A city in Illyria, and the seacoast near it*]

1.1   *Enter Orsino Duke of Illyria, Curio, and other lords [with musicians].*

ORSINO
If music be the food of love, play on;
Give me excess of it, that surfeiting,
The appetite may sicken and so die.
That strain again! It had a dying fall;   4
O, it came o'er my ear like the sweet sound
That breathes upon a bank of violets,
Stealing and giving odor. Enough, no more.
'Tis not so sweet now as it was before.
O spirit of love, how quick and fresh art thou,   9
That, notwithstanding thy capacity

1.1. Location: Orsino's court.
s.d. Illyria Nominally on the east coast of the Adriatic Sea, but with a suggestion also of "illusion" and "delirium."   **4 fall** cadence
9 quick and fresh keen and hungry

Receiveth as the sea, naught enters there,
Of what validity and pitch soe'er,   12
But falls into abatement and low price   13
Even in a minute! So full of shapes is fancy   14
That it alone is high fantastical.   15
CURIO
Will you go hunt, my lord?
ORSINO   What, Curio?
CURIO   The hart.
ORSINO
Why, so I do, the noblest that I have.   17
O, when mine eyes did see Olivia first,
Methought she purged the air of pestilence.
That instant was I turned into a hart,
And my desires, like fell and cruel hounds,   21
E'er since pursue me.

Enter Valentine.

                        How now, what news from her? 22
VALENTINE
So please my lord, I might not be admitted,
But from her handmaid do return this answer:
The element itself, till seven years' heat,   25
Shall not behold her face at ample view;
But like a cloistress she will veilèd walk,   27
And water once a day her chamber round
With eye-offending brine—all this to season   29
A brother's dead love, which she would keep fresh   30
And lasting in her sad remembrance.
ORSINO
O, she that hath a heart of that fine frame   32
To pay this debt of love but to a brother,
How will she love, when the rich golden shaft   34
Hath killed the flock of all affections else   35
That live in her; when liver, brain, and heart,   36
These sovereign thrones, are all supplied, and filled   37
Her sweet perfections, with one self king!   38
Away before me to sweet beds of flowers.
Love-thoughts lie rich when canopied with bowers.

                                              Exeunt.

❦

---

12 **validity** value. **pitch** superiority. (Literally, the highest point of a falcon's flight.)   13 **abatement** depreciation. (The lover's brain entertains innumerable fantasies but soon tires of them all.)   14 **shapes** imagined forms.   **fancy** love   15 **it . . . fantastical** it surpasses everything else in imaginative power   17 **the noblest . . . have** i.e., my noblest part, my heart (punning on *hart*)   21 **fell** fierce   22 **pursue me** (Alludes to the story in Ovid of Actaeon, who, having seen Diana bathing, was transformed into a stag and killed by his own hounds.) 25 **element** sky.   **seven years' heat** seven summers   27 **cloistress** nun secluded in a religious community   29 **season** keep fresh (playing on the idea of the salt in her tears)   30 **A brother's dead love** her love for her dead brother and the memory of his love for her 32 **frame** construction   34 **golden shaft** Cupid's golden-tipped arrow, causing love. (His lead-tipped arrow causes aversion.)   35 **affections else** other feelings   36 **liver, brain, and heart** (In medieval and Elizabethan psychology, these organs were the seats of the passions, of thought, and of feeling.)   37 **supplied** filled   37–38 **and . . . perfections** and her sweet perfections filled   38 **self king** single lord (the object of her entire affection)

1.2   *Enter Viola, a Captain, and sailors.*

VIOLA   What country, friends, is this?
CAPTAIN   This is Illyria, lady.
VIOLA
And what should I do in Illyria?
My brother he is in Elysium.   4
Perchance he is not drowned. What think you,
   sailors?   5
CAPTAIN
It is perchance that you yourself were saved.   6
VIOLA
O, my poor brother! And so perchance may he be.
CAPTAIN
True, madam, and to comfort you with chance,   8
Assure yourself, after our ship did split,
When you and those poor number saved with you
Hung on our driving boat, I saw your brother,   11
Most provident in peril, bind himself,
Courage and hope both teaching him the practice,
To a strong mast that lived upon the sea;   14
Where, like Arion on the dolphin's back,   15
I saw him hold acquaintance with the waves
So long as I could see.
VIOLA   For saying so, there's gold. [*She gives money.*]
Mine own escape unfoldeth to my hope,   19
Whereto thy speech serves for authority,   20
The like of him. Know'st thou this country?   21
CAPTAIN
Ay, madam, well, for I was bred and born
Not three hours' travel from this very place.
VIOLA   Who governs here?
CAPTAIN
A noble duke, in nature as in name.
VIOLA   What is his name?
CAPTAIN   Orsino.
VIOLA
Orsino! I have heard my father name him.
He was a bachelor then.
CAPTAIN
And so is now, or was so very late;
For but a month ago I went from hence,
And then 'twas fresh in murmur—as, you know,   32
What great ones do the less will prattle of—   33
That he did seek the love of fair Olivia.
VIOLA   What's she?
CAPTAIN
A virtuous maid, the daughter of a count
That died some twelvemonth since, then leaving her
In the protection of his son, her brother,

1.2 Location: The seacoast.
4 **Elysium** classical abode of the blessed dead   5–6 **Perchance . . . perchance** perhaps . . . by mere chance   8 **chance** i.e., what one may hope that chance will bring about   11 **driving** drifting, driven by the seas   14 **lived** i.e., kept afloat   15 **Arion** a Greek poet who so charmed the dolphins with his lyre that they saved him when he leaped into the sea to escape murderous sailors   19–21 **unfoldeth . . . him** offers a hopeful example that he may have escaped similarly, to which hope your speech provides support   32 **murmur** rumor   33 **less** social inferiors

Who shortly also died; for whose dear love,
They say, she hath abjured the sight
And company of men.
VIOLA   O, that I served that lady,
And might not be delivered to the world   42
Till I had made mine own occasion mellow,   43
What my estate is!
CAPTAIN   That were hard to compass,   44
Because she will admit no kind of suit,
No, not the Duke's.   46
VIOLA
There is a fair behavior in thee, Captain,
And though that nature with a beauteous wall   48
Doth oft close in pollution, yet of thee
I will believe thou hast a mind that suits
With this thy fair and outward character.   51
I prithee, and I'll pay thee bounteously,
Conceal me what I am, and be my aid
For such disguise as haply shall become   54
The form of my intent. I'll serve this duke.   55
Thou shalt present me as an eunuch to him.   56
It may be worth thy pains, for I can sing
And speak to him in many sorts of music
That will allow me very worth his service.   59
What else may hap, to time I will commit;
Only shape thou thy silence to my wit.   61
CAPTAIN
Be you his eunuch, and your mute I'll be;   62
When my tongue blabs, then let mine eyes not see.
VIOLA I thank thee. Lead me on.   *Exeunt.*

♣

1.3 *Enter Sir Toby [Belch] and Maria.*

SIR TOBY   What a plague means my niece to take the
death of her brother thus? I am sure care's an enemy
to life.
MARIA   By my troth, Sir Toby, you must come in earlier
o' nights. Your cousin, my lady, takes great exceptions 5
to your ill hours.
SIR TOBY   Why, let her except before excepted.   7
MARIA   Ay, but you must confine yourself within the
modest limits of order.   9
SIR TOBY   Confine? I'll confine myself no finer than I am. 10
These clothes are good enough to drink in, and so be

these boots too. An they be not, let them hang them-   12
selves in their own straps.
MARIA   That quaffing and drinking will undo you. I
heard my lady talk of it yesterday, and of a foolish
knight that you brought in one night here to be her
wooer.
SIR TOBY   Who, Sir Andrew Aguecheek?
MARIA   Ay, he.
SIR TOBY   He's as tall a man as any's in Illyria.   20
MARIA   What's that to the purpose?
SIR TOBY   Why, he has three thousand ducats a year.   22
MARIA   Ay, but he'll have but a year in all these ducats. 23
He's a very fool and a prodigal.
SIR TOBY   Fie, that you'll say so! He plays o' the viol-de- 25
gamboys, and speaks three or four languages word 26
for word without book, and hath all the good gifts of 27
nature.
MARIA   He hath indeed, almost natural, for, besides that 29
he's a fool, he's a great quarreler, and but that he hath
the gift of a coward to allay the gust he hath in quar- 31
reling, 'tis thought among the prudent he would
quickly have the gift of a grave.
SIR TOBY   By this hand, they are scoundrels and sub- 34
stractors that say so of him. Who are they?   35
MARIA   They that add, moreover, he's drunk nightly in
your company.
SIR TOBY   With drinking healths to my niece. I'll drink
to her as long as there is a passage in my throat and
drink in Illyria. He's a coward and a coistrel that will 40
not drink to my niece till his brains turn o' the toe like
a parish top. What, wench? *Castiliano vulgo!* For here 42
comes Sir Andrew Agueface.   43

Enter Sir Andrew [Aguecheek].

SIR ANDREW   Sir Toby Belch! How now, Sir Toby Belch?
SIR TOBY   Sweet Sir Andrew!
SIR ANDREW   [*to Maria*]   Bless you, fair shrew.   46
MARIA   And you too, sir.
SIR TOBY   Accost, Sir Andrew, accost.   48
SIR ANDREW   What's that?
SIR TOBY   My niece's chambermaid.   50
SIR ANDREW   Good Mistress Accost, I desire better
acquaintance.

---

42 delivered revealed, made known (with suggestion of "born")
43 mellow ready or convenient (to be made known) **44 estate** position in society. **compass** bring about, encompass **46 not** not even
48 though that though **51 character** face or features as indicating
moral qualities **54–55 as haply . . . intent** as may suit the nature of
my purpose **56 eunuch** castrato, high-voiced singer **59 allow**
prove **61 wit** plan, invention **62 mute** silent attendant (sometimes
used of nonspeaking actors)
1.3. Location: Olivia's house.
5 cousin kinswoman **7 let . . . excepted** i.e., let her take exception
to my conduct all she wants; I don't care. (Plays on the legal phrase
exceptis excipiendis, "with the exceptions before named.") **9 modest**
moderate **10 I'll . . . finer** (1) I'll constrain myself no more rigorously (2) I'll dress myself no more finely

12 An if **20 tall** brave. (But Maria pretends to take the word in the
common sense.) **22 ducats** coins worth about four or five shillings
23 he'll . . . ducats he'll spend all his money within a year **25–
26 viol-de-gamboys** viola da gamba, leg-viol, bass viol **27 without
book** by heart **29 natural** (with a play on the sense "born idiot")
31 gift natural ability. (But shifted to mean "present" in line 33.) **allay the gust** moderate the taste **34–35 substractors** i.e., detractors
40 coistrel horse-groom, base fellow **42 parish top** a large top provided by the parish to be spun by whipping, apparently for exercise.
Castiliano vulgo (Of uncertain meaning. Possibly Sir Toby is saying
"Speak of the devil!" Castiliano is the name adopted by a devil in
Haughton's *Grim the Collier of Croydon*.) **43 Agueface** (Like
Aguecheek, this name betokens the thin, pale countenance of one suffering from an ague.) **46 shrew** i.e., diminutive creature (but with
probably unintended suggestion of shrewishness) **48 Accost** go
alongside (a nautical term), i.e., greet her, address her **50 chambermaid** lady-in-waiting (a gentlewoman, not one who would do menial
tasks)

MARIA My name is Mary, sir.

SIR ANDREW Good Mistress Mary Accost—

SIR TOBY You mistake, knight. "Accost" is front her, board her, woo her, assail her. 55 56

SIR ANDREW By my troth, I would not undertake her in this company. Is that the meaning of "accost"? 57

MARIA Fare you well, gentlemen.   [Going.]

SIR TOBY An thou let part so, Sir Andrew, would thou mightst never draw sword again. 60

SIR ANDREW An you part so, mistress, I would I might never draw sword again. Fair lady, do you think you have fools in hand? 64

MARIA Sir, I have not you by the hand.

SIR ANDREW Marry, but you shall have, and here's my hand.   [He gives her his hand.] 66

MARIA Now, sir, thought is free. I pray you, bring your hand to the buttery-bar, and let it drink. 68 69

SIR ANDREW Wherefore, sweetheart? What's your metaphor?

MARIA It's dry, sir. 72

SIR ANDREW Why, I think so. I am not such an ass but I can keep my hand dry. But what's your jest?

MARIA A dry jest, sir. 75

SIR ANDREW Are you full of them?

MARIA Ay, sir, I have them at my fingers' ends. Marry, now I let go your hand, I am barren. 77 78
          [She lets go his hand.] Exit Maria.

SIR TOBY O knight, thou lack'st a cup of canary! When did I see thee so put down? 79

SIR ANDREW Never in your life, I think, unless you see canary put me down. Methinks sometimes I have no more wit than a Christian or an ordinary man has. But I am a great eater of beef, and I believe that does harm to my wit. 82

SIR TOBY No question.

SIR ANDREW An I thought that, I'd forswear it. I'll ride home tomorrow, Sir Toby.

SIR TOBY Pourquoi, my dear knight? 89

SIR ANDREW What is "pourquoi"? Do or not do? I would I had bestowed that time in the tongues that I have in fencing, dancing, and bearbaiting. O, had I but followed the arts! 91 93

SIR TOBY Then hadst thou had an excellent head of hair.

SIR ANDREW Why, would that have mended my hair? 95

SIR TOBY Past question, for thou seest it will not curl by nature.

SIR ANDREW But it becomes me well enough, does 't not?

SIR TOBY Excellent. It hangs like flax on a distaff; and I hope to see a huswife take thee between her legs and spin it off. 100 102

SIR ANDREW Faith, I'll home tomorrow, Sir Toby. Your niece will not be seen, or if she be, it's four to one she'll none of me. The Count himself here hard by woos her. 105

SIR TOBY She'll none o' the Count. She'll not match above her degree, neither in estate, years, nor wit; I have heard her swear 't. Tut, there's life in 't, man. 108 109

SIR ANDREW I'll stay a month longer. I am a fellow o' the strangest mind i' the world; I delight in masques and revels sometimes altogether.

SIR TOBY Art thou good at these kickshawses, knight? 113

SIR ANDREW As any man in Illyria, whatsoever he be, under the degree of my betters, and yet I will not compare with an old man. 115 116

SIR TOBY What is thy excellence in a galliard, knight? 117

SIR ANDREW Faith, I can cut a caper. 118

SIR TOBY And I can cut the mutton to 't.

SIR ANDREW And I think I have the back-trick simply as strong as any man in Illyria. 120

SIR TOBY Wherefore are these things hid? Wherefore have these gifts a curtain before 'em? Are they like to take dust, like Mistress Mall's picture? Why dost thou not go to church in a galliard and come home in a coranto? My very walk should be a jig; I would not so much as make water but in a sink-a-pace. What dost thou mean? Is it a world to hide virtues in? I did think, by the excellent constitution of thy leg, it was formed under the star of a galliard. 123 124 126 127 128 130

SIR ANDREW Ay, 'tis strong, and it does indifferent well in a dun-colored stock. Shall we set about some revels? 131 132

SIR TOBY What shall we do else? Were we not born under Taurus? 135

55 front confront, come alongside 56 board greet, approach (as though preparing to board in a naval encounter) 57 undertake have to do with (here with unintended sexual suggestion, to which Maria mirthfully replies with her jokes about dry jests, barren, and buttery-bar) 60 An . . . part if you let her leave 64 have . . . hand i.e., have to deal with fools. (But Maria puns on the literal sense.) 66 Marry i.e., indeed. (Originally, "By the Virgin Mary.") 68 thought is free i.e., I may think what I like. (Proverbial; replying to do you think . . . in hand, above.) 69 buttery-bar ledge on top of the half-door to the buttery or the wine cellar 72 dry thirsty; also dried up, a sign of age and sexual debility 75 dry (1) ironic (2) dull, barren (referring to Sir Andrew) 77 at my fingers' ends (1) at the ready (2) by the hand 78 barren i.e., empty of jests and of Sir Andrew's hand 79 thou . . . canary i.e., you look as if you need a drink. (Canary is a sweet wine from the Canary Islands.) 82 put me down (1) baffle my wits (2) lay me out flat 89 Pourquoi why 91 tongues languages. (Sir Toby then puns on "tongs," curling irons.) 93 the arts the liberal arts, learning. (But Sir Toby plays on the phrase as meaning "artifice," the antithesis of nature.) 95 mended improved

100 distaff a staff for holding the flax, tow, or wool in spinning 102 spin it off i.e., (1) treat your flaxen hair as though it were flax on a distaff to be spun (2) cause you to lose hair as a result of venereal disease. (Huswife suggests "hussy," "whore.") 105 Count i.e., Duke Orsino, sometimes referred to as Count. hard near 108 degree social position. estate fortune, social position 109 there's life in 't i.e., while there's life there's hope 113 kickshawses delicacies, fancy trifles. (From the French, quelque chose.) 115 under . . . betters excepting those who are above me 116 old man i.e., one experienced through age 117 galliard lively dance in triple time 118 cut a caper make a lively leap. (But Sir Toby puns on the caper used to make a sauce served with mutton. Mutton, in turn, suggests "whore.") 120 back-trick backward step in the galliard 123–124 like to take likely to collect 124 Mistress Mall's picture i.e., perhaps the portrait of some woman protected from light and dust, as many pictures were, by curtains 126 coranto lively running dance 127 sink-a-pace dance like the galliard. (French cinquepace.) 128 virtues talents 130 under . . . galliard i.e., under a star favorable to dancing 131 indifferent well well enough. (Said complacently.) 132 dun-colored stock mouse-colored stocking 135 Taurus zodiacal sign. (Sir Andrew is mistaken, since Leo governed sides and hearts in medical astrology. Taurus governed legs and thighs, or, more commonly, neck and throat.)

SIR ANDREW   Taurus? That's sides and heart.

SIR TOBY   No, sir, it is legs and thighs. Let me see thee caper. [*Sir Andrew capers.*] Ha, higher! Ha, ha, excellent! *Exeunt.*

❖

1.4   *Enter Valentine, and Viola in man's attire.*

VALENTINE   If the Duke continue these favors towards you, Cesario, you are like to be much advanced. He hath known you but three days, and already you are no stranger.

VIOLA   You either fear his humor or my negligence, that you call in question the continuance of his love. Is he inconstant, sir, in his favors? 5

VALENTINE   No, believe me.

Enter Duke [Orsino], Curio, and attendants.

VIOLA   I thank you. Here comes the Count.

ORSINO   Who saw Cesario, ho?

VIOLA   On your attendance, my lord, here. 11

ORSINO
Stand you awhile aloof. [*The others stand aside.*] Cesario,
Thou know'st no less but all. I have unclasped
To thee the book even of my secret soul.
Therefore, good youth, address thy gait unto her; 15
Be not denied access, stand at her doors,
And tell them, there thy fixèd foot shall grow 17
Till thou have audience.

VIOLA   Sure, my noble lord,
If she be so abandoned to her sorrow
As it is spoke, she never will admit me.

ORSINO
Be clamorous and leap all civil bounds 21
Rather than make unprofited return.

VIOLA
Say I do speak with her, my lord, what then?

ORSINO
O, then unfold the passion of my love;
Surprise her with discourse of my dear faith. 25
It shall become thee well to act my woes; 26
She will attend it better in thy youth
Than in a nuncio's of more grave aspect. 28

VIOLA
I think not so, my lord.

ORSINO   Dear lad, believe it;
For they shall yet belie thy happy years
That say thou art a man. Diana's lip
Is not more smooth and rubious; thy small pipe 32
Is as the maiden's organ, shrill and sound, 33
And all is semblative a woman's part. 34

I know thy constellation is right apt 35
For this affair.—Some four or five attend him.
All, if you will, for I myself am best
When least in company.—Prosper well in this,
And thou shalt live as freely as thy lord,
To call his fortunes thine.

VIOLA   I'll do my best
To woo your lady. [*Aside.*] Yet a barful strife! 41
Whoe'er I woo, myself would be his wife.   *Exeunt.*

❖

1.5   *Enter Maria and Clown [Feste].*

MARIA   Nay, either tell me where thou hast been, or I will not open my lips so wide as a bristle may enter in way of thy excuse. My lady will hang thee for thy absence.

FESTE   Let her hang me. He that is well hanged in this world needs to fear no colors. 6

MARIA   Make that good. 7

FESTE   He shall see none to fear. 8

MARIA   A good Lenten answer. I can tell thee where that saying was born, of "I fear no colors." 9

FESTE   Where, good Mistress Mary?

MARIA   In the wars, and that may you be bold to say in your foolery. 12,13

FESTE   Well, God give them wisdom that have it; and those that are fools, let them use their talents. 15

MARIA   Yet you will be hanged for being so long absent; or to be turned away, is not that as good as a hanging to you? 17

FESTE   Many a good hanging prevents a bad marriage; and for turning away, let summer bear it out. 19,20

MARIA   You are resolute, then?

FESTE   Not so, neither, but I am resolved on two points. 23

MARIA   That if one break, the other will hold; or if both break, your gaskins fall. 25

FESTE   Apt, in good faith, very apt. Well, go thy way. If Sir Toby would leave drinking, thou wert as witty a piece of Eve's flesh as any in Illyria. 27,28

35 constellation i.e., nature as determined by your horoscope
41 barful strife endeavor full of impediments
1.5. Location: Olivia's house.
6 fear no colors i.e., fear no foe, fear nothing (with pun on *colors*, worldly deceptions, and "collars," halters or nooses)   **7 Make that good** explain that   **8 He . . . fear** i.e., he'll be dead and unable to see anything   **9 Lenten** meager, scanty (like Lenten fare), and morbid   **12 In the wars** (where *colors* would mean "military standards, enemy flags"—the literal meaning of the proverb)   **12–13 that . . . foolery** that's an answer you may be bold to use in your fool's conundrums   **15 talents** abilities (also alluding to the parable of the talents, Matthew 25:14–29, and to "talons," claws)   **17 turned away** dismissed (possibly also meaning "turned off," "hanged")   **19 good hanging** (with possible bawdy pun on "being well hung")   **20 for** as for.   **let . . . out** i.e., let mild weather make dismissal endurable   **23 points** (Maria plays on the meaning "laces used to hold up hose or breeches.")   **25 gaskins** wide breeches   **27–28 thou . . . Illyria** (Feste may be observing ironically that Maria is as likely to prove witty as Sir Toby is to give up drinking; or he may hint at a match between the two.)

1.4. Location: Orsino's court.
5 humor changeableness   **11 On your attendance** ready to do you service   **15 address thy gait** go   **17 them** i.e., Olivia's servants   **21 civil bounds** bounds of civility   **25 Surprise** take by storm. (A military term.)   **dear** heartfelt   **26 become** suit   **28 nuncio's** messenger's   **32 rubious** ruby red.   **pipe** voice, throat   **33 shrill and sound** high and clear, uncracked   **34 semblative** resembling, like

MARIA Peace, you rogue, no more o' that. Here comes my lady. Make your excuse wisely, you were best. 30

[Exit.]

Enter Lady Olivia with Malvolio, [and attendants].

FESTE *[aside]* Wit, an 't be thy will, put me into good 31 fooling! Those wits that think they have thee do very oft prove fools, and I that am sure I lack thee may pass for a wise man. For what says Quinapalus? "Better a 34 witty fool than a foolish wit." —God bless thee, lady!

OLIVIA *[to attendants]* Take the fool away.

FESTE Do you not hear, fellows? Take away the lady.

OLIVIA Go to, you're a dry fool. I'll no more of you. 38 Besides, you grow dishonest.

FESTE Two faults, madonna, that drink and good 40 counsel will amend. For give the dry fool drink, then is the fool not dry. Bid the dishonest man mend himself; if he mend, he is no longer dishonest; if he cannot, let the botcher mend him. Anything that's 44 mended is but patched; virtue that transgresses is but 45 patched with sin, and sin that amends is but patched with virtue. If that this simple syllogism will serve, so; 47 if it will not, what remedy? As there is no true cuckold 48 but calamity, so beauty's a flower. The lady bade take 49 away the fool; therefore I say again, take her away.

OLIVIA Sir, I bade them take away you.

FESTE Misprision in the highest degree! Lady, *cucullus* 52 *non facit monachum;* that's as much to say as I wear not 53 motley in my brain. Good madonna, give me leave to 54 prove you a fool.

OLIVIA Can you do it?

FESTE Dexterously, good madonna.

OLIVIA Make your proof.

FESTE I must catechize you for it, madonna. Good my 59 mouse of virtue, answer me. 60

OLIVIA Well, sir, for want of other idleness, I'll bide 61 your proof.

FESTE Good madonna, why mourn'st thou?

OLIVIA Good fool, for my brother's death.

FESTE I think his soul is in hell, madonna.

OLIVIA I know his soul is in heaven, fool.

FESTE The more fool, madonna, to mourn for your brother's soul, being in heaven. Take away the fool, gentlemen.

OLIVIA What think you of this fool, Malvolio? Doth he not mend? 71

MALVOLIO Yes, and shall do till the pangs of death shake him. Infirmity, that decays the wise, doth ever make the better fool.

FESTE God send you, sir, a speedy infirmity for the better increasing your folly! Sir Toby will be sworn that I am no fox, but he will not pass his word for 77 twopence that you are no fool.

OLIVIA How say you to that, Malvolio?

MALVOLIO I marvel your ladyship takes delight in such a barren rascal. I saw him put down the other day with an ordinary fool that has no more brain than a 82 stone. Look you now, he's out of his guard already. 83 Unless you laugh and minister occasion to him, he is 84 gagged. I protest I take these wise men that crow so at 85 these set kind of fools no better than the fools' zanies. 86

OLIVIA O, you are sick of self-love, Malvolio, and taste with a distempered appetite. To be generous, guiltless, 88 and of free disposition is to take those things for bird- 89 bolts that you deem cannon bullets. There is no slan- 90 der in an allowed fool, though he do nothing but rail; 91 nor no railing in a known discreet man, though he do 92 nothing but reprove. 93

FESTE Now Mercury endue thee with leasing, for thou 94 speak'st well of fools!

Enter Maria.

MARIA Madam, there is at the gate a young gentleman much desires to speak with you.

OLIVIA From the Count Orsino, is it?

MARIA I know not, madam. 'Tis a fair young man, and well attended.

OLIVIA Who of my people hold him in delay?

MARIA Sir Toby, madam, your kinsman.

OLIVIA Fetch him off, I pray you. He speaks nothing but madman. Fie on him! *[Exit Maria.]* Go you, Mal- 104 volio. If it be a suit from the Count, I am sick, or not at home; what you will, to dismiss it. *(Exit Malvolio.)* Now you see, sir, how your fooling grows old, and people dislike it.

FESTE Thou hast spoke for us, madonna, as if thy eldest son should be a fool; whose skull Jove cram with brains, for—here he comes—

Enter Sir Toby.

one of thy kin has a most weak *pia mater.* 112

OLIVIA By mine honor, half drunk. What is he at the gate, cousin?

SIR TOBY A gentleman.

OLIVIA A gentleman? What gentleman?

---

30 you were best it would be best for you **31 an 't** if it
34 Quinapalus (Feste's invented authority.) **38 Go to** (An expression of annoyance or expostulation.) **dry** dull **40 madonna** my lady
44 botcher mender of old clothes and shoes (playing on two senses of *mend:* "reform" and "repair") **44–45 Anything . . . patched** i.e., life is patched or parti-colored like the Fool's garment, a mix of good and bad **47 so** well and good **48–49 As . . . flower** i.e., Olivia has wedded calamity but will not be faithful to it, for the natural course is to seize the moment of youth and beauty before we lose it
52 Misprision mistake, misunderstanding. (A legal term meaning a wrongful action or misdemeanor.) **52–53 cucullus . . . monachum** the cowl does not make the monk **54 motley** the many-colored garment of jesters **59–60 Good . . . virtue** my good, virtuous mouse. (A term of endearment.) **61 idleness** pastime. **bide** endure
71 mend i.e., improve, grow more amusing. (But Malvolio uses the word to mean "grow more like a fool.")

77 pass give **82 with** by **83 out of his guard** defenseless, unprovided with a witty answer **84 minister occasion** provide opportunity (for his fooling) **85 protest** avow, declare. **crow** laugh stridently **86 set** artificial, stereotyped. **zanies** assistants, aping attendants
88 distempered diseased. **generous** noble-minded **89 free** magnanimous **89–90 bird-bolts** blunt arrows for shooting small birds
91 allowed licensed (to speak freely) **92–93 nor . . . reprove** (Olivia gently chides Malvolio for not reproving more civilly, while at the same time tactfully complimenting his sobriety). **94 Now . . . leasing** i.e., may Mercury, the god of deception, make you a skillful liar **104 madman** i.e., the words of madness **112 pia mater** i.e., brain (actually the soft membrane enclosing the brain)

SIR TOBY   'Tis a gentleman here—[*He belches.*] A plague
o' these pickle-herring! [*To Feste.*] How now, sot?   118
FESTE   Good Sir Toby.
OLIVIA   Cousin, cousin, how have you come so early by   120
this lethargy?
SIR TOBY   Lechery? I defy lechery. There's one at the
gate.
OLIVIA   Ay, marry, what is he?
SIR TOBY   Let him be the devil an he will, I care not.
Give me faith, say I. Well, it's all one.   *Exit.*   126
OLIVIA   What's a drunken man like, Fool?
FESTE   Like a drowned man, a fool, and a madman.
One draft above heat makes him a fool, the second   129
mads him, and a third drowns him.
OLIVIA   Go thou and seek the crowner, and let him sit   131
o' my coz; for he's in the third degree of drink, he's   132
drowned. Go, look after him.
FESTE   He is but mad yet, madonna; and the fool shall
look to the madman.   [*Exit.*]

Enter Malvolio.

MALVOLIO   Madam, yond young fellow swears he will
speak with you. I told him you were sick; he takes on
him to understand so much, and therefore comes to
speak with you. I told him you were asleep; he seems
to have a foreknowledge of that too, and therefore
comes to speak with you. What is to be said to him,
lady? He's fortified against any denial.
OLIVIA   Tell him he shall not speak with me.
MALVOLIO   He's been told so; and he says he'll stand at
your door like a sheriff's post, and be the supporter to   145
a bench, but he'll speak with you.
OLIVIA   What kind o' man is he?
MALVOLIO   Why, of mankind.
OLIVIA   What manner of man?
MALVOLIO   Of very ill manner. He'll speak with you,
will you or no.
OLIVIA   Of what personage and years is he?
MALVOLIO   Not yet old enough for a man, nor young
enough for a boy; as a squash is before 'tis a peascod,   154
or a codling when 'tis almost an apple. 'Tis with him in   155
standing water between boy and man. He is very   156
well-favored, and he speaks very shrewishly. One   157
would think his mother's milk were scarce out
of him.
OLIVIA   Let him approach. Call in my gentlewoman.
MALVOLIO   Gentlewoman, my lady calls.   *Exit.*

Enter Maria.

OLIVIA
Give me my veil. Come, throw it o'er my face.

We'll once more hear Orsino's embassy. [*Olivia veils.*]

Enter Viola.

VIOLA   The honorable lady of the house, which is she?
OLIVIA   Speak to me; I shall answer for her. Your will?
VIOLA   Most radiant, exquisite, and unmatchable
beauty —I pray you, tell me if this be the lady of the
house, for I never saw her. I would be loath to cast
away my speech; for besides that it is excellently well
penned, I have taken great pains to con it. Good   170
beauties, let me sustain no scorn; I am very comptible,   171
even to the least sinister usage.   172
OLIVIA   Whence came you, sir?
VIOLA   I can say little more than I have studied, and
that question's out of my part. Good gentle one, give
me modest assurance if you be the lady of the house,   176
that I may proceed in my speech.
OLIVIA   Are you a comedian?   178
VIOLA   No, my profound heart; and yet, by the very   179
fangs of malice, I swear I am not that I play. Are you   180
the lady of the house?
OLIVIA   If I do not usurp myself, I am.   182
VIOLA   Most certain, if you are she, you do usurp your-   183
self; for what is yours to bestow is not yours to reserve.   184
But this is from my commission. I will on with my   185
speech in your praise, and then show you the heart of
my message.
OLIVIA   Come to what is important in 't. I forgive you   188
the praise.
VIOLA   Alas, I took great pains to study it, and 'tis
poetical.
OLIVIA   It is the more like to be feigned. I pray you,
keep it in. I heard you were saucy at my gates, and
allowed your approach rather to wonder at you than
to hear you. If you be not mad, begone; if you have   195
reason, be brief. 'Tis not that time of moon with me to   196
make one in so skipping a dialogue.   197
MARIA   Will you hoist sail, sir? Here lies your way.
VIOLA   No, good swabber, I am to hull here a little   199
longer.—Some mollification for your giant, sweet   200
lady. Tell me your mind; I am a messenger.
OLIVIA   Sure you have some hideous matter to deliver,
when the courtesy of it is so fearful. Speak your office.   203

118 sot (1) fool (2) drunkard   120 Cousin kinsman (here, uncle)
126 Give me faith i.e., to resist the devil.   it's all one it doesn't matter   129 draft drinking portion.   above heat above the point needed
to make him normally warm   131 crowner coroner   131–132 sit o'
my coz hold an inquest on my kinsman (Sir Toby)   145 sheriff's
post post before the sheriff's door to mark a residence of authority
154 squash unripe pea pod.   peascod pea pod   155 codling unripe
apple   155–156 in standing water at the turn of the tide   157 well-
favored good-looking.   shrewishly sharply

170 con learn by heart   171 comptible susceptible, sensitive
172 least sinister slightest discourteous   176 modest reasonable
178 comedian actor   179 my profound heart my most wise lady; or,
in all sincerity   179–180 by . . . I play i.e., I swear, whatever people may maliciously suppose, I am not what I impersonate   182 do
. . . myself am not an impostor   183–184 usurp yourself i.e., mis-
appropriate yourself, by withholding yourself from love and marriage
185 from outside of   188 forgive you excuse you from repeating
195 If . . . mad i.e., if you don't have madness to excuse your saucy
behavior, or, if you be not altogether mad(?). Possibly an error for *If
. . . but mad* (?)   196 reason sanity.   moon (The moon was thought
to affect lunatics according to its changing phases.)   197 make one
take part   199 swabber one in charge of washing the decks. (A nautical retort to *hoist sail.*)   hull lie with sails furled   200 Some . . . for
i.e., please mollify, pacify.   giant i.e., the diminutive Maria who,
like many giants in medieval romances, is guarding the lady
203 courtesy i.e., complimentary, "poetical" introduction. (Or Olivia
may refer to Cesario's importunate manner at her gate, as reported by
Malvolio.)   office commission, business

VIOLA   It alone concerns your ear. I bring no overture of 204
war, no taxation of homage. I hold the olive in my 205
hand; my words are as full of peace as matter.
OLIVIA   Yet you began rudely. What are you? What 207
would you?
VIOLA   The rudeness that hath appeared in me have I
learned from my entertainment. What I am and what 210
I would are as secret as maidenhead—to your ears,
divinity; to any other's, profanation. 212
OLIVIA   Give us the place alone. We will hear this
divinity. [*Exeunt Maria and attendants.*] Now, sir, what
is your text?
VIOLA   Most sweet lady—
OLIVIA   A comfortable doctrine, and much may be said 217
of it. Where lies your text?
VIOLA   In Orsino's bosom.
OLIVIA   In his bosom? In what chapter of his bosom?
VIOLA   To answer by the method, in the first of his 221
heart.
OLIVIA   O, I have read it. It is heresy. Have you no
more to say?
VIOLA   Good madam, let me see your face.
OLIVIA   Have you any commission from your lord to
negotiate with my face? You are now out of your text. 227
But we will draw the curtain and show you the
picture. [*Unveiling.*] Look you, sir, such a one I was 229
this present. Is 't not well done? 230
VIOLA   Excellently done, if God did all.
OLIVIA   'Tis in grain, sir; 'twill endure wind and 232
weather.
VIOLA
'Tis beauty truly blent, whose red and white 234
Nature's own sweet and cunning hand laid on. 235
Lady, you are the cruel'st she alive
If you will lead these graces to the grave
And leave the world no copy. 238
OLIVIA   O, sir, I will not be so hardhearted. I will give
out divers schedules of my beauty. It shall be inven- 240
toried, and every particle and utensil labeled to my 241
will: as, item, two lips, indifferent red; item, two gray 242
eyes, with lids to them; item, one neck, one chin, and
so forth. Were you sent hither to praise me? 244
VIOLA
I see you what you are: you are too proud.
But, if you were the devil, you are fair. 246
My lord and master loves you. O, such love

Could be but recompensed, though you were
crowned 248
The nonpareil of beauty!
OLIVIA   How does he love me?
VIOLA
With adorations, fertile tears, 250
With groans that thunder love, with sighs of fire.
OLIVIA
Your lord does know my mind; I cannot love him.
Yet I suppose him virtuous, know him noble,
Of great estate, of fresh and stainless youth,
In voices well divulged, free, learned, and valiant, 255
And in dimension and the shape of nature 256
A gracious person. But yet I cannot love him. 257
He might have took his answer long ago.
VIOLA
If I did love you in my master's flame, 259
With such a suffering, such a deadly life, 260
In your denial I would find no sense;
I would not understand it.
OLIVIA   Why, what would you?
VIOLA
Make me a willow cabin at your gate 263
And call upon my soul within the house; 264
Write loyal cantons of contemnèd love 265
And sing them loud even in the dead of night;
Hallow your name to the reverberate hills, 267
And make the babbling gossip of the air 268
Cry out "Olivia!" O, you should not rest
Between the elements of air and earth
But you should pity me!
OLIVIA   You might do much.
What is your parentage?
VIOLA
Above my fortunes, yet my state is well: 273
I am a gentleman.
OLIVIA   Get you to your lord.
I cannot love him. Let him send no more—
Unless, perchance, you come to me again
To tell me how he takes it. Fare you well.
I thank you for your pains. Spend this for me.
[*She offers a purse.*]
VIOLA
I am no fee'd post, lady. Keep your purse. 279
My master, not myself, lacks recompense.
Love make his heart of flint that you shall love, 281
And let your fervor, like my master's, be
Placed in contempt! Farewell, fair cruelty.   *Exit.*
OLIVIA   "What is your parentage?"
"Above my fortunes, yet my state is well:

---

204 overture declaration. (Literally, opening.)   **205 taxation** demand
for the payment.   **olive** olive-branch (signifying peace)   **207 Yet . . .
rudely** i.e., yet you were saucy at my gates   **210 entertainment** reception   **212 divinity** sacred discourse   **217 comfortable** comforting
221 To . . . method i.e., to continue the metaphor (of delivering a
sermon, begun with *divinity* and *what is your text* and continued in
doctrine, heresy, etc.)   **227 out of** straying from   **229–230 such . . .
present** this is a recent portrait of me. (Since it was customary to hang
curtains in front of pictures, Olivia in unveiling speaks as if she were
displaying a picture of herself.)   **232 in grain** fast dyed   **234 blent**
blended   **235 cunning** skillful   **238 copy** i.e., a child. (But Olivia
uses the word to mean "transcript.")   **240 schedules** inventories
241 utensil article, item.   **labeled** added as a codicil   **242 indifferent**
somewhat   **244 praise** (with pun on "appraise")   **246 if** even if

248 but . . . though no more than evenly repaid even though
250 fertile copious   **255 In . . . divulged** well spoken of.   **free** generous   **256 in . . . nature** in his physical form   **257 gracious** graceful, attractive   **259 flame** passion   **260 deadly** deathlike   **263 willow
cabin** shelter, hut. (Willow was a symbol of unrequited love.)
264 my soul i.e., Olivia   **265 cantons** songs.   **contemnèd** rejected
267 Hallow (1) halloo (2) bless   **268 babbling . . . air** echo
273 state social standing   **279 fee'd post** messenger to be tipped
281 Love . . . love may Love make the heart of the man you love as
hard as flint

I am a gentleman." I'll be sworn thou art!
Thy tongue, thy face, thy limbs, actions, and spirit
Do give thee fivefold blazon. Not too fast! Soft, soft!   288
Unless the master were the man. How now?   289
Even so quickly may one catch the plague?
Methinks I feel this youth's perfections
With an invisible and subtle stealth
To creep in at mine eyes. Well, let it be.
What ho, Malvolio!

Enter Malvolio.

MALVOLIO   Here, madam, at your service.
OLIVIA
Run after that same peevish messenger,
The County's man. He left this ring behind him,   296
                              [*giving a ring*]
Would I or not. Tell him I'll none of it.   297
Desire him not to flatter with his lord,   298
Nor hold him up with hopes; I am not for him.
If that the youth will come this way tomorrow,
I'll give him reasons for 't. Hie thee, Malvolio.
MALVOLIO   Madam, I will.   *Exit*
OLIVIA
I do I know not what, and fear to find
Mine eye too great a flatterer for my mind.   304
Fate, show thy force. Ourselves we do not owe.   305
What is decreed must be; and be this so.   [*Exit.*]

2.1   *Enter Antonio and Sebastian.*

ANTONIO   Will you stay no longer? Nor will you not   1
that I go with you?
SEBASTIAN   By your patience, no. My stars shine darkly   3
over me. The malignancy of my fate might perhaps   4
distemper yours; therefore I shall crave of you your   5
leave that I may bear my evils alone. It were a bad
recompense for your love to lay any of them on you.
ANTONIO   Let me yet know of you whither you are
bound.
SEBASTIAN   No, sooth, sir; my determinate voyage is   10
mere extravagancy. But I perceive in you so excellent   11
a touch of modesty that you will not extort from me
what I am willing to keep in; therefore it charges me in   13
manners the rather to express myself. You must know   14
of me then, Antonio, my name is Sebastian, which I

called Roderigo. My father was that Sebastian of
Messaline whom I know you have heard of. He left   17
behind him myself and a sister, both born in an hour.   18
If the heavens had been pleased, would we had so
ended! But you, sir, altered that, for some hour before   20
you took me from the breach of the sea was my sister   21
drowned.
ANTONIO   Alas the day!
SEBASTIAN   A lady, sir, though it was said she much resembled me, was yet of many accounted beautiful. But
though I could not with such estimable wonder over-   26
far believe that, yet thus far I will boldly publish her: 27
she bore a mind that envy could not but call fair. She   28
is drowned already, sir, with salt water, though I seem
to drown her remembrance again with more.
ANTONIO   Pardon me, sir, your bad entertainment.   31
SEBASTIAN   O good Antonio, forgive me your trouble.   32
ANTONIO   If you will not murder me for my love, let me   33
be your servant.
SEBASTIAN   If you will not undo what you have done,
that is, kill him whom you have recovered, desire it   36
not. Fare ye well at once. My bosom is full of
kindness, and I am yet so near the manners of my   38
mother that upon the least occasion more mine eyes   39
will tell tales of me. I am bound to the Count Orsino's
court. Farewell.   *Exit.*
ANTONIO
The gentleness of all the gods go with thee!
I have many enemies in Orsino's court,
Else would I very shortly see thee there.
But come what may, I do adore thee so
That danger shall seem sport, and I will go.   *Exit.*

❖

2.2   *Enter Viola and Malvolio, at several doors.*

MALVOLIO   Were not you even now with the Countess
Olivia?
VIOLA   Even now, sir. On a moderate pace I have since
arrived but hither.
MALVOLIO   She returns this ring to you, sir. You might
have saved me my pains, to have taken it away   6
yourself. She adds, moreover, that you should put
your lord into a desperate assurance she will none of   8
him. And one thing more: that you be never so hardy   9
to come again in his affairs, unless it be to report your   10
lord's taking of this. Receive it so.

---

288 **blazon** heraldic description.   **Soft** wait a minute   289 **Unless
. . . man** i.e., unless Cesario and Orsino changed places   296 **County's** Count's, i.e., Duke's   297 **Would I or not** whether I wanted it or
not   298 **flatter with** encourage   304 **Mine . . . mind** i.e., that my
eyes (through which love enters the soul) have betrayed my reason by
giving a flattering view of Cesario   305 **owe** own, control
2.1. Location: Somewhere in Illyria.
1 **Nor will you not** do you not wish   3 **patience** leave   4 **malignancy**
malevolence (of the stars; also in a medical sense)   5 **distemper** infect
10 **sooth** truly.   **determinate** intended, determined upon   11 **extravagancy** aimless wandering   13 **am willing . . . in** wish to keep secret
13–14 **it . . . . manners** it is incumbent upon me in all courtesy
14 **express** reveal

17 **Messaline** possibly Messina, or, more likely, Massila (the modern
Marseilles). In Plautus' *Menaechmi*, Massilians and Illyrians are mentioned together.   18 **in an hour** in the same hour   20 **some hour**
about an hour   21 **breach of the sea** surf   26 **estimable wonder** admiring judgment   27 **publish** proclaim   28 **envy** even malice   31 **entertainment** reception, hospitality   32 **your trouble** the trouble I put
you to   33 **murder me for** i.e., be the cause of my death in return for
36 **recovered** rescued, restored   38 **kindness** tenderness, natural emotion (of grief)   38–39 **manners of my mother** i.e., womanly inclination to weep
2.2. Location: Outside Olivia's house.
s.d. several different   6 **to have taken** by taking   8 **desperate** without
hope   9–10 **hardy to come** bold as to come

VIOLA   She took the ring of me. I'll none of it.   12
MALVOLIO   Come, sir, you peevishly threw it to her, and her will is it should be so returned. [*He throws down the ring.*] If it be worth stooping for, there it lies, in your eye; if not, be it his that finds it.   *Exit.*   16
VIOLA [*picking up the ring*]
I left no ring with her. What means this lady?
Fortune forbid my outside have not charmed her!   18
She made good view of me, indeed so much
That sure methought her eyes had lost her tongue,   20
For she did speak in starts, distractedly.
She loves me, sure! The cunning of her passion
Invites me in this churlish messenger.   23
None of my lord's ring? Why, he sent her none.
I am the man. If it be so—as 'tis—   25
Poor lady, she were better love a dream.
Disguise, I see, thou art a wickedness
Wherein the pregnant enemy does much.   28
How easy is it for the proper false   29
In women's waxen hearts to set their forms!   30
Alas, our frailty is the cause, not we,
For such as we are made of, such we be.   32
How will this fadge? My master loves her dearly,   33
And I, poor monster, fond as much on him;   34
And she, mistaken, seems to dote on me.
What will become of this? As I am man,
My state is desperate for my master's love;
As I am woman—now, alas the day!—
What thriftless sighs shall poor Olivia breathe!   39
O Time, thou must untangle this, not I;
It is too hard a knot for me t' untie.   [*Exit.*]

❧

2.3   *Enter Sir Toby and Sir Andrew.*

SIR TOBY   Approach, Sir Andrew. Not to be abed after midnight is to be up betimes; and *diluculo surgere,* thou know'st—   2
SIR ANDREW   Nay, by my troth, I know not, but I know to be up late is to be up late.
SIR TOBY   A false conclusion. I hate it as an unfilled can.   6
To be up after midnight and to go to bed then, is early; so that to go to bed after midnight is to go to bed betimes. Does not our lives consist of the four elements?   9
   10
SIR ANDREW   Faith, so they say, but I think it rather consists of eating and drinking.

SIR TOBY   Thou'rt a scholar; let us therefore eat and drink. Marian, I say, a stoup of wine!   14

   Enter Clown [Feste].

SIR ANDREW   Here comes the Fool, i' faith.
FESTE   How now, my hearts! Did you never see the picture of "we three"?   17
SIR TOBY   Welcome, ass. Now let's have a catch.   18
SIR ANDREW   By my troth, the Fool has an excellent breast. I had rather than forty shillings I had such a   20
leg, and so sweet a breath to sing, as the fool has. In sooth, thou wast in very gracious fooling last night, when thou spok'st of Pigrogromitus, of the Vapians   23
passing the equinoctial of Queubus. 'Twas very good,   24
i' faith. I sent thee sixpence for thy leman. Hadst it?   25
FESTE   I did impeticos thy gratillity; for Malvolio's nose   26
is no whipstock. My lady has a white hand, and the   27
Myrmidons are no bottle-ale houses.   28
SIR ANDREW   Excellent! Why, this is the best fooling, when all is done. Now, a song.
SIR TOBY   Come on, there is sixpence for you. [*He gives money.*] Let's have a song.
SIR ANDREW   There's a testril of me too. [*He gives money.*]   33
If one knight give a—
FESTE   Would you have a love song, or a song of good   35
life?   36
SIR TOBY   A love song, a love song.
SIR ANDREW   Ay, ay, I care not for good life.
FESTE (*sings*)
   O mistress mine, where are you roaming?
   O, stay and hear, your true love 's coming,
      That can sing both high and low.
   Trip no further, pretty sweeting;
   Journeys end in lovers' meeting,
      Every wise man's son doth know.

SIR ANDREW   Excellent good, i' faith.
SIR TOBY   Good, good.
FESTE [*sings*]
   What is love? 'tis not hereafter;
   Present mirth hath present laughter;
      What's to come is still unsure.   49
   In delay there lies no plenty.
   Then come kiss me, sweet and twenty;   51
      Youth's a stuff will not endure.

SIR ANDREW   A mellifluous voice, as I am true knight.
SIR TOBY   A contagious breath.   54

---

12 She . . . it (Viola tells a quick and friendly lie to shield Olivia.) **16 in your eye** in plain sight **18 charmed** enchanted **20 lost** caused her to lose **23 in** in the person of **25 the man** the man of her choice **28 pregnant** quick, resourceful. **enemy** i.e., Satan **29 proper false** men who are handsome and deceitful **30 waxen** i.e., malleable, impressionable. **set their forms** stamp their images (as of a seal) **32 such as . . . be** being made of frail material, we are frail **33 fadge** turn out **34 monster** i.e., being both man and woman. **fond** dote **39 thriftless** unprofitable
2.3. Location: Olivia's house.
2 betimes early. **diluculo surgere [saluberrimum est]** to rise early is most healthful. (A sentence from Lilly's *Latin Grammar*.) **6 can** tankard **9–10 four elements** i.e., fire, air, water, and earth, the elements that were thought to make up all matter

14 stoup drinking vessel **17 picture of "we three"** picture of two fools or asses inscribed "we three," the spectator being the third **18 catch** round **20 breast** voice **23–24 Pigrogromitus . . . Queubus** (Feste's mock erudition.) **25 leman** sweetheart **26 impeticos thy gratillity** (Suggests "impetticoat, or pocket up, thy gratuity.") **27 whipstock** whip handle. (Possibly suggests that Malvolio can't be led by the nose; or, just nonsense.) **has a white hand** i.e., is ladylike. (But Feste's speech may be mere nonsense.) **28 Myrmidons** followers of Achilles. **bottle-ale houses** (Used contemptuously of taverns because they sold low-class drink.) **33 testril** tester, a coin worth sixpence **35–36 good life** virtuous living. (Or perhaps Feste means simply "life's pleasures," but is misunderstood by Sir Andrew to mean "virtuous living.") **49 still** always **51 sweet and twenty** i.e., sweet and twenty times sweet **54 A contagious breath** (1) a catchy voice (2) an infected or contagious breath

SIR ANDREW Very sweet and contagious, i' faith.

SIR TOBY To hear by the nose, it is dulcet in contagion. 56
But shall we make the welkin dance indeed? Shall we 57
rouse the night owl in a catch that will draw three 58
souls out of one weaver? Shall we do that? 59

SIR ANDREW An you love me, let's do 't. I am dog at a 60
catch. 61

FESTE By 'r Lady, sir, and some dogs will catch well. 62

SIR ANDREW Most certain. Let our catch be "Thou 63
knave." 64

FESTE "Hold thy peace, thou knave," knight? I shall be
constrained in 't to call thee knave, knight.

SIR ANDREW 'Tis not the first time I have constrained
one to call me knave. Begin, Fool. It begins, "Hold thy
peace."

FESTE I shall never begin if I hold my peace.

SIR ANDREW Good, i' faith. Come, begin. *Catch sung.*

Enter Maria.

MARIA What a caterwauling do you keep here! If my
lady have not called up her steward Malvolio and bid
him turn you out of doors, never trust me.

SIR TOBY My lady's a Cataian, we are politicians, 75
Malvolio's a Peg-o'-Ramsey, and [*he sings*] "Three 76
merry men be we." Am not I consanguineous? Am I 77
not of her blood? Tillyvally! Lady! [*He sings.*] "There 78
dwelt a man in Babylon, lady, lady." 79

FESTE Beshrew me, the knight's in admirable fooling. 80

SIR ANDREW Ay, he does well enough if he be disposed, and so do I too. He does it with a better grace,
but I do it more natural. 83

SIR TOBY [*sings*]
"O' the twelfth day of December"— 84

MARIA For the love o' God, peace!

Enter Malvolio.

MALVOLIO My masters, are you mad? Or what are you?
Have you no wit, manners, nor honesty but to gabble 87
like tinkers at this time of night? Do ye make an alehouse of my lady's house, that ye squeak out your coz- 89
iers' catches without any mitigation or remorse of 90
voice? Is there no respect of place, persons, nor time in
you?

SIR TOBY We did keep time, sir, in our catches. Sneck 93
up! 94

MALVOLIO Sir Toby, I must be round with you. My 95
lady bade me tell you that though she harbors you as
her kinsman, she's nothing allied to your disorders. If
you can separate yourself and your misdemeanors,
you are welcome to the house; if not, an it would
please you to take leave of her, she is very willing to
bid you farewell.

SIR TOBY [*sings*]
"Farewell, dear heart, since I must needs be gone." 102

MARIA Nay, good Sir Toby.

FESTE [*sings*]
"His eyes do show his days are almost done."

MALVOLIO Is 't even so?

SIR TOBY [*sings*]
"But I will never die."

FESTE
"Sir Toby, there you lie."

MALVOLIO This is much credit to you.

SIR TOBY [*sings*]
"Shall I bid him go?"

FESTE [*sings*]
"What an if you do?"

SIR TOBY [*sings*]
"Shall I bid him go, and spare not?"

FESTE [*sings*]
"O, no, no, no, no, you dare not."

SIR TOBY Out o' tune, sir? Ye lie. Art any more than a 113
steward? Dost thou think, because thou art virtuous,
there shall be no more cakes and ale?

FESTE Yes, by Saint Anne, and ginger shall be hot i' the 116
mouth, too.

SIR TOBY Thou'rt i' the right.—Go, sir, rub your chain 118
with crumbs.—A stoup of wine, Maria! 119

MALVOLIO Mistress Mary, if you prized my lady's
favor at anything more than contempt, you would not
give means for this uncivil rule. She shall know of it, 122
by this hand. *Exit.*

MARIA Go shake your ears. 124

SIR ANDREW 'Twere as good a deed as to drink when a
man's a-hungry to challenge him the field and then to 126
break promise with him and make a fool of him.

SIR TOBY Do 't, knight. I'll write thee a challenge, or I'll

---

56 To . . . contagion i.e., if we were to describe hearing in olfactory terms, we could say it is sweet in stench. (Sir Toby may be mocking Sir Andrew's uncritical acceptance of the word *contagious*, missing the pun.) **57 make . . . dance** i.e., drink till the sky seems to turn around **58–59 draw three souls** (Refers to the threefold nature of the soul—vegetal, sensible, and intellectual—or to the three singers of the three-part catch; or, just a comic exaggeration.) **59 weaver** (Weavers were often associated with psalm singing.) **60 dog at** very clever at. (But Feste uses the word literally.) **61 catch** round. (But Feste uses it to mean "seize.") **62 By 'r Lady** (An oath, originally, "by the Virgin Mary.") **63–64 Thou knave** (This popular round is arranged so that the three singers repeatedly sing to one another, "Thou knave." "Knight and knave" is a common antithesis, like "rich and poor.") **75 Catian** Cathayan, i.e., Chinese, a trickster or inscrutable; or, just nonsense. **politicians** schemers, intriguers **76 Peg-o'-Ramsey** character in a popular song. (Used here contemptuously.) **76–77 Three . . . we** (A snatch of an old song.) **77 consanguineous** i.e., a blood relative of Olivia **78 Tillyvally** nonsense, fiddle-faddle **78–79 There . . . lady** (The first line of a ballad, "The Constancy of Susanna," together with the refrain, "Lady, lady.") **80 Beshrew** i.e., devil take. (A mild curse.) **83 natural** naturally (but unconsciously suggesting idiocy.) **84 O' . . . December** (Possibly part of a ballad about the Battle of Musselburgh Field, or Toby's error for the "twelfth day of Christmas," i.e., Twelfth Night.) **87 wit** common sense. **honesty** decency

89–90 coziers' cobblers' **90 mitigation or remorse** i.e., considerate lowering **93–94 Sneck up** go hang **95 round** blunt **102 Farewell . . . gone** (From the ballad "Corydon's Farewell to Phyllis.") **113 Out o' tune** (Perhaps a quibbling reply—"We did too keep time in our tune"—to Malvolio's accusation of having no respect for place or time, line 91. Often emended to *Out o' time*, easily misread in secretary hand.) **116 Saint Anne** mother of the Virgin Mary. (Her cult was derided in the Reformation, much as Puritan reformers also derided the tradition of *cakes and ale* at church feasts.) **ginger** (Commonly used to spice ale.) **118–119 Go . . . crumbs** i.e., scour or polish your steward's chain; attend to your own business and remember your station **122 give means** i.e., supply drink. **rule** conduct **124 your ears** i.e., your ass's ears **126 the field** i.e., to a duel deliver thy indignation to him by word of mouth.

MARIA Sweet Sir Toby, be patient for tonight. Since the youth of the Count's was today with my lady, she is much out of quiet. For Monsieur Malvolio, let me 132 alone with him. If I do not gull him into a nayword 133 and make him a common recreation, do not think I 134 have wit enough to lie straight in my bed. I know I can do it.

SIR TOBY Possess us, possess us. Tell us something of 137 him.

MARIA Marry, sir, sometimes he is a kind of puritan. 139

SIR ANDREW O, if I thought that, I'd beat him like a dog.

SIR TOBY What, for being a puritan? Thy exquisite reason, dear knight?

SIR ANDREW I have no exquisite reason for 't, but I have reason good enough.

MARIA The devil a puritan that he is, or anything con- 146 stantly, but a time-pleaser; an affectioned ass, that cons 147 state without book and utters it by great swaths; the 148 best persuaded of himself, so crammed, as he thinks, 149 with excellencies, that it is his grounds of faith that all 150 that look on him love him; and on that vice in him will my revenge find notable cause to work.

SIR TOBY What wilt thou do?

MARIA I will drop in his way some obscure epistles of love, wherein by the color of his beard, the shape of his leg, the manner of his gait, the expressure of his 156 eye, forehead, and complexion, he shall find himself 157 most feelingly personated. I can write very like my 158 lady your niece; on a forgotten matter we can hardly 159 make distinction of our hands.

SIR TOBY Excellent! I smell a device.

SIR ANDREW I have 't in my nose too.

SIR TOBY He shall think, by the letters that thou wilt drop, that they come from my niece, and that she's in love with him.

MARIA My purpose is indeed a horse of that color.

SIR ANDREW And your horse now would make him an ass.

MARIA Ass, I doubt not. 169

SIR ANDREW O, 'twill be admirable!

MARIA Sport royal, I warrant you. I know my physic 171 will work with him. I will plant you two, and let the Fool make a third, where he shall find the letter.

Observe his construction of it. For this night, to bed, 174 and dream on the event. Farewell. *Exit.* 175

SIR TOBY Good night, Penthesilea. 176

SIR ANDREW Before me, she's a good wench. 177

SIR TOBY She's a beagle true-bred and one that adores 178 me. What o' that?

SIR ANDREW I was adored once, too.

SIR TOBY Let's to bed, knight. Thou hadst need send for more money.

SIR ANDREW If I cannot recover your niece, I am a foul 183 way out. 184

SIR TOBY Send for money, knight. If thou hast her not i' the end, call me cut. 186

SIR ANDREW If I do not, never trust me, take it how you will.

SIR TOBY Come, come, I'll go burn some sack. 'Tis too 189 late to go to bed now. Come, knight; come, knight. 190

Exeunt.

❧

2.4 *Enter Duke [Orsino] Viola, Curio, and others.*

ORSINO
Give me some music. Now, good morrow, friends. 1
Now, good Cesario, but that piece of song, 2
That old and antique song we heard last night. 3
Methought it did relieve my passion much,
More than light airs and recollected terms 5
Of these most brisk and giddy-pacèd times.
Come, but one verse.

CURIO He is not here, so please your lordship, that should sing it.

ORSINO Who was it?

CURIO Feste the jester, my lord, a fool that the Lady Olivia's father took much delight in. He is about the house.

ORSINO
Seek him out, and play the tune the while.
[Exit Curio.] Music plays.
[To Viola.] Come hither, boy. If ever thou shalt love,
In the sweet pangs of it remember me;
For such as I am, all true lovers are,
Unstaid and skittish in all motions else 18
Save in the constant image of the creature
That is beloved. How dost thou like this tune?

VIOLA
It gives a very echo to the seat 21
Where Love is throned.

---

132 For as for **132–133 let . . . him** leave him to me **133 gull** trick. **nayword** byword. (His name will be synonymous with "dupe.") **134 recreation** sport **137 Possess** inform **139 puritan** (Maria's point is that Malvolio is sometimes a *kind* of Puritan, insofar as he is precise about moral conduct and censorious of others for immoral conduct, but that he is nothing consistently except a time-server. He is not, then, simply a satirical type of the Puritan sect. The extent of the resemblance is left unstated.) **146–147 constantly** consistently **147 time-pleaser** time-server, sycophant. **affectioned** affected **147–148 cons . . . book** learns by heart the phrases and mannerisms of the great **148 by great swaths** in great sweeps, like rows of mown grain **149 best persuaded** having the best opinion **150 grounds of faith** creed, belief **156 expressure** expression **157 complexion** countenance **158 personated** represented **159 on a forgotten matter** when we've forgotten which of us wrote something or what it was about **169 Ass, I** (with a pun on "as I") **171 physic** medicine

174 construction interpretation **175 event** outcome **176 Penthesilea** Queen of the Amazons. (Another ironical allusion to Maria's diminutive stature.) **177 Before me** i.e., on my soul **178 beagle** a small, intelligent hunting dog **183 recover** win **183–184 foul way out** i.e., miserably out of pocket. (Literally, out of my way and in the mire.) **186 cut** a horse with a docked tail; also, a gelding, or the female genital organ **189 burn some sack** warm some Spanish wine **190 s.d. Exeunt** (Feste may have left earlier; he says nothing after line 117 and is perhaps referred to without his being present at 172–173.) **2.4. Location:** Orsino's court.
1 morrow morning **2 but** i.e., I ask only **3 antique** old, quaint, fantastic **5 recollected terms** studied and artificial expressions **18 motions else** other thoughts and emotions **21 the seat** i.e., the heart

ORSINO   Thou dost speak masterly.
My life upon 't, young though thou art, thine eye
Hath stayed upon some favor that it loves.   24
Hath it not, boy?
VIOLA   A little, by your favor.   25
ORSINO
What kind of woman is 't?
VIOLA   Of your complexion.
ORSINO
She is not worth thee, then. What years, i' faith?
VIOLA   About your years, my lord.
ORSINO
Too old, by heaven. Let still the woman take   29
An elder than herself. So wears she to him;   30
So sways she level in her husband's heart.   31
For, boy, however we do praise ourselves,
Our fancies are more giddy and unfirm,
More longing, wavering, sooner lost and worn,   34
Than women's are.
VIOLA   I think it well, my lord.
ORSINO
Then let thy love be younger than thyself,
Or thy affection cannot hold the bent;   37
For women are as roses, whose fair flower
Being once displayed, doth fall that very hour.   39
VIOLA
And so they are. Alas that they are so,
To die even when they to perfection grow!   41

Enter Curio and Clown [Feste].

ORSINO
O fellow, come, the song we had last night.
Mark it, Cesario, it is old and plain;
The spinsters and the knitters in the sun,   44
And the free maids that weave their thread with   45
    bones,
Do use to chant it. It is silly sooth,   46
And dallies with the innocence of love,   47
Like the old age.   48
FESTE   Are you ready, sir?
ORSINO   Ay, prithee, sing.   *Music.*

The Song.

FESTE [*sings*]
        Come away, come away, death,   51
            And in sad cypress let me be laid.   52
        Fly away, fly away, breath;
            I am slain by a fair cruel maid.

My shroud of white, stuck all with yew,   55
    O, prepare it!
My part of death, no one so true   57
    Did share it.   58

Not a flower, not a flower sweet
    On my black coffin let there be strown;   60
Not a friend, not a friend greet
    My poor corpse, where my bones shall be
        thrown.
A thousand thousand sighs to save,
    Lay me, O, where
Sad true lover never find my grave,
    To weep there!

ORSINO [*offering money*]   There's for thy pains.
FESTE   No pains, sir. I take pleasure in singing, sir.
ORSINIO   I'll pay thy pleasure then.
FESTE   Truly, sir, and pleasure will be paid, one time   70
or another.   71
ORSINO   Give me now leave to leave thee.   72
FESTE   Now, the melancholy god protect thee, and the   73
tailor make thy doublet of changeable taffeta, for thy   74
mind is a very opal. I would have men of such con-   75
stancy put to sea, that their business might be every-   76
thing and their intent everywhere, for that's it that   77
always makes a good voyage of nothing. Farewell.   78
                                                  Exit.
ORSINO
Let all the rest give place. [*Curio and attendants
    withdraw.*] Once more, Cesario,   79
Get thee to yond same sovereign cruelty.
Tell her, my love, more noble than the world,
Prizes not quantity of dirty lands;
The parts that fortune hath bestowed upon her,   83
Tell her, I hold as giddily as fortune;   84
But 'tis that miracle and queen of gems   85
That nature pranks her in attracts my soul.   86
VIOLA   But if she cannot love you, sir?
ORSINO
I cannot be so answered.
VIOLA   Sooth, but you must.   88
Say that some lady, as perhaps there is,
Hath for your love as great a pang of heart
As you have for Olivia. You cannot love her;

---

24 **stayed . . . favor** rested upon some face   25 **by your favor** if you
please (but also hinting at "like you in feature")   29 **still** always
30 **wears she** she adapts herself   31 **sways she level** she keeps a perfect equipoise and steady affection   34 **worn** exhausted. (Sometimes
emended to **won**.)   37 **hold the bent** hold steady, stand the strain
(like the tension of a bow)   39 **displayed** full blown   41 **even when**
just as   44 **spinsters** spinners   45 **free** carefree, innocent.   **bones**
bobbins on which bone-lace was made   46 **Do use** are accustomed.
silly sooth simple truth   47 **dallies with** dwells lovingly on, sports
with   48 **Like . . . age** as in the good old times   51 **Come away**
come hither   52 **cypress** i.e., a coffin of cypress wood, or bier strewn
with sprigs of cypress

55 **yew** yew sprigs. (Emblematic of mourning, like cypress.)
57–58 **My . . . it** no one died for love so true to love as I
60 **strown** strewn   70–71 **pleasure . . . another** sooner or later one
must pay for indulgence   72 **leave to leave** permission to take leave
of, dismiss   73 **the melancholy god** i.e., Saturn, whose planet was
thought to control the melancholy temperament   74 **doublet** close-fitting jacket.   **changeable taffeta** a silk so woven of various-colored
threads that its color shifts with changing perspective   75 **opal** an iridescent precious stone that changes color when seen from various angles or in different lights   76–77 **that . . . everywhere** i.e., so that in
the changeableness of the sea their inconstancy could always be exercised   77 **intent** destination   77–78 **for . . . nothing** because that's
the quality that succeeds in making a "good" voyage come to nothing
79 **give place** withdraw   83 **parts** attributes such as wealth or rank
84 **I . . . fortune** I esteem as carelessly as I do fortune, that fickle
goddess   85 **that miracle . . . gems** i.e., her beauty   86 **pranks**
adorns.   **attracts** that attracts   88 **Sooth** in truth

You tell her so. Must she not then be answered? 92
ORSINO   There is no woman's sides
　Can bide the beating of so strong a passion 94
　As love doth give my heart; no woman's heart
　So big, to hold so much. They lack retention. 96
　Alas, their love may be called appetite,
　No motion of the liver, but the palate, 98
　That suffer surfeit, cloyment, and revolt; 99
　But mine is all as hungry as the sea,
　And can digest as much. Make no compare 101
　Between that love a woman can bear me
　And that I owe Olivia.
VIOLA   Ay, but I know— 103
ORSINO   What dost thou know?
VIOLA
　Too well what love women to men may owe.
　In faith, they are as true of heart as we.
　My father had a daughter loved a man
　As it might be, perhaps, were I a woman,
　I should your lordship.
ORSINO   And what's her history?
VIOLA
　A blank, my lord. She never told her love,
　But let concealment, like a worm i' the bud,
　Feed on her damask cheek. She pined in thought, 112
　And with a green and yellow melancholy 113
　She sat like Patience on a monument, 114
　Smiling at grief. Was not this love indeed?
　We men may say more, swear more, but indeed
　Our shows are more than will; for still we prove 117
　Much in our vows, but little in our love.
ORSINO
　But died thy sister of her love, my boy?
VIOLA
　I am all the daughters of my father's house,
　And all the brothers too—and yet I know not.
　Sir, shall I to this lady?
ORSINO   Ay, that's the theme.
　To her in haste; give her this jewel. [*He gives a jewel.*]
　Say
　My love can give no place, bide no denay. 124
                              Exeunt [separately].

❧

2.5   *Enter Sir Toby, Sir Andrew, and Fabian.*

SIR TOBY   Come thy ways, Signor Fabian. 1
FABIAN   Nay, I'll come. If I lose a scruple of this sport, 2
　let me be boiled to death with melancholy. 3

SIR TOBY   Wouldst thou not be glad to have the nig-
　gardly rascally sheep-biter come by some notable 5
　shame?
FABIAN   I would exult, man. You know he brought me
　out o' favor with my lady about a bearbaiting here. 8
SIR TOBY   To anger him we'll have the bear again, and
　we will fool him black and blue. Shall we not, Sir An- 10
　drew?
SIR ANDREW   An we do not, it is pity of our lives. 12

Enter Maria [with a letter].

SIR TOBY   Here comes the little villain.—How now, my 13
　metal of India! 14
MARIA   Get ye all three into the boxtree. Malvolio's 15
　coming down this walk. He has been yonder i' the sun
　practicing behavior to his own shadow this half hour.
　Observe him, for the love of mockery, for I know this
　letter will make a contemplative idiot of him. Close, in 19
　the name of jesting! [*The others hide.*] Lie thou there
　[*throwing down a letter*]; for here comes the trout that
　must be caught with tickling.   *Exit.* 22

Enter Malvolio.

MALVOLIO   'Tis but fortune; all is fortune. Maria once
　told me she did affect me; and I have heard herself 24
　come thus near, that should she fancy, it should be 25
　one of my complexion. Besides, she uses me with a
　more exalted respect than anyone else that follows 27
　her. What should I think on 't?
SIR TOBY   Here's an overweening rogue!
FABIAN   O, peace! Contemplation makes a rare turkey- 30
　cock of him. How he jets under his advanced plumes! 31
SIR ANDREW   'Slight, I could so beat the rogue! 32
SIR TOBY   Peace, I say.
MALVOLIO   To be Count Malvolio.
SIR TOBY   Ah, rogue!
SIR ANDREW   Pistol him, pistol him.
SIR TOBY   Peace, peace!
MALVOLIO   There is example for 't. The lady of the Stra- 38
　chy married the yeoman of the wardrobe. 39
SIR ANDREW   Fie on him, Jezebel! 40
FABIAN   O, peace! Now he's deeply in. Look how imag-
　ination blows him. 42
MALVOLIO   Having been three months married to her,
　sitting in my state— 44
SIR TOBY   O, for a stone-bow, to hit him in the eye! 45
MALVOLIO   Calling my officers about me, in my

---

92 be answered accept your answer   **94 bide** withstand   **96 to hold** as to contain.   **retention** constancy, the power of retaining   **98 motion** impulse.   **liver . . . palate** (Real love is a passion of the liver, whereas fancy, light love, is born in the eye and nourished in the palate.)   **99 cloyment** satiety.   **revolt** sickness, revulsion   **101 compare** comparison   **103 owe** have for   **112 damask** pink and white like the damask rose   **113 green and yellow** pale and sallow   **114 on a monument** carved in statuary on a tomb   **117 shows** displays of passion.   **more than will** greater than our feelings.   **still** always   **124 can . . . denay** cannot yield or endure denial
2.5. Location: Olivia's garden.
1 Come thy ways come along   **2 a scruple** the least bit   **3 boiled** (with a pun on "biled"; black bile was the "humor" of melancholy and was thought to be a cold humor)

5 sheep-biter a dog that bites sheep, i.e., a sneak and a censorious fellow   **8 bearbaiting** (A special target of Puritan disapproval.)   **10 fool . . . blue** mock him until he is figuratively black and blue   **12 An** if.   **pity of our lives** a pity we should live   **13 villain** (Here, a term of endearment.)   **14 metal** gold, i.e., priceless one   **15 boxtree** an evergreen shrub   **19 contemplative** i.e., from his musings.   **Close** i.e., keep close, stay hidden   **22 tickling** (1) stroking gently about the gills—an actual method of fishing (2) flattery   **24 she** Olivia.   **affect** have fondness for   **25 fancy** fall in love   **27 follows** serves   **30 rare** excellent   **31 jets** struts.   **advanced** raised   **32 'Slight** by His (God's) light   **38 example** precedent   **38–39 lady of the Strachy** (Apparently a lady who had married below her station; no certain identification.)   **40 Jezebel** the proud queen of Ahab, King of Israel   **42 blows** puffs up   **44 state** chair of state   **45 stone-bow** crossbow that shoots stones

branched velvet gown; having come from a daybed, 47
where I have left Olivia sleeping—

SIR TOBY   Fire and brimstone!

FABIAN   O, peace, peace!

MALVOLIO   And then to have the humor of state; and 51
after a demure travel of regard, telling them I know 52
my place as I would they should do theirs, to ask for
my kinsman Toby. 54

SIR TOBY   Bolts and shackles!

FABIAN   O, peace, peace, peace! Now, now.

MALVOLIO   Seven of my people, with an obedient start,
make out for him. I frown the while, and perchance
wind up my watch, or play with my—some rich 59
jewel. Toby approaches; curtsies there to me— 60

SIR TOBY   Shall this fellow live?

FABIAN   Though our silence be drawn from us with 62
cars, yet peace. 63

MALVOLIO   I extend my hand to him thus, quenching
my familiar smile with an austere regard of control— 65

SIR TOBY   And does not Toby take you a blow o' the lips 66
then?

MALVOLIO   Saying, "Cousin Toby, my fortunes having
cast me on your niece give me this prerogative of
speech—"

SIR TOBY   What, what?

MALVOLIO   "You must amend your drunkenness."

SIR TOBY   Out, scab! 73

FABIAN   Nay, patience, or we break the sinews of our 74
plot.

MALVOLIO   "Besides, you waste the treasure of your
time with a foolish knight—"

SIR ANDREW   That's me, I warrant you.

MALVOLIO   "One Sir Andrew."

SIR ANDREW   I knew 'twas I, for many do call me fool.

MALVOLIO   What employment have we here? 81
                              [*Taking up the letter.*]

FABIAN   Now is the woodcock near the gin. 82

SIR TOBY   O, peace, and the spirit of humors intimate 83
reading aloud to him!

MALVOLIO   By my life, this is my lady's hand. These be
her very c's, her u's, and her t's; and thus makes she 86
her great P's. It is in contempt of question her hand. 87

SIR ANDREW   Her c's, her u's, and her t's. Why that?

MALVOLIO [*reads*]   "To the unknown beloved, this,
and my good wishes."—Her very phrases! By your 90
leave, wax. Soft! And the impressure her Lucrece, 91

with which she uses to seal. 'Tis my lady. To whom 92
should this be?   [*He opens the letter.*]

FABIAN   This wins him, liver and all. 94

MALVOLIO [*reads*]
      "Jove knows I love,
         But who?
      Lips, do not move;
         No man must know."
"No man must know." What follows? The numbers 99
altered! "No man must know." If this should be thee, 100
Malvolio?

SIR TOBY   Marry, hang thee, brock! 102

MALVOLIO [*reads*]
      "I may command where I adore,
         But silence, like a Lucrece knife,
      With bloodless stroke my heart doth gore;
         M.O.A.I. doth sway my life."

FABIAN   A fustian riddle! 107

SIR TOBY   Excellent wench, say I.

MALVOLIO   "M.O.A.I. doth sway my life." Nay, but
first, let me see, let me see, let me see.

FABIAN   What dish o' poison has she dressed him! 111

SIR TOBY   And with what wing the staniel checks 112
at it! 113

MALVOLIO   "I may command where I adore." Why, she
may command me; I serve her, she is my lady. Why,
this is evident to any formal capacity. There is no 116
obstruction in this. And the end—what should that
alphabetical position portend? If I could make that 118
resemble something in me! Softly! M.O.A.I.—

SIR TOBY   O, ay, make up that. He is now at a cold scent. 120

FABIAN   Sowter will cry upon 't for all this, though it be 121
as rank as a fox. 122

MALVOLIO   M—Malvolio. M! Why, that begins my
name!

FABIAN   Did not I say he would work it out? The cur is
excellent at faults. 126

MALVOLIO   M—But then there is no consonancy in the 127
sequel that suffers under probation: A should follow, 128
but O does.

FABIAN   And O shall end, I hope. 130

SIR TOBY   Ay, or I'll cudgel him, and make him cry "O!"

MALVOLIO   And then I comes behind.

FABIAN   Ay, an you had any eye behind you, you 133

---

47 branched adorned with a figured pattern suggesting branched leaves or flowers. **daybed** sofa, couch **51 have . . . state** adopt the imperious manner of authority **52 demure . . . regard** grave survey of the company. **telling** indicating to **54 Toby** (Malvolio omits the title *Sir*.) **59 play with my** (Malvolio perhaps means his steward's chain but checks himself in time; as "Count Malvolio," he would not be wearing it. A bawdy meaning of playing with himself is also suggested.) **60 curtsies** bows **62–63 with cars** with chariots, i.e., by force **65 familiar** friendly. **regard of control** look of authority **66 take** deliver **73 scab** scurvy fellow **74 break . . . of** hamstring, disable **81 employment** business **82 woodcock** (A bird proverbial for its stupidity.) **gin** snare **83 humors** whim, caprice **86 c's . . . t's** i.e., *cut*, slang for the female pudenda **87 great** (1) uppercase (2) copious. (*P* suggests "pee.") **in contempt of** beyond **90–91 By . . . wax** (Addressed to the seal on the letter.) **91 Soft** softly, not so fast. **impressure** device imprinted on the seal. **Lucrece** Lucretia, chaste matron who, ravished by Tarquin, committed suicide

92 uses is accustomed **94 liver** i.e., the seat of passion
99–100 The numbers altered more verses, in a different meter
102 brock badger. (Used contemptuously.) **107 fustian** bombastic, ridiculously pompous **111 What** what a. **dressed** prepared for **112 wing** i.e., speed. **staniel** kestrel, a sparrow hawk. (The word is used contemptuously because of the uselessness of the staniel for falconry.) **112–113 checks at it** turns to fly at it **116 formal capacity** normal understanding **118 position** arrangement **120 O, ay** (playing on *O.I.* of *M.O.A.I.*) **make up** work out **121–122 Sowter . . . fox** i.e., the hound, having lost the *cold scent* of the hare, will "give tongue" in picking up the rank new scent of the fox and will dash away on this false trail **121 Sowter** cobbler. (Here, the name for a hound.) **126 at faults** i.e., at maneuvering his way past breaks in the line of scent—in this case, on a false trail **127–128 consonancy . . . probation** pattern in the following letters that stands up under examination. (In fact, the letters "M.O.A.I." represent the first, last, second, and next to last letters of Malvolio's name.) **130 O shall end** (1) O ends Malvolio's name (2) a noose shall end his life (3) *omega* ends the Greek alphabet (4) his cry of pain will end the joke **133 eye** (punning on the "I" of "O, ay" and "M.O.A.I.")

might see more detraction at your heels than fortunes 134
before you.

MALVOLIO　M.O.A.I. This simulation is not as the 136
former. And yet, to crush this a little, it would bow to
me, for every one of these letters are in my name. Soft!
Here follows prose.
[*He reads.*] "If this fall into thy hand, revolve. In my 140
stars I am above thee, but be not afraid of greatness. 141
Some are born great, some achieve greatness, and
some have greatness thrust upon 'em. Thy Fates open 143
their hands; let thy blood and spirit embrace them; 144
and, to inure thyself to what thou art like to be, cast 145
thy humble slough and appear fresh. Be opposite with 146
a kinsman, surly with servants. Let thy tongue tang 147
arguments of state; put thyself into the trick of 148
singularity. She thus advises thee that sighs for thee. 149
Remember who commended thy yellow stockings,
and wished to see thee ever cross-gartered. I say, 151
remember. Go to, thou art made, if thou desir'st to be 152
so. If not, let me see thee a steward still, the fellow of
servants, and not worthy to touch Fortune's fingers.
Farewell. She that would alter services with thee, 155
　　　　　　　　　　　The Fortunate-Unhappy."
Daylight and champaign discovers not more! This is 157
open. I will be proud, I will read politic authors, I will 158
baffle Sir Toby, I will wash off gross acquaintance, I 159
will be point-devise the very man. I do not now fool 160
myself, to let imagination jade me; for every reason 161
excites to this, that my lady loves me. She did com- 162
mend my yellow stockings of late, she did praise my
leg being cross-gartered; and in this she manifests her- 164
self to my love, and with a kind of injunction drives
me to these habits of her liking. I thank my stars, I am 166
happy. I will be strange, stout, in yellow stockings 167
and cross-gartered, even with the swiftness of putting
on. Jove and my stars be praised! Here is yet a postscript. [*He reads.*] "Thou canst not choose but know who
I am. If thou entertain'st my love, let it appear in thy 171
smiling; thy smiles become thee well. Therefore in my
presence still smile, dear my sweet, I prithee." 173
Jove, I thank thee. I will smile; I will do everything that
thou wilt have me. 　　　　　　　　　　　　*Exit.*

[*Sir Toby, Sir Andrew, and Fabian come from hiding.*]

FABIAN　I will not give my part of this sport for a

pension of thousands to be paid from the Sophy. 177
SIR TOBY　I could marry this wench for this device.
SIR ANDREW　So could I too.
SIR TOBY　And ask no other dowry with her but such
another jest.

　　　　　Enter Maria.

SIR ANDREW　Nor I neither.
FABIAN　Here comes my noble gull-catcher. 183
SIR TOBY　Wilt thou set thy foot o' my neck?
SIR ANDREW　Or o' mine either?
SIR TOBY　Shall I play my freedom at tray-trip, and 186
become thy bondslave?
SIR ANDREW　I' faith, or I either?
SIR TOBY　Why, thou hast put him in such a dream that
when the image of it leaves him he must run mad.
MARIA　Nay, but say true, does it work upon him?
SIR TOBY　Like aqua vitae with a midwife. 192
MARIA　If you will then see the fruits of the sport, mark
his first approach before my lady. He will come to her
in yellow stockings, and 'tis a color she abhors, and
cross-gartered, a fashion she detests; and he will smile
upon her, which will now be so unsuitable to her
disposition, being addicted to a melancholy as she is,
that it cannot but turn him into a notable contempt. If 199
you will see it, follow me.
SIR TOBY　To the gates of Tartar, thou most excellent 201
devil of wit!
SIR ANDREW　I'll make one too. 　　　　　　*Exeunt.* 203

3.1　*Enter Viola, and Clown [Feste, playing his pipe*
　　　and tabor].

VIOLA　Save thee, friend, and thy music. Dost thou live 1
by thy tabor? 　　　　　　　　　　　　　　　　　　2
FESTE　No, sir, I live by the church.
VIOLA　Art thou a churchman?
FESTE　No such matter, sir. I do live by the church, for
I do live at my house, and my house doth stand by the
church.
VIOLA　So thou mayst say the king lies by a beggar if 8
a beggar dwell near him, or the church stands by thy 9
tabor if thy tabor stand by the church. 　　　　　10
FESTE　You have said, sir. To see this age! A sentence is 11
but a cheveril glove to a good wit. How quickly the 12
wrong side may be turned outward!

134 **detraction** defamation.　**at your heels** pursuing you　136 **simu-**
lation disguise, puzzle　140 **revolve** consider　141 **stars** fortune
143–144 **open their hands** offer their bounty　145 **inure** accustom.
like likely.　**cast** cast off　146 **slough** skin of a snake; hence, former
demeanor of humbleness.　**opposite** contradictory　147 **tang** sound
loud with　148 **state** politics, statecraft　148–149 **trick of singularity**
eccentricity of manner　151 **cross-gartered** wearing garters above
and below the knee so as to cross behind it　152 **Go to** (An expression of remonstrance.)　155 **alter services** i.e., exchange place of
mistress and servant　157 **champaign** open country.　**discovers** discloses　158 **politic** dealing with state affairs　159 **baffle** deride, degrade. (A technical chivalric term used to describe the disgrace of a
perjured knight.)　**gross** base　160 **point-devise** correct to the letter
161 **to let** by letting.　**jade** trick (as an unruly horse does)　162 **ex-**
cites to this prompts this conclusion　164 **this** this letter　166 **these**
habits this attire　167 **happy** fortunate.　**strange** aloof.　**stout**
haughty　171 **thou entertain'st** you accept　173 **still** continually

177 **Sophy** Shah of Persia　183 **gull-catcher** tricker of *gulls* or dupes
186 **play** gamble.　**tray-trip** a game of dice, success in which depended on throwing a three (*tray*)　192 **aqua vitae** brandy or other
distilled liquors　199 **notable contempt** notorious object of contempt
201 **Tartar** Tartarus, the infernal regions　203 **make one** i.e., tag
along
3.1. Location: Olivia's garden.
1 **Save** God save　1–2 **live by** earn your living with. (But Feste uses
the phrase to mean "dwell near.")　2 **tabor** small drum　8 **lies by** (1)
lies sexually with (2) dwells near　9–10 **stands by . . . stand by** (1) is
maintained by (2) is placed near　11 **You have said** you've expressed
your opinion.　**sentence** maxim, judgment, opinion　12 **cheveril**
kidskin

VIOLA   Nay, that's certain. They that dally nicely with 14
words may quickly make them wanton.   15

FESTE   I would therefore my sister had had no name,
sir.

VIOLA   Why, man?

FESTE   Why, sir, her name's a word, and to dally with
that word might make my sister wanton. But indeed,
words are very rascals since bonds disgraced them. 21

VIOLA   Thy reason, man?

FESTE   Troth, sir, I can yield you none without words,
and words are grown so false I am loath to prove
reason with them.

VIOLA   I warrant thou art a merry fellow and car'st for 26
nothing.   27

FESTE   Not so, sir, I do care for something; but in my
conscience, sir, I do not care for you. If that be to care
for nothing, sir, I would it would make you invisible. 30

VIOLA   Art not thou the Lady Olivia's fool?

FESTE   No indeed, sir. The Lady Olivia has no folly. She
will keep no fool, sir, till she be married, and fools are
as like husbands as pilchers are to herrings—the 34
husband's the bigger. I am indeed not her fool but
her corrupter of words.

VIOLA   I saw thee late at the Count Orsino's.   37

FESTE   Foolery, sir, does walk about the orb like the 38
sun; it shines everywhere. I would be sorry, sir, but 39
the fool should be as oft with your master as with my
mistress. I think I saw your wisdom there.   41

VIOLA   Nay, an thou pass upon me, I'll no more with 42
thee. Hold, there's expenses for thee.
                              [She gives a coin.]

FESTE   Now Jove, in his next commodity of hair, send 44
thee a beard!

VIOLA   By my troth, I'll tell thee, I am almost sick for 46
one—[aside] though I would not have it grow on my 47
chin.—Is thy lady within?

FESTE   Would not a pair of these have bred, sir?

VIOLA   Yes, being kept together and put to use.   50

FESTE   I would play Lord Pandarus of Phrygia, sir, to 51
bring a Cressida to this Troilus.

VIOLA   I understand you, sir. 'Tis well begged.
                         [She gives another coin.]

FESTE   The matter, I hope, is not great, sir, begging 54
but a beggar; Cressida was a beggar. My lady is 55

within, sir. I will conster to them whence you come. 56
Who you are and what you would are out of my
welkin—I might say "element," but the word is 58
overworn.   Exit.

VIOLA
This fellow is wise enough to play the fool,
And to do that well craves a kind of wit.
He must observe their mood on whom he jests,
The quality of persons, and the time,   63
And, like the haggard, check at every feather   64
That comes before his eye. This is a practice   65
As full of labor as a wise man's art;
For folly that he wisely shows is fit,   67
But wise men, folly-fall'n, quite taint their wit.   68

Enter Sir Toby and [Sir] Andrew.

SIR TOBY   Save you, gentleman.

VIOLA   And you, sir.

SIR ANDREW   *Dieu vous garde, monsieur.*   71

VIOLA   *Et vous aussi; votre serviteur.*   72

SIR ANDREW   I hope, sir, you are, and I am yours.

SIR TOBY   Will you encounter the house? My niece is 74
desirous you should enter, if your trade be to her. 75

VIOLA   I am bound to your niece, sir; I mean, she is the 76
list of my voyage.   77

SIR TOBY   Taste your legs, sir. Put them to motion. 78

VIOLA   My legs do better understand me, sir, than I un- 79
derstand what you mean by bidding me taste my legs.

SIR TOBY   I mean, to go, sir, to enter.

VIOLA   I will answer you with gait and entrance.—But 82
we are prevented.   83

Enter Olivia and gentlewoman [Maria].

Most excellent accomplished lady, the heavens rain
odors on you!

SIR ANDREW   That youth's a rare courtier. "Rain
odors"—well.

VIOLA   My matter hath no voice, lady, but to your own 88
most pregnant and vouchsafed ear.   89

SIR ANDREW   "Odors," "pregnant," and "vouchsafed."
I'll get 'em all three all ready.   91

OLIVIA   Let the garden door be shut, and leave me to
my hearing. [*Exeunt Sir Toby, Sir Andrew, and Maria.*]
Give me your hand, sir.

14 dally nicely (1) play subtly (2) toy amorously   **15 wanton** (1)
equivocal (2) licentious, unchaste. (Feste then "dallies" with the word
in its sexual sense; see line 20.)   **21 since . . . them** i.e., since bonds
have been needed to make sworn statements good   **26–27 car'st for
nothing** are without any worries. (But Feste puns on *care for* in lines
29–30 in the sense of "like.")   **30 invisible** i.e., nothing; absent
34 pilchers pilchards, fish resembling herring   **37 late** recently
38 orb earth   **39–41 I would . . . mistress** (1) I should be sorry not
to visit Orsino's house often (2) it would be a shame if folly were no
less common there than in Olivia's household   **39 but** unless
41 your wisdom i.e., you. (A title of mock courtesy.)   **42 an . . . me**
if you fence (verbally) with me, pass judgment on me   **44 commodity**
supply   **46–47 sick for one** (1) eager to have a beard (2) in love with
a bearded man   **50 put to use** put out at interest   **51 Pandarus** the
go-between in the love story of Troilus and Cressida; uncle to Cressida   **54–55 begging . . . beggar** (A reference to Henryson's *Testament of Cresseid* in which Cressida became a leper and a beggar.
Feste desires another coin to be the mate of the one he has, as Cressida, the beggar, was mate to Troilus.)

56 conster construe, explain   **58 welkin** sky.   **element** (The word
can be synonymous with *welkin*, but the common phrase *out of my
element* means "beyond my scope.")   **63 quality** character, rank
64 haggard untrained adult hawk, hence unmanageable   **64–
65 check . . . eye** strike at every bird it sees, i.e., dart adroitly from
subject to subject   **65 practice** exercise of skill   **67 folly . . . fit** the
folly he displays is a proper skill   **68 folly-fall'n** having fallen into
folly.   **taint their wit** infect and impugn their own intelligence
71 Dieu . . . monsieur God keep you, sir   **72 Et . . . serviteur** and
you, too; (I am) your servant. (Sir Andrew is not quite up to a reply in
French.)   **74 encounter** (High-sounding word to express "approach.")
75 trade business (suggesting also a commercial venture)   **76 I am
bound** (1) I am on a journey. (Continuing Sir Toby's metaphor in
trade.) (2) I am obliged   **77 list** limit, destination   **78 Taste** try
79 understand stand under, support   **82 gait and entrance** going and
entering (with a pun on *gate*: [1] stride [2] entryway)   **83 prevented**
anticipated   **88 hath no voice** cannot be uttered   **89 pregnant** receptive.   **vouchsafed** proffered, i.e., attentive   **91 all ready** committed to memory for future use

VIOLA
My duty, madam, and most humble service.

OLIVIA   What is your name?

VIOLA
Cesario is your servant's name, fair princess.

OLIVIA
My servant, sir? 'Twas never merry world   98
Since lowly feigning was called compliment.   99
You're servant to the Count Orsino, youth.

VIOLA
And he is yours, and his must needs be yours;   101
Your servant's servant is your servant, madam.

OLIVIA
For him, I think not on him. For his thoughts,   103
Would they were blanks, rather than filled with me!   104

VIOLA
Madam, I come to whet your gentle thoughts
On his behalf.

OLIVIA   O, by your leave, I pray you.   106
I bade you never speak again of him.
But, would you undertake another suit,
I had rather hear you to solicit that
Than music from the spheres.

VIOLA   Dear lady—   110

OLIVIA
Give me leave, beseech you. I did send,
After the last enchantment you did here,
A ring in chase of you; so did I abuse   113
Myself, my servant, and, I fear me, you.
Under your hard construction must I sit,   115
To force that on you in a shameful cunning   116
Which you knew none of yours. What might you
    think?
Have you not set mine honor at the stake   118
And baited it with all th' unmuzzled thoughts   119
That tyrannous heart can think? To one of your
    receiving   120
Enough is shown; a cypress, not a bosom,   121
Hides my heart. So, let me hear you speak.

VIOLA
I pity you.

OLIVIA   That's a degree to love.

VIOLA
No, not a grece; for 'tis a vulgar proof   124
That very oft we pity enemies.

OLIVIA
Why then, methinks 'tis time to smile again.   126

O world, how apt the poor are to be proud!   127
If one should be a prey, how much the better
To fall before the lion than the wolf!   *Clock strikes.*   129
The clock upbraids me with the waste of time.
Be not afraid, good youth, I will not have you;
And yet, when wit and youth is come to harvest
Your wife is like to reap a proper man.   133
There lies your way, due west.

VIOLA   Then westward ho!   134
Grace and good disposition attend your ladyship.   135
You'll nothing, madam, to my lord by me?

OLIVIA   Stay.
I prithee, tell me what thou think'st of me.

VIOLA
That you do think you are not what you are.   139

OLIVIA
If I think so, I think the same of you.   140

VIOLA
Then think you right. I am not what I am.

OLIVIA
I would you were as I would have you be!

VIOLA
Would it be better, madam, than I am?
I wish it might, for now I am your fool.   144

OLIVIA [*aside*]
O, what a deal of scorn looks beautiful
In the contempt and anger of his lip!
A murderous guilt shows not itself more soon
Than love that would seem hid; love's night is
    noon.—   148
Cesario, by the roses of the spring,
By maidhood, honor, truth, and everything,
I love thee so that, maugre all thy pride,   151
Nor wit nor reason can my passion hide.   152
Do not extort thy reasons from this clause,   153
For that I woo, thou therefore hast no cause.   154
But rather reason thus with reason fetter: 155
Love sought is good, but given unsought is better.

VIOLA
By innocence I swear, and by my youth,
I have one heart, one bosom, and one truth,
And that no woman has, nor never none
Shall mistress be of it save I alone.
And so adieu, good madam. Nevermore
Will I my master's tears to you deplore.   162

98–99 'Twas . . . compliment things have never been the same since affected humility (like calling oneself another's servant) began to be mistaken for courtesy   101 yours your servant.   his those belonging to him   103 For as for   104 blanks blank coins ready to be stamped or empty sheets of paper   106 by your leave i.e., allow me to interrupt   110 music from the spheres (The heavenly bodies were thought to be fixed in hollow concentric spheres that revolved one about the other, producing a harmony too exquisite to be heard by human ears.)   113 abuse wrong, mislead   115 hard construction harsh interpretation   116 To force for forcing   118 at the stake (The figure is from bearbaiting.)   119 baited harassed. (Literally, set the dogs on to bite the bear.)   120 receiving capacity, intelligence   121 cypress a thin, gauzelike, black material   124 grece step. (Synonymous with *degree* in the preceding line.)   vulgar proof common experience   126 smile i.e., cast off love's melancholy

127 how . . . proud how ready the unfortunate and rejected (like myself) are to find something to be proud of in their distress   129 To fall . . . wolf i.e., to fall before a noble adversary   133 like likely. proper handsome, worthy   134 westward ho (The cry of Thames watermen to attract westward-bound passengers from London to Westminster.)   135 Grace . . . ladyship may you enjoy God's blessing and a happy frame of mind   139 That . . . are i.e., that you think you are in love with a man, and you are mistaken   140 If . . . you (Olivia may interpret Viola's cryptic statement as suggesting that Olivia "does not know herself," i.e., is distracted with passion; she may also hint at her suspicion that "Cesario" is higher born than he admits.)   144 fool butt   148 love's . . . noon i.e., love, despite its attempt to be secret, reveals itself as plain as day   151 maugre in spite of   152 Nor neither   153–154 Do . . . cause do not rationalize your indifference along these lines, that because I am the wooer you have no cause to reciprocate   155 But . . . fetter but instead control your reasoning with the following reason   162 deplore beweep

OLIVIA
Yet come again, for thou perhaps mayst move
That heart, which now abhors, to like his love.

Exeunt [*separately*].

3.2   *Enter Sir Toby, Sir Andrew, and Fabian.*

SIR ANDREW   No, faith, I'll not stay a jot longer.

SIR TOBY   Thy reason, dear venom, give thy reason.   2

FABIAN   You must needs yield your reason, Sir Andrew.

SIR ANDREW   Marry, I saw your niece do more favors to the Count's servingman than ever she bestowed upon me. I saw 't i' the orchard.   6

SIR TOBY   Did she see thee the while, old boy? Tell me that.

SIR ANDREW   As plain as I see you now.

FABIAN   This was a great argument of love in her toward you.   10

SIR ANDREW   'Slight, will you make an ass o' me?   12

FABIAN   I will prove it legitimate, sir, upon the oaths of judgment and reason.   13

SIR TOBY   And they have been grand-jurymen since before Noah was a sailor.

FABIAN   She did show favor to the youth in your sight only to exasperate you, to awake your dormouse valor, to put fire in your heart and brimstone in your liver. You should then have accosted her, and with some excellent jests, fire-new from the mint, you should have banged the youth into dumbness. This was looked for at your hand, and this was balked. The double gilt of this opportunity you let time wash off, and you are now sailed into the north of my lady's opinion, where you will hang like an icicle on a Dutchman's beard unless you do redeem it by some laudable attempt either of valor or policy.   18 22 23 24 25 26 27 28

SIR ANDREW   An 't be any way, it must be with valor, for policy I hate. I had as lief be a Brownist as a politician.   30 31

SIR TOBY   Why, then, build me thy fortunes upon the basis of valor. Challenge me the Count's youth to fight with him; hurt him in eleven places. My niece shall take note of it; and assure thyself, there is no love-broker in the world can more prevail in man's commendation with woman than report of valor.   32 36

FABIAN   There is no way but this, Sir Andrew.

SIR ANDREW   Will either of you bear me a challenge to him?

SIR TOBY   Go, write it in a martial hand. Be curst and brief; it is no matter how witty, so it be eloquent and full of invention. Taunt him with the license of ink. If thou "thou"-est him some thrice, it shall not be amiss; and as many lies as will lie in thy sheet of paper, although the sheet were big enough for the bed of Ware in England, set 'em down. Go, about it. Let there be gall enough in thy ink, though thou write with a goose pen, no matter. About it.   41 43 44 45 46 47 48 49

SIR ANDREW   Where shall I find you?

SIR TOBY   We'll call thee at the cubiculo. Go.   51

Exit Sir Andrew.

FABIAN   This is a dear manikin to you, Sir Toby.   52

SIR TOBY   I have been dear to him, lad, some two thousand strong or so.   53

FABIAN   We shall have a rare letter from him; but you'll not deliver 't?

SIR TOBY   Never trust me, then; and by all means stir on the youth to an answer. I think oxen and wainropes cannot hale them together. For Andrew, if he were opened and you find so much blood in his liver as will clog the foot of a flea, I'll eat the rest of th' anatomy.   58 59 60 61

FABIAN   And his opposite, the youth, bears in his visage no great presage of cruelty.   62

Enter Maria.

SIR TOBY   Look where the youngest wren of nine comes.   64

MARIA   If you desire the spleen, and will laugh yourselves into stitches, follow me. Yond gull Malvolio is turned heathen, a very renegado; for there is no Christian that means to be saved by believing rightly can ever believe such impossible passages of grossness. He's in yellow stockings.   66 68 70 71

SIR TOBY   And cross-gartered?

MARIA   Most villainously, like a pedant that keeps a school i' the church. I have dogged him like his murderer. He does obey every point of the letter that I dropped to betray him. He does smile his face into more lines than is in the new map with the augmentation of the Indies. You have not seen such a thing as 'tis. I can hardly forbear hurling things at him. I know   73 77

3.2. Location: Olivia's house.
2 venom i.e., person filled with venom. (Sir Andrew professes to be angry.) **6 orchard** garden **10 argument** proof **12 'Slight** by his (God's) light **13 it** my contention.   **oaths** i.e., testimony under oath **18 dormouse** i.e., sleepy and timid **22 banged** struck **23 balked** missed, neglected **23–24 double gilt** thick layer of gold, i.e., rare worth **25 north** i.e., out of the warmth and sunshine of her favor **26–27 icicle . . . beard** (Alludes to the arctic voyage of William Barentz in 1596–1597.) **28 policy** stratagem **30 Brownist** (An early name of the Congregationalists, from the name of the founder, Robert Browne.) **30–31 politician** intriguer. (Sir Andrew misinterprets Sir Toby's more neutral use of *policy*, "clever stratagem.") **32 build me** i.e., build **36 love-broker** agent between lovers

41 curst fierce **43 with . . . ink** i.e., with the freedom that may be risked in writing but not in conversation. **44 "thou"-est** ("Thou" was used only between friends or to inferiors.) **45 lies** charges of lying **46–47 bed of Ware** A famous bedstead capable of holding twelve persons, about eleven feet square, said to have been at the Stag Inn in Ware, Hertfordshire. **48 gall** (1) bitterness, rancor (2) a growth found on certain oaks, used as an ingredient of ink **49 goose pen** (1) goose quill (2) foolish style **51 call thee** call for you.   **cubiculo** little chamber **52 manikin** puppet **53 dear** expensive (playing on *dear*, "a source of pleasure," in the previous speech) **58 wainropes** wagon ropes **59 hale** haul.   **For** as for **60 liver** (A pale and bloodless liver was a sign of cowardice.) **61 anatomy** cadaver **62 opposite** adversary **64 youngest . . . nine** the last hatched and smallest of a nest of wrens **66 the spleen** a laughing fit. (The spleen was thought to be the seat of immoderate laughter.) **68 renegado** renegade, deserter of his religion **70–71 impossible passages of grossness** gross impossibilities (i.e., in the letter) **73 villainously** i.e., abominably.   **pedant** schoolmaster **77 new map** (Probably a reference to a map made by Emmeric Mollineux in 1599 for the purchasers of Hakluyt's *Voyages*, showing more of the East Indies, including Japan, than had ever been mapped before.)

my lady will strike him. If she do, he'll smile and
take 't for a great favor.

SIR TOBY   Come, bring us, bring us where he is.

Exeunt omnes.

❖

3.3   *Enter Sebastian and Antonio.*

SEBASTIAN
I would not by my will have troubled you,
But since you make your pleasure of your pains,
I will no further chide you.

ANTONIO
I could not stay behind you. My desire,
More sharp than filèd steel, did spur me forth,
And not all love to see you—though so much   6
As might have drawn one to a longer voyage—
But jealousy what might befall your travel,   8
Being skilless in these parts, which to a stranger,   9
Unguided and unfriended, often prove
Rough and unhospitable. My willing love,
The rather by these arguments of fear,   12
Set forth in your pursuit.

SEBASTIAN   My kind Antonio,
I can no other answer make but thanks,
And thanks; and ever oft good turns   15
Are shuffled off with such uncurrent pay.   16
But were my worth, as is my conscience, firm,   17
You should find better dealing. What's to do?   18
Shall we go see the relics of this town?   19

ANTONIO
Tomorrow, sir. Best first go see your lodging.

SEBASTIAN
I am not weary, and 'tis long to night.
I pray you, let us satisfy our eyes
With the memorials and the things of fame
That do renown this city.

ANTONIO   Would you'd pardon me.   24
I do not without danger walk these streets.
Once in a sea fight 'gainst the Count his galleys   26
I did some service, of such note indeed
That were I ta'en here it would scarce be answered. 28

SEBASTIAN
Belike you slew great number of his people?   29

ANTONIO
Th' offense is not of such a bloody nature,
Albeit the quality of the time and quarrel
Might well have given us bloody argument.   32
It might have since been answered in repaying   33

What we took from them, which for traffic's sake   34
Most of our city did. Only myself stood out,
For which, if I be lapsèd in this place,   36
I shall pay dear.

SEBASTIAN   Do not then walk too open.

ANTONIO
It doth not fit me. Hold, sir, here's my purse.
                              [*He gives his purse.*]
In the south suburbs, at the Elephant,   39
Is best to lodge. I will bespeak our diet,   40
Whiles you beguile the time and feed your knowl-
edge
With viewing of the town. There shall you have me.

SEBASTIAN   Why I your purse?

ANTONIO
Haply your eye shall light upon some toy   44
You have desire to purchase; and your store   45
I think is not for idle markets, sir.   46

SEBASTIAN
I'll be your purse-bearer and leave you
For an hour.

ANTONIO   To th' Elephant.

SEBASTIAN   I do remember.
                              Exeunt [separately].

❖

3.4   *Enter Olivia and Maria.*

OLIVIA [*aside*]
I have sent after him; he says he'll come.   1
How shall I feast him? What bestow of him?   2
For youth is bought more oft than begged or
borrowed.
I speak too loud.—
Where's Malvolio? He is sad and civil,   5
And suits well for a servant with my fortunes.
Where is Malvolio?

MARIA   He's coming, madam, but in very strange
manner. He is, sure, possessed, madam.   9

OLIVIA   Why, what's the matter? Does he rave?

MARIA   No, madam, he does nothing but smile. Your
ladyship were best to have some guard about you if he
come, for sure the man is tainted in 's wits.   13

OLIVIA
Go call him hither. [*Maria summons Malvolio.*] I am as
mad as he,
If sad and merry madness equal be.

        *Enter Malvolio, [cross-gartered and in yellow
        stockings].*

How now, Malvolio?

3.3. Location: A street.
6 all only, merely.   **so much** i.e., that was great enough   **8 jealousy**
anxiety   **9 skilless in** unacquainted with   **12 The rather** made all the
more willing   **15 And . . . turns** (This probably corrupt line is usually
made to read, "And thanks and ever thanks; and oft good turns.")
16 shuffled off turned aside.   **uncurrent** worthless (such as mere
thanks)   **17 worth** wealth.   **conscience** i.e., moral inclination to assist   **18 dealing** treatment, payment   **19 relics** antiquities   **24 renown** make famous   **26 Count his** Count's, i.e., Duke's   **28 it . . .
answered** I'd be hard put to offer a defense   **29 Belike** perhaps
32 bloody argument cause for bloodshed   **33 answered** compensated

34 traffic's trade's   **36 lapsèd** caught off guard, surprised   **39 Elephant** the name of an inn   **40 bespeak our diet** order our food
44 Haply perhaps.   **toy** trifle   **45 store** store of money   **46 idle markets** unnecessary purchases, luxuries
3.4. Location: Olivia's garden.
1 he . . . come i.e., suppose he says he'll come   **2 of** on   **5 sad and
civil** sober and decorous   **9 possessed** i.e., possessed with an evil
spirit   **13 in 's** in his

MALVOLIO   Sweet lady, ho, ho!

OLIVIA   Smil'st thou? I sent for thee upon a sad 18 occasion.

MALVOLIO   Sad, lady? I could be sad. This does make 20 some obstruction in the blood, this cross-gartering, but what of that? If it please the eye of one, it is with me as the very true sonnet is, "Please one and please 23 all." 24

OLIVIA   Why, how dost thou, man? What is the matter with thee?

MALVOLIO   Not black in my mind, though yellow in my 27 legs. It did come to his hands, and commands shall be 28 executed. I think we do know the sweet roman hand. 29

OLIVIA   Wilt thou go to bed, Malvolio? 30

MALVOLIO   To bed! "Ay, sweetheart, and I'll come to 31 thee." 32

OLIVIA   God comfort thee! Why dost thou smile so and kiss thy hand so oft?

MARIA   How do you, Malvolio?

MALVOLIO   At your request? Yes, nightingales answer 36 daws. 37

MARIA   Why appear you with this ridiculous boldness before my lady?

MALVOLIO   "Be not afraid of greatness." 'Twas well writ.

OLIVIA   What mean'st thou by that, Malvolio?

MALVOLIO   "Some are born great—"

OLIVIA   Ha?

MALVOLIO   "Some achieve greatness—"

OLIVIA   What sayst thou?

MALVOLIO   "And some have greatness thrust upon them."

OLIVIA   Heaven restore thee!

MALVOLIO   "Remember who commended thy yellow stockings—"

OLIVIA   Thy yellow stockings?

MALVOLIO   "And wished to see thee cross-gartered."

OLIVIA   Cross-gartered?

MALVOLIO   "Go to, thou art made, if thou desir'st to be so—"

OLIVIA   Am I made?

MALVOLIO   "If not, let me see thee a servant still."

OLIVIA   Why, this is very midsummer madness. 58

Enter Servant.

SERVANT   Madam, the young gentleman of the Count Orsino's is returned. I could hardly entreat him back. He attends your ladyship's pleasure.

OLIVIA   I'll come to him. [*Exit Servant.*] Good Maria, let this fellow be looked to. Where's my cousin Toby? Let some of my people have a special care of him. I would not have him miscarry for the half of my dowry. 65

Exeunt [Olivia and Maria, different ways].

MALVOLIO   Oho, do you come near me now? No worse 66 man than Sir Toby to look to me! This concurs directly with the letter. She sends him on purpose that I may appear stubborn to him, for she incites me to that in the letter. "Cast thy humble slough," says she; "be opposite with a kinsman, surly with servants; let thy tongue tang with arguments of state; put thyself into the trick of singularity." And consequently sets down 73 the manner how: as, a sad face, a reverend carriage, a 74 slow tongue, in the habit of some sir of note, and so 75 forth. I have limed her, but it is Jove's doing, and Jove 76 make me thankful! And when she went away now, "Let this fellow be looked to." "Fellow!" Not "Malvo- 78 lio," nor after my degree, but "fellow." Why, every- 79 thing adheres together, that no dram of a scruple, no 80 scruple of a scruple, no obstacle, no incredulous or un- 81 safe circumstance—what can be said?—nothing that 82 can be can come between me and the full prospect of my hopes. Well, Jove, not I, is the doer of this, and he is to be thanked.

Enter [Sir] Toby, Fabian, and Maria.

SIR TOBY   Which way is he, in the name of sanctity? If all the devils of hell be drawn in little, and Legion him- 87 self possessed him, yet I'll speak to him.

FABIAN   Here he is, here he is. —How is 't with you, sir? How is 't with you, man?

MALVOLIO   Go off. I discard you. Let me enjoy my private. Go off. 92

MARIA   Lo, how hollow the fiend speaks within him! Did not I tell you? Sir Toby, my lady prays you to have a care of him.

MALVOLIO   Aha, does she so?

SIR TOBY   Go to, go to! Peace, peace, we must deal gently with him. Let me alone.—How do you, 98 Malvolio? How is 't with you? What, man, defy the 99 devil! Consider, he's an enemy to mankind.

MALVOLIO   Do you know what you say?

MARIA   La you, an you speak ill of the devil, how he 102 takes it at heart! Pray God he be not bewitched!

FABIAN   Carry his water to the wisewoman. 104

MARIA   Marry, and it shall be done tomorrow morning, if I live. My lady would not lose him for more than I'll say.

MALVOLIO   How now, mistress?

---

18 **sad** serious   20 **sad** (1) serious (2) melancholy   23 **sonnet** song, ballad   23–24 **Please . . . all** to please one special person is as good as to please everybody. (The refrain of a ballad.)   27 **black** i.e., melancholic   28 **It** i.e., the letter.   **his** Malvolio's   29 **roman hand** fashionable italic style of handwriting   30 **go to bed** i.e., try to sleep off your mental distress   31–32 **Ay . . . thee** (Malvolio quotes from a popular song of the day.)   36–37 **nightingales answer daws** i.e., (to Maria), do you suppose a fine fellow like me would answer a lowly creature (a *daw*, a "crow") like you   58 **midsummer madness** (A proverbial phrase; the midsummer moon was supposed to cause madness.)

65 **miscarry** come to harm   66 **come near** understand, appreciate   73 **consequently** thereafter   74 **sad** serious   75 **habit . . . note** attire suited to a man of distinction   76 **limed** caught like a bird with birdlime (a sticky substance spread on branches)   78 **Fellow** (Malvolio takes the original meaning, "companion.")   79 **after my degree** according to my position   80 **dram** (Literally, one-eighth of a fluid ounce.)   **scruple** (Literally, one-third of a dram.)   81 **incredulous** incredible   81–82 **unsafe** uncertain, unreliable   87 **drawn in little** (1) portrayed in miniature (2) gathered into a small space, i.e., in Malvolio's heart.   **Legion** an unclean spirit. ("My name is Legion, for we are many," Mark 5:9.)   92 **private** privacy   98 **Let me alone** leave him to me   99 **defy** renounce   102 **La you** look you   104 **water** urine (for medical analysis)

MARIA   O Lord!

SIR TOBY   Prithee, hold thy peace; this is not the way. Do you not see you move him? Let me alone with 111 him.

FABIAN   No way but gentleness, gently, gently. The fiend is rough, and will not be roughly used.

SIR TOBY   Why, how now, my bawcock! How dost 115 thou, chuck? 116

MALVOLIO   Sir!

SIR TOBY   Ay, biddy, come with me. What, man, 'tis 118 not for gravity to play at cherry-pit with Satan. Hang 119 him, foul collier! 120

MARIA   Get him to say his prayers, good Sir Toby, get him to pray.

MALVOLIO   My prayers, minx?

MARIA   No, I warrant you, he will not hear of godliness.

MALVOLIO   Go hang yourselves all! You are idle, shal- 125 low things; I am not of your element. You shall know 126 more hereafter.   *Exit.* 127

SIR TOBY   Is 't possible?

FABIAN   If this were played upon a stage, now, I could condemn it as an improbable fiction.

SIR TOBY   His very genius hath taken the infection of 131 the device, man.

MARIA   Nay, pursue him now, lest the device take air 133 and taint. 134

FABIAN   Why, we shall make him mad indeed.

MARIA   The house will be the quieter.

SIR TOBY   Come, we'll have him in a dark room and 137 bound. My niece is already in the belief that he's mad. 138 We may carry it thus for our pleasure and his penance 139 till our very pastime, tired out of breath, prompt us to have mercy on him, at which time we will bring the device to the bar and crown thee for a finder of 142 madmen. But see, but see! 143

Enter Sir Andrew [with a letter].

FABIAN   More matter for a May morning. 144

SIR ANDREW   Here's the challenge. Read it. I warrant there's vinegar and pepper in 't.

FABIAN   Is 't so saucy? 147

SIR ANDREW   Ay, is 't, I warrant him. Do but read.

SIR TOBY   Give me. [*He reads.*] "Youth, whatsoever thou art, thou art but a scurvy fellow."

FABIAN   Good, and valiant.

SIR TOBY [*reads*]   "Wonder not, nor admire not in thy 152 mind, why I do call thee so, for I will show thee no reason for 't."

FABIAN   A good note, that keeps you from the blow of 155 the law.

SIR TOBY [*reads*]   "Thou com'st to the Lady Olivia, and in my sight she uses thee kindly. But thou liest in thy throat; that is not the matter I challenge thee for."

FABIAN   Very brief, and to exceeding good sense—less.

SIR TOBY [*reads*]   "I will waylay thee going home, where if it be thy chance to kill me—"

FABIAN   Good.

SIR TOBY [*reads*]   "Thou kill'st me like a rogue and a villain."

FABIAN   Still you keep o' the windy side of the law. 166 Good.

SIR TOBY [*reads*]   "Fare thee well, and God have mercy upon one of our souls! He may have mercy upon mine, but my hope is better, and so look to thyself. 170 Thy friend, as thou usest him, and thy sworn enemy, Andrew Aguecheek." If this letter move him not, his legs cannot. I'll give 't 173 him.

MARIA   You may have very fit occasion for 't. He is now in some commerce with my lady, and will by and by 176 depart.

SIR TOBY   Go, Sir Andrew. Scout me for him at the 178 corner of the orchard like a bum-baily. So soon as ever 179 thou seest him, draw, and as thou draw'st, swear hor- 180 rible; for it comes to pass oft that a terrible oath, with 181 a swaggering accent sharply twanged off, gives man-hood more approbation than ever proof itself would 183 have earned him. Away!

SIR ANDREW   Nay, let me alone for swearing.   *Exit.* 185

SIR TOBY   Now will not I deliver his letter, for the behav-ior of the young gentleman gives him out to be of good capacity and breeding; his employment between his lord and my niece confirms no less. Therefore this letter, being so excellently ignorant, will breed no ter-ror in the youth. He will find it comes from a clodpoll. 191 But, sir, I will deliver his challenge by word of mouth, set upon Aguecheek a notable report of valor, and drive the gentleman—as I know his youth will aptly 194 receive it—into a most hideous opinion of his rage, 195 skill, fury, and impetuosity. This will so fright them both that they will kill one another by the look, like cockatrices. 198

Enter Olivia and Viola.

FABIAN   Here he comes with your niece. Give them way 199 till he take leave, and presently after him. 200

---

111 **move** upset, excite   115 **bawcock** fine fellow. (From the French *beau-coq*.)   116 **chuck** (A form of "chick," term of endearment.) 118 **biddy** chicken   119 **for gravity** suitable for a man of your dig-nity.   **cherry-pit** a children's game consisting of throwing cherry stones into a little hole   120 **collier** i.e., Satan. (Literally, a coal ven-dor.)   125 **idle** foolish   126 **element** sphere of existence 126–127 **know more** i.e., hear about this   131 **genius** i.e., soul, spirit   133–134 **take . . . taint** become exposed to air (i.e., become known) and thus spoil   137–138 **in . . . bound** (The standard treat-ment for insanity at this time.)   139 **carry** manage   142 **bar** i.e., bar of judgment   142–143 **finder of madmen** member of a jury charged with "finding" if the accused is insane   144 **matter . . . morning** sport for Mayday plays or games   147 **saucy** (1) spicy (2) insolent 152 **admire** marvel

155 **note** observation, remark   166 **windy** windward, i.e., safe, where one is less likely to be driven onto legal rocks and shoals 170 **my hope is better** (Sir Andrew's comically inept way of saying he hopes to be the survivor; instead, he seems to say, "May I be damned.")   173 **move** (1) stir up (2) set in motion   176 **commerce** transaction   178 **Scout me** keep watch   179 **bum-baily** minor sher-iff's officer employed in making arrests   180–181 **horrible** horribly 183 **approbation** reputation (for courage).   **proof** performance 185 **let . . . swearing** don't worry about my ability in swearing 191 **clodpoll** blockhead   194–195 **his . . . it** his inexperience will make him all the more ready to believe it   198 **cockatrices** basilisks, fabulous serpents reputed to be able to kill by a mere look   199 **Give them way** stay out of their way   200 **presently** immediately

SIR TOBY   I will meditate the while upon some horrid 201
message for a challenge.
                    [*Exeunt Sir Toby, Fabian, and Maria.*]
OLIVIA
I have said too much unto a heart of stone
And laid mine honor too unchary on 't.   204
There's something in me that reproves my fault,
But such a headstrong potent fault it is
That it but mocks reproof.
VIOLA
With the same havior that your passion bears
Goes on my master's griefs.
OLIVIA [*giving a locket*]
Here, wear this jewel for me. 'Tis my picture.   210
Refuse it not; it hath no tongue to vex you.
And I beseech you come again tomorrow.
What shall you ask of me that I'll deny,
That honor, saved, may upon asking give?   214
VIOLA
Nothing but this: your true love for my master.
OLIVIA
How with mine honor may I give him that
Which I have given to you?
VIOLA   I will acquit you.   217
OLIVIA
Well, come again tomorrow. Fare thee well.
A fiend like thee might bear my soul to hell.   [*Exit.*] 219

Enter [Sir] Toby and Fabian.

SIR TOBY   Gentleman, God save thee.
VIOLA   And you, sir.
SIR TOBY   That defense thou hast, betake thee to 't. Of
what nature the wrongs are thou hast done him, I
know not, but thy intercepter, full of despite, bloody 224
as the hunter, attends thee at the orchard end. 225
Dismount thy tuck, be yare in thy preparation, for thy 226
assailant is quick, skillful, and deadly.
VIOLA   You mistake sir. I am sure no man hath any
quarrel to me. My remembrance is very free and clear 229
from any image of offense done to any man.
SIR TOBY   You'll find it otherwise, I assure you. Therefore, if you hold your life at any price, betake you to
your guard, for your opposite hath in him what youth, 233
strength, skill, and wrath can furnish man withal. 234
VIOLA   I pray you, sir, what is he?
SIR TOBY   He is knight, dubbed with unhatched rapier 236
and on carpet consideration, but he is a devil in 237
private brawl. Souls and bodies hath he divorced
three, and his incensement at this moment is so implacable that satisfaction can be none but by pangs of

death and sepulcher. Hob, nob is his word; give 't or 241
take 't.
VIOLA   I will return again into the house and desire
some conduct of the lady. I am no fighter. I have 244
heard of some kind of men that put quarrels purposely on others, to taste their valor. Belike this is a 246
man of that quirk. 247
SIR TOBY   Sir, no. His indignation derives itself out of a
very competent injury; therefore, get you on and give 249
him his desire. Back you shall not to the house unless
you undertake that with me which with as much 251
safety you might answer him. Therefore, on, or strip
your sword stark naked; for meddle you must, that's 253
certain, or forswear to wear iron about you. 254
VIOLA   This is as uncivil as strange. I beseech you, do
me this courteous office, as to know of the knight what 256
my offense to him is. It is something of my negligence,
nothing of my purpose.
SIR TOBY   I will do so.—Signor Fabian, stay you by this
gentleman till my return.   *Exit [Sir] Toby.*
VIOLA   Pray you, sir, do you know of this matter?
FABIAN   I know the knight is incensed against you,
even to a mortal arbitrament, but nothing of the 263
circumstance more.
VIOLA   I beseech you, what manner of man is he?
FABIAN   Nothing of that wonderful promise, to read 266
him by his form, as you are like to find him in the 267
proof of his valor. He is, indeed, sir, the most skillful,
bloody, and fatal opposite that you could possibly
have found in any part of Illyria. Will you walk 270
towards him, I will make your peace with him if I can.
VIOLA   I shall be much bound to you for 't. I am one
that had rather go with Sir Priest than Sir Knight. I 273
care not who knows so much of my mettle.   *Exeunt.*

Enter [Sir] Toby and [Sir] Andrew.

SIR TOBY   Why, man, he's a very devil; I have not seen
such a firago. I had a pass with him, rapier, scabbard, 276
and all, and he gives me the stuck in with such a 277
mortal motion that it is inevitable; and on the answer, 278
he pays you as surely as your feet hits the ground they
step on. They say he has been fencer to the Sophy. 280
SIR ANDREW   Pox on 't, I'll not meddle with him.
SIR TOBY   Ay, but he will not now be pacified. Fabian
can scarce hold him yonder.
SIR ANDREW   Plague on 't, an I thought he had been
valiant and so cunning in fence, I'd have seen him
damned ere I'd have challenged him. Let him let the
matter slip and I'll give him my horse, gray Capilet. 287

---

201 horrid terrifying. (Literally, "bristling.")   **204 laid** hazarded.   **unchary on 't** recklessly on it   **210 jewel** (Any piece of jewelry; here, seemingly, a locket.)   **214 That . . . give** that can be granted without compromising your honor   **217 acquit you** release you of your promise   **219 like** resembling   **224 intercepter** he who lies in wait.   **despite** defiance   **224–225 bloody as the hunter** bloodthirsty as a hunting dog   **226 Dismount thy tuck** draw your rapier.   **yare** ready, nimble   **229 to** with   **233 opposite** opponent.   **what** whatsoever   **234 withal** with   **236 unhatched** unhacked, unused in battle   **237 carpet consideration** (A carpet knight was one whose title was obtained, not in battle, but through connections at court.)

241 Hob, nob have or have not, i.e., give it or take it, kill or be killed.   **word** motto   **224 conduct** escort   **246 taste** test. **Belike** probably   **247 quirk** peculiar humor   **249 competent** sufficient   **251 that** i.e., to give satisfaction in a duel   **253 meddle** engage (in conflict)   **254 forswear . . . iron** give up your right to wear a sword   **256 know of** inquire from   **263 mortal arbitrament** trial to the death   **266–267 read . . . form** judge him by his appearance   **267 like** likely   **270 Will you** if you will   **273 go with** associate with.   **Sir Priest** (*Sir* was a courtesy title for priests.)   **276 firago** virago.   **pass** bout   **277 stuck in** stoccado, a thrust in fencing   **278 answer** return hit   **280 to** in the service of   **287 Capilet** i.e., "little horse." (From "capel," a nag.)

SIR TOBY   I'll make the motion. Stand here, make a 288
good show on 't. This shall end without the perdition 289
of souls. [*Aside, as he crosses to meet Fabian.*] Marry, I'll 290
ride your horse as well as I ride you.

Enter Fabian and Viola.

[*Aside to Fabian.*] I have his horse to take up the 292
quarrel. I have persuaded him the youth's a devil.
FABIAN   He is as horribly conceited of him, and pants 294
and looks pale as if a bear were at his heels.
SIR TOBY [*to Viola*]   There's no remedy, sir, he will
fight with you for 's oath's sake. Marry, he hath
better bethought him of his quarrel, and he finds
that now scarce to be worth talking of. Therefore
draw, for the supportance of his vow; he protests he 300
will not hurt you.
VIOLA [*aside*]   Pray God defend me! A little thing
would make me tell them how much I lack of a man.
FABIAN   Give ground, if you see him furious.
SIR TOBY [*crossing to Sir Andrew*]   Come, Sir Andrew,
there's no remedy. The gentleman will, for his
honor's sake, have one bout with you. He cannot by
the *duello* avoid it. But he has promised me, as he is 308
a gentleman and a soldier, he will not hurt you.
Come on, to 't.
SIR ANDREW   Pray God he keep his oath!

Enter Antonio.

VIOLA   I do assure you, 'tis against my will.
[*They draw.*]
ANTONIO [*drawing, to Sir Andrew*]
Put up your sword. If this young gentleman
Have done offense, I take the fault on me;
If you offend him, I for him defy you.
SIR TOBY   You, sir? Why, what are you?
ANTONIO
One, sir, that for his love dares yet do more
Than you have heard him brag to you he will.
SIR TOBY [*drawing*]
Nay, if you be an undertaker, I am for you. 319

Enter Officers.

FABIAN   O good Sir Toby, hold! Here come the officers.
SIR TOBY [*to Antonio*]   I'll be with you anon.
VIOLA [*to Sir Andrew*]   Pray, sir, put your sword up, if
you please.
SIR ANDREW   Marry, will I, sir; and for that I promised 324
you, I'll be as good as my word. He will bear you 325
easily, and reins well.
FIRST OFFICER   This is the man. Do thy office.
SECOND OFFICER
Antonio, I arrest thee at the suit
Of Count Orsino.
ANTONIO   You do mistake me, sir.

FIRST OFFICER
No, sir, no jot. I know your favor well, 330
Though now you have no sea-cap on your head.—
Take him away. He knows I know him well.
ANTONIO
I must obey. [*To Viola.*] This comes with seeking you.
But there's no remedy; I shall answer it. 334
What will you do, now my necessity
Makes me to ask you for my purse? It grieves me
Much more for what I cannot do for you
Than what befalls myself. You stand amazed,
But be of comfort.
SECOND OFFICER   Come, sir, away.
ANTONIO [*to Viola*]
I must entreat of you some of that money.
VIOLA   What money, sir?
For the fair kindness you have showed me here,
And part being prompted by your present trouble, 343
Out of my lean and low ability
I'll lend you something. My having is not much; 345
I'll make division of my present with you. 346
Hold, there's half my coffer.   [*She offers money.*] 347
ANTONIO   Will you deny me now?
Is 't possible that my deserts to you 349
Can lack persuasion? Do not tempt my misery, 350
Lest that it make me so unsound a man 351
As to upbraid you with those kindnesses
That I have done for you.
VIOLA   I know of none,
Nor know I you by voice or any feature.
I hate ingratitude more in a man
Than lying, vainness, babbling drunkenness, 356
Or any taint of vice whose strong corruption
Inhabits our frail blood.
ANTONIO   O heavens themselves!
SECOND OFFICER   Come, sir, I pray you, go.
ANTONIO
Let me speak a little. This youth that you see here
I snatched one half out of the jaws of death,
Relieved him with such sanctity of love, 363
And to his image, which methought did promise 364
Most venerable worth, did I devotion. 365
FIRST OFFICER
What 's that to us? The time goes by. Away!
ANTONIO
But, O, how vile an idol proves this god!
Thou hast, Sebastian, done good feature shame. 368
In nature there's no blemish but the mind;
None can be called deformed but the unkind. 370

---

288 **motion** offer   289–290 **perdition of souls** i.e., loss of lives
292 **take up** settle, make up   294 **He . . . him** i.e., Cesario has as
horrible a conception of Sir Andrew   300 **supportance** upholding
308 **duello** dueling code   319 **undertaker** one who takes upon himself a task or business; here, a challenger.   **for you** ready for you
324 **for that** as for what   325 **He** i.e., the horse

330 **favor** face   334 **answer it** stand trial and make reparation for it
343 **part** partly   345 **having** wealth   346 **present** present store
347 **coffer** purse. (Literally, strongbox.)   349–350 **deserts . . . persuasion** claims on you can fail to persuade you to help me
350 **tempt** try too severely   351 **unsound** morally weak, lacking in
self-control   356 **vainness** vaingloriousness   363 **such** much
364 **image** what he appeared to be (playing on the idea of a religious
icon to be venerated)   365 **venerable worth** worthiness of being venerated   368 **Thou . . . shame** i.e., you have shamed physical beauty
by showing that it does not always reflect inner beauty   370 **unkind**
ungrateful, unnatural

Virtue is beauty, but the beauteous evil 371
Are empty trunks o'erflourished by the devil. 372

FIRST OFFICER
The man grows mad. Away with him! Come, come,
sir.

ANTONIO Lead me on.   *Exit [with Officers].*

VIOLA *[aside]*
Methinks his words do from such passion fly
That he believes himself. So do not I. 376
Prove true, imagination, O, prove true,
That I, dear brother, be now ta'en for you!

SIR TOBY Come hither, knight. Come hither, Fabian.
We'll whisper o'er a couplet or two of most sage saws. 380
    [They gather apart from Viola.]

VIOLA
He named Sebastian. I my brother know 381
Yet living in my glass; even such and so 382
In favor was my brother, and he went
Still in this fashion, color, ornament, 384
For him I imitate. O, if it prove, 385
Tempests are kind, and salt waves fresh in love!
       [Exit.]

SIR TOBY A very dishonest paltry boy, and more a 387
coward than a hare. His dishonesty appears in leaving 388
his friend here in necessity and denying him; and for 389
his cowardship, ask Fabian.

FABIAN A coward, a most devout coward, religious in it. 391

SIR ANDREW 'Slid, I'll after him again and beat him. 392

SIR TOBY Do, cuff him soundly, but never draw thy
sword.

SIR ANDREW An I do not—   *[Exit.]*

FABIAN Come, let's see the event. 396

SIR TOBY I dare lay any money 'twill be nothing yet. 397
      Exeunt.

❖

4.1 *Enter Sebastian and Clown [Feste].*

FESTE Will you make me believe that I am not sent for
you?

SEBASTIAN Go to, go to, thou art a foolish fellow. Let
me be clear of thee.

FESTE Well held out, i' faith! No, I do not know you, 5
nor I am not sent to you by my lady to bid you come
speak with her, nor your name is not Master Cesario,
nor this is not my nose, neither. Nothing that is so is so.

SEBASTIAN I prithee, vent thy folly somewhere else. 9
Thou know'st not me.

FESTE Vent my folly! He has heard that word of some 11
great man, and now applies it to a fool. Vent my folly!
I am afraid this great lubber, the world, will prove a 13
cockney. I prithee now, ungird thy strangeness and 14
tell me what I shall vent to my lady. Shall I vent to her
that thou art coming?

SEBASTIAN I prithee, foolish Greek, depart from me. 17
There's money for thee. [*He gives money.*] If you tarry
longer, I shall give worse payment.

FESTE By my troth, thou hast an open hand. These 20
wise men that give fools money get themselves a good
report—after fourteen years' purchase. 22

Enter [Sir] Andrew, [Sir] Toby, and Fabian.

SIR ANDREW Now, sir, have I met you again? There 's
for you!   [*He strikes Sebastian.*]

SEBASTIAN Why, there's for thee, and there, and there!
 [*He beats Sir Andrew with the hilt of his dagger.*]
Are all the people mad?

SIR TOBY Hold, sir, or I'll throw your dagger o'er the
house.

FESTE This will I tell my lady straight. I would not be in 29
some of your coats for twopence. [*Exit.*]

SIR TOBY Come on, sir, hold! [*He grips Sebastian.*]

SIR ANDREW Nay, let him alone. I'll go another way to
work with him. I'll have an action of battery against 33
him, if there be any law in Illyria. Though I struck him
first, yet it's no matter for that.

SEBASTIAN Let go thy hand!

SIR TOBY Come, sir, I will not let you go. Come, my
young soldier, put up your iron. You are well fleshed. 38
Come on.

SEBASTIAN
I will be free from thee. [*He breaks free and draws his
 sword.*] What wouldst thou now?
If thou dar'st tempt me further, draw thy sword. 41

SIR TOBY What, what? Nay, then I must have an ounce
or two of this malapert blood from you. [*He draws.*] 43

Enter Olivia.

OLIVIA
Hold, Toby! On thy life I charge thee, hold!

SIR TOBY Madam—

OLIVIA
Will it be ever thus? Ungracious wretch,
Fit for the mountains and the barbarous caves,
Where manners ne'er were preached! Out of my
 sight!—

Be not offended, dear Cesario.—
Rudesby, begone!
        [*Exeunt Sir Toby, Sir Andrew, and Fabian.*]
              I prithee, gentle friend,   50
Let thy fair wisdom, not thy passion, sway
In this uncivil and unjust extent   52
Against thy peace. Go with me to my house,
And hear thou there how many fruitless pranks
This ruffian hath botched up, that thou thereby   55
Mayst smile at this. Thou shalt not choose but go.   56
Do not deny. Beshrew his soul for me!   57
He started one poor heart of mine, in thee.   58

SEBASTIAN [*aside*]
What relish is in this? How runs the stream?   59
Or I am mad, or else this is a dream.   60
Let fancy still my sense in Lethe steep;   61
If it be thus to dream, still let me sleep!

OLIVIA
Nay, come, I prithee. Would thou'dst be ruled by
   me!

SEBASTIAN
Madam, I will.

OLIVIA   O, say so, and so be!   *Exeunt.*

❖

4.2   *Enter Maria [with a gown and a false beard], and*
        Clown [Feste].

MARIA   Nay, I prithee, put on this gown and this beard;
   make him believe thou art Sir Topas the curate. Do it   2
   quickly. I'll call Sir Toby the whilst.   [*Exit.*]   3

FESTE   Well, I'll put it on, and I will dissemble myself   4
in 't, and I would I were the first that ever dissembled
in such a gown. [*He disguises himself in gown and
beard.*] I am not tall enough to become the function   7
well, nor lean enough to be thought a good student;   8
but to be said an honest man and a good housekeeper   9
goes as fairly as to say a careful man and a great   10
scholar. The competitors enter.   11

        Enter [Sir] Toby [and Maria].

---

50 Rudesby ruffian   **52 extent** attack   **55 botched up** clumsily contrived   **56 Thou . . . go** I insist on your going with me   **57 deny**
refuse.   **Beshrew** curse. (A mild oath.)   **for me** on my account
58 He . . . thee i.e., he alarmed half of my heart, which lies in your
bosom. (To *start* is also to drive an animal such as a *hart* [*heart*] from
its cover, though the term is more usually applied to rabbits.)
59 What . . . this? i.e., what am I to make of this? (*Relish* means
"taste.")   **60 Or** either   **61 fancy** imagination.   **still** ever.   **Lethe** the
river of forgetfulness in the underworld; i.e., forgetfulness

4.2. Location: Olivia's house.
2 Sir (An honorific title for priests.)   **Topas** (A name perhaps derived
from Chaucer's comic knight in the "Rime of Sir Thopas" or from a
similar character in Lyly's *Endymion*. Topaz, a semiprecious stone,
was believed to be a cure for lunacy.)   **3 the whilst** in the meantime
4 dissemble disguise (with a play on "feign")   **7 become** grace,
adorn.   **function** priestly office   **8 lean** (Scholars were proverbially
sparing of diet.)   **student** scholar (in divinity)   **9 said** called, known
as.   **housekeeper** household manager, hospitable person   **10 goes as
fairly as** sounds just as honorable as.   **careful** painstaking in studies.
(Feste suggests that honesty and charity are found as often in ordinary
men as in clerics.)   **11 competitors** associates, partners (in this plot)

SIR TOBY   Jove bless thee, Master Parson.

FESTE   *Bonos dies*, Sir Toby. For, as the old hermit of   13
Prague, that never saw pen and ink, very wittily said   14
to a niece of King Gorboduc, "That that is, is"; so I,   15
being Master Parson, am Master Parson; for what is
"that" but "that," and "is" but "is"?

SIR TOBY   To him, Sir Topas.

FESTE   What, ho, I say! Peace in this prison!
             [*He approaches the door
            behind which Malvolio is confined.*]

SIR TOBY   The knave counterfeits well; a good knave.

MALVOLIO   (*within*) Who calls there?

FESTE   Sir Topas the curate, who comes to visit Malvolio
the lunatic.

MALVOLIO   Sir Topas, Sir Topas, good Sir Topas, go to
my lady—

FESTE   Out, hyperbolical fiend! How vexest thou this   26
man! Talkest thou nothing but of ladies?

SIR TOBY   Well said, Master Parson.

MALVOLIO   Sir Topas, never was man thus wronged.
Good Sir Topas, do not think I am mad. They have
laid me here in hideous darkness.

FESTE   Fie, thou dishonest Satan! I call thee by the most
modest terms, for I am one of those gentle ones that   33
will use the devil himself with courtesy. Sayst thou
that house is dark?   35

MALVOLIO   As hell, Sir Topas.

FESTE   Why, it hath bay windows transparent as barri-   37
cadoes, and the clerestories toward the south north   38
are as lustrous as ebony; and yet complainest thou of
obstruction?

MALVOLIO   I am not mad, Sir Topas. I say to you this
house is dark.

FESTE   Madman, thou errest. I say there is no darkness
but ignorance, in which thou art more puzzled than
the Egyptians in their fog.   45

MALVOLIO   I say this house is as dark as ignorance,
though ignorance were as dark as hell; and I say there
was never man thus abused. I am no more mad than
you are. Make the trial of it in any constant question.   49

FESTE   What is the opinion of Pythagoras concerning   50
wildfowl?   51

MALVOLIO   That the soul of our grandam might haply   52
inhabit a bird.

FESTE   What think'st thou of his opinion?

MALVOLIO   I think nobly of the soul, and no way
approve his opinion.

---

13 Bonos dies good day   **13–14 hermit of Prague** (Probably another
invented authority.)   **15 King Gorboduc** a legendary king of ancient
Britain, protagonist in the English tragedy *Gorboduc* (1562)   **26 hyperbolical** vehement, boisterous.   **fiend** i.e., the devil supposedly
possessing Malvolio   **33 modest terms** mild terms (such as "dishonest" instead of "lying")   **35 house** i.e., room   **37–38 barricadoes**
barricades (which are opaque. Feste speaks comically in impossible
paradoxes, but Malvolio seems not to notice.)   **38 clerestories** windows in an upper wall   **45 Egyptians . . . fog** (Alluding to the darkness brought upon Egypt by Moses; see Exodus 10:21–23.)   **49 constant question** problem that requires consecutive reasoning   **50–
51 Pythagoras . . . wildfowl** (An opening for the discussion of
transmigration of souls, a doctrine held by Pythagoras.)   **52 haply**
perhaps

FESTE Fare thee well. Remain thou still in darkness.
Thou shalt hold th' opinion of Pythagoras ere I will
allow of thy wits, and fear to kill a woodcock lest thou   59
dispossess the soul of thy grandam. Fare thee well.
          [*He moves away from Malvolio's prison.*]
MALVOLIO Sir Topas, Sir Topas!
SIR TOBY My most exquisite Sir Topas!
FESTE Nay, I am for all waters.   63
MARIA Thou mightst have done this without thy beard
and gown. He sees thee not.
SIR TOBY To him in thine own voice, and bring me
word how thou find'st him. I would we were well rid
of this knavery. If he may be conveniently delivered, I   68
would he were, for I am now so far in offense with
my niece that I cannot pursue with any safety this
sport to the upshot. Come by and by to my chamber.   71
                    Exit [*with Maria*].
FESTE [*singing as he approaches Malvolio's prison*]
      "Hey, Robin, jolly Robin,   72
      Tell me how thy lady does."   73
MALVOLIO Fool!
FESTE "My lady is unkind, pardie."   75
MALVOLIO Fool!
FESTE "Alas, why is she so?"
MALVOLIO Fool, I say!
FESTE "She loves another—" Who calls, ha?
MALVOLIO Good Fool, as ever thou wilt deserve well at
my hand, help me to a candle, and pen, ink, and
paper. As I am a gentleman, I will live to be thankful
to thee for 't.
FESTE Master Malvolio?
MALVOLIO Ay, good Fool.
FESTE Alas, sir, how fell you beside your five wits?   86
MALVOLIO Fool, there was never man so notoriously 87
abused. I am as well in my wits, Fool, as thou art.   88
FESTE But as well? Then you are mad indeed, if you be 89
no better in your wits than a fool.
MALVOLIO They have here propertied me, keep me in 91
darkness, send ministers to me—asses—and do all
they can to face me out of my wits.   93
FESTE Advise you what you say. The minister is here. 94
[*He speaks as Sir Topas.*] Malvolio, Malvolio, thy wits
the heavens restore! Endeavor thyself to sleep, and
leave thy vain bibble-babble.
MALVOLIO Sir Topas!
FESTE [*in Sir Topas' voice*] Maintain no words with
him, good fellow. [*In his own voice.*] Who, I, sir? Not
I, sir. God b' wi' you, good Sir Topas. [*In Sir Topas'* 101
voice.] Marry, amen. [*In his own voice.*] I will, sir, I will.

MALVOLIO Fool! Fool! Fool, I say!
FESTE Alas, sir, be patient. What say you, sir? I am
shent for speaking to you.   105
MALVOLIO Good Fool, help me to some light and some
paper. I tell thee I am as well in my wits as any man in
Illyria.
FESTE Welladay that you were, sir!   109
MALVOLIO By this hand, I am. Good Fool, some ink,
paper, and light; and convey what I will set down to
my lady. It shall advantage thee more than ever the
bearing of letter did.
FESTE I will help you to 't. But tell me true, are you
not mad indeed, or do you but counterfeit?
MALVOLIO Believe me, I am not. I tell thee true.
FESTE Nay, I'll ne'er believe a madman till I see his
brains. I will fetch you light and paper and ink.
MALVOLIO Fool, I'll requite it in the highest degree. I
prithee, begone.
FESTE [*sings*]
      I am gone, sir,
      And anon, sir,
      I'll be with you again,
      In a trice,
      Like to the old Vice,   125
   Your need to sustain;

      Who, with dagger of lath,   127
      In his rage and his wrath,
   Cries, "Aha!" to the devil;
      Like a mad lad,
      "Pare thy nails, dad?   131
   Adieu, goodman devil!"   *Exit.* 132

                    ❖

4.3   *Enter Sebastian* [*with a pearl*].

SEBASTIAN
   This is the air; that is the glorious sun;
   This pearl she gave me, I do feel 't and see 't;
   And though 'tis wonder that enwraps me thus,
   Yet 'tis not madness. Where's Antonio, then?
   I could not find him at the Elephant;
   Yet there he was, and there I found this credit,   6
   That he did range the town to seek me out.
   His counsel now might do me golden service;
   For though my soul disputes well with my sense   9
   That this may be some error, but no madness,
   Yet doth this accident and flood of fortune   11
   So far exceed all instance, all discourse,   12

59 allow of thy wits certify your sanity. **woodcock** (A proverbially
stupid bird, easily caught.) **63 Nay . . . waters** i.e., indeed, I can
turn my hand to anything **68 delivered** i.e., delivered from prison
71 upshot conclusion **72–73 Hey, Robin . . . does** (Another fragment of an old song, a version of which is attributed to Sir Thomas
Wyatt.) **75 pardie** i.e., by God, certainly **86 beside** out of. **five
wits** The intellectual faculties, usually listed as common wit, imagination, fantasy, judgment, and memory **87–88 notoriously abused**
egregiously ill treated **89 But** only **91 propertied me** i.e., treated
me as property and thrown me into the lumber-room **93 face . . .
wits** brazenly represent me as having lost my wits **94 Advise you**
take care **101 God b' wi' you** God be with you

105 shent scolded, rebuked **109 Welladay** alas, would that
125 Vice comic tempter of the "old" morality plays **127 dagger of
lath** comic weapon of the Vice in at least some morality plays
131 Pare thy nails (Evidently a comic routine in Tudor morality
drama, though no samples survive.) **132 goodman** title for a person
of substance but not of gentle birth. (This line could be Feste's farewell to Malvolio and his "devil.")
4.3. Location: Olivia's garden.
6 was was previously. **credit** report **9 my soul . . . sense** i.e., both
my rational faculties and my physical senses come to the conclusion
11 accident unexpected event **12 instance** precedent. **discourse**
reason

That I am ready to distrust mine eyes
And wrangle with my reason that persuades me
To any other trust but that I am mad,   15
Or else the lady's mad. Yet if 'twere so,
She could not sway her house, command her
    followers,   17
Take and give back affairs and their dispatch   18
With such a smooth, discreet, and stable bearing
As I perceive she does. There's something in 't
That is deceivable. But here the lady comes.   21

Enter Olivia and Priest.

OLIVIA
Blame not this haste of mine. If you mean well,
Now go with me and with this holy man
Into the chantry by. There, before him,   24
And underneath that consecrated roof,
Plight me the full assurance of your faith,
That my most jealous and too doubtful soul   27
May live at peace. He shall conceal it
Whiles you are willing it shall come to note,   29
What time we will our celebration keep   30
According to my birth. What do you say?   31

SEBASTIAN
I'll follow this good man, and go with you,
And having sworn truth, ever will be true.

OLIVIA
Then lead the way, good Father, and heavens so
    shine
That they may fairly note this act of mine! *Exeunt.* 35

5.1 *Enter Clown [Feste] and Fabian.*

FABIAN Now, as thou lov'st me, let me see his letter.
FESTE Good Master Fabian, grant me another request.
FABIAN Anything.
FESTE Do not desire to see this letter.
FABIAN This is to give a dog and in recompense desire 5
my dog again.   6

Enter Duke [Orsino], Viola, Curio, and lords.

ORSINO Belong you to the Lady Olivia, friends?
FESTE Ay, sir, we are some of her trappings.   8
ORSINO I know thee well. How dost thou, my good fellow?
FESTE Truly, sir, the better for my foes and the worse 10
for my friends.
ORSINO Just the contrary—the better for thy friends.

FESTE No, sir, the worse.
ORSINO How can that be?
FESTE Marry, sir, they praise me, and make an ass of 15
me. Now my foes tell me plainly I am an ass, so that 16
by my foes, sir, I profit in the knowledge of myself,
and by my friends I am abused; so that, conclusions to 18
be as kisses, if your four negatives make your two 19
affirmatives, why then the worse for my friends and 20
the better for my foes.
ORSINO Why, this is excellent.
FESTE By my troth, sir, no, though it please you to be 23
one of my friends.   24
ORSINO Thou shalt not be the worse for me. There's gold.
                                      [*He gives a coin.*]
FESTE But that it would be double-dealing, sir, I would 26
you could make it another.
ORSINO O, you give me ill counsel.
FESTE Put your grace in your pocket, sir, for this once, 29
and let your flesh and blood obey it.   30
ORSINO Well, I will be so much a sinner to be a 31
double-dealer. There's another. [*He gives another coin.*]
FESTE *Primo, secundo, tertio,* is a good play, and the old 33
saying is, the third pays for all. The triplex, sir, is a 34
good tripping measure; or the bells of Saint Bennet, 35
sir, may put you in mind—one, two, three.
ORSINO You can fool no more money out of me at this
throw. If you will let your lady know I am here to 38
speak with her, and bring her along with you, it may
awake my bounty further.
FESTE Marry, sir, lullaby to your bounty till I come
again. I go, sir, but I would not have you to think that
my desire of having is the sin of covetousness. But as
you say, sir, let your bounty take a nap. I will awake
it anon.   *Exit.*

Enter Antonio and Officers.

VIOLA
Here comes the man, sir, that did rescue me.
ORSINO
That face of his I do remember well,
Yet when I saw it last it was besmeared
As black as Vulcan in the smoke of war.   49
A baubling vessel was he captain of,   50
For shallow draft and bulk unprizable,   51

15 **trust** belief 17 **sway** rule 18 **Take . . . dispatch** receive reports on matters of household business and see to their execution 21 **deceivable** deceptive 24 **chantry by** privately endowed chapel nearby 27 **jealous** anxious, mistrustful. **doubtful** full of doubts 29 **Whiles** until. **come to note** become known 30 **What time** at which time. **our celebration** i.e., the actual marriage. (What they are about to perform is a binding betrothal.) 31 **birth** social position 35 **fairly note** look upon with favor
5.1. Location: Before Olivia's house.
5–6 This . . . again (Apparently a reference to a well-known reply of Dr. Bulleyn when Queen Elizabeth asked for his dog and promised a gift of his choosing in return; he asked to have his dog back.) 8 **trappings** ornaments, decorations 10 **for** because of

15–16 **make an ass of me** i.e., flatter me into foolishly thinking well of myself 18 **abused** flatteringly deceived 18–20 **conclusions . . . affirmatives** i.e., as when a young lady, asked for a kiss, says "no, no" really meaning "yes"; or, as in grammar, two negatives make an affirmative 19 **your four negatives** the four negatives that people talk about 23 **though** even though 24 **friends** i.e., those who, according to Feste's syllogism, flatter him 26 **But** except for the fact. **double-dealing** (1) giving twice (2) deceit, duplicity 29 **Put . . . pocket** (1) pocket up your virtue, your grace before God (2) reach in your pocket or purse and show your customary grace or munificence. (*Your Grace* is also the formal way of addressing a duke.) 30 **it** i.e., my "ill counsel" 31 **to be** as to be 33 **play** (Perhaps a mathematical game or game of dice.) 34 **the third . . . all** the third time is lucky. (Proverbial.) **triplex** triple time in music 35 **Saint Bennet** church of St. Benedict 38 **throw** (1) time (2) throw of the dice 49 **Vulcan** Roman god of fire and smith to the other gods; his face was blackened by the fire. 50 **baubling** insignificant, trifling 51 **For** because of. **draft** depth of water a ship draws. **unprizable** of value too slight to be estimated, not worth taking as a "prize"

With which such scatheful grapple did he make 52
With the most noble bottom of our fleet 53
That very envy and the tongue of loss 54
Cried fame and honor on him. What's the matter?

FIRST OFFICER
Orsino, this is that Antonio
That took the *Phoenix* and her freight from Candy, 57
And this is he that did the *Tiger* board
When your young nephew Titus lost his leg.
Here in the streets, desperate of shame and state, 60
In private brabble did we apprehend him. 61

VIOLA
He did me kindness, sir, drew on my side,
But in conclusion put strange speech upon me. 63
I know not what 'twas but distraction. 64

ORSINO
Notable pirate, thou saltwater thief,
What foolish boldness brought thee to their mercies 65
Whom thou in terms so bloody and so dear 67
Hast made thine enemies?

ANTONIO   Orsino, noble sir,
Be pleased that I shake off these names you give me. 69
Antonio never yet was thief or pirate,
Though, I confess, on base and ground enough 71
Orsino's enemy. A witchcraft drew me hither.
That most ingrateful boy there by your side
From the rude sea's enraged and foamy mouth
Did I redeem; a wreck past hope he was. 75
His life I gave him, and did thereto add
My love, without retention or restraint, 77
All his in dedication. For his sake 78
Did I expose myself—pure for his love— 79
Into the danger of this adverse town, 80
Drew to defend him when he was beset;
Where being apprehended, his false cunning,
Not meaning to partake with me in danger,
Taught him to face me out of his acquaintance 84
And grew a twenty years' removèd thing 85
While one would wink; denied me mine own purse, 86
Which I had recommended to his use 87
Not half an hour before.

VIOLA   How can this be?
ORSINO   When came he to this town?

ANTONIO
Today, my lord; and for three months before,
No interim, not a minute's vacancy,
Both day and night did we keep company.

Enter Olivia and attendants.

ORSINO
Here comes the Countess. Now heaven walks on
    earth.
But for thee, fellow—fellow, thy words are madness. 95
Three months this youth hath tended upon me;
But more of that anon. Take him aside.

OLIVIA [*to Orsino*]
What would my lord—but that he may not have— 98
Wherein Olivia may seem serviceable?—
Cesario, you do not keep promise with me.

VIOLA   Madam?
ORSINO   Gracious Olivia—

OLIVIA
What do you say, Cesario?—Good my lord— 103

VIOLA
My lord would speak. My duty hushes me.

OLIVIA
If it be aught to the old tune, my lord,
It is as fat and fulsome to mine ear 106
As howling after music.

ORSINO   Still so cruel?
OLIVIA   Still so constant, lord.

ORSINO
What, to perverseness? You uncivil lady,
To whose ingrate and unauspicious altars 111
My soul the faithfull'st offerings have breathed out
That e'er devotion tendered! What shall I do?

OLIVIA
Even what it please my lord that shall become him. 114

ORSINO
Why should I not, had I the heart to do it,
Like to th' Egyptian thief at point of death 116
Kill what I love?—a savage jealousy
That sometimes savors nobly. But hear me this: 118
Since you to nonregardance cast my faith, 119
And that I partly know the instrument 120
That screws me from my true place in your favor, 121
Live you the marble-breasted tyrant still.
But this your minion, whom I know you love, 123
And whom, by heaven I swear, I tender dearly, 124
Him will I tear out of that cruel eye
Where he sits crowned in his master's spite.— 126
Come, boy, with me. My thoughts are ripe in
    mischief.
I'll sacrifice the lamb that I do love, 128
To spite a raven's heart within a dove.   [*Going.*] 129

52 **scatheful** destructive 53 **bottom** ship 54 **very envy** i.e., even those who had most reason to hate him, his enemies. **loss** i.e., the losers 57 **from Candy** on her return from Candia, or Crete 60 **desperate . . . state** recklessly disregarding the disgrace that public quarreling would bring on him and his dangerous status as a wanted man 61 **brabble** brawl 63 **put . . . me** spoke to me strangely 64 **but distraction** unless (it was) madness 65 **Notable** notorious 67 **in terms so bloody** in so bloodthirsty a manner. **dear** costly, grievous 69 **Be pleased that I** allow me to 71 **base and ground** solid grounds 75 **wreck** person cast ashore from a wrecked vessel 77 **retention** reservation 78 **All . . . dedication** devoted wholly to him 79 **pure** entirely, purely 80 **adverse** hostile 84 **face . . . acquaintance** brazenly deny he knew me 85–86 **grew . . . wink** in the twinkling of an eye acted as though we had been estranged for twenty years 87 **recommended** consigned

95 **for** as for 98 **but . . . have** except that which he may not have—i.e., my love 103 **Good my lord** (Olivia urges Orsino to listen to Cesario.) 106 **fat and fulsome** gross and offensive 111 **ingrate** ungrateful. **unauspicious** unpropitious, not disposed to be favorable 114 **become** suit 116 **Egyptian thief** (An allusion to the story of Theagenes and Chariclea in the *Ethiopica*, a Greek romance by Heliodorus. The robber chief, Thyamis of Memphis, having captured Chariclea and fallen in love with her, is attacked by a larger band of robbers; threatened with death, he attempts to slay her first.) 118 **savors nobly** is not without nobility 119 **nonregardance** neglect 120 **that** since 121 **screws** pries, forces 123 **minion** darling, favorite 124 **tender** regard 126 **in . . . spite** to the vexation of his master 128–129 **I'll . . . dove** i.e., I'll kill Cesario, whom I love, to revenge myself on this beautiful but black-hearted lady

VIOLA
And I, most jocund, apt, and willingly, 130
To do you rest, a thousand deaths would die. 131
[Going.]

OLIVIA
Where goes Cesario?

VIOLA   After him I love
More than I love these eyes, more than my life,
More by all mores than e'er I shall love wife. 134
If I do feign, you witnesses above
Punish my life for tainting of my love! 136

OLIVIA
Ay me, detested! How am I beguiled! 137

VIOLA
Who does beguile you? Who does do you wrong?

OLIVIA
Hast thou forgot thyself? Is it so long?
Call forth the holy father.   [Exit an attendant.]

ORSINO [to Viola]   Come, away!

OLIVIA
Whither, my lord? Cesario, husband, stay.

ORSINO
Husband?

OLIVIA   Ay, husband. Can he that deny?

ORSINO [to Viola]
Her husband, sirrah?

VIOLA   No, my lord, not I. 143

OLIVIA
Alas, it is the baseness of thy fear
That makes thee strangle thy propriety. 145
Fear not, Cesario, take thy fortunes up;
Be that thou know'st thou art, and then thou art 147
As great as that thou fear'st.

Enter Priest.

                      O, welcome, Father! 148
Father, I charge thee by thy reverence
Here to unfold—though lately we intended
To keep in darkness what occasion now
Reveals before 'tis ripe—what thou dost know
Hath newly passed between this youth and me.

PRIEST
A contract of eternal bond of love,
Confirmed by mutual joinder of your hands, 155
Attested by the holy close of lips, 156
Strengthened by interchangement of your rings,
And all the ceremony of this compact
Sealed in my function, by my testimony; 159
Since when, my watch hath told me, toward my
        grave
I have traveled but two hours.

ORSINO [to Viola]
O thou dissembling cub! What wilt thou be
When time hath sowed a grizzle on thy case? 163
Or will not else thy craft so quickly grow
That thine own trip shall be thine overthrow? 165
Farewell, and take her, but direct thy feet
Where thou and I henceforth may never meet.

VIOLA
My Lord, I do protest—

OLIVIA   O, do not swear!
Hold little faith, though thou hast too much fear. 169

Enter Sir Andrew.

SIR ANDREW   For the love of God, a surgeon! Send one
presently to Sir Toby. 171

OLIVIA   What's the matter?

SIR ANDREW   He's broke my head across, and has given 173
Sir Toby a bloody coxcomb too. For the love of God, 174
your help! I had rather than forty pound I were at
home.

OLIVIA   Who has done this, Sir Andrew?

SIR ANDREW   The Count's gentleman, one Cesario. We
took him for a coward, but he's the very devil
incarnate. 180

ORSINO   My gentleman, Cesario?

SIR ANDREW   'Od's lifelings, here he is!—You broke my 182
head for nothing, and that that I did I was set on to
do 't by Sir Toby.

VIOLA
Why do you speak to me? I never hurt you.
You drew your sword upon me without cause,
But I bespake you fair, and hurt you not. 187

SIR ANDREW   If a bloody coxcomb be a hurt, you have
hurt me. I think you set nothing by a bloody cox- 189
comb.

Enter [Sir] Toby and Clown [Feste].

Here comes Sir Toby, halting. You shall hear more. 191
But if he had not been in drink, he would have tickled
you othergates than he did. 193

ORSINO   How now, gentleman? How is 't with you?

SIR TOBY   That's all one. He's hurt me, and there's th' 195
end on 't. —Sot, didst see Dick surgeon, sot? 196

FESTE   O, he's drunk, Sir Toby, an hour agone; his eyes 197
were set at eight i' the morning. 198

SIR TOBY   Then he's a rogue, and a passy measures 199
pavane. I hate a drunken rogue. 200

130 apt readily 131 do you rest give you ease. die (with possible
suggestion of "have an orgasm") 134 by all mores by all such comparisons 136 Punish . . . love punish me with death for being disloyal to the love I feel 137 detested hated and denounced by another 143 sirrah (The normal way of addressing an inferior.)
145 strangle thy propriety i.e., deny what you are 147 that that
which 148 that thou fear'st him you fear, i.e., Orsino 155 joinder
joining 156 close meeting 159 Sealed in my function ratified
through my carrying out of my priestly office

163 a grizzle scattering of gray hair. case skin 165 trip wrestling
trick used to throw an opponent. (You'll get overclever and trip yourself up.) 169 Hold little faith keep at least a little part of what you
promised 171 presently immediately 173 broke broken the skin,
cut 174 coxcomb fool's cap resembling the crest of a cock; here,
head 180 incardinate (For "incarnate.") 182 'Od's lifelings by
God's little lives 187 bespake you fair addressed you courteously
189 set nothing by regard as insignificant 191 halting limping
193 othergates otherwise 195 That's all one it doesn't matter; never
mind 195–196 there's . . . on 't that's all there is to it 196 Sot (1)
fool (2) drunkard 197 agon ago 198 set fixed or closed 199–
200 passy measures pavane passe-measure pavane, a slow-moving,
stately dance (suggesting Sir Toby's impatience to have his wounds
dressed)

OLIVIA   Away with him! Who hath made this havoc
with them?

SIR ANDREW   I'll help you, Sir Toby, because we'll be 203
dressed together. 204

SIR TOBY   Will you help? An ass-head and a coxcomb
and a knave, a thin-faced knave, a gull!

OLIVIA
Get him to bed, and let his hurt be looked to.
                    [*Exeunt Feste, Fabian, Sir Toby, and Sir*
                                        Andrew.]

        Enter Sebastian.

SEBASTIAN
I am sorry, madam, I have hurt your kinsman;
But, had it been the brother of my blood, 209
I must have done no less with wit and safety.— 210
You throw a strange regard upon me, and by that 211
I do perceive it hath offended you.
Pardon me, sweet one, even for the vows
We made each other but so late ago.

ORSINO
One face, one voice, one habit, and two persons, 215
A natural perspective, that is and is not! 216

SEBASTIAN
Antonio, O my dear Antonio!
How have the hours racked and tortured me 218
Since I have lost thee!

ANTONIO   Sebastian are you?

SEBASTIAN   Fear'st thou that, Antonio? 221

ANTONIO
How have you made division of yourself?
An apple cleft in two is not more twin
Than these two creatures. Which is Sebastian?

OLIVIA   Most wonderful!

SEBASTIAN   [*seeing Viola*]
Do I stand there? I never had a brother;
Nor can there be that deity in my nature
Of here and everywhere. I had a sister, 228
Whom the blind waves and surges have devoured. 229
Of charity, what kin are you to me? 230
What countryman? What name? What parentage?

VIOLA
Of Messaline. Sebastian was my father.
Such a Sebastian was my brother, too.
So went he suited to his watery tomb. 234
If spirits can assume both form and suit, 235
You come to fright us.

SEBASTIAN   A spirit I am indeed,
But am in that dimension grossly clad 237

Which from the womb I did participate. 238
Were you a woman, as the rest goes even, 239
I should my tears let fall upon your cheek
And say, "Thrice welcome, drownèd Viola!"

VIOLA
My father had a mole upon his brow.

SEBASTIAN   And so had mine.

VIOLA
And died that day when Viola from her birth
Had numbered thirteen years.

SEBASTIAN
O, that record is lively in my soul! 246
He finishèd indeed his mortal act
That day that made my sister thirteen years.

VIOLA
If nothing lets to make us happy both 249
But this my masculine usurped attire,
Do not embrace me till each circumstance
Of place, time, fortune, do cohere and jump 252
That I am Viola—which to confirm
I'll bring you to a captain in this town
Where lie my maiden weeds, by whose gentle help 255
I was preserved to serve this noble count.
All the occurrence of my fortune since
Hath been between this lady and this lord.

SEBASTIAN   [*to Olivia*]
So comes it, lady, you have been mistook.
But nature to her bias drew in that. 260
You would have been contracted to a maid,
Nor are you therein, by my life, deceived.
You are betrothed both to a maid and man. 263

ORSINO   [*to Olivia*]
Be not amazed; right noble is his blood.
If this be so, as yet the glass seems true, 265
I shall have share in this most happy wreck. 266
[*To Viola.*] Boy, thou hast said to me a thousand
    times
Thou never shouldst love woman like to me. 268

VIOLA
And all those sayings will I over swear, 269
And all those swearings keep as true in soul
As doth that orbèd continent the fire 271
That severs day from night.

ORSINO   Give me thy hand,
And let me see thee in thy woman's weeds.

VIOLA
The captain that did bring me first on shore
Hath my maid's garments. He upon some action 275
Is now in durance, at Malvolio's suit, 276
A gentleman and follower of my lady's.

203–204 **be dressed** have our wounds surgically dressed   **209 the brother of my blood** my own brother   **210 with wit and safety** with intelligent concern for my own safety   **211 strange regard** look such as one directs at a stranger   **215 habit** dress   **216 A natural perspective** an optical device or illusion created in this instance by nature   **218 racked** tortured   **221 Fear'st thou that** do you doubt that   **228 here and everywhere** omnipresence   **229 blind** heedless, indiscriminating   **230 Of charity** (tell me) in kindness   **234 suited** dressed; clad in human form   **235 form and suit** physical appearance and dress   **237 in . . . clad** clothed in that fleshly shape

238 **participate** possess in common with all humanity   **239 as . . . even** since everything else agrees   **246 record** recollection   **249 lets** hinders   **252 jump** coincide, fit exactly   **255 weeds** clothes   **260 nature . . . that** nature followed her bent in that. (The metaphor is from the game of bowls.)   **263 a maid** i.e., a virgin man   **265 the glass** i.e., the *natural perspective* of line 216   **266 wreck** shipwreck, accident   **268 like to me** as well as you love me   **269 over swear** swear again   **271 As . . . fire** i.e., as the sphere of the sun keeps the fire   **275 action** legal charge   **276 durance** imprisonment

OLIVIA
He shall enlarge him. Fetch Malvolio hither.   278
And yet, alas, now I remember me,
They say, poor gentleman, he's much distract.

Enter Clown [Feste] with a letter, and Fabian.

A most extracting frenzy of mine own   281
From my remembrance clearly banished his.   282
How does he, sirrah?
FESTE   Truly, madam, he holds Beelzebub at the stave's   284
end as well as a man in his case may do. He's here   285
writ a letter to you; I should have given 't you today
morning. But as a madman's epistles are no gospels,   287
so it skills not much when they are delivered.   288
OLIVIA   Open 't and read it.
FESTE   Look then to be well edified when the fool
delivers the madman. [*He reads loudly.*] "By the Lord,   291
madam—"
OLIVIA   How now, art thou mad?
FESTE   No, madam, I do but read madness. An your
ladyship will have it as it ought to be, you must allow
vox.   296
OLIVIA   Prithee, read i' thy right wits.
FESTE   So I do, madonna; but to read his right wits is to   298
read thus. Therefore perpend, my princess, and give   299
ear.
OLIVIA [*to Fabian*]   Read it you, sirrah.
FABIAN [*reads*]   "By the Lord, madam, you wrong me,
and the world shall know it. Though you have put me
into darkness and given your drunken cousin rule
over me, yet have I the benefit of my senses as well
as your ladyship. I have your own letter that induced
me to the semblance I put on, with the which I   307
doubt not but to do myself much right or you much
shame. Think of me as you please. I leave my duty   309
a little unthought of, and speak out of my injury.   310
                              The madly used Malvolio."
OLIVIA   Did he write this?
FESTE   Ay, madam.
ORSINO   This savors not much of distraction.
OLIVIA
See him delivered, Fabian. Bring him hither.   315
                                        [*Exit Fabian.*]
My lord, so please you, these things further thought
on,   316

To think me as well a sister as a wife,   317
One day shall crown th' alliance on 't, so please you, 318
Here at my house and at my proper cost.   319
ORSINO
Madam, I am most apt t' embrace your offer.   320
[*To Viola.*] Your master quits you; and for your
service done him,   321
So much against the mettle of your sex,   322
So far beneath your soft and tender breeding,
And since you called me master for so long,
Here is my hand. You shall from this time be
Your master's mistress.
OLIVIA   A sister! You are she.

Enter [Fabian, with] Malvolio.

ORSINO
Is this the madman?
OLIVIA   Ay, my lord, this same.
How now, Malvolio?
MALVOLIO   Madam, you have done me wrong,
Notorious wrong.
OLIVIA   Have I, Malvolio? No.
MALVOLIO [*showing a letter*]
Lady, you have. Pray you, peruse that letter.
You must not now deny it is your hand.
Write from it, if you can, in hand or phrase,   332
Or say 'tis not your seal, not your invention.   333
You can say none of this. Well, grant it then,
And tell me, in the modesty of honor,   335
Why you have given me such clear lights of favor,   336
Bade me come smiling and cross-gartered to you,
To put on yellow stockings, and to frown
Upon Sir Toby and the lighter people?   339
And, acting this in an obedient hope,   340
Why have you suffered me to be imprisoned,
Kept in a dark house, visited by the priest,   342
And made the most notorious geck and gull   343
That e'er invention played on? Tell me why?   344
OLIVIA
Alas, Malvolio, this is not my writing,
Though, I confess, much like the character;   346
But out of question 'tis Maria's hand.   347
And now I do bethink me, it was she
First told me thou wast mad; then cam'st in smiling, 349
And in such forms which here were presupposed   350
Upon thee in the letter. Prithee, be content.
This practice hath most shrewdly passed upon thee; 352
But when we know the grounds and authors of it,

278 enlarge release   281 extracting i.e., that obsessed me and drew all thoughts except of Cesario from my mind   282 his i.e., his madness   284–285 holds . . . end i.e., keeps the devil at a safe distance. (The metaphor is of fighting with quarterstaffs or long poles.)   287 a madman's . . . gospels i.e., there is no truth in a madman's letters. (An allusion to readings in the church service of selected passages from the epistles and the gospels.)   288 skills matters.   delivered (1) delivered to their recipient (2) read aloud   291 delivers speaks the words of   296 vox voice, i.e., an appropriately loud voice   298 to read . . . wits to express his true state of mind   299 perpend consider, attend. (A deliberately lofty word.)   307 the which i.e., the letter   309–310 I leave . . . injury i.e., in saying this, I speak for the moment not as your steward should, but as an injured party   315 delivered released   316 so . . . on if you are pleased on further consideration of all that has happened

317 To . . . wife to regard me as favorably as a sister-in-law as you had hoped to regard me as a wife   318 crown . . . on 't i.e., serve as occasion for two marriages confirming our new relationship   319 proper own   320 apt ready   321 quits releases   322 mettle natural disposition   332 from it differently   333 invention composition   335 in . . . honor in the name of all that is decent and honorable   336 clear lights evident signs   339 lighter lesser   340 acting . . . hope when I acted thus out of obedience to you and in hope of your favor   342 priest i.e., Feste   343 geck dupe   344 invention played on contrivance sported with   346 the character my handwriting   347 out of beyond   349 cam'st you came   350 presupposed specified beforehand   352 practice plot.   shrewdly mischievously.   passed been perpetrated

Thou shalt be both the plaintiff and the judge
Of thine own cause.

FABIAN   Good madam, hear me speak,
And let no quarrel nor no brawl to come   356
Taint the condition of this present hour,   357
Which I have wondered at. In hope it shall not,
Most freely I confess, myself and Toby
Set this device against Malvolio here,
Upon some stubborn and uncourteous parts   361
We had conceived against him. Maria writ   362
The letter at Sir Toby's great importance,   363
In recompense whereof he hath married her.
How with a sportful malice it was followed   365
May rather pluck on laughter than revenge,   366
If that the injuries be justly weighed   367
That have on both sides passed.

OLIVIA [to Malvolio]
Alas, poor fool, how have they baffled thee!   369

FESTE   Why, "Some are born great, some achieve
greatness, and some have greatness thrown upon
them." I was one, sir, in this interlude, one Sir Topas, 372
sir, but that's all one. "By the Lord, fool, I am not   373
mad." But do you remember? "Madam, why laugh
you at such a barren rascal? An you smile not, he's
gagged." And thus the whirligig of time brings in his   376
revenges.

MALVOLIO   I'll be revenged on the whole pack of you!
[Exit.]

OLIVIA
He hath been most notoriously abused.

ORSINO
Pursue him, and entreat him to a peace.
He hath not told us of the captain yet.
When that is known, and golden time convents,   382
A solemn combination shall be made
Of our dear souls. Meantime, sweet sister,
We will not part from hence. Cesario, come—
For so you shall be, while you are a man;
But when in other habits you are seen,   387
Orsino's mistress and his fancy's queen.   388
                         Exeunt [all, except Feste].

FESTE (sings)
When that I was and a little tiny boy,   389
    With hey, ho, the wind and the rain,
A foolish thing was but a toy,   391
    For the rain it raineth every day.

But when I came to man's estate,
    With hey, ho, the wind and the rain,
'Gainst knaves and thieves men shut their gate,
    For the rain it raineth every day.

But when I came, alas, to wive,
    With hey, ho, the wind and the rain,
By swaggering could I never thrive,
    For the rain it raineth every day.

But when I came unto my beds,   401
    With hey, ho, the wind and the rain,
With tosspots still had drunken heads,   403
    For the rain it raineth every day.

A great while ago the world begun,
    With hey, ho, the wind and the rain,
But that's all one, our play is done,
    And we'll strive to please you every day.
                                              [Exit.]

401 unto my beds i.e., (1) drunk to bed, or, perhaps, (2) in the
evening of life   **403 tosspots** drunkards

356 to come in the future   **357 condition** (happy) nature   **361 Upon**
on account of.   **parts** qualities, deeds   **362 conceived against him**
seen and resented in him   **363 importance** importunity   **365 followed** carried out   **366 pluck on** induce   **367 If that** if   **369 baffled**
disgraced, quelled   **372 interlude** little play   **373 that's all one** no
matter for that   **376 whirligig** spinning top   **382 convents** (1) summons, calls together (2) suits   **387 habits** attire   **388 fancy's** love's
389 and a little a little   **391 toy** trifle

All's Well That Ends Well

All's Well That Ends Well belongs to that period of Shakespeare's creative life when he concentrated on his great tragedies and wrote little comedy. The few apparent exceptions do not fit readily into conventional dramatic genres. *Measure for Measure* (1603–1604), usually called a problem play, is darkly preoccupied with human carnality and injustice. *Troilus and Cressida* (c. 1601–1602), printed between the histories and the tragedies in the Folio of 1623, is a disillusioning satire of love and war somewhat akin to the black comedy of our modern theater. *All's Well* shares, to an extent, the satiric and brooding spirit of these two plays. Its "bed trick," in which one woman is substituted for another in an assignation with the protagonist, Bertram, poses ethical problems for the audience (as does a similar trick in *Measure for Measure*). Helena, in arranging the substitution, may seem too much of a schemer. The relations between the sexes are problematic in this play, written, as it seemingly was, at a time when Shakespeare was preoccupied with tragedies that are haunted by images of destructive femaleness and of debasing sexuality. The action of *All's Well* is, to a large extent, controlled by an admirable and attractive woman, and yet the play dwells more than any previous comedy on the potential hazards of sexuality. For these and other reasons, *All's Well* is often grouped with the problem plays.

At the same time, the play also looks forward to Shakespeare's late romances, *Pericles, Cymbeline, The Winter's Tale,* and *The Tempest.* Here the mode of comedy turns toward the miraculous and tragicomic, with journeys of separation ending in tearful reunion, and sinful error ending in spiritual rebirth. This mode was not unknown in Shakespeare's comedies of the late 1590s: *As You Like It* ends with the sudden and implausible conversion of its villains, and *Much Ado About Nothing* offers forgiveness to the undeserving Claudio while restoring his traduced fiancée, Hero, to a new life. *Measure for Measure* follows a similar pattern of redemptive pardon for the corrupted Angelo and providential deliverance for Isabella. Both *All's Well* and *Measure for Measure* contain features of this comedy of forgiveness, even if admittedly the ironies surrounding the gesture of forgiving are far less controlled than in the late romances.

Certainly, in any case, *All's Well* occupies a central position in the line of development from the early comedies to the late romances. Helena points back to earlier comic women in her role as engineer of the love plot and points forward to women of the late romances in her role as daughter, victim, and savior (though early comedy and late romance are, to be sure, not as neatly distinguishable as this antithesis suggests). Bertram, who is virtually without precedent in earlier comedies, anticipates, to a degree, Posthumus in *Cymbeline,* Florizel in *The Winter's Tale,* and Ferdinand in *The Tempest* in that he takes part in a marriage sanctioned and defined largely by paternal intervention. *All's Well,* like the romances and unlike the earlier comedies, affords a remarkably prominent role to the older generation.

The probable date of *All's Well* is consistent with such a transitional function. Its dates are hard to fix by external evidence, for it was neither registered nor printed until 1623, and allusions to it are scarce. Some scholars think that it is the *Love's Labor's Won* intriguingly mentioned by Francis Meres in *Palladis Tamia* in 1598, which Shakespeare might then have revised some time around 1601–1604. Portions of the play do feature the rhymed couplets, letters in sonnet form, and witty conceits that we normally associate with Shakespeare's early style. These old-fashioned effects may have been deliberate on Shakespeare's part, however, not unlike the anachronisms he later introduces in *Pericles* and *Cymbeline.* Certainly, a major portion of the play dates stylistically from 1601–1604 or even later. Here the language is elliptical and compact, the images complexly interwoven, the verse rhythms free.

In any event, with its two contrasting styles poised between romance and satire, *All's Well* plaintively seeks comic reassurance amid the pessimistic ironies of Shakespeare's tragic period. It lacks many of the felicities we associate with the festive comedies of the 1590s: the love songs, the innocently hedonistic joy, and the well-mated young lovers escaping from stern parents or an envious court. *All's Well* has too often been judged negatively for its failure to achieve a festive mood that Shakespeare probably did not intend it to have. The hero, Bertram, is undeniably a cad, and Helena is perhaps wrong to force Bertram to marry her against his will. As the undeserving hero, forgiven in spite of his waywardness, however, Bertram plays an essential role in the play's problematic resolution—or failure to achieve complete resolution. He is, in the common Renaissance view of all humanity, unworthy of the forgiveness he receives, whereas Helena's generosity in forgiving him (however flawed by her aggressiveness) suggests at least a capability in humanity for decency and compassion. We are left, as in *Measure for Measure,* with a sense of the perennially unbridgeable gap between human ideals and their achievement, and yet we view this dilemma in a comic context where second chances and hope are bestowed even on those who appear to deserve them least.

The satiric mode in *All's Well* is conveyed chiefly through Lavatch the clown and through Parolles, the boastful, cowardly knave who accompanies Bertram to the wars. Lavatch, with the bitter and riddling wit of the professional fool, gives expression to many of the satirical themes that are also illustrated by the exposure of Parolles. Lavatch jests about cuckoldry and the other marital difficulties that cause men to flee from women; he pokes fun at court manners and apes the prodigal disobedience of his master Bertram. He is, like Parolles, called a "foulmouthed and calumnious knave" (1.3.56–57), although the inversion of appearance and reality is evident here, as with all Shakespearean fools: Parolles is truly more fool and knave than his mocking counterpart. Parolles is all pretense. Full of sound, but hollow like the drum to which he is compared, he is a swaggerer and a fashionmonger whose clothes conceal his lack of inner substance. He is a recognizable satiric type that goes back to the Latin dramatists Plautus and Terence: the braggart soldier. He is, to be sure, endearing in his outrageousness; Shakespeare endows him with that vitality we find also in those earlier braggart soldiers, Falstaff and Pistol. Yet, because Parolles lacks the self-awareness of Falstaff, we merely laugh at him rather than with him. To the impressionable young Bertram, hungry for fame, Parolles represents smartness and military style. Bertram rejects the true worth of Helena because she lacks family position and, ironically, embraces the false worth of a parvenu. Parolles and Helena are foils from their first encounter, when the braggart sardonically derides virginity as unnatural and out of fashion. Parolles stands opposite also to Lafew, the Countess, and the King—those dignified embodiments of a traditional chivalrous order, whose generous teachings Bertram rejects for the company of Parolles and of attractive young women. By disguising his slick insolence in the guise of fashionable manliness, Parolles is able to win Bertram's friendship for a time. Parolles is not really a tempter, for we never see him bending Bertram from his true inclination; rather, Bertram is himself too much in love with sham reputation, too rebellious against the civilized decencies of his elders. He is the Prodigal Son, or Youth in the old morality play, perversely eager to prove his own worst enemy.

Yet Bertram is not without a redeeming nobleness—he bears himself bravely in the Florentine wars—and cannot be fooled indefinitely by his roguish companion. The exposure of Parolles is one of satiric humiliation, like that of Malvolio in *Twelfth Night* or one of Ben Jonson's humorous gulls. The engineers of Parolles' exposure use the language of Jonsonian satire in their devices to outwit him: their game is a "sport" done "for the love of laughter," employing a snare whereby the "fox" or the "woodcock" will entrap himself (3.6.34–102 and 4.1.92). The device of public

humiliation is particularly appropriate, because Parolles is himself a railing slanderer, like Lucio in *Measure for Measure,* caustically brilliant in his invective but nonetheless a slayer of men's reputations. The punishment of ridicule fits his particular crime. His callous disregard for the good name of various French military commanders is parallel to Bertram's indifference to the public shame he has heaped upon his virtuous wife. Once Parolles' bluff has been called, Bertram is, in part, disabused of his folly; but other means are needed to convince him of the wrong he has done to Helena. Indeed, Bertram's very coldness in turning away from Parolles shows a lack of humility. Bertram must learn to know himself better by being tricked, exposed, and humiliated.

The fabulous romancelike aspect of *All's Well* is conveyed chiefly through its folktale plot and through the character of Helena. The story is derived from the third "day" of Giovanni Boccaccio's *Decameron,* a day devoted to tales of lovers obliged to overcome seemingly impossible obstacles in order to achieve love's happiness. The story was translated into English by William Painter in *The Palace of Pleasure* (1566). To win the nobly born Beltramo, Giletta of Narbona must cure the French king with her physician-father's secret remedy and then must perform the riddling tasks assigned her by Beltramo as his means of being rid of her. Both these motifs have ancient antecedents in folklore, and, as in his late romances, Shakespeare puts great stress on the wondrous and improbable nature of these events.

All common sense warns against the likelihood of Helena's success. She is vastly below Bertram in social station or in "blood," even though she excels in "virtue." (This low station is unique among Shakespeare's comic heroines, and it contributes to what is so unusual about this play.) Her only hope is a desperate gamble: to cure the ailing King and so win Bertram as her reward. No one supposes at first she will even be admitted to the King, who has given up all hope of living; his "congregated college" of learned doctors "have concluded / That laboring art can never ransom nature / From her inaidible estate" (2.1.119–121). Helena transcends these rational doubts through resourcefulness and, above all, through a faith in help from above. She is willing to "hazard" all for love. She senses that her father's legacy will "be sanctified / By th' luckiest stars in heaven" (1.3.243–244), and she manages to convince not only the Countess and Lafew (persons who do not appear in Boccaccio) but also the King himself. Believing, like George Bernard Shaw's Saint Joan, that God will perform his greatest works through the humblest of his creatures, Helena inspires her listeners with faith in the impossible. Lafew is so moved by her simple eloquence that he proclaims to the King, "I have seen a medicine / That's able to breathe life into a stone" (2.1.73–74). Soon the King, too, is persuaded that in Helena "some blessèd spirit doth speak / His powerful sound within an organ weak" (lines 177–178). Once the

King's cure has been effected, even Parolles and Bertram must agree with Lafew that the age of miracles, long thought to have passed, is with them again. The King's cure by the "Very hand of heaven," through the agency of a "weak—/ And debile minister," is matter for a pious ballad or an old tale (2.3.31–34). At the same time, Helena is very determined and is willing to use whatever means are necessary to get what she wants.

Helena's aggressiveness is a problem for Bertram. He nominally objects to her lower social station, but that is a matter the King can remedy. Evidently, Bertram is daunted by something else: by the very prospect of marriage with a virtuous and attractive young woman who unmistakably wants him. He reacts with subterfuge and flight, subscribing to Parolles' notion that it is better to be a soldier than to be one who "hugs his kicky-wicky here at home, / Spending his manly marrow in her arms" (2.3.281–282). War gives Bertram his excuse to evade the responsibilities of marriage. In Italy, to be sure, he finds the prospect of sexual encounter with Diana irresistible, since he thinks he can obtain and then discard her when the affair is done. He is prepared to cheapen "available" women this way but not to commit himself to the complex and mutual commitment that marriage requires. In these terms, Helena's task is to bring Bertram to the point of understanding that sexuality and deep friendship can and should exist in a single relationship, and that women must not be bifurcated by his imagination into those who are respectable but untouchable (like his mother) or cheap and violable. Bertram's unself-knowing friendship with Parolles is symptomatic of his immaturity, and hence the exposure of Parolles is a necessary part of Bertram's education, but Helena must also find a way to help Bertram get over his mistrust of her sexuality.

The impossible tasks Helena must perform are stated as riddles, as is usual in a folktale, and must be solved by riddling or paradoxical means. Bertram writes that she must "get the ring upon my finger, which never shall come off, and show me a child begotten of thy body that I am father to" (3.2.57–59). Such a challenge invites ingenuity, as in Boccaccio, but in Shakespeare the solution also requires providential aid. Helena's first sad response is to set Bertram free and renounce her audacious pretentions. Her pilgrimage of grief takes her to Florence, where Bertram happens to be serving in the wars. This cannot be mere coincidence, and yet we do not accuse her of scheming in any opprobrious sense. Throughout, her motives are at once virtuous and deceitful, lawful and sinful, just as her very sexuality is wholesome and yet is seen by us in a context of debased human nature (as is generally not the case with Shakespeare's earlier heroines). Her acts are prompted at once by providence and by shrewd calculation. Even if providence must be credited with introducing her to Diana, the very lady whom Bertram is importuning in love, Helena makes the most of such opportunities afforded her, never doubting that "heaven" has "fated" her both to help Diana and simultaneously to serve her own turn (4.4.18–20). The bed trick is a "plot," but a virtuous one, a "deceit" that is "lawful," a deed that is "not sin, and yet a sinful fact" (3.7.38–47). Diana repeatedly plays upon these same riddles in accusing Bertram before the King: he is "guilty, and he is not guilty" (5.3.290).

The conundrums, although playful and entertaining in Shakespeare's highly complicated denouement (not found in Boccaccio), also hint at paradoxes in the nature of humanity. Bertram's typically human waywardness justifies a cunning response. "I think 't no sin," argues Diana, "To cozen him that would unjustly win" (4.2.75–76). Justice on earth, as in Measure for Measure, must take forms only roughly approximating those of heavenly justice, for human depravity sometimes requires a harsh remedy in kind. Yet, by a providential paradox, humanity's thwarted and evil nature, seemingly so fatal, leads instead to regeneration: by being humbled, humanity is enabled to rise. "The web of our life is of a mingled yarn, good and ill together," says a sympathetic observer of Bertram. "Our virtues would be proud if our faults whipped them not, and our crimes would despair if they were not cherished by our virtues" (4.3.70–73). Human perversity accentuates the need for divine grace.

Helena is a romantic heroine, only metaphorically the "angel" who must "Bless this unworthy husband," reprieving him by her "prayers" from "the wrath / Of greatest justice" (3.4.25–29). Indeed, she is capable of being quite threatening to Bertram. If Bertram typifies the "Natural rebellion" of all youth and Helena, the "herb of grace" whom he has willfully rejected (5.3.6 and 4.5.17), Helena is also an aggressive woman whose clever plans to win Bertram against his will produce an understandable reluctance in the young man. Still, the spiritual overtones are not extraneous to this bittersweet comedy. However much we may sympathize with his desire to choose in love for himself, Bertram's revolt is incomprehensible to every witness except Parolles. Bertram himself concedes, too late it seems, that he has recognized Helena's precious worth. This note of "love that comes too late," wherein the penitent sinner confesses "That's good that's gone," hovers over the play with its tragicomic mood (5.3.58–61). Helena is a "jewel" thrown away and seemingly forever lost (5.3.1). The semblance of her death is, in fact, only another one of her inventive schemes, along with the bewildering contretemps of the final scene. Yet, when she reappears, setting all to rights, she comes as "one that's dead" but is now "quick," alive again, merely a "shadow" of her former self (5.3.304–308). Bertram has not actually committed the evil he intended; by a providential sophistry, he is innocent, like Claudio in Much Ado or Angelo in Measure for Measure, and so is reconciled to the goodness he has failed to merit. Even Parolles is given a second chance by the magnanimous Lafew. As the play's title implies, all might have miscarried through humanity's "rash faults" that "Make trivial price of serious things we have" (5.3.61–62), were it not for a forgiving power that can make people's worst failings an instrument of their penitence and recovery. This resolution fleetingly comforts us in the final scene, even though it must do battle with such manifest imbalances as the prolonged shaming of Bertram and the scant attention paid to his reunion with Helena. The web of human life remains a mingled yarn.

All's Well That Ends Well

[*Dramatis Personae*

COUNTESS OF ROSSILLION, *Bertram's mother and Helena's guardian*
BERTRAM, *Count of Rossillion*
HELENA (*or* HELEN), *orphaned daughter of the Countess's physician*
PAROLLES, *a follower of Bertram*
RINALDO, *a steward,* }
LAVATCH, *a clown or fool,* } *servants of the Countess*
PAGE, } *of Rossillion*

KING OF FRANCE
LAFEW, *an old lord*
Two FRENCH LORDS, *the brothers Dumain, later captains in the Florentine army*
Other LORDS
Two FRENCH SOLDIERS
A GENTLEMAN
A MESSENGER

DUKE OF FLORENCE
WIDOW CAPILET *of Florence*
DIANA, *her daughter*
MARIANA, *neighbor and friend of the Widow*

Lords, Attendants, Soldiers, Citizens

SCENE: *Rossillion; Paris; Florence; Marseilles*]

1.1   *Enter young Bertram, Count of Rossillion, his mother* [*the Countess*], *and Helena,* [*with*] *Lord Lafew, all in black.*

COUNTESS   In delivering my son from me, I bury a ₁ second husband.
BERTRAM   And I in going, madam, weep o'er my father's death anew. But I must attend His Majesty's ₄ command, to whom I am now in ward, evermore in ₅ subjection.
LAFEW   You shall find of the King a husband, madam; ₇ you, sir, a father. He that so generally is at all times ₈

1.1. Location: Rossillion, i.e., Roussillon, in southern France, on the Spanish border near the Mediterranean. The Count's residence.
1 delivering sending (with play on "giving birth to" and "freeing")
4 attend heed   **5 in ward** (According to a feudal custom, the King became the guardian of orphaned heirs to estates, who remained "in ward" so long as they were minors. The King's jurisdiction extended even so far as the bestowal of his ward in marriage, but only to someone of equal rank.)   **7 of** in the person of.   **husband** i.e., guardian, patron   **8 generally** to all people

good must of necessity hold his virtue to you, whose 9
worthiness would stir it up where it wanted rather 10
than lack it where there is such abundance. 11

COUNTESS   What hope is there of His Majesty's amend- 12
ment? 13

LAFEW   He hath abandoned his physicians, madam,
under whose practices he hath persecuted time with 15
hope, and finds no other advantage in the process but 16
only the losing of hope by time.

COUNTESS   This young gentlewoman had a father—O,
that "had," how sad a passage 'tis!—whose skill was 19
almost as great as his honesty; had it stretched so far, 20
would have made nature immortal, and death should
have play for lack of work. Would for the King's sake 22
he were living! I think it would be the death of the
King's disease.

LAFEW   How called you the man you speak of, madam?

COUNTESS   He was famous, sir, in his profession, and it
was his great right to be so: Gerard de Narbonne.

LAFEW   He was excellent indeed, madam. The King
very lately spoke of him admiringly and mourningly.
He was skillful enough to have lived still, if knowl- 30
edge could be set up against mortality.

BERTRAM   What is it, my good lord, the King lan-
guishes of?

LAFEW   A fistula, my lord. 34

BERTRAM   I heard not of it before.

LAFEW   I would it were not notorious.—Was this
gentlewoman the daughter of Gerard de Narbonne?

COUNTESS   His sole child, my lord, and bequeathed to
my overlooking. I have those hopes of her good that 39
her education promises her dispositions she inherits, 40
which makes fair gifts fairer; for where an unclean 41
mind carries virtuous qualities, there commendations 42
go with pity—they are virtues and traitors too. In her 43
they are the better for their simpleness. She derives 44
her honesty and achieves her goodness. 45

LAFEW   Your commendations, madam, get from her
tears.

COUNTESS   'Tis the best brine a maiden can season her 48
praise in. The remembrance of her father never
approaches her heart but the tyranny of her sorrows
takes all livelihood from her cheek.—No more of this, 51

Helena.   Go to, no more, lest it be rather thought you 52
affect a sorrow than to have— 53

HELENA   I do affect a sorrow indeed, but I have it too. 54

LAFEW   Moderate lamentation is the right of the dead, 55
excessive grief the enemy to the living.

COUNTESS   If the living be enemy to the grief, the excess 57
makes it soon mortal. 58

BERTRAM   Madam, I desire your holy wishes.

LAFEW   How understand we that? 60

COUNTESS
Be thou blest, Bertram, and succeed thy father
In manners as in shape! Thy blood and virtue 62
Contend for empire in thee, and thy goodness 63
Share with thy birthright! Love all, trust a few, 64
Do wrong to none. Be able for thine enemy 65
Rather in power than use, and keep thy friend 66
Under thy own life's key. Be checked for silence 67
But never taxed for speech. What heaven more will, 68
That thee may furnish and my prayers pluck down, 69
Fall on thy head! Farewell. [To Lafew.] My lord,
'Tis an unseasoned courtier; good my lord, 71
Advise him.

LAFEW   He cannot want the best 72
That shall attend his love. 73

COUNTESS   Heaven bless him!—Farewell, Bertram.

BERTRAM   The best wishes that can be forged in your 75
thoughts be servants to you!   [Exit Countess.]
[To Helena.] Be comfortable to my mother, your 77
mistress, and make much of her. 78

LAFEW   Farewell, pretty lady. You must hold the credit 79
of your father.   [Exeunt Bertram and Lafew.]

HELENA
O, were that all! I think not on my father,
And these great tears grace his remembrance more 82
Than those I shed for him. What was he like? 83
I have forgot him. My imagination
Carries no favor in 't but Bertram's. 85
I am undone. There is no living, none,
If Bertram be away. 'Twere all one
That I should love a bright particular star

---

9 **hold** continue to devote   9–11 **whose . . . abundance** you whose
virtue is such that it would inspire generosity even in those who normally lack it, and who therefore cannot fail to find it in a king who is
so abundantly generous   10 **wanted** is lacking   12–13 **amendment**
recovery   15–16 **hath . . . hope** has tormented his time with painful
treatments in vain hope of cure   19 **passage** (1) phrase, expression (2)
passing away   20 **honesty** integrity of character   22 **Would** if only
30 **still** (1) now as before (2) forever   34 **fistula** ulcerous sore
39 **overlooking** supervision   39–41 **I have . . . fairer** I have high
hopes of her coming to great good, since her upbringing adds to her
natural gifts those qualities that will make her innate abilities even
more attractive   41–43 **where . . . pity** i.e., when an innately evil
disposition is given the accomplishments of a good education, in that
instance praises are mingled with regrets   43 **virtues and traitors too**
i.e., accomplishments that serve evil purposes.   **In her** i.e., in Helena   44 **simpleness** purity, being unmixed with vice.   **derives** inherits   45 **achieves** i.e., acquires by her own efforts in response to her
upbringing   48 **season** preserve (as with salt)   51 **livelihood**
animation

52 **Go to** i.e., come, come   53 **affect** are enamored of, make an exaggerated show of.   **than** rather than   54 **do affect** (1) am drawn to
(2) put on, feign. (Helena riddlingly means more than the Countess
understands.)   55 **right** rightful due   57–58 **If . . . mortal** if those
who live resist excessive grief, the excess will soon wear itself out
60 **How . . . that** (Lafew may be reacting to Bertram's unmannerly interruption of the talk about Helena's grief.)   62 **manners** moral conduct.   **Thy blood** may your noble birth   63–64 **thy goodness . . .
birthright** may the good qualities you achieve share with your inherited qualities in ruling your life   65–66 **Be able . . . use** be powerful
enough to resist your enemy without having to use that power
66–67 **keep . . . key** hold your friend's life as dearly as your own
67 **checked** reproved   68 **taxed for speech** rebuked for idle talk.
will may bestow   69 **pluck** draw   71 **unseasoned** inexperienced
72 **want the best** lack the best advice   73 **attend his love** accompany
my love for him   75 **forged** devised   77 **comfortable** comforting, serviceable   78 **make much of** be devoted to   79 **hold** uphold.   **credit**
reputation   82 **his** i.e., Bertram's (?) (Helena seems to be contrasting
her misunderstood tears of this present occasion with those few tears
shed for her father's death. Perhaps her present tears remember her father chiefly in terms of the man she now loves in her father's stead.)
83 **for him** i.e., for my father when he died   85 **favor** (1) face (2)
love token (3) preference

And think to wed it, he is so above me.
In his bright radiance and collateral light   90
Must I be comforted, not in his sphere.
Th' ambition in my love thus plagues itself;
The hind that would be mated by the lion   93
Must die for love. 'Twas pretty, though a plague,   94
To see him every hour, to sit and draw
His archèd brows, his hawking eye, his curls,   96
In our heart's table—heart too capable   97
Of every line and trick of his sweet favor.   98
But now he's gone, and my idolatrous fancy   99
Must sanctify his relics. Who comes here?

Enter Parolles.

[*Aside.*]   One that goes with him. I love him for his
sake;   101
And yet I know him a notorious liar,
Think him a great way fool, solely a coward.   103
Yet these fixed evils sit so fit in him   104
That they take place when virtue's steely bones   105
Looks bleak i' th' cold wind. Withal, full oft we see   106
Cold wisdom waiting on superfluous folly.   107
PAROLLES   Save you, fair queen!   108
HELENA   And you, monarch!
PAROLLES   No.
HELENA   And no.
PAROLLES   Are you meditating on virginity?
HELENA   Ay. You have some stain of soldier in you; let   113
me ask you a question. Man is enemy to virginity;
how may we barricado it against him?   115
PAROLLES   Keep him out.
HELENA   But he assails, and our virginity, though
valiant, in the defense yet is weak. Unfold to us some   118
warlike resistance.
PAROLLES   There is none. Man setting down before you   120
will undermine you and blow you up.   121
HELENA   Bless our poor virginity from underminers and
blowers-up! Is there no military policy how virgins   123
might blow up men?
PAROLLES   Virginity being blown down, man will
quicklier be blown up. Marry, in blowing him down   126

again, with the breach yourselves made you lose your   127
city. It is not politic in the commonwealth of nature to   128
preserve virginity. Loss of virginity is rational in-   129
crease, and there was never virgin got till virginity was   130
first lost. That you were made of is metal to make vir-   131
gins. Virginity by being once lost may be ten times   132
found; by being ever kept, it is ever lost. 'Tis too cold   133
a companion. Away with 't!
HELENA   I will stand for 't a little, though therefore I die 135
a virgin.
PAROLLES   There's little can be said in 't; 'tis against the 137
rule of nature. To speak on the part of virginity is to   138
accuse your mothers, which is most infallible disobedience. He that hangs himself is a virgin; virginity   140
murders itself, and should be buried in highways out   141
of all sanctified limit, as a desperate offendress against 142
nature. Virginity breeds mites, much like a cheese,
consumes itself to the very paring, and so dies with   144
feeding his own stomach. Besides, virginity is pee-   145
vish, proud, idle, made of self-love, which is the most
inhibited sin in the canon. Keep it not; you cannot   147
choose but lose by 't. Out with 't! Within th' one year   148
it will make itself two, which is a goodly increase, and
the principal itself not much the worse. Away with 't!   150
HELENA   How might one do, sir, to lose it to her own   151
liking?
PAROLLES   Let me see. Marry, ill, to like him that ne'er   153
it likes. 'Tis a commodity will lose the gloss with lying; 154
the longer kept, the less worth. Off with 't while 'tis
vendible; answer the time of request. Virginity, like   156
an old courtier, wears her cap out of fashion, richly
suited, but unsuitable, just like the brooch and the   158
toothpick, which wear not now. Your date is better in   159
your pie and your porridge than in your cheek; and   160
your virginity, your old virginity, is like one of our
French withered pears—it looks ill, it eats drily. Mar-   162

126–128 in blowing . . . city i.e., in satisfying his desire by making a breach in your virginity, you will be forced to surrender entirely, paying the loss of your virginity for the subsiding of his erection **128 politic** expedient **129–130 rational increase** (1) an increase by the law of nature (2) an increase of rational beings **130 got** begotten **131 That** that which. **metal** substance, as in minting of coins or compounding of interest (with idea also of *mettle*, "spirit," "temperament") **132–133 may . . . found** i.e., may reproduce itself tenfold **135 stand** fight, stand up (with a sexual quibble). **die** (with probable quibble on "experience orgasm") **137 in 't** in its behalf **138 on the part of** in behalf of **140 is a virgin** i.e., is like a virgin, since virginity is a kind of suicide **141–142 buried . . . limit** (Suicides were customarily buried at crossroads of highways, not in consecrated ground.) **144 paring** covering rind **145 his** its. **stomach** (1) maw (2) pride **147 inhibited** prohibited. **canon** catalogue of sins. (Pride is the first of the Deadly Sins.) **Keep** hoard **148 Out with 't** (1) away with it (2) put it out at interest **150 the principal** the original investment, i.e., the former virgin **151 How** what **153–154 ill . . . likes** i.e., one must do ill, by liking a man that dislikes virginity **154 will** that will. **gloss** gloss of newness. **with lying** with being unused (with quibble on "lying down") **156 vendible** marketable. **the time of request** when there is demand **158 unsuitable** unfashionable **159 wear not** are not in fashion. (Brooches in hats and the affectation of using toothpicks, once fashionable, are no longer so.) **159–160 Your . . . cheek** i.e., the date does better as an ingredient in cooking than as an emblem of withering in your cheek. (*Date* also suggests age.) **162 withered pears** i.e., pears that have become unappetizing through age and atrophying, and that physically resemble the aging female genitalia (as does the date). **eats drily** is dry to eat

90 collateral distant and parallel, shed from a different sphere. (The different Ptolemaic spheres were said to move collaterally, the implication here being that the distance cannot be closed.) **93 hind** female deer **94 pretty** pleasing **96 hawking** keen **97 table** drawing board **97–98 capable Of** susceptible to **98 trick** characteristic expression. **favor** face **99 fancy** love **101 his** i.e., Bertram's **103 a great way** in large measure a. **solely** completely **104 fixed** ineradicable, firmly established. **sit so fit** are so natural and plausible (in him) **105–106 take . . . wind** find acceptance and take precedence, while virtue, in its uncompromising severity, is left out in the cold **106 Withal** consequently **107 Cold . . . folly** naked and unprovided wisdom being forced to defer to overdressed folly **108 Save** i.e., God save. **queen** (A hyperbolical compliment, which Helena answers in kind, whereupon they both deny their titles.) **113 stain** tinge **115 barricado** barricade **118 Unfold** reveal **120–121 setting . . . you** laying siege (as though to a town, but with bawdy quibbling that is elaborated in the following lines. To *undermine* is to "impair your resistances" and "tunnel into your lower regions"; to *blow up* is to "explode with mines" and "impregnate.") **123 policy** stratagem **126 be blown up** i.e., achieve orgasm. **Marry** (A mild oath derived from "by the Virgin Mary.")

ry, 'tis a withered pear; it was formerly better; marry, yet 'tis a withered pear. Will you anything with it?

HELENA

Not my virginity, yet . . .   165
There shall your master have a thousand loves,   166
A mother, and a mistress, and a friend,   167
A phoenix, captain, and an enemy,   168
A guide, a goddess, and a sovereign,
A counselor, a traitress, and a dear;
His humble ambition, proud humility,
His jarring concord, and his discord dulcet,
His faith, his sweet disaster, with a world   173
Of pretty, fond, adoptious christendoms   174
That blinking Cupid gossips. Now shall he—   175
I know not what he shall. God send him well!
The court's a learning place, and he is one—

PAROLLES   What one, i' faith?

HELENA   That I wish well. 'Tis pity—

PAROLLES   What's pity?

HELENA

That wishing well had not a body in 't   181
Which might be felt, that we, the poorer born,   182
Whose baser stars do shut us up in wishes,   183
Might with effects of them follow our friends   184
And show what we alone must think, which never   185
Returns us thanks.   186

Enter Page.

PAGE   Monsieur Parolles, my lord calls for you. [*Exit.*]

PAROLLES   Little Helen, farewell. If I can remember thee, I will think of thee at court.

HELENA   Monsieur Parolles, you were born under a charitable star.

PAROLLES   Under Mars, I.

HELENA   I especially think under Mars.

PAROLLES   Why under Mars?

HELENA   The wars hath so kept you under that you   195
must needs be born under Mars.

PAROLLES   When he was predominant.   197

HELENA   When he was retrograde, I think rather.   198

PAROLLES   Why think you so?

HELENA   You go so much backward when you fight.

PAROLLES   That's for advantage.   201

HELENA   So is running away, when fear proposes the safety. But the composition that your valor and fear 203 makes in you is a virtue of a good wing, and I like the 204 wear well.   205

PAROLLES   I am so full of businesses I cannot answer thee acutely. I will return perfect courtier, in the which 207 my instruction shall serve to naturalize thee, so thou 208 wilt be capable of a courtier's counsel and understand 209 what advice shall thrust upon thee; else thou diest in thine unthankfulness, and thine ignorance makes thee 211 away. Farewell. When thou hast leisure, say thy pray- 212 ers; when thou hast none, remember thy friends. Get 213 thee a good husband, and use him as he uses thee. So, farewell.   [*Exit.*]

HELENA

Our remedies oft in ourselves do lie
Which we ascribe to heaven. The fated sky   217
Gives us free scope, only doth backward pull
Our slow designs when we ourselves are dull.   219
What power is it which mounts my love so high,   220
That makes me see and cannot feed mine eye?   221
The mightiest space in fortune nature brings   222
To join like likes and kiss like native things.   223
Impossible be strange attempts to those   224
That weigh their pains in sense and do suppose   225
What hath been cannot be. Who ever strove   226
To show her merit that did miss her love?   227
The King's disease—my project may deceive me,
But my intents are fixed and will not leave me.   *Exit.*

1.2   *Flourish cornets. Enter the King of France, with letters, and [two Lords and] divers attendants.*

KING

The Florentines and Senoys are by th' ears,   1
Have fought with equal fortune and continue
A braving war.

---

165 **Not . . . yet** the moment for surrendering my virginity has not yet arrived (?) (There may be a textual omission here.) 166 **There** i.e., at court 167–173 **A mother . . . disaster** (Helena here provides a catalogue of the various emotional relationships and paradoxical emotional attitudes found in Elizabethan courtly love poetry.) 168 **phoenix** i.e., nonpareil. (Literally, a fabulous bird of which only one exists at any given time.) 173 **disaster** unlucky star 174 **fond** foolish. **adoptious christendoms** pet names 175 **blinking . . . gossips** blind Cupid is godfather to, sponsors 181–182 **That . . . felt** that good wishing does not have a tangible body which could be perceived by the object (Bertram) of this wishing 183 **Whose . . . wishes** whose lower births (owing to the aspect of less fortunate stars) confine us to mere wishing 184 **Might . . . them** might with the assistance of our fulfilled wishes 185–186 **And show . . . thanks** and reveal to them what we must confine to our private thoughts, and for which we receive no return 195 **under** down, in an inferior position (playing on Parolles' *Under*, line 192, in the sense of "governed by") 197 **predominant** in the ascendant, ruling 198 **retrograde** moving backward (i.e., in a direction from east to west relative to the fixed positions of the signs of the zodiac)

201 **for advantage** to gain tactical advantage. (But Helena caustically interprets it as "craven self-protection.") 203 **composition** mixture 204 **of a good wing** strong in flight (and hence useful in rapid retreat; with a quibble on a sartorial sense of *wing*, meaning "an ornamental shoulder flap") 205 **wear** fashion 207 **perfect** complete. **in the which** i.e., in which courtly behavior 208 **naturalize** familiarize; also, deflower. **so** provided that 209 **capable** receptive (with bawdy double meaning, continued in *understand*, *thrust*, and *diest*) 211–212 **makes thee away** destroys, puts an end to you 213 **when . . . friends** i.e., (patronizingly) don't forget to say your prayers, but remember also that you have friends 217 **fated** invested with the power of destiny 219 **dull** slow, sluggish 220 **so high** to so exalted an object, i.e., to Bertram 221 **That . . . eye** i.e., that puts a desirable object in my mind but will not let me feed my longings in his presence 222–223 **The . . . things** natural affection can cause even those separated by the widest diversity in social status to come together as if they belonged together 224–226 **Impossible . . . be** extraordinary attempts (at surmounting social barriers) seem impossible to those who too carefully calculate the extent and cost of their difficulties and suppose something to be impossible even though it has been done before (?) 227 **miss** fail to achieve

1.2. Location: Paris. The royal court.

1 **Senoys** natives of Siena. **by th' ears** at variance, quarreling

FIRST LORD   So 'tis reported, sir.   3

KING

Nay, 'tis most credible. We here receive it
A certainty, vouched from our cousin Austria,   5
With caution that the Florentine will move us   6
For speedy aid, wherein our dearest friend   7
Prejudicates the business, and would seem   8
To have us make denial.

FIRST LORD   His love and wisdom,   9
Approved so to Your Majesty, may plead   10
For amplest credence.

KING   He hath armed our answer,   11
And Florence is denied before he comes.
Yet for our gentlemen that mean to see   13
The Tuscan service, freely have they leave
To stand on either part.

SECOND LORD   It well may serve   15
A nursery to our gentry, who are sick   16
For breathing and exploit.

KING   What's he comes here?   17

Enter Bertram, Lafew, and Parolles.

FIRST LORD

It is the Count Rossillion, my good lord,
Young Bertram.

KING   Youth, thou bear'st thy father's face.
Frank nature, rather curious than in haste,   20
Hath well composed thee. Thy father's moral parts   21
Mayst thou inherit too! Welcome to Paris.

BERTRAM

My thanks and duty are Your Majesty's.

KING

I would I had that corporal soundness now   24
As when thy father and myself in friendship
First tried our soldiership! He did look far   26
Into the service of the time, and was   27
Discipled of the bravest. He lasted long,   28
But on us both did haggish age steal on,   29
And wore us out of act. It much repairs me   30
To talk of your good father. In his youth
He had the wit which I can well observe
Today in our young lords; but they may jest
Till their own scorn return to them unnoted   34
Ere they can hide their levity in honor.   35

So like a courtier, contempt nor bitterness   36
Were in his pride or sharpness; if they were,   37
His equal had awaked them, and his honor,   38
Clock to itself, knew the true minute when   39
Exception bid him speak, and at this time   40
His tongue obeyed his hand. Who were below him   41
He used as creatures of another place   42
And bowed his eminent top to their low ranks,   43
Making them proud of his humility   44
In their poor praise he humbled. Such a man   45
Might be a copy to these younger times,   46
Which, followed well, would demonstrate them now   47
But goers backward.

BERTRAM   His good remembrance, sir,   48
Lies richer in your thoughts than on his tomb.
So in approof lives not his epitaph   50
As in your royal speech.

KING

Would I were with him! He would always say—
Methinks I hear him now; his plausive words   53
He scattered not in ears, but grafted them   54
To grow there and to bear. "Let me not live—"
This his good melancholy oft began
On the catastrophe and heel of pastime,   57
When it was out—"Let me not live," quoth he,   58
"After my flame lacks oil, to be the snuff   59
Of younger spirits, whose apprehensive senses   60
All but new things disdain, whose judgments are   61
Mere fathers of their garments, whose constancies   62
Expire before their fashions." This he wished.
I, after him, do after him wish too,   64
Since I nor wax nor honey can bring home,   65
I quickly were dissolvèd from my hive   66
To give some laborers room.

SECOND LORD   You're lovèd, sir.
They that least lend it you shall lack you first.   68

KING

I fill a place, I know 't.—How long is 't, Count,
Since the physician at your father's died?
He was much famed.

---

3 braving war war of mutual defiance   **5 our cousin** my fellow sovereign of   **6 move** petition   **7 friend** i.e., the Duke of Austria   **8 Prejudicates** prejudges   **8–9 would . . . denial** appears to wish that we deny aid (to the Florentines)   **10 Approved** demonstrated, proved   **11 credence** belief.   **armed** fortified (against denial)   **13 for** as for.   **see** i.e., participate in   **15 stand** serve, fight.   **part** side.   **serve** serve as   **16 nursery** training school   **16–17 sick For breathing** longing for vigorous exercise, or, sick for lack of exercise   **20 Frank** generous, bountiful.   **curious** careful, skillful   **21 parts** qualities   **24 corporal soundness** physical health   **26 tried** tested   **26–27 He did . . . time** he had a deep understanding of the affairs of war   **28 Discipled of** followed by (or, perhaps, "taught by")   **29 haggish** like a hag, malevolent   **30 wore . . . act** wore us down into inactivity.   **repairs** restores   **34 Till . . . unnoted** i.e., until people stop paying attention to their scornful remarks other than to respond with scorn   **35 Ere . . . honor** sooner than they can cover their frivolous jesting of youth with truly honorable action

36–37 So . . . sharpness so like a true courtier as he was, he showed no contemptuousness in his proper self-esteem or bitterness of tongue in his sharpness of wit   **37 if they were** i.e., if he ever spoke sharply   **38 equal** i.e., social equal, not an inferior   **39 Clock to itself** i.e., self-governing.   **true** exact   **40 Exception** disapproval   **41 obeyed his hand** i.e., would speak only what his hand was ready to back up with action, much as a clock rings when the hand of the clock tells it to do so.   **Who** those who   **42 creatures . . . place** people of a different (i.e., more elevated) station   **43 top** head   **44–45 Making . . . humbled** i.e., making them proud that he should humble his own eminence in praise of them   **46 copy** model   **47–48 demonstrate . . . backward** show today's young men to be inferior to him   **50 So . . . epitaph** the epitaph on his tomb is nowhere so amply confirmed   **53 plausive** praiseworthy   **54 scattered not** did not strew haphazardly   **57–58 On . . . out** at the drawing to a close of some sport (such as hunting), when the sport was over   **59 snuff** burned wick that interferes with proper burning of the candle, hence, hindrance   **60 apprehensive** quick to perceive, keen but impatient   **61–62 whose . . . garments** i.e., whose wisdom produces nothing but new fashions   **62 constancies** loyalties   **64 I . . . too** I, surviving him, wish as he did (with a suggestion also of wishing to follow him in death)   **65 nor . . . nor** neither . . . nor   **66 dissolvèd** separated   **68 lend it you** give love to you.   **lack** miss

BERTRAM   Some six months since, my lord.

KING
If he were living, I would try him yet.—
Lend me an arm.—The rest have worn me out   73
With several applications. Nature and sickness   74
Debate it at their leisure. Welcome, Count;   75
My son's no dearer.

BERTRAM   Thank Your Majesty.

Exeunt. Flourish.

✣

1.3   *Enter Countess, Steward [Rinaldo], and Clown
[Lavatch].*

COUNTESS   I will now hear. What say you of this
gentlewoman?

RINALDO   Madam, the care I have had to even your con-   3
tent I wish might be found in the calendar of my past   4
endeavors; for then we wound our modesty, and
make foul the clearness of our deservings, when of
ourselves we publish them.   7

COUNTESS   What does this knave here?—Get you
gone, sirrah. The complaints I have heard of you I do   9
not all believe. 'Tis my slowness that I do not, for I
know you lack not folly to commit them and have
ability enough to make such knaveries yours.

LAVATCH   'Tis not unknown to you, madam, I am a
poor fellow.

COUNTESS   Well, sir.

LAVATCH   No, madam, 'tis not so well that I am poor,   16
though many of the rich are damned; but if I may have
your ladyship's good will to go to the world, Isbel   18
the woman and I will do as we may.   19

COUNTESS   Wilt thou needs be a beggar?

LAVATCH   I do beg your good will in this case.

COUNTESS   In what case?

LAVATCH   In Isbel's case and mine own. Service is no   23
heritage, and I think I shall never have the blessing of   24
God till I have issue o' my body; for they say bairns are   25
blessings.

COUNTESS   Tell me thy reason why thou wilt marry.

LAVATCH   My poor body, madam, requires it. I am
driven on by the flesh, and he must needs go that the   29
devil drives.

COUNTESS   Is this all your worship's reason?   31

LAVATCH   Faith, madam, I have other holy reasons,   32
such as they are.

COUNTESS   May the world know them?

LAVATCH   I have been, madam, a wicked creature, as
you and all flesh and blood are, and indeed I do marry
that I may repent.   37

COUNTESS   Thy marriage, sooner than thy wickedness.   38

LAVATCH   I am out o' friends, madam, and I hope to
have friends for my wife's sake.

COUNTESS   Such friends are thine enemies, knave.

LAVATCH   You're shallow, madam, in great friends, for   42
the knaves come to do that for me which I am aweary
of. He that ears my land spares my team and gives me   44
leave to in the crop. If I be his cuckold, he's my   45
drudge. He that comforts my wife is the cherisher of   46
my flesh and blood; he that cherishes my flesh and
blood loves my flesh and blood; he that loves my flesh
and blood is my friend. Ergo, he that kisses my wife
is my friend. If men could be contented to be what   50
they are, there were no fear in marriage; for young   51
Charbon the puritan and old Poysam the papist, how-   52
soe'er their hearts are severed in religion, their heads
are both one—they may jowl horns together like any   54
deer i' the herd.

COUNTESS   Wilt thou ever be a foulmouthed and ca-   56
lumnious knave?   57

LAVATCH   A prophet I, madam, and I speak the truth
the next way: 59
For I the ballad will repeat
Which men full true shall find:
Your marriage comes by destiny,
Your cuckoo sings by kind.   63

COUNTESS   Get you gone, sir. I'll talk with you more
anon.

RINALDO   May it please you, madam, that he bid Helen
come to you. Of her I am to speak.

COUNTESS   Sirrah, tell my gentlewoman I would speak
with her—Helen, I mean.

LAVATCH [*sings*]
"Was this fair face the cause," quoth she,   70
"Why the Grecians sackèd Troy?
Fond done, done fond,   72
Was this King Priam's joy?"   73
With that she sighèd as she stood,
With that she sighèd as she stood,
And gave this sentence then: 76
"Among nine bad if one be good,   77
Among nine bad if one be good,
There's yet one good in ten."

---

73 The rest i.e., my physicians   **74 several applications** various medical treatments   **75 Debate . . . leisure** i.e., contend over my condition at length
1.3. Location: Rossillion.
3–4 to . . . content to meet your expectations   **4 calendar** record
7 publish make known   **9 sirrah** (Form of address to a social inferior.)
16 well (The Clown plays on the Countess's "Well" in line 15, i.e., "Well, go ahead"; he means "satisfactory." He also plays on *poor* in lines 14 and 16: [1] wretched [2] impoverished.)   **18 go . . . world** i.e., marry   **19 do** (1) get along (2) copulate   **23 case** (with a bawdy pun on "female pudenda")   **23–24 Service is no heritage** i.e., being a servant gives me little to bequeath to my heirs   **25 bairns** children
29 needs necessarily   **31 your worship's** (The Countess uses a mock title.)   **32 holy reasons** i.e., reasons sanctioned by the marriage service (with obscene puns on "holey" and "raisings")

37 repent i.e., (1) atone for my carnal ways by making them legitimate (2) regret marrying   **38 Thy marriage** i.e., you'll repent your marriage (since proverbially hasty marriage leads to regret)   **42 shallow . . . in** a superficial judge of   **44–45 He . . . crop** i.e., he that plows (*ears*) my wife sexually takes the load off my *team*, my sexual organs, and provides me with a *crop* of children   **45 in** bring in, harvest.   **cuckold** a man whose wife is unfaithful   **46 drudge** menial laborer   **50–51 what they are** i.e., cuckolds   **52 Charbon, Poysam** (Corruptions of *chairbonne*, good meat, and *poisson*, fish, the fast-day diets of Puritans and Catholics, respectively.)   **54 both one** alike (in having cuckolds' horns).   **jowl** dash, knock   **56 ever** always   **56–57 calumnious** slandering   **59 next** nearest, most direct   **63 kind** nature (since cuckoldry is natural)   **70 fair face** i.e., Helen of Troy's face.   **she** i.e., Hecuba, wife of Priam (?)   **72 Fond** foolishly
73 Priam's joy i.e., Paris, son of King Priam of Troy   **76 sentence** maxim   **77 Among** along with

COUNTESS   What, one good in ten? You corrupt the 80
song, sirrah. 81

LAVATCH   One good woman in ten, madam, which is a
purifying o' the song. Would God would serve the 83
world so all the year! We'd find no fault with the tithe- 84
woman if I were the parson. One in ten, quoth 'a? An 85
we might have a good woman born but or every blaz- 86
ing star, or at an earthquake, 'twould mend the lottery 87
well. A man may draw his heart out ere 'a pluck one. 88

COUNTESS   You'll be gone, sir knave, and do as I
command you?

LAVATCH   That man should be at woman's command,
and yet no hurt done! Though honesty be no Puritan, 92
yet it will do no hurt; it will wear the surplice of hu- 93
mility over the black gown of a big heart. I am going, 94
forsooth. The business is for Helen to come hither.

Exit.

COUNTESS   Well, now.

RINALDO   I know, madam, you love your gentlewoman
entirely.

COUNTESS   Faith, I do. Her father bequeathed her to
me, and she herself, without other advantage, may 100
lawfully make title to as much love as she finds. There 101
is more owing her than is paid, and more shall be paid
her than she'll demand.

RINALDO   Madam, I was very late more near her than I 104
think she wished me. Alone she was, and did
communicate to herself her own words to her own
ears; she thought, I dare vow for her, they touched not
any stranger sense. Her matter was, she loved your 108
son. Fortune, she said, was no goddess, that had put 109
such difference betwixt their two estates; Love no god,
that would not extend his might only where qualities 111
were level; Dian no queen of virgins, that would suffer 112
her poor knight surprised without rescue in the first 113
assault or ransom afterward. This she delivered in the 114

most bitter touch of sorrow that e'er I heard virgin 115
exclaim in, which I held my duty speedily to acquaint
you withal, sithence, in the loss that may happen, it 117
concerns you something to know it. 118

COUNTESS   You have discharged this honestly. Keep it 119
to yourself. Many likelihoods informed me of this 120
before, which hung so tottering in the balance that I
could neither believe nor misdoubt. Pray you, leave 122
me. Stall this in your bosom, and I thank you for your 123
honest care. I will speak with you further anon.

Exit Steward [Rinaldo].

Enter Helena.

Even so it was with me when I was young. 125
    If ever we are nature's, these are ours. This thorn 126
Doth to our rose of youth rightly belong;
    Our blood to us, this to our blood is born. 128
It is the show and seal of nature's truth, 129
Where love's strong passion is impressed in youth. 130
By our remembrances of days forgone,
Such were our faults, or then we thought them
    none. 132
Her eye is sick on 't. I observe her now. 133

HELENA   What is your pleasure, madam?

COUNTESS
You know, Helen, I am a mother to you.

HELENA
Mine honorable mistress.

COUNTESS   Nay, a mother.
Why not a mother? When I said "a mother,"
Methought you saw a serpent. What's in "mother"
That you start at it? I say I am your mother,
And put you in the catalogue of those
That were enwombèd mine. 'Tis often seen
Adoption strives with nature, and choice breeds 142
A native slip to us from foreign seeds. 143
You ne'er oppressed me with a mother's groan, 144
Yet I express to you a mother's care.
God's mercy, maiden, does it curd thy blood
To say I am thy mother? What's the matter,
That this distempered messenger of wet, 148
The many-colored Iris, rounds thine eye? 149
Why? That you are my daughter?

HELENA   That I am not. 150

80–81 You . . . song (The song must have had "nine good in ten,"
or "one bad in ten," referring probably to Paris as Priam's one bad
son; but the Clown indicates he is singing of women, for whom one
good in ten is a *purifying* or improvement.)   83 Would if only   84–
85 tithe-woman (An allusion to the practice of paying tithes, or a
tenth part of one's farm produce, in kind rather than in money. The
parson ought to be satisfied with one good woman in ten.)   85 quoth
'a said he, i.e., forsooth.   An if   86–87 but . . . earthquake only as
commonly as a comet or an earthquake occurs (both of which are
rare)   87 mend the lottery improve the current odds   88 pluck one
i.e., draw one good woman by lottery   92–94 Though . . . heart
i.e., though my frank nature (my *honesty*) makes no pretensions to
virtue (is *no Puritan*), it will not offend authority; it will, like the Puritan, hide its proud spirit (*big heart*) beneath the guise of humble obedience. (The metaphor concerns those Puritans who demurred at obedience to some of the rubrics and canons pertaining to public
worship; some of them, to *do no hurt*, conformed in some respect by
wearing the surplice; nevertheless, they wore it over the black Gene-
van gown customarily worn by Calvinistic Protestants on the Continent.)   100 without even without.   advantage i.e., interest accrued.
(The Countess's metaphor is of the inheritance of a valuable property
that is entitled to high regard in its own right.)   101 make title lay
claim   104 late recently   108 any stranger sense any other person's
sense of hearing.   matter theme   109 was no goddess i.e., was a
thing of accident only, not divine   111 extend his might only exercise his (Love's) power except   111–112 qualities were level social
rank was equal   112 Dian Diana, goddess of chastity   112–113 suffer . . . surprised allow her hapless devotee to be captured   114 delivered spoke

115 touch note, pang   117 withal with.   sithence since.   in . . .
happen in view of the harm that may come of this (such as Helena's
despondency)   118 something somewhat   119 discharged performed
120 likelihoods indications   122 misdoubt doubt   123 Stall lodge
125 Even so (The Countess speaks without being heard by Helena,
who has entered.)   126 these i.e., these pangs of love (signs of which
the Countess sees manifested in Helena)   128 blood natural feeling,
especially *love's strong passion,* line 130, and linked to the sexual
suggestion of *thorn* and *rose* in lines 126–127   129 show and seal
sign and guarantee   130 impressed imprinted (as by a seal in wax, or
a thorn)   132 or . . . none or rather things we didn't consider faults
at the time   133 on 't with it.   observe her see what is troubling her
142 strives vies (in strength of attachment)   142–143 choice . . .
seeds choice of a grafting or scion grown from an unrelated stock
makes wholly ours what was originally foreign   144 with a mother's
groan i.e., in childbirth   148 distempered . . . wet inclement and
distracted tear   149 Iris Juno's messenger; also the rainbow (which
appears refracted in Helena's tears).   rounds encircles   150 not i.e.,
not daughter-in-law

COUNTESS
I say I am your mother.
HELENA   Pardon, madam;
The Count Rossillion cannot be my brother.
I am from humble, he from honored name;
No note upon my parents, his all noble.   154
My master, my dear lord he is, and I
His servant live and will his vassal die.
He must not be my brother.
COUNTESS   Nor I your mother?
HELENA
You are my mother, madam. Would you were—
So that my lord your son were not my brother—
Indeed my mother! Or were you both our mothers,   160
I care no more for than I do for heaven,   161
So I were not his sister. Can 't no other   162
But, I your daughter, he must be my brother?   163
COUNTESS
Yes, Helen, you might be my daughter-in-law.
God shield you mean it not! "Daughter" and
    "mother"   165
So strive upon your pulse. What, pale again?
My fear hath catched your fondness. Now I see   167
The mystery of your loneliness and find
Your salt tears' head. Now to all sense 'tis gross: 169
You love my son. Invention is ashamed,   170
Against the proclamation of thy passion,   171
To say thou dost not. Therefore tell me true,
But tell me then 'tis so, for look, thy cheeks
Confess it th' one to th' other, and thine eyes
See it so grossly shown in thy behaviors
That in their kind they speak it. Only sin   176
And hellish obstinacy tie thy tongue,
That truth should be suspected. Speak, is 't so?   178
If it be so, you have wound a goodly clew;   179
If it be not, forswear 't. Howe'er, I charge thee,   180
As heaven shall work in me for thine avail,   181
To tell me truly.
HELENA   Good madam, pardon me!
COUNTESS
Do you love my son?
HELENA   Your pardon, noble mistress!
COUNTESS
Love you my son?
HELENA   Do not you love him, madam?
COUNTESS
Go not about. My love hath in 't a bond   185

Whereof the world takes note. Come, come, disclose   186
The state of your affection, for your passions
Have to the full appeached.
HELENA [kneeling]   Then I confess   188
Here on my knee, before high heaven and you,
That before you, and next unto high heaven,   190
I love your son.
My friends were poor but honest, so's my love.   192
Be not offended, for it hurts not him
That he is loved of me. I follow him not
By any token of presumptuous suit,   195
Nor would I have him till I do deserve him,
Yet never know how that desert should be.
I know I love in vain, strive against hope;
Yet in this captious and intenible sieve   199
I still pour in the waters of my love
And lack not to lose still. Thus, Indian-like,   201
Religious in mine error, I adore
The sun, that looks upon his worshiper
But knows of him no more. My dearest madam,   204
Let not your hate encounter with my love   205
For loving where you do; but if yourself,
Whose agèd honor cites a virtuous youth,   207
Did ever in so true a flame of liking   208
Wish chastely and love dearly, that your Dian   209
Was both herself and Love, O, then, give pity   210
To her whose state is such that cannot choose
But lend and give where she is sure to lose;
That seeks not to find that her search implies,   213
But riddle-like lives sweetly where she dies.   214
COUNTESS
Had you not lately an intent—speak truly—
To go to Paris?
HELENA   Madam, I had.
COUNTESS   Wherefore?   216
Tell true.
HELENA
I will tell truth, by grace itself I swear.
You know my father left me some prescriptions
Of rare and proved effects, such as his reading
And manifest experience had collected   221
For general sovereignty; and that he willed me   222
In heedfull'st reservation to bestow them,   223
As notes whose faculties inclusive were   224
More than they were in note. Amongst the rest   225

---

154 note mark of distinction. parents ancestors   160 both our
mothers mother of us both   161 I . . . heaven (Helena ambiguously
suggests [1] she wouldn't care much for this [2] she would care for it
as much as she longs for heaven.)   162 So so long as   162–163 Can
't . . . daughter must it be that if I'm your daughter   165 shield forbid. (But the construction with not is ambiguous.)   167 catched
caught. fondness love (of Bertram); or foolishness. (The Countess
speaks ambiguously while she tests Helena.)   169 head   source.
sense perception. gross palpable, apparent   170 Invention i.e., your
ability to invent excuses   171 Against in the face of   176 in their
kind in their natural way, i.e., by weeping   178 suspected surmised
(by me) rather than openly declared; or, rendered suspect, brought
into disrepute   179 wound . . . clew wound up a fine ball of thread,
i.e., snarled things up beautifully   180 forswear 't deny it under
oath. Howe'er in any case   181 avail benefit   185 Go not about
don't evade me.   bond i.e., maternal bond

186 Whereof . . . note which society acknowledges   188 appeached
informed against (you)   190 before you even more than (I love) you;
or, even more than you love him   192 friends kinfolk   195 By . . .
suit with any indication of my presumptuous love   199 captious deceptive; also, capacious.   intenible incapable of holding   201 lack
. . . still still have enough to keep pouring without diminishing my
supply; also, continually lose.   Indian-like idolatrously, like the savage (who worships the sun)   204 no more nothing else   205 encounter with oppose   207 agèd honor cites honorable old age bespeaks,
gives evidence of   208 liking love   209 that so that   210 both . . .
Love i.e., both Diana and Venus, chaste and passionate   213 that
. . . implies what her search is for   214 riddle-like paradoxically,
with an unguessed mystery   216 Wherefore why   221 manifest experience i.e., the practice, in antithesis to the theory (reading)
222 general sovereignty general efficacy and use   223 In . . . them
to employ them only with the greatest care   224–225 As . . . note
as prescriptions whose power was greater than recognized

There is a remedy, approved, set down,   226
To cure the desperate languishings whereof
The King is rendered lost.   228
COUNTESS
This was your motive for Paris, was it? Speak.
HELENA
My lord your son made me to think of this,
Else Paris and the medicine and the King
Had from the conversation of my thoughts   232
Haply been absent then.
COUNTESS   But think you, Helen,   233
If you should tender your supposèd aid,   234
He would receive it? He and his physicians
Are of a mind: he, that they cannot help him,
They, that they cannot help. How shall they credit   237
A poor unlearnèd virgin, when the schools,
Emboweled of their doctrine, have left off   239
The danger to itself?
HELENA   There's something in 't
More than my father's skill, which was the great'st
Of his profession, that his good receipt   242
Shall for my legacy be sanctified
By th' luckiest stars in heaven; and would your
   honor   244
But give me leave to try success, I'd venture   245
The well-lost life of mine on His Grace's cure   246
By such a day and hour.   247
COUNTESS   Dost thou believe 't?
HELENA   Ay, madam, knowingly.   249
COUNTESS
Why, Helen, thou shalt have my leave and love,
Means and attendants, and my loving greetings
To those of mine in court. I'll stay at home
And pray God's blessing into thy attempt.   253
Begone tomorrow, and be sure of this:
What I can help thee to thou shalt not miss.   *Exeunt.* 255

❖

2.1   *Enter the King [in his chair] with divers young
Lords taking leave for the Florentine war, [Bertram]
Count Rossillion, and Parolles. Flourish cornets.*

KING
Farewell, young lords. These warlike principles   1
Do not throw from you. And you, my lords,
   farewell.   2

Share the advice betwixt you; if both gain all,   3
The gift doth stretch itself as 'tis received,   4
And is enough for both.
FIRST LORD   'Tis our hope, sir,
After well-entered soldiers, to return   6
And find Your Grace in health.
KING
No, no, it cannot be; and yet my heart
Will not confess he owes the malady   9
That doth my life besiege. Farewell, young lords.
Whether I live or die, be you the sons
Of worthy Frenchmen. Let higher Italy—   12
Those bated that inherit but the fall   13
Of the last monarchy—see that you come   14
Not to woo honor, but to wed it. When   15
The bravest questant shrinks, find what you seek,   16
That fame may cry you loud. I say, farewell.   17
SECOND LORD
Health at your bidding serve Your Majesty!
KING
Those girls of Italy, take heed of them.
They say our French lack language to deny
If they demand. Beware of being captives   21
Before you serve.
BOTH   Our hearts receive your warnings. 22
KING
Farewell.—Come hither to me.   *[The King converses
                               privately with various lords; Bertram and his
                                     companions move apart.]*
FIRST LORD
O my sweet lord, that you will stay behind us!
PAROLLES
'Tis not his fault, the spark.
SECOND LORD   O, 'tis brave wars!   25
PAROLLES   Most admirable. I have seen those wars.
BERTRAM   I am commanded here and kept a coil with   27
"Too young" and "The next year" and "'Tis too early."
PAROLLES   An thy mind stand to 't, boy, steal away   29
   bravely.   30
BERTRAM
I shall stay here the forehorse to a smock,   31
Creaking my shoes on the plain masonry,   32
Till honor be bought up, and no sword worn   33
But one to dance with. By heaven, I'll steal away!   34

226 **approved** tested   228 **rendered lost** reckoned to be incurable
232 **conversation** movement, train   233 **Haply** perhaps   234 **tender**
offer   237 **credit** trust   239 **Emboweled** emptied.   **left off** abandoned   242 **that** whereby.   **receipt** prescription   244 **luckiest** i.e.,
most able to confer luck   245 **try success** test the outcome.   **venture**
risk, wager   246 **well-lost** i.e., well lost in such a cause, worthless
otherwise   247 **such a** i.e., a specific   249 **knowingly** knowing what
I'm doing, or, knowing with certainty rather than simply believing
253 **into** upon   255 **miss** be lacking
2.1. Location: Paris. The royal court.
1–2 These . . . you i.e., remember this military advice   **2 And you**
(Said perhaps to a second group of lords, one intending to fight on the
other side in this war of Florentines and Sienese.)

3–4 **if . . . received** i.e., if both sides wish to follow all of my advice, it will stretch to accommodate the demand   6 **After . . . sol-**
diers after having become seasoned soldiers; or, in the manner of experienced soldiers   9 **he owes** it owns   12 **higher Italy** (1) the
knightly class of Italy, corresponding to *worthy Frenchmen*, or (2) Tus-
cany, of which Florence and Siena are cities   13–14 **Those . . .**
monarchy i.e., except those who have basely profited from the fall of
the Holy Roman Empire (or some such absolutist authority?)   15 **woo**
flirt with.   **wed** possess as your own   16 **questant** seeker   17 **cry**
you loud proclaim you loudly   21–22 **captives . . . serve** (Both
terms describe love in terms of military encounters.)   25 **spark** elegant young man.   **brave** splendid   27 **here** i.e., to remain here.
kept a coil pestered, fussed over   29 **An** if   30 **bravely** (1) worthily
(2) valiantly   31 **the forehorse . . . smock** the lead horse of a team
driven by a woman   32 **plain masonry** smooth masonry floor (instead
of a battlefield)   33 **Till . . . up** till opportunity for winning honor in
the wars is past, all consumed   34 **one . . . with** i.e., a light ornamental weapon

FIRST LORD
There's honor in the theft.

PAROLLES   Commit it, Count.

SECOND LORD
I am your accessory. And so, farewell.

BERTRAM   I grow to you, and our parting is a tortured 37
body.   38

FIRST LORD   Farewell, Captain.

SECOND LORD   Sweet Monsieur Parolles!

PAROLLES   Noble heroes, my sword and yours are kin.
Good sparks and lustrous, a word, good metals: you 42
shall find in the regiment of the Spinii one Captain
Spurio, with his cicatrice, an emblem of war, here on 44
his sinister cheek; it was this very sword entrenched it. 45
Say to him I live, and observe his reports for me.   46

FIRST LORD   We shall, noble Captain.

PAROLLES   Mars dote on you for his novices!   48
                                          [*Exeunt Lords.*]

[*To Bertram.*]   What will ye do?

BERTRAM   Stay the King.   50

PAROLLES [*to Bertram*]   Use a more spacious ceremony 51
to the noble lords; you have restrained yourself within
the list of too cold an adieu. Be more expressive to 53
them, for they wear themselves in the cap of the time; 54
there do muster true gait, eat, speak, and move under 55
the influence of the most received star; and, though the 56
devil lead the measure, such are to be followed. After 57
them, and take a more dilated farewell.   58

BERTRAM   And I will do so.

PAROLLES   Worthy fellows, and like to prove most sin- 60
ewy swordmen.   *Exeunt* [*Bertram and Parolles*]. 61

Enter Lafew [and approaches the King].

LAFEW [*kneeling*]
Pardon, my lord, for me and for my tidings.   62

KING   I'll fee thee to stand up.   63

LAFEW [*rising*]
Then here's a man stands that has brought his
pardon.   64
I would you had kneeled, my lord, to ask me mercy,
And that at my bidding you could so stand up.

KING
I would I had, so I had broke thy pate   67
And asked thee mercy for 't.

LAFEW   Good faith, across!   68
But, my good lord, 'tis thus: will you be cured
Of your infirmity?

KING   No.

LAFEW   O, will you eat   70
No grapes, my royal fox? Yes, but you will   71
My noble grapes, an if my royal fox   72
Could reach them. I have seen a medicine   73
That's able to breathe life into a stone,
Quicken a rock, and make you dance canary   75
With sprightly fire and motion, whose simple touch   76
Is powerful to araise King Pepin, nay,   77
To give great Charlemain a pen in 's hand
And write to her a love line.

KING   What "her" is this?   79

LAFEW
Why, Doctor She! My lord, there's one arrived,
If you will see her. Now by my faith and honor,
If seriously I may convey my thoughts
In this my light deliverance, I have spoke   83
With one that in her sex, her years, profession,   84
Wisdom, and constancy hath amazed me more   85
Than I dare blame my weakness. Will you see her,   86
For that is her demand, and know her business?
That done, laugh well at me.

KING   Now, good Lafew,
Bring in the admiration, that we with thee   89
May spend our wonder too, or take off thine   90
By wondering how thou took'st it.

LAFEW   Nay, I'll fit you,   91
And not be all day neither.   [*He goes to the door.*]

KING
Thus he his special nothing ever prologues.   93

LAFEW   Nay, come your ways.   94

Enter Helena.

KING   This haste hath wings indeed.

LAFEW   Nay, come your ways.
This is His Majesty. Say your mind to him.
A traitor you do look like, but such traitors   98
His Majesty seldom fears. I am Cressid's uncle,   99
That dare leave two together. Fare you well.   *Exit.*

---

37 grow to grow deeply attached to, become as one with   **37–38 a tortured body** i.e., as painful as a body being torn apart by torture
42 metals i.e., "blades"; spirits of mettle   **44 Spurio** (This name suggests "spurious," "counterfeit.")   **cicatrice** scar   **45 sinister** left
46 reports reply   **48 Mars** may Mars.   **novices** devotees   **50 Stay the King** support or wait on the King. (But also interpreted, with different punctuation, as "Stay; the King wills it" or "Stay; the King approaches.")   **51 spacious ceremony** effusive courtesy   **53 list** boundary. (Literally, the selvage or finished edge of cloth.)   **54 wear . . . time** stand out as ornaments of the fashionable world   **55 muster true gait** set the right pace, move gracefully   **56 received** fashionable   **57 measure** dance   **58 dilated** protracted; expansive   **60 like** likely
60–61 sinewy energetic, forceful   **62 tidings** news, information   **63 I'll . . . up** i.e., I bid you rise; or, I will rather reward you for rising   **64 pardon** i.e., something to win the King's indulgence
67–68 so . . . for 't i.e., that would be like wounding you on the head and begging your pardon for it

68 across i.e., a weak jest. (A metaphor derived from tilting, where to break a lance *across* an opponent was to strike awkwardly and ineffectively instead of directly with the point.)   **70–71 will . . . fox** i.e., will you be like the fox in Aesop's fable and call the grapes sour because they are beyond your reach   **72 an if** if   **73 medicine** i.e., physician   **75 Quicken** bring to life.   **canary** a lively Spanish dance   **76 simple** (1) mere (2) medicinal, making use of "simples" or herbs   **77 araise** raise from the dead.   **King Pepin** French king of the eighth century, father of Charlemagne   **79 love line** (Some of Lafew's terms, such as *stone, quicken, fire and motion, touch, araise,* and *pen in 's hand,* have possible erotic undertones that link recovery to restored potency.)   **83 deliverance** manner of speaking   **84 profession** what she professes to be able to do   **85–86 more . . . weakness** more than I can attribute to my feebleness or susceptibility as an old man   **89 admiration** wonder   **90 spend** expend.   **take off** dispel, reduce   **91 took'st** conceived (with a play on *take* in the previous line).   **fit** satisfy   **93 special nothing** particular trifles.   **prologues** introduces   **94 come your ways** come along   **98 traitor** (Lafew's joke depends on the idea that it is dangerous to leave an unknown person alone with a king, for fear of a plot.)   **99 Cressid's uncle** Pandarus, go-between for the lovers Troilus and Cressida

KING
Now, fair one, does your business follow us?   101
HELENA   Ay, my good lord.
Gerard de Narbonne was my father;
In what he did profess, well found.
KING   I knew him.   104
HELENA
The rather will I spare my praises towards him;
Knowing him is enough. On 's bed of death
Many receipts he gave me, chiefly one   107
Which, as the dearest issue of his practice,   108
And of his old experience th' only darling,   109
He bade me store up as a triple eye   110
Safer than mine own two, more dear. I have so;   111
And, hearing Your High Majesty is touched
With that malignant cause wherein the honor   113
Of my dear father's gift stands chief in power,   114
I come to tender it and my appliance   115
With all bound humbleness.
KING   We thank you, maiden,   116
But may not be so credulous of cure   117
When our most learnèd doctors leave us and
The congregated college have concluded   119
That laboring art can never ransom nature   120
From her inaidible estate. I say we must not
So stain our judgment, or corrupt our hope,   122
To prostitute our past-cure malady   123
To empirics, or to dissever so   124
Our great self and our credit, to esteem   125
A senseless help when help past sense we deem.   126
HELENA
My duty then shall pay me for my pains.   127
I will no more enforce mine office on you,   128
Humbly entreating from your royal thoughts
A modest one to bear me back again.   130
KING
I cannot give thee less, to be called grateful.
Thou thought'st to help me, and such thanks I give
As one near death to those that wish him live.
But what at full I know, thou know'st no part,   134
I knowing all my peril, thou no art.
HELENA
What I can do can do no hurt to try,
Since you set up your rest 'gainst remedy.   137

He that of greatest works is finisher
Oft does them by the weakest minister.
So holy writ in babes hath judgment shown,
When judges have been babes; great floods have
   flown   141
From simple sources, and great seas have dried   142
When miracles have by the great'st been denied.
Oft expectation fails, and most oft there
Where most it promises, and oft it hits   145
Where hope is coldest and despair most fits.
KING
I must not hear thee. Fare thee well, kind maid.
Thy pains, not used, must by thyself be paid;   148
Proffers not took reap thanks for their reward.   149
HELENA
Inspirèd merit so by breath is barred.   150
It is not so with Him that all things knows
As 'tis with us that square our guess by shows;   152
But most it is presumption in us when
The help of heaven we count the act of men.   154
Dear sir, to my endeavors give consent;
Of heaven, not me, make an experiment.   156
I am not an impostor that proclaim   157
Myself against the level of mine aim;   158
But know I think, and think I know most sure,   159
My art is not past power, nor you past cure.   160
KING
Art thou so confident? Within what space   161
Hop'st thou my cure?
HELENA   The great'st grace lending grace, 162
Ere twice the horses of the sun shall bring
Their fiery torcher his diurnal ring,   164
Ere twice in murk and occidental damp   165
Moist Hesperus hath quenched her sleepy lamp,   166
Or four-and-twenty times the pilot's glass   167
Hath told the thievish minutes how they pass,
What is infirm from your sound parts shall fly,
Health shall live free, and sickness freely die.
KING
Upon thy certainty and confidence
What dar'st thou venture?
HELENA   Tax of impudence,   172
A strumpet's boldness, a divulgèd shame
Traduced by odious ballads; my maiden's name   174

---

101 follow concern   **104 well found** found to be skilled   **107 receipts** remedies   **108–109 the dearest . . . darling** the favorite child or product of his many years of practice   **110 triple** third   **111 Safer** more safely   **113–114 cause . . . power** disease for which my father's honored gift to me is most particularly effective   **115 tender** offer. **appliance** treatment   **116 bound** dutiful   **117 credulous of** ready to believe in   **119 congregated college** college of physicians   **120 art** skill, i.e., medicine   **122 stain** pervert   **123–126 To . . . deem** by basely submitting my past-cure illness to quack doctors, or by divorcing my kingly greatness from my reputation to such an extent as to put credulous faith in a cure too improbable to be believed when the disease exceeds all reasonable hope   **127 My duty** i.e., having tried to do my duty, or, the respect and love I owe you, in any case   **128 office** dutiful service   **130 A modest one** i.e., a favorable regard commensurate with my humble station and with my maidenly modesty.   **bear me back** bear back with me   **134 no part** not at all   **137 set . . . rest** stake your all. (A figure from the gambling game of primero.)

141 babes i.e., babyish, foolish. (The inversion of babes and wise men appears often in the Bible.)   **142 simple** small, insignificant. **great seas** (Probably the Red Sea; *the great'st* in line 143 is presumably Pharaoh.)   **145 hits** succeeds, is confirmed   **148 by . . . paid** i.e., be their own reward   **149 thanks** i.e., nothing but thanks   **150 Inspirèd . . . barred** divinely inspired virtue is thus denied by mere spoken words   **152 square . . . shows** support our conjectures on the basis of appearances   **154 count** account   **156 experiment** trial   **157–158 proclaim . . . aim** claim to be a sure marksman even before I take aim   **159–160 But . . . cure** but I am one who knows what she thinks and am confident that my skill has the power to cure you   **161 space** period of time   **162 Hop'st thou** do you hope for. **The great'st . . . grace** i.e., with God's help   **164 torcher** torchbearer. **his diurnal ring** on his daily round   **165 occidental** western, sunset   **166 Hesperus** evening star (actually Venus)   **167 glass** hourglass   **172 venture** risk, wager. **Tax** accusation   **174 Traduced** slandered

Seared otherwise; nay, worse of worst, extended   175
With vilest torture let my life be ended.

KING
Methinks in thee some blessèd spirit doth speak
His powerful sound within an organ weak;
And what impossibility would slay   179
In common sense, sense saves another way.   180
Thy life is dear, for all that life can rate   181
Worth name of life in thee hath estimate: 182
Youth, beauty, wisdom, courage, all
That happiness and prime can happy call.   184
Thou this to hazard needs must intimate   185
Skill infinite, or monstrous desperate.   186
Sweet practicer, thy physic I will try,   187
That ministers thine own death if I die.   188

HELENA
If I break time or flinch in property   189
Of what I spoke, unpitied let me die,
And well deserved. Not helping, death's my fee;   191
But, if I help, what do you promise me?

KING
Make thy demand.

HELENA   But will you make it even?   193

KING
Ay, by my scepter and my hopes of heaven.

HELENA
Then shalt thou give me with thy kingly hand
What husband in thy power I will command.
Exempted be from me the arrogance
To choose from forth the royal blood of France,
My low and humble name to propagate
With any branch or image of thy state;
But such a one, thy vassal, whom I know
Is free for me to ask, thee to bestow.

KING
Here is my hand. The premises observed,
Thy will by my performance shall be served.
So make the choice of thy own time, for I,
Thy resolved patient, on thee still rely.   206
More should I question thee, and more I must—
Though more to know could not be more to trust—
From whence thou cam'st, how tended on; but rest   209
Unquestioned welcome and undoubted blest.—   210
Give me some help here, ho!—If thou proceed
As high as word, my deed shall match thy meed.   212
        Flourish. Exeunt, [the King carried in].

175 **Seared otherwise** branded in other ways as well. **extended** stretched out on the rack; or, drawn out in time 179–180 **what . . . way** what common sense would regard as impossible, a higher sense (faith) can regard as possible 181 **rate** reckon, consider 182 **estimate** value 184 **happiness** good fortune. **prime** the "springtime" of youth 185 **Thou . . . intimate** that you are prepared to hazard all this argues 186 **monstrous desperate** (that you are) extremely reckless 187 **physic** medicine 188 **ministers** administers 189 **break** infringe, fail to keep. **flinch in property** fall short in any respect 191 **Not helping** if I do not help 193 **make it even** carry it out 206 **still** continually 209 **tended on** attended 210 **Unquestioned** (1) without being questioned (2) unquestionably 212 **high as word** fully as you have promised

2.2   *Enter Countess and Clown [Lavatch].*

COUNTESS   Come on, sir. I shall now put you to the 1
height of your breeding. 2
LAVATCH   I will show myself highly fed and lowly 3
taught. I know my business is but to the court. 4
COUNTESS   "To the court"? Why, what place make you 5
special, when you put off that with such contempt? 6
"But to the court"!
LAVATCH   Truly, madam, if God have lent a man any
manners, he may easily put it off at court. He that 9
cannot make a leg, put off 's cap, kiss his hand, and 10
say nothing has neither leg, hands, lip, nor cap; and
indeed such a fellow, to say precisely, were not for the
court. But for me, I have an answer will serve all men.
COUNTESS   Marry, that's a bountiful answer that fits all
questions.
LAVATCH   It is like a barber's chair that fits all buttocks:
the pin-buttock, the quatch-buttock, the brawn-but- 17
tock, or any buttock.
COUNTESS   Will your answer serve fit to all questions?
LAVATCH   As fit as ten groats is for the hand of an 20
attorney, as your French crown for your taffety punk, 21
as Tib's rush for Tom's forefinger, as a pancake for 22
Shrove Tuesday, a morris for May Day, as the nail to 23
his hole, the cuckold to his horn, as a scolding quean 24
to a wrangling knave, as the nun's lip to the friar's
mouth, nay, as the pudding to his skin. 26
COUNTESS   Have you, I say, an answer of such fitness
for all questions?
LAVATCH   From below your duke to beneath your
constable, it will fit any question.
COUNTESS   It must be an answer of most monstrous
size that must fit all demands.
LAVATCH   But a trifle neither, in good faith, if the 33
learned should speak truth of it. Here it is, and all that
belongs to 't. Ask me if I am a courtier. It shall do you
no harm to learn.
COUNTESS   To be young again, if we could! I will be a
fool in question, hoping to be the wiser by your
answer. I pray you, sir, are you a courtier?
LAVATCH   O, Lord, sir!—There's a simple putting off. 40
More, more, a hundred of them.

2.2. Location: Rossillion.
1–2 put . . . breeding test your good manners **3–4 highly . . . taught** overfed and underdisciplined. ("Better fed than taught" was proverbial for a spoiled child.) **5–6 make you special** do you consider special **6 put off** dismiss **9 put it off** carry it off (with a play on *put off* in line 6 and anticipating the meaning "doff" in line 10) **10 leg** respectful bow or curtsy **17 pin** narrow, pointed. **quatch** fat, wide. **brawn** hefty, fleshy **20 ten groats** forty pence **21 French crown** (1) coin (2) *corona veneris*, a scab on the head symptomatic of syphilis, the "French disease." **taffety punk** prostitute finely dressed **22 Tib's rush** (Refers to a folk custom of exchanging rings made of rushes in a marriage without benefit of clergy.) **pancake** (Traditionally eaten as a last feast on the final day before Lent, Shrove Tuesday.) **23 morris** morris dance, country dance common at May Day celebrations **24 his** its. **quean** wench **26 pudding** sausage. **his** its **33 But . . . neither** on the contrary, it's only a trifle **40 O, Lord, sir** (A foppish phrase currently in vogue at court. Here it suggests, "I do indeed presume to be a courtier; isn't that plain enough from my appearance?") **putting off** evasion

COUNTESS Sir, I am a poor friend of yours, that loves you.

LAVATCH O, Lord, sir!—Thick, thick, spare not me. 44

COUNTESS I think, sir, you can eat none of this homely 45 meat. 46

LAVATCH O Lord, sir!—Nay, put me to 't, I warrant you.

COUNTESS You were lately whipped, sir, as I think.

LAVATCH O Lord, sir!—Spare not me.

COUNTESS Do you cry, "O Lord, sir!" at your whipping, and "spare not me"? Indeed your "O Lord, sir!" is very sequent to your whipping. You would answer 52 very well to a whipping, if you were but bound to 't. 53

LAVATCH I ne'er had worse luck in my life in my "O Lord, sir!" I see things may serve long, but not serve ever.

COUNTESS
I play the noble huswife with the time,
To entertain it so merrily with a fool.

LAVATCH O Lord, sir!—Why, there 't serves well again.

COUNTESS
An end, sir! To your business. Give Helen this,
                    [*giving a letter*]
And urge her to a present answer back. 61
Commend me to my kinsmen and my son.
This is not much.

LAVATCH Not much commendation to them?

COUNTESS Not much employment for you. You understand me?

LAVATCH Most fruitfully. I am there before my legs.

COUNTESS Haste you again.   *Exeunt [separately].* 68

❧

2.3 *Enter Count [Bertram], Lafew, and Parolles.*

LAFEW They say miracles are past, and we have our philosophical persons to make modern and familiar 2 things supernatural and causeless. Hence is it that we 3 make trifles of terrors, ensconcing ourselves into seem- 4 ing knowledge when we should submit ourselves to an unknown fear. 6

PAROLLES Why, 'tis the rarest argument of wonder 7 that hath shot out in our latter times. 8

BERTRAM And so 'tis.

LAFEW To be relinquished of the artists— 10

PAROLLES So I say, both of Galen and Paracelsus. 11

LAFEW Of all the learned and authentic fellows— 12

PAROLLES Right, so I say.

LAFEW That gave him out incurable— 14

PAROLLES Why, there 'tis; so say I too.

LAFEW Not to be helped.

PAROLLES Right! As 'twere a man assured of a—

LAFEW Uncertain life and sure death.

PAROLLES Just, you say well; so would I have said. 19

LAFEW I may truly say it is a novelty to the world.

PAROLLES It is, indeed. If you will have it in showing, 21 you shall read it in—what-do-ye-call there?
          [*He points to a ballad in Lafew's hand.*]

LAFEW [*reading*] "A showing of a heavenly effect in an earthly actor."

PAROLLES That's it, I would have said the very same.

LAFEW Why, your dolphin is not lustier. 'Fore me, I 26 speak in respect— 27

PAROLLES Nay, 'tis strange, 'tis very strange, that is the 28 brief and the tedious of it; and he's of a most facinor- 29 ous spirit that will not acknowledge it to be the— 30

LAFEW Very hand of heaven.

PAROLLES Ay, so I say.

LAFEW In a most weak—

PAROLLES And debile minister; great power, great 34 transcendence, which should indeed give us a further use to be made than alone the recovery of the King, as to be—

LAFEW Generally thankful. 38

Enter King, Helena, and attendants. [The King sits.]

PAROLLES I would have said it; you say well. Here comes the King.

LAFEW Lustig, as the Dutchman says. I'll like a maid 41 the better whilst I have a tooth in my head. Why, he's 42 able to lead her a coranto. 43

PAROLLES *Mort du vinaigre!* Is not this Helen? 44

LAFEW 'Fore God, I think so. 45

KING
Go, call before me all the lords in court.
          [*Exit one or more attendants.*]
Sit, my preserver, by thy patient's side,   [*She sits.*]
And with this healthful hand, whose banished sense 48
Thou hast repealed, a second time receive 49
The confirmation of my promised gift,
Which but attends thy naming. 51

Enter four Lords.

44 Thick quickly **45–46 homely meat** plain fare **52 is very sequent to** is a pertinent response to (because it would be a plea for mercy) **52–53 answer . . . to** (1) reply cleverly to (2) serve as a suitable subject for **53 bound to 't** (1) obliged to reply (2) tied up for it **61 present** immediate **68 again** back again
2.3. Location: Paris. The royal court.
2–3 philosophical . . . causeless scientists who can make supernatural things, inexplicable by any natural cause, seem commonplace and familiar **4 ensconcing** taking refuge, fortifying **6 unknown fear** awe of the unknown **7 rarest argument** most extraordinary theme **8 shot out** suddenly appeared. **latter** recent **10 relinquished of** abandoned by. **artists** i.e., physicians **11 Galen** Greek physician of the second century; the traditional authority. **Paracelsus** Swiss physician of the sixteenth century; the new and more radical authority **12 authentic fellows** those properly licensed to practice

14 gave him out proclaimed him **19 Just** exactly **21 showing** i.e., print **26 dolphin** (A sportive and vigorous sea animal; with a pun perhaps on *dauphin*, "French crown prince.") **'Fore me** i.e., upon my soul **27 in respect** intending no disrespect **28–29 the brief . . . it** i.e., the short and the long of it **29–30 facinorous** infamous, wicked **34 debile minister** weak agent **38 Generally** universally **41 Lustig** lusty, sportive. **Dutchman** i.e., from any Germanic country **42 have a tooth** (with a play on the meaning "have a sweet tooth, a taste for the pleasures of the senses") **43 coranto** lively dance **44 Mort du vinaigre** (Possibly an oath by the vinegar in Christ's wounds; literally, "death of vinegar.") **45 I think so** i.e., I should say it is. (Lafew knows it is Helena.) **48 banished sense** loss of feeling **49 repealed** recalled (from the banishment of illness) **51 attends** waits upon

Fair maid, send forth thine eye. This youthful parcel   52
Of noble bachelors stand at my bestowing,   53
O'er whom both sovereign power and father's voice
I have to use. Thy frank election make;   55
Thou hast power to choose, and they none to
    forsake.   56

HELENA
To each of you one fair and virtuous mistress
Fall, when Love please! Marry, to each but one!

LAFEW [aside]
I'd give bay Curtal and his furniture   59
My mouth no more were broken than these boys',   60
And writ as little beard.

KING   Peruse them well.   61
Not one of those but had a noble father.

HELENA   Gentlemen,
Heaven hath through me restored the King to
    health.

ALL THE LORDS
We understand it, and thank heaven for you.

HELENA
I am a simple maid, and therein wealthiest
That I protest I simply am a maid.—
Please it Your Majesty, I have done already.
The blushes in my cheeks thus whisper me,
"We blush that thou shouldst choose; but, be
    refused,   70
Let the white death sit on thy cheek forever,   71
We'll ne'er come there again."

KING   Make choice and see.
Who shuns thy love shuns all his love in me.   73

HELENA
Now, Dian, from thy altar do I fly,   74
And to imperial Love, that god most high,   75
Do my sighs stream. (She addresses her to a Lord.) Sir,
will you hear my suit?

FIRST LORD
And grant it.

HELENA   Thanks, sir. All the rest is mute.   77

LAFEW [aside]   I had rather be in this choice than
throw ambs-ace for my life.   79

HELENA [to Second Lord]
The honor, sir, that flames in your fair eyes
Before I speak too threateningly replies.
Love make your fortunes twenty times above   82
Her that so wishes, and her humble love!   83

SECOND LORD
No better, if you please.

HELENA   My wish receive,   84
Which great Love grant! And so I take my leave.

LAFEW [aside]   Do all they deny her? An they were   86
sons of mine, I'd have them whipped, or I would
send them to the Turk to make eunuchs of.

HELENA [to Third Lord]
Be not afraid that I your hand should take;
I'll never do you wrong for your own sake.
Blessing upon your vows, and in your bed
Find fairer fortune, if you ever wed!

LAFEW [aside]   These boys are boys of ice; they'll none
have her. Sure they are bastards to the English; the   94
French ne'er got 'em.   95

HELENA [to Fourth Lord]
You are too young, too happy, and too good
To make yourself a son out of my blood.

FOURTH LORD   Fair one, I think not so.

LAFEW [aside]   There's one grape yet; I am sure thy fa-   99
ther drunk wine. But if thou be'st not an ass, I am a   100
youth of fourteen; I have known thee already.   101

HELENA [to Bertram]
I dare not say I take you, but I give
Me and my service, ever whilst I live,
Into your guiding power.—This is the man.

KING
Why, then, young Bertram, take her; she's thy wife.

BERTRAM
My wife, my liege? I shall beseech Your Highness,
In such a business give me leave to use
The help of mine own eyes.

KING   Know'st thou not, Bertram,
What she has done for me?

BERTRAM   Yes, my good lord,
But never hope to know why I should marry her.

KING
Thou know'st she has raised me from my sickly bed.

BERTRAM
But follows it, my lord, to bring me down   112
Must answer for your raising? I know her well;
She had her breeding at my father's charge.
A poor physician's daughter my wife? Disdain   115
Rather corrupt me ever!   116

KING
'Tis only title thou disdain'st in her, the which   117
I can build up. Strange is it that our bloods,
Of color, weight, and heat, poured all together,

52 parcel group   53 stand . . . bestowing i.e., are my wards, whom
I may give in marriage   55 frank election free choice   56 forsake
refuse   59 bay . . . furniture i.e., my dock-tailed bay horse and his
trappings   60 My . . . broken i.e., (1) that I had lost no more teeth
(2) that I, like a young horse, were no more "broken to the bit"
61 writ i.e., and that I laid claim to. (Lafew wishes he were young
enough to be a suitor of Helena.)   70 be refused i.e., if you are refused   71 the white death i.e., death in its pallor   73 Who he who
74 Dian Diana, the goddess of chastity   75 imperial Love i.e., the
god of love, Cupid   77 All . . . mute I have nothing more to say to
you   79 ambs-ace two aces, the lowest possible throw in dice. (To
throw ambs-ace with one's life at stake is to risk all on a throw.)
82 Love make may Love make   83 Her . . . love her that speaks this
wish—i.e., myself—and the humble love I deserve or can give

84 No better i.e., I wish for nothing better than your humble love.
My wish receive i.e., take my wish for your fortunate marriage, rather
than me   86 Do . . . her (Lafew, unable to hear, misinterprets her
passing from one to another.)   An if   94 Sure certainly.   bastards to
i.e., illegitimate children of   95 got begot   99 grape i.e., scion of a good
family.   thy i.e., Bertram's   100 drunk wine i.e., was red-blooded
100–101 But . . . fourteen i.e., but for all that, I bet anything you'll
prove to be as stubborn and foolish as the rest   101 known i.e., seen
through   112 bring me down i.e., lower me to a socially inferior
wife, to the (marriage) bed   115–116 Disdain . . . ever i.e., rather
let my disdain for her ruin me forever in your favor   117 title i.e.,
her lack of title

Would quite confound distinction, yet stands off   120
In differences so mighty. If she be   121
All that is virtuous save what thou dislik'st—
A poor physician's daughter—thou dislik'st
Of virtue for the name. But do not so.   124
From lowest place when virtuous things proceed,   125
The place is dignified by th' doer's deed.
Where great additions swell 's, and virtue none,   127
It is a dropsied honor. Good alone   128
Is good without a name; vileness is so;   129
The property by what it is should go,   130
Not by the title. She is young, wise, fair;
In these to nature she's immediate heir,   132
And these breed honor. That is honor's scorn   133
Which challenges itself as honor's born   134
And is not like the sire. Honors thrive   135
When rather from our acts we them derive
Than our foregoers. The mere word's a slave
Debauched on every tomb, on every grave   138
A lying trophy, and as oft is dumb   139
Where dust and damned oblivion is the tomb
Of honored bones indeed. What should be said?   141
If thou canst like this creature as a maid,
I can create the rest. Virtue and she   143
Is her own dower; honor and wealth from me.   144

BERTRAM
I cannot love her, nor will strive to do 't.

KING
Thou wrong'st thyself, if thou shouldst strive to
    choose.   146

HELENA
That you are well restored, my lord, I'm glad.
Let the rest go.

KING
My honor's at the stake, which to defeat,   149
I must produce my power. Here, take her hand,
Proud, scornful boy, unworthy this good gift,
That dost in vile misprision shackle up   152
My love and her desert; that canst not dream,   153
We, poising us in her defective scale,   154
Shall weigh thee to the beam; that wilt not know   155

It is in us to plant thine honor where   156
We please to have it grow. Check thy contempt;   157
Obey our will, which travails in thy good;   158
Believe not thy disdain, but presently   159
Do thine own fortunes that obedient right   160
Which both thy duty owes and our power claims,
Or I will throw thee from my care forever
Into the staggers and the careless lapse   163
Of youth and ignorance, both my revenge and hate
Loosing upon thee in the name of justice   165
Without all terms of pity. Speak; thine answer.   166

BERTRAM
Pardon, my gracious lord, for I submit
My fancy to your eyes. When I consider   168
What great creation and what dole of honor   169
Flies where you bid it, I find that she, which late   170
Was in my nobler thoughts most base, is now
The praisèd of the King, who, so ennobled,
Is as 'twere born so.

KING   Take her by the hand,
And tell her she is thine, to whom I promise
A counterpoise, if not to thy estate,   175
A balance more replete.

BERTRAM   I take her hand.   176

KING
Good fortune and the favor of the King
Smile upon this contract, whose ceremony   178
Shall seem expedient on the now-born brief   179
And be performed tonight. The solemn feast   180
Shall more attend upon the coming space,   181
Expecting absent friends. As thou lov'st her,   182
Thy love's to me religious; else, does err.   183

Exeunt. Parolles and Lafew stay behind,
commenting of this wedding.

LAFEW   Do you hear, monsieur? A word with you.
PAROLLES   Your pleasure, sir?
LAFEW   Your lord and master did well to make his re-
cantation.
PAROLLES   Recantation? My lord? My master?
LAFEW   Ay. Is it not a language I speak?
PAROLLES   A most harsh one, and not to be understood
without bloody succeeding. My master?   191
LAFEW   Are you companion to the Count Rossillion?   192

---

120 Would . . . distinction could not be distinguished at all.   **stands off** stand separated   **121 differences** i.e., social differences   **124 name** i.e., lack of a name (title)   **125 proceed** emanate   **127 great . . . swell 's** pompous titles puff us up   **128 dropsied** unhealthily swollen   **128–129 Good . . . name** i.e., what is in itself good is so without a title   **129 so** the same   **130 property** quality. **go** i.e., be judged, be valued   **132 In . . . heir** in these qualities she inherits directly from nature   **133–135 That . . . sire** true honor is scornful of any claim to honor based only on the fact of noble birth rather than on action derived from the noble behavior of one's forebears   **138 Debauched** corrupted, disparaged   **139 trophy** memorial. **dumb** silent   **141 honored bones indeed** i.e., the remains of those who were genuinely honorable   **143–144 Virtue . . . dower** i.e., her marriage gift to you will be her virtue and herself   **146 strive to choose** try to assert your own choice   **149 which** i.e., which threat to my honor   **152 misprision** contempt and poor judgment (with a play on "undeserved imprisonment").   **shackle up** confine, limit   **153–155 that . . . beam** you who cannot imagine that I, weighing my royal self on her underweight (defective) side of the scales, will outweigh yours and pull it up to the cross-beam

156 in us within my royal power   **157 Check** curb, restrain   **158 travails in** labors for   **159 Believe not** do not place faith in or obey. **presently** at once   **160 obedient right** right of obedience   **163 staggers** giddy decline. (Literally, a horse disease.)   **careless lapse** irresponsible fall   **165 Loosing** turning loose   **166 all . . . pity** pity in any form   **168 fancy** affection   **169 great creation** creating of greatness.   **dole** share, doling out   **170 which late** who lately   **175–176 A counterpoise . . . replete** i.e., an equal weight of money as dowry, if not an amount even exceeding your estate   **178–179 whose . . . brief** i.e., the consecration of which will expeditiously and properly give ceremonial form to the contract just made (?)   **180 solemn** solemnizing   **181–182 more . . . friends** be delayed for a time until absent friends and relatives can arrive. (Following the formal betrothal just completed onstage, there is to be a wedding tonight and a celebratory feast later on when all can gather.)   **182–183 As . . . err** to the extent that you love her, to that extent I acknowledge the sacred validity of your love to me; otherwise, you are a heretic   **183 s.d. of** on   **191 succeeding** consequences; i.e., a fight   **192 companion** (1) comrade (2) rascally knave

PAROLLES To any count, to all counts, to what is man. 193

LAFEW To what is count's man. Count's master is of 194
another style.

PAROLLES You are too old, sir; let it satisfy you, you are 196
too old.

LAFEW I must tell thee, sirrah, I write man, to which 198
title age cannot bring thee.

PAROLLES What I dare too well do, I dare not do. 200

LAFEW I did think thee, for two ordinaries, to be a 201
pretty wise fellow; thou didst make tolerable vent of 202
thy travel; it might pass. Yet the scarves and the 203
bannerets about thee did manifoldly dissuade me 204
from believing thee a vessel of too great a burden. I 205
have now found thee. When I lose thee again, I care 206
not; yet art thou good for nothing but taking up, and 207
that thou'rt scarce worth.

PAROLLES Hadst thou not the privilege of antiquity
upon thee—

LAFEW Do not plunge thyself too far in anger, lest thou
hasten thy trial; which if—Lord have mercy on thee 212
for a hen! So, my good window of lattice, fare thee 213
well. Thy casement I need not open, for I look through 214
thee. Give me thy hand.

PAROLLES My lord, you give me most egregious indig- 216
nity.

LAFEW Ay, with all my heart, and thou art worthy of it.

PAROLLES I have not, my lord, deserved it.

LAFEW Yes, good faith, every dram of it, and I will not 220
bate thee a scruple. 221

PAROLLES Well, I shall be wiser. 222

LAFEW Even as soon as thou canst, for thou hast to pull 223
at a smack o' the contrary. If ever thou be'st bound in 224
thy scarf and beaten, thou shall find what it is to be
proud of thy bondage. I have a desire to hold my ac- 226
quaintance with thee, or rather my knowledge, that I

may say in the default, "He is a man I know." 228

PAROLLES My lord, you do me most insupportable
vexation.

LAFEW I would it were hell-pains for thy sake, and my 231
poor doing eternal; for doing I am past, as I will by 232
thee, in what motion age will give me leave.   Exit. 233

PAROLLES Well, thou hast a son shall take this disgrace 234
off me—scurvy, old, filthy, scurvy lord! Well, I must 235
be patient; there is no fettering of authority. I'll beat 236
him, by my life, if I can meet him with any convenience, an he were double and double a lord. I'll have 238
no more pity of his age than I would have of—I'll beat
him, an if I could but meet him again. 240

Enter Lafew.

LAFEW Sirrah, your lord and master's married; there's
news for you. You have a new mistress.

PAROLLES I most unfeignedly beseech your lordship to
make some reservation of your wrongs. He is my 244
good lord; whom I serve above is my master. 245

LAFEW Who? God?

PAROLLES Ay, sir.

LAFEW The devil it is that's thy master. Why dost thou 248
garter up thy arms o' this fashion? Dost make hose of 249
thy sleeves? Do other servants so? Thou wert best set 250
thy lower part where thy nose stands. By mine honor,
if I were but two hours younger, I'd beat thee.
Methink'st thou art a general offense, and every man
should beat thee. I think thou wast created for men to
breathe themselves upon thee. 255

PAROLLES This is hard and undeserved measure, my
lord.

LAFEW Go to, sir. You were beaten in Italy for picking 258
a kernel out of a pomegranate. You are a vagabond 259
and no true traveler. You are more saucy with lords
and honorable personages than the commission of 261
your birth and virtue gives you heraldry. You are not 262
worth another word, else I'd call you knave. I leave
you.   *Exit.*

PAROLLES Good, very good! It is so then. Good, very
good. Let it be concealed awhile.

Enter [Bertram] Count Rossillion.

BERTRAM Undone, and forfeited to cares forever!

PAROLLES What's the matter, sweetheart?

---

193 **what is man** i.e., any true man; or, what is manly   194 **count's man** i.e., servant. (Said belittlingly.)   196 **too old** i.e., for me to duel with.   **let . . . you** i.e., take that as a satisfaction instead of a duel   198 **write man** i.e., account myself a man, lay claim to that title   200 **What . . . not do** i.e., what I could too easily accomplish—beat you—I must not do because of your age   201 **for two ordinaries** during the space of two meals   202 **didst . . . of** discoursed tolerably upon   203–204 **scarves, bannerets** i.e., soldiers' scarves, reminding Lafew of a ship's pennants   205 **burden** cargo, capacity   206 **found** found out.   **lose thee,** forget you, get rid of you (with a play on the antithesis of "find" and "lose")   207 **taking up** contradicting; arresting; enlisting; picking up (as opposed to *losing*)   212 **thy trial** i.e., the testing of your supposed valor   213 **hen** i.e., cackling, cowardly female.   **window of lattice** wooden frame with cross-hatched slats (instead of glass), often painted red and used as the sign of an alehouse; something easily seen through and common, disreputable   214 **casement** window sash   216 **give** offer. (But Lafew mockingly replies as though he were indeed making a valuable gift. He plays with *deserved* the same way in lines 219–220: "Oh, you *deserved* it, all right.")   **egregious** outrageous, flagrant   220 **dram** bit. (Literally, one-eighth of an ounce.)   221 **bate** abate, remit.   **scruple** smallest bit. (Literally, one-third of a dram.)   222 **wiser** i.e., wiser than to deal with such dotards in the future. (But Lafew jestingly answers that Parolles indeed has to learn to be wise, i.e., less foolish.)   223–224 **for . . . contrary** i.e., because it's necessary for you to have a taste of your own folly before you can be called self-knowing and wise   226 **bondage** i.e., the scarf, in which you would be bound and of which you are now vainly proud.   **hold** continue

228 **in the default** when you default, i.e., show your emptiness on being brought to trial   231–232 **my poor doing** i.e., my inadequate power to teach you a lesson   232 **for doing** for energetic activity (with a sexual suggestion)   232–233 **will by thee** i.e., will pass by you (punning on *past*, "passed")   233 **in . . . leave** with whatever speed age will allow me   234–235 **shall . . . me** i.e., on whom I will vindicate myself for these insults   236 **fettering** restraining   238 **an** even if   240 **an if** if   244 **make . . . wrongs** put some restraint upon your insults, qualify the insults you've given me   245 **good lord** i.e., patron (not master, as Lafew has insultingly said).   **whom** i.e., he whom (God)   248–250 **Why . . . sleeves** (Parolles apparently has decorative scarves tied around the sleeves of his outfit.)   249 **o'** of, in   255 **breathe** exercise   258–259 **for . . . pomegranate** i.e., for some petty offense, or, on a slight pretext   261 **commission** warrant   262 **gives you heraldry** entitles you to be

BERTRAM　Although before the solemn priest I have
sworn, I will not bed her.

PAROLLES　What, what, sweetheart?

BERTRAM
O my Parolles, they have married me!
I'll to the Tuscan wars, and never bed her.

PAROLLES　France is a dog-hole, and it no more merits
the tread of a man's foot. To the wars!

BERTRAM　There's letters from my mother. What th' 276
import is I know not yet.

PAROLLES　Ay, that would be known. To the wars, my
boy, to the wars!
He wears his honor in a box unseen
That hugs his kicky-wicky here at home,　　　　281
Spending his manly marrow in her arms,　　　　282
Which should sustain the bound and high curvet　283
Of Mars's fiery steed. To other regions!
France is a stable, we that dwell in 't jades.　　285
Therefore, to th' war!

BERTRAM
It shall be so. I'll send her to my house,
Acquaint my mother with my hate to her
And wherefore I am fled, write to the King
That which I durst not speak. His present gift
Shall furnish me to those Italian fields　　　　291
Where noble fellows strike. War is no strife
To the dark house and the detested wife.　　　293

PAROLLES
Will this capriccio hold in thee? Art sure?　　294

BERTRAM
Go with me to my chamber and advise me.
I'll send her straight away. Tomorrow　　　　296
I'll to the wars, she to her single sorrow.

PAROLLES
Why, these balls bound; there's noise in it. 'Tis hard! 298
A young man married is a man that's marred.
Therefore away, and leave her bravely. Go.
The King has done you wrong, but hush, 'tis so.

　　　　　　　　　　　　　　　　　　　Exeunt.

2.4　*Enter Helena [with a letter], and Clown [Lavatch].*

HELENA
My mother greets me kindly. Is she well?

LAVATCH　She is not well, but yet she has her health. 2
She's very merry, but yet she is not well. But thanks

be given, she's very well and wants nothing i' the
world; but yet she is not well.

HELENA　If she be very well, what does she ail that she's
not very well?

LAVATCH　Truly, she's very well indeed, but for two
things.

HELENA　What two things?

LAVATCH　One, that she's not in heaven, whither God
send her quickly. The other, that she's in earth, from
whence God send her quickly.

　　　　　　　Enter Parolles.

PAROLLES　Bless you, my fortunate lady!

HELENA　I hope, sir, I have your good will to have mine
own good fortunes.

PAROLLES　You had my prayers to lead them on, and to 17
keep them on have them still.—O my knave, how 18
does my old lady?

LAVATCH　So that you had her wrinkles and I her
money, I would she did as you say.　　　　21

PAROLLES　Why, I say nothing.

LAVATCH　Marry, you are the wiser man, for many a
man's tongue shakes out his master's undoing. To say 24
nothing, to do nothing, to know nothing, and to have
nothing is to be a great part of your title, which is 26
within a very little of nothing.

PAROLLES　Away! Thou'rt a knave.

LAVATCH　You should have said, sir, "Before a knave 29
thou'rt a knave"; that's, "Before me thou'rt a knave." 30
This had been truth, sir.

PAROLLES　Go to, thou art a witty fool. I have found 32
thee.　　　　33

LAVATCH　Did you find me in yourself, sir? Or were 34
you taught to find me? The search, sir, was profitable;
and much fool may you find in you, even to the
world's pleasure and the increase of laughter.

PAROLLES
A good knave, i' faith, and well fed.　　　　38
Madam, my lord will go away tonight;
A very serious business calls on him.
The great prerogative and rite of love,
Which, as your due, time claims, he does
　acknowledge,　　　　42
But puts it off to a compelled restraint;　　　43
Whose want and whose delay is strewed with
　sweets,　　　　44

276 **letters** i.e., a letter　281 **kicky-wicky** woman (with sexual suggestion, as also in *box* in the previous line and *Spending* and *marrow* in
the following line)　282 **manly marrow** masculine essence, semen
283 **curvet** leap　285 **jades** worn-out horses　291 **furnish me** (Knights
customarily provided themselves with trappings and armed retainers
when enlisting in warlike enterprises.)　293 **To . . . house** i.e., compared to the madhouse (of marriage)　294 **capriccio** caprice
296 **straight** at once　298 **Why . . . hard** i.e., now you're talking;
that's the way to behave. (*Balls* here are tennis balls.)
2.4. Location: Paris. The royal court.
2 **not well** (Referring to the Elizabethan euphemism by which the
dead were spoken of as "well," i.e., well rid of this life and well off
in heaven.)

17 **them** i.e., your good fortunes. (A plural concept.)　**17–18 to . . .
still** to maintain your good fortune, you have my prayers continually
21 **did as you say** i.e., became as nothing. (*Did* may pun on "died";
the words were sometimes spelled alike.)　24 **man's** servant's.
shakes out i.e., brings about by talking too freely　26 **title** claim to
possessions or status (with a play on "tittle," minute amount)　29 **Before** in presence of　30 **Before me** i.e., upon my soul. (But, by substituting *me* for *knave*, Lavatch suggests that Parolles call himself a
knave.)　32–33 **found thee** found you out, found you to be a fool
34 **in yourself** (1) by your own efforts (2) in your reflection　38 **well
fed** (Referring to the proverb "better fed than taught," as at 2.2.3.)
42 **time** i.e., the present time　43 **to** owing to　44 **Whose want** the
lack of which (rite of love). The postponing of love's rites makes them
sweeter, like perfume made sweeter by distillation.　**sweets** sweet-
smelling flowers

Which they distill now in the curbèd time,   45
To make the coming hour o'erflow with joy
And pleasure drown the brim.
HELENA   What's his will else?   47
PAROLLES
That you will take your instant leave o' the King
And make this haste as your own good proceeding,   49
Strengthened with what apology you think
May make it probable need.
HELENA   What more commands he?   51
PAROLLES
That, having this obtained, you presently
Attend his further pleasure.   53
HELENA
In every thing I wait upon his will.
PAROLLES   I shall report it so.   *Exit Parolles.*
HELENA   I pray you.—Come, sirrah.
                                            Exit [with Lavatch].

2.5   *Enter Lafew and Bertram.*

LAFEW   But I hope your lordship thinks not him a
soldier.
BERTRAM   Yes, my lord, and of very valiant approof.   3
LAFEW   You have it from his own deliverance.   4
BERTRAM   And by other warranted testimony.
LAFEW   Then my dial goes not true. I took this lark for 6
a bunting.   7
BERTRAM   I do assure you, my lord, he is very great in
knowledge, and accordingly valiant.   9
LAFEW   I have then sinned against his experience and
transgressed against his valor; and my state that way   11
is dangerous, since I cannot yet find in my heart to   12
repent. Here he comes. I pray you, make us friends; I
will pursue the amity.

        Enter Parolles.

PAROLLES [*to Bertram*]   These things shall be done, sir.
LAFEW [*to Bertram*]   Pray you, sir, who's his tailor?   16
PAROLLES   Sir?
LAFEW   O, I know him well. Ay, sir, he, sir, 's a good   18
workman, a very good tailor.   19
BERTRAM [*aside to Parolles*]   Is she gone to the King?

PAROLLES   She is.
BERTRAM   Will she away tonight?
PAROLLES   As you'll have her.
BERTRAM
I have writ my letters, casketed my treasure,
Given order for our horses; and tonight,
When I should take possession of the bride,
End ere I do begin.
LAFEW   A good traveler is something at the latter end of 28
a dinner; but one that lies three thirds, and uses a   29
known truth to pass a thousand nothings with, should
be once heard and thrice beaten. God save you, Cap-
tain.
BERTRAM [*to Parolles*]   Is there any unkindness between 33
my lord and you, monsieur?
PAROLLES   I know not how I have deserved to run into
my lord's displeasure.
LAFEW   You have made shift to run into 't, boots and   37
spurs and all, like him that leapt into the custard; and 38
out of it you'll run again, rather than suffer question   39
for your residence.   40
BERTRAM   It may be you have mistaken him, my lord.   41
LAFEW   And shall do so ever, though I took him at 's
prayers. Fare you well, my lord, and believe this of
me: there can be no kernel in this light nut. The soul
of this man is his clothes. Trust him not in matter of
heavy consequence. I have kept of them tame, and   46
know their natures.—Farewell, monsieur. I have
spoken better of you than you have or will to deserve   48
at my hand; but we must do good against evil.
                                            [*Exit.*]
PAROLLES   An idle lord, I swear.   50
BERTRAM   I think so.   51
PAROLLES   Why, do you not know him?
BERTRAM
Yes, I do know him well, and common speech
Gives him a worthy pass. Here comes my clog.   54

        Enter Helena.

HELENA
I have, sir, as I was commanded from you,
Spoke with the King, and have procured his leave
For present parting; only he desires
Some private speech with you.
BERTRAM   I shall obey his will.
You must not marvel, Helen, at my course,

---

45 they i.e., the lack and delay.   **curbèd time** period of restraint (and
also of distillation, as in the making of perfume from *curbing* flowers
or *sweets*, line 44, in a still)   **47 else** besides   **49 make** represent.
proceeding course of action   **51 probable need** a plausible necessity
53 Attend await.   **pleasure** command.
2.5. Location: Paris. The royal court.
3 valiant approof proven valor   **4 deliverance** testimony, word
6 dial clock, compass, i.e., judgment   **6–7 I . . . bunting** i.e., I underestimated him. (The bunting resembles the lark but lacks the lark's
beautiful song.)   **9 accordingly** correspondingly   **11 my state** i.e., the
state of my soul. (Lafew uses an elaborate metaphor of religious penitence ironically.)   **12 find in** find it in   **16 who's his tailor** i.e., what
tailor made this stuffed (bombast) figure? (Lafew ironically suggests that Parolles is all show and
no substance.   **16 who's his tailor** i.e., what
tailor made this stuffed (bombast) figure? (Lafew is talking to Bertram
but is taunting Parolles, who replies indignantly.)   **18–19 O . . . tailor** (Lafew mockingly takes Parolles' *Sir* in line 17 as the name of his
tailor.)

28–29 A good . . . dinner i.e., a person with many traveling experiences is an asset as a storyteller after dinner   **29 three thirds** i.e., all
the time   **33 unkindness** ill will   **37 made shift** contrived (at our previous meeting)   **38 like . . . custard** i.e., like a clown at an annual
city entertainment jumping into a large, deep custard   **39 you'll run**
you will want to run   **39–40 suffer . . . residence** undergo questioning about your being there, i.e., explain how your cowardice displeased me   **41 mistaken him** misjudged or misidentified him. (But
Lafew deliberately takes the phrase in the sense of "taken exception
to his behavior.")   **46 heavy** serious.   **I . . . tame** I have kept tame
creatures of this kind (for the amusement they provide)   **48 have . . .
deserve** have deserved or are likely to deserve   **50 idle** foolish   **51 I
think so** i.e., I suppose you're right. (Parolles emphasizes *know* in the
next line to contrast with *think*.)   **54 pass** reputation.   **clog** a heavy
weight attached to the leg or neck of a man or animal to prevent freedom of movement

Which holds not color with the time, nor does   60
The ministration and requirèd office   61
On my particular. Prepared I was not   62
For such a business; therefore am I found
So much unsettled. This drives me to entreat you
That presently you take your way for home;
And rather muse than ask why I entreat you,   66
For my respects are better than they seem,   67
And my appointments have in them a need   68
Greater than shows itself at the first view
To you that know them not. This to my mother.

                                    [*He gives a letter.*]

'Twill be two days ere I shall see you, so
I leave you to your wisdom.

HELENA   Sir, I can nothing say
But that I am your most obedient servant.

BERTRAM
Come, come, no more of that.

HELENA   And ever shall
With true observance seek to eke out that   75
Wherein toward me my homely stars have failed   76
To equal my great fortune.

BERTRAM   Let that go.
My haste is very great. Farewell. Hie home.   78

                                    [*He starts to go.*]

HELENA
Pray, sir, your pardon.

BERTRAM   Well, what would you say?

HELENA
I am not worthy of the wealth I owe,   80
Nor dare I say 'tis mine, and yet it is;
But, like a timorous thief, most fain would steal   82
What law does vouch mine own.

BERTRAM   What would you have?   83

HELENA
Something, and scarce so much; nothing, indeed.
I would not tell you what I would, my lord. Faith,
  yes—
Strangers and foes do sunder, and not kiss.   86

BERTRAM
I pray you, stay not, but in haste to horse.   87

HELENA
I shall not break your bidding, good my lord.

BERTRAM
Where are my other men, monsieur?—Farewell.

                                    Exit [*Helena*].

Go thou toward home, where I will never come
Whilst I can shake my sword or hear the drum.
Away, and for our flight.

PAROLLES   Bravely, *coraggio!* [*Exeunt.*] 92

❧

3.1

Flourish. Enter the Duke of Florence [*attended*];
the two Frenchmen, with a troop of soldiers.

DUKE
So that from point to point now have you heard
The fundamental reasons of this war,
Whose great decision hath much blood let forth,   3
And more thirsts after.

FIRST LORD   Holy seems the quarrel
Upon Your Grace's part, black and fearful
On the opposer.   6

DUKE
Therefore we marvel much our cousin France   7
Would in so just a business shut his bosom
Against our borrowing prayers.

SECOND LORD   Good my lord,   9
The reasons of our state I cannot yield   10
But like a common and an outward man   11
That the great figure of a council frames   12
By self-unable motion, therefore dare not   13
Say what I think of it, since I have found
Myself in my incertain grounds to fail
As often as I guessed.

DUKE   Be it his pleasure.   16

FIRST LORD
But I am sure the younger of our nature,   17
That surfeit on their ease, will day by day   18
Come here for physic.

DUKE   Welcome shall they be,   19
And all the honors that can fly from us   20
Shall on them settle. You know your places well;
When better fall, for your avails they fell.   22
Tomorrow to the field.   *Flourish.* [*Exeunt.*]

❧

3.2

Enter Countess and Clown [*Lavatch*].

COUNTESS   It hath happened all as I would have had it,
  save that he comes not along with her.

LAVATCH   By my troth, I take my young lord to be a   3
  very melancholy man.

COUNTESS   By what observance, I pray you?   5

LAVATCH   Why, he will look upon his boot and sing,
  mend the ruff and sing, ask questions and sing, pick 7
  his teeth and sing. I know a man that had this trick of 8

60–62 Which . . . particular which does not appear to suit with the
occasion (of our marriage), nor does it fulfill what is incumbent upon
me as a husband   **66 muse** wonder   **67 my respects** the circumstances prompting me   **68 appointments** purposes   **75 observance**
dutiful and reverential service.   **eke out** add to   **76 homely stars** i.e.,
lowly origin   **78 Hie** hasten   **80 owe** own   **82 fain** gladly
83 vouch affirm to be   **86 sunder** separate   **87 stay** delay   **92 coraggio** courage, bravo

3.1. Location: Florence.
3 decision combat to decide an issue   **6 the opposer** i.e., the opposer's part   **7 cousin** i.e., fellow sovereign   **9 borrowing prayers**
prayers for assistance   **10 yield** communicate, produce   **11 But** except.   **outward** not having intimate knowledge of things   **12 figure**
scheme.   **frames** constructs   **13 self-unable motion** i.e., one's own
imperfect guess   **16 Be . . . pleasure** i.e., be it as the King of France
wishes   **17 nature** outlook, disposition   **18 surfeit** grow sick
19 physic i.e., cure of their surfeit (through bloodletting)   **20 can fly
from us** i.e., we can grant   **22 better fall** i.e., better places fall vacant.   **fell** will have fallen
3.2. Location: Rossillion.
3 troth faith   **5 observance** observation   **7 mend the ruff** adjust the
loose turned-over flap at the top of his boot   **7–8 pick his teeth** (An
affected mannerism, as at 1.1.159.)

melancholy sold a goodly manor for a song.   9

COUNTESS   Let me see what he writes and when he
means to come.   [*Opening a letter.*]

LAVATCH   I have no mind to Isbel since I was at court.
Our old lings and our Isbels o' the country are nothing   13
like your old ling and your Isbels o' the court. The
brains of my Cupid's knocked out, and I begin to love
as an old man loves money, with no stomach.   16

COUNTESS   What have we here?

LAVATCH   E'en that you have there.   *Exit.*   18

COUNTESS [*reads*] *a letter.*   "I have sent you a daughter-
in-law. She hath recovered the King and undone me.   20
I have wedded her, not bedded her, and sworn to
make the 'not' eternal. You shall hear I am run away;   22
know it before the report come. If there be breadth
enough in the world, I will hold a long distance. My   24
duty to you.

                        Your unfortunate son,
                                    Bertram."

This is not well, rash and unbridled boy,
To fly the favors of so good a king,
To pluck his indignation on thy head   30
By the misprizing of a maid too virtuous   31
For the contempt of empire.   32

Enter Clown [*Lavatch*].

LAVATCH   O madam, yonder is heavy news within   33
between two soldiers and my young lady!

COUNTESS   What is the matter?

LAVATCH   Nay, there is some comfort in the news,
some comfort. Your son will not be killed so soon as I
thought he would.

COUNTESS   Why should he be killed?

LAVATCH   So say I, madam, if he run away, as I hear he
does. The danger is in standing to 't; that's the loss of   41
men, though it be the getting of children. Here they   42
come will tell you more. For my part, I only hear your
son was run away.   [*Exit.*]   44

Enter Helena and [*the*] *two* [*French*] *Gentlemen*
[*or Lords*].

SECOND LORD   Save you, good madam.

HELENA
Madam, my lord is gone, forever gone!

FIRST LORD   Do not say so.

COUNTESS
Think upon patience. Pray you, gentlemen,
I have felt so many quirks of joy and grief

That the first face of neither, on the start,   50
Can woman me unto 't. Where is my son, I pray
you?   51

FIRST LORD
Madam, he's gone to serve the Duke of Florence.
We met him thitherward; for thence we came,   53
And, after some dispatch in hand at court,   54
Thither we bend again.

HELENA
Look on his letter, madam; here's my passport.   56
[*She reads.*] "When thou canst get the ring upon my
finger, which never shall come off, and show me a
child begotten of thy body that I am father to, then call
me husband; but in such a 'then' I write a 'never.' "
This is a dreadful sentence.   61

COUNTESS
Brought you this letter, gentlemen?

FIRST LORD   Ay, madam,
And for the contents' sake are sorry for our pains.

COUNTESS
I prithee, lady, have a better cheer.
If thou engrossest all the griefs are thine,   65
Thou robb'st me of a moi'ty. He was my son,   66
But I do wash his name out of my blood,
And thou art all my child.—Towards Florence is he?   68

FIRST LORD
Ay, madam.

COUNTESS   And to be a soldier?

FIRST LORD
Such is his noble purpose; and, believe 't,
The Duke will lay upon him all the honor
That good convenience claims.

COUNTESS   Return you thither?   72

SECOND LORD
Ay, madam, with the swiftest wing of speed.

HELENA [*reading*]
"Till I have no wife, I have nothing in France."
'Tis bitter.

COUNTESS   Find you that there?

HELENA   Ay, madam.

SECOND LORD
'Tis but the boldness of his hand, haply,   76
Which his heart was not consenting to.

COUNTESS
Nothing in France, until he have no wife!
There's nothing here that is too good for him
But only she, and she deserves a lord
That twenty such rude boys might tend upon
And call her, hourly, mistress. Who was with him?

SECOND LORD
A servant only, and a gentleman
Which I have sometime known.

---

9 sold who sold   **13 old lings** i.e., salacious old men. (Literally,
salted cod, but with a bawdy meaning referring to the penis.)
16 stomach appetite   **18 E'en . . . there** (The Clown is playfully literal: to the Countess's "What's this?" he replies, "It looks like a letter.")   **20 recovered** cured   **22 not** (with a pun on "knot")
24 hold a long distance stay far away   **30 pluck** bring down   **31 misprizing** scorning, failing to appreciate   **32 of empire** of even an emperor   **33 heavy** sad   **41 standing to 't** standing one's ground (with
sexual pun. The Clown jests on running from a battle and running
from a woman; in both cases, a soldier can avoid the *danger* of dying, with its suggestion of sexual climax.)   **42 getting** begetting
44 was has

50–51 That . . . unto 't i.e., that neither joy nor grief, no matter how
suddenly either appears, can make me weep as women are supposed
to do   **53 thitherward** on his way there   **54 dispatch in hand** business to be taken care of   **56 passport** license to wander as a beggar
61 sentence (1) sentence of punishment (2) statement, utterance
65 thou engrossest you monopolize.   **are** that are   **66 moi'ty** half
68 all my my only   **72 convenience** propriety, fitness   **76 haply**
perhaps

COUNTESS   Parolles, was it not?
SECOND LORD   Ay, my good lady, he.
COUNTESS
A very tainted fellow, and full of wickedness.
My son corrupts a well-derivèd nature
With his inducement.
SECOND LORD   Indeed, good lady,   89
The fellow has a deal of that too much   90
Which holds him much to have.   91
COUNTESS   You're welcome, gentlemen.
I will entreat you, when you see my son,
To tell him that his sword can never win
The honor that he loses. More I'll entreat you
Written to bear along.
FIRST LORD   We serve you, madam,   96
In that and all your worthiest affairs.
COUNTESS
Not so, but as we change our courtesies.   98
Will you draw near?   *Exit [with Gentlemen].*   99
HELENA
"Till I have no wife, I have nothing in France."
Nothing in France, until he has no wife!
Thou shalt have none, Rossillion, none in France;   102
Then hast thou all again. Poor lord, is 't I
That chase thee from thy country and expose
Those tender limbs of thine to the event   105
Of the none-sparing war? And is it I
That drive thee from the sportive court, where thou   107
Wast shot at with fair eyes, to be the mark   108
Of smoky muskets? O you leaden messengers,   109
That ride upon the violent speed of fire,
Fly with false aim; move the still-piecing air,   111
That sings with piercing; do not touch my lord!   112
Whoever shoots at him, I set him there;
Whoever charges on his forward breast,   114
I am the caitiff that do hold him to 't;   115
And, though I kill him not, I am the cause
His death was so effected. Better 'twere
I met the ravin lion when he roared   118
With sharp constraint of hunger; better 'twere
That all the miseries which nature owes   120
Were mine at once. No, come thou home,
    Rossillion,
Whence honor but of danger wins a scar,   122
As oft it loses all. I will be gone.   123
My being here it is that holds thee hence.
Shall I stay here to do 't? No, no, although

The air of paradise did fan the house
And angels officed all. I will be gone,   127
That pitiful rumor may report my flight   128
To consolate thine ear. Come, night; end, day!   129
For with the dark, poor thief, I'll steal away.   *Exit.*

❖

3.3   *Flourish. Enter the Duke of Florence, [Bertram,
        Count] Rossillion, drum and trumpets, soldiers,
        Parolles.*

DUKE
The General of our Horse thou art, and we,
Great in our hope, lay our best love and credence   2
Upon thy promising fortune.
BERTRAM   Sir, it is
A charge too heavy for my strength, but yet
We'll strive to bear it for your worthy sake
To th' extreme edge of hazard.
DUKE   Then go thou forth,   6
And Fortune play upon thy prosperous helm,   7
As thy auspicious mistress!
BERTRAM   This very day,
Great Mars, I put myself into thy file.   9
Make me but like my thoughts, and I shall prove   10
A lover of thy drum, hater of love.   *Exeunt omnes.*

❖

3.4   *Enter Countess and Steward [Rinaldo].*

COUNTESS
Alas! And would you take the letter of her?
Might you not know she would do as she has done,
By sending me a letter? Read it again.
RINALDO *[reads the] letter*
"I am Saint Jaques' pilgrim, thither gone.   4
    Ambitious love hath so in me offended
That barefoot plod I the cold ground upon,
    With sainted vow my faults to have amended.   7
Write, write, that from the bloody course of war
    My dearest master, your dear son, may hie.   9
Bless him at home in peace, whilst I from far
    His name with zealous fervor sanctify.
His taken labors bid him me forgive;   12
    I, his despiteful Juno, sent him forth   13

89 **With his inducement** i.e., by Parolles' corrupt influence
90–91 has . . . have i.e., has considerably too much of that ingratiating and persuasive quality which stands him in good stead   **96 Written** in writing   **98 but . . . courtesies** i.e., only if I can repay or exchange your courtesy with my own   **99 draw near** come with me
102 Rossillion i.e., Bertram (whom Helena refers to by his title)
105 event hazard, outcome   **107 sportive** amorous   **108 mark** target
109 leaden messengers i.e., bullets   **111 still-piecing** always closing
or repairing itself again. (The Folio reading, *still-peering,* is possible in
the sense of "always observing.")   **112 sings with piercing** i.e., whistles when a bullet passes through it   **114 forward** facing forward in
battle, in the van   **115 caitiff** base wretch   **118 ravin** ravenous
120 nature owes human nature possesses, suffers   **122–123 Whence
. . . all** i.e., from war, in which honor is at best rewarded for danger
with a scar, and often loses life itself

127 **officed all** performed all domestic duties   **128 pitiful** compassionate   **129 consolate** console
3.3. Location: Florence.
2 Great pregnant, expectant.   **lay** wager.   **credence** trust   **6 edge of
hazard** limit of peril   **7 helm** helmet   **9 file** battle line; ranks, catalogue   **10 like my thoughts** i.e., as valiant as I aspire to be
3.4. Location: Rossillion.
4–17 (The letter is in the form of a sonnet.)   **4 Saint Jaques' pilgrim**
i.e., a pilgrim to the shrine of Saint James, presumably the famous
shrine of Santiago de Compostella in Spain   **7 sainted vow** a vow to
a saint   **9 hie** hasten   **12 His taken labors** the labors he has undertaken   **13 despiteful** spiteful.   **Juno** goddess who persecuted Hercules by assigning him the twelve labors

From courtly friends, with camping foes to live   14
  Where death and danger dogs the heels of worth.
He is too good and fair for death and me;
Whom I myself embrace, to set him free."   17

COUNTESS
Ah, what sharp stings are in her mildest words!
Rinaldo, you did never lack advice so much   19
As letting her pass so. Had I spoke with her,
I could have well diverted her intents,
Which thus she hath prevented.

RINALDO   Pardon me, madam.   22
If I had given you this at overnight,   23
She might have been o'erta'en; and yet she writes
Pursuit would be but vain.

COUNTESS   What angel shall
Bless this unworthy husband? He cannot thrive,
Unless her prayers, whom heaven delights to hear   27
And loves to grant, reprieve him from the wrath
Of greatest justice. Write, write, Rinaldo,
To this unworthy husband of his wife.   30
Let every word weigh heavy of her worth   31
That he does weigh too light. My greatest grief,
Though little he do feel it, set down sharply.
Dispatch the most convenient messenger.
When haply he shall hear that she is gone,
He will return; and hope I may that she,
Hearing so much, will speed her foot again,
Led hither by pure love. Which of them both
Is dearest to me, I have no skill in sense   39
To make distinction. Provide this messenger.
My heart is heavy and mine age is weak;
Grief would have tears, and sorrow bids me speak.
                                        Exeunt.

♣

3.5 *A tucket afar off. Enter old Widow of Florence, her
        daughter [Diana], and Mariana, with other
        citizens.*

WIDOW   Nay, come, for if they do approach the city we
shall lose all the sight.   2
DIANA   They say the French count has done most
honorable service.
WIDOW   It is reported that he has taken their great'st 5
commander, and that with his own hand he slew the
Duke's brother. [*Tucket.*] We have lost our labor; they
are gone a contrary way. Hark! You may know by
their trumpets.
MARIANA   Come, let's return again and suffice our-   10
selves with the report of it.—Well, Diana, take heed of

this French earl. The honor of a maid is her name, and   12
no legacy is so rich as honesty.   13
WIDOW [*to Diana*]   I have told my neighbor how you   14
have been solicited by a gentleman, his companion.
MARIANA   I know that knave, hang him! One Parolles,
a filthy officer he is in those suggestions for the young   17
earl. Beware of them, Diana; their promises, enticements, oaths, tokens, and all these engines of lust are   19
not the things they go under. Many a maid hath been   20
seduced by them; and the misery is, example, that so   21
terrible shows in the wreck of maidenhood, cannot for   22
all that dissuade succession, but that they are limed   23
with the twigs that threatens them. I hope I need not   24
to advise you further, but I hope your own grace will   25
keep you where you are, though there were no fur-   26
ther danger known but the modesty which is so lost.   27
DIANA   You shall not need to fear me.   28

                Enter Helena [disguised like a pilgrim].

WIDOW   I hope so.—Look, here comes a pilgrim. I
know she will lie at my house; thither they send one   30
another. I'll question her.—God save you, pilgrim!
Whither are bound?   32
HELENA   To Saint Jaques le Grand.
Where do the palmers lodge, I do beseech you?   34
WIDOW
At the Saint Francis here beside the port.   35
HELENA   Is this the way?   (*A march afar.*)
WIDOW
Ay, marry, is 't. Hark you, they come this way.
If you will tarry, holy pilgrim,
But till the troops come by,
I will conduct you where you shall be lodged,
The rather for I think I know your hostess
As ample as myself.   42
HELENA   Is it yourself?
WIDOW   If you shall please so, pilgrim.
HELENA
I thank you, and will stay upon your leisure.   45
WIDOW
You came, I think, from France?
HELENA   I did so.
WIDOW
Here you shall see a countryman of yours
That has done worthy service.
HELENA   His name, I pray you?
DIANA
The Count Rossillion. Know you such a one?

---

14 camping encamped, contending (playing on the antithesis of court
and military camp)   **17 Whom** i.e., death   **19 advice** judgment
22 prevented forestalled   **23 at overnight** last night   **27 her** i.e., Helena's. (Helena is likened to the Virgin Mary and other saints who can
intercede with heaven on behalf of a sinner.)   **30 unworthy . . . wife**
husband unworthy of his wife   **31 weigh heavy of** emphasize   **39 in
sense** in perception
3.5. Location: Florence. Outside the walls.
s.d. tucket a trumpet fanfare   **2 lose . . . sight** miss seeing them
5 their i.e., the Sienese's   **10 suffice** content

12 earl i.e., Count Bertram.   **her name** her reputation (for chastity)
13 honesty chastity   **14 my neighbor** i.e., Mariana   **17 officer** agent.
suggestions for solicitings on behalf of, or, temptations of   **19 engines**
artifices, devices   **20 go under** pretend to be   **21–23 example . . .
succession** the dreadful example of what happens with the loss of virginity nonetheless cannot dissuade another from a similar course
23–24 they . . . twigs i.e., other maidens are caught in the traps.
(Birdlime was smeared on twigs to ensnare birds.)   **25 grace** virtue
26 though even though   **26–27 further danger** i.e., pregnancy
27 modesty chastity and chaste reputation   **28 fear** worry about
30 lie lodge   **32 are** are you   **34 palmers** pilgrims   **35 the Saint
Francis** the inn with the sign of Saint Francis.   **port** city gate   **42 ample** fully, completely   **45 stay . . . leisure** await your convenience

HELENA
But by the ear, that hears most nobly of him.
His face I know not.
DIANA   Whatsoe'er he is,
He's bravely taken here. He stole from France,   52
As 'tis reported, for the King had married him   53
Against his liking. Think you it is so?
HELENA
Ay, surely, mere the truth. I know his lady.   55
DIANA
There is a gentleman that serves the Count
Reports but coarsely of her.
HELENA   What's his name?
DIANA
Monsieur Parolles.
HELENA   O, I believe with him.   58
In argument of praise, or to the worth   59
Of the great Count himself, she is too mean   60
To have her name repeated. All her deserving   61
Is a reservèd honesty, and that   62
I have not heard examined.
DIANA   Alas, poor lady!   63
'Tis a hard bondage to become the wife
Of a detesting lord.
WIDOW
I warrant, good creature, wheresoe'er she is,
Her heart weighs sadly. This young maid might do
    her
A shrewd turn, if she pleased.
HELENA   How do you mean?   68
Maybe the amorous Count solicits her
In the unlawful purpose?
WIDOW   He does indeed,
And brokes with all that can in such a suit   71
Corrupt the tender honor of a maid.
But she is armed for him and keeps her guard
In honestest defense.   74

> *Drum and colors. Enter [Bertram] Count
> Rossillion, Parolles, and the whole army.*

MARIANA   The gods forbid else!   75
WIDOW   So, now they come.
That is Antonio, the Duke's eldest son;
That, Escalus.
HELENA   Which is the Frenchman?
DIANA   He,
That with the plume. 'Tis a most gallant fellow.
I would he loved his wife. If he were honester   80
He were much goodlier. Is 't not a handsome
    gentleman?
HELENA   I like him well.
DIANA
'Tis pity he is not honest. Yond's that same knave

That leads him to these places. Were I his lady
I would poison that vile rascal.
HELENA   Which is he?
DIANA
That jackanapes with scarves. Why is he
    melancholy?   86
HELENA   Perchance he's hurt i' the battle.
PAROLLES   Lose our drum? Well.
MARIANA   He's shrewdly vexed at something. Look, he   89
    has spied us.
WIDOW [*to Parolles*]   Marry, hang you!
MARIANA [*to Parolles*]   And your courtesy, for a ring-   92
    carrier!   93

> *Exeunt [Bertram, Parolles, and army].*

WIDOW
The troop is past. Come, pilgrim, I will bring you
Where you shall host. Of enjoined penitents   95
There's four or five, to great Saint Jaques bound,
Already at my house.
HELENA   I humbly thank you.
Please it this matron and this gentle maid   98
To eat with us tonight, the charge and thanking   99
Shall be for me; and, to requite you further,
I will bestow some precepts of this virgin   101
Worthy the note.
BOTH   We'll take your offer kindly. 102

> *Exeunt.*

❧

3.6   *Enter [Bertram] Count Rossillion and the [two]
           Frenchmen, as at first.*

FIRST LORD   Nay, good my lord, put him to 't. Let him   1
    have his way.
SECOND LORD   If your lordship find him not a hilding,   3
    hold me no more in your respect.
FIRST LORD   On my life, my lord, a bubble.
BERTRAM   Do you think I am so far deceived in him?
FIRST LORD   Believe it, my lord, in mine own direct
    knowledge, without any malice, but to speak of him   8
    as my kinsman, he's a most notable coward, an infi-   9
    nite and endless liar, an hourly promise-breaker, the
    owner of no one good quality worthy your lordship's
    entertainment.   12
SECOND LORD   It were fit you knew him, lest, reposing   13
    too far in his virtue, which he hath not, he might at
    some great and trusty business in a main danger fail   15
    you.
BERTRAM   I would I knew in what particular action to
    try him.   18

---

86 jackanapes monkey **89 shrewdly** sorely **92 courtesy** ceremonious bow **92–93 ring-carrier** go-between **95 host** lodge. **enjoined
penitents** those bound by oath to undertake a pilgrimage as penance
for sin **98 Please it** if it please **99–100 the charge . . . me** i.e., I
will bear the expense and be grateful at the same time **101 of** on
102 kindly gratefully
3.6. Location: The Florentine camp.
1 to 't i.e., to the test **3 hilding** good-for-nothing **8–9 to speak
. . . kinsman** i.e., to put it charitably **12 entertainment** patronage
13 reposing trusting **15 trusty** demanding trustworthiness **18 try** test

---

52 bravely taken highly regarded **53 for** because **55 mere** absolutely **58 believe** agree **59 In argument of** as a subject for. **to**
compared to **60 mean** lowly **61–62 All . . . honesty** her only
merit is a well-guarded chastity **63 examined** doubted, questioned
68 shrewd malicious, hurtful **71 brokes** bargains **74 honestest** most
chaste **75 else** that it should be otherwise **80 honester** more honorable (and more chaste)

SECOND LORD   None better than to let him fetch off his 19
drum, which you hear him so confidently undertake
to do.

FIRST LORD   I, with a troop of Florentines, will suddenly
surprise him; such I will have whom I am sure 23
he knows not from the enemy. We will bind and
hoodwink him so, that he shall suppose no other but 25
that he is carried into the leaguer of the adversary's, 26
when we bring him to our own tents. Be but your
lordship present at his examination. If he do not, for
the promise of his life and in the highest compulsion
of base fear, offer to betray you and deliver all the in- 30
telligence in his power against you, and that with the 31
divine forfeit of his soul upon oath, never trust my
judgment in anything.

SECOND LORD   O, for the love of laughter, let him fetch
his drum. He says he has a stratagem for 't. When your
lordship sees the bottom of his success in 't, and to 36
what metal this counterfeit lump of ore will be melted,
if you give him not John Drum's entertainment, your 38
inclining cannot be removed. Here he comes. 39

Enter Parolles.

FIRST LORD [*aside to Bertram*]   O, for the love of
laughter, hinder not the honor of his design. Let him
fetch off his drum in any hand. 42

BERTRAM   How now, monsieur? This drum sticks sorely 43
in your disposition. 44

SECOND LORD   A pox on 't, let it go. 'Tis but a drum.

PAROLLES   But a drum! Is 't but a drum? A drum so lost!
There was excellent command—to charge in with our
horse upon our own wings and to rend our own 48
soldiers!

SECOND LORD   That was not to be blamed in the com- 50
mand of the service. It was a disaster of war that 51
Caesar himself could not have prevented, if he had
been there to command.

BERTRAM   Well, we cannot greatly condemn our suc- 54
cess. Some dishonor we had in the loss of that drum, 55
but it is not to be recovered.

PAROLLES   It might have been recovered.

BERTRAM   It might, but it is not now.

PAROLLES   It is to be recovered. But that the merit of 59
service is seldom attributed to the true and exact
performer, I would have that drum or another, or *hic* 61
jacet. 62

BERTRAM   Why, if you have a stomach, to 't, monsieur! 63
If you think your mystery in stratagem can bring this 64
instrument of honor again into his native quarter, be 65

magnanimous in the enterprise and go on. I will grace 66
the attempt for a worthy exploit. If you speed well in 67
it, the Duke shall both speak of it and extend to you
what further becomes his greatness, even to the 69
utmost syllable of your worthiness.

PAROLLES   By the hand of a soldier, I will undertake it.

BERTRAM   But you must not now slumber in it.

PAROLLES   I'll about it this evening, and I will presently 73
pen down my dilemmas, encourage myself in my 74
certainty, put myself into my mortal preparation; and 75
by midnight look to hear further from me.

BERTRAM   May I be bold to acquaint His Grace you are
gone about it?

PAROLLES   I know not what the success will be, my
lord, but the attempt I vow.

BERTRAM   I know thou'rt valiant, and to the possibility 81
of thy soldiership will subscribe for thee. Farewell. 82

PAROLLES   I love not many words.   *Exit.*

FIRST LORD   No more than a fish loves water. Is not this
a strange fellow, my lord, that so confidently seems to
undertake this business, which he knows is not to be
done, damns himself to do, and dares better be 87
damned than to do 't?

SECOND LORD   You do not know him, my lord, as we
do. Certain it is that he will steal himself into a man's
favor and for a week escape a great deal of discover- 91
ies; but when you find him out, you have him ever 92
after.

BERTRAM   Why, do you think he will make no deed at 94
all of this that so seriously he does address himself
unto?

FIRST LORD   None in the world, but return with an
invention, and clap upon you two or three probable 98
lies. But we have almost embossed him. You shall see 99
his fall tonight; for indeed he is not for your lordship's
respect.

SECOND LORD   We'll make you some sport with the fox
ere we case him. He was first smoked by the old lord 103
Lafew. When his disguise and he is parted, tell me 104
what a sprat you shall find him, which you shall see 105
this very night.

FIRST LORD
I must go look my twigs. He shall be caught. 107

BERTRAM
Your brother he shall go along with me. 108

FIRST LORD
As 't please your lordship. I'll leave you.   [*Exit.*]

19 **fetch off** recapture   23 **surprise** capture   25 **hoodwink** blindfold
26 **leaguer** camp   30–31 **intelligence in his power** information at his
command   36 **bottom** extent   38 **John Drum's entertainment** (Slang
phrase for a thorough beating and unceremonious dismissal.)   39 **inclining** partiality (for Parolles)   42 **in any hand** in any case   43–
44 **sticks . . . disposition** i.e., greatly troubles you   48 **wings** flanks.
rend cut up, attack   50–51 **in . . . service** upon the orders given for
the action   51 **disaster** accident   54–55 **we . . . success** i.e., we
were successful enough   59 **But that** were it not that   61–62 **hic
jacet** Latin for *here lies,* the beginning phrase of tomb inscriptions.
Hence, Parolles means "I would die in the attempt."   63 **stomach**
appetite   64 **mystery** skill   65 **again . . . quarter** back home again

66 **grace** honor   67 **speed** succeed   69 **becomes** suits, is worthy of
73 **presently** immediately   74 **pen . . . dilemmas** i.e., reflect on my
choices or uncertainties   75 **my mortal preparation** spiritual preparedness for my death; or, death-dealing readiness   81 **possibility**
capacity   82 **subscribe** vouch   87 **damns** condemns.   **better** rather
91–92 **escape . . . discoveries** i.e., almost get away with it   92 **have
him** have a true knowledge of him   94 **deed** attempt   98 **invention**
fabrication.   **probable** plausible   99 **embossed** driven to exhaustion,
cornered. (A hunting term.)   103 **case** skin, strip, unmask.   **smoked**
smelled out; smoked out into the open   104 **is parted** are separated
105 **sprat** a small fish; a contemptible creature   107 **look my twigs**
i.e., see to my trap (as in catching birds with birdlime on twigs)
108 **Your brother** i.e., the Second Lord

BERTRAM
Now will I lead you to the house and show you
The lass I spoke of.
SECOND LORD   But you say she's honest.   111
BERTRAM
That's all the fault. I spoke with her but once
And found her wondrous cold; but I sent to her,
By this same coxcomb that we have i' the wind,   114
Tokens and letters, which she did re-send,   115
And this is all I have done. She's a fair creature.
Will you go see her?
SECOND LORD   With all my heart, my lord.
                                        Exeunt.

❧

3.7   *Enter Helena and Widow.*

HELENA
If you misdoubt me that I am not she,   1
I know not how I shall assure you further
But I shall lose the grounds I work upon.   3
WIDOW
Though my estate be fall'n, I was well born,   4
Nothing acquainted with these businesses,
And would not put my reputation now
In any staining act.
HELENA   Nor would I wish you.
First give me trust the Count he is my husband,   8
And what to your sworn counsel I have spoken   9
Is so from word to word; and then you cannot,   10
By the good aid that I of you shall borrow,   11
Err in bestowing it.
WIDOW   I should believe you,
For you have showed me that which well approves   13
You're great in fortune.
HELENA [*giving money*]   Take this purse of gold,
And let me buy your friendly help thus far,
Which I will overpay and pay again
When I have found it. The Count he woos your
   daughter,   17
Lays down his wanton siege before her beauty,
Resolved to carry her. Let her in fine consent,   19
As we'll direct her how 'tis best to bear it.   20
Now his important blood will naught deny   21
That she'll demand. A ring the County wears,   22
That downward hath succeeded in his house
From son to son some four or five descents
Since the first father wore it. This ring he holds

In most rich choice, yet, in his idle fire,   26
To buy his will it would not seem too dear,   27
Howe'er repented after.
WIDOW
Now I see the bottom of your purpose.
HELENA
You see it lawful, then. It is no more
But that your daughter, ere she seems as won,
Desires this ring; appoints him an encounter;   32
In fine, delivers me to fill the time,
Herself most chastely absent. After,
To marry her, I'll add three thousand crowns   35
To what is passed already.
WIDOW   I have yielded.
Instruct my daughter how she shall persever,
That time and place with this deceit so lawful
May prove coherent. Every night he comes   39
With musics of all sorts, and songs composed   40
To her unworthiness. It nothing steads us   41
To chide him from our eaves, for he persists   42
As if his life lay on 't.
HELENA   Why then tonight   43
Let us essay our plot, which, if it speed,   44
Is wicked meaning in a lawful deed,   45
And lawful meaning in a wicked act,
Where both not sin, and yet a sinful fact.   47
But let's about it.   [*Exeunt.*]

❧

4.1   *Enter one of the Frenchmen [the First Lord] with five or six other Soldiers, in ambush.*

FIRST LORD   He can come no other way but by this
hedge corner. When you sally upon him, speak what   2
terrible language you will. Though you understand it   3
not yourselves, no matter; for we must not seem to
understand him, unless someone among us whom   5
we must produce for an interpreter.
FIRST SOLDIER   Good Captain, let me be th' interpreter.
FIRST LORD   Art not acquainted with him? Knows he
not thy voice?
FIRST SOLDIER   No, sir, I warrant you.
FIRST LORD   But what linsey-woolsey hast thou to   11
speak to us again?   12
FIRST SOLDIER   E'en such as you speak to me.

---

111 honest chaste   **114 coxcomb** fool.   **have i' the wind** have to our
downwind side, whom we are tracking   **115 re-send** send back
3.7. Location: Florence. The Widow's house.
1 misdoubt doubt   **3 But . . . upon** unless (by revealing myself to
Bertram) I forfeit the ground upon which my plans are built   **4 estate**
worldly condition   **8 give me trust** believe me (that)   **9 to . . . counsel** to your private understanding, guarded by your oath of secrecy
10 so . . . word true in every word   **11 By** with regard to   **13 approves** proves   **17 found it** i.e., received your help with success
19 carry win.   **in fine** finally, or, to sum up (as also in line 33)
20 bear manage   **21 important blood** importunate passion   **22 That**
what.   **County** Count

26 choice estimation, regard.   **idle fire** foolish passion   **27 will** sexual desire   **32 appoints him an encounter** arranges a meeting   **35 To
marry her** as her dowry   **39 coherent** suitable   **40 musics** musicians
41 To her unworthiness to her, my humble daughter; or, to the end
of persuading her to do an unworthy deed.   **nothing steads** profits
not at all   **42 chide** drive   **43 lay** depended   **44 essay** try.   **speed**
succeed   **45 wicked meaning** sinful intention (on Bertram's part, as
contrasted with Helena's *lawful meaning* in the next line, just as
wicked act may glance at the ethical dubiety of Helena's plot)
47 fact deed (which would have been sinful as Bertram intended it)
4.1. Location: Outside the Florentine camp.
2 sally rush out   **3 terrible** terrifying   **5 unless** except for   **11 linsey-
woolsey** a fabric woven from wool and flax; figuratively, a hodge-
podge   **12 again** in reply

FIRST LORD   He must think us some band of strangers 14
i' th' adversary's entertainment. Now he hath a smack 15
of all neighboring languages. Therefore we must every 16
one be a man of his own fancy, not to know what we 17
speak one to another; so we seem to know is to know 18
straight our purpose: choughs' language, gabble 19
enough and good enough. As for you, interpreter,
you must seem very politic. But couch, ho! Here he 21
comes, to beguile two hours in a sleep, and then to 22
return and swear the lies he forges.   [*They hide.*]

               Enter Parolles.

PAROLLES   Ten o'clock. Within these three hours 'twill
be time enough to go home. What shall I say I have
done? It must be a very plausive invention that carries 26
it. They begin to smoke me, and disgraces have of late 27
knocked too often at my door. I find my tongue is too
foolhardy; but my heart hath the fear of Mars before it, 29
and of his creatures, not daring the reports of my 30
tongue.   31
FIRST LORD [*aside*]   This is the first truth that e'er thine
own tongue was guilty of.
PAROLLES   What the devil should move me to undertake the recovery of this drum, being not ignorant of
the impossibility, and knowing I had no such purpose? I must give myself some hurts, and say I got
them in exploit. Yet slight ones will not carry it—they
will say, "Came you off with so little?"—and great
ones I dare not give. Wherefore? What's the instance? 40
Tongue, I must put you into a butter-woman's mouth 41
and buy myself another of Bajazeth's mule, if you 42
prattle me into these perils.
FIRST LORD [*aside*]   Is it possible he should know what
he is, and be that he is?
PAROLLES   I would the cutting of my garments would
serve the turn, or the breaking of my Spanish sword. 47
FIRST LORD [*aside*]   We cannot afford you so.   48
PAROLLES   Or the baring of my beard, and to say it was 49
in stratagem.   50
FIRST LORD [*aside*]   'Twould not do.
PAROLLES   Or to drown my clothes, and say I was
stripped.
FIRST LORD [*aside*]   Hardly serve.
PAROLLES   Though I swore I leapt from the window of
the citadel—

FIRST LORD [*aside*]   How deep?
PAROLLES   Thirty fathom.   58
FIRST LORD [*aside*]   Three great oaths would scarce
make that be believed.
PAROLLES   I would I had any drum of the enemy's. I
would swear I recovered it.
FIRST LORD [*aside*]   You shall hear one anon.   63
PAROLLES   A drum now of the enemy's—   64
                         Alarum within.
FIRST LORD [*coming forward*]   *Throca movousus, cargo,
cargo, cargo.*
ALL   *Cargo, cargo, cargo, villianda par corbo, cargo.*
                         [*They seize and blindfold him.*]
PAROLLES
O, ransom, ransom! Do not hide mine eyes.
FIRST SOLDIER   *Boskos thromuldo boskos.*
PAROLLES
I know you are the Muskos' regiment,   70
And I shall lose my life for want of language.   71
If there be here German, or Dane, Low Dutch,
Italian, or French, let him speak to me,   73
I'll discover that which shall undo the Florentine.   74
FIRST SOLDIER   *Boskos vauvado.* I understand thee and
can speak thy tongue. *Kerelybonto.* Sir, betake thee to 76
thy faith, for seventeen poniards are at thy bosom. 77
PAROLLES   O!
FIRST SOLDIER   O, pray, pray, pray! *Manka revania
dulche.*
FIRST LORD   *Oscorbidulchos volivorco.*
FIRST SOLDIER
The General is content to spare thee yet,
And, hoodwinked as thou art, will lead thee on   83
To gather from thee. Haply thou mayst inform   84
Something to save thy life.
PAROLLES   O, let me live,
And all the secrets of our camp I'll show,
Their force, their purposes; nay, I'll speak that
Which you will wonder at.
FIRST SOLDIER   But wilt thou faithfully?
PAROLLES
If I do not, damn me.
FIRST SOLDIER   *Acordo linta.*
Come on; thou art granted space.   90
           Exit [*with Parolles guarded*]. *A short alarum within.*
FIRST LORD
Go tell the Count Rossillion and my brother
We have caught the woodcock and will keep him
    muffled   92
Till we do hear from them.
SECOND SOLDIER   Captain, I will.
FIRST LORD
'A will betray us all unto ourselves.
Inform on that.   95

SECOND SOLDIER   So I will, sir.

FIRST LORD

Till then I'll keep him dark and safely locked. *Exeunt.*

❧

4.2   *Enter Bertram and the maid called Diana.*

BERTRAM

They told me that your name was Fontibell.

DIANA

No, my good lord, Diana.

BERTRAM   Titled goddess,   2
And worth it, with addition! But, fair soul,   3
In your fine frame hath love no quality?   4
If the quick fire of youth light not your mind,   5
You are no maiden, but a monument.   6
When you are dead, you should be such a one
As you are now; for you are cold and stern,
And now you should be as your mother was
When your sweet self was got.   10

DIANA

She then was honest.

BERTRAM   So should you be.

DIANA   No.   11
My mother did but duty—such, my lord,
As you owe to your wife.

BERTRAM   No more o' that.
I prithee, do not strive against my vows.   14
I was compelled to her, but I love thee
By love's own sweet constraint and will forever
Do thee all rights of service.

DIANA   Ay, so you serve us
Till we serve you; but when you have our roses,   18
You barely leave our thorns to prick ourselves   19
And mock us with our bareness.

BERTRAM   How have I sworn!   20

DIANA

'Tis not the many oaths that makes the truth,
But the plain single vow that is vowed true.
What is not holy, that we swear not by,   23
But take the High'st to witness. Then pray you,
tell me,   24
If I should swear by Jove's great attributes
I loved you dearly, would you believe my oaths
When I did love you ill? This has no holding,   27
To swear by Him whom I protest to love   28

That I will work against Him. Therefore your oaths   29
Are words and poor conditions but unsealed,   30
At least in my opinion.

BERTRAM   Change it, change it!   31
Be not so holy-cruel. Love is holy,   32
And my integrity ne'er knew the crafts   33
That you do charge men with. Stand no more off,
But give thyself unto my sick desires,   35
Who then recovers. Say thou art mine, and ever   36
My love as it begins shall so persever.

DIANA

I see that men may rope 's in such a snare   38
That we'll forsake ourselves. Give me that ring.

BERTRAM

I'll lend it thee, my dear, but have no power
To give it from me.

DIANA   Will you not, my lord?

BERTRAM

It is an honor 'longing to our house,
Bequeathèd down from many ancestors,
Which were the greatest obloquy i' the world   44
In me to lose.

DIANA   Mine honor's such a ring.
My chastity's the jewel of our house,
Bequeathèd down from many ancestors,
Which were the greatest obloquy i' the world
In me to lose. Thus your own proper wisdom   49
Brings in the champion Honor on my part   50
Against your vain assault.

BERTRAM   Here, take my ring!
My house, mine honor, yea, my life, be thine,
And I'll be bid by thee.   [*He gives the ring.*]   53

DIANA

When midnight comes, knock at my chamber
window.
I'll order take my mother shall not hear.   55
Now will I charge you in the bond of truth,
When you have conquered my yet maiden bed,
Remain there but an hour, nor speak to me.
My reasons are most strong, and you shall know
them   59
When back again this ring shall be delivered.   60
And on your finger in the night I'll put
Another ring, that what in time proceeds   62
May token to the future our past deeds.   63
Adieu till then; then, fail not. You have won
A wife of me, though there my hope be done.   65

---

29 work against Him oppose His will by my sinful action   **30 words . . . unsealed** mere words and invalid provisos, unratified and hence lacking in legally binding force   **31 it** i.e., your opinion   **32 holy-cruel** i.e., cruel to me in your holiness   **33 crafts** deceits   **35 sick** i.e., unfulfilled and in need of Helena's ministrations   **36 Who** which.   **recovers** recover   **38 rope 's** rope us, entrap us. (The Folio reads *make rope 's in such a scarre.*)   **44 obloquy** disgrace (as also in line 48)   **49 proper** personal   **50 part** side   **53 bid** commanded   **55 order take** make provision   **59–60 you . . . delivered** (Diana hints obscurely at the eventual return of Bertram's ring, when he will understand everything; see 5.3.192 ff.)   **62 Another ring** i.e., the ring the King gave Helena; see 5.3.77 ff.)   **that . . . proceeds** which, whatever may happen   **63 token** betoken, indicate   **65 A wife . . . done** i.e., me as your love partner, although all hope of marriage is thereby destroyed for me

4.2. Location: Florence. The Widow's house.
2–3 Titled . . . addition you who have the name of a goddess, and who deserve that and more   **4 quality** position   **5 quick** lively   **6 monument** statue, lifeless effigy   **10 got** begotten   **11 honest** chaste, true to marriage vows. (But Bertram uses it to mean "frank.")   **14 vows** i.e., vows to live apart from Helena   **18 serve you** i.e., serve you sexually. (The sexual suggestion is continued in *roses* and in *prick,* line 19.)   **19 You . . . thorns** you leave us with only the bare thorns (of shame and guilt)   **20 our bareness** i.e., the loss of our rose of virginity   **23–24 What . . . witness** when we swear an oath, we do so not in the name of unholy things, but with God as our witness   **27 ill** perfidiously and hence contrary to the purport of an oath sworn to God.   **holding** power to bind; consistency   **28 protest** profess

BERTRAM
A heaven on earth I have won by wooing thee.
                                                        [*Exit.*]

DIANA
For which live long to thank both heaven and me!
You may so in the end.
My mother told me just how he would woo,
As if she sat in 's heart. She says all men
Have the like oaths. He had sworn to marry me   71
When his wife's dead; therefore I'll lie with him
When I am buried. Since Frenchmen are so braid,   73
Marry that will, I live and die a maid.   74
Only in this disguise I think 't no sin
To cozen him that would unjustly win.   *Exit.* 76

4.3 *Enter the two French Captains and some two or*
       three Soldiers.

FIRST LORD You have not given him his mother's letter?

SECOND LORD I have delivered it an hour since. There 2
is something in 't that stings his nature, for on the
reading it he changed almost into another man.

FIRST LORD He has much worthy blame laid upon him 5
for shaking off so good a wife and so sweet a lady.

SECOND LORD Especially he hath incurred the everlasting displeasure of the King, who had even tuned his 8
bounty to sing happiness to him. I will tell you a 9
thing, but you shall let it dwell darkly with you. 10

FIRST LORD When you have spoken it, 'tis dead, and I
am the grave of it.

SECOND LORD He hath perverted a young gentlewoman 13
here in Florence, of a most chaste renown, and this
night he fleshes his will in the spoil of her honor. He 15
hath given her his monumental ring and thinks him- 16
self made in the unchaste composition. 17

FIRST LORD Now, God delay our rebellion! As we are 18
ourselves, what things are we! 19

SECOND LORD Merely our own traitors. And as in the 20
common course of all treasons we still see them reveal 21
themselves till they attain to their abhorred ends, so 22
he that in this action contrives against his own 23
nobility, in his proper stream o'erflows himself. 24

FIRST LORD Is it not meant damnable in us to be 25
trumpeters of our unlawful intents? We shall not then
have his company tonight?

SECOND LORD Not till after midnight, for he is dieted 28
to his hour. 29

FIRST LORD That approaches apace. I would gladly have
him see his company anatomized, that he might take 31
a measure of his own judgments wherein so curiously 32
he had set this counterfeit. 33

SECOND LORD We will not meddle with him till he 34
come, for his presence must be the whip of the other. 35

FIRST LORD In the meantime, what hear you of these
wars?

SECOND LORD I hear there is an overture of peace.

FIRST LORD Nay, I assure you, a peace concluded.

SECOND LORD What will Count Rossillion do then?
Will he travel higher or return again into France? 41

FIRST LORD I perceive, by this demand, you are not 42
altogether of his council. 43

SECOND LORD Let it be forbid, sir! So should I be a great
deal of his act. 45

FIRST LORD Sir, his wife some two months since fled
from his house. Her pretense is a pilgrimage to Saint 47
Jaques le Grand, which holy undertaking with most
austere sanctimony she accomplished. And, there 49
residing, the tenderness of her nature became as a
prey to her grief; in fine, made a groan of her last 51
breath, and now she sings in heaven.

SECOND LORD How is this justified? 53

FIRST LORD The stronger part of it by her own letters,
which makes her story true even to the point of her 55
death. Her death itself, which could not be her office
to say is come, was faithfully confirmed by the rector
of the place.

SECOND LORD Hath the Count all this intelligence?

FIRST LORD Ay, and the particular confirmations, point
from point, to the full arming of the verity. 61

SECOND LORD I am heartily sorry that he'll be glad of
this.

FIRST LORD How mightily sometimes we make us 64
comforts of our losses! 65

SECOND LORD And how mightily some other times we 66
drown our gain in tears! The great dignity that his 67
valor hath here acquired for him shall at home be
encountered with a shame as ample.

FIRST LORD The web of our life is of a mingled yarn,
good and ill together. Our virtues would be proud if 71

---

71 had has (?) would have (?)   **73 braid** i.e., deceitful. (A *braid* is a
trick.)   **74 Marry** let those marry   **76 cozen** cheat
4.3. Location: The Florentine camp.
2 since ago   **5 worthy** deserved   **8–9 who . . . to him** i.e., who
previously had prepared to be bountiful to Bertram, carefully tuning
his generosity as though it were an instrument to accompany his song
of good fortune   **10 darkly** secretly   **13 perverted** seduced
15 fleshes his will gratifies his lust (like a hunter giving some meat to
his hounds from the hunted animal, the quarry or *spoil*)   **16 monumental** i.e., serving as a token of his identity   **17 made** a made man.
composition bargain   **18 delay our rebellion** make us slow to rebel,
assuage our lustful appetites   **18–19 are ourselves** i.e., unaided by
God   **20 Merely** absolutely, entirely   **21–22 still . . . themselves** always see traitors express their true natures   **23–24 he . . . himself**
i.e., Bertram, who thus seduces a woman, subverts his own nobility
by abusing the qualities that should channel and perpetuate it. (Like
all traitors, indeed like all people, Bertram is most of all a traitor to
himself, betraying in himself those very qualities that otherwise seem
noble in him.)

25 meant damnable designed as a mortal sin   **28–29 dieted to his
hour** tied to his schedule   **31 his company** the company he keeps,
his companion.   **anatomized** dissected, exposed   **32 curiously** carefully, elaborately   **33 counterfeit** false jewel, i.e., Parolles   **34 he
. . . he** i.e., Parolles . . . Bertram   **35 his . . . the other** i.e., Bertram's . . . Parolles   **41 higher** farther   **42 demand** question   **43 of
his council** in his confidence   **45 of his act** an accessory to his misdeeds   **47 pretense** intent   **49 sanctimony** holiness   **51 in fine** at last
53 justified made certain   **55 point** time, moment   **61 arming** cor-
roboration, strengthening.   **verity** truth   **64–67 make . . . tears** perversely take comfort in misfortune and at other times weep when we
are fortunate. (Bertram is glad to lose Helena and grieved at gaining
her.)   **71–73 Our . . . virtues** i.e., we would be fatally proud of our
virtue if we were not continually humbled by our failings and, conversely, we would despair of being so sinful if our better natures did
not take pity on our failings

our faults whipped them not, and our crimes would 72
despair if they were not cherished by our virtues.   73

Enter a [Servant as] messenger.

How now? Where's your master?

SERVANT   He met the Duke in the street, sir, of whom
he hath taken a solemn leave. His lordship will next 76
morning for France. The Duke hath offered him letters
of commendations to the King.

SECOND LORD   They shall be no more than needful 79
there, if they were more than they can commend.   80

Enter [Bertram] Count Rossillion.

FIRST LORD   They cannot be too sweet for the King's
tartness. Here's his lordship now.—How now, my
lord, is 't not after midnight?

BERTRAM   I have tonight dispatched sixteen businesses,
a month's length apiece, by an abstract of success: I 85
have congeed with the Duke, done my adieu with his 86
nearest, buried a wife, mourned for her, writ to my 87
lady mother I am returning, entertained my convoy, 88
and between these main parcels of dispatch effected 89
many nicer needs. The last was the greatest, but that 90
I have not ended yet.

SECOND LORD   If the business be of any difficulty, and
this morning your departure hence, it requires haste
of your lordship.

BERTRAM   I mean, the business is not ended, as fearing
to hear of it hereafter. But shall we have this dialogue
between the fool and the soldier? Come, bring forth
this counterfeit module; he's deceived me like a 98
double-meaning prophesier.   99

SECOND LORD   Bring him forth. *[Exit one or more.]* He's
sat i' the stocks all night, poor gallant knave.

BERTRAM   No matter; his heels have deserved it, in
usurping his spurs so long. How does he carry
himself?

SECOND LORD   I have told your lordship already, the
stocks carry him. But to answer you as you would be
understood, he weeps like a wench that had shed her 107
milk. He hath confessed himself to Morgan, whom he
supposes to be a friar, from the time of his remem- 109
brance to this very instant disaster of his setting i' the 110
stocks. And what think you he hath confessed?

BERTRAM   Nothing of me, has 'a?

SECOND LORD   His confession is taken, and it shall be
read to his face. If your lordship be in 't, as I believe
you are, you must have the patience to hear it.

*Enter Parolles [guarded and blindfolded] with
[First Soldier as] his interpreter.*

BERTRAM   A plague upon him! Muffled! He can say 116
nothing of me.

FIRST LORD   Hush, hush! Hoodman comes!—*Portotar-* 118
tarosa.

FIRST SOLDIER   He calls for the tortures. What will you
say without 'em?

PAROLLES   I will confess what I know without constraint. If ye pinch me like a pasty, I can say no more. 123

FIRST SOLDIER   *Bosko chimurcho.*

FIRST LORD   *Boblibindo chicurmurco.*

FIRST SOLDIER   You are a merciful general.—Our general bids you answer to what I shall ask you out of a note. 127

PAROLLES   And truly, as I hope to live.

FIRST SOLDIER   *[as if reading]* "First demand of him how
many horse the Duke is strong." What say you to that? 130

PAROLLES   Five or six thousand, but very weak and
unserviceable. The troops are all scattered and the
commanders very poor rogues, upon my reputation
and credit and as I hope to live.

FIRST SOLDIER   Shall I set down your answer so?
                                        [He makes as though to write.]

PAROLLES   Do. I'll take the Sacrament on 't, how and
which way you will.

BERTRAM *[aside to the Lords]*   All's one to him. What a
past-saving slave is this!

FIRST LORD *[aside to Bertram]*   You're deceived, my lord.
This is Monsieur Parolles, the gallant militarist—that
was his own phrase—that had the whole theoric of 142
war in the knot of his scarf, and the practice in the
chape of his dagger.   144

SECOND LORD *[aside]*   I will never trust a man again
for keeping his sword clean, nor believe he can have 146
everything in him by wearing his apparel neatly.

FIRST SOLDIER *[to Parolles]*   Well, that's set down.

PAROLLES   "Five or six thousand horse," I said—I will
say true—"or thereabouts," set down, for I'll speak
truth.

FIRST LORD *[aside]*   He's very near the truth in this.

BERTRAM *[aside]*   But I con him no thanks for 't, in the 153
nature he delivers it.   154

PAROLLES   "Poor rogues," I pray you, say.

FIRST SOLDIER   Well, that's set down.

PAROLLES   I humbly thank you, sir. A truth's a truth.
The rogues are marvelous poor.

FIRST SOLDIER *[as if reading]*   "Demand of him of what
strength they are afoot." What say you to that?

PAROLLES   By my troth, sir, if I were to live this present 161
hour, I will tell true. Let me see: Spurio, a hundred and
fifty; Sebastian, so many; Corambus, so many; Jaques, 163
so many; Guiltian, Cosmo, Lodowick, and Gratii, two
hundred fifty each; mine own company, Chitopher,

---

76 will i.e., will depart   **79–80 They . . . commend** even if they
were stronger than any recommendation could be, they would still be
no more than what is needed (to calm the King's anger at Bertram)
85 by . . . success by a series of successful moves, as follows, or, by
a series of moves that may be summarized as follows   **86 congeed
with** taken leave of   **86–87 his nearest** those persons nearest him
88 entertained my convoy hired my transportation   **89 main . . . dispatch** major items to be settled   **90 nicer** more delicate.   **The last**
i.e., the affair with Diana (which Bertram fears he will hear of again
in the form of a claim on him as husband)   **98 module** mere image
99 double-meaning ambiguous, equivocating   **107 shed** spilled
109–110 the time . . . remembrance as far back as he can recall
110 instant present

116 Muffled blindfolded   **118 Hoodman comes** (Customary call in
the game of blindman's buff.)   **123 pasty** meat pie   **127 note** memorandum or list   **130 horse** horsemen, cavalry troops   **142 theoric** theory   **144 chape** scabbard tip   **146 clean** polished   **153 con** offer. (Literally, "know.")   **153–154 in . . . it** considering what sort of
truth it is that he tells   **161 live** i.e., live only   **163 so many** the same
number

Vaumond, Bentii, two hundred fifty each; so that the muster-file, rotten and sound, upon my life, amounts not to fifteen thousand poll, half of the which dare not shake the snow from off their cassocks, lest they shake themselves to pieces. 167 168 169

BERTRAM [*aside to the Lords*] What shall be done to him?

FIRST LORD [*aside*] Nothing, but let him have thanks.— Demand of him my condition and what credit I have with the Duke.

FIRST SOLDIER Well, that's set down. [*As if reading.*] "You shall demand of him whether one Captain Dumain be i' the camp, a Frenchman; what his reputation is with the Duke; what his valor, honesty, and expertness in wars; or whether he thinks it were not possible, with well-weighing sums of gold, to corrupt him to a revolt." What say you to this? What do you know of it? 181

PAROLLES I beseech you, let me answer to the particular of the inter'gatories. Demand them singly. 185

FIRST SOLDIER Do you know this Captain Dumain?

PAROLLES I know him. 'A was a botcher's prentice in Paris, from whence he was whipped for getting the sheriff's fool with child—a dumb innocent that could not say him nay. 187 189

BERTRAM [*aside to First Lord, who makes as if to strike Parolles*] Nay, by your leave, hold your hands— though I know his brains are forfeit to the next tile that falls. 193 194

FIRST SOLDIER Well, is this captain in the Duke of Florence's camp?

PAROLLES Upon my knowledge, he is, and lousy. 197

FIRST LORD [*aside to Bertram*] Nay, look not so upon me. We shall hear of your lordship anon.

FIRST SOLDIER What is his reputation with the Duke?

PAROLLES The Duke knows him for no other but a poor officer of mine, and writ to me this other day to turn him out o' the band. I think I have his letter in my pocket.

FIRST SOLDIER Marry, we'll search.

[*They search his pockets.*]

PAROLLES In good sadness, I do not know; either it is there, or it is upon a file with the Duke's other letters in my tent. 206

FIRST SOLDIER Here 'tis, here's a paper. Shall I read it to you?

PAROLLES I do not know if it be it or no.

BERTRAM [*aside*] Our interpreter does it well.

FIRST LORD [*aside*] Excellently.

FIRST SOLDIER [*reads*]
"Dian, the Count's a fool, and full of gold—"

PAROLLES That is not the Duke's letter, sir. That is an advertisement to a proper maid in Florence, one 216

Diana, to take heed of the allurement of one Count Rossillion, a foolish idle boy, but for all that very ruttish. I pray you, sir, put it up again. 219

FIRST SOLDIER Nay, I'll read it first, by your favor.

PAROLLES My meaning in 't, I protest, was very honest in the behalf of the maid, for I knew the young Count to be a dangerous and lascivious boy, who is a whale to virginity, and devours up all the fry it finds. 224

BERTRAM [*aside*] Damnable both-sides rogue!

FIRST SOLDIER [*reads the*] letter
"When he swears oaths, bid him drop gold, and
    take it; 226
    After he scores, he never pays the score. 227
Half won is match well made; match, and well make
    it. 228
    He ne'er pays after-debts; take it before. 229
And say a soldier, Dian, told thee this:
Men are to mell with, boys are not to kiss. 231
For count of this, the Count's a fool, I know it, 232
Who pays before, but not when he does owe it. 233
    Thine, as he vowed to thee in thine ear,
                                        Parolles."

BERTRAM [*aside*] He shall be whipped through the army with this rhyme in 's forehead.

SECOND LORD [*aside*] This is your devoted friend, sir, the manifold linguist and the armipotent soldier. 239

BERTRAM [*aside*] I could endure anything before but a cat, and now he's a cat to me. 241

FIRST SOLDIER I perceive, sir, by our general's looks, we shall be fain to hang you. 243

PAROLLES My life, sir, in any case! Not that I am afraid to die, but that, my offenses being many, I would repent out the remainder of nature. Let me live, sir, in a dungeon, i' the stocks, or anywhere, so I may live. 246

FIRST SOLDIER We'll see what may be done, so you confess freely. Therefore, once more to this Captain Dumain. You have answered to his reputation with the Duke, and to his valor. What is his honesty?

PAROLLES He will steal, sir, an egg out of a cloister. For rapes and ravishments he parallels Nessus. He professes not keeping of oaths; in breaking 'em he is stronger than Hercules. He will lie, sir, with such volubility that you would think truth were a fool. Drunkenness is his best virtue, for he will be swine-drunk, and in his sleep he does little harm, save to his bedclothes about him; but they know his conditions, 253 254 256 259

167 file roll **168 poll** heads **169 cassocks** cloaks **181 well-weighing** heavy and persuasive **185 inter'gatories** questions **187 botcher's** mender's, especially a tailor or cobbler who makes repairs **189 sheriff's fool** feeble-minded girl in the sheriff's custody **193–194 his . . . falls** i.e., such a liar is headed straight for sudden and violent death **197 lousy** (1) contemptible (2) infested with lice **206 sadness** seriousness **216 advertisement** warning. **proper** respectable

219 ruttish lecherous **224 fry** small fish **226 drop** i.e., offer, pay. **take it** i.e., you should take it **227 scores** (1) buys on credit (2) hits the mark, scores sexually. **score** bill **228 Half . . . make it** one is halfway to success if the *match* or bargain is well stated with clearly defined agreements, so be sure to do this **229 after-debts** debts payable after the goods are received. **it** i.e., payment **231 Men . . . kiss** i.e., don't fool around with mere boys like Bertram, but with real men (like me) **232 For count of** on account of, or, therefore take note of **233 before** in advance (when he is required to do so). **owe it** (1) owe payment for something already received (2) possess it, i.e., her maidenhood **239 manifold linguist** speaker of many languages. **armipotent** powerful in arms **241 cat** (A term of contempt.) **243 fain** obliged **246 the remainder of nature** what is left of my natural life **253 Nessus** a centaur who attempted to rape the wife of Hercules **253–254 professes** makes a practice of **256 volubility** fluency, facility. **truth were a fool** i.e., truth here seems so easily put down and made to look foolish **259 they** i.e., his servants. **conditions** habits and lay him in straw. I have but little more to say, sir, of his honesty. He has everything that an honest man should not have; what an honest man should have, he has nothing.

FIRST LORD [aside]   I begin to love him for this.

BERTRAM [aside]   For this description of thine honesty? A pox upon him for me, he's more and more a cat.

FIRST SOLDIER   What say you to his expertness in war?

PAROLLES   Faith, sir, he's led the drum before the 268 English tragedians. To belie him I will not, and more 269 of his soldiership I know not, except in that country he had the honor to be the officer at a place there called Mile End, to instruct for the doubling of files. I would 272 do the man what honor I can, but of this I am not certain.

FIRST LORD [aside]   He hath out-villained villainy so far that the rarity redeems him.   276

BERTRAM [aside]   A pox on him, he's a cat still.

FIRST SOLDIER   His qualities being at this poor price, I need not to ask you if gold will corrupt him to revolt.

PAROLLES   Sir, for a cardecu he will sell the fee simple of 280 his salvation, the inheritance of it, and cut th' entail 281 from all remainders, and a perpetual succession for it 282 perpetually.   283

FIRST SOLDIER   What's his brother, the other Captain Dumain?

SECOND LORD [aside]   Why does he ask him of me?

FIRST SOLDIER   What's he?

PAROLLES   E'en a crow o' the same nest; not altogether so great as the first in goodness, but greater a great deal in evil. He excels his brother for a coward, yet his brother is reputed one of the best that is. In a retreat he outruns any lackey; marry, in coming on he has the 292 cramp.

FIRST SOLDIER   If your life be saved, will you undertake to betray the Florentine?

PAROLLES   Ay, and the Captain of his Horse, Count 296 Rossillion.

FIRST SOLDIER   I'll whisper with the General and know his pleasure.

PAROLLES [to himself]   I'll no more drumming. A plague of all drums! Only to seem to deserve well, and to beguile the supposition of that lascivious young boy, 302 the Count, have I run into this danger. Yet who would have suspected an ambush where I was taken?

FIRST SOLDIER   There is no remedy, sir, but you must die. The General says, you that have so traitorously discovered the secrets of your army and made such 307 pestiferous reports of men very nobly held can serve 308 the world for no honest use; therefore you must

die.—Come, headsman, off with his head.

PAROLLES   O Lord, sir, let me live, or let me see my death!

FIRST SOLDIER   That shall you, and take your leave of all your friends. [Unblinding him.] So, look about you. Know you any here?

BERTRAM   Good morrow, noble Captain.

SECOND LORD   God bless you, Captain Parolles.

FIRST LORD   God save you, noble Captain.

SECOND LORD   Captain, what greeting will you to my 319 Lord Lafew? I am for France.   320

FIRST LORD   Good Captain, will you give me a copy of the sonnet you writ to Diana in behalf of the Count Rossillion? An I were not a very coward, I'd compel it 323 of you; but fare you well.   Exeunt [Bertram and Lords].

FIRST SOLDIER   You are undone, Captain, all but your scarf; that has a knot on 't yet.

PAROLLES   Who cannot be crushed with a plot?

FIRST SOLDIER   If you could find out a country where but women were that had received so much shame, you might begin an impudent nation. Fare ye well, sir. 330 I am for France too. We shall speak of you there.

Exit [with Soldiers].

PAROLLES
Yet am I thankful. If my heart were great,
'Twould burst at this. Captain I'll be no more,
But I will eat and drink, and sleep as soft
As captain shall. Simply the thing I am
Shall make me live. Who knows himself a braggart, 336
Let him fear this, for it will come to pass
That every braggart shall be found an ass.
Rust, sword! Cool, blushes! And, Parolles, live
Safest in shame! Being fooled, by foolery thrive! 340
There's place and means for every man alive.
I'll after them.   Exit.

❖

4.4   *Enter Helena, Widow, and Diana.*

HELENA
That you may well perceive I have not wronged you,
One of the greatest in the Christian world
Shall be my surety; 'fore whose throne 'tis needful, 3
Ere I can perfect mine intents, to kneel.
Time was, I did him a desirèd office,
Dear almost as his life, which gratitude   6
Through flinty Tartar's bosom would peep forth
And answer thanks. I duly am informed
His Grace is at Marseilles, to which place
We have convenient convoy. You must know   10
I am supposèd dead. The army breaking,   11

268–269 led . . . tragedians (It was a custom of actors entering a village or town to parade in the street before the performance of a play.) 272 Mile End place near London where citizen militiamen were regularly exercised.   doubling of files simple drill maneuver in which the soldiers stand in a row two deep   276 rarity unique excellence 280 cardecu quart d'écu, one-quarter of a French crown.   fee simple total and perpetual ownership   281–283 cut . . . perpetually prevent it from being passed on successively to subsequent heirs 292 lackey running footman.   coming on moving forward   296 Captain of his Horse cavalry commander   302 supposition judgment 307 discovered revealed   308 pestiferous malicious, pernicious. held regarded

319 will you do you wish to send   320 for bound for, off to   323 An if   330 impudent shameless   336 Who he who   340 Being . . . thrive i.e., since they have made a fool of me, I will now thrive by playing the fool
4.4. Location: Florence. The Widow's house.
3 surety guarantee   6 which gratitude gratitude for which   10 convenient convoy suitable transport   11 breaking disbanding

My husband hies him home, where, heaven aiding,   12
And by the leave of my good lord the King,
We'll be before our welcome.
WIDOW   Gentle madam,   14
You never had a servant to whose trust
Your business was more welcome.
HELENA   Nor you, mistress,
Ever a friend whose thoughts more truly labor
To recompense your love. Doubt not but heaven
Hath brought me up to be your daughter's dower,   19
As it hath fated her to be my motive   20
And helper to a husband. But O, strange men!
That can such sweet use make of what they hate,
When saucy trusting of the cozened thoughts   23
Defiles the pitchy night; so lust doth play   24
With what it loathes for that which is away.   25
But more of this hereafter. You, Diana,
Under my poor instructions yet must suffer   27
Something in my behalf.
DIANA   Let death and honesty   28
Go with your impositions, I am yours   29
Upon your will to suffer.
HELENA   Yet, I pray you;   30
But with the word the time will bring on summer,   31
When briers shall have leaves as well as thorns,   32
And be as sweet as sharp. We must away;
Our wagon is prepared, and time revives us.   34
All's well that ends well. Still the fine's the crown;   35
Whate'er the course, the end is the renown.   *Exeunt.*   36

4.5   *Enter Clown [Lavatch], Old Lady [Countess], and Lafew.*

LAFEW   No, no, no, your son was misled with a   1
snipped-taffeta fellow there, whose villainous saffron   2
would have made all the unbaked and doughy youth   3
of a nation in his color. Your daughter-in-law had

been alive at this hour, and your son here at home,
more advanced by the King than by that red-tailed
humble-bee I speak of.   7
COUNTESS   I would I had not known him! It was the
death of the most virtuous gentlewoman that ever
nature had praise for creating. If she had partaken of
my flesh, and cost me the dearest groans of a mother,   11
I could not have owed her a more rooted love.   12
LAFEW   'Twas a good lady, 'twas a good lady. We may
pick a thousand salads ere we light on such another
herb.
LAVATCH   Indeed, sir, she was the sweet marjoram of
the salad, or rather the herb of grace.   17
LAFEW   They are not herbs, you knave, they are nose-   18
herbs.   19
LAVATCH   I am no great Nebuchadnezzar, sir. I have   20
not much skill in grass.   21
LAFEW   Whether dost thou profess thyself, a knave or a   22
fool?
LAVATCH   A fool, sir, at a woman's service, and a knave
at a man's.
LAFEW   Your distinction?
LAVATCH   I would cozen the man of his wife and do his   27
service.   28
LAFEW   So you were a knave at his service, indeed.
LAVATCH   And I would give his wife my bauble, sir, to   30
do her service.
LAFEW   I will subscribe for thee, thou art both knave   32
and fool.
LAVATCH   At your service.
LAFEW   No, no, no!   35
LAVATCH   Why, sir, if I cannot serve you, I can serve as
great a prince as you are.
LAFEW   Who's that, a Frenchman?
LAVATCH   Faith, sir, 'a has an English name, but his   39
physnomy is more hotter in France than there.   40
LAFEW   What prince is that?
LAVATCH   The black prince, sir, alias the prince of
darkness, alias the devil.
LAFEW   Hold thee, there's my purse. [*He gives money.*] I
give thee not this to suggest thee from thy master thou   45
talk'st of; serve him still.
LAVATCH   I am a woodland fellow, sir, that always   47
loved a great fire, and the master I speak of ever keeps
a good fire. But sure he is the prince of the world; let
his nobility remain in 's court. I am for the house with

---

12 **hies him** hastens   14 **be . . . welcome** i.e., arrive before we are expected   19 **Hath . . . dower** i.e., has groomed me for the role of providing a dowry for your daughter   20 **motive** means
23–24 **When . . . night** when lascivious yielding to the deceptions of lust makes blacker the already black night   25 **for that** believing it to be that.   **away** absent. (Helena describes how Bertram has lustfully enjoyed Helena, making *sweet use* of what he hates, believing her to be the absent Diana.)   27 **yet** for a time yet   28 **Let death and honesty** i.e., even if death (provided my honor be maintained)   29 **your impositions** what you impose or command   30 **Upon . . . suffer** to face whatever suffering you ask of me.   **Yet** yet a little longer
31–32 **with . . . thorns** i.e., if we go on yet a little longer, as the saying goes, time will bring on a happier state of affairs, with rewards to compensate for our suffering. (Helena refers to the sweetbrier or eglantine, a species of small rose, which has prickly stems and highly aromatic leaves.)   34 **revives** will revive   35 **the fine's the crown** the end is the crown of all   36 **is the renown** will determine how well and how widely we are regarded
4.5. Location: Rossillion.
1 with by   **2 snipped-taffeta** wearing taffeta silk garments with slashes to allow the under material to be visible (suggestive of Parolles' hollow flashiness).   **saffron** bright yellow spice used in making pastry and also in dyeing starched ruffs and collars   **3 unbaked and doughy** raw and unformed

7 **humble-bee** bumblebee (noisy and useless)   11 **dearest** (1) direst (2) most loving.   **groans of a mother** i.e., pains of childbirth   12 **rooted** firm   17 **herb of grace** rue   18 **not herbs** i.e., not edible salad herbs or greens   18–19 **nose-herbs** fragrant herbs used for bouquets, not salads   20–21 **Nebuchadnezzar . . . grass** (In Daniel 4:28–37, King Nebuchadnezzar is reported to have gone mad and eaten grass like an ox.)   21 **grass** (with a pun on *grace;* the word in the Folio is *grace*)   22 **Whether** which of the two   27 **cozen** cheat   27–28 **do his service** i.e., usurp his sexual role   30 **bauble** stick carried by a court fool (with bawdy suggestion)   32 **subscribe** vouch   35 **No, no, no** i.e., not under the terms of service you have described   39 **English name** i.e., the Black Prince, a widely known name for the eldest son of Edward III who defeated the French   40 **physnomy** physiognomy.   **more hotter** (1) more choleric in the fury of fighting (2) more susceptible to the "French disease," syphilis   45 **suggest** tempt
47 **woodland** rustic

the narrow gate, which I take to be too little for pomp 51
to enter. Some that humble themselves may, but the
many will be too chill and tender, and they'll be for the 53
flowery way that leads to the broad gate and the great 54
fire.

LAFEW   Go thy ways. I begin to be aweary of thee; and 56
I tell thee so before, because I would not fall out with 57
thee. Go thy ways. Let my horses be well looked to,
without any tricks.

LAVATCH   If I put any tricks upon 'em, sir, they shall be
jades' tricks, which are their own right by the law of 61
nature.   *Exit.*

LAFEW   A shrewd knave and an unhappy.   63

COUNTESS   So 'a is. My lord that's gone made himself
much sport out of him. By his authority he remains
here, which he thinks is a patent for his sauciness; and
indeed he has no pace, but runs where he will.   67

LAFEW   I like him well; 'tis not amiss. And I was about
to tell you, since I heard of the good lady's death, and
that my lord your son was upon his return home, I
moved the King my master to speak in the behalf of
my daughter, which, in the minority of them both, His 72
Majesty, out of a self-gracious remembrance, did first 73
propose. His Highness hath promised me to do it, and
to stop up the displeasure he hath conceived against
your son, there is no fitter matter. How does your
ladyship like it?

COUNTESS   With very much content, my lord, and I
wish it happily effected.

LAFEW   His Highness comes post from Marseilles, of as 80
able body as when he numbered thirty. 'A will be here 81
tomorrow, or I am deceived by him that in such 82
intelligence hath seldom failed.   83

COUNTESS   It rejoices me that I hope I shall see him ere 84
I die. I have letters that my son will be here tonight. I
shall beseech your lordship to remain with me till they
meet together.

LAFEW   Madam, I was thinking with what manners I
might safely be admitted.   89

COUNTESS   You need but plead your honorable privi- 90
lege.   91

LAFEW   Lady, of that I have made a bold charter, but I 92
thank my God it holds yet.

Enter Clown [Lavatch].

LAVATCH   O madam, yonder's my lord your son with a
patch of velvet on 's face. Whether there be a scar
under 't or no, the velvet knows, but 'tis a goodly
patch of velvet. His left cheek is a cheek of two pile 97
and a half, but his right cheek is worn bare.   98

LAFEW   A scar nobly got, or a noble scar, is a good livery 99
of honor; so belike is that.   100

LAVATCH   But it is your carbonadoed face.   101

LAFEW   Let us go see your son, I pray you. I long to talk
with the young noble soldier.

LAVATCH   Faith, there's a dozen of 'em, with delicate
fine hats, and most courteous feathers, which bow the
head and nod at every man.   *Exeunt.*

5.1   *Enter Helena, Widow, and Diana, with two attendants.*

HELENA
But this exceeding posting day and night   1
Must wear your spirits low. We cannot help it.
But since you have made the days and nights as one
To wear your gentle limbs in my affairs,   4
Be bold you do so grow in my requital   5
As nothing can unroot you.

Enter a Gentleman.

                                    In happy time!   6
This man may help me to His Majesty's ear,
If he would spend his power.—God save you, sir.   8

GENTLEMAN   And you.

HELENA
Sir, I have seen you in the court of France.

GENTLEMAN   I have been sometimes there.

HELENA
I do presume, sir, that you are not fallen
From the report that goes upon your goodness;
And therefore, goaded with most sharp occasions   14
Which lay nice manners by, I put you to   15
The use of your own virtues, for the which
I shall continue thankful.

GENTLEMAN   What's your will?

HELENA   That it will please you
To give this poor petition to the King
                              [*showing a petition*]
And aid me with that store of power you have
To come into his presence.

GENTLEMAN
The King's not here.

HELENA   Not here, sir?
GENTLEMAN   Not indeed.
  He hence removed last night, and with more haste   23
  Than is his use.
WIDOW   Lord, how we lose our pains!   24
HELENA   All's well that ends well yet,
  Though time seem so adverse and means unfit.
  I do beseech you, whither is he gone?
GENTLEMAN
  Marry, as I take it, to Rossillion,
  Whither I am going.
HELENA   I do beseech you, sir,
  Since you are like to see the King before me,
  Commend the paper to his gracious hand,   31
                          [giving the petition]
  Which I presume shall render you no blame
  But rather make you thank your pains for it.
  I will come after you with what good speed
  Our means will make us means.
GENTLEMAN   This I'll do for you.   35
HELENA
  And you shall find yourself to be well-thanked,
  Whate'er falls more. We must to horse again.—   37
  Go, go, provide.   [Exeunt separately.]

❧

5.2   *Enter Clown [Lavatch], and Parolles.*

PAROLLES   Good Monsieur Lavatch, give my Lord
  Lafew this letter. [He offers a letter.] I have ere now, sir,
  been better known to you, when I have held familiarity with fresher clothes; but I am now, sir, muddied in
  Fortune's mood, and smell somewhat strong of her
  strong displeasure.
LAVATCH   Truly, Fortune's displeasure is but sluttish if
  it smell so strongly as thou speak'st of. I will henceforth eat no fish of Fortune's buttering. Prithee, allow   9
  the wind.   10
PAROLLES   Nay, you need not to stop your nose, sir. I
  spake but by a metaphor.
LAVATCH   Indeed, sir, if your metaphor stink, I will
  stop my nose, or against any man's metaphor.
  Prithee, get thee further.
PAROLLES   Pray you, sir, deliver me this paper.
LAVATCH   Foh! Prithee, stand away. A paper from
  Fortune's close-stool to give to a nobleman! Look, here   18
  he comes himself.

                     Enter Lafew.

  Here is a purr of Fortune's, sir, or of Fortune's cat—but   20

not a musk cat—that has fallen into the unclean fish-   21
  pond of her displeasure, and, as he says, is muddied
  withal. Pray you, sir, use the carp as you may, for he   23
  looks like a poor, decayed, ingenious, foolish, rascally   24
  knave. I do pity his distress in my similes of comfort,   25
  and leave him to your lordship.   [Exit.]
PAROLLES   My lord, I am a man whom Fortune hath
  cruelly scratched.
LAFEW   And what would you have me to do? 'Tis too
  late to pare her nails now. Wherein have you played
  the knave with Fortune that she should scratch you,
  who of herself is a good lady and would not have
  knaves thrive long under her? There's a cardecu for   33
  you. [He gives money.] Let the justices make you and   34
  Fortune friends; I am for other business.
                            [He starts to leave.]
PAROLLES   I beseech your honor to hear me one single
  word.
LAFEW   You beg a single penny more. Come, you shall
  ha 't. Save your word.
PAROLLES   My name, my good lord, is Parolles.
LAFEW   You beg more than "word," then. Cox my   41
  passion! Give me your hand. How does your drum?   42
PAROLLES   O my good lord, you were the first that
  found me!   44
LAFEW   Was I, in sooth? And I was the first that lost   45
  thee.
PAROLLES   It lies in you, my lord, to bring me in some
  grace, for you did bring me out.   48
LAFEW   Out upon thee, knave! Dost thou put upon me
  at once both the office of God and the devil? One
  brings thee in grace and the other brings thee out.
  [Trumpets sound.] The King's coming; I know by his
  trumpets. Sirrah, inquire further after me. I had talk of
  you last night. Though you are a fool and a knave, you
  shall eat. Go to, follow.
PAROLLES   I praise God for you.   [Exeunt.]

❧

5.3   *Flourish. Enter King, Old Lady [Countess],
        Lafew, the two French Lords, with attendants.*

KING
  We lost a jewel of her, and our esteem   1
  Was made much poorer by it; but your son,

---

23 **removed** departed   24 **use** usual practice   31 **Commend** present
as worthy of favorable consideration   35 **Our . . . means** our resources will allow us   37 **falls more** else may happen
5.2. Location: Rossillion.
9 **of Fortune's buttering** i.e., prepared and served by Fortune
9–10 **allow the wind** let me have the windward side of you (since
you have been befouled by evil-smelling Fortune)   18 **close-stool**
privy   20 **purr** (The multiple pun here may include "male child,"
"piece of dung," "the purr of a cat," and the name given to the jack
or knave in the card game post and pair.)

21 **musk cat** musk deer, prized for its musk scent   23 **carp** (1) a fish
often bred in sewage-rich fish ponds or moats (2) a chatterer   24 **ingenious** stupid, lacking in genius or intellect (?)   25 **similes of comfort** comforting or instructive similes   33 **cardecu** quart d'écu, one-
quarter of a French crown   34 **justices** i.e., Justices of the Peace,
responsible in Elizabethan England for tending to the deserving poor
41 **more than "word"** i.e., many words; *Parolles* suggests a plural of
the French *parole*, "word"   41–42 **Cox my passion** i.e., by God's
(Christ's) passion on the cross   44 **found me** found me out   45 **lost**
abandoned (playing on *lost* and *found*)   48 **grace** favor.   **out** out of
favor
5.3. Location: Rossillion.
s.d. Lafew (Lafew may remain onstage from the end of the previous
scene.)   1 **of** in.   **our esteem** my own value

As mad in folly, lacked the sense to know   3
Her estimation home.

COUNTESS   'Tis past, my liege,   4
And I beseech Your Majesty to make it   5
Natural rebellion, done i' the blade of youth,   6
When oil and fire, too strong for reason's force,
O'erbears it and burns on.

KING   My honored lady,
I have forgiven and forgotten all,
Though my revenges were high bent upon him   10
And watched the time to shoot.

LAFEW   This I must say—   11
But first I beg my pardon—the young lord   12
Did to His Majesty, his mother, and his lady
Offense of mighty note, but to himself
The greatest wrong of all. He lost a wife
Whose beauty did astonish the survey   16
Of richest eyes, whose words all ears took captive,   17
Whose dear perfection hearts that scorned to serve
Humbly called mistress.

KING   Praising what is lost
Makes the remembrance dear. Well, call him hither.
We are reconciled, and the first view shall kill
All repetition. Let him not ask our pardon.   22
The nature of his great offense is dead,   23
And deeper than oblivion we do bury
Th' incensing relics of it. Let him approach   25
A stranger, no offender; and inform him   26
So 'tis our will he should.

GENTLEMAN   I shall, my liege.   [Exit.] 27

KING [to Lafew]
What says he to your daughter? Have you spoke?

LAFEW
All that he is hath reference to Your Highness.   29

KING
Then shall we have a match. I have letters sent me
That sets him high in fame.

Enter Count Bertram.

LAFEW   He looks well on 't.
KING   I am not a day of season,   33
For thou mayst see a sunshine and a hail
In me at once. But to the brightest beams
Distracted clouds give way; so stand thou forth.   36
The time is fair again.

BERTRAM   My high-repented blames,   37
Dear sovereign, pardon to me.

KING   All is whole;   38
Not one word more of the consumèd time.   39
Let's take the instant by the forward top;   40
For we are old, and on our quick'st decrees
Th' inaudible and noiseless foot of Time
Steals ere we can effect them. You remember
The daughter of this lord?

BERTRAM   Admiringly, my liege. At first
I stuck my choice upon her, ere my heart   46
Durst make too bold a herald of my tongue;
Where the impression of mine eye infixing,   48
Contempt his scornful perspective did lend me,   49
Which warped the line of every other favor,   50
Scorned a fair color, or expressed it stolen,   51
Extended or contracted all proportions   52
To a most hideous object. Thence it came   53
That she whom all men praised and whom myself,   54
Since I have lost, have loved, was in mine eye
The dust that did offend it.

KING   Well excused.   56
That thou didst love her strikes some scores away
From the great compt. But love that comes too late,   58
Like a remorseful pardon slowly carried,   59
To the great sender turns a sour offense,   60
Crying, "That's good that's gone." Our rash faults
Make trivial price of serious things we have,   62
Not knowing them until we know their grave.   63
Oft our displeasures, to ourselves unjust,   64
Destroy our friends, and after weep their dust;   65
Our own love waking cries to see what's done,
While shameful hate sleeps out the afternoon.   67
Be this sweet Helen's knell, and now forget her.
Send forth your amorous token for fair Maudlin.   69
The main consents are had; and here we'll stay
To see our widower's second marriage day.

COUNTESS
Which better than the first, O dear heaven, bless!
Or, ere they meet, in me, O nature, cesse!   73

LAFEW
Come on, my son, in whom my house's name
Must be digested: give a favor from you   75

3–4 know . . . home appreciate her value fully   5 make account, consider   6 Natural rebellion rebellion by the passions. blade greenness, freshness   10 high bent i.e., as with a fully drawn bow   11 watched waited for   12 But . . . pardon (Lafew ceremoniously begs pardon for expressing an opinion that may seem critical.) 16 astonish the survey dazzle the sight   17 richest i.e., richest in experience   22 repetition rehearsing what is past   23 dead i.e., forgotten   25 incensing relics reminders that kindle anger   26 A stranger i.e., as one whose story is unknown   27 s.p. Gentleman (This could be one of the two French lords or some other person in attendance.) 29 hath reference to defers to   33 of season i.e., of one consistent kind of weather   36 Distracted . . . way clouds disperse and give way   37 high-repented blames sorely repented failings

38 whole mended, well   39 consumèd past   40 take . . . top take time by the forelock   46 stuck fixed   48 Where . . . infixing i.e., the image of her entering first at my eye and then fixing itself in my heart. (Bertram seems to say that he loved Lafew's daughter some time ago but dared not speak of his love and that, on her account, he came to despise all women, especially Helena, who was like an offending speck in his eye, though since then he has learned to love the memory of the wife he lost.)   49 perspective an optical glass for producing distorted images   50 favor face   51 expressed it stolen declared it to be painted cosmetically   52–53 Extended . . . object elongated or compressed all other forms until they made a hideous sight   54 she i.e., Helena   56 offend it (1) give it offense (2) blur its vision   58 compt account, reckoning (with a suggestion of the Day of Judgment)   59 remorseful compassionate. slowly carried i.e., arriving too late   60 turns . . . offense i.e., turns sour on him   62 Make trivial price of greatly undervalue   63 knowing i.e., appreciating. know their grave i.e., are aware of their irrevocable loss   64 displeasures offenses   65 weep their dust mourn over their remains   67 sleeps . . . afternoon i.e., sleeps at ease having done its work   69 Maudlin i.e., Magdalen, the daughter of Lafew   73 ere they meet i.e., before the two marriages come to resemble one another in unhappiness. cesse cease   75 digested swallowed up. favor token

To sparkle in the spirits of my daughter,   76
That she may quickly come. [*Bertram gives a ring.*]
  By my old beard,
And every hair that's on 't, Helen that's dead
Was a sweet creature; such a ring as this,
The last that e'er I took her leave at court,   80
I saw upon her finger.

BERTRAM   Hers it was not.

KING
Now, pray you, let me see it; for mine eye,
While I was speaking, oft was fastened to 't.
                          [*The ring is given to the King.*]
This ring was mine, and when I gave it Helen
I bade her, if her fortunes ever stood   85
Necessitied to help, that by this token   86
I would relieve her. Had you that craft to reave her   87
Of what should stead her most?

BERTRAM   My gracious sovereign, 88
Howe'er it pleases you to take it so,
The ring was never hers.

COUNTESS   Son, on my life,
I have seen her wear it, and she reckoned it
At her life's rate.

LAFEW   I am sure I saw her wear it.   92

BERTRAM
You are deceived, my lord; she never saw it.
In Florence was it from a casement thrown me,
Wrapped in a paper, which contained the name
Of her that threw it. Noble she was, and thought
I stood engaged; but when I had subscribed   97
To mine own fortune, and informed her fully   98
I could not answer in that course of honor   99
As she had made the overture, she ceased   100
In heavy satisfaction, and would never   101
Receive the ring again.

KING   Plutus himself,   102
That knows the tinct and multiplying med'cine,   103
Hath not in nature's mystery more science   104
Than I have in this ring. 'Twas mine, 'twas Helen's,
Whoever gave it you. Then, if you know   106
That you are well acquainted with yourself,   107
Confess 'twas hers, and by what rough enforcement
You got it from her. She called the saints to surety   109
That she would never put it from her finger
Unless she gave it to yourself in bed,
Where you have never come, or sent it us
Upon her great disaster.

BERTRAM   She never saw it. 113

KING
Thou speak'st it falsely, as I love mine honor,
And mak'st conjectural fears to come into me   115
Which I would fain shut out. If it should prove   116
That thou art so inhuman—'twill not prove so,
And yet I know not. Thou didst hate her deadly,
And she is dead, which nothing but to close
Her eyes myself could win me to believe,
More than to see this ring. Take him away.
My forepast proofs, howe'er the matter fall,   122
Shall tax my fears of little vanity,   123
Having vainly feared too little. Away with him!   124
We'll sift this matter further.

BERTRAM   If you shall prove
This ring was ever hers, you shall as easy
Prove that I husbanded her bed in Florence,
Where yet she never was.   [*Exit, guarded.*]

       Enter a Gentleman.

KING
I am wrapped in dismal thinkings.

GENTLEMAN   Gracious sovereign,
Whether I have been to blame or no, I know not.
Here's a petition from a Florentine,   [*giving petition*]
Who hath for four or five removes come short   132
To tender it herself. I undertook it,   133
Vanquished thereto by the fair grace and speech   134
Of the poor suppliant, who by this I know   135
Is here attending. Her business looks in her   136
With an importing visage, and she told me,   137
In a sweet verbal brief, it did concern   138
Your Highness with herself.

KING [*reads*] *a letter* "Upon his many protestations to
  marry me when his wife was dead, I blush to say it,
  he won me. Now is the Count Rossillion a widower,
  his vows are forfeited to me, and my honor's paid to
  him. He stole from Florence, taking no leave, and I
  follow him to his country for justice. Grant it me, O
  King! In you it best lies; otherwise a seducer flourishes, and a poor maid is undone.   Diana Capilet"

LAFEW   I will buy me a son-in-law in a fair, and toll for 148
this. I'll none of him.   149

KING
The heavens have thought well on thee, Lafew,
To bring forth this discovery.—Seek these suitors.   151
Go speedily and bring again the Count.
               [*Exeunt one or more attendants.*]

---

76 To sparkle in i.e., to cheer with its luster   **80 The last** the last
time.   **took her leave** took leave of her   **85 bade her** i.e., bade her
remember   **86 Necessitied to** in need of   **87 reave** deprive, rob
88 stead help   **92 rate** value   **97 engaged** i.e., pledged to her; or,
possibly, not pledged to another. (The Folio spelling, *ingag'd*, may
suggest a negative prefix.)   **97–98 subscribed . . . fortune** i.e., explained my true situation (of my marriage)   **99–100 answer . . .
overture** respond honorably to the proposal (of marriage) that she
honorably made   **101 heavy satisfaction** doleful resignation
102 Plutus the god of wealth   **103 the tinct . . . med'cine** the alchemical elixir for transmuting base metals into gold   **104 science**
knowledge   **106–107 if . . . yourself** i.e., if you are secure in self-
knowledge and are willing to take responsibility for your own
actions (?)   **109 to surety** to witness

113 Upon . . . disaster on the occasion of a disaster to her   **115 conjectural fears** fearful conjectures   **116 fain** willingly   **122 My forepast proofs** the evidence I already have.   **fall** turn out   **123–
124 Shall . . . too little** will hardly censure my fears (concerning
Helena) as inconsequential; indeed, I have foolishly been too little apprehensive   **132 for . . . short** on account of four or five shifts of residence of the court (as it moved from Marseilles to Rossillion) come
too late   **133 tender** offer   **134 Vanquished** won   **135 by this** by this
time   **136 looks** manifests itself   **137 importing** urgent and full of import   **138 brief** summary   **148 in a fair** i.e., where stolen and disreputable merchandise are common. (Lafew says he can do better at
such a place than with Bertram.)   **148–149 toll for this** i.e., put Bertram up for sale. (Merchants wishing to sell at market paid a toll or
fee in order to enter their goods in a register.)   **151 suitors** petitioners

I am afeard the life of Helen, lady,
Was foully snatched.
COUNTESS   Now, justice on the doers!

Enter Bertram [guarded].

KING
I wonder, sir, since wives are monsters to you,
And that you fly them as you swear them lordship,   156
Yet you desire to marry.

Enter Widow [and] Diana.

                          What woman's that?   157
DIANA
I am, my lord, a wretched Florentine,
Derivèd from the ancient Capilet.   159
My suit, as I do understand, you know,
And therefore know how far I may be pitied.
WIDOW
I am her mother, sir, whose age and honor
Both suffer under this complaint we bring,
And both shall cease, without your remedy.   164
KING
Come hither, Count. Do you know these women?
BERTRAM
My lord, I neither can nor will deny
But that I know them. Do they charge me further?
DIANA
Why do you look so strange upon your wife?
BERTRAM
She's none of mine, my lord.
DIANA   If you shall marry,
You give away this hand, and that is mine;   170
You give away heaven's vows, and those are mine;
You give away myself, which is known mine;
For I by vow am so embodied yours
That she which marries you must marry me,
Either both or none.
LAFEW [*to Bertram*]   Your reputation comes too short
for my daughter; you are no husband for her.
BERTRAM
My lord, this is a fond and desperate creature,   178
Whom sometime I have laughed with. Let Your
    Highness
Lay a more noble thought upon mine honor
Than for to think that I would sink it here.
KING
Sir, for my thoughts, you have them ill to friend   182
Till your deeds gain them. Fairer prove your honor
Than in my thought it lies!
DIANA   Good my lord,
Ask him upon his oath if he does think
He had not my virginity.
KING   What sayst thou to her?
BERTRAM   She's impudent, my lord,   188

And was a common gamester to the camp.   189
DIANA
He does me wrong, my lord. If I were so,
He might have bought me at a common price.
Do not believe him. O, behold this ring,
                          [*showing a ring*]
Whose high respect and rich validity   193
Did lack a parallel; yet for all that
He gave it to a commoner o' the camp,
If I be one.
COUNTESS   He blushes, and 'tis hit.   196
Of six preceding ancestors, that gem,
Conferred by testament to th' sequent issue,   198
Hath it been owed and worn. This is his wife;   199
That ring's a thousand proofs.
KING [*to Diana*]   Methought you said
You saw one here in court could witness it.
DIANA
I did, my lord, but loath am to produce
So bad an instrument. His name's Parolles.
LAFEW
I saw the man today, if man he be.
KING
Find him, and bring him hither.   [*Exit an Attendant.*]
BERTRAM   What of him?
He's quoted for a most perfidious slave,   206
With all the spots o' the world taxed and
    debauched,   207
Whose nature sickens but to speak a truth.
Am I or that or this for what he'll utter,   209
That will speak anything?
KING   She hath that ring of yours.
BERTRAM
I think she has. Certain it is I liked her,
And boarded her i' the wanton way of youth.   212
She knew her distance and did angle for me,   213
Madding my eagerness with her restraint,   214
As all impediments in fancy's course   215
Are motives of more fancy; and, in fine,   216
Her infinite cunning, with her modern grace,   217
Subdued me to her rate. She got the ring,   218
And I had that which any inferior might
At market price have bought.
DIANA   I must be patient.
You that have turned off a first so noble wife
May justly diet me. I pray you yet—   222
Since you lack virtue, I will lose a husband—
Send for your ring, I will return it home,
And give me mine again.
BERTRAM   I have it not.
KING [*to Diana*]   What ring was yours, I pray you?

156 as . . . lordship as soon as you swear to be their lord and husband   157 Yet still   159 Derivèd descended   164 both i.e., both
age and honor. (I will die dishonored.)   170 this hand i.e., Bertram's
hand   178 fond foolish   182 for as for.   you . . . friend they are
not well disposed toward you   188 impudent shameless

189 gamester prostitute   193 validity value   196 'tis hit i.e., that
point scored   198 sequent issue next heir   199 owed owned
206 quoted for set down as   207 With . . . debauched censured for
being debauched with all the vices in the world   209 Am I am I to
be considered.   or . . . or either . . . or.   for because of
212 boarded accosted (with sexual meaning)   213 knew her distance
i.e., knew how to keep her distance, knew her value   214 Madding
making mad, exciting   215 fancy's love's   216 motives causes.   fine
conclusion   217 modern commonplace   218 her rate her terms
222 diet restrain

DIANA
Sir, much like the same upon your finger.

KING
Know you this ring? This ring was his of late.

DIANA
And this was it I gave him, being abed.

KING
The story then goes false you threw it him   231
Out of a casement?

DIANA   I have spoke the truth.

Enter Parolles [attended].

BERTRAM
My lord, I do confess the ring was hers.

KING
You boggle shrewdly; every feather starts you.—   234
Is this the man you speak of?

DIANA   Ay, my lord.

KING [*to Parolles*]
Tell me, sirrah—but tell me true, I charge you,
Not fearing the displeasure of your master,
Which on your just proceeding I'll keep off—   238
By him and by this woman here what know you?   239

PAROLLES   So please Your Majesty, my master hath been an honorable gentleman. Tricks he hath had in him, which gentlemen have.

KING   Come, come, to the purpose. Did he love this woman?

PAROLLES   Faith, sir, he did love her; but how?

KING   How, I pray you?

PAROLLES   He did love her, sir, as a gentleman loves a woman.   248

KING   How is that?

PAROLLES   He loved her, sir, and loved her not.   250

KING   As thou art a knave and no knave. What an equivocal companion is this!   252

PAROLLES   I am a poor man, and at Your Majesty's command.

LAFEW   He's a good drum, my lord, but a naughty or- 255
ator.

DIANA   Do you know he promised me marriage?

PAROLLES   Faith, I know more than I'll speak.

KING   But wilt thou not speak all thou know'st?

PAROLLES   Yes, so please Your Majesty. I did go between them, as I said; but more than that, he loved her, for indeed he was mad for her, and talked of Satan and of Limbo and of Furies and I know not what. Yet I was in that credit with them at that time that I knew of 264
their going to bed, and of other motions, as promising 265
her marriage, and things which would derive me ill 266
will to speak of. Therefore I will not speak what I know.

231 The story . . . false the story then is not true that   **234 boggle shrewdly** shy away violently.   **starts** startles   **238 on . . . proceeding** if you speak honestly   **239 By** concerning   **248 woman** i.e., not a gentlewoman   **250 loved her not** i.e., desired her only sexually **252 equivocal companion** equivocating knave   **255 drum** drummer (capable of mere noise).   **naughty** worthless   **264 in . . . with them** so much in their confidence   **265 motions** proposals   **266 derive** gain

KING   Thou hast spoken all already, unless thou canst say they are married. But thou art too fine in thy 269
evidence; therefore stand aside.—
This ring, you say, was yours?

DIANA   Ay, my good lord.

KING
Where did you buy it? Or who gave it you?

DIANA
It was not given me, nor I did not buy it.

KING
Who lent it you?

DIANA   It was not lent me neither.

KING
Where did you find it, then?

DIANA   I found it not.

KING
If it were yours by none of all these ways,
How could you give it him?

DIANA   I never gave it him.

LAFEW   This woman's an easy glove, my lord; she goes off and on at pleasure.

KING
This ring was mine. I gave it his first wife.

DIANA
It might be yours or hers, for aught I know.

KING
Take her away; I do not like her now.
To prison with her. And away with him.—
Unless thou tell'st me where thou hadst this ring,
Thou diest within this hour.

DIANA   I'll never tell you.

KING
Take her away.

DIANA   I'll put in bail, my liege.   286

KING
I think thee now some common customer.   287

DIANA
By Jove, if ever I knew man, 'twas you.   288

KING
Wherefore hast thou accused him all this while?   289

DIANA
Because he's guilty, and he is not guilty.
He knows I am no maid, and he'll swear to 't;
I'll swear I am a maid, and he knows not.
Great King, I am no strumpet, by my life;
I am either maid or else this old man's wife.
                  [*Pointing to Lafew.*]

KING
She does abuse our ears. To prison with her!

DIANA
Good Mother, fetch my bail. [*Exit Widow.*] Stay, royal sir.
The jeweler that owes the ring is sent for,   297
And he shall surety me. But for this lord,   298
Who hath abused me, as he knows himself,

269 fine subtle   **286 put in bail** make bail, i.e., produce evidence to assure my liberty   **287 customer** i.e., prostitute   **288 knew** i.e., sexually   **289 Wherefore** why   **297 owes** owns   **298 surety me** be my security

Though yet he never harmed me, here I quit him.   300
He knows himself my bed he hath defiled,
And at that time he got his wife with child.
Dead though she be, she feels her young one kick.
So there's my riddle: one that's dead is quick—   304
And now behold the meaning.

Enter Helena and Widow.

KING   Is there no exorcist   305
Beguiles the truer office of mine eyes?
Is 't real that I see?

HELENA   No, my good lord,
'Tis but the shadow of a wife you see,
The name and not the thing.

BERTRAM   Both, both. O, pardon!

HELENA
O my good lord, when I was like this maid,   310
I found you wondrous kind. There is your ring,   311
And, look you, here's your letter. [*She produces a
    letter.*] This it says:
"When from my finger you can get this ring
And are by me with child," et cetera. This is done.
Will you be mine, now you are doubly won?

BERTRAM
If she, my liege, can make me know this clearly,
I'll love her dearly, ever, ever dearly.

HELENA
If it appear not plain and prove untrue,
Deadly divorce step between me and you!—   319
O my dear Mother, do I see you living?

LAFEW
Mine eyes smell onions; I shall weep anon.
[*To Parolles.*] Good Tom Drum, lend me a handkerchief.
So, I thank thee. Wait on me home, I'll make sport
with thee. Let thy curtsies alone; they are scurvy ones.

KING
Let us from point to point this story know,
To make the even truth in pleasure flow.   326
[*To Diana.*] If thou be'st yet a fresh uncroppèd
    flower,
Choose thou thy husband, and I'll pay thy dower;
For I can guess that by thy honest aid
Thou kept'st a wife herself, thyself a maid.
Of that and all the progress, more and less,
Resolvedly more leisure shall express.   332
All yet seems well, and if it end so meet,   333
The bitter past, more welcome is the sweet. *Flourish.*   334

300 quit (1) acquit (2) repay   **304 quick** alive (and pregnant)
305 exorcist one who conjures up spirits   **310 like this maid** i.e., disguised as Diana   **311 There** i.e., on Diana's finger (unless Diana has
returned the ring to Helena)   **319 Deadly divorce** divorcing death
326 even precise, plain   **332 Resolvedly** so that all doubts are removed   **333 meet** fittingly   **334 past** being past

[Epilogue]

KING [*advancing*]
The king's a beggar, now the play is done.
All is well ended, if this suit be won,
That you express content; which we will pay,   3
With strife to please you, day exceeding day.   4
Ours be your patience then, and yours our parts;   5
Your gentle hands lend us, and take our hearts.   6
                     Exeunt omnes.

Epilogue
3 express content i.e., applaud   **4 strife** effort   **5 Ours . . . parts**
i.e., we will patiently attend, like an audience, while you undertake
the active role by applauding   **6 hearts** i.e., gratitude

Measure for Measure

"A play Caled Mesur for Mesur" by "Shaxberd" was performed at court, for the new King James I, by "his Maiesties plaiers" on December 26, 1604. Probably it had been composed that same year or in late 1603. The play dates from the very height of Shakespeare's tragic period, three years or so after *Hamlet,* contemporary with *Othello,* shortly before *King Lear* and *Macbeth.* This period includes very little comedy of any sort, and what there is differs markedly from the festive comedy of the 1590s. *Troilus and Cressida* (c. 1601–1602), hovering between satire and tragedy, bleakly portrays a hopeless love affair caught in the toils of a pointless and stalemated war. *All's Well That Ends Well* (c. 1601–1604) resembles *Measure for Measure* in its portrayal of an undeserving protagonist who must be deceived into marriage by the ethically ambiguous trick of substituting one woman for another in the protagonist's bed. *Measure for Measure,* the last such comedy from the tragic period, illustrates most clearly of all what critics usually mean by "problem comedy" or "problem play."

Its chief concern is not with the triumphs of love, as in the happy comedies, but with moral and social problems: "filthy vices" arising from sexual desire and the abuses of judicial authority. Images of disease abound in this play. We see corruption in Vienna "boil and bubble / Till it o'errun the stew" (5.1.326–327). The protagonist, Angelo, is for most of the play a deeply torn character, abhorring his own perverse sinfulness, compulsively driven to an attempted murder in order to cover up his lust for the heroine, Isabella. His soliloquies are introspective, tortured, focused on the psychological horror of an intelligent mind succumbing to criminal desire. The disguised Duke Vincentio, witnessing this fall into depravity and despair, can offer Angelo's intended victims no better philosophical counsel than Christian renunciation of the world and all its vain hopes. Tragedy is averted only by providential intervention and by the harsh trickery of "Craft against vice" (3.2.270), in which the Duke becomes involved as chief manipulator and stage manager. Of the concluding marriages, two are foisted on the bridegrooms (Angelo and Lucio) against their wills, whereas that of the Duke and Isabella jars oddly with his stoical teachings and with her previous determination to be a nun. The end-

ing thus seems arbitrary; both justice and romantic happiness are so perilously achieved in this play that they seem inconsistent with the injustice and lechery that have prevailed until the last.

Yet the very improbability of the ending and the sense of tragedy narrowly averted are perhaps intentional. These features are appropriate, not only for problem comedy, but also for tragicomedy or comedy of forgiveness, overlapping genres toward which Shakespeare gravitated in his late romances. Angelo is, like Leontes in *The Winter's Tale* (or, earlier, like Bertram in *All's Well That Ends Well* or Claudio in *Much Ado About Nothing*), an erring protagonist forgiven in excess of his deserving, spared by a benign, overseeing providence from destroying that which is most precious to him.

The play's title, *Measure for Measure,* introduces a paradox of human justice which this "problem" play cannot wholly resolve. How are fallible humans to judge the sins of their fellow mortals and still obey Christ's injunction of the Sermon on the Mount: "Judge not that ye be not judged"? Three positions emerge from the debate: absolute justice at one extreme, mercy at the other, and equity as a middle ground. Isabella speaks for mercy, and her words ring with biblical authority. Since all humanity would be condemned to eternal darkness were God not merciful as well as just, should not humans also be merciful? The difficulty, however, is that Vienna shows all too clearly the effects of leniency under the kindly Duke. Vice is rampant; stern measures are needed. Though he has not wished to crack the whip himself, the Duke firmly endorses "strict statutes and most biting laws, / The needful bits and curbs to headstrong steeds" (1.3.19–20). To carry out necessary reform, the Duke has chosen Angelo, spokesman for absolute justice, to represent him. Angelo's position is cold but consistent. Only by a literal and impartial administering of the statutes, he maintains, can the law deter potential offenders. If the judge is found guilty, he must pay the penalty as well. One difficulty here, however, is that literal enforcement of the statute on fornication seems ironically to catch the wrong culprits. Claudio and Juliet, who are about to be married and are already joined by a "true contract" of betrothal, are sentenced to the severest limit of the law, whereas the pimps and whores of Vienna's suburbs manage at first to evade punishment entirely. Angelo's deputy, Escalus, can only shake his head in dismay at this unjust result of strict justice. Angelo has not remembered fully the terms of his commission from the Duke: to practice both "Mortality and mercy" in Vienna, to "enforce or qualify the laws / As to your soul seems good." The attributes of a ruler, like those of God, must include "terror" but also "love" (1.1.20–67).

Escalus' compassionate and pragmatic approach to law illustrates equity or the flexible application of the law to particular cases. Because Claudio is only technically guilty (though still guilty), Escalus would pronounce for him a light sentence. Pompey and Mistress Overdone, on the other hand, require vigorous prosecution. The problem of policing vice is compounded by the law's inefficiency, as well as by erring human nature, which will never be wholly tamed. Constable Elbow, like Dogberry in *Much Ado,* is a pompous user of malapropisms, less clever by far than the criminals he would arrest. His evidence against Pompey is so absurdly circumstantial that Escalus is first obliged to let off this engaging pimp with a stern warning. Yet Escalus patiently and tenaciously attends to such proceedings, unlike Angelo, whose interest in the law is too theoretical. Escalus deals with day-to-day problems effectively. He orders reforms of the system by which constables are selected, instructs Elbow in the rudiments of his office, and so proceeds, ultimately, to an effective arrest. Vice is not eliminated; as Pompey defiantly points out, unless someone plans to "geld and splay all the youth of the city," they "will to 't then" (2.1.229–233). Still, vice is held in check. Law can shape the outer person and hope for some inner reform. Even Pompey is taught a trade, albeit a grisly one, as an apprentice hangman. The law must use both "correction" and "instruction."

The solutions arrived at in the comic subplot do not fit the case of Angelo, for he is powerful enough to be above the Viennese law. Indeed, he tries finally to brazen it out, pitting his authority against that of the seemingly friendless Isabella, much like the biblical Elders when justly accused of immorality by the innocent Susannah. Society is on Angelo's side—even the well-meaning Escalus; only providence can rescue the defenseless. The Duke of Vienna, hovering in the background and seeing all that happens, intervenes just at those points when tragedy threatens to become irreversible. Moreover, the Duke is testing those he observes. As he says to Friar Thomas, explaining why he has delegated his power to Angelo: "Hence shall we see, / If power change purpose, what our seemers be" (1.3.53–54). The Duke obviously expects Angelo to fall. Indeed, he has known all along that Angelo had dishonorably repudiated his solemn contract to Mariana when her marriage dowry disappeared at sea (3.1.215–225). Like an all-seeing deity who keeps a reckoning of humanity's good and evil deeds, the Duke has found out Angelo's great weakness. As Angelo confesses, "I perceive Your Grace, like power divine, / Hath looked upon my passes" (5.1.377–378). Paradoxically, however, this seemingly tragic story of temptation and fall yields precious benefits of remorse and humility. Angelo is rescued from his self-made nightmare of seduction, murder, and tyranny. Knowing now that he is prone like other mortals to fleshly weakness, he knows also that he needs spiritual assistance and that, as judge, he ought to use mercy. Seen in retrospect, his panic, despair, and humiliation are curative.

The Duke is no less a problematic character than Angelo, Isabella, and the rest. Vienna's deep corruption is, in part, the result of his unwillingness to bear down on vice, and yet, rather than undertake to remedy the failure himself, this strange "Duke of dark corners" (4.3.157) elects to leave the business to one he suspects will make matters worse. The Duke has a great deal to learn about his own dislike of crowds, his complacent tolerance of human weakness, and his naive supposition that all his subjects speak well of him. He is a highly manipulative character, the one most responsible in the play for the ethically dubious solutions through which craft must be employed against vice. The comforting words of spiritual counsel he offers Claudio, Juliet, and the rest are spoken by a secular ruler fraudulently disguised as a friar. Certainly, the Duke is no allegorized god-figure, for all his omniscience and final role as both punisher and forgiver. As *deux ex machina* of this problem comedy, the Duke is human, frail, and vulnerable—as indeed he ought to be in a play that explores with such rich complexity the ironic distance between divine and human justice.

Yet, for all his manifest and even comic weaknesses, the Duke is finally the authority figure who must attempt to bring order to the imperfect world of Vienna. The devices he employs, including the bed trick, seem morally questionable and yet are palpable comic fictions that unmistakably notify us what genre we are watching. If the Duke's role is more that of artist than ruler or diety, his being so is appropriate to the artistically contrived and theatrical world that Shakespeare presents to us. Within the world of this play, the disguised Duke's chief function is to test the other characters and to mislead them intentionally into expecting the worst, in order to try their resolve. On a comic level, he exposes the amiable but loose-tongued Lucio as a slanderer against the Duke himself and devises for Lucio a suitably satirical exposure and witty punishment. More seriously, as confessor to Juliet, he assures her that her beloved Claudio must die on the morrow. As she ought, she penitentially accepts "shame with joy" and so is cleansed (2.3.37). Because the Duke is not really a friar, he does not have the spiritual authority to do this, and the ruse strikes us as theatrical, employing devices of illusion that actors and dramatists use. Even so, it provides real comfort for Juliet. The very theatricality of the illusion, by reminding us that we are in the theater, enables us to see the Duke as a kind of morally persuasive playwright who can change the lives of his characters for the better.

Similarly, the counsel of Christian renunciation offered to Claudio by the bogus friar (3.1) is at once illusory and comforting. The Duke's poignant reflection on the vanity of human striving is made ironic but not invalid by our awareness that we are viewing a deception with an ultimately benign purpose—that of persuading Claudio to see matters in their true perspective. The Duke characterizes life as a breath, a dreamlike "after-dinner's sleep," a fever of inconstancy in which timorous humans long fretfully for what they do not have and spurn those things they have. Claudio responds as he ought, resolving to "find life" by "seeking death" (3.1.5–43). He achieves this calm, however, in the face of certain execution; ironically, what he must then learn to overmaster is the desperate hope of living by means of his sister's dishonor. Claudio is broken by this test and perversely begs for a few years of guilty life at the cost of eternal shame for himself and Isabella. From this harrowing experience, he emerges at length with a better understanding of his own weakness and a greater compassion toward the weakness of others.

The searing encounter between Claudio and Isabella puts her to the test as well, and her response seems hysterical and no doubt prudish to modern audiences. She has much to learn about the complexities of human behavior. Although she is sincere in protesting that she would lay down her life for her brother and is correct, in the play's terms, to prefer virtue to mere existence, her tone is too strident. Like other major characters, she must be humbled before she can rise. She and Claudio must heed the Duke's essential admonition: "Do not satisfy your resolution with hopes that are fallible" (3.1.170–171). Only then, paradoxically, can Isabella and Claudio go on to achieve earthly happiness.

Isabella and Angelo are paradoxically alike. Both have retreated from the world of carnal pleasure into havens they regard as safe but that turn out not to work in the way they had hoped. Isabella longs for the restraints of the sisterhood into which she is about to enter. Her suspicions about human frailty can be seen in her testing of her brother; she fears he will fail her by begging life at the cost of her eternal shame, and when he does just that, she reacts with shrill condemnation and even hatred. This is a dark moment for Isabella, and she needs the spiritual counsel of the disguised Duke to enable her to forgive not only her brother but also herself. Angelo, meanwhile, has attempted to put down the rebellion of the flesh by suppressing and denying all such feeling in himself. We see him at first as the workaholic official who is not hesitant to condemn in others what he believes he is free of personally. He cherishes restraint as much as Isabella does, and that is why he is so terrified when the apparent absence of his only superior, the Duke, opens up to him the abyss of his own licentiousness. Once his word is law, Angelo perceives that he can play the tyrant and seducer without check. He is horrified to discover, not only that he has ungovernable sexual longings within him, but also that they perversely direct themselves toward a woman who is virginal and saintly. Why does he yearn to "raze the sanctuary" thus (2.2.178)? The revelation to him of his own innate evil is virtually tragic in the intensity of his self-loathing, and yet, in this strange comedy, this revelation is a first step toward coming to terms with his reprobate self. Until Angelo acknowledges the carnal within, he cannot begin looking for a way to understand and accept this frailty. The Duke's test provides the means of self-discovery that Angelo cannot fashion on his own.

In her final testing, Isabella shows greatness of spirit. Here, Shakespeare significantly alters his chief sources, George Whetstone's *Promos and Cassandra* (1578), Giovanni Baptista Giraldi Cinthio's *Hecatommithi*, and Whetstone's *Heptameron of Civil Discourses*. In all these versions, the character corresponding to Angelo does actually ravish the heroine, and in the *Hecatommithi* he also murders her brother. Shakespeare, by withholding these irreversible acts, not only gives to Angelo a technical innocence, but also allows the Duke, as *deus ex machina*, to practice virtuous deception on Isabella one more time. Can she forgive the supposed murderer of her brother? Her affirmative answer confutes the Old Testament ethic of "An Angelo for Claudio, death for death" whereby "Like doth quit like, and measure still for measure" (5.1.417–419). Although Angelo concedes that he deserves to die for what he intended, the forfeit need not be paid so long as humanity can reveal itself capable of Isabella's godlike mercy.

With its apparently unsuitable marriages and its improbable plotting, *Measure for Measure* does end by dealing directly with the problems of human nature confronted in the earlier scenes. The bed trick (switching Mariana for Isabella) may seem a legalistic and contrived way to bring Angelo to terms with his own carnality, but it is instructive, not only to him, but also to Isabella; she, like Angelo, must learn to accept the realities of the human condition. By helping Mariana to achieve her legitimate desire to couple and marry, Isabella sees into her own need. Her begging for Angelo's life is not merely an act of forgiveness to an enemy; it is a gift of continued marriage to Mariana. This realization helps to prepare Isabella herself for a marriage that, although dramatically surprising on stage (and even rejected by her in some modern productions), may be intended to demonstrate her having given up the cloistered life for all that marriage signifies. *Measure for Measure* is thus essentially comic (unlike *Troilus and Cressida*), despite its harrowing scenes of conflict and its awareness of vice everywhere in human nature. The play celebrates the *felix culpa* of human nature, the fall from grace that is an integral part of humanity's rise to happiness and self-knowledge. Throughout, in the play's finest scenes, poignancy is tempered by a wit and humor that are ultimately gracious. The formal and substantive emphasis on marriage stresses not just the benefits of remorse and humility but also the real possibility of psychic and spiritual growth: Isabella can acknowledge that she is a woman, Angelo can be genuinely freed from repression, and Claudio can value life more intensely because he has confronted death. All these recognitions affirm the acceptance and proper use of the physical and sexual side of human nature, and yet they are achieved only through charity and forgiveness. Humanity can learn, however slowly and painfully, that the talents entrusted to it by providence are to be used wisely.

Measure
for
Measure

The Names of All the Actors

VINCENTIO, *the Duke*
ANGELO, *the deputy*
ESCALUS, *an ancient lord*
CLAUDIO, *a young gentleman*
LUCIO, *a fantastic*
Two other like GENTLEMEN
PROVOST
THOMAS, } *two friars*
PETER, }
[A JUSTICE]
[VARRIUS, *a friend of the Duke*]

ELBOW, *a simple constable*
FROTH, *a foolish gentleman*
CLOWN [POMPEY, *a servant to Mistress Overdone*]
ABHORSON, *an executioner*
BARNARDINE, *a dissolute prisoner*

ISABELLA, *sister to Claudio*
MARIANA, *betrothed to Angelo*
JULIET, *beloved of Claudio*
FRANCISCA, *a nun*
MISTRESS OVERDONE, *a bawd*

[A SERVANT *of Angelo*
BOY *singer*
A MESSENGER *from Angelo*

Lords, Officers, Citizens, Servants, and other Attendants]

SCENE: *Vienna*

1.1 *Enter Duke, Escalus, lords, [and attendants].*

DUKE Escalus.
ESCALUS My lord.
DUKE
Of government the properties to unfold   3
Would seem in me t' affect speech and discourse,   4
Since I am put to know that your own science   5
Exceeds, in that, the lists of all advice   6

My strength can give you. Then no more remains   7
But that to your sufficiency   8
 . . . . as your worth is able,   9
And let them work. The nature of our people,
Our city's institutions, and the terms   11
For common justice, you're as pregnant in
As art and practice hath enrichèd any   13
That we remember. There is our commission,
  [*giving a paper*]
From which we would not have you warp.—Call
  hither,   15
I say, bid come before us Angelo.   [*Exit one.*]
What figure of us think you he will bear?   17
For you must know, we have with special soul   18
Elected him our absence to supply,   19
Lent him our terror, dressed him with our love,   20
And given his deputation all the organs   21
Of our own power. What think you of it?
ESCALUS
If any in Vienna be of worth
To undergo such ample grace and honor,   24
It is Lord Angelo.

    Enter Angelo.

DUKE   Look where he comes.
ANGELO
Always obedient to Your Grace's will,
I come to know your pleasure.
DUKE   Angelo,
There is a kind of character in thy life   28
That to th' observer doth thy history
Fully unfold. Thyself and thy belongings   30
Are not thine own so proper as to waste   31
Thyself upon thy virtues, they on thee.   32
Heaven doth with us as we with torches do,   33
Not light them for themselves; for if our virtues
Did not go forth of us, 'twere all alike   35
As if we had them not. Spirits are not finely touched   36
But to fine issues, nor Nature never lends   37
The smallest scruple of her excellence   38
But, like a thrifty goddess, she determines   39
Herself the glory of a creditor,   40
Both thanks and use. But I do bend my speech   41

1.1. Location: Vienna. The court of Duke Vincentio.
3 Of . . . unfold to explain the qualities needed in governing well
4 seem . . . discourse i.e., make me seem enamored of the sound of
my own voice **5 put to know** obliged to admit. **science** knowledge
6 that i.e., properties of government (line 3). **lists** limits

7 strength power of mind **8–9 But . . . able** (The passage appears
in the Folio as a single line. Several attempts at emendation have
been made, but the most plausible explanation is that something has
been deleted or inadvertently omitted.) **11 terms** terms of court; or,
modes of procedure **13 art** learning, theory **15 warp** deviate
17 What . . . bear i.e., how do you think he will do as my substitute
18 special soul all the powers of the mind; whole heart **19 Elected**
chosen. **supply** fill, make up for **20 terror** power to inspire awe
and fear **21 his deputation** him as deputy. **organs** instruments
24 undergo bear the weight of **28 character** writing **30 belongings**
attributes, endowments **31 proper** exclusively **31–32 as to . . .
thee** that you can expend all your efforts on your own talents or use
them solely for your own advantage **33 torches** (Compare Jesus'
command that we not hide our light under a bushel, Matthew 5:14–
16.) **35 forth of us** out of us and into the world. **'twere all alike** it
would be exactly the same **36 Spirits** souls. **finely touched** excellently endowed and tested **37 fine issues** noble purposes **38 scruple** bit. (Literally, a small weight.) **39 determines** assumes **40 Herself** for herself. **glory** privileges **41 use** interest. **bend** direct

To one that can my part in him advertise.   42
Hold, therefore, Angelo:
In our remove be thou at full ourself.   44
Mortality and mercy in Vienna   45
Live in thy tongue and heart. Old Escalus,
Though first in question, is thy secondary.   47
Take thy commission.   [*He gives a paper.*]

ANGELO   Now, good my lord,
Let there be some more test made of my mettle   49
Before so noble and so great a figure
Be stamped upon it.

DUKE   No more evasion.
We have with a leavened and preparèd choice   52
Proceeded to you; therefore take your honors.
Our haste from hence is of so quick condition   54
That it prefers itself and leaves unquestioned   55
Matters of needful value. We shall write to you,
As time and our concernings shall importune,   57
How it goes with us, and do look to know   58
What doth befall you here. So, fare you well.
To th' hopeful execution do I leave you   60
Of your commissions.

ANGELO   Yet give leave, my lord,   61
That we may bring you something on the way.   62

DUKE   My haste may not admit it;   63
Nor need you, on mine honor, have to do   64
With any scruple. Your scope is as mine own,   65
So to enforce or qualify the laws
As to your soul seems good. Give me your hand.
I'll privily away. I love the people   68
But do not like to stage me to their eyes;   69
Though it do well, I do not relish well   70
Their loud applause and "aves" vehement,   71
Nor do I think the man of safe discretion   72
That does affect it. Once more, fare you well.   73

ANGELO
The heavens give safety to your purposes!

ESCALUS
Lead forth and bring you back in happiness!   75

DUKE   I thank you. Fare you well.   *Exit.*

ESCALUS
I shall desire you, sir, to give me leave
To have free speech with you; and it concerns me   78

To look into the bottom of my place.   79
A power I have, but of what strength and nature
I am not yet instructed.

ANGELO
'Tis so with me. Let us withdraw together,
And we may soon our satisfaction have
Touching that point.

ESCALUS   I'll wait upon your honor.

                                              Exeunt.

❖

1.2   *Enter Lucio and two other Gentlemen.*

LUCIO   If the Duke with the other dukes come not to
composition with the King of Hungary, why then all   2
the dukes fall upon the King.   3

FIRST GENTLEMAN   Heaven grant us its peace, but not
the King of Hungary's!

SECOND GENTLEMAN   Amen.

LUCIO   Thou conclud'st like the sanctimonious pirate
that went to sea with the Ten Commandments but
scraped one out of the table.   9

SECOND GENTLEMAN   "Thou shalt not steal"?

LUCIO   Ay, that he razed.   11

FIRST GENTLEMAN   Why, 'twas a commandment to
command the captain and all the rest from their function; they put forth to steal. There's not a soldier of   14
us all that, in the thanksgiving before meat, do relish   15
the petition well that prays for peace.

SECOND GENTLEMAN   I never heard any soldier dislike it.

LUCIO   I believe thee, for I think thou never wast where
grace was said.

SECOND GENTLEMAN   No? A dozen times at least.

FIRST GENTLEMAN   What, in meter?

LUCIO   In any proportion or in any language.   22

FIRST GENTLEMAN   I think, or in any religion.

LUCIO   Ay, why not? Grace is grace, despite of all   24
controversy; as, for example, thou thyself art a wicked
villain, despite of all grace.

FIRST GENTLEMAN   Well, there went but a pair of shears   27
between us.   28

LUCIO   I grant; as there may between the lists and the   29
velvet. Thou art the list.   30

FIRST GENTLEMAN   And thou the velvet. Thou art good
velvet; thou'rt a three-piled piece, I warrant thee. I had   32

42 that . . . advertise who can instruct that part of me now vested in him, i.e., who knows already what I have to say   **44 remove** absence.   **at full** in every respect.   **ourself** i.e., myself. (The royal plural.)   **45 Mortality** the full rigor of the law, the death sentence   **47 first in question** senior and first appointed   **49 mettle** substance, quality (with play on "metal," a common variant spelling, continued in the coining imagery of lines 50–51)   **52 leavened** i.e., carefully considered (just as yeast is given time to leaven dough)   **54–55 Our . . . itself** the cause for my hasty departure is so urgent (*quick*) that it takes precedence over all other matters   **55 unquestioned** not yet considered   **57 concernings** affairs.   **importune** urge   **58 look to know** expect to be informed   **60 hopeful** exciting hopes of success.   **execution** carrying out   **61 leave** permission   **62 bring you something** accompany you for a short distance   **63 admit** permit   **64 have to do** have concern   **65 scruple** misgiving   **68 I'll privily away** I'll go away secretly   **69 stage me** make a show of myself   **70 do well** i.e., serves a political purpose   **71 aves** hails of acclamation   **72 safe** sound   **73 affect** desire, court   **75 Lead** may they conduct you   **78 free** frank

79 the bottom of my place the extent of my commission
1.2. Location: A public place.
2 composition agreement   **3 fall upon** attack   **9 table** tablet
11 razed scraped out. (The word may also suggest *rased*, "erased.")
14 put forth set out to sea   **15 thanksgiving** prayer of thanksgiving, grace.   **meat** the meal   **22 proportion** form   **24 Grace is grace** (Refers to the Catholic-Protestant *controversy*, line 25, as to whether humanity can be saved by works or by grace alone; with punning on *grace* as "thanks for a meal," line 19, and "gracefulness" or "becomingness," line 26.)   **27–28 there . . . between us** i.e., we're cut from the same cloth   **29–30 as . . . list** (Lucio jokes that the shears might also cut between, i.e., distinguish between, the mere *lists* or selvages, edges of a woven fabric, and the *velvet* betokening a true gentleman. Lucio wittily asserts himself to be a true gentleman; the other, not.)   **32 three-piled** having a threefold pile or nap (the best grade of velvet)

as lief be a list of an English kersey as be piled, as thou 33
art piled, for a French velvet. Do I speak feelingly now? 34

LUCIO   I think thou dost, and indeed with most painful
feeling of thy speech. I will, out of thine own confession, learn to begin thy health but, whilst I live, forget 37
to drink after thee. 38

FIRST GENTLEMAN   I think I have done myself wrong, 39
have I not?

SECOND GENTLEMAN   Yes, that thou hast, whether
thou art tainted or free. 42

Enter bawd [Mistress Overdone].

LUCIO   Behold, behold, where Madam Mitigation 43
comes! I have purchased as many diseases under her
roof as come to—

SECOND GENTLEMAN   To what, I pray?

LUCIO   Judge. 47

SECOND GENTLEMAN   To three thousand dolors a year. 48

FIRST GENTLEMAN   Ay, and more.

LUCIO   A French crown more. 50

FIRST GENTLEMAN   Thou art always figuring diseases in 51
me, but thou art full of error. I am sound.

LUCIO   Nay, not, as one would say, healthy, but so
sound as things that are hollow. Thy bones are 54
hollow; impiety has made a feast of thee. 55

FIRST GENTLEMAN [*to Mistress Overdone*]   How now,
which of your hips has the most profound sciatica? 57

MISTRESS OVERDONE   Well, well; there's one yonder
arrested and carried to prison was worth five thousand of you all.

SECOND GENTLEMAN   Who's that, I pray thee?

MISTRESS OVERDONE   Marry, sir, that's Claudio, Signor 62
Claudio.

FIRST GENTLEMAN   Claudio to prison? 'Tis not so.

MISTRESS OVERDONE   Nay, but I know 'tis so. I saw him
arrested, saw him carried away; and, which is more, 66
within these three days his head to be chopped off.

LUCIO   But, after all this fooling, I would not have it so. 68
Art thou sure of this?

MISTRESS OVERDONE   I am too sure of it; and it is for
getting Madam Julietta with child.

LUCIO   Believe me, this may be. He promised to meet
me two hours since, and he was ever precise in 73
promise-keeping.

SECOND GENTLEMAN   Besides, you know, it draws 75
something near to the speech we had to such a 76
purpose.

FIRST GENTLEMAN   But most of all agreeing with the
proclamation.

LUCIO   Away! Let's go learn the truth of it.
                 Exit [Lucio with the Gentlemen].

MISTRESS OVERDONE   Thus, what with the war, what
with the sweat, what with the gallows, and what with 82
poverty, I am custom-shrunk. 83

Enter Clown [Pompey].

How now, what's the news with you?

POMPEY   Yonder man is carried to prison.

MISTRESS OVERDONE   Well, what has he done? 86

POMPEY   A woman.

MISTRESS OVERDONE   But what's his offense?

POMPEY   Groping for trouts in a peculiar river. 89

MISTRESS OVERDONE   What? Is there a maid with child
by him?

POMPEY   No, but there's a woman with maid by him. 92
You have not heard of the proclamation, have you?

MISTRESS OVERDONE   What proclamation, man?

POMPEY   All houses in the suburbs of Vienna must be 95
plucked down.

MISTRESS OVERDONE   And what shall become of those
in the city?

POMPEY   They shall stand for seed. They had gone 99
down too, but that a wise burgher put in for them. 100

MISTRESS OVERDONE   But shall all our houses of resort
in the suburbs be pulled down?

POMPEY   To the ground, mistress.

MISTRESS OVERDONE   Why, here's a change indeed in
the commonwealth! What shall become of me?

POMPEY   Come, fear not you. Good counselors lack no 106
clients. Though you change your place, you need not
change your trade; I'll be your tapster still. Courage! 108
There will be pity taken on you. You that have worn 109
your eyes almost out in the service, you will be con- 110
sidered.

---

33 **as lief** as soon, rather.   **kersey** a coarse woolen fabric. (The First
Gentleman turns the joke on Lucio by saying he would rather be a
plain, homespun Englishman than a Frenchified velvet gentleman in
decay and threadbare. *Velvet* suggests prostitutes and venereal disease, as in the following notes.)   **be piled** (1) have a cloth nap (2)
suffer from hemorrhoids (3) be pilled or peeled, i.e., hairless, bald, as
a result of mercury treatment for venereal disease (known as the
"French disease"; see *French velvet* in the next line and *French
crown*, line 50)   **34 feelingly** with pathos, so as to hit home. (But
Lucio's reply quibbles on "painfully," meaning the Gentleman's
mouth is affected by the French disease; hence, Lucio will not drink
from the same cup after him.)   **37 begin thy health** begin drinking to
your health   **37–38 forget . . . thee** take care not to drink from your
cup   **39 done myself wrong** i.e., asked for that   **42 tainted** infected
43 Mitigation (So called because her function is to relieve desire.)
47 Judge guess   **48 dolors** (quibbling on *dollars;* spelled *Dollours* in
the Folio)   **50 French crown** (1) gold coin (2) bald head incurred
through syphilis, the "French disease"   **51 figuring** (1) imagining (2)
reckoning (recalling the monetary puns of lines 48 and 50)   **54 sound**
(1) healthy (2) resounding (because of hollow bones caused by syphilis)   **55 impiety** wickedness   **57 sciatica** a disease affecting the sciatic
nerve in the hip and thigh, thought to be a symptom of syphilis
62 Marry i.e., by the Virgin Mary   **66 which** what   **68 after**
notwithstanding

73 **ever** always   **75–76 draws . . . near to** approaches, sounds
somewhat like   **76–77 to . . . purpose** on that topic   **82 sweat**
sweating sickness; a form of the plague   **83 custom-shrunk** having
fewer customers   **86 done** (Pompey quibbles in line 87 on a sexual
sense of the word, present also in Mistress Overdone's name.)
89 peculiar privately owned (with bawdy suggestion)   **92 woman
with maid** (Pompey playfully corrects Mistress Overdone's use of the
word "maid," joking that a pregnant woman cannot be a virgin
[*maid*] though the child she carries is one.)   **95 houses** i.e., brothels.
suburbs (Location of the brothels in Shakespeare's London, as in other
walled cities.)   **99 for seed** to preserve the species (with ribald pun)
100 burgher citizen.   **put . . . them** interceded on their behalf, offered to acquire them   **106 counselors** counseling lawyers   **108 tapster** one who draws beer in an alehouse   **109–110 worn . . . out**
i.e., worked so hard (perhaps with an ironic reference to the traditional image of the blind Cupid)

MISTRESS OVERDONE   What's to do here, Thomas Tapster? Let's withdraw.
POMPEY   Here comes Signor Claudio, led by the Pro-   114
vost to prison; and there's Madam Juliet.   *Exeunt.*   115

*Enter Provost, Claudio, Juliet, Officers; Lucio and
two Gentlemen [follow].*

CLAUDIO [*to the Provost*]
paraoling around
Fellow, why dost thou show me thus to the world?
Bear me to prison, where I am committed.
PROVOST
I do it not in evil disposition
But from Lord Angelo by special charge.
CLAUDIO
Thus can the demigod Authority
Make us pay down for our offense, by weight,   121
The words of heaven. On whom it will, it will;   122
On whom it will not, so; yet still 'tis just.   123
LUCIO
Why, how now, Claudio? Whence comes this
restraint?
CLAUDIO
From too much liberty, my Lucio, liberty.
As surfeit is the father of much fast,   126
So every scope, by the immoderate use,   127
Turns to restraint. Our natures do pursue,
Like rats that ravin down their proper bane,   129
A thirsty evil, and when we drink we die.
LUCIO   If I could speak so wisely under an arrest, I
would send for certain of my creditors. And yet, to say   132
the truth, I had as lief have the foppery of freedom as   133
the morality of imprisonment. What's thy offense,
Claudio?
CLAUDIO
What but to speak of would offend again.
LUCIO
What, is 't murder?
CLAUDIO   No.
LUCIO   Lechery?
CLAUDIO
Call it so.
PROVOST   Away, sir, you must go.
CLAUDIO
One word, good friend.—Lucio, a word with you.
LUCIO
A hundred, if they'll do you any good.
Is lechery so looked after?   141
CLAUDIO
Thus stands it with me: upon a true contract   142

I got possession of Julietta's bed.
You know the lady; she is fast my wife,   144
Save that we do the denunciation lack   145
Of outward order. This we came not to,   146
Only for propagation of a dower   147
Remaining in the coffer of her friends,   148
From whom we thought it meet to hide our love
Till time had made them for us. But it chances   150
The stealth of our most mutual entertainment
With character too gross is writ on Juliet.   152
LUCIO
With child, perhaps?
CLAUDIO   Unhappily, even so.
And the new deputy now for the Duke—
Whether it be the fault and glimpse of newness,   155
Or whether that the body public be
A horse whereon the governor doth ride,   *injustice*
Who, newly in the seat, that it may know
He can command, lets it straight feel the spur;   159
Whether the tyranny be in his place,   160
Or in his eminence that fills it up,   161
I stagger in—but this new governor   162
Awakes me all the enrollèd penalties   163
Which have, like unscoured armor, hung by the wall
So long that nineteen zodiacs have gone round   165
And none of them been worn; and for a name   166
Now puts the drowsy and neglected act
Freshly on me. 'Tis surely for a name.
LUCIO   I warrant it is, and thy head stands so tickle on   169
thy shoulders that a milkmaid, if she be in love, may
sigh it off. Send after the Duke and appeal to him.
CLAUDIO
I have done so, but he's not to be found.
I prithee, Lucio, do me this kind service:
This day my sister should the cloister enter   174
And there receive her approbation.   175
Acquaint her with the danger of my state;
Implore her, in my voice, that she make friends
To the strict deputy; bid herself assay him.   178
I have great hope in that, for in her youth
There is a prone and speechless dialect   180
Such as move men; besides, she hath prosperous art   181
When she will play with reason and discourse,
And well she can persuade.
LUCIO   I pray she may, as well for the encouragement of
the like, which else would stand under grievous im-   185
position, as for the enjoying of thy life, who I would   186

114–115 **Provost** officer charged with apprehension, custody, and
punishment of offenders   **121–123 pay . . . so** pay the full penalty
for our offense called for in the Bible (Romans 9:18): "Therefore hath
he [God] mercy on whom he will have mercy, and whom he will
hardeneth"   **126 surfeit** excess.   **fast** abstinence   **127 scope** freedom   **129 ravin . . . bane** greedily devour what is poisonous to
them   **132 creditors** (who would arrest me for debt)   **133 lief** willingly.   **foppery** folly   **141 looked after** kept under observation
142 a true contract i.e., one made in the presence of witnesses,
though without a religious ceremony. (Such a precontract was binding
but, in the eyes of the Church, did not confer the right of sexual consummation before the nuptials.)

144 **fast my wife** i.e., firmly bound by precontract   **145 denunciation**
formal declaration   **146 outward order** public ceremony   **147 propa-**
gation increase, begetting   **148 friends** relatives   **150 made . . . us**
disposed them in our favor   **152 character too gross** writing too evident   **155 the fault . . . newness** the faulty flashiness of novelty
159 straight at once   **160 in his place** inherent in the office   **161 his**
eminence the eminence of him   **162 I stagger in** I am uncertain
163 Awakes me i.e., awakes, activates. (*Me* is used colloquially.)
enrollèd written on a roll or deed   **165 zodiacs** i.e., years   **166 for a**
name for reputation's sake   **169 tickle** uncertain, unstable   **174 clois-**
ter i.e., convent   **175 approbation** novitiate, period of probation
178 To with.   **assay** try, test   **180 prone** eager, apt, supplicating.
dialect language   **181 prosperous art** skill or ability to gain favorable
results   **185 the like** i.e., similar offenders.   **else** otherwise   **185–**
186 imposition accusation

be sorry should be thus foolishly lost at a game of tick- 187
tack. I'll to her.   188

CLAUDIO   I thank you, good friend Lucio.
LUCIO   Within two hours.
CLAUDIO   Come, officer, away!   *Exeunt.*

❧

1.3   *Enter Duke and Friar Thomas.*

DUKE
No, holy Father, throw away that thought;
Believe not that the dribbling dart of love   2
Can pierce a complete bosom. Why I desire thee   3
To give me secret harbor hath a purpose   4
More grave and wrinkled than the aims and ends   5
Of burning youth.
FRIAR THOMAS   May Your Grace speak of it?
DUKE
My holy sir, none better knows than you
How I have ever loved the life removed   8
And held in idle price to haunt assemblies   9
Where youth and cost witless bravery keeps.   10
I have delivered to Lord Angelo,
A man of stricture and firm abstinence,   12
My absolute power and place here in Vienna,
And he supposes me traveled to Poland;
For so I have strewed it in the common ear,
And so it is received. Now, pious sir,
You will demand of me why I do this.
FRIAR THOMAS   Gladly, my lord.
DUKE
We have strict statutes and most biting laws,
The needful bits and curbs to headstrong steeds, 20
Which for this fourteen years we have let slip, 21
Even like an o'ergrown lion in a cave   22
That goes not out to prey. Now, as fond fathers, 23
Having bound up the threatening twigs of birch
Only to stick it in their children's sight
For terror, not to use, in time the rod
Becomes more mocked than feared, so our decrees,
Dead to infliction, to themselves are dead;   28
And liberty plucks justice by the nose,   29
The baby beats the nurse, and quite athwart   30
Goes all decorum.
FRIAR THOMAS   It rested in Your Grace   31
To unloose this tied-up justice when you pleased;

And it in you more dreadful would have seemed
Than in Lord Angelo.
DUKE   I do fear, too dreadful.
Sith 'twas my fault to give the people scope,   35
'Twould be my tyranny to strike and gall them   36
For what I bid them do; for we bid this be done 37
When evil deeds have their permissive pass   38
And not the punishment. Therefore indeed, my
   father,
I have on Angelo imposed the office,   40
Who may in th' ambush of my name strike home,   41
And yet my nature never in the fight   42
To do in slander. And to behold his sway   43
I will, as 'twere a brother of your order,
Visit both prince and people. Therefore, I prithee,
Supply me with the habit, and instruct me
How I may formally in person bear   47
Like a true friar. More reasons for this action
At our more leisure shall I render you.   49
Only this one: Lord Angelo is precise,   50
Stands at a guard with envy, scarce confesses   51
That his blood flows or that his appetite   52
Is more to bread than stone. Hence shall we see, 53
If power change purpose, what our seemers be.
                                        Exeunt.

❧

1.4   *Enter Isabella and Francisca, a nun.*

ISABELLA
And have you nuns no farther privileges?
FRANCISCA   Are not these large enough?
ISABELLA
Yes, truly. I speak not as desiring more,
But rather wishing a more strict restraint
Upon the sisterhood, the votarists of Saint Clare. 5
LUCIO (*within*)
Ho! Peace be in this place!
ISABELLA   Who's that which calls?
FRANCISCA
It is a man's voice. Gentle Isabella,
Turn you the key, and know his business of him.
You may, I may not; you are yet unsworn.   9
When you have vowed, you must not speak with
   men
But in the presence of the prioress;

Then if you speak you must not show your face,
Or if you show your face you must not speak.
He calls again. I pray you, answer him.   [*Exit.*]

ISABELLA
Peace and prosperity! Who is 't that calls?

[*She opens the door. Enter Lucio.*]

LUCIO
Hail, virgin, if you be, as those cheek roses   16
Proclaim you are no less. Can you so stead me   17
As bring me to the sight of Isabella,   18
A novice of this place, and the fair sister
To her unhappy brother Claudio?   20

ISABELLA
Why "her unhappy brother"? Let me ask,
The rather for I now must make you know   22
I am that Isabella, and his sister.

LUCIO
Gentle and fair, your brother kindly greets you.
Not to be weary with you, he's in prison.   25

ISABELLA   Woe me! For what?

LUCIO
For that which, if myself might be his judge,
He should receive his punishment in thanks:
He hath got his friend with child.

ISABELLA
Sir, make me not your story.

LUCIO   'Tis true.   30
I would not—though 'tis my familiar sin   31
With maids to seem the lapwing, and to jest,   32
Tongue far from heart—play with all virgins so.
I hold you as a thing enskied and sainted   34
By your renouncement, an immortal spirit
And to be talked with in sincerity
As with a saint.

ISABELLA
You do blaspheme the good in mocking me.   38

LUCIO
Do not believe it. Fewness and truth, 'tis thus: 39
Your brother and his lover have embraced.
As those that feed grow full, as blossoming time   41
That from the seedness the bare fallow brings   42
To teeming foison, even so her plenteous womb   43
Expresseth his full tilth and husbandry.   44

ISABELLA
Someone with child by him? My cousin Juliet?

LUCIO   Is she your cousin?

ISABELLA
Adoptedly, as schoolmaids change their names   47
By vain though apt affection.

LUCIO   She it is.   48

ISABELLA
O, let him marry her.

LUCIO   This is the point.
The Duke is very strangely gone from hence;
Bore many gentlemen, myself being one,   51
In hand and hope of action; but we do learn,   52
By those that know the very nerves of state,
His givings-out were of an infinite distance   54
From his true-meant design. Upon his place,   55
And with full line of his authority,   56
Governs Lord Angelo, a man whose blood
Is very snow broth; one who never feels   58
The wanton stings and motions of the sense,   59
But doth rebate and blunt his natural edge   60
With profits of the mind, study, and fast.
He—to give fear to use and liberty,   62
Which have for long run by the hideous law
As mice by lions—hath picked out an act,
Under whose heavy sense your brother's life   65
Falls into forfeit. He arrests him on it
And follows close the rigor of the statute
To make him an example. All hope is gone,
Unless you have the grace by your fair prayer
To soften Angelo. And that's my pith of business   70
Twixt you and your poor brother.

ISABELLA   Doth he so
Seek his life?

LUCIO   He's censured him already,   72
And, as I hear, the Provost hath a warrant
For 's execution.

ISABELLA   Alas, what poor
Ability's in me to do him good?

LUCIO   Assay the power you have.   76

ISABELLA
My power? Alas, I doubt.

LUCIO   Our doubts are traitors,
And makes us lose the good we oft might win,   78
By fearing to attempt. Go to Lord Angelo,
And let him learn to know, when maidens sue
→ Men give like gods, but when they weep and kneel,
All their petitions are as freely theirs   82
As they themselves would owe them.   83

ISABELLA   I'll see what I can do.

LUCIO   But speedily.

---

16 **cheek roses** i.e., blushes   17 **stead** help   18 **As** as to   20 **un-happy** unfortunate   22 **The rather for** the more so because
25 **weary** wearisome   30 **story** subject for mirth   31 **familiar** customary   32 **lapwing** peewit or plover. (The lapwing runs away from its nest in order to draw away enemies from its young, much as Lucio throws up smokescreens in his seductive talk with young women.)
34 **enskied** placed in heaven   38 **You . . . me** you blaspheme goodness itself when you mockingly praise me, unworthy as I am, for saintliness   39 **it** i.e., that I am mocking.   **Fewness and truth** in few words and truly   41–43 **as . . . foison** as the blossoming season brings the bare untilled land from a state of being sown to abundant harvest (?) (The grammatical construction is unclear.)   44 **tilth** tillage.
husbandry (1) tillage (2) duties of a husband and sexual partner

47 **change** exchange   48 **vain though apt** girlish though natural and suitable   51–52 **Bore . . . action** i.e., he misleadingly kept us in expectation of some military action   54 **givings-out** public statements   55 **Upon** in, on the strength of   56 **line** extent   58 **snow broth** melted snow (i.e., ice water)   59 **motions** promptings.   **the sense** sexual passion   60 **rebate** dull, abate.   **his** its.   **edge** sharpness of desire   62 **use and liberty** habitual licentiousness   65 **heavy sense** severe interpretation   70 **my pith of business** the essence of my business   72 **censured** sentenced   76 **Assay** try   78 **makes** i.e., make   82 **their petitions** i.e., the things the maidens ask for   83 **As . . . them** as they themselves would wish to have them

ISABELLA   I will about it straight,
No longer staying but to give the Mother   87
Notice of my affair. I humbly thank you.
Commend me to my brother. Soon at night   89
I'll send him certain word of my success.   90
LUCIO
I take my leave of you.
ISABELLA   Good sir, adieu.
                              Exeunt [separately].

❖

2.1   *Enter Angelo, Escalus, and servants, [a] Justice.*

ANGELO
We must not make a scarecrow of the law,
Setting it up to fear the birds of prey,
And let it keep one shape till custom make it   2
Their perch and not their terror.
ESCALUS   Ay, but yet   *why be lenient?*
Let us be keen and rather cut a little   5
Than fall and bruise to death. Alas, this gentleman   6
Whom I would save had a most noble father!
Let but your honor know,   8
Whom I believe to be most strait in virtue,   9
That, in the working of your own affections,   10
Had time cohered with place, or place with wishing,
Or that the resolute acting of your blood   12
Could have attained th' effect of your own purpose, 13
Whether you had not sometime in your life   14
Erred in this point which now you censure him,   15
And pulled the law upon you.
ANGELO
'Tis one thing to be tempted, Escalus,
Another thing to fall. I not deny
The jury, passing on the prisoner's life,
May in the sworn twelve have a thief or two
Guiltier than him they try. What's open made to
  justice,
That justice seizes. What knows the laws   22
That thieves do pass on thieves? 'Tis very pregnant, 23
The jewel that we find, we stoop and take 't
Because we see it; but what we do not see
We tread upon and never think of it.
You may not so extenuate his offense
For I have had such faults; but rather tell me,   28
When I that censure him do so offend,
Let mine own judgment pattern out my death   30
And nothing come in partial. Sir, he must die.   31

Enter Provost.

ESCALUS
Be it as your wisdom will.
ANGELO   Where is the Provost?
PROVOST
Here, if it like your honor.
ANGELO   See that Claudio   33
Be executed by nine tomorrow morning.
Bring him his confessor; let him be prepared.
For that's the utmost of his pilgrimage.   36
                              [*Exit Provost.*]
ESCALUS
Well, heaven forgive him, and forgive us all!
Some rise by sin, and some by virtue fall;
Some run from breaks of ice and answer none,   39
And some condemnèd for a fault alone.   40

Enter Elbow, Froth, Clown [Pompey], officers.

ELBOW   Come, bring them away. If these be good   41
people in a commonweal that do nothing but use their   42
abuses in common houses, I know no law. Bring them   43
away.
ANGELO   How now, sir, what's your name? And what's
the matter?
ELBOW   If it please your honor, I am the poor Duke's   47
constable, and my name is Elbow. I do lean upon   48
justice, sir, and do bring in here before your good
honor two notorious benefactors.
ANGELO   Benefactors? Well, what benefactors are they?
Are they not malefactors?
ELBOW   If it please your honor, I know not well what
they are; but precise villains they are, that I am sure of,   54
and void of all profanation in the world that good   55
Christians ought to have.
ESCALUS [*to Angelo*]   This comes off well. Here's a
wise officer.
ANGELO   Go to. What quality are they of?—Elbow is   59
your name? Why dost thou not speak, Elbow?
POMPEY   He cannot, sir; he's out at elbow.   61
ANGELO   What are you, sir?
ELBOW   He, sir? A tapster, sir, parcel-bawd, one that   63
serves a bad woman, whose house, sir, was, as they
say, plucked down in the suburbs; and now she

---

87 **but** than.   **Mother** Mother Superior, prioress   89 **Soon at night**
early tonight   90 **my success** how I have succeeded
2.1. Location: A court of justice.
2 **fear** frighten   5 **keen** sharp   6 **fall** let fall heavily.   **bruise** i.e.,
crush   8 **know** consider   9 **strait** strict   10 **affections** desires
12 **blood** passion   13 **effect** realization   14 **had** would have.   **sometime** on some occasion   15 **censure him** sentence him for
22–23 **What . . . on thieves** i.e., what cognizance can the laws take
of the possibility that thieves may pass sentence upon thieves
23 **pregnant** clear   28 **For** because   30 **judgment pattern out** sentence (imposed in this and similar cases) serve as a model for
31 **nothing . . . partial** let no partiality be allowed

33 **like** please   36 **utmost** furthest point.   **pilgrimage** i.e., life
39 **Some . . . none** i.e., some run away from imminent danger, not
staying to answer for their sins (?) (A famous crux; the Folio reads
brakes of ice.)   **40 a fault alone** one single infraction   41 **away** onward   42–43 **use . . . houses** practice their vices in bawdy houses
47 **poor Duke's** i.e., Duke's poor   48 **lean upon** rely on, appeal to
(with an unintended comic reference to the idea of leaning on one's
elbow)   54 **precise** complete (or perhaps a blunder for "precious"—a word that unintentionally recalls the description of Angelo
as *precise,* i.e., strict or puritanical, at 1.3.50)   55 **profanation** (A
blunder for "profession," or a word meaning "irreverence" where Elbow intends "reverence." Elbow already has used several seeming
malapropisms, including *lean upon, benefactors,* and *precise.*)
59 **Go to** an expression of impatience or reproof.   **quality** occupation
61 **out at elbow** (1) impoverished, threadbare, hence without any
ideas (2) missing his cue, i.e., silent (or *out*) after being called by his
name   63 **parcel-bawd** part-time bawd (and part-time tapster)

professes a hothouse, which I think is a very ill house 66
too.

ESCALUS   How know you that?

ELBOW   My wife, sir, whom I detest before heaven and 69
your honor—

ESCALUS   How? Thy wife?

ELBOW   Ay, sir; whom I thank heaven is an honest
woman—

ESCALUS   Dost thou detest her therefore?

ELBOW   I say, sir, I will detest myself also, as well as
she, that this house, if it be not a bawd's house, it is
pity of her life, for it is a naughty house.   77

ESCALUS   How dost thou know that, Constable?

ELBOW   Marry, sir, by my wife, who, if she had been a
woman cardinally given, might have been accused in 80
fornication, adultery, and all uncleanliness there.

ESCALUS   By the woman's means?

ELBOW   Ay, sir, by Mistress Overdone's means; but as
she spit in his face, so she defied him.   84

POMPEY   Sir, if it please your honor, this is not so.

ELBOW   Prove it before these varlets here, thou honor- 86
able man, prove it.   87

ESCALUS [to Angelo]   Do you hear how he misplaces?

POMPEY   Sir, she came in great with child, and longing,
saving your honor's reverence, for stewed prunes. Sir, 90
we had but two in the house, which at that very
distant time stood, as it were, in a fruit dish, a 92
dish of some threepence. Your honors have seen such
dishes; they are not China dishes, but very good
dishes—

ESCALUS   Go to, go to. No matter for the dish, sir.

POMPEY   No, indeed, sir, not of a pin; you are therein 97
in the right. But to the point. As I say, this Mistress
Elbow, being, as I say, with child, and being great-
bellied, and longing, as I said, for prunes; and having
but two in the dish, as I said, Master Froth here, this
very man, having eaten the rest, as I said, and, as I
say, paying for them very honestly—for, as you
know, Master Froth, I could not give you threepence
again.   105

FROTH   No, indeed.

POMPEY   Very well. You being then, if you be
remembered, cracking the stones of the foresaid 108
prunes—

FROTH   Ay, so I did indeed.

POMPEY   Why, very well; I telling you then, if you be
remembered, that such a one and such a one were
past cure of the thing you wot of, unless they kept 113
very good diet, as I told you—

FROTH   All this is true.

POMPEY   Why, very well, then—

ESCALUS   Come, you are a tedious fool. To the purpose.
What was done to Elbow's wife, that he hath cause to
complain of? Come me to what was done to her.   119

POMPEY   Sir, your honor cannot come to that yet.

ESCALUS   No, sir, nor I mean it not.

POMPEY   Sir, but you shall come to it, by your honor's
leave. And, I beseech you, look into Master Froth here,
sir, a man of fourscore pound a year, whose father 124
died at Hallowmas.—Was 't not at Hallowmas, Mas- 125
ter Froth?

FROTH   All-hallond eve.   127

POMPEY   Why, very well. I hope here be truths. He, sir,
sitting, as I say, in a lower chair, sir—'twas in the 129
Bunch of Grapes, where indeed you have a delight to 130
sit, have you not?

FROTH   I have so, because it is an open room and good 132
for winter.

POMPEY   Why, very well, then. I hope here be truths.

ANGELO
This will last out a night in Russia,
When nights are longest there. I'll take my leave
And leave you to the hearing of the cause,   137
Hoping you'll find good cause to whip them all.

ESCALUS
I think no less. Good morrow to your lordship.   139
                                        Exit [Angelo].
Now, sir, come on. What was done to Elbow's wife, 140
once more?

POMPEY   Once, sir? There was nothing done to her
once.

ELBOW   I beseech you, sir, ask him what this man did
to my wife.

POMPEY   I beseech your honor, ask me.

ESCALUS   Well, sir, what did this gentleman to her?

POMPEY   I beseech you, sir, look in this gentleman's
face. Good Master Froth, look upon his honor; 'tis for
a good purpose. Doth your honor mark his face?   150

ESCALUS   Ay, sir, very well.

POMPEY   Nay, I beseech you, mark it well.

ESCALUS   Well, I do so.

POMPEY   Doth your honor see any harm in his face?

ESCALUS   Why, no.

POMPEY   I'll be supposed upon a book, his face is the 156
worst thing about him. Good, then; if his face be the
worst thing about him, how could Master Froth do the
Constable's wife any harm? I would know that of your
honor.

---

66 professes a hothouse professes to run a bathhouse   **69 detest** (For
"protest.")   **77 pity of her life** a great pity.   **naughty** wicked
80 cardinally (For "carnally.")   **given** inclined   **84 his** i.e., Pompey's, who was carrying out Mistress Overdone's wishes and was
therefore her *means*   **86–87 varlets . . . honorable** (Elbow reverses
or *misplaces* these epithets.)   **90 saving . . . reverence** i.e., begging
your pardon for what I'm about to say.   **stewed prunes** (Commonly
served in houses of prostitution, or *stews*, and therefore suggesting
prostitutes. The bawdy double entendre continues in *stood, dish, pin,
point, cracking the stones*, etc.)   **92 distant** (Blunder for "instant"?)
97 a pin i.e., an insignificant trifle   **105 again** back   **108 stones** pits.
(With suggestion also of "testicles.")   **113 the thing . . . of** you
know what I mean (i.e., venereal disease)

119 Come me i.e., come. (*Me* is used colloquially. Pompey makes a
vulgar joke on the words *come* and *done*; see note at line 140.)
124 of . . . year i.e., well off   **125 Hallowmas** All Saints' Day, November 1   **127 All-hallond eve** Halloween, October 31   **129 a
lower chair** i.e., an easy chair (?)   **130 Bunch of Grapes** (It was not
uncommon to designate particular rooms in inns by such names.)
132 open public   **137 cause** case (with a play on *cause*, "reason," in
the next line. See also the play on *leave* in 136–137.)   **139 I . . .
less** I think so, too   **140 done** (Pompey, in his answer, uses *done* in a
sexual sense.)   **150 mark** observe   **156 supposed** (A malapropism
for "deposed," i.e., sworn.)   **book** i.e., Bible

ESCALUS   He's in the right, Constable. What say you to it?

ELBOW   First, an it like you, the house is a respected 163 house; next, this is a respected fellow; and his mistress is a respected woman.

POMPEY   By this hand, sir, his wife is a more respected person than any of us all.

ELBOW   Varlet, thou liest! Thou liest, wicked varlet! The time is yet to come that she was ever respected with man, woman, or child.

POMPEY   Sir, she was respected with him before he married with her.

ESCALUS   Which is the wiser here, Justice or Iniquity?— 173 Is this true?

ELBOW   O thou caitiff! O thou varlet! O thou wicked 175 Hannibal! I respected with her before I was married to 176 her?—If ever I was respected with her, or she with me, let not your worship think me the poor Duke's officer.—Prove this, thou wicked Hannibal, or I'll have mine action of battery on thee. 180

ESCALUS   If he took you a box o' th' ear, you might have 181 your action of slander too.

ELBOW   Marry, I thank your good worship for it. What is 't your worship's pleasure I shall do with this wicked caitiff?

ESCALUS   Truly, officer, because he hath some offenses in him that thou wouldst discover if thou couldst, let 187 him continue in his courses till thou know'st what 188 they are.

ELBOW   Marry, I thank your worship for it.—Thou seest, thou wicked varlet, now, what's come upon thee: thou art to continue now, thou varlet, thou art to continue. 192

ESCALUS   [to Froth]   Where were you born, friend?

FROTH   Here in Vienna, sir.

ESCALUS   Are you of fourscore pounds a year? 195

FROTH   Yes, an 't please you, sir.

ESCALUS   So. [To Pompey.] What trade are you of, sir?

POMPEY   A tapster, a poor widow's tapster.

ESCALUS   Your mistress' name?

POMPEY   Mistress Overdone.

ESCALUS   Hath she had any more than one husband?

POMPEY   Nine, sir. Overdone by the last. 202

ESCALUS   Nine?—Come hither to me, Master Froth. Master Froth, I would not have you acquainted with tapsters. They will draw you, Master Froth, and you 205 will hang them. Get you gone, and let me hear no 206 more of you.

FROTH   I thank your worship. For mine own part, I never come into any room in a taphouse but I am 209 drawn in. 210

ESCALUS   Well, no more of it, Master Froth. Farewell. [Exit Froth.] Come you hither to me, Master Tapster. What's your name, Master Tapster?

POMPEY   Pompey.

ESCALUS   What else?

POMPEY   Bum, sir.

ESCALUS   Troth, and your bum is the greatest thing about you, so that in the beastliest sense you are Pompey the Great. Pompey, you are partly a bawd, Pompey, howsoever you color it in being a tapster, are you 220 not? Come, tell me true. It shall be the better for you.

POMPEY   Truly, sir, I am a poor fellow that would live.

ESCALUS   How would you live, Pompey? By being a 223 bawd? What do you think of the trade, Pompey? Is it a lawful trade?

POMPEY   If the law would allow it, sir.

ESCALUS   But the law will not allow it, Pompey; nor it shall not be allowed in Vienna.

POMPEY   Does your worship mean to geld and splay all 229 the youth of the city?

ESCALUS   No, Pompey.

POMPEY   Truly, sir, in my poor opinion, they will to 't then. If your worship will take order for the drabs and 233 the knaves, you need not to fear the bawds.

ESCALUS   There is pretty orders beginning, I can tell you. It is but heading and hanging. 236

POMPEY   If you head and hang all that offend that way but for ten year together, you'll be glad to give out a 238 commission for more heads. If this law hold in Vienna 239 ten year, I'll rent the fairest house in it after threepence 240 a bay. If you live to see this come to pass, say Pompey 241 told you so.

ESCALUS   Thank you, good Pompey. And, in requital of 243 your prophecy, hark you: I advise you let me not find you before me again upon any complaint whatsoever; no, not for dwelling where you do. If I do, Pompey, I shall beat you to your tent and prove a shrewd Caesar 247 to you; in plain dealing, Pompey, I shall have you whipped. So for this time, Pompey, fare you well.

POMPEY   I thank your worship for your good counsel. [Aside.] But I shall follow it as the flesh and fortune shall better determine.
Whip me? No, no, let carman whip his jade. 253
The valiant heart's not whipped out of his trade.
Exit.

ESCALUS   Come hither to me, Master Elbow; come hither, Master Constable. How long have you been in this place of constable?

163 an it like if it please. respected (For "suspected.") 173 Justice or Iniquity (Personified characters in a morality play.) 175 caitiff knave, villain 176 Hannibal (A blunder for "cannibal," perhaps also suggested by the fact that Hannibal and Pompey were both famous generals in the classical world.) 180 battery (An error for "slander," as Escalus amusedly points out.) 181 took gave. o' on 187 discover (1) detect (2) reveal 188 courses courses of action 192 continue (Elbow may confuse the word with its opposite.) 195 of possessed of 202 Overdone . . . last (1) her name, Overdone, was given her by her last husband (2) she has been worn out (overdone) by the last one 205 draw (1) cheat, take in (2) empty, deplete (with a pun on the tapster's trade of drawing liquor from a barrel, and on Froth's name) (3) disembowel, or drag to execution 206 will hang them will be the cause of their hanging

209 taphouse alehouse 210 drawn in enticed. (Still another meaning of draw, line 205.) 220 color disguise 223 live make a living 229 splay spay 233 take order take measures. drabs prostitutes 236 but heading neither more nor less than beheading 238 year together years at a stretch 239 commission order. hold remain in force 240 after at the rate of 241 bay division of a house included under one gable 243 requital of return for 247 shrewd harsh, severe. Caesar (Escalus refers to Julius Caesar's defeat of Pompey at Pharsalia in 48 B.C.) 253 carman one who drives a cart. jade broken-down horse

ELBOW   Seven year and a half, sir.

ESCALUS   I thought, by your readiness in the office, you 259
had continued in it some time. You say, seven years
together?

ELBOW   And a half, sir.

ESCALUS   Alas, it hath been great pains to you. They do
you wrong to put you so oft upon 't. Are there not
men in your ward sufficient to serve it? 265

ELBOW   Faith, sir, few of any wit in such matters. As
they are chosen, they are glad to choose me for them. 267
I do it for some piece of money and go through with 268
all. 269

ESCALUS   Look you bring me in the names of some six 270
or seven, the most sufficient of your parish.

ELBOW   To your worship's house, sir?

ESCALUS   To my house. Fare you well.   [Exit Elbow.]
What's o'clock, think you?

JUSTICE   Eleven, sir.

ESCALUS   I pray you home to dinner with me. 276

JUSTICE   I humbly thank you.

ESCALUS
It grieves me for the death of Claudio;
But there's no remedy.

JUSTICE
Lord Angelo is severe.

ESCALUS   It is but needful.
Mercy is not itself, that oft looks so; 281
Pardon is still the nurse of second woe. 282
But yet—poor Claudio! There is no remedy.
Come, sir.   Exeunt.

❧

2.2   *Enter Provost [and a] Servant.*

SERVANT
He's hearing of a cause; he will come straight. 1
I'll tell him of you.

PROVOST   Pray you, do. [Exit Servant.] I'll know
His pleasure; maybe he will relent. Alas,
He hath but as offended in a dream! 4
All sects, all ages smack of this vice—and he 5
To die for 't!

Enter Angelo.

ANGELO   Now, what's the matter, Provost?

PROVOST
Is it your will Claudio shall die tomorrow?

ANGELO
Did not I tell thee yea? Hadst thou not order?
Why dost thou ask again?

PROVOST   Lest I might be too rash.
Under your good correction, I have seen 11
When, after execution, judgment hath
Repented o'er his doom. 13

ANGELO   Go to; let that be mine. 14
Do you your office, or give up your place,
And you shall well be spared. 16

PROVOST   I crave your honor's pardon.
What shall be done, sir, with the groaning Juliet? 18
She's very near her hour.

ANGELO   Dispose of her 19
To some more fitter place, and that with speed.

[Enter a Servant.]

SERVANT
Here is the sister of the man condemned
Desires access to you.

ANGELO   Hath he a sister? 22

PROVOST
Ay, my good lord, a very virtuous maid,
And to be shortly of a sisterhood,
If not already.

ANGELO   Well, let her be admitted.
[Exit Servant.]
See you the fornicatress be removed.
Let her have needful but not lavish means.
There shall be order for 't.

Enter Lucio and Isabella.

PROVOST   Save your honor! 28

ANGELO [to Provost]
Stay a little while. [To Isabella.] You're welcome.
What's your will?

ISABELLA
I am a woeful suitor to your honor,
Please but your honor hear me.

ANGELO   Well, what's your suit? 31

ISABELLA
There is a vice that most I do abhor,
And most desire should meet the blow of justice,
For which I would not plead, but that I must;
For which I must not plead, but that I am
At war twixt will and will not.

ANGELO   Well, the matter?

ISABELLA
I have a brother is condemned to die.
I do beseech you, let it be his fault, 38
And not my brother.

PROVOST [aside]   Heaven give thee moving graces!

259 **readiness** proficiency, alacrity 265 **sufficient** able 267 **for them** i.e., to take their place 268–269 **go . . . all** i.e., perform my duties thoroughly 270 **Look** see to it that 276 **dinner** (Dinner was customarily eaten just before midday.) 281 **Mercy . . . so** i.e., what seems merciful may not really be so (since it may encourage crime and hence lead to more punishment) 282 **still** always
2.2. Location: Adjacent to the court of justice, perhaps at Angelo's official residence.
1 **hearing . . . cause** listening to a case. **straight** immediately 4 **He** i.e., Claudio. **but as offended** offended only as if 5 **sects** classes of people, ranks. **ages** i.e., ages of history or of life. **smack** partake

11 **Under . . . correction** i.e., allow me to say 13 **doom** sentence 14 **mine** my business 16 **well be spared** easily be done without 18 **groaning** (with labor pains) 19 **hour** time of delivery 22 **Desires** who desires 28 **Save** may God save 31 **Please . . . me** if only it will please you to hear me 38 **let . . . fault** i.e., let the fault die, be condemned

ANGELO
Condemn the fault, and not the actor of it?
Why, every fault's condemned ere it be done.
Mine were the very cipher of a function,
To fine the faults whose fine stands in record   43
And let go by the actor.
ISABELLA   O just but severe law!
I had a brother, then. Heaven keep your honor!
LUCIO [aside to Isabella]
Give 't not o'er so. To him again, entreat him!   47
Kneel down before him; hang upon his gown.
You are too cold. If you should need a pin,   49
You could not with more tame a tongue desire it.
To him, I say!
ISABELLA [to Angelo]
Must he needs die?
ANGELO   Maiden, no remedy.
ISABELLA
Yes, I do think that you might pardon him,
And neither heaven nor man grieve at the mercy.
ANGELO
I will not do 't.
ISABELLA   But can you, if you would?
ANGELO
Look what I will not, that I cannot do.   56
ISABELLA
But might you do 't, and do the world no wrong,
If so your heart were touched with that remorse   58
As mine is to him?
ANGELO   He's sentenced. 'Tis too late.
LUCIO [aside to Isabella]   You are too cold.
ISABELLA
Too late? Why, no; I that do speak a word
May call it back again. Well, believe this:
No ceremony that to great ones 'longs,   64
Not the king's crown, nor the deputed sword,   65
The marshal's truncheon, nor the judge's robe,   66
Become them with one half so good a grace
As mercy does.
If he had been as you, and you as he,
You would have slipped like him; but he, like you,   70
Would not have been so stern.
ANGELO   Pray you, begone.
ISABELLA
I would to heaven I had your potency,
And you were Isabel! Should it then be thus?
No, I would tell what 'twere to be a judge   74
And what a prisoner.
LUCIO [aside to Isabella]   Ay, touch him; there's the vein.   75
ANGELO
Your brother is a forfeit of the law,   76

And you but waste your words.
ISABELLA   Alas, alas!
Why, all the souls that were were forfeit once,   78
And He that might the vantage best have took   79
Found out the remedy. How would you be,   80
If He, which is the top of judgment, should   81
But judge you as you are? O, think on that,
And mercy then will breathe within your lips,
Like man new-made.
ANGELO   Be you content, fair maid.   84
It is the law, not I, condemn your brother.
Were he my kinsman, brother, or my son,
It should be thus with him. He must die tomorrow.
ISABELLA
Tomorrow! O, that's sudden! Spare him, spare him!
He's not prepared for death. Even for our kitchens
We kill the fowl of season. Shall we serve heaven   90
With less respect than we do minister
To our gross selves? Good, good my lord, bethink
  you:
Who is it that hath died for this offense?
There's many have committed it.
LUCIO [aside to Isabella]   Ay, well said.
ANGELO
The law hath not been dead, though it hath slept.
Those many had not dared to do that evil
If the first that did th' edict infringe
Had answered for his deed. Now 'tis awake,
Takes note of what is done, and like a prophet
Looks in a glass that shows what future evils,   100
Either now, or by remissness new-conceived   101
And so in progress to be hatched and born,   102
Are now to have no successive degrees,   103
But ere they live, to end.
ISABELLA   Yet show some pity.   104
ANGELO
I show it most of all when I show justice;
For then I pity those I do not know,
Which a dismissed offense would after gall,   107
And do him right that, answering one foul wrong,   108
Lives not to act another. Be satisfied;
Your brother dies tomorrow. Be content.
ISABELLA
So you must be the first that gives this sentence,
And he that suffers. O, it is excellent
To have a giant's strength, but it is tyrannous
To use it like a giant.
LUCIO [aside to Isabella]   That's well said.

43 fine . . . fine punish . . . penalty. in record in the statutes
47 Give 't . . . so don't give up so soon 49 need a pin i.e., ask for
the smallest trifle 56 Look what whatever 58 remorse pity
64 'longs is fitting, belongs 65 deputed sword sword of justice entrusted to the ruler 66 truncheon staff borne by military officers
70 like you in your situation 74 tell make known 75 there's the
vein i.e., that's the right approach. (Vein means "lode to be profitably
mined," or perhaps "vein for bloodletting.") 76 a forfeit one who
must incur the penalty

78–80 Why . . . remedy (A reference to God's redemption of sinful
humanity when He would have been justified in destroying humankind.) 81 top of judgment supreme judge 84 new-made i.e., created new by salvation, born again 90 of season that is in season and
properly mature 100 glass magic crystal 101 Either . . . new-conceived i.e., both evils already hatched and those that would be encouraged by continued laxity of enforcement 102 in progress in the
course of time 103 successive degrees successors or future stages.
(Future evils are to be aborted before they are born and propagate.)
104 ere they live i.e., before they can be committed 107 dismissed
forgiven. gall irritate, injure 108 do . . . answering do justice to
that person who, by paying the penalty for

ISABELLA   Could great men thunder
As Jove himself does, Jove would never be quiet,   116
For every pelting, petty officer   117
Would use his heaven for thunder,
Nothing but thunder! Merciful Heaven,
Thou rather with thy sharp and sulfurous bolt   120
Splits the unwedgeable and gnarlèd oak   121
Than the soft myrtle; but man, proud man,
Dressed in a little brief authority,
Most ignorant of what he's most assured,   124
His glassy essence, like an angry ape   125
Plays such fantastic tricks before high heaven
As makes the angels weep; who, with our spleens,   127
Would all themselves laugh mortal.   128

LUCIO [aside to Isabella]
O, to him, to him, wench! He will relent.
He's coming, I perceive 't.

PROVOST [aside]   Pray heaven she win him!   130

ISABELLA
We cannot weigh our brother with ourself.   131
Great men may jest with saints; 'tis wit in them,
But in the less, foul profanation.   133

LUCIO [aside to Isabella]
Thou'rt i' the right, girl. More o' that.

ISABELLA
That in the captain's but a choleric word   135
Which in the soldier is flat blasphemy.   136

LUCIO [aside to Isabella] Art advised o' that? More on 't.   137

ANGELO
Why do you put these sayings upon me?   138

ISABELLA
Because authority, though it err like others,
Hath yet a kind of medicine in itself
That skins the vice o' the top. Go to your bosom;   141
Knock there, and ask your heart what it doth know
That's like my brother's fault. If it confess
A natural guiltiness such as is his,
Let it not sound a thought upon your tongue
Against my brother's life.

ANGELO [aside]   She speaks, and 'tis such sense   147
That my sense breeds with it.—Fare you well.   148

[He starts to go.]

ISABELLA   Gentle my lord, turn back.   149

ANGELO
I will bethink me. Come again tomorrow.   150

ISABELLA
Hark how I'll bribe you. Good my lord, turn back.

ANGELO   How? Bribe me?

ISABELLA
Ay, with such gifts that heaven shall share with
you.   153

LUCIO [aside to Isabella]   You had marred all else.   154

ISABELLA
Not with fond sicles of the tested gold,   155
Or stones whose rate are either rich or poor   156
As fancy values them, but with true prayers
That shall be up at heaven and enter there
Ere sunrise—prayers from preservèd souls,   159
From fasting maids whose minds are dedicate   160
To nothing temporal.

ANGELO   Well, come to me tomorrow.

LUCIO [aside to Isabella]   Go to, 'tis well. Away!

ISABELLA
Heaven keep your honor safe!

ANGELO [aside]   Amen!
For I am that way going to temptation,
Where prayers cross.

ISABELLA   At what hour tomorrow   165
Shall I attend your lordship?

ANGELO   At any time 'fore noon.

ISABELLA   Save your honor!   168

[Exeunt Isabella, Lucio, and Provost.]

ANGELO   From thee, even from thy virtue!
What's this, what's this? Is this her fault or mine?
The tempter or the tempted, who sins most, ha?
Not she, nor doth she tempt; but it is I
That, lying by the violet in the sun,
Do, as the carrion does, not as the flower,   174
Corrupt with virtuous season. Can it be   175
That modesty may more betray our sense   176
Than woman's lightness? Having waste ground
enough,   177
Shall we desire to raze the sanctuary
And pitch our evils there? O, fie, fie, fie!   179
What dost thou, or what art thou, Angelo?
Dost thou desire her foully for those things
That make her good? O, let her brother live!
Thieves for their robbery have authority
When judges steal themselves. What, do I love her,
That I desire to hear her speak again
And feast upon her eyes? What is 't I dream on?

116 be quiet have any quiet   117 pelting paltry   120 bolt thunderbolt   121 unwedgeable unable to be split   124–125 of what . . . essence i.e., of his own spiritual essence, his natural infirmity and need for God's grace, something his faith should make him certain of   125 glassy i.e., reflected from God but also fragile and illusory, like the image in a mirror.   angry ape i.e., ludicrous buffoon   127 with our spleens i.e., if they laughed at folly as we do. (The spleen was thought to be the seat of laughter.)   128 themselves laugh mortal laugh themselves out of immortality (by indulging in uncharitable laughter)   130 coming coming around   131 cannot . . . ourself cannot judge our fellow men by the same standards we blindly use in judging ourselves   133 in the less in ordinary persons (it is)   135 That . . . word i.e., we treat the abusive language a commanding officer uses in anger merely as an outburst; we are indulgent toward the failings of great men. (As in lines 131–133, Isabella's point seems to be that our judgments are biased by our inordinate regard for authority.)   136 blasphemy defamation   137 advised informed, aware.   on 't of it   138 put . . . me apply these sayings to me   141 skins . . . top covers over the sore with skin, leaving it unhealed. (The medicine of line 140 is thus only a palliative.)   147–148 sense . . . sense import . . . sensuality

149 Gentle my lord my noble lord   150 bethink me consider   153 that as   154 else otherwise   155 fond i.e., foolishly valued. sicles shekels (Hebrew coins).   tested purest, tested by the touchstone   156 rate values   159 preservèd protected (from the world)   160 dedicate dedicated   165 cross are at cross purposes   168 Save may God save   174 carrion decaying flesh   175 Corrupt . . . season i.e., putrefy while all else flourishes. (The warmth of flowering time causes the violet, Isabella, to blossom but causes the carrion lying beside it, Angelo, to rot.)   176 modesty virtue, chastity.   sense sensual nature   177 lightness immodesty, lust   179 pitch our evils there i.e., erect a privy, not on waste ground (line 177), but on sanctified ground. (Evils also has the more common meaning of "wickedness.")

O cunning enemy that, to catch a saint,   187
With saints dost bait thy hook! Most dangerous
Is that temptation that doth goad us on
To sin in loving virtue. Never could the strumpet,
With all her double vigor—art and nature—   191
Once stir my temper; but this virtuous maid   192
Subdues me quite. Ever till now,
When men were fond, I smiled and wondered how.   194

Exit.

❖

2.3 *Enter, [meeting,] Duke [disguised as a friar] and*
Provost.

DUKE
Hail to you, Provost—so I think you are.

PROVOST
I am the Provost. What's your will, good Friar?

DUKE
Bound by my charity and my blest order,
I come to visit the afflicted spirits
Here in the prison. Do me the common right   5
To let me see them and to make me know
The nature of their crimes, that I may minister
To them accordingly.

PROVOST
I would do more than that, if more were needful.

Enter Juliet.

Look, here comes one: a gentlewoman of mine,
Who, falling in the flaws of her own youth,   11
Hath blistered her report. She is with child,   12
And he that got it, sentenced—a young man   13
More fit to do another such offense
Than die for this.

DUKE
When must he die?

PROVOST   As I do think, tomorrow.
[*To Juliet.*] I have provided for you. Stay awhile,   17
And you shall be conducted.   18

DUKE
Repent you, fair one, of the sin you carry?

JULIET
I do, and bear the shame most patiently.

DUKE
I'll teach you how you shall arraign your conscience,   21
And try your penitence, if it be sound   22
Or hollowly put on.   23

JULIET   I'll gladly learn.

DUKE   Love you the man that wronged you?

JULIET
Yes, as I love the woman that wronged him.

DUKE
So then it seems your most offenseful act
Was mutually committed?

JULIET   Mutually.

DUKE
Then was your sin of heavier kind than his.

JULIET
I do confess it and repent it, Father.

DUKE
'Tis meet so, daughter. But lest you do repent   31
As that the sin hath brought you to this shame,   32
Which sorrow is always toward ourselves, not
  heaven,   33
Showing we would not spare heaven as we love it,   34
But as we stand in fear—

JULIET
I do repent me as it is an evil,
And take the shame with joy.

DUKE   There rest.   37
Your partner, as I hear, must die tomorrow,
And I am going with instruction to him.
Grace go with you. *Benedicite!*   *Exit.* 40

JULIET
Must die tomorrow? O injurious law,
That respites me a life whose very comfort   42
Is still a dying horror!

PROVOST   'Tis pity of him.   *Exeunt.* 43

❖

2.4 *Enter Angelo.*

ANGELO
When I would pray and think, I think and pray
To several subjects. Heaven hath my empty words,   2
Whilst my invention, hearing not my tongue,   3
Anchors on Isabel; Heaven in my mouth,
As if I did but only chew His name,   5
And in my heart the strong and swelling evil
Of my conception. The state, whereon I studied,   7
Is like a good thing, being often read,
Grown sere and tedious. Yea, my gravity,   9
Wherein—let no man hear me—I take pride,
Could I with boot change for an idle plume,   11

---

187 **enemy** i.e., Satan   191 **double . . . nature** twofold power (of alluring men) through artifice and a sensuous nature   192 **temper** mental balance, temperament   194 **fond** foolishly in love
2.3. Location: A prison.
5 **common right** i.e., right of all clerics   11 **flaws** sudden gusts (of
passion)   12 **blistered her report** marred her reputation   13 **got** begot
17 **provided** provided a place to stay   18 **conducted** taken there
21 **arraign** accuse   22 **try** test   23 **hollowly** falsely

31 **'Tis meet so** it is fitting that you do so   32 **As that** because
33 **toward ourselves** i.e., narrowly self-concerned rather than loving
virtue for its own sake   34 **spare heaven** i.e., spare heaven the sorrow felt there for unconfessed sins; or, forbear to offend heaven.   **as**
because. (Also in lines 35 and 36.)   37 **There rest** hold fast to that
truth   40 **Benedicite** blessings on you   42 **respites** prolongs, does
not forfeit. (Juliet laments that her life is spared through Angelo's cruel
kindness while Claudio's is not.)   42–43 **whose . . . horror** whose
greatest comfort will always be a deadly horror   43 **pity of** a pity
about
2.4. Location: Angelo's official residence.
2 **several** separate   3 **invention** imagination   5 **His** i.e., Heaven's,
God's   7 **conception** thought.   **The state** statecraft   9 **sere** withered,
old   11–12 **Could . . . vain** I could profitably exchange for a frivolous feather, one that the air beats in reproof of its vanity

Which the air beats for vain. O place, O form,   12
How often dost thou with thy case, thy habit,   13
Wrench awe from fools and tie the wiser souls   14
To thy false seeming! Blood, thou art blood.   15
Let's write "good angel" on the devil's horn,   16
'Tis not the devil's crest.

Enter Servant.

How now? Who's there?   17

SERVANT
One Isabel, a sister, desires access to you.

ANGELO
Teach her the way. [*Exit Servant.*] O heavens!   19
Why does my blood thus muster to my heart,   20
Making both it unable for itself   21
And dispossessing all my other parts
Of necessary fitness?
So play the foolish throngs with one that swoons,   24
Come all to help him, and so stop the air
By which he should revive; and even so
The general subject to a well-wished king   27
Quit their own part and in obsequious fondness   28
Crowd to his presence, where their untaught love   29
Must needs appear offense.

Enter Isabella.

How now, fair maid?   30

ISABELLA   I am come to know your pleasure.

ANGELO
That you might know it would much better
    please me   32
Than to demand what 'tis. Your brother cannot live.   33

ISABELLA
Even so. Heaven keep your honor!   34

[*She turns to leave.*]

ANGELO
Yet may he live awhile; and, it may be,
As long as you or I. Yet he must die.

ISABELLA   Under your sentence?

ANGELO   Yea.

ISABELLA
When, I beseech you? That in his reprieve,
Longer or shorter, he may be so fitted   40
That his soul sicken not.

ANGELO
Ha? Fie, these filthy vices! It were as good   42
To pardon him that hath from nature stolen   43
A man already made, as to remit   44
Their saucy sweetness that do coin heaven's image   45
In stamps that are forbid. 'Tis all as easy   46
Falsely to take away a life true made
As to put metal in restrainèd means   48
To make a false one.

ISABELLA
'Tis set down so in heaven, but not in earth.   50

ANGELO
Say you so? Then I shall pose you quickly: 51
Which had you rather, that the most just law
Now took your brother's life, or, to redeem him,
Give up your body to such sweet uncleanness
As she that he hath stained?

ISABELLA   Sir, believe this,
I had rather give my body than my soul.   56

ANGELO
I talk not of your soul. Our compelled sins   57
Stand more for number than for account.

ISABELLA   How say you?   58

ANGELO
Nay, I'll not warrant that, for I can speak   59
Against the thing I say. Answer to this:
I, now the voice of the recorded law,
Pronounce a sentence on your brother's life;
Might there not be a charity in sin
To save this brother's life?

ISABELLA   Please you to do 't,   64
I'll take it as a peril to my soul;   65
It is no sin at all, but charity.

ANGELO
Pleased you to do 't at peril of your soul   67
Were equal poise of sin and charity.   68

ISABELLA
That I do beg his life, if it be sin,
Heaven let me bear it! You granting of my suit,
If that be sin, I'll make it my morn prayer
To have it added to the faults of mine,
And nothing of your answer.

ANGELO   Nay, but hear me.   73
Your sense pursues not mine. Either you are
    ignorant

---

12 place official position, rank. **form** dignity of office, ceremony
13 case mere outward appearance. **habit** garb **14–15 Wrench
. . . seeming** intimidate ordinary foolish men and allure even the wise
to the seeming virtue of authority **15 Blood . . . blood** i.e., passions
are inherent in human nature, under all these outward appearances
16 Let's write i.e., if we were to write. **good angel** (with a play on
Angelo's name) **17 'Tis . . . crest** that still would not make it a true
sign of the devil's identity (i.e., it would not make the devil an angel
merely to write "good angel" on his horn). The *crest* is an identifying
emblem worn on the helmet or coat of arms. **19 Teach** show
20 muster to assemble like soldiers in **21 unable** ineffectual
24 play act **27 general subject** i.e., commoners, subjects. **well-
wished** attended by good wishes **28 Quit . . . part** abandon their
proper function and (politely distant) place **29 untaught** ignorant,
unmannerly **30 Must needs** will necessarily **32 know it** i.e., know
my pleasure, my desire. (Angelo is thinking of his desire for Isabella;
know suggests "have carnal knowledge.") **33 Than to demand** than
for you to ask **34 Even so** i.e., so be it **40 fitted** prepared

42–46 It were . . . forbid one might as well pardon the murderer of
a man already alive as pardon the wanton pleasures of those persons
who produce illegitimate offspring, like counterfeit coiners. (*Heaven's
image* is humankind, made in God's likeness; Genesis 1:27.)
48 metal (with a play on *mettle*, a variant spelling, and as it is
spelled in the Folio; i.e., substance). **restrainèd** prohibited, illicit
50 'Tis . . . earth i.e., equating murder and bastardizing accords with
divine law but not with human law, according to which murder is
more heinous **51 pose** nonplus with a question **56 give** i.e., give to
death or punishment. (Isabella doesn't understand the drift of the
question.) **57–58 Our . . . account** our sins committed under compulsion are recorded but not charged to our spiritual account **59 I'll
. . . that** i.e., I'm not necessarily endorsing the view I just expressed
64 Please you if you please **65 take** accept **67 Pleased** if it pleased
68 Were equal poise there would be equal balance **73 of your answer** to which you will have to answer

Or seem so craftily; and that's not good.

ISABELLA
Let me be ignorant, and in nothing good,
But graciously to know I am no better.   77

ANGELO
Thus wisdom wishes to appear most bright
When it doth tax itself, as these black masks   79
Proclaim an enshield beauty ten times louder   80
Than beauty could, displayed. But mark me.
To be receivèd plain, I'll speak more gross: 82
Your brother is to die.

ISABELLA   So.

ANGELO
And his offense is so, as it appears,
Accountant to the law upon that pain.   86

ISABELLA   True.

ANGELO
Admit no other way to save his life—   88
As I subscribe not that, nor any other,   89
But in the loss of question—that you, his sister,   90
Finding yourself desired of such a person   91
Whose credit with the judge, or own great place,
Could fetch your brother from the manacles
Of the all-binding law; and that there were
No earthly means to save him, but that either
You must lay down the treasures of your body
To this supposed, or else to let him suffer.   97
What would you do?

ISABELLA
As much for my poor brother as myself:
That is, were I under the terms of death,
Th' impression of keen whips I'd wear as rubies,   100
And strip myself to death as to a bed
That longing have been sick for, ere I'd yield   103
My body up to shame.

ANGELO   Then must your brother die.

ISABELLA   And 'twere the cheaper way.
Better it were a brother died at once   107
Than that a sister, by redeeming him,
Should die forever.

ANGELO
Were not you then as cruel as the sentence
That you have slandered so?

ISABELLA
Ignomy in ransom and free pardon   112
Are of two houses. Lawful mercy   113
Is nothing kin to foul redemption.   114

ANGELO
You seemed of late to make the law a tyrant,
And rather proved the sliding of your brother   116
A merriment than a vice.

ISABELLA
O, pardon me, my lord. It oft falls out,
To have what we would have, we speak not what
  we mean.
I something do excuse the thing I hate   120
For his advantage that I dearly love.

ANGELO
We are all frail.

ISABELLA   Else let my brother die,
If not a fedary but only he   123
Owe and succeed thy weakness.   124

ANGELO   Nay, women are frail too.

ISABELLA
Ay, as the glasses where they view themselves,   126
Which are as easy broke as they make forms.   127
Women? Help, Heaven! Men their creation mar   128
In profiting by them. Nay, call us ten times frail,   129
For we are soft as our complexions are,   130
And credulous to false prints.

ANGELO   I think it well.   131
And from this testimony of your own sex—   132
Since I suppose we are made to be no stronger   133
Than faults may shake our frames—let me be bold.   134
I do arrest your words. Be that you are,   135
That is, a woman; if you be more, you're none.   136
If you be one, as you are well expressed   137
By all external warrants, show it now
By putting on the destined livery. be sexual!   139

ISABELLA
I have no tongue but one. Gentle my lord,   140
Let me entreat you speak the former language.   141

ANGELO   Plainly conceive, I love you.

ISABELLA   My brother did love Juliet,
And you tell me that he shall die for 't.

ANGELO
He shall not, Isabel, if you give me love.

ISABELLA
I know your virtue hath a license in 't,   146
Which seems a little fouler than it is   147

---

77 **graciously** through divine grace   79 **tax itself** accuse itself (of ignorance).   **these** (Generically referring to any.)   80 **enshield** enshielded, protected from view behind the black masks   82 **receivèd plain** plainly understood.   **gross** openly   86 **Accountant** accountable.   **pain** penalty   88 **Admit** suppose   89–90 **As . . . question** since I will admit no alternative possibility in our discussion. (*Loss of question* means "forfeiting the terms of our debate.")   91 **of** by   97 **supposed** hypothetical person.   **him** i.e., Claudio   100 **terms** sentence   103 **That . . . for** i.e., that I have been sick with longing for. (Isabella's images are of love, death, and flagellation.)   107 **died at once** should die once for all, rather than *die forever* (line 109) in the death of the soul through sin   112 **Ignomy** ignominy   113 **of two houses** i.e., unrelated   114 **nothing** not at all

116 **proved** argued   120 **something** to some extent   123 **fedary** confederate, companion who is equally guilty   124 **Owe . . . weakness** possess and inherit the weakness you speak of, or the weakness to which all men as a class are prone. (Isabella argues that Claudio should die only if he is the only man who is frail.)   126 **glasses** mirrors   127 **forms** (1) images (2) copies of themselves, i.e., children   128–129 **Men . . . them** men mar their creation in God's likeness by taking advantage of women   130 **complexions** constitutions, appearance   131 **credulous . . . prints** susceptible to false impressions. (The metaphor is from the stamping of metal.)   132 **of** about   133 **we** i.e., men and women   134 **Than** than that   135 **arrest your words** take what you have said and hold you to it.   **that** what   136 **if . . . none** i.e., if you claim to be perfect, you are no longer a woman as we have defined that term   137 **expressed** shown to be   139 **putting . . . livery** i.e., assuming the characteristic frailty that all women possess   140 **tongue** language   141 **former** i.e., customary   146–148 **your . . . others** i.e., you, although virtuous, are pretending foul purposes in order to mislead (*pluck on*) me

To pluck on others.
ANGELO   Believe me, on mine honor,   148
My words express my purpose.
ISABELLA
Ha! Little honor to be much believed,
And most pernicious purpose! Seeming, seeming!
I will proclaim thee, Angelo, look for 't!
Sign me a present pardon for my brother,   153
Or with an outstretched throat I'll tell the world
aloud
What man thou art.
ANGELO   Who will believe thee, Isabel?
My unsoiled name, th' austereness of my life,
My vouch against you, and my place i' the state   157
Will so your accusation overweigh
That you shall stifle in your own report
And smell of calumny. I have begun,   160
And now I give my sensual race the rein.   161
Fit thy consent to my sharp appetite;
Lay by all nicety and prolixious blushes   163
That banish what they sue for. Redeem thy brother   164
By yielding up thy body to my will,
Or else he must not only die the death,   166
But thy unkindness shall his death draw out
To ling'ring sufferance. Answer me tomorrow,   168
Or, by the affection that now guides me most,   169
I'll prove a tyrant to him. As for you,
Say what you can, my false o'erweighs your true.
                                            Exit.

ISABELLA
To whom should I complain? Did I tell this,   172
Who would believe me? O perilous mouths,
That bear in them one and the selfsame tongue,
Either of condemnation or approof,   175
Bidding the law make curtsy to their will,
Hooking both right and wrong to th' appetite,   177
To follow as it draws! I'll to my brother.   178
Though he hath fall'n by prompture of the blood,   179
Yet hath he in him such a mind of honor
That, had he twenty heads to tender down   181
On twenty bloody blocks, he'd yield them up
Before his sister should her body stoop
To such abhorred pollution.
Then, Isabel, live chaste, and, brother, die;
More than our brother is our chastity.
I'll tell him yet of Angelo's request,
And fit his mind to death, for his soul's rest.   *Exit.*

♣

3.1   *Enter Duke [disguised as before], Claudio, and*
         Provost.

DUKE
So then you hope of pardon from Lord Angelo?
CLAUDIO
The miserable have no other medicine
But only hope.
I have hope to live and am prepared to die.
DUKE
Be absolute for death. Either death or life
Shall thereby be the sweeter. Reason thus with life:
If I do lose thee, I do lose a thing
That none but fools would keep. A breath thou art,
Servile to all the skyey influences   9
That dost this habitation where thou keep'st   10
Hourly afflict. Merely, thou art death's fool,   11
For him thou labor'st by thy flight to shun,
And yet runn'st toward him still. Thou art not
noble,   13
For all th' accommodations that thou bear'st   14
Are nursed by baseness. Thou'rt by no means
valiant,   15
For thou dost fear the soft and tender fork   16
Of a poor worm. Thy best of rest is sleep,   17
And that thou oft provok'st, yet grossly fear'st   18
Thy death, which is no more. Thou art not thyself,
For thou exists on many a thousand grains
That issue out of dust. Happy thou art not,
For what thou hast not, still thou striv'st to get,
And what thou hast, forget'st. Thou art not certain,   23
For thy complexion shifts to strange effects,   24
After the moon. If thou art rich, thou'rt poor,   25
For, like an ass whose back with ingots bows,
Thou bear'st thy heavy riches but a journey,
And death unloads thee. Friend hast thou none,
For thine own bowels which do call thee sire,   29
The mere effusion of thy proper loins,   30
Do curse the gout, serpigo, and the rheum   31
For ending thee no sooner. Thou hast nor youth
nor age,   32
But as it were an after-dinner's sleep   33
Dreaming on both, for all thy blessèd youth
Becomes as agèd and doth beg the alms   35
Of palsied eld; and, when thou art old and rich,   36
Thou hast neither heat, affection, limb, nor beauty   37

153 **present** immediate   157 **vouch** testimony   160 **calumny** slander
161 **race** natural or inherited disposition (with a probable quibble on
"horse race")   163 **by** aside.   **nicety** coyness, reserve.   **prolixious**
time-wasting   164 **banish . . . for** (1) i.e., seem to repulse the sensual pleasure you must really want, or (2) banish all hope of saving
Claudio   166 **die the death** be put to death   168 **sufferance** torture
169 **affection** passion   172 **Did I tell** if I told   175 **approof** approval,
sanction   177 **Hooking** attaching   178 **as it draws** wherever it drags
179 **prompture** prompting, suggestion   181 **tender down** lay down in
payment

3.1. Location: The prison
9 **skyey influences** influence of the stars   10 **this habitation** i.e., the
earth (and the body as well).   **keep'st** dwell   11 **Merely** utterly, only
13 **still** always   14 **accommodations** conveniences, civilized comforts
15 **nursed by baseness** nurtured by ignoble means   16 **fork** forked
tongue   17 **worm** (1) snake (2) grave worm   18 **thou oft provok'st**
you often invoke, summon   23 **certain** steadfast   24 **complexion**
constitution.   **strange effects** new appearances, manifestations
25 **After** in obedience to, under the influence of   29 **bowels** i.e., offspring   30 **mere** very.   **proper** own   31 **serpigo** a skin eruption.
rheum catarrh   32 **nor youth** neither youth   33 **after-dinner's** i.e., afternoon's   35 **as agèd** like old age, having to depend on it. (Youth is
penniless and dependent on the aged, whereas the old lack the physical capacity of youth.)   36 **eld** old age   37 **heat** vigor.   **affection**
passion

To make thy riches pleasant. What's yet in this
That bears the name of life? Yet in this life
Lie hid more thousand deaths; yet death we fear,
That makes these odds all even.
CLAUDIO   I humbly thank you. 41
To sue to live, I find I seek to die,   42
And, seeking death, find life. Let it come on.

Enter Isabella.

ISABELLA
What, ho! Peace here; grace and good company!   44
PROVOST
Who's there? Come in. The wish deserves a welcome.
                                    [*He goes to greet her.*]
DUKE [*to Claudio*]
Dear sir, ere long I'll visit you again.
CLAUDIO   Most holy sir, I thank you.
ISABELLA
My business is a word or two with Claudio.
PROVOST
And very welcome.—Look, signor, here's your sister.
DUKE [*aside to the Provost*]   Provost, a word with you.
PROVOST   As many as you please.
DUKE
Bring me to hear them speak, where I may be
Concealed.   [*The Duke and the Provost withdraw.*]
CLAUDIO   Now, sister, what's the comfort?
ISABELLA   Why,
As all comforts are: most good, most good indeed.
Lord Angelo, having affairs to heaven,
Intends you for his swift ambassador,
Where you shall be an everlasting leiger.   57
Therefore your best appointment make with speed; 58
Tomorrow you set on.
CLAUDIO   Is there no remedy?   59
ISABELLA
None but such remedy as, to save a head,
To cleave a heart in twain.
CLAUDIO   But is there any?
ISABELLA   Yes, brother, you may live.
There is a devilish mercy in the judge,
If you'll implore it, that will free your life
But fetter you till death.
CLAUDIO   Perpetual durance?   66
ISABELLA
Ay, just; perpetual durance, a restraint,   67
Though all the world's vastidity you had,   68
To a determined scope.
CLAUDIO   But in what nature?   69
ISABELLA
In such a one as, you consenting to 't,

Would bark your honor from that trunk you bear   71
And leave you naked.
CLAUDIO   Let me know the point.
ISABELLA
O, I do fear thee, Claudio, and I quake   73
Lest thou a feverous life shouldst entertain,   74
And six or seven winters more respect   75
Than a perpetual honor. Dar'st thou die?
The sense of death is most in apprehension,   77
And the poor beetle that we tread upon
In corporal sufferance finds a pang as great
As when a giant dies.
CLAUDIO   Why give you me this shame?
Think you I can a resolution fetch   82
From flowery tenderness? If I must die,   83
I will encounter darkness as a bride
And hug it in mine arms.
ISABELLA
There spake my brother! There my father's grave
Did utter forth a voice. Yes, thou must die.
Thou art too noble to conserve a life
In base appliances. This outward-sainted deputy, 89
Whose settled visage and deliberate word   90
Nips youth i' the head, and follies doth enew   91
As falcon doth the fowl, is yet a devil;
His filth within being cast, he would appear   93
A pond as deep as hell.
CLAUDIO   The prenzie Angelo?   94
ISABELLA
O, 'tis the cunning livery of hell,   95
The damned'st body to invest and cover   96
In prenzie guards! Dost thou think, Claudio: 97
If I would yield him my virginity,
Thou mightst be freed!
CLAUDIO   O heavens, it cannot be.
ISABELLA
Yes, he would give 't thee, from this rank offense, 100
So to offend him still. This night's the time   101
That I should do what I abhor to name,
Or else thou diest tomorrow.
CLAUDIO   Thou shalt not do 't.
ISABELLA   O, were it but my life,
I'd throw it down for your deliverance
As frankly as a pin.
CLAUDIO   Thanks, dear Isabel.   107

---

41 makes . . . even makes all equal **42 To sue** suing **44 grace . . . company** may God's grace and the companionship of the angels be yours **57 leiger** resident ambassador **58 appointment** preparation **59 set on** set forward **66 durance** imprisonment **67 just** just so **67–69 a restraint . . . scope** a confinement to fixed limits or bounds (i.e., to certain damnation and perpetual remorse for the sinful bargain you had struck), even if you had the entire vastness of the world to wander in

71 bark strip off (as one strips bark from a tree *trunk*) **73 fear** fear for **74 feverous** feverish. **entertain** maintain, desire **75 respect** value **77 apprehension** anticipation **82 resolution** fixity of purpose. **fetch** derive **83 flowery tenderness** i.e., comforting figures of speech **89 In base appliances** by means of ignoble devices, remedies. **outward-sainted** outwardly holy **90 settled visage** composed features **91 Nips . . . head** i.e., strikes at the head, like a falcon swooping upon its prey. **enew** drive prey down into the water or into covert **93 cast** vomited; cleared out; reckoned up (?) **94, 97 prenzie** (A word unknown elsewhere, perhaps meaning "princely" or "precise.") **95–97 'tis . . . guards** it is the cunning disguise of the devil to clothe and conceal the wickedest man imaginable in decorously proper trimmings **97 Dost thou think** i.e., would you believe **100 give 't thee** i.e., grant you license. **from** in return for, as a result of **101 So . . . still** i.e., to continue with your fornication **107 frankly** freely

ISABELLA
Be ready, Claudio, for your death tomorrow.

CLAUDIO
Yes. Has he affections in him,   109
That thus can make him bite the law by the nose   110
When he would force it? Sure it is no sin,   111
Or of the deadly seven it is the least.

ISABELLA   Which is the least?

CLAUDIO
If it were damnable, he being so wise,
Why would he for the momentary trick   115
Be perdurably fined? O Isabel!   116

ISABELLA
What says my brother?

CLAUDIO   Death is a fearful thing.

ISABELLA   And shamèd life a hateful.

CLAUDIO
Ay, but to die, and go we know not where,
To lie in cold obstruction and to rot,   120
This sensible warm motion to become   121
A kneaded clod, and the delighted spirit   122
To bathe in fiery floods, or to reside
In thrilling region of thick-ribbèd ice;   124
To be imprisoned in the viewless winds   125
And blown with restless violence round about
The pendent world; or to be worse than worst   127
Of those that lawless and incertain thought   128
Imagine howling—'tis too horrible!
The weariest and most loathèd worldly life
That age, ache, penury, and imprisonment   131
Can lay on nature is a paradise
To what we fear of death.   133

ISABELLA   Alas, alas!

CLAUDIO   Sweet sister, let me live.
What sin you do to save a brother's life,
Nature dispenses with the deed so far   137
That it becomes a virtue.

ISABELLA   O you beast!
O faithless coward! O dishonest wretch!   139
Wilt thou be made a man out of my vice?
Is 't not a kind of incest, to take life
From thine own sister's shame? What should I
   think?
Heaven shield my mother played my father fair!   143
For such a warpèd slip of wilderness   144
Ne'er issued from his blood. Take my defiance,
Die, perish! Might but my bending down   146

Reprieve thee from thy fate, it should proceed.
I'll pray a thousand prayers for thy death,
No word to save thee.

CLAUDIO
Nay, hear me, Isabel.

ISABELLA   O, fie, fie, fie!
Thy sin's not accidental, but a trade.   151
Mercy to thee would prove itself a bawd;   152
'Tis best that thou diest quickly.

CLAUDIO   O, hear me, Isabella!

[The Duke comes forward.]

DUKE
Vouchsafe a word, young sister, but one word.   155

ISABELLA   What is your will?

DUKE   Might you dispense with your leisure, I would
by and by have some speech with you. The satisfaction I would require is likewise your own benefit.   159

ISABELLA   I have no superfluous leisure—my stay
must be stolen out of other affairs—but I will attend   161
you awhile.   *[She walks apart.]*

DUKE   Son, I have overheard what hath passed between
you and your sister. Angelo had never the purpose to
corrupt her; only he hath made an assay of her virtue   165
to practice his judgment with the disposition of na-   166
tures. She, having the truth of honor in her, hath made   167
him that gracious denial which he is most glad to re-   168
ceive. I am confessor to Angelo, and I know this to be
true; therefore prepare yourself to death. Do not satisfy
your resolution with hopes that are fallible. Tomorrow
you must die. Go to your knees and make ready.

CLAUDIO   Let me ask my sister pardon. I am so out of
love with life that I will sue to be rid of it.

DUKE   Hold you there. Farewell. *[Claudio retires.]* Pro-   175
vost, a word with you.

[The Provost comes forward.]

PROVOST   What's your will, Father?

DUKE   That now you are come, you will be gone. Leave
me awhile with the maid. My mind promises with my   179
habit no loss shall touch her by my company.   180

PROVOST   In good time.   *Exit [Provost with Claudio].*   181

[Isabella comes forward.]

DUKE   The hand that hath made you fair hath made you
good. The goodness that is cheap in beauty makes   183
beauty brief in goodness; but grace, being the soul of   184
your complexion, shall keep the body of it ever fair.   185
The assault that Angelo hath made to you, fortune
hath conveyed to my understanding; and, but that   187

---

109 affections passions   **110 bite . . . nose** i.e., flout the law
111 force enforce. (Claudio wonders that lust can drive Angelo to
make a mockery of the law even while seeking to enforce it.)
115 trick trifle   **116 perdurably fined** everlastingly punished
120 obstruction cessation of vital functions   **121 sensible** endowed
with feeling.   **motion** organism   **122 kneaded clod** shapeless lump of
earth.   **delighted spirit** spirit attended with delight; or, beloved spirit
124 thrilling piercingly cold   **125 viewless** invisible   **127 pendent**
hanging in space. (A Ptolemaic concept.)   **128 lawless . . . thought**
i.e., wild conjecture   **131 penury** extreme poverty   **133 To** compared to   **137 dispenses with** grants a dispensation for, excuses
139 dishonest dishonorable   **143 shield** forfend, forbid   **144 warpèd
. . . wilderness** perverse, licentious scion, one that reverts to the original wild stock   **146 but** merely

151 accidental casual.   **trade** established habit   **152 prove . . .
bawd** i.e., provide opportunity for sexual license   **155 Vouchsafe** allow   **159 require** ask   **161 attend** await; listen to   **165 only he hath**
he has only.   **assay** test   **166–167 to practice . . . natures** to test
his ability to judge and control people's characters   **168 gracious** virtuous   **175 Hold you there** hold fast to that resolution
179–180 with my habit as well as my priestly garb (that)   **181 In
good time** i.e., very well   **183–184 The goodness . . . in goodness**
i.e., the physical graces that come easily with beauty make beauty
soon cease to be morally good   **185 complexion** character and appearance   **187 but that** were it not that

frailty hath examples for his falling, I should wonder 188
at Angelo. How will you do to content this substitute 189
and to save your brother?

ISABELLA   I am now going to resolve him. I had rather 191
my brother die by the law than my son should be
unlawfully born. But, O, how much is the good Duke
deceived in Angelo! If ever he return and I can speak
to him, I will open my lips in vain, or discover his 195
government. 196

DUKE   That shall not be much amiss. Yet, as the matter
now stands, he will avoid your accusation; he made 198
trial of you only. Therefore fasten your ear on my
advisings. To the love I have in doing good a remedy
presents itself. I do make myself believe that you may
most uprightously do a poor wronged lady a merited
benefit, redeem your brother from the angry law, do
no stain to your own gracious person, and much
please the absent Duke, if peradventure he shall ever
return to have hearing of this business.

ISABELLA   Let me hear you speak farther. I have spirit 207
to do anything that appears not foul in the truth of my 208
spirit. 209

DUKE   Virtue is bold, and goodness never fearful. Have 210
you not heard speak of Mariana, the sister of Frederick, the great soldier who miscarried at sea?

ISABELLA   I have heard of the lady, and good words
went with her name.

DUKE   She should this Angelo have married, was 215
affianced to her by oath, and the nuptial appointed;
between which time of the contract and limit of the 217
solemnity, her brother Frederick was wrecked at sea, 218
having in that perished vessel the dowry of his sister.
But mark how heavily this befell to the poor gentlewoman. There she lost a noble and renowned brother,
in his love toward her ever most kind and natural;
with him, the portion and sinew of her fortune, her 223
marriage dowry; with both, her combinate husband, 224
this well-seeming Angelo.

ISABELLA   Can this be so? Did Angelo so leave her?

DUKE   Left her in her tears, and dried not one of them
with his comfort; swallowed his vows whole, pretend- 228
ing in her discoveries of dishonor; in few, bestowed 229
her on her own lamentation, which she yet wears for 230
his sake; and he, a marble to her tears, is washed with 231
them but relents not.

ISABELLA   What a merit were it in death to take this
poor maid from the world! What corruption in this

life, that it will let this man live! But how out of this can
she avail? 236

DUKE   It is a rupture that you may easily heal, and the
cure of it not only saves your brother but keeps you
from dishonor in doing it.

ISABELLA   Show me how, good Father.

DUKE   This forenamed maid hath yet in her the continuance of her first affection; his unjust unkindness, that
in all reason should have quenched her love, hath, like
an impediment in the current, made it more violent
and unruly. Go you to Angelo; answer his requiring
with a plausible obedience; agree with his demands to 246
the point. Only refer yourself to this advantage: first, 247
that your stay with him may not be long, that the time
may have all shadow and silence in it, and the place 249
answer to convenience. This being granted in
course—and now follows all—we shall advise this
wronged maid to stead up your appointment, go in 252
your place. If the encounter acknowledge itself here- 253
after, it may compel him to her recompense. And here, 254
by this, is your brother saved, your honor untainted,
the poor Mariana advantaged, and the corrupt deputy
scaled. The maid will I frame and make fit for his at- 257
tempt. If you think well to carry this as you may, the
doubleness of the benefit defends the deceit from reproof. What think you of it?

ISABELLA   The image of it gives me content already,
and I trust it will grow to a most prosperous perfection.

DUKE   It lies much in your holding up. Haste you speed- 264
ily to Angelo. If for this night he entreat you to his
bed, give him promise of satisfaction. I will presently
to Saint Luke's; there, at the moated grange, resides 267
this dejected Mariana. At that place call upon me; and
dispatch with Angelo, that it may be quickly. 269

ISABELLA   I thank you for this comfort. Fare you well,
good Father.   *Exit. [The Duke remains.]*

3.2   *Enter [to the Duke] Elbow, Clown [Pompey, and]*
          officers.

ELBOW   Nay, if there be no remedy for it but that you
will needs buy and sell men and women like beasts,
we shall have all the world drink brown and white
bastard. 4

DUKE   O heavens, what stuff is here?

POMPEY   'Twas never merry world since, of two usur- 6
ies, the merriest was put down, and the worser al- 7

---

188 examples precedents   **189 this substitute** i.e., the deputy, Angelo
191 resolve him set his mind at rest   **195–196 discover his government** i.e., expose Angelo's misconduct   **198 avoid** evade, refute.   **he
made** i.e., he will say that he made   **207 spirit** courage   **208 truth**
righteousness   **209 spirit** soul   **210 fearful** afraid   **215 She . . . married** Angelo was supposed to have married her.   **was** i.e., he was
217–218 limit . . . solemnity date set for the ceremony   **223 sinew**
i.e., mainstay   **224 combinate husband** i.e., betrothed   **228–
229 pretending** falsely alleging   **229 in her** i.e., to have found in her.
in few in short   **229–230 bestowed . . . lamentation** left her to her
grief (with quibble on *bestowed,* meaning ''gave in marriage'')
230 wears i.e., carries in her heart   **231 a marble to** i.e., unmoved by

236 avail benefit   **246–247 to the point** precisely   **247 refer . . .
advantage** obtain these conditions   **249 shadow** darkness, secrecy
252 stead . . . appointment go in your stead   **253–254 If the . . .
hereafter** i.e., if she should become pregnant   **257 scaled** weighed
(and found wanting).   **frame** prepare   **264 holding up** ability to
carry it off   **267 moated grange** country house surrounded by a ditch
269 dispatch settle, conclude (business)
3.2. Location: Scene continues. The Duke remains onstage.
4 bastard sweet Spanish wine. (Used quibblingly.)   **6–7 two usuries**
i.e., moneylending (the *worser*) and procuring for fornication (the
merriest), both of which yield increase

lowed by order of law a furred gown to keep him 8
warm, and furred with fox on lambskins too, to signify that craft, being richer than innocency, stands 10
for the facing. 11

ELBOW Come your way, sir.—Bless you, good Father
Friar.

DUKE And you, good Brother Father. What offense hath 14
this man made you, sir?

ELBOW Marry, sir, he hath offended the law; and, sir,
we take him to be a thief too, sir, for we have found
upon him, sir, a strange picklock, which we have sent 18
to the deputy.

DUKE [to Pompey]
Fie, sirrah, a bawd, a wicked bawd!
The evil that thou causest to be done,
That is thy means to live. Do thou but think
What 'tis to cram a maw or clothe a back 23
From such a filthy vice; say to thyself,
From their abominable and beastly touches 25
I drink, I eat, array myself, and live.
Canst thou believe thy living is a life,
So stinkingly depending? Go mend, go mend. 28

POMPEY Indeed, it does stink in some sort, sir. But yet,
sir, I would prove— 30

DUKE
Nay, if the devil have given thee proofs for sin, 31
Thou wilt prove his.—Take him to prison, officer. 32
Correction and instruction must both work
Ere this rude beast will profit.

ELBOW He must before the deputy, sir; he has given 35
him warning. The deputy cannot abide a whoremaster. If he be a whoremonger and comes before him, he 37
were as good go a mile on his errand. 38

DUKE
That we were all, as some would seem to be, 39
From our faults, as faults from seeming, free! 40

Enter Lucio.

ELBOW His neck will come to your waist—a cord, sir. 41

POMPEY I spy comfort, I cry bail. Here's a gentleman
and a friend of mine.

LUCIO How now, noble Pompey? What, at the wheels
of Caesar? Art thou led in triumph? What, is there 45
none of Pygmalion's images, newly made woman, to 46

be had now, for putting the hand in the pocket and
extracting it clutched? What reply, ha? What sayst thou 48
to this tune, matter, and method? Is 't not drowned i' 49
the last rain, ha? What sayst thou, trot? Is the world 50
as it was, man? Which is the way? Is it sad, and few 51
words? Or how? The trick of it? 52

DUKE Still thus, and thus; still worse!

LUCIO How doth my dear morsel, thy mistress? Procures she still, ha?

POMPEY Troth, sir, she hath eaten up all her beef, and 56
she is herself in the tub. 57

LUCIO Why, 'tis good. It is the right of it, it must be so.
Ever your fresh whore and your powdered bawd; an 59
unshunned consequence, it must be so. Art going to 60
prison, Pompey?

POMPEY Yes, faith, sir.

LUCIO Why, 'tis not amiss, Pompey. Farewell. Go, say
I sent thee thither. For debt, Pompey? Or how?

ELBOW For being a bawd, for being a bawd.

LUCIO Well, then, imprison him. If imprisonment be
the due of a bawd, why, 'tis his right. Bawd is he
doubtless, and of antiquity too; bawd-born. Farewell, 68
good Pompey. Commend me to the prison, Pompey.
You will turn good husband now, Pompey; you will 70
keep the house. 71

POMPEY I hope, sir, your good worship will be my bail.

LUCIO No, indeed, will I not, Pompey; it is not the
wear. I will pray, Pompey, to increase your bondage. 74
If you take it not patiently, why, your mettle is the 75
more. Adieu, trusty Pompey.—Bless you, Friar. 76

DUKE And you.

LUCIO Does Bridget paint still, Pompey, ha? 78

ELBOW [to Pompey] Come your ways, sir, come. 79

POMPEY [to Lucio] You will not bail me, then, sir?

LUCIO Then, Pompey, nor now.—What news abroad, 81
Friar? What news?

ELBOW Come your ways, sir, come.

LUCIO Go to kennel, Pompey, go. [*Exeunt Elbow,
Pompey, and Officers.*] What news, Friar, of the Duke?

DUKE I know none. Can you tell me of any?

LUCIO Some say he is with the Emperor of Russia; other 87
some, he is in Rome. But where is he, think you? 88

DUKE I know not where; but wheresoever, I wish him
well.

---

8 furred gown (Characteristic attire of usurers.) **10–11 stands . . .
facing** represents the outer covering. (Fox symbolizes *craft* or craftiness, lambskin, *innocency*.) **14 Brother Father** (The Duke's retort to
Elbow's *Father Friar*, i.e., Father Brother.) **18 strange picklock** (referring to a chastity belt) **23 cram a maw** fill a stomach **25 touches**
sexual encounters **28 depending** supported **30 prove** i.e., argue,
demonstrate **31 proofs for** arguments in defense of **32 prove** turn
out to be **35 must** must go. **deputy** i.e., Angelo (though Escalus
gave Pompey the warning) **37–38 he . . . errand** i.e., he will have
a hard road to travel **39 That** would that **40 From . . . free** i.e.,
free from faults, and our faults free from dissembling **41 His . . .
cord** i.e., he is likely to hang by a cord like that around your waist.
(The Duke is habited like a friar.) **45 Caesar** (who defeated Pompey
at Pharsalia and led his sons in triumph after defeating them at
Munda) **46 Pygmalion's images** i.e., prostitutes, so called because
they "painted" with cosmetics like a painted statue. (Pygmalion was a
sculptor, according to legend, whose female statue came to life
"newly made.")

48 clutched i.e., with money in it (but also with sexual suggestion)
48–50 What sayst . . . rain i.e., what do you say now to this latest
turn of events? Are our prospects a little dampened? **50 trot** old
bawd **51–52 Which . . . words?** i.e., what is the latest fashion? Is
melancholy now in vogue? (A wry comment on Pompey's silence.)
52 trick fashion **56 eaten . . . beef** i.e., run through all her prostitutes **57 in the tub** being treated for venereal disease by the sweating-tub treatment (much as beef was salted down in a tub to preserve
it) **59 Ever . . . bawd** i.e., it always happens that young whores turn
into old bawds, "powdered" like beef in a tub and caked with cosmetics **60 unshunned** unshunnable, unavoidable **68 antiquity** long
continuance. **bawd-born** a born bawd and born of a bawd
70 good husband thrifty manager **71 keep the house** stay indoors
(with pun on the pimp's function as doorkeeper) **74 wear** fashion
75–76 your . . . more (1) your spirit is revealed all the more (2) your
shackles will be made heavier (playing on *mettle/metal*) **78 paint** use
cosmetics **79 Come your ways** come along **81 Then** neither then
87–88 other some some others

LUCIO It was a mad fantastical trick of him to steal from 91
the state and usurp the beggary he was never born to. 92
Lord Angelo dukes it well in his absence; he puts 93
transgression to 't.   94

DUKE He does well in 't.

LUCIO A little more lenity to lechery would do no harm
in him. Something too crabbed that way, Friar.   97

DUKE It is too general a vice, and severity must cure it.

LUCIO Yes, in good sooth, the vice is of a great kindred; 99
it is well allied. But it is impossible to extirp it quite, 100
Friar, till eating and drinking be put down. They say
this Angelo was not made by man and woman after 102
this downright way of creation. Is it true, think you? 103

DUKE How should he be made, then?

LUCIO Some report a sea maid spawned him; some, 105
that he was begot between two stockfishes. But it is 106
certain that when he makes water his urine is congealed ice; that I know to be true. And he is a motion 108
ungenerative; that's infallible.   109

DUKE You are pleasant, sir, and speak apace.   110

LUCIO Why, what a ruthless thing is this in him, for the
rebellion of a codpiece to take away the life of a man! 112
Would the Duke that is absent have done this? Ere he
would have hanged a man for the getting a hundred
bastards, he would have paid for the nursing a
thousand. He had some feeling of the sport; he knew
the service, and that instructed him to mercy.   117

DUKE I never heard the absent Duke much detected for 118
women. He was not inclined that way.

LUCIO O, sir, you are deceived.

DUKE 'Tis not possible.

LUCIO Who, not the Duke? Yes, your beggar of fifty;
and his use was to put a ducat in her clack-dish. The 123
Duke had crotchets in him. He would be drunk too, 124
that let me inform you.

DUKE You do him wrong, surely.

LUCIO Sir, I was an inward of his. A shy fellow was the 127
Duke, and I believe I know the cause of his with-
drawing.

DUKE What, I prithee, might be the cause?

LUCIO No, pardon. 'Tis a secret must be locked within
the teeth and the lips. But this I can let you understand: the greater file of the subject held the Duke to 133
be wise.

DUKE Wise? Why, no question but he was.

LUCIO A very superficial, ignorant, unweighing fellow. 136

DUKE Either this is envy in you, folly, or mistaking. The 137
very stream of his life and the business he hath helmed 138
must, upon a warranted need, give him a better proc- 139
lamation. Let him be but testimonied in his own 140
bringings-forth, and he shall appear to the envious a 141
scholar, a statesman, and a soldier. Therefore you
speak unskillfully; or, if your knowledge be more, it is 143
much darkened in your malice.

LUCIO Sir, I know him, and I love him.

DUKE Love talks with better knowledge, and knowledge with dearer love.

LUCIO Come, sir, I know what I know.

DUKE I can hardly believe that, since you know not
what you speak. But if ever the Duke return, as our
prayers are he may, let me desire you to make your
answer before him. If it be honest you have spoke,
you have courage to maintain it. I am bound to call
upon you; and, I pray you, your name?

LUCIO Sir, my name is Lucio, well known to the Duke.

DUKE He shall know you better, sir, if I may live to report you.

LUCIO I fear you not.

DUKE O, you hope the Duke will return no more, or
you imagine me too unhurtful an opposite. But indeed 160
I can do you little harm; you'll forswear this again.   161

LUCIO I'll be hanged first. Thou art deceived in me,
Friar. But no more of this. Canst thou tell if Claudio
die tomorrow or no?

DUKE Why should he die, sir?

LUCIO Why? For filling a bottle with a tundish. I would 166
the Duke we talk of were returned again. This ungen- 167
itured agent will unpeople the province with conti- 168
nency. Sparrows must not build in his house eaves, 169
because they are lecherous. The Duke yet would have
dark deeds darkly answered; he would never bring 171
them to light. Would he were returned! Marry, this
Claudio is condemned for untrussing. Farewell, good 173
Friar. I prithee, pray for me. The Duke, I say to thee,
again, would eat mutton on Fridays. He's now past it, 175
yet, and I say to thee, he would mouth with a beggar, 176
though she smelt brown bread and garlic. Say that I 177
said so. Farewell.   *Exit.*

DUKE
No might nor greatness in mortality   179
Can censure scape; back-wounding calumny   180
The whitest virtue strikes. What king so strong   181

---

91 **steal** steal away   92 **beggary** i.e., status of a wanderer or traveler (with unconscious ironic appropriateness; Lucio clearly does not see through the Duke's disguise as a mendicant friar)   93–94 **puts . . . to 't** puts lawbreaking under severe restraint   97 **Something** somewhat.   **crabbed** harsh   99 **kindred** i.e., family, numerous and well connected   100 **extirp** eradicate   102 **after** in accordance with   103 **downright** straightforward, usual   105 **sea maid** mermaid   106 **stockfishes** dried codfish   108–109 **motion ungenerative** masculine puppet, without sexual potency   110 **pleasant** jocose.   **apace** fast and idly   112 **codpiece** An appendage to the front of close-fitting hose or breeches worn by men, often ornamented and indelicately conspicuous; hence, slang for "penis."   117 **the service** i.e., prostitution   118 **detected** accused   123 **use** custom.   **clack-dish** beggar's wooden dish with a lid, which was "clacked" to attract attention; probably used metaphorically here for the female pudenda   136 **unweighing** injudicious

137 **envy** malice   138 **helmed** steered   139 **upon . . . need** if a warrant were needed   139–140 **give . . . proclamation** proclaim him better (than you assert)   140–141 **in . . . bringings-forth** by his own public actions   141 **to the envious** even to the malicious   143 **unskillfully** in ignorance   160 **too . . . opposite** too harmless an adversary   161 **forswear this** deny under oath what you've said.   **again** another time   166 **tundish** funnel (here representing the penis)   167–168 **ungenitured agent** sexless deputy   169 **Sparrows** (Proverbially lecherous birds.)   171 **darkly** secretly   173 **untrussing** undressing. (Specifically, untying the points used to fasten hose to doublet.)   175 **eat . . . Fridays** i.e., frequent loose women in flagrant disregard of the law. (Literally, violate religious observance by eating meat on fast days).   **past it** beyond the age for it   176 **mouth** kiss   177 **smelt brown bread** smelled of coarse bran bread   179 **mortality** humankind; human life   180 **scape** escape.   **back-wounding calumny** backbiting slander   181 **so** be he never so

Can tie the gall up in the slanderous tongue?   182
But who comes here?

Enter Escalus, Provost, and [officers with] bawd
[Mistress Overdone].

ESCALUS   Go, away with her to prison.

MISTRESS OVERDONE   Good my lord, be good to me.
Your honor is accounted a merciful man. Good my
lord.

ESCALUS   Double and treble admonition, and still forfeit   188
in the same kind! This would make mercy swear and   189
play the tyrant.

PROVOST   A bawd of eleven years' continuance, may it
please your honor.

MISTRESS OVERDONE   My lord, this is one Lucio's infor-   193
mation against me. Mistress Kate Keepdown was with   194
child by him in the Duke's time; he promised her marriage. His child is a year and a quarter old, come Philip   196
and Jacob. I have kept it myself; and see how he goes   197
about to abuse me!   198

ESCALUS   That fellow is a fellow of much license. Let
him be called before us. Away with her to prison! Go
to, no more words. [*Exeunt Officers with Mistress Ov-*
erdone.] Provost, my brother Angelo will not be al-   202
tered; Claudio must die tomorrow. Let him be furnished with divines and have all charitable   204
preparation. If my brother wrought by my pity, it   205
should not be so with him.

PROVOST   So please you, this friar hath been with him,
and advised him for th' entertainment of death.   208

ESCALUS   Good even, good Father.

DUKE   Bliss and goodness on you!

ESCALUS   Of whence are you?

DUKE
Not of this country, though my chance is now
To use it for my time. I am a brother   213
Of gracious order, late come from the See   214
In special business from His Holiness.

ESCALUS   What news abroad i' the world?

DUKE   None but that there is so great a fever on goodness that the dissolution of it must cure it. Novelty is   218
only in request, and, as it is, as dangerous to be aged   219
in any kind of course as it is virtuous to be constant   220
in any undertaking. There is scarce truth enough alive   221

to make societies secure, but security enough to make   222
fellowships accursed. Much upon this riddle runs the   223
wisdom of the world. This news is old enough, yet it
is every day's news. I pray you, sir, of what disposition was the Duke?

ESCALUS   One that, above all other strifes, contended   227
especially to know himself.

DUKE   What pleasure was he given to?

ESCALUS   Rather rejoicing to see another merry than
merry at anything which professed to make him re-   231
joice—a gentleman of all temperance. But leave we
him to his events, with a prayer they may prove pros-   233
perous, and let me desire to know how you find Claudio prepared. I am made to understand that you have
lent him visitation.   236

DUKE   He professes to have received no sinister measure   237
from his judge but most willingly humbles himself to
the determination of justice; yet had he framed to him-   239
self, by the instruction of his frailty, many deceiving   240
promises of life, which I, by my good leisure, have
discredited to him, and now is he resolved to die.

ESCALUS   You have paid the heavens your function, and
the prisoner the very debt of your calling. I have la-   244
bored for the poor gentleman to the extremest shore of   245
my modesty, but my brother justice have I found so   246
severe that he hath forced me to tell him he is indeed
Justice.

DUKE   If his own life answer the straitness of his   249
proceeding, it shall become him well; wherein if he
chance to fail, he hath sentenced himself.

ESCALUS   I am going to visit the prisoner. Fare you well.

DUKE   Peace be with you!

[Exeunt Escalus and Provost.]

He who the sword of heaven will bear
Should be as holy as severe;
Pattern in himself to know,   256
Grace to stand, and virtue go;   257
More nor less to others paying   258
Than by self-offenses weighing.   259
Shame to him whose cruel striking
Kills for faults of his own liking!
Twice treble shame on Angelo,
To weed my vice and let his grow!   263
O, what may man within him hide,
Though angel on the outward side!

182 Can i.e., that he can   **188–189 forfeit . . . kind** guilty of the
same offense   **189 mercy** i.e., even mercy   **193–194 information**
accusation   **196–197 Philip and Jacob** the Feast of Saint Philip and
Saint James (*Jacobus* in Latin), May 1   **197–198 goes about** busies
himself   **202 brother** i.e., fellow officer of state   **204 divines** clergymen   **205 wrought . . . pity** acted in accord with my impulses of
pity   **208 entertainment** reception, acceptance   **213 use** dwell in.
time present occasion   **214 the See** Rome   **218 the dissolution . . .
cure it** i.e., only by dying can goodness be rid of the disease   **218–
219 is only in request** is the only thing people seek   **219–221 as it
. . . undertaking** as things currently stand, (it is) as dangerous to be
constant in any undertaking as it is virtuous to be thus constant
221–223 There . . . accursed i.e., there is hardly enough integrity
and trust extant to bind men in sincere affection, but binding contrac-
tual obligations enough to make ordinary transactions intolerable.
(The Duke thus puns on *security* [1] a sense of trust [2] financial
pledge required to borrow money, and on *fellowship* [1] friendship
[2] corporations formed for trading ventures.)

223 upon this riddle in this riddling fashion   **227 strifes** endeavors
231 professed attempted   **233 his events** the outcome of his affairs
236 lent him visitation paid him a visit   **237 sinister measure** unfair
treatment meted out to him   **239–240 framed to himself** formulated
in his mind   **240 by . . . frailty** at the prompting of his natural human weakness   **244 the prisoner . . . calling** what your calling as a
friar obliges you to give the prisoner, i.e., the comforts of spiritual
counsel   **245–246 shore . . . modesty** limit of propriety   **249 straitness** strictness   **256 Pattern . . . know** to find an example or *pattern*
in himself by which to conduct himself or judge others   **257 Grace
. . . go** (to find in himself) grace to keep himself upright and virtue to
guide himself in the straight path   **258–259 More . . . weighing** in-
flicting no more and no less punishment on others than conscience
teaches him after weighing his own offenses   **263 my vice** i.e., vice
in everyone else

How may likeness made in crimes, 266
Making practice on the times, 267
To draw with idle spiders' strings 268
Most ponderous and substantial things! 269
Craft against vice I must apply.
With Angelo tonight shall lie
His old betrothèd but despisèd;
So disguise shall, by the disguisèd, 273
Pay with falsehood false exacting 274
And perform an old contracting.   *Exit.* 275

❖

4.1   *Enter Mariana, and Boy singing.*

Song.

BOY
Take, O, take those lips away,
That so sweetly were forsworn,
And those eyes, the break of day,
Lights that do mislead the morn; 4
But my kisses bring again, bring again, 5
Seals of love, but sealed in vain, sealed in vain. 6

Enter Duke [disguised as before].

MARIANA
Break off thy song, and haste thee quick away.
Here comes a man of comfort, whose advice
Hath often stilled my brawling discontent. [*Exit Boy.*] 9
I cry you mercy, sir, and well could wish 10
You had not found me here so musical.
Let me excuse me, and believe me so,
My mirth it much displeased, but pleased my woe. 13
DUKE
'Tis good; though music oft hath such a charm
To make bad good, and good provoke to harm. 15
I pray you, tell me, hath anybody inquired for me here
today? Much upon this time have I promised here 17
to meet.
MARIANA You have not been inquired after. I have sat
here all day.

Enter Isabella.

DUKE I do constantly believe you. The time is come 21
even now. I shall crave your forbearance a little. May- 22
be I will call upon you anon, for some advantage to 23
yourself.
MARIANA I am always bound to you.   *Exit.*
DUKE Very well met, and welcome.
What is the news from this good deputy?
ISABELLA
He hath a garden circummured with brick, 28
Whose western side is with a vineyard backed;
And to that vineyard is a planchèd gate, 30
That makes his opening with this bigger key. 31
[*She shows keys.*]
This other doth command a little door
Which from the vineyard to the garden leads;
There have I made my promise, upon the 34
Heavy middle of the night, to call upon him.
DUKE
But shall you on your knowledge find this way?
ISABELLA
I have ta'en a due and wary note upon 't.
With whispering and most guilty diligence,
In action all of precept, he did show me 39
The way twice o'er.
DUKE   Are there no other tokens
Between you 'greed concerning her observance? 41
ISABELLA
No, none, but only a repair i' the dark, 42
And that I have possessed him my most stay 43
Can be but brief; for I have made him know
I have a servant comes with me along,
That stays upon me, whose persuasion is 46
I come about my brother.
DUKE   'Tis well borne up. 47
I have not yet made known to Mariana
A word of this.—What, ho, within! Come forth!

Enter Mariana.

I pray you, be acquainted with this maid;
She comes to do you good.
ISABELLA   I do desire the like.
DUKE
Do you persuade yourself that I respect you? 52
MARIANA
Good Friar, I know you do, and have found it. 53
DUKE
Take then this your companion by the hand,
Who hath a story ready for your ear.
I shall attend your leisure. But make haste;
The vaporous night approaches.
MARIANA Will 't please you walk aside?
          Exit [with Isabella].

266–269 How . . . things (Seemingly a corrupt passage, perhaps missing two lines. The meaning may be: how can false seeming, composed of guilt within, practicing deception on the world, draw away in time with the web of legal deception the very substance of social order?) 273–275 So . . . contracting so shall disguise, by means of a disguised person, pay back with illusion (Mariana's disguise) the false exaction (of Angelo), and thus fulfill an old contract
4.1. Location: The moated grange at Saint Luke's.
4 Lights . . . morn i.e., eyes that mislead the morn into thinking the sun has risen 5 again back 6 Seals confirmations, pledges
9 brawling clamorous 10 cry you mercy beg your pardon 13 My . . . woe i.e., it suited not a merry but a melancholy mood 15 bad good i.e., bad seem good, attractive. (The Duke, echoing Renaissance conceptions of the psychological effects of music, warns that music may soothe melancholy at times but may also produce unvirtuous effects on the mind.) 17 Much upon pretty nearly about 21 constantly confidently

22 crave . . . little i.e., ask you to withdraw briefly 23 anon presently 28 circummured walled about 30 planchèd made of boards, planks 31 his its 34 upon during, at 39 In action . . . precept i.e., teaching by demonstration 41 her observance what she is supposed to do 42 repair act of going or coming to a place 43 possessed informed. my most stay my stay at the longest 46 stays upon waits for. persuasion belief 47 borne up sustained, carried out 52 respect you are concerned for your welfare 53 found it i.e., found it to be true

DUKE
O place and greatness! Millions of false eyes
Are stuck upon thee. Volumes of report   60
Run with these false and most contrarious quests   61
Upon thy doings; thousand escapes of wit   62
Make thee the father of their idle dream   63
And rack thee in their fancies.

Enter Mariana and Isabella.

Welcome. How agreed?   64

ISABELLA
She'll take the enterprise upon her, Father,
If you advise it.   It is not my consent,
DUKE   66
But my entreaty too.
ISABELLA   Little have you to say   67
When you depart from him but, soft and low,
"Remember now my brother."
MARIANA   Fear me not.   69
DUKE
Nor, gentle daughter, fear you not at all.
He is your husband on a precontract;   71
To bring you thus together, 'tis no sin,
Sith that the justice of your title to him   73
Doth flourish the deceit. Come, let us go.   74
Our corn's to reap, for yet our tithe's to sow. *Exeunt.* 75

4.2   *Enter Provost and Clown [Pompey].*

PROVOST   Come hither, sirrah. Can you cut off a man's
head?
POMPEY   If the man be a bachelor, sir, I can; but if he be
a married man, he's his wife's head, and I can never   4
cut off a woman's head.   5
PROVOST   Come, sir, leave me your snatches, and yield 6
me a direct answer. Tomorrow morning are to die
Claudio and Barnardine. Here is in our prison a com-   8
mon executioner, who in his office lacks a helper. If 9
you will take it on you to assist him, it shall redeem
you from your gyves; if not, you shall have your full 11
time of imprisonment and your deliverance with an
unpitied whipping, for you have been a notorious
bawd.

POMPEY   Sir, I have been an unlawful bawd time out of
mind, but yet I will be content to be a lawful hangman. I would be glad to receive some instruction from
my fellow partner.
PROVOST   What, ho, Abhorson! Where's Abhorson,
there?

Enter Abhorson.

ABHORSON   Do you call, sir?
PROVOST   Sirrah, here's a fellow will help you tomorrow
in your execution. If you think it meet, compound   23
with him by the year, and let him abide here with
you; if not, use him for the present and dismiss him.
He cannot plead his estimation with you; he hath   26
been a bawd.
ABHORSON   A bawd, sir? Fie upon him! He will discredit our mystery.   29
PROVOST   Go to, sir, you weigh equally; a feather will
turn the scale.   *Exit.*
POMPEY   Pray, sir, by your good favor—for surely, sir, 32
a good favor you have, but that you have a hanging 33
look—do you call, sir, your occupation a mystery?   34
ABHORSON   Ay, sir, a mystery.
POMPEY   Painting, sir, I have heard say, is a mystery, 36
and your whores, sir, being members of my occupation, using painting, do prove my occupation a
mystery. But what mystery there should be in hanging, if I should be hanged, I cannot imagine.
ABHORSON   Sir, it is a mystery.
POMPEY   Proof?
ABHORSON   Every true man's apparel fits your thief. If it 43
be too little for your thief, your true man thinks it big 44
enough; if it be too big for your thief, your thief thinks 45
it little enough. So every true man's apparel fits your 46
thief.

Enter Provost.

PROVOST   Are you agreed?
POMPEY   Sir, I will serve him, for I do find your hangman is a more penitent trade than your bawd: he doth 50
oftener ask forgiveness.   51
PROVOST   You, sirrah, provide your block and your ax
tomorrow four o'clock.
ABHORSON   Come on, bawd. I will instruct thee in my
trade. Follow!
POMPEY   I do desire to learn, sir; and I hope, if you have

---

60 stuck fastened   **60–62 Volumes . . . doings** innumerable rumors
follow a false scent and hunt counter in pursuing your activities
62 escapes sallies   **63 Make . . . dream** credit you with being the
source of their fantasies   **64 rack** stretch as on the rack, distort
66 not not only   **67 Little . . . say** say little   **69 Fear me not** i.e.,
don't worry about my carrying out my part   **71 precontract** legally
binding agreement entered into before any church ceremony. (Compare
Claudio's and Juliet's *true contract* at 1.2.142.)   **73 Sith that**
since   **74 flourish** adorn, make fair   **75 Our corn's . . . sow** we
must first sow grain before we can expect to reap a harvest; i.e., we
must get started.   **tithe** grain sown for tithe dues; or, an error for
"tilth"

4.2. Location: The prison.
4 wife's head (Compare Ephesians 5:23: "The husband is the head of
the wife.")   **5 head** i.e., maidenhead   **6 leave . . . snatches** leave off
your quips   **8–9 common** public   **11 gyves** fetters, shackles

23 compound make an agreement   **26 plead his estimation** claim any
respect on account of his reputation   **29 mystery** craft, occupation
32–33 favor . . . favor leave . . . face   **33–34 hanging look** (1)
downcast look (2) look of a hangman   **36 Painting** (1) painting of pictures (2) applying cosmetics   **43–46 Every . . . enough** (Just as Pompey argues that whores belong to a skilled craft because they are like
painters, Abhorson implies that hangmen are skilled craftsmen because they are like thieves, who, in turn, are like tailors; both thieves
and tailors "fit" honest men's apparel, by stealing or adjusting it.
Hangmen, in turn, are like thieves because they receive the garments
of the men they execute.)   **44–45 big enough** i.e., enough of a loss
46 little enough little enough for his efforts   **50–51 he doth . . .
forgiveness** (The executioner perfunctorily asked forgiveness of those
whose lives he was about to take.)

occasion to use me for your own turn, you shall find ₅₇
me yare. For truly, sir, for your kindness I owe you a ₅₈
good turn.
PROVOST
Call hither Barnardine and Claudio.
                                    Exit [Pompey, with Abhorson].
Th' one has my pity; not a jot the other,
Being a murderer, though he were my brother.

                    Enter Claudio.

Look, here's the warrant, Claudio, for thy death.
'Tis now dead midnight, and by eight tomorrow
Thou must be made immortal. Where's Barnardine? ₆₅
CLAUDIO
As fast locked up in sleep as guiltless labor   ₆₆
When it lies starkly in the traveler's bones.   ₆₇
He will not wake.
PROVOST   Who can do good on him?
Well, go, prepare yourself. [*Knocking within.*] But
    hark, what noise?
Heaven give your spirits comfort! [*Exit Claudio.*] By
    and by.—
I hope it is some pardon or reprieve
For the most gentle Claudio.

                Enter Duke [disguised as before].

                                        Welcome, Father.
DUKE
The best and wholesom'st spirits of the night
Envelop you, good Provost! Who called here of late?
PROVOST   None since the curfew rung.
DUKE
Not Isabel?
PROVOST   No.
DUKE   They will, then, ere 't be long.
PROVOST   What comfort is for Claudio?
DUKE
There's some in hope.
PROVOST   It is a bitter deputy.
DUKE
Not so, not so. His life is paralleled   ₇₉
Even with the stroke and line of his great justice. ₈₀
He doth with holy abstinence subdue
That in himself which he spurs on his power   ₈₂
To qualify in others. Were he mealed with that   ₈₃
Which he corrects, then were he tyrannous;
But this being so, he's just. [*Knocking within.*] Now
    are they come.   [*The Provost goes to the door.*]
This is a gentle provost; seldom when   ₈₆
The steelèd jailer is the friend of men.   ₈₇
                                    [*Knocking within.*]

How now? What noise? That spirit's possessed with
    haste
That wounds th' unsisting postern with these
    strokes.   ₈₉
PROVOST [*speaking at the door*]
There he must stay until the officer
Arise to let him in. He is called up.
                            [*He returns to the Duke.*]
DUKE
Have you no countermand for Claudio yet,
But he must die tomorrow?
PROVOST   None, sir, none.
DUKE
As near the dawning, Provost, as it is,
You shall hear more ere morning.
PROVOST   Happily   ₉₅
You something know, yet I believe there comes
No countermand. No such example have we;   ₉₇
Besides, upon the very siege of justice   ₉₈
Lord Angelo hath to the public ear
Professed the contrary.

                Enter a Messenger.

                            This is his lordship's man.
DUKE
And here comes Claudio's pardon.
MESSENGER [*giving a paper*]   My lord hath sent you
    this note, and by me this further charge, that you
    swerve not from the smallest article of it, neither in
    time, matter, or other circumstance. Good morrow;
    for, as I take it, it is almost day.
PROVOST   I shall obey him.   [*Exit Messenger.*]
DUKE [*aside*]
This is his pardon, purchased by such sin
For which the pardoner himself is in.   ₁₀₉
Hence hath offense his quick celerity,   ₁₁₀
When it is borne in high authority.   ₁₁₁
When vice makes mercy, mercy's so extended
That for the fault's love is th' offender friended.— ₁₁₃
Now, sir, what news?
PROVOST   I told you. Lord Angelo, belike thinking me ₁₁₅
    remiss in mine office, awakens me with this un- ₁₁₆
    wonted putting-on—methinks strangely, for he hath ₁₁₇
    not used it before.
DUKE   Pray you, let's hear.
PROVOST [*reads*] *the letter* "Whatsoever you may hear
    to the contrary, let Claudio be executed by four of
    the clock, and in the afternoon Barnardine. For my
    better satisfaction, let me have Claudio's head sent ₁₂₃
    me by five. Let this be duly performed, with a
    thought that more depends on it than we must yet

---

57 **for . . . turn** (1) as a pimp to provide for your sexual needs (2) as
your hangman when it is your turn to be hanged or "turned off" the
ladder   **58 yare** ready, alacritous   **65 made immortal** i.e., executed
66 fast firmly, soundly.   **guiltless labor** (A personification of the well-
earned weariness that tires the innocent laborer.)   **67 starkly** stiffly.
traveler's bones bones of one who travails or labors   **79–80 is paralleled . . . with** runs parallel and in exact conformity with   **80 stroke
and line** rigorous and exact course   **82 spurs on** encourages, urges
83 qualify mitigate.   **86 seldom when** i.e.,
it is seldom that   **87 steelèd** hardened

89 **unsisting** unassisting, unresting, or unresisting (?).   **postern** small
door   **95 Happily** haply, perhaps   **97 example** precedent   **98 siege**
seat   **109 in** engaged   **110–111 Hence . . . authority** i.e., any offense of which the person in authority is himself guilty will spread
quickly. (*His* means "its own.")   **113 the fault's love** love of the
fault.   **friended** befriended, countenanced   **115 belike** perchance
116–117 unwonted putting-on unaccustomed urging   **123 better satisfaction** greater assurance

deliver. Thus fail not to do your office, as you will 126
answer it at your peril."
What say you to this, sir?

DUKE   What is that Barnardine who is to be executed in
th' afternoon?

PROVOST   A Bohemian born, but here nursed up and 131
bred; one that is a prisoner nine years old. 132

DUKE   How came it that the absent Duke had not either
delivered him to his liberty or executed him? I have
heard it was ever his manner to do so.

PROVOST   His friends still wrought reprieves for him;
and indeed his fact, till now in the government of Lord 137
Angelo, came not to an undoubtful proof.

DUKE   It is now apparent?

PROVOST   Most manifest, and not denied by himself.

DUKE   Hath he borne himself penitently in prison? How
seems he to be touched? 142

PROVOST   A man that apprehends death no more dread- 143
fully but as a drunken sleep—careless, reckless, and 144
fearless of what's past, present, or to come; insensible 145
of mortality, and desperately mortal. 146

DUKE   He wants advice. 147

PROVOST   He will hear none. He hath evermore had the 148
liberty of the prison; give him leave to escape hence, 149
he would not. Drunk many times a day, if not many
days entirely drunk. We have very oft awaked him, as
if to carry him to execution, and showed him a
seeming warrant for it; it hath not moved him at all.

DUKE   More of him anon. There is written in your brow,
Provost, honesty and constancy; if I read it not truly,
my ancient skill beguiles me, but, in the boldness of 156
my cunning, I will lay myself in hazard. Claudio, 157
whom here you have warrant to execute, is no greater
forfeit to the law than Angelo who hath sentenced him.
To make you understand this in a manifested effect, I 160
crave but four days' respite, for the which you are to
do me both a present and a dangerous courtesy. 162

PROVOST   Pray, sir, in what?

DUKE   In the delaying death.

PROVOST   Alack, how may I do it, having the hour
limited, and an express command, under penalty, to 166
deliver his head in the view of Angelo? I may make
my case as Claudio's, to cross this in the smallest.

DUKE   By the vow of mine order I warrant you, if my
instructions may be your guide. Let this Barnardine
be this morning executed, and his head borne to Angelo.

PROVOST   Angelo hath seen them both and will dis- 173
cover the favor. 174

DUKE   O, death's a great disguiser, and you may add to

it. Shave the head, and tie the beard, and say it was 176
the desire of the penitent to be so bared before his
death. You know the course is common. If anything
fall to you upon this more than thanks and good 179
fortune, by the saint whom I profess, I will plead 180
against it with my life.

PROVOST   Pardon me, good Father, it is against my oath.

DUKE   Were you sworn to the Duke or to the deputy?

PROVOST   To him, and to his substitutes.

DUKE   You will think you have made no offense if the
Duke avouch the justice of your dealing? 186

PROVOST   But what likelihood is in that?

DUKE   Not a resemblance, but a certainty. Yet since I see 188
you fearful, that neither my coat, integrity, nor
persuasion can with ease attempt you, I will go further 190
than I meant, to pluck all fears out of you. Look you,
sir, here is the hand and seal of the Duke. [*He shows a
letter.*] You know the character, I doubt not, and the 193
signet is not strange to you. 194

PROVOST   I know them both.

DUKE   The contents of this is the return of the Duke.
You shall anon overread it at your pleasure, where
you shall find within these two days he will be here.
This is a thing that Angelo knows not, for he this very
day receives letters of strange tenor, perchance of the
Duke's death, perchance entering into some monas- 201
tery, but by chance nothing of what is writ. Look, th' 202
unfolding star calls up the shepherd. Put not yourself 203
into amazement how these things should be; all difficulties are but easy when they are known. Call your
executioner, and off with Barnardine's head. I will
give him a present shrift and advise him for a better 207
place. Yet you are amazed, but this shall absolutely 208
resolve you. Come away; it is almost clear dawn. 209

Exit [*with Provost*].

4.3   *Enter Clown* [*Pompey*].

POMPEY   I am as well acquainted here as I was in our 1
house of profession. One would think it were Mistress
Overdone's own house, for here be many of her old
customers. First, here's young Master Rash; he's in for 4
a commodity of brown paper and old ginger, nine- 5

---

126 deliver make known   **131 here** i.e., in Vienna   **132 a prisoner
. . . old** nine years a prisoner   **137 fact** crime   **142 touched** affected
143–144 no more dreadfully but with no more dread than   **145–
146 insensible . . . mortal** incapable of comprehending the meaning
of death, and without hope of immortality or of escaping execution
147 wants advice needs spiritual counsel   **148 evermore** constantly
148–149 the liberty . . . prison freedom to go anywhere within the
prison   **156–157 in the . . . hazard** confident in my knowledge (of
human character), I will put myself at risk   **160 in . . . effect** by
means of concrete proof   **162 present** immediate   **166 limited** fixed,
set   **173–174 discover the favor** recognize the face

176 tie trim, or tie in preparation for beheading (?)   **179 fall to** befall
180 profess acknowledge   **186 avouch** confirm   **188 resemblance**
seeming   **190 attempt** win, tempt   **193 character** handwriting
194 strange unknown   **201 entering** of his entering   **202 writ** i.e.,
written here   **203 unfolding star** i.e., morning star, Venus, which
bids the shepherd lead his sheep from the fold   **207 present shrift** immediate absolution for sins (after confession)   **208 Yet** still   **209 resolve you** dispel your uncertainties

4.3. Location: The prison.
1 well widely   **4 Rash** (All the names mentioned by Pompey apparently glance at contemporary social affectations and defects. *Rash*
means "reckless.")   **5 a commodity . . . ginger** (To circumvent the
laws against excessive rates of interest, moneylenders often advanced
cheap commodities to gullible borrowers in lieu of cash at a high rate
of interest. Master Rash, having agreed to a valuation of one hundred
ninety-seven pounds for such merchandise, has been able to resell it
for five marks, each mark worth about two-thirds of a pound, and has
been thrown into prison for debt.)

score and seventeen pounds, of which he made five marks, ready money. Marry, then ginger was not much in request, for the old women were all dead. 8 Then is there here one Master Caper, at the suit of 9 Master Three-pile the mercer, for some four suits of 10 peach-colored satin, which now peaches him a beg- 11 gar. Then have we here young Dizzy, and young 12 Master Deep-vow, and Master Copper-spur, and 13 Master Starve-lackey the rapier and dagger man, and 14 young Drop-heir that killed lusty Pudding, and Mas- 15 ter Forthlight the tilter, and brave Master Shoe-tie the 16 great traveler, and wild Half-can that stabbed Pots, 17 and I think forty more, all great doers in our trade, and are now "for the Lord's sake." 19

Enter Abhorson.

ABHORSON   Sirrah, bring Barnardine hither.
POMPEY   Master Barnardine! You must rise and be 21 hanged, Master Barnardine! 22
ABHORSON   What, ho, Barnardine!
BARNARDINE (*within*) A pox o' your throats! Who makes that noise there? What are you?
POMPEY   Your friends, sir, the hangman. You must be so good, sir, to rise and be put to death.
BARNARDINE [*within*]   Away, you rogue, away! I am sleepy.
ABHORSON   Tell him he must awake, and that quickly, too.
POMPEY   Pray, Master Barnardine, awake till you are ex-ecuted, and sleep afterwards.
ABHORSON   Go in to him, and fetch him out.
POMPEY   He is coming, sir, he is coming. I hear his straw rustle.

Enter Barnardine.

ABHORSON   Is the ax upon the block, sirrah?
POMPEY   Very ready, sir.
BARNARDINE   How now, Abhorson? What's the news with you?
ABHORSON   Truly, sir, I would desire you to clap into 41 your prayers; for, look you, the warrant's come.
BARNARDINE   You rogue, I have been drinking all night. I am not fitted for 't.

POMPEY   O, the better, sir, for he that drinks all night and is hanged betimes in the morning may sleep the 46 sounder all the next day.

Enter Duke [disguised as before].

ABHORSON   Look you, sir, here comes your ghostly 48 father. Do we jest now, think you?
DUKE   Sir, induced by my charity, and hearing how hastily you are to depart, I am come to advise you, comfort you, and pray with you.
BARNARDINE   Friar, not I. I have been drinking hard all night, and I will have more time to prepare me, or they shall beat out my brains with billets. I will not 55 consent to die this day, that's certain.
DUKE
O, sir, you must, and therefore I beseech you
Look forward on the journey you shall go.
BARNARDINE   I swear I will not die today for any man's persuasion.
DUKE   But hear you—
BARNARDINE   Not a word. If you have anything to say to me, come to my ward, for thence will not I today. 63
                                              Exit.

Enter Provost.

DUKE
Unfit to live or die. O gravel heart!   64
After him, fellows. Bring him to the block.
                   [*Exeunt Abhorson and Pompey.*]
PROVOST
Now, sir, how do you find the prisoner?
DUKE
A creature unprepared, unmeet for death;   67
And to transport him in the mind he is   68
Were damnable.
PROVOST   Here in the prison, Father,
There died this morning of a cruel fever
One Ragozine, a most notorious pirate,
A man of Claudio's years, his beard and head
Just of his color. What if we do omit   73
This reprobate till he were well inclined,
And satisfy the deputy with the visage
Of Ragozine, more like to Claudio?
DUKE
O, 'tis an accident that heaven provides!
Dispatch it presently; the hour draws on   78
Prefixed by Angelo. See this be done,   79
And sent according to command, whiles I
Persuade this rude wretch willingly to die.   81
PROVOST
This shall be done, good Father, presently.
But Barnardine must die this afternoon.
And how shall we continue Claudio,   84

---

8 **old women** (Proverbially fond of ginger.)   9 **Caper** (To *caper* was to dance or leap gracefully.)   10 **Three-pile** the thickest nap and most expensive grade of velvet.   **mercer** cloth merchant.   **suits** (with a play on *suit*, line 9)   11 **peaches him** denounces him as (with a play on *peach*)   12 **Dizzy** i.e., giddy, foolish?   13 **Deep-vow** One who swears earnestly and often.   **Copper-spur** (Copper was often used fraudulently to simulate gold.)   14 **Starve-lackey** (Spendthrift gallants often virtually starve their pages.)   15 **Drop-heir** (Perhaps referring to those who disinherited or preyed on unsuspecting heirs; or else *Drop-hair*, losing hair from syphilis.)   **lusty** vigorous.   **Pudding** i.e., sausage   16 **Forthlight** (Unexplained; perhaps an error for *Forthright*, referring to a style of tilting.)   **tilter** jouster.   **brave** showy, splendidly dressed.   **Shoe-tie** (Evidently a nickname for travelers and others who affected the foreign fashion of elaborate rosettes on the tie of the shoe.)   17 **Half-can** i.e., a small drinking tankard.   **Pots** i.e., ale pots   19 **for . . . sake** (The cry of prisoners from jail grates to passers-by to give them food or alms.)   21–22 **be hanged** (with a play on the im-precation; compare "go to the devil")   41 **clap into** quickly begin

46 **betimes** early   48 **ghostly** spiritual   55 **billets** cudgels, blocks of wood   63 **ward** cell   64 **gravel** stony   67 **unmeet** unready, unfit 68 **transport him** i.e., send him to his doom.   **he is** he is in   73 **omit** ignore, overlook   78 **presently** immediately (as also in line 82) 79 **Prefixed** appointed beforehand, stipulated   81 **rude** uncivilized 84 **continue** preserve

To save me from the danger that might come
If he were known alive?
DUKE   Let this be done:
Put them in secret holds, both Barnardine and
    Claudio.   87
Ere twice the sun hath made his journal greeting   88
To yond generation, you shall find   89
Your safety manifested.
PROVOST   I am your free dependent.   91
DUKE
Quick, dispatch, and send the head to Angelo.
                                         Exit [Provost].
Now will I write letters to Varrius—   93
The Provost, he shall bear them—whose contents
Shall witness to him I am near at home,
And that, by great injunctions, I am bound   96
To enter publicly. Him I'll desire
To meet me at the consecrated fount   98
A league below the city; and from thence,   99
By cold gradation and well-balanced form,   100
We shall proceed with Angelo.

        Enter Provost [with Ragozine's head].

PROVOST
Here is the head. I'll carry it myself.
DUKE
Convenient is it. Make a swift return,   103
For I would commune with you of such things   104
That want no ear but yours.
PROVOST   I'll make all speed. *Exit.* 105
ISABELLA (*within*)   Peace, ho, be here!
DUKE
The tongue of Isabel. She's come to know
If yet her brother's pardon be come hither.
But I will keep her ignorant of her good,
To make her heavenly comforts of despair   110
When it is least expected.

        Enter Isabella.

ISABELLA   Ho, by your leave!
DUKE
Good morning to you, fair and gracious daughter.
ISABELLA
The better, given me by so holy a man.
Hath yet the deputy sent my brother's pardon?
DUKE
He hath released him, Isabel, from the world.
His head is off and sent to Angelo.

87 **holds** cells, dungeons   88 **journal** daily   89 **yond** i.e., beyond
these walls, outside the perpetually dark prison (?). Sometimes it is
emended to *th' under*, the people of the Antipodes, on the opposite
side of the earth, or, people under the sun, the human race.   91 **free
dependent** willing servant   93 **to Varrius** (The Folio reads *to Angelo*,
but see line 99 below and 4.5.12–14; evidently, the Duke's plan is
to meet Varrius "a league below the city" and then proceed to the
rendezvous with Angelo.)   96 **by great injunctions** by powerful precedent or for compelling reasons   98 **fount** spring   99 **league** (A
measure of varying length but usually about three miles.)   100 **cold
. . . form** i.e., moving deliberately and with proper observance of all
formalities   103 **Convenient** timely, fitting   104 **commune** converse
105 **want** require   110 **of** from, transformed out of

ISABELLA
Nay, but it is not so!
DUKE   It is no other.
Show your wisdom, daughter, in your close
    patience.   118
ISABELLA
O, I will to him and pluck out his eyes!
DUKE
You shall not be admitted to his sight.
ISABELLA
Unhappy Claudio! Wretched Isabel!
Injurious world! Most damnèd Angelo!
DUKE
This nor hurts him nor profits you a jot.   123
Forbear it therefore; give your cause to heaven.
Mark what I say, which you shall find
By every syllable a faithful verity.   126
The Duke comes home tomorrow. Nay, dry your
    eyes;
One of our convent, and his confessor,
Gives me this instance. Already he hath carried   129
Notice to Escalus and Angelo,
Who do prepare to meet him at the gates,
There to give up their pow'r. If you can, pace your
    wisdom   132
In that good path that I would wish it go,
And you shall have your bosom on this wretch,   134
Grace of the Duke, revenges to your heart,   135
And general honor.
ISABELLA   I am directed by you.
DUKE
This letter, then, to Friar Peter give.
                              [*He gives her a letter.*]
'Tis that he sent me of the Duke's return.   138
Say, by this token, I desire his company
At Mariana's house tonight. Her cause and yours
I'll perfect him withal, and he shall bring you   141
Before the Duke, and to the head of Angelo   142
Accuse him home and home. For my poor self,   143
I am combinèd by a sacred vow,   144
And shall be absent. Wend you with this letter.   145
Command these fretting waters from your eyes   146
With a light heart. Trust not my holy order
If I pervert your course. Who's here?

        Enter Lucio.

LUCIO   Good even. Friar, where's the Provost?
DUKE   Not within, sir.
LUCIO   O pretty Isabella, I am pale at mine heart to see 151
thine eyes so red. Thou must be patient. I am fain to 152

118 **close patience** silent enduring   123 **nor hurts** neither hurts
126 **By** with respect to   129 **instance** proof   132 **pace** teach to move
in response to your will, as with a horse   134 **bosom** desire
135 **Grace of** manifestation of favor from.   **to** in accord with
138 **that** that which.   **of** concerning   141 **perfect** acquaint completely.   **withal** with   142 **head** i.e., face   143 **home and home**
thoroughly   144 **combinèd** bound   145 **Wend** go   146 **fretting** cor-
roding   151 **pale . . . heart** i.e., pale from sighing, since sighs cost
the heart loss of blood   152 **fain** compelled (as also in line 171)

dine and sup with water and bran; I dare not for my 153
head fill my belly; one fruitful meal would set me 154
to 't. But they say the Duke will be here tomorrow. 155
By my troth, Isabel, I loved thy brother. If the old fantastical Duke of dark corners had been at home, he
had lived.   [*Exit Isabella.*]

DUKE   Sir, the Duke is marvelous little beholding to 159
your reports; but the best is, he lives not in them. 160

LUCIO   Friar, thou knowest not the Duke so well as I
do. He's a better woodman than thou tak'st him for. 162

DUKE   Well, you'll answer this one day. Fare ye well.
[*He starts to go.*]

LUCIO   Nay, tarry, I'll go along with thee. I can tell thee
pretty tales of the Duke.

DUKE   You have told me too many of him already, sir, if
they be true; if not true, none were enough.

LUCIO   I was once before him for getting a wench with
child.

DUKE   Did you such a thing?

LUCIO   Yes, marry, did I, but I was fain to forswear it.
They would else have married me to the rotten medlar. 172

DUKE   Sir, your company is fairer than honest. Rest you
well.

LUCIO   By my troth, I'll go with thee to the lane's end.
If bawdy talk offend you, we'll have very little of it.
Nay, Friar, I am a kind of burr; I shall stick. *Exeunt.*

❧

4.4   *Enter Angelo and Escalus, [reading letters].*

ESCALUS   Every letter he hath writ hath disvouched 1
other.

ANGELO   In most uneven and distracted manner. His
actions show much like to madness. Pray heaven his
wisdom be not tainted! And why meet him at the 5
gates and redeliver our authorities there?

ESCALUS   I guess not.   7

ANGELO   And why should we proclaim it in an hour be- 8
fore his entering, that if any crave redress of injustice,
they should exhibit their petitions in the street? 10

ESCALUS   He shows his reason for that: to have a
dispatch of complaints, and to deliver us from devices 12
hereafter, which shall then have no power to stand
against us.

ANGELO   Well, I beseech you, let it be proclaimed.
Betimes i' the morn I'll call you at your house. Give 16
notice to such men of sort and suit as are to meet him. 17

ESCALUS   I shall, sir. Fare you well.

ANGELO   Good night.   *Exit [Escalus].*
This deed unshapes me quite, makes me
unpregnant   20
And dull to all proceedings. A deflowered maid,
And by an eminent body that enforced   22
The law against it! But that her tender shame   23
Will not proclaim against her maiden loss,
How might she tongue me! Yet reason dares her no,   25
For my authority bears of a credent bulk   26
That no particular scandal once can touch
But it confounds the breather. He should have lived, 28
Save that his riotous youth, with dangerous sense, 29
Might in the times to come have ta'en revenge
By so receiving a dishonored life   31
With ransom of such shame. Would yet he had
lived!
Alack, when once our grace we have forgot,
Nothing goes right; we would, and we would not.
Exit.

4.5   *Enter Duke [in his own habit] and Friar Peter.*

DUKE
These letters at fit time deliver me.   [*Giving letters.*] 1
The Provost knows our purpose and our plot.
The matter being afoot, keep your instruction,   3
And hold you ever to our special drift,   4
Though sometimes you do blench from this to that 5
As cause doth minister. Go call at Flavius' house,   6
And tell him where I stay. Give the like notice
To Valencius, Rowland, and to Crassus,
And bid them bring the trumpets to the gate;   9
But send me Flavius first.

FRIAR PETER   It shall be speeded well.   [*Exit.*] 11

Enter Varrius.

DUKE
I thank thee, Varrius. Thou hast made good haste.
Come, we will walk. There's other of our friends
Will greet us here anon. My gentle Varrius!   *Exeunt.*

4.6   *Enter Isabella and Mariana.*

ISABELLA
To speak so indirectly I am loath.
I would say the truth, but to accuse him so,
That is your part. Yet I am advised to do it,

153–154 for my head i.e., on my life   **154 fruitful** abundant   **154–**
155 set me to 't i.e., awaken my lust and thus place me in danger of
Angelo's edict   **159 marvelous** marvelously.   **beholding** beholden
160 he . . . them i.e., he is not accurately described by them
162 woodman i.e., hunter (of women)   **172 medlar** A fruit that was
eaten after it had begun to rot; here, signifying a prostitute.
4.4. Location: In Vienna.
1 disvouched contradicted   **5 tainted** diseased   **7 guess not** cannot
guess   **8 in an hour** i.e., a full hour   **10 exhibit** present   **12 dispatch**
prompt settlement.   **devices** contrived complaints   **16 Betimes** early
17 sort rank.   **suit** such as owe attendance or are followed by a
retinue

20 unpregnant unapt   **22 body** person   **23 But that** were it not that
25 tongue i.e., reproach, accuse.   **dares her no** i.e., frightens her to
say nothing   **26 bears . . . bulk** bears such a huge credibility
28 But . . . breather without its confuting the person who speaks
29 sense passion, intention   **31 By** for, because of
4.5. Location: Outside the city.
1 me for me   **3 keep** keep to   **4 drift** plot   **5 blench** deviate   **6 min-**
ister prompt, provide occasion   **9 trumpets** trumpeters   **11 speeded**
accomplished, expedited
4.6. Location: Near the city gate.

He says, to veil full purpose.

MARIANA   Be ruled by him.

ISABELLA

Besides, he tells me that if peradventure   5
He speak against me on the adverse side,
I should not think it strange, for 'tis a physic   7
That's bitter to sweet end.

Enter [Friar] Peter.

MARIANA

I would Friar Peter—

ISABELLA   O, peace, the Friar is come.

FRIAR PETER

Come, I have found you out a stand most fit,   10
Where you may have such vantage on the Duke
He shall not pass you. Twice have the trumpets
  sounded.
The generous and gravest citizens   13
Have hent the gates, and very near upon   14
The Duke is entering. Therefore hence, away!

Exeunt.

❖

5.1   *Enter Duke, Varrius, lords, Angelo, Escalus,
          Lucio, [Provost, officers, and] citizens at several
          doors.*

DUKE

My very worthy cousin, fairly met!   1
Our old and faithful friend, we are glad to see you.

ANGELO, ESCALUS

Happy return be to Your Royal Grace!

DUKE

Many and hearty thankings to you both.
We have made inquiry of you, and we hear
Such goodness of your justice that our soul
Cannot but yield you forth to public thanks,   7
Forerunning more requital.   8

ANGELO   You make my bonds still greater.   9

DUKE

O, your desert speaks loud, and I should wrong it
To lock it in the wards of covert bosom,   11
When it deserves with characters of brass   12
A forted residence 'gainst the tooth of time   13
And razure of oblivion. Give me your hand,   14
And let the subject see, to make them know   15
That outward courtesies would fain proclaim   16
Favors that keep within. Come, Escalus,   17

You must walk by us on our other hand,
And good supporters are you.

Enter [Friar] Peter and Isabella.

FRIAR PETER

Now is your time. Speak loud, and kneel before him.

ISABELLA *[kneeling]*

Justice, O royal Duke! Vail your regard   21
Upon a wronged—I would fain have said a maid.
O worthy prince, dishonor not your eye
By throwing it on any other object
Till you have heard me in my true complaint
And given me justice, justice, justice, justice!

DUKE

Relate your wrongs. In what? By whom? Be brief.
Here is Lord Angelo shall give you justice.   28
Reveal yourself to him.

ISABELLA   O worthy Duke,
You bid me seek redemption of the devil.
Hear me yourself; for that which I must speak
Must either punish me, not being believed,   32
Or wring redress from you.
Hear me, O, hear me, hear!

ANGELO

My lord, her wits, I fear me, are not firm.
She hath been a suitor to me for her brother
Cut off by course of justice.

ISABELLA *[standing]*   By course of justice!

ANGELO

And she will speak most bitterly and strange.   38

ISABELLA

Most strange, but yet most truly, will I speak.
That Angelo's forsworn, is it not strange?
That Angelo's a murderer, is 't not strange?
That Angelo is an adulterous thief,
An hypocrite, a virgin-violator,
Is it not strange, and strange?

DUKE   Nay, it is ten times strange.

ISABELLA

It is not truer he is Angelo
Than this is all as true as it is strange.   47
Nay, it is ten times true, for truth is truth
To th' end of reck'ning.

DUKE   Away with her! Poor soul,
She speaks this in th' infirmity of sense.   50

ISABELLA

O prince, I conjure thee, as thou believ'st
There is another comfort than this world,
That thou neglect me not with that opinion   53
That I am touched with madness. Make not
  impossible   54
That which but seems unlike. 'Tis not impossible   55
But one the wicked'st caitiff on the ground   56

5 **peradventure** perhaps   7 **physic** remedy   10 **stand** place to stand
13 **generous** highborn   14 **hent** reached, occupied.   **very near upon**
almost immediately now
5.1. Location: The city gate.
s.d. several separate   1 **cousin** fellow nobleman. (Addressed to Angelo.)   7 **yield . . . to** call you forth to give you   8 **more requital** further reward   9 **bonds** obligations   11 **To lock . . . bosom** i.e., to
keep it locked up in my heart   12 **characters** writing, letters
13 **forted** fortified   14 **razure** effacement   15 **the subject** those who
are subjects   16 **fain** happily (as also in line 22)   17 **keep** reside.
within i.e., in the heart

21 **Vail your regard** look down   28 **shall** who shall   32 **not being** if
I am not   38 **strange** strangely   47 **Than** than that   50 **in . . . sense**
out of a sick mind, out of the weakness of passion   53 **with that
opinion** out of a supposition   54 **Make not** do not consider as
55 **unlike** unlikely   56 **But one the wicked'st caitiff** but that the most
wicked villain

May seem as shy, as grave, as just, as absolute   57
As Angelo; even so may Angelo,
In all his dressings, characts, titles, forms,   59
Be an archvillain. Believe it, royal prince,
If he be less, he's nothing; but he's more,   61
Had I more name for badness.

DUKE   By mine honesty,
If she be mad—as I believe no other—
Her madness hath the oddest frame of sense,   64
Such a dependency of thing on thing,   65
As e'er I heard in madness.

ISABELLA   O gracious Duke,
Harp not on that, nor do not banish reason   67
For inequality, but let your reason serve   68
To make the truth appear where it seems hid,
And hide the false seems true.   70

DUKE   Many that are not mad
Have, sure, more lack of reason. What would
    you say?

ISABELLA
I am the sister of one Claudio,
Condemned upon the act of fornication
To lose his head, condemned by Angelo.
I, in probation of a sisterhood,   76
Was sent to by my brother; one Lucio
As then the messenger—

LUCIO   That's I, an 't like Your Grace. 78
I came to her from Claudio and desired her
To try her gracious fortune with Lord Angelo
For her poor brother's pardon.

ISABELLA   That's he indeed.

DUKE [to Lucio]
You were not bid to speak.

LUCIO   No, my good lord,
Nor wished to hold my peace.

DUKE   I wish you now, then.
Pray you, take note of it. And when you have
A business for yourself, pray heaven you then
Be perfect.   86

LUCIO   I warrant your honor.   87

DUKE
The warrant's for yourself. Take heed to 't.

ISABELLA
This gentleman told somewhat of my tale—

LUCIO   Right.

DUKE
It may be right, but you are i' the wrong
To speak before your time.—Proceed.

ISABELLA   I went
To this pernicious caitiff deputy—

DUKE
That's somewhat madly spoken.

ISABELLA   Pardon it;
The phrase is to the matter.   95

DUKE   Mended again. The matter; proceed.   96

ISABELLA
In brief, to set the needless process by,   97
How I persuaded, how I prayed and kneeled,
How he refelled me, and how I replied—   99
For this was of much length—the vile conclusion
I now begin with grief and shame to utter.
He would not, but by gift of my chaste body
To his concupiscible intemperate lust,   103
Release my brother; and after much debatement   104
My sisterly remorse confutes mine honor,   105
And I did yield to him. But the next morn betimes,   106
His purpose surfeiting, he sends a warrant   107
For my poor brother's head.

DUKE   This is most likely!

ISABELLA
O, that it were as like as it is true!   109

DUKE   By heaven, fond wretch, thou know'st not what
    thou speak'st,   110
Or else thou art suborned against his honor   111
In hateful practice. First, his integrity   112
Stands without blemish. Next, it imports no reason   113
That with such vehemency he should pursue
Faults proper to himself. If he had so offended,   115
He would have weighed thy brother by himself   116
And not have cut him off. Someone hath set you on.
Confess the truth, and say by whose advice
Thou cam'st here to complain.

ISABELLA   And is this all?
Then, O you blessèd ministers above,
Keep me in patience, and with ripened time
Unfold the evil which is here wrapped up   122
In countenance! Heaven shield Your Grace
    from woe,   123
As I thus wronged hence unbelievèd go!

[She starts to leave.]

DUKE
I know you'd fain be gone. An officer!
To prison with her. Shall we thus permit
A blasting and a scandalous breath to fall   127

---

57 **shy** quietly dignified. **absolute** flawless 59 **dressings** ceremonial robes. **characts** insignia of office 61 **If . . . nothing** i.e., even if he were less than an archvillain, he would be worthless 64 **frame of sense** form of reason 65 **dependency . . : on thing** coherence 67–68 **do . . . inequality** i.e., do not assume lack of reason on my part because of the inconsistency between my story and Angelo's refutation, or because of the inequality in our reputations 70 **hide** put out of sight, remove from consideration, **seems** that seems 76 **in probation** i.e., a novice 78 **As then** being at that time. **an 't like** if it please 86 **perfect** prepared 87 **warrant** assure. (The Duke, however, quibbles in line 88 on the meaning "judicial writ.")

95 **to the matter** to the purpose 96 **Mended again** set right. **The matter** i.e., proceed to the main point 97 **to set . . . by** not to dwell on unnecessary details in the story 99 **refelled** refuted, repelled 103 **concupiscible** lustful 104 **debatement** argument, debate 105 **remorse** pity. **confutes** confounds, silences 106 **betimes** early 107 **surfeiting** becoming satiated 109 **like** likely 110 **fond** foolish 111 **suborned** induced to give false testimony 112 **practice** machination, conspiracy 113 **imports no reason** i.e., makes no sense 115 **proper to himself** of which he himself is guilty 116 **weighed** judged 122 **Unfold** disclose 122–123 **wrapped . . . countenance** concealed by means of authority, as well as by Angelo's hypocritically composed features and his partiality or favoritism 127 **blasting** blighting

On him so near us? This needs must be a practice.
Who knew of your intent and coming hither?

ISABELLA
One that I would were here, Friar Lodowick.

                                    [*Exit under guard.*]

DUKE
A ghostly father, belike. Who knows that Lodowick?

LUCIO
My lord, I know him; 'tis a meddling friar.
I do not like the man. Had he been lay, my lord,   133
For certain words he spake against Your Grace
In your retirement, I had swinged him soundly.   135

DUKE
Words against me? This' a good friar, belike!   136
And to set on this wretched woman here
Against our substitute! Let this friar be found.

                            [*Exit one or more attendants.*]

LUCIO
But yesternight, my lord, she and that friar,
I saw them at the prison. A saucy friar,
A very scurvy fellow.

FRIAR PETER   Blessed be Your Royal Grace!
I have stood by, my lord, and I have heard
Your royal ear abused. First, hath this woman
Most wrongfully accused your substitute,
Who is as free from touch or soil with her
As she from one ungot.   147

DUKE   We did believe no less.
Know you that Friar Lodowick that she speaks of?

FRIAR PETER
I know him for a man divine and holy,
Not scurvy, nor a temporary meddler,   151
As he's reported by this gentleman;
And, on my trust, a man that never yet
Did, as he vouches, misreport Your Grace.

LUCIO
My lord, most villainously, believe it.

FRIAR PETER
Well, he in time may come to clear himself;
But at this instant he is sick, my lord,
Of a strange fever. Upon his mere request,   158
Being come to knowledge that there was complaint   159
Intended 'gainst Lord Angelo, came I hither,
To speak, as from his mouth, what he doth know
Is true and false, and what he with his oath
And all probation will make up full clear,   163
Whensoever he's convented. First, for this woman,   164
To justify this worthy nobleman,
So vulgarly and personally accused,   166
Her shall you hear disprovèd to her eyes,   167
Till she herself confess it.

DUKE   Good Friar, let's hear it.
                    [*Friar Peter goes to bring in Mariana.*]
Do you not smile at this, Lord Angelo?

O heaven, the vanity of wretched fools!   170
Give us some seats.   [*Seats are provided.*]
                            Come, cousin Angelo,
In this I'll be impartial. Be you judge
Of your own cause.   [*The Duke and Angelo sit.*]

            Enter Mariana, [veiled].

                            Is this the witness, Friar?
First, let her show her face, and after speak.

MARIANA
Pardon, my lord, I will not show my face
Until my husband bid me.

DUKE   What, are you married?

MARIANA   No, my lord.

DUKE   Are you a maid?

MARIANA   No, my lord.

DUKE   A widow, then?

MARIANA   Neither, my lord.

DUKE   Why, you are nothing then, neither maid,
widow, nor wife?

LUCIO   My lord, she may be a punk, for many of them   185
are neither maid, widow, nor wife.

DUKE
Silence that fellow. I would he had some cause
To prattle for himself.   188

LUCIO   Well, my lord.

MARIANA
My lord, I do confess I ne'er was married,
And I confess besides I am no maid.
I have known my husband, yet my husband   192
Knows not that ever he knew me.

LUCIO   He was drunk then, my lord; it can be no better.

DUKE   For the benefit of silence, would thou wert so too!

LUCIO   Well, my lord.

DUKE
This is no witness for Lord Angelo.

MARIANA   Now I come to 't, my lord.
She that accuses him of fornication
In selfsame manner doth accuse my husband,
And charges him, my lord, with such a time   201
When, I'll depose, I had him in mine arms   202
With all th' effect of love.   203

ANGELO   Charges she more than me?   204

MARIANA   Not that I know.

DUKE   No? You say your husband?

MARIANA
Why, just, my lord, and that is Angelo,   207
Who thinks he knows that he ne'er knew my body,
But knows he thinks that he knows Isabel's.

ANGELO
This is a strange abuse. Let's see thy face.   210

MARIANA
My husband bids me. Now I will unmask.

                                    [*She unveils.*]

---

133 lay not a cleric   **135 In your retirement** during your absence.
had swinged would have beaten   **136 This'** this is   **147 ungot** unbegotten   **151 temporary meddler** meddler in temporal affairs
158 Upon . . . request solely at his request   **159 Being . . . knowledge** he having learned   **163 probation** proof   **164 convented** summoned   **166 vulgarly** publicly   **167 to her eyes** i.e., to her face

170 vanity folly   **185 punk** harlot   **188 To . . . himself** to speak in
his own defense. (The Duke hints that there might well be charges
pending against Lucio.)   **192 known** had sexual intercourse with
201 with . . . time with doing the deed at just the same time
202 depose testify under oath   **203 effect** manifestations
204 Charges . . . me does she (Isabella) bring charges against persons
besides myself   **207 just** just so   **210 abuse** deception

This is that face, thou cruel Angelo,
Which once thou swor'st was worth the looking on;
This is the hand which, with a vowed contract,
Was fast belocked in thine; this is the body   215
That took away the match from Isabel,   216
And did supply thee at thy garden house
In her imagined person.

DUKE [to Angelo]   Know you this woman?

LUCIO   Carnally, she says.

DUKE   Sirrah, no more!

LUCIO   Enough, my lord.

ANGELO
My lord, I must confess I know this woman,
And five years since there was some speech of
   marriage
Betwixt myself and her, which was broke off,
Partly for that her promisèd proportions   226
Came short of composition, but in chief   227
For that her reputation was disvalued   228
In levity. Since which time of five years   229
I never spake with her, saw her, nor heard from her,
Upon my faith and honor.

MARIANA [kneeling]   Noble prince,
As there comes light from heaven and words from
   breath,
As there is sense in truth and truth in virtue,
I am affianced this man's wife as strongly
As words could make up vows; and, my good lord,
But Tuesday night last gone in 's garden house
He knew me as a wife. As this is true,
Let me in safety raise me from my knees,
Or else forever be confixèd here,
A marble monument!

ANGELO   I did but smile till now.
Now, good my lord, give me the scope of justice.   242
My patience here is touched. I do perceive   243
These poor informal women are no more   244
But instruments of some more mightier member   245
That sets them on. Let me have way, my lord,
To find this practice out.

DUKE   Ay, with my heart,
And punish them to your height of pleasure.—
Thou foolish friar, and thou pernicious woman,
Compact with her that's gone, think'st thou thy
   oaths,   250
Though they would swear down each particular
   saint,   251
Were testimonies against his worth and credit
That's sealed in approbation?—You, Lord Escalus,   253
Sit with my cousin; lend him your kind pains
To find out this abuse, whence 'tis derived.
There is another friar that set them on;
Let him be sent for.

[The Duke rises; Escalus takes his chair.]

FRIAR PETER
Would he were here, my lord! For he indeed
Hath set the women on to this complaint.
Your Provost knows the place where he abides,
And he may fetch him.

DUKE   Go do it instantly.

[Exit Provost.]
And you, my noble and well-warranted cousin,
Whom it concerns to hear this matter forth,   263
Do with your injuries as seems you best,   264
In any chastisement. I for a while
Will leave you; but stir not you till you have
Well determined upon these slanderers.   267

ESCALUS   My lord, we'll do it throughly.   Exit [Duke].   268
Signor Lucio, did not you say you knew that Friar
Lodowick to be a dishonest person?

LUCIO   Cucullus non facit monachum; honest in noth-   271
ing but in his clothes, and one that hath spoke most
villainous speeches of the Duke.

ESCALUS   We shall entreat you to abide here till he come,
and enforce them against him. We shall find this friar 275
a notable fellow.   276

LUCIO   As any in Vienna, on my word.

ESCALUS   Call that same Isabel here once again. I would
speak with her. [Exit an attendant.] Pray you, my lord,
give me leave to question. You shall see how I'll handle
her.

LUCIO   Not better than he, by her own report.

ESCALUS   Say you?

LUCIO   Marry, sir, I think, if you handled her privately, 284
she would sooner confess; perchance publicly she'll be
ashamed.

ESCALUS   I will go darkly to work with her.   287

LUCIO   That's the way, for women are light at midnight.   288

Enter Duke [disguised as a friar], Provost, Isabella,
[and officers].

ESCALUS   Come on, mistress. Here's a gentlewoman
denies all that you have said.

LUCIO   My lord, here comes the rascal I spoke of, here
with the Provost.

ESCALUS   In very good time. Speak not you to him till
we call upon you.

LUCIO   Mum.

ESCALUS   Come, sir, did you set these women on to
slander Lord Angelo? They have confessed you did.

DUKE   'Tis false.

ESCALUS   How? Know you where you are?

DUKE
Respect to your great place! And let the devil   300
Be sometimes honored for his burning throne!   301

---

215 fast belocked firmly locked   216 match assignation   226 for
that because.   proportions dowry   227 composition agreement
228–229 disvalued In levity discredited for lightness   239 confixèd
firmly fixed   242 scope full authority   243 touched injured, affected
244 informal rash, distracted   245 But than   250 Compact in collusion   251 swear . . . saint call down to witness every single saint
253 sealed in approbation ratified by proof

263 forth through   264 Do . . . best respond to the wrongs done you
as seems best to you   267 determined reached judgment
268 throughly thoroughly   271 Cucullus . . . monachum a cowl
doesn't make a monk   275 enforce them forcefully urge your charges
276 notable notorious   284 if . . . privately (with sexual suggestion,
punning on Escalus' use of handle in line 280)   287 darkly subtly,
slyly   288 light wanton, unchaste   300–301 let . . . throne i.e.,
may all authority be respected, even the devil's. (Said sardonically.)

Where is the Duke? 'Tis he should hear me speak.

ESCALUS
The Duke's in us, and we will hear you speak.
Look you speak justly.

DUKE
Boldly, at least. But O, poor souls,
Come you to seek the lamb here of the fox?
Good night to your redress! Is the Duke gone?
Then is your cause gone too. The Duke's unjust,
Thus to retort your manifest appeal,   309
And put your trial in the villain's mouth
Which here you come to accuse.

LUCIO
This is the rascal. This is he I spoke of.

ESCALUS
Why, thou unreverend and unhallowed friar,
Is 't not enough thou hast suborned these women
To accuse this worthy man, but, in foul mouth
And in the witness of his proper ear,   316
To call him villain? And then to glance from him
To th' Duke himself, to tax him with injustice?   318
Take him hence. To th' rack with him! We'll
    touse you   319
Joint by joint, but we will know his purpose.
What, "unjust"?

DUKE   Be not so hot. The Duke
Dare no more stretch this finger of mine than he
Dare rack his own. His subject am I not,
Nor here provincial. My business in this state   324
Made me a looker-on here in Vienna,
Where I have seen corruption boil and bubble
Till it o'errun the stew; laws for all faults,   327
But faults so countenanced that the strong statutes   328
Stand like the forfeits in a barber's shop,   329
As much in mock as mark.

ESCALUS   Slander to th' state!   330
Away with him to prison.

ANGELO
What can you vouch against him, Signor Lucio?
Is this the man that you did tell us of?

LUCIO   'Tis he, my lord.—Come hither, Goodman 334
Baldpate. Do you know me?   335

DUKE   I remember you, sir, by the sound of your voice.
I met you at the prison, in the absence of the Duke.

LUCIO   O, did you so? And do you remember what you
said of the Duke?

DUKE   Most notedly, sir.   340

LUCIO   Do you so, sir? And was the Duke a flesh-
monger, a fool, and a coward, as you then reported him to be?

DUKE   You must, sir, change persons with me ere you   344

309 **retort** turn back. **manifest** obviously just 316 **in . . . ear**
within his own hearing 318 **tax him with** accuse him of 319 **touse**
tear 324 **provincial** subject to the religious authority of this province
or state 327 **stew** (1) stewpot (2) brothel 328 **countenanced** allowed 329 **forfeits** cautionary displays, or lists of rules and fines for
handling razors, etc., which barbers (who also acted as dentists and
surgeons) hung in their shops 330 **As . . . mark** as often flouted as
observed 334–335 **Goodman Baldpate** (Lucio refers to the tonsure
he assumes this "friar" must have.) 340 **notedly** particularly
344 **change** exchange

make that my report. You indeed spoke so of him, and
much more, much worse.

LUCIO   O thou damnable fellow! Did not I pluck thee by
the nose for thy speeches?

DUKE   I protest I love the Duke as I love myself.

ANGELO   Hark how the villain would close now, after 350
his treasonable abuses!

ESCALUS   Such a fellow is not to be talked withal. Away
with him to prison! Where is the Provost? Away with
him to prison! Lay bolts enough upon him. Let him 354
speak no more. Away with those giglots too, and with 355
the other confederate companion!   356
                    [The Provost lays hands on the Duke.]

DUKE [to Provost]   Stay, sir, stay awhile.

ANGELO   What, resists he? Help him, Lucio.

LUCIO   Come, sir, come, sir, come, sir; foh, sir! Why,
you bald-pated, lying rascal, you must be hooded,
must you? Show your knave's visage, with a pox to
you! Show your sheep-biting face, and be hanged an 362
hour! Will 't not off?   363
            [He pulls off the friar's hood, and discovers
                the Duke. Angelo and Escalus rise.]

DUKE
Thou art the first knave that e'er mad'st a duke.
First, Provost, let me bail these gentle three.   365
[To Lucio.] Sneak not away, sir, for the Friar
    and you
Must have a word anon.—Lay hold on him.

LUCIO   This may prove worse than hanging.

DUKE [to Escalus]
What you have spoke I pardon. Sit you down.
We'll borrow place of him. [To Angelo.] Sir, by your
    leave.   [He takes Angelo's seat. Escalus also sits.]
Hast thou or word, or wit, or impudence,   371
That yet can do thee office? If thou hast,   372
Rely upon it till my tale be heard,
And hold no longer out.

ANGELO [kneeling]   O my dread lord,   374
I should be guiltier than my guiltiness
To think I can be undiscernible,
When I perceive Your Grace, like power divine,
Hath looked upon my passes. Then, good prince,   378
No longer session hold upon my shame,
But let my trial be mine own confession.
Immediate sentence then and sequent death   381
Is all the grace I beg.

DUKE   Come hither, Mariana.
Say, wast thou e'er contracted to this woman?

ANGELO   I was, my lord.

DUKE
Go take her hence and marry her instantly.
Do you the office, Friar, which consummate,   386

350 **close** come to terms, compromise 354 **bolts** iron fetters 355 **giglots** wanton women 356 **confederate companion** i.e., Friar Peter
362 **sheep-biting** knavish (from the action of wolves or dogs that prey
on sheep) 362–363 **hanged an hour** (A sardonic way of saying
"hanged.") 365 **gentle three** i.e., Mariana, Isabella, and Friar Peter
371 **or word** either word 372 **office** service 374 **hold . . . out**
then persist no longer 378 **passes** actions, trespasses 381 **sequent**
subsequent 386 **Do . . . office** you perform the service. **consummate** being completed

Return him here again. Go with him, Provost.
        Exit [*Angelo, with Mariana, Friar Peter, and*
                                        Provost].

ESCALUS
  My lord, I am more amazed at his dishonor
  Than at the strangeness of it.
DUKE   Come hither, Isabel.
  Your friar is now your prince. As I was then
  Advertising and holy to your business,   391
  Not changing heart with habit, I am still
  Attorneyed at your service.
ISABELLA   O, give me pardon,   393
  That I, your vassal, have employed and pained   394
  Your unknown sovereignty!
DUKE   You are pardoned, Isabel.
  And now, dear maid, be you as free to us.   396
  Your brother's death, I know, sits at your heart;
  And you may marvel why I obscured myself,
  Laboring to save his life, and would not rather
  Make rash remonstrance of my hidden power   400
  Than let him so be lost. O most kind maid,
  It was the swift celerity of his death,
  Which I did think with slower foot came on,
  That brained my purpose. But peace be with him!   404
  That life is better life past fearing death
  Than that which lives to fear. Make it your comfort,
  So happy is your brother.

        Enter Angelo, Mariana, [*Friar*] *Peter,* [*and*]
        Provost.

ISABELLA   I do, my lord.   407
DUKE
  For this new-married man approaching here,
  Whose salt imagination yet hath wronged   409
  Your well-defended honor, you must pardon
  For Mariana's sake. But as he adjudged your
    brother—
  Being criminal, in double violation
  Of sacred chastity and of promise-breach   413
  Thereon dependent, for your brother's life—   414
  The very mercy of the law cries out   415
  Most audible, even from his proper tongue,   416
  "An Angelo for Claudio, death for death!"
  Haste still pays haste, and leisure answers leisure;   418
  Like doth quit like, and measure still for measure.   419
  Then, Angelo, thy fault's thus manifested,
  Which, though thou wouldst deny, denies thee
    vantage.   421
  We do condemn thee to the very block
  Where Claudio stooped to death, and with like
    haste.

Away with him!
MARIANA   O my most gracious lord,
  I hope you will not mock me with a husband!
DUKE
  It is your husband mocked you with a husband.
  Consenting to the safeguard of your honor,
  I thought your marriage fit; else imputation,   428
  For that he knew you, might reproach your life   429
  And choke your good to come. For his possessions,   430
  Although by confiscation they are ours,
  We do instate and widow you withal,   432
  To buy you a better husband.
MARIANA   O my dear lord,
  I crave no other, nor no better man.
DUKE
  Never crave him; we are definitive.   435
MARIANA [*kneeling*]
  Gentle my liege—
DUKE   You do but lose your labor.
  Away with him to death! [*To Lucio.*] Now, sir,
    to you.
MARIANA
  O my good lord! Sweet Isabel, take my part!
  Lend me your knees, and all my life to come
  I'll lend you all my life to do you service.
DUKE
  Against all sense you do importune her.
  Should she kneel down in mercy of this fact,   442
  Her brother's ghost his pavèd bed would break,   443
  And take her hence in horror.
MARIANA   Isabel,
  Sweet Isabel, do yet but kneel by me!
  Hold up your hands, say nothing; I'll speak all.
  They say best men are molded out of faults,   447
  And, for the most, become much more the better   448
  For being a little bad. So may my husband.
  O Isabel, will you not lend a knee?
DUKE
  He dies for Claudio's death.
ISABELLA [*kneeling*]   Most bounteous sir,
  Look, if it please you, on this man condemned
  As if my brother lived. I partly think
  A due sincerity governed his deeds,
  Till he did look on me. Since it is so,
  Let him not die. My brother had but justice,
  In that he did the thing for which he died.
  For Angelo,
  His act did not o'ertake his bad intent,
  And must be buried but as an intent   460
  That perished by the way. Thoughts are no subjects,   461
  Intents but merely thoughts.
MARIANA   Merely, my lord.

---

391 Advertising attentive.   **holy** virtuously dedicated   **393 Attorneyed at** serving as agent in   **394 pained** put to trouble   **396 free to
us** i.e., generous in pardoning me   **400 rash remonstrance** sudden
manifestation   **404 brained** dashed, defeated   **407 So** thus   **409 salt**
lecherous   **413–414 promise-breach . . . dependent** i.e., breaking
his promise made in return for the yielding up of chastity   **415 The
very . . . law** i.e., even mercy itself   **416 his proper** its own
418 still always   **419 quit** requite   **421 though** even if.   **vantage**
i.e., any advantage. (Angelo must suffer the same penalty as Claudio.)

428 fit appropriate.   **imputation** accusation, slander   **429 For that**
because.   **knew** had sexual relations with   **430 For** as for   **432 instate . . . withal** grant to you the estate appropriate to a widow
435 definitive firmly resolved   **442 in . . . fact** pleading mercy for
this crime   **443 pavèd bed** grave covered with a stone slab
447 best men even the best of men   **448 most** most part   **460 buried**
i.e., forgotten   **461 no subjects** i.e., not subject to the state's
authority

DUKE
Your suit's unprofitable. Stand up, I say.   463
[They stand.]
I have bethought me of another fault.
Provost, how came it Claudio was beheaded
At an unusual hour?

PROVOST   It was commanded so.

DUKE
Had you a special warrant for the deed?

PROVOST
No, my good lord, it was by private message.

DUKE
For which I do discharge you of your office.
Give up your keys.

PROVOST   Pardon me, noble lord.
I thought it was a fault, but knew it not,   472
Yet did repent me after more advice;   473
For testimony whereof, one in the prison,
That should by private order else have died,
I have reserved alive.

DUKE   What's he?

PROVOST   His name is Barnardine.

DUKE
I would thou hadst done so by Claudio.
Go fetch him hither. Let me look upon him.
[Exit Provost.]

ESCALUS
I am sorry one so learnèd and so wise
As you, Lord Angelo, have still appeared,   482
Should slip so grossly, both in the heat of blood
And lack of tempered judgment afterward.

ANGELO
I am sorry that such sorrow I procure,
And so deep sticks it in my penitent heart
That I crave death more willingly than mercy.
'Tis my deserving, and I do entreat it.   488

*Enter Barnardine and Provost, Claudio [muffled],
[and] Juliet.*

DUKE
Which is that Barnardine?

PROVOST   This, my lord.

DUKE
There was a friar told me of this man.—
Sirrah, thou art said to have a stubborn soul
That apprehends no further than this world,
And squar'st thy life according. Thou'rt condemned; 493
But, for those earthly faults, I quit them all,   494
And pray thee take this mercy to provide
For better times to come.—Friar, advise him;
I leave him to your hand.—What muffled fellow's
that?

PROVOST
This is another prisoner that I saved,

Who should have died when Claudio lost his head,
As like almost to Claudio as himself.
[He unmuffles Claudio.]

DUKE *[to Isabella]*
If he be like your brother, for his sake
Is he pardoned, and for your lovely sake,
Give me your hand and say you will be mine;
He is my brother too. But fitter time for that.
By this Lord Angelo perceives he's safe;
Methinks I see a quickening in his eye.
Well, Angelo, your evil quits you well.   507
Look that you love your wife, her worth worth
yours.   508
I find an apt remission in myself;   509
And yet here's one in place I cannot pardon.   510
[To Lucio.] You, sirrah, that knew me for a fool, a
coward,
One all of luxury, an ass, a madman—   512
Wherein have I so deserved of you
That you extol me thus?

LUCIO   Faith, my lord, I spoke it but according to the
trick. If you will hang me for it, you may; but I had 516
rather it would please you I might be whipped.

DUKE
Whipped first, sir, and hanged after.
Proclaim it, Provost, round about the city,
If any woman wronged by this lewd fellow—
As I have heard him swear himself there's one
Whom he begot with child—let her appear,
And he shall marry her. The nuptial finished,
Let him be whipped and hanged.

LUCIO   I beseech Your Highness, do not marry me to a
whore. Your Highness said even now I made you a   526
duke; good my lord, do not recompense me in making
me a cuckold.

DUKE
Upon mine honor, thou shalt marry her.
Thy slanders I forgive and therewithal   530
Remit thy other forfeits.—Take him to prison,   531
And see our pleasure herein executed.   532

LUCIO   Marrying a punk, my lord, is pressing to death,   533
whipping, and hanging.

DUKE   Slandering a prince deserves it.
[Exeunt officers with Lucio.]
She, Claudio, that you wronged, look you restore.
Joy to you, Mariana! Love her, Angelo.
I have confessed her, and I know her virtue.
Thanks, good friend Escalus, for thy much
goodness;

---

463 unprofitable worthless   **472 knew it not** was not sure   **473 advice** consideration   **482 still** always   **488 s.d. muffled** wrapped up
so as to conceal identity (as also in line 497)   **493 squar'st** regulates
494 for as for.   **quit** pardon

507 quits rewards, requites   **508 her . . . yours** see to it that you are
worthy of her worth, since she deserves no less   **509 apt remission**
readiness to show mercy   **510 in place** present   **512 luxury** lechery
516 trick fashion   **526 even** just   **530–531 and therewithal . . .
forfeits** i.e., and therefore will not have you whipped and hanged
532 see . . . executed i.e., see that my order be carried out that Lucio marry Kate Keepdown (see 3.2.194–196)   **533 pressing to death**
i.e., by having heavy weights placed on the chest. (A standard form
of executing those who refused to plead to a felony charge.) Lucio
wryly complains that marrying a whore is as bad as death by torture.

There's more behind that is more gratulate.   540
Thanks, Provost, for thy care and secrecy;
We shall employ thee in a worthier place.
Forgive him, Angelo, that brought you home
The head of Ragozine for Claudio's;
Th' offense pardons itself. Dear Isabel,
I have a motion much imports your good,   546
Whereto if you'll a willing ear incline,
What's mine is yours, and what is yours is mine.—
So, bring us to our palace, where we'll show   549
What's yet behind, that's meet you all should know.   550
                                [Exeunt.]

540 behind in store, to come. **gratulate** gratifying **546 motion** proposal (which) **549 bring** escort **550 What's yet behind** what is still to be told

Troilus and Cressida

Shakespeare must have had some relative failures in the theater, as well as enormous successes. *Troilus and Cressida* seems to have been a relative failure. Perhaps it was performed publicly at the Globe Theatre for a brief run but of such short duration that a preface to a Second Quarto printing in 1603 could claim that the play had never been "staled with the stage" or "clapper-clawed with the palms of the vulgar." It is a bitter play about an inconclusive war and a failed love affair, quite unlike anything Shakespeare had written before in his romantic comedies and English history plays. Its bleak satire of political stalemate seems directed, in part, at the unhappy story of the abortive rebellion of the Earl of Essex in 1601; like many of the warriors in *Troilus and Cressida*, Essex was a tarnished hero whose charisma fell victim to his own egomaniacal ambitions and to the mood of anxious helplessness that hovered over Queen Elizabeth's last years. The play is unusually elliptical in its language, as though Shakespeare deliberately adopted a new, contorted style to express the unresolvable paradoxes of the political and psychological no-man's-land he wanted to describe. A major topic of the play is fame, or rather notoriety, for most of Shakespeare's major characters came to him in the story with full-blown legendary identities as antiheroes: Cressida, the faithless woman; Troilus, the rejected male; Pandarus, the go-between; and Achilles, the butcherer of Hector. Shakespeare's language has to deal with shattered identities, with the unstable subjectivity of human willfulness, and with spiritual exhaustion and neurosis. Perhaps some members of Shakespeare's audience were not quite prepared for all of this, and certainly the play was seldom seen onstage until the twentieth century.

Today, on the other hand, the play enjoys high critical esteem and has shown itself to be theatrically powerful. What we perceive is that its mordant wit, its satirical depiction of war, and its dispiriting portrayal of sexual infidelity call for a response very different from the one required for an appreciation of *A Midsummer Night's Dream* and *As You Like It* or *1 Henry IV*. *Troilus and Cressida*, written probably in 1601–1602, shortly before the Stationers' Register entry of 1603, is attuned to a new and darker mood emerging during this period in Shakespeare's work and in the work of his contemporaries.

In the early 1600s, dramatic satire enjoyed a sudden and highly visible notoriety. Catering, in large part, to select and courtly audiences, and given new impetus by the reopening of the boys' acting companies at the indoor theaters in 1599, satirical drama quickly employed the talents of Ben Jonson, John Marston, and George Chapman, as well as other sophisticated dramatists. Jonson launched a series of plays he called comical satires, in which he rebuked the London citizenry and presumed to teach manners to the court as well. The so-called War of the Theaters among Jonson, Marston, and Thomas Dekker, although partly a personality clash of no consequence, was also a serious debate between public and more courtly or select stages on the proper uses of satire. Public dramatists complained about the libelous boldness of the new satire and were galled by the preference of some audiences for this new theatrical phenomenon; even Shakespeare fretted in *Hamlet* (2.2.353–379) about the rivalry. Yet, as an artist in search of new forms, he also responded with positive interest. He experimented with a Jonsonian type of satirical plot in the exposure of Malvolio in *Twelfth Night* (1600–1602). *Troilus and Cressida* seems to have been another and more ambitious experiment, embracing a different kind of satire, not of witty exposure, but of disillusionment.

This satiric genre is hard to classify according to the conventional definitions of tragedy, comedy, or history but does have its own clearly defined rationale that makes special sense in terms of our modern theater. The play is nominally tragic in that it presents the fall of great Hector and adumbrates the fall of Troy, yet its love story merely dwindles into frustrated estrangement without the death of either lover. The play is comic only insofar as it is black comedy or comedy of the absurd. Its leering sexual titillation and its mood of spiritual paralysis link *Troilus and Cressida* to the problem comedies *All's Well That Ends Well* (c. 1601–1604) and *Measure for Measure* (1603–1604). The play is called a "history" on both its early title pages and assuredly deals with the great events of history's most famous war, but history has become essentially ironic. In this, *Troilus and Cressida* represents a culmination of Shakespeare's ironic exploration of history as begun in the impasses of *Richard II* or *Henry IV* and as portrayed more fully in the sustained ambiguities of *Julius Caesar* (1599). However much Shakespeare may have been influenced by the contemporary vogue of satire in the boys' theater, his own satire of disillusion is integral to his development as an artist. *Troilus and Cressida* is a fitting companion and contemporary for *Hamlet* (c. 1599–1601). Like that play, it evokes a universal disorder that may well reflect the Jacobean loss of an assured sense of philosophical reliance on the medieval hierarchies of the old Ptolemaic earth-centered cosmos.

Troilus and Cressida achieves its disillusioning effect through repeated ironic juxtaposition of heroic ideals and tarnished realities. Although it deals with the greatest war in history and a renowned love affair, we as audience know that Troy and the lovers will be overthrown by cunning and infidelity. Shakespeare partly inherited from his sources this duality of epic grandness and dispiriting conclusion. To learn of the war itself, he must have known George Chapman's translation of Homer's *Iliad* (of which seven books were published in 1598) and, of course, Virgil's account of the destruction of Troy, but he relied more particularly on medieval romances: Raoul Lefevre's *Recueil des Histoires de Troyes,* as translated and published by William Caxton, and perhaps John Lydgate's *Troy Book,* derived in part from Guido delle Colonne's *Historia Trojana.* These romances were Trojan in point of view and hence concerned with the fall of that city. For the bitter love story, Shakespeare went to Geoffrey Chaucer's *Troilus and Criseyde* (c. 1385–1386), which had been derived from the twelfth-century medieval romance of Benoit de Sainte-Maure, *Le Roman de Troie,* as amplified and retold in Boccaccio's *Il Filostrato.* Chaucer's Criseyde is an admirably self-possessed young woman, and her love for Troilus captures the spirit of the courtly love tradition upon which the story was based. After the late fourteenth century, however, Chaucer's heroine suffered a drastic decline in esteem. In Robert Henryson's *Testament of Cresseid,* for example, Cressida becomes a leper and beggar, the "lazar kite of Cressid's kind" to whom Pistol alludes in *Henry V.* Her name has become synonymous with womanly infidelity, as Shakespeare wryly points out in *Troilus and Cressida:* "Let all constant men be Troiluses, all false women Cressids, and all brokers-between Pandars" (3.2.201–203). Shakespeare is fascinated by this phenomenon of declining reputations. Just as the illustrious warrior Achilles must learn that envious time detracts from our best achievements and stigmatizes us for our worst failings, Troilus, Cressida, and Pandarus all anticipate the lasting consequences to their reputations of a failed love relationship. The passion to which they commit themselves eternally becomes not only an emblem of lost hopes and promises but also a caricature to later generations of enervating and frustrated desire, promiscuity, and pandering. Thus, Shakespeare finds in his materials both chivalric splendor and a deflation of it.

Stylistically, Shakespeare exploits this juxtaposition. He employs epic conventions more than is his custom. The narrative commences, as the chorus informs us, *in medias res,* "Beginning in the middle." Epic similes adorn the formal speeches of Ulysses, Agamemnon, and Nestor. The rhetoric of persuasion plays an important role, as in *Julius Caesar* and other Roman plays. The great names of antiquity are paraded past us in a roll call of heroes. Hector, above all, is an epic hero, although in the fashion of medieval romance he is also the prince of chivalry. He longs to resolve the war by a challenge to single combat, in tournament, with the breaking of lances and with each warrior defending the honor of his lady-fair (1.3.264–283). The Greeks respond for a time to this stirring call to arms. Yet, in the broader context of the war itself, with its unworthy causes, its frustrating irresolu-

tion, and its debilitating effect on the morale of both sides, Hector's idealism cannot prevail. On the Greek side, Ulysses' ennobling vision of "degree, priority, and place" (1.3.86), by which the heavens show to humanity the value of harmonious order, serves more to criticize and mock the present disorder of the Greek army than to offer guidance toward a restoration of that order. Epic convention becomes hollow travesty, as chivalric aspirations repeatedly dissolve into the sordid insinuations of Thersites or Pandarus. Despite the play's epic machinery, the gods are nowhere to be found.

A prevailing metaphor is that of disease (as also in *Hamlet*). Insubordinate conduct "infects" (1.3.187) the body politic. The Greek commanders hope to "physic" (1.3.377) Achilles lest his virtues, "like fair fruit in an unwholesome dish," rot untasted (2.3.119). Hector deplores the way his fellow Trojans "infectiously" enslave themselves to willful appetite (2.2.59). Elsewhere, love is described as an open ulcer and as an itch that must be scratched; Helen is "contaminated carrion" (4.1.73). Thersites, most of all, invites us to regard both love and war as disease-ridden, afflicted by boils, plagues, scabs, the "Neapolitan bone-ache" (syphilis), "lethargies, cold palsies, raw eyes, dirt-rotten livers, wheezing lungs, bladders full of imposthume [abscesses], sciaticas," and still more (2.3.18 and 5.1.19–21). Pandarus ends the play on a similarly tawdry note by jesting about prostitutes (Winchester geese, he calls them) and the "sweating" or venereal diseases.

The war is both glorious and absurd. It calls forth brave deeds and heroic sacrifices. Yet it is correctly labeled by the chorus as a "quarrel," begun over an "old aunt," whom the Greeks have held captive, and Helen, whom the Trojans abducted in reprisal. No one believes the original cause to justify the bloodletting that has ensued. Menelaus' cuckoldry is the subject of obscene mirth in the Greek camp. Among the Trojans, Troilus can argue only that one doesn't return soiled goods; since all Troy consented to Helen's abduction, Troy must continue the war to maintain its honor. The war thus assumes a grim momentum of its own. The combatants repeatedly discover that they are trapped in the ironies of a situation they helped make but can no longer unmake. Hector's challenge to single combat falls upon Ajax, his "father's sister's son." Achilles, too, has allegiances in the enemy's camp, since he is enamored of Priam's daughter Polyxena. In the parleys between the two sides, the warriors greet one another as long-lost brothers, though they vow to slaughter one another on the morrow. With fitting oxymoron, Paris comments on the paradox of this "most despiteful gentle greeting," this "noblest hateful love" (4.1.34–35). Only a barbarian could be free of regret for a peace that seems so near and is yet so far. The war offers insidious temptations to potentially worthy men, perverting Achilles' once-honorable quest for fame into maniacal ambition and an irresistible impulse to murder Hector. History and tradition, we know, will mock Achilles for this craven deed. It will put him down as a bully rather than as a brave soldier, just as Troilus, Cressida, and Pandarus will come to be regarded in time as stereotypes of the cheated man, the whore, and the procurer. Even before the murder of Hector, Achilles sees his reputation for bravery tarnished by his inaction, while Ajax is hoisted into prominence by the machinations of Ulysses and the other generals.

Hector's tragedy is, in its own way, no less ironic. Even though he emerges as the most thoughtful and courageous man on either side and advises his fellow Trojans to let Helen go in response to the "moral laws / Of nature and of nations," he nonetheless ends the Trojan council of war by resolving to fight on with them (2.2.184–185). This conclusion may represent, in part, a realization that the others will fight on, in any case, and that he must therefore be loyal to them, but the choice also reflects hubris. Hector is not unlike Julius Caesar in his proud repudiation of his wife Andromache's ominous dreams, his sister Cassandra's mad but oracular prophecies, and his own conviction that Troy's pursuit of honor stems from a sickened appetite. He goes to his death because "The gods have heard me swear" (5.3.15). His character is his fate. Even his humane compunctions, like Brutus', are held against him; he spares the life of Achilles and is murdered in reward. War is no place for men of scruple, as Troilus reminds his older brother. Yet, Hector, at least, is the better man for refusing to be corrupted by the savagery of war; we honor his memory, even if we also view him as senselessly victimized by a meaningless conflict.

The lovers, as well, are caught in war's trap—not only Troilus and Cressida, but also Paris and Helen, Achilles and Polyxena. Achilles vows to Polyxena not to fight and thereby misses his cherished opportunity for fame; ironically, he is aroused to vengeful action only by the death of a male friend, Patroclus, who is whispered to be his "male varlet" or "masculine whore" (5.1.15–17). Paris is obliged to ask his brother Troilus to return Cressida to the Greeks, so that Paris may continue to enjoy Helen. What else can Paris do? "There is no help," he complains. "The bitter disposition of the time / Will have it so" (4.1.50–51). Troilus prepares his own undoing when he argues in the Trojan council of war that Helen must be kept at all cost; the cost, it turns out, is his own Cressida. He sees this irony at once: "How my achievements mock me!" (4.2.71); that is, he has no sooner achieved her sexually than he must give her up so that the war may go on with Trojan honor intact and Helen still in Paris' bed. The love of Troilus and Cressida is dwarfed by the war, which has no regard for their private concerns. Troilus wins Cressida after many months of wooing, only to lose her the next day. Yet how could Cressida's father Calchas know of her personal situation? He wishes only to have his daughter back. And, although the Trojan leaders do know of Troilus' affair, they must pay heed first to such matters of state as the exchange of prisoners.

So, too, must Troilus. Perhaps the greatest irony is that he must himself choose to send Cressida to the Greeks, plac-

ing duty above personal longing. He appears to have no real choice, but the result is surrounded by absurdities, and it is something that Cressida cannot comprehend. She has determined to stay no matter what the world may think; passionate love is more important to her. Although Cressida was first introduced to us as a sardonic and worldly young woman, urbane, mocking, self-possessed, witty, unsentimental, even scheming and opportunistic, and, above all, wary of emotional commitment, her brief involvement with Troilus does touch deep emotion. For a moment, she catches a glimpse of something precious to which she would cling, something genuine in her unstable world. Yet Troilus, caught between love and duty, consents to her departure to the Greek camp. There she reverts to her former disillusioned self, behaving as is expected of her. Who has deserted whom? Cressida gives up, hating herself for doing so. She knows she cannot be true because, like too many women in her experience, she is led by "The error of our eye" and is thus a prey to male importunity (5.2.113). Sometimes she seems, to Ulysses at least, one of those "sluttish spoils of opportunity / And daughters of the game" (4.5.63–64). Still, this surrender to will and appetite in her is not unsympathetic, and does not happen without inner struggle. Her weakness is emblematic of a universal disorder and is partly caused by it. In the grim interplay of war and love, both men and women are powerless to assert their true selves. As the malcontent Thersites concludes, "Lechery, lechery, still wars and lechery; nothing else holds fashion."

The printing history of Troilus and Cressida is full of obscurities that may give some insight into the play's apparent lack of stage success. On February 7, 1603, the printer James Roberts entered his name on the Register of the Company of Stationers (i.e., publishers and booksellers) to print, "when he hath gotten sufficient authority for it, the book of Troilus and Cressida as it is acted by my Lord Chamberlain's Men." Evidently, the authority was not forthcoming, for in 1609 the play was reregistered to R. Bonian and H. Walley and published by them that year in quarto as The History of Troilus and Cressida. As it was acted by the King's Majesty's servants at the Globe. Written by William Shakespeare. Immediately afterward, and well before this first printing had sold out, a new title page was substituted as follows: The Famous History of Troilus and Cresseid. Excellently expressing the beginning of their loves, with the conceited wooing of Pandarus Prince of Lycia. Written by William Shakespeare. This second version had, moreover, a preface to the reader (something found in no other Shakespearean quarto) declaring Troilus and Cressida to be "a new play, never staled with the stage, never clapper-clawed with the palms of the vulgar," nor "sullied with the smoky breath of the multitude." The preface goes on to imply that the play's "grand possessors" (i.e., Shakespeare's acting company) had not wished to see the play released at all. What this substituted title page and added preface may suggest is that Bonian and Walley felt constrained to present their text as a new one—a literary rather than a theatrical text—and hence different from the version entered in the Stationers' Register "as it is acted by my Lord Chamberlain's Men." Because that version had been legally registered in the name of James Roberts, the new publishers made their case for legal possession by offering a "new" play.

Later, the editors of the First Folio in 1623 seemed to have had difficulty in obtaining permission to print *Troilus and Cressida*. Three pages of the play were actually printed to follow *Romeo and Juliet,* among the tragedies, but were then withdrawn to be replaced by *Timon of Athens*. Ultimately, the play appeared in the Folio almost without pagination, unlisted in the table of contents, and placed with fitting ambiguity between the histories and the tragedies.

This unusual printing history offers conflicting information about original stage performance. Against the evidence of the second version of the 1609 Quarto, with its preface proclaiming a play "never staled with the stage," we have the evidence of the first title page mentioning the King's Majesty's servants at the Globe and of the Stationers' Register entry in 1603 referring to the play "as it is acted." Since the 1609 preface may be part of a legal maneuver designed to represent the play as new, the case in favor of actual performance has some weight. We cannot be sure, however, that the performance was successful or that it reached a very large audience. Some scholars have hypothesized that Shakespeare's company mounted a special production of the play for a private audience at the Inns of Court (where young men studied law) or a similar place, even though an arrangement of this sort would have been most unusual, if not unique; Shakespeare's company often took its regular plays to court or other special audiences, but no instance is positively known in which Shakespeare wrote on commission for a private showing. More likely, *Troilus and Cressida* was performed publicly without great success. A sequel, promised in the closing lines of the play by Pandarus to be presented "some two months hence," evidently did not materialize, perhaps because public demand was insufficient. The 1609 Quarto, with its revised title page and added preface, may have attempted to capitalize on the play's public failure by touting it as sophisticated fare, to be appreciated only by discerning readers. Possibly, Shakespeare and his company took another look at *Troilus and Cressida* in 1608, after they had acquired the right to perform in their indoor theater at Blackfriars, where audiences tended to be more select, only to discover anew that the play was not a great success on the popular stage. Its subsequent stage history, in any case, is largely a blank until the twentieth century, except for a much changed Restoration adaptation by John Dryden (1679) in which Cressida remains true to Troilus and slays herself when accused of infidelity.

The following is a complete text of the preface to the reader from the 1609 Quarto.

A Never Writer, to an Ever Reader. News.

Eternal reader, you have here a new play, never staled with the stage, never clapper-clawed with the palms of the vulgar, and yet passing full of the palm comical; for it is a birth of your brain that never undertook anything comical vainly. And were but the vain names of comedies changed for the titles of commodities, or of plays for pleas, you should see all those grand censors, that now style them such vanities, flock to them for the main grace of their gravities, especially this author's comedies, that are so framed to the life that they serve for the most common commentaries of all the actions of our lives, showing such a dexterity and power of wit that the most displeased with plays are pleased with his comedies. And all such dull and heavy-witted worldlings as were never capable of the wit of a comedy, coming by report of them to his representations, have found that wit there that they never found in themselves and have parted better witted than they came, feeling an edge of wit set upon them more than ever they dreamed they had brain to grind it on. So much and such savored salt of wit is in his comedies that they seem, for their height of pleasure, to be born in that sea that brought forth Venus. Amongst all there is none more witty than this; and had I time I would comment upon it, though I know it needs not, for so much as will make you think your testern well bestowed, but for so much worth as even poor I know to be stuffed in it. It deserves such a labor as well as the best comedy in Terence or Plautus. And believe this, that when he is gone and his comedies out of sale, you will scramble for them and set up a new English Inquisition. Take this for a warning, and at the peril of your pleasure's loss, and judgment's, refuse not, nor like this the less for not being sullied with the smoky breath of the multitude; but thank fortune for the scape it hath made amongst you, since by the grand possessors' wills I believe you should have prayed for them rather than been prayed. And so I leave all such to be prayed for, for the states of their wits' healths, that will not praise it. *Vale.*

Troilus and Cressida

[*Dramatis Personae*

PROLOGUE

PRIAM, *King of Troy*
HECTOR,
TROILUS,
PARIS,
DEIPHOBUS,   } *his sons*
HELENUS, *a priest,*
MARGARETON, *a bastard,*
AENEAS   } *Trojan commanders*
ANTENOR
CALCHAS, *a Trojan priest, Cressida's father, and defector to the Greeks*
PANDARUS, *Cressida's uncle*
SERVANT *to Troilus*
SERVANT *to Paris*

CASSANDRA, *Priam's daughter, a prophetess*
ANDROMACHE, *Hector's wife*
HELEN, *former wife of Menelaus, now Paris' mistress*
CRESSIDA, *Calchas' daughter, loved by Troilus*
ALEXANDER, *Cressida's servant*

AGAMEMNON, *the Greek General*
MENELAUS, *brother of Agamemnon*
ACHILLES,
AJAX,
ULYSSES,   } *Greek commanders*
NESTOR,
DIOMEDES,
PATROCLUS, *Achilles' friend*
THERSITES, *a scurrilous fool*
SERVANT *to Diomedes*

Trojan and Greek Soldiers, and Attendants

SCENE: *Troy, and the Greek camp before it*]

Prologue

[*Enter the Prologue, in armor.*]

PROLOGUE
In Troy, there lies the scene. From isles of Greece
The princes orgulous, their high blood chafed,   2
Have to the port of Athens sent their ships,
Fraught with the ministers and instruments   4
Of cruel war. Sixty and nine, that wore
Their crownets regal, from th' Athenian bay   6
Put forth toward Phrygia, and their vow is made   7
To ransack Troy, within whose strong immures   8
The ravished Helen, Menelaus' queen,   9
With wanton Paris sleeps; and that's the quarrel.
To Tenedos they come,   11
And the deep-drawing barks do there disgorge   12
Their warlike freightage. Now on Dardan plains   13
The fresh and yet unbruisèd Greeks do pitch
Their brave pavilions. Priam's six-gated city—   15
Dardan, and Timbria, Helias, Chetas, Troien,   16
And Antenorides—with massy staples   17
And corresponsive and fulfilling bolts,   18
Spar up the sons of Troy.   19
Now expectation, tickling skittish spirits   20
On one and other side, Trojan and Greek,
Sets all on hazard. And hither am I come,   22
A prologue armed, but not in confidence   23
Of author's pen or actor's voice, but suited   24
In like conditions as our argument,   25
To tell you, fair beholders, that our play
Leaps o'er the vaunt and firstlings of those broils,   27
Beginning in the middle, starting thence away   28
To what may be digested in a play.
Like or find fault; do as your pleasures are;
Now, good or bad, 'tis but the chance of war.
[*Exit.*]

❖

1.1   *Enter Pandarus and Troilus.*

TROILUS
Call here my varlet; I'll unarm again.   1
Why should I war without the walls of Troy,
That find such cruel battle here within?
Each Trojan that is master of his heart,
Let him to field; Troilus, alas, hath none.   5
PANDARUS   Will this gear ne'er be mended?   6

4 Fraught laden.   **ministers** agents, i.e., soldiers   **6 crownets** coronets, crowns worn by nobles   **7 Phrygia** district in western Asia Minor, identified as Troy by the Roman poets, and hence in Renaissance poetry   **8 immures** walls   **9 ravished** abducted   **11 Tenedos** small island in the Aegean Sea off the coast of Asia Minor   **12 deep-drawing barks** ships lying low in the water (with their heavy cargo)   **13 Dardan** Trojan. (From *Dardanus*, son of Zeus and Electra, daughter of Atlas. According to legend, Dardanus was the ancestor of the Trojan race.)   **15 brave pavilions** splendid tents   **16–17 Dardan . . . Antenorides** (The names of Troy's six gates.)   **17–18 massy . . . bolts** i.e., massive posts fitted with sockets to receive matching and well-fitted bolts   **19 Spar** close   **20 skittish** lively   **22 Sets . . . hazard** puts all at risk   **23 armed** in armor   **23–24 not . . . voice** i.e., not overconfident in the value of the play or the acting   **24–25 suited . . . argument** i.e., dressed in armor to match the character of the military plot. (*Argument* means both "plot of the story" and "quarrel.")   **27 vaunt and firstlings** beginnings   **28 Beginning in the middle** (Alluding to the tradition of beginning epic poetry *in medias res*.)
1.1. Location: Troy.
1 varlet page or servant of a knight   **5 none** i.e., no heart to fight
6 gear business

Prologue
2 orgulous proud.   **chafed** heated, angered

TROILUS
The Greeks are strong, and skillful to their strength,   7
Fierce to their skill, and to their fierceness valiant;   8
But I am weaker than a woman's tear,
Tamer than sleep, fonder than ignorance,   10
Less valiant than the virgin in the night,
And skilless as unpracticed infancy.
PANDARUS   Well, I have told you enough of this. For
my part, I'll not meddle nor make no farther. He that   14
will have a cake out of the wheat must tarry the   15
grinding.
TROILUS   Have I not tarried?
PANDARUS   Ay, the grinding, but you must tarry the
bolting.   19
TROILUS   Have I not tarried?
PANDARUS   Ay, the bolting, but you must tarry the leav-
ening.
TROILUS   Still have I tarried.
PANDARUS   Ay, to the leavening, but here's yet in the
word "hereafter" the kneading, the making of the
cake, the heating the oven, and the baking; nay, you
must stay the cooling too, or ye may chance burn   27
your lips.
TROILUS
Patience herself, what goddess e'er she be,   29
Doth lesser blench at sufferance than I do.   30
At Priam's royal table do I sit,
And when fair Cressid comes into my thoughts—
So, traitor! When she comes? When is she thence?   33
PANDARUS   Well, she looked yesternight fairer than ever
I saw her look, or any woman else.
TROILUS
I was about to tell thee—when my heart,
As wedgèd with a sigh, would rive in twain,   37
Lest Hector or my father should perceive me,
I have, as when the sun doth light a-scorn,   39
Buried this sigh in wrinkle of a smile;
But sorrow that is couched in seeming gladness   41
Is like that mirth fate turns to sudden sadness.
PANDARUS   An her hair were not somewhat darker than   43
Helen's—well, go to—there were no more compari-   44
son between the women. But, for my part, she is my
kinswoman; I would not, as they term it, praise her.
But I would somebody had heard her talk yesterday,
as I did. I will not dispraise your sister Cassandra's
wit, but—
TROILUS
O Pandarus! I tell thee, Pandarus—

When I do tell thee there my hopes lie drowned,
Reply not in how many fathoms deep
They lie indrenched. I tell thee I am mad   53
In Cressid's love. Thou answer'st she is fair;
Pour'st in the open ulcer of my heart
Her eyes, her hair, her cheek, her gait, her voice;
Handlest in thy discourse—O!—that her hand,   57
In whose comparison all whites are ink   58
Writing their own reproach, to whose soft seizure   59
The cygnet's down is harsh, and spirit of sense   60
Hard as the palm of plowman. This thou tell'st me,
As true thou tell'st me, when I say I love her;
But saying thus, instead of oil and balm   63
Thou lay'st in every gash that love hath given me
The knife that made it.
PANDARUS   I speak no more than truth.
TROILUS   Thou dost not speak so much.   67
PANDARUS   Faith, I'll not meddle in it. Let her be as she
is. If she be fair, 'tis the better for her; an she be not,
she has the mends in her own hands.   70
TROILUS   Good Pandarus, how now, Pandarus?
PANDARUS   I have had my labor for my travail; ill   72
thought on of her and ill thought on of you; gone be-   73
tween and between, but small thanks for my labor.
TROILUS   What, art thou angry, Pandarus? What, with
me?
PANDARUS   Because she's kin to me, therefore she's not
so fair as Helen. An she were not kin to me, she would   78
be as fair o' Friday as Helen is on Sunday. But what   79
care I? I care not an she were a blackamoor. 'Tis all one   80
to me.
TROILUS   Say I she is not fair?
PANDARUS   I do not care whether you do or no. She's a
fool to stay behind her father. Let her to the Greeks,   84
and so I'll tell her the next time I see her. For my part,
I'll meddle nor make no more i' the matter.
TROILUS   Pandarus—
PANDARUS   Not I.
TROILUS   Sweet Pandarus—
PANDARUS   Pray you, speak no more to me. I will leave
all as I found it, and there an end.   *Exit.* 91
                                        Sound alarum.
TROILUS
Peace, you ungracious clamors! Peace, rude sounds!
Fools on both sides! Helen must needs be fair,
When with your blood you daily paint her thus.   94

7,8 to in addition to, in proportion to   **10 fonder** more foolish
14 meddle nor make have anything more to do with it   **15 tarry** wait
for   **19 bolting** sifting   **27 stay** wait for   **29 what . . . be** however
much a goddess; or, if she is a goddess   **30 Doth . . . sufferance**
flinches under suffering with less fortitude   **33 So, traitor . . . thence**
(Troilus rebukes himself as a traitor to Love for implying that Cressida
is ever out of his thoughts, as she would have to be before she could
come into them.)   **37 As wedgèd** as if cleft by a wedge.   **rive** split
39 a-scorn scorningly, mockingly. (Troilus compares his face to that
of the sun, putting on a false look of joviality.)   **41 couched** hidden
43 An if.   **darker** (A dark complexion was considered less handsome;
Helen is blonde.)   **44 go to** (An exclamation of impatience or irritation.)   **were** would be

53 indrenched drowned   **57 Handlest** you handle.   **that her hand**
that hand of hers   **58 In whose comparison** in comparison with
which   **59 to** in comparison with.   **seizure** clasp   **60 cygnet's** young
swan's.   **spirit of sense** the most delicate of all material substances.
(According to Renaissance physiology, spirits were the invisible vapors that transmitted sense impressions to the soul.)   **63 oil and balm**
ointments, salves   **67 so much** i.e., the whole truth about Cressida
(since she is indescribable)   **70 has . . . hands** i.e., can apply remedy, such as cosmetics   **72 had** had only   **73 of** by   **78 An . . . to
me** i.e., if I were free to praise her unreservedly, without appearing to
be biased (as in lines 45–46)   **79 as fair . . . Sunday** i.e., as attractive in her plainest attire as Helen in her Sunday best   **80 blackamoor**
dark-skinned African   **84 her father** i.e., Calchas, a Trojan priest,
who, advised by the oracle of Apollo that Troy would fall, fled to the
Greeks   **91 s.d. alarum** trumpet signal to arms   **94 paint** (As though
the blood were cosmetic, reddening her complexion.)

I cannot fight upon this argument;   95
It is too starved a subject for my sword.   96
But Pandarus—O gods, how do you plague me!
I cannot come to Cressid but by Pandar,
And he's as tetchy to be wooed to woo   99
As she is stubborn-chaste against all suit.
Tell me, Apollo, for thy Daphne's love,   101
What Cressid is, what Pandar, and what we?   102
Her bed is India, there she lies, a pearl;
Between our Ilium and where she resides,   104
Let it be called the wild and wandering flood,   105
Ourself the merchant, and this sailing Pandar
Our doubtful hope, our convoy, and our bark.

          Alarum. Enter Aeneas.

AENEAS
How now, Prince Troilus, wherefore not afield?
TROILUS
Because not there. This woman's answer sorts,   109
For womanish it is to be from thence.
What news, Aeneas, from the field today?
AENEAS
That Paris is returnèd home and hurt.
TROILUS
By whom, Aeneas?
AENEAS   Troilus, by Menelaus.
TROILUS
Let Paris bleed. 'Tis but a scar to scorn;   114
Paris is gored with Menelaus' horn.   *Alarum.* 115
AENEAS
Hark, what good sport is out of town today!   116
TROILUS
Better at home, if "would I might" were "may."   117
But to the sport abroad. Are you bound thither?
AENEAS
In all swift haste.
TROILUS   Come, go we then together. *Exeunt.*

1.2   *Enter Cressida and her man [Alexander].*

CRESSIDA
Who were those went by?
ALEXANDER   Queen Hecuba and Helen.
CRESSIDA
And whither go they?
ALEXANDER   Up to the eastern tower,
Whose height commands as subject all the vale,

To see the battle. Hector, whose patience
Is as a virtue fixed, today was moved.   5
He chid Andromache and struck his armorer,
And, like as there were husbandry in war,   7
Before the sun rose he was harnessed light,   8
And to the field goes he, where every flower
Did as a prophet weep what it foresaw   10
In Hector's wrath.
CRESSIDA   What was his cause of anger?
ALEXANDER
The noise goes, this: there is among the Greeks   12
A lord of Trojan blood, nephew to Hector;   13
They call him Ajax.
CRESSIDA   Good; and what of him?
ALEXANDER
They say he is a very man per se   15
And stands alone.   16
CRESSIDA So do all men, unless they are drunk, sick, or
have no legs.
ALEXANDER   This man, lady, hath robbed many beasts
of their particular additions. He is as valiant as the   20
lion, churlish as the bear, slow as the elephant; a man
into whom nature hath so crowded humors that his   22
valor is crushed into folly, his folly sauced with discretion. There is no man hath a virtue that he hath not a
glimpse of, nor any man an attaint but he carries some   25
stain of it. He is melancholy without cause and merry
against the hair. He hath the joints of everything, but   27
everything so out of joint that he is a gouty Briareus,   28
many hands and no use, or purblind Argus, all eyes   29
and no sight.
CRESSIDA   But how should this man, that makes me
smile, make Hector angry?
ALEXANDER   They say he yesterday coped Hector in the   33
battle and struck him down, the disdain and shame
whereof hath ever since kept Hector fasting and
waking.

                  Enter Pandarus.

CRESSIDA   Who comes here?
ALEXANDER   Madam, your uncle Pandarus.
CRESSIDA   Hector's a gallant man.
ALEXANDER   As may be in the world, lady.
PANDARUS   What's that? What's that?
CRESSIDA   Good morrow, uncle Pandarus.
PANDARUS   Good morrow, cousin Cressid. What do you   43

---

95 upon this argument for this cause, theme   **96 starved** empty, trivial. (Troilus would have to fight on an empty stomach, as it were.)
99 tetchy to be irritable at being   **101 Apollo** (The ardent pursuer
of the nymph Daphne who, coy like Cressida, was changed into a
bay tree to elude Apollo's pursuit.)   **102 we** i.e., I   **104 Ilium** i.e.,
Troy generally, but here Priam's palace   **105 flood** open sea
109 sorts is appropriate   **114 a scar to scorn** (1) a wound not sufficiently serious to be regarded (2) a scar in return for Paris' scorn of
Menelaus   **115 horn** i.e., cuckold's horn, since Paris had stolen
Helen from Menelaus   **116 out of town** outside the walls   **117 Better . . . may** if I had my wish, I'd have better entertainment at home
with Cressida
1.2. Location: Troy.

5 fixed steadfast.   **moved** angry (with wordplay on the antithesis between *fixed* and *moved*)   **7 like as** as if.   **husbandry** good management (by rising early and getting to work. Hector is a stern "husband"
in marriage and in war.)   **8 harnessed light** dressed in light armor
10 weep (The early morning dew on the flowers suggests tears and extends the metaphor of a husbandman or farmer going into the field.)
12 noise rumor   **13 nephew** i.e., relation   **15 per se** intrinsically
16 alone without peer. (But Cressida sardonically takes it to mean literally "all by himself, without support.")   **20 additions** qualities bestowing special distinction   **22 humors** temperamental characteristics
25 glimpse trace.   **attaint** defect, stain.   **but** but that   **27 against the
hair** contrary to natural tendency   **28 Briareus** Greek mythological
monster with fifty heads and one hundred hands; here, all those
hands are gouty   **29 Argus** a monster with one hundred eyes; here,
all are blind (*purblind*)   **33 coped** encountered, came to blows with
43 cousin kinswoman, i.e., niece

talk of?— Good morrow, Alexander.— How do you, cousin? When were you at Ilium? 45

CRESSIDA   This morning, uncle.

PANDARUS   What were you talking of when I came? Was Hector armed and gone ere ye came to Ilium? Helen was not up, was she?

CRESSIDA   Hector was gone, but Helen was not up?

PANDARUS   E'en so. Hector was stirring early.

CRESSIDA   That were we talking of, and of his anger.

PANDARUS   Was he angry?

CRESSIDA   So he says here.

PANDARUS   True, he was so. I know the cause too. He'll lay about him today, I can tell them that; and there's 56 Troilus will not come far behind him. Let them take heed of Troilus, I can tell them that too.

CRESSIDA   What, is he angry too?

PANDARUS   Who, Troilus? Troilus is the better man of the two.

CRESSIDA   O Jupiter! There's no comparison.

PANDARUS   What, not between Troilus and Hector? Do you know a man if you see him? 64

CRESSIDA   Ay, if I ever saw him before and knew him.

PANDARUS   Well, I say Troilus is Troilus. 66

CRESSIDA   Then you say as I say, for I am sure he is not Hector.

PANDARUS   No, nor Hector is not Troilus in some de- 69 grees.

CRESSIDA   'Tis just to each of them; he is himself. 71

PANDARUS   Himself? Alas, poor Troilus! I would he 72 were.

CRESSIDA   So he is.

PANDARUS   Condition, I had gone barefoot to India. 75

CRESSIDA   He is not Hector.

PANDARUS   Himself? No, he's not himself. Would 'a 77 were himself! Well, the gods are above; time must friend or end. Well, Troilus, well, I would my heart were in her body. No, Hector is not a better man than Troilus.

CRESSIDA   Excuse me. 82

PANDARUS   He is elder.

CRESSIDA   Pardon me, pardon me.

PANDARUS   Th' other's not come to 't. You shall tell me 85 another tale, when th' other's come to 't. Hector shall not have his wit this year. 87

CRESSIDA   He shall not need it, if he have his own.

PANDARUS   Nor his qualities.

CRESSIDA   No matter.

PANDARUS   Nor his beauty.

CRESSIDA   'Twould not become him; his own's better.

PANDARUS   You have no judgment, niece. Helen herself

swore th' other day that Troilus, for a brown favor— 94 for so 'tis, I must confess—not brown neither—

CRESSIDA   No, but brown. 96

PANDARUS   Faith, to say truth, brown and not brown.

CRESSIDA   To say the truth, true and not true.

PANDARUS   She praised his complexion above Paris'.

CRESSIDA   Why, Paris hath color enough.

PANDARUS   So he has.

CRESSIDA   Then Troilus should have too much. If she 102 praised him above, his complexion is higher than his. 103 He having color enough, and the other higher, is too flaming a praise for a good complexion. I had as lief 105 Helen's golden tongue had commended Troilus for a copper nose. 107

PANDARUS   I swear to you, I think Helen loves him better than Paris.

CRESSIDA   Then she's a merry Greek indeed. 110

PANDARUS   Nay, I am sure she does. She came to him th' other day into the compassed window—and, you 112 know, he has not past three or four hairs on his chin—

CRESSIDA   Indeed, a tapster's arithmetic may soon bring 114 his particulars therein to a total.

PANDARUS   Why, he is very young; and yet will he, within three pound, lift as much as his brother Hector.

CRESSIDA   Is he so young a man and so old a lifter? 118

PANDARUS   But to prove to you that Helen loves him: she came and puts me her white hand to his cloven chin— 120

CRESSIDA   Juno have mercy! How came it cloven?

PANDARUS   Why, you know, 'tis dimpled. I think his smiling becomes him better than any man in all Phrygia.

CRESSIDA   O, he smiles valiantly.

PANDARUS   Does he not?

CRESSIDA   O, yes, an 'twere a cloud in autumn. 127

PANDARUS   Why, go to, then. But to prove to you that Helen loves Troilus—

CRESSIDA   Troilus will stand to the proof, if you'll prove 130 it so.

PANDARUS   Troilus? Why, he esteems her no more than I esteem an addle egg. 133

CRESSIDA   If you love an addle egg as well as you love an idle head, you would eat chickens i' the shell. 135

PANDARUS   I cannot choose but laugh to think how she tickled his chin. Indeed, she has a marvelous white 137 hand, I must needs confess—

CRESSIDA   Without the rack. 139

---

94 for a brown favor considering he has a dark complexion **96 No, but brown** (Cressida mocks her uncle's hairsplitting: "It isn't brown, but it's brown.") **102 should** would of necessity **103 higher than his** i.e., ruddier than Paris' **105 flaming** (1) flamboyant (2) inflamed with pimples. **lief** willingly **107 copper** red (with drinking) **110 merry Greek** (Slang for a frivolous person, loose in morals.) **112 compassed** bay **114 tapster** barkeep. (Proverbially slow at simple addition.) **118 old** experienced. **lifter** (with a pun on the meaning "thief") **120 puts me** i.e., puts. (Me is merely an emphatic marker implying "listen to this.") **127 an** as if. **an . . . autumn** i.e., his smile is like a dark and threatening rain cloud in autumn. (Cressida is teasing her uncle by dispraising Troilus.) **130 stand . . . proof** i.e., not shrink from the test (with bawdy pun on stand, be erect) **133 addle** spoiled **135 idle** (with a play on addle) **137 marvelous** marvelously **139 rack** torture device (used to elicit confessions)

45 Ilium the palace **56 lay about him** fight fiercely **64 know a man** recognize a complete man. (But Cressida, pretending to misunderstand, takes it to mean simply "recognize.") **66 is Troilus** is that extraordinary individual known far and wide as Troilus. (But, again, Cressida reduces it to the literal.) **69 in some** by several **71 he** each **72 Himself** (Pandarus plays with the expression "not to be oneself," to be out of sorts.) **75 Condition . . . India** i.e., Troilus is about as likely to be himself again as I am to have walked barefoot on pilgrimage to India, which of course I haven't **77 'a** he **82 Excuse me** i.e., I beg to differ. (Line 84 means the same.) **85 to 't** i.e., to Hector's age, to maturity **87 his wit** i.e., Troilus' intelligence

PANDARUS   And she takes upon her to spy a white hair on his chin.

CRESSIDA   Alas, poor chin! Many a wart is richer.

PANDARUS   But there was such laughing! Queen Hecuba laughed that her eyes ran o'er.

CRESSIDA   With millstones.   145

PANDARUS   And Cassandra laughed.

CRESSIDA   But there was a more temperate fire under the pot of her eyes. Did her eyes run o'er too?

PANDARUS   And Hector laughed.

CRESSIDA   At what was all this laughing?

PANDARUS   Marry, at the white hair that Helen spied on Troilus' chin.

CRESSIDA   An 't had been a green hair, I should have laughed too.   153

PANDARUS   They laughed not so much at the hair as at his pretty answer.

CRESSIDA   What was his answer?

PANDARUS   Quoth she, "Here's but two-and-fifty hairs on your chin, and one of them is white."   158

CRESSIDA   This is her question.

PANDARUS   That's true, make no question of that. "Two-and-fifty hairs," quoth he, "and one white. That white hair is my father, and all the rest are his sons." "Jupiter!" quoth she, "which of these hairs is Paris my husband?" "The forked one," quoth he, "pluck 't out, and give it him." But there was such laughing! And Helen so blushed, and Paris so chafed, and all the rest so laughed, that it passed.   165 167 168

CRESSIDA   So let it now, for it has been a great while going by.   169

PANDARUS   Well, cousin, I told you a thing yesterday. Think on 't.

CRESSIDA   So I do.

PANDARUS   I'll be sworn 'tis true. He will weep you an 'twere a man born in April.   174 175

CRESSIDA   And I'll spring up in his tears an 'twere a nettle against May.   *Sound a retreat.*   176 177

PANDARUS   Hark, they are coming from the field. Shall we stand up here and see them as they pass toward Ilium? Good niece, do, sweet niece Cressida.

CRESSIDA   At your pleasure.

PANDARUS   Here, here, here's an excellent place; here we may see most bravely. I'll tell you them all by their names as they pass by, but mark Troilus above the rest.   183

Enter Aeneas [and passes across the stage].

---

145 With millstones i.e., mirthlessly, since nothing has been said funny enough to make the eyes weep tears of laughter. (To *weep millstones* is to be cruel and heartless.)   **153 An** if   **158 two-and-fifty** (Priam had fifty sons. Perhaps the forked hair is to count for two.) **hairs** (With a pun on "heirs"; the Quarto spelling is "heires.") **165 forked** (1) bifurcated (2) bearing a cuckold's horns. (The suggestion is that Helen will cheat Paris in love as she has done Menelaus.) **167 so chafed** was so angry   **168 it passed** it exceeded all description. (But Cressida puns on the sense of "passed by.")   **169 it** i.e., Pandarus' story   **174–175 an 'twere** as if he were   **175 April** i.e., the season of showers   **176–177 an 'twere . . . May** as if I were a nettle in anticipation of May. (Cressida will "nettle" Troilus.) **177 s.d. retreat** trumpet signal for withdrawal   **183 bravely** excellently

CRESSIDA   Speak not so loud.

PANDARUS   That's Aeneas. Is not that a brave man? He's one of the flowers of Troy, I can tell you. But mark Troilus; you shall see anon.   187

Enter Antenor [and passes across the stage].

CRESSIDA   Who's that?

PANDARUS   That's Antenor. He has a shrewd wit, I can tell you, and he's a man good enough. He's one o' the soundest judgments in Troy whosoever, and a proper man of person. When comes Troilus? I'll show you Troilus anon. If he see me, you shall see him nod at me.   193

CRESSIDA   Will he give you the nod?   197

PANDARUS   You shall see.

CRESSIDA   If he do, the rich shall have more.   199

Enter Hector [and passes across the stage].

PANDARUS   That's Hector, that, that, look you, that. There's a fellow! Go thy way, Hector! There's a brave man, niece. O brave Hector! Look how he looks! There's a countenance! Is 't not a brave man?

CRESSIDA   O, a brave man!

PANDARUS   Is 'a not? It does a man's heart good. Look you what hacks are on his helmet! Look you yonder, do you see? Look you there. There's no jesting; there's laying on, take 't off who will, as they say. There be hacks.   206 208

CRESSIDA   Be those with swords?

Enter Paris [and passes across the stage].

PANDARUS   Swords, anything, he cares not; an the devil come to him, it's all one. By God's lid, it does one's heart good. Yonder comes Paris, yonder comes Paris. Look ye yonder, niece. Is 't not a gallant man, too, is 't not? Why, this is brave now. Who said he came hurt home today? He's not hurt. Why, this will do Helen's heart good now, ha! Would I could see Troilus now! You shall see Troilus anon.   212

CRESSIDA   Who's that?

Enter Helenus [and passes across the stage].

PANDARUS   That's Helenus. I marvel where Troilus is. That's Helenus. I think he went not forth today. That's Helenus.   221

CRESSIDA   Can Helenus fight, uncle?

PANDARUS   Helenus? No. Yes, he'll fight indifferent well. I marvel where Troilus is. Hark, do you not hear the people cry "Troilus"? Helenus is a priest.   224 225

CRESSIDA   What sneaking fellow comes yonder?

Enter Troilus [and passes across the stage].

---

187 brave excellent   **193 proper** handsome   **197 nod** (with a pun on *noddy*, fool, simpleton)   **199 the rich . . . more** i.e., the fool will become more foolish (since foolish Pandarus will receive a nod or *noddy*)   **206 hacks** dents, gashes   **208 laying on** i.e., evidence of blows exchanged.   **take 't off who will** whatever anyone may say to the contrary (with a pun on *taking off* as contrasted with *laying on*) **212 all one** all the same to him.   **By God's lid** by God's eyelid. (An oath.)   **221 he** i.e., Troilus   **224 indifferent** moderately   **225 marvel** wonder

PANDARUS Where? Yonder? That's Deiphobus. 'Tis Troilus! There's a man, niece! Hem! Brave Troilus! The prince of chivalry!

CRESSIDA Peace, for shame, peace!

PANDARUS Mark him, note him. O brave Troilus! Look well upon him, niece. Look you how his sword is bloodied and his helm more hacked than Hector's, 234 and how he looks, and how he goes! O admirable 235 youth! He ne'er saw three-and-twenty. Go thy way, Troilus, go thy way! Had I a sister were a grace, or a 237 daughter a goddess, he should take his choice. O admirable man! Paris? Paris is dirt to him; and I warrant Helen, to change, would give an eye to 240 boot. 241

Enter common soldiers [and pass across the stage].

CRESSIDA Here comes more.

PANDARUS Asses, fools, dolts! Chaff and bran, chaff and bran! Porridge after meat! I could live and die i' 244 th' eyes of Troilus. Ne'er look, ne'er look. The eagles are gone; crows and daws, crows and daws! I had 246 rather be such a man as Troilus than Agamemnon and all Greece.

CRESSIDA There is among the Greeks Achilles, a better man than Troilus.

PANDARUS Achilles? A drayman, a porter, a very camel. 251

CRESSIDA Well, well.

PANDARUS "Well, well"! Why, have you any discretion? Have you any eyes? Do you know what a man is? Is not birth, beauty, good shape, discourse, manhood, learning, gentleness, virtue, youth, liberality, and so forth, the spice and salt that season a man?

CRESSIDA Ay, a minced man; and then to be baked 258 with no date in the pie, for then the man's date is out. 259

PANDARUS You are such another woman! One knows not at what ward you lie. 261

CRESSIDA Upon my back to defend my belly, upon my wit to defend my wiles, upon my secrecy to defend 263 mine honesty, my mask to defend my beauty, and 264 you to defend all these, and at all these wards I lie, at 265 a thousand watches. 266

PANDARUS Say one of your watches.

CRESSIDA Nay, I'll watch you for that; and that's one of the chiefest of them too. If I cannot ward what I would 269

not have hit, I can watch you for telling how I took the blow—unless it swell past hiding, and then it's past 271 watching. 272

PANDARUS You are such another!

Enter [Troilus'] Boy.

BOY Sir, my lord would instantly speak with you.

PANDARUS Where?

BOY At your own house. There he unarms him.

PANDARUS Good boy, tell him I come.   [*Exit Boy.*]
I doubt he be hurt. Fare ye well, good niece. 278

CRESSIDA Adieu, uncle.

PANDARUS I'll be with you, niece, by and by.

CRESSIDA To bring, uncle? 281

PANDARUS Ay, a token from Troilus.

CRESSIDA By the same token, you are a bawd.

Exit Pandarus.

Words, vows, gifts, tears, and love's full sacrifice
He offers in another's enterprise;
But more in Troilus thousandfold I see
Than in the glass of Pandar's praise may be. 287
Yet hold I off. Women are angels, wooing; 288
Things won are done, joy's soul lies in the doing.
That she beloved knows naught that knows not this: 290
Men prize the thing ungained more than it is. 291
That she was never yet that ever knew
Love got so sweet as when desire did sue. 293
Therefore this maxim out of love I teach: 294
Achievement is command; ungained, beseech. 295
Then though my heart's contents firm love doth
    bear, 296
Nothing of that shall from mine eyes appear.

Exit [with Alexander].

❧

1.3 *Sennet. Enter Agamemnon, Nestor, Ulysses, Diomedes, Menelaus, with others.*

AGAMEMNON Princes,
What grief hath set the jaundice on your cheeks?
The ample proposition that hope makes 3
In all designs begun on earth below
Fails in the promised largeness. Checks and disasters 5
Grow in the veins of actions highest reared, 6
As knots, by the conflux of meeting sap, 7

234 **helm** helmet 235 **goes** walks 237 **a grace** one of the three Graces, the personification of loveliness 240–241 **to change . . . boot** would give Paris plus one of her eyes besides to have Troilus in exchange 244 **Porridge** soup (usually eaten before the meat course; after, it would be an anticlimax) 246 **daws** jackdaws (glossy, black crowlike birds) 251 **drayman** one who draws a cart 258 **minced** (1) chopped up fine (2) affected, effeminate 259 **the man's date is out** (1) the man is like a pie without any dates, a common ingredient used for flavoring (2) the man is out of fashion (with a suggestion, too, of his being a sexual failure) 261 **at what . . . lie** what defensive postures you adopt. (*Ward* and *lie* are technical terms from fencing. Cressida picks up *lie* in a sexual sense.) 263 **secrecy** (with suggestion of the female anatomy) 264 **honesty** reputation for chastity. **mask** (Used to protect fair skin from sunburning, considered unhandsome.) 265–266 **at a thousand watches** i.e., guarding myself in a thousand ways. (Subsequently, in the wordplay, *watch* means "devotional exercises" or "night watches," line 267, "keep under observation," line 268, and "watch out lest you tell," line 270.) 269 **ward** shield

271 **swell** i.e., in pregnancy 271–272 **past watching** too late to be concerned about 278 **doubt** fear 281 **To bring** i.e., are you bringing something? (But Cressida's phrase also completes a colloquial expression, "be with you to bring," meaning roughly, "I'll get even with you.") 287 **glass** mirror 288 **wooing** being wooed 290 **That she** that woman. (Also in line 292.) 291 **than it is** than it is worth in essence, in objective reality 293 **got** obtained (by the man) 294 **out of** derived from 295 **Achievement . . . beseech** to achieve (to win a woman) is to command her; not yet won, she must be entreated 296 **though . . . bear** though I carry firm love in my heart 1.3. **Location: The Greek camp. Before Agamemnon's tent.** s.d. **Sennet** trumpet call signaling a processional entrance or exit 3 **proposition** offer, proposal 5 **Fails . . . largeness** fails to materialize fully as promised 5–6 **Checks . . . reared** i.e., hindrances and disaster attend great enterprises. (*Veins* are sap vessels in plants.) 7 **conflux** flowing together

Infects the sound pine and diverts his grain 8
Tortive and errant from his course of growth. 9
Nor, princes, is it matter new to us
That we come short of our suppose so far 11
That after seven years' siege yet Troy walls stand, 12
Sith every action that hath gone before, 13
Whereof we have record, trial did draw 14
Bias and thwart, not answering the aim 15
And that unbodied figure of the thought 16
That gave 't surmisèd shape. Why then, you
  princes, 17
Do you with cheeks abashed behold our works
And think them shames, which are indeed naught
  else
But the protractive trials of great Jove 20
To find persistive constancy in men? 21
The fineness of which metal is not found
In Fortune's love; for then the bold and coward, 23
The wise and fool, the artist and unread, 24
The hard and soft, seem all affined and kin. 25
But in the wind and tempest of her frown, 26
Distinction, with a loud and powerful fan, 27
Puffing at all, winnows the light away, 28
And what hath mass or matter by itself
Lies rich in virtue and unminglèd. 30
NESTOR
With due observance of thy godly seat, 31
Great Agamemnon, Nestor shall apply 32
Thy latest words. In the reproof of chance 33
Lies the true proof of men. The sea being smooth,
How many shallow bauble boats dare sail 35
Upon her patient breast, making their way
With those of nobler bulk!
But let the ruffian Boreas once enrage 38
The gentle Thetis, and anon behold 39
The strong-ribbed bark through liquid mountains
  cut,
Bounding between the two moist elements 41
Like Perseus' horse. Where's then the saucy boat 42
Whose weak untimbered sides but even now 43
Corrivaled greatness? Either to harbor fled

Or made a toast for Neptune. Even so 45
Doth valor's show and valor's worth divide 46
In storms of Fortune. For in her ray and brightness 47
The herd hath more annoyance by the breese 48
Than by the tiger; but when the splitting wind
Makes flexible the knees of knotted oaks,
And flies fled under shade, why, then the thing of
  courage, 51
As roused with rage, with rage doth sympathize, 52
And with an accent tuned in selfsame key
Retorts to chiding Fortune.
ULYSSES   Agamemnon,
Thou great commander, nerve and bone of Greece, 55
Heart of our numbers, soul and only sprite, 56
In whom the tempers and the minds of all 57
Should be shut up, hear what Ulysses speaks. 58
Besides th' applause and approbation 59
The which, [to Agamemnon] most mighty for thy
  place and sway,
[To Nestor] And thou most reverend for thy
  stretched-out life,
I give to both your speeches, which were such
As Agamemnon and the hand of Greece
Should hold up high in brass, and such again
As venerable Nestor, hatched in silver, 65
Should with a bond of air, strong as the axletree 66
On which the heavens ride, knit all Greeks' ears 67
To his experienced tongue, yet let it please both,
Thou great, and wise, to hear Ulysses speak.
AGAMEMNON
Speak, Prince of Ithaca, and be 't of less expect 70
That matter needless, of importless burden, 71
Divide thy lips, than we are confident, 72
When rank Thersites opes his mastic jaws, 73
We shall hear music, wit, and oracle. 74
ULYSSES
Troy, yet upon his basis, had been down, 75
And the great Hector's sword had lacked a master,
But for these instances.
The specialty of rule hath been neglected; 78
And look how many Grecian tents do stand 79
Hollow upon this plain, so many hollow factions. 80
When that the general is not like the hive 81

8,9 his its   9 Tortive and errant twisted and deviating   11 suppose expectation   12 yet still   13–17 Sith . . . shape since everything we've tried, according to the historical record, has gone awry in the doing of it, not corresponding to our aims and imaginings as to how it should go   20 protractive delaying, drawing out   21 persistive enduring   23 In Fortune's love i.e., when Fortune smiles   24 artist scholar   25 affined related   26 her Fortune's   27–28 Distinction . . . away (Fortune is a winnowing tool, blowing away like chaff those who do not persevere and leaving behind like grain those who do.)   30 virtue excellence.   unminglèd unalloyed, uncontaminated   31 observance of respect for.   seat throne, i.e., dignity of office   32 apply expore the implications of   33 reproof rebuke, defiance   35 bauble toylike   38 Boreas north wind   39 Thetis a sea deity, mother of Achilles; here, used for the sea itself. (Probably confused with Tethys, the wife of Oceanus.)   41 moist elements air and water   42 Perseus' horse Pegasus, a winged horse that sprang from the blood of Medusa when Perseus cut off her head. (The horse was given to Bellerophon by the gods. It is associated, however, with Perseus, probably because Ovid relates that the latter hero was mounted on Pegasus when he rescued Andromeda from the sea monster.)   43 but even now only a moment ago

45 toast rich morsel to be swallowed, like toasted bread floating in liquor   46 show mere appearance   47 storms of Fortune trials and tests visited by misfortune.   her Fortune's   48 breese gadfly   51 fled are fled.   the thing of courage any brave heart   52 As being.   sympathize correspond   55 nerve sinews   56 numbers armies   57 tempers dispositions   58 shut up gathered in, embodied   59 approbation approval   65 hatched in silver (1) adorned with silver hair, a sign of age and wisdom (2) born wise   66 bond of air i.e., his breath or words as speech, powerful oration   66–67 axletree . . . ride axis on which the heavens, in the Ptolemaic cosmology, revolve around the earth   70–74 be 't . . . oracle i.e., we should expect unimportant matter from you even less than we should expect music, wit, and truth from Thersites   70 expect expectation   73 rank disgusting, foul-smelling.   mastic gummy, abusive, scouring   75 yet . . . basis still standing on its foundations   78 specialty of rule particular rights and responsibilities of supreme authority   79 look how many however many, just as many   80 Hollow (1) empty, because of the present assembly (2) symbolizing faction   81 When that when.   like the hive i.e., serving as the focus of activity, the command center

To whom the foragers shall all repair,   82
What honey is expected? Degree being vizarded,   83
Th' unworthiest shows as fairly in the mask.   84
The heavens themselves, the planets, and this center   85
Observe degree, priority, and place,
Insisture, course, proportion, season, form,   87
Office, and custom, in all line of order.
And therefore is the glorious planet Sol   89
In noble eminence enthroned and sphered   90
Amidst the other, whose med'cinable eye   91
Corrects the ill aspects of planets evil   92
And posts, like the commandment of a king,   93
Sans check, to good and bad. But when the planets   94
In evil mixture to disorder wander,   95
What plagues and what portents, what mutiny,
What raging of the sea, shaking of earth,
Commotion in the winds, frights, changes, horrors,
Divert and crack, rend and deracinate   99
The unity and married calm of states
Quite from their fixure! O, when degree is shaked,   101
Which is the ladder to all high designs,
The enterprise is sick. How could communities,
Degrees in schools, and brotherhoods in cities,   104
Peaceful commerce from dividable shores,   105
The primogeneity and due of birth,   106
Prerogative of age, crowns, scepters, laurels,
But by degree stand in authentic place?
Take but degree away, untune that string,
And hark what discord follows. Each thing meets
In mere oppugnancy. The bounded waters   111
Should lift their bosoms higher than the shores
And make a sop of all this solid globe;   113
Strength should be lord of imbecility,   114
And the rude son should strike his father dead;   115
Force should be right; or rather, right and wrong,
Between whose endless jar justice resides,   117
Should lose their names, and so should justice too.
Then everything includes itself in power,   119
Power into will, will into appetite;
And appetite, an universal wolf,
So doubly seconded with will and power,

Must make perforce an universal prey   123
And last eat up himself. Great Agamemnon,
This chaos, when degree is suffocate,   125
Follows the choking.   126
And this neglection of degree it is   127
That by a pace goes backward in a purpose   128
It hath to climb. The general's disdained   129
By him one step below, he by the next,
That next by him beneath; so every step,
Exampled by the first pace that is sick   132
Of his superior, grows to an envious fever   133
Of pale and bloodless emulation.
And 'tis this fever that keeps Troy on foot,
Not her own sinews. To end a tale of length,
Troy in our weakness lives, not in her strength.

NESTOR
Most wisely hath Ulysses here discovered   138
The fever whereof all our power is sick.   139

AGAMEMNON
The nature of the sickness found, Ulysses,
What is the remedy?

ULYSSES
The great Achilles, whom opinion crowns
The sinew and the forehand of our host,   143
Having his ear full of his airy fame,   144
Grows dainty of his worth and in his tent   145
Lies mocking our designs. With him Patroclus
Upon a lazy bed the livelong day
Breaks scurril jests,
And with ridiculous and awkward action,
Which, slanderer, he imitation calls,
He pageants us. Sometimes, great Agamemnon,   151
Thy topless deputation he puts on,   152
And like a strutting player, whose conceit   153
Lies in his hamstring, and doth think it rich   154
To hear the wooden dialogue and sound   155
Twixt his stretched footing and the scaffoldage,   156
Such to-be-pitied and o'erwrested seeming   157
He acts thy greatness in; and when he speaks,
'Tis like a chime a-mending, with terms unsquared,   159
Which, from the tongue of roaring Typhon dropped,   160
Would seem hyperboles. At this fusty stuff   161
The large Achilles, on his pressed bed lolling,   162

---

82 repair return   **83 Degree being vizarded** when the hierarchical function of authority is masked   **84 shows as fairly** appears as attractive (as the most noble)   **85 this center** the earth, center of the Ptolemaic universe   **87 Insisture** steady continuance in their path, or apparent pausing when a planet seems from earth's perspective to reverse course   **89 Sol** sun (regarded as a planet because of its apparent movement around the earth)   **90 sphered** placed in its sphere   **91 other** others.   **med'cinable** healing   **92 aspects** relative positions of the heavenly bodies as they appear to an observer on the earth's surface at a given time, and the influence attributed thereto   **93 posts** speeds   **94 Sans check** without pause   **95 mixture** conjunction   **99 deracinate** uproot   **101 fixure** stability   **104 Degrees in schools** academic rank.   **brotherhoods** corporations, guilds   **105 dividable** separated, serving the function of dividing   **106 primogeneity** right of the eldest son to succeed to his father's estate   **111 mere oppugnancy** total strife   **113 sop** piece of bread or cake floating in liquor; pulp   **114 imbecility** weakness   **115 rude** brutal   **117 Between . . . resides** i.e., justice is arrived at only through an unceasing conflict between right and wrong. (*Jar* means "collision.")   **119 includes** subsumes

123 Must . . . prey must inevitably prey on everything   **125 suffocate** suffocated   **126 choking** act of suffocation   **127 neglection** neglect   **128 by a pace** step by step   **128–129 in . . . climb** when it intends to climb   **132–133 Exampled . . . superior** shown a precedent by the first envious step that his superior takes   **138 discovered** revealed   **139 power** army   **143 forehand** first in might.   **host** army   **144 airy fame** unsubstantial reputation   **145 dainty** fastidious   **151 pageants** mimics   **152 topless deputation** supreme power   **153–154 whose . . . hamstring** i.e., whose wits are in his thighs   **154 rich** admirable   **155–156 To hear . . . scaffoldage** i.e., to hear the echoing sound of his marching to and fro on the stage or scaffolding   **157 to-be-pitied . . . seeming** pitiful and exaggerated acting   **159 a-mending** being repaired or retuned.   **terms unsquared** expressions unadapted to their subject, ill-fitted (like unsquared timbers or stones in architecture)   **160 from** even if from.   **Typhon** Greek mythological monster with a hundred heads that breathed fire; he made war against the gods and was destroyed by one of Zeus' thunderbolts   **161 fusty** stale (and suggesting *fustian*, bombastic)   **162 pressed** weighed down (by its occupant)

From his deep chest laughs out a loud applause,
Cries, "Excellent! 'Tis Agamemnon just. 164
Now play me Nestor; hem, and stroke thy beard,
As he being dressed to some oration." 166
That's done, as near as the extremest ends 167
Of parallels, as like as Vulcan and his wife, 168
Yet god Achilles still cries, "Excellent!
'Tis Nestor right. Now play him me, Patroclus,
Arming to answer in a night alarm." 171
And then, forsooth, the faint defects of age 172
Must be the scene of mirth; to cough and spit,
And with a palsy, fumbling on his gorget, 174
Shake in and out the rivet. And at this sport
Sir Valor dies; cries, "O, enough, Patroclus,
Or give me ribs of steel! I shall split all
In pleasure of my spleen." And in this fashion, 178
All our abilities, gifts, natures, shapes,
Severals and generals of grace exact, 180
Achievements, plots, orders, preventions, 181
Excitements to the field, or speech for truce, 182
Success or loss, what is or is not, serves
As stuff for these two to make paradoxes. 184

NESTOR
And in the imitation of these twain—
Who, as Ulysses says, opinion crowns 186
With an imperial voice—many are infect. 187
Ajax is grown self-willed and bears his head
In such a rein, in full as proud a place 189
As broad Achilles; keeps his tent like him; 190
Makes factious feasts; rails on our state of war, 191
Bold as an oracle; and sets Thersites,
A slave whose gall coins slanders like a mint, 193
To match us in comparisons with dirt,
To weaken and discredit our exposure, 195
How rank soever rounded in with danger. 196

ULYSSES
They tax our policy and call it cowardice, 197
Count wisdom as no member of the war, 198
Forestall prescience, and esteem no act 199
But that of hand. The still and mental parts 200
That do contrive how many hands shall strike
When fitness calls them on and know by measure 202
Of their observant toil the enemy's weight— 203

Why, this hath not a finger's dignity. 204
They call this bed work, mappery, closet war; 205
So that the ram that batters down the wall,
For the great swinge and rudeness of his poise, 207
They place before his hand that made the engine, 208
Or those that with the fineness of their souls 209
By reason guide his execution. 210

NESTOR
Let this be granted, and Achilles' horse 211
Makes many Thetis' sons.   Tucket. 212

AGAMEMNON   What trumpet? Look, Menelaus.
MENELAUS   From Troy.

Enter Aeneas [with a trumpeter].

AGAMEMNON   What would you 'fore our tent?
AENEAS
Is this great Agamemnon's tent, I pray you?
AGAMEMNON   Even this.
AENEAS
May one that is a herald and a prince
Do a fair message to his kingly ears?
AGAMEMNON
With surety stronger than Achilles' arm 220
'Fore all the Greekish host, which with one voice 221
Call Agamemnon head and general.
AENEAS
Fair leave and large security. How may 223
A stranger to those most imperial looks
Know them from eyes of other mortals?
AGAMEMNON   How?
AENEAS
Ay. I ask, that I might waken reverence,
And bid the cheek be ready with a blush
Modest as morning when she coldly eyes 229
The youthful Phoebus. 230
Which is that god in office, guiding men?
Which is the high and mighty Agamemnon?
AGAMEMNON
This Trojan scorns us, or the men of Troy
Are ceremonious courtiers.
AENEAS
Courtiers as free, as debonair, unarmed, 235
As bending angels—that's their fame in peace. 236
But when they would seem soldiers, they have galls, 237
Good arms, strong joints, true swords, and—Jove's
   accord— 238
Nothing so full of heart. But peace, Aeneas, 239

164 just exactly   **166 dressed** addressed   **167–168 as near . . . parallels** (Parallel lines never meet, no matter how far they are extended.)   **168 Vulcan . . . wife** i.e., the ugliest god, and Venus, the most beautiful goddess   **171 answer in** respond to   **172 faint** weak   **174 palsy** tremor.   **gorget** piece of armor for the throat   **178 spleen** (Regarded as the seat of laughter.)   **180 Severals . . . exact** well-ordered gifts, individual and general   **181 preventions** defensive precautions   **182 Excitements** exhortations   **184 paradoxes** absurdities   **186–187 crowns . . . voice** i.e., regards most highly, adulates   **189 In . . . rein** i.e., so haughtily   **190 broad** hefty.   **keeps** keeps to   **191 factious** i.e., for his faction.   **our state of war** our state of preparedness for war; our soldiers in their readiness   **193 slave** contemptible person.   **gall** the seat of bile and rancor   **195 exposure** vulnerable situation   **196 rank** thickly.   **rounded in with** surrounded by   **197 tax our policy** censure our prudent management   **198 no member** no fit guide or companion   **199 Forestall prescience** condemn beforehand any attempts at foresight   **200 that of hand** any immediate physical response   **202 fitness** suitability of occasion   **202–203 know . . . weight** figure out by laborious calculation the enemy's strength

204 hath . . . dignity is not worth a snap of the fingers   **205 bed work** i.e., armchair strategy.   **mappery** mere making of maps.   **closet war** war planned in the study   **207 For . . . poise** because of the great impetus and roughness of its impact   **208 place before** give precedence to   **209 fineness . . . souls** subtle skill of their intelligence   **210 his execution** i.e., the use of the battering ram   **211–212 Let . . . sons** if this is granted, then Achilles' horse in its brute strength outvalues many an Achilles (the son of Thetis)   **212 s.d. Tucket** signal given on a trumpet   **220 surety** security   **221 'Fore** i.e., leading into battle   **223 Fair leave** courteous permission   **229 she** i.e., Aurora, the blushing dawn goddess   **230 Phoebus** Apollo, here referred to as the sun-god   **235 free** generous.   **debonair** gentle   **236 bending** bowing   **237 galls** i.e., spirit to resent injury. (See line 193.)   **238 Jove's accord** Jove being in full accord   **239 Nothing . . . heart** nothing is so full of heart (courage) as they

Peace, Trojan; lay thy finger on thy lips!
The worthiness of praise distains his worth,
If that the praised himself bring the praise forth.
But what the repining enemy commends,
That breath fame blows; that praise, sole pure,
   transcends.
AGAMEMNON
Sir, you of Troy, call you yourself Aeneas?
AENEAS   Ay, Greek, that is my name.
AGAMEMNON   What's your affair, I pray you?
AENEAS
Sir, pardon. 'Tis for Agamemnon's ears.
AGAMEMNON
He hears naught privately that comes from Troy.
AENEAS
Nor I from Troy come not to whisper him.
I bring a trumpet to awake his ear,
To set his sense on the attentive bent,
And then to speak.
AGAMEMNON   Speak frankly as the wind;
It is not Agamemnon's sleeping hour.
That thou shalt know, Trojan, he is awake,
He tells thee so himself.
AENEAS   Trumpet, blow loud;
Send thy brass voice through all these lazy tents,
And every Greek of mettle, let him know
What Troy means fairly shall be spoke aloud.
                          The trumpets sound.
We have, great Agamemnon, here in Troy
A prince called Hector—Priam is his father—
Who in this dull and long-continued truce
Is resty grown. He bade me take a trumpet
And to this purpose speak: Kings, princes, lords!
If there be one among the fair'st of Greece
That holds his honor higher than his ease,
That seeks his praise more than he fears his peril,
That knows his valor and knows not his fear,
That loves his mistress more than in confession
With truant vows to her own lips he loves,
And dare avow her beauty and her worth
In other arms than hers—to him this challenge.
Hector, in view of Trojans and of Greeks,
Shall make it good, or do his best to do it,
He hath a lady, wiser, fairer, truer,
Than ever Greek did compass in his arms,
And will tomorrow with his trumpet call
Midway between your tents and walls of Troy
To rouse a Grecian that is true in love.
If any come, Hector shall honor him;
If none, he'll say in Troy when he retires,
The Grecian dames are sunburnt and not worth

243
244

251
252

263

269
270

272

276

282

The splinter of a lance. Even so much.   283
AGAMEMNON
This shall be told our lovers, Lord Aeneas.
If none of them have soul in such a kind,   285
We left them all at home. But we are soldiers;
And may that soldier a mere recreant prove   287
That means not, hath not, or is not in love!   288
If then one is, or hath, or means to be,
That one meets Hector; if none else, I am he.
NESTOR
Tell him of Nestor, one that was a man
When Hector's grandsire sucked. He is old now,
But if there be not in our Grecian host
One noble man that hath one spark of fire
To answer for his love, tell him from me
I'll hide my silver beard in a gold beaver,   296
And in my vambrace put this withered brawn,   297
And meeting him will tell him that my lady
Was fairer than his grandam and as chaste   299
As may be in the world. His youth in flood,   300
I'll prove this truth with my three drops of blood.
AENEAS
Now heavens forbid such scarcity of youth!
ULYSSES   Amen.
AGAMEMNON
Fair Lord Aeneas, let me touch your hand;
To our pavilion shall I lead you first.
Achilles shall have word of this intent;
So shall each lord of Greece, from tent to tent.
Yourself shall feast with us before you go,
And find the welcome of a noble foe.   309
                  Exeunt. Mane[n]t Ulysses and Nestor.
ULYSSES   Nestor!
NESTOR   What says Ulysses?
ULYSSES
I have a young conception in my brain;
Be you my time to bring it to some shape.   313
NESTOR   What is 't?
ULYSSES   This 'tis:
Blunt wedges rive hard knots; the seeded pride   316
That hath to this maturity blown up   317
In rank Achilles must or now be cropped   318
Or, shedding, breed a nursery of like evil   319
To overbulk us all.
NESTOR   Well, and how?   320
ULYSSES
This challenge that the gallant Hector sends,
However it is spread in general name,
Relates in purpose only to Achilles.

241

283

285
287
288

296
297

299
300

309

313

316
317
318
319

320

---

283 Even so much (A formulaic conclusion to a delivered message, meaning, "that is the totality of what I am bid to say.")   **285 such a kind** such a spirit   **287 mere recreant** utter coward   **288 means not** intends not to be   **296 beaver** face guard of a helmet   **297 vambrace** armor for the front part of the arm.   **brawn** i.e., arm   **299 grandam** grandmother   **300 His . . . flood** i.e., though his manhood and vigor be at their height   **309 s.d. Mane[n]t** they remain   **313 Be . . . time** i.e., act as midwife to my newly conceived plan   **316 rive** split, break apart.   **seeded pride** pride that has gone to seed, overblown   **317 blown up** sprouted, puffed up   **318 rank** overripe, swollen.   **or** either   **319 shedding** if it scatters its seeds.   **nursery** (1) breeding ground (2) crop   **320 overbulk** overwhelm, outgrow

241 distains his sullies its own   **243 repining** begrudging   **244 That . . . blows** fame proclaims abroad that speech.   **sole** completely   **251 trumpet** trumpeter   **252 set . . . bent** i.e., bend his sense of hearing attentively toward me   **263 resty** sluggish, inactive, restive   **269–270 That . . . loves** i.e., who shows his love for his beloved more in deeds of arms than in sweet nothings promised lip to lip   **272 In . . . hers** i.e., in the arms of warfare rather than those of his mistress   **276 compass** encompass, embrace   **282 sunburnt** i.e., unattractive, according to Elizabethan tastes in beauty

NESTOR
The purpose is perspicuous even as substance,   324
Whose grossness little characters sum up;   325
And, in the publication, make no strain   326
But that Achilles, were his brain as barren
As banks of Libya—though, Apollo knows,   328
'Tis dry enough—will, with great speed of
judgment,   329
Ay, with celerity, find Hector's purpose   330
Pointing on him.
ULYSSES   And wake him to the answer, think you?
NESTOR
Yes, 'tis most meet. Who may you else oppose   333
That can from Hector bring his honor off
If not Achilles? Though 't be a sportful combat,
Yet in this trial much opinion dwells,   336
For here the Trojans taste our dear'st repute   337
With their fin'st palate. And trust to me, Ulysses,   338
Our imputation shall be oddly poised   339
In this wild action. For the success,   340
Although particular, shall give a scantling   341
Of good or bad unto the general;   342
And in such indices, although small pricks   343
To their subsequent volumes, there is seen   344
The baby figure of the giant mass
Of things to come at large. It is supposed
He that meets Hector issues from our choice;
And choice, being mutual act of all our souls,
Makes merit her election and doth boil,   349
As 'twere from forth us all, a man distilled
Out of our virtues; who miscarrying,   351
What heart from hence receives the conquering part,   352
To steel a strong opinion to themselves?   353
Which entertained, limbs are his instruments,   354
In no less working than are swords and bows   355
Directive by the limbs.   356
ULYSSES   Give pardon to my speech:
Therefore 'tis meet Achilles meet not Hector.   358
Let us, like merchants, show our foulest wares,
And think perchance they'll sell; if not,
The lustre of the better yet to show
Shall show the better. Do not consent

That ever Hector and Achilles meet;
For both our honor and our shame in this
Are dogged with two strange followers.
NESTOR
I see them not with my old eyes. What are they?
ULYSSES
What glory our Achilles shares from Hector,   367
Were he not proud, we all should wear with him.
But he already is too insolent,
And we were better parch in Afric sun   370
Than in the pride and salt scorn of his eyes,
Should he scape Hector fair. If he were foiled,   372
Why then we did our main opinion crush   373
In taint of our best man. No, make a lottery,   374
And, by device, let blockish Ajax draw
The sort to fight with Hector. Among ourselves   376
Give him allowance as the worthier man;   377
For that will physic the great Myrmidon   378
Who broils in loud applause, and make him fall   379
His crest that prouder than blue Iris bends.   380
If the dull brainless Ajax come safe off,
We'll dress him up in voices; if he fail,   382
Yet go we under our opinion still
That we have better men. But, hit or miss,
Our project's life this shape of sense assumes: 385
Ajax employed plucks down Achilles' plumes.
NESTOR
Now, Ulysses, I begin to relish thy advice;
And I will give a taste of it forthwith
To Agamemnon. Go we to him straight.
Two curs shall tame each other; pride alone
Must tar the mastiffs on, as 'twere their bone.   391
                                                    Exeunt.

2.1   *Enter Ajax and Thersites.*

AJAX   Thersites!
THERSITES   Agamemnon—how if he had boils, full, all
over, generally?
AJAX   Thersites!
THERSITES   And those boils did run? Say so. Did not the
General run, then? Were not that a botchy core?   6
AJAX   Dog!

324–325 perspicuous . . . up as perceivable as great wealth or matter, the size of which can be rendered in little figures   326 in . . .
strain when it is publicly announced, have no doubt   328 banks
sandbanks; shores   329 dry dull   330 celerity quickness   333 meet
fitting.   else oppose otherwise put forward as opponent   336 opinion
reputation   337 taste our dear'st repute i.e., put to the test Achilles,
our warrior of greatest reputation   338 their fin'st palate i.e., Hector
339 Our imputation what is imputed to us, our reputation.   oddly
poised unequally balanced   340 wild rash.   success outcome
341 particular relating to (two) particular men.   scantling specimen,
sample   342 general army at large   343 indices indications, table of
contents   343–344 small . . . volumes small indicators in comparison with the volumes that follow   349 election basis of choice
351 miscarrying i.e., if he should fail   352 What . . . part (1) what
cheer will the conquering party, i.e., the Trojans, receive from this, or
(2) what encouragement can anyone take from this   353 steel
strengthen   354–356 Which . . . limbs i.e., if one does entertain a
strong opinion of oneself, one's limbs become the instruments of that
strong opinion, no less efficacious and responsive to it than swords
and bows are subject to the direction of the limbs   358 meet fitting

367 shares from gains at the expense of   370 parch for us to parch,
to shrivel   372 scape Hector fair escape from Hector victoriously.
(Ulysses' argument is that Achilles, already too proud, will be insuffer-
able if he wins, and that, if he loses, the Greeks will undergo the humiliation of losing with their best-reputed warrior.)   373 main opinion crush destroy our general reputation   374 In taint in the dishonor
376 sort lot   377 allowance as acknowledgment as   378 physic
purge medically.   Myrmidon i.e., Achilles. (So called here because
accompanied by a band of Myrmidon warriors, from a tribe living in
Thessaly.)   379 broils in basks in.   fall let fall, bow   380 crest
plumes on helmet.   Iris the messenger of Juno, i.e., the rainbow, and
the blue flower.   bends arches   382 voices applause   385 life success   391 tar . . . on provoke, incite
2.1. Location: The Greek camp.
6 botchy core central hard mass of a boil or tumor

THERSITES   Then there would come some matter from 8
him. I see none now.

AJAX   Thou bitch-wolf's son, canst thou not hear?
Strikes him. Feel, then.

THERSITES   The plague of Greece upon thee, thou mon- 12
grel beef-witted lord! 13

AJAX   Speak then, thou vinewed'st leaven, speak. I will 14
beat thee into handsomeness.

THERSITES   I shall sooner rail thee into wit and holiness;
but I think thy horse will sooner con an oration than 17
thou learn a prayer without book. Thou canst strike, 18
canst thou? A red murrain o' thy jade's tricks! 19

AJAX   Toadstool, learn me the proclamation. 20

THERSITES   Dost thou think I have no sense, thou strik- 21
est me thus?

AJAX   The proclamation!

THERSITES   Thou art proclaimed a fool, I think.

AJAX   Do not, porcupine, do not. My fingers itch. 25

THERSITES   I would thou didst itch from head to foot.
An I had the scratching of thee, I would make thee the
loathsomest scab in Greece. When thou art forth in the
incursions, thou strikest as slow as another. 29

AJAX   I say, the proclamation!

THERSITES   Thou grumblest and railest every hour on
Achilles, and thou art as full of envy at his greatness as
Cerberus is at Proserpina's beauty, ay, that thou 33
bark'st at him.

AJAX   Mistress Thersites!

THERSITES   Thou shouldst strike him— 36

AJAX   Cobloaf! 37

THERSITES   He would pun thee into shivers with his 38
fist, as a sailor breaks a biscuit.

AJAX   [*beating him*]   You whoreson cur!

THERSITES   Do, do. 41

AJAX   Thou stool for a witch! 42

THERSITES   Ay, do, do, thou sodden-witted lord! Thou 43
hast no more brain than I have in mine elbows; an
asinego may tutor thee. Thou scurvy-valiant ass! Thou 45
art here but to thrash Trojans, and thou art bought 46
and sold among those of any wit, like a barbarian 47
slave. If thou use to beat me, I will begin at thy heel 48
and tell what thou art by inches, thou thing of no 49
bowels, thou! 50

AJAX   You dog!

THERSITES   You scurvy lord!

AJAX   [*beating him*]   You cur!

THERSITES   Mars his idiot! Do, rudeness, do, camel, 54
do, do.

Enter Achilles and Patroclus.

ACHILLES   Why, how now, Ajax, wherefore do ye thus? 56
How now, Thersites, what's the matter, man?

THERSITES   You see him there, do you?

ACHILLES   Ay; what's the matter?

THERSITES   Nay, look upon him.

ACHILLES   So I do. What's the matter?

THERSITES   Nay, but regard him well.

ACHILLES   Well, why, I do so.

THERSITES   But yet you look not well upon him; for,
whosoever you take him to be, he is Ajax. 65

ACHILLES   I know that, fool.

THERSITES   Ay, but that fool knows not himself. 67

AJAX   Therefore I beat thee.

THERSITES   Lo, lo, lo, lo, what modicums of wit he ut- 69
ters! His evasions have ears thus long. I have bobbed 70
his brain more than he has beat my bones. I will buy
nine sparrows for a penny, and his pia mater is not 72
worth the ninth part of a sparrow. This lord, Achilles—Ajax, who wears his wit in his belly and his guts
in his head—I'll tell you what I say of him.

ACHILLES   What?

THERSITES   I say, this Ajax—   [*Ajax threatens him.*]

ACHILLES   Nay, good Ajax.

THERSITES   Has not so much wit—

ACHILLES   Nay, I must hold you.

THERSITES   As will stop the eye of Helen's needle, for 81
whom he comes to fight.

ACHILLES   Peace, fool!

THERSITES   I would have peace and quietness, but the
fool will not—he there, that he. Look you there.

AJAX   O thou damned cur! I shall—

ACHILLES   Will you set your wit to a fool's? 87

THERSITES   No, I warrant you, for a fool's will shame it.

PATROCLUS   Good words, Thersites. 89

ACHILLES   What's the quarrel?

AJAX   I bade the vile owl go learn me the tenor of the
proclamation, and he rails upon me.

THERSITES   I serve thee not.

AJAX   Well, go to, go to.

THERSITES   I serve here voluntary. 95

ACHILLES   Your last service was sufferance, 'twas not 96
voluntary; no man is beaten voluntary. Ajax was here
the voluntary, and you as under an impress. 98

THERSITES   E'en so. A great deal of your wit, too, lies in 99
your sinews, or else there be liars. Hector shall have a

---

8 matter (1) sense (2) pus   **12–13 mongrel** (Ajax's mother was a Trojan, the sister of Priam; compare 2.2.77 [note], 4.5.84, and 4.5.121.)
13 beef-witted i.e., slow-witted. (Perhaps this refers to the belief that
eating beef made one dull, or Thersites may merely be calling Ajax a
"stupid ox.")   **14 vinewed'st** most moldy.   **leaven** dough   **17 con**
memorize   **18 without book** by heart   **19 murrain** plague.   **jade's
tricks** i.e., ill-tempered kicking and rearing, as of a worthless horse
20 learn me find out for me   **21 sense** feeling   **25 porcupine** (A term
of abuse for one who is prickly and small.)   **29 incursions** i.e., attacks upon the Trojan forces   **33 Cerberus** three-headed dog that
guarded the entrance to Hades.   **Proserpina** Queen of Hades
36 Thou if thou   **37 Cobloaf** small round loaf; a bun   **38 pun** pound.
shivers fragments   **41 Do** i.e., go ahead, I dare you   **42 stool** privy
43 sodden-witted boiled-brained   **45 asinego** little ass   **46–**
47 bought and sold i.e., treated like merchandise   **48 use** continue
49 by inches methodically, inch by inch   **50 bowels** sensitivity, human feeling

54 Mars his Mars'   **56 wherefore** why   **65 Ajax** (with probable pun
on *a jakes*, a latrine)   **67 that fool . . . himself** (Thersites answers as
though Achilles had said, "I know that fool.")   **69 modicums** small
amounts   **70 have . . . long** i.e., are those of an ass, are asinine.
bobbed thumped   **72 pia mater** (Literally, membrane cover of the
brain; used here for the brain.)   **81 stop** stop up, fill (perhaps with
bawdy sense)   **87 set your wit to** match wits with   **89 Good words**
i.e., speak gently   **95 voluntary** voluntarily   **96 sufferance** something
imposed   **98 impress** (1) impressment, military draft (2) imprint (of
blows)   **99 E'en so** exactly

great catch an 'a knock out either of your brains; 'a 101
were as good crack a fusty nut with no kernel.   102
ACHILLES   What, with me too, Thersites?
THERSITES   There's Ulysses and old Nestor, whose wit
    was moldy ere your grandsires had nails on their toes,
    yoke you like draft-oxen and make you plow up the
    war.
ACHILLES   What? What?
THERSITES   Yes, good sooth. To, Achilles! To, Ajax! To! 109
AJAX   I shall cut out your tongue.
THERSITES   'Tis no matter. I shall speak as much wit as
    thou afterwards.   112
PATROCLUS   No more words, Thersites. Peace!
THERSITES   I will hold my peace when Achilles' brach 114
    bids me, shall I?
ACHILLES   There's for you, Patroclus.
THERSITES   I will see you hanged like clodpolls ere I 117
    come any more to your tents. I will keep where there
    is wit stirring and leave the faction of fools.   *Exit.*
PATROCLUS   A good riddance.
ACHILLES
    Marry, this, sir, is proclaimed through all our host:
    That Hector, by the fifth hour of the sun,   122
    Will with a trumpet twixt our tents and Troy
    Tomorrow morning call some knight to arms
    That hath a stomach, and such a one that dare   125
    Maintain—I know not what, 'tis trash. Farewell.
AJAX   Farewell. Who shall answer him?
ACHILLES
    I know not. 'Tis put to lottery. Otherwise
    He knew his man.   [*Exit with Patroclus.*] 129
AJAX   O, meaning you? I will go learn more of it.
                                                       Exit.

❧

2.2   *Enter Priam, Hector, Troilus, Paris, and Helenus.*

PRIAM
    After so many hours, lives, speeches spent,
    Thus once again says Nestor from the Greeks:
    "Deliver Helen, and all damage else—
    As honor, loss of time, travail, expense,   4
    Wounds, friends, and what else dear that is
        consumed
    In hot digestion of this cormorant war—   6
    Shall be struck off." Hector, what say you to 't?   7
HECTOR
    Though no man lesser fears the Greeks than I

As far as toucheth my particular,   9
Yet, dread Priam,
There is no lady of more softer bowels,   11
More spongy to suck in the sense of fear,
More ready to cry out, "Who knows what follows?"
Than Hector is. The wound of peace is surety,   14
Surety secure; but modest doubt is called   15
The beacon of the wise, the tent that searches   16
To th' bottom of the worst. Let Helen go.
Since the first sword was drawn about this question,
Every tithe soul, 'mongst many thousand dismes,   19
Hath been as dear as Helen; I mean, of ours.
If we have lost so many tenths of ours
To guard a thing not ours—nor worth to us,
Had it our name, the value of one ten—   23
What merit's in that reason which denies
The yielding of her up?
TROILUS   Fie, fie, my brother!
Weigh you the worth and honor of a king
So great as our dread father in a scale
Of common ounces? Will you with counters sum   28
The past-proportion of his infinite,   29
And buckle in a waist most fathomless
With spans and inches so diminutive   31
As fears and reasons? Fie, for godly shame!
HELENUS [*to Troilus*]
No marvel, though you bite so sharp at reasons,   33
You are so empty of them. Should not our father   34
Bear the great sway of his affairs with reason,
Because your speech hath none that tell him so?   36
TROILUS
You are for dreams and slumbers, brother priest;
You fur your gloves with reason. Here are your
    reasons: 38
You know an enemy intends you harm;
You know a sword employed is perilous,
And reason flies the object of all harm.   41
Who marvels then, when Helenus beholds
A Grecian and his sword, if he do set
The very wings of reason to his heels
And fly like chidden Mercury from Jove   45
Or like a star disorbed? Nay, if we talk of reason,   46
Let's shut our gates and sleep. Manhood and honor

---

101 an 'a if he   **101–102 'a . . . good** he might as well   **102 fusty**
moldy   **109 To . . . To** (Thersites impersonates Nestor and Ulysses as
drivers of a team, urging Achilles and Ajax to plow.)   **112 afterwards**
i.e., even after my tongue is cut out   **114 brach** bitch hound. (The
Quarto reading, *brooch*, could mean "bauble, plaything," referring to
Patroclus.)   **117 clodpolls** blockheads   **122 fifth hour** eleven o'clock
125 stomach appetite (for fighting)   **129 knew** would know
2.2. Location: Troy. The palace.
4 travail strenuous effort   **6 cormorant** voracious (like the seabird)
7 struck off canceled

9 my particular me personally   **11 bowels** i.e., mercy, pity   **14 The
. . . surety** the danger of peace is in the sense of security it breeds
15 secure overconfident.   **modest doubt** a reasonable estimate of
danger   **16 beacon** warning signal.   **tent** surgical probe   **19 Every
tithe soul** every soul exacted by the war as a tithe.   **dismes** tenths (of
men sacrificed)   **23 Had . . . name** i.e., even if Helen were a Trojan.
one ten one tithe exacted by the war, one Trojan life   **28 counters**
pieces of coin-shaped metal used in calculation.   **sum** total up
29 The past-proportion . . . infinite his infinitude past all comparison
31 spans measures of nine inches spanning the hand from thumb to
little finger   **33 reasons** (Pronounced like "raisins," with pun.)
34 not our father our father not   **36 Because . . . so** i.e., simply because you unreasonably urge him to govern unreasonably   **38 fur**
line with soft fur. (Troilus accuses Helenus of using reason as a justification for personal comfort, explaining cowardly flight as prudence.)
41 the object . . . harm the sight of anything harmful   **45 chidden
Mercury** (Mercury as Jove's errand boy was subject to his chiding or
impatient bidding.)   **46 disorbed** removed from its sphere (like a
shooting star)

Should have hare hearts, would they but fat their
thoughts   48
With this crammed reason. Reason and respect   49
Make livers pale and lustihood deject.   50

HECTOR
Brother, she is not worth what she doth cost
The holding.

TROILUS   What's aught but as 'tis valued?

HECTOR
But value dwells not in particular will;   53
It holds his estimate and dignity   54
As well wherein 'tis precious of itself   55
As in the prizer. 'Tis mad idolatry   56
To make the service greater than the god;
And the will dotes that is inclinable   58
To what infectiously itself affects   59
Without some image of th' affected merit.   60

TROILUS
I take today a wife, and my election   61
Is led on in the conduct of my will—
My will enkindled by mine eyes and ears,
Two traded pilots twixt the dangerous shores   64
Of will and judgment. How may I avoid,   65
Although my will distaste what it elected,   66
The wife I chose? There can be no evasion
To blench from this and to stand firm by honor.   68
We turn not back the silks upon the merchant
When we have spoiled them, nor the remainder
viands   70
We do not throw in unrespective sieve   71
Because we now are full. It was thought meet
Paris should do some vengeance on the Greeks.   73
Your breath of full consent bellied his sails;   74
The seas and winds, old wranglers, took a truce   75
And did him service. He touched the ports desired,
And for an old aunt whom the Greeks held captive   77
He brought a Grecian queen, whose youth and
freshness
Wrinkles Apollo's and makes stale the morning.   79
Why keep we her? The Grecians keep our aunt.
Is she worth keeping? Why, she is a pearl

Whose price hath launched above a thousand ships   82
And turned crowned kings to merchants.   83
If you'll avouch 'twas wisdom Paris went—
As you must needs, for you all cried, "Go, go"—
If you'll confess he brought home noble prize—
As you must needs, for you all clapped your hands
And cried, "Inestimable!"—why do you now
The issue of your proper wisdoms rate   89
And do a deed that never Fortune did,   90
Beggar the estimation which you prized   91
Richer than sea and land? O, theft most base,
That we have stol'n what we do fear to keep!
But thieves unworthy of a thing so stol'n,   94
That in their country did them that disgrace   95
We fear to warrant in our native place!   96

CASSANDRA [within]
Cry, Trojans, cry!

PRIAM   What noise? What shriek is this?

TROILUS
'Tis our mad sister. I do know her voice.

CASSANDRA [within] Cry, Trojans!

HECTOR   It is Cassandra.

*Enter Cassandra, [raving,] with her hair about her
ears.*

CASSANDRA
Cry, Trojans, cry! Lend me ten thousand eyes,
And I will fill them with prophetic tears.

HECTOR   Peace, sister, peace!

CASSANDRA
Virgins and boys, mid-age and wrinkled old,   104
Soft infancy, that nothing canst but cry,   105
Add to my clamor! Let us pay betimes   106
A moiety of that mass of moan to come.   107
Cry, Trojans, cry! Practice your eyes with tears!
Troy must not be, nor goodly Ilium stand;
Our firebrand brother, Paris, burns us all.   110
Cry, Trojans, cry! A Helen and a woe!
Cry, cry! Troy burns, or else let Helen go. *Exit.*

HECTOR
Now, youthful Troilus, do not these high strains
Of divination in our sister work
Some touches of remorse? Or is your blood
So madly hot that no discourse of reason,
Nor fear of bad success in a bad cause,
Can qualify the same?

TROILUS   Why, brother Hector,   118

48–49 fat . . . reason i.e., fatten or cram their thoughts with this
reason   49 respect caution   50 livers pale (A bloodless liver was
thought to be a sign of cowardice.)   lustihood bodily vigor   53 particular will i.e., one person's preference merely   54 his its.   dignity
worth   55 of itself intrinsically   56 the prizer i.e., the opinion of
him who prizes it   58–60 the will . . . merit any will is mere willfulness that is derived from the will's own diseased affection without
some visible appearance of merit in the thing desired   61 I take today a wife (Troilus, in setting up a hypothetical case that applies to
Paris, is also stating his own credo about love.)   election choice
64 traded skillful in their trade; trafficking back and forth   65 avoid
rid myself of   66 distaste dislike (in time)   68 blench shrink.   and
and simultaneously   70 remainder viands leftover food   71 unrespective sieve undiscriminating receptacle, i.e., garbage can   73 vengeance i.e., in return for Hesione's abduction; see line 77 and note
74 bellied swelled   75 old wranglers traditional enemies   77 an old
aunt i.e., Hesione, Priam's sister, rescued from the wrath of Poseidon
by Hercules and bestowed by him on the Greek, Telamon, father of
Ajax; we learn in 4.5.84 and 4.5.121 that she was Ajax' mother
79 Wrinkles Apollo's makes Apollo's youthful countenance look old
and ugly by comparison

82 Whose . . . ships (Perhaps echoes the famous line from Marlowe's
Doctor Faustus: "Was this the face that launched a thousand ships?")
83 turned . . . merchants i.e., has made kings behave like merchants
seeking a rare pearl. (Compare Matthew 13:45.)   89 The issue . . .
rate condemn the results of your own wise deliberation   90 do . . .
did act more capriciously than Fortune ever did   91 Beggar . . .
which consider valueless the once esteemed object that   94 But i.e.,
we are but   95–96 That . . . place who disgraced the Greeks in
their own country through an act (the abducting of Helen) that we are
now too cowardly to justify right here in our own native land
104 old old persons   105 nothing canst can do nothing   106 betimes
before it is too late   107 moiety part   110 firebrand (Paris' mother,
Hecuba, dreamed when pregnant with Paris that she would be delivered of a firebrand destined to burn down Troy.)   118 qualify
moderate

We may not think the justness of each act 119
Such and no other than th' event doth form it, 120
Nor once deject the courage of our minds 121
Because Cassandra's mad. Her brainsick raptures 122
Cannot distaste the goodness of a quarrel 123
Which hath our several honors all engaged
To make it gracious. For my private part, 125
I am no more touched than all Priam's sons, 126
And Jove forbid there should be done amongst us 127
Such things as might offend the weakest spleen 128
To fight for and maintain! 129

PARIS
Else might the world convince of levity 130
As well my undertakings as your counsels. 131
But I attest the gods, your full consent 132
Gave wings to my propension and cut off 133
All fears attending on so dire a project.
For what, alas, can these my single arms? 135
What propugnation is in one man's valor 136
To stand the push and enmity of those
This quarrel would excite? Yet, I protest,
Were I alone to pass the difficulties, 139
And had as ample power as I have will,
Paris should ne'er retract what he hath done
Nor faint in the pursuit.

PRIAM   Paris, you speak
Like one besotted on your sweet delights. 143
You have the honey still, but these the gall.
So to be valiant is no praise at all. 145

PARIS
Sir, I propose not merely to myself
The pleasures such a beauty brings with it,
But I would have the soil of her fair rape 148
Wiped off in honorable keeping her.
What treason were it to the ransacked queen, 150
Disgrace to your great worths, and shame to me,
Now to deliver her possession up 152
On terms of base compulsion! Can it be
That so degenerate a strain as this
Should once set footing in your generous bosoms? 155
There's not the meanest spirit on our party 156
Without a heart to dare or sword to draw
When Helen is defended, nor none so noble
Whose life were ill bestowed or death unfamed 159
Where Helen is the subject. Then I say,
Well may we fight for her whom we know well
The world's large spaces cannot parallel.

HECTOR
Paris and Troilus, you have both said well,
And on the cause and question now in hand
Have glozed—but superficially, not much 165
Unlike young men, whom Aristotle thought
Unfit to hear moral philosophy. 167
The reasons you allege do more conduce 168
To the hot passion of distempered blood
Than to make up a free determination 170
Twixt right and wrong, for pleasure and revenge
Have ears more deaf than adders to the voice 172
Of any true decision. Nature craves 173
All dues be rendered to their owners. Now,
What nearer debt in all humanity
Than wife is to the husband? If this law
Of nature be corrupted through affection, 177
And that great minds, of partial indulgence 178
To their benumbèd wills, resist the same,
There is a law in each well-ordered nation
To curb those raging appetites that are
Most disobedient and refractory. 182
If Helen then be wife to Sparta's king,
As it is known she is, these moral laws
Of nature and of nations speak aloud
To have her back returned. Thus to persist
In doing wrong extenuates not wrong
But makes it much more heavy. Hector's opinion
Is this in way of truth; yet ne'ertheless, 189
My sprightly brethren, I propend to you 190
In resolution to keep Helen still,
For 'tis a cause that hath no mean dependence 192
Upon our joint and several dignities. 193

TROILUS
Why, there you touched the life of our design!
Were it not glory that we more affected 195
Than the performance of our heaving spleens, 196
I would not wish a drop of Trojan blood
Spent more in her defense. But, worthy Hector,
She is a theme of honor and renown,
A spur to valiant and magnanimous deeds,
Whose present courage may beat down our foes, 201
And fame in time to come canonize us; 202
For I presume brave Hector would not lose
So rich advantage of a promised glory
As smiles upon the forehead of this action 205
For the wide world's revenue.

HECTOR   I am yours,
You valiant offspring of great Priamus.
I have a roisting challenge sent amongst 208

119–122 We . . . mad we must not let our sense of the justice of our proceedings become merely pragmatic, nor abate our courage solely because of Cassandra's mad warnings   123 distaste render distasteful   125 gracious righteous, dignified (because our honorable selves "grace" the enterprise)   126 touched affected   127–129 Jove . . . maintain Jove forbid that any act done by any of Priam's sons (such as abducting Helen) should be such that even the least courageous among us would not willingly fight to maintain   130 convince convict   131 As well . . . as both . . . and   132 attest call to witness   133 propension propensity, inclination   135 can . . . arms can my arms alone accomplish   136 propugnation defense, might   139 pass experience, undergo   143 besotted drunk   145 So thus, under these circumstances.   praise merit   148 soil stain. rape abduction   150 ransacked carried off   152 her possession possession of her   155 generous noble   156 party part, side   159 bestowed employed

165 glozed commented on   167 moral philosophy (Aristotle says this of political philosophy in the Nichomachean Ethics.)   168 conduce lead, tend   170 free unbiased   172 adders (Psalms 58:4–5 speaks of adders as deaf.)   173 craves demands   177 affection passion   178 that if that, if. of partial out of self-interested   182 refractory obstinate   189 truth abstract principle   190 sprightly full of spirit. propend incline   192–193 'tis . . . dignities i.e., it is a cause upon which depend to no small degree our collective and individual honors   195 more affected desired more   196 heaving spleens i.e., aroused anger   201 Whose of which   202 canonize enroll among famous persons   205 forehead i.e., prospect, beginning   208 roisting roistering, clamorous

The dull and factious nobles of the Greeks
Will strike amazement to their drowsy spirits.   210
I was advertised their great general slept,   211
Whilst emulation in the army crept.   212
This, I presume, will wake him.   *Exeunt.*

❧

2.3   *Enter Thersites, solus.*

THERSITES   How now, Thersites? What, lost in the labyrinth of thy fury? Shall the elephant Ajax carry it   2
thus? He beats me, and I rail at him. O, worthy
satisfaction! Would it were otherwise, that I could beat
him whilst he railed at me. 'Sfoot, I'll learn to conjure   5
and raise devils but I'll see some issue of my spiteful   6
execrations. Then there's Achilles, a rare enginer! If   7
Troy be not taken till these two undermine it, the walls
will stand till they fall of themselves. O thou great
thunder-darter of Olympus, forget that thou art Jove,
the king of gods, and, Mercury, lose all the serpentine   11
craft of thy caduceus, if ye take not that little little less   12
than little wit from them that they have, which short-   13
armed ignorance itself knows is so abundant scarce it   14
will not in circumvention deliver a fly from a spider   15
without drawing their massy irons and cutting the   16
web! After this, the vengeance on the whole camp! Or
rather, the Neapolitan bone-ache! For that, methinks,   18
is the curse dependent on those that war for a placket.   19
I have said my prayers, and devil Envy say
"Amen."—What ho! My lord Achilles!

Enter Patroclus [at the door of the tent].

PATROCLUS   Who's there? Thersites? Good Thersites,
come in and rail.   [*Exit.*]
THERSITES   If I could ha' remembered a gilt counterfeit,   24
thou wouldst not have slipped out of my contemplation. But it is no matter; thyself upon thyself! The   26
common curse of mankind, folly and ignorance, be
thine in great revenue! Heaven bless thee from a tutor,   28
and discipline come not near thee! Let thy blood be   29

thy direction till thy death; then if she that lays thee
out says thou art a fair corpse, I'll be sworn and sworn
upon 't she never shrouded any but lazars.   32

[*Enter Patroclus.*]

Amen.—Where's Achilles?
PATROCLUS   What, art thou devout? Wast thou in
prayer?
THERSITES   Ay. The heavens hear me!
PATROCLUS   Amen.

Enter Achilles.

ACHILLES   Who's there?
PATROCLUS   Thersites, my lord.
ACHILLES   Where, where? O, where?—Art thou come?
Why, my cheese, my digestion, why hast thou not   41
served thyself in to my table so many meals? Come,
what's Agamemnon?
THERSITES   Thy commander, Achilles.—Then tell me,
Patroclus, what's Achilles?
PATROCLUS   Thy lord, Thersites. Then tell me, I pray
thee, what's thyself?
THERSITES   Thy knower, Patroclus. Then tell me, Patro-
clus, what art thou?
PATROCLUS   Thou mayst tell that knowest.
ACHILLES   O, tell, tell.
THERSITES   I'll decline the whole question. Agamemnon   52
commands Achilles, Achilles is my lord, I am Patro-
clus' knower, and Patroclus is a fool.
PATROCLUS   You rascal!
THERSITES   Peace, fool! I have not done.
ACHILLES   He is a privileged man.—Proceed, Thersites.   57
THERSITES   Agamemnon is a fool, Achilles is a fool,
Thersites is a fool, and, as aforesaid, Patroclus is a fool.
ACHILLES   Derive this. Come.   60
THERSITES   Agamemnon is a fool to offer to command
Achilles, Achilles is a fool to be commanded of
Agamemnon, Thersites is a fool to serve such a fool,
and Patroclus is a fool positive.   64
PATROCLUS   Why am I a fool?
THERSITES   Make that demand to the Creator. It suffices
me thou art. Look you, who comes here?

*Enter [at a distance] Agamemnon, Ulysses,
Nestor, Diomedes, Ajax, and Calchas.*

ACHILLES   Patroclus, I'll speak with nobody.—Come in
with me, Thersites.   *Exit.*
THERSITES   Here is such patchery, such juggling, and   70
such knavery! All the argument is a whore and a   71
cuckold, a good quarrel to draw emulous factions and   72
bleed to death upon. Now, the dry serpigo on the   73
subject, and war and lechery confound all!   [*Exit.*]

---

210 **Will** that will   211 **advertised** informed.   **their great general**
i.e., Achilles; or possibly Agamemnon   212 **emulation** ambitious or
jealous rivalry
2.3. Location: The Greek camp. Before Achilles' tent.
2 **carry it** carry off the honors   5 **'Sfoot** by His (God's) foot   6 **but I'll
see** unless I see.   **issue** result   7 **execrations** curses.   **enginer** one
who digs countermines or tunnels underneath the enemy's battle-
ments, or devises plans for such undertakings   11–12 **serpentine
. . . caduceus** (Alludes to Mercury's wand, having two serpents
twined round it.)   13–14 **short-armed** inadequate in its reach, finding everything beyond its grasp   15 **circumvention** craft, stratagem
16 **massy irons** massive swords (used with overkill on a mere spider's
web)   18 **Neapolitan bone-ache** i.e., venereal disease   19 **dependent
on** hanging over.   **placket** slit in a petticoat; hence (indecently) a
woman   24 **ha'** have.   **gilt counterfeit** counterfeit coin (often called
a "slip"; hence the quibble in line 25)   26 **thyself upon thyself** (Thersites, after alleging that he would have cursed Patroclus along with
Ajax and Achilles if he were not counterfeit and hence so easily overlooked, now undertakes to curse Patroclus with the most dire curse
imaginable: may Patroclus simply be himself, be plagued by himself.)
28 **great revenue** generous amounts.   **bless thee from** bless you by
protecting you from (so as to preserve your native ignorance)
29 **blood** violent passion

32 **lazars** lepers   41 **cheese** (Supposed, proverbially, to aid digestion.)
52 **decline** go through in order from beginning to end (as when declining a noun)   57 **privileged man** (Fools were permitted to speak
without restraint.)   60 **Derive** explain, give the origin of. (The grammatical metaphor is continued here and also in line 64.)   64 **positive**
absolute   70 **patchery** knavery   71 **All the argument** the issue of the
war   72 **draw** (1) attract (2) draw blood from; see line 73.   **emulous**
envious   73 **serpigo** skin eruption

AGAMEMNON   Where is Achilles?

PATROCLUS
Within his tent, but ill disposed, my lord.

AGAMEMNON
Let it be known to him that we are here.
He shent our messengers, and we lay by   78
Our appertainments, visiting of him.   79
Let him be told so, lest perchance he think
We dare not move the question of our place,   81
Or know not what we are.

PATROCLUS   I shall so say to him. [Exit.]

ULYSSES   We saw him at the opening of his tent. He is
not sick.

AJAX   Yes, lion-sick, sick of proud heart. You may call it 85
melancholy if you will favor the man, but, by my
head, 'tis pride. But why, why? Let him show us the
cause.—A word, my lord. [He takes Agamemnon aside.]

NESTOR   What moves Ajax thus to bay at him?

ULYSSES   Achilles hath inveigled his fool from him.

NESTOR   Who, Thersites?

ULYSSES   He.

NESTOR   Then will Ajax lack matter, if he have lost his 93
argument.   94

ULYSSES   No, you see, he is his argument that has his 95
argument—Achilles.   96

NESTOR   All the better; their fraction is more our wish 97
than their faction. But it was a strong council that a 98
fool could disunite.

ULYSSES   The amity that wisdom knits not, folly may
easily untie.

Enter Patroclus.

Here comes Patroclus.

NESTOR   No Achilles with him.

ULYSSES   The elephant hath joints, but none for cour- 104
tesy. His legs are legs for necessity, not for flexure.

PATROCLUS
Achilles bids me say he is much sorry
If anything more than your sport and pleasure
Did move your greatness and this noble state   108
To call upon him. He hopes it is no other
But for your health and your digestion's sake,
An after-dinner's breath.

AGAMEMNON   Hear you, Patroclus: 111
We are too well acquainted with these answers;
But his evasion, winged thus swift with scorn,
Cannot outfly our apprehensions.   114
Much attribute he hath, and much the reason   115

Why we ascribe it to him. Yet all his virtues,
Not virtuously on his own part beheld,   117
Do in our eyes begin to lose their gloss,
Yea, like fair fruit in an unwholesome dish,
Are like to rot untasted. Go and tell him   120
We come to speak with him. And you shall not sin   121
If you do say we think him overproud
And underhonest, in self-assumption greater   123
Than in the note of judgment; and worthier than
himself   124
Here tend the savage strangeness he puts on,   125
Disguise the holy strength of their command,
And underwrite in an observing kind   127
His humorous predominance—yea, watch   128
His pettish lunes, his ebbs, his flows, as if   129
The passage and whole carriage of this action
Rode on his tide. Go tell him this, and add
That if he overhold his price so much,   132
We'll none of him, but let him, like an engine   133
Not portable, lie under this report: 134
"Bring action hither, this cannot go to war."
A stirring dwarf we do allowance give   136
Before a sleeping giant. Tell him so.

PATROCLUS
I shall, and bring his answer presently.   138

AGAMEMNON
In second voice we'll not be satisfied.   139
We come to speak with him.—Ulysses, enter you.
Exit Ulysses [with Patroclus].

AJAX   What is he more than another?

AGAMEMNON   No more than what he thinks he is.

AJAX   Is he so much? Do you not think he thinks
himself a better man than I am?

AGAMEMNON   No question.

AJAX   Will you subscribe his thought and say he is?   146

AGAMEMNON   No, noble Ajax, you are as strong, as
valiant, as wise, no less noble, much more gentle, and
altogether more tractable.

AJAX   Why should a man be proud? How doth pride
grow? I know not what it is.

AGAMEMNON   Your mind is the clearer, Ajax, and your
virtues the fairer. He that is proud eats up himself.
Pride is his own glass, his own trumpet, his own 154
chronicle; and whatever praises itself but in the deed 155
devours the deed in the praise.

Enter Ulysses.

AJAX   I do hate a proud man as I hate the engendering
of toads.

78 shent sent back insultingly   79 appertainments rights, prerogatives
81 move the question insist upon the prerogatives   85 lion-sick i.e.,
sick with pride   93 matter subject matter (to rail upon)   93–94 his
argument i.e., the subject of his railing, Thersites   95–96 he . . .
Achilles Achilles, who now has Ajax' former subject of railing, Thersites, has himself become Ajax' new target of raillery   97–98 their
. . . faction i.e., this discord between Achilles and Ajax better suits
our wishes than would an alliance between them   98 council compact. (Said contemptuously.)   104 The elephant hath joints (Refers to
a common belief that elephants' joints did not enable them to lie
down.)   108 state council of state   111 breath i.e., stroll for a breath
of fresh air   114 apprehensions (1) power of arrest (2) understanding
115 attribute credit, reputation

117 Not . . . beheld not modestly borne   120 like likely   121 sin err
123 self-assumption self-importance   124 Than . . . judgment than
men of true judgment know him to be; or, than in qualities of wise
judgment   124–125 worthier . . . on worthier persons than himself
here stand in attendance while he assumes an uncivil aloofness
127–128 underwrite . . . predominance deferentially subscribe to
the humor now dominant in him—i.e., blood, leading to pride
129 pettish lunes ill-humored tantrums   132 overhold overvalue
133 engine military machine   134 lie under suffer under   136 allowance approbation, praise   138 presently right away   139 In second
voice i.e., with a mere messenger's report   146 subscribe concur in
154 glass mirror   155 but in the deed in any way other than doing
(praiseworthy) deeds

NESTOR [aside]   Yet he loves himself. Is 't not
strange?

ULYSSES
Achilles will not to the field tomorrow.

AGAMEMNON
What's his excuse?

ULYSSES   He doth rely on none,
But carries on the stream of his dispose   163
Without observance or respect of any,
In will peculiar and in self-admission.   165

AGAMEMNON
Why, will he not upon our fair request
Untent his person and share the air with us?

ULYSSES
Things small as nothing, for request's sake only, 168
He makes important. Possessed he is with greatness,
And speaks not to himself but with a pride
That quarrels at self-breath. Imagined worth   171
Holds in his blood such swoll'n and hot discourse
That twixt his mental and his active parts
Kingdomed Achilles in commotion rages   174
And batters down himself. What should I say?
He is so plaguey proud that the death tokens of it 176
Cry "No recovery."

AGAMEMNON   Let Ajax go to him.
Dear lord, go you and greet him in his tent.
'Tis said he holds you well and will be led,   179
At your request, a little from himself.   180

ULYSSES
O Agamemnon, let it not be so!
We'll consecrate the steps that Ajax makes
When they go from Achilles. Shall the proud lord
That bastes his arrogance with his own seam   184
And never suffers matter of the world   185
Enter his thoughts, save such as do revolve   186
And ruminate himself, shall he be worshiped   187
Of that we hold an idol more than he?   188
No, this thrice worthy and right valiant lord
Must not so stale his palm, nobly acquired,   190
Nor, by my will, assubjugate his merit,   191
As amply titled as Achilles' is,   192
By going to Achilles.
That were to enlard his fat-already pride
And add more coals to Cancer when he burns   195
With entertaining great Hyperion.   196
This lord go to him? Jupiter forbid,
And say in thunder, "Achilles, go to him."

163 **dispose** bent of mind   165 **will peculiar** his own independent
will.   **self-admission** self-approbation   168 **for . . . only** only because they are requested   171 **quarrels at self-breath** i.e., is almost
too proud to speak to himself   174 **Kingdomed** i.e., like a microcosm
of a state   176 **death tokens** fatal symptoms   179 **holds** regards
180 **from himself** i.e., from his usual arrogant behavior   184 **seam**
fat, grease (by means of which Achilles feeds his own pride)
185 **suffers** allows   186–187 **do . . . himself** serves for endless
self-contemplation   188 **Of that** by one whom (i.e., Ajax).   **idol**
thing worthy of worship   190 **stale . . . acquired** sully his nobly
won honor   191 **assubjugate** debase, reduce to subjection   192 **As
. . . is** having as great a name as Achilles'   195–196 **add . . . Hyperion** i.e., add a fire to the heat of summer. (Cancer is the sign of the
zodiac into which the sun [Hyperion] enters at the beginning of
summer.)

NESTOR [aside to Diomedes]
O, this is well. He rubs the vein of him.   199

DIOMEDES [aside to Nestor]
And how his silence drinks up this applause!

AJAX
If I go to him, with my armèd fist
I'll pash him o'er the face.   202

AGAMEMNON   O, no, you shall not go.

AJAX
An 'a be proud with me, I'll feeze his pride.   204
Let me go to him.

ULYSSES
Not for the worth that hangs upon our quarrel.   206

AJAX   A paltry, insolent fellow!

NESTOR [aside]   How he describes himself!

AJAX   Can he not be sociable?

ULYSSES [aside]   The raven chides blackness.

AJAX   I'll let his humor's blood.   211

AGAMEMNON [aside]   He will be the physician that
should be the patient.

AJAX   An all men were o' my mind—

ULYSSES [aside]   Wit would be out of fashion.

AJAX   'A should not bear it so. 'A should eat swords first. 216
Shall pride carry it?

NESTOR [aside]   An 'twould, you'd carry half.   218

ULYSSES [aside]   'A would have ten shares.   219

AJAX   I will knead him; I'll make him supple.

NESTOR [aside]   He's not yet through warm. Farce him 221
with praises. Pour in, pour in; his ambition is dry.

ULYSSES [to Agamemnon]
My lord, you feed too much on this dislike.   223

NESTOR
Our noble General, do not do so.

DIOMEDES
You must prepare to fight without Achilles.

ULYSSES
Why, 'tis this naming of him does him harm.   226
Here is a man—but 'tis before his face;
I will be silent.

NESTOR   Wherefore should you so?
He is not emulous, as Achilles is.   229

ULYSSES
Know the whole world, he is as valiant—

AJAX   A whoreson dog, that shall palter thus with us! 231
Would he were a Trojan!

NESTOR   What a vice were it in Ajax now—

ULYSSES   If he were proud—

DIOMEDES   Or covetous of praise—

ULYSSES   Ay, or surly borne—   236

DIOMEDES   Or strange, or self-affected!   237

199 **vein** humor, disposition   202 **pash** smash   204 **feeze** settle the
business of   206 **our quarrel** i.e., with the Trojans   211 **let . . .
blood** bleed him (as a physician would) to cure his excessive humors
216 **'A** he.   **eat swords** swallow my sword, i.e., be beaten in fight
218 **An** if   219 **ten shares** i.e., the whole without sharing
221 **through** thoroughly.   **Farce** stuff   223 **this dislike** i.e., Achilles'
truculence   226 **this . . . harm** this continual citing of him as our
chief hero that creates the difficulty   229 **emulous** envious, eager for
glory   231 **that shall palter** who thinks he can trifle, dodge
236 **surly borne** bearing himself in a surly fashion   237 **strange** distant.   **self-affected** in love with himself

ULYSSES [*to Ajax*]
Thank the heavens, lord, thou art of sweet
　　composure. 238
Praise him that got thee, she that gave thee suck; 239
Famed be thy tutor, and thy parts of nature 240
Thrice famed, beyond, beyond all erudition; 241
But he that disciplined thine arms to fight, 242
Let Mars divide eternity in twain
And give him half; and, for thy vigor,
Bull-bearing Milo his addition yield 245
To sinewy Ajax. I will not praise thy wisdom, 246
Which, like a bourn, a pale, a shore, confines 247
Thy spacious and dilated parts. Here's Nestor, 248
Instructed by the antiquary times; 249
He must, he is, he cannot but be wise.
But pardon, father Nestor, were your days
As green as Ajax' and your brain so tempered, 252
You should not have the eminence of him, 253
But be as Ajax.

AJAX   Shall I call you father?
ULYSSES
Ay, my good son.
DIOMEDES   Be ruled by him, Lord Ajax.
ULYSSES
There is no tarrying here; the hart Achilles
Keeps thicket. Please it our great General 257
To call together all his state of war. 258
Fresh kings are come to Troy; tomorrow
We must with all our main of power stand fast. 260
And here's a lord—come knights from east to west,
And cull their flower, Ajax shall cope the best. 262
AGAMEMNON
Go we to council. Let Achilles sleep.
Light boats sail swift, though greater hulks draw
　　deep. *Exeunt.* 264

❧

3.1 *Music sounds within. Enter Pandarus and a
Servant.*

PANDARUS Friend, you, pray you, a word. Do not you
follow the young Lord Paris? 2
SERVANT Ay, sir, when he goes before me. 3
PANDARUS You depend upon him, I mean? 4

238 **composure** temperament, constitution 239 **got** begot
240–241 **thy parts . . . erudition** i.e., your natural gifts thrice exceeding what erudition can add thereto (with an ironic double meaning, suggesting that erudition can add little) 242 **But he** but as for him 245 **Bull-bearing . . . yield** let bull-bearing Milo yield up his title. (Milo, a celebrated athlete of phenomenal strength, was able to carry a bull on his shoulders.) 246 **I will not** (1) I will forbear to (2) I won't 247 **bourn** boundary. **pale** fence 248 **dilated parts** extensive and well-known qualities (but also hinting at Ajax' beefy build) 249 **antiquary** ancient 252 **green** immature. **tempered** composed 253 **have . . . of** be reckoned superior to 257 **Keeps thicket** i.e., stays hidden. (A *thicket* is a dense growth of shrubs or trees.) 258 **state** council 260 **main** full force 262 **cull their flower** choose their flower of chivalry. **cope** prove a match for 264 **hulks** big, unwieldy ships
3.1. Location: Troy. The palace.
2 **follow** serve. (But the servant takes it in the sense of "follow after.") 3 **goes** walks 4 **depend upon** serve as dependent to. (The servant mockingly uses a more spiritual sense.)

SERVANT Sir, I do depend upon the lord. 5
PANDARUS You depend upon a notable gentleman; I
must needs praise him. 7
SERVANT The Lord be praised!
PANDARUS You know me, do you not?
SERVANT Faith, sir, superficially. 10
PANDARUS Friend, know me better. I am the Lord
Pandarus.
SERVANT I hope I shall know your honor better. 13
PANDARUS I do desire it.
SERVANT You are in the state of grace. 15
PANDARUS Grace? Not so, friend. "Honor" and "lordship" are my titles. What music is this?
SERVANT I do but partly know, sir. It is music in parts.
PANDARUS Know you the musicians?
SERVANT Wholly, sir.
PANDARUS Who play they to?
SERVANT To the hearers, sir.
PANDARUS At whose pleasure, friend?
SERVANT At mine, sir, and theirs that love music.
PANDARUS Command, I mean, friend.
SERVANT Who shall I command, sir?
PANDARUS Friend, we understand not one another; I
am too courtly and thou too cunning. At whose
request do these men play?
SERVANT That's to 't indeed, sir. Marry, sir, at the 30
request of Paris my lord, who's there in person; with
him, the mortal Venus, the heart-blood of beauty,
love's visible soul—
PANDARUS Who, my cousin Cressida?
SERVANT No, sir, Helen. Could not you find out that
by her attributes?
PANDARUS It should seem, fellow, that thou hast not
seen the Lady Cressida. I come to speak with Paris
from the Prince Troilus. I will make a complimental 39
assault upon him, for my business seethes. 40
SERVANT Sodden business! There's a stewed phrase, 41
indeed!

Enter Paris and Helen [attended].

PANDARUS Fair be to you, my lord, and to all this fair 43
company! Fair desires, in all fair measure, fairly guide 44
them! Especially to you, fair queen, fair thoughts be
your fair pillow!
HELEN Dear lord, you are full of fair words.
PANDARUS You speak your fair pleasure, sweet
queen.—Fair prince, here is good broken music. 49

5 **lord** (quibbling on *lord*, referring to Paris, and "Lord" as "God")
7 **needs** necessarily 10 **superficially** (1) by sight (2) not in depth
13 **know . . . better** (1) become better acquainted with you (2) see you become a better man. (*Your honor* is a polite form of address to one of social consequence.) 15 **in . . . grace** i.e., in the way of salvation because of desiring to be better. (Pandarus answers as though *grace* referred to the courtly title applicable to a duke or prince.)
30 **to 't** to the point 39 **complimental** courteous 40 **seethes** boils, requires haste 41 **Sodden, stewed** (A play on *seethes* and with quibbling reference to stews or brothels and to the sweating treatment for venereal disease.) 43 **Fair** fair wishes, good fortune (with wordplay in subsequent uses of *fair*: attractive, pleasing, just, clean) 44 **fairly** favorably 49 **broken music** music arranged for different families of instruments

PARIS You have broke it, cousin, and, by my life, you 50
shall make it whole again; you shall piece it out with 51
a piece of your performance.—Nell, he is full of harmony.

PANDARUS Truly, lady, no.

HELEN O, sir—

PANDARUS Rude, in sooth; in good sooth, very rude. 56

PARIS Well said, my lord. Well, you say so in fits. 57

PANDARUS I have business to my lord, dear
queen.—My lord, will you vouchsafe me a word? 59

HELEN Nay, this shall not hedge us out. We'll hear you 60
sing, certainly.

PANDARUS Well, sweet queen, you are pleasant with 62
me.—But, marry, thus, my lord: my dear lord and
most esteemed friend, your brother Troilus—

HELEN My lord Pandarus, honey-sweet lord—

PANDARUS Go to, sweet queen, go to—commends 66
himself most affectionately to you—

HELEN You shall not bob us out of our melody. If you 68
do, our melancholy upon your head!

PANDARUS Sweet queen, sweet queen, that's a sweet
queen, i' faith.

HELEN And to make a sweet lady sad is a sour offense.

PANDARUS Nay, that shall not serve your turn, that shall
it not, in truth, la. Nay, I care not for such words, no, 74
no.—And, my lord, he desires you, that if the King
call for him at supper you will make his excuse.

HELEN My lord Pandarus—

PANDARUS What says my sweet queen, my very very
sweet queen?

PARIS What exploit's in hand? Where sups he tonight?

HELEN Nay, but, my lord—

PANDARUS What says my sweet queen? My cousin will 82
fall out with you. 83

HELEN [to Paris] You must not know where he sups. 84

PARIS I'll lay my life, with my disposer Cressida. 85

PANDARUS No, no, no such matter; you are wide. 86
Come, your disposer is sick.

PARIS Well, I'll make 's excuse. 88

PANDARUS Ay, good my lord. Why should you say
Cressida? No, your poor disposer's sick.

PARIS I spy. 91

PANDARUS You spy! What do you spy?—Come, give
me an instrument. [He is handed a musical instrument.]
Now, sweet queen.

HELEN Why, this is kindly done.

PANDARUS My niece is horribly in love with a thing
you have, sweet queen.

HELEN She shall have it, my lord, if it be not my lord
Paris.

PANDARUS He? No, she'll none of him. They two are
twain. 101

HELEN Falling in, after falling out, may make them 102
three. 103

PANDARUS Come, come, I'll hear no more of this. I'll
sing you a song now.

HELEN Ay, ay, prithee. Now, by my troth, sweet lord,
thou hast a fine forehead.

PANDARUS Ay, you may, you may. 108

HELEN Let thy song be love. This love will undo us all.
O Cupid, Cupid, Cupid!

PANDARUS Love? Ay, that it shall, i' faith.

PARIS Ay, good now, "Love, love, nothing but love." 112

PANDARUS In good truth, it begins so: [He sings.]
Love, love, nothing but love, still love, still more!
  For, O, love's bow
  Shoots buck and doe. 116
  The shaft confounds 117
  Not that it wounds, 118
But tickles still the sore. 119
These lovers cry, "O! O!", they die! 120
  Yet that which seems the wound to kill 121
Doth turn "O! O!" to "ha, ha, he!"
  So dying love lives still. 123
  "O! O!" awhile, but "ha, ha, ha!"
  "O! O!" groans out for "ha! ha! ha!"—
Heigh-ho!

HELEN In love, i' faith, to the very tip of the nose.

PARIS He eats nothing but doves, love, and that breeds
hot blood, and hot blood begets hot thoughts, and hot
thoughts beget hot deeds, and hot deeds is love.

PANDARUS Is this the generation of love? Hot blood, hot 131
thoughts, and hot deeds? Why, they are vipers. Is love
a generation of vipers? Sweet lord, who's afield 133
today?

PARIS Hector, Deiphobus, Helenus, Antenor, and all
the gallantry of Troy. I would fain have armed today,
but my Nell would not have it so. How chance my
brother Troilus went not?

HELEN He hangs the lip at something. You know all, 139
Lord Pandarus.

PANDARUS Not I, honey-sweet queen. I long to hear
how they sped today.—You'll remember your broth- 142
er's excuse?

PARIS To a hair. 144

PANDARUS Farewell, sweet queen.

HELEN Commend me to your niece.

PANDARUS I will, sweet queen.   [Exit.]
Sound a retreat.

---

50 broke interrupted. **cousin** (Often used at court in addressing a so-cial equal.) **51 piece it out** mend it **56 Rude** (I am) unpolished **57 in fits** (1) by fits and starts (2) in divisions of a song, in stanzas **59 vouchsafe** permit **60 hedge** shut **62 pleasant** jocular **66 Go to** (An expression of mild protest.) **68 bob** cheat **74 la** (An exclamation accompanying a conventional phrase.) **82–83 My . . . you** i.e., Paris will be angry with you for interrupting so **84 You must not** i.e., Pandarus does not want you to. **he** i.e., Troilus **85 lay** wager. **my disposer** i.e., one who may do what she likes (with me or Troilus) **86 wide** wide of the mark **88 make 's excuse** make his (Troilus') excuse (to Priam) **91 I spy** I get it

101 twain not in accord **102–103 Falling . . . three** (Helen bawd-ily jokes that Cressida's game will result in the birth of a child, a third person.) **108 you may** go on, have your joke **112 good now** please **116 buck and doe** i.e., male and female **117 confounds** overwhelms **118 Not that** (1) not that which, or (2) not so much that. (The erotic suggestion is that love does its harm by penetrating and tickling.) **119 sore** (1) wound (2) buck in its fourth year **120, 123 die, dying** (quibbling on the idea of experiencing orgasm) **121 wound to kill** fa-tal wound **131 generation** genealogy **133 generation of vipers** (See Matthew 3:7, 12:34, and 23:33.) **139 hangs the lip** pouts, sulks **142 sped** succeeded **144 To a hair** to the last detail

PARIS
They're come from field. Let us to Priam's hall
To greet the warriors. Sweet Helen, I must woo you
To help unarm our Hector. His stubborn buckles,
With these your white enchanting fingers touched,
Shall more obey than to the edge of steel
Or force of Greekish sinews. You shall do more
Than all the island kings: disarm great Hector.   154
HELEN
'Twill make us proud to be his servant, Paris.
Yea, what he shall receive of us in duty
Gives us more palm in beauty than we have,   157
Yea, overshines ourself.
PARIS   Sweet, above thought I love thee.   *Exeunt.*

❖

3.2   *Enter Pandarus and Troilus' Man, [meeting].*

PANDARUS   How now, where's thy master? At my cousin Cressida's?
MAN   No, sir, he stays for you to conduct him thither.

Enter Troilus.

PANDARUS   O, here he comes.—How now, how now?
TROILUS   Sirrah, walk off.   *[Exit Man.]*
PANDARUS   Have you seen my cousin?
TROILUS
No, Pandarus. I stalk about her door,
Like a strange soul upon the Stygian banks   8
Staying for waftage. O, be thou my Charon,   9
And give me swift transportance to those fields   10
Where I may wallow in the lily beds
Proposed for the deserver! O gentle Pandar,   12
From Cupid's shoulder pluck his painted wings,
And fly with me to Cressid!
PANDARUS   Walk here i' th' orchard. I'll bring her   15
straight.   *Exit Pandarus.*
TROILUS
I am giddy; expectation whirls me round.
Th' imaginary relish is so sweet
That it enchants my sense. What will it be
When that the watery palates taste indeed   20
Love's thrice repurèd nectar? Death, I fear me,   21
Swooning destruction, or some joy too fine,
Too subtle-potent, tuned too sharp in sweetness
For the capacity of my ruder powers.
I fear it much; and I do fear besides
That I shall lose distinction in my joys,   26

As doth a battle, when they charge on heaps   27
The enemy flying.

Enter Pandarus.

PANDARUS   She's making her ready; she'll come
straight. You must be witty now. She does so blush, 30
and fetches her wind so short, as if she were frayed 31
with a spirit. I'll fetch her. It is the prettiest villain! She 32
fetches her breath as short as a new-ta'en sparrow.
                              Exit Pandarus.
TROILUS
Even such a passion doth embrace my bosom.
My heart beats thicker than a feverous pulse,   35
And all my powers do their bestowing lose,   36
Like vassalage at unawares encount'ring   37
The eye of majesty.

Enter Pandarus, and Cressida, [veiled].

PANDARUS   Come, come, what need you blush?
Shame's a baby.—Here she is now. Swear the oaths
now to her that you have sworn to me. [*Cressida draws
back.*] What, are you gone again? You must be watched 42
ere you be made tame, must you? Come your ways,
come your ways; an you draw backward, we'll put
you i' the thills.—Why do you not speak to her?—   45
Come, draw this curtain, and let's see your picture. 46
[*He draws back her veil.*] Alas the day, how loath you are
to offend daylight! An 'twere dark, you'd close sooner. 48
So, so, rub on, and kiss the mistress. [*They kiss.*] How 49
now, a kiss in fee-farm? Build there, carpenter, the air 50
is sweet. Nay, you shall fight your hearts out ere I part
you—the falcon as the tercel, for all the ducks i' the 52
river. Go to, go to.   53
TROILUS   You have bereft me of all words, lady.
PANDARUS   Words pay no debts; give her deeds. But
she'll bereave you o' the deeds too, if she call your ac- 56
tivity in question. What, billing again? Here's "In wit- 57
ness whereof the parties interchangeably"—Come in, 58
come in. I'll go get a fire.   *[Exit.]*   59
CRESSIDA   Will you walk in, my lord?
TROILUS   O Cressida, how often have I wished me thus!
CRESSIDA   Wished, my lord? The gods grant—O my
lord!

27 battle army   **30 witty** alert, resourceful in easy conversation
31 fetches . . . short is short of breath   **31–32 frayed . . . spirit**
frightened by a ghost   **32 villain** (Used endearingly.)   **35 thicker**
faster   **36 bestowing** proper use   **37 vassalage at unawares** vassals
unexpectedly   **42 watched** kept awake (like a hawk that is being
tamed through sleeplessness)   **45 thills** shafts of a cart or wagon
46 curtain veil. (Curtains were hung in front of pictures.)   **48 close**
(1) encounter (2) come to terms   **49 kiss the mistress** (In bowls, to
touch the central target; to *rub* is to maneuver obstacles as the ball
rolls; *mistress* is analogous to "master," short for "master bowl," a
small bowl placed as a mark for players to aim at.)   **50 in fee-farm**
i.e., unending, as with land that is held in perpetuity   **52–53 the falcon . . . river** i.e., I'll bet all the ducks in the river that the female
hawk will be as eager as the male. (Or, alternatively, the ducks are to
be the object of their striving.)   **56–57 activity** virility. (Pandarus
jests that Cressida will wear Troilus down in lovemaking.)   **57 billing**
kissing   **57–58 In . . . interchangeably** (A legal formula used for
contracts, ending "have set their hand and seals.")   **59 get a fire** order a fire (for the bedroom)

154 island kings i.e., Greek chieftains   **157 palm** i.e., honor
**3.2. Location: Troy. The garden of Cressida's house (where she lived
with her father Calchas until he left Troy.)**
s.d. Man servant. (Probably the *varlet* referred to in 1.1.1.)   **8–9 a
strange . . . Charon** (Refers to the Greek mythological conception of
the fate of departed souls who had to wait on the banks of the Styx or
Acheron until the boatman Charon ferried them across to the infernal
region.)   **10 fields** the Elysian fields   **12 Proposed for** promised to
15 orchard garden   **20 watery palates** i.e., sense of taste watering
with anticipation   **21 repurèd** refined, repurified   **26 lose . . . joys**
be unable to distinguish one delight from another

TROILUS What should they grant? What makes this
pretty abruption? What too curious dreg espies my ⁶⁵
sweet lady in the fountain of our love?

CRESSIDA More dregs than water, if my fears have eyes.

TROILUS Fears make devils of cherubins; they never see ⁶⁸
truly.

CRESSIDA Blind fear, that seeing reason leads, finds ⁷⁰
safer footing than blind reason stumbling without
fear. To fear the worst oft cures the worse.

TROILUS O, let my lady apprehend no fear. In all
Cupid's pageant there is presented no monster.

CRESSIDA Nor nothing monstrous neither?

TROILUS Nothing but our undertakings, when we vow ⁷⁶
to weep seas, live in fire, eat rocks, tame tigers, thinking it harder for our mistress to devise imposition ⁷⁸
enough than for us to undergo any difficulty imposed.
This is the monstrosity in love, lady, that the will is
infinite and the execution confined, that the desire is
boundless and the act a slave to limit.

CRESSIDA They say all lovers swear more performance
than they are able, and yet reserve an ability that they
never perform, vowing more than the perfection of ten ⁸⁵
and discharging less than the tenth part of one. They
that have the voice of lions and the act of hares, are
they not monsters?

TROILUS Are there such? Such are not we. Praise us as
we are tasted, allow us as we prove; our head shall go ⁹⁰
bare till merit crown it. No perfection in reversion shall ⁹¹
have a praise in present; we will not name desert before his birth, and, being born, his addition shall be ⁹³
humble. Few words to fair faith. Troilus shall be such ⁹⁴
to Cressid as what envy can say worst shall be a mock ⁹⁵
for his truth, and what truth can speak truest not truer ⁹⁶
than Troilus.

CRESSIDA Will you walk in, my lord?

Enter Pandarus.

PANDARUS What, blushing still? Have you not done
talking yet?

CRESSIDA Well, uncle, what folly I commit, I dedicate ¹⁰¹
to you.

PANDARUS I thank you for that. If my lord get a boy of
you, you'll give him me. Be true to my lord. If he
flinch, chide me for it.

TROILUS You know now your hostages: your uncle's
word and my firm faith.

PANDARUS Nay, I'll give my word for her too. Our
kindred, though they be long ere they are wooed,

they are constant being won. They are burrs, I can tell
you; they'll stick where they are thrown.   ¹¹¹

CRESSIDA
Boldness comes to me now and brings me heart.
Prince Troilus, I have loved you night and day
For many weary months.

TROILUS
Why was my Cressid then so hard to win?

CRESSIDA
Hard to seem won; but I was won, my lord,
With the first glance that ever—pardon me;
If I confess much, you will play the tyrant.
I love you now, but till now not so much
But I might master it. In faith, I lie;
My thoughts were like unbridled children, grown   ¹²¹
Too headstrong for their mother. See, we fools!
Why have I blabbed? Who shall be true to us,
When we are so unsecret to ourselves?
But, though I loved you well, I wooed you not;
And yet, good faith, I wished myself a man,
Or that we women had men's privilege
Of speaking first. Sweet, bid me hold my tongue,
For in this rapture I shall surely speak
The thing I shall repent. See, see, your silence,
Cunning in dumbness, in my weakness draws
My soul of counsel from me! Stop my mouth.   ¹³²

TROILUS
And shall, albeit sweet music issues thence.

                              [He kisses her.]

PANDARUS Pretty, i' faith.

CRESSIDA
My lord, I do beseech you, pardon me;
'Twas not my purpose thus to beg a kiss.
I am ashamed. O heavens, what have I done?
For this time will I take my leave, my lord.

TROILUS Your leave, sweet Cressid?

PANDARUS Leave? An you take leave till tomorrow ¹⁴⁰
morning—

CRESSIDA Pray you, content you.   ¹⁴²

TROILUS What offends you, lady?

CRESSIDA Sir, mine own company.

TROILUS You cannot shun yourself.

CRESSIDA Let me go and try.
I have a kind of self resides with you,
But an unkind self that itself will leave   ¹⁴⁸
To be another's fool. Where is my wit?   ¹⁴⁹
I would be gone. I speak I know not what.

TROILUS
Well know they what they speak that speak so
wisely.

CRESSIDA
Perchance, my lord, I show more craft than love,
And fell so roundly to a large confession   ¹⁵³
To angle for your thoughts. But you are wise,

65 **abruption** breaking off. **curious dreg** finicky and anxiety-causing
impurity 68 **make . . . cherubins** i.e., make things seem worst rather
than best 70 **that . . . leads** that is led by clear-sighted reason
76 **undertakings** vows 78 **to devise imposition** to think up tasks to
impose 85 **perfection of ten** accomplishment of ten perfect lovers
90 **tasted** tried, proved. **allow** acknowledge, approve 91 **No . . .
reversion** no promise of perfection to come 93 **addition** title
94 **Few . . . faith** (Compare the proverb: "Where many words are,
the truth goes by.") 95–96 **as what . . . truth** that the worst that
malice can do is to mock Troilus' loyalty 101 **folly** foolishness. (Pandarus understands it to mean "lechery.")

111 **thrown** (1) tossed (2) thrown down in the act of seduction
121 **unbridled** unrestrained 132 **My . . . counsel** my inmost
thoughts 140 **An** if 142 **content you** i.e., be quiet 148 **unkind** unnatural 148–149 **that . . . fool** that will desert its true nature to be
your dupe or plaything 153 **roundly** outspokenly. **large** free

Or else you love not, for to be wise and love   155
Exceeds man's might; that dwells with gods above.
TROILUS
  O, that I thought it could be in a woman—
  As, if it can, I will presume in you—   158
  To feed for aye her lamp and flames of love,
  To keep her constancy in plight and youth,   160
  Outliving beauty's outward, with a mind   161
  That doth renew swifter than blood decays!   162
  Or that persuasion could but thus convince me
  That my integrity and truth to you
  Might be affronted with the match and weight   165
  Of such a winnowed purity in love;   166
  How were I then uplifted! But, alas,
  I am as true as truth's simplicity,   168
  And simpler than the infancy of truth.   169
CRESSIDA
  In that I'll war with you.
TROILUS   O virtuous fight,
  When right with right wars who shall be most right!
  True swains in love shall in the world to come
  Approve their truth by Troilus. When their rhymes,   173
  Full of protest, of oath and big compare,   174
  Wants similes, truth tired with iteration—   175
  "As true as steel, as plantage to the moon,   176
  As sun to day, as turtle to her mate,   177
  As iron to adamant, as earth to the center"—   178
  Yet, after all comparisons of truth,   179
  As truth's authentic author to be cited,   180
  "As true as Troilus" shall crown up the verse   181
  And sanctify the numbers.
CRESSIDA   Prophet may you be!   182
  If I be false or swerve a hair from truth,
  When time is old and hath forgot itself,
  When waterdrops have worn the stones of Troy,
  And blind oblivion swallowed cities up,
  And mighty states characterless are grated   187
  To dusty nothing, yet let memory,
  From false to false, among false maids in love,
  Upbraid my falsehood! When they've said "as false
  As air, as water, wind, or sandy earth,
  As fox to lamb, or wolf to heifer's calf,
  Pard to the hind, or stepdame to her son,"   193
  Yea, let them say, to stick the heart of falsehood,   194
  "As false as Cressid."

155 **else** rather   158 **presume** presume that it is   160 **To . . . youth**
to keep her pledged constancy fresh   161 **outward** appearance
162 **blood decays** passions wane   165–166 **affronted . . . love**
matched with an equal quantity of purified love (in you).   **winnowed**
separated from the chaff   168 **truth's simplicity** the simple truth
169 **the infancy of truth** i.e., pure, innocent truth   173 **Approve** attest.   **by Troilus** i.e., using Troilus as an ideal comparison   174 **protest** protestation (of love).   **big compare** extravagant comparisons
175 **Wants** are without   176 **plantage** vegetation (waxing in growth
by the moon's influence)   177 **turtle** turtledove   178 **adamant** lodestone (magnetic).   **center** center of the earth, axis   179 **comparisons**
illustrative similes   180 **As . . . cited** when we want to cite as our
authority the very fountainhead of truth   181 **crown up** give the fin-
ishing touches to   182 **numbers** verses   187 **characterless** unre-
corded, without a mark left.   **grated** pulverized   193 **Pard** leopard or
panther.   **hind** doe.   **stepdame** stepmother   194 **stick the heart**
pierce the center of the target

PANDARUS   Go to, a bargain made. Seal it, seal it; I'll be
  the witness. Here I hold your hand, here my cousin's.
  If ever you prove false one to another, since I have
  taken such pains to bring you together, let all pitiful 199
  goers-between be called to the world's end after my
  name: call them all Pandars. Let all constant men be
  Troiluses, all false women Cressids, and all brokers-
  between Pandars! Say "Amen."
TROILUS   Amen.
CRESSIDA   Amen.
PANDARUS   Amen. Whereupon I will show you a chamber with a bed, which bed, because it shall not speak
  of your pretty encounters, press it to death. Away!   208
                    Exeunt [Troilus and Cressida].
  And Cupid grant all tongue-tied maidens here   209
  Bed, chamber, pander to provide this gear!   *Exit.* 210

                              ❖

3.3   *Flourish. Enter Ulysses, Diomedes, Nestor,*
         Agamemnon, [Ajax,] Menelaus, and Calchas.

CALCHAS
  Now, princes, for the service I have done you,
  Th' advantage of the time prompts me aloud   2
  To call for recompense. Appear it to your mind   3
  That, through the sight I bear in things to come,   4
  I have abandoned Troy, left my possession,
  Incurred a traitor's name, exposed myself
  From certain and possessed conveniences   7
  To doubtful fortunes, sequestering from me all   8
  That time, acquaintance, custom, and condition
  Made tame and most familiar to my nature;   10
  And here, to do you service, am become   11
  As new into the world, strange, unacquainted.
  I do beseech you, as in way of taste,   13
  To give me now a little benefit
  Out of those many registered in promise
  Which, you say, live to come in my behalf.   16
AGAMEMNON
  What wouldst thou of us, Trojan? Make demand.
CALCHAS
  You have a Trojan prisoner called Antenor
  Yesterday took. Troy holds him very dear.
  Oft have you—often have you thanks therefor—
  Desired my Cressid in right great exchange,   21
  Whom Troy hath still denied; but this Antenor,   22
  I know, is such a wrest in their affairs   23
  That their negotiations all must slack,

199 **pitiful** compassionate   208 **press . . . death** (Alludes to the
usual punishment by weights for accused persons refusing to plead or
"speak.")   209 **here** i.e., in the audience   210 **gear** equipment
3.3. Location: The Greek camp. Before Achilles' tent.
2 **advantage of** favorable opportunity offered by   3 **Appear it** let it
appear   4 **bear** am endowed with   7 **From** turning from   8 **sequestering** separating, removing   10 **tame** familiar, domestic   11 **am**
have   13 **taste** foretaste   16 **live to come** await fulfillment   21 **right
great exchange** exchange for distinguished captives   22 **still**
continually   23 **wrest** tuning key, i.e., one producing harmony and
order

Wanting his manage, and they will almost   25
Give us a prince of blood, a son of Priam,
In change of him. Let him be sent, great princes,   27
And he shall buy my daughter; and her presence
Shall quite strike off all service I have done
In most accepted pain.

AGAMEMNON   Let Diomedes bear him,   30
And bring us Cressid hither. Calchas shall have
What he requests of us. Good Diomed,
Furnish you fairly for this interchange.
Withal bring word if Hector will tomorrow   34
Be answered in his challenge. Ajax is ready.   35

DIOMEDES
This shall I undertake, and 'tis a burden
Which I am proud to bear.   *Exit [with Calchas].* 37

Achilles and Patroclus stand in their tent.

ULYSSES
Achilles stands i' th' entrance of his tent.
Please it our General pass strangely by him,   39
As if he were forgot; and, princes all,
Lay negligent and loose regard upon him.
I will come last. 'Tis like he'll question me
Why such unplausive eyes are bent, why turned, on
  him.   43
If so, I have derision medicinable   44
To use between your strangeness and his pride,   45
Which his own will shall have desire to drink.   46
It may do good. Pride hath no other glass   47
To show itself but pride, for supple knees   48
Feed arrogance and are the proud man's fees.   49

AGAMEMNON
We'll execute your purpose and put on
A form of strangeness as we pass along.
So do each lord, and either greet him not
Or else disdainfully, which shall shake him more
Than if not looked on. I will lead the way.

[They move in procession past Achilles' tent.]

ACHILLES
What, comes the General to speak with me?
You know my mind. I'll fight no more 'gainst Troy.

AGAMEMNON
What says Achilles? Would he aught with us?   57

NESTOR
Would you, my lord, aught with the General?

ACHILLES   No.

NESTOR   Nothing, my lord.

AGAMEMNON   The better.   61

[Exeunt Agamemnon and Nestor.]

ACHILLES [*to Menelaus*]   Good day, good day.
MENELAUS   How do you? How do you?   [*Exit.*]
ACHILLES   What, does the cuckold scorn me?
AJAX   How now, Patroclus!
ACHILLES   Good morrow, Ajax.
AJAX   Ha?
ACHILLES   Good morrow.
AJAX   Ay, and good next day too.
                        Exit. [*Ulysses remains behind, reading.*]
ACHILLES
What mean these fellows? Know they not Achilles?
PATROCLUS
They pass by strangely. They were used to bend,   71
To send their smiles before them to Achilles,
To come as humbly as they use to creep   73
To holy altars.
ACHILLES   What, am I poor of late?
'Tis certain, greatness, once fall'n out with fortune,
Must fall out with men too. What the declined is   76
He shall as soon read in the eyes of others
As feel in his own fall; for men, like butterflies,
Show not their mealy wings but to the summer,   79
And not a man, for being simply man,   80
Hath any honor but honor for those honors   81
That are without him—as place, riches, and favor,   82
Prizes of accident as oft as merit;
Which, when they fall, as being slippery standers,   84
The love that leaned on them, as slippery too,
Doth one pluck down another and together
Die in the fall. But 'tis not so with me;
Fortune and I are friends. I do enjoy
At ample point all that I did possess,   89
Save these men's looks, who do, methinks, find out
Something not worth in me such rich beholding   91
As they have often given. Here is Ulysses;
I'll interrupt his reading.—How now, Ulysses?
ULYSSES   Now, great Thetis' son!
ACHILLES
What are you reading?
ULYSSES   A strange fellow here
Writes me that man, how dearly ever parted,   97
How much in having, or without or in,   98
Cannot make boast to have that which he hath,
Nor feels not what he owes, but by reflection;   100
As when his virtues, shining upon others,
Heat them, and they retort that heat again   102
To the first givers.
ACHILLES   This is not strange, Ulysses.
The beauty that is borne here in the face
The bearer knows not, but commends itself   105
To others' eyes; nor doth the eye itself,

---

25 **Wanting** lacking.   **manage** management   27 **change of** exchange
for   30 **In . . . pain** in pains (troubles, hardships) which I have endured most willingly.   **bear** escort   34 **Withal** in addition   35 **Be answered in** meet the answerer of   37 **s.d. stand in** i.e., enter and stand
in the entrance of   39 **strangely** i.e., as one who pretends to be a
stranger   43 **unplausive** disapproving   44 **derision medicinable** scorn
that can be used medicinally   45 **use** i.e., make connection.
strangeness aloofness   46 **Which** i.e., which medicine   47 **glass** mirror   48 **To show . . . pride** in which to see its image except the pride
of others   48–49 **for supple . . . fees** i.e., obsequiousness merely
encourages arrogance by rewarding pride with the adulation it expects
57 **Would he aught** does he want anything   61 **The better** so much
the better

71 **used** accustomed   73 **use** are accustomed   76 **the declined** the
man brought low   79 **mealy** powdery   80–82 **not . . . him** no one
is honored for himself but, rather, for those marks of distinction that
are external to him   82 **as** such as   84 **being . . . standers** standing
on uncertain foundation   89 **At ample point** to the full   91 **Something . . . beholding** something in me not worthy of such high respect
97–98 **Writes . . . or in** writes that humanity, however richly endowed with natural good qualities both external and internal
100 **owes** owns.   **but by reflection** i.e., except as reflected in others'
opinions   102 **retort** reflect   105 **but** but instead

That most pure spirit of sense, behold itself,   107
Not going from itself, but eye to eye opposed   108
Salutes each other with each other's form.   109
For speculation turns not to itself   110
Till it hath traveled and is mirrored there
Where it may see itself. This is not strange at all.

ULYSSES
I do not strain at the position—   113
It is familiar—but at the author's drift,   114
Who, in his circumstance, expressly proves   115
That no man is the lord of anything,
Though in and of him there be much consisting,   117
Till he communicate his parts to others;
Nor doth he of himself know them for aught   119
Till he behold them formed in the applause
Where they're extended; who, like an arch,
   reverb'rate   121
The voice again, or, like a gate of steel
Fronting the sun, receives and renders back   123
His figure and his heat. I was much rapt in this   124
And apprehended here immediately
Th' unknown Ajax. Heavens, what a man is there!   126
A very horse, that has he knows not what.   127
Nature, what things there are
Most abject in regard and dear in use!   129
What things again most dear in the esteem   130
And poor in worth! Now shall we see tomorrow—
An act that very chance doth throw upon him—
Ajax renowned. O heavens, what some men do,
While some men leave to do!   134
How some men creep in skittish Fortune's hall,   135
Whiles others play the idiots in her eyes!   136
How one man eats into another's pride,   137
While pride is fasting in his wantonness!   138
To see these Grecian lords—why, even already
They clap the lubber Ajax on the shoulder,   140
As if his foot were on brave Hector's breast
And great Troy shrinking.

ACHILLES   I do believe it,
For they passed by me as misers do by beggars,
Neither gave to me good word nor look.
What, are my deeds forgot?

ULYSSES
Time hath, my lord, a wallet at his back,   146
Wherein he puts alms for oblivion,   147
A great-sized monster of ingratitudes.
Those scraps are good deeds past, which are
   devoured
As fast as they are made, forgot as soon
As done. Perseverance, dear my lord,
Keeps honor bright; to have done is to hang
Quite out of fashion, like a rusty mail   153
In monumental mock'ry. Take the instant way,   154
For honor travels in a strait so narrow
Where one but goes abreast. Keep then the path,
For emulation hath a thousand sons   157
That one by one pursue. If you give way,   158
Or hedge aside from the direct forthright,   159
Like to an entered tide they all rush by
And leave you hindmost;
Or, like a gallant horse fall'n in first rank,
Lie there for pavement to the abject rear,   163
O'errun and trampled on. Then what they do in
   present,
Though less than yours in past, must o'ertop yours;
For Time is like a fashionable host
That slightly shakes his parting guest by the hand,   167
And with his arms outstretched, as he would fly,
Grasps in the comer. The welcome ever smiles,   169
And farewell goes out sighing. Let not virtue seek
Remuneration for the thing it was;
For beauty, wit,
High birth, vigor of bone, desert in service,
Love, friendship, charity, are subjects all
To envious and calumniating Time.   175
One touch of nature makes the whole world kin,   176
That all with one consent praise newborn gauds,
Though they are made and molded of things past,   178
And give to dust that is a little gilt   179
More laud than gilt o'erdusted.   180
The present eye praises the present object.
Then marvel not, thou great and complete man,
That all the Greeks begin to worship Ajax,
Since things in motion sooner catch the eye
Than what not stirs. The cry went once on thee,   185
And still it might, and yet it may again,
If thou wouldst not entomb thyself alive
And case thy reputation in thy tent,   188

107 most . . . sense most exquisite of the five senses. (Compare 1.1.60.) 108–109 Not . . . form since it cannot go out from itself; instead, two persons' eyes gazing into each other must convey to both persons a sense of what they look like from another's point of view 110 speculation power of sight 113 strain at find difficulty in. position i.e., general stance of the writer 114 drift i.e., particular application 115 circumstance detailed argument 117 Though . . . consisting although in him there are qualities from which much may be expected 119 aught anything of value 121 Where they're extended of those persons to whom they are displayed. who i.e., the applauders 123 Fronting facing 124 His its, the sun's 126 Th' unknown Ajax i.e., the Ajax whose true worth is not yet generally known 127 that . . . what who does not know himself 129 abject . . . use lowly esteemed and yet valuable, of practical value 130 again on the other hand 134 to do undone 135 creep i.e., are unobtrusive, draw no attention to themselves. skittish fickle 136 Whiles . . . eyes while others attract the attention of the goddess Fortune by making fools of themselves 137–138 How . . . wantonness i.e., how one man, like Ajax, encroaches on another's glory, while that other man, like Achilles, starves his own glory through self-indulgence or caprice 140 lubber clumsy

146 wallet knapsack 147 alms for oblivion i.e., noble deeds to be forgotten 153 mail suit of armor 154 In . . . mock'ry serving as a mocking trophy of forgotten noble deeds. instant way way that lies immediately before you now 157 emulation envious rivalry 158 one by one pursue crowd after one another in single file, vying for supremacy 159 forthright straight path 163 abject rear inferior specimens who bring up the rear 167 slightly negligently 169 Grasps in welcomes, embraces 175 calumniating slandering 176 nature i.e., natural human weakness; here, the propensity of men to praise frivolous novelty (newborn gauds) 178 Though . . . past i.e., even though their apparent novelty is all derivative 179–180 And . . . o'erdusted i.e., and give more praise to trivial things that have been made to look glittering than to objects of true worth that have been covered by the dust of oblivion 185 cry acclaim 188 case box up, enclose

Whose glorious deeds but in these fields of late   189
Made emulous missions 'mongst the gods
   themselves   190
And drave great Mars to faction.

ACHILLES   Of this my privacy   191
I have strong reasons.

ULYSSES   But 'gainst your privacy
The reasons are more potent and heroical.   193
'Tis known, Achilles, that you are in love
With one of Priam's daughters.

ACHILLES   Ha! Known?   195

ULYSSES   Is that a wonder?
The providence that's in a watchful state   197
Knows almost every grain of Pluto's gold,   198
Finds bottom in th' uncomprehensive deeps,   199
Keeps place with thought and almost, like the gods,   200
Do thoughts unveil in their dumb cradles.   201
There is a mystery—with whom relation   202
Durst never meddle—in the soul of state,   203
Which hath an operation more divine
Than breath or pen can give expressure to.   205
All the commerce that you have had with Troy   206
As perfectly is ours as yours, my lord;   207
And better would it fit Achilles much
To throw down Hector than Polyxena.
But it must grieve young Pyrrhus now at home,   210
When Fame shall in our islands sound her trump,   211
And all the Greekish girls shall tripping sing,
"Great Hector's sister did Achilles win,
But our great Ajax bravely beat down him."   214
Farewell, my lord. I as your lover speak.   215
The fool slides o'er the ice that you should break.   216
                                  [*Exit.*]

PATROCLUS
To this effect, Achilles, have I moved you.
A woman impudent and mannish grown   218
Is not more loathed than an effeminate man
In time of action. I stand condemned for this;
They think my little stomach to the war   221
And your great love to me restrains you thus.
Sweet, rouse yourself, and the weak wanton Cupid
Shall from your neck unloose his amorous fold   224
And, like a dewdrop from the lion's mane,
Be shook to air.

ACHILLES   Shall Ajax fight with Hector?

PATROCLUS
Ay, and perhaps receive much honor by him.

ACHILLES
I see my reputation is at stake;
My fame is shrewdly gored.

PATROCLUS   O, then, beware!   229
Those wounds heal ill that men do give themselves.
Omission to do what is necessary
Seals a commission to a blank of danger;   232
And danger, like an ague, subtly taints   233
Even then when we sit idly in the sun.

ACHILLES
Go call Thersites hither, sweet Patroclus.
I'll send the fool to Ajax and desire him
T' invite the Trojan lords after the combat
To see us here unarmed. I have a woman's longing,
An appetite that I am sick withal,   239
To see great Hector in his weeds of peace,   240
To talk with him and to behold his visage,
Even to my full of view.

      Enter Thersites.

             A labor saved.   242

THERSITES   A wonder!
ACHILLES   What?
THERSITES   Ajax goes up and down the field, asking for
himself.   246
ACHILLES   How so?
THERSITES   He must fight singly tomorrow with Hector
and is so prophetically proud of an heroical cudgeling
that he raves in saying nothing.
ACHILLES   How can that be?
THERSITES   Why, 'a stalks up and down like a peacock—
a stride and a stand; ruminates like an hostess that   253
hath no arithmetic but her brain to set down her reck-   254
oning; bites his lip with a politic regard, as who   255
should say, "There were wit in this head, an 'twould
out"—and so there is, but it lies as coldly in him as
fire in a flint, which will not show without knocking.
The man's undone forever, for if Hector break not his
neck i' the combat, he'll break 't himself in vainglory.
He knows not me. I said, "Good morrow, Ajax," and
he replies, "Thanks, Agamemnon." What think you of
this man, that takes me for the General? He's grown a
very land-fish, languageless, a monster. A plague of   264
opinion! A man may wear it on both sides, like a   265
leather jerkin.   266
ACHILLES   Thou must be my ambassador to him, Thersites.
THERSITES   Who, I? Why, he'll answer nobody; he
professes not answering. Speaking is for beggars; he   270

---

189 **but . . . late** only recently on the battlefield   190–191 **Made
. . . faction** i.e., caused the gods themselves to join in the fighting
on opposing sides, emulously, and even drove the god of war to be
partisan   193 **heroical** suitable to a hero   195 **one . . . daughters**
i.e., Polyxena   197 **providence** foresight   198 **Pluto's** (Pluto, god of
the underworld, was often confused with Plutus, god of riches.)
199 **uncomprehensive** unfathomable   200 **Keeps . . . thought** keeps
up with what is being thought   201 **Do . . . cradles** discovers
thought before it is conceived in the mind and spoken
202–203 **with . . . meddle** that can never be talked about   205 **expressure** expression   206 **commerce** dealings (i.e., with Polyxena)
207 **is ours** is known to us of the Greek council   210 **Pyrrhus** Achilles' son, also called Neoptolemus   211 **trump** trumpet   214 **him**
i.e., Hector   215 **lover** friend   216 **The fool . . . break** i.e., the fool
easily escapes dangers that to a man of your dignity would be fatal
218 **impudent** shameless   221 **little stomach to** lack of enthusiasm
for   224 **fold** embrace

229 **shrewdly gored** severely wounded   232 **Seals . . . danger** i.e.,
gives danger unlimited license, a blank check. (Literally, a warrant
with blank spaces.)   233 **ague** fever.   **taints** infects. (Meat spoils
when left lying in the sun.)   239 **withal** with   240 **weeds** garments
242 **to . . . view** to the fullest satisfaction of my eyes   246 **himself**
i.e., "Ajax" (with a quibble on "a jakes" or latrine)   253–254 **hostess . . . arithmetic** (Tavern keepers were proverbially poor at addition; compare 1.2.114.)   255 **politic regard** assumption of a knowing
manner   264 **land-fish** i.e., monstrous creature   264–265 **of opinion** on reputation   266 **jerkin** close-fitting jacket   270 **professes** i.e.,
makes a point of

wears his tongue in 's arms. I will put on his presence. 271
Let Patroclus make demands to me; you shall see
the pageant of Ajax.
ACHILLES   To him, Patroclus. Tell him I humbly desire
the valiant Ajax to invite the most valorous Hector to
come unarmed to his tent, and to procure safe-conduct
for his person of the magnanimous and most illus-
trious six-or-seven-times-honored Captain-General of
the Grecian army, Agamemnon, et cetera. Do this.
PATROCLUS   Jove bless great Ajax!
THERSITES   Hum!
PATROCLUS   I come from the worthy Achilles—
THERSITES   Ha?
PATROCLUS   Who most humbly desires you to invite
Hector to his tent—
THERSITES   Hum!
PATROCLUS   And to procure safe-conduct from Aga-
memnon.
THERSITES   Agamemnon?
PATROCLUS   Ay, my lord.
THERSITES   Ha!
PATROCLUS   What say you to 't?
THERSITES   God b' wi' you, with all my heart.
PATROCLUS   Your answer, sir.
THERSITES   If tomorrow be a fair day, by eleven o' clock
it will go one way or other. Howsoever, he shall 296
pay for me ere he has me.
PATROCLUS   Your answer, sir.
THERSITES   Fare ye well, with all my heart.
ACHILLES   Why, but he is not in this tune, is he? 300
THERSITES   No, but he's out o' tune thus. What music
will be in him when Hector has knocked out his
brains, I know not; but, I am sure, none, unless the 303
fiddler Apollo get his sinews to make catlings on. 304
ACHILLES
Come, thou shalt bear a letter to him straight.
THERSITES   Let me carry another to his horse, for that's
the more capable creature. 307
ACHILLES
My mind is troubled, like a fountain stirred,
And I myself see not the bottom of it.
                                    [*Exeunt Achilles and Patroclus.*]
THERSITES   Would the fountain of your mind were clear
again, that I might water an ass at it! I had rather be a
tick in a sheep than such a valiant ignorance. [*Exit.*] 312

4.1   *Enter, at one door, Aeneas, with a torch; at
another, Paris, Deiphobus, Antenor, Diomedes the
Grecian [and others], with torches.*

PARIS   See, ho! Who is that there?
DEIPHOBUS   It is the Lord Aeneas.

AENEAS   Is the Prince there in person?
Had I so good occasion to lie long
As you, Prince Paris, nothing but heavenly business
Should rob my bedmate of my company.
DIOMEDES
That's my mind too. Good morrow, Lord Aeneas. 7
PARIS
A valiant Greek, Aeneas; take his hand.
Witness the process of your speech, wherein 9
You told how Diomed, a whole week by days, 10
Did haunt you in the field.
AENEAS   Health to you, valiant sir,
During all question of the gentle truce; 13
But when I meet you armed, as black defiance 14
As heart can think or courage execute.
DIOMEDES
The one and other Diomed embraces. 16
Our bloods are now in calm; and so long, health! 17
But when contention and occasion meet, 18
By Jove, I'll play the hunter for thy life
With all my force, pursuit, and policy. 20
AENEAS
And thou shalt hunt a lion that will fly
With his face backward. In humane gentleness, 22
Welcome to Troy! Now, by Anchises' life, 23
Welcome, indeed! By Venus' hand I swear, 24
No man alive can love in such a sort 25
The thing he means to kill more excellently.
DIOMEDES
We sympathize. Jove, let Aeneas live, 27
If to my sword his fate be not the glory,
A thousand complete courses of the sun!
But, in mine emulous honor, let him die 30
With every joint a wound, and that tomorrow!
AENEAS   We know each other well.
DIOMEDES
We do, and long to know each other worse.
PARIS
This is the most despiteful gentle greeting, 34
The noblest hateful love, that e'er I heard of.
What business, lord, so early?
AENEAS
I was sent for to the King, but why, I know not.
PARIS
His purpose meets you. 'Twas to bring this Greek 38
To Calchas' house, and there to render him, 39
For the enfreed Antenor, the fair Cressid.
Let's have your company, or, if you please,
Haste there before us. [*Aside to Aeneas.*] I constantly
do think— 42

---

271 **arms** weapons.   **put . . . presence** assume his demeanor
296 **Howsoever** in either case   300 **tune** i.e., mood, disposition
303–304 **the fiddler Apollo** i.e., Apollo, as god of music
304 **catlings** catgut, of which strings for instruments were made
307 **capable** able to understand   312 **ignorance** ignoramus, fool
4.1. Location: Troy. A street.
s.d. torch, torches (These directions may indicate torchbearers.)

7 **mind** opinion   9 **process** drift   10 **a whole . . . days** every day for
a week   13 **question** discussion, parley (allowed by the truce)   14 **as
black defiance** i.e., defiance as black   16 **The one and other** i.e.,
Aeneas' promises of *health* and *defiance*   17 **so long** for as long as
this truce lasts   18 **when . . . meet** i.e., when the battle gives us opportunity   20 **policy** cunning   22 **face backward** i.e., bravely facing
the enemy   23, 24 **Anchises, Venus** (Aeneas' parents)   25 **in . . .
sort** to such a degree   27 **sympathize** share your feeling   30 **emulous**
ambitious   34 **despiteful** contemptuous   38 **His . . . you** i.e., I can
tell you, since the matter is at hand   39 **render** give   42 **constantly**
confirmedly

Or rather, call my thought a certain knowledge—
My brother Troilus lodges there tonight.
Rouse him and give him note of our approach,   45
With the whole quality whereof. I fear   46
We shall be much unwelcome.
AENEAS   That I assure you.
Troilus had rather Troy were borne to Greece
Than Cressid borne from Troy.
PARIS   There is no help.
The bitter disposition of the time   50
Will have it so. On, lord; we'll follow you.
AENEAS   Good morrow, all.   *Exit Aeneas.*
PARIS
And tell me, noble Diomed, faith, tell me true,
Even in the soul of sound good-fellowship,   54
Who, in your thoughts, merits fair Helen most,
Myself or Menelaus?
DIOMEDES   Both alike.
He merits well to have her that doth seek her,
Not making any scruple of her soilure,   58
With such a hell of pain and world of charge;   59
And you as well to keep her that defend her,
Not palating the taste of her dishonor,   61
With such a costly loss of wealth and friends.
He, like a puling cuckold, would drink up   63
The lees and dregs of a flat 'tamèd piece;   64
You, like a lecher, out of whorish loins
Are pleased to breed out your inheritors.   66
Both merits poised, each weighs nor less nor more;   67
But he as he, the heavier for a whore.   68
PARIS
You are too bitter to your countrywoman.
DIOMEDES
She's bitter to her country. Hear me, Paris:
For every false drop in her bawdy veins
A Grecian's life hath sunk; for every scruple   72
Of her contaminated carrion weight   73
A Trojan hath been slain. Since she could speak,
She hath not given so many good words breath
As for her Greeks and Trojans suffered death.
PARIS
Fair Diomed, you do as chapmen do,   77
Dispraise the thing that you desire to buy.
But we in silence hold this virtue well:
We'll not commend what we intend not sell.
Here lies our way.   *Exeunt.*

❧

4.2   *Enter Troilus and Cressida.*

TROILUS
Dear, trouble not yourself. The morn is cold.
CRESSIDA
Then, sweet my lord, I'll call mine uncle down.
He shall unbolt the gates.
TROILUS   Trouble him not.
To bed, to bed! Sleep kill those pretty eyes,   4
And give as soft attachment to thy senses   5
As infants' empty of all thought!   6
CRESSIDA
Good morrow, then.
TROILUS   I prithee now, to bed.
CRESSIDA   Are you aweary of me?
TROILUS
O Cressida! But that the busy day,
Waked by the lark, hath roused the ribald crows,   10
And dreaming night will hide our joys no longer,
I would not from thee.
CRESSIDA   Night hath been too brief.
TROILUS
Beshrew the witch! With venomous wights she stays   13
As tediously as hell, but flies the grasps of love
With wings more momentary-swift than thought.
You will catch cold, and curse me.
CRESSIDA
Prithee, tarry. You men will never tarry.
O foolish Cressid! I might have still held off,
And then you would have tarried. Hark, there's
   one up.
PANDARUS [*within*]   What's all the doors open here?   20
TROILUS   It is your uncle.

Enter Pandarus.

CRESSIDA
A pestilence on him! Now will he be mocking.
I shall have such a life!
PANDARUS   How now, how now, how go maiden-   24
heads? Here, you maid! Where's my cousin Cressid?   25
CRESSIDA
Go hang yourself, you naughty mocking uncle!
You bring me to do—and then you flout me too.
PANDARUS   To do what, to do what?—Let her say
what.—What have I brought you to do?
CRESSIDA
Come, come, beshrew your heart! You'll ne'er be
   good,
Nor suffer others.   31
PANDARUS   Ha, ha! Alas, poor wretch! Ah, poor *capoc-*   32
chia! Has 't not slept tonight? Would he not—a   33

---

45 note news, notice   **46 the . . . whereof** all the causes thereof,
reasons why   **50 disposition** (1) temperament (2) arrangement, ordering   **54 soul** spirit   **58 Not . . . scruple** not worrying about.   **soilure**
dishonor, stain   **59 charge** cost   **61 Not palating** not tasting, being
insensible of   **63 puling** complaining   **64 flat 'tamèd piece** wine cask
so long opened that the wine is flat; hence, a used woman   **66 breed
out** exhaust the breed, degenerate.   **inheritors** descendants
67 poised weighed, balanced.   **nor less** neither less   **68 he as he** the
one like the other   **72 scruple** little bit. (Literally, one twenty-fourth
of an ounce.)   **73 carrion** putrefied and rotten, like a carcass
77 chapmen traders, merchants

4.2. Location: Troy. The courtyard of Cressida's house.
4 Sleep kill let sleep overpower, put to rest   **5 attachment** arrest, confinement   **6 infants'** i.e., infants' eyes   **10 ribald** offensively noisy, irreverent   **13 Beshrew** curse.   **the witch** i.e., the night.   **venomous
wights** malignant beings   **20 What's** why are   **24 how go** what
price   **25 Where's . . . Cressid** (Pandarus pretends not to recognize
Cressida now that she is no longer a virgin.)   **31 suffer others** allow
others (to be good)   **32–33 capocchia** dolt, simpleton. (Italian.)

naughty man—let it sleep? A bugbear take him!   34
CRESSIDA
Did not I tell you? Would he were knocked i' the
   head!   *One knocks.*
Who's that at door? Good uncle, go and see.—
My lord, come you again into my chamber.
You smile and mock me, as if I meant naughtily.
TROILUS   Ha, ha!
CRESSIDA
Come, you are deceived. I think of no such thing.
                                            Knock.
How earnestly they knock! Pray you, come in.
I would not for half Troy have you seen here.
                    Exeunt [Troilus and Cressida].
PANDARUS   Who's there? What's the matter? Will you
beat down the door? [*He opens the door.*] How now,
what's the matter?

           [*Enter Aeneas.*]

AENEAS   Good morrow, lord, good morrow.
PANDARUS   Who's there? My lord Aeneas? By my troth,
I knew you not. What news with you so early?
AENEAS   Is not Prince Troilus here?
PANDARUS   Here? What should he do here?   50
AENEAS
Come, he is here, my lord. Do not deny him.
It doth import him much to speak with me.   52
PANDARUS   Is he here, say you? It's more than I know,
I'll be sworn. For my own part, I came in late. What   54
should he do here?
AENEAS   Hoo!—Nay, then. Come, come, you'll do him
wrong ere you are ware. You'll be so true to him, to be   57
false to him. Do not you know of him, but yet go fetch   58
him hither. Go.

           Enter Troilus.

TROILUS   How now, what's the matter?
AENEAS
My lord, I scarce have leisure to salute you,
My matter is so rash. There is at hand   62
Paris your brother and Deiphobus,
The Grecian Diomed, and our Antenor
Delivered to us; and for him forthwith,
Ere the first sacrifice, within this hour,   66
We must give up to Diomedes' hand
The Lady Cressida.
TROILUS   Is it so concluded?
AENEAS
By Priam and the general state of Troy.   69
They are at hand and ready to effect it.

TROILUS
How my achievements mock me!
I will go meet them. And, my lord Aeneas,
We met by chance; you did not find me here.   73
AENEAS
Good, good, my lord, the secrets of nature
Have not more gift in taciturnity.
                    Exeunt [Troilus and Aeneas].
PANDARUS   Is 't possible? No sooner got but lost? The
devil take Antenor! The young prince will go mad. A
plague upon Antenor! I would they had broke 's neck!

           Enter Cressida.

CRESSIDA
How now? What's the matter? Who was here?
PANDARUS   Ah, ah!
CRESSIDA
Why sigh you so profoundly? Where's my lord?
Gone? Tell me, sweet uncle, what's the matter?
PANDARUS   Would I were as deep under the earth as I
am above!
CRESSIDA   O the gods! What's the matter?
PANDARUS   Pray thee, get thee in. Would thou hadst
ne'er been born! I knew thou wouldst be his death. O,
poor gentleman! A plague upon Antenor!
CRESSIDA   Good uncle, I beseech you, on my knees I
beseech you, what's the matter?
PANDARUS   Thou must be gone, wench, thou must be
gone. Thou art changed for Antenor. Thou must to thy   92
father and be gone from Troilus. 'Twill be his death,
'twill be his bane; he cannot bear it.   94
CRESSIDA
O you immortal gods! I will not go.
PANDARUS   Thou must.
CRESSIDA
I will not, uncle. I have forgot my father.
I know no touch of consanguinity;   98
No kin, no love, no blood, no soul so near me
As the sweet Troilus. O you gods divine!
Make Cressid's name the very crown of falsehood
If ever she leave Troilus! Time, force, and death,
Do to this body what extremity you can;
But the strong base and building of my love
Is as the very center of the earth,
Drawing all things to it. I'll go in and weep—
PANDARUS   Do, do.
CRESSIDA
Tear my bright hair and scratch my praisèd cheeks,
Crack my clear voice with sobs and break my heart
With sounding "Troilus." I will not go from Troy.   110
                                            Exeunt.

                    ♣

---

34 it (Used to refer to small children; Pandarus is teasing.) **bugbear**
hobgoblin   **50 should he do** would he be doing   **52 import** concern
54 late recently   **57–58 You'll . . . of him** i.e., in seeking to guard
Troilus' secret, you'll protect him from knowing of a matter that concerns him. Go ahead and pretend you don't know he is here.
62 rash urgent, pressing   **66 Ere . . . sacrifice** before the first religious ceremony of the day   **69 state** council

73 We met i.e., remember to say that we met. (This is the fiction to
which Aeneas agrees.)   **92 changed** exchanged   **94 bane** death
98 touch of consanguinity sense or tiniest bit of kinship   **110 sounding** uttering

4.3 *Enter Paris, Troilus, Aeneas, Deiphobus, Antenor, and Diomedes.*

PARIS
It is great morning, and the hour prefixed   1
For her delivery to this valiant Greek
Comes fast upon. Good my brother Troilus,
Tell you the lady what she is to do,
And haste her to the purpose.
TROILUS   Walk into her house.
I'll bring her to the Grecian presently;   6
And to his hand when I deliver her,
Think it an altar, and thy brother Troilus
A priest there offering to it his own heart.   [*Exit.*]
PARIS   I know what 'tis to love;
And would, as I shall pity, I could help!   11
Please you walk in, my lords?   *Exeunt.*

❖

4.4 *Enter Pandarus and Cressida.*

PANDARUS   Be moderate, be moderate.
CRESSIDA
Why tell you me of moderation?
The grief is fine, full, perfect, that I taste,   3
And violenteth in a sense as strong   4
As that which causeth it. How can I moderate it?
If I could temporize with my affection,   6
Or brew it to a weak and colder palate,   7
The like allayment could I give my grief.   8
My love admits no qualifying dross;   9
No more my grief, in such a precious loss.

Enter Troilus.

PANDARUS   Here, here, here he comes. Ah, sweet
ducks!
CRESSIDA   O Troilus! Troilus!   [*Embracing him.*]
PANDARUS   What a pair of spectacles is here! Let me em-   14
brace, too. "O heart," as the goodly saying is,
  "O heart, heavy heart,
  Why sigh'st thou without breaking?"
where he answers again,
  "Because thou canst not ease thy smart
  By friendship nor by speaking."
There was never a truer rhyme. Let us cast away noth-
ing, for we may live to have need of such a verse. We
see it, we see it. How now, lambs?
TROILUS
Cressid, I love thee in so strained a purity   24

That the blest gods, as angry with my fancy,   25
More bright in zeal than the devotion which
Cold lips blow to their deities, take thee from me.
CRESSIDA   Have the gods envy?
PANDARUS   Ay, ay, ay, ay; 'tis too plain a case.
CRESSIDA
And is it true that I must go from Troy?
TROILUS
A hateful truth.
CRESSIDA   What, and from Troilus too?
TROILUS
From Troy and Troilus.
CRESSIDA   Is 't possible?
TROILUS
And suddenly, where injury of chance   33
Puts back leave-taking, jostles roughly by   34
All time of pause, rudely beguiles our lips
Of all rejoindure, forcibly prevents   36
Our locked embrasures, strangles our dear vows   37
Even in the birth of our own laboring breath.
We two, that with so many thousand sighs
Did buy each other, must poorly sell ourselves
With the rude brevity and discharge of one.   41
Injurious Time now with a robber's haste
Crams his rich thiev'ry up, he knows not how.   43
As many farewells as be stars in heaven,
With distinct breath and consigned kisses to them,   45
He fumbles up into a loose adieu,   46
And scants us with a single famished kiss,   47
Distasted with the salt of broken tears.   48
AENEAS *(within)*   My lord, is the lady ready?
TROILUS
Hark! You are called. Some say the genius so   50
Cries "Come!" to him that instantly must die.—
Bid them have patience. She shall come anon.
PANDARUS   Where are my tears? Rain, to lay this wind,   53
or my heart will be blown up by the root.   [*Exit.*]   54
CRESSIDA
I must then to the Grecians?
TROILUS   No remedy.
CRESSIDA
A woeful Cressid 'mongst the merry Greeks!
When shall we see again?   57
TROILUS
Hear me, my love. Be thou but true of heart—
CRESSIDA
I true? How now? What wicked deem is this?   59

4.3. Location: Troy. Before Cressida's house.
1 great morning broad day.   **prefixed** earlier agreed upon   **6 presently** immediately   **11 as** as much as
4.4. Location: Troy. Cressida's house.
3 fine refined, pure   **4 violenteth** is violent   **6 temporize** compromise, come to terms   **7 brew** dilute.   **palate** taste   **8 allayment** dilu-
tion, mitigation   **9 qualifying dross** foreign matter making it less pure
14 spectacles sights (with suggestion of "eyeglasses")   **24 strained**
purified as by filtering

25 as as if.   **fancy** love   **33 injury of chance** injurious Fortune
34 Puts back forestalls, prevents   **36 rejoindure** reunion (in a farewell
kiss)   **37 embrasures** embraces   **41 discharge** (1) exhalation of a sigh
(2) payment in exchange of ourselves   **43 thievery** stolen property.
he . . . how every which way, distractedly   **45 With . . . them** with
the words of farewell and the kisses with which those words are confirmed, sealed   **46 fumbles** clumsily wraps   **47 scants** inadequately
supplies   **48 Distasted** rendered distasteful.   **broken** interrupted with
sobs   **50 genius** attendant spirit supposed to be assigned to a person
at birth   **53 Rain . . . wind** i.e., tears, to allay my sighs   **54 by the
root** i.e., as though the heart were a tree in a storm of sighs. (Sighs
were thought to deprive the heart of its blood.)   **57 see** see each
other   **59 deem** thought, surmise

TROILUS
Nay, we must use expostulation kindly,   60
For it is parting from us.   61
I speak not "Be thou true" as fearing thee,   62
For I will throw my glove to Death himself   63
That there's no maculation in thy heart;   64
But "Be thou true," say I, to fashion in   65
My sequent protestation: Be thou true,   66
And I will see thee.
CRESSIDA
O, you shall be exposed, my lord, to dangers
As infinite as imminent! But I'll be true.
TROILUS
And I'll grow friend with danger. Wear this sleeve.   70
                            [They exchange favors.]
CRESSIDA
And you this glove. When shall I see you?
TROILUS
I will corrupt the Grecian sentinels,
To give thee nightly visitation.
But yet, be true.
CRESSIDA   O heavens, "Be true" again?
TROILUS   Hear why I speak it, love.
The Grecian youths are full of quality;   76
Their loving well composed with gifts of nature,   77
And flowing o'er with arts and exercise.   78
How novelty may move, and parts with person,   79
Alas, a kind of godly jealousy—   80
Which, I beseech you, call a virtuous sin—
Makes me afeard.
CRESSIDA   O heavens! You love me not.
TROILUS   Die I a villain, then!
In this I do not call your faith in question
So mainly as my merit. I cannot sing,   85
Nor heel the high lavolt, nor sweeten talk,   86
Nor play at subtle games—fair virtues all,   87
To which the Grecians are most prompt and
    pregnant.   88
But I can tell that in each grace of these
There lurks a still and dumb-discoursive devil   90
That tempts most cunningly. But be not tempted.
CRESSIDA   Do you think I will?
TROILUS
No. But something may be done that we will not;   94
And sometimes we are devils to ourselves,

When we will tempt the frailty of our powers,   96
Presuming on their changeful potency.   97
AENEAS (within)
Nay, good my lord—
TROILUS   Come, kiss, and let us part.
PARIS (within)
Brother Troilus!
TROILUS   Good brother, come you hither,
And bring Aeneas and the Grecian with you.
CRESSIDA   My lord, will you be true?
TROILUS
Who, I? Alas, it is my vice, my fault.
Whiles others fish with craft for great opinion,   103
I with great truth catch mere simplicity;   104
Whilst some with cunning gild their copper crowns,
With truth and plainness I do wear mine bare.

        [Enter Aeneas, Paris, Antenor, Deiphobus, and
        Diomedes.]

Fear not my truth. The moral of my wit   107
Is "plain and true"; there's all the reach of it.—   108
Welcome, Sir Diomed. Here is the lady
Which for Antenor we deliver you.
At the port, lord, I'll give her to thy hand,   111
And by the way possess thee what she is.   112
Entreat her fair, and by my soul, fair Greek,   113
If e'er thou stand at mercy of my sword,
Name Cressid, and thy life shall be as safe
As Priam is in Ilium.
DIOMEDES   Fair Lady Cressid,
So please you, save the thanks this prince expects.   117
The luster in your eye, heaven in your cheek,
Pleads your fair usage; and to Diomed
You shall be mistress, and command him wholly.
TROILUS
Grecian, thou dost not use me courteously,
To shame the zeal of my petition to thee
In praising her. I tell thee, lord of Greece,
She is as far high-soaring o'er thy praises
As thou unworthy to be called her servant.
I charge thee use her well, even for my charge;   126
For, by the dreadful Pluto, if thou dost not,
Though the great bulk Achilles be thy guard,   128
I'll cut thy throat.
DIOMEDES   O, be not moved, Prince Troilus.   129
Let me be privileged by my place and message
To be a speaker free. When I am hence,
I'll answer to my lust. And know you, lord,   132

60–61 we must . . . from us i.e., we must expostulate gently, for soon even this opportunity for speech will be lost to us 62 as fearing thee i.e., if not trusting your constancy 63 throw . . . to i.e., challenge 64 maculation stain of impurity 65 fashion in serve as introduction for 66 sequent ensuing 70 sleeve (Sleeves were detachable and could be given as favors or tokens; gloves could be similarly given.) 76 quality good qualities 77 Their . . . composed i.e., their skill in lovemaking is well endowed 78 arts and exercise skills sharpened by practice 79 parts with person accomplishments with personal charm 80 godly divinely sanctioned, as in a marriage 85 mainly strongly.   merit (Troilus plays on the Protestant insistence on salvation through faith, line 84, not merit.) 86 lavolt lavolta, a lively dance for two 87 subtle (1) requiring skill (2) cunning, deceptive 88 pregnant ready 90 dumb-discoursive eloquently silent 94 will not do not desire

96 will tempt deliberately tempt 97 changeful potency power that may change to failure 103 craft cunning.   opinion reputation (for wisdom) 104 I . . . simplicity I, in my use of simple truth, earn a reputation for being simple and plain 107 moral maxim 108 all the reach full extent 111 port gate of the city 112 possess inform 113 Entreat her fair treat her with courtesy 117 So . . . expects i.e., please save yourself the trouble of thanking Troilus for your good treatment at my hands; I'll do it for your sake, not his 126 even . . . charge simply because I demand that you do so 128 bulk hulk 129 moved angry 132 answer to my lust do what I please—with Cressida, and in responding to your challenge

I'll nothing do on charge. To her own worth   133
She shall be prized; but that you say "Be 't so,"   134
I'll speak it in my spirit and honor, "No."   135

TROILUS
  Come, to the port.—I'll tell thee, Diomed,
  This brave shall oft make thee to hide thy head.—   137
  Lady, give me your hand, and, as we walk,
  To our own selves bend we our needful talk.
        [*Exeunt Troilus, Cressida, and Diomedes.*]
                Sound trumpet [*within*].

PARIS
  Hark! Hector's trumpet.

AENEAS   How have we spent this morning! 140
  The Prince must think me tardy and remiss,
  That swore to ride before him to the field.

PARIS
  'Tis Troilus' fault. Come, come, to field with him.

DEIPHOBUS   Let us make ready straight.

AENEAS
  Yea, with a bridegroom's fresh alacrity,
  Let us address to tend on Hector's heels.   146
  The glory of our Troy doth this day lie
  On his fair worth and single chivalry.   *Exeunt.* 148

❧

4.5   *Enter Ajax, armed, Achilles, Patroclus,
        Agamemnon, Menelaus, Ulysses, Nestor, etc.*

AGAMEMNON
  Here art thou in appointment fresh and fair,   1
  Anticipating time with starting courage.   2
  Give with thy trumpet a loud note to Troy,
  Thou dreadful Ajax, that the appallèd air   4
  May pierce the head of the great combatant
  And hale him hither.

AJAX   Thou, trumpet, there's my purse. 6
         [*He throws money to his trumpeter.*]
  Now crack thy lungs and split thy brazen pipe.
  Blow, villain, till thy spherèd bias cheek   8
  Outswell the colic of puffed Aquilon.   9
  Come, stretch thy chest, and let thy eyes spout
    blood;
  Thou blowest for Hector.   [*Trumpet sounds.*]

ULYSSES   No trumpet answers.

ACHILLES   'Tis but early days.   13

      [*Enter Diomedes, with Cressida.*]

AGAMEMNON
  Is not yond Diomed, with Calchas' daughter?

ULYSSES
  'Tis he. I ken the manner of his gait;   15
  He rises on the toe. That spirit of his
  In aspiration lifts him from the earth.

AGAMEMNON
  Is this the Lady Cressid?

DIOMEDES   Even she.

AGAMEMNON
  Most dearly welcome to the Greeks, sweet lady.
                [*He kisses her.*]

NESTOR
  Our General doth salute you with a kiss.

ULYSSES
  Yet is the kindness but particular;   21
  'Twere better she were kissed in general.   22

NESTOR
  And very courtly counsel. I'll begin.   [*He kisses her.*]
  So much for Nestor.

ACHILLES
  I'll take that winter from your lips, fair lady.   25
  Achilles bids you welcome.   [*He kisses her.*]

MENELAUS
  I had good argument for kissing once.   27

PATROCLUS
  But that's no argument for kissing now;
  For thus popped Paris in his hardiment,   29
  And parted thus you and your argument.
                [*He kisses her.*]

ULYSSES
  O deadly gall and theme of all our scorns,
  For which we lose our heads to gild his horns!   32

PATROCLUS
  The first was Menelaus' kiss; this, mine.
  Patroclus kisses you.   [*He kisses her again.*]

MENELAUS   O, this is trim!   34

PATROCLUS
  Paris and I kiss evermore for him.   35

MENELAUS
  I'll have my kiss, sir.—Lady, by your leave.

CRESSIDA
  In kissing, do you render or receive?

MENELAUS
  Both take and give.

CRESSIDA   I'll make my match to live,   38
  The kiss you take is better than you give;
  Therefore no kiss.

---

133 **on charge** because you command it **134–135 but that . . .
"No"** but (I swear it by my honor) not because you tell me to
137 brave boast, defiance **140 spent** consumed by using **146 address** get ready. **tend** attend **148 single chivalry** individual
prowess
4.5. Location: Near the Greek camp. Lists set out as an arena for
combat.
1 appointment equipment, accoutrement **2 starting** bold, eager to
begin **4 dreadful** inspiring dread **6 trumpet** trumpeter **8 bias**
puffed out (and shaped like a weighted bowling ball used in bowls)
9 colic i.e., swelling (like that caused by colic). **Aquilon** the north
wind (here personified as distended by colic) **13 days** in the day

15 ken recognize **21 particular** single, limited to one **22 in
general** by everyone (with a play on "by the general") **25 that winter** (Alludes to Nestor's old age.) **27 argument** theme (i.e., Helen;
but Patroclus answers in the sense of "supporting reason")
29 popped came in suddenly (with sexual suggestion). **hardiment**
bold exploits, boldness (with bawdy double meaning of "hardness")
32 horns i.e., cuckold's horns. (We fight and die, observes Ulysses,
only to celebrate Menelaus' cuckoldry.) **34 trim** fine. (Said ironically.) **35 Paris . . . him** i.e., I take the kiss Menelaus hoped for,
just as Paris does in kissing Helen **38 I'll . . . to live** I'll wager my
life

MENELAUS
I'll give you boot; I'll give you three for one.   41
CRESSIDA
You are an odd man; give even, or give none.   42
MENELAUS
An odd man, lady? Every man is odd.
CRESSIDA
No, Paris is not, for you know 'tis true
That you are odd, and he is even with you.
MENELAUS
You fillip me o' the head.
CRESSIDA   No, I'll be sworn.   46
ULYSSES
It were no match, your nail against his horn.   47
May I, sweet lady, beg a kiss of you?
CRESSIDA
You may.
ULYSSES   I do desire it.
CRESSIDA   Why, beg too.
ULYSSES
Why then for Venus' sake, give me a kiss
When Helen is a maid again, and his.   51
CRESSIDA
I am your debtor; claim it when 'tis due.
ULYSSES
Never's my day, and then a kiss of you.   53
DIOMEDES
Lady, a word. I'll bring you to your father.
                              [*They talk apart.*]
NESTOR
A woman of quick sense.
ULYSSES   Fie, fie upon her!   55
There's language in her eye, her cheek, her lip,
Nay, her foot speaks; her wanton spirits look out
At every joint and motive of her body.   58
O, these encounterers, so glib of tongue,
That give accosting welcome ere it comes,   60
And wide unclasp the tables of their thoughts   61
To every ticklish reader! Set them down   62
For sluttish spoils of opportunity   63
And daughters of the game.   64
                    Exeunt [*Diomedes and Cressida*].

*Flourish. Enter all of Troy: Hector, Paris, Aeneas,
Helenus,* [*Troilus,*] *and attendants.*

ALL
The Trojans' trumpet.
AGAMEMNON   Yonder comes the troop.

AENEAS
Hail, all you state of Greece! What shall be done   66
To him that victory commands? Or do you purpose   67
A victor shall be known? Will you the knights   68
Shall to the edge of all extremity   69
Pursue each other, or shall they be divided   70
By any voice or order of the field?   71
Hector bade ask.
AGAMEMNON   Which way would Hector have it?
AENEAS
He cares not; he'll obey conditions.   73
AGAMEMNON
'Tis done like Hector.
ACHILLES   But securely done,   74
A little proudly, and great deal disprising   75
The knight opposed.
AENEAS   If not Achilles, sir,
What is your name?
ACHILLES   If not Achilles, nothing.
AENEAS
Therefore Achilles. But, whate'er, know this:
In the extremity of great and little,   79
Valor and pride excel themselves in Hector,   80
The one almost as infinite as all,
The other blank as nothing. Weigh him well,
And that which looks like pride is courtesy.
This Ajax is half made of Hector's blood,   84
In love whereof half Hector stays at home;
Half heart, half hand, half Hector comes to seek
This blended knight, half Trojan and half Greek.
ACHILLES
A maiden battle, then? O, I perceive you.   88

[*Enter Diomedes.*]

AGAMEMNON
Here is Sir Diomed. Go, gentle knight,
Stand by our Ajax. As you and Lord Aeneas
Consent upon the order of their fight,   91
So be it, either to the uttermost,
Or else a breath. The combatants being kin   93
Half stints their strife before their strokes begin.
                    [*Ajax and Hector enter the lists.*]
ULYSSES   They are opposed already.
AGAMEMNON [*to Ulysses*]
What Trojan is that same that looks so heavy?   96
ULYSSES
The youngest son of Priam, a true knight,
Not yet mature, yet matchless firm of word,

---

41 boot odds, something in addition   **42 odd** The wordplay here and in lines 43–45 includes (1) strange (2) single, no longer having a wife (3) unique, standing alone (4) odd man out (5) the opposite of *even*   **46 fillip . . . head** i.e., touch a sensitive spot, by alluding to my cuckold's horns   **47 It . . . horn** i.e., it would be an uneven contest between the fingernail with which you tap his head and Menelaus' cuckold's horn   **51 his** Menelaus' wife   **53 and . . . you**, I'll never claim that kiss   **55 quick sense** lively wit   **58 motive** moving limb or organ   **60 accosting** approaching, sidling up to   **61 tables** tablets   **62 ticklish** easily tickled; fickle   **63 sluttish . . . opportunity** "corrupt wenches, of whose chastity every opportunity may make a prey" (Johnson)   **64 daughters of the game** i.e., prostitutes

66 state noble lords.   **What . . . done** i.e., what honors shall be afforded   **67 that . . . commands** that wins the victory   **68–71 Will . . . field** do you desire that the combatants fight to the death, or that they be required to separate on order of the marshals, according to set regulations of the field of honor?   **73 conditions** whatever conditions are agreed upon   **74 securely** overconfidently   **75 disprising** disdaining, underrating   **79–80 In . . . Hector** i.e., Hector's valor is extremely great; his pride, extremely little   **84 Ajax . . . blood** (Compare 2.2.77, note, and 4.5.121.)   **88 maiden battle** combat without bloodshed.   **perceive** understand   **91 Consent** agree.   **order** procedure, rules   **93 a breath** a pause in the fighting   **96 heavy** sad

Speaking in deeds and deedless in his tongue;   99
Not soon provoked, nor being provoked soon
  calmed;
His heart and hand both open and both free.   101
For what he has he gives; what thinks, he shows;
Yet gives he not till judgment guide his bounty,
Nor dignifies an impare thought with breath;   104
Manly as Hector, but more dangerous,
For Hector in his blaze of wrath subscribes   106
To tender objects, but he in heat of action   107
Is more vindicative than jealous love.   108
They call him Troilus, and on him erect
A second hope, as fairly built as Hector.
Thus says Aeneas, one that knows the youth
Even to his inches, and with private soul   112
Did in great Ilium thus translate him to me.   113
              Alarum. [Hector and Ajax fight.]
AGAMEMNON   They are in action.
NESTOR   Now, Ajax, hold thine own!
TROILUS   Hector, thou sleep'st. Awake thee!
AGAMEMNON
His blows are well disposed. There, Ajax!   117
                              Trumpets cease.
DIOMEDES
You must no more.
AENEAS   Princes, enough, so please you.
AJAX
I am not warm yet. Let us fight again.
DIOMEDES
As Hector pleases.
HECTOR   Why, then will I no more.
Thou art, great lord, my father's sister's son,
A cousin-german to great Priam's seed.   122
The obligation of our blood forbids
A gory emulation twixt us twain.   124
Were thy commixtion Greek and Trojan so   125
That thou couldst say, "This hand is Grecian all,
And this is Trojan; the sinews of this leg
All Greek, and this all Troy; my mother's blood
Runs on the dexter cheek, and this sinister   129
Bounds in my father's," by Jove multipotent,
Thou shouldst not bear from me a Greekish member
Wherein my sword had not impressure made   132
Of our rank feud. But the just gods gainsay   133
That any drop thou borrow'dst from thy mother,
My sacred aunt, should by my mortal sword
Be drained! Let me embrace thee, Ajax.
By him that thunders, thou hast lusty arms!   137
Hector would have them fall upon him thus.

Cousin, all honor to thee!   [*They embrace.*]
AJAX   I thank thee, Hector.
Thou art too gentle and too free a man.
I came to kill thee, cousin, and bear hence
A great addition earnèd in thy death.   142
HECTOR
Not Neoptolemus so mirable,   143
On whose bright crest Fame with her loud'st
  "Oyez"   144
Cries, "This is he," could promise to himself   145
A thought of added honor torn from Hector.   146
AENEAS
There is expectance here from both the sides   147
What further you will do.
HECTOR   We'll answer it;
The issue is embracement. Ajax, farewell.   149
                              [*They embrace.*]
AJAX
If I might in entreaties find success—
As seld I have the chance—I would desire   151
My famous cousin to our Grecian tents.
DIOMEDES
'Tis Agamemnon's wish, and great Achilles
Doth long to see unarmed the valiant Hector.
HECTOR
Aeneas, call my brother Troilus to me,
And signify this loving interview   156
To the expecters of our Trojan part;   157
Desire them home. Give me thy hand, my cousin.   158
I will go eat with thee and see your knights.
              [*Agamemnon and the rest approach them.*]
AJAX
Great Agamemnon comes to meet us here.
HECTOR [*to Aeneas*]
The worthiest of them tell me name by name;
But for Achilles, mine own searching eyes
Shall find him by his large and portly size.   163
AGAMEMNON
Worthy of arms! As welcome as to one   164
That would be rid of such an enemy—
But that's no welcome. Understand more clear:
What's past and what's to come is strewed with
  husks
And formless ruin of oblivion;
But in this extant moment, faith and troth,
Strained purely from all hollow bias-drawing,   170
Bids thee, with most divine integrity,
From heart of very heart, great Hector, welcome.

---

99 **deedless in his tongue** i.e., never boastful   101 **free** open, generous   104 **impare** unconsidered. (Or perhaps *impair*, "unsuitable," "unworthy," or "injurious.")   106–107 **subscribes . . . objects** yields mercy to those who awaken his pity   108 **vindicative** vindictive   112 **Even . . . inches** i.e., every inch of him.   **with private soul** in private confidence   113 **translate** interpret   117 **disposed** placed   122 **cousin-german** first cousin   124 **gory emulation** bloody rivalry   125 **commixtion** mixture   129 **dexter** right.   **sinister** left   132 **impressure** impression   133 **rank** hot, intemperate.   **gainsay** forbid   137 **By . . . thunders** i.e., by Jove

142 **addition** honorable title   143–146 **Not . . . Hector** i.e., not even the much-wondered-at Achilles, on whose heraldic badge Fame herself in the role of the public crier announces "This is the man," could assure himself of added honor by defeating Hector. (*Neoptolemus* is actually the name of Achilles' son.)   147 **expectance** expectation   149 **issue** outcome   151 **seld** seldom.   **desire** invite   156 **signify** announce   157 **the expecters . . . part** those awaiting the outcome on our Trojan side   158 **home** to go home   163 **portly** stately, dignified   164 **of arms** (1) to bear weapons (2) to receive embracements.   **as to one** as it is possible to one   170 **Strained** refined, purged.   **hollow bias-drawing** i.e., insincerities, obliquities, such as the bias gives the bowling ball in the game of bowls

HECTOR
I thank thee, most imperious Agamemnon.   173
AGAMEMNON [to Troilus]
My well-famed lord of Troy, no less to you.
MENELAUS
Let me confirm my princely brother's greeting.
You brace of warlike brothers, welcome hither.
HECTOR
Who must we answer?
AENEAS   The noble Menelaus.
HECTOR
O, you, my lord? By Mars his gauntlet, thanks!
Mock not that I affect th' untraded oath;   179
Your quondam wife swears still by Venus' glove.   180
She's well, but bade me not commend her to you.
MENELAUS
Name her not now, sir. She's a deadly theme.   182
HECTOR   O, pardon! I offend.
NESTOR
I have, thou gallant Trojan, seen thee oft,
Laboring for destiny, make cruel way   185
Through ranks of Greekish youth, and I have seen
    thee,
As hot as Perseus, spur thy Phrygian steed,   187
And seen thee scorning forfeits and subduements,   188
When thou hast hung thy advancèd sword i' th' air,   189
Not letting it decline on the declined,   190
That I have said unto my standers-by,   191
"Lo, Jupiter is yonder, dealing life!"
And I have seen thee pause and take thy breath,
When that a ring of Greeks have hemmed thee in,   194
Like an Olympian, wrestling. This have I seen;   195
But this thy countenance, still locked in steel,   196
I never saw till now. I knew thy grandsire   197
And once fought with him. He was a soldier good,
But, by great Mars, the captain of us all,
Never like thee. Let an old man embrace thee;
And, worthy warrior, welcome to our tents.
                    [They embrace.]
AENEAS   'Tis the old Nestor.
HECTOR
Let me embrace thee, good old chronicle,   203
That hast so long walked hand in hand with Time.
Most reverend Nestor, I am glad to clasp thee.
NESTOR
I would my arms could match thee in contention
As they contend with thee in courtesy.
HECTOR   I would they could.

NESTOR   Ha!
By this white beard, I'd fight with thee tomorrow.
Well, welcome, welcome! I have seen the time.   211
ULYSSES
I wonder now how yonder city stands
When we have here her base and pillar by us.
HECTOR
I know your favor, Lord Ulysses, well.   214
Ah, sir, there's many a Greek and Trojan dead
Since first I saw yourself and Diomed
In Ilium, on your Greekish embassy.
ULYSSES
Sir, I foretold you then what would ensue.
My prophecy is but half his journey yet,
For yonder walls, that pertly front your town,   220
Yon towers, whose wanton tops do buss the clouds,   221
Must kiss their own feet.
HECTOR   I must not believe you.
There they stand yet, and modestly I think   223
The fall of every Phrygian stone will cost
A drop of Grecian blood. The end crowns all,
And that old common arbitrator, Time,
Will one day end it.
ULYSSES   So to him we leave it.
Most gentle and most valiant Hector, welcome!
After the General, I beseech you next
To feast with me and see me at my tent.
ACHILLES
I shall forestall thee, Lord Ulysses, thou!   231
Now, Hector, I have fed mine eyes on thee;
I have with exact view perused thee, Hector,
And quoted joint by joint.
HECTOR   Is this Achilles?   234
ACHILLES   I am Achilles.
HECTOR
Stand fair, I pray thee. Let me look on thee.   236
ACHILLES
Behold thy fill.
HECTOR   Nay, I have done already.
ACHILLES
Thou art too brief. I will the second time,
As I would buy thee, view thee limb by limb.
HECTOR
O, like a book of sport thou'lt read me o'er;
But there's more in me than thou understand'st.
Why dost thou so oppress me with thine eye?
ACHILLES
Tell me, you heavens, in which part of his body
Shall I destroy him? Whether there, or there, or
    there?
That I may give the local wound a name
And make distinct the very breach whereout
Hector's great spirit flew. Answer me, heavens!

---

173 imperious imperial   **179 untraded** unhackneyed. (Hector insists that his oath, "by Mars' gauntlet," is suited to a war fought over a woman.)   **180 quondam** former   **182 deadly theme** subject for mortal strife   **185 Laboring for destiny** employed in the service of fate, putting people to death   **187 Perseus** (See the note for 1.3.42.)
188 scorning . . . subduements i.e., ignoring those already vanquished, whose lives were forfeit; refusing easy prey   **189 advancèd** raised aloft   **190 the declined** those already vanquished   **191 unto my standers-by** to some of my followers   **194 When that** when
195 Olympian Olympian god, or a wrestler in the Olympic games
196 still always   **197 grandsire** i.e., Laomedon, builder of the walls of Troy and defender of the city against an earlier Greek army under Hercules   **203 chronicle** i.e., storehouse of memories

211 I . . . time i.e., there was such a time   **214 favor** face
220 pertly front boldly stand before   **221 wanton** insolent, reckless (with suggestion of amorousness in the metaphor of kissing).   **buss** kiss   **223 modestly** without exaggeration   **231 forestall** prevent
234 quoted joint by joint scrutinized limb by limb   **236 fair** in full view

HECTOR
It would discredit the blest gods, proud man,
To answer such a question. Stand again.
Think'st thou to catch my life so pleasantly   250
As to prenominate in nice conjecture   251
Where thou wilt hit me dead?

ACHILLES   I tell thee, yea.

HECTOR
Wert thou the oracle to tell me so,
I'd not believe thee. Henceforth guard thee well;
For I'll not kill thee there, nor there, nor there,
But, by the forge that stithied Mars his helm,
I'll kill thee everywhere, yea, o'er and o'er.—   256
You wisest Grecians, pardon me this brag;
His insolence draws folly from my lips.
But I'll endeavor deeds to match these words,
Or may I never—

AJAX   Do not chafe thee, cousin.   261
And you, Achilles, let these threats alone,
Till accident or purpose bring you to 't.   263
You may have every day enough of Hector,
If you have stomach. The general state, I fear,   265
Can scarce entreat you to be odd with him.   266

HECTOR [to Achilles]
I pray you, let us see you in the field.
We have had pelting wars since you refused   268
The Grecians' cause.

ACHILLES   Dost thou entreat me, Hector?
Tomorrow do I meet thee, fell as death;   270
Tonight all friends.

HECTOR   Thy hand upon that match.
                [They grasp hands.]

AGAMEMNON
First, all you peers of Greece, go to my tent;
There in the full convive you. Afterwards,   273
As Hector's leisure and your bounties shall
Concur together, severally entreat him.   275
Beat loud the taborins, let the trumpets blow,   276
That this great soldier may his welcome know.
     [Flourish.] Exeunt [all except Troilus and Ulysses].

TROILUS
My lord Ulysses, tell me, I beseech you,
In what place of the field doth Calchas keep?   279

ULYSSES
At Menelaus' tent, most princely Troilus.
There Diomed doth feast with him tonight,
Who neither looks on heaven nor on earth
But gives all gaze and bent of amorous view
On the fair Cressid.

TROILUS
Shall I, sweet lord, be bound to you so much,
After we part from Agamemnon's tent,
To bring me thither?

ULYSSES   You shall command me, sir.
As gentle tell me, of what honor was   288
This Cressida in Troy? Had she no lover there
That wails her absence?

TROILUS
O, sir, to such as boasting show their scars   291
A mock is due. Will you walk on, my lord?
She was beloved, she loved; she is, and doth.
But still sweet love is food for fortune's tooth.   294
                 Exeunt.

❖

5.1   *Enter Achilles and Patroclus.*

ACHILLES
I'll heat his blood with Greekish wine tonight,
Which with my scimitar I'll cool tomorrow.   2
Patroclus, let us feast him to the height.

PATROCLUS
Here comes Thersites.

     Enter Thersites.

ACHILLES   How now, thou core of envy!   4
Thou crusty botch of nature, what's the news?   5

THERSITES   Why, thou picture of what thou seemest   6
and idol of idiot-worshipers, here's a letter for thee.

ACHILLES   From whence, fragment?   8

THERSITES   Why, thou full dish of fool, from Troy.
        [He gives a letter. Achilles reads it.]

PATROCLUS   Who keeps the tent now?   10

THERSITES   The surgeon's box, or the patient's wound.   11

PATROCLUS   Well said, adversity! And what need these   12
tricks?

THERSITES   Prithee, be silent, boy. I profit not by thy
talk. Thou art thought to be Achilles' male varlet.

PATROCLUS   Male varlet, you rogue? What's that?

THERSITES   Why, his masculine whore. Now, the rotten
diseases of the south, the guts-griping, ruptures,
catarrhs, loads o' gravel i' the back, lethargies, cold   19
palsies, raw eyes, dirt-rotten livers, wheezing lungs,
bladders full of imposthume, sciaticas, limekilns i' the   21
palm, incurable bone-ache, and the riveled fee simple   22
of the tetter, take and take again such preposterous   23
discoveries!   24

---

250 **pleasantly** easily   251 **prenominate** name beforehand.   **nice** precise   256 **stithied Mars his helm** forged Mars' helmet   261 **chafe thee** anger yourself   263 **to 't** i.e., to battle with Hector   265 **stomach** appetite (for fighting).   **general state** i.e., Greek commanders in council   266 **be odd** be at odds, undertake to fight   268 **pelting** paltry   270 **fell** fierce   273 **convive** feast together   275 **severally** individually.   **entreat** invite   276 **taborins** drums   279 **keep** dwell

288 As gentle be so courteous as to.   **honor** reputation   **291 such as** those who   **294 still** always
5.1. Location: The Greek camp. Before Achilles' tent.
2 scimitar sword. (Literally, a short, curved, single-bladed sword.)
4 core central hard mass of a boil or tumor   **5 crusty . . . nature** scabbed-over ulcer infecting the natural order   **6 picture** mere image
8 fragment crust of bread   **10 Who . . . now** (Patroclus may be pointing out that Achilles no longer keeps to his tent, thus depriving Thersites of an object of satirical humor.)   **11 surgeon's box** (Thersites puns on *tent* in the previous line, i.e., a probe for cleaning a wound.)
12 adversity perversity, contrariety   **19 gravel** stones.   **back** kidney. **lethargies** apoplexies, torpid languor   **21 imposthume** abscesses. **limekilns** burning sensations   **22 riveled** wrinkled.   **fee simple** absolute possession, i.e., incurable disease   **23 tetter** skin disease.   **take** afflict with disease   **23–24 preposterous discoveries** i.e., the revelation of such unnatural perversions as take place between Patroclus and Achilles

PATROCLUS   Why, thou damnable box of envy, thou, what mean'st thou to curse thus?

THERSITES   Do I curse thee?

PATROCLUS   Why, no, you ruinous butt, you whoreson 28
indistinguishable cur, no. 29

THERSITES   No? Why art thou then exasperate, thou idle 30
immaterial skein of sleave silk, thou green sarcenet 31
flap for a sore eye, thou tassel of a prodigal's purse,
thou? Ah, how the poor world is pestered with such
waterflies, diminutives of nature!

PATROCLUS   Out, gall! 35

THERSITES   Finch egg! 36

ACHILLES
My sweet Patroclus, I am thwarted quite
From my great purpose in tomorrow's battle.
Here is a letter from Queen Hecuba,
A token from her daughter, my fair love,
Both taxing me and gaging me to keep 41
An oath that I have sworn. I will not break it.
Fall, Greeks; fail, fame; honor, or go or stay. 43
My major vow lies here; this I'll obey.
Come, come, Thersites, help to trim my tent. 45
This night in banqueting must all be spent.
Away, Patroclus!   Exit [with Patroclus].

THERSITES   With too much blood and too little brain,
these two may run mad; but if with too much brain
and too little blood they do, I'll be a curer of madmen. 50
Here's Agamemnon, an honest fellow enough and
one that loves quails, but he has not so much brain as 52
earwax. And the goodly transformation of Jupiter 53
there, his brother, the bull—the primitive statue and 54
oblique memorial of cuckolds, a thrifty shoeing-horn 55
in a chain, hanging at his brother's leg—to what form 56
but that he is should wit larded with malice and malice farced with wit turn him to? To an ass were noth- 58
ing, he is both ass and ox; to an ox were nothing, he's
both ox and ass. To be a dog, a mule, a cat, a fit- 60
chew, a toad, a lizard, an owl, a puttock, or a herring 61
without a roe, I would not care; but to be Menelaus! I 62
would conspire against destiny. Ask me not what I
would be if I were not Thersites, for I care not to be 64
the louse of a lazar, so I were not Menelaus. Heyday! 65
Sprites and fires! 66

Enter Hector, [Troilus,] Ajax, Agamemnon,
Ulysses, Nestor, [Menelaus, and] Diomedes, with
lights.

AGAMEMNON
We go wrong, we go wrong.

AJAX   No, yonder 'tis,
There, where we see the light.

HECTOR   I trouble you.

AJAX
No, not a whit.

Enter Achilles.

ULYSSES   Here comes himself to guide you.

ACHILLES
Welcome, brave Hector; welcome, princes all.

AGAMEMNON
So now, fair Prince of Troy, I bid good night.
Ajax commands the guard to tend on you.

HECTOR
Thanks and good night to the Greeks' general.

MENELAUS   Good night, my lord.

HECTOR   Good night, sweet Lord Menelaus.

THERSITES [aside] Sweet draft. "Sweet," quoth 'a? 76
Sweet sink, sweet sewer. 77

ACHILLES
Good night and welcome, both at once, to those
That go or tarry.

AGAMEMNON   Good night.
                    Exeunt Agamemnon [and] Menelaus.

ACHILLES
Old Nestor tarries; and you too, Diomed,
Keep Hector company an hour or two.

DIOMEDES
I cannot, lord. I have important business,
The tide whereof is now. Good night, great Hector. 84

HECTOR   Give me your hand.

ULYSSES [aside to Troilus]
Follow his torch; he goes to Calchas' tent.
I'll keep you company.

TROILUS   Sweet sir, you honor me.

HECTOR
And so, good night.
            [Exit Diomedes; Ulysses and Troilus following.]

ACHILLES   Come, come, enter my tent.
            Exeunt [Achilles, Hector, Ajax, and Nestor].

THERSITES   That same Diomed's a false-hearted rogue, a
most unjust knave. I will no more trust him when he 90
leers than I will a serpent when he hisses. He will
spend his mouth and promise, like Brabbler the 92
hound, but when he performs, astronomers foretell it; 93
it is prodigious, there will come some change. The sun 94
borrows of the moon when Diomed keeps his word. 95

---

28 **ruinous butt** dilapidated cask   29 **indistinguishable** shapeless
30 **exasperate** exasperated, angry   31 **skein** coil.   **sleave silk** floss
silk, i.e., unwoven and hence worthless (*immaterial*).   **sarcenet** fine,
soft silk   35 **gall** (1) bitter railer (2) blister   36 **Finch egg** (The finch is
a small bird.)   41 **taxing** urging.   **gaging** binding, pledging   43 **or go**
either go   45 **trim** prepare   50 **I'll . . . madmen** (A most unlikely circumstance.)   52 **quails** i.e., prostitutes. (Cant term.)   53–54 **transformation . . . bull** (Alludes ironically to the myth of Jupiter's rape of
Europa, whom he encountered in a meadow after changing himself
into a bull. Thersites has in mind the bull's horns, which are like
Menelaus' cuckold's horns.)   54–55 **the primitive . . . cuckolds** i.e.,
the prototype and indirect reminder of cuckolds in having horns   55–
56 **a thrifty . . . leg** i.e., a convenient tool, always available to do
Agamemnon's will (the *shoeing-horn* having been suggested in Thersites' mind by the cuckold's horn)   58 **farced** covered, trimmed,
adorned   60–61 **fitchew** polecat   61 **puttock** bird of prey of the kite
kind   61–62 **herring . . . roe** i.e., least valuable kind of herring
64 **I care not to be** I wouldn't mind being   65 **lazar** leper.   **so** provided   66 **Sprites and fires** (Thersites sees those who are entering
with lights, reminding him of will-o'-the-wisps and other spirits.)

76 **draft** privy.   **'a** he   77 **sink** cesspool   84 **tide** time   90 **unjust**
dishonest, perfidious   92 **spend his mouth** bay loudly   92–93 **Brabbler the hound** a hound that makes a lot of noise (babbles) but often
loses the scent   93–94 **astronomers . . . change** i.e., it is a rare and
wondrous event   95 **borrows of** borrows reflected light from (reversing the natural superiority of the sun—something that will never
happen)

I will rather leave to see Hector than not to dog him. 96
They say he keeps a Trojan drab and uses the traitor 97
Calchas his tent. I'll after. Nothing but lechery! All 98
incontinent varlets!   [*Exit.*] 99

❖

5.2 *Enter Diomedes.*

DIOMEDES What, are you up here, ho? Speak.
CALCHAS [*within*] Who calls?
DIOMEDES
 Diomed. Calchas, I think. Where's your daughter?
CALCHAS [*within*] She comes to you.

  Enter Troilus and Ulysses [at a distance; after
  them, Thersites].

ULYSSES [*to Troilus*]
 Stand where the torch may not discover us. 5
  [*He and Troilus conceal themselves in one place,*
       Thersites in another.]

  Enter Cressida.

TROILUS
 Cressid comes forth to him.
DIOMEDES   How now, my charge?
CRESSIDA
 Now, my sweet guardian! Hark, a word with you.
      [*She whispers to him.*]
TROILUS Yea, so familiar?
ULYSSES She will sing any man at first sight. 9
THERSITES [*aside*] And any man may sing her, if he can
 take her clef. She's noted. 11
DIOMEDES Will you remember?
CRESSIDA Remember? Yes.
DIOMEDES Nay, but do, then,
 And let your mind be coupled with your words.
TROILUS What should she remember?
ULYSSES List. 17
CRESSIDA
 Sweet honey Greek, tempt me no more to folly.
THERSITES [*aside*] Roguery!
DIOMEDES Nay, then—
CRESSIDA I'll tell you what—
DIOMEDES
 Foh, foh! Come, tell a pin. You are forsworn. 22
CRESSIDA
 In faith, I cannot. What would you have me do? 23
THERSITES [*aside*] A juggling trick—to be secretly 24
open. 25

DIOMEDES
 What did you swear you would bestow on me?
CRESSIDA
 I prithee, do not hold me to mine oath.
 Bid me do anything but that, sweet Greek.
DIOMEDES Good night.   [*He starts to go.*]
TROILUS Hold, patience!
ULYSSES How now, Trojan?
CRESSIDA Diomed—
DIOMEDES
 No, no, good night. I'll be your fool no more. 33
TROILUS Thy better must. 34
CRESSIDA Hark, one word in your ear.
      [*She whispers to him.*]
TROILUS O plague and madness!
ULYSSES
 You are moved, Prince. Let us depart, I pray you,
 Lest your displeasure should enlarge itself
 To wrathful terms. This place is dangerous, 39
 The time right deadly. I beseech you, go.
    [*He tries to lead Troilus away.*]
TROILUS
 Behold, I pray you!
ULYSSES   Nay, good my lord, go off.
 You flow to great distraction. Come, my lord. 42
TROILUS
 I prithee, stay.
ULYSSES   You have not patience. Come.
TROILUS
 I pray you, stay. By hell and all hell's torments,
 I will not speak a word!
DIOMEDES
 And so, good night.
CRESSIDA   Nay, but you part in anger.
TROILUS
 Doth that grieve thee? O witherèd truth!
ULYSSES
 Why, how now, lord?
TROILUS   By Jove, I will be patient.
CRESSIDA
 Guardian!—Why, Greek!
DIOMEDES   Foh, foh! Adieu. You palter. 49
CRESSIDA
 In faith, I do not. Come hither once again.
ULYSSES
 You shake, my lord, at something. Will you go?
 You will break out.
TROILUS   She strokes his cheek!
ULYSSES   Come, Come.
TROILUS
 Nay, stay. By Jove, I will not speak a word.
 There is between my will and all offenses 54
 A guard of patience. Stay a little while.
THERSITES [*aside*] How the devil Luxury, with his fat 56

---

96 **leave to see** cease looking upon. **him** Diomedes 97 **drab**
whore. **uses** frequents 98 **Calchas his** Calchas' 98–99 **incontinent** (1) unchaste (2) incorrigible
5.2. **Location:** The Greek camp. Before Calchas' tent.
5 **discover** reveal 9 **sing** make music with, play upon 11 **clef** key
(with obscene pun on "cleft," i.e., vulva). **noted** set to music (with
pun on the meaning "known," i.e., notorious, or "used sexually")
17 **List** listen 22 **tell a pin** i.e., tell me no trifles 23 **I cannot** i.e. I
cannot do what I promised 24 **juggling trick** magic trick (since to be
secretly open is an apparent contradiction in terms) 25 **open** (1)
frank (2) sexually available

33 **fool** dupe 34 **Thy better must** i.e., better men than you (including myself) must play the fool to women like Cressida 39 **wrathful
terms** i.e., a fight 42 **You . . . distraction** your overfull heart will
vent itself in emotional turmoil 49 **palter** use trickery 54 **will** i.e.,
desire to speak and act 56 **Luxury** lechery

rump and potato finger, tickles these together! Fry, 57
lechery, fry!

DIOMEDES   But will you, then?

CRESSIDA
In faith, I will, la. Never trust me else.

DIOMEDES
Give me some token for the surety of it.

CRESSIDA   I'll fetch you one.   *Exit.*

ULYSSES
You have sworn patience.

TROILUS   Fear me not, sweet lord.
I will not be myself, nor have cognition
Of what I feel. I am all patience.

                    Enter Cressida, [with Troilus' sleeve].

THERSITES [*aside*]   Now the pledge; now, now, now!

CRESSIDA   Here, Diomed, keep this sleeve.
                                        [*She gives it to him.*]

TROILUS
O beauty! Where is thy faith?

ULYSSES   My lord—

TROILUS
I will be patient; outwardly I will.

CRESSIDA
You look upon that sleeve. Behold it well.
He loved me—O false wench!—Give 't me again.
                                        [*She takes it back again.*]

DIOMEDES   Whose was 't?

CRESSIDA
It is no matter, now I ha 't again.
I will not meet with you tomorrow night.
I prithee, Diomed, visit me no more.

THERSITES [*aside*]   Now she sharpens. Well said, whet- 76
stone!

DIOMEDES
I shall have it.

CRESSIDA   What, this?

DIOMEDES   Ay, that.

CRESSIDA
O all you gods! O pretty, pretty pledge!
Thy master now lies thinking on his bed
Of thee and me, and sighs, and takes my glove,
And gives memorial dainty kisses to it—   82

DIOMEDES   As I kiss thee.   [*He gets the sleeve from her.*]

CRESSIDA   Nay, do not snatch it from me;
He that takes that doth take my heart withal.   84

DIOMEDES
I had your heart before; this follows it.

TROILUS   I did swear patience.

CRESSIDA
You shall not have it, Diomed, faith, you shall not.
I'll give you something else.

DIOMEDES   I will have this. Whose was it?
                                        [*He gets the sleeve from her.*]

CRESSIDA   It is no matter.

DIOMEDES   Come, tell me whose it was.

CRESSIDA
'Twas one's that loved me better than you will.
But, now you have it, take it.

DIOMEDES   Whose was it?

CRESSIDA
By all Diana's waiting-women yond,   94
And by herself, I will not tell you whose.

DIOMEDES
Tomorrow will I wear it on my helm
And grieve his spirit that dares not challenge it.   97

TROILUS
Wert thou the devil, and wor'st it on thy horn,   98
It should be challenged.

CRESSIDA
Well, well, 'tis done, 'tis past. And yet it is not;
I will not keep my word.

DIOMEDES   Why, then, farewell.
Thou never shalt mock Diomed again.
                                        [*He starts to go.*]

CRESSIDA
You shall not go. One cannot speak a word
But it straight starts you.

DIOMEDES   I do not like this fooling.   104

TROILUS [*aside*]   Nor I, by Pluto; but that that likes not 105
you pleases me best.

DIOMEDES   What, shall I come? The hour?

CRESSIDA
Ay, come—O Jove!—do come—I shall be plagued.

DIOMEDES
Farewell till then.

CRESSIDA   Good night. I prithee, come.
                                        Exit [Diomedes].
Troilus, farewell! One eye yet looks on thee,
But with my heart the other eye doth see.
Ah, poor our sex! This fault in us I find:
The error of our eye directs our mind.
What error leads must err. O, then conclude:
Minds swayed by eyes are full of turpitude.   *Exit.* 115

THERSITES [*aside*]
A proof of strength she could not publish more,   116
Unless she said, "My mind is now turned whore."

ULYSSES
All's done, my lord.

TROILUS   It is.

ULYSSES   Why stay we, then?

TROILUS
To make a recordation to my soul   119
Of every syllable that here was spoke.
But if I tell how these two did coact,
Shall I not lie in publishing a truth?
Sith yet there is a credence in my heart,
An esperance so obstinately strong,   124
That doth invert th' attest of eyes and ears,   125

---

57 potato finger (Potatoes were accounted stimulants to lechery.)
Fry burn (with passion)   **76 sharpens** whets his appetite   **82 memorial** in loving remembrance   **84 withal** with it

94 Diana's . . . yond i.e., yonder stars. (Diana is the moon goddess
and, ironically, the goddess of chastity.)   **97 grieve** afflict   **98 wor'st**
wore   **104 straight starts you** immediately starts you off on some
abrupt action   **105 likes** pleases   **115 turpitude** wickedness   **116 A
proof . . . more** she could not state a stronger proof   **119 recordation** record   **124 esperance** hope   **125 attest** witness

As if those organs had deceptious functions   126
Created only to calumniate.   127
Was Cressid here?
ULYSSES   I cannot conjure, Trojan.
TROILUS
She was not, sure.
ULYSSES   Most sure she was.
TROILUS
Why, my negation hath no taste of madness.   130
ULYSSES
Nor mine, my lord. Cressid was here but now.
TROILUS
Let it not be believed, for womanhood!   132
Think, we had mothers. Do not give advantage
To stubborn critics, apt, without a theme   134
For depravation, to square the general sex   135
By Cressid's rule. Rather think this not Cressid.   136
ULYSSES
What hath she done, Prince, that can soil our
    mothers?
TROILUS
Nothing at all, unless that this were she.
THERSITES [aside]   Will 'a swagger himself out on 's own   139
eyes?   140
TROILUS
This she? No, this is Diomed's Cressida.
If beauty have a soul, this is not she;
If souls guide vows, if vows be sanctimonies,   143
If sanctimony be the gods' delight,
If there be rule in unity itself,   145
This is not she. O, madness of discourse,   146
That cause sets up with and against itself!   147
Bifold authority, where reason can revolt   148
Without perdition, and loss assume all reason   149
Without revolt! This is and is not Cressid.   150
Within my soul there doth conduce a fight   151
Of this strange nature, that a thing inseparate   152
Divides more wider than the sky and earth,
And yet the spacious breadth of this division
Admits no orifex for a point as subtle   155
As Ariachne's broken woof to enter.   156
Instance, O, instance, strong as Pluto's gates,   157

Cressid is mine, tied with the bonds of heaven;
Instance, O, instance, strong as heaven itself,
The bonds of heaven are slipped, dissolved, and
    loosed,
And with another knot, five-finger-tied,   161
The fractions of her faith, orts of her love,   162
The fragments, scraps, the bits and greasy relics
Of her o'ereaten faith, are bound to Diomed.   164
ULYSSES
May worthy Troilus be half attached   165
With that which here his passion doth express?
TROILUS
Ay, Greek; and that shall be divulgèd well
In characters as red as Mars his heart   168
Inflamed with Venus. Never did young man fancy   169
With so eternal and so fixed a soul.
Hark, Greek: as much as I do Cressid love,
So much by weight hate I her Diomed.   172
That sleeve is mine that he'll bear on his helm.
Were it a casque composed by Vulcan's skill,   174
My sword should bite it. Not the dreadful spout   175
Which shipmen do the hurricano call,
Constringed in mass by the almighty sun,   177
Shall dizzy with more clamor Neptune's ear   178
In his descent than shall my prompted sword
Falling on Diomed.
THERSITES [aside]   He'll tickle it for his concupy.   181
TROILUS
O Cressid! O false Cressid! False, false, false!
Let all untruths stand by thy stainèd name,
And they'll seem glorious.
ULYSSES   O, contain yourself.
Your passion draws ears hither.

        Enter Aeneas.

AENEAS
I have been seeking you this hour, my lord.
Hector, by this, is arming him in Troy;   187
Ajax, your guard, stays to conduct you home.
TROILUS
Have with you, Prince. My courteous lord, adieu.   189
Farewell, revolted fair! And, Diomed,
Stand fast, and wear a castle on thy head!   191
ULYSSES   I'll bring you to the gates.
TROILUS   Accept distracted thanks.
            Exeunt Troilus, Aeneas, and Ulysses.
THERSITES   Would I could meet that rogue Diomed! I

126 deceptious deceiving   **127 calumniate** slander, defame
130 negation denial   **132 for** for the sake of   **134 stubborn** hostile
134–136 apt . . . rule apt enough, even when they lack grounds for
negative comment, to make Cressida the standard by which all womankind is measured. (To *square* is to use a carpenter's square or measuring tool.)   **139–140 Will . . . eyes** i.e., will he succeed in denying the evidence of his own eyes?   **143 sanctimonies** sacred things
145 If . . . itself i.e., if an entity (like Cressida) can only be itself and
not two entities   **146 discourse** reason   **147 That . . . up** that sets up
a debate or argument   **148 Bifold** divided in two   **148–150 where
. . . Without revolt** where reason can revolt against itself (by denying
the testimony of the senses that this is indeed Cressida) without becoming madness, and where loss of reason can put on the appearance of reason without actually revolting against it   **151 conduce** take
place   **152 a thing inseparate** i.e., Cressida, an indivisible entity
155 orifex orifice   **156 Ariachne's broken woof** i.e., a thread of a
spider's web. (Arachne [the normal spelling] challenged Minerva to a
weaving contest; the goddess became angered, tore up Arachne's
work, and turned her into a spider.)   **157 Instance** proof, evidence

161 five-finger-tied i.e., tied by giving her hand to Diomedes
162 fractions fragments.   **orts** leftovers, fragments   **164 o'ereaten**
i.e., surfeiting through overfeeding, or begnawed, eaten away
165 half attached half as much affected (as it appears)   **168 red**
bloody. (Troilus will manifest his passion now in warlike deeds.)
Mars his Mars'   **169 fancy** love   **172 So . . . weight** to the same extent   **174 casque** headpiece, helmet   **175 spout** waterspout
177 Constringed compressed   **178 dizzy** make dizzy   **181 He'll . . .
concupy** he'll rain ineffectual blows on Diomed's helmet, fighting it
out with Diomed for the sake of his concupiscence (i.e., his lust) or
his concubine (i.e., Cressida)   **187 him** himself   **189 Have with you**
let us go together   **191 castle** fortress, i.e., strong helmet

would croak like a raven; I would bode, I would bode. 195
Patroclus will give me anything for the intelligence of 196
this whore. The parrot will not do more for an almond
than he for a commodious drab. Lechery, lechery, still 198
wars and lechery; nothing else holds fashion. A burn- 199
ing devil take them!   *Exit.* 200

❧

5.3   *Enter Hector, [armed,] and Andromache.*

ANDROMACHE
When was my lord so much ungently tempered
To stop his ears against admonishment?
Unarm, unarm, and do not fight today.
HECTOR
You train me to offend you. Get you in.   4
By all the everlasting gods, I'll go!
ANDROMACHE
My dreams will, sure, prove ominous to the day.   6
HECTOR
No more, I say.

          Enter Cassandra.

CASSANDRA   Where is my brother Hector?
ANDROMACHE
Here, sister, armed, and bloody in intent.
Consort with me in loud and dear petition;   9
Pursue we him on knees. For I have dreamt
Of bloody turbulence, and this whole night
Hath nothing been but shapes and forms of
     slaughter.
CASSANDRA
O, 'tis true.
HECTOR   Ho! Bid my trumpet sound.
CASSANDRA
No notes of sally, for the heavens, sweet brother.   14
HECTOR
Begone, I say. The gods have heard me swear.
CASSANDRA
The gods are deaf to hot and peevish vows.   16
They are polluted offerings, more abhorred
Than spotted livers in the sacrifice.   18
ANDROMACHE
O, be persuaded! Do not count it holy
To hurt by being just. It is as lawful,
For we would give much, to use violent thefts,   21
And rob in the behalf of charity.
CASSANDRA
It is the purpose that makes strong the vow,
But vows to every purpose must not hold.   24
Unarm, sweet Hector.

HECTOR   Hold you still, I say.
Mine honor keeps the weather of my fate.   26
Life every man holds dear, but the dear man   27
Holds honor far more precious-dear than life.

          Enter Troilus.

How now, young man, mean'st thou to fight today?
ANDROMACHE
Cassandra, call my father to persuade.   30

                              Exit Cassandra.
HECTOR
No, faith, young Troilus, doff thy harness, youth;   31
I am today i' the vein of chivalry.
Let grow thy sinews till their knots be strong,
And tempt not yet the brushes of the war.   34
Unarm thee, go, and doubt thou not, brave boy,
I'll stand today for thee and me and Troy.
TROILUS
Brother, you have a vice of mercy in you,
Which better fits a lion than a man.   38
HECTOR
What vice is that? Good Troilus, chide me for it.
TROILUS
When many times the captive Grecian falls,   40
Even in the fan and wind of your fair sword,
You bid them rise and live.
HECTOR
O, 'tis fair play.
TROILUS   Fool's play, by heaven, Hector.
HECTOR
How now, how now?
TROILUS   For th' love of all the gods,
Let's leave the hermit Pity with our mothers,
And when we have our armors buckled on,
The venomed vengeance ride upon our swords,
Spur them to ruthful work, rein them from ruth.   48
HECTOR
Fie, savage, fie!
TROILUS   Hector, then 'tis wars.   49
HECTOR
Troilus, I would not have you fight today.
TROILUS   Who should withhold me?
Not fate, obedience, nor the hand of Mars
Beck'ning with fiery truncheon my retire,   53
Not Priamus and Hecuba on knees,
Their eyes o'ergallèd with recourse of tears,   55
Nor you, my brother, with your true sword drawn
Opposed to hinder me, should stop my way,
But by my ruin.

          Enter Priam and Cassandra.

---

195 bode warn, prognosticate   **196 intelligence of** information about
198 commodious drab accommodating harlot   **199–200 A burning
devil** i.e., venereal disease
5.3. Location: Troy. The palace.
4 train tempt, induce   **6 ominous to** prophetic in respect of   **9 dear**
ardent   **14 sally** sallying, going forth to battle.   **for the heavens** for
heaven's sake   **16 peevish** headstrong   **18 spotted** tainted and hence
a bad omen   **21 For** because.   **would give** want to give   **24 vows
. . . hold** not every vow must be held sacred (since not all purposes
are valid)

26 keeps the weather of keeps to the windward side of, takes precedence over   **27 dear man** worthy man, man of nobility   **30 father** father-in-law, i.e., Priam   **31 doff thy harness** take off your armor
34 tempt attempt, assay.   **brushes** hostile encounters   **38 better fits a
lion** (Lions were thought to be merciful to submissive prey.)   **40 captive** overpowered in battle, wretched   **48 ruthful** lamentable, i.e.,
causing lamentation.   **ruth** pity, mercy   **49 then 'tis wars** i.e., war is
like that. (Troilus expresses his determination to fight.)   **53 truncheon**
staff of office.   **retire** withdrawal   **55 o'ergallèd** inflamed.   **recourse**
flowing down repeatedly

CASSANDRA
Lay hold upon him, Priam, hold him fast;
He is thy crutch. Now if thou loose thy stay,   60
Thou on him leaning, and all Troy on thee,
Fall all together.
PRIAM   Come, Hector, come. Go back.
Thy wife hath dreamt, thy mother hath had visions,
Cassandra doth foresee, and I myself
Am like a prophet suddenly enrapt   65
To tell thee that this day is ominous.
Therefore, come back.
HECTOR   Aeneas is afield,
And I do stand engaged to many Greeks,
Even in the faith of valor, to appear   69
This morning to them.
PRIAM   Ay, but thou shalt not go.
HECTOR   I must not break my faith.
You know me dutiful; therefore, dear sir,
Let me not shame respect, but give me leave   73
To take that course by your consent and voice
Which you do here forbid me, royal Priam.
CASSANDRA
O Priam, yield not to him!
ANDROMACHE   Do not, dear Father.
HECTOR
Andromache, I am offended with you.
Upon the love you bear me, get you in.
                                                    Exit Andromache.
TROILUS
This foolish, dreaming, superstitious girl
Makes all these bodements.
CASSANDRA   O, farewell, dear Hector! 80
Look how thou diest! Look how thy eye turns pale!
Look how thy wounds do bleed at many vents!
Hark, how Troy roars, how Hecuba cries out,
How poor Andromache shrills her dolors forth!   84
Behold, distraction, frenzy, and amazement,
Like witless antics, one another meet,   86
And all cry, "Hector! Hector's dead! O Hector!"
TROILUS   Away! away!
CASSANDRA
Farewell. Yet soft! Hector, I take my leave.   89
Thou dost thyself and all our Troy deceive.   *Exit.*
HECTOR
You are amazed, my liege, at her exclaim.   91
Go in and cheer the town. We'll forth and fight,
Do deeds of praise, and tell you them at night.
PRIAM
Farewell. The gods with safety stand about thee!
               [*Exeunt Priam and Hector separately.*] *Alarum.*
TROILUS
They are at it, hark! Proud Diomed, believe,
I come to lose my arm, or win my sleeve.

                    Enter Pandarus.

PANDARUS   Do you hear, my lord? Do you hear?
TROILUS   What now?
PANDARUS   Here's a letter come from yond poor girl.
                                              [*He gives a letter.*]
TROILUS   Let me read.
PANDARUS   A whoreson phthisic, a whoreson rascally 101
phthisic so troubles me, and the foolish fortune of this
girl, and what one thing, what another, that I shall
leave you one o' these days. And I have a rheum in 104
mine eyes, too, and such an ache in my bones that,
unless a man were cursed, I cannot tell what to think
on 't.—What says she there?
TROILUS
Words, words, mere words, no matter from the
    heart;
Th' effect doth operate another way.   109
                    [*He tears the letter and tosses it away.*]
Go, wind, to wind! There turn and change together. 110
My love with words and errors still she feeds,   111
But edifies another with her deeds.   *Exeunt.* 112

5.4   *Alarum. Enter Thersites. Excursions.*

THERSITES   Now they are clapper-clawing one another. 1
I'll go look on. That dissembling abominable varlet,
Diomed, has got that same scurvy doting foolish
young knave's sleeve of Troy there in his helm. I
would fain see them meet, that that same young
Trojan ass that loves the whore there might send that
Greekish whoremasterly villain with the sleeve back to
the dissembling luxurious drab, of a sleeveless errand. 8
O' th' other side, the policy of those crafty swearing
rascals—that stale old mouse-eaten dry cheese,
Nestor, and that same dog-fox, Ulysses—is proved
not worth a blackberry. They set me up, in policy, 12
that mongrel cur, Ajax, against that dog of as bad a
kind, Achilles. And now is the cur Ajax prouder than
the cur Achilles, and will not arm today, whereupon
the Grecians began to proclaim barbarism, and policy 16
grows into an ill opinion.

          Enter Diomedes, and Troilus [following].

Soft! Here comes Sleeve, and t'other.
TROILUS
Fly not, for shouldst thou take the River Styx, 19
I would swim after.

60 loose thy stay let go your prop   **65 enrapt** carried away, inspired
69 the faith of valor a warrior's honor   **73 shame respect** i.e., violate
my filial duty   **80 Makes** causes.   **bodements** omens of ill fortune
84 shrills her dolors wails her grief   **86 antics** fools   **89 soft** i.e.,
gently; wait   **91 amazed** dumbstruck.   **exclaim** outcry

101 phthisic consumptive cough   **104 rheum** watery discharge
109 Th' effect . . . way i.e., her actions belie her words   **110 Go,
wind, to wind** go, empty words, to the air   **111 errors** deceits
112 s.d. Exeunt (In the Folio version, Pandarus is angrily dismissed at
this point using the lines printed by the Quarto at 5.10.32–34.)
5.4. Location: Between Troy and the Greek camp. The battlefield is
the setting for the rest of the play.
s.d. Excursions sorties or issuings forth of soldiers   **1 clapper-clawing**
mauling, thrashing   **8 luxurious drab** lecherous slut.   **sleeveless** futile
12 set me set. (*Me* is used colloquially.)   **policy** craftiness   **16 proclaim barbarism** set up ignorance in place of authority; they will be
governed by *policy* or statecraft no longer   **19 take** enter (by way of
escape).   **Styx** river of the underworld

DIOMEDES   Thou dost miscall retire.   20
I do not fly, but advantageous care   21
Withdrew me from the odds of multitude.   22
Have at thee!   [*They fight.*]
THERSITES   Hold thy whore, Grecian!—Now for thy
whore, Trojan!—Now the sleeve, now the sleeve!
                    [*Exeunt Troilus and Diomedes, fighting.*]

Enter Hector.

HECTOR
What art thou, Greek? Art thou for Hector's match?
Art thou of blood and honor?   27
THERSITES   No, no, I am a rascal, a scurvy railing knave,
a very filthy rogue.
HECTOR   I do believe thee. Live.   [*Exit.*]
THERSITES   God-a-mercy, that thou wilt believe me; but   31
a plague break thy neck for frighting me! What's become of the wenching rogues? I think they have swallowed one another. I would laugh at that miracle—
yet, in a sort, lechery eats itself. I'll seek them.   *Exit.* 35

5.5   *Enter Diomedes and Servant.*

DIOMEDES
Go, go, my servant, take thou Troilus' horse;
Present the fair steed to my lady Cressid.
Fellow, commend my service to her beauty;
Tell her I have chastised the amorous Trojan
And am her knight by proof.
SERVANT   I go, my lord.   [*Exit.*] 5

Enter Agamemnon.

AGAMEMNON
Renew, renew! The fierce Polydamas   6
Hath beat down Menon; bastard Margareton
Hath Doreus prisoner,
And stands colossus-wise, waving his beam   9
Upon the pashèd corpses of the kings   10
Epistrophus and Cedius; Polyxenes is slain,
Amphimachus and Thoas deadly hurt,
Patroclus ta'en or slain, and Palamedes
Sore hurt and bruised. The dreadful Sagittary   14
Appals our numbers. Haste we, Diomed,   15
To reinforcement, or we perish all.

Enter Nestor [and soldiers].

NESTOR
Go, bear Patroclus' body to Achilles,

And bid the snail-paced Ajax arm for shame.
                          [*Exeunt some.*]
There is a thousand Hectors in the field.
Now here he fights on Galathe his horse,
And there lacks work; anon he's there afoot,
And there they fly or die, like scalèd schools   22
Before the belching whale; then is he yonder,
And there the strawy Greeks, ripe for his edge,   24
Fall down before him, like the mower's swath.
Here, there, and everywhere he leaves and takes,   26
Dexterity so obeying appetite
That what he will he does, and does so much
That proof is called impossibility.   29

Enter Ulysses.

ULYSSES
O, courage, courage, princes! Great Achilles
Is arming, weeping, cursing, vowing vengeance.
Patroclus' wounds have roused his drowsy blood,
Together with his mangled Myrmidons,   33
That noseless, handless, hacked and chipped, come
   to him,
Crying on Hector. Ajax hath lost a friend   35
And foams at mouth, and he is armed and at it,
Roaring for Troilus, who hath done today
Mad and fantastic execution,   38
Engaging and redeeming of himself   39
With such a careless force and forceless care   40
As if that luck, in very spite of cunning,   41
Bade him win all.   42

Enter Ajax.

AJAX
Troilus! Thou coward Troilus!   *Exit.*
DIOMEDES   Ay, there, there.   *Exit.*
NESTOR
So, so, we draw together.

Enter Achilles.

ACHILLES   Where is this Hector?   44
Come, come, thou boy-queller, show thy face!   45
Know what it is to meet Achilles angry.
Hector! Where's Hector? I will none but Hector.
                          Exit [with others].

5.6   *Enter Ajax.*

AJAX
Troilus, thou coward Troilus, show thy head!

---

20 miscall retire call my tactical withdrawal by the wrong name of
flight   **21–22 advantageous . . . multitude** desire for better military
advantage prompted me to withdraw from the general melee, where I
faced heavy odds   **27 blood** noble blood   **31 God-a-mercy** thank
God, thanks   **35 in a sort** in a way
5.5. Location: As before; the battle continues.
5 by proof by proof of arms   **6 Renew** get ready to attack again
9 colossus-wise like the Colossus (the great bronze statue of Apollo at
Rhodes, one of the seven wonders of the ancient world).   **beam**
lance   **10 pashèd** battered   **14 Sagittary** (Literally, the archer; a centaur, i.e., a monster half man, half horse, who according to medieval
legends fought in the Trojan War against the Greeks.)   **15 Appals
our numbers** dismays our troops

22 scalèd schools scattering schools of scaly fish   **24 strawy** like
straw ready for mowing.   **his edge** the edge of his sword   **26 leaves
and takes** spares and slays   **29 proof** fact, accomplished deed
33 Myrmidons soldiers of Thessaly (whom Achilles led to Troy)
35 Crying on complaining of, exclaiming against   **38 execution** deeds
39–42 Engaging . . . all committing himself to battle and emerging
unhurt with such nonchalant use of strength and effortless self-defense
as if Fortune herself cheered him on to victory, in defiance of (his enemies') skill in arms   **44 we draw together** i.e., at last we Greeks are
pulling together, with Ajax and Achilles engaged to fight   **45 boy-
queller** boy killer, i.e., slayer of Patroclus
5.6. Location: As before; the battle continues.

Enter Diomedes.

DIOMEDES
Troilus, I say! Where's Troilus?

AJAX   What wouldst thou?

DIOMEDES   I would correct him.

AJAX
Were I the general, thou shouldst have my office
Ere that correction.—Troilus, I say! What, Troilus!   5

Enter Troilus.

TROILUS
O traitor Diomed! Turn thy false face, thou traitor,
And pay the life thou owest me for my horse!

DIOMEDES   Ha, art thou there?

AJAX
I'll fight with him alone. Stand, Diomed.   9

DIOMEDES
He is my prize. I will not look upon.   10

TROILUS
Come, both you cogging Greeks, have at you both!   11
     Exit Troilus [with Ajax and Diomedes, fighting].

Enter Hector.

HECTOR
Yea, Troilus? O, well fought, my youngest brother!

Enter Achilles.

ACHILLES
Now do I see thee. Ha! Have at thee, Hector!
          [They fight; Achilles tires.]

HECTOR   Pause, if thou wilt.

ACHILLES
I do disdain thy courtesy, proud Trojan.
Be happy that my arms are out of use.
My rest and negligence befriends thee now,
But thou anon shalt hear of me again;
Till when, go seek thy fortune.   *Exit.*

HECTOR   Fare thee well.
I would have been much more a fresher man,
Had I expected thee.

Enter Troilus.

          How now, my brother!

TROILUS
Ajax hath ta'en Aeneas. Shall it be?
No, by the flame of yonder glorious heaven,
He shall not carry him. I'll be ta'en too,   24
Or bring him off. Fate, hear me what I say!   25
I reck not though thou end my life today.   *Exit.* 26

Enter one in armor.

HECTOR
Stand, stand, thou Greek! Thou art a goodly mark.   27
No? Wilt thou not? I like thy armor well;
I'll frush it and unlock the rivets all,   29

5 **Ere that correction** i.e., sooner than take from me the privilege of chastising Troilus   9 **Stand** i.e., stand aside   10 **look upon** remain an onlooker   11 **cogging** deceitful   24 **carry him** i.e., into captivity   25 **bring him off** rescue him   26 **reck** care   27 **mark** target   29 **frush** bruise, smash

But I'll be master of it. [*Exit one in armor.*] Wilt thou
   not, beast, abide?
Why then, fly on. I'll hunt thee for thy hide.   31
               Exit [in pursuit].

5.7   *Enter Achilles, with Myrmidons.*

ACHILLES
Come here about me, you my Myrmidons;
Mark what I say. Attend me where I wheel.   2
Strike not a stroke, but keep yourselves in breath,   3
And when I have the bloody Hector found,
Empale him with your weapons round about;   5
In fellest manner execute your arms.   6
Follow me, sirs, and my proceedings eye.   7
It is decreed Hector the great must die.   *Exeunt.*

Enter Thersites; Menelaus and Paris [fighting].

THERSITES   The cuckold and the cuckold maker are at it.
Now, bull! Now, dog! 'Loo, Paris, 'loo! Now my dou- 10
ble-horned Spartan! 'Loo, Paris, 'loo! The bull has the 11
game. Ware horns, ho!   12
         Exeunt Paris and Menelaus.

Enter Bastard [Margareton].

MARGARETON   Turn, slave, and fight.

THERSITES   What art thou?

MARGARETON   A bastard son of Priam's.

THERSITES   I am a bastard too; I love bastards. I am bastard begot, bastard instructed, bastard in mind, bastard in valor, in everything illegitimate. One bear will
not bite another, and wherefore should one bastard?
Take heed, the quarrel's most ominous to us. If the
son of a whore fight for a whore, he tempts judgment.
Farewell, bastard.   *[Exit.]*

MARGARETON   The devil take thee, coward!   *Exit.*

5.8   *Enter Hector, [dragging the one in armor he has slain].*

HECTOR
Most putrefièd core, so fair without,   1
Thy goodly armor thus hath cost thy life.
Now is my day's work done. I'll take good breath.
Rest, sword; thou hast thy fill of blood and death.
          [He disarms.]

Enter Achilles and his Myrmidons.

5.7. Location: As before; the battle continues.
2 **wheel** execute a turning maneuver   3 **in breath** in readiness   5 **Empale** fence   6 **fellest** fiercest.   **execute your arms** bring your weapons into operation   7 **my proceedings eye** watch what I do   10 **bull** i.e., Menelaus, a cuckold, a horned creature.   **'Loo** (A cry to incite a dog against the bull in the sport of bullbaiting in Shakespeare's England.)
11–12 has the game wins   12 **Ware** beware
5.8. Location: As before; the battle continues.
1 **core** i.e., the body of the Greek from whom Hector has taken the armor

ACHILLES
  Look, Hector, how the sun begins to set,
  How ugly night comes breathing at his heels.
  Even with the vail and dark'ning of the sun,   7
  To close the day up, Hector's life is done.
HECTOR
  I am unarmed. Forgo this vantage, Greek.
ACHILLES
  Strike, fellows, strike! This is the man I seek.
                      [*They fall upon Hector and kill him.*]
  So, Ilium, fall thou! Now, Troy, sink down!
  Here lies thy heart, thy sinews, and thy bone.
  On, Myrmidons, and cry you all amain,   13
  "Achilles hath the mighty Hector slain."
                                      Retreat [*sounded*].
  Hark! A retire upon our Grecian part.   15
MYRMIDON
  The Trojans trumpets sound the like, my lord.
ACHILLES
  The dragon wing of night o'erspreads the earth,
  And, stickler-like, the armies separates.   18
  My half-supped sword, that frankly would have fed,   19
  Pleased with this dainty bait, thus goes to bed.   20
                          [*He sheathes his sword.*]
  Come, tie his body to my horse's tail.
  Along the field I will the Trojan trail.
                          Exeunt [*with Hector's body*].

5.9 *Sound retreat. Enter Agamemnon, Ajax,*
         Menelaus, Nestor, Diomedes, and the rest,
         marching. Shout [*within*].

AGAMEMNON   Hark! Hark! What shout is that?
NESTOR   Peace, drums!
SOLDIERS   (*within*)
  Achilles! Achilles! Hector's slain! Achilles!
DIOMEDES
  The bruit is, Hector's slain, and by Achilles.   4
AJAX
  If it be so, yet bragless let it be;   5
  Great Hector was a man as good as he.
AGAMEMNON
  March patiently along. Let one be sent
  To pray Achilles see us at our tent.
  If in his death the gods have us befriended,
  Great Troy is ours, and our sharp wars are ended.
                                          Exeunt.

5.10 *Enter Aeneas, Paris, Antenor, and Deiphobus.*

AENEAS
  Stand, ho! Yet are we masters of the field.   1

7 **vail** going down   13 **amain** with all your might   15 **retire** call to
retreat   18 **stickler-like** like a referee   19 **frankly** freely   20 **dainty
bait** tasty snack
5.9. Location: The battlefield; the battle has concluded.
4 **bruit** rumor, noise   5 **bragless** without boasting
5.10. Location: The battlefield after the battle.
1 **Yet** still

  Never go home; here starve we out the night.   2
                      Enter Troilus.
TROILUS
  Hector is slain.
ALL   Hector! The gods forbid!
TROILUS
  He's dead, and at the murderer's horse's tail,
  In beastly sort, dragged through the shameful field.
  Frown on, you heavens, effect your rage with speed!
  Sit, gods, upon your thrones and smite at Troy!
  I say, at once: let your brief plagues be mercy,   8
  And linger not our sure destructions on!   9
AENEAS
  My lord, you do discomfort all the host.   10
TROILUS
  You understand me not that tell me so.
  I do not speak of flight, of fear of death,   12
  But dare all imminence that gods and men   13
  Address their dangers in. Hector is gone.   14
  Who shall tell Priam so, or Hecuba?
  Let him that will a screech owl aye be called
  Go in to Troy, and say their Hector's dead.
  There is a word will Priam turn to stone,
  Make wells and Niobes of the maids and wives,   19
  Cold statues of the youth, and, in a word,
  Scare Troy out of itself. But march away.
  Hector is dead. There is no more to say.
  Stay yet.—You vile abominable tents,
  Thus proudly pitched upon our Phrygian plains,
  Let Titan rise as early as he dare,   25
  I'll through and through you! And, thou great-sized
    coward,   26
  No space of earth shall sunder our two hates.   27
  I'll haunt thee like a wicked conscience still,
  That moldeth goblins swift as frenzy's thoughts.
  Strike a free march! To Troy with comfort go.   30
  Hope of revenge shall hide our inward woe.
                          [*They proceed to march away.*]

                      Enter Pandarus.

PANDARUS [*to Troilus*]   But hear you, hear you!
TROILUS
  Hence, broker-lackey! Ignomy and shame   33
  Pursue thy life, and live aye with thy name!
                          Exeunt all but Pandarus.
PANDARUS   A goodly medicine for my aching bones! O
  world, world, world! Thus is the poor agent despised.

2 **starve we out** let us endure, outlast   8 **let . . . mercy** let your afflictions end us quickly, be mercifully brief   9 **linger** draw out, protract   10 **discomfort** discourage.   **host** army   12 **of flight** merely of
disordered retreat   13 **imminence** impending evils, threats of imminent disaster   14 **Address . . . in** prepare to endanger me with
19 **Niobes** (Niobe boasted that her six sons and six daughters made
her superior to Latona, mother of Apollo and Diana, for which she
was punished by seeing them put to death by the arrows of these two
deities. While weeping, she was changed into a stone, but her tears
continued to flow from the rock.)   25 **Titan** i.e., Helios, the sun-god,
one of the Titans   26 **coward** i.e., Achilles, cowardly slayer of Hector
27 **sunder** keep apart   30 **free** unregimented, quick   33 **Ignomy**
ignominy

O traitors and bawds, how earnestly are you set
a-work, and how ill requited! Why should our endeavor be so desired and the performance so loathed?
What verse for it? What instance for it? Let me see: 40

Full merrily the humble-bee doth sing,   41
Till he hath lost his honey and his sting;
And being once subdued in armèd tail,   43
Sweet honey and sweet notes together fail.

Good traders in the flesh, set this in your painted   45
cloths: 46
As many as be here of Pandar's hall,   47
Your eyes, half out, weep out at Pandar's fall;   48
Or if you cannot weep, yet give some groans,
Though not for me, yet for your aching bones.   50
Brethren and sisters of the hold-door trade,   51
Some two months hence my will shall here be
    made.
It should be now, but that my fear is this:
Some gallèd goose of Winchester would hiss.   54
Till then I'll sweat and seek about for eases,   55
And at that time bequeath you my diseases.   [*Exit.*]

40 instance illustrative example   **41 humble-bee** bumblebee   **43 being . . . tail** having lost its sting (much as a lover is emptied and perhaps infected in the sexual act)   **45–46 painted cloths** cheap wall
hangings worked or painted with scenes and mottoes   **47 hall** fraternity   **48 half out** i.e., already half destroyed by venereal disease
50 aching bones (A symptom of venereal disease.)   **51 hold-door
trade** i.e., brothel keeping   **54 gallèd . . . Winchester** i.e., a prostitute having venereal disease; so called because the brothels of Southwark were under the jurisdiction of the Bishop of Winchester
55 sweat (A common treatment for venereal disease.)

The Histories

The First Part of King Henry the Sixth

Throughout much of the fifteenth century, England had suffered the ravages of civil war. From the long struggles between the Lancastrians and the Yorkists, the so-called Wars of the Roses, the country had emerged in 1485 shaken but united at last under the strong rule of the Tudors. To Elizabethans, this period of civil war was still a recent event that had tested and almost destroyed England's nationhood. They were, moreover, still troubled by political and dynastic uncertainties of their own. Queen Elizabeth, granddaughter of the first Tudor king, Henry VII, was unmarried and aging, and her successor unchosen. Her Catholic enemies at home and abroad plotted a return to the ancient faith renounced by Henry VIII in his reformation of the church. Spain had attempted an invasion of England with the great Armada in 1588, perhaps two years before Shakespeare began writing his *Henry VI* plays. It was in such an era of crisis and patriotic excitement that the *Henry VI* plays first appeared. Indeed, they helped to establish the vogue of the English history play, which was to flourish throughout the 1590s. England's civil wars could be studied and analyzed now, from a perspective of over one hundred years later, and perhaps could provide a key to the present time. At hand was a new edition of Raphael Holinshed's *Chronicles,* 1587, along with the earlier chronicle writings of Robert Fabyan, John Stow, and Richard Grafton, as well as Edward Hall's *Union of the Two Noble and Illustre Families of Lancaster and York,* John Foxe's *Acts and Monuments of Martyrs,* and *A Mirror for Magistrates.*

How had these wars begun? Elizabethans searched for an answer, not in economic or social terms, but in religious and moral ones. According to a traditional and government-sponsored explanation, reflected to a large extent (though with many contradictions) in the chronicles of Edward Hall, and familiar to Shakespeare whether he accepted it fully or not, the Wars of the Roses were a manifestation of God's wrath, a divine punishment inflicted on the English people for their wayward behavior. The people and their rulers had brought civil war on themselves by self-serving ambition, arrogance, and disloyalty. King Henry VI's grandfather, Henry IV, had come to the throne in 1399 by deposing and then executing his own cousin, Richard II (a momentous event, to be portrayed by Shakespeare in a later history play). Henry VI was himself an infant when he succeeded to the throne in 1422, owing to the untimely death of his father, Henry V. Too young at first to rule and never blessed with his father's ability to act decisively, Henry VI was utterly unable to halt the struggle for power that developed among members of his large but discordant family. Ultimately, his very title to the throne was challenged by his kinsman Richard Plantagenet, Duke of York, who claimed to be rightful king by virtue of his descent from Henry IV's uncle Lionel, Duke of Clarence. The Yorkist faction marched to battle against Henry VI's Lancastrian faction (so named because for generations the family had been possessors of the dukedom of Lancaster), and the war was on.

This official view was never wholly endorsed by the chroniclers and certainly not by Shakespeare. Edward Hall's overall scheme is undeniably providential, and yet, as a historian, he presents a multiplicity of detail that cumulatively raises difficult issues of interpretation. At the same time, the providential view made good propaganda for the Tudor regime, and as such it gave widespread currency to the theory of God's anger toward a rebellious people. The outcome of the war seemed to confirm this pattern: universal devastation and the deaths of those most responsible for the conflict led eventually, according to the theory, to appeasement of God's anger and a restoration of order. Richard Plantagenet died in the struggle, as did Henry VI, Henry's son Edward, and much of the English nobility. Richard's son Edward survived to become Edward IV, but his manner of obtaining the throne was so manifestly offensive to Providence that (according to the theory) he suffered a retributive death at the hands of an angry God and was succeeded by his younger brother, Richard III. This last Yorkist ruler governed only two years, 1483–1485, and it was through Richard's insane vengeance that God finally settled all his scores against the wayward English people. Having completed this purgation, God chose as his instrument of a new order Henry Tudor, Earl of Richmond, Henry VII. Although Henry's return to England and defeat of Richard at the battle of Bosworth Field might outwardly resemble Henry IV's seizure of power from Richard II, the difference was crucial to Tudor apologists. Richard III had to be seen, from the Tudor point of view, not as a flawed legitimate monarch, but as a mad usurper and tyrant; his defeat was not the disobedient act of one man but a rising up of the entire English nation at the prompting of divine command. Henry VII's accession to power was officially viewed not as a precedent for further rebellion but as a manifestation of divine will without parallel in human history.

The essence of this providential view of events was that divine retribution and eventual reconciliation revealed themselves in the history of the war. The theory, of course, served the interests of the Tudor state and was in part a propaganda weapon calculatedly employed by the ruling class.

Shakespeare's commitment to it should not be taken for granted, and indeed a number of recent studies have expressed a profound skepticism toward the theory as the basis of Shakespeare's dramaturgy. Especially in his later tetralogy, or four-play series, from *Richard II* to *Henry V*, Shakespeare reveals considerably more interest in the clash of personalities than in patterns of divine retribution. Shakespeare does not endorse the orthodox view that Bolingbroke's seizure of the throne is a violation of divine purpose for which he and England must be humbled; instead, Shakespeare portrays the issues as many-sided and subject to varying interpretations.

Throughout his history plays, indeed, Shakespeare avoids expressing the Tudor providential view of recent history through didactic narrators or chorus figures who might seem to represent the point of view of the entire plays; instead, he puts this providential interpretation into the mouths of avowedly biased and self-interested characters whose motives and testimony the audience can then evaluate as it sees fit. In *1 Henry VI*, for example, the most detailed exposition of the providential historical view is given to Mortimer (2.5), whose interpretation, though given special authority by the fact that a dying man is speaking, is self-interestedly consistent with his own frustrated claim to the English throne. His nephew, Richard Plantagenet, who of course endorses the providential logic of Mortimer's speech, is portrayed as consumed with ambition for the crown. In Shakespeare's depiction of the Lancastrian-Yorkist conflict, neither side maintains a consistent ideological position but, instead, shifts argument as required by the expediency of the moment. Although in his earlier tetralogy from *1 Henry VI* to *Richard III* Shakespeare does sometimes allow his contending characters to hearken back to the deposition of Richard II in order to explain the misfortunes of England's civil wars, those characters speak from self-interest and interpret history to their own advantage.

The individual plays of this earlier tetralogy, if seen or read separately, do not consistently comfort the spectator or reader with an assurance that all is working out according to God's plan. Even if a providential interpretation might argue in retrospect that the disasters afflicting England in the fifteenth century were an essential part of God's plan, the events themselves, seen from the immediate perspective of the moment, provide little comfort. At the end of *1 Henry VI*, King Henry has surrendered to a disastrous marriage and has lost most of France; at the end of *2 Henry VI*, the good Duke Humphrey of Gloucester is dead and his opportunistic political enemies are about to take King Henry off of his throne. The hostilities of Lancaster and York end at the conclusion of *3 Henry VI*, to be sure, but prospects for a stable peace are doubtful in view of Richard of Gloucester's baleful presence. The reciprocity of slaughter visited on both sides appears to stem as much from humanity's insane desire for vengeance as from God's evening of the score. Only in

Richard III do we retroactively see a pattern of divine anger, retribution, and eventual appeasement that can then be applied to the tetralogy as a continuous narrative. E. M. W. Tillyard's argument for a providential reading of these plays (in his *Shakespeare's History Plays*, 1944) is based not coincidentally on a view of the tetralogy as a cohesive whole. What about the playgoers who saw the plays one at a time? The plays, so far as we know, were written and produced singly and were never staged in a continuous series. Even though the tetralogy as a whole may harmonize in part with the chronicles of Edward Hall and others, written to glorify the Tudor state and to give thanks for its having ended the prolonged anarchy of the fifteenth century, we can see that Shakespeare is no apologist for the Tudor state. He gives expression to a widely felt distrust of political chaos. A pattern of divine wrath and appeasement, seen retrospectively in *Richard III*, at last provides a causal explanation of England's darkest hour. More immediately, in each individual play, the overriding cosmic irony stressing the gulf between foolish humanity and the inscrutable intentions of Providence offers a potentially stirring conflict of which Shakespeare makes rich use.

Shakespeare wrote his first tetralogy some time between 1589 and 1594. Just how much of this first tetralogy may have been planned out when Shakespeare began work is hard to say. In fact, the very order of composition has long been in dispute. Despite the commonsense pleading of Dr. Johnson that Part Two follows from Part One as a logical consequence, some scholars argue that Part One was composed last. One piece of evidence is that a corrupt version of Part Two was published in quarto version in 1594 as *The First Part of the Contention Betwixt the Two Famous Houses of York and Lancaster* and that a corrupt version of Part Three was published in octavo in 1595 as *The True Tragedy of Richard Duke of York*. Part One had to await publication in the Folio of 1623 and was registered for publication at that time as "The third part of Henry the sixth." It seems odd, moreover, that Parts Two and Three make no mention of Lord Talbot, so prominent in Part One. If, however, as seems likely, the early printed versions of Parts Two and Three were memorial reconstructions without the authority of the official playbook, the claim of Part Two to have been written first may be unsubstantial. The very fact of prior publication of Parts Two and Three could explain why Part One was called "The third part" in 1623. Although Talbot is not mentioned in Parts Two and Three, these texts do recall important aspects of Part One. It is certainly possible that Shakespeare wrote all three parts in normal order.

Equally vexing is the question of authorship. Many Elizabethan plays were written by teams of authors, and Shakespeare might have collaborated with others, especially at the beginning of his career. Perhaps he rewrote older works by such writers as Thomas Nashe, Robert Greene, and Christopher Marlowe. Theories of multiple authorship, once a commonplace of nineteenth-century scholarship and then discounted by much twentieth-century criticism, have recently been argued anew by the editors of the *Oxford Shakespeare* (1986). Yet there is much reason to believe that Shakespeare is essentially the author of the entire *Henry VI* series. Greene's famous resentment toward Shakespeare as the "upstart crow beautified with our feathers" seems more the envy of a lesser talent than the righteous indignation of one who has been plagiarized. The chief criteria used to "disintegrate" the plays into the hands of various supposed contributors are those of taste and style; for example, the low comic scenes of Joan of Arc were long held to be too coarse for Shakespeare's genius. Today most critics see a consistency of view throughout the *Henry VI* plays, despite minor inconsistencies of fact that might be the result of simple error or of using multiple sources, and they find nothing in these plays inimical to Shakespeare's budding genius. This belief confirms the judgment of Heminges and Condell, Shakespeare's fellow actors and editors of the 1623 Folio, who placed all the *Henry VI* plays among Shakespeare's collected works in their historical order.

If Shakespeare was at least chiefly responsible for the *Henry VI* series, he may also have been an important innovator in the new genre of the history play. Only the anonymous *Famous Victories of Henry V* is certainly earlier in dealing with recent English history. There were, to be sure, plays about legendary British history, such as *Gorboduc* or *The Misfortunes of Arthur,* or about far-off lands, such as *Cambises* or Marlowe's *Tamburlaine.* All these plays had explored by analogue political questions fascinating to Elizabethan England, and *Tamburlaine*'s immense success had certainly established a vogue for grand scenes of military conquest. Still, the English history play as a recognizable form came into being with *Henry VI.* The success was evidently tremendous and established Shakespeare as a major playwright.

1 Henry VI, like all the plays in Shakespeare's first tetralogy, comprises a large number of episodes, a sizable cast of characters, and a wide geographical range. The subject is England's loss of French territories because of political division at home. The structure of the play is one of sequential action displayed in great variety and in alternating scenes that are thematically juxtaposed and contrasted with one another. In the rapid shifting back and forth between the English and French court, for example, Shakespeare establishes a paradoxical theme: France triumphs in England's weakness, not in her own strength. The French court is merely one of debased sexual frivolity. The English are naturally superior but are torn apart by internal dissension, by a "jarring discord of nobility," and by a "shouldering of each other in the court" (4.1.188–189) among those attempting to take advantage of Henry VI's weak minority rule and his vulnerable genealogical claim. Two of young Henry's kinsmen jockeying for position are Humphrey, Duke of

Gloucester, and the Bishop of Winchester. Humphrey's intentions are virtuous, but he is unable to prevent the opportunistic scheming of his rival. Winchester, despite his ecclesiastical calling, is a man of evil ambition and corrupt life, wholly intent on destroying the right-minded Gloucester. Shakespeare employs derisive anticlerical humor against Winchester and enlists the Protestant sympathies of his Elizabethan audience against the meddling Catholic Church's attempts to exploit England's weak kingship for its own ulterior purposes.

Even so, the menace threatening England is not seen as a Catholic conspiracy throughout; Winchester is only one opportunist seeking to exploit the political vacillation and factionalism at court. Of greater danger in the long term is Richard Plantagenet, scion of the Yorkist claim. From the start, Shakespeare portrays him as cunning, able to ingratiate himself and bide his time, and ultimately ruthless. In these qualities, he ominously foreshadows his youngest son and namesake, Richard III. In this play, Plantagenet's strategy is to allow England to wear herself down by the various conflicts at court and military losses abroad; once the situation is reduced to anarchy, Plantagenet will be able to move in. The strategy works only too well.

Chief defender of England's military might in France, and eventual victim of the bickering among the English nobility, is Lord Talbot. He is the heroic figure of this play with whom Elizabethan audiences identified. He pleads for political and military unity against the French and demonstrates that with such unity England would be invincible. Talbot is "the terror of the French" (1.4.42), able to hold off a troop of French soldiers with his bare fists, and reputed to twist bars of steel. As the embodiment of chivalry, he delivers a richly deserved rebuke to Sir John Falstaff (historically "Fastolfe," but called "Falstaff" in the Folio text of this play), the cowardly soldier who foreshadows the fat knight of *1 Henry IV.* In *1 Henry VI,* cowardice and honor are rendered in black and white extremes. Talbot is a model general, illustrating all the qualities of great leadership advocated by the textbooks of the age: he is a stirring orator, fearless, witty, and concerned with a proper lasting fame. In the touching scenes with his son, Talbot rises triumphantly above death to become the immortal embodiment of brave soldiership. Yet, even if *1 Henry VI* offers this one important model of rhetoric and arts of leadership put to right use, Talbot's presence nonetheless lends itself more to a profound anxiety about historical events than to a reassuring confidence in divine assistance. Talbot's unnecessary death offers a devastating critique of the weak leadership that has allowed authority in France to be divided among political rivals.

The relations between men and women in this play are also used to create thematic contrasts. Talbot's chief military rival in France is Joan of Arc; and, although many earlier scholars have wanted to deny Shakespeare's authorship of the Joan of Arc scenes, their thematic function is central. As a woman in armor, Joan is the embodiment of the domineering Amazonian woman to whom the effete and self-indulgent dauphin, Charles, weakly capitulates. The sexual roles have been reversed; Venus triumphs over Mars. Joan's role as virgin-warrior, her trafficking in demonology, and her obscenely parodic resemblance to the Virgin Mary all suggest a profound male-oriented ambivalence toward women in positions of authority—including, by implication, Queen Elizabeth. Joan's sexuality is not only demonic but also obsessive in its promiscuity and seeming insatiability. The name by which she is known in France, *la Pucelle*, can mean both "virgin" and "slut." She even attempts to practice her witchcraft (with sexual overtones) on Talbot and his son, but in vain. Talbot's sense of duty never succumbs to Circean voluptuousness. In his encounter with the Countess of Auvergne, Talbot resourcefully outwits another woman who, like Joan, seeks to entrap him. The Countess finally submits to Talbot's courteous but firm authority, thereby re-establishing the traditional relationship of male and female. Talbot stands for every kind of decency and order that ought to prevail but is senselessly destroyed through England's political division.

The last woman introduced in the play, Margaret of Anjou, is another domineering female. Her adulterous relationship with the fleshly Suffolk, and her ascendancy over the weak Henry VI, are to be of fateful consequence in the ensuing plays. Her scenes, although once dismissed as an afterthought, linking *1 Henry VI* with the following plays, in fact recapitulate the motifs of female dominance with great dramatic effect. Young Henry VI is no Talbot; inexperienced in love and highly impressionable, he surrenders to the mere description of a woman he has not even seen and refuses a politically advantageous match arranged by Duke Humphrey in order that he may marry a conniving Frenchwoman without dowry. The marriage also anticipates that of Edward IV (in *3 Henry VI*) to a penniless widow who has caught his roving eye, when Edward could have obtained a handsome dowry and a favorable alliance by marrying the French King's sister-in-law. Such dismal triumphs of passion over reason are emblematic of the general decay among the English aristocracy. Despite Henry's weakness, he is the central character of this play after all, and his enervating surrender in love is a fitting anticlimax with which to end the first installment of England's decline. Events such as these are not necessarily incompatible with providential history in a long-term view, since they can be viewed as the process by which God tests humanity and eventually restores His grace, but in the theater we are left at the end of *1 Henry VI* with an appalling sense of dislocation and loss for which no remedies appear to be at hand.

The First Part of King Henry the Sixth

[*Dramatis Personae*

KING HENRY THE SIXTH
DUKE OF GLOUCESTER, *uncle of the King, and Lord Protector*
DUKE OF BEDFORD, *uncle of the King, and Regent of France*
DUKE OF EXETER, *Thomas Beaufort, great-uncle of the King*
BISHOP OF WINCHESTER, *Henry Beaufort, great-uncle of the King, later* CARDINAL
DUKE OF SOMERSET, *John Beaufort, formerly Earl of Somerset*
RICHARD PLANTAGENET, *son of Richard, late Earl of Cambridge, later* DUKE OF YORK *and Regent of France*
EARL OF WARWICK
EARL OF SALISBURY
EARL OF SUFFOLK, *William de la Pole*
LORD TALBOT, *later Earl of Shrewsbury*
JOHN TALBOT, *his son*
EDMUND MORTIMER
SIR JOHN FALSTAFF
SIR WILLIAM LUCY
SIR WILLIAM GLASDALE
SIR THOMAS GARGRAVE
MAYOR *of London*
WOODVILLE, *Lieutenant of the Tower of London*
VERNON, *of the White Rose or York faction*
BASSET, *of the Red Rose or Lancaster faction*
A LAWYER, *of the York faction*
A PAPAL LEGATE
MESSENGERS
WARDERS *of the Tower of London*
SERVINGMEN
AN OFFICER *serving the Lord Mayor*
A SOLDIER *in Talbot's army*
CAPTAINS
A KEEPER *or Jailer of Mortimer*
WATCH *at the gates of Rouen*

CHARLES, *Dauphin, and afterward King, of France*
REIGNIER, *Duke of Anjou, and titular King of Naples*
MARGARET, *his daughter*
DUKE OF ALENÇON
BASTARD OF ORLEANS
DUKE OF BURGUNDY

GENERAL *of the French forces at Bordeaux*
COUNTESS *of Auvergne*
PORTER *to the Countess*

MASTER GUNNER *of Orleans*
A BOY, *his son*
JOAN LA PUCELLE, *Joan of Arc*
SHEPHERD, *her father*
SERGEANT *of a French detachment*
SENTINEL *of a French detachment*
SOLDIER *with Pucelle at Rouen*
A SCOUT *in the Dauphin's army at Angiers*

English and French Heralds, Soldiers, Officers, Sen-
tinels, Servingmen, Keepers or Jailers, Atten-
dants, the Governor of Paris, Ambassadors,
Fiends attending on La Pucelle

SCENE: *Partly in England, and partly in France*]

1.1   *Dead march. Enter the funeral of King Henry the*
Fifth, attended on by the Duke of Bedford, Regent
of France; the Duke of Gloucester, Protector; the
Duke of Exeter, [the Earl of] Warwick, the Bishop
of Winchester, and the Duke of Somerset, [heralds,
etc.].

BEDFORD
  Hung be the heavens with black! Yield, day, to
    night!   1
  Comets, importing change of times and states,   2
  Brandish your crystal tresses in the sky,   3
  And with them scourge the bad revolting stars   4
  That have consented unto Henry's death—   5
  King Henry the Fifth, too famous to live long!
  England ne'er lost a king of so much worth.
GLOUCESTER
  England ne'er had a king until his time.   8
  Virtue he had, deserving to command.   9
  His brandished sword did blind men with his beams;10
  His arms spread wider than a dragon's wings;
  His sparkling eyes, replete with wrathful fire,
  More dazzled and drove back his enemies
  Than midday sun fierce bent against their faces.
  What should I say? His deeds exceed all speech.
  He ne'er lift up his hand but conquerèd.   16
EXETER
  We mourn in black. Why mourn we not in blood?
  Henry is dead and never shall revive.
  Upon a wooden coffin we attend,
  And death's dishonorable victory
  We with our stately presence glorify,
  Like captives bound to a triumphant car.   22

  What? Shall we curse the planets of mishap   23
  That plotted thus our glory's overthrow?
  Or shall we think the subtle-witted French
  Conjurers and sorcerers, that, afraid of him,
  By magic verses have contrived his end?   27
WINCHESTER
  He was a king blest of the King of kings.
  Unto the French the dreadful Judgment Day
  So dreadful will not be as was his sight.   30
  The battles of the Lord of hosts he fought;
  The Church's prayers made him so prosperous.   32
GLOUCESTER
  The Church? Where is it? Had not churchmen
    prayed,   33
  His thread of life had not so soon decayed.   34
  None do you like but an effeminate prince,   35
  Whom like a schoolboy you may overawe.
WINCHESTER
  Gloucester, whate'er we like, thou art Protector,   37
  And lookest to command the Prince and realm.
  Thy wife is proud. She holdeth thee in awe   39
  More than God or religious churchmen may.
GLOUCESTER
  Name not religion, for thou lov'st the flesh,
  And ne'er throughout the year to church thou go'st
  Except it be to pray against thy foes.
BEDFORD
  Cease, cease these jars and rest your minds in peace! 44
  Let's to the altar. Heralds, wait on us.   45
                              [*They prepare to leave.*]
  Instead of gold we'll offer up our arms,   46
  Since arms avail not now that Henry's dead.
  Posterity, await for wretched years,   48
  When at their mothers' moistened eyes babes shall
    suck,   49
  Our isle be made a nourish of salt tears,   50
  And none but women left to wail the dead.
  Henry the Fifth, thy ghost I invocate: 52
  Prosper this realm; keep it from civil broils;   53
  Combat with adverse planets in the heavens!
  A far more glorious star thy soul will make
  Than Julius Caesar or bright——

              Enter a Messenger.

FIRST MESSENGER
  My honorable lords, health to you all.

1.1. Location: Westminster Abbey.
1 Hung . . . black (A metaphor from the theatrical practice of draping
the "heavens" or roof projecting over the stage in black when a tragedy was to be performed.) **2 importing** foretelling, portending
3 crystal bright, shining. **tresses** hair, i.e., the trail of the comet
4 scourge (as if the tresses were whips). **revolting** rebelling **5 consented unto** conspired to bring about **8 a king** a king in the fullest
sense **9 Virtue** excellence, authority **10 his beams** its beams
16 lift lifted. **but conquerèd** without conquering **22 car** chariot

23 planets of mishap misfortune-causing planets **27 verses** spells
30 his sight the sight of him **32 prosperous** successful **33 prayed**
(with pun on "preyed"; also in line 43) **34 decayed** been destroyed
35 effeminate prince ineffectual, unmanly ruler **37 Protector** head
of state during the king's minority **39 Thy wife is proud** (A reference
to Gloucester's ambitious wife, Eleanor, whose inordinate desire for
greatness is depicted in *2 Henry VI*.) **holdeth . . . awe** overawes you
44 jars discords **45 wait on us** i.e., lead the procession **s.d. They
prepare to leave** (Here or later in the scene, the various members of
the funeral procession not specifically mentioned in the exits at lines
166–177, including Warwick, Somerset, and the heralds, must leave
the stage.) **46 arms** weapons **48 await for** expect **49 When . . .
suck** i.e., when mothers will feed their children with tears only
50 nourish . . . tears i.e., a nurse feeding with tears only **52 invocate** invoke, as one would call on a saint **53 Prosper** make
prosperous

Sad tidings bring I to you out of France,
Of loss, of slaughter, and discomfiture.
Guyenne, Champagne, Rouen, Rheims, Orleans,   60
Paris, Gisors, Poitiers, are all quite lost.

BEDFORD
What sayst thou, man, before dead Henry's corpse?
Speak softly, or the loss of those great towns
Will make him burst his lead and rise from death.   64

GLOUCESTER
Is Paris lost? Is Rouen yielded up?
If Henry were recalled to life again,
These news would cause him once more yield the
    ghost.

EXETER
How were they lost? What treachery was used?

FIRST MESSENGER
No treachery, but want of men and money.   69
Amongst the soldiers this is mutterèd,
That here you maintain several factions,   71
And whilst a field should be dispatched and fought,   72
You are disputing of your generals.   73
One would have lingering wars with little cost;
Another would fly swift, but wanteth wings;   75
A third thinks, without expense at all,
By guileful fair words peace may be obtained.
Awake, awake, English nobility!
Let not sloth dim your honors new-begot.
Cropped are the flower-de-luces in your arms;   80
Of England's coat one half is cut away.   [Exit.]

EXETER
Were our tears wanting to this funeral,   82
These tidings would call forth her flowing tides.   83

BEDFORD
Me they concern; Regent I am of France.   84
Give me my steelèd coat. I'll fight for France.
Away with these disgraceful wailing robes!
Wounds will I lend the French instead of eyes,   87
To weep their intermissive miseries.   88

Enter to them another Messenger, [with letters].

SECOND MESSENGER
Lords, view these letters, full of bad mischance.
France is revolted from the English quite,   90
Except some petty towns of no import.
The Dauphin Charles is crownèd king in Rheims;
The Bastard of Orleans with him is joined;

Reignier, Duke of Anjou, doth take his part;   94
The Duke of Alençon flieth to his side.   *Exit.*

EXETER
The Dauphin crownèd king? All fly to him?   96
O, whither shall we fly from this reproach?   97

GLOUCESTER
We will not fly but to our enemies' throats!   98
Bedford, if thou be slack, I'll fight it out.

BEDFORD
Gloucester, why doubt'st thou of my forwardness?
An army have I mustered in my thoughts,
Wherewith already France is overrun.

Enter another Messenger.

THIRD MESSENGER
My gracious lords, to add to your laments,
Wherewith you now bedew King Henry's hearse,
I must inform you of a dismal fight   105
Betwixt the stout Lord Talbot and the French.   106

WINCHESTER
What? Wherein Talbot overcame, is 't so?

THIRD MESSENGER
O, no! Wherein Lord Talbot was o'erthrown.
The circumstance I'll tell you more at large.   109
The tenth of August last, this dreadful lord,   110
Retiring from the siege of Orleans,
Having full scarce six thousand in his troop,   112
By three-and-twenty thousand of the French
Was round encompassèd and set upon.   114
No leisure had he to enrank his men.   115
He wanted pikes to set before his archers,   116
Instead whereof sharp stakes plucked out of hedges
They pitchèd in the ground confusedly,
To keep the horsemen off from breaking in.
More than three hours the fight continuèd,
Where valiant Talbot above human thought   121
Enacted wonders with his sword and lance.
Hundreds he sent to hell, and none durst stand
    him;   123
Here, there, and everywhere, enraged he slew.
The French exclaimed the devil was in arms;
All the whole army stood agazed on him.   126
His soldiers, spying his undaunted spirit,
"A Talbot! a Talbot!" crièd out amain   128
And rushed into the bowels of the battle.
Here had the conquest fully been sealed up   130
If Sir John Falstaff had not played the coward.   131
He, being in the vaward, placed behind   132

60 Champagne Compiègne **64 lead** leaden inner coffin or wrapping, inside the wooden coffin (line 19) **69 want** lack **71 several** separate (and divisive) **72 field** (1) battle (2) combat force **73 of** about **75 wanteth** lacks **80 Cropped** plucked. **flower-de-luces** the *fleur-de-lis*, or iris, national emblem of France. (According to the Treaty of Troyes, 1420, the crown of France was ceded to England but was nominally to belong to the French king, Charles VI, as long as he lived. Henry V's title was designated "King of England and Heir of France." At his death, this title passed to Henry VI, but, within two months after this took place, Charles VI died and his son Charles VII was proclaimed king. The loss of the French crown would deprive the English king of the right to display the *fleur-de-lis* in his coat of arms.) **82 wanting** lacking **83 her** i.e., England's **84 Regent** ruler in the king's absence **87–88 Wounds . . . weep** i.e., I'll make the French shed blood instead of weep tears **88 intermissive** intermittent but now to be resumed **90 quite** entirely

94 Reignier René **96–97 fly . . . fly** flock . . . flee **98 fly** (Gloucester turns the word to mean "fly at their throats.") **105 dismal** savage, terrible **106 stout** brave **109 circumstance** particulars. **at large** in full detail **110 dreadful** to be dreaded **112 full scarce** scarce full, barely **114 round encompassèd** surrounded **115 enrank** draw up in battle array **116 wanted pikes** lacked iron-bound stakes, sharpened at the ends and set in the ground in front of archers as protection against cavalry **121 above human thought** beyond imagining **123 stand him** stand up against him **126 agazed on** astounded at **128 A Talbot** rally to Talbot. **amain** with full force **130 sealed up** completed **131 Falstaff** ("Fastolfe" in the chronicles, but the Shakespearean spelling used here shows us the origin of the name used in the *Henry IV* plays.) **132 vaward** vanguard

With purpose to relieve and follow them,
Cowardly fled, not having struck one stroke.
Hence grew the general wrack and massacre.   135
Enclosèd were they with their enemies.   136
A base Walloon, to win the Dauphin's grace,   137
Thrust Talbot with a spear into the back,
Whom all France with their chief assembled strength
Durst not presume to look once in the face.

BEDFORD
Is Talbot slain then? I will slay myself
For living idly here in pomp and ease
Whilst such a worthy leader, wanting aid,
Unto his dastard foemen is betrayed.

THIRD MESSENGER
O no, he lives, but is took prisoner,
And Lord Scales with him, and Lord Hungerford;
Most of the rest slaughtered or took likewise.

BEDFORD
His ransom there is none but I shall pay.   148
I'll hale the Dauphin headlong from his throne;
His crown shall be the ransom of my friend.
Four of their lords I'll change for one of ours.   151
Farewell, my masters; to my task will I.
Bonfires in France forthwith I am to make,   153
To keep our great Saint George's feast withal.   154
Ten thousand soldiers with me I will take,
Whose bloody deeds shall make all Europe quake.

THIRD MESSENGER
So you had need, for Orleans is besieged;   157
The English army is grown weak and faint;
The Earl of Salisbury craveth supply   159
And hardly keeps his men from mutiny,
Since they, so few, watch such a multitude.   [Exit.] 161

EXETER
Remember, lords, your oaths to Henry sworn,
Either to quell the Dauphin utterly
Or bring him in obedience to your yoke.

BEDFORD
I do remember it, and here take my leave
To go about my preparation.   Exit Bedford.

GLOUCESTER
I'll to the Tower with all the haste I can   167
To view th' artillery and munition,
And then I will proclaim young Henry king.
                              Exit Gloucester.

EXETER
To Eltham will I, where the young King is,   170

Being ordained his special governor,
And for his safety there I'll best devise.   Exit.

WINCHESTER
Each hath his place and function to attend.
I am left out; for me nothing remains.
But long I will not be jack-out-of-office.   175
The King from Eltham I intend to steal
And sit at chiefest stern of public weal.   Exit. 177

❧

1.2 *Sound a flourish. Enter Charles, Alençon, and
Reignier, marching with drum and soldiers.*

CHARLES
Mars his true moving, even as in the heavens   1
So in the earth, to this day is not known.
Late did he shine upon the English side;   3
Now we are victors, upon us he smiles.
What towns of any moment but we have?   5
At pleasure here we lie near Orleans;   6
Otherwhiles the famished English, like pale ghosts, 7
Faintly besiege us one hour in a month.

ALENÇON
They want their porridge and their fat bull-beeves.
Either they must be dieted like mules   10
And have their provender tied to their mouths,
Or piteous they will look, like drownèd mice.

REIGNIER
Let's raise the siege. Why live we idly here?   13
Talbot is taken, whom we wont to fear.   14
Remaineth none but mad-brained Salisbury,
And he may well in fretting spend his gall;   16
Nor men nor money hath he to make war.   17

CHARLES
Sound, sound alarum! We will rush on them.   18
Now for the honor of the forlorn French!   19
Him I forgive my death that killeth me
When he sees me go back one foot or fly.   Exeunt.

*Here alarum. They are beaten back by the English
with great loss. Enter Charles, Alençon, and
Reignier.*

CHARLES
Who ever saw the like? What men have I!

---

135 **wrack** wreckage, destruction 136 **with** by 137 **Walloon** an in-habitant of that province, now a part of southern Belgium and the ad-joining part of France 148 **His . . . pay** i.e., I'll pay all the ransom there's going to be, by retaliating 151 **change** i.e., kill in exchange 153 **am** intend 154 **Saint George's feast** the twenty-third of April. (Saint George was the patron saint of England. To celebrate his day in France would be to assert England's claim to that territory.) 157 **Or-leans is besieged** (At line 60, a messenger says that Orleans has fallen; at 1.2.8 ff., an English siege to recover Orleans is under way. The messenger here may mean that the besieging English army needs help.) 159 **supply** reinforcements 161 **watch** find themselves face to face with 167 **Tower** Tower of London, ancient palace-fortress, later a prison for persons of eminence 170 **Eltham** a royal residence southeast of London

175 **jack-out-of-office** i.e., a dismissed fellow with nothing to do 177 **at chiefest stern** in the steersman's seat, in a position of supreme control
1.2. Location: France. Before Orleans.
s.d. flourish trumpet fanfare. **drum** drummer 1 **Mars . . . moving** Mars' precise orbit. (The planet's seemingly eccentric orbit was a source of perplexity in Shakespeare's day; here, its influence on earth in human affairs is likewise mysterious. Mars is also the god of war.) 3 **Late** lately, recently 5 **What . . . have** what towns of any conse-quence do we not possess 6 **lie** are encamped 7 **Otherwhiles** at times 10 **dieted** fed. (The eating of beef, line 9, was believed to con-fer courage.) 13 **raise the siege** drive off the besieging English 14 **wont** were accustomed 16 **spend** expend, waste. **gall** i.e., bit-terness of spirit 17 **Nor** neither 18 **alarum** call to arms 19 **forlorn** in extreme risk

Dogs, cowards, dastards! I would ne'er have fled
But that they left me 'midst my enemies.

REIGNIER
Salisbury is a desperate homicide;
He fighteth as one weary of his life.   26
The other lords, like lions wanting food,
Do rush upon us as their hungry prey.   28

ALENÇON
Froissart, a countryman of ours, records   29
England all Olivers and Rolands bred   30
During the time Edward the Third did reign.
More truly now may this be verified,
For none but Samsons and Goliases   33
It sendeth forth to skirmish. One to ten!
Lean raw-boned rascals! Who would e'er suppose   35
They had such courage and audacity?

CHARLES
Let's leave this town; for they are harebrained
  slaves,
And hunger will enforce them to be more eager.   38
Of old I know them. Rather with their teeth
The walls they'll tear down than forsake the siege.

REIGNIER
I think by some odd gimmers or device   41
Their arms are set, like clocks, still to strike on;   42
Else ne'er could they hold out so as they do.
By my consent, we'll even let them alone.   44

ALENÇON   Be it so.

Enter the Bastard of Orleans.

BASTARD
Where's the Prince Dauphin? I have news for him.

CHARLES
Bastard of Orleans, thrice welcome to us.

BASTARD
Methinks your looks are sad, your cheer appalled.   48
Hath the late overthrow wrought this offense?   49
Be not dismayed, for succor is at hand.
A holy maid hither with me I bring,
Which, by a vision sent to her from heaven,
Ordainèd is to raise this tedious siege
And drive the English forth the bounds of France.   54
The spirit of deep prophecy she hath,
Exceeding the nine sibyls of old Rome.   56
What's past and what's to come she can descry.
Speak, shall I call her in? Believe my words,
For they are certain and unfallible.

CHARLES
Go, call her in. [*Bastard goes to the door.*] But first, to
  try her skill,
Reignier, stand thou as Dauphin in my place.
Question her proudly; let thy looks be stern.
By this means shall we sound what skill she hath.   63
                                     [*They exchange places.*]

Enter Joan [la] Pucelle, [the Bastard escorting her].

REIGNIER
Fair maid, is 't thou wilt do these wondrous feats?

PUCELLE
Reignier, is 't thou that thinkest to beguile me?
Where is the Dauphin?—Come, come from behind;
I know thee well, though never seen before.
Be not amazed. There's nothing hid from me.
In private will I talk with thee apart.
Stand back, you lords, and give us leave awhile.
                                     [*The lords stand aside.*]

REIGNIER
She takes upon her bravely at first dash.   71

PUCELLE
Dauphin, I am by birth a shepherd's daughter,
My wit untrained in any kind of art.   73
Heaven and our Lady gracious hath it pleased
To shine on my contemptible estate.
Lo, whilst I waited on my tender lambs
And to sun's parching heat displayed my cheeks,
God's mother deignèd to appear to me,
And in a vision full of majesty
Willed me to leave my base vocation
And free my country from calamity.
Her aid she promised, and assured success.
In complete glory she revealed herself;
And, whereas I was black and swart before,   84
With those clear rays which she infused on me   85
That beauty am I blest with which you may see.
Ask me what question thou canst possible,
And I will answer unpremeditated.
My courage try by combat, if thou dar'st,
And thou shalt find that I exceed my sex.
Resolve on this: thou shalt be fortunate   91
If thou receive me for thy warlike mate.   92

CHARLES
Thou hast astonished me with thy high terms.   93
Only this proof I'll of thy valor make: 94
In single combat thou shalt buckle with me,   95
And if thou vanquishest, thy words are true.
Otherwise I renounce all confidence.   97

PUCELLE
I am prepared. Here is my keen-edged sword,
Decked with five flower-de-luces on each side,   99

---

26 **as one** like one who is   28 **hungry prey** of their hunger
29 **Froissart** a fourteenth-century French chronicler who wrote of contemporary events in Flanders, France, Spain, and England   30 **Olivers
and Rolands** paladins in the Charlemagne legends, the most famous of
the twelve for their daring exploits   33 **Samsons, Goliases** (i.e., Golia-
ths), biblical characters typifying great physical strength   35 **rascals**
young, lean, or inferior deer of a herd   38 **eager** (1) fierce (2) hungry
41 **gimmers** gimmals, joints or connecting parts for transmitting motion   42 **still** continually   44 **consent** advice.   **even** i.e., do nothing
but   48 **cheer appalled** countenances made pale   49 **late . . . offense** recent defeat brought about this harm   54 **forth** out of   56 **nine
. . . Rome** inspired women of the ancient world. (Not only of Rome,
however; the phrase here is probably owing to a confusion with the
Cumaean sibyl who came to Tarquin with nine prophetic books.)

63 **sound** test, determine.   **s.d. Pucelle** virgin   71 **takes . . . bravely**
plays her part well   73 **wit** mind, intelligence.   **art** learning
84 **black and swart** i.e., heavily tanned   85 **infused** poured   91 **Resolve on** be sure of   92 **warlike mate** (With sexual suggestion, as in
the military terms throughout this interview.)   93 **high** lofty   94 **proof**
trial, test   95 **buckle** join in close combat (with bawdy suggestion)
97 **confidence** (1) trust in your speech (2) intimacy   99 **Decked**
adorned

The which at Touraine, in Saint Katharine's
   churchyard,
Out of a great deal of old iron I chose forth.

CHARLES
Then come, i' God's name! I fear no woman.

PUCELLE
And while I live, I'll ne'er fly from a man.   103

Here they fight, and Joan la Pucelle overcomes.

CHARLES
Stay, stay thy hands! Thou art an Amazon,   104
And fightest with the sword of Deborah.   105

PUCELLE
Christ's mother helps me, else I were too weak.

CHARLES
Whoe'er helps thee, 'tis thou that must help me!
Impatiently I burn with thy desire.   108
My heart and hands thou hast at once subdued.
Excellent Pucelle, if thy name be so,
Let me thy servant and not sovereign be.   111
'Tis the French Dauphin sueth to thee thus.

PUCELLE
I must not yield to any rites of love,
For my profession's sacred from above.
When I have chasèd all thy foes from hence,
Then will I think upon a recompense.

CHARLES
Meantime, look gracious on thy prostrate thrall.

REIGNIER [*to the other lords apart*]
My lord, methinks, is very long in talk.

ALENÇON
Doubtless he shrives this woman to her smock,   119
Else ne'er could he so long protract his speech.

REIGNIER
Shall we disturb him, since he keeps no mean?   121

ALENÇON
He may mean more than we poor men do know.
These women are shrewd tempters with their
   tongues.   123

REIGNIER [*to Charles*]
My lord, where are you? What devise you on?   124
Shall we give o'er Orleans, or no?

PUCELLE
Why, no, I say. Distrustful recreants,   126
Fight till the last gasp. I'll be your guard.

CHARLES
What she says I'll confirm. We'll fight it out.

PUCELLE
Assigned am I to be the English scourge.
This night the siege assuredly I'll raise.

Expect Saint Martin's summer, halcyon days,   131
Since I have enterèd into these wars.
Glory is like a circle in the water,
Which never ceaseth to enlarge itself
Till by broad spreading it disperse to naught.
With Henry's death the English circle ends;
Dispersèd are the glories it included.
Now am I like that proud insulting ship   138
Which Caesar and his fortune bare at once.   139

CHARLES
Was Mahomet inspirèd with a dove?   140
Thou with an eagle art inspirèd then.
Helen, the mother of great Constantine,   142
Nor yet Saint Philip's daughters, were like thee.   143
Bright star of Venus, fall'n down on the earth,
How may I reverently worship thee enough?

ALENÇON
Leave off delays, and let us raise the siege.

REIGNIER
Woman, do what thou canst to save our honors.
Drive them from Orleans and be immortalized.

CHARLES
Presently we'll try. Come, let's away about it.   149
No prophet will I trust, if she prove false.   *Exeunt.*

❖

1.3   *Enter [the Duke of] Gloucester, with his
           Servingmen [in blue coats].*

GLOUCESTER
I am come to survey the Tower this day.   1
Since Henry's death, I fear, there is conveyance.   2
Where be these warders, that they wait not here?   3
Open the gates! 'Tis Gloucester that calls.

                                        [*They knock.*]

FIRST WARDER [*within*]
Who's there that knocks so imperiously?

FIRST SERVINGMAN
It is the noble Duke of Gloucester.

SECOND WARDER [*within*]
Whoe'er he be, you may not be let in.

FIRST SERVINGMAN
Villains, answer you so the Lord Protector?

FIRST WARDER [*within*]
The Lord protect him! So we answer him.

---

103 ne'er . . . man (With bawdy suggestion.)   **104 Amazon** race of
warrior women   **105 Deborah** Hebrew prophetess who "judged" Israel in the fourteenth century B.C. (She led an army against the
Canaanite oppressors, whom she overcame: Judges 4, 5.)   **108 thy
desire** desire for you   **111 servant** (With suggestion of a lover who
will fulfill his mistress's commands.)   **119 shrives** hears confession,
i.e., examines.   **to her smock** to her undergarment, i.e., completely
(with bawdy suggestion)   **121 keeps no mean** observes no moderation
123 shrewd cunning, mischievous   **124 where are you** i.e., what are
you up to.   **devise** decide   **126 Distrustful recreants** faithless
cowards

131 Saint Martin's summer i.e., Indian summer; Saint Martin's Day is
November 11.   **halcyon days** i.e., unseasonable calm. (The halcyon
is the kingfisher, which, according to fable, nested at midwinter on
the seas, which became calm for that purpose.)   **138–139 Now . . .
once** (North's translation of Plutarch relates how Caesar, encountering
a storm, said to the mariners, "Fear not, for thou hast Caesar and his
fortune with thee.")   **140 Was . . . dove** (Mohammed supposedly
claimed that he received divine inspiration from a dove whispering in
his ear.)   **142 Helen** mother of the emperor Constantine and supposed discoverer of the holy cross and sepulcher of the Lord
143 Saint Philip's daughters the four daughters of Philip the Evange-
list, said in Acts 21:9 to have the power of prophecy   **149 Presently**
immediately
1.3. Location: Before the Tower of London.
1 survey inspect   **2 conveyance** trickery   **3 warders** guards

We do no otherwise than we are willed.   10
GLOUCESTER
Who willèd you? Or whose will stands but mine?   11
There's none Protector of the realm but I.—
Break up the gates. I'll be your warrantize.   13
Shall I be flouted thus by dunghill grooms?   14

         Gloucester's men rush at the Tower gates,
         and Woodville the Lieutenant speaks within.

WOODVILLE [*within*]
What noise is this? What traitors have we here?
GLOUCESTER
Lieutenant, is it you whose voice I hear?
Open the gates. Here's Gloucester that would enter.
WOODVILLE [*within*]
Have patience, noble Duke. I may not open;
The Cardinal of Winchester forbids.   19
From him I have express commandement   20
That thou nor none of thine shall be let in.
GLOUCESTER
Fainthearted Woodville, prizest him 'fore me?
Arrogant Winchester, that haughty prelate,
Whom Henry, our late sovereign, ne'er could brook? 24
Thou art no friend to God or to the King.
Open the gates, or I'll shut thee out shortly.   26
SERVINGMEN
Open the gates unto the Lord Protector,
Or we'll burst them open, if that you come not
   quickly.   28

         Enter to the Protector at the Tower gates
         Winchester and his men in tawny coats.

WINCHESTER
How now, ambitious Humphrey, what means this?
GLOUCESTER
Peeled priest, dost thou command me to be shut
   out?   30
WINCHESTER
I do, thou most usurping proditor,   31
And not Protector, of the King or realm.
GLOUCESTER
Stand back, thou manifest conspirator,
Thou that contrivedst to murder our dead lord,   34
Thou that giv'st whores indulgences to sin.   35
I'll canvass thee in thy broad cardinal's hat   36

If thou proceed in this thy insolence.
WINCHESTER
Nay, stand thou back. I will not budge a foot.
This be Damascus, be thou cursèd Cain,   39
To slay thy brother Abel, if thou wilt.   40
GLOUCESTER
I will not slay thee, but I'll drive thee back.
Thy scarlet robes as a child's bearing cloth   42
I'll use to carry thee out of this place.
WINCHESTER
Do what thou dar'st! I beard thee to thy face.   44
GLOUCESTER
What, am I dared and bearded to my face?
Draw, men, for all this privilegèd place—   46
Blue coats to tawny coats. Priest, beware your
   beard.
I mean to tug it and to cuff you soundly.
Under my feet I stamp thy cardinal's hat.
In spite of Pope or dignities of Church,   50
Here by the cheeks I'll drag thee up and down.
WINCHESTER
Gloucester, thou wilt answer this before the Pope.   52
GLOUCESTER
Winchester goose! I cry, a rope, a rope!   53
[*To his Servingmen.*] Now beat them hence. Why do
   you let them stay?—
Thee I'll chase hence, thou wolf in sheep's array.
Out, tawny coats! Out, scarlet hypocrite!

         Here Gloucester's men beat out the Cardinal's
         men, and enter in the hurly-burly the Mayor of
         London and his Officers.

MAYOR
Fie, lords, that you, being supreme magistrates,   57
Thus contumeliously should break the peace!   58
GLOUCESTER
Peace, Mayor! Thou know'st little of my wrongs.
Here's Beaufort, that regards nor God nor king,   60
Hath here distrained the Tower to his use.   61
WINCHESTER
Here's Gloucester, a foe to citizens,
One that still motions war and never peace,   63
O'ercharging your free purses with large fines,   64
That seeks to overthrow religion
Because he is Protector of the realm,
And would have armor here out of the Tower
To crown himself king and suppress the Prince.   68

---

10 willed commanded   **11 stands** has authority   **13 warrantize** authorization   **14 dunghill grooms** i.e., base fellows. **s.d. rush . . . gates** (Gloucester's men assault the facade of the tiring-house wall backstage, which represents the Tower gates; Woodville and the warders are "within," or behind that wall, invisible to the audience.) **19 Cardinal** (An inconsistency with 5.1.28 ff., where Winchester has just been installed as cardinal.)   **20 commandement** commandment (pronounced in four syllables)   **24 brook** endure   **26 I'll . . . shortly** i.e., I'll take possession and shut you out   **28 if that** if   **30 Peeled** shaven, tonsured   **31 proditor** traitor   **34–35 Thou . . . sin** (Gloucester, in his bill of particulars against Winchester, charged that the cleric had suborned someone to attempt the murder of the prince who later became Henry V. Here he refers also to the fact that Winchester collected revenues from houses of prostitution on the south bank of the Thames.)   **35 indulgences** forgiveness of sins. (One could buy indulgences from the Church.)   **36 canvass** i.e., deal with severely. (The metaphor is that of tossing someone in a canvas or blanket as sport or punishment.)

39 This be let this be. **Damascus** a city reputed to have been built on the site of Cain's slaying of Abel   **40 thy brother** (Winchester is Gloucester's half-uncle.)   **42 bearing cloth** christening robe   **44 beard** openly defy   **46 for all this** in spite of this being a. **privilegèd place** (The Tower, as a royal residence, was one of the precincts where drawing of weapons was forbidden by the law of arms; compare with the note for 2.4.86.)   **50 dignities** dignitaries   **52 answer** render an account of, pay for   **53 Winchester goose** (Slang for a symptom of venereal disease.)` **a rope** i.e., a halter for hanging   **57 magistrates** rulers   **58 contumeliously** arrogantly, contemptuously   **60 regards nor** has a proper respect for neither   **61 distrained** confiscated   **63 still motions** incessantly advocates   **64 O'ercharging . . . fines** overburdening you with excessive taxation   **68 Prince** i.e., Henry VI

GLOUCESTER
I will not answer thee with words, but blows.
Here they skirmish again.

MAYOR
Naught rests for me in this tumultuous strife   70
But to make open proclamation.
Come, officer, as loud as e'er thou canst,
Cry.

OFFICER   All manner of men assembled here in arms
this day against God's peace and the King's, we charge
and command you, in His Highness' name, to repair
to your several dwelling places, and not to wear, han-   77
dle, or use any sword, weapon, or dagger henceforward, upon pain of death.   79

GLOUCESTER
Cardinal, I'll be no breaker of the law.
But we shall meet and break our minds at large.   81

WINCHESTER
Gloucester, we'll meet to thy cost, be sure.
Thy heart-blood I will have for this day's work.

MAYOR
I'll call for clubs, if you will not away.   84
This cardinal's more haughty than the devil.

GLOUCESTER
Mayor, farewell. Thou dost but what thou mayst.

WINCHESTER
Abominable Gloucester, guard thy head,
For I intend to have it ere long.
Exeunt, [separately, Gloucester and Winchester
with their Servingmen].

MAYOR
See the coast cleared, and then we will depart.
Good God, these nobles should such stomachs bear!   90
I myself fight not once in forty year.   *Exeunt.*

1.4   *Enter the Master Gunner of Orleans and his Boy.*

MASTER GUNNER
Sirrah, thou know'st how Orleans is besieged   1
And how the English have the suburbs won.

BOY
Father, I know, and oft have shot at them,
Howe'er unfortunate I missed my aim.   4

MASTER GUNNER
But now thou shalt not. Be thou ruled by me.
Chief master gunner am I of this town;
Something I must do to procure me grace.   7
The Prince's espials have informèd me   8
How the English, in the suburbs close entrenched,
Wont through a secret grate of iron bars   10

In yonder tower to overpeer the city
And thence discover how with most advantage
They may vex us with shot or with assault.
To intercept this inconvenience,   14
A piece of ordnance 'gainst it I have placed,   15
And even these three days have I watched,
If I could see them. Now do thou watch,
For I can stay no longer.
If thou spy'st any, run and bring me word,
And thou shalt find me at the governor's.   *Exit.*

BOY
Father, I warrant you; take you no care.   21
I'll never trouble you, if I may spy them.   *Exit.* 22

Enter Salisbury and Talbot on the turrets, with
[Sir William Glasdale, Sir Thomas Gargrave, and]
others.

SALISBURY
Talbot, my life, my joy, again returned?
How wert thou handled being prisoner?
Or by what means gott'st thou to be released?
Discourse, I prithee, on this turret's top.

TALBOT
The Duke of Bedford had a prisoner
Called the brave Lord Ponton de Santrailles;
For him was I exchanged and ransomèd.
But with a baser man-of-arms by far   30
Once in contempt they would have bartered me;
Which I disdaining scorned, and cravèd death
Rather than I would be so pilled esteemed.   33
In fine, redeemed I was as I desired.   34
But O, the treacherous Falstaff wounds my heart,
Whom with my bare fists I would execute
If I now had him brought into my power.

SALISBURY
Yet tell'st thou not how thou wert entertained.   38

TALBOT
With scoffs and scorns and contumelious taunts.   39
In open marketplace produced they me
To be a public spectacle to all.
"Here," said they, "is the terror of the French,
The scarecrow that affrights our children so."
Then broke I from the officers that led me
And with my nails digged stones out of the ground
To hurl at the beholders of my shame.
My grisly countenance made others fly;
None durst come near for fear of sudden death.
In iron walls they deemed me not secure;
So great fear of my name 'mongst them were spread
That they supposed I could rend bars of steel
And spurn in pieces posts of adamant.   52
Wherefore a guard of chosen shot I had   53

---

70 rests for me remains for me to do   **77 several** various   **79 pain**
punishment   **81 break our minds** (1) say what's on our minds (2)
crack heads.   **at large** at length   **84 call for clubs** i.e., sound the rallying cry for London apprentices armed with clubs   **90 these** that
these.   **stomachs** i.e., angry tempers
1.4. Location: France. Orleans.
1 Sirrah (Customary form of address to an inferior.)   **4 Howe'er un-**
fortunate although unfortunately   **7 grace** honor, credit   **8 espials**
spies   **10 Wont** are accustomed

14 inconvenience mischief   **15 'gainst** directed toward   **21 take you**
no care don't you worry   **22 s.d. turrets** i.e., some high point of vantage in the theater, above the main stage   **30 baser** of lower rank
33 pilled peeled, i.e., despoiled of honor   **34 In fine** finally.   **re-**
deemed ransomed   **38 entertained** treated   **39 contumelious** reproachful   **52 spurn** kick.   **adamant** a legendary substance supposedly of incredible hardness, like diamond, or like a magnet
53 chosen shot carefully selected marksmen

That walked about me every minute while;   54
And if I did but stir out of my bed,
Ready they were to shoot me to the heart.   56

Enter the Boy with a linstock.

SALISBURY
I grieve to hear what torments you endured.
But we will be revenged sufficiently.
Now it is suppertime in Orleans.
Here, through this grate, I count each one
And view the Frenchmen how they fortify.
Let us look in; the sight will much delight thee.
Sir Thomas Gargrave and Sir William Glasdale,
Let me have your express opinions   64
Where is best place to make our battery next.   65
GARGRAVE
I think at the north gate, for there stands lords.
GLASDALE
And I here, at the bulwark of the bridge.   67
TALBOT
For aught I see, this city must be famished   68
Or with light skirmishes enfeebled.   69

Here they shoot, and Salisbury falls down [together
with Gargrave].

SALISBURY
O Lord, have mercy on us, wretched sinners!
GARGRAVE
O Lord, have mercy on me, woeful man!
TALBOT
What chance is this that suddenly hath crossed us?   72
Speak, Salisbury—at least, if thou canst, speak.
How far'st thou, mirror of all martial men?   74
One of thy eyes and thy cheek's side struck off?
Accursèd tower! Accursèd fatal hand
That hath contrived this woeful tragedy!
In thirteen battles Salisbury o'ercame;
Henry the Fifth he first trained to the wars.
Whilst any trump did sound or drum struck up,
His sword did ne'er leave striking in the field.   81
Yet liv'st thou, Salisbury? Though thy speech doth
    fail,
One eye thou hast to look to heaven for grace.
The sun with one eye vieweth all the world.
Heaven, be thou gracious to none alive
If Salisbury wants mercy at thy hands!   86
Sir Thomas Gargrave, hast thou any life?
Speak unto Talbot. Nay, look up to him.—
Bear hence his body; I will help to bury it.

[Gargrave's body is borne off.]

Salisbury, cheer thy spirit with this comfort:
Thou shalt not die whiles—

He beckons with his hand and smiles on me,
As who should say, "When I am dead and gone,   93
Remember to avenge me on the French."
Plantagenet, I will; and Nero-like   95
Play on the lute, beholding the towns burn.
Wretched shall France be only in my name.   97

Here an alarum, and it thunders and lightens.

What stir is this? What tumult 's in the heavens?
Whence cometh this alarum and the noise?

Enter a Messenger.

MESSENGER
My lord, my lord, the French have gathered head!   100
The Dauphin, with one Joan la Pucelle joined,
A holy prophetess new risen up,
Is come with a great power to raise the siege.   103

Here Salisbury lifteth himself up and groans.

TALBOT
Hear, hear how dying Salisbury doth groan!
It irks his heart he cannot be revenged.
Frenchmen, I'll be a Salisbury to you.
Pucelle or pussel, Dauphin or dogfish,   107
Your hearts I'll stamp out with my horse's heels
And make a quagmire of your mingled brains.—
Convey me Salisbury into his tent,   110
And then we'll try what these dastard Frenchmen
    dare.   *Alarum. Exeunt, [bearing out Salisbury].*

1.5 *Here an alarum again, and Talbot pursueth the*
Dauphin and driveth him. Then enter Joan la
Pucelle, driving Englishmen before her [and exit
after them]. Then enter [again] Talbot.

TALBOT
Where is my strength, my valor, and my force?
Our English troops retire; I cannot stay them.   2
A woman clad in armor chaseth them.

Enter [Joan la] Pucelle.

Here, here she comes.—I'll have a bout with thee;   4
Devil or devil's dam, I'll conjure thee.   5
Blood will I draw on thee—thou art a witch—   6
And straightway give thy soul to him thou serv'st.   7
PUCELLE
Come, come, 'tis only I that must disgrace thee.

Here they fight.

93 As who as one who   **95 Plantagenet** (The Earl of Salisbury was
Thomas Montacute; he was descended from the Plantagenet Edward
I.)   **Nero-like** (Talbot is being compared to Nero, who played music
while Rome burned.)   **97 only in** at the mere sound of   **100 gathered
head** drawn their forces together   **103 power** army   **107 pussel** drab,
slut. (A punning spelling variant of *pucelle*, "maid.")   **Dauphin** (The
normal Folio Elizabethan spelling of *Dauphin* is *Dolphin*. The sea
mammal by that name is included in the meaning and is contrasted
with *dogfish*, a very low form of sea life.)   **110 Convey me** convey.
(*Me* is used colloquially.)
1.5. Location: Scene continues at Orleans.
2 stay halt   **4 bout** encounter in the fighting (but with sexual overtones)   **5 dam** dame, mother   **6 Blood . . . witch** (Anyone who succeeded in drawing blood from a witch was thought to be invulnerable
to her magic.)   **7 him** i.e., the devil

54 every minute while i.e., constantly, at minute intervals   **56 s.d.
linstock** forked stick used to hold a lighted match for firing cannon
64 express precise   **65 battery** attack   **67 bulwark** fortification (protecting the bridge)   **68 must be famished** will have to be reduced to
famine   **69 s.d. Here they shoot** i.e., the French (probably offstage,
though the Boy's appearance with the linstock at line 56 visually symbolizes the action of preparing to fire)   **72 chance** misfortune.
crossed afflicted   **74 mirror of** example to   **81 leave** leave off
86 wants lacks

TALBOT
Heavens, can you suffer hell so to prevail?
My breast I'll burst with straining of my courage
And from my shoulders crack my arms asunder
But I will chastise this high-minded strumpet.   12

They fight again.

PUCELLE
Talbot, farewell. Thy hour is not yet come.
I must go victual Orleans forthwith.   14

A short alarum. Then enter the town with soldiers.

O'ertake me if thou canst! I scorn thy strength.
Go, go, cheer up thy hungry starvèd men;
Help Salisbury to make his testament.
This day is ours, as many more shall be.   *Exit.*

TALBOT
My thoughts are whirlèd like a potter's wheel.
I know not where I am nor what I do.
A witch by fear, not force, like Hannibal   21
Drives back our troops and conquers as she lists.   22
So bees with smoke and doves with noisome stench   23
Are from their hives and houses driven away.
They called us, for our fierceness, English dogs;
Now, like to whelps, we crying run away.

A short alarum.

Hark, countrymen! Either renew the fight
Or tear the lions out of England's coat!   28
Renounce your soil; give sheep in lions' stead.   29
Sheep run not half so treacherous from the wolf,   30
Or horse or oxen from the leopard,
As you fly from your oft-subduèd slaves.

Alarum. Here another skirmish.

It will not be. Retire into your trenches.   33
You all consented unto Salisbury's death,
For none would strike a stroke in his revenge.   35
Pucelle is entered into Orleans
In spite of us or aught that we could do.
O, would I were to die with Salisbury!
The shame hereof will make me hide my head.   39

Exit Talbot. Alarum. Retreat.

1.6
Flourish. Enter, on the walls, Pucelle, Dauphin [Charles], Reignier, Alençon, and soldiers.

PUCELLE
Advance our waving colors on the walls;   1
Rescued is Orleans from the English!

12 But I will if I do not. **high-minded** arrogant **14 victual** supply with provisions. **s.d. enter** i.e., they, the French, enter Orleans; Joan follows four lines later **21 Hannibal** Carthaginian general who once repulsed a Roman army by tying firebrands to the horns of a herd of oxen and driving the animals toward the Romans **22 lists** pleases **23 noisome** noxious **28 lions . . . coat** i.e., the three lions passant displayed in the English coat of arms **29 soil** country (?) disgrace (?) **give** display (on coat of arms) **30 treacherous** i.e., cowardly **33 It will not be** i.e., it's hopeless **35 his revenge** revenge of him **39 s.d. Retreat** trumpet call to signal a withdrawal from the attack
1.6. Location: Scene continues at Orleans.
s.d. on the walls i.e., in the gallery backstage, above the main doors of the tiring-house facade. (When Joan enters Orleans at 1.5.14, she enters the tiring-house through one of its doors, and that tiring-house facade remains the visual equivalent of the walls of Orleans through 2.1.) **1 Advance** lift up

Thus Joan la Pucelle hath performed her word.
CHARLES
Divinest creature, Astraea's daughter,   4
How shall I honor thee for this success?
Thy promises are like Adonis' garden,   6
That one day bloomed and fruitful were the next.
France, triumph in thy glorious prophetess!
Recovered is the town of Orleans.
More blessèd hap did ne'er befall our state.   10
REIGNIER
Why ring not out the bells aloud throughout the
town?
Dauphin, command the citizens make bonfires
And feast and banquet in the open streets
To celebrate the joy that God hath given us.
ALENÇON
All France will be replete with mirth and joy
When they shall hear how we have played the men.   16
CHARLES
'Tis Joan, not we, by whom the day is won;
For which I will divide my crown with her,
And all the priests and friars in my realm
Shall in procession sing her endless praise.
A statelier pyramid to her I'll rear
Than Rhodope's of Memphis ever was.   22
In memory of her when she is dead,
Her ashes, in an urn more precious
Than the rich-jeweled coffer of Darius,   25
Transported shall be at high festivals
Before the kings and queens of France.
No longer on Saint Denis will we cry,   28
But Joan la Pucelle shall be France's saint.
Come in, and let us banquet royally
After this golden day of victory.   *Flourish. Exeunt.*

♣

2.1
Enter [on the walls] a [French] Sergeant of a band, with two Sentinels.

SERGEANT
Sirs, take your places and be vigilant.
If any noise or soldier you perceive
Near to the walls, by some apparent sign   3
Let us have knowledge at the court of guard.   4
A SENTINEL
Sergeant, you shall. [*Exit Sergeant.*] Thus are poor
servitors,   5

4 Astraea goddess of Justice **6 Adonis' garden** mythical garden of eternal fecundity **10 hap** event **16 played the men** showed manly courage **22 Rhodope** a Greek courtesan who became the wife of the king of Egypt. (A legend was current that she built the third pyramid.) **Memphis** an ancient city of Egypt near which stand the pyramids of Ramses II **25 Darius** King of Persia conquered by Alexander the Great. Alexander, according to legend, used Darius' *rich-jeweled coffer* to carry about the poems of Homer. **28 on** in the name of. **Saint Denis** patron saint of France
2.1. Location: Before Orleans, as in the previous scenes; the time is later that night.
s.d. band detachment of soldiers **3 apparent** plain **4 court of guard** guardhouse **5 servitors** soldiers

When others sleep upon their quiet beds,　6
Constrained to watch in darkness, rain, and cold.　7

Enter Talbot, Bedford, and Burgundy, [and
forces,] with scaling ladders.

TALBOT
Lord Regent, and redoubted Burgundy,
By whose approach the regions of Artois,　9
Walloon, and Picardy are friends to us,
This happy night the Frenchmen are secure,　11
Having all day caroused and banqueted.
Embrace we then this opportunity
As fitting best to quittance their deceit,　14
Contrived by art and baleful sorcery.　15

BEDFORD
Coward of France, how much he wrongs his fame,　16
Despairing of his own arm's fortitude,
To join with witches and the help of hell!

BURGUNDY
Traitors have never other company.
But what's that Pucelle whom they term so pure?

TALBOT
A maid, they say.

BEDFORD　　　　　　A maid, and be so martial?

BURGUNDY
Pray God she prove not masculine ere long,　22
If underneath the standard of the French
She carry armor as she hath begun.

TALBOT
Well, let them practice and converse with spirits.
God is our fortress, in whose conquering name
Let us resolve to scale their flinty bulwarks.

BEDFORD
Ascend, brave Talbot. We will follow thee.

TALBOT
Not all together. Better far, I guess,
That we do make our entrance several ways,　30
That, if it chance the one of us do fail,　31
The other yet may rise against their force.

BEDFORD
Agreed. I'll to yond corner.

BURGUNDY　　　　　　And I to this.

TALBOT
And here will Talbot mount, or make his grave.
Now, Salisbury, for thee, and for the right

Of English Henry, shall this night appear　36
How much in duty I am bound to both.

SENTINELS
Arm, arm! The enemy doth make assault!　38

[*The English scale the walls, Talbot in the center,*
and exeunt above into the city.]
Cry: "Saint George! A Talbot!"
The French leap o'er the walls in their shirts.
Enter, several ways, [the] Bastard [of Orleans],
Alençon, [and] Reignier, half ready, and half
unready.

ALENÇON
How now, my lords? What, all unready so?

BASTARD
Unready? Ay, and glad we scaped so well.

REIGNIER
'Twas time, I trow, to wake and leave our beds,　41
Hearing alarums at our chamber doors.

ALENÇON
Of all exploits since first I followed arms,
Ne'er heard I of a warlike enterprise
More venturous or desperate than this.

BASTARD
I think this Talbot be a fiend of hell.

REIGNIER
If not of hell, the heavens sure favor him.

ALENÇON
Here cometh Charles. I marvel how he sped.　48

Enter Charles and Joan [la Pucelle].

BASTARD
Tut, holy Joan was his defensive guard.

CHARLES
Is this thy cunning, thou deceitful dame?　50
Didst thou at first, to flatter us withal,　51
Make us partakers of a little gain
That now our loss might be ten times so much?

PUCELLE
Wherefore is Charles impatient with his friend?
At all times will you have my power alike?
Sleeping or waking must I still prevail,　56
Or will you blame and lay the fault on me?—
Improvident soldiers! Had your watch been good,
This sudden mischief never could have fall'n.

CHARLES
Duke of Alençon, this was your default,　60
That, being captain of the watch tonight,　61
Did look no better to that weighty charge.　62

ALENÇON
Had all your quarters been as safely kept
As that whereof I had the government,
We had not been thus shamefully surprised.

BASTARD
Mine was secure.

---

6 upon their quiet beds quietly in their beds　**7 s.d. Burgundy** the Duke of Burgundy, allied to the English by the Treaty of Troyes, 1420. (His support brought with it the cooperation of territories near to Burgundy, in the Low Countries, such as Walloon and Picardy.) **9 By whose approach** by means of whose joining our alliance　**11 secure** overconfident　**14 quittance** requite　**15 art** i.e., black magic **16 Coward of France** i.e., the Dauphin.　**fame** reputation　**22 prove not masculine** i.e., (1) proves not to be so manly after all (2) proves herself feminine by becoming pregnant. (The bawdy punning continues in *standard*, "that which stands up," *carry armor*, "bear the weight of a man," *practice and converse*, "engage in sexual contact," etc.)　**30 several ways** i.e., on ladders at different points. (The three leaders place their ladders against the tiring-house facade, one in the middle for Talbot and one on each wing, and actually ascend to the gallery or top of the "walls," where they surprise the French. Some of the French, thus surprised, leap from the gallery down onto the main stage, where the Bastard, Alençon, and others consult in a state of disorder about their situation.)　**31 That** so that

36 shall it shall　**38 s.d. unready** not fully clothed. (This scene is based on an incident occurring at Le Mans, a year prior to the siege of Orleans.)　**41 trow** believe　**48 marvel** wonder.　**sped** fared **50 cunning** skill　**51 flatter** lead on with false hopes.　**withal** with it **56 still prevail** always succeed　**60 default** failure　**61 tonight** this previous night　**62 charge** responsibility

REIGNIER   And so was mine, my lord.
CHARLES
And, for myself, most part of all this night
Within her quarter and mine own precinct   68
I was employed in passing to and fro
About relieving of the sentinels.
Then how or which way should they first break in?
PUCELLE
Question, my lords, no further of the case,
How or which way. 'Tis sure they found some place
But weakly guarded, where the breach was made.
And now there rests no other shift but this: 75
To gather our soldiers, scattered and dispersed,
And lay new platforms to endamage them.   77

> *Alarum. Enter a[n English] Soldier, crying "A*
> *Talbot! A Talbot!" They fly, leaving their clothes*
> *behind.*

SOLDIER
I'll be so bold to take what they have left.
The cry of "Talbot" serves me for a sword,
For I have loaden me with many spoils,   80
Using no other weapon but his name.
> *Exit, [bearing spoils].*

2.2   *Enter Talbot, Bedford, Burgundy, [a Captain, and*
soldiers].

BEDFORD
The day begins to break, and night is fled,
Whose pitchy mantle overveiled the earth.   2
Here sound retreat and cease our hot pursuit.   3
> *Retreat [is sounded].*
TALBOT
Bring forth the body of old Salisbury
And here advance it in the marketplace,   5
The middle center of this cursèd town.

> *[Enter a funeral procession with Salisbury's*
> *body,] their drums beating a dead march.*

Now have I paid my vow unto his soul:
For every drop of blood was drawn from him   8
There hath at least five Frenchmen died tonight.
And that hereafter ages may behold
What ruin happened in revenge of him,
Within their chiefest temple I'll erect
A tomb, wherein his corpse shall be interred;
Upon the which, that everyone may read,
Shall be engraved the sack of Orleans,
The treacherous manner of his mournful death,
And what a terror he had been to France.
> *[Exit funeral procession.]*

But, lords, in all our bloody massacre,
I muse we met not with the Dauphin's grace,   19
His new-come champion, virtuous Joan of Arc,   20
Nor any of his false confederates.
BEDFORD
'Tis thought, Lord Talbot, when the fight began,
Roused on the sudden from their drowsy beds,
They did amongst the troops of armèd men
Leap o'er the walls for refuge in the field.
BURGUNDY
Myself, as far as I could well discern
For smoke and dusky vapors of the night,
Am sure I scared the Dauphin and his trull,   28
When arm in arm they both came swiftly running,
Like to a pair of loving turtledoves
That could not live asunder day or night.
After that things are set in order here,
We'll follow them with all the power we have.

> *Enter a Messenger.*

MESSENGER
All hail, my lords! Which of this princely train
Call ye the warlike Talbot, for his acts
So much applauded through the realm of France?
TALBOT
Here is the Talbot. Who would speak with him?
MESSENGER
The virtuous lady, Countess of Auvergne,
With modesty admiring thy renown,
By me entreats, great lord, thou wouldst vouchsafe
To visit her poor castle where she lies,   41
That she may boast she hath beheld the man
Whose glory fills the world with loud report.   43
BURGUNDY
Is it even so? Nay, then, I see our wars
Will turn unto a peaceful comic sport,
When ladies crave to be encountered with.   46
You may not, my lord, despise her gentle suit.   47
TALBOT
Ne'er trust me then; for when a world of men   48
Could not prevail with all their oratory,
Yet hath a woman's kindness overruled.   50
And therefore tell her I return great thanks,
And in submission will attend on her.   52
Will not your honors bear me company?
BEDFORD
No, truly, 'tis more than manners will;   54
And I have heard it said unbidden guests
Are often welcomest when they are gone.
TALBOT
Well then, alone, since there's no remedy,
I mean to prove this lady's courtesy.   58

---

68 her i.e., Joan's (with a suggestion of sexual intercourse, continued in *passing to and fro*, line 69)   **75 rests** remains.   **shift** strategy
77 platforms plans   **80 loaden me** laden myself
2.2. Location: Orleans. Within the town.
2 pitchy pitch black   **3 retreat** pull back from the attack   **5 advance** raise aloft (on a bier)   **8 was** that was

19 muse wonder.   **the Dauphin's grace** His Grace the Dauphin
20 virtuous (Said ironically.)   **28 trull** strumpet (i.e., Joan)   **41 lies** dwells   **43 report** (1) acclaim (2) noise of battle   **46 encountered with** i.e., encountered socially, as an adversary in the battle of the sexes, and as the object of wooing   **47 gentle** gracious, courteous
48 a world of many   **50 overruled** prevailed   **52 in . . . on her** will visit her in compliance with her wishes   **54 will** require   **58 prove** test

Come hither, Captain. (*Whispers.*) You perceive my
mind?

CAPTAIN
I do, my lord, and mean accordingly.   *Exeunt.* 60

❧

2.3   *Enter [the] Countess [and her Porter].*

COUNTESS
Porter, remember what I gave in charge,   1
And when you have done so, bring the keys to me.

PORTER   Madam, I will.   *Exit.*

COUNTESS
The plot is laid. If all things fall out right,
I shall as famous be by this exploit
As Scythian Tomyris by Cyrus' death.   6
Great is the rumor of this dreadful knight,   7
And his achievements of no less account.
Fain would mine eyes be witness with mine ears,
To give their censure of these rare reports.   10

Enter Messenger and Talbot.

MESSENGER   Madam,
According as your ladyship desired,
By message craved, so is Lord Talbot come.

COUNTESS
And he is welcome. What? Is this the man?

MESSENGER
Madam, it is.

COUNTESS   Is this the scourge of France?
Is this the Talbot, so much feared abroad   16
That with his name the mothers still their babes?   17
I see report is fabulous and false.
I thought I should have seen some Hercules,   19
A second Hector, for his grim aspect   20
And large proportion of his strong-knit limbs.   21
Alas, this is a child, a silly dwarf!   22
It cannot be this weak and writhled shrimp   23
Should strike such terror to his enemies.

TALBOT
Madam, I have been bold to trouble you;
But since your ladyship is not at leisure,
I'll sort some other time to visit you.   [*Going.*] 27

COUNTESS
What means he now? Go ask him whither he goes.

MESSENGER
Stay, my Lord Talbot, for my lady craves
To know the cause of your abrupt departure.

TALBOT
Marry, for that she's in a wrong belief,   31
I go to certify her Talbot's here.   32

Enter Porter with keys.

COUNTESS
If thou be he, then art thou prisoner.

TALBOT
Prisoner? To whom?

COUNTESS   To me, bloodthirsty lord;
And for that cause I trained thee to my house.   35
Long time thy shadow hath been thrall to me,   36
For in my gallery thy picture hangs;
But now the substance shall endure the like,
And I will chain these legs and arms of thine
That hast by tyranny these many years   40
Wasted our country, slain our citizens,
And sent our sons and husbands captivate.   42

TALBOT   Ha, ha, ha!

COUNTESS
Laughest thou, wretch? Thy mirth shall turn to
   moan.

TALBOT
I laugh to see your ladyship so fond   45
To think that you have aught but Talbot's shadow
Whereon to practice your severity.

COUNTESS   Why, art not thou the man?

TALBOT   I am indeed.

COUNTESS   Then have I substance too.

TALBOT
No, no, I am but shadow of myself.
You are deceived. My substance is not here;
For what you see is but the smallest part
And least proportion of humanity.   54
I tell you, madam, were the whole frame here,   55
It is of such a spacious lofty pitch   56
Your roof were not sufficient to contain 't.

COUNTESS
This is a riddling merchant for the nonce!   58
He will be here, and yet he is not here.
How can these contrarieties agree?

TALBOT
That will I show you presently.   61

*Winds his horn. Drums strike up. A peal of
ordnance. Enter soldiers.*

How say you, madam? Are you now persuaded
That Talbot is but shadow of himself?
These are his substance, sinews, arms, and strength,
With which he yoketh your rebellious necks,
Razeth your cities, and subverts your towns,   66

---

60 mean intend to act
2.3. Location: Auvergne. The Countess' castle.
1 gave in charge commanded   **6 Scythian Tomyris** tribal queen of the
Massagetae, who slew Cyrus the Great when he invaded her territory
and, in revenge for her son's death, had the head of Cyrus placed in a
wineskin filled with blood   **7 rumor** reputation.   **dreadful** inspiring
dread   **10 censure** judgment.   **rare** remarkable   **16 abroad** everywhere   **17 still** quiet   **19–20 Hercules, Hector** (Types of great physical strength.)   **20 for** because of.   **aspect** facial appearance   **21 proportion** size   **22 silly** i.e., frail, mere   **23 writhled** wrinkled   **27 sort**
choose

31 Marry (A mild interjection; originally an oath, "by the Virgin
Mary.")   **for that** because   **32 I go . . . here** i.e., I leave as a way of
informing her that I am the real Talbot, not the legendary figure of
popular report   **35 trained** lured, enticed   **36 shadow** image, likeness.   **thrall** slave   **40 tyranny** cruelty   **42 captivate** into captivity
45 fond foolish   **54 proportion of humanity** (1) part of the whole
man (2) portion of my army   **55 frame** structure, construct, i.e., of
man and of the army   **56 pitch** height   **58 riddling merchant** dealer
in riddles.   **nonce** occasion   **61 presently** immediately.   **s.d. Winds**
sounds   **66 subverts** overthrows

And in a moment makes them desolate.

COUNTESS
Victorious Talbot, pardon my abuse.   68
I find thou art no less than fame hath bruited,   69
And more than may be gathered by thy shape.
Let my presumption not provoke thy wrath,
For I am sorry that with reverence
I did not entertain thee as thou art.   73

TALBOT
Be not dismayed, fair lady, nor misconster   74
The mind of Talbot, as you did mistake
The outward composition of his body.
What you have done hath not offended me;
Nor other satisfaction do I crave
But only, with your patience, that we may   79
Taste of your wine and see what cates you have;   80
For soldiers' stomachs always serve them well.   81

COUNTESS
With all my heart, and think me honorèd
To feast so great a warrior in my house.   *Exeunt.*

❧

2.4   *Enter Richard Plantagenet, Warwick, Somerset,*
[William de la] Pole, [Earl of Suffolk, Vernon],
and others [including a Lawyer. A rose-bush is
provided onstage.]

PLANTAGENET
Great lords and gentlemen, what means this silence?
Dare no man answer in a case of truth?

SUFFOLK
Within the Temple hall we were too loud.   3
The garden here is more convenient.

PLANTAGENET
Then say at once if I maintained the truth;
Or else was wrangling Somerset in th' error?   6

SUFFOLK
Faith, I have been a truant in the law   7
And never yet could frame my will to it,   8
And therefore frame the law unto my will.

SOMERSET
Judge you, my lord of Warwick, then, between us.

WARWICK
Between two hawks, which flies the higher pitch,   11
Between two dogs, which hath the deeper mouth,   12
Between two blades, which bears the better temper,

Between two horses, which doth bear him best,   14
Between two girls, which hath the merriest eye,
I have perhaps some shallow spirit of judgment;
But in these nice sharp quillets of the law,   17
Good faith, I am no wiser than a daw.   18

PLANTAGENET
Tut, tut, here is a mannerly forbearance.   19
The truth appears so naked on my side
That any purblind eye may find it out.   21

SOMERSET
And on my side it is so well appareled,
So clear, so shining, and so evident,
That it will glimmer through a blind man's eye.

PLANTAGENET
Since you are tongue-tied and so loath to speak,
In dumb significants proclaim your thoughts.   26
Let him that is a trueborn gentleman
And stands upon the honor of his birth,
If he suppose that I have pleaded truth,   29
From off this brier pluck a white rose with me.   30
          [He plucks a white rose.]

SOMERSET
Let him that is no coward nor no flatterer,
But dare maintain the party of the truth,   32
Pluck a red rose from off this thorn with me.   33
          [He plucks a red rose. The others similarly
pluck roses as they speak.]

WARWICK
I love no colors, and without all color   34
Of base insinuating flattery
I pluck this white rose with Plantagenet.   36

SUFFOLK
I pluck this red rose with young Somerset
And say withal I think he held the right.   38

VERNON
Stay, lords and gentlemen, and pluck no more
Till you conclude that he upon whose side
The fewest roses are cropped from the tree
Shall yield the other in the right opinion.   42

SOMERSET
Good Master Vernon, it is well objected.   43
If I have fewest, I subscribe in silence.   44

PLANTAGENET   And I.

VERNON
Then, for the truth and plainness of the case,
I pluck this pale and maiden blossom here,

---

68 **abuse** (1) error (2) deception   69 **fame** report.   **bruited** reported,
rumored   73 **entertain** receive   74 **misconster** misconstrue   79 **patience** permission   80 **cates** delicacies, dainty confections   81 **stomachs** (1) appetites (2) bravery
2.4. **Location: London. The Temple Garden, with rosebushes. (The
Temple was a district of London taking its name from the Knights
Templars, who owned it during the twelfth and thirteenth centuries.
Its buildings were converted into Inns of Court, housing the legal societies of London, including the Inner Temple and the Middle Temple, in the fourteenth century.)**
3 **were** would have been   6 **Or else** i.e., in other words (?) (Or Plantagenet may be saying, lines 5–6, with intended humor, ''Am I right,
or is Somerset wrong?'')   7 **a truant** a neglectful student   8 **frame**
adapt   11 **pitch** elevation in flight   12 **mouth** voice

14 **bear him** carry himself   17 **nice** subtle, precise.   **quillets** subtle
distinctions   18 **daw** jackdaw. (A type of foolishness.)   19 **here . . .
forbearance** (Plantagenet sardonically deplores this offering of polite
excuses.)   21 **purblind** dim-sighted   26 **dumb significants** silent tokens, signs   29 **pleaded** argued. (One of many legal terms occurring
throughout this scene.)   30 **white rose** badge of the Mortimers and
subsequently of the house of York   32 **party** side (in law)   33 **red
rose** badge of the house of Lancaster   34 **colors** pretexts (playing on
the literal meaning)   36 **Plantagenet** (The nickname of Geoffrey of
Anjou, founder of the Angevin dynasty, which ruled England from the
reign of Geoffrey's son, Henry II, to that of Richard III. None of Geoffrey's descendants assumed the name until Richard, Duke of York,
adopted it in order to proclaim his superior right to the crown.)
38 **withal** besides   42 **yield** concede. (Another legal term, like *objected* and *subscribe* in the following two lines and *verdict* at line 48.)
43 **objected** urged   44 **subscribe** submit, concur (literally, by
signature)

Giving my verdict on the white rose side.

SOMERSET
Prick not your finger as you pluck it off,
Lest, bleeding, you do paint the white rose red,
And fall on my side so against your will.

VERNON
If I, my lord, for my opinion bleed,
Opinion shall be surgeon to my hurt   53
And keep me on the side where still I am.

SOMERSET   Well, well, come on, who else?

LAWYER [to Somerset]
Unless my study and my books be false,
The argument you held was wrong in law;
In sign whereof I pluck a white rose too.

PLANTAGENET
Now, Somerset, where is your argument?

SOMERSET
Here in my scabbard, meditating that   60
Shall dye your white rose in a bloody red.

PLANTAGENET
Meantime your cheeks do counterfeit our roses;   62
For pale they look with fear, as witnessing
The truth on our side.

SOMERSET   No, Plantagenet,
'Tis not for fear, but anger, that thy cheeks
Blush for pure shame to counterfeit our roses,
And yet thy tongue will not confess thy error.

PLANTAGENET
Hath not thy rose a canker, Somerset?   68

SOMERSET
Hath not thy rose a thorn, Plantagenet?

PLANTAGENET
Ay, sharp and piercing, to maintain his truth,   70
Whiles thy consuming canker eats his falsehood.

SOMERSET
Well, I'll find friends to wear my bleeding roses
That shall maintain what I have said is true,
Where false Plantagenet dare not be seen.

PLANTAGENET
Now, by this maiden blossom in my hand,
I scorn thee and thy fashion, peevish boy.   76

SUFFOLK
Turn not thy scorns this way, Plantagenet.

PLANTAGENET
Proud Pole, I will, and scorn both him and thee.   78

SUFFOLK
I'll turn my part thereof into thy throat.   79

SOMERSET
Away, away, good William de la Pole!
We grace the yeoman by conversing with him.   81

WARWICK
Now, by God's will, thou wrong'st him, Somerset.
His grandfather was Lionel, Duke of Clarence,   83
Third son to the third Edward, King of England.
Spring crestless yeomen from so deep a root?   85

PLANTAGENET
He bears him on the place's privilege,   86
Or durst not, for his craven heart, say thus.

SOMERSET
By him that made me, I'll maintain my words
On any plot of ground in Christendom.
Was not thy father, Richard, Earl of Cambridge,
For treason executed in our late king's days?   91
And by his treason stand'st not thou attainted,   92
Corrupted, and exempt from ancient gentry?   93
His trespass yet lives guilty in thy blood,
And till thou be restored, thou art a yeoman.

PLANTAGENET
My father was attachèd, not attainted,   96
Condemned to die for treason, but no traitor;
And that I'll prove on better men than Somerset,
Were growing time once ripened to my will.   99
For your partaker Pole, and you yourself,   100
I'll note you in my book of memory
To scourge you for this apprehension.   102
Look to it well, and say you are well warned.

SOMERSET
Ah, thou shalt find us ready for thee still,   104
And know us by these colors for thy foes,   105
For these my friends in spite of thee shall wear.   106

PLANTAGENET
And, by my soul, this pale and angry rose,
As cognizance of my blood-drinking hate,   108
Will I forever, and my faction, wear
Until it wither with me to my grave
Or flourish to the height of my degree.   111

SUFFOLK
Go forward, and be choked with thy ambition!
And so farewell until I meet thee next.   *Exit.*

SOMERSET
Have with thee, Pole.—Farewell, ambitious Richard. 114
                                                Exit.

---

53 **Opinion** public opinion, i.e., my reputation (punning on *opinion* in the sense of "conviction" in the previous line)   **60 that** that which   **62 counterfeit** imitate   **68 canker** cankerworm (that feeds on buds)   **70 his** its. (Also in line 71.)   **76 fashion** sort, or, the fashion of wearing red roses.   **peevish** silly   **78 Pole** family name of the Duke of Suffolk. (See also line 80.)   **79 I'll . . . throat** I'll throw the lies or slanders back into the throat from which they proceeded   **81 grace** do honor to.   **yeoman** a small freeholder, below the rank of landed gentleman. (A gibe at Plantagenet for having lost his lands and titles when his father, Richard, Earl of Cambridge, was executed in 1415 by Henry V for treason.)

83 His . . . Clarence (Lionel was actually Richard's maternal great-great-grandfather, but Edmund, Duke of York, fifth son of Edward III, was his paternal grandfather. Richard thus could trace his descent from Edward III through both Lionel and Edmund.)   **85 crestless** lacking heraldic titles (with a suggestion also of cowardice)   **86 He . . . privilege** i.e., Somerset presumes upon the safety of a privileged place (since engaging in quarrels with drawn weapons was prohibited in certain precincts, including the official residences of the sovereign; in fact, however, the Inns of Court were not thus privileged)   **91 late king's** i.e., Henry V's   **92 attainted** convicted and condemned. (According to law, the heirs of a person so attainted were deprived of all the rights and titles of their forebears; their blood was pronounced *corrupted*.)   **93 exempt** excluded.   **ancient gentry** hereditary rank   **96 attached, not attainted** (Historically, as Plantagenet insists, his father was *attached*, i.e., arrested, and summarily executed for treason without a bill of attainder.)   **99 Were . . . will** i.e., if the unfolding of time provides me opportunity   **100 For your partaker** as for your supporter   **102 apprehension** conception   **104 still** always   **105 know . . . foes** i.e., recognize us by these red badges as your enemies   **106 these . . . wear** my supporters will wear these (red roses) in spite of you   **108 cognizance** badge   **111 degree** noble rank   **114 Have with thee** I'll go along with you

PLANTAGENET
How I am braved and must perforce endure it!   115

WARWICK
This blot that they object against your house   116
Shall be wiped out in the next parliament,
Called for the truce of Winchester and Gloucester;   118
And if thou be not then created York,
I will not live to be accounted Warwick.
Meantime, in signal of my love to thee,   121
Against proud Somerset and William Pole,
Will I upon thy party wear this rose.
And here I prophesy: this brawl today,
Grown to this faction in the Temple Garden,
Shall send, between the red rose and the white,
A thousand souls to death and deadly night.

PLANTAGENET
Good Master Vernon, I am bound to you
That you on my behalf would pluck a flower.

VERNON
In your behalf still will I wear the same.

LAWYER   And so will I.

PLANTAGENET   Thanks, gentlemen.
Come, let us four to dinner. I dare say
This quarrel will drink blood another day.   *Exeunt.*

♣

2.5   *Enter Mortimer, brought in a chair, and Jailers.*

MORTIMER
Kind keepers of my weak decaying age,
Let dying Mortimer here rest himself.
Even like a man new-halèd from the rack,
So fare my limbs with long imprisonment;
And these gray locks, the pursuivants of death,   5
Nestor-like agèd in an age of care,   6
Argue the end of Edmund Mortimer.   7
These eyes, like lamps whose wasting oil is spent,
Wax dim, as drawing to their exigent;   9
Weak shoulders, overborne with burdening grief,
And pithless arms, like to a withered vine   11
That droops his sapless branches to the ground.
Yet are these feet, whose strengthless stay is numb,   13
Unable to support this lump of clay,
Swift-wingèd with desire to get a grave,
As witting I no other comfort have.   16
But tell me, keeper, will my nephew come?   17

FIRST KEEPER
Richard Plantagenet, my lord, will come.
We sent unto the Temple, unto his chamber,
And answer was returned that he will come.

MORTIMER
Enough. My soul shall then be satisfied.
Poor gentleman, his wrong doth equal mine.   22
Since Henry Monmouth first began to reign,   23
Before whose glory I was great in arms,
This loathsome sequestration have I had;   25
And even since then hath Richard been obscured,
Deprived of honor and inheritance.
But now the arbitrator of despairs,   28
Just Death, kind umpire of men's miseries,
With sweet enlargement doth dismiss me hence.   30
I would his troubles likewise were expired,   31
That so he might recover what was lost.

Enter Richard [Plantagenet].

FIRST KEEPER
My lord, your loving nephew now is come.

MORTIMER
Richard Plantagenet, my friend, is he come?

PLANTAGENET
Ay, noble uncle, thus ignobly used,
Your nephew, late despisèd Richard, comes.   36

MORTIMER
Direct mine arms I may embrace his neck,   37
And in his bosom spend my latter gasp.   38
O, tell me when my lips do touch his cheeks,
That I may kindly give one fainting kiss.
[*He embraces Richard.*]
And now declare, sweet stem from York's great
     stock,
Why didst thou say of late thou wert despised?

PLANTAGENET
First, lean thine agèd back against mine arm,
And, in that ease, I'll tell thee my disease.   44
This day, in argument upon a case,
Some words there grew twixt Somerset and me;
Among which terms he used his lavish tongue
And did upbraid me with my father's death;
Which obloquy set bars before my tongue,
Else with the like I had requited him.
Therefore, good uncle, for my father's sake,
In honor of a true Plantagenet,
And for alliance' sake, declare the cause   53
My father, Earl of Cambridge, lost his head.

MORTIMER
That cause, fair nephew, that imprisoned me
And hath detained me all my flowering youth
Within a loathsome dungeon, there to pine,
Was cursèd instrument of his decease.

---

115 **braved** defied.   **perforce** necessarily   116 **object** urge, allege
118 **Called . . . of** assembled to make peace between   121 **signal**
token
2.5. Location: The Tower of London.
5 **pursuivants** heralds   6 **Nestor-like** i.e., extremely old. (Nestor, the
oldest of the Greek chieftains at the siege of Troy, came to represent a
type of old age.)   7 **Argue** portend   9 **exigent** end   11 **pithless** marrowless, weak   13 **stay** support   16 **As witting** as if knowing
17 **nephew** (Richard was son of the fifth Earl of March's sister, Anne
Mortimer, who married Richard, Earl of Cambridge.)

22 **his wrong** the wrong done him   23 **Henry Monmouth** i.e., Henry
V   25 **sequestration** imprisonment. (Shakespeare, following the
chroniclers, confuses Edmund Mortimer, fifth Earl of March and great-
grandson of Lionel, Duke of Clarence, hence potential heir to the
throne, with his uncle Sir Edmund Mortimer, who was imprisoned by
Glendower, and also with the Earl of March's cousin, Sir John Mortimer, who was imprisoned and finally executed for agitating in behalf
of Edmund's royal claim. The Earl of March remained loyal to Henry
V.)   28 **arbitrator** bringer about of a definite issue   30 **enlargement**
release from confinement   31 **his** i.e., Richard's   36 **late** lately   37 **I
may** so that I may   38 **latter** last   44 **disease** unease, trouble, grievance   53 **alliance'** kinship's

PLANTAGENET
Discover more at large what cause that was,   59
For I am ignorant and cannot guess.

MORTIMER
I will, if that my fading breath permit
And death approach not ere my tale be done.
Henry the Fourth, grandfather to this king,
Deposed his nephew Richard, Edward's son,   64
The first-begotten and the lawful heir
Of Edward king, the third of that descent;
During whose reign the Percys of the north,   67
Finding his usurpation most unjust,
Endeavored my advancement to the throne.
The reason moved these warlike lords to this   70
Was for that—young King Richard thus removed,   71
Leaving no heir begotten of his body—
I was the next by birth and parentage;
For by my mother I derivèd am   74
From Lionel, Duke of Clarence, third son
To King Edward the Third; whereas he   76
From John of Gaunt doth bring his pedigree,
Being but fourth of that heroic line.
But mark. As in this haughty great attempt   79
They labored to plant the rightful heir,   80
I lost my liberty and they their lives.
Long after this, when Henry the Fifth,
Succeeding his father Bolingbroke, did reign,
Thy father, Earl of Cambridge then, derived
From famous Edmund Langley, Duke of York,
Marrying my sister that thy mother was,
Again, in pity of my hard distress,
Levied an army, weening to redeem   88
And have installed me in the diadem.   89
But, as the rest, so fell that noble earl
And was beheaded. Thus the Mortimers,
In whom the title rested, were suppressed.

PLANTAGENET
Of which, my lord, your honor is the last.

MORTIMER
True, and thou seest that I no issue have,
And that my fainting words do warrant death.   95
Thou art my heir. The rest I wish thee gather;   96
But yet be wary in thy studious care.   97

PLANTAGENET
Thy grave admonishments prevail with me.
But yet methinks my father's execution
Was nothing less than bloody tyranny.

MORTIMER
With silence, nephew, be thou politic.   101
Strong-fixèd is the house of Lancaster

And like a mountain, not to be removed.
But now thy uncle is removing hence,   104
As princes do their courts, when they are cloyed
With long continuance in a settled place.

PLANTAGENET
O uncle, would some part of my young years
Might but redeem the passage of your age!   108

MORTIMER
Thou dost then wrong me, as that slaughterer doth
Which giveth many wounds when one will kill.
Mourn not, except thou sorrow for my good;   111
Only give order for my funeral.   112
And so farewell, and fair be all thy hopes,
And prosperous be thy life in peace and war!   Dies.

PLANTAGENET
And peace, no war, befall thy parting soul!
In prison hast thou spent a pilgrimage
And like a hermit overpassed thy days.   117
Well, I will lock his counsel in my breast,
And what I do imagine, let that rest.   119
Keepers, convey him hence, and I myself
Will see his burial better than his life.
            Exeunt [Keepers, bearing out the body of
                                Mortimer].
Here dies the dusky torch of Mortimer,
Choked with ambition of the meaner sort.   123
And for those wrongs, those bitter injuries,   124
Which Somerset hath offered to my house,
I doubt not but with honor to redress;
And therefore haste I to the parliament,
Either to be restorèd to my blood   128
Or make mine ill th' advantage of my good.   Exit. 129

❦

3.1   *Flourish. Enter King, Exeter, Gloucester,
Winchester, Warwick, Somerset, Suffolk, Richard
Plantagenet, [and others]. Gloucester offers to put
up a bill; Winchester snatches it, [and] tears it.*

WINCHESTER
Com'st thou with deep premeditated lines,
With written pamphlets studiously devised?
Humphrey of Gloucester, if thou canst accuse,
Or aught intend'st to lay unto my charge,   4
Do it without invention, suddenly,   5
As I with sudden and extemporal speech
Purpose to answer what thou canst object.   7

59 **Discover** make known. **at large** at length 64 **nephew** kinsman. (Here, cousin.) 67 **whose** i.e., Henry IV's 70 **moved** that moved 71 **for that** that 74 **mother** (Shakespeare appears to confuse this Edmund with his uncle, Edmund Mortimer, second son of Lionel's daughter Philippa.) 76 **he** i.e., Henry IV, and, by extension of the family line, Henry VI. (See line 63.) 79 **haughty** proud, exalted 80 **They** the Percys and Mortimers 88 **weening** thinking. **redeem** rescue, free 89 **installed . . . diadem** crowned me king 95 **warrant** promise, assure 96 **gather** (1) infer (2) take as your own 97 **studious** diligent 101 **politic** prudent

104 **removing hence** departing from here, i.e., dying 108 **redeem the passage** buy back the passing 111 **except** unless 112 **give order** make arrangements 117 **overpassed** passed 119 **let that rest** leave it alone, i.e., let that be my business 123 **with** by. **meaner sort** those whose claim to the throne was inferior to his, i.e., the Lancastrians 124 **for** as for 128 **blood** hereditary rights 129 **Or . . . good** or make my wrongs the means of achieving my ambition
3.1. Location: London. The Parliament House.
s.d. **offers** tries, starts. **bill** (Here, a written accusation.) 4 **lay unto my charge** charge me with 5 **invention** premeditated design. **suddenly** extempore 7 **object** urge, present

GLOUCESTER
Presumptuous priest, this place commands my
  patience,   8
Or thou shouldst find thou hast dishonored me.
Think not, although in writing I preferred   10
The manner of thy vile outrageous crimes,
That therefore I have forged, or am not able
Verbatim to rehearse the method of my pen.   13
No, prelate, such is thy audacious wickedness,
Thy lewd, pestiferous, and dissentious pranks,   15
As very infants prattle of thy pride.   16
Thou art a most pernicious usurer,
Froward by nature, enemy to peace,   18
Lascivious, wanton, more than well beseems
A man of thy profession and degree.
And for thy treachery, what's more manifest?   21
In that thou laidst a trap to take my life,
As well at London Bridge as at the Tower.   23
Besides, I fear me, if thy thoughts were sifted,
The King, thy sovereign, is not quite exempt
From envious malice of thy swelling heart.
WINCHESTER
Gloucester, I do defy thee. Lords, vouchsafe
To give me hearing what I shall reply.
If I were covetous, ambitious, or perverse,
As he will have me, how am I so poor?
Or how haps it I seek not to advance   31
Or raise myself, but keep my wonted calling?   32
And for dissension, who preferreth peace
More than I do, except I be provoked?   34
No, my good lords, it is not that offends;   35
It is not that that hath incensed the Duke.
It is because no one should sway but he,   37
No one but he should be about the King;   38
And that engenders thunder in his breast
And makes him roar these accusations forth.
But he shall know I am as good—
GLOUCESTER   As good?
Thou bastard of my grandfather!   42
WINCHESTER
Ay, lordly sir! For what are you, I pray,
But one imperious in another's throne?   44
GLOUCESTER
Am I not Protector, saucy priest?
WINCHESTER
And am not I a prelate of the Church?

GLOUCESTER
Yes, as an outlaw in a castle keeps   47
And useth it to patronage his theft.   48
WINCHESTER
Unreverent Gloucester!
GLOUCESTER   Thou art reverend   49
Touching thy spiritual function, not thy life.   50
WINCHESTER
Rome shall remedy this.
WARWICK   Roam thither, then.
SOMERSET [to Warwick]
My lord, it were your duty to forbear.   52
WARWICK
Ay, see the Bishop be not overborne.   53
SOMERSET
Methinks my lord should be religious   54
And know the office that belongs to such.   55
WARWICK
Methinks his lordship should be humbler.   56
It fitteth not a prelate so to plead.
SOMERSET
Yes, when his holy state is touched so near.   58
WARWICK
State holy or unhallowed, what of that?
Is not His Grace Protector to the King?   60
PLANTAGENET [aside]
Plantagenet, I see, must hold his tongue,
Lest it be said, "Speak, sirrah, when you should;
Must your bold verdict enter talk with lords?"   63
Else would I have a fling at Winchester.
KING
Uncles of Gloucester and of Winchester,
The special watchmen of our English weal,   66
I would prevail, if prayers might prevail,
To join your hearts in love and amity.
O, what a scandal is it to our crown
That two such noble peers as ye should jar!   70
Believe me, lords, my tender years can tell   71
Civil dissension is a viperous worm
That gnaws the bowels of the commonwealth.
        A noise within, "Down with the tawny coats!"
What tumult's this?
WARWICK   An uproar, I dare warrant,
Begun through malice of the Bishop's men.
        A noise again, "Stones! Stones!"

        Enter Mayor.

8 **this place** i.e., Parliament, with the King presiding **10 preferred** put forward. (See 1.3.34–35 and note.) **13 Verbatim . . . pen** orally to recount what I have written **15 lewd** wicked. **pestiferous** deadly **16 As** that **18 Froward** perverse **21 for** as for. (Also in line 33.) **23 at London Bridge** (Gloucester's articles of accusation against Winchester presented to the Parliament stated that the latter had "set men-of-arms and archers at the end of London Bridge next Southwark," to prevent Gloucester's going to Eltham to interfere with the Bishop's plans regarding the young King.) **31 haps** happens **32 wonted calling** customary profession **34 except** unless **35 that** that that **37 sway** govern **38 about** near to **42 Thou bastard** (Winchester, son of John of Gaunt and Katharine Swynford before their marriage, was, with his two brothers and one sister, legitimatized by act of Parliament in Richard II's reign.) **44 imperious** (1) exercising rule (2) domineering

47 **keeps** dwells **48 patronage** maintain **49 Unreverent . . . reverend** irreverent, hostile to spiritual authority . . . respected, revered. (The Folio spellings, *Vnreuerent* and *reuerent*, accentuate the wordplay.) **50 Touching . . . function** i.e., in ecclesiastical title only **52 were** should be **53 overborne** prevailed over **54 my lord** i.e., Winchester. **should be** i.e., should be regarded as. (But Warwick, two lines below, uses the phrase in the sense "ought to be." Alternatively, Somerset here criticizes Warwick or Gloucester for showing disrespect toward a bishop.) **55 office** duty **56 his lordship** i.e., Winchester **58 state** degree, rank. **touched so near** so closely concerned **60 His Grace** i.e., Gloucester **63 bold verdict** audacious opinion. **enter talk** hold conversation **66 weal** common good **70 jar** quarrel **71 my tender years** (The King was actually five years old at the time of this episode.)

MAYOR
O my good lords, and virtuous Henry,
Pity the city of London, pity us!
The Bishop and the Duke of Gloucester's men,   80
Forbidden late to carry any weapon,   81
Have filled their pockets full of pebblestones
And, banding themselves in contrary parts,   83
Do pelt so fast at one another's pate
That many have their giddy brains knocked out.
Our windows are broke down in every street,
And we for fear compelled to shut our shops.

*Enter [Servingmen of both parties], in skirmish
with bloody pates.*

KING
We charge you, on allegiance to ourself,
To hold your slaughtering hands and keep the peace!
Pray, uncle Gloucester, mitigate this strife.
FIRST SERVINGMAN   Nay, if we be forbidden stones,
we'll fall to it with our teeth.
SECOND SERVINGMAN
Do what ye dare, we are as resolute.   *Skirmish again.*
GLOUCESTER
You of my household, leave this peevish broil   94
And set this unaccustomed fight aside.   95
THIRD SERVINGMAN
My lord, we know Your Grace to be a man
Just and upright, and for your royal birth
Inferior to none but to His Majesty;
And ere that we will suffer such a prince,   99
So kind a father of the commonweal,
To be disgracèd by an inkhorn mate,   101
We and our wives and children all will fight
And have our bodies slaughtered by thy foes.
FIRST SERVINGMAN
Ay, and the very parings of our nails
Shall pitch a field when we are dead.   *Begin again.*
GLOUCESTER   Stay, stay, I say! 105
An if you love me, as you say you do,
Let me persuade you to forbear awhile.
KING
O, how this discord doth afflict my soul!
Can you, my lord of Winchester, behold
My sighs and tears and will not once relent?
Who should be pitiful, if you be not?
Or who should study to prefer a peace,   112
If holy churchmen take delight in broils?
WARWICK
Yield, my Lord Protector; yield, Winchester,
Except you mean with obstinate repulse   115
To slay your sovereign and destroy the realm.
You see what mischief, and what murder too,

Hath been enacted through your enmity.
Then be at peace, except ye thirst for blood.
WINCHESTER
He shall submit, or I will never yield.
GLOUCESTER
Compassion on the King commands me stoop,
Or I would see his heart out ere the priest
Should ever get that privilege of me.   123
WARWICK
Behold, my lord of Winchester, the Duke
Hath banished moody discontented fury,   125
As by his smoothèd brows it doth appear.
Why look you still so stern and tragical?
GLOUCESTER
Here, Winchester, I offer thee my hand.
[He offers his hand, which Winchester refuses.]
KING
Fie, uncle Beaufort! I have heard you preach
That malice was a great and grievous sin;
And will not you maintain the thing you teach,
But prove a chief offender in the same?
WARWICK
Sweet King! The Bishop hath a kindly gird.   133
For shame, my lord of Winchester, relent!
What, shall a child instruct you what to do?
WINCHESTER
Well, Duke of Gloucester, I will yield to thee.
Love for thy love and hand for hand I give.
[They clasp hands.]
GLOUCESTER *[aside]*
Ay, but, I fear me, with a hollow heart.—   138
See here, my friends and loving countrymen,
This token serveth for a flag of truce   140
Betwixt ourselves and all our followers.
So help me God, as I dissemble not!
WINCHESTER *[aside]*
So help me God, as I intend it not!
KING
O loving uncle, kind Duke of Gloucester,
How joyful am I made by this contract!
[To Servingmen.] Away, my masters. Trouble us no
    more,   146
But join in friendship, as your lords have done.
FIRST SERVINGMAN
Content. I'll to the surgeon's.
SECOND SERVINGMAN   And so will I.
THIRD SERVINGMAN
And I will see what physic the tavern affords.   149
Exeunt [Servingmen and Mayor].
WARWICK *[proferring scroll]*
Accept this scroll, most gracious sovereign,
Which in the right of Richard Plantagenet
We do exhibit to Your Majesty.   152

80 Bishop Bishop's **81 late** lately **83 contrary parts** contending factions **94 peevish** petty, senseless **95 unaccustomed** contrary to custom and normality **99 ere that** before **101 inkhorn mate** scribbler. (Alludes scornfully to Winchester as a cleric or clerk.) **105 pitch a field** fight a battle, set in array for fighting (with defensive stakes) **112 prefer** propose, assist in arranging **115 Except** unless. **repulse** refusal

123 privilege of advantage over **125 moody** haughty **133 kindly gird** appropriate rebuke **138 hollow** treacherous **140 This token** i.e., the handshake **146 masters** (Condescending term of address to social inferiors.) **149 physic** medicine, remedy **152 exhibit** present for official consideration

GLOUCESTER
Well urged, my lord of Warwick. For, sweet prince,
An if Your Grace mark every circumstance,   154
You have great reason to do Richard right,
Especially for those occasions   156
At Eltham Place I told Your Majesty.

KING
And those occasions, uncle, were of force.   158
Therefore, my loving lords, our pleasure is
That Richard be restorèd to his blood.   160

WARWICK
Let Richard be restorèd to his blood.
So shall his father's wrongs be recompensed.

WINCHESTER
As will the rest, so willeth Winchester.

KING
If Richard will be true, not that alone
But all the whole inheritance I give
That doth belong unto the house of York,
From whence you spring by lineal descent.

PLANTAGENET
Thy humble servant vows obedience
And humble service till the point of death.

KING
Stoop then and set your knee against my foot.
                                    [Richard kneels.]
And in reguerdon of that duty done,   171
I gird thee with the valiant sword of York.
Rise, Richard, like a true Plantagenet,
And rise created princely Duke of York.

PLANTAGENET [rising]
And so thrive Richard as thy foes may fall!
And as my duty springs, so perish they
That grudge one thought against Your Majesty!   177

ALL
Welcome, high prince, the mighty Duke of York!

SOMERSET [aside]
Perish, base prince, ignoble Duke of York!

GLOUCESTER
Now will it best avail Your Majesty
To cross the seas and to be crownèd in France.
The presence of a king engenders love
Amongst his subjects and his loyal friends,
As it disanimates his enemies.   184

KING
When Gloucester says the word, King Henry goes,
For friendly counsel cuts off many foes.

GLOUCESTER
Your ships already are in readiness.   187
                    Sennet. Flourish. Exeunt. Manet Exeter.

EXETER
Ay, we may march in England or in France,
Not seeing what is likely to ensue.
This late dissension grown betwixt the peers   190

Burns under feignèd ashes of forged love   191
And will at last break out into a flame.
As festered members rot but by degree
Till bones and flesh and sinews fall away,
So will this base and envious discord breed.
And now I fear that fatal prophecy
Which in the time of Henry named the Fifth
Was in the mouth of every sucking babe:
That Henry born at Monmouth should win all   199
And Henry born at Windsor lose all;   200
Which is so plain that Exeter doth wish
His days may finish ere that hapless time.   Exit.

3.2   *Enter [Joan la] Pucelle disguised, with four
Soldiers with sacks upon their backs.*

PUCELLE
These are the city gates, the gates of Rouen,   1
Through which our policy must make a breach.   2
Take heed, be wary how you place your words;
Talk like the vulgar sort of marketmen   4
That come to gather money for their corn.   5
If we have entrance, as I hope we shall,
And that we find the slothful watch but weak,   7
I'll by a sign give notice to our friends,
That Charles the Dauphin may encounter them.   9

FIRST SOLDIER
Our sacks shall be a mean to sack the city,   10
And we be lords and rulers over Rouen.
Therefore we'll knock.   Knock.

WATCH [within]   *Qui là?*   13

PUCELLE
Paysans, la pauvre gens de France,
Poor market folks that come to sell their corn.

WATCH [opening the gates]
Enter, go in. The market bell is rung.

PUCELLE [aside]
Now, Rouen, I'll shake thy bulwarks to the ground.
                              Exeunt [to the town].

        *Enter Charles, [the] Bastard [of Orleans], Alençon,
        [Reignier, and forces].*

CHARLES
Saint Denis bless this happy stratagem!
And once again we'll sleep secure in Rouen.

BASTARD
Here entered Pucelle and her practisants.   20

---

154 **An if** if   156 **occasions** reasons which   158 **of force** compelling
160 **blood** hereditary right, inherited from his father   171 **reguerdon**
reward   177 **grudge one thought** harbor one grudging thought
184 **disanimates** discourages   187 **s.d. Sennet** set of notes played on
a trumpet as a signal for the approach or departure of processions.
Manet he remains onstage   190 **late** recent

191 **forged** feigned   199 **Henry born at Monmouth** i.e., Henry V
200 **Henry born at Windsor** i.e., Henry VI
3.2. Location: France. Before Rouen.
1 **Rouen** (As at Orleans in 1.5 through 2.1, the city gates here are represented by doors in the tiring-house facade, the "walls" of Rouen.
Appearances "on the walls," as at line 40 s.d., take place on the gallery backstage.)   2 **policy** stratagem   4 **vulgar** common   5 **corn** grain
7 **that** if   9 **them** i.e., the English soldiers guarding Rouen   10 **mean**
means   13 *Qui là qui est là,* who is there. (Rustic French.)   20 **practisants** conspirators

Now she is there, how will she specify
Here is the best and safest passage in?   22

REIGNIER
By thrusting out a torch from yonder tower,
Which, once discerned, shows that her meaning is,
No way to that, for weakness, which she entered.   25

*Enter Pucelle on the top, thrusting out a torch
burning.*

PUCELLE
Behold, this is the happy wedding torch
That joineth Rouen unto her countrymen,
But burning fatal to the Talbonites!   28

BASTARD
See, noble Charles, the beacon of our friend!
The burning torch in yonder turret stands.

CHARLES
Now shine it like a comet of revenge,   31
A prophet to the fall of all our foes!

REIGNIER
Defer no time! Delays have dangerous ends.
Enter, and cry "The Dauphin!" presently,   34
And then do execution on the watch.   35

Alarum. [They storm the gates.]

*An alarum. [Enter] Talbot in an excursion [from
within].*

TALBOT
France, thou shalt rue this treason with thy tears,
If Talbot but survive thy treachery.
Pucelle, that witch, that damnèd sorceress,
Hath wrought this hellish mischief unawares,   39
That hardly we escaped the pride of France.   *Exit.*   40

*An alarum. Excursions. Bedford, brought in sick
in a chair. Enter Talbot and Burgundy without;
within, Pucelle, Charles, Bastard, [Alençon,] and
Reignier, on the walls.*

PUCELLE
Good morrow, gallants. Want ye corn for bread?
I think the Duke of Burgundy will fast   42
Before he'll buy again at such a rate.   43
'Twas full of darnel. Do you like the taste?   44

BURGUNDY
Scoff on, vile fiend and shameless courtesan!

I trust ere long to choke thee with thine own   46
And make thee curse the harvest of that corn.

CHARLES
Your Grace may starve, perhaps, before that time.

BEDFORD
O, let no words, but deeds, revenge this treason!

PUCELLE
What will you do, good graybeard, break a lance
And run atilt at Death within a chair?   51

TALBOT
Foul fiend of France and hag of all despite,   52
Encompassed with thy lustful paramours!   53
Becomes it thee to taunt his valiant age
And twit with cowardice a man half dead?
Damsel, I'll have a bout with you again,   56
Or else let Talbot perish with this shame.

PUCELLE
Are ye so hot, sir?—Yet, Pucelle, hold thy peace.   58
If Talbot do but thunder, rain will follow.   59
        They [the English] whisper together in council.
God speed the parliament! Who shall be the speaker? 60

TALBOT
Dare ye come forth and meet us in the field?

PUCELLE
Belike your lordship takes us then for fools,   62
To try if that our own be ours or no.

TALBOT
I speak not to that railing Hecate,   64
But unto thee, Alençon, and the rest.
Will ye, like soldiers, come and fight it out?

ALENÇON   Seigneur, no.

TALBOT
Seigneur, hang! Base muleteers of France!   68
Like peasant footboys do they keep the walls   69
And dare not take up arms like gentlemen.

PUCELLE
Away, captains. Let's get us from the walls,
For Talbot means no goodness by his looks.
Good-bye, my lord. We came but to tell you
That we are here.   *Exeunt from the walls.*

TALBOT
And there will we be too, ere it be long,
Or else reproach be Talbot's greatest fame!   76
Vow, Burgundy, by honor of thy house,
Pricked on by public wrongs sustained in France,   78
Either to get the town again or die.
And I, as sure as English Henry lives
And as his father here was conqueror,   81
As sure as in this late-betrayèd town   82

22 **Here . . . in** i.e., that here (the same spot she entered) is the best and safest place for us to enter as well   25 **No . . . entered** no other place can be compared to the one where she entered for weakness; it is the most weakly defended.   **s.d. on the top** i.e., at some upper vantage point in the theater   28 **Talbonites** followers of Talbot   31 **shine it** may it shine   34 **presently** immediately   35 **do . . . watch** kill all the guards.   **s.d. excursion** skirmish, sortie   39 **unawares** unexpectedly   40 **pride** princely power.   **s.d. Bedford . . . sick** (Actually, Bedford outlived Joan of Arc by four years. The entire episode of the capture of Rouen, as presented here, is unhistorical; the English did not relinquish the city until 1449, some eighteen years after Joan's death.)   **without** i.e., on the main stage.   **within** i.e., in the gallery backstage   42–43 **will fast . . . rate** i.e., will be hesitant to do business with us again, having been sold a bill of goods   44 **darnel** injurious weed

46 **thine own** i.e., your own bread   51 **run atilt at** joust with.   **within** i.e., sitting in   52 **hag of all despite** malicious witch   53 **Encompassed with** surrounded by   56 **bout** encounter with weapons (with sexual overtones, as earlier at 1.5.4)   58 **hot** (1) hot-tempered (2) lustful   59 **If . . . follow** (A proverb, suggesting that angry talk is to be followed by fighting.)   60 **speaker** spokesman (playing on the sense of "parliamentary leader")   62 **Belike** perhaps   64 **Hecate** goddess of night and of black magic   68 **muleteers** mule drivers   69 **keep** keep safely within   76 **fame** reputation   78 **Pricked on** goaded   81 **father . . . conqueror** (Henry V captured Rouen in 1419.)   82 **late-betrayèd** recently lost to the enemy through treachery

Great Coeur de Lion's heart was buried,   83
So sure I swear to get the town or die.

BURGUNDY
My vows are equal partners with thy vows.

TALBOT
But ere we go, regard this dying prince,   86
The valiant Duke of Bedford.—Come, my lord,
We will bestow you in some better place,
Fitter for sickness and for crazy age.   89

BEDFORD
Lord Talbot, do not so dishonor me.
Here will I sit before the walls of Rouen
And will be partner of your weal or woe.   92

BURGUNDY
Courageous Bedford, let us now persuade you.

BEDFORD
Not to be gone from hence; for once I read
That stout Pendragon in his litter sick   95
Came to the field and vanquishèd his foes.
Methinks I should revive the soldiers' hearts,
Because I ever found them as myself.

TALBOT
Undaunted spirit in a dying breast!
Then be it so. Heavens keep old Bedford safe!
And now no more ado, brave Burgundy,
But gather we our forces out of hand   102
And set upon our boasting enemy.

> *Exeunt [all but Bedford and attendants].*

> *An alarum. Excursions. Enter Sir John Falstaff
> and a Captain.*

CAPTAIN
Whither away, Sir John Falstaff, in such haste?

FALSTAFF
Whither away? To save myself by flight.
We are like to have the overthrow again.   106

CAPTAIN
What? Will you fly, and leave Lord Talbot?

FALSTAFF   Ay,
All the Talbots in the world, to save my life.   *Exit.*

CAPTAIN
Cowardly knight, ill fortune follow thee!   *Exit.*

> *Retreat. Excursions. Pucelle, Alençon, and
> Charles fly.*

BEDFORD
Now, quiet soul, depart when heaven please,   110
For I have seen our enemies' overthrow.   111

What is the trust or strength of foolish man?
They that of late were daring with their scoffs
Are glad and fain by flight to save themselves.   114

> *Bedford dies, and is carried in by two in his chair.*

> *An alarum. Enter Talbot, Burgundy, and the rest
> [of the English soldiers].*

TALBOT
Lost and recovered in a day again!
This is a double honor, Burgundy.
Yet heavens have glory for this victory!

BURGUNDY
Warlike and martial Talbot, Burgundy
Enshrines thee in his heart and there erects
Thy noble deeds as valor's monuments.

TALBOT
Thanks, gentle Duke. But where is Pucelle now?   121
I think her old familiar is asleep.   122
Now where's the Bastard's braves, and Charles his
    gleeks?   123
What, all amort? Rouen hangs her head for grief   124
That such a valiant company are fled.
Now will we take some order in the town,   126
Placing therein some expert officers,
And then depart to Paris to the King,
For there young Henry with his nobles lie.

BURGUNDY
What wills Lord Talbot pleaseth Burgundy.

TALBOT
But yet, before we go, let's not forget
The noble Duke of Bedford late deceased,
But see his exequies fulfilled in Rouen.   133
A braver soldier never couchèd lance;   134
A gentler heart did never sway in court.   135
But kings and mightiest potentates must die,
For that's the end of human misery.   *Exeunt.*

❦

3.3   *Enter Charles, [the] Bastard [of Orleans], Alençon,
          Pucelle, [and French soldiers].*

PUCELLE
Dismay not, princes, at this accident,   1
Nor grieve that Rouen is so recoverèd.
Care is no cure, but rather corrosive,   3
For things that are not to be remedied.
Let frantic Talbot triumph for a while
And like a peacock sweep along his tail;
We'll pull his plumes and take away his train,   7
If Dauphin and the rest will be but ruled.

---

83 Great . . . heart (According to Holinshed, Richard Coeur de Lion, "the lion-hearted" King of England 1189–1199, had willed that "his heart be conveyed unto Rouen and there buried, in testimony of the love which he had ever borne unto that city.")   **86 regard** attend to   **89 crazy** decrepit   **92 weal** welfare   **95 Pendragon** (According to Holinshed, it was the brother of Uther Pendragon who, "even sick as he was, caused himself to be carried forth in a litter; with whose presence his people were so encouraged that, encountering with the Saxons, they won the victory." Geoffrey of Monmouth, on the other hand, credits this feat to Uther himself. Uther was father of King Arthur.)   **102 out of hand** at once   **106 like to . . . overthrow** likely to be overthrown   **110–111 Now . . . overthrow** (A secular version of Luke 2:29–30, "Lord, now lettest thou thy servant depart in peace," etc., sung as the *Nunc dimittis* in evensong in the Book of Common Prayer.)

114 fain eager.   **s.d. carried in** carried offstage   **121 gentle** noble   **122 old familiar** customary attendant demon   **123 braves** boasts. **Charles his gleeks** Charles's gibes, jests   **124 amort** sick to death, dispirited   **126 take some order** establish order and government   **133 exequies** funeral rites   **134 couchèd lance** carried his lance lowered, in the position of attack   **135 gentler** more noble.   **sway** exercise influence
3.3. Location: Near Rouen.
1 Dismay not be not dismayed, disheartened.   **accident** bad luck, untoward event   **3 Care** sorrow   **7 train** (1) peacock's tail (2) army

CHARLES
We have been guided by thee hitherto,
And of thy cunning had no diffidence.   10
One sudden foil shall never breed distrust.   11

BASTARD
Search out thy wit for secret policies,   12
And we will make thee famous through the world.

ALENÇON
We'll set thy statue in some holy place
And have thee reverenced like a blessèd saint.
Employ thee then, sweet virgin, for our good.

PUCELLE
Then thus it must be; this doth Joan devise:
By fair persuasions, mixed with sugared words,
We will entice the Duke of Burgundy
To leave the Talbot and to follow us.

CHARLES
Ay, marry, sweeting, if we could do that,
France were no place for Henry's warriors,
Nor should that nation boast it so with us,
But be extirpèd from our provinces.   24

ALENÇON
Forever should they be expulsed from France
And not have title of an earldom here.

PUCELLE
Your honors shall perceive how I will work
To bring this matter to the wishèd end.
                        Drum sounds afar off.
Hark, by the sound of drum you may perceive
Their powers are marching unto Paris-ward.   30
                    Here sounds an English march.
There goes the Talbot, with his colors spread,
And all the troops of English after him.
                                French march.
Now in the rearward comes the Duke and his.
Fortune in favor makes him lag behind.   34
Summon a parley. We will talk with him.   35
                        Trumpets sound a parley.

[*Enter the Duke of Burgundy.*]

CHARLES
A parley with the Duke of Burgundy!

BURGUNDY
Who craves a parley with the Burgundy?

PUCELLE
The princely Charles of France, thy countryman.

BURGUNDY
What sayst thou, Charles? For I am marching hence.

CHARLES
Speak, Pucelle, and enchant him with thy words.   40

PUCELLE
Brave Burgundy, undoubted hope of France,   41
Stay. Let thy humble handmaid speak to thee.

BURGUNDY
Speak on, but be not overtedious.

PUCELLE
Look on thy country, look on fertile France,
And see the cities and the towns defaced
By wasting ruin of the cruel foe.
As looks the mother on her lowly babe   47
When death doth close his tender-dying eyes,   48
See, see the pining malady of France!   49
Behold the wounds, the most unnatural wounds,   50
Which thou thyself hast given her woeful breast.
O, turn thy edgèd sword another way!
Strike those that hurt, and hurt not those that help!
One drop of blood drawn from thy country's bosom
Should grieve thee more than streams of foreign
   gore.
Return thee therefore with a flood of tears
And wash away thy country's stainèd spots.   57

BURGUNDY [*aside*]
Either she hath bewitched me with her words,
Or nature makes me suddenly relent.

PUCELLE
Besides, all French and France exclaims on thee,   60
Doubting thy birth and lawful progeny.   61
Who join'st thou with but with a lordly nation
That will not trust thee but for profit's sake?
When Talbot hath set footing once in France
And fashioned thee that instrument of ill,   65
Who then but English Henry will be lord,
And thou be thrust out like a fugitive?   67
Call we to mind, and mark but this for proof: 68
Was not the Duke of Orleans thy foe?
And was he not in England prisoner?
But when they heard he was thine enemy,
They set him free without his ransom paid,
In spite of Burgundy and all his friends.
See, then, thou fight'st against thy countrymen
And join'st with them will be thy slaughtermen.   75
Come, come, return. Return, thou wandering lord!
Charles and the rest will take thee in their arms.

BURGUNDY [*aside*]
I am vanquished. These haughty words of hers   78
Have battered me like roaring cannon-shot
And made me almost yield upon my knees.—
Forgive me, country, and sweet countrymen!
And, lords, accept this hearty kind embrace.
My forces and my power of men are yours.
So farewell, Talbot. I'll no longer trust thee.

PUCELLE
Done like a Frenchman—[*aside*] turn and turn again!

CHARLES
Welcome, brave Duke! Thy friendship makes us
   fresh.

47 **lowly** little, or humbled by misfortune, lying low   48 **tender-dying** dying at a tender age   49 **malady of France** (With comic double meaning; the phrase normally refers to venereal disease.)   50 **unnatural** i.e., turned against the doer's own country   57 **thy . . . spots** blemishes to your country's reputation   60 **exclaims on** denounces, accuses   61 **progeny** ancestry   65 **fashioned thee** turned you into   67 **fugitive** renegade, deserter of your own nation   68 **Call we to mind** let us remember   75 **them** those who   78 **I am vanquished** (Historically, Burgundy did not desert the English alliance until four years after Joan's death. This desertion occurred five years before the Duke of Orleans was released by the English; see lines 69–73.) **haughty** lofty

10 **diffidence** distrust   11 **foil** repulse, defeat   12 **policies** stratagems   24 s.d. **extirpèd** rooted out   30 s.d. **Here . . . march** (Probably the English are heard from offstage, and the French at line 32, but conceivably soldiers could pass over the stage.)   34 **in favor** benevolently, i.e., in our favor   35 **Summon a parley** sound a trumpet signal requesting negotiations   40 **enchant** put spells on   41 **undoubted** i.e., whose bravery and strength are sure bulwarks

BASTARD
And doth beget new courage in our breasts.

ALENÇON
Pucelle hath bravely played her part in this   88
And doth deserve a coronet of gold.

CHARLES
Now let us on, my lords, and join our powers,   90
And seek how we may prejudice the foe.   *Exeunt.* 91

❖

3.4   *Enter the King, Gloucester, Winchester, [Richard, Duke of] York, Suffolk, Somerset, Warwick, Exeter, [Vernon, wearing a white rose, Basset, wearing a red rose, and others]. To them, with his soldiers, Talbot.*

TALBOT
My gracious prince, and honorable peers,
Hearing of your arrival in this realm,
I have awhile given truce unto my wars
To do my duty to my sovereign;   4
In sign whereof, this arm, that hath reclaimed
To your obedience fifty fortresses,
Twelve cities, and seven walled towns of strength,
Besides five hundred prisoners of esteem,
Lets fall his sword before Your Highness' feet,
And with submissive loyalty of heart
Ascribes the glory of his conquest got
First to my God and next unto Your Grace.
                                        [He kneels.]

KING
Is this the Lord Talbot, uncle Gloucester,
That hath so long been resident in France?

GLOUCESTER
Yes, if it please Your Majesty, my liege.

KING
Welcome, brave captain and victorious lord!
When I was young—as yet I am not old—
I do remember how my father said   18
A stouter champion never handled sword.   19
Long since we were resolvèd of your truth,   20
Your faithful service, and your toil in war;
Yet never have you tasted our reward
Or been reguerdoned with so much as thanks,   23
Because till now we never saw your face.
Therefore, stand up. *[Talbot rises.]* And for these
    good deserts   25
We here create you Earl of Shrewsbury;
And in our coronation take your place.   27
            Sennet. Flourish. Exeunt. Manent Vernon and
                                        Basset.

VERNON
Now, sir, to you, that were so hot at sea,   28
Disgracing of these colors that I wear   29
In honor of my noble lord of York:
Dar'st thou maintain the former words thou spak'st?

BASSET
Yes, sir, as well as you dare patronage   32
The envious barking of your saucy tongue
Against my lord the Duke of Somerset.

VERNON
Sirrah, thy lord I honor as he is.   35

BASSET
Why, what is he? As good a man as York.

VERNON
Hark ye, not so. In witness, take ye that.
                                        Strikes him.

BASSET
Villain, thou knowest the law of arms is such   38
That whoso draws a sword, 'tis present death,   39
Or else this blow should broach thy dearest blood.   40
But I'll unto His Majesty and crave
I may have liberty to venge this wrong,   42
When thou shalt see I'll meet thee to thy cost.

VERNON
Well, miscreant, I'll be there as soon as you,
And after meet you, sooner than you would. *Exeunt.* 45

4.1   *Enter King, Gloucester, Winchester, [Richard, Duke of] York, Suffolk, Somerset, Warwick, Talbot, Exeter, Governor [of Paris, and others].*

GLOUCESTER
Lord Bishop, set the crown upon his head.

WINCHESTER
God save King Henry, of that name the sixth!
                                [The King is crowned.]

GLOUCESTER
Now, Governor of Paris, take your oath,
                                [The governor kneels.]
That you elect no other king but him,   4
Esteem none friends but such as are his friends,
And none your foes but such as shall pretend   6
Malicious practices against his state.   7
This shall ye do, so help you righteous God!
                                [The Governor retires.]

            Enter [Sir John] Falstaff.

---

88 bravely courageously and excellently   **90 powers** armed forces
91 prejudice harm
3.4. Location: Paris. The royal court.
4 duty homage   **18** I . . . **said** (Historically, Henry VI was an infant of nine months at his father's death.)   **19 stouter** more intrepid
20 we i.e., I. (The royal "we.")   **resolvèd** convinced.   **truth** loyalty
23 reguerdoned rewarded   **25 deserts** deservings   **27 s.d. Manent** they remain onstage

28 so hot at sea (The details of this quarrel are given below, at 4.1.87–97.)   **29 Disgracing of** insulting.   **these colors** i.e., the white rose of York   **32 patronage** defend   **35 as he is** i.e., for what he is—a person of no worth   **38 law of arms** (This law forbade the drawing of weapons near a royal residence; see 1.3.46 and note, and 2.4.86 and note.)   **39 present** instant   **40 broach** tap, draw.   **dearest blood** i.e., lifeblood   **42 wrong** insult   **45 after** i.e., once the royal permission to fight a duel has been obtained
4.1. Location: Paris. Scene continues. (The action appears to go on immediately after the events of 3.4.)
s.d. York i.e., Richard Plantagenet, created Duke of York in 3.1 and hereafter identified by the speech prefix YORK   **4 elect** acknowledge
6 pretend purpose, intend   **7 practices** stratagems

FALSTAFF
My gracious sovereign, as I rode from Calais
To haste unto your coronation,
A letter was delivered to my hands,
Writ to Your Grace from th' Duke of Burgundy.
                              [*He presents a letter.*]

TALBOT
Shame to the Duke of Burgundy and thee!
I vowed, base knight, when I did meet thee next,
To tear the Garter from thy craven's leg,   15
                              [*plucking it off*]
Which I have done, because unworthily
Thou wast installèd in that high degree.—
Pardon me, princely Henry, and the rest.
This dastard, at the battle of Poitiers,   19
When but in all I was six thousand strong   20
And that the French were almost ten to one,   21
Before we met or that a stroke was given,
Like to a trusty squire did run away;   23
In which assault we lost twelve hundred men.
Myself and divers gentlemen besides
Were there surprised and taken prisoners.
Then judge, great lords, if I have done amiss,
Or whether that such cowards ought to wear
This ornament of knighthood, yea or no?

GLOUCESTER
To say the truth, this fact was infamous   30
And ill beseeming any common man,
Much more a knight, a captain, and a leader.

TALBOT
When first this order was ordained, my lords,
Knights of the Garter were of noble birth,
Valiant and virtuous, full of haughty courage,   35
Such as were grown to credit by the wars—   36
Not fearing death, nor shrinking for distress,
But always resolute in most extremes.   38
He then that is not furnished in this sort   39
Doth but usurp the sacred name of knight,
Profaning this most honorable order,
And should, if I were worthy to be judge,
Be quite degraded, like a hedge-born swain   43
That doth presume to boast of gentle blood.   44

KING [*to Falstaff*]
Stain to thy countrymen, thou hear'st thy doom.   45
Be packing, therefore, thou that wast a knight.   46
Henceforth we banish thee, on pain of death.
                              [*Exit Falstaff.*]
And now, my Lord Protector, view the letter

Sent from our uncle Duke of Burgundy.   49
GLOUCESTER [*taking the letter*]
What means His Grace, that he hath changed his
    style?   50
No more but, plain and bluntly, "To the King"?
Hath he forgot he is his sovereign?
Or doth this churlish superscription   53
Pretend some alteration in good will?   54
What's here? [*He reads.*] "I have, upon especial
    cause,
Moved with compassion of my country's wrack,   56
Together with the pitiful complaints
Of such as your oppression feeds upon,
Forsaken your pernicious faction
And joined with Charles, the rightful King of
    France."
O monstrous treachery! Can this be so,
That in alliance, amity, and oaths
There should be found such false dissembling guile?

KING
What? Doth my uncle Burgundy revolt?   64
GLOUCESTER
He doth, my lord, and is become your foe.
KING
Is that the worst this letter doth contain?
GLOUCESTER
It is the worst, and all, my lord, he writes.
KING
Why, then, Lord Talbot there shall talk with him
And give him chastisement for this abuse.   69
[*To Talbot.*] How say you, my lord? Are you not
    content?
TALBOT
Content, my liege? Yes. But that I am prevented,   71
I should have begged I might have been employed.
KING
Then gather strength and march unto him straight.   73
Let him perceive how ill we brook his treason,   74
And what offense it is to flout his friends.
TALBOT
I go, my lord, in heart desiring still   76
You may behold confusion of your foes.   [*Exit.*]   77

          Enter Vernon and Basset, [wearing a white and a
          red rose respectively, as before].

VERNON
Grant me the combat, gracious sovereign.   78
BASSET
And me, my lord. Grant me the combat too.
YORK
This is my servant. Hear him, noble prince.   80

---

15 **Garter** badge of the Knights of the Garter, a ribbon of blue velvet edged and buckled with gold, worn below the left knee. (Historically, the Garter was apparently taken from Fastolfe by the Duke of Bedford; Talbot, who was a captive of the French at the time of Henry VI's coronation in Paris, was opposed to the restoration of the Garter to Fastolfe.)   19 **Poitiers** (Seemingly confused with Patay.)   20 **but in all** all told   21 **And that** and   23 **trusty squire** (Said contemptuously.)
30 **fact** deed   35 **haughty** exalted   36 **were grown to credit** had achieved renown   38 **most** greatest   39 **furnished . . . sort** endowed thus   43 **degraded** lowered in rank.   **hedge-born swain** lowly born rustic   44 **gentle** noble   45 **doom** sentence   46 **Be packing** be off

49 **uncle** (The Lancastrian and Burgundian houses were allied by the marriage of the Duke of Bedford, the King's uncle, to Anne, sister of the Duke of Burgundy.)   50 **style** form of address   53 **churlish superscription** insolent form of address on the outside of the letter
54 **Pretend** portend, import   56 **wrack** ruin   64 **revolt** fall away to the other side   69 **abuse** deception   71 **prevented** anticipated
73 **straight** immediately   74 **brook** endure   76 **still** always   77 **confusion** destruction   78 **the combat** permission to fight a trial by duel
80 **servant** follower

SOMERSET
And this is mine. Sweet Henry, favor him.
KING
Be patient, lords, and give them leave to speak.
Say, gentlemen, what makes you thus exclaim?
And wherefore crave you combat, or with whom?
VERNON
With him, my lord, for he hath done me wrong.
BASSET
And I with him, for he hath done me wrong.
KING
What is that wrong whereof you both complain?
First let me know, and then I'll answer you.
BASSET
Crossing the sea from England into France,
This fellow here, with envious carping tongue,   90
Upbraided me about the rose I wear,
Saying the sanguine color of the leaves   92
Did represent my master's blushing cheeks,
When stubbornly he did repugn the truth   94
About a certain question in the law
Argued betwixt the Duke of York and him;
With other vile and ignominious terms.
In confutation of which rude reproach,
And in defense of my lord's worthiness,
I crave the benefit of law of arms.   100
VERNON
And that is my petition, noble lord.
For though he seem with forgèd quaint conceit   102
To set a gloss upon his bold intent,   103
Yet know, my lord, I was provoked by him,
And he first took exceptions at this badge,
Pronouncing that the paleness of this flower
Bewrayed the faintness of my master's heart.   107
YORK
Will not this malice, Somerset, be left?   108
SOMERSET
Your private grudge, my lord of York, will out,   109
Though ne'er so cunningly you smother it.
KING
Good Lord, what madness rules in brainsick men,
When for so slight and frivolous a cause
Such factious emulations shall arise!   113
Good cousins both, of York and Somerset,   114
Quiet yourselves, I pray, and be at peace.
YORK
Let this dissension first be tried by fight,
And then Your Highness shall command a peace.
SOMERSET
The quarrel toucheth none but us alone;   118
Betwixt ourselves let us decide it then.
YORK
There is my pledge. Accept it, Somerset.   120
                    [*He throws down a gage.*]

VERNON
Nay, let it rest where it began at first.   121
BASSET
Confirm it so, mine honorable lord.   122
GLOUCESTER
Confirm it so? Confounded be your strife!
And perish ye, with your audacious prate!
Presumptuous vassals, are you not ashamed
With this immodest clamorous outrage   126
To trouble and disturb the King and us?
And you, my lords, methinks you do not well   128
To bear with their perverse objections,   129
Much less to take occasion from their mouths
To raise a mutiny betwixt yourselves.   131
Let me persuade you take a better course.
EXETER
It grieves His Highness. Good my lords, be friends.
KING
Come hither, you that would be combatants:
Henceforth I charge you, as you love our favor,
Quite to forget this quarrel and the cause.
And you, my lords: remember where we are—
In France, amongst a fickle wavering nation.
If they perceive dissension in our looks
And that within ourselves we disagree,   140
How will their grudging stomachs be provoked   141
To willful disobedience, and rebel!
Besides, what infamy will there arise
When foreign princes shall be certified   144
That for a toy, a thing of no regard,   145
King Henry's peers and chief nobility
Destroyed themselves and lost the realm of France!
O, think upon the conquest of my father,
My tender years, and let us not forgo
That for a trifle that was bought with blood!   150
Let me be umpire in this doubtful strife.   151
I see no reason, if I wear this rose,
                    [*putting on a red rose*]
That anyone should therefore be suspicious
I more incline to Somerset than York.
Both are my kinsmen, and I love them both.
As well they may upbraid me with my crown
Because, forsooth, the King of Scots is crowned.
But your discretions better can persuade
Than I am able to instruct or teach;
And therefore, as we hither came in peace,
So let us still continue peace and love.   161
Cousin of York, we institute Your Grace
To be our regent in these parts of France.
And, good my lord of Somerset, unite
Your troops of horsemen with his bands of foot;   165

90 envious malicious   **92 sanguine** bloodred.   **leaves** petals   **94 repugn** oppose, resist   **100 benefit . . . arms** right to protect my honor in a duel   **102 forgèd quaint conceit** false ingenious rhetoric **103 gloss** speciously fair appearance   **107 Bewrayed** revealed **108 left** given up, forgotten   **109 out** appear, be revealed   **113 factious emulations** contentions between rivals   **114 cousins** kinsmen **118 toucheth** concerns   **120 pledge** i.e., a glove or gauntlet flung down as a gage in a duel

121 let . . . first i.e., let the quarrel remain with me and Basset, who began it. (Said perhaps to York or to the King.)   **122 Confirm . . . lord** i.e., confirm the suggestion that Vernon and I be allowed to fight it out between ourselves. (Said perhaps to Somerset or to the King.) **126 immodest** arrogant, impudent   **128 my lords** i.e., York and Somerset. (Also in line 137.)   **129 objections** charges, accusations **131 mutiny** quarrel, strife   **140 within** among   **141 grudging stomachs** resentful tempers   **144 certified** informed   **145 toy** trifle **150 That . . . that** for a trifle that which   **151 doubtful** causing apprehension   **161 still** ever   **165 bands of foot** troops of infantry

And like true subjects, sons of your progenitors,
Go cheerfully together and digest   167
Your angry choler on your enemies.
Ourself, my Lord Protector, and the rest
After some respite will return to Calais;
From thence to England, where I hope ere long
To be presented, by your victories,
With Charles, Alençon, and that traitorous rout.   173
Flourish. Exeunt. Manent York, Warwick,
Exeter, [and] Vernon.

WARWICK
My lord of York, I promise you, the King   174
Prettily, methought, did play the orator.

YORK
And so he did; but yet I like it not
In that he wears the badge of Somerset.

WARWICK
Tush, that was but his fancy. Blame him not.
I dare presume, sweet prince, he thought no harm.

YORK
An if I wist he did—But let it rest.   180
Other affairs must now be managèd.
Exeunt. Manet Exeter.

EXETER
Well didst thou, Richard, to suppress thy voice;
For, had the passions of thy heart burst out,
I fear we should have seen deciphered there   184
More rancorous spite, more furious raging broils,
Than yet can be imagined or supposed.
But howsoe'er, no simple man that sees   187
This jarring discord of nobility,
This shouldering of each other in the court,
This factious bandying of their favorites,   190
But that it doth presage some ill event.   191
'Tis much when scepters are in children's hands,
But more when envy breeds unkind division.   193
There comes the ruin, there begins confusion.   *Exit.*

❧

4.2   *Enter Talbot, with trump and drum [and forces],*
before Bordeaux.

TALBOT
Go to the gates of Bordeaux, trumpeter.   1
Summon their general unto the wall.

[Trumpet] sounds. Enter General, aloft.

English John Talbot, captains, calls you forth,
Servant in arms to Harry King of England,
And thus he would: Open your city gates,   5

Be humble to us, call my sovereign yours,
And do him homage as obedient subjects,
And I'll withdraw me and my bloody power.   8
But if you frown upon this proffered peace,
You tempt the fury of my three attendants,
Lean famine, quartering steel, and climbing fire,   11
Who in a moment even with the earth   12
Shall lay your stately and air-braving towers,   13
If you forsake the offer of their love.   14

GENERAL
Thou ominous and fearful owl of death,   15
Our nation's terror and their bloody scourge,   16
The period of thy tyranny approacheth.   17
On us thou canst not enter but by death,
For I protest we are well fortified
And strong enough to issue out and fight.
If thou retire, the Dauphin, well appointed,   21
Stands with the snares of war to tangle thee.
On either hand thee there are squadrons pitched, 23
To wall thee from the liberty of flight;
And no way canst thou turn thee for redress
But death doth front thee with apparent spoil   26
And pale destruction meets thee in the face.   27
Ten thousand French have ta'en the Sacrament   28
To rive their dangerous artillery   29
Upon no Christian soul but English Talbot.
Lo, there thou stand'st, a breathing valiant man
Of an invincible unconquered spirit.
This is the latest glory of thy praise   33
That I, thy enemy, due thee withal;   34
For ere the glass that now begins to run   35
Finish the process of his sandy hour,   .   36
These eyes, that see thee now well colorèd,   37
Shall see thee withered, bloody, pale, and dead.
Drum afar off.
Hark, hark! The Dauphin's drum, a warning bell,
Sings heavy music to thy timorous soul,
And mine shall ring thy dire departure out.   *Exit.* 41

TALBOT
He fables not. I hear the enemy.
Out, some light horsemen, and peruse their wings. 43
[Exeunt some.]
O, negligent and heedless discipline!   44
How are we parked and bounded in a pale—   45
A little herd of England's timorous deer,
Mazed with a yelping kennel of French curs!   47
If we be English deer, be then in blood: 48

---

167 **digest** disperse, dissipate 173 **rout** rabble. **s.d. Manent** they remain onstage 174 **promise** assure 180 **An . . . wist** if I knew for
certain 184 **deciphered** detected, expressed 187 **simple** common
190 **bandying** contending. **favorites** followers 191 **But that** i.e., but
sees that. **event** outcome 193 **envy** malice. **unkind** unnatural
4.2. Location: France. Before Bordeaux.
s.d. trump and drum trumpeter and drummer **1 gates** (As before at
Orleans and Rouen, these city gates are represented by a door in the
tiring-house facade, which is imagined to be the walls of Bordeaux.
Occupants of Bordeaux appearing *aloft* or on the walls are seen in the
gallery backstage.) **5 would** wishes

8 **bloody power** bloodthirsty army 11 **quartering** dismembering
12 **even** level 13 **air-braving** defying the heavens (by their height)
14 **forsake** refuse. **their** i.e., *famine, steel,* and *fire* 15 **owl** i.e.,
portent 16 **their** our people's 17 **period** termination. **tyranny** cruelty 21 **appointed** equipped 23 **thee** of you. **pitched** set in battle
array 26 **front** face. **apparent spoil** obvious destruction 27 **pale**
(because Death is portrayed as pale) 28 **ta'en the Sacrament** i.e.,
confirmed their solemn oaths by taking the Sacrament 29 **rive** burst,
fire 33 **latest** final 34 **due** endue, invest 35 **glass** hourglass
36 **sandy hour** hour as measured by the running of the sand 37 **well
colorèd** in the pink of health 41 **departure** i.e., death 43 **peruse**
survey, reconnoiter. **wings** flanks 44 **discipline** military tactics
45 **parked** enclosed. **pale** fenced-in space 47 **Mazed with** (1) bewildered, amazed by (2) enclosed by, as in a labyrinth (?) 48 **in
blood** in prime condition

Not rascal-like to fall down with a pinch,   49
But rather, moody-mad and desperate stags,   50
Turn on the bloody hounds with heads of steel   51
And make the cowards stand aloof at bay.
Sell every man his life as dear as mine
And they shall find dear deer of us, my friends.   54
God and Saint George, Talbot and England's right,
Prosper our colors in this dangerous fight!   [*Exeunt.*] 56

❧

4.3   *Enter a Messenger that meets York. Enter York*
         with trumpet and many soldiers.

YORK
   Are not the speedy scouts returned again
   That dogged the mighty army of the Dauphin?
MESSENGER
   They are returned, my lord, and give it out   3
   That he is marched to Bordeaux with his power   4
   To fight with Talbot. As he marched along,
   By your espials were discoverèd   6
   Two mightier troops than that the Dauphin led,
   Which joined with him and made their march for
      Bordeaux.
YORK
   A plague upon that villain Somerset,
   That thus delays my promisèd supply   10
   Of horsemen that were levied for this siege!
   Renownèd Talbot doth expect my aid,
   And I am louted by a traitor villain   13
   And cannot help the noble chevalier.
   God comfort him in this necessity!
   If he miscarry, farewell wars in France.   16

   Enter another Messenger, [Sir William Lucy].

LUCY
   Thou princely leader of our English strength,
   Never so needful on the earth of France,
   Spur to the rescue of the noble Talbot,
   Who now is girdled with a waist of iron
   And hemmed about with grim destruction.
   To Bordeaux, warlike Duke! To Bordeaux, York!
   Else, farewell Talbot, France, and England's honor.
YORK
   O God, that Somerset, who in proud heart
   Doth stop my cornets, were in Talbot's place!   25
   So should we save a valiant gentleman
   By forfeiting a traitor and a coward.
   Mad ire and wrathful fury makes me weep
   That thus we die while remiss traitors sleep.

LUCY
   O, send some succor to the distressed lord!   30
YORK
   He dies, we lose; I break my warlike word;
   We mourn, France smiles; we lose, they daily get;
   All 'long of this vile traitor Somerset.   33
LUCY
   Then God take mercy on brave Talbot's soul,
   And on his son young John, who two hours since
   I met in travel toward his warlike father.
   This seven years did not Talbot see his son,
   And now they meet where both their lives are done.
YORK
   Alas, what joy shall noble Talbot have
   To bid his young son welcome to his grave?
   Away! Vexation almost stops my breath,   41
   That sundered friends greet in the hour of death.
   Lucy, farewell. No more my fortune can   43
   But curse the cause I cannot aid the man.
   Maine, Blois, Poitiers, and Tours are won away,
   'Long all of Somerset and his delay.
                                   Exit [with his soldiers].
LUCY
   Thus, while the vulture of sedition
   Feeds in the bosom of such great commanders,
   Sleeping neglection doth betray to loss
   The conquest of our scarce-cold conqueror,
   That ever-living man of memory,   51
   Henry the Fifth. Whiles they each other cross,
   Lives, honors, lands, and all hurry to loss.

4.4   *Enter Somerset, with his army; [a Captain of*
         Talbot's with him].

SOMERSET
   It is too late. I cannot send them now.
   This expedition was by York and Talbot
   Too rashly plotted. All our general force   3
   Might with a sally of the very town   4
   Be buckled with. The overdaring Talbot   5
   Hath sullied all his gloss of former honor
   By this unheedful, desperate, wild adventure.
   York set him on to fight and die in shame,
   That, Talbot dead, great York might bear the name.   9
CAPTAIN
   Here is Sir William Lucy, who with me
   Set from our o'ermatched forces forth for aid.

   [Sir William Lucy comes forward.]

---

30 distressed in difficulties **33 'long of** on account of **41 Vexation** anguish **43 can** is able to do **51 ever-living . . . memory** man of ever living memory
4.4. Location: France. Scene continues. Lucy does not leave the stage.
3–5 All . . . with i.e., our entire army might be successfully encountered by a sortie of the mere French garrison in Bordeaux, unsupported by the other French armies coming to the relief of Bordeaux **9 That** so that. **bear the name** i.e., receive all honor as supreme commander in France

49 rascal-like (1) like young or inferior deer (2) like rascals. **pinch** nip **50 moody-mad** high-spirited and mad with rage **51 heads of steel** (1) swordlike antlers (2) helmeted heads **54 dear** (1) costly (in terms of casualties) (2) precious **56 colors** banners
4.3. Location: France. Plains in Gascony.
3 give it out report **4 power** army **6 espials** spies **10 supply** reinforcements **13 louted** made a fool of, mocked **16 miscarry** come to grief **25 stop** hold back. **cornets** cavalry units

SOMERSET
How now, Sir William, whither were you sent?

LUCY
Whither, my lord? From bought and sold Lord
  Talbot,
Who, ringed about with bold adversity,
Cries out for noble York and Somerset
To beat assailing death from his weak legions;
And whiles the honorable captain there
Drops bloody sweat from his war-wearied limbs
And, in advantage lingering, looks for rescue,   19
You, his false hopes, the trust of England's honor,   20
Keep off aloof with worthless emulation.   21
Let not your private discord keep away
The levied succors that should lend him aid,   23
While he, renownèd noble gentleman,
Yield up his life unto a world of odds.   25
Orleans the Bastard, Charles, Burgundy,
Alençon, Reignier, compass him about,
And Talbot perisheth by your default.   28

SOMERSET
York set him on. York should have sent him aid.

LUCY
And York as fast upon Your Grace exclaims,   30
Swearing that you withhold his levied horse
Collected for this expedition.

SOMERSET
York lies. He might have sent and had the horse.   33
I owe him little duty and less love,
And take foul scorn to fawn on him by sending.   35

LUCY
The fraud of England, not the force of France,
Hath now entrapped the noble-minded Talbot.
Never to England shall he bear his life,
But dies betrayed to fortune by your strife.

SOMERSET
Come, go. I will dispatch the horsemen straight.
Within six hours they will be at his aid.

LUCY
Too late comes rescue. He is ta'en or slain;
For fly he could not, if he would have fled;
And fly would Talbot never, though he might.

SOMERSET
If he be dead, brave Talbot, then adieu!

LUCY
His fame lives in the world, his shame in you.
                    Exeunt [separately].

❧

4.5   *Enter Talbot and his son [John].*

TALBOT
O young John Talbot, I did send for thee

To tutor thee in stratagems of war,
That Talbot's name might be in thee revived
When sapless age and weak unable limbs
Should bring thy father to his drooping chair.   5
But, O malignant and ill-boding stars!
Now thou art come unto a feast of death,
A terrible and unavoided danger.   8
Therefore, dear boy, mount on my swiftest horse,
And I'll direct thee how thou shalt escape
By sudden flight. Come, dally not, begone.

JOHN
Is my name Talbot, and am I your son,
And shall I fly? O, if you love my mother,
Dishonor not her honorable name
To make a bastard and a slave of me!   15
The world will say he is not Talbot's blood
That basely fled when noble Talbot stood.

TALBOT
Fly to revenge my death if I be slain.

JOHN
He that flies so will ne'er return again.

TALBOT
If we both stay, we both are sure to die.

JOHN
Then let me stay, and, Father, do you fly.
Your loss is great; so your regard should be.   22
My worth unknown, no loss is known in me.   23
Upon my death the French can little boast;
In yours they will, in you all hopes are lost.
Flight cannot stain the honor you have won;
But mine it will, that no exploit have done.   27
You fled for vantage, everyone will swear,   28
But if I bow they'll say it was for fear.
There is no hope that ever I will stay,
If the first hour I shrink and run away.
Here on my knee I beg mortality,   32
Rather than life preserved with infamy.

TALBOT
Shall all thy mother's hopes lie in one tomb?

JOHN
Ay, rather than I'll shame my mother's womb.

TALBOT
Upon my blessing I command thee go.

JOHN
To fight I will, but not to fly the foe.

TALBOT
Part of thy father may be saved in thee.

JOHN
No part of him but will be shame in me.

TALBOT
Thou never hadst renown, nor canst not lose it.

JOHN
Yes, your renownèd name. Shall flight abuse it?   41

---

19 in advantage lingering making the best he can out of delaying tactics, or finding every way he can to delay matters   **20 trust** guardian
21 worthless emulation ignoble rivalry   **23 levied succors** raised reinforcements   **25 a world of** huge   **28 default** failure   **30 upon . . .
exclaims** accuses Your Grace   **33 might . . . had** i.e., had and could
have sent   **35 take foul scorn** consider it humiliating
4.5. Location: France. A field of battle near Bordeaux.

5 drooping invalid   **8 unavoided** unavoidable   **15 To . . . me** by
prompting me to act the part of a bastard and contemptible low person   **22 Your loss is great** the loss of you would be a severe setback.
regard heed for yourself   **23 no loss . . . me** the loss of me would
scarcely be noticed   **27 that** I who   **28 vantage** military advantage
32 mortality death   **41 abuse** dishonor

TALBOT

Thy father's charge shall clear thee from that stain. 42

JOHN

You cannot witness for me, being slain. 43
If death be so apparent, then both fly.

TALBOT

And leave my followers here to fight and die?
My age was never tainted with such shame. 46

JOHN

And shall my youth be guilty of such blame?
No more can I be severed from your side
Than can yourself yourself in twain divide.
Stay, go, do what you will—the like do I;
For live I will not, if my father die.

TALBOT

Then here I take my leave of thee, fair son,
Born to eclipse thy life this afternoon. 53
Come, side by side together live and die,
And soul with soul from France to heaven fly.

Exeunt.

4.6 *Alarum. Excursions, wherein Talbot's son is hemmed about, and Talbot rescues him.*

TALBOT

Saint George and victory! Fight, soldiers, fight!
The Regent hath with Talbot broke his word 2
And left us to the rage of France his sword. 3
Where is John Talbot?—Pause, and take thy breath.
I gave thee life and rescued thee from death.

JOHN

O, twice my father, twice am I thy son!
The life thou gav'st me first was lost and done
Till with thy warlike sword, despite of fate, 8
To my determined time thou gav'st new date. 9

TALBOT

When from the Dauphin's crest thy sword struck
    fire, 10
It warmed thy father's heart with proud desire
Of boldfaced victory. Then leaden age,
Quickened with youthful spleen and warlike rage, 13
Beat down Alençon, Orleans, Burgundy,
And from the pride of Gallia rescued thee. 15
The ireful bastard Orleans, that drew blood
From thee, my boy, and had the maidenhood
Of thy first fight, I soon encountered,
And interchanging blows, I quickly shed
Some of his bastard blood; and in disgrace 20

Bespoke him thus: "Contaminated, base,
And misbegotten blood I spill of thine,
Mean and right poor, for that pure blood of mine 23
Which thou didst force from Talbot, my brave boy."
Here, purposing the Bastard to destroy, 25
Came in strong rescue. Speak, thy father's care.
Art thou not weary, John? How dost thou fare?
Wilt thou yet leave the battle, boy, and fly,
Now thou art sealed the son of chivalry? 29
Fly, to revenge my death when I am dead.
The help of one stands me in little stead.
O, too much folly is it, well I wot, 32
To hazard all our lives in one small boat!
If I today die not with Frenchmen's rage,
Tomorrow I shall die with mickle age. 35
By me they nothing gain an if I stay;
'Tis but the shortening of my life one day.
In thee thy mother dies, our household's name,
My death's revenge, thy youth, and England's fame.
All these and more we hazard by thy stay;
All these are saved if thou wilt fly away.

JOHN

The sword of Orleans hath not made me smart; 42
These words of yours draw lifeblood from my heart.
On that advantage, bought with such a shame, 44
To save a paltry life and slay bright fame,
Before young Talbot from old Talbot fly,
The coward horse that bears me fall and die! 47
And like me to the peasant boys of France, 48
To be shame's scorn and subject of mischance!
Surely, by all the glory you have won,
An if I fly, I am not Talbot's son.
Then talk no more of flight. It is no boot. 52
If son to Talbot, die at Talbot's foot.

TALBOT

Then follow thou thy desperate sire of Crete,
Thou Icarus. Thy life to me is sweet. 55
If thou wilt fight, fight by thy father's side;
And, commendable proved, let's die in pride.

Exeunt.

4.7 *Alarum. Excursions. Enter old Talbot led [by a Servant].*

TALBOT

Where is my other life? Mine own is gone.
O, where's young Talbot? Where is valiant John?
Triumphant Death, smeared with captivity, 3

---

42 charge giving you an order **43 being slain** you having been slain
46 age lifetime **53 eclipse** (suggesting a pun on *son, sun* in the previous line)
4.6. Location: The battlefield still, moments later; the scene is continuous.
2 The Regent i.e., the Duke of York. (Compare this with 4.1.162–163.) **3 France his** France's **8 despite of fate** defying what fate had seemingly decreed **9 determined** having been determined to end.
date limit, termination **10 crest** i.e., helmet **13 Quickened** revived.
spleen i.e., courage, ardor **15 Gallia** France **20 in disgrace** by way of insult

23 Mean base, inferior **25 purposing** as I purposed **29 sealed** certified **32 wot** know **35 mickle** great **42 smart** feel pain **44 On that advantage** i.e., to gain that advantage of safety **47 fall** i.e., may it fall **48 like** liken **52 boot** use **55 Thou Icarus** (Daedalus of Crete and his son Icarus escaped from the labyrinth by means of wings that the father's ingenuity had devised. As they flew across the sea, Icarus mounted too high, the sun's heat melted the wax by which his wings were attached, and he fell into the sea, hence called the Icarian Sea, and was lost.)
4.7. Location: The battlefield still; the scene is continuous.
3 smeared with captivity i.e., stained with the blood of your captives. (The image is of a triumphal procession.)

Young Talbot's valor makes me smile at thee.
When he perceived me shrink and on my knee,   5
His bloody sword he brandished over me,
And like a hungry lion did commence
Rough deeds of rage and stern impatience.
But when my angry guardant stood alone,   9
Tend'ring my ruin and assailed of none,   10
Dizzy-eyed fury and great rage of heart   11
Suddenly made him from my side to start
Into the clustering battle of the French,   13
And in that sea of blood my boy did drench   14
His overmounting spirit; and there died
My Icarus, my blossom, in his pride.   16

Enter [soldiers], with John Talbot, borne.

SERVANT
O my dear lord, lo, where your son is borne!

TALBOT
Thou antic Death, which laugh'st us here to scorn,   18
Anon, from thy insulting tyranny,
Coupled in bonds of perpetuity,
Two Talbots, wingèd through the lither sky,   21
In thy despite shall scape mortality.—   22
O thou, whose wounds become hard-favored Death,   23
Speak to thy father ere thou yield thy breath!
Brave Death by speaking, whether he will or no;   25
Imagine him a Frenchman and thy foe.—
Poor boy! He smiles, methinks, as who should say,   27
"Had Death been French, then Death had died to-
  day."
Come, come, and lay him in his father's arms.
  [John is laid in his father's arms.]
My spirit can no longer bear these harms.
Soldiers, adieu! I have what I would have,
Now my old arms are young John Talbot's grave.   32
  Dies. [Exeunt soldiers.]

*Enter Charles, Alençon, Burgundy, Bastard, and
Pucelle.*

CHARLES
Had York and Somerset brought rescue in,
We should have found a bloody day of this.

BASTARD
How the young whelp of Talbot's, raging wood,   35
Did flesh his puny sword in Frenchmen's blood!   36

PUCELLE
Once I encountered him, and thus I said:
"Thou maiden youth, be vanquished by a maid."   38
But with a proud, majestical high scorn
He answered thus: "Young Talbot was not born
To be the pillage of a giglot wench."   41
So, rushing in the bowels of the French,
He left me proudly, as unworthy fight.   43

BURGUNDY
Doubtless he would have made a noble knight.
See where he lies inhearsèd in the arms   45
Of the most bloody nurser of his harms!   46

BASTARD
Hew them to pieces, hack their bones asunder,
Whose life was England's glory, Gallia's wonder.

CHARLES
O, no, forbear! For that which we have fled
During the life, let us not wrong it dead.

*Enter [Sir William] Lucy [attended; Herald of the
French preceding].*

LUCY
Herald, conduct me to the Dauphin's tent,
To know who hath obtained the glory of the day.

CHARLES
On what submissive message art thou sent?

LUCY
Submission, Dauphin? 'Tis a mere French word.
We English warriors wot not what it means.
I come to know what prisoners thou hast ta'en
And to survey the bodies of the dead.

CHARLES
For prisoners ask'st thou? Hell our prison is.   58
But tell me whom thou seek'st.

LUCY
But where's the great Alcides of the field,   60
Valiant Lord Talbot, Earl of Shrewsbury,
Created for his rare success in arms
Great Earl of Wexford, Waterford, and Valence,
Lord Talbot of Goodrich and Urchinfield,
Lord Strange of Blackmere, Lord Verdun of Alton,
Lord Cromwell of Wingfield, Lord Furnival of
  Sheffield,
The thrice-victorious Lord of Falconbridge,
Knight of the noble order of Saint George,
Worthy Saint Michael, and the Golden Fleece,
Great Marshal to Henry the Sixth
Of all his wars within the realm of France?

PUCELLE
Here is a silly, stately style indeed!   72
The Turk, that two-and-fifty kingdoms hath,   73
Writes not so tedious a style as this.

---

5 shrink retire in battle   **9 guardant** guardian   **10 Tend'ring** being concerned for.   **of** by   **11 Dizzy-eyed** (Staring, dazzled eyes were thought of as a conventional feature of wrath.)   **13 clustering battle** swarming army   **14 drench** drown   **16 pride** glory   **18 antic** i.e., grinning. (A personification probably suggested by grotesque pictorial representations in the Middle Ages and early Renaissance, such as the Dance of Death.)   **here** here on earth   **21 lither** yielding   **22 In thy despite** in spite of you.   **scape mortality** escape the bonds of death (through immortality)   **23 thou** i.e., John.   **become . . . Death** make Death, otherwise hideous, seem beautiful   **25 Brave** defy   **27 as who** as if one   **32 s.d. Dies** (Historically, Talbot did not die until some twenty-two years after Henry VI's coronation in Paris. Talbot's campaign in the Bordeaux region was successful and included the taking of the city.)   **35 whelp of Talbot's** (Talbot is the name of a species of hound.)   **wood** mad   **36 flesh** use for the first time in battle.   **puny** inexperienced (in bloodshed)

38 maiden i.e., not yet initiated in warfare   **41 giglot** wanton   **43 unworthy** unworthy of   **45 inhearsèd** as in a coffin   **46 Of . . . harms** of the father who gave him his capacity for doing harm to the enemy   **58 Hell . . . is** i.e., we have slain and thus sent our enemies to hell rather than take any prisoners   **60 Alcides** Hercules. (Literally, descendant of Alcaeus, who was the father of Hercules' stepfather.)   **72 style** list of titles, manner of address   **73 The Turk** i.e., the Sultan of Turkey

Him that thou magnifi'st with all these titles
Stinking and flyblown lies here at our feet.

LUCY
Is Talbot slain, the Frenchmen's only scourge,   77
Your kingdom's terror and black nemesis?   78
O, were mine eyeballs into bullets turned,
That I in rage might shoot them at your faces!
O, that I could but call these dead to life!
It were enough to fright the realm of France.
Were but his picture left amongst you here,
It would amaze the proudest of you all.   84
Give me their bodies, that I may bear them hence
And give them burial as beseems their worth.   86

PUCELLE
I think this upstart is old Talbot's ghost,
He speaks with such a proud commanding spirit.
For God's sake, let him have them! To keep them
  here,
They would but stink and putrefy the air.

CHARLES   Go, take their bodies hence.

LUCY
I'll bear them hence; but from their ashes shall be
  reared
A phoenix that shall make all France afeard.   93

CHARLES
So we be rid of them, do with them what thou wilt.   94
      [Exeunt Lucy, Herald, and attendants with the bodies.]
And now to Paris in this conquering vein.
All will be ours, now bloody Talbot's slain.   Exeunt

5.1   *Sennet. Enter King, Gloucester, and Exeter,*
          [and others].

KING
Have you perused the letters from the Pope,   1
The Emperor, and the Earl of Armagnac?   2

GLOUCESTER
I have, my lord, and their intent is this:
They humbly sue unto your excellence
To have a godly peace concluded of
Between the realms of England and of France.

KING
How doth Your Grace affect their motion?   7

GLOUCESTER
Well, my good lord, and as the only means
To stop effusion of our Christian blood
And stablish quietness on every side.

KING
Ay, marry, uncle; for I always thought
It was both impious and unnatural
That such immanity and bloody strife   13
Should reign among professors of one faith.

GLOUCESTER
Besides, my lord, the sooner to effect
And surer bind this knot of amity,
The Earl of Armagnac, near knit to Charles,   17
A man of great authority in France,
Proffers his only daughter to Your Grace
In marriage, with a large and sumptuous dowry.

KING
Marriage, uncle! Alas, my years are young,
And fitter is my study and my books
Than wanton dalliance with a paramour.
Yet call th' ambassadors. [*Exit one or more.*] And, as
  you please,
So let them have their answers every one.
I shall be well content with any choice
Tends to God's glory and my country's weal.   27

      Enter Winchester [in cardinal's habit], and three
      Ambassadors, [one a Papal Legate].

EXETER [*aside*]
What? Is my lord of Winchester installed
And called unto a cardinal's degree?   29
Then I perceive that will be verified
Henry the Fifth did sometime prophesy: 31
"If once he come to be a cardinal,
He'll make his cap coequal with the crown."   33

KING
My Lords Ambassadors, your several suits   34
Have been considered and debated on.
Your purpose is both good and reasonable,
And therefore are we certainly resolved
To draw conditions of a friendly peace,   38
Which by my lord of Winchester we mean
Shall be transported presently to France.   40

GLOUCESTER [*to the Ambassadors from Armagnac*]
And for the proffer of my lord your master,   41
I have informed His Highness so at large   42
As, liking of the lady's virtuous gifts,
Her beauty, and the value of her dower,
He doth intend she shall be England's queen.

KING
In argument and proof of which contract,
Bear her this jewel, pledge of my affection.
      [*A jewel is presented to the Ambassadors.*]
And so, my Lord Protector, see them guarded
And safely brought to Dover, wherein shipped,   49
Commit them to the fortune of the sea.
      Exeunt [all but Winchester and Legate].

---

77 **only** supreme   78 **nemesis** agent for retribution or punishment
84 **amaze** stun, throw into confusion   86 **beseems their worth** befits
their rank   93 **phoenix** fabulous bird, the only one of its kind, which
every five hundred years built itself a funeral pile and died upon it;
from the ashes a new phoenix arose   94 **So** as long as
5.1. Location: London. The royal court.
1–2 Pope . . . Armagnac (During the years 1434–1435, efforts were
made by the Emperor Sigismund and other potentates to effect a
peace. The marriage proposal of the King to the Earl of Armagnac's
daughter, however, was made eight or nine years later.)   7 **affect**
their motion incline toward their proposal

13 **immanity** atrocious savagery   17 **knit** i.e., by ties of kinship
27 **Tends** that tends   29 **called . . . degree** (Winchester's newly being
made a cardinal is inconsistent with 1.3.19 and 36.)   31 **sometime** at
one time   33 **cap** i.e., cardinal's skullcap   34 **several** various
38 **draw** draw up   40 **presently** immediately   41 **for** as for, regarding
42 **at large** in full   49 **shipped** embarked

WINCHESTER
Stay, my Lord Legate. You shall first receive
The sum of money which I promisèd
Should be delivered to His Holiness
For clothing me in these grave ornaments.   54

LEGATE
I will attend upon your lordship's leisure.
                                       [He steps aside.]

WINCHESTER [aside]
Now Winchester will not submit, I trow,
Or be inferior to the proudest peer.
Humphrey of Gloucester, thou shalt well perceive
That neither in birth or for authority
The Bishop will be overborne by thee.
I'll either make thee stoop and bend thy knee,
Or sack this country with a mutiny.   Exeunt. 62

❧

5.2
Enter Charles, Burgundy, Alençon, Bastard,
Reignier, and Joan [la Pucelle].

CHARLES
These news, my lords, may cheer our drooping
        spirits:
'Tis said the stout Parisians do revolt   2
And turn again unto the warlike French.

ALENÇON
Then march to Paris, royal Charles of France,
And keep not back your powers in dalliance.   5

PUCELLE
Peace be amongst them, if they turn to us;
Else, ruin combat with their palaces!   7

        Enter Scout.

SCOUT
Success unto our valiant general,
And happiness to his accomplices!   9

CHARLES
What tidings send our scouts? I prithee, speak.

SCOUT
The English army, that divided was
Into two parties, is now conjoined in one
And means to give you battle presently.

CHARLES
Somewhat too sudden, sirs, the warning is,
But we will presently provide for them.

BURGUNDY
I trust the ghost of Talbot is not there.
Now he is gone, my lord, you need not fear.

PUCELLE
Of all base passions, fear is most accurst.
Command the conquest, Charles, it shall be thine,
Let Henry fret and all the world repine.

54 grave ornaments i.e., solemn robes of ecclesiastical office
62 mutiny rebellion
5.2. Location: France. Fields before Angiers.
2 stout courageous   5 powers forces   7 Else . . . palaces otherwise,
let ruin destroy their palaces   9 accomplices allies

CHARLES
Then on, my lords, and France be fortunate!

                                       Exeunt.

5.3
Alarum. Excursions. Enter Joan la Pucelle.

PUCELLE
The Regent conquers, and the Frenchmen fly.   1
Now help, ye charming spells and periapts,   2
And ye choice spirits that admonish me   3
And give me signs of future accidents.   Thunder. 4
You speedy helpers, that are substitutes   5
Under the lordly monarch of the north,   6
Appear and aid me in this enterprise!

        Enter Fiends.

This speedy and quick appearance argues proof   8
Of your accustomed diligence to me.
Now, ye familiar spirits, that are culled
Out of the powerful regions under earth,
Help me this once, that France may get the field.   12
                        They walk, and speak not.
O, hold me not with silence overlong!
Where I was wont to feed you with my blood,   14
I'll lop a member off and give it you
In earnest of a further benefit,   16
So you do condescend to help me now.   17
                        They hang their heads.
No hope to have redress? My body shall
Pay recompense, if you will grant my suit.
                        They shake their heads.
Cannot my body nor blood sacrifice
Entreat you to your wonted furtherance?   21
Then take my soul—my body, soul, and all—
Before that England give the French the foil.   23
                        They depart.
See, they forsake me! Now the time is come
That France must vail her lofty-plumèd crest   25
And let her head fall into England's lap.
My ancient incantations are too weak,   27
And hell too strong for me to buckle with.   28
Now, France, thy glory droopeth to the dust.   Exit.

        Excursions. Burgundy and York fight hand to
        hand. French fly. [Joan la Pucelle is taken.]

YORK
Damsel of France, I think I have you fast.

5.3. Location: Before Angiers still. The scene is continuous.
1 The Regent i.e., the Duke of York   2 charming working by charms.
periapts amulets   3 admonish forewarn   4 accidents occurrences
5 substitutes deputies, agents   6 north (Evil spirits were frequently associated with the North.)   8 argues proof gives evidence   12 get the
field win the battle   14 Where (1) whereas (2) where   16 earnest advance payment.   further benefit (With sexual suggestion, as in member, line 15, and Pay recompense, line 19.)   17 So provided.   condescend agree   21 wonted furtherance customary aid   23 Before
that before.   foil defeat   25 vail lower.   lofty-plumèd crest plume
proudly waving at the top of the helmet (in token of arrogant pride)
27 ancient former   28 buckle with do combat with (continuing the
sexual suggestion of lines 15–19)

Unchain your spirits now with spelling charms,   31
And try if they can gain your liberty.
A goodly prize, fit for the devil's grace!   33
See how the ugly witch doth bend her brows
As if, with Circe, she would change my shape!   35
PUCELLE
Changed to a worser shape thou canst not be.
YORK
O, Charles the Dauphin is a proper man!   37
No shape but his can please your dainty eye.   38
PUCELLE
A plaguing mischief light on Charles and thee!   39
And may ye both be suddenly surprised   40
By bloody hands in sleeping on your beds!
YORK
Fell banning hag! Enchantress, hold thy tongue!   42
PUCELLE
I prithee, give me leave to curse awhile.
YORK
Curse, miscreant, when thou com'st to the stake.   44

Exeunt.

Alarum. Enter Suffolk, with Margaret in his hand.

SUFFOLK
Be what thou wilt, thou art my prisoner.

Gazes on her.

O fairest beauty, do not fear nor fly!
For I will touch thee but with reverent hands.
I kiss these fingers for eternal peace   48
And lay them gently on thy tender side.   49
Who art thou? Say, that I may honor thee.
MARGARET
Margaret my name, and daughter to a king,
The King of Naples, whosoe'er thou art.
SUFFOLK
An earl I am, and Suffolk am I called.
Be not offended, nature's miracle,
Thou art allotted to be ta'en by me.   55
So doth the swan her downy cygnets save,
Keeping them prisoner underneath her wings.
Yet if this servile usage once offend,   58
Go and be free again as Suffolk's friend. *She is going.* 59
O, stay! [*Aside.*] I have no power to let her pass;
My hand would free her, but my heart says no.
As plays the sun upon the glassy streams,   62
Twinkling another counterfeited beam,   63

So seems this gorgeous beauty to mine eyes.
Fain would I woo her, yet I dare not speak.
I'll call for pen and ink and write my mind.
Fie, de la Pole, disable not thyself!   67
Hast not a tongue? Is she not here?   68
Wilt thou be daunted at a woman's sight?   69
Ay, beauty's princely majesty is such
Confounds the tongue and makes the senses rough.   71
MARGARET
Say, Earl of Suffolk—if thy name be so—
What ransom must I pay before I pass?
For I perceive I am thy prisoner.
SUFFOLK [*aside*]
How canst thou tell she will deny thy suit
Before thou make a trial of her love?
MARGARET
Why speak'st thou not? What ransom must I pay?
SUFFOLK [*aside*]
She's beautiful, and therefore to be wooed;
She is a woman, therefore to be won.
MARGARET
Wilt thou accept of ransom, yea or no?
SUFFOLK [*aside*]
Fond man, remember that thou hast a wife.   81
Then how can Margaret be thy paramour?
MARGARET
I were best to leave him, for he will not hear.
SUFFOLK [*aside*]
There all is marred; there lies a cooling card.   84
MARGARET
He talks at random. Sure the man is mad.
SUFFOLK [*aside*]
And yet a dispensation may be had.   86
MARGARET
And yet I would that you would answer me.
SUFFOLK [*aside*]
I'll win this Lady Margaret. For whom?
Why, for my king. Tush, that's a wooden thing!   89
MARGARET
He talks of wood. It is some carpenter.
SUFFOLK [*aside*]
Yet so my fancy may be satisfied,   91
And peace establishèd between these realms.
But there remains a scruple in that too;
For though her father be the King of Naples,
Duke of Anjou and Maine, yet is he poor,
And our nobility will scorn the match.
MARGARET
Hear ye, captain, are you not at leisure?
SUFFOLK [*aside*]
It shall be so, disdain they ne'er so much.
Henry is youthful and will quickly yield.—
Madam, I have a secret to reveal.

---

31 spirits i.e., the demons—"familiars"—attending on Joan. (Compare with line 10.) **spelling charms** charms that cast a spell **33 the devil's grace** His Grace the devil. (Said sardonically.) **35 with** like. **Circe** sorceress celebrated for her power to change men into swine **37 proper** handsome. (Said sardonically.) **38 dainty** fastidious **39 mischief** misfortune **40 surprised** assailed, taken **42 Fell** fierce, cruel. **banning** cursing **44 s.d. in his hand** by the hand **48–49 I kiss . . . side** i.e., I kiss your hand (which I am holding) in token of eternal peace between us, and then I release your hand to hang by your side in token of giving you your freedom. (See line 61, where Suffolk speaks of wishing to free her hand, even though his heart tells him to keep her.) **55 allotted** destined **58 servile usage** being treated as a captive **59 friend** (With suggestion of "lover.") **62 As . . . streams** just as the sun plays upon the glassy surface of a stream **63 Twinkling** causing to twinkle. **counterfeited** i.e., reflected

67 disable disparage **68 here** i.e., here with me, ready to be wooed **69 a woman's sight** the sight of a woman **71 Confounds** that it confounds. **rough** dull **81 Fond** foolish **84 cooling card** something that cools one's ardor or dashes one's hopes. (A metaphor from card playing.) **86 dispensation** papal permission (to divorce a wife) **89 wooden** stupid (i.e., either King Henry, or Suffolk's plan) **91 fancy** desire in love

MARGARET [*aside*]
  What though I be enthralled? He seems a knight,   101
  And will not any way dishonor me.
SUFFOLK
  Lady, vouchsafe to listen what I say.
MARGARET [*aside*]
  Perhaps I shall be rescued by the French,
  And then I need not crave his courtesy.
SUFFOLK
  Sweet madam, give me hearing in a cause—
MARGARET [*aside*]
  Tush, women have been captive ere now.   107
SUFFOLK
  Lady, wherefore talk you so?
MARGARET
  I cry you mercy, 'tis but quid for quo.   109
SUFFOLK
  Say, gentle Princess, would you not suppose
  Your bondage happy, to be made a queen?   111
MARGARET
  To be a queen in bondage is more vile
  Than is a slave in base servility,
  For princes should be free.
SUFFOLK   And so shall you,   114
  If happy England's royal king be free.   115
MARGARET
  Why, what concerns his freedom unto me?
SUFFOLK
  I'll undertake to make thee Henry's queen,
  To put a golden scepter in thy hand,
  And set a precious crown upon thy head,
  If thou wilt condescend to be my—
MARGARET   What?   120
SUFFOLK   His love.
MARGARET
  I am unworthy to be Henry's wife.
SUFFOLK
  No, gentle madam. I unworthy am
  To woo so fair a dame to be his wife
  And have no portion in the choice myself.   125
  How say you, madam, are ye so content?
MARGARET
  An if my father please, I am content.   127
SUFFOLK
  Then call our captains and our colors forth.   128
  And, madam, at your father's castle walls
  We'll crave a parley, to confer with him.   130

      Sound [a parley]. Enter Reignier on the walls.

  See, Reignier, see thy daughter prisoner!
REIGNIER
  To whom?
SUFFOLK   To me.
REIGNIER   Suffolk, what remedy?
  I am a soldier, and unapt to weep
  Or to exclaim on fortune's fickleness.   134
SUFFOLK
  Yes, there is remedy enough, my lord.
  Consent, and for thy honor give consent,   136
  Thy daughter shall be wedded to my king,
  Whom I with pain have wooed and won thereto;   138
  And this her easy-held imprisonment   139
  Hath gained thy daughter princely liberty.
REIGNIER
  Speaks Suffolk as he thinks?
SUFFOLK   Fair Margaret knows
  That Suffolk doth not flatter, face, or feign.   142
REIGNIER
  Upon thy princely warrant, I descend   143
  To give thee answer of thy just demand.
                    [Exit from the walls.]
SUFFOLK
  And here I will expect thy coming.   145

     Trumpets sound. Enter Reignier [below].

REIGNIER
  Welcome, brave earl, into our territories.
  Command in Anjou what your honor pleases.
SUFFOLK
  Thanks, Reignier, happy for so sweet a child,   148
  Fit to be made companion with a king.
  What answer makes Your Grace unto my suit?
REIGNIER
  Since thou dost deign to woo her little worth   151
  To be the princely bride of such a lord,
  Upon condition I may quietly
  Enjoy mine own, the country Maine and Anjou,   154
  Free from oppression or the stroke of war,
  My daughter shall be Henry's, if he please.
SUFFOLK
  That is her ransom. I deliver her,   157
  And those two counties I will undertake
  Your Grace shall well and quietly enjoy.
REIGNIER
  And I again, in Henry's royal name,   160
  As deputy unto that gracious king,   161
  Give thee her hand for sign of plighted faith.
SUFFOLK
  Reignier of France, I give thee kingly thanks,

---

101 enthralled captured   **107 captive** taken captive   **109 cry you mercy** beg your pardon.   **quid for quo** tit for tat   **111 to be** if you were to be   **114 princes** i.e., men or women of royal birth   **115 happy** fortunate   **120 condescend** consent   **125 And have . . . myself** (Suffolk seems to say to Margaret that he is only the unworthy agent, not deserving to have any other role, but his double meaning points to his having a "piece" out of this for himself.)   **choice** (1) choosing (2) person chosen   **127 An if** if   **128 Then . . . forth** (Suffolk probably calls offstage to attendants.)   **130 s.d. on the walls** (As in previous sieges, the "walls" of Angiers are here represented by the tiring-house facade, with Reignier appearing above, in the gallery backstage.)

134 exclaim on complain against   **136 Consent . . . consent** consent, and do so for the sake of your honor   **138 Whom** i.e., Margaret   **139 easy-held** easily endured   **142 face** show a false face, deceive   **143 warrant** assurance   **145 expect** await   **148 happy for** fortunate in having   **151 her little worth** her, little worthy as she is   **154 country** i.e., district or region including   **157 deliver** free. (Her ransom having been agreed upon, Suffolk releases her.)   **160 again** in return. (In return for promises made in the name of King Henry, Reignier gives back his daughter into the hands of Suffolk, who released her to her father three lines earlier.)   **161 As deputy** i.e., to you, Suffolk, as deputy

Because this is in traffic of a king.   164
[*Aside.*] And yet methinks I could be well content
To be mine own attorney in this case.—
I'll over then to England with this news
And make this marriage to be solemnized.
So farewell, Reignier. Set this diamond safe
In golden palaces, as it becomes.   170

REIGNIER
I do embrace thee, as I would embrace
The Christian prince, King Henry, were he here.
                                    [*He embraces Suffolk.*]

MARGARET
Farewell, my lord. Good wishes, praise, and prayers
Shall Suffolk ever have of Margaret.   *She is going.*

SUFFOLK
Farewell, sweet madam. But hark you, Margaret—
No princely commendations to my king?

MARGARET
Such commendations as becomes a maid,
A virgin, and his servant, say to him.

SUFFOLK
Words sweetly placed and modestly directed.   179
But, madam, I must trouble you again—
No loving token to His Majesty?

MARGARET
Yes, my good lord: a pure unspotted heart,
Never yet taint with love, I send the King.   183

SUFFOLK   And this withal.   *Kiss her.* 184

MARGARET
That for thyself. I will not so presume
To send such peevish tokens to a king.   186
                            [*Exeunt Reignier and Margaret.*]

SUFFOLK
O, wert thou for myself! But, Suffolk, stay.
Thou mayest not wander in that labyrinth;   188
There Minotaurs and ugly treasons lurk.
Solicit Henry with her wondrous praise;   190
Bethink thee on her virtues that surmount,
And natural graces that extinguish art;   192
Repeat their semblance often on the seas,   193
That, when thou com'st to kneel at Henry's feet,
Thou mayest bereave him of his wits with wonder.
                                                                        Exit.

❖

5.4   *Enter York, Warwick, Shepherd, [and] Pucelle
[guarded].*

YORK
Bring forth that sorceress condemned to burn.

SHEPHERD
Ah, Joan, this kills thy father's heart outright!
Have I sought every country far and near,   3
And, now it is my chance to find thee out,   4
Must I behold thy timeless cruel death?   5
Ah, Joan, sweet daughter Joan, I'll die with thee!

PUCELLE
Decrepit miser, base ignoble wretch!   7
I am descended of a gentler blood.   8
Thou art no father nor no friend of mine.   9

SHEPHERD
Out, out! My lords, an please you, 'tis not so.   10
I did beget her, all the parish knows.
Her mother liveth yet, can testify
She was the first fruit of my bach'lorship.   13

WARWICK
Graceless, wilt thou deny thy parentage?

YORK
This argues what her kind of life hath been,
Wicked and vile; and so her death concludes.   16

SHEPHERD
Fie, Joan, that thou wilt be so obstacle!   17
God knows thou art a collop of my flesh,   18
And for thy sake have I shed many a tear.
Deny me not, I prithee, gentle Joan.

PUCELLE
Peasant, avaunt!—You have suborned this man   21
Of purpose to obscure my noble birth.   22

SHEPHERD
'Tis true, I gave a noble to the priest   23
The morn that I was wedded to her mother.
Kneel down and take my blessing, good my girl.
Wilt thou not stoop? Now cursèd be the time
Of thy nativity! I would the milk
Thy mother gave thee when thou suckedst her
       breast
Had been a little ratsbane for thy sake!   29
Or else, when thou didst keep my lambs afield,   30
I wish some ravenous wolf had eaten thee!
Dost thou deny thy father, cursèd drab?   32
O, burn her, burn her! Hanging is too good.   *Exit.*

YORK [*to guards*]
Take her away, for she hath lived too long,
To fill the world with vicious qualities.

PUCELLE
First, let me tell you whom you have condemned:
Not me begotten of a shepherd swain,
But issued from the progeny of kings,
Virtuous and holy, chosen from above
By inspiration of celestial grace
To work exceeding miracles on earth.   41

---

164 **traffic** business   170 **as it becomes** as befits such a jewel
179 **placed** arranged   183 **taint** tainted   184 **withal** in addition
186 **peevish** trivial   188 **labyrinth** a structure built by Daedalus consisting of intricate passageways where the Minotaur—a monster born
from the union of the Cretan king's wife with a bull—was confined
190 **her wondrous praise** praise of her wondrous beauty   192 **extinguish** eclipse   193 **Repeat their semblance** rehearse mentally the image of her virtues
5.4. Location: France. Camp of the Duke of York in Anjou.

3 **country** district   4 **chance** fortune.   **find thee out** discover you
5 **timeless** premature   7 **miser** wretch   8 **gentler** more noble
9 **friend** kinsman   10 **an please you** if you please   13 **was . . .
bach'lorship** i.e., was conceived out of wedlock, was the first product
of my endeavor as a young man   16 **concludes** (1) confirms (2) ends
17 **obstacle** (For "obstinate.")   18 **collop** slice   21 **suborned** induced
to commit perjury   22 **Of** on   23 **noble** coin worth six shillings eight
pence   29 **ratsbane** rat poison   30 **keep** tend   32 **drab** whore
41 **exceeding** exceptional

I never had to do with wicked spirits.
But you, that are polluted with your lusts,
Stained with the guiltless blood of innocents,
Corrupt and tainted with a thousand vices—
Because you want the grace that others have,   46
You judge it straight a thing impossible   47
To compass wonders but by help of devils.   48
No, misconceivèd! Joan of Arc hath been   49
A virgin from her tender infancy,
Chaste and immaculate in very thought,
Whose maiden blood, thus rigorously effused,   52
Will cry for vengeance at the gates of heaven.
YORK
Ay, ay.—Away with her to execution.
WARWICK
And hark ye, sirs: because she is a maid,
Spare for no faggots. Let there be enough.
Place barrels of pitch upon the fatal stake,   57
That so her torture may be shortenèd.
PUCELLE
Will nothing turn your unrelenting hearts?
Then, Joan, discover thine infirmity,   60
That warranteth by law to be thy privilege: 61
I am with child, ye bloody homicides.
Murder not then the fruit within my womb,
Although ye hale me to a violent death.
YORK
Now heaven forfend! The holy maid with child?   65
WARWICK
The greatest miracle that e'er ye wrought.
Is all your strict preciseness come to this?   67
YORK
She and the Dauphin have been juggling.   68
I did imagine what would be her refuge.
WARWICK
Well, go to. We'll have no bastards live,
Especially since Charles must father it.   71
PUCELLE
You are deceived. My child is none of his.
It was Alençon that enjoyed my love.
YORK
Alençon, that notorious Machiavel?   74
It dies an if it had a thousand lives.
PUCELLE
O, give me leave, I have deluded you.
'Twas neither Charles nor yet the Duke I named,
But Reignier, King of Naples, that prevailed.

WARWICK
A married man! That's most intolerable.
YORK
Why, here's a girl! I think she knows not well,
There were so many, whom she may accuse.
WARWICK
It's sign she hath been liberal and free.   82
YORK
And yet, forsooth, she is a virgin pure!
Strumpet, thy words condemn thy brat and thee.
Use no entreaty, for it is in vain.
PUCELLE
Then lead me hence; with whom I leave my curse.
May never glorious sun reflex his beams   87
Upon the country where you make abode,
But darkness and the gloomy shade of death
Environ you, till mischief and despair   90
Drive you to break your necks or hang yourselves!
                                                Exit [guarded].

Enter [Winchester, now] Cardinal [Beaufort, with
letters, attended].

YORK [to Joan as she exits]
Break thou in pieces and consume to ashes,   92
Thou foul accursèd minister of hell!   93
CARDINAL
Lord Regent, I do greet your excellence
With letters of commission from the King.
For know, my lords, the states of Christendom,
Moved with remorse of these outrageous broils,   97
Have earnestly implored a general peace
Betwixt our nation and the aspiring French;
And here at hand the Dauphin and his train   100
Approacheth, to confer about some matter.
YORK
Is all our travail turned to this effect?   102
After the slaughter of so many peers,
So many captains, gentlemen, and soldiers,
That in this quarrel have been overthrown
And sold their bodies for their country's benefit,
Shall we at last conclude effeminate peace?
Have we not lost most part of all the towns,
By treason, falsehood, and by treachery,
Our great progenitors had conquerèd?
O, Warwick, Warwick! I foresee with grief
The utter loss of all the realm of France.
WARWICK
Be patient, York. If we concluded a peace,
It shall be with such strict and severe covenants   114
As little shall the Frenchmen gain thereby.   115

Enter Charles, Alençon, Bastard, Reignier.

46 want lack   47 straight straightway, at once   48 compass encompass, bring about   49 misconceivèd you who have a wrong idea. (The word has an ironic application to Joan.)   52 rigorously effused mercilessly shed   57 pitch (Pitch would produce heavy smoke, asphyxiating the person being burned and thereby shortening the suffering. Warwick may be speaking sardonically, however: "We're going to give her a nice quick death.")   60 discover reveal   61 warranteth guarantees.   privilege i.e., to be spared until the birth of her supposed child   65 forfend forbid. (Said sardonically.)   67 preciseness propriety, modesty   68 juggling playing conjuring tricks (with sexual suggestion)   71 must father it is evidently the father   74 Machiavel (In the popular Elizabethan conception, Niccolò Machiavelli, Italian political philosopher, symbolized political immorality and ruthless ambition.)

82 liberal unrestrained, licentious (with a mocking glance at a more innocent meaning, "generous")   87 reflex reflect, shed   90 mischief misfortune   92–93 Break . . . hell (Winchester's entrance in time to hear these lines seemingly directed at Joan provides added irony, since Winchester is also a villain.)   97 remorse of pity for   100 train entourage   102 travail labor   114 convenants articles of agreement   115 As that

CHARLES
    Since, lords of England, it is thus agreed
    That peaceful truce shall be proclaimed in France,
    We come to be informèd by yourselves
    What the conditions of that league must be.
YORK
    Speak, Winchester, for boiling choler chokes   120
    The hollow passage of my poisoned voice
    By sight of these our baleful enemies.   122
CARDINAL
    Charles, and the rest, it is enacted thus:
    That, in regard King Henry gives consent,   124
    Of mere compassion and of lenity,   125
    To ease your country of distressful war
    And suffer you to breathe in fruitful peace,
    You shall become true liegemen to his crown.   128
    And, Charles, upon condition thou wilt swear
    To pay him tribute and submit thyself,
    Thou shalt be placed as viceroy under him,
    And still enjoy thy regal dignity.
ALENÇON
    Must he be then as shadow of himself?
    Adorn his temples with a coronet,
    And yet in substance and authority   135
    Retain but privilege of a private man?
    This proffer is absurd and reasonless.
CHARLES
    'Tis known already that I am possessed
    With more than half the Gallian territories   139
    And therein reverenced for their lawful king.
    Shall I, for lucre of the rest unvanquished,   141
    Detract so much from that prerogative   142
    As to be called but viceroy of the whole?   143
    No, Lord Ambassador, I'll rather keep
    That which I have than, coveting for more,
    Be cast from possibility of all.   146
YORK
    Insulting Charles, hast thou by secret means
    Used intercession to obtain a league,
    And, now the matter grows to compromise,   149
    Stand'st thou aloof upon comparison?   150
    Either accept the title thou usurp'st,
    Of benefit proceeding from our king   152
    And not of any challenge of desert,   153
    Or we will plague thee with incessant wars.
REIGNIER [aside to Charles]
    My lord, you do not well in obstinacy
    To cavil in the course of this contract.   156
    If once it be neglected, ten to one
    We shall not find like opportunity.

ALENÇON [aside to Charles]
    To say the truth, it is your policy   159
    To save your subjects from such massacre
    And ruthless slaughters as are daily seen
    By our proceeding in hostility;
    And therefore take this compact of a truce,
    Although you break it when your pleasure serves.
WARWICK
    How sayst thou, Charles? Shall our condition stand?   165
CHARLES   It shall;
    Only reserved, you claim no interest   167
    In any of our towns of garrison.   168
YORK
    Then swear allegiance to His Majesty,
    As thou art knight, never to disobey
    Nor be rebellious to the crown of England,
    Thou nor thy nobles, to the crown of England.
      [Charles and his nobles give tokens of fealty.]
    So, now dismiss your army when ye please.
    Hang up your ensigns, let your drums be still,
    For here we entertain a solemn peace.   Exeunt. 175

5.5   *Enter Suffolk in conference with the King,*
          Gloucester, and Exeter.

KING
    Your wondrous rare description, noble earl,
    Of beauteous Margaret hath astonished me.
    Her virtues gracèd with external gifts
    Do breed love's settled passions in my heart;   4
    And like as rigor of tempestuous gusts   5
    Provokes the mightiest hulk against the tide,   6
    So am I driven by breath of her renown   7
    Either to suffer shipwreck or arrive
    Where I may have fruition of her love.
SUFFOLK
    Tush, my good lord, this superficial tale
    Is but a preface of her worthy praise.   11
    The chief perfections of that lovely dame,
    Had I sufficient skill to utter them,
    Would make a volume of enticing lines
    Able to ravish any dull conceit;   15
    And, which is more, she is not so divine,
    So full replete with choice of all delights,   17
    But with as humble lowliness of mind
    She is content to be at your command—
    Command, I mean, of virtuous chaste intents,
    To love and honor Henry as her lord.
KING
    And otherwise will Henry ne'er presume.

---

120 **choler** i.e., anger 122 **By** at the 124 **in regard** inasmuch as
125 **Of mere** out of pure 128 **true liegemen** loyal subjects 135 **in
. . . authority** in actual power 139 **Gallian** French 141 **for lucre of**
in order to gain 142 **Detract . . . prerogative** i.e., yield up my right
to be called king in the territories I already possess 143 **As** so as, in
order to 146 **cast** excluded 149 **grows to compromise** moves toward a peaceful settlement 150 **upon comparison** i.e., quibbling
about the proposed articles 152 **Of benefit** as a feudal bestowal
153 **challenge of desert** claim of inherent right 156 **cavil . . . contract** raise frivolous or fault-finding objections during this period of
negotiation

159 **policy** politic course 165 **condition** treaty, contract 167 **Only
reserved** with this single proviso, that 168 **towns of garrison** fortified
towns 175 **entertain** accept
5.5. Location: London. The royal court.
4 **settled** fixed, rooted 5 **like as rigor** just as the severity 6 **Provokes**
drives. **hulk** vessel 7 **breath** (1) report (2) wind in the sails 11 **her
worthy praise** the praise she is truly worth 15 **conceit** imagination
17 **full** fully

Therefore, my Lord Protector, give consent
That Margaret may be England's royal queen.

GLOUCESTER
So should I give consent to flatter sin.   25
You know, my lord, Your Highness is betrothed
Unto another lady of esteem.   27
How shall we then dispense with that contract
And not deface your honor with reproach?

SUFFOLK
As doth a ruler with unlawful oaths,
Or one that, at a triumph having vowed   31
To try his strength, forsaketh yet the lists   32
By reason of his adversary's odds.
A poor earl's daughter is unequal odds,
And therefore may be broke without offense.   35

GLOUCESTER
Why, what, I pray, is Margaret more than that?
Her father is no better than an earl,
Although in glorious titles he excel.

SUFFOLK
Yes, my lord, her father is a king,
The King of Naples and Jerusalem,
And of such great authority in France
As his alliance will confirm our peace   42
And keep the Frenchmen in allegiance.

GLOUCESTER
And so the Earl of Armagnac may do,
Because he is near kinsman unto Charles.

EXETER
Besides, his wealth doth warrant a liberal dower,   46
Where Reignier sooner will receive than give.   47

SUFFOLK
A dower, my lords? Disgrace not so your king
That he should be so abject, base, and poor
To choose for wealth and not for perfect love.
Henry is able to enrich his queen,
And not to seek a queen to make him rich.
So worthless peasants bargain for their wives,   53
As marketmen for oxen, sheep, or horse.
Marriage is a matter of more worth
Than to be dealt in by attorneyship.   56
Not whom we will, but whom His Grace affects,   57
Must be companion of his nuptial bed.
And therefore, lords, since he affects her most,
That most of all these reasons bindeth us
In our opinions she should be preferred.
For what is wedlock forcèd but a hell,
An age of discord and continual strife?   63
Whereas the contrary bringeth bliss,
And is a pattern of celestial peace.   65
Whom should we match with Henry, being a king,
But Margaret, that is daughter to a king?
Her peerless feature, joinèd with her birth,   68

Approves her fit for none but for a king.
Her valiant courage and undaunted spirit,
More than in women commonly is seen,
Will answer our hope in issue of a king;   72
For Henry, son unto a conqueror,
Is likely to beget more conquerors,
If with a lady of so high resolve
As is fair Margaret he be linked in love.
Then yield, my lords, and here conclude with me
That Margaret shall be queen, and none but she.

KING
Whether it be through force of your report,
My noble lord of Suffolk, or for that   80
My tender youth was never yet attaint   81
With any passion of inflaming love,
I cannot tell; but this I am assured,
I feel such sharp dissension in my breast,
Such fierce alarums both of hope and fear,
As I am sick with working of my thoughts.
Take therefore shipping; post, my lord, to France.   87
Agree to any covenants, and procure   88
That Lady Margaret do vouchsafe to come
To cross the seas to England and be crowned
King Henry's faithful and anointed queen.
For your expenses and sufficient charge,   92
Among the people gather up a tenth.   93
Begone, I say, for till you do return
I rest perplexèd with a thousand cares.   95
And you, good uncle, banish all offense.   96
If you do censure me by what you were,   97
Not what you are, I know it will excuse   98
This sudden execution of my will.
And so, conduct me where, from company,   100
I may revolve and ruminate my grief.   101
                                        Exit [*with Exeter*].

GLOUCESTER
Ay, grief, I fear me, both at first and last.   102
                                        Exit Gloucester.

SUFFOLK
Thus Suffolk hath prevailed; and thus he goes,
As did the youthful Paris once to Greece,   104
With hope to find the like event in love,   105
But prosper better than the Trojan did.
Margaret shall now be Queen and rule the King;
But I will rule both her, the King, and realm.   *Exit.*

72 **Will . . . king** i.e., will fulfill our hopes of royal progeny   **80 for that** because   **81 attaint** infected   **87 post** hasten   **88 procure** bring it about   **92 charge** money   **93 gather up a tenth** levy a tax of ten percent of the produce of lands and industry   **95 rest** remain   **96 offense** feeling of resentment and disapproval   **97–98 censure . . . are** i.e., judge me (in my lovesickness) in comparison to your own youthful ways, not to your present wisdom   **100 from company** alone   **101–102 grief . . . grief** love melancholy . . . remorse   **104 Paris** Trojan prince whose abduction of Helen of Sparta instigated the Trojan war   **105 the like event** a similar outcome

25 **flatter** countenance, excuse   27 **another lady** i.e., the Earl of Armagnac's daughter. (See 5.1.17 ff.)   31 **triumph** tournament   32 **lists** place of combat in a tournament   35 **may be broke** i.e., the contract with her may be broken   42 **As** that.   **confirm** strengthen   46 **warrant** guarantee   47 **Where** whereas   53 **So** thus do   56 **attorneyship** haggling proxies   57 **affects** desires   63 **age** lifetime   65 **pattern** image.   **peace** harmony   68 **feature** figure

The Second Part of King Henry the Sixth

Henry VI, Part Two is at once a continuation of the historical narrative begun in *1 Henry VI* (based indeed on the same chronicle sources) and an independent play that must have been staged on a separate occasion in Shakespeare's theater. As the second play of a four-play series, it is open-ended, commencing in a state of political flux and concluding with a civil war in its early phase. Providential consolation seems far away, even if there are signs of divine wrath at work in human affairs. At the same time, this play has its own integrity of theme and dramatic form.

2 Henry VI picks up where *1 Henry VI* ends (in the year 1445) and continues down to the very eve of actual civil war at the Battle of St. Albans (1455). The major events portrayed are the downfall of Humphrey, Duke of Gloucester, and the angry stirrings of the commoners, leading finally to Jack Cade's rebellion. Popular agitation brings about the death of the Duke of Suffolk, thereby claiming the life of one of those most cynically responsible for England's troubles. The villainous Cardinal of Winchester also dies a horrible and edifying death, suggesting that divine retribution is beginning to reveal its inexorable force. Yet throughout this declining action we witness in countermovement the ominous rise of Richard Plantagenet, Duke of York.

Richard's strategy, like that of his namesake in *Richard III*, is to exploit antagonisms at the English court, turning feuding nobles against one another until his potential rivals for power have destroyed themselves. In particular, he takes advantage of the animosity between the new Queen Margaret and Duke Humphrey. Margaret, daughter of a foreign prince, is a consort in the autocratic European style. She haughtily insists on the privileges of her exalted rank and spurns those who govern in the name of justice. "Is this the guise, / Is this the fashion in the court of England?" she incredulously inquires of Suffolk, her lover and political ally (1.3.42–43). Suffolk is an apt mate for Margaret, since he, too, oppresses the commoners. A petition "against the Duke of Suffolk, for enclosing the commons of Melford" (lines 23–24) is one of many heartfelt grievances brought to the attention of the throne by the common people. Margaret

naturally resents the moderate and fair-minded counsel of Duke Humphrey, who urges King Henry to remedy the distress of the commoners.

Richard of York has no inherent admiration for Suffolk and Margaret but cynically backs them as a way of destroying the good Duke of Gloucester. He advises his partners Salisbury and Warwick, "Wink at the Duke of Suffolk's insolence, / At Beaufort's pride, at Somerset's ambition, / At Buckingham, and all the crew of them, / Till they have snared the shepherd of the flock, / That virtuous prince, the good Duke Humphrey" (2.2.70–74). And Humphrey has, in fact, a fatal weakness through which he can be pulled down: the ambition of his wife, Eleanor. Intent on being first lady of the land, Eleanor comes into inevitable conflict with the remorseless Queen Margaret. Winchester and Suffolk, knowing Eleanor's self-blinding pride, find it pathetically easy to plant spies in her household who will encourage her penchant for witchcraft. Humphrey is never contaminated personally by his wife's pride but is doomed nonetheless. King Henry knows of Humphrey's goodness but cannot save him. This fall of a courageous moderate, highlighted in the title of the 1594 Quarto text ("with the death of the good Duke Humphrey"), singles Humphrey out as the most prominent victim of the second play, like Talbot in Part One. He is cut down by an insincere and temporary alliance of extremists from both sides: those such as Margaret and Suffolk who cling to despotic privilege and those such as York who wish to stir up the commoners for their own ulterior purposes. In times of confrontation, the middle position is inherently vulnerable, and its destruction leads to escalating polarization.

As York both foresees and desires, the commoners are indeed unruly when deprived of Humphrey's moderating leadership. Shakespeare has already shown that they tend to ape the quarrels of their elders (as in the ludicrous duel between Horner the Armorer and his man Peter Thump) and are superstitiously gullible (as in the episode of Simpcox the fraudulent blind man). Now, no longer able to petition through channels, their voice becomes importunate. "The commons, like an angry hive of bees / That want their leader, scatter up and down / And care not who they sting in his revenge" (3.2.125–127). At first, their grievances are plausible and their wrath directed at guilty objects. They suspect rightly that their hero, Humphrey, has been destroyed by Suffolk and the Cardinal, and they demand Suffolk's banishment. The request is laudable, but the peremptory tone suggests that the people are beginning to feel their own political power. Unless Suffolk is banished, they warn, they will take him by force from the palace. Poor King Henry, lamenting the lost conciliatory authority of Humphrey, aptly points up the central issue of royal prerogative: "And had I not been cited so by them, / Yet did I purpose as they do entreat" (3.2.281–282). In the perspective of this play, Henry's yielding to popular force is regrettable, but he has no alternative. Equally lamentable is the execution of Suffolk by private citizens taking justice into their own hands. However much this despot deserves to be condemned, his murder is an affront to justice. Servant has turned against master; the commoners have begun to feel their own power.

The popular rebellion itself, Cade's uprising, is a travesty of popular longings for social justice and suggests that any movement of this sort is bound to end in absurdity. Shakespeare, for all his appreciative depiction of individual commoners, never credits them with collective political sagacity once they are demonstrating for their rights. Although Cade's rebellion did, in the view of most historians, arise from deplorable economic conditions of poverty and oppression, Shakespeare ignores any circumstances that might give sympathy to the plight of those who strike back at their masters. To the contrary, he accentuates the dangers of popular agitation by unhistorically bringing together the worst excesses of the Cade rebellion itself (1450) and the famous Peasants' Revolt of 1381. The Cade scenes abound in degrading comedy in the shape of lower-class self-assertion. We laugh at the contrast between Cade's professed Utopian notions of abundance for all and his petty ambition to be king. He kills those who refer to him as Jack Cade rather than by his pretended title of Lord Mortimer. His movement is fiercely anti-intellectual. Yet the sour joke does not indict the commoners alone. Cade's insolent pretentions and his claptrap genealogical claims are an exaggerated but recognizable parody of aristocratic behavior. More important, we remember that Cade was whetted on to his rebellion by the demagogic York. That schemer has "seduced" Cade to make commotion while York himself raises a huge personal army and advances his fortunes in Ireland. "This devil here shall be my substitute" (3.1.371). The commoners can indeed prove irresponsible when goaded, but, throughout 2 Henry VI, feuding aristocrats must bear the chief blame for causing popular discontent.

In view of the need for some kind of coherence amid this universal decline into anarchy and strife, prophecy assumes a structural importance in 2 Henry VI that is to be accentuated in later plays of the tetralogy. As in ancient Greek drama, prophecies are always eventually fulfilled. They reveal divine necessity but in such ambiguous and riddling language that the persons affected by the prophecy do not comprehend the true nature of the utterance until the event itself is upon them. In this play, for example, the spirit conjured to appear before the Duchess of Gloucester (1.4) predicts that Suffolk will die "by water" and that Somerset should "shun castles." What sorts of warnings are these? When his time comes, Suffolk dies at the hands of a man named Walter (pronounced "water," though Suffolk tries desperately to insist on the French "Gualtier"), whereas Somerset dies at the Castle Inn near St. Albans, at the play's end. Through such paltry quibbles, as in Macbeth, great men are misled into a false security. No less riddling is the

prophecy about King Henry and his political antagonist: "The duke yet lives that Henry shall depose, / But him outlive, and die a violent death" (1.4.31–32). The first phrase of this oracle is perfectly ambiguous: it can mean that a still living duke will depose Henry or that Henry will depose this duke. Both interpretations turn out to be valid; during the wars of Lancaster and York shown in 3 Henry VI, King Henry and his Yorkist opponent will, by turns, take the throne from each other. Eventually, too, in 3 Henry VI and Richard III, Edward of York will outlive Henry only to die a retributive death. In such prophecy, there is already the concept of an eye for an eye, a Lancastrian for a Yorkist, through which Providence will finally impose its penalty on a rebellious people. Prophecy then serves not to allow human beings to escape their destiny, which is unavoidable, but to give them the opportunity to perceive at last the pattern of divine justice. The audience realizes that prophecy is a divine warning too often unheeded by foolish human beings, and acknowledges the necessity of a fulfillment that is tragic and dispiriting but also comforting to the extent that it shows the heavens to be just.

The role of prophecy is thus central in 2 Henry VI in that it gives to the play a dominant pattern of prediction and eventual fulfillment. Yet the experience of 2 Henry VI is one of turbulence. Events increasingly take on their own unstoppable momentum. Ceremonies and institutions employed to control the flux are not successful. Abstract ideas conflict with stern realities; the idea of kingship is appealed to as a rallying cry for authority and stability, but the fact of King Henry's inept leadership and the self-serving ambitions of his antagonists invite continual disarray. As a work of art, 2 Henry VI thus grapples with the problem of making something artistically coherent out of chaos. It does so, as does 3 Henry VI, by containing the instability within the recurring pattern of an eye for an eye.

Any sense of comfort is slow to arrive in this play. England's political and moral decline remains unchecked. The commoners' rebellion, cynically fomented by Richard, Duke of York, has established the precedent for further rebellion. Knowing his enemies to be weak and divided, Richard no longer conceals the ambition that has led him to accept an assignment in Ireland and thereby raise an army. His excuse for returning to England in arms, to rid King Henry of the hated adviser Somerset, is similarly shown to be no more than a pretext for declaring open civil war. His final justification for challenging King Henry, despite all the fine talk about genealogies, is that Richard has the ambition and the raw power to carry out his plan. Henry's assertions of right are no less governed by expediency, for he privately confesses the weakness of his claim. The admirable example, shown late in this play, of a Kentish gentleman named Iden who is content to live peaceably on his estate, serves as a contrast to the dismaying ambitions that have infected not only Richard of York and his allies but also the remorseless

Queen Margaret and those loyal to her. If, as A. P. Rossiter has cogently argued, *2 Henry VI* is a "morality of state" in which forces of good and evil struggle for the soul of that beleaguered heroine, Respublica or the commonwealth, then the play must ultimately be viewed as one in which the forces of good do not fare well. To be sure, the haughty Suffolk meets his dire fate, though by a means that encourages further private revenge; Somerset falls as predicted at St. Albans; and Winchester suffers a death of edifying horror. Still, Richard of York and Queen Margaret, having profited from the victimization of the virtuous Duke Humphrey, are more powerful than ever, and Richard's son and namesake is only beginning to make his presence felt. Many scores remain to be settled at the close of *2 Henry VI*.

The Second Part of King Henry the Sixth

[*Dramatis Personae*

KING HENRY THE SIXTH
QUEEN MARGARET
Humphrey, DUKE OF GLOUCESTER, *King Henry's uncle, and Lord Protector*
DUCHESS OF GLOUCESTER, *Dame Eleanor Cobham*
CARDINAL BEAUFORT, *Bishop of Winchester, the King's great-uncle*
DUKE OF SOMERSET
DUKE OF SUFFOLK, *William de la Pole, earlier Marquess of Suffolk*
DUKE OF BUCKINGHAM
LORD CLIFFORD
YOUNG CLIFFORD, *his son*

RICHARD PLANTAGENET, DUKE OF YORK, *leader of the York faction*
EDWARD, *Earl of March, his eldest son*
RICHARD, *his son*
EARL OF SALISBURY, } *supporters of the*
EARL OF WARWICK, *his son,* } *Yorkist claim*

LORD SCALES,
LORD SAYE,
SIR HUMPHREY STAFFORD,
WILLIAM STAFFORD, *his* BROTHER, } *supporters of King Henry against Cade's rebellion*

SIR JOHN STANLEY, *custodian of the Duchess of Gloucester*
SHERIFF *of London, custodian of the Duchess of Gloucester*

SIR JOHN HUME, *a priest*
JOHN SOUTHWELL, *a priest*
MARGERY JORDAN, *a witch*
ROGER BOLINGBROKE, *a conjurer*
A SPIRIT *named* ASNATH

Two or Three PETITIONERS
THOMAS HORNER, *the Armorer*
PETER THUMP, *the Armorer's man*
Three NEIGHBORS *of Horner*
Three Fellow PRENTICES *of Peter*

A TOWNSMAN *of St. Albans*
SIMPCOX *or Simon, supposedly restored to sight*
His WIFE
MAYOR *of St. Albans*

A BEADLE *of St. Albans*

LIEUTENANT *or Captain of a ship*
MASTER *of the ship*
WALTER WHITMORE
Two GENTLEMEN *prisoners*

JACK CADE, *rebel leader from Kent*
GEORGE BEVIS,
JOHN HOLLAND,
DICK, *the butcher,* } *followers of Cade*
SMITH, *the weaver,*
MICHAEL,

MESSENGERS
Two SERVINGMEN, *of Gloucester and York*
A HERALD
POST *or Messenger to Parliament*
Two MURDERERS *of Gloucester*
VAUX, *a messenger*
A CLERK *of Chartham*
ALEXANDER IDEN, *a gentleman of Kent*

*Falconers, Townsmen and Aldermen, Commoners,
Rebels, a Sawyer, Soldiers, Servingmen, Attendants, Guards, Officers, Matthew Gough*

SCENE: *England*]

1.1   *Flourish of trumpets, then hautboys. Enter [the]
King, Duke Humphrey [of Gloucester], Salisbury,
Warwick, and [Cardinal] Beaufort, on the one side;
the Queen, Suffolk, York, Somerset, and
Buckingham, on the other.*

SUFFOLK
As by Your High Imperial Majesty
I had in charge at my depart for France,   2
As procurator to Your Excellence,   3
To marry Princess Margaret for Your Grace,
So, in the famous ancient city Tours,
In presence of the Kings of France and Sicil,   6
The Dukes of Orleans, Calaber, Brittaine, and
    Alençon,   7
Seven earls, twelve barons, and twenty reverend
    bishops,
I have performed my task and was espoused;
And humbly now upon my bended knee, [*kneeling*]
In sight of England and her lordly peers,
Deliver up my title in the Queen
To your most gracious hands, that are the substance
Of that great shadow I did represent: 14

The happiest gift that ever marquess gave,   15
The fairest queen that ever king received.
KING
Suffolk, arise. Welcome, Queen Margaret.
                                        [*Suffolk rises.*]
I can express no kinder sign of love   18
Than this kind kiss. [*He kisses her.*] O Lord, that
    lends me life,   19
Lend me a heart replete with thankfulness!
For thou hast given me in this beauteous face
A world of earthly blessings to my soul,
If sympathy of love unite our thoughts.
QUEEN
Great King of England and my gracious lord,
The mutual conference that my mind hath had   25
By day, by night, waking and in my dreams,
In courtly company or at my beads,   27
With you, mine alderliefest sovereign,   28
Makes me the bolder to salute my king
With ruder terms, such as my wit affords   30
And overjoy of heart doth minister.   31
KING
Her sight did ravish, but her grace in speech,   32
Her words yclad with wisdom's majesty,   33
Makes me from wondering fall to weeping joys,   34
Such is the fullness of my heart's content.
Lords, with one cheerful voice welcome my love.
ALL (*kneeling*)
Long live Queen Margaret, England's happiness!
QUEEN   We thank you all.   *Flourish.* [*They all rise.*]
SUFFOLK
My Lord Protector, so it please Your Grace,
Here are the articles of contracted peace
Between our sovereign and the French king Charles,
For eighteen months concluded by consent.
GLOUCESTER (*reads*) "Imprimis, it is agreed between   43
the French king Charles and William de la Pole, Mar-   44
quess of Suffolk, ambassador for Henry, King of En-   45
gland, that the said Henry shall espouse the Lady Mar-
garet, daughter unto Reignier, King of Naples, Sicilia,
and Jerusalem, and crown her Queen of England ere
the thirtieth of May next ensuing. Item, that the duchy   49
of Anjou and the county of Maine shall be released and
delivered to the King her father"—
                                        [*He lets the paper fall.*]
KING
Uncle, how now?
GLOUCESTER   Pardon me, gracious lord.
Some sudden qualm hath struck me at the heart
And dimmed mine eyes, that I can read no further.   54

1.1. **Location: London. The royal court.**
s.d. Flourish fanfare. **hautboys** oboelike instruments **2 had in
charge** was commissioned. **depart** departure **3 procurator to**
agent, proxy for **6 Sicil** Sicily. (Titularly ruled by Margaret's father,
the Duke of Anjou.) **7 Calaber** Calabria, in southern Italy
14 shadow image, i.e., of royalty

15 happiest most fortunate **18 kinder** more natural **19 kind** loving
25 mutual conference intimate communication (of the mind with itself) **27 In . . . beads** in courtly society or at my prayers (with the
rosary) **28 alderliefest** most loved **30 ruder** less polished. **wit** intelligence **31 minister** supply **32 Her sight** the sight of her
33 yclad clad, clothed **34 wondering** admiring **43 Imprimis** in the
first place **44–45 Marquess** (William de la Pole was fourth Earl and
then first Duke of Suffolk. Edward Hall writes that he was elevated
from earl to marquess "when the marriage contract was agreed.")
49 Item also **54 that** so that

KING
Uncle of Winchester, I pray, read on.   55
CARDINAL [*reads*]   "Item, it is further agreed between
them that the duchies of Anjou and Maine shall be   57
released and delivered over to the King her father, and
she sent over of the King of England's own proper cost   59
and charges, without having any dowry."
KING
They please us well. Lord Marquess, kneel down.
                                                        [*Suffolk kneels.*]
We here create thee the first Duke of Suffolk,
And gird thee with the sword. [*Suffolk rises.*] Cousin
   of York,   63
We here discharge Your Grace from being regent
I' the parts of France, till term of eighteen months   65
Be full expired. Thanks, uncle Winchester,
Gloucester, York, Buckingham, Somerset,
Salisbury, and Warwick;
We thank you all for this great favor done
In entertainment to my princely queen.   70
Come, let us in, and with all speed provide
To see her coronation be performed.   72
                                  Exeunt King, Queen, and Suffolk.
                                  Manent the rest.
GLOUCESTER
Brave peers of England, pillars of the state,
To you Duke Humphrey must unload his grief,
Your grief, the common grief of all the land.
What? Did my brother Henry spend his youth,   76
His valor, coin, and people in the wars?
Did he so often lodge in open field,
In winter's cold and summer's parching heat,
To conquer France, his true inheritance?
And did my brother Bedford toil his wits   81
To keep by policy what Henry got?   82
Have you yourselves, Somerset, Buckingham,
Brave York, Salisbury, and victorious Warwick,
Received deep scars in France and Normandy?
Or hath mine uncle Beaufort and myself,
With all the learnèd Council of the realm,
Studied so long, sat in the Council House
Early and late, debating to and fro
How France and Frenchmen might be kept in awe,   90
And had His Highness in his infancy
Crowned in Paris in despite of foes?
And shall these labors and these honors die?
Shall Henry's conquest, Bedford's vigilance,
Your deeds of war, and all our counsel die?
O peers of England, shameful is this league!
Fatal this marriage, canceling your fame,
Blotting your names from books of memory,   98

Razing the characters of your renown,   99
Defacing monuments of conquered France,
Undoing all, as all had never been!   101
CARDINAL
Nephew, what means this passionate discourse,
This peroration with such circumstance?   103
For France, 'tis ours; and we will keep it still.   104
GLOUCESTER
Ay, uncle, we will keep it if we can,
But now it is impossible we should.
Suffolk, the new-made duke that rules the roast,   107
Hath given the duchy of Anjou, and Maine,
Unto the poor King Reignier, whose large style   109
Agrees not with the leanness of his purse.
SALISBURY
Now, by the death of Him that died for all,
These counties were the keys of Normandy.
But wherefore weeps Warwick, my valiant son?
WARWICK
For grief that they are past recovery;
For, were there hope to conquer them again,
My sword should shed hot blood, mine eyes no
   tears.
Anjou and Maine? Myself did win them both!
Those provinces these arms of mine did conquer.
And are the cities that I got with wounds
Delivered up again with peaceful words?
Mort Dieu!   121
YORK
For Suffolk's duke, may he be suffocate,   122
That dims the honor of this warlike isle!
France should have torn and rent my very heart
Before I would have yielded to this league.   125
I never read but England's kings have had
Large sums of gold and dowries with their wives;
And our King Henry gives away his own
To match with her that brings no vantages.   129
GLOUCESTER
A proper jest, and never heard before,
That Suffolk should demand a whole fifteenth   131
For costs and charges in transporting her!
She should have stayed in France and starved in
   France
Before—
CARDINAL
My lord of Gloucester, now ye grow too hot.
It was the pleasure of my lord the King.
GLOUCESTER
My lord of Winchester, I know your mind.
'Tis not my speeches that you do mislike,
But 'tis my presence that doth trouble ye.

---

55 Uncle (Actually, great-uncle.)   **57 duchies . . . Maine** i.e., the
duchy of Anjou and the county of Maine, as in lines 49–50 above.
(Perhaps the text is in error.)   **59 of** at.   **proper** personal   **63 Cousin**
(An appropriate title for the King to use toward any peer, but York is
also his distant cousin.)   **65 parts** territories.   **term . . . months** i.e.,
the period of the truce between England and France   **70 entertainment to** gracious reception of   **72 s.d. Manent** they remain onstage
76 Henry i.e., Henry V   **81 Bedford** (As portrayed in *1 Henry VI*.)
82 policy prudent management   **90 awe** subjection   **98 books of
memory** i.e., chronicles

99 Razing the characters scraping away the records, or *rasing*, "erasing"   **101 as** as if   **103 circumstance** detail   **104 For** as for.   **still** always   **107 rules the roast** i.e., domineers. (The Folio spelling, "rost,"
may also suggest "roost," but the etymology is uncertain.)   **109 large
style** lavish title   **121 Mort Dieu** by God's (Christ's) death   **122 For**
as for.   **suffocate** (punning on *Suffolk*)   **125 yielded** consented
129 vantages benefits, profits   **131 whole fifteenth** i.e., tax levy consisting of one-fifteenth of the produce of lands and industry. (Compare
this with *1 Henry VI*, 5.5.92–93, where the figure is put at
one-tenth.)

Rancor will out. Proud prelate, in thy face
I see thy fury. If I longer stay,
We shall begin our ancient bickerings.
Lordings, farewell; and say, when I am gone,   143
I prophesied France will be lost ere long.
                                   Exit Humphrey.
CARDINAL
So, there goes our Protector in a rage.
'Tis known to you he is mine enemy,
Nay, more, an enemy unto you all,
And no great friend, I fear me, to the King.
Consider, lords, he is the next of blood   149
And heir apparent to the English crown.
Had Henry got an empire by his marriage,
And all the wealthy kingdoms of the west,   152
There's reason he should be displeased at it.   153
Look to it, lords; let not his smoothing words   154
Bewitch your hearts. Be wise and circumspect.
What though the common people favor him,
Calling him "Humphrey, the good Duke of
     Gloucester,"
Clapping their hands and crying with loud voice,
"Jesu maintain Your Royal Excellence!"
With "God preserve the good Duke Humphrey!"
I fear me, lords, for all this flattering gloss,   161
He will be found a dangerous Protector.
BUCKINGHAM
Why should he, then, protect our sovereign,
He being of age to govern of himself?   164
Cousin of Somerset, join you with me,   165
And all together, with the Duke of Suffolk,
We'll quickly hoist Duke Humphrey from his seat.
CARDINAL
This weighty business will not brook delay;   168
I'll to the Duke of Suffolk presently.   *Exit Cardinal.* 169
SOMERSET
Cousin of Buckingham, though Humphrey's pride   170
And greatness of his place be grief to us,   171
Yet let us watch the haughty Cardinal.
His insolence is more intolerable
Than all the princes in the land besides.   174
If Gloucester be displaced, he'll be Protector.
BUCKINGHAM
Or thou or I, Somerset, will be Protector,   176
Despite Duke Humphrey or the Cardinal.
               Exeunt Buckingham and Somerset.
SALISBURY
Pride went before, Ambition follows him.   178
While these do labor for their own preferment,   179
Behooves it us to labor for the realm.
I never saw but Humphrey, Duke of Gloucester,

Did bear him like a noble gentleman.   182
Oft have I seen the haughty Cardinal,
More like a soldier than a man o' the Church,
As stout and proud as he were lord of all,   185
Swear like a ruffian and demean himself   186
Unlike the ruler of a commonweal.
Warwick, my son, the comfort of my age,
Thy deeds, thy plainness, and thy housekeeping   189
Hath won thee greatest favor of the commons,
Excepting none but good Duke Humphrey.   191
And, brother York, thy acts in Ireland,   192
In bringing them to civil discipline,
Thy late exploits done in the heart of France,
When thou wert regent for our sovereign,
Have made thee feared and honored of the people.
Join we together for the public good,
In what we can, to bridle and suppress
The pride of Suffolk and the Cardinal,
With Somerset's and Buckingham's ambition;
And, as we may, cherish Duke Humphrey's deeds,   201
While they do tend the profit of the land.   202
WARWICK
So God help Warwick, as he loves the land
And common profit of his country!
YORK
And so says York—[*aside*] for he hath greatest cause. 205
SALISBURY
Then let's away and look unto the main.   206
WARWICK
Unto the main? O Father, Maine is lost!
That Maine which by main force Warwick did win,
And would have kept so long as breath did last!
Main chance, Father, you meant; but I meant Maine,
Which I will win from France, or else be slain.   211
          Exeunt Warwick and Salisbury. Manet York.
YORK
Anjou and Maine are given to the French;
Paris is lost; the state of Normandy
Stands on a tickle point now they are gone.   214
Suffolk concluded on the articles,   215
The peers agreed, and Henry was well pleased
To change two dukedoms for a duke's fair daughter.
I cannot blame them all. What is 't to them?
'Tis thine they give away, and not their own.   219
Pirates may make cheap pennyworths of their
     pillages,   220
And purchase friends, and give to courtesans,   221
Still reveling like lords till all be gone;   222

182 him himself   **185 stout** haughty.   **as** as if   **186 demean** conduct
189 plainness plain dealing.   **housekeeping** hospitality   **191 Excepting none but** second only to   **192 brother** i.e., brother-in-law; see
note to line 238 below   **201 cherish** support   **202 tend** tend to, serve
205 greatest cause i.e., as hopeful claimant to the throne   **206 unto
the main** to the most important business (with several puns in the following lines: [1] *Maine*, a French province lost in the treaty [2] *main
force*, brute force [3] *Main chance*, a gambling term from the dice
game called hazard)   **211 s.d. Manet** he remains onstage   **214 tickle**
unstable, insecure   **215 concluded on the articles** negotiated the exact terms (of the marriage agreement)   **219 thine** (York speaks to himself.)   **220 make cheap pennyworths of** i.e., practically give away
221 purchase friends i.e., win friends through reckless generosity
222 Still continually

143 Lordings my lords, gentlemen   **149 next of blood** i.e., in line to
succeed to the throne, as Henry's eldest uncle. (Henry was as yet
childless.)   **152 the wealthy . . . west** (Seemingly an anachronistic
reference to New World possessions.)   **153 he** i.e., Gloucester
154 smoothing flattering   **161 flattering gloss** attractive appearance
164 He i.e., King Henry   **165 join you** if you join   **168 brook** endure, permit   **169 presently** immediately   **170 Cousin** kinsman, fellow peer   **171 grief** grievance   **174 Than** i.e., than that of.   **princes**
peers   **176 Or** either   **178 Pride** i.e., Winchester.   **Ambition** i.e.,
Buckingham and Somerset   **179 preferment** advancement

Whileas the silly owner of the goods   223
Weeps over them, and wrings his hapless hands,
And shakes his head, and trembling stands aloof,   225
While all is shared and all is borne away,
Ready to starve and dare not touch his own.   227
So York must sit and fret and bite his tongue,
While his own lands are bargained for and sold.
Methinks the realms of England, France, and Ireland
Bear that proportion to my flesh and blood   231
As did the fatal brand Althaea burnt   232
Unto the Prince's heart of Calydon.   233
Anjou and Maine both given unto the French!
Cold news for me, for I had hope of France,
Even as I have of fertile England's soil.
A day will come when York shall claim his own;
And therefore I will take the Nevilles' parts   238
And make a show of love to proud Duke
    Humphrey,
And, when I spy advantage, claim the crown,   240
For that's the golden mark I seek to hit.   241
Nor shall proud Lancaster usurp my right,   242
Nor hold the scepter in his childish fist,
Nor wear the diadem upon his head,
Whose churchlike humors fits not for a crown.   245
Then, York, be still awhile, till time do serve.
Watch thou and wake when others be asleep,
To pry into the secrets of the state,
Till Henry, surfeiting in joys of love
With his new bride and England's dear-bought
    queen,
And Humphrey with the peers be fall'n at jars.   251
Then will I raise aloft the milk-white rose,   252
With whose sweet smell the air shall be perfumed,
And in my standard bear the arms of York,   254
To grapple with the house of Lancaster;
And force perforce I'll make him yield the crown,   256
Whose bookish rule hath pulled fair England down.   257

                                        Exit York.

                          ✜

1.2   *Enter Duke Humphrey and his wife Eleanor.*

DUCHESS
Why droops my lord, like overripened corn,   1

Hanging the head at Ceres' plenteous load?   2
Why doth the great Duke Humphrey knit his
    brows,
As frowning at the favors of the world?   4
Why are thine eyes fixed to the sullen earth,
Gazing on that which seems to dim thy sight?
What seest thou there? King Henry's diadem,
Enchased with all the honors of the world?   8
If so, gaze on, and grovel on thy face,
Until thy head be circled with the same.
Put forth thy hand; reach at the glorious gold.
What, is 't too short? I'll lengthen it with mine;   12
And having both together heaved it up,   13
We'll both together lift our heads to heaven
And nevermore abase our sight so low
As to vouchsafe one glance unto the ground.
GLOUCESTER
O Nell, sweet Nell, if thou dost love thy lord,
Banish the canker of ambitious thoughts!   18
And may that hour when I imagine ill
Against my king and nephew, virtuous Henry,
Be my last breathing in this mortal world!
My troublous dream this night doth make me sad.   22
DUCHESS
What dreamed my lord? Tell me, and I'll requite it
With sweet rehearsal of my morning's dream.   24
GLOUCESTER
Methought this staff, mine office badge in court,   25
Was broke in twain—by whom, I have forgot,
But, as I think, it was by the Cardinal—
And on the pieces of the broken wand
Were placed the heads of Edmund, Duke of
    Somerset,
And William de la Pole, first Duke of Suffolk.
This was my dream. What it doth bode, God
    knows.
DUCHESS
Tut, this was nothing but an argument   32
That he that breaks a stick of Gloucester's grove   33
Shall lose his head for his presumption.
But list to me, my Humphrey, my sweet duke: 35
Methought I sat in seat of majesty
In the cathedral church of Westminster,
And in that chair where kings and queens are
    crowned,
Where Henry and Dame Margaret kneeled to me
And on my head did set the diadem.
GLOUCESTER
Nay, Eleanor, then must I chide outright.
Presumptuous dame, ill-nurtured Eleanor,   42
Art thou not second woman in the realm,
And the Protector's wife, beloved of him?
Hast thou not worldly pleasure at command

---

223 **Whileas** while. **silly** wretched, helpless   **225 stands aloof**
stands to one side (unable to intervene)   **227 Ready . . . and** he being on the point of starvation and yet   **231 proportion** relationship
232 Althaea mother of Meleager, prince of Calydon. (At his birth, she
was told that her son would live only as long as a brand of wood remained unconsumed. She snatched the brand from the fire, but years
later, when Meleager quarreled with Althaea's brothers and slew
them, she resentfully threw the fatal brand into the fire, thus causing
his death.)   **233 Unto . . . Calydon** to the heart of the Prince of Calydon   **238 the Nevilles'** i.e., Salisbury's and his son Warwick's (to
whom Richard of York was allied by marriage, having married Cecille
or Cicely Neville, Salisbury's sister)   **240 advantage** opportunity
241 mark archery target   **242 Lancaster** i.e., Henry VI, here demoted
to his title of duke   **245 humors** temperament   **251 at jars** in discords, quarreling   **252 milk-white rose** (Emblem of the Yorkist dynasty.)   **254 standard** battle standard, ensign.   **arms** coat of arms
256 force perforce by violent compulsion   **257 bookish** scholarly and
ineffectual
1.2. Location: The Duke of Gloucester's house.
1 corn grain

2 **Ceres** goddess of the harvest and agriculture   **4 As** as if   **8 Enchased** adorned as with gems   **12 is 't** i.e., is your arm   **13 heaved it**
i.e., lifted the crown   **18 canker** ulcer   **22 this night** this past night
24 rehearsal recounting.   **morning's dream** (Morning dreams were,
in folklore, regarded as foretelling true things.)   **25 mine office badge**
the symbol of my office of Protector   **32 argument** proof, evidence
33 breaks . . . grove i.e., harms Gloucester in the slightest. (The image of the stick is suggested by the broken staff.)   **35 list** listen
42 ill-nurtured ill-bred

Above the reach or compass of thy thought?   46
And wilt thou still be hammering treachery,   47
To tumble down thy husband and thyself
From top of honor to disgrace's feet?
Away from me, and let me hear no more!

DUCHESS
What, what, my lord? Are you so choleric
With Eleanor for telling but her dream?
Next time I'll keep my dreams unto myself,
And not be checked.   54

GLOUCESTER
Nay, be not angry. I am pleased again.

Enter Messenger.

MESSENGER
My Lord Protector, 'tis His Highness' pleasure
You do prepare to ride unto Saint Albans,
Whereas the King and Queen do mean to hawk.   58

GLOUCESTER
I go. Come, Nell, thou wilt ride with us?

DUCHESS
Yes, my good lord, I'll follow presently.   60
             Exit Humphrey [with Messenger].
Follow I must; I cannot go before   61
While Gloucester bears this base and humble mind.
Were I a man, a duke, and next of blood,
I would remove these tedious stumbling blocks
And smooth my way upon their headless necks;
And, being a woman, I will not be slack
To play my part in Fortune's pageant.—   67
Where are you there? Sir John! Nay, fear not, man,   68
We are alone; here's none but thee and I.

Enter Hume.

HUME
Jesus preserve Your Royal Majesty!

DUCHESS
What sayst thou? "Majesty"? I am but "Grace."   71

HUME
But by the grace of God and Hume's advice
Your Grace's title shall be multiplied.

DUCHESS
What sayst thou, man? Hast thou as yet conferred
With Margery Jordan, the cunning witch,
With Roger Bolingbroke, the conjurer?
And will they undertake to do me good?

HUME
This they have promisèd: to show Your Highness
A spirit raised from depth of underground
That shall make answer to such questions
As by Your Grace shall be propounded him.

DUCHESS
It is enough. I'll think upon the questions.
When from Saint Albans we do make return,
We'll see these things effected to the full.

Here, Hume, take this reward. [*She gives money.*]
  Make merry, man,
With thy confederates in this weighty cause.
                  Exit Eleanor.

HUME
Hume must make merry with the Duchess' gold.
Marry, and shall! But, how now, Sir John Hume?   88
Seal up your lips, and give no words but mum;
The business asketh silent secrecy.
Dame Eleanor gives gold to bring the witch;
Gold cannot come amiss, were she a devil.
Yet have I gold flies from another coast—   93
I dare not say, from the rich Cardinal
And from the great and new-made Duke of Suffolk,
Yet I do find it so; for, to be plain,
They, knowing Dame Eleanor's aspiring humor,   97
Have hirèd me to undermine the Duchess
And buzz these conjurations in her brain.
They say "A crafty knave does need no broker,"   100
Yet am I Suffolk and the Cardinal's broker.
Hume, if you take not heed, you shall go near   102
To call them both a pair of crafty knaves.   103
Well, so it stands; and thus, I fear, at last
Hume's knavery will be the Duchess' wrack,   105
And her attainture will be Humphrey's fall.   106
Sort how it will, I shall have gold for all.   *Exit.* 107

❖

1.3   *Enter three or four Petitioners, [Peter,] the*
        Armorer's man, being one.

FIRST PETITIONER   My masters, let's stand close. My 1
Lord Protector will come this way by and by, and then
we may deliver our supplications in the quill.   3

SECOND PETITIONER   Marry, the Lord protect him, for
he's a good man! Jesu bless him!

Enter Suffolk and Queen.

FIRST PETITIONER   Here 'a comes, methinks, and the 6
Queen with him. I'll be the first, sure.
                    [*He starts forward.*]

SECOND PETITIONER   Come back, fool. This is the Duke
of Suffolk, and not my Lord Protector.

SUFFOLK   How now, fellow? Wouldst anything with
me?

FIRST PETITIONER   I pray, my lord, pardon me. I took
ye for my Lord Protector.

QUEEN [*reads*]   "To my Lord Protector"? Are your sup- 14
plications to his lordship? Let me see them. What is
thine?   [*She takes the petition.*]

---

88 Marry, and shall i.e., indeed he will. (*Marry* was originally an oath, "by the Virgin Mary.") **93 flies** i.e., that flies, approaches. **coast** quarter, source **97 humor** temperament, fancy **100 They say** people say. **broker** agent **102–103 go near To call** come close to calling **105 wrack** destruction, ruin **106 attainture** conviction and disgrace **107 Sort . . . will** turn out which way it will. **for all** i.e., in any case

1.3. Location: London. The royal court.
1 close near together **3 in the quill** i.e., simultaneously, in a body **6 'a** he **14 s.d. reads** (The Queen evidently reads the superscription while the First Petitioner is holding his petition.)

---

46 compass encompassing   47 hammering i.e., devising
54 checked rebuked   58 Whereas where. hawk hunt with hawks
60 presently at once   61 go before i.e., advance my own ambitions
to be second to none   67 pageant spectacular entertainment   68 Sir
John (Conventional form of addressing a priest.)   71 Grace (Appropriate address to a duchess.)

FIRST PETITIONER   Mine is, an 't please Your Grace, 17
against John Goodman, my Lord Cardinal's man, for
keeping my house, and lands, and wife and all, from
me.

SUFFOLK   Thy wife too? That's some wrong, indeed.—
What's yours? What's here? [*He takes a petition.*]
"Against the Duke of Suffolk, for enclosing the 23
commons of Melford." How now, sir knave?   24

SECOND PETITIONER   Alas, sir, I am but a poor petitioner of our whole township.   26

PETER [*giving his petition*]   Against my master, Thomas
Horner, for saying that the Duke of York was
rightful heir to the crown.

QUEEN   What sayst thou? Did the Duke of York say he
was rightful heir to the crown?

PETER   That my master? No, forsooth; my master
said that he was, and that the King was an usurper.

SUFFOLK   Who is there? (*Enter Servant.*) Take this fellow
in, and send for his master with a pursuivant pres- 35
ently. We'll hear more of your matter before the King. 36
                              Exit [Servant with Peter].

QUEEN [*to the Petitioners*]
And as for you, that love to be protected
Under the wings of our Protector's grace,
Begin your suits anew and sue to him.
                              Tear the supplication.
Away, base cullions! Suffolk, let them go.   40

ALL   Come, let's be gone.   *Exeunt [Petitioners].*

QUEEN
My lord of Suffolk, say, is this the guise,   42
Is this the fashions in the court of England?
Is this the government of Britain's isle,
And this the royalty of Albion's king?   45
What, shall King Henry be a pupil still
Under the surly Gloucester's governance?
Am I a queen in title and in style,
And must be made a subject to a duke?
I tell thee, Pole, when in the city Tours   50
Thou rann'st atilt in honor of my love   51
And stol'st away the ladies' hearts of France,
I thought King Henry had resembled thee
In courage, courtship, and proportion.   54
But all his mind is bent to holiness,
To number Ave Marys on his beads.
His champions are the prophets and apostles,
His weapons holy saws of sacred writ,   58
His study is his tiltyard, and his loves   59
Are brazen images of canonized saints.   60
I would the College of the Cardinals
Would choose him Pope and carry him to Rome

And set the triple crown upon his head;   63
That were a state fit for his holiness.   64

SUFFOLK
Madam, be patient. As I was cause
Your Highness came to England, so will I
In England work Your Grace's full content.

QUEEN
Besides the haughty Protector, have we Beaufort
The imperious churchman, Somerset, Buckingham,
And grumbling York; and not the least of these
But can do more in England than the King.

SUFFOLK
And he of these that can do most of all
Cannot do more in England than the Nevilles.
Salisbury and Warwick are no simple peers.

QUEEN
Not all these lords do vex me half so much
As that proud dame, the Lord Protector's wife.
She sweeps it through the court with troops of
ladies,   77
More like an empress than Duke Humphrey's wife.
Strangers in court do take her for the Queen.   79
She bears a duke's revenues on her back,   80
And in her heart she scorns our poverty.
Shall I not live to be avenged on her?
Contemptuous baseborn callet as she is,   83
She vaunted 'mongst her minions t' other day   84
The very train of her worst wearing gown   85
Was better worth than all my father's lands,   86
Till Suffolk gave two dukedoms for his daughter.   87

SUFFOLK
Madam, myself have limed a bush for her,   88
And placed a choir of such enticing birds   89
That she will light to listen to the lays   90
And never mount to trouble you again.   91
So let her rest. And, madam, list to me,   92
For I am bold to counsel you in this:
Although we fancy not the Cardinal,   94
Yet must we join with him and with the lords
Till we have brought Duke Humphrey in disgrace.
As for the Duke of York, this late complaint   97
Will make but little for his benefit.

---

17 an 't if it   **23–24 enclosing the commons** the action of a lord of a manor in enclosing or converting into private property lands formerly undivided and used by the community as a whole   **26 of** on behalf of   **35 pursuivant** minor messenger or officer with authority to execute warrants   **35–36 presently** at once   **40 cullions** base fellows. (Originally, *cullion* meant "testicle.")   **42 guise** custom, manner   **45 Albion's** England's   **50 Pole** i.e., Suffolk   **51 rann'st atilt** jousted in a tournament   **54 courtship** courtly manners.   **proportion** carriage, build   **58 saws** sayings   **59 tiltyard** enclosed space for tilts or tournaments   **60 brazen images** bronze statues

63 the triple crown i.e., the diadem of the papacy—a large hat enriched by three gold crowns symbolizing perhaps the Church militant, suffering, and triumphant   **64 state** status.   **his holiness** Henry's piety (but playing on the Pope's title, "His Holiness")   **77 sweeps it** moves majestically, with trailing garments   **79 Strangers** visiting foreigners   **80 on her back** i.e., in her garments   **83 Contemptuous** (1) contemptible (2) full of contempt.   **callet** lewd woman   **84 vaunted** boasted.   **minions** followers, attendants (with overtones of "saucy women")   **85–87 The very . . . daughter** i.e., (Eleanor boasted that) the mere trailing part of her least expensive gown was worth more than all the lands possessed by Reignier until Suffolk arranged a dowry whereby the Duke received two rich dukedoms (Anjou and Maine) in return for the marriage of me, his daughter, to King Henry   **88 limed a bush** set a trap. (A metaphor from the practice of catching birds by putting sticky birdlime on twigs of trees.)   **89 enticing birds** i.e., decoys   **90 light** alight.   **lays** songs   **91 mount** (1) fly off, fly aloft (2) aspire   **92 let her rest** i.e., forget about her   **94 fancy not** do not like   **97 late complaint** i.e., recent allegation made by Peter that his master, the armorer, had spoken of York as the proper King of England

So one by one we'll weed them all at last,
And you yourself shall steer the happy helm.   100

Sound a sennet. Enter the King, Duke Humphrey
[of Gloucester], Cardinal [Beaufort], Buckingham,
York, [Somerset,] Salisbury, Warwick, and the
Duchess [of Gloucester].

KING
For my part, noble lords, I care not which;   101
Or Somerset or York, all's one to me.   102
YORK
If York have ill demeaned himself in France,   103
Then let him be denied the regentship.
SOMERSET
If Somerset be unworthy of the place,
Let York be regent. I will yield to him.
WARWICK
Whether Your Grace be worthy, yea or no,
Dispute not that. York is the worthier.
CARDINAL
Ambitious Warwick, let thy betters speak.
WARWICK
The Cardinal's not my better in the field.   110
BUCKINGHAM
All in this presence are thy betters, Warwick.
WARWICK
Warwick may live to be the best of all.
SALISBURY
Peace, son!—And show some reason, Buckingham,
Why Somerset should be preferred in this.
QUEEN
Because the King, forsooth, will have it so.
GLOUCESTER
Madam, the King is old enough himself
To give his censure. These are no women's matters.   117
QUEEN
If he be old enough, what needs Your Grace
To be Protector of His Excellence?
GLOUCESTER
Madam, I am Protector of the realm,
And at his pleasure will resign my place.
SUFFOLK
Resign it then, and leave thine insolence.
Since thou wert king—as who is king but thou?—
The commonwealth hath daily run to wrack,
The Dauphin hath prevailed beyond the seas,   125
And all the peers and nobles of the realm
Have been as bondmen to thy sovereignty.   127
CARDINAL
The commons hast thou racked; the clergy's bags   128

Are lank and lean with thy extortions.
SOMERSET
Thy sumptuous buildings and thy wife's attire
Have cost a mass of public treasury.
BUCKINGHAM
Thy cruelty in execution
Upon offenders hath exceeded law,
And left thee to the mercy of the law.
QUEEN
Thy sale of offices and towns in France—
If they were known, as the suspect is great—   136
Would make thee quickly hop without thy head.
          Exit Humphrey. [The Queen drops her fan.]
Give me my fan. What, minion, can ye not?   138
          She gives the Duchess a box on the ear.
I cry you mercy, madam. Was it you?   139
DUCHESS
Was 't I? Yea, I it was, proud Frenchwoman.
Could I come near your beauty with my nails,
I'd set my ten commandments in your face.   142
KING
Sweet aunt, be quiet. 'Twas against her will.   143
DUCHESS
Against her will, good King? Look to 't in time.
She'll hamper thee and dandle thee like a baby.   145
Though in this place most master wear no breeches,   146
She shall not strike Dame Eleanor unrevenged.
                              Exit Eleanor.
BUCKINGHAM [*aside to the Cardinal*]
Lord Cardinal, I will follow Eleanor,
And listen after Humphrey, how he proceeds.   149
She's tickled now; her fume needs no spurs.   150
She'll gallop far enough to her destruction.
                          Exit Buckingham.

Enter Humphrey.

GLOUCESTER
Now, lords, my choler being overblown   152
With walking once about the quadrangle,
I come to talk of commonwealth affairs.
As for your spiteful false objections,
Prove them, and I lie open to the law;
But God in mercy so deal with my soul
As I in duty love my king and country!
But, to the matter that we have in hand:
I say, my sovereign, York is meetest man   160
To be your regent in the realm of France.
SUFFOLK
Before we make election, give me leave   162
To show some reason, of no little force,

---

100 s.d. sennet trumpet signal for the approach or departure of processions   **101 For my part** (The Quarto stage direction makes it clear that York and Somerset enter "on both sides of the King, whispering with him." The King is answering their requests.)   **102 Or** either   **103 have . . . himself** has conducted himself badly   **110 field** field of combat   **117 censure** opinion, judgment   **125 Dauphin** (Suffolk here uses the title of the heir apparent of France to refer to King Charles VII because Suffolk, like all Englishmen, considers Henry the rightful King of France.)   **127 bondmen** slaves   **128 racked** (Literally, tortured; here, strained beyond endurance in matters of taxation.)   **bags** money bags

136 suspect suspicion   **138 minion** hussy   **139 cry you mercy** beg your pardon. (The Queen pretends that she thought she was merely slapping one of her ladies in attendance for being slow to obey.)   **142 ten commandments** i.e., ten fingernails (like the fingernails Moses, or God, is proverbially thought to have used in inscribing the ten commandments)   **143 against her will** unintentional   **145 hamper** (1) fetter (2) cradle   **146 most master** the one most in command (i.e., the Queen)   **149 listen** inquire   **150 tickled** (1) vexed, irritated (2) like a fish about to be caught by tickling.   **fume** smoke, i.e., rage   **152 choler . . . overblown** anger being dissipated   **160 meetest** fittest   **162 election** choice

That York is most unmeet of any man.

YORK
I'll tell thee, Suffolk, why I am unmeet:
First, for I cannot flatter thee in pride;   166
Next, if I be appointed for the place,
My lord of Somerset will keep me here
Without discharge, money, or furniture   169
Till France be won into the Dauphin's hands.
Last time I danced attendance on his will   171
Till Paris was besieged, famished, and lost.

WARWICK
That can I witness, and a fouler fact   173
Did never traitor in the land commit.

SUFFOLK   Peace, headstrong Warwick!

WARWICK
Image of pride, why should I hold my peace?   176

Enter [Horner, the] Armorer, and his man [Peter, guarded].

SUFFOLK
Because here is a man accused of treason.
Pray God the Duke of York excuse himself!

YORK
Doth anyone accuse York for a traitor?   179

KING
What mean'st thou, Suffolk? Tell me, what are
these?   180

SUFFOLK
Please it Your Majesty, this is the man
That doth accuse his master of high treason.
His words were these: that Richard, Duke of York,
Was rightful heir unto the English crown,
And that Your Majesty was an usurper.

KING   Say, man, were these thy words?

HORNER   An 't shall please Your Majesty, I never said 187
nor thought any such matter. God is my witness, I am
falsely accused by the villain.

PETER   By these ten bones, my lords, he did speak them 190
to me in the garret one night as we were scouring
my lord of York's armor.

YORK
Base dunghill villain and mechanical,   193
I'll have thy head for this thy traitor's speech!
[*To the King.*] I do beseech Your Royal Majesty,
Let him have all the rigor of the law.

HORNER   Alas, my lord, hang me if ever I spake the
words. My accuser is my prentice; and when I did
correct him for his fault the other day, he did vow 199
upon his knees he would be even with me. I have
good witness of this. Therefore I beseech Your Majesty,
do not cast away an honest man for a villain's accusa- 202
tion.

KING [*to Gloucester*]
Uncle, what shall we say to this in law?

GLOUCESTER
This doom, my lord, if I may judge: 205
Let Somerset be regent o'er the French,
Because in York this breeds suspicion;   207
And let these have a day appointed them   208
For single combat in convenient place,   209
For he hath witness of his servant's malice.
This is the law, and this Duke Humphrey's doom.

KING
Then be it so. My lord of Somerset,
We make Your Grace regent over the French.

SOMERSET
I humbly thank Your Royal Majesty.

HORNER   And I accept the combat willingly.

PETER   Alas, my lord, I cannot fight; for God's sake, pity
my case. The spite of man prevaileth against me. O
Lord, have mercy upon me! I shall never be able to
fight a blow. O Lord, my heart!

GLOUCESTER
Sirrah, or you must fight or else be hanged.   220

KING   Away with them to prison; and the day of combat
shall be the last of the next month. Come, Somerset,
we'll see thee sent away.   *Flourish. Exeunt.*

❖

1.4   *Enter [Margery Jordan] the Witch, the two priests [Hume and Southwell], and Bolingbroke.*

HUME   Come, my masters. The Duchess, I tell you, ex- 1
pects performance of your promises.

BOLINGBROKE   Master Hume, we are therefore pro- 3
vided. Will her ladyship behold and hear our exor- 4
cisms?   5

HUME   Ay, what else? Fear you not her courage.   6

BOLINGBROKE   I have heard her reported to be a woman
of an invincible spirit. But it shall be convenient, Master Hume, that you be by her aloft, while we be busy
below; and so, I pray you, go in God's name and
leave us. (*Exit Hume.*) Mother Jordan, be you prostrate and grovel on the earth. John Southwell, read 12
you; and let us to our work.   13

[*Margery Jordan lies face downward.*]

Enter [Duchess] Eleanor aloft, [Hume following].

DUCHESS   Well said, my masters, and welcome all. To 14
this gear, the sooner the better.   15

BOLINGBROKE
Patience, good lady; wizards know their times.
Deep night, dark night, the silent of the night,

166 **for** because   169 **discharge** payment of what is owed.   **furniture** military equipment   171 **Last time** (See *1 Henry VI,* 4.3.)   173 **fact** crime, deed   176 **Image** i.e., symbol   179 **for** of being   180 **what** who   187 **An 't** if it   190 **bones** i.e., fingers   193 **mechanical** common workman   199 **correct** punish.   **fault** mistake   202 **for** because of

205 **doom** judgment   207 **in York . . . suspicion** i.e., this arouses suspicions about York's loyalty   208 **these** i.e., Peter and Horner   209 **single combat** combat one-on-one   220 **Sirrah** (Customary form of address to servants.)   **or you** either you
1.4. Location: Gloucester's house.
1 **my masters** sirs   3 **therefore** for that very purpose   4–5 **exorcisms** conjurations   6 **Fear** doubt   12–13 **read you** (In the stage direction at line 23, Southwell or Bolingbroke *reads* or recites a black magic spell.)   13 **s.d. aloft** (The Quarto specifies that the Duchess "goes up to the tower," i.e., some elevated place in the theater.)   14 **Well said** well done   14–15 **To this gear** get on with this business

The time of night when Troy was set on fire, 18
The time when screech owls cry and bandogs howl, 19
And spirits walk, and ghosts break up their graves—
That time best fits the work we have in hand.
Madam, sit you and fear not. Whom we raise
We will make fast within a hallowed verge. 23

*Here [they] do the ceremonies belonging, and make
the circle. Bolingbroke or Southwell reads* Conjuro
te, *etc. It thunders and lightens terribly; then the
Spirit riseth.*

SPIRIT *Adsum.* 24
MARGERY JORDAN Asnath, 25
By the eternal God, whose name and power
Thou tremblest at, answer that I shall ask, 27
For till thou speak thou shalt not pass from hence.
SPIRIT
Ask what thou wilt. That I had said and done! 29
BOLINGBROKE [*reading out of a paper*]
"First, of the King: what shall of him become?"
SPIRIT
The duke yet lives that Henry shall depose, 31
But him outlive, and die a violent death. 32
[*As the Spirit speaks, Southwell writes the answer.*]
BOLINGBROKE
"What fates await the Duke of Suffolk?"
SPIRIT
By water shall he die and take his end. 34
BOLINGBROKE
"What shall befall the Duke of Somerset?"
SPIRIT Let him shun castles; 36
Safer shall he be upon the sandy plains
Than where castles mounted stand. 38
Have done, for more I hardly can endure. 39
BOLINGBROKE
Descend to darkness and the burning lake!
False fiend, avoid! 41
*Thunder and lightning. Exit Spirit, [sinking down
again].*

*Enter the Duke of York and the Duke of
Buckingham with their guard and break in. [They
seize Jordan and her cohorts, with their papers.]*

YORK
Lay hands upon these traitors and their trash.

[*To Jordan.*] Beldam, I think we watched you at an
inch. 43
[*To the Duchess.*] What, madam, are you there? The
King and commonweal
Are deeply indebted for this piece of pains. 45
My Lord Protector will, I doubt it not,
See you well guerdoned for these good deserts. 47
DUCHESS
Not half so bad as thine to England's king,
Injurious Duke, that threatest where's no cause. 49
BUCKINGHAM
True, madam, none at all. What call you this?
[*He shows her the papers he has seized.*]
Away with them! Let them be clapped up close 51
And kept asunder. You, madam, shall with us.
Stafford, take her to thee. 53
[*Exeunt above Duchess and Hume, guarded.*]
We'll see your trinkets here all forthcoming. 54
All away!   *Exit [guard with Jordan, Southwell, and
Bolingbroke].*
YORK
Lord Buckingham, methinks you watched her well. 56
A pretty plot, well chosen to build upon! 57
Now, pray, my lord, let's see the devil's writ.
What have we here?   *Reads.*
"The duke yet lives that Henry shall depose;
But him outlive, and die a violent death."
Why, this is just "*Aio te, Aeacida,* 62
Romanos vincere posse." Well, to the rest: 63
"Tell me what fate awaits the Duke of Suffolk?"
"By water shall he die and take his end."
"What shall betide the Duke of Somerset?"
"Let him shun castles;
Safer shall he be upon the sandy plains
Than where castles mounted stand."
Come, come, my lords, these oracles
Are hardly attained and hardly understood. 71
The King is now in progress towards Saint Albans; 72
With him the husband of this lovely lady.
Thither goes these news, as fast as horse can carry
them—
A sorry breakfast for my Lord Protector.
BUCKINGHAM
Your Grace shall give me leave, my lord of York,
To be the post, in hope of his reward. 77

18 set on fire (i.e., by the Greeks concealed in the Trojan horse; described in Virgil, *Aeneid*, Book 2) **19 bandogs** leashed watchdogs **23 hallowed verge** magic circle. **s.d. the ceremonies belonging** i.e., the "hocus-pocus" necessary to conjure spirits, such as drawing a magic circle and reciting a formula. **Conjuro te** I conjure you. **riseth** (Presumably a trapdoor is used on the main stage.) **24 Adsum** I am here **25 Asnath** (An anagram for *Sathan*.) **27 that** that which **29 That** would that. (The Spirit is reluctant to answer questions.) **31–32 The duke . . . death** (The first line of the prophecy, as is characteristic of such utterances, is capable of a double construction: "whom Henry will depose" or "who will depose Henry." The second line is fulfilled in *3 Henry VI* and *Richard III*. "The duke" may refer ambiguously both to Edward IV and to his father, who preceded him as Duke of York.) **34 By water** (See 4.1.31–35 for an explanation of this riddle.) **36 Let him shun castles** (The warning is riddlingly fulfilled in 5.2.65 ff.) **38 mounted** on a mount **39 Have done** finish up **41 False** treacherous. **avoid** begone

43 Beldam witch, hag. **at an inch** i.e., closely **45 piece of pains** trouble undergone. (Said ironically.) **47 guerdoned** rewarded. **deserts** deserving acts. (Said ironically.) **49 Injurious** insulting **51 clapped up close** imprisoned securely **53 Stafford** (Presumably one of Buckingham's kinsmen, perhaps Sir Humphrey Stafford, acting as an officer of the arresting guard.) **54 trinkets** trifles, rubbish (used in performing magical acts, and now confiscated to be *forthcoming*, used as legal evidence) **56 watched** kept surveillance over **57 plot** clever plan (with pun on the sense of "plot of ground"). **build upon** erect a scheme on (continuing the architectural pun) **62 just** precisely **62–63 Aio . . . posse** I say that you, Aeacides, the Romans can conquer. (This prophecy, given by the Delphic oracle to Pyrrhus, descendant of Aeacus, is grammatically ambiguous in just the same fashion as the English oracle about Henry and the Yorkists, lines 31–32.) **71 hardly attained** with difficulty obtained, or comprehended **72 in progress** on a state journey **77 post** messenger

YORK
At your pleasure, my good lord.   [*Exit Buckingham.*]
Who's within there, ho!

       Enter a Servingman.

Invite my lords of Salisbury and Warwick
To sup with me tomorrow night. Away!   *Exeunt.*

❖

2.1   *Enter the King, Queen [with her hawk on her fist],*
Protector [Gloucester], Cardinal, and Suffolk, with
falconers halloing.

QUEEN
Believe me, lords, for flying at the brook   1
I saw not better sport these seven years' day.   2
Yet, by your leave, the wind was very high,
And ten to one old Joan had not gone out.   4
KING [*to Gloucester*]
But what a point, my lord, your falcon made,   5
And what a pitch she flew above the rest!   6
To see how God in all his creatures works!
Yea, man and birds are fain of climbing high.   8
SUFFOLK
No marvel, an it like Your Majesty,   9
My Lord Protector's hawks do tower so well;   10
They know their master loves to be aloft
And bears his thoughts above his falcon's pitch.
GLOUCESTER
My lord, 'tis but a base ignoble mind
That mounts no higher than a bird can soar.
CARDINAL
I thought as much. He would be above the clouds.
GLOUCESTER
Ay, my Lord Cardinal, how think you by that?
Were it not good Your Grace could fly to heaven?
KING
The treasury of everlasting joy.
CARDINAL [*to Gloucester*]
Thy heaven is on earth; thine eyes and thoughts
Beat on a crown, the treasure of thy heart.   20
Pernicious Protector, dangerous peer,
That smooth'st it so with King and commonweal!   22
GLOUCESTER
What, Cardinal, is your priesthood grown
   peremptory?
Tantaene animis caelestibus irae?   24

Churchmen so hot? Good uncle, hide such malice.
With such holiness, can you do it?
SUFFOLK
No malice, sir, no more than well becomes
So good a quarrel and so bad a peer.
GLOUCESTER
As who, my lord?
SUFFOLK   Why, as you, my lord,
An 't like your lordly Lord-Protectorship.
GLOUCESTER
Why, Suffolk, England knows thine insolence.
QUEEN
And thy ambition, Gloucester.
KING   I prithee, peace,
Good Queen, and whet not on these furious peers;   33
For blessèd are the peacemakers on earth.   34
CARDINAL
Let me be blessèd for the peace I make
Against this proud Protector with my sword!
GLOUCESTER [*aside to Cardinal*]
Faith, holy uncle, would 'twere come to that!
CARDINAL [*aside to Gloucester*]   Marry, when thou dar'st.
GLOUCESTER [*aside to Cardinal*]
Make up no factious numbers for the matter;   39
In thine own person answer thy abuse.   40
CARDINAL [*aside to Gloucester*]
Ay, where thou dar'st not peep. An if thou dar'st,   41
This evening, on the east side of the grove.
KING
How now, my lords?
CARDINAL [*aloud*]   Believe me, cousin Gloucester,
Had not your man put up the fowl so suddenly,   44
We had had more sport. [*Aside to Gloucester.*] Come
   with thy two-hand sword.
GLOUCESTER [*aloud*]   True, uncle.
[*Aside to Cardinal.*] Are ye advised? The east side of
   the grove.   47
CARDINAL [*aside to Gloucester*]
I am with you.
KING   Why, how now, uncle Gloucester?
GLOUCESTER
Talking of hawking; nothing else, my lord.
[*Aside to Cardinal.*] Now by God's mother, priest, I'll
   shave your crown for this,   50
Or all my fence shall fail.
CARDINAL [*aside to Gloucester*]   *Medice, teipsum*—   51
Protector, see to 't well. Protect yourself.   52
KING
The winds grow high; so do your stomachs, lords.   53
How irksome is this music to my heart!
When such strings jar, what hope of harmony?

2.1. Location: St. Albans.
1 flying . . . brook i.e., hawking for waterfowl   **2 these . . . day** in
seven years' time   **4 old . . . out** i.e., the hawk named old Joan
would not have flown in such a high wind   **5 point** advantageous position from which the hawk attacks the bird   **6 pitch** height to which
a hawk soars before descending on its prey   **8 fain** fond   **9 an it like**
if it please. (Also lines 30 and 78.)   **10 hawks** (Refers not only to the
hawks flown by Gloucester in this hunt but also to the falcon with a
maiden's head portrayed on his heraldic badge.)   **tower** rise wheeling
up to the *point* from which the hawk swoops down   **20 Beat on**
dwell on, think about constantly   **22 smooth'st it** flatters   **24 Tantaene . . . irae** can there be such resentment in heavenly minds? (Virgil, *Aeneid,* 1.11.)

33 whet not on do not encourage   **34 blessèd . . . earth** (King Henry
cites the Sermon on the Mount, Matthew 5:9.)   **39 Make . . . matter**
do not bring a party of your quarrelsome supporters into the quarrel
40 abuse offense, insult   **41 peep** i.e., show your face.   **An if** if
44 man i.e., falconer.   **put . . . fowl** startled the game into flight
47 advised agreed   **50 I'll shave your crown** (Since a priest is already tonsured, this would be to give him a close shave indeed.)
51 fence skill in fighting with a sword.   **Medice, teipsum** physician,
(heal) thyself. (Luke 4:23.)   **52 Protect** (with a pun on *Protector*)
53 stomachs tempers

I pray, my lords, let me compound this strife.   56

*Enter one [a Townsman of Saint Albans] crying
"A miracle!"*

GLOUCESTER   What means this noise?
Fellow, what miracle dost thou proclaim?
TOWNSMAN   A miracle! A miracle!
SUFFOLK
Come to the King and tell him what miracle.
TOWNSMAN
Forsooth, a blind man at Saint Albans' shrine
Within this half hour hath received his sight—
A man that ne'er saw in his life before.
KING
Now, God be praised, that to believing souls
Gives light in darkness, comfort in despair!   65

*Enter the Mayor of Saint Albans and his brethren,
bearing the man [Simpcox] between two in a chair,
[Simpcox's Wife and others following].*

CARDINAL
Here comes the townsmen on procession,   66
To present Your Highness with the man.
KING
Great is his comfort in this earthly vale,
Although by his sight his sin be multiplied.   69
GLOUCESTER
Stand by, my masters. Bring him near the King;
His Highness' pleasure is to talk with him.
KING
Good fellow, tell us here the circumstance,
That we for thee may glorify the Lord.
What, hast thou been long blind and now restored?
SIMPCOX   Born blind, an 't please Your Grace.
WIFE   Ay, indeed, was he.
SUFFOLK   What woman is this?
WIFE   His wife, an 't like your worship.
GLOUCESTER   Hadst thou been his mother, thou couldst
have better told.
KING   Where wert thou born?
SIMPCOX
At Berwick in the north, an 't like Your Grace.
KING
Poor soul, God's goodness hath been great to thee.
Let never day nor night unhallowed pass,   84
But still remember what the Lord hath done.   85
QUEEN
Tell me, good fellow, cam'st thou here by chance,
Or of devotion, to this holy shrine?
SIMPCOX
God knows, of pure devotion, being called
A hundred times and oftener in my sleep

By good Saint Alban, who said, "Simon, come,   90
Come, offer at my shrine and I will help thee."   91
WIFE
Most true, forsooth; and many time and oft
Myself have heard a voice to call him so.
CARDINAL   What, art thou lame?
SIMPCOX   Ay, God Almighty help me!
SUFFOLK   How cam'st thou so?
SIMPCOX   A fall off of a tree.
WIFE   A plum tree, master.   98
GLOUCESTER   How long hast thou been blind?
SIMPCOX   O, born so, master.
GLOUCESTER   What, and wouldst climb a tree?
SIMPCOX   But that in all my life, when I was a youth.   102
WIFE
Too true, and bought his climbing very dear.
GLOUCESTER   Mass, thou lov'dst plums well, that   104
wouldst venture so.
SIMPCOX   Alas, good master, my wife desired some
damsons and made me climb, with danger of my life.   107
GLOUCESTER
A subtle knave! But yet it shall not serve.   108
Let me see thine eyes. Wink now. Now open them.   109
In my opinion yet thou seest not well.
SIMPCOX   Yes, master, clear as day, I thank God and
Saint Alban.
GLOUCESTER
Sayst thou me so? What color is this cloak of?
SIMPCOX   Red, master, red as blood.
GLOUCESTER
Why, that's well said. What color is my gown of?
SIMPCOX   Black, forsooth, coal black as jet.
KING
Why, then, thou know'st what color jet is of?
SUFFOLK
And yet, I think, jet did he never see.
GLOUCESTER
But cloaks and gowns, before this day, a many.   119
WIFE
Never, before this day, in all his life.
GLOUCESTER   Tell me, sirrah, what's my name?
SIMPCOX   Alas, master, I know not.
GLOUCESTER [*pointing*]   What's his name?
SIMPCOX   I know not.
GLOUCESTER [*pointing to another*]   Nor his?
SIMPCOX   No, indeed, master.
GLOUCESTER   What's thine own name?
SIMPCOX   Sander Simpcox, an if it please you, master.
GLOUCESTER   Then, Sander, sit there, the lying'st   129
knave in Christendom. If thou hadst been born
blind, thou mightst as well have known all our names
as thus to name the several colors we do wear. Sight

---

56 **compound** settle.   **s.d. Saint Albans** a shrine and a town named for Saint Alban, supposedly the first Christian martyr in Britain, executed under the edicts of Diocletian in A.D. 304 for sheltering a Christian priest   65 **s.d. brethren** aldermen, fellow members of the corporation or guild   66 **on** in   69 **by his sight . . . multiplied** i.e., he may now be subject to more temptations, being able to see   84 **unhallowed** unblessed by your prayers   85 **still** continually

90 **Simon** (His proper name; *Simpcox* is a variant.)   91 **offer** make an offering   98 **plum tree** (A slang phrase for the female pudenda that sets up an elaborate ribald joke here about a husband risking his life to try to satisfy his wife's craving.)   102 **But that** only that once   104 **Mass** by the Mass. (An oath.)   107 **damsons** a variety of plum (commonly used as a slang phrase for testicles)   108 **shall not serve** won't serve to fool me   109 **Wink** close your eyes   119 **many** multitude   129 **sit there** there you sit

may distinguish of colors, but suddenly to nominate 133
them all, it is impossible.—My lords, Saint Alban here
hath done a miracle; and would ye not think his
cunning to be great that could restore this cripple to
his legs again?

SIMPCOX   O master, that you could!

GLOUCESTER   My masters of Saint Albans, have you not
beadles in your town, and things called whips?   140

MAYOR   Yes, my lord, if it please Your Grace.

GLOUCESTER   Then send for one presently.   142

MAYOR   Sirrah, go fetch the beadle hither straight.   143
Exit [an Attendant].

GLOUCESTER   Now fetch me a stool hither by and by. [*A* 144
stool is brought.] Now, sirrah, if you mean to save
yourself from whipping, leap me over this stool and 146
run away.

SIMPCOX   Alas, master, I am not able to stand alone. You
go about to torture me in vain.

Enter a Beadle with whips.

GLOUCESTER   Well, sir, we must have you find your legs.
Sirrah beadle, whip him till he leap over that same
stool.

BEADLE   I will, my lord.—Come on, sirrah, off with
your doublet quickly.   154

SIMPCOX   Alas, master, what shall I do? I am not able to
stand.

*After the Beadle hath hit him once, he leaps over
the stool and runs away; and they follow and cry,
"A miracle!"*

KING
O God, seest Thou this, and bearest so long?   157

QUEEN
It made me laugh to see the villain run.

GLOUCESTER [*to the Beadle*]
Follow the knave, and take this drab away.   159

WIFE   Alas, sir, we did it for pure need.

GLOUCESTER   Let them be whipped through every market town till they come to Berwick, from whence they
came.   *Exit [Wife, with Beadle, Mayor, etc.].*

CARDINAL
Duke Humphrey has done a miracle today.

SUFFOLK
True; made the lame to leap and fly away.

GLOUCESTER
But you have done more miracles than I;
You made in a day, my lord, whole towns to fly.   167

Enter Buckingham.

KING
What tidings with our cousin Buckingham?

BUCKINGHAM
Such as my heart doth tremble to unfold:

A sort of naughty persons, lewdly bent,   170
Under the countenance and confederacy   171
Of Lady Eleanor, the Protector's wife,
The ringleader and head of all this rout,   173
Have practiced dangerously against your state,   174
Dealing with witches and with conjurers,
Whom we have apprehended in the fact,   176
Raising up wicked spirits from under ground,
Demanding of King Henry's life and death   178
And other of Your Highness' Privy Council,
As more at large Your Grace shall understand.   180

CARDINAL
And so, my Lord Protector, by this means
Your lady is forthcoming yet at London.   182
[*Aside to Gloucester*] This news, I think, hath turned
your weapon's edge;
'Tis like, my lord, you will not keep your hour.   184

GLOUCESTER
Ambitious churchman, leave to afflict my heart.   185
Sorrow and grief have vanquished all my powers;
And, vanquished as I am, I yield to thee
Or to the meanest groom.   188

KING
O God, what mischiefs work the wicked ones,
Heaping confusion on their own heads thereby!   190

QUEEN
Gloucester, see here the tainture of thy nest,   191
And look thyself be faultless, thou wert best.   192

GLOUCESTER
Madam, for myself, to heaven I do appeal   193
How I have loved my king and commonweal;
And, for my wife, I know not how it stands.   195
Sorry I am to hear what I have heard.
Noble she is; but if she have forgot
Honor and virtue, and conversed with such   198
As, like to pitch, defile nobility,
I banish her my bed and company
And give her as a prey to law and shame
That hath dishonored Gloucester's honest name.

KING
Well, for this night we will repose us here;
Tomorrow toward London back again,
To look into this business thoroughly,
And call these foul offenders to their answers,
And poise the cause in Justice' equal scales,   207
Whose beam stands sure, whose rightful cause
prevails.   *Flourish. Exeunt.* 208

❧

133 **nominate** call by name   140 **beadles** minor parish officers who
might punish petty offenses   142 **presently** immediately   143 **straight**
immediately   144 **by and by** at once   146 **me** for me   154 **doublet**
close-fitting jacket   157 **bearest** do you endure (such sinfulness)
159 **drab** slut   167 **You . . . fly** i.e., you gave away French towns in
a day, as part of Queen Margaret's dowry

170 **sort** lot, gang.   **naughty** wicked.   **lewdly** evilly   171 **Under . . .**
confederacy with the authorization and even complicity   173 **rout**
crew   174 **practiced** conspired   176 **fact** crime, deed   178 **De-**
manding of inquiring about   180 **at large** in detail   182 **forthcoming**
ready to appear (in court)   184 **like** likely.   **hour** appointment (for
the duel between Gloucester and the Cardinal)   185 **leave to afflict**
cease afflicting   188 **meanest** of lowest degree   190 **confusion** destruction   191 **tainture** defilement   192 **look** take care, see to it.
thou wert best you'd be well advised   193, 195 **for** as for   198 **con-**
versed had to do with   207 **poise** weigh   208 **beam stands sure**
cross-bar is perfectly level

2.2   *Enter York, Salisbury, and Warwick.*

YORK
Now, my good lords of Salisbury and Warwick,
Our simple supper ended, give me leave,
In this close walk, to satisfy myself   3
In craving your opinion of my title,
Which is infallible, to England's crown.

SALISBURY
My lord, I long to hear it at full.

WARWICK
Sweet York, begin; and if thy claim be good,
The Nevilles are thy subjects to command.

YORK   Then thus:
Edward the Third, my lords, had seven sons:
The first, Edward the Black Prince, Prince of Wales;
The second, William of Hatfield, and the third,
Lionel, Duke of Clarence; next to whom
Was John of Gaunt, the Duke of Lancaster;
The fifth was Edmund Langley, Duke of York;
The sixth was Thomas of Woodstock, Duke of
    Gloucester;
William of Windsor was the seventh and last.
Edward the Black Prince died before his father
And left behind him Richard, his only son,   19
Who after Edward the Third's death reigned as king
Till Henry Bolingbroke, Duke of Lancaster,
The eldest son and heir of John of Gaunt,
Crowned by the name of Henry the Fourth,
Seized on the realm, deposed the rightful king,
Sent his poor queen to France, from whence she
    came,
And him to Pomfret; where, as all you know,
Harmless Richard was murdered traitorously.

WARWICK
Father, the Duke hath told the truth.
Thus got the house of Lancaster the crown.

YORK
Which now they hold by force and not by right;
For Richard, the first son's heir, being dead,
The issue of the next son should have reigned.   32

SALISBURY
But William of Hatfield died without an heir.

YORK
The third son, Duke of Clarence, from whose line
I claim the crown, had issue, Philippe, a daughter,
Who married Edmund Mortimer, Earl of March.
Edmund had issue, Roger Earl of March;
Roger had issue, Edmund, Anne, and Eleanor.

SALISBURY
This Edmund, in the reign of Bolingbroke,   39
As I have read, laid claim unto the crown,

And, but for Owen Glendower, had been king,
Who kept him in captivity till he died.   42
But to the rest.

YORK   His eldest sister, Anne,
My mother, being heir unto the crown,
Married Richard, Earl of Cambridge, who was son
To Edmund Langley, Edward the Third's fifth son.
By her I claim the kingdom. She was heir
To Roger, Earl of March, who was the son
Of Edmund Mortimer, who married Philippe,
Sole daughter unto Lionel, Duke of Clarence.
So, if the issue of the elder son
Succeed before the younger, I am king.

WARWICK
What plain proceeding is more plain than this?
Henry doth claim the crown from John of Gaunt,
The fourth son; York claims it from the third.
Till Lionel's issue fails, his should not reign.   56
It fails not yet, but flourishes in thee   57
And in thy sons, fair slips of such a stock.   58
Then, father Salisbury, kneel we together,
And in this private plot be we the first   60
That shall salute our rightful sovereign
With honor of his birthright to the crown.

BOTH [*kneeling*]
Long live our sovereign Richard, England's king!

YORK
We thank you, lords. [*They rise.*] But I am not your
    king   64
Till I be crowned, and that my sword be stained   65
With heart-blood of the house of Lancaster;
And that's not suddenly to be performed,
But with advice and silent secrecy.   68
Do you as I do in these dangerous days:
Wink at the Duke of Suffolk's insolence,   70
At Beaufort's pride, at Somerset's ambition,
At Buckingham, and all the crew of them,
Till they have snared the shepherd of the flock,
That virtuous prince, the good Duke Humphrey.
'Tis that they seek, and they in seeking that
Shall find their deaths, if York can prophesy.

SALISBURY
My lord, break we off. We know your mind at full.

WARWICK
My heart assures me that the Earl of Warwick
Shall one day make the Duke of York a king.

YORK
And, Neville, this I do assure myself: 80
Richard shall live to make the Earl of Warwick
The greatest man in England but the King.   *Exeunt.*

❖

2.2. Location: London. The Duke of York's garden.
3 close private   19 Richard i.e., Richard II   32 issue offspring
39 This Edmund (A historical error, found also in the chronicles, of confusing Edmund Mortimer, fifth Earl of March, who was named heir to the throne by Richard II, with his uncle Edmund, brother of Roger, who married Glendower's daughter. See *1 Henry VI*, 2.5, and *1 Henry IV*, 1.3.)

42 Who i.e., Glendower   56 his i.e., John of Gaunt's   57 It fails not i.e., Lionel's line of descent has not died out   58 slips cuttings   60 plot plot of ground   64 We (The royal "we"!)   65 and that and until the time that   68 advice careful reflection   70 Wink at shut your eyes to   80 Neville (York addresses Warwick by his family name.)

2.3   *Sound trumpets. Enter the King and state, [the*
Queen, Gloucester, York, Suffolk, Salisbury, and
others,] with guard, to banish the Duchess [of
Gloucester, who is brought on under guard with
Margery Jordan, Southwell, Hume, and
Bolingbroke].

KING
　Stand forth, Dame Eleanor Cobham, Gloucester's
　　wife.
　In sight of God and us, your guilt is great.
　Receive the sentence of the law for sins
　Such as by God's book are adjudged to death.   4
　[*To Margery and the others.*] You four, from hence to
　　prison back again;
　From thence unto the place of execution.
　The witch in Smithfield shall be burnt to ashes,
　And you three shall be strangled on the gallows.
　[*To the Duchess.*] You, madam, for you are more
　　nobly born,   9
　Despoilèd of your honor in your life,   10
　Shall, after three days' open penance done,
　Live in your country here in banishment
　With Sir John Stanley in the Isle of Man.   13
DUCHESS
　Welcome is banishment. Welcome were my death.   14
GLOUCESTER
　Eleanor, the law, thou seest, hath judged thee.
　I cannot justify whom the law condemns.
　　　　　[*Exeunt Duchess and other prisoners, guarded.*]
　Mine eyes are full of tears, my heart of grief.
　Ah, Humphrey, this dishonor in thine age
　Will bring thy head with sorrow to the grave!
　I beseech Your Majesty, give me leave to go;
　Sorrow would solace, and mine age would ease.   21
KING
　Stay, Humphrey, Duke of Gloucester. Ere thou go,
　Give up thy staff. Henry will to himself   23
　Protector be; and God shall be my hope,
　My stay, my guide, and lantern to my feet.
　And go in peace, Humphrey, no less beloved
　Than when thou wert Protector to thy king.
QUEEN
　I see no reason why a king of years   28
　Should be to be protected like a child.   29
　God and King Henry govern England's realm!
　Give up your staff, sir, and the King his realm. 31
GLOUCESTER
　My staff? Here, noble Henry, is my staff.
　　　　　　　　　　　　[*He lays down his staff.*]

As willingly do I the same resign
As ere thy father Henry made it mine;
And even as willingly at thy feet I leave it   34
As others would ambitiously receive it.
Farewell, good King. When I am dead and gone,
May honorable peace attend thy throne!
　　　　　　　　　　　　　　　Exit Gloucester.
QUEEN
　Why, now is Henry king and Margaret queen,
　And Humphrey, Duke of Gloucester scarce himself,
　That bears so shrewd a maim. Two pulls at once: 41
　His lady banished, and a limb lopped off.   42
　This staff of honor raught, there let it stand   43
　Where it best fits to be, in Henry's hand.
SUFFOLK
　Thus droops this lofty pine and hangs his sprays; 45
　Thus Eleanor's pride dies in her youngest days.   46
YORK
　Lords, let him go. Please it Your Majesty,
　This is the day appointed for the combat,
　And ready are the appellant and defendant—   49
　The armorer and his man—to enter the lists,
　So please Your Highness to behold the fight.
QUEEN
　Ay, good my lord, for purposely therefor
　Left I the court, to see this quarrel tried.
KING
　I' God's name, see the lists and all things fit.
　Here let them end it, and God defend the right!
YORK
　I never saw a fellow worse bestead,   56
　Or more afraid to fight, than is the appellant,
　The servant of this armorer, my lords.   58

　　Enter at one door, the Armorer [Horner] and his
　　Neighbors, drinking to him so much that he is
　　drunk; and he enters with a drum before him and
　　his staff with a sandbag fastened to it; and at the
　　other door his man [Peter], with a drum and
　　sandbag, and Prentices drinking to him.

FIRST NEIGHBOR   Here, neighbor Horner, I drink to
　you in a cup of sack; and fear not, neighbor, you shall 60
　do well enough.
SECOND NEIGHBOR   And here, neighbor, here's a cup
　of charneco.   63
THIRD NEIGHBOR   And here's a pot of good double   64
　beer, neighbor. Drink, and fear not your man.
HORNER   Let it come, i' faith, and I'll pledge you all; and 66
　a fig for Peter!   67

2.3. Location: London. A place of justice.
s.d. and others (In the Quarto, the Cardinal, Buckingham, and Warwick are also named. Warwick, York, and Salisbury enter ''to them,''
i.e., meeting the royal party.)   **4 by God's book** i.e., according to the
commandments in the Bible against witches, Exodus 22:18, and en-
chantments, Leviticus 19:26, among other passages   **9 for** because
10 Despoiled deprived.   **in your life** during the remainder of your
life   **13 With . . . Stanley** (An error for Sir Thomas Stanley, the
Duchess's custodian and the Lord Stanley of *Richard III*.)   **With** in the
custody of   **14 were** would be   **21 would** wishes to have   **23 staff**
staff of office   **28 of years** who is of age   **29 be to be** need to be
31 King his King's

34 ere at an earlier time. (The Quarto reading, ''erst,'' conveys the
same meaning.)   **41 bears . . . maim** endures so grievous a mutilation.   **pulls** pluckings   **42 a limb lopped off** i.e., his staff of office
taken away, so much a part of him that the severing was like an am-
putation   **43 raught** attained, seized   **45 lofty pine** (An emblem
adopted by Henry IV, Gloucester's father.)   **sprays** branches   **46 in
her youngest days** i.e., when her ambition and pride were at their
height   **49 appellant** challenger   **56 bestead** prepared   **58 s.d. drinking to him** offering toasts to him (to which he is obliged to drink in return, drink for drink).   **drum** drummer   **60 sack** a dry Spanish or Canary wine   **63 charneco** a sweet Portuguese wine   **64 double** strong
66 Let it come i.e., let the drink be passed around.   **pledge you** drink
your health   **67 a fig** (An obscene insult, accompanied by the gesture
of putting the thumb between the first and second fingers.)

FIRST PRENTICE　　Here, Peter, I drink to thee, and be not afraid.

SECOND PRENTICE　　Be merry, Peter, and fear not thy master. Fight for credit of the prentices.　71

PETER　　I thank you all. Drink, and pray for me, I pray you, for I think I have taken my last draft in this world. Here, Robin, an if I die, I give thee my apron; and Will, thou shalt have my hammer; and here, Tom, take all the money that I have. [*He gives away his things.*] O Lord bless me, I pray God, for I am never able to deal with my master, he hath learned so much fence 78 already.

SALISBURY　　Come, leave your drinking and fall to blows. Sirrah, what's thy name?

PETER　　Peter, forsooth.

SALISBURY　　Peter? What more?

PETER　　Thump.

SALISBURY　　Thump! Then see thou thump thy master well.

HORNER　　Masters, I am come hither, as it were, upon my man's instigation, to prove him a knave and myself an honest man; and touching the Duke of York, I will take my death, I never meant him any ill, 90 nor the King, nor the Queen. And therefore, Peter, have at thee with a downright blow!　92

YORK
Dispatch. This knave's tongue begins to double.　93
Sound, trumpets, alarum to the combatants!　94
　　　　[*Alarum.*] *They fight, and Peter strikes him down.*

HORNER　　Hold, Peter, hold! I confess, I confess treason.
　　　　　　　　　　　　　　　　　　　　　[*He dies.*]

YORK　　Take away his weapon. Fellow, thank God and the good wine in thy master's way.　97

PETER　　O God, have I overcome mine enemies in this presence? O Peter, thou hast prevailed in right!

KING
Go, take hence that traitor from our sight;　100
For by his death we do perceive his guilt,
And God in justice hath revealed to us
The truth and innocence of this poor fellow,
Which he had thought to have murdered wrongfully. 104
[*To Peter.*] Come, fellow, follow us for thy reward.
　　　　　Sound a flourish. Exeunt [*with Horner's body*].

❧

2.4　*Enter Duke Humphrey* [*of Gloucester*] *and his Men in mourning cloaks.*

GLOUCESTER
Thus sometimes hath the brightest day a cloud,
And after summer evermore succeeds
Barren winter, with his wrathful nipping cold;

So cares and joys abound, as seasons fleet.　4
Sirs, what's o'clock?

SERVANT　　Ten, my lord.

GLOUCESTER
Ten is the hour that was appointed me
To watch the coming of my punished duchess.
Uneath may she endure the flinty streets,　9
To tread them with her tender-feeling feet.
Sweet Nell, ill can thy noble mind abrook　11
The abject people gazing on thy face,　12
With envious looks laughing at thy shame,　13
That erst did follow thy proud chariot wheels　14
When thou didst ride in triumph through the streets.
But, soft! I think she comes, and I'll prepare　16
My tearstained eyes to see her miseries.　17

　　　Enter the Duchess [*of Gloucester, barefoot*], *in a white sheet,* [*with verses pinned upon her back,*] *and a taper burning in her hand; with* [*Sir John Stanley,*] *the Sheriff, and officers* [*with bills and halberds*].

SERVANT
So please Your Grace, we'll take her from the sheriff. 18

GLOUCESTER
No, stir not for your lives. Let her pass by.

DUCHESS
Come you, my lord, to see my open shame?
Now thou dost penance too. Look how they gaze!　21
See how the giddy multitude do point
And nod their heads and throw their eyes on thee!
Ah, Gloucester, hide thee from their hateful looks,　24
And, in thy closet pent up, rue my shame,　25
And ban thine enemies, both mine and thine!　26

GLOUCESTER
Be patient, gentle Nell. Forget this grief.

DUCHESS
Ah, Gloucester, teach me to forget myself!
For whilst I think I am thy married wife
And thou a prince, Protector of this land,
Methinks I should not thus be led along,
Mailed up in shame, with papers on my back,　32
And followed with a rabble that rejoice　33
To see my tears and hear my deep-fet groans.　34
The ruthless flint doth cut my tender feet,
And when I start, the envious people laugh　36
And bid me be advisèd how I tread.　37
Ah, Humphrey, can I bear this shameful yoke?
Trowest thou that e'er I'll look upon the world,　39

71 **credit** reputation, good name　78 **fence** skill in fencing　90 **take my death** i.e., take an oath on pain of death　92 **have at thee** here I come at you　93 **double** thicken and slur (with intoxication)　94 **alarum** call to arms　97 **in thy master's way** i.e., that marred your master's fighting ability　100 **that traitor** i.e., Horner　104 **Which he** i.e., whom Horner
2.4. Location: London. A street.

4 **fleet** flow by　9 **Uneath** with difficulty, scarcely　11 **abrook** endure
12 **abject** lowly born　13 **envious** full of malice　14 **erst** formerly
16 **soft** wait a minute　17 **s.d. with bills and halberds** with long-handled axlike weapons. (The bracketed stage directions are derived from the Quarto.)　18 **take her** rescue her by force　21 **Look how they gaze** (The crowd of commoners may be represented onstage, or the Duchess may gesture offstage.)　24 **hateful** full of hate　25 **closet** private room　26 **ban** curse　32 **Mailed up** enveloped. (Used in hawking to prevent the hawk from struggling, just as Eleanor is wrapped in a white sheet.)　**papers on my back** (The verses pinned upon her back describe the sin for which she is doing penance.)
33 **with** by　34 **deep-fet** fetched from the depths　36 **start** flinch, wince. **envious** malicious　37 **advisèd** careful　39 **Trowest thou** do you believe

Or count them happy that enjoys the sun?
No, dark shall be my light and night my day;
To think upon my pomp shall be my hell.
Sometimes I'll say I am Duke Humphrey's wife,
And he a prince and ruler of the land;
Yet so he ruled, and such a prince he was,
As he stood by whilst I, his forlorn duchess,   46
Was made a wonder and a pointing-stock   47
To every idle rascal follower.
But be thou mild and blush not at my shame,
Nor stir at nothing till the ax of death
Hang over thee, as, sure, it shortly will.
For Suffolk, he that can do all in all
With her that hateth thee and hates us all,   53
And York and impious Beaufort, that false priest,
Have all limed bushes to betray thy wings,   55
And fly thou how thou canst, they'll tangle thee.   56
But fear not thou until thy foot be snared,   57
Nor never seek prevention of thy foes.   58

GLOUCESTER
Ah, Nell, forbear! Thou aimest all awry.
I must offend before I be attainted;   60
And had I twenty times so many foes,
And each of them had twenty times their power,
All these could not procure me any scathe   63
So long as I am loyal, true, and crimeless.
Wouldst have me rescue thee from this reproach?
Why, yet thy scandal were not wiped away,   66
But I in danger for the breach of law.
Thy greatest help is quiet, gentle Nell.   68
I pray thee, sort thy heart to patience;   69
These few days' wonder will be quickly worn.   70

        Enter a Herald.

HERALD
I summon Your Grace to His Majesty's Parliament,
Holden at Bury the first of this next month.   72

GLOUCESTER
And my consent ne'er asked herein before?
This is close dealing. Well, I will be there.   74
                               [Exit Herald.]
My Nell, I take my leave. And, Master Sheriff,
Let not her penance exceed the King's commission.

SHERIFF
An 't please Your Grace, here my commission stays,   77
And Sir John Stanley is appointed now
To take her with him to the Isle of Man.

GLOUCESTER
Must you, Sir John, protect my lady here?

STANLEY
So am I given in charge, may 't please Your Grace.   81

GLOUCESTER
Entreat her not the worse in that I pray   82
You use her well. The world may laugh again,   83
And I may live to do you kindness if
You do it her. And so, Sir John, farewell.
                          [He starts to leave.]

DUCHESS
What, gone, my lord, and bid me not farewell?

GLOUCESTER
Witness my tears, I cannot stay to speak.
                    Exit Gloucester [with his men].

DUCHESS
Art thou gone too? All comfort go with thee!
For none abides with me. My joy is death—
Death, at whose name I oft have been afeard,
Because I wished this world's eternity.   91
Stanley, I prithee, go, and take me hence.
I care not whither, for I beg no favor;
Only convey me where thou art commanded.

STANLEY
Why, madam, that is to the Isle of Man,
There to be used according to your state.   96

DUCHESS
That's bad enough, for I am but reproach;   97
And shall I then be used reproachfully?

STANLEY
Like to a duchess and Duke Humphrey's lady,
According to that state you shall be used.

DUCHESS
Sheriff, farewell, and better than I fare,   101
Although thou hast been conduct of my shame.   102

SHERIFF
It is my office; and, madam, pardon me.

DUCHESS
Ay, ay, farewell. Thy office is discharged.
                        [Exit Sheriff and his men.]
Come, Stanley, shall we go?

STANLEY
Madam, your penance done, throw off this sheet,
And go we to attire you for our journey.

DUCHESS
My shame will not be shifted with my sheet.   108
No, it will hang upon my richest robes
And show itself, attire me how I can.
Go, lead the way. I long to see my prison.   Exeunt.

❧

46 As that   47 pointing-stock one pointed at in scorn   53 her i.e.,
Queen Margaret   55 limed put out sticky birdlime as a trap on
56 fly . . . thee no matter how you try to fly away, they will ensnare
you   57 fear not thou i.e., you are not properly wary. (Or the Duchess may be ironically urging him to wait until it is too late.)   58 prevention forestalling   60 attainted condemned for treason or other serious wrongdoing   63 scathe injury   66 were not would not be
68 quiet i.e., patient endurance   69 sort adapt   70 These . . . wonder i.e., this passing notoriety (as in the phrase "a nine-days' wonder").   worn worn out, i.e., forgotten   72 Holden at Bury to be held
at Bury St. Edmunds (in Suffolk)   74 close secret, underhand
77 stays stops, ends

81 given in charge commanded   82 Entreat treat.   in that merely
because   83 The world . . . again i.e., we may see happier times.
(Proverbial.)   91 this world's eternity endless worldly success
96 state noble rank. (But Eleanor plays on state in the sense of "condition.")   97 I . . . reproach I am the embodiment of reproach or
disgrace, deserve only my shame   101 better . . . fare may you fare
better than I   102 conduct conductor   108 shifted changed (with a
pun on shift, "a chemise")

3.1 *Sound a sennet. Enter King, Queen, Cardinal [Beaufort], Suffolk, York, Buckingham, Salisbury, and Warwick to the Parliament.*

KING
I muse my lord of Gloucester is not come.   1
'Tis not his wont to be the hindmost man,   2
Whate'er occasion keeps him from us now.

QUEEN
Can you not see, or will ye not observe,
The strangeness of his altered countenance?   5
With what a majesty he bears himself?
How insolent of late he is become?
How proud, how peremptory, and unlike himself?
We know the time since he was mild and affable,   9
And if we did but glance a far-off look,
Immediately he was upon his knee,
That all the court admired him for submission;   12
But meet him now, and, be it in the morn,
When everyone will give the time of day,   14
He knits his brow and shows an angry eye
And passeth by with stiff unbowèd knee,
Disdaining duty that to us belongs.   17
Small curs are not regarded when they grin,   18
But great men tremble when the lion roars—
And Humphrey is no little man in England.
First note that he is near you in descent,
And should you fall, he is the next will mount.   22
Me seemeth then it is no policy,   23
Respecting what a rancorous mind he bears   24
And his advantage following your decease,
That he should come about your royal person
Or be admitted to Your Highness' Council.
By flattery hath he won the commons' hearts;
And when he please to make commotion,   29
'Tis to be feared they all will follow him.
Now 'tis the spring, and weeds are shallow-rooted;
Suffer them now, and they'll o'ergrow the garden
And choke the herbs for want of husbandry.   33
The reverent care I bear unto my lord
Made me collect these dangers in the Duke.   35
If it be fond, call it a woman's fear—   36
Which fear, if better reasons can supplant,   37
I will subscribe and say I wronged the Duke.   38
My lord of Suffolk, Buckingham, and York,
Reprove my allegation if you can,   40
Or else conclude my words effectual.   41

SUFFOLK
Well hath Your Highness seen into this duke,
And, had I first been put to speak my mind,
I think I should have told Your Grace's tale.
The Duchess by his subornation,   45
Upon my life, began her devilish practices;   46
Or if he were not privy to those faults,   47
Yet, by reputing of his high descent—   48
As next the King he was successive heir,
And such high vaunts of his nobility—   50
Did instigate the bedlam brainsick Duchess   51
By wicked means to frame our sovereign's fall.   52
Smooth runs the water where the brook is deep,
And in his simple show he harbors treason.   54
The fox barks not when he would steal the lamb.
No, no, my sovereign, Gloucester is a man
Unsounded yet and full of deep deceit.   57

CARDINAL
Did he not, contrary to form of law,
Devise strange deaths for small offenses done?

YORK
And did he not, in his protectorship,
Levy great sums of money through the realm
For soldiers' pay in France, and never sent it,
By means whereof the towns each day revolted?   63

BUCKINGHAM
Tut, these are petty faults to faults unknown,   64
Which time will bring to light in smooth Duke
   Humphrey.

KING
My lords, at once: the care you have of us   66
To mow down thorns that would annoy our foot   67
Is worthy praise; but, shall I speak my conscience,   68
Our kinsman Gloucester is as innocent
From meaning treason to our royal person
As is the sucking lamb or harmless dove.
The Duke is virtuous, mild, and too well given   72
To dream on evil or to work my downfall.

QUEEN
Ah, what's more dangerous than this fond affiance?   74
Seems he a dove? His feathers are but borrowed,
For he's disposèd as the hateful raven.   76
Is he a lamb? His skin is surely lent him,
For he's inclined as is the ravenous wolves.
Who cannot steal a shape that means deceit?   79
Take heed, my lord. The welfare of us all
Hangs on the cutting short that fraudful man.   81

Enter Somerset.

3.1. Location: A hall for a session of Parliament at Bury St. Edmunds (historically, the Abbey).
s.d. Sound a sennet (The Quarto stage direction specifies that two heralds enter first, leading a formal procession.) **1 muse** wonder why **2 wont** custom **5 strangeness** aloofness **9 know** remember. **since when 12 admired** wondered at **14 give . . . day** say good morning **17 Disdaining . . . belongs** disdaining to show the ceremonial respect that is our (or my) due **18 grin** bare their teeth **22 will mount** who will mount the throne **23 Me seemeth** it seems to me. **policy** prudent course **24 Respecting** considering **29 make commotion** foment unrest **33 husbandry** proper cultivation **35 collect** gather, infer **36 fond** foolish **37 Which . . . supplant** if better reasons can supplant which fear **38 subscribe** agree. (Literally, "undersign.") **40 Reprove** disprove **41 effectual** decisive

45 subornation instigation **46 Upon my life** i.e., I swear this on pain of death. **practices** intrigues **47 privy to those faults** informed as to those crimes **48 reputing** boasting, overvaluing **50 vaunts** boasts **51 bedlam** crazy **52 frame** devise **54 simple show** innocent outward appearance **57 Unsounded** with depths still undiscovered **63 By means whereof** on which account **64 to** compared with **66 at once** answering all of you; or, without more ado; or, once and for all **67 annoy** injure **68 shall I speak** if I may speak in accordance with **72 well given** kindly disposed **74 fond affiance** foolish confidence **76 he's disposèd as** he has the disposition of **79 Who . . . deceit** who is there, intending to deceive, that cannot assume an appropriate disguise? **81 cutting short** (with a grisly suggestion of beheading)

SOMERSET
  All health unto my gracious sovereign!
KING
  Welcome, Lord Somerset. What news from France?
SOMERSET
  That all your interest in those territories
  Is utterly bereft you. All is lost.
KING
  Cold news, Lord Somerset; but God's will be done!
YORK [*aside*]
  Cold news for me, for I had hope of France
  As firmly as I hope for fertile England.
  Thus are my blossoms blasted in the bud,
  And caterpillars eat my leaves away;
  But I will remedy this gear ere long,   91
  Or sell my title for a glorious grave.

          Enter Gloucester.

GLOUCESTER
  All happiness unto my lord the King!
  Pardon, my liege, that I have stayed so long.   94
SUFFOLK
  Nay, Gloucester, know that thou art come too soon,
  Unless thou wert more loyal than thou art.
  I do arrest thee of high treason here.
GLOUCESTER
  Well, Suffolk, thou shalt not see me blush
  Nor change my countenance for this arrest.
  A heart unspotted is not easily daunted.
  The purest spring is not so free from mud
  As I am clear from treason to my sovereign.
  Who can accuse me? Wherein am I guilty?
YORK
  'Tis thought, my lord, that you took bribes of France
  And, being Protector, stayed the soldiers' pay,   105
  By means whereof His Highness hath lost France.
GLOUCESTER
  Is it but thought so? What are they that think it?   107
  I never robbed the soldiers of their pay,
  Nor ever had one penny bribe from France.
  So help me God as I have watched the night,   110
  Ay, night by night, in studying good for England!
  That doit that e'er I wrested from the King,   112
  Or any groat I hoarded to my use,   113
  Be brought against me at my trial day!   114
  No, many a pound of mine own proper store,   115
  Because I would not tax the needy commons,
  Have I dispursèd to the garrisons   117
  And never asked for restitution.
CARDINAL
  It serves you well, my lord, to say so much.
GLOUCESTER
  I say no more than truth, so help me God!
YORK
  In your protectorship you did devise

Strange tortures for offenders, never heard of,
That England was defamed by tyranny.   123
GLOUCESTER
  Why, 'tis well known that, whiles I was Protector,
  Pity was all the fault that was in me;
  For I should melt at an offender's tears,   126
  And lowly words were ransom for their fault.   127
  Unless it were a bloody murderer,
  Or foul felonious thief that fleeced poor passengers,   129
  I never gave them condign punishment.   130
  Murder indeed, that bloody sin, I tortured
  Above the felon or what trespass else.   132
SUFFOLK
  My lord, these faults are easy, quickly answered;   133
  But mightier crimes are laid unto your charge
  Whereof you cannot easily purge yourself.
  I do arrest you in His Highness' name,
  And here commit you to my Lord Cardinal
  To keep until your further time of trial.   138
KING
  My lord of Gloucester, 'tis my special hope
  That you will clear yourself from all suspense.   140
  My conscience tells me you are innocent.
GLOUCESTER
  Ah, gracious lord, these days are dangerous!
  Virtue is choked with foul ambition,
  And charity chased hence by rancor's hand;
  Foul subornation is predominant,   145
  And equity exiled Your Highness' land.   146
  I know their complot is to have my life,   147
  And if my death might make this island happy
  And prove the period of their tyranny,   149
  I would expend it with all willingness.
  But mine is made the prologue to their play;   151
  For thousands more, that yet suspect no peril,
  Will not conclude their plotted tragedy.   153
  Beaufort's red sparkling eyes blab his heart's malice,
  And Suffolk's cloudy brow his stormy hate;   155
  Sharp Buckingham unburdens with his tongue
  The envious load that lies upon his heart;
  And dogged York, that reaches at the moon,   158
  Whose overweening arm I have plucked back,
  By false accuse doth level at my life.   160
  [*To the Queen.*] And you, my sovereign lady, with
      the rest,
  Causeless have laid disgraces on my head,
  And with your best endeavor have stirred up
  My liefest liege to be mine enemy.   164

91 **gear** business   94 **stayed** delayed   105 **stayed** held back
107 **What** who   110 **watched the night** remained awake all night
112, 113 **doit, groat** coins of small value   114 **Be** may it be.   **trial day** i.e., Day of Judgment before God   115 **proper** personal
117 **dispursèd** disbursed

123 **That** so that.   **was defamed by** became notorious for
126 **should** would   127 **lowly** humble.   **their fault** the offenders' crimes   129 **fleeced poor passengers** robbed unfortunate travelers
130 **condign** worthily deserved   132 **Above . . . else** beyond any other kind of felony or misdemeanor   133 **easy** slight   138 **further** future   140 **suspense** i.e., doubt as to your innocence   145 **subornation** instigating others to commit crimes, including perjury   146 **exiled** exiled from   147 **complot** plot, conspiracy   149 **prove the period** turn out to be the end   151 **mine** i.e., my death   153 **Will . . . tragedy** will not suffice to bring to an end this tragedy they have devised. (With a suggestion of plotting a play.)   155 **cloudy** threatening
158 **dogged** (1) relentless (2) currish   160 **accuse** accusation.   **level** aim   164 **liefest liege** dearest sovereign

Ay, all of you have laid your heads together—
Myself had notice of your conventicles—   166
And all to make away my guiltless life.
I shall not want false witness to condemn me   168
Nor store of treasons to augment my guilt.
The ancient proverb will be well effected: 170
"A staff is quickly found to beat a dog."
CARDINAL
My liege, his railing is intolerable.
If those that care to keep your royal person   173
From treason's secret knife and traitors' rage
Be thus upbraided, chid, and rated at,   175
And the offender granted scope of speech,   176
'Twill make them cool in zeal unto Your Grace.
SUFFOLK
Hath he not twit our sovereign lady here   178
With ignominious words, though clerkly couched,   179
As if she had suborned some to swear
False allegations to o'erthrow his state?
QUEEN
But I can give the loser leave to chide.   182
GLOUCESTER
Far truer spoke than meant. I lose, indeed;
Beshrew the winners, for they played me false!   184
And well such losers may have leave to speak.
BUCKINGHAM
He'll wrest the sense and hold us here all day.   186
Lord Cardinal, he is your prisoner.
CARDINAL [to his attendants]
Sirs, take away the Duke and guard him sure.
GLOUCESTER
Ah, thus King Henry throws away his crutch
Before his legs be firm to bear his body.
Thus is the shepherd beaten from thy side,
And wolves are gnarling who shall gnaw thee first.   192
Ah, that my fear were false; ah, that it were!
For, good King Henry, thy decay I fear.   194
     Exit Gloucester [guarded by the Cardinal's men].
KING [*rising*]
My lords, what to your wisdoms seemeth best
Do or undo, as if ourself were here.
QUEEN
What, will Your Highness leave the Parliament?
KING
Ay, Margaret. My heart is drowned with grief,
Whose flood begins to flow within mine eyes,
My body round engirt with misery;
For what's more miserable than discontent?
Ah, uncle Humphrey, in thy face I see
The map of honor, truth, and loyalty;
And yet, good Humphrey, is the hour to come
That e'er I proved thee false or feared thy faith.   205
What louring star now envies thy estate,
That these great lords and Margaret our queen

Do seek subversion of thy harmless life?
Thou never didst them wrong nor no man wrong.
And as the butcher takes away the calf
And binds the wretch and beats it when it strains,   211
Bearing it to the bloody slaughterhouse,
Even so remorseless have they borne him hence;
And as the dam runs lowing up and down,   214
Looking the way her harmless young one went,
And can do naught but wail her darling's loss,
Even so myself bewails good Gloucester's case
With sad unhelpful tears, and with dimmed eyes
Look after him and cannot do him good,
So mighty are his vowèd enemies.
His fortunes I will weep, and twixt each groan
Say "Who's a traitor? Gloucester he is none."   222
     Exeunt [King, Buckingham, Salisbury, and
     Warwick with attendants; Somerset remains
     apart].
QUEEN
Free lords, cold snow melts with the sun's hot
     beams.   223
Henry my lord is cold in great affairs,   224
Too full of foolish pity; and Gloucester's show   225
Beguiles him, as the mournful crocodile   226
With sorrow snares relenting passengers,   227
Or as the snake, rolled in a flowering bank,   228
With shining checkered slough, doth sting a child   229
That for the beauty thinks it excellent.
Believe me, lords, were none more wise than I—   231
And yet herein I judge mine own wit good—   232
This Gloucester should be quickly rid the world,   233
To rid us from the fear we have of him.
CARDINAL
That he should die is worthy policy,   235
But yet we want a color for his death.   236
'Tis meet he be condemned by course of law.
SUFFOLK
But, in my mind, that were no policy.   238
The King will labor still to save his life,   239
The commons haply rise to save his life;   240
And yet we have but trivial argument,   241
More than mistrust, that shows him worthy death.   242
YORK
So that, by this, you would not have him die.   243

166 conventicles private or secret meetings **168 want** lack **170 effected** fulfilled, realized **173 care** take care **175 rated** scolded **176 scope** freedom **178 twit** twitted **179 clerkly couched** learnedly and cleverly phrased **182 leave** permission **184 Beshrew** curse **186 wrest the sense** twist the meaning **192 gnarling** snarling over **194 decay** downfall **205 feared thy faith** doubted your loyalty

211 strains strives. (The Folio reading, *strays,* is perhaps possible if *binds* means "pens in.") **214 dam** mother **222 s.d. Exeunt** (The Quarto version has Salisbury and Warwick exit here with the King. Buckingham, with no further role in the scene, possibly leaves, too. But the Folio reads *Exit,* and it is possible the King departs alone, leaving the others in little groups, trying to conduct a parliament without a king.) **223 Free** noble **224 cold** i.e., faint, neglectful, and ready to melt or give way **225 show** false appearance **226 mournful crocodile** i.e., animal famous for its "crocodile tears" **227 relenting passengers** gullible passersby **228 rolled** coiled **229 slough** skin **231 were . . . than I** i.e., I would venture my opinion, were there not wiser heads than I **232 wit** intelligence **233 rid** removed from **235 is worthy policy** is a sound scheme **236 color** pretext **238 were no policy** would be a poor stratagem **239 still** continually **240 haply rise** perhaps rise in rebellion **241 argument** evidence **242 More than mistrust** other than suspicion **243 by this** i.e., by this reasoning

SUFFOLK
Ah, York, no man alive so fain as I!   244
YORK
'Tis York that hath more reason for his death.
But, my Lord Cardinal, and you, my lord of Suffolk,
Say as you think, and speak it from your souls:
Were 't not all one an empty eagle were set   248
To guard the chicken from a hungry kite   249
As place Duke Humphrey for the King's Protector?
QUEEN
So the poor chicken should be sure of death.
SUFFOLK
Madam, 'tis true; and were 't not madness then
To make the fox surveyor of the fold?   253
Who, being accused a crafty murderer,
His guilt should be but idly posted over   255
Because his purpose is not executed.
No, let him die in that he is a fox,
By nature proved an enemy to the flock,
Before his chaps be stained with crimson blood,   259
As Humphrey, proved by reasons, to my liege.   260
And do not stand on quillets how to slay him—   261
Be it by gins, by snares, by subtlety,   262
Sleeping or waking, 'tis no matter how,
So he be dead. For that is good deceit   264
Which mates him first that first intends deceit.   265
QUEEN
Thrice-noble Suffolk, 'tis resolutely spoke.
SUFFOLK
Not resolute, except so much were done,   267
For things are often spoke and seldom meant;
But that my heart accordeth with my tongue,   269
Seeing the deed is meritorious,
And to preserve my sovereign from his foe,
Say but the word and I will be his priest.   272
CARDINAL
But I would have him dead, my lord of Suffolk,
Ere you can take due orders for a priest.   274
Say you consent and censure well the deed,   275
And I'll provide his executioner,
I tender so the safety of my liege.   277
SUFFOLK
Here is my hand. The deed is worthy doing.
QUEEN   And so say I.
YORK   And I. And now we three have spoke it,

It skills not greatly who impugns our doom.   281

Enter a Post.

POST
Great lords, from Ireland am I come amain   282
To signify that rebels there are up   283
And put the Englishmen unto the sword.
Send succors, lords, and stop the rage betimes,   285
Before the wound do grow uncurable;
For, being green, there is great hope of help.   [*Exit.*] 287
CARDINAL
A breach that craves a quick expedient stop!
What counsel give you in this weighty cause?
YORK
That Somerset be sent as regent thither.
'Tis meet that lucky ruler be employed—   291
Witness the fortune he hath had in France.
SOMERSET [*coming forward*]
If York, with all his far-fet policy,   293
Had been the regent there instead of me,
He never would have stayed in France so long.
YORK
No, not to lose it all, as thou hast done.
I rather would have lost my life betimes   297
Than bring a burden of dishonor home
By staying there so long till all were lost.   299
Show me one scar charactered on thy skin.   300
Men's flesh preserved so whole do seldom win.   301
QUEEN
Nay, then, this spark will prove a raging fire
If wind and fuel be brought to feed it with.
No more, good York; sweet Somerset, be still.
Thy fortune, York, hadst thou been regent there,
Might happily have proved far worse than his.   306
YORK
What, worse than naught? Nay, then a shame take
all!
SOMERSET
And, in the number, thee that wishest shame!   308
CARDINAL
My lord of York, try what your fortune is.
Th' uncivil kerns of Ireland are in arms   310
And temper clay with blood of Englishmen.   311
To Ireland will you lead a band of men,
Collected choicely, from each county some,
And try your hap against the Irishmen?   314

244 fain glad, eager   248 all one all the same, the same thing that.
empty hungry   249 kite scavenger bird, a kind of hawk   253 surveyor guardian.   fold sheepfold   255 idly posted over foolishly ignored or hastened over. (Suffolk argues that it would be foolish to
place a fox in charge of a sheepfold and then exonerate it of being a
killer simply because it hasn't yet killed the sheep.)   259 chaps jaws
260 proved i.e., proved to be an enemy.   by reasons by arguments
261 quillets subtle distinctions or disputes   262 gins engines, traps
264 So so long as   265 mates checkmates, foils (i.e., strikes quickly
before the enemy can move first)   267 except . . . done unless what
I've spoken is converted into action   269 that i.e., to prove that
272 be his priest i.e., perform the last rites for him, preside over his
death   274 take . . . priest (1) make arrangements to have a priest
there (2) prepare yourself for the priesthood   275 censure well approve   277 tender am concerned for, care for

281 skills not makes no great difference.   impugns our doom questions our decision.   s.d. Post messenger   282 amain with full speed
283 signify report.   up up in arms   285 betimes early, swiftly
287 green fresh   291 meet fitting. (Said ironically; York is hostile toward Somerset.)   293 far-fet farfetched, artful, deep. (Said ironically;
Somerset comes forward to defend himself against York's insulting
way of speaking, as though Somerset were not there.)   297 betimes
forthwith, sooner   299 staying . . . long temporizing   300 charactered inscribed   301 Men's . . . win men who can show no wounds
are seldom victors   306 happily haply, perhaps   308 in . . . shame
i.e., among the "all" to whom you wish shame, may you be included
310 uncivil kerns disorderly and irregular light-armed Irish soldiers
311 temper clay moisten the soil   314 hap fortune

YORK
I will, my lord, so please His Majesty.

SUFFOLK
Why, our authority is his consent,
And what we do establish he confirms.
Then, noble York, take thou this task in hand.

YORK
I am content. Provide me soldiers, lords,
Whiles I take order for mine own affairs. 320

SUFFOLK
A charge, Lord York, that I will see performed.
But now return we to the false Duke Humphrey. 322

CARDINAL
No more of him; for I will deal with him
That henceforth he shall trouble us no more.
And so, break off. The day is almost spent. 325
Lord Suffolk, you and I must talk of that event. 326

YORK
My lord of Suffolk, within fourteen days
At Bristol I expect my soldiers,
For there I'll ship them all for Ireland.

SUFFOLK
I'll see it truly done, my lord of York. 330
Exeunt. Manet York.

YORK
Now, York, or never, steel thy fearful thoughts 331
And change misdoubt to resolution. 332
Be that thou hop'st to be, or what thou art 333
Resign to death; it is not worth th' enjoying.
Let pale-faced fear keep with the mean-born man 335
And find no harbor in a royal heart.
Faster than springtime show'rs comes thought on
   thought,
And not a thought but thinks on dignity. 338
My brain, more busy than the laboring spider,
Weaves tedious snares to trap mine enemies. 340
Well, nobles, well, 'tis politicly done 341
To send me packing with an host of men. 342
I fear me you but warm the starvèd snake, 343
Who, cherished in your breasts, will sting your
   hearts.
'Twas men I lacked, and you will give them me;
I take it kindly. Yet be well assured
You put sharp weapons in a madman's hands.
Whiles I in Ireland nourish a mighty band,
I will stir up in England some black storm
Shall blow ten thousand souls to heaven or hell; 350
And this fell tempest shall not cease to rage 351
Until the golden circuit on my head, 352

Like to the glorious sun's transparent beams,
Do calm the fury of this mad-bred flaw. 354
And, for a minister of my intent, 355
I have seduced a headstrong Kentishman,
John Cade of Ashford,
To make commotion, as full well he can,
Under the title of John Mortimer. 359
In Ireland have I seen this stubborn Cade
Oppose himself against a troop of kerns,
And fought so long till that his thighs with darts 362
Were almost like a sharp-quilled porcupine;
And in the end being rescued, I have seen
Him caper upright like a wild Morisco, 365
Shaking the bloody darts as he his bells. 366
Full often, like a shag-haired crafty kern,
Hath he conversèd with the enemy,
And undiscovered come to me again
And given me notice of their villainies.
This devil here shall be my substitute;
For that John Mortimer, which now is dead, 372
In face, in gait, in speech, he doth resemble.
By this I shall perceive the commons' mind,
How they affect the house and claim of York. 375
Say he be taken, racked, and torturèd, 376
I know no pain they can inflict upon him
Will make him say I moved him to those arms. 378
Say that he thrive, as 'tis great like he will, 379
Why then from Ireland come I with my strength
And reap the harvest which that rascal sowed.
For, Humphrey being dead, as he shall be,
And Henry put apart, the next for me. *Exit.* 383

❧

3.2 *Enter two or three running over the stage, from
   the murder of Duke Humphrey.*

FIRST MURDERER
Run to my lord of Suffolk. Let him know
We have dispatched the Duke, as he commanded.

SECOND MURDERER
O, that it were to do! What have we done? 3

354 **mad-bred** produced by madness. **flaw** squall, tempest
355 **minister** agent 359 **Mortimer** (The name of a powerful family claiming descent from Lionel, Duke of Clarence, and hence entitled to the crown. See *1 Henry VI*, 2.5.) 362 **till that** until. **darts** light spears or arrows 365 **Morisco** morris dancer, always fancily or grotesquely dressed; or the dance itself 366 **he** i.e., the morris dancer, with bells on his shins 372 **For that** because 375 **affect** incline toward 376 **Say he be taken** if he were to be captured 378 **Will** that will. **moved** incited, prompted 379 **great like** very likely 383 **put apart** ousted
3.2. Location: Bury St. Edmunds, in a room of state adjoining the place of imprisonment where Gloucester has been murdered. Seats are prepared, as for his trial.
s.d. from the murder (In the Quarto version, "the curtains being drawn, Duke Humphrey is discovered in his bed, and two men lying on his breast and smothering him in his bed." Suffolk enters to them. The curtains are closed as the Murderers exit at line 14.) **3 that . . . do** i.e., would that it were not yet done and thus could be avoided

320 **take order for** arrange 322 **return we** let's get back to talking about 325 **break off** cease conversation 326 **event** affair, business
330 **s.d. Manet** he remains onstage 331 **fearful** timid 332 **misdoubt** suspicion, fear 333 **that** that which 335 **keep** dwell. **mean-born** lowly born 338 **dignity** i.e., the dignity of high office—kingship
340 **tedious** intricate 341 **politicly** shrewdly. (Said ironically.)
342 **packing** away, a-journeying 343 **starvèd** i.e., deathlike with cold. (One of Aesop's fables is about a man who puts a snake next to his chest to warm it and is stung by it.) 350 **Shall** that shall 351 **fell** fierce 352 **circuit** circlet, crown

Didst ever hear a man so penitent?

Enter Suffolk.

FIRST MURDERER　　Here comes my lord.

SUFFOLK

Now, sirs, have you dispatched this thing?

FIRST MURDERER　　Ay, my good lord, he's dead.

SUFFOLK

Why, that's well said. Go get you to my house.　　8
I will reward you for this venturous deed.
The King and all the peers are here at hand.
Have you laid fair the bed? Is all things well,　　11
According as I gave directions?

FIRST MURDERER　　'Tis, my good lord.

SUFFOLK　　Away! Begone.　　　　　*Exeunt [Murderers].*

Sound trumpets. Enter the King, the Queen,
Cardinal [Beaufort], Somerset, with attendants.

KING

Go call our uncle to our presence straight.　　15
Say we intend to try His Grace today
If he be guilty, as 'tis publishèd.　　17

SUFFOLK

I'll call him presently, my noble lord.　　*Exit.* 18

KING

Lords, take your places; and, I pray you all,
Proceed no straiter 'gainst our uncle Gloucester　　20
Than from true evidence of good esteem　　21
He be approved in practice culpable.　　22
　　　　　　　　　　　　[They take their places.]

QUEEN

God forbid any malice should prevail
That faultless may condemn a nobleman!　　24
Pray God he may acquit him of suspicion!　　25

KING

I thank thee, Meg. These words content me much.

Enter Suffolk.

How now? Why look'st thou pale? Why tremblest
thou?
Where is our uncle? What's the matter, Suffolk?

SUFFOLK

Dead in his bed, my lord. Gloucester is dead.

QUEEN　　Marry, God forfend!　　　　　30

CARDINAL

God's secret judgment. I did dream tonight　　31
The Duke was dumb and could not speak a word.
　　　　　　　　　　　　　King swoons.

QUEEN

How fares my lord? Help, lords, the King is dead!

SOMERSET

Rear up his body. Wring him by the nose.　　34

QUEEN

Run, go, help, help! O Henry, ope thine eyes!
　　　　　　　　　　　[They revive the King.]

SUFFOLK

He doth revive again. Madam, be patient.

KING

O heavenly God!

QUEEN　　　　　How fares my gracious lord?

SUFFOLK

Comfort, my sovereign! Gracious Henry, comfort!

KING

What, doth my lord of Suffolk comfort me?
Came he right now to sing a raven's note,　　40
Whose dismal tune bereft my vital powers,
And thinks he that the chirping of a wren,
By crying comfort from a hollow breast,　　43
Can chase away the first-conceivèd sound?　　44
Hide not thy poison with such sugared words.
Lay not thy hands on me. Forbear, I say!
Their touch affrights me as a serpent's sting.
Thou baleful messenger, out of my sight!
Upon thy eyeballs murderous Tyranny
Sits in grim majesty to fright the world.
Look not upon me, for thine eyes are wounding.
Yet do not go away. Come, basilisk,　　52
And kill the innocent gazer with thy sight;
For in the shade of death I shall find joy,　　54
In life but double death, now Gloucester's dead.

QUEEN

Why do you rate my lord of Suffolk thus?　　56
Although the Duke was enemy to him,
Yet he most Christian-like laments his death.
And for myself, foe as he was to me,　　59
Might liquid tears or heart-offending groans　　60
Or blood-consuming sighs recall his life,　　61
I would be blind with weeping, sick with groans,
Look pale as primrose with blood-drinking sighs,　　63
And all to have the noble Duke alive.
What know I how the world may deem of me?　　65
For it is known we were but hollow friends.
It may be judged I made the Duke away;
So shall my name with slander's tongue be wounded
And princes' courts be filled with my reproach.　　69
This get I by his death. Ay me, unhappy,
To be a queen, and crowned with infamy!

KING

Ah, woe is me for Gloucester, wretched man!

QUEEN

Be woe for me, more wretched than he is.　　73
What, dost thou turn away and hide thy face?
I am no loathsome leper. Look on me.
What? Art thou, like the adder, waxen deaf?　　76

---

8 well said well done　**11 laid fair the bed** i.e., straightened the bed linen to conceal the signs of struggle　**15 straight** straightway　**17 If** whether.　**publishèd** publicly proclaimed　**18 presently** at once **20 straiter** more severely　**21 of good esteem** worthy of belief **22 approved in** proved guilty of　**24 faultless** (Modifies *nobleman*.) **25 acquit him** exonerate himself　**30 forfend** forbid　**31 tonight** this past night　**34 Wring . . . nose** (Evidently a common first-aid remedy for restoring consciousness; compare with *Venus and Adonis*, line 475.)

40 right now just now.　**raven's note** a supposed omen of death **43 hollow** deceitful　**44 first-conceivèd sound** sound that was perceived first　**52 basilisk** fabulous reptile, said to kill by its look **54 shade** shadow　**56 rate** berate　**59 for** as for　**60, 61, 63 heart-offending, blood-consuming, blood-drinking** (It was commonly believed that groans and sighs cost the heart a drop of blood.) **65 deem** judge　**69 my reproach** blame of me　**73 woe** sorry **76 waxen deaf** grown deaf. (Snakes were popularly supposed to be deaf.)

Be poisonous too, and kill thy forlorn queen.
Is all thy comfort shut in Gloucester's tomb?
Why, then, Dame Margaret was ne'er thy joy.
Erect his statue and worship it,
And make my image but an alehouse sign.
Was I for this nigh wrecked upon the sea
And twice by awkward wind from England's bank   83
Drove back again unto my native clime?   84
What boded this, but well forewarning wind   85
Did seem to say, "Seek not a scorpion's nest,
Nor set no footing on this unkind shore"?
What did I then but cursed the gentle gusts
And he that loosed them forth their brazen caves,   89
And bid them blow towards England's blessèd shore
Or turn our stern upon a dreadful rock?
Yet Aeolus would not be a murderer,
But left that hateful office unto thee.
The pretty-vaulting sea refused to drown me,   94
Knowing that thou wouldst have me drowned on
    shore
With tears as salt as sea, through thy unkindness.
The splitting rocks cow'red in the sinking sands   97
And would not dash me with their ragged sides,
Because thy flinty heart, more hard than they,   99
Might in thy palace perish Margaret.   100
As far as I could ken thy chalky cliffs,   101
When from thy shore the tempest beat us back,
I stood upon the hatches in the storm,
And when the dusky sky began to rob
My earnest-gaping sight of thy land's view,   105
I took a costly jewel from my neck—
A heart it was, bound in with diamonds—
And threw it towards thy land. The sea received it,
And so I wished thy body might my heart.
And even with this I lost fair England's view,
And bid mine eyes be packing with my heart,   111
And called them blind and dusky spectacles   112
For losing ken of Albion's wishèd coast.   113
How often have I tempted Suffolk's tongue,   114
The agent of thy foul inconstancy,   115
To sit and witch me, as Ascanius did   116
When he to madding Dido would unfold   117
His father's acts commenced in burning Troy!

Am I not witched like her, or thou not false like
    him?   119
Ay me, I can no more. Die, Margaret!
For Henry weeps that thou dost live so long.

*Noise within. Enter Warwick, [Salisbury,] and
many Commons.*

WARWICK
    It is reported, mighty sovereign,
    That good Duke Humphrey traitorously is murdered
    By Suffolk and the Cardinal Beaufort's means.
    The commons, like an angry hive of bees
    That want their leader, scatter up and down   126
    And care not who they sting in his revenge.   127
    Myself have calmed their spleenful mutiny,   128
    Until they hear the order of his death.   129
KING
    That he is dead, good Warwick, 'tis too true;
    But how he died God knows, not Henry.
    Enter his chamber, view his breathless corpse,
    And comment then upon his sudden death.   133
WARWICK
    That shall I do, my liege.—Stay, Salisbury,
    With the rude multitude till I return.   [*Exit.*] 135
                    [*Exit Salisbury with the Commons.*]
KING
    O Thou that judgest all things, stay my thoughts, 136
    My thoughts that labor to persuade my soul
    Some violent hands were laid on Humphrey's life!
    If my suspect be false, forgive me, God,   139
    For judgment only doth belong to Thee.
    Fain would I go to chafe his paly lips   141
    With twenty thousand kisses, and to drain
    Upon his face an ocean of salt tears,
    To tell my love unto his dumb deaf trunk
    And with my fingers feel his hand unfeeling.
    But all in vain are these mean obsequies.   146

    *Bed put forth [bearing Gloucester's body. Enter
    Warwick.]*

    And to survey his dead and earthy image,
    What were it but to make my sorrow greater?
WARWICK
    Come hither, gracious sovereign. View this body.
KING
    That is to see how deep my grave is made.
    For with his soul fled all my worldly solace;
    For seeing him I see my life in death.   152
WARWICK
    As surely as my soul intends to live

83 **awkward** adverse. **bank** shore 84 **Drove** driven. **clime** country
85 **but** but that 89 **he** i.e., Aeolus, god of the winds. **forth** forth
from. **brazen** (In Homer's *Odyssey*, 10.3–4, the floating island of
Aeolus is enclosed by a rampart of bronze.) 94 **pretty-vaulting** handsomely rising and falling 97 **splitting rocks** rocks on which ships
split. **sinking sands** sandbars on which ships founder and sink
99 **Because** so that 100 **perish** cause to perish 101 **ken** discern
105 **My earnest-gaping . . . view** my ardently peering eyesight of the
view of your land 111 **be packing** begone. **my heart** (1) my affection, left behind in England (2) my heart-shaped jewel 112 **spectacles** instruments of sight 113 **Albion's** England's. **wished** longed
for 114 **tempted** (Queen Margaret's point is that, by her beauty, she
has innocently induced Suffolk to practice witchcraft on her in behalf
of King Henry.) 115 **agent** i.e., arranger of the marriage agreement
between Henry and Margaret 116 **witch** bewitch. **Ascanius** young
son of Aeneas. (In Virgil's *Aeneid*, Book 1, during Aeneas' narration
of his adventures and misfortunes to Queen Dido, Aeneas' mother,
Venus, sends Cupid disguised as Ascanius to afflict the Queen with
love for Aeneas.) 117 **madding** becoming frantic (with love). **unfold** disclose, narrate

119 **witched** bewitched. **him** i.e., Aeneas 126 **want** lack 127 **his
revenge** revenge of him 128 **spleenful mutiny** wrathful uprising
129 **order** manner 133 **comment . . . upon** explain 135 **rude** turbulent, unpolished 136 **stay** hold back 139 **suspect** suspicion
141 **Fain** gladly. **chafe** rub, warm. **paly** pale 146 **mean obsequies**
deficient funeral rites. **s.d. Bed put forth** (In the Quarto version,
Warwick need not leave the stage [see line 135] to view Gloucester's
dead body; he simply "draws the curtain and shows Duke Humphrey
in his bed." In the present Folio version, the bed must be thrust forth
onto the stage with Humphrey in it.) 152 **For . . . death** i.e., for in
his death I see an image of my own

With that dread King that took our state upon Him   154
To free us from His Father's wrathful curse,
I do believe that violent hands were laid
Upon the life of this thrice-famèd duke.   157

SUFFOLK
A dreadful oath, sworn with a solemn tongue!
What instance gives Lord Warwick for his vow?   159

WARWICK
See how the blood is settled in his face.
Oft have I seen a timely-parted ghost,   161
Of ashy semblance, meager, pale, and bloodless,
Being all descended to the laboring heart,   163
Who, in the conflict that it holds with death,   164
Attracts the same for aidance 'gainst the enemy,   165
Which with the heart there cools and ne'er returneth   166
To blush and beautify the cheek again.   167
But see, his face is black and full of blood;
His eyeballs further out than when he lived,
Staring full ghastly, like a strangled man;
His hair upreared, his nostrils stretched with
    struggling;   171
His hands abroad displayed, as one that grasped   172
And tugged for life and was by strength subdued.
Look, on the sheets his hair, you see, is sticking;
His well-proportioned beard made rough and rugged,
Like to the summer's corn by tempest lodged.   176
It cannot be but he was murdered here.
The least of all these signs were probable.   178

SUFFOLK
Why, Warwick, who should do the Duke to death?
Myself and Beaufort had him in protection,
And we, I hope, sir, are no murderers.

WARWICK
But both of you were vowed Duke Humphrey's foes,
[To Cardinal] And you, forsooth, had the good Duke
    to keep.   183
'Tis like you would not feast him like a friend,   184
And 'tis well seen he found an enemy.   185

QUEEN
Then you, belike, suspect these noblemen   186
As guilty of Duke Humphrey's timeless death.   187

WARWICK
Who finds the heifer dead and bleeding fresh
And sees fast by a butcher with an ax,   189
But will suspect 'twas he that made the slaughter?
Who finds the partridge in the puttock's nest   191
But may imagine how the bird was dead,
Although the kite soar with unbloodied beak?
Even so suspicious is this tragedy.

QUEEN
Are you the butcher, Suffolk? Where's your knife?
Is Beaufort termed a kite? Where are his talons?

SUFFOLK
I wear no knife to slaughter sleeping men;
But here's a vengeful sword, rusted with ease,   198
That shall be scourèd in his rancorous heart
That slanders me with murder's crimson badge.
Say, if thou dar'st, proud lord of Warwickshire,
That I am faulty in Duke Humphrey's death.   202
    [Exeunt Cardinal, Somerset, and others.]

WARWICK
What dares not Warwick, if false Suffolk dare him?

QUEEN
He dares not calm his contumelious spirit,   204
Nor cease to be an arrogant controller,   205
Though Suffolk dare him twenty thousand times.

WARWICK
Madam, be still—with reverence may I say—
For every word you speak in his behalf
Is slander to your royal dignity.

SUFFOLK
Blunt-witted lord, ignoble in demeanor!
If ever lady wronged her lord so much,
Thy mother took into her blameful bed
Some stern untutored churl, and noble stock   213
Was graft with crab-tree slip—whose fruit thou art   214
And never of the Nevilles' noble race.

WARWICK
But that the guilt of murder bucklers thee   216
And I should rob the deathsman of his fee,   217
Quitting thee thereby of ten thousand shames,   218
And that my sovereign's presence makes me mild,   219
I would, false murderous coward, on thy knee
Make thee beg pardon for thy passèd speech   221
And say it was thy mother that thou meant'st,   222
That thou thyself wast born in bastardy;
And after all this fearful homage done,   224
Give thee thy hire and send thy soul to hell,   225
Pernicious bloodsucker of sleeping men!   226

SUFFOLK
Thou shalt be waking while I shed thy blood,   227
If from this presence thou dar'st go with me.   228

---

154 King i.e., Christ. state i.e., human nature   157 thrice-famèd very famous   159 instance proof   161 a timely-parted ghost the remains of one having died in the natural course of events   163 Being all descended i.e., the blood having all descended   164 Who i.e., the heart   165 the same i.e., the blood. aidance aid. the enemy i.e., death   166 Which i.e., the blood   167 blush cause to take on sanguine color   171 upreared standing on end   172 abroad displayed spread apart   176 corn grain. lodged beaten down   178 were probable would be sufficient confirmation   183 to keep in your custody   184 like likely   185 well seen obvious   186 belike perchance   187 timeless untimely   189 fast by close by   191 puttock's kite's

198 ease i.e., disuse   202 faulty in guilty of.   s.d. Exeunt . . . others (The Cardinal's exit is marked in the Quarto, not in the Folio. Somerset's exit here is even more uncertain, but he is not needed for the ensuing quarrel and may help the ailing and guilt-ridden Cardinal offstage. Also, at some point, the bed and its dead occupant must be withdrawn or concealed by curtains.)   204 contumelious contemptuous, contentious   205 controller critic, detractor   213 stern rough   214 graft grafted.   slip cutting (with a possible play on the sense of "moral lapse")   216 But that were it not that.   bucklers shields   217 deathsman executioner   218 Quitting ridding   219 that were it not that   221 passèd just spoken   222 And . . . thy mother i.e., and force you to admit it was your own mother. (The emphasis is on thy.)   224 fearful homage craven submission   225 Give i.e., I would give.   hire reward (i.e., death)   226 bloodsucker . . . men (Warwick accuses Suffolk of killing Gloucester in his sleep, suggesting further that he is a sort of vampire.)   227 waking (Suffolk responds sarcastically to the accusation of killing sleeping men.)   *228 this presence (Drawing swords is not allowed in the King's presence, as also at lines 237–238.)

WARWICK
Away, even now, or I will drag thee hence!
Unworthy though thou art, I'll cope with thee   230
And do some service to Duke Humphrey's ghost.
                              Exeunt [Suffolk and Warwick].

KING
What stronger breastplate than a heart untainted?
Thrice is he armed that hath his quarrel just,
And he but naked, though locked up in steel,   234
Whose conscience with injustice is corrupted.
                              A noise within.

QUEEN   What noise is this?

               *Enter Suffolk and Warwick with their weapons
               drawn.*

KING
Why, how now, lords? Your wrathful weapons
     drawn
Here in our presence? Dare you be so bold?
Why, what tumultuous clamor have we here?
SUFFOLK
The traitorous Warwick, with the men of Bury,
Set all upon me, mighty sovereign.

               Enter Salisbury.

SALISBURY [*to the Commons, within*]
Sirs, stand apart. The King shall know your mind.—
Dread lord, the commons send you word by me,
Unless Lord Suffolk straight be done to death   244
Or banishèd fair England's territories,
They will by violence tear him from your palace
And torture him with grievous lingering death.
They say, by him the good Duke Humphrey died;
They say, in him they fear Your Highness' death;
And mere instinct of love and loyalty,   250
Free from a stubborn opposite intent,   251
As being thought to contradict your liking,   252
Makes them thus forward in his banishment.   253
They say, in care of your most royal person,
That if Your Highness should intend to sleep,
And charge that no man should disturb your rest
In pain of your dislike or pain of death,   257
Yet, notwithstanding such a strait edict,   258
Were there a serpent seen with forkèd tongue
That slyly glided towards Your Majesty,
It were but necessary you were waked,
Lest, being suffered in that harmful slumber,   262
The mortal worm might make the sleep eternal.   263
And therefore do they cry, though you forbid,
That they will guard you, whe'er you will or no,   265
From such fell serpents as false Suffolk is—   266
With whose envenomèd and fatal sting   267

Your loving uncle, twenty times his worth,   268
They say, is shamefully bereft of life.   269
COMMONS (*within*)
An answer from the King, my lord of Salisbury!
SUFFOLK
'Tis like the commons, rude unpolished hinds,   271
Could send such message to their sovereign!
[*To Salisbury.*] But you, my lord, were glad to be
     employed,
To show how quaint an orator you are.   274
But all the honor Salisbury hath won
Is that he was the lord ambassador
Sent from a sort of tinkers to the King.   277
COMMONS (*within*)
An answer from the King, or we will all break in!
KING
Go, Salisbury, and tell them all from me,
I thank them for their tender loving care;
And had I not been cited so by them,   281
Yet did I purpose as they do entreat.
For, sure, my thoughts do hourly prophesy
Mischance unto my state by Suffolk's means.   284
And therefore, by His majesty I swear,   285
Whose far unworthy deputy I am,
He shall not breathe infection in this air   287
But three days longer, on the pain of death.
                              [*Exit Salisbury.*]
QUEEN
O Henry, let me plead for gentle Suffolk!   289
KING
Ungentle queen, to call him gentle Suffolk!
No more, I say! If thou dost plead for him,
Thou wilt but add increase unto my wrath.
Had I but said, I would have kept my word,   293
But when I swear, it is irrevocable.
[*To Suffolk.*] If, after three days' space, thou here
     be'st found
On any ground that I am ruler of,
The world shall not be ransom for thy life.
Come, Warwick, come, good Warwick, go with me.
I have great matters to impart to thee.   299
               Exit [with all but Queen and Suffolk].
QUEEN
Mischance and sorrow go along with you!
Heart's discontent and sour affliction
Be playfellows to keep you company!
There's two of you; the devil make a third,   303
And threefold vengeance tend upon your steps!   304
SUFFOLK
Cease, gentle Queen, these execrations,
And let thy Suffolk take his heavy leave.   306
QUEEN
Fie, coward woman and softhearted wretch!

230 **cope with** encounter 234 **naked** i.e., unprotected 244 **straight** at once 250 **mere instinct** pure impulse 251–252 **Free . . . liking** innocent of any stubborn willfulness that might be interpreted as crossing your wishes 253 **forward in** bold, insistent upon 257 **In pain** under penalty 258 **strait** strict 262 **being suffered** you being permitted to remain 263 **mortal worm** deadly serpent 265 **whe'er** whether 266 **fell** cruel 267–269 **With . . . life** with whose venomous and fatal sting, they say, your uncle (who is twenty times more worthy than Suffolk) is deprived of life

271 **like** likely. (Said ironically.) **hinds** boors, rustics 274 **quaint** skilled, clever 277 **sort** gang 281 **cited** incited, urged 284 **Mischance** disaster 285 **His** i.e., God's 287 **breathe** breathe out, spread 289 **gentle** noble 293 **but said** merely spoken, without an oath 299 **s.d. Exit** (Possibly the bed and Gloucester's body are concealed or withdrawn at this point; see line 202 s.d.) 303 **two** i.e., the King and Warwick 304 **tend upon** follow 306 **heavy** sorrowful

Hast thou not spirit to curse thine enemies?

SUFFOLK

A plague upon them, wherefore should I curse
  them?
Could curses kill, as doth the mandrake's groan,   310
I would invent as bitter searching terms,   311
As curst, as harsh, and horrible to hear,   312
Delivered strongly through my fixèd teeth,
With full as many signs of deadly hate,
As lean-faced Envy in her loathsome cave.
My tongue should stumble in mine earnest words,
Mine eyes should sparkle like the beaten flint,
My hair be fixed on end, as one distract;   318
Ay, every joint should seem to curse and ban;   319
And even now my burdened heart would break,
Should I not curse them. Poison be their drink!
Gall, worse than gall, the daintiest that they taste!
Their sweetest shade a grove of cypress trees!   323
Their chiefest prospect murdering basilisks!   324
Their softest touch as smart as lizards' stings!   325
Their music frightful as the serpent's hiss,
And boding screech owls make the consort full!   327
All the foul terrors in dark-seated hell—

QUEEN

Enough, sweet Suffolk. Thou torment'st thyself,
And these dread curses, like the sun 'gainst glass,
Or like an overchargèd gun, recoil   331
And turn the force of them upon thyself.

SUFFOLK

You bade me ban, and will you bid me leave?   333
Now, by the ground that I am banished from,
Well could I curse away a winter's night,
Though standing naked on a mountain top,
Where biting cold would never let grass grow,
And think it but a minute spent in sport.

QUEEN

O, let me entreat thee cease! Give me thy hand,
That I may dew it with my mournful tears;
Nor let the rain of heaven wet this place
To wash away my woeful monuments.   342

        [*She kisses his hand.*]

O, could this kiss be printed in thy hand,
That thou mightst think upon these by the seal,   344
Through whom a thousand sighs are breathed for
  thee!   345
So, get thee gone, that I may know my grief;   346
'Tis but surmised whiles thou art standing by,
As one that surfeits thinking on a want.   348

310 **mandrake's groan** (Folk belief held that when the forked and
man-shaped mandrake root was pulled from the ground, it uttered a
shriek that was fatal to the hearer or would drive him or her mad;
compare with *Romeo and Juliet*, 4.3.47–48.) 311 **searching** probing, cutting 312 **curst** malignant 318 **distract** mad 319 **ban** curse
323 **cypress trees** (Associated with death because they were often
planted near graveyards.) 324 **prospect** view. **basilisks** (See line 52
above.) 325 **smart** stinging 327 **boding** portending evil. **consort**
ensemble of musicians 331 **overchargèd** overloaded 333 **leave**
leave off 342 **monuments** i.e., tears as memorials of sorrow
344 **these** i.e., my lips. **seal** imprint 345 **Through whom** i.e.,
through which lips 346 **know** fully comprehend 348 **As . . . want**
like a person (such as myself) who, enjoying plenty, anticipates a time
of deprivation

I will repeal thee, or, be well assured,   349
Adventure to be banishèd myself;   350
And banishèd I am, if but from thee.
Go, speak not to me. Even now, begone!
O, go not yet! Even thus two friends condemned
Embrace and kiss and take ten thousand leaves,
Loather a hundred times to part than die.

        [*They embrace.*]

Yet now farewell, and farewell life with thee!

SUFFOLK

Thus is poor Suffolk ten times banishèd,
Once by the King, and three times thrice by thee.
'Tis not the land I care for, wert thou thence.
A wilderness is populous enough,
So Suffolk had thy heavenly company;   361
For where thou art, there is the world itself,
With every several pleasure in the world,   363
And where thou art not, desolation.
I can no more. Live thou to joy thy life;   365
Myself no joy in naught but that thou liv'st.

        Enter Vaux.

QUEEN

Whither goes Vaux so fast? What news, I prithee?

VAUX

To signify unto His Majesty   368
That Cardinal Beaufort is at point of death;
For suddenly a grievous sickness took him
That makes him gasp and stare and catch the air,
Blaspheming God and cursing men on earth.
Sometimes he talks as if Duke Humphrey's ghost
Were by his side; sometimes he calls the King,
And whispers to his pillow as to him
The secrets of his overchargèd soul;   376
And I am sent to tell His Majesty
That even now he cries aloud for him.

QUEEN

Go tell this heavy message to the King.   *Exit* [*Vaux*].
Ay me, what is this world? What news are these!
But wherefore grieve I at an hour's poor loss,   381
Omitting Suffolk's exile, my soul's treasure?   382
Why only, Suffolk, mourn I not for thee,
And with the southern clouds contend in tears—   384
Theirs for the earth's increase, mine for my sorrows?
Now get thee hence. The King, thou know'st, is
  coming.
If thou be found by me, thou art but dead.   387

SUFFOLK

If I depart from thee, I cannot live,
And in thy sight to die, what were it else
But like a pleasant slumber in thy lap?
Here could I breathe my soul into the air,
As mild and gentle as the cradle babe
Dying with mother's dug between its lips—   393

349 **repeal thee** bring about your recall 350 **Adventure** risk 361 **So**
so long as 363 **several** distinct 365 **joy** enjoy 368 **signify** report
376 **overchargèd** overburdened with guilt 381 **an hour's** (i.e., the
Cardinal has figuratively but an hour left to live in any case)
382 **Omitting** neglecting 384 **southern** i.e., especially moist 387 **by
me** near me 393 **dug** breast

Where, from thy sight, I should be raging mad   394
And cry out for thee to close up mine eyes,
To have thee with thy lips to stop my mouth.
So shouldst thou either turn my flying soul,   397
Or I should breathe it so into thy body,
And then it lived in sweet Elysium.   399
To die by thee were but to die in jest;   400
From thee to die were torture more than death.   401
O, let me stay, befall what may befall!

QUEEN
Away! Though parting be a fretful corrosive,   403
It is applièd to a deathful wound.   404
To France, sweet Suffolk. Let me hear from thee,
For wheresoe'er thou art in this world's globe,
I'll have an Iris that shall find thee out.   407

SUFFOLK   I go.

QUEEN   And take my heart with thee.

SUFFOLK
A jewel, locked into the woefull'st cask   410
That ever did contain a thing of worth.
Even as a splitted bark, so sunder we.   412
This way fall I to death.

QUEEN   This way for me.   413

Exeunt [separately].

♣

3.3   *Enter the King, Salisbury, and Warwick, to the*
          Cardinal in bed, [raving and staring as if he were
          mad].

KING
How fares my lord? Speak, Beaufort, to thy
    sovereign.

CARDINAL
If thou be'st Death, I'll give thee England's treasure,
Enough to purchase such another island,
So thou wilt let me live and feel no pain.   4

KING
Ah, what a sign it is of evil life,
Where death's approach is seen so terrible!

WARWICK
Beaufort, it is thy sovereign speaks to thee.

CARDINAL
Bring me unto my trial when you will.
Died he not in his bed? Where should he die?   9
Can I make men live, whe'er they will or no?   10
O, torture me no more! I will confess.
Alive again? Then show me where he is.
I'll give a thousand pound to look upon him.
He hath no eyes! The dust hath blinded them.
Comb down his hair. Look, look! It stands upright,
Like lime-twigs set to catch my wingèd soul.   16
Give me some drink, and bid the apothecary
Bring the strong poison that I bought of him.   18

KING
O thou eternal mover of the heavens,
Look with a gentle eye upon this wretch!
O, beat away the busy meddling fiend
That lays strong siege unto this wretch's soul,
And from his bosom purge this black despair!

WARWICK
See, how the pangs of death do make him grin!   24

SALISBURY
Disturb him not. Let him pass peaceably.

KING
Peace to his soul, if God's good pleasure be!
Lord Card'nal, if thou think'st on heaven's bliss,
Hold up thy hand. Make signal of thy hope.
                        [The Cardinal dies.]
He dies and makes no sign. O God, forgive him!

WARWICK
So bad a death argues a monstrous life.

KING
Forbear to judge, for we are sinners all.
Close up his eyes and draw the curtain close,   32
And let us all to meditation. *[The curtains are closed.]*
                                            Exeunt.

♣

4.1   *Alarum [within]. Fight at sea. Ordnance goes off.*
          Enter Lieutenant, [a Master, a Master's Mate,
          Walter Whitmore, and others; with them] Suffolk
          [disguised], and others, [prisoners].

LIEUTENANT
The gaudy, blabbing, and remorseful day   1
Is crept into the bosom of the sea,

---

394 Where whereas.   **from** out of   **397 turn** turn back, i.e., prevent the soul's escape, preserve my life. (The soul was thought to leave the body through the mouth.)   **399 lived** would live.   **Elysium** classical abode after death of those favored by the gods   **400 die in jest** i.e., not truly to die at all. (*To die* carries the suggestion of experiencing orgasm.)   **401 From** away from   **403 fretful corrosive** painful and caustic course of treatment   **404 deathful** fatal (since Suffolk's remaining would prove fatal)   **407 Iris** Juno's messenger   **410 cask** casket   **412 splitted bark** sailing vessel split in two   **413 s.d. Exeunt** (Gloucester's body in its bed is probably concealed or removed earlier, perhaps at line 202 or line 299; since the bed is needed immediately in the next scene, it almost certainly does not remain onstage until the end of this scene.)
3.3. Location: The Cardinal's bedchamber.
s.d. in bed (In the Quarto version, the curtains are drawn and the Cardinal "is discovered in his bed," raving and staring; compare with 3.2.0 s.d.)   **4 So** provided

9 he i.e., Gloucester   **10 whe'er** whether   **16 lime-twigs** twigs smeared with sticky birdlime to trap birds   **18 of** from   **24 grin** bare his teeth   **32 curtain** (The bed itself, presumably "thrust out" onstage for this brief scene, would have to be removed at this point; the curtains here are presumably bed curtains, although in the Quarto version they are drawn open at line 1 in such a way that the Cardinal is brought into view without having to bring on a bed, i.e., using a curtained area backstage.)
4.1. Location: The coast of Kent.
1 s.p. Lieutenant i.e., captain in charge of the fighting; see lines 65 and 107. (He is called "Captain of the ship" in the Quarto stage direction, but the Master is the mariner in charge of sailing the vessel.)
1 blabbing telltale, revealing.   **remorseful** compassionate (as contrasted with the menacing night)

And now loud-howling wolves arouse the jades   3
That drag the tragic melancholy night,
Who, with their drowsy, slow, and flagging wings   5
Clip dead men's graves, and from their misty jaws   6
Breathe foul contagious darkness in the air.
Therefore bring forth the soldiers of our prize;   8
For, whilst our pinnace anchors in the Downs,   9
Here shall they make their ransom on the sand,
Or with their blood stain this discolored shore.   11
Master, this prisoner freely give I thee;   12
And thou that art his mate, make boot of this;   13
The other, Walter Whitmore, is thy share.   14

[Three gentlemen prisoners, one of them Suffolk,
are apportioned and handed over.]

FIRST GENTLEMAN
What is my ransom, Master? Let me know.

MASTER
A thousand crowns, or else lay down your head.

MATE *[to the Second Gentleman]*
And so much shall you give, or off goes yours.

LIEUTENANT
What, think you much to pay two thousand crowns,
And bear the name and port of gentlemen?   19
Cut both the villains' throats, for die you shall.
The lives of those which we have lost in fight   21
Be counterpoised with such a petty sum?   22

FIRST GENTLEMAN
I'll give it, sir, and therefore spare my life.

SECOND GENTLEMAN
And so will I, and write home for it straight.

WHITMORE *[to Suffolk]*
I lost mine eye in laying the prize aboard,   25
And therefore to revenge it shalt thou die;
And so should these, if I might have my will.

LIEUTENANT
Be not so rash. Take ransom; let him live.   28

SUFFOLK
Look on my George; I am a gentleman.   29
Rate me at what thou wilt, thou shalt be paid.   30

WHITMORE
And so am I. My name is Walter Whitmore.   31

[Suffolk starts.]

How now, why starts thou? What, doth death
affright?

SUFFOLK
Thy name affrights me, in whose sound is death.   33
A cunning man did calculate my birth   34
And told me that by water I should die.
Yet let not this make thee be bloody-minded;
Thy name is Gualtier, being rightly sounded.

WHITMORE
Gualtier or Walter, which it is, I care not.
Never yet did base dishonor blur our name
But with our sword we wiped away the blot.
Therefore, when merchantlike I sell revenge,   41
Broke be my sword, my arms torn and defaced,   42
And I proclaimed a coward through the world!

SUFFOLK *[revealing his face]*
Stay, Whitmore, for thy prisoner is a prince,
The Duke of Suffolk, William de la Pole.

WHITMORE
The Duke of Suffolk muffled up in rags?

SUFFOLK
Ay, but these rags are no part of the Duke.
Jove sometime went disguised, and why not I?

LIEUTENANT
But Jove was never slain, as thou shalt be.

SUFFOLK
Obscure and lousy swain, King Henry's blood,   50
The honorable blood of Lancaster,
Must not be shed by such a jaded groom.   52
Hast thou not kissed thy hand and held my stirrup?
Bareheaded plodded by my footcloth mule   54
And thought thee happy when I shook my head?   55
How often hast thou waited at my cup,
Fed from my trencher, kneeled down at the board,   57
When I have feasted with Queen Margaret?
Remember it, and let it make thee crestfall'n,   59
Ay, and allay this thy abortive pride.   60
How in our voiding lobby hast thou stood   61
And duly waited for my coming forth?   62
This hand of mine hath writ in thy behalf,   63
And therefore shall it charm thy riotous tongue.   64

WHITMORE
Speak, Captain, shall I stab the forlorn swain?   65

---

3 the jades i.e., the winged dragons of Hecate that draw the chariot of the night   **5 flagging** drooping   **6 Clip** embrace, or strike a shearing blow.   **their** i.e., the graves'   **8 soldiers . . . prize** i.e., those taken from the vessel we have captured   **9 pinnace** one-masted vessel.   **Downs** anchorage off the Kentish coast   **11 discolored** i.e., to be discolored by blood   **12 this prisoner** i.e., the First Gentleman   **13 his** i.e., the shipmaster's.   **make . . . this** i.e., make a profit by ransoming this Second Gentleman   **14 The other** i.e., Suffolk   **19 port** demeanor   **21–22 The lives . . . sum** (An indignant question, and one that should perhaps be spoken by Whitmore rather than the Lieutenant; see lines 25–28.)   **25 laying . . . aboard** boarding the captured ship   **28 Be . . . live** (The Lieutenant's caution about killing the prisoners seems to contradict his threatening speech at lines 20–22. Perhaps those lines should be assigned to Whitmore, but it's also possible that the Lieutenant is simply being pragmatic in line 28, advising against killing the goose with the golden egg.)   **29 George** the gold or jeweled figure of Saint George, worn as the insignium of the Order of the Knights of the Garter   **30 Rate** value, assess   **31 am I** i.e., am I a gentleman. (Whitmore denies Suffolk's assertion of distinction in rank.)

33 Thy name (i.e., *Walter*, pronounced like "water." In line 37 below, Suffolk tries to avert the prophecy referred to in lines 34–35 [compare with 1.4.33–34] by urging the French form of the name, *Gualtier* or *Gaultier*.)   **34 A . . . birth** a fortune-teller cast my horoscope   **41 sell revenge** i.e., give up revenge (for my lost eye) in return for ransom money   **42 arms** coat of arms   **50 lousy** louse-infested, scurvy.   **King Henry's blood** (Suffolk's claim to be connected to the house of Lancaster is a dubious one.)   **52 jaded** ignoble (with a play in the next line on one who deals with *jades*, or "horses")   **54 footcloth** with a large, richly ornamented cloth laid over the back of a horse or mule, hanging down to the ground on each side   **55 happy** fortunate.   **shook** i.e., nodded   **57 trencher** wooden dish or plate.   **board** dining table   **59 it** all this.   **crestfall'n** (1) downcast, abashed (2) deprived of the coat of arms boasted of in line 42   **60 abortive** monstrous   **61 our voiding lobby** my anteroom   **62 duly** dutifully   **63 writ . . . behalf** i.e., written to recommend you or because you cannot write   **64 charm** put a spell on, silence   **65 Captain** (Appropriate courtesy title for the Lieutenant, since he is the military commander.)   **forlorn swain** desolate, wretched fellow

LIEUTENANT
First let my words stab him, as he hath me.
SUFFOLK
Base slave, thy words are blunt, and so art thou.   67
LIEUTENANT
Convey him hence, and on our longboat's side
Strike off his head.
SUFFOLK   Thou dar'st not, for thy own.   69
LIEUTENANT
Yes, Pole.
SUFFOLK   Pole?
LIEUTENANT   Pool! Sir Pool! Lord!   70
Ay, kennel, puddle, sink, whose filth and dirt   71
Troubles the silver spring where England drinks.
Now will I dam up this thy yawning mouth   73
For swallowing the treasure of the realm.   74
Thy lips that kissed the Queen shall sweep the
    ground,
And thou that smiledst at good Duke Humphrey's
    death
Against the senseless winds shalt grin in vain,   77
Who in contempt shall hiss at thee again.   78
And wedded be thou to the hags of hell   79
For daring to affy a mighty lord   80
Unto the daughter of a worthless king,
Having neither subject, wealth, nor diadem.   82
By devilish policy art thou grown great,   83
And, like ambitious Sylla, overgorged   84
With gobbets of thy mother's bleeding heart.   85
By thee Anjou and Maine were sold to France.
The false revolting Normans thorough thee   87
Disdain to call us lord, and Picardy
Hath slain their governors, surprised our forts,
And sent the ragged soldiers wounded home.
The princely Warwick, and the Nevilles all,
Whose dreadful swords were never drawn in vain,
As hating thee, are rising up in arms;
And now the house of York, thrust from the crown
By shameful murder of a guiltless king   95
And lofty, proud, encroaching tyranny,
Burns with revenging fire, whose hopeful colors
Advance our half-faced sun, striving to shine,   98
Under the which is writ, "*Invitis nubibus.*"   99
The commons here in Kent are up in arms,

And, to conclude, reproach and beggary
Is crept into the palace of our King,
And all by thee.—Away! Convey him hence.
SUFFOLK
O, that I were a god, to shoot forth thunder
Upon these paltry, servile, abject drudges!
Small things make base men proud. This villain
    here,
Being captain of a pinnace, threatens more
Than Bargulus, the strong Illyrian pirate.   108
Drones suck not eagles' blood, but rob beehives.   109
It is impossible that I should die
By such a lowly vassal as thyself.
Thy words move rage and not remorse in me.
I go of message from the Queen to France;   113
I charge thee waft me safely cross the Channel.   114
LIEUTENANT   Walter—
WHITMORE
Come, Suffolk, I must waft thee to thy death.
SUFFOLK
Paene gelidus timor occupat artus.   117
It is thee I fear.
WHITMORE
Thou shalt have cause to fear before I leave thee.
What, are ye daunted now? Now will ye stoop.
FIRST GENTLEMAN [*to Suffolk*]
My gracious lord, entreat him, speak him fair.   121
SUFFOLK
Suffolk's imperial tongue is stern and rough,
Used to command, untaught to plead for favor.
Far be it we should honor such as these
With humble suit. No, rather let my head
Stoop to the block than these knees bow to any
Save to the God of heaven and to my king;
And sooner dance upon a bloody pole   128
Than stand uncovered to the vulgar groom.   129
True nobility is exempt from fear.
More can I bear than you dare execute.
LIEUTENANT
Hale him away, and let him talk no more.   132
SUFFOLK
Come, soldiers, show what cruelty ye can,
That this my death may never be forgot!
Great men oft die by vile bezonians: 135
A Roman sworder and banditto slave   136
Murdered sweet Tully; Brutus' bastard hand   137
Stabbed Julius Caesar; savage islanders   138

67 blunt blunted like an arrow with no point, harmless **69 for thy own** i.e., for fear of losing your own head **70 Pole, Pool** (with verbal play on *poll*, head, *Pole*, Suffolk's family name, and *pool*, a pool of water, all similar in pronunciation) **71 kennel** gutter. **sink** cesspool **73 yawning** greedily gaping **74 For swallowing** (1) lest it swallow (2) for having swallowed **77 senseless** insensible. (Suffolk's head is to be put up on display.) **78 Who** which, i.e., the winds. **again** in return **79 the hags of hell** i.e., the Furies **80 affy** betroth. **lord** i.e., King Henry **82 Having** i.e., he, Reignier, having **83 policy** political cunning **84 ambitious Sylla** i.e., Sulla (138–78 B.C.), Roman dictator, notorious for his cruel proceedings against his adversaries **85 gobbets** pieces of raw flesh. **mother's** i.e., England's **87 thorough** through, because of **95 shameful . . . king** i.e., the murder of Richard II by Bolingbroke, who thereupon sidestepped the Yorkist claim and became King Henry IV **98 Advance** raise, display. **half-faced sun** (Edward III's and Richard II's banner displayed the rays of the sun dispersing themselves out of a cloud.) **99 Invitis nubibus** in spite of the clouds

108 Bargulus (A pirate, Bardulis, mentioned in Cicero's *De Officiis*, 2.11.) **109 Drones** beetles, worthless parasites. (The legends referred to here, that beetles suck the blood of eagles and that drone bees rob beehives of honey, are typical of much imaginary natural history during the Renaissance.) **113 of message** as messenger **114 waft** transport, convey **117 Paene . . . artus** cold fear takes hold of my limbs almost entirely **121 fair** courteously **128 And . . . pole** i.e., and rather have my head stuck on a bloodstained pole on London Bridge for treason **129 uncovered** bareheaded **132 Hale** drag **135 bezonians** needy beggars, rascals **136 sworder** gladiator. **banditto** bandit **137 Tully** Cicero. **bastard** (According to an unreliable tradition, Brutus was thought to be Caesar's bastard son.) **138 savage islanders** i.e., inhabitants of Lesbos. (But Plutarch reports, quite to the contrary, that Pompey the Great was stabbed by his former officers at the instigation of Ptolemy, in Egypt after his defeat by Caesar at Pharsalus.)

Pompey the Great; and Suffolk dies by pirates.
                    Exit Walter [Whitmore and others] with Suffolk.
LIEUTENANT
    And as for these whose ransom we have set,
    It is our pleasure one of them depart;
    Therefore [*to the Second Gentleman*] come you with us
    and let him go.   *Exeunt Lieutenant and the rest.* 142
                                    Manet the First Gentleman.

        *Enter Walter [Whitmore] with the body [and
        severed head of Suffolk].*

WHITMORE
    There let his head and lifeless body lie,
    Until the Queen his mistress bury it.   *Exit Walter.*
FIRST GENTLEMAN
    O barbarous and bloody spectacle!
    His body will I bear unto the King.
    If he revenge it not, yet will his friends;   147
    So will the Queen, that living held him dear.   148
                    [*Exit with the body and head.*]

                            ♣

4.2 *Enter [George] Bevis and John Holland, [with long
        staves].*

BEVIS Come, and get thee a sword, though made of a
    lath. They have been up these two days.   2
HOLLAND They have the more need to sleep now, then.   3
BEVIS I tell thee, Jack Cade the clothier means to dress   4
    the commonwealth, and turn it, and set a new nap   5
    upon it.
HOLLAND So he had need, for 'tis threadbare. Well, I   7
    say it was never merry world in England since gentle-
    men came up.   9
BEVIS O miserable age! Virtue is not regarded in handi-   10
    craftsmen.
HOLLAND The nobility think scorn to go in leather   12
    aprons.
BEVIS Nay, more, the King's Council are no good
    workmen.   15
HOLLAND True. And yet it is said, "Labor in thy vocation,"
    which is as much to say as, "Let the magistrates be la-
    boring men." And therefore should we be magistrates.
BEVIS Thou hast hit it, for there's no better sign of a   19
    brave mind than a hard hand.   20

HOLLAND I see them, I see them! There's Best's son,
    the tanner of Wingham—   22
BEVIS He shall have the skins of our enemies to make
    dog's leather of.   24
HOLLAND And Dick the butcher—
BEVIS Then is sin struck down like an ox, and iniquity's
    throat cut like a calf.
HOLLAND And Smith the weaver—
BEVIS Argo, their thread of life is spun.   29
HOLLAND Come, come, let's fall in with them.   30

        *Drum. Enter Cade, Dick [the] butcher, Smith the
        weaver, and a Sawyer, with infinite numbers,
        [bearing long staves].*

CADE We, John Cade, so termed of our supposed   31
    father—
DICK [*aside*] Or rather, of stealing a cade of herrings.   33
CADE For our enemies shall fall before us, inspired   34
    with the spirit of putting down kings and princes—
    command silence.
DICK Silence!
CADE My father was a Mortimer—   38
DICK [*aside*] He was an honest man, and a good
    bricklayer.   40
CADE My mother a Plantagenet—
DICK [*aside*] I knew her well. She was a midwife.
CADE My wife descended of the Lacys—   43
DICK [*aside*] She was, indeed, a peddler's daughter,
    and sold many laces.
SMITH [*aside*] But now of late, not able to travel with 46
    her furred pack, she washes bucks here at home.   47
CADE Therefore am I of an honorable house.
DICK [*aside*] Ay, by my faith, the field is honorable;   49
    and there was he born, under a hedge, for his father
    had never a house but the cage.   51
CADE Valiant I am.
SMITH [*aside*] 'A must needs, for beggary is valiant.   53
CADE I am able to endure much.
DICK [*aside*] No question of that; for I have seen him
    whipped three market days together.   56
CADE I fear neither sword nor fire.
SMITH [*aside*] He need not fear the sword, for his coat
    is of proof.   59

---

142 **him** i.e., the First Gentleman. **s.d. Manet** he remains onstage
147 **his** i.e., Suffolk's **148 living** while he was living
4.2. Location: Blackheath, a heath in Kent near London.
s.d. John Holland (The name of the actor assigned to a bit part in this
scene; probably *George Bevis* is similarly a hired man in the company.) **2 lath** wood strip. (A dagger of lath was often used by the
comic Vice character in morality plays.) **up** i.e., up in arms
3 They . . . then (Holland's joke is that if they've been *up*, awake, for
two days, they must be sleepy.) **4 dress** (1) clothe, array (2) remedy
5 turn (1) turn inside out (as a way of refurbishing old cloth) (2) turn
upside down socially. **nap** (1) fuzz or down on the surface of cloth
(2) surface of the social structure **7 threadbare** (1) shabby (2) down-
at-heels **9 came up** came into fashion, rose to prominence **10 regarded** esteemed **12 think scorn** disdain **15 workmen** (1) laborers
(2) masters of their calling **19 hit it** hit the nail on the head
20 brave noble. **hard** callused

22 **Wingham** a village near Canterbury **24 dog's leather** (Used in the
manufacture of gloves.) **29 Argo** i.e., ergo, therefore **30 s.d. infinite numbers** i.e., as many supers as the theater can provide **31 We**
(The royal "we," fatuously misappropriated.) **so termed of** named
after **33 of** on account of. **cade** barrel, cask **34 For** because. **fall**
(with a pun on the Latin *cado*, I fall) **38 Mortimer** (See 3.1.359 and
note.) **40 bricklayer** (with a play on *Mortimer* and "mortarer")
43 Lacys the family name of the Earls of Lincoln. (But Dick makes an
obvious pun on *laces*.) **46 travel** (suggesting also *travail*, "work")
47 furred pack peddler's pack made of hides turned hair outward
(with a pun on "herd of deer"). **bucks** soiled clothes treated with
buck or lye. (There is a bawdy suggestion of a loose woman, a vagabond's daughter, who has given up streetwalking with her *furred
pack*, her genital organs, to service men [*bucks*] at home.) **49 field**
(1) field in a coat of arms (2) out in the fields **51 cage** prison for
petty malefactors **53 'A must needs** he must be. **valiant** sturdy,
able to work. (Ordinances forbade those who were sturdy to beg.)
56 whipped i.e., for vagabondage **59 of proof** (1) impenetrable,
tried by experience and hence reliable (2) well-worn

DICK [*aside*]   But methinks he should stand in fear of fire, being burnt i' the hand for stealing of sheep.   61

CADE   Be brave, then, for your captain is brave, and vows reformation. There shall be in England seven halfpenny loaves sold for a penny, the three-hooped 64 pot shall have ten hoops, and I will make it felony to 65 drink small beer. All the realm shall be in common, 66 and in Cheapside shall my palfry go to grass. And 67 when I am king, as king I will be—

ALL   God save Your Majesty!

CADE   I thank you, good people—there shall be no money. All shall eat and drink on my score; and I will 71 apparel them all in one livery, that they may agree like brothers and worship me their lord.

DICK   The first thing we do, let's kill all the lawyers.

CADE   Nay, that I mean to do. Is not this a lamentable thing, that of the skin of an innocent lamb should be made parchment? That parchment, being scribbled o'er, should undo a man? Some say the bee stings, but I say 'tis the bee's wax; for I did but seal once to a 79 thing, and I was never mine own man since. How now? Who's there?

Enter [some, bringing forward] a Clerk [of Chartham].

SMITH   The clerk of Chartham. He can write and read 82 and cast account.   83

CADE   O, monstrous!

SMITH   We took him setting of boys' copies.   85

CADE   Here's a villain!

SMITH   H'as a book in his pocket with red letters in 't.   87

CADE   Nay, then, he is a conjurer.

DICK   Nay, he can make obligations and write court 89 hand.   90

CADE   I am sorry for 't. The man is a proper man, of 91 mine honor; unless I find him guilty, he shall not die. Come hither, sirrah, I must examine thee. What is thy name?

CLERK   Emmanuel.   95

DICK   They use to write it on the top of letters. 'Twill go 96 hard with you.

CADE   Let me alone.—Dost thou use to write thy 98 name? Or hast thou a mark to thyself, like an honest, plain-dealing man?

CLERK   Sir, I thank God, I have been so well brought up that I can write my name.

ALL   He hath confessed. Away with him! He's a villain and a traitor.

CADE   Away with him, I say! Hang him with his pen and inkhorn about his neck.   *Exit one with the Clerk.*

Enter Michael.

MICHAEL   Where's our general?

CADE   Here I am, thou particular fellow.   108

MICHAEL   Fly, fly, fly! Sir Humphrey Stafford and his brother are hard by, with the King's forces.

CADE   Stand, villain, stand, or I'll fell thee down. He shall be encountered with a man as good as himself. He is but a knight, is 'a?

MICHAEL   No.   114

CADE   To equal him, I will make myself a knight presently. [*He kneels.*] Rise up Sir John Mortimer. [*He 116 rises.*] Now have at him!   117

Enter Sir Humphrey Stafford and his Brother, with drum and soldiers.

STAFFORD
Rebellious hinds, the filth and scum of Kent,   118
Marked for the gallows, lay your weapons down!
Home to your cottages, forsake this groom.   120
The King is merciful, if you revolt.   121

BROTHER
But angry, wrathful, and inclined to blood
If you go forward. Therefore yield, or die.

CADE
As for these silken-coated slaves, I pass not.   124
It is to you, good people, that I speak,
Over whom, in time to come, I hope to reign;
For I am rightful heir unto the crown.

STAFFORD
Villain, thy father was a plasterer,
And thou thyself a shearman, art thou not?   129

CADE
And Adam was a gardener.

BROTHER   And what of that?

CADE
Marry, this: Edmund Mortimer, Earl of March,
Married the Duke of Clarence' daughter, did he not?

STAFFORD   Ay, sir.

CADE
By her he had two children at one birth.

BROTHER   That's false.

CADE
Ay, there's the question. But I say 'tis true.
The elder of them, being put to nurse,
Was by a beggar-woman stol'n away,
And, ignorant of his birth and parentage,
Became a bricklayer when he came to age.

61 burnt i' the hand branded   **64–65 three-hooped pot** wooden quart-pot made with three metal bands or staves. (A ten-hooped pot would presumably hold a lot more.)   **66 small** weak. (Cade intends that everyone shall drink strong beer.)   **be in common** belong to everyone, be free from enclosure. (See 1.3.23–24 and note.)   **67 Cheapside** chief location for markets in London (which Cade wishes to abolish)   **71 on my score** at my expense   **79 seal** i.e., sign and seal (with sealing wax) a legal agreement   **82 Chartham** a town near Canterbury; or perhaps Chatham, near Rochester   **83 cast account** i.e., do arithmetic   **85 setting . . . copies** setting out passages to be reproduced by schoolboys   **87 H'as** he has.   **book . . . in 't** a schoolbook, probably a primer, with "rubricated" or red-lettered capitals   **89 make obligations** draw up bonds   **89–90 court hand** professional hand used in preparing legal documents   **91 proper** handsome-looking.   **of** upon   **95 Emmanuel** i.e., God with us. (Used frequently as heading for letters and documents.)   **96 use** make it a practice   **98 Let me alone** let me handle this

108 particular private (as opposed to *general* in the previous line)   **114 No** i.e., he is only a knight   **116 presently** immediately   **117 have at him** let me at him.   **s.d. drum** drummer   **118 hinds** peasants   **120 groom** i.e., low wretch   **121 revolt** turn back   **124 pass** care   **129 shearman** one who shears the excess nap (see line 5) from woolen cloth during its manufacture

His son am I. Deny it if you can.

DICK
Nay, 'tis too true. Therefore he shall be king.   142

SMITH   Sir, he made a chimney in my father's house,   143
and the bricks are alive at this day to testify it.
Therefore deny it not.

STAFFORD
And will you credit this base drudge's words,
That speaks he knows not what?

ALL
Ay, marry, will we. Therefore get ye gone.

BROTHER
Jack Cade, the Duke of York hath taught you this.

CADE [aside]   He lies, for I invented it myself.—Go to,
sirrah, tell the King from me that for his father's
sake, Henry the Fifth, in whose time boys went to
span-counter for French crowns, I am content he   153
shall reign; but I'll be Protector over him.

DICK   And furthermore, we'll have the Lord Saye's   155
head for selling the dukedom of Maine.

CADE   And good reason; for thereby is England
mained, and fain to go with a staff, but that my   158
puissance holds it up. Fellow kings, I tell you that that   159
Lord Saye hath gelded the commonwealth and made
it an eunuch; and more than that, he can speak
French, and therefore he is a traitor.

STAFFORD
O gross and miserable ignorance!

CADE   Nay, answer, if you can. The Frenchmen are our
enemies. Go to, then, I ask but this: can he that speaks
with the tongue of an enemy be a good counselor,
or no?

ALL   No, no! And therefore we'll have his head.

BROTHER [to Stafford]
Well, seeing gentle words will not prevail,
Assail them with the army of the King.

STAFFORD
Herald, away, and throughout every town
Proclaim them traitors that are up with Cade,
That those which fly before the battle ends   173
May, even in their wives' and children's sight,
Be hanged up for example at their doors.
And you that be the King's friends, follow me.
Exeunt [the two Staffords, and soldiers].

CADE
And you that love the commons, follow me.
Now show yourselves men; 'tis for liberty!
We will not leave one lord, one gentleman;
Spare none but such as go in clouted shoon,   180
For they are thrifty honest men and such
As would, but that they dare not, take our parts.

DICK   They are all in order and march toward us.   183

CADE   But then are we in order when we are most out
of order. Come, march forward.   [Exeunt.]

4.3   *Alarums to the fight, wherein both the Staffords
are slain. Enter Cade and the rest.*

CADE   Where's Dick, the butcher of Ashford?

DICK   Here, sir.

CADE   They fell before thee like sheep and oxen, and
thou behavedst thyself as if thou hadst been in thine
own slaughterhouse. Therefore thus will I reward
thee: the Lent shall be as long again as it is, and thou   6
shalt have a license to kill for a hundred lacking one.   7

DICK   I desire no more.

CADE   And, to speak truth, thou deserv'st no less. This
monument of the victory will I bear [putting on Sir   10
Humphrey's armor]; and the bodies shall be dragged at
my horse heels till I do come to London, where we
will have the Mayor's sword borne before us.

DICK   If we mean to thrive and do good, break open the   14
jails and let out the prisoners.

CADE   Fear not that, I warrant thee. Come, let's march   16
towards London.   *Exeunt [with the Staffords' bodies].*

❖

4.4   *Enter the King with a supplication, and the Queen
with Suffolk's head, the Duke of Buckingham, and
the Lord Saye.*

QUEEN [to herself]
Oft have I heard that grief softens the mind
And makes it fearful and degenerate.
Think therefore on revenge and cease to weep.
But who can cease to weep and look on this?
Here may his head lie on my throbbing breast,
But where's the body that I should embrace?

BUCKINGHAM   What answer makes Your Grace to the
rebels' supplication?

KING
I'll send some holy bishop to entreat,
For God forbid so many simple souls
Should perish by the sword! And I myself,
Rather than bloody war shall cut them short,
Will parley with Jack Cade their general.
But stay, I'll read it over once again.   [He reads.]

---

142 **too** very   143 **he** i.e., Cade's father   153 **span-counter** a boys'
game, in which one throws a counter or a piece of money that the
other wins if he can throw another that hits it or falls within a span
(nine inches) of it.   **crowns** (1) coins (2) kingdoms   155 **Lord Saye** (A
peer implicated with Suffolk in the loss of Anjou and Maine.)
158 **mained** maimed (with a pun on *Maine*).   **fain to go** obliged to
walk   158–159 **but . . . puissance** were it not that my power
173 **That . . . fly** i.e., so that those cowardly traitors who will surely
flee   180 **clouted shoon** hobnailed or patched shoes

183 **in order** in battle array. (But Cade, in reply, plays on the contrast
between public order and rebellion.)
4.3. Location: Scene continues at Blackheath.
s.d. (The bodies of the slain Staffords must be removed at some point.)
6–7 **Lent . . . one** (For Dick the butcher's benefit, Cade proposes to
double the length of Lent, during which animals could be butchered
only by special license in order to supply the sick and others with
particular needs; during this period, Dick is to have license to kill
ninety-nine animals a week, or to supply ninety-nine persons, or for
ninety-nine years.)   10 **monument** memorial   14 **do good** succeed
16 **Fear** doubt
4.4. Location: London. The royal court.

QUEEN [*to herself*]
Ah, barbarous villains! Hath this lovely face
Ruled, like a wandering planet, over me,   16
And could it not enforce them to relent
That were unworthy to behold the same?

KING
Lord Saye, Jack Cade hath sworn to have thy head.

SAYE
Ay, but I hope Your Highness shall have his.

KING   How now, madam?
Still lamenting and mourning for Suffolk's death?
I fear me, love, if that I had been dead,
Thou wouldst not have mourned so much for me.

QUEEN
No, my love, I should not mourn, but die for thee.

Enter a Messenger.

KING
How now, what news? Why com'st thou in such
   haste?

FIRST MESSENGER
The rebels are in Southwark. Fly, my lord!   27
Jack Cade proclaims himself Lord Mortimer,
Descended from the Duke of Clarence' house,
And calls Your Grace usurper, openly,
And vows to crown himself in Westminster.
His army is a ragged multitude
Of hinds and peasants, rude and merciless.
Sir Humphrey Stafford and his brother's death
Hath given them heart and courage to proceed.
All scholars, lawyers, courtiers, gentlemen,
They call false caterpillars and intend their death.

KING
O graceless men! They know not what they do.   38

BUCKINGHAM
My gracious lord, retire to Killingworth   39
Until a power be raised to put them down.   40

QUEEN
Ah, were the Duke of Suffolk now alive,
These Kentish rebels would be soon appeased!   42

KING
Lord Saye, the traitors hateth thee;
Therefore away with us to Killingworth.

SAYE
So might Your Grace's person be in danger.
The sight of me is odious in their eyes;
And therefore in this city will I stay
And live alone as secret as I may.

Enter another Messenger.

SECOND MESSENGER
Jack Cade hath gotten London Bridge!
The citizens fly and forsake their houses.
The rascal people, thirsting after prey,
Join with the traitor, and they jointly swear

To spoil the city and your royal court.   53

BUCKINGHAM
Then linger not, my lord. Away, take horse!

KING
Come, Margaret. God, our hope, will succor us.

QUEEN
My hope is gone, now Suffolk is deceased.

KING [*to Saye*]
Farewell, my lord. Trust not the Kentish rebels.

BUCKINGHAM
Trust nobody, for fear you be betrayed.

SAYE
The trust I have is in mine innocence,
And therefore am I bold and resolute.   *Exeunt.*

❖

4.5   *Enter Lord Scales upon the Tower, walking. Then
        enter two or three Citizens below.*

SCALES   How now, is Jack Cade slain?

FIRST CITIZEN   No, my lord, nor likely to be slain; for
   they have won the bridge, killing all those that withstand them. The Lord Mayor craves aid of your honor
   from the Tower to defend the city from the rebels.

SCALES
Such aid as I can spare you shall command.
But I am troubled here with them myself;
The rebels have essayed to win the Tower.
But get you to Smithfield and gather head,   9
And thither I will send you Matthew Gough.
Fight for your king, your country, and your lives.
And so, farewell, for I must hence again.   *Exeunt.*

❖

4.6   *Enter Jack Cade and the rest, and strikes his staff
        on London Stone.*

CADE   Now is Mortimer lord of this city. And here,
   sitting upon London Stone, I charge and command
   that, of the city's cost, the Pissing Conduit run nothing   3
   but claret wine this first year of our reign. And now
   henceforward it shall be treason for any that calls me
   other than Lord Mortimer.

Enter a Soldier, running.

SOLDIER   Jack Cade! Jack Cade!

CADE   Knock him down there.   *They kill him.*

SMITH   If this fellow be wise, he'll never call ye Jack
   Cade more. I think he hath a very fair warning.

---

16 **wandering** i.e., not fixed, like the stars   27 **Southwark** suburb on
the south bank of the Thames, just across the river from London
38 **They . . . do** (An echo of Christ's "Father, forgive them, for they
know not what they do," Luke 23:34.)   39 **Killingworth** Kenilworth
(in Warwickshire)   40 **power** army   42 **appeased** pacified

53 **spoil** despoil, sack
4.5. Location: The Tower of London.
s.d. upon the Tower i.e., probably in the rear gallery above the main
stage   9 **Smithfield** area of open fields to the northwest, just outside
London's walls.   **head** an armed force
4.6. Location: London.
s.d. London Stone ancient landmark, located in Cannon Street   3 **of**
at.   **Pissing Conduit** popular name of a conduit, or common fountain,
near the Royal Exchange

DICK   My lord, there's an army gathered together in Smithfield.

CADE   Zounds, then, let's go fight with them. But first go and set London Bridge on fire, and, if you can, burn down the Tower too. Come, let's away.

Exeunt omnes.

4.7

Alarums. Matthew Gough is slain, and all the rest. Then enter Jack Cade, with his company.

CADE   So, sirs. Now go some and pull down the Savoy; 1
others to th' Inns of Court. Down with them all. 2

DICK   I have a suit unto your lordship.

CADE   Be it a lordship, thou shalt have it for that word. 4

DICK   Only that the laws of England may come out of your mouth.

HOLLAND *[aside]*   Mass, 'twill be sore law then, for he was thrust in the mouth with a spear, and 'tis not whole yet.

SMITH *[aside]*   Nay, John, it will be stinking law, for his breath stinks with eating toasted cheese.

CADE   I have thought upon it. It shall be so. Away! Burn all the records of the realm. My mouth shall be the Parliament of England.

HOLLAND *[aside]*   Then we are like to have biting statutes, unless his teeth be pulled out.

CADE   And henceforward all things shall be in common.

Enter a Messenger.

MESSENGER   My lord, a prize, a prize! Here's the Lord Saye, which sold the towns in France; he that made us pay one-and-twenty fifteens, and one shilling to the 20
pound, the last subsidy. 21

Enter George [Bevis], with the Lord Saye.

CADE   Well, he shall be beheaded for it ten times.—Ah, thou say, thou serge, nay, thou buckram lord! Now 23
art thou within point-blank of our jurisdiction regal. 24
What canst thou answer to My Majesty for giving up of Normandy unto Monsieur Basimecu, the Dau- 26
phin of France? Be it known unto thee by these 27
presence, even the presence of Lord Mortimer, that I 28
am the besom that must sweep the court clean of such 29
filth as thou art. Thou hast most traitorously corrupted

the youth of the realm in erecting a grammar school; and whereas, before, our forefathers had no other books but the score and the tally, thou hast caused 33
printing to be used, and contrary to the King his crown 34
and dignity thou hast built a paper mill. It will be proved to thy face that thou hast men about thee that usually talk of a noun and a verb and such abomin- 37
able words as no Christian ear can endure to hear. Thou hast appointed justices of peace to call poor men be- fore them about matters they were not able to answer. Moreover, thou hast put them in prison, and because they could not read thou hast hanged them, when in- 42
deed only for that cause they have been most worthy to 43
live. Thou dost ride on a footcloth, dost thou not? 44

SAYE   What of that?

CADE   Marry, thou oughtst not to let thy horse wear a cloak, when honester men than thou go in their hose 47
and doublets. 48

DICK   And work in their shirt too—as myself, for example, that am a butcher.

SAYE   You men of Kent—

DICK   What say you of Kent?

SAYE   Nothing but this: 'tis *bona terra, mala gens.* 53

CADE   Away with him, away with him! He speaks Latin.

SAYE

Hear me but speak, and bear me where you will.
Kent, in the *Commentaries* Caesar writ,
Is termed the civil'st place of all this isle.
Sweet is the country, because full of riches,
The people liberal, valiant, active, wealthy, 60
Which makes me hope you are not void of pity.
I sold not Maine, I lost not Normandy,
Yet to recover them would lose my life.
Justice with favor have I always done; 64
Prayers and tears have moved me, gifts could never.
When have I aught exacted at your hands 66
But to maintain the King, the realm, and you?
Large gifts have I bestowed on learnèd clerks, 68
Because my book preferred me to the King; 69
And, seeing ignorance is the curse of God,
Knowledge the wing wherewith we fly to heaven,
Unless you be possessed with devilish spirits
You cannot but forbear to murder me.
This tongue hath parleyed unto foreign kings 74
For your behoof— 75

4.7. Location: London. The rebellion continues. (The historical location moves from Cannon Street to Smithfield, but onstage the action is continuous.)
s.d. all the rest i.e., the King's forces. (The bodies of Gough and other slain must be removed at some point.) **1 the Savoy** (This palace, res- idence of the Duke of Lancaster, was actually destroyed during Wat Tyler's rebellion in 1381 and was not rebuilt until the sixteenth cen- tury.) **2 Inns of Court** sets of buildings in London belonging to legal societies training persons in the law **4 lordship** title and estates of a noble lord (playing on the honorific *your lordship* in line 3, by which Cade is flattered) **20–21 one . . . pound** (An exaggeratedly inflated estimate of personal property.) **21 subsidy** tax levied on special oc- casions; see 1.1.131–134.) **23 say, serge, buckram** kinds of cloth, of silk, wool, and coarse linen, respectively (with a pun on "say/ Saye") **24 point-blank** so close that a missile will travel straight to the target **26 Basimecu** *baise mon cul* (French), "kiss my ass" **27– 28 these presence** i.e., Cade's error, or joke, for "these presents, this present document." (A legal phrase.) **29 besom** broom

33 score . . . tally means of reckoning accounts or keeping score, in which a stick was notched and then split lengthwise, thereby giving both debtor and creditor a record of what was owed **34 printing** (An anachronism; the first printing press was set up in England twenty- seven years after Cade's rebellion, and the first paper mill was set up in 1495.) **King his** King's **37 usually** habitually **42 could not read** i.e., could not demonstrate their literacy in Latin and thereby claim exemption from criminal prosecution through "benefit of clergy" **43 only . . . cause** for that reason alone **44 footcloth** richly orna- mented horse covering; see the note for 4.1.54 **47–48 hose and doublets** breeches and jacket (without a cloak) **53 bona . . . gens** good land, bad people **60 liberal** generous, free, refined **64 favor** compassion **66 aught . . . hands** taken any taxes from you (in my capacity as Lord Treasurer) **68 clerks** scholars **69 book** learning. **preferred . . . King** gave me advancement at court **74 parleyed unto** entered into negotiations with **75 behoof** benefit

CADE Tut, when struck'st thou one blow in the field?

SAYE

Great men have reaching hands. Oft have I struck   77
Those that I never saw, and struck them dead.

BEVIS O monstrous coward! What, to come behind
folks?

SAYE

These cheeks are pale for watching for your good.   81

CADE Give him a box o' the ear, and that will make 'em
red again.

SAYE

Long sitting to determine poor men's causes   84
Hath made me full of sickness and diseases.

CADE Ye shall have a hempen caudle, then, and the   86
help of hatchet.   87

DICK Why dost thou quiver, man?

SAYE

The palsy, and not fear, provokes me.

CADE Nay, he nods at us, as who should say, "I'll be   90
even with you." I'll see if his head will stand steadier
on a pole or no. Take him away and behead him.

SAYE

Tell me wherein have I offended most?
Have I affected wealth or honor? Speak.   94
Are my chests filled up with extorted gold?
Is my apparel sumptuous to behold?
Whom have I injured, that ye seek my death?
These hands are free from guiltless blood-shedding,   98
This breast from harboring foul deceitful thoughts.
O, let me live!

CADE [aside] I feel remorse in myself with his words,
but I'll bridle it. He shall die, an it be but for   102
pleading so well for his life.—Away with him! He
has a familiar under his tongue; he speaks not i'   104
God's name. Go, take him away, I say, and strike
off his head presently; and then break into his   106
son-in-law's house, Sir James Cromer, and strike off
his head, and bring them both upon two poles hither.

ALL It shall be done.

SAYE

Ah, countrymen! If when you make your prayers,
God should be so obdurate as yourselves,
How would it fare with your departed souls?   112
And therefore yet relent, and save my life.

CADE

Away with him! And do as I command ye.
      [Exeunt some with Lord Saye.]
The proudest peer in the realm shall not wear a head
on his shoulders unless he pay me tribute. There shall
not a maid be married but she shall pay to me her

maidenhead ere they have it. Men shall hold of me *in*   118
capite; and we charge and command that their wives   119
be as free as heart can wish or tongue can tell.   120

DICK My lord, when shall we go to Cheapside and take   121
up commodities upon our bills?   122

CADE Marry, presently.

ALL O, brave!   124

Enter one with the heads [of Lord Saye and Sir
John Cromer upon two poles].

CADE But is not this braver? Let them kiss one another,
for they loved well when they were alive. [*The heads*
are made to touch one another.] Now part them again,
lest they consult about the giving up of some more
towns in France. Soldiers, defer the spoil of the city   129
until night, for with these borne before us instead of
maces will we ride through the streets, and at every   131
corner have them kiss. Away!   *Exeunt.*

4.8 *Alarum and retreat. Enter again Cade and all his*
rabblement.

CADE Up Fish Street! Down Saint Magnus' Corner! Kill   1
and knock down! Throw them into Thames! (*Sound a*
parley.) What noise is this I hear? Dare any be so bold   3
to sound retreat or parley when I command them kill?

Enter Buckingham and old Clifford [attended].

BUCKINGHAM

Ay, here they be that dare and will disturb thee.
Know, Cade, we come ambassadors from the King
Unto the commons, whom thou hast misled,
And here pronounce free pardon to them all   8
That will forsake thee and go home in peace.

CLIFFORD

What say ye, countrymen? Will ye relent,
And yield to mercy whilst 'tis offered you,
Or let a rebel lead you to your deaths?
Who loves the King and will embrace his pardon,   13
Fling up his cap and say "God save His Majesty!"
Who hateth him and honors not his father,
Henry the Fifth, that made all France to quake,
Shake he his weapon at us and pass by.   17

77 **reaching** far-reaching 81 **for watching** from remaining awake, on
watch 84 **sitting** i.e., on the judge's bench. **determine** settle, decide 86 **caudle** warm gruel, given to sick people. (*Hempen caudle*
means that his restorative is to be a hanging.) 86–87 **the help of**
hatchet i.e., the assistance of the executioner's ax. (Possibly a variant
of, or error for, "pap with a hatchet," the administering of punishment under the ironical guise of kindly correction.) 90 **as who**
should as one might 94 **affected** preferred, striven for 98 **guiltless**
blood-shedding shedding of guiltless blood 102 **an it be but** if only
104 **familiar** familiar spirit, attendant demon 106 **presently** immediately 112 **your departed souls** your souls when you die

118 **maidenhead** (Cade claims the *droit de seigneur,* presumed customary right of a feudal lord to be the first to enjoy a bride sexually
on her marriage night.) **hold** hold property 118–119 **in capite** as
tenant in chief, i.e., directly from the crown. (The Latin *caput,*
"head," also puns on *maidenhead.*) 120 **free** (1) legally unencum-
bered (2) licentious 121–122 **take . . . bills** obtain goods on credit
(with a pun on *bills,* military weapons having wooden handles and a
blade or ax-shaped head) 124 **brave** fine, splendid 129 **spoil** plundering 131 **maces** staves of office carried by sergeants
4.8. Location: Southwark. The rebellion continues. (The historical location moves from Smithfield to Southwark, but the onstage action is
uninterrupted.)
s.d. retreat signal to cease attack 1 **Fish Street, Saint Magnus' Cor-**
ner locations in London near London Bridge, directly across from
Southwark 3 **s.d. parley** trumpet signal requesting a conference between the contending forces. (Also in line 4.) 8 **pronounce** proclaim
13 **Who** anyone who. (Also in line 15.) 17 **Shake he** let him shake
(in a gesture of defiance)

ALL   God save the King! God save the King!

[*They fling up their caps.*]

CADE   What, Buckingham and Clifford, are ye so brave? 19
And you, base peasants, do ye believe him? Will you
needs be hanged with your pardons about your necks? 21
Hath my sword therefore broke through London
gates, that you should leave me at the White Hart in 23
Southwark? I thought ye would never have given out 24
these arms till you had recovered your ancient freedom. But you are all recreants and dastards, and de- 26
light to live in slavery to the nobility. Let them break
your backs with burdens, take your houses over your
heads, ravish your wives and daughters before your
faces. For me, I will make shift for one, and so God's 30
curse light upon you all!

ALL   We'll follow Cade, we'll follow Cade!

CLIFFORD
Is Cade the son of Henry the Fifth,
That thus you do exclaim you'll go with him?
Will he conduct you through the heart of France
And make the meanest of you earls and dukes? 36
Alas, he hath no home, no place to fly to,
Nor knows he how to live but by the spoil, 38
Unless by robbing of your friends and us.
Were 't not a shame that, whilst you live at jar, 40
The fearful French, whom you late vanquishèd, 41
Should make a start o'er seas and vanquish you? 42
Methinks already in this civil broil
I see them lording it in London streets,
Crying *"Villiago!"* unto all they meet. 45
Better ten thousand baseborn Cades miscarry 46
Than you should stoop unto a Frenchman's mercy.
To France, to France, and get what you have lost!
Spare England, for it is your native coast.
Henry hath money; you are strong and manly;
God on our side, doubt not of victory.

ALL   A Clifford! A Clifford! We'll follow the King and 52
Clifford!

CADE [*aside*]   Was ever feather so lightly blown to and
fro as this multitude? The name of Henry the Fifth
hales them to an hundred mischiefs and makes them 56
leave me desolate. I see them lay their heads together
to surprise me. My sword make way for me, for here 58
is no staying.—In despite of the devils and hell, have 59
through the very middest of you! And heavens and 60
honor be witness that no want of resolution in me, but
only my followers' base and ignominious treasons,
makes me betake me to my heels. 63

Exit [*Cade, running through the crowd,
weapon in hand*].

BUCKINGHAM
What, is he fled? Go some, and follow him,
And he that brings his head unto the King
Shall have a thousand crowns for his reward.

Exeunt some of them.

Follow me, soldiers. We'll devise a means
To reconcile you all unto the King.   *Exeunt omnes.*

❖

4.9   *Sound trumpets. Enter King, Queen, and
Somerset, on the terrace [aloft].*

KING
Was ever king that joyed an earthly throne   1
And could command no more content than I?
No sooner was I crept out of my cradle
But I was made a king, at nine months old.
Was never subject longed to be a king
As I do long and wish to be a subject.

Enter Buckingham and [old] Clifford.

BUCKINGHAM
Health and glad tidings to Your Majesty!

KING
Why, Buckingham, is the traitor Cade surprised?   8
Or is he but retired to make him strong?

*Enter [below] multitudes, with halters about their
necks.*

CLIFFORD
He is fled, my lord, and all his powers do yield,   10
And humbly thus, with halters on their necks,
Expect Your Highness' doom, of life or death.   12

KING
Then, heaven, set ope thy everlasting gates
To entertain my vows of thanks and praise!   14
Soldiers, this day have you redeemed your lives
And showed how well you love your prince and
country.
Continue still in this so good a mind,
And Henry, though he be infortunate,
Assure yourselves, will never be unkind.
And so, with thanks and pardon to you all,
I do dismiss you to your several countries.   21

ALL   God save the King! God save the King!

[*Exeunt the multitudes.*]

Enter a Messenger.

19 **brave** haughty   21 **pardons . . . necks** (because the pardons
would be not only worthless but also the very means of their hanging)
23 **that** to the end that.   **White Hart** a famous inn in Southwark
24 **out** up   26 **recreants** those who break faith, cowards   30 **For** as
for.   **make shift for one** manage for myself   36 **meanest** lowest born
38 **the spoil** pillaging   40 **at jar** in discord   41 **fearful** timid.   **late**
lately   42 **make a start** suddenly arouse themselves   45 **Villiago** rascal, villain. (Italian.)   46 **miscarry** encounter misfortune   52 **A Clifford** rally to Clifford   56 **hales** draws   58 **surprise** capture   59 **despite** spite   59–60 **have through** i.e., here I come through   63 **s.d.
Exit** (In the Quarto version, Cade "runs through them with his staff
and flies away.")

4.9. **Location:** A castle, historically identified as Kenilworth Castle in
Warwickshire, though in the theater we only know that the King receives the submission of the rebels shortly after the fighting in London.
s.d. on the terrace i.e., probably in the gallery to the rear above the
main stage   1 **joyed** enjoyed   8 **surprised** captured   10 **powers**
troops. (Also at line 25.)   12 **Expect** await.   **doom** judgment   14 **entertain** receive   21 **several countries** various localities

MESSENGER
Please it Your Grace to be advertisèd   23
The Duke of York is newly come from Ireland,
And with a puissant and a mighty power
Of gallowglasses and stout kerns   26
Is marching hitherward in proud array,
And still proclaimeth, as he comes along,   28
His arms are only to remove from thee
The Duke of Somerset, whom he terms a traitor.

KING
Thus stands my state, twixt Cade and York
    distressed,
Like to a ship that, having scaped a tempest,
Is straightway calmed and boarded with a pirate.   33
But now is Cade driven back, his men dispersed,   34
And now is York in arms to second him.
I pray thee, Buckingham, go and meet him,
And ask him what's the reason of these arms.
Tell him I'll send Duke Edmund to the Tower;   38
And, Somerset, we will commit thee thither,
Until his army be dismissed from him.

SOMERSET   My lord,
I'll yield myself to prison willingly,
Or unto death, to do my country good.

KING [to Buckingham]
In any case, be not too rough in terms,
For he is fierce and cannot brook hard language.   45

BUCKINGHAM
I will, my lord, and doubt not so to deal
As all things shall redound unto your good.

KING
Come, wife, let's in, and learn to govern better,
For yet may England curse my wretched reign.   49
                          Flourish. Exeunt.

❖

4.10   *Enter Cade.*

CADE   Fie on ambitions! Fie on myself, that have a
sword and yet am ready to famish! These five days
have I hid me in these woods and durst not peep out,
for all the country is laid for me. But now am I so   4
hungry that, if I might have a lease of my life for a
thousand years, I could stay no longer. Wherefore, o'er 6
a brick wall have I climbed into this garden to see if I
can eat grass or pick a sallet another while, which is   8
not amiss to cool a man's stomach this hot weather.
And I think this word "sallet" was born to do me
good; for many a time, but for a sallet, my brainpan
had been cleft with a brown bill; and many a time,   12
when I have been dry and bravely marching, it hath

served me instead of a quart pot to drink in; and now
the word "sallet" must serve me to feed on.   15

Enter Iden [and his men].

IDEN
Lord, who would live turmoilèd in the court,
And may enjoy such quiet walks as these?
This small inheritance my father left me
Contenteth me, and worth a monarchy.
I seek not to wax great by others' waning,
Or gather wealth, I care not with what envy.
Sufficeth that I have maintains my state   22
And sends the poor well pleasèd from my gate.   23

CADE [*aside*]   Zounds, here's the lord of the soil come to
seize me for a stray, for entering his fee simple without 25
leave.—Ah, villain, thou wilt betray me and get a
thousand crowns of the King by carrying my head to
him; but I'll make thee eat iron like an ostrich and
swallow my sword like a great pin, ere thou and I part.

IDEN
Why, rude companion, whatsoe'er thou be,   30
I know thee not. Why then should I betray thee?
Is 't not enough to break into my garden,
And like a thief to come to rob my grounds,
Climbing my walls in spite of me the owner,
But thou wilt brave me with these saucy terms?   35

CADE   Brave thee? Ay, by the best blood that ever was   36
broached, and beard thee too. Look on me well. I have 37
eat no meat these five days, yet come thou and thy   38
five men, an if I do not leave you all as dead as a
doornail, I pray God I may never eat grass more.

IDEN
Nay, it shall ne'er be said, while England stands,
That Alexander Iden, an esquire of Kent,
Took odds to combat a poor famished man.   43
Oppose thy steadfast-gazing eyes to mine;
See if thou canst outface me with thy looks.
Set limb to limb, and thou art far the lesser;   46
Thy hand is but a finger to my fist,
Thy leg a stick comparèd with this truncheon;   48
My foot shall fight with all the strength thou hast;
And if mine arm be heavèd in the air,   50
Thy grave is digged already in the earth.   51
As for words, whose greatness answers words,   52
Let this my sword report what speech forbears.   53

CADE   By my valor, the most complete champion that   54
ever I heard! Steel, if thou turn the edge, or cut not out 55

---

23 **advertisèd** informed   26 **gallowglasses, kerns** Irish horsemen and
foot soldiers, armed with heavy and light weapons, respectively
28 **still** continually   33 **calmed** becalmed.   **with** by   34 **But now**
even now, just now   38 **Duke Edmund** i.e., Edmund Beaufort, the
Duke of Somerset   45 **brook** endure   49 **yet** until now
4.10. Location: Kent. Iden's garden.
4 **is laid** is lying in wait   6 **stay** wait   8 **sallet** salad greens (with a
pun in the following lines on *sallet*, "light helmet")   12 **brown bill**
brown-handled weapon with a blade or ax-shaped head

15 **s.d. and his men** (The Quarto reads, "Enter Jack Cade at one door,
and at the other Master Alexander Eyden and his men," and at lines
38–39 Cade refers to Iden's "five men.")   22 **Sufficeth . . . state** it
suffices that what I have supports my manner of life   23 **And . . .
gate** i.e., and also provides enough to feed the poor who come to my
gate   25 **stray** trespasser.   **fee simple** estate belonging to an owner
and his heirs forever   30 **rude companion** base fellow   35 **brave**
defy, taunt.   **saucy** insolent   36 **best blood** i.e., Christ's blood
37 **broached** tapped, shed.   **beard** defy   38 **eat** eaten. (Pronounced
"et.")   43 **odds** advantage   46 **Set** compare   48 **truncheon** heavy
staff (i.e., Iden's leg)   50–51 **And . . . earth** i.e., if I but lift my arm,
you're as good as dead already   52 **whose . . . words** i.e., I whose
might is more than a match for your words   53 **report . . . forbears**
i.e., speak through actions in place of words   54 **complete** accomplished   55 **turn the edge** fail to cut

the burly-boned clown in chines of beef ere thou sleep 56
in thy sheath, I beseech God on my knees thou mayst
be turned to hobnails.   *Here they fight. [Cade falls.]* 58
O, I am slain! Famine and no other hath slain me. Let
ten thousand devils come against me, and give me but
the ten meals I have lost, and I'd defy them all. Wither,
garden, and be henceforth a burying place to all that
do dwell in this house, because the unconquered soul
of Cade is fled.

IDEN
Is 't Cade that I have slain, that monstrous traitor?
Sword, I will hallow thee for this thy deed
And hang thee o'er my tomb when I am dead.
Ne'er shall this blood be wipèd from thy point,
But thou shalt wear it as a herald's coat
To emblaze the honor that thy master got.   70

CADE   Iden, farewell, and be proud of thy victory. Tell
Kent from me she hath lost her best man, and exhort
all the world to be cowards; for I, that never feared
any, am vanquished by famine, not by valor.   *Dies.*

IDEN
How much thou wrong'st me, heaven be my judge.
Die, damnèd wretch, the curse of her that bare thee! 76
And as I thrust thy body in with my sword,
                              [stabbing Cade's body]
So wish I, I might thrust thy soul to hell.
Hence will I drag thee headlong by the heels   79
Unto a dunghill, which shall be thy grave,
And there cut off thy most ungracious head,
Which I will bear in triumph to the King,
Leaving thy trunk for crows to feed upon.
                   Exit, [dragging out the body].

❧

5.1   *Enter York and his army of Irish, with drum and*
        colors.

YORK
From Ireland thus comes York to claim his right
And pluck the crown from feeble Henry's head.
Ring, bells, aloud! Burn, bonfires, clear and bright
To entertain great England's lawful king!   4
Ah, *sancta maiestas,* who would not buy thee dear?   5
Let them obey that knows not how to rule;
This hand was made to handle naught but gold.
I cannot give due action to my words
Except a sword or scepter balance it.   9

A scepter shall it have, have I a soul,   10
On which I'll toss the flower-de-luce of France.   11

   Enter Buckingham.

Whom have we here? Buckingham, to disturb me?
The King hath sent him, sure. I must dissemble.
BUCKINGHAM
York, if thou meanest well, I greet thee well.
YORK
Humphrey of Buckingham, I accept thy greeting.
Art thou a messenger, or come of pleasure?
BUCKINGHAM
A messenger from Henry, our dread liege,
To know the reason of these arms in peace;
Or why thou, being a subject as I am,
Against thy oath and true allegiance sworn
Should raise so great a power without his leave,   21
Or dare to bring thy force so near the court.
YORK *[aside]*
Scarce can I speak, my choler is so great.
O, I could hew up rocks and fight with flint,
I am so angry at these abject terms!   25
And now, like Ajax Telamonius,   26
On sheep or oxen could I spend my fury.
I am far better born than is the King,
More like a king, more kingly in my thoughts.
But I must make fair weather yet awhile,   30
Till Henry be more weak and I more strong.—
Buckingham, I prithee, pardon me,
That I have given no answer all this while;
My mind was troubled with deep melancholy.
The cause why I have brought this army hither
Is to remove proud Somerset from the King,
Seditious to His Grace and to the state.
BUCKINGHAM
That is too much presumption on thy part.
But if thy arms be to no other end,
The King hath yielded unto thy demand:
The Duke of Somerset is in the Tower.
YORK
Upon thine honor, is he prisoner?
BUCKINGHAM
Upon mine honor, he is prisoner.
YORK
Then, Buckingham, I do dismiss my powers.
Soldiers, I thank you all. Disperse yourselves;
Meet me tomorrow in Saint George's field;   46
You shall have pay and everything you wish.
                          [Exeunt soldiers.]

---

56 **chines** roasts   58 **turned to hobnails** i.e., melted down and recast
as boot nails   70 **emblaze** proclaim as by a heraldic device   76 **her**
i.e., your mother.   **bare** bore, gave birth to   79 **headlong** precipi-
tately

5.1. **Location:** In the theater, Act 5 appears to take place in one continuous sweep, though historically the action begins between Dart-
ford and Blackheath just southeast of London in 1452–1453 (see
line 46) and then shifts to a battlefield between London and St. Albans, near the Castle Inn, in 1455.

s.d. drum and colors drummer and flag bearer   4 **entertain** welcome
5 **sancta maiestas** sacred majesty   9 **Except** unless.   **balance it** i.e.,
give due weight to my action

10 **have I** i.e., just as sure as I have   11 **On which** i.e., my sword-
holding hand, my action. (The *it* of line 10.)   **toss** carry aloft on the
point of a sword.   **flower-de-luce** the heraldic emblem of France's
royal coat of arms   21 **power** armed force   25 **abject terms** degrading, insulting words   26 **Ajax Telamonius** Ajax, the son of Telamon,
one of the Greek heroes of the Trojan War, who, when the weapons
of Achilles were allotted to Odysseus, slaughtered in his fury a flock
of sheep, mistaking them for the enemy   30 **make fair weather** i.e.,
dissemble   46 **Saint George's field** an open area south of the Thames
River near Southwark

And let my sovereign, virtuous Henry,
Command my eldest son, nay, all my sons,   49
As pledges of my fealty and love;   50
I'll send them all as willing as I live.
Lands, goods, horse, armor, anything I have
Is his to use, so Somerset may die.   53

BUCKINGHAM
York, I commend this kind submission.
We twain will go into His Highness' tent.
                               [*They walk arm in arm.*]

Enter King and attendants.

KING
Buckingham, doth York intend no harm to us,
That thus he marcheth with thee arm in arm?

YORK
In all submission and humility
York doth present himself unto Your Highness.

KING
Then what intends these forces thou dost bring?

YORK
To heave the traitor Somerset from hence
And fight against that monstrous rebel Cade,
Who since I heard to be discomfited.   63

Enter Iden, with Cade's head.

IDEN
If one so rude and of so mean condition   64
May pass into the presence of a king,
Lo, I present Your Grace a traitor's head,
The head of Cade, whom I in combat slew.

KING
The head of Cade? Great God, how just art Thou!
O, let me view his visage, being dead,
That living wrought me such exceeding trouble.
Tell me, my friend, art thou the man that slew him?

IDEN   I was, an 't like Your Majesty.   72

KING
How art thou called, and what is thy degree?   73

IDEN
Alexander Iden, that's my name,
A poor esquire of Kent that loves his king.

BUCKINGHAM [*to the King*]
So please it you, my lord, 'twere not amiss
He were created knight for his good service.

KING
Iden, kneel down. [*He kneels.*] Rise up a knight.
                                      [*Iden rises.*]
We give thee for reward a thousand marks,   79
And will that thou henceforth attend on us.   80

IDEN
May Iden live to merit such a bounty,
And never live but true unto his liege!

Enter Queen and Somerset.

49 Command demand   50 pledges hostages   53 so as long as
63 discomfited routed   64 rude uncultivated. mean condition low
rank   72 an 't like if it please   73 degree social rank   79 marks (Valued at two-thirds of a pound.)   80 will command

KING
See, Buckingham, Somerset comes with th' Queen.
Go bid her hide him quickly from the Duke.   84

QUEEN
For thousand Yorks he shall not hide his head,
But boldly stand and front him to his face.   86

YORK
How now? Is Somerset at liberty?
Then, York, unloose thy long-imprisoned thoughts
And let thy tongue be equal with thy heart.
Shall I endure the sight of Somerset?
False king, why hast thou broken faith with me,
Knowing how hardly I can brook abuse?   92
"King" did I call thee? No, thou art not king,
Not fit to govern and rule multitudes,
Which dar'st not—no, nor canst not—rule a traitor.   95
That head of thine doth not become a crown;
Thy hand is made to grasp a palmer's staff,   97
And not to grace an awful princely scepter.   98
That gold must round engirt these brows of mine,
Whose smile and frown, like to Achilles' spear,   100
Is able with the change to kill and cure.
Here is a hand to hold a scepter up
And with the same to act controlling laws.   103
Give place. By heaven, thou shalt rule no more
O'er him whom heaven created for thy ruler.

SOMERSET
O monstrous traitor! I arrest thee, York,
Of capital treason 'gainst the King and crown.
Obey, audacious traitor. Kneel for grace.

YORK
Wouldst have me kneel? First let me ask of these,   109
If they can brook I bow a knee to man.   110
[*To an attendant.*] Sirrah, call in my sons to be my
     bail.   [*Exit attendant.*]
I know, ere they will have me go to ward,   112
They'll pawn their swords for my enfranchisement.   113

QUEEN [*to Buckingham*]
Call hither Clifford. Bid him come amain,   114
To say if that the bastard boys of York
Shall be the surety for their traitor father.   116
                              [*Exit Buckingham.*]

YORK [*to the Queen*]
O blood-bespotted Neapolitan,   117
Outcast of Naples, England's bloody scourge!
The sons of York, thy betters in their birth,

84 the Duke i.e., of York   86 front confront   92 brook abuse tolerate deception   95 Which who   97 palmer's pilgrim's   98 awful
awe-inspiring   100 Achilles' spear (Telephus, wounded by Achilles'
spear, learned from an oracle that he could be cured only by the
agent that had wounded him. He was eventually cured by an application of rust from the point of the spear.)   103 act enact   109 these
i.e., his sons, who are waiting outside, or attendants, or possibly his
hands or weapons   110 brook . . . man tolerate that I should bow
my knee in submission to anyone   112 to ward into custody
113 pawn pledge. enfranchisement freedom   114 amain swiftly
116 s.d. Exit Buckingham (Buckingham must exit somewhere before
an attendant is sent to find him at line 192, and here seems a likely
place.)   117 Neapolitan (Margaret's father Reignier, or René, was titular King of Naples.)

Shall be their father's bail, and bane to those 120
That for my surety will refuse the boys! 121

Enter Edward and Richard [Plantagenet, with drum and soldiers, at one door].

See where they come. I'll warrant they'll make it
good.

Enter [old] Clifford [and his Son, with drum and soldiers, at the other door].

QUEEN
And here comes Clifford to deny their bail.
CLIFFORD [*kneeling before King Henry*]
Health and all happiness to my lord the King!
[*He rises.*]
YORK
I thank thee, Clifford. Say, what news with thee?
Nay, do not fright us with an angry look.
We are thy sovereign, Clifford, kneel again.
For thy mistaking so, we pardon thee.
CLIFFORD
This is my king, York. I do not mistake,
But thou mistakes me much to think I do.—
To Bedlam with him! Is the man grown mad? 131
KING
Ay, Clifford, a bedlam and ambitious humor 132
Makes him oppose himself against his king.
CLIFFORD
He is a traitor. Let him to the Tower,
And chop away that factious pate of his. 135
QUEEN
He is arrested, but will not obey.
His sons, he says, shall give their words for him.
YORK Will you not, sons?
EDWARD
Ay, noble Father, if our words will serve.
RICHARD
And if words will not, then our weapons shall.
CLIFFORD
Why, what a brood of traitors have we here!
YORK
Look in a glass, and call thy image so. 142
I am thy king, and thou a false-heart traitor.
Call hither to the stake my two brave bears, 144
That with the very shaking of their chains
They may astonish these fell-lurking curs.—
Bid Salisbury and Warwick come to me.
[*An attendant goes to summon them.*]

Enter the Earls of Warwick and Salisbury, [with drum and soldiers].

CLIFFORD
Are these thy bears? We'll bait thy bears to death
And manacle the bearherd in their chains, 149
If thou dar'st bring them to the baiting place. 150
RICHARD
Oft have I seen a hot o'erweening cur 151
Run back and bite, because he was withheld, 152
Who, being suffered with the bear's fell paw, 153
Hath clapped his tail between his legs and cried;
And such a piece of service will you do,
If you oppose yourselves to match Lord Warwick. 156
CLIFFORD
Hence, heap of wrath, foul indigested lump, 157
As crooked in thy manners as thy shape!
YORK
Nay, we shall heat you thoroughly anon. 159
CLIFFORD
Take heed, lest by your heat you burn yourselves.
KING
Why, Warwick, hath thy knee forgot to bow?
Old Salisbury, shame to thy silver hair,
Thou mad misleader of thy brainsick son!
What, wilt thou on thy deathbed play the ruffian,
And seek for sorrow with thy spectacles? 165
O, where is faith? O, where is loyalty?
If it be banished from the frosty head,
Where shall it find a harbor in the earth?
Wilt thou go dig a grave to find out war,
And shame thine honorable age with blood?
Why art thou old and want'st experience? 171
Or wherefore dost abuse it if thou hast it? 172
For shame! In duty bend thy knee to me
That bows unto the grave with mickle age. 174
SALISBURY
My lord, I have considered with myself
The title of this most renownèd duke,
And in my conscience do repute His Grace
The rightful heir to England's royal seat.
KING
Hast thou not sworn allegiance unto me?
SALISBURY I have.
KING
Canst thou dispense with heaven for such an oath? 181
SALISBURY
It is great sin to swear unto a sin,

120 **bane** destruction 121 **s.d. drum** drummer. **at one door** (The Quarto version is explicit that Plantagenet's sons enter "at one door" and Clifford with his son and forces "at the other.") 131 **Bedlam** hospital of St. Mary of Bethlehem in London, used as an asylum for the mentally deranged 132 **bedlam** mad. **humor** disposition 135 **factious pate** rebellious head 142 **glass** looking glass 144 **brave bears** i.e., Salisbury and his son Warwick. (Compare with lines 202–203 below, where Warwick describes the badge of his house as a *rampant bear chained to the ragged staff*. The image is from bearbaiting, in which bears were chained to a stake and attacked by *fell-lurking curs*, "cruelly waiting dogs," line 146.)

149 **bearherd** bear handler, keeper (i.e., York) 150 **baiting place** bearbaiting pit 151 **hot o'erweening** hot-tempered and overconfident 152 **bite** i.e., at its trainer, who is restraining it. 153 **suffered with** permitted to do battle with, or, injured by. **fell** fierce, terrible 156 **oppose yourselves** set yourselves up as opponents 157 **indigested** ill-formed. **lump** (Bear cubs were supposedly born unformed and had to be licked into shape by their mother. See *3 Henry VI*, 3.2.161, where Richard's hunched back and other deformities are compared with those of *an unlicked bear whelp*.) 159 **heat you** i.e., warm you in the fighting 165 **spectacles** (A sign of advanced age, like *silver hair*, line 162, and *frosty*, "white-haired," line 167.) 171 **want'st** lack. (Why are you old before you are wise?) 172 **Or . . . it** or why do you put wisdom and experience to such bad use if you have them? 174 **That bows** you that bow or your knee that bows. **mickle** great 181 **dispense with heaven for** expect or obtain dispensation from heaven for breaking

But greater sin to keep a sinful oath.
Who can be bound by any solemn vow
To do a murderous deed, to rob a man,
To force a spotless virgin's chastity,
To reave the orphan of his patrimony,   187
To wring the widow from her customed right,   188
And have no other reason for this wrong
But that he was bound by a solemn oath?

QUEEN
A subtle traitor needs no sophister.   191

KING [to an attendant]
Call Buckingham, and bid him arm himself.
                    [Exit attendant.]

YORK [to King Henry]
Call Buckingham and all the friends thou hast,   193
I am resolved for death or dignity.   194

CLIFFORD
The first I warrant thee, if dreams prove true.

WARWICK
You were best to go to bed and dream again,   196
To keep thee from the tempest of the field.

CLIFFORD
I am resolved to bear a greater storm
Than any thou canst conjure up today;
And that I'll write upon thy burgonet,   200
Might I but know thee by thy household badge.   201

WARWICK
Now, by my father's badge, old Neville's crest,   202
The rampant bear chained to the ragged staff,
This day I'll wear aloft my burgonet,   204
As on a mountaintop the cedar shows   205
That keeps his leaves in spite of any storm,   206
Even to affright thee with the view thereof.

CLIFFORD
And from thy burgonet I'll rend thy bear
And tread it underfoot with all contempt,
Despite the bearherd that protects the bear.

YOUNG CLIFFORD
And so to arms, victorious Father,
To quell the rebels and their complices.   212

RICHARD
Fie! Charity, for shame! Speak not in spite,
For you shall sup with Jesu Christ tonight.

YOUNG CLIFFORD
Foul stigmatic, that's more than thou canst tell.   215

RICHARD
If not in heaven, you'll surely sup in hell.
                    Exeunt [separately].

---

187 reave bereave   **188 customed right** i.e., right to inherit a portion of her husband's estate   **191 sophister** equivocator, expert in casuistry   **193 Call** even if you call   **194 resolved for** determined to have.   **dignity** exalted rank   **196 You were best** you had better **200 burgonet** light helmet or steel cap (upon which the wearer's heraldic device was often mounted)   **201 Might . . . badge** if I can identify you in the battle by your family crest   **202 old Neville's crest** (The Nevilles' crest was, in fact, a bull; Warwick inherited his badge of a chained bear from his wife's family, the Beauchamps.)   **204 aloft** on high   **205 shows** shows itself   **206 leaves** i.e., needles   **212 complices** accomplices   **215 stigmatic** one branded with the mark of his crime (just as Richard is marked by his deformities)

5.2   [Alarums to the battle.] Enter Warwick.

WARWICK
Clifford of Cumberland, 'tis Warwick calls!
And if thou dost not hide thee from the bear,
Now, when the angry trumpet sounds alarum
And dead men's cries do fill the empty air,   4
Clifford, I say, come forth and fight with me!
Proud northern lord, Clifford of Cumberland,
Warwick is hoarse with calling thee to arms.

      Enter York.

How now, my noble lord? What, all afoot?

YORK
The deadly-handed Clifford slew my steed,
But match to match I have encountered him
And made a prey for carrion kites and crows
Even of the bonny beast he loved so well.

      Enter [old] Clifford.

WARWICK [to Clifford]
Of one or both of us the time is come.

YORK
Hold, Warwick, seek thee out some other chase,   14
For I myself must hunt this deer to death.

WARWICK
Then, nobly, York! 'Tis for a crown thou fight'st.—
As I intend, Clifford, to thrive today,
It grieves my soul to leave thee unassailed.
                    Exit Warwick.

CLIFFORD
What seest thou in me, York? Why dost thou pause?

YORK
With thy brave bearing should I be in love,   20
But that thou art so fast mine enemy.   21

CLIFFORD
Nor should thy prowess want praise and esteem,   22
But that 'tis shown ignobly and in treason.

YORK
So let it help me now against thy sword
As I in justice and true right express it.

CLIFFORD
My soul and body on the action both!   26

YORK
A dreadful lay! Address thee instantly.   27
              [They fight, and Clifford falls.]

CLIFFORD
La fin couronne les oeuvres.   [He dies.] 28

YORK
Thus war hath given thee peace, for thou art still.
Peace with his soul, heaven, if it be thy will!   [Exit.]

      Enter young Clifford.

YOUNG CLIFFORD
Shame and confusion! All is on the rout.   31

5.2. Location: Scene continues at the battlefield near the Castle Inn. **4 dead** dying   **14 chase** game, prey   **20 bearing** demeanor   **21 fast** unalterably, completely   **22 want** lack   **26 action** outcome of action **27 lay** wager, oath.   **Address thee** prepare yourself   **28 La . . . oeuvres** the end crowns the work   **31 confusion** destruction.   **on the rout** i.e., in disorderly retreat

Fear frames disorder, and disorder wounds   32
Where it should guard. O war, thou son of hell,
Whom angry heavens do make their minister,   34
Throw in the frozen bosoms of our part   35
Hot coals of vengeance! Let no soldier fly.
He that is truly dedicate to war   37
Hath no self-love, nor he that loves himself   38
Hath not essentially but by circumstance   39
The name of valor. [*Seeing his dead father.*] O, let
     the vile world end   40
And the premisèd flames of the last day   41
Knit earth and heaven together!
Now let the general trumpet blow his blast,   43
Particularities and petty sounds   44
To cease! Wast thou ordained, dear Father,   45
To lose thy youth in peace, and to achieve   46
The silver livery of advisèd age,   47
And in thy reverence and thy chair days, thus   48
To die in ruffian battle? Even at this sight
My heart is turned to stone, and while 'tis mine
It shall be stony. York not our old men spares;
No more will I their babes. Tears virginal   52
Shall be to me even as the dew to fire,   53
And beauty, that the tyrant oft reclaims,   54
Shall to my flaming wrath be oil and flax.
Henceforth I will not have to do with pity.
Meet I an infant of the house of York,   57
Into as many gobbets will I cut it   58
As wild Medea young Absyrtus did.   59
In cruelty will I seek out my fame.   60
Come, thou new ruin of old Clifford's house.
As did Aeneas old Anchises bear,   62
So bear I thee upon my manly shoulders;
But then Aeneas bare a living load,   64
Nothing so heavy as these woes of mine.   65
                 [*Exit, bearing off his father.*]

Enter Richard and Somerset to fight. [Somerset is
killed under the sign of the Castle Inn.]

RICHARD   So, lie thou there;
For underneath an alehouse' paltry sign,

---

32 **frames** causes   **32–33 disorder . . . guard** i.e., disorderly retreat makes for casualties instead of effective defense   **34 minister** agent   **35 frozen** i.e., unwarmed by wrathful courage.   **part** party, faction   **37 dedicate** dedicated   **38 Hath no self-love** i.e., gives no thought to his own safety.   **nor** conversely   **39–40 Hath . . . valor** is valiant only by happenstance, not in essence. (Such a person is not truly courageous.)   **41 premisèd** foreordained.   **last day** Day of Judgment   **43 general** i.e., summmoning all humanity   **44 Particularities** individual affairs   **45 cease** bring to an end.   **ordained** chosen, fated   **46 lose** expend   **47 silvery livery** i.e., white hair, worn as though part of a uniform.   **advisèd** wise, prudent   **48 reverence** revered old age.   **chair days** i.e., inactive years of old age   **52 virginal** of young maidens   **53 dew to fire** (Water finely sprayed on a fire was thought to cause it to burn hotter.)   **54 that . . . reclaims** which often softens the temper of the tyrant   **57 Meet I** if I should meet   **58 gobbets** pieces or lumps of flesh   **59 Medea** daughter of Aeetes, King of Colchis, who helped Jason recover the Golden Fleece and fled with him. (To delay her father's pursuit, she killed her brother Absyrtus and left pieces of his dismembered body in the father's path.)   **60 fame** reputation   **62 Aeneas, Anchises** (In Virgil's *Aeneid*, Aeneas, fleeing from Troy, carried his aged father on his shoulders.)   **64 bare** bore   **65 Nothing** not at all.   **heavy** (1) weighty (2) sorrowful

---

The Castle in Saint Albans, Somerset
Hath made the wizard famous in his death.   69
Sword, hold thy temper; heart, be wrathful still.   70
Priests pray for enemies, but princes kill.   [*Exit.*] 71

       Fight. Excursions. Enter King, Queen, and others.

QUEEN
Away, my lord! You are slow. For shame, away!
KING
Can we outrun the heavens? Good Margaret, stay.
QUEEN
What are you made of? You'll nor fight nor fly.   74
Now is it manhood, wisdom, and defense
To give the enemy way, and to secure us   76
By what we can, which can no more but fly.   77
                     Alarum afar off.
If you be ta'en, we then should see the bottom
Of all our fortunes; but if we haply scape,
As well we may, if not through your neglect,   80
We shall to London get, where you are loved
And where this breach now in our fortunes made
May readily be stopped.

       Enter [young] Clifford.

YOUNG CLIFFORD
But that my heart's on future mischief set,
I would speak blasphemy ere bid you fly;
But fly you must. Uncurable discomfit   86
Reigns in the hearts of all our present parts.   87
Away, for your relief! And we will live
To see their day and them our fortune give.   89
Away, my lord, away!   *Exeunt.*

5.3   *Alarum. Retreat. Enter York, Richard, Warwick,*
        and soldiers, with drum and colors.

YORK
Of Salisbury, who can report of him,
That winter lion, who in rage forgets   2
Agèd contusions and all brush of time,   3
And like a gallant in the brow of youth   4
Repairs him with occasion? This happy day   5
Is not itself, nor have we won one foot,
If Salisbury be lost.
RICHARD   My noble Father,
Three times today I holp him to his horse,   8

---

69 Hath . . . death i.e., has confirmed by his death the prophecy that he would die *where castles mounted stand*. (See 1.4.36–38.)   **70 still** always   **71 s.d. Exit** (The body of the slain Somerset must be removed at some point.)   **s.d. Excursions** sorties   **74 nor . . . nor** neither . . . nor   **76 secure us** save ourselves   **77 what** whatever means.   **which** (we) who   **80 if not** unless   **86 Uncurable discomfit** hopeless discouragement   **87 our present parts** those forces still remaining to us   **89 To . . . give** to see a day of success like theirs and let them experience our misfortune
5.3. Location: Scene continues at the battlefield.
2 winter i.e., aged   **3 brush** assault, collision   **4 gallant** young man of fashion.   **brow** i.e., crown, height   **5 Repairs . . . occasion** i.e., renews his strength with the opportunity of further military action
8 holp helped

Three times bestrid him; thrice I led him off,   9
Persuaded him from any further act.
But still, where danger was, still there I met him,   11
And like rich hangings in a homely house,   12
So was his will in his old feeble body.
But, noble as he is, look where he comes.

    Enter Salisbury.

SALISBURY
Now, by my sword, well hast thou fought today!
By th' Mass, so did we all. I thank you, Richard.
God knows how long it is I have to live,
And it hath pleased Him that three times today
You have defended me from imminent death.
Well, lords, we have not got that which we have;   20
'Tis not enough our foes are this time fled,
Being opposites of such repairing nature.   22
YORK
I know our safety is to follow them;
For, as I hear, the King is fled to London
To call a present court of Parliament.   25
Let us pursue him ere the writs go forth.   26
What says Lord Warwick? Shall we after them?
WARWICK
After them? Nay, before them, if we can.
Now, by my faith, lords, 'twas a glorious day.
Saint Albans battle won by famous York
Shall be eternized in all age to come.   31
Sound drum and trumpets, and to London all,
And more such days as these to us befall!
         [Flourish.] Exeunt.

9 bestrid him i.e., stood over him to defend him when he was down
11 still continually   **12 hangings** tapestries.   **homely** modest   **20 not
. . . have** i.e., not decisively overwhelmed the forces we today defeated in order to secure the whole country   **22 Being . . . nature**
they being adversaries with such ability to recover quickly
25 present immediate   **26 writs** official summonses issued by the
King to members of Parliament   **31 eternized** immortalized

The Third Part of King Henry the Sixth

Henry VI, Part III, must be regarded not only as a part of Shakespeare's first historical four-play series, but also as a play in its own right, presumably seen on its first showing by an Elizabethan audience who, though aware of a larger context, witnessed this dramatic action as a self-contained event. Because *3 Henry VI* represents nearly the entire military phase of the civil war, it is the most crowded and bustling play of the series. Historically, it covers the period from the battles of Wakefield and second St. Albans (1460–1461) to the decisive Yorkist victories at Barnet and Tewkesbury (1471). These and other battles are actually represented onstage. The conventional method of representing armed conflict is by means of alarums and excursions (i.e., sudden assaults and forays by armed soldiers in response to a signal to attack), employing as many soldiers as the acting company could muster, with martial music and numerous entrances and exits in rapid succession. Battles are usually preceded by florid boastful rhetorical exchanges, or *flytings*, between the combatants. The military contests focus on heroic confrontations between individual leaders. Staging of battles often uses the Elizabethan playhouse to its physical capacity, with appearances "on the walls" of some town (i.e., from the upper gallery), scaling operations, sieges, and the like. *3 Henry VI* abounds in spectacular deaths, often performed as gruesome rituals. Young Rutland is dragged from his tutor by the implacable Clifford, and Richard of York is mocked with a paper crown by Queen Margaret; Clifford dies with an arrow in his neck, and Warwick the kingmaker dies lamenting the vanity of all earthly achievement; King Henry dies in the Tower, a defenseless prisoner in the hands of Richard of Gloucester. The play is perhaps confusing to the reader, but it breathes with violent energy onstage.

Symbolic of the chaos is the lack of a single central character. The title of the 1595 Octavo edition pairs the deaths of Richard of York and King Henry as the play's most memorable episodes; and in this dual focus we see the dominant motif of reciprocity, a Yorkist death for a Lancastrian death. This pattern will continue into *Richard III*, for *3 Henry VI*

ends with an ominous amount of unfinished business; Clarence, for example, later sees that he must die in atonement for his part in the slaughter of Edward, the Lancastrian Prince of Wales. Just as the deaths are balanced and contrasted with one another, the military action also seesaws back and forth. Both Henry VI and Edward IV are at times imprisoned. The wheel of fortune elevates one side and then the other. Political alliances shift the balance of power one way and then the other. The action is painfully indecisive, the carnage leading pointlessly only to further violence. The spectacle is made infinitely more agonizing by the realization that all this is a family quarrel. The commoners suffer accordingly: we witness the grief of a father who has mistakenly killed his son in battle and of a son who has killed his father (2.5). The people, seldom seen, are no longer political troublemakers (as they were briefly in *2 Henry VI*) but mere victims, waiting patiently for an end. A recurrent emblem used to convey the utter futility of this war is the molehill. York is mockingly crowned before his execution on a molehill, and King Henry retires from a battle to a molehill in order to meditate on the happy contemplative life he has been denied. The molehill suggests the ironic perversity of humanity's quest for worldly power, whereby those who possess power are incapable of exercising it wisely and those who burn with ambition are denied legitimate opportunity.

One sure sign of moral chaos throughout this play is the phenomenon of oath breaking. In the opening scene, Richard of York accepts under oath an obligation to honor Henry VI as his king in return for being named king after Henry's death, but he is soon talked out of his promise by his son Richard on the specious grounds that the oath was not made before "a true and lawful magistrate" (1.2.23). This masterful equivocation, anticipated in the perfidies of the Duke of Suffolk in *1* and *2 Henry VI*, prepares us for Richard's later perfidies in *Richard III*. (In Shakespeare's sources, especially Edward Hall, Parliament plays a major role in working out the compromise between York and Henry; Shakespeare shows us, instead, a personal agreement made between two contending leaders on the basis of private will and assertion of military power—an agreement that is easily broken on the same pragmatic grounds.) King Henry is no less forsworn in denying to his own son the crown bestowed on him as birthright by sacred law and custom. Lewis, the French King, excuses his shifting of alliance from King Henry to the Yorkists on the grounds of simple expediency. Clarence forswears his oaths made to his brother Edward and changes sides in the wars, offended at Edward's perfidy in having renounced his intent to marry the French King's sister-in-law. Soon Clarence is back again in the Yorkist camp, having now betrayed the promises he made to the Lancastrians. Warwick the kingmaker forswears his oaths to Edward because Edward has undermined Warwick's embassy to France. Where, in fact, do truth and justice reside, now that England is governed by two kings who are both forsworn?

The common people sense this dilemma, as revealed in the attitudes of two gamekeepers; they capture Henry to whom they were once loyal, because they are now "sworn in all allegiance" to Edward but would be true subjects again to Henry "If he were seated as King Edward is" (3.1.70, 95). Political and military reality governs political ethics; the ruler to be acknowledged is he who can establish control.

Another sign of moral decay in this play is the dominance of vengeful purpose. *3 Henry VI,* indeed, can be viewed as a kind of revenge play in which Richard of Gloucester finally emerges as the consummate avenger in a society of avengers. In the opening confrontation between the Yorkists and the Lancastrians, Warwick taunts the Lancastrians with having lost many of their fathers in the recent military action at St. Albans; the fathers of Northumberland, Westmorland, and Clifford have all fallen in that one battle. (Historically, Westmorland and Clifford appear to be the same man with the same father, Old Clifford of *2 Henry VI;* Shakespeare gives us more fatherless sons by this division of one man into two.) The sons, of course, vow vengeance. Clifford, renowned as "the butcher" for his cruelty, exacts a terrible price for his father's death through the slaughter of the defenseless young Rutland and the mocking execution of Rutland's father, the Duke of York. York's surviving sons take vengeance, not only on Clifford, but also on King Henry, his son Edward, and many others. Warwick turns against Edward of York more to avenge an insult than to aid Henry and is himself cut down by the Yorkists at Barnet (4.2). The implacable pattern of an eye for an eye eventually takes on a providential meaning, especially as seen from the hindsight of *Richard III,* but, as we experience this play in the theater, the reality is chiefly one of much brutality and horror.

As in earlier plays of the series, the relationships between men and women echo the discord of the English nation and contribute, in turn, to further discord. Margaret of Anjou, the remorseless defender of her son Edward's claim, acts with increasingly masculine authority, while her ineffectual husband abdicates responsibility. She is the Lancastrian general, resourceful in battle and often victorious, implacable in vengeance. This inversion of male and female roles is reflected on the Yorkist side by Edward IV's disastrous marriage with Lady Elizabeth Grey. She is the widow of a Lancastrian soldier with no family position or political power to bring to the marriage—nothing, in fact, but her ambition on behalf of her kinsmen. Edward's attraction to her is fleshly and imprudent. To make matters worse, Warwick is at that very moment negotiating a highly favorable marriage treaty for Edward with the King of France. Edward IV thus unconsciously apes the earlier willfulness of his counterpart, Henry VI. Edward IV's snubbing of Warwick leads to the defection of that powerful leader and through him to the defection of Edward's brother Clarence, who has succumbed to the charms of Warwick's daughter Isabel. And whereas *1 Henry VI* at least counterbalances the uxoriousness of

Henry with the positive example of Lord Talbot, *3 Henry VI* fails to discover any such central noble character. (To be sure, we are briefly introduced to the young Earl of Richmond, who is to be Henry VII, but only as a glimpse of a hopeful future.) The almost total lack of any distinctly virtuous character gives to *3 Henry VI* its predominantly dismaying and helpless mood. The heroes have been destroyed.

Richard of Gloucester alone seems to profit from England's decline. Like his father, York, his strategy has been to let England flay herself into anarchic vulnerability. Once the father York has disappeared from the scene, young Richard's malevolent character becomes increasingly apparent. No longer merely one of York's brave sons, Richard is the new genius of discord. As the youngest of three sons who will eventually supplant his older brothers and their rights of inheritance, Richard is a supreme example of inversion in a world turned upside down. His bravura soliloquy in 3.2 is often included in performances of *Richard III,* for it yields rich clues to his emerging character: he is ambitious, ruthless, deformed from birth, and, above all, a consummate deceiver. To the audience he boasts of his ability, claiming that as a hypocrite he will excel the combined talents of Nestor, Ulysses, Sinon, Proteus, and Machiavelli. The superb self-assurance is arresting, the heartless consistency admirable even though despicable. In a second soliloquy, virtually at the end of the play, having already dispatched Henry VI and his son Edward, Richard confides to the audience that Clarence is to be his next victim. And, although Richard pledges fealty to his young nephew, Edward, the Yorkist crown prince, at the Yorkist victory celebration with which the play ends, we know that Richard's kiss of peace is no more trustworthy than Judas' kiss given to Christ. All those standing between Richard and the throne are to be eliminated. Clearly, the pious longings for peace expressed by King Edward IV are to be cruelly violated.

The Third Part of King Henry The Sixth

[Dramatis Personae

KING HENRY THE SIXTH
QUEEN MARGARET
PRINCE EDWARD, *their son*
DUKE OF EXETER,
EARL OF NORTHUMBERLAND,
EARL OF WESTMORLAND,
EARL OF OXFORD,
LORD CLIFFORD,
SIR JOHN SOMERVILLE,
A HUNTSMAN *guarding Edward*
} *supporters of the house of Lancaster*

DUKE OF YORK, *Richard Plantagenet*
EDWARD, *Earl of March, later Duke of York and* KING EDWARD IV,
GEORGE, *later Duke of Clarence,*
RICHARD, *later Duke of Gloucester,*
EARL OF RUTLAND,
} *York's sons*
LADY GREY, *later Edward IV's queen*
PRINCE EDWARD, *her infant son*
EARL RIVERS, *her brother*
SIR JOHN MORTIMER,
SIR HUGH MORTIMER,
} *York's uncles*
DUKE OF NORFOLK,
EARL OF PEMBROKE,
LORD HASTINGS,
LORD STAFFORD,
SIR WILLIAM STANLEY,
SIR JOHN MONTGOMERY,
A NOBLEMAN,
} *supporters of the house of York*
TUTOR *of the Earl of Rutland*
Two KEEPERS *or gamekeepers*
Three WATCHMEN *guarding Edward's tent*
A SOLDIER *in the Yorkist army*

EARL OF WARWICK,
MARQUESS MONTAGUE,
DUKE OF SOMERSET,
} *supporters of York and then of Lancaster*
HENRY, EARL OF RICHMOND
LIEUTENANT *of the Tower of London*
MAYOR OF YORK
MAYOR OF COVENTRY
A SON *that has killed his father*
A FATHER *that has killed his son*
MESSENGERS
POSTS

KING LEWIS *of France*
LADY BONA, *his sister-in-law*
LORD BOURBON, *French Admiral*

English and French Soldiers, Attendants, Aldermen, a Nurse to Prince Edward

SCENE: *England and France*]

1.1

Alarum. Enter [Richard] Plantagenet [Duke of York], Edward, Richard, Norfolk, Montague, Warwick, [with drum] and soldiers, [wearing white roses in their hats. A chair of state is onstage.]

WARWICK
I wonder how the King escaped our hands.
YORK
While we pursued the horsemen of the north,
He slyly stole away and left his men;
Whereat the great lord of Northumberland,
Whose warlike ears could never brook retreat,   5
Cheered up the drooping army, and himself,
Lord Clifford, and Lord Stafford, all abreast,
Charged our main battle's front and, breaking in,   8
Were by the swords of common soldiers slain.   9
EDWARD
Lord Stafford's father, Duke of Buckingham,
Is either slain or wounded dangerous;   11
I cleft his beaver with a downright blow.   12
That this is true, Father, behold his blood.
                    [*He shows his bloody sword.*]
MONTAGUE [*to York*]
And, brother, here's the Earl of Wiltshire's blood,   14
Whom I encountered as the battles joined.   15
                    [*He shows his sword.*]
RICHARD [*showing the Duke of Somerset's head*]
Speak thou for me and tell them what I did.
YORK
Richard hath best deserved of all my sons.
But is Your Grace dead, my lord of Somerset?   18
NORFOLK
Such hap have all the line of John of Gaunt!   19

1.1. Location: London. The Parliament House (see lines 35–39, 71, etc.), also referred to as King Henry VI's palace, line 25, since in the fifteenth and sixteenth centuries the Parliament House and Westminster Palace were part of the same complex. The throne is onstage, seemingly on a raised platform.
s.d. **Alarum** trumpet call to arms. (York and his followers, in hot pursuit of King Henry, have just arrived from St. Albans.)   **drum** drummer.   **white roses** (The badge of the house of York.)   **5 brook** endure.   **retreat** the call sounding withdrawal from the attack
8 battle's army's   **9 Were . . . slain** (In *2 Henry VI*, 5.2, it is York who kills old Clifford.)   **11 dangerous** dangerously   **12 beaver** face guard of a helmet, i.e., here the helmet itself   **14 brother** (Montague was actually brother to Warwick, but his father, Salisbury of *2 Henry VI*, was brother-in-law of York.)   **15 battles joined** battalions joined in combat   **18 But . . . Somerset** i.e., are you really dead, my lord? (Like his son, York contemptuously addresses his slain enemy.)
19 Such . . . Gaunt (The descendants of John of Gaunt, to whom Norfolk wishes ill luck, include King Henry VI, as well as Somerset, who is already dead.)

RICHARD
  Thus do I hope to shake King Henry's head.
WARWICK
  And so do I. Victorious prince of York,
  Before I see thee seated in that throne   22
  Which now the house of Lancaster usurps,
  I vow by heaven these eyes shall never close.
  This is the palace of the fearful King,   25
  And this the regal seat. Possess it, York,
  For this is thine and not King Henry's heirs'.
YORK
  Assist me, then, sweet Warwick, and I will,
  For hither we have broken in by force.
NORFOLK
  We'll all assist you. He that flies shall die.
YORK
  Thanks, gentle Norfolk. Stay by me, my lords,   31
  And soldiers, stay and lodge by me this night.   32
                    They go up [to the chair of state].
WARWICK
  And when the King comes, offer him no violence,
  Unless he seek to thrust you out perforce.   34
                    [*The soldiers withdraw.*]
YORK
  The Queen this day here holds her Parliament,
  But little thinks we shall be of her council.   36
  By words or blows here let us win our right.
RICHARD
  Armed as we are, let's stay within this house.
WARWICK
  The Bloody Parliament shall this be called,
  Unless Plantagenet, Duke of York, be king   40
  And bashful Henry deposed, whose cowardice
  Hath made us bywords to our enemies.   42
YORK
  Then leave me not, my lords. Be resolute.
  I mean to take possession of my right.
WARWICK
  Neither the King, nor he that loves him best,
  The proudest he that holds up Lancaster,   46
  Dares stir a wing if Warwick shake his bells.   47
  I'll plant Plantagenet, root him up who dares.
  Resolve thee, Richard; claim the English crown.   49
                    [*York seats himself in the throne.*]

  Flourish. Enter King Henry, Clifford,
  Northumberland, Westmorland, Exeter, and the
  rest. [All wear red roses.]

KING HENRY
  My lords, look where the sturdy rebel sits,   50
  Even in the chair of state! Belike he means,   51
  Backed by the power of Warwick, that false peer,
  To aspire unto the crown and reign as king.
  Earl of Northumberland, he slew thy father,
  And thine, Lord Clifford, and you both have vowed
      revenge
  On him, his sons, his favorites, and his friends.
NORTHUMBERLAND
  If I be not, heavens be revenged on me!   57
CLIFFORD
  The hope thereof makes Clifford mourn in steel.   58
WESTMORLAND
  What, shall we suffer this? Let's pluck him down.
  My heart for anger burns. I cannot brook it.
KING HENRY
  Be patient, gentle Earl of Westmorland.
CLIFFORD
  Patience is for poltroons, such as he.   62
  He durst not sit there, had your father lived.
  My gracious lord, here in the Parliament
  Let us assail the family of York.
NORTHUMBERLAND
  Well hast thou spoken, cousin. Be it so.   66
KING HENRY
  Ah, know you not the city favors them,   67
  And they have troops of soldiers at their beck?
EXETER
  But when the Duke is slain, they'll quickly fly.
KING HENRY
  Far be the thought of this from Henry's heart,
  To make a shambles of the Parliament House!   71
  Cousin of Exeter, frowns, words, and threats
  Shall be the war that Henry means to use.—
  Thou factious Duke of York, descend my throne
  And kneel for grace and mercy at my feet!
  I am thy sovereign.
YORK   I am thine.
EXETER
  For shame, come down. He made thee Duke of
      York.   77
YORK
  It was my inheritance, as the earldom was.   78
EXETER
  Thy father was a traitor to the crown.   79
WARWICK
  Exeter, thou art a traitor to the crown
  In following this usurping Henry.

---

22 Before i.e., until **25 fearful** timid **31 gentle** noble **32 s.d. They go up** i.e., Plantagenet, his sons, Norfolk, Montague, and Warwick, all seemingly go up onto the dais or raised platform supporting the throne. (The soldiers may withdraw at this point; they must reenter later at line 169.) **34 perforce** by force **36 of her council** (1) taking part in the Privy Council meeting (2) serving as confidential advisers **40 be** become **42 bywords** i.e., objects of scorn. **our enemies** i.e., the French **46 he . . . up** person that supports **47 shake his bells** (Bells were sometimes fastened to the legs of a falcon to incite it to greater ferocity and to terrify its victims.) **49 Resolve thee** be resolute. **s.d. Flourish** trumpet fanfare. **red roses** (The badge of the house of Lancaster.)

50 sturdy self-assured **51 chair of state** throne. **Belike** evidently **57 be not** i.e., be not avenged **58 in steel** i.e., in armor, not in mourning attire **62 poltroons** arrant cowards. **he** i.e., York, who must not be impatient for the throne, in Clifford's view **66 cousin** kinsman. (Also in line 72.) **67 the city** i.e., London **71 shambles** slaughterhouse **77–78 He . . . was** (Compare with *1 Henry VI*, 3.1.161–174, where the King restored to Richard the whole inheritance of the house of York, which included the earldom of March.) **79 Thy . . . crown** (On the execution of Richard, Earl of Cambridge, for treason by Henry V, see *Henry V*, 2.2, and *1 Henry VI*, 2.4.90–94, 2.5.84–91.)

CLIFFORD
  Whom should he follow but his natural king?
WARWICK
  True, Clifford. That's Richard, Duke of York.
KING HENRY [to York]
  And shall I stand, and thou sit in my throne?
YORK
  It must and shall be so. Content thyself.
WARWICK [to King Henry]
  Be Duke of Lancaster. Let him be king.
WESTMORLAND
  He is both King and Duke of Lancaster,
  And that the lord of Westmorland shall maintain.
WARWICK
  And Warwick shall disprove it. You forget
  That we are those which chased you from the field
  And slew your fathers, and with colors spread   91
  Marched through the city to the palace gates.
NORTHUMBERLAND
  Yes, Warwick, I remember it to my grief;
  And, by his soul, thou and thy house shall rue it.   94
WESTMORLAND
  Plantagenet, of thee and these thy sons,
  Thy kinsmen and thy friends, I'll have more lives
  Than drops of blood were in my father's veins.   97
CLIFFORD
  Urge it no more, lest that, instead of words,   98
  I send thee, Warwick, such a messenger
  As shall revenge his death before I stir.   100
WARWICK
  Poor Clifford, how I scorn his worthless threats!
YORK
  Will you we show our title to the crown?   102
  If not, our swords shall plead it in the field.
KING HENRY
  What title hast thou, traitor, to the crown?
  Thy father was, as thou art, Duke of York,   105
  Thy grandfather, Roger Mortimer, Earl of March.
  I am the son of Henry the Fifth,
  Who made the Dauphin and the French to stoop
  And seized upon their towns and provinces.
WARWICK
  Talk not of France, sith thou hast lost it all.   110
KING HENRY
  The Lord Protector lost it, and not I.   111
  When I was crowned I was but nine months old.
RICHARD
  You are old enough now, and yet, methinks, you
    lose.—

91 colors battle flags   94 his i.e., the second Earl of Northumberland's, who fell at St. Albans on the Lancastrian side. (This event is
not shown in 2 Henry VI.) The speaker is the third Earl.   97 my father's (Three noble fathers died on the Lancastrian side at St. Albans,
according to Hall: Northumberland, old Clifford, and Somerset. Westmorland's father was not a casualty in that battle, but Shakespeare
may be replacing Somerset here to keep the symmetry of three.)
98 lest that lest   100 his i.e., old Clifford's; see note at line 97
102 Will you do you desire   105 Thy . . . York (Shakespeare's historical inaccuracy; Richard's father was never Duke of York. That title
belonged to his oldest brother, Edward, who died at Agincourt; it was
given by Henry VI to Richard.)   110 sith since   111 Lord Protector
i.e., Humphrey, Duke of Gloucester

  Father, tear the crown from the usurper's head.
EDWARD
  Sweet father, do so. Set it on your head.
MONTAGUE [to York]
  Good brother, as thou lov'st and honorest arms,
  Let's fight it out and not stand caviling thus.
RICHARD
  Sound drums and trumpets, and the King will fly.
YORK   Sons, peace!
NORTHUMBERLAND
  Peace, thou! And give King Henry leave to speak.
WARWICK
  Plantagenet shall speak first. Hear him, lords,
  And be you silent and attentive too,
  For he that interrupts him shall not live.
KING HENRY
  Think'st thou that I will leave my kingly throne,
  Wherein my grandsire and my father sat?
  No! First shall war unpeople this my realm;
  Ay, and their colors, often borne in France,
  And now in England to our heart's great sorrow,
  Shall be my winding-sheet. Why faint you, lords?   129
  My title's good, and better far than his.
WARWICK
  Prove it, Henry, and thou shalt be king.
KING HENRY
  Henry the Fourth by conquest got the crown.
YORK
  'Twas by rebellion against his king.
KING HENRY [aside]
  I know not what to say; my title's weak.—
  Tell me, may not a king adopt an heir?
YORK   What then?
KING HENRY
  An if he may, then am I lawful king;   137
  For Richard, in the view of many lords,
  Resigned the crown to Henry the Fourth,
  Whose heir my father was, and I am his.
YORK
  He rose against him, being his sovereign,   141
  And made him to resign his crown perforce.
WARWICK
  Suppose, my lords, he did it unconstrained,
  Think you 'twere prejudicial to his crown?   144
EXETER
  No, for he could not so resign his crown
  But that the next heir should succeed and reign.
KING HENRY
  Art thou against us, Duke of Exeter?
EXETER
  His is the right, and therefore pardon me.   148
YORK
  Why whisper you, my lords, and answer not?
EXETER
  My conscience tells me he is lawful king.

129 winding-sheet sheet in which a corpse was wrapped.   faint lose
heart   137 An if if   141 him, being i.e., Richard, who was   144
'twere . . . crown it would invalidate his, Richard's, entitlement to
the throne   148 His i.e., York's

KING HENRY [*aside*]
  All will revolt from me and turn to him.

NORTHUMBERLAND
  Plantagenet, for all the claim thou lay'st,
  Think not that Henry shall be so deposed.

WARWICK
  Deposed he shall be, in despite of all.   154

NORTHUMBERLAND
  Thou art deceived. 'Tis not thy southern power   155
  Of Essex, Norfolk, Suffolk, nor of Kent,
  Which makes thee thus presumptuous and proud,
  Can set the Duke up in despite of me.

CLIFFORD
  King Henry, be thy title right or wrong,
  Lord Clifford vows to fight in thy defense.
  May that ground gape and swallow me alive
  Where I shall kneel to him that slew my father!

KING HENRY
  O Clifford, how thy words revive my heart!

YORK
  Henry of Lancaster, resign thy crown.
  What mutter you, or what conspire you, lords?

WARWICK
  Do right unto this princely Duke of York,   166
  Or I will fill the house with armèd men
  And over the chair of state, where now he sits,
  Write up his title with usurping blood.   169
          He stamps with his foot, and the soldiers show
                                        themselves.

KING HENRY
  My lord of Warwick, hear but one word:
  Let me for this my lifetime reign as king.

YORK
  Confirm the crown to me and to mine heirs,
  And thou shalt reign in quiet while thou liv'st.   173

KING HENRY
  I am content. Richard Plantagenet,
  Enjoy the kingdom after my decease.

CLIFFORD
  What wrong is this unto the Prince your son!

WARWICK
  What good is this to England and himself!   177

WESTMORLAND
  Base, fearful, and despairing Henry!

CLIFFORD
  How hast thou injured both thyself and us!

WESTMORLAND
  I cannot stay to hear these articles.   180

NORTHUMBERLAND   Nor I.

CLIFFORD
  Come, cousin, let us tell the Queen these news.

WESTMORLAND
  Farewell, fainthearted and degenerate King,
  In whose cold blood no spark of honor bides.   184
              [*Exit with his men.*]

NORTHUMBERLAND
  Be thou a prey unto the house of York
  And die in bonds for this unmanly deed!   186
              [*Exit with his men.*]

CLIFFORD
  In dreadful war mayst thou be overcome,
  Or live in peace abandoned and despised!
              [*Exit with his men.*]

WARWICK
  Turn this way, Henry, and regard them not.

EXETER
  They seek revenge and therefore will not yield.   190

KING HENRY
  Ah, Exeter!

WARWICK   Why should you sigh, my lord?

KING HENRY
  Not for myself, Lord Warwick, but my son,
  Whom I unnaturally shall disinherit.
  But be it as it may: [*to York*] I here entail   194
  The crown to thee and to thine heirs forever,
  Conditionally, that here thou take an oath
  To cease this civil war, and whilst I live
  To honor me as thy king and sovereign,
  And neither by treason nor hostility
  To seek to put me down and reign thyself.

YORK
  This oath I willingly take and will perform.

WARWICK
  Long live King Henry! Plantagenet, embrace him.
              [*York descends and embraces Henry.*]

KING HENRY
  And long live thou and these thy forward sons!   203

YORK
  Now York and Lancaster are reconciled.

EXETER
  Accursed be he that seeks to make them foes!   205
              Sennet. Here they come down.

YORK
  Farewell, my gracious lord. I'll to my castle.   206
              [*Exeunt York and his sons with their men.*]

WARWICK
  And I'll keep London with my soldiers.
              [*Exit Warwick with his men.*]

NORFOLK
  And I to Norfolk with my followers.
              [*Exit Norfolk with his men.*]

MONTAGUE
  And I unto the sea from whence I came.   209
              [*Exit Montague with his men.*]

---

154 **despite** spite. (Also in line 158.)   155 **deceived** mistaken
166 **Do right unto** deal justly with   169 **usurping blood** i.e., the
blood of usurping Henry VI   173 **while** as long as   177 **What . . . to**
i.e., what a good thing for. (Warwick welcomes Henry's decision.)
180 **articles** terms of agreement   184 **cold** listless, cowardly

186 **bonds** fetters   190 **revenge** i.e., for their fathers' deaths   194 **entail** bequeath irrevocably   203 **forward** precocious, zealous, promising   205 **s.d. Sennet** trumpet notes signaling a procession.   **Here they come down** (York and his sons, together with Norfolk, Montague, and Warwick, have evidently been on the dais around the throne since line 32. Once York has descended and embraced Henry, formalizing their agreement, the rest of the York faction can descend and prepare to depart.)   206 **castle** i.e., Sandal Castle in Yorkshire. (See the next scene.)   209 **unto the sea** (Actually, Montague appears in scene 2 at Sandal Castle, not at the sea; possibly he is confused here with his uncle, William Neville, Baron Falconbridge. See line 239 below.)

KING HENRY
And I, with grief and sorrow, to the court.

Enter the Queen [Margaret and Edward, Prince of Wales].

EXETER
Here comes the Queen, whose looks bewray her anger.   211
I'll steal away.

KING HENRY   Exeter, so will I.   [*They start to leave.*]

QUEEN MARGARET
Nay, go not from me. I will follow thee.

KING HENRY
Be patient, gentle Queen, and I will stay.

QUEEN MARGARET
Who can be patient in such extremes?
Ah, wretched man! Would I had died a maid
And never seen thee, never borne thee son,
Seeing thou hast proved so unnatural a father!   218
Hath he deserved to lose his birthright thus?
Hadst thou but loved him half so well as I,
Or felt that pain which I did for him once,
Or nourished him as I did with my blood,
Thou wouldst have left thy dearest heart-blood
    there,
Rather than have made that savage duke thine heir
And disinherited thine only son.

PRINCE
Father, you cannot disinherit me.
If you be king, why should not I succeed?

KING HENRY
Pardon me, Margaret. Pardon me, sweet son.
The Earl of Warwick and the Duke enforced me.

QUEEN MARGARET
Enforced thee? Art thou king, and wilt be forced?
I shame to hear thee speak. Ah, timorous wretch!
Thou hast undone thyself, thy son, and me,
And given unto the house of York such head   233
As thou shalt reign but by their sufferance.   234
To entail him and his heirs unto the crown,
What is it but to make thy sepulcher
And creep into it far before thy time?
Warwick is Chancellor and the lord of Calais;
Stern Falconbridge commands the narrow seas;   239
The Duke is made Protector of the realm;   240
And yet shalt thou be safe? Such safety finds
The trembling lamb environèd with wolves.   242
Had I been there, which am a silly woman,   243
The soldiers should have tossed me on their pikes   244
Before I would have granted to that act.   245
But thou preferr'st thy life before thine honor;
And seeing thou dost, I here divorce myself
Both from thy table, Henry, and thy bed,
Until that act of Parliament be repealed

Whereby my son is disinherited.
The northern lords that have forsworn thy colors   251
Will follow mine, if once they see them spread;
And spread they shall be, to thy foul disgrace
And utter ruin of the house of York.
Thus do I leave thee.—Come, son, let's away.
Our army is ready. Come, we'll after them.

KING HENRY
Stay, gentle Margaret, and hear me speak.

QUEEN MARGARET
Thou hast spoke too much already. Get thee gone.

KING HENRY
Gentle son Edward, thou wilt stay with me?

QUEEN MARGARET
Ay, to be murdered by his enemies!

PRINCE
When I return with victory from the field,
I'll see Your Grace. Till then I'll follow her.

QUEEN MARGARET
Come, son, away. We may not linger thus.
          [*Exeunt Queen Margaret and the Prince.*]

KING HENRY
Poor Queen! How love to me and to her son
Hath made her break out into terms of rage!   265
Revenged may she be on that hateful duke,
Whose haughty spirit, wingèd with desire,
Will cost my crown, and like an empty eagle   268
Tire on the flesh of me and of my son!   269
The loss of those three lords torments my heart.   270
I'll write unto them and entreat them fair.   271
Come, cousin, you shall be the messenger.

EXETER
And I, I hope, shall reconcile them all.

                                        Flourish. Exeunt.

1.2   *Enter Richard, Edward, and Montague.*

RICHARD
Brother, though I be youngest, give me leave.   1

EDWARD
No, I can better play the orator.

MONTAGUE
But I have reasons strong and forcible.

          Enter the Duke of York.

YORK
Why, how now, sons and brother, at a strife?   4
What is your quarrel? How began it first?

---

211 bewray betray, reveal   **218 unnatural** i.e., showing no feeling for a son   **233 head** i.e., free rein   **234 As** that   **239 Falconbridge** i.e., William Neville or his son Thomas. (See line 209 above and note.) **narrow seas** i.e., English Channel   **240 Duke** i.e., Duke of York **242 environèd** surrounded   **243 silly** helpless   **244 tossed** impaled. **pikes** long steel-pointed or axlike weapons   **245 granted** yielded

251 The northern lords i.e., Northumberland, Westmorland, and Clifford (as also in the *three lords* of line 270)   **265 terms** words **268 cost** i.e., deprive me of (with a pun on *coast*, "attack," "fly from the straight course," a metaphor that generates the image of the eagle).   **empty** hungry   **269 Tire** feed ravenously   **270 those three lords** i.e., Westmorland, Northumberland, and Clifford; see lines 176–188   **271 fair** civilly, kindly
1.2. Location: Sandal Castle (the Duke of York's castle) in Yorkshire. **1 give me leave** permit me (to speak first)   **4 brother** (See the note for 1.1.14.)

EDWARD
No quarrel, but a slight contention.

YORK   About what?

RICHARD
About that which concerns Your Grace and us:
The crown of England, Father, which is yours.

YORK
Mine, boy? Not till King Henry be dead.

RICHARD
Your right depends not on his life or death.

EDWARD
Now you are heir; therefore enjoy it now.
By giving the house of Lancaster leave to breathe,   13
It will outrun you, Father, in the end.

YORK
I took an oath that he should quietly reign.

EDWARD
But for a kingdom any oath may be broken.
I would break a thousand oaths to reign one year.

RICHARD
No. God forbid Your Grace should be forsworn.

YORK
I shall be, if I claim by open war.

RICHARD
I'll prove the contrary, if you'll hear me speak.

YORK
Thou canst not, son. It is impossible.

RICHARD
An oath is of no moment, being not took   22
Before a true and lawful magistrate
That hath authority over him that swears.
Henry had none, but did usurp the place.
Then, seeing 'twas he that made you to depose,   26
Your oath, my lord, is vain and frivolous.
Therefore, to arms! And, Father, do but think
How sweet a thing it is to wear a crown,
Within whose circuit is Elysium   30
And all that poets feign of bliss and joy.   31
Why do we linger thus? I cannot rest
Until the white rose that I wear be dyed
Even in the lukewarm blood of Henry's heart.

YORK
Richard, enough. I will be king, or die.
[To Montague.] Brother, thou shalt to London
    presently   36
And whet on Warwick to this enterprise.
Thou, Richard, shalt to the Duke of Norfolk
And tell him privily of our intent.   39
You, Edward, shall unto my Lord Cobham,
With whom the Kentishmen will willingly rise.
In them I trust, for they are soldiers,
Witty, courteous, liberal, full of spirit.   43
While you are thus employed, what resteth more   44
But that I seek occasion how to rise,

And yet the King not privy to my drift,   46
Nor any of the house of Lancaster?

        Enter a Messenger.

But stay, what news? Why com'st thou in such
    post?   48

MESSENGER
The Queen with all the northern earls and lords
Intend here to besiege you in your castle.
She is hard by with twenty thousand men,
And therefore fortify your hold, my lord.   52

YORK
Ay, with my sword. What, think'st thou that we
    fear them?
Edward and Richard, you shall stay with me;
My brother Montague shall post to London.
Let noble Warwick, Cobham, and the rest,
Whom we have left protectors of the King,
With powerful policy strengthen themselves   58
And trust not simple Henry nor his oaths.

MONTAGUE
Brother, I go. I'll win them, fear it not.
And thus most humbly I do take my leave.

                            Exit Montague.

    *Enter [Sir John] Mortimer and [Sir Hugh,] his
    brother.*

YORK
Sir John and Sir Hugh Mortimer, mine uncles,
You are come to Sandal in a happy hour.
The army of the Queen mean to besiege us.   63

SIR JOHN
She shall not need. We'll meet her in the field.

YORK   What, with five thousand men?

RICHARD
Ay, with five hundred, Father, for a need.   67
A woman's general. What should we fear?

                            A march afar off.

EDWARD
I hear their drums. Let's set our men in order,
And issue forth and bid them battle straight.   70

YORK
Five men to twenty! Though the odds be great,
I doubt not, uncle, of our victory.
Many a battle have I won in France
Whenas the enemy hath been ten to one.   74
Why should I not now have the like success?

                            Alarum. Exeunt.

1.3   [*Alarums.*] *Enter Rutland and his Tutor.*

RUTLAND
Ah, whither shall I fly to scape their hands?

---

46 privy to aware of   **48 post** haste   **52 hold** stronghold, castle
58 policy stratagem, cunning   **63 in a happy hour** opportunely
67 for a need if necessary   **70 straight** immediately   **74 Whenas**
when

**1.3. Location: Field of battle between Sandal Castle and Wakefield.
The action follows continuously from the previous scene.**
s.d. Alarums calls to arms (signaling by sound effects a battle fought
offstage)

---

13 to breathe i.e., to enjoy a respite   **22 moment** significance
26 depose take an oath   **30 Elysium** the classical abode after life of
those beloved of the gods   **31 feign** portray imaginatively   **36 presently** immediately   **39 privily** secretly   **43 Witty** intelligent.
liberal large-minded   **44 what resteth more** what else remains

Ah, tutor, look where bloody Clifford comes!

Enter Clifford [and soldiers].

CLIFFORD
Chaplain, away! Thy priesthood saves thy life.
As for the brat of this accursèd duke,   4
Whose father slew my father, he shall die.
TUTOR
And I, my lord, will bear him company.
CLIFFORD   Soldiers, away with him!
TUTOR
Ah, Clifford, murder not this innocent child,
Lest thou be hated both of God and man!
                    Exit [dragged off by soldiers].
CLIFFORD
How now, is he dead already? Or is it fear
That makes him close his eyes? I'll open them.
RUTLAND
So looks the pent-up lion o'er the wretch   12
That trembles under his devouring paws;
And so he walks, insulting o'er his prey,   14
And so he comes, to rend his limbs asunder.
Ah, gentle Clifford, kill me with thy sword   16
And not with such a cruel threatening look!
Sweet Clifford, hear me speak before I die!
I am too mean a subject for thy wrath.   19
Be thou revenged on men, and let me live.
CLIFFORD
In vain thou speak'st, poor boy. My father's blood
Hath stopped the passage where thy words should
    enter.
RUTLAND
Then let my father's blood open it again.
He is a man, and, Clifford, cope with him.   24
CLIFFORD
Had I thy brethren here, their lives and thine
Were not revenge sufficient for me;
No, if I digged up thy forefathers' graves
And hung their rotten coffins up in chains,
It could not slake mine ire nor ease my heart.   29
The sight of any of the house of York
Is as a fury to torment my soul;
And till I root out their accursèd line
And leave not one alive, I live in hell.
Therefore—   *[Lifting his sword.]*
RUTLAND
O, let me pray before I take my death!
To thee I pray. Sweet Clifford, pity me!
CLIFFORD
Such pity as my rapier's point affords.
RUTLAND
I never did thee harm. Why wilt thou slay me?

CLIFFORD
Thy father hath.
RUTLAND   But 'twas ere I was born.
Thou hast one son. For his sake pity me,
Lest in revenge thereof, sith God is just,   41
He be as miserably slain as I.
Ah, let me live in prison all my days,
And when I give occasion of offense,   44
Then let me die, for now thou hast no cause.
CLIFFORD   No cause?
Thy father slew my father. Therefore, die.
                        [He stabs him.]
RUTLAND
Di faciant laudis summa sit ista tuae!   *[He dies.]* 48
CLIFFORD
Plantagenet, I come, Plantagenet!
And this thy son's blood cleaving to my blade
Shall rust upon my weapon, till thy blood,
Congealed with this, do make me wipe off both.
                Exit [with soldiers, bearing off Rutland's body].

1.4   *Alarum. Enter Richard, Duke of York.*

YORK
The army of the Queen hath got the field.   1
My uncles both are slain in rescuing me,   2
And all my followers to the eager foe
Turn back and fly, like ships before the wind   4
Or lambs pursued by hunger-starvèd wolves.
My sons—God knows what hath bechancèd them;
But this I know, they have demeaned themselves   7
Like men born to renown by life or death.
Three times did Richard make a lane to me,
And thrice cried, "Courage, Father, fight it out!"
And full as oft came Edward to my side,
With purple falchion painted to the hilt   12
In blood of those that had encountered him.
And when the hardiest warriors did retire,
Richard cried, "Charge, and give no foot of
    ground!"
And cried, "A crown, or else a glorious tomb!   16
A scepter, or an earthly sepulcher!"
With this, we charged again, but, out, alas!   18
We budged again, as I have seen a swan   19
With bootless labor swim against the tide   20
And spend her strength with overmatching waves.   21
                    A short alarum within.

41 sith since   **44 occasion of** cause for   **48 Di . . . tuae** The gods
grant that this may be the height of your glory, the deed for which
you will be best known. (Ovid, *Heroides,* 2.66.)
1.4. Location: The battle of Wakefield continues.
1 got the field won the battle   **2 uncles** i.e., Sir John and Sir Hugh
Mortimer   **4 Turn back** turn their backs   **7 demeaned** conducted
12 purple purple with blood.   **falchion** curved sword   **16 And cried**
(Some text may be missing here; the parallelism of lines 9–13 suggests that Edward is quoted as speaking after Richard.)   **18 out** (An
expression of reproach.)   **19 budged** gave way   **20 bootless** fruitless
21 with against

4 duke i.e., Duke of York, who killed old Clifford in *2 Henry VI,* 5.2
12 pent-up caged, hence fierce and hungry   **14 insulting** gloating, exulting   **16 gentle** noble (with ironic suggestion of "free from harshness")   **19 mean** lowly. (Rutland appeals to the popular notion that,
because the lion was a royal beast, it would show compassion to
women and children. See 2.2.11–12.)   **24 cope with** engage in
combat with   **29 slake** lessen

Ah, hark! The fatal followers do pursue,   22
And I am faint and cannot fly their fury;
And, were I strong, I would not shun their fury.
The sands are numbered that makes up my life.   25
Here must I stay, and here my life must end.

Enter the Queen [Margaret], Clifford,
Northumberland, the young Prince, and soldiers.

Come, bloody Clifford, rough Northumberland,
I dare your quenchless fury to more rage.   28
I am your butt, and I abide your shot.   29
NORTHUMBERLAND
Yield to our mercy, proud Plantagenet.   30
CLIFFORD
Ay, to such mercy as his ruthless arm,
With downright payment, showed unto my father.
Now Phaëton hath tumbled from his car   33
And made an evening at the noontide prick.   34
YORK
My ashes, as the phoenix, may bring forth   35
A bird that will revenge upon you all;
And in that hope I throw mine eyes to heaven,
Scorning whate'er you can afflict me with.
Why come you not? What? Multitudes, and fear?
CLIFFORD
So cowards fight when they can fly no further;
So doves do peck the falcon's piercing talons;
So desperate thieves, all hopeless of their lives,
Breathe out invectives 'gainst the officers.
YORK
O Clifford, but bethink thee once again,   44
And in thy thought o'errun my former time;   45
And, if thou canst for blushing, view this face,   46
And bite thy tongue, that slanders him with
   cowardice
Whose frown hath made thee faint and fly ere this!
CLIFFORD
I will not bandy with thee word for word,   49
But buckler with thee blows, twice two for one.   50
[He threatens with his sword.]
QUEEN MARGARET
Hold, valiant Clifford! For a thousand causes
I would prolong awhile the traitor's life.
Wrath makes him deaf.—Speak thou,
   Northumberland.   53
NORTHUMBERLAND
Hold, Clifford! Do not honor him so much
To prick thy finger, though to wound his heart.
What valor were it, when a cur doth grin,   56
For one to thrust his hand between his teeth,

When he might spurn him with his foot away?   58
It is war's prize to take all vantages,   59
And ten to one is no impeach of valor.   60
[They capture York, who struggles.]
CLIFFORD
Ay, ay, so strives the woodcock with the gin.   61
NORTHUMBERLAND
So doth the coney struggle in the net.   62
YORK
So triumph thieves upon their conquered booty;
So true men yield, with robbers so o'ermatched.   64
NORTHUMBERLAND *[to the Queen]*
What would Your Grace have done unto him now?
QUEEN MARGARET
Brave warriors, Clifford and Northumberland,
Come, make him stand upon this molehill here,
That raught at mountains with outstretchèd arms   68
Yet parted but the shadow with his hand.—   69
What, was it you that would be England's king?
Was 't you that reveled in our Parliament   71
And made a preachment of your high descent?   72
Where are your mess of sons to back you now,   73
The wanton Edward and the lusty George?
And where's that valiant crookback prodigy,   75
Dicky, your boy, that with his grumbling voice
Was wont to cheer his dad in mutinies?   77
Or, with the rest, where is your darling Rutland?
Look, York, I stained this napkin with the blood   79
That valiant Clifford, with his rapier's point,
Made issue from the bosom of the boy;
And if thine eyes can water for his death,
I give thee this to dry thy cheeks withal.   83
[She gives him the bloodstained cloth.]
Alas, poor York, but that I hate thee deadly,   84
I should lament thy miserable state.
I prithee, grieve, to make me merry, York.
What, hath thy fiery heart so parched thine entrails
That not a tear can fall for Rutland's death?
Why art thou patient, man? Thou shouldst be mad;
And I, to make thee mad, do mock thee thus.
Stamp, rave, and fret, that I may sing and dance.
Thou wouldst be fee'd, I see, to make me sport.   92
York cannot speak, unless he wear a crown.—
A crown for York! And, lords, bow low to him.
Hold you his hands, whilst I do set it on.
[She puts a paper crown on his head.]
Ay, marry, sir, now looks he like a king!   96
Ay, this is he that took King Henry's chair,   97
And this is he was his adopted heir.
But how is it that great Plantagenet

22 followers pursuing troops 25 sands (of the hourglass) 28 dare defy. more even more 29 butt target 30 Yield . . . mercy put yourself at our mercy 33 Phaëton son of the sun god, who begged his father to allow him to drive the chariot of the sun; he drove it so near the earth that Zeus destroyed him with a thunderbolt 34 noontide prick exact point of noon on a sundial 35 phoenix fabulous bird that was consumed through spontaneous combustion and was reborn from its own ashes 44 but bethink thee only call to mind 45 o'errun review 46 for despite 49 bandy exchange 50 buckler join in close combat, grapple 53 him i.e., Clifford 56 grin show its teeth

58 spurn kick 59 prize reward, benefit 60 impeach calling in question 61 woodcock (A proverbially stupid bird.) gin snare, trap 62 coney rabbit 64 true honest 68 That raught he that reached 69 parted but only divided. (The prize York reached for turned out to be illusory.) 71 reveled rioted 72 preachment of sermon about 73 mess group of four 75 prodigy monster 77 cheer urge on. mutinies rebellions 79 napkin handkerchief 83 withal with 84 but were it not 92 fee'd paid 96 marry i.e., indeed. (Originally an oath, "by the Virgin Mary.") 97 chair throne

Is crowned so soon, and broke his solemn oath?
As I bethink me, you should not be king
Till our King Henry had shook hands with death.
And will you pale your head in Henry's glory,   103
And rob his temples of the diadem,
Now, in his life, against your holy oath?   105
O, 'tis a fault too-too unpardonable!
Off with the crown, and, with the crown, his head!
And whilst we breathe, take time to do him dead.   108

CLIFFORD
That is my office, for my father's sake.

QUEEN MARGARET
Nay, stay. Let's hear the orisons he makes.   110

YORK
She-wolf of France, but worse than wolves of
    France,
Whose tongue more poisons than the adder's tooth!
How ill-beseeming is it in thy sex
To triumph, like an Amazonian trull   114
Upon their woes whom fortune captivates!   115
But that thy face is, vizardlike, unchanging,   116
Made impudent with use of evil deeds,
I would essay, proud Queen, to make thee blush.   118
To tell thee whence thou cam'st, of whom derived,
Were shame enough to shame thee, wert thou not
    shameless.
Thy father bears the type of King of Naples,   121
Of both the Sicils and Jerusalem,   122
Yet not so wealthy as an English yeoman.   123
Hath that poor monarch taught thee to insult?   124
It needs not, nor it boots thee not, proud Queen,   125
Unless the adage must be verified
That beggars mounted run their horse to death.
'Tis beauty that doth oft make women proud;
But, God he knows, thy share thereof is small.
'Tis virtue that doth make them most admired;
The contrary doth make thee wondered at.
'Tis government that makes them seem divine;   132
The want thereof makes thee abominable.   133
Thou art as opposite to every good
As the Antipodes are unto us,   135
Or as the south to the Septentrion.   136
O tiger's heart wrapped in a woman's hide!
How couldst thou drain the lifeblood of the child,
To bid the father wipe his eyes withal,
And yet be seen to bear a woman's face?
Women are soft, mild, pitiful, and flexible;   141

Thou stern, obdurate, flinty, rough, remorseless.
Bidd'st thou me rage? Why, now thou hast thy wish.
Wouldst have me weep? Why, now thou hast thy
    will.
For raging wind blows up incessant showers,
And, when the rage allays, the rain begins.   146
                                                   [He weeps.]
These tears are my sweet Rutland's obsequies,   147
And every drop cries vengeance for his death
'Gainst thee, fell Clifford, and thee, false
    Frenchwoman.   149

NORTHUMBERLAND
Beshrew me, but his passions moves me so   150
That hardly can I check my eyes from tears.   151

YORK
That face of his the hungry cannibals
Would not have touched, would not have stained
    with blood.
But you are more inhuman, more inexorable,
O, ten times more, than tigers of Hyrcania.   155
See, ruthless Queen, a hapless father's tears!
This cloth thou dippedst in blood of my sweet boy,
And I with tears do wash the blood away.
Keep thou the napkin, and go boast of this;
And if thou tell'st the heavy story right,   160
Upon my soul, the hearers will shed tears.
Yea, even my foes will shed fast-falling tears
And say, "Alas, it was a piteous deed!"
There, take the crown, and with the crown my
    curse;   164
And in thy need such comfort come to thee
As now I reap at thy too cruel hand!
Hardhearted Clifford, take me from the world.
My soul to heaven, my blood upon your heads!

NORTHUMBERLAND
Had he been slaughterman to all my kin,
I should not for my life but weep with him,   170
To see how inly sorrow gripes his soul.   171

QUEEN MARGARET
What, weeping-ripe, my Lord Northumberland?   172
Think but upon the wrong he did us all,
And that will quickly dry thy melting tears.

CLIFFORD [stabbing him]
Here's for my oath. Here's for my father's death.

QUEEN MARGARET [stabbing him]
And here's to right our gentlehearted king.

YORK
Open Thy gate of mercy, gracious God!
My soul flies through these wounds to seek out
    Thee.   [He dies.]

103 pale encircle   105 life lifetime   108 breathe rest.   do him dead
kill him   110 orisons prayers   114 triumph exult.   Amazonian from
the race of legendary female warriors.   trull wench, whore
115 Upon . . . captivates upon the woes of those whom fortune
takes captive   116 But that were it not that.   vizardlike masklike
118 essay attempt   121 type title   122 both the Sicils i.e., Sicily and
Naples (known as the Kingdom of the Two Sicilies)   123 yeoman
landowner below rank of gentleman   124 insult triumph scornfully
125 needs not is unnecessary.   boots profits   132 government self-
government   133 want lack   135 Antipodes people dwelling on the
opposite side of the world   136 Septentrion the seven stars, i.e., the
Big Dipper, representing the north   141 pitiful capable of pity

146 allays abates   147 obsequies funeral observances   149 fell cruel
150 Beshrew curse   151 check restrain   155 Hyrcania region of the
ancient Persian empire, reputed to abound in wild beasts. (See the
Aeneid, 4.366–367.)   160 heavy sorrowful   164 There . . . crown
(Unless his hands are restrained, as at line 95, York probably removes
his paper crown and throws it to them, as with the handkerchief at
line 159.)   170 for my life if my life depended on it   171 inly inward.   gripes grieves (with suggestion also of grips, "seizes")
172 weeping-ripe ready to weep

QUEEN MARGARET
Off with his head and set it on York gates,
So York may overlook the town of York.
                    Flourish. Exeunt [with the body].

2.1   *A march. Enter Edward, Richard, and their power.*

EDWARD
I wonder how our princely father scaped,
Or whether he be scaped away or no
From Clifford's and Northumberland's pursuit.
Had he been ta'en, we should have heard the news;
Had he been slain, we should have heard the news;
Or had he scaped, methinks we should have heard
The happy tidings of his good escape.
How fares my brother? Why is he so sad?

RICHARD
I cannot joy until I be resolved   9
Where our right valiant father is become.   10
I saw him in the battle range about
And watched him how he singled Clifford forth.
Methought he bore him in the thickest troop   13
As doth a lion in a herd of neat,   14
Or as a bear encompassed round with dogs,
Who having pinched a few and made them cry,   16
The rest stand all aloof and bark at him.
So fared our father with his enemies;
So fled his enemies my warlike father.   19
Methinks 'tis prize enough to be his son.
See how the morning opes her golden gates
And takes her farewell of the glorious sun!   22
How well resembles it the prime of youth,
Trimmed like a younker prancing to his love!   24

EDWARD
Dazzle mine eyes, or do I see three suns?   25

RICHARD
Three glorious suns, each one a perfect sun,
Not separated with the racking clouds,   27
But severed in a pale clear-shining sky.
See, see! They join, embrace, and seem to kiss,
As if they vowed some league inviolable.
Now are they but one lamp, one light, one sun.
In this the heaven figures some event.   32

EDWARD
'Tis wondrous strange, the like yet never heard of.
I think it cites us, brother, to the field,   34
That we, the sons of brave Plantagenet,
Each one already blazing by our meeds,   36
Should notwithstanding join our lights together
And overshine the earth as this the world.   38
Whate'er it bodes, henceforward will I bear
Upon my target three fair-shining suns.   40

RICHARD
Nay, bear three daughters. By your leave I speak it,   41
You love the breeder better than the male.   42

            Enter one [a Messenger] blowing [a horn].

But what art thou, whose heavy looks foretell   43
Some dreadful story hanging on thy tongue?

MESSENGER
Ah, one that was a woeful looker-on
Whenas the noble Duke of York was slain,   46
Your princely father and my loving lord!

EDWARD
O, speak no more, for I have heard too much.

RICHARD
Say how he died, for I will hear it all.

MESSENGER
Environèd he was with many foes,   50
And stood against them, as the hope of Troy   51
Against the Greeks that would have entered Troy.
But Hercules himself must yield to odds;
And many strokes, though with a little ax,
Hews down and fells the hardest-timbered oak.
By many hands your father was subdued,
But only slaughtered by the ireful arm   57
Of unrelenting Clifford and the Queen,
Who crowned the gracious Duke in high despite,
Laughed in his face; and when with grief he wept,
The ruthless Queen gave him to dry his cheeks
A napkin steepèd in the harmless blood
Of sweet young Rutland, by rough Clifford slain.
And after many scorns, many foul taunts,
They took his head, and on the gates of York
They set the same; and there it doth remain,
The saddest spectacle that e'er I viewed.

EDWARD
Sweet Duke of York, our prop to lean upon,
Now thou art gone, we have no staff, no stay.   69
O Clifford, boisterous Clifford! Thou hast slain   70
The flower of Europe for his chivalry;
And treacherously hast thou vanquished him,
For hand to hand he would have vanquished thee.
Now my soul's palace is become a prison.   74

2.1. **Location**: Fields near the Welsh border or marches (line 140), historically identified as near Mortimer's Cross in Herefordshire, several days after the battle of Wakefield.
s.d. power army   **9 resolved** informed   **10 Where . . . become** what is become of our very valiant father   **13 bore him** conducted himself   **14 neat** cattle   **16 pinched** bit   **19 fled his enemies** his enemies fled from   **22 farewell** (The dawn is pictured as remaining behind while the sun ascends the sky.)   **24 Trimmed** dressed up. **younker** young man   **25 three suns** (According to the chronicles, it was because Edward saw three suns as a favorable omen before the battle of Mortimer's Cross, in which he triumphed, that he chose the bright sun as his badge.)   **27 with** by.   **racking** driving, scudding   **32 figures** prefigures

34 cites incites, impels   **36 meeds** worth, deserts   **38 overshine** (1) shine upon (2) surpass in shining.   **this** i.e., this phenomenon   **40 target** shield   **41 daughters** i.e., instead of sons or *suns*   **42 breeder** female. (Richard jokes about Edward's weakness for women, to be demonstrated in 3.2 and following.)   **s.d. blowing a horn** (Express riders thus announced themselves.)   **43 heavy** sorrowful   **46 Whenas** when   **50 Environèd** surrounded   **51 the hope of Troy** i.e., Hector   **57 ireful** angry   **69 stay** support   **70 boisterous** savage   **74 soul's palace** i.e., body

Ah, would she break from hence, that this my body
Might in the ground be closèd up in rest!
For never henceforth shall I joy again.
Never, O, never, shall I see more joy!   78

RICHARD
I cannot weep, for all my body's moisture
Scarce serves to quench my furnace-burning heart;
Nor can my tongue unload my heart's great burden,
For selfsame wind that I should speak withal   82
Is kindling coals that fires all my breast,
And burns me up with flames that tears would
    quench.
To weep is to make less the depth of grief.
Tears, then, for babes; blows and revenge for me!
Richard, I bear thy name. I'll venge thy death,
Or die renownèd by attempting it.

EDWARD
His name that valiant duke hath left with thee;
His dukedom and his chair with me is left.   90

RICHARD
Nay, if thou be that princely eagle's bird,   91
Show thy descent by gazing 'gainst the sun;   92
For "chair" and "dukedom," "throne" and
    "kingdom" say;
Either that is thine, or else thou wert not his.   94

*March. Enter Warwick, Marquess Montague, and
their army.*

WARWICK
How now, fair lords? What fare? What news
    abroad?   95

RICHARD
Great lord of Warwick, if we should recount
Our baleful news, and at each word's deliverance
Stab poniards in our flesh till all were told,   98
The words would add more anguish than the
    wounds.
O valiant lord, the Duke of York is slain!

EDWARD
O Warwick, Warwick! That Plantagenet,
Which held thee dearly as his soul's redemption,
Is by the stern Lord Clifford done to death.

WARWICK
Ten days ago I drowned these news in tears;
And now, to add more measure to your woes,   105
I come to tell you things sith then befallen.   106
After the bloody fray at Wakefield fought,
Where your brave father breathed his latest gasp,   108
Tidings, as swiftly as the posts could run,   109
Were brought me of your loss and his depart.   110

I, then in London, keeper of the King,   111
Mustered my soldiers, gathered flocks of friends,
And very well appointed, as I thought,   113
Marched toward Saint Albans to intercept the
    Queen,
Bearing the King in my behalf along;   115
For by my scouts I was advertisèd   116
That she was coming with a full intent
To dash our late decree in Parliament   118
Touching King Henry's oath and your succession. 119
Short tale to make, we at Saint Albans met,
Our battles joined, and both sides fiercely fought. 121
But whether 'twas the coldness of the King,
Who looked full gently on his warlike queen,
That robbed my soldiers of their heated spleen,   124
Or whether 'twas report of her success,
Or more than common fear of Clifford's rigor,   126
Who thunders to his captives blood and death,
I cannot judge; but, to conclude with truth,
Their weapons like to lightning came and went;
Our soldiers', like the night owl's lazy flight,
Or like an idle thresher with a flail,   131
Fell gently down, as if they struck their friends.
I cheered them up with justice of our cause,
With promise of high pay and great rewards,
But all in vain. They had no heart to fight,
And we in them no hope to win the day,
So that we fled: the King unto the Queen;
Lord George your brother, Norfolk, and myself   138
In haste, posthaste, are come to join with you.
For in the marches here we heard you were,   140
Making another head to fight again.   141

EDWARD
Where is the Duke of Norfolk, gentle Warwick?   142
And when came George from Burgundy to England?

WARWICK
Some six miles off the Duke is with his soldiers;
And for your brother, he was lately sent   145
From your kind aunt, Duchess of Burgundy,   146
With aid of soldiers to this needful war.

RICHARD
'Twas odds, belike, when valiant Warwick fled.   148
Oft have I heard his praises in pursuit,   149
But ne'er till now his scandal of retire.   150

WARWICK
Nor now my scandal, Richard, dost thou hear;
For thou shalt know this strong right hand of mine
Can pluck the diadem from faint Henry's head

78 **see more joy** see joy any more   **82 For . . . withal** for that very
breath that I should use in speaking   **90 his chair** i.e., his ducal seat,
but also the claim to the throne   **91 bird** i.e., offspring   **92 gazing
. . . sun** (According to Pliny and other writers, eagles could gaze unblinkingly at the sun and would test their young by forcing them to do
so.)   **94 that** i.e., the throne, symbolized by the sun.   **his** i.e., Plantagenet's son.   **s.d. army** (The Octavo text specifies drum, i.e., drummer, and ensign along with soldiers.)   **95 What fare** how are things
faring   **98 poniards** daggers   **105 measure** quantity   **106 sith** since
108 latest last   **109 posts** messengers   **110 depart** departure, i.e.,
death

111 **keeper** jailer   **113 appointed** equipped   **115 in my behalf** for my
advantage   **116 advertised** informed   **118 dash** overthrow.   **late** recent   **119 Touching** regarding   **121 battles** armies   **124 heated
spleen** i.e., courage roused to a high pitch   **126 rigor** fierceness
131 flail threshing tool   **138 Lord George** i.e., George, later Duke of
Clarence, brother to Edward and Richard   **140 marches** borders (of
Wales)   **141 Making another head** raising another armed force
142 gentle noble   **145 for** as for   **146 Duchess of Burgundy** (A
granddaughter of John of Gaunt and distant relative of Richard of
York, to whom, according to the chroniclers, both George and Richard were sent for protection after York's execution.)   **148 'Twas odds,
belike** i.e., no doubt the odds were very heavy   **149 in pursuit** i.e.,
for pursuing the enemy   **150 his . . . retire** i.e., condemnation of
him for retreating

And wring the awful scepter from his fist,   154
Were he as famous and as bold in war
As he is famed for mildness, peace, and prayer.
RICHARD
I know it well, Lord Warwick. Blame me not.
'Tis love I bear thy glories make me speak.   158
But in this troublous time what's to be done?
Shall we go throw away our coats of steel
And wrap our bodies in black mourning gowns,
Numb'ring our Ave Marys with our beads?   162
Or shall we on the helmets of our foes
Tell our devotion with revengeful arms?   164
If for the last, say ay, and to it, lords.
WARWICK
Why, therefore Warwick came to seek you out,
And therefore comes my brother Montague.
Attend me, lords. The proud insulting Queen,   168
With Clifford and the haught Northumberland,   169
And of their feather many more proud birds,
Have wrought the easy-melting King like wax.   171
He swore consent to your succession,
His oath enrollèd in the Parliament,   173
And now to London all the crew are gone
To frustrate both his oath and what besides   175
May make against the house of Lancaster.   176
Their power, I think, is thirty thousand strong.
Now, if the help of Norfolk and myself,
With all the friends that thou, brave Earl of March,   179
Amongst the loving Welshmen canst procure,   180
Will but amount to five-and-twenty thousand,
Why, *via*! To London will we march,   182
And once again bestride our foaming steeds,
And once again cry "Charge!" upon our foes,
But never once again turn back and fly.   185
RICHARD
Ay, now methinks I hear great Warwick speak.
Ne'er may he live to see a sunshine day   187
That cries "Retire!" if Warwick bid him stay.   188
EDWARD
Lord Warwick, on thy shoulder will I lean;
And when thou fail'st—as God forbid the hour!—
Must Edward fall, which peril heaven forfend!   191
WARWICK
No longer Earl of March, but Duke of York;
The next degree is England's royal throne.   193
For King of England shalt thou be proclaimed
In every borough as we pass along;
And he that throws not up his cap for joy
Shall for the fault make forfeit of his head.
King Edward, valiant Richard, Montague,

Stay we no longer, dreaming of renown,   199
But sound the trumpets and about our task.
RICHARD
Then, Clifford, were thy heart as hard as steel,
As thou hast shown it flinty by thy deeds,
I come to pierce it or to give thee mine.
EDWARD
Then strike up drums. God and Saint George for us!   204

Enter a Messenger.

WARWICK   How now? What news?
MESSENGER
The Duke of Norfolk sends you word by me
The Queen is coming with a puissant host;   207
And craves your company for speedy counsel.
WARWICK
Why then it sorts. Brave warriors, let's away.   209
                                                        Exeunt omnes.

❖

2.2   *Flourish. Enter the King [Henry], the Queen*
          [Margaret], Clifford, Northumberland, and young
          Prince, with drum and trumpets. [York's head is
          set above the gates.]

QUEEN MARGARET
Welcome, my lord, to this brave town of York.   1
Yonder's the head of that archenemy
That sought to be encompassed with your crown.
Doth not the object cheer your heart, my lord?
KING HENRY
Ay, as the rocks cheer them that fear their wreck.   5
To see this sight, it irks my very soul.
Withhold revenge, dear God! 'Tis not my fault,
Nor wittingly have I infringed my vow.
CLIFFORD
My gracious liege, this too much lenity
And harmful pity must be laid aside.
To whom do lions cast their gentle looks?
Not to the beast that would usurp their den.
Whose hand is that the forest bear doth lick?
Not his that spoils her young before her face.   14
Who scapes the lurking serpent's mortal sting?
Not he that sets his foot upon her back.
The smallest worm will turn, being trodden on,
And doves will peck in safeguard of their brood.   18
Ambitious York did level at thy crown,   19
Thou smiling while he knit his angry brows.
He, but a duke, would have his son a king
And raise his issue, like a loving sire;   22
Thou, being a king, blest with a goodly son,
Didst yield consent to disinherit him,
Which argued thee a most unloving father.   25

154 **awful** awe-inspiring 158 **make** that makes 162 **beads** rosary
beads (used in reciting *Ave Marys*, i.e., Ave Marias or Hail Marys)
164 **Tell our devotion** (1) count off our prayers (2) proclaim our love.
(Said ironically.) 168 **Attend** listen to. **insulting** scornfully triumphing 169 **haught** haughty 171 **wrought** worked on, manipulated
173 **enrolled** recorded on official rolls 175 **frustrate** annul. **what
besides** anything else 176 **make** be effective 179 **Earl of March**
i.e., Edward, who, at his father's death, inherited this with other titles
180 **loving** loyal, friendly 182 **via** forward 185 **turn back** turn our
backs 187 **he** i.e., anyone 188 **stay** stand firm 191 **forfend** forbid
193 **degree** step, rank

199 **Stay we** let us remain 204 **Saint George** patron saint of England
207 **puissant** powerful 209 **sorts** is fitting, is working out
2.2. Location: Before the walls of York.
s.d. drum drummer. **trumpets** trumpeters 1 **brave** fine 5 **wreck**
shipwreck, destruction 14 **spoils** destroys, seizes as prey 18 **safeguard of** safeguarding 19 **level** aim 22 **raise** raise in dignity. **issue**
offspring 25 **argued thee** showed you to be

Unreasonable creatures feed their young;   26
And though man's face be fearful to their eyes,   27
Yet, in protection of their tender ones,
Who hath not seen them, even with those wings
Which sometimes they have used with fearful flight,
Make war with him that climbed unto their nest,
Offering their own lives in their young's defense?
For shame, my liege, make them your precedent!
Were it not pity that this goodly boy
Should lose his birthright by his father's fault,
And long hereafter say unto his child,
"What my great-grandfather and grandsire got,
My careless father fondly gave away"?   38
Ah, what a shame were this! Look on the boy,
And let his manly face, which promiseth
Successful fortune, steel thy melting heart
To hold thine own and leave thine own with him.

KING HENRY
Full well hath Clifford played the orator,
Inferring arguments of mighty force.   44
But, Clifford, tell me, didst thou never hear
That things ill got had ever bad success?   46
And happy always was it for that son   47
Whose father for his hoarding went to hell?   48
I'll leave my son my virtuous deeds behind;
And would my father had left me no more!
For all the rest is held at such a rate   51
As brings a thousandfold more care to keep
Than in possession any jot of pleasure.
Ah, cousin York, would thy best friends did know
How it doth grieve me that thy head is here!

QUEEN MARGARET
My lord, cheer up your spirits. Our foes are nigh,
And this soft courage makes your followers faint. 57
You promised knighthood to our forward son.   58
Unsheathe your sword and dub him presently.   59
Edward, kneel down.   [The Prince kneels.]

KING HENRY
Edward Plantagenet, arise a knight,
And learn this lesson: Draw thy sword in right.

PRINCE [rising]
My gracious Father, by your kingly leave,
I'll draw it as apparent to the crown,   64
And in that quarrel use it to the death.

CLIFFORD
Why, that is spoken like a toward prince.   66

Enter a Messenger.

MESSENGER
Royal commanders, be in readiness,
For with a band of thirty thousand men
Comes Warwick, backing of the Duke of York,   69
And in the towns, as they do march along,

Proclaims him king, and many fly to him.
Darraign your battle, for they are at hand.   72

CLIFFORD
I would Your Highness would depart the field.
The Queen hath best success when you are absent.

QUEEN MARGARET
Ay, good my lord, and leave us to our fortune.

KING HENRY
Why, that's my fortune too. Therefore I'll stay.

NORTHUMBERLAND
Be it with resolution then to fight.

PRINCE
My royal Father, cheer these noble lords
And hearten those that fight in your defense.
Unsheathe your sword, good Father; cry "Saint
  George!"   80

March. Enter Edward, Warwick, Richard, [George
of] Clarence, Norfolk, Montague, and soldiers.

EDWARD
Now, perjured Henry, wilt thou kneel for grace   81
And set thy diadem upon my head,
Or bide the mortal fortune of the field?   83

QUEEN MARGARET
Go rate thy minions, proud insulting boy!   84
Becomes it thee to be thus bold in terms   85
Before thy sovereign and thy lawful king?

EDWARD
I am his king, and he should bow his knee.
I was adopted heir by his consent.
Since when, his oath is broke; for, as I hear,
You, that are king, though he do wear the crown,   90
Have caused him, by new act of Parliament,
To blot out me and put his own son in.

CLIFFORD   And reason too.
Who should succeed the father but the son?

RICHARD
Are you there, butcher? O, I cannot speak!   95

CLIFFORD
Ay, crookback, here I stand to answer thee,
Or any he the proudest of thy sort.   97

RICHARD
'Twas you that killed young Rutland, was it not?

CLIFFORD
Ay, and old York, and yet not satisfied.

RICHARD
For God's sake, lords, give signal to the fight.

WARWICK
What sayst thou, Henry, wilt thou yield the crown?

QUEEN MARGARET
Why, how now, long-tongued Warwick, dare you
  speak?
When you and I met at Saint Albans last,

---

26 **Unreasonable** not endowed with reason 27 **fearful** causing fear
38 **fondly** foolishly 44 **Inferring** alleging, adducing 46 **success** outcome 47–48 **And . . . hell** i.e., the son may be fortunate in inheriting wealth, but the father who obtained that wealth by hoarding and
miserly grasping will go to hell 51 **rate** cost 57 **faint** fainthearted
58 **forward** promising 59 **presently** at once 64 **apparent** heir
66 **toward** ready, bold, promising 69 **Duke of York** i.e., Edward

72 **Darraign your battle** set your army in battle array 80 s.d.
George of Clarence (Actually, George is not made Duke of Clarence
until 2.6.104.) 81 **grace** mercy, pardon 83 **bide** await. **mortal** fatal 84 **rate thy minions** chide your followers or favorites 85 **terms**
language 90 **You, that are king** i.e., you, Margaret, who, in fact,
rule 95 **butcher** (Clifford was nicknamed "the butcher" for his cruelty.) 97 **any he** any man. **sort** gang

Your legs did better service than your hands.

WARWICK
Then 'twas my turn to fly, and now 'tis thine.

CLIFFORD
You said so much before, and yet you fled.

WARWICK
'Twas not your valor, Clifford, drove me thence.

NORTHUMBERLAND
No, nor your manhood that durst make you stay.

RICHARD
Northumberland, I hold thee reverently.　109
Break off the parley, for scarce I can refrain　110
The execution of my big-swoll'n heart　111
Upon that Clifford, that cruel child-killer.

CLIFFORD
I slew thy father. Call'st thou him a child?

RICHARD
Ay, like a dastard and a treacherous coward,
As thou didst kill our tender brother Rutland;
But ere sunset I'll make thee curse the deed.

KING HENRY
Have done with words, my lords, and hear me
　speak.

QUEEN MARGARET
Defy them, then, or else hold close thy lips.

KING HENRY
I prithee, give no limits to my tongue.　119
I am a king, and privileged to speak.

CLIFFORD
My liege, the wound that bred this meeting here
Cannot be cured by words. Therefore be still.

RICHARD
Then, executioner, unsheathe thy sword.
By Him that made us all, I am resolved　124
That Clifford's manhood lies upon his tongue.　125

EDWARD
Say, Henry, shall I have my right or no?
A thousand men have broke their fasts today　127
That ne'er shall dine unless thou yield the crown.

WARWICK
If thou deny, their blood upon thy head,　129
For York in justice puts his armor on.

PRINCE
If that be right which Warwick says is right,
There is no wrong, but everything is right.

RICHARD
Whoever got thee, there thy mother stands;　133
For, well I wot, thou hast thy mother's tongue.　134

QUEEN MARGARET
But thou art neither like thy sire nor dam,
But like a foul misshapen stigmatic,
Marked by the destinies to be avoided,　136

As venom toads or lizards' dreadful stings.　138

RICHARD
Iron of Naples hid with English gilt,　139
Whose father bears the title of a king—
As if a channel should be called the sea—　141
Sham'st thou not, knowing whence thou art
　extraught,　142
To let thy tongue detect thy baseborn heart?　143

EDWARD
A wisp of straw were worth a thousand crowns　144
To make this shameless callet know herself.　145
Helen of Greece was fairer far than thou,
Although thy husband may be Menelaus;　147
And ne'er was Agamemnon's brother wronged　148
By that false woman, as this king by thee.
His father reveled in the heart of France,　150
And tamed the King, and made the Dauphin stoop;
And had he matched according to his state,　152
He might have kept that glory to this day.
But when he took a beggar to his bed
And graced thy poor sire with his bridal day,　155
Even then that sunshine brewed a shower for him
That washed his father's fortunes forth of France　157
And heaped sedition on his crown at home.
For what hath broached this tumult but thy pride?　159
Hadst thou been meek, our title still had slept,　160
And we, in pity of the gentle King,
Had slipped our claim until another age.　162

GEORGE
But when we saw our sunshine made thy spring,　163
And that thy summer bred us no increase,　164
We set the ax to thy usurping root;
And though the edge hath something hit ourselves,　166
Yet know thou, since we have begun to strike,
We'll never leave till we have hewn thee down　168
Or bathed thy growing with our heated bloods.　169

EDWARD
And in this resolution I defy thee,
Not willing any longer conference,
Since thou deniedst the gentle King to speak.
Sound trumpets! Let our bloody colors wave!
And either victory, or else a grave.

QUEEN MARGARET　Stay, Edward.

---

138 venom venomous　**139 Iron . . . gilt** i.e., you cheap product of Naples (being daughter of the titular King of Naples), being gilded over by an English marriage　**141 As . . . sea** i.e., comparing your father to a king is like comparing a gutter (*channel*) to the sea　**142 extraught** descended, extracted　**143 detect** expose　**144 wisp of straw** (A traditional way of marking or branding a scolding woman.)　**145 callet** lewd woman　**147 Menelaus** husband of Helen of Greece, whose abduction led to the Trojan War. (By implication, King Henry is the cuckolded husband, just as Menelaus was.)　**148 Agamemnon** brother of Menelaus and leader of the Greeks in the Trojan War　**150 His father** i.e., Henry V　**152 had . . . state** i.e., if Henry VI had married someone equal to him in social position　**155 graced** honored.　**thy poor sire** i.e., Reignier, King of Naples.　**his** i.e., Henry VI's　**157 of** out of　**159 broached** set flowing, started　**160 title** claim to the throne　**162 Had slipped** would have postponed　**163 But . . . spring** i.e., but when we saw you reaping all the benefit of what should be ours　**164 increase** harvest　**166 something** somewhat　**168 leave** leave off　**169 bathed thy growing** have watered your growth

---

109 hold thee reverently hold you in the greatest respect　**110 refrain** give up, hold back　**111 execution** i.e., giving practical effect to my passion　**119 give** set　**124 resolved** convinced　**125 lies . . . tongue** i.e., consists only in words　**127 broke their fasts** i.e., had breakfast　**129 deny** refuse.　**upon** be upon　**133 got** begot, sired　**134 wot** know　**136 stigmatic** one branded with the mark of his crime or deformity. (See *2 Henry VI*, 5.1.215.)

EDWARD
No, wrangling woman, we'll no longer stay.
These words will cost ten thousand lives this day.   177

Exeunt omnes.

2.3   *Alarum. Excursions. Enter Warwick.*

WARWICK
Forspent with toil, as runners with a race,   1
I lay me down a little while to breathe;   2
For strokes received and many blows repaid
Have robbed my strong-knit sinews of their strength,
And, spite of spite, needs must I rest awhile.   5

Enter Edward, running.

EDWARD
Smile, gentle heaven, or strike, ungentle death!   6
For this world frowns, and Edward's sun is clouded.

WARWICK
How now, my lord, what hap? What hope of good?   8

Enter [George of] Clarence.

GEORGE
Our hap is loss, our hope but sad despair,
Our ranks are broke, and ruin follows us.
What counsel give you? Whither shall we fly?

EDWARD
Bootless is flight. They follow us with wings,   12
And weak we are and cannot shun pursuit.

Enter Richard.

RICHARD
Ah, Warwick, why hast thou withdrawn thyself?
Thy brother's blood the thirsty earth hath drunk,   15
Broached with the steely point of Clifford's lance;   16
And in the very pangs of death he cried,
Like to a dismal clangor heard from far,
"Warwick, revenge! Brother, revenge my death!"
So, underneath the belly of their steeds,
That stained their fetlocks in his smoking blood,
The noble gentleman gave up the ghost.

WARWICK
Then let the earth be drunken with our blood!
I'll kill my horse, because I will not fly.
Why stand we like softhearted women here,
Wailing our losses, whiles the foe doth rage,
And look upon, as if the tragedy   27
Were played in jest by counterfeiting actors?   28

Here on my knee I vow to God above   *[kneeling]*
I'll never pause again, never stand still,
Till either death hath closed these eyes of mine
Or fortune given me measure of revenge.   32

EDWARD *[kneeling]*
O Warwick, I do bend my knee with thine,
And in this vow do chain my soul to thine!
And, ere my knee rise from the earth's cold face,
I throw my hands, mine eyes, my heart to Thee,   36
Thou setter-up and plucker-down of kings,
Beseeching Thee, if with Thy will it stands   38
That to my foes this body must be prey,
Yet that Thy brazen gates of heaven may ope
And give sweet passage to my sinful soul!

[They rise.]

Now, lords, take leave until we meet again,
Where'er it be, in heaven or in earth.

RICHARD
Brother, give me thy hand; and, gentle Warwick,   44
Let me embrace thee in my weary arms.

[They embrace.]

I, that did never weep, now melt with woe
That winter should cut off our springtime so.

WARWICK
Away, away! Once more, sweet lords, farewell.

GEORGE
Yet let us all together to our troops,
And give them leave to fly that will not stay,
And call them pillars that will stand to us;   51
And, if we thrive, promise them such rewards
As victors wear at the Olympian games.
This may plant courage in their quailing breasts,
For yet is hope of life and victory.
Forslow no longer! Make we hence amain.   *Exeunt.* 56

2.4   *Excursions. Enter Richard and Clifford [meeting].*

RICHARD
Now, Clifford, I have singled thee alone.   1
Suppose this arm is for the Duke of York,
And this for Rutland—both bound to revenge,
Wert thou environed with a brazen wall.   4

CLIFFORD
Now, Richard, I am with thee here alone.
This is the hand that stabbed thy father York,
And this the hand that slew thy brother Rutland,
And here's the heart that triumphs in their death
And cheers these hands that slew thy sire and
        brother   9
To execute the like upon thyself.
And so, have at thee!   11

They fight. Warwick comes; Clifford flies.

177 s.d. omnes all
2.3. Location: The field of battle near York, immediately following the preceding scene. (Historically, the field of battle was between Towton and Saxton in Yorkshire.)
s.d. Excursions sorties, forays of armed soldiers   **1 Forspent** exhausted   **2 breathe** rest   **5 spite of spite** i.e., come what may.   **needs must I** I must   **6 ungentle** ignoble   **8 hap** fortune   **12 Bootless** useless   **15 Thy brother's blood** (Warwick's half-brother, the Bastard of Salisbury, not among the *Dramatis Personae* of this play, was killed at Ferrybridge shortly before the battle of Towton.)   **16 Broached with** set flowing by   **27 upon** on   **28 counterfeiting actors** actors performing roles

32 measure full quantity   **36 Thee** i.e., God   **38 stands** agrees
44 gentle noble   **51 stand to** support   **56 Forslow** delay.   **amain** with full speed
2.4. Location: Scene continues at the battlefield.
1 singled singled out, chosen   **4 environed** surrounded   **9 cheers** urges on   **11 have at thee** i.e., on guard, here I come

RICHARD

Nay, Warwick, single out some other chase,   12
For I myself will hunt this wolf to death.   *Exeunt.*

2.5   *Alarum. Enter King Henry alone.*

KING HENRY

This battle fares like to the morning's war,
When dying clouds contend with growing light,
What time the shepherd, blowing of his nails,   3
Can neither call it perfect day nor night.
Now sways it this way, like a mighty sea
Forced by the tide to combat with the wind;
Now sways it that way, like the selfsame sea
Forced to retire by fury of the wind.
Sometimes the flood prevails, and then the wind;
Now one the better, then another best;
Both tugging to be victors, breast to breast,
Yet neither conqueror nor conquerèd.
So is the equal poise of this fell war.   13
Here on this molehill will I sit me down.   [*He sits.*]
To whom God will, there be the victory!
For Margaret my queen, and Clifford too,
Have chid me from the battle, swearing both
They prosper best of all when I am thence.
Would I were dead, if God's good will were so!
For what is in this world but grief and woe?
O God! Methinks it were a happy life
To be no better than a homely swain,   22
To sit upon a hill, as I do now,
To carve out dials quaintly, point by point,   24
Thereby to see the minutes how they run:
How many makes the hour full complete,
How many hours brings about the day,
How many days will finish up the year,
How many years a mortal man may live.
When this is known, then to divide the times:
So many hours must I tend my flock,
So many hours must I take my rest,
So many hours must I contemplate,
So many hours must I sport myself,   34
So many days my ewes have been with young,
So many weeks ere the poor fools will ean,   36
So many years ere I shall shear the fleece.
So minutes, hours, days, months, and years,
Passed over to the end they were created,   39
Would bring white hairs unto a quiet grave.
Ah, what a life were this, how sweet, how lovely!
Gives not the hawthorn bush a sweeter shade
To shepherds looking on their silly sheep   43
Than doth a rich embroidered canopy
To kings that fear their subjects' treachery?

O, yes, it doth, a thousandfold it doth.
And to conclude, the shepherd's homely curds,
His cold thin drink out of his leather bottle,
His wonted sleep under a fresh tree's shade,   49
All which secure and sweetly he enjoys,
Is far beyond a prince's delicates—   51
His viands sparkling in a golden cup,
His body couchèd in a curious bed—   53
When care, mistrust, and treason waits on him.

*Alarum. Enter a Son that hath killed his father, at
one door [bearing in the dead body].*

SON

Ill blows the wind that profits nobody.
This man, whom hand to hand I slew in fight,
May be possessèd with some store of crowns;   57
And I, that haply take them from him now,   58
May yet ere night yield both my life and them
To some man else, as this dead man doth me.—
Who's this? O God! It is my father's face,
Whom in this conflict I unwares have killed.
O, heavy times, begetting such events!   63
From London by the King was I pressed forth;   64
My father, being the Earl of Warwick's man,   65
Came on the part of York, pressed by his master;   66
And I, who at his hands received my life,
Have by my hands of life bereavèd him.
Pardon me, God, I knew not what I did!   69
And pardon, Father, for I knew not thee!
My tears shall wipe away these bloody marks;
And no more words till they have flowed their fill.
                                        [*He weeps.*]

KING HENRY

O piteous spectacle! O bloody times!
Whiles lions war and battle for their dens,
Poor harmless lambs abide their enmity.   75
Weep, wretched man. I'll aid thee tear for tear;
And let our hearts and eyes, like civil war,
Be blind with tears, and break o'ercharged with
        grief.   [*He weeps.*] 78

*Enter at another door, a Father that hath killed his
son, bearing of his son.*

FATHER

Thou that so stoutly hath resisted me,   79
Give me thy gold, if thou hast any gold;
For I have bought it with an hundred blows.
But let me see: is this our foeman's face?
Ah, no, no, no, it is mine only son!
Ah, boy, if any life be left in thee,
Throw up thine eye! See, see what showers arise,
Blown with the windy tempest of my heart,
Upon thy wounds, that kills mine eye and heart!

---

12 chase prey
2.5. Location: The battlefield, as before.
3 What time when.   **of** on (to warm them)   **13 poise** balance.   **fell**
cruel   **22 homely** simple   **24 dials** sundials.   **quaintly** artfully, intricately   **34 sport** amuse   **36 ean** bring forth (lambs)   **39 end they** end
for which they   **43 silly** innocent, helpless

49 wonted accustomed   **51 delicates** luxuries   **53 curious** skillfully
and daintily made, decorated   **57 crowns** i.e., coins, money
58 haply by chance   **63 heavy** sorrowful   **64 pressed forth** impressed
into military service   **65 man** retainer, servant   **66 part** party, side
69 Pardon . . . did (An echo of Luke 23:34, "Father, forgive them,
for they know not what they do.")   **75 abide** endure, pay for
78 o'ercharged overfilled   **79 stoutly** bravely

O, pity, God, this miserable age!   [*He weeps.*]
What stratagems, how fell, how butcherly,   89
Erroneous, mutinous, and unnatural,   90
This deadly quarrel daily doth beget!
O boy, thy father gave thee life too soon,
And hath bereft thee of thy life too late!   93

KING HENRY
Woe above woe, grief more than common grief!   94
O, that my death would stay these ruthful deeds!   95
O, pity, pity, gentle heaven, pity!
The red rose and the white are on his face,
The fatal colors of our striving houses.
The one his purple blood right well resembles;
The other his pale cheeks, methinks, presenteth.   100
Wither one rose, and let the other flourish;
If you contend, a thousand lives must wither.

SON
How will my mother for a father's death
Take on with me and ne'er be satisfied!   104

FATHER
How will my wife for slaughter of my son
Shed seas of tears and ne'er be satisfied!

KING HENRY
How will the country for these woeful chances   107
Misthink the King and not be satisfied!   108

SON
Was ever son so rued a father's death?

FATHER
Was ever father so bemoaned his son?

KING HENRY
Was ever king so grieved for subjects' woe?
Much is your sorrow; mine ten times so much.

SON
I'll bear thee hence, where I may weep my fill.
              [*Exit with the body.*]

FATHER
These arms of mine shall be thy winding-sheet;   114
My heart, sweet boy, shall be thy sepulcher,
For from my heart thine image ne'er shall go.
My sighing breast shall be thy funeral bell;
And so obsequious will thy father be,   118
E'en for the loss of thee, having no more,
As Priam was for all his valiant sons.   120
I'll bear thee hence, and let them fight that will,
For I have murdered where I should not kill.
              Exit [*with the body*].

KING HENRY
Sad-hearted men, much overgone with care,   123
Here sits a king more woeful than you are.

Alarums. Excursions. Enter the Queen
[*Margaret*], *the Prince, and Exeter.*

PRINCE
Fly, Father, fly! For all your friends are fled,
And Warwick rages like a chafèd bull.   126
Away! For death doth hold us in pursuit.

QUEEN MARGARET
Mount you, my lord. Towards Berwick post amain.   128
Edward and Richard, like a brace of greyhounds   129
Having the fearful flying hare in sight,
With fiery eyes sparkling for very wrath,
And bloody steel grasped in their ireful hands,
Are at our backs; and therefore hence amain.

EXETER
Away! For vengeance comes along with them.
Nay, stay not to expostulate. Make speed!
Or else come after. I'll away before.

KING HENRY
Nay, take me with thee, good sweet Exeter.
Not that I fear to stay, but love to go
Whither the Queen intends. Forward! Away! *Exeunt.*

2.6   *A loud alarum. Enter Clifford, wounded,* [*with an
arrow in his neck*].

CLIFFORD
Here burns my candle out; ay, here it dies,
Which, whiles it lasted, gave King Henry light.
O Lancaster, I fear thy overthrow
More than my body's parting with my soul!
My love and fear glued many friends to thee;   5
And, now I fall, thy tough commixture melts,   6
Impairing Henry, strengthening misproud York.   7
The common people swarm like summer flies;
And whither fly the gnats but to the sun?   9
And who shines now but Henry's enemies?
O Phoebus, hadst thou never given consent
That Phaëthon should check thy fiery steeds,   12
Thy burning car never had scorched the earth!   13
And, Henry, hadst thou swayed as kings should do,   14
Or as thy father and his father did,
Giving no ground unto the house of York,
They never then had sprung like summer flies;
I and ten thousand in this luckless realm
Had left no mourning widows for our death,
And thou this day hadst kept thy chair in peace.   20
For what doth cherish weeds but gentle air?   21
And what makes robbers bold but too much lenity?
Bootless are plaints, and cureless are my wounds;   23

---

126 chafèd enraged   **128 Berwick** Berwick-on-Tweed, on the Scottish
border at the North Sea shore.   **post amain** hasten with full speed
129 brace pair
2.6. Location: The battlefield, as before.
5 My love and fear love and fear of me   **6 now** now that.   **commixture** compound (in which many friends have been glued together)
7 Impairing weakening.   **misproud** falsely proud   **9 the sun** (Refers
to Edward's emblem.)   **12 Phaëthon** (See the note for 1.4.33.)
check control, manage   **13 car** chariot   **14 swayed** reigned
20 chair throne   **21 cherish** foster, encourage   **23 Bootless** fruitless.
plaints lamentations

---

89 stratagems deeds of violence.   **fell** cruel   **90 Erroneous** criminal
93 late lately   **94 above** piled on   **95 stay** put a halt to.   **ruthful**
pitiful   **100 presenteth** represents   **104 Take on with** cry out against.
satisfied comforted   **107 chances** happenings   **108 Misthink** think ill
of   **114 winding-sheet** shroud, burial cloth   **118 obsequious** dutiful
in manifesting regard for the dead   **120 Priam** King of Troy, whose
fifty sons fell in the war against the Greeks   **123 overgone** overcome

No way to fly, nor strength to hold out flight.   24
The foe is merciless, and will not pity,
For at their hands I have deserved no pity.
The air hath got into my deadly wounds,
And much effuse of blood doth make me faint.   28
Come, York and Richard, Warwick and the rest;
I stabbed your fathers' bosoms. Split my breast.   30
                                [He faints.]

Alarum and retreat. Enter Edward, Warwick,
Richard, and soldiers, Montague, and [George of]
Clarence.

EDWARD
Now breathe we, lords. Good fortune bids us pause   31
And smooth the frowns of war with peaceful looks.
Some troops pursue the bloody-minded Queen,
That led calm Henry, though he were a king,
As doth a sail, filled with a fretting gust,   35
Command an argosy to stem the waves.   36
But think you, lords, that Clifford fled with them?
WARWICK
No, 'tis impossible he should escape;
For, though before his face I speak the words,   39
Your brother Richard marked him for the grave,
And wheresoe'er he is, he's surely dead.
                         Clifford groans [and dies].
RICHARD
Whose soul is that which takes her heavy leave?
A deadly groan, like life and death's departing.   43
See who it is.
EDWARD   And, now the battle's ended,
If friend or foe, let him be gently used.   45
RICHARD
Revoke that doom of mercy, for 'tis Clifford,   46
Who not contented that he lopped the branch   47
In hewing Rutland when his leaves put forth,
But set his murdering knife unto the root
From whence that tender spray did sweetly
    spring—   50
I mean our princely father, Duke of York.
WARWICK
From off the gates of York fetch down the head,
Your father's head, which Clifford placèd there;
Instead whereof let this supply the room.   54
Measure for measure must be answerèd.   55
EDWARD
Bring forth that fatal screech owl to our house,   56
That nothing sung but death to us and ours.
   [Soldiers drag Clifford's body in front of York gates.]

24 hold out sustain **28 effuse** effusion **30 s.d. retreat** signal to
cease the attack **31 breathe we** let us pause for breath **35 fretting**
blowing in gusts (with a suggestion also of "nagging") **36 Command**
compel forward. **argosy** large merchant vessel. **stem** make headway against, cut through **39 his** i.e., Richard's **43 departing** parting
45 If whether. **gently used** treated in death with dignity **46 doom**
judgment **47 Who not contented** who did not rest contented
50 spray small and tender twig **54 this** i.e., Clifford's head. **supply**
the room take the place **55 answerèd** given in return **56 screech**
owl (A conventional omen of death, here likened to Clifford.) **house**
family

Now death shall stop his dismal threatening sound,
And his ill-boding tongue no more shall speak.
WARWICK
I think his understanding is bereft.   60
Speak, Clifford, dost thou know who speaks to
    thee?—
Dark cloudy death o'ershades his beams of life,
And he nor sees nor hears us what we say.   63
RICHARD
O, would he did! And so perhaps he doth.
'Tis but his policy to counterfeit,   65
Because he would avoid such bitter taunts
Which in the time of death he gave our father.
GEORGE
If so thou think'st, vex him with eager words.   68
RICHARD
Clifford, ask mercy and obtain no grace.
EDWARD
Clifford, repent in bootless penitence.
WARWICK
Clifford, devise excuses for thy faults.
GEORGE
While we devise fell tortures for thy faults.   72
RICHARD
Thou didst love York, and I am son to York.
EDWARD
Thou pitiedst Rutland. I will pity thee.
GEORGE
Where's Captain Margaret to fence you now?   75
WARWICK
They mock thee, Clifford. Swear as thou wast wont.   76
RICHARD
What, not an oath? Nay, then the world goes hard
When Clifford cannot spare his friends an oath.
I know by that he's dead; and, by my soul,
If this right hand would buy two hours' life
That I in all despite might rail at him,   81
This hand should chop it off, and with the issuing
    blood   82
Stifle the villain whose unstanchèd thirst   83
York and young Rutland could not satisfy.
WARWICK
Ay, but he's dead. Off with the traitor's head,
And rear it in the place your father's stands.
And now to London with triumphant march,
There to be crownèd England's royal king;
From whence shall Warwick cut the sea to France
And ask the Lady Bona for thy queen.   90
So shalt thou sinew both these lands together,   91
And, having France thy friend, thou shalt not dread 92
The scattered foe that hopes to rise again;
For though they cannot greatly sting to hurt,

60 bereft taken from him **63 nor . . . nor** neither . . . nor **65 pol-**
icy stratagem **68 eager** biting, bitter **72 fell** cruel. **faults** crimes
75 fence defend **76 wont** accustomed to **81 despite** spite, contempt **82 This hand** i.e., this left hand **83 unstanchèd** unquenchable **90 Lady Bona** daughter of the Duke of Savoy and sister to the
Queen of France **91 sinew** join (as with sinew) **92 France** the King
of France

Yet look to have them buzz to offend thine ears.
First will I see the coronation,
And then to Brittany I'll cross the sea
To effect this marriage, so it please my lord.

EDWARD
Even as thou wilt, sweet Warwick, let it be;
For in thy shoulder do I build my seat,   100
And never will I undertake the thing
Wherein thy counsel and consent is wanting.
Richard, I will create thee Duke of Gloucester,
And George, of Clarence. Warwick, as ourself,
Shall do and undo as him pleaseth best.

RICHARD
Let me be Duke of Clarence, George of Gloucester;
For Gloucester's dukedom is too ominous.   107

WARWICK
Tut, that's a foolish observation.
Richard, be Duke of Gloucester. Now to London,
To see these honors in possession.   *Exeunt.* 110

❧

3.1   *Enter [two Keepers] with crossbows in their hands.*

FIRST KEEPER
Under this thick-grown brake we'll shroud
    ourselves,   1
For through this laund anon the deer will come;   2
And in this covert will we make our stand,
Culling the principal of all the deer.   4

SECOND KEEPER
I'll stay above the hill, so both may shoot.

FIRST KEEPER
That cannot be. The noise of thy crossbow
Will scare the herd, and so my shoot is lost.
Here stand we both, and aim we at the best;   8
And, for the time shall not seem tedious,   9
I'll tell thee what befell me on a day
In this self place where now we mean to stand.   11

SECOND KEEPER
Here comes a man. Let's stay till he be past.
                    [They remain concealed.]

*Enter the King [Henry, disguised,] with a prayer
book.*

KING HENRY
From Scotland am I stol'n, even of pure love,   13
To greet mine own land with my wishful sight.   14
No, Harry, Harry, 'tis no land of thine!
Thy place is filled, thy scepter wrung from thee,

Thy balm washed off wherewith thou wast
    anointed.
No bending knee will call thee Caesar now,
No humble suitors press to speak for right,   19
No, not a man comes for redress of thee;   20
For how can I help them, and not myself?

FIRST KEEPER *[aside to Second Keeper]*
Ay, here's a deer whose skin's a keeper's fee: 22
This is the quondam king. Let's seize upon him.   23

KING HENRY
Let me embrace thee, sour adversity,
For wise men say it is the wisest course.

SECOND KEEPER *[aside]*
Why linger we? Let us lay hands upon him.

FIRST KEEPER *[aside]*
Forbear awhile. We'll hear a little more.

KING HENRY
My queen and son are gone to France for aid;
And, as I hear, the great commanding Warwick
Is thither gone, to crave the French King's sister
To wife for Edward. If this news be true,   31
Poor Queen and son, your labor is but lost,
For Warwick is a subtle orator,
And Lewis a prince soon won with moving words.
By this account, then, Margaret may win him,
For she's a woman to be pitied much.
Her sighs will make a battery in his breast;   37
Her tears will pierce into a marble heart.
The tiger will be mild whiles she doth mourn,
And Nero will be tainted with remorse   40
To hear and see her plaints, her brinish tears.   41
Ay, but she's come to beg, Warwick to give;
She, on his left side, craving aid for Henry,
He, on his right, asking a wife for Edward.
She weeps and says her Henry is deposed;
He smiles and says his Edward is installed;
That she, poor wretch, for grief can speak no more,   47
Whiles Warwick tells his title, smooths the wrong,   48
Inferreth arguments of mighty strength,   49
And in conclusion wins the King from her
With promise of his sister, and what else,   51
To strengthen and support King Edward's place.   52
O Margaret, thus 'twill be, and thou, poor soul,
Art then forsaken, as thou went'st forlorn!
                    [The Keepers come forward.]

SECOND KEEPER
Say, what art thou that talk'st of kings and queens?   55

KING HENRY
More than I seem, and less than I was born to.
A man at least, for less I should not be;
And men may talk of kings, and why not I?

---

100 in thy shoulder i.e., with your support.   **seat** throne
107 Gloucester's . . . ominous (Three dukes of Gloucester had met with violent deaths: Hugh Spenser, a favorite of Edward II, Thomas of Woodstock, youngest son of Edward III [see *Richard II*, 1.1], and Humphrey, uncle of Henry VI [see *2 Henry VI*, 3.2].)   **110 in possession** i.e., in our possession
3.1. Location: A forest in the north of England, near the Scottish border.
s.d. Keepers gamekeepers   **1 brake** thicket   **2 laund** glade   **4 Culling . . . deer** selecting the best deer   **8 at the best** as best we can
9 for so that   **11 self** same, very   **13 of** out of   **14 wishful** longing

19 speak for right plead for justice   **20 of** from   **22 fee** perquisite. (The gamekeeper will get a reward for capturing the King, just as gamekeepers were customarily awarded the horn and skins of a slain deer.)   **23 quondam** onetime, former   **31 To** as a   **37 a battery in** an assault upon   **40 Nero** Roman emperor famed for his cruelty. **tainted** touched, affected   **41 brinish** salty   **47 That** so that   **48 his title** i.e., Edward's royal claim.   **smooths** explains away   **49 Inferreth** adduces   **51 what else** other things also   **52 place** position of authority   **55 what** who

SECOND KEEPER
Ay, but thou talk'st as if thou wert a king.

KING HENRY
Why, so I am, in mind, and that's enough.

SECOND KEEPER
But, if thou be a king, where is thy crown?

KING HENRY
My crown is in my heart, not on my head;
Not decked with diamonds and Indian stones,   63
Nor to be seen. My crown is called content;
A crown it is that seldom kings enjoy.

SECOND KEEPER
Well, if you be a king crowned with content,
Your crown content and you must be contented
To go along with us. For, as we think,
You are the king King Edward hath deposed;
And we his subjects sworn in all allegiance
Will apprehend you as his enemy.   71

KING HENRY
But did you never swear, and break an oath?

SECOND KEEPER
No, never such an oath, nor will not now.

KING HENRY
Where did you dwell when I was King of England?

SECOND KEEPER
Here in this country where we now remain.   75

KING HENRY
I was anointed king at nine months old;
My father and my grandfather were kings,
And you were sworn true subjects unto me.
And tell me, then, have you not broke your oaths?

FIRST KEEPER
No, for we were subjects but while you were king.   80

KING HENRY
Why, am I dead? Do I not breathe a man?
Ah, simple men, you know not what you swear!   82
Look, as I blow this feather from my face,   83
And as the air blows it to me again,
Obeying with my wind when I do blow,   85
And yielding to another when it blows,
Commanded always by the greater gust—
Such is the lightness of you common men.
But do not break your oaths, for of that sin
My mild entreaty shall not make you guilty.
Go where you will, the King shall be commanded;
And be you kings, command, and I'll obey.

FIRST KEEPER
We are true subjects to the King, King Edward.

KING HENRY
So would you be again to Henry,
If he were seated as King Edward is.

FIRST KEEPER
We charge you, in God's name, and the King's,
To go with us unto the officers.

KING HENRY
In God's name, lead. Your king's name be obeyed,

And what God will, that let your king perform;
And what he will, I humbly yield unto.   *Exeunt.*

❖

3.2 *Enter King Edward, Gloucester, Clarence, [and]*
      Lady Grey.

KING EDWARD
Brother of Gloucester, at Saint Albans field
This lady's husband, Sir Richard Grey, was slain,   2
His land then seized on by the conqueror.
Her suit is now to repossess those lands,
Which we in justice cannot well deny,
Because in quarrel of the house of York
The worthy gentleman did lose his life.

GLOUCESTER
Your Highness shall do well to grant her suit.
It were dishonor to deny it her.

KING EDWARD
It were no less, but yet I'll make a pause.

GLOUCESTER [*aside to Clarence*] Yea, is it so?
I see the lady hath a thing to grant   12
Before the King will grant her humble suit.

CLARENCE [*aside to Gloucester*]
He knows the game. How true he keeps the wind!   14

GLOUCESTER [*aside to Clarence*] Silence!

KING EDWARD
Widow, we will consider of your suit;
And come some other time to know our mind.

LADY GREY
Right gracious lord, I cannot brook delay.   18
May it please Your Highness to resolve me now,   19
And what your pleasure is shall satisfy me.   20

GLOUCESTER [*aside to Clarence*]
Ay, widow? Then I'll warrant you all your lands,   21
An if what pleases him shall pleasure you.   22
Fight closer, or, good faith, you'll catch a blow.   23

CLARENCE [*aside to Gloucester*]
I fear her not, unless she chance to fall.   24

GLOUCESTER [*aside to Clarence*]
God forbid that! For he'll take vantages.

KING EDWARD
How many children hast thou, widow? Tell me.

---

63 Indian stones gems   **71 apprehend** arrest   **75 country** region
80 but only   **82 simple** foolish   **83 this feather** (Henry may take a
feather from his hat.)   **85 wind** breath

3.2. Location: London. The royal court.
s.d. Gloucester, Clarence i.e., Richard and George, King Edward's
brothers, made dukes in 2.6.103–104   **2 Sir Richard Grey** (An error
for Sir John Grey, who fell at the second battle of St. Albans fighting
on the Lancastrian side; compare with *Richard III,* 1.3.127–130.)
12 a thing (With a sexual double entendre that runs through much of
this scene.)   **14 game** (1) quarry in hunting (2) game of seduction.
keeps the wind hunts downwind (to prevent the game from catching
the scent)   **18 brook** tolerate   **19 resolve me** answer me, end my uncertainty   **20 And . . . me** and whatever you please to grant will
content me. (But Richard, in the next speech, plays on sexual meanings of *pleasure* and *satisfy*.)   **21 warrant** guarantee   **22 An if** if.
pleasure please   **23 Fight closer . . . catch a blow** (The dueling
terms here are used with sexual double meaning, as also in *fall* and
vantages, lines 24, 25. See also *a thing,* line 12, *beg a child,* line 27,
crutch, i.e., crotch, line 35, *service,* line 43, *do,* line 48, and *shift,*
i.e., a woman's smock, line 108, for other sexual double entendres.)
24 fear i.e., fear for

CLARENCE [*aside to Gloucester*]
  I think he means to beg a child of her.   27
GLOUCESTER [*aside to Clarence*]
  Nay, whip me, then; he'll rather give her two.   28
LADY GREY   Three, my most gracious lord.
GLOUCESTER [*aside to Clarence*]
  You shall have four, if you'll be ruled by him.   30
KING EDWARD
  'Twere pity they should lose their father's lands.
LADY GREY
  Be pitiful, dread lord, and grant it then.
KING EDWARD
  Lords, give us leave. I'll try this widow's wit.   33
GLOUCESTER [*aside to Clarence*]
  Ay, good leave have you; for you will have leave   34
  Till youth take leave and leave you to the crutch.   35
                        [*Gloucester and Clarence stand apart.*]
KING EDWARD
  Now tell me, madam, do you love your children?
LADY GREY
  Ay, full as dearly as I love myself.
KING EDWARD
  And would you not do much to do them good?
LADY GREY
  To do them good I would sustain some harm.
KING EDWARD
  Then get your husband's lands, to do them good.
LADY GREY
  Therefore I came unto Your Majesty.
KING EDWARD
  I'll tell you how these lands are to be got.
LADY GREY
  So shall you bind me to Your Highness' service.
KING EDWARD
  What service wilt thou do me if I give them?
LADY GREY
  What you command that rests in me to do.   45
KING EDWARD
  But you will take exceptions to my boon.   46
LADY GREY
  No, gracious lord, except I cannot do it.   47
KING EDWARD
  Ay, but thou canst do what I mean to ask.
LADY GREY
  Why, then, I will do what Your Grace commands.
GLOUCESTER [*aside to Clarence*]
  He plies her hard; and much rain wears the marble.
CLARENCE [*aside to Gloucester*]
  As red as fire! Nay then, her wax must melt.   51

LADY GREY
  Why stops my lord? Shall I not hear my task?
KING EDWARD
  An easy task. 'Tis but to love a king.
LADY GREY
  That's soon performed, because I am a subject.
KING EDWARD
  Why, then, thy husband's lands I freely give thee.
LADY GREY
  I take my leave with many thousand thanks.
                        [*She curtsies, preparing to go.*]
GLOUCESTER [*aside to Clarence*]
  The match is made; she seals it with a curtsy.   57
KING EDWARD
  But stay thee. 'Tis the fruits of love I mean.
LADY GREY
  The fruits of love I mean, my loving liege.   59
KING EDWARD
  Ay, but, I fear me, in another sense.
  What love, think'st thou, I sue so much to get?
LADY GREY
  My love till death, my humble thanks, my
    prayers—
  That love which virtue begs and virtue grants.
KING EDWARD
  No, by my troth, I did not mean such love.   64
LADY GREY
  Why then you mean not as I thought you did.
KING EDWARD
  But now you partly may perceive my mind.
LADY GREY
  My mind will never grant what I perceive
  Your Highness aims at, if I aim aright.   68
KING EDWARD
  To tell thee plain, I aim to lie with thee.
LADY GREY
  To tell you plain, I had rather lie in prison.   70
KING EDWARD
  Why, then, thou shalt not have thy husband's
    lands.
LADY GREY
  Why, then, mine honesty shall be my dower,   72
  For by that loss I will not purchase them.   73
KING EDWARD
  Therein thou wrong'st thy children mightily.
LADY GREY
  Herein Your Highness wrongs both them and me.
  But, mighty lord, this merry inclination
  Accords not with the sadness of my suit.   77
  Please you dismiss me, either with ay or no.
KING EDWARD
  Ay, if thou wilt say ay to my request;
  No, if thou dost say no to my demand.

---

27 beg a child i.e., seek to be appointed guardian of her child, or to be guardian of some rich young ward—a lucrative sinecure (with sexual double meaning)   **28 whip me** i.e., I'll bet a whipping the King has other designs.   **give her two** make her pregnant twice   **30 have four** (Her fourth child would be sired by Edward.)   **33 give us leave** pardon us, i.e., leave us to confer alone.   **wit** intelligence **34–35 Ay . . . crutch** yes, may you be pardoned, for you will take liberties, until your youth bids you farewell and leaves you hobbling on a crutch, too old for lovemaking (with a pun on *crutch, crotch,* the loins)   **45 rests in me** lies in my power   **46 take . . . boon** object to the request I ask   **47 except** unless   **51 As red as fire** i.e., Edward is hotly importunate

57 seals confirms (as in affixing a seal to a document)   **59 fruits of love** (Lady Grey interprets the King's sexual phrase in the innocent sense of ''loyal feelings of affection toward the monarch.'')   **64 troth** faith   **68 aim** guess   **70 lie** be confined (with a play on King Edward's *lie* in sexual embrace)   **72 honesty** chastity, virtue   **73 that loss** loss of that   **77 sadness** seriousness

LADY GREY
　Then, no, my lord. My suit is at an end.
GLOUCESTER [*aside to Clarence*]
　The widow likes him not. She knits her brows.
CLARENCE [*aside to Gloucester*]
　He is the bluntest wooer in Christendom.
KING EDWARD [*aside*]
　Her looks doth argue her replete with modesty;　84
　Her words doth show her wit incomparable;
　All her perfections challenge sovereignty.　86
　One way or other, she is for a king,
　And she shall be my love, or else my queen.—
　Say that King Edward take thee for his queen?
LADY GREY
　'Tis better said than done, my gracious lord.
　I am a subject fit to jest withal,
　But far unfit to be a sovereign.
KING EDWARD
　Sweet widow, by my state I swear to thee　93
　I speak no more than what my soul intends,
　And that is, to enjoy thee for my love.
LADY GREY
　And that is more than I will yield unto.
　I know I am too mean to be your queen,　97
　And yet too good to be your concubine.
KING EDWARD
　You cavil, widow. I did mean my queen.
LADY GREY
　'Twill grieve Your Grace my sons should call you
　　father.
KING EDWARD
　No more than when my daughters call thee mother.
　Thou art a widow, and thou hast some children;
　And, by God's mother, I, being but a bachelor,
　Have other some. Why, 'tis a happy thing　104
　To be the father unto many sons.
　Answer no more, for thou shalt be my queen.
GLOUCESTER [*aside to Clarence*]
　The ghostly father now hath done his shrift.　107
CLARENCE [*aside to Gloucester*]
　When he was made a shriver, 'twas for shift.　108
KING EDWARD
　Brothers, you muse what chat we two have had.　109
　　　　[*Gloucester and Clarence come forward.*]
GLOUCESTER
　The widow likes it not, for she looks very sad.
KING EDWARD
　You'd think it strange if I should marry her.
CLARENCE
　To who, my lord?
KING EDWARD　　　　Why, Clarence, to myself.　112

GLOUCESTER
　That would be ten days' wonder at the least.　113
CLARENCE
　That's a day longer than a wonder lasts.
GLOUCESTER
　By so much is the wonder in extremes.　115
KING EDWARD
　Well, jest on, brothers. I can tell you both
　Her suit is granted for her husband's lands.

　　　Enter a Nobleman.

NOBLEMAN
　My gracious lord, Henry your foe is taken
　And brought your prisoner to your palace gate.
KING EDWARD
　See that he be conveyed unto the Tower.
　And go we, brothers, to the man that took him,
　To question of his apprehension.　122
　Widow, go you along. Lords, use her honorably.
　　　　Exeunt. Manet Richard [*of Gloucester*].
GLOUCESTER
　Ay, Edward will use women honorably.
　Would he were wasted, marrow, bones, and all,　125
　That from his loins no hopeful branch may spring
　To cross me from the golden time I look for!　127
　And yet, between my soul's desire and me—
　The lustful Edward's title burièd—　129
　Is Clarence, Henry, and his son young Edward,
　And all the unlooked-for issue of their bodies,　131
　To take their rooms ere I can place myself.　132
　A cold premeditation for my purpose!　133
　Why, then, I do but dream on sovereignty,
　Like one that stands upon a promontory
　And spies a far-off shore where he would tread,
　Wishing his foot were equal with his eye,　137
　And chides the sea that sunders him from thence,
　Saying he'll lade it dry to have his way.　139
　So do I wish the crown, being so far off,
　And so I chide the means that keeps me from it,　141
　And so I say I'll cut the causes off,　142
　Flattering me with impossibilities.　143
　My eye's too quick, my heart o'erweens too much,　144
　Unless my hand and strength could equal them.
　Well, say there is no kingdom then for Richard;
　What other pleasure can the world afford?
　I'll make my heaven in a lady's lap,
　And deck my body in gay ornaments,
　And witch sweet ladies with my words and looks.　150
　O miserable thought, and more unlikely

---

113 ten days' wonder (One day longer than the proverbial "nine days' wonder," i.e., an event of sudden notoriety. Clarence points out the exaggeration in the next line.)　**115 in extremes** an unusual wonder indeed　**122 of his apprehension** about his being taken
125 wasted wasted with disease—syphilis, in particular　**127 cross** thwart, frustrate　**129 The . . . burièd** i.e., even after lustful Edward's title to the throne is eliminated by his death　**131 unlooked-for** unforeseeable and undesirable　**132 rooms** places　**133 cold premeditation** discouraging prospect　**137 equal with his eye** i.e., able to achieve what he views　**139 lade** empty (by ladling, scooping)
141 means obstacles　**142 causes** i.e., causes of my impatience
143 Flattering . . . impossibilities deceiving myself with vain hopes
144 o'erweens presumes　**150 witch** bewitch

---

84 argue her show her to be　**86 challenge** lay claim to　**93 state** i.e., kingship　**97 mean** low in social rank　**104 other some** some others.　**happy** fortunate　**107 ghostly father** spiritual father, confessor.　**done his shrift** finished hearing confession　**108 for shift** (1) to serve a devious purpose (2) for a woman's smock or chemise
109 muse wonder　**112 To who** (Edward might *marry her* in the sense of giving her in marriage to a wealthy subject; he might then take her as his mistress.)

Than to accomplish twenty golden crowns!   152
Why, love forswore me in my mother's womb;
And, for I should not deal in her soft laws,   154
She did corrupt frail nature with some bribe
To shrink mine arm up like a withered shrub;
To make an envious mountain on my back,   157
Where sits deformity to mock my body;
To shape my legs of an unequal size;
To disproportion me in every part,
Like to a chaos, or an unlicked bear whelp   161
That carries no impression like the dam.   162
And am I then a man to be beloved?
O monstrous fault, to harbor such a thought!
Then, since this earth affords no joy to me
But to command, to check, to o'erbear such   166
As are of better person than myself,   167
I'll make my heaven to dream upon the crown,
And, whiles I live, t' account this world but hell,
Until my misshaped trunk that bears this head
Be round impalèd with a glorious crown.   171
And yet I know not how to get the crown,
For many lives stand between me and home;   173
And I—like one lost in a thorny wood,
That rends the thorns and is rent with the thorns,
Seeking a way and straying from the way,
Not knowing how to find the open air,
But toiling desperately to find it out—
Torment myself to catch the English crown;
And from that torment I will free myself
Or hew my way out with a bloody ax.
Why, I can smile, and murder whiles I smile,
And cry "Content" to that which grieves my heart,
And wet my cheeks with artificial tears,
And frame my face to all occasions.
I'll drown more sailors than the mermaid shall;   186
I'll slay more gazers than the basilisk;   187
I'll play the orator as well as Nestor,   188
Deceive more slyly than Ulysses could,   189
And, like a Sinon, take another Troy.   190
I can add colors to the chameleon,
Change shapes with Proteus for advantages,   192
And set the murderous Machiavel to school.   193
Can I do this, and cannot get a crown?
Tut, were it farther off, I'll pluck it down.   *Exit.*

❖

152 **accomplish** get possession of   154 **for** so that   157 **envious** spiteful, detested   161 **unlicked bear whelp** (It was a popular notion that bears licked their shapeless newly born cubs into a proper shape.) 162 **impression** shape   166 **check** control, rebuke.   **o'erbear** dominate   167 **better person** handsomer appearance   171 **impalèd** enclosed   173 **home** i.e., the goal   186 **mermaid** (Mermaids allegedly had the power to lure sailors to destruction by their singing or weeping.)   187 **basilisk** fabulous reptile said to kill by its gaze   188–189 **Nestor, Ulysses** Greek leaders in the Trojan War, noted, respectively, for aged wisdom and cunning   190 **Sinon** Greek warrior who allowed himself to be taken captive by the Trojans and who then, feigning resentment toward his Greek companions, persuaded Priam to bring the wooden horse within the city walls, by which Troy was taken   192 **Proteus** old man of the sea, able to assume different shapes.   **for advantages** to suit my purpose   193 **set . . . school** teach Machiavelli how to be ruthless. (In the popular imagination, Machiavelli was the archetype of ruthless political cunning and atheism.)

3.3 *Flourish. Enter Lewis the French King, his sister Bona, his Admiral, called Bourbon, Prince Edward, Queen Margaret, and the Earl of Oxford. Lewis sits, and riseth up again.*

KING LEWIS
Fair Queen of England, worthy Margaret,
Sit down with us. It ill befits thy state   2
And birth that thou shouldst stand while Lewis
    doth sit.
QUEEN MARGARET
No, mighty King of France. Now Margaret
Must strike her sail and learn awhile to serve   5
Where kings command. I was, I must confess,
Great Albion's queen in former golden days.   7
But now mischance hath trod my title down
And with dishonor laid me on the ground,
Where I must take like seat unto my fortune,   10
And to my humble state conform myself.
KING LEWIS
Why, say, fair Queen, whence springs this deep
    despair?
QUEEN MARGARET
From such a cause as fills mine eyes with tears
And stops my tongue, while heart is drowned in
    cares.
KING LEWIS
Whate'er it be, be thou still like thyself,   15
And sit thee by our side. (*Seats her by him.*) Yield
    not thy neck
To fortune's yoke, but let thy dauntless mind
Still ride in triumph over all mischance.
Be plain, Queen Margaret, and tell thy grief.   19
It shall be eased, if France can yield relief.   20
QUEEN MARGARET
Those gracious words revive my drooping thoughts
And give my tongue-tied sorrows leave to speak.
Now, therefore, be it known to noble Lewis
That Henry, sole possessor of my love,
Is, of a king, become a banished man   25
And forced to live in Scotland a forlorn,   26
While proud, ambitious Edward, Duke of York,
Usurps the regal title and the seat
Of England's true-anointed lawful king.
This is the cause that I, poor Margaret,
With this my son, Prince Edward, Henry's heir,
Am come to crave thy just and lawful aid;
And if thou fail us, all our hope is done.
Scotland hath will to help, but cannot help;
Our people and our peers are both misled,
Our treasure seized, our soldiers put to flight,
And, as thou seest, ourselves in heavy plight.   37
KING LEWIS
Renownèd Queen, with patience calm the storm,

3.3. Location: France. The royal court. A throne and a seat or seats are provided.
2 **state** rank   5 **strike her sail** lower her sail, i.e., act deferentially, as the captain of a sea vessel does to one of higher rank   7 **Albion's** England's   10 **like seat unto** a place befitting   15 **like thyself** i.e., as befits your title   19 **grief** grievances   20 **France** i.e., the King of France   25 **of** from being   26 **forlorn** outcast   37 **heavy** sorrowful

While we bethink a means to break it off.   39

QUEEN MARGARET
The more we stay, the stronger grows our foe.   40

KING LEWIS
The more I stay, the more I'll succor thee.   41

QUEEN MARGARET
O, but impatience waiteth on true sorrow.   42
And see where comes the breeder of my sorrow!

Enter Warwick.

KING LEWIS
What's he approacheth boldly to our presence?   44

QUEEN MARGARET
Our Earl of Warwick, Edward's greatest friend.

KING LEWIS
Welcome, brave Warwick! What brings thee to
    France?   *He descends. She ariseth.*

QUEEN MARGARET
Ay, now begins a second storm to rise,
For this is he that moves both wind and tide.

WARWICK
From worthy Edward, King of Albion,
My lord and sovereign, and thy vowèd friend,
I come in kindness and unfeignèd love,
First, to do greetings to thy royal person,
And then to crave a league of amity;
And lastly, to confirm that amity
With nuptial knot, if thou vouchsafe to grant
That virtuous Lady Bona, thy fair sister,   56
To England's king in lawful marriage.

QUEEN MARGARET [*aside*]
If that go forward, Henry's hope is done.

WARWICK (*speaking to Bona*)
And, gracious madam, in our king's behalf
I am commanded, with your leave and favor,   60
Humbly to kiss your hand, and with my tongue
To tell the passion of my sovereign's heart—
Where fame, late entering at his heedful ears,   63
Hath placed thy beauty's image and thy virtue.

QUEEN MARGARET
King Lewis and Lady Bona, hear me speak
Before you answer Warwick. His demand   66
Springs not from Edward's well-meant honest love,
But from deceit bred by necessity.
For how can tyrants safely govern home
Unless abroad they purchase great alliance?
To prove him tyrant this reason may suffice,
That Henry liveth still; but were he dead,
Yet here Prince Edward stands, King Henry's son.
Look, therefore, Lewis, that by this league and
    marriage
Thou draw not on thy danger and dishonor.   75
For though usurpers sway the rule awhile,   76
Yet heavens are just, and time suppresseth wrongs.

WARWICK
Injurious Margaret!

PRINCE   And why not "Queen"?   78

WARWICK
Because thy father Henry did usurp,
And thou no more art prince than she is queen.

OXFORD
Then Warwick disannuls great John of Gaunt,   81
Which did subdue the greatest part of Spain;   82
And after John of Gaunt, Henry the Fourth,
Whose wisdom was a mirror to the wisest;   84
And after that wise prince, Henry the Fifth,
Who by his prowess conquerèd all France.
From these our Henry lineally descends.

WARWICK
Oxford, how haps it in this smooth discourse   88
You told not how Henry the Sixth hath lost
All that which Henry the Fifth had gotten?
Methinks these peers of France should smile at that.
But for the rest: you tell a pedigree
Of threescore-and-two years—a silly time   93
To make prescription for a kingdom's worth.   94

OXFORD
Why, Warwick, canst thou speak against thy liege,
Whom thou obeyèd'st thirty-and-six years,
And not bewray thy treason with a blush?   97

WARWICK
Can Oxford, that did ever fence the right,   98
Now buckler falsehood with a pedigree?   99
For shame! Leave Henry, and call Edward king.

OXFORD
Call him my king by whose injurious doom   101
My elder brother, the Lord Aubrey Vere,   102
Was done to death? And more than so, my father,   103
Even in the downfall of his mellowed years,
When nature brought him to the door of death?
No, Warwick, no! While life upholds this arm,
This arm upholds the house of Lancaster.

WARWICK   And I the house of York.

KING LEWIS
Queen Margaret, Prince Edward, and Oxford,
Vouchsafe, at our request, to stand aside
While I use further conference with Warwick.   111
                              They stand aloof.

QUEEN MARGARET
Heavens grant that Warwick's words bewitch
    him not!

KING LEWIS
Now, Warwick, tell me, even upon thy conscience,
Is Edward your true king? For I were loath
To link with him that were not lawful chosen.

---

39 break it off i.e., cease the storm of grief   **40 stay** delay   **41 The . . . thee** i.e., the longer preparation I make, the greater help I can give you   **42 waiteth on** attends, accompanies   **44 he** he who   **56 sister** i.e., sister-in-law   **60 leave and favor** kind permission   **63 fame** report. **late** lately   **66 demand** request   **75 draw not on** do not bring about   **76 sway** exercise

78 Injurious insulting   **81 disannuls** cancels, takes no account of   **82 Which** who   **84 a mirror** a model for emulation   **88 haps it** does it happen that   **93 threescore-and-two** i.e., from 1399, the date of Henry IV's accession, to 1461, that of Edward's.   **silly** i.e., ridiculously short   **94 prescription** claim founded upon long use and de facto possession   **97 bewray** reveal   **98 fence** defend   **99 buckler** shield, protect   **101 doom** judgment   **102 Lord Aubrey Vere** the eldest son of the twelfth Earl of Oxford, John de Vere. (Both he and his father were attainted and executed for treason by the Yorkists in 1462.)   **103 more than so** even more than that   **111 use further conference** hold further conversation.   **s.d. aloof** to one side

WARWICK
Thereon I pawn my credit and mine honor.   116
KING LEWIS
But is he gracious in the people's eye?
WARWICK
The more that Henry was unfortunate.
KING LEWIS
Then further, all dissembling set aside,
Tell me for truth the measure of his love   120
Unto our sister Bona.
WARWICK   Such it seems
As may beseem a monarch like himself.   122
Myself have often heard him say and swear
That this his love was an eternal plant,
Whereof the root was fixed in virtue's ground,
The leaves and fruit maintained with beauty's sun,
Exempt from envy, but not from disdain,   127
Unless the Lady Bona quit his pain.   128
KING LEWIS
Now, sister, let us hear your firm resolve.
BONA
Your grant, or your denial, shall be mine.   130
(Speaks to Warwick.) Yet I confess that often ere this
     day,
When I have heard your king's desert recounted, 132
Mine ear hath tempted judgment to desire.   133
KING LEWIS
Then, Warwick, thus: our sister shall be Edward's.
And now forthwith shall articles be drawn   135
Touching the jointure that your king must make, 136
Which with her dowry shall be counterpoised.—   137
Draw near, Queen Margaret, and be a witness
That Bona shall be wife to the English King.
          [Margaret, Edward, and Oxford come forward.]
PRINCE
To Edward, but not to the English King.
QUEEN MARGARET
Deceitful Warwick! It was thy device   141
By this alliance to make void my suit.
Before thy coming, Lewis was Henry's friend.
KING LEWIS
And still is friend to him and Margaret.
But if your title to the crown be weak,
As may appear by Edward's good success,
Then 'tis but reason that I be released
From giving aid which late I promisèd.   148
Yet shall you have all kindness at my hand
That your estate requires and mine can yield.   150
WARWICK [to Queen Margaret]
Henry now lives in Scotland at his ease,

Where, having nothing, nothing can he lose.
And as for you yourself, our quondam queen,   153
You have a father able to maintain you,
And better 'twere you troubled him than France.
QUEEN MARGARET
Peace, impudent and shameless Warwick,
Proud setter-up and puller-down of kings!
I will not hence till, with my talk and tears,
Both full of truth, I make King Lewis behold
Thy sly conveyance and thy lord's false love;   160
For both of you are birds of selfsame feather.   161
               Post blowing a horn within.
KING LEWIS
Warwick, this is some post to us or thee.

          Enter the Post.

POST (speaks to Warwick)
My Lord Ambassador, these letters are for you,
Sent from your brother, Marquess Montague.
(To Lewis.) These from our king unto Your Majesty.
(To Margaret.) And, madam, these for you; from
     whom I know not.   They all read their letters.
OXFORD [to Edward]
I like it well that our fair queen and mistress
Smiles at her news, while Warwick frowns at his.
PRINCE [to Oxford]
Nay, mark how Lewis stamps, as he were nettled. 169
I hope all's for the best.
KING LEWIS
Warwick, what are thy news? And yours, fair
     Queen?
QUEEN MARGARET
Mine, such as fill my heart with unhoped joys.
WARWICK
Mine, full of sorrow and heart's discontent.
KING LEWIS
What, has your king married the Lady Grey?
And now, to soothe your forgery and his,   175
Sends me a paper to persuade me patience?   176
Is this th' alliance that he seeks with France?
Dare he presume to scorn us in this manner?
QUEEN MARGARET
I told Your Majesty as much before.
This proveth Edward's love and Warwick's honesty.
WARWICK
King Lewis, I here protest, in sight of heaven
And by the hope I have of heavenly bliss,
That I am clear from this misdeed of Edward's—   183
No more my king, for he dishonors me,
But most himself, if he could see his shame.
Did I forget that by the house of York   186
My father came untimely to his death?   187
Did I let pass th' abuse done to my niece?   188

116 pawn my credit stake my reputation 120 for truth truly. measure extent 122 beseem befit 127 envy ill will, malice. but . . . disdain i.e., his love will wither if the lady disdains him. (Warwick uses the stock hyperbole of Petrarchan devotion.) 128 quit requite, alleviate 130 grant granting, agreeing 132 desert deserving 133 Mine . . . desire what I have heard has prompted my judgment to desire him 135 articles i.e., articles of a marriage contract 136 Touching concerning. jointure marriage settlement made by the groom in behalf of the bride 137 counterpoised matched, balanced in amount 141 device stratagem 148 late lately 150 estate rank, condition

153 quondam former 160 conveyance underhand dealing 161 s.d. Post messenger 169 as as if 175 soothe gloss over. forgery deceit 176 persuade advise 183 clear from innocent of 186 by owing to 187 My father i.e., Salisbury (who, according to the chronicles, was captured at Wakefield and beheaded by the Lancastrians) 188 abuse . . . niece (The chronicles report that Edward attempted to "deflower" Warwick's niece while she was a guest in his house.)

Did I impale him with the regal crown? 189
Did I put Henry from his native right?
And am I guerdoned at the last with shame? 191
Shame on himself! For my desert is honor; 192
And to repair my honor lost for him,
I here renounce him and return to Henry.
My noble Queen, let former grudges pass,
And henceforth I am thy true servitor. 196
I will revenge his wrong to Lady Bona
And replant Henry in his former state.

QUEEN MARGARET
Warwick, these words have turned my hate to love;
And I forgive and quite forget old faults,
And joy that thou becom'st King Henry's friend.

WARWICK
So much his friend, ay, his unfeignèd friend,
That, if King Lewis vouchsafe to furnish us
With some few bands of chosen soldiers,
I'll undertake to land them on our coast
And force the tyrant from his seat by war. 206
'Tis not his new-made bride shall succor him. 207
And as for Clarence, as my letters tell me,
He's very likely now to fall from him, 209
For matching more for wanton lust than honor, 210
Or than for strength and safety of our country.

BONA
Dear brother, how shall Bona be revenged
But by thy help to this distressèd queen?

QUEEN MARGARET
Renownèd prince, how shall poor Henry live,
Unless thou rescue him from foul despair?

BONA
My quarrel and this English queen's are one.

WARWICK
And mine, fair Lady Bona, joins with yours.

KING LEWIS
And mine with hers, and thine, and Margaret's.
Therefore at last I firmly am resolved
You shall have aid.

QUEEN MARGARET
Let me give humble thanks for all at once.

KING LEWIS [to the Post]
Then, England's messenger, return in post 222
And tell false Edward, thy supposèd king,
That Lewis of France is sending over masquers 224
To revel it with him and his new bride.
Thou seest what's passed. Go fear thy king withal. 226

BONA
Tell him, in hope he'll prove a widower shortly,
I'll wear the willow garland for his sake. 228

QUEEN MARGARET
Tell him my mourning weeds are laid aside 229

And I am ready to put armor on. 189
WARWICK
Tell him from me that he hath done me wrong,
And therefore I'll uncrown him ere 't be long.
There's thy reward. [He gives money.] Begone.
                                        Exit Post.
KING LEWIS   But Warwick,
Thou and Oxford, with five thousand men,
Shall cross the seas and bid false Edward battle;
And, as occasion serves, this noble queen
And prince shall follow with a fresh supply. 237
Yet, ere thou go, but answer me one doubt: 238
What pledge have we of thy firm loyalty?
WARWICK
This shall assure my constant loyalty,
That, if our queen and this young prince agree,
I'll join mine eldest daughter and my joy 242
To him forthwith in holy wedlock bands.
QUEEN MARGARET
Yes, I agree, and thank you for your motion. 244
Son Edward, she is fair and virtuous;
Therefore delay not. Give thy hand to Warwick,
And, with thy hand, thy faith irrevocable
That only Warwick's daughter shall be thine.
PRINCE
Yes, I accept her, for she well deserves it;
And here, to pledge my vow, I give my hand.
                        He gives his hand to Warwick.
KING LEWIS
Why stay we now? These soldiers shall be levied, 251
And thou, Lord Bourbon, our high admiral,
Shall waft them over with our royal fleet. 253
I long till Edward fall by war's mischance
For mocking marriage with a dame of France. 255
                        Exeunt. Manet Warwick.
WARWICK
I came from Edward as ambassador,
But I return his sworn and mortal foe.
Matter of marriage was the charge he gave me,
But dreadful war shall answer his demand.
Had he none else to make a stale but me? 260
Then none but I shall turn his jest to sorrow.
I was the chief that raised him to the crown,
And I'll be chief to bring him down again—
Not that I pity Henry's misery,
But seek revenge on Edward's mockery.   Exit.

❖

4.1 Enter Richard [Duke of Gloucester], Clarence,
        Somerset, and Montague.

GLOUCESTER
Now tell me, brother Clarence, what think you

189 **impale him** i.e., encircle his head   191 **guerdoned** rewarded
192 **my desert** what I deserve   196 **true servitor** loyal servant
206 **tyrant** usurper   207 **'Tis . . . him** i.e., no newly chosen bride
like Lady Grey is going to be enough to save him   209 **fall from**
desert   210 **matching** marrying   222 **in post** in haste   224 **masquers**
dancers in a masque or court revels. (Said ironically.)   226 **fear**
frighten.   **withal** with this   228 **willow garland** (Symbol of a forsaken
lover; said here contemptuously. The leaves are from the great willow
herb, or loosestrife, not from the willow tree.)   229 **weeds** garments

237 **supply** reinforcements   238 **but** only   242 **eldest daughter** (A
historical inaccuracy; Prince Edward was betrothed to a younger
daughter of Warwick, Anne, who later married Richard of Gloucester;
the eldest daughter, Isabella, was already the wife of the Duke of
Clarence.)   244 **motion** proposal   251 **stay** delay   253 **waft** convey
by water   255 **s.d. Manet** he remains onstage   260 **stale** dupe,
laughingstock
4.1. Location: London. The royal court.

Of this new marriage with the Lady Grey?
Hath not our brother made a worthy choice?

CLARENCE
Alas, you know, 'tis far from hence to France;
How could he stay till Warwick made return?   5

SOMERSET
My lords, forbear this talk. Here comes the King.   6

*Flourish. Enter King Edward, Lady Grey [as
Queen Elizabeth], Pembroke, Stafford, Hastings.
Four stand on one side and four on the other.*

GLOUCESTER   And his well-chosen bride.

CLARENCE
I mind to tell him plainly what I think.   8

KING EDWARD
Now, brother of Clarence, how like you our choice,
That you stand pensive, as half malcontent?   10

CLARENCE
As well as Lewis of France, or the Earl of Warwick,
Which are so weak of courage and in judgment   12
That they'll take no offense at our abuse.   13

KING EDWARD
Suppose they take offense without a cause;
They are but Lewis and Warwick, I am Edward,
Your king and Warwick's, and must have my will.   16

GLOUCESTER
And shall have your will, because our king.
Yet hasty marriage seldom proveth well.

KING EDWARD
Yea, brother Richard, are you offended too?

GLOUCESTER   Not I.
No, God forbid that I should wish them severed
Whom God hath joined together! Ay, and 'twere
pity
To sunder them that yoke so well together.   23

KING EDWARD
Setting your scorns and your mislike aside,   24
Tell me some reason why the Lady Grey
Should not become my wife and England's queen.
And you too, Somerset and Montague,
Speak freely what you think.

CLARENCE
Then this is mine opinion: that King Lewis
Becomes your enemy for mocking him
About the marriage of the Lady Bona.

GLOUCESTER
And Warwick, doing what you gave in charge,   32
Is now dishonorèd by this new marriage.

KING EDWARD
What if both Lewis and Warwick be appeased
By such invention as I can devise?   35

MONTAGUE
Yet, to have joined with France in such alliance
Would more have strengthened this our
commonwealth
'Gainst foreign storms than any homebred marriage.

HASTINGS
Why, knows not Montague that of itself
England is safe, if true within itself?

MONTAGUE
But the safer when 'tis backed with France.

HASTINGS
'Tis better using France than trusting France.
Let us be backed with God and with the seas
Which He hath given for fence impregnable,
And with their helps only defend ourselves;   45
In them and in ourselves our safety lies.

CLARENCE
For this one speech Lord Hastings well deserves
To have the heir of the Lord Hungerford.   48

KING EDWARD
Ay, what of that? It was my will and grant,
And for this once my will shall stand for law.

GLOUCESTER
And yet methinks Your Grace hath not done well
To give the heir and daughter of Lord Scales
Unto the brother of your loving bride.   53
She better would have fitted me or Clarence.
But in your bride you bury brotherhood.

CLARENCE
Or else you would not have bestowed the heir
Of the Lord Bonville on your new wife's son,   57
And leave your brothers to go speed elsewhere.   58

KING EDWARD
Alas, poor Clarence! Is it for a wife
That thou art malcontent? I will provide thee.

CLARENCE
In choosing for yourself you showed your judgment,
Which being shallow, you shall give me leave
To play the broker in mine own behalf;   63
And to that end I shortly mind to leave you.   64

KING EDWARD
Leave me or tarry, Edward will be king,   65
And not be tied unto his brother's will.

QUEEN ELIZABETH
My lords, before it pleased His Majesty
To raise my state to title of a queen,
Do me but right, and you must all confess
That I was not ignoble of descent;
And meaner than myself have had like fortune.   71
But as this title honors me and mine,
So your dislikes, to whom I would be pleasing,   73

5 stay wait. (Clarence speaks ironically.)   6 s.d. Four stand i.e., the four already onstage. Edward is seemingly in the middle.   8 mind intend   10 malcontent discontented   12 Which who   13 abuse insult. (Clarence speaks with scornful irony, as does Gloucester in lines 21–23.)   16 have my will (1) have my way (2) fulfill my lust   23 yoke are bound in marriage. (But Gloucester parodies the language of the marriage service in such a way as to suggest sexual coupling and the yoking of oxen.)   24 mislike displeasure   32 gave in charge commissioned   35 invention scheme, plan

45 only alone   48 To . . . Hungerford (Clarence objects to the marriage of Lord Hastings to the daughter of Lord Hungerford.)   53 brother i.e., Lord Anthony Rivers (whose marriage to the daughter of Lord Scales was one of the advancements of Queen Elizabeth's kindred so much resented by Edward's brothers and other noble supporters)   57 son i.e., Sir Thomas Grey, Marquess Dorset, another of the Queen's upstart relatives advanced by Edward   58 speed prosper   63 broker agent, go-between   64 mind intend   65 Leave whether you leave   71 meaner more lowly   73 would wish to

Doth cloud my joys with danger and with sorrow.   74
KING EDWARD
My love, forbear to fawn upon their frowns.   75
What danger or what sorrow can befall thee
So long as Edward is thy constant friend
And their true sovereign, whom they must obey?
Nay, whom they shall obey, and love thee too,
Unless they seek for hatred at my hands;
Which if they do, yet will I keep thee safe,
And they shall feel the vengeance of my wrath.
GLOUCESTER [*aside*]
I hear, yet say not much, but think the more.

Enter a Post.

KING EDWARD
Now, messenger, what letters or what news
From France?
POST
My sovereign liege, no letters, and few words,
But such as I, without your special pardon,
Dare not relate.   87
KING EDWARD
Go to, we pardon thee. Therefore, in brief,   89
Tell me their words as near as thou canst guess
them.   90
What answer makes King Lewis unto our letters?
POST
At my depart, these were his very words: 92
"Go tell false Edward, thy supposèd king,
That Lewis of France is sending over masquers
To revel it with him and his new bride."
KING EDWARD
Is Lewis so brave? Belike he thinks me Henry.   96
But what said Lady Bona to my marriage?
POST
These were her words, uttered with mild disdain:
"Tell him, in hope he'll prove a widower shortly,
I'll wear the willow garland for his sake."
KING EDWARD
I blame not her, she could say little less;
She had the wrong. But what said Henry's queen?
For I have heard that she was there in place.
POST
"Tell him," quoth she, "my mourning weeds are
done,
And I am ready to put armor on."   104
KING EDWARD
Belike she minds to play the Amazon.   106
But what said Warwick to these injuries?   107
POST
He, more incensed against Your Majesty
Than all the rest, discharged me with these words: 109
"Tell him from me that he hath done me wrong,
And therefore I'll uncrown him ere 't be long."

KING EDWARD
Ha! Durst the traitor breathe out so proud words?
Well, I will arm me, being thus forewarned.
They shall have wars and pay for their presumption.
But say, is Warwick friends with Margaret?
POST
Ay, gracious sovereign, they are so linked in
friendship
That young Prince Edward marries Warwick's
daughter.
CLARENCE
Belike the elder; Clarence will have the younger.   118
Now, brother king, farewell, and sit you fast,   119
For I will hence to Warwick's other daughter,
That, though I want a kingdom, yet in marriage   121
I may not prove inferior to yourself.
You that love me and Warwick, follow me.
Exit Clarence, and Somerset follows.
GLOUCESTER [*aside*]   Not I.
My thoughts aim at a further matter. I
Stay not for the love of Edward, but the crown.
KING EDWARD
Clarence and Somerset both gone to Warwick?
Yet am I armed against the worst can happen;   128
And haste is needful in this desperate case.
Pembroke and Stafford, you in our behalf
Go levy men and make prepare for war.   131
They are already, or quickly will be, landed.
Myself in person will straight follow you.   133
Exeunt Pembroke and Stafford.
But ere I go, Hastings and Montague,
Resolve my doubt. You twain, of all the rest,
Are near to Warwick by blood and by alliance.
Tell me if you love Warwick more than me.
If it be so, then both depart to him;
I rather wish you foes than hollow friends.
But if you mind to hold your true obedience,   140
Give me assurance with some friendly vow,
That I may never have you in suspect.   142
MONTAGUE
So God help Montague as he proves true!
HASTINGS
And Hastings as he favors Edward's cause!
KING EDWARD
Now, brother Richard, will you stand by us?
GLOUCESTER
Ay, in despite of all that shall withstand you.   146
KING EDWARD
Why, so. Then am I sure of victory.
Now therefore let us hence, and lose no hour
Till we meet Warwick with his foreign power.
Exeunt.

❖

74 danger apprehension   **75 forbear . . . frowns** stop trying to overcome their disapproval by ingratiating yourself   **87 pardon** i.e., permission   **89 Go to** (An expression of remonstrance.)   **90 guess** i.e.,
reproduce from memory   **92 depart** departure   **96 Belike** perhaps
104 done i.e., no longer needed   **106 Amazon** mythical female warrior   **107 injuries** insults   **109 discharged** dismissed

118 the elder (Compare with the note for 3.3.242.)   **119 sit you fast**
i.e., hold on tight to your throne   **121 want** lack   **128 can** that can
131 prepare preparation   **133 straight** immediately   **140 mind** intend
142 suspect suspicion   **146 despite** spite

4.2   *Enter Warwick and Oxford in England, with French soldiers.*

WARWICK
Trust me, my lord, all hitherto goes well.
The common people by numbers swarm to us.

Enter Clarence and Somerset.

But see where Somerset and Clarence comes!
Speak suddenly, my lords, are we all friends?
CLARENCE   Fear not that, my lord.
WARWICK
Then, gentle Clarence, welcome unto Warwick;   6
And welcome, Somerset! I hold it cowardice
To rest mistrustful where a noble heart   8
Hath pawned an open hand in sign of love;   9
Else might I think that Clarence, Edward's brother,
Were but a feignèd friend to our proceedings.
But welcome, sweet Clarence. My daughter shall be
    thine.
And now what rests but, in night's coverture,   13
Thy brother being carelessly encamped,
His soldiers lurking in the towns about,   15
And but attended by a simple guard,   16
We may surprise and take him at our pleasure?   17
Our scouts have found the adventure very easy;   18
That as Ulysses and stout Diomed   19
With sleight and manhood stole to Rhesus' tents   20
And brought from thence the Thracian fatal steeds,   21
So we, well covered with the night's black mantle,
At unawares may beat down Edward's guard   23
And seize himself. I say not "slaughter him,"
For I intend but only to surprise him.   25
You that will follow me to this attempt,
Applaud the name of Henry with your leader.
            They all cry, "Henry!"
Why, then, let's on our way in silent sort.   28
For Warwick and his friends, God and Saint George!
                                    Exeunt.

❧

4.3   *Enter three Watchmen to guard the King's tent.*

FIRST WATCH
Come on, my masters, each man take his stand.
The King by this is set him down to sleep.   2
SECOND WATCH   What, will he not to bed?

4.2. Location: Fields in Warwickshire.
6 gentle noble   **8 rest** remain   **9 pawned** pledged   **13 rests** remains.
in night's coverture under cover of night   **15 lurking** idling, lodging
16 simple mere   **17 at our pleasure** whenever we wish   **18 adventure** venturing (into Edward's camp)   **19–21 Ulysses . . . steeds** (In Book 10 of the *Iliad*, Ulysses and Diomedes under cover of night stealthily enter the camp of the Thracian leader Rhesus, slay him and twelve of his men, and lead away his horses. The horses are called *fatal steeds* because of a prophecy foretelling that Troy would not fall as long as these horses drank from the River Xanthus and grazed on the Trojan plain.)   **19 stout** brave   **20 sleight** cunning   **23 At unawares** unexpectedly, suddenly   **25 surprise** capture   **28 sort** fashion
4.3. Location: Edward's camp near Warwick.
2 by this by this time.   **is set him** has settled himself

FIRST WATCH
Why, no, for he hath made a solemn vow
Never to lie and take his natural rest
Till Warwick or himself be quite suppressed.
SECOND WATCH
Tomorrow then belike shall be the day,
If Warwick be so near as men report.
THIRD WATCH
But say, I pray, what nobleman is that
That with the King here resteth in his tent?
FIRST WATCH
'Tis the Lord Hastings, the King's chiefest friend.
THIRD WATCH
O, is it so? But why commands the King
That his chief followers lodge in towns about him,   13
While he himself keeps in the cold field?   14
SECOND WATCH
'Tis the more honor, because more dangerous.
THIRD WATCH
Ay, but give me worship and quietness;   16
I like it better than a dangerous honor.
If Warwick knew in what estate he stands,   18
'Tis to be doubted he would waken him.   19
FIRST WATCH
Unless our halberds did shut up his passage.   20
SECOND WATCH
Ay. Wherefore else guard we his royal tent
But to defend his person from night foes?

Enter Warwick, Clarence, Oxford, Somerset, and French soldiers, silent all.

WARWICK
This is his tent, and see where stand his guard.
Courage, my masters! Honor now or never!
But follow me, and Edward shall be ours.   25
FIRST WATCH   Who goes there?
SECOND WATCH   Stay, or thou diest!
            *Warwick and the rest cry all, "Warwick!
            Warwick!" and set upon the guard, who
            fly, crying, "Arm! Arm!" Warwick and
            the rest following them.*

The drum playing and trumpet sounding, enter Warwick, Somerset, and the rest, bringing the King [Edward] out in his gown, sitting in a chair. Richard [of Gloucester] and Hastings fly over the stage.

SOMERSET   What are they that fly there?
WARWICK
Richard and Hastings. Let them go. Here is
The Duke.
KING EDWARD   "The Duke"? Why, Warwick, when we
    parted
Thou calledst me King.

13 about round about   **14 keeps** remains, lodges   **16 worship** ease and dignity   **18 estate** situation.   **he** i.e., King Edward   **19 doubted** feared   **20 halberds** long-handled weapons bearing axlike heads.
shut up his passage prevent Warwick's getting through   **25 But** only

WARWICK   Ay, but the case is altered.
When you disgraced me in my ambassade,   32
Then I degraded you from being king,
And come now to create you Duke of York.
Alas, how should you govern any kingdom,
That know not how to use ambassadors,
Nor how to be contented with one wife,
Nor how to use your brothers brotherly,
Nor how to study for the people's welfare,
Nor how to shroud yourself from enemies?   40

KING EDWARD
Yea, brother of Clarence, art thou here too?
Nay, then I see that Edward needs must down.   42
Yet, Warwick, in despite of all mischance,
Of thee thyself and all thy complices,   44
Edward will always bear himself as king.
Though Fortune's malice overthrow my state,
My mind exceeds the compass of her wheel.   47

WARWICK
Then, for his mind, be Edward England's king.   48
                    Takes off his [Edward's] crown.
But Henry now shall wear the English crown
And be true king indeed, thou but the shadow.
My lord of Somerset, at my request
See that forthwith Duke Edward be conveyed
Unto my brother, Archbishop of York.   53
When I have fought with Pembroke and his fellows,
I'll follow you, and tell what answer
Lewis and the Lady Bona send to him.
Now, for a while farewell, good Duke of York.
                    They [begin to] lead him out forcibly.

KING EDWARD
What fates impose, that men must needs abide.
It boots not to resist both wind and tide.   59
                    Exeunt [Edward, Somerset, and soldiers].

OXFORD
What now remains, my lords, for us to do
But march to London with our soldiers?

WARWICK
Ay, that's the first thing that we have to do,
To free King Henry from imprisonment
And see him seated in the regal throne.   *Exeunt.*

❖

4.4   *Enter Rivers and Lady Grey [Queen Elizabeth].*

RIVERS
Madam, what makes you in this sudden change?   1

QUEEN ELIZABETH
Why, brother Rivers, are you yet to learn
What late misfortune is befallen King Edward?   3

RIVERS
What? Loss of some pitched battle against Warwick?

QUEEN ELIZABETH
No, but the loss of his own royal person.

RIVERS   Then is my sovereign slain?

QUEEN ELIZABETH
Ay, almost slain, for he is taken prisoner,
Either betrayed by falsehood of his guard
Or by his foe surprised at unawares;
And, as I further have to understand,   10
Is new committed to the Bishop of York,   11
Fell Warwick's brother, and by that our foe.   12

RIVERS
These news I must confess are full of grief.
Yet, gracious madam, bear it as you may.
Warwick may lose, that now hath won the day.

QUEEN ELIZABETH
Till then fair hope must hinder life's decay.   16
And I the rather wean me from despair
For love of Edward's offspring in my womb.
This is it that makes me bridle passion   19
And bear with mildness my misfortune's cross.
Ay, ay, for this I draw in many a tear   21
And stop the rising of bloodsucking sighs,   22
Lest with my sighs or tears I blast or drown   23
King Edward's fruit, true heir to th' English crown.

RIVERS
But, madam, where is Warwick then become?

QUEEN ELIZABETH
I am informed that he comes towards London,
To set the crown once more on Henry's head.
Guess thou the rest. King Edward's friends must
    down.   28
But, to prevent the tyrant's violence—   29
For trust not him that hath once broken faith—
I'll hence forthwith unto the sanctuary,   31
To save at least the heir of Edward's right.   32
There shall I rest secure from force and fraud.
Come, therefore, let us fly while we may fly.
If Warwick take us we are sure to die.   *Exeunt.*

❖

4.5   *Enter Richard [Duke of Gloucester], Lord
Hastings, and Sir William Stanley.*

GLOUCESTER
Now, my Lord Hastings and Sir William Stanley,
Leave off to wonder why I drew you hither   2
Into this chiefest thicket of the park.   3

---

32 **ambassade** ambassadorial mission 40 **shroud** conceal, shield 42 **needs must down** must fall of necessity 44 **complices** accomplices 47 **My . . . wheel** i.e., my spirit rises above the misery of Fortune and her wheel. **compass** range, circumference 48 **for his mind** i.e., in his own thoughts 53 **Archbishop of York** i.e., George Neville 59 **boots** avails
4.4. Location: London. The royal court.
1 **makes . . . change** causes this sudden change (of mood) in you
3 **late** recent

10 **have to** am given to 11 **new** newly. **Bishop** i.e., Archbishop 12 **Fell** cruel. **by that** i.e., by that token 16 **hope . . . decay** i.e., only hope can hold off my downfall and death 19 **bridle passion** control my grief 21 **draw in** hold back 22 **bloodsucking sighs** (Sighs were thought to cost the heart a drop of blood.) 23 **blast** wither, blight 28 **must down** are destined to fall 29 **prevent** forestall 31 **the sanctuary** residence inside a church building, providing immunity from law 32 **right** royal claim
4.5. Location: A park belonging to the Archbishop of York, historically identified as Middleham Castle in Yorkshire.
2 **Leave off** cease 3 **chiefest thicket** thickest copse

Thus stands the case: you know our king, my
   brother,
Is prisoner to the Bishop here, at whose hands
He hath good usage and great liberty,
And, often but attended with weak guard,   7
Comes hunting this way to disport himself.   8
I have advertised him by secret means   9
That if about this hour he make this way   10
Under the color of his usual game,   11
He shall here find his friends with horse and men
To set him free from his captivity.

Enter King Edward and a Huntsman with him.

HUNTSMAN
This way, my lord, for this way lies the game.   14
KING EDWARD
Nay, this way, man. See where the huntsmen
   stand.—
Now, brother of Gloucester, Lord Hastings, and the
   rest,
Stand you thus close to steal the Bishop's deer?   17
GLOUCESTER
Brother, the time and case requireth haste.   18
Your horse stands ready at the park corner.
KING EDWARD
But whither shall we then?
HASTINGS   To Lynn, my lord—   20
And shipped from thence to Flanders?
GLOUCESTER
Well guessed, believe me, for that was my meaning.
KING EDWARD
Stanley, I will requite thy forwardness.   23
GLOUCESTER
But wherefore stay we? 'Tis no time to talk.
KING EDWARD
Huntsman, what sayst thou? Wilt thou go along? 25
HUNTSMAN
Better do so than tarry and be hanged.
GLOUCESTER
Come then, away. Let's ha' no more ado.
KING EDWARD
Bishop, farewell! Shield thee from Warwick's frown,
And pray that I may repossess the crown.   *Exeunt.*

❖

4.6 *Flourish. Enter King Henry the Sixth, Clarence,*
Warwick, Somerset, young Henry [Earl of
Richmond], Oxford, Montague, and Lieutenant [of
the Tower].

KING HENRY
Master Lieutenant, now that God and friends

Have shaken Edward from the regal seat
And turned my captive state to liberty,
My fear to hope, my sorrows unto joys,
At our enlargement what are thy due fees?   5
LIEUTENANT
Subjects may challenge nothing of their sovereigns; 6
But if an humble prayer may prevail,
I then crave pardon of Your Majesty.
KING HENRY
For what, Lieutenant? For well using me?
Nay, be thou sure I'll well requite thy kindness,
For that it made my imprisonment a pleasure—   11
Ay, such a pleasure as encagèd birds
Conceive when, after many moody thoughts,
At last by notes of household harmony   14
They quite forget their loss of liberty.
But, Warwick, after God, thou sett'st me free,
And chiefly therefore I thank God and thee.
He was the author, thou the instrument.
Therefore, that I may conquer fortune's spite
By living low, where fortune cannot hurt me,   20
And that the people of this blessèd land
May not be punished with my thwarting stars,   22
Warwick, although my head still wear the crown,
I here resign my government to thee,
For thou art fortunate in all thy deeds.
WARWICK
Your Grace hath still been famed for virtuous,   26
And now may seem as wise as virtuous
By spying and avoiding fortune's malice,   28
For few men rightly temper with the stars.   29
Yet in this one thing let me blame Your Grace:
For choosing me when Clarence is in place.   31
CLARENCE
No, Warwick, thou art worthy of the sway,   32
To whom the heavens in thy nativity
Adjudged an olive branch and laurel crown,   34
As likely to be blest in peace and war;
And therefore I yield thee my free consent.   36
WARWICK
And I choose Clarence only for Protector.   37
KING HENRY
Warwick and Clarence, give me both your hands.
               [The King joins their hands.]
Now join your hands, and with your hands your
   hearts,
That no dissension hinder government.
I make you both Protectors of this land,
While I myself will lead a private life
And in devotion spend my latter days,   43
To sin's rebuke and my Creator's praise.

---

7 but attended with attended only by **8 disport** amuse **9 advertised** notified **10 make** come **11 color** pretext. **his usual game** his usual custom of the hunt **14 game** quarry **17 close** concealed **18 case** circumstance **20 Lynn** King's Lynn, a seaport in Norfolk **23 requite** repay. **forwardness** zeal **25 go along** come along with us
4.6. Location: The Tower of London.
s.d. Enter . . . Tower (In the Octavo stage direction, Warwick and Clarence enter first "with the crown," and then Henry, Oxford, Somerset, and "the young Earl of Richmond.")

5 enlargement release from confinement **6 challenge** claim as a right **11 For that** because **14 household harmony** harmonious song suited to a domestic life **20 low** humbly **22 thwarting** crossing (in their astrological influence) **26 still** always. **famed for virtuous** reputed to be virtuous **28 spying** spying out, foreseeing **29 temper . . . stars** i.e., blend or accord with their destiny **31 in place** present **32 sway** rule **34 olive branch** (Symbol of peace.) **laurel crown** (Symbol of honor in war.) **36 free** freely given **37 only for** as sole **43 latter** last

WARWICK
    What answers Clarence to his sovereign's will?
CLARENCE
    That he consents, if Warwick yield consent;
    For on thy fortune I repose myself.   47
WARWICK
    Why, then, though loath, yet must I be content.
    We'll yoke together, like a double shadow
    To Henry's body, and supply his place—
    I mean, in bearing weight of government
    While he enjoys the honor and his ease.
    And, Clarence, now then it is more than needful
    Forthwith that Edward be pronounced a traitor,
    And all his lands and goods be confiscate.
CLARENCE
    What else? And that succession be determined.   56
WARWICK
    Ay, therein Clarence shall not want his part.   57
KING HENRY
    But with the first of all your chief affairs,
    Let me entreat—for I command no more—
    That Margaret your queen and my son Edward
    Be sent for, to return from France with speed;
    For till I see them here, by doubtful fear
    My joy of liberty is half eclipsed.
CLARENCE
    It shall be done, my sovereign, with all speed.
KING HENRY
    My lord of Somerset, what youth is that
    Of whom you seem to have so tender care?
SOMERSET
    My liege, it is young Henry, Earl of Richmond.   67
KING HENRY
    Come hither, England's hope. (*Lays his hand on his
       head.*) If secret powers
    Suggest but truth to my divining thoughts,   69
    This pretty lad will prove our country's bliss.
    His looks are full of peaceful majesty,
    His head by nature framed to wear a crown,
    His hand to wield a scepter, and himself
    Likely in time to bless a regal throne.
    Make much of him, my lords, for this is he
    Must help you more than you are hurt by me.

              Enter a Post.

WARWICK   What news, my friend?
POST
    That Edward is escapèd from your brother   78
    And fled, as he hears since, to Burgundy.   79
WARWICK
    Unsavory news! But how made he escape?
POST
    He was conveyed by Richard, Duke of Gloucester,   81

And the Lord Hastings, who attended him   82
    In secret ambush on the forest side
    And from the Bishop's huntsmen rescued him;
    For hunting was his daily exercise.
WARWICK
    My brother was too careless of his charge.
    But let us hence, my sovereign, to provide
    A salve for any sore that may betide.   88
         Exeunt. Manent Somerset, Richmond, and
                                Oxford.
SOMERSET [*to Oxford*]
    My lord, I like not of this flight of Edward's;   89
    For doubtless Burgundy will yield him help,
    And we shall have more wars before 't be long.
    As Henry's late presaging prophecy
    Did glad my heart with hope of this young
       Richmond,
    So doth my heart misgive me, in these conflicts
    What may befall him, to his harm and ours.
    Therefore, Lord Oxford, to prevent the worst,
    Forthwith we'll send him hence to Brittany,
    Till storms be past of civil enmity.
OXFORD
    Ay, for if Edward repossess the crown,
    'Tis like that Richmond with the rest shall down.   100
SOMERSET
    It shall be so. He shall to Brittany.
    Come, therefore, let's about it speedily.   *Exeunt.*

                      ❖

4.7   *Flourish. Enter [King] Edward, Richard [Duke of
       Gloucester], Hastings, and soldiers, [a troop of
       Hollanders].*

KING EDWARD
    Now, brother Richard, Lord Hastings, and the rest,
    Yet thus far fortune maketh us amends
    And says that once more I shall interchange
    My wanèd state for Henry's regal crown.
    Well have we passed and now repassed the seas,
    And brought desirèd help from Burgundy.
    What then remains, we being thus arrived
    From Ravenspurgh haven before the gates of York,   8
    But that we enter, as into our dukedom?
                           [*One knocks.*]
GLOUCESTER
    The gates made fast? Brother, I like not this;
    For many men that stumble at the threshold
    Are well foretold that danger lurks within.
KING EDWARD
    Tush, man, abodements must not now affright us.   13
    By fair or foul means we must enter in,
    For hither will our friends repair to us.

---

47 repose myself rely   **56 What else** i.e., yes, certainly. **succession
be determined** the order of succession to the throne (in view of Edward's removal) be definitely established   **57 want** lack. (Clarence
would have an interest in the crown previously claimed by his brother
and willed to him after Henry's death.)   **67 Henry . . . Richmond**
Henry Tudor, later Henry VII and founder of the Tudor dynasty
69 divining foreseeing the future   **78 your brother** i.e., the Archbishop of York   **79 he** i.e., your brother   **81 conveyed** spirited away

82 attended awaited **88 betide** occur, develop. **s.d. Manent** they
remain onstage **89 like not of** am displeased by **100 like** likely.
down fall
4.7. Location: Before the walls of York.
8 Ravenspurgh former seaport on the Yorkshire coast, at the mouth of
the River Humber **13 abodements** omens (such as stumbling at the
threshold, a conventional sign of bad luck)

HASTINGS
My liege, I'll knock once more to summon them.   16
                              [*He knocks.*]

          Enter, on the walls, the Mayor of York and his
          brethren [the aldermen].

MAYOR
My lords, we were forewarnèd of your coming
And shut the gates for safety of ourselves;
For now we owe allegiance unto Henry.

KING EDWARD
But, Master Mayor, if Henry be your king,
Yet Edward at the least is Duke of York.

MAYOR
True, my good lord, I know you for no less.

KING EDWARD
Why, and I challenge nothing but my dukedom,   23
As being well content with that alone.

GLOUCESTER [*aside*]
But when the fox hath once got in his nose,
He'll soon find means to make the body follow.

HASTINGS
Why, Master Mayor, why stand you in a doubt?
Open the gates. We are King Henry's friends.

MAYOR
Ay, say you so? The gates shall then be opened.   29
                    He descends [with the aldermen].

GLOUCESTER
A wise stout captain, and soon persuaded!   30

HASTINGS
The good old man would fain that all were well,   31
So 'twere not long of him; but being entered,   32
I doubt not, I, but we shall soon persuade
Both him and all his brothers unto reason.

          Enter [below] the Mayor and two aldermen.

KING EDWARD
So, Master Mayor, these gates must not be shut
But in the night or in the time of war.
What, fear not, man, but yield me up the keys.
                              Takes his keys.
For Edward will defend the town and thee,
And all those friends that deign to follow me.   39

          March. Enter Montgomery, with drum and
          soldiers.

GLOUCESTER
Brother, this is Sir John Montgomery,   40
Our trusty friend, unless I be deceived.

KING EDWARD
Welcome, Sir John! But why come you in arms?

MONTGOMERY
To help King Edward in his time of storm,
As every loyal subject ought to do.

KING EDWARD
Thanks, good Montgomery; but we now forget
Our title to the crown, and only claim
Our dukedom till God please to send the rest.

MONTGOMERY
Then fare you well, for I will hence again.
I came to serve a king and not a duke.
Drummer, strike up, and let us march away.   50
                    The drum begins to march.

KING EDWARD
Nay, stay, Sir John, awhile, and we'll debate
By what safe means the crown may be recovered.

MONTGOMERY
What talk you of debating? In few words,
If you'll not here proclaim yourself our king,
I'll leave you to your fortune and be gone
To keep them back that come to succor you.
Why shall we fight, if you pretend no title?   57

GLOUCESTER
Why, brother, wherefore stand you on nice points?   58

KING EDWARD
When we grow stronger, then we'll make our claim;
Till then, 'tis wisdom to conceal our meaning.   60

HASTINGS
Away with scrupulous wit! Now arms must rule.   61

GLOUCESTER
And fearless minds climb soonest unto crowns.
Brother, we will proclaim you out of hand;   63
The bruit thereof will bring you many friends.   64

KING EDWARD
Then be it as you will. For 'tis my right,
And Henry but usurps the diadem.

MONTGOMERY
Ay, now my sovereign speaketh like himself,
And now will I be Edward's champion.

HASTINGS
Sound trumpet! Edward shall be here proclaimed.
Come, fellow soldier, make thou proclamation.
          [*He gives a soldier a paper.*] *Flourish. Sound.*
SOLDIER [*reads*] "Edward the Fourth, by the grace of
God, King of England and France, and lord of
Ireland, etc."

MONTGOMERY
And whosoe'er gainsays King Edward's right,   74
By this I challenge him to single fight.
                    Throws down his gauntlet.
ALL   Long live Edward the Fourth!

KING EDWARD
Thanks, brave Montgomery, and thanks unto you
    all.
If fortune serve me, I'll requite this kindness.
Now, for this night, let's harbor here in York;

---

16 s.d. on the walls (In this scene, the back wall of the stage, or tiring-house facade, is imagined to be the walls of York; a door in the
facade represents the gates; and persons in the rear gallery above the
stage are *on the walls*.) 23 **challenge** claim 29 s.d. **descends** (The
Mayor and aldermen descend from the rear gallery behind the scenes
and then enter below through the door representing the gates of
York.) 30 **stout** brave 31 **fain** be glad 32 **So . . . him** as long as
he does not bear the responsibility 39 **deign** are willing. s.d. **drum**
drummer 40 **Sir John Montgomery** (Called "Sir Thomas" in the
chronicles.)

50 s.d. **drum . . . march** drummer strikes up a marching beat
57 **pretend** claim 58 **nice points** overscrupulous details 60 **meaning**
intentions 61 **scrupulous wit** cautious or prudent reasoning 63 **out
of hand** at once 64 **bruit** rumor, report 74 **gainsays** denies

And when the morning sun shall raise his car   80
Above the border of this horizon,
We'll forward towards Warwick and his mates;
For well I wot that Henry is no soldier.   83
Ah, froward Clarence, how evil it beseems thee   84
To flatter Henry and forsake thy brother!
Yet, as we may, we'll meet both thee and Warwick.
Come on, brave soldiers. Doubt not of the day,   87
And, that once gotten, doubt not of large pay.

                                        Exeunt.

❖

4.8   *Flourish. Enter the King [Henry], Warwick,*
          Montague, Clarence, Oxford, and Exeter.

WARWICK
What counsel, lords? Edward from Belgia,   1
With hasty Germans and blunt Hollanders,   2
Hath passed in safety through the narrow seas   3
And with his troops doth march amain to London,   4
And many giddy people flock to him.   5

KING HENRY
Let's levy men and beat him back again.

CLARENCE
A little fire is quickly trodden out
Which, being suffered, rivers cannot quench.   8

WARWICK
In Warwickshire I have truehearted friends,
Not mutinous in peace, yet bold in war.
Those will I muster up. And thou, son Clarence,   11
Shalt stir up in Suffolk, Norfolk, and in Kent,
The knights and gentlemen to come with thee.
Thou, brother Montague, in Buckingham,
Northampton, and in Leicestershire, shalt find
Men well inclined to hear what thou command'st.
And thou, brave Oxford, wondrous well beloved,
In Oxfordshire shalt muster up thy friends.
My sovereign, with the loving citizens,
Like to his island girt in with the ocean,
Or modest Dian circled with her nymphs,   21
Shall rest in London till we come to him.   22
Fair lords, take leave and stand not to reply.   23
Farewell, my sovereign.

KING HENRY
Farewell, my Hector, and my Troy's true hope.   25

CLARENCE [*kissing the King's hand*]
In sign of truth, I kiss Your Highness' hand.

KING HENRY
Well-minded Clarence, be thou fortunate!   27

MONTAGUE [*kissing the King's hand*]
Comfort, my lord; and so I take my leave.

OXFORD [*kissing the King's hand*]
And thus I seal my truth, and bid adieu.   29

KING HENRY
Sweet Oxford, and my loving Montague,
And all at once, once more a happy farewell.   31

WARWICK
Farewell, sweet lords. Let's meet at Coventry.
            Exeunt [all but King Henry and Exeter].

KING HENRY
Here at the palace will I rest awhile.   33
Cousin of Exeter, what thinks your lordship?   34
Methinks the power that Edward hath in field
Should not be able to encounter mine.

EXETER
The doubt is that he will seduce the rest.   37

KING HENRY
That's not my fear. My meed hath got me fame.   38
I have not stopped mine ears to their demands,
Nor posted off their suits with slow delays.   40
My pity hath been balm to heal their wounds,
My mildness hath allayed their swelling griefs,
My mercy dried their water-flowing tears.   43
I have not been desirous of their wealth,
Nor much oppressed them with great subsidies,   45
Nor forward of revenge, though they much erred.   46
Then why should they love Edward more than me?
No, Exeter, these graces challenge grace;   48
And when the lion fawns upon the lamb,
The lamb will never cease to follow him.   50
            Shout within, "A Lancaster!" "A York!"

EXETER
Hark, hark, my lord! What shouts are these?

            Enter [King] Edward and his soldiers [with
            Gloucester].

KING EDWARD
Seize on the shamefaced Henry, bear him hence,   52
And once again proclaim us king of England!
You are the fount that makes small brooks to flow.
Now stops thy spring; my sea shall suck them dry   55
And swell so much the higher by their ebb.
Hence with him to the Tower. Let him not speak.
            Exit [guard] with King Henry.
And, lords, towards Coventry bend we our course,
Where peremptory Warwick now remains.   59
The sun shines hot, and, if we use delay,   60
Cold biting winter mars our hoped-for hay.   61

---

80 his car i.e., Phoebus' chariot **83 wot** know **84 froward** perverse. **evil** ill **87 the day** the day's outcome
4.8. Location: The Bishop of London's palace.
1 Belgia i.e., the Low Countries **2 hasty** quick-tempered. **blunt** harsh, merciless **3 narrow seas** English Channel **4 amain** with full speed **5 giddy** fickle **8 suffered** allowed **11 son** i.e., son-in-law **21 modest Dian** chaste Diana, goddess of the moon and of chastity **22 rest** remain **23 stand** wait **25 Hector** i.e., chief protector of Troy. (England derived its legendary descent from Troy, through Brutus, great-grandson of Aeneas, supposed founder of the English nation.) **27 Well-minded** virtuously inclined

29 seal my truth confirm my loyalty (as though putting a seal to a document) **31 at once** together **33 palace** i.e., Bishop's palace **34 Cousin** (Form of address from the King to his peers.) **37 doubt** fear, danger **38 My . . . fame** my merits (for dealing generously and justly) have established my reputation **40 posted off** put off **43 water-flowing tears** tears flowing like water **45 subsidies** taxes **46 forward of** eager for **48 challenge grace** claim favor **50 s.d. A Lancaster! A York!** (Conflicting rallying cries for both sides.)
52 shamefaced shy, shamefast **55 thy spring** i.e., the source of your power **59 peremptory** overbearing **60–61 The sun . . . hay** i.e., make hay while the sun shines

GLOUCESTER
   Away betimes, before his forces join,   62
   And take the great-grown traitor unawares.
   Brave warriors, march amain towards Coventry.
                   Exeunt.

❖

5.1   *Enter Warwick, the Mayor of Coventry, two*
       Messengers, and others upon the walls.

WARWICK
   Where is the post that came from valiant Oxford?—   1
   How far hence is thy lord, mine honest fellow?
FIRST MESSENGER
   By this at Dunsmore, marching hitherward.   3
WARWICK
   How far off is our brother Montague?
   Where is the post that came from Montague?
SECOND MESSENGER
   By this at Daintry, with a puissant troop.   6

     Enter [Sir John] Somerville [to them, aloft].

WARWICK
   Say, Somerville, what says my loving son?   7
   And, by thy guess, how nigh is Clarence now?
SOMERVILLE
   At Southam I did leave him with his forces,   9
   And do expect him here some two hours hence.
                  [A march afar off.]
WARWICK
   Then Clarence is at hand. I hear his drum.
SOMERVILLE
   It is not his, my lord. Here Southam lies. *[He points.]*
   The drum your honor hears marcheth from
     Warwick.   13
WARWICK
   Who should that be? Belike unlooked-for friends.
SOMERVILLE
   They are at hand, and you shall quickly know.

     March. Flourish. Enter [King] Edward, Richard
     [Duke of Gloucester], and soldiers [below].

KING EDWARD
   Go, trumpet, to the walls and sound a parle.   16
                 [A parley is sounded.]
GLOUCESTER
   See how the surly Warwick mans the wall!
WARWICK
   O unbid spite! Is sportful Edward come?   18
   Where slept our scouts, or how are they seduced,
   That we could hear no news of his repair?   20

62 betimes quickly. **join** unite
5.1. Location: Before the walls of Coventry.
s.d. upon the walls (As in 4.7, the *walls* of this town are the tiring-house facade backstage, and those appearing *on the walls* are in the rear gallery above the stage.) **1 post** messenger. (Also at line 5.)
3 By this by this time **3, 6, 9, 13 Dunsmore, Daintry** (i.e., Daventry), **Southam, Warwick** (Towns within a day's march of Coventry.)
6 puissant powerful **7 son** i.e., son-in-law **16 trumpet** trumpeter. **parle** trumpet call for a parley **18 unbid** unwelcome. **spite** vexatious circumstance. **sportful** lascivious **20 repair** approach

KING EDWARD
   Now, Warwick, wilt thou ope the city gates,
   Speak gentle words, and humbly bend thy knee,
   Call Edward king, and at his hands beg mercy?
   And he shall pardon thee these outrages.
WARWICK
   Nay, rather, wilt thou draw thy forces hence,   25
   Confess who set thee up and plucked thee down,
   Call Warwick patron, and be penitent?
   And thou shalt still remain the Duke of York.
GLOUCESTER
   I thought at least he would have said "the King";
   Or did he make the jest against his will?
WARWICK
   Is not a dukedom, sir, a goodly gift?
GLOUCESTER
   Ay, by my faith, for a poor earl to give.
   I'll do thee service for so good a gift.   33
WARWICK
   'Twas I that gave the kingdom to thy brother.
KING EDWARD
   Why, then, 'tis mine, if but by Warwick's gift.
WARWICK
   Thou art no Atlas for so great a weight;   36
   And, weakling, Warwick takes his gift again,
   And Henry is my king, Warwick his subject.
KING EDWARD
   But Warwick's king is Edward's prisoner.
   And, gallant Warwick, do but answer this:
   What is the body when the head is off?
GLOUCESTER
   Alas, that Warwick had no more forecast,   42
   But, whiles he thought to steal the single ten,   43
   The King was slyly fingered from the deck!
   You left poor Henry at the Bishop's palace,
   And ten to one you'll meet him in the Tower.   46
KING EDWARD
   'Tis even so. Yet you are Warwick still.   47
GLOUCESTER
   Come, Warwick, take the time. Kneel down, kneel
     down.   48
   Nay, when? Strike now, or else the iron cools.   49
WARWICK
   I had rather chop this hand off at a blow,
   And with the other fling it at thy face,
   Than bear so low a sail to strike to thee.
KING EDWARD
   Sail how thou canst, have wind and tide thy friend,

25 draw withdraw **33 do thee service** i.e., pay feudal homage. (Said ironically.) **36 Atlas** the Titan's son in classical myth who carried the world on his shoulders **42 forecast** forethought **43 single ten** mere ten card. (Less valuable than the king card. Gloucester sardonically remarks that, while Warwick has been desperately trying to shore up his defenses, he has left his prize card, King Henry, inadequately guarded; see 4.8.) **46 you'll . . . Tower** i.e., you'll soon be imprisoned in the Tower with King Henry **47 Yet . . . still** i.e., you are still the Earl of Warwick and still have time to change before disaster strikes **48 time** opportunity **49 when** i.e., when are you going to act. (An expression of impatience.) **Strike . . . cools** i.e., strike while the iron is hot. (But *strike* also means to "lower sail," "yield"; hence, Warwick's refusal to *bear so low a sail,* i.e., offer tokens of submission, in line 52. Compare with the note for 3.3.5.)

This hand, fast wound about thy coal black hair,
Shall, whiles thy head is warm and new cut off,
Write in the dust this sentence with thy blood:
"Wind-changing Warwick now can change no
    more."   57

Enter Oxford, with drum and colors.

WARWICK
O cheerful colors! See where Oxford comes!
OXFORD
Oxford, Oxford, for Lancaster!
                [He and his forces enter the city.]
GLOUCESTER
The gates are open. Let us enter too.
KING EDWARD
So other foes may set upon our backs.   61
Stand we in good array, for they no doubt
Will issue out again and bid us battle.
If not, the city being but of small defense,
We'll quickly rouse the traitors in the same. 65
            [Oxford appears above, on the walls.]
WARWICK
O, welcome, Oxford, for we want thy help.

Enter Montague, with drum and colors.

MONTAGUE
Montague, Montague, for Lancaster!
                [He and his forces enter the city.]
GLOUCESTER
Thou and thy brother both shall buy this treason 68
Even with the dearest blood your bodies bear.
KING EDWARD
The harder matched, the greater victory.   70
My mind presageth happy gain and conquest.   71

Enter Somerset, with drum and colors.

SOMERSET
Somerset, Somerset, for Lancaster!
                [He and his forces enter the city.]
GLOUCESTER
Two of thy name, both Dukes of Somerset,   73
Have sold their lives unto the house of York,
And thou shalt be the third, if this sword hold.

Enter Clarence, with drum and colors.

WARWICK
And lo, where George of Clarence sweeps along,
Of force enough to bid his brother battle;   77
With whom an upright zeal to right prevails   78

More than the nature of a brother's love!   79
        [Gloucester and Clarence whisper together.]
Come, Clarence, come; thou wilt, if Warwick call.
CLARENCE
Father of Warwick, know you what this means?   81
            *[He takes his red rose out of his hat
                        and throws it at Warwick.]*
Look here, I throw my infamy at thee.
I will not ruinate my father's house,   83
Who gave his blood to lime the stones together, 84
And set up Lancaster. Why, trowest thou, Warwick, 85
That Clarence is so harsh, so blunt, unnatural,
To bend the fatal instruments of war   87
Against his brother and his lawful king?
Perhaps thou wilt object my holy oath.   89
To keep that oath were more impiety
Than Jephthah when he sacrificed his daughter. 91
I am so sorry for my trespass made
That, to deserve well at my brother's hands,
I here proclaim myself thy mortal foe,
With resolution, wheresoe'er I meet thee—
As I will meet thee, if thou stir abroad—   96
To plague thee for thy foul misleading me.
And so, proudhearted Warwick, I defy thee,
And to my brother turn my blushing cheeks.
Pardon me, Edward, I will make amends;
And, Richard, do not frown upon my faults,
For I will henceforth be no more unconstant.
KING EDWARD
Now welcome more, and ten times more beloved,
Than if thou never hadst deserved our hate!
GLOUCESTER
Welcome, good Clarence. This is brotherlike.
WARWICK
O passing traitor, perjured and unjust!   106
KING EDWARD
What, Warwick, wilt thou leave the town and fight?
Or shall we beat the stones about thine ears?
WARWICK
Alas, I am not cooped here for defense!
I will away towards Barnet presently,   110
And bid thee battle, Edward, if thou dar'st.
KING EDWARD
Yes, Warwick, Edward dares, and leads the way.
Lords, to the field! Saint George and victory!

*Exeunt [King Edward and his company]. March.
Warwick and his company follows [out of the city].*

---

57 **Wind-changing** i.e., shifting, like a weathervane. **s.d. drum** drummer. **colors** flags borne by flag carriers 61 **So** in that case. **set . . . backs** attack us from the rear 65 **rouse** cause (an animal) to rise from its lair 68 **buy** pay dearly for 70 **The harder . . . victory** the more powerful the enemy, the greater the victory. (Proverbial.) 71 **happy** fortunate 73 **Two of thy name** i.e., Edmund Beaufort, second Duke of Somerset, killed at St. Albans in 1455, and his son Henry (not a character in this play), beheaded in 1464 for his Lancastrian sympathies. (The Duke addressed here is Henry's brother Edmund, fourth Duke.) 77 **Of force enough** with a powerful enough army 78 **to right** on behalf of justice

79 **nature** natural feeling. **s.d. Gloucester . . . together** (This stage direction, and that at line 81, are basically from the Octavo text.) 81 **Father** i.e., father-in-law 83 **ruinate** bring into ruin 84 **lime** cement 85 **trowest thou** do you think 87 **bend** direct 89 **object** urge 91 **Jephthah** (See Judges 11:30 ff. for the account of Jephthah's vow to sacrifice, if victorious, the first living creature that came to meet him on his return. His daughter was the victim.) 96 **abroad** from home, i.e., outside the city walls 106 **passing** surpassing 110 **Barnet** a town in Hertfordshire, about ten miles north of London. (Warwick's illogical proposal that the armies meet at Barnet, some seventy-five miles from Coventry, is a result of Shakespeare's telescoping and rearranging of historical events.) **presently** immediately

5.2   *Alarum and excursions. Enter [King] Edward, bringing forth Warwick wounded.*

KING EDWARD
So, lie thou there. Die thou, and die our fear,
For Warwick was a bug that feared us all.   2
Now, Montague, sit fast. I seek for thee,   3
That Warwick's bones may keep thine company.
                                                    Exit.

WARWICK
Ah, who is nigh? Come to me, friend or foe,
And tell me who is victor, York or Warwick?
Why ask I that? My mangled body shows,
My blood, my want of strength, my sick heart
   shows,
That I must yield my body to the earth
And, by my fall, the conquest to my foe.
Thus yields the cedar to the ax's edge,
Whose arms gave shelter to the princely eagle,   12
Under whose shade the ramping lion slept,   13
Whose top branch overpeered Jove's spreading tree   14
And kept low shrubs from winter's powerful wind.
These eyes, that now are dimmed with death's black
   veil,
Have been as piercing as the midday sun
To search the secret treasons of the world.
The wrinkles in my brows, now filled with blood,
Were likened oft to kingly sepulchers;
For who lived king, but I could dig his grave?
And who durst smile when Warwick bent his brow?   22
Lo, now my glory smeared in dust and blood!
My parks, my walks, my manors that I had,
Even now forsake me, and of all my lands
Is nothing left me but my body's length.
Why, what is pomp, rule, reign, but earth and dust?
And, live we how we can, yet die we must.

                Enter Oxford and Somerset.

SOMERSET
Ah, Warwick, Warwick! Wert thou as we are,
We might recover all our loss again.
The Queen from France hath brought a puissant
   power;   31
Even now we heard the news. Ah, couldst thou fly!
WARWICK
Why, then I would not fly. Ah, Montague,
If thou be there, sweet brother, take my hand,
And with thy lips keep in my soul awhile!   35
Thou lov'st me not, for, brother, if thou didst,
Thy tears would wash this cold congealèd blood
That glues my lips and will not let me speak.
Come quickly, Montague, or I am dead.

SOMERSET
Ah, Warwick, Montague hath breathed his last,
And to the latest gasp cried out for Warwick   41
And said, "Commend me to my valiant brother."
And more he would have said, and more he spoke,
Which sounded like a cannon in a vault,
That mought not be distinguished; but at last   45
I well might hear, delivered with a groan,
"O, farewell, Warwick!"
WARWICK
Sweet rest his soul! Fly, lords, and save yourselves,
For Warwick bids you all farewell, to meet in
   heaven.   *[He dies.]*
OXFORD
Away, away, to meet the Queen's great power!
                Here they bear away his body. Exeunt.

5.3   *Flourish. Enter King Edward in triumph, with Richard [Duke of Gloucester], Clarence, and the rest.*

KING EDWARD
Thus far our fortune keeps an upward course,
And we are graced with wreaths of victory.
But in the midst of this bright-shining day
I spy a black, suspicious, threatening cloud
That will encounter with our glorious sun   5
Ere he attain his easeful western bed:
I mean, my lords, those powers that the Queen
Hath raised in Gallia have arrived our coast   8
And, as we hear, march on to fight with us.
CLARENCE
A little gale will soon disperse that cloud
And blow it to the source from whence it came.
The very beams will dry those vapors up,   12
For every cloud engenders not a storm.
GLOUCESTER
The Queen is valued thirty thousand strong,
And Somerset, with Oxford, fled to her.
If she have time to breathe, be well assured   16
Her faction will be full as strong as ours.
KING EDWARD
We are advertised by our loving friends   18
That they do hold their course toward Tewkesbury.   19
We, having now the best at Barnet field,
Will thither straight, for willingness rids way;   21
And, as we march, our strength will be augmented
In every county as we go along.
Strike up the drum, cry "Courage!" and away.
                                                  Exeunt.

                      ❧

5.2. Location: A field of battle near Barnet. (Despite the distance from Coventry to Barnet, the sense here is of virtually continuous action.)
2 bug bugbear, goblin.   **feared** frightened   **3 sit fast** position yourself as securely as you can   **12, 13 eagle, lion** (Royal emblems; Warwick, the lofty *cedar* in this metaphor, has at times given his protection to both Edward and Henry.)   **13 ramping** rampant, upreared. (A heraldic term.)   **14 Jove's spreading tree** i.e., the oak   **22 bent his brow** frowned   **31 puissant** powerful   **35 with thy lips** i.e., with a kiss. (The soul was thought to leave the body through the mouth at death.)

41 latest last   **45 mought** might
5.3. Location: The field of battle near Barnet, as before.
5 sun i.e., the heraldic sun on the Yorkist coat of arms   **8 Gallia** France.   **arrived** reached   **12 very** mere   **16 breathe** i.e., pause and muster her strength   **18 advertised** notified   **19 Tewkesbury** a town in Gloucestershire   **21 straight** immediately.   **rids way** annihilates distance, makes the way seem short

5.4   *Flourish. March. Enter the Queen [Margaret], young [Prince] Edward, Somerset, Oxford, and soldiers.*

QUEEN MARGARET
Great lords, wise men ne'er sit and wail their loss,
But cheerly seek how to redress their harms.   2
What though the mast be now blown overboard,
The cable broke, the holding-anchor lost,
And half our sailors swallowed in the flood?   5
Yet lives our pilot still. Is 't meet that he   6
Should leave the helm and, like a fearful lad,
With tearful eyes add water to the sea
And give more strength to that which hath too
    much,
Whiles, in his moan, the ship splits on the rock,   10
Which industry and courage might have saved?
Ah, what a shame, ah, what a fault were this!
Say Warwick was our anchor. What of that?
And Montague our topmast. What of him?
Our slaughtered friends the tackles. What of these?   15
Why, is not Oxford here another anchor?
And Somerset another goodly mast?
The friends of France our shrouds and tacklings?   18
And, though unskillful, why not Ned and I
For once allowed the skillful pilot's charge?   20
We will not from the helm to sit and weep,   21
But keep our course, though the rough wind say no,
From shelves and rocks that threaten us with wreck.   23
As good to chide the waves as speak them fair.   24
And what is Edward but a ruthless sea?
What Clarence but a quicksand of deceit?
And Richard but a ragged fatal rock?
All these the enemies to our poor bark.
Say you can swim, alas, 'tis but a while;
Tread on the sand, why, there you quickly sink;
Bestride the rock, the tide will wash you off,
Or else you famish—that's a threefold death.
This speak I, lords, to let you understand,
If case some one of you would fly from us,   34
That there's no hoped-for mercy with the brothers
More than with ruthless waves, with sands and
    rocks.
Why, courage then! What cannot be avoided
'Twere childish weakness to lament or fear.

PRINCE
Methinks a woman of this valiant spirit
Should, if a coward heard her speak these words,
Infuse his breast with magnanimity
And make him, naked, foil a man at arms.   42
I speak not this as doubting any here;
For did I but suspect a fearful man,
He should have leave to go away betimes,   45

Lest in our need he might infect another
And make him of like spirit to himself.
If any such be here—as God forbid!—
Let him depart before we need his help.

OXFORD
Women and children of so high a courage,
And warriors faint! Why, 'twere perpetual shame.
O brave young Prince! Thy famous grandfather   52
Doth live again in thee. Long mayst thou live
To bear his image and renew his glories!   54

SOMERSET
And he that will not fight for such a hope,
Go home to bed, and, like the owl by day,
If he arise, be mocked and wondered at.

QUEEN MARGARET
Thanks, gentle Somerset; sweet Oxford, thanks.

PRINCE
And take his thanks that yet hath nothing else.   59

Enter a Messenger.

MESSENGER
Prepare you, lords, for Edward is at hand,
Ready to fight. Therefore be resolute.

OXFORD
I thought no less. It is his policy   62
To haste thus fast, to find us unprovided.   63

SOMERSET
But he's deceived. We are in readiness.

QUEEN MARGARET
This cheers my heart, to see your forwardness.   65

OXFORD
Here pitch our battle. Hence we will not budge.   66

Flourish and march. Enter [King] Edward, Richard [Duke of Gloucester], Clarence, and soldiers.

KING EDWARD
Brave followers, yonder stands the thorny wood
Which, by the heavens' assistance and your
    strength,
Must by the roots be hewn up yet ere night.
I need not add more fuel to your fire,
For well I wot ye blaze to burn them out.   71
Give signal to the fight, and to it, lords!

QUEEN MARGARET
Lords, knights, and gentlemen, what I should say
My tears gainsay; for every word I speak,   74
Ye see, I drink the water of mine eye.   75
Therefore, no more but this: Henry, your sovereign,
Is prisoner to the foe, his state usurped,   77
His realm a slaughterhouse, his subjects slain,
His statutes canceled, and his treasure spent;
And yonder is the wolf that makes this spoil.   80

5.4. Location: Near Tewkesbury.
2 cheerly cheerfully   **5 flood** water, sea   **6 our pilot** i.e., King Henry.   **meet** fitting   **10 in his moan** as he makes lamentation   **15 tackles** rigging   **18 shrouds** ropes or cables supporting the mast   **20 charge** responsibility   **21 from** go away from   **23 shelves** sandbanks, shoals   **24 As good to** i.e., one might as well.   **speak them fair** address them courteously   **34 If** in   **42 naked** unarmed.   **foil** defeat.   **man at arms** armed soldier   **45 betimes** at once

52 grandfather i.e., Henry V   **54 image** likeness   **59 his . . . else** i.e., my thanks, I who as yet have nothing else to give   **62 policy** stratagem   **63 unprovided** unprepared   **65 forwardness** eagerness   **66 pitch our battle** draw up our armies   **71 wot** know   **74 gainsay** forbid   **74–75 for . . . eye** (Margaret's point is that this is no time for words; they will only distract her from the fury expressed in her tears.)   **77 state** royal status as king   **80 spoil** plunder, destruction

You fight in justice. Then, in God's name, lords,
Be valiant, and give signal to the fight.   82
            Alarum. Retreat. Excursions [in which
            Queen Margaret, Prince Edward, Oxford,
            and Somerset are taken]. Exeunt.

5.5   *Flourish. Enter [King] Edward, Richard [Duke of*
            Gloucester]; Queen [Margaret, as prisoner];
            Clarence; Oxford, Somerset [as prisoners].

KING EDWARD
  Now here a period of tumultuous broils.   1
  Away with Oxford to Hames Castle straight.   2
  For Somerset, off with his guilty head.   3
  Go, bear them hence. I will not hear them speak.
OXFORD
  For my part, I'll not trouble thee with words.
SOMERSET
  Nor I, but stoop with patience to my fortune.
            Exeunt [Oxford and Somerset, guarded].
QUEEN MARGARET
  So part we sadly in this troublous world,
  To meet with joy in sweet Jerusalem.   8
KING EDWARD
  Is proclamation made that who finds Edward   9
  Shall have a high reward, and he his life?
GLOUCESTER
  It is. And lo, where youthful Edward comes!

            Enter [soldiers, with] the Prince [Edward].

KING EDWARD
  Bring forth the gallant. Let us hear him speak.
  What, can so young a thorn begin to prick?
  Edward, what satisfaction canst thou make   14
  For bearing arms, for stirring up my subjects,
  And all the trouble thou hast turned me to?
PRINCE
  Speak like a subject, proud ambitious York!
  Suppose that I am now my father's mouth;
  Resign thy chair, and where I stand kneel thou,   19
  Whilst I propose the selfsame words to thee,
  Which, traitor, thou wouldst have me answer to.
QUEEN MARGARET
  Ah, that thy father had been so resolved!
GLOUCESTER
  That you might still have worn the petticoat
  And ne'er have stol'n the breech from Lancaster.   24
PRINCE
  Let Aesop fable in a winter's night;   25

His currish riddles sorts not with this place.   26
GLOUCESTER
  By heaven, brat, I'll plague ye for that word.
QUEEN MARGARET
  Ay, thou wast born to be a plague to men.
GLOUCESTER
  For God's sake, take away this captive scold.
PRINCE
  Nay, take away this scolding crookback rather.
KING EDWARD
  Peace, willful boy, or I will charm your tongue.   31
CLARENCE
  Untutored lad, thou art too malapert.   32
PRINCE
  I know my duty. You are all undutiful.
  Lascivious Edward, and thou perjured George,
  And thou misshapen Dick, I tell ye all
  I am your better, traitors as ye are,
  And thou usurp'st my father's right and mine.
KING EDWARD
  Take that, thou likeness of this railer here!   38
            Stabs him.
GLOUCESTER
  Sprawl'st thou? Take that, to end thy agony.   39
            Richard stabs him.
CLARENCE
  And there's for twitting me with perjury.
            Clarence stabs him. [Prince Edward dies.]
QUEEN MARGARET O, kill me too!
GLOUCESTER Marry, and shall.   *Offers to kill her.* 42
KING EDWARD
  Hold, Richard, hold, for we have done too much.
GLOUCESTER
  Why should she live, to fill the world with words?
            [Margaret swoons.]
KING EDWARD
  What, doth she swoon? Use means for her recovery.
GLOUCESTER *[aside to Clarence]*
  Clarence, excuse me to the King my brother;
  I'll hence to London on a serious matter.
  Ere ye come there, be sure to hear some news.   48
CLARENCE *[aside to Gloucester]*   What? What?
GLOUCESTER *[aside to Clarence]*   The Tower, the Tower.
            Exit.
QUEEN MARGARET *[reviving]*
  O Ned, sweet Ned, speak to thy mother, boy!
  Canst thou not speak? O traitors, murderers!
  They that stabbed Caesar shed no blood at all,
  Did not offend, nor were not worthy blame,
  If this foul deed were by to equal it.   55
  He was a man; this, in respect, a child,   56
  And men ne'er spend their fury on a child.
  What's worse than murderer, that I may name it?
  No, no, my heart will burst an if I speak;

82 s.d. Alarum (The Octavo version provides that *chambers*, or short cannon, are "discharged," after which King Edward and his brothers and allies enter with "a great shout," and cry "For York! For York!" and take the Queen and her son.)
5.5. Location: Scene continues at the battlefield near Tewkesbury.
1 period termination **2 Hames Castle** i.e., Hammes Castle near Calais (where Oxford was indeed confined, but not until his capture some three years after Tewkesbury). **straight** at once **3 For** as for
8 sweet Jerusalem i.e., the heavenly Jerusalem **9 who** anyone who
14 satisfaction recompense **19 chair** throne **24 breech** breeches, symbol of male authority **25 Aesop** Greek teller of fables (who, like Gloucester, was reputed to have been deformed). **in . . . night** i.e., in a setting fitted for such childish tales

26 His . . . place his mean riddles are inappropriate to this place. (Prince Edward is retorting to Gloucester's gibe, denying the allegation that his father was henpecked.) **31 charm** cast a spell upon, i.e., silence **32 malapert** saucy **38 this railer here** i.e., Queen Margaret **39 Sprawl'st thou** i.e., are you twitching in the throes of death **42 Marry, and shall** i.e., indeed, I will. **s.d. Offers to** is about to **48 be sure** expect **55 equal** compare with **56 respect** comparison

And I will speak, that so my heart may burst.
Butchers and villains, bloody cannibals!
How sweet a plant have you untimely cropped!
You have no children, butchers; if you had,
The thought of them would have stirred up
    remorse.
But if you ever chance to have a child,
Look in his youth to have him so cut off
As, deathsmen, you have rid this sweet young
    prince!   67

KING EDWARD
Away with her. Go, bear her hence perforce.   68

QUEEN MARGARET
Nay, never bear me hence. Dispatch me here!
Here sheathe thy sword. I'll pardon thee my death.
What, wilt thou not? Then, Clarence, do it thou.

CLARENCE
By heaven, I will not do thee so much ease.   72

QUEEN MARGARET
Good Clarence, do. Sweet Clarence, do thou do it.

CLARENCE
Didst thou not hear me swear I would not do it?

QUEEN MARGARET
Ay, but thou usest to forswear thyself.   75
'Twas sin before, but now 'tis charity.
What, wilt thou not? Where is that devil's butcher,
Hard-favored Richard? Richard, where art thou?   78
Thou art not here. Murder is thy almsdeed;   79
Petitioners for blood thou ne'er putt'st back.   80

KING EDWARD
Away, I say! I charge ye, bear her hence.

QUEEN MARGARET
So come to you and yours as to this prince!   82
                                        Exit Queen, [guarded].

KING EDWARD   Where's Richard gone?

CLARENCE
To London, all in post—[aside] and, as I guess,   84
To make a bloody supper in the Tower.

KING EDWARD
He's sudden, if a thing comes in his head.
Now march we hence. Discharge the common sort   87
With pay and thanks, and let's away to London
And see our gentle queen how well she fares.
By this, I hope, she hath a son for me.   Exeunt. 90

❧

5.6   *Enter Henry the Sixth and Richard [Duke of
           Gloucester], with the Lieutenant [of the Tower],
           on the walls.*

GLOUCESTER
Good day, my lord. What, at your book so hard?   1

KING HENRY
Ay, my good lord—"my lord," I should say rather.
'Tis sin to flatter. "Good" was little better.   3
"Good Gloucester" and "good devil" were alike,   4
And both preposterous; therefore, not "good lord."   5

GLOUCESTER [*to the Lieutenant*]
Sirrah, leave us to ourselves. We must confer.   6
                                            [*Exit Lieutenant.*]

KING HENRY
So flies the reckless shepherd from the wolf;   7
So first the harmless sheep doth yield his fleece
And next his throat unto the butcher's knife.
What scene of death hath Roscius now to act?   10

GLOUCESTER
Suspicion always haunts the guilty mind;
The thief doth fear each bush an officer.   12

KING HENRY
The bird that hath been limèd in a bush,   13
With trembling wings misdoubteth every bush;   14
And I, the hapless male to one sweet bird,   15
Have now the fatal object in my eye
Where my poor young was limed, was caught, and
    killed.

GLOUCESTER
Why, what a peevish fool was that of Crete,   18
That taught his son the office of a fowl!
And yet, for all his wings, the fool was drowned.

KING HENRY
I, Daedalus; my poor boy, Icarus;
Thy father, Minos, that denied our course;   22
The sun that seared the wings of my sweet boy,   23
Thy brother Edward; and thyself, the sea
Whose envious gulf did swallow up his life.   25
Ah, kill me with thy weapon, not with words!
My breast can better brook thy dagger's point   27
Than can my ears that tragic history.   28
But wherefore dost thou come? Is 't for my life?

GLOUCESTER
Think'st thou I am an executioner?

KING HENRY
A persecutor I am sure thou art.
If murdering innocents be executing,
Why, then thou art an executioner.

GLOUCESTER
Thy son I killed for his presumption.

KING HENRY
Hadst thou been killed when first thou didst
    presume,

67 **rid** removed, killed   **68 perforce** by force   **72 ease** i.e., easing of
your grief in death   **75 thou usest** you are accustomed   **78 Hard-favored** ugly   **79 almsdeed** act of charity   **80 Petitioners . . . back**
you never turn away persons asking for blood   **82 So come** may it
happen   **84 post** haste   **87 common sort** ordinary soldiers   **90 this**
this time
5.6. Location: The Tower of London.
1 book i.e., book of devotion

3 little better i.e., little more than flattery   **4 were** would be   **5 preposterous** unnatural   **6 Sirrah** (Customary form of address to inferiors.)   **7 reckless** heedless   **10 Roscius** celebrated Roman actor much
admired by Cicero and regarded by the Elizabethans as a model of
tragic acting   **12 an officer** to be an arresting officer   **13 limèd**
snared with birdlime, a sticky substance smeared on branches
14 misdoubteth is mistrustful of   **15 male** father, begetter.   **bird**
chick, offspring   **18 peevish** silly.   **that of Crete** (Daedalus escaped
from Crete, where he had fashioned for King Minos a labyrinth to
contain the Minotaur, by devising wings for himself and his son
Icarus, but Icarus flew too near the sun, which melted the wax in his
wings, thus causing him to fall into the sea.)   **22 course** i.e., departure   **23 sun** (with reference to the Yorkist heraldic badge, as at
2.1.25)   **25 envious gulf** malicious whirlpool   **27 brook** endure
28 history story

Thou hadst not lived to kill a son of mine.
And thus I prophesy, that many a thousand,
Which now mistrust no parcel of my fear,   38
And many an old man's sigh and many a widow's,
And many an orphan's water-standing eye—   40
Men for their sons', wives for their husbands',
Orphans for their parents' timeless death—   42
Shall rue the hour that ever thou wast born.
The owl shrieked at thy birth—an evil sign;
The night crow cried, aboding luckless time;   45
Dogs howled, and hideous tempest shook down
    trees;
The raven rooked her on the chimney's top;   47
And chattering pies in dismal discords sung.   48
Thy mother felt more than a mother's pain,
And yet brought forth less than a mother's hope,
To wit, an indigested and deformèd lump,   51
Not like the fruit of such a goodly tree.
Teeth hadst thou in thy head when thou wast born,
To signify thou cam'st to bite the world;
And if the rest be true which I have heard,
Thou cam'st—

GLOUCESTER
I'll hear no more. Die, prophet, in thy speech.
                                            Stabs him.
For this, amongst the rest, was I ordained.

KING HENRY
Ay, and for much more slaughter after this.
O, God forgive my sins, and pardon thee!   Dies.

GLOUCESTER
What, will the aspiring blood of Lancaster
Sink in the ground? I thought it would have
    mounted.
See how my sword weeps for the poor King's death!
O, may such purple tears be always shed   64
From those that wish the downfall of our house!
If any spark of life be yet remaining,
Down, down to hell, and say I sent thee thither,
                                        Stabs him again
I, that have neither pity, love, nor fear.
Indeed, 'tis true that Henry told me of;   69
For I have often heard my mother say
I came into the world with my legs forward.
Had I not reason, think ye, to make haste
And seek their ruin that usurped our right?
The midwife wondered and the women cried,
"O, Jesus bless us, he is born with teeth!"
And so I was, which plainly signified
That I should snarl and bite and play the dog.
Then, since the heavens have shaped my body so,
Let hell make crook'd my mind to answer it.   79
I have no brother, I am like no brother;
And this word "love," which graybeards call divine,
Be resident in men like one another
And not in me. I am myself alone.

Clarence, beware. Thou keep'st me from the light;
But I will sort a pitchy day for thee;   85
For I will buzz abroad such prophecies
That Edward shall be fearful of his life,   87
And then, to purge his fear, I'll be thy death.
King Henry and the Prince his son are gone;
Clarence, thy turn is next, and then the rest,
Counting myself but bad till I be best.   91
I'll throw thy body in another room
And triumph, Henry, in thy day of doom.
                              Exit [with the body].

❧

5.7   *Flourish. Enter King [Edward], Queen [Elizabeth],*
        Clarence, Richard [Duke of Gloucester], Hastings,
        Nurse [with the young Prince], and attendants.
        [King Edward sits on his throne.]

KING EDWARD
Once more we sit in England's royal throne,
Repurchased with the blood of enemies.
What valiant foemen, like to autumn's corn,   3
Have we mowed down in tops of all their pride!   4
Three Dukes of Somerset, threefold renowned
For hardy and undoubted champions;   6
Two Cliffords, as the father and the son;   7
And two Northumberlands—two braver men
Ne'er spurred their coursers at the trumpet's sound;   9
With them, the two brave bears, Warwick and
    Montague,   10
That in their chains fettered the kingly lion
And made the forest tremble when they roared.
Thus have we swept suspicion from our seat   13
And made our footstool of security.
Come hither, Bess, and let me kiss my boy.
                              [He kisses his son.]
Young Ned, for thee, thine uncles and myself
Have in our armors watched the winter's night,   17
Went all afoot in summer's scalding heat,
That thou mightst repossess the crown in peace;
And of our labors thou shalt reap the gain.

GLOUCESTER [aside]
I'll blast his harvest, if your head were laid;   21
For yet I am not looked on in the world.   22
This shoulder was ordained so thick to heave,
And heave it shall some weight, or break my back.
Work thou the way, and thou shalt execute.   25

KING EDWARD
Clarence and Gloucester, love my lovely queen,
And kiss your princely nephew, brothers both.

---

85 sort select.   **pitchy** black   **87 of** for   **91 bad** unfortunate
5.7. Location: London. The royal court. A throne is provided onstage.
3 corn grain   **4 in tops** at the height   **6 undoubted** fearless   **7 as** to
wit   **9 coursers** horses   **10 bears** (Refers to the Neville family emblem.)   **13 seat** throne   **17 watched** stayed awake throughout
21 blast blight.   **if . . . laid** i.e., once you are laid out on the bier in
death (with a suggestion also of grain flattened by a storm)
22 looked on heeded, respected   **25 Work thou** (Addressed to himself, indicating his head.)   **thou shalt** (Addressed to his shoulder and
arm.)

---

38 mistrust . . . fear i.e., feel none of the suspicion that I feel
40 water-standing i.e., filled with tears   **42 timeless** untimely
45 night crow nightjar or owl.   **aboding** foreboding   **47 rooked her**
couched, roosted   **48 pies** magpies   **51 indigested** shapeless, chaotic   **64 purple** bloodred   **69 that** what   **79 answer** match

CLARENCE
    The duty that I owe unto Your Majesty
    I seal upon the lips of this sweet babe.
                            [He kisses the Prince.]

QUEEN ELIZABETH
    Thanks, noble Clarence; worthy brother, thanks.   30

GLOUCESTER
    And, that I love the tree from whence thou
        sprang'st,
    Witness the loving kiss I give the fruit.
                         [He kisses the Prince.]
    [Aside.] To say the truth, so Judas kissed his master,
    And cried "All hail!" whenas he meant all harm.

KING EDWARD
    Now am I seated as my soul delights,
    Having my country's peace and brothers' loves.

CLARENCE
    What will Your Grace have done with Margaret?
    Reignier, her father, to the King of France
    Hath pawned the Sicils and Jerusalem,   39
    And hither have they sent it for her ransom.   40

KING EDWARD
    Away with her, and waft her hence to France.   41
    And now what rests but that we spend the time   42
    With stately triumphs, mirthful comic shows,   43
    Such as befits the pleasure of the court?
    Sound drums and trumpets! Farewell sour annoy!
    For here, I hope, begins our lasting joy.   46
                     [Flourish.] Exeunt omnes.

---

30 brother i.e., brother-in-law   **39 the Sicils** (See the note to
1.4.122.)   **40 it** i.e., the money raised by "pawn"   **41 waft** convey
by water   **42 rests** remains   **43 triumphs** festivities   **46 s.d. omnes**
all

The Tragedy of King Richard the Third

Richard III begins where *3 Henry VI* has left off, with the return of Edward IV to the throne in 1471, and ends with the defeat of Richard III, the last Yorkist king, at the battle of Bosworth (1485). It thus completes the action of the four-play series begun with *1 Henry VI*. Because of its close relation in subject to passages in *3 Henry VI* and its similar Senecan style, the play appears to have been written soon after its predecessors, sometime between 1591 and 1594. It greatly condenses events of fourteen years, particularly at the beginning, when King Henry's funeral rites (1471), Richard's courtship of Lady Anne (1472), Clarence's murder in the Tower (1478), and Edward's death (1483) are made to take place at the same time. Similarly, Buckingham's rebellion (1483), Richmond's thwarted sailing (1483), and his landing at Milford Haven (1485) are also compressed. Queen Margaret's role is a nonhistorical addition to the play, for the widowed Queen never left France after her ransom in 1475 by Louis XI.

Richard's evil character, already taking clear shape in the last of the *Henry VI* plays, stands fully revealed in *Richard III*. With a bold stroke, Shakespeare opens the play with his arresting soliloquy; Richard takes over the stage in a way that has aroused fascinated interest ever since Burbage first performed the role. Richard announces his determination to "prove a villain," both defying and fulfilling Nature, which made his body deformed. In fact, he has already begun his treacherous course, and we see at once how his plot against Clarence, founded on something so trivial as the letter G, has manipulated the King and has ensnared Clarence. Then, with outrageous hypocrisy, he "comforts" Clarence. Within less than a hundred lines, Shakespeare makes us feel how brilliant, cynical, charming, and dangerous Richard of Gloucester is. Richard proceeds to dominate the other characters—and the whole play—to an extraordinary degree.

By organizing this play firmly around Richard, Shakespeare solved the problems of giving form to his drama and of concluding the series of plays about the dynastic rivalry of York and Lancaster. *Richard III* begins and ends with a peace, yet the recent peace of the Yorkist King Edward is scorned and sabotaged by Richard as soon as it is introduced. It is vulnerable to factions at court and is bitterly denounced by that memoir of the cruel and violent past, Queen Margaret. There can be no peace in England while Richard lives to undermine it. Still, as the plot moves through Richard's exhilarating rise to the throne and the events of his tragic fall—when his conscience, the spirits of those he murdered, and the Earl of Richmond punish and defeat him—we see that his career is part of a larger order, a seemingly providential plan of retribution for wickedness and injustice and for reconciling England's divisions. For all its specific reminders of past warfare and atrocity on both Yorkist and Lancastrian sides, *Richard III* dramatizes an archetypal struggle between good and evil, personified in Richard the villain-hero and Richmond his opponent, who is dramatized as the righteous agent of divine and poetic justice.

Dramatically, Richmond, like Queen Margaret, is more a symbol than a fully developed character. It is Richard who is the exciting figure as he deceives and manipulates others and finally faces the chillingly isolated condition into which he has brought himself by being so truly a villain. He climbs to power by deceit, and so he is constantly acting a part. Richard's ability as an actor is seemingly limitless. He has already boasted, in *3 Henry VI,* that he can deceive more slyly than Ulysses, Sinon, or Machiavelli and can put on more false shapes than Proteus. To us as audience, he is cynically candid and boastful, setting us up in advance to watch his unbelievable performances. In an instant, before our eyes, he is the concerned younger brother of Clarence, sharing a hatred of Queen Elizabeth and her kindred; he is the jocular uncle of the little princes; or he is the pious recluse studying divinity with his clerical teachers, reluctant to accept the responsibilities of state that are thrust upon him by his importunate subjects (i.e., by Catesby and Buckingham, who are also actors in this staged scene).

None of these bravura performances, however, matches the wooing of Lady Anne. Richard himself sees it as the great test of his powers and is suitably impressed by his victory. The wooing scene, to some critics, challenges credibility. One key to credibility must lie in superb acting. The actor who plays Richard must transform himself from the gloating villain we know in soliloquy to the grief-stricken lover. Richard's argument is, after all, speciously plausible: that he has killed Anne's husband and father-in-law out of desperate love for her. The argument appeals to vanity, that most fatal of human weaknesses. What power Anne suddenly appears to have over Richard! She can kill him or spare his life. Richard shrewdly judges her as one who is not able to kill, and so he risks offering her his sword. As stage manager, he has altered her role from that of sincere mourner to the stereotype of the proud woman worshiped by her groveling servant in love. With superb irony, Richard has inverted the appearance and the reality of control in this struggle between man and woman, winning mastery by flattering Anne that she has such power over his emotions and his life. From his amazing success, Richard concludes that ordinary men and women can be made to believe anything and to betray their own instincts by "the plain devil and dissembling looks" (1.2.239). Richard is indeed devil-like; his role as actor stems from that of the Vice in the morality play, brilliantly comic and sinister. Yet even the devil can prevail over his victims only when they acquiesce in evil. The devil can deceive the senses, but acceptance of evil is still an act of the perverted will. Anne is guilty, however much we can appreciate the mesmerizing power of Richard's personality. By the end of the scene, she has violated everything she holds sacred.

The image of Richard as devil or Vice raises questions of motivation and of symbolic meaning. Is Richard a human character, propelled toward the throne by his insatiable ambition, like Macbeth? Is there a clue to his behavior in his ugliness and misanthropy? One might argue that he compensates for his ugliness and unlovability by resolving to domineer. Feeling unwanted, he despises all humans and undertakes to prove them weak and corrupt in order to affirm himself. He expresses a universal human penchant for cruelty and senseless domination. Yet the proposition that Richard is evil *because* he was born ugly logically can be reversed as well: he was born ugly *because* he is evil.

This concept, owing much to Renaissance notions of platonic correspondence between outer appearances and inner qualities, is grounded on the idea of a vast struggle in the cosmos between the forces of absolute good and the forces of absolute evil, one in which every event in human life has divine meaning and cause. Richard's birth is a physical manifestation of that divine meaning. Providential destiny, having determined the need for a genius of evil at this point in English history, decrees that Richard shall be born. The teeth and hunched back merely give evidence of what is already predetermined. In the apt words of the choric Queen Margaret, Richard was "sealed in thy nativity / The slave of nature and the son of hell" (1.3.229–230). Though he devotes himself to selfish ambition and evildoing, Richard ultimately serves the righteous purpose of divine Providence in human affairs. He functions as a scourge of God, whose plots or tyranny are permitted in order to bring just retribution upon offenders of the moral law. He is fundamentally unlike Shakespeare's more human villains, such as Macbeth or Claudius, but belongs, instead, to a special group of villains, including Iago in *Othello* and Edmund in *King Lear*. Like them, Richard is driven both by human motivation and by his preexistent evil genius; he displays the "motiveless malignity" ascribed by Coleridge to Iago.

Such a reading helps explain not only Richard's delight in evil but also the necessity for so much evil and suffering in England's civil wars. This theory of history owes much to Edward Hall's *Union of the Two Noble and Illustre Families of Lancaster and York* (1542), Shakespeare's chief source, along with Raphael Holinshed's *Chronicles* (1578),

for his *Henry VI* plays. Shakespeare's treatment of Richard is ultimately indebted to Polydore Vergil's *Anglica Historia* (1534) and especially to *The History of King Richard the Third*, attributed to Sir Thomas More (published 1557). This latter work, adopted in turn by Edward Hall, Richard Grafton, and Raphael Holinshed, purposefully blackens Richard's character. He becomes a study in the nature of tyranny, an object lesson to future rulers and their subjects. He is, moreover, a result of the curse placed by God on the English people for their sinful disobedience.

Richmond, in this Tudor explanation, becomes God's minister, chosen to destroy the scourge and thereafter to fulfill a new and happy covenant between God and humanity as King Henry VII. Thus, the play hardly touches on the sensitive matter of his somewhat remote Lancastrian claim to the crown. His victory at Bosworth is not one more turn of Fortune's wheel raising or deposing Lancastrian or Yorkist kings, but the end of a long cycle of unnatural violence, and his marriage to the Yorkist Princess Elizabeth is the restoration and the symbol of unity and peace in England's fair land. Although modern historians more impartially regard the defeat of Richard III at Bosworth Field in 1485 as a political overthrow not unlike Henry IV's overthrow of Richard II and stress that Richard III was a talented administrator guilty of no worse political crimes than those of his more fortunate successor, Elizabethan audiences (under constant promptings of the Tudor state) could not have found sufficient meaning in such a neutral interpretation. They were taught to see history as revealing God's intention and to view Henry VII's accession not as a parallel to the deposing of Richard II by Henry IV but, instead, as a divinely sanctioned deliverance of the English nation, to which Elizabeth's subjects were the happy heirs. Accordingly, the Tudor myth stressed the tyrannical nature of Richard III's seizure of power and conversely minimized the political element in Henry VII's takeover. Bosworth Field was seen as an act of God, a rising up of some irresistible force, and under no circumstances as a precedent for future rebellion.

In the *Henry VI* plays, Shakespeare puts considerable distance between himself and the Tudor orthodox reading of history, allowing the grim realities of civil war to speak for themselves. In *Richard III*, however, the pattern shown in the chronicles provides Shakespeare with an essential structural device. Viewing the civil wars in retrospect, *Richard III* potentially manifests a cohesive sense in which England's suffering has fulfilled a necessary plan of fall from innocence, leading through sin and penitence to regeneration. Evil is seen at last as something through which good triumphs, in English history, as in the story of humankind's fall and a restoration by divine grace.

This providential scheme imposes a double irony on *Richard III*. In the short run, Richard appears to be complete master over his victims. "Your imprisonment shall not be long," Richard assures his brother Clarence. "I will deliver you, or else lie for you" (1.1.114–115). The audience, already let in on the secret, can shiver at the grisly humor of these double entendres. Clarence will indeed soon be delivered—to his death. Richard's henchmen are fond of such jokes, too. When Lord Hastings is on his way to the Tower, Buckingham observes aside, "And supper too, although thou know'st it not" (3.2.122). Shortly before, Catesby has assured Hastings of Richard's and Buckingham's favor: "The princes both make high account of you— / [Aside.] For they account his head upon the Bridge" (3.2.69–70). Richard has a phrase for such wit: "Thus, like the formal Vice, Iniquity, I moralize two meanings in one word" (3.1.82–83). The point of such ironies is always the same: the devil is cleverer than his victims, deceiving them through equivocation and triumphing in their spriritual blindness.

The delayed irony of the play, however, ultimately offers another possible explanation for the seemingly nihilistic conclusions of the early scenes; that is, there may be a larger plan at work, of which Richard is unconscious and in which he plays a role quite unlike the one he creates for himself. Perhaps Shakespeare's Richard is, as he was regarded in the chronicles of Edward Hall and others, the scourge of God, fulfilling a divine plan, even in the process of what he gloatingly regards as his own self-aggrandizement. Divine plans are always complex, inscrutable to the minds of mortals, and understood least by those who unwittingly execute them. In attempting to prove his own contention that human nature is bestial and that a Machiavellian man of utter self-confidence can force his way to the top, flouting all conventions of morality, he succeeds in demonstrating the opposite. From the moment he takes the throne, he feels it insecure beneath him; opposition and betrayal spring up from every quarter, and, in his last moments, a mere horse is worth his whole kingdom. With sardonic comedy and poetic justice, Richard becomes the proverbial beguiler who is beguiled.

Certainly the play offers for our consideration a theory of divine causality in which virtually all of Richard's victims deserve their fate because they have offended God. Prophecies and dreams give structure to the sequence of retributive actions and keep grim score. As the choric Margaret observes, a York must pay for a Lancaster, eye for an eye: Edward IV for Henry VI, young Edward V for Henry VI's son Edward. Thus, the Yorkist princes, though guiltless, die for their family's sins. The Yorkist Queen Elizabeth, like the Lancastrian Margaret, must outlive her husband into impotent old age, bewailing her children's cruel deaths. Clarence sees his death as punishment for breaking his oath at the battle of Tewkesbury and for his part in murdering Henry VI's son, Prince Edward. The Queen's kindred have been guilty of ambition, and Lord Hastings, in turn, is vulnerable because he has been willing to plot with Richard against the Queen's kindred. Margaret's curses serve both to warn the characters of their fates (a warning they blindly ignore) and to invite each person to curse himself or herself unwittingly but with ironic appropriateness. Lady Anne wishes unhappiness on any woman so insane as to marry Richard. Buckingham protests in a most sacred oath that whenever he turns again on the Queen's kindred, he will deserve to be punished by the treachery of his dearest friend (i.e., Richard). Dreams serve the same purpose of divine warning, giving Clarence a grotesque intimation of his death by drowning (in a butt of malmsey wine) and warning Hastings (through Stanley's dream) that the boar, Richard, will cut off his head. Thus, the English court punishes itself through Richard. He is the essence of the courtiers' factionalism, able to succeed as he does only because they forswear their most holy vows and conspire to destroy one another. They deserve to be outwitted at their own dismal game. Yet their falls are curative as well; Richard's victims acknowledge the justice of their undoings and penitently implore divine forgiveness. Richard contrastingly finds conscience a torment, rather than a voice of comfort and wisdom.

Richard III is not without its ironies and historical anxieties. Richard's own successful career of evil through much of the play demonstrates how rhetoric and theater can be used to dupe and to corrupt. The political process seems endlessly prone to cynical manipulation, and triumph comes chiefly to those who know how to use rhetoric to calculated effect. The Lord Mayor and his London associates are as pliable as the aristocracy. For all the belated assurances of providential meaning in Richard's rise to power and overthrow, we are allowed to speculate uncomfortably about the pragmatic action of history and its seeming ability to thrust forward into prominence an evil king or a good one, as individual temperament happens to dictate. Finally, there is the question of how Richard is supplanted. Whatever the reasons for Richard's baleful emergence, the process of his overthrow requires human agency and a rebellion against established (even if tyrannical) royal authority. To thoughtful observers in the sixteenth century, including Queen Elizabeth, any such rebellion, no matter how seemingly necessary, established a disturbing precedent and a threat to Tudor monarchical stability. If *Richard III* finds reassuring answers in the victory of Henry Tudor, Earl of Richmond, it does so in the face of pressing and troublesome circumstances.

Still, belief in the eventual triumph of good over evil is at last affirmed, if only because some Englishmen have the patience and common sense to endure a presumably deserved punishment and wait for deliverance. As in *3 Henry VI*, the common people have little to do with the action of the play. They are choric spokesmen and bystanders, virtuous in their attitude (except for the two suborned murderers of Clarence). In their plain folk wisdom, they see the folly and evil their betters ignore: "O, full of danger is the Duke of Gloucester, / And the Queen's sons and brothers haught and proud" (2.3.28–29). And, although they accept Richard as ruler, they do so most reluctantly; Buckingham's first attempt to persuade the people to this course meets with apathy and silence. Their wisdom is to "leave it all to God" (line 46). In the fullness of time, this faith in goodness brings its just reward.

The Tragedy of King Richard the Third

[*Dramatis Personae*

KING EDWARD THE FOURTH
QUEEN ELIZABETH, *wife of King Edward*
EDWARD, PRINCE OF WALES, } *sons of Edward*
RICHARD, DUKE OF YORK, } *and Elizabeth*
GEORGE, DUKE OF CLARENCE, } *brothers of the King*
RICHARD, DUKE OF GLOUCESTER, } *the King*
  later King Richard III,
DUCHESS OF YORK, *mother of Edward IV, Clarence, and Richard, Duke of Gloucester*
LADY ANNE, *widow of Edward, Prince of Wales (son of Henry VI); later wife of Richard, Duke of Gloucester*
MARGARET, *widow of King Henry VI*
BOY, *son of Clarence (Edward Plantagenet, Earl of Warwick)*
GIRL, *daughter of Clarence (Margaret Plantagenet, Countess of Salisbury)*

ANTHONY WOODVILLE, EARL RIVERS, *brother of Queen Elizabeth*
MARQUESS OF DORSET, } *sons of Queen*
LORD GREY, } *Elizabeth*
SIR THOMAS VAUGHAN, *executed with Rivers and Grey*

WILLIAM, LORD HASTINGS, *the Lord Chamberlain*
DUKE OF BUCKINGHAM, *Richard's supporter, later in opposition*
SIR WILLIAM CATESBY, }
SIR RICHARD RATCLIFFE, } *Richard's supporters*
LORD LOVELL, } *and henchmen*
SIR JAMES TYRREL, }
DUKE OF NORFOLK, } *Richard's*
EARL OF SURREY, } *generals*

HENRY, EARL OF RICHMOND, *later King Henry VII*
LORD STANLEY, EARL OF DERBY, }
EARL OF OXFORD, }
SIR JAMES BLUNT, } *supporters of*
SIR WALTER HERBERT, } *Richmond*
SIR WILLIAM BRANDON, }
CHRISTOPHER URSWICK, *a priest,* }

CARDINAL BOURCHIER, *Archbishop of Canterbury*
ARCHBISHOP OF YORK (*Thomas Rotherham*)
BISHOP OF ELY (*John Morton*)
GHOSTS *of King Henry VI, Edward Prince of Wales, and others murdered by Richard (Clarence, Rivers, Grey, Vaughan, Hastings, the two young princes, Anne, and Buckingham)*

SIR ROBERT BRACKENBURY, *Lieutenant of the Tower*
TRESSEL,
BERKELEY,   } *attending the*
HALBERDIER,   *Lady Anne*
GENTLEMAN,
Two MURDERERS
KEEPER *in the Tower*
Three CITIZENS
MESSENGER *to Queen Elizabeth*
LORD MAYOR OF LONDON
MESSENGER *to Lord Hastings*
PURSUIVANT
PRIEST
SCRIVENER
Two BISHOPS
PAGE *to Richard III*
Four MESSENGERS *to Richard III*
SHERIFF OF WILTSHIRE

Lords, Attendants, Aldermen, Citizens, Councilors, Soldiers

SCENE: *England.*]

1.1   *Enter Richard, Duke of Gloucester, solus.*

RICHARD
Now is the winter of our discontent
Made glorious summer by this son of York,   2
And all the clouds that loured upon our house   3
In the deep bosom of the ocean buried.
Now are our brows bound with victorious wreaths,   5
Our bruisèd arms hung up for monuments,   6
Our stern alarums changed to merry meetings,   7
Our dreadful marches to delightful measures.   8
Grim-visaged War hath smoothed his wrinkled
   front;   9
And now, instead of mounting barbèd steeds   10
To fright the souls of fearful adversaries,   11
He capers nimbly in a lady's chamber
To the lascivious pleasing of a lute.
But I, that am not shaped for sportive tricks,   14
Nor made to court an amorous looking glass;
I, that am rudely stamped, and want love's majesty   16
To strut before a wanton ambling nymph;   17
I, that am curtailed of this fair proportion,   18
Cheated of feature by dissembling Nature,   19
Deformed, unfinished, sent before my time

Into this breathing world scarce half made up,
And that so lamely and unfashionable   22
That dogs bark at me as I halt by them—   23
Why, I, in this weak piping time of peace,   24
Have no delight to pass away the time,
Unless to see my shadow in the sun
And descant on mine own deformity.   27
And therefore, since I cannot prove a lover
To entertain these fair well-spoken days,   29
I am determinèd to prove a villain
And hate the idle pleasures of these days.
Plots have I laid, inductions dangerous,   32
By drunken prophecies, libels, and dreams,
To set my brother Clarence and the King
In deadly hate the one against the other;
And if King Edward be as true and just
As I am subtle, false, and treacherous,
This day should Clarence closely be mewed up   38
About a prophecy, which says that G   39
Of Edward's heirs the murderer shall be.
Dive, thoughts, down to my soul; here Clarence
   comes.

Enter Clarence, guarded, and Brackenbury,
[Lieutenant of the Tower].

Brother, good day. What means this armèd guard
That waits upon Your Grace?
CLARENCE   His Majesty,   43
Tend'ring my person's safety, hath appointed   44
This conduct to convey me to the Tower.   45
RICHARD
Upon what cause?
CLARENCE   Because my name is George.
RICHARD
Alack, my lord, that fault is none of yours.
He should, for that, commit your godfathers.
O, belike His Majesty hath some intent   49
That you should be new christened in the Tower.   50
But what's the matter, Clarence, may I know?   51
CLARENCE
Yea, Richard, when I know; for I protest
As yet I do not. But, as I can learn,
He hearkens after prophecies and dreams,
And from the crossrow plucks the letter G,   55
And says a wizard told him that by G
His issue disinherited should be;   57
And, for my name of George begins with G,   58
It follows in his thought that I am he.

1.1. Location: London. Near the Tower.
s.d. solus alone   **2 son** Edward IV was the son of Richard, Duke of York. (With a pun on "sun"; Edward IV used the sun on his badge.)
3 loured looked threateningly   **5 brows** foreheads   **6 arms** armor.
monuments trophies   **7 alarums** calls to arms, or assaults   **8 dreadful**
formidable, awe-inspiring.   **measures** stately dances   **9 wrinkled**
front furrowed forehead   **10 barbèd** armored   **11 fearful** frightened
14 sportive amorous   **16 rudely stamped** roughly fashioned, coined.
want lack   **17 ambling** walking affectedly, i.e., wantonly   **18 cur-**
tailed cut short, denied.   **proportion** shape   **19 feature** shapeliness
of body

22 unfashionable badly fashioned   **23 halt** limp   **24 piping time**
i.e., a time when the music heard is that of pipes and not fifes and
drums   **27 descant** compose variations, comment on   **29 entertain**
pass away pleasurably.   **well-spoken** refined, elegant   **32 inductions**
preparations   **38 mewed up** confined (like a hawk)   **39 prophecy**
. . . G (The prophecy is mentioned in the chronicles; the quibble is
that G stands for *Gloucester* and not for *George*, the given name of
the Duke of Clarence.)   **43 waits** attends   **44 Tend'ring** having care
for   **45 conduct** escort   **49 belike** probably   **50 new christened** (Anticipates, ironically, Clarence's death by drowning in 1.4.)   **51 matter**
reason, cause   **55 crossrow** Christ-crossrow, or alphabet (so called
from the cross printed before the alphabet in the hornbook)   **57 issue**
offspring   **58 for** because

These, as I learn, and suchlike toys as these   60
Hath moved His Highness to commit me now.   61
RICHARD
Why, this it is when men are ruled by women.
'Tis not the King that sends you to the Tower;
My Lady Grey his wife, Clarence, 'tis she   64
That tempers him to this extremity.   65
Was it not she, and that good man of worship,
Anthony Woodville, her brother there,   67
That made him send Lord Hastings to the Tower,
From whence this present day he is delivered?
We are not safe, Clarence, we are not safe.
CLARENCE
By heaven, I think there is no man secure
But the Queen's kindred and night-walking heralds   72
That trudge betwixt the King and Mistress Shore.   73
Heard you not what an humble suppliant
Lord Hastings was to her for his delivery?   75
RICHARD
Humbly complaining to Her Deity   76
Got my Lord Chamberlain his liberty.   77
I'll tell you what: I think it is our way,   78
If we will keep in favor with the King,
To be her men and wear her livery.   80
The jealous, o'erworn widow and herself,   81
Since that our brother dubbed them gentlewomen,   82
Are mighty gossips in our monarchy.   83
BRACKENBURY
I beseech Your Graces both to pardon me:
His Majesty hath straitly given in charge   85
That no man shall have private conference,
Of what degree soever, with your brother.   87
RICHARD
Even so? An 't please your worship, Brackenbury,   88
You may partake of anything we say.
We speak no treason, man. We say the King
Is wise and virtuous, and his noble queen
Well struck in years, fair, and not jealous.   92
We say that Shore's wife hath a pretty foot,
A cherry lip, a bonny eye, a passing pleasing
  tongue;   94
And that the Queen's kindred are made gentlefolks.

How say you, sir? Can you deny all this?
BRACKENBURY
With this, my lord, myself have naught to do.
RICHARD
Naught to do with Mistress Shore? I tell thee, fellow, 98
He that doth naught with her, excepting one,
Were best to do it secretly, alone.
BRACKENBURY   What one, my lord?
RICHARD
Her husband, knave. Wouldst thou betray me?   102
BRACKENBURY
I beseech Your Grace to pardon me, and withal   103
Forbear your conference with the noble Duke.
CLARENCE
We know thy charge, Brackenbury, and will obey.
RICHARD
We are the Queen's abjects, and must obey.   106
Brother, farewell. I will unto the King;
And whatsoe'er you will employ me in,
Were it to call King Edward's widow sister,   109
I will perform it to enfranchise you.   110
Meantime, this deep disgrace in brotherhood
Touches me deeper than you can imagine.   112
CLARENCE
I know it pleaseth neither of us well.
RICHARD
Well, your imprisonment shall not be long;
I will deliver you, or else lie for you.   115
Meantime, have patience.
CLARENCE   I must perforce. Farewell. 116
          Exit Clarence [*with Brackenbury and guard*].
RICHARD
Go tread the path that thou shalt ne'er return.
Simple, plain Clarence, I do love thee so
That I will shortly send thy soul to heaven,
If heaven will take the present at our hands.
But who comes here? The new-delivered Hastings?   121

          Enter Lord Hastings.

HASTINGS
Good time of day unto my gracious lord.
RICHARD
As much unto my good Lord Chamberlain.
Well are you welcome to the open air.
How hath your lordship brooked imprisonment?   125
HASTINGS
With patience, noble lord, as prisoners must.
But I shall live, my lord, to give them thanks   127
That were the cause of my imprisonment.

60 toys trifles **61 commit** arrest **64 My Lady Grey** (A disrespectful reference to the Queen, whose maiden name was Elizabeth Woodville and who, when the King married her, was the widow of Sir John Grey.) **65 tempers** governs, directs **67 Woodville** i.e., Earl Rivers (whom Richard also disrespectfully refers to by his family name rather than by his recently acquired title) **72 night-walking heralds** i.e., secret messengers for an assignation **73 Mistress Shore** Jane Shore, the King's mistress, and wife of a goldsmith in Lombard Street. (The title *Mistress* is a respectful form of address for any woman, married or unmarried.) **75 her** i.e., Jane Shore **76 Her Deity** (A mock title for Jane Shore, suggesting she is even more elevated than "Her Grace" or "Her Majesty.") **77 Lord Chamberlain** i.e., Lord Hastings **78 our way** i.e., our only way (to succeed) **80 men** servants **81 widow** i.e., Queen Elizabeth. (See the note for line 64.) **herself** i.e., Jane Shore **82 Since that** since. **gentlewomen** (A sneer at the Queen's family, which was gentle but not noble until after her marriage with the King; Jane Shore was, of course, neither gentle nor noble.) **83 mighty gossips** i.e., influential busybodies **85 straitly . . . charge** strictly ordered **87 degree** rank **88 An 't** if it **92 Well struck** i.e., well along. **not jealous** (Implies there are things she might be jealous about.) **94 passing** surpassingly

98 Naught (Richard quibbles on the meanings "nothing" and "the sexual act.") **102 betray me** i.e., into naming the King as a person who does "naught" with Mistress Shore **103 withal** furthermore **106 abjects** abjectly servile subjects **109 King Edward's widow** i.e., the widow whom Edward has made queen **110 enfranchise** release from imprisonment **112 Touches . . . imagine** (1) distresses me more than can be imagined (2) concerns me (in my personal ambition) more than you could possibly guess **115 lie for you** (1) take your place in prison (2) tell lies about you **116 perforce** necessarily **121 new-delivered** recently released **125 brooked** endured **127 give them thanks** i.e., pay them back. (Said ironically.)

RICHARD
No doubt, no doubt; and so shall Clarence too,
For they that were your enemies are his,
And have prevailed as much on him as you.
HASTINGS
More pity that the eagles should be mewed,
Whiles kites and buzzards prey at liberty.   133
RICHARD   What news abroad?   134
HASTINGS
No news so bad abroad as this at home:
The King is sickly, weak, and melancholy,
And his physicians fear him mightily.   137
RICHARD
Now, by Saint John, that news is bad indeed!
O, he hath kept an evil diet long   139
And overmuch consumed his royal person.
'Tis very grievous to be thought upon.
Where is he, in his bed?
HASTINGS   He is.
RICHARD
Go you before, and I will follow you.   *Exit Hastings.*
He cannot live, I hope, and must not die
Till George be packed with post-horse up to heaven.   146
I'll in, to urge his hatred more to Clarence
With lies well steeled with weighty arguments;   148
And, if I fail not in my deep intent,
Clarence hath not another day to live.
Which done, God take King Edward to his mercy
And leave the world for me to bustle in!
For then I'll marry Warwick's youngest daughter.   153
What though I killed her husband and her father?   154
The readiest way to make the wench amends
Is to become her husband and her father,
The which will I; not all so much for love
As for another secret close intent   158
By marrying her which I must reach unto.
But yet I run before my horse to market.
Clarence still breathes, Edward still lives and reigns;
When they are gone, then must I count my gains.
                                                Exit.

❧

1.2   *Enter the corpse of [King] Henry the Sixth, with
Halberds to guard it; Lady Anne being the
mourner [attended by Tressel and Berkeley].*

ANNE
Set down, set down your honorable load—
If honor may be shrouded in a hearse—   2

133 **kites** scavengers of the hawk family   134 **abroad** at large, circu-
lating   137 **fear** fear for   139 **diet** course of life, regimen   146 **with
post-horse** by post-horses, i.e., by swiftest possible means
148 **steeled** reinforced   153 **Warwick's youngest daughter** the Lady
Anne Neville, widow of Edward, Prince of Wales, son of King Henry
VI   154 **father** i.e., father-in-law (Henry VI)   158 **intent** design (i.e.,
Richard hopes to ally himself with the house of Lancaster to bolster
his claim to the throne)
1.2. Location: London. A street.
s.d. **Halberds** halberdiers, guards with halberds, or long poleaxes
2 **hearse** (probably here an open coffin on a bier)

Whilst I awhile obsequiously lament   3
Th' untimely fall of virtuous Lancaster.
                    [*The bearers set down the coffin.*]
Poor key-cold figure of a holy king,   5
Pale ashes of the house of Lancaster,
Thou bloodless remnant of that royal blood,
Be it lawful that I invocate thy ghost   8
To hear the lamentations of poor Anne,
Wife to thy Edward, to thy slaughtered son,
Stabbed by the selfsame hand that made these
    wounds!
Lo, in these windows that let forth thy life   12
I pour the helpless balm of my poor eyes.   13
O, cursèd be the hand that made these holes!
Cursèd the heart that had the heart to do it!
Cursèd the blood that let this blood from hence!
More direful hap betide that hated wretch   17
That makes us wretched by the death of thee
Than I can wish to wolves, to spiders, toads,
Or any creeping venomed thing that lives!
If ever he have child, abortive be it,   21
Prodigious, and untimely brought to light,   22
Whose ugly and unnatural aspect   23
May fright the hopeful mother at the view,
And that be heir to his unhappiness!   25
If ever he have wife, let her be made
More miserable by the life of him
Than I am made by my young lord and thee!—   28
Come now towards Chertsey with your holy load,   29
Taken from Paul's to be interrèd there.   30
                    [*The bearers take up the hearse.*]
And still as you are weary of this weight,   31
Rest you, whiles I lament King Henry's corpse.

Enter Richard, Duke of Gloucester.

RICHARD
Stay, you that bear the corpse, and set it down.
ANNE
What black magician conjures up this fiend
To stop devoted charitable deeds?   35
RICHARD
Villains, set down the corpse, or, by Saint Paul,
I'll make a corpse of him that disobeys.
HALBERDIER [*advancing with his halberd lowered*]
My lord, stand back, and let the coffin pass.
RICHARD
Unmannered dog, stand thou when I command!   39
Advance thy halberd higher than my breast,   40
Or, by Saint Paul, I'll strike thee to my foot
And spurn upon thee, beggar, for thy boldness.   42
                    [*The bearers set down the hearse.*]

3 **obsequiously** as befits a funeral, mournfully   5 **key-cold** extremely
cold, cold as a metal key. (Proverbial.)   8 **invocate** invoke   12 **windows** i.e., wounds   13 **helpless** useless, unavailing   17 **hap betide**
fortune befall   21 **abortive** misshapen, monstrous   22 **Prodigious**
monstrous, unnatural   23 **aspect** appearance   25 **unhappiness** evil
nature   28 **by . . . thee** i.e., by the deaths of Prince Edward and
King Henry VI   29 **Chertsey** monastery in Surrey, near London,
where King Henry's body is to be buried   30 **Paul's** Saint Paul's Cathedral in London   31 **still as** as often as   35 **devoted** holy   39 **stand**
halt   40 **Advance . . . breast** raise your halberd upright   42 **spurn**
trample

ANNE
What do you tremble? Are you all afraid?   43
Alas, I blame you not, for you are mortal,
And mortal eyes cannot endure the devil.—
Avaunt, thou dreadful minister of hell!   46
Thou hadst but power over his mortal body;
His soul thou canst not have. Therefore, begone.

RICHARD
Sweet saint, for charity, be not so curst.   49

ANNE
Foul devil, for God's sake hence and trouble us not, 50
For thou hast made the happy earth thy hell,
Filled it with cursing cries and deep exclaims.   52
If thou delight to view thy heinous deeds,
Behold this pattern of thy butcheries.   54
                    [She uncovers the corpse.]
O, gentlemen, see, see dead Henry's wounds
Open their congealed mouths and bleed afresh!   56
Blush, blush, thou lump of foul deformity;
For 'tis thy presence that exhales this blood   58
From cold and empty veins where no blood dwells.
Thy deeds inhuman and unnatural
Provokes this deluge most unnatural.
O God, which this blood mad'st, revenge his death!
O earth, which this blood drink'st, revenge his
    death!
Either heav'n with lightning strike the murd'rer
    dead,
Or earth gape open wide and eat him quick,   65
As thou dost swallow up this good king's blood,
Which his hell-governed arm hath butcherèd!

RICHARD
Lady, you know no rules of charity,
Which renders good for bad, blessings for curses.

ANNE
Villain, thou know'st nor law of God nor man.   70
No beast so fierce but knows some touch of pity.   71

RICHARD
But I know none, and therefore am no beast.

ANNE
O, wonderful, when devils tell the truth!   73

RICHARD
More wonderful, when angels are so angry.
Vouchsafe, divine perfection of a woman,   75
Of these supposèd crimes to give me leave
By circumstance but to acquit myself.   77

ANNE
Vouchsafe, defused infection of a man,   78
Of these known evils but to give me leave
By circumstance t' accuse thy cursèd self.

RICHARD
Fairer than tongue can name thee, let me have
Some patient leisure to excuse myself.

ANNE
Fouler than heart can think thee, thou canst make
No excuse current but to hang thyself.   84

RICHARD
By such despair I should accuse myself.

ANNE
And by despairing shalt thou stand excused
For doing worthy vengeance on thyself
That didst unworthy slaughter upon others.

RICHARD   Say that I slew them not?

ANNE   Then say they were not slain.
But dead they are, and, devilish slave, by thee.

RICHARD   I did not kill your husband.

ANNE   Why, then he is alive.

RICHARD
Nay, he is dead, and slain by Edward's hand.

ANNE
In thy foul throat thou liest! Queen Margaret saw
Thy murderous falchion smoking in his blood,   96
The which thou once didst bend against her breast,   97
But that thy brothers beat aside the point.

RICHARD
I was provokèd by her slanderous tongue,
That laid their guilt upon my guiltless shoulders.

ANNE
Thou wast provokèd by thy bloody mind,
That never dream'st on aught but butcheries.   102
Didst thou not kill this king?

RICHARD   I grant ye.

ANNE
Dost grant me, hedgehog? Then God grant me too   104
Thou mayst be damnèd for that wicked deed!
O, he was gentle, mild, and virtuous!

RICHARD
The better for the King of Heaven that hath him.

ANNE
He is in heaven, where thou shalt never come.

RICHARD
Let him thank me that holp to send him thither;   109
For he was fitter for that place than earth.

ANNE
And thou unfit for any place but hell.

RICHARD
Yes, one place else, if you will hear me name it.

ANNE   Some dungeon.

RICHARD   Your bedchamber.

ANNE
Ill rest betide the chamber where thou liest!   115

RICHARD
So will it, madam, till I lie with you.

ANNE
I hope so.

43 **What** why   46 **Avaunt** begone   49 **curst** spiteful, shrewish
50 **hence** go hence, depart   52 **exclaims** exclamations   54 **pattern**
example   56 **bleed afresh** (A phenomenon popularly supposed to occur in the presence of the murderer.)   58 **exhales** draws out
65 **quick** alive   70 **nor . . . nor** neither . . . nor   71 **so fierce but
knows** is so savage that it has not   73 **O . . . truth** (Anne bitterly re-
interprets Richard's *am no beast,* "am not beastly," to mean that he is
neither man nor beast, but devil.)   75 **Vouchsafe** deign, consent
77 **circumstance** detailed argument   78 **defused** diffused, disordered,
shapeless; *defused infection* means "spreading plague"

84 **current** genuine, acceptable (as in coinage)   96 **falchion** curved
sword   97 **bend** direct, aim   102 **aught** anything   104 **hedgehog** (Richard's heraldic emblem featured a boar or wild hog.)   109 **holp**
helped   115 **betide** befall

RICHARD   I know so. But, gentle Lady Anne,
To leave this keen encounter of our wits
And fall something into a slower method,   119
Is not the causer of the timeless deaths   120
Of these Plantagenets, Henry and Edward,
As blameful as the executioner?

ANNE
Thou wast the cause and most accurst effect.   123

RICHARD
Your beauty was the cause of that effect—   124
Your beauty, that did haunt me in my sleep
To undertake the death of all the world,
So I might live one hour in your sweet bosom.

ANNE
If I thought that, I tell thee, homicide,   128
These nails should rend that beauty from my cheeks.   129

RICHARD
These eyes could not endure that beauty's wrack;   130
You should not blemish it, if I stood by.
As all the world is cheerèd by the sun,
So I by that. It is my day, my life.

ANNE
Black night o'ershade thy day, and death thy life!

RICHARD
Curse not thyself, fair creature—thou art both.

ANNE
I would I were, to be revenged on thee.   136

RICHARD
It is a quarrel most unnatural
To be revenged on him that loveth thee.

ANNE
It is a quarrel just and reasonable
To be revenged on him that killed my husband.

RICHARD
He that bereft thee, lady, of thy husband
Did it to help thee to a better husband.

ANNE
His better doth not breathe upon the earth.

RICHARD
He lives that loves thee better than he could.   144

ANNE
Name him.

RICHARD   Plantagenet.

ANNE   Why, that was he.   145

RICHARD
The selfsame name, but one of better nature.

ANNE
Where is he?

RICHARD   Here.   [She] spits at him.
Why dost thou spit at me?

ANNE
Would it were mortal poison for thy sake!

RICHARD
Never came poison from so sweet a place.

ANNE
Never hung poison on a fouler toad.   150
Out of my sight! Thou dost infect mine eyes.

RICHARD
Thine eyes, sweet lady, have infected mine.   152

ANNE
Would they were basilisks, to strike thee dead!   153

RICHARD
I would they were, that I might die at once;
For now they kill me with a living death.
Those eyes of thine from mine have drawn salt
    tears,
Shamed their aspects with store of childish drops;   157
These eyes, which never shed remorseful tear—
No, when my father York and Edward wept
To hear the piteous moan that Rutland made   160
When black-faced Clifford shook his sword at him;   161
Nor when thy warlike father, like a child,   162
Told the sad story of my father's death
And twenty times made pause to sob and weep,
That all the standers-by had wet their cheeks   165
Like trees bedashed with rain—in that sad time
My manly eyes did scorn an humble tear;
And what these sorrows could not thence exhale,   168
Thy beauty hath, and made them blind with
    weeping.
I never sued to friend nor enemy;   170
My tongue could never learn sweet smoothing
    words;   171
But now thy beauty is proposed my fee,   172
My proud heart sues and prompts my tongue to
    speak.   She looks scornfully at him.
Teach not thy lip such scorn, for it was made
For kissing, lady, not for such contempt.
If thy revengeful heart cannot forgive,
Lo, here I lend thee this sharp-pointed sword,
Which if thou please to hide in this true breast
And let the soul forth that adoreth thee,
I lay it naked to the deadly stroke
And humbly beg the death upon my knee.   181
    He [kneels and] lays his breast open; she offers at [it]
                                      with his sword.
Nay, do not pause; for I did kill King Henry—
But 'twas thy beauty that provokèd me.
Nay, now dispatch; 'twas I that stabbed young
    Edward—

---

119 **something into a** into a somewhat   120 **timeless** untimely
123 **effect** agent   124 **effect** result   128 **homicide** murderer
129 **rend** tear   130 **wrack** destruction   136 **I would I were** (If Anne
were truly both Richard's day and his life, she could terminate both.)
144 **He lives** i.e., there is a man.   **he** i.e., Prince Edward   145 **Plantagenet** (Richard's father, the Duke of York, adopted this name when
he made his claim to the English throne—see *I Henry VI*,
2.4.36—but the name had been in the family of England's Angevin
rulers since the time of Henry II and thus could also be claimed by
Henry VI.)

150 **poison . . . toad** (Toads were popularly regarded as poisonous.)
152 **infected** i.e., with love (since love was thought to enter through
the eyes)   153 **basilisks** mythical reptiles reputed to kill by their looks
157 **aspects** appearance   160 **Rutland** second son of Richard, Duke
of York. (See *3 Henry VI*, 1.3, for his death scene.)   161 **black-faced**
i.e., foreboding in appearance   162 **thy warlike father** i.e., the Earl
of Warwick   165 **That** so that   168 **exhale** draw out   170 **sued** sup-
plicated, appealed   171 **smoothing** flattering   172 **now** now that.
proposed my fee offered as my reward   181 **the death** death after
sentencing.   **s.d. offers** aims

But 'twas thy heavenly face that set me on.   185
                                    She falls the sword.
Take up the sword again, or take up me.
ANNE
Arise, dissembler. Though I wish thy death,
I will not be thy executioner.
RICHARD [*rising*]
Then bid me kill myself, and I will do it.
ANNE
I have already.
RICHARD   That was in thy rage.
Speak it again, and even with the word
This hand, which for thy love did kill thy love,
Shall for thy love kill a far truer love.
To both their deaths shalt thou be accessory.
ANNE   I would I knew thy heart.   195
RICHARD   'Tis figured in my tongue.   196
ANNE   I fear me both are false.
RICHARD   Then never man was true.
ANNE   Well, well, put up your sword.
RICHARD   Say, then, my peace is made.
ANNE   That shalt thou know hereafter.
RICHARD   But shall I live in hope?
ANNE   All men, I hope, live so.
RICHARD   Vouchsafe to wear this ring.   204
ANNE   To take is not to give.   205
            [*He slips the ring on her finger.*]
RICHARD
Look how my ring encompasseth thy finger,   206
Even so thy breast encloseth my poor heart;
Wear both of them, for both of them are thine.
And if thy poor devoted servant may   209
But beg one favor at thy gracious hand,
Thou dost confirm his happiness forever.
ANNE   What is it?
RICHARD
That it may please you leave these sad designs
To him that hath most cause to be a mourner,
And presently repair to Crosby House,   215
Where, after I have solemnly interred
At Chertsey monast'ry this noble king
And wet his grave with my repentant tears,
I will with all expedient duty see you.   219
For divers unknown reasons, I beseech you,   220
Grant me this boon.
ANNE
With all my heart, and much it joys me, too,
To see you are become so penitent.
Tressel and Berkeley, go along with me.
RICHARD
Bid me farewell.
ANNE   'Tis more than you deserve;
But since you teach me how to flatter you,

Imagine I have said farewell already.
                    Exeunt two [Tressel and Berkeley] with Anne.
RICHARD
Sirs, take up the corpse.
GENTLEMAN   Towards Chertsey, noble lord?
RICHARD
No, to Whitefriars. There attend my coming.   229
                            Exeunt [bearers with] corpse.
Was ever woman in this humor wooed?
Was ever woman in this humor won?
I'll have her, but I will not keep her long.
What? I, that killed her husband and his father,
To take her in her heart's extremest hate,
With curses in her mouth, tears in her eyes,
The bleeding witness of my hatred by,
Having God, her conscience, and these bars
    against me,   237
And I no friends to back my suit withal
But the plain devil and dissembling looks?
And yet to win her! All the world to nothing!   240
Ha!
Hath she forgot already that brave prince,
Edward, her lord, whom I, some three months
    since,
Stabbed in my angry mood at Tewkesbury?
A sweeter and a lovelier gentleman,
Framed in the prodigality of nature,   246
Young, valiant, wise, and, no doubt, right royal,
The spacious world cannot again afford.   248
And will she yet abase her eyes on me,   249
That cropped the golden prime of this sweet prince   250
And made her widow to a woeful bed?
On me, whose all not equals Edward's moiety?   252
On me, that halts and am misshapen thus?   253
My dukedom to a beggarly denier,   254
I do mistake my person all this while.
Upon my life, she finds, although I cannot,
Myself to be a marvelous proper man.   257
I'll be at charges for a looking glass   258
And entertain a score or two of tailors   259
To study fashions to adorn my body.
Since I am crept in favor with myself,
I will maintain it with some little cost.
But first I'll turn yon fellow in his grave,   263
And then return lamenting to my love.
Shine out, fair sun, till I have bought a glass,   265
That I may see my shadow as I pass.   *Exit.*

185 s.d. **falls** lets fall   195 **would** wish   196 **figured** portrayed
204 **Vouchsafe** consent   205 **To take . . . give** i.e., I accept the ring
but I make no promises   206 **Look how** just as   209 **servant** i.e.,
lover, one whom she may command   215 **presently** at once.
Crosby House (One of Richard's London dwellings; built originally by
Sir John Crosby.)   219 **expedient** expeditious   220 **unknown** secret

229 **Whitefriars** the Carmelite priory in London.   **attend** await
237 **bars** obstacles   240 **All . . . nothing** i.e., against infinite odds
246 **Framed . . . nature** i.e., formed in nature's most lavish mood
248 **afford** (because Nature was so lavish)   249 **abase** lower, devalue
250 **cropped** cut short.   **prime** springtime, early manhood   252 **moiety** half (of Edward's virtues)   253 **halts** limps   254 **denier** small copper coin, the twelfth part of a sou   257 **proper** handsome   258 **be
. . . for** undertake the expense of   259 **entertain** retain, employ
263 **in** into   265 **glass** mirror

1.3   *Enter the Queen Mother [Elizabeth], Lord Rivers,*
[Marquess of Dorset,] and Lord Grey.

RIVERS
    Have patience, madam. There's no doubt His
        Majesty
    Will soon recover his accustomed health.
GREY
    In that you brook it ill, it makes him worse.   3
    Therefore, for God's sake, entertain good comfort,   4
    And cheer His Grace with quick and merry eyes.
QUEEN ELIZABETH
    If he were dead, what would betide on me?   6
GREY
    No other harm but loss of such a lord.
QUEEN ELIZABETH
    The loss of such a lord includes all harms.
GREY
    The heavens have blessed you with a goodly son
    To be your comforter when he is gone.
QUEEN ELIZABETH
    Ah, he is young, and his minority
    Is put unto the trust of Richard Gloucester,
    A man that loves not me, nor none of you.
RIVERS
    Is it concluded he shall be Protector?
QUEEN ELIZABETH
    It is determined, not concluded yet;   15
    But so it must be, if the King miscarry.   16

        Enter Buckingham and [Lord Stanley Earl of]
        Derby.

GREY
    Here come the lords of Buckingham and Derby.
BUCKINGHAM
    Good time of day unto Your Royal Grace!
STANLEY
    God make Your Majesty joyful, as you have been!
QUEEN ELIZABETH
    The Countess Richmond, good my lord of Derby,   20
    To your good prayer will scarcely say amen.
    Yet, Derby, notwithstanding she's your wife
    And loves not me, be you, good lord, assured
    I hate not you for her proud arrogance.   24
STANLEY
    I do beseech you, either not believe
    The envious slanders of her false accusers,   26
    Or, if she be accused on true report,
    Bear with her weakness, which I think proceeds
    From wayward sickness and no grounded malice.   29

QUEEN ELIZABETH
    Saw you the King today, my lord of Derby?
STANLEY
    But now the Duke of Buckingham and I   31
    Are come from visiting His Majesty.
QUEEN ELIZABETH
    What likelihood of his amendment, lords?   33
BUCKINGHAM
    Madam, good hope; His Grace speaks cheerfully.
QUEEN ELIZABETH
    God grant him health! Did you confer with him?
BUCKINGHAM
    Ay, madam. He desires to make atonement   36
    Between the Duke of Gloucester and your brothers,   37
    And between them and my Lord Chamberlain,
    And sent to warn them to his royal presence.   39
QUEEN ELIZABETH
    Would all were well! But that will never be.
    I fear our happiness is at the height.

        Enter Richard [Duke of Gloucester, and Lord
        Hastings].

RICHARD
    They do me wrong, and I will not endure it!
    Who is it that complains unto the King
    That I, forsooth, am stern and love them not?
    By holy Paul, they love His Grace but lightly
    That fill his ears with such dissentious rumors.   46
    Because I cannot flatter and look fair,   47
    Smile in men's faces, smooth, deceive, and cog,   48
    Duck with French nods and apish courtesy,   49
    I must be held a rancorous enemy.
    Cannot a plain man live and think no harm,
    But thus his simple truth must be abused
    With silken, sly, insinuating Jacks?   53
GREY
    To whom in all this presence speaks Your Grace?   54
RICHARD
    To thee, that hast nor honesty nor grace.   55
    When have I injured thee? When done thee wrong?
    Or thee? Or thee? Or any of your faction?
    A plague upon you all! His Royal Grace—
    Whom God preserve better than you would wish!—
    Cannot be quiet scarce a breathing while   60
    But you must trouble him with lewd complaints.   61
QUEEN ELIZABETH
    Brother of Gloucester, you mistake the matter.
    The King, of his own royal disposition,   63
    And not provoked by any suitor else,
    Aiming, belike, at your interior hatred,   65

1.3. Location: London. The royal court.
3 brook endure   **4 comfort** cheer   **6 betide on** become of   **15 determined, not concluded** i.e., decided though not officially passed   **16 miscarry** perish   **20 The Countess Richmond** i.e., Margaret Beaufort (1443–1509), who married, successively, Edmund Tudor (Earl of Richmond), Lord Henry Stafford, and Thomas Lord Stanley (here called the Earl of Derby), to whom she is currently married. By the Earl of Richmond, she was mother of the future Henry VII.   **24 arrogance** i.e., ambition for her son   **26 envious** malicious   **29 wayward** not yielding readily to treatment.   **grounded** firmly fixed

31 But now just now   **33 amendment** recovery   **36 atonement** reconciliation   **37 brothers** (Only one brother, Earl Rivers, is mentioned in the play, though historically Elizabeth had others; Shakespeare may be thinking of other kinsmen, including her sons, whom she helped to advance.)   **39 warn** summon   **46 dissentious** quarrelsome, discordant   **47 fair** courteously   **48 smooth** flatter.   **cog** fawn   **49 Duck . . . nods** i.e., bow affectedly   **53 With** by.   **Jacks** lowbred persons   **54 presence** company   **55 grace** sense of duty or propriety (playing upon *Your Grace* in the preceding line)   **60 breathing while** i.e., brief time   **61 lewd** vile, base   **63 disposition** inclination   **65 Aiming** guessing.   **belike** probably

That in your outward action shows itself
Against my children, brothers, and myself,
Makes him to send, that he may learn the ground   68
Of your ill will, and thereby to remove it.

RICHARD
I cannot tell. The world is grown so bad   70
That wrens make prey where eagles dare not perch.
Since every Jack became a gentleman,
There's many a gentle person made a Jack.

QUEEN ELIZABETH
Come, come, we know your meaning, brother
   Gloucester;
You envy my advancement and my friends'.   75
God grant we never may have need of you!

RICHARD
Meantime, God grants that I have need of you.
Our brother is imprisoned by your means,   78
Myself disgraced, and the nobility
Held in contempt, while great promotions
Are daily given to ennoble those
That scarce some two days since were worth a
   noble.   82

QUEEN ELIZABETH
By Him that raised me to this careful height   83
From that contented hap which I enjoyed,   84
I never did incense His Majesty
Against the Duke of Clarence, but have been
An earnest advocate to plead for him.
My lord, you do me shameful injury
Falsely to draw me in these vile suspects.   89

RICHARD
You may deny that you were not the means
Of my Lord Hastings' late imprisonment.

RIVERS   She may, my lord, for—

RICHARD
She may, Lord Rivers! Why, who knows not so?
She may do more, sir, than denying that:
She may help you to many fair preferments,   95
And then deny her aiding hand therein,
And lay those honors on your high desert.   97
What may she not? She may, ay, marry, may she—   98

RIVERS   What, marry, may she?

RICHARD
What, marry, may she? Marry with a king,
A bachelor, and a handsome stripling too!   101
Iwis your grandam had a worser match.   102

QUEEN ELIZABETH
My lord of Gloucester, I have too long borne
Your blunt upbraidings and your bitter scoffs.
By heaven, I will acquaint His Majesty
Of those gross taunts that oft I have endured.
I had rather be a country servant maid

Than a great queen with this condition,
To be so baited, scorned, and stormèd at.   109

Enter old Queen Margaret [behind].

Small joy have I in being England's queen.

QUEEN MARGARET *[aside]*
And lessened be that small, God I beseech him!
Thy honor, state, and seat is due to me.   112

RICHARD
What? Threat you me with telling of the King?   113
Tell him, and spare not. Look what I have said   114
I will avouch 't in presence of the King.
I dare adventure to be sent to the Tower.   116
'Tis time to speak; my pains are quite forgot.   117

QUEEN MARGARET *[aside]*
Out, devil! I do remember them too well: 118
Thou killedst my husband Henry in the Tower,
And Edward, my poor son, at Tewkesbury.

RICHARD
Ere you were queen, ay, or your husband king,
I was a packhorse in his great affairs,   122
A weeder-out of his proud adversaries,
A liberal rewarder of his friends.
To royalize his blood I spent mine own.

QUEEN MARGARET *[aside]*
Ay, and much better blood than his or thine.

RICHARD
In all which time you and your husband Grey
Were factious for the house of Lancaster;   128
And, Rivers, so were you. Was not your husband   129
In Margaret's battle at Saint Albans slain?
Let me put in your minds, if you forget,
What you have been ere this, and what you are;
Withal, what I have been, and what I am.   133

QUEEN MARGARET *[aside]*
A murderous villain, and so still thou art.

RICHARD
Poor Clarence did forsake his father, Warwick,   135
Ay, and forswore himself—which Jesu pardon!—

QUEEN MARGARET *[aside]*   Which God revenge!

RICHARD
To fight on Edward's party for the crown;
And for his meed, poor lord, he is mewed up.   139
I would to God my heart were flint, like Edward's,
Or Edward's soft and pitiful, like mine.
I am too childish-foolish for this world.

---

68 Makes him causes him. (The implied subject is "The king's own disposition.") **ground** cause (of your ill will) **70 I cannot tell** i.e., I don't know what to think. (Richard plays the role of the exasperated moralist.) **75 friends'** i.e., kinsmen's **78 Our brother** i.e., Clarence **82 noble** (1) gold coin worth six shillings eight pence (2) nobleman **83 careful** full of cares **84 hap** fortune **89 in** into. **suspects** suspicions **95 preferments** advantages, promotions **97 lay . . . on** attribute these high honors to **98 marry** i.e., indeed (followed by a pun on "wed") **101 stripling** young man **102 Iwis** certainly

109 baited harassed. **s.d. Queen Margaret** (Historically, Queen Margaret was held prisoner in England for five years following the battle of Tewkesbury and then was sent to France; see the note to line 167 below.) **112 state** degree, high rank. **seat** throne **113 Threat** threaten **114 Look what** whatever **116 adventure to be** risk being **117 pains** efforts (in King Edward's behalf) **118 Out** (An exclamation of anger.) **122 packhorse** workhorse, beast of burden **128 factious** promoting dissension. **for** on the side of **129 husband** (Queen Elizabeth's first husband, Sir John Grey, fell fighting on the Lancastrian side at Saint Albans.) **133 Withal** in addition **135 father** i.e., father-in-law. (See *3 Henry VI*, 4.1, when Clarence deserted his brothers to marry Warwick's daughter Isabella and supported the Lancastrian cause for a time; thereafter, he forswore his oath to Warwick by returning to fight on Edward's *party* [line 138] or side.) **139 meed** reward. **mewed** caged (like a hawk)

QUEEN MARGARET [aside]
    Hie thee to hell for shame, and leave this world,   143
    Thou cacodemon! There thy kingdom is.   144
RIVERS
    My lord of Gloucester, in those busy days
    Which here you urge to prove us enemies,   146
    We followed then our lord, our sovereign king.
    So should we you, if you should be our king.
RICHARD
    If I should be? I had rather be a peddler.
    Far be it from my heart, the thought thereof!
QUEEN ELIZABETH
    As little joy, my lord, as you suppose
    You should enjoy were you this country's king,
    As little joy you may suppose in me
    That I enjoy, being the queen thereof.
QUEEN MARGARET [aside]
    Ah, little joy enjoys the queen thereof,
    For I am she, and altogether joyless.
    I can no longer hold me patient.   [Advancing.]
    Hear me, you wrangling pirates, that fall out
    In sharing that which you have pilled from me!   159
    Which of you trembles not that looks on me?
    If not, that I am queen, you bow like subjects,   161
    Yet that, by you deposed, you quake like rebels?   162
    [To Richard.] Ah, gentle villain, do not turn away!   163
RICHARD
    Foul wrinkled witch, what mak'st thou in my sight?   164
QUEEN MARGARET
    But repetition of what thou hast marred;   165
    That will I make before I let thee go.
RICHARD
    Wert thou not banishèd on pain of death?   167
QUEEN MARGARET
    I was; but I do find more pain in banishment
    Than death can yield me here by my abode.
    A husband and a son thou ow'st to me,   170
    And thou a kingdom; all of you allegiance.   171
    This sorrow that I have by right is yours,
    And all the pleasures you usurp are mine.
RICHARD
    The curse my noble father laid on thee   174
    When thou didst crown his warlike brows with
        paper
    And with thy scorns drew'st rivers from his eyes,
    And then, to dry them, gav'st the Duke a clout   177
    Steeped in the faultless blood of pretty Rutland—   178
    His curses then, from bitterness of soul

Denounced against thee, are all fall'n upon thee;   180
    And God, not we, hath plagued thy bloody deed.
QUEEN ELIZABETH
    So just is God, to right the innocent.
HASTINGS
    O, 'twas the foulest deed to slay that babe,   183
    And the most merciless, that e'er was heard of!
RIVERS
    Tyrants themselves wept when it was reported.   185
DORSET
    No man but prophesied revenge for it.   186
BUCKINGHAM
    Northumberland, then present, wept to see it.
QUEEN MARGARET
    What? Were you snarling all before I came,
    Ready to catch each other by the throat,
    And turn you all your hatred now on me?
    Did York's dread curse prevail so much with heaven
    That Henry's death, my lovely Edward's death,
    Their kingdom's loss, my woeful banishment,
    Should all but answer for that peevish brat?   194
    Can curses pierce the clouds and enter heaven?
    Why, then, give way, dull clouds, to my quick
        curses!   196
    Though not by war, by surfeit die your king,   197
    As ours by murder, to make him a king!
    Edward thy son, that now is Prince of Wales,
    For Edward our son, that was Prince of Wales,
    Die in his youth by like untimely violence!
    Thyself a queen, for me that was a queen,
    Outlive thy glory, like my wretched self!
    Long mayst thou live to wail thy children's death
    And see another, as I see thee now,
    Decked in thy rights, as thou art stalled in mine!   206
    Long die thy happy days before thy death,
    And, after many lengthened hours of grief,
    Die neither mother, wife, nor England's queen!
    Rivers and Dorset, you were standers-by,   210
    And so wast thou, Lord Hastings, when my son   211
    Was stabbed with bloody daggers: God, I pray him,
    That none of you may live his natural age,   213
    But by some unlooked accident cut off!   214
RICHARD
    Have done thy charm, thou hateful withered hag!   215
QUEEN MARGARET
    And leave out thee? Stay, dog, for thou shalt
        hear me.
    If heaven have any grievous plague in store
    Exceeding those that I can wish upon thee,
    O, let them keep it till thy sins be ripe,   219

---

143 Hie hasten **144 cacodemon** evil spirit **146 urge** cite
159 pilled pillaged, robbed **161–162 If . . . rebels** i.e., even if you
do not bow low to me as your queen, you quake as rebels who have
deposed me **163 gentle** nobly born. *Gentle villain* is an oxymoron,
since *villain* can mean "one ignobly born." **164 mak'st thou** are you
doing **165 But . . . marred** only reciting your crimes **167 banishèd** (Margaret was banished in 1464, returned to England in 1471,
and after the Battle of Tewkesbury was confined in the Tower until
1476, when she returned to France, dying there in 1482, one year
before the historical time of this scene.) **170 thou** i.e., Richard
171 thou i.e., Elizabeth **174 The curse** (See *3 Henry VI*, 1.4.164–
166.) **177 clout** cloth, handkerchief **178 faultless** innocent

180 Denounced proclaimed vengefully **183 that babe** i.e., Rutland
185 Tyrants pitiless men **186 No . . . prophesied** there was no one
who did not prophesy **194 but answer for** merely atone for, equal.
peevish silly, senseless **196 quick** lively, piercing **197 surfeit** dissipated living **206 Decked** dressed. **stalled** installed **210–211 Rivers, Dorset, Hastings** (Not present in Shakespeare's dramatization of
the event in *3 Henry VI*, 5.5, but named in the chronicles as having
been present.) **213 natural age** full course of life **214 unlooked** unexpected **215 charm** magic curse, pronounced by a witch
219 them i.e., the heavens, heaven

And then hurl down their indignation
On thee, the troubler of the poor world's peace!
The worm of conscience still begnaw thy soul!   222
Thy friends suspect for traitors while thou liv'st,
And take deep traitors for thy dearest friends!
No sleep close up that deadly eye of thine,
Unless it be while some tormenting dream
Affrights thee with a hell of ugly devils!
Thou elvish-marked, abortive, rooting hog,   228
Thou that wast sealed in thy nativity   229
The slave of nature and the son of hell!   230
Thou slander of thy heavy mother's womb,   231
Thou loathèd issue of thy father's loins,
Thou rag of honor, thou detested—   233

RICHARD
Margaret.

QUEEN MARGARET   Richard!

RICHARD   Ha?

QUEEN MARGARET   I call thee not.

RICHARD
I cry thee mercy then, for I did think   235
That thou hadst called me all these bitter names.

QUEEN MARGARET
Why, so I did, but looked for no reply.
O, let me make the period to my curse!   238

RICHARD
'Tis done by me, and ends in "Margaret."

QUEEN ELIZABETH   [to Queen Margaret]
Thus have you breathed your curse against yourself.

QUEEN MARGARET
Poor painted queen, vain flourish of my fortune!   241
Why strew'st thou sugar on that bottled spider,   242
Whose deadly web ensnareth thee about?
Fool, fool, thou whet'st a knife to kill thyself.
The day will come that thou shalt wish for me
To help thee curse this poisonous bunch-backed
    toad.   246

HASTINGS
False-boding woman, end thy frantic curse,   247
Lest to thy harm thou move our patience.

QUEEN MARGARET
Foul shame upon you! You have all moved mine.

RIVERS
Were you well served, you would be taught your
    duty.   250

QUEEN MARGARET
To serve me well, you all should do me duty,   251

Teach me to be your queen, and you my subjects.   252
O, serve me well, and teach yourselves that duty!

DORSET
Dispute not with her. She is lunatic.

QUEEN MARGARET
Peace, Master Marquess, you are malapert.   255
Your fire-new stamp of honor is scarce current.   256
O, that your young nobility could judge
What 'twere to lose it and be miserable!
They that stand high have many blasts to shake
    them,   259
And if they fall, they dash themselves to pieces.

RICHARD
Good counsel, marry! Learn it, learn it, Marquess.

DORSET
It touches you, my lord, as much as me.

RICHARD
Ay, and much more; but I was born so high.
Our aerie buildeth in the cedar's top,   264
And dallies with the wind and scorns the sun.

QUEEN MARGARET
And turns the sun to shade; alas, alas!   266
Witness my son, now in the shade of death,
Whose bright outshining beams thy cloudy wrath
Hath in eternal darkness folded up.
Your aerie buildeth in our aerie's nest.
O God, that seest it, do not suffer it!
As it is won with blood, lost be it so!

BUCKINGHAM
Peace, peace, for shame, if not for charity!

QUEEN MARGARET
Urge neither charity nor shame to me.
                                        [Turning to the others.]
Uncharitably with me have you dealt,
And shamefully my hopes by you are butchered.
My charity is outrage, life my shame,   277
And in that shame still live my sorrow's rage!

BUCKINGHAM   Have done, have done.

QUEEN MARGARET
O princely Buckingham, I'll kiss thy hand
In sign of league and amity with thee.
Now fair befall thee and thy noble house!   282
Thy garments are not spotted with our blood,
Nor thou within the compass of my curse.   284

BUCKINGHAM
Nor no one here; for curses never pass   285
The lips of those that breathe them in the air.   286

QUEEN MARGARET
I will not think but they ascend the sky   287

---

222 **still begnaw** continually gnaw   228 **elvish-marked** marked by
elves at birth.   **hog** (Alludes to Richard's badge, the wild boar.)
229 **sealed** stamped   230 **slave of nature** i.e., wretch made by the
malignancy of nature (as seen in his deformity)   231 **heavy** sorrowful
233 **rag** tattered remnant   235 **cry thee mercy** beg your pardon. (Said
sarcastically.)   238 **period** conclusion   241 **painted** counterfeit.
vain . . . fortune i.e., mere ornament of a position that is mine by
right   242 **bottled** bottle-shaped, swollen   246 **bunch-backed** hunchbacked   247 **False-boding** falsely prophesying   250 **well served**
treated as you deserve. (But Margaret turns the phrase around to mean
"served as befitting one of royal rank.")   **your duty** your place (i.e.,
to be obedient)   251 **duty** reverence

252 **Teach me** i.e., show by your obedience what is my role
255 **malapert** impudent   256 **fire-new** newly coined.   **current** genuine as legal tender   259 **blasts** strong gusts of wind   264 **aerie** eagle's
brood   266 **sun** (with a play on *son* in the next line)   277 **My . . .
shame** i.e., instead of charity I receive outrage, and the only life
given me is one of shame; or, outrage is all the charity I feel, and
shame is my only life   282 **fair befall** good luck to   284 **compass**
scope, boundary   285–286 **curses . . . air** i.e., curses have no effect on others, though they may return upon the heads of those who
utter them   287 **I . . . but** I must believe that

And there awake God's gentle-sleeping peace.
O Buckingham, take heed of yonder dog!
Look when he fawns, he bites; and when he bites,   290
His venom tooth will rankle to the death.   291
Have not to do with him, beware of him;
Sin, death, and hell have set their marks on him,
And all their ministers attend on him.

RICHARD
What doth she say, my lord of Buckingham?

BUCKINGHAM
Nothing that I respect, my gracious lord.   296

QUEEN MARGARET
What, dost thou scorn me for my gentle counsel?
And soothe the devil that I warn thee from?   298
O, but remember this another day,
When he shall split thy very heart with sorrow,
And say poor Margaret was a prophetess!
Live each of you the subjects to his hate,   302
And he to yours, and all of you to God's!   Exit.

BUCKINGHAM
My hair doth stand on end to hear her curses.

RIVERS
And so doth mine. I muse why she's at liberty.   305

RICHARD
I cannot blame her. By God's holy mother,
She hath had too much wrong, and I repent
My part thereof that I have done to her.

QUEEN ELIZABETH
I never did her any, to my knowledge.

RICHARD
Yet you have all the vantage of her wrong.   310
I was too hot to do somebody good   311
That is too cold in thinking of it now.   312
Marry, as for Clarence, he is well repaid;
He is franked up to fatting for his pains—   314
God pardon them that are the cause thereof!

RIVERS
A virtuous and a Christian-like conclusion,
To pray for them that have done scathe to us.   317

RICHARD
So do I ever—(speaks to himself) being well advised.
For had I cursed now, I had cursed myself.

        Enter Catesby.

CATESBY
Madam, His Majesty doth call for you,
And for Your Grace, and yours, my gracious lord.

QUEEN ELIZABETH
Catesby, I come.—Lords, will you go with me?

RIVERS
We wait upon Your Grace.   323
        Exeunt all but [Richard Duke of] Gloucester.

RICHARD
I do the wrong, and first begin to brawl.
The secret mischiefs that I set abroach   325
I lay unto the grievous charge of others.   326
Clarence, who I indeed have cast in darkness,
I do beweep to many simple gulls—   328
Namely, to Derby, Hastings, Buckingham—
And tell them 'tis the Queen and her allies
That stir the King against the Duke my brother.
Now they believe it, and withal whet me   332
To be revenged on Rivers, Dorset, Grey.
But then I sigh and, with a piece of Scripture,
Tell them that God bids us do good for evil.   335
And thus I clothe my naked villainy
With odd old ends stol'n forth of Holy Writ,   337
And seem a saint when most I play the devil.

        Enter two Murderers.

But soft! Here come my executioners.   339
How now, my hardy, stout, resolvèd mates,   340
Are you now going to dispatch this thing?

FIRST MURDERER
We are, my lord, and come to have the warrant
That we may be admitted where he is.

RICHARD
Well thought upon. I have it here about me.
                        [He gives the warrant.]
When you have done, repair to Crosby Place.   345
But sirs, be sudden in the execution,
Withal obdurate; do not hear him plead;   347
For Clarence is well-spoken, and perhaps
May move your hearts to pity if you mark him.   349

FIRST MURDERER
Tut, tut, my lord, we will not stand to prate;
Talkers are no good doers.   Be assured
We go to use our hands and not our tongues.

RICHARD
Your eyes drop millstones when fools' eyes fall
    tears.   353
I like you, lads. About your business straight.
Go, go, dispatch.

FIRST MURDERER   We will, my noble lord.   [Exeunt.]

                        ♣

1.4   Enter Clarence and Keeper.

KEEPER
Why looks Your Grace so heavily today?   1

CLARENCE
O, I have passed a miserable night,
So full of fearful dreams, of ugly sights,

---

290 **Look when** whenever   291 **venom** envenomed.   **rankle** cause a festering wound   296 **respect** heed   298 **soothe** flatter   302 **the subjects to** subjugated to   305 **muse** wonder   310 **vantage of her wrong** advantage derived from the wrongs she has suffered   311 **hot** eager (in helping Edward to the throne)   312 **That . . . cold** who is too ungrateful   314 **franked up** shut up in a frank or sty.   **to fatting** to be fattened (for slaughter)   317 **scathe** harm   323 **wait upon** attend

325 **set abroach** set flowing, begin   326 **lay . . . of** impute as a serious accusation against   328 **gulls** credulous persons   332 **withal** furthermore.   **whet** urge, incite   335 **for** in return for   337 **ends** fragments, tags   339 **soft** gently; wait a minute   340 **resolvèd mates** resolute fellows   345 **repair** betake yourselves   347 **Withal** at the same time   349 **mark** pay attention to   353 **millstones** heavy stone disks used for grinding. (To *drop millstones* was proverbially to show signs of hardheartedness.)   **fall** let fall
1.4. Location: London. The Tower.
1 heavily sad

That, as I am a Christian faithful man,
I would not spend another such a night
Though 'twere to buy a world of happy days,
So full of dismal terror was the time!

KEEPER
What was your dream, my lord? I pray you, tell me.

CLARENCE
Methought that I had broken from the Tower   9
And was embarked to cross to Burgundy,   10
And in my company my brother Gloucester,
Who from my cabin tempted me to walk
Upon the hatches. Thence we looked toward
    England   13
And cited up a thousand heavy times,   14
During the wars of York and Lancaster,
That had befall'n us. As we paced along
Upon the giddy footing of the hatches,   17
Methought that Gloucester stumbled, and in falling
Struck me, that thought to stay him, overboard   19
Into the tumbling billows of the main.   20
O Lord, methought what pain it was to drown!
What dreadful noise of waters in my ears!
What sights of ugly death within my eyes!
Methought I saw a thousand fearful wracks;   24
Ten thousand men that fishes gnawed upon;
Wedges of gold, great anchors, heaps of pearl,   26
Inestimable stones, unvalued jewels,   27
All scattered in the bottom of the sea.
Some lay in dead men's skulls, and in the holes
Where eyes did once inhabit there were crept,
As 'twere in scorn of eyes, reflecting gems,
That wooed the slimy bottom of the deep   32
And mocked the dead bones that lay scattered by.

KEEPER
Had you such leisure in the time of death
To gaze upon these secrets of the deep?

CLARENCE
Methought I had, and often did I strive
To yield the ghost; but still the envious flood   37
Stopped in my soul and would not let it forth   38
To seek the empty, vast, and wandering air,
But smothered it within my panting bulk,   40
Which almost burst to belch it in the sea.

KEEPER
Awaked you not in this sore agony?

CLARENCE
No, no, my dream was lengthened after life.
O, then began the tempest to my soul!
I passed, methought, the melancholy flood,   45
With that sour ferryman which poets write of,   46

Unto the kingdom of perpetual night.
The first that there did greet my stranger soul   48
Was my great father-in-law, renownèd Warwick,
Who spake aloud, "What scourge for perjury
Can this dark monarchy afford false Clarence?"
And so he vanished. Then came wandering by
A shadow like an angel, with bright hair   53
Dabbled in blood, and he shrieked out aloud,
"Clarence is come—false, fleeting, perjured Clarence,   55
That stabbed me in the field by Tewkesbury.
Seize on him, Furies, take him unto torment!"
With that, methought, a legion of foul fiends
Environed me and howlèd in mine ears
Such hideous cries that with the very noise
I trembling waked, and for a season after   61
Could not believe but that I was in hell,
Such terrible impression made my dream.

KEEPER
No marvel, my lord, though it affrighted you.
I am afraid, methinks, to hear you tell it.

CLARENCE
Ah, keeper, keeper, I have done these things,
That now give evidence against my soul,
For Edward's sake, and see how he requites me!   68
O God! If my deep prayers cannot appease thee,
But thou wilt be avenged on my misdeeds,
Yet execute thy wrath in me alone!
O, spare my guiltless wife and my poor children!
Keeper, I prithee, sit by me awhile.
My soul is heavy, and I fain would sleep.   74

KEEPER
I will, my lord. God give Your Grace good rest!
                                        [Clarence sleeps.]

Enter Brackenbury, the Lieutenant.

BRACKENBURY
Sorrow breaks seasons and reposing hours,   76
Makes the night morning and the noontide night.
Princes have but their titles for their glories,
An outward honor for an inward toil,
And, for unfelt imaginations,   80
They often feel a world of restless cares;
So that between their titles and low name   82
There's nothing differs but the outward fame.   83

Enter two Murderers.

FIRST MURDERER   Ho! Who's here?
BRACKENBURY
What would'st thou, fellow, and how cam'st thou
    hither?
FIRST MURDERER   I would speak with Clarence, and I
came hither on my legs.
BRACKENBURY   What, so brief?

---

9 Methought it seemed to me   **10 Burgundy** (Clarence and Richard, according to the chronicles, had been sent to Burgundy for protection following their father's death.)   **13 hatches** movable planks forming a deck   **14 cited up** recalled   **17 giddy** dizzying   **19 stay** hold, steady   **20 main** ocean   **24 wracks** shipwrecked vessels   **26 Wedges** ingots   **27 Inestimable** precious and innumerable.   **unvalued** priceless   **32 wooed** (These lifeless eyes have nothing to flirt with but the murky depths.)   **37 envious flood** malicious water   **38 Stopped** held   **40 bulk** body   **45 melancholy flood** i.e., River Styx   **46 ferryman** i.e., Charon, who ferried souls to Hades, *the kingdom of perpetual night* (line 47)

48 stranger i.e., newly arrived   **53 shadow** i.e., ghost of Edward, Prince of Wales, son of Henry VI   **55 fleeting** fickle, deceitful   **61 season** time   **68 requites** repays   **74 fain** willingly   **76 breaks seasons** i.e., disrupts the normal rhythms of life.   **reposing hours** i.e., hours properly devoted to sleep   **80 for unfelt imaginations** in return for glories that are merely illusory   **82 low name** i.e., the lowly position of ordinary men   **83 fame** reputation

SECOND MURDERER   'Tis better, sir, than to be tedious.—
Let him see our commission, and talk no more.
                              [*Brackenbury*] *reads* [*it*].
BRACKENBURY
I am in this commanded to deliver
The noble Duke of Clarence to your hands.
I will not reason what is meant hereby,
Because I will be guiltless from the meaning.   94
There lies the Duke asleep, and there the keys.
                              [*He gives keys.*]
I'll to the King and signify to him
That thus I have resigned to you my charge.
FIRST MURDERER   You may, sir; 'tis a point of wisdom.
Fare you well.   *Exit* [*Brackenbury with Keeper*].
SECOND MURDERER   What, shall I stab him as he
sleeps?
FIRST MURDERER   No. He'll say 'twas done cowardly,
when he wakes.
SECOND MURDERER   Why, he shall never wake until the
great Judgment Day.
FIRST MURDERER   Why, then he'll say we stabbed him
sleeping.
SECOND MURDERER   The urging of that word "judg-
ment" hath bred a kind of remorse in me.
FIRST MURDERER   What, art thou afraid?
SECOND MURDERER   Not to kill him, having a warrant,
but to be damned for killing him, from the which no
warrant can defend me.
FIRST MURDERER   I thought thou hadst been resolute.
SECOND MURDERER   So I am—to let him live.
FIRST MURDERER   I'll back to the Duke of Gloucester
and tell him so.
SECOND MURDERER   Nay, I prithee, stay a little. I hope
this passionate humor of mine will change. It was   119
wont to hold me but while one tells twenty.   120
FIRST MURDERER   How dost thou feel thyself now?
SECOND MURDERER   Faith, some certain dregs of con-
science are yet within me.
FIRST MURDERER   Remember our reward when the
deed 's done.
SECOND MURDERER   Zounds, he dies! I had forgot the   126
reward.
FIRST MURDERER   Where's thy conscience now?
SECOND MURDERER   O, in the Duke of Gloucester's
purse.
FIRST MURDERER   When he opens his purse to give us
our reward, thy conscience flies out.
SECOND MURDERER   'Tis no matter; let it go. There's few
or none will entertain it.   134
FIRST MURDERER   What if it come to thee again?
SECOND MURDERER   I'll not meddle with it; it makes a
man a coward. A man cannot steal but it accuseth him;
a man cannot swear but it checks him; a man cannot   138
lie with his neighbor's wife but it detects him. 'Tis a
blushing, shamefaced spirit that mutinies in a man's
bosom. It fills a man full of obstacles. It made me once
restore a purse of gold that by chance I found. It

beggars any man that keeps it. It is turned out of
towns and cities for a dangerous thing, and every man
that means to live well endeavors to trust to himself
and live without it.
FIRST MURDERER   Zounds, 'tis even now at my elbow,
persuading me not to kill the Duke.
SECOND MURDERER   Take the devil in thy mind, and   149
believe him not. He would insinuate with thee but to   150
make thee sigh.
FIRST MURDERER   Tut, I am strong-framed; he cannot
prevail with me.
SECOND MURDERER   Spoke like a tall man that respects 154
thy reputation. Come, shall we fall to work?
FIRST MURDERER   Take him on the costard with the hilts 156
of thy sword, and then throw him into the malmsey   157
butt in the next room.   158
SECOND MURDERER   O, excellent device! And make a sop 159
of him.
FIRST MURDERER   Soft, he wakes.
SECOND MURDERER   Strike!
FIRST MURDERER   No, we'll reason with him.   163
CLARENCE [*waking*]
Where art thou, keeper? Give me a cup of wine.
SECOND MURDERER
You shall have wine enough, my lord, anon.
CLARENCE   In God's name, what art thou?
FIRST MURDERER   A man, as you are.
CLARENCE   But not, as I am, royal.
FIRST MURDERER   Nor you, as we are, loyal.
CLARENCE
Thy voice is thunder, but thy looks are humble.
FIRST MURDERER
My voice is now the King's, my looks mine own.
CLARENCE
How darkly and how deadly dost thou speak!   172
Your eyes do menace me. Why look you pale?
Who sent you hither? Wherefore do you come?
SECOND MURDERER   To, to, to—
CLARENCE   To murder me?
BOTH   Ay, ay.
CLARENCE
You scarcely have the hearts to tell me so,
And therefore cannot have the hearts to do it.
Wherein, my friends, have I offended you?
FIRST MURDERER
Offended us you have not, but the King.
CLARENCE
I shall be reconciled to him again.
SECOND MURDERER
Never, my lord; therefore prepare to die.
CLARENCE
Are you drawn forth among a world of men   184
To slay the innocent? What is my offense?
Where is the evidence that doth accuse me?

94 **will be** wish to be   119 **passionate humor** compassionate mood
120 **tells** counts   126 **Zounds** i.e., by God's (Christ's) wounds
134 **entertain it** receive it, give it welcome   138 **checks** reproves

149–150 **Take . . . not** i.e., listen to the devil and pay no heed to
conscience. **in** into. **him** conscience   150 **insinuate** ingratiate himself   154 **tall** brave   156 **Take** strike. **costard** head. (Literally, a
kind of apple.)   157–158 **malmsey butt** wine barrel. (Malmsey is a
sweet wine.)   159 **sop** bread or cake soaked in wine   163 **reason**
talk   172 **darkly** ominously   184 **drawn . . . men** especially selected from the whole human race

What lawful quest have given their verdict up 187
Unto the frowning judge? Or who pronounced
The bitter sentence of poor Clarence' death
Before I be convict by course of law? 190
To threaten me with death is most unlawful.
I charge you, as you hope to have redemption
By Christ's dear blood shed for our grievous sins,
That you depart and lay no hands on me.
The deed you undertake is damnable.

FIRST MURDERER
What we will do, we do upon command.

SECOND MURDERER
And he that hath commanded is our king.

CLARENCE
Erroneous vassals! The great King of kings 198
Hath in the table of his law commanded 199
That thou shalt do no murder. Will you then
Spurn at his edict and fulfill a man's?
Take heed; for he holds vengeance in his hand
To hurl upon their heads that break his law.

SECOND MURDERER
And that same vengeance doth he hurl on thee
For false forswearing and for murder, too.
Thou didst receive the Sacrament to fight 206
In quarrel of the house of Lancaster.

FIRST MURDERER
And, like a traitor to the name of God,
Didst break that vow, and with thy treacherous
   blade
Unrippedst the bowels of thy sovereign's son. 210

SECOND MURDERER
Whom thou wast sworn to cherish and defend.

FIRST MURDERER
How canst thou urge God's dreadful law to us
When thou hast broke it in such dear degree? 213

CLARENCE
Alas! For whose sake did I that ill deed?
For Edward, for my brother, for his sake.
He sends you not to murder me for this,
For in that sin he is as deep as I.
If God will be avengèd for the deed,
O, know you yet he doth it publicly!
Take not the quarrel from his powerful arm.
He needs no indirect or lawless course
To cut off those that have offended him.

FIRST MURDERER
Who made thee, then, a bloody minister 223
When gallant-springing brave Plantagenet, 224
That princely novice, was struck dead by thee? 225

CLARENCE
My brother's love, the devil, and my rage. 226

FIRST MURDERER
Thy brother's love, our duty, and thy faults

Provoke us hither now to slaughter thee.

CLARENCE
If you do love my brother, hate not me!
I am his brother, and I love him well.
If you are hired for meed, go back again, 231
And I will send you to my brother Gloucester,
Who shall reward you better for my life
Than Edward will for tidings of my death.

SECOND MURDERER
You are deceived. Your brother Gloucester hates
   you.

CLARENCE
O, no, he loves me, and he holds me dear.
Go you to him from me.

FIRST MURDERER   Ay, so we will.

CLARENCE
Tell him, when that our princely father York
Blessed his three sons with his victorious arm
And charged us from his soul to love each other,
He little thought of this divided friendship.
Bid Gloucester think of this, and he will weep.

FIRST MURDERER
Ay, millstones, as he lessoned us to weep. 243

CLARENCE
O, do not slander him, for he is kind.

FIRST MURDERER
Right, as snow in harvest. Come, you deceive
   yourself. 245
'Tis he that sends us to destroy you here.

CLARENCE
It cannot be, for he bewept my fortune,
And hugged me in his arms, and swore with sobs
That he would labor my delivery. 249

FIRST MURDERER
Why, so he doth, when he delivers you
From this earth's thralldom to the joys of heaven. 251

SECOND MURDERER
Make peace with God, for you must die, my lord.

CLARENCE
Have you that holy feeling in your souls
To counsel me to make my peace with God,
And are you yet to your own souls so blind
That you will war with God by murdering me?
O, sirs, consider, they that set you on
To do this deed will hate you for the deed.

SECOND MURDERER [to First Murderer]
What shall we do?

CLARENCE   Relent, and save your souls.
Which of you, if you were a prince's son,
Being pent from liberty, as I am now, 261
If two such murderers as yourselves came to you,
Would not entreat for life?

FIRST MURDERER
Relent? No. 'Tis cowardly and womanish.

CLARENCE
Not to relent is beastly, savage, devilish.

---

187 quest inquest, i.e., jury   **190 convict** convicted   **198 Erroneous vassals** sinful and mistaken wretches   **199 table** tablet   **206 receive the Sacrament** i.e., swear upon the Sacrament   **210 sovereign's son** i.e., Prince Edward, son of Henry VI   **213 dear** grievous   **223 minister** agent of God   **224 gallant-springing** i.e., gallant and sprightly, aspiring.   **Plantagenet** i.e., the Lancastrian Prince Edward, killed in *3 Henry VI*, 5.5. (See the note at 1.2.145 on Edward's claim to this name.)   **225 novice** youth   **226 My brother's love** i.e., my love for my brother

231 meed financial reward   **243 lessoned** taught   **245 Right . . . harvest** i.e., he's just as kind and natural—that is, both affectionate and with the natural feelings of a brother—as is snow at harvest time   **249 labor my delivery** work for my release   **251 thralldom** bondage, captivity   **261 pent** shut up

My friend [*to Second Murderer*], I spy some pity in
  thy looks.
O, if thine eye be not a flatterer,
Come thou on my side, and entreat for me,
As you would beg, were you in my distress.
A begging prince what beggar pities not?

SECOND MURDERER Look behind you, my lord.

FIRST MURDERER
Take that, and that! (*Stabs him.*) If all this will
  not do,
I'll drown you in the malmsey butt within.
                      Exit [*with the body*].

SECOND MURDERER
A bloody deed, and desperately dispatched!
How fain, like Pilate, would I wash my hands 275
Of this most grievous murder!

        Enter First Murderer.

FIRST MURDERER
How now? What mean'st thou that thou help'st
  me not?
By heaven, the Duke shall know how slack you
  have been.

SECOND MURDERER
I would he knew that I had saved his brother!
Take thou the fee, and tell him what I say,
For I repent me that the Duke is slain.   *Exit.*

FIRST MURDERER
So do not I. Go, coward as thou art.—
Well, I'll go hide his body in some hole
Till that the Duke give order for his burial;
And when I have my meed, I will away,
For this will out, and then I must not stay. *Exit.* 286

❧

2.1   *Flourish. Enter the King [Edward], sick, the
    Queen [Elizabeth], Lord Marquess Dorset, [Grey,]
    Rivers, Hastings, Catesby, Buckingham, [and
    others].*

KING EDWARD
Why, so. Now have I done a good day's work.
You peers, continue this united league.
I every day expect an embassage
From my Redeemer to redeem me hence;
And more in peace my soul shall part to heaven,
Since I have made my friends at peace on earth.
Rivers and Hastings, take each other's hand;
Dissemble not your hatred, swear your love. 8

RIVERS [*taking Hastings' hand*]
By heaven, my soul is purged from grudging hate,
And with my hand I seal my true heart's love.

HASTINGS
So thrive I, as I truly swear the like!

KING EDWARD
Take heed you dally not before your king, 12
Lest he that is the supreme King of kings
Confound your hidden falsehood, and award 14
Either of you to be the other's end. 15

HASTINGS
So prosper I, as I swear perfect love!

RIVERS
And I, as I love Hastings with my heart!

KING EDWARD
Madam, yourself is not exempt from this,
Nor you, son Dorset, Buckingham, nor you; 19
You have been factious one against the other. 20
Wife, love Lord Hastings; let him kiss your hand;
And what you do, do it unfeignedly.

QUEEN ELIZABETH
There, Hastings, I will never more remember
Our former hatred, so thrive I and mine! 24
            [*Hastings kisses her hand.*]

KING EDWARD
Dorset, embrace him. Hastings, love Lord Marquess.

DORSET
This interchange of love, I here protest,
Upon my part shall be inviolable.

HASTINGS And so swear I.   [*They embrace.*]

KING EDWARD
Now, princely Buckingham, seal thou this league
With thy embracements to my wife's allies,
And make me happy in your unity.

BUCKINGHAM [*to the Queen*]
Whenever Buckingham doth turn his hate
Upon Your Grace, but with all duteous love 33
Doth cherish you and yours, God punish me
With hate in those where I expect most love!
When I have most need to employ a friend,
And most assurèd that he is a friend,
Deep, hollow, treacherous, and full of guile 38
Be he unto me! This do I beg of God,
When I am cold in love to you or yours.
                   [*They*] *embrace.*

KING EDWARD
A pleasing cordial, princely Buckingham, 41
Is this thy vow unto my sickly heart.
There wanteth now our brother Gloucester here 43
To make the blessèd period of this peace. 44

BUCKINGHAM And, in good time,
Here comes Sir Richard Ratcliffe and the Duke.

    Enter Ratcliffe and [Richard Duke of] Gloucester.

RICHARD
Good morrow to my sovereign king and queen;
And, princely peers, a happy time of day!

---

275 fain gladly   **286 this will out** ("Murder will out" was a proverbial saying.)
2.1. Location: London. The royal court.
s.d. Flourish trumpet call to announce the arrival of a distinguished
person **8 Dissemble** conceal, disguise (under a false appearance of
love)

12 dally trifle **14 Confound** defeat **15 Either . . . end** i.e., each of
you to be the agent of death of the other **19 son** i.e., stepson
20 factious quarrelsome **24 mine** my family and children **33 but**
i.e., nor **38 Deep** subtle, crafty **41 cordial** restorative **43 wanteth**
is lacking **44 period** conclusion

KING EDWARD
Happy, indeed, as we have spent the day.
Gloucester, we have done deeds of charity,
Made peace of enmity, fair love of hate,
Between these swelling wrong-incensèd peers.   52
RICHARD
A blessèd labor, my most sovereign lord.
Among this princely heap, if any here,   54
By false intelligence, or wrong surmise,   55
Hold me a foe;
If I unwittingly, or in my rage,
Have aught committed that is hardly borne   58
By any in this presence, I desire
To reconcile me to his friendly peace.
'Tis death to me to be at enmity;
I hate it, and desire all good men's love.
First, madam, I entreat true peace of you,
Which I will purchase with my duteous service;
Of you, my noble cousin Buckingham,
If ever any grudge were lodged between us;
Of you and you, Lord Rivers, and of Dorset,
That all without desert have frowned on me;   68
Dukes, earls, lords, gentlemen—indeed, of all.
I do not know that Englishman alive
With whom my soul is any jot at odds
More than the infant that is born tonight.   72
I thank my God for my humility.
QUEEN ELIZABETH
A holy day shall this be kept hereafter.
I would to God all strifes were well compounded.   75
My sovereign lord, I do beseech Your Highness
To take our brother Clarence to your grace.
RICHARD
Why, madam, have I offered love for this,
To be so flouted in this royal presence?   79
Who knows not that the gentle Duke is dead?
                        They all start.
You do him injury to scorn his corpse.
KING EDWARD
Who knows not he is dead? Who knows he is?
QUEEN ELIZABETH
All-seeing heaven, what a world is this!
BUCKINGHAM
Look I so pale, Lord Dorset, as the rest?
DORSET
Ay, my good lord, and no man in the presence   85
But his red color hath forsook his cheeks.
KING EDWARD
Is Clarence dead? The order was reversed.
RICHARD
But he, poor man, by your first order died,
And that a wingèd Mercury did bear;   89
Some tardy cripple bare the countermand,   90

That came too lag to see him buried.   91
God grant that some, less noble and less loyal,   92
Nearer in bloody thoughts but not in blood,   93
Deserve not worse than wretched Clarence did,   94
And yet go current from suspicion!   95
    Enter [Lord Stanley] Earl of Derby.
STANLEY [kneeling]
A boon, my sovereign, for my service done!   96
KING EDWARD
I prithee, peace. My soul is full of sorrow.
STANLEY
I will not rise unless Your Highness hear me.
KING EDWARD
Then say at once what is it thou requests.
STANLEY
The forfeit, sovereign, of my servant's life,   100
Who slew today a riotous gentleman
Lately attendant on the Duke of Norfolk.
KING EDWARD
Have I a tongue to doom my brother's death,   103
And shall that tongue give pardon to a slave?   104
My brother killed no man; his fault was thought,
And yet his punishment was bitter death.
Who sued to me for him? Who, in my wrath,
Kneeled at my feet, and bid me be advised?   108
Who spoke of brotherhood? Who spoke of love?
Who told me how the poor soul did forsake
The mighty Warwick and did fight for me?
Who told me, in the field at Tewkesbury,
When Oxford had me down, he rescued me   113
And said, "Dear brother, live, and be a king"?
Who told me, when we both lay in the field
Frozen almost to death, how he did lap me   116
Even in his garments, and did give himself,
All thin and naked, to the numb-cold night?   118
All this from my remembrance brutish wrath
Sinfully plucked, and not a man of you
Had so much grace to put it in my mind.
But when your carters or your waiting vassals   122
Have done a drunken slaughter and defaced   123
The precious image of our dear Redeemer,   124
You straight are on your knees for pardon, pardon;   125
And I, unjustly too, must grant it you.
                        [Stanley rises.]
But for my brother not a man would speak,
Nor I, ungracious, speak unto myself
For him, poor soul. The proudest of you all
Have been beholding to him in his life;   130

52 swelling i.e., with anger or rivalry 54 heap assembly 55 false
intelligence being misinformed 58 hardly borne taken amiss, deeply
resented 68 all without desert wholly without my having deserved it
72 More than the infant i.e., more than is that infant's soul 75 compounded settled 79 flouted mocked 85 presence i.e., royal presence 89 Mercury messenger of the classical gods 90 tardy cripple
(Richard privately shares with the audience a jest on his own role in
this.) bare bore

91 lag late 92–95 God . . . suspicion i.e., (ironically) pray God
there be not persons who deserve worse than Clarence got, persons
less noble or related by blood to the King than he, although closely
involved in bloody plots, who yet go undetected. (Richard means the
Queen and her kindred.) 95 go current are accepted at face value
(like legal currency). from free from 96 A boon (I crave) a favor
100 The forfeit i.e., the remission of the forfeit 103 doom decree
104 slave wretch 108 advised cautious 113 Oxford (See 3 Henry
VI, 5.5.2; this episode has no historical basis.) 116 lap wrap
118 thin thinly clad 122 carters cart drivers 123–124 defaced . . .
Redeemer i.e., killed a man. (God made humanity in his own image;
Genesis 1:27.) 125 straight at once 130 beholding beholden

Yet none of you would once beg for his life.
O God, I fear thy justice will take hold
On me and you, and mine and yours, for this!
Come, Hastings, help me to my closet. Ah, poor
    Clarence!   *Exeunt some with King and Queen.* 134
RICHARD
This is the fruits of rashness. Marked you not
How that the guilty kindred of the Queen
Looked pale when they did hear of Clarence' death?
O, they did urge it still unto the King.   138
God will revenge it. Come, lords, will you go
To comfort Edward with our company?
BUCKINGHAM   We wait upon Your Grace.   *Exeunt.*

❦

2.2   *Enter the old Duchess of York, with the two
           children of Clarence, [Edward and Margaret
           Plantagenet].*

BOY
Good grandam, tell us, is our father dead?
DUCHESS   No, boy.
GIRL
Why do you weep so oft, and beat your breast,
And cry, "O Clarence, my unhappy son"?
BOY
Why do you look on us, and shake your head,
And call us orphans, wretches, castaways,
If that our noble father were alive?   7
DUCHESS
My pretty cousins, you mistake me both.   8
I do lament the sickness of the King,
As loath to lose him, not your father's death;
It were lost sorrow to wail one that's lost.
BOY
Then, you conclude, my grandam, he is dead.
The King mine uncle is to blame for it.
God will revenge it, whom I will importune   14
With earnest prayers all to that effect.
GIRL   And so will I.
DUCHESS
Peace, children, peace! The King doth love you well.
Incapable and shallow innocents,   18
You cannot guess who caused your father's death.
BOY
Grandam, we can; for my good uncle Gloucester
Told me the King, provoked to it by the Queen,
Devised impeachments to imprison him;   22
And when my uncle told me so, he wept,
And pitied me, and kindly kissed my cheek;
Bade me rely on him as on my father,
And he would love me dearly as his child.
DUCHESS
Ah, that deceit should steal such gentle shape,

And with a virtuous visor hide deep vice!   28
He is my son—ay, and therein my shame;
Yet from my dugs he drew not this deceit.   30
BOY
Think you my uncle did dissemble, grandam?
DUCHESS   Ay, boy.
BOY
I cannot think it. Hark, what noise is this?   33

    *Enter the Queen [Elizabeth], with her hair about
    her ears; Rivers and Dorset after her.*

QUEEN ELIZABETH
Ah, who shall hinder me to wail and weep,
To chide my fortune and torment myself?
I'll join with black despair against my soul,
And to myself become an enemy.
DUCHESS
What means this scene of rude impatience?   38
QUEEN ELIZABETH
To make an act of tragic violence.   39
Edward, my lord, thy son, our king, is dead!   40
Why grow the branches when the root is gone?
Why wither not the leaves that want their sap?
If you will live, lament; if die, be brief,   43
That our swift-wingèd souls may catch the King's
Or, like obedient subjects, follow him
To his new kingdom of ne'er-changing night.
DUCHESS
Ah, so much interest have I in thy sorrow
As I had title in thy noble husband!   48
I have bewept a worthy husband's death
And lived with looking on his images;   50
But now two mirrors of his princely semblance   51
Are cracked in pieces by malignant death,
And I for comfort have but one false glass,   53
That grieves me when I see my shame in him.
Thou art a widow; yet thou art a mother,
And hast the comfort of thy children left;
But death hath snatched my husband from mine
    arms
And plucked two crutches from my feeble hands,
Clarence and Edward. O, what cause have I,   59
Thine being but a moiety of my moan,   60
To overgo thy woes and drown thy cries!   61
BOY
Ah, aunt! You wept not for our father's death.
How can we aid you with our kindred tears?   63
GIRL
Our fatherless distress was left unmoaned;
Your widow-dolor likewise be unwept!   65

134 **closet** private chambers   138 **still** continually
2.2. Location: London. The royal court.
7 **If that** if   8 **cousins** kinsmen   14 **importune** solicit, beg   18 **Incapable** unable to understand   22 **impeachments** accusations

28 **visor** mask   30 **dugs** breasts   33 **s.d. with her . . . ears** (A conventional sign of grief.)   38 **rude impatience** violent unwillingness to accept misfortune   39 **make** perform. (Continues the theatrical metaphor in the previous line.)   40 **Edward . . . dead** (Clarence's death, February 1478, and Edward IV's death, April 1483, are treated as if they had occurred nearly together.)   43 **brief** quick   48 **title** i.e., as mother of the King   50 **images** likenesses; here, children   51 **two mirrors** i.e., Edward and Clarence. (She does not count Rutland.)   53 **false glass** i.e., Richard   59 **what . . . I** what a cause I have   60 **moiety of my moan** half (the cause) of my grief   61 **overgo** exceed   63 **kindred tears** i.e., tears of kinsmen   65 **widow-dolor** widow's grief

QUEEN ELIZABETH
Give me no help in lamentation;
I am not barren to bring forth complaints.   67
All springs reduce their currents to mine eyes,   68
That I, being governed by the watery moon,   69
May send forth plenteous tears to drown the world!
Ah for my husband, for my dear lord Edward!

CHILDREN
Ah for our father, for our dear lord Clarence!

DUCHESS
Alas for both, both mine, Edward and Clarence!

QUEEN ELIZABETH
What stay had I but Edward? And he's gone.   74

CHILDREN
What stay had we but Clarence? And he's gone.

DUCHESS
What stays had I but they? And they are gone.

QUEEN ELIZABETH
Was never widow had so dear a loss!   77

CHILDREN
Were never orphans had so dear a loss!

DUCHESS
Was never mother had so dear a loss!
Alas, I am the mother of these griefs;
Their woes are parceled, mine is general.   81
She for an Edward weeps, and so do I;
I for a Clarence weep, so doth not she.
These babes for Clarence weep, and so do I;
I for an Edward weep, so do not they.
Alas, you three, on me, threefold distressed,
Pour all your tears! I am your sorrow's nurse,
And I will pamper it with lamentation.   88

DORSET [to Queen Elizabeth]
Comfort, dear Mother. God is much displeased
That you take with unthankfulness his doing.
In common worldly things 'tis called ungrateful
With dull unwillingness to repay a debt   92
Which with a bounteous hand was kindly lent;
Much more to be thus opposite with heaven   94
For it requires the royal debt it lent you.   95

RIVERS
Madam, bethink you like a careful mother
Of the young Prince your son. Send straight for him;
Let him be crowned. In him your comfort lives.
Drown desperate sorrow in dead Edward's grave
And plant your joys in living Edward's throne.

Enter Richard [Duke of Gloucester], Buckingham,
[Lord Stanley Earl of] Derby, Hastings, and
Ratcliffe.

RICHARD
Sister, have comfort. All of us have cause
To wail the dimming of our shining star,

But none can help our harms by wailing them.—
Madam, my mother, I do cry you mercy;   104
I did not see Your Grace. Humbly on my knee
I crave your blessing.   [*He kneels.*]

DUCHESS
God bless thee, and put meekness in thy breast,
Love, charity, obedience, and true duty!

RICHARD
Amen! [*Aside.*] And make me die a good old man!
That is the butt end of a mother's blessing;   110
I marvel that Her Grace did leave it out.

BUCKINGHAM
You cloudy princes and heart-sorrowing peers,   112
That bear this heavy mutual load of moan,   113
Now cheer each other in each other's love.
Though we have spent our harvest of this king,
We are to reap the harvest of his son.
The broken rancor of your high-swoll'n hates,
But lately splintered, knit, and joined together,   118
Must gently be preserved, cherished, and kept.   119
Me seemeth good that with some little train   120
Forthwith from Ludlow the young Prince be fet   121
Hither to London, to be crowned our king.

RIVERS
Why with some little train, my lord of Buckingham?

BUCKINGHAM
Marry, my lord, lest by a multitude   124
The new-healed wound of malice should break out,
Which would be so much the more dangerous
By how much the estate is green and yet
    ungoverned.   127
Where every horse bears his commanding rein   128
And may direct his course as please himself,   129
As well the fear of harm, as harm apparent,   130
In my opinion, ought to be prevented.

RICHARD
I hope the King made peace with all of us;
And the compact is firm and true in me.

RIVERS
And so in me, and so, I think, in all.
Yet since it is but green, it should be put
To no apparent likelihood of breach,
Which haply by much company might be urged.   137
Therefore I say with noble Buckingham
That it is meet so few should fetch the Prince.   139

HASTINGS   And so say I.

RICHARD
Then be it so; and go we to determine
Who they shall be that straight shall post to Ludlow.   142

---

67 **barren to** i.e., unable to. (She is pregnant with grief.) 68 **All
springs reduce** let all springs bring back 69 **I . . . moon** (Her grief
is now a sea, fed by springs and her tides governed by the moon.)
74 **stay** support 77 **dear** grievous 81 **Their . . . parceled** i.e., the
woes of Queen Elizabeth and these children are single 88 **pamper**
feed luxuriously 92 **dull** sluggish 94 **opposite with** hostile toward
95 **For it requires** because it calls back

104 **cry you mercy** beg your pardon 110 **butt end** concluding portion. (The *butt* is the end of a spear shaft.) 112 **cloudy** clouded with
grief 113 **moan** lamentation 118 **But lately splintered** only recently
bound together (as with a splint) 119 **Must . . . preserved** i.e., the
recent mending of differences must be preserved 120 **Me seemeth** it
seems to me. **train** entourage 121 **Ludlow** royal castle in Shrop-
shire, near the Welsh border. **fet** fetched 124 **multitude** i.e., large
train or entourage 127 **estate** state, government. **green** unripe, i.e.,
newly established 128 **bears . . . rein** controls the reins that ought
to control him 129 **as please** as it pleases 130 **As well . . . as** both
. . . and. **apparent** evident, real 137 **haply** perhaps. **urged** encouraged, provoked 139 **meet** fitting 142 **post** hasten

Madam, and you, my sister, will you go
To give your censures in this business?   144
QUEEN ELIZABETH, DUCHESS   With all our hearts.   145
    Exeunt. Manent Buckingham and Richard.
BUCKINGHAM
My lord, whoever journeys to the Prince,
For God's sake let not us two stay at home;
For by the way I'll sort occasion,   148
As index to the story we late talked of,   149
To part the Queen's proud kindred from the Prince.
RICHARD
My other self, my counsel's consistory,   151
My oracle, my prophet! My dear cousin,
I, as a child, will go by thy direction.
Toward Ludlow then, for we'll not stay behind.
              Exeunt.

❖

2.3 *Enter one Citizen at one door, and another at the other.*

FIRST CITIZEN
Good morrow, neighbor. Whither away so fast?
SECOND CITIZEN
I promise you, I scarcely know myself.   2
Hear you the news abroad?
FIRST CITIZEN Yes, that the King is dead.
SECOND CITIZEN
Ill news, by 'r Lady; seldom comes the better.   5
I fear, I fear 'twill prove a giddy world.   6

    Enter another Citizen.

THIRD CITIZEN
Neighbors, God speed!
FIRST CITIZEN Give you good morrow, sir.
THIRD CITIZEN
Doth the news hold of good King Edward's death?   8
SECOND CITIZEN
Ay, sir, it is too true, God help the while!
THIRD CITIZEN
Then, masters, look to see a troublous world.   10
FIRST CITIZEN
No, no; by God's good grace his son shall reign.
THIRD CITIZEN
Woe to that land that's governed by a child!   12
SECOND CITIZEN
In him there is a hope of government,
Which in his nonage, council under him,   14
And in his full and ripened years, himself,
No doubt shall then, and till then, govern well.

FIRST CITIZEN
So stood the state when Henry the Sixth
Was crowned in Paris but at nine months old.
THIRD CITIZEN
Stood the state so? No, no, good friends, God wot,   19
For then this land was famously enriched
With politic, grave counsel; then the King   21
Had virtuous uncles to protect His Grace.
FIRST CITIZEN
Why, so hath this, both by his father and mother.
THIRD CITIZEN
Better it were they all came by his father,
Or by his father there were none at all;
For emulation who shall now be nearest   26
Will touch us all too near, if God prevent not.
O, full of danger is the Duke of Gloucester,
And the Queen's sons and brothers haught and
  proud!   29
And were they to be ruled, and not to rule,
This sickly land might solace as before.   31
FIRST CITIZEN
Come, come, we fear the worst. All will be well.
THIRD CITIZEN
When clouds are seen, wise men put on their cloaks;
When great leaves fall, then winter is at hand;
When the sun sets, who doth not look for night?
Untimely storms makes men expect a dearth.
All may be well; but if God sort it so,   37
'Tis more than we deserve or I expect.
SECOND CITIZEN
Truly, the hearts of men are full of fear.
You cannot reason almost with a man   40
That looks not heavily and full of dread.   41
THIRD CITIZEN
Before the days of change, still is it so.   42
By a divine instinct men's minds mistrust   43
Ensuing danger; as, by proof, we see   44
The water swell before a boisterous storm.
But leave it all to God. Whither away?
SECOND CITIZEN
Marry, we were sent for to the justices.
THIRD CITIZEN
And so was I. I'll bear you company. *Exeunt.*

❖

2.4 *Enter [the] Archbishop [of York], [the] young [Duke of] York, the Queen [Elizabeth], and the Duchess [of York].*

ARCHBISHOP
Last night, I hear, they lay at Stony Stratford,   1

---

144 censures judgments **145 s.d. Manent** they remain onstage
148 by on. **sort** find, contrive **149 index** prologue. **late** lately
151 consistory council chamber
2.3. Location: London. A street.
2 promise assure **5 by 'r Lady** by Our Lady. **seldom comes the better** i.e., rarely is change for the better **6 giddy** mad **8 Doth the news hold** is the news true **10 masters** sirs. **troublous** troubled, disorderly **12 Woe . . . child** (Compare with Ecclesiastes 10:16: "Woe to thee, O land, when thy king is a child.") **14 nonage** minority. **council under him** i.e., with the Privy Council governing in his name

19 wot knows **21 politic** sagacious **26 emulation** ambitious rivalry **29 haught** haughty **31 solace** be happy, have comfort **37 sort** dispose **40 You . . . man** there is scarcely anyone with whom you can talk **41 heavily** sad **42 still** ever **43 mistrust** suspect, fear **44 proof** experience
2.4. Location: London. The royal court.
1 Stony Stratford town in Buckinghamshire

And at Northampton they do rest tonight.   2
Tomorrow, or next day, they will be here.
DUCHESS
I long with all my heart to see the Prince.
I hope he is much grown since last I saw him.
QUEEN ELIZABETH
But I hear, no; they say my son of York
Has almost overta'en him in his growth.
YORK
Ay, Mother, but I would not have it so.
DUCHESS
Why, my young cousin? It is good to grow.
YORK
Grandam, one night as we did sit at supper,
My uncle Rivers talked how I did grow
More than my brother. "Ay," quoth my uncle
    Gloucester,
"Small herbs have grace; great weeds do grow
    apace."   13
And since, methinks, I would not grow so fast,   14
Because sweet flowers are slow and weeds make
    haste.
DUCHESS
Good faith, good faith, the saying did not hold   16
In him that did object the same to thee.   17
He was the wretched'st thing when he was young,
So long a-growing and so leisurely,
That, if his rule were true, he should be gracious.
ARCHBISHOP
And so no doubt he is, my gracious madam.
DUCHESS
I hope he is, but yet let mothers doubt.
YORK
Now, by my troth, if I had been remembered,   23
I could have given my uncle's Grace a flout   24
To touch his growth nearer than he touched mine.   25
DUCHESS
How, my young York? I prithee, let me hear it.
YORK
Marry, they say my uncle grew so fast
That he could gnaw a crust at two hours old;
'Twas full two years ere I could get a tooth.
Grandam, this would have been a biting jest.   30
DUCHESS
I prithee, pretty York, who told thee this?
YORK   Grandam, his nurse.
DUCHESS
His nurse? Why, she was dead ere thou wast born.
YORK
If 'twere not she, I cannot tell who told me.

QUEEN ELIZABETH
A parlous boy! Go to, you are too shrewd.   35
DUCHESS
Good madam, be not angry with the child.
QUEEN ELIZABETH   Pitchers have ears.   37

                Enter a Messenger.

ARCHBISHOP
Here comes a messenger. What news?
MESSENGER
Such news, my lord, as grieves me to report.
QUEEN ELIZABETH
How doth the Prince?
MESSENGER   Well, madam, and in health.
DUCHESS   What is thy news?
MESSENGER
Lord Rivers and Lord Grey are sent to Pomfret,   42
And with them Sir Thomas Vaughan, prisoners.
DUCHESS
Who hath committed them?
MESSENGER   The mighty dukes
Gloucester and Buckingham.
ARCHBISHOP   For what offense?
MESSENGER
The sum of all I can, I have disclosed.   46
Why or for what the nobles were committed
Is all unknown to me, my gracious lord.
QUEEN ELIZABETH
Ay me, I see the ruin of my house!
The tiger now hath seized the gentle hind;   50
Insulting tyranny begins to jut   51
Upon the innocent and aweless throne.   52
Welcome, destruction, blood, and massacre!
I see, as in a map, the end of all.   54
DUCHESS
Accursèd and unquiet wrangling days,
How many of you have mine eyes beheld!
My husband lost his life to get the crown,
And often up and down my sons were tossed   58
For me to joy and weep their gain and loss;
And being seated, and domestic broils   60
Clean overblown, themselves the conquerors
Make war upon themselves, brother to brother,
Blood to blood, self against self. O preposterous   63
And frantic outrage, end thy damnèd spleen,   64
Or let me die, to look on death no more!
QUEEN ELIZABETH
Come, come, my boy, we will to sanctuary.   66
Madam, farewell.
DUCHESS   Stay, I will go with you.

---

2 **Northampton** town in Northamptonshire and hence farther from
London than Stony Stratford. The Prince was taken back to Northampton after the arrest of Rivers, Grey, and Vaughan. The Archbishop
does not yet know of that arrest, but the Folio version of his speech,
followed here, is based misleadingly on historical information of subsequent events. (The quartos reverse the order in which the two towns
are named.) **13 grace** virtuous qualities. **apace** rapidly **14 since**
ever since **16 hold** pertain **17 In him** i.e., in Richard. **object . . .
to** i.e., apply this saying to **23 troth** truth, faith. **been remembered** considered, recollected **24 my . . . flout** His Grace, my uncle, a mocking gibe **25 touch . . . nearer** i.e., taunt him about his
growth more tellingly **30 biting** (With a play on the idea of teething.)

35 **parlous** cunning, precocious. **Go to** (An expression of remonstrance.) **shrewd** sharp-tongued **37 Pitchers have ears** i.e., little
pitchers have large ears. (Proverbial.) **42 Pomfret** the castle at Pontefract in Yorkshire **46 can** know **50 hind** doe **51 Insulting** scornfully triumphing. **jut** encroach **52 aweless** inspiring no awe (because of the youth of the King) **54 map** i.e., of future events **58 up
. . . tossed** i.e., my sons were raised and then lowered on fortune's
wheel **60 seated** i.e., on the throne **63 preposterous** monstrous,
perverse **64 spleen** i.e., malice, hatred **66 sanctuary** (Queen Elizabeth, with her son, daughters, and kinsmen, lodged in the precincts
of Westminster Abbey, which served as a legal refuge for criminals
and persons in danger of their lives.)

QUEEN ELIZABETH
You have no cause.
ARCHBISHOP [*to the Queen*]   My gracious lady, go,
And thither bear your treasure and your goods.
For my part, I'll resign unto Your Grace
The seal I keep; and so betide to me   71
As well I tender you and all of yours!   72
Go, I'll conduct you to the sanctuary.   *Exeunt.*

❧

3.1   *The trumpets sound. Enter [the] young Prince*
[Edward], the Dukes of Gloucester and
Buckingham, [Lord] Cardinal [Bourchier, Catesby],
etc.

BUCKINGHAM
Welcome, sweet Prince, to London, to your
    chamber.   1
RICHARD
Welcome, dear cousin, my thoughts' sovereign!
The weary way hath made you melancholy.
PRINCE EDWARD
No, uncle, but our crosses on the way   4
Have made it tedious, wearisome, and heavy.
I want more uncles here to welcome me.   6
RICHARD
Sweet Prince, the untainted virtue of your years
Hath not yet dived into the world's deceit.
Nor more can you distinguish of a man
Than of his outward show—which, God he knows,
Seldom or never jumpeth with the heart.   11
Those uncles which you want were dangerous.
Your Grace attended to their sugared words
But looked not on the poison of their hearts.
God keep you from them, and from such false
    friends!
PRINCE EDWARD
God keep me from false friends! But they were
    none.
RICHARD
My lord, the Mayor of London comes to greet you.

Enter [the] Lord Mayor [and his train].

MAYOR
God bless Your Grace with health and happy days!
PRINCE EDWARD
I thank you, good my lord, and thank you all.
                [The Mayor and his train stand aside.]
I thought my mother and my brother York
Would long ere this have met us on the way.

Fie, what a slug is Hastings, that he comes not   22
To tell us whether they will come or no!

Enter Lord Hastings.

BUCKINGHAM
And, in good time, here comes the sweating lord.
PRINCE EDWARD
Welcome, my lord. What, will our mother come?
HASTINGS
On what occasion God he knows, not I,   26
The Queen your mother and your brother York
Have taken sanctuary. The tender Prince
Would fain have come with me to meet Your Grace,
But by his mother was perforce withheld.   30
BUCKINGHAM
Fie, what an indirect and peevish course   31
Is this of hers! Lord Cardinal, will Your Grace
Persuade the Queen to send the Duke of York
Unto his princely brother presently?   34
If she deny, Lord Hastings, go with him,
And from her jealous arms pluck him perforce.   36
CARDINAL
My lord of Buckingham, if my weak oratory
Can from his mother win the Duke of York,
Anon expect him here; but if she be obdurate   39
To mild entreaties, God in heaven forbid
We should infringe the holy privilege
Of blessèd sanctuary! Not for all this land
Would I be guilty of so deep a sin.
BUCKINGHAM
You are too senseless-obstinate, my lord,
Too ceremonious and traditional.   45
Weigh it but with the grossness of this age,   46
You break not sanctuary in seizing him.
The benefit thereof is always granted
To those whose dealings have deserved the place
And those who have the wit to claim the place.
This Prince hath neither claimed it nor deserved it,
And therefore, in mine opinion, cannot have it.
Then, taking him from thence that is not there,   53
You break no privilege nor charter there.
Oft have I heard of sanctuary men,
But sanctuary children never till now.
CARDINAL
My lord, you shall o'errule my mind for once.
Come on, Lord Hastings, will you go with me?
HASTINGS   I go, my lord.
PRINCE EDWARD
Good lords, make all the speedy haste you may.
                [Exeunt Cardinal and Hastings.]
Say, uncle Gloucester, if our brother come,
Where shall we sojourn till our coronation?   62
RICHARD
Where it seems best unto your royal self.

---

71 seal seal of office i.e., the Great Seal of England. (The Archbishop's giving the Great Seal to Elizabeth is an unusual and extra-legal action.)   **71–72 so . . . you** may my fortunes be measured by the care I take of you
3.1. Location: London. A street.
1 chamber (London was called the *camera regis*, or King's chamber.)
4 crosses vexations (i.e., the arrests of the Queen's kindred)   **6 want** (1) lack (2) wish   **11 jumpeth** agrees

22 slug sluggard   **26 On what occasion** for what reason   **30 perforce** by force   **31 peevish** perverse   **34 presently** at once   **36 jealous** suspicious   **39 Anon** shortly   **45 ceremonious** bound by formalities   **46 grossness** lack of moral refinement   **53 taking . . . there** i.e., taking the Prince from a place that cannot properly be called a sanctuary in his case   **62 sojourn** reside

If I may counsel you, some day or two
Your Highness shall repose you at the Tower;   65
Then where you please, and shall be thought
    most fit
For your best health and recreation.

PRINCE EDWARD
I do not like the Tower, of any place.   68
Did Julius Caesar build that place, my lord?

BUCKINGHAM
He did, my gracious lord, begin that place,
Which, since, succeeding ages have re-edified.   71

PRINCE EDWARD
Is it upon record, or else reported   72
Successively from age to age, he built it?

BUCKINGHAM   Upon record, my gracious lord.

PRINCE EDWARD
But say, my lord, it were not registered,   75
Methinks the truth should live from age to age,
As 'twere retailed to all posterity,   77
Even to the general all-ending day.   78

RICHARD [aside]
So wise so young, they say, do never live long.

PRINCE EDWARD   What say you, uncle?

RICHARD
I say, without characters fame lives long.   81
[Aside.] Thus, like the formal Vice, Iniquity,   82
I moralize two meanings in one word.   83

PRINCE EDWARD
That Julius Caesar was a famous man;
With what his valor did enrich his wit,   85
His wit set down to make his valor live.   86
Death makes no conquest of this conqueror,
For now he lives in fame, though not in life.
I'll tell you what, my cousin Buckingham—

BUCKINGHAM   What, my gracious lord?

PRINCE EDWARD
An if I live until I be a man,   91
I'll win our ancient right in France again
Or die a soldier, as I lived a king.

RICHARD [aside]
Short summers lightly have a forward spring.   94

Enter young York, Hastings, [and the] Cardinal.

BUCKINGHAM
Now, in good time, here comes the Duke of York.

PRINCE EDWARD
Richard of York, how fares our loving brother?   96

YORK
Well, my dread lord—so must I call you now.   97

PRINCE EDWARD
Ay, brother, to our grief, as it is yours.
Too late he died that might have kept that title, 99
Which by his death hath lost much majesty.

RICHARD
How fares our cousin, noble lord of York?

YORK
I thank you, gentle uncle. O my lord,
You said that idle weeds are fast in growth;   103
The Prince my brother hath outgrown me far.

RICHARD
He hath, my lord.

YORK   And therefore is he idle?

RICHARD
O my fair cousin, I must not say so.

YORK
Then he is more beholding to you than I.   107

RICHARD
He may command me as my sovereign,
But you have power in me as in a kinsman.

YORK
I pray you, uncle, give me this dagger.

RICHARD
My dagger, little cousin? With all my heart.   111

PRINCE EDWARD   A beggar, brother?

YORK
Of my kind uncle, that I know will give;   113
And being but a toy, which is no grief to give. 114

RICHARD
A greater gift than that I'll give my cousin.

YORK
A greater gift? O, that's the sword to it.

RICHARD
Ay, gentle cousin, were it light enough.

YORK
O, then I see you will part but with light gifts. 118
In weightier things you'll say a beggar nay.

RICHARD
It is too heavy for Your Grace to wear.

YORK
I weigh it lightly, were it heavier.   121

RICHARD
What, would you have my weapon, little lord?

YORK
I would, that I might thank you as you call me.

RICHARD   How?

YORK   Little.   125

---

65 **Tower** (Although in the fifteenth century—the historical time this play represents—the Tower of London was a royal palace, by Shakespeare's day it had acquired a sinister reputation.)   68 **of any place** of all places   71 **re-edified** rebuilt   72 **upon record** in the written record.   **reported** i.e., by oral tradition   75 **say** suppose.   **registered** written down   77 **retailed** repeated, handed down from one to another   78 **general . . . day** Day of Judgment   81 **without characters** even lacking written records   82 **formal Vice** i.e., the conventional Vice figure of the morality play, a comic tempter to evil, who would habitually *moralize two meanings in one word,* that is, play on double meanings in a single phrase, as Richard does in the phrase *live long*   83 **moralize** interpret, discover   85–86 **With . . . live** i.e., taking his military achievements, whereby his bravery as a soldier added stature to his understanding, he used his understanding to set down in writing an account (the *Gallic Wars*) that would make his valor immortal.   **With what** with that with which   91 **An if** if   94 **lightly** commonly, often.   **forward** early. (Alludes to Edward's precociousness.)

96 **our** i.e., my. (The royal "we.")   97 **dread** inspiring reverential fear (as King)   99 **late** lately   103 **idle** useless   107 **beholding** beholden   111 **With . . . heart** willingly. (Richard combines in one phrase an overt generosity and a hidden threat.)   113 **that** who   114 **toy** trifle   118 **light** trivial   121 **I weigh . . . heavier** I consider it a trifle (playing on the literal meanings of "light" and "heavy") and would do so even if it were heavier   125 **Little** (York saucily suggests that he would give little thanks for such a "light" gift.)

PRINCE EDWARD
My lord of York will still be cross in talk.   126
Uncle, Your Grace knows how to bear with him.
YORK
You mean, to bear me, not to bear with me.
Uncle, my brother mocks both you and me:
Because that I am little, like an ape,
He thinks that you should bear me on your
    shoulders.   131
BUCKINGHAM [aside to Hastings]
With what a sharp-provided wit he reasons!   132
To mitigate the scorn he gives his uncle,
He prettily and aptly taunts himself.
So cunning and so young is wonderful.
RICHARD [to the Prince]
My lord, will 't please you pass along?
Myself and my good cousin Buckingham
Will to your mother, to entreat of her
To meet you at the Tower and welcome you.
YORK [to the Prince]
What, will you go unto the Tower, my lord?
PRINCE EDWARD
My Lord Protector needs will have it so.
YORK
I shall not sleep in quiet at the Tower.
RICHARD   Why, what should you fear?
YORK
Marry, my uncle Clarence' angry ghost.
My grandam told me he was murdered there.
PRINCE EDWARD   I fear no uncles dead.
RICHARD   Nor none that live, I hope.
PRINCE EDWARD
An if they live, I hope I need not fear.   148
But come, my lord; with a heavy heart,
Thinking on them, go I unto the Tower.   150
          [A sennet.] Exeunt Prince, York, Hastings,
                    [Cardinal, and others]. Manent
                    Richard, Buckingham, [and Catesby].
BUCKINGHAM
Think you, my lord, this little prating York   151
Was not incensèd by his subtle mother   152
To taunt and scorn you thus opprobriously?
RICHARD
No doubt, no doubt. O, 'tis a parlous boy,   154
Bold, quick, ingenious, forward, capable.
He is all the mother's, from the top to toe.
BUCKINGHAM
Well, let them rest.—Come hither, Catesby.   157
Thou art sworn as deeply to effect what we intend
As closely to conceal what we impart.

Thou know'st our reasons urged upon the way.   160
What think'st thou? Is it not an easy matter
To make William Lord Hastings of our mind
For the installment of this noble Duke   163
In the seat royal of this famous isle?
CATESBY
He for his father's sake so loves the Prince   165
That he will not be won to aught against him.
BUCKINGHAM
What think'st thou, then, of Stanley? Will not he?
CATESBY
He will do all in all as Hastings doth.
BUCKINGHAM
Well, then, no more but this: go, gentle Catesby,
And, as it were far off, sound thou Lord Hastings   170
How he doth stand affected to our purpose,   171
And summon him tomorrow to the Tower
To sit about the coronation.   173
If thou dost find him tractable to us,
Encourage him, and tell him all our reasons.
If he be leaden, icy, cold, unwilling,
Be thou so too; and so break off the talk,
And give us notice of his inclination.
For we tomorrow hold divided councils,   179
Wherein thyself shalt highly be employed.
RICHARD
Commend me to Lord William. Tell him, Catesby,   181
His ancient knot of dangerous adversaries   182
Tomorrow are let blood at Pomfret Castle;   183
And bid my lord, for joy of this good news,
Give Mistress Shore one gentle kiss the more.   185
BUCKINGHAM
Good Catesby, go, effect this business soundly.   186
CATESBY
My good lords both, with all the heed I can.   187
RICHARD
Shall we hear from you, Catesby, ere we sleep?
CATESBY   You shall, my lord.
RICHARD
At Crosby House, there shall you find us both.
          Exit Catesby.
BUCKINGHAM
Now, my lord, what shall we do if we perceive
Lord Hastings will not yield to our complots?   192
RICHARD
Chop off his head. Something we will determine.
And look when I am king, claim thou of me   194
The earldom of Hereford and all the movables   195
Whereof the King my brother was possessed.

126 **still** always.   **cross in talk** perverse in twisting words   131 **bear me . . . shoulders** (At fairs, the bear commonly carried an ape on his back. The speech is doubtless an allusion to Richard's hump and puns triply on *bear with*, "put up with," *bear*, "carry," and *bear*, "an animal.")   132 **sharp-provided** nimble and ready   148 **An if** if.   **they** i.e., Rivers and Grey. (Grey was, in fact, Edward's stepbrother, not his uncle. See the note to 1.3.37.)   150 **s.d. sennet** trumpet call to announce the approach or departure of processions.   **Manent** they remain onstage   151 **prating** babbling   152 **incensèd** incited   154 **parlous** clever, but also dangerous   157 **let them rest** leave them for the moment

160 **the way** i.e., the journey to London from Ludlow   163 **installment** installation   165 **He . . . sake** i.e., Hastings for King Edward IV's sake   170 **sound** sound out   171 **doth stand affected** is disposed   173 **sit** sit in council   179 **divided councils** (While the regular Council meets about the coronation, Richard plans also to have his own private consultation at Crosby House.)   181 **Lord William** i.e., Hastings   182 **knot** group, company   183 **are let blood** will be bled, i.e., executed   185 **Mistress Shore** (According to Thomas More, Jane Shore had become the mistress of Hastings after the death of Edward IV.)   186 **soundly** thoroughly   187 **heed** attention, care   192 **complots** conspiracies   194 **look when** as soon as   195 **movables** personal property, other than real estate

BUCKINGHAM
I'll claim that promise at Your Grace's hand.
RICHARD
And look to have it yielded with all kindness.
Come, let us sup betimes, that afterwards   199
We may digest our complots in some form.   *Exeunt.*   200

❖

3.2   *Enter a Messenger to the door of Hastings.*

MESSENGER   My lord! My lord!
HASTINGS [*within*]   Who knocks?
MESSENGER   One from the Lord Stanley.
HASTINGS [*within*]   What is 't o'clock?   4
MESSENGER   Upon the stroke of four.

Enter Lord Hastings.

HASTINGS
Cannot my Lord Stanley sleep these tedious nights?
MESSENGER
So it appears by that I have to say.
First, he commends him to your noble self.
HASTINGS   What then?
MESSENGER
Then certifies your lordship that this night   10
He dreamt the boar had razèd off his helm.   11
Besides, he says there are two councils kept,
And that may be determined at the one
Which may make you and him to rue at th' other.   14
Therefore he sends to know your lordship's
    pleasure,
If you will presently take horse with him   16
And with all speed post with him toward the north,
To shun the danger that his soul divines.
HASTINGS
Go, fellow, go, return unto thy lord.
Bid him not fear the separated councils.
His honor and myself are at the one,   21
And at the other is my good friend Catesby,
Where nothing can proceed that toucheth us
Whereof I shall not have intelligence.   24
Tell him his fears are shallow, without instance.   25
And for his dreams, I wonder he's so simple
To trust the mockery of unquiet slumbers.   27
To fly the boar before the boar pursues   28
Were to incense the boar to follow us,
And make pursuit where he did mean no chase.
Go, bid thy master rise and come to me,
And we will both together to the Tower,
Where he shall see the boar will use us kindly.

MESSENGER
I'll go, my lord, and tell him what you say.   *Exit.*

Enter Catesby.

CATESBY
Many good morrows to my noble lord!
HASTINGS
Good morrow, Catesby. You are early stirring.
What news, what news, in this our tottering state?
CATESBY
It is a reeling world, indeed, my lord,
And I believe will never stand upright
Till Richard wear the garland of the realm.
HASTINGS
How? Wear the garland? Dost thou mean the
    crown?
CATESBY   Ay, my good lord.
HASTINGS
I'll have this crown of mine cut from my shoulders   43
Before I'll see the crown so foul misplaced.
But canst thou guess that he doth aim at it?
CATESBY
Ay, on my life, and hopes to find you forward   46
Upon his party for the gain thereof;   47
And thereupon he sends you this good news,
That this same very day your enemies,
The kindred of the Queen, must die at Pomfret.
HASTINGS
Indeed, I am no mourner for that news,
Because they have been still my adversaries.   52
But that I'll give my voice on Richard's side
To bar my master's heirs in true descent,
God knows I will not do it, to the death.   55
CATESBY
God keep your lordship in that gracious mind!
HASTINGS
But I shall laugh at this a twelvemonth hence,
That they which brought me in my master's hate,   58
I live to look upon their tragedy.   59
Well, Catesby, ere a fortnight make me older,
I'll send some packing that yet think not on 't.
CATESBY
'Tis a vile thing to die, my gracious lord,
When men are unprepared and look not for it.
HASTINGS
O, monstrous, monstrous! And so falls it out   64
With Rivers, Vaughan, Grey; and so 'twill do
With some men else, that think themselves as safe
As thou and I—who, as thou know'st, are dear
To princely Richard and to Buckingham.
CATESBY
The princes both make high account of you—   69

---

199 **betimes** soon   200 **digest** arrange, perfect.   **form** good order
3.2. Location: Before Lord Hastings' house.
4 What is 't o'clock what time is it   **10 certifies** informs   **11 boar**
i.e., Richard.   **razèd** torn, slashed   **14 th' other** i.e., the regular
Council meeting in the Tower, in which Hastings and Stanley will
participate   **16 presently** immediately   **21 His honor** Lord Stanley
24 intelligence information   **25 without instance** lacking evidence
27 To as to   **28 fly** flee

43 crown i.e., head. (Recalls Stanley's dream in line 11 and anticipates Hastings' execution by beheading.)   **46 forward** inclined
47 Upon his party on his side   **52 still** always   **55 to the death** i.e.,
though I lose my life. (A common asseveration, but here with ironic
meaning.)   **58–59 That . . . tragedy** that I will live to see the fatal
end of those who brought me out of favor with King Edward IV
64 so . . . out so it has happened   **69 high account** great estimation.
(The quibble on *high* appears in the next line.)

[*Aside.*] For they account his head upon the Bridge.   70
HASTINGS
  I know they do, and I have well deserved it.

      Enter Lord Stanley [Earl of Derby].

  Come on, come on, where is your boar spear, man?
  Fear you the boar, and go so unprovided?
STANLEY
  My lord, good morrow. Good morrow, Catesby.
  You may jest on, but, by the Holy Rood,   75
  I do not like these several councils, I.   76
HASTINGS   My lord,
  I hold my life as dear as you do yours,
  And never in my days, I do protest,
  Was it so precious to me as 'tis now.
  Think you, but that I know our state secure,
  I would be so triumphant as I am?
STANLEY
  The lords at Pomfret, when they rode from London,   83
  Were jocund and supposed their states were sure,   84
  And they indeed had no cause to mistrust;
  But yet you see how soon the day o'ercast.   86
  This sudden stab of rancor I misdoubt.   87
  Pray God, I say, I prove a needless coward!
  What, shall we toward the Tower? The day is spent. 89
HASTINGS
  Come, come, have with you. Wot you what, my
    lord?   90
  Today the lords you talk of are beheaded.
STANLEY
  They, for their truth, might better wear their heads   92
  Than some that have accused them wear their hats.   93
  But come, my lord, let's away.   94

      Enter a Pursuivant.

HASTINGS
  Go on before. I'll talk with this good fellow.
      Exit Lord Stanley [Earl of Derby] and Catesby.
  How now, sirrah? How goes the world with thee?   96
PURSUIVANT
  The better that your lordship please to ask.
HASTINGS
  I tell thee, man, 'tis better with me now
  Than when thou mett'st me last where now we
    meet.
  Then was I going prisoner to the Tower,
  By the suggestion of the Queen's allies;   101
  But now, I tell thee—keep it to thyself—
  This day those enemies are put to death,
  And I in better state than e'er I was.

---

70 **account** expect, reckon (punning on *account* in the previous line).
the Bridge London Bridge, on a tower of which the heads of traitors
were exposed   75 **Rood** cross   76 **several** separate   83 **London** (An
error for "Ludlow"?)   84 **jocund** merry   86 **o'ercast** became overcast
87 **This . . . misdoubt** i.e., I fear more such sudden attacks
89 **spent** i.e., well advanced (although the scene began at 4:00 A.M.)
90 **have with you** I'll go with you.   **Wot** know   92 **for their truth**
as far as their honesty is concerned.   **better** more justly   93 **wear**
their hats i.e., hold their offices   94 **s.d. Pursuivant** attendant on a
herald with authority to serve warrants   96 **sirrah** (Form of address to
inferiors.)   101 **suggestion** instigation

PURSUIVANT
  God hold it, to your honor's good content!   105
HASTINGS
  Gramercy, fellow. There, drink that for me.   106
                              Throws him his purse.
PURSUIVANT   I thank your honor.   *Exit Pursuivant.*

      Enter a Priest.

PRIEST
  Well met, my lord. I am glad to see your honor.
HASTINGS
  I thank thee, good Sir John, with all my heart.   109
  I am in your debt for your last exercise;   110
  Come the next Sabbath, and I will content you.   111
                              [*He whispers in his ear.*]
PRIEST   I'll wait upon your lordship.

      Enter Buckingham.

BUCKINGHAM
  What, talking with a priest, Lord Chamberlain?
  Your friends at Pomfret, they do need the priest;
  Your honor hath no shriving work in hand.   115
HASTINGS
  Good faith, and when I met this holy man,
  The men you talk of came into my mind.
  What, go you toward the Tower?
BUCKINGHAM
  I do, my lord, but long I cannot stay there.
  I shall return before your lordship thence.
HASTINGS
  Nay, like enough, for I stay dinner there.   121
BUCKINGHAM [*aside*]
  And supper too, although thou know'st it not.—
  Come, will you go?
HASTINGS   I'll wait upon your lordship.
                                          Exeunt.

❖

3.3   *Enter Sir Richard Ratcliffe, with Halberds, carrying
          the nobles [Rivers, Grey, and Vaughan] to death
          at Pomfret.*

RATCLIFFE   Come, bring forth the prisoners.
RIVERS
  Sir Richard Ratcliffe, let me tell thee this:
  Today shalt thou behold a subject die
  For truth, for duty, and for loyalty.
GREY
  God bless the Prince from all the pack of you!   5
  A knot you are of damnèd bloodsuckers.   6
VAUGHAN
  You live that shall cry woe for this hereafter.

---

105 **hold it** continue it (i.e., the better state)   106 **Gramercy** much
thanks   109 **Sir** (Common title for addressing any priest.)   110 **exer-**
cise sermon or devotional exercise   111 **content** compensate
115 **shriving work** confession and absolution   121 **stay** stay for
3.3. Location: Pomfret (Pontefract) Castle.
5 **pack** gang   6 **knot** group

RATCLIFFE
    Dispatch. The limit of your lives is out.   8
RIVERS
    O Pomfret, Pomfret! O thou bloody prison,
    Fatal and ominous to noble peers!
    Within the guilty closure of thy walls   11
    Richard the Second here was hacked to death;
    And, for more slander to thy dismal seat,   13
    We give to thee our guiltless blood to drink.
GREY
    Now Margaret's curse is fall'n upon our heads,
    When she exclaimed on Hastings, you, and I,
    For standing by when Richard stabbed her son.
RIVERS
    Then cursed she Richard, then cursed she
        Buckingham,
    Then cursed she Hastings. O, remember, God,
    To hear her prayer for them, as now for us!
    And for my sister and her princely sons,
    Be satisfied, dear God, with our true blood,
    Which, as thou know'st, unjustly must be spilt.
RATCLIFFE
    Make haste. The hour of death is expiate.   24
RIVERS
    Come, Grey, come, Vaughan, let us here embrace.
                                    [*They embrace.*]
    Farewell, until we meet again in heaven.   *Exeunt.*

❧

3.4   *Enter Buckingham, [Lord Stanley Earl of] Derby,
        Hastings, Bishop of Ely, Norfolk, Ratcliffe, Lovell,
        with others, at a table.*

HASTINGS
    Now, noble peers, the cause why we are met
    Is to determine of the coronation.   2
    In God's name, speak. When is the royal day?
BUCKINGHAM
    Is all things ready for the royal time?
STANLEY
    It is, and wants but nomination.   5
ELY
    Tomorrow, then, I judge a happy day.   6
BUCKINGHAM
    Who knows the Lord Protector's mind herein?
    Who is most inward with the noble Duke?   8
ELY
    Your Grace, methinks, should soonest know his
        mind.
BUCKINGHAM
    We know each other's faces; for our hearts,   10
    He knows no more of mine than I of yours,

    Or I of his, my lord, than you of mine.
    Lord Hastings, you and he are near in love.
HASTINGS
    I thank His Grace, I know he loves me well;
    But, for his purpose in the coronation,
    I have not sounded him, nor he delivered
    His gracious pleasure any way therein.
    But you, my honorable lords, may name the time,
    And in the Duke's behalf I'll give my voice,   19
    Which I presume he'll take in gentle part.   20

            Enter [Richard Duke of] Gloucester.

ELY
    In happy time, here comes the Duke himself.
RICHARD
    My noble lords and cousins all, good morrow.   22
    I have been long a sleeper; but I trust
    My absence doth neglect no great design   24
    Which by my presence might have been concluded.
BUCKINGHAM
    Had you not come upon your cue, my lord,
    William Lord Hastings had pronounced your part,
    I mean your voice for crowning of the King.
RICHARD
    Than my Lord Hastings no man might be bolder.
    His lordship knows me well, and loves me well.—
    My lord of Ely, when I was last in Holborn,   31
    I saw good strawberries in your garden there.
    I do beseech you send for some of them.
ELY
    Marry, and will, my lord, with all my heart.
                                    Exit Bishop.
RICHARD
    Cousin of Buckingham, a word with you.
                                    [*Drawing him aside.*]
    Catesby hath sounded Hastings in our business,
    And finds the testy gentleman so hot
    That he will lose his head ere give consent
    His master's child, as worshipfully he terms it,   39
    Shall lose the royalty of England's throne.
BUCKINGHAM
    Withdraw yourself awhile. I'll go with you.
                                    Exeunt [Richard and Buckingham].
STANLEY
    We have not yet set down this day of triumph.
    Tomorrow, in my judgment, is too sudden,
    For I myself am not so well provided   44
    As else I would be, were the day prolonged.   45

            Enter the Bishop of Ely.

ELY
    Where is my lord the Duke of Gloucester?
    I have sent for these strawberries.
HASTINGS
    His Grace looks cheerfully and smooth this morning;   48

---

8 Dispatch hurry.   **is out** has been reached   **11 closure** enclosure
13 for . . . seat i.e., to add further to the evil reputation of this place
24 expiate fully come
3.4. Location: London. The Tower.
2 determine of decide upon   **5 nomination** naming of a date
6 happy favorable   **8 inward** intimate   **10 for** as for

19 voice vote   **20 in gentle part** with gracious approval   **22 cousins**
i.e., peers   **24 neglect** cause the neglect of   **31 Holborn** (location of
the Bishop's London palace)   **39 worshipfully** reverently. (Said contemptuously.)   **44 provided** equipped   **45 prolonged** postponed
48 smooth pleasant

There's some conceit or other likes him well   49
When that he bids good morrow with such spirit.
I think there's never a man in Christendom
Can lesser hide his love or hate than he,
For by his face straight shall you know his heart.

STANLEY
What of his heart perceive you in his face
By any likelihood he showed today?

HASTINGS
Marry, that with no man here he is offended;
For, were he, he had shown it in his looks.

STANLEY   I pray God he be not, I say.

Enter Richard and Buckingham.

RICHARD
I pray you all, tell me what they deserve
That do conspire my death with devilish plots
Of damnèd witchcraft, and that have prevailed
Upon my body with their hellish charms?

HASTINGS
The tender love I bear Your Grace, my lord,   63
Makes me most forward in this princely presence
To doom th' offenders, whosoe'er they be:
I say, my lord, they have deservèd death.

RICHARD
Then be your eyes the witness of their evil.
    [*He bares his arm.*]
Look how I am bewitched! Behold, mine arm
Is like a blasted sapling withered up.   69
And this is Edward's wife, that monstrous witch,
Consorted with that harlot strumpet Shore,   71
That by their witchcraft thus have markèd me.

HASTINGS
If they have done this deed, my noble lord—

RICHARD
If? Thou protector of this damnèd strumpet,
Talk'st thou to me of "ifs"? Thou art a traitor.
Off with his head! Now, by Saint Paul I swear,
I will not dine until I see the same.
Lovell and Ratcliffe, look that it be done.   78
The rest that love me, rise and follow me.   79
    Exeunt. Manent Lovell and Ratcliffe,
    with the Lord Hastings.

HASTINGS
Woe, woe for England! Not a whit for me,
For I, too fond, might have prevented this.   81
Stanley did dream the boar did raze our helms,
And I did scorn it and disdain to fly.
Three times today my footcloth horse did stumble,   84
And started, when he looked upon the Tower,
As loath to bear me to the slaughterhouse.
O, now I need the priest that spake to me!
I now repent I told the pursuivant,
As too triumphing, how mine enemies
Today at Pomfret bloodily were butchered,

And I myself secure in grace and favor.
O Margaret, Margaret, now thy heavy curse
Is lighted on poor Hastings' wretched head!

RATCLIFFE
Come, come, dispatch. The Duke would be at
    dinner.
Make a short shrift. He longs to see your head.   95

HASTINGS
O momentary grace of mortal men,   96
Which we more hunt for than the grace of God!
Who builds his hope in air of your good looks   98
Lives like a drunken sailor on a mast,
Ready with every nod to tumble down
Into the fatal bowels of the deep.

LOVELL
Come, come, dispatch. 'Tis bootless to exclaim.   102

HASTINGS
O bloody Richard! Miserable England!
I prophesy the fearfull'st time to thee
That ever wretched age hath looked upon.
Come, lead me to the block; bear him my head.
They smile at me who shortly shall be dead.
    Exeunt.

3.5   *Enter Richard [Duke of Gloucester] and*
    Buckingham in rotten armor, marvelous
    ill-favored.

RICHARD
Come, cousin, canst thou quake and change thy
    color,
Murder thy breath in middle of a word,   2
And then again begin, and stop again,
As if thou wert distraught and mad with terror?

BUCKINGHAM
Tut, I can counterfeit the deep tragedian,
Speak and look back, and pry on every side,   6
Tremble and start at wagging of a straw;
Intending deep suspicion, ghastly looks   8
Are at my service, like enforcèd smiles;
And both are ready in their offices,   10
At any time, to grace my stratagems.
But what, is Catesby gone?

RICHARD
He is; and, see, he brings the Mayor along.

Enter the Mayor and Catesby.

BUCKINGHAM   Lord Mayor—
RICHARD   Look to the drawbridge there!
BUCKINGHAM   Hark, a drum!
RICHARD   Catesby, o'erlook the walls.   [*Exit Catesby.*]   17

---

49 conceit fancy, idea. **likes** pleases   **63 tender** dear   **69 blasted** shriveled   **71 Consorted** associated   **78 look** see to it   **79 s.d. Manent** they remain onstage   **81 fond** foolish   **84 footcloth** large, richly ornamented cloth laid over the back of a horse and hanging to the ground on each side.   **stumble** (An omen of misfortune.)

95 shrift confession   **96 grace** favor, fortune   **98 Who** he who.   **in . . . looks** on the insubstantial foundation of your favor   **102 bootless** useless
3.5. Location: London. The Tower.
s.d. rotten rusty.   **marvelous ill-favored** remarkably unattractive
2 Murder i.e., stop, catch   **6 back** over my shoulder.   **pry** peer
8 Intending pretending   **10 offices** uses, functions   **17 o'erlook** inspect

BUCKINGHAM
Lord Mayor, the reason we have sent—
RICHARD
Look back, defend thee, here are enemies!
BUCKINGHAM
God and our innocence defend and guard us!

Enter Lovell and Ratcliffe, with Hastings' head.

RICHARD
Be patient. They are friends, Ratcliffe and Lovell.
LOVELL
Here is the head of that ignoble traitor,
The dangerous and unsuspected Hastings.
RICHARD
So dear I loved the man that I must weep.
I took him for the plainest harmless creature
That breathed upon the earth a Christian,
Made him my book wherein my soul recorded   27
The history of all her secret thoughts.
So smooth he daubed his vice with show of virtue
That, his apparent open guilt omitted—   30
I mean, his conversation with Shore's wife—   31
He lived from all attainder of suspects.   32
BUCKINGHAM
Well, well, he was the covert'st sheltered traitor   33
That ever lived. Look ye, my Lord Mayor,
Would you imagine, or almost believe,   35
Were 't not that by great preservation   36
We live to tell it, that the subtle traitor
This day had plotted, in the Council House,
To murder me and my good lord of Gloucester?
MAYOR   Had he done so?   39
RICHARD
What, think you we are Turks or infidels?
Or that we would, against the form of law,
Proceed thus rashly in the villain's death,
But that the extreme peril of the case,
The peace of England, and our persons' safety,
Enforced us to this execution?
MAYOR
Now fair befall you! He deserved his death,   47
And your good graces both have well proceeded   48
To warn false traitors from the like attempts.
BUCKINGHAM
I never looked for better at his hands
After he once fell in with Mistress Shore.
Yet had we not determined he should die
Until your lordship came to see his end,
Which now the loving haste of these our friends,
Something against our meanings, have prevented;   55
Because, my lord, we would have had you heard   56
The traitor speak and timorously confess

The manner and the purpose of his treasons,
That you might well have signified the same
Unto the citizens, who haply may   60
Misconster us in him and wail his death.   61
MAYOR
But, my good lord, Your Grace's words shall serve
As well as I had seen and heard him speak.   63
And do not doubt, right noble princes both,
But I'll acquaint our duteous citizens
With all your just proceedings in this cause.
RICHARD
And to that end we wished your lordship here,
T' avoid the censures of the carping world.
BUCKINGHAM
Which, since you come too late of our intent,   69
Yet witness what you hear we did intend.   70
And so, my good Lord Mayor, we bid farewell.

Exit Mayor.

RICHARD
Go, after, after, cousin Buckingham.
The Mayor towards Guildhall hies him in all post.   73
There, at your meet'st advantage of the time,   74
Infer the bastardy of Edward's children.   75
Tell them how Edward put to death a citizen
Only for saying he would make his son
Heir to the Crown—meaning indeed his house,   78
Which, by the sign thereof, was termèd so.
Moreover, urge his hateful luxury   80
And bestial appetite in change of lust,   81
Which stretched unto their servants, daughters,
    wives,   82
Even where his raging eye or savage heart,
Without control, lusted to make a prey.
Nay, for a need, thus far come near my person: 85
Tell them, when that my mother went with child   86
Of that insatiate Edward, noble York   87
My princely father then had wars in France,
And by true computation of the time
Found that the issue was not his begot—
Which well appearèd in his lineaments,   91
Being nothing like the noble Duke my father.
Yet touch this sparingly, as 'twere far off,
Because, my lord, you know my mother lives.
BUCKINGHAM
Doubt not, my lord, I'll play the orator
As if the golden fee for which I plead   96
Were for myself. And so, my lord, adieu.

---

27 **book** i.e., table book or diary   30 **his . . . omitted** apart from his manifest open guilt   31 **conversation** sexual intimacy   32 **from** free from.   **attainder of suspects** stain of suspicion   33 **covert'st** most secret.   **sheltered** most hidden   35 **almost** even   36 **great preservation** providential protection   39 **Had he** would he have   47 **fair** good fortune   48 **proceeded** done   55 **Something . . . meanings** somewhat contrary to our intent.   **have prevented** has anticipated   56 **we . . . heard** we would have wished you to have heard

60 **haply** perhaps   61 **Misconster . . . him** i.e., misconstrue our intentions regarding him   63 **as** as if   69 **of** regarding   70 **witness** bear witness to   73 **Guildhall** central hall for municipal affairs.   **hies** hastens.   **post** haste   74 **meet'st advantage** most suitable opportunity   75 **Infer** allege, adduce   78 **the Crown** i.e., a tavern in Cheapside identified by the sign of the Crown. (King Edward is portrayed as having been so sensitive to possible rivals that he put to death a man merely for naming his son heir to "the Crown," even though the poor fellow innocently meant nothing more than his own tavern. The story is from Sir Thomas More's *History of King Richard III*.)   80 **luxury** lechery   81 **in . . . lust** i.e., constantly desiring new mistresses   82 **their** i.e., the citizens'   85 **for a need** if necessary   86 **when that** when   86–87 **went . . . Of** was pregnant with   91 **lineaments** features   96 **golden fee** i.e., crown

RICHARD
If you thrive well, bring them to Baynard's Castle,   98
Where you shall find me well accompanied
With reverend fathers and well-learnèd bishops.
BUCKINGHAM
I go; and towards three or four o'clock
Look for the news that the Guildhall affords.
                                        Exit Buckingham.
RICHARD
Go, Lovell, with all speed to Doctor Shaw.   103
[*To Ratcliffe.*] Go thou to Friar Penker. Bid them both   104
Meet me within this hour at Baynard's Castle.
                              Exeunt [all but Richard].
Now will I go to take some privy order   106
To draw the brats of Clarence out of sight,
And to give order that no manner person   108
Have any time recourse unto the princes.   *Exit.* 109

3.6   *Enter a Scrivener [with a paper in his hand].*

SCRIVENER
Here is the indictment of the good Lord Hastings,
Which in a set hand fairly is engrossed   2
That it may be today read o'er in Paul's.   3
And mark how well the sequel hangs together: 4
Eleven hours I have spent to write it over,
For yesternight by Catesby was it sent me;
The precedent was full as long a-doing.   7
And yet within these five hours Hastings lived,
Untainted, unexamined, free, at liberty.   9
Here's a good world the while! Who is so gross   10
That cannot see this palpable device?
Yet who's so bold but says he sees it not?
Bad is the world, and all will come to naught
When such ill dealing must be seen in thought.   14
                                              Exit.

3.7   *Enter Richard [Duke of Gloucester] and*
          Buckingham, at several doors.

RICHARD
How now, how now, what say the citizens?
BUCKINGHAM
Now, by the holy mother of our Lord,

The citizens are mum, say not a word.
RICHARD
Touched you the bastardy of Edward's children?   4
BUCKINGHAM
I did; with his contract with Lady Lucy   5
And his contract by deputy in France;   6
Th' insatiate greediness of his desire   7
And his enforcement of the city wives;   8
His tyranny for trifles; his own bastardy,   9
As being got, your father then in France,   10
And his resemblance, being not like the Duke.
Withal I did infer your lineaments,   12
Being the right idea of your father   13
Both in your form and nobleness of mind;
Laid open all your victories in Scotland,   15
Your discipline in war, wisdom in peace,   16
Your bounty, virtue, fair humility;
Indeed, left nothing fitting for your purpose
Untouched or slightly handled in discourse.
And when mine oratory drew toward end,
I bid them that did love their country's good
Cry, "God save Richard, England's royal king!"
RICHARD   And did they so?
BUCKINGHAM
No, so God help me, they spake not a word,
But, like dumb statues or breathing stones,
Stared each on other and looked deadly pale.
Which when I saw, I reprehended them,
And asked the Mayor what meant this willful
    silence.
His answer was, the people were not used
To be spoke to but by the Recorder.   30
Then he was urged to tell my tale again:
"Thus saith the Duke, thus hath the Duke
    inferred"—   32
But nothing spake in warrant from himself.   33
When he had done, some followers of mine own,
At lower end of the hall, hurled up their caps,
And some ten voices cried, "God save King
    Richard!"
And thus I took the vantage of those few: 37
"Thanks, gentle citizens and friends," quoth I,
"This general applause and cheerful shout
Argues your wisdoms and your love to Richard"—
And even here brake off and came away.   41
RICHARD
What tongueless blocks were they! Would they not
    speak?

---

98 Baynard's Castle Richard's residence on the north bank of the Thames. It was founded by Baynard, a nobleman in the time of the Conquest, and had belonged to Richard's father.   **103, 104 Doctor Shaw, Friar Penker** (Well-known divines who delivered sermons in Richard's favor.)   **106 take . . . order** make some secret disposition **108 no manner person** no one at all   **109 any time** at any time.   **recourse** access, admittance
3.6. Location: London. A street.
2 in . . . engrossed is written out in a style of script used for legal documents   **3 Paul's** i.e., Saint Paul's Cathedral   **4 the sequel** what follows   **7 precedent** prepared indictment serving as a first draft
9 Untainted unaccused   **10 the while** meanwhile.   **gross** dull, stupid
14 seen in thought i.e., perceived in silence
3.7. Location: The courtyard of Baynard's Castle.
s.d. several separate

4 Touched you did you deal with, touch upon, discuss   **5 contract** betrothal.   **Lady Lucy** Elizabeth Lucy (by whom Edward had a child, though there was no formal contract of betrothal)   **6 deputy** (See *3 Henry VI,* 3.3.49 ff., where Warwick, as deputy, contracts with Louis XI of France for the marriage of King Edward to Lady Bona, sister of the French queen.)   **7 insatiate** insatiable   **8 enforcement** forcible seduction   **9 tyranny for trifles** harsh punishment of minor offenses, or cruel behavior over trifles   **10 got** begot   **12 Withal** in addition.   **infer** mention, relate.   **lineaments** features   **13 right idea** exact image **15 victories in Scotland** (Richard had commanded the English forces in the Scottish expedition of 1482.)   **16 discipline** skill, training
30 the Recorder a city official   **32 inferred** alleged, asserted   **33 in . . . himself** on his own authority   **37 vantage of** opportunity from **41 brake** broke

BUCKINGHAM   No, by my troth, my lord.

RICHARD
Will not the Mayor, then, and his brethren come?

BUCKINGHAM
The Mayor is here at hand. Intend some fear; 45
Be not you spoke with but by mighty suit. 46
And look you get a prayer book in your hand,
And stand between two churchmen, good my lord,
For on that ground I'll make a holy descant; 49
And be not easily won to our requests.
Play the maid's part: still answer nay and take it.

RICHARD
I go; and if you plead as well for them
As I can say nay to thee for myself,
No doubt we'll bring it to a happy issue. 54

BUCKINGHAM
Go, go, up to the leads. The Lord Mayor knocks. 55

[Exit Richard.]

Enter the Mayor, [aldermen,] and citizens.

Welcome, my lord. I dance attendance here; 56
I think the Duke will not be spoke withal. 57

Enter Catesby.

Now, Catesby, what says your lord to my request?

CATESBY
He doth entreat Your Grace, my noble lord,
To visit him tomorrow or next day.
He is within, with two right reverend fathers,
Divinely bent to meditation,
And in no worldly suits would he be moved
To draw him from his holy exercise.

BUCKINGHAM
Return, good Catesby, to the gracious Duke.
Tell him myself, the Mayor and aldermen,
In deep designs, in matter of great moment,
No less importing than our general good, 68
Are come to have some conference with His Grace.

CATESBY
I'll signify so much unto him straight.   *Exit.*

BUCKINGHAM
Aha, my lord, this prince is not an Edward!
He is not lolling on a lewd love bed
But on his knees at meditation;
Not dallying with a brace of courtesans 74
But meditating with two deep divines; 75
Not sleeping, to engross his idle body, 76
But praying, to enrich his watchful soul.
Happy were England, would this virtuous prince
Take on His Grace the sovereignty thereof;
But sure I fear we shall not win him to it.

MAYOR
Marry, God defend His Grace should say us nay! 81

BUCKINGHAM
I fear he will.—Here Catesby comes again.

Enter Catesby.

Now, Catesby, what says His Grace?

CATESBY   My lord,
He wonders to what end you have assembled
Such troops of citizens to come to him,
His Grace not being warned thereof before.
He fears, my lord, you mean no good to him.

BUCKINGHAM
Sorry I am my noble cousin should
Suspect me that I mean no good to him.
By heaven, we come to him in perfect love,
And so once more return and tell His Grace.

Exit [Catesby].

When holy and devout religious men
Are at their beads, 'tis much to draw them thence, 93
So sweet is zealous contemplation. 94

Enter Richard aloft, between two bishops. [Catesby returns to the main stage.]

MAYOR
See where His Grace stands, 'tween two clergymen!

BUCKINGHAM
Two props of virtue for a Christian prince,
To stay him from the fall of vanity. 97
And, see, a book of prayer in his hand,
True ornaments to know a holy man.— 99
Famous Plantagenet, most gracious prince,
Lend favorable ear to our requests,
And pardon us the interruption
Of thy devotion and right Christian zeal.

RICHARD
My lord, there needs no such apology.
I do beseech Your Grace to pardon me,
Who, earnest in the service of my God,
Deferred the visitation of my friends.
But, leaving this, what is Your Grace's pleasure?

BUCKINGHAM
Even that, I hope, which pleaseth God above,
And all good men of this ungoverned isle.

RICHARD
I do suspect I have done some offense
That seems disgracious in the city's eye, 112
And that you come to reprehend my ignorance.

BUCKINGHAM
You have, my lord. Would it might please Your
    Grace,
On our entreaties, to amend your fault!

RICHARD
Else wherefore breathe I in a Christian land? 116

---

45 **Intend** pretend 46 **mighty suit** importunate entreaty 49 **ground** the plainsong or melody on which a *descant* or melodious accompaniment is raised 54 **issue** outcome 55 **leads** flat lead coverings for roof; hence, the roof itself 56 **dance attendance** i.e., am kept waiting 57 **withal** with 68 **No less importing** concerned with nothing less 74 **brace** pair 75 **deep** learned 76 **engross** fatten 81 **defend** forbid

93 **beads** i.e., prayers. **much** hard 94 **s.d. aloft** i.e., on the gallery above the stage, rear. (The tiring-house facade in this scene is imagined to be the facade of Baynard's Castle.) 97 **stay** steady. **of** caused by 99 **ornaments** i.e., the bishops as well as the prayer book 112 **disgracious** unbecoming, displeasing 116 **Else . . . land** i.e., how otherwise could I claim to be a good Christian, living in a Christian land

BUCKINGHAM
  Know then, it is your fault that you resign
  The supreme seat, the throne majestical,
  The sceptered office of your ancestors,
  Your state of fortune and your due of birth,   120
  The lineal glory of your royal house,
  To the corruption of a blemished stock;   122
  Whiles, in the mildness of your sleepy thoughts,   123
  Which here we waken to our country's good,
  The noble isle doth want her proper limbs;   125
  Her face defaced with scars of infamy,
  Her royal stock graft with ignoble plants,   127
  And almost shouldered in the swallowing gulf   128
  Of dark forgetfulness and deep oblivion.
  Which to recure, we heartily solicit   130
  Your gracious self to take on you the charge
  And kingly government of this your land—
  Not as protector, steward, substitute,
  Or lowly factor for another's gain,   134
  But as successively from blood to blood,   135
  Your right of birth, your empery, your own.   136
  For this, consorted with the citizens,   137
  Your very worshipful and loving friends,
  And by their vehement instigation,
  In this just cause come I to move Your Grace.
RICHARD
  I cannot tell if to depart in silence
  Or bitterly to speak in your reproof
  Best fitteth my degree or your condition.   143
  If not to answer, you might haply think   144
  Tongue-tied ambition, not replying, yielded   145
  To bear the golden yoke of sovereignty,
  Which fondly you would here impose on me.   147
  If to reprove you for this suit of yours,
  So seasoned with your faithful love to me,   149
  Then on the other side I checked my friends.   150
  Therefore, to speak, and to avoid the first,
  And then, in speaking, not to incur the last,
  Definitively thus I answer you.   153
  Your love deserves my thanks, but my desert
  Unmeritable shuns your high request.   155
  First, if all obstacles were cut away,
  And that my path were even to the crown   157
  As the ripe revenue and due of birth,   158
  Yet so much is my poverty of spirit,
  So mighty and so many my defects,
  That I would rather hide me from my greatness—   161

  Being a bark to brook no mighty sea—   162
  Than in my greatness covet to be hid   163
  And in the vapor of my glory smothered.
  But, God be thanked, there is no need of me,
  And much I need to help you, were there need.   166
  The royal tree hath left us royal fruit,
  Which, mellowed by the stealing hours of time,   168
  Will well become the seat of majesty
  And make, no doubt, us happy by his reign.
  On him I lay that you would lay on me,   171
  The right and fortune of his happy stars,
  Which God defend that I should wring from him!   173
BUCKINGHAM
  My lord, this argues conscience in Your Grace;
  But the respects thereof are nice and trivial,   175
  All circumstances well considerèd.
  You say that Edward is your brother's son.
  So say we too, but not by Edward's wife;
  For first was he contract to Lady Lucy—   179
  Your mother lives a witness to his vow—   180
  And afterward by substitute betrothed   181
  To Bona, sister to the King of France.   182
  These both put off, a poor petitioner,
  A care-crazed mother to a many sons,
  A beauty-waning and distressèd widow,
  Even in the afternoon of her best days,
  Made prize and purchase of his wanton eye,   187
  Seduced the pitch and height of his degree   188
  To base declension and loathed bigamy.   189
  By her, in his unlawful bed, he got
  This Edward, whom our manners call the Prince.   191
  More bitterly could I expostulate,   192
  Save that, for reverence to some alive,   193
  I give a sparing limit to my tongue.
  Then, good my lord, take to your royal self   195
  This proffered benefit of dignity;
  If not to bless us and the land withal,
  Yet to draw forth your noble ancestry   198
  From the corruption of abusing times
  Unto a lineal true-derivèd course.
MAYOR
  Do, good my lord. Your citizens entreat you.

---

120 state of fortune position to which fortune entitles you
122 blemished i.e., through bastardy; see lines 177–191 below
123 sleepy reposeful **125 want her proper limbs** lack its own limbs, is crippled **127 graft** engrafted **128 shouldered in** jostled into, or immersed up to the shoulders in **130 recure** restore, make whole
134 factor agent **135 successively** in order of succession **136 empery** realm of your sole rule **137 consorted** associated, leagued
143 degree rank. **condition** social status **144 haply** perhaps
145 Tongue-tied silent. (Silence gives consent.) **yielded** consented
147 fondly foolishly **149 seasoned** i.e., made agreeable or palatable
150 checked rebuked, i.e., would rebuke **153 Definitively** once and for all **155 Unmeritable** undeserving **157 even** smooth **158 ripe revenue** possession ready to be inherited **161 my greatness** i.e., my claim to the throne

162 bark ship. **brook** endure **163 Than . . . hid** than wish to be enveloped in and overwhelmed by my greatness, i.e., the throne
166 I need I lack the requisite ability **168 stealing** stealthily moving
171 that what **173 defend** forbid **175 respects thereof** considerations by which you support your argument. **nice** overscrupulous
179 contract contracted **180 Your . . . vow** (According to the chronicles, Richard's mother, in opposing Edward's intention of marrying Lady Grey because it was interfering with the negotiations for his marriage to Lady Bona of Savoy, asserted that Lady Elizabeth Lucy was already Edward's trothplight wife. Compare with 3.5.75 and 3.7.6.) **181 substitute** proxy **182 sister** i.e., sister-in-law, the Queen's sister **187 purchase** booty **188 Seduced** debased. **pitch** height, highest point (as in falconry). **degree** rank **189 declension** falling away from a high standard. **bigamy** (Edward was not only bound by previous contracts, as indicated in lines 178–182 above, but also, by marrying a widow, entered into a union that was widely regarded as bigamous.) **191 manners** sense of politeness **192 expostulate** discuss, dilate **193 some alive** i.e., the Duchess of York. (See 3.5.93–94.) **195 good my lord** my good lord **198 draw forth** rescue

BUCKINGHAM
Refuse not, mighty lord, this proffered love.
CATESBY
O, make them joyful. Grant their lawful suit!
RICHARD
Alas, why would you heap this care on me?
I am unfit for state and majesty.
I do beseech you, take it not amiss;
I cannot nor I will not yield to you.
BUCKINGHAM
If you refuse it—as, in love and zeal,   208
Loath to depose the child, your brother's son,
As well we know your tenderness of heart   210
And gentle, kind, effeminate remorse,   211
Which we have noted in you to your kindred
And equally indeed to all estates—   213
Yet know, whe'er you accept our suit or no,   214
Your brother's son shall never reign our king,
But we will plant some other in the throne
To the disgrace and downfall of your house.
And in this resolution here we leave you.—
Come, citizens. Zounds! I'll entreat no more.   219
RICHARD
O, do not swear, my lord of Buckingham.
          Exeunt [Buckingham,
          Mayor, aldermen, and the citizens].
CATESBY
Call him again, sweet prince. Accept their suit.
If you deny them, all the land will rue it.
RICHARD
Will you enforce me to a world of cares?
Call them again. I am not made of stone,
But penetrable to your kind entreaties,
Albeit against my conscience and my soul.

          Enter Buckingham and the rest.

Cousin of Buckingham, and sage, grave men,
Since you will buckle fortune on my back,
To bear her burden, whe'er I will or no,
I must have patience to endure the load.
But if black scandal or foul-faced reproach
Attend the sequel of your imposition,   232
Your mere enforcement shall acquittance me   233
From all the impure blots and stains thereof;
For God doth know, and you may partly see,
How far I am from the desire of this.
MAYOR
God bless Your Grace! We see it and will say it.
RICHARD
In saying so, you shall but say the truth.
BUCKINGHAM
Then I salute you with this royal title:
Long live Richard, England's worthy king!
MAYOR AND CITIZENS   Amen.

BUCKINGHAM
Tomorrow may it please you to be crowned?
RICHARD
Even when you please, for you will have it so.
BUCKINGHAM
Tomorrow, then, we will attend Your Grace.
And so most joyfully we take our leave.
RICHARD [*to the Bishops*]
Come, let us to our holy work again.—
Farewell, my cousin. Farewell, gentle friends. *Exeunt.*

          ♣

4.1   *Enter [at one door] the Queen [Elizabeth], the*
          Duchess of York, and Marquess [of] Dorset; [at
          another door] Anne, Duchess of Gloucester,
          [leading Lady Margaret Plantagenet, Clarence's
          young daughter].

DUCHESS
Who meets us here? My niece Plantagenet   1
Led in the hand of her kind aunt of Gloucester?
Now, for my life, she's wandering to the Tower,   3
On pure heart's love to greet the tender Prince.   4
Daughter, well met.
ANNE   God give Your Graces both   5
A happy and a joyful time of day!
QUEEN ELIZABETH
As much to you, good sister. Whither away?   7
ANNE
No farther than the Tower, and, as I guess,
Upon the like devotion as yourselves,   9
To gratulate the gentle princes there.   10
QUEEN ELIZABETH
Kind sister, thanks. We'll enter all together.

          Enter [Brackenbury] the Lieutenant.

And, in good time, here the Lieutenant comes.
Master Lieutenant, pray you, by your leave,
How doth the Prince and my young son of York?
BRACKENBURY
Right well, dear madam. By your patience,
I may not suffer you to visit them;   16
The King hath strictly charged the contrary.
QUEEN ELIZABETH
The King! Who's that?
BRACKENBURY   I mean the Lord Protector.
QUEEN ELIZABETH
The Lord protect him from that kingly title!
Hath he set bounds between their love and me?   20
I am their mother; who shall bar me from them?
DUCHESS
I am their father's mother; I will see them.
ANNE
Their aunt I am in law, in love their mother;

---

208 as from being   **210 As . . . know** since we know well
211 kind, effeminate remorse natural, tender pity   **213 estates** ranks.
(This virtue of pity is found in Richard's treatment of everyone.)
214 whe'er whether   **219 Zounds** by His (God's) wounds   **232 your
imposition** the duty that you lay upon me   **233 mere** absolute, downright.   **acquittance** acquit

4.1. Location: London. Before the Tower.
1 niece i.e., granddaughter   **3 for** on   **4 On** out of.   **tender** young
5 Daughter i.e., daughter-in-law   **7 sister** i.e., sister-in-law   **9 like
devotion** same devout errand   **10 gratulate** greet, salute   **16 suffer**
permit   **20 bounds** barriers

Then bring me to their sights. I'll bear thy blame
And take thy office from thee, on my peril.   25
BRACKENBURY
No, madam, no; I may not leave it so.   26
I am bound by oath, and therefore pardon me.
                                        Exit Lieutenant.

        Enter [Lord] Stanley [Earl of Derby].

STANLEY
Let me but meet you, ladies, one hour hence,
And I'll salute Your Grace of York as mother,   29
And reverend looker-on, of two fair queens.   30
[*To Anne.*] Come, madam, you must straight to
        Westminster,
There to be crownèd Richard's royal queen.
QUEEN ELIZABETH   Ah, cut my lace asunder,   33
That my pent heart may have some scope to beat,
Or else I swoon with this dead-killing news!
ANNE
Despiteful tidings! O unpleasing news!   36
DORSET
Be of good cheer. Mother, how fares Your Grace?
QUEEN ELIZABETH
O Dorset, speak not to me. Get thee gone!
Death and destruction dogs thee at thy heels;
Thy mother's name is ominous to children.
If thou wilt outstrip death, go cross the seas
And live with Richmond, from the reach of hell.   42
Go, hie thee, hie thee from this slaughterhouse,   43
Lest thou increase the number of the dead
And make me die the thrall of Margaret's curse,   45
Nor mother, wife, nor England's counted queen.   46
STANLEY
Full of wise care is this your counsel, madam.
[*To Dorset.*] Take all the swift advantage of the
        hours.
You shall have letters from me to my son   49
In your behalf, to meet you on the way.   50
Be not ta'en tardy by unwise delay.   51
DUCHESS
O ill-dispersing wind of misery!   52
O my accursèd womb, the bed of death!
A cockatrice hast thou hatched to the world,   54
Whose unavoided eye is murderous.
STANLEY [*to Anne*]
Come, madam, come. I in all haste was sent.
ANNE
And I with all unwillingness will go.

O, would to God that the inclusive verge   58
Of golden metal that must round my brow
Were red-hot steel, to sear me to the brains!
Anointed let me be with deadly venom   61
And die ere men can say, "God save the Queen!"
QUEEN ELIZABETH
Go, go, poor soul. I envy not thy glory.
To feed my humor, wish thyself no harm.   64
ANNE
No? Why? When he that is my husband now
Came to me, as I followed Henry's corpse,
When scarce the blood was well washed from his
        hands
Which issued from my other angel husband
And that dear saint which then I weeping
        followed—
O, when, I say, I looked on Richard's face,
This was my wish: "Be thou," quoth I, "accurst
For making me, so young, so old a widow!   72
And, when thou wedd'st, let sorrow haunt thy bed;
And be thy wife—if any be so mad—
More miserable by the life of thee
Than thou hast made me by my dear lord's death!"
Lo, ere I can repeat this curse again,
Within so small a time, my woman's heart
Grossly grew captive to his honey words   79
And proved the subject of mine own soul's curse,
Which hitherto hath held mine eyes from rest;
For never yet one hour in his bed
Did I enjoy the golden dew of sleep,
But with his timorous dreams was still awaked.   84
Besides, he hates me for my father Warwick,   85
And will, no doubt, shortly be rid of me.
QUEEN ELIZABETH
Poor heart, adieu! I pity thy complaining.
ANNE
No more than with my soul I mourn for yours.
DORSET
Farewell, thou woeful welcomer of glory!
ANNE
Adieu, poor soul, that tak'st thy leave of it!
DUCHESS [*to Dorset*]
Go thou to Richmond, and good fortune guide thee!
[*To Anne.*] Go thou to Richard, and good angels
        tend thee!
[*To Queen Elizabeth.*] Go thou to sanctuary, and good
        thoughts possess thee!
I to my grave, where peace and rest lie with me!
Eighty-odd years of sorrow have I seen,
And each hour's joy wracked with a week of teen.   96
                                        [*They start to go.*]

25 take . . . thee i.e., relieve you of the responsibility   26 leave it
i.e., fail to perform my office   29 mother i.e., mother-in-law (of Elizabeth as widow of Edward and of Anne as wife of King Richard)
30 looker-on beholder.   two fair queens i.e., Elizabeth and Anne,
since Anne's husband, Richard, is about to be crowned   33 lace cord
used to lace the bodice   36 Despiteful cruel   42 with Richmond i.e.,
with Henry Tudor, Earl of Richmond, at this time in Brittany   43 hie
hasten   45 thrall subject, victim   46 Nor neither.   counted accepted, esteemed   49–50 You . . . way i.e., I'll give you a letter to
my son George Stanley (or possibly to the Earl of Richmond, Stanley's
stepson) asking for protection and assistance on your journey
51 ta'en taken, caught   52 ill-dispersing scattering ill fortune
54 cockatrice basilisk. (See the note for 1.2.153.)

58 inclusive verge enclosing circle, i.e., the crown, here likened to
an instrument of torture used to punish regicides or other criminals
61 Anointed (Anne desires to be anointed with poison rather than
with holy oil, as in the ceremony of coronation.)   64 To . . . harm
do not curse yourself (or, possibly, I do not wish you harm) just to
satisfy my vengeful mood   72 so old a widow i.e., destined to live so
long as a widow   79 Grossly stupidly   84 timorous full of fears.
still continually   85 for on account of   96 wracked destroyed, or,
racked, tortured.   teen woe

QUEEN ELIZABETH
Stay, yet look back with me unto the Tower.
Pity, you ancient stones, those tender babes
Whom envy hath immured within your walls—   99
Rough cradle for such little pretty ones!
Rude ragged nurse, old sullen playfellow   101
For tender princes, use my babies well!
So foolish sorrows bids your stones farewell.   *Exeunt.*

❧

4.2   *Sound a sennet. Enter Richard, in pomp;*
       Buckingham, Catesby, Ratcliffe, Lovell, [a Page,
       and others].

KING RICHARD
Stand all apart. Cousin of Buckingham!   1
            [The others stand aside, out of earshot.]
BUCKINGHAM   My gracious sovereign?
KING RICHARD
Give me thy hand.
            Sound [trumpets. Here he ascends the throne.]
                 Thus high, by thy advice
And thy assistance, is King Richard seated.
But shall we wear these glories for a day?
Or shall they last, and we rejoice in them?
BUCKINGHAM
Still live they, and forever let them last!
KING RICHARD
Ah, Buckingham, now do I play the touch,   8
To try if thou be current gold indeed: 9
Young Edward lives. Think now what I would
   speak.
BUCKINGHAM   Say on, my loving lord.
KING RICHARD
Why, Buckingham, I say I would be king.
BUCKINGHAM
Why, so you are, my thrice-renownèd lord.
KING RICHARD
Ha! Am I king? 'Tis so. But Edward lives.
BUCKINGHAM
True, noble prince.
KING RICHARD   O bitter consequence,   15
That Edward still should live "true, noble prince"!   16
Cousin, thou wast not wont to be so dull.   17
Shall I be plain? I wish the bastards dead,
And I would have it suddenly performed.   19
What sayst thou now? Speak suddenly; be brief.
BUCKINGHAM   Your Grace may do your pleasure.
KING RICHARD
Tut, tut, thou art all ice; thy kindness freezes.
Say, have I thy consent that they shall die?

BUCKINGHAM
Give me some little breath, some pause, dear lord,
Before I positively speak in this.
I will resolve you herein presently.   *Exit Buckingham.* 26
CATESBY *[to those standing aside]*
The King is angry. See, he gnaws his lip.
KING RICHARD *[aside]*
I will converse with iron-witted fools   28
And unrespective boys. None are for me   29
That look into me with considerate eyes.   30
High-reaching Buckingham grows circumspect.—   31
Boy!
PAGE *[approaching]*   My lord?
KING RICHARD
Know'st thou not any whom corrupting gold
Will tempt unto a close exploit of death?   35
PAGE
My lord, I know a discontented gentleman
Whose humble means match not his haughty spirit.
Gold were as good as twenty orators,
And will, no doubt, tempt him to anything.
KING RICHARD
What is his name?
PAGE   His name, my lord, is Tyrrel.
KING RICHARD
I partly know the man. Go call him hither, boy.
                                   Exit [Page].
[Aside.] The deep-revolving, witty Buckingham   42
No more shall be the neighbor to my counsels.
Hath he so long held out with me untired,
And stops he now for breath? Well, be it so.

                Enter [Lord] Stanley [Earl of Derby].

How now, Lord Stanley? What's the news?
STANLEY   Know, my loving lord,
The Marquess Dorset, as I hear, is fled
To Richmond, in the parts where he abides.
                                   [He stands apart.]
KING RICHARD
Come hither, Catesby. Rumor it abroad
That Anne my wife is very grievous sick;
I will take order for her keeping close.   52
Inquire me out some mean poor gentleman,   53
Whom I will marry straight to Clarence' daughter.
The boy is foolish, and I fear not him.   55
Look how thou dream'st! I say again, give out
That Anne my queen is sick and like to die.   57
About it, for it stands me much upon   58
To stop all hopes whose growth may damage me.
                                   [Exit Catesby.]
I must be married to my brother's daughter,   60

---

99 **envy** malice   101 **Rude** rough
4.2. Location: London. The royal court.
1 apart aside   **8 play the touch** play the part of a touchstone (to test
the quality of gold)   **9 current** sterling, genuine   **15 bitter consequence** i.e., intolerable answer to my words, and an intolerable fact
16 "true, noble prince" (Richard mockingly repeats Buckingham's
evasive reply in line 15 and applies it to the irritating fact that young
Edward still lives and is a noble prince.)   **17 wast not wont** used not
19 suddenly swiftly

26 **resolve** answer   28 **converse** associate.   **iron-witted** unfeeling,
stupid   29 **unrespective** thoughtless   30 **considerate** deliberate, reflective   31 **High-reaching** ambitious.   **circumspect** cautious
35 **close** secret   42 **deep-revolving** deeply scheming.   **witty** cunning
52 **take** give.   **close** imprisoned, confined   53 **mean poor** of low degree   55 **boy** i.e., Clarence's eldest son, Edward Plantagenet, Earl of
Warwick   57 **like** likely   58 **stands . . . upon** is a matter of the utmost importance to me   60 **brother's daughter** i.e., Elizabeth of
York, daughter to Edward IV, who will, in fact, later become the
queen of Henry VII; see 4.5.7–9 and 5.5.29–31

Or else my kingdom stands on brittle glass.
Murder her brothers, and then marry her—
Uncertain way of gain! But I am in
So far in blood that sin will pluck on sin.   64
Tear-falling pity dwells not in this eye.   65

Enter [Page, with] Tyrrel.

Is thy name Tyrrel?
TYRREL
James Tyrrel, and your most obedient subject.
KING RICHARD
Art thou, indeed?
TYRREL   Prove me, my gracious lord.   68
KING RICHARD
Dar'st thou resolve to kill a friend of mine?
TYRREL   Please you;   70
But I had rather kill two enemies.
KING RICHARD
Why, there thou hast it: two deep enemies,
Foes to my rest and my sweet sleep's disturbers
Are they that I would have thee deal upon—   74
Tyrrel, I mean those bastards in the Tower.
TYRREL
Let me have open means to come to them,   76
And soon I'll rid you from the fear of them.
KING RICHARD
Thou sing'st sweet music. Hark, come hither, Tyrrel.
Go, by this token. [*He gives him a token.*] Rise, and
lend thine ear.   *Whispers.*
There is no more but so. Say it is done,
And I will love thee and prefer thee for it.   81
TYRREL   I will dispatch it straight.   *Exit.*

Enter Buckingham.

BUCKINGHAM
My lord, I have considered in my mind
The late request that you did sound me in.   84
KING RICHARD
Well, let that rest. Dorset is fled to Richmond.
BUCKINGHAM   I hear the news, my lord.
KING RICHARD
Stanley, he is your wife's son. Well, look to it.   87
BUCKINGHAM
My lord, I claim the gift, my due by promise,
For which your honor and your faith is pawned: 89
Th' earldom of Hereford and the movables
Which you have promisèd I shall possess.
KING RICHARD
Stanley, look to your wife. If she convey
Letters to Richmond, you shall answer it.   93
BUCKINGHAM
What says Your Highness to my just request?
KING RICHARD
I do remember me, Henry the Sixth
Did prophesy that Richmond should be king,

When Richmond was a little peevish boy.
A king! Perhaps, perhaps—
BUCKINGHAM   My lord!
KING RICHARD
How chance the prophet could not at that time   100
Have told me, I being by, that I should kill him?   101
BUCKINGHAM
My lord, your promise for the earldom!
KING RICHARD
Richmond! When last I was at Exeter,
The Mayor in courtesy showed me the castle
And called it Rougemont, at which name I started,   105
Because a bard of Ireland told me once
I should not live long after I saw Richmond.
BUCKINGHAM   My lord!
KING RICHARD   Ay, what's o'clock?   109
BUCKINGHAM
I am thus bold to put Your Grace in mind
Of what you promised me.
KING RICHARD   Well, but what's o'clock?
BUCKINGHAM   Upon the stroke of ten.
KING RICHARD   Well, let it strike.
BUCKINGHAM   Why let it strike?
KING RICHARD
Because that, like a jack, thou keep'st the stroke   116
Betwixt thy begging and my meditation.
I am not in the giving vein today.   118
BUCKINGHAM
May it please you to resolve me in my suit.   119
KING RICHARD
Thou troublest me. I am not in the vein.
                Exit [with all but Buckingham].
BUCKINGHAM
And is it thus? Repays he my deep service
With such contempt? Made I him king for this?
O, let me think on Hastings, and be gone
To Brecknock, while my fearful head is on!   *Exit.* 124

❖

4.3   *Enter Tyrrel.*

TYRREL
The tyrannous and bloody act is done,
The most arch deed of piteous massacre   2
That ever yet this land was guilty of.
Dighton and Forrest, whom I did suborn   4
To do this piece of ruthless butchery,
Albeit they were fleshed villains, bloody dogs,   6

---

64 **pluck on** draw on   65 **Tear-falling** tear-dropping   68 **Prove** test
70 **Please** if it please   74 **deal upon** proceed against   76 **open** un-
hampered   81 **prefer** promote, advance   84 **late** recent.   **sound me
in** ask me about   87 **he** i.e., Richmond   89 **pawned** pledged   93 **it**
for it

100 **the prophet** i.e., Henry VI   101 **by** nearby.   **him** (The word applies to Richmond and Henry VI.)   105 **Rougemont** i.e., Red Hill
(with a play on "Richmond")   109 **what's o'clock** what time is it
116 **jack** the figure of a man that strikes the bell on the outside of a
clock (with a play on the meaning "lowbred fellow." Richard's complaint is that Buckingham, like the jack of a clock, being on the point
of striking the hour—i.e., speaking his request—breaks the continuity
of Richard's reflections.)   118 **vein** mood   119 **resolve me** give me a
final answer   124 **Brecknock** i.e., Brecon, Buckingham's family seat
in Wales.   **fearful** full of fears
4.3. Location: London. The royal court.
2 **arch deed** i.e., chief or notorious act   4 **suborn** bribe   6 **fleshed**
experienced in bloodshed

Melted with tenderness and mild compassion,
Wept like to children in their deaths' sad story.   8
"O, thus," quoth Dighton, "lay the gentle babes."
"Thus, thus," quoth Forrest, "girdling one another
Within their alabaster innocent arms.
Their lips were four red roses on a stalk,
Which in their summer beauty kissed each other.
A book of prayers on their pillow lay,
Which once," quoth Forrest, "almost changed my
   mind;
But O! the devil"—there the villain stopped;
When Dighton thus told on: "We smotherèd
The most replenishèd sweet work of Nature   18
That from the prime creation e'er she framed."   19
Hence both are gone; with conscience and remorse   20
They could not speak; and so I left them both,
To bear this tidings to the bloody king.

   Enter [King] Richard.

And here he comes.—All health, my sovereign lord!
KING RICHARD
   Kind Tyrrel, am I happy in thy news?
TYRREL
   If to have done the thing you gave in charge   25
   Beget your happiness, be happy then,
   For it is done.
KING RICHARD   But didst thou see them dead?
TYRREL
   I did, my lord.
KING RICHARD   And buried, gentle Tyrrel?
TYRREL
   The chaplain of the Tower hath buried them;
   But where, to say the truth, I do not know.
KING RICHARD
   Come to me, Tyrrel, soon at after-supper,   31
   When thou shalt tell the process of their death.   32
   Meantime, but think how I may do thee good,
   And be inheritor of thy desire.   34
   Farewell till then.
TYRREL   I humbly take my leave.   [*Exit.*]
KING RICHARD
   The son of Clarence have I pent up close,   36
   His daughter meanly have I matched in marriage,   37
   The sons of Edward sleep in Abraham's bosom,   38
   And Anne my wife hath bid this world good night.
   Now, for I know the Breton Richmond aims   40
   At young Elizabeth, my brother's daughter,   41
   And by that knot looks proudly on the crown,   42

To her go I, a jolly thriving wooer.

   Enter Ratcliffe.

RATCLIFFE   My lord!
KING RICHARD
   Good or bad news, that thou com'st in so bluntly?
RATCLIFFE
   Bad news, my lord. Morton is fled to Richmond,   46
   And Buckingham, backed with the hardy Welshmen,
   Is in the field, and still his power increaseth.   48
KING RICHARD
   Ely with Richmond troubles me more near   49
   Than Buckingham and his rash-levied strength.   50
   Come, I have learned that fearful commenting   51
   Is leaden servitor to dull delay;   52
   Delay leads impotent and snail-paced beggary.   53
   Then fiery expedition be my wing,   54
   Jove's Mercury, and herald for a king!   55
   Go muster men. My counsel is my shield;   56
   We must be brief when traitors brave the field.   57
                                          Exeunt.

❦

4.4   *Enter old Queen Margaret.*

QUEEN MARGARET
   So now prosperity begins to mellow   1
   And drop into the rotten mouth of death.
   Here in these confines slyly have I lurked   3
   To watch the waning of mine enemies.
   A dire induction am I witness to,   5
   And will to France, hoping the consequence   6
   Will prove as bitter, black, and tragical.
   Withdraw thee, wretched Margaret. Who comes
      here?   [*She steps aside.*]

   Enter Duchess [of York] and Queen [Elizabeth].

QUEEN ELIZABETH
   Ah, my poor princes! Ah, my tender babes!
   My unblown flowers, new-appearing sweets!   10
   If yet your gentle souls fly in the air
   And be not fixed in doom perpetual,   12
   Hover about me with your airy wings
   And hear your mother's lamentation!
QUEEN MARGARET [*aside*]
   Hover about her; say that right for right   15

---

8 in their . . . story in telling the story of their deaths   **18 replenishèd** complete, perfect   **19 prime** first   **20 gone** undone, unnerved. **with** due to   **25 gave in charge** ordered, commanded   **31 aftersupper** dessert after supper   **32 process** story   **34 be . . . desire** expect to get what you ask   **36 pent up close** strictly confined   **37 His . . . marriage** (Margaret Plantagenet was about twelve years old when Richard died. Shakespeare may have confused her with Lady Cicely, a daughter of Edward IV, whom Richard, according to Holinshed, intended to marry to "a man found in a cloud, and of an unknown lineage and family.")   **38 Abraham's bosom** (See Luke 16:22.) **40 for** because.   **Breton** located in Brittany   **41 my brother's** Edward's   **42 by that knot** by virtue of that alliance

46 Morton i.e., John Morton, Bishop of Ely, who had been prisoner at Brecknock (or Brecon) Castle; he is the Ely of 3.4   **48 power** army   **49 near** deeply   **50 rash-levied** hastily recruited   **51 fearful commenting** timorous talk   **52 leaden servitor** sluggish attendant **53 leads** leads to.   **beggary** ruin   **54 expedition** speed   **55 Mercury** messenger of the gods   **56 My . . . shield** i.e., I will take counsel by arming myself   **57 brave** challenge
4.4. Location: London. Near the royal court.
1 mellow mature   **3 confines** regions.   **slyly** stealthily   **5 induction** beginning (as of a play)   **6 will** will go.   **the consequence** what follows, the sequel and conclusion (as in a play)   **10 unblown** unopened.   **sweets** flowers   **12 doom perpetual** i.e., eternal punishment or reward   **15 right for right** i.e., a just punishment for an offense against justice

Hath dimmed your infant morn to agèd night. 16

DUCHESS
So many miseries have crazed my voice 17
That my woe-wearied tongue is still and mute.
Edward Plantagenet, why art thou dead?

QUEEN MARGARET [aside]
Plantagenet doth quit Plantagenet. 20
Edward for Edward pays a dying debt. 21

QUEEN ELIZABETH
Wilt thou, O God, fly from such gentle lambs 22
And throw them in the entrails of the wolf?
When didst thou sleep when such a deed was done? 24

QUEEN MARGARET [aside]
When holy Harry died, and my sweet son. 25

DUCHESS
Dead life, blind sight, poor mortal-living ghost, 26
Woe's scene, world's shame, grave's due by life
  usurped, 27
Brief abstract and record of tedious days, 28
Rest thy unrest on England's lawful earth,
  [sitting down]
Unlawfully made drunk with innocent blood!

QUEEN ELIZABETH
Ah, that thou wouldst as soon afford a grave 31
As thou canst yield a melancholy seat!
Then would I hide my bones, not rest them here.
Ah, who hath any cause to mourn but we?
  [Sitting down by her.]

QUEEN MARGARET [coming forward]
If ancient sorrow be most reverend, 35
Give mine the benefit of seniory 36
And let my griefs frown on the upper hand. 37
If sorrow can admit society,   [sitting down with them]
Tell o'er your woes again by viewing mine:
I had an Edward, till a Richard killed him; 40
I had a Harry, till a Richard killed him: 41
Thou hadst an Edward, till a Richard killed him; 42
Thou hadst a Richard, till a Richard killed him. 43

DUCHESS
I had a Richard too, and thou didst kill him; 44
I had a Rutland too, thou holp'st to kill him. 45

QUEEN MARGARET
Thou hadst a Clarence too, and Richard killed him.
From forth the kennel of thy womb hath crept
A hellhound that doth hunt us all to death.

That dog, that had his teeth before his eyes 49
To worry lambs and lap their gentle blood, 50
That foul defacer of God's handiwork,
That excellent grand tyrant of the earth 52
That reigns in gallèd eyes of weeping souls, 53
Thy womb let loose, to chase us to our graves.
O upright, just, and true-disposing God,
How do I thank thee that this carnal cur 56
Preys on the issue of his mother's body 57
And makes her pew-fellow with others' moan! 58

DUCHESS
O Harry's wife, triumph not in my woes!
God witness with me, I have wept for thine.

QUEEN MARGARET
Bear with me. I am hungry for revenge,
And now I cloy me with beholding it. 62
Thy Edward he is dead that killed my Edward; 63
Thy other Edward dead, to quit my Edward; 64
Young York he is but boot, because both they 65
Matched not the high perfection of my loss.
Thy Clarence he is dead that stabbed my Edward;
And the beholders of this frantic play, 68
Th' adulterate Hastings, Rivers, Vaughan, Grey, 69
Untimely smothered in their dusky graves. 70
Richard yet lives, hell's black intelligencer, 71
Only reserved their factor to buy souls 72
And send them thither; but at hand, at hand
Ensues his piteous and unpitied end. 74
Earth gapes, hell burns, fiends roar, saints pray,
To have him suddenly conveyed from hence.
Cancel his bond of life, dear God, I pray,
That I may live and say, "The dog is dead!"

QUEEN ELIZABETH
O, thou didst prophesy the time would come
That I should wish for thee to help me curse
That bottled spider, that foul bunch-backed toad! 81

QUEEN MARGARET
I called thee then vain flourish of my fortune; 82
I called thee then poor shadow, painted queen,
The presentation of but what I was, 84
The flattering index of a direful pageant, 85
One heaved a-high to be hurled down below,
A mother only mocked with two fair babes,
A dream of what thou wast, a garish flag 88
To be the aim of every dangerous shot; 89

---

16 dimmed . . . night i.e., brought the youthful promise of your children to ruin and death   17 crazed cracked   20 quit requite   21 Edward for Edward i.e., Edward V, the Yorkist Prince, for Edward, the son of Margaret and Henry VI.   dying debt debt paid through death   22 fly from abandon   24 When i.e., whenever till now   25 Harry i.e., Henry VI   26 mortal-living ghost i.e., a dead person still among the living   27 grave's . . . usurped i.e., one who, by living too long, deprives the grave of its due   28 abstract epitome   31 that would that.   thou i.e., the earth   35 reverend worthy of respect   36 seniory seniority of claim   37 on . . . hand i.e., from a place of precedence   40 Edward i.e., my son, the former Prince of Wales   41 Harry i.e., my husband, King Henry VI   42 Thou i.e., Queen Elizabeth.   Edward i.e., Edward V   43 Richard i.e., the young Duke of York   44 Richard i.e., Duke of York, the Duchess's husband and father of Richard III, killed by Margaret's army at the Battle of Wakefield in 1460   45 Rutland i.e., Edmund, son of the Duke of York, also killed at Wakefield

49 teeth (Richard was supposedly born with teeth.)   50 worry tear to pieces   52 excellent unparalleled   53 gallèd sore with weeping   56 carnal flesh-eating   57 issue offspring   58 pew-fellow i.e., intimate associate   62 cloy me satiate myself   63 Thy Edward Edward IV.   my Edward the son of Henry VI   64 other Edward Edward V.   quit requite   65 Young York Richard, Duke of York, the younger of the princes murdered in the Tower.   but boot merely into the bargain   68 frantic insane   69 adulterate adulterous   70 smothered covered up   71 intelligencer agent, go-between, spy   72 Only . . . factor chosen above all others as their (hell's) agent, and sent to earth for no other purpose   74 piteous deplorable   81 bottled bottle-shaped, swollen (as at 1.3.242).   bunch-backed hunchbacked   82 flourish ornament, embellishment   84 presentation representation, semblance   85 index argument, preface, prologue.   pageant spectacular entertainment   88–89 garish . . . shot i.e., standard-bearer, conspicuous in appearance, and thus the target of enemy fire

A sign of dignity, a breath, a bubble,   90
A queen in jest, only to fill the scene.
Where is thy husband now? Where be thy brothers?
Where be thy two sons? Wherein dost thou joy?
Who sues and kneels and says, "God save the
    Queen"?
Where be the bending peers that flattered thee?   95
Where be the thronging troops that followed thee?   96
Decline all this, and see what now thou art: 97
For happy wife, a most distressèd widow;
For joyful mother, one that wails the name;
For one being sued to, one that humbly sues;
For queen, a very caitiff crowned with care;   101
For she that scorned at me, now scorned of me;   102
For she being feared of all, now fearing one;   103
For she commanding all, obeyed of none.   104
Thus hath the course of justice whirled about
And left thee but a very prey to time,
Having no more but thought of what thou wast
To torture thee the more, being what thou art.
Thou didst usurp my place, and dost thou not
Usurp the just proportion of my sorrow?
Now thy proud neck bears half my burdened yoke,   111
From which even here I slip my weary head
And leave the burden of it all on thee.
Farewell, York's wife, and queen of sad mischance!
These English woes shall make me smile in France.
                                             [*She starts to leave.*]
QUEEN ELIZABETH
O thou well skilled in curses, stay awhile,
And teach me how to curse mine enemies!
QUEEN MARGARET
Forbear to sleep the nights, and fast the days;
Compare dead happiness with living woe;
Think that thy babes were sweeter than they were
And he that slew them fouler than he is.
Bett'ring thy loss makes the bad causer worse;   122
Revolving this will teach thee how to curse.   123
QUEEN ELIZABETH
My words are dull. O, quicken them with thine!   124
QUEEN MARGARET
Thy woes will make them sharp, and pierce like
    mine.   *Exit Margaret.*
DUCHESS
Why should calamity be full of words?
QUEEN ELIZABETH
Windy attorneys to their client's woes,   127
Airy succeeders of intestate joys,   128
Poor breathing orators of miseries,   129
Let them have scope! Though what they will impart
Help nothing else, yet do they ease the heart.

90 **sign** mere token   95 **bending** bowing   96 **troops** supporters, followers   97 **Decline** go through in order. (A grammatical metaphor.)
101 **caitiff** wretch, slave   102, 103, 104 **of** by   111 **burdened** burdensome   122 **Bett'ring** magnifying   123 **Revolving** meditating on
124 **quicken** put life into   127 **Windy . . . woes** i.e., words, which
are airy pleaders on behalf of one who is suffering   128 **Airy . . .
joys** insubstantial words, all that is left of joys that died unfulfilled
(literally, having died without anything to bequeath)   129 **breathing**
speaking

DUCHESS
If so, then be not tongue-tied. Go with me,
And in the breath of bitter words let's smother
My damnèd son that thy two sweet sons smothered.
                                             [*Sound trumpet.*]
The trumpet sounds. Be copious in exclaims.   135

        Enter KING RICHARD *and his train* [*marching, with
            drums and trumpets*].

KING RICHARD
Who intercepts me in my expedition?   136
DUCHESS
O, she that might have intercepted thee,
By strangling thee in her accursèd womb,
From all the slaughters, wretch, that thou hast done!
QUEEN ELIZABETH
Hid'st thou that forehead with a golden crown
Where should be branded, if that right were right,
The slaughter of the prince that owed that crown   142
And the dire death of my poor sons and brothers?
Tell me, thou villain slave, where are my children?
DUCHESS
Thou toad, thou toad, where is thy brother Clarence?
And little Ned Plantagenet, his son?   146
QUEEN ELIZABETH
Where is the gentle Rivers, Vaughan, Grey?
DUCHESS   Where is kind Hastings?
KING RICHARD
A flourish, trumpets! Strike alarum, drums!   149
Let not the heavens hear these telltale women   150
Rail on the Lord's anointed. Strike, I say!
                                             Flourish. Alarums.
Either be patient and entreat me fair,   152
Or with the clamorous report of war   153
Thus will I drown your exclamations.
DUCHESS   Art thou my son?
KING RICHARD
Ay, I thank God, my father, and yourself.
DUCHESS
Then patiently hear my impatience.
KING RICHARD
Madam, I have a touch of your condition,   158
That cannot brook the accent of reproof.
DUCHESS
O, let me speak!
KING RICHARD   Do then, but I'll not hear.
DUCHESS
I will be mild and gentle in my words.
KING RICHARD
And brief, good Mother, for I am in haste.
DUCHESS
Art thou so hasty? I have stayed for thee,   163
God knows, in torment and in agony.
KING RICHARD
And came I not at last to comfort you?

135 **exclaims** exclamations   136 **expedition** (1) haste (2) military undertaking   142 **owed** owned   146 **Ned Plantagenet** (See 4.3.36.)
149 **alarum** the cry or signal "allarme" (to arms)   150 **telltale** tattling, gabbling   152 **entreat me fair** treat me with courtesy   153 **report** noise   158 **condition** disposition   163 **stayed** waited

DUCHESS
  No, by the Holy Rood, thou know'st it well,   166
  Thou cam'st on earth to make the earth my hell.
  A grievous burden was thy birth to me;
  Tetchy and wayward was thy infancy;   169
  Thy schooldays frightful, desperate, wild, and
    furious;   170
  Thy prime of manhood daring, bold, and venturous;
  Thy age confirmed, proud, subtle, sly, and bloody,   172
  More mild, but yet more harmful—kind in hatred.   173
  What comfortable hour canst thou name
  That ever graced me with thy company?
KING RICHARD
  Faith, none, but Humphrey Hour, that called Your
    Grace   176
  To breakfast once forth of my company.   177
  If I be so disgracious in your eye,   178
  Let me march on and not offend you, madam.—
  Strike up the drum.
DUCHESS   I prithee, hear me speak.
KING RICHARD
  You speak too bitterly.
DUCHESS   Hear me a word,
  For I shall never speak to thee again.
KING RICHARD   So.
DUCHESS
  Either thou wilt die by God's just ordinance
  Ere from this war thou turn a conqueror,   185
  Or I with grief and extreme age shall perish
  And nevermore behold thy face again.
  Therefore take with thee my most grievous curse,
  Which in the day of battle tire thee more
  Than all the complete armor that thou wear'st!
  My prayers on the adverse party fight,   191
  And there the little souls of Edward's children
  Whisper the spirits of thine enemies   193
  And promise them success and victory!
  Bloody thou art, bloody will be thy end;
  Shame serves thy life and doth thy death attend.   196
                                          Exit.
QUEEN ELIZABETH
  Though far more cause, yet much less spirit to curse
  Abides in me; I say amen to her.
KING RICHARD
  Stay, madam. I must talk a word with you.
QUEEN ELIZABETH
  I have no more sons of the royal blood
  For thee to slaughter. For my daughters, Richard,   201
  They shall be praying nuns, not weeping queens,
  And therefore level not to hit their lives.   203
KING RICHARD
  You have a daughter called Elizabeth,

Virtuous and fair, royal and gracious.
QUEEN ELIZABETH
  And must she die for this? O, let her live,
  And I'll corrupt her manners, stain her beauty,   207
  Slander myself as false to Edward's bed,
  Throw over her the veil of infamy;
  So she may live unscarred of bleeding slaughter,   210
  I will confess she was not Edward's daughter.
KING RICHARD
  Wrong not her birth. She is a royal princess.
QUEEN ELIZABETH
  To save her life, I'll say she is not so.
KING RICHARD
  Her life is safest only in her birth.   214
QUEEN ELIZABETH
  And only in that safety died her brothers.
KING RICHARD
  Lo, at their birth good stars were opposite.   216
QUEEN ELIZABETH
  No, to their lives ill friends were contrary.   217
KING RICHARD
  All unavoided is the doom of destiny.   218
QUEEN ELIZABETH
  True, when avoided grace makes destiny.   219
  My babes were destined to a fairer death,
  If grace had blessed thee with a fairer life.
KING RICHARD
  You speak as if that I had slain my cousins.   222
QUEEN ELIZABETH
  Cousins, indeed, and by their uncle cozened   223
  Of comfort, kingdom, kindred, freedom, life.
  Whose hand soever lanced their tender hearts,   225
  Thy head, all indirectly, gave direction.   226
  No doubt the murderous knife was dull and blunt
  Till it was whetted on thy stone-hard heart,
  To revel in the entrails of my lambs.
  But that still use of grief makes wild grief tame,   230
  My tongue should to thy ears not name my boys
  Till that my nails were anchored in thine eyes;
  And I, in such a desperate bay of death,   233
  Like a poor bark of sails and tackling reft,   234
  Rush all to pieces on thy rocky bosom.
KING RICHARD
  Madam, so thrive I in my enterprise   236
  And dangerous success of bloody wars   237
  As I intend more good to you and yours
  Than ever you or yours by me were harmed!
QUEEN ELIZABETH
  What good is covered with the face of heaven,   240
  To be discovered, that can do me good?

---

166 **Holy Rood** Christ's cross   169 **Tetchy** fretful, peevish
170 **frightful** frightening   172 **age confirmed** riper manhood
173 **kind in hatred** concealing hatred under pretense of kindness
176 **Humphrey Hour** (To "dine with Duke Humphrey" was to go
hungry. The passage is obscure.)   177 **forth of** away from   178 **disgracious** unpleasing, disliked   185 **turn** return   191 **party** side
193 **Whisper** whisper to   196 **serves** accompanies   201 **For my** as
for my   203 **level** aim

207 **manners** morals   210 **So** provided.   **of** by   214 **is safest . . .
birth** is most safe because of her high birth   216 **opposite** hostile,
antagonistic   217 **contrary** opposed   218 **unavoided** unavoidable
219 **avoided grace** i.e., Richard, in whom grace is void or lacking
222 **as if that** as if   223 **cozened** cheated   225 **Whose hand soever**
whoever it was whose hand   226 **all indirectly** by indirect means,
and wrongly   230 **But** except.   **still** continual   233 **bay** (1) inlet (2)
position of a hunted animal turning to face the hounds   234 **bark**
sailing vessel.   **reft** bereft   236 **so thrive I** may I so thrive   237 **success** sequel, result   240 **covered with** hidden by (and therefore not
yet revealed to humanity)

KING RICHARD
Th' advancement of your children, gentle lady.
QUEEN ELIZABETH
Up to some scaffold, there to lose their heads.
KING RICHARD
Unto the dignity and height of fortune,
The high imperial type of this earth's glory.   245
QUEEN ELIZABETH
Flatter my sorrow with report of it;
Tell me what state, what dignity, what honor,
Canst thou demise to any child of mine?   248
KING RICHARD
Even all I have—ay, and myself and all—
Will I withal endow a child of thine,
So in the Lethe of thy angry soul   251
Thou drown the sad remembrance of those wrongs
Which thou supposest I have done to thee.
QUEEN ELIZABETH
Be brief, lest that the process of thy kindness   254
Last longer telling than thy kindness' date.   255
KING RICHARD
Then know that from my soul I love thy daughter.   256
QUEEN ELIZABETH
My daughter's mother thinks it with her soul.
KING RICHARD   What do you think?
QUEEN ELIZABETH
That thou dost love my daughter from thy soul.
So from thy soul's love didst thou love her brothers,   260
And from my heart's love I do thank thee for it.
KING RICHARD
Be not so hasty to confound my meaning.   262
I mean that with my soul I love thy daughter
And do intend to make her Queen of England.
QUEEN ELIZABETH
Well then, who dost thou mean shall be her king?
KING RICHARD
Even he that makes her queen. Who else should be?
QUEEN ELIZABETH
What, thou?
KING RICHARD   Even so. How think you of it?
QUEEN ELIZABETH
How canst thou woo her?
KING RICHARD   That would I learn of you,
As one being best acquainted with her humor.   269
QUEEN ELIZABETH
And wilt thou learn of me?
KING RICHARD   Madam, with all my heart.
QUEEN ELIZABETH
Send to her, by the man that slew her brothers,
A pair of bleeding hearts; thereon engrave
"Edward" and "York"; then haply will she weep.   273
Therefore present to her—as sometime Margaret   274

Did to thy father, steeped in Rutland's blood—   275
A handkerchief, which, say to her, did drain
The purple sap from her sweet brothers' body;
And bid her wipe her weeping eyes withal.
If this inducement move her not to love,
Send her a letter of thy noble deeds.
Tell her thou mad'st away her uncle Clarence,
Her uncle Rivers, ay, and for her sake
Mad'st quick conveyance with her good aunt Anne.   283
KING RICHARD
You mock me, madam. This is not the way
To win your daughter.
QUEEN ELIZABETH   There is no other way,
Unless thou couldst put on some other shape
And not be Richard that hath done all this.
KING RICHARD
Say that I did all this for love of her.
QUEEN ELIZABETH
Nay, then indeed she cannot choose but hate thee,
Having bought love with such a bloody spoil.   290
KING RICHARD
Look what is done cannot be now amended.   291
Men shall deal unadvisedly sometimes,   292
Which after-hours gives leisure to repent.
If I did take the kingdom from your sons,
To make amends I'll give it to your daughter.
If I have killed the issue of your womb,
To quicken your increase I will beget   297
Mine issue of your blood upon your daughter.
A grandam's name is little less in love
Than is the doting title of a mother;
They are as children but one step below,
Even of your metal, of your very blood,   302
Of all one pain, save for a night of groans   303
Endured of her for whom you bid like sorrow.   304
Your children were vexation to your youth,
But mine shall be a comfort to your age.
The loss you have is but a son being king,
And by that loss your daughter is made queen.
I cannot make you what amends I would;
Therefore accept such kindness as I can.   310
Dorset your son, that with a fearful soul
Leads discontented steps in foreign soil,
This fair alliance quickly shall call home
To high promotions and great dignity.
The king that calls your beauteous daughter wife
Familiarly shall call thy Dorset brother;   316
Again shall you be mother to a king,
And all the ruins of distressful times
Repaired with double riches of content.
What? We have many goodly days to see.
The liquid drops of tears that you have shed
Shall come again, transformed to orient pearl,   322

245 **imperial type** symbol of rule   248 **demise** convey, transmit, lease 251 **So** provided that.   **Lethe** river in the underworld, the waters of which produce forgetfulness   254 **process** story   255 **date** duration 256 **from** with. (But Queen Elizabeth, in lines 259–261, sarcastically uses the word in the sense "apart from," "at variance with.") 260 **So** just so. (Said ironically.)   262 **confound** deliberately miscon-strue   269 **humor** temperament   273 **haply** perhaps   274 **sometime** once

275 **Rutland's** (See *3 Henry VI*, 1.4.79–83.)   283 **conveyance** with disposal of   290 **spoil** slaughter. (A hunting term.)   291 **Look what** whatever   292 **shall deal** cannot but act   297 **quicken your increase** give new life to your progeny   302 **metal** substance (with a sugges-tion also of *mettle*, "spirit." The Folio reads *mettall*.)   303 **pain** labor, effort   304 **of** by.   **bid** endured, bided   310 **can** am able (to give) 316 **Familiarly** familially   322 **orient** bright, shining

Advantaging their love with interest   323
Of ten times double gain of happiness.
Go then, my mother, to thy daughter go.
Make bold her bashful years with your experience;
Prepare her ears to hear a wooer's tale;
Put in her tender heart th' aspiring flame
Of golden sovereignty; acquaint the Princess
With the sweet silent hours of marriage joys.
And when this arm of mine hath chastisèd
The petty rebel, dull-brained Buckingham,
Bound with triumphant garlands will I come
And lead thy daughter to a conqueror's bed;
To whom I will retail my conquest won,   335
And she shall be sole victoress, Caesar's Caesar.

QUEEN ELIZABETH
What were I best to say? Her father's brother
Would be her lord? Or shall I say her uncle?
Or, he that slew her brothers and her uncles?
Under what title shall I woo for thee
That God, the law, my honor, and her love
Can make seem pleasing to her tender years?

KING RICHARD
Infer fair England's peace by this alliance.   343

QUEEN ELIZABETH
Which she shall purchase with still-lasting war.   344

KING RICHARD
Tell her the King, that may command, entreats.

QUEEN ELIZABETH
That at her hands which the King's King forbids.   346

KING RICHARD
Say she shall be a high and mighty queen.

QUEEN ELIZABETH
To vail the title, as her mother doth.   348

KING RICHARD
Say I will love her everlastingly.

QUEEN ELIZABETH
But how long shall that title "ever" last?

KING RICHARD
Sweetly in force unto her fair life's end.

QUEEN ELIZABETH
But how long fairly shall her sweet life last?   352

KING RICHARD
As long as heaven and nature lengthens it.

QUEEN ELIZABETH
As long as hell and Richard likes of it.

KING RICHARD
Say I, her sovereign, am her subject low.

QUEEN ELIZABETH
But she, your subject, loathes such sovereignty.

KING RICHARD
Be eloquent in my behalf to her.

QUEEN ELIZABETH
An honest tale speeds best being plainly told.   358

KING RICHARD
Then plainly to her tell my loving tale.

QUEEN ELIZABETH
Plain and not honest is too harsh a style.

KING RICHARD
Your reasons are too shallow and too quick.   361

QUEEN ELIZABETH
O, no, my reasons are too deep and dead—
Too deep and dead, poor infants, in their graves.

KING RICHARD
Harp not on that string, madam. That is past.

QUEEN ELIZABETH
Harp on it still shall I till heartstrings break.

KING RICHARD
Now, by my George, my Garter, and my crown—   366

QUEEN ELIZABETH
Profaned, dishonored, and the third usurped.

KING RICHARD
I swear—

QUEEN ELIZABETH   By nothing, for this is no oath.
Thy George, profaned, hath lost his lordly honor;   369
Thy Garter, blemished, pawned his knightly virtue;
Thy crown, usurped, disgraced his kingly glory.
If something thou wouldst swear to be believed,
Swear then by something that thou hast not
    wronged.

KING RICHARD
Then, by myself—

QUEEN ELIZABETH   Thyself is self-misused.

KING RICHARD
Now, by the world—

QUEEN ELIZABETH   'Tis full of thy foul wrongs.

KING RICHARD
My father's death—

QUEEN ELIZABETH   Thy life hath it dishonored.

KING RICHARD
Why then, by God—

QUEEN ELIZABETH   God's wrong is most of all.
If thou didst fear to break an oath with Him,
The unity the King my husband made   379
Thou hadst not broken, nor my brothers died.
If thou hadst feared to break an oath by Him,
Th' imperial metal circling now thy head
Had graced the tender temples of my child,
And both the princes had been breathing here,
Which now, two tender bedfellows for dust,
Thy broken faith hath made the prey for worms.
What canst thou swear by now?

KING RICHARD   The time to come.

QUEEN ELIZABETH
That thou hast wrongèd in the time o'erpast;
For I myself have many tears to wash
Hereafter time, for time past wronged by thee.   390

---

323 **Advantaging** augmenting.   **their love** i.e., the love that prompted
tears   335 **retail** relate   343 **Infer** allege, adduce (as a reason)
344 **still-lasting war** i.e., perpetual domestic strife   346 **forbids** (*The
Book of Common Prayer*, echoing the injunctions of Leviticus 18, prohibits the marriage of a man with his brother's daughter.)   348 **vail**
lower, abase as a sign of submission   352 **fairly** without foul play
358 **speeds** succeeds

361 **quick** hasty (with a pun on the meaning "alive," contrasted with
dead in the next line, just as *shallow* is punningly contrasted with
deep)   366 **George . . . Garter** (The George, a badge showing Saint
George slaying the dragon, was not added to the insignia of the Order
of the Garter until the reign of Henry VII or Henry VIII.)   369 **his** its
(as also in lines 370, 371)   379 **The unity** i.e., the reconciliation between Queen Elizabeth and her enemies   390 **Hereafter time** the
future

The children live whose fathers thou hast
  slaughtered,
Ungoverned youth, to wail it in their age;   392
The parents live whose children thou hast butchered,
Old barren plants, to wail it with their age.
Swear not by time to come, for that thou hast
Misused ere used, by times ill-used o'erpast.   396

KING RICHARD
As I intend to prosper and repent,   397
So thrive I in my dangerous affairs
Of hostile arms! Myself myself confound!   399
Heaven and fortune bar me happy hours!
Day, yield me not thy light, nor, night, thy rest!
Be opposite all planets of good luck   402
To my proceeding if, with dear heart's love,
Immaculate devotion, holy thoughts,
I tender not thy beauteous, princely daughter!   405
In her consists my happiness and thine;
Without her follows to myself and thee,
Herself, the land, and many a Christian soul,
Death, desolation, ruin, and decay.
It cannot be avoided but by this;
It will not be avoided but by this.
Therefore, dear Mother—I must call you so—
Be the attorney of my love to her.
Plead what I will be, not what I have been,
Not my deserts, but what I will deserve.
Urge the necessity and state of times,   416
And be not peevish-fond in great designs.   417

QUEEN ELIZABETH
Shall I be tempted of the devil thus?

KING RICHARD
Ay, if the devil tempt you to do good.

QUEEN ELIZABETH
Shall I forget myself to be myself?   420

KING RICHARD
Ay, if yourself's remembrance wrong yourself.   421

QUEEN ELIZABETH
Yet thou didst kill my children.

KING RICHARD
But in your daughter's womb I bury them,
Where in that nest of spicery they will breed   424
Selves of themselves, to your recomforture.   425

QUEEN ELIZABETH
Shall I go win my daughter to thy will?

KING RICHARD
And be a happy mother by the deed.

QUEEN ELIZABETH
I go. Write to me very shortly,
And you shall understand from me her mind.

KING RICHARD
Bear her my true love's kiss; and so, farewell.
                    Exit Queen [Elizabeth].
Relenting fool, and shallow, changing woman!

Enter Ratcliffe; [Catesby following].

How now, what news?

RATCLIFFE
Most mighty sovereign, on the western coast
Rideth a puissant navy; to our shores   434
Throng many doubtful, hollow-hearted friends,   435
Unarmed and unresolved to beat them back.
'Tis thought that Richmond is their admiral;   437
And there they hull, expecting but the aid   438
Of Buckingham to welcome them ashore.

KING RICHARD
Some light-foot friend post to the Duke of Norfolk: 440
Ratcliffe, thyself, or Catesby; where is he?

CATESBY
Here, my good lord.

KING RICHARD   Catesby, fly to the Duke.

CATESBY
I will, my lord, with all convenient haste.   443

KING RICHARD
Ratcliffe, come hither. Post to Salisbury.
When thou com'st thither—[*To Catesby.*] Dull,
  unmindful villain,
Why stay'st thou here, and go'st not to the Duke?

CATESBY
First, mighty liege, tell me Your Highness' pleasure,
What from Your Grace I shall deliver to him.

KING RICHARD
O, true, good Catesby. Bid him levy straight
The greatest strength and power that he can make,   450
And meet me suddenly at Salisbury.   451

CATESBY   I go.   *Exit.*

RATCLIFFE
What, may it please you, shall I do at Salisbury?

KING RICHARD
Why, what wouldst thou do there before I go?

RATCLIFFE
Your Highness told me I should post before.   455

KING RICHARD
My mind is changed.

Enter Lord Stanley [Earl of Derby].

                    Stanley, what news with you?

STANLEY
None good, my liege, to please you with the
  hearing,
Nor none so bad but well may be reported.

KING RICHARD
Heyday, a riddle! Neither good nor bad!
What need'st thou run so many miles about,

---

392 Ungoverned i.e., without a father's guidance or rule   **396 Misused . . . o'erpast** misused even before it came time to be used, by your ill use of past times   **397 As . . . repent** i.e., I swear that as I hope to thrive and intend to repent   **399 Myself . . . confound** may I destroy myself   **402 opposite** opposed, adverse   **405 tender** have a tender regard for   **416 state of times** state of affairs   **417 peevishfond** childishly foolish   **420 myself . . . myself** the person wronged by Richard . . . the queen-mother   **421 wrong yourself** i.e., interferes with what is to your advantage   **424 nest of spicery** (The fabled phoenix arose anew from the nest of spices, its funeral pyre.)   **425 recomforture** comfort, consolation

434 puissant powerful   **435 doubtful** apprehensive   **437 their admiral** i.e., of the *puissant navy*, named three lines earlier   **438 hull** drift with the sails furled   **440 light-foot** swift-footed.   **post** hasten   **443 convenient** appropriate, suitable   **450 make** raise   **451 suddenly** swiftly   **455 post** hasten

When thou mayst tell thy tale the nearest way?   461
Once more, what news?
STANLEY   Richmond is on the seas.
KING RICHARD
  There let him sink, and be the seas on him!
  White-livered runagate, what doth he there?   464
STANLEY
  I know not, mighty sovereign, but by guess.
KING RICHARD   Well, as you guess?
STANLEY
  Stirred up by Dorset, Buckingham, and Morton,
  He makes for England, here to claim the crown.
KING RICHARD
  Is the chair empty? Is the sword unswayed?   469
  Is the King dead? The empire unpossessed?   470
  What heir of York is there alive but we?
  And who is England's king but great York's heir?
  Then tell me, what makes he upon the seas?   473
STANLEY
  Unless for that, my liege, I cannot guess.
KING RICHARD
  Unless for that he comes to be your liege,
  You cannot guess wherefore the Welshman comes.   476
  Thou wilt revolt and fly to him, I fear.
STANLEY
  No, my good lord; therefore mistrust me not.
KING RICHARD
  Where is thy power, then, to beat him back?   479
  Where be thy tenants and thy followers?
  Are they not now upon the western shore,
  Safe-conducting the rebels from their ships?
STANLEY
  No, my good lord, my friends are in the north.
KING RICHARD
  Cold friends to me! What do they in the north
  When they should serve their sovereign in the west?
STANLEY
  They have not been commanded, mighty King.
  Pleaseth Your Majesty to give me leave,   487
  I'll muster up my friends and meet Your Grace
  Where and what time Your Majesty shall please.
KING RICHARD
  Ay, thou wouldst be gone to join with Richmond.
  But I'll not trust thee.
STANLEY   Most mighty sovereign,
  You have no cause to hold my friendship doubtful.
  I never was nor never will be false.
KING RICHARD
  Go then and muster men, but leave behind
  Your son, George Stanley. Look your heart be firm,
  Or else his head's assurance is but frail.   496
STANLEY
  So deal with him as I prove true to you.
            Exit Stanley [Earl of Derby].

Enter a Messenger.

FIRST MESSENGER
  My gracious sovereign, now in Devonshire,
  As I by friends am well advertisèd,   499
  Sir Edward Courtney and the haughty prelate,
  Bishop of Exeter, his elder brother,   501
  With many more confederates, are in arms.

Enter another Messenger.

SECOND MESSENGER
  In Kent, my liege, the Guildfords are in arms,
  And every hour more competitors   504
  Flock to the rebels, and their power grows strong.

Enter another Messenger.

THIRD MESSENGER
  My lord, the army of great Buckingham—
KING RICHARD
  Out on ye, owls! Nothing but songs of death?   507
                       He striketh him.
  There, take thou that, till thou bring better news.
THIRD MESSENGER
  The news I have to tell Your Majesty
  Is that by sudden floods and fall of waters
  Buckingham's army is dispersed and scattered,
  And he himself wandered away alone,
  No man knows whither.
KING RICHARD   I cry thee mercy.
  There is my purse to cure that blow of thine.
                       [He gives money.]
  Hath any well-advisèd friend proclaimed   515
  Reward to him that brings the traitor in?
THIRD MESSENGER
  Such proclamation hath been made, my lord.

Enter another Messenger.

FOURTH MESSENGER
  Sir Thomas Lovell and Lord Marquess Dorset,   518
  'Tis said, my liege, in Yorkshire are in arms.
  But this good comfort bring I to Your Highness:
  The Breton navy is dispersed by tempest.
  Richmond, in Dorsetshire, sent out a boat
  Unto the shore, to ask those on the banks
  If they were his assistants, yea or no,
  Who answered him they came from Buckingham
  Upon his party. He, mistrusting them,
  Hoised sail and made his course again for Brittany.   527
KING RICHARD
  March on, march on, since we are up in arms,
  If not to fight with foreign enemies,
  Yet to beat down these rebels here at home.

Enter Catesby.

CATESBY

My liege, the Duke of Buckingham is taken!
That is the best news. That the Earl of Richmond
Is with a mighty power landed at Milford   533
Is colder tidings, yet they must be told.

KING RICHARD

Away towards Salisbury! While we reason here,   535
A royal battle might be won and lost.
Someone take order Buckingham be brought
To Salisbury. The rest march on with me.
                              Flourish. Exeunt.

❦

4.5   *Enter [Lord Stanley Earl of] Derby and Sir
             Christopher [Urswick, a priest].*

STANLEY

Sir Christopher, tell Richmond this from me:
That in the sty of the most deadly boar
My son George Stanley is franked up in hold.   3
If I revolt, off goes young George's head;
The fear of that holds off my present aid.
So get thee gone; commend me to thy lord.
Withal say that the Queen hath heartily consented   7
He should espouse Elizabeth her daughter.   8
But tell me, where is princely Richmond now?

CHRISTOPHER

At Pembroke, or at Ha'rfordwest, in Wales.   10

STANLEY   What men of name resort to him?   11

CHRISTOPHER

Sir Walter Herbert, a renownèd soldier,
Sir Gilbert Talbot, Sir William Stanley,
Oxford, redoubted Pembroke, Sir James Blunt,   14
And Rice ap Thomas, with a valiant crew,
And many other of great name and worth;
And towards London do they bend their power,   17
If by the way they be not fought withal.

STANLEY

Well, hie thee to thy lord; I kiss his hand.   19
My letter will resolve him of my mind.   20
                              [He gives a letter.]
Farewell.   *Exeunt.*

❦

5.1   *Enter Buckingham, with [Sheriff and] halberds, led
             to execution.*

BUCKINGHAM

Will not King Richard let me speak with him?

SHERIFF

No, my good lord. Therefore be patient.

BUCKINGHAM

Hastings, and Edward's children, Grey, and Rivers,
Holy King Henry, and thy fair son Edward,   4
Vaughan, and all that have miscarried   5
By underhand corrupted foul injustice:
If that your moody, discontented souls   7
Do through the clouds behold this present hour,
Even for revenge mock my destruction!
This is All Souls' Day, fellow, is it not?   10

SHERIFF   It is, my lord.

BUCKINGHAM

Why, then All Souls' Day is my body's doomsday.
This is the day which, in King Edward's time,
I wished might fall on me when I was found
False to his children and his wife's allies;
This is the day wherein I wished to fall
By the false faith of him whom most I trusted;
This, this All Souls' Day to my fearful soul
Is the determined respite of my wrongs.   19
That high All-Seer which I dallied with
Hath turned my feignèd prayer on my head
And given in earnest what I begged in jest.
Thus doth he force the swords of wicked men
To turn their own points in their masters' bosoms.
Thus Margaret's curse falls heavy on my neck:
"When he," quoth she, "shall split thy heart with
    sorrow,
Remember Margaret was a prophetess."
Come lead me, officers, to the block of shame.
Wrong hath but wrong, and blame the due of
    blame.   *Exeunt Buckingham with officers.*

❦

5.2   *Enter Richmond, Oxford, [Sir James] Blunt, [Sir
             Walter] Herbert, and others, with drum and
             colors.*

RICHMOND

Fellows in arms, and my most loving friends
Bruised underneath the yoke of tyranny,
Thus far into the bowels of the land   3
Have we marched on without impediment;
And here receive we from our father Stanley   5
Lines of fair comfort and encouragement.
The wretched, bloody, and usurping boar,
That spoiled your summer fields and fruitful vines,   8
Swills your warm blood like wash, and makes his
    trough   9
In your emboweled bosoms, this foul swine   10

---

533 **Milford** i.e., Milford Haven on the coast of Wales in the county
of Pembroke. (A gap of two years is bridged here. Richmond's first
fruitless expedition was in October 1483; his landing at Milford was
in August 1485.) 535 **reason** talk
4.5. Location: London. The house of Lord Stanley, Earl of Derby.
s.d. Sir (Honorific title for a clergyman.) 3 **franked up in hold** shut
up in custody, as in a pigpen 7 **Withal** in addition 8 **espouse** marry
10 **Ha'rfordwest** Haverfordwest, in Wales 11 **name** rank 14 **redoubted** dreaded. **Pembroke** i.e., Jasper Tudor, Earl of Pembroke,
uncle to Richmond 17 **bend their power** direct their forces 19 **hie**
hasten 20 **resolve him of** inform him concerning
5.1. Location: Salisbury. An open place.

4 **thy** i.e., Henry's 5 **miscarried** perished 7 **moody** angry. **discontented** i.e., still seeking vengeance 10 **All Souls' Day** November 2,
the day on which the Roman Catholic Church intercedes for all Christian souls 19 **determined . . . wrongs** i.e., the ordained date to
which the punishment of my evil practices was respited or postponed
5.2. Location: A camp near Tamworth.
3 **bowels** i.e., center 5 **father** i.e., stepfather, Lord Stanley, Earl of
Derby 8 **spoiled** despoiled 9 **Swills** gulps. **wash** hogwash, swill
10 **emboweled** disemboweled

Is now even in the center of this isle,
Near to the town of Leicester, as we learn.
From Tamworth thither is but one day's march.
In God's name, cheerly on, courageous friends,   14
To reap the harvest of perpetual peace
By this one bloody trial of sharp war.

OXFORD
Every man's conscience is a thousand swords
To fight against this guilty homicide.

HERBERT
I doubt not but his friends will turn to us.

BLUNT
He hath no friends but what are friends for fear,   20
Which in his dearest need will fly from him.   21

RICHMOND
All for our vantage. Then, in God's name, march!
True hope is swift and flies with swallow's wings;
Kings it makes gods and meaner creatures kings.   24

                              Exeunt omnes.

5.3   *Enter King Richard in arms, with Norfolk,
Ratcliffe, and the Earl of Surrey [and others].*

KING RICHARD
Here pitch our tent, even here in Bosworth Field.
My lord of Surrey, why look you so sad?

SURREY
My heart is ten times lighter than my looks.

KING RICHARD
My lord of Norfolk—

NORFOLK   Here, most gracious liege.

KING RICHARD
Norfolk, we must have knocks; ha! Must we not?   5

NORFOLK
We must both give and take, my loving lord.

KING RICHARD
Up with my tent! Here will I lie tonight.
           [*Soldiers begin to set up King Richard's tent.*]
But where tomorrow? Well, all's one for that.   8
Who hath descried the number of the traitors?   9

NORFOLK
Six or seven thousand is their utmost power.

KING RICHARD
Why, our battalia trebles that account.   11
Besides, the King's name is a tower of strength,
Which they upon the adverse faction want.   13
Up with the tent! Come, noble gentlemen,
Let us survey the vantage of the ground.   15
Call for some men of sound direction.   16
Let's lack no discipline, make no delay,

For, lords, tomorrow is a busy day.   *Exeunt.*

    *Enter [on the other side of the stage] Richmond,
    Sir William Brandon, Oxford, and Dorset, [Blunt,
    Herbert, and others. Some of the soldiers pitch
    Richmond's tent.]*

RICHMOND
The weary sun hath made a golden set,
And, by the bright track of his fiery car,   20
Gives token of a goodly day tomorrow.
Sir William Brandon, you shall bear my standard.
Give me some ink and paper in my tent.
I'll draw the form and model of our battle,
Limit each leader to his several charge,   25
And part in just proportion our small power.   26
My lord of Oxford, you, Sir William Brandon,
And you, Sir Walter Herbert, stay with me.
The Earl of Pembroke keeps his regiment;   29
Good Captain Blunt, bear my good-night to him,
And by the second hour in the morning
Desire the Earl to see me in my tent.
Yet one thing more, good Captain, do for me:
Where is Lord Stanley quartered, do you know?

BLUNT
Unless I have mista'en his colors much,
Which well I am assured I have not done,
His regiment lies half a mile at least
South from the mighty power of the King.   38

RICHMOND
If without peril it be possible,
Sweet Blunt, make some good means to speak with
   him,
And give him from me this most needful note.
                              [*He gives a letter.*]

BLUNT
Upon my life, my lord, I'll undertake it.
And so, God give you quiet rest tonight!

RICHMOND
Good night, good Captain Blunt. [*Exit Blunt.*] Come,
   gentlemen,
Let us consult upon tomorrow's business.
Into my tent; the dew is raw and cold.
                   They withdraw into the tent.

    *Enter [to his tent, King] Richard, Ratcliffe,
    Norfolk, and Catesby.*

KING RICHARD
What is 't o'clock?

CATESBY   It's suppertime, my lord;
It's nine o'clock.

KING RICHARD   I will not sup tonight.
Give me some ink and paper.
What, is my beaver easier than it was,   50
And all my armor laid into my tent?

CATESBY
It is, my liege, and all things are in readiness.

---

14 **cheerly** cheerily, heartily   20 **for fear** i.e., out of fearing Richard
21 **dearest** direst   24 **meaner** of lower degree.   **s.d. omnes** all
5.3. Location: Bosworth Field.
5 **knocks** blows   8 **all's . . . that** be that as it may   9 **descried** re-
connoitred   11 **battalia** army   13 **want** lack   15 **vantage of the
ground** i.e., way in which the field can best be used for tactical advantage   16 **direction** judgment, military skill

20 **car** chariot (of Phoebus)   25 **Limit** appoint.   **several charge** individual command   26 **power** army   29 **keeps** i.e., is with   38 **power**
army   50 **beaver** face-guard or visor of helmet.   **easier** looser, better
fitting

KING RICHARD
Good Norfolk, hie thee to thy charge.
Use careful watch; choose trusty sentinels.
NORFOLK   I go, my lord.
KING RICHARD
Stir with the lark tomorrow, gentle Norfolk.
NORFOLK   I warrant you, my lord.   [Exit.] 57
KING RICHARD   Catesby!
CATESBY
My lord?
KING RICHARD   Send out a pursuivant at arms   59
To Stanley's regiment. Bid him bring his power   60
Before sunrising, lest his son George fall
Into the blind cave of eternal night.   [Exit Catesby.]
Fill me a bowl of wine. Give me a watch.   63
Saddle white Surrey for the field tomorrow.   64
Look that my staves be sound and not too heavy.   65
Ratcliffe!
RATCLIFFE   My lord?
KING RICHARD
Sawst thou the melancholy Lord Northumberland?
RATCLIFFE
Thomas the Earl of Surrey and himself,
Much about cockshut time, from troop to troop   70
Went through the army, cheering up the soldiers.
KING RICHARD
So, I am satisfied. Give me a bowl of wine.
I have not that alacrity of spirit
Nor cheer of mind that I was wont to have.   74
                          [Wine is brought.]
Set it down. Is ink and paper ready?
RATCLIFFE
It is, my lord.
KING RICHARD   Bid my guard watch. Leave me.
Ratcliffe, about the mid of night come to my tent
And help to arm me. Leave me, I say.
                  Exit Ratcliffe. [Richard sleeps.]

Enter [Lord Stanley Earl of] Derby, to Richmond
in his tent, [lords and others attending].

STANLEY
Fortune and victory sit on thy helm!   79
RICHMOND
All comfort that the dark night can afford
Be to thy person, noble father-in-law!   81
Tell me, how fares our loving mother?
STANLEY
I, by attorney, bless thee from thy mother,   83
Who prays continually for Richmond's good.
So much for that. The silent hours steal on,
And flaky darkness breaks within the east.   86

In brief—for so the season bids us be—   87
Prepare thy battle early in the morning,   88
And put thy fortune to the arbitrament   89
Of bloody strokes and mortal-staring war.   90
I, as I may—that which I would I cannot—   91
With best advantage will deceive the time   92
And aid thee in this doubtful shock of arms.   93
But on thy side I may not be too forward,   94
Lest, being seen, thy brother, tender George,   95
Be executed in his father's sight.
Farewell. The leisure and the fearful time   97
Cuts off the ceremonious vows of love
And ample interchange of sweet discourse
Which so long sundered friends should dwell upon.
God give us leisure for these rites of love!
Once more, adieu. Be valiant, and speed well!   102
RICHMOND
Good lords, conduct him to his regiment.
I'll strive with troubled thoughts to take a nap,   104
Lest leaden slumber peise me down tomorrow,   105
When I should mount with wings of victory.
Once more, good night, kind lords and gentlemen.
              Exeunt. [Richmond remains.]
O Thou whose captain I account myself,
Look on my forces with a gracious eye;
Put in their hands thy bruising irons of wrath,
That they may crush down with a heavy fall
The usurping helmets of our adversaries!
Make us thy ministers of chastisement,
That we may praise thee in the victory!
To thee I do commend my watchful soul
Ere I let fall the windows of mine eyes.   116
Sleeping and waking, O, defend me still!   117
                          [He sleeps.]

Enter the Ghost of young Prince Edward, son [of]
Harry the Sixth, to Richard.

GHOST (to Richard)
Let me sit heavy on thy soul tomorrow!   118
Think, how thou stabbedst me in my prime of youth
At Tewkesbury. Despair therefore and die!
(To Richmond.) Be cheerful, Richmond, for the
   wrongèd souls
Of butchered princes fight in thy behalf.
King Henry's issue, Richmond, comforts thee. [Exit.]

Enter the Ghost of Henry the Sixth.

GHOST (to Richard)
When I was mortal, my anointed body   124
By thee was punchèd full of deadly holes.

57 warrant guarantee 59 pursuivant at arms junior officer attendant
on a herald 60 power forces 63 watch watch light, candle marked
into equal divisions to show time; or, perhaps, sentinel 64 white
Surrey (The name seems to be Shakespeare's invention. The chroniclers say that Richard was mounted on a "great white courser.")
65 staves lance shafts 70 cockshut time evening twilight; possibly,
the time at which the poultry are shut up 74 was wont used
79 helm helmet 81 father-in-law i.e., stepfather 83 by attorney as
proxy 86 flaky streaked with light

87 season time of day 88 battle troops 89 arbitrament arbitration
90 mortal-staring fatal-visaged 91 that . . . cannot i.e., I cannot
fight openly on your side, though I want to 92 With . . . time i.e.,
as best I can I will work for your side without seeming to do so
93 shock encounter 94 forward zealous 95 brother i.e., stepbrother. tender young, of tender years 97 leisure i.e., brief time allowed 102 speed well may you succeed 104 with against, in spite
of 105 peise weigh 116 windows i.e., eyelids 117 still continually 118 sit heavy on be oppressive to 124 anointed i.e., with the
sacred oil used in the coronation ceremony; compare with 4.4.151

Think on the Tower and me. Despair and die!   126
Harry the Sixth bids thee despair and die!
(*To Richmond.*) Virtuous and holy, be thou
    conqueror!
Harry, that prophesied thou shouldst be king,   129
Doth comfort thee in thy sleep. Live and flourish!
                                            [*Exit.*]

Enter the Ghost of Clarence.

GHOST [*to Richard*]
Let me sit heavy in thy soul tomorrow,
I, that was washed to death with fulsome wine,   132
Poor Clarence, by thy guile betrayed to death!
Tomorrow in the battle think on me,
And fall thy edgeless sword. Despair and die!   135
(*To Richmond.*) Thou offspring of the house of
    Lancaster,
The wrongèd heirs of York do pray for thee.
Good angels guard thy battle! Live and flourish!   138
                                            [*Exit.*]

Enter the Ghosts of Rivers, Grey, [and] Vaughan.

GHOST OF RIVERS [*to Richard*]
Let me sit heavy in thy soul tomorrow,
Rivers that died at Pomfret! Despair and die!
GHOST OF GREY [*to Richard*]
Think upon Grey, and let thy soul despair!
GHOST OF VAUGHAN [*to Richard*]
Think upon Vaughan, and, with guilty fear,
Let fall thy lance. Despair and die!
ALL (*to Richmond*)
Awake, and think our wrongs in Richard's bosom
Will conquer him! Awake, and win the day!
                                        [*Exeunt Ghosts.*]

Enter the Ghost of Hastings.

GHOST [*to Richard*]
Bloody and guilty, guiltily awake
And in a bloody battle end thy days!
Think on Lord Hastings. Despair and die!
(*To Richmond.*) Quiet untroubled soul, awake,
    awake!
Arm, fight, and conquer for fair England's sake!
                                            [*Exit.*]

Enter the Ghosts of the two young Princes.

GHOSTS (*to Richard*)
Dream on thy cousins smothered in the Tower.   151
Let us be lead within thy bosom, Richard,
And weigh thee down to ruin, shame, and death!
Thy nephews' souls bid thee despair and die!
(*To Richmond.*) Sleep, Richmond, sleep in peace, and
    wake in joy.
Good angels guard thee from the boar's annoy!   156

Live, and beget a happy race of kings!
Edward's unhappy sons do bid thee flourish.
                                        [*Exeunt Ghosts.*]

Enter the Ghost of Lady Anne, his wife.

GHOST [*to Richard*]
Richard, thy wife, that wretched Anne thy wife,
That never slept a quiet hour with thee,
Now fills thy sleep with perturbations.
Tomorrow in the battle think on me,
And fall thy edgeless sword. Despair and die!
(*To Richmond.*) Thou quiet soul, sleep thou a quiet
    sleep;
Dream of success and happy victory!
Thy adversary's wife doth pray for thee.   [*Exit.*]

Enter the Ghost of Buckingham.

GHOST [*to Richard*]
The first was I that helped thee to the crown;
The last was I that felt thy tyranny.
O, in the battle think on Buckingham,
And die in terror of thy guiltiness!
Dream on, dream on of bloody deeds and death;
Fainting, despair; despairing, yield thy breath!   172
(*To Richmond.*) I died for hope ere I could lend thee
    aid,   173
But cheer thy heart, and be thou not dismayed.
God and good angels fight on Richmond's side,
And Richard fall in height of all his pride.   [*Exit.*] 176
                Richard starteth up out of a dream.
KING RICHARD
Give me another horse! Bind up my wounds!
Have mercy, Jesu!—Soft, I did but dream.
O coward conscience, how dost thou afflict me!
The lights burn blue. It is now dead midnight.   180
Cold fearful drops stand on my trembling flesh.
What do I fear? Myself? There's none else by.
Richard loves Richard; that is, I am I.   183
Is there a murderer here? No. Yes, I am.
Then fly. What, from myself? Great reason why: 185
Lest I revenge. What, myself upon myself?
Alack, I love myself. Wherefore? For any good   187
That I myself have done unto myself?
O, no! Alas, I rather hate myself
For hateful deeds committed by myself!
I am a villain. Yet I lie, I am not.
Fool, of thyself speak well. Fool, do not flatter.
My conscience hath a thousand several tongues,   193
And every tongue brings in a several tale,
And every tale condemns me for a villain.
Perjury, perjury, in the highest degree,
Murder, stern murder, in the direst degree,
All several sins, all used in each degree,   198

---

126 **Tower** (Where Henry VI was supposed to have been murdered.)
129 **prophesied** (See *3 Henry VI*, 4.6.68 ff.)   132 **washed to death**
i.e., drowned in a butt of malmsey.   **fulsome** cloying   135 **fall** let
fall.   **edgeless** blunt, useless   138 **battle** troops   151 **cousins** i.e.,
nephews   156 **the boar's annoy** i.e., Richard's attack

172 **Fainting** losing heart   173 **for hope** i.e., for hoping to support
you, or for want of hope, hoping in vain to help   176 **Richard fall**
may Richard fall   180 **lights burn blue** (Superstitiously regarded as
evidence of the presence of ghosts.)   183 **I am I** (A blasphemy of
God's "ego sum.")   185 **fly** flee   187 **Wherefore** why   193 **several**
different, separate   198 **used . . . degree** committed in every degree
of infamy, from bad to worst

Throng to the bar, crying all, "Guilty! Guilty!"   199
I shall despair. There is no creature loves me,   200
And if I die no soul will pity me.
And wherefore should they, since that I myself
Find in myself no pity to myself?
Methought the souls of all that I had murdered
Came to my tent, and every one did threat
Tomorrow's vengeance on the head of Richard.

Enter Ratcliffe.

RATCLIFFE   My lord!
KING RICHARD   Zounds! Who is there?
RATCLIFFE
My lord, 'tis I. The early village cock
Hath twice done salutation to the morn.
Your friends are up and buckle on their armor.
KING RICHARD
O Ratcliffe, I have dreamed a fearful dream!
What think'st thou, will our friends prove all true?
RATCLIFFE
No doubt, my lord.
KING RICHARD   O Ratcliffe, I fear, I fear!
RATCLIFFE
Nay, good my lord, be not afraid of shadows.
KING RICHARD
By the apostle Paul, shadows tonight
Have struck more terror to the soul of Richard
Than can the substance of ten thousand soldiers
Armèd in proof and led by shallow Richmond.   219
'Tis not yet near day. Come, go with me;
Under our tents I'll play the eavesdropper,
To see if any mean to shrink from me.
                        Exeunt [Richard and Ratcliffe].

Enter the Lords to Richmond, [sitting in his tent].

LORDS   Good morrow, Richmond!
RICHMOND
Cry mercy, lords and watchful gentlemen,   224
That you have ta'en a tardy sluggard here.
A LORD   How have you slept, my lord?
RICHMOND
The sweetest sleep and fairest-boding dreams
That ever entered in a drowsy head
Have I since your departure had, my lords.
Methought their souls whose bodies Richard
    murdered
Came to my tent and cried on victory.   231
I promise you, my soul is very jocund   232
In the remembrance of so fair a dream.
How far into the morning is it, lords?
A LORD   Upon the stroke of four.
RICHMOND
Why, then 'tis time to arm and give direction.

His oration to his soldiers.

More than I have said, loving countrymen,   237
The leisure and enforcement of the time   238
Forbids to dwell upon. Yet remember this:
God and our good cause fight upon our side.
The prayers of holy saints and wrongèd souls,
Like high-reared bulwarks, stand before our faces.
Richard except, those whom we fight against   243
Had rather have us win than him they follow.
For what is he they follow? Truly, gentlemen,
A bloody tyrant and a homicide;
One raised in blood, and one in blood established; 247
One that made means to come by what he hath,   248
And slaughtered those that were the means to help
    him;
A base, foul stone, made precious by the foil   250
Of England's chair, where he is falsely set;   251
One that hath ever been God's enemy.
Then if you fight against God's enemy,
God will in justice ward you as his soldiers;   254
If you do sweat to put a tyrant down,
You sleep in peace, the tyrant being slain;
If you do fight against your country's foes,
Your country's fat shall pay your pains the hire; 258
If you do fight in safeguard of your wives,
Your wives shall welcome home the conquerors;
If you do free your children from the sword,
Your children's children quits it in your age.   262
Then, in the name of God and all these rights,
Advance your standards! Draw your willing swords! 264
For me, the ransom of my bold attempt   265
Shall be this cold corpse on the earth's cold face; 266
But if I thrive, the gain of my attempt
The least of you shall share his part thereof.
Sound drums and trumpets boldly and cheerfully;
God and Saint George! Richmond and victory!
                                    [Exeunt.]

Enter King Richard, Ratcliffe, [attendants and forces].

KING RICHARD
What said Northumberland as touching Richmond?
RATCLIFFE
That he was never trainèd up in arms.
KING RICHARD
He said the truth. And what said Surrey then?
RATCLIFFE
He smiled and said, "The better for our purpose."
KING RICHARD
He was in the right, and so indeed it is.
                            The clock striketh.
Tell the clock there. Give me a calendar.   276

199 **bar** i.e., bar of justice 200 **despair** (Considered the only unforgivable sin.) 219 **proof** armor that is proof against weapons 224 **Cry mercy** I beg your pardon 231 **cried on victory** invoked victory, cried out to it 232 **jocund** cheerful

237 **have said** have already said before 238 **leisure** i.e., brief time allowed 243 **except** excepted 247 **in blood** by bloodshed 248 **made means** i.e., has taken advantage, created opportunity 250 **foil** a thin leaf of metal placed under a gem to set it off to advantage 251 **chair** throne. **set** (1) seated (2) set like a jewel 254 **ward** protect 258 **fat** prosperity, wealth. **pains** efforts. **hire** reward 262 **quits** requite. **in your age** when you are old 264 **Advance** raise 265–266 **the ransom . . . face** i.e., if I fail, there will be no question of ransom, but only death 276 **Tell** count the strokes of. **calendar** almanac

Who saw the sun today?   [*He takes an almanac.*]
RATCLIFFE   Not I, my lord.
KING RICHARD
Then he disdains to shine, for by the book   278
He should have braved the east an hour ago.   279
A black day will it be to somebody.
Ratcliffe!
RATCLIFFE
My lord?
KING RICHARD   The sun will not be seen today;
The sky doth frown and lour upon our army.   283
I would these dewy tears were from the ground.
Not shine today? Why, what is that to me
More than to Richmond? For the selfsame heaven
That frowns on me looks sadly upon him.

Enter Norfolk.

NORFOLK
Arm, arm, my lord, the foe vaunts in the field!   288
KING RICHARD
Come, bustle, bustle! Caparison my horse.   289
Call up Lord Stanley; bid him bring his power.
I will lead forth my soldiers to the plain,
And thus my battle shall be orderèd: 292
My foreward shall be drawn out all in length,   293
Consisting equally of horse and foot;
Our archers shall be placèd in the midst.
John Duke of Norfolk, Thomas Earl of Surrey,
Shall have the leading of this foot and horse.
They thus directed, we will follow   298
In the main battle, whose puissance on either side   299
Shall be well wingèd with our chiefest horse.   300
This, and Saint George to boot! What think'st thou,
Norfolk?   301
NORFOLK
A good direction, warlike sovereign.
This found I on my tent this morning.
                              He showeth him a paper.
KING RICHARD [*reads*]
"Jockey of Norfolk, be not so bold,   304
For Dickon thy master is bought and sold."   305
A thing devisèd by the enemy.
Go, gentlemen, every man unto his charge.
Let not our babbling dreams affright our souls;
Conscience is but a word that cowards use,
Devised at first to keep the strong in awe.
Our strong arms be our conscience, swords our law!
March on, join bravely! Let us to it pell-mell;   312
If not to heaven, then hand in hand to hell.

His oration to his army.

278 **the book** i.e., the almanac   279 **braved** made splendid
283 **lour** look threateningly   288 **vaunts** boasts his strength   289 **Caparison** put on the battle trappings of   292 **battle** troops   293 **foreward** vanguard   298 **directed** deployed   299 **main battle** main
body of troops.   **puissance** strength   300 **wingèd** flanked.   **horse**
cavalry   301 **to boot** i.e., to give us aid in addition   304 **Jockey** i.e.,
Jack, John   305 **Dickon** i.e., Dick, Richard.   **bought and sold** i.e.,
betrayed for a bribe, brought to confusion   312 **join** join battle.
pell-mell headlong, recklessly

What shall I say more than I have inferred?   314
Remember whom you are to cope withal:
A sort of vagabonds, rascals, and runaways,   316
A scum of Bretons and base lackey peasants,   317
Whom their o'ercloyèd country vomits forth   318
To desperate adventures and assured destruction.
You sleeping safe, they bring to you unrest;
You having lands, and blest with beauteous wives,
They would restrain the one, distain the other.   322
And who doth lead them but a paltry fellow,
Long kept in Brittany at our mother's cost?   324
A milksop, one that never in his life
Felt so much cold as over shoes in snow?   326
Let's whip these stragglers o'er the seas again.
Lash hence these overweening rags of France,   328
These famished beggars, weary of their lives,
Who, but for dreaming on this fond exploit,   330
For want of means, poor rats, had hanged
themselves.   331
If we be conquered, let men conquer us,
And not these bastard Bretons, whom our fathers
Have in their own land beaten, bobbed, and
thumped,   334
And in record left them the heirs of shame.   335
Shall these enjoy our lands? Lie with our wives?
Ravish our daughters? [*Drum afar off.*] Hark! I hear
their drum.
Fight, gentlemen of England! Fight, bold yeomen!
Draw, archers, draw your arrows to the head!
Spur your proud horses hard, and ride in blood;
Amaze the welkin with your broken staves!   341

[*Enter a Messenger.*]

What says Lord Stanley? Will he bring his power?
MESSENGER   My lord, he doth deny to come.   343
KING RICHARD   Off with his son George's head!
NORFOLK
My lord, the enemy is past the marsh.
After the battle let George Stanley die.
KING RICHARD
A thousand hearts are great within my bosom.
Advance our standards! Set upon our foes!   348
Our ancient word of courage, fair Saint George,   349
Inspire us with the spleen of fiery dragons!   350
Upon them! Victory sits on our helms!   *Exeunt.*

314 **inferred** stated   316 **sort** gang   317 **lackey** servile
318 **o'ercloyèd** satiated, glutted   322 **restrain** deprive you of.   **distain** defile, sully   324 **our mother's** (Richmond's mother was not Richard's. This error occurs in the second edition of Holinshed's *Chronicles*. The first edition reads "brothers," the reference being to the fact
that Richmond had been supported at the court of the Duke of Brittany at the cost of Charles, Duke of Burgundy, Richard's brother-in-
law.)   326 **over shoes** i.e., over his shoe-tops   328 **rags** ragged fellows   330 **fond** foolish   331 **want of means** poverty   334 **bobbed**
thrashed   335 **And . . . shame** and left them with nothing but the
promise of a shameful record in history   341 **Amaze the welkin** fright
the skies   343 **deny** refuse   348 **Advance** raise   349 **word of courage** battle cry   350 **dragons** (Richard ironically identifies with the
dragon slain by Saint George.)

5.4   *Alarum. Excursions. [Norfolk and forces continue to make forays, entering and exiting.] Enter [in the melee] Catesby.*

CATESBY
Rescue, my lord of Norfolk, rescue, rescue!
The King enacts more wonders than a man,   2
Daring an opposite to every danger.   3
His horse is slain, and all on foot he fights,
Seeking for Richmond in the throat of death.
Rescue, fair lord, or else the day is lost!

[Alarums.] Enter [King] Richard.

KING RICHARD
A horse! A horse! My kingdom for a horse!
CATESBY
Withdraw, my lord. I'll help you to a horse.
KING RICHARD
Slave, I have set my life upon a cast,   9
And I will stand the hazard of the die.   10
I think there be six Richmonds in the field;   11
Five have I slain today instead of him.
A horse! A horse! My kingdom for a horse! *[Exeunt.]*

5.5   *Alarum. Enter Richard and Richmond; they fight. Richard is slain. [Exit Richmond.] Then, retreat being sounded, [flourish, and] enter Richmond, [Lord Stanley Earl of] Derby bearing the crown, with other lords, etc.*

RICHMOND
God and your arms be praised, victorious friends!
The day is ours; the bloody dog is dead.
STANLEY *[offering him the crown]*
Courageous Richmond, well hast thou acquit thee.
Lo, here this long-usurpèd royalty
From the dead temples of this bloody wretch
Have I plucked off, to grace thy brows withal.   6
Wear it, enjoy it, and make much of it.
RICHMOND
Great God of heaven, say amen to all!
But, tell me, is young George Stanley living?
STANLEY
He is, my lord, and safe in Leicester town,
Whither, if it please you, we may now withdraw us.
RICHMOND
What men of name are slain on either side?
STANLEY
John Duke of Norfolk, Walter Lord Ferrers,

Sir Robert Brackenbury, and Sir William Brandon.
RICHMOND
Inter their bodies as becomes their births.
Proclaim a pardon to the soldiers fled
That in submission will return to us,
And then, as we have ta'en the Sacrament,   18
We will unite the white rose and the red.
Smile heaven upon this fair conjunction,   20
That long have frowned upon their enmity!
What traitor hears me and says not amen?
England hath long been mad, and scarred herself;
The brother blindly shed the brother's blood,
The father rashly slaughtered his own son,
The son, compelled, been butcher to the sire.
All this divided York and Lancaster,
Divided in their dire division.
O, now let Richmond and Elizabeth,
The true succeeders of each royal house,
By God's fair ordinance conjoin together!   31
And let their heirs, God, if thy will be so,
Enrich the time to come with smooth-faced peace,
With smiling plenty, and fair prosperous days!
Abate the edge of traitors, gracious Lord,   35
That would reduce these bloody days again   36
And make poor England weep in streams of blood!
Let them not live to taste this land's increase
That would with treason wound this fair land's peace!
Now civil wounds are stopped, peace lives again.   40
That she may long live here, God say amen! *Exeunt.*

18 ta'en the Sacrament sworn a sacred oath on the Sacrament (to marry Princess Elizabeth, daughter of Edward IV, thereby uniting the houses of York and of Lancaster, white rose and red rose)   **20 conjunction** union. (An astrological metaphor.)   **31 ordinance** decree   **35 Abate** blunt, render ineffective   **36 reduce** bring back   **40 stopped** closed up

5.4. Location: Bosworth Field, as before; the action is continuous.
s.d. Excursions sorties   **2 than a man** than seems possible for a human being   **3 Daring . . . danger** boldly facing every danger in battle   **9 cast** throw of the dice   **10 die** (Singular of *dice*.)   **11 six Richmonds** i.e., Richmond himself and five men dressed like him as a safety precaution
5.5. Location: Action continues at Bosworth Field.
s.d. retreat trumpet signal to withdraw, cease the attack   **6 withal** with

The Life and Death of King John

The Life and Death of King John is usually dated on grounds of style between Shakespeare's two historical tetralogies, perhaps shortly before *Richard II* in 1594 or 1595. In structure and characterization, it is also transitional from the episodic first series *(Henry VI* through *Richard III)* to the more tightly organized second series *(Richard II* through *Henry V).* It stands alone among Shakespeare's history plays of the 1590s in choosing the early thirteenth century for its subject, rather than the fifteenth century. Yet the political problems are familiar.

Foremost is the uncertainty of John's claim to the English throne. He occupies that throne by "strong possession" and also seemingly by the last will and testament of his deceased eldest brother, King Richard I. But could such a will disinherit Arthur, the son of John's older brother Geoffrey? English primogeniture specified that property must descend to the eldest son; after Richard's death, without direct heirs, his next brother, Geoffrey, would inherit and then Geoffrey's son, Arthur. Significantly, even John's mother, Queen Eleanor, who publicly supports John's claim, privately admits that "strong possession" is much more on their side than "right" (1.1.39–40). All parties concede, then, that young Arthur's claim is legally superior.

Yet such a claim raises serious practical questions, because it challenges the status quo. John is de facto king, and Arthur a child. To make the dilemma complete, Arthur has no ambitions to rule and seemingly no talent for leadership. Without the unremitting zeal of his widowed mother, Constance, Arthur would retire into the private world of kindness and love, where his virtues shine. Moreover, Constance's uncompromising defense of her son's true claim requires her to seek alliance with the French for an invasion of England. Such an appalling prospect of invasion and civil war inevitably poses the question: is the replacement of John by Arthur worth the price? Which is better—an ongoing regime flawed by uncertain claim and political compromises or restitution of the "right" by violent and potentially self-destructive means?

Shakespeare refuses to simplify the issues. John is neither a monstrous tyrant nor a martyred hero, although both interpretations were available to Shakespeare in sixteenth-century historical writings. Catholic historians of the late Middle Ages, such as Polydore Vergil, had uniformly condemned John, partly, at least, because of his interference with the Church. The English Reformation brought about a conscious rewriting of history, and, in John Bale's play *King Johan* (1538, with later revisions), the protagonist is unassailably a champion of the right. Centuries ahead of his time, this King John comprehends the true interests of the state in fending off the encroachments of the international Church. He fails only because his people are superstitious and his aristocrats are the dupes of Catholic meddling. Bale's play is transparently a warning to Tudor England. This portrait of John as a martyr continues unabated in John Foxe's *Acts and Monuments* and in the chronicles of Richard Grafton and Raphael Holinshed, which were based on Foxe. Most virulent of all is the play called *The Troublesome Reign of King John* (c. 1587–1591), once thought to be by Shakespeare and analyzed by some recent editors as a bad quarto of Shakespeare's text but now generally regarded as the work of some more chauvinistic playwright, such as George Peele. Although generally close to Shakespeare's play in its narrative of events, it also contains scenes of the most degraded anti-Catholic humor, featuring gross abbots who conceal nuns in their private rooms, and the like. Against such a corrupt institution, the plundering undertaken by King John's loyal follower, Philip the Bastard (also known as Sir Richard Plantagenet), is wholly justifiable. John and the Bastard would be invincible, were it not for the base Catholic loyalties of the nobility.

Shakespeare consciously declines to endorse either the Catholic or the Protestant interpretation of the reign of King John. (Interestingly, neither side showed any interest in Magna Carta; not until the seventeenth century was that event interpreted as a famous precedent for constitutional restraints imposed on the monarchy.) To be sure, some anticlericalism still remains in the play. John grandly proclaims that "no Italian priest / Shall tithe or toll in our dominions." John is "supreme head" of Church and State (the actual title claimed by Henry VIII), defending his people against "this meddling priest" with his "juggling witchcraft" (3.1.153–169). Yet Shakespeare's King John is not vindictive against the Church. He seizes some of its wealth, not as a reprisal, but to support his costly military campaigns; when he is poisoned by a monk, neither John nor anyone else assumes that a Catholic conspiracy is responsible—as it is in *Troublesome Reign.* Similarly, the baronial opposition to John is motivated not by secret leanings toward Rome but by understandable revulsion at the apparent murder of Arthur.

Shakespeare's balanced treatment need not merely reflect his own political allegiances, whatever they were. Artistically, *King John* is a study of impasse, of tortured political dilemmas to which there can be no clear answer. How do people behave under such trying circumstances? Shakespeare's play is remarkable for its sensitivity and compassion toward all sides. His most completely sympathetic characters are those innocently caught in the political cross fire, such as Arthur and the Lady Blanche. Among the major contenders for power, all except the ruthless Dauphin Lewis are guided by worthy intentions and yet are forced to make unfortunate and self-contradictory compromises. Constance, for all her virtuous singleness of mind, must seek a French invasion of England. King Philip of France, bound to Constance's cause by all the holy vows of heaven, changes his purpose when England offers a profitable marriage alliance and then shifts quickly back again when the papacy demands in the name of the Church that Philip punish King John for heresy. Philip's conscience is troubled about both decisions, but what is a king to do when faced with practical choices affecting his people's welfare and his own political safety?

Even Pandulph, the papal legate, can be viewed as a well-intentioned statesman caught in the web of political compromise. Presumably, he is sincere in his belief that King John's defiance of the papacy—in particular, his refusal to accept the Pope's choice, Stephen Langton, as Archbishop of Canterbury—represents a grave threat to Catholic Christendom. Yet Pandulph reveals an unprincipled cunning when he teaches King Philip how to equivocate a sacred vow, or instructs the apt young Lewis in Machiavellian intrigue. As Pandulph explains, the French can exploit King John's capture of Arthur by invading England in Arthur's name, thereby forcing John to murder his nephew in order to terminate the rival claim to the throne. Arthur's death will, in turn, drive the English nobility over to the French side. By this stratagem, the seemingly bad luck of Arthur's capture can neatly be turned to the advantage of France and the international Church (3.4.126–181). Lewis learns his lesson only too well. What Pandulph has failed to take into account is the insincerity of Lewis' alliance with papal power. When the legate has achieved through the invasion what he wants—the submission of John—and then tries to call off Lewis' army, Pandulph discovers too late that the young Frenchman cares only for war on his own terms. Pandulph's cunning becomes a weapon turned against himself.

John is, like his enemies, a talented man justly punished by his own perjuries. His failings are serious, but they are also understandable. Given the fact that he is king, his desire to maintain rule serves both his own interests and those of political order generally. The deal by which John bargains away his French territories of Angiers, Touraine, Maine, Poitiers, and the rest, in order to win peace with France, is prudent under the circumstances but a blow to those English dreams of greatness that John professes to uphold. When France immediately repudiates this treaty, John merely gets what he deserves for entering such a deal. His surrender of the crown to the papacy is again the canny result of yielding to the least dangerous of the alternatives available but diminishes John's already shaky authority nonetheless.

Most heinous is John's determination to be rid of Arthur. He has compelling reasons, to be sure. As Pandulph predicts, the French invasion of England, using Arthur's claim as its pretext, forces John to consider Arthur as an immediate threat to himself. (Queen Elizabeth had long agonized over a similar problem with her captive, Mary, Queen of Scots; so long as Mary lived, a Catholic and claimant to the throne, English Catholics had a perennial rallying point.) What is a ruling king to do with a rival claimant in his captivity? As Henry IV also discovers once he has captured Richard II, the logic demanding death is inexorable. Yet such a deed is not only murder but also murder of one's close kinsman and murder of the Lord's anointed in the eyes of those believing the captive, in this case Arthur, to be rightful king. Furthermore, it is sure to backfire and punish the doer by arousing national resentment and rebellion. John quickly regrets Arthur's death, but we suspect that the regret is, in part, motivated by fear of the consequences. The same unseen power that protects John against his own worst instincts, momentarily saving the boy from Hubert's instruments of torture, also justly prevents John from obtaining any political benefit from this brief reprieve; Hubert is too late, Arthur dies in a fall, and the lords are convinced of John's guilt. With fitting irony, John is punished for his crime after he has decided not to do it and after the murder itself has failed to take place.

The word used to sum up the universal political scheming and oath breaking in this play is *commodity*, or self-interest (2.1.574). The word is introduced by the Bastard, the fascinating choric figure of *King John,* whose reactions to the events of the play are so important in shaping our own. The Bastard is an outsider from birth and so not beholden to society for its usual tawdry benefits. As the natural son of the great King Richard Coeur de Lion, the Bastard is a kind of folk hero: he is instinctively royal and yet a commoner, a projection of the Elizabethan audience's sentimental fondness for monarchy and at the same time a hero representing all of society. He is a fictional character in a largely historical world. His quarrel with his effete brother Robert over the inheritance of their father's property comically mirrors the futility of the dynastic quarrel between King John and Arthur. In both contentions, a will left by the deceased confuses the issue of genealogical priority. Thus John, who defends the Bastard's unconventional claim to his inheritance, discovers a natural ally.

The Bastard is strangely drawn to commodity at first. He finds it exhilarating to trust his fortune to war and the King's favor, rather than to the easy comfort of a landed estate. The wars enable him to pursue a quest for self-identity. After learning from his reluctant mother who his real father was, the Bastard must venge himself upon the Duke of Austria, who killed his father. When first confronted with the moral ambiguity of the war, the Bastard's response is mischievous, almost Vicelike. He makes the cunning suggestion, for example, that France and England join against the city of Angiers until it surrenders, after which they may resume fighting one another. Clearly, this Machiavellian proposal embodies, even satirizes, the spirit of commodity. Yet the Bastard is not motivated by self-interest or a cynical delight in duping people, as is the bastard Edmund in *King Lear*. This Bastard's illegitimacy has no such ominous cosmic import. Instead, he is at first the detached witty observer, wryly amused at the seemingly inherent absurdity of politics. Although he does protest also that he will worship commodity for his own gain, we never see him doing so. Despite his philosophic detachment, he remains loyal to England and to John. In fact, he is the play's greatest patriot.

The supreme test for the Bastard, as for all well-meaning characters and for the audience as well, is the death of Arthur. The Bastard must experience disaffection and even revulsion if he is to retain our sympathy as choric interpreter. Yet his chief function is to triumph over that revulsion and, in so doing, to act as counterpart to the more rash English lords. They have come hastily to the conclusion that John is guilty of Arthur's death. This is, of course, true in the main, but they do not know all the circumstances, and truth, as always, is more complicated than they suppose. Only the Bastard consistently phrases his condemnation in qualified terms: "It is a damnèd and a bloody work . . . If that it be the work of any hand" (4.3.57–59). Moreover, the lords have concluded that John's guilt justifies their rebellion. Yet they stoop to commodity of the very sort they condemn. They fight for the supposed good of England by allying themselves with Lewis of France. Once again, the ironies of cosmic justice demand that such commodity be repaid by treachery. The lords are luckily saved just in time by Lord Melun's revelation of Lewis' plan, just as John had been saved from his own headstrong folly by the kindness of Hubert. The Bastard's decision to remain loyal to John thus proves not only prudent but also right-minded. He has led our sympathies through disaffection to acceptance. Rebellion only worsens matters by playing into the hands of opportunists. Loyalty to John is still, in a sense, a kind of commodity, for it involves compromise and acceptance of politics as morally a world unto itself. Nevertheless, loyalty is a conscientious choice and is rewarded finally by the accession of young Henry III, who at last combines political legitimacy and the will to act.

The ending of *King John* is not without its ironies. England, having suffered through the dynastic uncertainties of a child claimant to the throne (as also in the *Henry VI* plays, *Richard III, Richard II,* and Christopher Marlowe's *Edward II*), must now face a new destiny under the young and unproven Henry III. The irony is often underscored, in modern productions at least, by doubling the parts of Arthur and Henry III for the same juvenile actor. Is there sufficient reason to suppose that the problem will not recur? The Bastard's role in seeking affirmation is a crucial one, and yet he does

so from his vantage point as the play's most visibly unhistorical personage. As a fictional character, the Bastard is free to invent fictions around him, to instruct King John in the playing of a part that will benefit England, and to fashion a concluding speech in which there can be hope for the future. What sort of consolation does this fiction provide? To dwell on the conflict between history and fiction is not to subvert all hope by labeling fiction as mere fantasy, but it does call attention to the fruitfully ambiguous relation between Shakespeare's stubbornly historical subject matter and his function as creative artist.

The Life and Death of King John

[Dramatis Personae

KING JOHN
QUEEN ELEANOR, *his mother*
PRINCE HENRY, *his son, afterward King Henry III*
ARTHUR, *Duke of Brittaine (Brittany), King John's nephew*
CONSTANCE, *Arthur's mother, widow of King John's elder brother, Geoffrey*
BLANCHE *of Spain, niece of King John*

LADY FAULCONBRIDGE, *widow of Sir Robert Faulconbridge*
Philip the BASTARD, *afterward knighted as Sir Richard Plantagenet, her illegitimate son by Richard I (Richard Coeur de Lion)*
ROBERT FAULCONBRIDGE, *her legitimate son*
JAMES GURNEY, *her attendant*

EARL OF PEMBROKE
EARL OF ESSEX
EARL OF SALISBURY
LORD BIGOT
HUBERT DE BURGH, *in the service of King John*
PETER OF POMFRET, *a prophet*
An English HERALD
Two MESSENGERS *to King John*
FIRST EXECUTIONER

KING PHILIP *of France (Philip II)*
LEWIS, *the Dauphin*
DUKE OF AUSTRIA *(Limoges)*
MELUN, *a French lord*
CHATILLON, *ambassador from France to King John*
A French HERALD
A MESSENGER *to the Dauphin*
CITIZEN *of Angiers*

CARDINAL PANDULPH, *the Pope's legate*

Lords, a Sheriff, Soldiers, Citizens of Angiers, Executioners, and Attendants

SCENE: *Partly in England and partly in France*]

1.1 *Enter King John, Queen Eleanor, Pembroke, Essex, and Salisbury, with the[m] Chatillon of France.*

KING JOHN
Now, say, Chatillon, what would France with us? 1
CHATILLON
Thus, after greeting, speaks the King of France,
In my behavior, to the majesty— 3
The borrowed majesty—of England here. 4
ELEANOR
A strange beginning: "borrowed majesty"!
KING JOHN
Silence, good Mother. Hear the embassy. 6
CHATILLON
Philip of France, in right and true behalf
Of thy deceasèd brother Geoffrey's son,
Arthur Plantagenet, lays most lawful claim
To this fair island and the territories,
To Ireland, Poitiers, Anjou, Touraine, Maine,
Desiring thee to lay aside the sword
Which sways usurpingly these several titles, 13
And put the same into young Arthur's hand,
Thy nephew and right royal sovereign.
KING JOHN
What follows if we disallow of this? 16
CHATILLON
The proud control of fierce and bloody war, 17
To enforce these rights so forcibly withheld.
KING JOHN
Here have we war for war and blood for blood,
Controlment for controlment. So answer France.
CHATILLON
Then take my king's defiance from my mouth,
The farthest limit of my embassy.
KING JOHN
Bear mine to him, and so depart in peace.
Be thou as lightning in the eyes of France;
For ere thou canst report I will be there, 25
The thunder of my cannon shall be heard. 26
So, hence! Be thou the trumpet of our wrath
And sullen presage of your own decay.— 28
An honorable conduct let him have. 29
Pembroke, look to 't.—Farewell, Chatillon.
Exeunt Chatillon and Pembroke.
ELEANOR
What now, my son? Have I not ever said
How that ambitious Constance would not cease 32
Till she had kindled France and all the world
Upon the right and party of her son? 34
This might have been prevented and made whole 35

1.1. Location: England. The court of King John.
1 what . . . us what does the King of France want with us **3 In my behavior** in my person and conduct, through me **4 borrowed** i.e., not belonging by true right **6 embassy** message **13 sways** manages, directs. **several titles** distinct possessions **16 disallow of** reject **17 control** compulsion **25 report** (1) deliver your message (2) sound like thunder **26 cannon** (An anachronism, since gunpowder was not employed in Europe until the fourteenth century.) **28 sullen presage** dismal portent, omen. **decay** ruin **29 conduct** escort, guard **32 How that** how **34 Upon** in behalf of. **party** cause **35 prevented** foreseen. **made whole** set right

With very easy arguments of love,   36
Which now the manage of two kingdoms must   37
With fearful bloody issue arbitrate.   38

KING JOHN
Our strong possession and our right for us.

ELEANOR [aside to King John]
Your strong possession much more than your right,
Or else it must go wrong with you and me—
So much my conscience whispers in your ear,
Which none but heaven and you and I shall hear.

    Enter a Sheriff, [who whispers to Essex].

ESSEX
My liege, here is the strangest controversy,   44
Come from the country to be judged by you,
That e'er I heard. Shall I produce the men?

KING JOHN   Let them approach.
              [The Sheriff goes to summon the men.]
Our abbeys and our priories shall pay
This expeditious charge.

    Enter Robert Faulconbridge and Philip, [his
    bastard brother].

                  What men are you?   49

BASTARD
Your faithful subject I, a gentleman,
Born in Northamptonshire, and eldest son,
As I suppose, to Robert Faulconbridge,
A soldier, by the honor-giving hand
Of Coeur de Lion knighted in the field.   54

KING JOHN   What art thou?

ROBERT
The son and heir to that same Faulconbridge.

KING JOHN
Is that the elder, and art thou the heir?
You came not of one mother then, it seems.

BASTARD
Most certain of one mother, mighty King—
That is well known—and, as I think, one father.
But for the certain knowledge of that truth
I put you o'er to heaven and to my mother.   62
Of that I doubt, as all men's children may.

ELEANOR
Out on thee, rude man! Thou dost shame thy
    mother   64
And wound her honor with this diffidence.   65

BASTARD
I, madam? No, I have no reason for it.
That is my brother's plea and none of mine—
The which if he can prove, 'a pops me out   68
At least from fair five hundred pound a year.
Heaven guard my mother's honor and my land!

KING JOHN
A good blunt fellow.—Why, being younger born,
Doth he lay claim to thine inheritance?

BASTARD
I know not why, except to get the land.
But once he slandered me with bastardy.   74
But whe'er I be as true begot or no,   75
That still I lay upon my mother's head;   76
But that I am as well begot, my liege—
Fair fall the bones that took the pains for me!—   78
Compare our faces and be judge yourself.
If old Sir Robert did beget us both
And were our father, and this son like him,
O old Sir Robert, Father, on my knee
I give heaven thanks I was not like to thee!

KING JOHN
Why, what a madcap hath heaven lent us here!

ELEANOR
He hath a trick of Coeur de Lion's face;   85
The accent of his tongue affecteth him.   86
Do you not read some tokens of my son
In the large composition of this man?   88

KING JOHN
Mine eye hath well examinèd his parts
And finds them perfect Richard. [To Robert.] Sirrah,
    speak.   90
What doth move you to claim your brother's land?

BASTARD
Because he hath a half-face like my father.   92
With half that face would he have all my land—   93
A half-faced groat five hundred pound a year!   94

ROBERT
My gracious liege, when that my father lived,   95
Your brother did employ my father much—   96

BASTARD
Well, sir, by this you cannot get my land.
Your tale must be how he employed my mother.

ROBERT
—And once dispatched him in an embassy
To Germany, there with the Emperor
To treat of high affairs touching that time.   101
Th' advantage of his absence took the King   102
And in the meantime sojourned at my father's;
Where how he did prevail I shame to speak,
But truth is truth. Large lengths of seas and shores
Between my father and my mother lay,
As I have heard my father speak himself,
When this same lusty gentleman was got.   108
Upon his deathbed he by will bequeathed

36 arguments of love amicable negotiation   37 manage government
38 issue consequence   44 liege feudal master, lord   49 expeditious
charge sudden expense   54 Coeur de Lion Lion-heart, i.e., Richard I
62 put you o'er refer you   64 Out on thee (An expression of reproach.)   65 diffidence distrust, suspicion   68 'a he

74 once in short   75 whe'er whether   76 lay . . . head leave to my
mother to give account   78 Fair fall may good fortune befall.   the
bones i.e., the man, now dead   85 trick characteristic look   86 affecteth resembles   88 large composition (1) general constitution (2)
big build   90 Sirrah (Customary form of address to inferiors.)
92 half-face (1) profile (2) defective, scant face   93 With half that
face i.e., with only half his father's thin face (but with plenty of
cheek)   94 half-faced groat i.e., coin bearing the sovereign's profile,
and perhaps also clipped and devalued. (The groat, worth four pence,
is a figure for Robert's insignificance, in antithesis to his fortune, five
hundred pounds a year.)   95 when that when   96 Your brother i.e.,
Richard Coeur de Lion   101 To . . . time to discuss matters that were
currently of first importance   102 Th' advantage . . . King the King
(Richard) took advantage of his (Sir Robert's) absence   108 lusty
merry.   got begotten

His lands to me, and took it on his death   110
That this my mother's son was none of his;
And if he were, he came into the world
Full fourteen weeks before the course of time.
Then, good my liege, let me have what is mine,
My father's land, as was my father's will.

KING JOHN
Sirrah, your brother is legitimate.
Your father's wife did after wedlock bear him,
And if she did play false, the fault was hers—
Which fault lies on the hazards of all husbands   119
That marry wives. Tell me, how if my brother,
Who, as you say, took pains to get this son,
Had of your father claimed this son for his?
In sooth, good friend, your father might have kept
This calf, bred from his cow, from all the world;
In sooth he might. Then, if he were my brother's,   125
My brother might not claim him, nor your father,
Being none of his, refuse him. This concludes: 127
My mother's son did get your father's heir;
Your father's heir must have your father's land.

ROBERT
Shall then my father's will be of no force
To dispossess that child which is not his?

BASTARD
Of no more force to dispossess me, sir,
Than was his will to get me, as I think.

ELEANOR [to the Bastard]
Whether hadst thou rather be: a Faulconbridge   134
And like thy brother, to enjoy thy land,
Or the reputed son of Coeur de Lion,
Lord of thy presence, and no land besides?   137

BASTARD
Madam, an if my brother had my shape   138
And I had his, Sir Robert's his, like him,   139
And if my legs were two such riding-rods,   140
My arms such eel skins stuffed, my face so thin
That in mine ear I durst not stick a rose   142
Lest men should say "Look, where three-farthings
    goes!"
And, to his shape, were heir to all this land,   144
Would I might never stir from off this place,   145
I would give it every foot to have this face;   146
I would not be Sir Nob in any case.   147

ELEANOR   110
I like thee well. Wilt thou forsake thy fortune,
Bequeath thy land to him, and follow me?
I am a soldier and now bound to France.

BASTARD
Brother, take you my land. I'll take my chance.
Your face hath got five hundred pound a year,
Yet sell your face for five pence and 'tis dear.—   153
Madam, I'll follow you unto the death.

ELEANOR
Nay, I would have you go before me thither.

BASTARD
Our country manners give our betters way.   156

KING JOHN   What is thy name?

BASTARD
Philip, my liege, so is my name begun;
Philip, good old Sir Robert's wife's eldest son.

KING JOHN
From henceforth bear his name whose form thou
    bearest.
Kneel thou down Philip, but rise more great:
            [The Bastard kneels and is knighted.]
Arise Sir Richard, and Plantagenet.

            [The Bastard rises.]
BASTARD
Brother by th' mother's side, give me your hand.
My father gave me honor; yours gave land.
Now blessèd be the hour, by night or day,   165
When I was got, Sir Robert was away!   166

ELEANOR
The very spirit of Plantagenet!
I am thy grandam, Richard. Call me so.

BASTARD
Madam, by chance but not by truth; what though?   169
Something about, a little from the right,   170
    In at the window, or else o'er the hatch.   171
Who dares not stir by day must walk by night,
    And have is have, however men do catch.   173
Near or far off, well won is still well shot,   174
And I am I, howe'er I was begot.

KING JOHN
Go, Faulconbridge. Now hast thou thy desire:
A landless knight makes thee a landed squire.—   177
Come, madam, and come, Richard, we must speed
For France, for France, for it is more than need.

BASTARD
Brother, adieu. Good fortune come to thee!

110 took . . . death i.e., swore solemnly (the most solemn oath being an oath on one's deathbed)   **119 lies on the hazards** is one of the risks   **125 if** even if   **127 Being . . . his** i.e., even if the Bastard were not sired by him.   **refuse** disclaim.   **concludes** settles the problem **134 Whether** which of the two   **137 Lord of thy presence** i.e., royal-blooded master of your own person   **138 an if** if   **139 I had . . . him** i.e., if I had Sir Robert's shape as my brother now has. (*Sir Robert's his* means "Sir Robert's.")   **140 riding-rods** switches (probably with a suggestion of sexual emaciation and insufficiency, as also in *eel skins stuffed*, line 141, and *Sir Nob in any case*, line 147)   **142 stick a rose** (The Queen's likeness on the three-farthing coin was distinguished from that on the three-halfpence by a rose behind her head. The Bastard's taunt is based on the thinness of the coin.)   **144 to his shape** in addition to (inheriting) his physical characteristics   **145 Would . . . place** i.e., may I never stir from this spot if I am not speaking the truth **146 it every foot** every foot of it.   **this face** my own appearance **147 Nob** (Diminutive of "Robert"; with a possible play on "knob," "head" in a sexual sense and as head of the family.)

153 dear expensive   **156 give . . . way** yield precedence to our superiors. (The Bastard jokes that he will not upset social precedence to rush before Queen Eleanor to death.)   **165–166 Now . . . away** i.e., I thank God that, at the blessed time when I was conceived, whether by night or day, Sir Robert was absent   **169 not by truth** not honorably, not chastely.   **what though** what of that   **170 Something about** somewhat roundabout, clandestinely   **171 hatch** lower half door. (*O'er the hatch* means clandestinely, out of wedlock.)   **173 have is . . . catch** possession is what matters, however it is achieved **174 Near . . . shot** i.e., in archery, hitting the target is what matters, whatever the distance. (With sexual suggestion.)   **177 A landless knight** i.e., the Bastard, who is willing to trade his inheritance for a knighthood

For thou wast got i' the way of honesty.
                                        Exeunt all but [the] Bastard.
A foot of honor better than I was,   182
But many a many foot of land the worse!
Well, now can I make any Joan a lady.   184
"Good e'en, Sir Richard!"—"God-a-mercy,
    fellow!"—   185
And if his name be George, I'll call him Peter,
For new-made honor doth forget men's names;
'Tis too respective and too sociable   188
For your conversion. Now your traveler,   189
He and his toothpick at my worship's mess,   190
And when my knightly stomach is sufficed,
Why then I suck my teeth and catechize   192
My pickèd man of countries: "My dear sir,"   193
Thus, leaning on mine elbow, I begin,
"I shall beseech you"—that is Question now;
And then comes Answer like an Absey book: 196
"O sir," says Answer, "at your best command;
At your employment; at your service, sir."
"No sir," says Question, "I, sweet sir, at yours";
And so, ere Answer knows what Question would,   200
Saving in dialogue of compliment,   201
And talking of the Alps and Apennines,
The Pyrenean and the river Po,
It draws toward supper in conclusion so.
But this is worshipful society
And fits the mounting spirit like myself,
For he is but a bastard to the time   207
That doth not smack of observation.   208
And so am I—whether I smack or no,   209
And not alone in habit and device,   210
Exterior form, outward accoutrement,
But from the inward motion—to deliver   212
Sweet, sweet, sweet poison for the age's tooth;   213
Which, though I will not practice to deceive,   214
Yet, to avoid deceit, I mean to learn;   215
For it shall strew the footsteps of my rising.   216

But who comes in such haste in riding robes?
What woman-post is this? Hath she no husband   218
That will take pains to blow a horn before her?   219

Enter Lady Faulconbridge and James Gurney.

O me! 'Tis my mother. How now, good lady?
What brings you here to court so hastily?
LADY FAULCONBRIDGE
Where is that slave, thy brother? Where is he,
That holds in chase mine honor up and down?   223
BASTARD
My brother Robert, old Sir Robert's son?
Colbrand the Giant, that same mighty man?   225
Is it Sir Robert's son that you seek so?
LADY FAULCONBRIDGE
Sir Robert's son, ay, thou unreverent boy,
Sir Robert's son. Why scorn'st thou at Sir Robert?
He is Sir Robert's son, and so art thou.
BASTARD
James Gurney, wilt thou give us leave awhile?   230
GURNEY
Good leave, good Philip.
BASTARD   Philip? Sparrow! James,   231
There's toys abroad. Anon I'll tell thee more.   232
                                        Exit James.
Madam, I was not old Sir Robert's son;
Sir Robert might have eat his part in me   234
Upon Good Friday and ne'er broke his fast.
Sir Robert could do well—marry, to confess—   236
Could he get me! Sir Robert could not do it;   237
We know his handiwork. Therefore, good Mother,
To whom am I beholding for these limbs?   239
Sir Robert never holp to make this leg.   240
LADY FAULCONBRIDGE
Hast thou conspirèd with thy brother too,
That for thine own gain shouldst defend mine
    honor?
What means this scorn, thou most untoward knave?   243
BASTARD
Knight, knight, good Mother, Basilisco-like.   244
What! I am dubbed; I have it on my shoulder.   245
But, Mother, I am not Sir Robert's son.
I have disclaimed Sir Robert and my land;
Legitimation, name, and all is gone.
Then, good my Mother, let me know my father;

182 foot degree **184 Joan** (Frequently used to designate any girl, usually of the lower class.) **185 Good e'en** good evening, good afternoon. (The Bastard imagines himself, in his new title, encountering a lower-class person.) **God-a-mercy** God reward you **188 respective** considerate **189 conversion** change of status, acquisition of *new-made honor.* (The Bastard wryly jokes that remembering names is too considerate a thing for a newly made knight to bother about.) **190 toothpick** (An affectation associated with foreign travel and the latest courtly fashion.) **my worship's mess** i.e., my dinner table. (A knight was formally addressed as "your worship.") **192 suck my teeth** i.e., in contrast to the use of toothpick by the *traveler* **193 pickèd** (1) refined (2) having picked his teeth **196 Absey** ABC, primer **200 would** intends, asks **201 Saving . . . compliment** except in polite but inane conversation **207–208 but a bastard . . . observation** i.e., not a true son of the times unless he observes and practices courtly obsequiousness **209 And so . . . no** and so I intend, whether or not I have a true smack of obsequiousness **210 habit and device** attire and outward appearance (with a suggestion, too, of "coat of arms") **212 from . . . motion** from my own inclination. (The Bastard is partly attracted to the use of flattery for self-advancement, even though he also laughs at it.) **213 Sweet . . . poison** flattery. **tooth** i.e., sweet tooth, appetite **214 practice to deceive** deliberately plan to deceive others **215 deceit** being deceived **216 it . . . rising** i.e., deceitful flattery will inevitably make easy my rise in importance, just as rushes are strewn on the floors of great men

218 woman-post female messenger **219 blow a horn** (The ordinary signal of approach; with a punning reference to the horn of cuckoldry.) **223 holds in chase** pursues **225 Colbrand the Giant** legendary Danish giant slain by Guy of Warwick in a popular romance named after its hero. (Said mockingly.) **230 give us leave** leave us alone **231 Philip? Sparrow!** call me Philip no more, a name commonly used for sparrows (because of their "Phip"-like chirp), since I'm now Sir Richard **232 There's toys abroad** trifling little things are going on. (A suggestive understatement.) **234 eat** eaten. (Pronounced "et.") **236 do** (With sexual suggestion.) **marry, to confess** indeed, to speak truly. (*Marry* was originally an oath, "by the Virgin Mary.") **237 Could he get** if he could beget **239 beholding** beholden **240 holp** helped **243 untoward** unmannerly **244 Basilisco-like** (The character Basilisco in the play *Solyman and Perseda,* presumably by Thomas Kyd, insists braggartlike on his knighthood but nevertheless is called "Knave" by his servant.) **245 dubbed** made a knight by a touch of the sword on the shoulder

Some proper man, I hope. Who was it, Mother?   250

LADY FAULCONBRIDGE
Hast thou denied thyself a Faulconbridge?

BASTARD
As faithfully as I deny the devil.

LADY FAULCONBRIDGE
King Richard Coeur de Lion was thy father.
By long and vehement suit I was seduced
To make room for him in my husband's bed.
Heaven lay not my transgression to my charge!
Thou art the issue of my dear offense,   257
Which was so strongly urged past my defense.

BASTARD
Now, by this light, were I to get again,   259
Madam, I would not wish a better father.
Some sins do bear their privilege on earth,   261
And so doth yours. Your fault was not your folly.   262
Needs must you lay your heart at his dispose,   263
Subjected tribute to commanding love,
Against whose fury and unmatchèd force
The aweless lion could not wage the fight,   266
Nor keep his princely heart from Richard's hand.
He that perforce robs lions of their hearts   268
May easily win a woman's. Ay, my Mother,
With all my heart I thank thee for my father!
Who lives and dares but say thou didst not well
When I was got, I'll send his soul to hell.
Come, lady, I will show thee to my kin;
    And they shall say, when Richard me begot,
If thou hadst said him nay, it had been sin.
    Who says it was, he lies; I say 'twas not.   *Exeunt.*

❖

2.1   *Enter, before Angiers, Philip King of France,
Lewis [the] Dauphin, Austria, Constance, Arthur,
[and soldiers].*

KING PHILIP
Before Angiers well met, brave Austria.—
Arthur, that great forerunner of thy blood,   2
Richard, that robbed the lion of his heart
And fought the holy wars in Palestine,   4
By this brave duke came early to his grave;   5

And, for amends to his posterity,
At our importance hither is he come   7
To spread his colors, boy, in thy behalf,   8
And to rebuke the usurpation   9
Of thy unnatural uncle, English John.
Embrace him, love him, give him welcome hither.

ARTHUR [*to Austria*]
God shall forgive you Coeur de Lion's death
The rather that you give his offspring life,
Shadowing their right under your wings of war.   14
I give you welcome with a powerless hand,
But with a heart full of unstainèd love.
Welcome before the gates of Angiers, Duke.

KING PHILIP
A noble boy! Who would not do thee right?

AUSTRIA [*kissing Arthur*]
Upon thy cheek lay I this zealous kiss,
As seal to this indenture of my love: 20
That to my home I will no more return
Till Angiers and the right thou hast in France,
Together with that pale, that white-faced shore,   23
Whose foot spurns back the ocean's roaring tides
And coops from other lands her islanders,   25
Even till that England, hedged in with the main,   26
That water-wallèd bulwark, still secure   27
And confident from foreign purposes,
Even till that utmost corner of the west
Salute thee for her king. Till then, fair boy,
Will I not think of home, but follow arms.

CONSTANCE
O, take his mother's thanks, a widow's thanks,
Till your strong hand shall help to give him strength
To make a more requital to your love!   34

AUSTRIA
The peace of heaven is theirs that lift their swords
In such a just and charitable war.

KING PHILIP
Well then, to work. Our cannon shall be bent   37
Against the brows of this resisting town.
Call for our chiefest men of discipline,   39
To cull the plots of best advantages.   40
We'll lay before this town our royal bones,
Wade to the marketplace in Frenchmen's blood,
But we will make it subject to this boy.   43

CONSTANCE
Stay for an answer to your embassy,
Lest unadvised you stain your swords with blood.   45
My Lord Chatillon may from England bring
That right in peace which here we urge in war,
And then we shall repent each drop of blood

---

250 proper handsome, fine   **257 dear** (1) precious, costly (2) loving
259 get be conceived   **261 do . . . earth** i.e., are excusable, venial
262 Your . . . folly you were morally at fault but not foolish (in
whom you yielded to)   **263 dispose** disposal   **266 aweless lion** (During
his imprisonment by the Duke of Austria, according to legend,
Coeur de Lion slew the Duke's son and as punishment was given to a
hungry lion. When the lion attacked him, he slew it by thrusting his
hand down its throat and tearing out its heart, which he is supposed
to have eaten.)   **268 perforce** forcibly
**2.1. Location: France. Before Angiers. (The French and Austrian
forces enter from opposite sides before the "gates" of Angiers seen
backstage.)**
s.d. Austria (The Duke of Austria wears a lion skin that he supposedly
took from Coeur de Lion; see note 5 and line 292.)   **2 forerunner** ancestor. (Richard was actually not a direct ancestor of Arthur, but his
uncle.)   **4 fought . . . Palestine** (Richard took part in the third Crusade in 1191–1192.)   **5 By . . . duke** (A confusion of the Duke of
Austria with Viscount Limoges, before whose castle Richard was mortally wounded. The roles of the two were combined in *The Troublesome Reign of King John*, as they are in this play.)

7 importance importunity   **8 spread his colors** display his military
colors, his battle ensigns   **9 rebuke** put down   **14 Shadowing** sheltering.   **their right** i.e., the cause of Arthur and his supporters   **20 indenture** contract   **23 pale . . . shore** i.e., the chalk cliffs at Dover
25 coops encloses for defense   **26 main** ocean   **27 still** perpetually
34 more greater   **37 bent** directed   **39 men of discipline** men trained
in military strategy   **40 To . . . advantages** to select positions that are
most favorable for attack   **43 But we will** i.e., if necessary to, or, if
we do not   **45 unadvised** rashly

That hot rash haste so indirectly shed.   49

Enter Chatillon.

KING PHILIP
A wonder, lady! Lo, upon thy wish,
Our messenger Chatillon is arrived.—
What England says, say briefly, gentle lord;   52
We coldly pause for thee. Chatillon, speak.   53

CHATILLON
Then turn your forces from this paltry siege
And stir them up against a mightier task.
England, impatient of your just demands,
Hath put himself in arms. The adverse winds,
Whose leisure I have stayed, have given him time   58
To land his legions all as soon as I.
His marches are expedient to this town,   60
His forces strong, his soldiers confident.
With him along is come the Mother-Queen,
An Ate, stirring him to blood and strife;   63
With her her niece, the Lady Blanche of Spain;   64
With them a bastard of the King's deceased;   65
And all th' unsettled humors of the land—   66
Rash, inconsiderate, fiery voluntaries,   67
With ladies' faces and fierce dragons' spleens—   68
Have sold their fortunes at their native homes,
Bearing their birthrights proudly on their backs,   70
To make a hazard of new fortunes here.
In brief, a braver choice of dauntless spirits   72
Than now the English bottoms have waft o'er   73
Did never float upon the swelling tide
To do offense and scathe in Christendom.   75

Drum beats.

The interruption of their churlish drums   76
Cuts off more circumstance. They are at hand,   77
To parley or to fight. Therefore prepare.

KING PHILIP
How much unlooked-for is this expedition!   79

AUSTRIA
By how much unexpected, by so much
We must awake endeavor for defense,
For courage mounteth with occasion.   82
Let them be welcome, then. We are prepared.

*Enter King [John] of England, [the] Bastard,
Queen [Eleanor], Blanche, Pembroke, and others.*

KING JOHN
Peace be to France, if France in peace permit

Our just and lineal entrance to our own.   85
If not, bleed France, and peace ascend to heaven,
Whiles we, God's wrathful agent, do correct   87
Their proud contempt that beats His peace to
   heaven.

KING PHILIP
Peace be to England, if that war return
From France to England, there to live in peace.
England we love, and for that England's sake   91
With burden of our armor here we sweat.
This toil of ours should be a work of thine;   93
But thou from loving England art so far
That thou hast underwrought his lawful king,   95
Cut off the sequence of posterity,   96
Outfacèd infant state, and done a rape   97
Upon the maiden virtue of the crown.
Look here upon thy brother Geoffrey's face:
These eyes, these brows, were molded out of his;
This little abstract doth contain that large   101
Which died in Geoffrey, and the hand of time   102
Shall draw this brief into as huge a volume.   103
That Geoffrey was thy elder brother born,
And this his son. England was Geoffrey's right,
And this is Geoffrey's. In the name of God,   106
How comes it then that thou art called a king,
When living blood doth in these temples beat
Which owe the crown that thou o'ermasterest?   109

KING JOHN
From whom hast thou this great commission,
   France,
To draw my answer from thy articles?   111

KING PHILIP
From that supernal judge that stirs good thoughts   112
In any breast of strong authority
To look into the blots and stains of right.
That judge hath made me guardian to this boy,
Under whose warrant I impeach thy wrong   116
And by whose help I mean to chastise it.

KING JOHN
Alack, thou dost usurp authority.

KING PHILIP
Excuse it is to beat usurping down.   119

ELEANOR
Who is it thou dost call usurper, France?

CONSTANCE
Let me make answer: thy usurping son.

---

49 indirectly wrongfully, misdirectedly   **52 England** the King of England (also in line 56 and perhaps line 46).   **gentle** noble   **53 coldly** calmly   **58 leisure** convenience.   **stayed** waited for   **60 expedient** speedy   **63 Ate** Greek goddess of discord   **64 niece** i.e., granddaughter   **65 of . . . deceased** of the deceased King, i.e., Richard   **66 unsettled humors** i.e., disgruntled individuals   **67 inconsiderate** reckless, heedless.   **voluntaries** volunteers   **68 With ladies' faces** i.e., beardless.   **fierce dragons' spleens** i.e., utmost fierceness. (The spleen was thought to be the seat of the passions.)   **70 Bearing . . . backs** i.e., having sold everything to obtain armor   **72 choice** picked company   **73 bottoms** i.e., ships.   **waft** wafted   **75 scathe** harm   **76 churlish** uncouth, rude   **77 circumstance** detailed reporting   **79 expedition** (1) speed (2) military force   **82 occasion** emergency

85 lineal by right of birth   **87 correct** chastise   **91 England's** i.e., Arthur's, whose claim to England the French King is supporting   **93 This . . . thine** i.e., you should be supporting our cause also, since it is your duty   **95 underwrought his** undermined its   **96 sequence of posterity** lawful succession   **97 Outfacèd infant state** defied the majesty of a boy king   **101 little abstract** abridgment or epitome   **101–102 doth . . . Geoffrey** contains that which, in its complete form, died in Geoffrey   **103 draw this brief** enlarge this epitome   **106 this** i.e., Arthur himself, or Angiers, or the English crown   **109 owe** own   **111 draw . . . articles** i.e., claim the right to demand of me an answer to the items in your indictment   **112 supernal** celestial, supreme   **116 whose** i.e., the supreme judge's, God's.   **impeach** accuse   **119 Excuse . . . down** i.e., the excuse for what you call my usurping of authority is that I am, in fact, resisting and defeating usurpation

ELEANOR
Out, insolent! Thy bastard shall be king,   122
That thou mayst be a queen and check the world!   123
CONSTANCE
My bed was ever to thy son as true
As thine was to thy husband, and this boy
Liker in feature to his father Geoffrey
Than thou and John in manners—being as like
As rain to water, or devil to his dam.   128
My boy a bastard? By my soul, I think
His father never was so true begot.
It cannot be, an if thou wert his mother.   131
ELEANOR [to Arthur]
There's a good mother, boy, that blots thy father.   132
CONSTANCE [to Arthur]
There's a good grandam, boy, that would blot thee.   133
AUSTRIA
Peace!
BASTARD   Hear the crier!
AUSTRIA   What the devil art thou?   134
BASTARD
One that will play the devil, sir, with you,
An 'a may catch your hide and you alone.   136
You are the hare of whom the proverb goes,   137
Whose valor plucks dead lions by the beard.
I'll smoke your skin coat an I catch you right.   139
Sirrah, look to 't. I' faith I will, i' faith.
BLANCHE
O, well did he become that lion's robe   141
That did disrobe the lion of that robe!
BASTARD
It lies as sightly on the back of him   143
As great Alcides' shows upon an ass.   144
But, ass, I'll take that burden from your back,
Or lay on that shall make your shoulders crack.   146
AUSTRIA
What cracker is this same that deafs our ears   147
With this abundance of superfluous breath?
King Philip, determine what we shall do straight.   149
KING PHILIP
Women and fools, break off your conference.—   150
King John, this is the very sum of all:

England and Ireland, Anjou, Touraine, Maine,
In right of Arthur do I claim of thee.
Wilt thou resign them and lay down thy arms?
KING JOHN
My life as soon. I do defy thee, France.—
Arthur of Brittaine, yield thee to my hand,   156
And out of my dear love I'll give thee more
Than e'er the coward hand of France can win.
Submit thee, boy.
ELEANOR   Come to thy grandam, child.
CONSTANCE
Do, child, go to it grandam, child;   160
Give grandam kingdom, and it grandam will
Give it a plum, a cherry, and a fig.
There's a good grandam.
ARTHUR   Good my Mother, peace!
I would that I were low laid in my grave.
I am not worth this coil that's made for me.   165

                                                      [He weeps.]
ELEANOR
His mother shames him so, poor boy, he weeps.
CONSTANCE
Now shame upon you, whe'er she does or no!   167
His grandam's wrongs, and not his mother's
   shames,   168
Draws those heaven-moving pearls from his poor
   eyes,
Which heaven shall take in nature of a fee.   170
Ay, with these crystal beads heaven shall be bribed   171
To do him justice and revenge on you.
ELEANOR
Thou monstrous slanderer of heaven and earth!
CONSTANCE
Thou monstrous injurer of heaven and earth!
Call not me slanderer. Thou and thine usurp
The dominations, royalties, and rights   176
Of this oppressèd boy. This is thy eldest son's son,   177
Infortunate in nothing but in thee.   178
Thy sins are visited in this poor child;   179
The canon of the law is laid on him,   180
Being but the second generation
Removèd from thy sin-conceiving womb.
KING JOHN
Bedlam, have done.
CONSTANCE   I have but this to say,   183
That he is not only plaguèd for her sin,   184
But God hath made her sin and her the plague   185

---

122 Out (An exclamation of remonstrance.)   **123 check** control
128 dam mother. (Constance says that Arthur is more like his father,
and therefore no bastard, than John is like his mother—a resemblance that would not rule out bastardy, especially when the two are
as alike as the devil and his mother. Constance goes on to wonder if
John's brother Geoffrey might also be a bastard.)   **131 an if** if
132 blots slanders   **133 blot** (with a pun on "obliterate, efface")
134 Hear the crier (A mocking suggestion by the Bastard that Austria's call for silence likens him to the town crier.)   **136 An 'a** if he.
hide i.e., the lion's skin Austria wears in celebration of his triumph
over Richard Coeur de Lion   **137 the proverb** i.e., "even hares may
insult the dead lion." (This proverb occurs in Erasmus' *Adages*.)
139 smoke thrash, beat.   **your skin coat** your own skin   **141 he** i.e.,
Richard Coeur de Lion   **143 sightly** suitably. (Said ironically.)   **him**
i.e., the Duke of Austria   **144 Alcides** Hercules, who slew the Nemean lion as one of his twelve labors and thereafter wore its pelt
146 lay on that i.e., beat you with a club that   **147 cracker** i.e.,
boaster (with a play on *crack*, line 146)   **149 straight** at once
150 fools children

156 Brittaine Brittany   **160 Do . . . grandam** (Contemptuous baby
talk.)   **it** its (also in line 161)   **165 coil** disturbance, fuss
167 whe'er whether   **168 wrongs** wrongdoings.   **shames** insults
170 a fee i.e., the fee paid to heaven in return for pleading as
Arthur's advocate   **171 beads** i.e., tears, here as gifts used to curry favor, or prayer beads   **176 dominations** dominions, sovereignties.
royalties royal prerogatives   **177 eldest son's son** i.e., eldest grandchild, not son of the eldest son   **178 Infortunate** unfortunate
179 visited punished   **180 canon . . . law** i.e., that the sins of parents shall be visited upon their children to the third and fourth generation; see Exodus 20:5   **183 Bedlam** lunatic   **184 he** i.e., Arthur.
her sin i.e., Eleanor's alleged adultery when she conceived John. (See
lines 124 ff.)   **185 her sin** i.e., John, the issue of her sin

On this removèd issue, plagued for her   186
And with her plague; her sin his injury,   187
Her injury the beadle to her sin,   188
All punished in the person of this child,
And all for her. A plague upon her!

ELEANOR
Thou unadvisèd scold, I can produce   191
A will that bars the title of thy son.   192

CONSTANCE
Ay, who doubts that? A will, a wicked will,
A woman's will, a cankered grandam's will!

KING PHILIP
Peace, lady! Pause, or be more temperate.
It ill beseems this presence to cry aim   196
To these ill-tunèd repetitions.—   197
Some trumpet summon hither to the walls   198
These men of Angiers. Let us hear them speak
Whose title they admit, Arthur's or John's.   200

Trumpet sounds. Enter a Citizen upon the walls.

CITIZEN
Who is it that hath warned us to the walls?   201

KING PHILIP
'Tis France, for England.

KING JOHN   England, for itself.   202
You men of Angiers, and my loving subjects—

KING PHILIP
You loving men of Angiers, Arthur's subjects,
Our trumpet called you to this gentle parle—   205

KING JOHN
For our advantage; therefore hear us first.
These flags of France, that are advancèd here   207
Before the eye and prospect of your town,
Have hither marched to your endamagement.
The cannons have their bowels full of wrath,
And ready mounted are they to spit forth
Their iron indignation 'gainst your walls.
All preparation for a bloody siege
And merciless proceeding by these French
Confronts your city's eyes, your winking gates;   215
And but for our approach those sleeping stones,
That as a waist doth girdle you about,
By the compulsion of their ordinance   218
By this time from their fixèd beds of lime

Had been dishabited, and wide havoc made   220
For bloody power to rush upon your peace.
But on the sight of us your lawful king,
Who painfully, with much expedient march,   223
Have brought a countercheck before your gates
To save unscratched your city's threatened cheeks,
Behold, the French, amazed, vouchsafe a parle;   226
And now, instead of bullets wrapped in fire   227
To make a shaking fever in your walls,
They shoot but calm words folded up in smoke   229
To make a faithless error in your ears.   230
Which trust accordingly, kind citizens,   231
And let us in, your king, whose labored spirits,   232
Forwearied in this action of swift speed,   233
Craves harborage within your city walls.

KING PHILIP
When I have said, make answer to us both.   235
Lo, in this right hand, whose protection   236
Is most divinely vowed upon the right   237
Of him it holds, stands young Plantagenet,   238
Son to the elder brother of this man
And king o'er him and all that he enjoys.   240
For this downtrodden equity we tread   241
In warlike march these greens before your town,
Being no further enemy to you
Than the constraint of hospitable zeal   244
In the relief of this oppressèd child
Religiously provokes. Be pleasèd then
To pay that duty which you truly owe
To him that owes it, namely this young prince;   248
And then our arms, like to a muzzled bear,
Save in aspect, hath all offense sealed up.   250
Our cannons' malice vainly shall be spent
Against th' invulnerable clouds of heaven;
And with a blessèd and unvexed retire,   253
With unhacked swords and helmets all unbruised,
We will bear home that lusty blood again
Which here we came to spout against your town,
And leave your children, wives, and you in peace.
But if you fondly pass our proffered offer,   258
'Tis not the roundure of your old-faced walls   259
Can hide you from our messengers of war,   260
Though all these English and their discipline   261
Were harbored in their rude circumference.   262
Then tell us, shall your city call us lord

---

186 removèd issue descendant at one remove, i.e., Arthur. **for her** on her account   **187 with her plague** i.e., by the offspring, John, with whom she was cursed. **his injury** i.e., the wrong done to Arthur   **188 Her injury** Eleanor's wrong deeds, which act as the officer *(beadle)* to incite her son John *(her sin)* on to further wrongs **191 unadvisèd** rash   **192 A will** i.e., according to Holinshed and other chroniclers, the final testament of Richard Coeur de Lion, naming John as his heir and disinheriting Arthur, who had been named heir in a previous will. (But Constance deliberately takes *will* to mean "willfulness.")   **196 ill . . . presence** is not proper in the presence of royalty   **196–197 cry aim To** encourage. (An archery term.) **197 repetitions** recitals   **198 trumpet** trumpeter   **200 s.d. upon the walls** i.e., in the upper gallery rearstage. (Throughout this scene, the tiring-house facade is visualized as the walls of Angiers.) **201 warned** summoned   **202 'Tis France, for England** i.e., it is the French King, on behalf of Arthur, true King of England   **205 parle** parley   **207 advancèd** raised   **215 winking** closed   **218 their** i.e., of *these French* (line 214).   **ordinance** ordnance, artillery

220 dishabited dislodged   **223 painfully** having taken great pains or care. **expedient** swift   **226 amazed** stunned   **227 bullets** cannonballs   **229 folded up in smoke** i.e., using the deceptive concealment of rhetoric   **230 faithless error** perfidious lie   **231 trust accordingly** trust as such lies deserve, i.e., not at all   **232 labored** oppressed with labor   **233 Forwearied in** exhausted by   **235 said** finished speaking **236–238 in . . . holds** i.e., led by my right hand, which hand is most sacredly committed to defend the right of the person whose hand it now holds   **240 enjoys** possesses, rules over   **241 For** on behalf of. **equity** justice, right   **244 constraint** necessity   **248 owes** owns, has a right to   **250 Save . . . up** except in appearance, will see to it that all capacity for injury to you is sealed up   **253 blessèd and unvexed retire** peaceful and unhindered withdrawal   **258 fondly pass** foolishly pass up   **259 roundure** roundness, enclosure, circumference   **260 messengers** i.e., cannonballs   **261 discipline** military skill   **262 rude** rough

In that behalf which we have challenged it,   264
Or shall we give the signal to our rage
And stalk in blood to our possession?

CITIZEN
In brief, we are the King of England's subjects.
For him, and in his right, we hold this town.

KING JOHN
Acknowledge then the King, and let me in.

CITIZEN
That can we not. But he that proves the King,   270
To him will we prove loyal. Till that time
Have we rammed up our gates against the world.

KING JOHN
Doth not the crown of England prove the King?
And if not that, I bring you witnesses,
Twice fifteen thousand hearts of England's breed—

BASTARD   Bastards, and else.   276

KING JOHN
To verify our title with their lives.

KING PHILIP
As many and as wellborn bloods as those—   278

BASTARD   Some bastards too.

KING PHILIP
Stand in his face to contradict his claim.   280

CITIZEN
Till you compound whose right is worthiest,   281
We for the worthiest hold the right from both.   282

KING JOHN
Then God forgive the sin of all those souls
That to their everlasting residence,
Before the dew of evening fall, shall fleet,   285
In dreadful trial of our kingdom's king!   286

KING PHILIP
Amen, amen! Mount, chevaliers! To arms!

BASTARD
Saint George, that swinged the dragon, and e'er
    since   288
Sits on 's horseback at mine hostess' door,   289
Teach us some fence! [To Austria.] Sirrah, were I at
    home,   290
At your den, sirrah, with your lioness,   291
I would set an ox head to your lion's hide,   292
And make a monster of you.

AUSTRIA   Peace! No more.

BASTARD
O, tremble, for you hear the lion roar.

KING JOHN
Up higher to the plain, where we'll set forth
In best appointment all our regiments.   296

BASTARD
Speed then, to take advantage of the field.   297

KING PHILIP
It shall be so; and at the other hill
Command the rest to stand. God and our right!   299
    Exeunt [separately. The citizens remain above, on the
                                              walls.]

    Here after excursions, enter the Herald of France,
                with trumpets, to the gates.

FRENCH HERALD
You men of Angiers, open wide your gates,
And let young Arthur, Duke of Brittaine, in,
Who by the hand of France this day hath made   302
Much work for tears in many an English mother,   303
Whose sons lie scattered on the bleeding ground.
Many a widow's husband groveling lies,
Coldly embracing the discolored earth,
And victory, with little loss, doth play
Upon the dancing banners of the French,
Who are at hand, triumphantly displayed,   309
To enter conquerors and to proclaim
Arthur of Brittaine England's king and yours.   311

    Enter English Herald, with trumpet.

ENGLISH HERALD
Rejoice, you men of Angiers, ring your bells!
King John, your king and England's, doth approach,
Commander of this hot malicious day.   314
Their armors, that marched hence so silver bright,
Hither return all gilt with Frenchmen's blood.   316
There stuck no plume in any English crest   317
That is removèd by a staff of France.   318
Our colors do return in those same hands   319
That did display them when we first marched forth;   320
And like a jolly troop of huntsmen come
Our lusty English, all with purpled hands   322
Dyed in the dying slaughter of their foes.   323
Open your gates and give the victors way.

CITIZEN
Heralds, from off our towers we might behold,
From first to last, the onset and retire   326
Of both your armies, whose equality   327
By our best eyes cannot be censurèd.   328
Blood hath bought blood, and blows have answered
    blows,
Strength matched with strength, and power
    confronted power.

264 In . . . which on behalf of him for whom   **270 proves** i.e.,
proves himself, proves to be   **276 else** others, suchlike   **278 bloods**
men of mettle and of good breeding   **280 in his face** opposite to him
281 compound settle, agree   **282 for** in the interests of.   **hold** withhold   **285 fleet** fly, leave (their bodies)   **286 dreadful trial** fearful
encounter, contest (with a suggestion, too, of the soul's *dreadful trial*
before God.)   **of . . . king** to determine who is king of our kingdom
288 swinged whipped, thrashed   **289 Sits . . . door** (One of the
most common signs at tavern doors was that of Saint George and the
dragon.)   **290 fence** skill in swordsmanship   **291 lioness** (With a suggestion of "whore.")   **292 set an ox head** i.e., give you the horns of
a cuckold   **296 appointment** order, readiness

297 take . . . field gain tactical position   **299 the rest** i.e., our reserve forces.   **s.d. excursions** skirmishes, sorties   **302 by . . . France**
with the aid of the French King   **303 work** cause   **309 triumphantly
displayed** deployed or arranged for a triumphal celebration   **311 s.d.
trumpet** trumpeter   **314 Commander** victor.   **hot malicious day** a
day hotly and violently contested   **316 gilt** gilded in red   **317–
318 There . . . France** i.e., no English helmet was so dishonored as
to have the plume of its crest struck off by a French spear.   **staff**
spear   **319–320 Our . . . forth** i.e., we have not been obliged to
strike our colors   **322 lusty** vigorous   **323 Dyed . . . foes** (Huntsmen
dipped their hands in the blood of a slain deer to celebrate the
slaughter.)   **326 onset and retire** attack and withdrawal   **327–
328 whose . . . censurèd** which are so evenly matched that our keenest observations cannot determine any difference

Both are alike, and both alike we like.
One must prove greatest. While they weigh so even,
We hold our town for neither, yet for both.   333

Enter the two Kings, with their powers, at several
doors: [King John with Queen Eleanor, Blanche,
the Bastard, and forces at one door, King Philip
with Lewis, Austria, and forces at the other].

KING JOHN
France, hast thou yet more blood to cast away?
Say, shall the current of our right run on,
Whose passage, vexed with thy impediment,
Shall leave his native channel and o'erswell   337
With course disturbed even thy confining shores,   338
Unless thou let his silver water keep
A peaceful progress to the ocean?

KING PHILIP
England, thou hast not saved one drop of blood
In this hot trial more than we of France;
Rather, lost more. And by this hand I swear,   343
That sways the earth this climate overlooks,   344
Before we will lay down our just-borne arms,
We'll put thee down, 'gainst whom these arms we
    bear,
Or add a royal number to the dead,   347
Gracing the scroll that tells of this war's loss
With slaughter coupled to the name of kings.

BASTARD
Ha, majesty! How high thy glory towers   350
When the rich blood of kings is set on fire!
O, now doth Death line his dead chaps with steel;   352
The swords of soldiers are his teeth, his fangs;
And now he feasts, mousing the flesh of men   354
In undetermined differences of kings.   355
Why stand these royal fronts amazèd thus?   356
Cry havoc, Kings! Back to the stainèd field,   357
You equal potents, fiery-kindled spirits!   358
Then let confusion of one part confirm   359
The other's peace. Till then, blows, blood, and
    death!

KING JOHN
Whose party do the townsmen yet admit?   361

KING PHILIP
Speak, citizens, for England. Who's your king?

CITIZEN
The King of England, when we know the king.

KING PHILIP
Know him in us, that here hold up his right.   364

KING JOHN
In us, that are our own great deputy
And bear possession of our person here,   366
Lord of our presence, Angiers, and of you.   367

CITIZEN
A greater power than we denies all this,
And, till it be undoubted, we do lock
Our former scruple in our strong-barred gates,
Kinged of our fear, until our fears, resolved,   371
Be by some certain king purged and deposed.

BASTARD
By heaven, these scroyles of Angiers flout you,
    Kings,   373
And stand securely on their battlements
As in a theater, whence they gape and point
At your industrious scenes and acts of death.
Your royal presences be ruled by me: 377
Do like the mutines of Jerusalem,   378
Be friends awhile, and both conjointly bend   379
Your sharpest deeds of malice on this town.
By east and west let France and England mount
Their battering cannon, chargèd to the mouths,   382
Till their soul-fearing clamors have brawled down   383
The flinty ribs of this contemptuous city.
I'd play incessantly upon these jades,   385
Even till unfencèd desolation   386
Leave them as naked as the vulgar air.   387
That done, dissever your united strengths,
And part your mingled colors once again;
Turn face to face and bloody point to point.
Then, in a moment, Fortune shall cull forth
Out of one side her happy minion,   392
To whom in favor she shall give the day,   393
And kiss him with a glorious victory.
How like you this wild counsel, mighty states?   395
Smacks it not something of the policy?   396

KING JOHN
Now, by the sky that hangs above our heads,
I like it well. France, shall we knit our powers
And lay this Angiers even with the ground,
Then after fight who shall be king of it?

BASTARD [*to King Philip*]
An if thou hast the mettle of a king,
Being wronged as we are by this peevish town,   402
Turn thou the mouth of thy artillery,
As we will ours, against these saucy walls;
And when that we have dashed them to the
    ground,   405

333 **s.d. powers** armies. **several** separate   337 **his native** its normal
338 **even . . . shores** (John hints that his might, fully roused in defense of what he claims for his own right, will spill over into French
territory.)   343 **this hand** i.e., my own royal hand   344 **climate** portion of the sky   347 **a royal number** i.e., a king's name. (King Philip
will win or die in the attempt and perhaps take other kings with him.)
350 **How . . . towers** to what height the glory-seeking spirit of majesty soars. (An image from hawking.)   352 **chaps** jaws   354 **mousing** tearing, gnawing   355 **undetermined differences** unsettled quarrels   356 **royal fronts** i.e., faces of kings   357 **Cry havoc** proclaim a
general slaughter with no taking of prisoners   358 **potents** potentates
359 **confusion** destruction, overthrow.   **part** faction, party   361 **yet**
now   364 **hold up his right** support his (Arthur's) claim

366 **bear . . . person** embody the claims of sovereignty in my own
person, needing no deputy   367 **Lord of our presence** my own master   371 **Kinged of** ruled by   373 **scroyles** scoundrels   377 **Your
royal presences** may Your Majesties   378 **mutines** mutineers.   **Jerusalem** (During the siege of Jerusalem by Titus, A.D. 70, rival Jewish
factions united to resist the Romans.)   379 **conjointly bend** together
aim   382 **chargèd to the mouths** filled to the brim with shot
383 **soul-fearing** inspiring fear in the soul.   **brawled down** i.e., noisily leveled   385 **play . . . jades** i.e., (1) fire cannon repeatedly upon
these wretches (2) torment these nags. (*Jades* are ill-conditioned
horses.)   386 **unfencèd** defenseless   387 **vulgar** common   392 **minion** favorite   393 **give the day** award the victory   395 **states** kings
396 **something** somewhat.   **the policy** the art of politics, a canny
maneuver   402 **peevish** stubborn   405 **when that** when

Why, then defy each other, and pell-mell   406
Make work upon ourselves, for heaven or hell.

KING PHILIP

Let it be so. Say, where will you assault?

KING JOHN

We from the west will send destruction
Into this city's bosom.

AUSTRIA   I from the north.

KING PHILIP   Our thunder from the south
Shall rain their drift of bullets on this town.   413

BASTARD [to King John]

O prudent discipline! From north to south   414
Austria and France shoot in each other's mouth.
I'll stir them to it.—Come, away, away!

[The armies start to move.]

CITIZEN

Hear us, great kings! Vouchsafe awhile to stay,
And I shall show you peace and fair-faced league,
Win you this city without stroke or wound,
Rescue those breathing lives to die in beds
That here come sacrifices for the field.
Persever not, but hear me, mighty kings.   422

KING JOHN

Speak on with favor. We are bent to hear.   423

CITIZEN

That daughter there of Spain, the Lady Blanche,
Is near to England. Look upon the years   425
Of Lewis the Dauphin and that lovely maid.
If lusty love should go in quest of beauty,
Where should he find it fairer than in Blanche?
If zealous love should go in search of virtue,   429
Where should he find it purer than in Blanche?
If love ambitious sought a match of birth,   431
Whose veins bound richer blood than Lady Blanche? 432
Such as she is, in beauty, virtue, birth,
Is the young Dauphin every way complete.   434
If not complete of, say he is not she,   435
And she again wants nothing, to name want,   436
If want it be not that she is not he.   437
He is the half part of a blessèd man,
Left to be finishèd by such as she,
And she a fair divided excellence,
Whose fullness of perfection lies in him.
O, two such silver currents, when they join,
Do glorify the banks that bound them in;
And two such shores to two such streams
    made one,
Two such controlling bounds, shall you be, Kings,
To these two princes, if you marry them.
This union shall do more than battery can   447

To our fast-closèd gates; for at this match,   448
With swifter spleen than powder can enforce,   449
The mouth of passage shall we fling wide ope
And give you entrance. But without this match,
The sea enragèd is not half so deaf,
Lions more confident, mountains and rocks
More free from motion, no, not Death himself
In mortal fury half so peremptory,   455
As we to keep this city.

BASTARD   Here's a stay   456
That shakes the rotten carcass of old Death   457
Out of his rags! Here's a large mouth, indeed,   458
That spits forth Death and mountains, rocks and
    seas,
Talks as familiarly of roaring lions
As maids of thirteen do of puppy dogs.
What cannoneer begot this lusty blood?   462
He speaks plain cannon: fire and smoke and
    bounce.   463
He gives the bastinado with his tongue.   464
Our ears are cudgeled; not a word of his
But buffets better than a fist of France.
Zounds! I was never so bethumped with words   467
Since I first called my brother's father Dad.   468

[The French confer apart.]

ELEANOR [to King John]

Son, list to this conjunction; make this match.   469
Give with our niece a dowry large enough,
For by this knot thou shalt so surely tie
Thy now unsured assurance to the crown
That yon green boy shall have no sun to ripe   473
The bloom that promiseth a mighty fruit.
I see a yielding in the looks of France;
Mark how they whisper. Urge them while their
    souls
Are capable of this ambition,   477
Lest zeal, now melted by the windy breath   478
Of soft petitions, pity, and remorse,   479
Cool and congeal again to what it was.

CITIZEN

Why answer not the double majesties
This friendly treaty of our threatened town?   482

KING PHILIP

Speak England first, that hath been forward first
To speak unto this city. What say you?

---

448 **match** (1) marriage (2) fire used to ignite gunpowder   449 **spleen** i.e., eager, violent energy   455 **peremptory** determined   456–458 **Here's . . . rags** i.e., here's a pause for consideration, one that shakes things up so that the skeleton of Death itself is shaken out of its rags and tatters   456 **stay** hindrance, obstacle   458 **mouth** i.e., like the mouth of a cannon but spewing forth rhetoric   462 **lusty blood** hot-blooded chap. (Said sardonically.)   463 **bounce** i.e., the noise of the cannon   464 **bastinado** beating with a cudgel   467 **Zounds** by God's (Christ's) wounds   468 **Since . . . Dad** i.e., since I learned to speak. (Colloquial, but here with particular fitness to the Bastard's illegitimacy.)   469 **list** listen   473 **green** youthful, hence unripe.   **boy** i.e., Arthur. (Seemingly not onstage.)   477 **capable of** susceptible to.   **ambition** i.e., scheme that might seem to their advantage   478 **zeal** i.e., the French King's zeal in Arthur's behalf. (The metaphor is one of melting and hardening wax.)   479 **remorse** compassion   482 **treaty** proposal

---

406 **pell-mell** headlong   413 **drift** shower.   **bullets** cannonballs   414 **prudent discipline** fine military skill. (Said sarcastically.)   422 **Persever** persevere   423 **favor** permission.   **bent** inclined   425 **near to England** a near relative of King John, i.e., his niece   429 **zealous** virtue-seeking   431 **of birth** i.e., of equal royal rank   432 **bound** contain   434 **complete** accomplished, perfect in   435–437 **If . . . he** (The idea here appears to be that the two young people lack only each other to be perfect in themselves.)   436 **wants** lacks   437 **If . . . he** unless it is called a lack that she is not he   447 **battery** artillery

KING JOHN
If that the Dauphin there, thy princely son,   485
Can in this book of beauty read "I love,"   486
Her dowry shall weigh equal with a queen;   487
For Anjou and fair Touraine, Maine, Poitiers,
And all that we upon this side the sea—
Except this city now by us besieged—
Find liable to our crown and dignity,   491
Shall gild her bridal bed and make her rich
In titles, honors, and promotions,   493
As she in beauty, education, blood,
Holds hand with any princess of the world.   495

KING PHILIP
What sayst thou, boy? Look in the lady's face.

LEWIS
I do, my lord, and in her eye I find
A wonder, or a wondrous miracle,
The shadow of myself formed in her eye,   499
Which, being but the shadow of your son,   500
Becomes a sun and makes your son a shadow.   501
I do protest I never loved myself
Till now infixèd I beheld myself
Drawn in the flattering table of her eye.   504
                              Whispers with Blanche.

BASTARD
Drawn in the flattering table of her eye!   505
  Hanged in the frowning wrinkle of her brow
And quartered in her heart! He doth espy   507
  Himself love's traitor. This is pity now,
That, hanged and drawn and quartered, there
  should be
In such a love so vile a lout as he.   510

BLANCHE [*to Lewis*]
My uncle's will in this respect is mine.
If he see aught in you that makes him like,
That anything he sees which moves his liking   513
I can with ease translate it to my will;   514
Or if you will, to speak more properly,   515
I will enforce it easely to my love.
Further I will not flatter you, my lord,
That all I see in you is worthy love,
Than this: that nothing do I see in you,

Though churlish thoughts themselves should be
  your judge,   520
That I can find should merit any hate.

KING JOHN
What say these young ones? What say you, my
  niece?

BLANCHE
That she is bound in honor still to do   523
What you in wisdom still vouchsafe to say.   524

KING JOHN
Speak then, Prince Dauphin. Can you love this
  lady?

LEWIS
Nay, ask me if I can refrain from love,
For I do love her most unfeignedly.

KING JOHN
Then do I give Volquessen, Touraine, Maine,
Poitiers, and Anjou, these five provinces,
With her to thee, and this addition more,
Full thirty thousand marks of English coin.   531
Philip of France, if thou be pleased withal,   532
Command thy son and daughter to join hands.   533

KING PHILIP
It likes us well. Young princes, close your hands.   534
            [*Lewis and Blanche exchange pledges of love.*]

AUSTRIA
And your lips too, for I am well assured
That I did so when I was first assured.   [*They kiss.*]   536

KING PHILIP
Now, citizens of Angiers, ope your gates.
Let in that amity which you have made,
For at Saint Mary's chapel presently   539
The rites of marriage shall be solemnized.
Is not the Lady Constance in this troop?
I know she is not, for this match made up   542
Her presence would have interrupted much.
Where is she and her son? Tell me, who knows.   544

LEWIS
She is sad and passionate at Your Highness' tent.   545

KING PHILIP
And, by my faith, this league that we have made
Will give her sadness very little cure.
Brother of England, how may we content
This widow lady? In her right we came,
Which we, God knows, have turned another way,
To our own vantage.

KING JOHN   We will heal up all,
For we'll create young Arthur Duke of Brittaine
And Earl of Richmond, and this rich, fair town
We make him lord of. Call the Lady Constance.
Some speedy messenger bid her repair   555
To our solemnity. I trust we shall,   556

485 If that if   **486 book . . . "I love"** (An allusion to William Lilly's famous Latin grammar, in which the verb *amo*, "I love," was used as a paradigm.)   **487 dowry** (What John offers as a wedding dowry is precisely Arthur's inheritance, none of his own.)   **491 Find liable** regard as subject   **493 promotions** elevations, advancements in courtly degree   **495 Holds hand with** equals   **499 shadow** image, reflection **500 being** from being.   **shadow** pale and substanceless imitation   **501 a shadow** i.e., a mere shaded area contrasted with the sun's brightness. (The Dauphin poetically describes a *miracle*, in which his new self, formed in Blanche's eye, casts into the shade his former self.)   **504 Drawn** pictured.   **table** tablet or flat surface on which the picture is painted   **505 Drawn** (With a pun on the meaning "disemboweled." The pun is continued in the next two lines in *Hanged* and *quartered*; Elizabethan punishment for traitors specified that they be *hanged*, taken down while still alive, *drawn*, or disemboweled, and *quartered*, or cut up.)   **507 quartered** (With a pun on the meaning "lodged" and, in heraldry, "placed quarterly on a shield or coat of arms.")   **510 love** (1) profession of love (2) lover   **513 That anything** whatever   **514 will** desire   **515 properly** exactly

520 churlish sparing of praise   **523, 524 still** always   **531 marks** (A mark was the equivalent of thirteen shillings four pence.)   **532 withal** with this   **533 daughter** i.e., future daughter-in-law   **534 likes** pleases.   **close** clasp   **536 assured** betrothed (with a play on *assured*, "certain," in line 535)   **539 presently** at once   **542 made up** arranged, concluded   **544 who** whoever   **545 passionate** filled with passionate sorrow   **555 repair** come   **556 our solemnity** i.e., the wedding

If not fill up the measure of her will,   557
Yet in some measure satisfy her so   558
That we shall stop her exclamation.   559
Go we, as well as haste will suffer us,   560
To this unlooked-for, unpreparèd pomp.

Exeunt [all but the Bastard].

BASTARD
Mad world, mad kings, mad composition!   562
John, to stop Arthur's title in the whole,
Hath willingly departed with a part;   564
And France, whose armor conscience buckled on,
Whom zeal and charity brought to the field
As God's own soldier, rounded in the ear   567
With that same purpose-changer, that sly devil,   568
That broker that still breaks the pate of faith,   569
That daily break-vow, he that wins of all,   570
Of kings, of beggars, old men, young men, maids—
Who, having no external thing to lose   572
But the word "maid," cheats the poor maid of
    that—   573
That smooth-faced gentleman, tickling Commodity,   574
Commodity, the bias of the world—   575
The world, who of itself is peisèd well,   576
Made to run even upon even ground,
Till this advantage, this vile-drawing bias,   578
This sway of motion, this Commodity,   579
Makes it take head from all indifferency,   580
From all direction, purpose, course, intent.
And this same bias, this Commodity,
This bawd, this broker, this all-changing word,   583
Clapped on the outward eye of fickle France,   584
Hath drawn him from his own determined aid,   585
From a resolved and honorable war,   586
To a most base and vile-concluded peace.
And why rail I on this Commodity?
But for because he hath not wooed me yet.   589
Not that I have the power to clutch my hand   590
When his fair angels would salute my palm,   591

But for my hand, as unattempted yet,   592
Like a poor beggar, raileth on the rich.
Well, whiles I am a beggar, I will rail
And say there is no sin but to be rich;
And being rich, my virtue then shall be
To say there is no vice but beggary.
Since kings break faith upon Commodity,   598
Gain, be my lord, for I will worship thee.   *Exit.*

3.1   *Enter Constance, Arthur, and Salisbury.*

CONSTANCE
Gone to be married? Gone to swear a peace?
False blood to false blood joined! Gone to be friends?
Shall Lewis have Blanche, and Blanche those
    provinces?
It is not so; thou hast misspoke, misheard.
Be well advised; tell o'er thy tale again.   5
It cannot be; thou dost but say 'tis so.
I trust I may not trust thee, for thy word
Is but the vain breath of a common man.   8
Believe me, I do not believe thee, man;
I have a king's oath to the contrary.
Thou shalt be punished for thus frighting me,
For I am sick and capable of fears,   12
Oppressed with wrongs, and therefore full of fears,
A widow, husbandless, subject to fears,
A woman, naturally born to fears;
And though thou now confess thou didst but jest,
With my vexed spirits I cannot take a truce,   17
But they will quake and tremble all this day.
What dost thou mean by shaking of thy head?
Why dost thou look so sadly on my son?
What means that hand upon that breast of thine?
Why holds thine eye that lamentable rheum,   22
Like a proud river peering o'er his bounds?   23
Be these sad signs confirmers of thy words?
Then speak again—not all thy former tale,
But this one word: whether thy tale be true.

SALISBURY
As true as I believe you think them false   27
That give you cause to prove my saying true.

CONSTANCE
O, if thou teach me to believe this sorrow,
Teach thou this sorrow how to make me die!
And let belief and life encounter so
As doth the fury of two desperate men
Which in the very meeting fall and die.
Lewis marry Blanche? *[To Arthur.]* O boy, then
    where art thou?
France friend with England, what becomes of me?

557 **the measure** the full measure and extent   558 **so** in such a way
559 **exclamation** complaint   560 **as well** in as suitable a fashion.
suffer allow   562 **composition** agreement, compromise   564 **departed with** given up   567 **rounded** whispered to   568 **With** by
569 **broker** go-between (with a pun on "one who breaks").   **still . . .
faith** continually knocks loyalty and truth over the head   570 **wins of**
gets the better of   572 **Who** i.e., the maids   573 **cheats** i.e., he,
Commodity, cheats   574 **smooth-faced** bland, plausible.   **tickling
Commodity** flattering self-interest   575 **bias** swaying influence. (From
the game of bowls, in which a weight in the side of a bowl causes it
to curve.)   576 **peisèd** balanced, in equilibrium   578 **advantage** ad-
vantage-seeking Commodity.   **vile-drawing** attracting to evil
579 **sway of motion** swaying or controlling of motion from its intended course   580 **take . . . indifferency** rush away from all balanced, equal motion   583 **all-changing** causing change in everything
584 **Clapped on** stuck on, presented to.   **outward eye** (1) eyeball (2)
hole in the bowling ball in which the lead creating the "bias" was inserted.   **France** i.e., the King of France. (Commodity, presented to
King Philip's eye in the guise of the marriage treaty, has acted like the
bias in a bowling ball to divert him from his former intention.)
585 **his . . . aid** i.e., the aid he had determined to give Arthur
586 **resolved** resolved upon   589 **But for** merely   590 **clutch** clench
(in a gesture of refusal)   591 **angels** coins bearing the figure of an angel, worth ten shillings.   **salute** kiss (with a pun on the idea of an angelic salutation)

592 **unattempted** untempted   598 **upon** because of
3.1. Location: France. The French King's quarters.
5 **Be well advised** be sure of what you are saying   8 **a common man**
i.e., a subject, not a king   12 **capable of** susceptible to   17 **take a
truce** make peace   22 **lamentable rheum** sad moisture, i.e., tears
23 **peering o'er his** i.e., overflowing its   27 **them** i.e., the French

[*To Salisbury.*] Fellow, begone! I cannot brook thy
  sight.   36
This news hath made thee a most ugly man.
SALISBURY
What other harm have I, good lady, done,
But spoke the harm that is by others done?
CONSTANCE
Which harm within itself so heinous is
As it makes harmful all that speak of it.
ARTHUR
I do beseech you, madam, be content.   42
CONSTANCE
If thou that bidd'st me be content wert grim,
Ugly, and slanderous to thy mother's womb,   44
Full of unpleasing blots and sightless stains,   45
Lame, foolish, crooked, swart, prodigious,   46
Patched with foul moles and eye-offending marks,   47
I would not care, I then would be content,
For then I should not love thee, no, nor thou
Become thy great birth nor deserve a crown.   50
But thou art fair, and at thy birth, dear boy,
Nature and Fortune joined to make thee great.
Of Nature's gifts thou mayst with lilies boast,
And with the half-blown rose. But Fortune, O,   54
She is corrupted, changed, and won from thee.
Sh' adulterates hourly with thine uncle John,   56
And with her golden hand hath plucked on France   57
To tread down fair respect of sovereignty,   58
And made his majesty the bawd to theirs.   59
France is a bawd to Fortune and King John,
That strumpet Fortune, that usurping John!
[*To Salisbury.*] Tell me, thou fellow, is not France
  forsworn?   62
Envenom him with words, or get thee gone   63
And leave those woes alone which I alone   64
Am bound to underbear.
SALISBURY   Pardon me, madam,   65
I may not go without you to the kings.
CONSTANCE
Thou mayst, thou shalt. I will not go with thee.
I will instruct my sorrows to be proud,
For grief is proud and makes his owner stoop.
                          [*She sits on the ground.*]
To me and to the state of my great grief   70
Let kings assemble, for my grief's so great
That no supporter but the huge, firm earth
Can hold it up. Here I and sorrows sit.
Here is my throne; bid kings come bow to it.

*Enter King John, [King Philip of] France, [Lewis
the] Dauphin, Blanche, Eleanor, Philip [the
Bastard], Austria, [and attendants]. [The two
kings are arm in arm.]*

KING PHILIP [*to Blanche*]
'Tis true, fair daughter, and this blessèd day   75
Ever in France shall be kept festival.
To solemnize this day the glorious sun
Stays in his course and plays the alchemist,   78
Turning with splendor of his precious eye
The meager cloddy earth to glittering gold.
The yearly course that brings this day about
Shall never see it but a holy day.
CONSTANCE [*rising*]
A wicked day, and not a holy day!
What hath this day deserved? What hath it done,
That it in golden letters should be set   85
Among the high tides in the calendar?   86
Nay, rather turn this day out of the week,
This day of shame, oppression, perjury.
Or if it must stand still, let wives with child   89
Pray that their burdens may not fall this day,
Lest that their hopes prodigiously be crossed.   91
But on this day let seamen fear no wreck;   92
No bargains break that are not this day made.   93
This day, all things begun come to ill end,
Yea, faith itself to hollow falsehood change!
KING PHILIP
By heaven, lady, you shall have no cause
To curse the fair proceedings of this day.
Have I not pawned to you my majesty?   98
CONSTANCE
You have beguiled me with a counterfeit
Resembling majesty, which, being touched and
  tried,   100
Proves valueless. You are forsworn, forsworn!
You came in arms to spill mine enemies' blood,   102
But now in arms you strengthen it with yours.   103
The grappling vigor and rough frown of war
Is cold in amity and painted peace,   105
And our oppression hath made up this league.   106
Arm, arm, you heavens, against these perjured
  kings!
A widow cries; be husband to me, heavens!   108
Let not the hours of this ungodly day   109
Wear out the day in peace, but ere sunset   110

36 brook endure   **42 content** calm   **44 slanderous** disgraceful
45 sightless unsightly   **46 swart** swarthy.   **prodigious** monstrous, an
evil omen   **47 Patched** blotched   **50 Become** befit   **54 half-blown**
only partly opened, still young   **56 adulterates** commits adultery
57 golden i.e., offering gold   **57–59 hath plucked on . . . theirs** i.e.,
she, Fortune, has induced the King of France to tread underfoot
Arthur's rights of sovereignty and has made the King of France the
bawd between Fortune and King John   **62 is not France forsworn**
hasn't the French King broken his oath   **63 Envenom . . . words** i.e.,
curse him for being forsworn, as I do.   **Envenom** poison   **64 leave
those woes alone** leave behind only those woes   **65 underbear** endure   **70 state** majesty, as in a chair of state

75 'Tis true (King Philip is in mid-conversation with Blanche.)
78 Stays in his course stands still.   **his** its   **85 golden** i.e., red
86 high tides i.e., great festivals   **89 stand still** remain   **91 prodigiously be crossed** be thwarted by some monstrous birth defect
92 But except, other than (since this is the most evil of days).   **wreck**
shipwreck   **93 No . . . made** break only agreements made on this
day   **98 pawned** pledged.   **my majesty** i.e., my kingly word
100 touched tested (as one tests gold by rubbing it on a touchstone)
102 in arms in armor   **103 in arms** embracing.   **with yours** i.e., by
uniting your enemies to your royal house in marriage   **105 Is cold in
amity** i.e., have lost all vigor in this new friendship.   **painted** specious, unreal   **106 our oppression** our being oppressed   **108 A
widow cries** it is a widow that cries   **109–110 Let . . . peace** do not
let this wicked day pass by peaceably

Set armèd discord twixt these perjured kings!
Hear me, O, hear me!

AUSTRIA   Lady Constance, peace!

CONSTANCE

War, war, no peace! Peace is to me a war.
O Limoges, O Austria, thou dost shame   114
That bloody spoil. Thou slave, thou wretch, thou
    coward!   115
Thou little valiant, great in villainy!
Thou ever strong upon the stronger side!
Thou Fortune's champion, that dost never fight
But when her humorous ladyship is by   119
To teach thee safety! Thou art perjured too,   120
And sooth'st up greatness. What a fool art thou, 121
A ramping fool, to brag and stamp and swear   122
Upon my party! Thou cold-blooded slave,   123
Hast thou not spoke like thunder on my side,
Been sworn my soldier, bidding me depend
Upon thy stars, thy fortune, and thy strength?
And dost thou now fall over to my foes?   127
Thou wear a lion's hide! Doff it for shame,
And hang a calfskin on those recreant limbs.   129

AUSTRIA

O, that a man should speak those words to me!

BASTARD

And hang a calfskin on those recreant limbs.

AUSTRIA

Thou dar'st not say so, villain, for thy life.

BASTARD

And hang a calfskin on those recreant limbs.

KING JOHN [to the Bastard]

We like not this. Thou dost forget thyself.   134

Enter Pandulph.

KING PHILIP

Here comes the holy legate of the Pope.

PANDULPH

Hail, you anointed deputies of heaven!
To thee, King John, my holy errand is.
I Pandulph, of fair Milan cardinal,
And from Pope Innocent the legate here,
Do in his name religiously demand
Why thou against the Church, our holy mother,
So willfully dost spurn, and force perforce   142
Keep Stephen Langton, chosen Archbishop   143
Of Canterbury, from that Holy See.

This, in our foresaid Holy Father's name,
Pope Innocent, I do demand of thee.

KING JOHN

What earthy name to interrogatories   147
Can task the free breath of a sacred king?   148
Thou canst not, Cardinal, devise a name
So slight, unworthy, and ridiculous,
To charge me to an answer, as the Pope.   151
Tell him this tale, and from the mouth of England
Add thus much more: that no Italian priest
Shall tithe or toll in our dominions;   154
But as we, under God, are supreme head,   155
So, under Him, that great supremacy
Where we do reign we will alone uphold
Without th' assistance of a mortal hand.
So tell the Pope, all reverence set apart
To him and his usurped authority.

KING PHILIP

Brother of England, you blaspheme in this.

KING JOHN

Though you and all the kings of Christendom
Are led so grossly by this meddling priest,   163
Dreading the curse that money may buy out,   164
And by the merit of vile gold, dross, dust,
Purchase corrupted pardon of a man
Who in that sale sells pardon from himself,   167
Though you and all the rest, so grossly led,
This juggling witchcraft with revenue cherish, 169
Yet I alone, alone do me oppose
Against the Pope, and count his friends my foes.

PANDULPH

Then, by the lawful power that I have,
Thou shalt stand cursed and excommunicate;
And blessèd shall he be that doth revolt
From his allegiance to an heretic;
And meritorious shall that hand be called,
Canonizèd and worshiped as a saint,
That takes away by any secret course
Thy hateful life.

CONSTANCE   O, lawful let it be
That I have room with Rome to curse awhile!   180
Good father Cardinal, cry thou "Amen"
To my keen curses, for without my wrong   182
There is no tongue hath power to curse him right.

114 **Limoges** (Compare with the note for 2.1.5.)   115 **spoil** booty, i.e., the lion's pelt that Austria wears   119 **humorous** capricious   120 **safety** i.e., how to choose the safe side   121 **sooth'st up greatness** flatter the influential   122 **ramping** making a fierce show   123 **Upon my party** in my behalf   127 **fall over** go over, desert   129 **calfskin** (Customarily used to make coats for the fools kept to amuse great families.)   **recreant** cowardly, having deserted his cause   134 **Thou . . . thyself** i.e., remember your place, and be silent   142 **spurn** oppose scornfully. (Literally, "kick.")   **force perforce** by compulsion   143 **Stephen Langton** Pope Innocent's choice to be Archbishop of Canterbury, whose rejection by King John led to a papal bull of deposition and eventual resolution only after John had been forced to pay tribute and acknowledge England to be a papal fiefdom

147–148 **What . . . king?** what earth-born official can take to task the free breath of a sacred king by asking it to submit to formal questioning? (John denies any divine authority in the Pope's office.)   151 **charge . . . answer** command me to answer   154 **tithe** impose tithes, a tenth of one's income given to the Church.   **toll** collect taxes   155 **supreme head** (The title assumed by Henry VIII at the time of the Reformation.)   163 **led** led astray.   **this meddling priest** i.e., the Pope   164 **the curse . . . out** i.e., excommunication, which a bribe to Rome can fix   167 **Who . . . himself** i.e., who, in selling indulgences, incurs his own damnation. (*From himself* may also suggest that the pardon stems only from him, not from God, and is therefore invalid.)   169 **juggling** cheating, deceiving.   **cherish** maintain   180 **room, Rome** (An obvious pun, pronounced alike in Elizabethan England.)   182 **without my wrong** i.e., (1) without recognition of the wrong done to me (2) without the motive of suffering wrongs as I have suffered

PANDULPH
  There's law and warrant, lady, for my curse.
CONSTANCE
  And for mine too. When law can do no right,   185
  Let it be lawful that law bar no wrong.   186
  Law cannot give my child his kingdom here,
  For he that holds his kingdom holds the law;   188
  Therefore, since law itself is perfect wrong,
  How can the law forbid my tongue to curse?
PANDULPH
  Philip of France, on peril of a curse,   191
  Let go the hand of that arch-heretic,
  And raise the power of France upon his head
  Unless he do submit himself to Rome.
ELEANOR
  Look'st thou pale, France? Do not let go thy hand.
CONSTANCE [to Eleanor]
  Look to it, devil, lest that France repent,   196
  And by disjoining hands, hell lose a soul.
AUSTRIA
  King Philip, listen to the Cardinal.
BASTARD
  And hang a calfskin on his recreant limbs.
AUSTRIA
  Well, ruffian, I must pocket up these wrongs,   200
  Because—
BASTARD   Your breeches best may carry them.
KING JOHN
  Philip, what sayst thou to the Cardinal?
CONSTANCE
  What should he say, but as the Cardinal?   203
LEWIS
  Bethink you, Father, for the difference   204
  Is purchase of a heavy curse from Rome
  Or the light loss of England for a friend.
  Forgo the easier.
BLANCHE   That's the curse of Rome.
CONSTANCE
  O Lewis, stand fast! The devil tempts thee here
  In likeness of a new, untrimmèd bride.   209
BLANCHE
  The Lady Constance speaks not from her faith   210
  But from her need.
CONSTANCE [to King Philip]   O, if thou grant my need,
  Which only lives but by the death of faith,   212
  That need must needs infer this principle: 213

That faith would live again by death of need.   214
O, then tread down my need, and faith mounts up;   215
Keep my need up, and faith is trodden down!
KING JOHN
  The King is moved, and answers not to this.
CONSTANCE [to King Philip]
  O, be removed from him, and answer well!   218
AUSTRIA
  Do so, King Philip. Hang no more in doubt.
BASTARD
  Hang nothing but a calfskin, most sweet lout.   220
KING PHILIP
  I am perplexed and know not what to say.
PANDULPH
  What canst thou say but will perplex thee more,
  If thou stand excommunicate and cursed?
KING PHILIP
  Good Reverend Father, make my person yours,   224
  And tell me how you would bestow yourself.   225
  This royal hand and mine are newly knit,
  And the conjunction of our inward souls
  Married in league, coupled and linked together
  With all religious strength of sacred vows.
  The latest breath that gave the sound of words   230
  Was deep-sworn faith, peace, amity, true love
  Between our kingdoms and our royal selves;
  And even before this truce, but new before,   233
  No longer than we well could wash our hands
  To clap this royal bargain up of peace,   235
  Heaven knows, they were besmeared and
    overstained
  With slaughter's pencil, where revenge did paint   237
  The fearful difference of incensèd kings.   238
  And shall these hands, so lately purged of blood,
  So newly joined in love, so strong in both,   240
  Unyoke this seizure and this kind regreet?   241
  Play fast and loose with faith? So jest with heaven,
  Make such unconstant children of ourselves,
  As now again to snatch our palm from palm,
  Unswear faith sworn, and on the marriage bed
  Of smiling peace to march a bloody host,
  And make a riot on the gentle brow
  Of true sincerity? O holy sir,
  My Reverend Father, let it not be so!
  Out of your grace, devise, ordain, impose
  Some gentle order; and then we shall be blest
  To do your pleasure and continue friends.
PANDULPH
  All form is formless, order orderless,
  Save what is opposite to England's love.

185–186 When . . . wrong i.e., when the law itself is powerless to remedy evils, people must be free to pursue wrongful remedies (such as cursing)   188 holds the law i.e., holds the law hostage   191 a curse excommunication   196 Look to it see to it, take care.   devil i.e., Eleanor, or the devil himself.   lest that lest   200 pocket up submit to. (But the Bastard plays on the literal sense of putting in one's breeches pocket, perhaps suggesting further that Austria will get a swift kick in the breeches.)   203 but as the Cardinal except what the Cardinal has already spoken and as he would be expected to speak   204 difference choice   209 untrimmèd i.e., freshly married, unshorn (suggesting she is still a virgin). (This alludes to the temptation of Saint Anthony by the devil in the form of a naked woman.)   210 not from her faith not what she truly believes   212 Which . . . faith i.e., which need is so strong only because I have lost faith in you   213 needs infer necessarily imply

214 That . . . need i.e., my faith will be rekindled once my prior and compelling necessity, Arthur's claim, has been satisfied   215 tread down i.e., put down by satisfying, subdue   218 removed separated (playing on moved in line 217)   220 Hang i.e., wear (playing on Hang, "hesitate," in line 219)   224 make . . . yours put yourself in my place   225 bestow conduct   230 latest most recent   233 even before just before.   but new immediately   235 clap . . . up i.e., conclude with a grasping of hands   237 pencil paintbrush.   paint picture, represent   238 difference dissension   240 both i.e., blood and love   241 Unyoke this seizure disjoin this handclasp.   regreet returned salutation, counterclasp

Therefore to arms! Be champion of our Church,
Or let the Church, our mother, breathe her curse,
A mother's curse, on her revolting son.　　　　　　257
France, thou mayst hold a serpent by the tongue,　258
A chafèd lion by the mortal paw,　　　　　　　　　259
A fasting tiger safer by the tooth,
Than keep in peace that hand which thou dost hold.

KING PHILIP
I may disjoin my hand, but not my faith.

PANDULPH
So mak'st thou faith an enemy to faith,　　　　　263
And like a civil war sett'st oath to oath,
Thy tongue against thy tongue. O, let thy vow
First made to heaven, first be to heaven performed,
That is, to be the champion of our Church!
What since thou swor'st is sworn against thyself　268
And may not be performèd by thyself,
For that which thou hast sworn to do amiss
Is not amiss when it is truly done;　　　　　　　271
And being not done where doing tends to ill,
The truth is then most done not doing it.
The better act of purposes mistook　　　　　　　274
Is to mistake again; though indirect,　　　　　　275
Yet indirection thereby grows direct,
And falsehood falsehood cures, as fire cools fire　277
Within the scorchèd veins of one new-burned.　　278
It is religion that doth make vows kept,
But thou hast sworn against religion;
By what thou swear'st against the thing thou
　　swear'st,　　　　　　　　　　　　　　　　　281
And mak'st an oath the surety for thy truth
Against an oath. The truth thou art unsure　　　283
To swear, swears only not to be forsworn,　　　　284
Else what a mockery should it be to swear!
But thou dost swear only to be forsworn,　　　　286
And most forsworn to keep what thou dost swear.
Therefore thy later vows against thy first
Is in thyself rebellion to thyself;
And better conquest never canst thou make
Than arm thy constant and thy nobler parts
Against these giddy loose suggestions,　　　　　292
Upon which better part our prayers come in,　　293
If thou vouchsafe them. But if not, then know　294

257 **revolting** rebellious　258 **mayst hold** may sooner hold
259 **mortal** deadly　263 **So . . . to faith** i.e., you are trying to set
your promise to John against your religious vow to the Church
268 **since** since then　271 **truly done** i.e., not done at all (since, as
Pandulph explains two lines later, an ill-considered vow is best performed by not performing it. This is an example of equivocation,
much deplored by many Elizabethans and regarded as typical of Catholic duplicity.)　274–275 **The better . . . again** i.e., the best thing to
do when one has made a wrong turn is to turn again　277–278 **as
fire . . . new-burned** (Burns were commonly treated with heat, on the
proverbial theory that one fire drives out another.)　281 **By . . . thing
thou swear'st** you swear against the very thing by which you swear;
i.e., by your oath of allegiance to John you directly violate your prior
vows given to the Church　283–284 **The truth . . . forsworn** i.e.,
your oath of allegiance to the true faith, which you are now hesitant
to affirm, is above all a promise not to break your oath　286 **But . . .
forsworn** i.e., but you are now proposing an oath to John in which
you will indeed break your prior oath　292 **suggestions** temptations
293 **Upon . . . part** in support of which better side　294 **vouchsafe**
accept, agree to

The peril of our curses light on thee
So heavy as thou shalt not shake them off,　　　296
But in despair die under their black weight.

AUSTRIA
Rebellion, flat rebellion!

BASTARD　　　　　　　　　　Will 't not be?　　　298
Will not a calfskin stop that mouth of thine?

LEWIS
Father, to arms!

BLANCHE　　　　　　Upon thy wedding day?
Against the blood that thou hast married?　　　301
What, shall our feast be kept with slaughtered men?
Shall braying trumpets and loud churlish drums,
Clamors of hell, be measures to our pomp?　　　304
[*Kneeling.*] O husband, hear me! Ay, alack, how new
Is "husband" in my mouth! Even for that name,
Which till this time my tongue did ne'er pronounce,
Upon my knee I beg, go not to arms
Against mine uncle.

CONSTANCE [*kneeling*]　O, upon my knee,
Made hard with kneeling, I do pray to thee,
Thou virtuous Dauphin, alter not the doom
Forethought by heaven!　　　　　　　　　　　312

BLANCHE [*to Lewis*]
Now shall I see thy love. What motive may
Be stronger with thee than the name of wife?

CONSTANCE
That which upholdeth him that thee upholds:　315
His honor. O, thine honor, Lewis, thine honor!

LEWIS [*to King Philip*]
I muse Your Majesty doth seem so cold,　　　　317
When such profound respects do pull you on.　318

PANDULPH
I will denounce a curse upon his head.　　　　　319

KING PHILIP [*letting go of King John's hand*]
Thou shalt not need. England, I will fall from thee.

CONSTANCE [*rising*]
O, fair return of banished majesty!

ELEANOR
O, foul revolt of French inconstancy!

KING JOHN
France, thou shalt rue this hour within this hour.

BASTARD
Old Time the clock setter, that bald sexton Time,
Is it as he will? Well then, France shall rue.　　325

BLANCHE [*rising*]
The sun's o'ercast with blood. Fair day, adieu!
Which is the side that I must go withal?　　　　327
I am with both: each army hath a hand,
And in their rage, I having hold of both,
They whirl asunder and dismember me.
Husband, I cannot pray that thou mayst win;
Uncle, I needs must pray that thou mayst lose;

296 **as** that　298 **Will 't not be** i.e., will nothing serve (to keep you
quiet)　301 **blood** (Blanche is related by blood to King John.)
304 **measures** musical accompaniment.　**pomp** i.e., wedding ceremony　312 **Forethought** destined　315 **that thee upholds** who supports you　317 **muse** wonder　318 **respects** considerations　319 **denounce** proclaim, call down　325 **France shall rue** i.e., if Time is to
decide, France will rue sooner or later　327 **withal** with

Father, I may not wish the fortune thine;   333
Grandam, I will not wish thy wishes thrive.
Whoever wins, on that side shall I lose;
Assurèd loss before the match be played.

LEWIS
Lady, with me, with me thy fortune lies.

BLANCHE
There where my fortune lives, there my life dies.

KING JOHN [to the Bastard]
Cousin, go draw our puissance together.   339
                                    [Exit the Bastard.]
France, I am burned up with inflaming wrath,
A rage whose heat hath this condition,
That nothing can allay, nothing but blood—
The blood, and dearest-valued blood, of France.

KING PHILIP
Thy rage shall burn thee up, and thou shalt turn
To ashes, ere our blood shall quench that fire.
Look to thyself. Thou art in jeopardy.

KING JOHN
No more than he that threats. To arms let's hie!   347
                                    Exeunt [separately].

3.2   *Alarums, excursions. Enter [the] Bastard, with*
          Austria's head.

BASTARD
Now, by my life, this day grows wondrous hot.
Some airy devil hovers in the sky   2
And pours down mischief. Austria's head lie there,
While Philip breathes.   [He puts down the head.] 4

          Enter [King] John, Arthur, [and] Hubert.

KING JOHN
Hubert, keep this boy. Philip, make up!   5
My mother is assailèd in our tent,
And ta'en, I fear.

BASTARD   My lord, I rescued her;
Her Highness is in safety, fear you not.
But on, my liege! For very little pains
Will bring this labor to an happy end.
                              Exeunt [with Austria's head].

3.3   *Alarums, excursions, retreat. Enter [King] John,*
          Eleanor, Arthur, [the] Bastard, Hubert, [and]
          lords.

KING JOHN [to Eleanor]
So shall it be; Your Grace shall stay behind   1

So strongly guarded. [To Arthur.] Cousin, look not
  sad.   2
Thy grandam loves thee, and thy uncle will
As dear be to thee as thy father was.

ARTHUR
O, this will make my mother die with grief!

KING JOHN [to the Bastard]
Cousin, away for England! Haste before,
And, ere our coming, see thou shake the bags
Of hoarding abbots; imprisoned angels   8
Set at liberty. The fat ribs of peace   9
Must by the hungry now be fed upon.
Use our commission in his utmost force.   11

BASTARD
Bell, book, and candle shall not drive me back   12
When gold and silver becks me to come on.   13
I leave Your Highness.—Grandam, I will pray,
If ever I remember to be holy,
For your fair safety. So I kiss your hand.

ELEANOR
Farewell, gentle cousin.

KING JOHN   Coz, farewell.   17
                              [Exit the Bastard.]

ELEANOR
Come hither, little kinsman. Hark, a word.
                              [She takes Arthur aside.]

KING JOHN
Come hither, Hubert. O my gentle Hubert,
We owe thee much! Within this wall of flesh   20
There is a soul counts thee her creditor   21
And with advantage means to pay thy love;   22
And, my good friend, thy voluntary oath   23
Lives in this bosom, dearly cherishèd.   24
Give me thy hand. I had a thing to say,
But I will fit it with some better tune.   26
By heaven, Hubert, I am almost ashamed
To say what good respect I have of thee.   28

HUBERT
I am much bounden to Your Majesty.   29

KING JOHN
Good friend, thou hast no cause to say so yet,
But thou shalt have; and, creep time ne'er so slow,
Yet it shall come for me to do thee good.
I had a thing to say—but let it go.
The sun is in the heaven, and the proud day,
Attended with the pleasures of the world,
Is all too wanton and too full of gauds   36
To give me audience. If the midnight bell   37
Did with his iron tongue and brazen mouth
Sound on into the drowsy race of night;   39

---

333 **Father** i.e., father-in-law, King Philip   **339 Cousin** kinsman.
puissance armed force   **347 hie** hasten
**3.2. Location: France. Plains near Angiers. The battle is seen as fol-
lowing immediately upon the previous scene.**
s.d. Alarums calls to arms.   **excursions** sorties   **2 airy devil** (Aerial
spirits or devils were thought to be the cause of tempests, thunder,
lightning, etc.)   **4 breathes** gets his breath   **5 make up** advance,
press on
3.3. Location: Scene continues on the plains near Angiers.
s.d. retreat signal for withdrawal of forces   **1 stay behind** i.e., remain
here in charge of the English territories

2 So thus   **8 angels** gold coins (with a common pun)   **9 fat ribs of
peace** (i.e., in contrast to the skeleton of war, the *bare-ribbed Death*
of 5.2.177)   **11 his** its   **12 Bell, book, and candle** (Articles used in
the office of excommunication.)   **13 becks** beckon   **17 Coz** cousin,
i.e., kinsman   **20 Within . . . flesh** i.e., within me   **21 counts** that
counts   **22 advantage** interest   **23 thy voluntary oath** your freely
given allegiance   **24 Lives in this bosom** is vividly felt in my heart
26 some better tune i.e., better words and some better reward
28 respect opinion   **29 bounden** obligated   **36 gauds** showy ornaments, trifles   **37 To give me audience** i.e., for you to hearken to my
words   **39 race** running, course. ("Face" and "ear" have been suggested as emendations.)

If this same were a churchyard where we stand,
And thou possessèd with a thousand wrongs;   41
Or if that surly spirit, melancholy,
Had baked thy blood and made it heavy, thick,
Which else runs tickling up and down the veins,
Making that idiot, laughter, keep men's eyes   45
And strain their cheeks to idle merriment,   46
A passion hateful to my purposes;   47
Or if that thou couldst see me without eyes,
Hear me without thine ears, and make reply
Without a tongue, using conceit alone,   50
Without eyes, ears, and harmful sound of words—   51
Then, in despite of brooded watchful day,   52
I would into thy bosom pour my thoughts.
But, ah, I will not! Yet I love thee well,
And, by my troth, I think thou lov'st me well.

HUBERT
So well that what you bid me undertake,   56
Though that my death were adjunct to my act,   57
By heaven, I would do it.

KING JOHN   Do not I know thou wouldst?
Good Hubert, Hubert, Hubert, throw thine eye
On yon young boy. I'll tell thee what, my friend,
He is a very serpent in my way,
And wheresoe'er this foot of mine doth tread
He lies before me. Dost thou understand me?
Thou art his keeper.

HUBERT   And I'll keep him so
That he shall not offend Your Majesty.

KING JOHN   Death.

HUBERT
My lord?

KING JOHN A grave.

HUBERT   He shall not live.

KING JOHN   Enough.
I could be merry now. Hubert, I love thee.
Well, I'll not say what I intend for thee.
Remember.—Madam, fare you well.
I'll send those powers o'er to Your Majesty.   70

ELEANOR
My blessing go with thee!

KING JOHN   For England, cousin, go.   71
Hubert shall be your man, attend on you
With all true duty.—On toward Calais, ho!   *Exeunt.*

❧

3.4   *Enter [King Philip of] France, [Lewis the]
Dauphin, Pandulph, [and] attendants.*

KING PHILIP
So, by a roaring tempest on the flood,   1

A whole armada of convicted sail   2
Is scattered and disjoined from fellowship.

PANDULPH
Courage and comfort! All shall yet go well.

KING PHILIP
What can go well when we have run so ill?
Are we not beaten? Is not Angiers lost?
Arthur ta'en prisoner? Divers dear friends slain?
And bloody England into England gone,   8
O'erbearing interruption, spite of France?   9

LEWIS
What he hath won, that hath he fortified.
So hot a speed, with such advice disposed,   11
Such temperate order in so fierce a cause,
Doth want example. Who hath read or heard   13
Of any kindred action like to this?   14

KING PHILIP
Well could I bear that England had this praise,
So we could find some pattern of our shame.   16

Enter Constance, [with her hair about her ears].

Look who comes here! A grave unto a soul,   17
Holding th' eternal spirit, against her will,
In the vile prison of afflicted breath.—   19
I prithee, lady, go away with me.

CONSTANCE
Lo, now! Now see the issue of your peace.   21

KING PHILIP
Patience, good lady. Comfort, gentle Constance.

CONSTANCE
No, I defy all counsel, all redress,   23
But that which ends all counsel, true redress:
Death. Death, O amiable, lovely Death!
Thou odoriferous stench! Sound rottenness!   26
Arise forth from the couch of lasting night,
Thou hate and terror to prosperity,
And I will kiss thy detestable bones,
And put my eyeballs in thy vaulty brows,   30
And ring these fingers with thy household worms,   31
And stop this gap of breath with fulsome dust,   32
And be a carrion monster like thyself.
Come, grin on me, and I will think thou smil'st,
And buss thee as thy wife. Misery's love,   35
O, come to me!

KING PHILIP   O fair affliction, peace!   36

CONSTANCE
No, no, I will not, having breath to cry.   37
O, that my tongue were in the thunder's mouth!

41 possessèd with obsessed by   **45 idiot** jester.   **keep** hold captive, possess   **46 strain** stretch (in laughter)   **47 passion** emotion   **50 conceit** the mental faculty   **51 harmful** (Because it is dangerous to speak of such matters.)   **52 brooded** brooding (and hence vigilant in defense of its young)   **56 what** whatever   **57 adjunct to** consequent upon   **70 those powers** i.e., the troops already agreed upon for the defense of England's French territories; see lines 1–2.   **o'er** i.e., from England to France   **71 cousin** i.e., Arthur
3.4. Location: France. The French King's quarters.
1 flood seas

2 armada (With probable allusion to the scattering of the Spanish Armada in 1588.)   **convicted** doomed   **8 bloody England** the blood-stained King of England   **9 O'erbearing interruption** overcoming all resistance.   **spite** in spite   **11 with . . . disposed** directed with such judgment   **13 Doth want example** lacks parallel instance   **14 kindred** comparable   **16 So** provided.   **pattern** precedent   **17 A grave . . . soul** i.e., a mere shell of a body without the will to live   **19 prison . . . breath** (The soul was thought to leave the body from the mouth with the last expiring breath.)   **21 issue** outcome   **23 defy** reject.   **redress** comfort   **26 odoriferous** sweet-smelling.   **Sound** wholesome   **30 vaulty** arched and hollow   **31 these** i.e., my.   **thy household worms** the worms of your retinue   **32 this gap of breath** i.e., my mouth.   **fulsome** loathsome   **35 buss** kiss.   **Misery's love** you whom those in misery love (as a way of ending their misery)   **36 affliction** afflicted one   **37 having** so long as I have

Then with a passion would I shake the world,
And rouse from sleep that fell anatomy   40
Which cannot hear a lady's feeble voice,
Which scorns a modern invocation.   42

PANDULPH
Lady, you utter madness and not sorrow.

CONSTANCE
Thou art not holy to belie me so.
I am not mad. This hair I tear is mine;
My name is Constance; I was Geoffrey's wife;
Young Arthur is my son; and he is lost.
I am not mad; I would to heaven I were,
For then 'tis like I should forget myself!   49
O, if I could, what grief should I forget?
Preach some philosophy to make me mad,
And thou shalt be canonized, Cardinal;
For, being not mad but sensible of grief,   53
My reasonable part produces reason   54
How I may be delivered of these woes,   55
And teaches me to kill or hang myself.
If I were mad, I should forget my son,
Or madly think a babe of clouts were he.   58
I am not mad. Too well, too well I feel
The different plague of each calamity.   60

KING PHILIP
Bind up those tresses. O, what love I note
In the fair multitude of those her hairs!
Where but by chance a silver drop hath fallen,   63
Even to that drop ten thousand wiry friends   64
Do glue themselves in sociable grief,   65
Like true, inseparable, faithful loves,
Sticking together in calamity.

CONSTANCE
To England, if you will.

KING PHILIP   Bind up your hairs.   68

CONSTANCE
Yes, that I will. And wherefore will I do it?
I tore them from their bonds and cried aloud,
"O, that these hands could so redeem my son,   71
As they have given these hairs their liberty!"
But now I envy at their liberty,
And will again commit them to their bonds,
Because my poor child is a prisoner.
                         [She binds up her hair.]
And, father Cardinal, I have heard you say
That we shall see and know our friends in heaven.
If that be true, I shall see my boy again;
For since the birth of Cain, the first male child,
To him that did but yesterday suspire,   80
There was not such a gracious creature born.

But now will canker sorrow eat my bud   82
And chase the native beauty from his cheek,   83
And he will look as hollow as a ghost,
As dim and meager as an ague's fit,
And so he'll die; and, rising so again,   86
When I shall meet him in the court of heaven
I shall not know him. Therefore never, never
Must I behold my pretty Arthur more.

PANDULPH
You hold too heinous a respect of grief.   90

CONSTANCE
He talks to me that never had a son.

KING PHILIP
You are as fond of grief as of your child.   92

CONSTANCE
Grief fills the room up of my absent child,   93
Lies in his bed, walks up and down with me,
Puts on his pretty looks, repeats his words,
Remembers me of all his gracious parts,   96
Stuffs out his vacant garments with his form;
Then, have I reason to be fond of grief?
Fare you well! Had you such a loss as I,
I could give better comfort than you do.
                         [She unbinds her hair again.]
I will not keep this form upon my head   101
When there is such disorder in my wit.   102
O Lord! My boy, my Arthur, my fair son!
My life, my joy, my food, my all the world!
My widow-comfort, and my sorrows' cure!   Exit.

KING PHILIP
I fear some outrage, and I'll follow her.   106
                         Exit [attended].

LEWIS
There's nothing in this world can make me joy.
Life is as tedious as a twice-told tale
Vexing the dull ear of a drowsy man;   109
And bitter shame hath spoiled the sweet world's
    taste,
That it yields naught but shame and bitterness.   111

PANDULPH
Before the curing of a strong disease,
Even in the instant of repair and health,
The fit is strongest. Evils that take leave,   114
On their departure most of all show evil.
What have you lost by losing of this day?   116

LEWIS
All days of glory, joy, and happiness.

PANDULPH
If you had won it, certainly you had.
No, no. When Fortune means to men most good,   119
She looks upon them with a threatening eye.
'Tis strange to think how much King John hath lost

---

40 fell anatomy fierce skeleton (the usual figure of Death in pictorial representations) **42 modern** everyday, commonplace. **invocation** entreaty **49 like** likely **53 sensible of** capable of feeling **54 reasonable part** i.e., brain **55 delivered of** (1) freed from (2) delivered of, as in childbirth **58 babe of clouts** rag doll **60 different plague** distinct affliction **63 silver drop** i.e., tear **64 wiry friends** i.e., hairs **65 Do . . . grief** i.e., cling together in sympathy of grief, bound to one another by the tears falling on them **68 To England** (Perhaps an answer to Philip's invitation at line 20; perhaps evidence of textual revision.) **71 redeem** free from imprisonment **80 suspire** breathe his first breath

82 canker like a cankerworm, feeding on buds **83 native** natural **86 so . . . so** thus . . . thus **90 heinous a respect** calamitous a view **92 fond of** foolishly doting on **93 room** place **96 Remembers** reminds **101 form** coiffure (with idea of order, contrasted with *disorder* in line 102) **102 wit** i.e., brain **106 outrage** i.e., outrage upon herself, suicide **109 dull** inattentive **111 That** so that **114 fit** bout of illness **116 this day** this day's battle. (But the Dauphin replies bitterly, using *day* in the more common meaning.) **119 means** intends

In this which he accounts so clearly won.
Are not you grieved that Arthur is his prisoner?
LEWIS
As heartily as he is glad he hath him.
PANDULPH
Your mind is all as youthful as your blood.
Now hear me speak with a prophetic spirit;
For even the breath of what I mean to speak
Shall blow each dust, each straw, each little rub,   128
Out of the path which shall directly lead
Thy foot to England's throne. And therefore mark.
John hath seized Arthur, and it cannot be
That, whiles warm life plays in that infant's veins,   132
The misplaced John should entertain an hour,   133
One minute, nay, one quiet breath of rest.
A scepter snatched with an unruly hand   135
Must be as boisterously maintained as gained;   136
And he that stands upon a slippery place
Makes nice of no vile hold to stay him up.   138
That John may stand, then Arthur needs must fall;
So be it, for it cannot be but so.
LEWIS
But what shall I gain by young Arthur's fall?
PANDULPH
You, in the right of Lady Blanche your wife,
May then make all the claim that Arthur did.
LEWIS
And lose it, life and all, as Arthur did.
PANDULPH
How green you are and fresh in this old world!
John lays you plots; the times conspire with you,   146
For he that steeps his safety in true blood   147
Shall find but bloody safety, and untrue.   148
This act so evilly borne shall cool the hearts   149
Of all his people and freeze up their zeal,
That none so small advantage shall step forth   151
To check his reign but they will cherish it;
No natural exhalation in the sky,   153
No scope of nature, no distempered day,   154
No common wind, no customèd event,   155
But they will pluck away his natural cause   156
And call them meteors, prodigies, and signs,
Abortives, presages, and tongues of heaven   158
Plainly denouncing vengeance upon John.   159
LEWIS
Maybe he will not touch young Arthur's life,
But hold himself safe in his prisonment.   161

PANDULPH
O, sir, when he shall hear of your approach,
If that young Arthur be not gone already,
Even at that news he dies; and then the hearts
Of all his people shall revolt from him,   165
And kiss the lips of unacquainted change,   166
And pick strong matter of revolt and wrath   167
Out of the bloody fingers' ends of John.   168
Methinks I see this hurly all on foot;   169
And, O, what better matter breeds for you   170
Than I have named! The bastard Faulconbridge
Is now in England, ransacking the Church,
Offending charity. If but a dozen French
Were there in arms, they would be as a call   174
To train ten thousand English to their side,   175
Or as a little snow, tumbled about,
Anon becomes a mountain. O noble Dauphin,
Go with me to the King. 'Tis wonderful
What may be wrought out of their discontent,
Now that their souls are topful of offense.   180
For England go. I will whet on the King.
LEWIS
Strong reasons make strange actions. Let us go.   182
If you say ay, the King will not say no.   *Exeunt.*

4.1   *Enter Hubert and Executioners [with irons and
rope].*

HUBERT
Heat me these irons hot, and look thou stand   1
Within the arras. When I strike my foot   2
Upon the bosom of the ground, rush forth
And bind the boy which you shall find with me
Fast to the chair. Be heedful. Hence, and watch.
FIRST EXECUTIONER
I hope your warrant will bear out the deed.   6
HUBERT
Uncleanly scruples! Fear not you. Look to 't.   7
                    [The Executioners withdraw.]
Young lad, come forth. I have to say with you.   8

        Enter Arthur.

ARTHUR
Good morrow, Hubert.
HUBERT   Good morrow, little prince.

---

128 rub obstacle. (From the game of bowls.)   **132 whiles** while.
warm life i.e., blood   **133 misplaced** i.e., usurping   **135 unruly** violating proper rule   **136 boisterously** violently   **138 Makes nice of no**
is not scrupulous about any   **146 lays you plots** i.e., makes plots by
which you may profit   **147 true blood** blood of a true prince
148 untrue uncertain, insecure   **149 borne** carried out   **151 none
. . . advantage** no opportunity, however small   **153 exhalation** meteor   **154 scope of nature** i.e., one of those prodigious phenomena
within nature's power.   **distempered** stormy   **155 customèd** customary   **156 pluck away his** discard its.   **cause** explanation   **158 Abortives** untimely or monstrous births   **159 denouncing** calling down
161 But . . . prisonment but regard himself as safe so long as Arthur
is imprisoned

165 him i.e., John   **166 kiss . . . change** i.e., welcome any change.
unacquainted unfamiliar   **167 pick strong matter of** find compelling
reason for   **168 Out . . . John** i.e., out of John's bloody-handed
deeds   **169 hurly** commotion.   **on foot** in motion   **170 breeds** is ripening   **174 call** (1) decoy (2) call to arms   **175 train** attract
180 topful of offense brimful of grievance and sated with John's offenses   **182 strange actions** i.e., an invasion of England—something
that, a moment ago, the Dauphin would have considered incredible
4.1. Location: England. A room in a castle. A chair is provided.
1 look take care   **2 Within the arras** behind the wall hangings. (Evidently, the Executioners go out as though to heat their irons and then
conceal themselves behind the arras, ready at line 71 to come forth.)
6 bear out provide sufficient authority for   **7 Uncleanly** improper, unbecoming   **8 to say** something to speak about

ARTHUR
As little prince, having so great a title   10
To be more prince, as may be. You are sad.   11
HUBERT
Indeed, I have been merrier.
ARTHUR   Mercy on me!
Methinks nobody should be sad but I.
Yet I remember, when I was in France,
Young gentlemen would be as sad as night,
Only for wantonness. By my christendom,   16
So I were out of prison and kept sheep,   17
I should be as merry as the day is long;
And so I would be here, but that I doubt   19
My uncle practices more harm to me.   20
He is afraid of me, and I of him.
Is it my fault that I was Geoffrey's son?
No, indeed, is 't not; and I would to heaven
I were your son, so you would love me, Hubert.   24
HUBERT [aside]
If I talk to him, with his innocent prate   25
He will awake my mercy, which lies dead.
Therefore I will be sudden, and dispatch.
ARTHUR
Are you sick, Hubert? You look pale today.
In sooth, I would you were a little sick,   29
That I might sit all night and watch with you.   30
I warrant I love you more than you do me.
HUBERT [aside]
His words do take possession of my bosom.—
Read here, young Arthur.   [Showing a paper.]
                    [Aside.] How now, foolish rheum? 33
Turning dispiteous torture out of door?   34
I must be brief, lest resolution drop
Out at mine eyes in tender womanish tears.—
Can you not read it? Is it not fair writ?   37
ARTHUR
Too fairly, Hubert, for so foul effect.   38
Must you with hot irons burn out both mine eyes?
HUBERT
Young boy, I must.
ARTHUR   And will you?
HUBERT   And I will.
ARTHUR
Have you the heart? When your head did but ache,
I knit my handkerchief about your brows—   42
The best I had, a princess wrought it me—   43
And I did never ask it you again;   44
And with my hand at midnight held your head,
And like the watchful minutes to the hour   46
Still and anon cheered up the heavy time,   47

Saying, "What lack you?" and "Where lies your
  grief?"
Or "What good love may I perform for you?"   49
Many a poor man's son would have lain still
And ne'er have spoke a loving word to you,
But you at your sick service had a prince.   52
Nay, you may think my love was crafty love,
And call it cunning. Do, an if you will.   54
If heaven be pleased that you must use me ill,
Why then you must. Will you put out mine eyes?
These eyes that never did nor never shall
So much as frown on you?
HUBERT   I have sworn to do it,
And with hot irons must I burn them out.
ARTHUR
Ah, none but in this iron age would do it!   60
The iron of itself, though heat red-hot,   61
Approaching near these eyes, would drink my tears
And quench his fiery indignation   63
Even in the matter of mine innocence;   64
Nay, after that, consume away in rust
But for containing fire to harm mine eye.   66
Are you more stubborn-hard than hammered iron?
An if an angel should have come to me   68
And told me Hubert should put out mine eyes,
I would not have believed him—no tongue but
  Hubert's.
HUBERT
Come forth!   [He stamps his foot.]

[Executioners come forth, with a cord, irons, etc.]

          Do as I bid you do.
ARTHUR
O, save me, Hubert, save me! My eyes are out
Even with the fierce looks of these bloody men.
HUBERT
Give me the iron, I say, and bind him here.
               [They start to bind Arthur to a chair.]
ARTHUR
Alas, what need you be so boisterous-rough?   75
I will not struggle; I will stand stone-still.
For heaven's sake, Hubert, let me not be bound!
Nay, hear me, Hubert: drive these men away,
And I will sit as quiet as a lamb;
I will not stir, nor wince, nor speak a word,
Nor look upon the iron angerly.   81
Thrust but these men away, and I'll forgive you,
Whatever torment you do put me to.
HUBERT
Go stand within. Let me alone with him.
FIRST EXECUTIONER
I am best pleased to be from such a deed.   85
                              [Exeunt Executioners.]

10–11 As . . . be I am as little a prince, despite my being entitled to be greater, as is possible **16 for wantonness** out of affected behavior. **By my christendom** as I am a Christian **17 So** provided **19 would be** would like to be. **but** except. **doubt** fear **20 practices** plots **24 so** provided **25 prate** prattle **29 sooth** truth **30 watch with** stay awake tending to **33 rheum** i.e., tears. (Literally, a fluid discharge.) **34 Turning . . . door** i.e., banishing pitiless torture **37 fair** handsomely, legibly **38 effect** purpose, meaning **42 knit** bound **43 wrought** i.e., embroidered. **me** for me **44 did . . . you** never asked for it back from you **46 like . . . hour** i.e., as regularly as clockwork **47 Still and anon** continually

49 love loving assistance **52 at your sick service** to serve you in your sickness **54 an if** if **60 iron age** degenerate time (with play on *hot irons*) **61 heat** heated **63 his** its **64 matter . . . innocence** substance betokening my innocence, i.e., my tears **66 But for containing** merely because it had contained **68 An if** if. **should have** had **75 what** why **81 angerly** angrily, complainingly **85 from** away from

ARTHUR
Alas, I then have chid away my friend!
He hath a stern look, but a gentle heart.
Let him come back, that his compassion may
Give life to yours.
HUBERT   Come, boy, prepare yourself.
ARTHUR
Is there no remedy?
HUBERT   None but to lose your eyes.
ARTHUR
O heaven, that there were but a mote in yours,   91
A grain, a dust, a gnat, a wandering hair,
Any annoyance in that precious sense!   93
Then feeling what small things are boisterous there, 94
Your vile intent must needs seem horrible.
HUBERT
Is this your promise? Go to, hold your tongue.   96
ARTHUR
Hubert, the utterance of a brace of tongues   97
Must needs want pleading for a pair of eyes.   98
Let me not hold my tongue. Let me not, Hubert!   99
Or, Hubert, if you will, cut out my tongue,
So I may keep mine eyes. O, spare mine eyes,   101
Though to no use but still to look on you!   102
Lo, by my troth, the instrument is cold   103
And would not harm me.
HUBERT   I can heat it, boy.
ARTHUR
No, in good sooth. The fire is dead with grief,   105
Being create for comfort, to be used   106
In undeserved extremes. See else yourself.   107
There is no malice in this burning coal;
The breath of heaven hath blown his spirit out
And strewed repentant ashes on his head.   110
HUBERT
But with my breath I can revive it, boy.
ARTHUR
An if you do, you will but make it blush
And glow with shame of your proceedings, Hubert.
Nay, it perchance will sparkle in your eyes,   114
And, like a dog that is compelled to fight,
Snatch at his master that doth tarre him on.   116
All things that you should use to do me wrong
Deny their office. Only you do lack   118
That mercy which fierce fire and iron extends,   119
Creatures of note for mercy-lacking uses.   120
HUBERT
Well, see to live. I will not touch thine eye   121

For all the treasure that thine uncle owes.   122
Yet am I sworn, and I did purpose, boy,
With this same very iron to burn them out.
ARTHUR
O, now you look like Hubert! All this while
You were disguisèd.
HUBERT   Peace! No more. Adieu.
Your uncle must not know but you are dead.   127
I'll fill these doggèd spies with false reports.   128
And, pretty child, sleep doubtless and secure   129
That Hubert, for the wealth of all the world,
Will not offend thee.
ARTHUR   O heaven! I thank you, Hubert.   131
HUBERT
Silence! No more. Go closely in with me.   132
Much danger do I undergo for thee.   *Exeunt.*

❖

4.2   *Enter [King] John, Pembroke, Salisbury, and other
lords. [The King sits on his throne.]*

KING JOHN
Here once again we sit, once again crowned,
And looked upon, I hope, with cheerful eyes.
PEMBROKE
This "once again," but that Your Highness pleased,
Was once superfluous. You were crowned before,
And that high royalty was ne'er plucked off,
The faiths of men ne'er stainèd with revolt.
Fresh expectation troubled not the land
With any longed-for change or better state.
SALISBURY
Therefore, to be possessed with double pomp,   9
To guard a title that was rich before,   10
To gild refinèd gold, to paint the lily,
To throw a perfume on the violet,
To smooth the ice, or add another hue
Unto the rainbow, or with taper light
To seek the beauteous eye of heaven to garnish,   15
Is wasteful and ridiculous excess.
PEMBROKE
But that your royal pleasure must be done,
This act is as an ancient tale new told,
And in the last repeating troublesome,
Being urgèd at a time unseasonable.
SALISBURY
In this the antique and well-noted face   21
Of plain old form is much disfigurèd;   22
And, like a shifted wind unto a sail,   23
It makes the course of thoughts to fetch about,   24
Startles and frights consideration,   25

91 **mote** minute particle of anything   93 **precious sense** i.e., sight
94 **boisterous** painful, irritating   96 **Go to** (An exclamation of remonstrance.)   97 **of a brace** of even a pair   98 **Must . . . pleading** must
be inadequate to plead sufficiently   99 **Let me not** don't make me,
don't hold me to my promise to   101 **So** provided, if thereby
102 **still** always   103 **troth** faith   105 **in good sooth** certainly
106 **create** created   107 **extremes** i.e., extreme cruelties.   **See else
yourself** see for yourself if it isn't true   110 **on his head** i.e., like a
penitent sinner heaping ashes on his head   114 **sparkle in** scatter
sparks into   116 **Snatch** snap.   **tarre** provoke, incite   118 **Deny**
refuse to do.   **office** function   119 **extends** proffer   120 **Creatures
. . . uses** things (i.e., fire and iron) noted as instruments of torture
121 **see to live** i.e., live, and continue to see

122 **owes** owns   127 **but** other than that   128 **doggèd** fierce, malicious   129 **doubtless** fearless   131 **offend** harm   132 **closely** secretly
4.2. Location: England. The court of King John.
9 **be possessed with** have possession of (the crown)   10 **guard** trim,
ornament; also, protect   15 **eye of heaven** i.e., the sun (much too fair
and bright to be enhanced by a *taper light* or candle)   21 **well-noted**
familiar   22 **form** custom   23 **a shifted wind** a wind that shifts direction   24 **fetch about** change direction, tack   25 **frights consideration**
i.e., frightens everyone into anxious reflection

Makes sound opinion sick and truth suspected,   26
For putting on so new a fashioned robe.   27

PEMBROKE
When workmen strive to do better than well,
They do confound their skill in covetousness;   29
And oftentimes excusing of a fault
Doth make the fault the worse by th' excuse,
As patches set upon a little breach   32
Discredit more in hiding of the fault
Than did the fault before it was so patched.

SALISBURY
To this effect, before you were new-crowned,
We breathed our counsel. But it pleased Your
    Highness   36
To overbear it, and we are all well pleased,   37
Since all and every part of what we would
Doth make a stand at what Your Highness will.   39

KING JOHN
Some reasons of this double coronation
I have possessed you with, and think them strong;   41
And more, more strong, when lesser is my fear,   42
I shall endue you with. Meantime but ask   43
What you would have reformed that is not well,
And well shall you perceive how willingly
I will both hear and grant you your requests.

PEMBROKE
Then I, as one that am the tongue of these   47
To sound the purposes of all their hearts,   48
Both for myself and them—but chief of all
Your safety, for the which myself and them   50
Bend their best studies—heartily request   51
Th' enfranchisement of Arthur, whose restraint   52
Doth move the murmuring lips of discontent
To break into this dangerous argument:
If what in rest you have in right you hold,   55
Why then your fears—which, as they say, attend   56
The steps of wrong—should move you to mew up   57
Your tender kinsman, and to choke his days
With barbarous ignorance, and deny his youth
The rich advantage of good exercise.   60
That the time's enemies may not have this   61
To grace occasions, let it be our suit   62
That you have bid us ask his liberty,   63

Which for our goods we do no further ask   64
Than whereupon our weal, on you depending,   65
Counts it your weal he have his liberty.   66

    Enter Hubert.

KING JOHN
Let it be so. I do commit his youth
To your direction.—Hubert, what news with you?
                              [*He takes Hubert aside.*]

PEMBROKE
This is the man should do the bloody deed;
He showed his warrant to a friend of mine.
The image of a wicked heinous fault
Lives in his eye; that close aspect of his   72
Doth show the mood of a much troubled breast,
And I do fearfully believe 'tis done
What we so feared he had a charge to do.   75

SALISBURY
The color of the King doth come and go
Between his purpose and his conscience,
Like heralds twixt two dreadful battles set.   78
His passion is so ripe it needs must break.   79

PEMBROKE
And when it breaks, I fear will issue thence
The foul corruption of a sweet child's death.

KING JOHN [*coming forward*]
We cannot hold mortality's strong hand.
Good lords, although my will to give is living,   83
The suit which you demand is gone and dead.
He tells us Arthur is deceased tonight.   85

SALISBURY
Indeed we feared his sickness was past cure.

PEMBROKE
Indeed we heard how near his death he was
Before the child himself felt he was sick.
This must be answered, either here or hence.   89

KING JOHN
Why do you bend such solemn brows on me?
Think you I bear the shears of destiny?
Have I commandment on the pulse of life?

SALISBURY
It is apparent foul play, and 'tis shame   93
That greatness should so grossly offer it.   94
So thrive it in your game! And so, farewell.   95

PEMBROKE
Stay yet, Lord Salisbury. I'll go with thee,
And find th' inheritance of this poor child,
His little kingdom of a forcèd grave.   98
That blood which owed the breadth of all this isle,   99
Three foot of it doth hold; bad world the while!   100

26–27 Makes . . . robe i.e., leads to the weakening of sound loyalty and to suspicions about the truth of John's dynastic claims, in that the English throne has dressed itself in this strange new ceremony 29 confound destroy, disrupt. in covetousness i.e., by their greedy desire to do better 32 breach hole 36 breathed spoke 37 overbear overrule 39 Doth . . . will may go no further than what Your Highness desires 41 possessed you with informed you of 42–43 And . . . with i.e., and I shall provide you with even more and stronger reasons when the emergency is past and can be talked about 47 tongue spokesman 48 sound express 50 them i.e., they 51 Bend direct. studies efforts 52 enfranchisement freeing from imprisonment 55 If . . . hold if, in fact, you hold by right of law what you now possess in peace. in rest in security, peaceably, or, possibly, in arrest (referring to Arthur) 56 Why then i.e., why is it, then, that 56–57 attend . . . wrong i.e., are evidence of wrongdoing, follow in the train of wrongdoing 57 mew up shut up. (A falconing term.) 60 exercise i.e., exercise in arms and other gentlemanly accomplishments 61 the time's enemies enemies of the present state of affairs 62 grace occasions i.e., suit their purposes, lend credence to their criticisms 62–63 let . . . liberty let the concession that you invited us to ask for (lines 43–46) be Arthur's liberty

64 our goods our personal benefit 65 whereupon to the extent that. weal welfare 66 Counts . . . liberty i.e., considers that it will be good for your welfare to have Arthur at liberty and therefore for ours, too, since we depend on you 72 Lives in his eye shows itself in the look of his eye. close aspect furtive appearance 75 charge commission 78 battles armies in battle order 79 ripe (like a boil full of pus, the *foul corruption* of line 81) 83 give i.e., grant your suit 85 tonight last night 89 answered atoned for. hence i.e., in heaven or perhaps on the field of battle 93 apparent evident, blatant 94 That . . . it i.e., that a king should flaunt foul play so flagrantly 95 So . . . game may your schemes lead to the same (bad) end 98 forcèd imposed by violence 99 owed owned 100 the while while such things occur

This must not be thus borne. This will break out
To all our sorrows, and ere long, I doubt.   102
                                                Exeunt [*lords*].
KING JOHN
They burn in indignation. I repent.
There is no sure foundation set on blood,
No certain life achieved by others' death.

                    Enter Messenger.

A fearful eye thou hast. Where is that blood   106
That I have seen inhabit in those cheeks?
So foul a sky clears not without a storm.
Pour down thy weather: how goes all in France?   109
MESSENGER
From France to England. Never such a power
For any foreign preparation   111
Was levied in the body of a land.   112
The copy of your speed is learned by them;   113
For when you should be told they do prepare,
The tidings comes that they are all arrived.
KING JOHN
O, where hath our intelligence been drunk?   116
Where hath it slept? Where is my mother's care,
That such an army could be drawn in France   118
And she not hear of it?
MESSENGER   My liege, her ear
Is stopped with dust. The first of April died
Your noble mother; and, as I hear, my lord,
The Lady Constance in a frenzy died
Three days before. But this from rumor's tongue
I idly heard; if true or false I know not.   124
KING JOHN
Withhold thy speed, dreadful Occasion!   125
O, make a league with me till I have pleased
My discontented peers! What, Mother dead?
How wildly then walks my estate in France!   128
Under whose conduct came those powers of France   129
That thou for truth giv'st out are landed here?   130
MESSENGER
Under the Dauphin.

          Enter [*the*] *Bastard and Peter of Pomfret.*

KING JOHN   Thou hast made me giddy
With these ill tidings. [*To the Bastard.*] Now, what
   says the world
To your proceedings? Do not seek to stuff   133
My head with more ill news, for it is full.
BASTARD
But if you be afeard to hear the worst,   135
Then let the worst unheard fall on your head.   136

KING JOHN
Bear with me, cousin, for I was amazed   137
Under the tide; but now I breathe again
Aloft the flood, and can give audience   139
To any tongue, speak it of what it will.
BASTARD
How I have sped among the clergymen,   141
The sums I have collected shall express.
But as I traveled hither through the land,
I find the people strangely fantasied,   144
Possessed with rumors, full of idle dreams,
Not knowing what they fear, but full of fear.
And here's a prophet that I brought with me
From forth the streets of Pomfret, whom I found   148
With many hundreds treading on his heels,
To whom he sung, in rude harsh-sounding rhymes,
That ere the next Ascension Day at noon   151
Your Highness should deliver up your crown.
KING JOHN
Thou idle dreamer, wherefore didst thou so?
PETER
Foreknowing that the truth will fall out so.
KING JOHN
Hubert, away with him! Imprison him,
And on that day at noon, whereon he says
I shall yield up my crown, let him be hanged.
Deliver him to safety, and return,   158
For I must use thee.[*Exit Hubert with Peter of Pomfret.*]
                    O my gentle cousin,   159
Hear'st thou the news abroad, who are arrived?
BASTARD
The French, my lord. Men's mouths are full of it.
Besides, I met Lord Bigot and Lord Salisbury,
With eyes as red as new-enkindled fire,
And others more, going to seek the grave
Of Arthur, whom they say is killed tonight   165
On your suggestion.
KING JOHN   Gentle kinsman, go   166
And thrust thyself into their companies.
I have a way to win their loves again.
Bring them before me.
BASTARD   I will seek them out.
KING JOHN
Nay, but make haste, the better foot before.   170
O, let me have no subject enemies
When adverse foreigners affright my towns   172
With dreadful pomp of stout invasion!   173
Be Mercury, set feathers to thy heels,   174
And fly like thought from them to me again.   175
BASTARD
The spirit of the time shall teach me speed.   *Exit.*

---

102 doubt fear   **106 fearful** full of fear and prompting fear in others
109 weather storm, tempest.   **goes all** is it all going. (But the Messenger replies literally in the sense that everything is physically going from France to England in an invasion.)   **111 preparation** expedition
112 body i.e., length and breadth   **113 copy** example.   **your speed** (As when John proceeded to Angiers; see 2.1.56 ff.)   **116 our intelligence** our spies, spy network   **118 drawn** mustered, assembled
124 idly by chance   **125 Occasion** course of events   **128 estate** power   **129 conduct** command   **130 for truth giv'st out** claim to be true   **133 proceedings** i.e., mission against the monasteries; see 3.3.6 ff.   **135–136 But . . . head** but if you are afraid to listen to bad news, misfortune will come upon you unawares (and be much more dangerous)

137 amazed bewildered   **139 Aloft the flood** riding on the sea's surface (continuing the metaphor of *tide*, line 138)   **141 sped** succeeded
144 strangely fantasied full of strange fancies   **148 Pomfret** Pontefract, in Yorkshire   **151 Ascension Day** the Thursday forty days after Easter celebrating the ascent of Christ into heaven   **158 safety** safekeeping   **159 gentle** noble   **165 is killed tonight** was killed last night
166 suggestion instigation   **170 the better foot before** i.e., as quickly as you can   **172 adverse** hostile   **173 stout** bold   **174 feathers** (Mercury, messenger of the gods, had winged sandals.)   **175 like thought** as swift as thought

KING JOHN
Spoke like a sprightful noble gentleman!   *177*
[*To the Messenger.*] Go after him, for he perhaps shall need
Some messenger betwixt me and the peers;
And be thou he.
MESSENGER   With all my heart, my liege.   [*Exit.*]
KING JOHN   My mother dead!

Enter Hubert.

HUBERT
My lord, they say five moons were seen tonight:
Four fixèd, and the fifth did whirl about
The other four in wondrous motion.
KING JOHN
Five moons!
HUBERT   Old men and beldams in the streets   *186*
Do prophesy upon it dangerously.   *187*
Young Arthur's death is common in their mouths,
And, when they talk of him, they shake their heads
And whisper one another in the ear;
And he that speaks doth grip the hearer's wrist,
Whilst he that hears makes fearful action,   *192*
With wrinkled brows, with nods, with rolling eyes.
I saw a smith stand with his hammer, thus,
The whilst his iron did on the anvil cool,
With open mouth swallowing a tailor's news;
Who, with his shears and measure in his hand,
Standing on slippers, which his nimble haste
Had falsely thrust upon contrary feet,   *199*
Told of a many thousand warlike French   *200*
That were embattlèd and ranked in Kent.   *201*
Another lean unwashed artificer   *202*
Cuts off his tale and talks of Arthur's death.
KING JOHN
Why seek'st thou to possess me with these fears?   *204*
Why urgest thou so oft young Arthur's death?
Thy hand hath murdered him. I had a mighty cause
To wish him dead, but thou hadst none to kill him.
HUBERT
No had, my lord? Why, did you not provoke me?   *208*
KING JOHN
It is the curse of kings to be attended
By slaves that take their humors for a warrant   *210*
To break within the bloody house of life,   *211*
And on the winking of authority   *212*
To understand a law, to know the meaning   *213*
Of dangerous majesty, when perchance it frowns
More upon humor than advised respect.   *215*

HUBERT [*showing his warrant*]
Here is your hand and seal for what I did.
KING JOHN
O, when the last account twixt heaven and earth
Is to be made, then shall this hand and seal
Witness against us to damnation!
How oft the sight of means to do ill deeds   *220*
Make deeds ill done! Hadst not thou been by,   *221*
A fellow by the hand of nature marked,
Quoted, and signed to do a deed of shame,   *223*
This murder had not come into my mind.
But, taking note of thy abhorred aspect,
Finding thee fit for bloody villainy,
Apt, liable to be employed in danger,   *227*
I faintly broke with thee of Arthur's death,   *228*
And thou, to be endearèd to a king,
Made it no conscience to destroy a prince.   *230*
HUBERT   My lord—
KING JOHN
Hadst thou but shook thy head or made a pause
When I spake darkly what I purposèd,   *233*
Or turned an eye of doubt upon my face,
As bid me tell my tale in express words,   *235*
Deep shame had struck me dumb, made me break off,
And those thy fears might have wrought fears in me.
But thou didst understand me by my signs
And didst in signs again parley with sin,
Yea, without stop didst let thy heart consent,
And consequently thy rude hand to act
The deed which both our tongues held vile to name.
Out of my sight, and never see me more!
My nobles leave me, and my state is braved,   *244*
Even at my gates, with ranks of foreign powers.
Nay, in the body of this fleshly land,   *246*
This kingdom, this confine of blood and breath,   *247*
Hostility and civil tumult reigns
Between my conscience and my cousin's death.
HUBERT
Arm you against your other enemies;
I'll make a peace between your soul and you.
Young Arthur is alive. This hand of mine
Is yet a maiden and an innocent hand,
Not painted with the crimson spots of blood.
Within this bosom never entered yet
The dreadful motion of a murderous thought;   *256*
And you have slandered nature in my form,   *257*
Which, howsoever rude exteriorly,   *258*

---

177 sprightful spirited **186 beldams** old women **187 prophesy upon it** make predictions from it, expound its meaning for the future. **dangerously** in terms of future danger, or threateningly to public order **192 action** gestures **199 upon contrary feet** the left slipper on the right foot and vice versa **200 a many thousand** many thousands of **201 embattled and ranked** drawn up in orderly battle array **202 artificer** artisan **204 possess . . . fears** give me these fearful tidings **208 No had** had I not. **provoke** incite **210 humors** whims **211 the bloody . . . life** the body, animated by lifeblood and made bloody by murder **212 winking** closing the eyes (i.e., when the person in authority closes his eyes to the law or gives the merest hint of approving illegality) **213 understand a law** i.e., infer what is being commanded **215 upon humor** through whim. **advised respect** careful consideration

220–221 How . . . done how often seeing a way to do ill deeds prompts us to go ahead **223 Quoted, and signed** particularly designated and marked out **227 liable** suitable. **danger** something dangerous to the victim **228 faintly broke with** hesitatingly broached the subject with **230 conscience** matter of conscience **233 darkly** indirectly **235 As** as though to. **express** explicit **244 my state is braved** my authority is challenged **246 body . . . land** i.e., John's own body. (Uses the figure of the microcosm, in which man is conceived as the epitome of the universe.) **247 confine** (1) territorial limit (2) prison **256 motion** impulse **257 slandered . . . form** i.e., slandered my nature by judging me harshly in terms of my unattractive appearance; or, slandered human nature in my person **258 rude** rough

Is yet the cover of a fairer mind
Than to be butcher of an innocent child.

KING JOHN
Doth Arthur live? O, haste thee to the peers!
Throw this report on their incensèd rage,   262
And make them tame to their obedience.
Forgive the comment that my passion made
Upon thy feature, for my rage was blind,   265
And foul imaginary eyes of blood   266
Presented thee more hideous than thou art.
O, answer not, but to my closet bring   268
The angry lords with all expedient haste.
I conjure thee but slowly; run more fast!   270
Exeunt [separately].

❖

4.3 *Enter Arthur, on the walls, [disguised as a
shipboy].*

ARTHUR
The wall is high, and yet will I leap down.
Good ground, be pitiful and hurt me not!
There's few or none do know me; if they did,
This shipboy's semblance hath disguised me quite.   4
I am afraid, and yet I'll venture it.
If I get down, and do not break my limbs,
I'll find a thousand shifts to get away.   7
As good to die and go as die and stay.
[He leaps down.]
O me! My uncle's spirit is in these stones.
Heaven take my soul, and England keep my bones!
Dies.

*Enter Pembroke, Salisbury [with a letter], and
Bigot.*

SALISBURY
Lords, I will meet him at Saint Edmundsbury.   11
It is our safety, and we must embrace   12
This gentle offer of the perilous time.   13

PEMBROKE
Who brought that letter from the Cardinal?

SALISBURY
The Count Melun, a noble lord of France,
Whose private with me of the Dauphin's love   16
Is much more general than these lines import.   17

BIGOT
Tomorrow morning let us meet him then.

SALISBURY
Or rather, then set forward, for 'twill be

Two long days' journey, lords, or ere we meet.   20

Enter [the] Bastard.

BASTARD
Once more today well met, distempered lords!   21
The King by me requests your presence straight.   22

SALISBURY
The King hath dispossessed himself of us.
We will not line his thin bestainèd cloak   24
With our pure honors, nor attend the foot   25
That leaves the print of blood where'er it walks.
Return and tell him so. We know the worst.

BASTARD
Whate'er you think, good words, I think, were best.

SALISBURY
Our griefs, and not our manners, reason now.   29

BASTARD
But there is little reason in your grief.
Therefore 'twere reason you had manners now.

PEMBROKE
Sir, sir, impatience hath his privilege.   32

BASTARD
'Tis true—to hurt his master, no man else.   33

SALISBURY
This is the prison. *[He sees Arthur's body.]* What is he
lies here?

PEMBROKE
O death, made proud with pure and princely
beauty!
The earth had not a hole to hide this deed.

SALISBURY
Murder, as hating what himself hath done,   37
Doth lay it open to urge on revenge.

BIGOT
Or, when he doomed this beauty to a grave,   39
Found it too precious-princely for a grave.

SALISBURY *[to the Bastard]*
Sir Richard, what think you? You have beheld.   41
Or have you read or heard, or could you think,   42
Or do you almost think, although you see,   43
That you do see? Could thought, without this object,   44
Form such another? This is the very top,   45
The height, the crest, or crest unto the crest,
Of murder's arms. This is the bloodiest shame,   47
The wildest savagery, the vilest stroke
That ever walleyed wrath or staring rage   49
Presented to the tears of soft remorse.   50

---

262 Throw . . . rage i.e., tell them this news as though throwing water on their burning rage **265 feature** outward appearance
266 imaginary . . . blood your eyes, which I imagined to be bloody in thought, or, more probably, my eyes made bloodshot with rage at imagined wrong **268 closet** private chamber **270 conjure** adjure, urge
4.3. Location: England. Before the walls of a castle.
s.d. on the walls in the gallery rearstage **4 semblance** disguise
7 shifts (1) stratagems (2) changes of costume **11 him** i.e., the Dauphin. **Saint Edmundsbury** Bury St. Edmunds, in Suffolk **12 our safety** our only means of safety **13 gentle** gracious. **of the** i.e., made in such a **16 private** private communication **17 general** all-embracing

20 or ere before **21 distempered** disaffected **22 straight** at once
24 line provide a lining for, reinforce **25 attend the foot** follow in the footsteps of one, serve one **29 griefs** grievances. **reason** speak. (But the Bastard answers in the sense of "rationality," line 30, and "common sense," line 31.) **32, 33 his** its **33 'Tis . . . else** i.e., perhaps anger must be allowed to speak, as you say, but it is apt to hurt the speaker more than his listeners. You'll be sorry for what you say.
37 as as if **39 he** i.e., murder **41 Sir Richard** i.e., the Bastard **42–43 Or . . . think** have you either read or heard (of anything like this), or could you believe or even begin to believe **44 That** that which
44–45 Could . . . another could you possibly imagine another sight like this without its actually being set before you? **47 arms** coat of arms. (This deed is the crest on top of the crest of murder's coat of arms.) **49 walleyed** glaring fiercely **50 tears** i.e., tearful view. **remorse** pity

PEMBROKE
All murders past do stand excused in this;   51
And this, so sole and so unmatchable,   52
Shall give a holiness, a purity,
To the yet unbegotten sin of times,   54
And prove a deadly bloodshed but a jest,   55
Exampled by this heinous spectacle.   56
BASTARD
It is a damnèd and a bloody work,
The graceless action of a heavy hand—   58
If that it be the work of any hand.
SALISBURY
If that it be the work of any hand?
We had a kind of light what would ensue.   61
It is the shameful work of Hubert's hand,
The practice and the purpose of the King,   63
From whose obedience I forbid my soul,
Kneeling before this ruin of sweet life,   [he kneels]
And breathing to his breathless excellence
The incense of a vow, a holy vow,   67
Never to taste the pleasures of the world,
Never to be infected with delight,   69
Nor conversant with ease and idleness,
Till I have set a glory to this hand   71
By giving it the worship of revenge.   72
PEMBROKE, BIGOT [kneeling]
Our souls religiously confirm thy words. [All rise.]

        Enter Hubert.

HUBERT
Lords, I am hot with haste in seeking you.
Arthur doth live. The King hath sent for you.
SALISBURY
O, he is bold and blushes not at death.
Avaunt, thou hateful villain! Get thee gone!   77
HUBERT
I am no villain.
SALISBURY [drawing his sword]   Must I rob the law?   78
BASTARD
Your sword is bright, sir. Put it up again.   79
SALISBURY
Not till I sheathe it in a murderer's skin.
HUBERT [drawing]
Stand back, Lord Salisbury, stand back, I say!
By heaven, I think my sword's as sharp as yours.
I would not have you, lord, forget yourself,
Nor tempt the danger of my true defense,   84
Lest I, by marking of your rage, forget   85
Your worth, your greatness, and nobility.

51 **in this** in comparison to this   52 **sole** unique   54 **times** i.e., future times   55 **but** to be only   56 **Exampled by** compared with   58 **graceless** unholy. **heavy** wicked   61 **light** premonition   63 **practice** plot, treachery   67 **The incense of a vow** i.e., a vow that ascends to heaven, like incense   69 **infected** tainted, imbued   71 **this hand** i.e., either Arthur's hand or Salisbury's own hand, which he raises in taking an oath   72 **worship** honor, sacred function   77 **Avaunt** begone   78 **Must . . . law** must I deprive the law of its intended victim by killing you myself?   79 **bright** i.e., unused   84 **tempt** risk, test   85 **by marking of your rage** paying attention only to your wrath

BIGOT
Out, dunghill! Dar'st thou brave a nobleman?   87
HUBERT
Not for my life. But yet I dare defend
My innocent life against an emperor.
SALISBURY
Thou art a murderer.
HUBERT   Do not prove me so;   90
Yet I am none. Whose tongue soe'er speaks false,
Not truly speaks; who speaks not truly, lies.
PEMBROKE
Cut him to pieces!
BASTARD [drawing]   Keep the peace, I say!
SALISBURY
Stand by, or I shall gall you, Faulconbridge.   94
BASTARD
Thou wert better gall the devil, Salisbury.
If thou but frown on me, or stir thy foot,
Or teach thy hasty spleen to do me shame,   97
I'll strike thee dead. Put up thy sword betimes, 98
Or I'll so maul you and your toasting iron   99
That you shall think the devil is come from hell.
BIGOT
What wilt thou do, renownèd Faulconbridge?
Second a villain and a murderer?
HUBERT
Lord Bigot, I am none.
BIGOT   Who killed this prince?
HUBERT
'Tis not an hour since I left him well.
I honored him, I loved him, and will weep
My date of life out for his sweet life's loss. [He weeps.] 106
SALISBURY
Trust not those cunning waters of his eyes,
For villainy is not without such rheum,   108
And he, long traded in it, makes it seem   109
Like rivers of remorse and innocency.
Away with me, all you whose souls abhor
Th' uncleanly savors of a slaughterhouse!   112
For I am stifled with this smell of sin.
BIGOT
Away toward Bury, to the Dauphin there!
PEMBROKE
There, tell the King, he may inquire us out.
                              Exeunt lords.
BASTARD
Here's a good world! Knew you of this fair work?
Beyond the infinite and boundless reach
Of mercy, if thou didst this deed of death,
Art thou damned, Hubert.
HUBERT   Do but hear me, sir.
BASTARD   Ha! I'll tell thee what;
Thou'rt damned as black—nay, nothing is so black;
Thou art more deep damned than Prince Lucifer.
There is not yet so ugly a fiend of hell

87 **brave** insult   90 **prove me so** i.e., make me a murderer by tempting me to kill you   94 **Stand by** stand aside. **gall** wound   97 **spleen** i.e., wrath   98 **betimes** promptly   99 **toasting iron** sword. (Used contemptuously.)   106 **date** duration   108 **rheum** watery discharge, i.e., tears   109 **traded** experienced   112 **savors** odors

As thou shalt be, if thou didst kill this child.

HUBERT
Upon my soul—

BASTARD   If thou didst but consent
To this most cruel act, do but despair;   126
And if thou want'st a cord, the smallest thread
That ever spider twisted from her womb
Will serve to strangle thee; a rush will be a beam   129
To hang thee on; or wouldst thou drown thyself,
Put but a little water in a spoon
And it shall be as all the ocean,
Enough to stifle such a villain up.
I do suspect thee very grievously.

HUBERT
If I in act, consent, or sin of thought
Be guilty of the stealing that sweet breath
Which was embounded in this beauteous clay,   137
Let hell want pains enough to torture me.   138
I left him well.

BASTARD   Go, bear him in thine arms.
I am amazed, methinks, and lose my way   140
Among the thorns and dangers of this world.
                [*Hubert picks up Arthur.*]
How easy dost thou take all England up!
From forth this morsel of dead royalty,
The life, the right, and truth of all this realm
Is fled to heaven; and England now is left
To tug and scamble and to part by th' teeth   146
The unowed interest of proud-swelling state.   147
Now for the bare-picked bone of majesty
Doth doggèd war bristle his angry crest,   149
And snarleth in the gentle eyes of peace.
Now powers from home and discontents at home   151
Meet in one line; and vast confusion waits,   152
As doth a raven on a sick-fall'n beast,
The imminent decay of wrested pomp.   154
Now happy he whose cloak and cincture can   155
Hold out this tempest! Bear away that child,
And follow me with speed. I'll to the King.
A thousand businesses are brief in hand,   158
And heaven itself doth frown upon the land.
                        Exeunt.

❖

5.1   *Enter King John and Pandulph, [with] attendants.*

KING JOHN [*giving Pandulph the crown*]
Thus have I yielded up into your hand
The circle of my glory.

---

126 **but** nothing but   129 **rush** reed   137 **clay** i.e., Arthur's body
138 **want** lack   140 **amazed** stunned   146 **scamble** scramble. **part
by th' teeth** tear apart by the teeth, as a ravenous animal would do
147 **unowed interest** disputed ownership or control   149 **doggèd**
fierce. (War is viewed as a pack of dogs fighting over a bone and bristling their hackles, continuing the metaphor of line 146.)   151 **powers from home** foreign armies   152 **in one line** in united purpose.
vast confusion waits limitless chaos awaits   154 **wrested pomp**
usurped majesty   155 **cincture** belt   158 **are brief in hand** demand
immediate action
5.1. Location: England. The court of King John.

PANDULPH [*giving back the crown*]   Take again
From this my hand, as holding of the Pope   3
Your sovereign greatness and authority.

KING JOHN
Now keep your holy word. Go meet the French,
And from His Holiness use all your power
To stop their marches 'fore we are inflamed.
Our discontented counties do revolt;   8
Our people quarrel with obedience,
Swearing allegiance and the love of soul   10
To stranger blood, to foreign royalty.   11
This inundation of mistempered humor   12
Rests by you only to be qualified.   13
Then pause not, for the present time's so sick
That present med'cine must be ministered,   15
Or overthrow incurable ensues.

PANDULPH
It was my breath that blew this tempest up,
Upon your stubborn usage of the Pope;   18
But since you are a gentle convertite,   19
My tongue shall hush again this storm of war
And make fair weather in your blustering land.
On this Ascension Day, remember well,
Upon your oath of service to the Pope,
Go I to make the French lay down their arms.
                  Exit [*with attendants*].

KING JOHN
Is this Ascension Day? Did not the prophet
Say that before Ascension Day at noon
My crown I should get off? Even so I have.
I did suppose it should be on constraint;
But, heav'n be thanked, it is but voluntary.

        Enter [the] Bastard.

BASTARD
All Kent hath yielded. Nothing there holds out
But Dover Castle. London hath received,
Like a kind host, the Dauphin and his powers.   32
Your nobles will not hear you, but are gone
To offer service to your enemy,
And wild amazement hurries up and down
The little number of your doubtful friends.   36

KING JOHN
Would not my lords return to me again
After they heard young Arthur was alive?

BASTARD
They found him dead and cast into the streets,
An empty casket, where the jewel of life
By some damned hand was robbed and ta'en away.

KING JOHN
That villain Hubert told me he did live.

BASTARD
So, on my soul, he did, for aught he knew.

---

3 **as . . . Pope** as signifying that you receive the crown from the Pope
8 **counties** shires; possibly, nobles   10 **love of soul** most sincere love
11 **stranger** foreign   12–13 **This . . . qualified** this erratic behavior
(thought to be caused by the excess of one of the bodily humors) can
be brought back to normal only by you   15 **present** prompt
18 **Upon** following   19 **convertite** convert   32 **powers** army
36 **doubtful** not to be relied on; fearful

But wherefore do you droop? Why look you sad?
Be great in act, as you have been in thought.
Let not the world see fear and sad distrust   46
Govern the motion of a kingly eye.
Be stirring as the time; be fire with fire;   48
Threaten the threat'ner, and outface the brow
Of bragging horror. So shall inferior eyes,
That borrow their behaviors from the great,
Grow great by your example and put on
The dauntless spirit of resolution.
Away, and glister like the god of war
When he intendeth to become the field!   55
Show boldness and aspiring confidence.
What, shall they seek the lion in his den,
And fright him there? And make him tremble there?
O, let it not be said! Forage, and run   59
To meet displeasure farther from the doors,
And grapple with him ere he come so nigh.

KING JOHN
The legate of the Pope hath been with me,
And I have made a happy peace with him;
And he hath promised to dismiss the powers
Led by the Dauphin.

BASTARD   O inglorious league!
Shall we, upon the footing of our land,   66
Send fair-play orders and make compromise,   67
Insinuation, parley, and base truce
To arms invasive? Shall a beardless boy,   69
A cockered silken wanton, brave our fields   70
And flesh his spirit in a warlike soil,   71
Mocking the air with colors idly spread,   72
And find no check? Let us, my liege, to arms!   73
Perchance the Cardinal cannot make your peace;
Or if he do, let it at least be said
They saw we had a purpose of defense.   76

KING JOHN
Have thou the ordering of this present time.

BASTARD
Away, then, with good courage! Yet, I know,   78
Our party may well meet a prouder foe.   Exeunt. 79

❖

5.2   *Enter, in arms, [Lewis the] Dauphin, Salisbury,*
Melun, Pembroke, Bigot, soldiers.

LEWIS
My Lord Melun, let this be copied out,   1

And keep it safe for our remembrance.
                              [*He gives a document.*]
Return the precedent to these lords again,   3
That, having our fair order written down,   4
Both they and we, perusing o'er these notes,
May know wherefore we took the Sacrament,   6
And keep our faiths firm and inviolable.

SALISBURY
Upon our sides it never shall be broken.
And, noble Dauphin, albeit we swear
A voluntary zeal and an unurged faith   10
To your proceedings, yet believe me, Prince,
I am not glad that such a sore of time   12
Should seek a plaster by contemned revolt,   13
And heal the inveterate canker of one wound   14
By making many. O, it grieves my soul
That I must draw this metal from my side   16
To be a widow maker! O, and there
Where honorable rescue and defense
Cries out upon the name of Salisbury!   19
But such is the infection of the time
That, for the health and physic of our right,   21
We cannot deal but with the very hand   22
Of stern injustice and confusèd wrong.
And is 't not pity, O my grievèd friends,
That we, the sons and children of this isle,
Were born to see so sad an hour as this,
Wherein we step after a stranger, march   27
Upon her gentle bosom, and fill up
Her enemies' ranks—I must withdraw and weep
Upon the spot of this enforcèd cause—   30
To grace the gentry of a land remote   31
And follow unacquainted colors here?   [*He weeps.*] 32
What, here? O nation, that thou couldst remove!   33
That Neptune's arms, who clippeth thee about,   34
Would bear thee from the knowledge of thyself,
And grapple thee unto a pagan shore,
Where these two Christian armies might combine   37
The blood of malice in a vein of league,   38
And not to spend it so unneighborly!

LEWIS
A noble temper dost thou show in this,
And great affections wrestling in thy bosom   41
Doth make an earthquake of nobility.   42

46 distrust lack of confidence, fainting courage   48 as the time as the state of affairs demands   55 become grace, adorn   59 Forage seek out the enemy as prey   66 upon . . . land standing on our native soil   67 fair-play orders chivalric conditions   69 invasive invading   70 cockered . . . wanton spoiled, dandified youngster.   brave (1) arrogantly display his splendor in (2) defy   71 flesh initiate in bloodshed or inure to bloodshed   72 idly carelessly, insolently   73 check restraint   76 of defense to defend ourselves   78–79 Yet . . . foe i.e., yet this call for courage is scarcely necessary, since our side is ready to take on a more spirited and fierce foe than this one. (Or he could mean, to himself, that he fears the enemy will prove too much for them.)
5.2. Location: England. The Dauphin's camp at St. Edmundsbury.
1 this i.e., the agreement with the English lords. (See lines 33–34 of the preceding scene.)

3 precedent original document, first draft   **4 order** proposal   **6 took the Sacrament** i.e., received communion to confirm the sacredness of our vows   **10 unurged** uncompelled   **12–13 that . . . revolt** i.e., that the ills of this troublesome time should seek out the despised remedy of rebellion.   **plaster** dressing for a wound.   **contemned** reviled   **14 inveterate canker** chronic and deep-seated ulcer   **16 metal** i.e., sword   **19 Cries out upon** appeal to, or, exclaim against   **21 physic** medical cure   **22 We . . . hand** i.e., we are obliged to use the very means (which we otherwise deplore). The nobles must fight fire with fire.   **27 step after** follow (as in a march).   **stranger** foreign (leader)   **30 spot** (1) stain (2) place.   **enforcèd cause** cause into which I am forced   **31 grace . . . remote** honor the aristocracy of a foreign land (France)   **32 unacquainted colors** the banners of a foreign power   **33 remove** depart, change location, i.e., go from this scene of civil carnage to a crusade against pagan enemies   **34 clippeth** embraces   **37–38 combine . . . league** i.e., unite the malice they now expend on one another in a league of hostility, a crusade, against a pagan foe   **41 affections** passions   **42 Doth . . . nobility** i.e., produces tumult in your noble nature

O, what a noble combat hast thou fought
Between compulsion and a brave respect!   44
Let me wipe off this honorable dew,
That silverly doth progress on thy cheeks.
                    [*He wipes away Salisbury's tears.*]
My heart hath melted at a lady's tears,
Being an ordinary inundation;
But this effusion of such manly drops,
This shower, blown up by tempest of the soul,
Startles mine eyes, and makes me more amazed
Than had I seen the vaulty top of heaven   52
Figured quite o'er with burning meteors.   53
Lift up thy brow, renownèd Salisbury,
And with a great heart heave away this storm.
Commend these waters to those baby eyes   56
That never saw the giant world enragèd,
Nor met with fortune other than at feasts,
Full warm of blood, of mirth, of gossiping.
Come, come, for thou shalt thrust thy hand as deep
Into the purse of rich prosperity
As Lewis himself. So, nobles, shall you all,
That knit your sinews to the strength of mine.

            Enter Pandulph.

And even there, methinks, an angel spake.   64
Look where the holy legate comes apace,
To give us warrant from the hand of heaven,
And on our actions set the name of right
With holy breath.
PANDULPH   Hail, noble prince of France!
The next is this: King John hath reconciled
Himself to Rome. His spirit is come in   70
That so stood out against the holy Church,
The great metropolis and See of Rome.
Therefore thy threatening colors now wind up,   73
And tame the savage spirit of wild war,
That, like a lion fostered up at hand,   75
It may lie gently at the foot of peace
And be no further harmful than in show.
LEWIS
Your Grace shall pardon me; I will not back.   78
I am too highborn to be propertied,   79
To be a secondary at control,   80
Or useful servingman and instrument
To any sovereign state throughout the world.
Your breath first kindled the dead coal of wars
Between this chastised kingdom and myself,
And brought in matter that should feed this fire;   85

And now 'tis far too huge to be blown out
With that same weak wind which enkindled it.
You taught me how to know the face of right,   88
Acquainted me with interest to this land,   89
Yea, thrust this enterprise into my heart.
And come ye now to tell me John hath made
His peace with Rome? What is that peace to me?
I, by the honor of my marriage bed,   93
After young Arthur, claim this land for mine;
And, now it is half conquered, must I back
Because that John hath made his peace with Rome?
Am I Rome's slave? What penny hath Rome borne,
What men provided, what munition sent,
To underprop this action? Is 't not I   99
That undergo this charge? Who else but I,   100
And such as to my claim are liable,   101
Sweat in this business and maintain this war?
Have I not heard these islanders shout out
"Vive le roi!" as I have banked their towns?   104
Have I not here the best cards for the game
To win this easy match played for a crown?   106
And shall I now give o'er the yielded set?   107
No, no, on my soul, it never shall be said.
PANDULPH
You look but on the outside of this work.
LEWIS
Outside or inside, I will not return
Till my attempt so much be glorified
As to my ample hope was promisèd
Before I drew this gallant head of war,   113
And culled these fiery spirits from the world
To outlook conquest and to win renown   115
Even in the jaws of danger and of death.
                         [*A trumpet sounds.*]
What lusty trumpet thus doth summon us?   117

            Enter [the] Bastard.

BASTARD
According to the fair play of the world,   118
Let me have audience. I am sent to speak.
My holy lord of Milan, from the King
I come, to learn how you have dealt for him;
And, as you answer, I do know the scope
And warrant limited unto my tongue.
PANDULPH
The Dauphin is too willful-opposite,   124
And will not temporize with my entreaties.   125
He flatly says he'll not lay down his arms.

44 **compulsion** what you are compelled to do (by the hard necessities of the times).   **brave respect** gallant consideration (of your country's need)   52 **had I seen** if I had seen   53 **Figured** adorned   56 **Commend** entrust, bequeath. (Leave tears to babies, says the Dauphin, that have never known the fury of the world at large and have had no worse fortune than to be well fed and entertained.)   64 **an angel spake** (1) i.e., Pandulph comes with warrant from "the hand of heaven" (2) a pun on *angel* meaning a coin, in "the purse of rich prosperity." A trumpet may sound at this point.   70 **is come in** has submitted   73 **wind up** furl   75 **at hand** by hand (and hence tame)   78 **shall** must.   **back** go back   79 **propertied** made a tool of   80 **secondary at control** subordinate under someone else's command   85 **matter** fuel

88 **right** my true claim   89 **interest** title, right   93 **by the . . . bed** i.e., in the name of Blanche, my wife   99 **underprop** support   100 **charge** expense   101 **claim** demand for service.   **liable** subject   104 **Vive le roi** long live the king. (Also a term in card playing; the metaphor continues in *banked*, "won by putting in the bank," *game, match, crown,* "a five-shilling stake," *set,* "round in a game," etc.)   **banked** coasted, skirted   106 **crown** (1) symbol of monarchy (2) stake in a game   107 **give o'er** abandon.   **the yielded set** the round or rubber already won   113 **drew** assembled.   **head of war** army   115 **outlook** stare down   117 **lusty** vigorous   118 **fair play** i.e., rules of chivalry   124 **willful-opposite** stubbornly opposed   125 **temporize** come to an agreement

BASTARD
By all the blood that ever fury breathed,   127
The youth says well. Now hear our English king,
For thus his royalty doth speak in me.
He is prepared, and reason too he should.   130
This apish and unmannerly approach,
This harnessed masque and unadvisèd revel,   132
This unhaired sauciness and boyish troops,   133
The King doth smile at, and is well prepared
To whip this dwarfish war, these pygmy arms,
From out the circle of his territories.
That hand which had the strength, even at your
    door,
To cudgel you and make you take the hatch,   138
To dive like buckets in concealèd wells,   139
To crouch in litter of your stable planks,   140
To lie like pawns locked up in chests and trunks,   141
To hug with swine, to seek sweet safety out   142
In vaults and prisons, and to thrill and shake   143
Even at the crying of your nation's crow,   144
Thinking his voice an armèd Englishman—
Shall that victorious hand be feebled here
That in your chambers gave you chastisement?   147
No! Know the gallant monarch is in arms,
And like an eagle o'er his aerie towers   149
To souse annoyance that comes near his nest.   150
And you degenerate, you ingrate revolts,   151
You bloody Neroes, ripping up the womb   152
Of your dear mother England, blush for shame!
For your own ladies and pale-visaged maids
Like Amazons come tripping after drums,   155
Their thimbles into armèd gauntlets change,   156
Their needles to lances, and their gentle hearts
To fierce and bloody inclination.
LEWIS
There end thy brave, and turn thy face in peace.   159
We grant thou canst outscold us. Fare thee well.
We hold our time too precious to be spent
With such a brabbler.
PANDULPH   Give me leave to speak.   162
BASTARD
No, I will speak.
LEWIS   We will attend to neither.   163
Strike up the drums, and let the tongue of war
Plead for our interest and our being here.

127 **blood** bold warriors   130 **reason . . . should** with good reason
132 **harnessed** in armor.   **unadvisèd revel** ill-considered entertainment   133 **unhaired** beardless, youthful   138 **take the hatch** leap
over the lower-half door; i.e., make a hasty and undignified retreat
139 **concealèd wells** wells offering a place to hide   140 **crouch** i.e.,
hide.   **litter** straw bedding for animals.   **planks** floors   141 **pawns**
articles in pawn   142 **hug** i.e., bed down   143 **thrill** shiver
144 **crying . . . crow** i.e., crowing of the rooster, a French national
symbol   147 **your chambers** i.e., your own terrain   149 **aerie** nest.
towers soars   150 **souse** swoop down upon   151 **revolts** rebels
152 **Neroes** (The Roman emperor Nero allegedly ripped open the
womb of his mother after having murdered her.)   155 **Amazons** female warriors of ancient mythology   156 **armèd gauntlets** steel-plated
gloves worn as part of the armor   159 **brave** defiant boast.   **turn thy
face** go back the way you came   162 **brabbler** noisy, quarrelsome
person   163 **attend to** (1) listen to (2) wait for

BASTARD
Indeed, your drums, being beaten, will cry out;
And so shall you, being beaten. Do but start
An echo with the clamor of thy drum,
And even at hand a drum is ready braced   169
That shall reverberate all as loud as thine.
Sound but another, and another shall,
As loud as thine, rattle the welkin's ear   172
And mock the deep-mouthed thunder. For at
    hand—
Not trusting to this halting legate here,
Whom he hath used rather for sport than need—
Is warlike John; and in his forehead sits
A bare-ribbed Death, whose office is this day   177
To feast upon whole thousands of the French.
LEWIS
Strike up our drums, to find this danger out.
BASTARD
And thou shalt find it, Dauphin, do not doubt.   180
                    [*Drums beat.*] *Exeunt* [*separately*].

5.3   *Alarums. Enter [King] John and Hubert.*

KING JOHN
How goes the day with us? O, tell me, Hubert.
HUBERT
Badly, I fear. How fares Your Majesty?
KING JOHN
This fever that hath troubled me so long
Lies heavy on me. O, my heart is sick!

            Enter a Messenger.

MESSENGER
My lord, your valiant kinsman, Faulconbridge,
Desires Your Majesty to leave the field
And send him word by me which way you go.
KING JOHN
Tell him, toward Swinstead, to the abbey there.   8
MESSENGER
Be of good comfort, for the great supply   9
That was expected by the Dauphin here
Are wrecked three nights ago on Goodwin Sands.   11
This news was brought to Richard but even now.   12
The French fight coldly and retire themselves.   13
KING JOHN
Ay me, this tyrant fever burns me up
And will not let me welcome this good news.
Set on toward Swinstead. To my litter straight;
Weakness possesseth me, and I am faint.   *Exeunt.*

169 **ready braced** i.e., tightened, ready to be struck   172 **welkin's**
heaven's, sky's   177 **bare-ribbed Death** i.e., Death envisaged as a
skeleton.   **office** function   180 **find it** i.e., find it with a vengeance
5.3. Location: England. The field of battle.
8 **Swinstead** (In Lincolnshire; an error for Swineshead.)   9 **supply** reinforcement   11 **Goodwin Sands** dangerous shoals off Kent   12 **Richard** i.e., the Bastard   13 **retire themselves** retreat

5.4   *Enter Salisbury, Pembroke, and Bigot.*

SALISBURY
I did not think the King so stored with friends.   1
PEMBROKE
Up once again! Put spirit in the French.
If they miscarry, we miscarry too.
SALISBURY
That misbegotten devil, Faulconbridge,
In spite of spite, alone upholds the day.   5
PEMBROKE
They say King John, sore sick, hath left the field.

     Enter Melun, wounded, [led by a soldier].

MELUN
Lead me to the revolts of England here.   7
SALISBURY
When we were happy we had other names.
PEMBROKE
It is the Count Melun.
SALISBURY   Wounded to death.
MELUN
Fly, noble English, you are bought and sold!   10
Unthread the rude eye of rebellion   11
And welcome home again discarded faith.
Seek out King John and fall before his feet;
For if the French be lords of this loud day,
He means to recompense the pains you take   15
By cutting off your heads. Thus hath he sworn,
And I with him, and many more with me,
Upon the altar at Saint Edmundsbury,
Even on that altar where we swore to you
Dear amity and everlasting love.
SALISBURY
May this be possible? May this be true?
MELUN
Have I not hideous death within my view,
Retaining but a quantity of life,   23
Which bleeds away, even as a form of wax
Resolveth from his figure 'gainst the fire?   25
What in the world should make me now deceive,
Since I must lose the use of all deceit?   27
Why should I then be false, since it is true
That I must die here and live hence by truth?   29
I say again, if Lewis do win the day,
He is forsworn if e'er those eyes of yours
Behold another day break in the east.
But even this night, whose black contagious breath   33
Already smokes about the burning crest   34
Of the old, feeble, and day-wearied sun,
Even this ill night, your breathing shall expire,

Paying the fine of rated treachery   37
Even with a treacherous fine of all your lives,   38
If Lewis by your assistance win the day.
Commend me to one Hubert with your king;
The love of him, and this respect besides,   41
For that my grandsire was an Englishman,   42
Awakes my conscience to confess all this.
In lieu whereof, I pray you, bear me hence   44
From forth the noise and rumor of the field,   45
Where I may think the remnant of my thoughts
In peace, and part this body and my soul
With contemplation and devout desires.
SALISBURY
We do believe thee, and beshrew my soul   49
But I do love the favor and the form   50
Of this most fair occasion, by the which
We will untread the steps of damnèd flight,   52
And like a bated and retirèd flood,   53
Leaving our rankness and irregular course,   54
Stoop low within those bounds we have o'erlooked   55
And calmly run on in obedience
Even to our ocean, to our great King John.
My arm shall give thee help to bear thee hence,
For I do see the cruel pangs of death
Right in thine eye. Away, my friends! New flight,   60
And happy newness, that intends old right!   61
         Exeunt [leading off Melun].

❧

5.5   *Enter [Lewis the] Dauphin and his train.*

LEWIS
The sun of heaven, methought, was loath to set,
But stayed and made the western welkin blush,
When English measure backward their own ground   3
In faint retire. O, bravely came we off,   4
When with a volley of our needless shot,   5
After such bloody toil, we bid good night,
And wound our tattering colors clearly up,   7
Last in the field, and almost lords of it!

     Enter a Messenger.

37 fine penalty.   **rated** (1) assessed, evaluated (2) rebuked, chided **38 fine** end (with a pun on *fine* of the previous line)   **41 respect** consideration   **42 For that** because, in that   **44 In lieu whereof** in payment for which (information)   **45 rumor** noise   **49 beshrew** curse **50 But** if.   **favor . . . form** i.e., attractive appearance   **52 untread** retrace.   **damnèd flight** cursed breaking away from proper obedience **53 bated . . . flood** river that has abated and receded   **54 rankness** overgrowth, i.e., flooding, exceeding of proper bounds   **55 Stoop low** (1) subside, like a river (2) kneel.   **o'erlooked** (1) overflowed (2) disregarded   **60 Right** unmistakably.   **New flight** i.e., another change of allegiance (see line 52)   **61 happy newness** a change for the better.   **intends old right** intends to reestablish an ancient right or just cause
5.5. Location: England. The French camp.
3 measure traverse   **4 faint retire** fainthearted retreat.   **bravely . . . off** we left the field of battle in fine fettle   **5 needless** i.e., fired toward a disappearing enemy that needed no encouragement to flee **7 tattering** flying in tatters (because of the day's fierce engagement). **clearly** free from entanglement, without enemy interference

5.4. Location: The field of battle, as before.
1 stored supplied   **5 In spite of spite** i.e., despite anything we do **7 revolts** rebels   **10 bought and sold** i.e., betrayed   **11 Unthread . . . eye** i.e., withdraw from the hazardous undertaking in which you are engaged, just as you would withdraw thread from a needle's eye **15 He** i.e., the French Dauphin   **23 quantity** small quantity   **25 Resolveth from his figure** melts and loses its shape   **27 use** profit **29 hence** in the next world   **33 contagious** (Night air was thought to be noxious.)   **34 smokes** grows misty

MESSENGER
Where is my prince, the Dauphin?
LEWIS   Here. What news?
MESSENGER
The Count Melun is slain. The English lords
By his persuasion are again fall'n off;   11
And your supply, which you have wished so long,
Are cast away and sunk on Goodwin Sands.
LEWIS
Ah, foul shrewd news! Beshrew thy very heart!   14
I did not think to be so sad tonight
As this hath made me. Who was he that said
King John did fly an hour or two before
The stumbling night did part our weary powers?   18
MESSENGER
Whoever spoke it, it is true, my lord.
LEWIS
Well, keep good quarter and good care tonight.   20
The day shall not be up so soon as I,
To try the fair adventure of tomorrow.   *Exeunt.* 22

❖

5.6   *Enter [the] Bastard and Hubert, severally.*

HUBERT
Who's there? Speak, ho! Speak quickly, or I shoot.
BASTARD
A friend. What art thou?
HUBERT   Of the part of England.   2
BASTARD
Whither dost thou go?
HUBERT   What's that to thee?
Why may not I demand of thine affairs
As well as thou of mine?
BASTARD   Hubert, I think?
HUBERT   Thou hast a perfect thought.   7
I will upon all hazards well believe   8
Thou art my friend, that know'st my tongue so well.
Who art thou?
BASTARD   Who thou wilt. And if thou please,
Thou mayst befriend me so much as to think
I come one way of the Plantagenets.
HUBERT
Unkind remembrance! Thou and eyeless night   13
Have done me shame. Brave soldier, pardon me,
That any accent breaking from thy tongue   15
Should scape the true acquaintance of mine ear.
BASTARD
Come, come; sans compliment, what news abroad?   17

11 are again fall'n off have withdrawn allegiance once again
14 shrewd of evil import   **18 stumbling** causing one to stumble
20 quarter watch   **22 adventure** hazard, fortune
5.6. Location: England. An open place in the neighborhood of Swinstead (or, more correctly, Swineshead) Abbey.
s.d. severally at separate doors   **2 Of the part** on the side   **7 perfect** correct   **8 upon all hazards** against any odds   **13 Unkind remembrance** (Hubert chides his own faulty memory.)   **Thou** i.e., my memory   **15 accent** speech   **17 sans compliment** without the usual civilities

HUBERT
Why, here walk I in the black brow of night,
To find you out.
BASTARD   Brief, then; and what's the news?
HUBERT
O, my sweet sir, news fitting to the night,
Black, fearful, comfortless, and horrible.
BASTARD
Show me the very wound of this ill news.
I am no woman; I'll not swoon at it.
HUBERT
The King, I fear, is poisoned by a monk.
I left him almost speechless, and broke out   25
To acquaint you with this evil, that you might
The better arm you to the sudden time   27
Than if you had at leisure known of this.   28
BASTARD
How did he take it? Who did taste to him?   29
HUBERT
A monk, I tell you, a resolvèd villain,
Whose bowels suddenly burst out. The King
Yet speaks and peradventure may recover.
BASTARD
Who didst thou leave to tend His Majesty?
HUBERT
Why, know you not? The lords are all come back,
And brought Prince Henry in their company,   35
At whose request the King hath pardoned them,
And they are all about His Majesty.
BASTARD
Withhold thine indignation, mighty heaven,
And tempt us not to bear above our power!   39
I'll tell thee, Hubert, half my power this night,   40
Passing these flats, are taken by the tide;   41
These Lincoln Washes have devourèd them.
Myself, well mounted, hardly have escaped.
Away before! Conduct me to the King.   44
I doubt he will be dead or ere I come.   *Exeunt.* 45

❖

5.7   *Enter Prince Henry, Salisbury, and Bigot.*

PRINCE HENRY
It is too late. The life of all his blood   1
Is touched corruptibly, and his pure brain,   2
Which some suppose the soul's frail dwelling-house,

25 out away   **27 to the sudden time** for this emergency   **28 at leisure** i.e., later, because of a leisurely report   **29 it** i.e., the poison.
Who did taste to him (A "taster" was supposed to eat a portion of everything the King was to eat in order to protect him from poisoning. The monk who did so here took the poison knowingly—as a *resolvèd villain*—to ensure the King's death.)   **35 Prince Henry** i.e., John's son, the future Henry III   **39 tempt . . . power** don't try us beyond our power of endurance   **40 power** army   **41 Passing** traversing.
flats tidal flatlands in the large inlet called the Wash, between Lincolnshire and Norfolk   **44 Away before** lead the way   **45 doubt** fear.
or ere before
5.7. Location: England. The orchard of Swinstead (or, more correctly, Swineshead) Abbey.
1 life essence   **2 touched** infected.   **corruptibly** leading to corruption and death.   **pure** clear

Doth by the idle comments that it makes   4
Foretell the ending of mortality.   5

Enter Pembroke.

PEMBROKE
His Highness yet doth speak, and holds belief
That, being brought into the open air,
It would allay the burning quality
Of that fell poison which assaileth him.   9

PRINCE HENRY
Let him be brought into the orchard here.

                                          [*Exit Bigot.*]

Doth he still rage?

PEMBROKE   He is more patient
Than when you left him. Even now he sung.

PRINCE HENRY
O vanity of sickness! Fierce extremes   13
In their continuance will not feel themselves.   14
Death, having preyed upon the outward parts,
Leaves them invisible, and his siege is now   16
Against the mind, the which he pricks and wounds
With many legions of strange fantasies,   18
Which, in their throng and press to that last hold, 19
Confound themselves. 'Tis strange that Death should
     sing.   20
I am the cygnet to this pale faint swan,   21
Who chants a doleful hymn to his own death,
And from the organ pipe of frailty sings
His soul and body to their lasting rest.

SALISBURY
Be of good comfort, Prince, for you are born
To set a form upon that indigest   26
Which he hath left so shapeless and so rude.   27

[*King*] *John brought in* [*in a chair, attended by
Bigot*].

KING JOHN
Ay, marry, now my soul hath elbowroom;
It would not out at windows nor at doors.
There is so hot a summer in my bosom
That all my bowels crumble up to dust.
I am a scribbled form, drawn with a pen   32
Upon a parchment, and against this fire
Do I shrink up.

PRINCE HENRY   How fares Your Majesty?

KING JOHN
Poisoned—ill fare! Dead, forsook, cast off;   35
And none of you will bid the winter come

To thrust his icy fingers in my maw,
Nor let my kingdom's rivers take their course
Through my burned bosom, nor entreat the north
To make his bleak winds kiss my parchèd lips
And comfort me with cold. I do not ask you
     much—
I beg cold comfort; and you are so strait   42
And so ingrateful, you deny me that.

PRINCE HENRY
O, that there were some virtue in my tears   44
That might relieve you!

KING JOHN   The salt in them is hot.
Within me is a hell, and there the poison
Is as a fiend confined to tyrannize
On unreprievable condemnèd blood.

Enter [*the*] *Bastard.*

BASTARD
O, I am scalded with my violent motion
And spleen of speed to see Your Majesty!   50

KING JOHN
O cousin, thou art come to set mine eye.   51
The tackle of my heart is cracked and burnt,   52
And all the shrouds wherewith my life should sail 53
Are turnèd to one thread, one little hair.
My heart hath one poor string to stay it by,   55
Which holds but till thy news be utterèd,
And then all this thou seest is but a clod
And module of confounded royalty.   58

BASTARD
The Dauphin is preparing hitherward,   59
Where God He knows how we shall answer him!   60
For in a night the best part of my power,   61
As I upon advantage did remove,   62
Were in the Washes all unwarily
Devourèd by the unexpected flood.   [*The King dies.*] 64

SALISBURY
You breathe these dead news in as dead an ear.—
My liege! My lord!—But now a king, now thus.

PRINCE HENRY
Even so must I run on, and even so stop.
What surety of the world, what hope, what stay,   68
When this was now a king and now is clay?

BASTARD [*to the King*]
Art thou gone so? I do but stay behind
To do the office for thee of revenge,
And then my soul shall wait on thee to heaven,   72
As it on earth hath been thy servant still.—   73

---

4 idle comments babble **5 mortality** life **9 fell** cruel **13 vanity** absurdity **14 In . . . themselves** i.e., by the very intensity of their continuation produce a loss of sensation **16 invisible** imperceptibly (?), insensate (?) **his** its, Death's **18 legions** (1) vast numbers (2) armies **19 hold** stronghold (the mind) **20 Confound** destroy, i.e., make incoherent and senseless **21 cygnet** young swan. (It was a popular belief that the swan sang only once in its life, just before it died, as its spirit attempted to pass through its long neck, the *organ pipe of frailty,* of line 23.) **26 indigest** shapeless mass, i.e., the confused state **27 rude** shapeless, i.e., ungoverned **32 a scribbled form** a hastily drafted document, i.e., a perishable being **35 fare** (1) food (2) fortune

42 cold comfort (1) the comfort of cold to my burning (2) empty consolation (since real consolation is no longer possible). **strait** niggardly **44 virtue** healing power **50 spleen** i.e., eagerness **51 set mine eye** close my eyes (in death) **52 tackle** rigging of a ship **53 shrouds** ropes giving support to masts (with a suggestion also of burial garments) **55 string** (1) heartstring (2) rope, as in lines 53–54. **stay it** support itself **58 module** counterfeit, mere image. **confounded** destroyed **59 preparing** repairing, coming **60 answer** meet and oppose **61 in a night** during the night. **power** army **62 upon advantage** to gain, or taking, favorable opportunity. **remove** shift position **64 flood** i.e., tide **68 stay** support **72 wait on** attend **73 still** always

Now, now, you stars that move in your right
   spheres,   74
Where be your powers? Show now your mended
   faiths,   75
And instantly return with me again
To push destruction and perpetual shame
Out of the weak door of our fainting land.
Straight let us seek, or straight we shall be sought;   79
The Dauphin rages at our very heels.

SALISBURY
It seems you know not, then, so much as we.
The Cardinal Pandulph is within at rest,
Who half an hour since came from the Dauphin,
And brings from him such offers of our peace
As we with honor and respect may take,   85
With purpose presently to leave this war.

BASTARD
He will the rather do it when he sees
Ourselves well sinewèd to our defense.   88

SALISBURY
Nay, 'tis in a manner done already,
For many carriages he hath dispatched   90
To the seaside, and put his cause and quarrel
To the disposing of the Cardinal,
With whom yourself, myself, and other lords,
If you think meet, this afternoon will post   94
To consummate this business happily.

BASTARD
Let it be so. And you, my noble Prince,
With other princes that may best be spared,
Shall wait upon your father's funeral.   98

PRINCE HENRY
At Worcester must his body be interred,
For so he willed it.

BASTARD   Thither shall it then.
And happily may your sweet self put on   101
The lineal state and glory of the land,   102
To whom, with all submission, on my knee
I do bequeath my faithful services   104
And true subjection everlastingly.   [He kneels.]

SALISBURY
And the like tender of our love we make,   106
To rest without a spot for evermore.   107
            [All kneel to Prince Henry, and then rise.]

PRINCE HENRY
I have a kind soul that would give you thanks
And knows not how to do it but with tears.

BASTARD
O, let us pay the time but needful woe,   110
Since it hath been beforehand with our griefs.
This England never did, nor never shall,
Lie at the proud foot of a conqueror

But when it first did help to wound itself.
Now these her princes are come home again,   115
Come the three corners of the world in arms   116
And we shall shock them. Naught shall make us
   rue,   117
If England to itself do rest but true.
            Exeunt [with the King's body].

115 **Now** now that.   **home** i.e., back to true faith and allegiance
116 **three . . . world** i.e., all the world except England, the fourth
corner   117 **shock** meet with force

74 **stars** i.e., nobles.   **right spheres** proper orbits (around the throne,
like heavenly bodies around the earth)   75 **faiths** loyalties (to the
crown)   79 **Straight** at once   85 **respect** self-respect   88 **well sinewèd to our** well strengthened in our own   90 **carriages** baggage ve-
hicles   94 **post** hasten   98 **wait upon** act as escorts and pallbearers
in   101 **happily** propitiously   102 **lineal state** crown by right of succession   104 **bequeath** give   106 **tender** offer   107 **rest** remain.
spot stain   110 **but needful woe** no more weeping than necessary

The Tragedy of King Richard the Second

Richard II (c. 1595–1596) is the first play in Shakespeare's great four-play historical saga, or tetralogy, that continues with the two parts of *Henry IV* (c. 1596–1598) and concludes with *Henry V* (1599). In this, his second, tetralogy, Shakespeare dramatizes the beginnings of the great conflict called the Wars of the Roses, having already dramatized the conclusion of that civil war in his earlier tetralogy on Henry VI and Richard III (c. 1589–1594). Both sequences move from an outbreak of civil faction to the eventual triumph of political stability. Together, they comprise the story of England's long century of political turmoil from the 1390s until Henry Tudor's victory over Richard III in 1485. Yet Shakespeare chose to tell the two halves of this chronicle in reverse order. His crowning statement about kingship in *Henry V* focuses on the earlier historical period, on the education and kingly success of Prince Hal.

With *Richard II*, then, Shakespeare turns to the events that had launched England's century of crisis. These events were still fresh and relevant to Elizabethan minds. Richard and Bolingbroke's contest for the English crown provided a sobering example of political wrongdoing and, at least by implication, a rule for political right conduct. One prominent reason for studying history, to an Elizabethan, was to avoid the errors of the past. The relevance of such historical analogy was, in fact, vividly underscored some six years after Shakespeare wrote the play: in 1601, followers of the Earl of Essex commissioned Shakespeare's acting company to perform a revived play about Richard II on the eve of what was to be an abortive rebellion, evidently with the intention of inciting a riot. Whether the play was Shakespeare's is not certain, but it seems likely. The acting company was ultimately exonerated, but not before Queen Elizabeth concluded that she was being compared to Richard II. When he wrote the play, Shakespeare presumably did not know that it would be used for such a purpose, but he must have known that the overthrow of Richard II was, in any case, a controversial subject because of its potential use as a precedent for rebellion. The scene of Richard's deposition (4.1) was considered so provocative by Elizabeth's government that it was censored in the printed quartos of Shakespeare's play during the Queen's lifetime.

In view of the startling relevance of this piece of history to Shakespeare's own times, then, what are the rights and wrongs of Richard's deposition, and to what extent can political lessons be drawn from Shakespeare's presentation?

To begin with, we should not underestimate Richard's attractive qualities, as a man and even as a king. Throughout the play, Richard is consistently more impressive and majestic in appearance than his rival, Bolingbroke. Richard fascinates us with his verbal sensitivity, his poetic insight, and his dramatic self-consciousness. He eloquently expounds a sacramental view of kingship, according to which "Not all the water in the rough rude sea / Can wash the balm off from an anointed king" (3.2.54–55). Bolingbroke can depose Richard but can never capture the aura of majesty Richard possesses; Bolingbroke may succeed politically but only at the expense of desecrating an idea. Richard is much more interesting to us as a man than Bolingbroke, more capable of grief, more tender in his personal relationships, and more in need of being understood. Indeed, a major factor in Richard's tragedy is the conflict between his public role (wherein he sees himself as divinely appointed, almost superhuman) and his private role (wherein he is emotionally dependent and easily hurt). He confuses what the medieval and Renaissance world knew as the king's "two bodies," the sacramental body of kingship, which is eternal, and the human body of a single occupant of the throne, whose frail mortal condition is subject to time and fortune. Richard's failure to perceive and to act wisely on this difference is part of his tragic predicament, but his increasing insight, through suffering, into the truth of the distinction is also part of his spiritual growth. His dilemma, however poignantly individual, lies at the heart of kingship. Richard is thus very much a king. Although he sometimes indulges in childish sentimentality, at his best he is superbly refined, perceptive, and poetic.

These qualities notwithstanding, Richard is an incompetent ruler, compared with the man who supplants him. Richard himself confesses to the prodigal expense of "too great a court." In order to raise funds, he has been obliged to "farm our royal realm"; that is, to sell for ready cash the right of collecting taxes to individual courtiers, who are then free to extort what the market will bear (1.4.43–45). Similarly, Richard proposes to issue "blank charters" (line 48) to his minions, who will then be authorized to fill in the amount of tax to be paid by any hapless subject. These abuses were infamous to Elizabethan audiences as symbols of autocratic misgovernment. No less heinous is Richard's seizure of the dukedom of Lancaster from his cousin Bolingbroke. Although Richard does receive the consent of his Council to banish Bolingbroke, he violates the very idea of inheritance of property when he takes away Bolingbroke's title and lands. And, as his uncle the Duke of York remonstrates, Richard's own right to the throne depends on that idea of due inheritance. By offending against the most sacred concepts of order and degree, he teaches others to rebel.

Richard's behavior even prior to the commencement of the play arouses suspicion. The nature of his complicity in the death of his uncle Thomas of Woodstock, Duke of Gloucester, is perhaps never entirely clear, and Gloucester may have given provocation. Indeed, one can sympathize with the predicament of a young ruler prematurely thrust into the center of power by the untimely death of his father, the crown prince, now having to cope with an array of worldly-wise, advice-giving uncles. Nevertheless, Richard is unambiguously guilty of murder in the eyes of Gloucester's widow and of her brother-in-law John of Gaunt, Duke of Lancaster. Apparently, too, Gaunt's son Bolingbroke believes Richard to be a murderer, and he brings accusation against Thomas Mowbray, Duke of Norfolk, partly as a means of embarrassing the King, whom he cannot accuse directly. Mowbray's lot is an unenviable one: he was in command at Calais when Gloucester was executed there, and he hints that Richard ordered the execution (even though Mowbray alleges that he himself did not carry out the order). For his part, Richard is only too glad to banish the man suspected of having been his agent in murder. Mowbray is a convenient scapegoat.

The polished, ceremonial tone of the play's opening is vitiated, then, by our growing awareness of dirty politics going on behind the display. Our first impression of Richard is of a king devoted to the public display of conciliatory even-handedness. He listens to the rival claims of Bolingbroke and Mowbray, and, when he cannot reconcile them peacefully, he orders a trial by combat. This trial (1.3) is replete with ceremonial repetition and ritual. The combatants are duly sworn in the justice of their cause, and God is to decide the quarrel by awarding victory to the champion who speaks the truth. Richard, the presiding officer, assumes the role of God's anointed deputy on earth. Yet it becomes evident in due course that Richard is a major perpetrator of injustice rather than an impartial judge, that Bolingbroke is after greater objectives than he acknowledges even to himself, and that Richard's refusal to let the trial by combat take place and his banishment of the two contenders are his desperate ways of burying a problem he cannot deal with forthrightly. His uncles reluctantly consent to the banishment only because they, too, see that disaffection has reached alarming proportions.

Bolingbroke's motivation in these opening scenes is perhaps even more obscure than Richard's. Our first impression of Bolingbroke is of forthrightness, moral indignation, and patriotic zeal. In fact, we never really question the earnestness of his outrage at Richard's misgovernance, his longing to avenge a family murder (for Gloucester was his uncle, too), or his bitter disappointment at being banished. Yet we are prompted to ask further: what is the essential cause of the enmity between Bolingbroke and Richard? If Mowbray is only a stalking-horse, is not Gloucester's death also the excuse for pursuing a preexistent animosity? Richard, for one, appears to think so. His portrayal of Bolingbroke as a scheming politician, who curries favor with the populace in order to build a widely based alliance against the King himself, is telling and prophetic. Bolingbroke, says Richard, acts "As were our England in reversion his, / And he our subjects' next degree in hope" (1.4.35–36). This unflattering appraisal might be ascribed to malicious envy on Richard's part, were it not proved by subsequent events to be wholly accurate.

Paradoxically, Richard is far the more prescient of the two contenders for the English throne. It is he, in fact, who perceives from the start that the conflict between them is irreconcilable. He banishes Bolingbroke as his chief rival and does not doubt what motives will call Bolingbroke home again. Meanwhile, Bolingbroke disclaims any motive for his deed other than love of country and hatred of injustice. Although born with a political canniness that Richard lacks, Bolingbroke does not reflect (out loud, at least) upon the consequences of his own acts. As a man of action, he lives in the present. Richard, conversely, a person of exquisite contemplative powers and poetic imagination, does not deign to cope with the practical. He both envies and despises Bolingbroke's easy way with the commoners. Richard cherishes kingship for the majesty and the royal prerogative it confers, not for the power to govern wisely. Thus it is that, despite his perception of what will follow, Richard habitually indulges his worst instincts, buying a moment of giddy pleasure at the expense of future disaster.

Granted Richard's incompetence as a ruler, is Bolingbroke justified in armed rebellion against him? According to Bolingbroke's uncle, the Duke of York (who later, to be sure, shifts his allegiance), and to the Bishop of Carlisle, Bolingbroke is not justified in the rebellion. The attitude of these men can be summed up by the phrase "passive obedience." And, although Bolingbroke's own father, John of Gaunt, dies before his son returns to England to seize power, Gaunt, too, is opposed to such human defiances of the sacred institution of kingship. "God's is the quarrel," he insists (1.2.37). Because Richard is God's anointed deputy on earth, as Gaunt sees the matter, only God may punish the King's wrongdoing. Gaunt does not question Richard's guilt, but neither does he question God's ability to avenge. Gaunt sees human intervention in God's affair as blasphemous: "for I may never lift / An angry arm against His minister" (1.2.40–41). To be sure, Gaunt does acknowledge a solemn duty to offer frank advice to extremists of both sides, and he does so unsparingly. He consents to the banishment of his son, and he rebukes Richard with his dying breath.

This doctrine of passive obedience was familiar to Elizabethans, for they heard it in church periodically in official homilies against rebellion. It was the Tudor state's answer to those who asserted a right to overthrow reputedly evil kings.

The argument was logically ingenious. Why are evil rulers permitted to govern from time to time? Presumably, because God wishes to test a people or to punish them for waywardness. Any king performing such chastisement is a divine scourge. Accordingly, the worst thing a people can do is to rebel against God's scourge, thereby manifesting more waywardness. Instead, they must attempt to remedy the insolence in their hearts, advise the King to mend his ways, and patiently await God's pardon. If they do so, they will not long be disappointed. The doctrine is essentially conservative, defending the status quo. It is reinforced in this play by the Bishop of Carlisle's prophecy that God will avenge through civil war the deposition of his anointed (4.1.126– 150); an Elizabethan audience would have appreciated the irony of the prophecy's having come true and having been the subject of Shakespeare's first historical tetralogy. Moreover, in *Richard II* the doctrine of passive obedience is a moderate position between the extremes of tyranny and rebellion, and is expressed by thoughtful, selfless characters. We might be tempted to label it Shakespeare's view if we did not also perceive that the doctrine is continually placed in ironic conflict with harsh political realities. The character who most reflects the ironies and even ludicrous incongruities of the position is the Duke of York.

York is to an extent a choric character, that is, one who helps direct our viewpoint, because his transfer of loyalties from Richard to Bolingbroke structurally delineates the decline of Richard's fortunes and the concurrent rise of Bolingbroke's. At first York shares his brother Gaunt's unwillingness to act, despite their dismay at Richard's willfulness. It is only when Richard seizes the dukedom of Lancaster that York can no longer hold his tongue. His condemnation is as bitter as that of Gaunt, hinting even at loss of allegiance (2.1.200–208). Still, he accepts the responsibility, so cavalierly bestowed by Richard, of governing England in the King's absence. He musters what force he can to oppose Bolingbroke's advance and lectures against this rebellion with the same vehemence he had used against Richard's despotism. Yet, when faced with Bolingbroke's overwhelming military superiority, he accedes rather than fights in behalf of a lost cause. However much this may resemble cowardice or mere expediency, it also displays a pragmatic logic. Once Bolingbroke has become de facto king, in York's view, he must be acknowledged and obeyed. By a kind of analogy to the doctrine of passive obedience (which more rigorous theorists would never allow), York accepts the status quo as inevitable. He is vigorously ready to defend the new regime, just as he earlier defended Richard's de jure rule. York's inconsistent loyalty helps define the structure of the play.

When, however, this conclusion brings York to the point of turning in his own son, Aumerle, for a traitor and quarreling with his wife as to whether their son shall live, the ironic absurdity is apparent. Bolingbroke, now King Henry, himself is amused, in one of the play's rare lighthearted moments (5.3.79–80). At the same time, the comedy deals with serious issues, especially the conflict between public responsibility urged by York and private or emotional satisfaction urged by his Duchess—a conflict seen earlier, for example, in the debate between Gaunt and his sister-in-law, the widowed Duchess of Gloucester (1.2). When a family and a kingdom are divided against one another, there can be no really satisfactory resolution.

We are never entirely convinced that all the fine old medieval theories surrounding kingship—divine right, passive obedience, trial by combat, and the like—can ever wholly explain or remedy the complex and nasty political situation afflicting England. The one man capable of decisive action, in fact, is he who never theorizes at all: Bolingbroke. As we have seen, his avowed motive for opposing Mowbray— simple patriotic indignation—is uttered with such earnestness that we wonder if indeed Bolingbroke has examined those political ambitions in himself that are so plainly visible to Richard and others. This same discrepancy between surface and depth applies to Bolingbroke's motives in returning to England. We cannot be sure at what time he begins to plot that return; the conspiracy announced by Northumberland (2.1.224–300) follows so closely after Richard's violation of Bolingbroke's hereditary rights and is already so well advanced that we gain the impression of an already existing plot, though some of this impression may be simply owing to Shakespeare's characteristic compression of historic time. When Bolingbroke arrives in England, in any case, he protests to York with seemingly passionate sincerity that he comes only for his dukedom of Lancaster (2.3.113–136). If so, why does he set about executing Richard's followers without legal authority and otherwise establishing his own claim to power? Why does he indulge in homophobic slurs against Richard, insinuating that Richard's favorites have "Broke the possession of a royal bed" (3.1.13), when, as far as we can see from the devotion Richard shows to his queen, the charges are trumped up and untrue? Does Bolingbroke seriously think he can reclaim his dukedom by force and then yield to Richard without either maintaining Richard as a puppet king or placing himself in intolerable jeopardy? And can he suppose that his allies, Northumberland and the rest, who have now openly defied the King, will countenance the return to power of one who would never trust them again? It is in this context that York protests, "Well, well, I see the issue of these arms" (2.3.152). The deposition of Richard and then Richard's death are unavoidable conclusions once Bolingbroke has succeeded in an armed rebellion. There can be no turning back. Yet Bolingbroke simply will not think in these terms. He permits Northumberland to proceed with almost sadistic harshness in the arrest and impeachment of Richard and then admonishes Northumberland in public for acting so harshly; the dirty work goes forward, with Northumberland taking the blame, while Bolingbroke assumes a statesmanlike pose. When the new King Henry discovers—to his surprise, evidently—that Richard's life is now a burden to the state, he ponders aloud, "Have I no friend will rid me of this living fear?" (5.4.2) and then rebukes Exton for proceeding on cue.

Bolingbroke's pragmatic spirit and new mode of governing are the embodiment of de facto rule. Ultimately, the justification for his authority is the very fact of its existence, its functioning. Bolingbroke is the man of the hour. In William Butler Yeats' fine maxim, Bolingbroke is the vessel of clay and Richard is the vessel of porcelain. One is durable and utilitarian, yet unattractive; the other is exquisite, fragile, and impractical. The comparison does not force us to prefer one to the other, even though Yeats himself characteristically sided with beauty against politics. Rather, Shakespeare gives us our choice, allowing us to see in ourselves an inclination toward political and social stability or toward artistic temperament.

The paradox may suggest that the qualities of a good administrator are not those of a sensitive, thoughtful man. However hopeless as a king, Richard stands before us increasingly as an introspective and fascinating person. The contradictions of his character are aptly focused in the business of breaking a mirror during his deposition: it is at once symbolic of a narcissistic, shallow concern for appearances and a quest for a deeper, inward truth, so that the smashing of the mirror is an act both of self-destruction and of self-discovery. When Richard's power crumbles, his spirit is enhanced, as though loss of power and royal identity were necessary for the discovery of true values.

In this there is a faint anticipation of King Lear's self-learning, fearfully and preciously bought. The trace is only slight here, because in good part Richard II is a political history play rather than a tragedy and because Richard's self-realization is imperfect. Nevertheless, when Richard faces deposition and separation from his queen, and especially when he is alone in prison expecting to die, he strives to understand his life and through it the general condition of humanity. He gains our sympathy in the wonderfully humane interchange between this deposed king and the poor groom of his stable, who once took care of Richard's horse, roan Barbary, now the possession of the new monarch (5.5.67–94). Richard perceives a contradiction in heaven's assurances about salvation: Christ promises to receive all God's children, and yet He also warns that it is as hard for a rich man to enter heaven as for a camel to be thread through a needle's eye (5.5.16–17). The paradox echoes the Beatitudes: the last shall be first, the meek shall inherit the earth. Richard, now one of the downtrodden, gropes for an understanding of the vanity of human achievement whereby he can aspire to the victory Christ promised. At his death, that victory seems to him assured: his soul will mount to its seat on high "Whilst my gross flesh sinks downward, here to die" (line 112).

In this triumph of spirit over flesh, the long downward motion of Richard's worldly fortune is crucially reversed. By the same token, the worldly success of Bolingbroke is shown to be no more than that: worldly success. His archetype is Cain, the primal murderer of a brother. To the extent that the play is a history, Bolingbroke's de facto success is still a matter of political relevance; but, in the belated movement toward Richard's personal tragedy, we experience a profound countermovement that partly achieves a purgative sense of atonement and reassurance. Whatever Richard may have lost, his gain is also great.

Balance and symmetry are unusually important in Richard II. The play begins and ends with elaborate ritual obeisance to the concept of social and monarchic order, and yet, in both cases, a note of personal disorder refuses to be subdued by the public ceremonial. Shakespeare keeps our response to both Richard and Bolingbroke ambivalent by clouding their respective responsibilities for murder. Just as Richard's role in Gloucester's death remains unclear, so Bolingbroke's role in the assassination of Richard remains equally unclear. Mowbray and Exton, as scapegoats, are in some respects parallel. Because Richard and Bolingbroke are both implicated in the deaths of near kinsmen, both are associated with Cain's murder of Abel. As Bolingbroke rises in worldly fortune, Richard falls; as Richard finds insight and release through suffering, Bolingbroke finds guilt and remorse through distasteful political necessity. Again and again, the ritual effects of staging and style draw our attention to the balanced conflicts between the two men and within Richard. Symmetry helps to focus these conflicts in visual and aural ways. In particular, the deposition scene, with its spectacle of a coronation in reverse, brings the sacramental and human sides of the central figure into poignant dramatic relationship.

Women play a subsidiary role in this play about male struggles for power, and yet the brief scenes in which women take part—the Duchess of Gloucester with Gaunt (1.2), Richard's queen with his courtiers and gardeners and then with Richard himself (2.2, 3.4, 5.1), the Duchess of York with her husband and son and King Henry (5.2–5.3)—highlight for us important thematic contrasts between the public and private spheres, power and powerlessness, political struggle and humane sensitivity, the state and the family. The women, excluded from roles of practical authority, offer, nonetheless, an invaluable critical perspective on the fateful and often self-consuming political games that men play among themselves.

The imagery of Richard II reinforces structure and meaning. The play is unlike the history plays that follow in its extensive use of blank verse and rhyme and in its interwoven sets of recurring images; Richard II is, in this respect, more typical of the so-called lyric period (c. 1594–1596) that also produced Romeo and Juliet and A Midsummer Night's Dream. Image patterns locate the play in our imaginations as a kind of lost Eden. England is a garden mismanaged by her royal gardener, so that weeds and caterpillars (e.g., Bushy, Bagot, and Green) flourish. The "garden" scene (3.4), located at the center of the play, offering a momentary haven of allegorical reflection on the play's hectic events, is central in the development of the garden metaphor. England is also a sick body, ill-tended by her royal physician, and a family divided against itself, yielding abortive and sterile progeny. Her political ills are attested to by disorders in the cosmos: comets, shooting stars, withered bay trees, and weeping rains. Night owls, associated with death, prevail over the larks of morning. The sun, royally associated at first with Richard, deserts him for Bolingbroke and leaves Richard as the Phaëthon who has mishandled the sun-god's chariot and so scorched the earth. Linked to the sun image is the prevalent leitmotif of ascent and descent. And, touching upon all these, a cluster of Biblical images sees England as a despoiled garden of Eden witnessing a second fall of humanity. Richard repeatedly brands his enemies and deserters as Judases and Pilates—not always fairly; nonetheless, in his last agony, he finds genuine consolation in Christ's example. For a man so self-absorbed in the drama of his existence, this poetic method is intensely suitable. Language and stage action have combined perfectly to express the conflict between a sensitive but flawed king and his efficient but unlovable successor.

The Tragedy of King Richard the Second

[*Dramatis Personae*

KING RICHARD THE SECOND
QUEEN, *Richard's wife*
JOHN OF GAUNT, *Duke of Lancaster, King Richard's uncle*
HENRY BOLINGBROKE, *John of Gaunt's son, Duke of Hereford and claimant to his father's dukedom of Lancaster, later King Henry IV*
DUKE OF YORK, *Edmund of Langley, King Richard's uncle*
DUCHESS OF YORK
DUKE OF AUMERLE, *York's son and the Earl of Rutland*
DUCHESS OF GLOUCESTER, *widow of Thomas of Woodstock, Duke of Gloucester (King Richard's uncle)*

THOMAS MOWBRAY, *Duke of Norfolk,*
EARL OF SALISBURY,
LORD BERKELEY,
DUKE OF SURREY,
BISHOP OF CARLISLE,   *supporters*
SIR STEPHEN SCROOP,   *of King*
ABBOT OF WESTMINSTER,   *Richard*
BUSHY,
BAGOT, *favorites of King Richard,*
GREEN,
CAPTAIN *of the Welsh Army,*

EARL OF NORTHUMBERLAND,
HARRY PERCY, *Northumberland's son,*
LORD ROSS,   *supporters*
LORD WILLOUGHBY,   *of Bolingbroke*
LORD FITZWATER,
SIR PIERCE OF EXTON,
Another LORD,

LORD MARSHAL
Two HERALDS
GARDENER
GARDENER'S MAN
LADY *attending the Queen*
KEEPER *of the prison*
A MAN *attending Exton*

SERVINGMAN *to York*
GROOM *of the stable*

Lords, Officers, Soldiers, Attendants, Ladies attending the Queen

SCENE: *England and Wales*]

1.1

Enter King Richard, John of Gaunt, with other nobles and attendants.

KING RICHARD

Old John of Gaunt, time-honored Lancaster,   1
Hast thou according to thy oath and bond
Brought hither Henry Hereford, thy bold son,
Here to make good the boisterous late appeal,   4
Which then our leisure would not let us hear,   5
Against the Duke of Norfolk, Thomas Mowbray?

GAUNT I have, my liege.   7

KING RICHARD

Tell me, moreover, hast thou sounded him   8
If he appeal the Duke on ancient malice,   9
Or worthily, as a good subject should,
On some known ground of treachery in him?

GAUNT

As near as I could sift him on that argument,   12
On some apparent danger seen in him   13
Aimed at Your Highness, no inveterate malice.

KING RICHARD

Then call them to our presence. [*Exit an attendant.*]
    Face to face,
And frowning brow to brow, ourselves will hear
The accuser and the accusèd freely speak.
High-stomached are they both, and full of ire;   18
In rage, deaf as the sea, hasty as fire.

Enter Bolingbroke and Mowbray.

BOLINGBROKE

Many years of happy days befall
My gracious sovereign, my most loving liege!

MOWBRAY

Each day still better others' happiness,   22
Until the heavens, envying earth's good hap,   23
Add an immortal title to your crown!

KING RICHARD

We thank you both. Yet one but flatters us,
As well appeareth by the cause you come: 26
Namely, to appeal each other of high treason.
Cousin of Hereford, what dost thou object   28
Against the Duke of Norfolk, Thomas Mowbray?

BOLINGBROKE

First—heaven be the record to my speech!—   30
In the devotion of a subject's love,
Tend'ring the precious safety of my prince,   32
And free from other misbegotten hate,

Come I appellant to this princely presence.   34
Now, Thomas Mowbray, do I turn to thee;
And mark my greeting well, for what I speak
My body shall make good upon this earth
Or my divine soul answer it in heaven.
Thou art a traitor and a miscreant,   39
Too good to be so and too bad to live,   40
Since the more fair and crystal is the sky,   41
The uglier seem the clouds that in it fly.
Once more, the more to aggravate the note,   43
With a foul traitor's name stuff I thy throat,
And wish, so please my sovereign, ere I move,
What my tongue speaks my right-drawn sword may
    prove.   46

MOWBRAY

Let not my cold words here accuse my zeal.   47
'Tis not the trial of a woman's war,   48
The bitter clamor of two eager tongues,   49
Can arbitrate this cause betwixt us twain;   50
The blood is hot that must be cooled for this.
Yet can I not of such tame patience boast
As to be hushed and naught at all to say.
First, the fair reverence of Your Highness curbs me
From giving reins and spurs to my free speech,
Which else would post until it had returned   56
These terms of treason doubled down his throat.
Setting aside his high blood's royalty,   58
And let him be no kinsman to my liege,   59
I do defy him, and I spit at him,
Call him a slanderous coward and a villain;
Which to maintain I would allow him odds
And meet him, were I tied to run afoot   63
Even to the frozen ridges of the Alps
Or any other ground inhabitable   65
Wherever Englishman durst set his foot.
Meantime, let this defend my loyalty:
By all my hopes, most falsely doth he lie.

BOLINGBROKE [*throwing down his gage*]

Pale trembling coward, there I throw my gage,   69
Disclaiming here the kindred of the King,   70
And lay aside my high blood's royalty,
Which fear, not reverence, makes thee to except.   72
If guilty dread have left thee so much strength
As to take up mine honor's pawn, then stoop.   74
By that, and all the rites of knighthood else,
Will I make good against thee, arm to arm,
What I have spoke or thou canst worse devise.   77

1.1 Location: A room of state. (Holinshed's *Chronicles* places this scene at Windsor, in 1398.)
1 Old John of Gaunt (Born in 1340 at Ghent; hence the surname *Gaunt.* In 1398 he was fifty-eight years old.) **4 late** recent. **appeal** accusation, formal challenge or impeachment that the accuser was obliged to maintain in combat **5 our, us** (The royal plural.) **leisure** i.e., lack of leisure **7 liege** i.e., sovereign **8 sounded** inquired of **9 appeal** accuse. **on . . . malice** on the grounds of a long-standing enmity **12 sift** discover by questioning. **argument** subject **13 apparent** obvious, manifest **18 High-stomached** haughty **22 Each . . . happiness** may each day improve on the happiness of other past days **23 hap** fortune **26 you come** i.e., about which you come **28 what . . . object** what accusation do you bring **30 record** witness **32 Tend'ring** watching over, holding dear

34 appellant as the accuser **39 miscreant** irreligious villain **40 good** i.e., noble, high-born **41 crystal** clear. (The image alludes to the crystal spheres in which, according to the Ptolemaic conception of the universe, the heavenly bodies were fixed.) **43 aggravate** emphasize. **note** reproach, stigma, i.e., charge of treason **46 right-drawn** justly or rightly drawn **47 accuse my zeal** cast doubt on my zeal or loyalty **48 woman's war** i.e., war of words **49 eager** sharp, biting **50 Can** that can **56 post** ride at high speed (by means of relays of horses) **58 Setting . . . royalty** disregarding Bolingbroke's royal blood (as grandson of Edward III) **59 let him be** suppose him to be **63 tied** obliged **65 inhabitable** uninhabitable **69 gage** a pledge to combat (usually a glove or gauntlet) **70 Disclaiming** relinquishing. **kindred** kinship **72 except** exempt, set aside **74 pawn** i.e., the gage **77 or . . . devise** or anything worse you can imagine to have been said about you

MOWBRAY [*taking up the gage*]
 I take it up; and by that sword I swear
 Which gently laid my knighthood on my shoulder,
 I'll answer thee in any fair degree
 Or chivalrous design of knightly trial;
 And when I mount, alive may I not light 82
 If I be traitor or unjustly fight!

KING RICHARD
 What doth our cousin lay to Mowbray's charge?
 It must be great that can inherit us 85
 So much as of a thought of ill in him.

BOLINGBROKE
 Look what I speak, my life shall prove it true: 87
 That Mowbray hath received eight thousand nobles 88
 In name of lendings for Your Highness' soldiers, 89
 The which he hath detained for lewd employments, 90
 Like a false traitor and injurious villain.
 Besides I say, and will in battle prove
 Or here or elsewhere to the furthest verge 93
 That ever was surveyed by English eye,
 That all the treasons for these eighteen years 95
 Complotted and contrivèd in this land 96
 Fetch from false Mowbray their first head and
  spring. 97
 Further I say, and further will maintain
 Upon his bad life to make all this good,
 That he did plot the Duke of Gloucester's death, 100
 Suggest his soon-believing adversaries, 101
 And consequently, like a traitor coward, 102
 Sluiced out his innocent soul through streams of
  blood— 103
 Which blood, like sacrificing Abel's, cries 104
 Even from the tongueless caverns of the earth 105
 To me for justice and rough chastisement.
 And, by the glorious worth of my descent,
 This arm shall do it or this life be spent.

KING RICHARD
 How high a pitch his resolution soars! 109
 Thomas of Norfolk, what sayst thou to this?

MOWBRAY
 O, let my sovereign turn away his face
 And bid his ears a little while be deaf,
 Till I have told this slander of his blood 113
 How God and good men hate so foul a liar!

KING RICHARD
 Mowbray, impartial are our eyes and ears.
 Were he my brother, nay, my kingdom's heir,
 As he is but my father's brother's son,
 Now, by my scepter's awe I make a vow, 118
 Such neighbor nearness to our sacred blood
 Should nothing privilege him nor partialize 120
 The unstooping firmness of my upright soul.
 He is our subject, Mowbray; so art thou.
 Free speech and fearless I to thee allow.

MOWBRAY
 Then, Bolingbroke, as low as to thy heart
 Through the false passage of thy throat thou liest!
 Three parts of that receipt I had for Calais 126
 Disbursed I duly to His Highness' soldiers;
 The other part reserved I by consent,
 For that my sovereign liege was in my debt 129
 Upon remainder of a dear account 130
 Since last I went to France to fetch his queen. 131
 Now swallow down that lie. For Gloucester's death, 132
 I slew him not, but to my own disgrace 133
 Neglected my sworn duty in that case. 134
 [*To Gaunt.*] For you, my noble lord of Lancaster,
 The honorable father to my foe,
 Once did I lay an ambush for your life,
 A trespass that doth vex my grievèd soul;
 But ere I last received the Sacrament
 I did confess it, and exactly begged 140
 Your Grace's pardon, and I hope I had it.
 This is my fault. As for the rest appealed, 142
 It issues from the rancor of a villain,
 A recreant and most degenerate traitor, 144
 Which in myself I boldly will defend, 145
 And interchangeably hurl down my gage 146
 Upon this overweening traitor's foot, 147
 To prove myself a loyal gentleman
 Even in the best blood chambered in his bosom. 149
 [*He throws down his gage. Bolingbroke picks it up.*]
 In haste whereof most heartily I pray 150
 Your Highness to assign our trial day.

KING RICHARD
 Wrath-kindled gentlemen, be ruled by me;
 Let's purge this choler without letting blood. 153
 This we prescribe, though no physician;
 Deep malice makes too deep incision.

82 light alight, dismount **85 inherit us** put us in possession of, make us have **87 Look what** whatever **88 nobles** gold coins worth six shillings eight pence **89 lendings** advances on pay **90 lewd** vile, base **93 Or** either **95 these eighteen years** i.e., ever since the Peasants' Revolt of 1381 **96 Complotted** plotted in a conspiracy **97 Fetch** derive. **head and spring** (Synonymous words meaning "origin.") **100 Duke of Gloucester's death** (Thomas of Woodstock, Duke of Gloucester, a younger son of Edward III and brother of John of Gaunt, was murdered at Calais in September 1397, while in Mowbray's custody.) **101 Suggest** prompt, incite. **soon-believing** easily persuaded, overcredulous **102 consequently** afterward **103 Sluiced out** let flow (as by the opening of a sluice, or valve) **104 Abel's** (For the story of Cain's murder of his brother Abel, the first such murder on earth and the archetype of the killing of a kinsman, see Genesis 4:3–12.) **105 tongueless** resonant but without articulate speech; echoing **109 pitch** highest reach of a falcon's flight **113 slander of** disgrace or reproach to

118 my scepter's awe the reverence due my scepter **120 nothing** not at all. **partialize** make partial, bias **126 receipt** money received **129 For that** because **130 Upon . . . account** for the balance of a heavy debt **131 Since . . . queen** (Mowbray went in 1395 to France to negotiate the King's marriage to Isabella, daughter of the French King Charles VI, but Richard himself escorted her to England.) **132 For** as for **132–134 For . . . case** (Mowbray speaks guardedly but seems to imply that he postponed the execution of Gloucester that he was ordered by Richard to carry out.) **140 exactly** (1) explicitly (2) fully **142 appealed** of which I am charged **144 recreant** cowardly; or, coward (used as a noun) **145 Which** which charge. **in myself** in my own person **146 interchangeably** in exchange, in turn **147 overweening** arrogant, proud **149 Even in** by shedding **150 In haste whereof** to hasten which proof of my innocence **153 Let's . . . blood** let's treat this wrath (caused by an excess of bile or choler) by purgation rather than by medical bloodletting (with a play on "bloodshed in combat")

Forget, forgive; conclude and be agreed;　　156
Our doctors say this is no month to bleed.—　157
Good uncle, let this end where it begun;
We'll calm the Duke of Norfolk, you your son.

GAUNT
To be a make-peace shall become my age.
Throw down, my son, the Duke of Norfolk's gage.

KING RICHARD
And Norfolk, throw down his.

GAUNT　　　　　　　　　　When, Harry, when?
Obedience bids I should not bid again.

KING RICHARD
Norfolk, throw down, we bid; there is no boot.　164

MOWBRAY [kneeling]
Myself I throw, dread sovereign, at thy foot.　165
My life thou shalt command, but not my shame.
The one my duty owes; but my fair name,
Despite of death that lives upon my grave,　168
To dark dishonor's use thou shalt not have.
I am disgraced, impeached, and baffled here,　170
Pierced to the soul with slander's venomed spear,
The which no balm can cure but his heart-blood
Which breathed this poison.

KING RICHARD　　　　　　　Rage must be withstood.　173
Give me his gage. Lions make leopards tame.　174

MOWBRAY
Yea, but not change his spots. Take but my shame,　175
And I resign my gage. My dear dear lord,
The purest treasure mortal times afford　177
Is spotless reputation; that away,
Men are but gilded loam or painted clay.
A jewel in a ten-times-barred-up chest
Is a bold spirit in a loyal breast.
Mine honor is my life; both grow in one;　182
Take honor from me, and my life is done.
Then, dear my liege, mine honor let me try;　184
In that I live, and for that will I die.

KING RICHARD [to Bolingbroke]
Cousin, throw up your gage; do you begin.　186

BOLINGBROKE
O, God defend my soul from such deep sin!
Shall I seem crestfallen in my father's sight?
Or with pale beggar-fear impeach my height　189
Before this out-dared dastard? Ere my tongue　190
Shall wound my honor with such feeble wrong,　191
Or sound so base a parle, my teeth shall tear　192

The slavish motive of recanting fear　　193
And spit it bleeding in his high disgrace,　194
Where shame doth harbor, even in Mowbray's face.　195
　　　　　　　　　　　　　　　[Exit Gaunt.]

KING RICHARD
We were not born to sue but to command;
Which since we cannot do to make you friends,
Be ready, as your lives shall answer it,
At Coventry upon Saint Lambert's day.　　199
There shall your swords and lances arbitrate
The swelling difference of your settled hate.
Since we cannot atone you, we shall see　　202
Justice design the victor's chivalry.　　203
Lord Marshal, command our officers at arms
Be ready to direct these home alarms.　　205
　　　　　　　　　　　　　　　Exeunt.

❖

1.2　*Enter John of Gaunt with the Duchess of
Gloucester.*

GAUNT
Alas, the part I had in Woodstock's blood　　1
Doth more solicit me than your exclaims　　2
To stir against the butchers of his life!　　3
But since correction lieth in those hands　　4
Which made the fault that we cannot correct,
Put we our quarrel to the will of heaven,
Who, when they see the hours ripe on earth,
Will rain hot vengeance on offenders' heads.

DUCHESS
Finds brotherhood in thee no sharper spur?
Hath love in thy old blood no living fire?
Edward's seven sons, whereof thyself art one,　11
Were as seven vials of his sacred blood
Or seven fair branches springing from one root.
Some of those seven are dried by nature's course,
Some of those branches by the Destinies cut;
But Thomas, my dear lord, my life, my Gloucester,
One vial full of Edward's sacred blood,
One flourishing branch of his most royal root,
Is cracked, and all the precious liquor spilt,
Is hacked down, and his summer leaves all faded,
By envy's hand and murder's bloody ax.　　21
Ah, Gaunt, his blood was thine! That bed, that
womb,

---

156 conclude come to a final agreement　**157 no month to bleed**
(Spring and autumn were regarded as the proper times to bleed patients.)　**164 boot** help for it　**165 Myself I throw** i.e., I throw myself, instead of my gage　**168 Despite . . . lives** that will live in spite
of death　**170 impeached** accused.　**baffled** publicly dishonored
173 Which breathed of him who uttered　**174 Lions . . . tame** (The
royal arms showed a lion rampant; Mowbray's emblem was a leopard.)　**175 spots** (1) leopard spots (2) stains of dishonor　**177 mortal
times** our earthly lives　**182 in one** inseparably　**184 try** put to the
test　**186 throw . . . gage** i.e., throw your gage up to me, thereby
ending the quarrel. (Richard is probably seated in an elevated position, as in scene 3.)　**189 impeach my height** discredit my high rank
190 out-dared dared down, cowed.　**dastard** coward　**191 feeble
wrong** dishonorable submission　**192 sound . . . parle** trumpet so
shameful a negotiation, i.e., consent to ask a truce

193 motive instrument, i.e., the tongue.　**recanting fear** i.e., fear that
makes one recant, or renounce one's vows　**194 in his** to its, the
tongue's　**195 s.d. Exit Gaunt** (A stage direction from the Folio,
adopted by most editors so that Gaunt will not be required to exit at
the end of scene 1 and then immediately reenter.)　**199 Saint Lambert's day** September 17　**202 atone** reconcile　**203 design** designate,
point out.　**chivalry** true knightly qualities (as demonstrated by victory
in trial by combat)　**205 home alarms** domestic conflicts
**1.2. Location: John of Gaunt's house (? No place is specified, and
the scene is not in Holinshed.)**
1 part . . . blood my kinship with Thomas of Woodstock, the Duke
of Gloucester (i.e., as his older brother)　**2 exclaims** exclamations
3 stir take action　**4 those hands** i.e., Richard's (whom Gaunt charges
with responsibility for Gloucester's death)　**11 Edward's** Edward III's
21 envy's malice's

240–279 • 290–318

THE TRAGEDY OF KING RICHARD THE SECOND: 1.3   **729**

That metal, that self mold that fashioned thee,
Made him a man; and though thou livest and
  breathest,
Yet art thou slain in him. Thou dost consent 25
In some large measure to thy father's death
In that thou seest thy wretched brother die,
Who was the model of thy father's life. 28
Call it not patience, Gaunt; it is despair.
In suffering thus thy brother to be slaughtered,
Thou showest the naked pathway to thy life, 31
Teaching stern murder how to butcher thee.
That which in mean men we entitle patience 33
Is pale cold cowardice in noble breasts.
What shall I say? To safeguard thine own life
The best way is to venge my Gloucester's death. 36

GAUNT
God's is the quarrel; for God's substitute, 37
His deputy anointed in His sight,
Hath caused his death; the which if wrongfully 39
Let heaven revenge, for I may never lift
An angry arm against His minister.

DUCHESS
Where then, alas, may I complain myself? 42

GAUNT
To God, the widow's champion and defense.

DUCHESS
Why, then, I will. Farewell, old Gaunt.
Thou goest to Coventry, there to behold
Our cousin Hereford and fell Mowbray fight. 46
O, sit my husband's wrongs on Hereford's spear, 47
That it may enter butcher Mowbray's breast!
Or if misfortune miss the first career, 49
Be Mowbray's sins so heavy in his bosom
That they may break his foaming courser's back
And throw the rider headlong in the lists,
A caitiff recreant to my cousin Hereford! 53
Farewell, old Gaunt. Thy sometime brother's wife 54
With her companion, Grief, must end her life.

GAUNT
Sister, farewell. I must to Coventry.
As much good stay with thee as go with me!

DUCHESS
Yet one word more. Grief boundeth where it falls, 58
Not with the empty hollowness, but weight. 59
I take my leave before I have begun, 60
For sorrow ends not when it seemeth done.
Commend me to thy brother, Edmund York. 62

Lo, this is all. Nay, yet depart not so!
Though this be all, do not so quickly go;
I shall remember more. Bid him—ah, what?—
With all good speed at Pleshey visit me. 66
Alack, and what shall good old York there see
But empty lodgings and unfurnished walls, 68
Unpeopled offices, untrodden stones, 69
And what hear there for welcome but my groans?
Therefore commend me; let him not come there
To seek out sorrow that dwells everywhere.
Desolate, desolate, will I hence and die.
The last leave of thee takes my weeping eye. *Exeunt.*

❖

1.3 *Enter Lord Marshal and the Duke [of] Aumerle.*

MARSHAL
My Lord Aumerle, is Harry Hereford armed?

AUMERLE
Yea, at all points, and longs to enter in. 2

MARSHAL
The Duke of Norfolk, sprightfully and bold, 3
Stays but the summons of the appellant's trumpet. 4

AUMERLE
Why then the champions are prepared, and stay
For nothing but His Majesty's approach.

*The trumpets sound, and the King enters with his
nobles [Gaunt, Bushy, Bagot, Green, and others].
When they are set, enter [Mowbray] the Duke of
Norfolk in arms, defendant, [with a herald].*

KING RICHARD
Marshal, demand of yonder champion
The cause of his arrival here in arms.
Ask him his name, and orderly proceed 9
To swear him in the justice of his cause.

MARSHAL
In God's name and the King's, say who thou art
And why thou comest thus knightly clad in arms,
Against what man thou com'st, and what thy
  quarrel. 13
Speak truly on thy knighthood and thy oath,
As so defend thee heaven and thy valor!

MOWBRAY
My name is Thomas Mowbray, Duke of Norfolk,
Who hither come engaged by my oath—
Which God defend a knight should violate!— 18
Both to defend my loyalty and truth
To God, my king, and my succeeding issue
Against the Duke of Hereford that appeals me,
And by the grace of God and this mine arm

---

23 metal substance out of which a person or a thing is made (with a
sense too of *mettle*, "temperament, disposition"). **self** selfsame
25 consent acquiesce **28 model** likeness, copy **31 naked** i.e., un-
defended **33 mean** lowly **36 venge** avenge **37 God's substitute**
i.e., the King, God's deputy on earth **39 his** i.e., Gloucester's
42 complain myself lodge a complaint on my own behalf **46 cousin**
kinsman. **fell** fierce **47 sit . . . wrongs** may my husband's wrongs
sit **49 misfortune** i.e., Mowbray's downfall. **career** charge of the
horse in a tourney or combat **53 caitiff** base, cowardly **54 sometime** late **58 boundeth** bounces, rebounds, returns. (The Duchess
apologizes for speaking yet again; her grief, she says, continues on
and on, like a bouncing tennis ball.) **59 Not . . . weight** (Grief is
not hollow, like a tennis ball, but continues to move because of its
heaviness.) **60 begun** i.e., begun to grieve **62 Edmund York** Edmund of Langley, fifth son of Edward III

66 Pleshey Gloucester's country seat, in Essex **68 unfurnished** bare
69 offices service quarters, workrooms
**1.3. Location: The lists at Coventry. Scaffolds or raised seats are pro-
vided for the King and his nobles, and chairs are provided for the
combatants.**
2 at all points completely. **in** i.e., into the lists, the space designed
for combat **3 sprightfully** with high spirit **4 Stays** awaits **9 orderly**
according to the rules **13 quarrel** complaint **18 defend** forbid

To prove him, in defending of myself,
A traitor to my God, my king, and me;
And as I truly fight, defend me heaven!

*The trumpets sound. Enter [Bolingbroke,] Duke of
Hereford, appellant, in armor, [with a herald].*

KING RICHARD
Marshal, ask yonder knight in arms
Both who he is and why he cometh hither
Thus plated in habiliments of war;   28
And formally, according to our law,
Depose him in the justice of his cause.   30

MARSHAL
What is thy name? And wherefore com'st thou
    hither,
Before King Richard in his royal lists?
Against whom comest thou? And what's thy
    quarrel?
Speak like a true knight, so defend thee heaven!

BOLINGBROKE
Harry of Hereford, Lancaster, and Derby
Am I, who ready here do stand in arms
To prove, by God's grace and my body's valor,
In lists, on Thomas Mowbray, Duke of Norfolk,
That he is a traitor foul and dangerous
To God of heaven, King Richard, and to me;
And as I truly fight, defend me heaven!

MARSHAL
On pain of death, no person be so bold
Or daring-hardy as to touch the lists,   43
Except the Marshal and such officers
Appointed to direct these fair designs.

BOLINGBROKE
Lord Marshal, let me kiss my sovereign's hand
And bow my knee before His Majesty;   47
For Mowbray and myself are like two men
That vow a long and weary pilgrimage.
Then let us take a ceremonious leave
And loving farewell of our several friends.   51

MARSHAL [*to King Richard*]
The appellant in all duty greets Your Highness
And craves to kiss your hand and take his leave.

KING RICHARD [*coming down*]
We will descend and fold him in our arms.
                           [*He embraces Bolingbroke.*]
Cousin of Hereford, as thy cause is right,   55
So be thy fortune in this royal fight!   56
Farewell, my blood—which if today thou shed,
Lament we may, but not revenge thee dead.

BOLINGBROKE
O, let no noble eye profane a tear   59
For me if I be gored with Mowbray's spear.   60

As confident as is the falcon's flight
Against a bird do I with Mowbray fight.
[*To the King.*] My loving lord, I take my leave of you;
[*To Aumerle.*] Of you, my noble cousin, Lord
    Aumerle;
Not sick, although I have to do with death,
But lusty, young, and cheerly drawing breath.   66
Lo, as at English feasts, so I regreet   67
The daintiest last, to make the end most sweet.   68
[*To Gaunt.*] O thou, the earthly author of my blood,
Whose youthful spirit, in me regenerate,   70
Doth with a twofold vigor lift me up   71
To reach at victory above my head,
Add proof unto mine armor with thy prayers,   73
And with thy blessings steel my lance's point
That it may enter Mowbray's waxen coat   75
And furbish new the name of John o' Gaunt   76
Even in the lusty havior of his son.   77

GAUNT
God in thy good cause make thee prosperous!
Be swift like lightning in the execution,
And let thy blows, doubly redoubled,
Fall like amazing thunder on the casque   81
Of thy adverse pernicious enemy.
Rouse up thy youthful blood, be valiant, and live.

BOLINGBROKE
Mine innocence and Saint George to thrive!   84

MOWBRAY
However God or fortune cast my lot,
There lives or dies, true to King Richard's throne,
A loyal, just, and upright gentleman.
Never did captive with a freer heart
Cast off his chains of bondage and embrace
His golden uncontrolled enfranchisement   90
More than my dancing soul doth celebrate
This feast of battle with mine adversary.
Most mighty liege, and my companion peers,
Take from my mouth the wish of happy years.   94
As gentle and as jocund as to jest   95
Go I to fight. Truth hath a quiet breast.   96

KING RICHARD
Farewell, my lord. Securely I espy   97
Virtue with valor couchèd in thine eye.—   98
Order the trial, Marshal, and begin.

MARSHAL
Harry of Hereford, Lancaster, and Derby,
Receive thy lance; and God defend the right!
                        [*A lance is given to Bolingbroke.*]

28 **plated** armored. **habiliments** the attire 30 **Depose him** take his sworn deposition 43 **daring-hardy** daringly bold, reckless. **touch** i.e., interfere in 47 **bow my knee** (Presumably Bolingbroke kneels to Richard and, at about line 69, to Gaunt.) 51 **several** various 55 **as** insofar as 56 **royal fight** i.e., a fight taking place in the presence of the King 59–60 **profane . . . For me** misuse tears by weeping for me

66 **lusty** full of vigor. **cheerly** cheerfully 67 **regreet** greet, salute 68 **The daintiest** i.e., the most tasty, the finest. (Bolingbroke refers to the custom of ending banquets with a sweet dessert.) 70 **regenerate** born anew 71 **twofold** i.e., of father and son 73 **proof** invulnerability 75 **enter . . . coat** pierce Mowbray's armor as though it were made of wax 76 **furbish** polish 77 **lusty havior** vigorous behavior, deportment 81 **amazing** bewildering. **casque** helmet 84 **to thrive** i.e., I rely on for my thriving 90 **enfranchisement** freedom 94 **Take . . . years** take from me the wish that you may enjoy many happy years 95 **gentle** unperturbed in spirit. **to jest** i.e., to a play or entertainment 96 **quiet** calm 97 **Securely** confidently 98 **couchèd** lodged, expressed, leveled in readiness (as with a lance)

BOLINGBROKE
Strong as a tower in hope, I cry "Amen!"   102
MARSHAL [*to an officer*]
Go bear this lance to Thomas, Duke of Norfolk.
                    [*A lance is given to Norfolk.*]
FIRST HERALD
Harry of Hereford, Lancaster, and Derby
Stands here for God, his sovereign, and himself,
On pain to be found false and recreant,
To prove the Duke of Norfolk, Thomas Mowbray,
A traitor to his God, his king, and him,   108
And dares him to set forward to the fight.
SECOND HERALD
Here standeth Thomas Mowbray, Duke of Norfolk,
On pain to be found false and recreant,
Both to defend himself and to approve   112
Henry of Hereford, Lancaster, and Derby,
To God, his sovereign, and to him disloyal,   114
Courageously and with a free desire
Attending but the signal to begin.   116
MARSHAL
Sound, trumpets, and set forward, combatants!
            [*A charge is sounded. Richard throws
                        down his baton.*]
Stay! The King hath thrown his warder down.   118
KING RICHARD
Let them lay by their helmets and their spears,
And both return back to their chairs again.
[*To his counselors.*] Withdraw with us, and let the
    trumpets sound
While we return these dukes what we decree.   122
        [*A long flourish. Richard consults apart with
                        Gaunt and others.*]
Draw near,
And list what with our council we have done.   124
For that our kingdom's earth should not be soiled   125
With that dear blood which it hath fostered;
And for our eyes do hate the dire aspect   127
Of civil wounds plowed up with neighbors' sword;
And for we think the eagle-wingèd pride
Of sky-aspiring and ambitious thoughts,
With rival-hating envy, set on you   131
To wake our peace, which in our country's cradle
Draws the sweet infant breath of gentle sleep,
Which, so roused up with boisterous untuned
    drums,   134
With harsh-resounding trumpets' dreadful bray
And grating shock of wrathful iron arms,
Might from our quiet confines fright fair peace
And make us wade even in our kindred's blood:

Therefore we banish you our territories.
You, cousin Hereford, upon pain of life,   140
Till twice five summers have enriched our fields,
Shall not regreet our fair dominions,
But tread the stranger paths of banishment.   143
BOLINGBROKE
Your will be done. This must my comfort be:
That sun that warms you here shall shine on me,
And those his golden beams to you here lent
Shall point on me and gild my banishment.
KING RICHARD
Norfolk, for thee remains a heavier doom,
Which I with some unwillingness pronounce:
The sly slow hours shall not determinate   150
The dateless limit of thy dear exile.   151
The hopeless word of "never to return"
Breathe I against thee, upon pain of life.
MOWBRAY
A heavy sentence, my most sovereign liege,
And all unlooked-for from Your Highness' mouth.
A dearer merit, not so deep a maim   156
As to be cast forth in the common air,
Have I deservèd at Your Highness' hands.
The language I have learned these forty years,
My native English, now I must forgo;
And now my tongue's use is to me no more
Than an unstringèd viol or a harp,   162
Or like a cunning instrument cased up,   163
Or, being open, put into his hands   164
That knows no touch to tune the harmony.
Within my mouth you have enjailed my tongue,
Doubly portcullised with my teeth and lips,   167
And dull unfeeling barren ignorance
Is made my jailer to attend on me.
I am too old to fawn upon a nurse,
Too far in years to be a pupil now.
What is thy sentence then but speechless death,
Which robs my tongue from breathing native
    breath?
KING RICHARD
It boots thee not to be compassionate.   174
After our sentence plaining comes too late.   175
MOWBRAY
Then thus I turn me from my country's light,
To dwell in solemn shades of endless night.
                            [*He starts to leave.*]
KING RICHARD
Return again, and take an oath with thee.
Lay on our royal sword your banished hands.
            [*They place their hands on Richard's sword.*]

---

102 **Strong . . . hope** (Alludes to Psalm 61:3: "for thou hast been my hope, and a strong tower for me against the face of the enemy.")
108 **him** himself, Bolingbroke. (See line 40.)   112 **approve** prove
114 **him** i.e., Mowbray. (See line 24.)   116 **Attending** awaiting
118 **warder** staff or truncheon borne by the King when presiding over a trial by combat   122 **While we return** until I inform.   **s.d. flourish** fanfare   124 **list** hear   125 **For that** in order that   127 **for** because (also in line 129)   131 **envy** enmity.   **set on you** set you on
134 **Which** i.e., which enmity, disturbance of the peace. (Although, in literal terms, the antecedent of *Which* is *peace* in line 132.)

140 **life** i.e., loss of life   143 **stranger** alien   150 **sly** stealthy. **determinate** put to an end   151 **dateless limit** unlimited term.   **dear** grievous   156 **dearer merit** more valued reward.   **maim** injury   162 **viol** a six-stringed instrument, related to the modern violin, played with a curved bow   163 **cunning** skillfully made   164 **open** taken from its case.   **his** that person's   167 **portcullised** shut in by a portcullis, an iron grating over a gateway that can be raised and lowered
174 **boots** avails.   **compassionate** full of laments   175 **plaining** complaining

Swear by the duty that you owe to God—
Our part therein we banish with yourselves—   181
To keep the oath that we administer:
You never shall, so help you truth and God,
Embrace each other's love in banishment,
Nor never look upon each other's face,
Nor never write, regreet, nor reconcile
This louring tempest of your homebred hate;   187
Nor never by advisèd purpose meet   188
To plot, contrive, or complot any ill   189
'Gainst us, our state, our subjects, or our land.

BOLINGBROKE   I swear.

MOWBRAY   And I, to keep all this.

BOLINGBROKE
Norfolk, so far as to mine enemy: 193
By this time, had the King permitted us,
One of our souls had wandered in the air,
Banished this frail sepulcher of our flesh,   196
As now our flesh is banished from this land.
Confess thy treasons ere thou fly the realm.
Since thou hast far to go, bear not along
The clogging burden of a guilty soul.   200

MOWBRAY
No, Bolingbroke. If ever I were traitor,
My name be blotted from the book of life,
And I from heaven banished as from hence!
But what thou art, God, thou, and I do know,
And all too soon, I fear, the King shall rue.
Farewell, my liege. Now no way can I stray;   206
Save back to England, all the world's my way.   *Exit.*

KING RICHARD [*to Gaunt*]
Uncle, even in the glasses of thine eyes   208
I see thy grievèd heart. Thy sad aspect
Hath from the number of his banished years
Plucked four away. [*To Bolingbroke.*] Six frozen
    winters spent,
Return with welcome home from banishment.

BOLINGBROKE
How long a time lies in one little word!
Four lagging winters and four wanton springs   214
End in a word; such is the breath of kings.

GAUNT
I thank my liege that in regard of me
He shortens four years of my son's exile.
But little vantage shall I reap thereby;
For, ere the six years that he hath to spend
Can change their moons and bring their times
    about,
My oil-dried lamp and time-bewasted light   221
Shall be extinct with age and endless night;
My inch of taper will be burnt and done,   223

And blindfold Death not let me see my son.   224

KING RICHARD
Why, uncle, thou hast many years to live.

GAUNT
But not a minute, King, that thou canst give.
Shorten my days thou canst with sullen sorrow,
And pluck nights from me, but not lend a morrow;
Thou canst help Time to furrow me with age,
But stop no wrinkle in his pilgrimage;   230
Thy word is current with him for my death,   231
But dead, thy kingdom cannot buy my breath.   232

KING RICHARD
Thy son is banished upon good advice,
Whereto thy tongue a party verdict gave.   234
Why at our justice seem'st thou then to lour?

GAUNT
Things sweet to taste prove in digestion sour.
You urged me as a judge, but I had rather
You would have bid me argue like a father.
O, had it been a stranger, not my child,
To smooth his fault I should have been more mild.   240
A partial slander sought I to avoid   241
And in the sentence my own life destroyed.
Alas, I looked when some of you should say   243
I was too strict, to make mine own away;   244
But you gave leave to my unwilling tongue
Against my will to do myself this wrong.

KING RICHARD
Cousin, farewell; and, uncle, bid him so.
Six years we banish him, and he shall go.
    [*Flourish. Exit King Richard with his train.*]

AUMERLE [*to Bolingbroke*]
Cousin, farewell. What presence must not know,   249
From where you do remain let paper show.   [*Exit.*] 250

MARSHAL [*to Bolingbroke*]
My lord, no leave take I, for I will ride,   251
As far as land will let me, by your side.
    [*Bolingbroke makes no answer. The Lord Marshal
                                      stands aside.*]

GAUNT [*to Bolingbroke*]
O, to what purpose dost thou hoard thy words,
That thou returnest no greeting to thy friends?

BOLINGBROKE
I have too few to take my leave of you,
When the tongue's office should be prodigal   256
To breathe the abundant dolor of the heart.   257

---

181 **Our part therein** i.e., the duty you owe me as King   187 **louring** threatening, scowling   188 **advisèd** deliberate, premeditated   189 **complot** plot with others   193 **so far** let me say this much   196 **sepulcher of our flesh** i.e., body, the temple or tomb of the soul   200 **clogging** (A clog was a wooden block attached to the leg to hinder movement.)   206 **stray** take the wrong road   208 **glasses** mirrors (here glistening with tears)   214 **wanton** luxuriant   221 **oil-dried** empty of oil   223 **taper** candle

224 **blindfold Death** i.e., *blindfold* because *Death* deprives its victims of their sight and because it is often pictured as an eyeless skull   230 **in his pilgrimage** brought about in time's journey   231 **current** i.e., as good as current coin, valid   232 **dead** i.e., once I am dead. **buy** i.e., restore with a payment   234 **a party verdict** one person's share in a joint verdict   240 **smooth** extenuate   241 **partial slander** accusation of partiality (on behalf of my son)   243 **looked when** expected that, awaited the point at which   244 **to . . . away** in making away with my own (son)   249 **What . . . know** what I cannot learn from you in person   250 **s.d. Exit** (The exit is uncertain; see 1.4.1–4.)   251 **no leave take I** i.e., I will not take my leave of you, my lord; I will not say good-bye   256 **office** function. **prodigal** lavish   257 **To breathe** in breathing

GAUNT
Thy grief is but thy absence for a time.   258
BOLINGBROKE
Joy absent, grief is present for that time.   259
GAUNT
What is six winters? They are quickly gone.
BOLINGBROKE
To men in joy; but grief makes one hour ten.
GAUNT
Call it a travel that thou tak'st for pleasure.   262
BOLINGBROKE
My heart will sigh when I miscall it so,
Which finds it an enforcèd pilgrimage.
GAUNT
The sullen passage of thy weary steps   265
Esteem as foil wherein thou art to set   266
The precious jewel of thy home return.
BOLINGBROKE
Nay, rather every tedious stride I make
Will but remember me what a deal of world   269
I wander from the jewels that I love.
Must I not serve a long apprenticehood
To foreign passages, and in the end,   272
Having my freedom, boast of nothing else
But that I was a journeyman to grief?   274
GAUNT
All places that the eye of heaven visits
Are to a wise man ports and happy havens.
Teach thy necessity to reason thus:
There is no virtue like necessity.
Think not the King did banish thee,
But thou the King. Woe doth the heavier sit   280
Where it perceives it is but faintly borne.   281
Go, say I sent thee forth to purchase honor,   282
And not the King exiled thee; or suppose
Devouring pestilence hangs in our air
And thou art flying to a fresher clime.
Look what thy soul holds dear, imagine it   286
To lie that way thou goest, not whence thou com'st.
Suppose the singing birds musicians,
The grass whereon thou tread'st the presence
    strewed,
The flowers fair ladies, and thy steps no more   289
Than a delightful measure or a dance;   291
For gnarling sorrow hath less power to bite   292
The man that mocks at it and sets it light.   293

BOLINGBROKE
O, who can hold a fire in his hand
By thinking on the frosty Caucasus?   295
Or cloy the hungry edge of appetite
By bare imagination of a feast?
Or wallow naked in December snow
By thinking on fantastic summer's heat?   299
O, no, the apprehension of the good
Gives but the greater feeling to the worse.
Fell Sorrow's tooth doth never rankle more   302
Than when he bites but lanceth not the sore.   303
GAUNT
Come, come, my son, I'll bring thee on thy way.   304
Had I thy youth and cause, I would not stay.   305
BOLINGBROKE
Then, England's ground, farewell. Sweet soil, adieu,
My mother and my nurse that bears me yet!
Where'er I wander, boast of this I can:
Though banished, yet a trueborn Englishman.
                                                        Exeunt.

❦

1.4   *Enter the King, with Bagot, [Green,] etc. at one
            door, and the Lord Aumerle at another.*

KING RICHARD
We did observe.—Cousin Aumerle,   1
How far brought you high Hereford on his way?
AUMERLE
I brought high Hereford, if you call him so,
But to the next highway, and there I left him.   4
KING RICHARD
And say, what store of parting tears were shed?
AUMERLE
Faith, none for me, except the northeast wind,   6
Which then blew bitterly against our faces,
Awaked the sleeping rheum and so by chance   8
Did grace our hollow parting with a tear.   9
KING RICHARD
What said our cousin when you parted with him?
AUMERLE   "Farewell!"
And, for my heart disdainèd that my tongue   12
Should so profane the word, that taught me craft   13
To counterfeit oppression of such grief
That words seemed buried in my sorrow's grave.

---

258 **grief** grievance   259 **grief** unhappiness   262 **travel** (The Quarto spelling, *trauaile*, suggests an interchangeable meaning of "travel" and "labor.")   265 **sullen** (1) melancholy (2) dull   266 **foil** thin metal leaf set behind gems to show off their luster; hence, that which sets something off to advantage   269 **remember** remind.   **a deal of world** a great distance   272 **passages** wanderings, experiences   274 **journeyman** one who labors for daily wages (with a hint also of "one who makes a journey")   280 **But . . . King** i.e., but suppose that you are banishing the King to the moral wilderness his crimes deserve   280–281 **Woe . . . borne** woe itself is unhappy, and hence neutralized, when it perceives it is shrugged off   282 **purchase** acquire   286 **Look what** whatever   289 **the presence strewed** the royal presence chamber strewn with rushes   291 **measure** stately, formal dance   292 **gnarling** snarling, growling   293 **sets it light** regards it as trivial

295 **Caucasus** mountain range now located in the Soviet Union between the Black and Caspian seas   299 **fantastic** imagined   302 **Fell** fierce.   **rankle** cause irritation and festering   303 **lanceth not** does not open the wound (to permit the release of the infection; Bolingbroke's point is that sorrow should be openly confronted, not rationalized or covered over and thus allowed to fester)   304 **bring** escort   305 **stay** linger
1.4. Location: The court.
1 We did observe (The scene begins in the midst of a conversation.)
4 next nearest   **6 for me** on my part.   **except** except that   **8 rheum** watery discharge (i.e., tears)   **9 hollow** insincere   **12 for** because   **13 that** i.e., my disdain. (Aumerle says he pretended to be overcome by grief in order to avoid saying an insincere "Farewell" to Bolingbroke.)

Marry, would the word "farewell" have lengthened
   hours   16
And added years to his short banishment,
He should have had a volume of farewells;
But since it would not, he had none of me.   19

KING RICHARD
He is our cousin, cousin; but 'tis doubt,
When time shall call him home from banishment,
Whether our kinsman come to see his friends.   22
Ourself and Bushy, Bagot here, and Green
Observed his courtship to the common people,
How he did seem to dive into their hearts
With humble and familiar courtesy,
What reverence he did throw away on slaves,
Wooing poor craftsmen with the craft of smiles
And patient underbearing of his fortune,   29
As 'twere to banish their affects with him.   30
Off goes his bonnet to an oyster wench;
A brace of draymen bid God speed him well   32
And had the tribute of his supple knee,
With "Thanks, my countrymen, my loving friends,"
As were our England in reversion his,   35
And he our subjects' next degree in hope.   36

GREEN
Well, he is gone, and with him go these thoughts.   37
Now for the rebels which stand out in Ireland,   38
Expedient manage must be made, my liege,   39
Ere further leisure yield them further means
For their advantage and Your Highness' loss.

KING RICHARD
We will ourself in person to this war.
And, for our coffers with too great a court   43
And liberal largess are grown somewhat light,
We are enforced to farm our royal realm,   45
The revenue whereof shall furnish us
For our affairs in hand. If that come short,
Our substitutes at home shall have blank charters, 48
Whereto, when they shall know what men are rich,
They shall subscribe them for large sums of gold   50
And send them after to supply our wants;   51
For we will make for Ireland presently.   52

Enter Bushy.

Bushy, what news?

BUSHY
Old John of Gaunt is grievous sick, my lord,
Suddenly taken, and hath sent posthaste

To entreat Your Majesty to visit him.
KING RICHARD   Where lies he?
BUSHY   At Ely House.   58
KING RICHARD
Now put it, God, in the physician's mind
To help him to his grave immediately!
The lining of his coffers shall make coats   61
To deck our soldiers for these Irish wars.
Come, gentlemen, let's all go visit him.
Pray God we may make haste and come too late!
ALL   Amen.   *Exeunt.*

❖

2.1   *Enter John of Gaunt sick, with the Duke of York, etc.*

GAUNT
Will the King come, that I may breathe my last
In wholesome counsel to his unstaid youth?   2
YORK
Vex not yourself, nor strive not with your breath,   3
For all in vain comes counsel to his ear.
GAUNT
O, but they say the tongues of dying men
Enforce attention like deep harmony.
Where words are scarce, they are seldom spent in
   vain,
For they breathe truth that breathe their words in
   pain.   8
He that no more must say is listened more   9
   Than they whom youth and ease have taught to
     glose.   10
More are men's ends marked than their lives before. 11
   The setting sun, and music at the close,
As the last taste of sweets, is sweetest last,
Writ in remembrance more than things long past.
Though Richard my life's counsel would not hear,   15
My death's sad tale may yet undeaf his ear.   16
YORK
No, it is stopped with other, flattering sounds,
As praises, of whose taste the wise are fond;   18
Lascivious meters, to whose venom sound   19
The open ear of youth doth always listen;
Report of fashions in proud Italy,   21
Whose manners still our tardy-apish nation   22
Limps after in base imitation.
Where doth the world thrust forth a vanity—

So it be new, there's no respect how vile—   25
That is not quickly buzzed into his ears?
Then all too late comes counsel to be heard
Where will doth mutiny with wit's regard.   28
Direct not him whose way himself will choose.
'Tis breath thou lack'st, and that breath wilt thou
    lose.

GAUNT
Methinks I am a prophet new inspired,
And thus expiring do foretell of him:
His rash fierce blaze of riot cannot last,   33
For violent fires soon burn out themselves;
Small showers last long, but sudden storms are short;
He tires betimes that spurs too fast betimes;   36
With eager feeding food doth choke the feeder;
Light vanity, insatiate cormorant,   38
Consuming means, soon preys upon itself.   39
This royal throne of kings, this sceptered isle,
This earth of majesty, this seat of Mars,   41
This other Eden, demi-paradise,
This fortress built by Nature for herself
Against infection and the hand of war,   44
This happy breed of men, this little world,   45
This precious stone set in the silver sea,
Which serves it in the office of a wall   47
Or as a moat defensive to a house,
Against the envy of less happier lands,
This blessed plot, this earth, this realm, this
    England,
This nurse, this teeming womb of royal kings,   51
Feared by their breed and famous by their birth,   52
Renownèd for their deeds as far from home
For Christian service and true chivalry
As is the sepulcher in stubborn Jewry   55
Of the world's ransom, blessèd Mary's Son,
This land of such dear souls, this dear dear land,
Dear for her reputation through the world,
Is now leased out—I die pronouncing it—
Like to a tenement or pelting farm.   60
England, bound in with the triumphant sea,   61
Whose rocky shore beats back the envious siege
Of wat'ry Neptune, is now bound in with shame,   63
With inky blots and rotten parchment bonds.   64
That England that was wont to conquer others
Hath made a shameful conquest of itself.
Ah, would the scandal vanish with my life,
How happy then were my ensuing death!

*Enter King [Richard] and Queen, [Aumerle,
Bushy, Green, Bagot, Ross, and Willoughby,] etc.*

YORK
The King is come. Deal mildly with his youth,
For young hot colts being reined do rage the more.
QUEEN
How fares our noble uncle Lancaster?
KING RICHARD
What comfort, man? How is 't with agèd Gaunt?
GAUNT
O, how that name befits my composition!   73
Old Gaunt indeed, and gaunt in being old.
Within me grief hath kept a tedious fast,
And who abstains from meat that is not gaunt?   76
For sleeping England long time have I watched;   77
Watching breeds leanness, leanness is all gaunt.
The pleasure that some fathers feed upon
Is my strict fast—I mean, my children's looks—   80
And, therein fasting, hast thou made me gaunt.   81
Gaunt am I for the grave, gaunt as a grave,
Whose hollow womb inherits naught but bones.   83
KING RICHARD
Can sick men play so nicely with their names?   84
GAUNT
No, misery makes sport to mock itself.   85
Since thou dost seek to kill my name in me,   86
I mock my name, great King, to flatter thee.   87
KING RICHARD
Should dying men flatter with those that live?   88
GAUNT
No, no, men living flatter those that die.   89
KING RICHARD
Thou, now a-dying, sayest thou flatterest me.
GAUNT
O, no, thou diest, though I the sicker be.
KING RICHARD
I am in health, I breathe, and see thee ill.
GAUNT
Now He that made me knows I see thee ill;
Ill in myself to see, and in thee seeing ill.   94
Thy deathbed is no lesser than thy land,
Wherein thou liest in reputation sick;
And thou, too careless patient as thou art,
Commit'st thy anointed body to the cure
Of those physicians that first wounded thee.   99
A thousand flatterers sit within thy crown,
Whose compass is no bigger than thy head,   101
And yet, encagèd in so small a verge,   102
The waste is no whit lesser than thy land.   103

---

25 So so long as. **there's no respect** it makes no difference   **28 will
. . . regard** natural inclination rebels against what reason esteems
33 riot profligacy   **36 betimes** soon, early   **38 Light vanity** frivolous
dissipation.   **cormorant** glutton. (Literally, a voracious seabird.)
39 means i.e., means of sustenance   **41 earth of majesty** land fit for
kings.   **seat of Mars** residence of the god of war   **44 infection** (1)
plague (2) moral pollution   **45 breed** race   **47 office** function
51 teeming fruitful   **52 by their breed** for their ancestral reputation
for prowess   **55 stubborn Jewry** i.e., Judea, called stubborn because
it resisted Christianity   **60 tenement** land or property held by a tenant.   **pelting** paltry   **61 bound in** bordered, surrounded   **63 bound
in** legally constrained   **64 blots . . . bonds** i.e., the blank charters

73 composition constitution   **76 meat** food   **77 watched** kept watch
at night, been vigilant   **80 Is . . . fast** is something I must forgo
81 therein fasting i.e., since I am starved of that pleasure   **83 inherits**
possesses, will receive   **84 nicely** (1) ingeniously (2) triflingly   **85 to
mock** of mocking   **86 kill . . . me** i.e., by banishing my son   **87 I
. . . thee** i.e., I disparage what you seek to overcome in order to flatter your greatness   **88 flatter with** try to please   **89 flatter** i.e., are
attentive to, offer comfort to   **94 Ill . . . ill** I, seeing poorly, by virtue
of my failing sight, and seeing the evil in you   **99 physicians** i.e., the
King's favorites   **101 compass** circle, circumference   **102 verge** (1)
circle, ring (2) the compass about the King's court, which extended
for twelve miles   **103 waste** (1) waist, circumference (2) that which is
destroyed (with a quibble on the legal meaning of *waste*, "damage
done to property by a tenant").   **whit** bit, speck

O, had thy grandsire with a prophet's eye   104
Seen how his son's son should destroy his sons,   105
From forth thy reach he would have laid thy shame,   106
Deposing thee before thou wert possessed,   107
Which art possessed now to depose thyself.   108
Why, cousin, wert thou regent of the world,   109
It were a shame to let this land by lease;
But, for thy world enjoying but this land,   111
Is it not more than shame to shame it so?
Landlord of England art thou now, not king.   113
Thy state of law is bondslave to the law,   114
And thou—

KING RICHARD A lunatic lean-witted fool,
Presuming on an ague's privilege,   116
Darest with thy frozen admonition   117
Make pale our cheek, chasing the royal blood
With fury from his native residence.   119
Now, by my seat's right royal majesty,   120
Wert thou not brother to great Edward's son,
This tongue that runs so roundly in thy head   122
Should run thy head from thy unreverent shoulders.   123

GAUNT
O, spare me not, my brother Edward's son,
For that I was his father Edward's son!   125
That blood already, like the pelican,   126
Hast thou tapped out and drunkenly caroused.   127
My brother Gloucester, plain well-meaning soul—
Whom fair befall in heaven 'mongst happy souls!—   129
May be a precedent and witness good
That thou respect'st not spilling Edward's blood.   131
Join with the present sickness that I have,
And thy unkindness be like crooked age   133
To crop at once a too-long-withered flower.   134
Live in thy shame, but die not shame with thee!   135
These words hereafter thy tormentors be!—
Convey me to my bed, then to my grave.
Love they to live that love and honor have.   138

Exit [borne off by his attendants].

KING RICHARD
And let them die that age and sullens have,   139
For both hast thou, and both become the grave.   140

YORK
I do beseech Your Majesty, impute his words
To wayward sickliness and age in him.
He loves you, on my life, and holds you dear
As Harry Duke of Hereford, were he here.   144

KING RICHARD
Right, you say true. As Hereford's love, so his;   145
As theirs, so mine; and all be as it is.

[Enter Northumberland.]

NORTHUMBERLAND
My liege, old Gaunt commends him to Your
Majesty.

KING RICHARD
What says he?

NORTHUMBERLAND   Nay, nothing, all is said.
His tongue is now a stringless instrument;
Words, life, and all, old Lancaster hath spent.

YORK
Be York the next that must be bankrupt so!
Though death be poor, it ends a mortal woe.   152

KING RICHARD
The ripest fruit first falls, and so doth he;
His time is spent, our pilgrimage must be.   154
So much for that. Now for our Irish wars:
We must supplant those rough rug-headed kerns,   156
Which live like venom where no venom else   157
But only they have privilege to live.   158
And, for these great affairs do ask some charge,   159
Towards our assistance we do seize to us
The plate, coin, revenues, and movables   161
Whereof our uncle Gaunt did stand possessed.

YORK
How long shall I be patient? Ah, how long
Shall tender duty make me suffer wrong?
Not Gloucester's death, nor Hereford's banishment,
Nor Gaunt's rebukes, nor England's private wrongs,   166
Nor the prevention of poor Bolingbroke   167
About his marriage, nor my own disgrace,   168
Have ever made me sour my patient cheek
Or bend one wrinkle on my sovereign's face.   170
I am the last of noble Edward's sons,
Of whom thy father, Prince of Wales, was first.
In war was never lion raged more fierce,   173
In peace was never gentle lamb more mild,
Than was that young and princely gentleman.

---

104 **grandsire** i.e., Edward III   105 **destroy his sons** (1) destroy Edward III's sons, Richard's uncles (2) destroy Richard's own heritage   106 **From . . . shame** he would have put the matter you have shamefully handled out of your reach   107 **Deposing** dispossessing.   **possessed** put in possession of the crown   108 **possessed** seized by a diabolical spirit, an obsession   109 **cousin** kinsman.   **regent** ruler   111 **But . . . land** i.e., but since you enjoy as your domain only this land of England (rather than the whole world)   113 **Landlord** i.e., one who leases out a property   114 **Thy . . . the law** i.e., your legal status as King is now subservient to and at the mercy of the law governing contracts, such as blank charters   116 **an ague's privilege** i.e., a sick person's right to be testy   117 **frozen** (1) chilly (2) caused by a chill   119 **his** its   120 **seat's** throne's   122–123 **runs . . . run** runs on, talks . . . drive, chase   122 **roundly** unceremoniously, bluntly   123 **unreverent** irreverent, disrespectful   125 **For that** because   126 **pelican** (The pelican was thought to feed its ingrateful and murderous young with its own blood.   **tapped out** drawn as from a tapped barrel.   **caroused** gulped, quaffed   129 **Whom fair befall** to whom may good come   131 **thou respect'st not** you care nothing about   133 **unkindness** unnatural behavior   134 **crop** cut   135 **die . . . thee** i.e., may your shame live after you   138 **Love they** let them desire   139 **sullens** sullenness, melancholy   140 **become** suit

144 **As** i.e., as he would love. (But see the next note.)   145 **Right . . . his** (Richard deliberately takes the opposite of what York had intended to say; Richard gibes that Gaunt is as little fond of the King as is Hereford.)   152 **death** the state of being dead   154 **our . . . be** i.e., our journey through life is yet to be completed but will also end   156 **supplant** expel (from the English territories of Ireland).   **rug-headed** shaggy-haired.   **kerns** light-armed Irish foot soldiers   157–158 **where . . . live** (Allusion to the freedom of Ireland from snakes, traditionally ascribed to Saint Patrick.)   **no venom** no poisonous snakes   159 **for** because.   **ask some charge** require some expenditure   161 **movables** personal property   166 **Gaunt's rebukes** i.e., the rebukes given to Gaunt   167–168 **prevention . . . marriage** (The *Chronicles* report that Richard had forestalled Bolingbroke's intended marriage with the Duke de Berri's daughter.)   170 **bend . . . on** once frown at   173 **was . . . fierce** never was there a lion more fiercely enraged

His face thou hast, for even so looked he,
Accomplished with the number of thy hours;   177
But when he frowned, it was against the French
And not against his friends. His noble hand
Did win what he did spend, and spent not that
Which his triumphant father's hand had won.
His hands were guilty of no kindred blood,   182
But bloody with the enemies of his kin.
O Richard! York is too far gone with grief,
Or else he never would compare between.   185

KING RICHARD
Why, uncle, what's the matter?

YORK   O my liege,
Pardon me, if you please; if not, I, pleased
Not to be pardoned, am content withal.
Seek you to seize and grip into your hands   188
The royalties and rights of banished Hereford?   190
Is not Gaunt dead? And doth not Hereford live?
Was not Gaunt just? And is not Harry true?
Did not the one deserve to have an heir?
Is not his heir a well-deserving son?
Take Hereford's rights away, and take from Time   195
His charters and his customary rights;   196
Let not tomorrow then ensue today;   197
Be not thyself; for how art thou a king
But by fair sequence and succession?
Now, afore God—God forbid I say true!—
If you do wrongfully seize Hereford's rights,
Call in the letters patents that he hath   202
By his attorneys general to sue   203
His livery, and deny his offered homage,   204
You pluck a thousand dangers on your head,
You lose a thousand well-disposèd hearts,
And prick my tender patience to those thoughts   207
Which honor and allegiance cannot think.

KING RICHARD
Think what you will, we seize into our hands
His plate, his goods, his money, and his lands.

YORK
I'll not be by the while. My liege, farewell.   211
What will ensue hereof there's none can tell;
But by bad courses may be understood   213
That their events can never fall out good.   Exit. 214

KING RICHARD
Go, Bushy, to the Earl of Wiltshire straight.   215
Bid him repair to us to Ely House   216
To see this business. Tomorrow next   217
We will for Ireland, and 'tis time, I trow.   218

And we create, in absence of ourself,
Our uncle York Lord Governor of England,   177
For he is just and always loved us well.—
Come on, our queen. Tomorrow must we part.
Be merry, for our time of stay is short.   223
    [Flourish.] Exeunt King and Queen [with attendants].
    Manet Northumberland [with Willoughby and Ross].

NORTHUMBERLAND
Well, lords, the Duke of Lancaster is dead.

ROSS
And living too, for now his son is duke.

WILLOUGHBY
Barely in title, not in revenues.

NORTHUMBERLAND
Richly in both, if justice had her right.

ROSS
My heart is great, but it must break with silence,   228
Ere 't be disburdened with a liberal tongue.   229

NORTHUMBERLAND
Nay, speak thy mind; and let him ne'er speak more
That speaks thy words again to do thee harm!

WILLOUGHBY
Tends that thou wouldst speak to the Duke of
    Hereford?   232
If it be so, out with it boldly, man.
Quick is mine ear to hear of good towards him.

ROSS
No good at all that I can do for him,
Unless you call it good to pity him,
Bereft and gelded of his patrimony.   237

NORTHUMBERLAND
Now, afore God, 'tis shame such wrongs are borne
In him, a royal prince, and many more
Of noble blood in this declining land.
The King is not himself, but basely led
By flatterers; and what they will inform   242
Merely in hate 'gainst any of us all,   243
That will the King severely prosecute
'Gainst us, our lives, our children, and our heirs.

ROSS
The commons hath he pilled with grievous taxes,   246
And quite lost their hearts; the nobles hath he fined
For ancient quarrels, and quite lost their hearts.

WILLOUGHBY
And daily new exactions are devised,
As blanks, benevolences, and I wot not what.   250
But what i' God's name doth become of this?   251

NORTHUMBERLAND
Wars hath not wasted it, for warred he hath not,
But basely yielded upon compromise
That which his noble ancestors achieved with
    blows.

177 Accomplished . . . hours i.e., when he was your age   182 kindred blood blood of one's relatives   185 compare between draw comparisons   188 withal with that, nonetheless   190 royalties privileges granted through the King and belonging, in this case, to a member of the royal family   195 Take . . . and take i.e., if you take . . . you take   196 His Time's   197 ensue follow   202–204 Call . . . livery i.e., revoke the royal grant giving him the privilege to sue through his attorneys for possession of his inheritance   204 deny refuse. homage avowal of allegiance (by which ceremony he would be able legally to secure his inheritance)   207 prick i.e., incite   211 by nearby, present   213 by concerning   214 events outcomes   215 Earl of Wiltshire (The King's Lord Treasurer and one of his notorious favorites.)   216 repair go   217 see see to.   Tomorrow next tomorrow   218 trow believe

223 s.d. Manet remains onstage   228 great i.e., great with sorrow   229 liberal unrestrained, freely speaking   232 Tends . . . to does what you wish to say concern   237 gelded i.e., deprived. (Literally, castrated.)   242 inform charge, report as spies   243 Merely in hate out of pure hatred   246 pilled plundered   250 blanks blank charters. benevolences forced loans to the crown (not actually employed until considerably later, in 1473).   wot know   251 this i.e., this unjustly collected revenue

More hath he spent in peace than they in wars.

ROSS
The Earl of Wiltshire hath the realm in farm.   256

WILLOUGHBY
The King's grown bankrupt, like a broken man.   257

NORTHUMBERLAND
Reproach and dissolution hangeth over him.

ROSS
He hath not money for these Irish wars,
His burdenous taxations notwithstanding,
But by the robbing of the banished Duke.

NORTHUMBERLAND
His noble kinsman. Most degenerate king!
But, lords, we hear this fearful tempest sing,
Yet seek no shelter to avoid the storm;
We see the wind sit sore upon our sails,   265
And yet we strike not, but securely perish.   266

ROSS
We see the very wrack that we must suffer,   267
And unavoided is the danger now   268
For suffering so the causes of our wrack.   269

NORTHUMBERLAND
Not so. Even through the hollow eyes of death   270
I spy life peering; but I dare not say
How near the tidings of our comfort is.

WILLOUGHBY
Nay, let us share thy thoughts, as thou dost ours.

ROSS
Be confident to speak, Northumberland.
We three are but thyself, and speaking so
Thy words are but as thoughts. Therefore be bold.

NORTHUMBERLAND
Then thus: I have from Port le Blanc,
A bay in Brittany, received intelligence
That Harry Duke of Hereford, Rainold Lord
   Cobham,
. . . .   280
That late broke from the Duke of Exeter,   281
His brother, Archbishop late of Canterbury,   282
Sir Thomas Erpingham, Sir John Ramston,
Sir John Norbery, Sir Robert Waterton, and Francis
   Coint,
All these well furnished by the Duke of Brittany
With eight tall ships, three thousand men of war,   286
Are making hither with all due expedience   287
And shortly mean to touch our northern shore.

Perhaps they had ere this, but that they stay   289
The first departing of the King for Ireland.   290
If then we shall shake off our slavish yoke,
Imp out our drooping country's broken wing,   292
Redeem from broking pawn the blemished crown,   293
Wipe off the dust that hides our scepter's gilt,   294
And make high majesty look like itself,
Away with me in post to Ravenspurgh;   296
But if you faint, as fearing to do so,   297
Stay and be secret, and myself will go.

ROSS
To horse, to horse! Urge doubts to them that fear.

WILLOUGHBY
Hold out my horse, and I will first be there.   *Exeunt.* 300

2.2   *Enter the Queen, Bushy, [and] Bagot.*

BUSHY
Madam, Your Majesty is too much sad.
You promised, when you parted with the King,   2
To lay aside life-harming heaviness   3
And entertain a cheerful disposition.   4

QUEEN
To please the King I did; to please myself
I cannot do it. Yet I know no cause
Why I should welcome such a guest as grief,
Save bidding farewell to so sweet a guest
As my sweet Richard. Yet again methinks
Some unborn sorrow ripe in Fortune's womb
Is coming towards me, and my inward soul
With nothing trembles. At some thing it grieves
More than with parting from my lord the King.

BUSHY
Each substance of a grief hath twenty shadows,   14
Which shows like grief itself but is not so;
For sorrow's eyes, glazèd with blinding tears,
Divides one thing entire to many objects,   17
Like perspectives, which rightly gazed upon   18
Show nothing but confusion, eyed awry   19
Distinguish form. So your sweet Majesty,   20
Looking awry upon your lord's departure,   21

---

256 **in farm** on lease   257 **broken** financially ruined   265 **sore** sorely, grievously   266 **strike** (1) furl the sails (2) strike blows.   **securely** heedlessly, overconfidently   267 **wrack** ruin   268 **unavoided** unavoidable   269 **suffering** permitting   270 **eyes** eye sockets   280 . . . (A line is probably missing here, perhaps because of censorship. From information contained in Holinshed, it may have read something like ''Thomas, son and heir to the Earl of Arundel'' or ''The son of Richard, Earl of Arundel.'')   281 **late broke from** lately escaped from the custody of. (Holinshed records that ''the Earl of Arundel's son, named Thomas, which was kept in the Duke of Exeter's house, escaped out of the realm . . . and went to his uncle Thomas Arundel, late Archbishop of Canterbury.'')   282 **His** i.e., the Earl of Arundel's.   **late** until recently   286 **tall** stately.   **men of war** troops   287 **expedience** expedition, speed

289–290 **stay . . . King** wait until the King departs   292 **Imp out** piece out. (A term from falconry, meaning to attach new feathers to a disabled wing of a bird.)   293 **broking pawn** the security held by a pawnbroker   294 **gilt** gold (with pun on *guilt*)   296 **post** haste.   **Ravenspurgh** a busy seaport in Yorkshire on the Humber River, destroyed since by the sea   297 **faint** are fainthearted   300 **Hold . . .** and if my horse holds out
2.2. Location: The court. According to Holinshed, the Queen remained at Windsor Castle when Richard left for Ireland.
2 **with** from   3 **heaviness** melancholy   4 **entertain** put on   14 **Each . . . shadows** i.e., for every real grief there exist twenty imagined ones   17 **thing entire to** complete thing into   18 **perspectives** (In lines 16–17, Bushy seems to have in mind a glass with a multifaceted lens, multiplying images of the object being viewed; in lines 18–20, *perspectives* are pictures of figures made to appear distorted or confused, except when viewed obliquely, *eyed awry*.)   **rightly** directly, straight   19 **awry** obliquely   20 **Distinguish form** make the form distinct and normal   21 **awry** i.e., mistakenly, distortedly

Find shapes of grief more than himself to wail, 22
Which, looked on as it is, is naught but shadows
Of what it is not. Then, thrice-gracious Queen,
More than your lord's departure weep not. More is
    not seen,
Or if it be, 'tis with false sorrow's eye,
Which for things true weeps things imaginary. 27

QUEEN
It may be so, but yet my inward soul
Persuades me it is otherwise. Howe'er it be,
I cannot but be sad—so heavy sad
As, though on thinking on no thought I think, 31
Makes me with heavy nothing faint and shrink. 32

BUSHY
'Tis nothing but conceit, my gracious lady. 33

QUEEN
'Tis nothing less. Conceit is still derived 34
From some forefather grief. Mine is not so,
For nothing hath begot my something grief, 36
Or something hath the nothing that I grieve. 37
'Tis in reversion that I do possess; 38
But what it is, that is not yet known what, 39
I cannot name. 'Tis nameless woe, I wot. 40

[Enter Green.]

GREEN
God save Your Majesty! And well met, gentlemen.
I hope the King is not yet shipped for Ireland.

QUEEN
Why hopest thou so? 'Tis better hope he is,
For his designs crave haste, his haste good hope.
Then wherefore dost thou hope he is not shipped?

GREEN
That he, our hope, might have retired his power, 46
And driven into despair an enemy's hope,
Who strongly hath set footing in this land.
The banished Bolingbroke repeals himself 49
And with uplifted arms is safe arrived 50
At Ravenspurgh.

QUEEN   Now God in heaven forbid!

GREEN
Ah, madam, 'tis too true; and that is worse, 52
The lord Northumberland, his son young Harry
    Percy,
The lords of Ross, Beaumont, and Willoughby,
With all their powerful friends, are fled to him.

BUSHY
Why have you not proclaimed Northumberland

And all the rest revolted faction traitors? 57

GREEN
We have, whereupon the Earl of Worcester
Hath broken his staff, resigned his stewardship, 59
And all the household servants fled with him
To Bolingbroke.

QUEEN
So, Green, thou art the midwife to my woe,
And Bolingbroke my sorrow's dismal heir. 63
Now hath my soul brought forth her prodigy, 64
And I, a gasping new-delivered mother,
Have woe to woe, sorrow to sorrow joined.

BUSHY
Despair not, madam.

QUEEN   Who shall hinder me?
I will despair, and be at enmity
With cozening hope. He is a flatterer, 69
A parasite, a keeper-back of death
Who gently would dissolve the bonds of life 71
Which false hope lingers in extremity. 72

[Enter York.]

GREEN   Here comes the Duke of York.

QUEEN
With signs of war about his agèd neck. 74
O, full of careful business are his looks! 75
Uncle, for God's sake, speak comfortable words. 76

YORK
Should I do so, I should belie my thoughts.
Comfort's in heaven, and we are on the earth,
Where nothing lives but crosses, cares, and grief. 79
Your husband, he is gone to save far off, 80
Whilst others come to make him lose at home.
Here am I left to underprop his land, 82
Who, weak with age, cannot support myself.
Now comes the sick hour that his surfeit made;
Now shall he try his friends that flattered him. 85

[Enter a Servingman.]

SERVINGMAN
My lord, your son was gone before I came. 86

YORK
He was? Why, so. Go all which way it will!
The nobles they are fled, the commons they are
    cold,
And will, I fear, revolt on Hereford's side.
Sirrah, get thee to Pleshey, to my sister Gloucester; 90
Bid her send me presently a thousand pound. 91

---

22 **himself** i.e., the grief itself. **wail** bewail 27 **for** in place of. **weeps** weeps for 31–32 **As . . . shrink** that, though I seem to be thinking of nothing, my "nothing" is so *heavy* or saddening that I faint and fall back under the weight 33 **conceit** fancy 34 **'Tis nothing less** i.e., it is anything but that. **still** always 36 **something** i.e., substantial 37 **something . . . grieve** the unsubstantial grief, the nothing, that I grieve about has something to it, some substance 38–40 **'Tis . . . name** i.e., my grief is like a legacy that will come to me at some future time, but I cannot tell its nature yet 40 **wot** know, assume 46 **retired** drawn back. **power** army 49 **repeals** recalls (from exile) 50 **uplifted arms** brandished weapons 52 **that** what

57 **rest** rest of the 59 **broken his staff** broken his badge of office (in token of resignation as Lord High Steward. Worcester is brother of the Earl of Northumberland.) 63 **heir** offspring 64 **prodigy** monstrous birth 69 **cozening** cheating. **He** i.e., false hope 71 **Who** i.e., death 72 **lingers** causes to linger 74 **signs of war** i.e., a piece of armor called the gorget, an iron collar that could be worn with ordinary clothes 75 **careful business** worried preoccupation 76 **comfortable** affording comfort 79 **crosses** obstacles, obstructions 80 **save far off** i.e., defend his rule in Ireland 82 **underprop** prop up, support 85 **try** test 86 **your son** i.e., the Duke of Aumerle 90 **sister** i.e., sister-in-law 91 **presently** immediately

Hold, take my ring.   92

SERVINGMAN
My lord, I had forgot to tell your lordship:
Today, as I came by, I callèd there—
But I shall grieve you to report the rest.

YORK   What is 't, knave?   96

SERVINGMAN
An hour before I came, the Duchess died.

YORK
God for his mercy, what a tide of woes
Comes rushing on this woeful land at once!
I know not what to do. I would to God,
So my untruth had not provoked him to it,   101
The King had cut off my head with my brother's.   102
What, are there no posts dispatched for Ireland?
How shall we do for money for these wars?
Come, sister—cousin, I would say—pray pardon
   me.
Go, fellow, get thee home. Provide some carts
And bring away the armor that is there.
                         [Exit Servingman.]
Gentlemen, will you go muster men?
If I know how or which way to order these affairs
Thus disorderly thrust into my hands,
Never believe me. Both are my kinsmen:
Th' one is my sovereign, whom both my oath
And duty bids defend; t'other again
Is my kinsman, whom the King hath wronged,
Whom conscience and my kindred bids to right.   115
Well, somewhat we must do. Come, cousin,   116
I'll dispose of you. Gentlemen,   117
Go, muster up your men, and meet me presently
At Berkeley. I should to Pleshey too,   119
But time will not permit. All is uneven,
And everything is left at six and seven.   121
                  Exeunt Duke [of York], Queen.
                  Manent Bushy, [Bagot,] Green.

BUSHY
The wind sits fair for news to go to Ireland,
But none returns. For us to levy power
Proportionable to the enemy
Is all unpossible.

GREEN
Besides, our nearness to the King in love
Is near the hate of those love not the King.   127

BAGOT
And that is the wavering commons, for their love
Lies in their purses, and whoso empties them
By so much fills their hearts with deadly hate.

BUSHY
Wherein the King stands generally condemned.

BAGOT
If judgment lie in them, then so do we,   132
Because we ever have been near the King.   133

GREEN
Well, I will for refuge straight to Bristol Castle.
The Earl of Wiltshire is already there.

BUSHY
Thither will I with you, for little office   136
Will the hateful commons perform for us,   137
Except like curs to tear us all to pieces.
[To Bagot.] Will you go along with us?

BAGOT
No, I will to Ireland to His Majesty.
Farewell. If heart's presages be not vain,
We three here part that ne'er shall meet again.

BUSHY
That's as York thrives to beat back Bolingbroke.   143

GREEN
Alas, poor duke! The task he undertakes
Is numbering sands and drinking oceans dry.
Where one on his side fights, thousands will fly.
Farewell at once, for once, for all, and ever.

BUSHY
Well, we may meet again.

BAGOT   I fear me, never.
                            [Exeunt.]

❧

2.3   *Enter [Bolingbroke, Duke of] Hereford, [and]*
         Northumberland [with forces].

BOLINGBROKE
How far is it, my lord, to Berkeley now?

NORTHUMBERLAND   Believe me, noble lord,
I am a stranger here in Gloucestershire.
These high wild hills and rough uneven ways
Draws out our miles and makes them wearisome;
And yet your fair discourse hath been as sugar,
Making the hard way sweet and delectable.
But I bethink me what a weary way
From Ravenspurgh to Cotswold will be found   9
In Ross and Willoughby, wanting your company,   10
Which, I protest, hath very much beguiled
The tediousness and process of my travel.   12
But theirs is sweetened with the hope to have
The present benefit which I possess;
And hope to joy is little less in joy
Than hope enjoyed. By this the weary lords   16
Shall make their way seem short, as mine hath done
By sight of what I have: your noble company.

BOLINGBROKE
Of much less value is my company
Than your good words. But who comes here?

Enter Harry Percy.

NORTHUMBERLAND
It is my son, young Harry Percy,
Sent from my brother Worcester whencesoever.   22
Harry, how fares your uncle?   23
PERCY
I had thought, my lord, to have learned his health
of you.
NORTHUMBERLAND   Why, is he not with the Queen?
PERCY
No, my good lord. He hath forsook the court,
Broken his staff of office, and dispersed
The household of the King.
NORTHUMBERLAND   What was his reason?
He was not so resolved when last we spake
together.
PERCY
Because your lordship was proclaimèd traitor.
But he, my lord, is gone to Ravenspurgh
To offer service to the Duke of Hereford,
And sent me over by Berkeley to discover
What power the Duke of York had levied there,
Then with directions to repair to Ravenspurgh.   35
NORTHUMBERLAND
Have you forgot the Duke of Hereford, boy?   36
PERCY
No, my good lord, for that is not forgot
Which ne'er I did remember. To my knowledge
I never in my life did look on him.
NORTHUMBERLAND
Then learn to know him now. This is the Duke.
PERCY
My gracious lord, I tender you my service,   41
Such as it is, being tender, raw, and young,
Which elder days shall ripen and confirm
To more approvèd service and desert.   44
BOLINGBROKE
I thank thee, gentle Percy, and be sure
I count myself in nothing else so happy
As in a soul remembering my good friends;   47
And as my fortune ripens with thy love,
It shall be still thy true love's recompense.   49
My heart this covenant makes, my hand thus
seals it.   *[He offers Percy his hand.]*
NORTHUMBERLAND
How far is it to Berkeley? And what stir   51
Keeps good old York there with his men of war?

PERCY
There stands the castle by yon tuft of trees,
Manned with three hundred men, as I have heard,
And in it are the lords of York, Berkeley, and
Seymour,
None else of name and noble estimate.   56

[Enter Ross and Willoughby.]

NORTHUMBERLAND
Here come the lords of Ross and Willoughby,
Bloody with spurring, fiery red with haste.   58
BOLINGBROKE
Welcome, my lords. I wot your love pursues   59
A banished traitor. All my treasury
Is yet but unfelt thanks, which, more enriched,   61
Shall be your love and labor's recompense.
ROSS
Your presence makes us rich, most noble lord.
WILLOUGHBY
And far surmounts our labor to attain it.
BOLINGBROKE
Evermore thank's the exchequer of the poor,   65
Which, till my infant fortune comes to years,   66
Stands for my bounty. But who comes here?   67

[Enter Berkeley.]

NORTHUMBERLAND
It is my lord of Berkeley, as I guess.
BERKELEY
My lord of Hereford, my message is to you.
BOLINGBROKE
My lord, my answer is—to "Lancaster";   70
And I am come to seek that name in England,
And I must find that title in your tongue
Before I make reply to aught you say.
BERKELEY
Mistake me not, my lord, 'tis not my meaning
To raze one title of your honor out.   75
To you, my lord, I come, what lord you will,
From the most gracious regent of this land,
The Duke of York, to know what pricks you on   78
To take advantage of the absent time   79
And fright our native peace with self-borne arms.   80

[Enter York.]

BOLINGBROKE
I shall not need transport my words by you;

---

56 estimate rank   **58 spurring** i.e., hard riding   **59 wot** am aware that. (Bolingbroke graciously indicates his awareness of the risk they are taking in supporting him.)   **61 unfelt** impalpable, expressed in words, not gifts.   **which** i.e., which treasury.   **more enriched** i.e., with still more thanks added, or, with substantial gifts at a later date   **65 Evermore . . . poor** "thank you" is always the exchequer of the poor, i.e., the only means they have to repay favors   **66 comes to years** reaches maturity   **67 Stands for** serves in place of   **70 "Lancaster"** (Bolingbroke will enter into no negotiations unless his proper title, taken away by Richard, is given him.)   **75 raze** scrape (or perhaps *rase*, "erase")   **78 pricks you on** incites you   **79 the absent time** i.e., the time of the King's absence   **80 self-borne** i.e., borne for oneself, not for the King (also *self-born*, "originating in the self")

22 whencesoever from wherever he is   **23 your uncle** i.e., the Earl of Worcester   **35 directions** instructions.   **repair** go   **36 boy** (A rebuke for not respectfully greeting Bolingbroke, though historically Percy was two years Bolingbroke's senior.)   **41 my service** (Presumably Percy kneels to Bolingbroke, and so do Ross and Willoughby when they enter.)   **44 approvèd** proven, demonstrated   **47 in a** in my   **49 still** always   **51 stir** action

Here comes His Grace in person.—My noble uncle!
                                        [*He kneels.*]
YORK
  Show me thy humble heart, and not thy knee,
  Whose duty is deceivable and false.   84
BOLINGBROKE   My gracious uncle—
YORK   Tut, tut!
  Grace me no grace, nor uncle me no uncle.
  I am no traitor's uncle; and that word "grace"
  In an ungracious mouth is but profane.
  Why have those banished and forbidden legs
  Dared once to touch a dust of England's ground?   91
  But then more "why?" Why have they dared to
    march
  So many miles upon her peaceful bosom,
  Frighting her pale-faced villages with war
  And ostentation of despisèd arms?   95
  Com'st thou because the anointed King is hence?
  Why, foolish boy, the King is left behind,
  And in my loyal bosom lies his power.
  Were I but now the lord of such hot youth
  As when brave Gaunt, thy father, and myself
  Rescued the Black Prince, that young Mars of men,   101
  From forth the ranks of many thousand French,
  O, then how quickly should this arm of mine,
  Now prisoner to the palsy, chastise thee
  And minister correction to thy fault!
BOLINGBROKE
  My gracious uncle, let me know my fault.
  On what condition stands it and wherein?   107
YORK
  Even in condition of the worst degree:
  In gross rebellion and detested treason.
  Thou art a banished man, and here art come
  Before the expiration of thy time
  In braving arms against thy sovereign.   112
BOLINGBROKE [*standing*]
  As I was banished, I was banished Hereford;
  But as I come, I come for Lancaster.   114
  And, noble uncle, I beseech Your Grace
  Look on my wrongs with an indifferent eye.   116
  You are my father, for methinks in you
  I see old Gaunt alive. O, then, my father,
  Will you permit that I shall stand condemned   119
  A wandering vagabond, my rights and royalties   120
  Plucked from my arms perforce and given away
  To upstart unthrifts? Wherefore was I born?   122
  If that my cousin king be King in England,
  It must be granted I am Duke of Lancaster.
  You have a son, Aumerle, my noble cousin;
  Had you first died, and he been thus trod down,   126

  He should have found his uncle Gaunt a father
  To rouse his wrongs and chase them to the bay.   128
  I am denied to sue my livery here,   129
  And yet my letters patents give me leave.   130
  My father's goods are all distrained and sold,   131
  And these, and all, are all amiss employed.
  What would you have me do? I am a subject,
  And I challenge law. Attorneys are denied me,   134
  And therefore personally I lay my claim
  To my inheritance of free descent.   136
NORTHUMBERLAND
  The noble Duke hath been too much abused.
ROSS
  It stands Your Grace upon to do him right.   138
WILLOUGHBY
  Base men by his endowments are made great.   139
YORK
  My lords of England, let me tell you this:
  I have had feeling of my cousin's wrongs
  And labored all I could to do him right;
  But in this kind to come, in braving arms,   143
  Be his own carver, and cut out his way   144
  To find out right with wrong—it may not be;
  And you that do abet him in this kind
  Cherish rebellion and are rebels all.
NORTHUMBERLAND
  The noble Duke hath sworn his coming is
  But for his own, and for the right of that
  We all have strongly sworn to give him aid;
  And let him never see joy that breaks that oath!
YORK
  Well, well, I see the issue of these arms.   152
  I cannot mend it, I must needs confess,
  Because my power is weak and all ill-left;   154
  But if I could, by Him that gave me life,
  I would attach you all and make you stoop   156
  Unto the sovereign mercy of the King.
  But since I cannot, be it known unto you
  I do remain as neuter. So fare you well—   159
  Unless you please to enter in the castle
  And there repose you for this night.
BOLINGBROKE
  An offer, uncle, that we will accept.
  But we must win Your Grace to go with us   163
  To Bristol Castle, which they say is held
  By Bushy, Bagot, and their complices,   165
  The caterpillars of the commonwealth,
  Which I have sworn to weed and pluck away.

---

84 duty gesture of obeisance.   **deceivable** deceitful, deceptive
91 dust particle of dust   **95 ostentation** display.   **despisèd** despicable   **101 the Black Prince** i.e., Edward, the eldest son of Edward III and King Richard's father   **107 condition** i.e., defect in me.
wherein in what does it consist   **112 braving** defiant (also at line 143)
114 for Lancaster i.e., under the title of Lancaster and in order to claim it   **116 indifferent** impartial   **119 condemned** condemned as
120 royalties privileges granted by the King   **122 unthrifts** spend-thrifts   **126 first** i.e., before Gaunt

128 rouse chase from cover, expose.   **the bay** the extremity where the hunted animal turns on its pursuers   **129 denied** denied the right.
sue my livery sue for possession of hereditary rights. (See 2.1.202–204 and note.)   **130 letters patents** i.e., letters from the King indicating Bolingbroke's legal rights   **131 distrained** seized officially   **134 challenge law** claim my legal rights   **136 of free descent** by legal succession   **138 stands . . . upon** is incumbent upon Your Grace   **139 his endowments** i.e., the properties that rightly belong to Bolingbroke   **143 kind** fashion   **144 Be . . . carver** i.e., act on his own authority, help himself   **152 issue** outcome   **154 power** army.
ill-left left with inadequate means   **156 attach** arrest   **159 as neuter** neutral   **163 win** persuade   **165 Bagot** (According to 2.2.140, Bagot had gone to Ireland.)

YORK
It may be I will go with you; but yet I'll pause,
For I am loath to break our country's laws.
Nor friends nor foes, to me welcome you are.   170
Things past redress are now with me past care.
                                                  Exeunt.

♣

2.4   *Enter Earl of Salisbury and a Welsh Captain.*

WELSH CAPTAIN
My lord of Salisbury, we have stayed ten days   1
And hardly kept our countrymen together,   2
And yet we hear no tidings from the King.   3
Therefore we will disperse ourselves. Farewell.

SALISBURY
Stay yet another day, thou trusty Welshman.
The King reposeth all his confidence in thee.

WELSH CAPTAIN
'Tis thought the King is dead. We will not stay.
The bay trees in our country are all withered,
And meteors fright the fixèd stars of heaven;
The pale-faced moon looks bloody on the earth,
And lean-looked prophets whisper fearful change;   11
Rich men look sad, and ruffians dance and leap,
The one in fear to lose what they enjoy,
The other to enjoy by rage and war.   14
These signs forerun the death or fall of kings.   15
Farewell. Our countrymen are gone and fled,
As well assured Richard their king is dead. [*Exit.*] 17

SALISBURY
Ah, Richard! With the eyes of heavy mind
I see thy glory like a shooting star
Fall to the base earth from the firmament.
Thy sun sets weeping in the lowly west,
Witnessing storms to come, woe, and unrest.   22
Thy friends are fled to wait upon thy foes,   23
And crossly to thy good all fortune goes.   [*Exit.*] 24

♣

3.1   *Enter [Bolingbroke,] Duke of Hereford, York,*
         Northumberland, [with] Bushy and Green,
         prisoners.

BOLINGBROKE   Bring forth these men.
Bushy and Green, I will not vex your souls—
Since presently your souls must part your bodies—   3
With too much urging your pernicious lives,   4
For 'twere no charity; yet, to wash your blood
From off my hands, here in the view of men
I will unfold some causes of your deaths.

You have misled a prince, a royal king,
A happy gentleman in blood and lineaments,   9
By you unhappied and disfigured clean.   10
You have in manner with your sinful hours   11
Made a divorce betwixt his queen and him,
Broke the possession of a royal bed,
And stained the beauty of a fair queen's cheeks
With tears drawn from her eyes by your foul
    wrongs.
Myself—a prince by fortune of my birth,
Near to the King in blood, and near in love
Till you did make him misinterpret me—
Have stooped my neck under your injuries
And sighed my English breath in foreign clouds,   20
Eating the bitter bread of banishment,
Whilst you have fed upon my seigniories,   22
Disparked my parks and felled my forest woods,   23
From my own windows torn my household coat,   24
Razed out my imprese, leaving me no sign,   25
Save men's opinions and my living blood,
To show the world I am a gentleman.
This and much more, much more than twice all this,
Condemns you to the death.—See them delivered
    over
To execution and the hand of death.

BUSHY
More welcome is the stroke of death to me
Than Bolingbroke to England. Lords, farewell.

GREEN
My comfort is that heaven will take our souls
And plague injustice with the pains of hell.

BOLINGBROKE
My lord Northumberland, see them dispatched.
    [*Exeunt Northumberland with the prisoners, guarded.*]
Uncle, you say the Queen is at your house.
For God's sake, fairly let her be entreated.   37
Tell her I send to her my kind commends.   38
Take special care my greetings be delivered.

YORK
A gentleman of mine I have dispatched
With letters of your love to her at large.   41

BOLINGBROKE
Thanks, gentle uncle. Come, lords, away,
To fight with Glendower and his complices.   43
Awhile to work, and after holiday.   *Exeunt.* 44

♣

170 **Nor** neither as
2.4. Location: A camp in Wales.
1 **stayed** waited   2 **hardly** with difficulty   3 **yet** still   11 **lean-looked**
lean-looking   14 **to . . . rage** in hopes of possessing by violence
15 **forerun** anticipate   17 **As** as being   22 **Witnessing** betokening
23 **wait upon** attend, offer allegiance to   24 **crossly** adversely
3.1. Location: Bristol. The castle.
3 **presently** immediately   4 **urging** emphasizing as reasons (for your
executions)

9 **happy** fortunate.   **blood and lineaments** birth and natural characteristics   10 **unhappied** made wretched, ruined.   **clean** completely
11 **in manner** as it were   20 **foreign clouds** i.e., the air of foreign
lands (and adding to the clouds with his sighs)   22 **seigniories** estates
23 **Disparked** thrown open to uses other than hunting and forestry
24 **household coat** coat of arms (frequently emblazoned on stained or
painted windows)   25 **Razed** scraped (or perhaps *rased*, "erased").
imprese heraldic device, emblematic design   37 **entreated** treated
38 **commends** regards, commendations   41 **at large** conveyed in full
43 **Glendower** (Owen Glendower was not, according to Holinshed's
Chronicles, at this time in arms against Bolingbroke. Possibly he is to
be identified here with the Welsh captain of the preceding scene.)
44 **after** afterwards

3.2 [*Drums. Flourish and colors.*] *Enter the King,*
Aumerle, [*the Bishop of*] *Carlisle, etc.* [*with*
soldiers].

KING RICHARD
Barkloughly Castle call they this at hand?   1
AUMERLE
Yea, my lord. How brooks Your Grace the air   2
After your late tossing on the breaking seas?   3
KING RICHARD
Needs must I like it well. I weep for joy   4
To stand upon my kingdom once again.
Dear earth, I do salute thee with my hand,
          [*He bends and touches the ground.*]
Though rebels wound thee with their horses' hoofs.
As a long-parted mother with her child   8
Plays fondly with her tears and smiles in meeting,
So, weeping, smiling, greet I thee, my earth,
And do thee favors with my royal hands.
Feed not thy sovereign's foe, my gentle earth,
Nor with thy sweets comfort his ravenous sense,   13
But let thy spiders, that suck up thy venom,   14
And heavy-gaited toads lie in their way,
Doing annoyance to the treacherous feet
Which with usurping steps do trample thee.
Yield stinging nettles to mine enemies;
And when they from thy bosom pluck a flower,
Guard it, I pray thee, with a lurking adder,   20
Whose double tongue may with a mortal touch   21
Throw death upon thy sovereign's enemies.—
Mock not my senseless conjuration, lords.   23
This earth shall have a feeling, and these stones
Prove armèd soldiers, ere her native king   25
Shall falter under foul rebellion's arms.
CARLISLE
Fear not, my lord. That Power that made you king
Hath power to keep you king in spite of all.
The means that heavens yield must be embraced
And not neglected; else heaven would,   30
And we will not. Heaven's offer we refuse,   31
The proffered means of succor and redress.   32
AUMERLE
He means, my lord, that we are too remiss,
Whilst Bolingbroke through our security   34
Grows strong and great in substance and in power.
KING RICHARD
Discomfortable cousin, know'st thou not   36
That when the searching eye of heaven is hid   37
Behind the globe that lights the lower world,   38

Then thieves and robbers range abroad unseen
In murders and in outrage boldly here;
But when from under this terrestrial ball   41
He fires the proud tops of the eastern pines   42
And darts his light through every guilty hole,
Then murders, treasons, and detested sins,
The cloak of night being plucked from off their
          backs,
Stand bare and naked, trembling at themselves?   46
So when this thief, this traitor, Bolingbroke,
Who all this while hath reveled in the night
Whilst we were wand'ring with the Antipodes,   49
Shall see us rising in our throne, the east,
His treasons will sit blushing in his face,
Not able to endure the sight of day,
But, self-affrighted, tremble at his sin.
Not all the water in the rough rude sea
Can wash the balm off from an anointed king;   55
The breath of worldly men cannot depose   56
The deputy elected by the Lord.   57
For every man that Bolingbroke hath pressed   58
To lift shrewd steel against our golden crown,   59
God for his Richard hath in heavenly pay
A glorious angel. Then, if angels fight,
Weak men must fall, for heaven still guards the
          right.   62

          Enter Salisbury.

Welcome, my lord. How far off lies your power?
SALISBURY
Nor near nor farther off, my gracious lord,   64
Than this weak arm. Discomfort guides my tongue   65
And bids me speak of nothing but despair.
One day too late, I fear me, noble lord,
Hath clouded all thy happy days on earth.
O, call back yesterday, bid time return,
And thou shalt have twelve thousand fighting men!
Today, today, unhappy day too late,
O'erthrows thy joys, friends, fortune, and thy state;   72
For all the Welshmen, hearing thou wert dead,
Are gone to Bolingbroke, dispersed, and fled.
AUMERLE
Comfort, my liege. Why looks Your Grace so pale?
KING RICHARD
But now the blood of twenty thousand men   76
     Did triumph in my face, and they are fled;   77
And till so much blood thither come again,
     Have I not reason to look pale and dead?   79
All souls that will be safe, fly from my side,
For time hath set a blot upon my pride.

3.2. Location: The coast of Wales, near Harlech Castle.
1 Barkloughly i.e., Harlech **2 brooks** enjoys **3 late** recent **4 Needs must** necessarily **8 a long-parted mother with** a mother long parted from **13 sweets** i.e., bounty. **sense** appetite **14 suck . . . venom** (Alludes to the belief that spiders drew their poison from the earth.) **20 Guard** (1) watch over (2) trim, decorate with braid **21 double** forked. **mortal** deadly **23 senseless conjuration** solemn entreaty of senseless things **25 native** entitled (to the crown) by birth, rightful. (Richard was born at Bordeaux.) **30–31 else . . . not** i.e., otherwise, we spurn heaven's will **32 succor and redress** help and remedy **34 security** overconfidence **36 Discomfortable** uncomforting, discouraging **37–38 when . . . world** i.e., when the sun is hid behind the earth, lighting its lower side

41 this terrestrial ball the earth **42 He fires** the sun lights up. (Literally, "sets on fire.") **46 at themselves** i.e., at being caught in their crimes **49 Antipodes** people on the other side of the world; here, the Irish **55 balm** consecrated oil used in anointing a king **56 worldly** earthly **57 elected** chosen **58 pressed** impressed, forced into the ranks **59 shrewd** keen, biting **62 still** always **64 Nor near** neither nearer **65 Discomfort** discouragement **72 state** royal power **76 But now** even now. **twenty** (A seeming discrepancy with *twelve* in line 70; perhaps the result of Richard's hyperbole.) **77 triumph** i.e., shine forth **79 pale and dead** deathly pale

AUMERLE

Comfort, my liege. Remember who you are.

KING RICHARD

I had forgot myself. Am I not king?
Awake, thou coward majesty, thou sleepest!
Is not the king's name twenty thousand names?
Arm, arm, my name! A puny subject strikes
At thy great glory. Look not to the ground,
Ye favorites of a king. Are we not high?
High be our thoughts. I know my uncle York
Hath power enough to serve our turn. But who
  comes here?

Enter Scroop.

SCROOP

More health and happiness betide my liege   91
Than can my care-tuned tongue deliver him!   92

KING RICHARD

Mine ear is open and my heart prepared.
The worst is worldly loss thou canst unfold.
Say, is my kingdom lost? Why, 'twas my care,   95
And what loss is it to be rid of care?
Strives Bolingbroke to be as great as we?
Greater he shall not be; if he serve God,
We'll serve Him too, and be his fellow so.   99
Revolt our subjects? That we cannot mend;
They break their faith to God as well as us.
Cry woe, destruction, ruin, and decay;
The worst is death, and death will have his day.

SCROOP

Glad am I that Your Highness is so armed   104
To bear the tidings of calamity.
Like an unseasonable stormy day,
Which makes the silver rivers drown their shores
As if the world were all dissolved to tears,
So high above his limits swells the rage   109
Of Bolingbroke, covering your fearful land   110
With hard bright steel and hearts harder than steel.
Whitebeards have armed their thin and hairless
  scalps   112
Against Thy Majesty; boys with women's voices
Strive to speak big, and clap their female joints   114
In stiff unwieldy arms against thy crown.   115
Thy very beadsmen learn to bend their bows   116
Of double-fatal yew against thy state;   117
Yea, distaff-women manage rusty bills   118
Against thy seat. Both young and old rebel,   119
And all goes worse than I have power to tell.

KING RICHARD

Too well, too well thou tell'st a tale so ill.
Where is the Earl of Wiltshire? Where is Bagot?   122
What is become of Bushy? Where is Green,
That they have let the dangerous enemy
Measure our confines with such peaceful steps?   125
If we prevail, their heads shall pay for it.
I warrant they have made peace with Bolingbroke.

SCROOP

Peace have they made with him indeed, my lord.

KING RICHARD

O villains, vipers, damned without redemption!
Dogs easily won to fawn on any man!
Snakes in my heart-blood warmed, that sting my
  heart!
Three Judases, each one thrice worse than Judas!
Would they make peace? Terrible hell
Make war upon their spotted souls for this!   134

SCROOP

Sweet love, I see, changing his property,   135
Turns to the sourest and most deadly hate.
Again uncurse their souls. Their peace is made
With heads and not with hands. Those whom you
  curse   138
Have felt the worst of death's destroying wound
And lie full low, graved in the hollow ground.   140

AUMERLE

Is Bushy, Green, and the Earl of Wiltshire dead?

SCROOP

Ay, all of them at Bristol lost their heads.

AUMERLE

Where is the Duke my father with his power?

KING RICHARD

No matter where. Of comfort no man speak!
Let's talk of graves, of worms, and epitaphs,
Make dust our paper, and with rainy eyes
Write sorrow on the bosom of the earth.
Let's choose executors and talk of wills.
And yet not so, for what can we bequeath
Save our deposèd bodies to the ground?   150
Our lands, our lives, and all are Bolingbroke's,
And nothing can we call our own but death
And that small model of the barren earth   153
Which serves as paste and cover to our bones.   154
For God's sake, let us sit upon the ground
And tell sad stories of the death of kings—
How some have been deposed, some slain in war,
Some haunted by the ghosts they have deposed,   158
Some poisoned by their wives, some sleeping killed,
All murdered. For within the hollow crown

---

91 **More . . . betide** may more health and happiness befall   92 **care-tuned** i.e., tuned by sorrow and to the key of sorrow.   **deliver** deliver to   95 **care** trouble   99 **his fellow** his (Bolingbroke's) equal   104 **armed** prepared   109 **his limits** (1) its banks (2) the limits properly allowed to Bolingbroke's rage   110 **fearful** full of fears   112 **Whitebeards** old men.   **thin** sparsely haired   114 **clap** thrust.   **female** i.e., weak and delicate   115 **arms** armor   116 **beadsmen** old almsmen or pensioners whose duty it was to pray for a benefactor; here, for the king   117 **double-fatal** doubly fatal (since the wood of the yew was used for bows and since its foliage and berries are poisonous)   118–119 **distaff-women . . . seat** spinning women wield unused and hence rusty pikes (long-handled axes) against your throne

122 **Bagot** (Although the King names Bagot here, he mentions only *three Judases* in line 132 and Aumerle does not ask about Bagot in line 141; in 3.4 we learn that Bagot is not executed along with the other three but reappears instead in 4.1.)   125 **Measure our confines** travel over my kingdom.   **peaceful** unopposed   134 **spotted** stained with treason   135 **his property** its distinctive quality   138 **hands** (Used in swearing oaths, surrendering, etc.)   140 **graved** buried   150 **deposèd** (1) dethroned, as in 4.1 (2) deprived of those functions carried out by the body in this transitory life (3) deposited   153 **model** microcosm or mold, i.e., the body   154 **paste** pastry, pie crust   158 **deposed** deprived of life

That rounds the mortal temples of a king   161
Keeps Death his court, and there the antic sits,   162
Scoffing his state and grinning at his pomp,   163
Allowing him a breath, a little scene,   164
To monarchize, be feared, and kill with looks,   165
Infusing him with self and vain conceit,   166
As if this flesh which walls about our life
Were brass impregnable; and humored thus,   168
Comes at the last and with a little pin
Bores through his castle wall, and—farewell, king!
Cover your heads, and mock not flesh and blood   171
With solemn reverence. Throw away respect,
Tradition, form, and ceremonious duty,
For you have but mistook me all this while.
I live with bread like you, feel want,
Taste grief, need friends. Subjected thus,   176
How can you say to me I am a king?

CARLISLE
My lord, wise men ne'er sit and wail their woes,
But presently prevent the ways to wail.   179
To fear the foe, since fear oppresseth strength,   180
Gives in your weakness strength unto your foe,   181
And so your follies fight against yourself.
Fear, and be slain. No worse can come to fight;   183
And fight and die is death destroying death,   184
Where fearing dying pays death servile breath.   185

AUMERLE
My father hath a power. Inquire of him,   186
And learn to make a body of a limb.   187

KING RICHARD
Thou chid'st me well. Proud Bolingbroke, I come
To change blows with thee for our day of doom.   189
This ague fit of fear is overblown;   190
An easy task it is to win our own.   191
Say, Scroop, where lies our uncle with his power?
Speak sweetly, man, although thy looks be sour.

SCROOP
Men judge by the complexion of the sky   194
    The state and inclination of the day.
So may you by my dull and heavy eye;
    My tongue hath but a heavier tale to say.

I play the torturer, by small and small   198
To lengthen out the worst that must be spoken:
Your uncle York is joined with Bolingbroke,
And all your northern castles yielded up,
And all your southern gentlemen in arms
Upon his party.
KING RICHARD   Thou hast said enough.   203
[To Aumerle.] Beshrew thee, cousin, which didst lead
    me forth   204
Of that sweet way I was in to despair.
What say you now? What comfort have we now?
By heaven, I'll hate him everlastingly
That bids me be of comfort any more.
Go to Flint Castle. There I'll pine away;   209
A king, woe's slave, shall kingly woe obey.
That power I have, discharge, and let them go
To ear the land that hath some hope to grow,   212
For I have none. Let no man speak again
To alter this, for counsel is but vain.

AUMERLE
My liege, one word.
KING RICHARD   He does me double wrong   215
That wounds me with the flatteries of his tongue.
Discharge my followers. Let them hence away,
From Richard's night to Bolingbroke's fair day.
                                                    [Exeunt.]

❖

3.3   *Enter [with drum and colors] Bolingbroke, York,
Northumberland, [attendants, and forces].*

BOLINGBROKE
So that by this intelligence we learn   1
The Welshmen are dispersed, and Salisbury
Is gone to meet the King, who lately landed
With some few private friends upon this coast.

NORTHUMBERLAND
The news is very fair and good, my lord:
Richard not far from hence hath hid his head.

YORK
It would beseem the Lord Northumberland   7
To say "King Richard." Alack the heavy day
When such a sacred king should hide his head!

NORTHUMBERLAND
Your Grace mistakes. Only to be brief
Left I his title out.
YORK   The time hath been,
Would you have been so brief with him, he would
Have been so brief with you to shorten you,   13
For taking so the head, your whole head's length.   14

BOLINGBROKE
Mistake not, uncle, further than you should.

161 **rounds** encircles   162 **antic** grotesque figure, jester
163 **Scoffing his state** scoffing at the king's regality.   164 **breath**
breathing space, moment   165 **monarchize** play the monarch.   **kill
with looks** i.e., order someone's death with a mere glance   166 **self
and vain conceit** vain conceit of himself   168 **humored thus** having
satisfied his humor or whim (referring to Death), or, having thus indulged the King, having led him on in this humor   171 **Cover your
heads** replace your hats (which have been removed out of respect for
the King)   176 **Subjected** made subject to grief, want, etc. (with pun
on "being treated like a subject")   179 **presently** immediately.   **prevent . . . wail** block off the paths leading to grief   180–181 **To fear
. . . foe** i.e., to be afraid of the foe is merely a weakness that, by oppressing your own resolve, gives advantage to the foe   183 **Fear . . .
fight** i.e., if you fear, you are sure to be slain, and no worse fate can
come to you if you fight   184–185 **fight . . . breath** to die fighting is
to conquer death in the very act of dying, whereas to die fearfully
pays to death the tribute of servility   186 **power** army (as also in line
192).   **of** about, or from   187 **learn . . . limb** i.e., discover how to
make a partial force substitute for a complete one   189 **change** exchange.   **for . . . doom** i.e., in order to settle our fates, which of us
is to die now   190 **ague fit** paroxysm of shivering (as with malarial
fever).   **is overblown** has blown over   191 **our own** i.e., my own
kingdom   194 **complexion** appearance

198 **by small and small** little by little   203 **Upon his party** on his side
204 **Beshrew** confound. (Literally, *curse*.)   **forth** out   209 **Flint Castle** (Near Chester.)   212 **ear** plow   215 **double wrong** i.e., in deceiving me and in again leading me into false hope
3.3. Location: Wales. Before Flint Castle.
1 **intelligence** information   7 **beseem** be appropriate for, be seemly
behavior in   13 **to** as to   14 **taking so the head** i.e., (1) presumptu-
ously omitting thus his title (2) being headstrong

YORK
Take not, good cousin, further than you should,
Lest you mistake the heavens are over our heads.   17
BOLINGBROKE
I know it, uncle, and oppose not myself
Against their will. But who comes here?

    Enter Percy.

Welcome, Harry. What, will not this castle yield?
PERCY
The castle royally is manned, my lord,
Against thy entrance.
BOLINGBROKE
Royally? Why, it contains no king?
PERCY   Yes, my good lord,
It doth contain a king. King Richard lies   25
Within the limits of yon lime and stone,
And with him are the Lord Aumerle, Lord
   Salisbury,
Sir Stephen Scroop, besides a clergyman
Of holy reverence—who, I cannot learn.
NORTHUMBERLAND
O, belike it is the Bishop of Carlisle.   30
BOLINGBROKE [*to Northumberland*]   Noble lord,
Go to the rude ribs of that ancient castle;   32
Through brazen trumpet send the breath of parley   33
Into his ruined ears, and thus deliver: 34
Henry Bolingbroke
On both his knees doth kiss King Richard's hand
And sends allegiance and true faith of heart
To his most royal person, hither come
Even at his feet to lay my arms and power,
Provided that my banishment repealed   40
And lands restored again be freely granted.   41
If not, I'll use the advantage of my power,   42
And lay the summer's dust with showers of blood
Rained from the wounds of slaughtered
   Englishmen—
The which how far off from the mind of Bolingbroke
It is such crimson tempest should bedrench   46
The fresh green lap of fair King Richard's land,
My stooping duty tenderly shall show.   48
Go, signify as much while here we march
Upon the grassy carpet of this plain.
   [*Northumberland and attendants advance to the castle.*]
Let's march without the noise of threatening drum,
That from this castle's tottered battlements   52
Our fair appointments may be well perused.   53
Methinks King Richard and myself should meet
With no less terror than the elements

Of fire and water, when their thundering shock   56
At meeting tears the cloudy cheeks of heaven.
Be he the fire, I'll be the yielding water;
The rage be his, whilst on the earth I rain   59
My waters—on the earth, and not on him.   60
March on, and mark King Richard how he looks.   61

   [*Bolingbroke's forces march about the stage.*] *The
   trumpets sound* [*a parley without and answer
   within, then a flourish. King*] *Richard appeareth
   on the walls* [*with the Bishop of Carlisle, Aumerle,
   Scroop, and Salisbury*].

See, see, King Richard doth himself appear,
As doth the blushing discontented sun   63
From out the fiery portal of the east
When he perceives the envious clouds are bent   65
To dim his glory and to stain the track
Of his bright passage to the occident.
YORK
Yet looks he like a king. Behold, his eye,   68
As bright as is the eagle's, lightens forth   69
Controlling majesty. Alack, alack, for woe,
That any harm should stain so fair a show!
KING RICHARD [*to Northumberland*]
We are amazed; and thus long have we stood
To watch the fearful bending of thy knee,   73
Because we thought ourself thy lawful king.
And if we be, how dare thy joints forget
To pay their awful duty to our presence?   76
If we be not, show us the hand of God   77
That hath dismissed us from our stewardship;
For well we know, no hand of blood and bone
Can grip the sacred handle of our scepter,
Unless he do profane, steal, or usurp.   81
And though you think that all, as you have done,
Have torn their souls by turning them from us,   83
And we are barren and bereft of friends,   84
Yet know, my master, God omnipotent,   85
Is mustering in his clouds on our behalf
Armies of pestilence; and they shall strike
Your children yet unborn and unbegot,
That lift your vassal hands against my head   89
And threat the glory of my precious crown.   90
Tell Bolingbroke—for yon methinks he stands—
That every stride he makes upon my land
Is dangerous treason. He is come to open   93
The purple testament of bleeding war;   94
But ere the crown he looks for live in peace,

---

17 mistake fail to perceive that. (Plays on Bolingbroke's use of *mistake*, just as York has punned on *brief* and *head*.) **25 lies** resides
30 belike probably **32 rude ribs** i.e., rugged walls **33 brazen** (1) brass (2) bold. **breath of parley** i.e., call for a conference **34 his ruined ears** i.e., its (the castle's) ancient and battered loopholes
40 my banishment repealed the revocation of my banishment
41 lands restored again the restoration of my lands **42 advantage of my power** superiority of my army **46 is** is that **48 stooping duty** submissive kneeling **52 tottered** in tottering condition, or dilapidated
53 appointments equipment

56 fire and water i.e., lightning and rain **59–60 rain . . . earth** i.e., weep contritely as I kneel **61 s.d. parley** trumpet summons to a negotiation. **on the walls** i.e., in the gallery of the tiring-house, above, to the rear of the stage **63 blushing** i.e., turning red with anger
65 he i.e., the sun. **envious** hostile **68 Yet** still, or nevertheless.
he i.e., King Richard **69 lightens forth** flashes out, like lightning
73 watch wait for **76 awful** reverential, full of awe **77 hand** signature **81 Unless he do profane** without committing sacrilege **83 torn . . . us** turned traitor to me at peril to their souls **84 And** and that
85 know know that **89 That** of you that. **vassal** subject **90 threat** threaten **93–94 open . . . testament** begin to carry out a bequest of blood to England. (Blood was often said to be purple.)

Ten thousand bloody crowns of mothers' sons 96
Shall ill become the flower of England's face, 97
Change the complexion of her maid-pale peace 98
To scarlet indignation, and bedew
Her pastures' grass with faithful English blood.
NORTHUMBERLAND
The King of heaven forbid our lord the King
Should so with civil and uncivil arms 102
Be rushed upon! Thy thrice-noble cousin
Harry Bolingbroke doth humbly kiss thy hand;
And by the honorable tomb he swears
That stands upon your royal grandsire's bones,
And by the royalties of both your bloods,
Currents that spring from one most gracious head, 108
And by the buried hand of warlike Gaunt,
And by the worth and honor of himself,
Comprising all that may be sworn or said,
His coming hither hath no further scope 112
Than for his lineal royalties, and to beg 113
Enfranchisement immediate on his knees; 114
Which on thy royal party granted once, 115
His glittering arms he will commend to rust, 116
His barbèd steeds to stables, and his heart 117
To faithful service of Your Majesty.
This swears he, as he is a prince and just,
And as I am a gentleman I credit him.
KING RICHARD
Northumberland, say thus the King returns: 121
His noble cousin is right welcome hither,
And all the number of his fair demands
Shall be accomplished without contradiction. 124
With all the gracious utterance thou hast
Speak to his gentle hearing kind commends. 126
[Northumberland and attendants retire to Bolingbroke and York.]
[To Aumerle.] We do debase ourself, cousin, do we not,
To look so poorly and to speak so fair? 128
Shall we call back Northumberland, and send
Defiance to the traitor, and so die?
AUMERLE
No, good my lord. Let's fight with gentle words
Till time lend friends, and friends their helpful swords.
KING RICHARD
O God, O God, that e'er this tongue of mine,
That laid the sentence of dread banishment
On yon proud man, should take it off again
With words of sooth! O, that I were as great 136
As is my grief, or lesser than my name!
Or that I could forget what I have been,

Or not remember what I must be now!
Swell'st thou, proud heart? I'll give thee scope to beat, 140
Since foes have scope to beat both thee and me. 141
[Northumberland returns to the castle walls.]
AUMERLE
Northumberland comes back from Bolingbroke.
KING RICHARD
What must the King do now? Must he submit?
The King shall do it. Must he be deposed?
The King shall be contented. Must he lose
The name of king? I' God's name, let it go.
I'll give my jewels for a set of beads, 147
My gorgeous palace for a hermitage,
My gay apparel for an almsman's gown, 149
My figured goblets for a dish of wood, 150
My scepter for a palmer's walking-staff, 151
My subjects for a pair of carvèd saints,
And my large kingdom for a little grave,
A little, little grave, an obscure grave;
Or I'll be buried in the King's highway,
Some way of common trade, where subjects' feet 156
May hourly trample on their sovereign's head;
For on my heart they tread now whilst I live,
And, buried once, why not upon my head? 159
Aumerle, thou weep'st, my tenderhearted cousin.
We'll make foul weather with despisèd tears;
Our sighs and they shall lodge the summer corn 162
And make a dearth in this revolting land. 163
Or shall we play the wantons with our woes 164
And make some pretty match with shedding tears? 165
As thus, to drop them still upon one place, 166
Till they have fretted us a pair of graves 167
Within the earth; and, therein laid—there lies
Two kinsmen digged their graves with weeping eyes. 169
Would not this ill do well? Well, well, I see
I talk but idly, and you laugh at me.—
Most mighty prince, my lord Northumberland,
What says King Bolingbroke? Will His Majesty
Give Richard leave to live till Richard die?
You make a leg, and Bolingbroke says ay. 175
NORTHUMBERLAND
My lord, in the base court he doth attend 176
To speak with you, may it please you to come down. 177
KING RICHARD
Down, down I come, like glistering Phaëthon, 178

96 crowns heads (playing on crown in line 95) 97 flower . . . face blooming face of England 98 maid-pale i.e., pale like the complexion of a young English maid 102 civil used in civil strife. uncivil barbarous, violent 108 head source 112 scope purpose, aim 113 lineal royalties hereditary rights as one of royal blood 114 Enfranchisement freedom (from banishment) 115 party part 116 commend give over 117 barbèd armored 121 returns answers 124 accomplished fulfilled 126 commends regards 128 poorly abject. fair courteously 136 sooth cajolery, flattery

140 scope freedom, space 141 scope capacity, opportunity 147 set of beads rosary 149 almsman's gown plain attire of one who lives on alms or charity 150 figured ornamented, embossed 151 palmer's pilgrim's 156 trade passage 159 buried once once I am buried 162 lodge beat down. corn grain 163 revolting rebelling 164 play the wantons sport, frolic 165 match game, contest 166 still continually 167 fretted us eaten away for us, worn (with a play on "complained") 169 digged who dug 175 a leg an obeisance 176 base court outer or lower court of a castle 177 may it please you if you please 178 glistering glistening, glittering. Phaëthon son of the sun-god, whose chariot he attempted to steer across the sky; unable to control the horses of the sun, he was hurled from the chariot by Jupiter

Wanting the manage of unruly jades.   179
In the base court? Base court, where kings grow
    base,
To come at traitors' calls and do them grace.   181
In the base court? Come down? Down, court!
    Down, king!
For night owls shriek where mounting larks should
    sing.   [*Exeunt from above.*]

    [*Northumberland rejoins Bolingbroke.*]

BOLINGBROKE
What says His Majesty?
NORTHUMBERLAND   Sorrow and grief of heart
Makes him speak fondly, like a frantic man.   185
Yet he is come.

    [*Enter King Richard and his attendants below.*]

BOLINGBROKE   Stand all apart,   187
And show fair duty to His Majesty.   *He kneels down.* 188
My gracious lord!
KING RICHARD
Fair cousin, you debase your princely knee   190
To make the base earth proud with kissing it.   191
Me rather had my heart might feel your love   192
Than my unpleased eye see your courtesy.
Up, cousin, up. Your heart is up, I know,
Thus high at least [*touching his crown*], although your
    knee be low.
BOLINGBROKE [*rising*]
My gracious lord, I come but for mine own.
KING RICHARD
Your own is yours, and I am yours, and all.
BOLINGBROKE
So far be mine, my most redoubted lord,   198
As my true service shall deserve your love.
KING RICHARD
Well you deserve. They well deserve to have
That know the strong'st and surest way to get.
[*To York, who weeps.*] Uncle, give me your hands.
    Nay, dry your eyes;
Tears show their love, but want their remedies.   203
[*To Bolingbroke.*] Cousin, I am too young to be your
    father,   204
Though you are old enough to be my heir.
What you will have, I'll give, and willing too,
For do we must what force will have us do.
Set on towards London, cousin, is it so?
BOLINGBROKE
Yea, my good lord.
KING RICHARD   Then I must not say no.
                                          [*Flourish. Exeunt.*]

❦

179 **Wanting . . . jades** lacking the skill in horsemanship to control
unruly nags   181 **do them grace** (1) bow to them (2) treat them graciously   185 **fondly** foolishly,   **frantic** mad   187 **apart** aside
188 **fair duty** respect   190–191 **debase . . . base** (Continues the
wordplay on *base* in line 180.)   192 **Me rather had** I had rather
198 **redoubted** dread   203 **want their remedies** lack remedies for
what caused them   204 **too young** (Historically, Richard and Bolingbroke were both thirty-three.)

3.4   *Enter the Queen with [two Ladies,] her attendants.*

QUEEN
What sport shall we devise here in this garden,
To drive away the heavy thought of care?
LADY   Madam, we'll play at bowls.   3
QUEEN
'Twill make me think the world is full of rubs,   4
And that my fortune runs against the bias.   5
LADY   Madam, we'll dance.
QUEEN
My legs can keep no measure in delight   7
When my poor heart no measure keeps in grief.   8
Therefore, no dancing, girl; some other sport.
LADY   Madam, we'll tell tales.
QUEEN
Of sorrow or of joy?
LADY   Of either, madam.
QUEEN   Of neither, girl;
For if of joy, being altogether wanting,   13
It doth remember me the more of sorrow;   14
Or if of grief, being altogether had,
It adds more sorrow to my want of joy.
For what I have I need not to repeat,
And what I want it boots not to complain.   18
LADY
Madam, I'll sing.
QUEEN   'Tis well that thou hast cause,
But thou shouldst please me better wouldst thou
    weep.   20
LADY
I could weep, madam, would it do you good.
QUEEN
And I could sing, would weeping do me good,   22
And never borrow any tear of thee.   23

        Enter Gardeners [a Master and two Men].

But stay, here come the gardeners.
Let's step into the shadow of these trees.
My wretchedness unto a row of pins,   26
They will talk of state, for everyone doth so   27
Against a change; woe is forerun with woe.   28
                          [*The Queen and Ladies stand apart.*]
GARDENER [*to one Man*]
Go bind thou up young dangling apricots
Which, like unruly children, make their sire
Stoop with oppression of their prodigal weight.   31
Give some supportance to the bending twigs.
[*To the other.*] Go thou, and like an executioner
Cut off the heads of too-fast-growing sprays

3.4. Location: The Duke of York's garden.
3 bowls i.e., lawn bowling, a common Elizabethan game   **4 rubs** impediments (in the game of bowls)   **5 against the bias** i.e., contrary,
athwart. (Literally, not following the naturally curved path of a bowl.)
7 measure a stately slow dance   **8 measure** moderation   **13 wanting**
lacking   **14 remember** remind   **18 boots** helps   **20 wouldst thou** if
you would   **22 would . . . good** i.e., if my troubles were merely the
kind that could be helped by weeping   **23 never borrow** never need
to borrow   **26 My . . . unto** i.e., I'll wager my wretchedness against
27 state statecraft, politics   **28 Against** anticipating.   **forerun with**
heralded by   **31 prodigal** excessive

That look too lofty in our commonwealth.
All must be even in our government. 36
You thus employed, I will go root away
The noisome weeds which without profit suck 38
The soil's fertility from wholesome flowers.
MAN
Why should we in the compass of a pale 40
Keep law and form and due proportion,
Showing as in a model our firm estate, 42
When our sea-wallèd garden, the whole land,
Is full of weeds, her fairest flowers choked up,
Her fruit trees all unpruned, her hedges ruined,
Her knots disordered, and her wholesome herbs 46
Swarming with caterpillars?
GARDENER   Hold thy peace.
He that hath suffered this disordered spring 48
Hath now himself met with the fall of leaf. 49
The weeds which his broad-spreading leaves did
    shelter,
That seemed in eating him to hold him up, 51
Are plucked up root and all by Bolingbroke:
I mean the Earl of Wiltshire, Bushy, Green.
MAN
What, are they dead?
GARDENER   They are; and Bolingbroke
Hath seized the wasteful King. O, what pity is it
That he had not so trimmed and dressed his land
As we this garden! We at time of year 57
Do wound the bark, the skin of our fruit trees,
Lest being overproud in sap and blood 59
With too much riches it confound itself;
Had he done so to great and growing men,
They might have lived to bear and he to taste
Their fruits of duty. Superfluous branches
We lop away, that bearing boughs may live; 64
Had he done so, himself had borne the crown 65
Which waste of idle hours hath quite thrown down.
MAN
What, think you the King shall be deposed?
GARDENER
Depressed he is already, and deposed 68
'Tis doubt he will be. Letters came last night 69
To a dear friend of the good Duke of York's,
That tell black tidings.
QUEEN [coming forward]   O, I am pressed to death 71
Through want of speaking! Thou, old Adam's
    likeness, 72
Set to dress this garden, how dares 73
Thy harsh rude tongue sound this unpleasing news?
What Eve, what serpent, hath suggested thee 75

To make a second fall of cursèd man?
Why dost thou say King Richard is deposed?
Dar'st thou, thou little better thing than earth,
Divine his downfall? Say where, when, and how 79
Cam'st thou by this ill tidings? Speak, thou wretch.
GARDENER
Pardon me, madam. Little joy have I
To breathe this news, yet what I say is true.
King Richard, he is in the mighty hold
Of Bolingbroke. Their fortunes both are weighed.
In your lord's scale is nothing but himself
And some few vanities that make him light;
But in the balance of great Bolingbroke,
Besides himself, are all the English peers,
And with that odds he weighs King Richard down.
Post you to London and you will find it so; 90
I speak no more than everyone doth know.
QUEEN
Nimble mischance, that art so light of foot,
Doth not thy embassage belong to me, 93
And am I last that knows it? O, thou thinkest
To serve me last, that I may longest keep .
Thy sorrow in my breast. Come, ladies, go 96
To meet at London London's king in woe.
What, was I born to this, that my sad look
Should grace the triumph of great Bolingbroke? 99
Gard'ner, for telling me these news of woe,
Pray God the plants thou graft'st may never grow.
                                    Exit [with Ladies].
GARDENER
Poor queen! So that thy state might be no worse, 102
I would my skill were subject to thy curse.
Here did she fall a tear; here in this place 104
I'll set a bank of rue, sour herb of grace. 105
Rue even for ruth here shortly shall be seen, 106
In the remembrance of a weeping queen.   Exeunt.

❖

4.1   *Enter Bolingbroke with the Lords [Aumerle,*
Northumberland, Harry Percy, Fitzwater, Surrey,
the Bishop of Carlisle, the Abbot of Westminster,
and another Lord, Herald, officers] to Parliament.
[The throne is provided on stage.]

BOLINGBROKE   Call forth Bagot.

Enter [officers with] Bagot.

Now, Bagot, freely speak thy mind,
What thou dost know of noble Gloucester's death,
Who wrought it with the King, and who performed 4

---

36 **even** equal   38 **noisome** harmful   40 **pale** enclosure, enclosed
garden   42 **firm** stable   46 **knots** flower beds laid out in patterns
48 **suffered** allowed   49 **fall of leaf** i.e., autumn   51 **in eating him**
i.e., while they were really eating his sustenance   57 **at . . . year** in
the appropriate season   59 **overproud in** swollen with   64 **bearing**
fruit-bearing   65 **crown** (1) royal crown (2) crown of a tree   68 **De-**
pressed brought low   69 **'Tis doubt** there is fear   71 **pressed to death**
(Allusion to the *peine forte et dure*, inflicted by pressure of heavy
weights upon the chests of indicted persons who refused to plead and
remained silent.)   72 **old Adam** (In his role as the first gardener.)
73 **dress** cultivate   75 **suggested** tempted

79 **Divine** prophesy   90 **Post** hasten. (See the note at 1.1.56.)
93 **embassage** message.   **belong to** i.e., concern   96 **Thy sorrow** the
sorrow that you (mischance) report   99 **triumph** triumphal procession.   **Bolingbroke** (The original spelling, *Bullingbrooke*, indicates the
rhyme with *look* in the previous line, pronounced something like
"bruke" and "luke.")   102 **So that** provided   104 **fall** let fall
105 **rue** "herb of grace," a plant symbolical of repentance, ruth, or
sorrow for another's misery   106 **ruth** pity
4.1. Location: Westminster Hall.
4 **Who . . . King** who prevailed upon the King to have the murder
performed

The bloody office of his timeless end.   5

BAGOT
Then set before my face the Lord Aumerle.

BOLINGBROKE [*to Aumerle*]
Cousin, stand forth, and look upon that man.
                              [*Aumerle comes forward.*]

BAGOT
My lord Aumerle, I know your daring tongue
Scorns to unsay what once it hath delivered.   9
In that dead time when Gloucester's death was
    plotted,   10
I heard you say, "Is not my arm of length,   11
That reacheth from the restful English court   12
As far as Calais, to mine uncle's head?"
Amongst much other talk that very time   14
I heard you say that you had rather refuse
The offer of an hundred thousand crowns
Than Bolingbroke's return to England—   17
Adding withal how blest this land would be   18
In this your cousin's death.

AUMERLE   Princes and noble lords,
What answer shall I make to this base man?
Shall I so much dishonor my fair stars   22
On equal terms to give him chastisement?   23
Either I must, or have mine honor soiled
With the attainder of his slanderous lips.   25
                              [*He throws down his gage.*]
There is my gage, the manual seal of death,   26
That marks thee out for hell. I say thou liest,
And will maintain what thou hast said is false
In thy heart-blood, though being all too base
To stain the temper of my knightly sword.

BOLINGBROKE
Bagot, forbear. Thou shalt not take it up.

AUMERLE
Excepting one, I would he were the best   32
In all this presence that hath moved me so.

FITZWATER [*throwing down a gage*]
If that thy valor stand on sympathy,   34
There is my gage, Aumerle, in gage to thine.   35
By that fair sun which shows me where thou
    stand'st,
I heard thee say, and vauntingly thou spak'st it,   37
That thou wert cause of noble Gloucester's death.
If thou deny'st it twenty times, thou liest,
And I will turn thy falsehood to thy heart,   40
Where it was forgèd, with my rapier's point.

AUMERLE [*taking up the gage*]
Thou dar'st not, coward, live to see that day.

FITZWATER
Now, by my soul, I would it were this hour.

AUMERLE
Fitzwater, thou art damned to hell for this.

PERCY
Aumerle, thou liest. His honor is as true
In this appeal as thou art all unjust;   46
And that thou art so, there I throw my gage
                              [*throwing down a gage*]
To prove it on thee to the extremest point   48
Of mortal breathing. Seize it if thou dar'st.   49

AUMERLE [*taking up the gage*]
An if I do not, may my hands rot off   50
And never brandish more revengeful steel   51
Over the glittering helmet of my foe!

ANOTHER LORD [*throwing down a gage*]
I task the earth to the like, forsworn Aumerle,   53
And spur thee on with full as many lies   54
As may be holloed in thy treacherous ear
From sun to sun. There is my honor's pawn;   56
Engage it to the trial, if thou darest.   57

AUMERLE [*taking up the gage*]
Who sets me else? By heaven, I'll throw at all!   58
I have a thousand spirits in one breast
To answer twenty thousand such as you.

SURREY
My lord Fitzwater, I do remember well
The very time Aumerle and you did talk.

FITZWATER
'Tis very true. You were in presence then,   63
And you can witness with me this is true.

SURREY
As false, by heaven, as heaven itself is true.

FITZWATER
Surrey, thou liest.

SURREY   Dishonorable boy!
That lie shall lie so heavy on my sword
That it shall render vengeance and revenge,   68
Till thou the lie-giver and that lie do lie
In earth as quiet as thy father's skull.
In proof whereof, there is my honor's pawn.
                              [*He throws down a gage.*]
Engage it to the trial if thou dar'st.

FITZWATER [*taking up the gage*]
How fondly dost thou spur a forward horse!   73
If I dare eat, or drink, or breathe, or live,
I dare meet Surrey in a wilderness   75
And spit upon him whilst I say he lies,
And lies, and lies. There is my bond of faith,
To tie thee to my strong correction.
                              [*He throws down a gage.*]

---

5 **office** function.   **timeless** untimely   9 **unsay** deny, take back
10 **dead** (1) deadly (2) dark, silent   11 **of length** long   12 **restful** i.e.,
untroubled by Gloucester   14 **that very time** (An inconsistency;
Gloucester's death occurred before Bolingbroke left England.)
17 **Than . . . return** than have Bolingbroke return   18 **withal** in addition   22 **stars** i.e., fortune, rank   23 **On . . . chastisement** as to
challenge him as my equal   25 **attainder** dishonoring accusation
26 **manual . . . death** death warrant sealed by my hand   32 **one** i.e.,
Bolingbroke.   **best** highest in rank   34 **stand on sympathy** i.e., insists
on correspondence of rank in your opponent   35 **in gage** engaged
37 **vauntingly** boastfully   40 **turn** turn back

46 **appeal** accusation (as also in line 80).   **all unjust** totally false
48–49 **to . . . breathing** to the death   50 **An if** if   51 **more** any
more, again   53 **I . . . like** I burden the ground in the same way
54 **lies** accusations of lying   56 **sun to sun** sunrise to sunset   57 **Engage . . . trial** take it up as a pledge to combat   58 **sets me** puts up
stakes against me, i.e., challenges me to a game.   **throw** (1) throw
dice (2) throw down gages   63 **in presence** present   68 **it** i.e., my
sword   73 **fondly** foolishly.   **forward** willing   75 **in a wilderness**
i.e., where fighting might go on uninterrupted to the death

As I intend to thrive in this new world,   79
Aumerle is guilty of my true appeal.   80
Besides, I heard the banished Norfolk say
That thou, Aumerle, didst send two of thy men
To execute the noble Duke at Calais.

AUMERLE
Some honest Christian trust me with a gage.
  [He borrows a gage and throws it down.]
That Norfolk lies, here do I throw down this,
If he may be repealed, to try his honor.   86

BOLINGBROKE
These differences shall all rest under gage   87
Till Norfolk be repealed. Repealed he shall be,
And, though mine enemy, restored again
To all his lands and seigniories. When he is returned,
Against Aumerle we will enforce his trial.

CARLISLE
That honorable day shall never be seen.
Many a time hath banished Norfolk fought
For Jesu Christ in glorious Christian field,
Streaming the ensign of the Christian cross   95
Against black pagans, Turks, and Saracens;
And, toiled with works of war, retired himself   97
To Italy, and there at Venice gave
His body to that pleasant country's earth
And his pure soul unto his captain, Christ,
Under whose colors he had fought so long.

BOLINGBROKE   Why, Bishop, is Norfolk dead?
CARLISLE   As surely as I live, my lord.

BOLINGBROKE
Sweet peace conduct his sweet soul to the bosom   104
Of good old Abraham! Lords appellants,   105
Your differences shall all rest under gage
Till we assign you to your days of trial.   107

    Enter York.

YORK
Great Duke of Lancaster, I come to thee
From plume-plucked Richard, who with willing soul
Adopts thee heir, and his high scepter yields
To the possession of thy royal hand.
Ascend his throne, descending now from him,
And long live Henry, fourth of that name!

BOLINGBROKE
In God's name, I'll ascend the regal throne.

CARLISLE   Marry, God forbid!
Worst in this royal presence may I speak,   116
Yet best beseeming me to speak the truth.   117
Would God that any in this noble presence
Were enough noble to be upright judge
Of noble Richard! Then true noblesse would   120

Learn him forbearance from so foul a wrong.   121
What subject can give sentence on his king?
And who sits here that is not Richard's subject?
Thieves are not judged but they are by to hear,   124
Although apparent guilt be seen in them;   125
And shall the figure of God's majesty,   126
His captain, steward, deputy elect,
Anointed, crownèd, planted many years,
Be judged by subject and inferior breath,
And he himself not present? O, forfend it God   130
That in a Christian climate souls refined   131
Should show so heinous, black, obscene a deed!   132
I speak to subjects, and a subject speaks,
Stirred up by God thus boldly for his king.
My lord of Hereford here, whom you call king,
Is a foul traitor to proud Hereford's king.
And if you crown him, let me prophesy:
The blood of English shall manure the ground
And future ages groan for this foul act;
Peace shall go sleep with Turks and infidels,
And in this seat of peace tumultuous wars
Shall kin with kin and kind with kind confound;   142
Disorder, horror, fear, and mutiny
Shall here inhabit, and this land be called
The field of Golgotha and dead men's skulls.   145
O, if you raise this house against this house,   146
It will the woefullest division prove
That ever fell upon this cursèd earth.
Prevent it, resist it, let it not be so,
Lest child, child's children, cry against you woe!

NORTHUMBERLAND
Well have you argued, sir, and for your pains
Of capital treason we arrest you here.   152
My lord of Westminster, be it your charge
To keep him safely till his day of trial.
         [Carlisle is taken into custody.]
May it please you, lords, to grant the commons'
   suit?   155

BOLINGBROKE
Fetch hither Richard, that in common view
He may surrender; so we shall proceed   157
Without suspicion.

YORK   I will be his conduct.   Exit. 158

BOLINGBROKE
Lords, you that here are under our arrest,
Procure your sureties for your days of answer.   160
Little are we beholding to your love,   161

79 in . . . world i.e., under the new king 80 appeal accusation
86 repealed recalled from exile. try test 87 under gage as challenges 95 Streaming flying 97 toiled wearied 104–105 bosom
. . . Abraham i.e., heaven. (See Luke 16:22.) 105 Lords appellants
lords who appear as formal accusers 107 s.d. Enter York (Some editors suggest that Richard's scepter, etc., are brought in at line 162,
but York here invites Bolingbroke to ascend the throne with the surrendered scepter, and so perhaps the regalia are brought on here.)
116 Worst least in rank 117 best beseeming me i.e., most befitting
to me as a clergyman 120 noblesse nobleness

121 Learn him forbearance teach him to forbear 124 judged . . . by
condemned unless they are present 125 apparent manifest
126 figure image 130 forfend forbid 131 souls refined civilized
people 132 obscene odious, repulsive 142 Shall . . . confound
shall destroy kinsmen by means of kinsmen and fellow countrymen by
means of fellow countrymen 145 Golgotha Calvary, the hill outside
of Jerusalem called "the place of dead men's skulls" (see Mark 15:22
and John 19:17) where Jesus was crucified 146 this house . . . this
house i.e., Lancaster against York. (See Mark 3:25.) 152 Of on a
charge of 155 the commons' suit request of the commons (i.e., that
Richard be formally tried and the causes of his deposition made public. This line begins the abdication passage omitted in early quartos of
the play.) 157 surrender i.e., surrender the crown, abdicate
158 conduct escort 160 sureties persons who will guarantee your
appearance. your days of answer the time when you must appear to
stand trial 161 beholding beholden, indebted

And little looked for at your helping hands.   162

Enter Richard and York.

KING RICHARD
Alack, why am I sent for to a king,
Before I have shook off the regal thoughts
Wherewith I reigned? I hardly yet have learned
To insinuate, flatter, bow, and bend my knee.
Give sorrow leave awhile to tutor me
To this submission. Yet I well remember
The favors of these men. Were they not mine?   169
Did they not sometime cry, "All hail!" to me?
So Judas did to Christ. But he, in twelve,
Found truth in all but one; I, in twelve thousand,
    none.
God save the King! Will no man say amen?
Am I both priest and clerk? Well then, amen.   174
God save the King, although I be not he;
And yet, amen, if heaven do think him me.
To do what service am I sent for hither?
YORK
To do that office of thine own good will
Which tired majesty did make thee offer:
The resignation of thy state and crown
To Henry Bolingbroke.
KING RICHARD
Give me the crown. [*He takes the crown.*] Here,
    cousin, seize the crown.
Here, cousin,
On this side my hand, and on that side thine.
Now is this golden crown like a deep well
That owes two buckets, filling one another,   186
The emptier ever dancing in the air,
The other down, unseen, and full of water.
That bucket down and full of tears am I,
Drinking my griefs, whilst you mount up on high.
BOLINGBROKE
I thought you had been willing to resign.
KING RICHARD
My crown I am, but still my griefs are mine.
You may my glories and my state depose,
But not my griefs; still am I king of those.
BOLINGBROKE
Part of your cares you give me with your crown.
KING RICHARD
Your cares set up do not pluck my cares down.   196
My care is loss of care, by old care done;   197
Your care is gain of care, by new care won.   198
The cares I give I have, though given away;   199
They 'tend the crown, yet still with me they stay.   200

BOLINGBROKE
Are you contented to resign the crown?
KING RICHARD
Ay, no; no, ay; for I must nothing be;   202
Therefore no, no, for I resign to thee.   203
Now mark me how I will undo myself: 204
    [*He yields his crown and scepter.*]
I give this heavy weight from off my head
And this unwieldy scepter from my hand,
The pride of kingly sway from out my heart;
With mine own tears I wash away my balm,
With mine own hands I give away my crown,
With mine own tongue deny my sacred state,
With mine own breath release all duteous oaths.   211
All pomp and majesty I do forswear;
My manors, rents, revenues I forgo;
My acts, decrees, and statutes I deny.
God pardon all oaths that are broke to me!
God keep all vows unbroke are made to thee!   216
Make me, that nothing have, with nothing grieved,   217
And thou with all pleased, that hast all achieved!
Long mayst thou live in Richard's seat to sit,
And soon lie Richard in an earthy pit!
God save King Henry, unkinged Richard says,
And send him many years of sunshine days!—
What more remains?
NORTHUMBERLAND [*presenting a paper*]
            No more but that you read   223
These accusations and these grievous crimes
Committed by your person and your followers
Against the state and profit of this land;
That, by confessing them, the souls of men
May deem that you are worthily deposed.
KING RICHARD
Must I do so? And must I ravel out   229
My weaved-up follies? Gentle Northumberland,
If thy offenses were upon record,
Would it not shame thee in so fair a troop   232
To read a lecture of them? If thou wouldst,   233
There shouldst thou find one heinous article
Containing the deposing of a king
And cracking the strong warrant of an oath,
Marked with a blot, damned in the book of heaven.
Nay, all of you that stand and look upon me,
Whilst that my wretchedness doth bait myself,   239
Though some of you, with Pilate, wash your hands,   240
Showing an outward pity, yet you Pilates
Have here delivered me to my sour cross,   242
And water cannot wash away your sin.

---

162 **little . . . hands** i.e., did not expect this from you, thinking you were on our side   169 **favors** (1) faces (2) support, good will   174 **priest and clerk** (In religious services, the clerk or assistant would say "Amen" to the priest's prayers.)   186 **owes** owns, has.   **filling one another** (The raising of the full bucket lowers the other to be filled in turn.)   196–200 **Your . . . stay** i.e., Your assuming the cares of office does not assuage my griefs. My grief is loss of kingly responsibility, destroyed by a failure in diligence; your concern is gaining of kingly responsibility, won by zealous effort. The anxieties I transfer to you I also keep for myself, despite my giving them to you; they accompany the crown and yet still remain with me.

202 **Ay** (1) yes (2) I. (But, says Richard, I am nothing, and therefore "Ay" is "I" or "nothing," that is, "no.")   203 **no, no . . . thee** (Richard plays on the logic that a double negative equals a positive.)   204 **undo** (1) undress (2) unmake   211 **release . . . oaths** release my subjects from their oaths of duty   216 **are** that are   217 **Make** i.e., God make.   **with nothing grieved** (1) grieved at nothing (2) grieved at having nothing   223 **read** i.e., read aloud   229 **ravel out** unravel   232 **troop** company   233 **read a lecture** give a public reading (as a warning)   239 **bait** torment, harass (as in bearbaiting)   240 **wash your hands** (See Matthew 27:24. Richard persistently compares himself to Christ; see also 3.2.132; 4.1.171.)   242 **sour** bitter

NORTHUMBERLAND
    My lord, dispatch. Read o'er these articles.   244

KING RICHARD
    Mine eyes are full of tears; I cannot see.
    And yet salt water blinds them not so much
    But they can see a sort of traitors here.   247
    Nay, if I turn mine eyes upon myself,
    I find myself a traitor with the rest;
    For I have given here my soul's consent
    T' undeck the pompous body of a king,   251
    Made glory base and sovereignty a slave,
    Proud majesty a subject, state a peasant.   253

NORTHUMBERLAND   My lord—

KING RICHARD
    No lord of thine, thou haught insulting man,   255
    Nor no man's lord. I have no name, no title,
    No, not that name was given me at the font,
    But 'tis usurped. Alack the heavy day,
    That I have worn so many winters out
    And know not now what name to call myself!
    O, that I were a mockery king of snow,
    Standing before the sun of Bolingbroke,
    To melt myself away in water drops!
    Good king, great king, and yet not greatly good,
    An if my word be sterling yet in England,   265
    Let it command a mirror hither straight,   266
    That it may show me what a face I have,
    Since it is bankrupt of his majesty.   268

BOLINGBROKE
    Go some of you and fetch a looking glass.   269
                              [Exit an Attendant.]

NORTHUMBERLAND
    Read o'er this paper while the glass doth come.

KING RICHARD
    Fiend, thou torments me ere I come to hell!

BOLINGBROKE
    Urge it no more, my lord Northumberland.

NORTHUMBERLAND
    The commons will not then be satisfied.

KING RICHARD
    They shall be satisfied. I'll read enough
    When I do see the very book indeed
    Where all my sins are writ, and that's myself.   276

        Enter one with a glass.

    Give me that glass, and therein will I read.
                              [He takes the mirror.]
    No deeper wrinkles yet? Hath sorrow struck
    So many blows upon this face of mine,
    And made no deeper wounds? O flattering glass,
    Like to my followers in prosperity,   281
    Thou dost beguile me! Was this face the face   282
    That every day under his household roof

Did keep ten thousand men? Was this the face
That, like the sun, did make beholders wink?   285
Is this the face which faced so many follies,   286
That was at last outfaced by Bolingbroke?   287
A brittle glory shineth in this face—
As brittle as the glory is the face,
                        [He throws down the mirror.]
For there it is, cracked in an hundred shivers.
Mark, silent king, the moral of this sport:
How soon my sorrow hath destroyed my face.

BOLINGBROKE
    The shadow of your sorrow hath destroyed   293
    The shadow of your face.

KING RICHARD   Say that again.   294
    The shadow of my sorrow? Ha! Let's see.
    'Tis very true, my grief lies all within;
    And these external manners of laments   297
    Are merely shadows to the unseen grief   298
    That swells with silence in the tortured soul.
    There lies the substance; and I thank thee, King,   300
    For thy great bounty, that not only giv'st   301
    Me cause to wail, but teachest me the way
    How to lament the cause. I'll beg one boon,   303
    And then be gone and trouble you no more.
    Shall I obtain it?

BOLINGBROKE   Name it, fair cousin.

KING RICHARD
    "Fair cousin"? I am greater than a king.
    For when I was a king, my flatterers
    Were then but subjects; being now a subject,
    I have a king here to my flatterer.   309
    Being so great, I have no need to beg.

BOLINGBROKE   Yet ask.

KING RICHARD   And shall I have?

BOLINGBROKE   You shall.

KING RICHARD   Then give me leave to go.

BOLINGBROKE   Whither?

KING RICHARD
    Whither you will, so I were from your sights.

BOLINGBROKE
    Go some of you, convey him to the Tower.   317

KING RICHARD
    O, good! "Convey"? Conveyers are you all,   318
    That rise thus nimbly by a true king's fall.
            [Exeunt King Richard, some lords, and a guard.]

BOLINGBROKE
    On Wednesday next we solemnly set down
    Our coronation. Lords, prepare yourselves.   321
            Exeunt. Manent [the Abbot of] Westminster, [the
                              Bishop of] Carlisle, Aumerle.

ABBOT
    A woeful pageant have we here beheld.

---

244 **dispatch** conclude, be done 247 **sort** gang 251 **pompous** stately, splendid 253 **state** high rank 255 **haught** haughty 265 **An if** if. **sterling** valid currency 266 **straight** immediately 268 **his** its 269 **some** i.e., someone 276 **s.d. glass** mirror 281 **in prosperity** i.e., in my prosperity 282 **Was this face** (An echo of Christopher Marlowe's *Doctor Faustus*, in which the protagonist addresses Helen of Troy.)

285 **wink** close the eyes, blink 286 **faced** countenanced 287 **outfaced** stared down, discountenanced 293 **shadow** outward show, or, overshadowing nature 294 **shadow** reflection (in the mirror) 297 **manners** forms 298 **shadows to** shadowings forth or embodiments of 300 **There** i.e., in the soul 301 **that** who 303 **boon** favor 309 **to** as 317 **convey** escort 318 **Convey** steal 321 **s.d. Manent** they remain onstage

CARLISLE
The woe's to come, the children yet unborn
Shall feel this day as sharp to them as thorn.   324

AUMERLE
You holy clergymen, is there no plot
To rid the realm of this pernicious blot?

ABBOT   My lord,
Before I freely speak my mind herein,
You shall not only take the Sacrament
To bury mine intents, but also to effect   330
Whatever I shall happen to devise.
I see your brows are full of discontent,
Your hearts of sorrow, and your eyes of tears.
Come home with me to supper; I'll lay
A plot shall show us all a merry day.   *Exeunt.* 335

❖

5.1   *Enter the Queen with [Ladies,] her attendants.*

QUEEN
This way the King will come. This is the way
To Julius Caesar's ill-erected tower,   2
To whose flint bosom my condemnèd lord
Is doomed a prisoner by proud Bolingbroke.
Here let us rest, if this rebellious earth
Have any resting for her true king's queen.

Enter Richard [and guard].

But soft, but see, or rather do not see
My fair rose wither. Yet look up, behold,
That you in pity may dissolve to dew,
And wash him fresh again with true-love tears.—
Ah, thou, the model where old Troy did stand,   11
Thou map of honor, thou King Richard's tomb,   12
And not King Richard! Thou most beauteous inn,   13
Why should hard-favored grief be lodged in thee   14
When triumph is become an alehouse guest?   15

KING RICHARD
Join not with grief, fair woman, do not so,
To make my end too sudden. Learn, good soul,
To think our former state a happy dream,
From which awaked, the truth of what we are
Shows us but this. I am sworn brother, sweet,
To grim Necessity, and he and I
Will keep a league till death. Hie thee to France,   22
And cloister thee in some religious house.   23
Our holy lives must win a new world's crown,   24
Which our profane hours here have thrown down.

QUEEN
What, is my Richard both in shape and mind
Transformed and weakened? Hath Bolingbroke
Deposed thine intellect? Hath he been in thy heart?
The lion dying thrusteth forth his paw
And wounds the earth, if nothing else, with rage
To be o'erpowered; and wilt thou, pupil-like,   31
Take the correction, mildly kiss the rod,
And fawn on rage with base humility,
Which art a lion and the king of beasts?

KING RICHARD
A king of beasts, indeed! If aught but beasts,   35
I had been still a happy king of men.
Good sometime queen, prepare thee hence for
France.   37
Think I am dead and that even here thou takest,
As from my deathbed, thy last living leave.
In winter's tedious nights sit by the fire
With good old folks, and let them tell thee tales
Of woeful ages long ago betid;   42
And ere thou bid good night, to quit their griefs   43
Tell thou the lamentable tale of me
And send the hearers weeping to their beds;
Forwhy the senseless brands will sympathize   46
The heavy accent of thy moving tongue,   47
And in compassion weep the fire out;
And some will mourn in ashes, some coal-black,   49
For the deposing of a rightful king.

Enter Northumberland.

NORTHUMBERLAND
My lord, the mind of Bolingbroke is changed;
You must to Pomfret, not unto the Tower.   52
And, madam, there is order ta'en for you: 53
With all swift speed you must away to France.

KING RICHARD
Northumberland, thou ladder wherewithal
The mounting Bolingbroke ascends my throne,
The time shall not be many hours of age
More than it is ere foul sin, gathering head,   58
Shall break into corruption. Thou shalt think,   59
Though he divide the realm and give thee half,
It is too little, helping him to all;   61
He shall think that thou, which knowest the way
To plant unrightful kings, wilt know again,
Being ne'er so little urged another way,
To pluck him headlong from the usurpèd throne.   65
The love of wicked men converts to fear,   66
That fear to hate, and hate turns one or both   67
To worthy danger and deservèd death.   68

---

324 Shall who shall   **330 To . . . intents** to conceal my plans
335 shall that shall
5.1. Location: London. A street leading to the Tower.
2 Julius . . . tower (The Tower of London, ascribed by tradition to
Julius Caesar, was built by William the Conqueror to hold the city in
subordination.) **ill-erected** erected for evil ends or with evil results
11 thou . . . stand i.e., you ruined majesty, pattern of fallen greatness
like the desolate waste where Troy once stood   **12 map of honor** i.e.,
the mere outline of a once-glorious honor   **13 inn** residence, house
14 hard-favored unpleasant-looking   **15 is . . . guest** lodges in such
a lowly tavern (i.e., in Bolingbroke)   **22 Hie** hasten   **23 religious
house** convent   **24 new world's** heaven's

31 To be at being   **35 king of beasts** (1) lion (2) ruler over beastly
men   **37 sometime** former   **42 Of . . . betid** of woe that happened
ages ago   **43 quit their griefs** requite their tales of woe   **46 Forwhy
. . . sympathize** because even the inanimate and unfeeling firebrands
will respond to   **47 moving** affecting, exciting sympathy   **49 some** (of
the brands)   **52 Pomfret** Pontefract Castle in Yorkshire   **53 order
ta'en** arrangement made   **58 gathering head** gathering to a head
59 corruption putrid matter, pus   **61 helping** since you helped
65 To how to   **66 converts** changes   **67 That fear** i.e., that fear
changes.   **one or both** i.e., the new king or his partner, or both
68 worthy well-merited

NORTHUMBERLAND
My guilt be on my head, and there an end.
Take leave and part, for you must part forthwith.   70
KING RICHARD
Doubly divorced! Bad men, you violate
A twofold marriage, twixt my crown and me,
And then betwixt me and my married wife.
[*To Queen.*] Let me unkiss the oath twixt thee and me; 74
And yet not so, for with a kiss 'twas made.—
Part us, Northumberland: I towards the north,
Where shivering cold and sickness pines the clime;   77
My wife to France, from whence, set forth in pomp,
She came adornèd hither like sweet May,
Sent back like Hallowmas or short'st of day.   80
QUEEN
And must we be divided? Must we part?
KING RICHARD
Ay, hand from hand, my love, and heart from
    heart.
QUEEN [*to Northumberland*]
Banish us both and send the King with me.
NORTHUMBERLAND
That were some love, but little policy.   84
QUEEN
Then whither he goes, thither let me go.
KING RICHARD
So two, together weeping, make one woe.
Weep thou for me in France, I for thee here;
Better far off than, near, be ne'er the near.   88
Go count thy way with sighs, I mine with groans.
QUEEN
So longest way shall have the longest moans.
KING RICHARD
Twice for one step I'll groan, the way being short,
And piece the way out with a heavy heart.   92
Come, come, in wooing sorrow let's be brief,
Since, wedding it, there is such length in grief.
One kiss shall stop our mouths, and dumbly part;   95
Thus give I mine, and thus take I thy heart.
                                [*They kiss.*]
QUEEN
Give me mine own again. 'Twere no good part   97
To take on me to keep and kill thy heart. [*They kiss.*] 98
So, now I have mine own again, begone,
That I may strive to kill it with a groan.
KING RICHARD
We make woe wanton with this fond delay.   101

Once more, adieu! The rest let sorrow say.
                Exeunt [*in two separate groups*].

5.2   *Enter Duke of York and the Duchess.*

DUCHESS
My lord, you told me you would tell the rest,
When weeping made you break the story off,
Of our two cousins coming into London.   3
YORK
Where did I leave?
DUCHESS   At that sad stop, my lord,   4
Where rude misgoverned hands from windows' tops 5
Threw dust and rubbish on King Richard's head.
YORK
Then, as I said, the Duke, great Bolingbroke,
Mounted upon a hot and fiery steed
Which his aspiring rider seemed to know,   9
With slow but stately pace kept on his course,
Whilst all tongues cried, "God save thee,
    Bolingbroke!"
You would have thought the very windows spake,
So many greedy looks of young and old
Through casements darted their desiring eyes
Upon his visage, and that all the walls
With painted imagery had said at once,   16
"Jesu preserve thee! Welcome, Bolingbroke!"
Whilst he, from the one side to the other turning,
Bareheaded, lower than his proud steed's neck,   19
Bespake them thus: "I thank you, countrymen."   20
And thus still doing, thus he passed along.   21
DUCHESS
Alack, poor Richard! Where rode he the whilst?
YORK
As in a theater the eyes of men,
After a well-graced actor leaves the stage,
Are idly bent on him that enters next,   25
Thinking his prattle to be tedious,
Even so, or with much more contempt, men's eyes
Did scowl on gentle Richard. No man cried, "God
    save him!"
No joyful tongue gave him his welcome home,
But dust was thrown upon his sacred head—
Which with such gentle sorrow he shook off,
His face still combating with tears and smiles,
The badges of his grief and patience,   33
That had not God for some strong purpose steeled
The hearts of men, they must perforce have melted, 35

70 **part . . . part** separate . . . depart   **74 unkiss** annul with a kiss (regarded as the seal of a ceremonial bond)   **77 pines** afflicts, distresses. **clime** region   **80 Hallowmas** All Saints' Day (November 1), regarded as the beginning of winter. **short'st of day** the winter solstice   **84 policy** political practicality   **88 Better . . . the near** i.e., better to be far apart than near and yet unable to meet. (The second *near* means "nearer.")   **92 piece . . . out** make the journey seem longer   **95 and dumbly part** and then let us part in silence   **97–98 'Twere . . . me** it would not be wise of me to take it upon myself   **·101 We . . . wanton** we sport with our grief.   **fond** (1) loving (2) pointless, foolish

5.2. Location: The Duke of York's house.
3 cousins kinsmen, i.e., nephews (Richard and Bolingbroke)   **4 leave** leave off   **5 misgoverned** unruly. **windows' tops** upper windows   **9 Which . . . know** which seemed to know its ambitious rider   **16 With painted imagery** i.e., showing crowds of people, as on a tapestry or painted cloth, depicting a procession. **at once** all together   **19 lower** bowing lower   **20 Bespake** addressed   **21 still** continually   **25 idly** indifferently   **33 badges** insignia, outward signs   **35 perforce** necessarily

And barbarism itself have pitied him.
But heaven hath a hand in these events,
To whose high will we bound our calm contents.
To Bolingbroke are we sworn subjects now,   38
Whose state and honor I for aye allow.   40

    [Enter Aumerle.]

DUCHESS
Here comes my son Aumerle.
YORK   Aumerle that was;   41
But that is lost for being Richard's friend,
And, madam, you must call him Rutland now.
I am in Parliament pledge for his truth   44
And lasting fealty to the new-made king.
DUCHESS
Welcome, my son. Who are the violets now   46
That strew the green lap of the new-come spring?   47
AUMERLE
Madam, I know not, nor I greatly care not.
God knows I had as lief be none as one.   49
YORK
Well, bear you well in this new spring of time,   50
Lest you be cropped before you come to prime.   51
What news from Oxford? Do these jousts and
    triumphs hold?   52
AUMERLE   For aught I know, my lord, they do.
YORK   You will be there, I know.
AUMERLE
If God prevent not, I purpose so.
YORK
What seal is that, that hangs without thy bosom?   56
Yea, look'st thou pale? Let me see the writing.
AUMERLE
My lord, 'tis nothing.
YORK   No matter, then, who see it.
I will be satisfied. Let me see the writing.
AUMERLE
I do beseech Your Grace to pardon me.   60
It is a matter of small consequence,
Which for some reasons I would not have seen.   62
YORK
Which for some reasons, sir, I mean to see.
I fear, I fear—
DUCHESS   What should you fear?
'Tis nothing but some bond that he is entered into
For gay apparel 'gainst the triumph day.   66

YORK
Bound to himself? What doth he with a bond   67
That he is bound to? Wife, thou art a fool.   68
Boy, let me see the writing.
AUMERLE
I do beseech you, pardon me. I may not show it.
YORK
I will be satisfied. Let me see it, I say.
    He plucks it out of his bosom and reads it.
Treason! Foul treason! Villain! Traitor! Slave!
DUCHESS   What is the matter, my lord?
YORK [*calling offstage*]
Ho! Who is within there? Saddle my horse!—
God for his mercy, what treachery is here?   75
DUCHESS   Why, what is it, my lord?
YORK [*calling offstage*]
Give me my boots, I say! Saddle my horse!—
Now, by mine honor, by my life, my troth,   78
I will appeach the villain.
DUCHESS   What is the matter?   79
YORK
Peace, foolish woman.
DUCHESS
I will not peace. What is the matter, Aumerle?
AUMERLE
Good Mother, be content. It is no more
Than my poor life must answer.
DUCHESS   Thy life answer?
YORK
Bring me my boots! I will unto the King.

    His Man enters with his boots.

DUCHESS
Strike him, Aumerle. Poor boy, thou art amazed.   85
[*To York's Man.*] Hence, villain! Never more come
    in my sight.
YORK   Give me my boots, I say.
    [*His Man helps him on with his boots, and exit.*]
DUCHESS   Why, York, what wilt thou do?
Wilt thou not hide the trespass of thine own?
Have we more sons? Or are we like to have?   90
Is not my teeming date drunk up with time?   91
And wilt thou pluck my fair son from mine age
And rob me of a happy mother's name?
Is he not like thee? Is he not thine own?
YORK   Thou fond mad woman,   95
Wilt thou conceal this dark conspiracy?
A dozen of them here have ta'en the Sacrament,   97

---

38 we . . . contents i.e., we bind ourselves to be calmly content
40 state i.e., royal title. allow acknowledge   41 Aumerle that was
(Aumerle, as a member of Richard's party, lost his dukedom, though
he remained Earl of Rutland.)   44 pledge the guarantor. truth loyalty   46–47 Who . . . spring i.e., who are the favorites of the new
king?   49 lief happily   50 bear you bear yourself   51 cropped cut
52 Do . . . hold are those tourneys and pageants going forward. (According to Holinshed, these tourneys at Oxford were part of a conspiracy against Bolingbroke by the Abbot of Westminster and others;
the new king was to be invited to attend and there be assassinated.)
56 seal i.e., seal attached to the border of a document   60 pardon
me i.e., excuse me if I don't comply   62 have seen wish to be seen
66 'gainst in anticipation of

67–68 What . . . bound to i.e., why should he have the bond instead of the creditor to whom the debt is owed?   75 God i.e., I pray
God   78 troth faith, allegiance   79 appeach inform against, publicly
accuse   85 Strike him i.e., strike the servant.   amazed confused, bewildered   90 Have we more sons (Historically, this Duchess of York
was the Duke's second wife and was not Aumerle's mother; she was,
however, the mother of another son, Richard, subsequently Earl of
Cambridge.)   91 teeming date period of childbearing   95 fond foolish   97–99 A dozen . . . Oxford ("Hereupon was an indenture sexti-
partite made, sealed with their seals and signed with their hands, in
the which each stood bound to other, to do their whole endeavor for
the accomplishment of their purposed exploit." [Holinshed])

And interchangeably set down their hands,
To kill the King at Oxford.

DUCHESS   He shall be none;   99
We'll keep him here. Then what is that to him?   100

YORK
Away, fond woman! Were he twenty times my son
I would appeach him.

DUCHESS   Hadst thou groaned for him   102
As I have done, thou wouldst be more pitiful.   103
But now I know thy mind. Thou dost suspect
That I have been disloyal to thy bed,
And that he is a bastard, not thy son.
Sweet York, sweet husband, be not of that mind!
He is as like thee as a man may be,
Not like to me, or any of my kin,
And yet I love him.

YORK   Make way, unruly woman! *Exit.*

DUCHESS
After, Aumerle! Mount thee upon his horse,   111
Spur post, and get before him to the King,   112
And beg thy pardon ere he do accuse thee.
I'll not be long behind. Though I be old,
I doubt not but to ride as fast as York.
And never will I rise up from the ground
Till Bolingbroke have pardoned thee. Away, begone!
                 [Exeunt separately.]

❖

5.3   *Enter [Bolingbroke, now] King [Henry], with his*
nobles [Harry Percy and others].

KING HENRY
Can no man tell me of my unthrifty son?   1
'Tis full three months since I did see him last.
If any plague hang over us, 'tis he.
I would to God, my lords, he might be found.
Inquire at London, 'mongst the taverns there,
For there, they say, he daily doth frequent
With unrestrainèd loose companions,
Even such, they say, as stand in narrow lanes
And beat our watch, and rob our passengers—   9
While he, young wanton and effeminate boy,   10
Takes on the point of honor to support   11
So dissolute a crew.

PERCY
My lord, some two days since I saw the Prince,
And told him of those triumphs held at Oxford.   14

KING HENRY   And what said the gallant?

PERCY
His answer was, he would unto the stews,   16
And from the common'st creature pluck a glove,

And wear it as a favor, and with that   18
He would unhorse the lustiest challenger.   19

KING HENRY
As dissolute as desperate! Yet through both
I see some sparks of better hope, which elder years
May happily bring forth. But who comes here?   22

         Enter Aumerle, amazed.

AUMERLE   Where is the King?

KING HENRY
What means our cousin, that he stares and looks
So wildly?

AUMERLE
God save Your Grace! I do beseech Your Majesty
To have some conference with Your Grace alone.

KING HENRY *[to his nobles]*
Withdraw yourselves, and leave us here alone.
               [Exeunt Percy and lords.]
What is the matter with our cousin now?

AUMERLE *[kneeling]*
Forever may my knees grow to the earth,
My tongue cleave to the roof within my mouth,   31
Unless a pardon ere I rise or speak.

KING HENRY
Intended or committed was this fault?
If on the first, how heinous e'er it be,   34
To win thy after-love I pardon thee.

AUMERLE *[rising]*
Then give me leave that I may turn the key,
That no man enter till my tale be done.

KING HENRY   Have thy desire.
       [Aumerle locks the door.] The Duke of York
              knocks at the door and crieth.

YORK *[within]*
My liege, beware! Look to thyself.
Thou hast a traitor in thy presence there.

KING HENRY *[drawing]*   Villain, I'll make thee safe.   41

AUMERLE
Stay thy revengeful hand. Thou hast no cause
to fear.

YORK *[within]*
Open the door, secure, foolhardy King!   43
Shall I for love speak treason to thy face?   44
Open the door, or I will break it open.
             [King Henry unlocks the door.]

         [Enter York.]

KING HENRY
What is the matter, uncle? Speak.
Recover breath; tell us how near is danger,
That we may arm us to encounter it.

YORK *[giving letter]*
Peruse this writing here, and thou shalt know

---

100 that i.e., the plot   **102 groaned for** i.e., given birth to (but see note, line 90)   **103 pitiful** pitying   **111 After** go after him.   **his horse** i.e., one of York's horses   **112 Spur post** ride as fast as possible
5.3. Location: The court (i.e., Windsor Castle).
1 unthrifty profligate   **9 watch** night watchmen.   **passengers** passers-by, wayfarers   **10 wanton** pampered youth.   **effeminate** self-indulgent   **11 Takes on the** i.e., makes it a   **14 held** i.e., to be held   **16 stews** brothels

18 with that i.e., wearing that as a favor   **19 lustiest** most vigorous and brave   **22 happily** with good fortune.   **s.d. amazed** stunned, bewildered   **31 My . . . mouth** (See Psalm 137:6: "If I do not remember thee, let my tongue cleave to the roof of my mouth.")   **34 If on the first** i.e., if intended only   **41 safe** harmless   **43 secure** unsuspecting, heedless   **44 speak . . . face** i.e., speak so disrespectfully as to call you *secure* and *foolhardy*

The treason that my haste forbids me show.   50

AUMERLE
Remember, as thou read'st, thy promise passed.
I do repent me. Read not my name there;
My heart is not confederate with my hand.   53

YORK
It was, villain, ere thy hand did set it down.
I tore it from the traitor's bosom, King;
Fear, and not love, begets his penitence.
Forget to pity him, lest thy pity prove   57
A serpent that will sting thee to the heart.

KING HENRY
O, heinous, strong, and bold conspiracy!
O loyal father of a treacherous son,
Thou sheer, immaculate, and silver fountain,   61
From whence this stream through muddy passages
Hath held his current and defiled himself,
Thy overflow of good converts to bad,   64
And thy abundant goodness shall excuse
This deadly blot in thy digressing son.   66

YORK
So shall my virtue be his vice's bawd,
And he shall spend mine honor with his shame,
As thriftless sons their scraping fathers' gold.   69
Mine honor lives when his dishonor dies,
Or my shamed life in his dishonor lies.
Thou kill'st me in his life; giving him breath,
The traitor lives, the true man's put to death.

DUCHESS [within]
What ho, my liege! For God's sake, let me in.

KING HENRY
What shrill-voiced suppliant makes this eager cry?

DUCHESS [within]
A woman, and thy aunt, great King. 'Tis I.
Speak with me, pity me, open the door!
A beggar begs that never begged before.

KING HENRY
Our scene is altered from a serious thing,
And now changed to "The Beggar and the King."   80
My dangerous cousin, let your mother in.
I know she is come to pray for your foul sin.

[Aumerle opens the door. Enter the Duchess. She kneels.]

YORK
If thou do pardon whosoever pray,
More sins for this forgiveness prosper may.   84
This festered joint cut off, the rest rest sound;
This let alone will all the rest confound.   86

DUCHESS
O King, believe not this hardhearted man.
Love loving not itself, none other can.   88

YORK
Thou frantic woman, what dost thou make here?   89
Shall thy old dugs once more a traitor rear?   90

DUCHESS
Sweet York, be patient.—Hear me, gentle liege.

KING HENRY
Rise up, good aunt.

DUCHESS   Not yet, I thee beseech.
Forever will I walk upon my knees,
And never see day that the happy sees,   94
Till thou give joy, until thou bid me joy,
By pardoning Rutland, my transgressing boy.

AUMERLE [kneeling]
Unto my mother's prayers I bend my knee.   97

YORK [kneeling]
Against them both my true joints bended be.
Ill mayst thou thrive, if thou grant any grace!

DUCHESS
Pleads he in earnest? Look upon his face.
His eyes do drop no tears, his prayers are in jest;
His words come from his mouth, ours from our
    breast.
He prays but faintly and would be denied;
We pray with heart and soul and all beside.   104
His weary joints would gladly rise, I know;
Our knees still kneel till to the ground they grow.   106
His prayers are full of false hypocrisy,
Ours of true zeal and deep integrity.
Our prayers do outpray his; then let them have
That mercy which true prayer ought to have.

KING HENRY
Good aunt, stand up.

DUCHESS   Nay, do not say "stand up."
Say "pardon" first, and afterwards "stand up."
An if I were thy nurse, thy tongue to teach,   113
"Pardon" should be the first word of thy speech.
I never longed to hear a word till now;
Say "pardon," King; let pity teach thee how.
The word is short, but not so short as sweet;
No word like "pardon" for kings' mouths so meet.

YORK
Speak it in French, King: say "pardonne moy."   119

DUCHESS
Dost thou teach pardon pardon to destroy?
Ah, my sour husband, my hardhearted lord,
That sets the word itself against the word!
Speak "pardon" as 'tis current in our land;
The chopping French we do not understand.   124
Thine eye begins to speak; set thy tongue there,
Or in thy piteous heart plant thou thine ear,
That hearing how our plaints and prayers do pierce,
Pity may move thee "pardon" to rehearse.   128

KING HENRY
Good aunt, stand up.

50 haste . . . show i.e., breathlessness prevents me from revealing **53 hand** signature **57 Forget** forget your promise **61 sheer** clear, pure **64 converts** changes **66 digressing** deviating from his proper course, transgressing **69 scraping** parsimonious **80 The Beggar . . . King** (Probably one of Shakespeare's many allusions to the ballad of King Cophetua and the Beggar Maid.) **84 for** because of **86 alone** untreated. **confound** ruin **88 Love . . . can** i.e., he who does not love himself in his own son can love no one else, not even the King

89 make do **90 once . . . rear** i.e., give life again by now redeeming Aumerle from death **94 never . . . sees** i.e., never partake of the bliss that happy people enjoy **97 Unto** in support of **104 beside** besides **106 still** continually **113 An if** if **119 pardonne moy** pardonnez-moi, excuse me. (An affectedly polite refusal.) **124 chopping** logic chopping, changing the sense **128 rehearse** repeat

DUCHESS   I do not sue to stand.
  Pardon is all the suit I have in hand.
KING HENRY
  I pardon him, as God shall pardon me.
DUCHESS
  O happy vantage of a kneeling knee!   132
  Yet am I sick for fear. Speak it again;
  Twice saying "pardon" doth not pardon twain
  But makes one pardon strong.
KING HENRY   With all my heart
  I pardon him.   [All rise.]
DUCHESS   A god on earth thou art.
KING HENRY
  But for our trusty brother-in-law and the Abbot,   137
  With all the rest of that consorted crew,   138
  Destruction straight shall dog them at the heels.
  Good uncle, help to order several powers   140
  To Oxford, or where'er these traitors are.
  They shall not live within this world, I swear,
  But I will have them, if I once know where.
  Uncle, farewell, and, cousin, adieu.
  Your mother well hath prayed; and prove you true.   145
DUCHESS
  Come, my old son. I pray God make thee new.   146
                          Exeunt [in two groups].

❧

5.4   *Enter Sir Pierce [of] Exton [and his Men].*

EXTON
  Didst thou not mark the King, what words he
    spake,
  "Have I no friend will rid me of this living fear?"   2
  Was it not so?
MAN   These were his very words.
EXTON
  "Have I no friend?" quoth he. He spake it twice,
  And urged it twice together, did he not?
MAN   He did.
EXTON
  And speaking it, he wishtly looked on me,   7
  As who should say, "I would thou wert the man
  That would divorce this terror from my heart"—
  Meaning the King at Pomfret. Come, let's go.
  I am the King's friend, and will rid his foe.   11
                          [Exeunt.]

❧

132 **happy vantage** fortunate gain   137 **But for** but as for.   **brother-
in-law** i.e., the Duke of Exeter, who had married Bolingbroke's sister
138 **consorted** conspiring, confederate   140 **powers** forces
145 **prove you true** may you prove loyal   146 **old** unregenerate
5.4. Location: The court. The opening stage direction in the Quarto
reads *Manet Sir Pierce Exton, etc.,* **suggesting continuity of action
with the preceding scene.**
2 **will** who will   7 **wishtly** intently   11 **rid** rid him of

5.5   *Enter Richard alone.*

KING RICHARD
  I have been studying how I may compare
  This prison where I live unto the world;
  And, for because the world is populous,   3
  And here is not a creature but myself,
  I cannot do it. Yet I'll hammer it out.   5
  My brain I'll prove the female to my soul,
  My soul the father, and these two beget
  A generation of still-breeding thoughts;   8
  And these same thoughts people this little world,   9
  In humors like the people of this world,   10
  For no thought is contented. The better sort,
  As thoughts of things divine, are intermixed
  With scruples and do set the word itself   13
  Against the word, as thus, "Come, little ones,"   14
  And then again,
  "It is as hard to come as for a camel
  To thread the postern of a small needle's eye."   17
  Thoughts tending to ambition, they do plot
  Unlikely wonders—how these vain weak nails
  May tear a passage through the flinty ribs
  Of this hard world, my ragged prison walls,   21
  And, for they cannot, die in their own pride.   22
  Thoughts tending to content flatter themselves
  That they are not the first of fortune's slaves,
  Nor shall not be the last—like seely beggars   25
  Who, sitting in the stocks, refuge their shame   26
  That many have and others must sit there;
  And in this thought they find a kind of ease,
  Bearing their own misfortunes on the back
  Of such as have before endured the like.
  Thus play I in one person many people,
  And none contented. Sometimes am I king;
  Then treason makes me wish myself a beggar,   33
  And so I am. Then crushing penury   34
  Persuades me I was better when a king;
  Then am I kinged again, and by and by
  Think that I am unkinged by Bolingbroke,
  And straight am nothing. But whate'er I be,
  Nor I, nor any man that but man is,   39
  With nothing shall be pleased till he be eased   40
  With being nothing. (*The music plays.*) Music do I
    hear?   41
  Ha, ha, keep time! How sour sweet music is,
  When time is broke and no proportion kept!
  So is it in the music of men's lives.
  And here have I the daintiness of ear

5.5. **Location: Pomfret Castle. A dungeon.**
3 **for because** because   5 **hammer** i.e., work, puzzle   8 **still-breeding** constantly breeding   9 **this little world** this prison as a microcosm
of the world   10 **humors** temperaments, peculiar fancies   13 **scruples**
doubts   13–14 **do set . . . word** i.e., oppose one scriptural passage
against its apparent opposite   14–17 **Come . . . eye** (See Matthew
19:14, 24.)   17 **postern** narrow gate   21 **ragged** rugged   22 **for** because.   **pride** prime   25 **seely** simpleminded   26 **refuge their shame**
i.e., rationalize their disgrace by reflecting   33 **treason** i.e., thinking
about treason   34 **penury** poverty   39 **Nor** neither   40 **nothing** anything   41 **being nothing** i.e., being dead

To check time broke in a disordered string; 46
But for the concord of my state and time
Had not an ear to hear my true time broke.
I wasted time, and now doth time waste me;
For now hath Time made me his numbering clock. 50
My thoughts are minutes, and with sighs they jar 51
Their watches on unto mine eyes, the outward
    watch 52
Whereto my finger, like a dial's point, 53
Is pointing still in cleansing them from tears.
Now sir, the sounds that tell what hour it is
Are clamorous groans that strike upon my heart,
Which is the bell. So sighs and tears and groans
Show minutes, hours, and times. But my time 58
Runs posting on in Bolingbroke's proud joy, 59
While I stand fooling here, his jack of the clock. 60
This music mads me. Let it sound no more, 61
For though it have holp madmen to their wits, 62
In me it seems it will make wise men mad.
                              [*The music ceases.*]
Yet blessing on his heart that gives it me!
For 'tis a sign of love; and love to Richard
Is a strange brooch in this all-hating world. 66

                Enter a Groom of the stable.

GROOM
    Hail, royal prince!
KING RICHARD   Thanks, noble peer.
    The cheapest of us is ten groats too dear. 68
    What art thou, and how comest thou hither,
    Where no man never comes but that sad dog
    That brings me food to make misfortune live?
GROOM
    I was a poor groom of thy stable, King,
    When thou wert king; who, traveling towards York,
    With much ado at length have gotten leave
    To look upon my sometime royal master's face. 75
    O, how it earned my heart when I beheld 76
    In London streets, that coronation day,
    When Bolingbroke rode on roan Barbary,
    That horse that thou so often hast bestrid,
    That horse that I so carefully have dressed! 80
KING RICHARD
    Rode he on Barbary? Tell me, gentle friend,
    How went he under him?

46 check rebuke. **string** stringed instrument **50 numbering clock** i.e., a clock that numbers hours and minutes (not an hourglass) **51–52 My . . . watch** my sad thoughts, occurring every minute, are parts of an inner clock that, by means of the sighs they provoke, transfer their cares to my eyes, the face of the clock **53 dial's point** clock hand **58 times** quarters and halves **59 posting** hastening **60 jack of the clock** manikin that struck the bell on a clock **61 mads** maddens **62 holp** helped **66 strange brooch** rare ornament **68 ten groats too dear** (There is a pun on *royal* and *noble* in the preceding lines. A royal (ten shillings) is worth ten groats (ten times four pence) more than a noble (six shillings, eight pence) is; hence, Richard is saying that he, "the cheapest of us" because he is a prisoner, is worth no more than the groom, whom he greets as "noble.") **75 sometime** former **76 earned** grieved **80 dressed** tended, groomed

GROOM
    So proudly as if he disdained the ground.
KING RICHARD
    So proud that Bolingbroke was on his back!
    That jade hath eat bread from my royal hand; 85
    This hand hath made him proud with clapping him. 86
    Would he not stumble? Would he not fall down,
    Since pride must have a fall, and break the neck
    Of that proud man that did usurp his back?
    Forgiveness, horse! Why do I rail on thee,
    Since thou, created to be awed by man,
    Wast born to bear? I was not made a horse,
    And yet I bear a burden like an ass,
    Spur-galled and tired by jaucing Bolingbroke. 94

        Enter one [a Keeper] to Richard with meat.

KEEPER [*to Groom*]
    Fellow, give place. Here is no longer stay.
KING RICHARD [*to Groom*]
    If thou love me, 'tis time thou wert away.
GROOM
    What my tongue dares not, that my heart shall say.
                                    Exit Groom.
KEEPER
    My lord, will 't please you to fall to?
KING RICHARD
    Taste of it first, as thou art wont to do. 99
KEEPER
    My lord, I dare not. Sir Pierce of Exton, who
    Lately came from the King, commands the contrary.
KING RICHARD
    The devil take Henry of Lancaster and thee!
    Patience is stale, and I am weary of it.
                            [*He beats the Keeper.*]
KEEPER Help, help, help!

        The murderers [Exton and his men] rush in.

KING RICHARD
    How now, what means death in this rude assault?
    Villain, thy own hand yields thy death's instrument.
        [*He snatches a weapon from a man and kills him.*]
    Go thou, and fill another room in hell. 107
        [*He kills another.*] *Here Exton strikes him down.*
    That hand shall burn in never-quenching fire
    That staggers thus my person. Exton, thy fierce hand 109
    Hath with the King's blood stained the King's own
        land.
    Mount, mount, my soul! Thy seat is up on high,
    Whilst my gross flesh sinks downward, here to die.
                                        [*He dies.*]
EXTON
    As full of valor as of royal blood.
    Both have I spilled. O, would the deed were good!
    For now the devil, that told me I did well,

85 eat eaten. (Pronounced "et.") **86 clapping** patting, stroking **94 Spur-galled** made sore by the spur. **jauncing** prancing, hard-riding. **s.d. meat** food **99 Taste . . . first** i.e., to ensure that it isn't poisoned **107 room** place **109 staggers** causes to stagger

Says that this deed is chronicled in hell.
This dead king to the living king I'll bear.
Take hence the rest, and give them burial here.
                    [Exeunt, with the bodies.]

♣

5.6   *[Flourish.] Enter Bolingbroke [as King], with the
            Duke of York, [other lords, and attendants].*

KING HENRY
    Kind uncle York, the latest news we hear
    Is that the rebels have consumed with fire
    Our town of Ci'cester in Gloucestershire,   3
    But whether they be ta'en or slain we hear not.

            Enter Northumberland.

    Wecome, my lord. What is the news?
NORTHUMBERLAND
    First, to thy sacred state wish I all happiness.
    The next news is, I have to London sent
    The heads of Salisbury, Spencer, Blunt, and Kent.
    The manner of their taking may appear   9
    At large discoursèd in this paper here.   10
                    [He gives a paper.]
KING HENRY
    We thank thee, gentle Percy, for thy pains,
    And to thy worth will add right worthy gains.   12

            Enter Lord Fitzwater.

FITZWATER
    My lord, I have from Oxford sent to London
    The heads of Brocas and Sir Bennet Seely,
    Two of the dangerous consorted traitors   15
    That sought at Oxford thy dire overthrow.
KING HENRY
    Thy pains, Fitzwater, shall not be forgot;
    Right noble is thy merit, well I wot.   18

            *Enter Henry Percy [with the Bishop of Carlisle,
            guarded].*

PERCY
    The grand conspirator, Abbot of Westminster,
    With clog of conscience and sour melancholy   20
    Hath yielded up his body to the grave;
    But here is Carlisle living, to abide   22
    Thy kingly doom and sentence of his pride.   23
KING HENRY   Carlisle, this is your doom:
    Choose out some secret place, some reverent room,   25
    More than thou hast, and with it joy thy life.   26
    So as thou liv'st in peace, die free from strife;
    For though mine enemy thou hast ever been,
    High sparks of honor in thee have I seen.

            Enter Exton, with [attendants bearing] the coffin.

5.6. Location: The court.
3 Ci'cester Cirencester   **9 taking** capture   **10 At large discoursèd** related in full   **12 worth** (1) deserving (2) present worth   **15 consorted**
conspiring   **18 wot** know   **20 clog** burden   **22 abide** await
23 doom judgment   **25 reverent room** place suitable for religious retirement   **26 More than thou hast** i.e., larger than your present cell,
or more worthy of reverence.   **joy** gladden, enjoy

EXTON
    Great King, within this coffin I present
    Thy buried fear. Herein all breathless lies
    The mightiest of thy greatest enemies,
    Richard of Bordeaux, by me hither brought.
KING HENRY
    Exton, I thank thee not, for thou hast wrought
    A deed of slander with thy fatal hand   35
    Upon my head and all this famous land.
EXTON
    From your own mouth, my lord, did I this deed.
KING HENRY
    They love not poison that do poison need,
    Nor do I thee. Though I did wish him dead,
    I hate the murderer, love him murderèd.
    The guilt of conscience take thou for thy labor,
    But neither my good word nor princely favor.
    With Cain go wander through the shades of night,   43
    And never show thy head by day nor light.
                    [Exeunt Exton and attendants.]
    Lords, I protest my soul is full of woe
    That blood should sprinkle me to make me grow.
    Come mourn with me for what I do lament,
    And put on sullen black incontinent.   48
    I'll make a voyage to the Holy Land
    To wash this blood off from my guilty hand.
    March sadly after. Grace my mournings here   51
    In weeping after this untimely bier.
                    [Exeunt in procession, following the coffin.]

35 deed of slander i.e., a deed sure to arouse slanderous talk about
the new King   **43 Cain** murderer of his brother Abel; see 1.1.104
48 incontinent immediately   **51 Grace** dignify

The First Part of King Henry the Fourth

The opening of *1 Henry IV* is taut and grave in tone. England is "shaken" and "wan with care." The troubles of *Richard II*, to which this play (c. 1596–1597) is a close sequel, have not been left behind. However much King Henry would prefer to unite his countrymen against a common foreign enemy in a crusade to the holy lands, he is prevented from doing so by continuing civil war. The impassioned rhetoric of his opening speech can only end in anticlimax, for the actual purpose of this meeting in council is to receive and assess reports of military action against the throne.

Henry's current troubles are in the far reaches of his kingdom: Scots in the north, Welsh in the west. Fighting for Henry on these two fronts are the nobles of the Percy family who helped him to power: Harry Percy ("Hotspur"), his father (Henry Percy) the Earl of Northumberland, his uncle the Earl of Worcester, and his brother-in-law Edmund Mortimer, the Earl of March. Apparently, they have fought bravely. Yet we soon sense that all is not well between the new King and those who rebelled with him against Richard II. A quarrel breaks out because Hotspur refuses to deliver to Henry some prisoners as required by feudal obedience. The matter of the ransom money is only a technicality; what is really at issue? In part, it is Henry's insistence on being obeyed on principle. Admiring Hotspur inordinately, the King feels he must discipline affectionately this fine young warrior as a father would discipline his son. Even more deeply, however, the issue of the prisoners galls Henry because of the proviso that he ransom Mortimer, captured by the Welsh. Henry does not forget that Mortimer is his chief rival for the English crown, being descended from the Duke of Clarence (elder brother to Henry's father, Gaunt) and having been proclaimed by Richard as heir to the throne. (Shakespeare accentuates the dynastic threat by combining two Edmund Mortimers from his historical sources: one who married Glendower's daughter and another who claimed the English throne; see 1.3.80–85 and note.) Mortimer is the last person Henry would wish ransomed. Moreover, the King suspects Mortimer of having fought with something less than total zeal against the Welsh Glendower. Mortimer's mar-

riage to Glendower's daughter confirms the King's worst fears. Henry knows Northumberland and Worcester to be expert in treasonous plotting, since they conspired with him to overthrow Richard. Now, Henry believes, these Percys are extending their alliance by a series of calculated marriages in order to seize power once again. This time their claimant is Mortimer.

Shakespeare's sympathies are many sided. The Percy clan is, in fact, organizing against Henry, but not without cause. As they see it, the man they helped to the throne has done little for them since. His manner of disciplining them sounds too much like hostility and ingratitude. Other counselors attend the King constantly while Worcester is banished from court. In such an atmosphere of distrust, suspicion breeds still more suspicion. The situation has deteriorated, surely more than either party originally intended.

Hotspur is the most attractive of the rebels—to us as well as to King Henry. He is outspoken, courageous, witty, and domineering in conversation. Above all, he is a disciple of manliness, loyalty, chivalry, bravery in battle—the attributes of an upstanding and somewhat old-fashioned sense of honor. Yet a fatal defect dwells even in these attractive qualities. Hotspur is impatient, proud, unwilling to tolerate a rival—be it Glendower or Prince Hal (Henry, Prince of Wales). In his first speech, purporting to explain his refusal to deliver the prisoners, he brilliantly satirizes an effete courtier who had come to him from King Henry in the midst of a battle. The satire betrays many harsh qualities in Hotspur: the self-indulgent wrath that returns fully to him even in recollection of the encounter, the pride in his own stoical indifference to suffering, and especially the obsessive nature (revealed in the repetitive pattern of the rhetoric) of his contempt for courtiers generally. Surely his scorn for stay-at-home politicians is directed in part at King Henry himself. To Hotspur, all courtiers are effeminate, perfume-wearing, affected in mannerism and speech, and scarcely masculine. This preoccupation of Hotspur's makes him extraordinarily prone to one-sided judgments. Like most excessive devotees of chivalry, he divides humanity into two categories: those who are gentlemen, like himself, and those who are beneath contempt. The "vile politician" Bolingbroke and his son, the "sword-and-buckler Prince of Wales" (1.3.240, 229) fall into the latter category.

Prone as he is to such an overly simple view of political behavior, Hotspur can see no good in the King's cause and no evil in his own. He is a poor listener because of his obsession and yet an easy prey to his uncle and father, who require his leadership for their cause. They need only implant the suggestion that King Henry is acting from a political motive in his refusal to ransom Mortimer, and Hotspur is ready to leap incautiously to the defense of their cause. The great irony is that Hotspur fails to see political motives in the machinations of his own relatives. While he fights for bright honor, they maneuver cautiously for position and prove to be uncertain allies when the hour of battle approaches. Most crucially, they betray Hotspur in the prebattle negotiations, at which he is not present. As Worcester explains to Vernon during their return to rebel headquarters (5.2.3–25), they cannot let Hotspur know of the King's offer to settle matters by a general pardon. Although, as they realize, the King could pardon Hotspur's youth, there can be no turning back for themselves. Thus, the honor for which Hotspur fights is at bottom a lie, and the mutual esteem that might have grown between him and a much-reformed Prince of Wales is thwarted by the polarization of attitudes in the two camps. Hotspur's brand of honor is the victim of its own excess and lends some credence to Falstaff's wry conclusion that honor "is a mere scutcheon" (5.1.139–140).

The contrasting of Falstaff and Hotspur on the theme of honor suggests that they are dramatic foils for each other, representing extremes between which Hal must choose. Shakespeare uses this foil device structurally and consciously; for example, he has considerably reduced the age of the Hotspur he found in Raphael Holinshed's *Chronicles* (1578) in order to stress the similarity between Hotspur and Prince Hal. Conversely, to emphasize the contrast between Falstaff and Hotspur, Shakespeare envisages Falstaff as old (nearly sixty, by his own admission), fat, humorous, and without honor. Falstaff's vices are Hotspur's virtues, and the reverse. Whereas Hotspur offers to Hal a model of chivalric striving and attention to duty, Falstaff is a highwayman and a liar. On the other hand, Hotspur is a fanatic, unbending and self-absorbed even in the company of his sprightly wife, Kate, and irritated by music and poetry; Falstaff is the epitome of merriment and joie de vivre. We excuse much in him because he lusts after life with such an appetite and ingratiates himself to others by inviting them to laugh at his expense.

Despite the nearly irresistible attractiveness of Falstaff as a jolly companion and butt of humorous joking, he and Prince Hal are perennially caught up in witty debate as to the importance of Falstaff in Hal's life and whether the young man will have to get rid of Falstaff once Hal is king. The bantering raillery of their first scene (1.2) seems designed to provide diverting entertainment for the Prince and for us, and yet, beneath the gay surface, we perceive that Hal and Falstaff are talking about the hanging of thieves and the question of whether or not Hal should give in to sinful temptation. Can the relationship of Hal and Falstaff continue unchanged into the reign of Henry V? Will there be gallows standing and justice for highwaymen? Will "Monsieur Remorse," as Poins calls Falstaff, ever sincerely repent? Will the Prince, for that matter? To allay our fears, Hal soliloquizes at scene's end, vowing his determination to use these scapegrace companions as mere foils for his triumphal reformation at the appropriate time. But this explanation raises an opposite danger in our sympathies: is he callously using his companions merely to create a self-serving myth of Prince Hal, the Pol-

itician with the Common Touch? Is Francis the drawer no more to Hal than a butt for his raillery? Since the rejection of Falstaff is, by Hal's own words, already determined, can we credit him with a serious friendship? Where do Shakespeare's sympathies lie—with the need for political order or with the hedonistic spirit of youth? Perhaps he recognizes the validity of both, and accordingly shows us a prince who is genuinely fond of Falstaff's exuberant company but who also knows that he is a king's son and must sooner or later accept the consequences of that unsought role. Falstaff's gift to him is youthful irresponsibility, which must be cherished (by all of us), even though it cannot last.

In the Gad's Hill robbery, Falstaff reveals that his "cowardice" differs from the natural craven fear of Bardolph and Peto. He fights no longer than he sees "reason," that is, not against unfair odds such as two athletic young men in the dark (or later, at Shrewsbury, against the burly Scots giant, the Douglas). A man could get killed that way. Falstaff's cowardice, then, is philosophic, seen by himself in a humorous perspective. The same is true of his lying about the robbery. However much Hal exults in exposing Falstaff as a fraud, we cannot dismiss the possibility that Falstaff may see through the Prince's scheme, and may then feed Hal the expectedly outlandish lie (two men in buckram become eleven men) as a means of begging for affection. Falstaff's only way of pleading his cause is to tickle the Prince's fancy, in his role as a kind of court fool. What Falstaff most wants is to be loved and retained for what he is, and that, poignantly enough, is the one thing the mature Henry V cannot grant.

Throughout *1 Henry IV*, Shakespeare seems interested in the relationships between fathers and sons. These relationships help structure the comparisons and contrasts among foil characters. Falstaff is a foil, not only for Hotspur, but also for Henry IV; that is, despite all his insistence on youthful irresponsibility, Falstaff acts as a kind of parental figure to Hal. In the tavern scene (2.4), Falstaff and Hal take turns playing king and crown prince, and in both roles Falstaff wittily argues his case as companion and guide to the heir to the throne. Is it better to be old and merry, fat and loved, or to be hated like Pharaoh's lean kine? Falstaff argues against the gravity of council meetings with the same amused fervor that he later directs at the grinning honor of a dead hero. Hal, in his turn as king, questions the propriety of a "devil" haunting the crown prince "in the likeness of an old fat man," a "reverend Vice," a "gray Iniquity," a "father ruffian" (2.4.442–449). For all the good humor in this exchange, both men are asking whether Falstaff or King Henry serves Hal as the better model. Hal anticipates some of the very arguments his father will use against him next day at court, and, indeed, the insistent presence of that sober adult world makes itself felt even in the tavern. When, under the pressure of that looming responsibility, Falstaff's merrymaking turns to something like urgent self-justification in his moving litany of appeals that Hal "banish not him thy Harry's company—banish plump Jack, and banish all the world," the Prince seems aware that he must face the consequences of his destiny. "I do, I will," he answers (lines 472–476), in a tone that can vary onstage (depending on the actor) from sober resolution to fond regret to awakening as from a dream.

Hotspur, too, is regarded as a son by more than one father. King Henry only half-jokingly wishes it could be proved that some night-tripping fairy had exchanged his Harry in the cradle for Harry Percy (1.1.85–89). Paradoxically, the King admires Hotspur all the more for standing up to him, just as another imperious father figure, Owen Glendower, bestows grudging but real admiration on Hotspur for his outspokenness (3.1.1–185). Hotspur's rebellious ways are cherished because they seem to promise manliness and fame; Hal's rebellious ways are feared and despised because they seem to reject the values of duty and leadership on which King Henry bases his self-respect. In these terms, the play must resolve Hal's coming of age, his acceptance of his role as true son of the King, and his proving his worth to the King. Hal must find his adult self—a self that differs greatly from that of King Henry—but must do so in a way that preserves the integrity of their relationship and the real debt he owes his father.

Prince Hal's uncertain journey toward maturity does not involve him in any significant relationships with women. His task is to fulfill what is expected of him as his father's son in a world of political and military conflict. Women stand on the periphery of affairs, as in *Richard II,* and yet the scenes in which they appear offer important perspectives on male competitiveness and ambition. Hotspur's wife, Kate, must put up with being condescended to and told little about men's doings; yet Hotspur's genuine fondness for her shows the best side of his personality, and her worries about his obsessive ways indicate that she understands him better than he understands himself. Mortimer's Welsh wife, too, introduces into this play an element of tenderness and anxious concern that is notably lacking in the earlier part of 3.1, when Hotspur cannot stop himself from quarreling pointlessly with his senior ally, Glendower. Hotspur's insensitivity to the Welsh lady's beautiful song is perhaps a key to his impending tragedy, for he is never a good listener. On a lower social scale, Mistress Quickly devotedly looks after Falstaff, only to be repaid with misogynistic insults that she does not appear to understand and with mooching that she recognizes all too well. Prince Hal, meantime, plays the role of intelligent observer of the battle of the sexes, even while he postpones his own engagement in that merry war. He must first sort out who he is in terms of male goals of career and success.

These conflicts surrounding Hal reach their climax and resolution at the field of Shrewsbury in Act 5. Hal's worth must be proven at Hotspur's expense. The rivalry between the two has been intense throughout the play, as seen for example in Hal's brilliant mimicking of Hotspur's devotion to bloodshed (2.4.101–108). Aware that his tarnished reputation puts him at a disadvantage, Hal speaks nobly of his rival and impresses even the adversarial camp with his regal bearing (5.1.83–100, 5.2.51–68). He rescues his father in the battle, thereby proving to King Henry that his son does not wish to supplant him, as he had feared. After the battle, Hal frees his Scottish adversary the Douglas in a display of princely magnificence, doing so with a more generous motive than Hotspur had displayed in his earlier release of the Douglas as his prisoner (1.3.259–262). Meantime, Hal has put considerable distance between himself and Falstaff, though sensitive still to the warmth of old memories. When he sees Hotspur and Falstaff on the ground together, both seemingly dead, Hal views as in a tableau the contrasting models between which he has shaped his own identity. Yet Falstaff is not dead. He rises to mutilate Hotspur's body and to claim the honor due Hal for Hotspur's death. For all Falstaff's witty commentary at the expense of honor, his own opposite course is unsuited to a time of war or to Hal's new public role. Falstaff's abuse of military conscription, his carrying a bottle of sack in place of a pistol, show him at his wittiest still, but in a world that may not tolerate such pranks. The merry games are out of place and childish. With characteristic generosity and imprudence, Hal gives the credit for Hotspur's death to Falstaff, who claims it so cravenly. Even so, the magic of their association has vanished. The time of adulthood is upon Hal.

The First Part of King Henry The Fourth

[Dramatis Personae

KING HENRY THE FOURTH
PRINCE HENRY, *Prince of Wales*⎱ *sons of the King*
PRINCE JOHN OF LANCASTER,⎰
EARL OF WESTMORLAND
SIR WALTER BLUNT

EARL OF NORTHUMBERLAND, *Henry Percy,*
HARRY PERCY (HOTSPUR), *his son,*
EARL OF WORCESTER, *Northumberland's
    younger brother,*
LORD MORTIMER, *Edmund Mortimer,
    also referred to as the Earl of March,*
OWEN GLENDOWER,
EARL OF DOUGLAS, *Archibald Douglas,*
SIR RICHARD VERNON,
ARCHBISHOP OF YORK, *Richard Scroop,*
SIR MICHAEL, *a member of the
    Archbishop's household,*

*rebels
against
the King*

LADY PERCY, *Hotspur's wife and Mortimer's sister*
LADY MORTIMER, *Mortimer's wife and Glendower's
    daughter*

SIR JOHN FALSTAFF
NED POINS
BARDOLPH
PETO
GADSHILL, *arranger of the highway robbery*
HOSTESS *of the tavern, Mistress Quickly*
FRANCIS, *a drawer, or tapster*
VINTNER, *or tavern keeper*

FIRST CARRIER
SECOND CARRIER
HOSTLER
CHAMBERLAIN
FIRST TRAVELER
SHERIFF
SERVANT *to Hotspur*
MESSENGER
SECOND MESSENGER

Soldiers, Travelers, Lords, Attendants

SCENE: *England and Wales*]

1.1   *Enter the King, Lord John of Lancaster, [the] Earl
of Westmorland, [Sir Walter Blunt,] with others.*

KING
So shaken as we are, so wan with care,
Find we a time for frighted peace to pant,   2
And breathe short-winded accents of new broils   3
To be commenced in strands afar remote.   4
No more the thirsty entrance of this soil   5
Shall daub her lips with her own children's blood;   6
No more shall trenching war channel her fields   7
Nor bruise her flowerets with the armèd hoofs
Of hostile paces. Those opposèd eyes,   9
Which, like the meteors of a troubled heaven,
All of one nature, of one substance bred,
Did lately meet in the intestine shock   12
And furious close of civil butchery,   13
Shall now in mutual well-beseeming ranks
March all one way and be no more opposed
Against acquaintance, kindred, and allies.
The edge of war, like an ill-sheathèd knife,
No more shall cut his master. Therefore, friends,   18
As far as to the sepulcher of Christ—
Whose soldier now, under whose blessèd cross
We are impressèd and engaged to fight—   21
Forthwith a power of English shall we levy,   22
Whose arms were molded in their mother's womb   23
To chase these pagans in those holy fields
Over whose acres walked those blessèd feet
Which fourteen hundred years ago were nailed
For our advantage on the bitter cross.
But this our purpose now is twelve month old,
And bootless 'tis to tell you we will go.   29
Therefore we meet not now. Then let me hear
Of you, my gentle cousin Westmorland,   31
What yesternight our council did decree
In forwarding this dear expedience.   33
WESTMORLAND
My liege, this haste was hot in question,   34
And many limits of the charge set down   35
But yesternight, when all athwart there came   36
A post from Wales loaden with heavy news,   37
Whose worst was that the noble Mortimer,
Leading the men of Herefordshire to fight
Against the irregular and wild Glendower,
Was by the rude hands of that Welshman taken,
A thousand of his people butcherèd—

1.1. Location: The royal court.
2 Find we let us find.   **frighted** frightened   **3 breathe short-winded
accents** speak, even though we are out of breath.   **accents** words.
broils battles   **4 strands afar remote** far-off shores, i.e., of the Holy
Land (to which, at the end of *Richard II*, Henry has pledged himself to
a crusade)   **5 thirsty entrance** i.e., parched mouth   **6 daub** coat,
smear   **7 trenching** cutting   **9 paces** horses' tread   **12 intestine** internal   **13 close** hand-to-hand encounter.   **civil** (as in "civil war")
18 his its   **21 impressèd** conscripted   **22 power** army   **23 their
mother's** i.e., England's, but also suggesting *their mothers'*   **29 bootless** useless   **31 Of** from.   **gentle cousin** noble kinsman   **33 dear expedience** urgent expedition   **34 hot in question** being hotly debated
35 limits . . . charge particulars of military responsibility   **36 athwart**
at cross purposes, contrarily   **37 post** messenger.   **loaden** heavily
laden

Upon whose dead corpse there was such misuse,   43
Such beastly shameless transformation,   44
By those Welshwomen done as may not be
Without much shame retold or spoken of.

KING
It seems then that the tidings of this broil
Brake off our business for the Holy Land.

WESTMORLAND
This matched with other did, my gracious lord;   49
For more uneven and unwelcome news   50
Came from the north, and thus it did import:
On Holy Rood Day, the gallant Hotspur there,   52
Young Harry Percy, and brave Archibald,
That ever-valiant and approvèd Scot,   54
At Holmedon met, where they did spend   55
A sad and bloody hour,
As by discharge of their artillery   57
And shape of likelihood the news was told;   58
For he that brought them, in the very heat   59
And pride of their contention did take horse,   60
Uncertain of the issue any way.

KING
Here is a dear, a true industrious friend,
Sir Walter Blunt, new lighted from his horse,
Stained with the variation of each soil
Betwixt that Holmedon and this seat of ours;
And he hath brought us smooth and welcome news.   66
The Earl of Douglas is discomfited;   67
Ten thousand bold Scots, two-and-twenty knights,
Balked in their own blood, did Sir Walter see   69
On Holmedon's plains. Of prisoners, Hotspur took
Mordake, Earl of Fife and eldest son   71
To beaten Douglas, and the Earl of Atholl,
Of Murray, Angus, and Menteith.
And is not this an honorable spoil?
A gallant prize? Ha, cousin, is it not?

WESTMORLAND
In faith, it is a conquest for a prince to boast of.

KING
Yea, there thou mak'st me sad, and mak'st me sin
In envy that my lord Northumberland
Should be the father to so blest a son—
A son who is the theme of honor's tongue,
Amongst a grove the very straightest plant,   81
Who is sweet Fortune's minion and her pride,   82
Whilst I, by looking on the praise of him,
See riot and dishonor stain the brow   84
Of my young Harry. O, that it could be proved
That some night-tripping fairy had exchanged   86
In cradle clothes our children where they lay,
And called mine Percy, his Plantagenet!   88

Sons?

Then would I have his Harry, and he mine.
But let him from my thoughts. What think you, coz,   90
Of this young Percy's pride? The prisoners
Which he in this adventure hath surprised   92
To his own use he keeps, and sends me word   93
I shall have none but Mordake, Earl of Fife.   94

WESTMORLAND
This is his uncle's teaching. This is Worcester,
Malevolent to you in all aspects,   96
Which makes him prune himself and bristle up   97
The crest of youth against your dignity.

KING
But I have sent for him to answer this;
And for this cause awhile we must neglect
Our holy purpose to Jerusalem.
Cousin, on Wednesday next our council we
Will hold at Windsor. So inform the lords.
But come yourself with speed to us again,
For more is to be said and to be done
Than out of anger can be utterèd.

WESTMORLAND   I will, my liege.   *Exeunt.*

❖

1.2   *Enter Prince of Wales and Sir John Falstaff.*

FALSTAFF   Now, Hal, what time of day is it, lad?

PRINCE   Thou art so fat-witted with drinking of old sack,   2
and unbuttoning thee after supper, and sleeping upon
benches after noon, that thou hast forgotten to de-   4
mand that truly which thou wouldst truly know. What
a devil hast thou to do with the time of the day? Unless   6
hours were cups of sack, and minutes capons, and
clocks the tongues of bawds, and dials the signs of   8
leaping houses, and the blessed sun himself a fair hot   9
wench in flame-colored taffeta, I see no reason why   10
thou shouldst be so superfluous to demand the time   11
of the day.

FALSTAFF   Indeed, you come near me now, Hal, for we   13
that take purses go by the moon and the seven stars,   14
and not by Phoebus, "he, that wandering knight so   15
fair." And I prithee, sweet wag, when thou art king,   16
as, God save Thy Grace—Majesty I should say, for   17
grace thou wilt have none—

PRINCE   What, none?

---

43 **corpse** corpses   44 **transformation** mutilation   49 **other** i.e.,
other news   50 **uneven** disconcerting, distressing   52 **Holy Rood Day**
September 14   54 **approvèd** proved by experience   55 **Holmedon**
Humbleton in Northumberland   57 **by** i.e., judging from   58 **shape
of likelihood** likely outcome   59 **them** i.e., the news   60 **pride**
height   66 **smooth** pleasant   67 **discomfited** defeated   69 **Balked**
heaped up in balks, or ridges   71 **Mordake** i.e., Murdoch, son of the
Earl of Albany   81 **plant** i.e., young tree   82 **minion** favorite   84 **riot**
debauchery   86 **night-tripping** i.e., moving nimbly in the night
88 **Plantagenet** (Family name of English royalty since Henry II.)

90 **let him** let him go.   **coz** cousin, i.e., kinsman   92 **surprised** am-
bushed, captured   93 **To . . . use** i.e., to collect ransom for them
94 **none but Mordake** (Since Mordake was of royal blood, being
grandson to Robert II of Scotland, Hotspur could not claim him as his
prisoner according to the law of arms.)   96 **Malevolent, aspects** (Astrological terms.)   97 **Which . . . himself** i.e., which teaching makes
Hotspur preen himself (as a falcon preens its feathers)
1.2. **Location: London, perhaps in an apartment of the Prince's.**
2 **sack** a Spanish white wine   4 **forgotten** forgotten how   6 **a devil** in
the devil   8 **dials** clocks   9 **leaping houses** houses of prostitution
10 **taffeta** (Commonly worn by prostitutes.)   11 **superfluous** (1) unnecessarily concerned (2) self-indulgent   13 **you . . . now** i.e.,
you've scored a point on me   14 **go by** (1) travel by the light of (2)
tell time by.   **the seven stars** the Pleiades   15–16 **Phoebus . . . fair**
(Phoebus, god of the sun, is here equated with the wandering knight
of a ballad or popular romance.)   17 **Grace** royal highness (with pun
on spiritual *grace* and also on the *grace* or blessing before a meal)

FALSTAFF   No, by my troth, not so much as will serve to 20
be prologue to an egg and butter. 21
PRINCE   Well, how then? Come, roundly, roundly. 22
FALSTAFF   Marry, then, sweet wag, when thou art 23
king, let not us that are squires of the night's body be 24
called thieves of the day's beauty. Let us be Diana's for- 25
esters, gentlemen of the shade, minions of the moon, 26
and let men say we be men of good government, 27
being governed, as the sea is, by our noble and chaste
mistress the moon, under whose countenance we steal. 29
PRINCE   Thou sayest well, and it holds well too, for the 30
fortune of us that are the moon's men doth ebb and
flow like the sea, being governed, as the sea is, by the
moon. As, for proof, now: a purse of gold most
resolutely snatched on Monday night and most dissolutely spent on Tuesday morning, got with swearing
"Lay by" and spent with crying "Bring in," now in as 36
low an ebb as the foot of the ladder and by and by in 37
as high a flow as the ridge of the gallows. 38
FALSTAFF   By the Lord, thou sayst true, lad. And is not
my hostess of the tavern a most sweet wench?
PRINCE   As the honey of Hybla, my old lad of the castle. 41
And is not a buff jerkin a most sweet robe of durance? 42
FALSTAFF   How now, how now, mad wag, what, in thy
quips and thy quiddities? What a plague have I to do 44
with a buff jerkin?
PRINCE   Why, what a pox have I to do with my hostess 46
of the tavern?
FALSTAFF   Well, thou hast called her to a reckoning many 48
a time and oft.
PRINCE   Did I ever call for thee to pay thy part?
FALSTAFF   No, I'll give thee thy due, thou hast paid all
there.
PRINCE   Yea, and elsewhere, so far as my coin would
stretch, and where it would not I have used my credit.
FALSTAFF   Yea, and so used it that, were it not here
apparent that thou art heir apparent—But I prithee,
sweet wag, shall there be gallows standing in England
when thou art king? And resolution thus fubbed as it 58
is with the rusty curb of old father Antic the law? Do 59

not thou, when thou art king, hang a thief.
PRINCE   No, thou shalt.
FALSTAFF   Shall I? O rare! By the Lord, I'll be a brave 62
judge.
PRINCE   Thou judgest false already. I mean, thou shalt
have the hanging of the thieves, and so become a rare 65
hangman.
FALSTAFF   Well, Hal, well; and in some sort it jumps 67
with my humor as well as waiting in the court, I can 68
tell you.
PRINCE   For obtaining of suits? 70
FALSTAFF   Yea, for obtaining of suits, whereof the
hangman hath no lean wardrobe. 'Sblood, I am as 72
melancholy as a gib cat or a lugged bear. 73
PRINCE   Or an old lion, or a lover's lute.
FALSTAFF   Yea, or the drone of a Lincolnshire bagpipe.
PRINCE   What sayest thou to a hare, or the melancholy 76
of Moorditch? 77
FALSTAFF   Thou hast the most unsavory similes, and art
indeed the most comparative, rascalliest, sweet young 79
prince. But Hal, I prithee, trouble me no more with
vanity. I would to God thou and I knew where a com- 81
modity of good names were to be bought. An old lord 82
of the council rated me the other day in the street 83
about you, sir, but I marked him not; and yet he talked
very wisely, but I regarded him not; and yet he talked
wisely, and in the street too.
PRINCE   Thou didst well, for wisdom cries out in the 87
streets and no man regards it. 88
FALSTAFF   O, thou hast damnable iteration, and art 89
indeed able to corrupt a saint. Thou hast done much
harm upon me, Hal, God forgive thee for it. Before I
knew thee, Hal, I knew nothing; and now am I, if a 92
man should speak truly, little better than one of the
wicked. I must give over this life, and I will give it
over. By the Lord, an I do not I am a villain. I'll be 95
damned for never a king's son in Christendom.
PRINCE   Where shall we take a purse tomorrow, Jack?
FALSTAFF   Zounds, where thou wilt, lad, I'll make one. 98
An I do not, call me villain and baffle me. 99
PRINCE   I see a good amendment of life in thee—from
praying to purse taking.
FALSTAFF   Why, Hal, 'tis my vocation, Hal. 'Tis no sin
for a man to labor in his vocation.

Enter Poins.

20 troth faith   **21 prologue . . . butter** i.e., grace before a brief meal
22 roundly i.e., out with it   **23 Marry** indeed. (Literally, "by the Virgin Mary.")   **wag** joker   **24–25 let . . . beauty** i.e., let not us who
are attendants on the goddess of night, members of her household, be
blamed for stealing daylight by sleeping in the daytime   **25–26
Diana's foresters** (An elegant name for thieves by night; Diana is goddess of the moon and the hunt.)   **26 minions** favorites   **27 government** (1) conduct (2) commonwealth   **29 countenance** (1) face (2) patronage, approval.   **steal** (1) move stealthily (2) rob   **30 it holds well**
the comparison is apt   **36 Lay by** (A cry of highwaymen, like "Hands
up!").   **Bring in** (An order given to a waiter in a tavern.)   **37 ladder**
(1) pier ladder (2) gallows ladder   **38 ridge** crossbar   **41 Hybla** (A
town, famed for its honey, in Sicily near Syracuse.)   **old . . . castle**
(1) a roisterer (2) the name, Sir John Oldcastle, borne by Falstaff in the
earlier version of the Henry IV plays   **42 buff jerkin** a leather jacket
worn by officers of the law.   **durance** (1) imprisonment (2) durability,
durable cloth   **44 quiddities** subtleties of speech   **46 pox** syphilis.
(Here, *what a pox* is used as an expletive, like "what the devil.")
48 reckoning settlement of the bill (with bawdy suggestion that is continued in *pay thy part* and *my coin would stretch*)   **58 resolution**
courage (of a highwayman).   **fubbed** cheated   **59
Antic** buffoon

62 brave excellent   **65 have . . . thieves** (1) be in charge of hanging
thieves (or protecting them from hanging) (2) hang like other thieves.
rare (1) rarely used (2) excellent   **67–68 jumps . . . humor** suits my
temperament   **68 waiting in the court** being in attendance at the
royal court   **70 suits** petitions. (But Falstaff uses the word to mean
suits of clothes; clothes belonging to an executed man were given to
the executioner.)   **72 'Sblood** by his (Christ's) blood   **73 gib cat** tomcat.   **lugged bear** bear led by a chain and baited by dogs   **76 hare**
(A proverbially melancholy animal.)   **77 Moorditch** (A foul ditch
draining Moorfields, outside London walls.)   **79 comparative** given to
abusive comparisons   **81 vanity** worldliness   **81–82 commodity** supply   **82 names** reputations   **83 rated** chastised   **87–88 wisdom . . .
it** (An allusion to Proverbs 1:20–24.)   **89 iteration** repetition (of biblical texts, with a neat twist)   **92 nothing** i.e., no evil   **95 an** if
98 Zounds by his (Christ's) wounds.   **make one** be one of the party
99 baffle publicly disgrace

Poins! Now shall we know if Gadshill have set a 104
match. O, if men were to be saved by merit, what 105
hole in hell were hot enough for him? This is the
most omnipotent villain that ever cried "Stand!" to a 107
true man. 108

PRINCE Good morrow, Ned.

POINS Good morrow, sweet Hal.—What says Monsieur Remorse? What says Sir John, Sack-and-Sugar
Jack? How agrees the devil and thee about thy soul
that thou soldest him on Good Friday last for a cup of
Madeira and a cold capon's leg?

PRINCE Sir John stands to his word; the devil shall have 115
his bargain, for he was never yet a breaker of
proverbs. He will give the devil his due.

POINS Then art thou damned for keeping thy word with
the devil.

PRINCE [to Falstaff] Else he had been damned for 120
cozening the devil. 121

POINS But my lads, my lads, tomorrow morning, by
four o'clock early, at Gad's Hill, there are pilgrims 123
going to Canterbury with rich offerings and traders
riding to London with fat purses. I have vizards for 125
you all; you have horses for yourselves. Gadshill lies 126
tonight in Rochester. I have bespoke supper tomorrow 127
night in Eastcheap. We may do it as secure as sleep. If
you will go, I will stuff your purses full of crowns; if
you will not, tarry at home and be hanged.

FALSTAFF Hear ye, Yedward, if I tarry at home and go 131
not, I'll hang you for going. 132

POINS You will, chops? 133

FALSTAFF Hal, wilt thou make one?

PRINCE Who, I rob? I a thief? Not I, by my faith.

FALSTAFF There's neither honesty, manhood, nor
good fellowship in thee, nor thou cam'st not of the
blood royal, if thou darest not stand for ten shillings. 138

PRINCE Well then, once in my days I'll be a madcap.

FALSTAFF Why, that's well said.

PRINCE Well, come what will, I'll tarry at home.

FALSTAFF By the Lord, I'll be a traitor then, when thou
art king.

PRINCE I care not.

POINS Sir John, I prithee leave the Prince and me alone.
I will lay him down such reasons for this adventure
that he shall go.

FALSTAFF Well, God give thee the spirit of persuasion
and him the ears of profiting, that what thou speakest
may move and what he hears may be believed, that
the true prince may, for recreation's sake, prove a false

thief; for the poor abuses of the time want counte- 152
nance. Farewell. You shall find me in Eastcheap. 153

PRINCE Farewell, thou latter spring! Farewell, All- 154
hallown summer! [Exit Falstaff.] 155

POINS Now, my good sweet honey lord, ride with us
tomorrow. I have a jest to execute that I cannot
manage alone. Falstaff, Peto, Bardolph, and Gadshill
shall rob those men that we have already waylaid— 159
yourself and I will not be there—and when they have
the booty, if you and I do not rob them, cut this head
off from my shoulders.

PRINCE How shall we part with them in setting forth?

POINS Why, we will set forth before or after them and
appoint them a place of meeting, wherein it is at our
pleasure to fail; and then will they adventure upon the 166
exploit themselves, which they shall have no sooner
achieved but we'll set upon them.

PRINCE Yea, but 'tis like that they will know us by our 169
horses, by our habits, and by every other appoint- 170
ment, to be ourselves. 171

POINS Tut, our horses they shall not see—I'll tie them
in the wood; our vizards we will change after we leave
them; and, sirrah, I have cases of buckram for the 174
nonce, to immask our noted outward garments. 175

PRINCE Yea, but I doubt they will be too hard for us. 176

POINS Well, for two of them, I know them to be as
true-bred cowards as ever turned back; and for the 178
third, if he fight longer than he sees reason, I'll forswear arms. The virtue of this jest will be the incompre- 180
hensible lies that this same fat rogue will tell us when 181
we meet at supper—how thirty at least he fought
with, what wards, what blows, what extremities he 183
endured; and in the reproof of this lives the jest. 184

PRINCE Well, I'll go with thee. Provide us all things necessary and meet me tomorrow night in Eastcheap.
There I'll sup. Farewell.

POINS Farewell, my lord. Exit Poins.

PRINCE
I know you all, and will awhile uphold
The unyoked humor of your idleness. 190
Yet herein will I imitate the sun,
Who doth permit the base contagious clouds 192
To smother up his beauty from the world,
That when he please again to be himself, 194
Being wanted he may be more wondered at 195

---

104 Gadshill (The name of one of the highwaymen.) 104–105 set a
match arranged a robbery 105 by merit i.e., according to their deservings rather than by God's grace 107 omnipotent unparalleled,
utter 108 true honest 115 stands to keeps 120 Else otherwise
121 cozening cheating 123 Gad's Hill (Location near Rochester on
the road from London to Canterbury; one of the highwaymen is called
Gadshill.) 125 vizards masks 126 lies lodges 127 bespoke ordered 131 Yedward (Nickname for *Edward*, Poins' first name.)
132 hang you have you hanged 133 chops i.e., fat jaws or cheeks
138 stand . . . shillings (1) stand up and fight for money (2) be worth
ten shillings, the value of the *royal*, the gold coin alluded to in *blood
royal* (line 138)

152–153 want countenance lack encouragement and protection
(from men of rank) 154–155 All-hallown summer (Compare with
"Indian summer." Falstaff's summer or *latter spring*, i.e., his youth,
has lasted to All Saints' Day, November 1.) 159 waylaid set an ambush for 166 pleasure choice, discretion 169 like likely 170 habits garments 170–171 appointment accoutrement 174 sirrah (Usually addressed to an inferior; here, a sign of intimacy.)
174–175 cases . . . nonce suits of buckram, a stiff-finished heavily
sized fabric, for the purpose 175 immask hide, disguise. noted
known 176 doubt fear. too hard too formidable 178 turned back
turned their backs and ran away 180–181 incomprehensible boundless 183 wards parries 184 reproof disproof 190 unyoked . . .
idleness unbridled inclination of your frivolity 192 contagious noxious 194 That so that 195 wanted missed, lacked

By breaking through the foul and ugly mists
Of vapors that did seem to strangle him.
If all the year were playing holidays,
To sport would be as tedious as to work;
But when they seldom come, they wished-for come,
And nothing pleaseth but rare accidents.   201
So when this loose behavior I throw off
And pay the debt I never promisèd,
By how much better than my word I am,
By so much shall I falsify men's hopes;   205
And like bright metal on a sullen ground,   206
My reformation, glittering o'er my fault,
Shall show more goodly and attract more eyes
Than that which hath no foil to set it off.   209
I'll so offend to make offense a skill,   210
Redeeming time when men think least I will.   *Exit.*   211

❧

1.3   *Enter the King, Northumberland, Worcester,*
      Hotspur, Sir Walter Blunt, with others.

KING
My blood hath been too cold and temperate,
Unapt to stir at these indignities,
And you have found me, for accordingly   3
You tread upon my patience. But be sure
I will from henceforth rather be myself,   5
Mighty and to be feared, than my condition,   6
Which hath been smooth as oil, soft as young
   down,
And therefore lost that title of respect
Which the proud soul ne'er pays but to the proud.
WORCESTER
Our house, my sovereign liege, little deserves   10
The scourge of greatness to be used on it—
And that same greatness too which our own hands
Have holp to make so portly.   13
NORTHUMBERLAND [*to the King*]   My lord—
KING
Worcester, get thee gone, for I do see
Danger and disobedience in thine eye.
O sir, your presence is too bold and peremptory,
And majesty might never yet endure
The moody frontier of a servant brow.   19
You have good leave to leave us. When we need   20
Your use and counsel, we shall send for you.
                                            Exit Worcester.
[*To Northumberland.*] You were about to speak.

NORTHUMBERLAND   Yea, my good lord.
Those prisoners in Your Highness' name demanded,
Which Harry Percy here at Holmedon took,
Were, as he says, not with such strength denied
As is delivered to Your Majesty.   26
Either envy, therefore, or misprision   27
Is guilty of this fault, and not my son.
HOTSPUR [*to the King*]
My liege, I did deny no prisoners.
But I remember when the fight was done,
When I was dry with rage and extreme toil,
Breathless and faint, leaning upon my sword,
Came there a certain lord, neat and trimly dressed,
Fresh as a bridegroom, and his chin new reaped   34
Showed like a stubble land at harvest home.   35
He was perfumèd like a milliner,   36
And twixt his finger and his thumb he held
A pouncet box, which ever and anon   38
He gave his nose and took 't away again,
Who therewith angry, when it next came there,   40
Took it in snuff; and still he smiled and talked,   41
And as the soldiers bore dead bodies by
He called them untaught knaves, unmannerly,
To bring a slovenly unhandsome corpse
Betwixt the wind and his nobility.
With many holiday and lady terms   46
He questioned me, amongst the rest demanded   47
My prisoners in Your Majesty's behalf.
I then, all smarting with my wounds being cold,
To be so pestered with a popinjay,   50
Out of my grief and my impatience   51
Answered neglectingly I know not what,
He should, or he should not; for he made me mad
To see him shine so brisk, and smell so sweet,
And talk so like a waiting-gentlewoman
Of guns and drums and wounds—God save the
   mark!—   56
And telling me the sovereignest thing on earth   57
Was parmacety for an inward bruise,   58
And that it was great pity, so it was,
This villainous saltpeter should be digged   60
Out of the bowels of the harmless earth,
Which many a good tall fellow had destroyed   62
So cowardly, and but for these vile guns
He would himself have been a soldier.
This bald unjointed chat of his, my lord,   65
I answered indirectly, as I said,   66

201 accidents events   **205 hopes** expectations   **206 sullen ground**
dark background, like a *foil.* (See line 209.)   **209 foil** metal sheet laid
contrastingly behind a jewel to set off its luster   **210 to** as to.   **skill**
i.e., clever tactic, piece of good policy   **211 Redeeming time** i.e.,
making amends for lost time
1.3. Location: London. The court (historically at Windsor).
3 found me found me so   **5 myself** i.e., my royal self   **6 my condition** my natural (mild) disposition   **10 Our house** i.e., the Percy family   **13 holp** helped.   **portly** majestic, prosperous   **19 moody frontier** i.e., angry brow, frown. (*Frontier* literally means "outwork" or
"fortification.")   **20 good leave** full permission

26 delivered reported   **27 envy** malice.   **misprision** misunderstanding
34 chin new reaped i.e., with beard freshly barbered according to the
latest fashion, not like a soldier's beard   **35 Showed** looked.   **harvest
home** end of harvest, fields being neat and bare   **36 milliner** man
dealing in fancy articles, such as gloves and hats   **38 pouncet box**
perfume box with perforated lid   **40 Who** i.e., his nose   **41 Took it
in snuff** (1) inhaled it (2) took offense.   **still** continually   **46 holiday
and lady** dainty and effeminate   **47 questioned** (1) conversed with
(2) put questions to   **50 popinjay** parrot   **51 grief** pain   **56 God . . .
mark** (Probably originally a formula to avert evil omen; here, an expression of impatience.)   **57 sovereignest** most efficacious   **58 parmacety** spermaceti, a fatty substance taken from the head of the
sperm whale, used as a medicinal ointment   **60 saltpeter** potassium
nitrate, used to make gunpowder and also used medicinally   **62 tall**
brave   **65 bald** trivial   **66 indirectly** inattentively, offhandedly

And I beseech you, let not his report
Come current for an accusation   68
Betwixt my love and your high majesty.

BLUNT [*to the King*]
The circumstance considered, good my lord,
Whate'er Lord Harry Percy then had said
To such a person and in such a place,
At such a time, with all the rest retold,
May reasonably die, and never rise
To do him wrong or any way impeach   75
What then he said, so he unsay it now.   76

KING
Why, yet he doth deny his prisoners,   77
But with proviso and exception   78
That we at our own charge shall ransom straight   79
His brother-in-law, the foolish Mortimer,   80
Who, on my soul, hath willfully betrayed
The lives of those that he did lead to fight
Against that great magician, damned Glendower,
Whose daughter, as we hear, that Earl of March   84
Hath lately married. Shall our coffers then
Be emptied to redeem a traitor home?
Shall we buy treason and indent with fears   87
When they have lost and forfeited themselves?
No, on the barren mountains let him starve!
For I shall never hold that man my friend
Whose tongue shall ask me for one penny cost
To ransom home revolted Mortimer.   92

HOTSPUR   Revolted Mortimer?
He never did fall off, my sovereign liege,   94
But by the chance of war. To prove that true
Needs no more but one tongue for all those
    wounds,
Those mouthèd wounds, which valiantly he took,   97
When on the gentle Severn's sedgy bank,   98
In single opposition, hand to hand,
He did confound the best part of an hour   100
In changing hardiment with great Glendower.   101
Three times they breathed, and three times did they
    drink,   102
Upon agreement, of swift Severn's flood,   103
Who then, affrighted with their bloody looks,   104
Ran fearfully among the trembling reeds

And hid his crisp head in the hollow bank,   106
Bloodstainèd with these valiant combatants.
Never did bare and rotten policy   108
Color her working with such deadly wounds,   109
Nor never could the noble Mortimer
Receive so many, and all willingly.
Then let not him be slandered with revolt.   112

KING
Thou dost belie him, Percy, thou dost belie him.
He never did encounter with Glendower.
I tell thee,
He durst as well have met the devil alone
As Owen Glendower for an enemy.
Art thou not ashamed? But, sirrah, henceforth
Let me not hear you speak of Mortimer.
Send me your prisoners with the speediest means,
Or you shall hear in such a kind from me   121
As will displease you. —My lord Northumberland,
We license your departure with your son.
Send us your prisoners, or you will hear of it.

                    Exit King [with Blunt, and train].

HOTSPUR
An if the devil come and roar for them   125
I will not send them. I will after straight   126
And tell him so, for I will ease my heart,
Albeit I make a hazard of my head.

NORTHUMBERLAND
What, drunk with choler? Stay and pause awhile.   129
Here comes your uncle.

                    Enter Worcester.

HOTSPUR   Speak of Mortimer?
Zounds, I will speak of him, and let my soul
Want mercy if I do not join with him!   132
Yea, on his part I'll empty all these veins,   133
And shed my dear blood drop by drop in the dust,
But I will lift the downtrod Mortimer
As high in the air as this unthankful king,
As this ingrate and cankered Bolingbroke.   137

NORTHUMBERLAND
Brother, the King hath made your nephew mad.

WORCESTER
Who struck this heat up after I was gone?

HOTSPUR
He will forsooth have all my prisoners;
And when I urged the ransom once again
Of my wife's brother, then his cheek looked pale,
And on my face he turned an eye of death,   143
Trembling even at the name of Mortimer.

WORCESTER
I cannot blame him. Was not he proclaimed   145
By Richard, that dead is, the next of blood?   146

---

68 Come current (1) be taken at face value (2) come rushing in
75 impeach discredit   **76 so** provided that   **77 yet** (emphatic) i.e.,
even now.   **deny** refuse to surrender   **78 proviso and exception** (synonymous terms)   **79 straight** straightway, at once   **80, 84 Mortimer,
Earl of March** (There were two Edmund Mortimers; Shakespeare confuses them and combines their stories. It was the uncle [1376–1409?]
who was captured by Glendower and married Glendower's daughter;
it was the nephew [1391–1425], fifth Earl of March, who was proclaimed heir presumptive to King Richard II after the death of his father, the fourth earl, whom Richard had named as his heir. The uncle
was brother to the fourth earl and to Hotspur's wife, Elizabeth, called
Kate in this play.)   **87 indent with fears** i.e., make a bargain or come
to terms with traitors whom we have reason to fear   **92 revolted** rebellious   **94 fall off** abandon his loyalty   **97 mouthèd** gaping and eloquent   **98 Severn's** (The Severn River flows from northern Wales
and western England into the Bristol Channel.)   **sedgy** bordered with
reeds   **100 confound** consume   **101 changing hardiment** exchanging
blows, matching valor   **102 breathed** paused for breath   **103 flood**
river   **104 Who** i.e., the river

106 crisp curly, i.e., rippled   **108 bare** paltry.   **policy** cunning
109 Color disguise   **112 revolt** i.e., the accusation of rebellion
121 kind manner   **125 An if** if   **126 will after straight** will go after
immediately   **129 choler** anger   **132 Want mercy** lack mercy, be
damned   **133 on his part** i.e., fighting on Mortimer's side   **137 cankered** spoiled, malignant.   **Bolingbroke** i.e., King Henry IV; Hotspur
pointedly refuses to acknowledge his royalty   **143 an eye of death** a
fearful look   **145 he** i.e., Mortimer   **146 next of blood** heir to the
throne

NORTHUMBERLAND
He was; I heard the proclamation.
And then it was when the unhappy king—   148
Whose wrongs in us God pardon!—did set forth   149
Upon his Irish expedition;   150
From whence he, intercepted, did return   151
To be deposed and shortly murderèd.

WORCESTER
And for whose death we in the world's wide mouth
Live scandalized and foully spoken of.

HOTSPUR
But, soft, I pray you, did King Richard then   155
Proclaim my brother Edmund Mortimer   156
Heir to the crown?

NORTHUMBERLAND   He did; myself did hear it.

HOTSPUR
Nay, then I cannot blame his cousin king,   158
That wished him on the barren mountains starve.
But shall it be that you that set the crown
Upon the head of this forgetful man,
And for his sake wear the detested blot
Of murderous subornation—shall it be   163
That you a world of curses undergo,
Being the agents, or base second means,   165
The cords, the ladder, or the hangman rather?
O, pardon me that I descend so low
To show the line and the predicament   168
Wherein you range under this subtle king!   169
Shall it for shame be spoken in these days,
Or fill up chronicles in time to come,
That men of your nobility and power
Did gage them both in an unjust behalf,   173
As both of you—God pardon it!—have done,
To put down Richard, that sweet lovely rose,
And plant this thorn, this canker, Bolingbroke?   176
And shall it in more shame be further spoken
That you are fooled, discarded, and shook off
By him for whom these shames ye underwent?
No! Yet time serves wherein you may redeem   180
Your banished honors and restore yourselves
Into the good thoughts of the world again;
Revenge the jeering and disdained contempt   183
Of this proud king, who studies day and night
To answer all the debt he owes to you   185
Even with the bloody payment of your deaths.
Therefore, I say—

WORCESTER   Peace, cousin, say no more.
And now I will unclasp a secret book,

And to your quick-conceiving discontents   189
I'll read you matter deep and dangerous,
As full of peril and adventurous spirit
As to o'erwalk a current roaring loud
On the unsteadfast footing of a spear.   193

HOTSPUR
If he fall in, good night, or sink or swim!   194
Send danger from the east unto the west,
So honor cross it from the north to south,   196
And let them grapple. O, the blood more stirs
To rouse a lion than to start a hare!

NORTHUMBERLAND [to Worcester]
Imagination of some great exploit
Drives him beyond the bounds of patience.

HOTSPUR
By heaven, methinks it were an easy leap
To pluck bright honor from the pale-faced moon,
Or dive into the bottom of the deep,
Where fathom line could never touch the ground,   204
And pluck up drownèd honor by the locks,
So he that doth redeem her thence might wear
Without corrival all her dignities;   207
But out upon this half-faced fellowship!   208

WORCESTER [to Northumberland]
He apprehends a world of figures here,   209
But not the form of what he should attend.—   210
Good cousin, give me audience for a while.

HOTSPUR
I cry you mercy.

WORCESTER   Those same noble Scots   212
That are your prisoners—

HOTSPUR   I'll keep them all.
By God, he shall not have a Scot of them,   214
No, if a scot would save his soul, he shall not!   215
I'll keep them, by this hand.

WORCESTER   You start away
And lend no ear unto my purposes.
Those prisoners you shall keep.

HOTSPUR   Nay, I will, that's flat.   218
He said he would not ransom Mortimer,
Forbade my tongue to speak of Mortimer,
But I will find him when he lies asleep,
And in his ear I'll holler "Mortimer!"
Nay, I'll have a starling shall be taught to speak
Nothing but "Mortimer," and give it him
To keep his anger still in motion.   225

WORCESTER   Hear you, cousin, a word.

HOTSPUR
All studies here I solemnly defy,   227

---

148 unhappy unfortunate   149 in us caused by our doings
150 Irish expedition (Richard was putting down a rebellion in Ireland
when Bolingbroke returned to England from exile.)   151 intercepted
interrupted   155 soft i.e., wait a minute   156 brother i.e., brother-
in-law   158 cousin (with a pun on cozen, "cheat")   163 murderous
subornation the suborning of, or inciting to, murder   165 second
means agents   168 line station, rank; also, hangman's rope.   predicament category; also, dangerous situation   169 range i.e., are classified   173 gage them engage, pledge themselves   176 canker (1) canker rose or dog rose, wild and unfragrant (2) ulcer   180 Yet still
183 Revenge i.e., wherein you may revenge yourself against.   disdained disdainful   185 answer satisfy, discharge

189 quick-conceiving comprehending quickly   193 spear i.e., spear
laid across a stream as a narrow bridge   194 If . . . swim i.e., such a
man will face a life-or-death challenge if he falls in   196 So provided
that. (Also at line 206.)   204 fathom line a weighted line marked at
fathom intervals (six feet), used for measuring the depth of water
207 corrival rival, competitor   208 out . . . fellowship down with
this paltry business of sharing glory with others   209 apprehends
snatches at.   figures figures of the imagination, or figures of speech
210 form essential nature.   attend give attention to   212 cry you
mercy beg your pardon   214–215 Scot . . . scot Scotsman . . . trifling amount   218 that's flat that's for sure   225 still continually
227 studies pursuits.   defy renounce

Save how to gall and pinch this Bolingbroke.
And that same sword-and-buckler Prince of Wales— 229
But that I think his father loves him not
And would be glad he met with some mischance—
I would have him poisoned with a pot of ale.

WORCESTER
Farewell, kinsman. I'll talk to you
When you are better tempered to attend.

NORTHUMBERLAND [to Hotspur]
Why, what a wasp-stung and impatient fool
Art thou to break into this woman's mood,
Tying thine ear to no tongue but thine own!

HOTSPUR
Why, look you, I am whipped and scourged with
    rods,
Nettled and stung with pismires, when I hear   239
Of this vile politician, Bolingbroke.   240
In Richard's time—what do you call the place?—
A plague upon it, it is in Gloucestershire;
'Twas where the madcap duke his uncle kept,   243
His uncle York; where I first bowed my knee
Unto this king of smiles, this Bolingbroke—
'Sblood, when you and he came back from
    Ravenspurgh.   246

NORTHUMBERLAND   At Berkeley Castle.   247

HOTSPUR   You say true.
Why, what a candy deal of courtesy   249
This fawning greyhound then did proffer me!
"Look when his infant fortune came to age,"   251
And "gentle Harry Percy," and "kind cousin"—
O, the devil take such cozeners!—God forgive me!   253
Good uncle, tell your tale; I have done.

WORCESTER
Nay, if you have not, to it again;
We will stay your leisure.

HOTSPUR   I have done, i' faith.   256

WORCESTER
Then once more to your Scottish prisoners.
Deliver them up without their ransom straight,   258
And make the Douglas' son your only means   259
For powers in Scotland, which, for divers reasons 260
Which I shall send you written, be assured
Will easily be granted. [To Northumberland.] You, my
    lord,
Your son in Scotland being thus employed,
Shall secretly into the bosom creep   264
Of that same noble prelate well beloved,
The Archbishop.

HOTSPUR   Of York, is it not?

WORCESTER   True, who bears hard   268
His brother's death at Bristol, the Lord Scroop.
I speak not this in estimation,   270
As what I think might be, but what I know
Is ruminated, plotted, and set down,
And only stays but to behold the face
Of that occasion that shall bring it on.

HOTSPUR
I smell it. Upon my life, it will do well.

NORTHUMBERLAND
Before the game is afoot thou still lett'st slip.   276

HOTSPUR
Why, it cannot choose but be a noble plot.   277
And then the power of Scotland and of York,   278
To join with Mortimer, ha?

WORCESTER   And so they shall.

HOTSPUR
In faith, it is exceedingly well aimed.   280

WORCESTER
And 'tis no little reason bids us speed,
To save our heads by raising of a head;   282
For, bear ourselves as even as we can,   283
The King will always think him in our debt,   284
And think we think ourselves unsatisfied
Till he hath found a time to pay us home.   286
And see already how he doth begin
To make us strangers to his looks of love.

HOTSPUR
He does, he does. We'll be revenged on him.

WORCESTER
Cousin, farewell. No further go in this
Than I by letters shall direct your course.
When time is ripe, which will be suddenly,   292
I'll steal to Glendower and Lord Mortimer,
Where you and Douglas and our powers at once,   294
As I will fashion it, shall happily meet   295
To bear our fortunes in our own strong arms,   296
Which now we hold at much uncertainty.

NORTHUMBERLAND
Farewell, good brother. We shall thrive, I trust.

HOTSPUR
Uncle, adieu. O, let the hours be short
Till fields and blows and groans applaud our sport! 300
                    Exeunt [in separate groups].

✽

2.1   Enter a Carrier with a lantern in his hand.

FIRST CARRIER   Heigh-ho! An it be not four by the day, 1
I'll be hanged. Charles's Wain is over the new   2

---

229 **sword-and-buckler** (Arms improper for a prince, who should
carry rapier and dagger.)   239 **pismires** ants. (From the urinous smell
of an anthill.)   240 **politician** deceitful schemer   243 **kept** dwelled
246 **Ravenspurgh** (A port at the mouth of the River Humber in Yorkshire, now covered by the sea, where Bolingbroke landed on his return from exile.)   247 **Berkeley Castle** castle near Bristol   249 **candy**
sugared, flattering   251 **Look when** when, as soon as   253 **cozeners**
cheats (with pun on *cousins*)   256 **stay** await   258 **Deliver them up**
free them   259 **the Douglas' son** i.e., Mordake. (See 1.1.71 and
note.)   **means** i.e., agent   260 **For powers** for raising an army
264 **secretly . . . creep** win the confidence

268 **bears hard** resents   270 **estimation** guesswork   276 **still lett'st
slip** always let loose the dogs   277 **cannot choose but be** cannot help
being   278 **power** army   280 **aimed** designed   282 **head** army
283 **even** carefully   284 **him** himself   286 **home** (1) fully (2) with a
thrust to the heart   292 **suddenly** soon   294 **at once** all together
295 **happily** fortunately   296 **arms** (1) limbs (2) military might
300 **fields** battlefields
2.1. Location: An innyard on the London-Canterbury road.
s.d. Carrier one whose trade was conveying goods, usually by packhorses   **1 An** if.   **by the day** in the morning   **2 Charles's Wain** i.e.,
Charlemagne's wagon; the constellation Ursa Major (the Big Dipper)

chimney, and yet our horse not packed. What, hostler! 3
HOSTLER [*within*]   Anon, anon.   4
FIRST CARRIER   I prithee, Tom, beat Cut's saddle, put a 5
few flocks in the point. Poor jade is wrung in the 6
withers out of all cess.   7

Enter another Carrier.

SECOND CARRIER   Peas and beans are as dank here as a 8
dog, and that is the next way to give poor jades the 9
bots. This house is turned upside down since Robin 10
Hostler died.
FIRST CARRIER   Poor fellow never joyed since the price
of oats rose. It was the death of him.
SECOND CARRIER   I think this be the most villainous
house in all London road for fleas. I am stung like a
tench.   16
FIRST CARRIER   Like a tench? By the Mass, there is ne'er
a king Christian could be better bit than I have been 18
since the first cock.   19
SECOND CARRIER   Why, they will allow us ne'er a jordan, 20
and then we leak in your chimney, and your chamber- 21
lye breeds fleas like a loach.   22
FIRST CARRIER   What, Hostler! Come away and be 23
hanged! Come away.
SECOND CARRIER   I have a gammon of bacon and two 25
races of ginger, to be delivered as far as Charing Cross. 26
FIRST CARRIER   God's body, the turkeys in my pannier 27
are quite starved. What, hostler! A plague on thee!
Hast thou never an eye in thy head? Canst not hear?
An 'twere not as good deed as drink to break the pate 30
on thee, I am a very villain. Come, and be hanged! 31
Hast no faith in thee?   32

Enter Gadshill.

GADSHILL   Good morrow, carriers. What's o'clock?
FIRST CARRIER   I think it be two o'clock.
GADSHILL   I prithee, lend me thy lantern to see my
gelding in the stable.
FIRST CARRIER   Nay, by God, soft, I know a trick worth 37
two of that, i' faith.
GADSHILL   I pray thee, lend me thine.
SECOND CARRIER   Ay, when, canst tell? Lend me thy 40
lantern, quoth he! Marry, I'll see thee hanged first.
GADSHILL   Sirrah carrier, what time do you mean to
come to London?

SECOND CARRIER   Time enough to go to bed with a
candle, I warrant thee. Come, neighbor Mugs, we'll
call up the gentlemen. They will along with company, 46
for they have great charge.   *Exeunt* [*Carriers*]. 47
GADSHILL   What, ho! Chamberlain!   48

Enter Chamberlain.

CHAMBERLAIN   At hand, quoth pickpurse.   49
GADSHILL   That's even as fair as—at hand, quoth the 50
chamberlain; for thou variest no more from picking of 51
purses than giving direction doth from laboring; thou 52
layest the plot how.   53
CHAMBERLAIN   Good morrow, Master Gadshill. It holds 54
current that I told you yesternight: there's a franklin in 55
the Weald of Kent hath brought three hundred marks 56
with him in gold. I heard him tell it to one of his company last night at supper—a kind of auditor, one that
hath abundance of charge too, God knows what. They
are up already, and call for eggs and butter. They will
away presently.   61
GADSHILL   Sirrah, if they meet not with Saint Nicholas' 62
clerks, I'll give thee this neck.   63
CHAMBERLAIN   No, I'll none of it. I pray thee, keep that 64
for the hangman, for I know thou worshipest Saint
Nicholas as truly as a man of falsehood may.
GADSHILL   What talkest thou to me of the hangman? If 67
I hang, I'll make a fat pair of gallows; for if I hang, old
Sir John hangs with me, and thou knowest he is no
starveling. Tut, there are other Trojans that thou 70
dream'st not of, the which for sport's sake are content
to do the profession some grace, that would, if matters 72
should be looked into, for their own credit's sake
make all whole. I am joined with no foot-landrakers, 74
no long-staff sixpenny strikers, none of these mad 75
mustachio purple-hued malt-worms, but with nobility 76
and tranquillity, burgomasters and great oneyers, such 77
as can hold in, such as will strike sooner than speak, 78
and speak sooner than drink, and drink sooner than
pray. And yet, zounds, I lie, for they pray continually
to their saint, the commonwealth, or rather not pray to
her but prey on her, for they ride up and down on her
and make her their boots.   83

3 **horse** horses. **hostler** groom   4 **Anon** right away, coming   5 **beat** soften.   **Cut's saddle** packsaddle of the horse named *Cut,* meaning "bobtailed"   6 **flocks** tufts of wool.   **point** pommel of the saddle. **jade** nag   6–7 **wrung . . . withers** chafed (by his saddle) on the ridge between his shoulder-blades   7 **cess** measure, estimate   8 **Peas and beans** i.e., horse fodder   8–9 **dank . . . dog** i.e., damp as can be   9 **next** nearest, quickest   10 **bots** intestinal maggots.   **house** inn   16 **tench** a spotted fish, whose spots may have been likened to flea bites   18 **king Christian** Christian king, accustomed to have the best of everything   19 **first cock** i.e., midnight   20 **jordan** chamberpot   21 **chimney** fireplace   21–22 **chamber-lye** urine   22 **loach** a small freshwater fish, thought to harbor parasites   23 **Come away** come along   25 **gammon of bacon** ham   26 **races** roots.   **Charing Cross** a market town lying between London and Westminster   27 **pannier** basket   30 **An** if   30–31 **to break . . . thee** to give you a blow on the head   31 **very** true   32 **faith** trustworthiness   37 **soft** i.e., wait a minute   40 **Ay . . . tell** i.e., you must be joking

46–47 **They . . . charge** i.e., they wish to travel in company, because they have lots of valuable cargo   48 **Chamberlain** (Male equivalent of a chambermaid. His entrance in the Quarto at line 47 may suggest that he is visible before Gadshill calls for him, giving point to his remark about being "At hand.")   49 **At . . . pickpurse** i.e., I am right beside you, as the pickpurse said   50 **fair** good, apt   51–53 **thou variest . . . how** i.e., you don't actually do the stealing, but you give directions, like a master workman to his apprentices   54–55 **holds current that** holds true what   55 **a franklin** a farmer owning his own land   56 **Weald** wooded region.   **marks** coins of the value of thirteen shillings four pence   61 **presently** immediately   62–63 **Saint Nicholas' clerks** highwaymen. (Saint Nicholas was popularly supposed the patron of thieves.)   64 **I'll none** I want none   67 **What** Why   70 **Trojans** i.e., slang for "sports" or "roisterers"   72 **profession** i.e., robbery.   **grace** credit, favor   74 **joined** associated.   **foot-landrakers** thieves who travel on foot   75 **long-staff sixpenny strikers** robbers with long staves who would knock down their victims for sixpence   76 **mustachio purple-hued malt-worms** purple-faced drunkards with huge mustaches   77 **tranquillity** those who lead easy lives.   **oneyers** ones (?)   78 **holds in** keep a secret; hold fast   83 **boots** booty (with pun on *boots,* "shoes")

CHAMBERLAIN   What, the commonwealth their boots? Will she hold out water in foul way? 85

GADSHILL   She will, she will. Justice hath liquored her. 86 We steal as in a castle, cocksure. We have the receipt 87 of fern seed; we walk invisible. 88

CHAMBERLAIN   Nay, by my faith, I think you are more beholding to the night than to fern seed for your 90 walking invisible.

GADSHILL   Give me thy hand. Thou shalt have a share in our purchase, as I am a true man. 93

CHAMBERLAIN   Nay, rather let me have it as you are a false thief.

GADSHILL   Go to; *homo* is a common name to all men. 96 Bid the hostler bring my gelding out of the stable. Farewell, you muddy knave.   [*Exeunt separately.*] 98

♣

2.2   *Enter Prince, Poins, Peto, [and Bardolph].*

POINS   Come, shelter, shelter! I have removed Falstaff's horse, and he frets like a gummed velvet. 2

PRINCE   Stand close.   [*They step aside.*] 3

Enter Falstaff.

FALSTAFF   Poins! Poins, and be hanged! Poins!

PRINCE [*coming forward*]   Peace, ye fat-kidneyed rascal! What a brawling dost thou keep! 6

FALSTAFF   Where's Poins, Hal?

PRINCE   He is walked up to the top of the hill. I'll go seek him.   [*He steps aside.*]

FALSTAFF   I am accursed to rob in that thief's company. The rascal hath removed my horse and tied him I know not where. If I travel but four foot by the square 12 further afoot, I shall break my wind. Well, I doubt not but to die a fair death for all this, if I scape hanging for 14 killing that rogue. I have forsworn his company hourly any time this two-and-twenty years, and yet I am bewitched with the rogue's company. If the rascal have not given me medicines to make me love him, I'll be 18 hanged; it could not be else—I have drunk medicines. Poins! Hal! A plague upon you both! Bardolph! Peto! I'll starve ere I'll rob a foot further. An 'twere not as good a deed as drink to turn true man and to leave 22 these rogues, I am the veriest varlet that ever chewed with a tooth. Eight yards of uneven ground is three-score-and-ten miles afoot with me, and the stony-hearted villains know it well enough. A plague upon

it when thieves cannot be true one to another! (*They whistle.*) Whew! A plague upon you all! Give me my 28 horse, you rogues, give me my horse, and be hanged!

PRINCE [*coming forward*]   Peace, ye fat-guts! Lie down. Lay thine ear close to the ground and list if thou 31 canst hear the tread of travelers.

FALSTAFF   Have you any levers to lift me up again, being down? 'Sblood, I'll not bear mine own flesh so far afoot again for all the coin in thy father's Exchequer. What a plague mean ye to colt me thus? 36

PRINCE   Thou liest. Thou art not colted, thou art uncolted.

FALSTAFF   I prithee, good Prince Hal, help me to my 39 horse, good king's son. 40

PRINCE   Out, ye rogue! Shall I be your hostler?

FALSTAFF   Go hang thyself in thine own heir-apparent garters! If I be ta'en, I'll peach for this. An I have not 43 ballads made on you all and sung to filthy tunes, let a cup of sack be my poison. When a jest is so forward, 45 and afoot too! I hate it. 46

Enter Gadshill.

GADSHILL   Stand. 47

FALSTAFF   So I do, against my will.

POINS [*coming forward with Bardolph and Peto*]   O, 'tis our setter. I know his voice. 50

BARDOLPH   What news?

GADSHILL   Case ye, case ye, on with your vizards! 52 There's money of the King's coming down the hill; 'tis going to the King's Exchequer.

FALSTAFF   You lie, ye rogue, 'tis going to the King's Tavern.

GADSHILL   There's enough to make us all. 57

FALSTAFF   To be hanged.

PRINCE   Sirs, you four shall front them in the narrow 59 lane; Ned Poins and I will walk lower. If they scape from your encounter, then they light on us.

PETO   How many be there of them?

GADSHILL   Some eight or ten.

FALSTAFF   Zounds, will they not rob us?

PRINCE   What, a coward, Sir John Paunch?

FALSTAFF   Indeed, I am not John of Gaunt, your 66 grandfather, but yet no coward, Hal.

PRINCE   Well, we leave that to the proof. 68

POINS   Sirrah Jack, thy horse stands behind the hedge. When thou need'st him, there thou shalt find him. Farewell, and stand fast.

85 Will . . . way will she let you go dry in muddy roads, i.e., will she protect you in tight places   **86 liquored** (1) made waterproof by oiling (2) bribed (3) made drunk   **87 as in a castle** i.e., in complete security.   **receipt** recipe, formula   **88 of fern seed** i.e., of becoming invisible (since fern seed, almost invisible itself, was popularly supposed to render its possessor invisible)   **90 beholding** beholden   **93 purchase** booty   **96 homo . . . men** i.e., the Latin name for man applies to all types   **98 muddy** stupid   **2.2. Location:** The highway, near Gad's Hill.   **2 frets** chafes (with pun on another meaning of the word, applying to *gummed velvet*, velvet stiffened with gum and therefore liable to *fret*, or "wear")   **3 close** concealed   **6 keep up** 12 square a measuring tool   **14 fair** exemplary.   **for all** despite all   **18 medicines** love potions   **22 turn true man** turn honest; turn informer

28 Whew (Perhaps Falstaff tries to answer the whistling he hears or mocks it.)   **31 list** listen   **36 colt** trick, cheat. (In lines 37–38, Prince Hal puns on the common meaning.)   **39–40 help . . . horse** help me to find my horse. (But in line 41, the Prince comically retorts as though having been asked to hold the stirrup while Falstaff mounted, as a hostler would do.)   **43 peach** inform on you.   **An if   45 so forward** (1) so far advanced (referring to the robbery plot) (2) so presumptuous (referring to the joke played on him)   **46 afoot** (1) in progress (2) on foot, i.e., not on horseback   **47 Stand** don't move. (But Falstaff answers in the sense of "stand on one's feet.")   **50 setter** arranger of the robbery. (See 1.2.104–105 and note.)   **52 Case ye** put on your masks   **57 make us all** make our fortunes (or, as Falstaff sees it, make us be hanged)   **59 front** confront   **66 Gaunt** i.e., Ghent (but punning on *gaunt*, "thin")   **68 proof** test

FALSTAFF Now cannot I strike him, if I should be 72
hanged. 73
PRINCE [*to Poins*] Ned, where are our disguises?
POINS [*to Prince*] Here, hard by. Stand close.
          [*Exeunt Prince and Poins.*]
FALSTAFF Now, my masters, happy man be his dole, 76
say I. Every man to his business. [*They stand aside.*]

    Enter the Travelers.

FIRST TRAVELER Come, neighbor. The boy shall lead
our horses down the hill; we'll walk afoot awhile, and
ease our legs.
THIEVES [*coming forward*] Stand!
TRAVELERS Jesus bless us!
FALSTAFF Strike! Down with them! Cut the villains'
throats! Ah, whoreson caterpillars, bacon-fed knaves! 84
They hate us youth. Down with them, fleece them!
TRAVELERS O, we are undone, both we and ours for-
ever!
FALSTAFF Hang ye, gorbellied knaves, are ye undone? 88
No, ye fat chuffs; I would your store were here. On, 89
bacons, on! What, ye knaves, young men must live. 90
You are grandjurors, are ye? We'll jure ye, 'faith. 91
    Here they rob them and bind them. Exeunt.

    Enter the Prince and Poins [in buckram].

PRINCE The thieves have bound the true men. Now
could thou and I rob the thieves and go merrily to
London, it would be argument for a week, laughter 94
for a month, and a good jest forever.
POINS Stand close. I hear them coming.
          [*They stand aside.*]

    Enter the thieves again.

FALSTAFF Come, my masters, let us share, and then to
horse before day. An the Prince and Poins be not two
arrant cowards, there's no equity stirring. There's no 99
more valor in that Poins than in a wild duck.
          [*The thieves begin to share the booty.*]
PRINCE Your money!
POINS Villains!
    *As they are sharing, the Prince and Poins set upon
    them. They all run away, and Falstaff, after a blow
    or two, runs away too, leaving the booty behind
                                          them.*

PRINCE
Got with much ease. Now merrily to horse.
The thieves are all scattered and possessed with fear
So strongly that they dare not meet each other;
Each takes his fellow for an officer.
Away, good Ned. Falstaff sweats to death

And lards the lean earth as he walks along. 108
Were 't not for laughing, I should pity him.
POINS How the fat rogue roared!   *Exeunt.*

2.3   *Enter Hotspur, solus, reading a letter.*

HOTSPUR "But, for mine own part, my lord, I could be
well contented to be there, in respect of the love I bear
your house." He could be contented; why is he not, 3
then? In respect of the love he bears our house! He
shows in this he loves his own barn better than he 5
loves our house. Let me see some more. "The purpose
you undertake is dangerous"—why, that's certain.
'Tis dangerous to take a cold, to sleep, to drink; but I
tell you, my lord fool, out of this nettle, danger, we
pluck this flower, safety. "The purpose you undertake
is dangerous, the friends you have named uncertain,
the time itself unsorted, and your whole plot too light 12
for the counterpoise of so great an opposition." Say 13
you so, say you so? I say unto you again, you are a
shallow, cowardly hind, and you lie. What a lack- 15
brain is this! By the Lord, our plot is a good plot as
ever was laid, our friends true and constant; a good
plot, good friends, and full of expectation; an excellent 18
plot, very good friends. What a frosty-spirited rogue is
this! Why, my lord of York commends the plot and 20
the general course of the action. Zounds, an I were 21
now by this rascal, I could brain him with his lady's
fan. Is there not my father, my uncle, and myself? Lord
Edmund Mortimer, my lord of York, and Owen Glendower? Is there not besides the Douglas? Have I not all
their letters to meet me in arms by the ninth of the next
month, and are they not some of them set forward
already? What a pagan rascal is this, an infidel! Ha, 28
you shall see now in very sincerity of fear and
cold heart will he to the King and lay open all our
proceedings. O, I could divide myself and go to buf- 31
fets for moving such a dish of skim milk with so hon- 32
orable an action! Hang him, let him tell the King, we
are prepared. I will set forward tonight.

    Enter his Lady.

How now, Kate? I must leave you within these two
hours.
LADY PERCY
O my good lord, why are you thus alone?
For what offense have I this fortnight been
A banished woman from my Harry's bed?
Tell me, sweet lord, what is 't that takes from thee

72–73 Now . . . hanged (Falstaff wishes he could hit Poins, who is too quick for him.) **76 happy . . . dole** may happiness be every man's portion or lot **84 whoreson** i.e., scurvy, abominable. **caterpillars** i.e., parasites. **bacon-fed** i.e., well-fed **88 gorbellied** big-bellied **89 chuffs** churls, rich but miserly. **store** total wealth **90 bacons** fat men **91 grandjurors** i.e., men of wealth, able to serve on juries **94 argument** a subject for conversation **99 arrant** notorious, unmitigated. **equity** judgment, discernment

108 lards drips fat, bastes
2.3. Location: Hotspur's estate (identified historically as Warkworth Castle in Northumberland).
s.d. solus alone **3 house** family **5 barn** (Hotspur refers derisively to the writer's residence, taking *house*, line 3, in its literal sense.)
12 unsorted unsuitable **13 for . . . of** to counterbalance **15 hind** menial, peasant **18 expectation** promise **20 lord of York** i.e., Archbishop Scroop. (Also in line 24.) **21 an** if **28 pagan** unbelieving **31–32 divide . . . buffets** i.e., fight with myself **32 moving** urging

Thy stomach, pleasure, and thy golden sleep? 41
Why dost thou bend thine eyes upon the earth
And start so often when thou sitt'st alone?
Why hast thou lost the fresh blood in thy cheeks
And given my treasures and my rights of thee 45
To thick-eyed musing and curst melancholy? 46
In thy faint slumbers I by thee have watched 47
And heard thee murmur tales of iron wars,
Speak terms of manage to thy bounding steed, 49
Cry, "Courage! To the field!" And thou hast talked
Of sallies and retires, of trenches, tents, 51
Of palisadoes, frontiers, parapets, 52
Of basilisks, of cannon, culverin, 53
Of prisoners' ransom, and of soldiers slain,
And all the currents of a heady fight. 55
Thy spirit within thee hath been so at war,
And thus hath so bestirred thee in thy sleep,
That beads of sweat have stood upon thy brow
Like bubbles in a late-disturbèd stream, 59
And in thy face strange motions have appeared,
Such as we see when men restrain their breath
On some great sudden hest. O, what portents are
   these? 62
Some heavy business hath my lord in hand, 63
And I must know it, else he loves me not.
HOTSPUR
What, ho!

         [Enter a Servant.]

        Is Gilliams with the packet gone?
SERVANT   He is, my lord, an hour ago.
HOTSPUR
Hath Butler brought those horses from the sheriff?
SERVANT
One horse, my lord, he brought even now. 68
HOTSPUR
What horse? A roan, a crop-ear, is it not?
SERVANT
It is, my lord.
HOTSPUR   That roan shall be my throne.
Well, I will back him straight. O, *Esperance!* 71
Bid Butler lead him forth into the park.
                     [Exit Servant.]
LADY PERCY   But hear you, my lord.
HOTSPUR   What sayst thou, my lady?
LADY PERCY   What is it carries you away? 75
HOTSPUR   Why, my horse, my love, my horse.
LADY PERCY   Out, you mad-headed ape!

A weasel hath not such a deal of spleen 78
As you are tossed with. In faith, 79
I'll know your business, Harry, that I will.
I fear my brother Mortimer doth stir
About his title, and hath sent for you 82
To line his enterprise; but if you go— 83
HOTSPUR
So far afoot, I shall be weary, love.
LADY PERCY
Come, come, you paraquito, answer me 85
Directly unto this question that I ask.
In faith, I'll break thy little finger, Harry,
An if thou wilt not tell me all things true. 88
HOTSPUR   Away,
Away, you trifler! Love? I love thee not;
I care not for thee, Kate. This is no world
To play with mammets and to tilt with lips. 92
We must have bloody noses and cracked crowns, 93
And pass them current too. Gods me, my horse! 94
What sayst thou, Kate? What wouldst thou have
   with me?
LADY PERCY
Do you not love me? Do you not, indeed?
Well, do not, then, for since you love me not
I will not love myself. Do you not love me?
Nay, tell me if you speak in jest or no.
HOTSPUR   Come, wilt thou see me ride?
And when I am a-horseback I will swear
I love thee infinitely. But hark you, Kate,
I must not have you henceforth question me
Whither I go, nor reason whereabout. 104
Whither I must, I must; and, to conclude,
This evening must I leave you, gentle Kate.
I know you wise, but yet no farther wise
Than Harry Percy's wife; constant you are,
But yet a woman; and for secrecy,
No lady closer, for I well believe 110
Thou wilt not utter what thou dost not know,
And so far will I trust thee, gentle Kate.
LADY PERCY   How, so far?
HOTSPUR
Not an inch further. But hark you, Kate:
Whither I go, thither shall you go too.
Today will I set forth, tomorrow you.
Will this content you, Kate?
LADY PERCY   It must, of force. *Exeunt.* 117

                    ❖

41 stomach appetite   45 And . . . thee i.e., and given what I treasure in you and have a right, as wife, to share   46 thick-eyed dull-sighted, vacant, abstracted.   curst ill-tempered   47 faint restless. watched lain awake   49 manage horsemanship   51 retires retreats 52 palisadoes stakes set in the ground for defense.   frontiers outworks, ramparts   53 basilisks large cannon.   culverin long cannon 55 heady headlong   59 late-disturbèd recently stirred up   62 hest command   63 heavy weighty; sorrowful   68 even just   71 back mount.   Esperance hope. (The motto of the Percy family.)   75 carries you away separates you from your judgment. (But Hotspur puns on the literal meaning.)

78 spleen (The spleen was thought to be the source of impulsive and irritable behavior.)   79 tossed tossed about, agitated   82 title claim to the throne   83 line strengthen   85 paraquito little parrot. (A term of endearment.)   88 An if if   92 mammets dolls (with a quibble on the Latin *mamma* meaning "breast")   93 crowns (1) heads (2) coins worth five shillings. (Cracked coins would not "pass current," as Hotspur jokes in the next line.)   94 Gods me God save me   104 reason whereabout discuss about what   110 closer more close-mouthed 117 of force perforce, of necessity

2.4   *Enter Prince and Poins.*

PRINCE   Ned, prithee, come out of that fat room, and ₁
lend me thy hand to laugh a little.

POINS   Where hast been, Hal?

PRINCE   With three or four loggerheads amongst three ₄
or four score hogsheads. I have sounded the very bass ₅
string of humility. Sirrah, I am sworn brother to a
leash of drawers, and can call them all by their Christian ₇
names, as Tom, Dick, and Francis. They take it already ₈
upon their salvation that, though I be but Prince of ₉
Wales, yet I am the king of courtesy, and tell me flatly
I am no proud Jack like Falstaff, but a Corinthian, a lad ₁₁
of mettle, a good boy—by the Lord, so they call me!—
and when I am King of England I shall command all
the good lads in Eastcheap. They call drinking deep ₁₄
"dyeing scarlet"; and when you breathe in your water- ₁₅
ing they cry "hem!" and bid you "play it off." To con- ₁₆
clude, I am so good a proficient in one quarter of an
hour that I can drink with any tinker in his own language during my life. I tell thee, Ned, thou hast lost
much honor that thou wert not with me in this action.
But, sweet Ned—to sweeten which name of Ned, I
give thee this pennyworth of sugar, clapped even now ₂₂
into my hand by an underskinker, one that never ₂₃
spake other English in his life than "Eight shillings
and sixpence," and "You are welcome," with this
shrill addition, "Anon, anon, sir! Score a pint of bas- ₂₆
tard in the Half-Moon," or so. But, Ned, to drive away ₂₇
the time till Falstaff come, I prithee do thou stand in
some by-room while I question my puny drawer to ₂₉
what end he gave me the sugar; and do thou never
leave calling "Francis," that his tale to me may be
nothing but "Anon." Step aside, and I'll show thee a
precedent.   [*Exit Poins.*] ₃₃

POINS [*within*]   Francis!

PRINCE   Thou art perfect.

POINS [*within*]   Francis!

Enter [Francis, a] drawer.

FRANCIS   Anon, anon, sir.—Look down into the Pom- ₃₇
garnet, Ralph.   ₃₈

PRINCE   Come hither, Francis.

FRANCIS   My lord?

2.4. Location: A tavern in Eastcheap, London, usually identified as the Boar's Head. Some tavern furniture, including stools, is provided onstage.
1 fat stuffy, or, a **vat** room   **4 loggerheads** blockheads   **5 hogsheads** wine barrels.   **bass** (With a pun on *base*.)   **7 leash of drawers** i.e., three waiters   **8–9 take . . . salvation** already maintain it as they hope to be saved   **11 Jack** (1) Jack Falstaff (2) fellow.   **Corinthian** i.e., gay blade, good sport. (Corinth was reputed to be licentious.)   **14–15 They . . . scarlet** (Either because excessive drinking causes a red complexion or because urine, produced by *drinking deep*, was sometimes used for fixing dyes.)   **15–16 breathe . . . watering** pause for breath in your drinking   **16 play it off** drink it up   **22 sugar** (Used to sweeten wine.)   **23 underskinker** assistant to a waiter or bartender   **26 Anon** right away, coming.   **Score** charge   **26–27 bastard** (A sweet Spanish wine.)   **27 Half-Moon** (The name of a room in the inn.)   **29 by-room** side-room.   **puny** inexperienced, raw.   **drawer** tapster, one who draws liquor   **33 precedent** example   **37–38 Pomgarnet** Pomegranate. (Another room in the inn.)

PRINCE   How long hast thou to serve, Francis? ₄₁

FRANCIS   Forsooth, five years, and as much as to—

POINS [*within*]   Francis!

FRANCIS   Anon, anon, sir.

PRINCE   Five year! By 'r Lady, a long lease for the ₄₅
clinking of pewter. But Francis, darest thou be so
valiant as to play the coward with thy indenture and ₄₇
show it a fair pair of heels and run from it?

FRANCIS   O Lord, sir, I'll be sworn upon all the books in ₄₉
England, I could find in my heart—

POINS [*within*]   Francis!

FRANCIS   Anon, sir.

PRINCE   How old art thou, Francis?

FRANCIS   Let me see, about Michaelmas next I shall ₅₄
be—

POINS [*within*]   Francis!

FRANCIS   Anon, sir. Pray, stay a little, my lord.

PRINCE   Nay, but hark you, Francis: for the sugar thou
gavest me, 'twas a pennyworth, was 't not?

FRANCIS   O Lord, I would it had been two!

PRINCE   I will give thee for it a thousand pound. Ask
me when thou wilt, and thou shalt have it.

POINS [*within*]   Francis!

FRANCIS   Anon, anon.

PRINCE   Anon, Francis? No, Francis; but tomorrow,
Francis, or, Francis, o' Thursday, or indeed, Francis,
when thou wilt. But, Francis—

FRANCIS   My lord?

PRINCE   Wilt thou rob this leathern-jerkin, crystal- ₆₉
button, not-pated, agate-ring, puke-stocking, caddis- ₇₀
garter, smooth-tongue, Spanish-pouch—   ₇₁

FRANCIS   O Lord, sir, who do you mean?

PRINCE   Why, then, your brown bastard is your only ₇₃
drink; for look you, Francis, your white canvas ₇₄
doublet will sully. In Barbary, sir, it cannot come to so ₇₅
much.   ₇₆

FRANCIS   What, sir?

POINS [*within*]   Francis!

PRINCE   Away, you rogue! Dost thou not hear them call?
Here they both call him; the drawer stands
amazed, not knowing which way to go.

Enter Vintner.

VINTNER   What stand'st thou still and hear'st such a ₈₀
calling? Look to the guests within. [*Exit Francis.*] My
lord, old Sir John, with half a dozen more, are at the
door. Shall I let them in?

PRINCE   Let them alone awhile, and then open the
door. [*Exit Vintner.*] Poins!

Enter Poins.

---

41 serve i.e., serve out your apprenticeship   **45 By 'r Lady** by Our Lady   **47 indenture** contract of apprenticeship   **49 books** i.e., Bibles   **54 Michaelmas** September 29   **69–71 Wilt . . . Spanish-pouch** i.e., will you rob your master of your services by running away, he who is characterized by a leather jacket, transparent buttons, cropped hair, a ring with small figures in an agate stone for a seal, dark woolen stockings, worsted garters, an ingratiating flattering manner of speech, wallet of Spanish leather   **73–76 Why . . . much** (The Prince talks seeming nonsense in order to bewilder Francis, but he also implies that Francis should stick to his trade, since he will not cut much of a figure in the world.)   **75 it** i.e., sugar   **80 What** why

POINS   Anon, anon, sir.

PRINCE   Sirrah, Falstaff and the rest of the thieves are at the door. Shall we be merry?

POINS   As merry as crickets, my lad. But hark ye, what cunning match have you made with this jest of the 90 drawer? Come, what's the issue? 91

PRINCE   I am now of all humors that have showed 92 themselves humors since the old days of Goodman 93 Adam to the pupil age of this present twelve o'clock at 94 midnight. 95

[Enter Francis, hurrying across the stage with wine.]

What's o'clock, Francis?

FRANCIS   Anon, anon, sir.   *[Exit.]*

PRINCE   That ever this fellow should have fewer words than a parrot, and yet the son of a woman! His industry is upstairs and downstairs, his eloquence the parcel 100 of a reckoning. I am not yet of Percy's mind, the Hot- 101 spur of the north, he that kills me some six or seven 102 dozen of Scots at a breakfast, washes his hands, and says to his wife, "Fie upon this quiet life! I want work." "O my sweet Harry," says she, "how many hast thou killed today?" "Give my roan horse a drench," says he, and answers, "Some fourteen," an 107 hour after, "a trifle, a trifle." I prithee, call in Falstaff. I'll play Percy, and that damned brawn shall play Dame 109 Mortimer his wife. "Rivo!" says the drunkard. Call in 110 ribs, call in tallow. 111

Enter Falstaff, [Gadshill, Bardolph, and Peto; Francis following with wine].

POINS   Welcome, Jack. Where hast thou been?

FALSTAFF   A plague of all cowards, I say, and a 113 vengeance too! Marry and amen! Give me a cup of sack, boy. Ere I lead this life long, I'll sew nether- 115 stocks, and mend them and foot them too. A plague 116 of all cowards! Give me a cup of sack, rogue. Is there no virtue extant?   *He drinketh.*

PRINCE   Didst thou never see Titan kiss a dish of butter, 119 pitiful-hearted Titan, that melted at the sweet tale of 120 the sun's? If thou didst, then behold that compound. 121

FALSTAFF   You rogue, here's lime in this sack too. There 122 is nothing but roguery to be found in villainous man, yet a coward is worse than a cup of sack with lime in it. A villainous coward! Go thy ways, old Jack, die when thou wilt. If manhood, good manhood, be not

forgot upon the face of the earth, then am I a shotten 127 herring. There lives not three good men unhanged in 128 England, and one of them is fat and grows old, God help the while! A bad world, I say. I would I were a 130 weaver; I could sing psalms or anything. A plague of 131 all cowards, I say still.

PRINCE   How now, woolsack, what mutter you? 133

FALSTAFF   A king's son! If I do not beat thee out of thy kingdom with a dagger of lath, and drive all thy 135 subjects afore thee like a flock of wild geese, I'll never wear hair on my face more. You, Prince of Wales!

PRINCE   Why, you whoreson round man, what's the matter?

FALSTAFF   Are not you a coward? Answer me to that. And Poins there?

POINS   Zounds, ye fat paunch, an ye call me coward, by 142 the Lord, I'll stab thee.

FALSTAFF   I call thee coward? I'll see thee damned ere I call thee coward, but I would give a thousand pound I could run as fast as thou canst. You are straight enough in the shoulders; you care not who sees your back. Call you that backing of your friends? A plague upon such backing! Give me them that will face me. Give me a cup of sack. I am a rogue if I drunk today.

PRINCE   O villain, thy lips are scarce wiped since thou drunk'st last.

FALSTAFF   All is one for that. *(He drinketh.)* A plague of 153 all cowards, still say I.

PRINCE   What's the matter?

FALSTAFF   What's the matter? There be four of us here have ta'en a thousand pound this day morning. 157

PRINCE   Where is it, Jack, where is it?

FALSTAFF   Where is it? Taken from us it is. A hundred upon poor four of us.

PRINCE   What, a hundred, man?

FALSTAFF   I am a rogue if I were not at half-sword with 162 a dozen of them two hours together. I have scaped by 163 miracle. I am eight times thrust through the doublet, 164 four through the hose, my buckler cut through and 165 through, my sword hacked like a handsaw—*ecce* 166 *signum!* I never dealt better since I was a man. All 167 would not do. A plague of all cowards! Let them 168 speak. If they speak more or less than truth, they are villains and the sons of darkness.

PRINCE   Speak, sirs, how was it?

GADSHILL   We four set upon some dozen—

FALSTAFF   Sixteen at least, my lord.

GADSHILL   And bound them.

PETO   No, no, they were not bound.

90 **match** game, contest   91 **issue** outcome, point   **92–95 I . . . midnight** i.e., I'm now in a mood for anything that has happened in the whole history of the world   93 **Goodman** (Title for a farmer.) 94 **pupil** youthful   100–101 **parcel . . . reckoning** items of a bill 102 **kills me** i.e., kills. (Me is used colloquially.)   107 **drench** draft (sometimes of medicine).   **says he** i.e., he tells a servant   109 **brawn** fat boar   110 **Rivo** (An exclamation of uncertain meaning, but related to drinking.)   111 **ribs** rib roast.   **tallow** fat drippings   113 **of** on 115–116 **netherstocks** stockings (the sewing or mending of which is a menial occupation)   116 **foot** make a new foot for   119 **Titan** i.e., the sun   120 **that** i.e., the butter   121 **compound** melting butter, i.e., Falstaff   122 **lime in this sack** i.e., lime added to make the wine sparkle

127–128 **a shotten herring** a herring that has cast its roe and is consequently thin   130 **the while** i.e., in these bad times   131 **weaver** (Many psalm-singing Protestant immigrants from the Low Countries were weavers.)   133 **woolsack** bale of wool   135 **dagger of lath** (The Vice, a stock comic figure in morality plays, was so armed.)   142 **an** if   153 **All . . . that** i.e., no matter   157 **this day morning** this morning   162 **at half-sword** fighting at close quarters   163 **scaped** escaped   164 **doublet** Elizabethan upper garment like a jacket 165 **hose** close-fitting breeches.   **buckler** shield   166–167 **ecce signum** behold the proof. (Familiar words from the Mass.)   167–168 **All . . . do** i.e., all that I did was of no use

FALSTAFF   You rogue, they were bound, every man of them, or I am a Jew else, an Hebrew Jew.

GADSHILL   As we were sharing, some six or seven fresh men set upon us—

FALSTAFF   And unbound the rest, and then come in the other.   181

PRINCE   What, fought you with them all?

FALSTAFF   All? I know not what you call all, but if I fought not with fifty of them, I am a bunch of radish. If there were not two- or three-and-fifty upon poor old Jack, then am I no two-legged creature.

PRINCE   Pray God you have not murdered some of them.

FALSTAFF   Nay, that's past praying for. I have peppered 188 two of them. Two I am sure I have paid, two rogues in buckram suits. I tell thee what, Hal, if I tell thee a lie, spit in my face, call me horse. Thou knowest my old ward. Here I lay, and thus I bore my point. [*He* 192 *demonstrates his stance.*] Four rogues in buckram let drive at me—

PRINCE   What, four? Thou saidst but two even now.   195

FALSTAFF   Four, Hal, I told thee four.

POINS   Ay, ay, he said four.

FALSTAFF   These four came all afront, and mainly thrust 198 at me. I made me no more ado but took all their seven 199 points in my target, thus.   200

PRINCE   Seven? Why, there were but four even now.

FALSTAFF   In buckram?

POINS   Ay, four, in buckram suits.

FALSTAFF   Seven, by these hilts, or I am a villain else.   204

PRINCE   [*aside to Poins*] Prithee, let him alone. We shall have more anon.

FALSTAFF   Dost thou hear me, Hal?

PRINCE   Ay, and mark thee too, Jack.   208

FALSTAFF   Do so, for it is worth the listening to. These nine in buckram that I told thee of—

PRINCE   So, two more already.

FALSTAFF   Their points being broken—   212

POINS   Down fell their hose.

FALSTAFF   Began to give me ground; but I followed me 214 close, came in foot and hand; and with a thought 215 seven of the eleven I paid.

PRINCE   O monstrous! Eleven buckram men grown out of two!

FALSTAFF   But, as the devil would have it, three misbegotten knaves in Kendal green came at my back 220 and let drive at me; for it was so dark, Hal, that thou couldst not see thy hand.

PRINCE   These lies are like their father that begets them, gross as a mountain, open, palpable. Why, thou claybrained guts, thou knotty-pated fool, thou whore- 225 son, obscene, greasy tallow-keech—   226

FALSTAFF   What, art thou mad? Art thou mad? Is not the truth the truth?

PRINCE   Why, how couldst thou know these men in Kendal green when it was so dark thou couldst not see thy hand? Come, tell us your reason. What sayest thou to this?

POINS   Come, your reason, Jack, your reason.

FALSTAFF   What, upon compulsion? Zounds, an I were at the strappado, or all the racks in the world, I would 235 not tell you on compulsion. Give you a reason on compulsion? If reasons were as plentiful as blackberries, 237 I would give no man a reason upon compulsion, I.

PRINCE   I'll be no longer guilty of this sin. This sanguine 239 coward, this bed-presser, this horse-backbreaker, this huge hill of flesh—

FALSTAFF   'Sblood, you starveling, you eel-skin, you dried neat's tongue, you bull's pizzle, you stockfish! 243 O, for breath to utter what is like thee! You tailor's yard, you sheath, you bowcase, you vile standing 245 tuck—   246

PRINCE   Well, breathe awhile, and then to it again, and when thou hast tired thyself in base comparisons, hear me speak but this.

POINS   Mark, Jack.

PRINCE   We two saw you four set on four and bound them, and were masters of their wealth. Mark now how a plain tale shall put you down. Then did we two set on you four, and, with a word, outfaced you from 254 your prize, and have it, yea, and can show it you here in the house. And, Falstaff, you carried your guts away as nimbly, with as quick dexterity, and roared for mercy, and still run and roared, as ever I heard bull calf. What a slave art thou, to hack thy sword as thou hast done, and then say it was in fight! What trick, what device, what starting-hole canst thou now find 261 out to hide thee from this open and apparent shame?

POINS   Come, let's hear, Jack. What trick hast thou now?

FALSTAFF   By the Lord, I knew ye as well as he that made ye. Why, hear you, my masters, was it for me to kill the heir apparent? Should I turn upon the true prince? Why, thou knowest I am as valiant as Hercules, but beware instinct. The lion will not touch the true prince. Instinct is a great matter; I was now a coward on instinct. I shall think the better of myself and thee during my life—I for a valiant lion, and thou for a true prince. But by the Lord, lads, I am glad you have the money. Hostess, clap to the doors! Watch 273 tonight, pray tomorrow. Gallants, lads, boys, hearts 274 of gold, all the titles of good fellowship come to you! What, shall we be merry? Shall we have a play extempore?

---

181 other others   **188 peppered** i.e., killed   **192 ward** defensive stance, parry. **lay** stood   **195 even** just   **198 afront** abreast. **mainly** powerfully   **199 made me** made. (*Me* is used colloquially.) **200 target** shield   **204 by these hilts** by my sword hilt. **villain** i.e., no gentleman   **208 mark** (1) pay heed (2) keep count   **212 points** sword points. (But Poins puns on the sense of laces, by which the hose were attached to the doublet.)   **214 followed me** followed **215 with a thought** quick as a thought   **220 Kendal** a town known for its textiles   **225 knotty-pated** thickheaded   **226 tallow-keech** lump of tallow

235 strappado a kind of torture   **237 reasons . . . blackberries** (Falstaff puns on *raisins*, pronounced nearly like *reasons*.)   **239 sanguine** ruddy   **243 neat's** ox's. **pizzle** penis. **stockfish** dried cod **245 yard** yardstick   **245–246 standing tuck** rapier standing on its point, or no longer pliant   **254 with a word** (1) in a word (2) with a minimum of speech. **outfaced** frightened   **261 starting-hole** point of shelter (like a rabbit's hole)   **273 Watch** (1) keep watchful vigil. (See Matthew 26:41.) (2) carouse   **274 pray** (1) pray to God (2) prey

PRINCE Content; and the argument shall be thy run- 278
ning away.

FALSTAFF Ah, no more of that, Hal, an thou lovest me!

Enter Hostess.

HOSTESS
O Jesu, my lord the Prince!

PRINCE How now, my lady the hostess, what sayst
thou to me?

HOSTESS Marry, my lord, there is a nobleman of the
court at door would speak with you. He says he
comes from your father.

PRINCE Give him as much as will make him a royal 287
man, and send him back again to my mother. 288

FALSTAFF What manner of man is he?

HOSTESS An old man.

FALSTAFF What doth Gravity out of his bed at mid- 291
night? Shall I give him his answer?

PRINCE Prithee, do, Jack.

FALSTAFF Faith, and I'll send him packing.   *Exit.*

PRINCE Now, sirs. By 'r Lady, you fought fair; so did
you, Peto; so did you, Bardolph. You are lions too,
you ran away upon instinct, you will not touch the
true prince; no, fie!

BARDOLPH Faith, I ran when I saw others run.

PRINCE Faith, tell me now in earnest, how came
Falstaff's sword so hacked?

PETO Why, he hacked it with his dagger, and said he
would swear truth out of England but he would make 303
you believe it was done in fight, and persuaded us to
do the like.

BARDOLPH Yea, and to tickle our noses with spear grass
to make them bleed, and then to beslubber our gar- 307
ments with it and swear it was the blood of true men.
I did that I did not this seven year before: I blushed to 309
hear his monstrous devices.

PRINCE O villain, thou stolest a cup of sack eighteen
years ago and wert taken with the manner, and ever 312
since thou hast blushed extempore. Thou hadst fire 313
and sword on thy side, and yet thou rann'st away.
What instinct hadst thou for it?

BARDOLPH My lord, do you see these meteors? Do you 316
behold these exhalations?   *[Pointing to his own face.]* 317

PRINCE I do.

BARDOLPH What think you they portend? 319

PRINCE Hot livers and cold purses. 320

BARDOLPH Choler, my lord, if rightly taken. 321

PRINCE No, if rightly taken, halter. 322

Enter Falstaff.

Here comes lean Jack, here comes bare-bone. How
now, my sweet creature of bombast? How long is 't 324
ago, Jack, since thou sawest thine own knee?

FALSTAFF My own knee? When I was about thy years,
Hal, I was not an eagle's talon in the waist; I could
have crept into any alderman's thumb ring. A plague
of sighing and grief! It blows a man up like a bladder.
There's villainous news abroad. Here was Sir John
Bracy from your father. You must to the court in the
morning. That same mad fellow of the north, Percy,
and he of Wales that gave Amamon the bastinado and 333
made Lucifer cuckold and swore the devil his true 334
liegeman upon the cross of a Welsh hook—what a 335
plague call you him?

POINS Owen Glendower.

FALSTAFF Owen, Owen, the same; and his son-in-law
Mortimer, and old Northumberland, and that
sprightly Scot of Scots, Douglas, that runs a-horseback
up a hill perpendicular—

PRINCE He that rides at high speed, and with his pistol
kills a sparrow flying.

FALSTAFF You have hit it. 344

PRINCE So did he never the sparrow.

FALSTAFF Well, that rascal hath good mettle in him; he
will not run. 347

PRINCE Why, what a rascal art thou then to praise him
so for running!

FALSTAFF A-horseback, ye cuckoo; but afoot he will not
budge a foot.

PRINCE Yes, Jack, upon instinct.

FALSTAFF I grant ye, upon instinct. Well, he is there too,
and one Mordake, and a thousand blue-caps more. 354
Worcester is stolen away tonight. Thy father's beard is
turned white with the news. You may buy land now
as cheap as stinking mackerel.

PRINCE Why, then, it is like, if there come a hot June 358
and this civil buffeting hold, we shall buy maiden- 359
heads as they buy hobnails, by the hundreds.

FALSTAFF By the mass, lad, thou sayest true; it is like
we shall have good trading that way. But tell me, Hal,
art not thou horrible afeard? Thou being heir apparent, could the world pick thee out three such enemies
again as that fiend Douglas, that spirit Percy, and that
devil Glendower? Art thou not horribly afraid? Doth
not thy blood thrill at it?

---

278 argument plot of the play **287–288 Give . . . man** (Prince Hal
puns on the value of coins: a *noble* was worth six shillings eight
pence; a *royal* was worth ten shillings.) **291 What doth** why is
303 but he would if he did not **307 beslubber** smear, cover
309 that something **312 taken . . . manner** caught with the goods
313 extempore without needing any occasion. (Bardolph is red-faced
whether he blushes or not.) **fire** i.e., a red nose and complexion
caused by heavy drinking **316, 317 meteors, exhalations** i.e., the
red blotches on Bardolph's face **319 portend** signify. (Continues the
metaphor of astrological influence begun in *meteors* and *exhalations*.)
320 Hot . . . purses i.e., livers inflamed by drink and purses made
empty by spending **321 Choler** a choleric or combative temperament. **taken** understood. (But the Prince, in his next speech, uses
the word to mean "arrested.")

322 halter hangman's noose. (The Prince plays on Bardolph's *choler,*
which he takes as *collar.*) **s.d.** (Falstaff's entry in the Quarto after
line 321 suggests he is visible to the audience while the Prince talks
of a hangman's halter.) **324 bombast** (1) cotton padding (2) fustian
speech **333 Amamon** (The name of a demon.) **bastinado** beating
on the soles of the feet **334 made . . . cuckold** i.e., gave Lucifer his
horns, the sign of cuckoldry **334–335 and swore . . . liegeman** and
made the devil take an oath of allegiance as a true subject
335 Welsh hook curved-bladed pike lacking the cross shape of the
sword on which such oaths were usually sworn **344 hit it** described
it exactly. (But the Prince takes *hit* literally in the next line.) **347 run**
flee. (But the Prince answers punningly in the sense of "ride at high
speed.") **354 blue-caps** Scottish soldiers **358 like** likely **359 hold**
continues

PRINCE Not a whit, i' faith. I lack some of thy instinct.

FALSTAFF Well, thou wilt be horribly chid tomorrow 369 when thou comest to thy father. If thou love me, practice an answer.

PRINCE Do thou stand for my father, and examine me upon the particulars of my life.

FALSTAFF Shall I? Content. This chair shall be my state, 374 this dagger my scepter, and this cushion my crown.

[Falstaff establishes himself on his "throne."]

PRINCE Thy state is taken for a joint stool, thy golden 376 scepter for a leaden dagger, and thy precious rich 377 crown for a pitiful bald crown.

FALSTAFF Well, an the fire of grace be not quite out of 379 thee, now shalt thou be moved. Give me a cup of sack to make my eyes look red, that it may be thought I have wept; for I must speak in passion, and I will do it in King Cambyses' vein.   383

PRINCE Well, here is my leg.   [He bows.]

FALSTAFF And here is my speech. Stand aside, nobility.

HOSTESS O Jesu, this is excellent sport, i' faith!

FALSTAFF
Weep not, sweet queen, for trickling tears are vain.

HOSTESS O, the Father, how he holds his countenance! 389

FALSTAFF
For God's sake, lords, convey my tristful queen,   390
For tears do stop the floodgates of her eyes.   391

HOSTESS O Jesu, he doth it as like one of these harlotry 392 players as ever I see!   393

FALSTAFF
Peace, good pint pot; peace, good tickle-brain.— 394 Harry, I do not only marvel where thou spendest thy time, but also how thou art accompanied; for though the camomile, the more it is trodden on the faster it 397 grows, yet youth, the more it is wasted the sooner it wears. That thou art my son I have partly thy mother's 399 word, partly my own opinion, but chiefly a villainous trick of thine eye and a foolish hanging of thy nether 401 lip that doth warrant me. If then thou be son to me, 402 here lies the point: why, being son to me, art thou so pointed at? Shall the blessed sun of heaven prove a micher and eat blackberries? A question not to be 405 asked. Shall the son of England prove a thief and take purses? A question to be asked. There is a thing, Harry, which thou hast often heard of, and it is known

to many in our land by the name of pitch. This pitch, 409 as ancient writers do report, doth defile; so doth the 410 company thou keepest. For, Harry, now I do not speak to thee in drink but in tears, not in pleasure but in passion, not in words only but in woes also. And yet there is a virtuous man whom I have often noted in thy company, but I know not his name.

PRINCE What manner of man, an it like Your Majesty? 416

FALSTAFF A goodly portly man, i' faith, and a corpulent; 417 of a cheerful look, a pleasing eye, and a most noble carriage; and, as I think, his age some fifty, or, by 'r Lady, inclining to threescore; and now I remember me, his name is Falstaff. If that man should be lewdly 421 given, he deceiveth me; for, Harry, I see virtue in his looks. If then the tree may be known by the fruit, as the 423 fruit by the tree, then peremptorily I speak it, there is 424 virtue in that Falstaff. Him keep with, the rest banish. And tell me now, thou naughty varlet, tell me, where hast thou been this month?

PRINCE Dost thou speak like a king? Do thou stand for me, and I'll play my father.

FALSTAFF Depose me? If thou dost it half so gravely, so majestically, both in word and matter, hang me up by the heels for a rabbit-sucker or a poulter's hare.   432

[Hal takes Falstaff's place on the "throne."]

PRINCE Well, here I am set.   433

FALSTAFF And here I stand. Judge, my masters.

PRINCE Now, Harry, whence come you?

FALSTAFF My noble lord, from Eastcheap.

PRINCE The complaints I hear of thee are grievous.

FALSTAFF 'Sblood, my lord, they are false.—Nay, I'll 438 tickle ye for a young prince, i' faith.   439

PRINCE Swearest thou, ungracious boy? Henceforth ne'er look on me. Thou art violently carried away from grace. There is a devil haunts thee in the likeness of an old fat man; a tun of man is thy companion. Why dost 443 thou converse with that trunk of humors, that bolting- 444 hutch of beastliness, that swollen parcel of dropsies, 445 that huge bombard of sack, that stuffed cloak-bag of 446 guts, that roasted Manningtree ox with the pudding in 447 his belly, that reverend Vice, that gray Iniquity, that 448 father ruffian, that vanity in years? Wherein is he good 449 but to taste sack and drink it? Wherein neat and cleanly but to carve a capon and eat it? Wherein 451 cunning but in craft? Wherein crafty but in villainy? 452

---

369 **chid** chided 374 **state** chair of state, throne 376 **joint stool** a stool made by a joiner or furniture maker. (To "take someone for a joint stool" is to offer an intentionally silly apology for overlooking that person, as in *King Lear*, 3.6.52. Prince Hal suggests that Falstaff's *state* is ridiculous [punning on *state*, "throne"].) 377 **leaden** of soft metal, hence inferior 379 **an** if 383 **in . . . vein** i.e., in the ranting and (by Shakespeare's time) old-fashioned style of Thomas Preston's *Cambyses*, an early Elizabethan tragedy 389 **the Father** i.e., in God's name. **holds his countenance** keeps a straight face 390 **convey** escort away. **tristful** sorrowing 391 **stop** fill 392 **harlotry** scurvy, vagabond 393 **players** actors 394 **tickle-brain** (A slang term for strong liquor, here applied as a nickname for the tavern hostess.) 397–399 **camomile . . . wears** (This parodies the style of Lyly's *Euphues* and exaggerates the balance and alliteration of the style.) **camomile** an aromatic creeping herb whose flowers and leaves are used medicinally 401 **trick** trait 402 **warrant** assure 405 **micher** truant

409–410 **This . . . defile** (An allusion to the familiar proverb from Ecclesiasticus 13:1 about the defilement of touching pitch.) **pitch** a sticky, black residue from the distillation of tar, used to seal wood from moisture 416 **an it like** if it please 417 **portly** (1) stately (2) corpulent 421 **lewdly** wickedly 423 **If . . . by the fruit** (See Matthew 12:33.) 424 **peremptorily** decisively 432 **rabbit-sucker** unweaned rabbit. **poulter's** poulterer's 433 **set** seated 438 **'Sblood** i.e., by Christ's blood 439 **tickle ye for** amuse you in the role of 443 **tun** (1) large barrel (2) ton 444 **converse** associate. **humors** body fluids, diseases 444–445 **bolting-hutch** large bin 446 **bombard** leathern drinking vessel. **cloak-bag** portmanteau 447 **Manningtree ox** (Manningtree, a town in Essex, had noted fairs where, no doubt, oxen were roasted whole.) **pudding** sausage 448 **Vice, Iniquity** (Allegorical names for the chief comic character and tempter in morality plays.) 449 **vanity** person given to worldly desires 451 **cleanly** (1) pure (2) deft 452 **cunning** (1) skillful (2) crafty

Wherein villainous but in all things? Wherein worthy but in nothing?

FALSTAFF   I would Your Grace would take me with 455
you. Whom means Your Grace? 456

PRINCE   That villainous abominable misleader of youth,
Falstaff, that old white-bearded Satan.

FALSTAFF   My lord, the man I know.

PRINCE   I know thou dost.

FALSTAFF   But to say I know more harm in him than in
myself were to say more than I know. That he is old,
the more the pity, his white hairs do witness it; but
that he is, saving your reverence, a whoremaster, that 464
I utterly deny. If sack and sugar be a fault, God help
the wicked! If to be old and merry be a sin, then many
an old host that I know is damned. If to be fat be to be 467
hated, then Pharaoh's lean kine are to be loved. No, 468
my good lord, banish Peto, banish Bardolph, banish
Poins; but for sweet Jack Falstaff, kind Jack Falstaff,
true Jack Falstaff, valiant Jack Falstaff, and therefore
more valiant being as he is old Jack Falstaff, banish not
him thy Harry's company, banish not him thy Harry's
company—banish plump Jack, and banish all the
world.

PRINCE   I do, I will.   [A knocking.
Exeunt Hostess, Francis, and Bardolph.]

Enter Bardolph, running.

BARDOLPH   O, my lord, my lord! The sheriff with a
most monstrous watch is at the door. 478

FALSTAFF   Out, ye rogue! Play out the play. I have
much to say in the behalf of that Falstaff.

Enter the Hostess.

HOSTESS   O Jesu, my lord, my lord!

PRINCE   Heigh, heigh! The devil rides upon a fiddle- 482
stick. What's the matter? 483

HOSTESS   The sheriff and all the watch are at the door.
They are come to search the house. Shall I let them in?

FALSTAFF   Dost thou hear, Hal? Never call a true piece 486
of gold a counterfeit. Thou art essentially made 487
without seeming so. 488

PRINCE   And thou a natural coward without instinct.

FALSTAFF   I deny your major. If you will deny the 490
sheriff, so; if not, let him enter. If I become not a cart 491
as well as another man, a plague on my bringing up! 492
I hope I shall as soon be strangled with a halter as
another.

PRINCE   Go hide thee behind the arras. The rest walk 495

up above. Now, my masters, for a true face and good 496
conscience.

FALSTAFF   Both which I have had, but their date is out, 498
and therefore I'll hide me.   [He hides behind the arras.]

PRINCE   Call in the sheriff.
[Exeunt all except the Prince and Peto.]

Enter Sheriff and the Carrier.

Now, Master Sheriff, what is your will with me?

SHERIFF
First, pardon me, my lord. A hue and cry 502
Hath followed certain men unto this house.

PRINCE   What men?

SHERIFF
One of them is well known, my gracious lord,
A gross, fat man.

CARRIER   As fat as butter.

PRINCE
The man, I do assure you, is not here,
For I myself at this time have employed him.
And, Sheriff, I will engage my word to thee 509
That I will, by tomorrow dinnertime, 510
Send him to answer thee, or any man,
For anything he shall be charged withal;
And so let me entreat you leave the house.

SHERIFF
I will, my lord. There are two gentlemen
Have in this robbery lost three hundred marks.

PRINCE
It may be so. If he have robbed these men,
He shall be answerable; and so farewell.

SHERIFF   Good night, my noble lord.

PRINCE
I think it is good morrow, is it not? 519

SHERIFF
Indeed, my lord, I think it be two o'clock.
Exit [with Carrier].

PRINCE   This oily rascal is known as well as Paul's. Go 521
call him forth.

PETO [discovering Falstaff]   Falstaff!—Fast asleep behind
the arras, and snorting like a horse.

PRINCE   Hark, how hard he fetches breath. Search his
pockets. (He searcheth his pockets, and findeth certain
papers.) What hast thou found?

PETO   Nothing but papers, my lord.

PRINCE   Let's see what they be. Read them.

PETO [reads]
Item, A capon, ...2s. 2d.
Item, Sauce, ...4d.
Item, Sack, two gallons,.......................5s. 8d.
Item, Anchovies and sack after
supper,...2s. 6d.
Item, Bread, ...ob. 534

PRINCE   O, monstrous! But one halfpennyworth of
bread to this intolerable deal of sack? What there is

455–456 take me with you let me catch up with your meaning
464 saving your reverence i.e., with my apology for using offensive
language   **467 host** innkeeper   **468 Pharaoh's lean kine** (See Genesis
41:3–4, 18–21.)   **478 watch** posse of constables   **482–483 The
. . . fiddlestick** i.e., here's much ado about nothing   **486–488 Dost
. . . seeming so** (In this difficult passage, Falstaff seems to suggest that
he is true gold, not counterfeit, and so should not be betrayed to the
watch by the Prince, who, he hopes, is not merely playacting at the
tavern but is truly one of its madcap members.)   **490 deny your major** reject your major premise.   **deny the** refuse entrance to the
491 become befit, adorn.   **cart** i.e., hangman's cart   **492 bringing
up** (1) upbringing (2) being brought before the authorities to be
hanged   **495 arras** wall hanging of tapestry

496 up above upstairs   **498 date is out** lease has run out   **502 hue
and cry** outcry calling for the pursuit of a felon   **509 engage** pledge
510 dinnertime i.e., about noon   **519 morrow** morning   **521 Paul's**
Saint Paul's Cathedral   **534 ob.** obolus, i.e., halfpenny

else, keep close; we'll read it at more advantage. There 537
let him sleep till day. I'll to the court in the morning.
We must all to the wars, and thy place shall be
honorable. I'll procure this fat rogue a charge of foot, 540
and I know his death will be a march of twelve score. 541
The money shall be paid back again with advantage. 542
Be with me betimes in the morning; and so, good 543
morrow, Peto.

PETO   Good morrow, good my lord.   545

Exeunt [separately. Falstaff is concealed
once more behind the arras.]

❧

3.1

Enter Hotspur, Worcester, Lord Mortimer, [and]
Owen Glendower.

MORTIMER
These promises are fair, the parties sure,
And our induction full of prosperous hope.   2

HOTSPUR
Lord Mortimer, and cousin Glendower,
Will you sit down? And uncle Worcester—
                                                    [They sit.]
A plague upon it, I have forgot the map.

GLENDOWER *[producing a map]*
No, here it is. Sit, cousin Percy,
Sit, good cousin Hotspur—for by that name
As oft as Lancaster doth speak of you   8
His cheek looks pale, and with a rising sigh
He wisheth you in heaven.

HOTSPUR   And you in hell,
As oft as he hears Owen Glendower spoke of.

GLENDOWER
I cannot blame him. At my nativity
The front of heaven was full of fiery shapes,   13
Of burning cressets, and at my birth   14
The frame and huge foundation of the earth
Shaked like a coward.

HOTSPUR   Why, so it would have done
At the same season, if your mother's cat
Had but kittened, though yourself had never been
  born.

GLENDOWER
I say the earth did shake when I was born.

HOTSPUR
And I say the earth was not of my mind,
If you suppose as fearing you it shook.

GLENDOWER
The heavens were all on fire; the earth did tremble.

HOTSPUR
O, then the earth shook to see the heavens on fire,
And not in fear of your nativity.
Diseasèd nature oftentimes breaks forth
In strange eruptions; oft the teeming earth
Is with a kind of colic pinched and vexed
By the imprisoning of unruly wind
Within her womb, which, for enlargement striving,   29
Shakes the old beldam earth and topples down   30
Steeples and moss-grown towers. At your birth
Our grandam earth, having this distemp'rature,   32
In passion shook.

GLENDOWER   Cousin, of many men   33
I do not bear these crossings. Give me leave   34
To tell you once again that at my birth
The front of heaven was full of fiery shapes,
The goats ran from the mountains, and the herds
Were strangely clamorous to the frighted fields.   38
These signs have marked me extraordinary,
And all the courses of my life do show
I am not in the roll of common men.
Where is he living, clipped in with the sea   42
That chides the banks of England, Scotland, Wales,
Which calls me pupil or hath read to me?   44
And bring him out that is but woman's son   45
Can trace me in the tedious ways of art   46
And hold me pace in deep experiments.   47

HOTSPUR
I think there's no man speaks better Welsh.   48
I'll to dinner.

MORTIMER
Peace, cousin Percy; you will make him mad.

GLENDOWER
I can call spirits from the vasty deep.   51

HOTSPUR
Why, so can I, or so can any man;
But will they come when you do call for them?

GLENDOWER
Why, I can teach you, cousin, to command the
  devil.

HOTSPUR
And I can teach thee, coz, to shame the devil
By telling truth. Tell truth and shame the devil.
If thou have power to raise him, bring him hither,
And I'll be sworn I have power to shame him
  hence.
O, while you live, tell truth and shame the devil!

---

537 close hidden.   **advantage** favorable opportunity   **540 charge of
foot** command of a company of infantry   **541 twelve score** i.e., two
hundred and forty yards   **542 advantage** interest   **543 betimes** early
545 s.d. Exeunt . . . arras (Onstage, the arras is evidently arranged so
that Falstaff can exit behind it once the scene is over.)
3.1. Location: Wales. Glendower's residence. (Holinshed places a
meeting of the rebel deputies at Bangor in the Archdeacon's house,
but in this present "unhistorical" scene, as invented by Shakespeare,
Glendower is host throughout.) Seats are provided onstage.
2 induction beginning.   **prosperous hope** hope of prospering   **8 Lancaster** i.e., King Henry, here demoted to Duke of Lancaster   **13 front**
brow, face (as also at line 36)   **14 cressets** lights burning in metal
baskets at the end of long poles or suspended; hence, meteors

29 enlargement release   **30 beldam** grandmother   **32 distemp'rature**
disorder   **33 passion** suffering.   **of** from   **34 crossings** contradictions
38 clamorous noisy   **42 he** anyone.   **clipped in with** enclosed by
44 Which who.   **read to** instructed   **45 bring him out** produce any
man   **46 Can . . . art** who can follow me in the laborious ways of
magic   **47 hold me pace** keep up with me.   **deep** occult   **48 speaks
better Welsh** (Hotspur hides an insult behind the literal meaning,
since "to speak Welsh" meant colloquially both "to boast" and "to
speak nonsense.")   **51 call** summon. (But Hotspur sardonically replies
in the sense of "call out to," whether or not there is any response.)
vasty deep lower world

MORTIMER
Come, come, no more of this unprofitable chat.
GLENDOWER
Three times hath Henry Bolingbroke made head   61
Against my power; thrice from the banks of Wye   62
And sandy-bottomed Severn have I sent him
Bootless home and weather-beaten back.   64
HOTSPUR
Home without boots, and in foul weather too!
How scapes he agues, in the devil's name?   66
GLENDOWER
Come, here is the map. Shall we divide our right
According to our threefold order ta'en?   68
MORTIMER
The Archdeacon hath divided it   69
Into three limits very equally: 70
England, from Trent and Severn hitherto,   71
By south and east is to my part assigned;
All westward, Wales beyond the Severn shore,
And all the fertile land within that bound,
To Owen Glendower; and, dear coz, to you
The remnant northward, lying off from Trent.
And our indentures tripartite are drawn,   77
Which being sealèd interchangeably—
A business that this night may execute—   79
Tomorrow, cousin Percy, you and I
And my good lord of Worcester will set forth
To meet your father and the Scottish power,
As is appointed us, at Shrewsbury.
My father Glendower is not ready yet,   84
Nor shall we need his help these fourteen days.
[*To Glendower.*] Within that space you may have
          drawn together   86
Your tenants, friends, and neighboring gentlemen.
GLENDOWER
A shorter time shall send me to you, lords;
And in my conduct shall your ladies come,   89
From whom you now must steal and take no leave,
For there will be a world of water shed
Upon the parting of your wives and you.
HOTSPUR [*consulting the map*]
Methinks my moiety, north from Burton here,   93
In quantity equals not one of yours.
See how this river comes me cranking in   95
And cuts me from the best of all my land
A huge half-moon, a monstrous cantle, out.   97
I'll have the current in this place dammed up,
And here the smug and silver Trent shall run   99

In a new channel, fair and evenly.
It shall not wind with such a deep indent
To rob me of so rich a bottom here.   102
GLENDOWER
Not wind? It shall, it must. You see it doth.
MORTIMER
Yea, but mark how he bears his course and runs
          me up   104
With like advantage on the other side,
Gelding the opposèd continent as much   106
As on the other side it takes from you.
WORCESTER
Yea, but a little charge will trench him here   108
And on this north side win this cape of land;
And then he runs straight and even.
HOTSPUR
I'll have it so. A little charge will do it.
GLENDOWER   I'll not have it altered.
HOTSPUR   Will not you?
GLENDOWER   No, nor you shall not.
HOTSPUR   Who shall say me nay?
GLENDOWER   Why, that will I.
HOTSPUR
Let me not understand you, then; speak it in Welsh.
GLENDOWER
I can speak English, lord, as well as you;
For I was trained up in the English court,
Where, being but young, I framèd to the harp   120
Many an English ditty lovely well,
And gave the tongue a helpful ornament—   122
A virtue that was never seen in you.
HOTSPUR
Marry, and I am glad of it with all my heart!
I had rather be a kitten and cry "mew"
Than one of these same meter balladmongers.
I had rather hear a brazen can'stick turned   127
Or a dry wheel grate on the axletree,   128
And that would set my teeth nothing on edge,   129
Nothing so much as mincing poetry.
'Tis like the forced gait of a shuffling nag.   131
GLENDOWER   Come, you shall have Trent turned.
HOTSPUR
I do not care. I'll give thrice so much land
To any well-deserving friend;
But in the way of bargain, mark ye me,
I'll cavil on the ninth part of a hair.   136
Are the indentures drawn? Shall we be gone?   137
GLENDOWER
The moon shines fair; you may away by night.

---

61 **made head** raised a force   62 **power** army   64 **Bootless** without
advantage. (But Hotspur quibbles on the sense of "barefoot.")
66 **agues** fevers   68 **order ta'en** arrangements made   69 **Archdeacon**
i.e., the Archdeacon of Bangor, in whose house, according to Holinshed, a meeting took place between deputies of the rebel leaders
70 **limits** regions   71 **hitherto** to this point   77 **tripartite** i.e., drawn
up in triplicate, each document sealed *interchangeably* (line 78) with
the seal of all signatories.   **drawn** drawn up   79 **this night may execute** may be carried out tonight   84 **father** i.e., father-in-law
86 **may** will be able to   89 **conduct** escort   93 **moiety** share
95 **comes me cranking in** comes bending in on my share. (The Trent,
by turning northward instead of continuing eastward into the Wash,
cuts Hotspur off from rich land in Lincolnshire and its vicinity.)
97 **cantle** piece   99 **smug** smooth

102 **bottom** valley   104 **runs me** runs. (*Me* is used colloquially.)
106 **Gelding . . . continent** cutting off from the land which it bounds
on the opposite side. (The Trent's southerly loop from Stoke to Burton
deprives Mortimer of a piece of land, just as its later northerly
course deprives Hotspur.)   108 **charge** expenditure.   **trench** provide a new channel   120 **framèd to the harp** set to harp accompaniment   122 **gave . . . ornament** i.e., added to the words a pleasing
ornament of music; also, gave to the English tongue the ornament of
music and poetry   127 **can'stick turned** candlestick turned on a lathe
128 **axletree** axle   129 **nothing** not at all   131 **shuffling** hobbled
136 **cavil . . . hair** i.e., argue about the most trivial detail
137 **drawn** drawn up

I'll haste the writer and withal   139
Break with your wives of your departure hence.   140
I am afraid my daughter will run mad,
So much she doteth on her Mortimer.   *Exit.*

MORTIMER
Fie, cousin Percy, how you cross my father!

HOTSPUR
I cannot choose. Sometimes he angers me
With telling me of the moldwarp and the ant,   145
Of the dreamer Merlin and his prophecies,   146
And of a dragon and a finless fish,
A clip-winged griffin and a moulten raven,   148
A couching lion and a ramping cat,   149
And such a deal of skimble-skamble stuff   150
As puts me from my faith. I tell you what: 151
He held me last night at least nine hours
In reckoning up the several devils' names   153
That were his lackeys. I cried "Hum," and "Well,
    go to,"   154
But marked him not a word. O, he is as tedious
As a tirèd horse, a railing wife,
Worse than a smoky house. I had rather live
With cheese and garlic in a windmill, far,
Than feed on cates and have him talk to me   159
In any summer house in Christendom.

MORTIMER
In faith, he is a worthy gentleman,
Exceedingly well read, and profited   162
In strange concealments, valiant as a lion   163
And wondrous affable, and as bountiful
As mines of India. Shall I tell you, cousin?
He holds your temper in a high respect   166
And curbs himself even of his natural scope   167
When you come 'cross his humor. Faith, he does.   168
I warrant you that man is not alive
Might so have tempted him as you have done   170
Without the taste of danger and reproof.
But do not use it oft, let me entreat you.

WORCESTER [*to Hotspur*]
In faith, my lord, you are too willful-blame,   173
And since your coming hither have done enough
To put him quite beside his patience.   175
You must needs learn, lord, to amend this fault.
Though sometimes it show greatness, courage,
    blood—   177

And that's the dearest grace it renders you—   178
Yet oftentimes it doth present harsh rage,   179
Defect of manners, want of government,   180
Pride, haughtiness, opinion, and disdain,   181
The least of which haunting a nobleman
Loseth men's hearts and leaves behind a stain
Upon the beauty of all parts besides,   184
Beguiling them of commendation.   185

HOTSPUR
Well, I am schooled. Good manners be your speed!   186
Here come our wives, and let us take our leave.

Enter Glendower with the ladies.

MORTIMER
This is the deadly spite that angers me: 188
My wife can speak no English, I no Welsh.

GLENDOWER
My daughter weeps she'll not part with you;
She'll be a soldier too, she'll to the wars.

MORTIMER
Good Father, tell her that she and my aunt Percy   192
Shall follow in your conduct speedily.
              Glendower speaks to her in Welsh,
              and she answers him in the same.

GLENDOWER
She is desperate here; a peevish self-willed harlotry,   194
One that no persuasion can do good upon.
                      The lady speaks in Welsh.

MORTIMER
I understand thy looks. That pretty Welsh   196
Which thou pourest down from these swelling
    heavens   197
I am too perfect in; and, but for shame,   198
In such a parley should I answer thee.   199
                      The lady again in Welsh.
I understand thy kisses and thou mine,
And that's a feeling disputation.   201
But I will never be a truant, love,
Till I have learned thy language; for thy tongue
Makes Welsh as sweet as ditties highly penned,   204
Sung by a fair queen in a summer's bower,
With ravishing division, to her lute.   206

GLENDOWER
Nay, if you melt, then will she run mad.   207
                      The lady speaks again in Welsh.

MORTIMER
O, I am ignorance itself in this!

---

139 writer i.e., scrivener who would be drawing the indentures.
withal also   **140 Break with** inform   **145 moldwarp** mole. (Holinshed tells us that the division was arranged because of a prophecy
that represented King Henry as the mole and the others as the dragon,
the lion, and the wolf, who should divide the land among them.)
146 Merlin the bard, prophet, and magician of Arthurian story, Welsh
in origin   **148 griffin** a fabulous beast, half lion, half eagle.   **moulten**
having molted   **149 couching** couchant, crouching. (Heraldic term.)
ramping rampant, advancing on its hind legs. (Hotspur is ridiculing
the heraldic emblems that Glendower holds so dear.)   **150 skimble-
skamble** foolish, nonsensical   **151 puts . . . faith** drives me from my
(Christian) faith   **153 several** various   **154 go to** i.e., you don't say
159 cates delicacies   **162 profited** proficient   **163 concealments** occult practices   **166 temper** temperament   **167 scope** freedom of
speech   **168 come 'cross** contradict   **170 Might** who could
173 too willful-blame blameworthy for too much self-will   **175 beside** out of   **177 blood** spirit

178 dearest grace best (and costliest) credit   **179 present** represent
180 want of government lack of self-control   **181 opinion** vanity, arrogance   **184 all parts besides** all other abilities   **185 Beguiling** depriving   **186 be your speed** give you good fortune   **188 spite** vexation   **192 aunt** (Percy's wife, here called Kate, was aunt of Edmund
Mortimer, the fifth Earl of March, but was sister-in-law to the Sir Edward Mortimer who married Glendower's daughter.)   **194 desperate
here** adamant on this point (i.e., her decision to accompany Mortimer).   **peevish self-willed harlotry** childish, willful, silly wench
196 That pretty Welsh i.e., your eloquent tears   **197 heavens** i.e.,
eyes   **198 perfect** proficient   **199 such a parley** i.e., the same language (of weeping)   **201 disputation** conversation, debate
204 highly eloquently, nobly   **206 division** variation, passage in
which rapid short notes vary a theme   **207 melt** i.e., weep

GLENDOWER

  She bids you on the wanton rushes lay you down   209
  And rest your gentle head upon her lap,
  And she will sing the song that pleaseth you
  And on your eyelids crown the god of sleep,   212
  Charming your blood with pleasing heaviness,   213
  Making such difference twixt wake and sleep
  As is the difference betwixt day and night
  The hour before the heavenly-harnessed team   216
  Begins his golden progress in the east.

MORTIMER

  With all my heart I'll sit and hear her sing.
  By that time will our book, I think, be drawn.   219

GLENDOWER   Do so;
  And those musicians that shall play to you
  Hang in the air a thousand leagues from hence,
  And straight they shall be here. Sit, and attend.

[Mortimer reclines with his head
in his wife's lap.]

HOTSPUR   Come, Kate, thou art perfect in lying down;
come, quick, quick, that I may lay my head in thy lap.

LADY PERCY   Go, ye giddy goose.

[Hotspur lies with his head
in Kate's lap.] The music plays.

HOTSPUR

  Now I perceive the devil understands Welsh;
  And 'tis no marvel he is so humorous.   228
  By 'r Lady, he is a good musician.

LADY PERCY   Then should you be nothing but musical,
for you are altogether governed by humors. Lie still,
ye thief, and hear the lady sing in Welsh.

HOTSPUR   I had rather hear Lady, my brach, howl in   233
Irish.

LADY PERCY   Wouldst thou have thy head broken?   235

HOTSPUR   No.

LADY PERCY   Then be still.

HOTSPUR   Neither, 'tis a woman's fault.   238

LADY PERCY   Now God help thee!   239

HOTSPUR   To the Welsh lady's bed.

LADY PERCY   What's that?

HOTSPUR   Peace, she sings.

Here the lady sings a Welsh song.

HOTSPUR   Come, Kate, I'll have your song too.

LADY PERCY   Not mine, in good sooth.

HOTSPUR   Not yours, in good sooth! Heart, you swear   245
like a comfit maker's wife. "Not you, in good sooth,"   246
and "as true as I live," and "as God shall mend me,"
and "as sure as day,"
  And givest such sarcenet surety for thy oaths   249

  As if thou never walk'st further than Finsbury.   250
  Swear me, Kate, like a lady as thou art,
  A good mouth-filling oath, and leave "in sooth,"
  And such protest of pepper-gingerbread,   253
  To velvet-guards and Sunday citizens.   254
  Come, sing.

LADY PERCY   I will not sing.

HOTSPUR   'Tis the next way to turn tailor, or be redbreast   257
teacher. An the indentures be drawn, I'll away within   258
these two hours; and so, come in when ye will. *Exit.*

GLENDOWER

  Come, come, Lord Mortimer. You are as slow
  As hot Lord Percy is on fire to go.
  By this our book is drawn; we'll but seal,   262
  And then to horse immediately.

MORTIMER   With all my heart.   *Exeunt.*

❖

3.2
Enter the King, Prince of Wales, and others.

KING

  Lords, give us leave. The Prince of Wales and I
  Must have some private conference; but be near at
    hand,
  For we shall presently have need of you.
                 Exeunt Lords.
  I know not whether God will have it so
  For some displeasing service I have done,
  That in his secret doom out of my blood   6
  He'll breed revengement and a scourge for me;
  But thou dost in thy passages of life   8
  Make me believe that thou art only marked   9
  For the hot vengeance and the rod of heaven   10
  To punish my mistreadings. Tell me else,   11
  Could such inordinate and low desires,   12
  Such poor, such bare, such lewd, such mean
    attempts,   13
  Such barren pleasures, rude society,
  As thou art matched withal and grafted to,   15
  Accompany the greatness of thy blood
  And hold their level with thy princely heart?   17

PRINCE

  So please Your Majesty, I would I could
  Quit all offenses with as clear excuse   19

---

250 Finsbury a field just outside London frequented by the London citizenry. (Hotspur jokes with Kate as though she were a citizen's wife, using the pious and modest oaths of such people.)   **253 protest . . . gingerbread** i.e., mealy-mouthed protestations   **254 velvet-guards** i.e., wives who wear velvet trimming   **257 next** nearest, quickest.   **turn tailor** (Tailors were noted for singing and effeminacy.) **257–258 be redbreast teacher** i.e., teach birds to sing. (Hotspur is expressing his contempt for music.)   **262 By this** by this time.   **but** just

3.2. Location: The royal court (historically, Westminster).
6 doom judgment.   **blood** offspring   **8 passages** course, conduct **9–11 thou . . . mistreadings** (1) you are marked as the means of heaven's vengeance against me, or (2) you are marked to suffer heaven's vengeance because of my sins   **11 else** how otherwise   **12 inordinate** (1) immoderate (2) unworthy of your rank   **13 lewd** low, base. **attempts** undertakings   **15 withal** with   **17 hold their level** claim equality   **19 Quit** acquit myself of

---

209 wanton soft, luxurious.   **rushes** (Used as floor covering.) **212 crown** give sway to   **213 heaviness** drowsiness   **216 the heavenly-harnessed team** i.e., the team of horses drawing the chariot of the sun   **219 book** document, indentures   **228 humorous** whimsical, capricious   **233 brach** bitch hound   **235 broken** i.e., struck so as to break the skin   **238 Neither . . . fault** i.e., I won't do that either; it's womanish to be submissive   **239 help** amend. (But Hotspur answers in the sense of "assist with an amour.")   **245 Heart** i.e., by Christ's heart   **246 comfit maker's** confectioner's   **249 sarcenet** soft, flimsy (from the soft silken material known as *sarcenet*)

As well as I am doubtless I can purge   20
Myself of many I am charged withal.
Yet such extenuation let me beg
As, in reproof of many tales devised,   23
Which oft the ear of greatness needs must hear
By smiling pickthanks and base newsmongers,   25
I may, for some things true, wherein my youth
Hath faulty wandered and irregular,
Find pardon on my true submission.

KING
God pardon thee! Yet let me wonder, Harry,
At thy affections, which do hold a wing   30
Quite from the flight of all thy ancestors.   31
Thy place in Council thou hast rudely lost,   32
Which by thy younger brother is supplied,
And art almost an alien to the hearts
Of all the court and princes of my blood.
The hope and expectation of thy time   36
Is ruined, and the soul of every man
Prophetically do forethink thy fall.
Had I so lavish of my presence been,
So common-hackneyed in the eyes of men,   40
So stale and cheap to vulgar company,
Opinion, that did help me to the crown,   42
Had still kept loyal to possession   43
And left me in reputeless banishment,
A fellow of no mark nor likelihood.   45
By being seldom seen, I could not stir
But like a comet I was wondered at,
That men would tell their children, "This is he!"
Others would say, "Where, which is Bolingbroke?"
And then I stole all courtesy from heaven,   50
And dressed myself in such humility
That I did pluck allegiance from men's hearts,
Loud shouts and salutations from their mouths,
Even in the presence of the crownèd King.
Thus did I keep my person fresh and new,
My presence, like a robe pontifical,   56
Ne'er seen but wondered at; and so my state,   57
Seldom but sumptuous, showed like a feast   58
And won by rareness such solemnity.   59
The skipping King, he ambled up and down
With shallow jesters and rash bavin wits,   61
Soon kindled and soon burnt; carded his state,   62
Mingled his royalty with capering fools,
Had his great name profanèd with their scorns,   64

And gave his countenance, against his name,   65
To laugh at gibing boys and stand the push   66
Of every beardless vain comparative;   67
Grew a companion to the common streets,
Enfeoffed himself to popularity,   69
That, being daily swallowed by men's eyes,
They surfeited with honey and began
To loathe the taste of sweetness, whereof a little
More than a little is by much too much.
So when he had occasion to be seen,
He was but as the cuckoo is in June,
Heard, not regarded—seen, but with such eyes
As, sick and blunted with community,   77
Afford no extraordinary gaze,
Such as is bent on sunlike majesty
When it shines seldom in admiring eyes;
But rather drowsed and hung their eyelids down,
Slept in his face, and rendered such aspect   82
As cloudy men use to their adversaries,   83
Being with his presence glutted, gorged, and full.
And in that very line, Harry, standest thou;
For thou hast lost thy princely privilege
With vile participation. Not an eye   87
But is aweary of thy common sight,
Save mine, which hath desired to see thee more—
Which now doth that I would not have it do,   90
Make blind itself with foolish tenderness.   91

PRINCE
I shall hereafter, my thrice gracious lord,
Be more myself.
KING   For all the world   93
As thou art to this hour was Richard then
When I from France set foot at Ravenspurgh,
And even as I was then is Percy now.
Now, by my scepter, and my soul to boot,   97
He hath more worthy interest to the state   98
Than thou the shadow of succession.   99
For of no right, nor color like to right,   100
He doth fill fields with harness in the realm,   101
Turns head against the lion's armèd jaws,   102
And, being no more in debt to years than thou,   103
Leads ancient lords and reverend bishops on
To bloody battles and to bruising arms.
What never-dying honor hath he got
Against renownèd Douglas! Whose high deeds,   107
Whose hot incursions and great name in arms

---

20 doubtless certain   **23 in reproof** upon disproof   **25 By** from.
pickthanks flatterers.   **newsmongers** talebearers   **30 affections** inclinations.   **hold a wing** fly a course   **31 from** at variance with
32 rudely by violence. (According to an apocryphal story, Prince Hal
boxed the ears of the Lord Chief Justice and was sent to prison for it;
see *2 Henry IV*, 1.2.54–55, 192, and 5.2.70–71.)   **36 time** time of
life, youth   **40 common-hackneyed** cheapened, vulgarized
42 Opinion public opinion   **43 to possession** i.e., to Richard II's sovereignty   **45 mark** importance.   **likelihood** likelihood of success
50 I . . . heaven i.e., I assumed a bearing of the utmost graciousness
56 pontifical like that of a pope or archbishop   **57 state** magnificence
in public appearances   **58 Seldom** infrequent   **59 such solemnity**
i.e., the solemnity appropriate to a festival   **61 bavin** brushwood,
soon burnt out   **62 carded** debased. (A term applied to the adultera-
tion or combing of wool.)   **state** royal status   **64 with their scorns**
by the scornful opinion people had of these favorites

65 gave . . . name lent his authority, to the detriment of his royal dignity and reputation   **66 stand the push** put up with the impudence
67 comparative maker of comparisons, wisecracker   **69 Enfeoffed**
himself gave himself up   **77 community** commonness   **82 in his face**
right before his eyes.   **aspect** look   **83 cloudy** sullen. (Also refers to
the image of the sun.)   **87 vile participation** base association or companionship   **90 that** that which   **91 tenderness** i.e., tears   **93 For all**
the world in every way   **97 to boot** in addition   **98–99 He . . . suc-**
cession i.e., even this rebel Hotspur has a better claim to the throne
than you, the mere shadow of an heir   **100 of . . . to right** having no
rightful claim or even the pretext of one   **101 harness** armor, i.e.,
men in armor   **102 Turns head** leads an armed insurrection.   **lion's**
i.e., King's   **103 being . . . thou** i.e., being no older than you
(though historically Hotspur was twenty-three years older than the
Prince)   **107 Whose** i.e., Hotspur's

Holds from all soldiers chief majority 109
And military title capital 110
Through all the kingdoms that acknowledge Christ.
Thrice hath this Hotspur, Mars in swaddling clothes,
This infant warrior, in his enterprises
Discomfited great Douglas, ta'en him once, 114
Enlargèd him and made a friend of him, 115
To fill the mouth of deep defiance up 116
And shake the peace and safety of our throne.
And what say you to this? Percy, Northumberland,
The Archbishop's Grace of York, Douglas, Mortimer, 119
Capitulate against us and are up. 120
But wherefore do I tell these news to thee?
Why, Harry, do I tell thee of my foes,
Which art my nearest and dearest enemy? 123
Thou that art like enough, through vassal fear, 124
Base inclination, and the start of spleen, 125
To fight against me under Percy's pay,
To dog his heels and curtsy at his frowns,
To show how much thou art degenerate.

PRINCE
Do not think so. You shall not find it so.
And God forgive them that so much have swayed
Your Majesty's good thoughts away from me!
I will redeem all this on Percy's head
And in the closing of some glorious day
Be bold to tell you that I am your son,
When I will wear a garment all of blood
And stain my favors in a bloody mask,
Which, washed away, shall scour my shame with it. 136
And that shall be the day, whene'er it lights, 138
That this same child of honor and renown,
This gallant Hotspur, this all-praisèd knight,
And your unthought-of Harry chance to meet. 141
For every honor sitting on his helm,
Would they were multitudes, and on my head
My shames redoubled! For the time will come
That I shall make this northern youth exchange
His glorious deeds for my indignities.
Percy is but my factor, good my lord, 147
To engross up glorious deeds on my behalf; 148
And I will call him to so strict account
That he shall render every glory up,
Yea, even the slightest worship of his time, 151
Or I will tear the reckoning from his heart.
This in the name of God I promise here,
The which if He be pleased I shall perform,
I do beseech Your Majesty may salve 155
The long-grown wounds of my intemperance. 156
If not, the end of life cancels all bonds,

(handwritten margin note: pledges to fight Hotspur)

And I will die a hundred thousand deaths
Ere break the smallest parcel of this vow.

KING
A hundred thousand rebels die in this!
Thou shalt have charge and sovereign trust herein. 161

Enter Blunt.

How now, good Blunt? Thy looks are full of speed.

BLUNT
So hath the business that I come to speak of.
Lord Mortimer of Scotland hath sent word 164
That Douglas and the English rebels met
The eleventh of this month at Shrewsbury.
A mighty and a fearful head they are, 167
If promises be kept on every hand,
As ever offered foul play in a state.

KING
The Earl of Westmorland set forth today,
With him my son, Lord John of Lancaster;
For this advertisement is five days old. 172
On Wednesday next, Harry, you shall set forward;
On Thursday we ourselves will march. Our meeting 174
Is Bridgnorth. And, Harry, you shall march 175
Through Gloucestershire; by which account,
Our business valuèd, some twelve days hence 177
Our general forces at Bridgnorth shall meet.
Our hands are full of business. Let's away!
Advantage feeds him fat while men delay. *Exeunt.* 180

✤

3.3   *Enter Falstaff and Bardolph.*

FALSTAFF   Bardolph, am I not fallen away vilely since 1
this last action? Do I not bate? Do I not dwindle? Why, 2
my skin hangs about me like an old lady's loose gown;
I am withered like an old applejohn. Well, I'll repent, 4
and that suddenly, while I am in some liking. I shall be 5
out of heart shortly, and then I shall have no strength 6
to repent. An I have not forgotten what the inside of a 7
church is made of, I am a peppercorn, a brewer's 8
horse. The inside of a church! Company, villainous 9
company, hath been the spoil of me.

BARDOLPH   Sir John, you are so fretful you cannot live 11
long.

FALSTAFF   Why, there is it. Come sing me a bawdy
song; make me merry. I was as virtuously given as a 14
gentleman need to be, virtuous enough: swore little,

---

109 majority preeminence   **110 capital** chief, principal
114 Discomfited defeated   **115 Enlargèd** freed   **116 To . . . up** to
swell the roar of deep defiance   **119 The Archbishop's Grace** His
Grace the Archbishop   **120 Capitulate** form a league, draw up articles.   **up** up in arms   **123 dearest** (1) most precious (2) direst
124 like likely.   **vassal** slavish   **125 Base inclination** inclination for
baseness.   **start of spleen** fit of ill temper   **136 favors** features
138 lights dawns   **141 unthought-of** ignored, disregarded   **147 factor** agent   **148 engross up** amass, buy up   **151 worship of his time**
honor of his youthful lifetime   **155 salve** soothe, heal   **156 intemperance** dissolute living, sickness

161 charge command (of troops)   **164 Lord Mortimer of Scotland** (A
Scottish nobleman, unrelated to Glendower's son-in-law.)   **167 head**
armed force   **172 advertisement** tidings, news   **174 meeting** place of
rendezvous   **175 Bridgnorth** a town near Shrewsbury   **177 Our business valuèd** estimating how long our business will take   **180 Advantage . . . fat** opportunity (for rebellion) prospers.   **him** himself
3.3. Location: A tavern in Eastcheap, as in 2.4.
1 fallen away shrunk   **2 action** i.e., the robbery at Gad's Hill.   **bate**
lose weight   **4 applejohn** a kind of apple still in good eating condition when shriveled   **5 liking** (1) good bodily condition (2) inclination
6 out of heart (1) disinclined, disheartened (2) out of condition   **7 An**
if   **8 peppercorn** unground dried pepper berry   **8–9 brewer's horse**
i.e., one that is old, withered, and decrepit   **11 fretful** (1) anxious (2)
fretted, frayed   **14 given** inclined

diced not above seven times—a week, went to a
bawdy house not above once in a quarter—of an
hour, paid money that I borrowed—three or four
times, lived well and in good compass; and now I live 19
out of all order, out of all compass.

BARDOLPH   Why, you are so fat, Sir John, that you must
needs be out of all compass, out of all reasonable
compass, Sir John.

FALSTAFF   Do thou amend thy face, and I'll amend my
life. Thou art our admiral, thou bearest the lantern in 25
the poop, but 'tis in the nose of thee. Thou art the
Knight of the Burning Lamp.

BARDOLPH   Why, Sir John, my face does you no harm.

FALSTAFF   No, I'll be sworn, I make as good use of it as
many a man doth of a death's-head or a *memento mori.* 30
I never see thy face but I think upon hellfire and
Dives that lived in purple; for there he is in his robes, 32
burning, burning. If thou wert any way given to
virtue, I would swear by thy face; my oath should be
"By this fire, that's God's angel." But thou art 35
altogether given over, and wert indeed, but for the 36
light in thy face, the son of utter darkness. When thou
rann'st up Gad's Hill in the night to catch my horse, if
I did not think thou hadst been an *ignis fatuus* or a ball 39
of wildfire, there's no purchase in money. O, thou art 40
a perpetual triumph, an everlasting bonfire light! 41
Thou hast saved me a thousand marks in links and 42
torches, walking with thee in the night betwixt tavern
and tavern; but the sack that thou hast drunk me
would have bought me lights as good cheap at the 45
dearest chandler's in Europe. I have maintained that 46
salamander of yours with fire any time this two-and- 47
thirty years. God reward me for it!

BARDOLPH   'Sblood, I would my face were in your belly! 49

FALSTAFF   God-a-mercy! So should I be sure to be
heartburned.

Enter Hostess.

How now, Dame Partlet the hen? Have you inquired 52
yet who picked my pocket?

HOSTESS   Why, Sir John, what do you think, Sir John?
Do you think I keep thieves in my house? I have
searched, I have inquired, so has my husband, man
by man, boy by boy, servant by servant. The tithe of a 57
hair was never lost in my house before.

FALSTAFF   Ye lie, hostess. Bardolph was shaved and 59
lost many a hair; and I'll be sworn my pocket was 60
picked. Go to, you are a woman, go.

HOSTESS   Who, I? No, I defy thee! God's light, I was 62
never called so in mine own house before.

FALSTAFF   Go to, I know you well enough.

HOSTESS   No, Sir John, you do not know me, Sir John.
I know you, Sir John. You owe me money, Sir John,
and now you pick a quarrel to beguile me of it. I
bought you a dozen of shirts to your back.

FALSTAFF   Dowlas, filthy dowlas. I have given them 69
away to bakers' wives; they have made bolters of 70
them.

HOSTESS   Now, as I am a true woman, holland of eight 72
shillings an ell. You owe money here besides, Sir 73
John, for your diet and by-drinkings, and money lent 74
you, four-and-twenty pound.

FALSTAFF   He had his part of it. Let him pay.   76

HOSTESS   He? Alas, he is poor, he hath nothing.

FALSTAFF   How, poor? Look upon his face. What call
you rich? Let them coin his nose, let them coin his
cheeks. I'll not pay a denier. What, will you make a 80
younker of me? Shall I not take mine ease in mine inn 81
but I shall have my pocket picked? I have lost a seal
ring of my grandfather's worth forty mark.

HOSTESS   O Jesu, I have heard the Prince tell him, I
know not how oft, that that ring was copper.

FALSTAFF   How? The Prince is a Jack, a sneak-up. 86
'Sblood, an he were here, I would cudgel him like a
dog if he would say so.   88

*Enter the Prince [with Peto], marching, and
Falstaff meets him playing upon his truncheon like
a fife.*

How now, lad, is the wind in that door, i' faith? Must 89
we all march?

BARDOLPH   Yea, two and two, Newgate fashion.   91

HOSTESS   My lord, I pray you, hear me.

PRINCE   What sayst thou, Mistress Quickly? How doth
thy husband? I love him well; he is an honest man.

HOSTESS   Good my lord, hear me.

FALSTAFF   Prithee, let her alone and list to me.

PRINCE   What sayst thou, Jack?

FALSTAFF   The other night I fell asleep here behind the
arras and had my pocket picked. This house is turned
bawdy house; they pick pockets.

PRINCE   What didst thou lose, Jack?

FALSTAFF   Wilt thou believe me, Hal? Three or four
bonds of forty pound apiece and a seal ring of my
grandfather's.

---

19 good compass reasonable limits; also, in Bardolph's speech, girth,
circumference **25 admiral** flagship. **lantern** i.e., a light for the rest
of the fleet to follow; here applied to Bardolph's inflamed nose, red
from overdrinking **30 memento mori** reminder of death, such as a
death's head or a skull engraved on a seal ring **32 Dives** the rich
man who went to hell, referred to in Luke 16:19–31 **35 By . . . angel** (A biblical echo, perhaps to Psalms 104:4, Hebrews 1:7, or Exodus 3:2.) **36 given over** abandoned to wickedness **39 ignis fatuus**
will-o'-the-wisp **40 wildfire** fireworks; lightning; will-o'-the-wisp
41 triumph procession led by torches **42 links** torches, flares
45 good cheap cheap **46 dearest** most expensive. **chandler's** candle maker's **47 salamander** lizard reputed to be able to live in fire
49 I . . . belly (A proverb meaning "I wish I were rid of this irritation"; stock response to an insult based on physical deformity.)
52 Partlet (Traditional name of a hen.) **57 tithe** tenth part

59 was shaved (1) had his beard cut (2) was cheated and robbed
60 lost many a hair (1) was shaved (2) was made bald by syphilis
62 God's light (A mild oath.) **69 Dowlas** a coarse kind of linen
70 bolters cloths for sifting flour **72 holland** fine linen **73 an ell** a
measure of forty-five inches **74 diet** meals. **by-drinkings** drinks between meals **76 He** i.e., Bardolph **80 denier** one-twelfth of a
French sou; type of very small coin **81 younker** greenhorn **86 Jack**
knave, rascal. **sneak-up** sneak **88 s.d. truncheon** officer's staff
89 is . . . door i.e., is that the way the wind is blowing **91 Newgate**
(A famous city prison in London. Prisoners marched two by two.)

PRINCE A trifle, some eightpenny matter.

HOSTESS So I told him, my lord, and I said I heard Your Grace say so; and, my lord, he speaks most vilely of you, like a foulmouthed man as he is, and said he would cudgel you.

PRINCE What, he did not!

HOSTESS There's neither faith, truth, nor womanhood in me else.

FALSTAFF There's no more faith in thee than in a stewed 113 prune, nor no more truth in thee than in a drawn fox; 114 and for womanhood, Maid Marian may be the dep- 115 uty's wife of the ward to thee. Go, you thing, go.   116

HOSTESS Say, what thing, what thing?

FALSTAFF What thing? Why, a thing to thank God on. 118

HOSTESS I am no thing to thank God on, I would thou 119 shouldst know it! I am an honest man's wife, and, setting thy knighthood aside, thou art a knave to call 121 me so.

FALSTAFF Setting thy womanhood aside, thou art a 123 beast to say otherwise.

HOSTESS Say, what beast, thou knave, thou?

FALSTAFF What beast? Why, an otter.

PRINCE An otter, Sir John! Why an otter?

FALSTAFF Why? She's neither fish nor flesh; a man knows not where to have her.   129

HOSTESS Thou art an unjust man in saying so. Thou or any man knows where to have me, thou knave, thou.

PRINCE Thou sayst true, hostess, and he slanders thee most grossly.

HOSTESS So he doth you, my lord, and said this other day you owed him a thousand pound.

PRINCE Sirrah, do I owe you a thousand pound?

FALSTAFF A thousand pound, Hal? A million. Thy love is worth a million; thou owest me thy love.

HOSTESS Nay, my lord, he called you Jack and said he would cudgel you.

FALSTAFF Did I, Bardolph?

BARDOLPH Indeed, Sir John, you said so.

FALSTAFF Yea, if he said my ring was copper.

PRINCE I say 'tis copper. Darest thou be as good as thy word now?

FALSTAFF Why, Hal, thou knowest, as thou art but man, I dare; but as thou art prince, I fear thee as I fear the roaring of the lion's whelp.   148

PRINCE And why not as the lion?

FALSTAFF The King himself is to be feared as the lion. Dost thou think I'll fear thee as I fear thy father? Nay, an I do, I pray God my girdle break.

PRINCE O, if it should, how would thy guts fall about thy knees! But, sirrah, there's no room for faith, truth,

nor honesty in this bosom of thine; it is all filled up with guts and midriff. Charge an honest woman with picking thy pocket? Why, thou whoreson, impudent, embossed rascal, if there were anything in thy pocket 158 but tavern reckonings, memorandums of bawdy 159 houses, and one poor pennyworth of sugar candy to make thee long-winded, if thy pocket were enriched with any other injuries but these, I am a villain. And 162 yet you will stand to it; you will not pocket up wrong! 163 Art thou not ashamed?

FALSTAFF Dost thou hear, Hal? Thou knowest in the state of innocency Adam fell; and what should poor Jack Falstaff do in the days of villainy? Thou seest I have more flesh than another man, and therefore more frailty. You confess then you picked my pocket.

PRINCE It appears so by the story.   170

FALSTAFF Hostess, I forgive thee. Go make ready break-fast. Love thy husband, look to thy servants, cherish thy guests. Thou shalt find me tractable to any honest reason; thou seest I am pacified still. Nay, prithee, 174 begone. (Exit Hostess.) Now, Hal, to the news at court: for the robbery, lad, how is that answered?

PRINCE O my sweet beef, I must still be good angel to thee. The money is paid back again.

FALSTAFF O, I do not like that paying back. 'Tis a double labor.   180

PRINCE I am good friends with my father and may do anything.

FALSTAFF Rob me the exchequer the first thing thou dost, and do it with unwashed hands too.   184

BARDOLPH Do, my lord.

PRINCE I have procured thee, Jack, a charge of foot. 186

FALSTAFF I would it had been of horse. Where shall I find one that can steal well? O, for a fine thief, of the 188 age of two-and-twenty or thereabouts! I am heinously unprovided. Well, God be thanked for these rebels; 190 they offend none but the virtuous. I laud them, I 191 praise them.

PRINCE Bardolph!

BARDOLPH My lord?

PRINCE [giving letters]
    Go bear this letter to Lord John of Lancaster,
    To my brother John; this to my lord of Westmorland.
                                        [Exit Bardolph.]
    Go, Peto, to horse, to horse, for thou and I
    Have thirty miles to ride yet ere dinnertime.
                                        [Exit Peto.]

113–114 stewed prune (Customarily associated with bawdy houses.) 114 drawn fox fox driven from cover and wily in getting back 115–116 Maid . . . thee i.e., Maid Marian, a disreputable woman in Robin Hood ballads, morris dances, and the like, was a model of respectability compared with you 118, 119 What thing . . . no thing (With sexual quibbles.) 121, 123 setting . . . aside (Mistress Quickly means, "without wishing to offend your rank of knighthood," but Falstaff replies in line 123 with the meaning, "setting aside your womanhood as of no value or pertinence.")   129 have understand (with suggestion of enjoying sexually) 148 whelp cub

158 embossed (1) swollen with fat (2) foaming at the mouth and exhausted, like a hunted animal. rascal (1) scoundrel (2) immature and inferior deer 159 memorandums souvenirs 162 injuries i.e., those things you claim to have lost, thereby suffering harm 163 stand to it make a stand, insist on your supposed rights. pocket up endure silently 170 by according to 174 still always 180 double labor i.e., the taking and the returning 184 with unwashed hands without wasting any time 186 charge of foot command of a company of infantry 188 one i.e., a companion in thievery. (Falstaff sees war as the opportunity for stealing and conning.) 190 unprovided ill-equipped 191 they . . . virtuous i.e., the rebels, by providing the occasion of war, give dishonest men a chance to profiteer and hence offend only those who are honest

Jack, meet me tomorrow in the Temple Hall   199
At two o'clock in the afternoon.
There shalt thou know thy charge, and there receive
Money and order for their furniture.   202
The land is burning. Percy stands on high,
And either we or they must lower lie.   [*Exit.*]

FALSTAFF
Rare words! Brave world! Hostess, my breakfast,
    come!   205
O, I could wish this tavern were my drum!   [*Exit.*] 206

❖

4.1   [*Enter Hotspur, Worcester, and Douglas.*]

HOTSPUR
Well said, my noble Scot. If speaking truth
In this fine age were not thought flattery,
Such attribution should the Douglas have   3
As not a soldier of this season's stamp   4
Should go so general current through the world.   5
By God, I cannot flatter; I do defy   6
The tongues of soothers! But a braver place   7
In my heart's love hath no man than yourself.
Nay, task me to my word; approve me, lord.   9
DOUGLAS   Thou art the king of honor.
No man so potent breathes upon the ground
But I will beard him.

        Enter one [*a Messenger*] *with letters.*

HOTSPUR   Do so, and 'tis well.—   12
What letters hast thou there?—I can but thank you.   13
MESSENGER
These letters come from your father.
HOTSPUR
Letters from him? Why comes he not himself?
MESSENGER
He cannot come, my lord. He is grievous sick.
HOTSPUR
Zounds, how has he the leisure to be sick
In such a jostling time? Who leads his power?   18
Under whose government come they along?   19
MESSENGER
His letters bears his mind, not I, my lord.
                          [*Hotspur reads the letter.*]
WORCESTER
I prithee, tell me, doth he keep his bed?   21
MESSENGER
He did, my lord, four days ere I set forth,

And at the time of my departure thence
He was much feared by his physicians.   24
WORCESTER
I would the state of time had first been whole   25
Ere he by sickness had been visited.
His health was never better worth than now.
HOTSPUR
Sick now? Droop now? This sickness doth infect
The very life-blood of our enterprise;
'Tis catching hither, even to our camp.
He writes me here that inward sickness—
And that his friends by deputation   32
Could not so soon be drawn, nor did he think it
    meet   33
To lay so dangerous and dear a trust
On any soul removed but on his own.   35
Yet doth he give us bold advertisement   36
That with our small conjunction we should on,   37
To see how fortune is disposed to us;
For, as he writes, there is no quailing now,   39
Because the King is certainly possessed   40
Of all our purposes. What say you to it?
WORCESTER
Your father's sickness is a maim to us.   42
HOTSPUR
A perilous gash, a very limb lopped off.
And yet, in faith, it is not! His present want   44
Seems more than we shall find it. Were it good   45
To set the exact wealth of all our states   46
All at one cast? To set so rich a main   47
On the nice hazard of one doubtful hour?   48
It were not good, for therein should we read   49
The very bottom and the soul of hope,   50
The very list, the very utmost bound   51
Of all our fortunes.
DOUGLAS   Faith, and so we should;
Where now remains a sweet reversion,   53
We may boldly spend upon the hope
Of what is to come in.
A comfort of retirement lives in this.   56
HOTSPUR
A rendezvous, a home to fly unto,
If that the devil and mischance look big   58
Upon the maidenhead of our affairs.   59
WORCESTER
But yet I would your father had been here.
The quality and hair of our attempt   61
Brooks no division. It will be thought   62

---

199 Temple Hall i.e., at the Inner Temple, one of the Inns of Court
202 furniture equipment, furnishing **205 Brave** splendid **206 drum**
(Possibly Falstaff means that he wishes he could continue to enjoy this
tavern instead of risking his life in battle. He may also be punning on
tavern/taborn, i.e., *taborin*, a kind of drum.)
4.1. Location: The rebel camp near Shrewsbury.
3 attribution praise, tribute **4 stamp** coinage **5 go . . . current** be
so widely accepted and acclaimed. (Continues the metaphor of coinage.) **6 defy** proclaim against **7 soothers** flatterers. **braver** better,
dearer **9 task . . . word** challenge me to make good my word. **approve** test **12 But . . . him** but that I will defy him **13 I can . . .
you** (Said to Douglas.) **18 jostling** contending, clashing **19 government** command **21 keep** keep to

24 feared feared for **25 time** the times **32 by deputation** through
deputies **33 drawn** assembled. **meet** appropriate **35 On . . . own**
on anyone other than himself **36 advertisement** counsel, advice
37 conjunction joint force. **on** go on **39 quailing** losing heart
40 possessed informed **42 maim** injury **44 want** absence
45 more more serious **46 To . . . states** to stake the absolute total of
our resources **47 cast** throw of the dice. **main** stake in gambling;
also, an army **48 nice** precarious, delicate. **hazard** (1) game at dice
(2) venture **49–50 should . . . hope** we should discover the utmost
foundation and basis of our hopes, the most we could rely on **51 list**
limit **53 reversion** (Literally, part of an estate yet to be inherited.)
56 retirement something to fall back on **58 big** threatening
59 maidenhead i.e., commencement **61 hair** kind, nature
62 Brooks tolerates

By some that know not why he is away
That wisdom, loyalty, and mere dislike   64
Of our proceedings kept the Earl from hence.
And think how such an apprehension   66
May turn the tide of fearful faction   67
And breed a kind of question in our cause.
For well you know we of the offering side   69
Must keep aloof from strict arbitrament,   70
And stop all sight holes, every loop from whence   71
The eye of reason may pry in upon us.
This absence of your father's draws a curtain   73
That shows the ignorant a kind of fear
Before not dreamt of.

HOTSPUR   You strain too far.   75
I rather of his absence make this use:
It lends a luster and more great opinion,   77
A larger dare to our great enterprise,   78
Than if the Earl were here; for men must think,
If we without his help can make a head   80
To push against a kingdom, with his help
We shall o'erturn it topsy-turvy down.
Yet all goes well, yet all our joints are whole.   83

DOUGLAS
As heart can think. There is not such a word
Spoke of in Scotland as this term of fear.

Enter Sir Richard Vernon.

HOTSPUR
My cousin Vernon, welcome, by my soul.

VERNON
Pray God my news be worth a welcome, lord.
The Earl of Westmorland, seven thousand strong,
Is marching hitherwards; with him Prince John.

HOTSPUR
No harm. What more?

VERNON   And further I have learned
The King himself in person is set forth,
Or hitherwards intended speedily,   92
With strong and mighty preparation.

HOTSPUR
He shall be welcome too. Where is his son,
The nimble-footed madcap Prince of Wales,
And his comrades, that doffed the world aside   96
And bid it pass?

VERNON   All furnished, all in arms;   97
All plumed like estridges, that with the wind   98
Bated like eagles having lately bathed,   99
Glittering in golden coats, like images,   100
As full of spirit as the month of May
And gorgeous as the sun at midsummer,

Wanton as youthful goats, wild as young bulls.   103
I saw young Harry, with his beaver on,   104
His cuisses on his thighs, gallantly armed,   105
Rise from the ground like feathered Mercury,
And vaulted with such ease into his seat   107
As if an angel dropped down from the clouds
To turn and wind a fiery Pegasus   109
And witch the world with noble horsemanship.   110

HOTSPUR
No more, no more! Worse than the sun in March   111
This praise doth nourish agues. Let them come.   112
They come like sacrifices in their trim,   113
And to the fire-eyed maid of smoky war   114
All hot and bleeding will we offer them.
The mailèd Mars shall on his altar sit   116
Up to the ears in blood. I am on fire
To hear this rich reprisal is so nigh,   118
And yet not ours. Come, let me taste my horse,
Who is to bear me like a thunderbolt
Against the bosom of the Prince of Wales.
Harry to Harry shall, hot horse to horse,
Meet and ne'er part till one drop down a corse.
O, that Glendower were come!

VERNON   There is more news:
I learned in Worcester, as I rode along,
He cannot draw his power this fourteen days.   126

DOUGLAS
That's the worst tidings that I hear of yet.

WORCESTER
Ay, by my faith, that bears a frosty sound.

HOTSPUR
What may the King's whole battle reach unto?   129

VERNON
To thirty thousand.

HOTSPUR   Forty let it be!
My father and Glendower being both away,
The powers of us may serve so great a day.   132
Come, let us take a muster speedily.
Doomsday is near; die all, die merrily.

DOUGLAS
Talk not of dying. I am out of fear   135
Of death or death's hand for this one half year.

Exeunt.

❖

4.2   *Enter Falstaff, [and] Bardolph.*

FALSTAFF   Bardolph, get thee before to Coventry; fill me
a bottle of sack. Our soldiers shall march through; we'll
to Sutton Coldfield tonight.   3

64 loyalty i.e., to the crown. **mere** absolute **66 apprehension** (1)
perception (2) apprehensiveness **67 fearful faction** timid support
69 offering side side that attacks **70 strict arbitrament** just inquiry or
investigation **71 loop** loophole **73 draws** draws aside, opens
75 strain too far exaggerate **77 opinion** renown **78 dare** daring
80 make a head raise an armed force **83 Yet** still. **joints** limbs
92 intended on the verge of departure **96 doffed** put aside with a
gesture **97 furnished** equipped **98 estridges** ostriches. (Refers to ostrich plumes on crests.) **99 Bated** flapped their wings. (From falconry.) **100 coats** (1) coats of mail (2) heraldic coats of arms. **images** gilded statues

103 Wanton sportive, frolicsome **104 beaver** visor; hence, helmet
105 cuisses armor for the thighs **107 seat** saddle **109 wind** wheel
about. **Pegasus** winged horse of Greek mythology **110 witch** bewitch **111–112 Worse . . . agues** (The spring sun was believed to
give impetus to chills and fevers, by drawing up vapors. Vernon's
speech, says Hotspur, gives one the shudders.) **113 sacrifices** beasts
for sacrifice. **trim** fine apparel, trappings **114 maid** i.e., Bellona,
goddess of war **116 mailèd** dressed in mail, armor **118 reprisal**
prize **126 draw his power** muster his army **129 battle** army
132 The . . . us our forces **135 out of** free from
4.2. Location: A public road near Coventry.
3 Sutton Coldfield (In Warwickshire near Coventry.)

BARDOLPH Will you give me money, Captain?

FALSTAFF Lay out, lay out.   5

BARDOLPH This bottle makes an angel.   6

FALSTAFF An if it do, take it for thy labor; an if it make 7
twice on the coinage. Bid my 8
lieutenant Peto meet me at town's end.

BARDOLPH I will, Captain. Farewell.   *Exit.*

FALSTAFF If I be not ashamed of my soldiers, I am a
soused gurnet. I have misused the King's press dam- 12
nably. I have got, in exchange of a hundred and fifty
soldiers, three hundred and odd pounds. I press me 14
none but good householders, yeomen's sons, inquire 15
me out contracted bachelors, such as had been asked 16
twice on the banns—such a commodity of warm 17
slaves as had as lief hear the devil as a drum, such as 18
fear the report of a caliver worse than a struck fowl or 19
a hurt wild duck. I pressed me none but such toasts- 20
and-butter, with hearts in their bellies no bigger than 21
pins' heads, and they have bought out their services; 22
and now my whole charge consists of ancients, cor- 23
porals, lieutenants, gentlemen of companies—slaves 24
as ragged as Lazarus in the painted cloth, where the 25
glutton's dogs licked his sores, and such as indeed
were never soldiers, but discarded unjust servingmen, 27
younger sons to younger brothers, revolted tapsters, 28
and hostlers trade-fallen, the cankers of a calm world 29
and a long peace, ten times more dishonorable-ragged
than an old feazed ancient. And such have I, to fill up 31
the rooms of them as have bought out their services,
that you would think that I had a hundred and fifty tattered prodigals lately come from swine keeping, from 34
eating draff and husks. A mad fellow met me on the way 35
and told me I had unloaded all the gibbets and pressed 36
the dead bodies. No eye hath seen such scarecrows. I'll
not march through Coventry with them, that's flat. 38
Nay, and the villains march wide betwixt the legs as if
they had gyves on, for indeed I had the most of them 40
out of prison. There's not a shirt and a half in all my
company, and the half shirt is two napkins tacked together and thrown over the shoulders like a herald's

coat without sleeves; and the shirt, to say the truth,
stolen from my host at Saint Albans, or the red-nose 45
innkeeper of Daventry. But that's all one; they'll find 46
linen enough on every hedge.   47

Enter the Prince [and the] Lord of Westmorland.

PRINCE How now, blown Jack? How now, quilt?   48

FALSTAFF What, Hal? How now, mad wag? What a
devil dost thou in Warwickshire? My good lord of
Westmorland, I cry you mercy. I thought your honor 51
had already been at Shrewsbury.

WESTMORLAND Faith, Sir John, 'tis more than time that
I were there, and you too; but my powers are there 54
already. The King, I can tell you, looks for us all. We
must away all night.   56

FALSTAFF Tut, never fear me. I am as vigilant as a cat to 57
steal cream.

PRINCE I think, to steal cream indeed, for thy theft hath 59
already made thee butter. But tell me, Jack, whose 60
fellows are these that come after?

FALSTAFF Mine, Hal, mine.

PRINCE I did never see such pitiful rascals.

FALSTAFF Tut, tut, good enough to toss; food for 64
powder, food for powder. They'll fill a pit as well as 65
better. Tush, man, mortal men, mortal men.

WESTMORLAND Ay, but, Sir John, methinks they are
exceeding poor and bare, too beggarly.   68

FALSTAFF Faith, for their poverty, I know not where 69
they had that, and for their bareness, I am sure they
never learned that of me.

PRINCE No, I'll be sworn, unless you call three fingers 72
in the ribs bare. But, sirrah, make haste. Percy is 73
already in the field.   *Exit.*

FALSTAFF What, is the King encamped?

WESTMORLAND He is, Sir John. I fear we shall stay too
long.   [*Exit.*]

FALSTAFF Well,
To the latter end of a fray and the beginning of a
feast
Fits a dull fighter and a keen guest.   *Exit.* 80

❖

4.3   *Enter Hotspur, Worcester, Douglas, [and] Vernon.*

HOTSPUR
We'll fight with him tonight.

WORCESTER   It may not be.

5 Lay out i.e., pay for it yourself **6 makes an angel** i.e., makes ten shillings I've spent for you. (But Falstaff answers as though *makes* means "produces," implying that Bardolph has profited from the transaction.) **7 An if** if **8 answer** be responsible for. **the coinage** i.e., the money produced **12 soused gurnet** a kind of pickled fish. **King's press** royal warrant for the impressment of troops **14 press me** draft, conscript **15 good** i.e., wealthy. **yeomen's** small free-holders' **16 contracted** engaged to be married **17 banns** public an-nouncements, declared on three Sundays in succession, of an intent to marry. **warm** i.e., loving their comfort **18 lief** willingly **19 caliver** musket. **struck** wounded **20–21 toasts-and-butter** weak-lings **22 bought . . . services** i.e., paid, bribed, to be released from military duty **23 charge** company, troop. **ancients** ensigns, stan-dard-bearers. (By appointing a disproportionate number of junior of-ficers, Falstaff has made it possible to collect for himself their more substantial pay.) **24 gentlemen of companies** a kind of junior officer **25 painted cloth** cheap hangings for a room. (For the story of Lazarus the beggar and Dives the rich man, see Luke 16:19–31.) **27 unjust** dishonest **28 younger . . . brothers** (i.e., with no possibility of in-heritance.) **revolted** runaway **29 trade-fallen** whose business has fallen away. **cankers** cankerworms that destroy leaves and buds. (Used figuratively.) **31 feazed ancient** frayed flag **34 prodigals** (See Luke 15:15–16.) **35 draff** hogwash **36 gibbets** gallows **38 that's flat** that's for sure **40 gyves** fetters

45 my host the innkeeper **45, 46 Saint Albans, Daventry** (Towns north and west of London, on the road to Coventry.) **46 that's all one** no matter **47 hedge** (Where wet linen was spread out to dry.) **48 blown** swollen, inflated; also, short of wind **51 cry you mercy** beg your pardon **54 powers** soldiers **56 must away** must march **57 fear** worry about **59–60 thy . . . butter** i.e., all the cream (rich things) you have stolen has been churned into butterfat in your barrel-like belly **64 toss** toss on a pike **64–65 food for powder** cannon fodder **68 poor and bare** inferior and threadbare. (But Falstaff puns on the sense of "financially strapped and lean.") **69 for** as for **72–73 three . . . ribs** i.e., Falstaff's fat-covered ribs. (A *finger* was a measure of three-fourths of an inch.) **80 keen** with keen appetite **4.3. Location: The rebel camp near Shrewsbury.**

DOUGLAS
You give him then advantage.

VERNON   Not a whit.   2

HOTSPUR
Why say you so? Looks he not for supply?   3

VERNON
So do we.

HOTSPUR   His is certain; ours is doubtful.

WORCESTER
Good cousin, be advised, stir not tonight.

VERNON
Do not, my lord.

DOUGLAS   You do not counsel well.
You speak it out of fear and cold heart.

VERNON
Do me no slander, Douglas. By my life,
And I dare well maintain it with my life,
If well-respected honor bid me on,   10
I hold as little counsel with weak fear
As you, my lord, or any Scot that this day lives.
Let it be seen tomorrow in the battle
Which of us fears.

DOUGLAS   Yea, or tonight.

VERNON   Content.

HOTSPUR   Tonight, say I.

VERNON
Come, come, it may not be. I wonder much,
Being men of such great leading as you are,   19
That you foresee not what impediments
Drag back our expedition. Certain horse   21
Of my cousin Vernon's are not yet come up.
Your uncle Worcester's horse came but today,
And now their pride and mettle is asleep,   24
Their courage with hard labor tame and dull,
That not a horse is half the half of himself.

HOTSPUR
So are the horses of the enemy
In general journey-bated and brought low.   28
The better part of ours are full of rest.

WORCESTER
The number of the King exceedeth our.
For God's sake, cousin, stay till all come in.   31

                 The trumpet sounds a parley.

Enter Sir Walter Blunt.

BLUNT
I come with gracious offers from the King,
If you vouchsafe me hearing and respect.   33

HOTSPUR
Welcome, Sir Walter Blunt; and would to God
You were of our determination!   35
Some of us love you well; and even those some   36

Envy your great deservings and good name
Because you are not of our quality   38
But stand against us like an enemy.

BLUNT
And God defend but still I should stand so,   40
So long as out of limit and true rule   41
You stand against anointed majesty.
But to my charge. The King hath sent to know
The nature of your griefs and whereupon   44
You conjure from the breast of civil peace
Such bold hostility, teaching his duteous land
Audacious cruelty. If that the King   47
Have any way your good deserts forgot,
Which he confesseth to be manifold,
He bids you name your griefs, and with all speed
You shall have your desires with interest
And pardon absolute for yourself and these
Herein misled by your suggestion.   53

HOTSPUR
The King is kind; and well we know the King
Knows at what time to promise, when to pay.
My father and my uncle and myself
Did give him that same royalty he wears,
And when he was not six-and-twenty strong,
Sick in the world's regard, wretched and low,
A poor unminded outlaw sneaking home,
My father gave him welcome to the shore;
And when he heard him swear and vow to God
He came but to be Duke of Lancaster,
To sue his livery and beg his peace   64
With tears of innocency and terms of zeal,
My father, in kind heart and pity moved,
Swore him assistance, and performed it too.
Now when the lords and barons of the realm
Perceived Northumberland did lean to him,
The more and less came in with cap and knee,   70
Met him in boroughs, cities, villages,
Attended him on bridges, stood in lanes,   72
Laid gifts before him, proffered him their oaths,
Gave him their heirs as pages, followed him   74
Even at the heels in golden multitudes.   75
He presently, as greatness knows itself,   76
Steps me a little higher than his vow   77
Made to my father while his blood was poor   78
Upon the naked shore at Ravenspurgh,
And now, forsooth, takes on him to reform
Some certain edicts and some strait decrees   81
That lie too heavy on the commonwealth,
Cries out upon abuses, seems to weep

---

38 quality party   **40 defend** forbid.   **still** always   **41 limit** bounds of allegiance   **44 griefs** grievances   **47 If that** if   **53 suggestion** instigation   **64 sue his livery** sue as an heir come of age for the delivery of his lands.   **beg his peace** i.e., request to be reconciled to King Richard   **70 more and less** persons of all ranks.   **with . . . knee** i.e., with cap in hand and with bended knee   **72 Attended** waited for.   **stood in lanes** stood row-deep along the roads   **74 Gave . . . heirs** i.e., to serve him   **75 golden** (1) auspicious, celebrating (2) majestically attired   **76 knows itself** perceives its own strength   **77 Steps me** i.e., steps. (*Me* is used colloquially.)   **vow** i.e., Henry's vow to seek no more than his inheritance   **78 blood** spirit, temper.   **poor** i.e., unambitious   **81 strait** strict

---

2 then i.e., if you wait. (Addressed to Worcester, not Hotspur.)   **3 supply** reinforcements   **10 well-respected** well weighed or considered   **19 leading** leadership   **21 expedition** speedy progress.   **horse** cavalry (as also at line 23)   **24 pride and mettle** spirit   **28 journey-bated** tired from the journey   **31 s.d. parley** trumpet summons to a conference   **33 respect** attention   **35 determination** persuasion (in the fight)   **36 even those some** i.e., those same persons among us who love you

Over his country's wrongs; and by this face,   84
This seeming brow of justice, did he win
The hearts of all that he did angle for;
Proceeded further—cut me off the heads   87
Of all the favorites that the absent King
In deputation left behind him here
When he was personal in the Irish war.   90

BLUNT
Tut, I came not to hear this.

HOTSPUR   Then to the point.
In short time after, he deposed the King,
Soon after that, deprived him of his life,
And in the neck of that tasked the whole state;   94
To make that worse, suffered his kinsman March—
Who is, if every owner were well placed,   96
Indeed his king—to be engaged in Wales,   97
There without ransom to lie forfeited;   98
Disgraced me in my happy victories,   99
Sought to entrap me by intelligence;   100
Rated mine uncle from the Council board;   101
In rage dismissed my father from the court;
Broke oath on oath, committed wrong on wrong,
And in conclusion drove us to seek out
This head of safety, and withal to pry   105
Into his title, the which we find
Too indirect for long continuance.

BLUNT
Shall I return this answer to the King?

HOTSPUR
Not so, Sir Walter. We'll withdraw awhile.
Go to the King; and let there be impawned   110
Some surety for a safe return again,
And in the morning early shall mine uncle
Bring him our purposes. And so farewell.   113

BLUNT
I would you would accept of grace and love.

HOTSPUR
And maybe so we shall.

BLUNT   Pray God you do. [Exeunt.]

❧

4.4   *Enter [the] Archbishop of York, [and] Sir Michael.*

ARCHBISHOP [*giving letters*]
Hie, good Sir Michael, bear this sealèd brief   1
With wingèd haste to the Lord Marshal,   2
This to my cousin Scroop, and all the rest   3

To whom they are directed. If you knew   4
How much they do import, you would make haste.

SIR MICHAEL   My good lord, I guess their tenor.

ARCHBISHOP   Like enough you do.
Tomorrow, good Sir Michael, is a day
Wherein the fortune of ten thousand men
Must bide the touch; for, sir, at Shrewsbury,   10
As I am truly given to understand,
The King with mighty and quick-raised power
Meets with Lord Harry. And I fear, Sir Michael,
What with the sickness of Northumberland,
Whose power was in the first proportion,   15
And what with Owen Glendower's absence thence,
Who with them was a rated sinew too   17
And comes not in, o'erruled by prophecies,
I fear the power of Percy is too weak
To wage an instant trial with the King.   20

SIR MICHAEL
Why, my good lord, you need not fear;
There is Douglas and Lord Mortimer.

ARCHBISHOP   No, Mortimer is not there.

SIR MICHAEL
But there is Mordake, Vernon, Lord Harry Percy,
And there is my lord of Worcester, and a head   25
Of gallant warriors, noble gentlemen.

ARCHBISHOP
And so there is. But yet the King hath drawn
The special head of all the land together: 28
The Prince of Wales, Lord John of Lancaster,
The noble Westmorland, and warlike Blunt,
And many more corrivals and dear men   31
Of estimation and command in arms.   32

SIR MICHAEL
Doubt not, my lord, they shall be well opposed.

ARCHBISHOP
I hope no less, yet needful 'tis to fear;
And, to prevent the worst, Sir Michael, speed.
For if Lord Percy thrive not, ere the King
Dismiss his power he means to visit us,   37
For he hath heard of our confederacy,
And 'tis but wisdom to make strong against him.
Therefore make haste. I must go write again
To other friends; and so farewell, Sir Michael.
                                    Exeunt [separately].

❧

5.1   *Enter the King, Prince of Wales, Lord John of
          Lancaster, Sir Walter Blunt, [and] Falstaff.*

KING
How bloodily the sun begins to peer
Above yon bosky hill! The day looks pale   2
At his distemperature.

---

84 **face** show, pretense   87 **cut me** i.e., cut   90 **personal** physically,
in person   94 **in . . . that** next, immediately after.   **tasked** laid taxes
upon   96 **if . . . placed** if every claimant were given his proper place
97 **engaged** held as hostage   98 **lie forfeited** remain prisoner, unre-
claimed   99 **Disgraced me** (by demanding the prisoners; see
1.3.23 ff.)   **happy** fortunate   100 **intelligence** secret information, i.e.,
from spies   101 **Rated** scolded   105 **head of safety** armed force for
our protection.   **withal** also   110 **impawned** pledged   113 **purposes**
proposals
4.4. Location: York. The Archbishop's palace.
1 **brief** letter, dispatch   2 **Lord Marshal** i.e., Thomas Mowbray, son
of the Duke of Norfolk who is exiled in *Richard II,* and a longtime enemy of the new King   3 **Scroop** i.e., perhaps Sir Stephen Scroop of
Richard II, 3.2.91–218, or Lord Scroop of Masham of *Henry V,* 2.2

4 **To whom** to those persons to whom   10 **bide the touch** be put to
the test (like gold)   15 **in . . . proportion** of the largest size
17 **rated sinew** main strength or support reckoned upon   20 **instant**
immediate   25 **head** troop   28 **special head** notable leaders
31 **corrivals** partners in the enterprise   32 **estimation** reputation, importance   37 **he** i.e., the King
5.1. Location: The King's camp near Shrewsbury.
2 **bosky** bushy

PRINCE   The southern wind   3
Doth play the trumpet to his purposes,   4
And by his hollow whistling in the leaves
Foretells a tempest and a blustering day.
KING
Then with the losers let it sympathize,
For nothing can seem foul to those that win.
                                The trumpet sounds.

              Enter Worcester [and Vernon].

How now, my lord of Worcester? 'Tis not well
That you and I should meet upon such terms
As now we meet. You have deceived our trust
And made us doff our easy robes of peace   12
To crush our old limbs in ungentle steel.
This is not well, my lord, this is not well.
What say you to it? Will you again unknit
This churlish knot of all-abhorrèd war
And move in that obedient orb again   17
Where you did give a fair and natural light,
And be no more an exhaled meteor,   19
A prodigy of fear, and a portent   20
Of broachèd mischief to the unborn times?   21
WORCESTER   Hear me, my liege:
For mine own part, I could be well content
To entertain the lag end of my life   24
With quiet hours, for I protest
I have not sought the day of this dislike.   26
KING
You have not sought it? How comes it, then?
FALSTAFF   Rebellion lay in his way, and he found it.
PRINCE   Peace, chewet, peace!   29
WORCESTER
It pleased Your Majesty to turn your looks
Of favor from myself and all our house;
And yet I must remember you, my lord,   32
We were the first and dearest of your friends.
For you my staff of office did I break
In Richard's time, and posted day and night   35
To meet you on the way, and kiss your hand,
When yet you were in place and in account
Nothing so strong and fortunate as I.   38
It was myself, my brother, and his son
That brought you home and boldly did outdare   40
The dangers of the time. You swore to us,
And you did swear that oath at Doncaster,
That you did nothing purpose 'gainst the state,
Nor claim no further than your new-fall'n right, 44
The seat of Gaunt, dukedom of Lancaster.

To this we swore our aid. But in short space
It rained down fortune showering on your head,
And such a flood of greatness fell on you—
What with our help, what with the absent King,
What with the injuries of a wanton time,   50
The seeming sufferances that you had borne,   51
And the contrarious winds that held the King
So long in his unlucky Irish wars
That all in England did repute him dead—
And from this swarm of fair advantages
You took occasion to be quickly wooed   56
To grip the general sway into your hand;
Forgot your oath to us at Doncaster;
And being fed by us, you used us so
As that ungentle gull, the cuckoo's bird,   60
Useth the sparrow; did oppress our nest,
Grew by our feeding to so great a bulk
That even our love durst not come near your sight 63
For fear of swallowing; but with nimble wing
We were enforced, for safety's sake, to fly
Out of your sight and raise this present head,   66
Whereby we stand opposèd by such means   67
As you yourself have forged against yourself
By unkind usage, dangerous countenance,   69
And violation of all faith and troth
Sworn to us in your younger enterprise.
KING
These things indeed you have articulate,   72
Proclaimed at market crosses, read in churches,
To face the garment of rebellion   74
With some fine color that may please the eye   75
Of fickle changelings and poor discontents,   76
Which gape and rub the elbow at the news   77
Of hurly-burly innovation.   78
And never yet did insurrection want   79
Such water-colors to impaint his cause,   80
Nor moody beggars, starving for a time   81
Of pell-mell havoc and confusion.   82
PRINCE
In both your armies there is many a soul   83
Shall pay full dearly for this encounter,
If once they join in trial. Tell your nephew
The Prince of Wales doth join with all the world
In praise of Henry Percy. By my hopes—   87
This present enterprise set off his head—   88
I do not think a braver gentleman,
More active-valiant or more valiant-young,
More daring or more bold, is now alive

---

3 **his distemperature** i.e., the sun's unhealthy appearance   **4 trumpet**
trumpeter.   **his** its, the sun's   **12 easy** comfortable   **17 orb** orbit,
sphere of action. (The King's subjects, like planets and stars in the
Ptolemaic cosmos, were supposed to revolve around the kingly center, comparable to the earth, in fixed courses.)   **19 exhaled meteor**
(Meteors were believed to be vapors drawn up or *exhaled* by the sun
and visible as streaks of light; they were regarded as ill omens.)
20 prodigy of fear fearful omen   **21 broachèd** set flowing, already
begun   **24 entertain** occupy   **26 the . . . dislike** this time of discord
29 chewet chough, jackdaw. (Here, a chatterer.)   **32 remember** remind   **35 posted** rode swiftly   **38 Nothing** not at all   **40 brought** escorted   **44 new-fall'n** recently inherited (by the death of John of
Gaunt)

50 injuries abuses, evils.   **wanton** lawless   **51 sufferances** suffering,
distress   **56 occasion** the opportunity   **60 ungentle . . . bird** rude
nestling, the cuckoo's young offspring. (The cuckoo lays its eggs in
other birds' nests.)   **63 our love** we in our love   **66 head** armed force
67 opposèd . . . means goaded into opposition by such factors
69 dangerous countenance threatening behavior   **72 articulate** set
forth, specified   **74 face** trim, adorn   **75 color** (1) hue (2) specious
appearance   **76 changelings** turncoats   **77 rub the elbow** i.e., hug
themselves with delight   **78 innovation** rebellion   **79 want** lack
80 water-colors i.e., thin excuses. (See *color,* line 75.)   **his** its
81 moody sullen, angry   **82 havoc** plundering   **83 both your** i.e.,
your and our   **87 hopes** i.e., hopes of salvation   **88 This . . . head**
i.e., if this present rebellion is taken from his account, not held
against him

To grace this latter age with noble deeds.
For my part, I may speak it to my shame,
I have a truant been to chivalry;
And so I hear he doth account me too.
Yet this before my father's majesty:
I am content that he shall take the odds
Of his great name and estimation,   98
And will, to save the blood on either side,
Try fortune with him in a single fight.

KING
And, Prince of Wales, so dare we venture thee,   101
Albeit considerations infinite   102
Do make against it. No, good Worcester, no.
We love our people well; even those we love
That are misled upon your cousin's part;   105
And, will they take the offer of our grace,   106
Both he and they and you, yea, every man
Shall be my friend again, and I'll be his.
So tell your cousin, and bring me word
What he will do. But if he will not yield,
Rebuke and dread correction wait on us,   111
And they shall do their office. So, begone.
We will not now be troubled with reply.
We offer fair; take it advisedly.
                        Exeunt Worcester [and Vernon].

PRINCE
It will not be accepted, on my life.
The Douglas and the Hotspur both together
Are confident against the world in arms.

KING
Hence, therefore, every leader to his charge;
For on their answer will we set on them,
And God befriend us as our cause is just!   120
                        Exeunt. Manent Prince, Falstaff.

FALSTAFF   Hal, if thou see me down in the battle and
bestride me, so; 'tis a point of friendship.   122

PRINCE   Nothing but a colossus can do thee that friendship. Say thy prayers, and farewell.

FALSTAFF   I would 'twere bedtime, Hal, and all well.

PRINCE   Why, thou owest God a death.   [*Exit.*] 126

FALSTAFF   'Tis not due yet; I would be loath to pay him
before his day. What need I be so forward with him
that calls not on me? Well, 'tis no matter; honor pricks 129
me on. Yea, but how if honor prick me off when I   130
come on? How then? Can honor set to a leg? No. Or 131
an arm? No. Or take away the grief of a wound? No.   132
Honor hath no skill in surgery, then? No. What is
honor? A word. What is in that word "honor"? What is
that "honor"? Air. A trim reckoning! Who hath it? He
that died o' Wednesday. Doth he feel it? No. Doth he
hear it? No. 'Tis insensible, then? Yea, to the dead. But
will it not live with the living? No. Why? Detraction   138

will not suffer it. Therefore I'll none of it. Honor is a   139
mere scutcheon. And so ends my catechism.   140
                                                            Exit.

❧

5.2   *Enter Worcester [and] Sir Richard Vernon.*

WORCESTER
O, no, my nephew must not know, Sir Richard,
The liberal and kind offer of the King.

VERNON
'Twere best he did.

WORCESTER   Then are we all undone.
It is not possible, it cannot be,
The King should keep his word in loving us;
He will suspect us still and find a time
To punish this offense in other faults.   7
Suspicion all our lives shall be stuck full of eyes;   8
For treason is but trusted like the fox,
Who, never so tame, so cherished, and locked up,   10
Will have a wild trick of his ancestors.   11
Look how we can, or sad or merrily,   12
Interpretation will misquote our looks,
And we shall feed like oxen at a stall,
The better cherished still the nearer death.
My nephew's trespass may be well forgot;
It hath the excuse of youth and heat of blood,
And an adopted name of privilege—   18
A harebrained Hotspur, governed by a spleen.   19
All his offenses live upon my head
And on his father's. We did train him on,   21
And, his corruption being ta'en from us,   22
We as the spring of all shall pay for all.   23
Therefore, good cousin, let not Harry know
In any case the offer of the King.

                        Enter Hotspur [and Douglas, with soldiers].

VERNON
Deliver what you will; I'll say 'tis so.   26
Here comes your cousin.

HOTSPUR   My uncle is returned.
Deliver up my lord of Westmorland.   28
Uncle, what news?

WORCESTER
The King will bid you battle presently.

DOUGLAS
Defy him by the lord of Westmorland.   31

---

139 suffer allow   **140 scutcheon** heraldic emblem carried in funerals,
displayed on coaches, etc.; it was the lowest form of symbol, having
no pennon or other insignia.   **catechism** the principles of faith given
in the form of question and answer
5.2. Location: Near the rebel camp.
7 in in punishing   **8 stuck . . . eyes** i.e., provided with many eyes,
suspiciously inquisitive   **10 never so** be he never so   **11 trick** trait
12 or sad either sad   **18 an adopted . . . privilege** i.e., a nickname,
"hotspur," to justify his rashness   **19 spleen** intemperate impulse
21 train incite, draw   **22 his . . . us** i.e., since his guilt originated in
us   **23 spring** source   **26 Deliver** report   **28 Deliver up** release (as
hostage; see 4.3.110–111)   **31 Defy him by** send back your defiance
with

---

98 estimation reputation   **101 venture** hazard, risk   **102 Albeit** although it be that. (The subjunctive has the force of "were it not
that.")   **105 cousin's** i.e., nephew's   **106 grace** pardon   **111 wait
on us** are in attendance upon us   **120 s.d. Manent** they remain onstage   **122 bestride** stand over in order to defend.   **so** well and good
126 thou . . . death (Proverbial, with a pun on *debt*.)   **129 pricks**
spurs   **130 prick me off** mark me off (as one dead)   **131 set to** rejoin
or set   **132 grief** pain   **138 Detraction** slander

HOTSPUR
    Lord Douglas, go you and tell him so.
DOUGLAS
    Marry, and shall, and very willingly.   *Exit Douglas.*
WORCESTER
    There is no seeming mercy in the King.
HOTSPUR
    Did you beg any? God forbid!
WORCESTER
    I told him gently of our grievances,
    Of his oath breaking, which he mended thus,
    By now forswearing that he is forsworn.
    He calls us rebels, traitors, and will scourge
    With haughty arms this hateful name in us.

            Enter Douglas.

DOUGLAS
    Arm, gentlemen, to arms! For I have thrown
    A brave defiance in King Henry's teeth,   42
    And Westmorland, that was engaged, did bear it;   43
    Which cannot choose but bring him quickly on.
WORCESTER
    The Prince of Wales stepped forth before the King,
    And, nephew, challenged you to single fight.
HOTSPUR
    O, would the quarrel lay upon our heads,
    And that no man might draw short breath today
    But I and Harry Monmouth! Tell me, tell me,   49
    How showed his tasking? Seemed it in contempt?   50
VERNON
    No, by my soul. I never in my life
    Did hear a challenge urged more modestly,
    Unless a brother should a brother dare   52
    To gentle exercise and proof of arms.   54
    He gave you all the duties of a man,   55
    Trimmed up your praises with a princely tongue,   56
    Spoke your deservings like a chronicle,
    Making you ever better than his praise
    By still dispraising praise valued with you;   59
    And, which became him like a prince indeed,
    He made a blushing cital of himself,   61
    And chid his truant youth with such a grace
    As if he mastered there a double spirit
    Of teaching and of learning instantly.   64
    There did he pause. But let me tell the world,
    If he outlive the envy of this day,   66
    England did never owe so sweet a hope,   67
    So much misconstrued in his wantonness.   68
HOTSPUR
    Cousin, I think thou art enamorèd
    On his follies. Never did I hear

Of any prince so wild a liberty.   71
    But be he as he will, yet once ere night
    I will embrace him with a soldier's arm,
    That he shall shrink under my courtesy.   74
    Arm, arm with speed! And, fellows, soldiers, friends,
    Better consider what you have to do
    Than I, that have not well the gift of tongue,
    Can lift your blood up with persuasion.

            Enter a Messenger.

FIRST MESSENGER   My lord, here are letters for you.
HOTSPUR   I cannot read them now.
    O gentlemen, the time of life is short!
    To spend that shortness basely were too long
    If life did ride upon a dial's point,   83
    Still ending at the arrival of an hour.   84
    An if we live, we live to tread on kings;
    If die, brave death, when princes die with us!   86
    Now, for our consciences, the arms are fair   87
    When the intent of bearing them is just.

            Enter another [Messenger].

SECOND MESSENGER
    My lord, prepare. The King comes on apace.
HOTSPUR
    I thank him that he cuts me from my tale,
    For I profess not talking. Only this—
    Let each man do his best. And here draw I
    A sword, whose temper I intend to stain
    With the best blood that I can meet withal
    In the adventure of this perilous day.
    Now, *Esperance!* Percy! And set on.   96
    Sound all the lofty instruments of war,
    And by that music let us all embrace;
    For, heaven to earth, some of us never shall   99
    A second time do such a courtesy.
            Here they embrace. The trumpets sound. [Exeunt.]

5.3   *The King enters with his power [and passes over
           the stage]. Alarum to the battle. Then enter
           Douglas, and Sir Walter Blunt [dressed like King
           Henry].*

BLUNT
    What is thy name, that in the battle thus
    Thou crossest me? What honor dost thou seek
    Upon my head?
DOUGLAS   Know then my name is Douglas,
    And I do haunt thee in the battle thus
    Because some tell me that thou art a king.

---

42 **brave** proud   43 **engaged** held as hostage   49 **Monmouth** (A
name for the Prince, taken from the Welsh town where he was born.)
50 **showed his tasking** appeared his giving the challenge   52 **urged**
put forward   54 **gentle** befitting noble birth.   **proof of arms** test of
martial skill   55 **duties** due merits   56 **Trimmed . . . praises**
adorned his praise of you   59 **still . . . you** constantly disparaging
praise itself compared with your true worth   61 **cital** account, citation   64 **instantly** simultaneously   66 **envy** hostility   67 **owe** own
68 **wantonness** playful sportiveness

71 **liberty** licentiousness   74 **shrink under my courtesy** (1) be
daunted by my greater courtesy (2) fall back before my attack   83 **If**
even if.   **dial's point** hand of a watch   84 **Still . . . hour** ineluctably
concluding within an hour's time   86 **brave** glorious   87 **for** as for.
fair just   96 **Esperance** (The motto of the Percy family.)   99 **heaven
to earth** i.e., I'll wager heaven against earth
5.3. Location: Shrewsbury field. The scene is virtually continuous.
s.d. power army.   **Alarum** trumpet signal to advance

BLUNT   They tell thee true.

DOUGLAS
The lord of Stafford dear today hath bought   7
Thy likeness, for instead of thee, King Harry,   8
This sword hath ended him. So shall it thee,
Unless thou yield thee as my prisoner.

BLUNT
I was not born a yielder, thou proud Scot,
And thou shalt find a king that will revenge
Lord Stafford's death.   *They fight. Douglas kills Blunt.*

     Then enter Hotspur.

HOTSPUR
O Douglas, hadst thou fought at Holmedon thus,
I never had triumphed upon a Scot.

DOUGLAS
All's done, all's won; here breathless lies the King.   16

HOTSPUR   Where?

DOUGLAS   Here.

HOTSPUR
This, Douglas? No. I know this face full well.
A gallant knight he was; his name was Blunt,
Semblably furnished like the King himself.   21

DOUGLAS
A fool go with thy soul, whither it goes!   22
A borrowed title hast thou bought too dear.
Why didst thou tell me that thou wert a king?

HOTSPUR
The King hath many marching in his coats.   25

DOUGLAS
Now, by my sword, I will kill all his coats!
I'll murder all his wardrobe, piece by piece,
Until I meet the King.

HOTSPUR   Up, and away!
Our soldiers stand full fairly for the day.   *[Exeunt.]* 29

     Alarum. Enter Falstaff, solus.

FALSTAFF   Though I could scape shot-free at London, I   30
fear the shot here; here's no scoring but upon the pate.   31
Soft, who are you? Sir Walter Blunt. There's honor for
you. Here's no vanity! I am as hot as molten lead, and   33
as heavy too. God keep lead out of me! I need no more
weight than mine own bowels. I have led my ragamuffins where they are peppered. There's not three of
my hundred and fifty left alive, and they are for the
town's end, to beg during life. But who comes here?   38

     Enter the Prince.

PRINCE
What, stands thou idle here? Lend me thy sword.

Many a nobleman lies stark and stiff
Under the hoofs of vaunting enemies,
Whose deaths are yet unrevenged. I prithee,
Lend me thy sword.

FALSTAFF   O Hal, I prithee, give me leave to breathe
awhile. Turk Gregory never did such deeds in arms as   45
I have done this day. I have paid Percy, I have made   46
him sure.   47

PRINCE
He is, indeed, and living to kill thee.
I prithee, lend me thy sword.

FALSTAFF   Nay, before God, Hal, if Percy be alive, thou
gets not my sword; but take my pistol, if thou wilt.

PRINCE
Give it me. What, is it in the case?

FALSTAFF   Ay, Hal, 'tis hot, 'tis hot. There's that will   53
sack a city.
     The Prince draws it out and finds it to be a bottle
                               of sack.

PRINCE
What, is it a time to jest and dally now?
           He throws the bottle at him. Exit.

FALSTAFF   Well, if Percy be alive, I'll pierce him. If he do   56
come in my way, so; if he do not, if I come in his   57
willingly, let him make a carbonado of me. I like not   58
such grinning honor as Sir Walter hath. Give me life,
which if I can save, so; if not, honor comes unlooked
for, and there's an end.   *[Exit.]* 61

5.4   *Alarum. Excursions. Enter the King, the Prince,*
Lord John of Lancaster, [and the] Earl of
Westmorland.

KING   I prithee,
Harry, withdraw thyself; thou bleedest too much.
Lord John of Lancaster, go you with him.

LANCASTER
Not I, my lord, unless I did bleed too.

PRINCE
I beseech Your Majesty, make up,   5
Lest your retirement do amaze your friends.   6

KING
I will do so. My lord of Westmorland,
Lead him to his tent.

---

7 dear dearly   **7–8 bought Thy likeness** paid for his resemblance to
you   **16 breathless** i.e., dead   **21 Semblably furnished** similarly accoutered   **22 A . . . soul** i.e., may the stigma of "fool" accompany
your soul (for having dressed as a decoy of King Henry)   **25 coats**
vests worn over armor embroidered with a coat of arms   **29 stand
. . . day** i.e., seem in an auspicious position, likely to win the victory
30 shot-free without paying the tavern bill   **31 scoring** (1) cutting (2)
marking up of charges, by notches on a stick or on the inn door
33 Here's no vanity i.e. (ironically), if this doesn't show what I was
saying about honor, then nothing does   **38 town's end** i.e., city gate,
frequented by beggars

45 Turk Gregory (*Turk* is an abusive term signifying a tyrant, and *Gregory* refers probably to Pope Gregory XIII, who was assumed to have
encouraged the Massacre of Saint Bartholomew [1572], in which
many French Protestants were slain, and to have encouraged plots
against Elizabeth.)   **46–47 made him sure** made sure of him. (But
Prince Hal takes *sure* in a different sense, meaning "safe.")   **53 hot**
(Falstaff implies he has been firing at the enemy.)   **56 Percy . . .
pierce** (Elizabethan pronunciation rendered the pun more obvious
than it is now.)   **57 so** well and good   **58 carbonado** meat scored
across for broiling   **61 there's an end** (1) that concludes the subject
of my catechism (see 5.1.129–140) (2) thus life ends
5.4. Location: Scene continues at Shrewsbury field.
s.d. Excursions sorties. (The fallen body of Blunt may be removed at
some point or may be onstage still at 5.4.77 when Hal kills Hotspur.)
5 make up go forward   **6 retirement** retreat.   **amaze** alarm

WESTMORLAND
Come, my lord, I'll lead you to your tent.

PRINCE
Lead me, my lord? I do not need your help.
And God forbid a shallow scratch should drive
The Prince of Wales from such a field as this,
Where stained nobility lies trodden on
And rebels' arms triumph in massacres!

LANCASTER
We breathe too long. Come, cousin Westmorland,   15
Our duty this way lies. For God's sake, come.
            [*Exeunt Prince John and Westmorland.*]

PRINCE
By God, thou hast deceived me, Lancaster!
I did not think thee lord of such a spirit.
Before, I loved thee as a brother, John,
But now I do respect thee as my soul.

KING
I saw him hold Lord Percy at the point   21
With lustier maintenance than I did look for   22
Of such an ungrown warrior.

PRINCE
O, this boy lends mettle to us all!   *Exit.*

            [*Enter Douglas.*]

DOUGLAS
Another king? They grow like Hydra's heads.   25
I am the Douglas, fatal to all those
That wear those colors on them. What art thou   27
That counterfeit'st the person of a king?

KING
The King himself, who, Douglas, grieves at heart
So many of his shadows thou hast met   30
And not the very King. I have two boys
Seek Percy and thyself about the field;   32
But, seeing thou fall'st on me so luckily,
I will assay thee; and defend thyself.   34

DOUGLAS
I fear thou art another counterfeit;
And yet, in faith, thou bearest thee like a king.
But mine I am sure thou art, whoe'er thou be,
And thus I win thee.
            They fight; the King being in danger,
                    enter Prince of Wales.

PRINCE
Hold up thy head, vile Scot, or thou art like   39
Never to hold it up again! The spirits
Of valiant Shirley, Stafford, Blunt, are in my arms.
It is the Prince of Wales that threatens thee,
Who never promiseth but he means to pay.   43
            They fight. Douglas flieth.
Cheerly, my lord. How fares Your Grace?
Sir Nicholas Gawsey hath for succor sent,

And so hath Clifton. I'll to Clifton straight.

KING   Stay and breathe awhile.
Thou hast redeemed thy lost opinion,   48
And showed thou mak'st some tender of my life   49
In this fair rescue thou hast brought to me.

PRINCE
O God, they did me too much injury
That ever said I hearkened for your death.   52
If it were so, I might have let alone
The insulting hand of Douglas over you,   54
Which would have been as speedy in your end
As all the poisonous potions in the world,
And saved the treacherous labor of your son.

KING
Make up to Clifton; I'll to Sir Nicholas Gawsey.   58
                            Exit King.

            Enter Hotspur.

HOTSPUR
If I mistake not, thou art Harry Monmouth.

PRINCE
Thou speak'st as if I would deny my name.

HOTSPUR
My name is Harry Percy.

PRINCE   Why then, I see
A very valiant rebel of the name.
I am the Prince of Wales; and think not, Percy,
To share with me in glory any more.
Two stars keep not their motion in one sphere,
Nor can one England brook a double reign   66
Of Harry Percy and the Prince of Wales.

HOTSPUR
Nor shall it, Harry, for the hour is come
To end the one of us; and would to God
Thy name in arms were now as great as mine!

PRINCE
I'll make it greater ere I part from thee,
And all the budding honors on thy crest
I'll crop to make a garland for my head.   73

HOTSPUR
I can no longer brook thy vanities.   *They fight.* 74

            Enter Falstaff.

FALSTAFF   Well said, Hal! To it, Hal! Nay, you shall find   75
no boy's play here, I can tell you.   76

            Enter Douglas. He fighteth with Falstaff, who falls
            down as if he were dead. [*Exit Douglas.*] *The*
            Prince killeth Percy.

HOTSPUR
O Harry, thou hast robbed me of my youth!
I better brook the loss of brittle life
Than those proud titles thou hast won of me;
They wound my thoughts worse than thy sword my
flesh.

---

15 **breathe** rest, pause for breath (as also at line 47)   21 **at the point**
at sword's point   22 **lustier maintenance** more vigorous bearing
25 **Hydra's heads** (The heads of the Lernaean Hydra grew again as
fast as they were cut off.)   27 **colors** i.e., the colors of the King's insignia   30 **shadows** having form without substance   32 **Seek** who
seek   34 **assay** put to the test   39 **like** likely   43 **pay** (1) settle a debt
(2) kill

48 **opinion** reputation   49 **thou . . . of** you have some care for
52 **hearkened** listened (as for welcome news)   54 **insulting** exulting
58 **Make up** advance   66 **brook** endure   73 **crop** pluck   74 **vanities**
empty boasts   75 **Well said** well done   76 s.d. **killeth** mortally
wounds

But thoughts, the slaves of life, and life, time's fool,   81
And time, that takes survey of all the world,
Must have a stop. O, I could prophesy,
But that the earthy and cold hand of death
Lies on my tongue. No, Percy, thou art dust,
And food for—   [*He dies.*]
PRINCE
For worms, brave Percy. Fare thee well, great heart.
Ill-weaved ambition, how much art thou shrunk!
When that this body did contain a spirit,
A kingdom for it was too small a bound;
But now two paces of the vilest earth
Is room enough. This earth that bears thee dead
Bears not alive so stout a gentleman.   93
If thou wert sensible of courtesy,   94
I should not make so dear a show of zeal;   95
But let my favors hide thy mangled face,   96
And, even in thy behalf, I'll thank myself
For doing these fair rites of tenderness.
             [*He covers Hotspur's face with a scarf*
                            or other favor.]
Adieu, and take thy praise with thee to heaven!
Thy ignominy sleep with thee in the grave,
But not remembered in thy epitaph!
             He spieth Falstaff on the ground.
What, old acquaintance, could not all this flesh
Keep in a little life? Poor Jack, farewell!
I could have better spared a better man.
O, I should have a heavy miss of thee   105
If I were much in love with vanity.   106
Death hath not struck so fat a deer today,
Though many dearer, in this bloody fray.
Emboweled will I see thee by and by.   109
Till then in blood by noble Percy lie.   *Exit.*
                   Falstaff riseth up.
FALSTAFF   Emboweled? If thou embowel me today, I'll
give you leave to powder me and eat me too tomor- 112
row. 'Sblood, 'twas time to counterfeit, or that hot ter- 113
magant Scot had paid me, scot and lot too. Counterfeit? 114
I lie, I am no counterfeit. To die is to be a counterfeit,
for he is but the counterfeit of a man who hath not the
life of a man; but to counterfeit dying, when a man
thereby liveth, is to be no counterfeit but the true and
perfect image of life indeed. The better part of valor is 119
discretion, in the which better part I have saved my
life. Zounds, I am afraid of this gunpowder Percy,
though he be dead. How if he should counterfeit too
and rise? By my faith, I am afraid he would prove the
better counterfeit. Therefore I'll make him sure; yea,
and I'll swear I killed him. Why may not he rise as well

as I? Nothing confutes me but eyes, and nobody sees 126
me. Therefore, sirrah [*stabbing him*], with a new
wound in your thigh, come you along with me.
              He takes up Hotspur on his back.
        Enter Prince [and] John of Lancaster.
PRINCE
Come, brother John; full bravely hast thou fleshed 129
Thy maiden sword.
LANCASTER   But soft, whom have we here?
Did you not tell me this fat man was dead?
PRINCE   I did; I saw him dead,
Breathless and bleeding on the ground.— Art thou
    alive?
Or is it fantasy that plays upon our eyesight?
I prithee, speak. We will not trust our eyes
Without our ears. Thou art not what thou seem'st.
FALSTAFF   No, that's certain, I am not a double man; but 137
if I be not Jack Falstaff, then am I a Jack. There is Percy 138
[*throwing the body down*]. If your father will do me
any honor, so; if not, let him kill the next Percy himself. I look to be either earl or duke, I can assure you.
PRINCE
Why, Percy I killed myself and saw thee dead.
FALSTAFF   Didst thou? Lord, Lord, how this world is
given to lying! I grant you I was down and out of
breath, and so was he; but we rose both at an instant 145
and fought a long hour by Shrewsbury clock. If I may
be believed, so; if not, let them that should reward
valor bear the sin upon their own heads. I'll take it 148
upon my death I gave him this wound in the thigh. 149
If the man were alive and would deny it, zounds, I
would make him eat a piece of my sword.
LANCASTER
This is the strangest tale that ever I heard.
PRINCE
This is the strangest fellow, brother John.—
Come, bring your luggage nobly on your back.
For my part, if a lie may do thee grace, 155
I'll gild it with the happiest terms I have. 156
                   A retreat is sounded.
The trumpet sounds retreat; the day is our.
Come, brother, let us to the highest of the field, 158
To see what friends are living, who are dead.
        Exeunt [Prince of Wales and Lancaster].
FALSTAFF   I'll follow, as they say, for reward. He that re-
wards me, God reward him! If I do grow great, I'll
grow less; for I'll purge, and leave sack, and live 162
cleanly as a nobleman should do.
               Exit [bearing off the body].

❖

81 thoughts . . . fool i.e., our mental consciousness, which is dependent on physical existence, and our life itself, which is subject to time
93 stout valiant   **94 sensible of courtesy** able to hear my praise
95 dear handsome, heartfelt.   **zeal** admiration   **96 favors** plume,
scarf, glove, or similar article   **105 heavy** (1) serious (2) corpulent
106 vanity frivolity   **109 Emboweled** disemboweled, i.e., for em-
balming and burial   **112 powder** salt   **113–114 termagant** violent
and blustering, like the heathen god of the Saracens in medieval and
Renaissance lore   **114 paid** i.e., killed.   **scot and lot** i.e., in full.
(Originally the phrase was the term for a parish tax.)   **119 part** con-
stituent part, quality, role

126 Nothing . . . eyes i.e., nothing can contradict me but an eyewitness   **129 fleshed** initiated (in battle)   **137 double man** (1) specter (2)
two men   **138 Jack** knave   **145 at an instant** simultaneously
148–149 take . . . death i.e., swear with my eternal soul at risk
155 a lie i.e., this lie of yours.   **grace** credit   **156 happiest** most felicitous   **158 highest** highest vantage point   **162 purge** (1) reduce in
weight, using laxatives (2) repent

5.5

The trumpets sound. Enter the King, Prince of
Wales, Lord John of Lancaster, Earl of
Westmorland, with Worcester and Vernon
prisoners.

KING
　Thus ever did rebellion find rebuke.
　Ill-spirited Worcester! Did not we send grace,
　Pardon, and terms of love to all of you?
　And wouldst thou turn our offers contrary?　　　　4
　Misuse the tenor of thy kinsman's trust?　　　　5
　Three knights upon our party slain today,
　A noble earl, and many a creature else
　Had been alive this hour,
　If like a Christian thou hadst truly borne
　Betwixt our armies true intelligence.　　　　10
WORCESTER
　What I have done my safety urged me to;
　And I embrace this fortune patiently,
　Since not to be avoided it falls on me.
KING
　Bear Worcester to the death and Vernon too.
　Other offenders we will pause upon.
　　　　　[*Exeunt Worcester and Vernon, guarded.*]
　How goest the field?
PRINCE
　The noble Scot, Lord Douglas, when he saw
　The fortune of the day quite turned from him,
　The noble Percy slain, and all his men
　Upon the foot of fear, fled with the rest;　　　　20
　And falling from a hill, he was so bruised
　That the pursuers took him. At my tent
　The Douglas is; and I beseech Your Grace
　I may dispose of him.
KING　　　　　　　　With all my heart.
PRINCE
　Then, brother John of Lancaster,
　To you this honorable bounty shall belong.　　　　26
　Go to the Douglas, and deliver him
　Up to his pleasure, ransomless and free.
　His valors shown upon our crests today　　　　29
　Have taught us how to cherish such high deeds
　Even in the bosom of our adversaries.
LANCASTER
　I thank Your Grace for this high courtesy,
　Which I shall give away immediately.　　　　33
KING
　Then this remains, that we divide our power.
　You, son John, and my cousin Westmorland
　Towards York shall bend you with your dearest
　　speed　　　　36
　To meet Northumberland and the prelate Scroop,

Who, as we hear, are busily in arms.
Myself and you, son Harry, will towards Wales,
To fight with Glendower and the Earl of March.
Rebellion in this land shall lose his sway,　　　　41
Meeting the check of such another day;
And since this business so fair is done,　　　　43
Let us not leave till all our own be won.　　　*Exeunt.* 44

41 his its　**43 fair** successfully　**44 leave** leave off

5.5. Location: The battlefield.
4 turn . . . contrary reverse the intention of our offers　**5 Misuse . . .
trust** i.e., abuse Hotspur's confidence (by concealing the generosity of
my offer, in your role as emissary)　**10 intelligence** information, report　**20 Upon . . . fear** fleeing in panic　**26 bounty** assignment, act
of benevolence　**29 crests** i.e., helmets　**33 give away** pass along,
confer on Douglas　**36 bend you** direct your course.　**dearest** most
urgent

The Second Part of King Henry the Fourth

Shakespeare wrote *2 Henry IV* quite soon after *1 Henry IV*, perhaps in 1597, partly, no doubt, to capitalize on the enormous theatrical success of Falstaff and partly to finish the story of Falstaff's rejection. In writing *2 Henry IV*, Shakespeare drew on materials similar to those used for *1 Henry IV*, notably Raphael Holinshed's *Chronicles* (1587) and the anonymous play *The Famous Victories of Henry V* (1583–1588). Moreover, he undertook to write a play that structurally is much like its predecessor, revealing more similarity between these plays than one can find elsewhere in Shakespeare. Even the three *Henry VI* plays do not reiterate structural patterns to the same degree. Is Shakespeare repeating himself, rewriting the earlier play, and, if so, why? Is *2 Henry IV* essentially a way of giving audiences more of what they had found so entertaining in the earlier play, or is it a way of reflecting on new and troublesome issues only partially raised in *1 Henry IV*?

The structural pattern runs as follows. In both plays, Shakespeare alternates between scenes of political seriousness and scenes of comic irresponsibility, juxtaposing a rebellion in the land with a rebellion in the King's own family. In *1 Henry IV*, we move from a council of war (1.1) to a planning of the robbery at Gad's Hill (1.2). The scenes comment on each other by their nearness and by their mutual concern with lawlessness. Similarly, in *2 Henry IV*, we are at first introduced to a political rebellion in the north of England, after which we encounter Falstaff and Prince Hal's page. In both plays, 2.2 shows us Hal with Poins, setting up a future meeting to embarrass Falstaff by means of a plot, and, in both plays, 2.4 is a long, centrally located scene at the tavern, involving Hal and Falstaff in a contest of wits devised to expose Falstaff as a resourceful liar. The festivities in both scenes are brought to an end by a knocking at the door. (The act-scene divisions are probably not Shakespeare's, for they do not appear in the early quartos of either play; nevertheless, the structural location of these scenes is similar.) Between these linked scenes of comic action, we turn in both plays to the rebel camp of the Percys for a discussion of military planning against King Henry (2.3). In both plays, Falstaff goes off supposedly to fight against the rebels, but instead manages to abuse his authority as recruiting officer and to garner undeserved honors, either through wounding the dead Hotspur in the leg or through capturing Coleville of the Dale with the aid of an inflated reputation. The battle scenes are punctuated by Falstaff's wry soliloquies; his disputation on wine in *2 Henry IV* (4.3.88–123) serves a function like that of his better-known catechism on honor in *1 Henry IV* (5.1.129–140). Both plays introduce a confrontation between Hal and his father: the son is penitent for his waywardness, the father lectures on statecraft, and the prodigal son is recovered into kingly grace. Prince Hal goes on thereafter to win public honor and to prove himself his father's true son. Even the rejection of Falstaff, with which the second play ends, finds its counterpart in *1 Henry IV* in Hal's impatience with Falstaff during the battle of Shrewsbury, his elegy over the seemingly dead body of his onetime companion, and his resolve to be henceforth a prince.

These resemblances, and still others, are further highlighted when we realize that Shakespeare continues to use in his second play the structural device of foils, or paired characters, around Hal, who help define alternative models of conduct. The father is, as before, an awesome figure of authority—one whose sternness Hal never fully adopts and yet one whose public role as king Hal must inherit. Falstaff, as before, offers himself as a companion in revelry, dissipation, and joie de vivre, and must be rejected, even though much of what he says offers insight into the coldness of King Henry and especially of Hal's dutiful brother Prince John. Yet the chief purpose of these recapitulations is to suggest profound differences. *2 Henry IV* does not simply go over familiar material. Repeatedly, the similarities of situations reveal how much Hal has still to learn, how much Falstaff has changed, and how much more complicated the political process is than it first appeared. The foil relationships in this play focus less on honor, as in *1 Henry IV*, than on two related matters: rumor or reputation, and justice.

Rumor begins the play—quite literally, since Rumor is presented to us in allegorized form as portrayed by Virgil, painted full of tongues, spreading false information about the battle of Shrewsbury just ended. Rumor takes particular delight in its most cruel trick of all—raising false hopes and then dashing them. In the scene following at the Percys' household, we see Rumor as it manifests itself in the real world of men, beguiling Northumberland with the "news" of his son Hotspur's triumph, only to disappoint him afterward with the stark truth of defeat and death. What is the function of the uncharacteristic allegory at the start of this play? It serves first to establish a new dispiriting tone. The rebels are in disarray, and their cause is in jeopardy. Hotspur is dead, and with him has died the bright honor of his cause. His kinsmen, always more Machiavellian than he, are now warier than ever. Northumberland is persuaded, in a later scene, to prevaricate to his allies and to withdraw to Scotland when they most need his support, waiting to come in on their side only when he can be sure of success. The atmosphere of realpolitik and of dealing in false appearances is a consequence of a world governed by rumor. The rebels' case is never as attractive in this play as in *1 Henry IV;* Hotspur's idealism and chivalry are sorely missed.

Rumor has profound consequences for the King's side as well, and for Falstaff and Prince Hal. Falstaff rides on false reputation through the early scenes of *2 Henry IV.* He evades arrest at the hands of the Lord Chief Justice because of his presumed deeds at Shrewsbury, which we know to be illusory. His day's service at Shrewsbury "hath a little gilded over" his "night's exploit on Gad's Hill," as the Lord Chief Justice reluctantly concedes (1.2.147–148). His reputation makes possible his capture of Coleville of the Dale at Gaultree Forest, even though, by this time, Falstaff's reputation is clearly beginning to wear thin.

Conversely, Hal discovers that his reputation for prodigality will not leave him. Hal begins to realize that, despite the fact that the King has severed Falstaff from him (1.2.201–202), so that Hal scarcely knows of Falstaff's whereabouts until he agrees to a kind of reunion for old times' sake at the tavern, everyone assumes the worst of Hal and expects his future reign to be one of continual riot. He himself characterizes his visit to the tavern, in order to see Falstaff again, as a base "transformation" like those Ovidian portrayals of Jove in lowly human disguise. Talking with Poins in 2.2.1–44, Hal professes to be "exceeding weary" of the "disgrace" it is in him to remember all his vile companions, including Poins, and he sardonically congratulates his companion on thinking like everyone else when Poins assumes that any weeping on Hal's part for his father's death would be no more than princely hypocrisy. "Let the end try the man," says Hal, in what should be a plain notice of his reformation, but no one credits him with sincerity. When his father does take to his deathbed, surrounded by hushed courtiers, Hal, until now notably absent from court, enters with exaggerated offhandedness, as though eschewing the show of mourning he knows cannot be believed in him. His taking the crown from the pillow of his seemingly dead father strikes King Henry and his courtiers as one last confirmation of Hal's desire to supplant his father, and indeed we, too, are forced to wonder at Hal's imprudence. (The patricidal overtones in one of Shakespeare's sources, *The Famous Victories of Henry V,* are much more overt than those in Shakespeare's play.)

The structural recapitulations of *2 Henry IV,* then, in which Hal first jests with Falstaff at the tavern and afterward confronts his father at court, are no mere repetitions; they stress the dreary fact that a reputation for riotous conduct persists, that the father's embracing of his son has lapsed into renewed distrust, and that "reformation" is not the simple process Hal once supposed. Reformation is first a matter of improving one's own conduct, but it is also a matter of improving one's image. This is not a happy revelation to a young man who is impatient of ceremony and public dis-

play, but it is the way of the world and an integral part of any successful kingship. King Henry's last advice to Hal, in fact, once they have been reconciled anew, concerns the manipulations of appearances in the name of statecraft; the father urges the son to resolve civil strife by going to war against some foreign enemy. He must "busy giddy minds / With foreign quarrels" (4.5.213–214). Hal will adopt this stratagem in *Henry V* by warring against the French. Meantime, in *2 Henry IV,* he must overcome his reputation, not only with his father, but also with the Lord Chief Justice, the nobles of the court, and his brother John. Not until the play's end do they believe other than that Hal will turn riot loose in his kingdom. The intransigent nature of false "rumor" or reputation does much to explain why the new King must reject Falstaff so publicly and so sharply. He has, in fact, already rejected Falstaff in the sense of leaving him, but no one has taken the point—least of all Falstaff, who now presses in upon the new King with hopes of reward and license to act as he pleases. "The laws of England are at my commandment," he exults (5.3.138–139). Only a public repudiation can meet the demands of kingship by making full use of the act's symbolic value. Hal must reject Falstaff, not only in his heart, but also in the view of his nation. It is a distasteful act, perhaps as much to him as to us, but it is made necessary by the political exigencies of the moment.

The play's concern with justice emerges in the first confrontation between the Lord Chief Justice and Falstaff (1.2.54–226). The one represents law; the other, license. Who is to represent and administer the law during Henry V's reign? The Lord Chief Justice is a firm and austere figure, a deputy or substitute for the father-king—one who has presumed to imprison Hal for resisting his authority. This Lord Chief Justice does not expect to remain in office once the new King is crowned; like other serious characters in the play, he longs for reassurance in the troubled times of civil war and of change of administration under a monarchy. In contrast to this somewhat awesome parental figure, Falstaff offers hedonism and irresponsibility. His wit is, in a sense, no less engaging than in *1 Henry IV.* His scenes with Shallow and Silence, as they choose soldiers for the upcoming campaign or prepare for the golden time they anticipate, are as funny as the best of Falstaff. The pairing of the Lord Chief Justice and Falstaff as foils might suggest at first that one is lacking where the other is strong and that Hal must steer between extremes.

Yet this play does not give us a genuine debate on justice, like that on honor in *1 Henry IV,* in which Falstaff's comments on honor strike home because of Hotspur's fanaticism. The Lord Chief Justice of this play is essentially in the right, however austere, and Falstaff is essentially in the wrong, however funny. The Lord Chief Justice sees through Falstaff and patiently bides his time. Falstaff's excesses are more pronounced than in the earlier play. We see him with Doll Tearsheet, a whore, in maudlin, drunken conversation.

He is associated with images of disease—gout, the pox, or syphilis, consumption, lameness—and of purging. His lying is not as consistently clever as before. Hal recalls the brilliant lie about the Gad's Hill robbery and credits Falstaff with having seen through the Prince's trick on that occasion (2.4.305–307), but, in the second tavern scene, Falstaff can only mutter incoherently that he had no idea that Hal was behind him in disguise, listening to his foulmouthed reproaches. Falstaff's rioting with Pistol disturbs the peace, and in such brawls homicides occur, necessitating arrest and punishment (5.4). When Falstaff appears with the diminutive page, as in 1.2, we are forcefully reminded of the grossness of his body, though he, too, laughs at this. His mooching off Mistress Quickly and his breach of promise of marriage to her, though hinted at in the earlier play, are much more open here; the humor is keen, but we cannot forget that Falstaff is victimizing a woman. Lawsuits and arrests are more prominent in this play than in its predecessor. Falstaff's abuse of authority to recruit soldiers, about which he discourses wittily in the earlier play, is here fully shown, both in its hilarity and in its lawless consequences.

Falstaff's new companions, Pistol, Doll, and then Justice Shallow and Justice Silence, sharpen our perception of Falstaff's increasingly flagrant lawlessness. Shallow and Silence are, by their very profession, counterparts to the Lord Chief Justice. In their complacent interest in their own prosperity ("How a good yoke of bullocks at Stamford fair?" 3.2.39), in their countenancing of influence peddling by their subordinates (5.1.37–52), and in Shallow's foxy aspirations to deceive Falstaff before Falstaff can deceive him, these pillars of rural respectability reveal how far injustice has permeated the English countryside. They are fit companions for Falstaff when he hears the news of his rejection and are suitably victimized by Falstaff's inability to repay a loan that Justice Shallow has advanced to him from motives of self-interest. These old men, myopically recollecting the jolly days of their youth, accentuate Falstaff's physical frailty and aging. Falstaff mocks the stories of their escapades, but he, too, as he confesses to Doll over his drink, is old. The necessary course of justice is made plain by the structural configurations of the play. Falstaff and his companions seek lawlessness and must be rebuked; the Lord Chief Justice, who fears rejection, must instead be embraced by Hal explicitly as a father figure ("You shall be as a father to my youth," 5.2.118) in order to reaffirm public decency. The Lord Chief Justice is to bear "the balance and the sword" (line 103) as emblems of justice and its stern role in maintaining order; Falstaff is dismissed as "The tutor and the feeder of my riots" (5.5.62). These necessities are plain, even though they do not answer the emotionally complicated issue of Hal's (and our) fondness for the companion of his youth.

Hal's brother, Prince John of Lancaster, is another opposite to Falstaff. Here the contrast is less prejudicial to Falstaff. Prince John takes charge of his ailing father's wars and engineers a surrender of the rebels at Gaultree Forest that is a triumph of equivocation and double-dealing. It also saves the nation from further civil conflict, at least for the time being, and establishes the peace that Hal inherits and turns to his advantage against France. What are we to make of what has been called (by Paul Jorgensen, PMLA, 1961) John's "dastardly treachery"? It seems all too much in keeping with the realpolitik that has characterized the conduct of both sides heretofore and may thus be said to be a suitable conclusion. The dismaying "revolution of the times" (3.1.46) brings with it the cooling of friendships and the recollection of dire prophecies from the days of Richard II. The only justification possible for what John does is that it succeeds. It surely lacks the glory and honor attendant on the conflict of Hal and Hotspur in 1 Henry IV. Not coincidentally, Hal is far away from Gaultree Forest when this dismal surrender is brought about. Prince John is a master at knowing how to "construe the times to their necessities" (4.1.104). His acts scarcely represent justice any more than honor. "Is this proceeding just and honorable?" ask the betrayed rebels and are answered merely "Is your assembly so?" (4.2.110–111). The end justifies the means. Falstaff's observations at Prince John's expense therefore have point. John is, as Falstaff characterizes him, "sober-blooded"; he drinks no wine and relies not on valor but on sagacity. Falstaff hopes that Hal will prove more valiant, tempering "the cold blood he did naturally inherit of his father" (4.3.87–117) with the imbibing of sherry and other pleasures learned from Falstaff. Whatever the merits of drinking as an inducement to courage, we do perceive that Prince John is too much his father's son and that Hal will avoid this cold extreme in his quest for a kingly identity that is both symbol and substance.

Hal has thus learned something from Falstaff, if only as a caution against extremes, and partly for this reason his rejection of Falstaff must come as a shock no matter how inevitable it is. Hal may well appear to dwindle in the process, for he has given up a good deal of his private self to adopt the public role thrust upon him. He accepts that public role not unwillingly, but may also perceive that he does so at some cost to himself—and to Falstaff. His terms of rejection are not wholly ungenerous—he allows the possibility of Falstaff's returning to court if he reforms, and makes financial allowance so that Falstaff will have no need to continue in crime—but the finality of the action remains stunning. We are left with a broken Falstaff, on his way to the Fleet prison by order of the Lord Chief Justice, trying to deceive himself into believing that all will be well. Hal and England have turned in a new direction; a war against the French is clearly in prospect already, which will absorb the energies of the new King and of his father's erstwhile political enemies as well. The emergence of Hal into his public role is complete.

The Second Part of King Henry the Fourth

The Actors' Names

RUMOR, *the Presenter*
KING HENRY THE FOURTH
PRINCE HENRY, *afterwards crowned* KING HENRY
  THE FIFTH
PRINCE JOHN OF LANCASTER ⎫ *sons to*
HUMPHREY [DUKE] OF GLOUCESTER ⎬ *Henry IV*
THOMAS [DUKE] OF CLARENCE ⎭ *and brethren*
                                   to Henry V

[EARL OF] NORTHUMBERLAND ⎫
[SCROOP,] THE ARCHBISHOP ⎪
  OF YORK ⎪
[LORD] MOWBRAY ⎪
[LORD] HASTING ⎬ *opposites against King*
LORD BARDOLPH ⎪   *Henry IV*
TRAVERS ⎪
MORTON ⎪
[SIR JOHN] COLEVILLE ⎭

[EARL OF] WARWICK ⎫
[EARL OF] WESTMORLAND ⎪
[EARL OF] SURREY ⎪
GOWER ⎬ *of the King's party*
HARCOURT ⎪
[BLUNT] ⎪
LORD CHIEF JUSTICE ⎪
[*His* SERVANT] ⎭

POINS ⎫
[SIR JOHN] FALSTAFF ⎪
BARDOLPH ⎬ *irregular humorists*
PISTOL ⎪
PETO ⎪
[FALSTAFF'S] PAGE ⎭

SHALLOW ⎫ *both country justices*
SILENCE ⎭
DAVY, *servant to Shallow*
FANG *and* SNARE, *two sergeants*
MOLDY, SHADOW, WART, FEEBLE, [*and*]
  BULLCALF, *country soldiers*
[FRANCIS, *a drawer*]

NORTHUMBERLAND'S WIFE
PERCY'S WIDOW [LADY PERCY]
HOSTESS QUICKLY
DOLL TEARSHEET
DRAWERS
BEADLES

GROOMS
[PORTER]

EPILOGUE

[*Lords, Attendants, Messengers, Pages, Musicians,
  Officers, etc.*]

[SCENE: *England*]

Induction

Enter Rumor, painted full of tongues.

RUMOR
Open your ears, for which of you will stop
The vent of hearing when loud Rumor speaks?
I, from the orient to the drooping west,
Making the wind my post-horse, still unfold   4
The acts commencèd on this ball of earth.
Upon my tongues continual slanders ride,
The which in every language I pronounce,
Stuffing the ears of men with false reports.
I speak of peace while covert enmity,
Under the smile of safety, wounds the world.
And who but Rumor, who but only I,
Make fearful musters and prepared defense,   12
Whiles the big year, swoll'n with some other grief, 13
Is thought with child by the stern tyrant War,
And no such matter? Rumor is a pipe   15
Blown by surmises, jealousies, conjectures,   16
And of so easy and so plain a stop   17
That the blunt monster with uncounted heads,   18
The still-discordant wavering multitude,
Can play upon it. But what need I thus   20
My well-known body to anatomize   21
Among my household? Why is Rumor here?   22
I run before King Harry's victory,
Who in a bloody field by Shrewsbury
Hath beaten down young Hotspur and his troops,
Quenching the flame of bold rebellion
Even with the rebels' blood. But what mean I
To speak so true at first? My office is
To noise abroad that Harry Monmouth fell   29
Under the wrath of noble Hotspur's sword,
And that the King before the Douglas' rage

Induction. Location: Although the allegory of Rumor, based ultimately on Virgil's depiction of Fama as full of eyes, ears, and tongues in the *Aeneid* (4.179–190), is timeless, Rumor is here represented as standing in front of Northumberland's castle, Warkworth. The play is supposed to open immediately after the battle of Shrewsbury, in which Henry Percy, or Hotspur, and the Scottish Earl of Douglas have been overthrown. We are concerned first of all with the news of the battle with which *1 Henry IV* ended.
4 post-horse horse kept at an inn or post-house for the use of travelers. **still** continually **12 musters** assemblies of soldiers **13 big** swollen, pregnant with disaster **15 And no such matter** and yet there is no substance in such rumors. **pipe** recorder (a wind instrument) **16 jealousies** suspicions **17 of . . . stop** whose stops or openings are so easily played on **18 blunt** stupid, dull-witted **20 what** why **21 anatomize** lay open minutely, explain **22 household** retinue, i.e., the audience **29 Harry Monmouth** Prince Hal (who was born at Monmouth in Wales)

Stooped his anointed head as low as death.
This have I rumored through the peasant towns   33
Between that royal field of Shrewsbury
And this worm-eaten hold of ragged stone,   35
Where Hotspur's father, old Northumberland,
Lies crafty-sick. The posts come tiring on,   37
And not a man of them brings other news
Than they have learned of me. From Rumor's tongues
They bring smooth comforts false, worse than true
wrongs.   *Exit Rumor.* 40

❖

1.1   *Enter the Lord Bardolph at one door.*

LORD BARDOLPH
Who keeps the gate here, ho?

[*Enter the Porter.*]

Where is the Earl?   1
PORTER
What shall I say you are?
LORD BARDOLPH   Tell thou the Earl
That the Lord Bardolph doth attend him here.   3
PORTER
His lordship is walked forth into the orchard.
Please it your honor knock but at the gate,
And he himself will answer.

*Enter the Earl [of] Northumberland [in a nightcap,
supporting himself with a crutch].*

LORD BARDOLPH   Here comes the Earl.
[*Exit Porter.*]

NORTHUMBERLAND
What news, Lord Bardolph? Every minute now
Should be the father of some stratagem.   8
The times are wild. Contention, like a horse
Full of high feeding, madly hath broke loose   10
And bears down all before him.
LORD BARDOLPH   Noble Earl,
I bring you certain news from Shrewsbury.   12
NORTHUMBERLAND
Good, an God will!
LORD BARDOLPH   As good as heart can wish.   13
The King is almost wounded to the death,
And, in the fortune of my lord your son,   15
Prince Harry slain outright; and both the Blunts
Killed by the hand of Douglas. Young Prince John
And Westmorland and Stafford fled the field,
And Harry Monmouth's brawn, the hulk Sir John,   19
Is prisoner to your son. O, such a day,

So fought, so followed, and so fairly won,   21
Came not till now to dignify the times
Since Caesar's fortunes!
NORTHUMBERLAND   How is this derived?   23
Saw you the field? Came you from Shrewsbury?
LORD BARDOLPH
I spake with one, my lord, that came from thence,
A gentleman well bred and of good name,
That freely rendered me these news for true.

Enter Travers.

NORTHUMBERLAND
Here comes my servant Travers, who I sent
On Tuesday last to listen after news.
LORD BARDOLPH
My lord, I overrode him on the way,   30
And he is furnished with no certainties
More than he haply may retail from me.   32
NORTHUMBERLAND
Now, Travers, what good tidings comes with you?
TRAVERS
My lord, Sir John Umfrevile turned me back   34
With joyful tidings and, being better horsed,
Outrode me. After him came spurring hard
A gentleman almost forspent with speed   37
That stopped by me to breathe his bloodied horse.   38
He asked the way to Chester, and of him
I did demand what news from Shrewsbury.
He told me that rebellion had ill luck
And that young Harry Percy's spur was cold.
With that, he gave his able horse the head,
And bending forward struck his armèd heels
Against the panting sides of his poor jade   45
Up to the rowel head, and starting so   46
He seemed in running to devour the way,
Staying no longer question.
NORTHUMBERLAND   Ha? Again: 48
Said he young Harry Percy's spur was cold?
Of Hotspur, Coldspur? That rebellion
Had met ill luck?
LORD BARDOLPH   My lord, I'll tell you what:
If my young lord your son have not the day,   52
Upon mine honor, for a silken point   53
I'll give my barony. Never talk of it.
NORTHUMBERLAND
Why should that gentleman that rode by Travers
Give then such instances of loss?
LORD BARDOLPH   Who, he?
He was some hilding fellow that had stol'n   57
The horse he rode on and, upon my life,
Spoke at a venture. Look, here comes more news.   59

Enter Morton.

33 peasant rural, provincial   **35 hold** stronghold, fortress   **37 crafty-sick** feigning sickness.   **The . . . on** the messengers gallop hard, exhausted by their effort   **40 worse . . . wrongs** i.e., false good news that is ultimately worse than hurtful truth
1.1. Location: Warkworth. Before Northumberland's castle.
s.d. Lord Bardolph (An ally of the Percys; not to be confused with Bardolph, Falstaff's red-faced companion.)   **1 keeps** guards   **3 attend** await   **8 stratagem** violence   **10 high feeding** too-rich fodder   **12 certain** reliable   **13 an** if   **15 in the fortune of** by the good fortune of, or, for what has befallen   **19 brawn** fat boar

21 followed carried through   **23 fortunes** successes.   **derived** learned, obtained   **30 overrode** outrode   **32 haply** perhaps.   **retail** relate   **34 Sir John Umfrevile** (Perhaps the name of Lord Bardolph in an earlier version of this scene.)   **37 forspent** exhausted   **38 breathe** rest.   **bloodied** i.e., with spurring   **45 jade** nag   **46 rowel head** the end of the spur, in which the barbed wheel turns.   **starting** springing forward   **48 Staying** waiting for   **52 day** victory   **53 point** tag for fastening clothes (i.e., something of very small value)   **57 hilding** good-for-nothing   **59 at a venture** at random, recklessly

NORTHUMBERLAND
Yea, this man's brow, like to a title leaf,   60
Foretells the nature of a tragic volume.
So looks the strand whereon the imperious flood   62
Hath left a witnessed usurpation.   63
Say, Morton, didst thou come from Shrewsbury?

MORTON
I ran from Shrewsbury, my noble lord,
Where hateful death put on his ugliest mask
To fright our party.

NORTHUMBERLAND   How doth my son and brother?
Thou tremblest, and the whiteness in thy cheek
Is apter than thy tongue to tell thy errand.
Even such a man, so faint, so spiritless,
So dull, so dead in look, so woebegone,
Drew Priam's curtain in the dead of night   72
And would have told him half his Troy was burnt;
But Priam found the fire ere he his tongue,
And I my Percy's death ere thou report'st it.
This thou wouldst say, "Your son did thus and
    thus;
Your brother thus; so fought the noble Douglas"—
Stopping my greedy ear with their bold deeds.   78
But in the end, to stop my ear indeed,   79
Thou hast a sigh to blow away this praise,
Ending with "Brother, son, and all are dead."

MORTON
Douglas is living, and your brother, yet;
But for my lord your son—

NORTHUMBERLAND   Why, he is dead.
See what a ready tongue suspicion hath!
He that but fears the thing he would not know
Hath by instinct knowledge from others' eyes
That what he feared is chancèd. Yet speak, Morton. 87
Tell thou an earl his divination lies,   88
And I will take it as a sweet disgrace
And make thee rich for doing me such wrong.

MORTON
You are too great to be by me gainsaid.   91
Your spirit is too true, your fears too certain. 92

NORTHUMBERLAND
Yet, for all this, say not that Percy's dead.   93
I see a strange confession in thine eye.
Thou shak'st thy head and hold'st it fear or sin
To speak a truth. If he be slain, say so.
The tongue offends not that reports his death;
And he doth sin that doth belie the dead,   98
Not he which says the dead is not alive.
Yet the first bringer of unwelcome news
Hath but a losing office, and his tongue   101
Sounds ever after as a sullen bell   102
Remembered tolling a departing friend.   103

LORD BARDOLPH
I cannot think, my lord, your son is dead.

MORTON [to Northumberland]
I am sorry I should force you to believe
That which I would to God I had not seen;
But these mine eyes saw him in bloody state,
Rend'ring faint quittance, wearied and outbreathed, 108
To Harry Monmouth, whose swift wrath beat down
The never-daunted Percy to the earth,
From whence with life he never more sprung up.
In few, his death, whose spirit lent a fire   112
Even to the dullest peasant in his camp,
Being bruited once, took fire and heat away   114
From the best-tempered courage in his troops;   115
For from his metal was his party steeled,   116
Which once in him abated, all the rest   117
Turned on themselves, like dull and heavy lead.   118
And as the thing that's heavy in itself
Upon enforcement flies with greatest speed,   120
So did our men, heavy in Hotspur's loss,
Lend to this weight such lightness with their fear
That arrows fled not swifter toward their aim
Than did our soldiers, aiming at their safety,
Fly from the field. Then was that noble Worcester
Too soon ta'en prisoner; and that furious Scot,
The bloody Douglas, whose well-laboring sword
Had three times slain th' appearance of the King, 128
'Gan vail his stomach and did grace the shame   129
Of those that turned their backs, and in his flight,
Stumbling in fear, was took. The sum of all
Is that the King hath won and hath sent out
A speedy power to encounter you, my lord,   133
Under the conduct of young Lancaster   134
And Westmorland. This is the news at full.   135

NORTHUMBERLAND
For this I shall have time enough to mourn.
In poison there is physic; and these news,   137
Having been well, that would have made me sick,   138
Being sick, have in some measure made me well.   139
And as the wretch whose fever-weakened joints
Like strengthless hinges buckle under life,   141
Impatient of his fit, breaks like a fire   142
Out of his keeper's arms, even so my limbs,   143
Weakened with grief, being now enraged with grief, 144
Are thrice themselves. Hence, therefore, thou nice
    crutch!   [He throws away his crutch.] 145

60 title leaf title page **62 strand** shore **63 a witnessed usurpation** evidence of its (the sea's) invasion, encroachment. (Morton's brow is furrowed like wrinkled sand.) **72 Priam** King of Troy. **curtain** bed-curtain **78 Stopping** filling **79 stop . . . indeed** prevent my ever hearing again **87 is chancèd** has occurred **88 divination** prophecy **91 gainsaid** contradicted **92 spirit** intuition, powers of perception **93 for** in spite of **98 belie** slander **101 losing office** i.e., thankless task **102 sullen** mournful **103 tolling** ringing the funeral bell for

108 quittance requital, i.e., resistance. **outbreathed** out of breath **112 In few** in few words **114 bruited** rumored, reported **115 best-tempered** i.e., like the highest quality steel **116 metal** (1) steel, continuing the metaphor of line 115 (2) mettle, courage **117 abated** (1) blunted (2) slackened **118 Turned on themselves** (1) bent backwards (2) turned and ran **120 Upon enforcement** when set forcibly in motion **128 appearance of the King** i.e., warriors dressed like the King. (See *1 Henry IV*, 5.3 and 5.4.25–38.) **129 'Gan . . . stomach** began to abate or lower his courage. **grace** sanction (by his own running away) **133 power** armed force **134 conduct** command **135 at** in **137 physic** medicine **138 Having . . . sick** that would have made me sick if I had been well **139 Being sick, have** I being sick, this same news has **141 buckle under life** bend under the weight of the living man **142 fit** attack of illness **143 keeper's** nurse's **144 grief . . . grief** pain and sickness . . . sorrow **145 nice** delicate, effeminate

A scaly gauntlet now with joints of steel   146
Must glove this hand. And hence, thou sickly coif!   147
  [*He takes off his nightcap.*]
Thou art a guard too wanton for the head   148
Which princes, fleshed with conquest, aim to hit.   149
Now bind my brows with iron, and approach
The ragged'st hour that time and spite dare bring   151
To frown upon th' enragèd Northumberland!
Let heaven kiss earth! Now let not Nature's hand
Keep the wild flood confined! Let order die,   154
And let this world no longer be a stage
To feed contention in a lingering act;   156
But let one spirit of the firstborn Cain   157
Reign in all bosoms, that, each heart being set   158
On bloody courses, the rude scene may end,
And darkness be the burier of the dead!

LORD BARDOLPH
This strainèd passion doth you wrong, my lord.   161

MORTON
Sweet Earl, divorce not wisdom from your honor.
The lives of all your loving complices   163
Lean on your health, the which, if you give o'er
To stormy passion, must perforce decay.   165
You cast th' event of war, my noble lord,   166
And summed the account of chance, before you said
"Let us make head." It was your presurmise   168
That in the dole of blows your son might drop.   169
You knew he walked o'er perils, on an edge,
More likely to fall in than to get o'er;
You were advised his flesh was capable   172
Of wounds and scars, and that his forward spirit   173
Would lift him where most trade of danger ranged.   174
Yet did you say, "Go forth." And none of this,
Though strongly apprehended, could restrain
The stiff-borne action. What hath then befall'n,   177
Or what hath this bold enterprise brought forth,
More than that being which was like to be?   179

LORD BARDOLPH
We all that are engagèd to this loss   180
Knew that we ventured on such dangerous seas
That if we wrought out life 'twas ten to one.   182
And yet we ventured, for the gain proposed
Choked the respect of likely peril feared;   184
And since we are o'erset, venture again.   185
Come, we will all put forth, body and goods.   186

MORTON
'Tis more than time. And, my most noble lord,
I hear for certain, and dare speak the truth,
The gentle Archbishop of York is up   189
With well-appointed powers. He is a man   190
Who with a double surety binds his followers.   191
My lord your son had only but the corpse,   192
But shadows and the shows of men, to fight;   193
For that same word "rebellion" did divide
The action of their bodies from their souls,
And they did fight with queasiness, constrained,
As men drink potions, that their weapons only   197
Seemed on our side. But, for their spirits and souls,   198
This word "rebellion," it had froze them up
As fish are in a pond. But now the Bishop
Turns insurrection to religion.   201
Supposed sincere and holy in his thoughts,   202
He's followed both with body and with mind,
And doth enlarge his rising with the blood   204
Of fair King Richard, scraped from Pomfret stones;   205
Derives from heaven his quarrel and his cause;
Tells them he doth bestride a bleeding land
Gasping for life under great Bolingbroke;   208
And more and less do flock to follow him.   209

NORTHUMBERLAND
I knew of this before, but, to speak truth,
This present grief had wiped it from my mind.
Go in with me, and counsel every man   212
The aptest way for safety and revenge.
Get posts and letters, and make friends with
  speed—   214
Never so few, and never yet more need.   *Exeunt.*

1.2   *Enter Sir John [Falstaff] alone, with his Page
          bearing his sword and buckler.*

FALSTAFF   Sirrah, you giant, what says the doctor to my   1
  water?   2
PAGE   He said, sir, the water itself was a good healthy
  water, but, for the party that owed it, he might have   4
  more diseases than he knew for.   5
FALSTAFF   Men of all sorts take a pride to gird at me.   6
  The brain of this foolish-compounded clay, man, is   7

---

146 **scaly** i.e., mailed   147 **sickly coif** close-fitting cap worn by an
invalid   148 **wanton** effeminate, luxurious   149 **fleshed** inflamed by
foretaste of blood and success   151 **ragged'st** roughest   154 **flood**
river   156 **in . . . act** in a drawn-out act (as of a play). (Northumberland wishes for an end to the lingering dissolution of a world in conflict.)   157 **of . . . Cain** i.e., of murder   158 **that** so that
161 **strainèd** excessive   163 **complices** allies   165 **perforce** necessarily   166 **cast th' event** calculated the outcome   168 **make head**
raise an army   169 **dole** dealing out, distribution   172 **advised** aware
173 **Of** of receiving.   **forward** eager, ardent   174 **trade** trafficking
177 **stiff-borne** obstinately carried out   179 **that . . . be** what was
likely to occur   180 **engagèd to** involved in   182 **if . . . one** if we
came out alive, we survived ten-to-one odds   184 **Choked the respect** suppressed the consideration   185 **o'erset** defeated, overthrown
186 **all put forth** (1) all set out, as though putting out to sea (2) stake
everything

189 **gentle** wellborn.   **Archbishop of York** i.e., Archbishop Scroop.
up in arms   190 **well-appointed powers** well-equipped armed forces
191 **a double surety** i.e., a bond of allegiance in terms of body and
soul   192 **only but** only.   **corpse** i.e., corpses, living bodies without
their souls   193 **But** only.   **to fight** to use for fighting   197 **potions**
medicine, poison   198 **for** as for   201 **to religion** into a sacred cause
202 **Supposed** i.e., rightly thought to be   204 **enlarge his rising** enhance the merit of his insurrection   205 **Pomfret** i.e., Pontefract Castle in Yorkshire, where Richard II was murdered   208 **Bolingbroke**
i.e., King Henry IV, here deprived of his title by the Archbishop
209 **more and less** all classes   212 **counsel every man** let every man
give advice as to   214 **posts** messengers.   **make** collect
1.2. Location: London. A street.
s.d. buckler shield   1 **Sirrah** (Form of address to a social inferior.)
1–2 **to my water** about my urine sample   4 **owed** owned   5 **knew
for** was aware of   6 **gird** jeer   7 **foolish-compounded** composed of
folly

not able to invent anything that tends to laughter more than I invent or is invented on me. I am not only witty in myself, but the cause that wit is in other men. I do here walk before thee like a sow that hath overwhelmed all her litter but one. If the Prince put thee into my service for any other reason than to set 13 me off, why then I have no judgment. Thou whoreson 14 mandrake, thou art fitter to be worn in my cap than to 15 wait at my heels. I was never manned with an agate 16 till now; but I will inset you neither in gold nor silver, but in vile apparel, and send you back again to your master, for a jewel—the juvenal, the Prince your 19 master, whose chin is not yet fledge. I will sooner 20 have a beard grow in the palm of my hand than he shall get one of his cheek, and yet he will not stick to 22 say his face is a face royal. God may finish it when he 23 will; 'tis not a hair amiss yet. He may keep it still at a 24 face royal, for a barber shall never earn sixpence out of it; and yet he'll be crowing as if he had writ man ever 26 since his father was a bachelor. He may keep his own grace, but he's almost out of mine, I can assure him. 28 What said Master Dommelton about the satin for my short cloak and my slops? 30

PAGE He said, sir, you should procure him better assurance than Bardolph. He would not take his bond 32 and yours; he liked not the security.

FALSTAFF Let him be damned, like the glutton! Pray 34 God his tongue be hotter! A whoreson Achitophel, a 35 rascally yea-forsooth knave, to bear a gentleman in 36 hand and then stand upon security! The whoreson 37 smoothy-pates do now wear nothing but high shoes 38 and bunches of keys at their girdles; and if a man is 39 through with them in honest taking up, then they 40 must stand upon security. I had as lief they would put 41 ratsbane in my mouth as offer to stop it with security. 42 I looked 'a should have sent me two-and-twenty 43 yards of satin, as I am a true knight, and he sends me

"security"! Well, he may sleep in security, for he hath 45 the horn of abundance, and the lightness of his wife 46 shines through it. And yet cannot he see, though he 47 have his own lantern to light him. Where's Bardolph? 48

PAGE He's gone into Smithfield to buy your worship a 49 horse.

FALSTAFF I bought him in Paul's, and he'll buy me a 51 horse in Smithfield. An I could get me but a wife in the 52 stews, I were manned, horsed, and wived. 53

Enter [the] Lord Chief Justice [and his Servant].

PAGE Sir, here comes the nobleman that committed the 54 Prince for striking him about Bardolph.

FALSTAFF Wait close; I will not see him. 56

[He tries to slip away.]

CHIEF JUSTICE What's he that goes there?

SERVANT Falstaff, an 't please your lordship.

CHIEF JUSTICE He that was in question for the robbery? 59

SERVANT He, my lord. But he hath since done good service at Shrewsbury, and, as I hear, is now going with some charge to the Lord John of Lancaster. 62

CHIEF JUSTICE What, to York? Call him back again.

SERVANT Sir John Falstaff!

FALSTAFF Boy, tell him I am deaf.

PAGE You must speak louder; my master is deaf.

CHIEF JUSTICE I am sure he is, to the hearing of anything good.—Go pluck him by the elbow; I must speak with him.

SERVANT Sir John!

FALSTAFF What, a young knave, and begging? Is there not wars? Is there not employment? Doth not the King lack subjects? Do not the rebels need soldiers? Though it be a shame to be on any side but one, it is worse shame to beg than to be on the worst side, were it worse than the name of rebellion can tell how to make it. 77

SERVANT You mistake me, sir.

FALSTAFF Why, sir, did I say you were an honest man? Setting my knighthood and my soldiership aside, I had lied in my throat if I had said so.

SERVANT I pray you, sir, then set your knighthood and your soldiership aside, and give me leave to tell you 83 you lie in your throat if you say I am any other than 84 an honest man.

13–14 set me off show me to the best advantage **14 whoreson** (A generalized term of abuse meaning "vile" or "detestable.") **15 mandrake** plant with a forked, man-shaped root. **fitter . . . cap** i.e., as small and decorous as a brooch worn in my hat **16 wait at my heels** i.e., wait in attendance on me, follow me about. **manned . . . agate** i.e., provided with a servant as small as the little figures cut in agate stone for jewelry and seal rings **19 juvenal** youth **20 fledge** covered with down **22 stick** hesitate **23 face royal** (Punning on the *royal*, a coin with the King's face stamped on it.) **24 a hair** (1) a single hair of the beard (2) a jot **at** at the value of **26 writ man** called himself man **28 grace** (1) title suited to his royal rank (2) favor **30 slops** loose breeches **32 assurance** guarantee. **Bardolph** (One of Falstaff's followers, not the Lord Bardolph of scene 1.) **34 the glutton** (A reference to the parable of Dives the rich man, who, sent to hell for his covetousness, cried out imploringly that Lazarus, the poor leper, might dip his finger in water to cool Dives' burning tongue, Luke 16:19–31.) **35 hotter** i.e., than Dives' tongue in hell. **Achitophel** abettor of Absalom's treason against David (2 Samuel 15–17) **36 yea-forsooth knave** i.e., Puritan tradesman who uses mild oaths but is a rascal for all that **36–37 bear . . . in hand** delude one with false hopes **37 stand upon security** insist upon guarantee of payment (as also at line 41) **38 smoothy-pates** (Alludes to the short hair of Puritan tradesmen.) **38–39 high shoes . . . keys** (Indications of their financial prosperity and putting on airs.) **39–40 is through . . . taking up** has agreed with them on an honest bargain **41 lief** willingly **42 ratsbane** rat poison **43 looked 'a** expected that he

45 in security i.e., in a false and complacent sense of security **46 horn of abundance** (1) cornucopia (2) cuckold's horn, a sign of his wife's infidelity. **lightness** (1) wantonness (2) light showing through a lantern (which would have windows of *horn*, thereby giving the cuckold a lantern in his own forehead) **47 cannot he see** i.e., he cannot see his own wife's infidelity **48 lantern** (The old spelling "lanthorn" preserves Falstaff's continued joke about cuckold's horns.) **49 Smithfield** district near Saint Paul's Cathedral, famous as a livestock market **51 Paul's** i.e., Saint Paul's Cathedral nave, resort of servingmen seeking employment **52 An** if **53 stews** brothels. **I . . . wived** (Proverbially, to be thus provided with a servant, a horse, and a wife at Saint Paul's, Smithfield, and Westminster, respectively, was to be taken for a sucker.) **54 committed** i.e., to prison. (According to an apocryphal story, Prince Hal boxed the ears of the Lord Chief Justice; see *1 Henry IV*, 3.2.32–33 and note, and *2 Henry IV*, 5.2.70–71.) **56 close** concealed **59 in question** under judicial examination **62 charge** command of soldiers **77 make** regard **83 leave** permission **84 in your throat** i.e., outrageously

FALSTAFF   I give thee leave to tell me so? I lay aside that which grows to me? If thou gett'st any leave of me, 87 hang me; if thou tak'st leave, thou wert better be hanged. You hunt counter. Hence! Avaunt!   89

SERVANT   Sir, my lord would speak with you.

CHIEF JUSTICE   Sir John Falstaff, a word with you.

FALSTAFF   My good lord! God give your lordship good time of day. I am glad to see your lordship abroad. I 93 heard say your lordship was sick. I hope your lordship goes abroad by advice. Your lordship, though not 95 clean past your youth, have yet some smack of age in you, some relish of the saltness of time in you, and I most humbly beseech your lordship to have a reverent care of your health.

CHIEF JUSTICE   Sir John, I sent for you before your expedition to Shrewsbury.

FALSTAFF   An 't please your lordship, I hear His Majesty is returned with some discomfort from Wales.

CHIEF JUSTICE   I talk not of His Majesty. You would not come when I sent for you.

FALSTAFF   And I hear, moreover, His Highness is fallen into this same whoreson apoplexy.

CHIEF JUSTICE   Well, God mend him! I pray you, let me speak with you.

FALSTAFF   This apoplexy, as I take it, is a kind of lethargy, an 't please your lordship, a kind of sleeping in the blood, a whoreson tingling.

CHIEF JUSTICE   What tell you me of it? Be it as it is.   113

FALSTAFF   It hath its original from much grief, from 114 study, and perturbation of the brain. I have read the cause of his effects in Galen. It is a kind of deafness.   116

CHIEF JUSTICE   I think you are fallen into the disease, for you hear not what I say to you.

FALSTAFF   Very well, my lord, very well. Rather, an 't please you, it is the disease of not listening, the malady of not marking, that I am troubled withal.

CHIEF JUSTICE   To punish you by the heels would 122 amend the attention of your ears, and I care not if I do become your physician.

FALSTAFF   I am as poor as Job, my lord, but not so patient. Your lordship may minister the potion of imprisonment to me in respect of poverty; but how I 127 should be your patient to follow your prescriptions, the wise may make some dram of a scruple, or indeed 129 a scruple itself.

CHIEF JUSTICE   I sent for you, when there were matters against you for your life, to come speak with me.   132

FALSTAFF   As I was then advised by my learned counsel in the laws of this land service, I did not come.   134

---

87 grows to is an integral part of   **89 hunt counter** i.e., run backward on the trail. (A hunting term.)   **93 abroad** out of doors   **95 by advice** by medical advice   **113 What** why   **114 its original** its origin **116 his** its.   **Galen** the famous Greek authority on medicine **122 punish . . . heels** i.e., set you in the stocks or fetters   **127 in . . . poverty** i.e., by reason of my being too poor to pay a fine **129 make . . . scruple** entertain some small portion of doubt. (*Dram* and *scruple* are small apothecaries' weights.)   **132 for your life** i.e., carrying the death penalty   **134 land service** military service (with a pun on avoiding the "service" of a legal summons and also on Falstaff's *land service* at Gad's Hill)

CHIEF JUSTICE   Well, the truth is, Sir John, you live in great infamy.

FALSTAFF   He that buckles himself in my belt cannot live in less.

CHIEF JUSTICE   Your means are very slender, and your 139 waste is great.

FALSTAFF   I would it were otherwise; I would my means were greater, and my waist slenderer.

CHIEF JUSTICE   You have misled the youthful Prince.

FALSTAFF   The young Prince hath misled me. I am the fellow with the great belly, and he my dog.

CHIEF JUSTICE   Well, I am loath to gall a new-healed wound. Your day's service at Shrewsbury hath a little gilded over your night's exploit on Gad's Hill. You 148 may thank th' unquiet time for your quiet o'erposting 149 that action.

FALSTAFF   My lord?

CHIEF JUSTICE   But since all is well, keep it so. Wake not a sleeping wolf.

FALSTAFF   To wake a wolf is as bad as smell a fox.   154

CHIEF JUSTICE   What, you are as a candle, the better part burnt out.

FALSTAFF   A wassail candle, my lord, all tallow. If I did 157 say of wax, my growth would approve the truth.   158

CHIEF JUSTICE   There is not a white hair on your face but should have his effect of gravity.   160

FALSTAFF   His effect of gravy, gravy, gravy.   161

CHIEF JUSTICE   You follow the young Prince up and down, like his ill angel.   163

FALSTAFF   Not so, my lord. Your ill angel is light, but I 164 hope he that looks upon me will take me without 165 weighing. And yet in some respects I grant I cannot 166 go. I cannot tell. Virtue is of so little regard in these 167 costermongers' times that true valor is turned bear- 168 ward; pregnancy is made a tapster, and his quick wit 169 wasted in giving reckonings. All the other gifts appur- 170 tenant to man, as the malice of this age shapes them, 171 are not worth a gooseberry. You that are old consider not the capacities of us that are young; you do measure the heat of our livers with the bitterness of your galls. 174

---

139 means financial resources   **148 exploit** i.e., the famous robbery in *1 Henry IV*, 2.2   **149 o'erposting** escaping the consequences of **154 smell a fox** suspect something. (Compare with "smell a rat.") **157 wassail candle** large candle lighted up at a feast.   **tallow** a mixture of animal fats (which Falstaff thinks is more appropriate for him than a candle made of bees' *wax*)   **158 wax** beeswax (with a pun on "growth").   **approve** prove   **160 his effect** its sign   **161 gravy** (Sweat was thought to be fat exuded from the flesh, like gravy from meat.)   **163 ill angel** evil attendant spirit. (But Falstaff quibbles on the meaning "a clipped angel," a coin worth six shillings eight pence.)   **164 light** i.e., underweight (because the coin is "clipped." Refers also to Satan, "an angel of light," 2 Corinthians 11:14.) **165 take me** accept me at face value   **166 weighing** (1) putting me on the scales (2) considering further, interpreting   **167 go** (1) walk (2) pass current.   **cannot tell** (1) don't know what to think (2) don't count as good money   **168 costermongers'** i.e., commercial. (A costermonger is a hawker of fruits or vegetables.)   **168–169 bearward** one who handles tame bears   **169 pregnancy** quickness (of wit), intellectual capacity   **170 reckonings** tavern bills   **170–171 appurtenant** belonging   **174 heat . . . galls** (The liver was thought to be the source of passion and to be active in youth; the gall was thought to be the seat of melancholy and rancor, and to be prevalent with age.)

And we that are in the vaward of our youth, I must ₁₇₅
confess, are wags too.

CHIEF JUSTICE Do you set down your name in the
scroll of youth, that are written down old with all the
characters of age? Have you not a moist eye, a dry ₁₇₉
hand, a yellow cheek, a white beard, a decreasing leg,
an increasing belly? Is not your voice broken, your
wind short, your chin double, your wit single, and ₁₈₂
every part about you blasted with antiquity? And will ₁₈₃
you yet call yourself young? Fie, fie, fie, Sir John!

FALSTAFF My lord, I was born about three of the clock
in the afternoon, with a white head and something a ₁₈₆
round belly. For my voice, I have lost it with halloing ₁₈₇
and singing of anthems. To approve my youth further, ₁₈₈
I will not. The truth is, I am only old in judgment and
understanding; and he that will caper with me for a ₁₉₀
thousand marks, let him lend me the money, and have ₁₉₁
at him! For the box of the ear that the Prince gave you, ₁₉₂
he gave it like a rude prince, and you took it like a
sensible lord. I have checked him for it, and the young ₁₉₄
lion repents—[aside] marry, not in ashes and sack- ₁₉₅
cloth, but in new silk and old sack. ₁₉₆

CHIEF JUSTICE Well, God send the Prince a better
companion!

FALSTAFF God send the companion a better prince! I
cannot rid my hands of him.

CHIEF JUSTICE Well, the King hath severed you and
Prince Harry. I hear you are going with Lord John of
Lancaster against the Archbishop and the Earl of
Northumberland.

FALSTAFF Yea, I thank your pretty sweet wit for it. But
look you pray, all you that kiss my lady Peace at home, ₂₀₆
that our armies join not in a hot day; for, by the Lord,
I take but two shirts out with me, and I mean not to
sweat extraordinarily. If it be a hot day, and I brandish
anything but a bottle, I would I might never spit white ₂₁₀
again. There is not a dangerous action can peep
out his head but I am thrust upon it. Well, I cannot last
ever. But it was alway yet the trick of our English ₂₁₃
nation, if they have a good thing, to make it too
common. If ye will needs say I am an old man, you
should give me rest. I would to God my name were
not so terrible to the enemy as it is. I were better to be
eaten to death with a rust than to be scoured to
nothing with perpetual motion.

CHIEF JUSTICE Well, be honest, be honest; and God
bless your expedition!

FALSTAFF Will your lordship lend me a thousand
pound to furnish me forth? ₂₂₃

CHIEF JUSTICE Not a penny, not a penny. You are too
impatient to bear crosses. Fare you well. Commend ₂₂₅
me to my cousin Westmorland.
[Exeunt Chief Justice and his Servant.]

FALSTAFF If I do, fillip me with a three-man beetle. A ₂₂₇
man can no more separate age and covetousness than
'a can part young limbs and lechery; but the gout galls
the one, and the pox pinches the other, and so both ₂₃₀
the degrees prevent my curses. Boy! ₂₃₁

PAGE Sir?

FALSTAFF What money is in my purse?

PAGE Seven groats and two pence. ₂₃₄

FALSTAFF I can get no remedy against this consumption
of the purse; borrowing only lingers and lingers it out, ₂₃₆
but the disease is incurable. [He gives letters.] Go bear
this letter to my lord of Lancaster, this to the Prince,
this to the Earl of Westmorland, and this to old Mistress Ursula, whom I have weekly sworn to marry
since I perceived the first white hair of my chin. About
it. You know where to find me. [Exit Page.] A pox of
this gout! Or, a gout of this pox! For the one or the
other plays the rogue with my great toe. 'Tis no matter
if I do halt; I have the wars for my color, and my ₂₄₅
pension shall seem the more reasonable. A good wit
will make use of anything. I will turn diseases to
commodity.   [Exit.] ₂₄₈

❖

1.3 Enter the Archbishop [of York], Thomas Mowbray
(Earl Marshal), the Lord Hastings, and [Lord]
Bardolph.

ARCHBISHOP
Thus have you heard our cause and known our
   means;
And, my most noble friends, I pray you all,
Speak plainly your opinions of our hopes.
And first, Lord Marshal, what say you to it?

MOWBRAY
I well allow the occasion of our arms, ₅
But gladly would be better satisfied
How in our means we should advance ourselves ₇
To look with forehead bold and big enough ₈
Upon the power and puissance of the King. ₉

HASTINGS
Our present musters grow upon the file ₁₀
To five-and-twenty thousand men of choice; ₁₁

---

175 **vaward** vanguard, forefront 179 **characters** (1) characteristics (2)
letters 182 **single** feeble 183 **blasted** withered, blighted 186 **something a** a somewhat 187 **halloing** shouting to hounds 188 **approve**
prove 190 **caper with me** compete with me in dancing 191 **marks**
coins worth thirteen shillings four pence 192 **For** as for. **box of the
ear** (See the note to line 54, above.) 194 **sensible** (1) intelligent (2)
capable of receiving physical sensations. **checked** rebuked
195 **marry** indeed. (Literally, "by the Virgin Mary.") 196 **sack** a
white Spanish wine 206 **look** be sure, take care 210 **spit white** i.e.,
from thirst 213 **alway** yet always. **trick** habit 223 **furnish** equip

225 **crosses** (1) afflictions (2) silver coins stamped with the figure of
the cross 227 **fillip** knock. **three-man beetle** a huge pile-driving
mallet requiring three men to wield it 230–231 **both . . . curses**
i.e., both age and youth, the one afflicted with gout and the other
with **pox**, or syphilis, have their own curses which anticipate mine
234 **groats** coins worth four pence 236 **lingers** prolongs, draws
245 **halt** limp. **color** excuse 248 **commodity** profit
1.3. Location: York. The Archbishop's palace.
s.d. Thomas Mowbray son of Thomas Mowbray, Duke of Norfolk,
who was banished by Richard II 5 **allow . . . arms** concede the justice of our arming 7 **in** with 8 **forehead** i.e., assurance, defiant
gaze 9 **puissance** strength 10 **file** roll 11 **men of choice** choice
men

And our supplies live largely in the hope 12
Of great Northumberland, whose bosom burns
With an incensèd fire of injuries.

LORD BARDOLPH
The question then, Lord Hastings, standeth thus:
Whether our present five-and-twenty thousand
May hold up head without Northumberland? 17

HASTINGS
With him, we may.

LORD BARDOLPH   Yea, marry, there's the point.
But if without him we be thought too feeble,
My judgment is we should not step too far
Till we had his assistance by the hand;
For in a theme so bloody-faced as this 22
Conjecture, expectation, and surmise
Of aids incertain should not be admitted.

ARCHBISHOP
'Tis very true, Lord Bardolph, for indeed
It was young Hotspur's case at Shrewsbury.

LORD BARDOLPH
It was, my lord; who lined himself with hope, 27
Eating the air on promise of supply, 28
Flatt'ring himself with project of a power 29
Much smaller than the smallest of his thoughts, 30
And so, with great imagination
Proper to madmen, led his powers to death 32
And winking leapt into destruction. 33

HASTINGS
But, by your leave, it never yet did hurt
To lay down likelihoods and forms of hope.

LORD BARDOLPH
Yes, if this present quality of war— 36
Indeed the instant action, a cause on foot— 37
Lives so in hope, as in an early spring 38
We see th' appearing buds, which to prove fruit 39
Hope gives not so much warrant as despair 40
That frosts will bite them. When we mean to build, 41
We first survey the plot, then draw the model; 42
And when we see the figure of the house, 43
Then must we rate the cost of the erection, 44
Which if we find outweighs ability, 45
What do we then but draw anew the model
In fewer offices, or at least desist 47
To build at all? Much more, in this great work,
Which is almost to pluck a kingdom down
And set another up, should we survey
The plot of situation and the model,

Consent upon a sure foundation, 52
Question surveyors, know our own estate, 53
How able such a work to undergo,
To weigh against his opposite; or else 55
We fortify in paper and in figures, 56
Using the names of men instead of men,
Like one that draws the model of an house
Beyond his power to build it, who, half through,
Gives o'er and leaves his part-created cost 60
A naked subject to the weeping clouds 61
And waste for churlish winter's tyranny.

HASTINGS
Grant that our hopes, yet likely of fair birth, 63
Should be stillborn, and that we now possessed
The utmost man of expectation, 65
I think we are a body strong enough,
Even as we are, to equal with the King.

LORD BARDOLPH
What, is the King but five-and-twenty thousand?

HASTINGS
To us no more, nay, not so much, Lord Bardolph.
For his divisions, as the times do brawl, 70
Are in three heads: one power against the French, 71
And one against Glendower; perforce a third 72
Must take up us. So is the unfirm King 73
In three divided, and his coffers sound 74
With hollow poverty and emptiness.

ARCHBISHOP
That he should draw his several strengths together 76
And come against us in full puissance
Need not be dreaded.

HASTINGS   If he should do so,
To French and Welsh he leaves his back unarmed,
They baying him at the heels. Never fear that. 80

LORD BARDOLPH
Who is it like should lead his forces hither? 81

HASTINGS
The Duke of Lancaster and Westmorland;
Against the Welsh, himself and Harry Monmouth.
But who is substituted 'gainst the French, 84
I have no certain notice.

ARCHBISHOP   Let us on,
And publish the occasion of our arms. 86
The commonwealth is sick of their own choice;
Their overgreedy love hath surfeited.
An habitation giddy and unsure
Hath he that buildeth on the vulgar heart. 90
O thou fond many, with what loud applause 91
Didst thou beat heaven with blessing Bolingbroke, 92

---

12 **supplies** reinforcements. **largely** abundantly **17 hold up head** i.e., succeed, be confident **22 theme** business **27 lined** strengthened **28 Eating . . . supply** i.e., living in false hopes of reinforcement **29 project . . . power** anticipation of the arrival of an armed force **30 Much smaller** i.e., that proved in fact to be much smaller **32 powers** forces **33 winking** shutting his eyes **36–41 Yes . . . them** i.e., Yes (replying to Lord Hastings), it can do hurt to be too hopeful about war; if, for example, this present business of war—indeed, the very campaign we anticipate, the matter that is now afoot—depends merely on such desperate hopes as we experience about buds appearing too early in the spring, since in reality hope gives us not so much warrant to expect their maturing into fruit as despair that frosts will bite them. (The text may be corrupt here.) **42 model** plan **43 figure** design **44 rate** estimate **45 ability** i.e., ability to pay **47 offices** rooms. **at least** at the worst

52 **Consent** agree **53 surveyors** architects. **estate** wealth **55 his opposite** adverse conditions **56 in paper** merely on paper **60 part-created cost** partly finished splendor **61 naked subject** exposed (i.e., helpless) victim **63 yet** still **65 The . . . expectation** i.e., all the men that we might hope to have **70 as . . . brawl** in accordance with the discordant necessity of the time **71 heads** armies **72 perforce** necessarily **73 take up** encounter, oppose **74 sound** resound, echo **76 several strengths** various armies **80 baying** pursuing (like hunting dogs) **81 Who . . . should** who is likely to **84 substituted** delegated **86 arms** hostilities **90 vulgar** common, plebeian **91 fond many** foolish multitude **92 beat heaven** assail heaven with prayers

Before he was what thou wouldst have him be!
And being now trimmed in thine own desires,   94
Thou, beastly feeder, art so full of him
That thou provok'st thyself to cast him up.
So, so, thou common dog, didst thou disgorge   97
Thy glutton bosom of the royal Richard;
And now thou wouldst eat thy dead vomit up,
And howl'st to find it. What trust is in these times?
They that, when Richard lived, would have him die,
Are now become enamored on his grave.
Thou, that threw'st dust upon his goodly head
When through proud London he came sighing on
After th' admirèd heels of Bolingbroke,
Criest now, "O earth, yield us that king again,
And take thou this!" O thoughts of men accurst!
Past and to come seems best; things present, worst.

MOWBRAY
Shall we go draw our numbers and set on?   109

HASTINGS
We are time's subjects, and time bids begone.

                                        Exeunt.

                        ❖

2.1   *Enter Hostess [Quickly] of the tavern and two
         officers: [Fang, followed by Snare].*

HOSTESS   Master Fang, have you entered the action?   1
FANG   It is entered.
HOSTESS   Where's your yeoman? Is 't a lusty yeoman?   3
Will 'a stand to 't?   4
FANG   [*looking around him*]   Sirrah—where's Snare?
HOSTESS   O Lord, ay, good Master Snare.
SNARE   [*from behind them*]   Here, here.
FANG   Snare, we must arrest Sir John Falstaff.
HOSTESS   Yea, good Master Snare, I have entered him   9
and all.
SNARE   It may chance cost some of us our lives, for he   11
will stab.
HOSTESS   Alas the day, take heed of him! He stabbed
me in mine own house, most beastly, in good faith. 'A
cares not what mischief he does; if his weapon be out,
he will foin like any devil; he will spare neither man,   16
woman, nor child.
FANG   If I can close with him, I care not for his thrust.   18
HOSTESS   No, nor I neither. I'll be at your elbow.
FANG   An I but fist him once, and 'a come but within   20
my vice—   21
HOSTESS   I am undone by his going, I warrant you; he's   22
an infinitive thing upon my score. Good Master Fang,   23

hold him sure. Good Master Snare, let him not scape.
'A comes continually to Pie Corner—saving your   25
manhoods—to buy a saddle; and he is indited to dinner   26
to the Lubber's Head in Lumbert street, to Master   27
Smooth's the silkman. I pray you, since my exion is en-   28
tered and my case so openly known to the world, let
him be brought in to his answer. A hundred mark is a   30
long one for a poor lone woman to bear; and I have   31
borne, and borne, and borne, and have been fubbed
off, and fubbed off, and fubbed off, from this day to
that day, that it is a shame to be thought on. There is
no honesty in such dealing, unless a woman should
be made an ass and a beast, to bear every knave's
wrong. Yonder he comes, and that arrant malmsey-   37
nose knave, Bardolph, with him. Do your offices, do   38
your offices. Master Fang and Master Snare, do me, do   39
me, do me your offices.

*Enter Sir John [Falstaff], and Bardolph, and the
Boy [Page].*

FALSTAFF   How now, whose mare's dead? What's the   41
matter?
FANG   Sir John, I arrest you at the suit of Mistress
Quickly.
FALSTAFF   Away, varlets! Draw, Bardolph. Cut me off
the villain's head. Throw the quean in the channel.   46
                                        [*They draw.*]
HOSTESS   Throw me in the channel? I'll throw thee in the
channel. Wilt thou? Wilt thou? Thou bastardly rogue!
Murder, murder! Ah, thou honeysuckle villain! Wilt   49
thou kill God's officers and the King's? Ah, thou hon-   50
eyseed rogue! Thou art a honeyseed, a man-queller,   51
and a woman-queller.   52
FALSTAFF   Keep them off, Bardolph.
OFFICERS   A rescue! A rescue!   54
HOSTESS   Good people, bring a rescue or two. Thou
woo't, woo't thou? Thou woo't, woo't ta? Do, do, thou   56
rogue! Do, thou hempseed!   57
PAGE   Away, you scullion, you rampallian, you fus-   58
tilarian! I'll tickle your catastrophe.   59

Enter [the] Lord Chief Justice and his men.

---

94 trimmed in furnished with, dressed in   **97 disgorge** vomit
109 draw our numbers assemble or muster our forces.   **set on** march
2.1. Location: London. A street.
1 entered the action begun the lawsuit   **3 yeoman** sheriff's man
4 Will . . . to 't will he fight boldly   **9 entered** brought action against
in court   **11 chance** possibly   **16 foin** thrust in fencing; with unintended sexual double meaning, as also in *stabbed, weapon, thrust,
entered, undone, saddle* (suggesting a prostitute), *case* (female pudendum), *openly known to the world, brought in, long one, borne,
fubbed off* (meaning also to be put off with excuses), *do me, stand to
me*, etc.   **18 close** grapple   **20 fist** i.e., seize   **21 vice** vise, grip
22 going i.e., going without paying   **23 infinitive** (Hostess Quickly's
malapropism for "infinite," endless.)   **score** accounts

25 continually (Perhaps a mixup of "continually" and "incontinently," immediately.)   **Pie Corner** a corner in the Smithfield district
of London, known for its cooks' shops   **25–26 saving your manhoods** i.e., with apologies for mentioning anything so indelicate
26 indited (For "invited.")   **27 Lubber's Head** i.e., Libbard's Head,
Leopard's Head Inn.   **Lumbert** i.e., Lombard   **28 exion** action, lawsuit   **30 mark** (Worth thirteen shillings four pence.)   **31 long one**
huge reckoning (with unconscious sexual suggestion)   **37–38
malmsey-nose** red-nosed (from drinking malmsey, a sweet red wine)
39 do me i.e., do your duty for me (with unintended sexual suggestion)   **41 whose mare's dead** i.e., what's all the fuss about   **46 quean**
slut, hussy.   **channel** street gutter   **49 honeysuckle** (For "homicidal.")   **50–51 honeyseed** (For "homicide.")   **51 man-queller** murderer   **52 woman-queller** destroyer of women (but with suggestion
also of "seducer")   **54 A rescue** i.e., come help the officers in their
rescue of the hostess. (Said to anyone within earshot.)   **56 woo't**
thou wilt thou.   **ta** thou   **57 hempseed** (Alludes to the hangman's
rope; Mistress Quickly probably means "homicide.")   **58 scullion**
kitchen wench.   **rampallian** scoundrel, ruffian   **58–59 fustilarian** fat,
frowsy woman   **59 catastrophe** i.e., backside

CHIEF JUSTICE
What is the matter? Keep the peace here, ho!

HOSTESS Good my lord, be good to me. I beseech you,
stand to me.   62

CHIEF JUSTICE
How now, Sir John? What are you brawling here?   63
Doth this become your place, your time, and
    business?
You should have been well on your way to York.—
Stand from him, fellow. Wherefore hang'st thou
    upon him?

HOSTESS O my most worshipful lord, an 't please Your
Grace, I am a poor widow of Eastcheap, and he is
arrested at my suit.

CHIEF JUSTICE For what sum?

HOSTESS It is more than for some, my lord, it is for all,
all I have. He hath eaten me out of house and home;
he hath put all my substance into that fat belly of his.
But I will have some of it out again, or I will ride thee
o' nights like the mare.   75

FALSTAFF I think I am as like to ride the mare, if I have
any vantage of ground to get up.   77

CHIEF JUSTICE How comes this, Sir John? Fie, what
man of good temper would endure this tempest of   79
exclamation? Are you not ashamed to enforce a poor
widow to so rough a course to come by her own?   81

FALSTAFF What is the gross sum that I owe thee?   82

HOSTESS Marry, if thou wert an honest man, thyself and
the money too. Thou didst swear to me upon a parcel- 84
gilt goblet, sitting in my Dolphin chamber, at the   85
round table, by a seacoal fire, upon Wednesday in   86
Wheeson week, when the Prince broke thy head for 87
liking his father to a singing-man of Windsor, thou   88
didst swear to me then, as I was washing thy wound,
to marry me and make me my lady thy wife. Canst
thou deny it? Did not goodwife Keech, the butcher's 91
wife, come in then and call me gossip Quickly?   92
Coming in to borrow a mess of vinegar, telling us she 93
had a good dish of prawns, whereby thou didst desire 94
to eat some, whereby I told thee they were ill for a
green wound? And didst thou not, when she was   96
gone downstairs, desire me to be no more so familiar- 97
ity with such poor people, saying that ere long they   98
should call me madam? And didst thou not kiss me
and bid me fetch thee thirty shillings? I put thee now
to thy book oath. Deny it if thou canst.   101

FALSTAFF My lord, this is a poor mad soul, and she
says up and down the town that her eldest son is like
you. She hath been in good case, and the truth is,   104
poverty hath distracted her. But for these foolish of- 105
ficers, I beseech you I may have redress against them.

CHIEF JUSTICE Sir John, Sir John, I am well acquainted
with your manner of wrenching the true cause the
false way. It is not a confident brow, nor the throng of
words that come with such more than impudent
sauciness from you, can thrust me from a level   111
consideration. You have, as it appears to me, practiced
upon the easy-yielding spirit of this woman and made
her serve your uses both in purse and in person.   114

HOSTESS Yea, in truth, my lord.

CHIEF JUSTICE Pray thee, peace.—Pay her the debt
you owe her, and unpay the villainy you have done
her. The one you may do with sterling money, and
the other with current repentance.   119

FALSTAFF My lord, I will not undergo this sneap   120
without reply. You call honorable boldness impudent
sauciness. If a man will make curtsy and say nothing, 122
he is virtuous. No, my lord, my humble duty remem- 123
bered, I will not be your suitor. I say to you, I do desire 124
deliverance from these officers, being upon hasty
employment in the King's affairs.

CHIEF JUSTICE You speak as having power to do wrong.
But answer in th' effect of your reputation, and satisfy 128
the poor woman.

FALSTAFF Come hither, hostess. [He takes her aside.]

Enter a messenger [Gower].

CHIEF JUSTICE Now, Master Gower, what news?

GOWER
The King, my lord, and Harry Prince of Wales
Are near at hand. The rest the paper tells.
    [He gives a letter. The Chief Justice reads.]

FALSTAFF [to Mistress Quickly] As I am a gentleman.

HOSTESS Faith, you said so before.

FALSTAFF As I am a gentleman. Come, no more words
of it.

HOSTESS By this heavenly ground I tread on, I must be
fain to pawn both my plate and the tapestry of my 139
dining chambers.

FALSTAFF Glasses, glasses, is the only drinking. And for 141
thy walls, a pretty slight drollery, or the story of the 142
Prodigal, or the German hunting in water work, is   143

---

62 **stand to** stand by (with bawdy suggestion) 63 **What** why
75 **o' nights** by night. **mare** nightmare 77 **vantage of ground** superior position. **get up** mount (with intended sexual suggestion, continued from *ride the mare* in line 76) 79 **temper** disposition 81 **come
by her own** get what is hers 82 **gross** whole 84–85 **parcel-gilt**
partly gilded 85 **Dolphin chamber** (The name of a room in her inn;
Dolphin means "Dauphin.") 86 **seacoal** bituminous coal, brought in
by sea 87 **Wheeson** Whitsun (Pentecost). **broke** hit, made a cut on
88 **liking** comparing. **singing-man** chorister 91 **goodwife** (Title of a
married woman.) **Keech** (Literally, "a lump of tallow.") 92 **gossip**
(Literally, a fellow godparent; hence, a female friend.) 93 **mess** small
quantity 94 **prawns** shrimps. **whereby** whereupon 96 **green** raw
97–98 **familiarity** (The hostess's word for "familiar.") 101 **book
oath** oath on a Bible

104 **in good case** well-to-do (perhaps with bawdy suggestion)
105 **distracted her** driven her mad. **for** as for 111 **level** fair-
minded, evenhanded 114 **serve your uses** (with erotic suggestion)
119 **current** genuine (with an allusion to current, or lawful, coin, the
sterling of line 118) 120 **sneap** reproof 122 **curtsy** bow
123–124 **my . . . remembered** i.e., with all due consideration of the
respect I owe to your position 128 **in . . . reputation** i.e., in a manner becoming a man of your reputation 139 **fain** obliged, content
141 **Glasses . . . drinking** i.e., glasses are all the fashion now for
drinking, instead of metal tankards 142 **drollery** comic picture
142–143 **the Prodigal** the Prodigal Son. (See Luke 15:11–32.)
143 **German hunting** hunting scene painted by a German or Dutch
artist. **water work** watercolor (painted on a wall to imitate tapestry)

worth a thousand of these bed-hangers and these 144
fly-bitten tapestries. Let it be ten pound, if thou canst.
Come, an 'twere not for thy humors, there's not a 146
better wench in England. Go wash thy face, and draw 147
the action. Come, thou must not be in this humor
with me. Dost not know me? Come, come, I know
thou wast set on to this.

HOSTESS Pray thee, Sir John, let it be but twenty
nobles. I' faith, I am loath to pawn my plate, so God 152
save me, la!

FALSTAFF Let it alone; I'll make other shift. You'll be a 154
fool still.

HOSTESS Well, you shall have it, though I pawn my
gown. I hope you'll come to supper. You'll pay me all
together?

FALSTAFF Will I live? [To Bardolph.] Go, with her, with 159
her; hook on, hook on. 160

HOSTESS Will you have Doll Tearsheet meet you at
supper?

FALSTAFF No more words. Let's have her.

Exeunt Hostess and Sergeant [Fang, Bardolph, and
others].

CHIEF JUSTICE [to Gower] I have heard better news.

FALSTAFF What's the news, my lord?

CHIEF JUSTICE [to Gower] Where lay the King tonight? 166

GOWER At Basingstoke, my lord. 167

FALSTAFF I hope, my lord, all's well. What is the news,
my lord?

CHIEF JUSTICE [to Gower] Come all his forces back?

GOWER
No, fifteen hundred foot, five hundred horse 171
Are marched up to my lord of Lancaster, 172
Against Northumberland and the Archbishop.

FALSTAFF Comes the King back from Wales, my noble
lord?

CHIEF JUSTICE [to Gower]
You shall have letters of me presently. 176
Come, go along with me, good Master Gower.

[They start to go.]

FALSTAFF My lord!

CHIEF JUSTICE What's the matter?

FALSTAFF Master Gower, shall I entreat you with me to
dinner?

GOWER I must wait upon my good lord here, I thank 182
you, good Sir John.

CHIEF JUSTICE Sir John, you loiter here too long, being 184
you are to take soldiers up in counties as you go. 185

FALSTAFF Will you sup with me, Master Gower?

CHIEF JUSTICE What foolish master taught you these
manners, Sir John?

FALSTAFF Master Gower, if they become me not, he was

a fool that taught them me.—This is the right fencing
grace, my lord: tap for tap, and so part fair. 191

CHIEF JUSTICE Now the Lord lighten thee! Thou art a 192
great fool. *[Exeunt separately.]*

2.2 *Enter the Prince [Henry, and] Poins.*

PRINCE Before God, I am exceeding weary.

POINS Is 't come to that? I had thought weariness durst
not have attached one of so high blood. 3

PRINCE Faith, it does me, though it discolors the 4
complexion of my greatness to acknowledge it. Doth it 5
not show vilely in me to desire small beer? 6

POINS Why, a prince should not be so loosely studied 7
as to remember so weak a composition. 8

PRINCE Belike then my appetite was not princely got, 9
for, by my troth, I do now remember the poor
creature, small beer. But indeed these humble considerations make me out of love with my greatness. What
a disgrace is it to me to remember thy name! Or to
know thy face tomorrow! Or to take note how many
pair of silk stockings thou hast, viz., these, and those 15
that were thy peach-colored ones! Or to bear the in- 16
ventory of thy shirts, as, one for superfluity, and an- 17
other for use! But that the tennis-court keeper knows 18
better than I; for it is a low ebb of linen with thee 19
when thou keepest not racket there, as thou hast not 20
done a great while, because the rest of the low coun- 21
tries have made a shift to eat up thy holland. And God 22
knows whether those that bawl out the ruins of thy 23
linen shall inherit His kingdom. But the midwives say 24
the children are not in the fault, whereupon the world 25
increases and kindreds are mightily strengthened. 26

POINS How ill it follows, after you have labored so hard,
you should talk so idly! Tell me, how many good

---

144 **bed-hangers** (Falstaff implies that the hostess's tapestries are only good enough to serve as curtains around a four-poster bed.) **146 an 'twere** if it were. **humors** whims, vagaries **147 draw** withdraw **152 nobles** coins current at six shillings eight pence **154 shift** expedient **159 Will I live** i.e., as sure as I live **160 hook on** i.e., follow her **166 tonight** this past night **167 Basingstoke** a town in Hampshire **171 foot** foot soldiers **172 to** i.e., led by **176 presently** immediately **182 wait upon** accompany **184–185 being . . . up** seeing that you are to levy soldiers

191 grace form, style. (Falstaff is saying that, by refusing to answer the Chief Justice's questions in lines 180 ff., Falstaff is only paying him back tit for tat for ignoring Falstaff's questions, lines 165–177.) **fair** on good terms **192 lighten** (1) enlighten (2) reduce in weight
2.2. Location: London. Prince Henry's dwelling.
3 attached seized **4–5 discolors . . . greatness** i.e., makes me blush or look pale with weariness, and casts a shadow over my princely greatness **6 show** appear. **small beer** weak kind of beer, hence inferior **7 studied** versed, inclined **8 so . . . composition** i.e., weak beer, trifles **9 Belike** probably. **got** begotten **15 viz.** namely. (An abbreviation of the Latin *videlicet.*) **16 bear** bear in mind **17 for superfluity** as a clean change (of shirt) **18–21 But . . . while** i.e., the keeper of the tennis court knows that your inventory of shirts is at a low ebb and that you do not have a spare clean shirt to shift into, because you have not been seen at the tennis court lately **21–22 the low countries** i.e., the brothels where you spend your money (with a pun on "the Netherlands") **22 made a shift** contrived (with a pun on *shift,* "shirt"). **eat . . . holland** i.e., use up all the money you would spend on a linen shirt (with a pun on *Holland* as one of the Low Countries) **23–24 those . . . linen** i.e., your bastards, who cry out from your cast-off shirts made into swaddling clothes **24 inherit His kingdom** i.e., go to heaven. (See Matthew 5:10, 25:34, or 19:14: "Suffer the little children . . . to come to me, for of such is the kingdom of heaven.") **25 in the fault** to be blamed (for being illegitimate) **26 kindreds** families. (The Prince's ironic point is that this is a fine way to increase family size.)

young princes would do so, their fathers being so sick as yours at this time is?

PRINCE   Shall I tell thee one thing, Poins?

POINS   Yes, faith, and let it be an excellent good thing.

PRINCE   It shall serve among wits of no higher breeding than thine.

POINS   Go to. I stand the push of your one thing that 35 you will tell.

PRINCE   Marry, I tell thee it is not meet that I should be 37 sad, now my father is sick. Albeit I could tell to thee, as to one it pleases me, for fault of a better, to call my friend, I could be sad, and sad indeed too.

POINS   Very hardly upon such a subject. 41

PRINCE   By this hand, thou thinkest me as far in the devil's book as thou and Falstaff for obduracy and persistency. Let the end try the man. But I tell thee, my heart bleeds inwardly that my father is so sick. And keeping such vile company as thou art hath in reason taken from me all ostentation of sorrow. 47

POINS   The reason?

PRINCE   What wouldst thou think of me if I should weep?

POINS   I would think thee a most princely hypocrite.

PRINCE   It would be every man's thought, and thou art a blessed fellow to think as every man thinks. Never a man's thought in the world keeps the roadway better 54 than thine. Every man would think me an hypocrite indeed. And what accites your most worshipful 56 thought to think so?

POINS   Why, because you have been so lewd and so 58 much engraffed to Falstaff. 59

PRINCE   And to thee.

POINS   By this light, I am well spoke on; I can hear it with mine own ears. The worst that they can say of me is that I am a second brother and that I am a proper 63 fellow of my hands, and those two things I confess I 64 cannot help. By the Mass, here comes Bardolph.

Enter Bardolph and Boy [Page].

PRINCE   And the boy that I gave Falstaff. 'A had him from me Christian, and look if the fat villain have not 67 transformed him ape. 68

BARDOLPH   God save Your Grace!

PRINCE   And yours, most noble Bardolph!

POINS   [*to Bardolph*] Come, you virtuous ass, you bashful fool, must you be blushing? Wherefore blush you 72 now? What a maidenly man-at-arms are you become! Is 't such a matter to get a pottle pot's maidenhead? 74

PAGE   'A calls me e'en now, my lord, through a red 75

lattice, and I could discern no part of his face from the 76 window. At last I spied his eyes, and methought he had made two holes in the alewife's petticoat and so 78 peeped through.

PRINCE   [*to Poins*]   Has not the boy profited?

BARDOLPH   Away, you whoreson upright rabbit, away!

PAGE   Away, you rascally Althaea's dream, away! 82

PRINCE   Instruct us, boy. What dream, boy?

PAGE   Marry, my lord, Althaea dreamt she was delivered of a firebrand, and therefore I call him her dream.

PRINCE   A crown's worth of good interpretation. There 86 'tis, boy.   [*He gives money.*]

POINS   O, that this blossom could be kept from cankers! 88 Well, there is sixpence to preserve thee. 89
[*He gives money.*]

BARDOLPH   An you do not make him be hanged among 90 you, the gallows shall have wrong.

PRINCE   And how doth thy master, Bardolph?

BARDOLPH   Well, my lord. He heard of Your Grace's coming to town. There's a letter for you.
[*He gives a letter.*]

POINS   Delivered with good respect. And how doth the 95 martlemas, your master? 96

BARDOLPH   In bodily health, sir.

POINS   Marry, the immortal part needs a physician, but that moves not him. Though that be sick, it dies not.

PRINCE   I do allow this wen to be as familiar with me as 100 my dog, and he holds his place, for look you how he 101 writes.   [*He shows the letter to Poins.*]

POINS   [*reading the superscription*] "John Falstaff, knight."—Every man must know that, as oft as he 104 has occasion to name himself, even like those that are kin to the King, for they never prick their finger but they say, "There's some of the King's blood spilt." "How comes that?" says he that takes upon 108 him not to conceive. The answer is as ready as a 109 borrower's cap: "I am the King's poor cousin, sir." 110

PRINCE   Nay, they will be kin to us, or they will fetch it 111 from Japheth. But the letter. [*He reads.*] "Sir John 112 Falstaff knight, to the son of the King nearest his father, Harry Prince of Wales, greeting."

POINS   Why, this is a certificate. 115

PRINCE   Peace! [*He reads.*] "I will imitate the honorable Romans in brevity."

---

35 push attack, thrust   **37 meet** fitting, appropriate   **41 Very hardly** scarcely, with difficulty   **47 ostentation** outward indication   **54 keeps the roadway** i.e., follows the common way of thinking   **56 accites** induces (with a quibble on "summons")   **58 lewd** base   **59 engraffed** closely attached   **63 second brother** i.e., a younger son, without inheritance   **63–64 proper . . . hands** i.e., good fighter   **67–68 have . . . ape** i.e., has not dressed him fantastically   **72 blushing** i.e., red-faced (from drink).   **Wherefore** why   **74 get . . . maidenhead** i.e., knock off a two-quart tankard of ale   **75 e'en now** just now, a moment ago   **75–76 red lattice** (Red lattices identified taverns.)

76 discern distinguish   **78 petticoat** i.e., red petticoat—a sign of disreputability   **82 Althaea's dream** (Althaea dreamed that her newborn son would live only so long as a brand on the fire lasted. The Page mistakenly relates Hecuba's dream: when pregnant with Paris, Hecuba dreamed she would be delivered of a firebrand that would destroy Troy.)   **86 A crown's** five shillings'   **88 cankers** cankerworms, worms that destroy buds and leaves   **89 to preserve thee** (Allusion to the cross on the sixpence.)   **90 An** if   **95 good respect** proper ceremony. (Said ironically.)   **96 martlemas** i.e., Martinmas beef, beef slaughtered on November 11 (and fattened beforehand)   **100 wen** swelling, tumor   **101 holds his place** stands upon his rank   **104 Every . . . that** i.e., Falstaff wants to make sure that everyone is aware of his knightly rank   **108–109 takes . . . conceive** pretends not to understand   **109–110 as ready . . . cap** i.e., as quick in coming forth as a cap is doffed by one seeking aid   **111–112 fetch . . . Japheth** i.e., trace their ancestry back to Japheth, third son of Noah and supposedly the ancestor of all Europeans (Genesis 10:2–5)   **115 certificate** legal document

POINS   Sure he means brevity in breath, short-winded.

PRINCE [*reads*]   "I commend me to thee, I commend thee, and I leave thee. Be not too familiar with Poins, for he misuses thy favors so much that he swears thou art to marry his sister Nell. Repent at idle times as thou mayst, and so farewell.

"Thine, by yea and no, which is as much as to say, as thou usest him, Jack Falstaff with my familiars, John with my brothers and sisters, and Sir John with all Europe." 124 126

POINS   My lord, I'll steep this letter in sack and make him eat it. 128

PRINCE   That's to make him eat twenty of his words. But do you use me thus, Ned? Must I marry your sister? 130

POINS   God send the wench no worse fortune! But I never said so.

PRINCE   Well, thus we play the fools with the time, and the spirits of the wise sit in the clouds and mock us.—Is your master here in London?

BARDOLPH   Yea, my lord.

PRINCE   Where sups he? Doth the old boar feed in the old frank? 139

BARDOLPH   At the old place, my lord, in Eastcheap.

PRINCE   What company?

PAGE   Ephesians, my lord, of the old church. 142

PRINCE   Sup any women with him?

PAGE   None, my lord, but old Mistress Quickly and Mistress Doll Tearsheet.

PRINCE   What pagan may that be? 146

PAGE   A proper gentlewoman, sir, and a kinswoman of my master's.

PRINCE   Even such kin as the parish heifers are to the town bull. Shall we steal upon them, Ned, at supper? 150

POINS   I am your shadow, my lord; I'll follow you.

PRINCE   Sirrah, you boy, and Bardolph, no word to your master that I am yet come to town. There's for your silence.   [*He gives money.*]

BARDOLPH   I have no tongue, sir.

PAGE   And for mine, sir, I will govern it.

PRINCE   Fare you well; go. [*Exeunt Bardolph and Page.*] This Doll Tearsheet should be some road. 158

POINS   I warrant you, as common as the way between Saint Albans and London.

PRINCE   How might we see Falstaff bestow himself 161 tonight in his true colors, and not ourselves be seen?

POINS   Put on two leathern jerkins and aprons, and wait 163 upon him at his table as drawers. 164

PRINCE   From a God to a bull? A heavy declension! It 165 was Jove's case. From a prince to a prentice? A low 166 transformation! That shall be mine, for in everything

the purpose must weigh with the folly. Follow me, 168 Ned.   *Exeunt.*

❖

2.3   *Enter Northumberland, his wife [Lady Northumberland], and the wife to Harry Percy [Lady Percy].*

NORTHUMBERLAND
I pray thee, loving wife and gentle daughter,   1
Give even way unto my rough affairs.   2
Put not you on the visage of the times   3
And be like them to Percy troublesome.   4

LADY NORTHUMBERLAND
I have given over; I will speak no more.
Do what you will; your wisdom be your guide.

NORTHUMBERLAND
Alas, sweet wife, my honor is at pawn,
And, but my going, nothing can redeem it.   8

LADY PERCY
O, yet, for God's sake, go not to these wars!
The time was, Father, that you broke your word,
When you were more endeared to it than now,   11
When your own Percy, when my heart's dear Harry,
Threw many a northward look to see his father
Bring up his powers; but he did long in vain.   14
Who then persuaded you to stay at home?
There were two honors lost, yours and your son's.
For yours, the God of heaven brighten it!   17
For his, it stuck upon him as the sun
In the gray vault of heaven, and by his light   19
Did all the chivalry of England move   20
To do brave acts. He was indeed the glass   21
Wherein the noble youth did dress themselves.
He had no legs that practiced not his gait;   23
And speaking thick, which nature made his
  blemish,   24
Became the accents of the valiant,
For those that could speak low and tardily
Would turn their own perfection to abuse   27
To seem like him. So that in speech, in gait,
In diet, in affections of delight,   29
In military rules, humors of blood,   30
He was the mark and glass, copy and book,   31
That fashioned others. And him, O, wondrous him!
O, miracle of men! Him did you leave,
Second to none, unseconded by you,   34
To look upon the hideous god of war

---

124 **by yea and no** (A mild Puritan oath.)   126 **familiars** intimate friends   128 **steep** soak   130 **twenty** i.e., a considerable number
139 **frank** sty, pen. (Often thought to refer to the Boar's Head Tavern.)
142 **Ephesians . . . church** i.e., good fellows of the usual, disreputable fellowship   146 **pagan** i.e., harlot   150 **town bull** a communally owned bull that local farmers could mate with their heifers
158 **should** must.   **road** i.e., common whore   161 **bestow** behave
163 **jerkins** jackets   164 **drawers** tapsters, tavern waiters   165 **heavy declension** grievous descent   166 **Jove's case** (Jupiter, for the love of Europa, transformed himself into a bull.)

168 **weigh with** match, counterbalance
2.3. Location: Warkworth. Before Northumberland's castle.
1 **daughter** i.e., daughter-in-law   2 **Give . . . affairs** i.e., make things as easy for me as you can at this difficult time   3 **Put . . . times** i.e., don't look as bleak or troubled as are the times   4 **to Percy** i.e., to me   8 **but** except for   11 **endeared** pledged, bound by affection
14 **powers** armed forces   17 **For** as for   19 **gray** sky-blue   20 **chivalry** men-at-arms   21 **glass** mirror   23 **He . . . gait** i.e., there was no man alive and able to walk who did not imitate Hotspur's stride
24 **thick** impulsively, impetuously   27 **turn . . . abuse** i.e., debase their own manner of speech and adopt his   29 **affections of delight** tastes for pleasure   30 **humors of blood** temperament   31 **mark** mark to aim at   34 **unseconded** unsupported

In disadvantage, to abide a field   36
Where nothing but the sound of Hotspur's name
Did seem defensible. So you left him.   38
Never, O, never do his ghost the wrong
To hold your honor more precise and nice   40
With others than with him! Let them alone.
The Marshal and the Archbishop are strong.
Had my sweet Harry had but half their numbers,
Today might I, hanging on Hotspur's neck,
Have talked of Monmouth's grave.
NORTHUMBERLAND   Beshrew your heart,   45
Fair daughter, you do draw my spirits from me
With new lamenting ancient oversights.   47
But I must go and meet with danger there,
Or it will seek me in another place
And find me worse provided.
LADY NORTHUMBERLAND   O, fly to Scotland,   50
Till that the nobles and the armèd commons
Have of their puissance made a little taste.   52
LADY PERCY
If they get ground and vantage of the King,   53
Then join you with them like a rib of steel,
To make strength stronger; but, for all our loves,
First let them try themselves. So did your son;   56
He was so suffered. So came I a widow,   57
And never shall have length of life enough
To rain upon remembrance with mine eyes,   59
That it may grow and sprout as high as heaven
For recordation to my noble husband.   61
NORTHUMBERLAND
Come, come, go in with me. 'Tis with my mind
As with the tide swelled up unto his height,
That makes a still-stand, running neither way.   64
Fain would I go to meet the Archbishop,   65
But many thousand reasons hold me back.
I will resolve for Scotland. There am I,   67
Till time and vantage crave my company.   Exeunt. 68

❖

2.4   *Enter a Drawer, [Francis, and another].*

FRANCIS What the devil hast thou brought there?
Applejohns? Thou knowest Sir John cannot endure 2
an applejohn.
SECOND DRAWER Mass, thou sayst true. The Prince 4
once set a dish of applejohns before him, and told

---

36 In disadvantage i.e., outnumbered. **abide a field** face a battle
38 defensible able to make defense **40 To . . . nice** to be more
punctilious in honoring your commitments **45 Monmouth's** i.e.,
Prince Hal's (since he was born at Monmouth). **Beshrew your heart**
(A reproachful oath.) **47 new lamenting** lamenting anew **50 provided** prepared **52 taste** trial **53 get . . . of** achieve a military advantage over **56 try** test **57 suffered** allowed to proceed. **came**
became **59 rain . . . eyes** water remembrance with my tears, as
though it were a plant like rosemary **61 recordation** remembrance,
memorial **64 still-stand** point of balance, standstill **65 Fain** gladly
67 resolve for decide to go to **68 vantage** opportunity
**2.4. Location: London. A tavern in Eastcheap, usually identified as
the Boar's Head. Some tavern furniture is provided.**
2 Applejohns a kind of apple eaten when shriveled and withered
4 Mass i.e., by the Mass

---

him there were five more Sir Johns, and, putting off
his hat, said, "I will now take my leave of these six
dry, round, old, withered knights." It angered him to
the heart. But he hath forgot that.
FRANCIS Why, then, cover, and set them down. And 10
see if thou canst find out Sneak's noise; Mistress Tear- 11
sheet would fain hear some music.

Enter Will [a third Drawer].

THIRD DRAWER Dispatch! The room where they 13
supped is too hot; they'll come in straight.   14
FRANCIS Sirrah, here will be the Prince and Master
Poins anon, and they will put on two of our jerkins
and aprons, and Sir John must not know of it.
Bardolph hath brought word.
THIRD DRAWER By the Mass, here will be old utas. It 19
will be an excellent stratagem.
SECOND DRAWER I'll see if I can find out Sneak. *Exit.*

*Enter Mistress Quickly [the Hostess] and Doll
Tearsheet.*

HOSTESS I' faith, sweetheart, methinks now you are in
an excellent good temperality. Your pulsidge beats as 23
extraordinarily as heart would desire, and your color, 24
I warrant you, is as red as any rose, in good truth, la!
But, i' faith, you have drunk too much canaries, and 26
that's a marvelous searching wine, and it perfumes 27
the blood ere one can say, "What's this?" How do you
now?
DOLL Better than I was. Hem!
HOSTESS Why, that's well said. A good heart's worth
gold. Lo, here comes Sir John.

Enter Sir John [Falstaff].

FALSTAFF [singing] "When Arthur first in court"— 33
Empty the jordan. [Exit a Drawer.]—[Singing.] "And 34
was a worthy king." How now, Mistress Doll?
HOSTESS Sick of a calm, yea, good faith.   36
FALSTAFF So is all her sect. An they be once in a calm, 37
they are sick.
DOLL A pox damn you, you muddy rascal, is that all
the comfort you give me?
FALSTAFF You make fat rascals, Mistress Doll.   41
DOLL I make them! Gluttony and diseases make them;
I make them not.
FALSTAFF If the cook help to make the gluttony, you
help to make the diseases, Doll. We catch of you, Doll,
we catch of you. Grant that, my poor virtue, grant that.
DOLL Yea, joy, our chains and our jewels.   47
FALSTAFF "Your brooches, pearls, and ouches." For to 48
serve bravely is to come halting off, you know; to

---

10 cover spread the cloth, set the table **11 noise** band of musicians
13 Dispatch hurry up **14 straight** very soon **19 old utas** i.e., rare
fun **23 temperality** i.e., temper. **pulsidge** i.e., pulse **24 extraordinarily** i.e., ordinarily **26 canaries** (A light, sweet wine from the Canary Islands.) **27 searching** potent **33 When . . . court** (A fragment
from the ballad "Sir Launcelot du Lake.") **34 jordan** chamber pot
36 calm i.e., qualm **37 sect** sex **41 rascals** (1) lean deer (2) good-
for-nothings **47 Yea . . . jewels** i.e., yes, indeed, you *catch* or steal
our valuables **48 ouches** jewels. (The line is from a ballad.)

come off the breach with his pike bent bravely, and to
surgery bravely; to venture upon the charged cham- 51
bers bravely— 52

DOLL　Hang yourself, you muddy conger, hang yourself!

HOSTESS　By my troth, this is the old fashion. You two
never meet but you fall to some discord. You are both,
i' good truth, as rheumatic as two dry toasts; you 57
cannot one bear with another's confirmities. What the 58
goodyear! One must bear, and that [to Doll] must be 59
you. You are the weaker vessel, as they say, the
emptier vessel.

DOLL　Can a weak empty vessel bear such a huge full
hogshead? There's a whole merchant's venture of Bor- 63
deaux stuff in him; you have not seen a hulk better 64
stuffed in the hold. Come, I'll be friends with thee,
Jack. Thou art going to the wars, and whether I shall
ever see thee again or no there is nobody cares.

Enter Drawer.

DRAWER　Sir, Ancient Pistol's below, and would speak 68
with you.

DOLL　Hang him, swaggering rascal! Let him not come
hither. It is the foul-mouth'st rogue in England.

HOSTESS　If he swagger, let him not come here. No, by
my faith, I must live among my neighbors. I'll no 73
swaggerers. I am in good name and fame with the
very best. Shut the door; there comes no swaggerers
here. I have not lived all this while to have swaggering
now. Shut the door, I pray you.

FALSTAFF　Dost thou hear, Hostess?

HOSTESS　Pray ye, pacify yourself, Sir John. There comes
no swaggerers here.

FALSTAFF　Dost thou hear? It is mine ancient.

HOSTESS　Tilly-fally, Sir John, ne'er tell me. Your ancient 82
swaggerer comes not in my doors. I was before Master
Tisick, the debuty, tother day, and, as he said to me, 84
'twas no longer ago than Wednesday last, i' good faith,
"Neighbor Quickly," says he—Master Dumbe, our
minister, was by then—"Neighbor Quickly," says he,
"receive those that are civil, for," said he, "you are in 88
an ill name." Now 'a said so, I can tell whereupon. 89
"For," says he, "you are an honest woman, and well
thought on; therefore take heed what guests you receive. Receive," says he, "no swaggering compan- 92
ions." There comes none here. You would bless you 93
to hear what he said. No, I'll no swaggerers.

FALSTAFF　He's no swaggerer, hostess; a tame cheater, 95
i' faith; you may stroke him as gently as a puppy
greyhound. He'll not swagger with a Barbary hen, if 97
her feathers turn back in any show of resistance.—
Call him up, drawer.　　　　　[Exit Drawer.]

HOSTESS　Cheater, call you him? I will bar no honest 100
man my house, nor no cheater, but I do not love
swaggering, by my troth. I am the worse when one
says "swagger." Feel, masters, how I shake; look you,
I warrant you.

DOLL　So you do, hostess.

HOSTESS　Do I? Yea, in very truth, do I, an 'twere an 106
aspen leaf. I cannot abide swaggerers.

Enter Ancient Pistol, [Bardolph,] and Boy [Page].

PISTOL　God save you, Sir John!

FALSTAFF　Welcome, Ancient Pistol. Here, Pistol, I
charge you with a cup of sack. Do you discharge upon 110
mine hostess.

PISTOL　I will discharge upon her, Sir John, with two
bullets.

FALSTAFF　She is pistol-proof, sir; you shall not hardly 114
offend her. 115

HOSTESS　Come, I'll drink no proofs nor no bullets. I'll
drink no more than will do me good, for no man's
pleasure, I.

PISTOL　Then to you, Mistress Dorothy; I will charge
you.

DOLL　Charge me? I scorn you, scurvy companion.
What, you poor, base, rascally, cheating, lack-linen 122
mate? Away, you moldy rogue, away! I am meat for 123
your master.

PISTOL　I know you, Mistress Dorothy.

DOLL　Away, you cutpurse rascal! You filthy bung, 126
away! By this wine, I'll thrust my knife in your moldy
chops an you play the saucy cuttle with me. Away, 128
you bottle-ale rascal! You basket-hilt stale juggler, you! 129
Since when, I pray you, sir? God's light, with two 130
points on your shoulder? Much! 131

PISTOL　God let me not live, but I will murder your ruff 132
for this.

FALSTAFF　No more, Pistol, I would not have you go off
here. Discharge yourself of our company, Pistol.

51–52 charged chambers small cannon; with bawdy double meaning, as also in *breach, pike, surgery* (venereal treatment), *conger* (eel,
with sexual connotation), *bear* **57 rheumatic** (Blunder for "choleric"
or "splenetic"?) **58 confirmities** (For "infirmities.") **58–59 What
the goodyear** (An expletive, meaning something like "what the
devil.") **59 bear** (1) put up with another's infirmities (2) bear the
weight of a lover (3) bear children **63 hogshead** large cask. **venture**
cargo **63–64 Bordeaux stuff** i.e., wine **64 hulk** large, unwieldy
cargo ship **68 Ancient** ensign, standard-bearer **73 I'll no** I'll have
no **82 Tilly-fally** i.e., fiddlesticks **84 Tisick** (Literally, phthisic, a
cough or consumption.) **debuty** deputy, deputy alderman
88–89 are . . . name have a bad reputation **89 whereupon** upon
what grounds **92–93 companions** ruffians **93 bless you** i.e., feel
yourself fortunate

95 tame cheater decoy in a team of confidence men **97 Barbary hen**
guinea hen. (Slang term for a prostitute.) **100 Cheater** (Mistress
Quickly may understand the word as *escheator*, "an officer of the
King's exchequer.") **106 an 'twere** i.e., as if I were **110 charge**
pledge, drink to. **discharge upon** toast; with bawdy double meaning;
see also *charge, Pistol, bullets* (testicles), *meat* (slang for "whore"),
etc. **114 pistol-proof** (1) invulnerable to the charms of Pistol (2) sexually impregnable to the *discharge* of *bullets* (testicles). **shall not
hardly** i.e., shall scarcely. (A colloquial expression.) **115 offend her**
do her any harm (with sexual suggestion) **122 lack-linen** i.e., without a shirt to your name **123 mate** low fellow. **meat** (with a pun
on "mate"; pronounced alike) **126 bung** (1) pickpocket (2) something that fills a hole **128 chops** cheeks. **play . . . cuttle** i.e., try
any of your tricks **129 basket-hilt** basketlike hilt or handguard, often
used on a practice weapon; see the note for 3.2.65. (Doll mocks Pistol for his pretense of swashbuckling.) **stale juggler** out-of-date imposter **130 Since when** i.e., since when do you claim to be so brave
and military? **131 points** lace tags (for securing armor to the shoulders). **Much** (An exclamation of scornful incredulity.) **132 murder**
i.e., tear. **ruff** pleated, starched collar

HOSTESS   No, good Captain Pistol, not here, sweet Captain.

DOLL   Captain? Thou abominable damned cheater, art thou not ashamed to be called captain? An captains were of my mind, they would truncheon you out for 140 taking their names upon you before you have earned them. You a captain? You slave, for what? For tearing a poor whore's ruff in a bawdy house? He a captain? Hang him, rogue! He lives upon moldy stewed 144 prunes and dried cakes. A captain? God's light, these 145 villains will make the word as odious as the word "occupy," which was an excellent good word before it 147 was ill sorted. Therefore captains had need look to 't. 148

BARDOLPH   Pray thee, go down, good Ancient.   149

FALSTAFF   Hark thee hither, Mistress Doll.

PISTOL   Not I. I tell thee what, Corporal Bardolph, I could tear her. I'll be revenged of her.

PAGE   Pray thee, go down.

PISTOL   I'll see her damned first, to Pluto's damned 154 lake, by this hand, to th' infernal deep,   155
With Erebus and tortures vile also.   156
Hold hook and line, say I.
Down, down, dogs! Down, faitors!   158
Have we not Hiren here?   159

HOSTESS   Good Captain Peesel, be quiet; 'tis very late, i' faith. I beseek you now, aggravate your choler.   161

PISTOL
These be good humors, indeed! Shall packhorses 162
And hollow pampered jades of Asia,
Which cannot go but thirty mile a day,
Compare with Caesars, and with cannibals,   165
And Troiant Greeks? Nay, rather damn them with 166
King Cerberus, and let the welkin roar.   167
Shall we fall foul for toys?   168

HOSTESS   By my troth, Captain, these are very bitter words.

BARDOLPH   Begone, good Ancient. This will grow to a brawl anon.

PISTOL
Die men like dogs! Give crowns like pins! Have we not Hiren here?   173

HOSTESS   O' my word, Captain, there's none such 174 here. What the goodyear, do you think I would deny 175 her? For God's sake, be quiet.   176

PISTOL
Then feed and be fat, my fair Calipolis.   177
Come, give 's some sack.
Si fortune me tormente, sperato me contento.   179
Fear we broadsides? No, let the fiend give fire.   180
Give me some sack, and, sweetheart, lie thou there.
      [*He lays down his sword.*]
Come we to full points here, and are etceteras nothings?   182

FALSTAFF   Pistol, I would be quiet.

PISTOL
Sweet knight, I kiss thy neaf.   184
What, we have seen the seven stars.   185

DOLL   For God's sake, thrust him downstairs. I cannot endure such a fustian rascal.   187

PISTOL
Thrust him downstairs? Know we not Galloway nags?   188

FALSTAFF   Quoit him down, Bardolph, like a shove- 189 groat shilling. Nay, an 'a do nothing but speak 190 nothing, 'a shall be nothing here.   191

BARDOLPH   Come, get you downstairs.

PISTOL [*snatching up his sword*]
What, shall we have incision? Shall we imbrue?   193
Then death rock me asleep, abridge my doleful days!   194
Why then, let grievous, ghastly, gaping wounds
Untwine the Sisters Three. Come, Atropos, I say!   196

HOSTESS   Here's goodly stuff toward!   197

FALSTAFF   Give me my rapier, boy.

DOLL   I pray thee, Jack, I pray thee, do not draw.

FALSTAFF [*to Pistol*]   Get you downstairs.   [*They fight.*]

HOSTESS   Here's a goodly tumult! I'll forswear keeping house afore I'll be in these tirrits and frights. So, 202 murder, I warrant now. Alas, alas, put up your naked weapons, put up your naked weapons.
      [*Exit Bardolph, driving Pistol out.*]

---

140 truncheon you out cudgel you out of the service with their officers' batons   **144–145 stewed prunes** (Associated with brothels.) **147 occupy** fornicate   **148 ill sorted** corrupted, put in such bad company.   **had need** would do well to   **149 go down** calm down, or, go downstairs and leave   **154–155 Pluto's damned lake** a river of the underworld   **156 Erebus** the underworld   **158 faitors** imposters, cheats   **159 Hiren** i.e., Pistol's fanciful name for his sword, with a seeming allusion to a lost play by Peele, *The Turkish Mahomet and Hiren the Fair Greek. Hiren* means "Irene." (Throughout, Pistol's colorful speech is full of echoes of the contemporary theater.)   **161 beseek** beseech.   **aggravate** (For "moderate.")   **162 good humors** i.e., fine goings-on   **162–166 Shall . . . Greeks** (Misquotation from Marlowe's *2 Tamburlaine,* 4.4.1–2.)   **165 cannibals** (The association here with Caesar would seem to suggest "Hannibals," but *cannibals* appears in the apparent source for this passage, John Eliot's *Orthoepia Gallica,* 1593. Pistol is ready to take on cannibals, Trojan Greeks, or anybody.)   **166 Troiant** Trojan   **167 Cerberus** three-headed dog guarding the entrance to Hades.   **welkin** heavens   **168 fall . . . toys** fall out over trifles   **173 Give crowns like pins** pass out kingdoms as if they were of the value of a pin (as Tamburlaine does to his followers)

174–175 there's none such here (The hostess seems to think that Pistol is asking after Hiren or Irene as though she were a boarder or habitué of the tavern.)   **175–176 deny her** deny that she was here, if she were   **177 Then . . . Calipolis** (Garbled version of a line in Peele's *The Battle of Alcazar,* 2.3.70.)   **179 Si . . . contento** if fortune torments me, hope contents me. (An ignorant medley of Spanish and Italian.)   **180 broadsides** volleys fired from one side of a ship. **give fire** shoot   **182 full points** full stops, periods; also, swords' points.   **etceteras nothings** (Both words suggest the female sexual anatomy.)   **184 neaf** fist   **185 the seven stars** the Pleiades, or Big Dipper. (Pistol means they have enjoyed themselves at night.) **187 fustian** bombast, worthless   **188 Galloway nags** a Scottish breed of small but swift horses (here used abusively to mean "harlots") **189 Quoit** throw   **189–190 shove-groat shilling** an Edward VI shilling used in shove-groat, a game in which the coins were shoved toward a mark   **190 an 'a** if he   **190–191 speak nothing** speak nonsense   **191 nothing here** gone from here   **193 incision** bloodshed. **imbrue** shed blood   **194 death . . . asleep** (Quotation from a poem written by Anne Boleyn or her brother as they awaited execution.) **196 Sisters Three** i.e., the three Fates: Clotho, Lachesis, and Atropos. Atropos severed the thread of life.   **197 toward** forthcoming   **202 tirrits** agitations, fits

DOLL I pray thee, Jack, be quiet; the rascal's gone. Ah, you whoreson little valiant villain, you!

HOSTESS Are you not hurt i' the groin? Methought 'a made a shrewd thrust at your belly.   208

[Enter Bardolph.]

FALSTAFF Have you turned him out o' doors?

BARDOLPH Yea, sir. The rascal's drunk. You have hurt him, sir, i' the shoulder.

FALSTAFF A rascal! To brave me?

DOLL Ah, you sweet little rogue, you! Alas, poor ape, how thou sweat'st! Come, let me wipe thy face. Come on, you whoreson chops. Ah, rogue, i' faith, I love 215 thee. Thou art as valorous as Hector of Troy, worth 216 five of Agamemnon, and ten times better than the 217 Nine Worthies. Ah, villain!   218

FALSTAFF A rascally slave! I will toss the rogue in a blanket.

DOLL Do, an thou dar'st for thy heart. An thou dost, I'll 221 canvass thee between a pair of sheets.   222

Enter Music.

PAGE The music is come, sir.

FALSTAFF Let them play. Play, sirs. Sit on my knee, Doll. A rascal bragging slave! The rogue fled from me like quicksilver.

DOLL [sitting on his knee] I' faith, and thou followedst him like a church. Thou whoreson little tidy Bartholo- 228 mew boar-pig, when wilt thou leave fighting o' days 229 and foining o' nights, and begin to patch up thine old 230 body for heaven?

Enter [behind] Prince and Poins [disguised as drawers].

FALSTAFF Peace, good Doll, do not speak like a death's-head; do not bid me remember mine end.   233

DOLL Sirrah, what humor's the Prince of?   234

FALSTAFF A good shallow young fellow. 'A would have made a good pantler, 'a would ha' chipped bread well. 236

DOLL They say Poins has a good wit.

FALSTAFF He a good wit? Hang him, baboon! His wit's as thick as Tewkesbury mustard. There's no more con- 239 ceit in him than is in a mallet.   240

DOLL Why does the Prince love him so, then?

FALSTAFF Because their legs are both of a bigness, and 242 'a plays at quoits well, and eats conger and fennel, and 243 drinks off candles' ends for flapdragons, and rides the 244 wild mare with the boys, and jumps upon joint 245 stools, and swears with a good grace, and wears his 246 boots very smooth like unto the sign of the Leg, and 247 breeds no bate with telling of discreet stories; and such 248 other gambol faculties 'a has that show a weak mind 249 and an able body, for the which the Prince admits him. For the Prince himself is such another; the weight of a hair will turn the scales between their avoirdupois.   253

PRINCE [to Poins] Would not this nave of a wheel 254 have his ears cut off?   255

POINS Let's beat him before his whore.   256

PRINCE Look whe'er the withered elder hath not his 257 poll clawed like a parrot.   258

POINS Is it not strange that desire should so many years outlive performance?

FALSTAFF Kiss me, Doll.

PRINCE [to Poins] Saturn and Venus this year in 262 conjunction? What says th' almanac to that?   263

POINS And look whether the fiery Trigon, his man, be 264 not lisping to his master's old tables, his notebook, his 265 counsel keeper.

FALSTAFF [to Doll] Thou dost give me flattering busses. 267

DOLL By my troth, I kiss thee with a most constant heart.

FALSTAFF I am old, I am old.

DOLL I love thee better than I love e'er a scurvy young boy of them all.

FALSTAFF What stuff wilt have a kirtle of? I shall 273 receive money o' Thursday; shalt have a cap tomor-row. A merry song, come. It grows late; we'll to bed. Thou'lt forget me when I am gone.

DOLL By my troth, thou'lt set me a-weeping an thou 277

---

208 shrewd vicious **215 chops** fat jaws **216 Hector of Troy** leader of the Trojans; the type of valor **217 Agamemnon** leader of the Greeks at Troy **218 Nine Worthies** Hector, Alexander, Julius Caesar; Joshua, David, Judas Maccabaeus; Arthur, Charlemagne, Godfrey of Boulogne **221 for thy heart** to save your life **222 canvass** toss. (Doll gives a sexual interpretation to Falstaff's phrase, *toss . . . in a blanket,* which means to subject a coward to ignominious treatment.) **s.d. Music** musicians **228 a church** i.e., a ponderous structure (?) **tidy** plump, tender **228–229 Bartholomew boar-pig** (Allusion to the serving of roast pig at Bartholomew Fair, August 24, in Smithfield.) **230 foining** thrusting, fornicating **233 death's-head** skull, used emblematically as a reminder of the inevitability of death **234 what . . . of** what is the Prince's disposition, temperament, mood **236 pantler** pantry worker. **chipped bread** cut off the hard bread crusts **239 Tewkesbury mustard** (Tewkesbury in Gloucestershire was famous for mustard.) **239–240 conceit** wit **240 mallet** wooden hammer, heavy and not at all sharp

242 of a bigness of equal size **243 conger and fennel** conger eel seasoned with a yellow-flowered herb. (Rich fare, likely to dull the wits.) **244 drinks . . . flapdragons** i.e., drinks liquor with a lighted candle floating in it, or extinguishes the candle with his mouth. (An act of bravado.) **245 wild mare** seesaw, or a game in which boys pile on top of one another until the *mare* collapses **245–246 joint stools** stools made by a joiner or craftsman **247 smooth** i.e., well-fitting. **sign . . . Leg** sign over a bootmaker's shop **248 breeds no bate** causes no strife. (Falstaff may be saying sardonically that Poins is not one to bore his listeners by limiting himself to discreet stories.) **249 gambol** sportive **253 avoirdupois** weight **254 nave** hub. (Refers to Falstaff's rotundity; with a pun on "knave.") **255 have . . . off** i.e., as the punishment for slandering royalty **256 before** in front of **257 elder** (1) elder tree (2) old man **258 poll . . . parrot** (Doll is probably rumpling the hair on Falstaff's head, his *poll.*) **262–263 Saturn . . . conjunction** i.e., will the planets that govern old age and love be near one another in the heavens? **264 fiery Trigon** (The twelve signs of the zodiac were divided into four *trigons* or triangles, one of which, consisting of Aries, Leo, and Sagittarius, was characterized as fiery. These three form a triangle because they are not contiguous on the circle of the zodiac but occur at points equivalent roughly to April, August, and December, at 120-degree intervals. The other three *trigons* were characterized as watery, airy, and earthy. The joke here is directed against Bardolph's fiery face.) **265 lisping . . . notebook** whispering lovingly to Falstaff's old confidante, i.e., Mistress Quickly. **tables** notebook (for assignations) **267 busses** kisses **273 stuff** material. **kirtle** skirt **277 an** if

sayst so. Prove that ever I dress myself handsome till
thy return—well, hearken a' th' end.   279

FALSTAFF   Some sack, Francis.

PRINCE, POINS [*coming forward*]   Anon, anon, sir.   281

FALSTAFF   Ha? A bastard son of the King's? And art not
thou Poins his brother?

PRINCE   Why, thou globe of sinful continents, what a   284
life dost thou lead!

FALSTAFF   A better than thou. I am a gentleman; thou
art a drawer.

PRINCE   Very true, sir, and I come to draw you out by   288
the ears.   289

HOSTESS   O, the Lord preserve Thy Grace! By my troth,
welcome to London. Now, the Lord bless that sweet
face of thine! O Jesu, are you come from Wales?

FALSTAFF   Thou whoreson mad compound of majesty,   293
by this light flesh and corrupt blood, thou art wel-   294
come.

DOLL   How, you fat fool! I scorn you.

POINS   My lord, he will drive you out of your revenge
and turn all to a merriment, if you take not the heat.   298

PRINCE   You whoreson candle-mine you, how vilely   299
did you speak of me even now before this honest,   300
virtuous, civil gentlewoman!

HOSTESS   God's blessing of your good heart! And so
she is, by my troth.

FALSTAFF   Didst thou hear me?

PRINCE   Yea, and you knew me, as you did when you   305
ran away by Gad's Hill. You knew I was at your back,   306
and spoke it on purpose to try my patience.

FALSTAFF   No, no, no, not so, I did not think thou wast
within hearing.

PRINCE   I shall drive you then to confess the willful
abuse, and then I know how to handle you.

FALSTAFF   No abuse, Hal, o' mine honor, no abuse.

PRINCE   Not? To dispraise me, and call me pantler and   313
bread-chipper and I know not what?

FALSTAFF   No abuse, Hal.

POINS   No abuse?

FALSTAFF   No abuse, Ned, i' the world, honest Ned,
none. I dispraised him before the wicked, that the
wicked might not fall in love with thee [*to Hal*]; in
which doing, I have done the part of a careful friend
and a true subject, and thy father is to give me thanks
for it. No abuse, Hal. None, Ned, none. No, faith,
boys, none.

PRINCE   See now whether pure fear and entire coward-   324
ice doth not make thee wrong this virtuous gentle-

woman to close with us. Is she of the wicked? Is thine   326
hostess here of the wicked? Or is thy boy of the
wicked? Or honest Bardolph, whose zeal burns in his
nose, of the wicked?

POINS   Answer, thou dead elm, answer.

FALSTAFF   The fiend hath pricked down Bardolph irre-   331
coverable, and his face is Lucifer's privy kitchen,   332
where he doth nothing but roast maltworms. For the   333
boy, there is a good angel about him, but the devil
blinds him too.   335

PRINCE   For the women?

FALSTAFF   For one of them, she's in hell already and
burns poor souls. For th' other, I owe her money, and   338
whether she be damned for that I know not.   339

HOSTESS   No, I warrant you.

FALSTAFF   No, I think thou art not; I think thou art quit 341
for that. Marry, there is another indictment upon thee,   342
for suffering flesh to be eaten in thy house, contrary to   343
the law, for the which I think thou wilt howl.   344

HOSTESS   All victuallers do so. What's a joint of mutton   345
or two in a whole Lent?

PRINCE   You, gentlewoman—

DOLL   What says Your Grace?

FALSTAFF   His Grace says that which his flesh rebels   349
against.   *Peto knocks at door.* 350

HOSTESS   Who knocks so loud at door? Look to the
door there, Francis.

[Francis goes to the door. Enter Peto.]

PRINCE   Peto, how now, what news?

PETO
The King your father is at Westminster,
And there are twenty weak and wearied posts   355
Come from the north. And as I came along
I met and overtook a dozen captains,
Bareheaded, sweating, knocking at the taverns,
And asking everyone for Sir John Falstaff.

PRINCE
By heaven, Poins, I feel me much to blame,
So idly to profane the precious time
When tempest of commotion, like the south   362
Borne with black vapor, doth begin to melt   363
And drop upon our bare unarmèd heads.
Give me my sword and cloak. Falstaff, good night.
Exeunt Prince and Poins, [and Peto].

279 hearken a' th' end i.e., wait to see how it turns out   **281 Anon, anon** (The cry of the drawer, or tapster, in answering his customers' demands for service, as in *1 Henry IV*, 2.4.21 ff.)   **284 globe** (1) terrestrial globe (2) sphere.   **continents** (1) the continents of the earth (2) contents (3) containers (of sin)   **288–289 draw . . . ears** (as one might grab by the ears a naughty child caught in some mischief)   **293 compound** lump, mass   **294 by . . . blood** (An extension of the oath, "by this light," here reworded to apply to Doll.)   **298 if . . . heat** if you don't strike while the iron is hot   **299 candle-mine** magazine or storehouse of tallow   **300 honest** chaste   **305–306 Yea . . . Gad's Hill** (See *1 Henry IV*, 2.4.)   **313 Not** i.e., you mean it's not abuse?   **324 entire** sheer

326 close come to terms, agree   **331 pricked down** marked, or designated   **332 privy** private   **333 maltworms** topers, drunkards.   **For** as for   **335 blinds** (A textual crux. The Folio reads *outbids*; it sometimes is emended to *attends* or *binds*.)   **338 burns** i.e., infects with venereal disease   **339 damned** (since usury was condemned by the church as well as the state)   **341–342 quit for that** (1) acquitted of that charge (2) repaid (as much as you are ever likely to be)   **343 flesh to be eaten** (Allusion to enactments to prevent the sale of meat in Lent; with sexual double entendre on *mutton*, "whore.")   **344 howl** (like damned souls in hell)   **345 victuallers** i.e., innkeepers   **349–350 His Grace . . . against** i.e., the Prince may call Doll "gentlewoman" all he likes, but his rebellious flesh looks at her in a different way. (With a pun on *Grace* as royal grace and inclination toward spiritual grace.)   **355 posts** messengers   **362 commotion** insurrection.   **south** south wind (regarded as a breeder of tempests)   **363 Borne** laden

FALSTAFF Now comes in the sweetest morsel of the night, and we must hence and leave it unpicked. [*Knocking within. Bardolph goes to the door.*] More knocking at the door!

[*Bardolph returns.*]

How now, what's the matter?

BARDOLPH
You must away to court, sir, presently.   371
A dozen captains stay at door for you.   372

FALSTAFF [*to the Page*] Pay the musicians, sirrah. Farewell, hostess; farewell, Doll. You see, my good wenches, how men of merit are sought after. The undeserver may sleep, when the man of action is called on. Farewell, good wenches. If I be not sent away post, 377 I will see you again ere I go.

DOLL I cannot speak. If my heart be not ready to burst—well, sweet Jack, have a care of thyself.

FALSTAFF Farewell, farewell.
                                        Exit [*with Bardolph and Page*].

HOSTESS Well, fare thee well. I have known thee these twenty-nine years come peascod time, but an honest- 383 er and truer-hearted man—well, fare thee well.

BARDOLPH [*at the door*] Mistress Tearsheet!

HOSTESS What's the matter?

BARDOLPH Bid Mistress Tearsheet come to my master.

HOSTESS O, run, Doll, run; run, good Doll. Come.— She comes blubbered.—Yea, will you come, Doll?   390
                                                    Exeunt.

❧

3.1 *Enter the King in his nightgown, alone* [*with a Page*].

KING
Go call the Earls of Surrey and of Warwick;
But ere they come, bid them o'erread these letters   2
And well consider of them. Make good speed.
                        [*He gives letters. Exit Page.*]
How many thousand of my poorest subjects
Are at this hour asleep! O sleep, O gentle sleep,
Nature's soft nurse, how have I frighted thee,
That thou no more wilt weigh my eyelids down
And steep my senses in forgetfulness?
Why rather, sleep, liest thou in smoky cribs,   9
Upon uneasy pallets stretching thee,   10
And hushed with buzzing night-flies to thy slumber,
Than in the perfumed chambers of the great,
Under the canopies of costly state,   13
And lulled with sound of sweetest melody?
O thou dull god, why liest thou with the vile   15

In loathsome beds, and leavest the kingly couch
A watch-case or a common 'larum bell?   17
Wilt thou upon the high and giddy mast
Seal up the shipboy's eyes, and rock his brains
In cradle of the rude imperious surge   20
And in the visitation of the winds,   21
Who take the ruffian billows by the top,   22
Curling their monstrous heads and hanging them
With deafing clamor in the slippery clouds,   24
That, with the hurly, death itself awakes?   25
Canst thou, O partial sleep, give thy repose
To the wet sea-boy in an hour so rude,
And, in the calmest and most stillest night,
With all appliances and means to boot,   29
Deny it to a king? Then happy low, lie down!   30
Uneasy lies the head that wears a crown.   31

Enter Warwick, Surrey, and Sir John Blunt.

WARWICK
Many good morrows to Your Majesty!

KING Is it good morrow, lords?

WARWICK 'Tis one o'clock, and past.

KING
Why, then, good morrow to you all, my lords.
Have you read o'er the letters that I sent you?

WARWICK We have, my liege.

KING
Then you perceive the body of our kingdom,
How foul it is, what rank diseases grow,   39
And with what danger near the heart of it.

WARWICK
It is but as a body yet distempered,   41
Which to his former strength may be restored   42
With good advice and little medicine.   43
My Lord Northumberland will soon be cooled.

KING
O God, that one might read the book of fate,
And see the revolution of the times   46
Make mountains level, and the continent,   47
Weary of solid firmness, melt itself
Into the sea, and other times to see
The beachy girdle of the ocean
Too wide for Neptune's hips, how chance's mocks   51
And changes fill the cup of alteration
With divers liquors! O, if this were seen,
The happiest youth, viewing his progress through,   54
What perils past, what crosses to ensue,   55
Would shut the book, and sit him down and die.

---

371 presently immediately **372 stay** wait **377 post** immediately **383 peascod time** i.e., early summer, when peas are still unripe **390 blubbered** disfigured with weeping **3.1. Location:** Westminster. The royal court. **s.d. nightgown** dressing gown **2 o'erread** read over **9 cribs** hovels **10 uneasy** uncomfortable. **thee** thyself **13 state** magnificence **15 dull** drowsy. **vile** low in rank

17 watch-case sentry box, or a space in which the occupant is restlessly aware of the passage of time **20 rude** turbulent **21 visitation** violent onset **22 Who** which, i.e., the winds **24 deafing** deafening. **slippery** quickly slipping by **25 That** so that. **hurly** tumult **29 appliances** devices. **to boot** as well, besides **30 low** humble persons **31 s.d. Sir John Blunt** (Since he says nothing and is omitted from the Folio, his presence may be unnecessary, but see line 35, "to you all.") **39 rank** festering **41 distempered** sick **42 his** its **43 little** a little **46 revolution of the times** changes brought by the passage of time **47 continent** dry land **51 Too wide** i.e., vast in expanse, when the ocean recedes. **chance's mocks** (A textual crux. The Quarto and Folio read *chances mocks;* sometimes emended to *chances mock*.) **54 progress through** life's progress from beginning to end **55 crosses** afflictions

'Tis not ten years gone
Since Richard and Northumberland, great friends,
Did feast together, and in two years after
Were they at wars. It is but eight years since
This Percy was the man nearest my soul,   61
Who like a brother toiled in my affairs
And laid his love and life under my foot,   63
Yea, for my sake, even to the eyes of Richard   64
Gave him defiance. But which of you was by—
[*To Warwick*] You, cousin Nevil, as I may
      remember—   66
When Richard, with his eye brimful of tears,
Then checked and rated by Northumberland,   68
Did speak these words, now proved a prophecy?
"Northumberland, thou ladder by the which   70
My cousin Bolingbroke ascends my throne"—
Though then, God knows, I had no such intent,
But that necessity so bowed the state
That I and greatness were compelled to kiss—
"The time shall come," thus did he follow it,
"The time will come, that foul sin, gathering head,
Shall break into corruption"— so went on,   77
Foretelling this same time's condition   78
And the division of our amity.

WARWICK
There is a history in all men's lives,
Figuring the nature of the times deceased,   81
The which observed, a man may prophesy,
With a near aim, of the main chance of things   83
As yet not come to life, who in their seeds   84
And weak beginnings lie intreasurèd.   85
Such things become the hatch and brood of time,   86
And by the necessary form of this   87
King Richard might create a perfect guess
That great Northumberland, then false to him,
Would of that seed grow to a greater falseness,
Which should not find a ground to root upon
Unless on you.

KING   Are these things then necessities?
Then let us meet them like necessities;
And that same word even now cries out on us.   94
They say the Bishop and Northumberland
Are fifty thousand strong.

WARWICK   It cannot be, my lord.
Rumor doth double, like the voice and echo,
The numbers of the feared. Please it Your Grace
To go to bed. Upon my soul, my lord,
The powers that you already have sent forth
Shall bring this prize in very easily.
To comfort you the more, I have received
A certain instance that Glendower is dead.   103

Your Majesty hath been this fortnight ill,
And these unseasoned hours perforce must add   105
Unto your sickness.
KING   I will take your counsel.
And were these inward wars once out of hand,   107
We would, dear lords, unto the Holy Land. *Exeunt.*

3.2   *Enter Justice Shallow and Justice Silence.*

SHALLOW   Come on, come on, come on, give me your
   hand, sir, give me your hand, sir. An early stirrer, by
   the rood! And how doth my good cousin Silence?   3
SILENCE   Good morrow, good cousin Shallow.
SHALLOW   And how doth my cousin your bedfellow?
   And your fairest daughter and mine, my goddaughter
   Ellen?
SILENCE   Alas, a black ouzel, cousin Shallow!   8
SHALLOW   By yea and no, sir. I dare say my cousin
   William is become a good scholar. He is at Oxford still,
   is he not?
SILENCE   Indeed, sir, to my cost.
SHALLOW   'A must then to the Inns o' Court shortly. I 13
   was once of Clement's Inn, where I think they will talk 14
   of mad Shallow yet.
SILENCE   You were called "lusty Shallow" then, cousin. 16
SHALLOW   By the Mass, I was called anything, and I
   would have done anything indeed too, and roundly   18
   too. There was I, and Little John Doit of Staffordshire,
   and black George Barnes, and Francis Pickbone, and
   Will Squele, a Cotswold man. You had not four such 21
   swinge-bucklers in all the Inns o' Court again. And I 22
   may say to you, we knew where the bona-robas were 23
   and had the best of them all at commandment. Then 24
   was Jack Falstaff, now Sir John, a boy, and page to   25
   Thomas Mowbray, Duke of Norfolk.   26
SILENCE   This Sir John, cousin, that comes hither anon
   about soldiers?
SHALLOW   The same Sir John, the very same. I see him 29
   break Scoggin's head at the court gate, when 'a was a 30
   crack not thus high. And the very same day did I fight 31
   with one Sampson Stockfish, a fruiterer, behind
   Gray's Inn. Jesu, Jesu, the mad days that I have spent! 33

61 This Percy i.e., Northumberland   **63 under my foot** i.e., under
my control   **64 to the eyes** i.e., face to face   **66 Nevil** (An error; this
Earl of Warwick's surname is Beauchamp.)   **68 checked and rated** rebuked   **70–77 Northumberland . . . corruption** (See *Richard II,*
5.1.55 ff.)   **78 same** present   **81 Figuring** depicting, reproducing.
deceased past   **83 main chance** probable outcome   **84 who** which
85 intreasurèd stored up   **86 hatch and brood** offspring   **87 necessary form** inevitable pattern   **94 cries out on** denounces   **103 certain instance** unquestionable proof

105 unseasoned unseasonable, late   **107 inward** civil.   **out of hand**
done with
**3.2. Location: Gloucestershire. Before Justice Shallow's house. A ta-
ble and chairs must be provided onstage.**
3 rood cross.   **cousin** kinsman (as also at lines 4, 5, and 9)   **8 ouzel**
blackbird. (Ellen is *black* or dark-complexioned, not fair.)   **13 Inns o'
Court** legal societies of London   **14 Clement's Inn** one of the Inns of
Chancery; in Shallow's time, these institutions prepared one for the
Inns of Court   **16 lusty** merry, lascivious   **18 roundly** thoroughly,
without ceremony   **21 Cotswold** from the Cotswold Hills in Gloucestershire   **22 swinge-bucklers** swashbucklers, roisterers   **23 bona-
robas** good-looking wenches, smart-looking prostitutes   **24 at commandment** at our beck and call   **25–26 page to Thomas Mowbray**
(Both Sir John Oldcastle, Falstaff's original, and Sir John Fastolfe, for
whom Falstaff was renamed, were pages to the Duke of Norfolk, who
figures in the play *Richard II.*)   **29 see** saw   **30 Scoggin** (Perhaps John
Scogan, court jester to Edward IV and protagonist of an Elizabethan
jestbook known as "Scogan's Jests.")   **31 crack** pert little boy
33 Gray's Inn one of the Inns of Court

And to see how many of my old acquaintance are dead!

SILENCE We shall all follow, cousin.

SHALLOW Certain, 'tis certain, very sure, very sure. Death, as the Psalmist saith, is certain to all, all shall 38 die. How a good yoke of bullocks at Stamford fair? 39

SILENCE By my troth, I was not there.

SHALLOW Death is certain. Is old Double of your town living yet?

SILENCE Dead, sir.

SHALLOW Jesu, Jesu, dead! 'A drew a good bow; and dead? 'A shot a fine shoot. John o' Gaunt loved him 45 well, and betted much money on his head. Dead? 'A would have clapped i' the clout at twelve score, and 47 carried you a forehand shaft a fourteen and fourteen 48 and a half, that it would have done a man's heart good 49 to see. How a score of ewes now?

SILENCE Thereafter as they be; a score of good ewes 51 may be worth ten pounds.

SHALLOW And is old Double dead?

SILENCE Here come two of Sir John Falstaff's men, as I think.

Enter Bardolph and one with him.

SHALLOW Good morrow, honest gentlemen.

BARDOLPH I beseech you, which is Justice Shallow?

SHALLOW I am Robert Shallow, sir, a poor esquire of 58 this county, and one of the King's justices of the peace. What is your good pleasure with me?

BARDOLPH My captain, sir, commends him to you, my 61 captain, Sir John Falstaff, a tall gentleman, by heaven, 62 and a most gallant leader.

SHALLOW He greets me well, sir. I knew him a good backsword man. How doth the good knight? May I 65 ask how my lady his wife doth?

BARDOLPH Sir, pardon; a soldier is better accommo- 67 dated than with a wife. 68

SHALLOW It is well said, in faith, sir, and it is well said indeed too. "Better accommodated"! It is good, yea, indeed is it. Good phrases are surely, and ever were, very commendable. "Accommodated"! It comes of *"accommodo."* Very good, a good phrase.

BARDOLPH Pardon sir, I have heard the word. "Phrase" call you it? By this day, I know not the phrase. But I will maintain the word with my sword to be a soldierlike word, and a word of exceeding good 77 command, by heaven. "Accommodated"; that is, 78 when a man is, as they say, accommodated; or when

a man is being whereby 'a may be thought to be accommodated, which is an excellent thing.

Enter Falstaff.

SHALLOW It is very just.—Look, here comes good Sir 82 John.—Give me your good hand, give me your worship's good hand. By my troth, you like well and 84 bear your years very well. Welcome, good Sir John.

FALSTAFF I am glad to see you well, good Master Robert Shallow.—Master Surecard, as I think?

SHALLOW No, Sir John, it is my cousin Silence, in 88 commission with me. 89

FALSTAFF Good Master Silence, it well befits you should be of the peace. 91

SILENCE Your good worship is welcome.

FALSTAFF Fie, this is hot weather, gentlemen. Have you provided me here half a dozen sufficient men? 94

SHALLOW Marry, have we, sir. Will you sit?

[They sit at a table.]

FALSTAFF Let me see them, I beseech you.

SHALLOW Where's the roll? Where's the roll? Where's the roll? Let me see, let me see, let me see. So, so, so, so, so, so, so; yea, marry, sir. Ralph Moldy! Let them appear as I call; let them do so, let them do so. Let me see, where is Moldy?

[Enter Moldy.]

MOLDY Here, an 't please you. 102

SHALLOW What think you, Sir John? A good-limbed fellow, young, strong, and of good friends. 104

FALSTAFF Is thy name Moldy?

MOLDY Yea, an 't please you.

FALSTAFF 'Tis the more time thou wert used.

SHALLOW Ha, ha, ha! Most excellent, i' faith! Things that are moldy lack use. Very singular good, in faith, well said, Sir John, very well said.

FALSTAFF Prick him. *[Shallow writes on the muster roll.]* 111

MOLDY I was pricked well enough before, an you could 112 have let me alone. My old dame will be undone now 113 for one to do her husbandry and her drudgery. You 114 need not to have pricked me. There are other men fitter to go out than I.

FALSTAFF Go to. Peace, Moldy, you shall go, Moldy, it is time you were spent. 118

MOLDY Spent?

SHALLOW Peace, fellow, peace. Stand aside. Know you where you are? For th' other, Sir John, let me see: 121 Simon Shadow!

[Enter Shadow.]

38–39 **Death . . . die** (See Psalm 89:48.) 39 **How** how much (is the asking price for) 45 **John o' Gaunt** (Father of Henry IV.) 47 **clapped . . . score** hit the bull's-eye at two hundred and forty yards 48–49 **carried . . . half** i.e., could shoot a heavy arrow in a straight line rather than in a curved trajectory for a distance of two hundred and eighty to two hundred and ninety yards 51 **Thereafter . . . be** according to their quality 58 **esquire** (A social rank between gentleman and knight.) 61 **commends him** sends his respects 62 **tall** valiant 65 **backsword** stick with a basket hilt used for fencing practice. (See the note for 2.4.129.) 67–68 **accommodated** furnished, equipped. (A bit of fine language on Bardolph's part.) 77–78 **a word . . . command** a perfectly good military term

82 **just** true 84 **like well** are in good condition, thrive 88–89 **in . . . me** a fellow justice of the peace 91 **of the peace** i.e., a magistrate (with a play on the name *Silence*, "peace") 94 **sufficient** fit for service 102 **an 't** if it (also in line 106) 104 **of good friends** well connected by family 111 **Prick him** mark him down on the list 112 **pricked** i.e., (1) vexed, grieved (2) turning sour or moldy (with sexual suggestion also, continued in *undone, husbandry,* and *spent,* "sexually used up") 113 **dame** mother, or, more probably in view of the sexual punning, "wife" 114 **husbandry** farm work. (But see the note at line 112.) 118 **spent** used up. (But see the note at line 112.) 121 **other** others

FALSTAFF   Yea, marry, let me have him to sit under. He's like to be a cold soldier. 124

SHALLOW   Where's Shadow?

SHADOW   Here, sir.

FALSTAFF   Shadow, whose son art thou?

SHADOW   My mother's son, sir.

FALSTAFF   Thy mother's son! Like enough, and thy 129 father's shadow. So the son of the female is the 130 shadow of the male. It is often so, indeed; but much of the father's substance.

SHALLOW   Do you like him, Sir John?

FALSTAFF   Shadow will serve for summer. Prick him 134 [aside], for we have a number of shadows fill up the 135 muster book.

SHALLOW   Thomas Wart!

[Enter Wart.]

FALSTAFF   Where's he?

WART   Here, sir.

FALSTAFF   Is thy name Wart?

WART   Yea, sir.

FALSTAFF   Thou art a very ragged wart.

SHALLOW   Shall I prick him, Sir John?

FALSTAFF   It were superfluous, for his apparel is built upon his back and the whole frame stands upon pins. 145 Prick him no more.

SHALLOW   Ha, ha, ha! You can do it, sir, you can do it. 147 I commend you well.—Francis Feeble!

[Enter Feeble.]

FEEBLE   Here, sir.

SHALLOW   What trade art thou, Feeble?

FEEBLE   A woman's tailor, sir. 151

SHALLOW   Shall I prick him, sir?

FALSTAFF   You may. But if he had been a man's tailor, he'd a' pricked you.—Wilt thou make as many holes 154 in an enemy's battle as thou hast done in a woman's 155 petticoat?

FEEBLE   I will do my good will, sir. You can have no more.

FALSTAFF   Well said, good woman's tailor! Well said, courageous Feeble! Thou wilt be as valiant as the wrathful dove or most magnanimous mouse. Prick the 161 woman's tailor. Well, Master Shallow, deep, Master Shallow.

FEEBLE   I would Wart might have gone, sir.

FALSTAFF   I would thou wert a man's tailor, that thou mightst mend him and make him fit to go. I cannot put him to a private soldier that is the leader of so 167 many thousands. Let that suffice, most forcible Feeble. 168

FEEBLE   It shall suffice, sir.

FALSTAFF   I am bound to thee, reverend Feeble. Who is 170 next?

SHALLOW   Peter Bullcalf o' the green!

[Enter Bullcalf.]

FALSTAFF   Yea, marry, let's see Bullcalf.

BULLCALF   Here, sir.

FALSTAFF   'Fore God, a likely fellow! Come, prick me Bullcalf till he roar again.

BULLCALF   O Lord! Good my lord Captain—

FALSTAFF   What, dost thou roar before thou art pricked?

BULLCALF   O Lord, sir! I am a diseased man.

FALSTAFF   What disease hast thou?

BULLCALF   A whoreson cold, sir, a cough, sir, which I caught with ringing in the King's affairs upon his 182 coronation day, sir. 183

FALSTAFF   Come, thou shalt go to the wars in a gown. 184 We will have away thy cold, and I will take such order 185 that thy friends shall ring for thee.—Is here all? 186

SHALLOW   Here is two more called than your number; you must have but four here, sir. And so, I pray you, go in with me to dinner.

FALSTAFF   Come, I will go drink with you, but I cannot tarry dinner. I am glad to see you, by my troth, Master 191 Shallow.

SHALLOW   O, Sir John, do you remember since we lay 193 all night in the Windmill in Saint George's Field? 194

FALSTAFF   No more of that, good Master Shallow, no more of that.

SHALLOW   Ha! 'Twas a merry night. And is Jane Nightwork alive?

FALSTAFF   She lives, Master Shallow.

SHALLOW   She never could away with me. 200

FALSTAFF   Never, never; she would always say she could not abide Master Shallow.

SHALLOW   By the Mass, I could anger her to the heart. She was then a bona-roba. Doth she hold her own well?

FALSTAFF   Old, old, Master Shallow.

SHALLOW   Nay, she must be old. She cannot choose but be old. Certain she's old, and had Robin Nightwork by old Nightwork before I came to Clement's Inn.

SILENCE   That's fifty-five year ago.

SHALLOW   Ha, cousin Silence, that thou hadst seen that that this knight and I have seen! Ha, Sir John, said I well?

124 like likely. cold (1) cool, deliberate (2) cowardly 129 son (With play on "sun.") 130 shadow i.e., image and namesake. (But, Falstaff jests, the father is only uncertainly copied in his son, since no man can ever be sure of his paternity the way a mother is sure that a child is truly hers. Yet the child consumes much of the father's substance.) 134 serve (1) suffice (2) be inducted. for summer (when shade is desirable) 135 shadows i.e., fictitious names for which the officer in charge receives pay. fill to fill 145 the whole . . . pins i.e., he's pinned together, badly made physically, and therefore needs no more pinpricks. (In a carpentry metaphor, the pins are also pegs for joining timber.) 147 can do it know how to make a joke 151 woman's tailor (Often regarded as an effeminate occupation.) 154 a' pricked (1) have attired (2) have thrust you through. (The word has a sexual suggestion also. Tailor could mean the male or female sex organ.) 155 battle army 161 magnanimous stouthearted

167 put him to enlist him as 168 thousands i.e., of vermin, lice 170 bound obliged 182–183 ringing . . . day i.e., ringing the church bells to celebrate the anniversary of the King's coronation 184 gown dressing gown 185 have away do away with. take such order provide 186 for thee (1) in your place (2) at your death 191 tarry wait for 193 since when 194 the Windmill a brothel, or an inn in a brothel district. Saint George's Field a popular place of resort on the south bank of the Thames 200 away with tolerate

FALSTAFF We have heard the chimes at midnight, Master Shallow.

SHALLOW That we have, that we have, that we have, in faith, Sir John, we have. Our watchword was "Hem boys!" Come, let's to dinner, come, let's to dinner. Jesus, the days that we have seen! Come, come. 217
218

Exeunt [Falstaff and the Justices].

BULLCALF Good Master Corporate Bardolph, stand my friend, and here's four Harry ten shillings in French crowns for you. [*He gives money.*] In very truth, sir, I had as lief be hanged, sir, as go. And yet for mine own part, sir, I do not care, but rather because I am unwilling, and for mine own part have a desire to stay with my friends. Else, sir, I did not care, for mine own part, so much. 220
221
223

BARDOLPH Go to, stand aside.

MOLDY And, good Master Corporal Captain, for my old dame's sake, stand my friend. She has nobody to do anything about her when I am gone, and she is old and cannot help herself. [*He gives money.*] You shall have forty, sir. 233

BARDOLPH Go to, stand aside.

FEEBLE By my troth, I care not. A man can die but once. We owe God a death. I'll ne'er bear a base mind. An 't be my destiny, so; an 't be not, so. No man's too good to serve 's prince. And let it go which way it will, he that dies this year is quit for the next. 239

BARDOLPH Well said. Thou'rt a good fellow.

FEEBLE Faith, I'll bear no base mind. 241

Enter Falstaff and the Justices.

FALSTAFF Come, sir, which men shall I have?

SHALLOW Four of which you please.

BARDOLPH [*to Falstaff*] Sir, a word with you. [*Aside.*] I have three pound to free Moldy and Bullcalf.

FALSTAFF Go to, well. 246

SHALLOW Come, Sir John, which four will you have?

FALSTAFF Do you choose for me.

SHALLOW Marry, then, Moldy, Bullcalf, Feeble, and Shadow.

FALSTAFF Moldy and Bullcalf: for you, Moldy, stay at home till you are past service; and for your part, Bullcalf, grow till you come unto it. I will none of you. 251
252
253

SHALLOW Sir John, Sir John, do not yourself wrong. They are your likeliest men, and I would have you served with the best.

FALSTAFF Will you tell me, Master Shallow, how to choose a man? Care I for the limb, the thews, the stature, bulk, and big assemblance of a man? Give me 258
259

the spirit, Master Shallow. Here's Wart; you see what a ragged appearance it is. 'A shall charge you and discharge you with the motion of a pewterer's hammer, come off and on swifter than he that gibbets on the brewer's bucket. And this same half-faced fellow, Shadow; give me this man. He presents no mark to the enemy; the foeman may with as great aim level at the edge of a penknife. And for a retreat, how swiftly will this Feeble the woman's tailor run off! O, give me the spare men, and spare me the great ones.—Put me a caliver into Wart's hand, Bardolph. 261
262
263
264
266
270

BARDOLPH [*giving Wart a musket*] Hold, Wart, traverse. Thus, thus, thus. 271

FALSTAFF Come, manage me your caliver. So. [*Wart performs maneuvers with the musket.*] Very well. Go to. Very good, exceeding good. O, give me always a little, lean, old, chapped, bald shot. Well said, i' faith, Wart, thou'rt a good scab. Hold, there's a tester for thee. 276
277

[He gives sixpence.]

SHALLOW He is not his craft's master; he doth not do it right. I remember at Mile End Green, when I lay at Clement's Inn—I was then Sir Dagonet in Arthur's show—there was a little quiver fellow, and 'a would manage you his piece thus [*Shallow demonstrates*], and 'a would about and about, and come you in and come you in. "Ra-ta-ta!" would 'a say, "Bounce," would 'a say, and away again would 'a go, and again would 'a come. I shall ne'er see such a fellow. 279
280
281
282
283
284

FALSTAFF These fellows will do well, Master Shallow. God keep you, Master Silence. I will not use many words with you. Fare you well, gentlemen both. I thank you. I must a dozen mile tonight. Bardolph, give the soldiers coats.

SHALLOW Sir John, the Lord bless you! God prosper your affairs! God send us peace! At your return, visit our house; let our old acquaintance be renewed. Peradventure I will with ye to the court.

FALSTAFF 'Fore God, would you would.

SHALLOW Go to; I have spoke at a word. God keep you. 297

FALSTAFF Fare you well, gentle gentlemen. *Exeunt [Justices.]* On, Bardolph; lead the men away. [*Exeunt Bardolph, recruits, etc.*] As I return, I will fetch off these justices. I do see the bottom of Justice Shallow. 300

217–218 Hem boys i.e., down the hatch **220 Corporate** (For "Corporal.") **stand** be, act as **221 Harry ten shillings** i.e., money coined in the reign of Henry VII, current in late Elizabethan times at half the face value. The reference is anachronistic. Four such coins would be worth twenty shillings, or one pound. Bullcalf gives his bribe in *French crowns*, worth four shillings each; presumably he gives five such coins. **223 lief** willingly **233 forty** i.e., forty shillings **239 quit** free, clear **241 bear** have **246 Go to, well** i.e., all right, fine, say no more **251 for** as for **252 past service** (1) too old to serve militarily (2) too old for sexual functioning **253 come unto it** (1) are a man old enough to fight (2) have arrived at sexual maturity **258 thews** strength **259 assemblance** appearance, frame

261–262 charge . . . discharge you load and fire **262–263 motion . . . hammer** i.e., precise, quick motion **263–264 come . . . bucket** raise and lower his musket quicker than a brewer's man raises and lowers the beam (*bucket*) of the brewer's yoke across his shoulders **264 half-faced** thin-faced. (Alludes to the profile portraits on coins.) **266 as great aim** as much likelihood of hitting the target. **level** aim **270 caliver** light musket **271 traverse** march, or, perhaps, perform the manual of arms, an exercise drill with a musket **276 shot** marksman. **Well said** well done **277 scab** rascal (punning on the name *Wart*). **tester** sixpence **279 Mile End Green** a drilling ground for citizen soldiers, to the east of London. **lay** lodged **280–281 Sir . . . show** (An exhibition of archery was held annually at Mile End Green, called "Arthur's show," in which each archer took the name of one of King Arthur's knights; Shallow played the part of Sir Dagonet, Arthur's fool.) **281 quiver** nimble **282 piece** firearm **283–284 'a would . . . you in** i.e., he was skillful at firing and then running around to the rear rank of musketeers to reload while the next rank fired, and so on **284 Bounce** bang **297 I have . . . word** I mean what I say **300 fetch off** get the better of

Lord, Lord, how subject we old men are to this vice of
lying! This same starved justice hath done nothing but
prate to me of the wildness of his youth and the feats
he hath done about Turnbull Street, and every third *305*
word a lie, duer paid to the hearer than the Turk's *306*
tribute. I do remember him at Clement's Inn like a *307*
man made after supper of a cheese paring. When 'a
was naked, he was, for all the world, like a forked radish, with a head fantastically carved upon it with a
knife. 'A was so forlorn that his dimensions to any *311*
thick sight were invisible. 'A was the very genius of *312*
famine, yet lecherous as a monkey, and the whores
called him mandrake. 'A came ever in the rearward of *314*
the fashion, and sung those tunes to the overscutched *315*
huswives that he heard the carmen whistle, and sware *316*
they were his fancies or his good-nights. And now is *317*
this Vice's dagger become a squire, and talks as *318*
familiarly of John o' Gaunt as if he had been sworn *319*
brother to him, and I'll be sworn 'a ne'er saw him but *320*
once in the tilt-yard, and then he burst his head for *321*
crowding among the marshal's men. I saw it, and told
John o' Gaunt he beat his own name, for you might *323*
have thrust him and all his apparel into an eelskin; the *324*
case of a treble hautboy was a mansion for him, a *325*
court. And now has he land and beefs. Well, I'll be *326*
acquainted with him if I return, and 't shall go hard
but I'll make him a philosopher's two stones to me. If *328*
the young dace be a bait for the old pike, I see no *329*
reason in the law of nature but I may snap at him. Let
time shape, and there an end.   [*Exit.*]

❖

4.1   *Enter the Archbishop [of York], Mowbray, [Lord]
Bardolph, Hastings, [and others,] within the Forest
of Gaultree.*

ARCHBISHOP   What is this forest called?

HASTINGS
'Tis Gaultree Forest, an 't shall please Your Grace.   2

305 **Turnbull Street** a street in Clerkenwell, ill-reputed   306 **duer**
more promptly   306–307 **Turk's tribute** tribute money paid annually
to the Sultan of Turkey by merchants and others   311 **forlorn** meager,
thin   312 **thick** imperfect.   **invisible** (Some editors retain the reading
of the Quarto and the Folio, *invincible*, as meaning ''invisible'' or ''in-
determinable.'')   **genius** spirit, personification   314 **mandrake** root of
a plant, said to resemble the body of a man   315–316 **overscutched
huswives** outworn and often-whipped prostitutes   316 **carmen** wag-
oners   317 **fancies . . . good-nights** fantasies and serenades (of
which he claimed authorship)   318 **Vice's dagger** (The Vice, or
comic character of the morality plays, was sometimes armed with a
wooden dagger.)   319–320 **sworn brother** companion in arms who
has taken a chivalric oath to share his fortunes   321 **tilt-yard** tournament ground at Westminster.   **he burst his head** he, Shallow, had his
head beaten so that he bled   323 **beat his own name** i.e., was
thrashing a gaunt person   324 **him** Shallow   325 **case** instrument
case.   **hautboy** ancestor of the oboe. (The *treble hautboy* was the
smallest and narrowest of this family of instruments.)   326 **beefs** oxen
328 **a philosopher's two stones** i.e., as valuable as the philosopher's
stones that supposedly changed ordinary metal into gold and preserved youth and health. (*Two stones* also suggests ''testicles.'')
329 **dace** small fish used for live bait
4.1. Location: Yorkshire. Gaultree Forest.
2 an 't if it

ARCHBISHOP
Here stand, my lords, and send discoverers forth   3
To know the numbers of our enemies.   4

HASTINGS
We have sent forth already.

ARCHBISHOP   'Tis well done.
My friends and brethren in these great affairs,
I must acquaint you that I have received
New-dated letters from Northumberland,   8
Their cold intent, tenor, and substance, thus: 9
Here doth he wish his person, with such powers   10
As might hold sortance with his quality,   11
The which he could not levy. Whereupon
He is retired, to ripe his growing fortunes,   13
To Scotland, and concludes in hearty prayers
That your attempts may overlive the hazard   15
And fearful meeting of their opposite.   16

MOWBRAY
Thus do the hopes we have in him touch ground   17
And dash themselves to pieces.

Enter Messenger.

HASTINGS   Now, what news?

MESSENGER
West of this forest, scarcely off a mile,
In goodly form comes on the enemy,   20
And, by the ground they hide, I judge their number
Upon or near the rate of thirty thousand.   22

MOWBRAY
The just proportion that we gave them out.   23
Let us sway on and face them in the field.   24

ARCHBISHOP
What well-appointed leader fronts us here?   25

Enter Westmorland.

MOWBRAY
I think it is my lord of Westmorland.

WESTMORLAND
Health and fair greeting from our general,
The Prince, Lord John and Duke of Lancaster.

ARCHBISHOP
Say on, my lord of Westmorland, in peace,
What doth concern your coming.

WESTMORLAND   Then, my lord,   30
Unto Your Grace do I in chief address
The substance of my speech. If that rebellion
Came like itself, in base and abject routs,   33
Led on by bloody youth, guarded with rags,   34
And countenanced by boys and beggary,   35
I say, if damned commotion so appeared   36
In his true, native, and most proper shape,

3 **discoverers** scouts   4 **know** learn   8 **New** recently   9 **cold** dispiriting, gloomy   10 **powers** forces   11 **hold sortance** accord.   **quality**
rank   13 **ripe** make ripe   15 **overlive** outlive   16 **opposite** adversary
17 **touch ground** hit bottom   20 **form** military formation   22 **rate** estimate   23 **just . . . out** precise number that we estimated   24 **sway
on** advance   25 **well-appointed** well-armed.   **fronts** confronts
30 **What . . . coming** what your coming means   33 **routs** mobs
34 **bloody** passionate.   **guarded** adorned, trimmed   35 **countenanced**
supported.   **beggary** beggars   36 **commotion** tumult, sedition

You, reverend father, and these noble lords
Had not been here to dress the ugly form
Of base and bloody insurrection
With your fair honors. You, Lord Archbishop,
Whose see is by a civil peace maintained,   42
Whose beard the silver hand of peace hath touched,
Whose learning and good letters peace hath tutored,   44
Whose white investments figure innocence,   45
The dove and very blessèd spirit of peace,
Wherefore do you so ill translate yourself   47
Out of the speech of peace that bears such grace
Into the harsh and boisterous tongue of war,
Turning your books to graves, your ink to blood,
Your pens to lances, and your tongue divine
To a loud trumpet and a point of war?   52

ARCHBISHOP
Wherefore do I this? So the question stands.
Briefly to this end: we are all diseased,
And with our surfeiting and wanton hours   55
Have brought ourselves into a burning fever,
And we must bleed for it; of which disease   57
Our late King Richard, being infected, died.
But, my most noble lord of Westmorland,
I take not on me here as a physician,   60
Nor do I as an enemy to peace
Troop in the throngs of military men,
But rather show awhile like fearful war   63
To diet rank minds, sick of happiness,   64
And purge th' obstructions which begin to stop
Our very veins of life. Hear me more plainly.
I have in equal balance justly weighed   67
What wrongs our arms may do, what wrongs we
    suffer,
And find our griefs heavier than our offenses.   69
We see which way the stream of time doth run,
And are enforced from our most quiet there   71
By the rough torrent of occasion,   72
And have the summary of all our griefs,
When time shall serve, to show in articles;   74
Which long ere this we offered to the King,
And might by no suit gain our audience.
When we are wronged and would unfold our griefs,
We are denied access unto his person
Even by those men that most have done us wrong.   79
The dangers of the days but newly gone,
Whose memory is written on the earth
With yet-appearing blood, and the examples
Of every minute's instance, present now,   83

Hath put us in these ill-beseeming arms,
Not to break peace, or any branch of it,
But to establish here a peace indeed,
Concurring both in name and quality.   87
WESTMORLAND
Whenever yet was your appeal denied?
Wherein have you been gallèd by the King?   89
What peer hath been suborned to grate on you,   90
That you should seal this lawless bloody book   91
Of forged rebellion with a seal divine   92
And consecrate commotion's bitter edge?
ARCHBISHOP
My brother general, the commonwealth,   94
To brother born an household cruelty,   95
I make my quarrel in particular.   96
WESTMORLAND
There is no need of any such redress;
Or if there were, it not belongs to you.
MOWBRAY
Why not to him in part, and to us all
That feel the bruises of the days before,
And suffer the condition of these times
To lay a heavy and unequal hand   102
Upon our honors?
WESTMORLAND   O my good Lord Mowbray,
Construe the times to their necessities,   104
And you shall say indeed it is the time,
And not the King, that doth you injuries.
Yet for your part, it not appears to me
Either from the King or in the present time
That you should have an inch of any ground
To build a grief on. Were you not restored
To all the Duke of Norfolk's seigniories,   111
Your noble and right well remembered father's?
MOWBRAY
What thing, in honor, had my father lost,
That need to be revived and breathed in me?   114
The King that loved him, as the state stood then,   115
Was force perforce compelled to banish him;   116
And then that Henry Bolingbroke and he,
Being mounted and both rousèd in their seats,   118
Their neighing coursers daring of the spur,   119
Their armèd staves in charge, their beavers down, 120
Their eyes of fire sparkling through sights of steel, 121

42 **see** diocese. **civil** orderly, law-abiding 44 **good letters** scholarship 45 **investments** vestments. **figure** symbolize 47 **translate** (1) change from one language to another (2) transform 52 **point of war** trumpet signal of war 55–79 **And . . . wrong** (Omitted from the Quarto probably because of censorship, since these lines plead the cause of rebellion; also lines 103–139.) 55 **wanton** self-indulgent 57 **bleed** (1) be bled by a doctor (2) bleed in war 60 **take . . . as** do not now undertake the role of 63 **show** appear 64 **rank . . . happiness** those who are bloated with indolent luxury 67 **equal balance** balanced scales. **justly** exactly 69 **griefs** grievances 71 **our . . . there** our greatest quiet therein, i.e., in the stream of time 72 **occasion** circumstances 74 **articles** specified items 83 **Of . . . instance** presented every minute

87 **Concurring . . . quality** i.e., a peace that will be both in name and in fact 89 **gallèd** injured, made sore with chafing 90 **suborned . . . on** induced to annoy, harass 91–92 **That . . . divine** i.e., that you should put your seal of approval on this lawless and forged rebellion, much as if a bishop were to license a troublesome book 94–96 **My brother . . . particular** (The text is perhaps corrupt here, but the general sense seems to be: the grievances of my brother-Englishmen and the cruelty shown to my blood brother Scroop [who was executed at Bristol by Henry IV; see *1 Henry IV,* 1.3.269] provoke me to make this cause my own.) 102 **unequal** unjust 104 **to** according to. **their necessities** i.e., that which is necessary in a time of disorder and civil strife 111 **seigniories** properties, estates 114 **breathed** given the breath of life 115 **state** condition of things 116 **force perforce** willy-nilly. (For the banishment of Mowbray by Richard II, see *Richard II,* 1.1 and 1.3.) 118 **rousèd** raised. **seats** saddles 119 **daring of the spur** i.e., eager to be urged on 120 **armèd . . . charge** lances ready for the charge. **beavers** movable visors of helmets 121 **sights** eye slits

And the loud trumpet blowing them together,
Then, then, when there was nothing could have
stayed
My father from the breast of Bolingbroke,
O, when the King did throw his warder down—   125
His own life hung upon the staff he threw—
Then threw he down himself and all their lives
That by indictment and by dint of sword
Have since miscarried under Bolingbroke.

WESTMORLAND
You speak, Lord Mowbray, now you know not
what.
The Earl of Hereford was reputed then   131
In England the most valiant gentleman.
Who knows on whom fortune would then have
smiled?
But if your father had been victor there,
He ne'er had borne it out of Coventry;   135
For all the country in a general voice
Cried hate upon him, and all their prayers and love
Were set on Hereford, whom they doted on,
And blessed, and graced, indeed more than the King.
But this is mere digression from my purpose.
Here come I from our princely general
To know your griefs, to tell you from His Grace
That he will give you audience; and wherein   143
It shall appear that your demands are just,
You shall enjoy them, everything set off   145
That might so much as think you enemies.   146

MOWBRAY
But he hath forced us to compel this offer,
And it proceeds from policy, not love.

WESTMORLAND
Mowbray, you overween to take it so.   149
This offer comes from mercy, not from fear.
For, lo, within a ken our army lies,   151
Upon mine honor, all too confident
To give admittance to a thought of fear.
Our battle is more full of names than yours,   154
Our men more perfect in the use of arms,
Our armor all as strong, our cause the best.
Then reason will our hearts should be as good.   157
Say you not then our offer is compelled.

MOWBRAY
Well, by my will we shall admit no parley.   159

WESTMORLAND
That argues but the shame of your offense.
A rotten case abides no handling.   161

HASTINGS
Hath the Prince John a full commission,
In very ample virtue of his father,   163

To hear and absolutely to determine   164
Of what conditions we shall stand upon?   165

WESTMORLAND
That is intended in the General's name.   166
I muse you make so slight a question.   167

ARCHBISHOP [giving a document]
Then take, my lord of Westmorland, this schedule,
For this contains our general grievances.
Each several article herein redressed,   170
All members of our cause, both here and hence,
That are insinewed to this action,   172
Acquitted by a true substantial form   173
And present execution of our wills   174
To us and to our purposes confined,   175
We come within our awful banks again   176
And knit our powers to the arm of peace.

WESTMORLAND
This will I show the General. Please you, lords,
In sight of both our battles we may meet,   179
And either end in peace—which God so frame!—   180
Or to the place of difference call the swords   181
Which must decide it.

ARCHBISHOP   My lord, we will do so.
                                        Exit Westmorland.

MOWBRAY
There is a thing within my bosom tells me
That no conditions of our peace can stand.

HASTINGS
Fear you not that. If we can make our peace
Upon such large terms and so absolute   186
As our conditions shall consist upon,   187
Our peace shall stand as firm as rocky mountains.

MOWBRAY
Yea, but our valuation shall be such   189
That every slight and false-derivèd cause,
Yea, every idle, nice, and wanton reason,   191
Shall to the King taste of this action,
That, were our royal faiths martyrs in love,   193
We shall be winnowed with so rough a wind
That even our corn shall seem as light as chaff   195
And good from bad find no partition.   196

ARCHBISHOP
No, no, my lord. Note this: the King is weary
Of dainty and such picking grievances;   198
For he hath found to end one doubt by death   199
Revives two greater in the heirs of life,   200
And therefore will he wipe his tables clean   201

And keep no telltale to his memory
That may repeat and history his loss 203
To new remembrance. For full well he knows
He cannot so precisely weed this land 205
As his misdoubts present occasion. 206
His foes are so enrooted with his friends
That, plucking to unfix an enemy,
He doth unfasten so and shake a friend.
So that this land, like an offensive wife
That hath enraged him on to offer strokes,
As he is striking, holds his infant up
And hangs resolved correction in the arm 213
That was upreared to execution.

HASTINGS
Besides, the King hath wasted all his rods 215
On late offenders, that he now doth lack 216
The very instruments of chastisement,
So that his power, like to a fangless lion,
May offer, but not hold.

ARCHBISHOP   'Tis very true. 219
And therefore be assured, my good Lord Marshal,
If we do now make our atonement well, 221
Our peace will, like a broken limb united,
Grow stronger for the breaking.

MOWBRAY   Be it so.
Here is returned my lord of Westmorland.

Enter Westmorland.

WESTMORLAND
The Prince is here at hand. Pleaseth your lordship 225
To meet His Grace just distance 'tween our armies. 226

MOWBRAY
Your Grace of York, in God's name then set
    forward.

ARCHBISHOP
Before, and greet His Grace.—My lord, we come. 228

4.2   *Enter Prince John [of Lancaster] and his army.*

PRINCE JOHN
You are well encountered here, my cousin
    Mowbray.
Good day to you, gentle Lord Archbishop, 1
And so to you, Lord Hastings, and to all. 2
My lord of York, it better showed with you 4
When that your flock, assembled by the bell,
Encircled you to hear with reverence
Your exposition on the holy text

Than now to see you here an iron man, 8
Cheering a rout of rebels with your drum, 9
Turning the word to sword and life to death. 10
That man that sits within a monarch's heart
And ripens in the sunshine of his favor,
Would he abuse the countenance of the King, 13
Alack, what mischiefs might he set abroach 14
In shadow of such greatness! With you, Lord
    Bishop,
It is even so. Who hath not heard it spoken 16
How deep you were within the books of God, 17
To us the speaker in his parliament, 18
To us th' imagined voice of God himself,
The very opener and intelligencer 20
Between the grace, the sanctities, of heaven
And our dull workings? O, who shall believe 22
But you misuse the reverence of your place,
Employ the countenance and grace of heaven
As a false favorite doth his prince's name,
In deeds dishonorable? You have ta'en up, 26
Under the counterfeited zeal of God,
The subjects of his substitute, my father, 28
And both against the peace of heaven and him
Have here up-swarmed them.

ARCHBISHOP   Good my lord of Lancaster, 30
I am not here against your father's peace;
But, as I told my lord of Westmorland,
The time misordered doth, in common sense, 33
Crowd us and crush us to this monstrous form
To hold our safety up. I sent Your Grace
The parcels and particulars of our grief, 36
The which hath been with scorn shoved from the
    court,
Whereon this Hydra son of war is born, 38
Whose dangerous eyes may well be charmed asleep 39
With grant of our most just and right desires,
And true obedience, of this madness cured,
Stoop tamely to the foot of majesty.

MOWBRAY
If not, we ready are to try our fortunes
To the last man.

HASTINGS   And though we here fall down, 44
We have supplies to second our attempt; 45
If they miscarry, theirs shall second them, 46
And so success of mischief shall be born, 47

---

203 **history** record, chronicle   205 **precisely** thoroughly   206 **misdoubts** suspicions   213 **hangs resolved correction** suspends in midaction the punishment that was intended   215 **wasted** exhausted, spent.   **rods** whipping rods   216 **late** (other) recent   219 **offer . . . hold** threaten violence but not hold fast   221 **atonement** reconciliation   225 **Pleaseth** may it please   226 **just distance** halfway   228 **Before** i.e., go before

4.2. Location: This scene is apparently continuous with the previous scene. In the Quarto, Prince John and his army enter before the last two lines of 4.1.

1 **cousin** (Normal address of royal family to a duke.)   2 **gentle** noble   4 **it . . . you** it showed you to better advantage

8 **iron man** (1) warrior clad in armor (2) merciless fighter   9 **rout** mob   10 **the word** i.e., the word of God, the Scriptures   13 **Would he** if he should choose to.   **countenance** favor   14 **set abroach** set aflowing, begin   16 **even** just   17 **within . . . God** (1) versed in works of divinity (2) in God's good graces   18 **speaker** i.e., spokesman for God, just as the Speaker of Parliament spoke in the name of the King   20 **opener and intelligencer** interpreter and messenger   22 **dull workings** imperfect human perceptions   26 **ta'en up** enlisted   28 **his substitute** God's deputy   30 **up-swarmed** raised up in swarms   33 **time misordered** disorders of the time.   **in common sense** i.e., as anyone can see   36 **parcels** items, details.   **grief** grievances   38 **Hydra** (The Lernaean Hydra was a fabulous monster with several heads; when one was cut off, others grew in its place.)   39 **eyes** (The image here conflates Hydra with Argus, Juno's watchful guard with one hundred eyes, who was charmed asleep by Mercury's music.)   44 **though** even if   45 **supplies** forces in reserve   46 **miscarry** come to grief.   **theirs** i.e., their reinforcements   47 **success** succession

And heir from heir shall hold this quarrel up
Whiles England shall have generation.   49
PRINCE JOHN
You are too shallow, Hastings, much too shallow,
To sound the bottom of the aftertimes.   51
WESTMORLAND
Pleaseth Your Grace to answer them directly   52
How far forth you do like their articles.
PRINCE JOHN
I like them all, and do allow them well,   54
And swear here, by the honor of my blood,
My father's purposes have been mistook,
And some about him have too lavishly   57
Wrested his meaning and authority.
My lord, these griefs shall be with speed redressed,
Upon my soul, they shall. If this may please you,
Discharge your powers unto their several counties,   61
As we will ours; and here between the armies
Let's drink together friendly and embrace,
That all their eyes may bear those tokens home
Of our restorèd love and amity.
ARCHBISHOP
I take your princely word for these redresses.
PRINCE JOHN
I give it you, and will maintain my word,
And thereupon I drink unto Your Grace.
                               [They drink together, and embrace.]
HASTINGS
Go, Captain, and deliver to the army
This news of peace. Let them have pay, and part.   70
I know it will well please them. Hie thee, Captain.
                                          [Exit a Captain.]
ARCHBISHOP
To you, my noble lord of Westmorland.
WESTMORLAND
I pledge Your Grace; and, if you knew what pains
I have bestowed to breed this present peace,
You would drink freely. But my love to ye
Shall show itself more openly hereafter.
ARCHBISHOP
I do not doubt you.
WESTMORLAND   I am glad of it.
Health to my lord and gentle cousin, Mowbray.
MOWBRAY
You wish me health in very happy season,   79
For I am on the sudden something ill.   80
ARCHBISHOP
Against ill chances men are ever merry,   81
But heaviness foreruns the good event.   82
WESTMORLAND
Therefore be merry, coz, since sudden sorrow   83

Serves to say thus, "Some good thing comes
   tomorrow."
ARCHBISHOP
Believe me, I am passing light in spirit.   85
MOWBRAY
So much the worse, if your own rule be true.
                                      Shout [within].
PRINCE JOHN
The word of peace is rendered. Hark, how they
   shout!   87
MOWBRAY
This had been cheerful after victory.   88
ARCHBISHOP
A peace is of the nature of a conquest,
For then both parties nobly are subdued,
And neither party loser.
PRINCE JOHN [to Westmorland]   Go, my lord,
And let our army be dischargèd too.
                            [Exit Westmorland.]
And, good my lord, so please you, let our trains   93
March by us, that we may peruse the men
We should have coped withal.
ARCHBISHOP   Go, good Lord Hastings,   95
And ere they be dismissed, let them march by.
                              [Exit Hastings.]
PRINCE JOHN
I trust, lords, we shall lie tonight together.

                    Enter Westmorland.

Now cousin, wherefore stands our army still?   98
WESTMORLAND
The leaders, having charge from you to stand,
Will not go off until they hear you speak.
PRINCE JOHN   They know their duties.

                    Enter Hastings.

HASTINGS [to the Archbishop]
My lord, our army is dispersed already.
Like youthful steers unyoked, they take their
   courses
East, west, north, south, or, like a school broke up,
Each hurries toward his home and sporting-place.
WESTMORLAND
Good tidings, my lord Hastings, for the which
I do arrest thee, traitor, of high treason.
And you, Lord Archbishop, and you, Lord
   Mowbray,
Of capital treason I attach you both.   109
MOWBRAY
Is this proceeding just and honorable?
WESTMORLAND   Is your assembly so?
ARCHBISHOP
Will you thus break your faith?
PRINCE JOHN   I pawned thee none. 112
I promised you redress of these same grievances

---

49 **generation** issue, offspring 51 **sound . . . aftertimes** i.e., predict
what the future will bring. **sound the bottom** plumb the depths
52 **Pleaseth** may it please 54 **allow** approve, sanction 57 **lavishly**
loosely, negligently 61 **powers** forces. **several** respective 70 **part**
depart 79 **in . . . season** at an opportune moment 80 **something**
somewhat 81 **Against** when about to face 82 **heaviness . . . event**
sadness comes over men prior to a happy outcome 83 **coz** cousin,
kinsman

85 **passing** surpassingly 87 **rendered** proclaimed 88 **had been**
would have been 93 **trains** followers, armies 95 **coped withal** encountered, fought with 98 **wherefore** why 109 **capital** punishable
by death. **attach** arrest 112 **pawned** pledged

Whereof you did complain, which, by mine honor,
I will perform with a most Christian care.
But for you rebels, look to taste the due   116
Meet for rebellion and such acts as yours.   117
Most shallowly did you these arms commence,   118
Fondly brought here and foolishly sent hence.—   119
Strike up our drums; pursue the scattered stray.   120
God, and not we, hath safely fought today.
Some guard these traitors to the block of death,
Treason's true bed and yielder-up of breath.

                                     [Exeunt.]

4.3 *Alarum. Excursions. Enter Falstaff [and Sir John Coleville, meeting].*

FALSTAFF What's your name, sir? Of what condition   1
are you, and of what place?
COLEVILLE I am a knight, sir, and my name is Coleville
of the Dale.
FALSTAFF Well, then, Coleville is your name, a knight is
your degree, and your place the Dale. Coleville shall be
still your name, a traitor your degree, and the dungeon   7
your place, a place deep enough; so shall you be still
Coleville of the Dale.
COLEVILLE Are not you Sir John Falstaff?
FALSTAFF As good a man as he, sir, whoe'er I am. Do
ye yield, sir, or shall I sweat for you? If I do sweat,
they are the drops of thy lovers, and they weep for thy   13
death. Therefore rouse up fear and trembling, and do
observance to my mercy.   15
COLEVILLE I think you are Sir John Falstaff, and in that
thought yield me.
FALSTAFF I have a whole school of tongues in this belly   18
of mine, and not a tongue of them all speaks any other
word but my name. An I had but a belly of any indif-   20
ferency, I were simply the most active fellow in Eu-   21
rope. My womb, my womb, my womb undoes me.   22
Here comes our general.

    Enter [Prince] John [of Lancaster], Westmorland,
    [Blunt,] and the rest.

PRINCE JOHN
The heat is past; follow no further now.   24
Call in the powers, good cousin Westmorland.   25
              [Exit Westmorland. Sound] retreat.
Now, Falstaff, where have you been all this while?

When everything is ended, then you come.
These tardy tricks of yours will, on my life,
One time or other break some gallows' back.
FALSTAFF I would be sorry, my lord, but it should be   30
thus. I never knew yet but rebuke and check was the   31
reward of valor. Do you think me a swallow, an arrow,
or a bullet? Have I, in my poor and old motion, the
expedition of thought? I have speeded hither with the   34
very extremest inch of possibility. I have foundered   35
nine score and odd posts, and here, travel-tainted as I   36
am, have in my pure and immaculate valor taken Sir
John Coleville of the Dale, a most furious knight and
valorous enemy. But what of that? He saw me and
yielded, that I may justly say, with the hook-nosed fel-   40
low of Rome, "I came, saw, and overcame."   41
PRINCE JOHN It was more of his courtesy than your deserving.
FALSTAFF I know not. Here he is, and here I yield him.
And I beseech Your Grace, let it be booked with the   45
rest of this day's deeds, or, by the Lord, I will have it
in a particular ballad else, with mine own picture on   47
the top on 't, Coleville kissing my foot. To the which   48
course if I be enforced, if you do not all show like gilt   49
twopences to me, and I in the clear sky of fame   50
o'ershine you as much as the full moon doth the cin-   51
ders of the element, which show like pins' heads to   52
her, believe not the word of the noble. Therefore let
me have right, and let desert mount.   54
PRINCE JOHN Thine's too heavy to mount.
FALSTAFF Let it shine, then.
PRINCE JOHN Thine's too thick to shine.   57
FALSTAFF Let it do something, my good lord, that may
do me good, and call it what you will.
PRINCE JOHN Is thy name Coleville?
COLEVILLE It is, my lord.
PRINCE JOHN A famous rebel art thou, Coleville.
FALSTAFF And a famous true subject took him.
COLEVILLE
I am, my lord, but as my betters are
That led me hither. Had they been ruled by me,   65
You should have won them dearer than you have.   66
FALSTAFF I know not how they sold themselves. But
thou, like a kind fellow, gavest thyself away gratis, and
I thank thee for thee.

    Enter Westmorland.

PRINCE JOHN Now, have you left pursuit?

---

116 for as for. **look** expect **117 Meet** fitting **118 shallowly** without due consideration. **arms** hostilities **119 Fondly** foolishly **120 stray** stragglers
4.3. Location: Gaultree Forest, as before. The scene is continuous.
s.d. Alarum trumpet call to battle. **Excursions** sallies, sudden movements of troops. (The Quarto stage direction may suggest that Falstaff enters before Coleville.) **1 condition** rank **7 dungeon** (Falstaff jests that a deep dungeon can be thought of as a kind of *dale* or valley.) **13 drops** tears. **lovers** friends **15 observance** reverence, homage **18 school** crowd. (Falstaff jests that his belly eloquently identifies him.) **20 An** if **20–21 indifferency** moderate size **21 were** would be **22 womb** belly **24 heat** pursuit, race **25 powers** forces

30–31 but . . . thus if it were not thus. (It is fitting, Falstaff wryly says, that valor is never properly recognized, because that is how the world goes.) **31 check** reprimand **34 expedition** speed **35 very extremest inch** fullest extent. **foundered** made lame **36 posts** post-horses **40–41 hook-nosed . . . Rome** i.e., Julius Caesar **45 booked** recorded by the chroniclers **47 a particular ballad** a broadside ballad written and published on this particular episode. **else** otherwise **48 on 't** of it **49 show** look **49–50 gilt twopences** coins gilded to pass for half-crowns of the same size **50 to** compared to (also in line 52) **51–52 cinders . . . element** i.e., stars **54 desert mount** merit be promoted **57 thick** (1) opaque, dim (2) heavy **65 been ruled by me** listened to my advice **66 dearer** i.e., at greater military cost

WESTMORLAND

Retreat is made and execution stayed. 71

PRINCE JOHN

Send Coleville with his confederates
To York, to present execution. 73
Blunt, lead him hence, and see you guard him sure.
                               [*Exit Blunt with Coleville.*]
And now dispatch we toward the court, my lords. 75
I hear the King my father is sore sick.
Our news shall go before us to His Majesty,
Which, cousin, you shall bear to comfort him, 78
And we with sober speed will follow you. 79

FALSTAFF   My lord, I beseech you give me leave to go
through Gloucestershire, and, when you come to
court, stand my good lord in your good report. 82

PRINCE JOHN

Fare you well, Falstaff. I, in my condition, 83
Shall better speak of you than you deserve.
                             [*Exeunt all but Falstaff.*]

FALSTAFF   I would you had but the wit; 'twere better
than your dukedom. Good faith, this same young
sober-blooded boy doth not love me, nor a man cannot make him laugh. But that's no marvel; he drinks
no wine. There's never none of these demure boys
come to any proof, for thin drink doth so overcool 90
their blood, and making many fish meals, that they
fall into a kind of male greensickness, and then, when 92
they marry, they get wenches. They are generally fools 93
and cowards, which some of us should be too, but for
inflammation. A good sherris sack hath a twofold op- 95
eration in it. It ascends me into the brain, dries me 96
there all the foolish and dull and crudy vapors which 97
environ it, makes it apprehensive, quick, forgetive, 98
full of nimble, fiery, and delectable shapes, which, delivered o'er to the voice, the tongue, which is the birth,
becomes excellent wit. The second property of your 101
excellent sherris is the warming of the blood, which,
before cold and settled, left the liver white and pale, 103
which is the badge of pusillanimity and cowardice.
But the sherris warms it and makes it course from the 105
innards to the parts' extremes. It illumineth the face, 106
which as a beacon gives warning to all the rest of this
little kingdom, man, to arm; and then the vital com- 108
moners and inland petty spirits muster me all to their 109
captain, the heart, who, great and puffed up with this
retinue, doth any deed of courage; and this valor
comes of sherris. So that skill in the weapon is nothing

without sack, for that sets it a-work, and learning a 113
mere hoard of gold kept by a devil till sack com- 114
mences it and sets it in act and use. Hereof comes it 115
that Prince Harry is valiant, for the cold blood he did
naturally inherit of his father, he hath, like lean, ster- 117
ile, and bare land, manured, husbanded, and tilled 118
with excellent endeavor of drinking good and good
store of fertile sherris, that he is become very hot and
valiant. If I had a thousand sons, the first human 121
principle I would teach them should be to forswear
thin potations and to addict themselves to sack. 123

    Enter Bardolph.

How now, Bardolph?

BARDOLPH   The army is discharged all and gone.

FALSTAFF   Let them go. I'll through Gloucestershire, and
there will I visit Master Robert Shallow, Esquire. I have
him already tempering between my finger and my 128
thumb, and shortly will I seal with him. Come away. 129
                                         [*Exeunt.*]

4.4   *Enter the King, Warwick, Thomas Duke of
Clarence, Humphrey [Duke] of Gloucester, [and
others].*

KING

Now, lords, if God doth give successful end
To this debate that bleedeth at our doors, 2
We will our youth lead on to higher fields 3
And draw no swords but what are sanctified. 4
Our navy is addressed, our power collected, 5
Our substitutes in absence well invested, 6
And everything lies level to our wish. 7
Only we want a little personal strength, 8
And pause us till these rebels now afoot
Come underneath the yoke of government.

WARWICK

Both which we doubt not but Your Majesty
Shall soon enjoy.

KING   Humphrey, my son of Gloucester,
Where is the Prince your brother?

GLOUCESTER

I think he's gone to hunt, my lord, at Windsor.

KING

And how accompanied?

GLOUCESTER   I do not know, my lord.

---

71 **Retreat . . . stayed** the order for withdrawal has been sounded, and the slaughter has been stopped 73 **present** immediate 75 **dispatch we** let us hasten 78 **cousin** i.e., Westmorland 79 **sober** controlled, dignified 82 **stand my good lord** act as my patron 83 **condition** i.e., function as commander 90 **come to any proof** stand up well under testing, turn out well. **thin drink** i.e., beer 92 **greensickness** a kind of anemia thought to affect young women 93 **get wenches** beget girls 95 **inflammation** passions excited by liquor. **sherris sack** sherry 96 **ascends me** i.e., ascends. (*Me* is used colloquially, as also in line 109.) 97 **crudy** curded 98 **environ** surround. **apprehensive** quick to perceive. **forgetive** inventive 101 **wit** mental capacity 103 **liver** (Thought to be the seat of courage.) 105 **course** run 106 **extremes** extremities 108–109 **vital . . . spirits** vital spirits of the human internal region 109 **muster me** assemble

113 **learning** learning is 114 **kept by a devil** guarded by an evil spirit, like a dragon 114–115 **commences it** transforms its potential into actuality (as at a commencement) 117 **lean** barren 118 **husbanded** cultivated 121 **human** secular 123 **potations** drinks 128 **tempering** softening (like a piece of wax) 129 **seal with** i.e., shape him to my purposes; seal a bargain with (continuing the metaphor of sealing wax)

4.4. Location: King Henry's court at Westminster. The Jerusalem Chamber (adjoining Westminster Abbey), so called for its various inscriptions concerning Jerusalem.

2 **debate** strife 3 **higher fields** i.e., a crusade to Palestine 4 **what** those that 5 **addressed** ready, prepared 6 **substitutes** deputies. **invested** empowered 7 **level** conformable 8 **want** lack

KING
  Is not his brother Thomas of Clarence with him?

GLOUCESTER
  No, my good lord, he is in presence here.   17

CLARENCE What would my lord and father?   18

KING
  Nothing but well to thee, Thomas of Clarence.
  How chance thou art not with the Prince thy
    brother?
  He loves thee, and thou dost neglect him, Thomas;
  Thou hast a better place in his affection
  Than all thy brothers. Cherish it, my boy,
  And noble offices thou mayst effect   24
  Of mediation, after I am dead,
  Between his greatness and thy other brethren.
  Therefore omit him not, blunt not his love,   27
  Nor lose the good advantage of his grace   28
  By seeming cold or careless of his will.
  For he is gracious, if he be observed.   30
  He hath a tear for pity and a hand
  Open as day for melting charity.   32
  Yet notwithstanding, being incensed, he is flint,   33
  As humorous as winter, and as sudden   34
  As flaws congealèd in the spring of day.   35
  His temper, therefore, must be well observed.   36
  Chide him for faults, and do it reverently,
  When you perceive his blood inclined to mirth;
  But, being moody, give him time and scope,   39
  Till that his passions, like a whale on ground,
  Confound themselves with working. Learn this,
    Thomas,   41
  And thou shalt prove a shelter to thy friends,
  A hoop of gold to bind thy brothers in,
  That the united vessel of their blood,
  Mingled with venom of suggestion—   45
  As, force perforce, the age will pour it in—
  Shall never leak, though it do work as strong
  As aconitum or rash gunpowder.   48

CLARENCE
  I shall observe him with all care and love.

KING
  Why art thou not at Windsor with him, Thomas?

CLARENCE
  He is not there today; he dines in London.

KING
  And how accompanied? Canst thou tell that?

CLARENCE
  With Poins and other his continual followers.

KING
  Most subject is the fattest soil to weeds,   54
  And he, the noble image of my youth,
  Is overspread with them. Therefore my grief
  Stretches itself beyond the hour of death.
  The blood weeps from my heart when I do shape
  In forms imaginary th' unguided days
  And rotten times that you shall look upon
  When I am sleeping with my ancestors.
  For when his headstrong riot hath no curb,
  When rage and hot blood are his counselors,
  When means and lavish manners meet together,   64
  O, with what wings shall his affections fly   65
  Towards fronting peril and opposed decay!   66

WARWICK
  My gracious lord, you look beyond him quite.   67
  The Prince but studies his companions
  Like a strange tongue, wherein, to gain the
    language,   69
  'Tis needful that the most immodest word
  Be looked upon and learned, which, once attained,
  Your Highness knows, comes to no further use
  But to be known and hated. So, like gross terms,   73
  The Prince will in the perfectness of time
  Cast off his followers, and their memory
  Shall as a pattern or a measure live
  By which His Grace must mete the lives of other,   77
  Turning past evils to advantages.

KING
  'Tis seldom when the bee doth leave her comb   79
  In the dead carrion.

    Enter Westmorland.

                Who's here? Westmorland?   80

WESTMORLAND
  Health to my sovereign, and new happiness
  Added to that that I am to deliver!
  Prince John your son doth kiss Your Grace's hand.
  Mowbray, the Bishop Scroop, Hastings, and all
  Are brought to the correction of your law.
  There is not now a rebel's sword unsheathed,
  But Peace puts forth her olive everywhere.
  The manner how this action hath been borne
  Here at more leisure may Your Highness read,
  With every course in his particular.   90

                [He gives a document.]

KING
  O Westmorland, thou art a summer bird,
  Which ever in the haunch of winter sings   92

---

17 **in presence** present at court 18 **would** wishes 24 **offices** functions. **effect** perform, accomplish 27 **omit** neglect 28 **grace** favor 30 **observed** paid proper respect, humored 32 **melting** tender, compassionate 33 **flint** i.e., both in hardness and in giving off sparks 34 **humorous** unpredictable in mood 35 **flaws congealèd** snow squalls. **spring of day** early morning 36 **temper** disposition 39 **moody** angry 41 **Confound** exhaust, consume. **working** struggling 45 **suggestion** insinuation, suspicion. (The image in lines 43–48 is of a vessel of the brothers' combined blood, held together with golden hoops of affection and loyalty but threatened by the poison of mutual mistrust that their enemies will try to foment in them.) 48 **aconitum** a strong poison extracted from monkshood. **rash** quick-acting

54 **fattest** richest 64 **lavish** unrestrained, licentious 65 **affections** inclinations 66 **fronting . . . decay** danger and ruin that confront him 67 **look beyond** go too far in judging 69 **strange** foreign 73 **like gross terms** just as with coarse expressions 77 **mete** measure, appraise. **other** others 79–80 **'Tis . . . carrion** rarely does the bee that has placed her comb in dead carrion leave her honeycomb; i.e., the Prince will not forsake his corrupt delights 90 **course . . . particular** event or phase set forth in detail. **his** its 92 **haunch** latter end

The lifting up of day.

Enter Harcourt.

Look, here's more news.   93

HARCOURT
From enemies heaven keep Your Majesty,
And, when they stand against you, may they fall
As those that I am come to tell you of!
The Earl Northumberland and the Lord Bardolph,
With a great power of English and of Scots,
Are by the sheriff of Yorkshire overthrown.
The manner and true order of the fight
This packet, please it you, contains at large.   101
[He gives letters.]

KING
And wherefore should these good news make me
    sick?
Will Fortune never come with both hands full,
But write her fair words still in foulest letters?   104
She either gives a stomach and no food—   105
Such are the poor, in health; or else a feast
And takes away the stomach—such are the rich,
That have abundance and enjoy it not.
I should rejoice now at this happy news,
And now my sight fails and my brain is giddy.
O, me! Come near me. Now I am much ill.
[The King swoons. Several come to his aid.]

GLOUCESTER
Comfort, Your Majesty!

CLARENCE   O my royal Father!

WESTMORLAND
My sovereign lord, cheer up yourself, look up.

WARWICK
Be patient, princes. You do know these fits
Are with His Highness very ordinary.
Stand from him, give him air; he'll straight be well.

CLARENCE
No, no, he cannot long hold out these pangs.   117
Th' incessant care and labor of his mind
Hath wrought the mure that should confine it in   119
So thin that life looks through and will break out.

GLOUCESTER
The people fear me, for they do observe   121
Unfathered heirs and loathly births of nature.   122
The seasons change their manners, as the year   123
Had found some months asleep and leapt them over.

CLARENCE
The river hath thrice flowed, no ebb between,   125
And the old folk, time's doting chronicles,
Say it did so a little time before
That our great-grandsire, Edward, sicked and died.   128

WARWICK
Speak lower, princes, for the King recovers.

GLOUCESTER
This apoplexy will certain be his end.

KING
I pray you, take me up and bear me hence
Into some other chamber. Softly, pray.

4.5   *[The King is borne to another part of the stage, to bed.]*

KING
Let there be no noise made, my gentle friends,
Unless some dull and favorable hand   2
Will whisper music to my weary spirit.

WARWICK
Call for the music in the other room.

KING
Set me the crown upon my pillow here.

CLARENCE
His eye is hollow, and he changes much.   6

WARWICK
Less noise, less noise!
[The crown is placed on the King's pillow.]

Enter [Prince] Harry.

PRINCE   Who saw the Duke of Clarence?

CLARENCE
I am here, brother, full of heaviness.   8

PRINCE
How now, rain within doors, and none abroad?   9
How doth the King?

GLOUCESTER   Exceeding ill.

PRINCE
Heard he the good news yet? Tell it him.

GLOUCESTER
He altered much upon the hearing it.

PRINCE   If he be sick with joy, he'll recover without
physic.

WARWICK
Not so much noise, my lords. Sweet Prince,
    speak low.
The King your father is disposed to sleep.

CLARENCE
Let us withdraw into the other room.

WARWICK
Will 't please Your Grace to go along with us?

PRINCE
No, I will sit and watch here by the King.
[Exeunt all but the Prince and the King.]
Why doth the crown lie there upon his pillow,
Being so troublesome a bedfellow?
O polished perturbation, golden care,   23
That keep'st the ports of slumber open wide   24
To many a watchful night! Sleep with it now;   25

---

93 **lifting up** dawn   101 **at large** in full   104 **still** always   105 **stomach** appetite   117 **hold out** endure   119 **wrought the mure** made the wall   121 **fear** frighten   122 **Unfathered heirs** persons believed to be supernaturally conceived.   **loathly births** monstrous offspring   123 **as** as if   125 **river** i.e., Thames. (Holinshed records this event as having happened on October 12, 1412.)   128 **Edward** Edward III.   **sicked** fell sick

4.5. Location: The scene is continuous.
2 **dull** soft, soothing.   **favorable** kindly   6 **changes** changes color, turns pale   8 **heaviness** sadness   9 **rain** i.e., tears   23 **perturbation** cause of perturbation   24 **ports** gates   25 **watchful** wakeful.   **Sleep with it** i.e., may you (King Henry) sleep with this symbol of care beside you

Yet not so sound and half so deeply sweet   26
As he whose brow with homely biggen bound   27
Snores out the watch of night. O majesty,
When thou dost pinch thy bearer, thou dost sit   29
Like a rich armor worn in heat of day,
That scald'st with safety. By his gates of breath   31
There lies a downy feather which stirs not.
Did he suspire, that light and weightless down   33
Perforce must move. My gracious lord! My Father!
This sleep is sound indeed. This is a sleep
That from this golden rigol hath divorced   36
So many English kings. Thy due from me
Is tears and heavy sorrows of the blood,   38
Which nature, love, and filial tenderness
Shall, O dear Father, pay thee plenteously.
My due from thee is this imperial crown,
Which, as immediate from thy place and blood,   42
Derives itself to me. [*He puts on the crown.*] Lo,
  where it sits,   43
Which God shall guard. And put the world's whole
  strength
Into one giant arm, it shall not force
This lineal honor from me. This from thee   46
Will I to mine leave, as 'tis left to me.   *Exit.*

KING [*awakening*]   Warwick! Gloucester! Clarence!

    Enter Warwick, Gloucester, Clarence, [and others].

CLARENCE
Doth the King call?
WARWICK   What would Your Majesty?
KING
Why did you leave me here alone, my lords?
CLARENCE
We left the Prince my brother here, my liege,
Who undertook to sit and watch by you.
KING
The Prince of Wales? Where is he? Let me see him.
He is not here.
WARWICK
This door is open; he is gone this way.
GLOUCESTER
He came not through the chamber where we stayed.
KING
Where is the crown? Who took it from my pillow?
WARWICK
When we withdrew, my liege, we left it here.
KING
The Prince hath ta'en it hence. Go seek him out.
Is he so hasty that he doth suppose
My sleep my death?
Find him, my lord of Warwick; chide him hither.
                  [*Exit Warwick.*]
This part of his conjoins with my disease   63

And helps to end me. See, sons, what things
  you are!
How quickly Nature falls into revolt
When gold becomes her object!
For this the foolish overcareful fathers
Have broke their sleep with thoughts,   68
Their brains with care, their bones with industry;
For this they have engrossèd and piled up   70
The cankered heaps of strange-achievèd gold;   71
For this they have been thoughtful to invest   72
Their sons with arts and martial exercises—
When, like the bee, tolling from every flower   74
The virtuous sweets,
Our thighs packed with wax, our mouths with
  honey,
We bring it to the hive, and like the bees
Are murdered for our pains. This bitter taste   78
Yields his engrossments to the ending father.   79

      Enter Warwick.

Now, where is he that will not stay so long
Till his friend sickness have determined me?   81
WARWICK
My lord, I found the Prince in the next room,
Washing with kindly tears his gentle cheeks,   83
With such a deep demeanor in great sorrow   84
That tyranny, which never quaffed but blood,   85
Would, by beholding him, have washed his knife
With gentle eyedrops. He is coming hither.
KING
But wherefore did he take away the crown?

    Enter [Prince] Harry [with the crown].

Lo, where he comes. Come hither to me, Harry.—
Depart the chamber; leave us here alone.
          Exeunt [Warwick and the rest].
PRINCE
I never thought to hear you speak again.
KING
Thy wish was father, Harry, to that thought.
I stay too long by thee; I weary thee.
Dost thou so hunger for mine empty chair   94
That thou wilt needs invest thee with my honors   95
Before thy hour be ripe? O foolish youth,
Thou seek'st the greatness that will overwhelm thee.
Stay but a little, for my cloud of dignity   98
Is held from falling with so weak a wind   99
That it will quickly drop. My day is dim.
Thou hast stol'n that which after some few hours
Were thine without offense, and at my death
Thou hast sealed up my expectation.   103

68 thoughts cares   **70 engrossèd** amassed   **71 cankered** rusting and malignant.   **strange-achievèd** won by unusual effort or means, or in distant lands   **72 thoughtful** careful   **74 tolling** taking as toll, collecting   **78–79 This . . . father** his stored-up treasures yield this bitter taste to the dying father   **81 determined** ended, put an end to   **83 kindly** natural, filial   **84 deep** intense   **85 tyranny** cruelty.   **quaffed** drank   **94 chair** throne   **95 wilt needs** must   **98 my cloud of dignity** the fragile substance of my high estate   **99 so weak a wind** i.e., the King's failing breath, compared to the wind that was thought to hold up the clouds   **103 sealed up** confirmed

26 Yet not i.e., yet your sleep will nonetheless not be   **27 biggen** nightcap   **29 pinch** torment   **31 scald'st with safety** burns while providing safety.   **gates of breath** lips and nose   **33 suspire** breathe   **36 rigol** circle, i.e., crown   **38 blood** (1) heart (2) kinship   **42 as immediate from** as I am next in line to   **43 Derives itself** descends   **46 lineal** inherited   **63 part** act.   **conjoins** unites, joins

Thy life did manifest thou lovedst me not,
And thou wilt have me die assured of it.
Thou hid'st a thousand daggers in thy thoughts,
Which thou hast whetted on thy stony heart,
To stab at half an hour of my life.
What, canst thou not forbear me half an hour?   109
Then get thee gone and dig my grave thyself,
And bid the merry bells ring to thine ear
That thou art crownèd, not that I am dead.
Let all the tears that should bedew my hearse
Be drops of balm to sanctify thy head.   114
Only compound me with forgotten dust;   115
Give that which gave thee life unto the worms.
Pluck down my officers, break my decrees,
For now a time is come to mock at form.   118
Harry the Fifth is crowned. Up, vanity!   119
Down, royal state! All you sage counselors, hence!   120
And to the English court assemble now,
From every region, apes of idleness!
Now, neighbor confines, purge you of your scum.   123
Have you a ruffian that will swear, drink, dance,
Revel the night, rob, murder, and commit
The oldest sins the newest kind of ways?
Be happy; he will trouble you no more.
England shall double gild his treble guilt;
England shall give him office, honor, might;
For the fifth Harry from curbed license plucks
The muzzle of restraint, and the wild dog
Shall flesh his tooth on every innocent.   132
O my poor kingdom, sick with civil blows!
When that my care could not withhold thy riots,   134
What wilt thou do when riot is thy care?   135
O, thou wilt be a wilderness again,   136
Peopled with wolves, thy old inhabitants!
PRINCE [kneeling and returning the crown]
 O, pardon me, my liege! But for my tears,   138
The moist impediments unto my speech,
I had forestalled this dear and deep rebuke   140
Ere you with grief had spoke and I had heard
The course of it so far. There is your crown;
And He that wears the crown immortally
Long guard it yours! If I affect it more   144
Than as your honor and as your renown,
Let me no more from this obedience rise,   146
Which my most inward true and duteous spirit
Teacheth this prostrate and exterior bending.
God witness with me, when I here came in,
And found no course of breath within Your Majesty,   150
How cold it struck my heart! If I do feign,
O, let me in my present wildness die
And never live to show th' incredulous world

The noble change that I have purposèd!
Coming to look on you, thinking you dead,
And dead almost, my liege, to think you were,
I spake unto this crown as having sense,   157
And thus upbraided it: "The care on thee depending
Hath fed upon the body of my father;
Therefore, thou best of gold art worst of gold.
Other, less fine in carat, is more precious,
Preserving life in med'cine potable;   162
But thou, most fine, most honored, most renowned,
Hast eat thy bearer up." Thus, my most royal liege,   164
Accusing it, I put it on my head,
To try with it, as with an enemy   166
That had before my face murdered my father,
The quarrel of a true inheritor.   168
But if it did infect my blood with joy
Or swell my thoughts to any strain of pride,   170
If any rebel or vain spirit of mine
Did with the least affection of a welcome   172
Give entertainment to the might of it,
Let God forever keep it from my head
And make me as the poorest vassal is
That doth with awe and terror kneel to it!
KING O my son,
God put it in thy mind to take it hence,
That thou mightst win the more thy father's love,
Pleading so wisely in excuse of it!
Come hither, Harry, sit thou by my bed,
   [The Prince rises and sits by the bed.]
And hear, I think, the very latest counsel   182
That ever I shall breathe. God knows, my son,
By what bypaths and indirect crook'd ways
I met this crown, and I myself know well
How troublesome it sat upon my head.
To thee it shall descend with better quiet,
Better opinion, better confirmation,   188
For all the soil of the achievement goes   189
With me into the earth. It seemed in me
But as an honor snatched with boisterous hand,   191
And I had many living to upbraid
My gain of it by their assistances,
Which daily grew to quarrel and to bloodshed,
Wounding supposèd peace. All these bold fears   195
Thou seest with peril I have answerèd,
For all my reign hath been but as a scene
Acting that argument. And now my death   198
Changes the mood, for what in me was purchased   199
Falls upon thee in a more fairer sort;   200
So thou the garland wear'st successively.   201
Yet, though thou stand'st more sure than I could do,

---

109 **forbear** spare   114 **balm** consecrated oil used in anointing the
King at his coronation   115 **compound** mix   118 **form** ceremony, orderly usages   119 **vanity** folly   120 **state** ceremony   123 **neighbor
confines** territories of neighboring countries   132 **flesh his tooth on**
i.e., plunge his teeth into the flesh of. (To *flesh* means "to initiate into
bloodshed," "to make an animal eager for prey by the taste of
blood.")   134 **When that** when.   **care** careful maintenance of discipline   135 **care** concern   136 **thou** i.e., the Prince and his kingdom
138 **But for** were it not for   140 **had** would have.   **dear** severe,
grievous (because deeply felt emotionally)   144 **affect** desire
146 **obedience** obeisance   150 **course** current

157 **as having sense** as if it were capable of sense impressions
162 **med'cine potable** potable gold, an elixir, thought from Galen's
time to possess magical powers to cure   164 **eat** eaten. (Pronounced
"et.")   166 **try** struggle   168 **The quarrel . . . inheritor** (The Prince,
as the son and heir of a murdered man, has a quarrel to settle with
the murderer.)   170 **strain** feeling, tendency   172 **affection** inclination   182 **latest** last   188 **opinion** public support, reputation
189 **soil** stain   191 **boisterous** violent   195 **fears** objects of fear
198 **argument** theme   199 **mood** state of mind; mode, musical key.
purchased i.e., gained by transaction   200 **sort** manner, way
201 **So** thus.   **garland** crown.   **successively** by right of succession

Thou art not firm enough, since griefs are green.   203
And all my friends, which thou must make thy
    friends,
Have but their stings and teeth newly ta'en out,
By whose fell working I was first advanced   206
And by whose power I well might lodge a fear   207
To be again displaced. Which to avoid,
I cut them off, and had a purpose now
To lead out many to the Holy Land,
Lest rest and lying still might make them look   211
Too near unto my state. Therefore, my Harry,   212
Be it thy course to busy giddy minds
With foreign quarrels, that action, hence borne out,   214
May waste the memory of the former days.   215
More would I, but my lungs are wasted so
That strength of speech is utterly denied me.
How I came by the crown, O God forgive,
And grant it may with thee in true peace live!

PRINCE   My gracious liege,
You won it, wore it, kept it, gave it me.
Then plain and right must my possession be,
Which I with more than with a common pain   223
'Gainst all the world will rightfully maintain.

       Enter [Prince John of] Lancaster, [Warwick, and
       others].

KING
Look, look, here comes my John of Lancaster.
PRINCE JOHN
Health, peace, and happiness to my royal father!
KING
Thou bring'st me happiness and peace, son John;
But health, alack, with youthful wings is flown
From this bare withered trunk. Upon thy sight   229
My worldly business makes a period.   230
Where is my lord of Warwick?
PRINCE   My lord of Warwick!

       [Warwick comes forward.]

KING
Doth any name particular belong
Unto the lodging where I first did swoon?   233
WARWICK
'Tis called Jerusalem, my noble lord.
KING
Laud be to God! Even there my life must end.
It hath been prophesied to me many years
I should not die but in Jerusalem,
Which vainly I supposed the Holy Land.
But bear me to that chamber; there I'll lie.
In that Jerusalem shall Harry die.

       [Exeunt, bearing the King in his bed.]

5.1   *Enter Shallow, Falstaff, and Bardolph [and Page].*

SHALLOW   By Cock and pie, sir, you shall not away   1
tonight.—What, Davy, I say!
FALSTAFF   You must excuse me, Master Robert Shallow.
SHALLOW   I will not excuse you, you shall not be excused, excuses shall not be admitted, there is no excuse
shall serve, you shall not be excused.—Why, Davy!

       [Enter Davy.]

DAVY   Here, sir.
SHALLOW   Davy, Davy, Davy, Davy, let me see, Davy,
let me see, Davy, let me see. Yea, marry, William cook,   9
bid him come hither.—Sir John, you shall not be excused.
DAVY   Marry, sir, thus: those precepts cannot be   12
served. And, again, sir: shall we sow the headland   13
with wheat?
SHALLOW   With red wheat, Davy. But for William   15
cook—are there no young pigeons?
DAVY   Yes, sir. Here is now the smith's note for shoeing   17
and plow irons.   *[He gives a paper.]*
SHALLOW   Let it be cast and paid.—Sir John, you shall   19
not be excused.
DAVY   Now, sir, a new link to the bucket must needs be   21
had. And sir, do you mean to stop any of William's
wages about the sack he lost the other day at Hinckley   23
fair?
SHALLOW   'A shall answer it. Some pigeons, Davy, a   25
couple of short-legged hens, a joint of mutton, and
any pretty little tiny kickshaws, tell William cook.   27

       [Davy and Shallow confer privately.]

DAVY   Doth the man of war stay all night, sir?
SHALLOW   Yea, Davy. I will use him well. A friend i' the
court is better than a penny in purse. Use his men
well, Davy, for they are arrant knaves, and will
backbite.
DAVY   No worse than they are backbitten, sir, for they   33
have marvelous foul linen.   34
SHALLOW   Well conceited, Davy. About thy business,   35
Davy.
DAVY   I beseech you, sir, to countenance William Visor   37
of Wo'ncot against Clement Perkes o' the Hill.
SHALLOW   There is many complaints, Davy, against that
Visor. That Visor is an arrant knave, on my knowledge.
DAVY   I grant your worship that he is a knave, sir; but
yet, God forbid, sir, but a knave should have some
countenance at his friend's request. An honest man,

5.1. Location: Gloucestershire. Shallow's house.
1 By Cock and pie (A mild oath, meaning "By God and the ordinal or book of services for the Church.")   **9 William cook** William the cook
12 precepts writs, summonses   **13 headland** strip of unplowed land between two plowed fields   **15 red wheat** a variety of red-tinged wheat planted late in the summer   **17 note** bill   **19 cast** added up
21 link chain.   **bucket** yoke or pail   **23 Hinckley** market town not far from Coventry, famous for its fairs   **25 answer** pay for   **27 kickshaws** fancy dishes. (From the French *quelque chose*.)   **33 backbitten** (With pun on "bitten by vermin.")   **34 marvelous** marvelously   **35 Well conceited** ingeniously punned   **37 countenance** favor

---

203 griefs are green grievances are fresh   **206 fell working** fierce effort   **207 lodge** harbor   **211–212 look . . . state** examine too painstakingly my regal status, my claim   **214 action . . . out** military action, conducted in other lands   **215 waste** efface, obliterate
223 pain effort   **229 Upon thy sight** at the very moment of my seeing you   **230 makes a period** comes to an end, rounds out a whole
233 lodging room, chamber

sir, is able to speak for himself, when a knave is not.
I have served your worship truly, sir, this eight years;
an I cannot once or twice in a quarter bear out a knave   47
against an honest man, I have little credit with your
worship. The knave is mine honest friend, sir; therefore, I beseech you, let him be countenanced.

SHALLOW   Go to, I say he shall have no wrong. Look   51
about, Davy. [*Exit Davy.*] Where are you, Sir John?   52
Come, come, come, off with your boots. Give me your
hand, Master Bardolph.

BARDOLPH   I am glad to see your worship.

SHALLOW   I thank thee with all my heart, kind Master
Bardolph. [*To the Page.*] And welcome, my tall fellow.   57
—Come, Sir John.

FALSTAFF   I'll follow you, good Master Robert Shallow.
[*Exit Shallow.*] Bardolph, look to our horses. [*Exeunt
Bardolph and Page.*] If I were sawed into quantities, I   61
should make four dozen of such bearded hermits'
staves as Master Shallow. It is a wonderful thing to see
the semblable coherence of his men's spirits and his.   64
They, by observing of him, do bear themselves like
foolish justices; he, by conversing with them, is turned   66
into a justice-like servingman. Their spirits are so mar-   67
ried in conjunction with the participation of society   68
that they flock together in consent, like so many wild
geese. If I had a suit to Master Shallow, I would humor
his men with the imputation of being near their mas-   71
ter; if to his men, I would curry with Master Shallow   72
that no man could better command his servants. It is
certain that either wise bearing or ignorant carriage is   74
caught, as men take diseases, one of another. Therefore let men take heed of their company. I will devise
matter enough out of this Shallow to keep Prince
Harry in continual laughter the wearing out of six
fashions, which is four terms, or two actions, and 'a   79
shall laugh without intervallums. O, it is much that a   80
lie with a slight oath and a jest with a sad brow will   81
do with a fellow that never had the ache in his shoul-   82
ders! O, you shall see him laugh till his face be like a   83
wet cloak ill laid up.   84

SHALLOW [*within*]   Sir John!

FALSTAFF   I come, Master Shallow, I come, Master
Shallow.   [*Exit.*]

47 **bear out** support   51 **Go to** (An expression of remonstrance.)
51–52 **Look about** look sharp, be on the alert   57 **tall** brave (but also
with an ironic witticism about the page's small stature)   61 **quantities**
pieces   64 **semblable coherence** close correspondence   66 **conversing** associating   67–68 **married . . . society** united by close association   71 **with . . . near** by implying that I am friendly with, or that
they enjoy the confidence of. (Probably the latter.)   72 **curry with**
flatter   74 **carriage** demeanor, behavior   79 **four terms** i.e., of
court—Michaelmas, Hilary, Easter, and Trinity—all in all, comprising one legal year.   **actions** lawsuits (which proceed slowly at the
rate of two a year, unlike fashions, which do not last even one-quarter of a year)   80 **intervallums** intervals between terms of court
81 **sad** serious   82–83 **a fellow . . . shoulders** i.e., someone who is
inexperienced in the troubles and complexities of this world and
hence gullible   84 **ill laid up** carelessly put away wet so that it
wrinkles

5.2

*Enter Warwick [and the] Lord Chief Justice
[meeting].*

WARWICK
How now, my Lord Chief Justice, whither away?   1

CHIEF JUSTICE   How doth the King?

WARWICK
Exceeding well. His cares are now all ended.

CHIEF JUSTICE
I hope, not dead.

WARWICK   He's walked the way of nature,   4
And to our purposes he lives no more.

CHIEF JUSTICE
I would His Majesty had called me with him.
The service that I truly did his life   7
Hath left me open to all injuries.

WARWICK
Indeed I think the young King loves you not.

CHIEF JUSTICE
I know he doth not, and do arm myself
To welcome the condition of the time,
Which cannot look more hideously upon me
Than I have drawn it in my fantasy.

*Enter [Prince] John [of Lancaster], Thomas [of
Clarence], and Humphrey [of Gloucester, with
Westmorland, and others].*

WARWICK
Here come the heavy issue of dead Harry.   14
O, that the living Harry had the temper   15
Of he, the worst of these three gentlemen!   16
How many nobles then should hold their places
That must strike sail to spirits of vile sort!   18

CHIEF JUSTICE
O God, I fear all will be overturned.

PRINCE JOHN
Good morrow, cousin Warwick, good morrow.

GLOUCESTER, CLARENCE   Good morrow, cousin.

PRINCE JOHN
We meet like men that had forgot to speak.   22

WARWICK
We do remember, but our argument   23
Is all too heavy to admit much talk.

PRINCE JOHN
Well, peace be with him that hath made us heavy!

CHIEF JUSTICE
Peace be with us, lest we be heavier!

GLOUCESTER
O good my lord, you have lost a friend indeed,
And I dare swear you borrow not that face
Of seeming sorrow; it is sure your own.

PRINCE JOHN
Though no man be assured what grace to find,   30

5.2. Location: Westminster. The royal court.
1 **whither away** where are you going   4 **walked . . . nature** i.e., died
7 **truly** loyally   14 **heavy issue** grieving sons   15 **temper** disposition
16 **he, the worst** the least worthy   18 **strike sail** i.e., salute as a token
of submission. (A naval custom.)   22 **forgot** forgotten how   23 **argument** subject   30 **grace to find** favor he will find

You stand in coldest expectation.   31
I am the sorrier; would 'twere otherwise.

CLARENCE
Well, you must now speak Sir John Falstaff fair,   33
Which swims against your stream of quality.   34

CHIEF JUSTICE
Sweet princes, what I did I did in honor,
Led by th' impartial conduct of my soul,
And never shall you see that I will beg
A ragged and forestalled remission.   38
If truth and upright innocency fail me,
I'll to the King my master that is dead
And tell him who hath sent me after him.

WARWICK   Here comes the Prince.

*Enter the Prince [as King Henry the Fifth] and
Blunt.*

CHIEF JUSTICE
Good morrow, and God save Your Majesty!

KING
This new and gorgeous garment, majesty,
Sits not so easy on me as you think.
Brothers, you mix your sadness with some fear.
This is the English, not the Turkish court;
Not Amurath an Amurath succeeds,   48
But Harry Harry. Yet be sad, good brothers,
For, by my faith, it very well becomes you.
Sorrow so royally in you appears
That I will deeply put the fashion on
And wear it in my heart. Why then, be sad,
But entertain no more of it, good brothers,
Than a joint burden laid upon us all.
For me, by heaven, I bid you be assured,   56
I'll be your father and your brother too.
Let me but bear your love, I'll bear your cares.
Yet weep that Harry's dead, and so will I;
But Harry lives that shall convert those tears
By number into hours of happiness.   61

PRINCES
We hope no otherwise from Your Majesty.

KING
You all look strangely on me. [*To the Chief Justice.*]
And you most.
You are, I think, assured I love you not.

CHIEF JUSTICE
I am assured, if I be measured rightly,
Your Majesty hath no just cause to hate me.

KING   No?
How might a prince of my great hopes forget
So great indignities you laid upon me?
What? Rate, rebuke, and roughly send to prison   70
Th' immediate heir of England? Was this easy?   71

May this be washed in Lethe and forgotten?   72

CHIEF JUSTICE
I then did use the person of your father;   73
The image of his power lay then in me.
And in th' administration of his law,
Whiles I was busy for the commonwealth,
Your Highness pleasèd to forget my place,
The majesty and power of law and justice,
The image of the King whom I presented,   79
And struck me in my very seat of judgment;
Whereon, as an offender to your father,
I gave bold way to my authority
And did commit you. If the deed were ill,   83
Be you contented, wearing now the garland,   84
To have a son set your decrees at naught,
To pluck down justice from your awful bench,   86
To trip the course of law and blunt the sword
That guards the peace and safety of your person,
Nay, more, to spurn at your most royal image
And mock your workings in a second body?   90
Question your royal thoughts, make the case yours;
Be now the father and propose a son,   92
Hear your own dignity so much profaned,
See your most dreadful laws so loosely slighted,
Behold yourself so by a son disdained,
And then imagine me taking your part
And in your power soft silencing your son.   97
After this cold consideration sentence me,   98
And, as you are a king, speak in your state   99
What I have done that misbecame my place,
My person, or my liege's sovereignty.

KING
You are right justice, and you weigh this well.   102
Therefore still bear the balance and the sword;   103
And I do wish your honors may increase,
Till you do live to see a son of mine
Offend you and obey you, as I did.
So shall I live to speak my father's words:
"Happy am I, that have a man so bold
That dares do justice on my proper son;   109
And not less happy, having such a son
That would deliver up his greatness so
Into the hands of justice." You did commit me;
For which I do commit into your hand
Th' unstainèd sword that you have used to bear,   114
With this remembrance, that you use the same   115
With the like bold, just, and impartial spirit
As you have done 'gainst me. There is my hand.
You shall be as a father to my youth.
My voice shall sound as you do prompt mine ear,   119
And I will stoop and humble my intents

---

31 **coldest** most comfortless   33 **speak . . . fair** speak courteously to Sir John Falstaff   34 **swims . . . quality** runs counter to your natural inclination and position   38 **A . . . remission** a half-hearted (beggarly) pardon, which is sure to be refused or whose effect is gone before it is granted   48 **Amurath** a Turkish sultan who, upon succeeding his father, had his brothers strangled   56 **For** as for   61 **By number** i.e., for each of our many tears, there will be an hour of happiness   70 **Rate** chide   71 **easy** of small importance, easily forgotten

72 **Lethe** the river of forgetfulness in Hades   73 **use the person** act as representative   79 **presented** represented   83 **commit** i.e., to prison   84 **garland** crown   86 **awful** inspiring awe   90 **second body** representative, deputy   92 **propose** imagine, suppose   97 **soft** gently   98 **cold consideration** calm reflection   99 **state** royal capacity   102 **right** true, ideal   103 **balance** scale (which along with the *sword* was an emblem of justice)   109 **proper** own   114 **have used** were accustomed   115 **remembrance** reminder, admonition   119 **sound** speak

To your well-practiced wise directions.
And, princes all, believe me, I beseech you:
My father is gone wild into his grave,   123
For in his tomb lie my affections,   124
And with his spirits sadly I survive,   125
To mock the expectation of the world,
To frustrate prophecies, and to raze out
Rotten opinion, who hath writ me down   128
After my seeming. The tide of blood in me   129
Hath proudly flowed in vanity till now;   130
Now doth it turn and ebb back to the sea,
Where it shall mingle with the state of floods   132
And flow henceforth in formal majesty.
Now call we our high court of Parliament.
And let us choose such limbs of noble counsel
That the great body of our state may go
In equal rank with the best-governed nation;
That war, or peace, or both at once, may be
As things acquainted and familiar to us,
[*To Chief Justice*] In which you, father, shall have
    foremost hand.
Our coronation done, we will accite,   141
As I before remembered, all our state.   142
And, God consigning to my good intents,   143
No prince nor peer shall have just cause to say,
God shorten Harry's happy life one day!   *Exeunt.*

❧

5.3 [*A table and chairs are set out.*] *Enter Sir John
[Falstaff], Shallow, Silence, Davy, Bardolph, [and
the] Page. [Davy provides food and wine.]*

SHALLOW   Nay, you shall see my orchard, where, in an
arbor, we will eat a last year's pippin of mine own   2
grafting, with a dish of caraways, and so forth. Come, 3
cousin Silence. And then to bed.
FALSTAFF   'Fore God, you have here a goodly dwelling
and a rich.
SHALLOW   Barren, barren, barren. Beggars all, beggars
all, Sir John. Marry, good air. Spread, Davy, spread, 8
Davy. Well said, Davy.   9
FALSTAFF   This Davy serves you for good uses. He is
your servingman and your husband.   11
SHALLOW   A good varlet, a good varlet, a very good   12
varlet, Sir John. By the Mass, I have drunk too much
sack at supper. A good varlet. Now sit down, now sit
down. Come, cousin.   [*They sit.*]

SILENCE   Ah, sirrah, quoth 'a, we shall   16
    [*sings*] "Do nothing but eat, and make good cheer,
        And praise God for the merry year,
        When flesh is cheap and females dear,   19
        And lusty lads roam here and there
        So merrily,
        And ever among so merrily."   22
FALSTAFF   There's a merry heart, good Master Silence!
I'll give you a health for that anon.   24
SHALLOW   Give Master Bardolph some wine, Davy.
DAVY [*to the guests*]   Sweet sir, sit.—I'll be with you
anon.—Most sweet sir, sit. Master page, good
master page, sit. Proface! What you want in meat,   28
we'll have in drink. But you must bear, the heart's all. 29
                                            [*Exit.*]
SHALLOW   Be merry, Master Bardolph, and, my little
soldier there, be merry.
SILENCE [*sings*]
    "Be merry, be merry, my wife has all,
    For women are shrews, both short and tall.
    'Tis merry in hall when beards wags all,   34
    And welcome merry Shrovetide.   35
    Be merry, be merry."
FALSTAFF   I did not think Master Silence had been a
man of this mettle.   38
SILENCE   Who, I? I have been merry twice and once   39
ere now.

            Enter Davy.

DAVY [*to the guests*]   There's a dish of leather-coats for 41
you.
SHALLOW   Davy!
DAVY   Your worship? I'll be with you straight. [*To
Falstaff.*] A cup of wine, sir?
SILENCE [*sings*]
    "A cup of wine that's brisk and fine,
    And drink unto thee, leman mine,   47
    And a merry heart lives long-a."
FALSTAFF   Well said, Master Silence.
SILENCE   And we shall be merry; now comes in the
sweet o' the night.
FALSTAFF   Health and long life to you, Master Silence.
SILENCE [*sings*]
    "Fill the cup, and let it come,   53
    I'll pledge you a mile to the bottom."   54
SHALLOW   Honest Bardolph, welcome. If thou want'st
anything, and wilt not call, beshrew thy heart. [*To the
Page.*] Welcome, my little tiny thief, and welcome in-
deed, too. I'll drink to Master Bardolph, and to all the
cabileros about London.   59

123–124 **My . . . affections** i.e., my wildness, having disappeared
with my father's death, is buried along with my father **124 affections**
(wild) inclinations **125 spirits** soul, spiritual heritage. **sadly** soberly
128 who which **129 After my seeming** according to what I appeared to be. **blood** passion **130 vanity** folly **132 state of floods**
majesty of the ocean **141 accite** summon **142 remembered** mentioned. **state** peers, nobility **143 consigning to** sanctioning
5.3. Location: Gloucestershire. Shallow's orchard.
2 pippin a kind of apple **3 caraways** caraway seeds (often eaten with
apples) **8 Spread** spread the cloth **9 said** done **11 husband** steward **12 varlet** servant

16 quoth 'a said he **19 flesh** meat (with sexual suggestion) **22 ever
among** all the while **24 give you a health** drink you a toast
28 Proface (Formula of welcome to a meal, meaning "May it do you
good.") **want** lack. **meat** food **29 bear** be forbearing **34 beards
wags all** all the beards wag up and down (as men talk and laugh)
35 Shrovetide three-day period of merrymaking before Ash Wednesday and Lent **38 mettle** spirit **39 twice and once** i.e., now and
again **41 leather-coats** russet apples **47 leman** sweetheart **53 let it
come** i.e., pass it around **54 a mile** i.e., even if it were a mile
59 cabileros cavaliers, gallants

DAVY   I hope to see London once ere I die.   60

BARDOLPH   An I might see you there, Davy!

SHALLOW   By the Mass, you'll crack a quart together, 62
ha, will you not, Master Bardolph?

BARDOLPH   Yea, sir, in a pottle pot.   64

SHALLOW   By God's liggens, I thank thee. The knave 65
will stick by thee, I can assure thee that. 'A will not
out, 'a; 'tis true bred.   67

BARDOLPH   And I'll stick by him, sir.

SHALLOW   Why, there spoke a king. Lack nothing; be
merry. (*One knocks at door.*) Look who's at door there,
ho! Who knocks?   [*Davy goes to the door.*]

FALSTAFF   [*to Silence, seeing him drinking*] Why, now
you have done me right.   73

SILENCE   [*sings*]
    "Do me right,
    And dub me knight,
        Samingo."   76
Is 't not so?

FALSTAFF   'Tis so.

SILENCE   Is 't so? Why then, say an old man can do
somewhat.   80

DAVY   [*returning*]   An 't please your worship, there's
one Pistol come from the court with news.

FALSTAFF   From the court? Let him come in.

Enter Pistol.

How now, Pistol?

PISTOL   Sir John, God save you!

FALSTAFF   What wind blew you hither, Pistol?

PISTOL   Not the ill wind which blows no man to good.
Sweet knight, thou art now one of the greatest men in
this realm.

SILENCE   By 'r Lady, I think 'a be, but goodman Puff of 90
Bar'son.

PISTOL   Puff?
Puff i' thy teeth, most recreant coward base!   93
Sir John, I am thy Pistol and thy friend,
And helter-skelter have I rode to thee,
And tidings do I bring, and lucky joys,
And golden times, and happy news of price.   97

FALSTAFF   I pray thee now, deliver them like a man of 98
this world.   99

PISTOL
A foutre for the world and worldlings base!   100
I speak of Africa and golden joys.   101

FALSTAFF
O base Assyrian knight, what is thy news?   102

Let King Cophetua know the truth thereof.   103

SILENCE   [*sings*]
    "And Robin Hood, Scarlet, and John."   104

PISTOL
Shall dunghill curs confront the Helicons?   105
And shall good news be baffled?   106
Then, Pistol, lay thy head in Furies' lap.   107

SHALLOW   Honest gentleman, I know not your breed- 108
ing.   109

PISTOL   Why then, lament therefor.   110

SHALLOW   Give me pardon, sir. If, sir, you come with
news from the court, I take it there's but two ways:
either to utter them or conceal them. I am, sir, under
the King, in some authority.

PISTOL
Under which king, Besonian? Speak, or die.   115

SHALLOW
Under King Harry.

PISTOL   Harry the Fourth, or Fifth?

SHALLOW
Harry the Fourth.

PISTOL   A foutre for thine office!
Sir John, thy tender lambkin now is king;
Harry the Fifth's the man. I speak the truth.
When Pistol lies, do this, and fig me like   120
The bragging Spaniard.   [*Pistol makes a fig.*]

FALSTAFF   What, is the old King dead?

PISTOL
As nail in door. The things I speak are just.   123

FALSTAFF   Away, Bardolph, saddle my horse! Master
Robert Shallow, choose what office thou wilt in the
land, 'tis thine. Pistol, I will double-charge thee with 126
dignities.

BARDOLPH   O joyful day! I would not take a knighthood
for my fortune.

PISTOL   What, I do bring good news?

FALSTAFF   Carry Master Silence to bed. [*Exit Davy,
carrying Silence.*] Master Shallow, my lord Shallow—be what thou wilt, I am fortune's steward—get
on thy boots. We'll ride all night. O sweet Pistol!
Away, Bardolph! [*Exit Bardolph.*] Come, Pistol, utter
more to me, and withal devise something to do thyself
good. Boot, boot, Master Shallow! I know the young
King is sick for me. Let us take any man's horses; the
laws of England are at my commandment. Blessed are
they that have been my friends, and woe to my Lord
Chief Justice!

---

60 **once** one day   62 **crack** consume   64 **pottle pot** two-quart tankard   65 **liggens** (Unexplained.)   67 **out** drop out   73 **done me
right** i.e., kept up with me in drinking   76 **Samingo** Sir Mingo (from
the Latin *mingo*, "I urinate"), the hero of the song   80 **somewhat**
something   90 **but** except. (Silence interprets *greatest* in the sense of
"heaviest.")   **goodman** yeoman   93 **recreant** faithless   97 **price**
great value   98–99 **man of this world** ordinary man   100 **foutre**
(From the French *foutre*, "fornicate"; a very insulting phrase.)
101 **Africa** (Fabled for its wealth.)   102 **Assyrian** (Falstaff adopts Pistol's high-flown style and metrics.)

103 **Cophetua** (King Cophetua married a beggar maid, according to
the popular ballad "King Cophetua and the Beggar Maid.")   104 **And
. . . John** (A scrap from another ballad.)   105 **Helicons** i.e., poets.
(Mount Helicon was the abode of the Muses.) Pistol takes umbrage at
the drunken interruption of his poetically phrased announcement.
106 **baffled** disgraced   107 **lay . . . lap** (Pistol appeals his wrong to
the avenging goddesses of classical mythology.)   108–109
breeding parentage, rank   110 **therefor** for that   115 **Besonian** low,
beggarly rascal. (From Italian *bisogno*, "need.")   120 **fig** insult with a
vulgar gesture, consisting of thrusting the thumb between the index
and middle fingers. (The gesture originated in Spain, as line 121 suggests. It means much the same as *foutre*, lines 100 and 117.)
123 **just** true   126 **double-charge** (With a play on Pistol's name.)

PISTOL
Let vultures vile seize on his lungs also!
"Where is the life that late I led?" say they.   143
Why, here it is. Welcome these pleasant days!
Exeunt.

❧

5.4   *Enter Beadle and three or four officers [dragging in Hostess Quickly and Doll Tearsheet].*

HOSTESS   No, thou arrant knave! I would to God that I might die, that I might have thee hanged. Thou hast drawn my shoulder out of joint.

BEADLE   The constables have delivered her over to me, and she shall have whipping cheer, I warrant her.   5 There hath been a man or two killed about her.   6

DOLL   Nuthook, nuthook, you lie! Come on, I'll tell thee   7 what, thou damned tripe-visaged rascal, an the child I   8 go with do miscarry, thou wert better thou hadst struck thy mother, thou paper-faced villain!   10

HOSTESS   O the Lord, that Sir John were come! He would make this a bloody day to somebody. But I pray God the fruit of her womb miscarry!   13

BEADLE   If it do, you shall have a dozen of cushions again; you have but eleven now. Come, I charge you   15 both, go with me, for the man is dead that you and Pistol beat amongst you.

DOLL   I'll tell you what, you thin man in a censer, I will   18 have you as soundly swinged for this—you bluebottle   19 rogue, you filthy famished correctioner, if you be not swinged, I'll forswear half-kirtles!   21

BEADLE   Come, come, you she knight-errant, come.   22

HOSTESS   O God, that right should thus overcome   23 might! Well, of sufferance comes ease.   24

DOLL   Come, you rogue, come, bring me to a justice.

HOSTESS   Ay, come, you starved bloodhound.

DOLL   Goodman death, goodman bones!

HOSTESS   Thou atomy, thou!   28

DOLL   Come, you thin thing, come, you rascal!   29

BEADLE   Very well.   [*Exeunt.*]

❧

143 **Where . . . led** (Fragment of a ballad.)
5.4. Location: London. A street.
5 **whipping cheer** i.e., a whipping for supper   6 **about her** (1) in her company (2) on her account   7 **Nuthook** hook for pulling down branches in nutting; here, a constable   8, 10 **tripe-visaged, paper-faced** (Allusions to the pockmarked and sallow complexion of the Beadle.)   13 **miscarry** (The hostess must mean just the opposite of this.)   15 **eleven now** (The Beadle accuses Doll of using one of the cushions to make her appear pregnant; pregnant women were spared execution.)   18 **thin . . . censer** i.e., figure of a man on the lid of a censer or incense burner, embossed in low relief   19 **swinged** thrashed.   **bluebottle** (An allusion to the Beadle's blue coat.)
21 **half-kirtles** skirts   22 **she knight-errant** i.e., a woman who wanders about and sins at night   23–24 **right . . . might** (The hostess gets this backward.)   24 **sufferance** suffering. (Suffering now promises a better future, since one's luck is bound to change.)   28 **atomy** (For "anatomy," skeleton; an *atomy* is an "atom," "speck.")   29 **rascal** lean deer

---

5.5   *Enter [Grooms as] strewers of rushes.*

FIRST GROOM   More rushes, more rushes!   1

SECOND GROOM   The trumpets have sounded twice.

THIRD GROOM   'Twill be two o'clock ere they come from the coronation. Dispatch, dispatch.   [*Exeunt.*]   4

Trumpets sound, and the King and his train pass over the stage. After them enter Falstaff, Shallow, Pistol, Bardolph, and the Boy [Page].

FALSTAFF   Stand here by me, Master Shallow; I will make the King do you grace. I will leer upon him as   6 'a comes by, and do but mark the countenance that he will give me.

PISTOL   God bless thy lungs, good knight!

FALSTAFF   Come here, Pistol, stand behind me.—O, if I had had time to have made new liveries, I would   11 have bestowed the thousand pound I borrowed of   12 you. But 'tis no matter; this poor show doth better.   13 This doth infer the zeal I had to see him.   14

SHALLOW   It doth so.

FALSTAFF   It shows my earnestness of affection—

SHALLOW   It doth so.

FALSTAFF   My devotion—

SHALLOW   It doth, it doth, it doth.

FALSTAFF   As it were, to ride day and night, and not to deliberate, not to remember, not to have patience to shift me—   22

SHALLOW   It is best, certain.

FALSTAFF   But to stand stained with travel and sweating with desire to see him, thinking of nothing else, putting all affairs else in oblivion, as if there were nothing else to be done but to see him.

PISTOL   'Tis *semper idem*, for *obsque hoc nihil est*. 'Tis all in   28 every part.   29

SHALLOW   'Tis so, indeed.

PISTOL
My knight, I will inflame thy noble liver   31
And make thee rage.
Thy Doll, and Helen of thy noble thoughts,   33
Is in base durance and contagious prison,   34
Haled thither   35
By most mechanical and dirty hand.   36
Rouse up Revenge from ebon den with fell Alecto's snake,   37
For Doll is in. Pistol speaks naught but truth.   38

5.5. Location: A public place near Westminster Abbey.
1 **rushes** floor coverings, here used for strewing the streets in the King's path   4 **Dispatch** hurry   6 **grace** honor.   **leer** glance sideways and invitingly   11 **liveries** uniforms of a noble or royal household   12 **bestowed** spent   13 **you** i.e., Justice Shallow.   **poor show** appearing in inferior garments   14 **infer** imply   22 **shift me** change my apparel   28 **semper . . . est** "always the same," for "apart from this there is nothing." (Pistol approvingly rephrases Falstaff's dedication to put his loyalty to the Prince above all else.) *Obsque* is an error for *absque*.   28–29 **'Tis . . . part** (Perhaps a very free translation of the Latin.)   31 **liver** (The seat of the passions.)   33 **Helen** i.e., Helen of Troy, the type of womanly beauty   34 **durance** imprisonment.   **contagious** pestilential   35 **Haled** dragged   36 **mechanical** menial, base   37 **ebon** black.   **Alecto** one of the Furies, who were depicted with snakes twined in their hair   38 **in** i.e., in prison

FALSTAFF   I will deliver her.

[*Shouts within, and the trumpets sound.*]

PISTOL
There roared the sea, and trumpet-clangor sounds.

Enter the King and his train, [the Lord Chief Justice among them].

FALSTAFF
God save Thy Grace, King Hal, my royal Hal!

PISTOL
The heavens thee guard and keep, most royal imp
of fame!   42

FALSTAFF   God save thee, my sweet boy!

KING
My Lord Chief Justice, speak to that vain man.   44

CHIEF JUSTICE [*to Falstaff*]
Have you your wits? Know you what 'tis you
speak?

FALSTAFF
My King! My Jove! I speak to thee, my heart!

KING
I know thee not, old man. Fall to thy prayers.
How ill white hairs becomes a fool and jester!
I have long dreamt of such a kind of man,
So surfeit-swelled, so old, and so profane,
But being awaked I do despise my dream.   50
Make less thy body hence, and more thy grace;   52
Leave gormandizing. Know the grave doth gape   53
For thee thrice wider than for other men.
Reply not to me with a fool-born jest.
Presume not that I am the thing I was,
For God doth know, so shall the world perceive,
That I have turned away my former self;
So will I those that kept me company.
When thou dost hear I am as I have been,
Approach me, and thou shalt be as thou wast,
The tutor and the feeder of my riots.
Till then, I banish thee, on pain of death,
As I have done the rest of my misleaders,
Not to come near our person by ten mile.
For competence of life I will allow you,   66
That lack of means enforce you not to evils.
And, as we hear you do reform yourselves,
We will, according to your strengths and qualities,
Give you advancement.—Be it your charge, my lord,
To see performed the tenor of our word.
Set on.   [*Exeunt King and his train.*]

FALSTAFF   Master Shallow, I owe you a thousand
pound.

SHALLOW   Yea, marry, Sir John, which I beseech you to
let me have home with me.

FALSTAFF   That can hardly be, Master Shallow. Do not
you grieve at this. I shall be sent for in private to him.
Look you, he must seem thus to the world. Fear not
your advancements; I will be the man yet that shall
make you great.

SHALLOW   I cannot perceive how, unless you give me
your doublet and stuff me out with straw. I beseech
you, good Sir John, let me have five hundred of my
thousand.

FALSTAFF   Sir, I will be as good as my word. This that
you heard was but a color.   87

SHALLOW   A color that I fear you will die in, Sir John.   88

FALSTAFF   Fear no colors. Go with me to dinner. Come,   89
Lieutenant Pistol, come, Bardolph. I shall be sent for
soon at night.   91

*Enter [the Lord Chief] Justice and Prince John [of
Lancaster, with officers].*

CHIEF JUSTICE
Go carry Sir John Falstaff to the Fleet.   92
Take all his company along with him.

FALSTAFF   My lord, my lord—

CHIEF JUSTICE
I cannot now speak. I will hear you soon.
Take them away.

PISTOL
Si fortuna me tormenta, spero me contenta.   97

*Exeunt [all but Prince John
and the Chief Justice].*

PRINCE JOHN
I like this fair proceeding of the King's.
He hath intent his wonted followers
Shall all be very well provided for,
But all are banished till their conversations   101
Appear more wise and modest to the world.

CHIEF JUSTICE   And so they are.

PRINCE JOHN
The King hath called his parliament, my lord.

CHIEF JUSTICE   He hath.

PRINCE JOHN
I will lay odds that, ere this year expire,
We bear our civil swords and native fire   107
As far as France. I heard a bird so sing,
Whose music, to my thinking, pleased the King.
Come, will you hence?   [*Exeunt.*]

❖

Epilogue

[*Enter Epilogue.*]

EPILOGUE
First, my fear; then, my curtsy; last, my speech. My   1
fear is your displeasure; my curtsy, my duty; and my
speech, to beg your pardons. If you look for a good
speech now, you undo me, for what I have to say is of

---

42 imp scion   **44 vain** foolish   **50 surfeit-swelled** swollen from gluttony   **52 hence** henceforth   **53 gormandizing** gluttonous eating
66 competence of life modest allowance

87 color pretense. (But Shallow uses the word to mean *collar*, "hangman's noose.")   **88 die** (1) be hanged (2) be dyed   **89 colors** standards or flags (of the enemy). "Fear not," says Falstaff.   **91 soon at
night** early in the evening   **92 Fleet** a famous London prison   **97 Si
. . . contenta** (See the note for 2.4.179, above.)   **101 conversations**
conduct   **107 civil . . . fire** i.e., our weapons used recently in civil
war
Epilogue
1 curtsy bow, obeisance

mine own making, and what indeed I should say will,
I doubt, prove mine own marring. But to the purpose, 6
and so to the venture. Be it known to you, as it is very
well, I was lately here in the end of a displeasing play, 8
to pray your patience for it and to promise you a better. I meant indeed to pay you with this, which, if like
an ill venture it come unluckily home, I break, and 11
you, my gentle creditors, lose. Here I promised you I
would be, and here I commit my body to your mercies. Bate me some and I will pay you some and, as 14
most debtors do, promise you infinitely.

If my tongue cannot entreat you to acquit me, will
you command me to use my legs? And yet that were
but light payment, to dance out of your debt. But a
good conscience will make any possible satisfaction,
and so would I. All the gentlewomen here have forgiven me. If the gentlemen will not, then the gentlemen do not agree with the gentlewomen, which was
never seen before in such an assembly.

One word more, I beseech you. If you be not too
much cloyed with fat meat, our humble author will
continue the story, with Sir John in it, and make you 26
merry with fair Katharine of France. Where, for anything I know, Falstaff shall die of a sweat, unless al- 28
ready 'a be killed with your hard opinions; for Oldcas- 29
tle died a martyr, and this is not the man. My tongue 30
is weary; when my legs are too, I will bid you good
night; and so I kneel down before you, but, indeed, to
pray for the Queen.   [*Exit Epilogue.*]

6 doubt fear   **8 displeasing play** (No satisfactory identification has
ever been made.)   **11 ill venture** unlucky sending out of merchant
vessels.   **break** (1) break my promise (2) become bankrupt   **14 Bate
me some** let me off from some portion of the debt   **26 Sir John in it**
(Shakespeare evidently originally intended to introduce Falstaff into
Henry V; instead, only his death is reported there in 2.1 and 2.3.)
28 sweat i.e., plague, fever, or venereal disease   **29–30 Oldcastle
. . . man** i.e., Falstaff was not intended to resemble Sir John Oldcastle, the Lollard venerated by sixteenth-century Puritans as a martyr for
their beliefs. (This statement may have been intended to placate Lord
Cobham, descendant of Oldcastle, whose resentment of Shakespeare's
use of the Oldcastle name in an earlier version of the *Henry IV* plays
may have led to the change of the name to Falstaff.)

The Life of King Henry the Fifth

Henry V (1599) is Shakespeare's culminating statement in the genre of the English history play. Unlike the late and atypical *Henry VIII* (1613), which is separated from the rest of Shakespeare's history plays by some fourteen years, *Henry V* sums up the historical themes with which Shakespeare had been fascinated for an entire decade. The play, first published in a memorially reconstructed and abridged quarto in 1600, must have been written not long after *2 Henry IV*. To be sure, the play does not entirely fulfill the promise made in *2 Henry IV* to "continue the story, with Sir John in it, and make you merry with fair Katharine of France." Falstaff is missing. As before, Shakespeare apparently saw a grand design to his four-play sequence (which had started with *Richard II*) but improvised when he came to the writing of each part. Despite these minor adjustments in the overall plan, however, *Henry V* is clearly intended to bring to fulfillment the education of a politician-prince and to illustrate the arts of political kingship that Prince Hal had derived from his experiences in the earlier plays.

In a sense, too, *Henry V* sums up the achievement of the English history play, not only for Shakespeare, but also for other popular playwrights. The patriotic history play, born in the excitement of the Armada era (c. 1588), had nearly run its course by 1599 and was soon to be supplanted by other dramatic genres, such as satire and revenge tragedy. Dark and complex political realities were already changing the buoyant mood in which the history play had been born: the aging Queen Elizabeth was near death and without a Protestant heir, while fear of another invasion threatened. In *Henry V*, we sense the approaching end of an era, for the play both celebrates the achievements of the English monarchy and examines its limits.

Henry V has become a controversial play, chiefly because our recent experiences with war have led us to be wary of political leaders who, in the name of patriotism, lay claim to and invade another country. George Bernard Shaw is prominent among those who have deplored Henry as a priggish and complacent warmonger and imperialist. Many historically minded critics, on the other hand, warn of the dangers of reading anachronistically from a modern perspective, and they argue that Henry is an admirable model of conduct according to Renaissance notions of statecraft and military leadership. What is Shakespeare's attitude toward his war hero? Does he sympathize with Henry's condescension toward the French and his order to every soldier to kill his French prisoners? Or is Shakespeare's admiration qualified by ironic reservations? As is usual in Shakespeare's work, the perspective is complex and balanced. The play pulls us in two directions. Although the Chorus, which interprets the play for us, approves of Henry's military posture, the grandiose rhetoric of war is consistently undercut by matter-of-fact revelations of people's self-interested motives. This contrast between rhetorical illusion and political reality extends from the justification of Henry's French campaign to his state marriage with Katharine of France. On the ethical issue of killing the French prisoners, for example, the play offers us contradictory and seemingly irreconcilable impressions. At the end of 4.6, Henry orders that "every soldier" is to "kill his prisoners," evidently because the English are under attack and cannot spare men to guard those who have been captured. In 4.7 (lines 1–10 and 54–55), however, we are told by Gower that the King gave the order in retaliation for the massacre by the cowardly French of the boys guarding the English luggage. Similarly, on the eve of the battle of Agincourt, we are left to draw our own conclusions about King Henry's conversation with his soldiers (4.1. 98–227). Is he evading the question of whether his cause is just by turning to a really very different matter of responsibility for someone else's sins, or is he simply testing his men with hard questions to prepare them for battle? Ironic puzzles such as these probably never amount to open disillusionment in this play, although some modern critics and directors would argue otherwise; the ironies are perhaps, instead, the acknowledgment of a special kind of morality pertaining to kingship.

Skill in rhetoric is a key to Henry's success—in defying the French Dauphin, in preparing troops for battle, or in wooing the French princess for his queen. As the Archbishop of Canterbury notes approvingly, King Henry's versatility as a rhetorician applies to all the vital disciplines of kingship: Henry can "reason in divinity," "debate of commonwealth affairs," "discourse of war," handle "any cause of policy," and in all such matters speak in "sweet and honeyed sentences" (1.1.39–51). Through the arts of language, Henry displays piety, learning, administrative sagacity, political cunning, and military intrepidity. Like the contemporary play *Julius Caesar* (1599), *Henry V* is concerned with techniques of persuasion. (The earlier *Richard III* is also a highly rhetorical play, though chiefly through the negative example of tyrannical behavior.) Yet, however much we may be swayed emotionally by the rhetoric, we realize that the public figure of Henry V is a mask behind which we can perceive little. Only rarely do we glimpse the affable young companion of the *Henry IV* plays. King Henry has accepted the responsibility of playing a political role. It denies him a private and separate identity, even—or especially—in choosing a wife. And it complicates our task of assessing the sincerity of his utterances. Is he genuinely pious, or has he merely learned the usefulness of pious utterance in swaying people's hearts? What especially are his motives for going to war against France?

Shakespeare could have begun this play with the stirring scene (1.2) in which Henry, urged on by his advisers, issues a defiant challenge to the French ambassadors. Instead, Shakespeare treats us to a prior glimpse beneath the patriotic surface. It seems that the Archbishop of Canterbury, threatened with a bill in Parliament designed to take away the better half of the Church's possessions, has resolved to parry with a counterproposal, whereby the Church will give Henry a very substantial sum for his French campaign, provided the offensive tax bill can be conveniently forgotten. The Archbishop has already been negotiating with Henry and surmises that the plan will work. This revelation is not shocking to us; it merely reveals the political process at work. The faint undercurrent of anticlericalism suggests that Henry is to be admired for putting pressure on his clergy with such success; they are rich and can afford to support the war. In any case, the dramatic effect is to show how men's practical motives affect their rhetoric. When, in the subsequent scene, the Archbishop delivers a public lecture on the English claim to France, we know that this learned prelate has a prior and self-interested commitment to the war. His intricate dynastic argument, which he proclaims to be "as clear as is the summer's sun" (1.2.86), gives to the war a much-needed public justification. Henry's questions indicate not only his genuine concern about the legitimacy of his claim but also his political need for the Church's endorsement of his cause; he has already claimed certain French dukedoms and must have the Church's official approval of those claims before he can proceed. He similarly needs the backing of his nobles, who also have their own reasons for approving the campaign. Henry skillfully orchestrates the scene to produce the desired effect of unanimous and patriotic consent.

Although never directly stated, Henry's own motives for going to war must also combine sincere zeal with calculated self-interest. As king, he longs to recover the French territory that England governed in the great days of Poitiers and Crécy. As a man, he bristles at the contemptuous challenge of the Dauphin; Henry must still strive to overcome his reputation as a wastrel and must prove himself worthy of honorable comparison with his great ancestors. Politically (and this motive remains most hidden), Henry has absorbed his father's sage advice to "busy giddy minds / With foreign quarrels" (2 Henry IV, 4.5.213–214), to blunt political opposition at home by uniting English resentment against a foreign scapegoat.

The exigencies of war do indeed provide Henry with an opportunity for proceeding against his political enemies. He arrests the Earl of Cambridge, Lord Scroop, and Sir Thomas Grey at Southampton on charges of conspiring with France. The scene (2.2) is, for Shakespeare, uncharacteristically one-sided. We are never even told that Cambridge is the chief pretender to the English throne, son of the Duke of York, married to Anne Mortimer, and founder of the Yorkist claim in the York-Lancastrian wars—the sort of rival whom Shakespeare elsewhere portrays with understanding. Instead, the rhetoric of the Chorus to Act 2 blatantly warns us to expect "hell and treason" (line 29). These three conspirators, like Judases, says the Chorus, have bargained away their king for gold. (In fact, Cambridge insists that his motive was not financial, though he is not permitted to say what it was.) The playwright does not give them complex motives; they are sinners, so horrified by their own intents that they are actually grateful to be caught. The scene serves, by such rhetorical devices, to strengthen Henry's claim to the English throne, as well as to the territories in France. Opposition to his rule during wartime is, in the view of the Chorus, simply treasonous; all persuasive evidences of dynastic rival claims are hidden from our view.

Comedy also contributes to the rhetorical image making of the hero in *Henry V*. The tavern crew is on hand, though deprived of Falstaff's beguiling company and more distant from Henry than in the earlier history plays. Only briefly and in disguise, on the night before the battle, does the King encounter Pistol. The name of Bardolph comes to Henry as though in recollection of a distant past, when he hears that Bardolph is about to be executed for stealing from French churches. Henry confirms the sentence: "We would have all such offenders so cut off" (3.6.107). Whatever momentary pang Henry may feel, he remains constant to his banishment of Falstaff. And, although Shakespeare pleads for our sympathies in the seriocomic account of Falstaff's death, seen through the childlike naiveté of Mistress Quickly, there is no hope of reconciliation between Henry and his former mates. Pistol, despite his ornamental language, is little more than a boaster, coward, and thief. The tavern revelers are now the opportunists of war, troublemakers such as are found in every army, engaging rascals deserving to be cudgeled by more honorable men.

Pistol gets his comeuppance from Captain Fluellen, who replaces Falstaff as the chief comic figure, both in prominence (his role is second in length to that of Henry) and in proximity to the King. Fluellen is a Welshman, like Henry of Monmouth, and is proud of this kinship. Because Fluellen is loyal and valiant, he is a person worthy to be seen in Henry's company. Yet there is none of the brilliant duel of wits previously linking Henry and Falstaff. Fluellen is a humorous character, identified at once by such comically exaggerated features as his Welsh accent and mannerisms of speech, his old-fashioned and somewhat fanatical sense of military propriety, and his devotion to the ancient rules of military discipline. Fluellen is a caricature, subject to mild satirical laughter, and there is a note of condescension in Henry's habit of playing practical jokes on the captain. (Henry makes practical jokes at others' expense as well, such as the soldier named Williams, with whom he exchanges gloves.) Unlike Falstaff, Fluellen lacks perspective on his own pomposity. He is a zealot for duty, and one feels Henry is taking unfair advantage when he picks on one who is such an easy mark for laughter. We suspect that Henry is using people again, bolstering his public image as the king with the common touch, borrowing a little Welsh color for myth-making purposes. At the same time, Fluellen is steadfast, upright, and a credit to his countryman Henry. With his fellow captains from Scotland, Ireland, and England, he demonstrates that Britishers can fight together, even if they do antagonize one another with their proud regional customs. Those customs are to be cherished as part of the British character; because Pistol offers gratuitous insult to the Welsh tradition of wearing a leek in the cap on Saint Davy's Day, he must be thrashed.

As with the comic characters and Henry's political enemies, Henry V is rhetorically one-sided in its presentation of the French. Patriotism is a raw emotion, and Henry cannot appeal to it without awakening hostility toward the enemy. (Ironically enough, the great film version of Henry V by Laurence Olivier was created during World War II to arouse national feelings against the Germans rather than against the French, and with complete success. Any enemy will do in such patriotic moods.) The French are portrayed as haughty, vastly superior in numbers, envious of one another, contemptuous of their own leadership (especially the Dauphin), treacherous (attacking the boys with the luggage), and craven. Even their joking is characterized by an unattractively bestial kind of bawdry (3.7.48–68). The British—"we few, we happy few" (4.3.60)—are tired and outnumbered but invincible and seemingly protected by God. Henry's order to kill the French prisoners and his description of the rapes and pillages his soldiers will commit if Harfleur fails to surrender (3.3.1–27) do, to be sure, raise serious questions about the morality of war under the best of kings; the play may be caustic toward the French nobility but does not necessarily exonerate the English. Even here, however, we are led to believe that, because the French are so execrably governed, France will suffer less under English rule. Henry takes care that his soldiers will not despoil the French countryside except under conditions of military "necessity." Only in Montjoy, the Duke of Burgundy, and Katharine of France does Shakespeare offer redeeming portraits of the French character, and in these instances the terms of hierarchical ascendancy seem clear: masculine English dominance, gentle French submissiveness. Katharine becomes "la belle France," depicted in Burgundy's eloquent peacemaking speech as being so much in need of competent management.

Women exist only on the margins of this war play, as in Shakespeare's other historical plays. Mistress Quickly's role is chiefly as a reminder to us that men fight with one another for the possession of women; the ludicrous quarrel of Pistol and Nym over Mistress Quickly anticipates the way in which Katharine of France will be one of the chief spoils of the war itself. Women also wait patiently at home while their men fight, and tend them when they are sick. Mistress Quickly's recollection of the death of Falstaff (2.3.9–25) is masterful in its evocation of tender solicitude, illiterate piety, and unconscious eroticism. Later, in France, Pistol pauses with momentary regret over news of the death of his wife from venereal disease (5.1.80–81). Katharine of France, though vastly better born, finds her role as a woman no less circumscribed. We first see her learning English from Alice, her lady in waiting (3.4). Why is she learning English? The obvious political reason, never explicitly stated, emerges with a kind of violence: the scene of the English lesson follows immediately after King Henry's ultimatum to the citizens of Harfleur to surrender or see their women raped and their children impaled by English weapons (3.3.27–41). Katharine accepts her lot with good grace, as though she had any other choice but to do so. We gather from her scene with Alice that she is a women of spirit who can be imperious, vain, and curious about sex. Because she also is very French, the wooing scene in Act 5 can play comically on the differences of temperament between her and Henry, who is as English as she is French. These differences make Henry and Katharine potentially compatible through complementarity—male and female, soldier and lady, English and French—but the compact is patently a hierarchical one of conqueror and conquered. Historically, we know that the product of their sexual union, Henry VI, will bring to a dismal end the harmony of discords that presides uncertainly over the end of Henry V.

Henry woos Katharine with real flair, despite their unstated mutual recognition that their courtship is, above all, a matter of state, in which they must play predetermined roles. The individual within Henry V gives way to the public personality, but he never loses his style. He manages always to be true to himself, as a wooer or as a soldier. We see him in disguise, hobnobbing with common soldiers of his camp on the eve of battle, earnestly discussing with them the morality of war. We see him, with endearing human inconsistency, coveting all the glory of victory over the French and then adjuring his soldiers to give credit for that victory to God alone. Even if we are at times less attracted to this successful warrior and politician than to the carefree young man of 1 Henry IV, we can still honor Henry's choice of responsible maturity and see that it is even compassionately self-denying. A king cannot be like other men, and Henry is willing to accept this price of leadership.

The Chorus presents Henry V to us as if it were an epic as well as a drama. Henry is an epic hero, defined in terms of mythic allusions and abstractions. He is compared to

Mars, the god of war, with Famine, Sword, and Fire leashed at his heels, crouched and ready for employment. He is the "mirror of all Christian kings," and his followers are "English Mercurys" (2.0.6–7) with winged heels. Personified Expectation sits in the air, promising crowns and crownets to Henry and his followers. Henry's fleet of ships in the English Channel becomes "A city on th' inconstant billows dancing" (3.0.15). On the eve of battle, amidst his brothers, friends, and countrymen, Henry warms every heart with "cheerful semblance and sweet majesty" and with his "largess universal like the sun" (4.0.40-43). He forbids vainglorious pride and gives credit for his victory "Quite from himself to God" (5.0.22).

The action the Chorus describes is comparably epic, as it moves from England to France and back again, leaping over time, surveying all levels of society in the English nation, portraying famous military encounters seemingly more suited to epic narration (or to film, as both Laurence Olivier's 1944 film and Kenneth Branagh's more recent [1989] film version brilliantly demonstrate) than to the stage. The stage's limitation forms, indeed, a major burden of the Chorus' argument. He apologizes to the spectators for the "flat unraisèd spirits" that have dared to bring forth so vast an object "On this unworthy scaffold," in this "cockpit" or "wooden O" (Prologue). The play confines "mighty men" "In little room," "Mangling by starts the full course of their glory" (Epilogue).

This apology sounds like becoming modesty on Shakespeare's part, in conceding the truth of Ben Jonson's objection that a few hired actors with rusty swords can scarcely do justice to England's great wars of the past. *Henry V* is not a Jonsonian neoclassical play. Paradoxically, however, Shakespeare's acknowledgment of the limited means at his disposal to create mimetic spectacle amounts to a defense of his own theater of the imagination. Through the Chorus' repeated urgings that we use our "imaginary forces" to supply what the actors and the theater necessarily lack, Shakespeare invites us as spectators and partners into his world of art. The play becomes a journey of thought, of making "imaginary puissance." When Shakespeare and his acting company talk of horses, we are to "see them / Printing their proud hoofs i' the receiving earth" (Prologue). This is not to minimize the importance of the theatrical experience but, indeed, quite the opposite, since we are instructed to liberate ourselves through that theatrical experience and to re-create by means of Shakespeare's script an epic vision. Shakespeare's stage, bare of scenery, relying on good actors and the words they speak, becomes through its very flexibility more versatile in creating that vision than the most ornate and mechanically sophisticated illusionistic theater.

The Life of King Henry the Fifth

[*Dramatis Personae*

CHORUS

KING HENRY THE FIFTH
HUMPHREY, DUKE OF GLOUCESTER,   } the King's brothers
JOHN, DUKE OF BEDFORD,
DUKE OF CLARENCE,
DUKE OF EXETER, *the King's uncle*
DUKE OF YORK, *the King's cousin*
EARL OF SALISBURY
EARL OF WESTMORLAND
EARL OF WARWICK
EARL OF HUNTINGDON

ARCHBISHOP OF CANTERBURY
BISHOP OF ELY

RICHARD, EARL OF CAMBRIDGE,   } conspirators against the King
HENRY, LORD SCROOP OF MASHAM,
SIR THOMAS GREY,

SIR THOMAS ERPINGHAM,
CAPTAIN GOWER,
CAPTAIN FLUELLEN,   } officers in the King's army
CAPTAIN MACMORRIS,
CAPTAIN JAMY,
JOHN BATES,
ALEXANDER COURT,   } soldiers in the King's army
MICHAEL WILLIAMS,
An English HERALD

PISTOL,
NYM,   } *Falstaff's former tavern-mates*
BARDOLPH,
BOY, *formerly Falstaff's page*
HOSTESS, *formerly Mistress Quickly, now married to Pistol*

DUKE OF BURGUNDY

FRENCH KING, *Charles the Sixth*
QUEEN ISABEL *of France*
DAUPHIN, *Lewis*
KATHARINE, *Princess of France*
ALICE, *a lady attending Katharine*
DUKE OF ORLEANS
DUKE OF BERRI
BUKE OF BOURBON
DUKE OF BRITTANY
CONSTABLE OF FRANCE

LORD RAMBURES
LORD GRANDPRÉ
GOVERNOR OF HARFLEUR
MONSIEUR LE FER, *a French soldier*
MONTJOY, *the French herald*
French AMBASSADORS *to England*

Lords, Ladies, Officers, Soldiers, Citizens, Messengers, and Attendants

SCENE: *England, afterwards France*]

Prologue

Enter [Chorus as] Prologue.

CHORUS
O, for a Muse of fire, that would ascend   1
The brightest heaven of invention!   2
A kingdom for a stage, princes to act,
And monarchs to behold the swelling scene!   4
Then should the warlike Harry, like himself,   5
Assume the port of Mars; and at his heels,   6
Leashed in like hounds, should famine, sword, and
    fire
Crouch for employment. But pardon, gentles all,   8
The flat unraisèd spirits that hath dared   9
On this unworthy scaffold to bring forth   10
So great an object. Can this cockpit hold   11
The vasty fields of France? Or may we cram   12
Within this wooden O the very casques   13
That did affright the air at Agincourt?
O, pardon! Since a crooked figure may
Attest in little place a million;   15
And let us, ciphers to this great account,   16
On your imaginary forces work.   17
Suppose within the girdle of these walls   18
Are now confined two mighty monarchies,
Whose high uprearèd and abutting fronts   21
The perilous narrow ocean parts asunder.   22
Piece out our imperfections with your thoughts:
Into a thousand parts divide one man,
And make imaginary puissance.   25
Think, when we talk of horses, that you see them
Printing their proud hoofs i' the receiving earth.

[handwritten margin note: we can never show you how big this really was]

For 'tis your thoughts that now must deck our
    kings,   28
Carry them here and there, jumping o'er times,
Turning th' accomplishment of many years
Into an hourglass—for the which supply,   31
Admit me Chorus to this history,
Who, Prologue-like, your humble patience pray
Gently to hear, kindly to judge, our play.   *Exit.*

♣

1.1   *Enter the two bishops, [the Archbishop] of
          Canterbury and [the Bishop of] Ely.*

CANTERBURY
My lord, I'll tell you. That self bill is urged   1
Which in th' eleventh year of the last king's reign
Was like, and had indeed against us passed,   3
But that the scambling and unquiet time   4
Did push it out of farther question.   5
ELY
But how, my lord, shall we resist it now?
CANTERBURY
It must be thought on. If it pass against us,
We lose the better half of our possession.
For all the temporal lands which men devout   9
By testament have given to the Church
Would they strip from us, being valued thus:
As much as would maintain, to the King's honor,
Full fifteen earls and fifteen hundred knights,
Six thousand and two hundred good esquires,   14
And, to relief of lazars and weak age   15
Of indigent faint souls past corporal toil,   16
A hundred almshouses right well supplied;
And to the coffers of the King besides
A thousand pounds by th' year. Thus runs the bill.
ELY   This would drink deep.
CANTERBURY   'Twould drink the cup and all.
ELY   But what prevention?
CANTERBURY
The King is full of grace and fair regard.
ELY
And a true lover of the holy Church.
CANTERBURY
The courses of his youth promised it not.
The breath no sooner left his father's body
But that his wildness, mortified in him,   27
Seemed to die too; yea, at that very moment
Consideration like an angel came   29
And whipped th' offending Adam out of him,   30
Leaving his body as a paradise
T' envelop and contain celestial spirits.
Never was such a sudden scholar made;

Prologue.
1 Muse of fire (Of the four elements—earth, air, fire, and water—fire is the most sublime and mounting.)   **2 invention** poetic imagination   **4 swelling** splendid, magnificent   **5 like himself** i.e., presented in a fashion worthy of so great a king   **6 port** bearing   **8 gentles** gentlemen and gentlewomen   **9 flat unraisèd** uninspired, lifeless.   **spirits** i.e., actors and playwright.   **hath** (Elizabethan usage often pairs a plural subject with a singular verb.)   **10 scaffold** stage   **11 cockpit** (Elizabethan theaters were shaped rather like arenas for animal fighting.)   **12 vasty** vast, spacious   **13 O** (Refers to a round theater such as the Globe; the play may have been performed at the Curtain Theater.)   **casques** helmets   **15 crooked figure** cipher or zero (which, added to a number, will multiply its value tenfold)   **16 Attest** stand for   **17 account** (1) sum total (continuing the metaphor of *crooked figure*) (2) story   **18 imaginary forces** forces of imagination   **21 abutting** touching, bordering.   **fronts** (1) frontiers, i.e., the cliffs of Dover and Calais (2) foreheads   **22 perilous . . . ocean** i.e., English Channel   **25 puissance** armed might, army

28 deck dress, adorn   **31 the which supply** which service
1.1. Location: England. The royal court.
1 self same   **3 like** likely (to have passed)   **4 scambling** unsettled   **5 question** consideration   **9 temporal** used for secular purposes   **14 esquires** members of the gentry, ranking just below knights   **15 lazars** lepers   **16 corporal** physical   **27 mortified** killed   **29 Consideration** meditation, reflection   **30 offending Adam** original sin

Never came reformation in a flood
With such a heady currance, scouring faults;   35
Nor never Hydra-headed willfulness   36
So soon did lose his seat, and all at once,   37
As in this king.
ELY   We are blessed in the change.
CANTERBURY
Hear him but reason in divinity,
And, all-admiring, with an inward wish
You would desire the King were made a prelate.
Hear him debate of commonwealth affairs,
You would say it hath been all in all his study.
List his discourse of war, and you shall hear   44
A fearful battle rendered you in music.   45
Turn him to any cause of policy,   46
The Gordian knot of it he will unloose,   47
Familiar as his garter, that, when he speaks,   48
The air, a chartered libertine, is still,   49
And the mute wonder lurketh in men's ears   50
To steal his sweet and honeyed sentences;   51
So that the art and practic part of life   52
Must be the mistress to this theoric.   53
Which is a wonder how His Grace should glean it,
Since his addiction was to courses vain,   55
His companies unlettered, rude, and shallow,   56
His hours filled up with riots, banquets, sports,   57
And never noted in him any study,
Any retirement, any sequestration
From open haunts and popularity.   60
ELY
The strawberry grows underneath the nettle,
And wholesome berries thrive and ripen best
Neighbored by fruit of baser quality;
And so the Prince obscured his contemplation
Under the veil of wildness, which, no doubt,
Grew like the summer grass, fastest by night,
Unseen, yet crescive in his faculty.   67
CANTERBURY
It must be so, for miracles are ceased.   68
And therefore we must needs admit the means   69
How things are perfected.
ELY   But, my good lord,
How now for mitigation of this bill
Urged by the Commons? Doth His Majesty

Incline to it, or no?
CANTERBURY   He seems indifferent,   73
Or rather swaying more upon our part
Than cherishing th' exhibiters against us;   75
For I have made an offer to His Majesty,
Upon our spiritual convocation   77
And in regard of causes now in hand,   78
Which I have opened to His Grace at large,   79
As touching France, to give a greater sum
Than ever at one time the clergy yet
Did to his predecessors part withal.   82
ELY
How did this offer seem received, my lord?
CANTERBURY
With good acceptance of His Majesty,
Save that there was not time enough to hear,
As I perceived His Grace would fain have done,   86
The severals and unhidden passages   87
Of his true titles to some certain dukedoms,
And generally to the crown and seat of France,   89
Derived from Edward, his great-grandfather.   90
ELY
What was th' impediment that broke this off?
CANTERBURY
The French ambassador upon that instant
Craved audience; and the hour I think is come
To give him hearing. Is it four o'clock?
ELY   It is.
CANTERBURY
Then go we in to know his embassy,   96
Which I could with a ready guess declare
Before the Frenchman speak a word of it.
ELY
I'll wait upon you, and I long to hear it.   Exeunt.

❧

1.2   *Enter the King, Humphrey [Duke of Gloucester],*
        Bedford, Clarence, Warwick, Westmorland, and
        Exeter [with attendants].

KING
Where is my gracious lord of Canterbury?
EXETER
Not here in presence.
KING   Send for him, good uncle.
WESTMORLAND
Shall we call in th' ambassador, my liege?
KING
Not yet, my cousin. We would be resolved,   4
Before we hear him, of some things of weight
That task our thoughts, concerning us and France.   6

35 **heady currance** headlong current 36 **Hydra-headed** i.e., many-headed. (Alludes to the Lernaean Hydra, a monster of many heads overcome by Hercules.) 37 **his seat** its throne 44 **List** listen to 45 **rendered . . . music** i.e., eloquently narrated 46 **cause of policy** matter of statecraft 47 **Gordian knot** (It was foretold that whoever should untie the Gordian knot would rule Asia. Alexander solved the problem by cutting the knot.) 48 **Familiar** as offhandedly or routinely. **that** so that 49 **chartered libertine** free spirit, licensed to roam at will 50–51 **the mute . . . sentences** i.e., wonder makes men silent, eagerly listening to hear more of his sweetly profitable wise sayings 52–53 **So . . . theoric** so that experience in practical life must have been the teacher by which he acquired his theoretical conception 55 **addiction** inclination 56 **rude** coarse 57 **riots** reveling. **sports** amusements 60 **open . . . popularity** places of public resort and low company 67 **crescive . . . faculty** naturally inclined to grow 68 **miracles are ceased** (Protestants generally believed that no miracles occurred after the revelation of Christ.) 69 **means** i.e., natural causes

73 **indifferent** impartial 75 **exhibiters** those who introduce bills in Parliament 77 **Upon** on behalf of. **convocation** formal assembly of the clergy 78 **in hand** under consideration 79 **opened** expounded. **at large** in full 82 **withal** with 86 **fain** gladly 87 **severals** details. **unhidden passages** obvious lines of descent 89 **seat** throne 90 **Edward** i.e., Edward III 96 **embassy** message
1.2. Location: England. The royal court.
4 **cousin** (Correct form of address from royal family to nobles.) **be resolved** come to a decision 6 **task** engage, occupy

Enter two bishops, [the Archbishop of Canterbury and the Bishop of Ely].

CANTERBURY
God and his angels guard your sacred throne,
And make you long become it!
KING   Sure we thank you.   8
My learnèd lord, we pray you to proceed,
And justly and religiously unfold
Why the law Salic that they have in France   11
Or should or should not bar us in our claim.   12
And God forbid, my dear and faithful lord,
That you should fashion, wrest, or bow your
    reading,
Or nicely charge your understanding soul   15
With opening titles miscreate, whose right   16
Suits not in native colors with the truth;   17
For God doth know how many now in health
Shall drop their blood in approbation   19
Of what your reverence shall incite us to.
Therefore take heed how you impawn our person,   21
How you awake our sleeping sword of war.
We charge you in the name of God take heed;
For never two such kingdoms did contend
Without much fall of blood, whose guiltless drops
Are every one a woe, a sore complaint   26
'Gainst him whose wrongs gives edge unto the
    swords   27
That makes such waste in brief mortality.   28
Under this conjuration speak, my lord;   29
For we will hear, note, and believe in heart
That what you speak is in your conscience washed
As pure as sin with baptism.

CANTERBURY
Then hear me, gracious sovereign, and you peers,
That owe yourselves, your lives, and services
To this imperial throne. There is no bar
To make against Your Highness' claim to France
But this, which they produce from Pharamond: 37
"In terram Salicam mulieres ne succedant,"
"No woman shall succeed in Salic land."
Which Salic land the French unjustly gloze   40
To be the realm of France, and Pharamond
The founder of this law and female bar.
Yet their own authors faithfully affirm
That the land Salic is in Germany,
Between the floods of Saale and of Elbe;   45
Where, Charles the Great having subdued the
    Saxons,   46
There left behind and settled certain French,
Who, holding in disdain the German women

For some dishonest manners of their life,   49
Established then this law: to wit, no female
Should be inheritrix in Salic land—
Which Salic, as I said, twixt Elbe and Saale,
Is at this day in Germany called Meissen.
Then doth it well appear the Salic law
Was not devisèd for the realm of France;
Nor did the French possess the Salic land
Until four hundred one-and-twenty years
After defunction of King Pharamond,   58
Idly supposed the founder of this law,   59
Who died within the year of our redemption
Four hundred twenty-six; and Charles the Great
Subdued the Saxons, and did seat the French
Beyond the River Saale, in the year
Eight hundred five. Besides, their writers say,
King Pepin, which deposèd Childeric,   65
Did, as heir general, being descended   66
Of Blithild, which was daughter to King Clothair,
Make claim and title to the crown of France.
Hugh Capet also, who usurped the crown
Of Charles the Duke of Lorraine, sole heir male
Of the true line and stock of Charles the Great,
To find his title with some shows of truth,   72
Though, in pure truth, it was corrupt and naught,
Conveyed himself as th' heir to the Lady Lingard,   74
Daughter to Charlemagne, who was the son   75
To Lewis the Emperor, and Lewis the son
Of Charles the Great. Also King Lewis the Tenth,   77
Who was sole heir to the usurper Capet,
Could not keep quiet in his conscience,
Wearing the crown of France, till satisfied
That fair Queen Isabel, his grandmother,
Was lineal of the Lady Ermengard,   82
Daughter to Charles the foresaid Duke of Lorraine;
By the which marriage the line of Charles the Great
Was reunited to the crown of France.
So that, as clear as is the summer's sun,
King Pepin's title and Hugh Capet's claim,
King Lewis his satisfaction, all appear   88
To hold in right and title of the female;
So do the kings of France unto this day,
Howbeit they would hold up this Salic law   91
To bar Your Highness claiming from the female,
And rather choose to hide them in a net   93
Than amply to imbar their crooked titles   94
Usurped from you and your progenitors.
KING
May I with right and conscience make this claim?
CANTERBURY
The sin upon my head, dread sovereign!

8 **become** adorn, grace 11 **Salic** (See explanation at lines 39–45.) 12 **Or** either 15 **nicely charge** subtly and foolishly burden 16 **opening titles miscreate** expounding spurious claims 17 **Suits . . . colors** i.e., does not naturally harmonize 19 **approbation** support, proof 21 **impawn** pledge 26 **woe** grievance. **sore** severe, grievous 27 **wrongs** wrongdoings 28 **in brief mortality** i.e., among mortal, short-lived men 29 **conjuration** solemn adjuration 37 **Pharamond** legendary Frankish king 40 **gloze** deceptively explain away 45 **floods** rivers 46 **Charles the Great** Charlemagne

49 **dishonest** unchaste 58 **defunction** death 59 **Idly** foolishly 65 **which** who (as also in line 67) 66 **heir general** heir through male or female line 72 **find** provide 74 **Conveyed himself** passed himself off 75 **Charlemagne** (Holinshed's and Hall's error, followed by Shakespeare, for Charles the Bold.) 77 **Lewis the Tenth** (Actually, Louis IX; an error copied from Holinshed.) 82 **lineal of** descended from 88 **Lewis his satisfaction** Lewis' conviction 91 **Howbeit** notwithstanding 93 **hide . . . net** i.e., conceal the weakness of their case in a tangle of contradictions 94 **amply to imbar** frankly to bar claim to

For in the Book of Numbers is it writ,
When the man dies, let the inheritance   99
Descend unto the daughter. Gracious lord,   100
Stand for your own; unwind your bloody flag!   101
Look back into your mighty ancestors:
Go, my dread lord, to your great-grandsire's tomb,·   103
From whom you claim! Invoke his warlike spirit,
And your great-uncle's, Edward the Black Prince,
Who on the French ground played a tragedy,   106
Making defeat on the full power of France,   107
Whiles his most mighty father on a hill
Stood smiling to behold his lion's whelp
Forage in blood of French nobility.
O noble English, that could entertain   111
With half their forces the full pride of France
And let another half stand laughing by,
All out of work and cold for action!   114

ELY
Awake remembrance of these valiant dead,
And with your puissant arm renew their feats!
You are their heir; you sit upon their throne;
The blood and courage that renownèd them   118
Runs in your veins; and my thrice-puissant liege
Is in the very May morn of his youth,
Ripe for exploits and mighty enterprises.

EXETER
Your brother kings and monarchs of the earth
Do all expect that you should rouse yourself
As did the former lions of your blood.

WESTMORLAND
They know Your Grace hath cause, and means, and
     might;
So hath Your Highness. Never king of England   126
Had nobles richer and more loyal subjects,
Whose hearts have left their bodies here in England
And lie pavilioned in the fields of France.   129

CANTERBURY
O, let their bodies follow, my dear liege,
With blood, and sword, and fire to win your right!
In aid whereof we of the spiritualty   132
Will raise Your Highness such a mighty sum
As never did the clergy at one time
Bring in to any of your ancestors.

KING
We must not only arm t' invade the French,
But lay down our proportions to defend   137
Against the Scot, who will make road upon us   138
With all advantages.   139

CANTERBURY
They of those marches, gracious sovereign,   140
Shall be a wall sufficient to defend
Our inland from the pilfering borderers.

KING
We do not mean the coursing snatchers only,   143
But fear the main intendment of the Scot,   144
Who hath been still a giddy neighbor to us.   145
For you shall read that my great-grandfather
Never went with his forces into France
But that the Scot on his unfurnished kingdom   148
Came pouring like the tide into a breach
With ample and brim fullness of his force,   150
Galling the gleanèd land with hot assays,   151
Girding with grievous siege castles and towns;
That England, being empty of defense,
Hath shook and trembled at th' ill neighborhood.   154

CANTERBURY
She hath been then more feared than harmed, my
     liege.   155
For hear her but exampled by herself: 156
When all her chivalry hath been in France   157
And she a mourning widow of her nobles,
She hath herself not only well defended
But taken and impounded as a stray   160
The King of Scots, whom she did send to France   161
To fill King Edward's fame with prisoner kings
And make her chronicle as rich with praise
As is the ooze and bottom of the sea
With sunken wrack and sumless treasuries.   165

A LORD
But there's a saying very old and true:
     "If that you will France win,
     Then with Scotland first begin."
For once the eagle England being in prey,   169
To her unguarded nest the weasel Scot
Comes sneaking, and so sucks her princely eggs,
Playing the mouse in absence of the cat,
To 'tame and havoc more than she can eat.   173

EXETER
It follows then the cat must stay at home;
Yet that is but a crushed necessity,   175
Since we have locks to safeguard necessaries
And pretty traps to catch the petty thieves.   177
While that the armèd hand doth fight abroad,
Th' advisèd head defends itself at home;   179

99–100 When . . . daughter (This paraphrase leaves out an important phrase. Numbers 27:8 reads, "When a man dies leaving no son, his patrimony shall pass to his daughter.")   **101 unwind** unfurl   **103 great-grandsire's** i.e., Edward III's. His descent through his mother Isabella from the French King Philip IV is the basis of English claims to the French kingdom—a claim through female inheritance. Hence the importance of lines 39–55.   **106 tragedy** i.e., the Battle of Crécy, 1346, a major defeat for the French   **107 power** army   **111 entertain** engage, encounter   **114 for action** for want of action   **118 renownèd** brought renown to   **126 So** so indeed   **129 pavilioned** tented, encamped   **132 spiritualty** clergy   **137 lay . . . proportions** allocate our forces   **138 road** inroad, raid   **139 With all advantages** whenever a good opportunity presents itself

140 marches borderlands (here, in the north)   **143 coursing snatchers** mounted raiders   **144 intendment** plan, hostile intent   **145 still** always.   **giddy** unstable, fickle   **148 unfurnished** unprovided with defense   **150 brim** absolute, complete   **151 Galling . . . assays** worrying the land stripped of defenders with hot attacks   **154 neighborhood** neighborliness   **155 feared** frightened   **156 hear . . . herself** i.e., only listen how she can be instructed by an example from her own history   **157 chivalry** knights   **160 impounded as a stray** (David II of Scotland was captured and imprisoned in 1346 while Edward III was in France.)   **161 to France** (Historically, David II was imprisoned in London, not sent to France.)   **165 wrack** wreckage.   **sumless** inestimable   **169 in prey** absent in search of prey   **173 'tame** attame, break into.   **havoc** ravage   **175 crushed necessity** forced conclusion   **177 pretty** ingenious   **179 advisèd** wise, prudent

For government, though high, and low, and lower,   180
Put into parts, doth keep in one consent,   181
Congreeing in a full and natural close,   182
Like music.
CANTERBURY Therefore doth heaven divide
The state of man in divers functions,
Setting endeavor in continual motion,
To which is fixèd, as an aim or butt,   186
Obedience; for so work the honeybees,
Creatures that by a rule in nature teach
The act of order to a peopled kingdom.
They have a king, and officers of sorts,   190
Where some, like magistrates, correct at home;   191
Others, like merchants, venture trade abroad;
Others, like soldiers, armèd in their stings,
Make boot upon the summer's velvet buds,
Which pillage they with merry march bring home   194
To the tent royal of their emperor,
Who, busied in his majesty, surveys   197
The singing masons building roofs of gold,
The civil citizens kneading up the honey,
The poor mechanic porters crowding in   200
Their heavy burdens at his narrow gate,
The sad-eyed justice with his surly hum   202
Delivering o'er to executors pale   203
The lazy yawning drone. I this infer,
That many things, having full reference   205
To one consent, may work contrariously.   206
As many arrows loosèd several ways   207
Come to one mark, as many ways meet in one
    town,   208
As many fresh streams meet in one salt sea,
As many lines close in the dial's center,   210
So may a thousand actions once afoot
End in one purpose, and be all well borne   212
Without defeat. Therefore to France, my liege!
Divide your happy England into four,
Whereof take you one quarter into France,
And you withal shall make all Gallia shake.   216
If we with thrice such powers left at home
Cannot defend our own doors from the dog,
Let us be worried, and our nation lose   219
The name of hardiness and policy.   220
KING
Call in the messengers sent from the Dauphin.   221

[Exeunt some.]
Now are we well resolved, and by God's help
And yours, the noble sinews of our power,
France being ours, we'll bend it to our awe,   224
Or break it all to pieces. Or there we'll sit,   225
Ruling in large and ample empery   226
O'er France and all her almost kingly dukedoms,
Or lay these bones in an unworthy urn,
Tombless, with no remembrance over them.
Either our history shall with full mouth
Speak freely of our acts, or else our grave,
Like Turkish mute, shall have a tongueless mouth,
Not worshiped with a waxen epitaph.   233

Enter Ambassadors of France.

Now are we well prepared to know the pleasure
Of our fair cousin Dauphin; for we hear
Your greeting is from him, not from the King.
FIRST AMBASSADOR
May 't please Your Majesty to give us leave
Freely to render what we have in charge,
Or shall we sparingly show you far off   239
The Dauphin's meaning and our embassy?
KING
We are no tyrant, but a Christian king,
Unto whose grace our passion is as subject
As is our wretches fettered in our prisons.
Therefore with frank and with uncurbèd plainness
Tell us the Dauphin's mind.
FIRST AMBASSADOR   Thus, then, in few:
Your Highness, lately sending into France,
Did claim some certain dukedoms, in the right
Of your great predecessor, King Edward the Third.
In answer of which claim, the Prince our master
Says that you savor too much of your youth,
And bids you be advised there's naught in France
That can be with a nimble galliard won;   252
You cannot revel into dukedoms there.
He therefore sends you, meeter for your spirit,   254
This tun of treasure, and in lieu of this   255
Desires you let the dukedoms that you claim
Hear no more of you. This the Dauphin speaks.
          [A casket is presented;
          Exeter examines its contents.]
KING
What treasure, uncle?
EXETER   Tennis balls, my liege.
KING
We are glad the Dauphin is so pleasant with us.   259
His present and your pains we thank you for.
When we have matched our rackets to these balls,   261
We will in France, by God's grace, play a set

180 **though . . . lower** i.e., though composed of three broad social ranks 181 **Put into parts** separated into different functions. **one consent** mutual harmony 182 **Congreeing** agreeing together. **close** musical cadence 186 **aim or butt** target. (All endeavor is to direct itself toward obedience.) 190 **They . . . king** (A common error of early natural history, derived from Aristotle. The simile of the bees appears in Virgil, Sir Thomas Elyot, John Lyly, and others.) **of sorts** of various kinds 191 **correct** administer justice 194 **Make boot** prey 197 **majesty** royal office 200 **mechanic** engaged in manual labor 202 **sad-eyed** grave-eyed 203 **executors pale** executioners, pale in their terrible sternness 205–206 **having . . . consent** united by a common understanding 207 **loosèd several ways** shot from different directions 208 **ways** roads 210 **close** come together. **dial's** sundial's 212 **borne** carried out, sustained 216 **Gallia** France. (Latin name.) 219 **worried** torn apart, as by dogs 220 **hardiness and policy** bravery and statesmanship 221 **Dauphin** heir apparent to the French throne

224 **ours** i.e., ours by right. **our awe** submission to us 225 **Or there** either there 226 **empery** dominion 233 **Not . . . epitaph** i.e., with not even so much as a wax (as opposed to bronze) epitaph; one easily effaced 239 **sparingly** delicately. **far off** i.e., in general terms 252 **galliard** a lively dance 254 **meeter** more fitting 255 **tun** cask 259 **pleasant** jocular. (Also in line 281.) 261 **rackets** (1) tennis rackets (2) noisy military assaults

Shall strike his father's crown into the hazard. 263
Tell him he hath made a match with such a
　wrangler 264
That all the courts of France will be disturbed 265
With chases. And we understand him well, 266
How he comes o'er us with our wilder days, 267
Not measuring what use we made of them.
We never valued this poor seat of England, 269
And therefore, living hence, did give ourself 270
To barbarous license—as 'tis ever common
That men are merriest when they are from home. 272
But tell the Dauphin I will keep my state, 273
Be like a king, and show my sail of greatness 274
When I do rouse me in my throne of France.
For that I have laid by my majesty 276
And plodded like a man for working days, 277
But I will rise there with so full a glory
That I will dazzle all the eyes of France,
Yea, strike the Dauphin blind to look on us.
And tell the pleasant Prince this mock of his
Hath turned his balls to gunstones, and his soul 282
Shall stand sore chargèd for the wasteful vengeance 283
That shall fly with them; for many a thousand
　widows
Shall this his mock mock out of their dear husbands,
Mock mothers from their sons, mock castles down,
And some are yet ungotten and unborn 287
That shall have cause to curse the Dauphin's scorn.
But this lies all within the will of God,
To whom I do appeal, and in whose name
Tell you the Dauphin I am coming on
To venge me as I may, and to put forth
My rightful hand in a well-hallowed cause.
So get you hence in peace; and tell the Dauphin
His jest will savor but of shallow wit
When thousands weep more than did laugh at it.—
Convey them with safe conduct.—Fare you well. 297
　　　　　　　　　　　　Exeunt Ambassadors.

EXETER　This was a merry message.
KING
We hope to make the sender blush at it.
Therefore, my lords, omit no happy hour 300
That may give furtherance to our expedition;
For we have now no thought in us but France,
Save those to God, that run before our business.
Therefore let our proportions for these wars 304
Be soon collected, and all things thought upon

That may with reasonable swiftness add
More feathers to our wings; for, God before, 307
We'll chide this Dauphin at his father's door.
Therefore let every man now task his thought, 309
That this fair action may on foot be brought.
　　　　　　　　　　　　Flourish. Exeunt.

❧

2.0　*Enter Chorus.*

CHORUS
Now all the youth of England are on fire,
And silken dalliance in the wardrobe lies. 2
Now thrive the armorers, and honor's thought
Reigns solely in the breast of every man.
They sell the pasture now to buy the horse,
Following the mirror of all Christian kings, 6
With wingèd heels, as English Mercurys. 7
For now sits Expectation in the air
And hides a sword from hilts unto the point 9
With crowns imperial, crowns and coronets, 10
Promised to Harry and his followers.
The French, advised by good intelligence 12
Of this most dreadful preparation,
Shake in their fear, and with pale policy 14
Seek to divert the English purposes.
O England! Model to thy inward greatness, 16
Like little body with a mighty heart,
What mightst thou do, that honor would thee do, 18
Were all thy children kind and natural?
But see, thy fault France hath in thee found out,
A nest of hollow bosoms, which he fills
With treacherous crowns; and three corrupted men, 22
One, Richard Earl of Cambridge, and the second,
Henry Lord Scroop of Masham, and the third,
Sir Thomas Grey, knight, of Northumberland,
Have, for the gilt of France—O, guilt indeed!— 26
Confirmed conspiracy with fearful France, 27
And by their hands this grace of kings must die,
If hell and treason hold their promises,
Ere he take ship for France, and in Southampton.
Linger your patience on, and we'll digest 31
Th' abuse of distance, force a play. 32
The sum is paid, the traitors are agreed,
The King is set from London, and the scene
Is now transported, gentles, to Southampton.

---

263 **crown** (1) coin staked in a game (2) symbol of majesty.　**hazard** (1) in tennis of that time, an opening in the wall; hitting the ball into it meant that it was unplayable (2) jeopardy　264 **wrangler** adversary, disputant　265 **courts** (1) tennis courts (2) royal courts　266 **chases** (1) double bounce in tennis, an unsuccessful return (2) pursuits　267 **comes o'er us** taunts me. (*Us* is the royal plural.)　269 **seat** throne　270 **living hence** not frequenting the royal court　272 **from** away from　273 **keep my state** i.e., fulfill the role of king　274 **sail** full swell. (Henry says he has not yet revealed his full majesty in laying claim to France.)　276 **For that** i.e., in anticipation of that great event.　277 **for** suited and ready for　282 **gunstones** cannonballs　283 **sore chargèd** sorely burdened with responsibility.　**wasteful** destructive　287 **yet ungotten** not yet conceived　297 **Convey** escort　300 **omit . . . hour** lose no favorable opportunity　304 **proportions** levies of men

307 **God before** with God leading, helping　309 **task** tax, exercise
2.0. Chorus.
2 **silken . . . lies** i.e., silken apparel and idle pleasure are packed away　6 **the mirror . . . kings** i.e., the ideal or model to which all other kings should compare themselves　7 **Mercurys** (Mercury, classical messenger of the gods, always wears winged heels.)　9 **hides a sword** i.e., holds up a sword completely impaled with the prizes of war　10 **With . . . coronets** with the crowns of emperors, kings, and nobles　12 **intelligence** espionage　14 **pale policy** fear-inspired intrigue　16 **Model to** small replica of　18 **would** would have　22 **crowns** coins, money (as a bribe)　26 **gilt** gold　27 **fearful** frightened　31–32 **digest . . . distance** i.e., stomach the violations of the unity of place　32 **force a play** stuff the actions of a play into a small compass

There is the playhouse now, there must you sit,
And thence to France shall we convey you safe,
And bring you back, charming the narrow seas
To give you gentle pass; for, if we may,   39
We'll not offend one stomach with our play.   40
But, till the King come forth, and not till then,   41
Unto Southampton do we shift our scene.   *Exit.*   42

irony! ↓ young? eager to fight?

2.1   *Enter Corporal Nym and Lieutenant Bardolph.*

BARDOLPH   Well met, Corporal Nym.

NYM   Good morrow, Lieutenant Bardolph.

BARDOLPH   What, are Ancient Pistol and you friends   3
yet?

NYM   For my part, I care not. I say little; but when time
shall serve, there shall be smiles—but that shall be as
it may. I dare not fight, but I will wink and hold out   7
mine iron. It is a simple one, but what though? It will   8
toast cheese, and it will endure cold as another man's   9
sword will—and there's an end.   10

BARDOLPH   I will bestow a breakfast to make you
friends, and we'll be all three sworn brothers to
France. Let 't be so, good Corporal Nym.

NYM   Faith, I will live so long as I may, that's the certain
of it; and when I cannot live any longer, I will do as I
may. That is my rest; that is the rendezvous of it.   16

BARDOLPH   It is certain, Corporal, that he is married to
Nell Quickly, and certainly she did you wrong, for
you were trothplight to her.   19

NYM   I cannot tell. Things must be as they may. Men
may sleep, and they may have their throats about
them at that time, and some say knives have edges. It
must be as it may. Though Patience be a tired mare,   23
yet she will plod. There must be conclusions. Well, I   24
cannot tell.

Enter Pistol and [Hostess] Quickly.

BARDOLPH   Here comes Ancient Pistol and his wife.
Good Corporal, be patient here.

NYM   How now, mine host Pistol?

PISTOL
Base tike, call'st thou me host?   29
Now, by this hand, I swear, I scorn the term!
Nor shall my Nell keep lodgers.

HOSTESS   No, by my troth, not long; for we cannot lodge
and board a dozen or fourteen gentlewomen that live
honestly by the prick of their needles, but it will be   34
thought we keep a bawdy house straight. [*Nym and
Pistol draw.*] O welladay, Lady! If he be not hewn   36
now, we shall see willful adultery and murder com-   37
mitted.

BARDOLPH   Good Lieutenant! Good Corporal! Offer   39
nothing here.   40

NYM   Pish!

PISTOL
Pish for thee, Iceland dog!   42
Thou prick-eared cur of Iceland!

HOSTESS   Good Corporal Nym, show thy valor, and   44
put up your sword.   [*They sheathe their swords.*]

NYM   Will you shog off? I would have you solus.   46

PISTOL
Solus, egregious dog? O viper vile!
The solus in thy most mervailous face!   48
The solus in thy teeth, and in thy throat,
And in thy hateful lungs, yea, in thy maw, pardie,   50
And, which is worse, within thy nasty mouth!
I do retort the solus in thy bowels;
For I can take, and Pistol's cock is up,   53
And flashing fire will follow.

NYM   I am not Barbason; you cannot conjure me. I have 55
an humor to knock you indifferently well. If you grow
foul with me, Pistol, I will scour you with my rapier, as 57
I may, in fair terms. If you would walk off, I would   58
prick your guts a little, in good terms, as I may, and
that's the humor of it.   60

PISTOL
O braggart vile and damnèd furious wight!   61
The grave doth gape, and doting death is near.
Therefore exhale!   [*They draw.*]   63

BARDOLPH   Hear me, hear me what I say. He that strikes
the first stroke, I'll run him up to the hilts, as I am a
soldier.   [*He draws.*]

PISTOL
An oath of mickle might, and fury shall abate.   67
            [*Pistol and Nym sheathe their swords.*]
[*To Nym.*] Give me thy fist, thy forefoot to me give.
Thy spirits are most tall.   69

NYM   I will cut thy throat, one time or other, in fair
terms. That is the humor of it.

39 pass passage   **40 offend one stomach** (1) offend anyone's taste by
sudden shifts in scene (2) make anyone seasick   **41–42 But . . .
scene** i.e., the scene will be shifted to Southampton after a scene in
London. (These lines sound as though they were added as an afterthought, to accommodate the inclusion of the comic scene in 2.1.)
2.1. Location: London. A street.
3 Ancient ensign, standard-bearer   **7 wink** shut the eyes   **8 iron**
sword.   **though** of that   **9 endure cold** i.e., doesn't mind being
drawn from its sheath   **10 there's an end** that's all there is to it
16 rest last stake (in the gambling game of primero).   **rendezvous** last
resort   **19 trothplight** betrothed   **23–24 Though . . . plod** i.e., patient persistence will ultimately achieve its goal. (Nym hints, as he
does elsewhere, at violence toward Pistol.)   **24 conclusions** an end to
matters. (Nym hints darkly that the end must come soon.)   **29 tike**
cur

34 prick (With a bawdy double meaning, as also in *Pistol's cock*, line
53.)   **36 welladay** wellaway, alas.   **Lady** i.e., by Our Lady. (An
oath.)   **hewn** struck down   **37 adultery** (Blunder for "battery"?)
39–40 Offer nothing attempt no violence   **42 Iceland dog** a small,
shaggy dog often kept as a house pet. (Pistol's humor is to use extravagant epithets, like this one, tags from current plays, and scraps of
foreign languages.)   **44 valor** (She means "calm," "forbearance.")
46 shog off move along.   **solus** alone   **48 mervailous** marvelous
50 maw belly.   **pardie** *par Dieu*, by God   **53 take** (1) take fire (2)
strike.   **cock is up** trigger is cocked (with bawdy pun)   **55 Barbason**
(Presumably the name of a fiend. Pistol's preceding speech is a parody of the formula for exorcising spirits.)   **conjure** exorcize   **57 foul**
(1) foulmouthed (2) fouled from firing and in need of scouring   **58 in
fair terms** i.e., make no mistake about it. (*In good terms* at line 59
means the same.)   **walk off** walk aside (to fight)   **60 that's . . . it**
that's my mood   **61 wight** person   **63 exhale** draw (sword, much as
the sun draws forth vapors)   **67 mickle** great   **69 tall** valiant

PISTOL   *Couple a gorge!*   72
That is the word. I thee defy again.
O hound of Crete, think'st thou my spouse to get?   74
No, to the spital go,   75
And from the powdering tub of infamy   76
Fetch forth the lazar kite of Cressid's kind,   77
Doll Tearsheet she by name, and her espouse.
I have, and I will hold, the quondam Quickly   79
For the only she; and—*pauca!* There's enough.   80
Go to.

Enter the Boy.

BOY   Mine host Pistol, you must come to my master,
and you, hostess. He is very sick and would to bed.
Good Bardolph, put thy face between his sheets, and   84
do the office of a warming pan. Faith, he's very ill.
BARDOLPH   Away, you rogue!
HOSTESS   By my troth, he'll yield the crow a pudding   87
one of these days. The King has killed his heart. Good   88
husband, come home presently.   *Exit [with Boy].* 89
BARDOLPH   Come, shall I make you two friends? We
must to France together. Why the devil should we
keep knives to cut one another's throats?
PISTOL
Let floods o'erswell, and fiends for food howl on!
NYM   You'll pay me the eight shillings I won of you at
betting?
PISTOL   Base is the slave that pays.
NYM   That now I will have. That's the humor of it.
PISTOL   As manhood shall compound. Push home.   98
                                          [They] draw.
BARDOLPH *[drawing]* By this sword, he that makes
the first thrust, I'll kill him! By this sword, I will.
PISTOL
Sword is an oath, and oaths must have their course. 101
                              [He sheathes his sword.]
BARDOLPH   Corporal Nym, an thou wilt be friends, be 102
friends; an thou wilt not, why, then, be enemies with
me too. Prithee, put up.   104
NYM   I shall have my eight shillings I won of you at
betting?
PISTOL
A noble shalt thou have, and present pay;   107
And liquor likewise will I give to thee,
And friendship shall combine, and brotherhood.

I'll live by Nym, and Nym shall live by me.   110
Is not this just? For I shall sutler be   111
Unto the camp, and profits will accrue.
Give me thy hand.
NYM   I shall have my noble?
PISTOL   In cash most justly paid.
NYM   Well, then, that's the humor of 't.
                    [Nym and Bardolph sheathe their swords.]

Enter Hostess.

HOSTESS   As ever you come of women, come in quickly 117
to Sir John. Ah, poor heart, he is so shaked of a burn-
ing quotidian tertian that it is most lamentable to be- 119
hold. Sweet men, come to him.   *[Exit.]*
NYM   The King hath run bad humors on the knight,   121
that's the even of it.   122
PISTOL   Nym, thou hast spoke the right.
His heart is fracted and corroborate.   124
NYM   The King is a good king, but it must be as it may;
he passes some humors and careers.   126
PISTOL
Let us condole the knight, for, lambkins, we will
live.   *[Exeunt.]* 127

❖

2.2   *Enter Exeter, Bedford, and Westmorland.*

BEDFORD
'Fore God, His Grace is bold to trust these traitors.
EXETER
They shall be apprehended by and by.
WESTMORLAND
How smooth and even they do bear themselves!   3
As if allegiance in their bosoms sat,
Crownèd with faith and constant loyalty.
BEDFORD
The King hath note of all that they intend,
By interception which they dream not of.
EXETER
Nay, but the man that was his bedfellow,   8
Whom he hath dulled and cloyed with gracious
favors—   9
That he should, for a foreign purse, so sell
His sovereign's life to death and treachery!

*Sound trumpets. Enter the King, Scroop,
Cambridge, and Grey, [and attendants].*

---

72 Couple a gorge *couper la gorge,* "cut the throat"   **74 hound of Crete** (Parallel to *Iceland dog,* line 42.)   **75 spital** hospital   **76 powdering tub** (Originally a tub used for salting beef; here, alluding to a method of curing venereal disease by sweating.)   **77 lazar . . . kind** i.e., diseased, leprous whore (a *kite* is a bird of prey) like Cressida, the fallen woman, who, in Robert Henryson's *Testament of Cresseid,* is shown as being rejected by Diomede and infected with leprosy   **79 quondam** former   **80 only she** i.e., only woman in the world. **pauca** i.e., in brief   **84 face** (Bardolph's face is fiery with drinking.)   **87 he'll** (Refers to the Boy or perhaps Falstaff.)   **yield . . . pudding** i.e., be hanged on the gallows and eaten by carrion birds   **88 his** i.e., Falstaff's   **89 presently** immediately   **98 As . . . compound** as valor shall settle the matter (in fight)   **101 Sword is an oath** (Quibbling on *sword* as *'s word,* i.e., "God's word.")   **102 an** if   **104 put up** i.e., put up your sword   **107 A noble . . . pay** i.e., I'll settle for paying you six shillings eight pence ready money

110 Nym (Quibbles on *nim,* meaning "thief.")   **111 sutler** seller of liquor and provisions to the soldiers   **117 come of** were born of   **119 quotidian tertian** (A *quotidian* fever was one that came daily; a *tertian* fever, one that came on alternate days, though some authorities believed that different fevers might mix and intensify their effects.)   **121 run bad humors** i.e., vented his displeasure   **122 even** level truth   **124 fracted** broken.   **corroborate** (Blunder for "broken to pieces" or "corrupted"? The word means "strengthened, confirmed.")   **126 passes . . . careers** lets pass (i.e., indulges in) some idiosyncrasies and capers. (A *career* is a full gallop.)   **127 condole** express our commiseration of or sympathy with.   **lambkins** (A term of endearment.)
2.2. Location: Southampton, a seaport on England's southern coast.
3 smooth and even pleasant and calm   **8 bedfellow** i.e., constant companion. (Refers to Scroop.)   **9 dulled** dulled the appetite of

KING
Now sits the wind fair, and we will aboard.   12
My lord of Cambridge, and my kind lord of
  Masham,
And you, my gentle knight, give me your thoughts.
Think you not that the pow'rs we bear with us   15
Will cut their passage through the force of France,
Doing the execution and the act
For which we have in head assembled them?   18

SCROOP
No doubt, my liege, if each man do his best.

KING
I doubt not that, since we are well persuaded
We carry not a heart with us from hence
That grows not in a fair consent with ours,   22
Nor leave not one behind that doth not wish
Success and conquest to attend on us.

CAMBRIDGE
Never was monarch better feared and loved
Than is Your Majesty. There's not, I think, a subject
That sits in heart-grief and uneasiness
Under the sweet shade of your government.

GREY
True. Those that were your father's enemies
Have steeped their galls in honey, and do serve you   30
With hearts create of duty and of zeal.   31

KING
We therefore have great cause of thankfulness,
And shall forget the office of our hand   33
Sooner than quittance of desert and merit   34
According to the weight and worthiness.

SCROOP
So service shall with steelèd sinews toil,
And labor shall refresh itself with hope,
To do Your Grace incessant services.

KING
We judge no less.—Uncle of Exeter,
Enlarge the man committed yesterday   40
That railed against our person. We consider
It was excess of wine that set him on,
And on his more advice we pardon him.   43

SCROOP
That's mercy, but too much security.   44
Let him be punished, sovereign, lest example
Breed, by his sufferance, more of such a kind.   46

KING   O, let us yet be merciful.

CAMBRIDGE
So may Your Highness, and yet punish too.

GREY
Sir, you show great mercy if you give him life
After the taste of much correction.   51

KING
Alas, your too much love and care of me

Are heavy orisons 'gainst this poor wretch!   53
If little faults proceeding on distemper   54
Shall not be winked at, how shall we stretch our eye   55
When capital crimes, chewed, swallowed, and
  digested,   56
Appear before us? We'll yet enlarge that man,   57
Though Cambridge, Scroop, and Grey, in their dear
  care
And tender preservation of our person,
Would have him punished. And now to our French
  causes.
Who are the late commissioners?   61

CAMBRIDGE   I one, my lord.
Your Highness bade me ask for it today.   63

SCROOP   So did you me, my liege.

GREY   And I, my royal sovereign.

KING [giving them papers]
Then, Richard Earl of Cambridge, there is yours;
There yours, Lord Scroop of Masham; and sir
  knight,
Grey of Northumberland, this same is yours.
Read them, and know I know your worthiness.—
My lord of Westmorland, and uncle Exeter,
We will aboard tonight.—Why, how now,
  gentlemen?
What see you in those papers, that you lose
So much complexion?—Look ye how they change!   73
Their cheeks are paper.—Why, what read you there   74
That have so cowarded and chased your blood
Out of appearance?

CAMBRIDGE   I do confess my fault,   76
And do submit me to Your Highness' mercy.

GREY, SCROOP   To which we all appeal.

KING
The mercy that was quick in us but late   79
By your own counsel is suppressed and killed.
You must not dare, for shame, to talk of mercy,
For your own reasons turn into your bosoms,
As dogs upon their masters, worrying you.—   83
See you, my princes and my noble peers,
These English monsters! My lord of Cambridge
  here,
You know how apt our love was to accord   86
To furnish him with all appurtenants   87
Belonging to his honor; and this man
Hath for a few light crowns lightly conspired   89
And sworn unto the practices of France   90
To kill us here in Hampton. To the which
This knight, no less for bounty bound to us   92
Than Cambridge is, hath likewise sworn. But O,

---

53 heavy orisons weighty prayers, pleas   **54 proceeding on distemper** resulting from unstable condition (caused by excessive drinking)   **55 stretch** open wide, not wink   **56 capital** punishable by death.   **chewed . . . digested** i.e., premeditated   **57 yet** in spite of what you say   **61 late** recently appointed (to serve while Henry is in France)   **63 it** i.e., my commission   **73 complexion** color   **74 paper** i.e., white as a sheet   **76 appearance** (1) sight (2) your faces. (Presumably the traitors kneel at this point.)   **79 quick** alive   **83 worrying** tearing   **86 accord** consent   **87 appurtenants** appurtenances, accessories   **89 light** insignificant.   **lightly** readily; casually   **90 practices** plots   **92 This knight** i.e., Grey

---

12 sits . . . fair the wind blows from a favorable quarter   **15 pow'rs** armed forces   **18 in head** as an army   **22 grows . . . consent** does not act in harmony   **30 galls** i.e., resentment   **31 create** composed   **33 office** use, function   **34 quittance** requital   **40 Enlarge** set free   **43 more advice** thinking better of it   **44 security** overconfidence   **46 sufferance** being pardoned   **51 correction** punishment

What shall I say to thee, Lord Scroop, thou cruel,
Ingrateful, savage, and inhuman creature?
Thou that didst bear the key of all my counsels,
That knew'st the very bottom of my soul,
That almost mightst have coined me into gold,
Wouldst thou have practiced on me for thy use: 99
May it be possible that foreign hire
Could out of thee extract one spark of evil
That might annoy my finger? 'Tis so strange   102
That though the truth of it stands off as gross   103
As black and white, my eye will scarcely see it.
Treason and murder ever kept together,
As two yoke-devils sworn to either's purpose,   106
Working so grossly in a natural cause   107
That admiration did not whoop at them.   108
But thou, 'gainst all proportion, didst bring in   109
Wonder to wait on treason and on murder;   110
And whatsoever cunning fiend it was
That wrought upon thee so preposterously   112
Hath got the voice in hell for excellence.   113
All other devils that suggest by treasons   114
Do botch and bungle up damnation   115
With patches, colors, and with forms being fetched   116
From glistering semblances of piety;   117
But he that tempered thee bade thee stand up,   118
Gave thee no instance why thou shouldst do
   treason,   119
Unless to dub thee with the name of traitor.
If that same demon that hath gulled thee thus
Should with his lion gait walk the whole world,   122
He might return to vasty Tartar back   123
And tell the legions, "I can never win
A soul so easy as that Englishman's."
O, how hast thou with jealousy infected   126
The sweetness of affiance! Show men dutiful?   127
Why, so didst thou. Seem they grave and learnèd?
Why, so didst thou. Come they of noble family?
Why, so didst thou. Seem they religious?
Why, so didst thou. Or are they spare in diet,
Free from gross passion or of mirth or anger,   132
Constant in spirit, not swerving with the blood,   133
Garnished and decked in modest complement,   134

Not working with the eye without the ear,   135
And but in purgèd judgment trusting neither?   136
Such and so finely bolted didst thou seem.   137
And thus thy fall hath left a kind of blot
To mark the full-fraught man and best endued   139
With some suspicion. I will weep for thee;
For this revolt of thine, methinks, is like
Another fall of man.—Their faults are open.   142
Arrest them to the answer of the law;
And God acquit them of their practices!   144

EXETER   I arrest thee of high treason, by the name of
         Richard Earl of Cambridge.
I arrest thee of high treason, by the name of Henry Lord
         Scroop of Masham.
I arrest thee of high treason, by the name of Thomas
         Grey, knight, of Northumberland.

SCROOP
Our purposes God justly hath discovered,   151
And I repent my fault more than my death,
Which I beseech Your Highness to forgive,
Although my body pay the price of it.

CAMBRIDGE
For me, the gold of France did not seduce,
Although I did admit it as a motive   156
The sooner to effect what I intended.   157
But God be thankèd for prevention,
Which I in sufferance heartily will rejoice,   159
Beseeching God and you to pardon me.

GREY
Never did faithful subject more rejoice
At the discovery of most dangerous treason
Than I do at this hour joy o'er myself,
Prevented from a damnèd enterprise.
My fault, but not my body, pardon, sovereign.

KING
God quit you in his mercy! Hear your sentence.   166
You have conspired against our royal person,
Joined with an enemy proclaimed, and from his
   coffers
Received the golden earnest of our death,   169
Wherein you would have sold your king to
   slaughter,
His princes and his peers to servitude,
His subjects to oppression and contempt,
And his whole kingdom into desolation.
Touching our person seek we no revenge,
But we our kingdom's safety must so tender,   175
Whose ruin you have sought, that to her laws

99 practiced on plotted against.   **use** profit (with play on the meaning "interest derived from usury"; Scroop had served as Lord Treasurer) **102 annoy** injure   **103 stands . . . gross** appears as obvious **106 yoke-devils** partners in a diabolical cause   **107–108 Working . . . them** working together so manifestly toward a purpose suited to their evil natures that they provoked no outcry of wonder   **109 proportion** fitness of things   **110 Wonder** astonishment (that Scroop should be a murderer).   **wait on** attend, accompany   **112 wrought** worked.   **preposterously** unnaturally   **113 voice** vote   **114 suggest** tempt   **115–117 Do . . . piety** i.e., clumsily conceal their damnable temptation by tricking it out in attractive-looking semblances of virtue **118 tempered thee** molded you to his will.   **bade** ordered.   **stand up** rebel   **119 instance** reason   **122 lion gait** (The devil, according to 1 Peter 5:8, strides about the world like a roaring lion, "seeking whom he may devour.")   **123 vasty** vast.   **Tartar** Tartarus, the hell of classical mythology   **126 jealousy** suspicion   **127 affiance** trust. **Show** appear   **132 or of** either of   **133 swerving with the blood** sinning through passion   **134 decked . . . complement** wearing the look of modesty

135–136 Not . . . neither trusting neither eye nor ear alone except on the basis of refined judgment   **137 bolted** sifted, refined   **139 full-fraught** richly laden (with excellent qualities).   **endued** endowed **142 open** apparent, obvious   **144 practices** plots   **151 discovered** revealed   **156 did . . . motive** i.e., accepted money from France as a means   **157 The . . . intended** (Cambridge's real motive, barely hinted at here, was to assist his brother-in-law Edmund Mortimer, fifth Earl of March, to the throne as the standard-bearer of the Yorkist claim against the Lancastrian Henry.)   **159 sufferance** my suffering and patient endurance   **166 quit** pardon   **169 golden earnest** advance payment   **175 tender** regard, hold dear

We do deliver you. Get you therefore hence,
Poor miserable wretches, to your death,
The taste whereof God of his mercy give
You patience to endure, and true repentance
Of all your dear offenses!—Bear them hence.   181
        Exeunt [Cambridge, Scroop, and Grey, guarded].
Now, lords, for France, the enterprise whereof
Shall be to you, as us, like glorious.   183
We doubt not of a fair and lucky war,
Since God so graciously hath brought to light
This dangerous treason lurking in our way
To hinder our beginnings. We doubt not now
But every rub is smoothèd on our way.   188
Then forth, dear countrymen! Let us deliver
Our puissance into the hand of God,   190
Putting it straight in expedition.   191
Cheerly to sea! The signs of war advance!   192
No king of England, if not king of France!
                    Flourish. [Exeunt.]

❖

2.3   *Enter Pistol, Nym, Bardolph, Boy, and Hostess.*

HOSTESS   Prithee, honey-sweet husband, let me bring
thee to Staines.   2
PISTOL   No, for my manly heart doth earn. Bardolph, be 3
blithe; Nym, rouse thy vaunting veins; Boy, bristle thy
courage up; for Falstaff he is dead, and we must earn
therefore.
BARDOLPH   Would I were with him, wheresoe'er he is,
either in heaven or in hell!
HOSTESS   Nay, sure he's not in hell. He's in Arthur's 9
bosom, if ever man went to Arthur's bosom. 'A made 10
a finer end, and went away an it had been any 11
christom child. 'A parted ev'n just between twelve 12
and one, ev'n at the turning o' the tide. For after I saw
him fumble with the sheets, and play with flowers,
and smile upon his finger's end, I knew there was but
one way; for his nose was as sharp as a pen, and 'a 16
babbled of green fields. "How now, Sir John?" quoth I. 17
"What, man? Be o' good cheer." So 'a cried out, "God,
God, God!" three or four times. Now I, to comfort him,
bid him 'a should not think of God; I hoped there was
no need to trouble himself with any such thoughts yet.
So 'a bade me lay more clothes on his feet. I put my

hand into the bed and felt them, and they were as cold
as any stone; then I felt to his knees, and so upward
and upward, and all was as cold as any stone.
NYM   They say he cried out of sack.   26
HOSTESS   Ay, that 'a did.
BARDOLPH   And of women.
HOSTESS   Nay, that 'a did not.
BOY   Yes, that 'a did, and said they were devils incar-
nate.
HOSTESS   'A could never abide carnation; 'twas a color
he never liked.
BOY   'A said once the devil would have him about
women.
HOSTESS   'A did in some sort, indeed, handle women; 36
but then he was rheumatic, and talked of the Whore of 37
Babylon.
BOY   Do you not remember, 'a saw a flea stick upon
Bardolph's nose, and 'a said it was a black soul
burning in hell?
BARDOLPH   Well, the fuel is gone that maintained that 42
fire. That's all the riches I got in his service.
NYM   Shall we shog? The King will be gone from South- 44
ampton.
PISTOL
Come, let's away.—My love, give me thy lips.
                    [They kiss.]
Look to my chattels and my movables.   47
Let senses rule. The word is "Pitch and pay."   48
Trust none,
For oaths are straws, men's faiths are wafer cakes,   50
And Holdfast is the only dog, my duck.   51
Therefore, *caveto* be thy counselor.   52
Go, clear thy crystals.—Yokefellows in arms,   53
Let us to France, like horseleeches, my boys,
To suck, to suck, the very blood to suck!
BOY   And that's but unwholesome food, they say.
PISTOL   Touch her soft mouth, and march.
BARDOLPH   Farewell, hostess.   *[Kissing her.]*
NYM   I cannot kiss, that is the humor of it; but adieu.
PISTOL
Let huswifery appear. Keep close, I thee command.   60
HOSTESS   Farewell! Adieu!   *Exeunt [separately].*

❖

181 dear grievous, dire   **183 like** alike, equally   **188 But** but that.
rub obstacle. (A bowling term.)   **190 puissance** army   **191 straight
in expedition** immediately in action   **192 signs** ensigns, banners
2.3. London. A street.
2 Staines town on the road from London to Southampton   **3 earn**
grieve. (But in line 5 there may also be a play on the sense of "find
other employment," since Pistol and the others are now on their
own.)   **9–10 Arthur's bosom** (Malapropism for "Abraham's bosom";
see Luke 16:22.)   **10 'A** he   **11 an** as if   **12 christom** newly christened   **16–17 'a babbled of green fields** (This line contains
Theobald's famous emendation. The Folio has *and a Table of greene
fields*. Falstaff would seem to have been reciting the Twenty-third
Psalm.)

26 of sack against sack (a Spanish wine)   **36 handle** discuss (though
an unintended literal sense is also comically present)   **37 rheumatic**
feverish, or perhaps an error for "lunatic." (Because "Rome" was pronounced "room," *rheumatic* also prepares for the allusion to the
Whore of Babylon, i.e., the Church of Rome. See also Revelation
17:4–5.)   **42 fuel** i.e., liquor, supplied by Falstaff, that has given
Bardolph his red face   **44 shog** be off   **47 chattels . . . movables**
personal property   **48 Let . . . pay** i.e., keep your eyes and ears
open, and let your motto as hostess be "cash down"   **50 wafer cakes**
i.e., easily broken   **51 Holdfast** clamp, staple. (Compare this with the
proverb "Brag is a good dog, but Holdfast is a better.")   **52 caveto**
be cautious. (From the Latin imperative of *caveo*.)   **53 clear thy crystals** wipe your eyes.   **Yokefellows** companions   **60 Let . . . close**
i.e., be a thrifty housekeeper and stay at home

2.4 *Flourish. Enter the French King, the Dauphin, the Dukes of Berri and Brittany, [the Constable, and others].*

FRENCH KING
Thus comes the English with full power upon us,
And more than carefully it us concerns
To answer royally in our defenses.
Therefore the Dukes of Berri and of Brittany,
Of Brabant and of Orleans, shall make forth,
And you, Prince Dauphin, with all swift dispatch,
To line and new-repair our towns of war   7
With men of courage and with means defendant;   8
For England his approaches makes as fierce
As waters to the sucking of a gulf.   10
It fits us then to be as provident
As fear may teach us, out of late examples   12
Left by the fatal and neglected English   13
Upon our fields.
DAUPHIN   My most redoubted father,   14
It is most meet we arm us 'gainst the foe;   15
For peace itself should not so dull a kingdom,
Though war nor no known quarrel were in
    question,
But that defenses, musters, preparations,
Should be maintained, assembled, and collected
As were a war in expectation.   20
Therefore, I say 'tis meet we all go forth
To view the sick and feeble parts of France.
And let us do it with no show of fear—
No, with no more than if we heard that England
Were busied with a Whitsun morris dance.   25
For, my good liege, she is so idly kinged,   26
Her scepter so fantastically borne
By a vain, giddy, shallow, humorous youth,   28
That fear attends her not.
CONSTABLE   O, peace, Prince Dauphin!
You are too much mistaken in this king.
Question Your Grace the late ambassadors,
With what great state he heard their embassy,   32
How well supplied with noble counselors,
How modest in exception, and withal   34
How terrible in constant resolution,   35
And you shall find his vanities forespent   36
Were but the outside of the Roman Brutus,   37
Covering discretion with a coat of folly,
As gardeners do with ordure hide those roots   39
That shall first spring and be most delicate.

DAUPHIN
Well, 'tis not so, my Lord High Constable;
But though we think it so, it is no matter.
In cases of defense 'tis best to weigh
The enemy more mighty than he seems.
So the proportions of defense are filled,   45
Which of a weak and niggardly projection   46
Doth, like a miser, spoil his coat with scanting
A little cloth.
FRENCH KING   Think we King Harry strong;
And, princes, look you strongly arm to meet him.   49
The kindred of him hath been fleshed upon us;   50
And he is bred out of that bloody strain
That haunted us in our familiar paths.
Witness our too-much-memorable shame
When Crécy battle fatally was struck,   54
And all our princes captived by the hand
Of that black name, Edward, Black Prince of Wales;
Whiles that his mountain sire, on mountain
    standing,   57
Up in the air, crowned with the golden sun,
Saw his heroical seed and smiled to see him   59
Mangle the work of nature and deface
The patterns that by God and by French fathers
Had twenty years been made. This is a stem   62
Of that victorious stock; and let us fear
The native mightiness and fate of him.   64

Enter a Messenger.

MESSENGER
Ambassadors from Harry King of England
Do crave admittance to Your Majesty.
FRENCH KING
We'll give them present audience. Go and bring
    them.   [*Exit Messenger.*]
You see this chase is hotly followed, friends.
DAUPHIN
Turn head and stop pursuit; for coward dogs   69
Most spend their mouths when what they seem to
    threaten   70
Runs far before them. Good my sovereign,
Take up the English short, and let them know   72
Of what a monarchy you are the head.
Self-love, my liege, is not so vile a sin
As self-neglecting.

Enter Exeter [and others].

FRENCH KING   From our brother of England?

2.4. Location: France. The royal court.
7 line reinforce **8 defendant** defensive **10 gulf** whirlpool **12 late** recent **13 fatal and neglected** fatally underestimated **14 redoubted** respected **15 meet** appropriate **20 As were** as if there were **25 Whitsun morris dance** folk dance often performed during Whitsuntide, in early summer, by persons in fancy costumes and decked with bells **26 idly** frivolously **28 humorous** capricious **32 state** dignity **34 exception** making objections **35 terrible** awesome, terrifying **36 vanities forespent** follies used up and now a thing of the past **37 Brutus** i.e., the elder Brutus, Lucius Junius Brutus, who pretended to be stupid (*brutus*) as a ruse to allay the suspicions of the tyrant Tarquin until the time for overthrow was ripe **39 ordure** manure

45 So . . . filled thus an adequate and full defense is provided **46 Which . . . projection** which defense, if designed on too small and miserly a scale **49 look** be sure **50 kindred** i.e., his great-grandfather Edward III and great-uncle Edward the Black Prince. **fleshed** initiated in the shedding of blood, with foretaste of further success **54 Crécy** French defeat in 1346. **struck** waged **57 mountain sire** i.e., Edward III, born in mountainous Wales, and of sturdy proportions **59 seed** i.e., son **62 twenty years** (i.e., because the warriors thus mangled were born twenty years or so before) **64 fate** what he is destined to do **69 Turn head** stand at bay. (A hunting term.) **stop pursuit** put an end to their pursuit **70 Most . . . mouths** bay the loudest **72 Take . . . short** quickly dispose of the English

EXETER
From him, and thus he greets Your Majesty:
He wills you, in the name of God Almighty,
That you divest yourself and lay apart   78
The borrowed glories that by gift of heaven,
By law of nature and of nations, 'longs   80
To him and to his heirs, namely, the crown
And all wide-stretchèd honors that pertain   82
By custom and the ordinance of times   83
Unto the crown of France. That you may know
'Tis no sinister nor no awkward claim,   85
Picked from the wormholes of long-vanished days,
Nor from the dust of old oblivion raked,
He sends you this most memorable line,   88
                                          [giving a paper]
In every branch truly demonstrative,
Willing you overlook this pedigree.   90
And when you find him evenly derived   91
From his most famed of famous ancestors,
Edward the Third, he bids you then resign
Your crown and kingdom, indirectly held   94
From him the native and true challenger.   95
FRENCH KING   Or else what follows?
EXETER
Bloody constraint; for if you hide the crown   97
Even in your hearts, there will he rake for it.
Therefore in fierce tempest is he coming,
In thunder and in earthquake, like a Jove,
That if requiring fail, he will compel;   101
And bids you, in the bowels of the Lord,   102
Deliver up the crown, and to take mercy
On the poor souls for whom this hungry war
Opens his vasty jaws; and on your head
Turning the widows' tears, the orphans' cries,
The dead men's blood, the privy maidens' groans,   107
For husbands, fathers, and betrothèd lovers
That shall be swallowed in this controversy.
This is his claim, his threatening, and my message—
Unless the Dauphin be in presence here,
To whom expressly I bring greeting too.
FRENCH KING
For us, we will consider of this further.
Tomorrow shall you bear our full intent
Back to our brother of England.
DAUPHIN   For the Dauphin,
I stand here for him. What to him from England?
EXETER
Scorn and defiance, slight regard, contempt,
And anything that may not misbecome   118
The mighty sender, doth he prize you at.   119
Thus says my king: an if your father's Highness   120

Do not, in grant of all demands at large,   121
Sweeten the bitter mock you sent His Majesty,
He'll call you to so hot an answer of it   123
That caves and womby vaultages of France   124
Shall chide your trespass and return your mock
In second accent of his ordinance.   126
DAUPHIN
Say if my father render fair return   127
It is against my will, for I desire
Nothing but odds with England. To that end,   129
As matching to his youth and vanity,
I did present him with the Paris balls.   131
EXETER
He'll make your Paris Louvre shake for it,   132
Were it the mistress court of mighty Europe.
And be assured, you'll find a difference,
As we his subjects have in wonder found,
Between the promise of his greener days   136
And these he masters now. Now he weighs time
Even to the utmost grain. That you shall read   138
In your own losses, if he stay in France.
FRENCH KING
Tomorrow shall you know our mind at full.   140
                                          Flourish.
EXETER
Dispatch us with all speed, lest that our king
Come here himself to question our delay;
For he is footed in this land already.
FRENCH KING
You shall be soon dispatched with fair conditions.
A night is but small breath and little pause
To answer matters of this consequence.
                                   Flourish. Exeunt.

                              ♣

3.0   *Enter Chorus.*

CHORUS
Thus with imagined wing our swift scene flies   1
In motion of no less celerity   2
Than that of thought. Suppose that you have seen
The well-appointed King at Dover pier   4
Embark his royalty, and his brave fleet   5
With silken streamers the young Phoebus fanning.   6
Play with your fancies, and in them behold
Upon the hempen tackle shipboys climbing;
Hear the shrill whistle, which doth order give

---

78 **apart** aside   80 **'longs** belongs   82 **wide-stretchèd** stretching far
and wide   83 **ordinance of times** decrees of tradition   85 **sinister** illegitimate.   **awkward** oblique   88 **line** pedigree   90 **Willing you
overlook** desiring that you look over   91 **evenly** directly   94 **indirectly** wrongfully   95 **native** natural (by birthright).   **challenger**
claimant   97 **constraint** coercion, compulsion   101 **requiring** requesting   102 **bowels** mercy, or innermost being. (Compare with
Philippians 1:8.)   107 **privy maidens' groans** maidens' secret griev-
ings   118 **misbecome** be inappropriate for   119 **prize** value, appraise
120 **an if** if

121 **in grant of** in assenting to.   **at large** in full   123 **of it** for it
124 **womby vaultages** hollow recesses   126 **second accent** echo.
ordinance ordnance, cannon   127 **fair return** courteous reply
129 **odds** strife   131 **Paris balls** tennis balls   132 **Louvre** the French
royal palace   136 **greener** younger   138 **That . . . read** i.e., you
will see this new seriousness manifested   140 **s.d. Flourish** (This
trumpet call is sounded as the French King arises from his throne,
thereby dismissing the embassy, but Exeter boldly insists on speaking
further.)
3.0. Chorus.
1 **imagined wing** wings of imagination   2 **celerity** speed   4 **well-
appointed** well-equipped.   **Dover** (Seemingly an error for Hampton,
i.e., Southampton.)   5 **brave** handsome   6 **the . . . fanning** i.e., fluttering against the rising sun

To sounds confused; behold the threaden sails,   10
Borne with th' invisible and creeping wind,
Draw the huge bottoms through the furrowed sea,   12
Breasting the lofty surge. O, do but think   13
You stand upon the rivage and behold   14
A city on th' inconstant billows dancing;
For so appears this fleet majestical,
Holding due course to Harfleur. Follow, follow!
Grapple your minds to sternage of this navy,   18
And leave your England as dead midnight still,
Guarded with grandsires, babies, and old women,
Either past or not arrived to pith and puissance;   21
For who is he whose chin is but enriched
With one appearing hair that will not follow
These culled and choice-drawn cavaliers to France?   24
Work, work your thoughts, and therein see a siege;
Behold the ordnance on their carriages,
With fatal mouths gaping on girded Harfleur.   27
Suppose th' ambassador from the French comes
    back,
Tells Harry that the King doth offer him
Katharine his daughter, and with her, to dowry,
Some petty and unprofitable dukedoms.
The offer likes not; and the nimble gunner   32
With linstock now the devilish cannon touches,   33
            Alarum, and chambers go off.
And down goes all before them. Still be kind,
And eke out our performance with your mind.
                                    Exit.

♣

3.1 *Enter the King, Exeter, Bedford, and Gloucester.*
Alarum, [with soldiers carrying] scaling ladders at
Harfleur.

KING
Once more unto the breach, dear friends, once more,
Or close the wall up with our English dead!
In peace there's nothing so becomes a man
As modest stillness and humility.
But when the blast of war blows in our ears,
Then imitate the action of the tiger:
Stiffen the sinews, conjure up the blood,
Disguise fair nature with hard-favored rage.   8
Then lend the eye a terrible aspect: 9
Let it pry through the portage of the head   10
Like the brass cannon; let the brow o'erwhelm it   11
As fearfully as doth a gallèd rock   12

O'erhang and jutty his confounded base,   13
Swilled with the wild and wasteful ocean.   14
Now set the teeth and stretch the nostril wide,
Hold hard the breath, and bend up every spirit
To his full height. On, on, you noblest English,
Whose blood is fet from fathers of war-proof,   18
Fathers that, like so many Alexanders,   19
Have in these parts from morn till even fought,   20
And sheathed their swords for lack of argument.   21
Dishonor not your mothers; now attest
That those whom you called fathers did beget you.
Be copy now to men of grosser blood,   24
And teach them how to war. And you, good yeomen,
Whose limbs were made in England, show us here
The mettle of your pasture. Let us swear   27
That you are worth your breeding, which I doubt not,
For there is none of you so mean and base
That hath not noble luster in your eyes.
I see you stand like greyhounds in the slips,   31
Straining upon the start. The game's afoot.
Follow your spirit, and upon this charge   33
Cry, "God for Harry! England and Saint George!"   34
        Alarum, and chambers go off. [Exeunt.]

3.2 *Enter Nym, Bardolph, Pistol, and Boy.*

BARDOLPH   On, on, on, on, on! To the breach, to the
    breach!
NYM   Pray thee, Corporal, stay. The knocks are too hot,
    and for mine own part I have not a case of lives. The   4
    humor of it is too hot, that is the very plainsong of it.   5
PISTOL
    "The plainsong" is most just; for humors do abound.
    Knocks go and come; God's vassals drop and die;
    [*He sings.*] "And sword and shield
            In bloody field
            Doth win immortal fame."
BOY   Would I were in an alehouse in London! I would
    give all my fame for a pot of ale and safety.
PISTOL   And I: [*He sings.*]
    "If wishes would prevail with me,   14
        My purpose should not fail with me,
            But thither would I hie."   16
BOY [*sings*]
    "As duly, but not as truly,
        As bird doth sing on bough."

    Enter Fluellen.

---

10 threaden woven of thread **12 bottoms** hulls of ships **13 surge**
swell of the sea **14 rivage** shore **18 Grapple** attach, hook. **to sternage** to the sterns **21 pith** strength **24 choice-drawn** carefully selected **27 fatal** deadly. **girded** besieged **32 likes** pleases **33 linstock** staff holding a gunner's match. **s.d. Alarum** call to arms.
chambers small cannon (fired off backstage, or "within")
3.1. Location: France. Before Harfleur.
s.d. scaling ladders (Presumably these are set up against the facade of
the tiring-house, backstage, which is perceived to be the walls of Harfleur.) **8 hard-favored** unsightly, ugly **9 terrible aspect** terrifying appearance **10 portage** portholes, eyes **11 o'erwhelm** project over
12 fearfully frighteningly. **gallèd** washed away, undermined

13 jutty overhang. **his confounded** its ruined **14 Swilled** washed.
wasteful destructive **18 fet** fetched, derived. **of war-proof** proved
in war **19 Alexanders** (Alexander grieved that there were no new
worlds for him to conquer.) **20 even** evening **21 argument** opposition **24 copy** models **27 mettle . . . pasture** quality of your breeding. (Literally, *pasture* means "feeding.") **31 slips** leashes **33 Follow your spirit** i.e., obey the impulse of your vital powers (as also in
line 16) **34 Saint George** patron saint of England
**3.2. Location: Before Harfleur, as in the previous scene; the action is
essentially continuous.**
4 case set **5 plainsong** i.e., simple truth **14 with me** in my case
16 hie hasten

FLUELLEN   Up to the breach, you dogs! Avaunt, you cul- 19
lions!   [Driving them forward.] 20
PISTOL

Be merciful, great duke, to men of mold.   21
Abate thy rage, abate thy manly rage,
Abate thy rage, great duke!
Good bawcock, bate thy rage! Use lenity, sweet chuck! 24

NYM   These be good humors! Your honor runs bad 25
humors.   Exit [with all but Boy]. 26

BOY   As young as I am, I have observed these three
swashers. I am boy to them all three, but all they three, 28
though they would serve me, could not be man to me; 29
for indeed three such antics do not amount to a man. 30
For Bardolph, he is white-livered and red-faced, by the 31
means whereof 'a faces it out but fights not. For Pistol, 32
he hath a killing tongue and a quiet sword, by the
means whereof 'a breaks words and keeps whole 34
weapons. For Nym, he hath heard that men of few
words are the best men, and therefore he scorns to say
his prayers, lest 'a should be thought a coward; but
his few bad words are matched with as few good
deeds, for 'a never broke any man's head but his own,
and that was against a post when he was drunk. They
will steal anything and call it purchase. Bardolph 41
stole a lute case, bore it twelve leagues, and sold it for
three halfpence. Nym and Bardolph are sworn brothers in filching, and in Calais they stole a fire shovel. I
knew by that piece of service the men would carry 45
coals. They would have me as familiar with men's 46
pockets as their gloves or their handkerchiefs, which
makes much against my manhood, if I should take 48
from another's pocket to put into mine, for it is plain
pocketing up of wrongs. I must leave them and seek 50
some better service. Their villainy goes against my 51
weak stomach, and therefore I must cast it up.   Exit. 52

Enter Gower [and Fluellen, meeting].

GOWER   Captain Fluellen, you must come presently to
the mines. The Duke of Gloucester would speak with 54
you.

FLUELLEN   To the mines? Tell you the Duke it is not so
good to come to the mines; for look you, the mines is

not according to the disciplines of the war. The 58
concavities of it is not sufficient. For look you, th' 59
athversary, you may discuss unto the Duke, look you, 60
is digt himself four yard under the countermines. By 61
Cheshu, I think 'a will plow up all, if there is not better 62
directions.

GOWER   The Duke of Gloucester, to whom the order of
the siege is given, is altogether directed by an Irishman, a very valiant gentleman, i' faith.

FLUELLEN   It is Captain Macmorris, is it not?

GOWER   I think it be.

FLUELLEN   By Cheshu, he is an ass, as in the world! I
will verify as much in his beard. He has no more di- 70
rections in the true disciplines of the wars, look you,
of the Roman disciplines, than is a puppy dog.

Enter Macmorris and Captain Jamy.

GOWER   Here 'a comes, and the Scots captain, Captain
Jamy, with him.

FLUELLEN   Captain Jamy is a marvelous falorous gentleman, that is certain, and of great expedition and 76
knowledge in th' aunchient wars, upon my particular
knowledge of his directions. By Cheshu, he will
maintain his argument as well as any military man in
the world, in the disciplines of the pristine wars of the 80
Romans.

JAMY   I say gud day, Captain Fluellen.

FLUELLEN   Good e'en to your worship, good Captain 83
James.

GOWER   How now, Captain Macmorris, have you quit
the mines? Have the pioners given o'er?   86

MACMORRIS   By Chrish, la, 'tish ill done! The work ish
give over, the trompet sound the retreat. By my hand
I swear, and my father's soul, the work ish ill done; it
ish give over. I would have blowed up the town, so
Chrish save me, la, in an hour. O, 'tish ill done, 'tish
ill done! By my hand, 'tish ill done!

FLUELLEN   Captain Macmorris, I beseech you now, will
you voutsafe me, look you, a few disputations with 94
you, as partly touching or concerning the disciplines
of the war, the Roman wars, in the way of argument,
look you, and friendly communication—partly to satisfy my opinion, and partly for the satisfaction, look
you, of my mind, as touching the direction of the military discipline, that is the point.

JAMY   It sall be vary gud, gud feith, gud captens bath, 101
and I sall quite you with gud leve, as I may pick 102
occasion. That sall I, marry.   103

19 Avaunt begone   19–20 cullions rascals. (The original meaning
was "testicles.")   21 duke leader, commander. (Latin dux.) A flattering title for a captain.   men of mold mere mortals   24 bawcock fine
fellow. (French beau coq.)   chuck (A term of endearment.)
25–26 Your . . . humors i.e., you are behaving very idiosyncratically, your honor. (Addressed to Fluellen, who is doubtless threatening or beating them to make them go forward.)   28 swashers swashbucklers   29 man (1) servant (2) a manly, brave person   30 antics
buffoons, zanies   31 For as for (also in lines 32 and 35).   white-livered i.e., cowardly. (In extreme fear, the blood was thought to sink
below the liver, leaving it bloodless.)   32 'a faces it out i.e., he puts
on a brave front   34 breaks words (1) misuses language and fails to
keep his word (2) uses words as weapons   41 purchase (Thieves' cant
for "stolen goods.")   45–46 carry coals i.e., submit to insult or degradation (punning on the literal meaning)   48 makes goes   50 pocketing . . . wrongs (1) putting up with insults (2) receiving stolen goods
51–52 goes . . . stomach (1) goes against my inclination (2) makes
me sick   52 cast it up (1) cast it aside (2) vomit it.   s.d. Exit (A
scene break may occur here, though it is not marked as such in most
editions. Possibly Fluellen did not leave the stage at line 26.)
54 mines undermining operation in a siege

58 disciplines of the war science of warfare (about which there were
many books from Greek and Roman times down to the Renaissance;
Fluellen's humor involves an obsession with this study and a preference for traditional methods)   59 concavities i.e., depth   60 athversary (Fluellen's pronunciation of adversary.)   discuss explain
61 is digt . . . countermines has dug himself countermines four yards
beneath our mines   62 Cheshu Jesu, Jesus.   plow blow. (In Fluellen's
Welsh dialect, p is regularly substituted for b and f for v.)   70 in his
beard i.e., to his face   76 expedition readiness of argument, quickness of wit   80 pristine ancient   83 Good e'en good afternoon or
evening   86 pioners sappers, diggers   94 voutsafe vouchsafe, permit
101 bath both   102 quite requite, answer.   with gud leve with good
leave, with your kind permission   103 marry indeed. (Originally, "by
the Virgin Mary.")

MACMORRIS   It is no time to discourse, so Chrish save
me! The day is hot, and the weather, and the wars,
and the King, and the dukes. It is no time to discourse.
The town is beseeched, and the trumpet call us to the   107
breach, and we talk, and, be Chrish, do nothing. 'Tis   108
shame for us all. So God sa' me, 'tis shame to stand
still, it is shame, by my hand! And there is throats to
be cut, and works to be done, and there ish nothing
done, so Chrish sa' me, la!   112

JAMY   By the Mess, ere theise eyes of mine take   113
themselves to slomber, ay'll de gud service, or I'll lig i'   114
the grund for it, ay, or go to death! And I'll pay 't as
valorously as I may, that sall I suerly do, that is the
breff and the long. Marry, I wad full fain heard some   117
question 'tween you twae.   118

FLUELLEN   Captain Macmorris, I think, look you, under
your correction, there is not many of your nation—

MACMORRIS   Of my nation? What ish my nation? Ish a   121
villain, and a bastard, and a knave, and a rascal? What   122
ish my nation? Who talks of my nation?

FLUELLEN   Look you, if you take the matter otherwise
than is meant, Captain Macmorris, peradventure I
shall think you do not use me with that affability as in
discretion you ought to use me, look you, being as
good a man as yourself, both in the disciplines of war
and in the derivation of my birth, and in other particularities.

MACMORRIS   I do not know you so good a man as myself. So Chrish save me, I will cut off your head!

GOWER   Gentlemen both, you will mistake each other.   133

JAMY   Ah, that's a foul fault!   *A parley [is sounded].*   134

GOWER   The town sounds a parley.

FLUELLEN   Captain Macmorris, when there is more better opportunity to be required, look you, I will be so   137
bold as to tell you I know the disciplines of war; and
there is an end.   *Exit [with others].*

3.3   [*Enter the Governor and some citizens on the
walls.*] *Enter the King [Henry] and all his train
before the gates.*

KING
How yet resolves the Governor of the town?
This is the latest parle we will admit.   2

---

107 **beseeched** besieged   108 **be** by   112 **Chrish sa' me** Christ save
me   113 **Mess** Mass   114 **ay'll de** I'll do.   **lig** lie   117 **breff** brief.
wad full fain heard would very willingly have heard   118 **question**
discussion   121 **What ish** i.e., what about   121–122 **Ish a villain**
i.e., is my nation a villain (etc.)?, or Macmorris may be making a de-
clarative statement, saying that anyone who says anything against my
nation is a villain, etc.   133 **will mistake** (Two possible meanings: [1]
insist on misunderstanding [2] are going to misunderstand.)   134 **s.d.**
parley trumpet summons to a negotiation   137 **required** found
3.3. Location: Before the gates of Harfleur, as in the previous scene.
The action is essentially continuous, as it is usually in battle sequences; possibly some of the captains in 3.2 do not need to exit
here. The gates are represented by the tiring-house facade. Those
who appear *on the walls* are seen in the gallery backstage.
2 **latest parle** last parley

Therefore to our best mercy give yourselves,
Or, like to men proud of destruction,   4
Defy us to our worst; for as I am a soldier,
A name that in my thoughts becomes me best,
If I begin the battery once again   7
I will not leave the half-achievèd Harfleur
Till in her ashes she lie burièd.
The gates of mercy shall be all shut up,
And the fleshed soldier, rough and hard of heart,   11
In liberty of bloody hand shall range
With conscience wide as hell, mowing like grass   13
Your fresh fair virgins and your flowering infants.
What is it then to me if impious war,
Arrayed in flames like to the prince of fiends,
Do with his smirched complexion all fell feats   17
Enlinked to waste and desolation?
What is 't to me, when you yourselves are cause,
If your pure maidens fall into the hand
Of hot and forcing violation?
What rein can hold licentious wickedness
When down the hill he holds his fierce career?   23
We may as bootless spend our vain command   24
Upon th' enragèd soldiers in their spoil
As send precepts to the leviathan   26
To come ashore. Therefore, you men of Harfleur,
Take pity of your town and of your people
Whiles yet my soldiers are in my command,
Whiles yet the cool and temperate wind of grace   30
O'erblows the filthy and contagious clouds   31
Of heady murder, spoil, and villainy.   32
If not, why, in a moment look to see   33
The blind and bloody soldier with foul hand   34
Defile the locks of your shrill-shrieking daughters,
Your fathers taken by the silver beards,
And their most reverend heads dashed to the walls;
Your naked infants spitted upon pikes,
Whiles the mad mothers with their howls confused
Do break the clouds, as did the wives of Jewry   40
At Herod's bloody-hunting slaughtermen.   41
What say you? Will you yield, and this avoid,
Or, guilty in defense, be thus destroyed?   43

GOVERNOR
Our expectation hath this day an end.
The Dauphin, whom of succors we entreated,   45
Returns us that his powers are yet not ready   46
To raise so great a siege. Therefore, great King,
We yield our town and lives to thy soft mercy.
Enter our gates, dispose of us and ours,

---

4 **like . . . destruction** i.e., like men elated at the prospect of death
and glorying in destruction   7 **battery** attack   11 **fleshed** made fierce
with the taste of blood   13 **wide as hell** i.e., letting anything pass
17 **smirched** discolored, covered with grime.   **fell** savage   23 **he**
. . . career it makes its fierce gallop   24 **bootless** fruitlessly   26 **pre-**
cepts written summons.   **leviathan** whale   30 **grace** mercy   31 **O'er-**
blows blows away. (Contagion was thought to reside in clouds and
mists.)   32 **heady** violent; headstrong   33 **look** expect   34 **blind** i.e.,
blinded with lust and rage   40 **Jewry** Judea   41 **Herod's . . .**
slaughtermen (For the account of Herod's slaughter of the innocent
children in his attempt to murder the infant Jesus, see Matthew 2:16–
18.)   43 **in defense** i.e., by not surrendering   45 **of succors** for help
46 **Returns** replies to

For we no longer are defensible.   50
KING
Open your gates.   [*Exit Governor.*]
                    Come, uncle Exeter,
Go you and enter Harfleur; there remain,
And fortify it strongly 'gainst the French.
Use mercy to them all. For us, dear uncle,   54
The winter coming on and sickness growing
Upon our soldiers, we will retire to Calais.
Tonight in Harfleur will we be your guest;
Tomorrow for the march are we addressed.   58
                    Flourish, and enter the town.

✤

3.4 *Enter Katharine and [Alice,] an old gentlewoman.*

KATHARINE   Alice, tu as été en Angleterre, et tu bien 1
parles le langage.
ALICE   Un peu, madame.
KATHARINE   Je te prie, m'enseignez; il faut que
j'apprenne à parler. Comment appelez-vous la main
en anglais?
ALICE   La main? Elle est appelée de hand.
KATHARINE   De hand. Et les doigts?
ALICE   Les doigts? Ma foi, j'oublie les doigts; mais je me
souviendrai. Les doigts? Je pense qu'ils sont appelés 10
de fingres; oui, de fingres.
KATHARINE   La main, de hand; les doigts, de fingres. Je
pense que je suis le bon écolier; j'ai gagné deux
mots d'anglais vîtement. Comment appelez-vous les
ongles?
ALICE   Les ongles? Nous les appelons de nailes.
KATHARINE   De nailes. Écoutez, dites-moi si je parle
bien: de hand, de fingres, et de nailes.
ALICE   C'est bien dit, madame; il est fort bon anglais.
KATHARINE   Dites-moi l'anglais pour le bras.   20
ALICE   De arm, madame.
KATHARINE   Et le coude?
ALICE   D' elbow.

50 defensible able to defend ourselves **54 For** as for **58 addressed** prepared
3.4. Location: The French court at Rouen.
Translation:
KATHARINE Alice, you have been in England and speak the language well.
ALICE A little, my lady.
KATHARINE I pray you teach me; I have to learn to speak it. What do you call *la main* in English?
ALICE *La main?* It is called de hand.
KATHARINE De hand. And *les doigts?*
ALICE *Les doigts?* Dear me, I forget *les doigts;* but I shall remember. I think that they are called de fingres; yes, de fingres.
KATHARINE *La main,* de hand; *les doigts,* de fingres. I think that I am a clever scholar; I have learned two English words in no time. What do you call *les ongles?*
ALICE *Les ongles?* We call them de nailes.
KATHARINE De nailes. Listen; tell me whether or not I speak correctly: de hand, de fingres, and de nailes.
ALICE That is correct, my lady; it is very good English.
KATHARINE Tell me the English for *le bras.*
ALICE De arm, my lady.
KATHARINE And *le coude?*
ALICE D' elbow.

KATHARINE   D' elbow. Je m'en fais la répétition de tous
les mots que vous m'avez appris dès à présent.
ALICE   Il est trop difficile, madame, comme je pense.
KATHARINE   Excusez-moi, Alice; écoutez: d' hand, de
fingre, de nailes, d' arma, de bilbow.
ALICE   D' elbow, madame.
KATHARINE   O Seigneur Dieu, je m'en oublie! D' elbow. 30
Comment appelez-vous le col?
ALICE   De nick, madame.
KATHARINE   De nick. Et le menton?
ALICE   De chin.
KATHARINE   De sin. Le col, de nick; le menton, de sin.
ALICE   Oui. Sauf votre honneur, en vérité, vous pro-
noncez les mots aussi droit que les natifs d'Angleterre.
KATHARINE   Je ne doute point d'apprendre, par la grâce
de Dieu, et en peu de temps.
ALICE   N'avez-vous pas déjà oublié ce que je vous ai 40
enseigné?
KATHARINE   Non, je réciterai à vous promptement: d'
hand, de fingre, de mailes—
ALICE   De nailes, madame.
KATHARINE   De nailes, de arm, de ilbow.
ALICE   Sauf votre honneur, d' elbow.
KATHARINE   Ainsi dis-je; d' elbow, de nick, et de sin.
Comment appelez-vous le pied et la robe?
ALICE   Le foot, madame, et le count.
KATHARINE   Le foot et le count! O Seigneur Dieu! Ils 50
sont les mots de son mauvais, corruptible, gros, et
impudique, et non pour les dames d'honneur d'user.
Je ne voudrais prononcer ces mots devant les seig-
neurs de France pour tout le monde. Foh! Le foot et le
count! Néanmoins, je réciterai une autre fois ma leçon
ensemble: d' hand, de fingre, de nailes, de arm,
d' elbow, de nick, de sin, de foot, le count.

KATHARINE D' elbow. I am going to repeat all the words you have taught me so far.
ALICE It is too hard, my lady, I fear.
KATHARINE Pardon me, Alice; listen: d'hand, de fingre, de nailes, d'arma, de bilbow.
ALICE D' elbow, my lady.
KATHARINE O Lord, I can't remember! D' elbow. What do you call *le col?*
ALICE De nick, my lady.
KATHARINE De nick. And *le menton?*
ALICE De chin.
KATHARINE De sin. *Le col,* de nick; *le menton,* de sin.
ALICE Yes. If I may say so, really you pronounce the words just as correctly as native Englishmen.
KATHARINE I have no doubt that I shall learn, with God's help, in a very short time.
ALICE Haven't you already forgotten what I have taught you?
KATHARINE No. I shall recite to you at once: d' hand, de fingre, de mailes—
ALICE De nailes, my lady.
KATHARINE De nailes, de arm, de ilbow.
ALICE By your leave, d' elbow.
KATHARINE That's what I said; d' elbow, de nick, and de sin. What do you call *le pied* and *la robe?*
ALICE Le foot, my lady, and le count. [As she pronounces them, *foot* sounds to Katharine like *foutre,* fornicate, and *count* (for gown) sounds like French for the female sexual organ, *cunt* in English.]
KATHARINE Le foot and le count! O Lord! Those are naughty words, wicked, coarse, and immodest, and are not fit to be used by ladies. I wouldn't say those words before French gentlemen for the whole world. Bah! Le foot and le count! Nevertheless, I shall recite my whole lesson once more: d' hand, de fingre, de nailes, de arm, d' elbow, de nick, de sin, de foot, le count.

ALICE Excellent, madame!

KATHARINE C'est assez pour une fois. Allons-nous à
dîner.   *Exit [with Alice].* 60

❖

3.5 *Enter the King of France, the Dauphin, [the Duke
of Brittany,] the Constable of France, and others.*

FRENCH KING
'Tis certain he hath passed the River Somme.

CONSTABLE
And if he be not fought withal, my lord,   2
Let us not live in France; let us quit all
And give our vineyards to a barbarous people.

DAUPHIN
O Dieu vivant! Shall a few sprays of us,   5
The emptying of our fathers' luxury,   6
Our scions, put in wild and savage stock,   7
Spirt up so suddenly into the clouds   8
And overlook their grafters?   9

BRITTANY
Normans, but bastard Normans, Norman bastards!
Mort de ma vie, if they march along   11
Unfought withal, but I will sell my dukedom   12
To buy a slobbery and a dirty farm   13
In that nook-shotten isle of Albion.   14

CONSTABLE
Dieu de batailles, where have they this mettle?   15
Is not their climate foggy, raw, and dull,
On whom as in despite the sun looks pale,   17
Killing their fruit with frowns? Can sodden water,   18
A drench for sur-reined jades, their barley broth,   19
Decoct their cold blood to such valiant heat?   20
And shall our quick blood, spirited with wine,   21
Seem frosty? O, for honor of our land,
Let us not hang like roping icicles   23
Upon our houses' thatch, whiles a more frosty
   people
Sweat drops of gallant youth in our rich fields!
"Poor" may we call them in their native lords.   26

DAUPHIN By faith and honor,
Our madams mock at us and plainly say   28
Our mettle is bred out, and they will give   29
Their bodies to the lust of English youth
To new-store France with bastard warriors.   31

BRITTANY
They bid us to the English dancing schools,   32
And teach lavoltas high and swift corantos,   33
Saying our grace is only in our heels   34
And that we are most lofty runaways.   35

FRENCH KING
Where is Montjoy the herald? Speed him hence.   36
Let him greet England with our sharp defiance.
Up, princes, and with spirit of honor edged   38
More sharper than your swords, hie to the field!   39
Charles Delabreth, High Constable of France,
You Dukes of Orleans, Bourbon, and of Berri,
Alençon, Brabant, Bar, and Burgundy,
Jaques Chatillion, Rambures, Vaudemont,
Beaumont, Grandpré, Roussi, and Faulconbridge,
Foix, Lestrelles, Boucicault, and Charolais,
High dukes, great princes, barons, lords, and
   knights,
For your great seats now quit you of great shames.   47
Bar Harry England, that sweeps through our land   48
With pennons painted in the blood of Harfleur.   49
Rush on his host, as doth the melted snow   50
Upon the valleys, whose low vassal seat
The Alps doth spit and void his rheum upon.   52
Go down upon him—you have power enough—
And in a captive chariot into Rouen
Bring him our prisoner.

CONSTABLE   This becomes the great.   55
Sorry am I his numbers are so few,
His soldiers sick and famished in their march,
For I am sure, when he shall see our army,
He'll drop his heart into the sink of fear   59
And for achievement offer us his ransom.   60

FRENCH KING
Therefore, Lord Constable, haste on Montjoy,   61
And let him say to England that we send
To know what willing ransom he will give.
Prince Dauphin, you shall stay with us in Rouen.

DAUPHIN
Not so, I do beseech Your Majesty.

FRENCH KING
Be patient, for you shall remain with us.

ALICE Excellent, my lady.
KATHARINE That's enough for one time. Let's go to dinner.
3.5. Location: The French court at Rouen.
2 withal with (as also in line 12) **5 Dieu vivant** living God. **sprays**
offshoots, illegitimate stock. (Here and through line 11, the French refer to the Norman conquest in 1066 and the resulting admixture of
Norman and Saxon stock.) **6 fathers' luxury** ancestors' lust **7 scions**
grafts. **put in** grafted upon **8 Spirt** shoot, sprout **9 overlook** rise
above and look down upon. **grafters** trees from which scions are
taken **11 Mort de ma vie** death of my life, i.e., may my life end
12 but I will i.e., if I do not **13 slobbery** slovenly **14 nook-shotten**
full of nooks and angles. (Refers to the coastline.) **isle of Albion** island of England, Scotland, and Wales **15 Dieu de batailles** God of
battles. **where** from where **17 despite** contempt **18 sodden water**
boiled water **19 A drench . . . jades** i.e., stuff no better than what
they give their overridden horses to drink. **barley broth** ale **20 Decoct** warm up **21 quick** lively **23 roping** hanging down like a rope
26 "Poor" . . . lords i.e., our fields, though rich in themselves, may
be called poor in that they are owned by a spiritless aristocracy.
(*Them* refers to "our fields"; *in* means "in respect to.")

28 madams wives, ladies **29 bred out** exhausted by breeding
31 new-store newly supply **32 bid us** bid us go **33 lavoltas, corantos** fashionable dances **34 in our heels** (1) in dancing gracefully (2)
in running away **35 lofty** (1) noble (2) leaping. **runaways** cowards
(but referring also to the movements of the dances) **36 Montjoy** title
of the chief herald of France **38 edged** given a sharp edge **39 hie**
hasten **47 For** in the name of, in defense of. **seats** positions. **quit
you** rid, free yourselves **48 Bar** stop, bar the way of **49 pennons**
banners, streamers **50 host** army **52 rheum** watery discharge, i.e.,
stream **55 becomes the great** befits greatness **59 sink** pit **60 for
achievement** instead of achieving victory, as his sole accomplishment
61 haste prod, hurry

Now forth, Lord Constable and princes all,
And quickly bring us word of England's fall. *Exeunt.*

❖

3.6   *Enter Captains, English and Welsh: Gower and Fluellen, [meeting].*

GOWER   How now, Captain Fluellen? Come you from the bridge?   2

FLUELLEN   I assure you, there is very excellent services 3 committed at the bridge.

GOWER   Is the Duke of Exeter safe?

FLUELLEN   The Duke of Exeter is as magnanimous as Agamemnon, and a man that I love and honor with 7 my soul, and my heart, and my duty, and my live, 8 and my living, and my uttermost power. He is not— God be praised and blessed!—any hurt in the world, but keeps the bridge most valiantly, with excellent discipline. There is an aunchient lieutenant there at the 12 pridge, I think in my very conscience he is as valiant a man as Mark Antony, and he is a man of no estimation 14 in the world, but I did see him do as gallant 15 service.

GOWER   What do you call him?

FLUELLEN   He is called Aunchient Pistol.

GOWER   I know him not.

Enter Pistol.

FLUELLEN   Here is the man.

PISTOL
Captain, I thee beseech to do me favors.
The Duke of Exeter doth love thee well.

FLUELLEN   Ay, I praise God, and I have merited some love at his hands.

PISTOL
Bardolph, a soldier, firm and sound of heart,
And of buxom valor, hath, by cruel fate   26
And giddy Fortune's furious fickle wheel,
That goddess blind
That stands upon the rolling restless stone—

FLUELLEN   By your patience, Aunchient Pistol. Fortune is painted blind, with a muffler afore her eyes, to sig- 31 nify to you that Fortune is blind; and she is painted also with a wheel, to signify to you, which is the moral of it, that she is turning, and inconstant, and mutability, and variation; and her foot, look you, is fixed upon a spherical stone, which rolls, and rolls, and rolls. In good truth, the poet is make a most excellent descrip- 37 tion of it. Fortune is an excellent moral.   38

PISTOL
Fortune is Bardolph's foe, and frowns on him;   39
For he hath stol'n a pax,   40
And hangèd must 'a be—a damnèd death!
Let gallows gape for dog; let man go free,
And let not hemp his windpipe suffocate.
But Exeter hath given the doom of death   44
For pax of little price.
Therefore, go speak—the Duke will hear thy voice—
And let not Bardolph's vital thread be cut
With edge of penny cord and vile reproach.   48
Speak, Captain, for his life, and I will thee requite.   49

FLUELLEN   Aunchient Pistol, I do partly understand your meaning.

PISTOL   Why then rejoice therefor.

FLUELLEN   Certainly, Aunchient, it is not a thing to rejoice at. For if, look you, he were my brother, I would desire the Duke to use his good pleasure and put him to execution; for discipline ought to be used.

PISTOL
Die and be damned! And *figo* for thy friendship!   57

FLUELLEN   It is well.

PISTOL   The fig of Spain!   *Exit.*

FLUELLEN   Very good.

GOWER   Why, this is an arrant counterfeit rascal! I remember him now; a bawd, a cutpurse.

FLUELLEN   I'll assure you, 'a uttered as prave words at the pridge as you shall see in a summer's day. But it is very well. What he has spoke to me, that is well, I warrant you, when time is serve.

GOWER   Why, 'tis a gull, a fool, a rogue, that now and 67 then goes to the wars, to grace himself at his return into London under the form of a soldier. And such fellows are perfect in the great commanders' names, 70 and they will learn you by rote where services were 71 done—at such and such a sconce, at such a breach, at 72 such a convoy; who came off bravely, who was shot, who disgraced, what terms the enemy stood on—and 74 this they con perfectly in the phrase of war, which 75 they trick up with new-tuned oaths. And what a 76 beard of the General's cut and a horrid suit of the 77 camp will do among foaming bottles and ale-washed 78 wits is wonderful to be thought on. But you must learn to know such slanders of the age, or else you 80 may be marvelously mistook.   81

3.6. Location: The English camp in northern France.
2 bridge (According to Holinshed, the French were beaten in their attempt to break down the bridge over the Ternoise. The audience is not told this, however, and might assume the river to be the Somme, mentioned in 3.5.1.)   **3 services** exploits (as also in line 71)   **7 Agamemnon** leader of the Greeks against Troy   **8 live** life   **12 aunchient lieutenant** (Pistol is elsewhere given the rank of ancient, or ensign.)   **14–15 estimation** fame   **26 buxom** (1) vigorous (2) compliant, meek   **31 muffler** blindfold   **37 is make** has made   **38 moral** emblem

39 Fortune . . . foe (Probably alludes to the ballad "Fortune, my foe!")   **40 pax** metal disk with a crucifix stamped on it, kissed by the priest during Mass. (But Holinshed describes an incident in which the object stolen is a *pyx,* the vessel containing the consecrated host.) **44 doom** judgment, sentence   **48 cord** rope   **49 requite** repay **57 figo** gesture of contempt made by thrusting the thumb between the index and middle fingers   **67 gull** simpleton   **70 are perfect in** i.e., can recite perfectly   **71 learn** teach   **72 sconce** fortification **74 terms . . . stood on** conditions the enemy insisted on   **75 con** learn by heart   **76 trick** dress.   **new-tuned** i.e., of the latest fashion **77–78 horrid . . . camp** fierce battle costume   **80 slanders of the age** persons who are a disgrace to the times   **81 mistook** mistaken, deluded

FLUELLEN I tell you what, Captain Gower, I do perceive he is not the man that he would gladly make show to the world he is. If I find a hole in his coat, I will tell 84 him my mind. [*Drum heard.*] Hark you, the King is coming, and I must speak with him from the pridge. 86

Drum and colors. Enter the King and his poor soldiers [and Gloucester].

God pless Your Majesty!

KING   How now, Fluellen, cam'st thou from the bridge?

FLUELLEN   Ay, so please Your Majesty. The Duke of Exeter has very gallantly maintained the pridge. The French is gone off, look you, and there is gallant and most prave passages. Marry, th' athversary was have 93 possession of the pridge, but he is enforced to retire, and the Duke of Exeter is master of the pridge. I can tell Your Majesty, the Duke is a prave man.

KING   What men have you lost, Fluellen?

FLUELLEN   The perdition of th' athversary hath been very 98 great, reasonable great. Marry, for my part, I think the Duke hath lost never a man, but one that is like to be ex- 100 ecuted for robbing a church, one Bardolph, if Your Majesty know the man. His face is all bubukles, and whelks, 102 and knobs, and flames o' fire, and his lips blows at his nose, and it is like a coal of fire, sometimes plue and sometimes red; but his nose is executed, and his fire's out.

KING We would have all such offenders so cut off. And we give express charge that, in our marches through the country, there be nothing compelled from the villages, nothing taken but paid for, none of the French upbraided or abused in disdainful language; for when lenity and cruelty play for a kingdom, the gentler gamester 112 is the soonest winner. 113

Tucket. Enter Montjoy.

MONTJOY   You know me by my habit. 114

KING Well then, I know thee. What shall I know of thee?

MONTJOY   My master's mind.

KING   Unfold it.

MONTJOY   Thus says my King: "Say thou to Harry of England, though we seemed dead, we did but sleep. Advantage is a better soldier than rashness. Tell him 120 we could have rebuked him at Harfleur, but that we thought not good to bruise an injury till it were full 122 ripe. Now we speak upon our cue, and our voice is imperial. England shall repent his folly, see his 124 weakness, and admire our sufferance. Bid him there- 125 fore consider of his ransom, which must proportion 126 the losses we have borne, the subjects we have lost,

the disgrace we have digested; which in weight to re- 128 answer, his pettiness would bow under. For our losses, 129 his exchequer is too poor; for th' effusion of our blood, 130 the muster of his kingdom too faint a number; and for 131 our disgrace, his own person kneeling at our feet but a weak and worthless satisfaction. To this add defiance; and tell him, for conclusion, he hath betrayed his followers, whose condemnation is pronounced." So far 135 my King and master; so much my office.

KING
What is thy name? I know thy quality. 137

MONTJOY   Montjoy.

KING
Thou dost thy office fairly. Turn thee back
And tell thy King I do not seek him now,
But could be willing to march on to Calais
Without impeachment. For, to say the sooth, 142
Though 'tis no wisdom to confess so much
Unto an enemy of craft and vantage, 144
My people are with sickness much enfeebled,
My numbers lessened, and those few I have
Almost no better than so many French,
Who when they were in health, I tell thee, herald,
I thought upon one pair of English legs
Did march three Frenchmen. Yet, forgive me, God,
That I do brag thus! This your air of France
Hath blown that vice in me. I must repent. 152
Go, therefore, tell thy master here I am;
My ransom is this frail and worthless trunk, 154
My army but a weak and sickly guard.
Yet, God before, tell him we will come on,
Though France himself and such another neighbor
Stand in our way. There's for thy labor, Montjoy.
                    [*He gives a purse.*]
Go bid thy master well advise himself. 159
If we may pass, we will; if we be hindered,
We shall your tawny ground with your red blood
Discolor. And so, Montjoy, fare you well.
The sum of all our answer is but this:
We would not seek a battle as we are,
Nor, as we are, we say we will not shun it.
So tell your master.

MONTJOY
I shall deliver so. Thanks to Your Highness.   [*Exit.*]

GLOUCESTER
I hope they will not come upon us now.

KING
We are in God's hand, brother, not in theirs.
March to the bridge. It now draws toward night.
Beyond the river we'll encamp ourselves,
And on tomorrow bid them march away.   *Exeunt.* 172

---

84 **a hole . . . coat** i.e., a weak spot in him. (Proverbial.)   86 **from the pridge** with news concerning the bridge   93 **passages** deeds of arms.   **was** did   98 **perdition** losses   100 **like** likely   102 **bubukles** carbuncles.   **whelks** boils, pimples   112 **gamester** player   113 s.d. **Tucket** trumpet signal, fanfare   114 **habit** i.e., tabard, herald's coat   120 **Advantage** knowing how to wait for favorable circumstance   122 **bruise an injury** squeeze a boil or pimple   124 **England** i.e., King Henry   125 **admire our sufferance** wonder at our patience   126 **proportion** be proportional to

128–129 **which . . . under** i.e., to compensate for which his means are too slender   130 **exchequer** treasury   131 **muster** total population   135 **condemnation** death sentence   137 **quality** rank and profession   142 **impeachment** impediment.   **sooth** truth   144 **vantage** superiority in resources   152 **blown** brought to bloom   154 **trunk** body   159 **advise himself** consider   172 **bid . . . away** bid our army march toward Calais

3.7

Enter the Constable of France, the Lord Rambures, Orleans, Dauphin, with others.

CONSTABLE Tut, I have the best armor of the world. Would it were day!

ORLEANS You have an excellent armor; but let my horse have his due.

CONSTABLE It is the best horse of Europe.

ORLEANS Will it never be morning?

DAUPHIN My lord of Orleans and my Lord High Constable, you talk of horse and armor?

ORLEANS You are as well provided of both as any prince in the world.

DAUPHIN What a long night is this! I will not change my horse with any that treads but on four pasterns. 12 Ça, ha! He bounds from the earth as if his entrails 13 were hairs; *le cheval volant,* the Pegasus, *qui a les narines* 14 *de feu!* When I bestride him, I soar, I am a hawk. He 15 trots the air. The earth sings when he touches it. The basest horn of his hoof is more musical than the pipe 17 of Hermes. 18

ORLEANS He's of the color of the nutmeg.

DAUPHIN And of the heat of the ginger. It is a beast for Perseus. He is pure air and fire; and the dull elements 21 of earth and water never appear in him, but only in patient stillness while his rider mounts him. He is indeed a horse, and all other jades you may call beasts.

CONSTABLE Indeed, my lord, it is a most absolute and 25 excellent horse.

DAUPHIN It is the prince of palfreys. His neigh is like 27 the bidding of a monarch, and his countenance enforces homage.

ORLEANS No more, cousin.

DAUPHIN Nay, the man hath no wit that cannot, from the rising of the lark to the lodging of the lamb, vary 32 deserved praise on my palfrey. It is a theme as fluent as the sea; turn the sands into eloquent tongues, and my horse is argument for them all. 'Tis a subject for a 35 sovereign to reason on, and for a sovereign's sovereign 36 to ride on; and for the world, familiar to us and un- 37 known, to lay apart their particular functions and 38 wonder at him. I once writ a sonnet in his praise, and 39 began thus: "Wonder of nature—"

ORLEANS I have heard a sonnet begin so to one's mistress.

DAUPHIN Then did they imitate that which I composed

to my courser, for my horse is my mistress. 44

ORLEANS Your mistress bears well.

DAUPHIN Me well, which is the prescript praise and 46 perfection of a good and particular mistress. 47

CONSTABLE Nay, for methought yesterday your mistress shrewdly shook your back. 49

DAUPHIN So perhaps did yours.

CONSTABLE Mine was not bridled. 51

DAUPHIN O, then belike she was old and gentle, and 52 you rode like a kern of Ireland, your French hose off, 53 and in your strait strossers. 54

CONSTABLE You have good judgment in horsemanship.

DAUPHIN Be warned by me, then: they that ride so, and ride not warily, fall into foul bogs. I had rather have my horse to my mistress. 58

CONSTABLE I had as lief have my mistress a jade. 59

DAUPHIN I tell thee, Constable, my mistress wears his 60 own hair. 61

CONSTABLE I could make as true a boast as that, if I had a sow to my mistress.

DAUPHIN *"Le chien est retourné à son propre vomissement,* 64 *et la truie lavée au bourbier."* Thou mak'st use of 65 anything.

CONSTABLE Yet do I not use my horse for my mistress, or any such proverb so little kin to the purpose. 68

RAMBURES My Lord Constable, the armor that I saw in your tent tonight, are those stars or suns upon it?

CONSTABLE Stars, my lord.

DAUPHIN Some of them will fall tomorrow, I hope.

CONSTABLE And yet my sky shall not want. 73

DAUPHIN That may be, for you bear a many superflu- 74 ously, and 'twere more honor some were away. 75

CONSTABLE Even as your horse bears your praises, who would trot as well, were some of your brags dismounted.

DAUPHIN Would I were able to load him with his desert! Will it never be day? I will trot tomorrow a mile, and my way shall be paved with English faces.

CONSTABLE I will not say so, for fear I should be faced 82 out of my way. But I would it were morning, for I 83 would fain be about the ears of the English. 84

RAMBURES Who will go to hazard with me for twenty 85 prisoners?

3.7. Location: The French camp, near Agincourt.
12 pasterns i.e., hooves. (The *pastern* literally is the part of the horse's leg between the fetlock and the hoof.) **13–14 as . . . hairs** i.e., as if he were a tennis ball. (Tennis balls were stuffed with hair. Or perhaps *hairs* should read *hares.*) **14–15 le cheval . . . feu** the flying horse, Pegasus, with nostrils breathing fire **17 basest horn** (1) lowest part (2) hoofbeat **17–18 pipe of Hermes** (Hermes, messenger of the gods, charmed Argus of the hundred eyes asleep with playing on his pipe.) **21 Perseus** (According to some Greek legends and to Ovid, Perseus rode Pegasus when he rescued Andromeda from the dragon.) **25 absolute** perfect **27 palfreys** saddle horses **32 lodging** lying down. **vary** produce variations of **35 argument** subject **36 reason** discourse **37–39 for . . . him** for both the known and unknown worlds to put aside their differences and join in wondering

44 horse is my mistress (Here begins a series of bawdy double entendres involving human and animal sexuality: *bears, shook your back, rode, foul bogs, doing,* etc.) **46 prescript** prescribed **47 particular** acknowledging only one master **49 shrewdly** viciously **51 Mine . . . bridled** i.e., at least my mistress was not a horse **52 belike** probably **53 kern** Irish foot soldier. (Here it is used to mean "rustic" or "boor.") **French hose** wide breeches **54 strait strossers** tight trousers, i.e., bare-legged **58 to** as **59 lief** happily. **jade** (1) worn-out horse (2) slut **60–61 wears . . . hair** i.e., is not artificially wigged, like an elegant court lady, and perhaps bald from syphilis **64–65 Le chien . . . bourbier** the dog is returned to his own vomit, and the washed sow to the mire. (See 2 Peter 2:22.) **68 kin** related **73 sky** i.e., sky of honor. **want** be lacking (in honor) **74 a many** many. (Parallel to "a few.") **75 'twere . . . away** i.e., it would be more honest and proper if some of your stars were done away with **82–83 faced . . . way** braved out of my way, put to shame **84 fain** gladly. **about the ears** buffeting the heads **85 go to hazard** bet, play at dice. (But the Constable replies in the sense of "encounter danger.")

CONSTABLE   You must first go yourself to hazard, ere you have them.

DAUPHIN   'Tis midnight. I'll go arm myself.   *Exit.*

ORLEANS   The Dauphin longs for morning.

RAMBURES   He longs to eat the English.

CONSTABLE   I think he will eat all he kills.

ORLEANS   By the white hand of my lady, he's a gallant prince.

CONSTABLE   Swear by her foot, that she may tread out 95 the oath. 96

ORLEANS   He is simply the most active gentleman of France.

CONSTABLE   Doing is activity, and he will still be doing. 99

ORLEANS   He never did harm, that I heard of. 100

CONSTABLE   Nor will do none tomorrow. He will keep that good name still.

ORLEANS   I know him to be valiant.

CONSTABLE   I was told that by one that knows him better than you.

ORLEANS   What's he?

CONSTABLE   Marry, he told me so himself, and he said he cared not who knew it.

ORLEANS   He needs not; it is no hidden virtue in him. 109

CONSTABLE   By my faith, sir, but it is. Never anybody 110 saw it but his lackey. 'Tis a hooded valor, and when it 111 appears it will bate. 112

ORLEANS   Ill will never said well.

CONSTABLE   I will cap that proverb with "There is flattery in friendship."

ORLEANS   And I will take up that with "Give the devil 116 his due." 117

CONSTABLE   Well placed. There stands your friend for 118 the devil. Have at the very eye of that proverb with "A 119 pox of the devil."

ORLEANS   You are the better at proverbs by how much "A fool's bolt is soon shot." 122

CONSTABLE   You have shot over. 123

ORLEANS   'Tis not the first time you were overshot. 124

Enter a Messenger.

MESSENGER   My Lord High Constable, the English lie within fifteen hundred paces of your tents.

CONSTABLE   Who hath measured the ground?

MESSENGER   The Lord Grandpré.

CONSTABLE   A valiant and most expert gentleman. [*Exit Messenger.*] Would it were day! Alas, poor Harry of England! He longs not for the dawning as we do.

95–96 **tread . . . oath** (1) fulfill the oath by dancing (2) stamp on, spurn the oath   99 **Doing** i.e., acting, pretending.   **still** continually   100 **did harm** i.e., offended. (But the Constable uses it to mean ''hurt any enemy.'')   109 **He needs not** i.e., there is no need for him to proclaim it himself.   **it** i.e., valor   110–111 **Never . . . lackey** i.e., he shows ''valor'' only in beating his servant   111 **hooded valor** (The hawk was kept hooded to prevent it from beating its wings, or ''bating.'')   112 **bate** (1) beat its wings (2) abate, be downcast   116–117 **Give . . . due** give even the devil his due; everyone deserves some praise. (But the Constable turns this proverb against the Dauphin by likening him to the devil.)   118–119 **There . . . devil** i.e., you just called the Dauphin the devil   119 **Have . . . eye** shoot straight at the mark. (A sporting term appropriate to this verbal contest of ''capping proverbs.'')   122 **bolt** short, blunt arrow   123 **shot over** i.e., shot over the mark   124 **overshot** i.e., outshot, defeated

ORLEANS   What a wretched and peevish fellow is this King of England, to mope with his fat-brained follow- 133 ers so far out of his knowledge!

CONSTABLE   If the English had any apprehension, they 135 would run away.

ORLEANS   That they lack; for if their heads had any intellectual armor, they could never wear such heavy headpieces.

RAMBURES   That island of England breeds very valiant creatures; their mastiffs are of unmatchable courage.

ORLEANS   Foolish curs, that run winking into the mouth 142 of a Russian bear and have their heads crushed like rotten apples. You may as well say "That's a valiant flea that dare eat his breakfast on the lip of a lion."

CONSTABLE   Just, just! And the men do sympathize with 146 the mastiffs in robustious and rough coming on, leav- 147 ing their wits with their wives; and then give them great meals of beef and iron and steel, they will eat like wolves and fight like devils.

ORLEANS   Ay, but these English are shrewdly out of 151 beef.

CONSTABLE   Then shall we find tomorrow they have only stomachs to eat and none to fight. Now is it time 154 to arm. Come, shall we about it?

ORLEANS   It is now two o'clock; but let me see, by ten We shall have each a hundred Englishmen.   *Exeunt.*

4.0   [*Enter*] Chorus.

CHORUS

Now entertain conjecture of a time 1
When creeping murmur and the poring dark 2
Fills the wide vessel of the universe.
From camp to camp, through the foul womb of night,
The hum of either army stilly sounds, 5
That the fixed sentinels almost receive
The secret whispers of each other's watch.
Fire answers fire, and through their paly flames 8
Each battle sees the other's umbered face. 9
Steed threatens steed, in high and boastful neighs
Piercing the night's dull ear; and from the tents
The armorers, accomplishing the knights, 12
With busy hammers closing rivets up,
Give dreadful note of preparation.
The country cocks do crow, the clocks do toll,
And the third hour of drowsy morning name.
Proud of their numbers and secure in soul, 17
The confident and overlusty French 18

133 **mope** (1) wander about (2) be downcast   135 **apprehension** (1) sense (2) sense of danger   142 **winking** shutting their eyes   146 **Just** exactly.   **sympathize with** resemble   147 **robustious** violent, boisterous   151 **shrewdly out of** devilishly short of   154 **stomachs** appetites
4.0. Chorus.
1 **entertain conjecture of** i.e., imagine   2 **poring** in which one must strain the eyes to see   5 **stilly** softly   8 **paly** pale   9 **battle** army.   **umbered** shadowed   12 **accomplishing** equipping   17 **secure** overconfident   18 **overlusty** overly merry

Do the low-rated English play at dice,   19
And chide the cripple tardy-gaited night,
Who like a foul and ugly witch doth limp
So tediously away. The poor condemnèd English,
Like sacrifices, by their watchful fires
Sit patiently and inly ruminate   24
The morning's danger; and their gesture sad,   25
Investing lank-lean cheeks and war-worn coats,   26
Presenteth them unto the gazing moon
So many horrid ghosts. O, now, who will behold
The royal captain of this ruined band
Walking from watch to watch, from tent to tent,
Let him cry, "Praise and glory on his head!"
For forth he goes and visits all his host,   32
Bids them good morrow with a modest smile,
And calls them brothers, friends, and countrymen.
Upon his royal face there is no note
How dread an army hath enrounded him.   36
Nor doth he dedicate one jot of color   37
Unto the weary and all-watchèd night,   38
But freshly looks and overbears attaint   39
With cheerful semblance and sweet majesty;
That every wretch, pining and pale before,
Beholding him, plucks comfort from his looks.
A largess universal like the sun
His liberal eye doth give to everyone,
Thawing cold fear, that mean and gentle all   45
Behold, as may unworthiness define,   46
A little touch of Harry in the night.
And so our scene must to the battle fly;
Where—O, for pity!—we shall much disgrace
With four or five most vile and ragged foils,
Right ill-disposed in brawl ridiculous,
The name of Agincourt. Yet sit and see,
Minding true things by what their mockeries be.   53

Exit.

❖

4.1   *Enter the King, Bedford, and Gloucester.*

KING
Gloucester, 'tis true that we are in great danger;
The greater therefore should our courage be.
Good morrow, brother Bedford. God Almighty!
There is some soul of goodness in things evil,
Would men observingly distill it out;   5
For our bad neighbor makes us early stirrers,
Which is both healthful and good husbandry.   7
Besides, they are our outward consciences,
And preachers to us all, admonishing

That we should dress us fairly for our end.   10
Thus may we gather honey from the weed
And make a moral of the devil himself.

Enter Erpingham.

Good morrow, old Sir Thomas Erpingham.
A good soft pillow for that good white head
Were better than a churlish turf of France.   15
ERPINGHAM
Not so, my liege. This lodging likes me better,   16
Since I may say, "Now lie I like a king."
KING
'Tis good for men to love their present pains
Upon example; so the spirit is eased.   19
And when the mind is quickened, out of doubt
The organs, though defunct and dead before,
Break up their drowsy grave and newly move   22
With casted slough and fresh legerity.   23
Lend me thy cloak, Sir Thomas. [*The King puts on
Erpingham's cloak.*] Brothers both,   24
Commend me to the princes in our camp;
Do my good morrow to them, and anon
Desire them all to my pavilion.
GLOUCESTER   We shall, my liege.
ERPINGHAM   Shall I attend Your Grace?
KING   No, my good knight,
Go with my brothers to my lords of England.
I and my bosom must debate awhile,
And then I would no other company.
ERPINGHAM
The Lord in heaven bless thee, noble Harry!
Exeunt [all but the King].
KING
God-a-mercy, old heart! Thou speak'st cheerfully.

Enter Pistol.

PISTOL   *Che vous là?*   36
KING   A friend.
PISTOL
Discuss unto me: art thou officer,   38
Or art thou base, common, and popular?   39
KING   I am a gentleman of a company.   40
PISTOL   Trail'st thou the puissant pike?   41
KING   Even so. What are you?
PISTOL
As good a gentleman as the Emperor.   43
KING   Then you are a better than the King.
PISTOL
The King's a bawcock and a heart of gold,   45

19 **play** gamble for   24 **inly** inwardly   25 **gesture sad** serious bearing   26 **Investing** clothing   32 **host** army   36 **enrounded** surrounded   37 **dedicate** yield up.   **color** i.e., bright color of complexion   38 **all-watchèd** spent entirely in wakefulness and waiting   39 **overbears attaint** overcomes the effects of weariness and depression   45 **mean and gentle** those of low and of high birth   46 **as . . . define** as we can express to you only imperfectly   53 **Minding** bearing in mind.   **mockeries** inadequate imitations
4.1. Location: The English camp at Agincourt.
5 **observingly** observantly   7 **husbandry** economy, thrift

10 **dress us fairly** prepare ourselves well   15 **churlish** rough, hard   16 **likes** pleases   19 **Upon example** i.e., following or considering the example of persons such as King Henry and Erpingham   22 **Break . . . grave** i.e., break out of their lethargy   23 **With casted slough** as though having cast off their old skin, like a snake.   **legerity** nimbleness   24 **Brothers both** i.e., Bedford and Gloucester   36 **Che vous là** i.e., *qui va là,* "who goes there"; or *qui vous là,* "who are you there." (Pistol's imperfect French.)   38 **Discuss** declare   39 **popular** of low birth   40 **gentleman of a company** gentleman serving voluntarily and without pay   41 **Trail'st . . . pike** i.e., are you in the infantry   43 **Emperor** i.e., Holy Roman Emperor   45 **bawcock** fine fellow. (From the French *beau coq.*)

A lad of life, an imp of fame,   46
Of parents good, of fist most valiant.
I kiss his dirty shoe, and from heartstring
I love the lovely bully. What is thy name?   49
KING   Harry le Roy.
PISTOL
Le Roy? A Cornish name. Art thou of Cornish crew?
KING   No, I am a Welshman.   52
PISTOL   Know'st thou Fluellen?
KING   Yes.
PISTOL
Tell him I'll knock his leek about his pate   55
Upon Saint Davy's Day.   56
KING   Do not you wear your dagger in your cap that
day, lest he knock that about yours.
PISTOL   Art thou his friend?
KING   And his kinsman too.
PISTOL   The *figo* for thee, then!   61
KING   I thank you. God be with you!
PISTOL   My name is Pistol called.   *Exit.*
KING   It sorts well with your fierceness.   64
                              Manet King [standing apart].

          Enter Fluellen and Gower [meeting].

GOWER   Captain Fluellen!
FLUELLEN   So, in the name of Jesu Christ, speak fewer.   66
It is the greatest admiration in the universal world,   67
when the true and aunchient prerogatifes and laws of
the wars is not kept. If you would take the pains but
to examine the wars of Pompey the Great, you shall   70
find, I warrant you, that there is no tiddle-taddle nor   71
pibble-pabble in Pompey's camp. I warrant you, you   72
shall find the ceremonies of the wars, and the cares of
it, and the forms of it, and the sobriety of it, and the   74
modesty of it, to be otherwise.   75
GOWER   Why, the enemy is loud; you hear him all
night.
FLUELLEN   If the enemy is an ass and a fool and a prating   78
coxcomb, is it meet, think you, that we should also,   79
look you, be an ass and a fool and a prating coxcomb?
In your own conscience, now?
GOWER   I will speak lower.
FLUELLEN   I pray you and beseech you that you will.
                              Exit [with Gower].
KING
Though it appear a little out of fashion,
There is much care and valor in this Welshman.

          Enter three soldiers, John Bates, Alexander Court,
          and Michael Williams.

COURT   Brother John Bates, is not that the morning
which breaks yonder?
BATES   I think it be. But we have no great cause to
desire the approach of day.
WILLIAMS   We see yonder the beginning of the day, but
I think we shall never see the end of it.—Who goes
there?
KING   A friend.
WILLIAMS   Under what captain serve you?
KING   Under Sir Thomas Erpingham.
WILLIAMS   A good old commander and a most kind
gentleman. I pray you, what thinks he of our estate?   97
KING   Even as men wrecked upon a sand, that look to   98
be washed off the next tide.
BATES   He hath not told his thought to the King?
KING   No, nor it is not meet he should. For, though I   101
speak it to you, I think the King is but a man, as I am.
The violet smells to him as it doth to me; the element   103
shows to him as it doth to me; all his senses have but   104
human conditions. His ceremonies laid by, in his   105
nakedness he appears but a man; and though his
affections are higher mounted than ours, yet when   107
they stoop, they stoop with the like wing. Therefore
when he sees reason of fears, as we do, his fears, out
of doubt, be of the same relish as ours are. Yet, in   110
reason, no man should possess him with any appear-   111
ance of fear, lest he, by showing it, should dishearten
his army.
BATES   He may show what outward courage he will; but
I believe, as cold a night as 'tis, he could wish himself
in Thames up to the neck; and so I would he were,
and I by him, at all adventures, so we were quit here.   117
KING   By my troth, I will speak my conscience of the
King: I think he would not wish himself anywhere but
where he is.
BATES   Then I would he were here alone. So should he
be sure to be ransomed, and a many poor men's lives
saved.
KING   I dare say you love him not so ill to wish him here
alone, howsoever you speak this to feel other men's
minds. Methinks I could not die anywhere so contented as in the King's company, his cause being just
and his quarrel honorable.
WILLIAMS   That's more than we know.
BATES   Ay, or more than we should seek after; for we
know enough if we know we are the King's subjects.
If his cause be wrong, our obedience to the King
wipes the crime of it out of us.
WILLIAMS   But if the cause be not good, the King
himself hath a heavy reckoning to make, when all
those legs and arms and heads, chopped off in a
battle, shall join together at the Latter Day and cry all,   137

---

46 imp of fame child or scion of renown   **49 bully** (A term of endear-
ment meaning "fine fellow.")   **52 Welshman** (Henry was born at
Monmouth, then considered part of Wales.)   **55–56 leek . . . Day**
(On Saint David's Day, March 1, the leek was worn in memory of a
Welsh victory over the Saxons in 540 A.D ., since Saint David, the
Welsh leader, had commanded his followers to wear leeks in their
caps on that occasion.)   **61 figo** (A provoking gesture of contempt;
see the note for 3.6.57.)   **64 sorts** fits, agrees.   **s.d. Manet King** the
King remains   **66 fewer** i.e., calmly, more quietly   **67 admiration**
wonder   **70 Pompey the Great** Roman general defeated by Julius
Caesar   **71–72 tiddle-taddle nor pibble-pabble** tittle-tattle nor bibble-
babble   **74 sobriety** orderliness, decorum   **75 modesty** propriety
78–79 prating coxcomb chattering fool

97 estate condition   **98 wrecked** shipwrecked   **101 meet** fitting
103–104 element shows sky appears   **105 conditions** qualities, i.e.,
limitations.   **ceremonies** observances due royalty; royal robes
107 affections . . . mounted desires soar higher. (A falconry metaphor continued in *stoop*, "descend," "swoop down," and *with the
like wing*, "similarly.")   **110 relish** taste   **111 possess him with** induce in him   **117 at all adventures** at all events (since the Thames
would be less risky under any circumstances than the impending battle).   **quit here** out of this situation   **137 Latter Day** last day, Day of
Judgment

"We died at such a place"—some swearing, some crying for a surgeon, some upon their wives left poor behind them, some upon the debts they owe, some upon their children rawly left. I am afeard there are 141 few die well that die in a battle; for how can they charitably dispose of anything, when blood is their argument? Now, if these men do not die well, it will be a black matter for the King that led them to it; who 145 to disobey were against all proportion of subjection. 146

KING So, if a son that is by his father sent about merchandise do sinfully miscarry upon the sea, the 148 imputation of his wickedness, by your rule, should be 149 imposed upon his father that sent him; or if a servant, under his master's command transporting a sum of money, be assailed by robbers and die in many 152 irreconciled iniquities, you may call the business of the 153 master the author of the servant's damnation. But this is not so. The King is not bound to answer the par- 155 ticular endings of his soldiers, the father of his son, nor the master of his servant; for they purpose not their 157 deaths when they propose their services. Besides, there is no king, be his cause never so spotless, if it come to the arbitrament of swords, can try it out with 160 all unspotted soldiers. Some, peradventure, have on 161 them the guilt of premeditated and contrived murder; some, of beguiling virgins with the broken seals of 163 perjury; some, making the wars their bulwark, that 164 have before gored the gentle bosom of peace with pillage and robbery. Now, if these men have defeated 166 the law and outrun native punishment, though they 167 can outstrip men, they have no wings to fly from God. War is his beadle, war is his vengeance; so that here 169 men are punished for before-breach of the King's laws 170 in now the King's quarrel. Where they feared the 171 death, they have borne life away; and where they 172 would be safe, they perish. Then if they die unpro- 173 vided, no more is the King guilty of their damnation 174 than he was before guilty of those impieties for the which they are now visited. Every subject's duty is the 176 King's; but every subject's soul is his own. Therefore should every soldier in the wars do as every sick man in his bed, wash every mote out of his conscience; and 179 dying so, death is to him advantage, or not dying, the time was blessedly lost wherein such preparation was gained. And in him that escapes, it were not sin to think that, making God so free an offer, He let him outlive that day to see His greatness and to teach others how they should prepare.

WILLIAMS 'Tis certain, every man that dies ill, the ill 186

upon his own head, the King is not to answer it.

BATES I do not desire he should answer for me, and yet I determine to fight lustily for him.

KING I myself heard the King say he would not be ransomed.

WILLIAMS Ay, he said so, to make us fight cheerfully; but when our throats are cut, he may be ransomed and we ne'er the wiser.

KING If I live to see it, I will never trust his word after.

WILLIAMS You pay him then! That's a perilous shot out 196 of an elder-gun, that a poor and a private displeasure 197 can do against a monarch. You may as well go about to turn the sun to ice with fanning in his face with a peacock's feather. You'll never trust his word after! Come, 'tis a foolish saying.

KING Your reproof is something too round. I should be 202 angry with you, if the time were convenient.

WILLIAMS Let it be a quarrel between us, if you live.

KING I embrace it.

WILLIAMS How shall I know thee again?

KING Give me any gage of thine, and I will wear it in 207 my bonnet. Then if ever thou dar'st acknowledge it, I will make it my quarrel.

WILLIAMS Here's my glove. Give me another of thine.

KING There.   [They exchange gloves.]

WILLIAMS This will I also wear in my cap. If ever thou come to me and say, after tomorrow, "This is my glove," by this hand, I will take thee a box on the ear. 214

KING If ever I live to see it, I will challenge it.

WILLIAMS Thou dar'st as well be hanged.

KING Well, I will do it, though I take thee in the King's company.

WILLIAMS Keep thy word. Fare thee well.

BATES Be friends, you English fools, be friends. We have French quarrels enough, if you could tell how to 221 reckon.

KING Indeed, the French may lay twenty French crowns 223 to one they will beat us, for they bear them on their shoulders; but it is no English treason to cut French 225 crowns, and tomorrow the King himself will be a clipper.   Exeunt soldiers.

Upon the King! Let us our lives, our souls,
Our debts, our careful wives,   229
Our children, and our sins lay on the King!
We must bear all. O hard condition,
Twin-born with greatness, subject to the breath 232
Of every fool, whose sense no more can feel 233
But his own wringing! What infinite heartsease 234
Must kings neglect that private men enjoy!
And what have kings that privates have not too, 236

141 rawly without provision 145 who whom 146 proportion of subjection proper duty of a subject 148 sinfully miscarry die in his sins 149 imputation charge, accusation 152–153 in . . . iniquities with his wicked deeds unabsolved 155 answer answer for 157 purpose intend 160 arbitrament arbitration 161 unspotted innocent 163 seals (1) covenants (2) maidenheads 164 bulwark refuge from punishment (for offenses committed) 166 defeated broken 167 native at home 169 beadle parish officer responsible for punishing petty offenders 170 before-breach prior violation 171–173 Where . . . perish i.e., whereas before they feared execution but escaped punishment, here where they look for safety they die in battle 173–174 unprovided spiritually unprepared 176 visited i.e., by punishment 179 mote small impurity 186 dies ill dies in sin

196 You pay him then i.e., that will really pay him back for his perfidy, won't it. (Said sarcastically.) 197 elder-gun popgun made from a branch of elder with the pith hollowed out 202 round direct, brusque 207 gage pledge 214 take give, strike 221 could tell knew 223 crowns (1) coins (2) heads 225 English treason (It was a treasonable offense to clip or "cut" English coins; it obviously is no offense to slash French heads, and even King Henry will be such a "clipper.") 229 careful full of cares 232–234 Twin-born . . . wringing i.e., inseparable from the condition of being born of royal rank, a condition that makes one the subject of the idle gossip of every fool, even those whose sensibilities pay attention to nothing other than the rumbling of their own stomachs 236 privates private men

Save ceremony, save general ceremony?
And what art thou, thou idol ceremony?
What kind of god art thou, that suffer'st more
Of mortal griefs than do thy worshipers?
What are thy rents? What are thy comings-in?   241
O ceremony, show me but thy worth!
What is thy soul of adoration?   243
Art thou aught else but place, degree, and form,   244
Creating awe and fear in other men?
Wherein thou art less happy, being feared,
Than they in fearing.
What drink'st thou oft, instead of homage sweet,
But poisoned flattery? O, be sick, great greatness,
And bid thy ceremony give thee cure!
Thinks thou the fiery fever will go out   251
With titles blown from adulation?   252
Will it give place to flexure and low bending?   253
Canst thou, when thou command'st the beggar's
    knee,
Command the health of it? No, thou proud dream,
That play'st so subtly with a king's repose.
I am a king that find thee, and I know   257
'Tis not the balm, the scepter, and the ball,   258
The sword, the mace, the crown imperial,   259
The intertissued robe of gold and pearl,   260
The farcèd title running 'fore the king,   261
The throne he sits on, nor the tide of pomp
That beats upon the high shore of this world—
No, not all these, thrice-gorgeous ceremony,
Not all these, laid in bed majestical,
Can sleep so soundly as the wretched slave
Who, with a body filled and vacant mind,
Gets him to rest, crammed with distressful bread;   268
Never sees horrid night, the child of hell,
But like a lackey from the rise to set   270
Sweats in the eye of Phoebus, and all night   271
Sleeps in Elysium; next day after dawn   272
Doth rise and help Hyperion to his horse,   273
And follows so the ever-running year
With profitable labor to his grave.
And but for ceremony, such a wretch,
Winding up days with toil and nights with sleep,
Had the forehand and vantage of a king.   278
The slave, a member of the country's peace,   279
Enjoys it, but in gross brain little wots   280
What watch the King keeps to maintain the peace,   281
Whose hours the peasant best advantages.   282

Enter Erpingham.

ERPINGHAM
My lord, your nobles, jealous of your absence,   283
Seek through your camp to find you.
KING   Good old knight,
Collect them all together at my tent.
I'll be before thee.
ERPINGHAM   I shall do 't, my lord.   *Exit.* 286
KING
O God of battles, steel my soldiers' hearts;
Possess them not with fear! Take from them now
The sense of reckoning, ere th' opposèd numbers   289
Pluck their hearts from them. Not today, O Lord,
O, not today, think not upon the fault   291
My father made in compassing the crown!   292
I Richard's body have interrèd new,   293
And on it have bestowed more contrite tears
Than from it issued forcèd drops of blood.
Five hundred poor I have in yearly pay
Who twice a day their withered hands hold up
Toward heaven, to pardon blood; and I have built
Two chantries, where the sad and solemn priests   299
Sing still for Richard's soul. More will I do;   300
Though all that I can do is nothing worth,
Since that my penitence comes after all,   302
Imploring pardon.

Enter Gloucester.

GLOUCESTER   My liege!
KING   My brother Gloucester's voice? Ay;
I know thy errand. I will go with thee.
The day, my friends, and all things stay for me.
                                        Exeunt.

❖

4.2   *Enter the Dauphin, Orleans, Rambures, and
        Beaumont.*

ORLEANS
The sun doth gild our armor. Up, my lords!
DAUPHIN   *Monte cheval!* My horse! *Varlet! Lacquais!* Ha! 2
ORLEANS   O brave spirit!
DAUPHIN   *Via, les eaux et terre!*   4
ORLEANS   *Rien puis? L'air et feu?*   5
DAUPHIN   *Cieux,* cousin Orleans.   6

Enter Constable.

241 comings-in revenues   243 thy soul of adoration the essential quality that makes you so much admired   244 place rank   251–252 will . . . adulation will be extinguished by speeches breathed by flatterers. (*Blown* also suggests "inflated.")   253 Will . . . flexure i.e., will the sickness yield to bowing   257 find expose   258 balm consecrating oil used to anoint a king in his coronation. ball orb of sovereignty   259 mace ceremonial staff   260 intertissued interwoven   261 farcèd stuffed (with pompous phrases)   268 distressful earned by hard work   270 lackey constant attendant. rise to set sunrise to sunset   271 Phoebus the sun god   272 Elysium in Greek mythology, the abode of the blessed   273 Hyperion the father of the sun, or the sun itself. (The peasant is up before the sun.)   278 Had would have. forehand upper hand   279 member sharer   280 it i.e., peace. wots knows   281 watch wakeful guard   282 the peasant best advantages most benefit the peasant

283 jealous of apprehensive because of   286 be be there   289 sense of reckoning ability to reckon up the odds   291 the fault i.e., the deposition and murder of Richard II   292 compassing obtaining   293 new anew   299 chantries chapels in which masses for the dead were celebrated. sad grave   300 still continually   302 Since that i.e., as shown by the fact that
4.2. Location: The French camp.
s.d. Beaumont (The Folio text mentions Lord Beaumont but does not give him a speaking part.)   2 Monte cheval! to horse   4 Via . . . terre begone, waters and earth. (The Dauphin imagines himself riding above rivers and solid ground.)   5 Rien . . . feu nothing more? What about air and fire? (i.e., Why not soar above all four elements, not just water and earth?)   6 Cieux the heavens. (The Dauphin carries the metaphor one step further to its ultimate height.)

Now, my Lord Constable!

CONSTABLE
Hark, how our steeds for present service neigh!   8

DAUPHIN
Mount them, and make incision in their hides,   9
That their hot blood may spin in English eyes   10
And dout them with superfluous courage. Ha!   11

RAMBURES
What, will you have them weep our horses' blood?
How shall we then behold their natural tears?

Enter Messenger.

MESSENGER
The English are embattled, you French peers.   14

CONSTABLE
To horse, you gallant princes, straight to horse!
Do but behold yond poor and starvèd band,
And your fair show shall suck away their souls,   17
Leaving them but the shales and husks of men.   18
There is not work enough for all our hands,
Scarce blood enough in all their sickly veins
To give each naked curtal ax a stain   21
That our French gallants shall today draw out
And sheathe for lack of sport. Let us but blow on
    them,
The vapor of our valor will o'erturn them.
'Tis positive against all exceptions, lords,   25
That our superfluous lackeys and our peasants,
Who in unnecessary action swarm
About our squares of battle, were enough   28
To purge this field of such a hilding foe,   29
Though we upon this mountain's basis by   30
Took stand for idle speculation—   31
But that our honors must not. What's to say?   32
A very little little let us do
And all is done. Then let the trumpets sound
The tucket sonance and the note to mount;   35
For our approach shall so much dare the field   36
That England shall couch down in fear and yield.

Enter Grandpré.

GRANDPRÉ
Why do you stay so long, my lords of France?
Yond island carrions, desperate of their bones,   39
Ill-favoredly become the morning field.   40
Their ragged curtains poorly are let loose,   41
And our air shakes them passing scornfully.   42
Big Mars seems bankrupt in their beggared host   43

And faintly through a rusty beaver peeps.   44
The horsemen sit like fixèd candlesticks,
With torch staves in their hand, and their poor jades   46
Lob down their heads, drooping the hides and hips,   47
The gum down-roping from their pale-dead eyes,   48
And in their pale dull mouths the gimmaled bit   49
Lies foul with chewed grass, still and motionless;
And their executors, the knavish crows,   51
Fly o'er them all impatient for their hour.
Description cannot suit itself in words
To demonstrate the life of such a battle   54
In life so lifeless as it shows itself.

CONSTABLE
They have said their prayers, and they stay for
    death.   56

DAUPHIN
Shall we go send them dinners and fresh suits,
And give their fasting horses provender,   58
And after fight with them?

CONSTABLE
I stay but for my guard. On to the field!   60
I will the banner from a trumpet take,   61
And use it for my haste. Come, come, away!
The sun is high, and we outwear the day.   *Exeunt.* 63

❧

4.3   *Enter Gloucester, Bedford, Exeter, Erpingham,
          with all his host, Salisbury, and Westmorland.*

GLOUCESTER   Where is the King?

BEDFORD
The King himself is rode to view their battle.   2

WESTMORLAND
Of fighting men they have full threescore thousand.

EXETER
There's five to one. Besides, they all are fresh.

SALISBURY
God's arm strike with us! 'Tis a fearful odds.
God b' wi' you, princes all; I'll to my charge.   6
If we no more meet till we meet in heaven,
Then, joyfully, my noble lord of Bedford,
My dear lord Gloucester, and my good lord Exeter,
And my kind kinsman, warriors all, adieu!   10

BEDFORD
Farewell, good Salisbury, and good luck go with
    thee!

EXETER
Farewell, kind lord. Fight valiantly today!
And yet I do thee wrong to mind thee of it,   13

---

8 **service** action   9 **incision** i.e., with spurs   10 **spin** gush, spatter
11 **And . . . courage** i.e., and put out the English eyes with the
horses' superfluous blood, the proof of their excessive courage.   **dout**
put out   14 **embattled** arranged in battle order   17 **fair show** impressive appearance   18 **shales** shells   21 **curtal ax** cutlass, short sword
25 **exceptions** objections   28 **squares of battle** four-sided military formation   29 **hilding** worthless, base   30 **basis** foot.   **by** nearby
31 **speculation** looking on   32 **But that** except for the fact that
35 **tucket sonance** trumpet call   36 **dare** (1) defy (2) stupify with fear
39 **carrions** cadavers for the scavenger birds.   **desperate of** without
hope of saving   40 **Ill-favoredly become** i.e., are an eyesore to
41 **curtains** colors, banners   42 **passing** exceedingly   43 **Mars** the
god of war

44 **beaver** visor   46 **torch staves** i.e., tapers in place of lances. (The
horsemen themselves look like carved candle-holders.)   47 **Lob down**
hang down.   **drooping** letting droop   48 **gum** watery discharge.
down-roping hanging down ropelike   49 **gimmaled** jointed   51 **their
executors** the disposers of their remains   54 **battle** army   56 **stay for**
await   58 **provender** fodder   60 **guard** (including a standard-bearer)
61 **trumpet** trumpeter   63 **outwear** waste
4.3. Location: The English camp.
2 **battle** army   6 **charge** post, command   10 **kinsman** i.e., Westmorland, whose son had married Salisbury's daughter   13 **mind** remind

For thou art framed of the firm truth of valor.   14
                                         [*Exit Salisbury.*]
BEDFORD
He is as full of valor as of kindness,
Princely in both.

          Enter the King.

WESTMORLAND   O, that we now had here
But one ten thousand of those men in England
That do no work today!
KING   What's he that wishes so?   18
My cousin Westmorland? No, my fair cousin.
If we are marked to die, we are enough   20
To do our country loss; and if to live,   21
The fewer men, the greater share of honor.
God's will, I pray thee, wish not one man more.
By Jove, I am not covetous for gold,
Nor care I who doth feed upon my cost;   25
It yearns me not if men my garments wear;   26
Such outward things dwell not in my desires.
But if it be a sin to covet honor
I am the most offending soul alive.
No, faith, my coz, wish not a man from England.   30
God's peace, I would not lose so great an honor
As one man more, methinks, would share from me   32
For the best hope I have. O, do not wish one more!
Rather proclaim it, Westmorland, through my host   34
That he which hath no stomach to this fight,   35
Let him depart; his passport shall be made
And crowns for convoy put into his purse.   37
We would not die in that man's company
That fears his fellowship to die with us.   39
This day is called the Feast of Crispian.   40
He that outlives this day and comes safe home
Will stand a-tiptoe when this day is named
And rouse him at the name of Crispian.
He that shall see this day and live old age   44
Will yearly on the vigil feast his neighbors   45
And say, "Tomorrow is Saint Crispian."
Then will he strip his sleeve and show his scars,
And say, "These wounds I had on Crispin's Day."
Old men forget; yet all shall be forgot,   49
But he'll remember with advantages   50
What feats he did that day. Then shall our names,
Familiar in his mouth as household words—
Harry the King, Bedford and Exeter,
Warwick and Talbot, Salisbury and Gloucester—
Be in their flowing cups freshly remembered.   55
This story shall the good man teach his son;

And Crispin Crispian shall ne'er go by,
From this day to the ending of the world,
But we in it shall be rememberèd—
We few, we happy few, we band of brothers.
For he today that sheds his blood with me
Shall be my brother; be he ne'er so vile,   62
This day shall gentle his condition.   63
And gentlemen in England now abed
Shall think themselves accurst they were not here,
And hold their manhoods cheap whiles any speaks
That fought with us upon Saint Crispin's Day.

          Enter Salisbury.

SALISBURY
My sovereign lord, bestow yourself with speed.   68
The French are bravely in their battles set,   69
And will with all expedience charge on us.   70
KING
All things are ready, if our minds be so.
WESTMORLAND
Perish the man whose mind is backward now!   72
KING
Thou dost not wish more help from England, coz?
WESTMORLAND
God's will, my liege, would you and I alone,
Without more help, could fight this royal battle!
KING
Why, now thou hast unwished five thousand men,
Which likes me better than to wish us one.—   77
You know your places. God be with you all!

          Tucket. Enter Montjoy.

MONTJOY
Once more I come to know of thee, King Harry,
If for thy ransom thou wilt now compound   80
Before thy most assurèd overthrow;
For certainly thou art so near the gulf   82
Thou needs must be englutted. Besides, in mercy   83
The Constable desires thee thou wilt mind   84
Thy followers of repentance, that their souls
May make a peaceful and a sweet retire   86
From off these fields where, wretches, their poor
   bodies
Must lie and fester.
KING   Who hath sent thee now?
MONTJOY   The Constable of France.
KING
I pray thee, bear my former answer back:
Bid them achieve me, and then sell my bones.   91
Good God, why should they mock poor fellows
   thus?
The man that once did sell the lion's skin
While the beast lived was killed with hunting him.

14 **framed** made, built   18 **What's** who is   20–21 **enough . . . loss**
enough loss for our country to suffer   25 **upon my cost** at my expense   26 **yearns** grieves   30 **coz** cousin, kinsman   32 **share from
me** take from me as his share   34 **host** army   35 **stomach to** appetite
for   37 **crowns for convoy** travel money   39 **That . . . us** who is
afraid to risk his life in my company   40 **Feast of Crispian** Saint
Crispin's Day, October 25. (Crispinus and Crispianus were martyrs
who fled from Rome in the third century; according to legend, they
disguised themselves as shoemakers and afterward became the patron
saints of that craft.)   44 **live** live to see   45 **vigil** evening before a
feast day   49 **yet** in time   50 **advantages** additions of his own
55 **flowing** overflowing

62 **vile** lowly   63 **gentle his condition** raise him to the rank of gentleman   68 **bestow yourself** take up your battle position   69 **bravely
. . . set** finely arrayed in their battalions   70 **expedience** speed
72 **backward** reluctant   77 **likes** pleases   80 **compound** make terms
82 **gulf** whirlpool   83 **englutted** swallowed up   84 **mind** remind
86 **retire** retreat   91 **achieve** capture

A many of our bodies shall no doubt   95
Find native graves, upon the which, I trust,   96
Shall witness live in brass of this day's work.
And those that leave their valiant bones in France,
Dying like men, though buried in your dunghills,
They shall be famed; for there the sun shall greet
  them
And draw their honors reeking up to heaven,   101
Leaving their earthly parts to choke your clime,
The smell whereof shall breed a plague in France.
Mark then abounding valor in our English,   104
That, being dead, like to the bullets crazing   105
Break out into a second course of mischief,
Killing in relapse of mortality.   107
Let me speak proudly. Tell the Constable
We are but warriors for the working day.   109
Our gayness and our gilt are all besmirched
With rainy marching in the painful field.
There's not a piece of feather in our host—
Good argument, I hope, we will not fly—
And time hath worn us into slovenry.
But, by the Mass, our hearts are in the trim!
And my poor soldiers tell me, yet ere night
They'll be in fresher robes, or they will pluck   117
The gay new coats o'er the French soldiers' heads
And turn them out of service. If they do this—   119
As, if God please, they shall—my ransom then
Will soon be levied. Herald, save thou thy labor.   121
Come thou no more for ransom, gentle herald.   122
They shall have none, I swear, but these my joints,
Which if they have as I will leave 'em them,
Shall yield them little, tell the Constable.

MONTJOY
I shall, King Harry. And so fare thee well.
Thou never shalt hear herald any more.   *Exit.*

KING
I fear thou wilt once more come again for a ransom.

        Enter York [and kneels].

YORK
My lord, most humbly on my knee I beg
The leading of the vaward.   130

KING
Take it, brave York. Now, soldiers, march away.
And how thou pleasest, God, dispose the day!
                                            Exeunt.

                      ❖

95 **A many** many. (The phrase is an exact parallel to "a few.")
96 **native** in their own land (i.e., England)   101 **reeking** (1) breathing
(2) smelling   104 **abounding** overflowing, abundant   105 **crazing**
shattering, with a suggestion also of *grazing*, "ricocheting"   107 **Killing . . . mortality** killing (their foes) as they (the English) fall back (de-
compose) into their elements; also, like the bullet, with a deadly ricochet   109 **for the working day** to do serious work, not take a
holiday   117 **in fresher robes** i.e., in heavenly garb. (Or perhaps the
phrase *or they will* means "even if they have to.")   119 **turn . . .
service** send them away stripped of their finery, like dismissed servants stripped of their livery   121 **levied** collected   122 **gentle** noble
130 **vaward** vanguard

4.4

*Alarum. Excursions. Enter Pistol, French Soldier,
[and] Boy.*

PISTOL   Yield, cur!
FRENCH SOLDIER   *Je pense que vous êtes le gentilhomme de*   2
bonne qualité.   3
PISTOL
  Qualtitie calmie custure me!   4
  Art thou a gentleman? What is thy name? Discuss.   5
FRENCH SOLDIER   *O Seigneur Dieu!*   6
PISTOL
  O, Signieur Dew should be a gentleman.
  Perpend my words, O Signieur Dew, and mark: 8
  O Signieur Dew, thou diest on point of fox,   9
  Except, O signieur, thou do give to me   10
  Egregious ransom.   [*He threatens him with his sword.*]   11
FRENCH SOLDIER   *O, prenez miséricorde! Ayez pitié de*   12
moi!   13
PISTOL
  "Moy" shall not serve. I will have forty moys,   14
  Or I will fetch thy rim out at thy throat   15
  In drops of crimson blood.
FRENCH SOLDIER   *Est-il impossible d'échapper la force de ton*   17
bras?   18
PISTOL   Brass, cur?
  Thou damnèd and luxurious mountain goat,   20
  Offer'st me brass?
FRENCH SOLDIER   *O, pardonnez-moi!*
PISTOL
  Sayst thou me so? Is that a ton of moys?   23
  Come hither, boy. Ask me this slave in French
  What is his name.
BOY   *Écoutez: comment êtes-vous appelé?*   26
FRENCH SOLDIER   *Monsieur le Fer.*
BOY   He says his name is Master Fer.
PISTOL   Master Fer? I'll fer him, and firk him, and ferret   29
  him. Discuss the same in French unto him.
BOY   I do not know the French for fer, and ferret, and
  firk.
PISTOL
  Bid him prepare, for I will cut his throat.
FRENCH SOLDIER   *Que dit-il, monsieur?*   34
BOY   *Il me commande à vous dire que vous faites vous*   35
prêt; car ce soldat ici est disposé tout à cette heure de   36
couper votre gorge.   37

4.4. Location: The field of battle.
s.d. Excursions sorties   **2–3 Je . . . qualité** I think that you are a
gentleman of high rank   **4 calmie custure me** (These words are perhaps derived from the refrain of a popular song, supposed to be Irish,
"Calen o custure me.")   **5 Discuss** speak   **6 O Seigneur Dieu** O Lord
God   **8 Perpend** attend to, consider   **9 fox** sword   **10 Except** unless
11 Egregious huge   **12–13 O . . . moi** Oh, have mercy! Take pity
on me!   **14 Moy** (Pistol, not understanding, takes *moi* for the name of
a coin or a sum of money.)   **15 rim** midriff, diaphragm   **17–18 Est-il
. . . bras** is it impossible to escape the strength of your arm? (But Pistol takes *bras*, "arm," for *brass*.)   **20 luxurious** lecherous   **23 a ton of
moys** (This is what Pistol phonetically makes out of *pardonnez-moi*.)
26 Écoutez . . . appelé listen: what is your name   **29 firk** trounce.
ferret worry (like a ferret)   **34–37 Que . . . gorge** What does he say,
sir? BOY He bids me tell you that you must prepare yourself, because
this soldier intends to cut your throat immediately

PISTOL

Owy, cuppele gorge, permafoy,   38

Peasant, unless thou give me crowns, brave crowns,

Or mangled shalt thou be by this my sword.

FRENCH SOLDIER   *O, je vous supplie, pour l'amour de*   41

Dieu, me pardonner! Je suis le gentilhomme de bonne   42

maison. Gardez ma vie, et je vous donnerai deux cents   43

écus.   44

PISTOL   What are his words?

BOY   He prays you to save his life. He is a gentleman of

a good house, and for his ransom he will give you two   47

hundred crowns.

PISTOL

Tell him my fury shall abate, and I

The crowns will take.

FRENCH SOLDIER   *Petit monsieur, que dit-il?*   51

BOY   *Encore qu'il est contre son jurement de pardonner* 52

aucun prisonnier, néanmoins, pour les écus que vous   53

l'avez promis, il est content à vous donner la liberté, 54

le franchisement.   55

FRENCH SOLDIER [*kneeling*]   *Sur mes genoux je vous*   56

donne mille remercîments; et je m'estime heureux que   57

j'ai tombé entre les mains d'un chevalier, je pense,   58

le plus brave, vaillant, et très-distingué seigneur   59

d'Angleterre.   60

PISTOL   Expound unto me, boy.

BOY   He gives you, upon his knees, a thousand thanks,

and he esteems himself happy that he hath fallen into

the hands of one, as he thinks, the most brave, valor-

ous, and thrice-worthy signieur of England.

PISTOL

As I suck blood, I will some mercy show.

Follow me!

BOY   *Suivez-vous le grand capitaine.* [*Exeunt Pistol and* 68

French Soldier.] I did never know so full a voice issue

from so empty a heart! But the saying is true, "The

empty vessel makes the greatest sound." Bardolph and

Nym had ten times more valor than this roaring devil 72

i' the old play, that everyone may pare his nails with

a wooden dagger, and they are both hanged; and so

would this be, if he durst steal anything adventur-

ously. I must stay with the lackeys, with the luggage

of our camp. The French might have a good prey of   77

us, if he knew of it, for there is none to guard it but

boys.   *Exit.*

---

38 Owy *oui,* "yes." **permafoy** *per ma foi,* "by my faith"   **41–44 O
. . . écus** Oh, I pray you, for the love of God, to pardon me. I am a
gentleman of a good house; preserve my life, and I shall give you two
hundred crowns   **47 house** family   **51–55 Petit . . . franchisement**
What does he say, little sir? BOY Although it is against his oath to pardon any prisoner, nevertheless, for the sake of the crowns you have
promised, he is willing to give you your liberty, your freedom   **56–
60 Sur . . . d'Angleterre** On my knees, I give you a thousand thanks,
and I consider myself happy that I have fallen into the hands of a
knight, as I think, the bravest, most valiant, and very distinguished
gentleman in England   **68 Suivez-vous . . . capitaine** follow the great
captain   **72 roaring devil** i.e., the devil in the morality play, a
comic figure paired with the Vice who traditionally had a wooden
dagger   **77 a good prey** i.e., easy pickings

4.5   *Enter Constable, Orleans, Bourbon, Dauphin, and
Rambures.*

CONSTABLE   *O diable!*   1

ORLEANS   *O Seigneur! Le jour est perdu, tout est perdu!*   2

DAUPHIN

Mort de ma vie! All is confounded, all.   3

Reproach and everlasting shame

Sits mocking in our plumes.   *A short alarum.*

O méchante fortune! Do not run away.   6

CONSTABLE   Why, all our ranks are broke.

DAUPHIN

O perdurable shame! Let's stab ourselves.   8

Be these the wretches that we played at dice for?

ORLEANS

Is this the king we sent to for his ransom?

BOURBON

Shame and eternal shame, nothing but shame!

Let us die! In once more! Back again!

And he that will not follow Bourbon now,

Let him go hence, and with his cap in hand,

Like a base pander, hold the chamber door

Whilst by a slave, no gentler than my dog,   16

His fairest daughter is contaminated.

CONSTABLE

Disorder, that hath spoiled us, friend us now!   18

Let us on heaps go offer up our lives.   19

ORLEANS

We are enough yet living in the field

To smother up the English in our throngs,

If any order might be thought upon.

BOURBON

The devil take order now! I'll to the throng.

Let life be short, else shame will be too long.

Exeunt.

4.6   *Alarum. Enter the King and his train,* [*Exeter,
and others,*] *with prisoners.*

KING

Well have we done, thrice valiant countrymen!

But all's not done; yet keep the French the field.

EXETER

The Duke of York commends him to Your Majesty.

KING

Lives he, good uncle? Thrice within this hour

I saw him down, thrice up again and fighting.

From helmet to the spur all blood he was.

EXETER

In which array, brave soldier, doth he lie,

4.5. Location: The field of battle still.
1 O diable O the devil   **2 O . . . perdu** O Lord, the day is lost, all is
lost. (Or Orleans may be addressing the Constable as "Sir" or "my
lord.")   **3 Mort de ma vie** death of my life, i.e., may my life end.
confounded lost   **6 O méchante fortune** O malicious fortune   **8 perdurable** everlasting   **16 gentler** (1) more nobly born (2) tenderer
18 friend befriend   **19 on** in
4.6. Location: The field of battle still.

Larding the plain; and by his bloody side,   8
Yokefellow to his honor-owing wounds,   9
The noble Earl of Suffolk also lies.
Suffolk first died; and York, all haggled over,   11
Comes to him, where in gore he lay insteeped,   12
And takes him by the beard, kisses the gashes
That bloodily did yawn upon his face.   14
He cries aloud, "Tarry, my cousin Suffolk!
My soul shall thine keep company to heaven;
Tarry, sweet soul, for mine, then fly abreast,
As in this glorious and well-foughten field
We kept together in our chivalry!"
Upon these words I came and cheered him up.
He smiled me in the face, raught me his hand,   21
And with a feeble grip says, "Dear my lord,
Commend my service to my sovereign."
So did he turn, and over Suffolk's neck
He threw his wounded arm, and kissed his lips,
And so, espoused to death, with blood he sealed
A testament of noble-ending love.
The pretty and sweet manner of it forced
Those waters from me which I would have stopped;   29
But I had not so much of man in me,
And all my mother came into mine eyes   31
And gave me up to tears.
KING   I blame you not;
For, hearing this, I must perforce compound   33
With mistful eyes, or they will issue too.   *Alarum.* 34
But, hark, what new alarum is this same?
The French have reinforced their scattered men.
Then every soldier kill his prisoners!   37
Give the word through.   *Exeunt.*

4.7   *Enter Fluellen and Gower.*

FLUELLEN   Kill the poys and the luggage? 'Tis expressly   1
against the law of arms. 'Tis as arrant a piece of
knavery, mark you now, as can be offert; in your
conscience, now, is it not?
GOWER   'Tis certain there's not a boy left alive; and the
cowardly rascals that ran from the battle ha' done this
slaughter. Besides, they have burned and carried
away all that was in the King's tent, wherefore the
King most worthily hath caused every soldier to cut
his prisoner's throat. O, 'tis a gallant king!
FLUELLEN   Ay, he was porn at Monmouth, Captain   11

Gower. What call you the town's name where Alexander the Pig was born?
GOWER   Alexander the Great.
FLUELLEN   Why, I pray you, is not "pig" great? The pig,
or the great, or the mighty, or the huge, or the
magnanimous, are all one reckonings, save the phrase   17
is a little variations.
GOWER   I think Alexander the Great was born in
Macedon. His father was called Philip of Macedon, as
I take it.
FLUELLEN   I think it is e'en Macedon where Alexander is
porn. I tell you, Captain, if you look in the maps of the
'orld, I warrant you sall find, in the comparisons between Macedon and Monmouth, that the situations,
look you, is both alike. There is a river in Macedon,
and there is also moreover a river at Monmouth. It is
called Wye at Monmouth, but it is out of my prains
what is the name of the other river; but 'tis all one, 'tis
alike as my fingers is to my fingers, and there is sal-
mons in both. If you mark Alexander's life well, Harry
of Monmouth's life is come after it indifferent well, for   32
there is figures in all things. Alexander, God knows,   33
and you know, in his rages, and his furies, and his
wraths, and his cholers, and his moods, and his displeasures, and his indignations, and also being a little
intoxicates in his prains, did, in his ales and his an-   37
gers, look you, kill his best friend, Cleitus.   38
GOWER   Our King is not like him in that. He never killed
any of his friends.
FLUELLEN   It is not well done, mark you now, to take
the tales out of my mouth ere it is made and finished.
I speak but in the figures and comparisons of it. As
Alexander killed his friend Cleitus, being in his ales
and his cups, so also Harry Monmouth, being in his
right wits and his good judgments, turned away the
fat knight with the great-belly doublet. He was full of   47
jests, and gipes, and knaveries, and mocks. I have   48
forgot his name.
GOWER   Sir John Falstaff.
FLUELLEN   That is he. I'll tell you there is good men
porn at Monmouth.
GOWER   Here comes His Majesty.

> *Alarum. Enter King Harry, [Warwick, Gloucester,*
> *Exeter, and others,] and Bourbon, with [other]*
> *prisoners. Flourish.*

KING
I was not angry since I came to France
Until this instant. Take a trumpet, herald;   55
Ride thou unto the horsemen on yond hill.
If they will fight with us, bid them come down,
Or void the field. They do offend our sight.   58

If they'll do neither, we will come to them,
And make them skirr away as swift as stones   60
Enforcèd from the old Assyrian slings.   61
Besides, we'll cut the throats of those we have,
And not a man of them that we shall take
Shall taste our mercy. Go and tell them so.

Enter Montjoy.

EXETER
Here comes the herald of the French, my liege.
GLOUCESTER
His eyes are humbler than they used to be.
KING
How now, what means this, herald? Know'st
    thou not
That I have fined these bones of mine for ransom?   68
Com'st thou again for ransom?
MONTJOY   No, great King.
I come to thee for charitable license,
That we may wander o'er this bloody field
To book our dead and then to bury them,   72
To sort our nobles from our common men.
For many of our princes—woe the while!—
Lie drowned and soaked in mercenary blood;   75
So do our vulgar drench their peasant limbs   76
In blood of princes; and the wounded steeds
Fret fetlock-deep in gore and with wild rage
Yerk out their armèd heels at their dead masters,   79
Killing them twice. O, give us leave, great King,
To view the field in safety, and dispose
Of their dead bodies!
KING   I tell thee truly, herald,
I know not if the day be ours or no,
For yet a many of your horsemen peer   84
And gallop o'er the field.
MONTJOY   The day is yours.
KING
Praisèd be God, and not our strength, for it!
What is this castle called that stands hard by?
MONTJOY   They call it Agincourt.
KING
Then call we this the field of Agincourt,
Fought on the day of Crispin Crispianus.
FLUELLEN   Your grandfather of famous memory, an 't 91
    please Your Majesty, and your great-uncle Edward the
    Plack Prince of Wales, as I have read in the chronicles,
    fought a most prave pattle here in France.
KING   They did, Fluellen.
FLUELLEN   Your Majesty says very true. If Your Majes-
    ties is remembered of it, the Welshmen did good
    service in a garden where leeks did grow, wearing
    leeks in their Monmouth caps, which, Your Majesty   99
    know, to this hour is an honorable badge of the

---

service; and I do believe Your Majesty takes no scorn
to wear the leek upon Saint Tavy's Day.
KING
I wear it for a memorable honor,
For I am Welsh, you know, good countryman.
FLUELLEN   All the water in Wye cannot wash Your
    Majesty's Welsh plood out of your pody, I can tell you
    that. God pless it and preserve it, as long as it pleases
    His Grace, and His Majesty too!
KING   Thanks, good my countryman.
FLUELLEN   By Jeshu, I am Your Majesty's countryman,
    I care not who know it. I will confess it to all the 'orld.
    I need not to be ashamed of Your Majesty, praised be
    God, so long as Your Majesty is an honest man.
KING
God keep me so!

Enter Williams [with a glove in his cap].

                     Our heralds go with him.
Bring me just notice of the numbers dead   115
On both our parts.
        [Exeunt Heralds and Gower with Montjoy.]
                Call yonder fellow hither.
EXETER   Soldier, you must come to the King.
KING   Soldier, why wear'st thou that glove in thy cap?
WILLIAMS   An 't please Your Majesty, 'tis the gage of
    one that I should fight withal, if he be alive.
KING   An Englishman?
WILLIAMS   An 't please Your Majesty, a rascal that swag-
    gered with me last night, who, if 'a live and ever dare
    to challenge this glove, I have sworn to take him a box
    o' th' ear; or if I can see my glove in his cap, which he
    swore, as he was a soldier, he would wear if 'a lived, I
    will strike it out soundly.
KING   What think you, Captain Fluellen, is it fit this
    soldier keep his oath?
FLUELLEN   He is a craven and a villain else, an 't please 130
    Your Majesty, in my conscience.
KING   It may be his enemy is a gentleman of great sort,   132
    quite from the answer of his degree.   133
FLUELLEN   Though he be as good a gentleman as the
    devil is, as Lucifer and Beelzebub himself, it is
    necessary, look Your Grace, that he keep his vow and
    his oath. If he be perjured, see you now, his reputa-
    tion is as arrant a villain and a Jack-sauce as ever his 138
    black shoe trod upon God's ground and His earth, in
    my conscience, la!
KING   Then keep thy vow, sirrah, when thou meet'st
    the fellow.
WILLIAMS   So I will, my liege, as I live.
KING   Who serv'st thou under?
WILLIAMS   Under Captain Gower, my liege.
FLUELLEN   Gower is a good captain, and is good
    knowledge and literatured in the wars.   147
KING   Call him hither to me, soldier.
WILLIAMS   I will, my liege.   *Exit.*

---

60 **skirr** scurry 61 **Enforcèd** discharged 68 **fined . . . ransom** i.e.,
agreed to pay as a fine or ransom only these bones of mine and no
more 72 **book** record 75 **mercenary** i.e., of common soldiers,
who fought for pay 76 **vulgar** commoners 79 **Yerk** kick 84 **peer**
(1) look about anxiously (2) appear 91 **grandfather** i.e., great-grandfather, Edward III. **an 't** if it 99 **Monmouth caps** round and rimless
caps with a tapering crown, commonly worn by the Welsh

---

115 **just** exact 130 **craven** coward 132 **sort** rank 133 **quite . . .
degree** i.e., too high in rank to answer the challenge of one so low
138 **Jack-sauce** saucy knave 147 **literatured** well read

KING   Here, Fluellen, wear thou this favor for me and stick it in thy cap. [*He gives Fluellen Williams' glove.*] When Alençon and myself were down together, I plucked this glove from his helm. If any man challenge 153 this, he is a friend to Alençon and an enemy to our person. If thou encounter any such, apprehend him, an thou dost me love.   156

FLUELLEN [*putting the glove in his cap*] Your Grace doo's 157 me as great honors as can be desired in the hearts of his subjects. I would fain see the man that 159 has but two legs that shall find himself aggriefed at this glove, that is all. But I would fain see it once, an 161 't please God of his grace that I might see.   162

KING   Know'st thou Gower?

FLUELLEN He is my dear friend, an 't please you.

KING   Pray thee, go seek him and bring him to my tent.

FLUELLEN I will fetch him.   *Exit.*

KING

My lord of Warwick, and my brother Gloucester,
Follow Fluellen closely at the heels.
The glove which I have given him for a favor
May haply purchase him a box o' th' ear.   170
It is the soldier's; I by bargain should
Wear it myself. Follow, good cousin Warwick.
If that the soldier strike him, as I judge
By his blunt bearing he will keep his word,
Some sudden mischief may arise of it;
For I do know Fluellen valiant
And touched with choler, hot as gunpowder,   177
And quickly will return an injury.   178
Follow, and see there be no harm between them.
Go you with me, uncle of Exeter.   *Exeunt* [*separately*].

❦

4.8   *Enter Gower and Williams.*

WILLIAMS   I warrant it is to knight you, Captain.

Enter Fluellen.

FLUELLEN God's will and his pleasure, Captain, I beseech you now, come apace to the King. There is more good toward you, peradventure, than is in your 4 knowledge to dream of.

WILLIAMS   Sir, know you this glove?

FLUELLEN Know the glove? I know the glove is a glove.

WILLIAMS   I know this, and thus I challenge it.
                                        Strikes him.

FLUELLEN 'Sblood, an arrant traitor as any 's in the 9 universal world, or in France, or in England!

GOWER [*to Williams*]   How now, sir? You villain!

WILLIAMS   Do you think I'll be forsworn?

153 **helm** helmet   156 **an** if   157 **doo's** does   159 **fain** willingly
161–162 **an 't** if it (also in line 164)   170 **haply** perhaps
177 **touched with choler** hot-tempered   178 **return** repay.   **injury** insult
4.8. Location: The English camp.
4 **peradventure** by chance   9 **'Sblood** by His (Christ's) blood

FLUELLEN Stand away, Captain Gower. I will give treason his payment into plows, I warrant you.   14

WILLIAMS   I am no traitor.

FLUELLEN That's a lie in thy throat. I charge you in His 16 Majesty's name, apprehend him. He's a friend of the Duke Alençon's.

Enter Warwick and Gloucester.

WARWICK   How now, how now, what's the matter?

FLUELLEN My lord of Warwick, here is—praised be God for it!—a most contagious treason come to light, 21 look you, as you shall desire in a summer's day.— Here is His Majesty.

Enter King [Henry] and Exeter.

KING   How now, what's the matter?

FLUELLEN My liege, here is a villain and a traitor that, look Your Grace, has struck the glove which Your Majesty is take out of the helmet of Alençon.

WILLIAMS   My liege, this was my glove; here is the fellow of it. [*Showing his other glove.*] And he that I gave it to in change promised to wear it in his cap. I promised 30 to strike him, if he did. I met this man with my glove in his cap, and I have been as good as my word.

FLUELLEN Your Majesty hear now, saving Your Majesty's manhood, what an arrant, rascally, beggarly, lousy knave it is. I hope Your Majesty is pear me 35 testimony and witness, and will avouchment, that this 36 is the glove of Alençon that Your Majesty is give me, in your conscience, now.

KING   Give me thy glove, soldier. Look, here is the fellow of it.   [*He shows his other glove.*]
'Twas I indeed thou promisèd'st to strike,
And thou hast given me most bitter terms.   42

FLUELLEN An 't please Your Majesty, let his neck 43 answer for it, if there is any martial law in the world.

KING
How canst thou make me satisfaction?

WILLIAMS   All offenses, my lord, come from the heart. Never came any from mine that might offend Your Majesty.

KING   It was ourself thou didst abuse.

WILLIAMS   Your Majesty came not like yourself. You appeared to me but as a common man—witness the night, your garments, your lowliness. And what Your 52 Highness suffered under that shape, I beseech you take it for your own fault and not mine; for had you been as I took you for, I made no offense. Therefore I beseech Your Highness pardon me.

KING
Here, uncle Exeter, fill this glove with crowns,
And give it to this fellow.—Keep it, fellow,
And wear it for an honor in thy cap
Till I do challenge it.—Give him the crowns.
     [*Exeter gives the glove and gold to Williams.*]
And Captain, you must needs be friends with him.

14 **his** its.   **into plows** in blows   16 **lie in thy throat** i.e., inexcusable
lie   21 **contagious** noxious   30 **change** exchange   35 **is pear** will
bear   36 **avouchment** avouch   42 **terms** words   43 **An 't** if it (also
in line 117)   52 **lowliness** humble mien

FLUELLEN   By this day and this light, the fellow has
mettle enough in his belly.—Hold, there is twelve-
pence for you. [*He offers a coin.*] And I pray you to
serve God, and keep you out of prawls, and prabbles,   65
and quarrels, and dissensions, and I warrant you it is
the better for you.
WILLIAMS   I will none of your money.
FLUELLEN   It is with a good will. I can tell you, it will
serve you to mend your shoes. Come, wherefore
should you be so pashful? Your shoes is not so good.
'Tis a good silling, I warrant you, or I will change it.

Enter [an English] Herald.

KING   Now, herald, are the dead numbered?
HERALD [*giving a paper*]
   Here is the number of the slaughtered French.
KING
   What prisoners of good sort are taken, uncle?   75
EXETER
   Charles Duke of Orleans, nephew to the King;   76
   John Duke of Bourbon, and Lord Boucicault;
   Of other lords and barons, knights and squires,
   Full fifteen hundred, besides common men.
KING
   This note doth tell me of ten thousand French
   That in the field lie slain. Of princes, in this number,
   And nobles bearing banners, there lie dead   82
   One hundred twenty-six; added to these,
   Of knights, esquires, and gallant gentlemen,
   Eight thousand and four hundred, of the which
   Five hundred were but yesterday dubbed knights.
   So that in these ten thousand they have lost
   There are but sixteen hundred mercenaries;
   The rest are princes, barons, lords, knights, squires,
   And gentlemen of blood and quality.
   The names of those their nobles that lie dead:
   Charles Delabreth, High Constable of France;
   Jaques of Chatillion, Admiral of France;
   The Master of the Crossbows, Lord Rambures;
   Great-Master of France, the brave Sir Guichard
      Dauphin;   95
   John, Duke of Alençon; Anthony, Duke of Brabant,
   The brother to the Duke of Burgundy;
   And Edward, Duke of Bar; of lusty earls,   98
   Grandpré and Roussi, Faulconbridge and Foix,
   Beaumont and Marle, Vaudemont and Lestrelles.
   Here was a royal fellowship of death!
   Where is the number of our English dead?
                    [*He is given another paper.*]
   Edward the Duke of York, the Earl of Suffolk,
   Sir Richard Keighley, Davy Gam, esquire;
   None else of name, and of all other men   105
   But five-and-twenty. O God, thy arm was here!
   And not to us, but to thy arm alone,
   Ascribe we all. When, without stratagem,

   But in plain shock and even play of battle,   109
   Was ever known so great and little loss
   On one part and on th' other? Take it, God,
   For it is none but thine.
EXETER   'Tis wonderful.   112
KING
   Come, go we in procession to the village.
   And be it death proclaimèd through our host
   To boast of this or take that praise from God
   Which is his only.
FLUELLEN   Is it not lawful, an 't please Your Majesty, to
tell how many is killed?
KING
   Yes, Captain, but with this acknowledgment,
   That God fought for us.
FLUELLEN   Yes, in my conscience, he did us great good.
KING   Do we all holy rites.
   Let there be sung *Non nobis* and *Te Deum*,   123
   The dead with charity enclosed in clay;
   And then to Calais, and to England then,
   Where ne'er from France arrived more happy men.   126
                              Exeunt.

❖

5.0   *Enter Chorus.*

CHORUS
   Vouchsafe to those that have not read the story   1
   That I may prompt them; and of such as have,
   I humbly pray them to admit th' excuse   3
   Of time, of numbers, and due course of things,
   Which cannot in their huge and proper life
   Be here presented. Now we bear the King
   Toward Calais. Grant him there. There seen,
   Heave him away upon your wingèd thoughts
   Athwart the sea. Behold, the English beach
   Pales in the flood with men, wives, and boys,   10
   Whose shouts and claps outvoice the deep-mouthed
      sea,
   Which like a mighty whiffler 'fore the King   12
   Seems to prepare his way. So let him land,
   And solemnly see him set on to London.
   So swift a pace hath thought that even now
   You may imagine him upon Blackheath,   16
   Where that his lords desire him to have borne   17
   His bruisèd helmet and his bended sword
   Before him through the city. He forbids it,
   Being free from vainness and self-glorious pride,

109 **even** equal   123 **Non nobis** i.e., Psalm 115, beginning, "Not
unto us, O Lord, not unto us, but unto thy name give glory." **Te
Deum** a hymn of thanksgiving, beginning, "We praise thee O God"
126 **happy** fortunate
5.0. **(Between Acts 4 and 5, there is historically an interval of about
five years during which Henry made a second campaign in France
that brought the French to terms in the Treaty of Troyes, with which
the play ends.)**
1 **Vouchsafe** permit it   3 **admit th' excuse** excuse our handling
10 **Pales in** hems in, surrounds.   **flood** sea   12 **whiffler** an usher
heading the procession to clear the way   16 **Blackheath** open area
just outside London, to the southeast   17 **Where that** where

65 **prabbles** i.e., brabbles, scuffles   75 **good sort** high rank   76–
112 **Charles . . . thine** (The catalogue of the captured and slain is
from Holinshed.)   82 **bearing banners** i.e., with coats of arms
95 **Great-Master** grandmaster, i.e., the chief officer of the royal
household   98 **lusty** vigorous   105 **name** rank, social importance

Giving full trophy, signal, and ostent   21
Quite from himself to God. But now behold,
In the quick forge and working-house of thought,
How London doth pour out her citizens!
The Mayor and all his brethren, in best sort,   25
Like to the senators of th' antique Rome
With the plebeians swarming at their heels,
Go forth and fetch their conquering Caesar in;
As by a lower but loving likelihood,   29
Were now the General of our gracious Empress,   30
As in good time he may, from Ireland coming,
Bringing rebellion broachèd on his sword,   32
How many would the peaceful city quit
To welcome him! Much more, and much more
    cause,   34
Did they this Harry. Now in London place him;
As yet the lamentation of the French   36
Invites the King of England's stay at home;   37
The Emperor's coming in behalf of France,   38
To order peace between them . . . and omit   39
All the occurrences, whatever chanced,
Till Harry's back-return again to France.   41
There must we bring him; and myself have played
The interim by remembering you 'tis past.   43
Then brook abridgment, and your eyes advance,   44
After your thoughts, straight back again to France.
                           Exit.

❖

5.1   *Enter Fluellen [with a leek in his cap, and a*
        cudgel], and Gower.

GOWER   Nay, that's right. But why wear you your leek
today? Saint Davy's Day is past.
FLUELLEN   There is occasions and causes why and
wherefore in all things. I will tell you asse my friend,   4
Captain Gower. The rascally, scald, beggarly, lousy,   5
pragging knave, Pistol, which you and yourself and all
the world know to be no petter than a fellow, look you
now, of no merits, he is come to me and prings me
pread and salt yesterday, look you, and bid me eat my
leek. It was in a place where I could not breed no con-

tention with him; but I will be so bold as to wear it in
my cap till I see him once again, and then I will tell
him a little piece of my desires.

             Enter Pistol.

GOWER   Why, here he comes, swelling like a turkey-
cock.
FLUELLEN   'Tis no matter for his swellings nor his
turkey-cocks.—God pless you, Aunchient Pistol! You
scurvy, lousy knave, God pless you!
PISTOL
   Ha, art thou bedlam? Dost thou thirst, base Trojan,   19
   To have me fold up Parca's fatal web?   20
   Hence, I am qualmish at the smell of leek.   21
FLUELLEN   I peseech you heartily, scurvy, lousy knave,
at my desires, and my requests, and my petitions, to
eat, look you, this leek. [*He offers the leek.*] Because,
look you, you do not love it, nor your affections and
your appetites and your disgestions doo's not agree
with it, I would desire you to eat it.
PISTOL
   Not for Cadwallader and all his goats.   28
FLUELLEN   There is one goat for you. (*Strikes him.*) Will
you be so good, scald knave, as eat it?
PISTOL   Base Trojan, thou shalt die.
FLUELLEN   You say very true, scald knave, when God's
will is. I will desire you to live in the meantime and
eat your victuals. Come, there is sauce for it. [*He strikes
him.*] You called me yesterday mountain squire, but I   35
will make you today a squire of low degree. I pray   36
you, fall to. If you can mock a leek, you can eat a leek.
GOWER   Enough, Captain, you have astonished him.   38
FLUELLEN   By Jesu, I will make him eat some part of my
leek, or I will peat his pate four days. Bite, I pray you;   40
it is good for your green wound and your ploody   41
coxcomb.   42
PISTOL   Must I bite?
FLUELLEN   Yes, certainly, and out of doubt and out of
question too, and ambiguities.
PISTOL
   By this leek, I will most horribly revenge—
                  [*Fluellen threatens him.*]
   I eat and eat—I swear—
FLUELLEN   Eat, I pray you. Will you have some more
sauce to your leek? There is not enough leek to
swear by.
PISTOL
   Quiet thy cudgel; thou dost see I eat.
FLUELLEN   Much good do you, scald knave, heartily.
Nay, pray you, throw none away; the skin is good for

---

21 Giving . . . ostent giving every memorial, token, and display of
victory   **25 sort** array   **29–34 As . . . him** (Seemingly, an allusion to
the Earl of Essex, who left London on his Irish expedition on March
27, 1599, in an attempt to put down Tyrone's rebellion; he returned
unsuccessful and under a cloud on September 28 of the same year.
These lines, therefore, were probably written between the dates mentioned.)   **29 a . . . likelihood** a less exalted comparison but one that
shows much love   **30 Empress** i.e., Elizabeth   **32 broachèd** transfixed, spitted   **36–37 As . . . home** i.e., the French are so dejected
that Henry can stay in England without fear of loss in France   **38 Emperor's coming** (The Holy Roman Emperor, Sigismund, came to England on behalf of France in May 1416.)   **39 them . . . and omit**
(Something appears to be left out here. Possibly it should read,
"them, and the death / O' the Dauphin, leap we over, and omit
. . .")   **41 Harry's back-return** i.e., Henry's second campaign, commencing in 1417   **43 remembering** reminding   **44 brook** tolerate,
excuse
5.1. Location: France. The English camp.
4 asse as   **5 scald** scurvy

---

19 bedlam crazy.   **Trojan** i.e., rascal   **20 Parca's** (The Parcae, or
Fates, spun, drew out, and cut the thread of destiny.)   **21 qualmish**
squeamish, nauseated   **28 Cadwallader** seventh-century Welsh warrior king.   **goats** (Pistol makes the customary taunt that the Welsh
were goatherds.)   **35 mountain squire** i.e., a squire owning mountainous, poor land   **36 squire of low degree** (Allusion to a popular
medieval romance, *The Squire of Low Degree*. Fluellen threatens to
make Pistol into a lowly, contemptible figure, towered over by a
mountain squire.)   **38 astonished** dazed, terrified   **40 pate** head
41 green raw   **42 coxcomb** fool's cap; here, the scalp

your broken coxcomb. When you take occasions to see   54
leeks hereafter, I pray you, mock at 'em, that is all.
PISTOL   Good.
FLUELLEN   Ay, leeks is good. Hold you, there is a groat   57
to heal your pate.   [*He offers a coin.*]
PISTOL   Me, a groat?
FLUELLEN   Yes, verily, and in truth you shall take it, or
I have another leek in my pocket which you shall eat.
PISTOL
I take thy groat in earnest of revenge.   62
FLUELLEN   If I owe you anything, I will pay you in
cudgels. You shall be a woodmonger and buy nothing
of me but cudgels. God b' wi' you, and keep you, and
heal your pate.   *Exit.*
PISTOL   All hell shall stir for this.
GOWER   Go, go, you are a counterfeit cowardly knave.
Will you mock at an ancient tradition, begun upon an
honorable respect and worn as a memorable trophy of   70
predeceased valor, and dare not avouch in your deeds   71
any of your words? I have seen you gleeking and   72
galling at this gentleman twice or thrice. You thought   73
because he could not speak English in the native garb
he could not therefore handle an English cudgel. You
find it otherwise; and henceforth let a Welsh cor-
rection teach you a good English condition. Fare
ye well.   *Exit.*
PISTOL
Doth Fortune play the huswife with me now?   79
News have I that my Doll is dead   80
I' th' spital of a malady of France,   81
And there my rendezvous is quite cut off.   82
Old I do wax, and from my weary limbs   83
Honor is cudgeled. Well, bawd I'll turn,
And something lean to cutpurse of quick hand.   85
To England will I steal, and there I'll steal;
And patches will I get unto these cudgeled scars,
And swear I got them in the Gallia wars.   *Exit.* 88

5.2   *Enter, at one door, King Henry, Exeter, Bedford,*
        [Gloucester, Clarence,] Warwick, [Westmorland,]
        and other lords; at another, Queen Isabel, the
        [French] King, the Duke of Burgundy, [the
        Princess Katharine, Alice,] and other French.

KING HENRY
Peace to this meeting, wherefor we are met!
Unto our brother France and to our sister,
Health and fair time of day; joy and good wishes
To our most fair and princely cousin Katharine;

And, as a branch and member of this royalty,   5
By whom this great assembly is contrived,
We do salute you, Duke of Burgundy;
And princes French, and peers, health to you all!
FRENCH KING
Right joyous are we to behold your face,
Most worthy brother England. Fairly met!
So are you, princes English, every one.
QUEEN ISABEL
So happy be the issue, brother England,   12
Of this good day and of this gracious meeting,
As we are now glad to behold your eyes—
Your eyes, which hitherto have borne in them
Against the French that met them in their bent   16
The fatal balls of murdering basilisks.   17
The venom of such looks, we fairly hope,
Have lost their quality, and that this day
Shall change all griefs and quarrels into love.   20
KING HENRY
To cry amen to that, thus we appear.
QUEEN ISABEL
You English princes all, I do salute you.
BURGUNDY
My duty to you both, on equal love,
Great Kings of France and England! That I have
  labored
With all my wits, my pains, and strong endeavors
To bring your most imperial Majesties
Unto this bar and royal interview,   27
Your mightiness on both parts best can witness.
Since, then, my office hath so far prevailed
That, face to face and royal eye to eye,
You have congreeted, let it not disgrace me   31
If I demand, before this royal view,   32
What rub or what impediment there is   33
Why that the naked, poor, and mangled Peace,
Dear nurse of arts, plenties, and joyful births,
Should not in this best garden of the world,
Our fertile France, put up her lovely visage?   37
Alas, she hath from France too long been chased,
And all her husbandry doth lie on heaps,   39
Corrupting in its own fertility.
Her vine, the merry cheerer of the heart,
Unprunèd dies; her hedges even-pleached,   42
Like prisoners wildly overgrown with hair,
Put forth disordered twigs; her fallow leas   44
The darnel, hemlock, and rank fumitory   45
Doth root upon, while that the coulter rusts   46
That should deracinate such savagery.   47
The even mead, that erst brought sweetly forth   48

54 broken bleeding (not "fractured")   **57 groat** fourpenny coin
62 in earnest of as a down payment for   **70 respect** consideration
71 predeceased valor valor of those now dead   **72–73 gleeking and
galling** mocking and scoffing   **79 huswife** hussy, fickle jade   **80 Doll**
(An error for "Nell"; may indicate an earlier version in which the
speaker of these lines was Falstaff.)   **81 spital** hospital.   **malady of
France** venereal disease   **82 rendezvous** place of individual resort,
refuge   **83 wax** grow   **85 something lean to** incline somewhat to
88 Gallia French
5.2. Location: The French court.

5 royalty royal family   **12 issue** outcome   **16 in their bent** (1) as they
were directed (2) in their glance   **17 fatal balls** (1) cannonballs (2)
eyeballs.   **basilisks** (1) large cannon (2) monsters supposed to kill
with their gaze   **20 griefs** grievances   **27 bar** tribunal   **31 congreeted** greeted each other   **32 demand** ask   **33 rub** obstacle. (A
term from bowls.)   **37 put up** show, lift up   **39 husbandry** cultivated
fields, agricultural produce   **42 even-pleached** smoothly intertwined
44 fallow leas uncultivated open fields   **45 darnel . . . fumitory** i.e.,
weeds that grow in cultivated land   **46 coulter** cutting blade in front
of the plowshare   **47 deracinate** root out   **48 even mead** level
meadow.   **erst** formerly

The freckled cowslip, burnet, and green clover, 49
Wanting the scythe, all uncorrected, rank, 50
Conceives by idleness, and nothing teems 51
But hateful docks, rough thistles, kecksies, burrs, 52
Losing both beauty and utility.
And all our vineyards, fallows, meads, and hedges, 54
Defective in their natures, grow to wildness. 55
Even so our houses and ourselves and children 56
Have lost, or do not learn for want of time,
The sciences that should become our country, 58
But grow like savages—as soldiers will
That nothing do but meditate on blood—
To swearing and stern looks, diffused attire, 61
And everything that seems unnatural.
Which to reduce into our former favor 63
You are assembled, and my speech entreats
That I may know the let why gentle Peace 65
Should not expel these inconveniences
And bless us with her former qualities.

KING HENRY
If, Duke of Burgundy, you would the peace,
Whose want gives growth to th' imperfections 69
Which you have cited, you must buy that peace 68
With full accord to all our just demands,
Whose tenors and particular effects 72
You have enscheduled briefly in your hands. 73

BURGUNDY
The King hath heard them, to the which as yet
There is no answer made.

KING HENRY   Well then, the peace,
Which you before so urged, lies in his answer.

FRENCH KING
I have but with a cursitory eye 77
O'erglanced the articles. Pleaseth Your Grace 78
To appoint some of your council presently
To sit with us once more, with better heed
To re-survey them, we will suddenly 81
Pass our accept and peremptory answer. 82

KING HENRY
Brother, we shall. Go, uncle Exeter,
And brother Clarence, and you, brother Gloucester,
Warwick, and Huntingdon, go with the King,
And take with you free power to ratify,
Augment, or alter, as your wisdoms best
Shall see advantageable for our dignity, 88
Anything in or out of our demands,
And we'll consign thereto.—Will you, fair sister, 90
Go with the princes, or stay here with us?

QUEEN ISABEL
Our gracious brother, I will go with them.
Haply a woman's voice may do some good 93
When articles too nicely urged be stood on. 94

KING HENRY
Yet leave our cousin Katharine here with us.
She is our capital demand, comprised 96
Within the fore-rank of our articles. 97

QUEEN ISABEL
She hath good leave.
           Exeunt omnes. Manent King [Henry]
                    and Katharine [with Alice].

KING HENRY   Fair Katharine, and most fair, 98
Will you vouchsafe to teach a soldier terms
Such as will enter at a lady's ear
And plead his love suit to her gentle heart?

KATHARINE Your Majesty shall mock at me. I cannot
speak your England.

KING HENRY O fair Katharine, if you will love me
soundly with your French heart, I will be glad to hear
you confess it brokenly with your English tongue. Do
you like me, Kate?

KATHARINE *Pardonnez-moi*, I cannot tell wat is "like
me."

KING HENRY An angel is like you, Kate, and you are
like an angel.

KATHARINE [*to Alice*] *Que dit-il? Que je suis semblable à* 112
les anges? 113

ALICE *Oui, vraiment, sauf Votre Grâce, ainsi dit-il.* 114

KING HENRY I said so, dear Katharine, and I must not
blush to affirm it.

KATHARINE *O bon Dieu! Les langues des hommes sont
pleines de tromperies.*

KING HENRY What says she, fair one? That the tongues
of men are full of deceits?

ALICE *Oui*, dat de tongues of de mans is be full of
deceits. Dat is de Princess.

KING HENRY The Princess is the better Englishwoman. 123
I' faith, Kate, my wooing is fit for thy understanding.
I am glad thou canst speak no better English, for if
thou couldst, thou wouldst find me such a plain king
that thou wouldst think I had sold my farm to buy my
crown. I know no ways to mince it in love, but directly 128
to say, "I love you." Then if you urge me farther than
to say, "Do you in faith?" I wear out my suit. Give me 130
your answer, i' faith, do, and so clap hands and a 131
bargain. How say you, lady?

KATHARINE *Sauf votre honneur*, me understand well.

KING HENRY Marry, if you would put me to verses or
to dance for your sake, Kate, why, you undid me. For
the one I have neither words nor measure, and for the 136
other I have no strength in measure, yet a reasonable 137

49 **burnet** a herb 50 **Wanting** lacking 51 **Conceives** gives birth (to weeds). **teems** flourishes 52 **kecksies** dry-stemmed plants, possibly dried hemlock stalks 54 **fallows** land plowed and left lying 55 **Defective . . . natures** i.e., perverted from their natural function, which is to grow useful plants 56 **houses** households 58 **sciences** skills 61 **diffused** disordered 63 **reduce . . . favor** return to our former good appearance and good graces 65 **let** hindrance 68 **would** wish 69 **want** lack 72 **tenors** general purport. **particular effects** specific details 73 **enscheduled** drawn up in writing 77 **cursitory** cursory, hasty 78 **Pleaseth** may it please 81 **suddenly** speedily 82 **Pass . . . answer** deliver an answer acceptable to us and final, decisive 88 **advantageable** advantageous 90 **consign** agree, subscribe

93 **Haply** perhaps 94 **nicely** punctiliously, with insistence on detail. **stood on** insisted on 96 **capital** chief 97 **fore-rank** first row 98 **s.d. omnes** all. **Manent** they remain onstage 112–114 **Que . . . ainsi dit-il** What does he say? That I am like the angels? ALICE Yes, truly, save Your Grace, he says so 123 **is the better Englishwoman** i.e., has a true Englishwoman's modesty and mistrust of flattery 128 **mince it** speak coyly 130 **wear out my suit** expend all my resources as a wooer 131 **clap** clasp 136 **measure** (skill in) meter 137 **measure** dance

measure in strength. If I could win a lady at leapfrog, 138
or by vaulting into my saddle with my armor on my
back, under the correction of bragging be it spoken, I
should quickly leap into a wife. Or if I might buffet for 141
my love, or bound my horse for her favors, I could lay 142
on like a butcher and sit like a jackanapes, never off. 143
But before God, Kate, I cannot look greenly, nor gasp 144
out my eloquence, nor I have no cunning in protestation—only downright oaths, which I never use till 146
urged, nor never break for urging. If thou canst love a
fellow of this temper, Kate, whose face is not worth 148
sunburning, that never looks in his glass for love of 149
anything he sees there, let thine eye be thy cook. I 150
speak to thee plain soldier. If thou canst love me for
this, take me. If not, to say to thee that I shall die is
true; but for thy love, by the Lord, no. Yet I love thee
too. And while thou liv'st, dear Kate, take a fellow of
plain and uncoined constancy, for he perforce must 155
do thee right, because he hath not the gift to woo in
other places. For these fellows of infinite tongue that
can rhyme themselves into ladies' favors, they do
always reason themselves out again. What? A speaker
is but a prater, a rhyme is but a ballad. A good leg will
fall, a straight back will stoop, a black beard will turn 161
white, a curled pate will grow bald, a fair face will
wither, a full eye will wax hollow; but a good heart,
Kate, is the sun and the moon—or rather the sun and
not the moon, for it shines bright and never changes,
but keeps his course truly. If thou would have such a
one, take me. And take me, take a soldier; take a
soldier, take a king. And what sayst thou then to my
love? Speak, my fair, and fairly, I pray thee.

KATHARINE   Is it possible dat I sould love de *ennemi* of
France?

KING HENRY   No, it is not possible you should love the
enemy of France, Kate; but in loving me you should
love the friend of France, for I love France so well that
I will not part with a village of it. I will have it all mine.
And, Kate, when France is mine and I am yours, then
yours is France and you are mine.

KATHARINE   I cannot tell wat is dat.

KING HENRY   No, Kate? I will tell thee in French, which
I am sure will hang upon my tongue like a new-
married wife about her husband's neck, hardly to be
shook off. *Je quand sur le possession de France, et quand* 182
vous avez le possession de moi—let me see, what then? 183
Saint Denis be my speed!—*donc vôtre est France et vous* 184
êtes mienne. It is as easy for me, Kate, to conquer the 185
kingdom as to speak so much more French. I shall
never move thee in French, unless it be to laugh at
me.

KATHARINE   *Sauf votre honneur, le français que vous parlez,* 189
il est meilleur que l' anglais lequel je parle. 190

KING HENRY   No, faith, is 't not, Kate. But thy speaking
of my tongue, and I thine, most truly-falsely, must 192
needs be granted to be much at one. But, Kate, dost 193
thou understand thus much English: Canst thou
love me?

KATHARINE   I cannot tell.

KING HENRY   Can any of your neighbors tell, Kate? I'll
ask them. Come, I know thou lovest me. And at
night, when you come into your closet, you'll question 199
this gentlewoman about me; and I know, Kate, you
will to her dispraise those parts in me that you love
with your heart. But, good Kate, mock me mercifully,
the rather, gentle Princess, because I love thee cruelly.
If ever thou beest mine, Kate, as I have a saving faith
within me tells me thou shalt, I get thee with
scambling, and thou must therefore needs prove a 206
good soldier-breeder. Shall not thou and I, between
Saint Denis and Saint George, compound a boy, half
French, half English, that shall go to Constantinople
and take the Turk by the beard? Shall we not? What
sayst thou, my fair flower-de-luce? 211

KATHARINE   I do not know dat.

KING HENRY   No; 'tis hereafter to know, but now to
promise. Do but now promise, Kate, you will endeavor for your French part of such a boy, and for my
English moiety take the word of a king and a bachelor. 216
How answer you, *la plus belle Katharine du monde, mon* 217
très cher et devin déesse? 218

KATHARINE   Your Majestee 'ave *fausse* French enough 219
to deceive de most *sage demoiselle* dat is *en France.*

KING HENRY   Now, fie upon my false French! By mine
honor, in true English, I love thee, Kate; by which
honor I dare not swear thou lovest me, yet my blood
begins to flatter me that thou dost, notwithstanding
the poor and untempering effect of my visage. Now 225
beshrew my father's ambition! He was thinking of civil
wars when he got me; therefore was I created with a
stubborn outside, with an aspect of iron, that when I 228
come to woo ladies I fright them. But in faith, Kate, the
elder I wax the better I shall appear. My comfort is that
old age, that ill layer-up of beauty, can do no more
spoil upon my face. Thou hast me, if thou hast me, at
the worst; and thou shalt wear me, if thou wear me,
better and better. And therefore tell me, most fair
Katharine, will you have me? Put off your maiden
blushes; avouch the thoughts of your heart with the 236
looks of an empress; take me by the hand, and say,
"Harry of England, I am thine." Which word thou
shalt no sooner bless mine ear withal, but I will tell

---

138 **measure** amount, aptitude   141 **buffet** box   142 **bound** make
prance   143 **jackanapes** ape, monkey   144 **greenly** like a lovesick
youth   146 **downright** straightforward   148–149 **not worth sunburning** i.e., so ugly that the sun couldn't make it worse   150 **let . . .
cook** i.e., dress me with fine qualities as a cook dresses meat
155 **uncoined** (1) not coined for circulation (2) unalloyed, therefore
fixed, steady   161 **fall** shrink, lose its shapeliness   182–185 **Je . . .
mienne** (Henry haltingly translates into French the last sentence of his
previous speech.)   184 **Saint Denis** patron saint of France.   **be my
speed** help me

189–190 **Sauf . . . parle** saving your honor, the French that you
speak is better than the English that I speak   192 **truly-falsely** true-
heartedly but incorrectly   193 **at one** alike   199 **closet** private chamber   206 **scambling** scrambling, seizing in a scuffle   211 **flower-de-
luce** fleur-de-lis, the emblem of France   216 **moiety** half   217–
218 **la plus . . . déesse** the most beautiful Katharine in the world, my
very dear and divine goddess   219 **fausse** i.e., false (both "incorrect"
and "deceptive")   225 **untempering** unsoftening   228 **aspect** appearance   236 **avouch** guarantee, confirm

thee aloud, "England is thine, Ireland is thine, France is thine, and Henry Plantagenet is thine"—who, though I speak it before his face, if he be not fellow with the best king, thou shalt find the best king of good fellows. Come, your answer in broken music! 244 For thy voice is music, and thy English broken. Therefore, queen of all, Katharine, break thy mind to 246 me in broken English. Wilt thou have me?

KATHARINE   Dat is as it shall please de *roi mon père*. 248

KING HENRY   Nay, it will please him well, Kate. It shall please him, Kate.

KATHARINE   Den it sall also content me.

KING HENRY   Upon that I kiss your hand, and I call you my queen.   [*He attempts to kiss her hand.*]

KATHARINE   *Laissez, mon seigneur, laissez, laissez! Ma* 254 *foi, je ne veux point que vous abaissiez votre grandeur* 255 *en baisant la main d'une—Notre Seigneur!—indigne* 256 *serviteur. Excusez-moi, je vous supplie, mon très-* 257 *puissant seigneur.*   258

KING HENRY   Then I will kiss your lips, Kate.

KATHARINE   *Les dames et demoiselles pour être baisées* 260 *devant leur noces, il n'est pas la coutume de France.*   261

KING HENRY [*to Alice*]   Madam my interpreter, what says she?

ALICE   Dat it is not be de fashion *pour les* ladies of France—I cannot tell wat is *baiser* en Anglish.

KING HENRY   To kiss.

ALICE   Your Majestee *entend* bettre *que moi.*   267

KING HENRY   It is not a fashion for the maids in France to kiss before they are married, would she say?

ALICE   *Oui, vraiment.*   270

KING HENRY   O Kate, nice customs curtsy to great kings. 271 Dear Kate, you and I cannot be confined within the weak list of a country's fashion. We are the makers of 273 manners, Kate; and the liberty that follows our places 274 stops the mouth of all find-faults, as I will do yours, for upholding the nice fashion of your country in denying me a kiss. Therefore, patiently and yielding. [*He kisses her.*] You have witchcraft in your lips, Kate. There is more eloquence in a sugar touch of them than in the tongues of the French council, and they should sooner persuade Harry of England than a general petition of monarchs.—Here comes your father.

Enter the French power and the English lords.

BURGUNDY   God save Your Majesty! My royal cousin, teach you our princess English?

KING HENRY   I would have her learn, my fair cousin, how perfectly I love her, and that is good English.

BURGUNDY   Is she not apt?

KING HENRY   Our tongue is rough, coz, and my condi- 288 tion is not smooth; so that, having neither the voice 289 nor the heart of flattery about me, I cannot so conjure up the spirit of love in her that he will appear in his true likeness.

BURGUNDY   Pardon the frankness of my mirth, if I answer you for that. If you would conjure in her, you 294 must make a circle; if conjure up love in her in his true likeness, he must appear naked and blind. Can you 296 blame her then, being a maid yet rosed over with the 297 virgin crimson of modesty, if she deny the appearance 298 of a naked blind boy in her naked seeing self? It were, 299 my lord, a hard condition for a maid to consign to. 300

KING HENRY   Yet they do wink and yield, as love is 301 blind and enforces.   302

BURGUNDY   They are then excused, my lord, when they see not what they do.

KING HENRY   Then, good my lord, teach your cousin to consent winking.

BURGUNDY   I will wink on her to consent, my lord, if you will teach her to know my meaning; for maids, well summered and warm kept, are like flies at Bar- 309 tholomew-tide: blind, though they have their eyes, 310 and then they will endure handling, which before 311 would not abide looking on.

KING HENRY   This moral ties me over to time and a hot 313 summer; and so I shall catch the fly, your cousin, in 314 the latter end, and she must be blind too.

BURGUNDY   As love is, my lord, before it loves.   316

KING HENRY   It is so; and you may, some of you, thank love for my blindness, who cannot see many a fair 318 French city for one fair French maid that stands in 319 my way.   320

FRENCH KING   Yes, my lord, you see them perspectively, 321 the cities turned into a maid; for they are all girdled with maiden walls that war hath never entered.   323

KING HENRY   Shall Kate be my wife?

FRENCH KING   So please you.

KING HENRY   I am content, so the maiden cities you talk of may wait on her. So the maid that stood in the way 327

---

244 broken music (Henry quibbles on the term for music composed in parts for different instruments.) **246 break** open **248 de roi mon père** the King my father **254–258 Laissez . . . seigneur** don't, my lord, don't, don't; by my faith, I do not wish you to lower your greatness by kissing the hand of an—Our dear Lord!—unworthy servant; excuse me, I beg you, my most powerful lord **260–261 Les dames . . . France** it is not customary in France for ladies and young girls to be kissed before their marriage **267 entend . . . moi** understands better than I **270 Oui, vraiment** yes, truly **271 nice** fastidious **273 list** limit, barrier **274 follows our places** attends our (high) rank

288–289 condition personality **294 conjure in her** (with bawdy double meaning of raising up something within her *circle*, line 295) **296 naked and blind** (as Cupid is conventionally portrayed) **297 yet rosed over** still blushing **298–299 if . . . self** i.e., if she refuses to acknowledge the naked emotion of love within her by laying bare her innermost feelings. (The phrase also suggests her virginal sense of shame in nakedness, both her own and that of the blind, naked boy.) **300 a hard condition** (suggesting erection). **consign** agree **301 wink** close the eyes **301–302 love is blind** i.e., (1) the maid closes her eyes and yields (2) the soldier enforces love in his blind zeal **309 summered** nurtured **309–310 Bartholomew-tide** August 24 (when flies, bees, etc., are sluggish) **311 handling** (1) handling of the beehive (2) sexual handling **313–314 This moral . . . summer** the lesson of your fable would oblige me to wait for the heat of summer **316 As . . . loves** (Love is blind before it loves, because it cannot yet see the beloved and because love has not yet opened the lover's eyes.) **318–320 who . . . my way** i.e., since I am so preoccupied with Katharine that I have forgotten for the moment about all those French towns I want. (He is joking; he gets the French towns, along with her.) **321 perspectively** i.e., as in an optical device that presents different images when viewed from different angles **323 maiden** unbreached (with a sexual metaphor, continued in *entered*) **327 wait on her** attend her, go along with her (as part of her dowry)

for my wish shall show me the way to my will.   328
FRENCH KING
    We have consented to all terms of reason.
KING HENRY   Is 't so, my lords of England?
WESTMORLAND
    The King hath granted every article:
    His daughter first, and then in sequel all,
    According to their firm proposèd natures.   333
EXETER
    Only he hath not yet subscribèd this: 334
    Where Your Majesty demands that the King of France,
    having any occasion to write for matter of grant, shall   336
    name Your Highness in this form and with this ad-   337
    dition, in French, *Notre très cher fils Henri, Roi*   338
    d'Angleterre, Héritier de France; and thus in Latin,   339
    Praeclarissimus filius noster Henricus, Rex Angliae et
    Haeres Franciae.
FRENCH KING
    Nor this I have not, brother, so denied   342
    But your request shall make me let it pass.   343
KING HENRY
    I pray you then, in love and dear alliance,
    Let that one article rank with the rest,
    And thereupon give me your daughter.
FRENCH KING
    Take her, fair son, and from her blood raise up
    Issue to me, that the contending kingdoms
    Of France and England, whose very shores look pale
    With envy of each other's happiness,
    May cease their hatred, and this dear conjunction
    Plant neighborhood and Christian-like accord
    In their sweet bosoms, that never war advance
    His bleeding sword twixt England and fair France.
LORDS   Amen!
KING HENRY
    Now, welcome, Kate; and bear me witness all,
    That here I kiss her as my sovereign queen.
                              [*He kisses her.*] *Flourish.*
QUEEN ISABEL
    God, the best maker of all marriages,
    Combine your hearts in one, your realms in one!
    As man and wife, being two, are one in love,
    So be there twixt your kingdoms such a spousal   361
    That never may ill office, or fell jealousy,   362
    Which troubles oft the bed of blessèd marriage,
    Thrust in between the paction of these kingdoms   364
    To make divorce of their incorporate league;
    That English may as French, French Englishmen,
    Receive each other. God speak this "Amen"!
ALL   Amen!

KING HENRY
    Prepare we for our marriage, on which day,
    My lord of Burgundy, we'll take your oath,
    And all the peers', for surety of our leagues.
    Then shall I swear to Kate, and you to me;
    And may our oaths well kept and prosperous be!
                              Sennet.   Exeunt.

❖

Epilogue

Enter Chorus.
CHORUS
    Thus far, with rough and all-unable pen,
        Our bending author hath pursued the story,   2
    In little room confining mighty men,
        Mangling by starts the full course of their glory.   4
    Small time, but in that small most greatly lived   5
        This star of England. Fortune made his sword,
    By which the world's best garden he achieved,   7
        And of it left his son imperial lord.
    Henry the Sixth, in infant bands crowned King   9
        Of France and England, did this king succeed;
    Whose state so many had the managing,
        That they lost France and made his England bleed,
    Which oft our stage hath shown; and, for their sake,   13
    In your fair minds let this acceptance take.   [*Exit.*]   14

Epilogue.
2 bending i.e., under the weight of his task   **4 by starts** in fits and
starts, in fragments   **5 Small time** (Henry V ruled for only nine years,
dying at the age of thirty-five.)   **7 best garden** i.e., France   **9 infant
bands** swaddling clothes   **13 Which . . . shown** (Refers to the three
parts of *King Henry VI.*)   **for their sake** i.e., since you liked them, or,
for the sake of those who lost France. (This play redresses the balance.)   **14 this acceptance take** this play meet with your approval

---

328 will (1) intention of ruling France (2) sexual desire   **333 According . . . natures** exactly as specified in the proposals   **334 subscribèd**
agreed to, signed to   **336 for . . . grant** in official deeds, granting title to land and the like   **337–338 addition** title   **338–339 Notre
. . . France** our very dear son Henry, King of England, Heir of
France. (The Latin has *Praeclarissimus,* "most famous," instead of
Praecharissimus, "most dear," because that is the way Shakespeare
found it in Holinshed.)   **342 so** so firmly   **343 But** but that
361 spousal marriage   **362 ill office** unfriendly dealings.   **fell** cruel
364 paction alliance, compact

[handwritten marginal note: Henry V dies soon, Henry VI loses France and the throne]

The Life of King Henry the Eighth

However much we may like to think of *The Tempest* (c. 1610–1611) as Shakespeare's farewell to his art, celebrating his retirement to Stratford in 1611 or 1612, his career was, in fact, not quite finished. He probably wrote *The Famous History of the Life of King Henry the Eighth* in 1613, and he evidently collaborated with the playwright John Fletcher (and possibly Francis Beaumont) in *The Two Noble Kinsmen* (1613–1616). *Henry VIII* was performed by the King's men, Shakespeare's acting company, at the Globe playhouse on June 29, 1613, as a "new" play, though perhaps it had also been performed earlier that spring at the indoors Blackfriars playhouse. During the Globe performance, small cannon (called "chambers") were discharged to welcome Henry VIII and his fellow-masquers to Cardinal Wolsey's house (1.4.64 ff.), accidentally setting fire to the thatch roof and burning the Globe to the ground in less than an hour. (The theater was subsequently rebuilt.) The letter reporting this incident refers to the play by the title *All Is True*, but its identification with the extant play of *Henry VIII* is virtually certain.

Not everyone has always agreed that the entire play is by Shakespeare, although doubts did not arise until the nineteenth century. Alfred Lord Tennyson was the first to suspect that much of the play is metrically non-Shakespearean. His friend James Spedding took up the suggestion in his study *Who Wrote Shakespeare's Henry VIII?* His conclusions, based on the assumption that Fletcher's mannered blank verse is generally end-stopped and much given to double or "feminine" endings, assigned only 1.1–2, 2.3–4, 3.2 (through line 204), and 5.1 to Shakespeare, attributing all the rest to Fletcher. These metrical tests have been bolstered by subsequent researchers and augmented by methods of statistical analysis. The result is perhaps a more elaborate case for joint authorship than for most other plays of doubtful attribution. Some of the stylistic shifts noted by Tennyson are indeed discernible, as for example in the movement from the dense, elliptical grammar and compact images of the first two scenes to the conversational fluency of scenes 3 and 4.

Against these arguments, however, the case for Shakespeare as author of essentially the entire play is impressive. Although Shakespeare did apparently collaborate with Fletcher in *The Two Noble Kinsmen* during his last years, that play was excluded from the 1623 Folio, whereas *Henry VIII* was included as Shakespeare's final history play. Spedding's hypothesis of joint authorship would rob from Shakespeare several of the play's most famous scenes, such as the farewell speeches of the Duke of Buckingham, Cardinal Wolsey, and Queen Katharine, and conversely would credit Fletcher with a dramatic power not shown elsewhere. The "Fletcherian" style may well have been the result of Shakespeare's having known the work of the younger man who became Shakespeare's heir as chief writer for the King's men. Unquestionably, Shakespeare's style did change in his later years under the influence of a sophisticated courtly audience at the indoors Blackfriars theater; the Prologue to *Henry VIII* suggests that the play was written with the more exclusive audience of Blackfriars ("The first and happiest hearers of the town") particularly in mind. Even if *Henry VIII* is a different sort of history play from *1 Henry IV*, it is stylistically close to Shakespeare's late romances. The shift in texture from scenes 1 and 2 to scenes 3 and 4 makes good sense dramatically; scene 4, for example, dramatizing an evening party, is suitably conversational, whereas the dense first scene is largely expository. Neither external evidence nor tradition during Shakespeare's day links the play with Fletcher. Scholarly efforts to assign portions of the text to other authors date only from the nineteenth century, where they should be seen as part of a broader effort to reassign various parts of many other plays and thereby rescue Shakespeare from scenes presumed unworthy of his genius. The tendency to regard *Henry VIII* as defective and lacking in unity may well have been caused in part by eighteenth- and nineteenth-century productions of the play, which, although frequent and popular, treated the play as a vehicle for famous actors and actresses in the parts of Wolsey and Katharine (Thomas Betterton, John Philip Kemble, Sarah Siddons, Charles Kean, and, more recently, Sybil Thorndike, Charles Laughton, and Flora Robson), and accordingly cut Act 5 and sometimes much of Act 4 along with other "extraneous" parts. Productions and criticism during the last thirty years, on the other hand, have shown *Henry VIII* to possess an impressive cohesion and to be an integral product of the late years in which Shakespeare centered his attention on romance and tragicomedy. This is not to deny that Fletcher may have made contributions here and there, especially in the Prologue and Epilogue. Still, we are safest in assuming that nineteenth-century efforts to deny Shakespeare authorship of the play as a whole are now happily out of fashion and that the Folio editors knew what they were doing when they included *Henry VIII*.

What was Shakespeare's purpose in this unexpected return to the English history play? He had set it aside fourteen years earlier, in 1599, bringing to completion in *Henry V* a series of eight plays on England's civil wars of the fifteenth century and another on the reign of King John. Why turn in 1613 to a historical subject so separated in time from that of Shakespeare's earlier interest and potentially so controversial because of its relation to the religious battle between Catholics and Protestants? Earlier generations of critics and playgoers, as we have seen, generally regarded parts of *Henry VIII* as belonging to another author or as the product of Shakespeare's presumed dotage, especially Act 5, with its apparent anticlimax following the deaths of the play's central characters, Wolsey and Katharine. More recent efforts to understand the whole of *Henry VIII* regard it as an experimental work, blending conventional genres (history, tragedy, and romance) and stressing masquelike stage effects in the opulent manner of court entertainment. Since its thematic focus is also one of courtly celebration, expressing gratitude for Queen Elizabeth's Protestant rule and wary hopes that her successor James will follow suit, the play may best be seen as a reworking of the English history play to meet the new mood of 1613. This return to a type of drama long since abandoned by Shakespeare resembles his similar fascination during his late years with the once-forgotten genre of romance.

In some ways, *Henry VIII* is deliberately unlike Shakespeare's earlier history plays, and so should not be judged by their standards. The Prologue is at pains to stress that the play will contain no merriment or bawdry, no "fellow / In a long motley coat." And, indeed, the play is unusually lacking in a comic subplot devoted to the endearing antics of a tavern crew. To be sure, the views of the citizens are not ignored, for Queen Katharine champions their hatred of Wolsey's taxes. In Act 5, the people put in a brief appearance, crowding bumptiously forward at the christening of the Princess Elizabeth (5.4). Even here, however, the tone is one of condescending amusement at their childish eagerness to see their future queen. The common people do not provide choric commentary, as they do in *Richard III* or *Richard II*.

These factors may well reflect the increasing influence of the court on Shakespeare and the King's men. Ever since they had become the King's men in 1603, when James I came to the throne, Shakespeare's company had enjoyed a closer relationship with the throne than before. *Measure for Measure* and *Macbeth*, among other of Shakespeare's plays, seem to contain flattering allusions to the new monarch. Moreover, faced with increasing competition from the boys' acting companies, which, since reopening in 1599 after a hiatus of nearly a decade, had attracted a courtly and sophisticated clientele, Shakespeare's company acquired the lease of Blackfriars in 1608 and henceforth used this "private" theater as their winter playhouse. Shakespeare's late plays are staged with public, private, and courtly conditions of performance in mind. The late romances show the influence of Inigo Jones' lavish designs for court masques, as in *Cymbeline*'s use of machinery for celestial ascents and

descents. *Henry VIII* reflects similar conditions of staging in its masquing scene (1.4), in the pageantlike trial of Katharine and the baptism of Elizabeth, and in the vision of white-robed figures dancing before the dying Katharine (4.2). This affinity to courtly entertainment should not be overstressed, for Shakespeare's company remained a public company throughout his career, and its stage was always fluidly bare of scenery when compared with Jones' ingenious devices and use of scenic perspective. Nonetheless, *Henry VIII* should be viewed as a history play for a somewhat more select audience than that of his earlier histories. The play's ornate compliments to Elizabeth have a courtly flavor. The year 1613 saw the politically important marriage of the Elector Palatine to James' daughter Elizabeth, who was often flatteringly compared with her namesake Queen Elizabeth, and, although *Henry VIII* is not among the plays known to have been performed for this occasion, the marriage itself would have given added significance to the play

Shakespeare's earlier histories also honor, as well as examine critically, the institution of monarchy, but even here *Henry VIII* provides a different emphasis. Shakespeare's earlier histories had focused on such issues as the education of a prince and the dilemmas of power a ruler faces. *Henry VIII* is less a study of kingship and more a dramatic expression of gratitude. *Henry VIII* is not a patriotic play in a broadly popular sense. It lacks battles and triumphant oratory. It voices thanksgiving for a particular ruling family. *Henry VIII* is, above all, the remarkable story of Queen Elizabeth's birth. The story is certainly not without its ironies, for providence works in mysterious ways, and Elizabeth's parents were complex persons. Shakespeare's play reveals an increasing psychological interest in analysis of motive, as do other later history plays such as John Ford's *Perkin Warbeck*. Yet the unifying impulse of the play remains the celebration of the birth of Elizabeth.

This rising action in the play is counterpointed by a series of tragic falls, which indeed seem at first to be the play's chief concern. These falls proceed in remorseless succession—Buckingham, Katharine, Wolsey. In the edifying manner of that staple of medieval tragedy, the "Fall of Princes," these deaths offer useful lessons on statecraft and personal conduct. All these characters stoically exemplify the art of holy dying. One after another, they forgive their enemies and regret such sins as they have committed, and yet they also prophesy that God's retribution will light on offenders' heads. The prevailing mood in the falls of Buckingham and Katharine is one of pity, for both are victims of the ruthless Wolsey.

Cardinal Wolsey is the most interesting character of the three and best illustrates another convention of medieval tragedy, the Wheel of Fortune. Even as he topples one victim after another, dispatching Surrey to Ireland, wheedling his way into the King's favor, reversing England's foreign policy with bewildering speed from pro-French to pro-

Empire and back again, all the while amassing a vast personal fortune and negotiating for supreme power within the Roman church, we sense that he is preparing his own catastrophe. Fortune raises insolent worldly persons of this sort, but an overseeing power is at work and will manifest itself through the King. Wolsey, in a nobly contrite farewell, sees the moral of his fall: had he served God zealously, God would not "Have left me naked to mine enemies" (3.2.458). Wolsey knows he has ventured beyond his depth in scheming, "Like little wanton boys that swim on bladders" (line 360). Shakespeare's appraisal of this controversial man is mixed, partly because his chief source, Raphael Holinshed's *Chronicles* (1578), incorporated both anti-Wolseyan diatribes and George Cavendish's appreciative account of Wolsey's last days. Still, the portraiture remains consistent throughout, for Wolsey is always intelligent and munificent (as in his founding of Cardinal College, later Christ Church, at Oxford) even though he employs his talents for worldly ends. His chief wrongdoing is his meddling on behalf of Rome, his finagling to gain the papacy, and most of all his sending of England's wealth overseas for reasons of private gain. Yet even this corrupt behavior has a function in the rising action of the story, for, had not Wolsey schemed against Queen Katharine in his plot to marry King Henry to the French Duchess of Alençon, Katharine might never have fallen to make way for Anne Bullen, and had not Wolsey given a sumptuous party to impress the court with his magnificence (1.4), Henry might never have met Queen Elizabeth's mother. Wolsey's fate is to introduce Henry to the woman whose rise will mean Wolsey's fall and the birth of a future queen. An overriding cosmic irony converts the worst intents of traitors to beneficent ends.

King Henry and Anne Bullen, who, as Elizabeth's parents, play the roles essential to England's bright future, are largely unaware of the great destiny they are performing. Henry especially, like Wolsey, is examined with some skepticism. His pious insistence that "conscience" alone banishes him from Katharine's bed elicits a wry observation, sotto voce, from the Duke of Suffolk: "No, his conscience / Has crept too near another lady" (2.2.17–18). As Henry neglectfully condones Wolsey's abuse of authority and credulously accepts perjured testimony against Buckingham, we catch glimpses of the whimsical tyrant whom history has revealed to us. These criticisms are muted, however, for Henry is, after all, Elizabeth's father. He is not only exonerated from most wrongdoing but steps boldly forward at the play's end as champion of religious reform. Anne, too, is ambivalently treated. In her scene with the Old Lady (2.3), we are reminded of the all-too-apparent reasons there are for suspecting that Anne is a schemer, a high-class auctioneer of her beauty who knows that Henry will pay handsomely. An Elizabethan audience would be bound to recall her grim fate at the hands of the public executioner. Yet, in her own person, Anne resists these ironies. All the characters of the play,

whether they stand to profit or lose by Anne's marriage, speak admiringly of her beauty and honor. Although her speeches are few, her appearances are sumptuously staged, with Anne at the center of a meaningful pageant.

The religious issue is presented with a similar tact and ambiguity, for it, too, is both controversial and of significance to England's future. Our sympathies are charitably disposed toward Katharine, whose innocent fall is a sad price for England's larger happiness. Shakespeare refuses to associate her with the decaying order of Catholicism, as he might have done. On the other hand, Bishop Gardiner, the villain of Act 5, is undeniably a Catholic and persecutor of heretics, a dangerous man whose overthrow by Henry and the Protestant Cranmer signals the beginning of a new era in religion. Though Shakespeare tactfully omits the relationship between Katharine's divorce and the Reformation, his audience would have had little difficulty making the connection in Act 5 between Cranmer's Protestant victory and the birth of Elizabeth. These two rising actions coalesce and give perspective to the pitiable falls from greatness that have necessarily contributed to a happy and even miraculous conclusion. History and tragicomic romance fulfill a common purpose in *Henry VIII*.

Act 5 is thus central to the play's thematic concerns, despite the poor opinion in which it was held in the nineteenth century and despite the apparently episodic way in which it introduces new characters (notably Archbishop Cranmer) and new issues. The ending confirms a pattern seen earlier in the sad stories of Buckingham and especially Wolsey, in which we mortals "outrun / By violent swiftness that which we run at, / And lose by overrunning" (1.1.141–143). Vain human striving after fame overreaches itself and brings itself down. The process is, in *Henry VIII*, not primarily a punishment for villainy, for there are no real villains here, but a curative process by which frail, proud men ascend on Fortune's wheel, only to discover how illusory are her rewards and how comforting are Fortune's losses that bring us to ourselves. Not a moment of ease does Wolsey enjoy until he is ruined in worldly terms. He assures Thomas Cromwell, at the moment of his fall, that "I know myself now, and I feel within me / A peace above all earthly dignities" (3.2.379–380). His fall is thus a happy fall, an instructive one for himself and others: "Mark but my fall, and that that ruined me" (line 440). Even Katharine and her gentleman usher, Griffin, perceive a happiness in Wolsey's decline, not because it satisfies a desire for vengeance, but because it offers a comforting precedent of self-discovery through suffering: "His overthrow heaped happiness upon him; / For then, and not till then, he felt himself" (4.2.64–65). To know oneself in these terms, *nosce teipsum,* is to enjoy the inestimable gift of penance and the laying aside of worldly striving. Cranmer is a suitable protagonist in Act 5 and a substitute for Wolsey as the King's adviser because he cares so little for himself in a worldly sense. He is the instrument of a higher power that, having imposed various trials on members of the court for their individual and collective betterment, at last reveals a meaning in that suffering and a future happiness arising out of humanity's imperfect attempts to know itself. As Buckingham says earlier (2.1.124), "Heaven has an end in all."

As history play, *Henry VIII* accomplishes a lot. In relating the rise and fall of Buckingham, Wolsey, Queen Katharine, and the rest, the play touches on several weighty historical themes: the uneasy tenure of people in high places, the emergence of a powerful monarchy, the loss of authority of the old nobility (exemplified by Buckingham) during a time when persons of no hereditary pretensions (such as Wolsey and Cromwell) are coming into new prominence, the victory of Protestantism over Catholicism, the bitter factionalism accompanying such historical transitions (which must have seemed acutely relevant to observers of King James' court in 1613), and still more. To compare *Henry VIII* with Holinshed's chronicles is to see how expertly Shakespeare has selected and causally linked his materials from those voluminous pages of history without distorting the overall import of those materials. Among the myriad historical events chronicled are the Treaty of the Field of the Cloth of Gold (1520), the enmity between Wolsey and Buckingham ending in the latter's arrest and execution (1520–1521), French abrogation of the treaty (1523), Wolsey's illegal tax (1525), Henry's meeting Anne Bullen (1525), the arrival of Cardinal Campeius (1528), Queen Katharine's being brought to court (1528), the rise to favor of Gardiner (1529) and then of Cranmer (1533), Wolsey's being found out by Henry (1529) and his death (1530), the naming of Sir Thomas More as Lord Chancellor (1529), Anne's being made Marchioness of Pembroke (1532), her marriage to Henry, coronation, and giving birth to Elizabeth (1533), the christening of Elizabeth (1533), the death of Katharine (1536), the indictment and trial of Cranmer (1544), and much more. Yet, for all its manifold historical content, the play is also illustrative of a pattern of events found in Shakespeare's late romances: that of the providential rise and fall and of eventual restoration of divine promises of happiness.

The play when staged offers a visual contrast between ceremonial pomp and worldly loss leading to renunciation and death. The processions and public events, conveyed by unusually full stage directions, celebrate the ordered arrangement of a hierarchical society. Yet among the most powerful scenes are those of Wolsey bidding farewell to his wealth and power, and Katharine in her isolation and approaching death. The Prologue promises to give us noble scenes, "Sad, high, and working, full of state and woe," and in this we are not disappointed. The Prologue also promises that the audience "May here find truth too"; and, despite the necessary omission of much bloodshed (we are never told directly what will become of Anne Bullen and Sir Thomas More), the play does give a vivid account of Henry VIII's time. We "see / The very persons of our noble story / As they were

living." Our impression is of great political and religious change, of splendor and richness, above all of the insecurity of worldly felicity under such a king. Theatrically, the play is sumptuous, pageantlike; though it chooses not to amuse us with comedy, and eschews battle scenes, it abounds in personages from history. In *Henry VIII,* Shakespeare adapts the history play to his late world of romance.

The Life of King Henry the Eighth

[Dramatis Personae

KING HENRY THE EIGHTH

DUKE OF BUCKINGHAM
DUKE OF NORFOLK
DUKE OF SUFFOLK
EARL OF SURREY
LORD ABERGAVENNY
LORD SANDS (Sir Walter Sands)
LORD CHAMBERLAIN
LORD CHANCELLOR
SIR HENRY GUILDFORD
SIR THOMAS LOVELL
SIR ANTHONY DENNY
SIR NICHOLAS VAUX

CARDINAL WOLSEY
THOMAS CROMWELL, Wolsey's aide, later in King Henry's service
SECRETARY of Wolsey
SERVANT of Wolsey
CARDINAL CAMPEIUS
CAPUCHIUS, Ambassador from the Emperor Charles the Fifth
GARDINER, King Henry's secretary, later Bishop of Winchester
PAGE to Gardiner
THOMAS CRANMER, Archbishop of Canterbury
BISHOP OF LINCOLN

QUEEN KATHARINE, King Henry's wife, later divorced
PATIENCE, her attendant
GRIFFITH, her gentleman usher
GENTLEWOMAN, } attending
GENTLEMAN, } Queen Katharine

ANNE BULLEN, Queen Katharine's Maid of Honor, later Queen
OLD LADY, friend of Anne Bullen

BRANDON
SERGEANT AT ARMS
SURVEYOR to the Duke of Buckingham
Three GENTLEMEN
CRIER
SCRIBE
MESSENGER to Queen Katharine
DOCTOR BUTTS
KEEPER of the Council Chamber
PORTER

Porter's MAN
GARTER KING AT ARMS

Speaker of the PROLOGUE and EPILOGUE

Lords, Ladies, Gentlemen, Judges, Bishops, Priests, Vergers, Lord Mayor of London and Aldermen, Common People, Attendants, Guards, Tipstaves, Halberdiers, Scribes, Secretaries, Officers, Pursuivants, Pages, Guards, Queen Katharine's Women, Musicians, Choristers, and Dancers as spirits

SCENE: London; Westminster; Kimbolton]

Prologue

[Enter Prologue.]

I come no more to make you laugh. Things now
That bear a weighty and a serious brow,
Sad, high, and working, full of state and woe,   3
Such noble scenes as draw the eye to flow,
We now present. Those that can pity here
May, if they think it well, let fall a tear;
The subject will deserve it. Such as give
Their money out of hope they may believe
May here find truth too. Those that come to see
Only a show or two, and so agree   10
The play may pass, if they be still and willing,
I'll undertake may see away their shilling
Richly in two short hours. Only they   13
That come to hear a merry, bawdy play,
A noise of targets, or to see a fellow   15
In a long motley coat guarded with yellow,   16
Will be deceived. For, gentle hearers, know   17
To rank our chosen truth with such a show
As fool and fight is, besides forfeiting
Our own brains and the opinion that we bring   20
To make that only true we now intend,   21
Will leave us never an understanding friend.
Therefore, for goodness' sake, and as you are known
The first and happiest hearers of the town,   24
Be sad, as we would make ye. Think ye see   25
The very persons of our noble story
As they were living. Think you see them great,   27
And followed with the general throng and sweat
Of thousand friends; then, in a moment, see
How soon this mightiness meets misery.

Prologue.
3 Sad . . . working serious, lofty, and exciting the emotions. **state** dignity **10 show** spectacle **13 two short hours** (A conventional period of time for a play.) **15 targets** shields **16 motley coat** pied costume of the fool. (Probably a slighting reference to Will Summers, Henry VIII's fool, as portrayed in Samuel Rowley's *When You See Me You Know Me*, 1605, reprinted 1613. The play also features Patch, Wolsey's fool.) **guarded** trimmed **17 deceived** disappointed. **know** i.e., it must be acknowledged that **20 Our own brains** i.e., the labor of our brains **20–21 the opinion . . . intend** the reputation we have for presenting truthfully what we intend to play **24 first** foremost. **happiest hearers** best-qualified audience **25 sad** serious **27 As** as if. **great** in high position

And if you can be merry then, I'll say
A man may weep upon his wedding day.   [*Exit.*]

❧

1.1   *Enter the Duke of Norfolk at one door; at the other,*
the Duke of Buckingham and the Lord
Abergavenny.

BUCKINGHAM
Good morrow, and well met. How have ye done
Since last we saw in France?
NORFOLK   I thank Your Grace,   2
Healthful, and ever since a fresh admirer   3
Of what I saw there.
BUCKINGHAM   An untimely ague   4
Stayed me a prisoner in my chamber when   5
Those suns of glory, those two lights of men,
Met in the vale of Andren.
NORFOLK   Twixt Guynes and Arde.   7
I was then present, saw them salute on horseback,
Beheld them when they lighted, how they clung   9
In their embracement, as they grew together;   10
Which had they, what four throned ones could have
weighed   11
Such a compounded one?
BUCKINGHAM   All the whole time
I was my chamber's prisoner.
NORFOLK   Then you lost
The view of earthly glory. Men might say
Till this time pomp was single, but now married
To one above itself. Each following day   16
Became the next day's master, till the last   17
Made former wonders its. Today the French,   18
All clinquant, all in gold, like heathen gods,   19
Shone down the English; and tomorrow they   20
Made Britain India—every man that stood   21
Showed like a mine. Their dwarfish pages were
As cherubins, all gilt. The madams too,   23
Not used to toil, did almost sweat to bear
The pride upon them, that their very labor   25
Was to them as a painting. Now this masque   26
Was cried incomparable; and th' ensuing night   27
Made it a fool and beggar. The two kings,
Equal in luster, were now best, now worst,
As presence did present them; him in eye   30
Still him in praise; and being present both,   31

'Twas said they saw but one, and no discerner   32
Durst wag his tongue in censure. When these
suns—   33
For so they phrase 'em—by their heralds challenged
The noble spirits to arms, they did perform
Beyond thought's compass, that former fabulous
story,   36
Being now seen possible enough, got credit,   37
That *Bevis* was believed.
BUCKINGHAM   O, you go far.   38
NORFOLK
As I belong to worship and affect   39
In honor honesty, the tract of everything   40
Would by a good discourser lose some life
Which action's self was tongue to. All was royal;   42
To the disposing of it naught rebelled.   43
Order gave each thing view; the office did   44
Distinctly his full function.
BUCKINGHAM   Who did guide—   45
I mean, who set the body and the limbs
Of this great sport together, as you guess?   47
NORFOLK
One, certes, that promises no element   48
In such a business.
BUCKINGHAM   I pray you, who, my lord?
NORFOLK
All this was ordered by the good discretion
Of the right reverend Cardinal of York.   51
BUCKINGHAM
The devil speed him! No man's pie is freed   52
From his ambitious finger. What had he
To do in these fierce vanities? I wonder   54
That such a keech can with his very bulk   55
Take up the rays o' the beneficial sun   56
And keep it from the earth.
NORFOLK   Surely, sir,
There's in him stuff that puts him to these ends;   58
For being not propped by ancestry, whose grace
Chalks successors their way, nor called upon   60
For high feats done to the crown, neither allied   61
To eminent assistants, but spiderlike,   62
Out of his self-drawing web, 'a gives us note,   63
The force of his own merit makes his way—
A gift that heaven gives for him, which buys
A place next to the King.

1.1. Location: London. The royal court.
2 saw saw each other   **3 fresh** untired   **4 what I saw there** (Norfolk's description is of the famous meeting of Henry VIII and Francis I of France in 1520. It was near Calais, at the Field of the Cloth of Gold, so called because of the magnificence of the display.)   **ague** fever   **5 Stayed** kept   **7 vale of Andren** (The name, more properly *Ardres*, appears as *Andren* in Holinshed.)   **9 lighted** alighted, dismounted   **10 as** as if   **11 Which had they** i.e., if they had grown together. **weighed** equaled in weight   **16 following** succeeding   **17 master** teacher, model   **18 its** its own   **19 clinquant** glittering   **20 they** i.e., the English   **21 India** i.e., seem as wealthy as the West Indies or India   **23 gilt** (Carved statues of cherubim in churches were often gilded.)   **madams** ladies   **25 pride** finery.   **that** so that   **26 Was . . . painting** i.e., flushed them as though with cosmetics   **27 cried** declared, extolled as   **30 As . . . them** i.e., when they appeared   **30–31 him . . . praise** the one in view at the moment received the praise

32 discerner beholder   **33 Durst** dared.   **censure** judgment (of one above the other)   **36 that . . . story** so that stories previously thought fabulous   **37 got credit** gained credibility   **38 Bevis** the fourteenth-century romance *Bevis of Hampton*   **39–40 belong . . . honesty** am of noble rank and love truth with honorable regard   **40 tract** telling; course   **42 Which . . . to** which would be best described by the event itself   **43 rebelled** jarred   **44–45 Order . . . function** everything appeared in its proper place, and every official performed his function without confusion   **47 sport** entertainment   **48 certes** certainly.   **promises no element** i.e., is out of his element   **51 Cardinal of York** i.e., Cardinal Wolsey   **52 speed** prosper   **54 fierce** extravagant   **55 keech** (Literally, fat of a slaughtered animal rolled into a lump; applied to Wolsey, who was reputed to be a butcher's son.)   **56 sun** i.e., King Henry   **58 stuff . . . him** traits that whet him on   **60 Chalks . . . way** indicates the path noble descendants are to follow   **61 high feats** great services   **61–62 allied . . . assistants** connected with high officials of the crown   **63 self-drawing** spun out of his own entrails.   **'a . . . note** he lets us know

ABERGAVENNY   I cannot tell
 What heaven hath given him—let some graver eye
 Pierce into that—but I can see his pride
 Peep through each part of him. Whence has he that?
 If not from hell, the devil is a niggard,
 Or has given all before, and he begins   71
 A new hell in himself.
BUCKINGHAM   Why the devil,
 Upon this French going-out, took he upon him, 73
 Without the privity o' the King, t' appoint   74
 Who should attend on him? He makes up the file 75
 Of all the gentry, for the most part such
 To whom as great a charge as little honor   77
 He meant to lay upon; and his own letter,   78
 The honorable board of council out,   79
 Must fetch him in he papers.
ABERGAVENNY   I do know   80
 Kinsmen of mine, three at the least, that have
 By this so sickened their estates that never   82
 They shall abound as formerly.
BUCKINGHAM   O, many   83
 Have broke their backs with laying manors on 'em 84
 For this great journey. What did this vanity 85
 But minister communication of   86
 A most poor issue?
NORFOLK   Grievingly I think   87
 The peace between the French and us not values 88
 The cost that did conclude it.
BUCKINGHAM   Every man,
 After the hideous storm that followed, was   90
 A thing inspired, and, not consulting, broke 91
 Into a general prophecy: that this tempest,   92
 Dashing the garment of this peace, aboded 93
 The sudden breach on 't.
NORFOLK   Which is budded out; 94
 For France hath flawed the league and hath attached 95
 Our merchants' goods at Bordeaux.
ABERGAVENNY   Is it therefore
 Th' ambassador is silenced?
NORFOLK   Marry, is 't.   97
ABERGAVENNY
 A proper title of a peace, and purchased   98
 At a superfluous rate!
BUCKINGHAM   Why, all this business 99
 Our reverend cardinal carried.

---

71 **he** i.e., Wolsey 73 **going-out** expedition, display 74 **Without
. . . King** without the King's being privy (to his plan) 75 **file** list
77–78 **To . . . upon** (i.e., the Cardinal imposed charges for defraying
the expenses of the costly interview on those noblemen to whom he
gave places of little honor) 78 **letter** i.e., summons 79 **out** not consulted 80 **Must . . . papers** compels the cooperation of every person
he cites. **he papers** whomever he lists 82 **sickened** i.e., depleted
83 **abound** thrive 84 **laying . . . 'em** i.e., pawning estates for ward-
robes 85 **What . . . vanity** i.e., what did this extravagance accomplish 86–87 **minister . . . issue** provide occasion for a conference
that had little value, poor results 88 **not values** is not worth 90 **hideous storm** (Holinshed reports such a storm that interrupted the festivities and was taken as a prognostication.) 91 **consulting** i.e., each
other 92 **general** common to all 93 **aboded** foretold 94 **on 't** of it.
is budded out i.e., has come to pass 95 **flawed** broken. **attached**
seized 97 **Marry** (An oath, originally "by the Virgin Mary.") 98 **A
proper . . . peace** a fine business to give the name of peace to
99 **superfluous rate** excessive price

NORFOLK   Like it Your Grace, 100
 The state takes notice of the private difference
 Betwixt you and the Cardinal. I advise you—
 And take it from a heart that wishes towards you
 Honor and plenteous safety—that you read 104
 The Cardinal's malice and his potency
 Together; to consider further that   106
 What his high hatred would effect wants not 107
 A minister in his power. You know his nature, 108
 That he's revengeful, and I know his sword
 Hath a sharp edge; it's long, and 't may be said
 It reaches far, and where 'twill not extend,
 Thither he darts it. Bosom up my counsel; 112
 You'll find it wholesome. Lo, where comes that rock 113
 That I advise your shunning.   114

  *Enter Cardinal Wolsey, the purse borne before him,
  certain of the guard, and two Secretaries with
  papers. The Cardinal in his passage fixeth his eye
  on Buckingham, and Buckingham on him, both
  full of disdain.*

WOLSEY [*to a secretary*]
 The Duke of Buckingham's surveyor, ha? 115
 Where's his examination?
SECRETARY   Here, so please you. 116
         [*He gives a paper.*]
WOLSEY
 Is he in person ready?
SECRETARY   Ay, please your Grace.
WOLSEY
 Well, we shall then know more, and Buckingham
 Shall lessen this big look.   119
     Exeunt Cardinal and his train.
BUCKINGHAM
 This butcher's cur is venom-mouthed, and I 120
 Have not the power to muzzle him; therefore best
 Not wake him in his slumber. A beggar's book 122
 Outworths a noble's blood.
NORFOLK   What, are you chafed? 123
 Ask God for temp'rance; that's th' appliance only 124
 Which your disease requires.
BUCKINGHAM   I read in 's looks
 Matter against me, and his eye reviled   126
 Me as his abject object. At this instant   127
 He bores me with some trick. He's gone to the King; 128
 I'll follow and outstare him.
NORFOLK   Stay, my lord,
 And let your reason with your choler question 130
 What 'tis you go about. To climb steep hills
 Requires slow pace at first. Anger is like

---

100 **carried** supervised. **Like it** may it please 104 **read** estimate, interpret 106 **Together** i.e., as equally strong 107–108 **wants . . .
power** is not without an agent under his control 112 **Bosom up** take
to heart and shut up in your bosom 113 **wholesome** beneficial
114 **s.d. purse** i.e., containing the great seal, pertaining to Wolsey as
Lord Chancellor 115 **surveyor** overseer of a household or estate
116 **examination** deposition 119 **big** haughty 120 **butcher's cur**
(Another dig at Wolsey's reputed lowly origin.) 122 **book** book
learning 123 **blood** noble descent. **chafed** angry 124 **appliance
only** only remedy 126 **Matter against** quarrel with 127 **abject** cast-
off, rejected 128 **bores** undermines, cheats 130 **question** debate,
discuss

A full hot horse who, being allowed his way,   133
Self-mettle tires him. Not a man in England   134
Can advise me like you. Be to yourself
As you would to your friend.
BUCKINGHAM   I'll to the King,
And from a mouth of honor quite cry down   137
This Ipswich fellow's insolence, or proclaim   138
There's difference in no persons.
NORFOLK   Be advised;   139
Heat not a furnace for your foe so hot
That it do singe yourself. We may outrun
By violent swiftness that which we run at,
And lose by overrunning. Know you not
The fire that mounts the liquor till 't run o'er   144
In seeming to augment it wastes it? Be advised.
I say again there is no English soul
More stronger to direct you than yourself,
If with the sap of reason you would quench
Or but allay the fire of passion.
BUCKINGHAM   Sir,   149
I am thankful to you, and I'll go along
By your prescription. But this top-proud fellow,   151
Whom from the flow of gall I name not, but   152
From sincere motions, by intelligence,   153
And proofs as clear as founts in July when   154
We see each grain of gravel, I do know
To be corrupt and treasonous.
NORFOLK   Say not "treasonous."
BUCKINGHAM
To th' King I'll say 't, and make my vouch as strong   157
As shore of rock. Attend. This holy fox,
Or wolf, or both—for he is equal ravenous   159
As he is subtle, and as prone to mischief
As able to perform 't—his mind and place   161
Infecting one another, yea, reciprocally,
Only to show his pomp as well in France
As here at home, suggests the King our master   164
To this last costly treaty, th' interview   165
That swallowed so much treasure and like a glass
Did break i' the wrenching.
NORFOLK   Faith, and so it did.   167
BUCKINGHAM
Pray, give me favor, sir. This cunning cardinal   168
The articles o' the combination drew   169
As himself pleased; and they were ratified
As he cried "Thus let be," to as much end   171
As give a crutch to th' dead. But our count-cardinal   172
Has done this, and 'tis well; for worthy Wolsey,
Who cannot err, he did it. Now this follows,

Which, as I take it, is a kind of puppy
To th' old dam, treason: Charles the Emperor,   176
Under pretense to see the Queen his aunt—
For 'twas indeed his color, but he came   178
To whisper Wolsey—here makes visitation;   179
His fears were that the interview betwixt
England and France might through their amity
Breed him some prejudice, for from this league
Peeped harms that menaced him; privily   183
Deals with our cardinal, and, as I trow—   184
Which I do well, for I am sure the Emperor
Paid ere he promised, whereby his suit was granted
Ere it was asked—but when the way was made
And paved with gold, the Emperor thus desired
That he would please to alter the King's course   189
And break the foresaid peace. Let the King know,
As soon he shall by me, that thus the Cardinal
Does buy and sell his honor as he pleases,   192
And for his own advantage.
NORFOLK   I am sorry
To hear this of him, and could wish he were
Something mistaken in 't.
BUCKINGHAM   No, not a syllable.   195
I do pronounce him in that very shape
He shall appear in proof.   197

Enter Brandon, a Sergeant at Arms before him,
and two or three of the guard.

BRANDON
Your office, Sergeant: execute it.
SERGEANT   Sir,
My lord the Duke of Buckingham, and Earl
Of Hereford, Stafford, and Northampton, I
Arrest thee of high treason, in the name
Of our most sovereign king.
BUCKINGHAM [*to Norfolk*]   Lo, you, my lord,
The net has fall'n upon me! I shall perish
Under device and practice.
BRANDON   I am sorry   204
To see you ta'en from liberty, to look on   205
The business present. 'Tis His Highness' pleasure
You shall to the Tower.
BUCKINGHAM   It will help me nothing   207
To plead mine innocence, for that dye is on me
Which makes my whit'st part black. The will of
   heaven
Be done in this and all things! I obey.
O my Lord Aberga'nny, fare you well.
BRANDON
Nay, he must bear you company. [*To Abergavenny.*]
   The King
Is pleased you shall to the Tower, till you know

133 full hot high-spirited   **134 Self-mettle** his own ardent spirits
137 of honor i.e., of a gentleman   **138 Ipswich** (Wolsey's birthplace)
139 difference distinctions in rank.   **Be advised** take care
144 mounts causes (by boiling) to rise   **149 allay** temper, moderate
151 top-proud supremely proud   **152 from . . . gall** i.e., from
promptings of anger   **153 motions** motives.   **intelligence** secret information   **154 founts** springs   **157 vouch** assertion, allegation
159 equal equally   **161 place** office, rank   **164 suggests** incites
165 last latest, recent.   **interview** i.e., Field of the Cloth of Gold
167 wrenching rough handling, rinsing   **168 favor** attention   **169 articles o' the combination** terms of the peace treaty   **171 end** purpose
172 count-cardinal i.e., cardinal putting on the airs of an aristocrat

176 dam mother (used especially of animals).   **Charles** i.e., Charles
V, Holy Roman Emperor, nephew of Queen Katharine. (Charles had
much to fear from an English-French alliance.)   **178 color** pretext
179 whisper whisper to   **183 privily** secretly   **184 trow** believe
189 he Wolsey   **192 his** King Henry's.   **he** Wolsey   **195 Something
mistaken** somewhat misrepresented   **197 in proof** in experience
204 device and practice stratagems and plots   **205 to look on** i.e.,
and sorry to witness   **207 nothing** not at all

How he determines further.

ABERGAVENNY   As the Duke said,
The will of heaven be done and the King's pleasure
By me obeyed!

BRANDON   Here is a warrant from
The King t' attach Lord Montacute and the bodies   217
Of the Duke's confessor, John de la Car,   218
One Gilbert Perk, his chancellor—

BUCKINGHAM   So, so;   219
These are the limbs o' the plot. No more, I hope?

BRANDON
A monk o' the Chartreux.

BUCKINGHAM   O, Nicholas Hopkins?

BRANDON   He.   221

BUCKINGHAM
My surveyor is false. The o'er-great Cardinal
Hath showed him gold; my life is spanned already.   223
I am the shadow of poor Buckingham,   224
Whose figure even this instant cloud puts on,   225
By darkening my clear sun. My lord, farewell.   226
                                    Exeunt.

❖

1.2   *Cornets. Enter King Henry, leaning on the
          Cardinal's shoulder, the nobles, and Sir Thomas
          Lovell. The Cardinal places himself under the
          King's feet on his right side. [The Cardinal's
          Secretary attends him.]*

KING *[to Wolsey]*
My life itself, and the best heart of it,   1
Thanks you for this great care. I stood i' the level 2
Of a full-charged confederacy, and give thanks   3
To you that choked it. Let be called before us
That gentleman of Buckingham's. In person   5
I'll hear him his confessions justify,   6
And point by point the treasons of his master
He shall again relate.   8

          *A noise within, crying "Room for the Queen!"
          Enter the Queen [Katharine], ushered by the Duke
          of Norfolk, and [the Duke of] Suffolk. She kneels.
          [The] King riseth from his state, takes her up,
          kisses and placeth her by him.*

KATHARINE
Nay, we must longer kneel. I am a suitor.

KING
Arise, and take place by us. Half your suit

Never name to us; you have half our power.
The other moiety ere you ask is given.   12
Repeat your will and take it.

KATHARINE   Thank Your Majesty.   13
That you would love yourself, and in that love
Not unconsidered leave your honor nor
The dignity of your office, is the point
Of my petition.

KING   Lady mine, proceed.

KATHARINE
I am solicited, not by a few,
And those of true condition, that your subjects   19
Are in great grievance. There have been
     commissions   20
Sent down among 'em which hath flawed the heart   21
Of all their loyalties; wherein, although,
My good lord Cardinal, they vent reproaches
Most bitterly on you, as putter-on   24
Of these exactions, yet the King our master—
Whose honor heaven shield from soil!—even he
     escapes not   26
Language unmannerly, yea, such which breaks
The sides of loyalty and almost appears
In loud rebellion.

NORFOLK   Not "almost appears,"
It doth appear; for, upon these taxations,
The clothiers all, not able to maintain
The many to them 'longing, have put off   32
The spinsters, carders, fullers, weavers, who,   33
Unfit for other life, compelled by hunger
And lack of other means, in desperate manner
Daring th' event to th' teeth, are all in uproar,   36
And danger serves among them.

KING   Taxation?   37
Wherein? And what taxation? My lord Cardinal,
You that are blamed for it alike with us,
Know you of this taxation?

WOLSEY   Please you, sir,
I know but of a single part in aught   41
Pertains to the state, and front but in that file   42
Where others tell steps with me.

KATHARINE   No, my lord?   43
You know no more than others? But you frame   44
Things that are known alike, which are not
     wholesome   45
To those which would not know them and yet must   46
Perforce be their acquaintance. These exactions,   47

217 **attach** arrest   218, 219 **John de la Car, Gilbert Perk** (The names
are from Holinshed's account: "Master John de la Car, alias de la
Court, the Duke's confessor, and Sir Gilbert Perke, priest, the Duke's
chancellor.")   221 **Chartreux** Carthusian order   223 **spanned** measured   224–226 **I am . . . sun** I am the mere semblance of my
former self, whose form and future hopes are obscured in this sudden
cloud of affliction by the darkening of my king's favor
1.2. Location: London. The council chamber.
s.d. under . . . feet i.e., at the foot of the royal dais   1 **best heart**
most essential part   2 **level** aim, line of fire   3 **full-charged confederacy** fully loaded conspiracy   5 **That . . . Buckingham's** i.e., Buckingham's surveyor (1.1.115), whom Wolsey has induced to testify against
his master   6 **justify** prove, confirm   8 **s.d. state** chair of state, raised
seat with a canopy

12 **moiety** half   13 **Repeat your will** express your desire   19 **true
condition** disposition to loyalty   20 **grievance** distress.   **commissions**
writs authorizing a tax levy, and the agents to carry them out
21 **flawed** damaged, cracked   24 **putter-on** instigator   26 **soil** moral
stain   32 **to them 'longing** in their employ.   **put off** laid off
33 **spinsters** spinners.   **carders** those who comb wool for impurities.
fullers those who beat wool to clean it   36 **Daring . . . teeth** defiantly challenging the outcome   37 **danger . . . them** mischief has
joined in their unrest   41–42 **a single . . . state** one individual's
share in state affairs   42–43 **front . . . me** take my place merely in
the front rank with others who share the responsibility.   **tell steps**
keep step, march   44–47 **you frame . . . acquaintance** you devise
measures known to all (the Council) which are harmful to those who
would much prefer not to be acquainted with them and yet must perforce put up with them

Whereof my sovereign would have note, they are   48
Most pestilent to the hearing, and to bear 'em
The back is sacrifice to the load. They say   50
They are devised by you, or else you suffer
Too hard an exclamation.
KING   Still exaction!   52
The nature of it? In what kind, let's know,
Is this exaction?
KATHARINE   I am much too venturous
In tempting of your patience, but am boldened   55
Under your promised pardon. The subjects' grief   56
Comes through commissions, which compels from
    each
The sixth part of his substance, to be levied   58
Without delay; and the pretense for this   59
Is named your wars in France. This makes bold
    mouths,
Tongues spit their duties out, and cold hearts freeze
Allegiance in them. Their curses now
Live where their prayers did, and it's come to pass
This tractable obedience is a slave   64
To each incensèd will. I would Your Highness   65
Would give it quick consideration, for
There is no primer business.
KING   By my life,   67
This is against our pleasure.
WOLSEY   And for me,
I have no further gone in this than by   69
A single voice, and that not passed me but   70
By learnèd approbation of the judges. If I am   71
Traduced by ignorant tongues, which neither know   72
My faculties nor person, yet will be   73
The chronicles of my doing, let me say
'Tis but the fate of place, and the rough brake   75
That virtue must go through. We must not stint   76
Our necessary actions in the fear
To cope malicious censurers, which ever,   78
As ravenous fishes, do a vessel follow
That is new trimmed, but benefit no further   80
Than vainly longing. What we oft do best,   81
By sick interpreters, once weak ones, is   82
Not ours, or not allowed; what worst, as oft   83
Hitting a grosser quality, is cried up   84
For our best act. If we shall stand still,   85
In fear our motion will be mocked or carped at,   86
We should take root here where we sit,
Or sit, state-statues only.

KING   Things done well,   88
And with a care, exempt themselves from fear;
Things done without example, in their issue   90
Are to be feared. Have you a precedent
Of this commission? I believe, not any.   92
We must not rend our subjects from our laws   93
And stick them in our will. Sixth part of each?   94
A trembling contribution! Why, we take   95
From every tree lop, bark, and part o' the timber,   96
And though we leave it with a root, thus hacked,
The air will drink the sap. To every county
Where this is questioned send our letters with   99
Free pardon to each man that has denied
The force of this commission. Pray look to 't;   101
I put it to your care.
WOLSEY [aside to his Secretary]   A word with you.
Let there be letters writ to every shire
Of the King's grace and pardon. The grieved
    commons   104
Hardly conceive of me; let it be noised   105
That through our intercession this revokement
And pardon comes. I shall anon advise you   107
Further in the proceeding.   Exit Secretary.

    Enter Surveyor.

KATHARINE
I am sorry that the Duke of Buckingham
Is run in your displeasure.
KING   It grieves many.   110
The gentleman is learned, and a most rare speaker,
To nature none more bound; his training such   112
That he may furnish and instruct great teachers
And never seek for aid out of himself. Yet see,   114
When these so noble benefits shall prove
Not well disposed, the mind growing once corrupt,   116
They turn to vicious forms, ten times more ugly
Than ever they were fair. This man so complete,   118
Who was enrolled 'mongst wonders, and when we,
Almost with ravished listening, could not find
His hour of speech a minute—he, my lady,
Hath into monstrous habits put the graces   122
That once were his, and is become as black
As if besmeared in hell. Sit by us. You shall hear—
This was his gentleman in trust—of him
Things to strike honor sad.—Bid him recount
The fore-recited practices, whereof   127
We cannot feel too little, hear too much.   128
WOLSEY
Stand forth, and with bold spirit relate what you,

48 note knowledge **50 is sacrifice to** i.e., is bowed down under **52 exclamation** reproach **55 boldened** made bold **56 grief** grievance **58 substance** wealth **59 pretense** pretext **64 tractable** i.e., once docile **64–65 is . . . will** is overmastered by angry defiance **67 primer** more urgent **69–70 I have . . . voice** i.e., my part in this was only to cast one vote in the Council, or to act by unanimous consent **71 approbation** approval. **the judges** those making judgment in the King's Privy Council **72 Traduced** defamed **73 faculties** qualities **75 place** high office. **brake** thicket **76 stint** stop **78 To cope** of encountering. **ever** always **80 new trimmed** newly fitted out **81–85 What . . . act** often our best deeds are, by malicous or sometimes weak-witted critics, either not credited to us or else disapproved of; our worst efforts, meantime, appealing to vulgar natures, are called the best things we've done **86 In fear** for fear that

88 state-statues mere statues of statesmen **90 example** precedent. **issue** consequences **92 Of** for **93 rend** tear **94 stick . . . will** make them the victims of our caprice **95 trembling** fearful, causing to tremble **96 lop** branches **99 questioned** disputed **101 force** validity **104 grace** mercy. **grieved** aggrieved **105 Hardly conceive** have a bad opinion. **noised** reported, rumored **107 anon** soon **110 Is run in** has incurred **112 To . . . bound** none more indebted to nature for talents **114 out of** beyond **116 disposed** applied **118 complete** accomplished **122 habits** garments, i.e., shapes **127 practices** intrigues **127–128 whereof . . . much** i.e., of which it behooves us to hear for our own safety, however painful it is to feel

Most like a careful subject, have collected   130
Out of the Duke of Buckingham.
KING   Speak freely.
SURVEYOR
First, it was usual with him—every day
It would infect his speech—that if the King
Should without issue die, he'll carry it so   134
To make the scepter his. These very words
I've heard him utter to his son-in-law,
Lord Aberga'nny, to whom by oath he menaced
Revenge upon the Cardinal.
WOLSEY   Please Your Highness, note
This dangerous conception in this point.
Not friended by his wish to your high person,   140
His will is most malignant, and it stretches
Beyond you to your friends.
KATHARINE   My learned lord Cardinal,
Deliver all with charity.
KING   Speak on.   143
How grounded he his title to the crown
Upon our fail? To this point hast thou heard him   145
At any time speak aught?
SURVEYOR   He was brought to this
By a vain prophecy of Nicholas Henton.   147
KING
What was that Henton?
SURVEYOR   Sir, a Chartreux friar,
His confessor, who fed him every minute
With words of sovereignty.
KING   How know'st thou this?   150
SURVEYOR
Not long before Your Highness sped to France,
The Duke being at the Rose, within the parish   152
Saint Lawrence Poultney, did of me demand
What was the speech among the Londoners   154
Concerning the French journey. I replied,
Men feared the French would prove perfidious,
To the King's danger. Presently the Duke   157
Said, 'twas the fear indeed, and that he doubted   158
'Twould prove the verity of certain words
Spoke by a holy monk, "that oft," says he,
"Hath sent to me, wishing me to permit
John de la Car, my chaplain, a choice hour
To hear from him a matter of some moment;   163
Whom after under the confession's seal
He solemnly had sworn that what he spoke
My chaplain to no creature living but
To me should utter, with demure confidence   167
This pausingly ensued: 'Neither the King nor 's heirs,
Tell you the Duke, shall prosper. Bid him strive
To gain the love o' the commonalty; the Duke
Shall govern England.' "

KATHARINE   If I know you well,
You were the Duke's surveyor, and lost your office
On the complaint o' the tenants. Take good heed
You charge not in your spleen a noble person   174
And spoil your nobler soul. I say, take heed;
Yes, heartily beseech you.
KING   Let him on.—   176
Go forward.
SURVEYOR   On my soul, I'll speak but truth.
I told my lord the Duke, by the devil's illusions
The monk might be deceived, and that 'twas
dangerous
To ruminate on this so far until
It forged him some design, which, being believed,   181
It was much like to do. He answered, "Tush,   182
It can do me no damage," adding further
That, had the King in his last sickness failed,   184
The Cardinal's and Sir Thomas Lovell's heads
Should have gone off.
KING   Ha? What, so rank? Aha,
There's mischief in this man.—Canst thou say
further?
SURVEYOR
I can, my liege.
KING   Proceed.
SURVEYOR   Being at Greenwich,
After Your Highness had reproved the Duke
About Sir William Bulmer—
KING   I remember
Of such a time. Being my sworn servant,
The Duke retained him his. But on; what hence?   192
SURVEYOR
"If," quoth he, "I for this had been committed,
As to the Tower I thought, I would have played
The part my father meant to act upon   195
Th' usurper Richard, who, being at Salisbury,
Made suit to come in 's presence, which if granted,
As he made semblance of his duty, would   198
Have put his knife into him."
KING   A giant traitor!
WOLSEY
Now, madam, may His Highness live in freedom,   200
And this man out of prison?
KATHARINE   God mend all!
KING
There's something more would out of thee. What
sayst?
SURVEYOR
After "the Duke his father," with "the knife,"
He stretched him, and, with one hand on his dagger,   204
Another spread on 's breast, mounting his eyes,   205
He did discharge a horrible oath, whose tenor
Was, were he evil used, he would outgo   207

130 collected i.e., learned by spying   134 issue offspring.   carry it so manage affairs so as   140 Not . . . person his wish (that the King die childless) being ungratified   143 Deliver tell   145 fail i.e., dying without an heir   147 Henton (According to Holinshed, an alias for Nicholas Hopkins; see 1.1.221.)   150 of sovereignty about gaining sovereign power   152 the Rose (A manor house belonging to Buckingham.)   154 speech talk   157 Presently immediately   158 doubted feared, suspected   163 moment importance   167 demure grave, solemn

174 spleen malice   176 on go on   181 forged him caused him to fashion.   being believed i.e., if the Duke put faith in what the monk was telling him   182 much like very likely   184 failed died   192 his as his own   195 my father i.e., the Duke of Buckingham of Richard III's time   198 semblance of his duty a show of dutiful kneeling   200 may can   204 stretched him raised himself to his full height   205 mounting raising   207 evil used badly treated

His father by as much as a performance
Does an irresolute purpose.

KING   There's his period,   209
To sheathe his knife in us. He is attached;   210
Call him to present trial. If he may   211
Find mercy in the law, 'tis his; if none,
Let him not seek 't of us. By day and night,
He's traitor to the height.   *Exeunt.*   214

❧

1.3   *Enter Lord Chamberlain and Lord Sands.*

CHAMBERLAIN
Is 't possible the spells of France should juggle   1
Men into such strange mysteries?

SANDS   New customs,   2
Though they be never so ridiculous,
Nay, let 'em be unmanly, yet are followed.

CHAMBERLAIN
As far as I see, all the good our English
Have got by the late voyage is but merely   6
A fit or two o' the face; but they are shrewd ones,   7
For when they hold 'em, you would swear directly   8
Their very noses had been counselors
To Pepin or Clotharius, they keep state so.   10

SANDS
They have all new legs, and lame ones. One would
     take it,   11
That never see 'em pace before, the spavin   12
Or springhalt reigned among 'em.

CHAMBERLAIN   Death, my lord!   13
Their clothes are after such a pagan cut to 't   14
That sure they've worn out Christendom.

Enter Sir Thomas Lovell.

                  How now?   15
What news, Sir Thomas Lovell?

LOVELL   Faith, my lord,
I hear of none but the new proclamation
That's clapped upon the court gate.

CHAMBERLAIN   What is 't for?   18

LOVELL
The reformation of our traveled gallants,
That fill the court with quarrels, talk, and tailors.

CHAMBERLAIN
I'm glad 'tis there. Now I would pray our monsieurs

To think an English courtier may be wise
And never see the Louvre.

LOVELL   They must either—   23
For so run the conditions—leave those remnants
Of fool and feather that they got in France,   25
With all their honorable points of ignorance   26
Pertaining thereunto, as fights and fireworks,   27
Abusing better men than they can be
Out of a foreign wisdom, renouncing clean   29
The faith they have in tennis and tall stockings,
Short blistered breeches, and those types of travel,   31
And understand again like honest men,   32
Or pack to their old playfellows. There, I take it,   33
They may, *cum privilegio,* "oui" away   34
The lag end of their lewdness and be laughed at.   35

SANDS
'Tis time to give 'em physic, their diseases   36
Are grown so catching.

CHAMBERLAIN   What a loss our ladies
Will have of these trim vanities!

LOVELL   Ay, marry,   38
There will be woe indeed, lords. The sly whoresons
Have got a speeding trick to lay down ladies;   40
A French song and a fiddle has no fellow.   41

SANDS
The devil fiddle 'em! I am glad they are going,
For sure there's no converting of 'em. Now
An honest country lord, as I am, beaten
A long time out of play, may bring his plainsong   45
And have an hour of hearing, and, by 'r Lady,
Held current music too.

CHAMBERLAIN   Well said, Lord Sands.   47
Your colt's tooth is not cast yet?

SANDS   No, my lord,   48
Nor shall not while I have a stump.

CHAMBERLAIN   Sir Thomas,   49
Whither were you a-going?

LOVELL   To the Cardinal's.
Your lordship is a guest too.

CHAMBERLAIN   O, 'tis true.
This night he makes a supper, and a great one,   52
To many lords and ladies. There will be
The beauty of this kingdom, I'll assure you.

LOVELL
That churchman bears a bounteous mind indeed,
A hand as fruitful as the land that feeds us;   56

---

209 irresolute unaccomplished. **period** aim, goal   **210 attached** arrested   **211 present** immediate   **214 to the height** in the highest degree
1.3. Location: London. The royal court.
1 juggle beguile, bewitch   **2 mysteries** artificial fashions   **6 the late voyage** i.e., to the Field of the Cloth of Gold   **7 fit . . . face** affected ways of screwing up the face into a grimace   **8 hold 'em** i.e., maintain the grimaces   **10 Pepin, Clotharius** kings of ancient France in the sixth and seventh centuries. **keep state** i.e., behave with an affected dignity   **11 legs** mannerisms of walking and making obeisances   **12 see** saw. **pace** walk. **spavin** disease of horses causing swelling of joints and lameness   **13 springhalt** nervous twitching in a horse's hind legs. **Death** by God's death. (An oath.)   **14 after . . . to 't** made so after the pagan fashion, moreover   **15 they've . . . Christendom** they have exhausted the repertory of Christian fashions   **18 clapped** placed

23 Louvre royal palace in France, seat of the French court   **25 fool and feather** i.e., folly and fashion   **26 honorable . . . ignorance** i.e., what they ignorantly regard as honorable   **27 as** such as. **fireworks** (With added suggestion of "whores.")   **29 renouncing** i.e., as a way of leaving their folly   **31 blistered** puffed. **types** badges, marks   **32 understand** (1) comprehend (2) use their legs to "stand under" them   **33 pack** be off   **34 cum privilegio** with exclusive right, immunity   **34–35 "oui" . . . lewdness** i.e., in French manner pass the remainder of their worthless lives   **36 physic** purging medicine   **38 trim vanities** finely dressed but worthless dandies   **40 speeding** successful. **lay down** seduce   **41 fiddle** (With sexual suggestion of something to fiddle with.) **fellow** equal   **45 play** i.e., playing love games. **plainsong** simple melody or air   **47 Held current** regarded as fashionable   **48 colt's tooth** i.e., lecherousness of youth. **cast** shed, cast aside   **49 stump** i.e., of a tooth (with a bawdy pun)   **52 makes** gives   **56 fruitful** generous

His dews fall everywhere.

CHAMBERLAIN   No doubt he's noble;
He had a black mouth that said other of him.   58

SANDS
He may, my lord. H'as wherewithal: in him   59
Sparing would show a worse sin than ill doctrine.   60
Men of his way should be most liberal;   61
They are set here for examples.

CHAMBERLAIN   True, they are so;
But few now give so great ones. My barge stays;   63
Your lordship shall along. Come, good Sir Thomas,   64
We shall be late else, which I would not be,   65
For I was spoke to, with Sir Henry Guildford,   66
This night to be comptrollers.

SANDS   I am your lordship's.   67
                                    Exeunt.

❧

1.4   *Hautboys. A small table under a state for the
Cardinal, a longer table for the guests. Then enter
Anne Bullen and divers other ladies and gentlemen
as guests, at one door; at another door enter Sir
Henry Guildford.*

GUILDFORD
Ladies, a general welcome from His Grace
Salutes ye all. This night he dedicates
To fair content and you. None here, he hopes,
In all this noble bevy, has brought with her   4
One care abroad. He would have all as merry
As, first, good company, good wine, good welcome
Can make good people.

        *Enter Lord Chamberlain, Lord Sands, and [Sir
        Thomas] Lovell.*
                            O my lord, you're tardy.
The very thought of this fair company
Clapped wings to me.

CHAMBERLAIN   You are young, Sir Harry Guildford.

SANDS
Sir Thomas Lovell, had the Cardinal
But half my lay thoughts in him, some of these   11
Should find a running banquet ere they rested,   12
I think would better please 'em. By my life,   13
They are a sweet society of fair ones.

LOVELL
O, that your lordship were but now confessor
To one or two of these!

SANDS   I would I were;
They should find easy penance.

LOVELL   Faith, how easy?

SANDS
As easy as a down bed would afford it.

CHAMBERLAIN
Sweet ladies, will it please you sit? Sir Harry,
Place you that side; I'll take the charge of this.   20
        [*The guests are shown their places at table.*]
His Grace is entering. Nay, you must not freeze;
Two women placed together makes cold weather.
My Lord Sands, you are one will keep 'em waking;   23
Pray, sit between these ladies.

SANDS   By my faith,
And thank your lordship. By your leave, sweet
    ladies.   [*He takes a place between Anne Bullen
                            and another lady.*]
If I chance to talk a little wild, forgive me;
I had it from my father.

ANNE   Was he mad, sir?

SANDS
O, very mad, exceeding mad, in love too.
But he would bite none; just as I do now,
He would kiss you twenty with a breath.   30
                            [*He kisses her.*]

CHAMBERLAIN   Well said, my lord.   31
So, now you're fairly seated. Gentlemen,
The penance lies on you if these fair ladies
Pass away frowning.

SANDS   For my little cure,   34
Let me alone.   35

        *Hautboys. Enter Cardinal Wolsey and takes his
        state.*

WOLSEY
You're welcome, my fair guests. That noble lady
Or gentleman that is not freely merry
Is not my friend. This, to confirm my welcome;
And to you all, good health!   [*He drinks.*]

SANDS   Your Grace is noble.
Let me have such a bowl may hold my thanks   40
And save me so much talking.

WOLSEY   My Lord Sands,   41
I am beholding to you. Cheer your neighbors.   42
Ladies, you are not merry. Gentlemen,
Whose fault is this?

SANDS   The red wine first must rise
In their fair cheeks, my lord; then we shall have 'em
Talk us to silence.

ANNE   You are a merry gamester,   46
My Lord Sands.

SANDS   Yes, if I make my play.   47

58 **He . . . mouth** a person must have an evil habit of speech
59 **H'as wherewithal** he has the necessary means   60 **Sparing** frugality.   **show** appear.   **ill doctrine** heresy   61 **way** way of life   63 **ones**
examples.   **stays** waits for me   64 **along** come along   65 **else** otherwise   66 **spoke to** asked   67 **comptrollers** stewards, masters of ceremonies
1.4. Location: Westminster. A hall in York Place.
s.d. Hautboys reed instruments related to the modern oboe.   **state**
canopy   4 **bevy** company   11 **lay** secular   12 **running banquet** hasty
meal (with amorous suggestion of pursuit and sensuous indulgence,
found also in *lay*, line 11, *confessor, easy penance*, etc.)   13 **I think**
i.e., which I think

20 **Place you** assign places on   23 **waking** i.e., lively   30 **kiss you**
kiss. (*You* is used colloquially to acknowledge the person addressed.)
twenty i.e., twenty women.   **with a breath** at one breath   31 **said**
done   34 **For** as for.   **cure** (1) remedy to prevent frowning (2) cure of
souls (continuing the ecclesiastical metaphor of lines 15 and 33)
35 **Let me alone** leave it to me.   **s.d. state** chair of state   40 **may** as
may   41 **And . . . talking** i.e., and let me express my thanks by
drinking a toast   42 **beholding** beholden.   **Cheer** entertain
46 **gamester** sportful, frolicsome person. (But Sands, in his reply,
plays on the sense of "gambler.")   47 **make my play** win my game
(of love)

Here's to your ladyship; and pledge it, madam,   48
For 'tis to such a thing—
ANNE   You cannot show me.   49
SANDS [to Wolsey]
I told Your Grace they would talk anon.
                    Drum and trumpet. Chambers discharged.
WOLSEY   What's that?   50
CHAMBERLAIN
Look out there, some of ye.   [Exit a Servant.]
WOLSEY   What warlike voice,
And to what end, is this? Nay, ladies, fear not;
By all the laws of war you're privileged.   53

            Enter a Servant.

CHAMBERLAIN
How now? What is 't?
SERVANT   A noble troop of strangers,   54
For so they seem. They've left their barge and
    landed,
And hither make, as great ambassadors   56
From foreign princes.
WOLSEY   Good Lord Chamberlain,
Go give 'em welcome; you can speak the French
    tongue;
And, pray, receive 'em nobly and conduct 'em
Into our presence, where this heaven of beauty
Shall shine at full upon them. Some attend him.
                    [Exit Chamberlain, attended.]
                    All rise, and tables removed.
You have now a broken banquet, but we'll mend it.
A good digestion to you all! And once more
I shower a welcome on ye. Welcome all!

        Hautboys. Enter King and others, as masquers,
        habited like shepherds, ushered by the Lord
        Chamberlain. They pass directly before the
        Cardinal and gracefully salute him.

A noble company! What are their pleasures?
CHAMBERLAIN
Because they speak no English, thus they prayed
To tell Your Grace that, having heard by fame   67
Of this so noble and so fair assembly
This night to meet here, they could do no less,
Out of the great respect they bear to beauty,
But leave their flocks, and, under your fair conduct,   71
Crave leave to view these ladies and entreat
An hour of revels with 'em.
WOLSEY   Say, Lord Chamberlain,
They have done my poor house grace, for which I
    pay 'em
A thousand thanks, and pray 'em take their
    pleasures.
            Choose ladies; King and Anne Bullen.

48 **pledge it** drink in response to my toast   49 **'tis . . . thing** (Sands proposes his toast in an unfinished sentence that is erotically suggestive.)   **You . . . me** i.e., you can't teach me a lesson in how to drink a toast. (Anne parries the erotic suggestion of Sands by drinking to him.)   50 **s.d. Chambers** small cannon (the firing of which in 1613 probably started the fire that burned down the Globe playhouse)   53 **privileged** i.e., entitled to immunity in the event of conflict   54 **strangers** foreigners   56 **make** come   67 **fame** report   71 **fair conduct** kind permission

KING
The fairest hand I ever touched! O beauty,
Till now I never knew thee!   Music. Dance.
WOLSEY [to the Chamberlain]
My lord!
CHAMBERLAIN   Your Grace?
WOLSEY   Pray, tell 'em thus much from me:
There should be one amongst 'em, by his person,
More worthy this place than myself, to whom,   80
If I but knew him, with my love and duty
I would surrender it.
CHAMBERLAIN   I will, my lord.
                    Whisper [with the masquers].
WOLSEY
What say they?
CHAMBERLAIN   Such a one, they all confess,
There is indeed, which they would have Your Grace
Find out, and he will take it.
WOLSEY   Let me see, then.   85
                [He comes from his chair of state.]
By all your good leaves, gentlemen; here I'll make
My royal choice.   [He bows before the King.]
KING [unmasking]   Ye have found him, Cardinal.
You hold a fair assembly; you do well, lord.
You are a churchman, or I'll tell you, Cardinal,
I should judge now unhappily.
WOLSEY   I am glad   90
Your Grace is grown so pleasant.
KING   My Lord Chamberlain,   91
Prithee, come hither. What fair lady's that?
CHAMBERLAIN
An 't please Your Grace, Sir Thomas Bullen's
    daughter—   93
The Viscount Rochford—one of Her Highness'
    women.
KING
By heaven, she is a dainty one.—Sweetheart,
I were unmannerly to take you out   96
And not to kiss you. [He kisses Anne.] A health,
    gentlemen!   97
Let it go round.   [He offers a toast.]
WOLSEY
Sir Thomas Lovell, is the banquet ready
I' the privy chamber?
LOVELL   Yes, my lord.
WOLSEY   Your Grace,
I fear, with dancing is a little heated.
KING
I fear, too much.
WOLSEY   There's fresher air, my lord,
In the next chamber.
KING
Lead in your ladies every one.—Sweet partner,
I must not yet forsake you.—Let's be merry,
Good my lord Cardinal. I have half a dozen healths
To drink to these fair ladies, and a measure   107

80 **this place** i.e., this chair of state   85 **it** i.e., the chair of state   90 **unhappily** unfavorably (of such a display of wealth)   91 **pleasant** merry   93 **An 't** if it   96 **take you out** lead you out for a dance   97 **health** toast   107 **measure** stately dance

To lead 'em once again; and then let's dream
Who's best in favor. Let the music knock it.   109
                        Exeunt, with trumpets.

❖

2.1   *Enter two Gentlemen, at several doors.*

FIRST GENTLEMAN
    Whither away so fast?
SECOND GENTLEMAN   O, God save ye!
    Ev'n to the hall, to hear what shall become   2
    Of the great Duke of Buckingham.
FIRST GENTLEMAN   I'll save you
    That labor, sir. All's now done but the ceremony
    Of bringing back the prisoner.
SECOND GENTLEMAN   Were you there?
FIRST GENTLEMAN
    Yes, indeed was I.
SECOND GENTLEMAN Pray, speak what has happened.
FIRST GENTLEMAN
    You may guess quickly what.
SECOND GENTLEMAN   Is he found guilty?
FIRST GENTLEMAN
    Yes, truly is he, and condemned upon 't.
SECOND GENTLEMAN
    I am sorry for 't.
FIRST GENTLEMAN So are a number more.
SECOND GENTLEMAN   But pray, how passed it?   10
FIRST GENTLEMAN
    I'll tell you in a little. The great Duke   11
    Came to the bar, where to his accusations
    He pleaded still not guilty and alleged   13
    Many sharp reasons to defeat the law.   14
    The King's attorney on the contrary
    Urged on the examinations, proofs, confessions   16
    Of divers witnesses, which the Duke desired
    To have brought viva voce to his face;   18
    At which appeared against him his surveyor,
    Sir Gilbert Perk his chancellor, and John Car,   20
    Confessor to him, with that devil monk,
    Hopkins, that made this mischief.
SECOND GENTLEMAN   That was he
    That fed him with his prophecies?
FIRST GENTLEMAN   The same.
    All these accused him strongly, which he fain   24
    Would have flung from him, but indeed he could
        not;
    And so his peers, upon this evidence,
    Have found him guilty of high treason. Much
    He spoke, and learnedly, for life; but all
    Was either pitied in him or forgotten.   29

SECOND GENTLEMAN
    After all this, how did he bear himself?
FIRST GENTLEMAN
    When he was brought again to th' bar, to hear
    His knell rung out, his judgment, he was stirred   32
    With such an agony he sweat extremely,
    And something spoke in choler, ill and hasty.   34
    But he fell to himself again, and sweetly   35
    In all the rest showed a most noble patience.
SECOND GENTLEMAN
    I do not think he fears death.
FIRST GENTLEMAN   Sure he does not;
    He never was so womanish. The cause
    He may a little grieve at.
SECOND GENTLEMAN   Certainly
    The Cardinal is the end of this.
FIRST GENTLEMAN   'Tis likely,   40
    By all conjectures: first, Kildare's attainder,   41
    Then deputy of Ireland, who removed,   42
    Earl Surrey was sent thither, and in haste too,
    Lest he should help his father.
SECOND GENTLEMAN   That trick of state   44
    Was a deep envious one.
FIRST GENTLEMAN   At his return   45
    No doubt he will requite it. This is noted,   46
    And generally: whoever the King favors,   47
    The Cardinal instantly will find employment,
    And far enough from court too.
SECOND GENTLEMAN   All the commons
    Hate him perniciously and, o' my conscience,   50
    Wish him ten fathom deep. This duke as much
    They love and dote on, call him bounteous
        Buckingham,
    The mirror of all courtesy—   53

        Enter Buckingham from his arraignment, tipstaves
        before him, the ax with the edge towards him,
        halberds on each side, accompanied with Sir
        Thomas Lovell, Sir Nicholas Vaux, Sir Walter
        Sands, and common people, etc.

FIRST GENTLEMAN   Stay there, sir,
    And see the noble ruined man you speak of.
SECOND GENTLEMAN
    Let's stand close and behold him.
BUCKINGHAM   All good people,   55
    You that thus far have come to pity me,
    Hear what I say, and then go home and lose me.   57
    I have this day received a traitor's judgment,

---

109 **best in favor** best-looking, or, most in favor with the ladies.
knock it strike up
2.1. Location: Westminster. A street.
s.d. several separate   **2 the hall** i.e., Westminster Hall, where the
trial was held   **10 passed it** did it proceed   **11 in a little** in brief
13 alleged brought forward   **14 law** i.e., case against him   **16 examinations** depositions.   **proofs** testimonies   **18 viva voce** so that their
voices could be heard   **20 Sir** (A common courtesy title for a priest.)
24 which i.e., which accusations.   **fain** gladly   **29 Was . . . forgotten** either produced no effect or produced only ineffectual pity

32 **judgment** sentence   **34 choler** anger.   **ill** malevolent   **35 fell to**
recovered   **40 end** cause   **41 Kildare's attainder** i.e., the confiscation
of estates and sentencing to death of the Earl of Kildare, Lord Lieutenant of Ireland (whom Wolsey, according to Holinshed, removed to
make room for Thomas Howard, Earl of Surrey, son-in-law to Buckingham, and thereby to keep Surrey in effective exile)   **42 who removed** i.e., Kildare having been removed   **44 father** i.e., father-in-
law.   **trick of state** political stratagem   **45 envious** malicious
46 requite repay   **47 generally** by everybody   **50 perniciously** with
deadly hatred   **53 mirror** i.e., paragon.   **s.d. tipstaves** bailiffs.   **halberds** halberdiers, with long-handled weapons.   **Walter** ("William"
in Holinshed.)   **55 close** silently close together and out of view
57 lose forget

And by that name must die. Yet, heaven bear
   witness,
And if I have a conscience, let it sink me,   60
Even as the ax falls, if I be not faithful!
The law I bear no malice for my death;
'T has done, upon the premises, but justice;   63
But those that sought it I could wish more
   Christians.   64
Be what they will, I heartily forgive 'em.
Yet let 'em look they glory not in mischief,
Nor build their evils on the graves of great men,   67
For then my guiltless blood must cry against 'em.
For further life in this world I ne'er hope,
Nor will I sue, although the King have mercies
More than I dare make faults. You few that loved me 71
And dare be bold to weep for Buckingham,
His noble friends and fellows, whom to leave   73
Is only bitter to him, only dying,   74
Go with me like good angels to my end,
And as the long divorce of steel falls on me   76
Make of your prayers one sweet sacrifice,   77
And lift my soul to heaven. Lead on, i' God's name!

LOVELL
I do beseech Your Grace, for charity,
If ever any malice in your heart
Were hid against me, now to forgive me frankly.

BUCKINGHAM
Sir Thomas Lovell, I as free forgive you
As I would be forgiven. I forgive all.
There cannot be those numberless offenses
'Gainst me that I cannot take peace with; no black
   envy   85
Shall mark my grave. Commend me to His Grace,
And if he speak of Buckingham, pray tell him
You met him half in heaven. My vows and prayers
Yet are the King's and, till my soul forsake,   89
Shall cry for blessings on him. May he live
Longer than I have time to tell his years!   91
Ever beloved and loving may his rule be!
And when old Time shall lead him to his end,   93
Goodness and he fill up one monument!   94

LOVELL
To th' waterside I must conduct Your Grace,
Then give my charge up to Sir Nicholas Vaux,
Who undertakes you to your end.

VAUX   Prepare there;   97
The Duke is coming. See the barge be ready,
And fit it with such furniture as suits   99
The greatness of his person.

BUCKINGHAM   Nay, Sir Nicholas,
Let it alone; my state now will but mock me.   101

When I came hither, I was Lord High Constable
And Duke of Buckingham; now, poor Edward
   Bohun.   103
Yet I am richer than my base accusers,
That never knew what truth meant. I now seal it,   105
And with that blood will make 'em one day groan
   for 't.
My noble father, Henry of Buckingham,
Who first raised head against usurping Richard,   108
Flying for succor to his servant Banister,
Being distressed, was by that wretch betrayed,
And without trial fell; God's peace be with him!
Henry the Seventh succeeding, truly pitying
My father's loss, like a most royal prince
Restored me to my honors, and out of ruins
Made my name once more noble. Now his son,
Henry the Eighth, life, honor, name, and all
That made me happy, at one stroke has taken
Forever from the world. I had my trial,
And must needs say a noble one; which makes me
A little happier than my wretched father.   120
Yet thus far we are one in fortunes: both
Fell by our servants, by those men we loved most—
A most unnatural and faithless service!
Heaven has an end in all. Yet, you that hear me,   124
This from a dying man receive as certain:
Where you are liberal of your loves and counsels
Be sure you be not loose; for those you make friends 127
And give your hearts to, when they once perceive
The least rub in your fortunes, fall away   129
Like water from ye, never found again
But where they mean to sink ye. All good people,
Pray for me! I must now forsake ye. The last hour
Of my long weary life is come upon me.
Farewell! And when you would say something that
   is sad,
Speak how I fell. I have done; and God forgive me!
                   Exeunt Duke and train.

FIRST GENTLEMAN
O, this is full of pity! Sir, it calls,
I fear, too many curses on their heads
That were the authors.

SECOND GENTLEMAN   If the Duke be guiltless,
'Tis full of woe. Yet I can give you inkling
Of an ensuing evil, if it fall,
Greater than this.

FIRST GENTLEMAN   Good angels keep it from us!
What may it be? You do not doubt my faith, sir?   142

SECOND GENTLEMAN
This secret is so weighty, 'twill require
A strong faith to conceal it.

FIRST GENTLEMAN   Let me have it;
I do not talk much.

---

60 sink ruin, damn   **63 premises** evidence   **64 more** better   **67 Nor
. . . men** i.e., nor extend their own evil careers by extinguishing the
lives of noblemen. (*Evils* may suggest "hovels" or "privies.")
71 make faults commit offenses   **73–74 whom . . . dying** the loss of
whose dear company is the only cause of bitterness in death, the only
death that matters   **76 divorce of steel** i.e., separation of body and
soul effected by the executioner's ax   **77 sacrifice** offering   **85 take**
make.   **envy** malice   **89 Yet** still.   **forsake** leave my body   **91 tell**
count   **93 Time** age   **94 monument** tomb   **97 undertakes** takes
charge of   **99 furniture** furnishings   **101 state** rank

103 Bohun (The Duke's family name was actually Stafford;
Shakespeare follows the error in Holinshed.)   **105 seal** ratify, attest to
the truth of   **108 raised head** gathered an army   **120 happier** more
fortunate   **124 end** aim   **127 loose** wanting in restraint, careless
129 rub impediment. (A term from bowls.)   **142 faith** i.e., ability to
keep a secret

SECOND GENTLEMAN I am confident;   145
  You shall, sir. Did you not of late days hear   146
  A buzzing of a separation   147
  Between the King and Katharine?
FIRST GENTLEMAN   Yes, but it held not; 148
  For when the King once heard it, out of anger
  He sent command to the Lord Mayor straight
  To stop the rumor and allay those tongues   151
  That durst disperse it.
SECOND GENTLEMAN   But that slander, sir,
  Is found a truth now, for it grows again
  Fresher than e'er it was, and held for certain
  The King will venture at it. Either the Cardinal,
  Or some about him near, have, out of malice   156
  To the good Queen, possessed him with a scruple   157
  That will undo her. To confirm this too,
  Cardinal Campeius is arrived, and lately,   159
  As all think, for this business.
FIRST GENTLEMAN   'Tis the Cardinal;
  And merely to revenge him on the Emperor   161
  For not bestowing on him at his asking
  The archbishopric of Toledo, this is purposed.   163
SECOND GENTLEMAN
  I think you have hit the mark. But is 't not cruel
  That she should feel the smart of this? The Cardinal 165
  Will have his will, and she must fall.
FIRST GENTLEMAN   'Tis woeful.
  We are too open here to argue this;   167
  Let's think in private more.   *Exeunt.*

❧

2.2 *Enter Lord Chamberlain, reading this letter.*

CHAMBERLAIN "My lord, the horses your lordship sent
for, with all the care I had, I saw well chosen, ridden, 2
and furnished. They were young and handsome, and 3
of the best breed in the north. When they were ready
to set out for London, a man of my lord Cardinal's,
by commission and main power, took 'em from me 6
with this reason: his master would be served before a
subject, if not before the King; which stopped our
mouths, sir."
I fear he will indeed. Well, let him have them.
He will have all, I think.

145 **am confident** i.e., trust your discretion 146 **shall** i.e., shall hear
it. **late** recent 147 **buzzing** rumor 148 **held not** ceased; or perhaps was not believed 151 **allay** subdue, confute 156 **about him**
near close to him 157 **possessed . . . scruple** put into his mind a
doubt. (Katharine had been married to Henry's older brother, Prince
Arthur, who died, still in his early teens, a year after the marriage.
Such a precontract would normally invalidate a subsequent marriage
with any close relative of Arthur's, but Henry's marriage to Katharine
had been made possible by a papal dispensation.) 159 **Cardinal**
Campeius Cardinal Lorenzo Campeggio, sent from Rome to confer on
the legality of the King's marriage 161 **Emperor** (The Queen was the
aunt of Charles V, Holy Roman Emperor and King of Spain; see
1.1.176 and note.) 163 **purposed** intended 165 **smart** pain
167 **open** public
2.2. Location: London. The royal court.
2 **ridden** broken in, trained 3 **furnished** equipped 6 **commission**
warrant. **main power** sheer force

*Enter to the Lord Chamberlain the Dukes of
Norfolk and Suffolk.*

NORFOLK Well met, my Lord Chamberlain.
CHAMBERLAIN Good day to both Your Graces.
SUFFOLK
  How is the King employed?
CHAMBERLAIN   I left him private,   14
  Full of sad thoughts and troubles.
NORFOLK   What's the cause? 15
CHAMBERLAIN
  It seems the marriage with his brother's wife
  Has crept too near his conscience.
SUFFOLK   No, his conscience
  Has crept too near another lady.
NORFOLK   'Tis so.
  This is the Cardinal's doing. The king-cardinal,
  That blind priest, like the eldest son of Fortune,   20
  Turns what he list. The King will know him one
    day.   21
SUFFOLK
  Pray God he do! He'll never know himself else.
NORFOLK
  How holily he works in all his business,   23
  And with what zeal! For, now he has cracked the
    league
  Between us and the Emperor, the Queen's great-
    nephew,
  He dives into the King's soul and there scatters
  Dangers, doubts, wringing of the conscience,
  Fears, and despairs, and all these for his marriage.
  And out of all these to restore the King,
  He counsels a divorce, a loss of her
  That, like a jewel, has hung twenty years
  About his neck, yet never lost her luster;
  Of her that loves him with that excellence
  That angels love good men with; even of her
  That, when the greatest stroke of fortune falls,
  Will bless the King. And is not this course pious?   36
CHAMBERLAIN
  Heaven keep me from such counsel! 'Tis most true
  These news are everywhere; every tongue speaks
    'em,   38
  And every true heart weeps for 't. All that dare
  Look into these affairs see this main end,
  The French King's sister. Heaven will one day open 41
  The King's eyes, that so long have slept upon   42
  This bold bad man.
SUFFOLK   And free us from his slavery.
NORFOLK We had need pray,
  And heartily, for our deliverance,
  Or this imperious man will work us all
  From princes into pages. All men's honors   47

14 **private** alone 15 **sad** serious 20–21 **blind . . . list** (Wolsey is
the favored son of Fortune, conventionally depicted as blind and turning her wheel.) 21 **list** wishes 23 **he** i.e., Wolsey 36 **Will bless**
the King (Katharine does, in fact, bless the King who has brought
about her misfortune, at 4.2.163.) 38 **news are** (*News* was commonly considered a plural noun.) 41 **The . . . sister** i.e., the Duchess of Alençon; see 3.2.86–87 42 **slept upon** been blind to
47 **pages** attendants

Lie like one lump before him, to be fashioned   48
Into what pitch he please.

SUFFOLK   For me, my lords,   49
I love him not, nor fear him; there's my creed.
As I am made without him, so I'll stand,   51
If the King please. His curses and his blessings
Touch me alike; they're breath I not believe in.
I knew him, and I know him; so I leave him
To him that made him proud, the Pope.

NORFOLK   Let's in,
And with some other business put the King
From these sad thoughts that work too much upon
     him.
My lord, you'll bear us company?

CHAMBERLAIN   Excuse me;
The King has sent me otherwhere. Besides,   59
You'll find a most unfit time to disturb him.
Health to your lordships.

NORFOLK   Thanks, my good Lord Chamberlain. 61
     Exit Lord Chamberlain; and the King draws
     the curtain and sits reading pensively.

SUFFOLK
How sad he looks! Sure he is much afflicted.   62

KING
Who's there, ha?

NORFOLK   Pray God he be not angry.

KING
Who's there, I say? How dare you thrust yourselves
Into my private meditations?
Who am I? Ha?

NORFOLK
A gracious king that pardons all offenses
Malice ne'er meant. Our breach of duty this way   68
Is business of estate, in which we come   69
To know your royal pleasure.

KING   Ye are too bold.
Go to! I'll make ye know your times of business.
Is this an hour for temporal affairs, ha?

     Enter Wolsey and Campeius, with a commission.

Who's there? My good lord Cardinal? O my Wolsey,
The quiet of my wounded conscience,
Thou art a cure fit for a king. [*To Campeius.*] You're
     welcome,
Most learnèd reverend sir, into our kingdom.
Use us and it. [*To Wolsey.*] My good lord, have great
     care
I be not found a talker.

WOLSEY   Sir, you cannot.   78
I would Your Grace would give us but an hour

---

48 **lump** i.e., lump of clay   49 **pitch** height (literally, of a falcon's flight), i.e., degree of dignity. (In a mixed metaphor, the Cardinal is likened to one who reduces all men of rank to one lump, which he will refashion into creatures of whatever stature he pleases.)   **For** as for   51 **As . . . stand** i.e., inasmuch as my rank was conferred on me by the King, not by Wolsey, I'll stand firm   59 **otherwhere** elsewhere   61 s.d. **curtain** (The King is probably in a "discovery space" rear stage.)   62 **afflicted** troubled   68 **this way** in this respect   69 **estate** public weal   78 **I . . . talker** i.e., lest my offer of hospitality be only talk, not deeds

---

Of private conference.

KING [*to Norfolk and Suffolk*]   We are busy; go.

NORFOLK [*aside to Suffolk*]
This priest has no pride in him?

SUFFOLK [*aside to Norfolk*]   Not to speak of.
I would not be so sick, though, for his place.   82
But this cannot continue.

NORFOLK [*aside to Suffolk*]   If it do,
I'll venture one have-at-him.

SUFFOLK [*aside to Norfolk*]   I another.   84
                         Exeunt Norfolk and Suffolk.

WOLSEY
Your Grace has given a precedent of wisdom   85
Above all princes, in committing freely
Your scruple to the voice of Christendom.   87
Who can be angry now? What envy reach you?   88
The Spaniard, tied by blood and favor to her,   89
Must now confess, if they have any goodness,   90
The trial just and noble. All the clerks—   91
I mean the learnèd ones in Christian kingdoms—
Have their free voices. Rome, the nurse of
     judgment,   93
Invited by your noble self, hath sent
One general tongue unto us: this good man,   95
This just and learnèd priest, Card'nal Campeius,
Whom once more I present unto Your Highness.

KING [*embracing Campeius*]
And once more in mine arms I bid him welcome,
And thank the holy conclave for their loves.   99
They have sent me such a man I would have
     wished for.

CAMPEIUS
Your Grace must needs deserve all strangers' loves,   101
You are so noble. To Your Highness' hand
I tender my commission, by whose virtue,
The court of Rome commanding, you, my lord
Cardinal of York, are joined with me their servant
In the unpartial judging of this business.
                    [*He gives the King a document.*]

KING
Two equal men. The Queen shall be acquainted   107
Forthwith for what you come. Where's Gardiner?   108

WOLSEY
I know Your Majesty has always loved her
So dear in heart not to deny her that   110
A woman of less place might ask by law: 111
Scholars allowed freely to argue for her.

---

82 **sick** i.e., sick with pride.   **for his place** even to gain his high office   84 **have-at-him** i.e., thrust at him (Wolsey) in fencing   85 **precedent** example   87 **scruple** doubt.   **the voice of Christendom** i.e., the Pope, through his representative Campeius, and the clerics and scholars of various Continental universities to whom Henry submitted his problem of "conscience"   88 **envy** malice   89 **The Spaniard** i.e., Charles V and his court   90 **confess** concede   91 **clerks** clerics, scholars   93 **Have their free voices** may vote as they choose   95 **One general tongue** i.e., a spokesman   99 **conclave** College of Cardinals   101 **needs** necessarily.   **strangers'** foreigners'   107 **equal** impartial.   **acquainted** informed   108 **Gardiner** i.e., Stephen Gardiner, Wolsey's secretary; he later becomes one of the most influential members of the King's Council   110 **that** that which   111 **less place** lower rank

KING
    Ay, and the best she shall have, and my favor
To him that does best; God forbid else. Cardinal,
Prithee, call Gardiner to me, my new secretary.
I find him a fit fellow.   *[Wolsey goes to the door.]* 116

    Enter Gardiner.

WOLSEY *[aside to Gardiner]*
    Give me your hand. Much joy and favor to you;
You are the King's now.
GARDINER *[aside to Wolsey]*   But to be commanded
Forever by Your Grace, whose hand has raised me.
KING   Come hither, Gardiner.   *Walks and whispers.*
CAMPEIUS
    My lord of York, was not one Doctor Pace   121
In this man's place before him?
WOLSEY   Yes, he was.
CAMPEIUS
    Was he not held a learnèd man?
WOLSEY   Yes, surely.
CAMPEIUS
    Believe me, there's an ill opinion spread then
Even of yourself, Lord Cardinal.
WOLSEY   How? Of me?
CAMPEIUS
    They will not stick to say you envied him,   126
And, fearing he would rise, he was so virtuous,
Kept him a foreign man still, which so grieved him   128
That he ran mad and died.
WOLSEY   Heaven's peace be with him! 129
That's Christian care enough. For living murmurers   130
There's places of rebuke. He was a fool,
For he would needs be virtuous. That good fellow,
                        [indicating Gardiner]
If I command him, follows my appointment;   133
I will have none so near else. Learn this, brother: 134
We live not to be gripped by meaner persons.   135
KING *[to Gardiner]*
    Deliver this with modesty to the Queen.   136
                          Exit Gardiner.
The most convenient place that I can think of
For such receipt of learning is Blackfriars;   138
There ye shall meet about this weighty business.
My Wolsey, see it furnished. O my lord,
Would it not grieve an able man to leave   141
So sweet a bedfellow? But conscience, conscience!
O, 'tis a tender place, and I must leave her.   *Exeunt.*

                        ❖

2.3   *Enter Anne Bullen and an Old Lady.*

ANNE
    Not for that neither. Here's the pang that pinches:
His Highness having lived so long with her, and she
So good a lady that no tongue could ever
Pronounce dishonor of her—by my life,   4
She never knew harm-doing—O, now, after
So many courses of the sun enthroned,
Still growing in a majesty and pomp, the which   7
To leave a thousandfold more bitter than
'Tis sweet at first t' acquire—after this process,   9
To give her the avaunt! It is a pity   10
Would move a monster.
OLD LADY   Hearts of most hard temper
Melt and lament for her.
ANNE   O, God's will, much better
She ne'er had known pomp. Though 't be temporal, 13
Yet, if that quarrel, Fortune, do divorce   14
It from the bearer, 'tis a sufferance panging   15
As soul and body's severing.
OLD LADY   Alas, poor lady!
She's a stranger now again.
ANNE   So much the more 17
Must pity drop upon her. Verily,
I swear, 'tis better to be lowly born
And range with humble livers in content   20
Than to be perked up in a glistering grief   21
And wear a golden sorrow.
OLD LADY   Our content
Is our best having.
ANNE   By my troth and maidenhead, 23
I would not be a queen.
OLD LADY   Beshrew me, I would,
And venture maidenhead for 't; and so would you,
For all this spice of your hypocrisy.   26
You that have so fair parts of woman on you   27
Have too a woman's heart, which ever yet
Affected eminence, wealth, sovereignty;   29
Which, to say sooth, are blessings; and which gifts, 30
Saving your mincing, the capacity   31
Of your soft cheveril conscience would receive   32
If you might please to stretch it.
ANNE   Nay, good troth.
OLD LADY
    Yes, troth, and troth. You would not be a queen?
ANNE
    No, not for all the riches under heaven.

116 fit suitable   **121 Doctor Pace** i.e., Richard Pace, Dean of Saint Paul's and Secretary of State, who served King Henry and Wolsey on diplomatic missions   **126 stick** hesitate. **envied him** i.e., were hostile toward Pace   **128 Kept . . . still** kept him constantly abroad on diplomatic missions   **129 died** (Pace actually died in 1536, six years after Wolsey's death.)   **130 murmurers** grumblers, troublemakers   **133 appointment** bidding **134 none . . . else** i.e., no one besides him so close to the King **135 gripped** clutched at, grasped by the hand. **meaner** of lower social rank **136 Deliver . . . modesty** make this known gently   **138 receipt of learning** reception of learned opinion, or of learned men. **Blackfriars** monastic buildings in London surrendered to the crown in Henry VIII's time   **141 able** vigorous

2.3. Location: London. The Queen's apartments.
4 Pronounce speak   **7 Still** always   **9 process** course of events   **10 give . . . avaunt** bid her begone. **pity** pitiful situation   **13 temporal** merely worldly prosperity, not heavenly   **14 quarrel** quarreler, troublemaker   **15 sufferance panging** suffering as painful   **17 stranger** foreigner   **20 range** rank. **livers** persons **21 perked up** trimmed out   **23 having** possession. **troth** good faith **26 For all** in spite of. **spice** dash, touch **27 parts** qualities **29 Affected** loved, aspired to **30 sooth** truth **31 Saving your mincing** with all due respect to your affected coyness **32 cheveril** kid leather. (Used as a type of flexibility.)

OLD LADY
'Tis strange. A threepence bowed would hire me,   36
Old as I am, to queen it. But I pray you,
What think you of a duchess? Have you limbs
To bear that load of title?

ANNE   No, in truth.

OLD LADY
Then you are weakly made. Pluck off a little;   40
I would not be a young count in your way   41
For more than blushing comes to. If your back
Cannot vouchsafe this burden, 'tis too weak   43
Ever to get a boy.

ANNE   How you do talk!   44
I swear again, I would not be a queen
For all the world.

OLD LADY   In faith, for little England
You'd venture an emballing. I myself   47
Would for Caernarvonshire, although there 'longed   48
No more to the crown but that. Lo, who comes
here?

Enter Lord Chamberlain.

CHAMBERLAIN
Good morrow, ladies. What were 't worth to know
The secret of your conference?

ANNE   My good lord,   51
Not your demand; it values not your asking.   52
Our mistress' sorrows we were pitying.

CHAMBERLAIN
It was a gentle business, and becoming
The action of good women. There is hope
All will be well.

ANNE   Now I pray God, amen!

CHAMBERLAIN
You bear a gentle mind, and heavenly blessings
Follow such creatures. That you may, fair lady,
Perceive I speak sincerely, and high note's
Ta'en of your many virtues, the King's Majesty
Commends his good opinion of you, and   61
Does purpose honor to you no less flowing   62
Than Marchioness of Pembroke; to which title
A thousand pound a year, annual support,
Out of his grace he adds.

ANNE   I do not know   65
What kind of my obedience I should tender.
More than my all is nothing; nor my prayers   67
Are not words duly hallowed, nor my wishes   68
More worth than empty vanities; yet prayers and
wishes   69
Are all I can return. Beseech your lordship,
Vouchsafe to speak my thanks and my obedience,   71
As from a blushing handmaid, to His Highness,
Whose health and royalty I pray for.

CHAMBERLAIN   Lady,
I shall not fail t' approve the fair conceit   74
The King hath of you. [*Aside.*] I have perused her
well;
Beauty and honor in her are so mingled
That they have caught the King. And who knows
yet
But from this lady may proceed a gem
To lighten all this isle? [*To Anne.*] I'll to the King,   79
And say I spoke with you.

ANNE   My honored lord!   *Exit Lord Chamberlain.*

OLD LADY   Why, this it is! See, see,
I have been begging sixteen years in court,
Am yet a courtier beggarly, nor could   84
Come pat betwixt too early and too late   85
For any suit of pounds; and you—O fate!—   86
A very fresh fish here—fie, fie, fie upon
This compelled fortune!—have your mouth filled up 88
Before you open it.

ANNE   This is strange to me.

OLD LADY
How tastes it? Is it bitter? Forty pence, no.   90
There was a lady once—'tis an old story—
That would not be a queen, that would she not,
For all the mud in Egypt. Have you heard it?   93

ANNE
Come, you are pleasant.

OLD LADY   With your theme, I could   94
O'ermount the lark. The Marchioness of Pembroke?
A thousand pounds a year for pure respect?   96
No other obligation? By my life,
That promises more thousands. Honor's train   98
Is longer than his foreskirt. By this time   99
I know your back will bear a duchess. Say,
Are you not stronger than you were?

ANNE   Good lady,
Make yourself mirth with your particular fancy,   102
And leave me out on 't. Would I had no being,
If this salute my blood a jot. It faints me   104
To think what follows.
The Queen is comfortless, and we forgetful
In our long absence. Pray, do not deliver   107

---

36 bowed crooked and therefore worthless; with sexual pun on "bawd," continued in *queen* ("quean," "whore"), *bear, count* (female pudenda), *way, emballing* **40 Pluck off** come lower **41 count** (A rank below that of duke.) **43 vouchsafe this burden** i.e., accept this load of honors (with sexual suggestion of bearing a man) **44 get** beget **47 emballing** investiture with the ball as a royal emblem (with sexual suggestion) **48 Caernarvonshire** an especially impoverished and barren Welsh county. **'longed** belonged **51 conference** conversation **52 Not your demand** i.e., it is not even worth your inquiring. **values not** is not worth **61 Commends** expresses **62 purpose** intend. **flowing** abundant **65 grace** favor **67–69 More . . . vanities** even more than I can possibly offer (in the way of thankful obedience) would be as nothing; my prayers aren't holy enough, and my good wishes (for the King) are mere vain and worthless things

71 Vouchsafe be so kind as **74 approve . . . conceit** confirm the good opinion **79 lighten** give light to. (Refers to Queen Elizabeth.) **84 beggarly** still in need **85 pat** precisely at the opportune time **86 suit of pounds** request for money **88 compelled** unsought, forced upon one **90 Forty pence, no** i.e., I'll venture a small sum that it isn't bitter to you **93 the mud in Egypt** i.e., the wealth of Egypt resulting from its fecund land **94 pleasant** merry **96 pure** mere **98–99 Honor's . . . foreskirt** i.e., honors to come will exceed this present gift, just as an elongated robe trailing behind is longer than the front of a skirt **102 your . . . fancy** your own private imaginings **104 salute** acts upon, excites. **faints me** makes me faint **107 deliver** report

What here you've have heard to her.

OLD LADY   What do you think me?   *Exeunt.*

❧

2.4   *Trumpets, sennet, and cornets. Enter two Vergers,*
with short silver wands; next them two Scribes, in
the habit of doctors; after them the [Arch]bishop
of Canterbury alone; after him the Bishops of
Lincoln, Ely, Rochester, and Saint Asaph; next
them, with some small distance, follows a
Gentleman bearing the purse, with the great seal,
and a cardinal's hat; then two Priests, bearing each
a silver cross; then [Griffith,] a Gentleman Usher,
bareheaded, accompanied with a Sergeant at Arms
bearing a silver mace; then two Gentlemen bearing
two great silver pillars; after them, side by side, the
two Cardinals; two Noblemen with the sword and
mace. The King takes place under the cloth of state;
the two Cardinals sit under him as judges. The
Queen takes place some distance from the King.
The Bishops place themselves on each side the
court, in manner of a consistory; below them the
Scribes. The Lords sit next the Bishops. The rest of
the attendants stand in convenient order about the
stage.

WOLSEY
  Whilst our commission from Rome is read,
  Let silence be commanded.

KING   What's the need?
  It hath already publicly been read,
  And on all sides th' authority allowed;   4
  You may then spare that time.

WOLSEY   Be 't so. Proceed.

SCRIBE
  Say, "Henry King of England, come into the court."

CRIER
  Henry King of England, come into the court.

KING Here.

SCRIBE
  Say, "Katharine Queen of England, come into the
  court."

CRIER
  Katharine Queen of England, come into the court.
          The Queen makes no answer, rises out of her chair,
          goes about the court, comes to the King, and kneels at
                                        his feet; then speaks.

KATHARINE
  Sir, I desire you do me right and justice,
  And to bestow your pity on me; for
  I am a most poor woman, and a stranger,   13
  Born out of your dominions, having here
  No judge indifferent, nor no more assurance   15

Of equal friendship and proceeding. Alas, sir,   16
In what have I offended you? What cause
Hath my behavior given to your displeasure
That thus you should proceed to put me off   19
And take your good grace from me? Heaven
    witness,
I have been to you a true and humble wife,
At all times to your will conformable,
Ever in fear to kindle your dislike,   23
Yea, subject to your countenance—glad or sorry
As I saw it inclined. When was the hour
I ever contradicted your desire,
Or made it not mine too? Or which of your friends
Have I not strove to love, although I knew
He were mine enemy? What friend of mine
That had to him derived your anger did I   30
Continue in my liking, nay, gave notice
He was from thence discharged? Sir, call to mind
That I have been your wife in this obedience
Upward of twenty years, and have been blessed
With many children by you. If, in the course   35
And process of this time, you can report,
And prove it too, against mine honor aught—   37
My bond to wedlock, or my love and duty
Against your sacred person—in God's name   39
Turn me away, and let the foul'st contempt
Shut door upon me, and so give me up
To the sharp'st kind of justice. Please you, sir,
The King your father was reputed for
A prince most prudent, of an excellent
And unmatched wit and judgment. Ferdinand   45
My father, King of Spain, was reckoned one   46
The wisest prince that there had reigned by many   47
A year before. It is not to be questioned
That they had gathered a wise council to them
Of every realm, that did debate this business,
Who deemed our marriage lawful. Wherefore I
    humbly
Beseech you, sir, to spare me till I may
Be by my friends in Spain advised, whose counsel
I will implore. If not, i' the name of God,
Your pleasure be fulfilled!

WOLSEY   You have here, lady,
And of your choice, these reverend fathers, men
Of singular integrity and learning,
Yea, the elect o' the land, who are assembled
To plead your cause. It shall be therefore bootless   59
That longer you desire the court, as well   60
For your own quiet as to rectify   61
What is unsettled in the King.

CAMPEIUS   His Grace
Hath spoken well and justly. Therefore, madam,
It's fit this royal session do proceed,

2.4. Location: London. A hall in Blackfriars.
s.d. sennet trumpet call announcing a procession.   **Vergers** those
who carry the verge or emblem of office; particularly, attendants on a
church dignitary.   **habit of doctors** furred black gowns and flat caps
worn by doctors of law.   **cloth of state** canopy.   **consistory** ecclesiastical court   **4 allowed** conceded   **13 stranger** foreigner   **15 indifferent** impartial

16 equal fair   **19 put me off** discard me   **23 dislike** displeasure
30 to him derived drawn upon himself   **35 many children** (The
Queen gave birth to five children, only one of whom, later Queen
Mary, survived infancy.)   **37 aught** anything   **39 Against** toward
45 wit intelligence   **46–47 one The wisest** the very wisest   **59 bootless** profitless   **60 That . . . court** that you entreat the court to postpone its work   **61 quiet** peace of mind

And that without delay their arguments
Be now produced and heard.
KATHARINE   Lord Cardinal,
To you I speak.
WOLSEY   Your pleasure, madam?
KATHARINE   Sir,
I am about to weep; but, thinking that
We are a queen, or long have dreamed so, certain   69
The daughter of a king, my drops of tears
I'll turn to sparks of fire.
WOLSEY   Be patient yet.
KATHARINE
I will when you are humble; nay, before,   72
Or God will punish me. I do believe,
Induced by potent circumstances, that   74
You are mine enemy, and make my challenge   75
You shall not be my judge. For it is you
Have blown this coal betwixt my lord and me—   77
Which God's dew quench! Therefore I say again,
I utterly abhor, yea, from my soul   79
Refuse you for my judge, whom yet once more
I hold my most malicious foe, and think not
At all a friend to truth.
WOLSEY   I do profess   82
You speak not like yourself, who ever yet   83
Have stood to charity and displayed th' effects   84
Of disposition gentle and of wisdom
O'ertopping woman's pow'r. Madam, you do me
    wrong.
I have no spleen against you, nor injustice   87
For you or any. How far I have proceeded,
Or how far further shall, is warranted   89
By a commission from the consistory,
Yea, the whole consistory of Rome. You charge me
That I have blown this coal. I do deny it.
The King is present. If it be known to him
That I gainsay my deed, how may he wound,   94
And worthily, my falsehood, yea, as much   95
As you have done my truth! If he know
That I am free of your report, he knows   97
I am not of your wrong. Therefore in him   98
It lies to cure me, and the cure is to   99
Remove these thoughts from you; the which before   100
His Highness shall speak in, I do beseech   101
You, gracious madam, to unthink your speaking
And to say so no more.
KATHARINE   My lord, my lord,
I am a simple woman, much too weak

T' oppose your cunning. You're meek and humble-
    mouthed;
You sign your place and calling, in full seeming,   106
With meekness and humility; but your heart
Is crammed with arrogancy, spleen, and pride.
You have, by fortune and His Highness' favors,
Gone slightly o'er low steps and now are mounted   110
Where powers are your retainers, and your words,   111
Domestics to you, serve your will as 't please   112
Yourself pronounce their office. I must tell you,   113
You tender more your person's honor than   114
Your high profession spiritual, that again
I do refuse you for my judge, and here
Before you all appeal unto the Pope,
To bring my whole cause 'fore His Holiness,
And to be judged by him.
          She curtsies to the King and offers to depart.
CAMPEIUS   The Queen is obstinate,
Stubborn to justice, apt to accuse it, and   120
Disdainful to be tried by 't. 'Tis not well.
She's going away.
KING   Call her again.
CRIER
Katharine Queen of England, come into the court.
GRIFFITH   Madam, you are called back.
KATHARINE
What need you note it? Pray you, keep your way;   126
When you are called, return. Now, the Lord help!
They vex me past my patience. Pray you, pass on.
I will not tarry; no, nor ever more
Upon this business my appearance make
In any of their courts.
          Exeunt Queen and her attendants.
KING   Go thy ways, Kate.
That man i' the world who shall report he has
A better wife, let him in naught be trusted
For speaking false in that. Thou art alone—
If thy rare qualities, sweet gentleness,
Thy meekness saintlike, wifelike government,   136
Obeying in commanding, and thy parts   137
Sovereign and pious else, could speak thee out—   138
The queen of earthly queens.—She's noble born,
And like her true nobility she has
Carried herself towards me.
WOLSEY   Most gracious sir,   141
In humblest manner I require Your Highness   142
That it shall please you to declare, in hearing
Of all these ears—for where I am robbed and
    bound,

---

69 **certain** certainly   72 **before** i.e., sooner than that (which will never be)   74 **Induced** persuaded   75 **make my challenge** I raise my formal objection (that)   77 **Have blown this coal** i.e., who have stirred up this trouble   79 **abhor** protest against. (A technical term of canon law.)   82 **profess** affirm   83 **ever yet** always   84 **stood to** upheld   87 **spleen** malice   89 **warranted** justified   94 **gainsay my deed** deny my acts   95 **worthily** deservedly   97 **free** innocent.   **report** accusation   98 **am . . . wrong** am not free from being slandered by you   99 **cure me** i.e., make me better, not by rectifying my behavior, which is blameless, but by removing the distress you cause me   100–101 **before . . . in** i.e., before the King rebukes you for this

106 **sign** signify, show marks of.   **in full seeming** with great ostentation   110 **slightly** easily   111 **powers . . . retainers** i.e., you command the service of people of rank   111–113 **your words . . . office** i.e., your clever speeches serve your ends in any way you choose; or, your very words are immediately acted upon   114 **tender more** are more concerned for   120 **Stubborn** resistant.   **apt to accuse it** ready to find fault with it   126 **What** why.   **keep your way** move on   136 **government** self-control, behavior   137 **Obeying in commanding** i.e., combining the qualities of obedient wife and regal queen.   **parts** qualities   138 **else** besides.   **speak thee out** declare you as you are   141 **Carried** borne, behaved   142 **require** request

There must I be unloosed, although not there
At once and fully satisfied—whether ever I   146
Did broach this business to Your Highness, or
Laid any scruple in your way, which might
Induce you to the question on 't? Or ever
Have to you, but with thanks to God for such
A royal lady, spake one the least word that might   151
Be to the prejudice of her present state,
Or touch of her good person?
KING   My lord Cardinal,   153
I do excuse you; yea, upon mine honor,   154
I free you from 't. You are not to be taught   155
That you have many enemies that know not
Why they are so, but, like to village curs,
Bark when their fellows do. By some of these
The Queen is put in anger. You're excused.
But will you be more justified? You ever   160
Have wished the sleeping of this business, never
    desired
It to be stirred, but oft have hindered, oft,
The passages made toward it. On my honor,   163
I speak my good lord Cardinal to this point,   164
And thus far clear him. Now, what moved me to 't,
I will be bold with time and your attention;
Then mark th' inducement. Thus it came; give
    heed to 't:
My conscience first received a tenderness,
Scruple, and prick, on certain speeches uttered
By th' Bishop of Bayonne, then French ambassador,
Who had been hither sent on the debating
A marriage twixt the Duke of Orleans and
Our daughter Mary. I' the progress of this business,
Ere a determinate resolution, he—   174
I mean the Bishop—did require a respite   175
Wherein he might the King his lord advertise   176
Whether our daughter were legitimate,
Respecting this our marriage with the dowager,   178
Sometime our brother's wife. This respite shook   179
The bosom of my conscience, entered me,
Yea, with a spitting power, and made to tremble   181
The region of my breast, which forced such way
That many mazed considerings did throng   183
And pressed in with this caution. First, methought   184
I stood not in the smile of heaven, who had   185
Commanded nature that my lady's womb,
If it conceived a male child by me, should
Do no more offices of life to 't than   188
The grave does to the dead; for her male issue
Or died where they were made, or shortly after   190
This world had aired them. Hence I took a thought   191

This was a judgment on me that my kingdom,
Well worthy the best heir o' the world, should not
Be gladded in 't by me. Then follows that   194
I weighed the danger which my realms stood in
By this my issue's fail, and that gave to me   196
Many a groaning throe. Thus hulling in   197
The wild sea of my conscience, I did steer
Toward this remedy, whereupon we are
Now present here together; that's to say,
I meant to rectify my conscience—which
I then did feel full sick, and yet not well—   202
By all the reverend fathers of the land
And doctors learned. First I began in private
With you, my lord of Lincoln. You remember
How under my oppression I did reek   206
When I first moved you.
LINCOLN   Very well, my liege.   207
KING
I have spoke long. Be pleased yourself to say
How far you satisfied me.
LINCOLN   So please Your Highness,
The question did at first so stagger me—
Bearing a state of mighty moment in 't   211
And consequence of dread—that I committed   212
The daring'st counsel which I had to doubt   213
And did entreat Your Highness to this course
Which you are running here.
KING [to Canterbury]   I then moved you,
My lord of Canterbury, and got your leave
To make this present summons. Unsolicited
I left no reverend person in this court,
But by particular consent proceeded
Under your hands and seals. Therefore, go on,   220
For no dislike i' the world against the person
Of the good Queen, but the sharp thorny points
Of my allegèd reasons, drives this forward.
Prove but our marriage lawful, by my life
And kingly dignity, we are contented
To wear our mortal state to come with her,   226
Katharine our queen, before the primest creature   227
That's paragoned o' the world.
CAMPEIUS   So please Your Highness, 228
The Queen being absent, 'tis a needful fitness   229
That we adjourn this court till further day.   230
Meanwhile must be an earnest motion   231
    Made to the Queen to call back her appeal
She intends unto His Holiness.
KING [aside]   I may perceive

146 At . . . satisfied given full restitution 151 one the least a single
153 touch sullying 154 excuse exonerate 155 are not do not need
160 justified vindicated 163 passages proceedings 164 speak bear
witness for 174 determinate resolution final decision 175 require
request 176 advertise inform, confer with 178 dowager widow
179 Sometime formerly 181 spitting piercing 183 mazed considerings conflicting and confused thoughts 184 caution warning
185 smile i.e., favor 188 offices services 190 Or either 191 aired
given air to

194 gladded made happy 196 By . . . fail by my lacking a son
197 throe pang, pain. hulling drifting with sails furled 202 yet still,
even now 206 oppression distress. reek sweat 207 moved mentioned the business to 211–212 Bearing . . . dread relating to matters of the greatest consequence to the state and an outcome too fearful to contemplate 212–213 I committed . . . doubt i.e., I screwed
up my courage 220 Under . . . seals i.e., with your signed agreement 226 wear . . . her (1) share the state of human existence with
her till we die (2) share royal pomp with her 227 primest most excellent 228 paragoned set forth as a perfect model 229 needful fitness necessary and proper action 230 further future 231 motion
appeal, request

These cardinals trifle with me. I abhor
This dilatory sloth and tricks of Rome.
My learned and well-belovèd servant, Cranmer,
Prithee, return. With thy approach, I know,   237
My comfort comes along.—Break up the court!
I say, set on.   *Exeunt in manner as they entered.*   239

❖

3.1   *Enter Queen and her women, as at work.*

KATHARINE
Take thy lute, wench. My soul grows sad with
   troubles;
Sing, and disperse 'em if thou canst. Leave working.   2
               Song.

GENTLEWOMAN [*sings*]
   Orpheus with his lute made trees,   3
   And the mountain tops that freeze,
     Bow themselves when he did sing.
   To his music plants and flowers
   Ever sprung, as sun and showers   7
     There had made a lasting spring.

   Everything that heard him play,
   Even the billows of the sea,
     Hung their heads, and then lay by.   11
   In sweet music is such art,
   Killing care and grief of heart   13
     Fall asleep, or hearing, die.

         Enter a Gentleman.

KATHARINE   How now?
GENTLEMAN
An 't please Your Grace, the two great cardinals   16
Wait in the presence.
KATHARINE   Would they speak with me?   17
GENTLEMAN
They willed me say so, madam.
KATHARINE   Pray Their Graces   18
To come near. [*The Gentleman goes to the door.*] What
   can be their business
With me, a poor weak woman, fall'n from favor?
I do not like their coming. Now I think on 't,
They should be good men, their affairs as righteous.   22
But all hoods make not monks.

     Enter the two cardinals, Wolsey and Campeius.

WOLSEY   Peace to Your Highness!

KATHARINE
Your Graces find me here part of a huswife—   24
I would be all—against the worst may happen.   25
What are your pleasures with me, reverend lords?
WOLSEY
May it please you, noble madam, to withdraw
Into your private chamber, we shall give you
The full cause of our coming.
KATHARINE   Speak it here.
There's nothing I have done yet, o' my conscience,
Deserves a corner. Would all other women   31
Could speak this with as free a soul as I do!   32
My lords, I care not, so much I am happy   33
Above a number, if my actions   34
Were tried by ev'ry tongue, ev'ry eye saw 'em,
Envy and base opinion set against 'em,   36
I know my life so even. If your business   37
Seek me out, and that way I am wife in,   38
Out with it boldly. Truth loves open dealing.
WOLSEY   *Tanta est erga te mentis integritas, regina ser-*   40
enissima—   41
KATHARINE   O, good my lord, no Latin!
I am not such a truant since my coming
As not to know the language I have lived in.
A strange tongue makes my cause more strange,
   suspicious;   45
Pray, speak in English. Here are some will
   thank you,
If you speak truth, for their poor mistress' sake.
Believe me, she has had much wrong. Lord
   Cardinal,
The willing'st sin I ever yet committed   49
May be absolved in English.
WOLSEY   Noble lady,
I am sorry my integrity should breed—
And service to His Majesty and you—
So deep suspicion, where all faith was meant.
We come not by the way of accusation,   54
To taint that honor every good tongue blesses,
Nor to betray you any way to sorrow—
You have too much, good lady—but to know
How you stand minded in the weighty difference   58
Between the King and you, and to deliver,   59
Like free and honest men, our just opinions   60
And comforts to your cause.
CAMPEIUS   Most honored madam,
My lord of York, out of his noble nature,
Zeal, and obedience he still bore Your Grace,   63
Forgetting, like a good man, your late censure

---

237 Prithee, return (Henry apostrophizes the Protestant churchman, Thomas Cranmer, who at this time, though the play doesn't say so directly, is on the Continent collecting opinions on the King's marriage question. His return is mentioned at 3.2.401.) **239 set on** do it, proceed
3.1. Location: London. The Queen's apartments.
2 Leave stop   **3 Orpheus** legendary musician in Greek mythology. **made trees** i.e., caused trees to bow   **7 as** as if   **11 lay by** subsided **13 Killing care** (so that) care that kills   **16 An 't** if it   **17 presence** reception room   **18 willed** bade   **22 their . . . righteous** i.e., the business they come on should be, like themselves, good

24 part of a huswife i.e., in some measure tending to household duties   **25 I . . . all** i.e., I wish to be a complete housewife, in case I am divorced and forced to live alone.   **against** in anticipation of **31 a corner** i.e., secrecy   **32 free** innocent   **33 happy** fortunate (in virtue)   **34 a number** many   **36 Envy** malice.   **opinion** rumor **37 even** constant, upright   **38 Seek . . . in** concerns me regarding my conduct as a wife   **40–41 Tanta . . . serenissima** so great is the integrity of our intentions toward you, most royal queen   **45 strange** foreign   **49 willing'st** most deliberate   **54 by the way** for the purpose **58 minded** inclined, disposed.   **difference** quarrel   **59 deliver** declare   **60 free** frank, honorable   **63 still bore** has always borne

Both of his truth and him—which was too far—   65
Offers, as I do, in a sign of peace,   66
His service and his counsel.

KATHARINE [aside]   To betray me.—
My lords, I thank you both for your good wills.
Ye speak like honest men; pray God ye prove so!
But how to make ye suddenly an answer
In such a point of weight, so near mine honor—
More near my life, I fear—with my weak wit,   72
And to such men of gravity and learning,
In truth, I know not. I was set at work   74
Among my maids, full little, God knows, looking
Either for such men or such business.
For her sake that I have been—for I feel   77
The last fit of my greatness—good Your Graces,   78
Let me have time and counsel for my cause.
Alas, I am a woman, friendless, hopeless!

WOLSEY
Madam, you wrong the King's love with these fears.
Your hopes and friends are infinite.

KATHARINE   In England
But little for my profit. Can you think, lords,   83
That any Englishman dare give me counsel,
Or be a known friend, 'gainst His Highness'
    pleasure,
Though he be grown so desperate to be honest,   86
And live a subject? Nay, forsooth, my friends,   87
They that must weigh out my afflictions,   88
They that my trust must grow to, live not here.
They are, as all my other comforts, far hence
In mine own country, lords.

CAMPEIUS   I would Your Grace
Would leave your griefs and take my counsel.

KATHARINE   How, sir?

CAMPEIUS
Put your main cause into the King's protection;
He's loving and most gracious. 'Twill be much
Both for your honor better and your cause;
For if the trial of the law o'ertake ye,
You'll part away disgraced.

WOLSEY   He tells you rightly.   97

KATHARINE
Ye tell me what ye wish for both—my ruin.
Is this your Christian counsel? Out upon ye!
Heaven is above all yet; there sits a judge
That no king can corrupt.

CAMPEIUS   Your rage mistakes us.   101

KATHARINE
The more shame for ye! Holy men I thought ye,
Upon my soul, two reverend cardinal virtues;   103
But cardinal sins and hollow hearts I fear ye.   104

Mend 'em, for shame, my lords. Is this your
    comfort?
The cordial that ye bring a wretched lady,   106
A woman lost among ye, laughed at, scorned?
I will not wish ye half my miseries;
I have more charity. But say I warned ye;
Take heed, for heaven's sake take heed, lest at once   110
The burden of my sorrows fall upon ye.

WOLSEY
Madam, this is a mere distraction.   112
You turn the good we offer into envy.   113

KATHARINE
Ye turn me into nothing. Woe upon ye
And all such false professors! Would you have me—
If you have any justice, any pity,
If ye be anything but churchmen's habits—   117
Put my sick cause into his hands that hates me?
Alas, he's banished me his bed already,
His love too long ago! I am old, my lords,
And all the fellowship I hold now with him
Is only my obedience. What can happen
To me above this wretchedness? All your studies   123
Make me a curse like this!

CAMPEIUS   Your fears are worse.   124

KATHARINE
Have I lived thus long—let me speak myself,   125
Since virtue finds no friends—a wife, a true one?
A woman, I dare say without vainglory,
Never yet branded with suspicion—
Have I with all my full affections
Still met the King, loved him next heaven,
    obeyed him,
Been out of fondness superstitious to him,   130
Almost forgot my prayers to content him,   131
And am I thus rewarded? 'Tis not well, lords.
Bring me a constant woman to her husband,
One that ne'er dreamed a joy beyond his pleasure,
And to that woman, when she has done most,
Yet will I add an honor: a great patience.

WOLSEY
Madam, you wander from the good we aim at.   138

KATHARINE
My lord, I dare not make myself so guilty
To give up willingly that noble title
Your master wed me to. Nothing but death
Shall e'er divorce my dignities.

WOLSEY   Pray, hear me.

KATHARINE
Would I had never trod this English earth
Or felt the flatteries that grow upon it!
Ye have angels' faces, but heaven knows your
    hearts.
What will become of me now, wretched lady?

---

65 **far** severe   66 **in** as   72 **wit** understanding   74 **set** seated   77 **For . . . been** for the sake of the queenly person I once was   78 **fit** brief space, short spell   83 **profit** benefit   86 **so desperate** i.e., reckless enough as   87 **live a subject** be allowed to continue living in this realm   88 **weigh out** compensate for, counterbalance   97 **part away** depart   101 **mistakes** misjudges   103 **cardinal virtues** i.e., justice, temperance, fortitude, and prudence, constituting four of the seven virtues opposing the seven Deadly Sins   104 **cardinal sins** i.e., the seven Deadly Sins

106 **cordial** restorative medicine   110 **at once** all at once   112 **mere distraction** sheer frenzy   113 **envy** malice   117 **habits** garments   123 **above** more than   123–124 **All . . . this** i.e., I challenge you, in your clerical exertions, to devise a worse fate than I already have   124 **worse** i.e., than the reality   125 **speak** describe, speak for   130 **Still** always.   **next** next to   131 **superstitious** i.e., to the point of idolatry   138 **wander from** mistake

I am the most unhappy woman living.
[*To her women.*] Alas, poor wenches, where are now
   your fortunes?
Shipwrecked upon a kingdom where no pity,
No friends, no hope, no kindred weep for me?
Almost no grave allowed me? Like the lily,
That once was mistress of the field and flourished,
I'll hang my head and perish.

WOLSEY   If Your Grace
Could but be brought to know our ends are honest, 154
You'd feel more comfort. Why should we, good
   lady,
Upon what cause, wrong you? Alas, our places, 156
The way of our profession, is against it;
We are to cure such sorrows, not to sow 'em.
For goodness' sake, consider what you do,
How you may hurt yourself, ay, utterly
Grow from the King's acquaintance, by this carriage. 161
The hearts of princes kiss obedience,
So much they love it; but to stubborn spirits
They swell and grow as terrible as storms.
I know you have a gentle, noble temper, 165
A soul as even as a calm. Pray, think us 166
Those we profess, peacemakers, friends, and
   servants.

CAMPEIUS
Madam, you'll find it so. You wrong your virtues
With these weak women's fears. A noble spirit,
As yours was put into you, ever casts 170
Such doubts as false coin from it. The King
   loves you;
Beware you lose it not. For us, if you please 172
To trust us in your business, we are ready
To use our utmost studies in your service. 174

KATHARINE
Do what ye will, my lords, and pray forgive me
If I have used myself unmannerly; 176
You know I am a woman, lacking wit
To make a seemly answer to such persons.
Pray, do my service to His Majesty. 179
He has my heart yet, and shall have my prayers
While I shall have my life. Come, reverend fathers,
Bestow your counsels on me. She now begs
That little thought when she set footing here 183
She should have bought her dignities so dear.
                             Exeunt.

❖

3.2   *Enter the Duke of Norfolk, Duke of Suffolk, Lord*
        Surrey, and Lord Chamberlain.

NORFOLK
If you will now unite in your complaints,

And force them with a constancy, the Cardinal 2
Cannot stand under them. If you omit 3
The offer of this time, I cannot promise 4
But that you shall sustain more new disgraces
With these you bear already.

SURREY   I am joyful
To meet the least occasion that may give me
Remembrance of my father-in-law, the Duke, 8
To be revenged on him.

SUFFOLK   Which of the peers 9
Have uncontemned gone by him, or at least 10
Strangely neglected? When did he regard 11
The stamp of nobleness in any person
Out of himself?

CHAMBERLAIN   My lords, you speak your pleasures. 13
What he deserves of you and me I know;
What we can do to him, though now the time
Gives way to us, I much fear. If you cannot 16
Bar his access to th' King, never attempt 17
Anything on him, for he hath a witchcraft 18
Over the King in 's tongue.

NORFOLK   O, fear him not;
His spell in that is out. The King hath found 20
Matter against him that forever mars
The honey of his language. No, he's settled, 22
Not to come off, in his displeasure.

SURREY   Sir, 23
I should be glad to hear such news as this
Once every hour.

NORFOLK   Believe it, this is true.
In the divorce his contrary proceedings 26
Are all unfolded, wherein he appears 27
As I would wish mine enemy.

SURREY   How came
His practices to light?

SUFFOLK   Most strangely.

SURREY   O, how, how? 29

SUFFOLK
The Cardinal's letters to the Pope miscarried, 30
And came to th' eye o' the King, wherein was read
How that the Cardinal did entreat His Holiness
To stay the judgment o' the divorce; for if 33
It did take place, "I do," quoth he, "perceive
My king is tangled in affection to
A creature of the Queen's, Lady Anne Bullen." 36

SURREY
Has the King this?

SUFFOLK   Believe it.

SURREY   Will this work?

CHAMBERLAIN
The King in this perceives him, how he coasts 38
And hedges his own way. But in this point 39

---

154 ends intentions. honest honorable 156 places official positions 161 Grow from become estranged from. carriage conduct 165 temper disposition 166 even steadfast 170 As . . . you such as was given to you 172 For as for 174 studies efforts 176 used myself conducted myself 179 do my service pay my respects 183 That who. set footing here landed in England
3.2. Location: London. Antechamber to the King's apartments.

2 force urge 3–4 If . . . time if you let this opportunity pass 8 father-in-law i.e., Buckingham. (See 2.1.41–44 and notes.) 9 him Wolsey 10 uncontemned unscorned 11 Strangely neglected i.e., not been negligently disregarded 13 Out of excepting 16 Gives way to favors 17–18 attempt Anything on attack, move against 20 out finished 22 settled fixed 23 come off escape. his i.e., the King's 26 contrary contradictory, divisive 27 unfolded exposed 29 practices plots 30 miscarried went astray 33 stay stop, delay 36 creature dependent 38–39 coasts And hedges goes a roundabout way, as by coast and hedgerow

All his tricks founder, and he brings his physic   40
After his patient's death. The King already
Hath married the fair lady.

SURREY   Would he had!

SUFFOLK
May you be happy in your wish, my lord,
For I profess you have it.

SURREY   Now, all my joy
Trace the conjunction!

SUFFOLK   My amen to 't.

NORFOLK   All men's.   45

SUFFOLK
There's order given for her coronation.
Marry, this is yet but young, and may be left   47
To some ears unrecounted. But, my lords,
She is a gallant creature, and complete   49
In mind and feature. I persuade me, from her   50
Will fall some blessing to this land which shall
In it be memorized.

SURREY   But will the King   52
Digest this letter of the Cardinal's?   53
The Lord forbid!

NORFOLK   Marry, amen!

SUFFOLK   No, no;
There be more wasps that buzz about his nose
Will make this sting the sooner. Cardinal Campeius
Is stol'n away to Rome, hath ta'en no leave,
Has left the cause o' the King unhandled, and
Is posted, as the agent of our cardinal,   59
To second all his plot. I do assure you
The King cried "Ha!" at this.

CHAMBERLAIN   Now, God incense him,
And let him cry "Ha!" louder!

NORFOLK   But, my lord,
When returns Cranmer?

SUFFOLK
He is returned in his opinions, which   64
Have satisfied the King for his divorce,
Together with all famous colleges,
Almost, in Christendom. Shortly, I believe,
His second marriage shall be published, and   68
Her coronation. Katharine no more
Shall be called Queen, but Princess Dowager
And widow to Prince Arthur.

NORFOLK   This same Cranmer's
A worthy fellow, and hath ta'en much pain
In the King's business.

SUFFOLK   He has, and we shall see him
For it an archbishop.

NORFOLK   So I hear.

SUFFOLK   'Tis so.

Enter Wolsey and Cromwell.

The Cardinal!

NORFOLK   Observe, observe, he's moody.

                        [*The nobles stand aside and observe.*]

WOLSEY
The packet, Cromwell, gave 't you the King?   76

CROMWELL
To his own hand, in 's bedchamber.

WOLSEY   Looked he
O' th' inside of the paper?

CROMWELL   Presently   78
He did unseal them, and the first he viewed
He did it with a serious mind; a heed   80
Was in his countenance. You he bade
Attend him here this morning.

WOLSEY   Is he ready
To come abroad?

CROMWELL   I think by this he is.   84

WOLSEY Leave me awhile.   *Exit Cromwell.*
[*To himself.*] It shall be to the Duchess of Alençon,
The French King's sister; he shall marry her.
Anne Bullen? No, I'll no Anne Bullens for him;
There's more in 't than fair visage. Bullen?
No, we'll no Bullens. Speedily I wish
To hear from Rome. The Marchioness of Pembroke?

NORFOLK
He's discontented.

SUFFOLK   Maybe he hears the King
Does whet his anger to him.

SURREY   Sharp enough,
Lord, for thy justice!

WOLSEY [*to himself*]
The late Queen's gentlewoman, a knight's daughter,   95
To be her mistress' mistress? The Queen's queen?
This candle burns not clear; 'tis I must snuff it,   97
Then out it goes. What though I know her virtuous
And well deserving? Yet I know her for
A spleeny Lutheran, and not wholesome to   100
Our cause, that she should lie i' the bosom of
Our hard-ruled king. Again, there is sprung up   102
An heretic, an arch one, Cranmer, one
Hath crawled into the favor of the King   104
And is his oracle.

NORFOLK   He is vexed at something.   105

Enter King, reading of a schedule, [and Lovell.
Wolsey stands apart, not observing the King.]

SURREY
I would 'twere something that would fret the string, 106
The master cord on 's heart.

SUFFOLK   The King, the King!   107

KING [*to himself*]
What piles of wealth hath he accumulated
To his own portion! And what expense by th' hour
Seems to flow from him! How i' the name of thrift
Does he rake this together?—Now, my lords,
Saw you the Cardinal?

---

40 **physic** medicine, cure 45 **Trace** follow 47 **young** recent, new
49 **complete** perfect, excellent 50 **persuade me** am confident
52 **memorized** caused to be remembered. (Refers prophetically to
Queen Elizabeth.) 53 **Digest** put up with, "swallow" 59 **Is posted**
has gone in haste 64 **in his opinions** having sent ahead his written
opinions 68 **published** proclaimed

76 **packet** parcel of dispatches 78 **Presently** immediately 80 **heed**
concern 84 **this** this time 95 **late** former 97 **clear** bright. **snuff it**
trim its wick 100 **spleeny** hot-headed, contentious 102 **hard-ruled**
hard to manage 104 **Hath** who has 105 **s.d. schedule** scroll
106 **fret** gnaw through (with a pun on the musical sense of pressing
the string of a musical instrument against a "fret" or bar, continued in
the play on *cord/chord*) 107 **on 's** of his

NORFOLK   My lord, we have
Stood here observing him. Some strange commotion
Is in his brain. He bites his lip, and starts,
Stops on a sudden, looks upon the ground,
Then lays his finger on his temple; straight   116
Springs out into fast gait, then stops again,
Strikes his breast hard, and anon he casts
His eye against the moon. In most strange postures
We have seen him set himself.

KING   It may well be
There is a mutiny in 's mind. This morning
Papers of state he sent me to peruse,
As I required; and wot you what I found   123
There—on my conscience, put unwittingly?
Forsooth, an inventory, thus importing   125
The several parcels of his plate, his treasure,   126
Rich stuffs and ornaments of household, which
I find at such proud rate that it outspeaks   128
Possession of a subject.

NORFOLK   It's heaven's will.   129
Some spirit put this paper in the packet
To bless your eye withal.

KING   If we did think   131
His contemplation were above the earth
And fixed on spiritual object, he should still
Dwell in his musings; but I am afraid
His thinkings are below the moon, not worth   135
His serious considering.

King takes his seat; whispers [to] Lovell,
who goes to the Cardinal [Wolsey].

WOLSEY   Heaven forgive me!
Ever God bless Your Highness!

KING   Good my lord,
You are full of heavenly stuff and bear the inventory   138
Of your best graces in your mind, the which
You were now running o'er. You have scarce time
To steal from spiritual leisure a brief span
To keep your earthly audit. Sure in that
I deem you an ill husband, and am glad   143
To have you therein my companion.

WOLSEY   Sir,   144
For holy offices I have a time; a time
To think upon the part of business which
I bear i' the state; and nature does require
Her times of preservation, which perforce
I, her frail son, amongst my brethren mortal,
Must give my tendance to.

KING   You have said well.   150

WOLSEY
And ever may Your Highness yoke together,

As I will lend you cause, my doing well
With my well saying!

KING   'Tis well said again,
And 'tis a kind of good deed to say well;
And yet words are no deeds. My father loved you;
He said he did, and with his deed did crown   156
His word upon you. Since I had my office,   158
I have kept you next my heart, have not alone   158
Employed you where high profits might come home,
But pared my present havings, to bestow   160
My bounties upon you.

WOLSEY [*aside*]   What should this mean?

SURREY [*aside*]
The Lord increase this business!

KING   Have I not made you
The prime man of the state? I pray you, tell me   163
If what I now pronounce you have found true;   164
And if you may confess it, say withal
If you are bound to us or no. What say you?

WOLSEY
My sovereign, I confess your royal graces,   167
Show'red on me daily, have been more than could   168
My studied purposes requite, which went   169
Beyond all man's endeavors. My endeavors
Have ever come too short of my desires,
Yet filed with my abilities. Mine own ends   172
Have been mine so that evermore they pointed   173
To th' good of your most sacred person and
The profit of the state. For your great graces
Heaped upon me, poor undeserver, I
Can nothing render but allegiant thanks,   177
My prayers to heaven for you, my loyalty,
Which ever has and ever shall be growing,
Till death, that winter, kill it.

KING   Fairly answered.
A loyal and obedient subject is
Therein illustrated. The honor of it   182
Does pay the act of it, as, i' the contrary,   183
The foulness is the punishment. I presume   184
That, as my hand has opened bounty to you,   185
My heart dropped love, my power rained honor, more
On you than any, so your hand and heart,
Your brain, and every function of your power,
Should, notwithstanding that your bond of duty,   189
As 'twere in love's particular, be more   190
To me, your friend, than any.

WOLSEY   I do profess
That for Your Highness' good I ever labored
More than mine own; that am, have, and will be—   193

---

116 straight at once   **123 wot** know   **125 importing** signifying
126 several parcels various items.   **plate** precious metal in the form
of household plate   **128–129 outspeaks . . . subject** describes possessions exceeding what a subject should have   **131 withal** with
135 below the moon i.e., in the mortal sphere   **138 stuff . . . inventory** (The King chooses his words with sardonic irony to apply to spiritual contemplation and to the accumulation of wealth. The joke continues in *steal* and *audit*.)   **143 ill husband** unthrifty manager of your
affairs (but with ironic reference to his management of the King's marriage)   **143–144 am glad . . . companion** am glad to have such an
unacquisitive man as my adviser (but said with more ironic subtext)
150 tendance attention

156 crown i.e., fulfill (by appointing Wolsey chaplain in 1507 and
Dean of Lincoln in 1509)   **158 next** nearest   **160 pared . . . havings**
reduced my own wealth   **163 prime** principal   **164 pronounce** declare   **167 graces** favors   **168–169 more . . . requite** more than I
could devise means to repay   **172 filed** kept pace   **173 so that** only
to the extent that   **177 allegiant** loyal   **182 illustrated** made evident
182–183 The honor . . . it (Compare with "Virtue is its own reward.")   **184 The foulness . . . punishment** dishonor is the proper
punishment of disloyalty   **185 opened** granted   **189 that . . . duty**
i.e., your priestly vows   **190 in love's particular** in the special devotion of friendship   **193 have** have been

Though all the world should crack their duty to you 194
And throw it from their soul, though perils did
Abound as thick as thought could make 'em and
Appear in forms more horrid—yet my duty,
As doth a rock against the chiding flood,
Should the approach of this wild river break, 199
And stand unshaken yours.

KING　　　　　　　　　　　　　　'Tis nobly spoken.
Take notice, lords, he has a loyal breast,
For you have seen him open 't.—Read o'er this,
　　　　　　　　　　　　　　[giving him papers]
And after, this, and then to breakfast with
What appetite you have.
　　　　　　　Exit King, frowning upon the Cardinal
　　　　[Wolsey]; the nobles throng after him [the King],
　　　　　　smiling and whispering, [and so exeunt].

WOLSEY　　　　　　　　　　What should this mean?
What sudden anger's this? How have I reaped it? 205
He parted frowning from me, as if ruin
Leaped from his eyes. So looks the chafèd lion 207
Upon the daring huntsman that has galled him, 208
Then makes him nothing. I must read this paper— 209
I fear, the story of his anger. 'Tis so!
This paper has undone me. 'Tis th' account
Of all that world of wealth I have drawn together
For mine own ends—indeed, to gain the popedom
And fee my friends in Rome. O negligence, 214
Fit for a fool to fall by! What cross devil 215
Made me put this main secret in the packet 216
I sent the King? Is there no way to cure this?
No new device to beat this from his brains?
I know 'twill stir him strongly; yet I know
A way, if it take right, in spite of fortune 220
Will bring me off again. What's this? "To th' Pope"? 221
The letter, as I live, with all the business
I writ to 's Holiness. Nay then, farewell!
I have touched the highest point of all my greatness,
And, from that full meridian of my glory 225
I haste now to my setting. I shall fall
Like a bright exhalation in the evening, 227
And no man see me more.

　　　Enter to Wolsey the Dukes of Norfolk and Suffolk,
　　　the Earl of Surrey, and the Lord Chamberlain.

NORFOLK
Hear the King's pleasure, Cardinal, who commands
　　you
To render up the great seal presently 230
Into our hands, and to confine yourself
To Asher House, my lord of Winchester's,
Till you hear further from His Highness.

WOLSEY　　　　　　　　　　　　　　Stay,
Where's your commission, lords? Words cannot
　　carry 234

Authority so weighty.

SUFFOLK　　　　　　　　　Who dare cross 'em, 235
Bearing the King's will from his mouth expressly?

WOLSEY
Till I find more than will or words to do it— 237
I mean your malice—know, officious lords, 238
I dare and must deny it. Now I feel
Of what coarse metal ye are molded—envy; 240
How eagerly ye follow my disgraces
As if it fed ye, and how sleek and wanton 242
Ye appear in everything may bring my ruin!
Follow your envious courses, men of malice!
You have Christian warrant for 'em, and no doubt 245
In time will find their fit rewards. That seal
You ask with such a violence, the King,
Mine and your master, with his own hand gave me;
Bade me enjoy it, with the place and honors,
During my life; and, to confirm his goodness,
Tied it by letters patents. Now, who'll take it? 251

SURREY
The King that gave it.

WOLSEY　　　　　　It must be himself, then.

SURREY
Thou art a proud traitor, priest.

WOLSEY　　　　　　　　Proud lord, thou liest!
Within these forty hours Surrey durst better
Have burnt that tongue than said so.

SURREY　　　　　　　　　　　Thy ambition,
Thou scarlet sin, robbed this bewailing land 256
Of noble Buckingham, my father-in-law.
The heads of all thy brother cardinals,
With thee and all thy best parts bound together, 259
Weighed not a hair of his. Plague of your policy! 260
You sent me deputy for Ireland,
Far from his succor, from the King, from all
That might have mercy on the fault thou gav'st him; 263
Whilst your great goodness, out of holy pity,
Absolved him with an ax.

WOLSEY　　　　　　　　This, and all else
This talking lord can lay upon my credit, 266
I answer is most false. The Duke by law
Found his deserts. How innocent I was
From any private malice in his end 269
His noble jury and foul cause can witness.
If I loved many words, lord, I should tell you
You have as little honesty as honor,
That in the way of loyalty and truth 273
Toward the King, my ever royal master,
Dare mate a sounder man than Surrey can be, 275

---

194 crack violate　**199 break** resist　**205 reaped** i.e., deserved, incurred　**207 chafèd** angry　**208 galled** wounded　**209 makes him nothing** destroys him (the hunter)　**214 fee** bribe　**215 cross** perverse　**216 main** weighty　**220 take right** succeed　**221 bring me off** let me escape　**225 meridian** a star's highest point of altitude　**227 exhalation** any astronomical phenomenon, such as a meteor or a falling star　**230 presently** immediately　**234 commission** authorizing warrant

235 cross oppose　**237–238 Till . . . malice** until I find better reason than your professed verbal statement of the King's will—which is really your own malice—to do as you say　**240 metal** (meaning also "mettle").　**envy** malice　**242 sleek** fawning.　**wanton** reckless of justice　**245 Christian warrant** i.e., the example of other uncharitable Christians　**251 letters patents** formal and public bestowing of rights or powers　**256 Thou scarlet sin** (Refers to his cardinal's cassock, described as scarlet; see 3.1.103–104. See also Isaiah 1:18.)　**259 parts** qualities　**260 Weighed** equaled in weight.　**Plague of** a plague on.　**policy** scheming　**263 fault . . . him** offense you charged him (Buckingham) with　**266 lay . . . credit** charge against my good name　**269 From** of　**273 That** I that　**275 mate** vie with

And all that love his follies.

SURREY   By my soul,
Your long coat, priest, protects you; thou shouldst
  feel
My sword i' the lifeblood of thee else. My lords,
Can ye endure to hear this arrogance?
And from this fellow? If we live thus tamely,
To be thus jaded by a piece of scarlet,   281
Farewell nobility! Let His Grace go forward
And dare us with his cap, like larks.

WOLSEY   All goodness   283
Is poison to thy stomach.

SURREY   Yes, that goodness
Of gleaning all the land's wealth into one,
Into your own hands, Cardinal, by extortion;
The goodness of your intercepted packets
You writ to th' Pope against the King. Your
  goodness,
Since you provoke me, shall be most notorious.
My lord of Norfolk, as you are truly noble,
As you respect the common good, the state
Of our despised nobility, our issues,   292
Who, if he live, will scarce be gentlemen,   293
Produce the grand sum of his sins, the articles   294
Collected from his life. [*To Wolsey.*] I'll startle you
Worse than the sacring bell, when the brown wench   296
Lay kissing in your arms, Lord Cardinal.

WOLSEY
How much, methinks, I could despise this man,
But that I am bound in charity against it!

NORFOLK
Those articles, my lord, are in the King's hand;   300
But thus much, they are foul ones.

WOLSEY   So much fairer   301
And spotless shall mine innocence arise
When the King knows my truth.

SURREY   This cannot save you.   303
I thank my memory, I yet remember
Some of these articles, and out they shall.   305
Now, if you can blush and cry "guilty," Cardinal,
You'll show a little honesty.

WOLSEY   Speak on, sir;
I dare your worst objections. If I blush,   308
It is to see a nobleman want manners.   309

SURREY
I had rather want those than my head. Have at you!
First, that without the King's assent or knowledge
You wrought to be a legate, by which power   312
You maimed the jurisdiction of all bishops.

NORFOLK
Then, that in all you writ to Rome, or else

To foreign princes, "*Ego et Rex meus*"   315
Was still inscribed, in which you brought the King   316
To be your servant.

SUFFOLK   Then that, without the knowledge
Either of King or Council, when you went
Ambassador to the Emperor, you made bold
To carry into Flanders the great seal.

SURREY
Item, you sent a large commission   321
To Gregory de Cassado, to conclude,
Without the King's will or the state's allowance,   323
A league between His Highness and Ferrara.

SUFFOLK
That out of mere ambition you have caused   325
Your holy hat to be stamped on the King's coin.

SURREY
Then, that you have sent innumerable substance—   327
By what means got, I leave to your own
  conscience—
To furnish Rome, and to prepare the ways   329
You have for dignities, to the mere undoing   330
Of all the kingdom. Many more there are,
Which since they are of you, and odious,
I will not taint my mouth with.

CHAMBERLAIN   O my lord,
Press not a falling man too far! 'Tis virtue.   334
His faults lie open to the laws; let them,
Not you, correct him. My heart weeps to see him
So little of his great self.

SURREY   I forgive him.

SUFFOLK
Lord Cardinal, the King's further pleasure is—
Because all those things you have done of late
By your power legative within this kingdom   340
Fall into the compass of a praemunire—   341
That therefore such a writ be sued against you,   342
To forfeit all your goods, lands, tenements,   343
Chattels, and whatsoever, and to be   344
Out of the King's protection. This is my charge.

NORFOLK
And so we'll leave you to your meditations
How to live better. For your stubborn answer
About the giving back the great seal to us,
The King shall know it and, no doubt, shall
  thank you.

---

281 **jaded** intimidated, cowed   283 **dare . . . larks** dazzle us with his cardinal's hat as birds with a mirror or a piece of scarlet cloth   292 **issues** sons   293 **he** Wolsey   294 **articles** items of the indictment   296 **sacring bell** bell rung at the most solemn portions of the Mass. (Surrey imagines a scene in which Wolsey is in bed with a wench instead of attending Mass.)   300 **hand** possession   301 **thus much** (I can say) this much   303 **truth** loyalty   305 **shall** i.e., shall come   308 **dare** defy.   **objections** accusations   309 **want** lack   312 **wrought** connived, worked.   **legate** representative of the Pope

315 **Ego et Rex meus** my king and I. (Literally, "I and my king"; Norfolk accuses Wolsey of using the phrase in such a way as to make the King his "servant" by naming himself first, but the Latin construction requires that "ego" precede any nouns parallel with it.)   316 **still** always   321 **Item** i.e., another item is.   **large** with full power to act   323 **allowance** assent   325 **mere** sheer   327 **innumerable substance** uncountable wealth   329 **To furnish Rome** (Implies that Wolsey made gifts to Rome as bribes to obtain his own advancement.)   330 **mere** utter   334 **'Tis virtue** i.e., it's virtuous not to do so   340 **legative** as a papal legate   341 **Fall . . . praemunire** fall within the penalties for violating a writ of praemunire, i.e., a writ by which one could be charged with appealing to a foreign court (especially a papal court) in an action involving an English subject and hence relevant to the King's court   342 **sued** moved, issued   343 **tenements** properties not owned outright but held for some set term   344 **Chattels** personal possessions

So fare you well, my little good lord Cardinal.
Exeunt all but Wolsey.

WOLSEY
So farewell to the little good you bear me.
Farewell? A long farewell, to all my greatness!
This is the state of man: today he puts forth
The tender leaves of hopes; tomorrow blossoms,   354
And bears his blushing honors thick upon him;   355
The third day comes a frost, a killing frost,
And when he thinks, good easy man, full surely   357
His greatness is a-ripening, nips his root,
And then he falls as I do. I have ventured,
Like little wanton boys that swim on bladders,   360
This many summers in a sea of glory,
But far beyond my depth. My high-blown pride
At length broke under me and now has left me,
Weary and old with service, to the mercy
Of a rude stream that must forever hide me.   365
Vain pomp and glory of this world, I hate ye!
I feel my heart new opened. O, how wretched
Is that poor man that hangs on princes' favors!
There is betwixt that smile we would aspire to,
That sweet aspect of princes, and their ruin,   370
More pangs and fears than wars or women have;
And when he falls, he falls like Lucifer,
Never to hope again.

Enter Cromwell, standing amazed.

                                   Why, how now, Cromwell?   373
CROMWELL
I have no power to speak, sir.
WOLSEY   What, amazed
At my misfortunes? Can thy spirit wonder
A great man should decline? Nay, an you weep,   376
I am fall'n indeed.
CROMWELL   How does Your Grace?
WOLSEY   Why, well;
Never so truly happy, my good Cromwell.
I know myself now, and I feel within me
A peace above all earthly dignities,
A still and quiet conscience. The King has cured me,
I humbly thank His Grace, and from these shoulders,
These ruined pillars, out of pity, taken
A load would sink a navy—too much honor.
O, 'tis a burden, Cromwell, 'tis a burden
Too heavy for a man that hopes for heaven.
CROMWELL
I am glad Your Grace has made that right use of it.
WOLSEY
I hope I have. I am able now, methinks,
Out of a fortitude of soul I feel,
To endure more miseries and greater far
Than my weakhearted enemies dare offer.
What news abroad?
CROMWELL   The heaviest and the worst
Is your displeasure with the King.

WOLSEY   God bless him!   393
CROMWELL
The next is that Sir Thomas More is chosen
Lord Chancellor in your place.
WOLSEY   That's somewhat sudden.
But he's a learnèd man. May he continue
Long in His Highness' favor and do justice
For truth's sake and his conscience, that his bones,
When he has run his course and sleeps in blessings,
May have a tomb of orphans' tears wept on him!   400
What more?
CROMWELL   That Cranmer is returned with
   welcome,
Installed Lord Archbishop of Canterbury.
WOLSEY
That's news indeed.
CROMWELL   Last, that the Lady Anne,
Whom the King hath in secrecy long married,
This day was viewed in open as his queen,
Going to chapel, and the voice is now   406
Only about her coronation.
WOLSEY
There was the weight that pulled me down. O
   Cromwell,
The King has gone beyond me. All my glories   409
In that one woman I have lost forever.
No sun shall ever usher forth mine honors,
Or gild again the noble troops that waited   412
Upon my smiles. Go get thee from me, Cromwell!
I am a poor fall'n man, unworthy now
To be thy lord and master. Seek the King;
That sun, I pray, may never set! I have told him
What and how true thou art. He will advance thee;
Some little memory of me will stir him—
I know his noble nature—not to let
Thy hopeful service perish too. Good Cromwell,
Neglect him not; make use now, and provide   421
For thine own future safety.
CROMWELL   O my lord,
Must I then leave you? Must I needs forgo
So good, so noble, and so true a master?
Bear witness, all that have not hearts of iron,
With what a sorrow Cromwell leaves his lord.
The King shall have my service, but my prayers
Forever and forever shall be yours.
WOLSEY
Cromwell, I did not think to shed a tear
In all my miseries, but thou hast forced me,
Out of thy honest truth, to play the woman.   431
Let's dry our eyes. And thus far hear me, Cromwell,
And when I am forgotten, as I shall be,
And sleep in dull cold marble, where no mention
Of me more must be heard of, say I taught thee;
Say Wolsey, that once trod the ways of glory,
And sounded all the depths and shoals of honor,   437

354 **tender** young   355 **blushing** glowing   357 **easy** complacent,
credulous   360 **wanton** sportful   365 **rude** rough   370 **their ruin** the
ruin they bring about   373 **s.d. amazed** stunned   376 **an** if

393 **displeasure** disgrace   400 **orphans'** i.e., such as would be under
the legal guardianship of the Lord Chancellor   406 **voice** talk
409 **gone beyond** overreached   412 **troops** i.e., of retainers
421 **make use** take advantage   431 **play the woman** i.e., shed tears
437 **sounded** explored, fathomed

Found thee a way, out of his wreck, to rise in,   438
A sure and safe one, though thy master missed it.
Mark but my fall, and that that ruined me.
Cromwell, I charge thee, fling away ambition!   441
By that sin fell the angels; how can man, then,
The image of his Maker, hope to win by it?
Love thyself last; cherish those hearts that hate thee.
Corruption wins not more than honesty.
Still in thy right hand carry gentle peace   446
To silence envious tongues. Be just, and fear not.
Let all the ends thou aim'st at be thy country's,
Thy God's, and truth's; then if thou fall'st, O
    Cromwell,
Thou fall'st a blessed martyr.
Serve the King, and—prithee, lead me in.
There take an inventory of all I have,
To the last penny; 'tis the King's. My robe,   453
And my integrity to heaven, is all
I dare now call mine own. O Cromwell, Cromwell,
Had I but served my God with half the zeal
I served my king, he would not in mine age
Have left me naked to mine enemies.

CROMWELL
Good sir, have patience.

WOLSEY   So I have. Farewell
The hopes of court! My hopes in heaven do dwell.
                                                    Exeunt.

❧

4.1   *Enter two Gentlemen, meeting one another.*

FIRST GENTLEMAN
You're well met once again.

SECOND GENTLEMAN   So are you.   1

FIRST GENTLEMAN
You come to take your stand here and behold
The Lady Anne pass from her coronation?

SECOND GENTLEMAN
'Tis all my business. At our last encounter
The Duke of Buckingham came from his trial.

FIRST GENTLEMAN
'Tis very true. But that time offered sorrow;
This, general joy.

SECOND GENTLEMAN   'Tis well. The citizens,
I am sure, have shown at full their royal minds—   8
As, let 'em have their rights, they are ever
    forward—   9
In celebration of this day with shows,
Pageants, and sights of honor.

FIRST GENTLEMAN   Never greater,
Nor, I'll assure you, better taken, sir.   12

SECOND GENTLEMAN
May I be bold to ask what that contains,
That paper in your hand?

FIRST GENTLEMAN   Yes, 'tis the list
Of those that claim their offices this day
By custom of the coronation.
The Duke of Suffolk is the first, and claims
To be High Steward; next, the Duke of Norfolk,
He to be Earl Marshal. You may read the rest.
                                        [*He offers a paper.*]

SECOND GENTLEMAN
I thank you, sir. Had I not known those customs,
I should have been beholding to your paper.   21
But, I beseech you, what's become of Katharine,
The Princess Dowager? How goes her business?

FIRST GENTLEMAN
That I can tell you too. The Archbishop
Of Canterbury, accompanied with other
Learnèd and reverend fathers of his order,
Held a late court at Dunstable, six miles off   27
From Ampthill, where the Princess lay, to which   28
She was often cited by them, but appeared not;   29
And, to be short, for not-appearance and   30
The King's late scruple, by the main assent   31
Of all these learnèd men she was divorced,
And the late marriage made of none effect;   33
Since which she was removed to Kimbolton,
Where she remains now sick.

SECOND GENTLEMAN   Alas, good lady!
                                        [*Trumpets.*]
The trumpets sound. Stand close, the Queen is
    coming.   *Hautboys.* 36

            The Order of the Coronation.
1. *A lively flourish of Trumpets.*
2. *Then, two* Judges.
3. Lord Chancellor, *with purse and mace before him.*
4. Choristers, *singing. Music.*
5. Mayor of London, *bearing the mace. Then* Garter,
   *in his coat of arms, and on his head he wore a gilt
   copper crown.*
6. Marquess Dorset, *bearing a scepter of gold, on his
   head a demi-coronal of gold. With him, the* Earl of
   Surrey, *bearing the rod of silver with the dove,
   crowned with an earl's coronet. Collars of S's.*
7. Duke of Suffolk, *in his robe of estate, his coronet on
   his head, bearing a long white wand, as High
   Steward. With him, the* Duke of Norfolk, *with the
   rod of marshalship, a coronet on his head. Collars of
   S's.*

---

438 **wreck** shipwreck   441 **fling away ambition** (Audiences were probably aware that Cromwell failed to heed this advice and was beheaded in 1540.)   446 **Still** always   453 **robe** i.e., clerical robe
4.1. Location: A street in Westminster.
1 **You're well met** I am happy to see you   8 **royal minds** loyalty to the crown (but perhaps suggesting also their pride)   9 **let . . . rights** to give them due credit.   **forward** i.e., eager to do

12 **taken** received   21 **beholding** beholden   27 **late** recent (as also in lines 31 and 33)   28 **lay** lodged   29 **cited** summoned   30 **short** brief   31 **main assent** general agreement   33 **of none effect** void, invalid   36 **close** aside.   **s.d. The Order of the Coronation:** (3)   **Lord Chancellor** i.e., Sir Thomas More.   (4)   **Music** musicians (as also in line 91).   (5)   **Garter** i.e., Garter King at Arms, a chief herald of the College of Arms.   (6)   **Collars of S's** golden chains of office made of flat, broad S-shaped links, ornately decorated.

8. A canopy borne by four of the Cinque Ports;
   under it, the Queen *in her robe, in her hair, richly*
   adorned with pearl, crowned. On each side her, the
   Bishops of London *and* Winchester.
9. *The old* Duchess of Norfolk, *in a coronal of gold*
   wrought with flowers, bearing the Queen's train.
10. *Certain* Ladies *or* Countesses, *with plain circlets of*
    gold without flowers.
    Exeunt, first passing over the stage in order and state,
    and then a great flourish of trumpets.

SECOND GENTLEMAN
A royal train, believe me. These I know.   37
Who's that that bears the scepter?
FIRST GENTLEMAN   Marquess Dorset,
And that the Earl of Surrey, with the rod.
SECOND GENTLEMAN
A bold brave gentleman. That should be
The Duke of Suffolk?
FIRST GENTLEMAN   'Tis the same: High Steward.
SECOND GENTLEMAN
And that my Lord of Norfolk?
FIRST GENTLEMAN   Yes.
SECOND GENTLEMAN [*looking at the Queen*]
                                   Heaven bless thee!
Thou hast the sweetest face I ever looked on.
Sir, as I have a soul, she is an angel;
Our King has all the Indies in his arms,
And more, and richer, when he strains that lady.   46
I cannot blame his conscience.
FIRST GENTLEMAN   They that bear
The cloth of honor over her are four barons   48
Of the Cinque Ports.   49
SECOND GENTLEMAN
Those men are happy, and so are all are near her.   50
I take it she that carries up the train
Is that old noble lady, Duchess of Norfolk.
FIRST GENTLEMAN
It is, and all the rest are countesses.
SECOND GENTLEMAN
Their coronets say so. These are stars indeed.
FIRST GENTLEMAN
And sometimes falling ones.
SECOND GENTLEMAN   No more of that.   55
                    [*Exit the last of the procession.*]

     Enter a third Gentleman.

FIRST GENTLEMAN
God save you, sir! Where have you been broiling?   56
THIRD GENTLEMAN
Among the crowd i' th' Abbey, where a finger

Could not be wedged in more. I am stifled
With the mere rankness of their joy.
SECOND GENTLEMAN   You saw   59
The ceremony?
THIRD GENTLEMAN   That I did.
FIRST GENTLEMAN   How was it?
THIRD GENTLEMAN
Well worth the seeing.
SECOND GENTLEMAN   Good sir, speak it to us.   61
THIRD GENTLEMAN
As well as I am able. The rich stream
Of lords and ladies, having brought the Queen
To a prepared place in the choir, fell off   64
A distance from her, while Her Grace sat down
To rest awhile, some half an hour or so,
In a rich chair of state, opposing freely   67
The beauty of her person to the people.
Believe me, sir, she is the goodliest woman
That ever lay by man; which when the people
Had the full view of, such a noise arose
As the shrouds make at sea in a stiff tempest,   72
As loud, and to as many tunes. Hats, cloaks—
Doublets, I think—flew up; and had their faces   74
Been loose, this day they had been lost. Such joy
I never saw before. Great-bellied women,
That had not half a week to go, like rams   77
In the old time of war, would shake the press   78
And make 'em reel before 'em. No man living
Could say "This is my wife" there, all were woven
So strangely in one piece.
SECOND GENTLEMAN   But what followed?
THIRD GENTLEMAN
At length Her Grace rose and with modest paces
Came to the altar, where she kneeled, and saintlike
Cast her fair eyes to heaven and prayed devoutly,
Then rose again and bowed her to the people;
When by the Archbishop of Canterbury
She had all the royal makings of a queen,
As holy oil, Edward Confessor's crown,   88
The rod, and bird of peace, and all such emblems
Laid nobly on her; which performed, the choir,
With all the choicest music of the kingdom,   91
Together sung *Te Deum*. So she parted,   92
And with the same full state paced back again   93
To York Place, where the feast is held.
FIRST GENTLEMAN   Sir,
You must no more call it York Place; that's past,
For since the Cardinal fell that title's lost.
'Tis now the King's, and called Whitehall.
THIRD GENTLEMAN   I know it,

(8) **Cinque Ports** barons of the Cinque Ports, a group of seaport towns (originally Dover, Hastings, Sandwich, Hythe, and Romney) situated on the southeast coast of England, in ancient times furnishing the chief parts of the English navy, in return for which they had many privileges and franchises. **in her hair** with hair loosely hanging (customary for brides) **37 train** procession **46 strains** embraces **48 cloth of honor** canopy **49 Cinque Ports** (See line 36 s.d. and note.) **50 all** all who **55 falling** (With a sexual pun.) **56 broiling** sweating

59 mere rankness (1) sheer exuberance (2) smelliness **61 speak** describe **64 fell off** withdrew **67 opposing** presenting in full view **72 shrouds** sail ropes **74 Doublets** close-fitting jackets **77 rams** battering rams **78 press** crowd **88 As** such as, namely **91 music** musicians **92 Te Deum** (A hymn of thanksgiving, the opening words of which are, *Te Deum laudamus*, "Thee, God, we praise.") **parted** departed **93 state** dignity

But 'tis so lately altered that the old name   98
Is fresh about me.
SECOND GENTLEMAN What two reverend bishops
Were those that went on each side of the Queen?
THIRD GENTLEMAN
Stokesley and Gardiner, the one of Winchester,   101
Newly preferred from the King's secretary,   102
The other, London.
SECOND GENTLEMAN He of Winchester   103
Is held no great good lover of the Archbishop's,
The virtuous Cranmer.
THIRD GENTLEMAN   All the land knows that.
However, yet there is no great breach; when it
   comes,
Cranmer will find a friend will not shrink from him.   107
SECOND GENTLEMAN
Who may that be, I pray you?
THIRD GENTLEMAN   Thomas Cromwell,
A man in much esteem with the King, and truly
A worthy friend. The King has made him Master
O' the Jewel House,
And one already of the Privy Council.
SECOND GENTLEMAN
He will deserve more.
THIRD GENTLEMAN   Yes, without all doubt.
Come, gentlemen, ye shall go my way, which
Is to the court, and there ye shall be my guests.
Something I can command. As I walk thither,   116
I'll tell ye more.
BOTH   You may command us, sir.   *Exeunt.*

❧

4.2   *Enter Katharine, Dowager, sick, led between*
Griffith, her gentleman usher, and Patience, her
woman.

GRIFFITH
How does Your Grace?
KATHARINE   O Griffith, sick to death!
My legs like loaden branches bow to th' earth,   2
Willing to leave their burden. Reach a chair.[*She sits.*]
So; now, methinks, I feel a little ease.
Didst thou not tell me, Griffith, as thou ledst me,
That the great child of honor, Cardinal Wolsey,
Was dead?
GRIFFITH   Yes, madam; but I think Your Grace,
Out of the pain you suffered, gave no ear to 't.
KATHARINE
Prithee, good Griffith, tell me how he died.
If well, he stepped before me happily   10
For my example.

GRIFFITH   Well, the voice goes, madam;   11
For after the stout Earl Northumberland   12
Arrested him at York, and brought him forward,
As a man sorely tainted, to his answer,   14
He fell sick suddenly and grew so ill
He could not sit his mule.
KATHARINE   Alas, poor man!
GRIFFITH
At last, with easy roads, he came to Leicester,   17
Lodged in the abbey, where the reverend abbot,
With all his convent, honorably received him,   19
To whom he gave these words: "O father Abbot,
An old man, broken with the storms of state,
Is come to lay his weary bones among ye.
Give him a little earth for charity!"
So went to bed, where eagerly his sickness
Pursued him still; and three nights after this,
About the hour of eight, which he himself
Foretold should be his last, full of repentance,
Continual meditations, tears, and sorrows,
He gave his honors to the world again,
His blessèd part to heaven, and slept in peace.
KATHARINE
So may he rest; his faults lie gently on him!
Yet thus far, Griffith, give me leave to speak him,   32
And yet with charity. He was a man
Of an unbounded stomach, ever ranking   34
Himself with princes; one that by suggestion   35
Tied all the kingdom. Simony was fair play.   36
His own opinion was his law. I' the presence   37
He would say untruths, and be ever double   38
Both in his words and meaning. He was never,
But where he meant to ruin, pitiful.   40
His promises were, as he then was, mighty;
But his performance, as he is now, nothing.
Of his own body he was ill, and gave   43
The clergy ill example.
GRIFFITH   Noble madam,
Men's evil manners live in brass; their virtues
We write in water. May it please Your Highness
To hear me speak his good now?
KATHARINE   Yes, good Griffith;
I were malicious else.
GRIFFITH   This cardinal,
Though from an humble stock, undoubtedly
Was fashioned to much honor. From his cradle
He was a scholar, and a ripe and good one,
Exceeding wise, fair-spoken, and persuading;
Lofty and sour to them that loved him not,
But, to those men that sought him, sweet as
   summer.
And though he were unsatisfied in getting,   55
Which was a sin, yet in bestowing, madam,

98 **lately** recently   **101–102 Gardiner . . . secretary** (Gardiner, secretary to the King, was made Bishop of Winchester at the fall of Wolsey; he continued to act as secretary for several years.)   **102 preferred** promoted   **103 London** i.e., Bishop of London   **107 will not** who will not   **116 Something . . . command** i.e., I can order refreshment
4.2. Location: Kimbolton Castle in Huntingtonshire. The Queen's apartments.
2 loaden laden, weighted down   **10 happily** fittingly

11 the voice goes people say   **12 stout** brave   **14 sorely tainted** grievously discredited.   **answer** i.e., trial   **17 roads** stages (of a journey)   **19 convent** monastery   **32 speak** describe   **34 stomach** ambition   **35 suggestion** crafty dealing   **36 Tied** fettered, controlled. **Simony** the selling of ecclesiastical offices   **37 presence** i.e., of the King   **38 double** duplicitous   **40 pitiful** pitying, compassionate   **43 ill** depraved   **55 getting** acquiring wealth

He was most princely. Ever witness for him
Those twins of learning that he raised in you,   58
Ipswich and Oxford, one of which fell with him,   59
Unwilling to outlive the good that did it;   60
The other, though unfinished, yet so famous,
So excellent in art, and still so rising,   62
That Christendom shall ever speak his virtue.
His overthrow heaped happiness upon him;
For then, and not till then, he felt himself,   65
And found the blessedness of being little.   66
And, to add greater honors to his age
Than man could give him, he died fearing God.

KATHARINE
After my death I wish no other herald,
No other speaker of my living actions,   70
To keep mine honor from corruption
But such an honest chronicler as Griffith.
Whom I most hated living, thou hast made me,   73
With thy religious truth and modesty,   74
Now in his ashes honor. Peace be with him!
Patience, be near me still, and set me lower.
I have not long to trouble thee. Good Griffith,
Cause the musicians play me that sad note   78
I named my knell, whilst I sit meditating
On that celestial harmony I go to.
                      Sad and solemn music. [Katharine sleeps.]

GRIFFITH
She is asleep. Good wench, let's sit down quiet,
For fear we wake her. Softly, gentle Patience.   82
                                        [They sit.]

*The vision. Enter, solemnly tripping one after
another, six personages, clad in white robes,
wearing on their heads garlands of bays, and
golden vizards on their faces, branches of bays or
palm in their hands. They first congee unto her,
then dance; and, at certain changes, the first two
hold a spare garland over her head, at which the
other four make reverent curtsies. Then the two
that held the garland deliver the same to the other
next two, who observe the same order in their
changes, and holding the garland over her head;
which done, they deliver the same garland to the
last two, who likewise observe the same order; at
which, as it were by inspiration, she makes in her
sleep signs of rejoicing, and holdeth up her hands
to heaven; and so in their dancing vanish, carrying
the garland with them. The music continues.*

KATHARINE *[waking]*
Spirits of peace, where are ye? Are ye all gone,
And leave me here in wretchedness behind ye?

GRIFFITH
Madam, we are here.

KATHARINE   It is not you I call for.
Saw ye none enter since I slept?

GRIFFITH   None, madam.

KATHARINE
No? Saw you not, even now, a blessèd troop
Invite me to a banquet, whose bright faces
Cast thousand beams upon me, like the sun?
They promised me eternal happiness,
And brought me garlands, Griffith, which I feel
I am not worthy yet to wear. I shall, assuredly.

GRIFFITH
I am most joyful, madam, such good dreams
Possess your fancy.

KATHARINE   Bid the music leave;   94
They are harsh and heavy to me.   *Music ceases.*

PATIENCE *[to Griffith]*   Do you note
How much Her Grace is altered on the sudden?
How long her face is drawn? How pale she looks,
And of an earthy cold? Mark her eyes!

GRIFFITH
She is going, wench. Pray, pray.

PATIENCE   Heaven comfort her!

                      Enter a Messenger.

MESSENGER
An 't like Your Grace—

KATHARINE   You are a saucy fellow.   100
Deserve we no more reverence?

GRIFFITH *[to the Messenger]*   You are too blame,   101
Knowing she will not lose her wonted greatness,   102
To use so rude behavior. Go to, kneel.

MESSENGER *[kneeling]*
I humbly do entreat Your Highness' pardon;
My haste made me unmannerly. There is staying   105
A gentleman, sent from the King, to see you.

KATHARINE
Admit him entrance, Griffith. But this fellow
Let me ne'er see again.   *Exit Messenger.*

        Enter Lord Capuchius [admitted by Griffith].

                                     If my sight fail not,
You should be Lord Ambassador from the Emperor,   109
My royal nephew, and your name Capuchius.

CAPUCHIUS
Madam, the same; your servant.

KATHARINE   O, my lord,
The times and titles now are altered strangely
With me since first you knew me. But I pray you,
What is your pleasure with me?

CAPUCHIUS   Noble lady,
First, mine own service to Your Grace; the next,
The King's request that I would visit you,
Who grieves much for your weakness, and by me

58–59 **raised . . . Oxford** built in you, O Ipswich and Oxford. (Wolsey founded a college, no longer extant, at Ipswich, where he was born, and a college at Oxford that is now Christ Church.)   60 **good that did** goodness that founded   62 **art** learning   65 **felt** knew 66 **little** of humble station   70 **living** while alive   73 **Whom** he whom   74 **modesty** moderation   78 **note** tune   82 s.d. **The vision: bays** bay leaves.   **vizards** masks.   **congee** make a congé, a ceremonious bow.   **changes** figures in the dance

94 **fancy** imagination.   **music leave** musicians cease   100 **An 't like** if it please   101 **too blame** too blameworthy   102 **lose** forgo. **wonted** accustomed   105 **staying** waiting   109 **Emperor** i.e., Charles V

Sends you his princely commendations,
And heartily entreats you take good comfort.
KATHARINE
O, my good lord, that comfort comes too late;
'Tis like a pardon after execution.
That gentle physic, given in time, had cured me,   122
But now I am past all comforts here but prayers.
How does His Highness?
CAPUCHIUS   Madam, in good health.
KATHARINE
So may he ever do, and ever flourish,
When I shall dwell with worms, and my poor name
Banished the kingdom!—Patience, is that letter
I caused you write yet sent away?
PATIENCE   No, madam.
KATHARINE
Sir, I most humbly pray you to deliver
This to my lord the King.
            [The letter is given to Capuchius.]
CAPUCHIUS   Most willing, madam.
KATHARINE
In which I have commended to his goodness
The model of our chaste loves, his young
    daughter—   132
The dews of heaven fall thick in blessings on her!—
Beseeching him to give her virtuous breeding—   134
She is young, and of a noble modest nature;
I hope she will deserve well—and a little
To love her for her mother's sake, that loved him,
Heaven knows how dearly. My next poor petition
Is that His Noble Grace would have some pity
Upon my wretched women, that so long
Have followed both my fortunes faithfully;   141
Of which there is not one, I dare avow—
And now I should not lie—but will deserve,   143
For virtue and true beauty of the soul,
For honesty and decent carriage,   145
A right good husband. Let him be a noble;
And sure those men are happy that shall have 'em.
The last is for my men—they are the poorest,
But poverty could never draw 'em from me—
That they may have their wages duly paid 'em,
And something over to remember me by.   151
If heaven had pleased to have given me longer life
And able means, we had not parted thus.   153
These are the whole contents. And, good my lord,
By that you love the dearest in this world,
As you wish Christian peace to souls departed,
Stand these poor people's friend, and urge the King
To do me this last right.
CAPUCHIUS   By heaven, I will,
Or let me lose the fashion of a man!   159

KATHARINE
I thank you, honest lord. Remember me
In all humility unto His Highness.
Say his long trouble now is passing
Out of this world. Tell him in death I blessed him,
For so I will. Mine eyes grow dim. Farewell,
My lord. Griffith, farewell. Nay, Patience,
You must not leave me yet. I must to bed;
Call in more women. When I am dead, good wench,
Let me be used with honor. Strew me over
With maiden flowers, that all the world may know   169
I was a chaste wife to my grave. Embalm me,
Then lay me forth; although unqueened, yet like   171
A queen, and daughter to a king, inter me.
I can no more.   Exeunt, leading Katharine. 173

5.1 *Enter Gardiner, Bishop of Winchester, a Page with
a torch before him, met by Sir Thomas Lovell.*

GARDINER
It's one o'clock, boy, is 't not?
PAGE   It hath struck.
GARDINER
These should be hours for necessities,
Not for delights; times to repair our nature
With comforting repose, and not for us
To waste these times.—Good hour of night, Sir
    Thomas!
Whither so late?
LOVELL   Came you from the King, my lord?
GARDINER
I did, Sir Thomas, and left him at primero   7
With the Duke of Suffolk.
LOVELL   I must to him too,
Before he go to bed. I'll take my leave.
GARDINER
Not yet, Sir Thomas Lovell. What's the matter?
It seems you are in haste. An if there be   11
No great offense belongs to 't, give your friend
Some touch of your late business. Affairs that walk, 13
As they say spirits do, at midnight, have
In them a wilder nature than the business
That seeks dispatch by day.
LOVELL   My lord, I love you,   16
And durst commend a secret to your ear   17
Much weightier than this work. The Queen's in
    labor,   18
They say, in great extremity, and feared   19
She'll with the labor end.
GARDINER   The fruit she goes with
I pray for heartily, that it may find

122 physic remedy.   had would have   132 model image.   young
daughter i.e., Mary, the only one of Katharine's many children to live
to maturity; she became Queen of England (1553–1558) before her
half-sister Elizabeth (1558–1603)   134 breeding upbringing
141 both my fortunes i.e., good and ill   143 now i.e., on my deathbed, when true speaking is of utmost spiritual importance   145 honesty . . . carriage chastity and proper behavior   151 over in addition
153 able sufficient   159 fashion nature, characteristics

169 maiden flowers spring flowers, symbolic of chastity. (Compare
The Winter's Tale, 4.4.113–129.)   171 lay me forth lay me out for
burial   173 can can do
5.1. Location: London. A gallery in the palace.
7 primero gambling card game   11 An if if   13 touch hint.   late recent   16 dispatch accomplishment   17 commend entrust   18 this
work i.e., what I am involved in   19 feared i.e., it is feared that

Good time, and live; but for the stock, Sir Thomas,   22
I wish it grubbed up now.

LOVELL   Methinks I could   23
Cry the amen; and yet my conscience says   24
She's a good creature and, sweet lady, does
Deserve our better wishes.

GARDINER   But, sir, sir,
Hear me, Sir Thomas. You're a gentleman
Of mine own way. I know you wise, religious;   28
And, let me tell you, it will ne'er be well—
'Twill not, Sir Thomas Lovell, take 't of me—
Till Cranmer, Cromwell—her two hands—and she
Sleep in their graves.

LOVELL   Now, sir, you speak of two
The most remarked i' the kingdom. As for
   Cromwell,   33
Besides that of the Jewel House, is made Master   34
O' the Rolls, and the King's secretary; further, sir,   35
Stands in the gap and trade of more preferments   36
With which the time will load him. Th' Archbishop   37
Is the King's hand and tongue, and who dare speak
One syllable against him?

GARDINER   Yes, yes, Sir Thomas,
There are that dare, and I myself have ventured
To speak my mind of him; and indeed this day,
Sir, I may tell it you, I think—I have
Incensed the lords o' the Council that he is—   43
For so I know he is, they know he is—
A most arch heretic, a pestilence
That does infect the land; with which they, moved,   46
Have broken with the King, who hath so far   47
Given ear to our complaint, of his great grace
And princely care foreseeing those fell mischiefs   49
Our reasons laid before him, hath commanded   50
Tomorrow morning to the Council board
He be convented. He's a rank weed, Sir Thomas,   52
And we must root him out. From your affairs
I hinder you too long. Good night, Sir Thomas.

LOVELL
Many good nights, my lord. I rest your servant.   55

                    Exeunt Gardiner and Page.

          Enter King and Suffolk.

KING [*to Suffolk*]
Charles, I will play no more tonight.
My mind's not on 't; you are too hard for me.   57

SUFFOLK
Sir, I did never win of you before.

KING   But little, Charles,
Nor shall not, when my fancy's on my play.—   60
Now, Lovell, from the Queen what is the news?

LOVELL
I could not personally deliver to her
What you commanded me, but by her woman
I sent your message, who returned her thanks
In the great'st humbleness and desired Your
   Highness
Most heartily to pray for her.

KING   What sayst thou, ha?
To pray for her? What, is she crying out?

LOVELL
So said her woman, and that her sufferance made   68
Almost each pang a death.

KING   Alas, good lady!

SUFFOLK
God safely quit her of her burden, and   70
With gentle travail, to the gladding of
Your Highness with an heir!

KING   'Tis midnight, Charles.
Prithee, to bed, and in thy prayers remember
Th' estate of my poor queen. Leave me alone,   74
For I must think of that which company
Would not be friendly to.

SUFFOLK   I wish Your Highness
A quiet night, and my good mistress will   77
Remember in my prayers.

KING   Charles, good night.   78

                         Exit Suffolk.

          Enter Sir Anthony Denny.

Well, sir, what follows?

DENNY
Sir, I have brought my lord the Archbishop,
As you commanded me.

KING   Ha? Canterbury?

DENNY
Ay, my good lord.

KING   'Tis true. Where is he, Denny?

DENNY
He attends Your Highness' pleasure.

KING   Bring him to us.
                              [*Exit Denny.*]

LOVELL [*aside*]
This is about that which the Bishop spake.   84
I am happily come hither.   85

          Enter Cranmer and Denny.

KING
Avoid the gallery. (*Lovell seems to stay.*) Ha? I have
   said. Begone.   86
What?   *Exeunt Lovell and Denny.*

CRANMER [*aside*]   I am fearful. Wherefore frowns he
   thus?
'Tis his aspect of terror. All's not well.   88

KING
How now, my lord? You do desire to know

---

22 Good time good fortune, a good delivery.   **stock** trunk or main
stem (i.e., Queen Anne herself)   **23 grubbed up** rooted up   **24 Cry
the amen** give assent   **28 way** religious faith (opposed to Protestant
reform)   **33 remarked** under the public eye   **34–35 Master . . .
Rolls** judge of the Court of Appeal   **36 gap and trade** opening and
beaten path   **37 time** course of events   **43 Incensed** stirred up
46–47 with . . . King which they, moved to anger at the idea, have
disclosed to the King   **49 fell** terrible, cruel   **50 hath** (that) he has
52 convented summoned   **55 rest** remain   **57 hard** good a player
60 fancy's mind's

68 sufferance suffering   **70 God** may God.   **quit** release   **74 estate**
condition   **77–78 and my . . . Remember** and I will remember my
good mistress, the Queen   **84 the Bishop** i.e., Gardiner   **85 happily**
luckily   **86 Avoid** vacate   **88 aspect** expression

Wherefore I sent for you.
CRANMER [*kneeling*]   It is my duty   90
  T' attend Your Highness' pleasure.
KING   Pray you, arise,
  My good and gracious lord of Canterbury.
  Come, you and I must walk a turn together;
  I have news to tell you. Come, come, give me your
    hand.   [*Cranmer rises.*]
  Ah, my good lord, I grieve at what I speak
  And am right sorry to repeat what follows.
  I have, and most unwillingly, of late
  Heard many grievous—I do say, my lord,
  Grievous—complaints of you, which, being
    considered,
  Have moved us and our Council that you shall
  This morning come before us, where I know
  You cannot with such freedom purge yourself   102
  But that, till further trial in those charges
  Which will require your answer, you must take
  Your patience to you and be well contented
  To make your house our Tow'r. You a brother of us, 106
  It fits we thus proceed, or else no witness   107
  Would come against you.
CRANMER [*kneeling*]   I humbly thank Your Highness,
  And am right glad to catch this good occasion
  Most throughly to be winnowed, where my chaff   110
  And corn shall fly asunder. For I know   111
  There's none stands under more calumnious tongues 112
  Than I myself, poor man.
KING   Stand up, good Canterbury!
  Thy truth and thy integrity is rooted
  In us, thy friend. Give me thy hand, stand up.
                                 [*Cranmer rises.*]
  Prithee, let's walk. Now, by my halidom,   116
  What manner of man are you? My lord, I looked   117
  You would have given me your petition that
  I should have ta'en some pains to bring together
  Yourself and your accusers, and to have heard you
  Without endurance further.
CRANMER   Most dread liege,   121
  The good I stand on is my truth and honesty.
  If they shall fail, I, with mine enemies,
  Will triumph o'er my person, which I weigh not,   124
  Being of those virtues vacant. I fear nothing   125
  What can be said against me.
KING   Know you not
  How your state stands i' the world, with the whole
    world?
  Your enemies are many, and not small; their
    practices   128
  Must bear the same proportion, and not ever   129

The justice and the truth o' the question carries   130
The due o' the verdict with it. At what ease   131
Might corrupt minds procure knaves as corrupt
To swear against you? Such things have been done.
You are potently opposed, and with a malice
Of as great size. Ween you of better luck,   135
I mean in perjured witness, than your master,   136
Whose minister you are, whiles here he lived
Upon this naughty earth? Go to, go to,   138
You take a precipice for no leap of danger
And woo your own destruction.
CRANMER   God and Your Majesty
  Protect mine innocence! Or I fall into
  The trap is laid for me.
KING   Be of good cheer;   142
  They shall no more prevail than we give way to.   143
  Keep comfort to you, and this morning see
  You do appear before them. If they shall chance,
  In charging you with matters, to commit you,   146
  The best persuasions to the contrary
  Fail not to use, and with what vehemency
  Th' occasion shall instruct you. If entreaties
  Will render you no remedy, this ring
  Deliver them, and your appeal to us
  There make before them. [*He gives a ring.*] Look, the
    good man weeps!
  He's honest, on mine honor. God's blest mother,
  I swear he is truehearted, and a soul
  None better in my kingdom. Get you gone,
  And do as I have bid you. (*Exit Cranmer.*) He has
    strangled
  His language in his tears.

                    Enter Old Lady.

LOVELL (*within*)   Come back! What mean you?
OLD LADY
  I'll not come back. The tidings that I bring
  Will make my boldness manners.—Now, good
    angels   159
  Fly o'er thy royal head, and shade thy person
  Under their blessèd wings!
KING   Now, by thy looks
  I guess thy message. Is the Queen delivered?
  Say ay, and of a boy.
OLD LADY   Ay, ay, my liege,
  And of a lovely boy. The God of heaven
  Both now and ever bless her! 'Tis a girl
  Promises boys hereafter. Sir, your queen
  Desires your visitation, and to be
  Acquainted with this stranger. 'Tis as like you
  As cherry is to cherry.
KING   Lovell!
LOVELL   Sir?
KING
  Give her an hundred marks. I'll to the Queen.   170
                               Exit King.

90 **Wherefore** why   102 **freedom** ease and completeness.   **purge** excuse, clear   106 **a brother of us** being a fellow member of the Council   107 **fits** is appropriate   110 **throughly** thoroughly   111 **corn** grain   112 **stands under** is the object of.   **calumnious** slandering   116 **by my halidom** i.e., by something sacred   117 **looked** expected   121 **endurance** imprisonment   124–125 **which . . . vacant** i.e., which I do not value if it is void of those virtues (*truth* and *honesty*)   125 **nothing** not at all   128 **small** insignificant.   **practices** schemes, plots   129 **bear . . . proportion** be correspondingly numerous and mighty   129–131 **not . . . it** the innocence of a person does not always ensure his acquittal

131 **At what ease** how easily   135 **Ween you of** do you expect   136 **master** i.e., Christ   138 **naughty** wicked   142 **is** that is   143 **give way to** allow   146 **commit** i.e., to prison   159 **good angels** may good angels   170 **an hundred marks** i.e., about sixty-five pounds

OLD LADY
An hundred marks? By this light, I'll ha' more.
An ordinary groom is for such payment.   172
I will have more, or scold it out of him.
Said I for this the girl was like to him?
I'll have more, or else unsay 't; and now,
While 'tis hot, I'll put it to the issue.   176

              Exit Lady [with Lovell].

❖

5.2   *Enter Cranmer, Archbishop of Canterbury,*
         [pursuivants, pages, etc. attending at the door].

CRANMER
I hope I am not too late, and yet the gentleman
That was sent to me from the Council prayed me
To make great haste. All fast? What means this? Ho!   3
Who waits there?

         Enter Keeper.

             Sure you know me?
KEEPER   Yes, my lord,
But yet I cannot help you.
CRANMER   Why?
KEEPER
Your Grace must wait till you be called for.

         Enter Doctor Butts.

CRANMER   So.
BUTTS [aside]
This is a piece of malice. I am glad
I came this way so happily. The King   9
Shall understand it presently.   *Exit Butts.*
CRANMER [aside]   'Tis Butts,   10
The King's physician. As he passed along,
How earnestly he cast his eyes upon me!
Pray heaven he sound not my disgrace! For certain   13
This is of purpose laid by some that hate me—   14
God turn their hearts! I never sought their malice—
To quench mine honor. They would shame to make
    me   16
Wait else at door, a fellow councillor,
'Mong boys, grooms, and lackeys. But their
    pleasures
Must be fulfilled, and I attend with patience.   19

         Enter the King and Butts at a window above.

---

172 **for** suited for   176 **put it to** force
5.2. Location: London. Adjacent to the council chamber.
s.d. pursuivants messengers, subordinates (as also in line 24).   **at the door** i.e., at a stage door, as though guarding the entrance to the Council chamber   3 **fast** locked   9 **happily** luckily   10 **presently** at once   13 **sound** fathom; or proclaim   14 **laid** contrived as a trap   16 **quench mine honor** destroy my reputation   19 **s.d. at a window above** (The gallery over the stage, representing a peephole through which the Council could be spied upon. The Folio text makes no scene division between this and the following scene, so that the Council would assemble under the view and in the hearing of the King, and the main stage, imagined in scene 2 to be adjacent to the Council chamber, becomes in scene 3 the chamber itself.)

BUTTS
I'll show Your Grace the strangest sight—
KING   What's that, Butts?
BUTTS
I think Your Highness saw this many a day.
KING
Body o' me, where is it?
BUTTS   There, my lord:
The high promotion of His Grace of Canterbury,
Who holds his state at door, 'mongst pursuivants,   24
Pages, and footboys.
KING   Ha? 'Tis he, indeed.
Is this the honor they do one another?
'Tis well there's one above 'em yet. I had thought   27
They had parted so much honesty among 'em—   28
At least good manners—as not thus to suffer
A man of his place, and so near our favor,   30
To dance attendance on their lordships' pleasures,   31
And at the door too, like a post with packets.   32
By holy Mary, Butts, there's knavery!
Let 'em alone, and draw the curtain close.
We shall hear more anon.

       [They conceal themselves behind the curtain.
       Cranmer remains waiting at the door, below.]

5.3   *A council table brought in with chairs and stools,*
      and placed under the state. Enter Lord Chancellor;
      places himself at the upper end of the table on the
      left hand, a seat being left void above him, as for
      Canterbury's seat. Duke of Suffolk, Duke of
      Norfolk, Surrey, Lord Chamberlain, Gardiner, seat
      themselves in order on each side. Cromwell at
      lower end, as secretary. [Keeper at the door.]

CHANCELLOR
Speak to the business, Master Secretary.
Why are we met in council?
CROMWELL   Please your honors,
The chief cause concerns His Grace of Canterbury.
GARDINER
Has he had knowledge of it?
CROMWELL   Yes.
NORFOLK   Who waits there?
KEEPER
Without, my noble lords?
GARDINER   Yes.
KEEPER   My lord Archbishop,   5
And has done half an hour, to know your pleasures.
CHANCELLOR
Let him come in.

---

24 **holds his state** maintains his dignity   27 **one above** (Suggests Henry's role as a godlike figure.)   28 **parted** shared.   **honor** honesty, decency   30 **place** official position   31 **dance attendance** stand waiting around   32 **post** messenger.   **packets** letters
5.3. Location: The Council chamber. Scene is continuous with the previous.
s.d. state canopy   5 **Without** outside the door. (Although Cranmer seemingly has never exited, the stage has now become the room into which he has been waiting to be admitted.)

KEEPER   Your Grace may enter now.
Cranmer approaches the council table.

CHANCELLOR
My good Lord Archbishop, I'm very sorry
To sit here at this present and behold   9
That chair stand empty. But we all are men,
In our own natures frail, and capable   11
Of our flesh—few are angels—out of which frailty   12
And want of wisdom, you, that best should teach
     us,
Have misdemeaned yourself, and not a little,   14
Toward the King first, then his laws, in filling
The whole realm, by your teaching and your
     chaplains'—
For so we are informed—with new opinions,
Divers and dangerous, which are heresies
And, not reformed, may prove pernicious.   19

GARDINER
Which reformation must be sudden too,
My noble lords; for those that tame wild horses
Pace 'em not in their hands to make 'em gentle,   22
But stop their mouths with stubborn bits and spur
     'em
Till they obey the manage. If we suffer,   24
Out of our easiness and childish pity   25
To one man's honor, this contagious sickness,
Farewell all physic! And what follows then?   27
Commotions, uproars, with a general taint
Of the whole state, as of late days our neighbors,
The upper Germany, can dearly witness,   30
Yet freshly pitied in our memories.

CRANMER
My good lords, hitherto, in all the progress
Both of my life and office, I have labored,
And with no little study, that my teaching
And the strong course of my authority
Might go one way, and safely; and the end
Was ever to do well. Nor is there living—
I speak it with a single heart, my lords—   38
A man that more detests, more stirs against,   39
Both in his private conscience and his place,   40
Defacers of a public peace than I do.
Pray heaven the King may never find a heart
With less allegiance in it! Men that make
Envy and crooked malice nourishment
Dare bite the best. I do beseech your lordships
That in this case of justice, my accusers,
Be what they will, may stand forth face to face
And freely urge against me.

SUFFOLK   Nay, my lord,   48
That cannot be. You are a councillor,
And by that virtue no man dare accuse you.   50

GARDINER
My lord, because we have business of more
     moment,
We will be short with you. 'Tis His Highness'
     pleasure,
And our consent, for better trial of you,
From hence you be committed to the Tower,
Where, being but a private man again,
You shall know many dare accuse you boldly—
More than, I fear, you are provided for.   57

CRANMER
Ah, my good lord of Winchester, I thank you;
You are always my good friend. If your will pass,   59
I shall both find your lordship judge and juror,
You are so merciful. I see your end;
'Tis my undoing. Love and meekness, lord,
Become a churchman better than ambition.
Win straying souls with modesty again;   64
Cast none away. That I shall clear myself,
Lay all the weight ye can upon my patience,   66
I make as little doubt as you do conscience   67
In doing daily wrongs. I could say more,   68
But reverence to your calling makes me modest.

GARDINER
My lord, my lord, you are a sectary,   70
That's the plain truth. Your painted gloss discovers,   71
To men that understand you, words and weakness.   72

CROMWELL
My lord of Winchester, you're a little,
By your good favor, too sharp. Men so noble,   74
However faulty, yet should find respect   75
For what they have been. 'Tis a cruelty
To load a falling man.

GARDINER   Good Master Secretary,   77
I cry your honor mercy; you may worst   78
Of all this table say so.

CROMWELL   Why, my lord?

GARDINER
Do not I know you for a favorer
Of this new sect? Ye are not sound.

CROMWELL   Not sound?   81

GARDINER
Not sound, I say.

CROMWELL   Would you were half so honest!
Men's prayers then would seek you, not their fears.

GARDINER
I shall remember this bold language.

CROMWELL   Do.
Remember your bold life too.

CHANCELLOR   This is too much.
Forbear, for shame, my lords.

GARDINER   I have done.

CROMWELL   And I.

---

9 **present** present time   11–12 **capable . . . flesh** susceptible to the weaknesses of the flesh   14 **misdemeaned yourself** been guilty of misconduct   19 **pernicious** deadly   22 **Pace . . . hands** don't lead them gently through their paces   24 **manage** training, handling.   **suffer** allow   25 **easiness** laxness   27 **physic** medicine, cure   30 **upper Germany** (Refers to the Peasants' Wars, 1524; possibly refers to the massacre of the Anabaptists in 1535.)   38 **single** honest; not given to double-dealing   39 **stirs** is active   40 **place** official capacity   48 **urge** make accusation   50 **by that virtue** by virtue of that

57 **provided** prepared   59 **pass** prevail   64 **modesty** moderation   66 **Lay . . . can** i.e., no matter how hard you press   67–68 **I . . . In** I have as little doubt (of my blamelessness) as you have scruples against   70 **sectary** follower of a heretical Protestant sect   71 **painted gloss discovers** false exterior (in speech and acts) reveals   72 **words** i.e., mere words   74 **By . . . favor** i.e., begging your pardon   75 **find** be accorded   77 **load** burden   78 **I cry . . . mercy** I beg your pardon. (Said ironically.)   **worst** with least justification   81 **sound** orthodox

CHANCELLOR [*to Cranmer*]
Then thus for you, my lord: it stands agreed,
I take it, by all voices, that forthwith
You be conveyed to the Tower a prisoner,
There to remain till the King's further pleasure
Be known unto us. Are you all agreed, lords?
ALL
We are.
CRANMER Is there no other way of mercy,
But I must needs to the Tower, my lords?
GARDINER   What other 93
Would you expect? You are strangely troublesome. 94
Let some o' the guard be ready there.

Enter the guard.

CRANMER   For me?
Must I go like a traitor thither?
GARDINER [*to the guard*]   Receive him,
And see him safe i' the Tower.
CRANMER   Stay, good my lords,
I have a little yet to say. Look there, my lords.
                    [*He shows the King's ring.*]
By virtue of that ring, I take my cause
Out of the grips of cruel men and give it   100
To a most noble judge, the King my master.
CHAMBERLAIN
This is the King's ring.
SURREY   'Tis no counterfeit.
SUFFOLK
'Tis the right ring, by heaven! I told ye all,
When we first put this dangerous stone a-rolling,
'Twould fall upon ourselves.
NORFOLK   Do you think, my lords,
The King will suffer but the little finger
Of this man to be vexed?
CHAMBERLAIN   'Tis now too certain.
How much more is his life in value with him!   108
Would I were fairly out on 't!
CROMWELL   My mind gave me,   109
In seeking tales and informations
Against this man, whose honesty the devil
And his disciples only envy at,   112
Ye blew the fire that burns ye. Now have at ye! 113

Enter King, frowning on them; takes his seat.

GARDINER
Dread sovereign, how much are we bound to
    heaven
In daily thanks, that gave us such a prince,
Not only good and wise, but most religious;
One that in all obedience makes the Church
The chief aim of his honor, and, to strengthen
That holy duty out of dear respect,   119
His royal self in judgment comes to hear

The cause betwixt her and this great offender.
KING
You were ever good at sudden commendations,   122
Bishop of Winchester. But know I come not
To hear such flattery now, and in my presence
They are too thin and base to hide offenses.
To me you cannot reach. You play the spaniel,
And think with wagging of your tongue to win me;
But whatsoe'er thou tak'st me for, I'm sure
Thou hast a cruel nature and a bloody.
[*To Cranmer.*] Good man, sit down. [*Cranmer sits.*]
Now let me see the proudest
He, that dares most, but wag his finger at thee. 131
By all that's holy, he had better starve   132
Than but once think this place becomes thee not.
SURREY
May it please Your Grace—
KING   No, sir, it does not please me.
I had thought I had had men of some understanding
And wisdom of my Council, but I find none.
Was it discretion, lords, to let this man,
This good man—few of you deserve that title—
This honest man, wait like a lousy footboy
At chamber door? And one as great as you are?
Why, what a shame was this! Did my commission
Bid ye so far forget yourselves? I gave ye
Power as he was a councillor to try him,
Not as a groom. There's some of ye, I see,
More out of malice than integrity,
Would try him to the utmost, had ye means
Which ye shall never have while I live.
CHANCELLOR   Thus far,
My most dread sovereign, may it like Your Grace   148
To let my tongue excuse all. What was purposed
Concerning his imprisonment was rather,
If there be faith in men, meant for his trial
And fair purgation to the world than malice,   152
I'm sure, in me.
KING   Well, well, my lords, respect him.
Take him, and use him well; he's worthy of it.
I will say thus much for him: if a prince
May be beholding to a subject, I   156
Am, for his love and service, so to him.
Make me no more ado, but all embrace him.
Be friends, for shame, my lords! [*They all embrace
    Cranmer.*] My lord of Canterbury,
I have a suit which you must not deny me:
That is, a fair young maid that yet wants baptism;
You must be godfather and answer for her.
CRANMER
The greatest monarch now alive may glory
In such an honor. How may I deserve it,
That am a poor and humble subject to you?
KING
Come, come, my lord, you'd spare your spoons.
You shall have   166

93 **must needs to** must necessarily go to   94 **strangely** uncommonly
100 **grips** clutches   108 **in value with** valued by.   **him** i.e., the King
109 **on 't** of it (this trouble).   **gave** told   112 **envy at** hate   113 **have
at ye** i.e., on guard, watch out. (Said as one attacks an opponent.)
s.d. Enter King (The King has presumably come down behind the
scene from above. He enters on the main stage.)   119 **dear respect**
heartfelt piety

122 **sudden commendations** unrehearsed compliments   131 **He** person   132 **starve** die   148 **like** please   152 **purgation** clearing of
himself   156 **beholding** beholden   166 **you'd . . . spoons** (Said jestingly; spoons were a common christening gift.)

Two noble partners with you: the old Duchess of
    Norfolk
And Lady Marquess Dorset. Will these please
    you?—
Once more, my lord of Winchester, I charge you,
Embrace and love this man.

GARDINER   With a true heart
And brother-love I do it.   [*He embraces Cranmer.*]

CRANMER   And let heaven
Witness how dear I hold this confirmation.

KING
Good man, those joyful tears show thy true heart.
The common voice, I see, is verified   174
Of thee, which says thus, "Do my lord of
    Canterbury
A shrewd turn, and he's your friend forever."   176
Come, lords, we trifle time away; I long
To have this young one made a Christian.
As I have made ye one, lords, one remain;   179
So I grow stronger, you more honor gain.   *Exeunt.*

❖

5.4   *Noise and tumult within. Enter Porter and his
Man.*

PORTER   You'll leave your noise anon, ye rascals! Do 1
you take the court for Paris Garden? Ye rude slaves, 2
leave your gaping. 3
ONE (*within*) Good master porter, I belong to the larder. 4
PORTER   Belong to the gallows, and be hanged, ye rogue!
Is this a place to roar in?—Fetch me a dozen crab tree
staves, and strong ones; these are but switches to 7
'em.—I'll scratch your heads. You must be seeing 8
christenings? Do you look for ale and cakes here, you 9
rude rascals?
MAN
Pray, sir, be patient. 'Tis as much impossible—
Unless we sweep 'em from the door with cannons—
To scatter 'em as 'tis to make 'em sleep
On May Day morning, which will never be.   14
We may as well push against Paul's as stir 'em.   15
PORTER   How got they in, and be hanged?
MAN
Alas, I know not. How gets the tide in?
As much as one sound cudgel of four foot—   18
You see the poor remainder—could distribute,
I made no spare, sir.
PORTER   You did nothing, sir.   20

---

174 **voice** report, opinion 176 **shrewd** malicious 179 **one** united in
spirit
5.4. Location: London. The palace yard.
1 **leave** stop. **anon** immediately 2 **Paris Garden** a bear garden on
the Bankside 3 **gaping** shouting 4 **I . . . larder** i.e., I am a servant
of the palace household, in the pantry 7–8 **to 'em** compared to
them, i.e., to cudgels made of crab tree 9 **ale and cakes** (Refreshments appropriate to christenings and other festivals.) 14 **May Day
morning** (Allusion to the custom of rising before dawn on May Day
for early morning festivities.) 15 **Paul's** Saint Paul's Cathedral
18 **cudgel** club 20 **made no spare** exercised no frugality

MAN
I am not Samson, nor Sir Guy, nor Colbrand,   21
To mow 'em down before me; but if I spared any
That had a head to hit, either young or old,
He or she, cuckold or cuckold maker,
Let me ne'er hope to see a chine again;   25
And that I would not for a cow, God save her!   26
ONE (*within*)   Do you hear, master porter?
PORTER   I shall be with you presently, good master
puppy.—Keep the door close, sirrah.
MAN   What would you have me do?
PORTER   What should you do, but knock 'em down by
the dozens? Is this Moorfields to muster in? Or have 32
we some strange Indian with the great tool come to 33
court, the women so besiege us? Bless me, what a fry 34
of fornication is at door! On my Christian conscience, 35
this one christening will beget a thousand; here will
be father, godfather, and all together.
MAN   The spoons will be the bigger, sir. There is a fel- 38
low somewhat near the door—he should be a brazier 39
by his face, for, o' my conscience, twenty of the dog 40
days now reign in 's nose; all that stand about him are 41
under the line, they need no other penance. That fire- 42
drake did I hit three times on the head, and three 43
times was his nose discharged against me; he stands
there like a mortar-piece to blow us. There was a 45
haberdasher's wife of small wit near him that railed
upon me till her pinked porringer fell off her head for 47
kindling such a combustion in the state. I missed the 48
meteor once and hit that woman, who cried out 49
"Clubs!" when I might see from far some forty trun- 50
cheoners draw to her succor, which were the hope o' 51
the Strand, where she was quartered. They fell on; I 52
made good my place. At length they came to the 53
broomstaff to me. I defied 'em still, when suddenly a 54
file of boys behind 'em, loose shot, delivered such a 55
shower of pebbles that I was fain to draw mine honor 56

---

21 **Samson** biblical character of great strength. **Sir Guy, Colbrand**
(Colbrand was a legendary Danish giant slain by Guy of Warwick in
the popular English romance named after its hero.) 25 **chine** backbone; hence, a joint of beef or other meat 26 **for a cow** i.e., for
anything (*cow* perhaps being suggested by *chine*) 32 **Moorfields** an
open space outside London walls, used, among other things, as a
training ground for the militia 33 **tool** genitals. (This sentence alludes
to the Jacobean excitement over exhibited Indians.) 34–35 **fry of
fornication** swarm of would-be fornicators or of bastards 38 **spoons**
i.e., as christening presents. (See 5.3.166.) 39 **brazier** worker in
brass 40–41 **dog days** i.e., midsummer, when Sirius, the Dog Star,
rises at about the same time as the sun 42 **under the line** on the
equator 42–43 **firedrake** fiery dragon 45 **mortar-piece** short cannon. **blow us** (1) blow us up (2) blow his nose at us 47 **pinked
porringer** small close-fitting cap ornamented with perforations
48 **combustion** tumult. **in the state** (1) in the commonwealth (2) in
the brazier, whose inflamed complexion, comically likened here to a
miniature cosmos, seems made up of meteors and discharging cannons 48–49 **the meteor** i.e., the red-faced brazier 50 **Clubs** (The
rallying cry for London apprentices to join in or stop a brawl.) 50–
51 **truncheoners** men armed with cudgels 51 **hope** pride and joy
52 **the Strand** a prosperous street of shops and residences. **fell on**
made their assault 53 **made . . . place** stood my ground 54 **broomstaff** i.e., close quarters 55 **loose shot** throwers or marksmen not attached to a particular company 56 **fain** obliged 56–57 **draw . . .
in** i.e., withdraw from the fight

in and let 'em win the work. The devil was amongst 57
'em, I think, surely.

PORTER   These are the youths that thunder at a playhouse and fight for bitten apples, that no audience but
the tribulation of Tower Hill or the limbs of Lime- 61
house, their dear brothers, are able to endure. I have 62
some of 'em in *Limbo Patrum,* and there they are like 63
to dance these three days, besides the running ban- 64
quet of two beadles that is to come. 65

Enter Lord Chamberlain.

CHAMBERLAIN
Mercy o' me, what a multitude are here!
They grow still too; from all parts they are coming,
As if we kept a fair here. Where are these porters,
These lazy knaves? You've made a fine hand,
    fellows! 69
There's a trim rabble let in. Are all these 70
Your faithful friends o' the suburbs? We shall have 71
Great store of room, no doubt, left for the ladies, 72
When they pass back from the christening.

PORTER   An 't please your honor, 73
We are but men, and what so many may do,
Not being torn a-pieces, we have done.
An army cannot rule 'em.

CHAMBERLAIN   As I live, 76
If the King blame me for 't, I'll lay ye all 77
By th' heels, and suddenly, and on your heads 78
Clap round fines for neglect. You're lazy knaves, 79
And here ye lie baiting of bombards, when 80
Ye should do service. [*A trumpet.*] Hark, the
    trumpets sound.
They're come already from the christening.
Go break among the press, and find a way out 83
To let the troop pass fairly, or I'll find 84
A Marshalsea shall hold ye play these two months. 85

PORTER
Make way there for the Princess!

MAN   You great fellow,
Stand close up, or I'll make your head ache.

PORTER
You i' the camlet, get up o' the rail! 88
I'll peck you o'er the pales else.   *Exeunt.* 89

❧

57 **work** fort   61 **tribulation** troublemakers, gang.   **limbs** lads; here,
rowdies   61–62 **Limehouse** a dockyard area east of Tower Hill, a
rough neighborhood   63 **Limbo Patrum** resting place for the pre-
Christian patriarchs who had to remain there until the coming of
Christ; hence, prison.   **like** likely   64 **dance** kick their heels   64–
65 **running banquet** whipping through the streets following imprisonment (like a *banquet* or "dessert" after a meal)   65 **beadles** minor officials charged with punishing petty offenses   69 **fine hand** fine job.
(Said ironically.)   70 **trim** fine. (Said ironically.)   71 **suburbs** areas
outside London walls and hence outside its legal jurisdiction
72 **store** plenty   73 **An 't** if it   76 **rule** control   77–78 **lay . . .
heels** put you in the stocks or in chains   79 **round** heavy   80 **baiting
of bombards** drinking from leathern bottles   83 **press** crowd
84 **troop** royal retinue   85 **Marshalsea** prison in Southwark.   **hold ye
play** keep you engaged   88 **camlet** a kind of fabric made of silk and
goat's hair. (Since no "crowd" is onstage, the Porter may be speaking
to his audience here as though it were crowding to see the christening.)   89 **peck** pitch.   **pales** railings

5.5

*Enter trumpets, sounding; then two Aldermen, Lord
Mayor, Garter, Cranmer, Duke of Norfolk with his
marshal's staff, Duke of Suffolk, two noblemen
bearing great standing bowls for the christening
gifts; then four noblemen bearing a canopy, under
which the Duchess of Norfolk, godmother, bearing
the child richly habited in a mantle, etc., train
borne by a lady; then follows the Marchioness
Dorset, the other godmother, and ladies. The troop
pass once about the stage, and Garter speaks.*

GARTER   Heaven, from thy endless goodness, send
prosperous life, long, and ever happy, to the high and
mighty Princess of England, Elizabeth!

Flourish. Enter King and guard.

CRANMER [*kneeling*]
And to your royal Grace and the good Queen,
My noble partners and myself thus pray 5
All comfort, joy, in this most gracious lady
Heaven ever laid up to make parents happy 7
May hourly fall upon ye!

KING
Thank you, good Lord Archbishop.
What is her name?

CRANMER   Elizabeth.

KING   Stand up, lord.
[*Cranmer rises. The King kisses the child.*]
With this kiss take my blessing. God protect thee,
Into whose hand I give thy life.

CRANMER   Amen.

KING
My noble gossips, you've been too prodigal. 13
I thank ye heartily; so shall this lady,
When she has so much English.

CRANMER   Let me speak, sir,
For heaven now bids me; and the words I utter
Let none think flattery, for they'll find 'em truth.
This royal infant—heaven still move about her!— 18
Though in her cradle, yet now promises
Upon this land a thousand thousand blessings,
Which time shall bring to ripeness. She shall be—
But few now living can behold that goodness—
A pattern to all princes living with her,
And all that shall succeed. Saba was never 24
More covetous of wisdom and fair virtue
Than this pure soul shall be. All princely graces
That mold up such a mighty piece as this is, 27
With all the virtues that attend the good,
Shall still be doubled on her. Truth shall nurse her,
Holy and heavenly thoughts still counsel her.
She shall be loved and feared. Her own shall bless
    her; 31
Her foes shake like a field of beaten corn, 32

5.5. Location: London. The royal court.
s.d. Garter Garter King at Arms, a chief herald of the College of Arms
5 **partners** co-sponsors   7 **laid up** provided   13 **gossips** godparents
18 **still** ever   24 **Saba** the Queen of Sheba, who visited Solomon to
discover wisdom from him; see 1 Kings 10:1–10   27 **mighty piece**
princely person   31 **own** own people   32 **beaten corn** wind-beaten
grain

And hang their heads with sorrow. Good grows
   with her.
In her days every man shall eat in safety
Under his own vine what he plants, and sing
The merry songs of peace to all his neighbors.
God shall be truly known, and those about her   37
From her shall read the perfect ways of honor   38
And by those claim their greatness, not by blood.   39
Nor shall this peace sleep with her; but as when   40
The bird of wonder dies, the maiden phoenix,   41
Her ashes new-create another heir
As great in admiration as herself,   43
So shall she leave her blessedness to one,   44
When heaven shall call her from this cloud of
   darkness,   45
Who from the sacred ashes of her honor
Shall starlike rise, as great in fame as she was,
And so stand fixed. Peace, plenty, love, truth, terror, 48
That were the servants to this chosen infant,
Shall then be his, and like a vine grow to him.
Wherever the bright sun of heaven shall shine,
His honor and the greatness of his name
Shall be, and make new nations. He shall flourish,
And like a mountain cedar reach his branches
To all the plains about him. Our children's children
Shall see this and bless heaven.
KING   Thou speakest wonders.
CRANMER
   She shall be, to the happiness of England,
An agèd princess; many days shall see her,
And yet no day without a deed to crown it.   59
Would I had known no more! But she must die,
She must, the saints must have her; yet a virgin,
A most unspotted lily shall she pass
To th' ground, and all the world shall mourn her.
KING   O Lord Archbishop,
Thou hast made me now a man! Never, before
This happy child, did I get anything.   66
This oracle of comfort has so pleased me
That when I am in heaven I shall desire
To see what this child does, and praise my Maker.
I thank ye all. To you, my good Lord Mayor,
And you, good brethren, I am much beholding;   71
I have received much honor by your presence,
And ye shall find me thankful. Lead the way, lords.
Ye must all see the Queen, and she must thank ye;
She will be sick else. This day, no man think   75
H'as business at his house; for all shall stay.   76
This little one shall make it holiday.   Exeunt.

❧

37 **God . . . known** i.e., true religion shall prevail   38 **read** learn
39 **greatness** nobility   40 **sleep** i.e., die   41 **phoenix** mythical bird
believed to rise from its own ashes; a symbol of regeneration
43 **great in admiration** greatly wondered at   44 **she** i.e., Elizabeth.
one i.e., King James I   45 **cloud of darkness** i.e., mortal life   48 **terror** quality inspiring awe   59 **deed** good deed   66 **get** beget; achieve
71 **beholding** beholden   75 **sick** unhappy   76 **H'as** (that) he has.
stay i.e., cease work

The Epilogue

[Enter the Epilogue.]

'Tis ten to one this play can never please
All that are here. Some come to take their ease,
And sleep an act or two; but those, we fear,
We've frighted with our trumpets; so, 'tis clear,
They'll say 'tis naught. Others to hear the city   5
Abused extremely, and to cry "That's witty!"
Which we have not done neither; that I fear   7
All the expected good we're like to hear   8
For this play at this time is only in
The merciful construction of good women,   10
For such a one we showed 'em. If they smile
And say 'twill do, I know, within a while
All the best men are ours; for 'tis ill hap   13
If they hold when their ladies bid 'em clap.   *[Exit.]* 14

Epilogue.
5 **naught** worthless.   **the city** i.e., London and its citizens, the satirical objects of "city comedy" by Ben Jonson, Thomas Middleton, and
others   7 **that** so that   8 **expected good** anticipated approval, applause   10 **construction** interpretation   13 **ill hap** bad luck   14 **hold**
hold back

The Tragedies

Titus Andronicus

Titus Andronicus has drawn some unusually harsh criticism. Ben Jonson singled it out, in his Induction to *Bartholomew Fair* (1614), as a play loved by ignorant audiences for its bombastic rhetoric. T. S. Eliot called it "one of the stupidest and most uninspired plays ever written." Others have argued that it was not Shakespeare's at all, or his perfunctory revision of an old play by Christopher Marlowe, Thomas Kyd, Robert Greene, or George Peele, or an early experimental work, or even a burlesque of the revenge play then in vogue. Early it surely was; it appeared in quarto in 1594 as played by Derby's, Pembroke's, and Sussex's men, and could well have been written in 1590 or even before. The allusion in theater owner and manager Philip Henslowe's *Diary* for January 24, 1594, to a new production by Sussex's men of "Titus & Ondronicus" could refer to a new play or one newly revised or newly acquired by the company. Shakespeare's *Titus Andronicus* was widely separated in time from the great tragedies; *Romeo and Juliet* is the only other tragedy (excluding the English history plays) of the decade preceding 1599, and it probably followed *Titus Andronicus* by five years or so. Unquestionably, *Titus Andronicus* does fall short of the expectations we normally bring to Shakespearean tragedy. Such a judgment compares the play, however, with the greatest dramas of the English language. Probably its most serious critical liability is that it continually reminds us of the later Roman plays and of *Hamlet* and *King Lear*. By any other dramatist, the play would not seem so imperfect as it seems when assigned to Shakespeare. *Titus Andronicus* was an early success onstage and has shown its timeless theatrical appeal in brilliant productions at Stratford-upon-Avon, directed by Sir Laurence Olivier, in 1957, and at the Swan in Stratford-upon-Avon, directed by Deborah Warner, in 1987.

Titus Andronicus is studded with bookish references to classical authors—another likely indication of an early date. No other tragedy, and perhaps no other Shakespearean play, reveals such direct evidence of youthful learning. Some of its many untranslated Latin phrases are school children's favorites, such as the *"Integer vitae"* of Horace that is immediately recognized by Chiron. "I read it in the grammar long ago," he says (4.2.23). Classical allusions compare the chief characters of the play with Aeneas and Dido, Queen of Carthage; Hector, King Priam, and Queen Hecuba of Troy; Ajax and Odysseus among the Greeks; Hercules, Prometheus, Orpheus, Coriolanus, Semiramis the siren Queen of Assyria, Pyramus, Cornelia the mother of the Gracchi, Actaeon; and others. Yet these learned references are far from being a mere display of youthful learning; through a controlled and self-conscious artistry, they enable us to explore a tragic world whose moral dimensions are defined in terms of classical literary models. Especially significant are the references to victims of rape and vengeance: Virginia the Roman, killed by her father Virginius to save her from rape; the chaste Lucrece, ravished by Tarquin; Philomel, raped and deprived of her tongue by Tereus, whose name she then reveals by weaving the information into a tapestry; and Procne, her sister and the wife of Tereus, who avenges Philomel by serving Tereus' son Itys to him in a meal.

Ovid's *Metamorphoses* gave Shakespeare his source for many of the legends, especially that of Tereus, Philomel, and Procne. Seneca's *Thyestes* offered him in dramatic form a similar tale of vengeance, in which two sons are slain and served to their parent in a grisly banquet. Shakespeare appears to have used a chapbook called *The History of Titus Andronicus;* the only extant printed copy is from the eighteenth century, but it may give a reliable version of the original. Some scholars believe that one or even two plays about Titus may have existed prior to Shakespeare's and that we can deduce their contributions to his work by examining two later continental plays derived from them: *Tragaedia van Tito Andronico* (German, 1620) and *Aran en Titus* (Dutch, 1641). Possibly one of these earlier plays was the "Titus & Vespacia" entered in Henslowe's *Diary* for April 11, 1592, as acted by Lord Strange's men. Even if Shakespeare used such prose and dramatic sources, however, he also knew well the Ovidian and Senecan originals that had inspired them. Elizabethan revenge tragedy, containing some Senecan influences (though those Senecan elements should not be overstressed), was a strongly formative influence, especially Kyd's *The Spanish Tragedy* (c. 1587). The phenomenal recent stage successes of Marlowe had left their mark: Titus' killing of his son Mutius recalls *Tamburlaine Part II,* and Aaron's Vice-like boasting of wanton villainy recalls *The Jew of Malta.* Shakespeare's reading of Virgil is evident not only in repeated references to the tragic love story of Dido and Aeneas but also in his choice of the name Lavinia (*The Aeneid,* Book 7 ff.)

As this sizable list of influences suggests, Shakespeare's first tragedy remains close to its models. Although the play anticipates several motifs in the later tragedies—the ingratitude of Rome toward its honored general as in *Coriolanus,* Roman political factionalism as in *Julius Caesar,* infirm old age confronted by human bestiality as in *King Lear*—*Titus Andronicus* is the kind of revenge play one might expect of a gifted young playwright in the early 1590s. The successful models for tragic writing in those years were Kyd and Marlowe; Greene, Peele, and others paid these two the flattery of imitation. So, to an extent, did Shakespeare. We can best understand *Titus Andronicus* if we view it as a revenge play in the sensational vein of Shakespeare's immediate predecessors, with generous additions of Ovidian pathos. We should not look to *Titus Andronicus* for that humane and compassionate wisdom we expect in mature Shakespearean tragedy; as a revenge play, *Titus Andronicus* focuses on violence and horror, and its mood is one of revulsion. The style, too, requires some adjustment in our expectations. Owing much to Kyd, Marlowe, and Ovid, it is replete with rhetorical figures and classical allusions in the manner of Shakespeare's Ovidian poems from the early 1590s, *Venus and Adonis* and *The Rape of Lucrece*. Even if its "early" features are manifest, the style works to good dramatic effect in highly wrought scenes, as when Titus pleads for justice to the unresponsive senators (3.1.1–47) or lays a trap for Tamora and her sons under the guise of his supposed madness (5.2). The seeming incongruity of violent action and elaborately refined metaphor, as in Titus' florid lament for Lavinia's mutilation (3.1.65 ff.), is not, as Eugene Waith has shown (*Shakespeare Survey*, 1957, 39–49), without its purpose, for it evokes pathos on behalf of gruesome suffering in a deliberately Ovidian manner, abstracting and generalizing human torment. As in Ovid, the interest is not in moralizing lessons but in the "transforming power of intense states of emotion."

Violence is an enduring feature of *Titus Andronicus*, and its function must be understood if the play is not to be dismissed as merely hyperbolical in its bloodshed. We are constantly aware of ritual human sacrifice, murder, and maiming, as in Titus' sentencing of Tamora's son Alarbus and his slaying of his own son Mutius, the massacre by Tamora's sons of Bassianus and their ravishing of Lavinia, the subsequent execution of two of Titus' sons wrongfully accused of Bassianus' murder, the cutting off of Titus' hand, the feeding to Tamora of her sons' bodies ground into a fine paste, and still more. Savage mutilation is characteristic of many of these atrocities, especially in the lopping off of hands and tongue. The play's climax is, in the manner of revenge tragedy, a spectacle of blood, with the deaths in rapid succession of Lavinia, Tamora, Titus, and Saturninus. These multiple slaughters cause revulsion in some viewers, such as T. S. Eliot, but to others the violence reveals a pattern and offers its own ethical stance on vengeance. Although we do not sense in this early play the same controlled perspective on human evil as in *Hamlet*, for example, we see that Shakespeare is intensely aware of the conflict between order and disorder. In the final scenes, Aaron the Moor is caught and sentenced to execution, Tamora and Saturninus are slain, Titus' brother Marcus appeals to Roman justice for vindication on the grounds that his family had no alternative, and Titus' last remaining son Lucius vows as the new emperor to "heal Rome's harms and wipe away her woe"

(5.3.148). Even if this resolution does not fully satisfy the ethical dilemmas with which the play began, it reveals Shakespeare's disinclination to allow the fulfillment of private vengeance to be the play's ultimate concern. Shakespeare is interested throughout in the ethical problems generated by revenge, and the play's relentless horror may be a commentary on the self-defeating nature of a revenge code. Violence has its aesthetic dimension in the play as well, in a conscious theatrical design of vengeance and countervengeance that today seems admirably attuned to Artaud's theater of cruelty.

The first part of *Titus Andronicus* functions to give the avenger a motive for his bloody course of action. Ironically, Titus is himself responsible for setting in motion the events that will overwhelm him. His family, the Andronici, are the first to practice vengeance, a fact that diminishes the sympathy they might later have been able to enjoy as victims and exiles. In fact, it is Lucius, ultimately to become the restorer of political stability, who first demands the ritual slaying of a captive Goth, Tamora's son Alarbus, to appease the spirits of the Andronici slain in battle. Such a demand is understandable in terms of family honor, but it is also vengeful and pagan. Despite the Romans' claim to be superior to the barbarians they fight (see 1.1.379, for example), their acts too often do not justify that claim to moral superiority. This irony is complete when the Gothic Queen Tamora and her sons become the spokespersons for godlike mercy. As Tamora's son Chiron bitterly observes, "Was never Scythia half so barbarous" (1.1.131).

Equally violent and unnatural is Titus' slaying of his own son Mutius for assisting in the abduction of Titus' daughter, Lavinia. This tragic error stems, like the first, from Titus' narrow sense of family honor. Titus has unwisely refused the imperial crown, bestowing it instead on the treacherous Saturninus, and has promised Lavinia as bride to the new emperor, despite her prior betrothal to Saturninus' virtuous rival and brother, Bassianus. When Titus' sons and Bassianus are driven to the expedient of abducting the lady, Titus cannot endure the shame of his violated promise and so kills Mutius in the ensuing melee. Yet, for this sacrifice on behalf of the Emperor, Titus receives only ingratitude and hostility. Moreover, he has taught Tamora and her sons to seek vengeance.

Once the Andronici become the victims of Tamora and her supporters, they gain in sympathy. They suffer unspeakable atrocities. Hunted down by jeering sadists who amuse themselves through rape and mutilation, the Andronici band together in mutual tribulation and selflessly attempt to ease one another's agony. They discover Rome to be a "wilderness of tigers" (3.1.54) in which the law blindly condemns Titus' innocent sons for the murder of Bassianus. Still, Titus has committed the first barbarism and turns increasingly to barbarism in his desire for vengeance. Because the Andronici are too much like their enemies, the prevailing mood, as in most revenge plays, is more ironic than tragic.

There is no strong sense (despite the capture of Aaron) that moral order is restored along with political order. The Andronici are vindicated, and they have gained some wisdom through suffering, but they are still the avengers who gave the first offense.

Equally unsettling is the play's depiction of gender relations. Titus is a patriarchal figure who responds with violence toward his own son when that son challenges his authority to give away his daughter Lavinia to Saturninus. In the play's bloody conclusion, Titus is the slayer of his own daughter as well, lest she "survive her shame" and by her presence continually remind Titus of the disgrace he has suffered by her rape (5.3.41–42). The archaic code of male domination insists that a father's honor is paramount and that his daughter's death is preferable to shameful life even if, as in Lavinia's case, she is wholly innocent and victimized in losing her chastity. (In The Rape of Lucrece, an innocent wife must pay the same terrible price to vindicate her husband's honor.) At the opposite end of the spectrum, Tamora represents everything that most males dread in the transgressing female. Because she is both wanton and domineering, her sexuality is intolerable to most noble Romans; she captivates Saturninus and Aaron with her sensual beauty, but ultimately in this play such a dangerous woman must be tricked into the gruesomely appropriate crime of eating her own sons. Roman order is reestablished at last. Even so, its patriarchal ascendancy has been responsible for the carnage to no less an extent than has the more overtly erotic violence of the non-Roman "barbarians" like Tamora, her sons, and Aaron.

Titus Andronicus displays many conventions of the revenge play found earlier in The Spanish Tragedy. The avenger, Titus, is a man of high position conscientiously serving the state, like Kyd's Hieronimo, who discovers that the state itself is too corrupt to give him justice for the wrongs done to his family. The evildoers are members of the Emperor's family, protected by their royal connection. Private and public interests clash, and public welfare is the loser. The avenger has difficulty proving the identity of the villains but finds an ingenious way at last (through Lavinia's writing in the sand). Once he becomes the avenger, like Hieronimo, Titus grows as remorseless and canny as his enemies. He becomes a menace to public order, uttering enigmatic threats and blazoning forth the injustices of the state. Verging on true madness, he also employs madness as a cloak for his Machiavellian intrigues. His plotting succeeds in duping Queen Tamora into allowing him to arrange his gruesome banquet. The drama ends, like The Spanish Tragedy, in a kind of play-within-the-play, as Tamora's two sons take the roles of Rape and Murder, Tamora Revenge, and Titus the cook. Playacting turns deadly earnest with a rapid succession of slaughters. Titus and Lavinia, like Hieronimo and Bel-Imperia, do not outlive their act of vengeance.

This conventional pattern accepts revenge as self-justifying. As in The Spanish Tragedy, where the choric Revenge controls the action for his own sinister purposes and welcomes the suffering of innocents or the collapse of governments as grist for his mill, Titus Andronicus portrays a world in which the avenger can act seemingly only through violence. Even Lavinia and Titus' young grandson endorse plotting and murder. Titus practices cunning toward his enemies, vowing to "o'erreach them in their own devices" (5.2.143). Our attention is increasingly drawn to the artistry of the "devices" on both sides. The machinations of Aaron and Tamora demand ingenuity in return. An eye must pay for an eye; the punishment must fit the crime. To be sure, Titus and his family do struggle to understand the moral nature of their universe. "If any power pities wretched tears, / To that I call," prays Titus, lifting his mangled hand toward heaven and imploring divine assistance (3.1.208–209). Repeatedly, the Andronici ask if a divine justice exists, if it cares about savagery among humans, and if that justice will assist the defenseless. "O heavens," asks Marcus, "can you hear a good man groan / And not relent, or not compassion him?" (4.1.125–126). Why should such terrible evils afflict the human race "Unless the gods delight in tragedies?" (line 62). Marcus seeks the identities of his niece's ravishers, hoping that Lavinia will be able to "display at last / What God will have discovered for revenge" (lines 75–76). Is revenge to be God's or humanity's? In part, at least, Marcus sees himself and his family as agents of divine justice, like Hamlet, though Titus' own errors will also require his own destruction. Yet even these questionings about the cosmos are a part of the revenge tradition, for Hieronimo in The Spanish Tragedy implores the gods in similar terms. Titus, for all his pleas to the heavens, is ultimately the avenger in a revenge play. He does not, like Hamlet, submit himself to what he takes to be the will of Providence and wait for whatever opportunity heaven will provide. Titus swears an oath of revenge and proceeds with the most gruesome acts imaginable. In his death there is no talk of reconciliation between divine and human will. As the moment of climax approaches, revenge is seen to be a force from hell, from the "infernal kingdom," while true justice is employed "with Jove in heaven" (5.2.30; 4.3.40). Titus is a protagonist suited to a play in which revenge proceeds by its own pitiless rules, in which brutality is the dominant fact of life, and in which violence is the only apparent means of redress. Divine ideas of justice mock humanity's blind attempts at self-governance without offering reassurance and direction.

As a tragedy of evil, then, Titus Andronicus illuminates the nature of that evil more than it attempts to transcend evil through human nobility, as in the later tragedies. This distinctive quality is made especially manifest by the play's outward resemblance to King Lear. Titus is old, infirm of judgment, and victimized by his own decision to relinquish power to a person whose villainy he does not comprehend.

He is, as Lear says of himself, certainly more sinned against than sinning. Titus approaches madness and generalizes in his grief about the omnipresence of murder and ingratitude in nature (3.2.52–78). His reflections on human injustice suggest the inversion of appearance and reality ("Grief has so wrought on him / He takes false shadows for true substances," lines 79–80), a motif of illusion that reappears in the allegorical play-within-the-play. Queen Tamora reveals an innate viciousness and sexual depravity like that of Goneril and Regan. Aaron the Moor, perhaps the first of Shakespeare's gloating Vice-like villains, resembles Edmund in *King Lear* as well as Richard III, Don John (in *Much Ado About Nothing*), and Iago (in *Othello*). *Titus Andronicus* shows us, in embryonic form and close to their sources, many of Shakespeare's later tragic themes and methods.

Aaron the Moor is the most vital character in this early play. Like the Vice of the morality play or like Marlowe's stage Machiavel, Aaron takes delight in pure evil and displays his cunning for the admiration of the audience. Evil to him is "sport," "wit," "stratagem," and, above all, "policy" (5.1.96; 2.3.1; 2.1.104). His malice encompasses all humanity and proceeds from no motive other than the sinister pleasure he takes in devising plots. When he is finally captured, Aaron boasts triumphantly of the extent and variety of his cruel accomplishments:

> Even now I curse the day—and yet, I think,
> Few come within the compass of my curse—
> Wherein I did not some notorious ill,
> As kill a man, or else devise his death,
> Ravish a maid, or plot the way to do it,
> Accuse some innocent and forswear myself,
> Set deadly enmity between two friends,
> Make poor men's cattle break their necks,
> Set fire on barns and haystacks in the night
> And bid the owners quench them with their tears.
> Oft have I digged up dead men from their graves
> And set them upright at their dear friends' door,
> Even when their sorrows almost was forgot. (5.1.125–137)

Through its depiction of evil as both comic and diabolical, this portrait gives us a vivid insight into the origins of one type of Shakespearean villain.

The seemingly attractive side to Aaron, his fiercely protective instincts toward his bastard son born of Tamora, is part of the central evil of this play: pride of family turning to violent revenge. Aaron and his son in their blackness of complexion are equated with barbarism, pagan atheism (Aaron scoffs at those who believe in God), and diabolism. Racial issues are thus as painfully explicit as those of gender in this play: Rome claims superiority over black peoples as over the Scythians, and yet the play sees Rome as fatally violent in its patriarchal, sexist, and racist assumptions. Aaron and Tamora are not the moral opposites of Saturninus and his Roman subjects but are, instead, symbolic of the inner darkness and carnality shared by all sorts of people.

As a revenge play, *Titus Andronicus* is theatrically effective. To be appreciated properly, it should be seen or read in these terms, rather than with the expectations we bring to *King Lear*. Shakespeare here presents barbarism and civilization as polar opposites, but he refuses to equate Rome with civilization, and he allows Titus at last no escape from the barbarism that he himself sets in motion. No tragic self-awareness grows out of Titus' humiliation, as it does in *King Lear*, no regret other than for having relinquished power to Saturninus. Instead of tragic self-awareness, we are left with an overpowering impression of the human potential for brutality. This vision is unameliorated. The constant reminder of a better world of justice and compassion merely serves to heighten the play's ironic and futile sense of wasted goodness.

Titus Andronicus

[Dramatis Personae

SATURNINUS, *son of the late Emperor of Rome,*
and afterward declared Emperor
BASSIANUS, *his brother*

TITUS ANDRONICUS, *a noble Roman, general*
against the Goths
LUCIUS,
QUINTUS, } *his sons*
MARTIUS,
MUTIUS,
LAVINIA, *his daughter*
YOUNG LUCIUS, *a* BOY, *Lucius' son*
MARCUS ANDRONICUS, *tribune of the people, and*
Titus' brother
PUBLIUS, *Marcus' son*
SEMPRONIUS,
CAIUS, } *Titus' kinsmen*
VALENTINE,

TAMORA, *Queen of the Goths, afterward Empress*
of Rome
ALARBUS,
DEMETRIUS, } *her sons*
CHIRON,
AARON, *a Moor, her lover*
NURSE

A Roman CAPTAIN
MESSENGER *to Titus*
CLOWN
AEMILIUS, *a noble Roman*
GOTHS
A Roman LORD
A ROMAN

Senators, Tribunes, Judges, Goths, Soldiers, Atten-
dants, a Child of Aaron and Tamora

SCENE: *Rome, and the country near it*]

1.1   [*Flourish.*] *Enter the tribunes and senators aloft;*
and then enter [below] Saturninus and his
followers at one door, and Bassianus and his
followers [at the other,] with drums and trumpets.

1.1. Location: Rome. Before the Capitol. The tomb of the Andronici
is provided onstage, possibly as a large property backstage or at a
trapdoor.
s.d. Flourish trumpet call.   **aloft** i.e., probably in the gallery,
rearstage above the tiring-house, looking down on the main stage.
followers (including soldiers; see *Exeunt soldiers* at lines 55 s.d. and
59 s.d.)   **drums** drummers.   **trumpets** trumpeters

SATURNINUS
Noble patricians, patrons of my right,
Defend the justice of my cause with arms;
And, countrymen, my loving followers,
Plead my successive title with your swords.   4
I am his firstborn son that was the last   5
That ware the imperial diadem of Rome.   6
Then let my father's honors live in me,
Nor wrong mine age with this indignity.   8
BASSIANUS
Romans, friends, followers, favorers of my right,
If ever Bassianus, Caesar's son,
Were gracious in the eyes of royal Rome,   11
Keep then this passage to the Capitol,   12
And suffer not dishonor to approach
The imperial seat, to virtue consecrate,   14
To justice, continence, and nobility;   15
But let desert in pure election shine,   16
And, Romans, fight for freedom in your choice.

[*Enter*] *Marcus Andronicus,* [*aloft,*] *with the*
crown.

MARCUS
Princes, that strive by factions and by friends
Ambitiously for rule and empery,   19
Know that the people of Rome, for whom we stand
A special party, have by common voice   21
In election for the Roman empery
Chosen Andronicus, surnamèd Pius   23
For many good and great deserts to Rome.
A nobler man, a braver warrior,
Lives not this day within the city walls.
He by the Senate is accited home   27
From weary wars against the barbarous Goths,
That with his sons, a terror to our foes,   29
Hath yoked a nation strong, trained up in arms.   30
Ten years are spent since first he undertook
This cause of Rome, and chastisèd with arms
Our enemies' pride. Five times he hath returned
Bleeding to Rome, bearing his valiant sons
In coffins from the field.   35
And now at last, laden with honor's spoils,
Returns the good Andronicus to Rome,
Renownèd Titus, flourishing in arms.   38

4 successive title title to the succession   **5 his . . . that** the firstborn
son of him who   **6 ware** wore   **8 age** seniority.   **this indignity** i.e.,
the challenge of my right by a younger brother   **11 Were gracious**
found favor and acceptance   **12 Keep** guard, defend   **14 consecrate**
consecrated   **15 continence** self-restraint   **16 pure election** free
choice, i.e., of the Roman citizens. (Bassianus urges the Romans to
let merit, or *desert*, prevail, rather than inherited right.)   **19 empery**
rule (as emperor)   **21 A special party** i.e., a representative group specially chosen. (As a tribune, Marcus Andronicus has been elected by
the *people of Rome*, line 20, the plebeians, to represent their rights.)
23 Chosen i.e., nominated.   **surnamèd** given the honorary epithet of.
Pius dutiful, patriotic   **27 accited** summoned   **29 That** who, i.e., Titus   **30 yoked** subdued   **35 field** (The First Quarto follows with three
and one-half lines deleted from the Second and Third Quartos and the
Folio because they are inconsistent with lines 96–147 below and
probably represent a canceled first draft that the printer of the First
Quarto mistakenly included: "and at this day / To the monument of
the Andronici, / Done sacrifice of expiation, / And slain the noblest
prisoner of the Goths.")   **38 flourishing** eminent

Let us entreat, by honor of his name　　　　　　　39
Whom worthily you would have now succeed,　　40
And in the Capitol and Senate's right,
Whom you pretend to honor and adore,　　　　　42
That you withdraw you and abate your strength,
Dismiss your followers, and, as suitors should,
Plead your deserts in peace and humbleness.

SATURNINUS
How fair the tribune speaks to calm my thoughts!　46

BASSIANUS
Marcus Andronicus, so I do affy　　　　　　　47
In thy uprightness and integrity,
And so I love and honor thee and thine,
Thy noble brother Titus and his sons,
And her to whom my thoughts are humbled all,　51
Gracious Lavinia, Rome's rich ornament,
That I will here dismiss my loving friends,
And to my fortunes and the people's favor
Commit my cause in balance to be weighed.
　　　　　　　　　　　Exeunt soldiers [of Bassianus].

SATURNINUS
Friends, that have been thus forward in my right,
I thank you all and here dismiss you all,
And to the love and favor of my country
Commit myself, my person, and the cause.
　　　　　　　　　　[Exeunt the soldiers of Saturninus.]
Rome, be as just and gracious unto me
As I am confident and kind to thee.　　　　　61
Open the gates and let me in.

BASSIANUS
Tribunes, and me, a poor competitor.　　　　　63
　　　　　　[Flourish.] They [Saturninus and Bassianus]
　　　　　　　　go up into the Senate House.

　　　　　Enter a Captain.

CAPTAIN
Romans, make way! The good Andronicus,
Patron of virtue, Rome's best champion,　　　65
Successful in the battles that he fights,
With honor and with fortune is returned
From where he circumscribèd with his sword　68
And brought to yoke the enemies of Rome.　　69

　　　Sound drums and trumpets, and then enter two of
　　　Titus' sons, [Martius and Mutius]; and then two
　　　men bearing a coffin covered with black; then two
　　　other sons [Lucius and Quintus]; then Titus
　　　Andronicus; and then Tamora, the Queen of
　　　Goths, and her three sons [Alarbus,] Chiron, and

　　　Demetrius, with Aaron the Moor, and others as
　　　many as can be. Then set down the coffin, and
　　　Titus speaks.

TITUS
Hail, Rome, victorious in thy mourning weeds!　70
Lo, as the bark that hath discharged his freight　71
Returns with precious lading to the bay
From whence at first she weighed her anchorage,　73
Cometh Andronicus, bound with laurel boughs,
To re-salute his country with his tears,
Tears of true joy for his return to Rome.
Thou great defender of this Capitol,　　　　　77
Stand gracious to the rites that we intend!
Romans, of five-and-twenty valiant sons,
Half of the number that King Priam had,　　　80
Behold the poor remains, alive and dead.
These that survive let Rome reward with love;
These that I bring unto their latest home,　　83
With burial amongst their ancestors.　　　　　84
Here Goths have given me leave to sheathe my
　　　sword.　　　　　　　　　　　　　　　85
Titus, unkind and careless of thine own,　　　86
Why suffer'st thou thy sons, unburied yet,
To hover on the dreadful shore of Styx?　　　88
Make way to lay them by their brethren.
　　　　　　　　　　　　　They open the tomb.
There greet in silence, as the dead are wont,
And sleep in peace, slain in your country's wars!
O sacred receptacle of my joys,
Sweet cell of virtue and nobility,
How many sons hast thou of mine in store
That thou wilt never render to me more!　　　95

LUCIUS
Give us the proudest prisoner of the Goths,
That we may hew his limbs, and on a pile
Ad manes fratrum sacrifice his flesh　　　　　98
Before this earthy prison of their bones,
That so the shadows be not unappeased,　　　100
Nor we disturbed with prodigies on earth.　　101

TITUS
I give him you, the noblest that survives,
The eldest son of this distressèd queen.

TAMORA *[kneeling]*
Stay, Roman brethren! Gracious conqueror,　　104
Victorious Titus, rue the tears I shed,
A mother's tears in passion for her son;　　　106
And if thy sons were ever dear to thee,
O, think my son to be as dear to me!

Sufficeth not that we are brought to Rome 109
To beautify thy triumphs, and return 110
Captive to thee and to thy Roman yoke,
But must my sons be slaughtered in the streets
For valiant doings in their country's cause?
O, if to fight for king and commonweal 114
Were piety in thine, it is in these.
Andronicus, stain not thy tomb with blood! 116
Wilt thou draw near the nature of the gods?
Draw near them then in being merciful.
Sweet mercy is nobility's true badge.
Thrice noble Titus, spare my firstborn son.

TITUS [raising her]
Patient yourself, madam, and pardon me. 121
These are their brethren, whom your Goths beheld 122
Alive and dead, and for their brethren slain
Religiously they ask a sacrifice.
To this your son is marked, and die he must
T' appease their groaning shadows that are gone.

LUCIUS
Away with him! And make a fire straight, 127
And with our swords, upon a pile of wood,
Let's hew his limbs till they be clean consumed. 129
                Exeunt Titus' sons with Alarbus.

TAMORA
O cruel, irreligious piety!

CHIRON
Was never Scythia half so barbarous. 131

DEMETRIUS
Oppose not Scythia to ambitious Rome. 132
Alarbus goes to rest, and we survive
To tremble under Titus' threatening look.
Then, madam, stand resolved, but hope withal 135
The selfsame gods that armed the Queen of Troy 136
With opportunity of sharp revenge
Upon the Thracian tyrant in his tent
May favor Tamora, the Queen of Goths—
When Goths were Goths and Tamora was queen—
To quit the bloody wrongs upon her foes. 141

            Enter the sons of Andronicus again [with their
            swords bloody].

LUCIUS
See, lord and father, how we have performed
Our Roman rites. Alarbus' limbs are lopped,
And entrails feed the sacrificing fire,
Whose smoke, like incense, doth perfume the sky.
Remaineth naught but to inter our brethren
And with loud 'larums welcome them to Rome. 147

TITUS
Let it be so, and let Andronicus
Make this his latest farewell to their souls. 149
        Sound trumpets, and lay the coffin in the tomb.
In peace and honor rest you here, my sons;
Rome's readiest champions, repose you here in rest,
Secure from worldly chances and mishaps!
Here lurks no treason, here no envy swells,
Here grow no damnèd drugs; here are no storms, 154
No noise, but silence and eternal sleep.
In peace and honor rest you here, my sons!

        Enter Lavinia.

LAVINIA
In peace and honor live Lord Titus long;
My noble lord and father, live in fame!
Lo, at this tomb my tributary tears 159
I render for my brethren's obsequies, 160
And at thy feet I kneel, with tears of joy   [kneeling]
Shed on this earth for thy return to Rome.
O, bless me here with thy victorious hand,
Whose fortunes Rome's best citizens applaud!

TITUS
Kind Rome, that hast thus lovingly reserved
The cordial of mine age to glad my heart! 166
Lavinia, live; outlive thy father's days
And fame's eternal date, for virtue's praise! 168
                            [She rises.]
        [Marcus Andronicus speaks from above
        where he is accompanied by Saturninus,
        Bassianus, other tribunes, etc.]

MARCUS
Long live Lord Titus, my belovèd brother,
Gracious triumpher in the eyes of Rome!

TITUS
Thanks, gentle tribune, noble brother Marcus.

MARCUS
And welcome, nephews, from successful wars,
You that survive, and you that sleep in fame!
Fair lords, your fortunes are alike in all, 174
That in your country's service drew your swords;
But safer triumph is this funeral pomp
That hath aspired to Solon's happiness, 177
And triumphs over chance in honor's bed. 178
Titus Andronicus, the people of Rome,
Whose friend in justice thou hast ever been,
Send thee by me, their tribune and their trust, 181
This palliament of white and spotless hue, 182
And name thee in election for the empire 183

---

109 **Sufficeth not** doesn't it suffice   110 **triumphs** (1) successes (2) entry procession in honor of victory.   **return** i.e., accompany your return   114 **commonweal** state, community as a whole   116 **tomb** family tomb   121 **Patient** calm   122 **their brethren** i.e., the brothers of those who have been slain   127 **straight** at once   129 **clean** wholly   131 **Scythia** a region north of the Black Sea; its people were notorious for their savagery   132 **Oppose** compare   135 **withal** besides   136 **Queen of Troy** Hecuba, wife of Priam, who after the fall of Troy was carried to Greece as a slave; there she found occasion to avenge the death of her son Polydorus by killing the two sons of the murderer, Polymnestor, King of Thrace   141 **quit** requite   147 **'larums** trumpet calls

149 **s.d. the coffin** (Although there is presumably more than one dead son, the staging may have relied on one coffin for the sake of economy.)   154 **drugs** poisonous plants   159 **tributary** paid in tribute   160 **obsequies** acts performed in honor of the dead   166 **cordial** restorative; or comfort, pleasure   168 **date** duration   174 **your . . . all** i.e., you who are alive and you who are dead share a similar fame and good fortune in your victory   177 **aspired** risen.   **Solon's happiness** i.e., the happiness defined by Solon (a Greek sage and lawgiver): that no man may be called happy until after his death   178 **chance** the vicissitudes of existence.   **honor's bed** an honorable grave   181 **trust** trusted one   182 **palliament** gown or cloak   183 **in election** i.e., as a candidate

With these our late-deceasèd emperor's sons.
Be *candidatus* then, and put it on,　　　　　　　185
And help to set a head on headless Rome.
　　　　　　　[*A white cloak is brought to Titus.*]

TITUS
A better head her glorious body fits
Than his that shakes for age and feebleness.
What should I don this robe and trouble you?　　189
Be chosen with proclamations today,
Tomorrow yield up rule, resign my life,
And set abroad new business for you all?　　　192
Rome, I have been thy soldier forty years,
And led my country's strength successfully,
And buried one-and-twenty valiant sons,
Knighted in field, slain manfully in arms,
In right and service of their noble country.　　197
Give me a staff of honor for mine age,
But not a scepter to control the world.
Upright he held it, lords, that held it last.

MARCUS
Titus, thou shalt obtain and ask the empery.　　201

SATURNINUS
Proud and ambitious tribune, canst thou tell?　　202

TITUS　　Patience, Prince Saturninus.

SATURNINUS　　Romans, do me right.
Patricians, draw your swords, and sheathe them not
Till Saturninus be Rome's emperor.
Andronicus, would thou were shipped to hell
Rather than rob me of the people's hearts!

LUCIUS
Proud Saturnine, interrupter of the good
That noble-minded Titus means to thee!

TITUS [*to Saturninus*]
Content thee, Prince. I will restore to thee
The people's hearts, and wean them from
　　themselves.　　　　　　　　　　　　　　212

BASSIANUS
Andronicus, I do not flatter thee,
But honor thee, and will do till I die.
My faction if thou strengthen with thy friends,
I will most thankful be; and thanks to men
Of noble minds is honorable meed.　　　　　217

TITUS
People of Rome, and people's tribunes here,
I ask your voices and your suffrages.　　　　219
Will ye bestow them friendly on Andronicus?

TRIBUNES
To gratify the good Andronicus
And gratulate his safe return to Rome,　　　222
The people will accept whom he admits.

TITUS
Tribunes, I thank you, and this suit I make:
That you create our emperor's eldest son,　　225
Lord Saturnine, whose virtues will, I hope,

Reflect on Rome as Titan's rays on earth,　　227
And ripen justice in this commonweal.
Then, if you will elect by my advice,
Crown him and say, "Long live our emperor!"

MARCUS
With voices and applause of every sort,
Patricians and plebeians, we create
Lord Saturninus Rome's great emperor,
And say, "Long live our Emperor Saturnine!"
　　　[*Saturninus is crowned. A long flourish till they
　　　　　　　　　　　　　　　　　come down.*]

SATURNINUS
Titus Andronicus, for thy favors done
To us in our election this day,
I give thee thanks in part of thy deserts,　　237
And will with deeds requite thy gentleness.　238
And, for an onset, Titus, to advance　　　　239
Thy name and honorable family,
Lavinia will I make my empress,
Rome's royal mistress, mistress of my heart,
And in the sacred Pantheon her espouse.　　243
Tell me, Andronicus, doth this motion please thee?　244

TITUS
It doth, my worthy lord, and in this match
I hold me highly honored of Your Grace.　　246
And here in sight of Rome to Saturnine,
King and commander of our commonweal,
The wide world's emperor, do I consecrate
My sword, my chariot, and my prisoners,
Presents well worthy Rome's imperious lord.　251
Receive them, then, the tribute that I owe,
Mine honor's ensigns humbled at thy feet.　253
　　　　　[*A tribute is laid at Saturninus' feet.*]

SATURNINUS
Thanks, noble Titus, father of my life!
How proud I am of thee and of thy gifts
Rome shall record, and when I do forget
The least of these unspeakable deserts,　　257
Romans, forget your fealty to me.

TITUS [*to Tamora*]
Now, madam, are you prisoner to an emperor,
To him that for your honor and your state
Will use you nobly and your followers.

SATURNINUS [*aside*]
A goodly lady, trust me, of the hue
That I would choose, were I to choose anew.—
Clear up, fair Queen, that cloudy countenance.
Though chance of war hath wrought this change of
　　cheer,　　　　　　　　　　　　　　265
Thou com'st not to be made a scorn in Rome.
Princely shall be thy usage every way.
Rest on my word, and let not discontent　　268
Daunt all your hopes. Madam, he comforts you
Can make you greater than the Queen of Goths.　270

185 candidatus a candidate. (Literally, one clad in white.)　**189 What** why　**192 abroad** i.e., on foot　**197 In . . . of** serving the just cause of　**201 obtain and ask** obtain simply by asking　**202 canst thou tell** i.e., that's what you think　**212 from themselves** i.e., from their present intention　**217 meed** reward　**219 voices** votes.　**suffrages** votes　**222 gratulate** salute, rejoice in　**225 create** i.e., elect

227 Titan's (Helios, the sun god, was a descendant of the Titans.)　**237 in** as　**238 gentleness** nobleness　**239 onset** beginning　**243 Pantheon** Roman temple dedicated to all the gods　**244 motion** proposal　**246 hold me** consider myself.　**of** by　**251 imperious** imperial　**253 ensigns** tokens　**257 unspeakable** inexpressible　**265 cheer** countenance.　**268 Rest** rely　**270 Can** who can

Lavinia, you are not displeased with this?

LAVINIA
Not I, my lord, sith true nobility   272
Warrants these words in princely courtesy.   273

SATURNINUS
Thanks, sweet Lavinia. Romans, let us go.
Ransomless here we set our prisoners free.
Proclaim our honors, lords, with trump and drum.
                    [*Flourish. Saturninus starts to leave,*
                                        attended.]

BASSIANUS [*seizing Lavinia*]
Lord Titus, by your leave, this maid is mine.

TITUS
How, sir? Are you in earnest then, my lord?

BASSIANUS
Ay, noble Titus, and resolved withal
To do myself this reason and this right.

MARCUS
Suum cuique is our Roman justice.   281
This prince in justice seizeth but his own.

LUCIUS
And that he will and shall, if Lucius live.

TITUS
Traitors, avaunt! Where is the Emperor's guard?   284
Treason, my lord! Lavinia is surprised!   285

SATURNINUS
Surprised? By whom?

BASSIANUS   By him that justly may
Bear his betrothed from all the world away.

MUTIUS
Brothers, help to convey her hence away,
And with my sword I'll keep this door safe.
          [*Exeunt Bassianus, Marcus, Lucius, Quintus, and
                            Martius, with Lavinia.*]

TITUS [*to Saturninus*]
Follow, my lord, and I'll soon bring her back.

MUTIUS [*guarding the door*]
My lord, you pass not here.

TITUS   What, villain boy?
Barr'st me my way in Rome?   [*He stabs Mutius.*]

MUTIUS   Help, Lucius, help!   292
                                  [*He dies.*]
          [*During the fray, exeunt Saturninus, Tamora,
                      Demetrius, Chiron, and Aaron.*]

          [*Enter Lucius.*]

LUCIUS [*to Titus*]
My lord, you are unjust; and more than so,
In wrongful quarrel you have slain your son.

TITUS
Nor thou nor he are any sons of mine.   295
My sons would never so dishonor me.

Traitor, restore Lavinia to the Emperor.

LUCIUS
Dead, if you will, but not to be his wife
That is another's lawful promised love.   [*Exit.*] 299

          Enter aloft the Emperor [*Saturninus*] *with Tamora
          and her two sons and Aaron the Moor.*

SATURNINUS
No, Titus, no. The Emperor needs her not,
Nor her, nor thee, nor any of thy stock.
I'll trust by leisure him that mocks me once;   302
Thee never, nor thy traitorous haughty sons,
Confederates all thus to dishonor me.
Was none in Rome to make a stale   305
But Saturnine? Full well, Andronicus,
Agree these deeds with that proud brag of thine
That saidst I begged the empire at thy hands.

TITUS
O monstrous! What reproachful words are these?

SATURNINUS
But go thy ways; go, give that changing piece   310
To him that flourished for her with his sword.   311
A valiant son-in-law thou shalt enjoy,
One fit to bandy with thy lawless sons,   313
To ruffle in the commonwealth of Rome.   314

TITUS
These words are razors to my wounded heart.

SATURNINUS
And therefore, lovely Tamora, Queen of Goths,
That like the stately Phoebe 'mongst her nymphs   317
Dost overshine the gallant'st dames of Rome,
If thou be pleased with this my sudden choice,
Behold, I choose thee, Tamora, for my bride,
And will create thee Empress of Rome.
Speak, Queen of Goths, dost thou applaud my
     choice?
And here I swear by all the Roman gods,
Sith priest and holy water are so near,
And tapers burn so bright, and everything
In readiness for Hymenaeus stand,   326
I will not re-salute the streets of Rome,
Or climb my palace, till from forth this place   328
I lead espoused my bride along with me.

TAMORA
And here in sight of heaven to Rome I swear,
If Saturnine advance the Queen of Goths,
She will a handmaid be to his desires,
A loving nurse, a mother to his youth.

SATURNINUS
Ascend, fair Queen, Pantheon. Lords, accompany
Your noble emperor and his lovely bride,

---

272 **sith** since   273 **Warrants** justifies   281 **Suum cuique** to each his own   284–285 **Traitors . . . surprised** (Evidently, Saturninus, starting to leave, has not quite realized what has happened, and his guard, accompanying him, has been caught napping.)   **avaunt** begone. **surprised** taken   292 s.d. **During . . . Aaron** (Evidently Saturninus, realizing he has been dishonored by the seizure of Lavinia and having decided in any case that he prefers Tamora, lines 262–263, decides to ascend to the Capitol and proclaim forthwith his choice of Tamora and repudiation of Lavinia.)   295 **Nor** neither. (Also in line 301.)

299 s.d. **Exit** (Lucius may take Mutius' body with him and return with it at line 341, but the presence of the dead body onstage from lines 299 to 341 would not be an inappropriate horror.)   302 **by leisure** with caution, barely   305 **Was . . . stale** was there no one in Rome to be made a laughingstock   310 **changing piece** fickle wench   311 **flourished . . . sword** brandished his sword to obtain her   313 **bandy** brawl   314 **ruffle** swagger   317 **Phoebe** (One of the names of the moon goddess.)   326 **Hymenaeus** god of marriage   328 **climb** ascend the stairs to

Sent by the heavens for Prince Saturnine,
Whose wisdom hath her fortune conquerèd.   337
There shall we consummate our spousal rites.   338
                              Exeunt omnes [except Titus].

TITUS
I am not bid to wait upon this bride.   339
Titus, when wert thou wont to walk alone,
Dishonored thus and challengèd of wrongs?   341

            *Enter Marcus and Titus' sons [Lucius, Quintus,
            and Martius].*

MARCUS
O Titus, see, O, see what thou hast done!
In a bad quarrel slain a virtuous son.

TITUS
No, foolish tribune, no; no son of mine,
Nor thou, nor these, confederates in the deed
That hath dishonored all our family.
Unworthy brother, and unworthy sons!

LUCIUS
But let us give him burial as becomes,   348
Give Mutius burial with our brethren.

TITUS
Traitors, away! He rests not in this tomb.
This monument five hundred years hath stood,
Which I have sumptuously re-edified.   352
Here none but soldiers and Rome's servitors   353
Repose in fame, none basely slain in brawls.
Bury him where you can, he comes not here.

MARCUS
My lord, this is impiety in you.
My nephew Mutius' deeds do plead for him;
He must be buried with his brethren.

MARTIUS
And shall.

QUINTUS   Or him we will accompany.

TITUS
"And shall"? What villain was it spake that word?

MARTIUS
He that would vouch it in any place but here.   361

TITUS
What, would you bury him in my despite?   362

MARCUS
No, noble Titus, but entreat of thee
To pardon Mutius and to bury him.

TITUS
Marcus, even thou hast struck upon my crest,
And, with these boys, mine honor thou hast
   wounded.
My foes I do repute you every one.   367
So trouble me no more, but get you gone.

QUINTUS
He is not with himself. Let us withdraw.   369

MARTIUS
Not I, till Mutius' bones be buried.
            The brother [Marcus] and the sons kneel.

MARCUS
Brother, for in that name doth nature plead—

MARTIUS
Father, and in that name doth nature speak—

TITUS
Speak thou no more, if all the rest will speed.   373

MARCUS
Renownèd Titus, more than half my soul—

LUCIUS
Dear Father, soul and substance of us all—

MARCUS
Suffer thy brother Marcus to inter   376
His noble nephew here in virtue's nest,
That died in honor and Lavinia's cause.
Thou art a Roman; be not barbarous.
The Greeks upon advice did bury Ajax,   380
That slew himself, and wise Laertes' son
Did graciously plead for his funerals.
Let not young Mutius, then, that was thy joy,
Be barred his entrance here.

TITUS   Rise, Marcus, rise.
                                          [They rise.]
The dismal'st day is this that e'er I saw,
To be dishonored by my sons in Rome!
Well, bury him, and bury me the next.
            They put him [Mutius] in the tomb.

LUCIUS
There lie thy bones, sweet Mutius, with thy friends,
Till we with trophies do adorn thy tomb.   389
                              They all kneel.

ALL
No man shed tears for noble Mutius;
He lives in fame that died in virtue's cause.   391
            [They rise.] Exeunt all but Marcus and Titus.

MARCUS
My lord, to step out of these dreary dumps,   392
How comes it that the subtle Queen of Goths
Is of a sudden thus advanced in Rome?

TITUS
I know not, Marcus, but I know it is—
Whether by device or no, the heavens can tell.   396
Is she not then beholding to the man   397
That brought her for this high good turn so far?

MARCUS
Yes, and will nobly him remunerate.   399

373 if . . . speed if all is to succeed, or, possibly, if you remaining sons do not wish to be slain like Mutius   **376 Suffer** permit   **380 advice** deliberation.   **Ajax** Greek hero of the Trojan War who went mad because the armor of Achilles was awarded to Odysseus, slew a flock of sheep deludedly thinking them Greeks, and later committed suicide in shame; he was refused burial until *Laertes' son,* line 381, Odysseus, successfully pleaded for his funeral rites   **389 trophies** memorials. **s.d. They all kneel** (Some editors think it unlikely that Titus joins his sons in kneeling or in saying lines 390–391, but Titus has relented and is not without feeling for the son he has slain.)   **391 s.d. Exeunt** (Perhaps the sons go off in order to accompany Bassianus' entry at line 399, or they may simply stand aside.)   **392 dumps** melancholy **396 device** scheming   **397 beholding** beholden   **399 Yes . . . remunerate** (Said sarcastically; Tamora will show her gratitude in physical ways.)

337 Whose . . . conquerèd i.e., whose wise choice to be my queen has overcome her ill fortune of being conquered in battle   **338 s.d. omnes** all   **339 bid** invited   **341 challengèd** accused   **348 becomes** is fitting   **352 re-edified** rebuilt   **353 servitors** armed defenders **361 vouch** maintain.   **any place but here** i.e., anywhere but in this sacred place   **362 in my despite** in despite of me   **367 repute** think of   **369 not with himself** distracted

*[Flourish.] Enter the Emperor [Saturninus],
Tamora, and her two sons, with [Aaron] the
Moor, at one door. Enter at the other door
Bassianus and Lavinia, with others, [Lucius,
Martius, and Quintus].*

SATURNINUS
So, Bassianus, you have played your prize.   400
God give you joy, sir, of your gallant bride!
BASSIANUS
And you of yours, my lord! I say no more,
Nor wish no less; and so I take my leave.
SATURNINUS
Traitor, if Rome have law or we have power,   404
Thou and thy faction shall repent this rape.   405
BASSIANUS
"Rape" call you it, my lord, to seize my own,
My true-betrothèd love and now my wife?
But let the laws of Rome determine all;
Meanwhile am I possessed of that is mine.   409
SATURNINUS
'Tis good, sir. You are very short with us,
But if we live we'll be as sharp with you.
BASSIANUS
My lord, what I have done, as best I may
Answer I must, and shall do with my life.
Only thus much I give Your Grace to know:
By all the duties that I owe to Rome,
This noble gentleman, Lord Titus here,
Is in opinion and in honor wronged,   417
That, in the rescue of Lavinia,
With his own hand did slay his youngest son
In zeal to you, and highly moved to wrath
To be controlled in that he frankly gave.   421
Receive him, then, to favor, Saturnine,
That hath expressed himself in all his deeds
A father and a friend to thee and Rome.
TITUS
Prince Bassianus, leave to plead my deeds.   425
'Tis thou, and those, that have dishonored me.   426
Rome and the righteous heavens be my judge
How I have loved and honored Saturnine!
                                            [He kneels.]
TAMORA *[to Saturninus]*
My worthy lord, if ever Tamora
Were gracious in those princely eyes of thine,
Then hear me speak indifferently for all;   431
And at my suit, sweet, pardon what is past.
SATURNINUS
What, madam? Be dishonored openly,
And basely put it up without revenge?   434
TAMORA
Not so, my lord. The gods of Rome forfend   435
I should be author to dishonor you!   436

But on mine honor dare I undertake   437
For good Lord Titus' innocence in all,
Whose fury not dissembled speaks his griefs.   439
Then at my suit look graciously on him;
Lose not so noble a friend on vain suppose,   441
Nor with sour looks afflict his gentle heart.
[Aside to Saturninus.] My lord, be ruled by me, be
    won at last;
Dissemble all your griefs and discontents.
You are but newly planted in your throne;
Lest then the people, and patricians too,
Upon a just survey take Titus' part   447
And so supplant you for ingratitude,
Which Rome reputes to be a heinous sin,
Yield at entreats; and then let me alone.   450
I'll find a day to massacre them all
And raze their faction and their family,
The cruel father and his traitorous sons
To whom I suèd for my dear son's life,
And make them know what 'tis to let a queen
Kneel in the streets and beg for grace in vain.—
[Aloud.] Come, come, sweet Emperor; come,
    Andronicus;
Take up this good old man, and cheer the heart   458
That dies in tempest of thy angry frown.
SATURNINUS
Rise, Titus, rise. My empress hath prevailed.
TITUS *[rising]*
I thank Your Majesty and her, my lord.
These words, these looks, infuse new life in me.
TAMORA
Titus, I am incorporate in Rome,   463
A Roman now adopted happily,   464
And must advise the Emperor for his good.
This day all quarrels die, Andronicus.   466
And let it be mine honor, good my lord,
That I have reconciled your friends and you.
For you, Prince Bassianus, I have passed
My word and promise to the Emperor
That you will be more mild and tractable.
And fear not, lords, and you, Lavinia;
By my advice, all humbled on your knees,
You shall ask pardon of His Majesty.   474
        [Lucius, Martius, Quintus, and Lavinia kneel.]
LUCIUS
We do, and vow to heaven and to His Highness
That what we did was mildly as we might,
Tend'ring our sister's honor and our own.   477
MARCUS *[kneeling]*
That, on mine honor, here do I protest.

---

400 played your prize played and won your bout (as in fencing)
404 we I. (The royal plural; also at lines 410–411, etc.)   **405 rape**
forcible seizure   **409 that** that which   **417 opinion** reputation
421 controlled opposed, restrained.   **in . . . gave** i.e., in his free bestowal of Lavinia on Saturninus   **425 leave to plead** cease pleading
426 those those sons of mine   **431 indifferently** impartially   **434 put
it up** put up with it   **435 forfend** forbid   **436 author** agent

437 undertake assert, vouch   **439 Whose . . . griefs** whose unconcealed anger gives testimonial to his grievances   **441 vain suppose**
idle supposition   **447 survey** examination   **450 at entreats** to entreaty.   **let me alone** leave it to me   **458 Take up** raise from kneeling
463 am incorporate in have been admitted to the fellowship of
464 happily fortunately   **466 die** (Perhaps with a double sense of "let
them die"; *dies* in line 459 may contain a similarly sinister suggestion.)   **474 s.d. Lucius . . . kneel** (Perhaps Bassianus kneels also,
though his pardon seems to have been assured at line 469.)
477 Tend'ring having regard for

SATURNINUS [*turning away*]
  Away, and talk not! Trouble us no more.
TAMORA
  Nay, nay, sweet Emperor, we must all be friends.
  The tribune and his nephews kneel for grace;
  I will not be denied. Sweetheart, look back.
SATURNINUS
  Marcus, for thy sake and thy brother's here,
  And at my lovely Tamora's entreats,
  I do remit these young men's heinous faults.
  Stand up.   [*The Andronici rise.*]
  Lavinia, though you left me like a churl,
  I found a friend, and sure as death I swore
  I would not part a bachelor from the priest.   489
  Come, if the Emperor's court can feast two brides,
  You are my guest, Lavinia, and your friends.
  This day shall be a love-day, Tamora.   492
TITUS
  Tomorrow, an it please Your Majesty   493
  To hunt the panther and the hart with me,
  With horn and hound we'll give Your Grace *bonjour*. 495
SATURNINUS
  Be it so, Titus, and gramercy too.   496
        Exeunt. Sound trumpets. Manet [Aaron the] Moor.

2.1

AARON
  Now climbeth Tamora Olympus' top,   1
  Safe out of fortune's shot, and sits aloft,
  Secure of thunder's crack or lightning flash,   3
  Advanced above pale envy's threatening reach.
  As when the golden sun salutes the morn
  And, having gilt the ocean with his beams,
  Gallops the zodiac in his glistering coach   7
  And overlooks the highest-peering hills,   8
  So Tamora.
  Upon her wit doth earthly honor wait,   10
  And virtue stoops and trembles at her frown.   11
  Then, Aaron, arm thy heart and fit thy thoughts
  To mount aloft with thy imperial mistress,
  And mount her pitch whom thou in triumph long   14
  Hast prisoner held, fettered in amorous chains
  And faster bound to Aaron's charming eyes   16
  Than is Prometheus tied to Caucasus.   17

489 **part** depart 492 **love-day** (1) day appointed to settle disputes (2) day for love 493 **an** if 495 **bonjour** good day 496 **gramercy** great thanks. **s.d. Manet** he remains onstage. (The Folio has Aaron exiting with the rest and reentering. The tomb of Act 1 is possibly concealed by a curtain backstage.)
2.1. Location: Scene continues. Aaron remains onstage.
1 **Olympus** home of the Greek gods 3 **of** from 7 **Gallops** gallops through 8 **overlooks** looks down on from on high 10 **wit** intelligence. **wait** attend 11 **virtue . . . frown** (1) she commands all virtue (2) she terrifies and oppresses virtue 14 **pitch** height to which a falcon soars before descending on its prey. (The image of *mounting* has sexual connotations also.) 16 **charming** exerting a magic spell 17 **Prometheus** Titan, who stole fire from the chariot of the sun and gave it to humanity; as punishment, Zeus fastened him to a mountain in the Caucasus and sent a vulture to feast on his liver

  Away with slavish weeds and servile thoughts!   18
  I will be bright, and shine in pearl and gold,
  To wait upon this new-made empress.
  To wait, said I? To wanton with this queen,
  This goddess, this Semiramis, this nymph,   22
  This siren that will charm Rome's Saturnine
  And see his shipwreck and his commonweal's.
  Holla! What storm is this?   25

        Enter Chiron and Demetrius, braving.

DEMETRIUS
  Chiron, thy years wants wit, thy wits wants edge   26
  And manners, to intrude where I am graced   27
  And may, for aught thou knowest, affected be.   28
CHIRON
  Demetrius, thou dost overween in all,   29
  And so in this, to bear me down with braves.   30
  'Tis not the difference of a year or two
  Makes me less gracious or thee more fortunate;
  I am as able and as fit as thou
  To serve, and to deserve my mistress' grace,
  And that my sword upon thee shall approve,   35
  And plead my passions for Lavinia's love.
AARON [*aside*]
  Clubs, clubs! These lovers will not keep the peace.   37
DEMETRIUS
  Why, boy, although our mother, unadvised,   38
  Gave you a dancing-rapier by your side,   39
  Are you so desperate grown to threat your friends?   40
  Go to! Have your lath glued within your sheath   41
  Till you know better how to handle it.
CHIRON
  Meanwhile, sir, with the little skill I have,
  Full well shalt thou perceive how much I dare.
DEMETRIUS
  Ay, boy, grow ye so brave?   *They draw.*
AARON [*coming forward*]   Why, how now, lords?
  So near the Emperor's palace dare ye draw   46
  And maintain such a quarrel openly?
  Full well I wot the ground of all this grudge.   48
  I would not for a million of gold
  The cause were known to them it most concerns,
  Nor would your noble mother for much more
  Be so dishonored in the court of Rome.
  For shame, put up.
DEMETRIUS   Not I, till I have sheathed   53
  My rapier in his bosom, and withal   54
  Thrust those reproachful speeches down his throat
  That he hath breathed in my dishonor here.

18 **weeds** garments 22 **Semiramis** mythical Queen of Assyria, famous for her cruelty and lust 25 **s.d. braving** defying (each other) 26 **wants** lack. **edge** sharpness, incisiveness 27 **graced** favored 28 **affected** loved 29 **overween** arrogantly presume 30 **braves** threats 35 **approve** prove 37 **Clubs, clubs** (A cry summoning the apprentices of London to join in or to suppress a riot or rebellion.) 38 **unadvised** ill-advisedly 39 **a dancing-rapier** an ornamental weapon worn in dancing 40 **to** as to 41 **Go to** (An expression of impatience.) **lath** counterfeit stage weapon of wood 46 **So . . . palace** (It was usually against the law to draw a sword in the presence of the King or near his royal residence. See also line 64.) 48 **wot** know 53 **put up** sheathe your swords 54 **withal** besides

CHIRON

For that I am prepared and full resolved,
Foul-spoken coward, that thunderest with thy
  tongue
And with thy weapon nothing dar'st perform!

AARON   Away, I say!

Now, by the gods that warlike Goths adore,
This petty brabble will undo us all.   62
Why, lords, and think you not how dangerous
It is to jet upon a prince's right?   64
What, is Lavinia then become so loose,
Or Bassianus so degenerate,
That for her love such quarrels may be broached   67
Without controlment, justice, or revenge?   68
Young lords, beware! And should the Empress
  know
This discord's ground, the music would not please.   70

CHIRON

I care not, I, knew she and all the world.   71
I love Lavinia more than all the world.

DEMETRIUS

Youngling, learn thou to make some meaner choice.   73
Lavinia is thine elder brother's hope.

AARON

Why, are ye mad? Or know ye not in Rome
How furious and impatient they be,
And cannot brook competitors in love?   77
I tell you, lords, you do but plot your deaths
By this device.

CHIRON   Aaron, a thousand deaths
Would I propose to achieve her whom I love.   80

AARON

To achieve her? How?

DEMETRIUS   Why makes thou it so strange?   81
She is a woman, therefore may be wooed;
She is a woman, therefore may be won;
She is Lavinia, therefore must be loved.
What, man, more water glideth by the mill
Than wots the miller of, and easy it is   86
Of a cut loaf to steal a shive, we know.   87
Though Bassianus be the Emperor's brother,
Better than he have worn Vulcan's badge.   89

AARON [aside]

Ay, and as good as Saturninus may.

DEMETRIUS

Then why should he despair that knows to court it   91
With words, fair looks, and liberality?
What, hast not thou full often struck a doe
And borne her cleanly by the keeper's nose?   94

AARON

Why then, it seems some certain snatch or so   95
Would serve your turns.

CHIRON   Ay, so the turn were served.   96

DEMETRIUS

Aaron, thou hast hit it.

AARON   Would you had hit it too!   97
Then should not we be tired with this ado.
Why, hark ye, hark ye, and are you such fools
To square for this? Would it offend you then   100
That both should speed?   101

CHIRON

Faith, not me.

DEMETRIUS   Nor me, so I were one.   102

AARON

For shame, be friends, and join for that you jar.   103
'Tis policy and stratagem must do   104
That you affect, and so must you resolve   105
That what you cannot as you would achieve,   106
You must perforce accomplish as you may.   107
Take this of me: Lucrece was not more chaste   108
Than this Lavinia, Bassianus' love.
A speedier course than lingering languishment   110
Must we pursue, and I have found the path.
My lords, a solemn hunting is in hand;   112
There will the lovely Roman ladies troop.
The forest walks are wide and spacious,
And many unfrequented plots there are,   115
Fitted by kind for rape and villainy.   116
Single you thither then this dainty doe,   117
And strike her home by force, if not by words;   118
This way, or not at all, stand you in hope.
Come, come, our empress, with her sacred wit   120
To villainy and vengeance consecrate,   121
Will we acquaint withal what we intend;   122
And she shall file our engines with advice,   123
That will not suffer you to square yourselves,   124
But to your wishes' height advance you both.
The Emperor's court is like the house of Fame,   126
The palace full of tongues, of eyes, and ears;
The woods are ruthless, dreadful, deaf, and dull.

62 brabble quarrel, brawl   64 jet encroach   67 broached begun, set flowing   68 controlment restraint   70 ground basis (with a pun on the musical meaning ''bass upon which a melody is constructed'')   71 knew she if she knew   73 meaner of lower degree   77 brook endure   80 propose be ready to meet   81 Why . . . strange why do you act so surprised   86 wots knows   87 shive slice   89 Vulcan's badge i.e., cuckold's horns, alluding to the public shame to which Vulcan was exposed by his wife Venus' affair with Mars   91 knows knows how. court it play the wooer   94 cleanly by clean past, without being observed

95 snatch sudden or quick catch (with a bawdy pun: ''a quickie'')   96 serve your turns answer your purposes (with sexual suggestion of a turn in the bed that is underscored in Chiron's reply)   97 hit it . . . hit it hit the nail on the head . . . scored sexually   100 square quarrel   101 speed succeed   102 so so long as   103 join . . . jar conspire to obtain what you're quarreling over   104 policy contrivance, craft   105 That that which. affect desire   106–107 That . . . may that if you can't do this in the way you'd prefer, you must necessarily accomplish it as best you can, by whatever means   108 Lucrece a chaste Roman lady ravished by Tarquin, as told in Shakespeare's poem The Rape of Lucrece   110 languishment love distress   112 solemn ceremonial   115 plots i.e., plots of ground   116 by kind by nature   117 Single single out (as in hunting)   118 home effectually, thoroughly, to the desired place (with sexual suggestion)   120 sacred i.e., consecrated (to villainy)   121 consecrate dedicated   122 withal with   123 file our engines sharpen our devices   124 square yourselves quarrel with each other   126 house of Fame residence of rumor. (Described in Ovid's Metamorphoses, Book 12, and in Chaucer's Hous of Fame; see also Virgil, Aeneid, 4.179–190.)

There speak and strike, brave boys, and take your
 turns;
There serve your lust, shadowed from heaven's eye,
And revel in Lavinia's treasury.

CHIRON
Thy counsel, lad, smells of no cowardice.

DEMETRIUS
Sit fas aut nefas, till I find the stream   133
To cool this heat, a charm to calm these fits,
Per Stygia, per manes vehor.   *Exeunt.* 135

❖

2.2 *Enter Titus Andronicus and his three sons [and
 Marcus], making a noise with hounds and horns.*

TITUS
The hunt is up, the morn is bright and gray,   1
The fields are fragrant, and the woods are green.
Uncouple here, and let us make a bay   3
And wake the Emperor and his lovely bride,
And rouse the Prince, and ring a hunter's peal,   5
That all the court may echo with the noise.
Sons, let it be your charge, as it is ours,
To attend the Emperor's person carefully.
I have been troubled in my sleep this night,
But dawning day new comfort hath inspired.   10

> *Here a cry of hounds, and wind horns in a peal.
> Then enter Saturninus, Tamora, Bassianus,
> Lavinia, Chiron, Demetrius, and their attendants.*

Many good morrows to Your Majesty;
Madam, to you as many and as good.
I promisèd Your Grace a hunter's peal.

SATURNINUS
And you have rung it lustily, my lords—   14
Somewhat too early for new-married ladies.

BASSIANUS
Lavinia, how say you?

LAVINIA   I say no;
I have been broad awake two hours and more.

SATURNINUS
Come on, then, horse and chariots let us have,
And to our sport. [*To Tamora.*] Madam, now shall ye
 see
Our Roman hunting.

MARCUS   I have dogs, my lord,
Will rouse the proudest panther in the chase   21
And climb the highest promontory top.

TITUS
And I have horse will follow where the game   23
Makes way and run like swallows o'er the plain.   24

DEMETRIUS [*aside to Chiron*]
Chiron, we hunt not, we, with horse nor hound,
But hope to pluck a dainty doe to ground.   *Exeunt.*

❖

2.3 *Enter Aaron alone [with a bag of gold].*

AARON
He that had wit would think that I had none,
To bury so much gold under a tree
And never after to inherit it.   3
Let him that thinks of me so abjectly
Know that this gold must coin a stratagem   5
Which, cunningly effected, will beget
A very excellent piece of villainy.
And so repose, sweet gold, for their unrest   8
That have their alms out of the Empress' chest.   9
                        [*He hides the gold.*]

Enter Tamora alone to the Moor.

TAMORA
My lovely Aaron, wherefore look'st thou sad,
When everything doth make a gleeful boast?   11
The birds chant melody on every bush,
The snake lies rollèd in the cheerful sun,   13
The green leaves quiver with the cooling wind
And make a checkered shadow on the ground.
Under their sweet shade, Aaron, let us sit,
And whilst the babbling echo mocks the hounds,
Replying shrilly to the well-tuned horns,
As if a double hunt were heard at once,
Let us sit down and mark their yellowing noise;   20
And after conflict such as was supposed
The wandering prince and Dido once enjoyed   22
When with a happy storm they were surprised   23
And curtained with a counsel-keeping cave,   24
We may, each wreathèd in the other's arms,
Our pastimes done, possess a golden slumber,
Whiles hounds and horns and sweet melodious
 birds
Be unto us as is a nurse's song
Of lullaby to bring her babe asleep.

---

133 Sit fas aut nefas be it right or wrong **135 Per . . . vehor** I am
carried through the Stygian regions, through the realm of the shades.
(Adapted from Seneca's *Hippolytus,* line 1180.)
2.2. Location: The grounds of the Emperor's palace.
1 gray cold, sunless light of early morning **3 Uncouple** unleash the
hounds. **make a bay** keep up a deep, prolonged barking **5 ring a
hunter's peal** blow a peal on the hunting horns (to set the dogs going)
10 s.d. cry deep barking. **wind** blow **14 lustily** heartily **21 Will**
that will. **chase** hunting ground

23 horse will horses that will **24 run** (The First Quarto's *runs* is possible, in parallel to *Makes,* but the verb probably applies to the *horse*
rather than to the *game.*)
**2.3. Location: A forest near Rome. A pit is provided in the stage,
presumably at a trapdoor, and near it some representation of an elder tree.**
3 inherit possess **5 coin** fabricate (with a pun on the literal meaning)
8–9 for . . . chest i.e., to discomfit those who will find this gold
taken from Tamora's treasure chest **11 boast** display **13 rolled**
coiled **20 yellowing** baying **22 prince** i.e., Aeneas, who, taking
shelter from a storm with Dido in a cave during a hunt, made love to
her **23 happy** fortunate **24 curtained with** concealed by. **counsel-
keeping** secret-keeping

AARON
    Madam, though Venus govern your desires,
    Saturn is dominator over mine.   31
    What signifies my deadly-standing eye,   32
    My silence, and my cloudy melancholy,   33
    My fleece of woolly hair that now uncurls
    Even as an adder when she doth unroll
    To do some fatal execution?
    No, madam, these are no venereal signs.   37
    Vengeance is in my heart, death in my hand,
    Blood and revenge are hammering in my head.
    Hark, Tamora, the empress of my soul,
    Which never hopes more heaven than rests in thee,   41
    This is the day of doom for Bassianus:
    His Philomel must lose her tongue today,   43
    Thy sons make pillage of her chastity
    And wash their hands in Bassianus' blood.
    Seest thou this letter? Take it up, I pray thee,   46
                            [giving her a letter]
    And give the King this fatal-plotted scroll.
    Now question me no more; we are espied.
    Here comes a parcel of our hopeful booty,   49
    Which dreads not yet their lives' destruction.

            Enter Bassianus and Lavinia.

TAMORA
    Ah, my sweet Moor, sweeter to me than life!
AARON
    No more, great Empress. Bassianus comes.
    Be cross with him, and I'll go fetch thy sons   53
    To back thy quarrels, whatsoe'er they be.   [Exit.]
BASSIANUS
    Who have we here? Rome's royal empress,
    Unfurnished of her well-beseeming troop?   56
    Or is it Dian, habited like her,   57
    Who hath abandonèd her holy groves
    To see the general hunting in this forest?
TAMORA
    Saucy controller of my private steps!   60
    Had I the power that some say Dian had,
    Thy temples should be planted presently   62
    With horns, as was Actaeon's, and the hounds   63
    Should drive upon thy new-transformèd limbs,   64
    Unmannerly intruder as thou art!

31 Saturn . . . mine i.e., Saturn, as the dominant planet in my horoscope, governs my temperament and makes it cold and sullen (unlike
Venus' effect, which is amorous)   32 deadly-standing fixed with a
death-dealing stare   33 cloudy gloomy   37 venereal erotic, Venus-
like   41 Which . . . thee which hopes for no greater bliss than may
be found in you   43 Philomel (An allusion to the story in Ovid's
Metamorphoses of Philomela, raped by her brother-in-law, Tereus;
compare with 2.4.26 below. He cut out her tongue so that she could
not disclose his villainy. She succeeded in weaving the account of her
misfortune in a tapestry.)   46 Take it up take it   49 parcel part.
hopeful hoped-for   53 Be cross pick a quarrel   56 Unfurnished . . .
troop unprovided with a suitable escort   57 Dian Diana, huntress
and goddess of chastity. (Here used sarcastically.)   habited dressed
60 Saucy controller impudent critic, censurer   62 presently immediately   63 Actaeon's (An allusion to the story of Actaeon, who was
transformed into a stag by Diana and killed by his own hounds as
punishment for having watched her and her nymphs at their bath.)
64 drive rush

LAVINIA
    Under your patience, gentle Empress,   66
    'Tis thought you have a goodly gift in horning,   67
    And to be doubted that your Moor and you   68
    Are singled forth to try experiments.   69
    Jove shield your husband from his hounds today!
    'Tis pity they should take him for a stag.
BASSIANUS
    Believe me, Queen, your swart Cimmerian   72
    Doth make your honor of his body's hue,
    Spotted, detested, and abominable.
    Why are you sequestered from all your train,
    Dismounted from your snow-white goodly steed,
    And wandered hither to an obscure plot,
    Accompanied but with a barbarous Moor,
    If foul desire had not conducted you?
LAVINIA
    And, being intercepted in your sport,
    Great reason that my noble lord be rated   81
    For sauciness. [To Bassianus.] I pray you, let us
        hence,
    And let her joy her raven-colored love;   83
    This valley fits the purpose passing well.   84
BASSIANUS
    The King my brother shall have note of this.
LAVINIA
    Ay, for these slips have made him noted long.   86
    Good king, to be so mightily abused!   87
TAMORA
    Why have I patience to endure all this?

            Enter Chiron and Demetrius.

DEMETRIUS
    How now, dear sovereign, and our gracious mother,
    Why doth Your Highness look so pale and wan?
TAMORA
    Have I not reason, think you, to look pale?
    These two have 'ticed me hither to this place.   92
    A barren detested vale you see it is;
    The trees, though summer, yet forlorn and lean,
    Overcome with moss and baleful mistletoe;   95
    Here never shines the sun; here nothing breeds,
    Unless the nightly owl or fatal raven.   97
    And when they showed me this abhorrèd pit,
    They told me here at dead time of the night
    A thousand fiends, a thousand hissing snakes,
    Ten thousand swelling toads, as many urchins,   101
    Would make such fearful and confusèd cries
    As any mortal body hearing it
    Should straight fall mad or else die suddenly.
    No sooner had they told this hellish tale

66 Under your patience if you will allow my saying so.   gentle noble
and kind. (Said with ironic politeness.)   67 horning cuckolding
68 doubted suspected, feared   69 Are . . . experiments i.e., are
alone together to experiment with each other   72 Cimmerian i.e., of
black complexion. (The Cimmerii in the Odyssey live in perpetual
darkness.)   81 my noble lord i.e., Bassianus.   rated berated   83 joy
enjoy   84 passing surpassingly   86 slips offenses.   noted notorious,
stigmatized   87 abused deceived   92 'ticed enticed   95 Overcome
overgrown   97 fatal ominous   101 urchins hedgehogs

But straight they told me they would bind me here
Unto the body of a dismal yew
And leave me to this miserable death.
And then they called me foul adulteress,
Lascivious Goth, and all the bitterest terms   110
That ever ear did hear to such effect;
And had you not by wondrous fortune come,
This vengeance on me had they executed.
Revenge it, as you love your mother's life,
Or be ye not henceforth called my children.
DEMETRIUS
This is a witness that I am thy son.
                              Stab him [*Bassianus*].
CHIRON
And this for me, struck home to show my strength.
              [*He also stabs Bassianus, who dies.*]
LAVINIA
Ay, come, Semiramis, nay, barbarous Tamora,   118
For no name fits thy nature but thy own!
TAMORA
Give me the poniard. You shall know, my boys,   120
Your mother's hand shall right your mother's wrong.
DEMETRIUS
Stay, madam, here is more belongs to her.   122
First thresh the corn, then after burn the straw.   123
This minion stood upon her chastity,   124
Upon her nuptial vow, her loyalty,
And with that painted hope braves your mightiness;   126
And shall she carry this unto her grave?
CHIRON
An if she do, I would I were an eunuch.   128
Drag hence her husband to some secret hole
And make his dead trunk pillow to our lust.
TAMORA
But when ye have the honey ye desire,
Let not this wasp outlive, us both to sting.   132
CHIRON
I warrant you, madam, we will make that sure.—
Come, mistress, now perforce we will enjoy
That nice-preservèd honesty of yours.   135
LAVINIA
O Tamora! Thou bearest a woman's face—
TAMORA
I will not hear her speak. Away with her!
LAVINIA
Sweet lords, entreat her hear me but a word.
DEMETRIUS [*to Tamora*]
Listen, fair madam. Let it be your glory
To see her tears, but be your heart to them
As unrelenting flint to drops of rain.
LAVINIA
When did the tiger's young ones teach the dam?
O, do not learn her wrath; she taught it thee!   143

The milk thou suck'st from her did turn to marble;   144
Even at thy teat thou hadst thy tyranny.   145
Yet every mother breeds not sons alike;
[*To Chiron.*] Do thou entreat her show a woman's
     pity.
CHIRON
What, wouldst thou have me prove myself a
     bastard?   148
LAVINIA
'Tis true, the raven doth not hatch a lark.
Yet have I heard—O, could I find it now!—   150
The lion, moved with pity, did endure
To have his princely paws pared all away.   152
Some say that ravens foster forlorn children   153
The whilst their own birds famish in their nests;   154
O, be to me, though thy hard heart say no,
Nothing so kind, but something pitiful!   156
TAMORA
I know not what it means. Away with her!   157
LAVINIA
O, let me teach thee! For my father's sake,
That gave thee life when well he might have slain
     thee,
Be not obdurate; open thy deaf ears.
TAMORA
Hadst thou in person ne'er offended me,
Even for his sake am I pitiless.
Remember, boys, I poured forth tears in vain
To save your brother from the sacrifice,
But fierce Andronicus would not relent.
Therefore away with her, and use her as you will—
The worse to her, the better loved of me.
LAVINIA
O Tamora, be called a gentle queen,
And with thine own hands kill me in this place!
For 'tis not life that I have begged so long;
Poor I was slain when Bassianus died.
               [*She clutches Tamora imploringly.*]
TAMORA
What begg'st thou, then? Fond woman, let me go.   172
LAVINIA
'Tis present death I beg, and one thing more   173
That womanhood denies my tongue to tell: 174
O, keep me from their worse-than-killing lust,
And tumble me into some loathsome pit,
Where never man's eye may behold my body!
Do this, and be a charitable murderer.
TAMORA
So should I rob my sweet sons of their fee.
No, let them satisfy their lust on thee.
DEMETRIUS [*to Lavinia*]
Away! For thou hast stayed us here too long.
LAVINIA
No grace, no womanhood? Ah, beastly creature!

110 Goth (A quibble; pronounced somewhat like "goat," symbolic of lechery.) **118 Semiramis** (See the note to 2.1.22.) **120 poniard** dagger **122 belongs to her** that is to be her portion **123 corn** grain **124 minion** hussy, wench. **stood upon** preened herself upon **126 painted** specious, unreal **128 An if** if **132 outlive** survive. **sting** i.e., do harm to (us) **135 nice** fastidiously. **honesty** chastity **143 learn** teach

144 thou suck'st that you sucked **145 hadst thy tyranny** gained your cruelty **148 a bastard** i.e., false to my parentage, an unnatural son **150 find it** find it true **152 paws** claws **153 forlorn** abandoned (by other birds) **154 birds** chicks **156 Nothing . . . pitiful** not so kind as the raven, but still showing some pity **157 it** i.e., pity **172 Fond** foolish **173 present** immediate **174 denies** forbids

The blot and enemy to our general name!   183
Confusion fall—   184
CHIRON
Nay, then I'll stop your mouth. [*To Demetrius.*] Bring
    thou her husband.
This is the hole where Aaron bid us hide him.
        [*Demetrius and Chiron throw the body of Bassianus
            into the pit, then exeunt, dragging off Lavinia.*]
TAMORA
Farewell, my sons. See that you make her sure.   187
Ne'er let my heart know merry cheer indeed
Till all the Andronici be made away.   189
Now will I hence to seek my lovely Moor,
And let my spleenful sons this trull deflower. [*Exit.*] 191

        *Enter Aaron, with two of Titus' sons [Quintus
            and Martius].*

AARON
Come on, my lords, the better foot before.   192
Straight will I bring you to the loathsome pit
Where I espied the panther fast asleep.
QUINTUS
My sight is very dull, whate'er it bodes.
MARTIUS
And mine, I promise you. Were it not for shame,
Well could I leave our sport to sleep awhile.
                                    [*He falls into the pit.*]
QUINTUS
What, art thou fallen? What subtle hole is this,
Whose mouth is covered with rude-growing briers
Upon whose leaves are drops of new-shed blood
As fresh as morning dew distilled on flowers?
A very fatal place it seems to me.   202
Speak, brother. Hast thou hurt thee with the fall?
MARTIUS
O brother, with the dismal'st object hurt   204
That ever eye with sight made heart lament!   205
AARON [*aside*]
Now will I fetch the King to find them here,
That he thereby may have a likely guess
How these were they that made away his brother.
                                                    Exit.
MARTIUS
Why dost not comfort me and help me out
From this unhallowèd and bloodstained hole?
QUINTUS
I am surprisèd with an uncouth fear.   211
A chilling sweat o'erruns my trembling joints;
My heart suspects more than mine eye can see.
MARTIUS
To prove thou hast a true-divining heart,
Aaron and thou look down into this den
And see a fearful sight of blood and death.

QUINTUS
Aaron is gone, and my compassionate heart
Will not permit mine eyes once to behold
The thing whereat it trembles by surmise.   219
O, tell me who it is! For ne'er till now
Was I a child to fear I know not what.
MARTIUS
Lord Bassianus lies berayed in blood,   222
All on a heap, like to a slaughtered lamb,   223
In this detested, dark, blood-drinking pit.
QUINTUS
If it be dark, how dost thou know 'tis he?
MARTIUS
Upon his bloody finger he doth wear
A precious ring that lightens all this hole,   227
Which like a taper in some monument   228
Doth shine upon the dead man's earthy cheeks   229
And shows the ragged entrails of this pit.   230
So pale did shine the moon on Pyramus   231
When he by night lay bathed in maiden blood.   232
O brother, help me with thy fainting hand—
If fear hath made thee faint, as me it hath—
Out of this fell devouring receptacle,   235
As hateful as Cocytus' misty mouth.   236
QUINTUS [*offering to help*]
Reach me thy hand, that I may help thee out,
Or, wanting strength to do thee so much good,   238
I may be plucked into the swallowing womb
Of this deep pit, poor Bassianus' grave.
I have no strength to pluck thee to the brink.
MARTIUS
Nor I no strength to climb without thy help.
QUINTUS
Thy hand once more; I will not loose again
Till thou art here aloft or I below.
Thou canst not come to me—I come to thee.
                                        [*He falls in.*]

        *Enter the Emperor [Saturninus, with attendants],
            and Aaron the Moor.*

SATURNINUS
Along with me! I'll see what hole is here,   246
And what he is that now is leapt into it.
                                    [*He speaks into the pit.*]
Say, who art thou that lately didst descend
Into this gaping hollow of the earth?
MARTIUS [*from within the pit*]
The unhappy sons of old Andronicus,

---

183 **our general name** i.e., women's reputation 184 **Confusion** destruction 187 **sure** safe, incapable of revenge 189 **made away** murdered 191 **spleenful** lustful. **trull** whore, slut 192 **better foot before** best foot forward 202 **fatal** ill-omened 204 **object** sight 205 **with . . . lament** made heart lament to see 211 **surprisèd** overcome. **uncouth** strange

219 **by surmise** even to imagine 222 **berayed in** defiled by 223 **on a heap** prostrate 227 **ring** (Presumably the carbuncle, which was believed to emit light.) 228 **monument** tomb 229 **earthy** clay-colored, pale 230 **ragged entrails** rough interior 231 **Pyramus** the lover of Thisbe, who killed himself in the mistaken supposition that she was dead. (See *A Midsummer Night's Dream*, 1.2, 3.1, and 5.1.) 232 **maiden** i.e., that of an unmarried person. (Pyramus, who dies first, lies in his own blood, not that of Thisbe, though she soon joins him in death.) 235 **fell** savage 236 **Cocytus' misty mouth** i.e., the mouth of hell. *Cocytus* is the river of lamentations in Hades. 238 **wanting** lacking 246 **Along** come along

Brought hither in a most unlucky hour
To find thy brother Bassianus dead.
SATURNINUS
My brother dead! I know thou dost but jest.
He and his lady both are at the lodge
Upon the north side of this pleasant chase;   255
'Tis not an hour since I left them there.
MARTIUS
We know not where you left them all alive,
But, out alas! Here have we found him dead.   258

    Enter Tamora, [Titus] Andronicus, and Lucius.

TAMORA   Where is my lord the King?
SATURNINUS
Here, Tamora, though gripped with killing grief.
TAMORA
Where is thy brother Bassianus?
SATURNINUS
Now to the bottom dost thou search my wound.   262
Poor Bassianus here lies murderèd.
TAMORA
Then all too late I bring this fatal writ,
The complot of this timeless tragedy,   265
And wonder greatly that man's face can fold   266
In pleasing smiles such murderous tyranny.
                    She giveth Saturnine a letter.
SATURNINUS *(reads the letter)*
"An if we miss to meet him handsomely,   268
Sweet huntsman—Bassianus 'tis we mean—
Do thou so much as dig the grave for him.   270
Thou know'st our meaning. Look for thy reward
Among the nettles at the elder tree
Which overshades the mouth of that same pit
Where we decreed to bury Bassianus.   274
Do this, and purchase us thy lasting friends."   275
O Tamora, was ever heard the like?
This is the pit, and this the elder tree.
Look, sirs, if you can find the huntsman out
That should have murdered Bassianus here.   279
AARON [*finding the gold*]
My gracious lord, here is the bag of gold.
SATURNINUS [*to Titus*]
Two of thy whelps, fell curs of bloody kind,   281
Have here bereft my brother of his life.—
Sirs, drag them from the pit unto the prison!
There let them bide until we have devised
Some never-heard-of torturing pain for them.
    [*Martius and Quintus are dragged out of the pit,*
          and Bassianus' body is raised.]
TAMORA
What, are they in this pit? O wondrous thing!
How easily murder is discoverèd!

TITUS [*kneeling*]
High Emperor, upon my feeble knee
I beg this boon, with tears not lightly shed,
That this fell fault of my accursèd sons—
Accursèd if the fault be proved in them—
SATURNINUS
If it be proved? You see it is apparent.   292
Who found this letter? Tamora, was it you?
TAMORA
Andronicus himself did take it up.   294
TITUS
I did, my lord, yet let me be their bail.
For, by my fathers' reverend tomb, I vow   296
They shall be ready at Your Highness' will
To answer their suspicion with their lives.   298
SATURNINUS
Thou shalt not bail them. See thou follow me.
Some bring the murdered body, some the
   murderers.
Let them not speak a word—the guilt is plain;
For, by my soul, were there worse end than death,
That end upon them should be executed.
TAMORA
Andronicus, I will entreat the King.
Fear not thy sons; they shall do well enough.   305
TITUS [*rising*]
Come, Lucius, come. Stay not to talk with them.   306
    [*Exeunt bearing the dead body of Bassianus;*
       Martius and Quintus under guard.]

                    ❧

2.4   *Enter the Empress' sons with Lavinia, her hands*
      cut off, and her tongue cut out, and ravished.

DEMETRIUS
So, now go tell, an if thy tongue can speak,
Who 'twas that cut thy tongue and ravished thee.
CHIRON
Write down thy mind, bewray thy meaning so,   3
An if thy stumps will let thee play the scribe.
DEMETRIUS
See how with signs and tokens she can scrawl.   5
CHIRON
Go home, call for sweet water, wash thy hands.   6
DEMETRIUS
She hath no tongue to call, nor hands to wash;
And so let's leave her to her silent walks.
CHIRON
An 'twere my cause, I should go hang myself.   9

---

255 **chase** hunting ground 258 **out alas** alas. (*Out* intensifies the interjection.) 262 **search** probe 265 **complot** plot. **timeless** untimely
266 **fold** hide, enfold 268 **An if** if. **handsomely** conveniently
270 **Do . . . as** be so good as to. (Said with mock ceremoniousness.)
274 **decreed** decided 275 **purchase** win 279 **should** was to
281 **kind** nature

292 **apparent** evident 294 **take** pick 296 **fathers'** forefathers'
298 **their suspicion** the suspicion they are under 305 **Fear not** fear
not for 306 **them** i.e., Martius and Quintus
2.4. Location: The forest still.
3 **bewray** reveal 5 **scrawl** gesticulate. (But also anticipating her writing in 4.1.71–80.) 6 **sweet** perfumed 9 **cause** case

DEMETRIUS

If thou hadst hands to help thee knit the cord.   10

Exeunt [Chiron and Demetrius].

[Wind horns.] Enter Marcus from hunting.
[Lavinia flees from him.]

MARCUS

Who is this? My niece, that flies away so fast?
Cousin, a word. Where is your husband?   12

[He see her injuries.]

If I do dream, would all my wealth would wake me!   13
If I do wake, some planet strike me down,   14
That I may slumber an eternal sleep!
Speak, gentle niece, what stern ungentle hands   16
Hath lopped and hewed and made thy body bare
Of her two branches, those sweet ornaments
Whose circling shadows kings have sought to
    sleep in,   19
And might not gain so great a happiness   20
As half thy love? Why dost not speak to me?   21
Alas, a crimson river of warm blood,
Like to a bubbling fountain stirred with wind,
Doth rise and fall between thy rosèd lips,
Coming and going with thy honey breath.
But, sure, some Tereus hath deflowered thee   26
And, lest thou shouldst detect him, cut thy tongue.   27
Ah, now thou turn'st away thy face for shame!
And notwithstanding all this loss of blood,
As from a conduit with three issuing spouts,
Yet do thy cheeks look red as Titan's face   31
Blushing to be encountered with a cloud.   32
Shall I speak for thee? Shall I say 'tis so?
O, that I knew thy heart, and knew the beast,   34
That I might rail at him to ease my mind!
Sorrow concealèd, like an oven stopped,   36
Doth burn the heart to cinders where it is.
Fair Philomela, why, she but lost her tongue,
And in a tedious sampler sewed her mind;   39
But, lovely niece, that means is cut from thee.
A craftier Tereus, cousin, hast thou met,
And he hath cut those pretty fingers off
That could have better sewed than Philomel.
O, had the monster seen those lily hands
Tremble like aspen leaves upon a lute
And make the silken strings delight to kiss them,
He would not then have touched them for his life!
Or had he heard the heavenly harmony
Which that sweet tongue hath made,
He would have dropped his knife and fell asleep,

As Cerberus at the Thracian poet's feet.   51
Come, let us go and make thy father blind,
For such a sight will blind a father's eye.
One hour's storm will drown the fragrant meads;   54
What will whole months of tears thy father's eyes?
Do not draw back, for we will mourn with thee.
O, could our mourning ease thy misery!   *Exeunt.*

❧

3.1   *Enter the judges and senators [and tribunes] with*
Titus' two sons bound, passing over the stage to
the place of execution, and Titus going before,
pleading.

TITUS

Hear me, grave fathers! Noble tribunes, stay!
For pity of mine age, whose youth was spent
In dangerous wars whilst you securely slept;
For all my blood in Rome's great quarrel shed;   4
For all the frosty nights that I have watched,   5
And for these bitter tears which now you see
Filling the agèd wrinkles in my cheeks,
Be pitiful to my condemnèd sons,
Whose souls is not corrupted as 'tis thought.
For two-and-twenty sons I never wept,   10
Because they died in honor's lofty bed.

[Titus] Andronicus lieth down and the judges pass by
him. [Titus weeps.]

For these, tribunes, in the dust I write
My heart's deep languor and my soul's sad tears.   13
Let my tears stanch the earth's dry appetite;   14
My sons' sweet blood will make it shame and blush.   15

[Exeunt all but Titus.]

O earth, I will befriend thee more with rain
That shall distill from these two ancient urns,   17
Than youthful April shall with all his showers.
In summer's drought I'll drop upon thee still;   19
In winter with warm tears I'll melt the snow,
And keep eternal springtime on thy face,
So thou refuse to drink my dear sons' blood.   22

Enter Lucius, with his weapon drawn.

O reverend tribunes! O gentle, agèd men!
Unbind my sons, reverse the doom of death,   24
And let me say, that never wept before,
My tears are now prevailing orators.

LUCIUS

O noble Father, you lament in vain.
The tribunes hear you not. No man is by,
And you recount your sorrows to a stone.

---

10 **knit** tie the knot in.   s.d. **Wind horns** blow hunting horns (off-stage. The stage direction is from the Folio.)   12 **Cousin** kinswoman
13 **would . . . me** I would give all my wealth to have this be only a bad dream   14 **strike me down** exert its baleful influence on me
16 **stern** cruel   19 **shadows** i.e., protection, shelter   20–21 **And . . . thy love** and could find nowhere any happiness half so great as having your love   26 **Tereus** i.e., the ravisher of Philomela; see the note to 2.3.43   27 **detect** expose   31 **Titan's** the sun god's   32 **encountered with** thwarted by   34 **thy heart** the truth concealed in your heart   36 **stopped** closed too long, plugged up   39 **tedious sampler** laboriously contrived embroidered cloth or tapestry. (See the note to 2.3.43.)   **sewed her mind** put her story down in embroidery

51 **Cerberus . . . feet** (According to legend, Orpheus' sweet singing charmed even Cerberus, three-headed dog guarding the entrance to Hades.)   54 **meads** meadows
3.1. Location: Rome. A street.
4 **my blood** i.e., the blood of my sons   5 **watched** stayed awake
10 **two-and-twenty** (At 1.1.79 and 195, we are told that twenty-one of Titus' twenty-five sons died fighting. Mutius is the twenty-second to die, though scarcely "in honor's lofty bed," as Titus sees it.)   13 **languor** grief   14 **stanch** satisfy   15 **shame** be ashamed   17 **urns** i.e., tear-filled eyes   19 **still** continually   22 **So** so long as   24 **doom** sentence

TITUS

Ah, Lucius, for thy brothers let me plead.
Grave tribunes, once more I entreat of you—

LUCIUS

My gracious lord, no tribune hears you speak.

TITUS

Why, 'tis no matter, man. If they did hear,
They would not mark me; if they did mark,
They would not pity me; yet plead I must,
And bootless unto them.   36
Therefore I tell my sorrows to the stones,
Who, though they cannot answer my distress,
Yet in some sort they are better than the tribunes,
For that they will not intercept my tale.   40
When I do weep, they humbly at my feet
Receive my tears and seem to weep with me;
And, were they but attirèd in grave weeds,   43
Rome could afford no tribunes like to these.   44
A stone is soft as wax, tribunes more hard than
    stones;
A stone is silent and offendeth not,
And tribunes with their tongues doom men to
    death.   [*He rises.*]
But wherefore stand'st thou with thy weapon
    drawn?

LUCIUS

To rescue my two brothers from their death,
For which attempt the judges have pronounced
My everlasting doom of banishment.   51

TITUS

O happy man! They have befriended thee.
Why, foolish Lucius, dost thou not perceive
That Rome is but a wilderness of tigers?
Tigers must prey, and Rome affords no prey
But me and mine. How happy art thou then
From these devourers to be banishèd!
But who comes with our brother Marcus here?

Enter Marcus with Lavinia.

MARCUS

Titus, prepare thy agèd eyes to weep,
Or if not so, thy noble heart to break.
I bring consuming sorrow to thine age.

TITUS

Will it consume me? Let me see it, then.

MARCUS

This was thy daughter.

TITUS   Why, Marcus, so she is.

LUCIUS   Ay me, this object kills me!   64

TITUS

Fainthearted boy, arise, and look upon her.   65
Speak, Lavinia, what accursèd hand
Hath made thee handless in thy father's sight?
What fool hath added water to the sea,
Or brought a faggot to bright-burning Troy?
My grief was at the height before thou cam'st,

And now, like Nilus, it disdaineth bounds.   71
Give me a sword, I'll chop off my hands too,   72
For they have fought for Rome, and all in vain;
And they have nursed this woe in feeding life;   74
In bootless prayer have they been held up,
And they have served me to effectless use.   76
Now all the service I require of them
Is that the one will help to cut the other.
'Tis well, Lavinia, that thou hast no hands,
For hands to do Rome service is but vain.

LUCIUS

Speak, gentle sister, who hath martyred thee?   81

MARCUS

O, that delightful engine of her thoughts,   82
That blabbed them with such pleasing eloquence,   83
Is torn from forth that pretty hollow cage
Where, like a sweet melodious bird, it sung
Sweet varied notes, enchanting every ear.

LUCIUS

O, say thou for her, who hath done this deed?

MARCUS

O, thus I found her, straying in the park,
Seeking to hide herself, as doth the deer
That hath received some unrecuring wound.   90

TITUS

It was my dear, and he that wounded her   91
Hath hurt me more than had he killed me dead;
For now I stand as one upon a rock
Environed with a wilderness of sea,
Who marks the waxing tide grow wave by wave,
Expecting ever when some envious surge   96
Will in his brinish bowels swallow him.   97
This way to death my wretched sons are gone;
Here stands my other son, a banished man,
And here my brother, weeping at my woes;
But that which gives my soul the greatest spurn   101
Is dear Lavinia, dearer than my soul.
Had I but seen thy picture in this plight,
It would have madded me; what shall I do
Now I behold thy lively body so?   105
Thou hast no hands to wipe away thy tears,
Nor tongue to tell me who hath martyred thee.
Thy husband he is dead, and for his death   108
Thy brothers are condemned, and dead by this.   109
Look, Marcus! Ah, son Lucius, look on her!
When I did name her brothers, then fresh tears
Stood on her cheeks, as doth the honey-dew   112
Upon a gathered lily almost withered.

MARCUS

Perchance she weeps because they killed her
    husband;

---

36 **bootless** in vain   40 **For that** because.   **intercept** interrupt
43 **grave weeds** sober garments   44 **afford** provide   51 **doom** sentence   64 **object** i.e., object of sight   65 **arise** (Evidently, Lucius has collapsed or fallen to his knees in grief.)

71 **Nilus** the Nile   72 **Give** if you will give   74 **they . . . life** i.e., in sustaining Rome, my hands have merely prolonged the misery of the Andronici   76 **effectless** fruitless   81 **martyred** mutilated   82 **engine** instrument   83 **blabbed** uttered   90 **unrecuring** incurable   91 **dear** (With a familiar pun on *deer*, line 89.)   96 **Expecting ever when** continually awaiting the moment when.   **envious** spiteful   97 **his** its
101 **spurn** stroke, kick   105 **lively** living, actual (as contrasted with her picture)   108 **husband he** husband   109 **by this** by now
112 **honey-dew** sweet dewlike substance, or the dew itself

Perchance because she knows them innocent.

TITUS
If they did kill thy husband, then be joyful,
Because the law hath ta'en revenge on them.
No, no, they would not do so foul a deed;
Witness the sorrow that their sister makes.
Gentle Lavinia, let me kiss thy lips;
Or make some sign how I may do thee ease.   121
Shall thy good uncle, and thy brother Lucius,
And thou, and I, sit round about some fountain,   123
Looking all downwards to behold our cheeks
How they are stained, like meadows yet not dry
With miry slime left on them by a flood?
And in the fountain shall we gaze so long
Till the fresh taste be taken from that clearness, 128
And made a brine pit with our bitter tears?   129
Or shall we cut away our hands, like thine?
Or shall we bite our tongues, and in dumb shows   131
Pass the remainder of our hateful days?
What shall we do? Let us that have our tongues
Plot some device of further misery,   134
To make us wondered at in time to come.

LUCIUS
Sweet Father, cease your tears, for at your grief
See how my wretched sister sobs and weeps.

MARCUS
Patience, dear niece. Good Titus, dry thine eyes.

TITUS
Ah, Marcus, Marcus! Brother, well I wot   139
Thy napkin cannot drink a tear of mine,   140
For thou, poor man, hast drowned it with thine
own.   141

LUCIUS
Ah, my Lavinia, I will wipe thy cheeks.

TITUS
Mark, Marcus, mark! I understand her signs.
Had she a tongue to speak, now would she say
That to her brother which I said to thee.
His napkin, with his true tears all bewet,
Can do no service on her sorrowful cheeks.
O, what a sympathy of woe is this,   148
As far from help as Limbo is from bliss!   149

Enter Aaron the Moor alone.

AARON
Titus Andronicus, my lord the Emperor
Sends thee this word: that if thou love thy sons,
Let Marcus, Lucius, or thyself, old Titus,
Or any one of you, chop off your hand

And send it to the King. He for the same
Will send thee hither both thy sons alive,   155
And that shall be the ransom for their fault.   156

TITUS
O gracious Emperor! O gentle Aaron!
Did ever raven sing so like a lark,
That gives sweet tidings of the sun's uprise?
With all my heart I'll send the Emperor my hand.
Good Aaron, wilt thou help to chop it off?

LUCIUS
Stay, Father, for that noble hand of thine,
That hath thrown down so many enemies,
Shall not be sent. My hand will serve the turn.
My youth can better spare my blood than you,
And therefore mine shall save my brothers' lives.

MARCUS
Which of your hands hath not defended Rome   167
And reared aloft the bloody battle-ax,
Writing destruction on the enemy's castle?
O, none of both but are of high desert.
My hand hath been but idle; let it serve
To ransom my two nephews from their death.
Then have I kept it to a worthy end.

AARON
Nay, come, agree whose hand shall go along,
For fear they die before their pardon come.

MARCUS
My hand shall go.

LUCIUS   By heaven, it shall not go!

TITUS
Sirs, strive no more. Such withered herbs as these
Are meet for plucking up, and therefore mine.   178

LUCIUS
Sweet Father, if I shall be thought thy son,   179
Let me redeem my brothers both from death.

MARCUS
And for our father's sake and mother's care,
Now let me show a brother's love to thee.

TITUS
Agree between you. I will spare my hand.   183

LUCIUS   Then I'll go fetch an ax.

MARCUS   But I will use the ax.

Exeunt [Lucius and Marcus].

TITUS
Come hither, Aaron. I'll deceive them both.
Lend me thy hand, and I will give thee mine.   187

AARON [*aside*]
If that be called deceit, I will be honest,
And never whilst I live deceive men so;
But I'll deceive you in another sort,

121 **do thee ease** bring you comfort, relief   123 **fountain** spring
128 **taken** removed, destroyed.   **clearness** i.e., of the pure water
129 **And made** i.e., and the spring made   131 **bite** bite out.   **dumb
shows** mute pageants, as in dramatic action without dialogue
134 **device** dramatic representation   139 **wot** know   140 **napkin**
handkerchief   141 **drowned** saturated   148 **sympathy** agreement,
sharing   149 **Limbo** region bordering hell, where were confined the
souls of those barred from heaven through no fault of their own, such
as good persons who lived before the Christian era or who died un-
baptized

155 **Will . . . alive** (Aaron's secret double meaning may be, "will
send to you here, you being alive, both your sons.")   156 **that** (Secretly, *that* may refer to the sons being sent here—dead.)
167 **Which . . . hands** has either of you a hand that   178 **meet** fit
179 **shall** am to   183 **spare** (In a virtuous deception, Titus uses a double meaning for *spare;* ostensibly he means "save from being cut off,"
but secretly he means "do without.")   187 **Lend . . . mine** (Another
pun, on *hand:* "Give me your assistance, and I'll give you my
hand.")

And that you'll say, ere half an hour pass.

He cuts off Titus' hand.

Enter Lucius and Marcus again.

TITUS
Now stay your strife. What shall be is dispatched.
Good Aaron, give His Majesty my hand.
Tell him it was a hand that warded him   194
From thousand dangers. Bid him bury it.
More hath it merited; that let it have.   196
As for my sons, say I account of them
As jewels purchased at an easy price,
And yet dear too, because I bought mine own.   199

AARON
I go, Andronicus, and for thy hand
Look by and by to have thy sons with thee.   201
[*Aside.*] Their heads, I mean. O, how this villainy
Doth fat me with the very thoughts of it!   203
Let fools do good, and fair men call for grace;   204
Aaron will have his soul black like his face.   *Exit.*

TITUS [*kneeling*]
O, here I lift this one hand up to heaven
And bow this feeble ruin to the earth.
If any power pities wretched tears,
To that I call! [*To Lavinia, who kneels.*] What, wouldst
     thou kneel with me?
Do, then, dear heart, for heaven shall hear our
     prayers,
Or with our sighs we'll breathe the welkin dim   211
And stain the sun with fog, as sometimes clouds
When they do hug him in their melting bosoms.   213

MARCUS
O brother, speak with possibility,   214
And do not break into these deep extremes.

TITUS
Is not my sorrow deep, having no bottom?
Then be my passions bottomless with them.   217

MARCUS
But yet let reason govern thy lament.   218

TITUS
If there were reason for these miseries,   219
Then into limits could I bind my woes.
When heaven doth weep, doth not the earth
     o'erflow?
If the winds rage, doth not the sea wax mad,
Threat'ning the welkin with his big-swoll'n face?
And wilt thou have a reason for this coil?   224
I am the sea. Hark how her sighs doth blow!   225
She is the weeping welkin, I the earth.
Then must my sea be movèd with her sighs,

Then must my earth with her continual tears
Become a deluge overflowed and drowned,
Forwhy my bowels cannot hide her woes,   230
But like a drunkard must I vomit them.   231
Then give me leave, for losers will have leave
To ease their stomachs with their bitter tongues.   233

Enter a Messenger, with two heads and a hand.

MESSENGER
Worthy Andronicus, ill art thou repaid
For that good hand thou sent'st the Emperor.
Here are the heads of thy two noble sons,
And here's thy hand in scorn to thee sent back—
Thy grief their sports, thy resolution mocked,   238
That woe is me to think upon thy woes   239
More than remembrance of my father's death.
[*He sets down the heads and hand, and exit.*]

MARCUS
Now let hot Etna cool in Sicily,   241
And be my heart an ever-burning hell!
These miseries are more than may be borne.
To weep with them that weep doth ease some deal,   244
But sorrow flouted at is double death.   245

LUCIUS
Ah, that this sight should make so deep a wound,
And yet detested life not shrink thereat!   247
That ever death should let life bear his name,   248
Where life hath no more interest but to breathe!   249
[*Lavinia kisses Titus.*]

MARCUS
Alas, poor heart, that kiss is comfortless
As frozen water to a starvèd snake.   251

TITUS
When will this fearful slumber have an end?   252

MARCUS
Now, farewell, flattery! Die, Andronicus.   253
Thou dost not slumber. See thy two sons' heads,
Thy warlike hand, thy mangled daughter here,
Thy other banished son with this dear sight   256
Struck pale and bloodless, and thy brother, I,
Even like a stony image, cold and numb.
Ah, now no more will I control thy griefs!   259
Rend off thy silver hair, thy other hand
Gnawing with thy teeth, and be this dismal sight
The closing up of our most wretched eyes.   262
Now is a time to storm. Why art thou still?

194 **warded** guarded   196 **that** i.e., burial   199 **dear** (1) expensive
(2) precious.   **because . . . own** because I am buying back what was
mine to begin with, my own dear sons   201 **Look** expect   203 **fat**
fatten, feed   204 **fair** (1) fair-complexioned (2) fair-minded.   **grace**
virtue   211 **breathe . . . dim** make cloudy the sky with our sighs.
welkin sky   213 **melting** i.e., dissolving into teardroplike rain
214 **with** within the bounds of   217 **be my passions** let my passionate
expressions of grief be.   **them** i.e., my sorrows   218–219 **reason
. . . reason** rationality . . . necessity   224 **coil** noise, fuss   225 **her**
i.e., Lavinia's, personifying the winds' rage

230 **Forwhy** because.   **bowels** (Supposed to be the seat of compassion; also, the bowels of the earth.)   231 **vomit** (The double image is
of vomiting and of volcanic eruption. Grief is like a conflict of the
four elements of fire, air, water, and earth—anger, sighs, tears, and
bowels.)   233 **ease their stomachs** relieve their resentments (with a
play on *vomit*)   238 **sports** entertainment   239 **That** so that
241 **Etna** volcanic mountain on the island of Sicily (which will, compared to Marcus' burning heart, seem cool. Compare with the note to
line 231.)   244 **some deal** somewhat   245 **flouted at** mocked. (To
deny sorrow is to experience it again and again.)   247 **shrink** slip
away   248 **bear his name** i.e., still be called life   249 **Where . . .
breathe** i.e., where virtually nothing remains of life except the drawing of breath   251 **starvèd** benumbed with cold   252 **fearful slumber**
dreadful nightmare   253 **flattery** comforting deception   256 **dear**
grievous   259 **control** try to restrain   262 **closing up** closing in death

TITUS   Ha, ha, ha!
MARCUS
    Why dost thou laugh? It fits not with this hour.
TITUS
    Why, I have not another tear to shed.
    Besides, this sorrow is an enemy,
    And would usurp upon my watery eyes
    And make them blind with tributary tears.   269
    Then which way shall I find Revenge's cave?
    For these two heads do seem to speak to me
    And threat me I shall never come to bliss
    Till all these mischiefs be returned again   273
    Even in their throats that hath committed them.
    Come, let me see what task I have to do.
    You heavy people, circle me about,   276
    That I may turn me to each one of you
    And swear unto my soul to right your wrongs.
                         [They form a circle about Titus,
                                and he pledges each.]
    The vow is made. Come, brother, take a head,
    And in this hand the other will I bear.
                         [They pick up the two heads,
                           and give the hand to Lavinia.]
    And, Lavinia, thou shalt be employed:
    Bear thou my hand, sweet wench, between thy
        teeth.
    As for thee, boy, [to Lucius] go get thee from my
        sight;
    Thou art an exile, and thou must not stay.
    Hie to the Goths and raise an army there.
    And if ye love me, as I think you do,
    Let's kiss and part, for we have much to do.
              [They kiss.] Exeunt [Titus, Marcus, and Lavinia].
LUCIUS
    Farewell, Andronicus, my noble father,
    The woefull'st man that ever lived in Rome.
    Farewell, proud Rome, till Lucius come again!
    He loves his pledges dearer than his life.   291
    Farewell, Lavinia, my noble sister.
    O, would thou wert as thou tofore hast been!   293
    But now nor Lucius nor Lavinia lives
    But in oblivion and hateful griefs.
    If Lucius live, he will requite your wrongs
    And make proud Saturnine and his empress
    Beg at the gates, like Tarquin and his queen.   298
    Now will I to the Goths and raise a power   299
    To be revenged on Rome and Saturnine. Exit Lucius.

                              ❧

269 **tributary tears** tears paid as tribute (to sorrow, the usurping enemy) 273 **mischiefs** evils, injuries 276 **heavy** sorrowing 291 **He
. . . life** his vows are more important to him than his life; or, he loves
his family, left behind in Rome as hostages to fortune, more than his
life 293 **tofore** heretofore, formerly 298 **Tarquin** Tarquinius Superbus, seventh king of Rome, who, because his son had raped a Roman
lady, Lucretia, was banished and his kingdom overthrown; a republic
was then established 299 **power** army

3.2   *A banquet [set out]. Enter [Titus] Andronicus,
          Marcus, Lavinia, and the boy [young Lucius].*

TITUS
    So, so. Now sit, and look you eat no more
    Than will preserve just so much strength in us
    As will revenge these bitter woes of ours.
    Marcus, unknit that sorrow-wreathen knot.   4
    Thy niece and I, poor creatures, want our hands   5
    And cannot passionate our tenfold grief   6
    With folded arms. This poor right hand of mine
    Is left to tyrannize upon my breast,   8
    Who, when my heart, all mad with misery,   9
    Beats in this hollow prison of my flesh,
    Then thus I thump it down.   [He beats his breast.]
    [To Lavinia.] Thou map of woe, that thus dost talk in
        signs,   12
    When thy poor heart beats with outrageous beating,
    Thou canst not strike it thus to make it still.
    Wound it with sighing, girl, kill it with groans;   15
    Or get some little knife between thy teeth
    And just against thy heart make thou a hole,
    That all the tears that thy poor eyes let fall
    May run into that sink and, soaking in,   19
    Drown the lamenting fool in sea-salt tears.   20
MARCUS
    Fie, brother, fie! Teach her not thus to lay
    Such violent hands upon her tender life.
TITUS
    How now, has sorrow made thee dote already?   23
    Why, Marcus, no man should be mad but I.   24
    What violent hands can she lay on her life?
    Ah, wherefore dost thou urge the name of hands,
    To bid Aeneas tell the tale twice o'er   27
    How Troy was burnt and he made miserable?
    O, handle not the theme, to talk of hands,
    Lest we remember still that we have none.   30
    Fie, fie, how franticly I square my talk,   31
    As if we should forget we had no hands
    If Marcus did not name the word of hands!
    Come, let's fall to; and, gentle girl, eat this.
    Here is no drink! Hark, Marcus, what she says;
    I can interpret all her martyred signs.
    She says she drinks no other drink but tears,
    Brewed with her sorrow, mashed upon her cheeks.   38
    Speechless complainer, I will learn thy thought;
    In thy dumb action will I be as perfect   40

3.2. Location: Rome. Titus' house.
s.d. banquet a light repast, here set out on stage as the scene begins,
with appropriate furniture allowing for sitting **4 sorrow-wreathen
knot** arms folded in a conventional expression of grief **5 want** lack
6 passionate express passionately **8 tyrannize** i.e., by beating
9 Who which **12 map** picture **15 Wound it with sighing** (Each sigh
was believed to cost the heart a drop of blood.) **19 sink** receptacle
20 fool (Here a term of pity or endearment.) **23 dote** be deranged
24 no man . . . but I i.e., don't talk madly **27 Aeneas** (Aeneas tells
of the fall of Troy in Book 2 of Virgil's *Aeneid*.) **30 still** continually
31 square shape, regulate **38 mashed** mixed with hot water in a
mash, as for brewing **40 action** gesture. **perfect** thoroughly acquainted

As begging hermits in their holy prayers.   41
Thou shalt not sigh, nor hold thy stumps to heaven,
Nor wink, nor nod, nor kneel, nor make a sign,   43
But I of these will wrest an alphabet
And by still practice learn to know thy meaning.   45

BOY [*weeping*]
Good grandsire, leave these bitter deep laments!
Make my aunt merry with some pleasing tale.

MARCUS
Alas, the tender boy, in passion moved,   48
Doth weep to see his grandsire's heaviness.

TITUS
Peace, tender sapling! Thou art made of tears,   50
And tears will quickly melt thy life away.
                    Marcus strikes the dish with a knife.
What dost thou strike at, Marcus, with thy knife?

MARCUS
At that that I have killed, my lord: a fly.

TITUS
Out on thee, murderer! Thou kill'st my heart.
Mine eyes are cloyed with view of tyranny.
A deed of death done on the innocent
Becomes not Titus' brother. Get thee gone!
I see thou art not for my company.

MARCUS
Alas, my lord, I have but killed a fly.

TITUS
"But"? How if that fly had a father and mother?
How would he hang his slender gilded wings   61
And buzz lamenting doings in the air!   62
Poor harmless fly,
That, with his pretty buzzing melody,
Came here to make us merry! And thou hast
    killed him.

MARCUS
Pardon me, sir. It was a black ill-favored fly,   66
Like to the Empress' Moor. Therefore I killed him.

TITUS   O, O, O!
Then pardon me for reprehending thee,
For thou hast done a charitable deed.
Give me thy knife. I will insult on him,   71
Flattering myself as if it were the Moor   72
Come hither purposely to poison me.—
There's for thyself, and that's for Tamora!
                    [*He takes the knife and strikes.*]
Ah, sirrah!   75
Yet I think we are not brought so low   76
But that between us we can kill a fly
That comes in likeness of a coal black Moor.

MARCUS
Alas, poor man! Grief has so wrought on him

He takes false shadows for true substances.

TITUS
Come, take away. Lavinia, go with me.   81
I'll to thy closet and go read with thee   82
Sad stories chancèd in the times of old.   83
Come, boy, and go with me. Thy sight is young,
And thou shalt read when mine begin to dazzle.   85
                                          Exeunt.

❧

4.1 *Enter Lucius' son, and Lavinia running after him,*
         and the boy flies from her, with his books under his
         arm. Enter Titus and Marcus.

BOY
Help, grandsire, help! My aunt Lavinia
Follows me everywhere, I know not why.
Good uncle Marcus, see how swift she comes.
Alas, sweet aunt, I know not what you mean.
                                   [*He drops his books.*]

MARCUS
Stand by me, Lucius. Do not fear thine aunt.

TITUS
She loves thee, boy, too well to do thee harm.

BOY
Ay, when my father was in Rome she did.   7

MARCUS
What means my niece Lavinia by these signs?

TITUS
Fear her not, Lucius. Somewhat doth she mean.   9

MARCUS
See, Lucius, see how much she makes of thee;
Somewhither would she have thee go with her.
Ah, boy, Cornelia never with more care   12
Read to her sons than she hath read to thee   13
Sweet poetry and Tully's *Orator*.   14
Canst thou not guess wherefore she plies thee thus?   15

BOY
My lord, I know not, I, nor can I guess,
Unless some fit or frenzy do possess her;
For I have heard my grandsire say full oft,
Extremity of griefs would make men mad,
And I have read that Hecuba of Troy   20
Ran mad for sorrow. That made me to fear,
Although, my lord, I know my noble aunt
Loves me as dear as e'er my mother did,
And would not but in fury fright my youth—   24

41 **As . . . prayers** as hermits are with the subject of their prayerful
meditation   43 **wink** close the eyes   45 **still** continual   48 **passion**
sorrow   50 **made of tears** (See Genesis 3:16: "In sorrow thou shalt
bring forth children." Like a sapling, the child is soft, unformed.)
61 **he** i.e., the father   62 **buzz . . . doings** tell sad stories   66 **ill-favored** ugly   71 **insult on** exult over   72 **Flattering . . . if** deluding
myself into believing   75 **sirrah** (Ordinary term of address to inferiors.)   76 **Yet . . . not** I do not think we are yet

81 **take away** clear the table. (The "banquet" and furniture are removed from the stage as the scene ends.)   82 **closet** private room
83 **chancèd** that occurred   85 **dazzle** become dazzled, unable to see
4.1. Location: Rome. Titus' garden.
7 **when . . . Rome** i.e., when my father was here to protect me
9 **Somewhat** something   12 **Cornelia** the mother of the Gracchi
brothers, the two most famous tribunes in Roman history. (Her success in educating her sons was highly regarded.)   13 **Read** gave instruction   14 **Tully's Orator** a treatise on rhetoric by Cicero, either
De Oratore or *ad M. Brutum Orator*   15 **plies** importunes
20 **Hecuba** (See 1.1.136 and note.)   24 **but in fury** except in madness

Which made me down to throw my books and fly,
Causeless, perhaps. But pardon me, sweet aunt,
And, madam, if my uncle Marcus go,   27
I will most willingly attend your ladyship.

MARCUS   Lucius, I will.   29

*[Lavinia turns over with her stumps the books
that young Lucius has let fall.]*

TITUS
How now, Lavinia? Marcus, what means this?
Some book there is that she desires to see.
Which is it, girl, of these?—Open them, boy.
[To Lavinia.] But thou art deeper read and better
skilled;
Come and take choice of all my library,
And so beguile thy sorrow till the heavens
Reveal the damned contriver of this deed.—
Why lifts she up her arms in sequence thus?   37

MARCUS
I think she means that there were more than one
Confederate in the fact. Ay, more there was;   39
Or else to heaven she heaves them for revenge.

TITUS
Lucius, what book is that she tosseth so?   41

BOY
Grandsire, 'tis Ovid's *Metamorphoses*.
My mother gave it me.

MARCUS   For love of her that's gone,
Perhaps, she culled it from among the rest.

TITUS
Soft, so busily she turns the leaves!
Help her.
What would she find? Lavinia, shall I read?
This is the tragic tale of Philomel,   49
And treats of Tereus' treason and his rape;   50
And rape, I fear, was root of thy annoy.   51

MARCUS
See, brother, see! Note how she quotes the leaves.   52

TITUS
Lavinia, wert thou thus surprised, sweet girl,
Ravished and wronged as Philomela was,
Forced in the ruthless, vast, and gloomy woods?   55
See, see!
Ay, such a place there is, where we did hunt—
O, had we never, never hunted there!—
Patterned by that the poet here describes,   59
By nature made for murders and for rapes.

MARCUS
O, why should nature build so foul a den,
Unless the gods delight in tragedies?

TITUS
Give signs, sweet girl—for here are none but
friends—
What Roman lord it was durst do the deed.

Or slunk not Saturnine, as Tarquin erst,   65
That left the camp to sin in Lucrece' bed?

MARCUS
Sit down, sweet niece. Brother, sit down by me.
[They sit.]
Apollo, Pallas, Jove, or Mercury   68
Inspire me, that I may this treason find!
My lord, look here. Look here, Lavinia.

*He writes his name with his staff,
and guides it with feet and mouth.*

This sandy plot is plain; guide, if thou canst,   71
This after me. I have writ my name   72
Without the help of any hand at all.
Cursed be that heart that forced us to this shift!   74
Write thou, good niece, and here display at last
What God will have discovered for revenge.   76
Heaven guide thy pen to print thy sorrows plain,
That we may know the traitors and the truth!

*She takes the staff in her mouth,
and guides it with her stumps, and writes.*

O, do ye read, my lord, what she hath writ?

TITUS   "*Stuprum.* Chiron. Demetrius."   80

MARCUS
What, what! The lustful sons of Tamora
Performers of this heinous, bloody deed?

TITUS
Magni Dominator poli,   83
Tam lentus audis scelera? Tam lentus vides?   84

MARCUS
O, calm thee, gentle lord, although I know
There is enough written upon this earth
To stir a mutiny in the mildest thoughts
And arm the minds of infants to exclaims.   88
My lord, kneel down with me; Lavinia, kneel;
And kneel, sweet boy, the Roman Hector's hope.   90
[All kneel.]
And swear with me—as, with the woeful fere   91
And father of that chaste dishonored dame,
Lord Junius Brutus sware for Lucrece' rape—   93
That we will prosecute by good advice   94
Mortal revenge upon these traitorous Goths,
And see their blood or die with this reproach.   96
[They rise.]

TITUS
'Tis sure enough, an you knew how.   97
But if you hunt these bear whelps, then beware:
The dam will wake an if she wind ye once.   99

---

65 Or . . . Saturnine or was it Saturnine who slunk.   **Tarquin** (See
the notes at 2.1.108 and 3.1.298.)   **erst** once   **68 Pallas** Minerva,
Athene   **71 plain** level   **72 after me** following my example   **74 shift**
expedient   **76 will** wishes to.   **discovered** revealed, uncovered
80 Stuprum violation, rape   **83–84 Magni . . . vides?** Ruler of the
mighty heavens, are you so slow to see and hear crimes? (Derived
from Seneca, *Hippolytus*, 671–672.)   **88 exclaims** exclamations
90 the Roman Hector's hope i.e., the hope and future of Lucius,
whose deeds compare with those of Hector in Troy   **91 fere** spouse,
husband   **93 Brutus** (After Sextus Tarquinius had raped Lucretia—see
2.1.108 and Shakespeare's *Rape of Lucrece*— Junius Brutus led the
Romans to expel the Tarquin dynasty; see also 3.1.298 and *Julius
Caesar*, 2.1.53– 54.)   **sware** swore   **94 by good advice** after careful
deliberation, planning   **96 reproach** disgrace, infamy   **97 an** if
99 dam mother.   **wind** scent

27 go i.e., come with us. (See line 11.) The boy doesn't want to be
alone with his mad aunt.   **29 Lucius** young Lucius, the boy   **37 in
sequence** one after the other   **39 fact** deed, crime   **41 tosseth** clumsily turns the pages of   **49–50 Philomel, Tereus** (Compare with the
note for 2.3.43.)   **51 annoy** injury   **52 quotes** examines   **55 vast**
desolate   **59 Patterned by that** on the pattern of that which

She's with the lion deeply still in league,   100
And lulls him whilst she playeth on her back,   101
And when he sleeps will she do what she list.   102
You are a young huntsman, Marcus. Let alone,   103
And come, I will go get a leaf of brass,   104
And with a gad of steel will write these words,   105
And lay it by. The angry northern wind   106
Will blow these sands like Sibyl's leaves abroad,   107
And where's our lesson then? Boy, what say you?

BOY
I say, my lord, that if I were a man,
Their mother's bedchamber should not be safe   110
For these base bondmen to the yoke of Rome.   111

MARCUS
Ay, that's my boy! Thy father hath full oft
For his ungrateful country done the like.   113

BOY
And, uncle, so will I, an if I live.

TITUS
Come, go with me into mine armory.
Lucius, I'll fit thee, and withal my boy   116
Shall carry from me to the Empress' sons
Presents that I intend to send them both.
Come, come. Thou'lt do my message, wilt thou not?

BOY
Ay, with my dagger in their bosoms, grandsire.

TITUS
No, boy, not so. I'll teach thee another course.
Lavinia, come. Marcus, look to my house.
Lucius and I'll go brave it at the court.   123
Ay, marry, will we, sir, and we'll be waited on.   124
            Exeunt [Titus, Lavinia, and young Lucius].

MARCUS
O heavens, can you hear a good man groan
And not relent, or not compassion him?   126
Marcus, attend him in his ecstasy,   127
That hath more scars of sorrow in his heart   128
Than foemen's marks upon his battered shield,
But yet so just that he will not revenge.
Revenge the heavens for old Andronicus!   *Exit.* 131

4.2   *Enter Aaron, Chiron, and Demetrius, at one door,
            and at the other door young Lucius and another,
            with a bundle of weapons and verses writ upon
            them.*

CHIRON
Demetrius, here's the son of Lucius.
He hath some message to deliver us.

AARON
Ay, some mad message from his mad grandfather.

BOY
My lords, with all the humbleness I may,
I greet your honors from Andronicus—
[*Aside.*] And pray the Roman gods confound you
    both!   6

DEMETRIUS
Gramercy, lovely Lucius. What's the news?   7

BOY [*aside*]
That you are both deciphered, that's the news,   8
For villains marked with rape.—May it please you,
My grandsire, well advised, hath sent by me   10
The goodliest weapons of his armory
To gratify your honorable youth,   12
The hope of Rome; for so he bid me say.
And so I do, and with his gifts present
Your lordships, that, whenever you have need,
You may be armèd and appointed well.   16
            [*His attendant presents the bundle.*]
And so I leave you both—[*aside*] like bloody villains.
                        Exit [with attendant].

DEMETRIUS
What's here? A scroll, and written round about?   19
Let's see:
[*He reads.*] "Integer vitae, scelerisque purus,   20
            Non eget Mauri iaculis, nec arcu."   21

CHIRON
O, 'tis a verse in Horace; I know it well.
I read it in the grammar long ago.   23

AARON
Ay, just; a verse in Horace; right, you have it.   24
[*Aside.*] Now, what a thing it is to be an ass!
Here's no sound jest! The old man hath found their
    guilt,   26
And sends them weapons wrapped about with lines
That wound, beyond their feeling, to the quick.   28
But were our witty empress well afoot,   29

❧

---

100 **the lion** the royal beast, i.e., Saturninus. **still** always **101 playeth on her back** (1) sports playfully like a wild animal (2) provides sex
to Saturninus **102 list** choose, please (with a suggestion of sexual infidelity) **103 young** inexperienced. **Let alone** let it alone, be wary
104 leaf sheet **105 gad** stylus, spike **106 lay it by** i.e., put it in
safekeeping, where the words will be preserved, unlike the writing in
the sand **107 Sibyl's leaves** (The Cumaean Sibyl, an inspired
woman, wrote her prophecies on leaves, which she placed at the entrance to her cave. Those wishing to consult them had to do so before
they were scattered by the wind.) **110–111 Their . . . Rome** i.e.,
no place of hiding will be held sacred in my seeking to destroy these
men who cravenly thrive under the yoke of Rome's tyranny
113 done the like i.e., fought against tyranny **116 fit thee** provide
you with what you need. **withal** in addition **123 brave it** put on a
good show, cut a bold figure **124 marry** (A mild interjection, equivalent to "Indeed!"; originally an oath, "by the Virgin Mary.") **be
waited on** i.e., demand attention **126 compassion** have compassion
for **127 ecstasy** madness **128 That** who **131 Revenge the heavens**
may the heavens take revenge

4.2. Location: Rome. The Emperor's palace.
s.d. another (Presumably an attendant of Lucius, bearing the weapons
and verses; see line 16 s.d.) **6 confound** destroy **7 Gramercy**
many thanks **8 deciphered** detected **10 well advised** having considered carefully **12 gratify** grace, please **16 appointed** equipped
19 round about all around **20–21 Integer . . . arcu** (The opening
lines of perhaps the best known of the Odes of Horace, line 22: "He
who is spotless in life and free of crime needs not the Moorish javelin
or bow.") **23 grammar** i.e., Latin grammar book. (William Lilly's
grammar book, containing this passage, was widely used in Elizabethan England.) **24 just** precisely **26 Here's no sound jest** (Said ironically to mean its opposite: Here's a splendid joke indeed.) **28 beyond . . . quick** i.e., far beyond the capacity of Demetrius and
Chiron to be sensitive to the injury, yet to the very heart of the matter
29 witty clever. **afoot** up and about, i.e., not in childbed (as we
soon learn)

She would applaud Andronicus' conceit.   30
But let her rest in her unrest awhile.—   31
And now, young lords, was 't not a happy star
Led us to Rome, strangers, and, more than so,
Captives, to be advancèd to this height?
It did me good, before the palace gate
To brave the tribune in his brother's hearing.   36

DEMETRIUS
But me more good to see so great a lord
Basely insinuate and send us gifts.   38

AARON
Had he not reason, Lord Demetrius?
Did you not use his daughter very friendly?

DEMETRIUS
I would we had a thousand Roman dames
At such a bay, by turn to serve our lust.   42

CHIRON
A charitable wish, and full of love!

AARON
Here lacks but your mother for to say amen.

CHIRON
And that would she, for twenty thousand more.   45

DEMETRIUS
Come, let us go and pray to all the gods
For our belovèd mother in her pains.   47

AARON
Pray to the devils. The gods have given us over.   48
                        Trumpets sound [within].

DEMETRIUS
Why do the Emperor's trumpets flourish thus?

CHIRON
Belike for joy the Emperor hath a son.   50

DEMETRIUS
Soft, who comes here?

        Enter Nurse, with a blackamoor child [in her arms].

NURSE   Good morrow, lords.   51
O, tell me, did you see Aaron the Moor?

AARON
Well, more or less, or ne'er a whit at all,   53
Here Aaron is; and what with Aaron now?   54

NURSE
O gentle Aaron, we are all undone.
Now help, or woe betide thee evermore!

AARON
Why, what a caterwauling dost thou keep!   57
What dost thou wrap and fumble in thy arms?

NURSE
O, that which I would hide from heaven's eye,

Our empress' shame and stately Rome's disgrace!
She is delivered, lords, she is delivered.

AARON   To whom?   62
NURSE   I mean she is brought abed.

AARON
Well, God give her good rest! What hath he sent her?   64
NURSE   A devil.

AARON
Why, then she is the devil's dam. A joyful issue!   66

NURSE
A joyless, dismal, black, and sorrowful issue!   67
Here is the babe, as loathsome as a toad
Amongst the fair-faced breeders of our clime.
The Empress sends it thee, thy stamp, thy seal,   70
And bids thee christen it with thy dagger's point.

AARON
Zounds, ye whore, is black so base a hue?   72
[To the child.] Sweet blowze, you are a beauteous
        blossom, sure.   73

DEMETRIUS   Villain, what hast thou done?
AARON   That which thou canst not undo.
CHIRON   Thou hast undone our mother.
AARON   Villain, I have done thy mother.   77

DEMETRIUS
And therein, hellish dog, thou hast undone her.
Woe to her chance, and damned her loathèd choice!   79
Accurst the offspring of so foul a fiend!   80

CHIRON   It shall not live.
AARON   It shall not die.

NURSE
Aaron, it must. The mother wills it so.

AARON
What, must it, Nurse? Then let no man but I
Do execution on my flesh and blood.

DEMETRIUS
I'll broach the tadpole on my rapier's point.   86
Nurse, give it me. My sword shall soon dispatch it.

AARON [taking the child and drawing his sword]
Sooner this sword shall plow thy bowels up.
Stay, murderous villains, will you kill your brother?
Now, by the burning tapers of the sky
That shone so brightly when this boy was got,   91
He dies upon my scimitar's sharp point
That touches this my firstborn son and heir!
I tell you, younglings, not Enceladus   94
With all his threatening band of Typhon's brood,   95

---

30 **conceit** design   31 **her unrest** i.e., her labor of delivery   36 **To
. . . hearing** i.e., to taunt Marcus in Titus' presence   38 **insinuate** ingratiate himself by flattery   42 **At such a bay** cornered thus (as in
hunting).   **by turn** (1) one after the other (2) doing a sexual "turn"
45 **more** i.e., more Roman *dames*, or ladies, to be ravished   47 **pains**
labor pains. (Tamora is being delivered of a child sired by Aaron; see
lines 29–31 above.)   48 **Pray . . . over** (Said perhaps to Demetrius
and Chiron, or as a mocking aside.)   50 **Belike** probably   51 **Soft**
i.e., wait a minute   53–54 **more . . . Aaron is** (Punning on *more*
and *Moor*, line 52, with sardonic humor, Aaron suggests that whether
he is addressed as Aaron the Great or the Less or by no title at all, he
is who he is.)   57 **keep** keep up

62 **To whom** (Aaron plays on *delivered*, line 61, in the sense of
"handed over or transferred to another person," though he, of course,
knows that the Nurse means "delivered of a child.")   64 **God . . .
rest** (Again, Aaron jestingly pretends to misinterpret *brought abed*, line
63, in its literal sense.)   66 **dam** mother.   **issue** result   67 **issue** offspring   70 **thy stamp, thy seal** i.e., bearing your imprint   72 **Zounds**
by His (Christ's) wounds   73 **blowze** red-cheeked one. (Usually addressed to a wench or slattern; here, an affectionately abusive term
for the child.)   77 **done** i.e., had sexual intercourse with (playing on
undone in the previous line)   79 **chance** luck.   **damned** damned be
80 **Accurst** accursed be   86 **broach** impale   91 **got** begotten
94 **Enceladus** one of the giants who rose against the gods and were
defeated by them; Enceladus was buried under Mount Etna in Sicily
95 **Typhon** a terrible monster who attacked the gods and was flung
into Tartarus

Nor great Alcides, nor the god of war   96
Shall seize this prey out of his father's hands.
What, what, ye sanguine, shallow-hearted boys!   98
Ye white-limed walls! Ye alehouse painted signs!   99
Coal black is better than another hue
In that it scorns to bear another hue;
For all the water in the ocean
Can never turn the swan's black legs to white,
Although she lave them hourly in the flood.   104
Tell the Empress from me, I am of age
To keep mine own, excuse it how she can.   106

DEMETRIUS
Wilt thou betray thy noble mistress thus?

AARON
My mistress is my mistress, this myself,   108
The vigor and the picture of my youth.
This before all the world do I prefer;
This maugre all the world will I keep safe,   111
Or some of you shall smoke for it in Rome.   112

DEMETRIUS
By this our mother is forever shamed.

CHIRON
Rome will despise her for this foul escape.   114

NURSE
The Emperor in his rage will doom her death.

CHIRON
I blush to think upon this ignomy.   116

AARON
Why, there's the privilege your beauty bears.   117
Fie, treacherous hue, that will betray with blushing
The close enacts and counsels of thy heart!   119
Here's a young lad framed of another leer.   120
Look how the black slave smiles upon the father,
As who should say, "Old lad, I am thine own."   122
He is your brother, lords, sensibly fed   123
Of that self blood that first gave life to you,   124
And from that womb where you imprisoned were
He is enfranchisèd and come to light.
Nay, he is your brother by the surer side,   127
Although my seal be stampèd in his face.   128

NURSE
Aaron, what shall I say unto the Empress?

DEMETRIUS
Advise thee, Aaron, what is to be done,   130

And we will all subscribe to thy advice.   131
Save thou the child, so we may all be safe.   132

AARON
Then sit we down, and let us all consult.
My son and I will have the wind of you;   134
Keep there. Now talk at pleasure of your safety.
                                               [They sit.]

DEMETRIUS [to the Nurse]
How many women saw this child of his?

AARON
Why, so, brave lords! When we join in league,
I am a lamb; but if you brave the Moor,
The chafèd boar, the mountain lioness,   139
The ocean swells not so as Aaron storms.
[To the Nurse.] But say again, how many saw the
   child?

NURSE
Cornelia the midwife and myself,
And no one else but the delivered Empress.

AARON
The Empress, the midwife, and yourself.
Two may keep counsel when the third's away.
Go to the Empress, tell her this I said.   He kills her.
Wheak, wheak!—   147
So cries a pig preparèd to the spit.   148

DEMETRIUS
What mean'st thou, Aaron? Wherefore didst thou
   this?

AARON
O Lord, sir, 'tis a deed of policy.   150
Shall she live to betray this guilt of ours,
A long-tongued, babbling gossip? No, lords, no.
And now be it known to you my full intent.
Not far, one Muliteus my countryman   154
His wife but yesternight was brought to bed;   155
His child is like to her, fair as you are.
Go pack with him, and give the mother gold,   157
And tell them both the circumstance of all,   158
And how by this their child shall be advanced
And be receivèd for the Emperor's heir,
And substituted in the place of mine,
To calm this tempest whirling in the court;
And let the Emperor dandle him for his own.
Hark ye, lords, you see I have given her physic,   164
                               [pointing to the Nurse]
And you must needs bestow her funeral.   165
The fields are near, and you are gallant grooms.   166
This done, see that you take no longer days,   167
But send the midwife presently to me.   168
The midwife and the nurse well made away,
Then let the ladies tattle what they please.

---

96 Alcides Hercules, a descendant of Alcaeus   **98 sanguine** red-cheeked (as distinguished from black-complexioned).   **shallow-hearted** cowardly   **99 white-limed** whitewashed. (The image is of a fair exterior hiding darkness within.)   **alehouse painted signs** i.e., cheap painted imitations of men   **104 lave** wash.   **flood** stream   **106 excuse . . . can** i.e., no matter how she may wish to explain away the circumstance by getting rid of the evidence   **108 this myself** i.e., this child is a part of myself   **111 maugre** in spite of   **112 smoke** i.e., suffer. (The metaphor is from burning at the stake.)   **114 escape** escapade, outrageous transgression   **116 ignomy** ignominy, shame   **117 Why . . . bears** i.e., blushing is one of the benefits of your fair complexion. (Said ironically; Aaron prefers a hue that cannot incriminate itself.)   **119 close enacts** secret purposes   **120 framed** made.   **leer** countenance, complexion   **122 As . . . say** as if saying, as if one might say   **123 sensibly fed** given corporeal sustenance   **124 Of** by.   **self** same   **127 surer** i.e., mother's   **128 seal be stampèd** (See line 70 above; the child bears the imprint of the father in his looks.)   **130 Advise thee** consider

131 subscribe agree   **132 so** so long as   **134 have . . . you** i.e., remain at a safe distance and stay downwind of you (as in hunting, so as not to be scented by the game)   **139 chafèd** enraged   **147 Wheak** (Aaron mimics her dying cry.)   **148 preparèd to the spit** being spitted for roasting   **150 policy** prudent action   **154–155 one . . . wife** the wife of a certain Muliteus, a fellow countryman of mine   **157 pack** make a deal   **158 the circumstance of all** the full details   **164 physic** medicine   **165 bestow** provide, furnish   **166 grooms** fellows   **167 days** time   **168 presently** at once

CHIRON
Aaron, I see thou wilt not trust the air
With secrets.
DEMETRIUS   For this care of Tamora,
Herself and hers are highly bound to thee.
Exeunt [Demetrius and Chiron, bearing off the
Nurse's body].

AARON
Now to the Goths, as swift as swallow flies,
There to dispose this treasure in mine arms   175
And secretly to greet the Empress' friends.   176
Come on, you thick-lipped slave, I'll bear you
    hence,
For it is you that puts us to our shifts.   178
I'll make you feed on berries and on roots,
And feed on curds and whey, and suck the goat,
And cabin in a cave, and bring you up   181
To be a warrior and command a camp.
Exit [with the child].

❧

4.3 *Enter Titus, old Marcus, [his son Publius,] young*
Lucius, and other gentlemen [Sempronius, Caius],
with bows; and Titus bears the arrows with letters
on the ends of them.

TITUS
Come, Marcus, come. Kinsmen, this is the way.
Sir boy, let me see your archery.
Look ye draw home enough, and 'tis there straight.   3
Terras Astraea reliquit;   4
Be you remembered, Marcus, she's gone, she's fled.   5
Sirs, take you to your tools. You, cousins, shall
Go sound the ocean, and cast your nets;
Happily you may catch her in the sea.   8
Yet there's as little justice as at land.   9
No; Publius and Sempronius, you must do it;
'Tis you must dig with mattock and with spade,
And pierce the inmost center of the earth.
Then, when you come to Pluto's region,   13
I pray you, deliver him this petition.
Tell him it is for justice and for aid,
And that it comes from old Andronicus,
Shaken with sorrows in ungrateful Rome.
Ah, Rome! Well, well, I made thee miserable
What time I threw the people's suffrages   19
On him that thus doth tyrannize o'er me.
Go, get you gone, and pray be careful all,
And leave you not a man-of-war unsearched.

This wicked emperor may have shipped her hence,   23
And, kinsmen, then we may go pipe for justice.   24
MARCUS
O Publius, is not this a heavy case,   25
To see thy noble uncle thus distract?   26
PUBLIUS
Therefore, my lords, it highly us concerns
By day and night t' attend him carefully,
And feed his humor kindly as we may,   29
Till time beget some careful remedy.   30
MARCUS
Kinsmen, his sorrows are past remedy.   31
Join with the Goths, and with revengeful war
Take wreak on Rome for this ingratitude,   33
And vengeance on the traitor Saturnine.
TITUS
Publius, how now? How now, my masters?
What, have you met with her?   36
PUBLIUS
No, my good lord, but Pluto sends you word,
If you will have Revenge from hell, you shall.
Marry, for Justice, she is so employed,   39
He thinks, with Jove in heaven, or somewhere else,
So that perforce you must needs stay a time.   41
TITUS
He doth me wrong to feed me with delays.
I'll dive into the burning lake below   43
And pull her out of Acheron by the heels.   44
Marcus, we are but shrubs, no cedars we,
No big-boned men framed of the Cyclops' size,   46
But metal, Marcus, steel to the very back,
Yet wrung with wrongs more than our backs can
    bear.
And sith there's no justice in earth nor hell,   49
We will solicit heaven and move the gods
To send down Justice for to wreak our wrongs.   51
Come, to this gear. You are a good archer, Marcus.   52
He gives them the arrows.
"Ad Jovem," that's for you; here, "Ad Apollinem";   53
"Ad Martem," that's for myself;   54
Here, boy, "to Pallas"; here, "to Mercury";   55
"To Saturn," Caius—not "to Saturnine"!
You were as good to shoot against the wind.   57
To it, boy! Marcus, loose when I bid.   58
Of my word, I have written to effect;   59
There's not a god left unsolicited.

---

175 **dispose** dispose of   176 **greet . . . friends** i.e., join forces with the Goths, who presumably will defend Tamora's interests in Rome   178 **shifts** stratagems, tricks   181 **cabin** lodge
4.3. Location: Rome. A public place.
3 **home** to the full extent (of the bow).   **'tis there straight** it will reach the point aimed at forthwith   4 **Terras Astraea reliquit** Astraea (the goddess of justice) has abandoned the earth. (From Ovid, *Metamorphoses,* 1.150.)   5 **Be you remembered** remember.   **she's** Justice is   8 **Happily** haply, perhaps   9 **there's** i.e., there in the sea there is   13 **Pluto's region** the underworld, ruled over by Pluto   19 **What time** when.   **suffrages** assent

23 **her** i.e., Justice, the goddess Astraea. (In his madness, Titus imagines that Saturninus may ship Astraea out of the country in an armed naval vessel, a *man-of-war.*)   24 **pipe** whistle, i.e., look in vain   25 **heavy case** sad situation   26 **distract** distracted, crazed   29 **feed his humor** humor him   30 **careful** showing and requiring care   31 **remedy** (In the First Quarto, this word is followed by a catch word *But* at the foot of the page that is not repeated in the first line of the next page, possibly suggesting an omission in the text.)   33 **wreak** vengeance   36 **her** i.e., Justice   39 **for** as for   41 **stay a time** wait awhile   43 **burning lake** i.e., Phlegethon, the burning river of the underworld   44 **Acheron** a river in the underworld   46 **Cyclops** one-eyed giants in Homer's *Odyssey* (9)   49 **sith** since   51 **for to** to   52 **gear** business   53–54 **Ad Jovem, Ad Apollinem, Ad Martem** to Jove, to Apollo, to Mars   55 **Pallas** Minerva, Athene   57 **You . . . wind** you would do as much good shooting against the wind (as you would in appealing to Saturninus)   58 **loose** let fly, discharge   59 **Of** on

MARCUS
Kinsmen, shoot all your shafts into the court.
We will afflict the Emperor in his pride.

TITUS
Now, masters, draw. [*They shoot.*] O, well said,
   Lucius!   63
Good boy, in Virgo's lap! Give it Pallas.   64

MARCUS
My lord, I aim a mile beyond the moon;   65
Your letter is with Jupiter by this.

TITUS   Ha, ha!
Publius, Publius, what hast thou done?
See, see, thou hast shot off one of Taurus' horns.   69

MARCUS
This was the sport, my lord: when Publius shot,
The Bull, being galled, gave Aries such a knock   71
That down fell both the Ram's horns in the court;   72
And who should find them but the Empress' villain?   73
She laughed, and told the Moor he should not
   choose   74
But give them to his master for a present.   75

TITUS
Why, there it goes. God give his lordship joy!   76

       Enter the Clown, with a basket, and two pigeons
       in it.

News, news from heaven! Marcus, the post is come.—
Sirrah, what tidings? Have you any letters?
Shall I have justice? What says Jupiter?

CLOWN   Ho, the gibbet maker? He says that he hath   80
taken them down again, for the man must not be   81
hanged till the next week.

TITUS   But what says Jupiter, I ask thee?

CLOWN   Alas, sir, I know not Jupiter. I never drank
with him in all my life.

TITUS   Why, villain, art not thou the carrier?   86

CLOWN   Ay, of my pigeons, sir; nothing else.

TITUS   Why, didst thou not come from heaven?

CLOWN   From heaven! Alas, sir, I never came there.
God forbid I should be so bold to press to heaven in
my young days. Why, I am going with my pigeons to
the tribunal plebs, to take up a matter of brawl betwixt   92
my uncle and one of the Emperal's men.   93

MARCUS [*to Titus*]   Why, sir, that is as fit as can be to
serve for your oration; and let him deliver the
pigeons to the Emperor from you.

---

63 **said** done   64 **in Virgo's lap** in the constellation of the Virgin (the zodiacal sign representing Astraea, having fled from earth).   **Give it Pallas** i.e., shoot the arrow labeled "Pallas" there   65 **a mile . . . moon** (Marcus' literal meaning is intended to humor Titus' madness, but his expression also means "wild conjecture, far wide of the mark," thus commenting on the madness of their proceedings.)   69, 71 **Taurus, Aries** the Bull, the Ram; signs of the zodiac   71 **galled** slightly wounded   72 **horns** i.e., signs of being a cuckold, bestowed by Aaron on the Emperor   73 **villain** i.e., Aaron, both servant and villain in the modern sense   74–75 **should . . . But** must   76 **there it goes** (A hunting cry of encouragement.)   **s.d. Clown** rustic   80 **gibbet maker** (The Clown seems to have heard "Jupiter" as "gibbeter.")   81 **them** i.e., the gallows.   **must not be** is not to be   86 **carrier** postman. (But the Clown answers in the sense of "one who carries things.")   92 **tribunal plebs** i.e., *tribunus plebis*, tribune of the plebs. **take up** settle amicably   93 **Emperal's** (Malapropism for "Emperor's.")

TITUS [*to Clown*]
Sirrah, come hither. Make no more ado,   97
But give your pigeons to the Emperor.
By me thou shalt have justice at his hands.
Hold, hold; meanwhile here's money for thy
   charges.   [*He gives money.*] 100
Give me pen and ink.
Sirrah, can you with a grace deliver up a
   supplication?

CLOWN   Ay, sir.

TITUS [*writing and handing him a supplication*]   Then
here is a supplication for you. And when you come to
him, at the first approach you must kneel, then kiss
his foot, then deliver up your pigeons, and then look
for your reward. I'll be at hand, sir; see you do it
bravely.   109

CLOWN   I warrant you, sir. Let me alone.   110

TITUS
Sirrah, hast thou a knife? Come let me see it.
       [*He takes the knife and gives it to Marcus.*]
Here, Marcus, fold it in the oration,
For thou hast made it like an humble suppliant.—   113
And when thou hast given it to the Emperor,
Knock at my door and tell me what he says.

CLOWN   God be with you, sir. I will.   *Exit.*

TITUS   Come, Marcus, let us go. Publius, follow me.
                                    Exeunt.

                            ❖

4.4   *Enter Emperor [Saturninus] and Empress*
       [Tamora] and her two sons [and others, including
       guards]. The Emperor brings the arrows in his
       hand that Titus shot at him. [The Emperor and
       Empress sit.]

SATURNINUS
Why, lords, what wrongs are these! Was ever seen
An emperor in Rome thus overborne,   2
Troubled, confronted thus, and, for the extent   3
Of equal justice, used in such contempt?
My lords, you know, as know the mightful gods,
However these disturbers of our peace
Buzz in the people's ears, there naught hath passed
But even with law against the willful sons   8
Of old Andronicus. And what an if
His sorrows have so overwhelmed his wits?
Shall we be thus afflicted in his wreaks,   11
His fits, his frenzy, and his bitterness?
And now he writes to heaven for his redress.
See, here's "to Jove," and this "to Mercury,"

---

97 **Sirrah** (In the early texts, this line is preceded by four lines that appear to be a first draft of lines 102–103: "TITUS Tell me, can you deliver an oration to the Emperor with a grace? CLOWN. Nay, truly, sir, I could never say grace in all my life.")   100 **charges** expenses   109 **bravely** handsomely, stylishly   110 **Let me alone** leave it to me   113 **For . . . suppliant** (A puzzling and perhaps corrupt line. Titus may mean that Marcus has made the supplication seem humble enough, even though it conceals a knife.)

4.4. Location: Rome. Before or in the palace.
2 **overborne** oppressed   3 **for the extent** as his reward for the exercising   8 **even** conformable   11 **wreaks** revengeful acts

This "to Apollo," this to the god of war—
Sweet scrolls to fly about the streets of Rome!
What's this but libeling against the Senate
And blazoning our unjustice everywhere?   18
A goodly humor, is it not, my lords?   19
As who would say, in Rome no justice were.
But if I live, his feignèd ecstasies   21
Shall be no shelter to these outrages;
But he and his shall know that justice lives   23
In Saturninus' health, whom, if he sleep,   24
He'll so awake as he in fury shall   25
Cut off the proud'st conspirator that lives.

TAMORA
My gracious lord, my lovely Saturnine,
Lord of my life, commander of my thoughts,
Calm thee, and bear the faults of Titus' age,
Th' effects of sorrow for his valiant sons,
Whose loss hath pierced him deep and scarred his
  heart;
And rather comfort his distressèd plight
Than prosecute the meanest or the best   33
For these contempts. [Aside.] Why, thus it shall
  become
High-witted Tamora to gloze with all.   35
But, Titus, I have touched thee to the quick;
Thy lifeblood out, if Aaron now be wise,   37
Then is all safe, the anchor in the port.

        Enter Clown.

How now, good fellow, wouldst thou speak
  with us?
CLOWN Yea, forsooth, an your mistress-ship be emperial.
TAMORA   Empress I am, but yonder sits the Emperor.
CLOWN   'Tis he. [He kneels.] God and Saint Stephen give
  you good e'en. I have brought you a letter and a   43
  couple of pigeons here.
            He [Saturninus] reads the letter.
SATURNINUS
Go, take him away, and hang him presently.   45
CLOWN   How much money must I have?   46
TAMORA   Come, sirrah, you must be hanged.
CLOWN   Hanged! By 'r Lady, then I have brought up a 48
  neck to a fair end.   Exit [guarded].
SATURNINUS
Despiteful and intolerable wrongs!
Shall I endure this monstrous villainy?
I know from whence this same device proceeds.
May this be borne?—as if his traitorous sons,

That died by law for murder of our brother,
Have by my means been butchered wrongfully!
Go, drag the villain hither by the hair.
Nor age nor honor shall shape privilege.   57
For this proud mock I'll be thy slaughterman,
Sly frantic wretch, that holp'st to make me great   59
In hope thyself should govern Rome and me.   60

        Enter nuntius, Aemilius.

What news with thee, Aemilius?
AEMILIUS
Arm, my lords! Rome never had more cause.
The Goths have gathered head, and with a power   63
Of high-resolvèd men bent to the spoil   64
They hither march amain under conduct   65
Of Lucius, son to old Andronicus,
Who threats in course of this revenge to do
As much as ever Coriolanus did.   68
SATURNINUS
Is warlike Lucius general of the Goths?
These tidings nip me, and I hang the head
As flowers with frost or grass beat down with
  storms.
Ay, now begins our sorrows to approach.
'Tis he the common people love so much;
Myself hath often heard them say,
When I have walkèd like a private man,   75
That Lucius' banishment was wrongfully,   76
And they have wished that Lucius were their
  emperor.
TAMORA
Why should you fear? Is not your city strong?
SATURNINUS
Ay, but the citizens favor Lucius
And will revolt from me to succor him.
TAMORA
King, be thy thoughts imperious, like thy name.   81
Is the sun dimmed, that gnats do fly in it?   82
The eagle suffers little birds to sing
And is not careful what they mean thereby,   84
Knowing that with the shadow of his wings
He can at pleasure stint their melody;   86
Even so mayst thou the giddy men of Rome.   87
Then cheer thy spirit, for know, thou Emperor,
I will enchant the old Andronicus
With words more sweet and yet more dangerous
Than baits to fish or honey-stalks to sheep,   91
Whenas the one is wounded with the bait,   92
The other rotted with delicious feed.   93

18 blazoning proclaiming   **19 humor** whim, caprice   **21 ecstasies** fits of madness   **23 his** i.e., the Andronici   **23–24 justice . . . health** i.e., justice in Rome depends on Saturninus' thriving   **24–25 whom . . . shall** i.e., and, if Saturninus be asleep, Titus will so arouse him (by his outrages) that Saturninus will angrily. Or, if Justice be asleep, Saturninus will so rouse him to fury that he will. (The use of male pronouns for Justice is unusual—see 4.3.4–5 and 23—and some editors amend he in lines 24–25 to she.)   **33 the meanest or the best** those of low or high station   **35 High-witted** clever.   **gloze** deceive with smooth talk   **37 Thy lifeblood out** once your lifeblood is spilled.   **wise** i.e., wise enough to keep silent about the baby   **43 good e'en** good afternoon or evening   **45 presently** at once   **46 must I** am I to   **48 By 'r Lady** by Our Lady, the Virgin Mary

57 Nor neither.   **shape privilege** make for exemption   **59 holp'st** helped   **60 s.d. nuntius** messenger   **63 gathered head** raised an army.   **power** armed force   **64 bent to the spoil** intent on plunder   **65 amain** forcefully, swiftly.   **conduct** command   **68 Coriolanus** an early Roman hero turned enemy of Rome, about whom Shakespeare wrote one of his later tragedies   **75 walkèd . . . man** i.e., gone in disguise among the commoners, like Henry V or the Duke in *Measure for Measure*   **76 wrongfully** wrongfully imposed   **81 imperious** imperial   **82 that** merely because   **84 careful** full of concern   **86 stint** stop   **87 giddy** changeable in opinion and allegiance   **91 honey-stalks** clover. (Too much clover can make sheep ill.)   **92 Whenas** when   **93 rotted** afflicted by the rot, a liver disease in sheep

SATURNINUS
But he will not entreat his son for us.

TAMORA
If Tamora entreat him, then he will;
For I can smooth and fill his agèd ears   96
With golden promises, that were his heart
Almost impregnable, his old ears deaf,
Yet should both ear and heart obey my tongue.
[To Aemilius.] Go thou before to be our ambassador.
Say that the Emperor requests a parley
Of warlike Lucius, and appoint the meeting   102
Even at his father's house, the old Andronicus.

SATURNINUS
Aemilius, do this message honorably,
And if he stand on hostage for his safety,   105
Bid him demand what pledge will please him best. 106

AEMILIUS
Your bidding shall I do effectually.   Exit.

TAMORA
Now will I to that old Andronicus
And temper him with all the art I have   109
To pluck proud Lucius from the warlike Goths.
And now, sweet Emperor, be blithe again
And bury all thy fear in my devices.

SATURNINUS
Then go successantly, and plead to him.   Exeunt. 113

❧

5.1   [Flourish.] Enter Lucius with an army of Goths,
with drums and soldiers.

LUCIUS
Approvèd warriors and my faithful friends,   1
I have receivèd letters from great Rome   2
Which signifies what hate they bear their emperor
And how desirous of our sight they are.
Therefore, great lords, be as your titles witness, 5
Imperious, and impatient of your wrongs,
And wherein Rome hath done you any scath   7
Let him make treble satisfaction.   8

A GOTH
Brave slip, sprung from the great Andronicus,   9
Whose name was once our terror, now our comfort,
Whose high exploits and honorable deeds
Ingrateful Rome requites with foul contempt,
Be bold in us. We'll follow where thou lead'st,   13
Like stinging bees in hottest summer's day
Led by their master to the flowered fields,   15
And be avenged on cursèd Tamora.   16

ALL THE GOTHS
And as he saith, so say we all with him.

LUCIUS
I humbly thank him, and I thank you all.
But who comes here, led by a lusty Goth?   19

Enter a Goth, leading of Aaron with his child in
his arms.

ANOTHER GOTH
Renownèd Lucius, from our troops I strayed
To gaze upon a ruinous monastery,   21
And as I earnestly did fix mine eye
Upon the wasted building, suddenly   23
I heard a child cry underneath a wall.
I made unto the noise, when soon I heard   25
The crying babe controlled with this discourse: 26
"Peace, tawny slave, half me and half thy dam!   27
Did not thy hue bewray whose brat thou art,   28
Had nature lent thee but thy mother's look,
Villain, thou mightst have been an emperor.
But where the bull and cow are both milk white,
They never do beget a coal black calf.
Peace, villain, peace!"—even thus he rates the
  babe—   33
"For I must bear thee to a trusty Goth,
Who, when he knows thou art the Empress' babe,
Will hold thee dearly for thy mother's sake."
With this, my weapon drawn, I rushed upon him,
Surprised him suddenly, and brought him hither
To use as you think needful of the man.   39

LUCIUS
O worthy Goth, this is the incarnate devil
That robbed Andronicus of his good hand!
This is the pearl that pleased your empress' eye,
And here's the base fruit of her burning lust.—   43
Say, walleyed slave, whither wouldst thou convey   44
This growing image of thy fiendlike face?   45
Why dost not speak? What, deaf? Not a word?
A halter, soldiers! Hang him on this tree,
And by his side his fruit of bastardy.

AARON
Touch not the boy. He is of royal blood.

LUCIUS
Too like the sire for ever being good.   50
First hang the child, that he may see it sprawl—   51
A sight to vex the father's soul withal.
Get me a ladder.
                [A ladder is brought, which Aaron is made to
                                                   ascend.]

AARON   Lucius, save the child,
And bear it from me to the Empress.
If thou do this, I'll show thee wondrous things
That highly may advantage thee to hear.

---

96 smooth flatter **102 Of** with **105 stand** insist **106 demand** request **109 temper** work upon **113 successantly** at once
5.1. Location: Near Rome.
s.d. drums drummers **1 Approved** put to proof, tried **2 letters** a letter **5 be . . . witness** live up to the greatness your noble titles proclaim **7 scath** injury **8 him** Saturninus (who is to pay for all the wrongs Rome has done the Goths) **9 slip** offspring, scion **13 bold** confident **15 their master** (Bees were thought to be led by a king bee.) **16 cursèd Tamora** (The play permits us to speculate as to why Tamora was not popular in her own country.)

19 lusty valiant **21 ruinous** decayed **23 wasted** ruined **25 made unto** approached **26 controlled** calmed **27 slave** (Used affectionately, as also in brat, line 28, and villain, lines 30 and 33.) **dam** mother **28 bewray** reveal **33 rates** chides **39 use . . . man** deal with the man as you think fit **43 fruit** i.e., the baby **44 walleyed** glaring **45 image** likeness **50 for ever being** ever to be **51 sprawl** twitch convulsively in the death agony

If thou wilt not, befall what may befall,
I'll speak no more but "Vengeance rot you all!"

LUCIUS
Say on. An if it please me which thou speak'st, 59
Thy child shall live, and I will see it nourished. 60

AARON
An if it please thee! Why, assure thee, Lucius,
'Twill vex thy soul to hear what I shall speak;
For I must talk of murders, rapes, and massacres,
Acts of black night, abominable deeds,
Complots of mischief, treason, villainies, 65
Ruthful to hear, yet piteously performed. 66
And this shall all be buried in my death,
Unless thou swear to me my child shall live.

LUCIUS
Tell on thy mind. I say thy child shall live.

AARON
Swear that he shall, and then I will begin.

LUCIUS
Who should I swear by? Thou believest no god.
That granted, how canst thou believe an oath?

AARON
What if I do not? As, indeed, I do not.
Yet, for I know thou art religious 74
And hast a thing within thee callèd conscience,
With twenty popish tricks and ceremonies
Which I have seen thee careful to observe,
Therefore I urge thy oath. For that I know 78
An idiot holds his bauble for a god 79
And keeps the oath which by that god he swears,
To that I'll urge him. Therefore thou shalt vow
By that same god, what god soe'er it be
That thou adorest and hast in reverence,
To save my boy, to nourish and bring him up,
Or else I will discover naught to thee.

LUCIUS
Even by my god I swear to thee I will.

AARON
First know thou, I begot him on the Empress.

LUCIUS
O most insatiate and luxurious woman! 88

AARON
Tut, Lucius, this was but a deed of charity
To that which thou shalt hear of me anon. 90
'Twas her two sons that murdered Bassianus;
They cut thy sister's tongue, and ravished her,
And cut her hands, and trimmed her as thou
    sawest. 93

LUCIUS
O detestable villain! Call'st thou that trimming?

AARON
Why, she was washed and cut and trimmed, and
    'twas
Trim sport for them which had the doing of it. 96

LUCIUS
O barbarous, beastly villains, like thyself!

AARON
Indeed, I was their tutor to instruct them.
That codding spirit had they from their mother, 99
As sure a card as ever won the set; 100
That bloody mind I think they learned of me,
As true a dog as ever fought at head. 102
Well, let my deeds be witness of my worth.
I trained thy brethren to that guileful hole 104
Where the dead corpse of Bassianus lay;
I wrote the letter that thy father found,
And hid the gold within that letter mentioned,
Confederate with the Queen and her two sons;
And what not done, that thou hast cause to rue,
Wherein I had no stroke of mischief in it?
I played the cheater for thy father's hand, 111
And when I had it, drew myself apart
And almost broke my heart with extreme laughter.
I pried me through the crevice of a wall 114
When, for his hand, he had his two sons' heads,
Beheld his tears, and laughed so heartily
That both mine eyes were rainy like to his;
And when I told the Empress of this sport,
She swoonèd almost at my pleasing tale,
And for my tidings gave me twenty kisses.

A GOTH
What, canst thou say all this and never blush?

AARON
Ay, like a black dog, as the saying is. 122

LUCIUS
Art thou not sorry for these heinous deeds?

AARON
Ay, that I had not done a thousand more.
Even now I curse the day—and yet, I think,
Few come within the compass of my curse—
Wherein I did not some notorious ill,
As kill a man, or else devise his death,
Ravish a maid, or plot the way to do it,
Accuse some innocent and forswear myself,
Set deadly enmity between two friends,
Make poor men's cattle break their necks,
Set fire on barns and haystacks in the night
And bid the owners quench them with their tears.
Oft have I digged up dead men from their graves
And set them upright at their dear friends' door,
Even when their sorrows almost was forgot,
And on their skins, as on the bark of trees,
Have with my knife carvèd in Roman letters,
"Let not your sorrow die, though I am dead."
But I have done a thousand dreadful things 141
As willingly as one would kill a fly,

59 An if if   60 nourished cared for   65 Complots conspiracies
66 Ruthful lamentable, pitiable.   piteously in a way to excite pity
74 for because   78 urge insist on.   For that because   79 bauble
fool's stick   88 luxurious lecherous   90 To compared to
93 trimmed (1) decked out, made ready (2) cut off the excrescences
96 Trim fine (with a play on trimmed, lines 93–95)

99 codding lustful   100 set game   102 as . . . head as ever went for
the bear's head (in bearbaiting)   104 trained lured   111 cheater (1)
deceiver (2) escheater, one designated to take care of property forfeited to the crown   114 pried me peered   122 like a black dog ("To
blush like a black dog" is a proverb with ironic meaning, as here; at
4.2.117–119, Aaron is proud that, being black, he cannot blush.)
141 But i.e., but why go on with this recital. (Sometimes emended to
Tut, as in the Second Quarto.)

And nothing grieves me heartily indeed
But that I cannot do ten thousand more.

LUCIUS
Bring down the devil, for he must not die
So sweet a death as hanging presently.   146

[*Aaron is brought down.*]

AARON
If there be devils, would I were a devil,
To live and burn in everlasting fire,
So I might have your company in hell
But to torment you with my bitter tongue!

LUCIUS
Sirs, stop his mouth, and let him speak no more.

[*Aaron is gagged.*]

Enter Aemilius.

A GOTH
My lord, there is a messenger from Rome
Desires to be admitted to your presence.   153

LUCIUS   Let him come near.
Welcome, Aemilius. What's the news from Rome?

AEMILIUS
Lord Lucius, and you princes of the Goths,
The Roman Emperor greets you all by me;
And, for he understands you are in arms,   158
He craves a parley at your father's house,
Willing you to demand your hostages,
And they shall be immediately delivered.

A GOTH   What says our general?

LUCIUS
Aemilius, let the Emperor give his pledges
Unto my father and my uncle Marcus,
And we will come. March away.   [*Flourish. Exeunt.*]

❖

5.2   *Enter Tamora and her two sons, disguised.*

TAMORA
Thus, in this strange and sad habiliment,   1
I will encounter with Andronicus
And say I am Revenge, sent from below
To join with him and right his heinous wrongs.
Knock at his study, where they say he keeps   5
To ruminate strange plots of dire revenge.
Tell him Revenge is come to join with him
And work confusion on his enemies.   8

*They knock, and Titus [above] opens his study
door.*

TITUS
Who doth molest my contemplation?
Is it your trick to make me ope the door,
That so my sad decrees may fly away   11
And all my study be to no effect?
You are deceived, for what I mean to do,

See here, in bloody lines I have set down,
And what is written shall be executed.

[*He shows a paper.*]

TAMORA
Titus, I am come to talk with thee.

TITUS
No, not a word. How can I grace my talk,
Wanting a hand to give it action?   18
Thou hast the odds of me; therefore no more.   19

TAMORA
If thou didst know me, thou wouldst talk with me.

TITUS
I am not mad; I know thee well enough.
Witness this wretched stump, witness these crimson
lines,   22
Witness these trenches made by grief and care,   23
Witness the tiring day and heavy night,
Witness all sorrow, that I know thee well
For our proud empress, mighty Tamora.
Is not thy coming for my other hand?

TAMORA
Know, thou sad man, I am not Tamora;
She is thy enemy, and I thy friend.
I am Revenge, sent from th' infernal kingdom
To ease the gnawing vulture of thy mind
By working wreakful vengeance on thy foes.   32
Come down and welcome me to this world's light;
Confer with me of murder and of death.
There's not a hollow cave or lurking-place,
No vast obscurity or misty vale   36
Where bloody murder or detested rape
Can couch for fear, but I will find them out,   38
And in their ears tell them my dreadful name,
Revenge, which makes the foul offender quake.

TITUS
Art thou Revenge? And art thou sent to me
To be a torment to mine enemies?

TAMORA
I am. Therefore come down and welcome me.

TITUS
Do me some service ere I come to thee.
Lo, by thy side where Rape and Murder stands.
Now give some surance that thou art Revenge: 46
Stab them, or tear them on thy chariot wheels,
And then I'll come and be thy wagoner,
And whirl along with thee about the globe.
Provide thee two proper palfreys, black as jet,   50
To hale thy vengeful wagon swift away   51
And find out murderers in their guilty caves;
And when thy car is loaden with their heads,   53
I will dismount, and by thy wagon wheel
Trot like a servile footman all day long,
Even from Hyperion's rising in the east   56
Until his very downfall in the sea;

---

146 **presently** immediately 153 **Desires** who desires 158 **for** since
5.2. Location: Rome. The court of Titus' house.
1 **sad habiliment** somber garments 5 **keeps** dwells 8 **confusion** destruction 11 **sad decrees** solemn resolutions

18 **Wanting . . . action** lacking a hand to provide suitable gesture by
way of support 19 **odds of** advantage over 22 **crimson** i.e., bloody
(as in line 14) 23 **trenches** i.e., wrinkles 32 **wreakful** vengeful
36 **obscurity** place of darkness and desolation 38 **couch** lie hidden
46 **surance** assurance 50 **proper** excellent, handsome. **palfreys**
horses 51 **hale** pull 53 **car** chariot 56 **Hyperion's** the sun god's

And day by day I'll do this heavy task,
So thou destroy Rapine and Murder there.   59
TAMORA
These are my ministers, and come with me.
TITUS
Are they thy ministers? What are they called?
TAMORA
Rape and Murder, therefore callèd so
'Cause they take vengeance of such kind of men.   63
TITUS
Good Lord, how like the Empress' sons they are,
And you the Empress! But we worldly men   65
Have miserable, mad, mistaking eyes.
O sweet Revenge, now do I come to thee,
And if one arm's embracement will content thee,
I will embrace thee in it by and by.   [*Exit above.*]
TAMORA
This closing with him fits his lunacy.   70
Whate'er I forge to feed his brainsick humors   71
Do you uphold and maintain in your speeches,
For now he firmly takes me for Revenge;
And being credulous in this mad thought,
I'll make him send for Lucius his son,
And whilst I at a banquet hold him sure,   76
I'll find some cunning practice out of hand   77
To scatter and disperse the giddy Goths
Or at the least make them his enemies.
See, here he comes, and I must ply my theme.

[*Enter Titus below.*]

TITUS
Long have I been forlorn, and all for thee.
Welcome, dread Fury, to my woeful house.   82
Rapine and Murder, you are welcome too.
How like the Empress and her sons you are!
Well are you fitted, had you but a Moor.   85
Could not all hell afford you such a devil?
For well I wot the Empress never wags   87
But in her company there is a Moor;
And, would you represent our queen aright,
It were convenient you had such a devil.   90
But welcome as you are. What shall we do?
TAMORA
What wouldst thou have us do, Andronicus?
DEMETRIUS
Show me a murderer, I'll deal with him.
CHIRON
Show me a villain that hath done a rape,
And I am sent to be revenged on him.
TAMORA
Show me a thousand that hath done thee wrong,
And I will be revengèd on them all.

TITUS [*to Demetrius*]
Look round about the wicked streets of Rome,
And when thou find'st a man that's like thyself,
Good Murder, stab him; he's a murderer.
[*To Chiron.*] Go thou with him, and when it is
   thy hap   101
To find another that is like to thee,
Good Rapine, stab him; he is a ravisher.
[*To Tamora.*] Go thou with them, and in the
   Emperor's court
There is a queen, attended by a Moor;
Well shalt thou know her by thine own proportion,
For up and down she doth resemble thee.   107
I pray thee, do on them some violent death;
They have been violent to me and mine.
TAMORA
Well hast thou lessoned us; this shall we do.
But would it please thee, good Andronicus,
To send for Lucius, thy thrice-valiant son,
Who leads towards Rome a band of warlike Goths,
And bid him come and banquet at thy house,
When he is here, even at thy solemn feast,   115
I will bring in the Empress and her sons,
The Emperor himself, and all thy foes,
And at thy mercy shall they stoop and kneel,
And on them shalt thou ease thy angry heart.
What says Andronicus to this device?
TITUS [*calling*]
Marcus, my brother! 'Tis sad Titus calls.

Enter Marcus.

Go, gentle Marcus, to thy nephew Lucius;
Thou shalt inquire him out among the Goths.
Bid him repair to me and bring with him   124
Some of the chiefest princes of the Goths.
Bid him encamp his soldiers where they are.
Tell him the Emperor and the Empress too
Feast at my house, and he shall feast with them.
This do thou for my love; and so let him,
As he regards his agèd father's life.
MARCUS
This will I do, and soon return again.   [*Exit.*]
TAMORA
Now will I hence about thy business
And take my ministers along with me.
TITUS
Nay, nay, let Rape and Murder stay with me,
Or else I'll call my brother back again
And cleave to no revenge but Lucius.   136
TAMORA [*aside to her sons*]
What say you, boys? Will you abide with him
Whiles I go tell my lord the Emperor
How I have governed our determined jest?   139
Yield to his humor, smooth and speak him fair,   140
And tarry with him till I turn again.   141

---

59 **So** provided that   63 **of . . . men** i.e., upon rapists and murderers   65 **worldly** mortal   70 **closing** agreeing   71 **forge** invent. **humors** moods, whims   76 **hold him sure** detain Lucius where he can
do no harm   77 **practice** plot.   **out of hand** on the spur of the moment   82 **Fury** (The Furies were primeval beings devoted to avenging
certain crimes, especially against the ties of kinship.)   85 **fitted** i.e.,
fitted out to resemble the Empress   87 **wags** moves about   90 **were
convenient** would be fitting

101 **hap** chance   107 **up and down** from top to toe   115 **solemn**
stately   124 **repair** come   136 **but Lucius** i.e., but that which Lucius
and his army can provide   139 **governed . . . jest** managed the jest
we determined on   140 **smooth . . . fair** flatter and humor him
141 **turn** return

TITUS [*aside*]
I knew them all, though they supposed me mad,
And will o'erreach them in their own devices—
A pair of cursèd hellhounds and their dam!

DEMETRIUS
Madam, depart at pleasure. Leave us here.

TAMORA
Farewell, Andronicus. Revenge now goes
To lay a complot to betray thy foes.   147

TITUS
I know thou dost; and, sweet Revenge, farewell.
                                    [*Exit Tamora.*]

CHIRON
Tell us, old man, how shall we be employed?

TITUS
Tut, I have work enough for you to do.
Publius, come hither! Caius, and Valentine!

      [*Enter Publius, Caius, and Valentine.*]

PUBLIUS   What is your will?

TITUS   Know you these two?

PUBLIUS
The Empress' sons, I take them—Chiron,
Demetrius.   154

TITUS
Fie, Publius, fie! Thou art too much deceived.
The one is Murder, and Rape is the other's name;
And therefore bind them, gentle Publius.
Caius and Valentine, lay hands on them.
Oft have you heard me wish for such an hour,
And now I find it. Therefore bind them sure,   160
And stop their mouths if they begin to cry.   [*Exit.*] 161
      [*Publius, Caius, and Valentine lay hold on Chiron
                              and Demetrius.*]

CHIRON
Villains, forbear! We are the Empress' sons.

PUBLIUS
And therefore do we what we are commanded.   163
Stop close their mouths; let them not speak a word.
                    [*They gag and bind the two sons.*]
Is he sure bound? Look that you bind them fast.

      *Enter Titus Andronicus with a knife, and Lavinia
      with a basin.*

TITUS
Come, come, Lavinia. Look, thy foes are bound.
Sirs, stop their mouths. Let them not speak to me,
But let them hear what fearful words I utter.
O villains, Chiron and Demetrius!
Here stands the spring whom you have stained with
      mud,   170
This goodly summer with your winter mixed.
You killed her husband, and for that vile fault
Two of her brothers were condemned to death,
My hand cut off and made a merry jest;
Both her sweet hands, her tongue, and that more
      dear

Than hands or tongue, her spotless chastity,
Inhuman traitors, you constrained and forced.
What would you say if I should let you speak?
Villains, for shame. You could not beg for grace.   179
Hark, wretches, how I mean to martyr you.   180
This one hand yet is left to cut your throats,
Whiles that Lavinia 'tween her stumps doth hold   182
The basin that receives your guilty blood.
You know your mother means to feast with me,
And calls herself Revenge, and thinks me mad.
Hark, villains, I will grind your bones to dust,
And with your blood and it I'll make a paste,   187
And of the paste a coffin I will rear,   188
And make two pasties of your shameful heads,   189
And bid that strumpet, your unhallowed dam,
Like to the earth swallow her own increase.   191
This is the feast that I have bid her to,
And this the banquet she shall surfeit on;
For worse than Philomel you used my daughter,
And worse than Procne I will be revenged.   195
And now prepare your throats. Lavinia, come.
                            He cuts their throats.
Receive the blood, and when that they are dead,
Let me go grind their bones to powder small,
And with this hateful liquor temper it,   199
And in that paste let their vile heads be baked.
Come, come, be everyone officious   201
To make this banquet, which I wish may prove
More stern and bloody than the Centaurs' feast.   203
So, now bring them in, for I'll play the cook
And see them ready against their mother comes.   205
                Exeunt [*bearing the dead bodies*].

                         ❧

5.3   *Enter Lucius, Marcus, and the Goths* [*with Aaron
          prisoner, and an attendant bearing his child*].

LUCIUS
Uncle Marcus, since 'tis my father's mind
That I repair to Rome, I am content.   2

A GOTH
And ours with thine, befall what fortune will.   3

179 for shame . . . grace i.e., your colossal shame would not let you beg for mercy, would choke your plea   **180 martyr** torture, kill cruelly   **182 Whiles that** while   **187 paste** dough   **188 coffin** pie crust (probably also suggesting the container in which they will be buried)   **189 pasties** meat pies   **191 Like . . . increase** swallow her offspring, just as the earth devours all her children when they have died   **195 worse than Procne** (An allusion to Procne's revenge on Tereus for raping her sister Philomel; compare with the note for 2.3.43. She killed her son Itys and served his flesh to Tereus, his father. In Seneca's *Thyestes*, Atreus similarly sets before Thyestes a dish of his own children's flesh.)   **199 temper** moisten, mix   **201 officious** busy   **203 Centaurs' feast** i.e., the wedding feast of Pirithous and Hippodamia to which the Lapithae invited the Centaurs, fabulous creatures, half-men and half-horses. (The Centaurs attempted to carry off the women but were slaughtered by their hosts.)   **205 against** by the time that

5.3. Location: The scene appears to take place in a court in Titus' house; in the opening lines, Lucius speaks as if he and his soldiers have just arrived in Rome.
2 repair return   **3 ours with thine** i.e., our intentions are in agreement with yours

147 complot conspiracy   **154 take them** take them to be   **160 sure** securely   **161 cry** cry out   **163 therefore** for that very reason   **170 spring** i.e., Lavinia

LUCIUS
Good uncle, take you in this barbarous Moor,   4
This ravenous tiger, this accursed devil.
Let him receive no sust'nance. Fetter him
Till he be brought unto the Empress' face   7
For testimony of her foul proceedings.   8
And see the ambush of our friends be strong;   9
I fear the Emperor means no good to us.
AARON
Some devil whisper curses in my ear
And prompt me that my tongue may utter forth
The venomous malice of my swelling heart!
LUCIUS
Away, inhuman dog, unhallowed slave!
Sirs, help our uncle to convey him in.
                    [Exeunt Goths, with Aaron.]
                    Sound trumpets [within].
The trumpets show the Emperor is at hand.

      Enter Emperor [Saturninus] and Empress
      [Tamora], with [Aemilius,] tribunes, [senators],
      and others.

SATURNINUS
What, hath the firmament more suns than one?   17
LUCIUS
What boots it thee to call thyself a sun?   18
MARCUS
Rome's emperor, and nephew, break the parle.   19
These quarrels must be quietly debated.
The feast is ready which the careful Titus   21
Hath ordained to an honorable end,
For peace, for love, for league, and good to Rome.
Please you therefore draw nigh and take your
  places.
SATURNINUS   Marcus, we will.
          [A table is brought in. The company sit down.]

      Trumpets sounding, enter Titus like a cook,
      placing the dishes, and Lavinia with a veil over her
      face, [young Lucius, and others].

TITUS
Welcome, my gracious lord; welcome, dread Queen;
Welcome, ye warlike Goths; welcome, Lucius;
And welcome, all. Although the cheer be poor,   28
'Twill fill your stomachs. Please you eat of it.
SATURNINUS
Why art thou thus attired, Andronicus?
TITUS
Because I would be sure to have all well
To entertain Your Highness and your empress.
TAMORA
We are beholding to you, good Andronicus.   33
TITUS
An if Your Highness knew my heart, you were.   34

My lord the Emperor, resolve me this: 35
Was it well done of rash Virginius   36
To slay his daughter with his own right hand
Because she was enforced, stained, and deflowered?
SATURNINUS   It was, Andronicus.
TITUS   Your reason, mighty lord?
SATURNINUS
Because the girl should not survive her shame,   41
And by her presence still renew his sorrows.   42
TITUS
A reason mighty, strong, and effectual;
A pattern, precedent, and lively warrant
For me, most wretched, to perform the like.
Die, die, Lavinia, and thy shame with thee,
And with thy shame thy father's sorrow die!
                    [He kills Lavinia.]
SATURNINUS
What hast thou done, unnatural and unkind?   48
TITUS
Killed her for whom my tears have made me blind.
I am as woeful as Virginius was,
And have a thousand times more cause than he
To do this outrage, and it now is done.
SATURNINUS
What, was she ravished? Tell who did the deed.
TITUS
Will 't please you eat? Will 't please Your Highness
  feed?
TAMORA
Why hast thou slain thine only daughter thus?
TITUS
Not I; 'twas Chiron and Demetrius.
They ravished her and cut away her tongue,
And they, 'twas they that did her all this wrong.
SATURNINUS
Go fetch them hither to us presently.   59
TITUS
Why, there they are, both bakèd in this pie,
Whereof their mother daintily hath fed,
Eating the flesh that she herself hath bred.
'Tis true, 'tis true; witness my knife's sharp point.
                    He stabs the Empress.
SATURNINUS
Die, frantic wretch, for this accursèd deed!
                    [He kills Titus.]
LUCIUS
Can the son's eye behold his father bleed?
There's meed for meed, death for a deadly deed!   66
          [He kills Saturninus. A great tumult, during which
                    Marcus, Lucius, and others go aloft.]

4 in i.e., into Titus' house; see line 123   7 unto before   8 of regarding   9 ambush forces lying in wait to attack   17 What . . . than one
i.e., two suns cannot occupy the same heavenly sphere, and Rome
cannot have two kings at once   18 boots avails   19 break the parle
cease the dispute   21 careful full of sorrows; assiduous   28 cheer
fare   33 beholding beholden   34 were would be

35 resolve answer   36 Virginius (According to Livy, the Roman cen-
turion Virginius killed his daughter to prevent her from being raped.
Shakespeare chooses, instead, an alternate version that was also current in the Renaissance: Virginius kills his daughter after her rape to
preserve her honor. This version is closer to the action of
Shakespeare's play.)   41 Because in order that   42 still continually
48 unkind (1) unnatural (2) cruel   59 presently at once   66 meed for
meed measure for measure.   s.d. A great . . . aloft (In lines
130–134, Marcus and Lucius offer to throw themselves down from
where they are speaking.)

MARCUS
    You sad-faced men, people and sons of Rome,
    By uproars severed, as a flight of fowl   68
    Scattered by winds and high tempestuous gusts,
    O, let me teach you how to knit again
    This scattered corn into one mutual sheaf,   71
    These broken limbs again into one body.
A ROMAN LORD
    Let Rome herself be bane unto herself,   73
    And she whom mighty kingdoms curtsy to,
    Like a forlorn and desperate castaway,
    Do shameful execution on herself,
    But if my frosty signs and chaps of age,   77
    Grave witnesses of true experience,
    Cannot induce you to attend my words.   79
    [To Lucius.] Speak, Rome's dear friend, as erst our
            ancestor,   80
    When with his solemn tongue he did discourse
    To lovesick Dido's sad-attending ear   82
    The story of that baleful burning night
    When subtle Greeks surprised King Priam's Troy.
    Tell us what Sinon hath bewitched our ears,   85
    Or who hath brought the fatal engine in
    That gives our Troy, our Rome, the civil wound.   87
    My heart is not compact of flint nor steel,   88
    Nor can I utter all our bitter grief,
    But floods of tears will drown my oratory
    And break my utterance, even in the time
    When it should move ye to attend me most
    And force you to commiseration.
    Here's Rome's young captain. Let him tell the tale,
    While I stand by and weep to hear him speak.
LUCIUS
    Then, gracious auditory, be it known to you
    That Chiron and the damnèd Demetrius
    Were they that murderèd our emperor's brother,
    And they it were that ravishèd our sister.
    For their fell faults our brothers were beheaded,   100
    Our father's tears despised, and basely cozened   101
    Of that true hand that fought Rome's quarrel out   102
    And sent her enemies unto the grave;
    Lastly, myself unkindly banishèd,   104
    The gates shut on me, and turned weeping out
    To beg relief among Rome's enemies,
    Who drowned their enmity in my true tears
    And oped their arms to embrace me as a friend.
    I am the turned-forth, be it known to you,   109
    That have preserved her welfare in my blood   110
    And from her bosom took the enemy's point,   111

Sheathing the steel in my adventurous body.
    Alas, you know I am no vaunter, I;
    My scars can witness, dumb although they are,   114
    That my report is just and full of truth.
    But soft, methinks I do digress too much,
    Citing my worthless praise. O, pardon me,
    For when no friends are by, men praise themselves.
MARCUS
    Now is my turn to speak. Behold the child:
            [pointing to the child in the arms of an attendant]
    Of this was Tamora delivered,
    The issue of an irreligious Moor,
    Chief architect and plotter of these woes.
    The villain is alive in Titus' house,
    And as he is to witness, this is true.
    Now judge what cause had Titus to revenge
    These wrongs unspeakable, past patience,   126
    Or more than any living man could bear.
    Now have you heard the truth. What say you,
            Romans?
    Have we done aught amiss, show us wherein,   129
    And from the place where you behold us pleading
    The poor remainder of Andronici
    Will hand in hand all headlong hurl ourselves,
    And on the ragged stones beat forth our souls,   133
    And make a mutual closure of our house.   134
    Speak, Romans, speak, and if you say we shall,
    Lo, hand in hand, Lucius and I will fall.
AEMILIUS
    Come, come, thou reverend man of Rome,
    And bring our emperor gently in thy hand,
    Lucius our emperor; for well I know
    The common voice do cry it shall be so.
ALL
    Lucius, all hail, Rome's royal emperor!
MARCUS [to attendants]
    Go, go into old Titus' sorrowful house
    And hither hale that misbelieving Moor
    To be adjudged some direful slaughtering death
    As punishment for his most wicked life.
            [Exeunt attendants. Marcus, Lucius, and the others
                                                come down.]
ALL
    Lucius, all hail, Rome's gracious governor!
LUCIUS
    Thanks, gentle Romans. May I govern so
    To heal Rome's harms and wipe away her woe!
    But, gentle people, give me aim awhile,   149
    For nature puts me to a heavy task.
    Stand all aloof, but, uncle, draw you near
    To shed obsequious tears upon this trunk.—   152
    O, take this warm kiss on thy pale cold lips,
                            [kissing Titus]
    These sorrowful drops upon thy bloodstained face,
    The last true duties of thy noble son!

---

68 severed disunited   **71 corn** grain   **73 s.p. A Roman Lord** (Perhaps
Aemilius; compare with his speech at lines 137 ff.)   **bane** poison,
death   **77 But if** if.   **frosty signs** i.e., white hair.   **chaps** wrinkles
79 attend listen to   **80 erst** formerly, once.   **our ancestor** i.e., Aeneas   **82 sad-attending** seriously listening   **85 Sinon** the crafty Greek
who persuaded the Trojans to take the wooden horse (the *fatal engine*) into their city   **87 civil** incurred in civil strife   **88 compact**
composed   **100 fell** savage, cruel   **101 and basely cozened** and he
was basely cheated   **102 fought . . . out** fought to the finish on behalf of Rome's cause   **104 unkindly** unnaturally   **109 turned-forth**
exile   **110 in** by   **111 from . . . point** took in my own bosom the
sword's point aimed at her, Rome's, bosom

114 dumb . . . are (The scars are dumb mouths, giving mute testimony.)   **126 patience** endurance   **129 Have we** if we have
133 ragged rough, rugged   **134 closure** conclusion, death   **149 give
me aim** bear with me, give me encouragement   **152 obsequious** dutiful, mourning

MARCUS [*kissing Titus*]
    Tear for tear, and loving kiss for kiss,
    Thy brother Marcus tenders on thy lips.
    O, were the sum of these that I should pay
    Countless and infinite, yet would I pay them!
LUCIUS [*to young Lucius*]
    Come hither, boy. Come, come, and learn of us
    To melt in showers. Thy grandsire loved thee well.
    Many a time he danced thee on his knee,
    Sung thee asleep, his loving breast thy pillow;
    Many a story hath he told to thee,
    And bid thee bear his pretty tales in mind
    And talk of them when he was dead and gone.
MARCUS
    How many thousand times hath these poor lips,
    When they were living, warmed themselves on
        thine!
    O, now, sweet boy, give them their latest kiss.   169
    Bid him farewell; commit him to the grave.
    Do them that kindness, and take leave of them.   171
BOY [*kissing Titus*]
    O grandsire, grandsire! Ev'n with all my heart
    Would I were dead, so you did live again!
    O Lord, I cannot speak to him for weeping.
    My tears will choke me if I ope my mouth.

            [*Enter attendants with Aaron.*]

A ROMAN
    You sad Andronici, have done with woes.   176
    Give sentence on this execrable wretch
    That hath been breeder of these dire events.
LUCIUS
    Set him breast-deep in earth and famish him;
    There let him stand and rave and cry for food.
    If anyone relieves or pities him,
    For the offense he dies. This is our doom.   182
    Some stay to see him fastened in the earth.
AARON
    Ah, why should wrath be mute and fury dumb?
    I am no baby, I, that with base prayers
    I should repent the evils I have done.
    Ten thousand worse than ever yet I did
    Would I perform, if I might have my will.
    If one good deed in all my life I did,
    I do repent it from my very soul.
LUCIUS
    Some loving friends convey the Emperor hence,
    And give him burial in his father's grave.   192
    My father and Lavinia shall forthwith
    Be closèd in our household's monument.
    As for that ravenous tiger, Tamora,
    No funeral rite, nor man in mourning weed,
    No mournful bell shall ring her burial;
    But throw her forth to beasts and birds to prey.   198

    Her life was beastly and devoid of pity,
    And being dead, let birds on her take pity.   200
            Exeunt, [bearing the dead bodies].

200 pity (The First Quarto text closes the play with this line. The Second Quarto and subsequent texts add the following four lines:
    See justice done on Aaron, that damned Moor,
    By whom our heavy haps had their beginning.
    Then, afterwards, to order well the state,
    That like events may ne'er it ruinate.)

---

169 latest last   **171 them** i.e., the lips   **176 s.p. A Roman** (The speech is sometimes assigned to Aemilius.)   **182 doom** decision, judgment   **192 father's** (or possibly *fathers'*, "forefathers'")
198 prey prey upon

Romeo and Juliet

Though a tragedy, *Romeo and Juliet* is, in some ways, more closely comparable to Shakespeare's romantic comedies and early writings than to his later tragedies. Stylistically belonging to the years 1594–1596, it is in the lyric vein of the sonnets, *A Midsummer Night's Dream,* and *Richard II,* all of which are from the mid 1590s. Like them, it uses a variety of rhyme schemes (couplets, quatrains, octets, and even sonnets) and revels in punning, metaphor, and wit combat. It is separated in tone and in time from the earliest of the great tragedies, *Julius Caesar* and *Hamlet,* by almost half a decade, and, except for the experimental *Titus Andronicus,* it is the only tragedy (that is not also a history) that Shakespeare wrote in the first decade of his career—a period devoted otherwise to romantic comedy and English history.

Like many comedies, *Romeo and Juliet* is a love story, celebrating the exquisite, brief joy of youthful passion. Even its tragic ending stresses the poignancy of that brief beauty, not the bitter futility of love, as in *Troilus and Cressida* or *Othello.* The tragic ending of *Romeo and Juliet* underscores the observation made by a vexed lover in *A Midsummer Night's Dream* that "The course of true love never did run smooth" (1.1.134). True love in *Romeo and Juliet,* as in *A Midsummer Night's Dream,* is destined to be crossed by differences in blood or family background, differences in age, arbitrary choices of family or friends, or uncontrollable catastrophes, such as war, death, and sickness. Love is thus, as in *A Midsummer Night's Dream,* "momentary as a sound, / Swift as a shadow, short as any dream," swallowed up by darkness; "So quick bright things come to confusion" (1.1.143–149). A dominant pattern of imagery in *Romeo and Juliet* evokes a corresponding sense of suddenness and violence: fire, gunpowder, hot blood, lightning, the inconstant wind, the storm-tossed or shipwrecked vessel. The beauty of a love that is so threatened and so fragile is intensified by the brevity of the experience. A tragic outcome therefore affirms the uniqueness and pristine quality of youthful ecstasy. The flowering and fading of a joy "too rich for use, for earth too dear" (1.5.48), does not so much condemn the unfeeling world as welcome the martyrdom of literally dying for love.

As protagonists, Romeo and Juliet lack tragic stature by any classical definition or in terms of the medieval convention of the Fall of Princes. The lovers are not extraordinary except in their passionate attachment to one another. They belong to prominent merchant families rather than to the nobility. They (especially Juliet) are very young, more so than any other of Shakespeare's tragic protagonists, and are indeed younger than most couples marrying in England at the time the play was written: the average age for women was between twenty-one and twenty-four; for men it was between twenty-four and twenty-seven. Romeo and Juliet's dilemma of parental opposition is of the domestic sort often found in comedy. In fact, several characters in the play partly resemble the conventional character types of the Latin comic playwright Plautus or of Italian neoclassical comedy: the domineering father who insists that his daughter marry according to his choice, the unwelcome rival wooer, the garrulous and bawdy nurse, and, of course, the lovers. The Italian *novella,* to which Shakespeare often turned for his plots, made use of these same types and paid little attention to the classical precept that protagonists in a tragic story ought to be persons of high rank who are humbled through some inner flaw, or hamartia.

The story of Romeo and Juliet goes back ultimately to the fifth-century A.D. Greek romance of *Ephesiaca,* in which we find the motif of the sleeping potion as a means of escaping an unwelcome marriage. Masuccio of Salerno, in his *Il Novellino,* in 1476, combined the narrative of the heroine's deathlike trance and seeming burial alive with that of the hero's tragic failure to receive news from the friar that she is still alive. Luigi da Porto, in his *novella* (c. 1530), set the scene at Verona, provided the names of Romeo and Giulietta for the hero and heroine, added the account of their feuding families, the Montecchi and Cappelletti, introduced the killing of Tybalt (Theobaldo), and provided other important details. Luigi's version was followed by Matteo Bandello's famous *Novelle* of 1554, which was translated into French by Pierre Boaistuau (1559). The French version became the source for Arthur Brooke's long narrative poem in English, *The Tragical History of Romeus and Juliet* (1562). Brooke mentions having seen a play on the subject, but it is doubtful that Shakespeare knew this old play or, if he did know it, made use of it. Brooke's poem was his chief and probably only source. Shakespeare has condensed Brooke's action from nine months to less than a week, has greatly expanded the role of Mercutio, and has given to the Nurse a warmth and humorous richness not found in the usual Italian duenna, or *balia.* He has also tidied up the Friar's immorality and deleted the antipapal tone. Throughout all these changes, Shakespeare retains Brooke's romantic (rather than classically tragic) conception of love overwhelmed by external obstacles.

Like the romantic comedies, *Romeo and Juliet* is often funny and bawdy. Samson and Gregory in the first scene are slapstick cowards, hiding behind the law and daring to quarrel only when reinforcements arrive. The Nurse delights us with her earthy recollections of the day she weaned Juliet: the child tasting "the wormwood on the nipple / Of my dug" (1.3.31–32), the warm Italian sun, an earthquake, the Nurse's husband telling his lame but often-repeated bawdy joke about women falling on their backs. Mercutio employs his inventive and sardonic humor to twit Romeo for lovesickness and the Nurse for her pomposity. She, in turn, scolds Peter and plagues Juliet (who is breathlessly awaiting news from Romeo) with a history of her back ailments. Mercutio and the Nurse are among Shakespeare's bawdiest characters. Their wry and salacious view of love contrasts with the nobly innocent and yet physically passionate love of Romeo and Juliet. Mercutio and the Nurse cannot take part in the play's denouement; one dies, misinterpreting Romeo's appeasement of Tybalt, and the other proves insensitive to Juliet's depth of feeling. Yet the disappearance of these engaging companions takes from the play some of its vitality and most of its funniness.

The lovers, too, are at first well suited to Shakespearean romantic comedy. When we meet Romeo, he is not in love with Juliet at all, despite the play's title, but is mooning over a "hardhearted wench" (in Mercutio's words) named Rosaline. This "goddess" appropriately never appears in the play; she is almost a disembodied idea in Romeo's mind, a scornful beauty like Phoebe in *As You Like It*. Romeo's love for her is tedious and self-pitying, like that of the conventional wooer in a sonnet sequence by Francesco Petrarch or one of his imitators. Juliet, although not yet fourteen, must change all this by teaching him the nature of true love. She will have none of his shopworn clichés learned in the service of Rosaline, his flowery protestations and swearing by the moon, lest they prove to be love's perjuries. With her innocent candor, she insists (like many heroines of the romantic comedies) on dispelling the mask of pretense that lovers too often show one another. "Capulet" and "Montague" are mere labels, not the inner self. Although Juliet would have been more coy, she confesses, had she known that Romeo was overhearing her, she will now "prove more true / Than those that have more cunning to be strange" (2.2.100–101). She is more practical than he in assessing danger and making plans. Later she also proves herself remarkably able to bear misfortune.

The comedy of the play's first half is, to be sure, overshadowed by the certainty of disaster. The opening chorus plainly warns us that the lovers will die. They are "star-crossed," and they speak of themselves as such. Romeo fears "Some consequence yet hanging in the stars" when he reluctantly goes to the Capulets' feast (1.4.107); after he has slain Tybalt, he cries "O, I am fortune's fool!" (3.1.135); and, at the news of Juliet's supposed death, he proclaims "Then I defy you, stars!" (5.1.24). Yet in what sense are Romeo and Juliet "star-crossed"? The concept is deliberately broad in this play, encompassing many factors, such as hatred, bumbling, bad luck, and simple lack of awareness.

The first scene presents feuding as a major cause in the tragedy. The quarrel between the two families is so ancient that the original motives are no longer even discussed. Inspired by the "fiery" Tybalt, factionalism pursues its mindless course, despite the efforts of the Prince to end it. Although the elders of both families talk of peace, they call for their swords quickly enough when a fray begins. Still, this senseless hatred does not lead to tragedy until its effects are fatally complicated through misunderstanding. With poignant irony, good intentions are repeatedly undermined by lack of knowledge. We can see why Juliet does not tell her family of her secret marriage with a presumably hated Montague, but, in fact, Capulet has accepted Romeo as a guest in his house under the terms of chivalric hospitality, praising him as a "virtuous and well governed youth" (1.5.69). For all his dictatorial ways, and the manifest advantages he may see in marrying his daughter to an aristocrat, Capulet would, of course, never propose the match if he knew his daughter to be married already. Not knowing of Juliet's marriage, he and his wife can only interpret her refusal to marry Paris as caprice. Count Paris himself is victim of this tragedy of unawareness. He is an eminently suitable wooer for Juliet, rich and nobly born, yet considerate, peace-loving, and deeply fond of Juliet (as he shows by his private and sincere grief at her tomb). Certainly, he would never intentionally woo a married woman. Not knowing, he plays the unattractive role of the rival wooer and dies for it. Similarly, Mercutio cannot understand Romeo's seemingly craven behavior toward Tybalt and so begins the duel that leads to Romeo's banishment. The final scene, with Friar Laurence's retelling of the story, allows us to see the survivors confronted with what they have all unknowingly done.

Chance, or accident, plays a role of importance equal to that of hatred and unawareness. An outbreak of the plague prevents Friar John from conveying Friar Laurence's letter to Romeo at Mantua. Friar Laurence, going hurriedly to the Capulets' tomb, arrives in time for Juliet's awakening but some minutes after Romeo has killed Paris and taken poison. Juliet awakens only moments later. The Watch comes just too late to prevent her suicide. Friar Laurence expresses well the sense of frustration at plans gone awry by such narrow margins: "what an unkind hour / Is guilty of this lamentable chance!" (5.3.145–146). Earlier, Capulet's decision to move the wedding date up one day has crucially affected the timing. Human miscalculation contributes also to the catastrophe: Mercutio is killed under Romeo's arm, and Friar Laurence wonders unhappily if any of his complicated plans "Miscarried by my fault" (line 267). Character and human decision play a part in this tragedy, for Romeo should not have dueled with Tybalt, no matter what the provocation. In choosing to kill Tybalt, he has deliberately cast aside as "effeminate" the gentle and forgiving qualities he has learned from his love of Juliet (3.1.113) and thus is guilty of a rash and self-destructive action. To ascribe the cause of the tragedy in Aristotelian fashion to his and Juliet's impulsiveness is, however, to ignore much of the rest of the play.

Instead, the ending of the play brings a pattern out of the seeming welter of mistakes and animosities. "A greater power than we can contradict / Hath thwarted our intents," says Friar Laurence, suggesting that the seeming bad luck of the delayed letter was, in fact, the intent of a mysterious higher intelligence (5.3.153–154). Prince Escalus, too, finds a necessary meaning in the tragic event. "See what a scourge is laid upon your hate," he admonishes the Montagues and Capulets, "That heaven finds means to kill your joys with love." Romeo and Juliet are "Poor sacrifices of our enmity" (lines 292–304). As the Prologue had foretold, their deaths will "bury their parents' strife"; the families' feud is a stubborn evil force "Which, but their children's end, naught could remove." Order is preciously restored; the price is great, but the sacrifice nonetheless confirms a sense of a larger intention in what had appeared to be simply hatred and misfortune. Throughout the play, love and hate are interrelated opposites, yoked through the rhetorical device of oxymoron, or inherent contradiction. Romeo apostrophizes "O brawling love, O loving hate" (1.1.176), and Juliet later echoes his words: "My only love sprung from my only hate" (1.5.139). This paradox expresses a conflict in humankind, as in the universe itself. "Two such opposèd kings encamp them still / In man as well as herbs," says Friar Laurence, "grace and rude will" (2.3.27–28). Hatred is a condition of our corrupted wills, of our fall from grace, and it attempts to destroy what is gracious in human beings. In this cosmic strife, love must pay the sacrifice, as Romeo and Juliet do with their lives, but, because their deaths are finally perceived as the cost of so much hatred, the two families come to terms with their collective guilt and resolve henceforth to be worthy of the sacrifice.

Structurally, *Romeo and Juliet* gives considerable prominence to the feuding of the two families. Public scenes occur at key points—at beginning, middle, and end (1.1, 3.1, and 5.3)—and each such scene concerns violence and its consequences. The play begins with a brawl. Tybalt is a baleful presence in 1.1 and 3.1, implacably bent on vengeance. The three public scenes are alike, too, in that they bring into confrontation the entire families of Capulets and Montagues, who call for swords and demand reprisal from the state for what they themselves have set in motion. Prince Escalus dominates these three public scenes. He must offer judgment in each, giving the families fair warning, then exiling Romeo for Tybalt's death, and finally counseling the families on the meaning of their collective tragedy. He is a spokesman for public order and security ("Mercy but murders, pardoning those that kill," 3.1.196), even though he is also unable to prevent the tragedy. He stands above the conflict and yet is affected by it; his own kinsman, Mercutio, is

one of the casualties. For all his dignity and impartiality, Escalus' official function is somehow tangential to the central emotional experience of the play. The law does not provide a remedy. Still, it can preside and arbitrate. To Escalus is given the final speech promising both punishment and pardon, and it is he who sums up the paradoxical interdependence of love and hate. Onstage, his role is sometimes doubled with that of the Chorus. Although the morning after the catastrophe brings with it sorrow, it also brings peace, however "glooming." Escalus is master of ceremonies for a restored order through which the families and we are reconciled to what has occurred.

In good part, the public scenes of the play serve to frame the love plot and the increasing isolation of the separated lovers, but these public scenes have a function of their own to the extent that the tragedy has touched and altered everyone. The final tableau is not the kiss of the dying lovers but the handclasp of the reconciled fathers. The long, last public ceremonial is important because, although the private catastrophe of the lovers is unalterably complete, recognition occurs only when the whole story is known by all. As we watch the bereaved families responding with shock to the story of Romeo and Juliet's tragedy, we understand the reason for Friar Laurence's lengthy recounting of a story we already know; only when it is too late, do the families begin to comprehend their own complicity in the disaster that has occurred. This recognition is not that of the protagonists, as in the Aristotelian conception of recognition, nor does it accompany a reversal of the love tragedy; that reversal already has taken place in Romeo's banishment and the lovers' deaths. This lack of correspondence with an Aristotelian definition of tragedy is not, however, a structural flaw; rather, it is a manifestation of the dual focus of the tragedy on the lovers and on all Verona. The city itself is a kind of protagonist, suffering through its own violence and coming at last to the sad comfort that wisdom brings.

Romeo and Juliet

[*Dramatis Personae*

CHORUS

ESCALUS, *Prince of Verona*
MERCUTIO, *the Prince's kinsman and Romeo's friend*
PARIS, *a young count and kinsman of the Prince*
PAGE *to Count Paris*

MONTAGUE
MONTAGUE'S WIFE
ROMEO, *son of the Montagues*
BENVOLIO, *Montague's nephew and Romeo's friend*
ABRAHAM, *a servant of the Montague household*
BALTHASAR, *a servant of the Montague household attending Romeo*

CAPULET
CAPULET'S WIFE
JULIET, *daughter of the Capulets*
NURSE
TYBALT, *nephew of Capulet's Wife*
PETRUCHIO, *Capulet's kinsman*
SECOND CAPULET, *an old man, Capulet's kinsman*
PETER, *a servant of the Capulet household attending the Nurse*
SAMSON ⎫
GREGORY ⎪
ANTHONY ⎬ *servants of the Capulet household*
POTPAN ⎪
CLOWN *or* SERVANT ⎪
Other SERVANTS ⎭

FRIAR LAURENCE ⎫ *Franciscan friars*
FRIAR JOHN ⎭

APOTHECARY
Three MUSICIANS (*Simon Catling, Hugh Rebeck, and James Soundpost*)
Three WATCHMEN

Citizens, Maskers, Torchbearers, Guards, Servants, and Attendants

SCENE: *Verona; Mantua*]

The Prologue

[*Enter Chorus.*]

CHORUS
Two households, both alike in dignity,   1
   In fair Verona, where we lay our scene,
From ancient grudge break to new mutiny,   3
   Where civil blood makes civil hands unclean.   4
From forth the fatal loins of these two foes
   A pair of star-crossed lovers take their life;   6
Whose misadventured piteous overthrows   7
   Doth with their death bury their parents' strife.
The fearful passage of their death-marked love,   9
   And the continuance of their parents' rage,
Which, but their children's end, naught could remove,
   Is now the two hours' traffic of our stage;   12
The which if you with patient ears attend,
What here shall miss, our toil shall strive to mend.   14

[*Exit.*]

❖

1.1   *Enter Samson and Gregory, with swords and bucklers, of the house of Capulet.*

SAMSON   Gregory, on my word, we'll not carry coals.   1
GREGORY   No, for then we should be colliers.   2
SAMSON   I mean, an we be in choler, we'll draw.   3
GREGORY   Ay, while you live, draw your neck out of collar.   5
SAMSON   I strike quickly, being moved.   6
GREGORY   But thou art not quickly moved to strike.
SAMSON   A dog of the house of Montague moves me.   8
GREGORY   To move is to stir, and to be valiant is to stand. Therefore, if thou art moved, thou runn'st away.   10
SAMSON   A dog of that house shall move me to stand. I will take the wall of any man or maid of Montague's.   12
GREGORY   That shows thee a weak slave, for the   13 weakest goes to the wall.   14
SAMSON   'Tis true, and therefore women, being the weaker vessels, are ever thrust to the wall. Therefore I   16

Prologue.
1–14 (The Prologue is in the form of a sonnet.)   **1 dignity** rank, status   **3 mutiny** strife, discord   **4 Where . . . unclean** where citizens' hands uncivilly are stained in civil strife with their fellow citizens' blood   **6 star-crossed** thwarted by destiny, by adverse stars   **7 misadventured** unlucky   **9 passage** progress   **12 traffic** business   **14 miss** i.e., miss the mark (in this performance).   **our toil** the actors' efforts
1.1. Location: Verona. A public place.
s.d. bucklers small shields   **1 carry coals** i.e., endure insults   **2 colliers** (Coal carriers were regarded as dirty and of evil repute.)   **3 an** if. **choler** anger (produced by one of the four humors).   **draw** draw swords   **5 collar** i.e., hangman's noose (with pun on *colliers* and *choler*)   **6 moved** i.e., to anger (with pun in next line)   **8 moves** incites   **10 stand** i.e., stand one's ground   **12 take the wall** take the cleaner side of the walk nearest the wall, thus forcing others out into the gutter   **13–14 the weakest . . . wall** (A proverb expressing the idea that the weakest are always forced to give way.)   **16 weaker vessels** (Saint Paul bids husbands give honor to their wives "as unto the weaker vessel," 1 Peter 3:7.)   **thrust to the wall** (With suggestion of amorous assault.)

will push Montague's men from the wall and thrust his maids to the wall.

GREGORY   The quarrel is between our masters and us 19
their men.   20

SAMSON   'Tis all one. I will show myself a tyrant: when 21
I have fought with the men, I will be civil with the
maids—I will cut off their heads.

GREGORY   The heads of the maids?

SAMSON   Ay, the heads of the maids, or their maidenheads. Take it in what sense thou wilt.   26

GREGORY   They must take it in sense that feel it.   27

SAMSON   Me they shall feel while I am able to stand, 28
and 'tis known I am a pretty piece of flesh.   29

GREGORY   'Tis well thou art not fish; if thou hadst, thou 30
hadst been Poor John. Draw thy tool. Here comes of 31
the house of Montagues.

*Enter two other Servingmen [Abraham and
another].*

SAMSON   My naked weapon is out. Quarrel, I will back
thee.

GREGORY   How, turn thy back and run?

SAMSON   Fear me not.   36

GREGORY   No, marry. I fear thee!   37

SAMSON   Let us take the law of our side. Let them 38
begin.

GREGORY   I will frown as I pass by, and let them take it
as they list.   41

SAMSON   Nay, as they dare. I will bite my thumb at 42
them, which is disgrace to them if they bear it.

[Samson makes taunting gestures.]

ABRAHAM   Do you bite your thumb at us, sir?

SAMSON   I do bite my thumb, sir.

ABRAHAM   Do you bite your thumb at us, sir?

SAMSON *[aside to Gregory]*   Is the law of our side if I
say ay?

GREGORY *[aside to Samson]*   No.

SAMSON *[to Abraham]*   No, sir, I do not bite my thumb
at you, sir, but I bite my thumb, sir.

GREGORY   Do you quarrel, sir?

ABRAHAM   Quarrel, sir? No, sir.

SAMSON   But if you do, sir, I am for you. I serve as good
a man as you.

ABRAHAM   No better.

SAMSON   Well, sir.

Enter Benvolio.

19–20 between . . . men i.e., between the males of one household
and the males of the other household; we have no quarrel with the
women   **21 one** the same   **26 what sense** whatever meaning
27 They . . . feel it i.e., it is the maids who must receive by way of
physical sensation (*sense*) what I have to offer, because they are the
ones who can feel it   **28 stand** (With suggestion of "have an erection," continued in the next few lines in *draw thy tool* and *my naked
weapon is out.*)   **29–30 flesh . . . fish** (Refers to the proverbial
phrase, "neither fish nor flesh.")   **31 Poor John** hake salted and
dried—a poor Lenten kind of food (probably with a bawdy suggestion
of sexual insufficiency).   **comes of** i.e., come members of   **36 Fear**
mistrust. (But Gregory deliberately misunderstands in the next line,
saying, in effect, "No indeed, do you think I'd be afraid of you?")
37 marry i.e., indeed. (Originally an oath, "by the Virgin Mary.")
38 take the law of have the law on   **41 list** please   **42 bite my
thumb** i.e., make an insulting gesture

GREGORY *[to Samson]*   Say "better." Here comes one of
my master's kinsmen.

SAMSON *[to Abraham]*   Yes, better, sir.

ABRAHAM   You lie.

SAMSON   Draw, if you be men. Gregory, remember thy
washing blow.   *They fight.* 63

BENVOLIO   Part, fools!
Put up your swords. You know not what you do.

Enter Tybalt [with sword drawn].

TYBALT
What, art thou drawn among these heartless hinds? 66
Turn thee, Benvolio. Look upon thy death.

BENVOLIO
I do but keep the peace. Put up thy sword,
Or manage it to part these men with me.   69

TYBALT
What, drawn and talk of peace? I hate the word
As I hate hell, all Montagues, and thee.
Have at thee, coward!   *[They fight.]* 72

*Enter three or four Citizens with clubs or
partisans.*

CITIZENS
Clubs, bills, and partisans! Strike! Beat them down! 73
Down with the Capulets! Down with the
Montagues!   74

Enter old Capulet in his gown, and his Wife.

CAPULET
What noise is this? Give me my long sword, ho!   75

CAPULET'S WIFE
A crutch, a crutch! Why call you for a sword?

CAPULET
My sword, I say! Old Montague is come
And flourishes his blade in spite of me.   78

Enter old Montague and his Wife.

MONTAGUE
Thou villain Capulet!—Hold me not; let me go.

MONTAGUE'S WIFE
Thou shalt not stir one foot to seek a foe.

Enter Prince Escalus, with his train.

PRINCE
Rebellious subjects, enemies to peace,
Profaners of this neighbor-stainèd steel—   82
Will they not hear? What, ho! You men, you beasts,
That quench the fire of your pernicious rage
With purple fountains issuing from your veins,   85
On pain of torture, from those bloody hands

63 washing slashing with great force   **66 heartless hinds** cowardly
menials   **69 manage** use   **72 Have at thee** i.e., on guard, here I
come   **73 Clubs** rallying cry, summoning apprentices with their
clubs.   **bills** long-handled spears with hooked blades.   **partisans**
long-handled spears   **74 s.d. gown** nightgown, dressing gown
75 long sword heavy, old-fashioned sword   **78 spite** defiance, despite
82 Profaners . . . steel you who profane your weapons by staining
them with neighbors' blood   **85 purple** bloody, dark red

Throw your mistempered weapons to the ground 87
And hear the sentence of your movèd prince. 88
Three civil brawls, bred of an airy word, 89
By thee, old Capulet, and Montague,
Have thrice disturbed the quiet of our streets
And made Verona's ancient citizens
Cast by their grave-beseeming ornaments 93
To wield old partisans in hands as old,
Cankered with peace, to part your cankered hate. 95
If ever you disturb our streets again
Your lives shall pay the forfeit of the peace. 97
For this time all the rest depart away.
You, Capulet, shall go along with me,
And Montague, come you this afternoon,
To know our farther pleasure in this case,
To old Freetown, our common judgment-place. 102
Once more, on pain of death, all men depart.
Exeunt [all but Montague, Montague's Wife, and
Benvolio].

MONTAGUE
Who set this ancient quarrel new abroach? 104
Speak, nephew, were you by when it began? 105
BENVOLIO
Here were the servants of your adversary,
And yours, close fighting ere I did approach.
I drew to part them. In the instant came
The fiery Tybalt with his sword prepared, 109
Which, as he breathed defiance to my ears,
He swung about his head and cut the winds
Who, nothing hurt withal, hissed him in scorn. 112
While we were interchanging thrusts and blows,
Came more and more, and fought on part and part 114
Till the Prince came, who parted either part. 115
MONTAGUE'S WIFE
O, where is Romeo? Saw you him today?
Right glad I am he was not at this fray.
BENVOLIO
Madam, an hour before the worshiped sun
Peered forth the golden window of the east, 119
A troubled mind drave me to walk abroad, 120
Where, underneath the grove of sycamore
That westward rooteth from this city's side, 122
So early walking did I see your son.
Towards him I made, but he was ware of me 124
And stole into the covert of the wood. 125
I, measuring his affections by my own, 126

Which then most sought where most might not be
  found, 127
Being one too many by my weary self,
Pursued my humor, not pursuing his, 129
And gladly shunned who gladly fled from me. 130
MONTAGUE
Many a morning hath he there been seen,
With tears augmenting the fresh morning's dew,
Adding to clouds more clouds with his deep sighs;
But all so soon as the all-cheering sun
Should in the farthest east begin to draw
The shady curtains from Aurora's bed, 136
Away from light steals home my heavy son 137
And private in his chamber pens himself,
Shuts up his windows, locks fair daylight out,
And makes himself an artificial night.
Black and portentous must this humor prove
Unless good counsel may the cause remove.
BENVOLIO
My noble uncle, do you know the cause?
MONTAGUE
I neither know it nor can learn of him.
BENVOLIO
Have you importuned him by any means? 145
MONTAGUE
Both by myself and many other friends.
But he, his own affections' counselor,
Is to himself—I will not say how true, 148
But to himself so secret and so close, 149
So far from sounding and discovery, 150
As is the bud bit with an envious worm 151
Ere he can spread his sweet leaves to the air
Or dedicate his beauty to the sun.
Could we but learn from whence his sorrows grow,
We would as willingly give cure as know.

Enter Romeo.

BENVOLIO
See where he comes. So please you, step aside. 156
I'll know his grievance or be much denied.
MONTAGUE
I would thou wert so happy by thy stay 158
To hear true shrift. Come, madam, let's away. 159
Exeunt [Montague and his Wife].
BENVOLIO
Good morrow, cousin.
ROMEO   Is the day so young? 160
BENVOLIO
But new struck nine.
ROMEO   Ay me! Sad hours seem long.
Was that my father that went hence so fast?

87 **mistempered** (1) having been tempered, or hardened, to a wrong use (2) malignant 88 **movèd** angry 89 **airy** i.e., merely a breath, trivial 93 **grave-beseeming ornaments** i.e., staffs and other appurtenances suited to wise old age 95 **Cankered . . . cankered** corroded (from disuse) . . . malignant 97 **Your . . . peace** death will be the penalty for breaking the peace 102 **Freetown** (Brooke's translation, in his poem *Romeus and Juliet*, of *Villa Franca*, as found in the Italian story.) **common** public 104 **set . . . abroach** reopened this old quarrel, set it flowing 105 **by** near 109 **prepared** drawn, ready 112 **Who, nothing** which not at all. **withal** therewith. **hissed** hissed at 114 **on part and part** on one side and the other 115 **either part** both parties 119 **forth** from forth 120 **drave** drove. **abroad** outside 122 **That . . . side** that grows on the west side of this city 124 **made** moved. **ware** wary, aware 125 **covert** cover, hiding place 126 **affections** wishes, inclination

127 **Which . . . found** which then chiefly desired a place where I might be alone 129 **humor** mood 130 **who** him who 136 **Aurora** goddess of dawn 137 **heavy** (1) sad (2) the opposite of *light*. **son** (punning on *sun*, line 134) 145 **any means** every means possible 148 **true** trustworthy 149 **close** concealed 150 **sounding** being fathomed (to discover deep or inner secrets) 151 **envious** malicious 156 **So please you** if you please 158 **happy** fortunate, successful 159 **To** as to. **shrift** confession 160 **cousin** kinsman

BENVOLIO
    It was. What sadness lengthens Romeo's hours?
ROMEO
    Not having that which, having, makes them short.
BENVOLIO   In love?
ROMEO   Out—
BENVOLIO   Of love?
ROMEO
    Out of her favor where I am in love.
BENVOLIO
    Alas, that Love, so gentle in his view,   169
    Should be so tyrannous and rough in proof!   170
ROMEO
    Alas, that Love, whose view is muffled still,   171
    Should without eyes see pathways to his will!   172
    Where shall we dine?—O me! What fray was here?
    Yet tell me not, for I have heard it all.
    Here's much to do with hate, but more with love.
    Why, then, O brawling love, O loving hate,
    O anything of nothing first create,   177
    O heavy lightness, serious vanity,
    Misshapen chaos of well-seeming forms,
    Feather of lead, bright smoke, cold fire, sick health,
    Still-waking sleep, that is not what it is!   181
    This love feel I, that feel no love in this.
    Dost thou not laugh?
BENVOLIO   No, coz, I rather weep.   183
ROMEO
    Good heart, at what?
BENVOLIO   At thy good heart's oppression.
ROMEO
    Why, such is love's transgression.
    Griefs of mine own lie heavy in my breast,
    Which thou wilt propagate, to have it pressed   187
    With more of thine. This love that thou hast shown   188
    Doth add more grief to too much of mine own.
    Love is a smoke made with the fume of sighs;
    Being purged, a fire sparkling in lovers' eyes;   191
    Being vexed, a sea nourished with lovers' tears.
    What is it else? A madness most discreet,   193
    A choking gall, and a preserving sweet.
    Farewell, my coz.
BENVOLIO   Soft! I will go along.   195
    An if you leave me so, you do me wrong.   196
ROMEO
    Tut, I have lost myself. I am not here.
    This is not Romeo; he's some other where.
BENVOLIO
    Tell me in sadness, who is that you love?   199
ROMEO   What, shall I groan and tell thee?

BENVOLIO
    Groan? Why, no, but sadly tell me who.   201
ROMEO
    Bid a sick man in sadness make his will—
    A word ill urged to one that is so ill!   203
    In sadness, cousin, I do love a woman.
BENVOLIO
    I aimed so near when I supposed you loved.
ROMEO
    A right good markman! And she's fair I love.   206
BENVOLIO
    A right fair mark, fair coz, is soonest hit.   207
ROMEO
    Well, in that hit you miss. She'll not be hit
    With Cupid's arrow. She hath Dian's wit,   209
    And, in strong proof of chastity well armed,   210
    From love's weak childish bow she lives unharmed.
    She will not stay the siege of loving terms,   212
    Nor bide th' encounter of assailing eyes,   213
    Nor ope her lap to saint-seducing gold.
    O, she is rich in beauty, only poor
    That when she dies, with beauty dies her store.   216
BENVOLIO
    Then she hath sworn that she will still live chaste?   217
ROMEO
    She hath, and in that sparing makes huge waste,   218
    For beauty starved with her severity   219
    Cuts beauty off from all posterity.
    She is too fair, too wise, wisely too fair,
    To merit bliss by making me despair.   222
    She hath forsworn to love, and in that vow   223
    Do I live dead, that live to tell it now.
BENVOLIO
    Be ruled by me. Forget to think of her.
ROMEO
    O, teach me how I should forget to think!
BENVOLIO
    By giving liberty unto thine eyes:
    Examine other beauties.
ROMEO   'Tis the way
    To call hers, exquisite, in question more.   229
    These happy masks that kiss fair ladies' brows,
    Being black, puts us in mind they hide the fair;
    He that is strucken blind cannot forget
    The precious treasure of his eyesight lost.
    Show me a mistress that is passing fair: 234
    What doth her beauty serve but as a note

169 **Love** Cupid. **view** appearance 170 **in proof** in reality, in experience 171 **view . . . still** sight is blindfolded always. (Love is blind.) 172 **to his will** to what he wants 177 **create** created 181 **Still-waking** continually awake 183 **coz** cousin, kinsman 187–188 **propagate . . . thine** increase by having it, i.e., my own grief, oppressed or made still heavier with your grief on my account. (The image of propagating and pressing is appropriately sexual.) 191 **purged** i.e., of smoke 193 **discreet** judicious, prudent 195 **Soft** i.e., wait a moment 196 **An if** if 199 **sadness** seriousness. **is that** is it whom

201 **sadly** seriously. (But Romeo plays on the word, and on *in sadness*, in the sense of "sorrowfully.") 203 **A word** i.e., *sadly* or *in sadness*—too sad a word, says Romeo, for a melancholy lover 206 **fair** beautiful 207 **fair mark** clear, distinct target 209 **Dian** Diana, huntress and goddess of chastity 210 **proof** armor 212 **stay** submit to 213 **bide** abide, endure 216 **store** wealth. (She will die without children, and therefore her beauty will die with her.) 217 **still** always 218 **sparing** miserliness 219 **starved with** killed by 222 **To . . . despair** i.e., earning her own salvation through chaste living while driving me to the spiritually dangerous state of despair 223 **forsworn to** renounced, repudiated 229 **in question more** even more keenly to mind, into consideration 234 **passing** surpassingly

Where I may read who passed that passing fair?   236
Farewell. Thou canst not teach me to forget.

BENVOLIO
I'll pay that doctrine, or else die in debt.   *Exeunt.* 238

❧

1.2   *Enter Capulet, County Paris, and the Clown [a Servingman].*

CAPULET
But Montague is bound as well as I,   1
In penalty alike, and 'tis not hard, I think,
For men so old as we to keep the peace.

PARIS
Of honorable reckoning are you both,   4
And pity 'tis you lived at odds so long.
But now, my lord, what say you to my suit?

CAPULET
But saying o'er what I have said before: 7
My child is yet a stranger in the world;
She hath not seen the change of fourteen years.
Let two more summers wither in their pride
Ere we may think her ripe to be a bride.

PARIS
Younger than she are happy mothers made.

CAPULET
And too soon marred are those so early made.
The earth hath swallowed all my hopes but she;
She is the hopeful lady of my earth.   15
But woo her, gentle Paris, get her heart;
My will to her consent is but a part;
And, she agreed, within her scope of choice   18
Lies my consent and fair-according voice.   19
This night I hold an old accustomed feast,   20
Whereto I have invited many a guest
Such as I love; and you among the store,   22
One more, most welcome, makes my number more.
At my poor house look to behold this night
Earth-treading stars that make dark heaven light.
Such comfort as do lusty young men feel   26
When well-appareled April on the heel   27
Of limping winter treads, even such delight
Among fresh fennel buds shall you this night   29
Inherit at my house. Hear all, all see,   30
And like her most whose merit most shall be;
Which on more view of many, mine, being one,   32
May stand in number, though in reckoning none.   33

Come, go with me. [*To the Servingman, giving a paper.*] Go, sirrah, trudge about   34
Through fair Verona; find those persons out
Whose names are written there, and to them say,
My house and welcome on their pleasure stay.   37
                     Exit [with Paris].

SERVINGMAN   Find them out whose names are written
here! It is written that the shoemaker should meddle   39
with his yard and the tailor with his last, the fisher   40
with his pencil, and the painter with his nets; but I am   41
sent to find those persons whose names are here writ,   42
and can never find what names the writing person   43
hath here writ. I must to the learned.—In good time!   44

Enter Benvolio and Romeo.

BENVOLIO
Tut, man, one fire burns out another's burning,
   One pain is lessened by another's anguish;   46
Turn giddy, and be holp by backward turning;   47
   One desperate grief cures with another's languish.   48
Take thou some new infection to thy eye,
And the rank poison of the old will die.   50

ROMEO
Your plaintain leaf is excellent for that.   51

BENVOLIO
For what, I pray thee?

ROMEO   For your broken shin.

BENVOLIO   Why, Romeo, art thou mad?

ROMEO
Not mad, but bound more than a madman is;   54
Shut up in prison, kept without my food,
Whipped and tormented and—Good e'en, good
   fellow.   56

SERVINGMAN God gi' good e'en. I pray, sir, can you read?   57

ROMEO
Ay, mine own fortune in my misery.

SERVINGMAN   Perhaps you have learned it without   59
book. But, I pray, can you read anything you see?   60

ROMEO
Ay, if I know the letters and the language.

---

236 passed surpassed   **238 pay that doctrine** i.e., give that instruction. **die in debt** i.e., feel I've failed as a friend
1.2. Location: Verona. A street.
s.d. County Count   **1 bound** legally obligated (to keep the peace) **4 reckoning** estimation, repute   **7 o'er** again   **15 the hopeful . . . earth** i.e., my heir and hope for posterity. (*Earth* includes property and lands.)   **18 she** if she be   **19 according** agreeing   **20 old accustomed** traditional   **22 store** group   **26 lusty** lively   **27 well-appareled** newly clothed in green   **29 fennel** flowering herb thought to have the power of awakening passion   **30 Inherit** possess   **32–33 Which . . . none** i.e., when you have looked over many ladies, my daughter, being one of them, may be numerically counted among the lot, but you will not think her worth your notice. (Capulet refers to the proverbial saying, "one is no number.")

34 sirrah (Customary form of address to servants.)   **37 on . . . stay** wait to serve their pleasure   **39 meddle** (*Meddle* is often sexual in meaning; compare *medlar* at 2.1.35. *Yard* and *pencil*, lines 40–41, are often slang terms for the male sexual organ. But the sexual idea goes nowhere here, as in *last* and *nets*, and may be irrelevant.) **40–41 yard, last, pencil, nets** (The servingman humorously assigns these tools of a trade to the wrong person, to suggest how useless it is for him, an illiterate servant, to be given a written instruction.)   **yard** yardstick.   **last** a shoemaker's form.   **pencil** paint brush   **42–43 find . . . find** locate . . . learn   **44 In good time** i.e., here comes help **46 another's anguish** the anguish of another pain   **47 holp** helped. **backward** reverse   **48 cures . . . languish** is cured by the suffering of a second *grief* or pain   **50 rank** foul   **51 Your** i.e., the kind of thing people talk about. **plantain leaf** herb used for cuts and abrasions, such as a *broken* or bleeding shin. (Romeo undercuts Benvolio's sententiousness by taking his medical metaphor literally, as if curing love were like curing a minor cut.)   **54 bound** (The usual treatment for madness.)   **56 Good e'en** good evening. (Used after noon.)   **57 gi'** give you   **59–60 without book** by memory. (The servingman takes Romeo's flowery response to his simple question as though it were the title of a literary work; his comment also suggests that one can learn misery without knowing how to read.)

SERVINGMAN   Ye say honestly. Rest you merry!   62
                                    [*Going.*]

ROMEO   Stay, fellow, I can read.   *He reads the letter.*
    "Signor Martino and his wife and daughters,
    County Anselme and his beauteous sisters,
    The lady widow of Vitruvio,
    Signor Placentio and his lovely nieces,
    Mercutio and his brother Valentine,
    Mine uncle Capulet, his wife, and daughters,
    My fair niece Rosaline, and Livia,
    Signor Valentio and his cousin Tybalt,
    Lucio and the lively Helena."
    A fair assembly. Whither should they come?   73
SERVINGMAN   Up.
ROMEO   Whither? To supper?
SERVINGMAN   To our house.
ROMEO   Whose house?
SERVINGMAN   My master's.
ROMEO
    Indeed, I should have asked thee that before.
SERVINGMAN   Now I'll tell you without asking. My
    master is the great rich Capulet; and if you be not of
    the house of Montagues, I pray, come and crush a cup   82
    of wine. Rest you merry!   [*Exit.*]
BENVOLIO
    At this same ancient feast of Capulet's   84
    Sups the fair Rosaline whom thou so loves,
    With all the admirèd beauties of Verona.
    Go thither, and with unattainted eye   87
    Compare her face with some that I shall show,
    And I will make thee think thy swan a crow.
ROMEO
    When the devout religion of mine eye
    Maintains such falsehood, then turn tears to fires;   91
    And these who, often drowned, could never die,   92
    Transparent heretics, be burnt for liars!   93
    One fairer than my love? The all-seeing sun
    Ne'er saw her match since first the world begun.
BENVOLIO
    Tut, you saw her fair, none else being by,
    Herself poised with herself in either eye;   97
    But in that crystal scales let there be weighed   98
    Your lady's love against some other maid
    That I will show you shining at this feast,
    And she shall scant show well that now seems best.   101
ROMEO
    I'll go along, no such sight to be shown,
    But to rejoice in splendor of mine own.   [*Exeunt.*]   103

1.3   *Enter Capulet's Wife and Nurse.*

WIFE
    Nurse, where's my daughter? Call her forth to me.
NURSE
    Now, by my maidenhead at twelve year old,
    I bade her come. What, lamb! What, ladybird!   3
    God forbid. Where's this girl? What, Juliet!

                Enter Juliet.

JULIET   How now? Who calls?
NURSE   Your mother.
JULIET
    Madam, I am here. What is your will?
WIFE
    This is the matter.—Nurse, give leave awhile,   8
    We must talk in secret.—Nurse, come back again;
    I have remembered me, thou's hear our counsel.   10
    Thou knowest my daughter's of a pretty age.
NURSE
    Faith, I can tell her age unto an hour.
WIFE
    She's not fourteen.
NURSE   I'll lay fourteen of my teeth—
    And yet, to my teen be it spoken, I have but four—   14
    She's not fourteen. How long is it now
    To Lammastide?
WIFE   A fortnight and odd days.   16
NURSE
    Even or odd, of all days in the year,
    Come Lammas Eve at night shall she be fourteen.
    Susan and she—God rest all Christian souls!—   19
    Were of an age. Well, Susan is with God;
    She was too good for me. But, as I said,
    On Lammas Eve at night shall she be fourteen,
    That shall she, marry, I remember it well.   23
    'Tis since the earthquake now eleven years,
    And she was weaned—I never shall forget it—
    Of all the days of the year, upon that day;
    For I had then laid wormwood to my dug,   27
    Sitting in the sun under the dovehouse wall.
    My lord and you were then at Mantua—
    Nay, I do bear a brain! But, as I said,   30
    When it did taste the wormwood on the nipple
    Of my dug and felt it bitter, pretty fool,   32
    To see it tetchy and fall out wi' th' dug!   33
    "Shake" quoth the dovehouse. 'Twas no need, I
       trow,   34

1.3. Location: Verona. Capulet's house.
3 What (An expression of impatience.)   **ladybird** (This term of affection can also have a wanton suggestion. The Nurse's "God forbid" may be an apology for using such a word or may simply be an expression of petulance or concern.)   **8 give leave** leave us   **10 thou's** thou shalt   **14 teen** sorrow (playing on *teen* and *four* in *fourteen*) **16 Lammastide** the days near August 1   **19 Susan** i.e., the Nurse's own child, who has evidently died   **23 marry** i.e., by the Virgin Mary. (A mild oath.)   **27 wormwood** (A bitter-tasting plant used to wean the child from the *dug* or "teat.")   **30 bear a brain** maintain a keen memory   **32 fool** (A term of endearment here.)   **33 tetchy** fretful   **34 "Shake" . . . dovehouse** i.e., the dovehouse shook.   **trow** believe, assure you

---

62 Rest you merry i.e., farewell. (The servingman can see he is getting nowhere.)   **73 Whither** where   **82 crush** i.e., drink   **84 ancient** customary   **87 unattainted** unbiased   **91 Maintains** upholds **92 these** i.e., these my eyes.   **drowned** i.e., in tears   **93 Transparent** (1) self-evident (2) clear   **97 poised** weighed, balanced   **98 crystal scales** i.e., Romeo's eyes, in which the ladies are to be balanced and compared   **101 scant** scarcely   **103 mine own** i.e., the sight of my own Rosaline

To bid me trudge!   35
And since that time it is eleven years,
For then she could stand high-lone; nay, by the
   rood,   37
She could have run and waddled all about.
For even the day before, she broke her brow,   39
And then my husband—God be with his soul!
'A was a merry man—took up the child.   41
"Yea," quoth he, "dost thou fall upon thy face?
Thou wilt fall backward when thou hast more wit,   43
Wilt thou not, Jule?" and, by my halidom,   44
The pretty wretch left crying and said "Ay."
To see now how a jest shall come about!   46
I warrant, an I should live a thousand years,
I never should forget it. "Wilt thou not, Jule?" quoth
   he,
And, pretty fool, it stinted and said "Ay."   49

WIFE
Enough of this. I pray thee, hold thy peace.

NURSE
Yes, madam. Yet I cannot choose but laugh
To think it should leave crying and say "Ay."
And yet, I warrant, it had upon its brow
A bump as big as a young cockerel's stone—   54
A perilous knock—and it cried bitterly.
"Yea," quoth my husband, "fall'st upon thy face?
Thou wilt fall backward when thou comest to age,
Wilt thou not, Jule?" It stinted and said "Ay."

JULIET
And stint thou too, I pray thee, Nurse, say I.   59

NURSE
Peace, I have done. God mark thee to his grace!
Thou wast the prettiest babe that e'er I nursed.
An I might live to see thee married once,   62
I have my wish.

WIFE
Marry, that "marry" is the very theme
I came to talk of. Tell me, daughter Juliet,
How stands your disposition to be married?   66

JULIET
It is an honor that I dream not of.

NURSE
An honor? Were not I thine only nurse,
I would say thou hadst sucked wisdom from thy
   teat.   69

WIFE
Well, think of marriage now. Younger than you
Here in Verona, ladies of esteem,   71
Are made already mothers. By my count
I was your mother much upon these years   73
That you are now a maid. Thus then in brief:
The valiant Paris seeks you for his love.

NURSE
A man, young lady! Lady, such a man
As all the world—why, he's a man of wax.   77

WIFE
Verona's summer hath not such a flower.

NURSE
Nay, he's a flower, in faith, a very flower.   79

WIFE
What say you? Can you love the gentleman?
This night you shall behold him at our feast.
Read o'er the volume of young Paris' face,
And find delight writ there with beauty's pen;
Examine every married lineament,   84
And see how one another lends content;   85
And what obscured in this fair volume lies
Find written in the margent of his eyes.   87
This precious book of love, this unbound lover,   88
To beautify him, only lacks a cover.   89
The fish lives in the sea, and 'tis much pride   90
For fair without the fair within to hide.   91
That book in many's eyes doth share the glory,   92
That in gold clasps locks in the golden story;   93
So shall you share all that he doth possess
By having him, making yourself no less.

NURSE
No less? Nay, bigger. Women grow by men.   96

WIFE
Speak briefly, can you like of Paris' love?   97

JULIET
I'll look to like, if looking liking move;   98
But no more deep will I endart mine eye   99
Than your consent gives strength to make it fly.

     Enter Servingman.

SERVINGMAN   Madam, the guests are come, supper
served up, you called, my young lady asked for, the
Nurse cursed in the pantry, and everything in extrem-   103
ity. I must hence to wait. I beseech you, follow straight.   104

WIFE
We follow thee. [*Exit Servingman.*] Juliet, the County
   stays.   105

NURSE
Go, girl, seek happy nights to happy days.   *Exeunt.*

     ❖

35 **trudge** be off quickly   37 **high-lone** on her feet, without help.
rood cross   39 **broke her brow** bruised her forehead (by falling)
41 **'A** he   43 **wit** understanding   44 **halidom** a relic or holy thing
46 **come about** come true   49 **stinted** ceased   54 **cockerel's stone**
young rooster's testicle   59 **say I** (With a pun on *said "Ay"* of previous line.)   62 **once** someday   66 **disposition** inclination   69 **thy teat**
the teat that nourished you   71 **esteem** worth, nobility   73 **much
. . . years** at much the same age

77 **a man of wax** such as one would picture in wax, i.e., handsome
79 **Nay** i.e., indeed   84 **married** harmonized.   **lineament** facial feature   85 **content** (1) satisfaction (2) substance   87 **margent** commentary or marginal gloss   88 **unbound** i.e., because not bound in marriage (with a double meaning in the continuing metaphor of an
unbound book)   89 **a cover** i.e., marriage, an embracing wife
90–91 **The fish . . . hide** i.e., the fish has its own suitable environment, and similarly in marriage the fair Juliet (here imagined as a
beautiful book cover "binding" Paris) would suitably enhance Paris'
worth   92–93 **That book . . . story** i.e., in many person's eyes, a
good story is all the more admirable for being handsomely bound.
clasps (1) book fastenings (2) embraces   96 **bigger** i.e., by pregnancy
97 **like of** be pleased with   98 **liking move** may provoke affection
99 **endart mine eye** i.e., let my eyes shoot Love's darts   103 **cursed**
i.e., for not helping with the preparations   104 **straight** at once
105 **County stays** Count (Paris) waits for you

1.4

*Enter Romeo, Mercutio, Benvolio, with five or six
other masquers; torchbearers.*

ROMEO
What, shall this speech be spoke for our excuse? 1
Or shall we on without apology? 2
BENVOLIO
The date is out of such prolixity. 3
We'll have no Cupid hoodwinked with a scarf, 4
Bearing a Tartar's painted bow of lath, 5
Scaring the ladies like a crowkeeper, 6
Nor no without-book prologue, faintly spoke 7
After the prompter, for our entrance;
But let them measure us by what they will, 9
We'll measure them a measure, and be gone. 10
ROMEO
Give me a torch. I am not for this ambling.
Being but heavy, I will bear the light. 12
MERCUTIO
Nay, gentle Romeo, we must have you dance.
ROMEO
Not I, believe me. You have dancing shoes
With nimble soles; I have a soul of lead
So stakes me to the ground I cannot move.
MERCUTIO
You are a lover; borrow Cupid's wings,
And soar with them above a common bound. 18
ROMEO
I am too sore enpiercèd with his shaft 19
To soar with his light feathers, and so bound 20
I cannot bound a pitch above dull woe. 21
Under love's heavy burden do I sink.
MERCUTIO
And, to sink in it, should you burden love—
Too great oppression for a tender thing. 23
ROMEO
Is love a tender thing? It is too rough,
Too rude, too boisterous, and it pricks like thorn.
MERCUTIO
If love be rough with you, be rough with love;
Prick love for pricking, and you beat love down. 28
Give me a case to put my visage in. 29

[*He puts on a mask.*]

A visor for a visor! What care I 30
What curious eye doth quote deformities? 31
Here are the beetle brows shall blush for me.
BENVOLIO
Come, knock and enter, and no sooner in
But every man betake him to his legs. 34
ROMEO
A torch for me. Let wantons light of heart
Tickle the senseless rushes with their heels, 36
For I am proverbed with a grandsire phrase: 37
I'll be a candle holder and look on. 38
The game was ne'er so fair, and I am done. 39
MERCUTIO
Tut, dun's the mouse, the constable's own word. 40
If thou art dun, we'll draw thee from the mire
Of—save your reverence—love, wherein thou
    stickest 42
Up to the ears. Come, we burn daylight, ho! 43
ROMEO
Nay, that's not so.
MERCUTIO   I mean, sir, in delay
We waste our lights in vain, like lamps by day.
Take our good meaning, for our judgment sits 46
Five times in that ere once in our five wits. 47
ROMEO
And we mean well in going to this masque,
But 'tis no wit to go.
MERCUTIO   Why, may one ask? 49
ROMEO
I dreamt a dream tonight.
MERCUTIO   And so did I. 50
ROMEO
Well, what was yours?
MERCUTIO   That dreamers often lie. 51
ROMEO
In bed asleep, while they do dream things true.
MERCUTIO
O, then, I see Queen Mab hath been with you. 53
She is the fairies' midwife, and she comes

1.4. **Location: Verona. A street in the vicinity of Capulet's house.**
1 speech (Masquers were customarily preceded by a messenger or
"presenter" with a set speech of compliment.) **2 on** go on, approach
3 The date . . . prolixity such windy rhetoric is out of fashion **4 Cupid** i.e., messenger or "presenter," probably a boy, disguised as Cupid. **hoodwinked** blindfolded **5 Tartar's . . . bow** (Tartars' bows,
shorter and more curved than the English longbow, were thought to
have resembled the old Roman bow with which Cupid was pictured.)
lath flimsy wood **6 crowkeeper** scarecrow **7 without-book** memorized **9 measure** judge **10 measure . . . measure** mete out or tread
a dance for them **12 heavy** (1) sad (2) the opposite of *light* (as at
1.1.137) **18 common** ordinary. **bound** (1) leap in the dance (2)
limit **19 sore** sorely (with pun on *soar;* see also pun on *soles* and
soul in line 15) **20 bound** confined (with play in line 21 on the
sense of "leap") **21 pitch** height. (A term from falconry for the highest point of a hawk's flight.) **23 to sink . . . love** i.e., if you should
sink in love, you would prove a burden to it and to your love partner
28 Prick . . . down i.e., if love gets rough, fight back (but with
bawdy suggestion of *pricking* as a way to satisfy desire and cause it to
subside) **29 case** mask

30 A visor . . . visor i.e., a mask for an ugly masklike face **31 quote**
take notice of **34 to his legs** i.e., to dancing **36 senseless** lacking
sensation. **rushes** (Used for floor covering.) **37 proverbed . . .
phrase** furnished with an old proverb **38 candle holder** i.e., onlooker. (Alludes to the proverb, "A good candle holder is a good
gamester," i.e., he who merely looks on can't get in trouble.)
39 The game . . . done (Another proverbial notion, that it is wisest to
quit when the gambling is at its best.) **40 dun's the mouse** (A common phrase usually taken to mean "keep still." *Dun,* gray-brown
color, plays on *done,* "done for." *Dun* also alludes to a Christmas
game, "Dun [the gray-brown horse] is in the mire," in which a heavy
log, representing a horse, was hauled out of an imaginary mire by the
players.) **constable's own word** (A constable might caution his men
to keep still; Mercutio mocks Romeo's caution as lovesickness.)
42 save your reverence (An apology for an improper expression,
which Mercutio supposes "love" to be.) **43 burn daylight** i.e., waste
time. (But Romeo quibbles, protesting that it is not literally daytime.)
46–47 Take . . . wits i.e., try to understand what I intend to say, relying on common sense rather than on the exercise of wit, or the testimony of the five senses **49 wit** wisdom (playing on *wits* in line 47;
mean in line 48 plays on *meaning* in line 46) **50 tonight** last night
51 lie tell falsehoods. (But Mercutio answers with a pun on "lie down
in bed.") **53 Queen Mab** (Possibly a name of Celtic origin for the
Fairy Queen.)

In shape no bigger than an agate stone   55
On the forefinger of an alderman,   56
Drawn with a team of little atomi   57
Over men's noses as they lie asleep.
Her chariot is an empty hazelnut,
Made by the joiner squirrel or old grub,   60
Time out o' mind the fairies' coachmakers.
Her wagon spokes made of long spinners' legs,   62
The cover of the wings of grasshoppers,
Her traces of the smallest spider web,
Her collars of the moonshine's watery beams,
Her whip of cricket's bone, the lash of film,   66
Her wagoner a small gray-coated gnat,   67
Not half so big as a round little worm   68
Pricked from the lazy finger of a maid.
And in this state she gallops night by night   70
Through lovers' brains, and then they dream of love;
O'er courtiers' knees, that dream on curtsies straight;   72
O'er lawyers' fingers, who straight dream on fees;
O'er ladies' lips, who straight on kisses dream,
Which oft the angry Mab with blisters plagues
Because their breaths with sweetmeats tainted are.   76
Sometimes she gallops o'er a courtier's nose,
And then dreams he of smelling out a suit.   78
And sometimes comes she with a tithe-pig's tail   79
Tickling a parson's nose as 'a lies asleep;
Then dreams he of another benefice.   81
Sometimes she driveth o'er a soldier's neck,
And then dreams he of cutting foreign throats,
Of breaches, ambuscadoes, Spanish blades,   84
Of healths five fathom deep, and then anon   85
Drums in his ear, at which he starts and wakes,
And being thus frighted swears a prayer or two
And sleeps again. This is that very Mab
That plats the manes of horses in the night,   89
And bakes the elflocks in foul sluttish hairs,   90
Which once untangled much misfortune bodes.
This is the hag, when maids lie on their backs,
That presses them and learns them first to bear,   93
Making them women of good carriage.   94
This is she—

ROMEO   Peace, peace, Mercutio, peace!
Thou talk'st of nothing.
MERCUTIO   True, I talk of dreams,
Which are the children of an idle brain,
Begot of nothing but vain fantasy,   98
Which is as thin of substance as the air,
And more inconstant than the wind, who woos
Even now the frozen bosom of the north,
And being angered, puffs away from thence,
Turning his side to the dew-dropping south.
BENVOLIO
This wind you talk of blows us from ourselves.   104
Supper is done, and we shall come too late.
ROMEO
I fear, too early; for my mind misgives   106
Some consequence yet hanging in the stars
Shall bitterly begin his fearful date   108
With this night's revels, and expire the term   109
Of a despisèd life closed in my breast
By some vile forfeit of untimely death.
But He that hath the steerage of my course
Direct my suit! On, lusty gentlemen.   113
BENVOLIO   Strike, drum.   *They march about the stage,* 114
                                  and [*retire to one side*].

1.5   *Servingmen come forth with napkins.*

FIRST SERVINGMAN Where's Potpan, that he helps not to
take away? He shift a trencher? He scrape a trencher? 2
SECOND SERVINGMAN   When good manners shall lie all
in one or two men's hands, and they unwashed too,
'tis a foul thing.
FIRST SERVINGMAN   Away with the joint stools, remove 6
the court cupboard, look to the plate. Good thou, save 7
me a piece of marchpane, and, as thou loves me, let 8
the porter let in Susan Grindstone and Nell. [*Exit
Second Servingman.*] Anthony and Potpan!

[*Enter two more Servingmen.*]

THIRD SERVINGMAN   Ay, boy, ready.
FIRST SERVINGMAN   You are looked for and called for,
asked for and sought for, in the great chamber.
FOURTH SERVINGMAN   We cannot be here and there
too. Cheerly, boys! Be brisk awhile, and the longest 15
liver take all.   *Exeunt.* 16

Enter [*Capulet and family and*] *all the guests and
gentlewomen to the masquers.*

55 agate stone (Precious stone often carved with diminutive figures
and set in a ring.) **56 alderman** member of the municipal council
57 atomi tiny creatures (atoms) **60 joiner** furniture maker. **grub** insect larva (which bores holes in nuts) **62 spinners'** spiders' **66 film**
gossamer thread **67 wagoner** chariot driver **68 worm** (Alludes to
an ancient superstition that "worms breed in the fingers of the idle.")
70 state pomp, dignity **72 curtsies** bows, obeisances. **straight** immediately **76 sweetmeats** candies or candied preserves **78 smelling
. . . suit** i.e., finding a petitioner who will pay for the use of his influence at court **79 tithe-pig** pig given to the parson in lieu of money
as the parishioner's tithing, or granting of a tenth **81 benefice** ecclesiastical living **84 breaches** opening of gaps in fortifications. **ambuscadoes** ambushes. **Spanish blades** swords from Toledo, where
the best swords were made **85 healths** toasts. **five fathom deep** a
very deep or tall drink **89 plats . . . horses** (Alludes to the familiar
superstition that "witches' stirrups," tangles in the manes of horses.)
90 elflocks tangles. (Thought superstitiously to be the work of elves,
who would seek revenge if the elflocks were untangled.) **93 learns**
teaches **94 good carriage** (1) commendable deportment (2) skill in
bearing the weight of men in sexual intercourse (3) able subsequently
to carry a child

98 vain fantasy empty imagination **104 from ourselves** from our
plans **106 misgives** fears **108 date** appointed time **109 expire**
bring to an end **113 lusty** lively **114 drum** drummer
1.5. Location: The action, continuous from the previous scene, is
now imaginatively transferred to a hall in Capulet's house.
2 take away clear the table. **trencher** wooden dish or plate. **6 joint
stools** stools of which the parts are fitted by a joiner or furniture
maker **7 court cupboard** sideboard. **plate** silverware. **8 marchpane**
cake made from sugar and almonds, marzipan **15–16 the longest
. . . all** (A proverb, "the survivor takes all," here used to advocate
seizing the moment of pleasure.)

CAPULET [*to the masquers*]
    Welcome, gentlemen! Ladies that have their toes
    Unplagued with corns will walk a bout with you.   18
    Ah, my mistresses, which of you all
    Will now deny to dance? She that makes dainty,   20
    She, I'll swear, hath corns. Am I come near ye now?   21
    Welcome, gentlemen! I have seen the day
    That I have worn a visor and could tell
    A whispering tale in a fair lady's ear
    Such as would please. 'Tis gone, 'tis gone, 'tis gone.
    You are welcome, gentlemen! Come, musicians, play.
                        Music plays, and they dance.
    A hall, a hall! Give room! And foot it, girls.   27
    [*To Servingmen.*] More light, you knaves, and turn
        the tables up,   28
    And quench the fire; the room is grown too hot.
    [*To his cousin.*] Ah, sirrah, this unlooked-for sport
        comes well.   30
    Nay, sit, nay, sit, good cousin Capulet,   31
    For you and I are past our dancing days.
    How long is 't now since last yourself and I
    Were in a mask?
SECOND CAPULET   By 'r Lady, thirty years.
CAPULET
    What, man? 'Tis not so much, 'tis not so much;
    'Tis since the nuptial of Lucentio,
    Come Pentecost as quickly as it will,   37
    Some five-and-twenty years, and then we masked.
SECOND CAPULET
    'Tis more, 'tis more. His son is elder, sir;
    His son is thirty.
CAPULET   Will you tell me that?
    His son was but a ward two years ago.   41
ROMEO [*to a Servingman*]
    What lady's that which doth enrich the hand
    Of yonder knight?
SERVINGMAN   I know not, sir.
ROMEO
    O, she doth teach the torches to burn bright!
    It seems she hangs upon the cheek of night
    As a rich jewel in an Ethiop's ear—
    Beauty too rich for use, for earth too dear!   48
    So shows a snowy dove trooping with crows   49
    As yonder lady o'er her fellows shows.
    The measure done, I'll watch her place of stand,   51

    And, touching hers, make blessèd my rude hand.   52
    Did my heart love till now? Forswear it, sight!   53
    For I ne'er saw true beauty till this night.
TYBALT
    This, by his voice, should be a Montague.
    Fetch me my rapier, boy. What dares the slave   56
    Come hither, covered with an antic face,   57
    To fleer and scorn at our solemnity?   58
    Now, by the stock and honor of my kin,
    To strike him dead I hold it not a sin.
CAPULET
    Why, how now, kinsman? Wherefore storm you so?
TYBALT
    Uncle, this is a Montague, our foe,
    A villain that is hither come in spite   63
    To scorn at our solemnity this night.
CAPULET
    Young Romeo is it?
TYBALT   'Tis he, that villain Romeo.
CAPULET
    Content thee, gentle coz, let him alone.
    'A bears him like a portly gentleman,   67
    And, to say truth, Verona brags of him
    To be a virtuous and well governed youth.
    I would not for the wealth of all this town
    Here in my house do him disparagement.
    Therefore be patient; take no note of him.
    It is my will, the which if thou respect,
    Show a fair presence and put off these frowns,   74
    An ill-beseeming semblance for a feast.   75
TYBALT
    It fits when such a villain is a guest.
    I'll not endure him.
CAPULET   He shall be endured.
    What, goodman boy? I say he shall. Go to!   78
    Am I the master here, or you? Go to.
    You'll not endure him! God shall mend my soul,
    You'll make a mutiny among my guests!   81
    You will set cock-a-hoop! You'll be the man!   82
TYBALT
    Why, uncle, 'tis a shame.
CAPULET   Go to, go to,
    You are a saucy boy. Is 't so, indeed?
    This trick may chance to scathe you. I know what,   85
    You must contrary me. Marry, 'tis time.—   86
    Well said, my hearts!—You are a princox, go.   87
    Be quiet, or—More light, more light! —For shame!
    I'll make you quiet.—What, cheerly, my hearts!

---

18 walk a bout dance a turn **20 makes dainty** seems coyly reluctant (to dance) **21 Am . . . now** have I hit a sensitive point, struck home **27 A hall** i.e., clear the hall for dancing **28 turn the tables up** (Tables were probably made of hinged leaves and placed on trestles. They were put aside for dancing.) **30 sirrah** (Normally used in addressing social inferiors. Perhaps Capulet uses a jesting tone toward his kinsman or possibly addresses himself.) **unlooked-for sport** i.e., arrival of the masquers, providing more men for the dancing **31 cousin** (*Cousin* often means "kinsman"; at 1.2.69, "Mine uncle Capulet" is named on the invitation list.) **37 Pentecost** seventh Sunday after Easter (and never as late as mid-July, two weeks before Lammas or August 1, when, according to 1.3.16, the play takes place; a seeming inconsistency) **41 a ward** a minor under guardianship **48 dear** precious **49 shows** appears **51 The measure done** when this dance is over. **her place of stand** where she stands

52 hers i.e., her hand. **rude** rough **53 Forswear it** deny any previous oath **56 What** how **57 antic face** grotesque mask **58 fleer** jeer. **solemnity** time-honored festivity **63 spite** malice **67 portly** of good deportment **74 presence** demeanor **75 semblance** facial expression **78 goodman boy** (A belittling term for Tybalt; *Goodman* applied to one below the rank of gentleman but still of some substance, like a wealthy farmer.) **Go to** (An expression of irritation.) **81 mutiny** disturbance **82 You . . . cock-a-hoop** i.e., you will behave recklessly, abandon all restraint. **be the man** play the big man **85 scathe** harm. **what** what I'm doing, or what I'll do **86 contrary** oppose, thwart. **'tis time** i.e., it's time you were taught a lesson **87 Well said** well done. (Said to the dancers.) **princox** saucy boy

TYBALT
Patience perforce with willful choler meeting   90
Makes my flesh tremble in their different greeting.   91
I will withdraw. But this intrusion shall,
Now seeming sweet, convert to bitterest gall.   *Exit.*
ROMEO [*to Juliet*]
a If I profane with my unworthiest hand   94
b   This holy shrine, the gentle sin is this: 95
a My lips, two blushing pilgrims, ready stand
b   To smooth that rough touch with a tender kiss.
JULIET
c Good pilgrim, you do wrong your hand too much,
d   Which mannerly devotion shows in this;   99
c For saints have hands that pilgrims' hands do touch, 100
d   And palm to palm is holy palmers' kiss.   101
ROMEO
e Have not saints lips, and holy palmers too?
JULIET
f   Ay, pilgrim, lips that they must use in prayer.
ROMEO
e O, then, dear saint, let lips do what hands do.
f   They pray; grant thou, lest faith turn to despair. 105
JULIET
Saints do not move, though grant for prayers' sake.   106
ROMEO
Then move not, while my prayer's effect I take.   107
                       [*He kisses her.*]
Thus from my lips, by thine, my sin is purged.
JULIET
Then have my lips the sin that they have took.
ROMEO
Sin from my lips? O trespass sweetly urged!
Give me my sin again.   [*He kisses her.*]
JULIET   You kiss by th' book.   111
NURSE [*approaching*]
Madam, your mother craves a word with you.
                       [*Juliet retires.*]
ROMEO
What is her mother?
NURSE   Marry, bachelor,   113
Her mother is the lady of the house,
And a good lady, and a wise and virtuous.
I nursed her daughter that you talked withal.   116
I tell you, he that can lay hold of her
Shall have the chinks.
ROMEO [*aside*]   Is she a Capulet?   118
O dear account! My life is my foe's debt.   119

90 Patience perforce patience upon compulsion. **willful choler** passionate anger   **91 different greeting** antagonistic opposition **94–107**
(These lines are in the form of a Shakespearean sonnet; they are followed by a quatrain.) **95 shrine** i.e., Juliet's hand   **99 mannerly**
proper   **100 saints** i.e., images of saints that are venerated by pilgrims   **101 palmers** pilgrims who have been to the Holy Land and
have brought back a palm (with a pun on the palm of the hand)
105 grant thou you must answer their prayers   **106 move** take the
initiative.   **grant** they grant (through intercession with God)
107 move (Romeo quibbles on Juliet's word in the common sense of
"change place or position.")   **111 again** back again.   **by th' book** by
the rule, expertly   **113 What** who.   **Marry** i.e., by the Virgin Mary.
bachelor young man   **116 withal** with   **118 the chinks** i.e., plenty of
money   **119 dear account** heavy reckoning.   **my foe's debt** due to
my foe, at his mercy

BENVOLIO [*approaching*]
Away, begone! The sport is at the best.   120
ROMEO
Ay, so I fear; the more is my unrest.
                 [*The masquers prepare to leave.*]
CAPULET
Nay, gentlemen, prepare not to be gone.
We have a trifling foolish banquet towards.   123
                 [*One whispers in his ear.*]
Is it e'en so? Why, then, I thank you all.
I thank you, honest gentlemen. Good night.   125
More torches here! Come on then, let's to bed.   126
[*To his cousin.*] Ah, sirrah, by my fay, it waxes late. 127
I'll to my rest.
        [*All proceed to leave but Juliet and the Nurse.*]
JULIET
Come hither, Nurse. What is yond gentleman?
NURSE
The son and heir of old Tiberio.
JULIET
What's he that now is going out of door?
NURSE
Marry, that, I think, be young Petruchio.
JULIET
What's he that follows here, that would not dance?
NURSE   I know not.
JULIET
Go ask his name. [*The Nurse goes.*] If he be married,
My grave is like to be my wedding bed.   136
NURSE [*returning*]
His name is Romeo, and a Montague,
The only son of your great enemy.
JULIET
My only love sprung from my only hate!
Too early seen unknown, and known too late!
Prodigious birth of love it is to me   141
That I must love a loathèd enemy.
NURSE
What's tis? What's tis?
JULIET   A rhyme I learned even now 143
Of one I danced withal.   *One calls within* "Juliet."
NURSE   Anon, anon!   144
Come, let's away. The strangers all are gone. *Exeunt.*

❖

2.0   [*Enter*] Chorus.
CHORUS
Now old desire doth in his deathbed lie,   1
And young affection gapes to be his heir;   2

120 The sport . . . best i.e., it is time to leave. (Refers to the proverb,
"When play is at the best, it is time to leave," as at 1.4.39.)
123 foolish banquet towards insignificant light refreshment just ready
125 honest honorable   **126 torches** i.e., to light the guests as they
leave   **127 fay** faith   **136 like** likely   **141 Prodigious** ominous
143 tis this. (Dialect pronunciation.)   **144 Anon** i.e., we're coming
2.0. Chorus.
1–14 (This chorus is a sonnet.)   **2 gapes** waits open-mouthed

That fair for which love groaned for and would die,   3
   With tender Juliet matched, is now not fair.   4
Now Romeo is beloved and loves again,
   Alike bewitchèd by the charm of looks;   6
But to his foe supposed he must complain,   7
   And she steal love's sweet bait from fearful hooks.   8
Being held a foe, he may not have access
   To breathe such vows as lovers use to swear;   10
And she as much in love, her means much less
   To meet her new-belovèd anywhere.
But passion lends them power, time means, to
   meet,   13
Temp'ring extremities with extreme sweet.   [Exit.]   14

✿

2.1   *Enter Romeo alone.*

ROMEO
Can I go forward when my heart is here?   1
Turn back, dull earth, and find thy center out.   2
                    [*Romeo retires.*]

Enter Benvolio with Mercutio.

BENVOLIO
Romeo! My cousin Romeo! Romeo!
MERCUTIO   He is wise
And, on my life, hath stolen him home to bed.
BENVOLIO
He ran this way and leapt this orchard wall.
Call, good Mercutio.
MERCUTIO   Nay, I'll conjure too.   7
Romeo! Humors! Madman! Passion! Lover!   8
Appear thou in the likeness of a sigh.
Speak but one rhyme, and I am satisfied;
Cry but "Ay me!" Pronounce but "love" and
   "dove."
Speak to my gossip Venus one fair word,   12
One nickname for her purblind son and heir,   13
Young Abraham Cupid, he that shot so trim   14
When King Cophetua loved the beggar maid.—   15
He heareth not, he stirreth not, he moveth not;
The ape is dead, and I must conjure him.—   17
I conjure thee by Rosaline's bright eyes,
By her high forehead and her scarlet lip,
By her fine foot, straight leg, and quivering thigh,

And the demesnes that there adjacent lie,   21
That in thy likeness thou appear to us.
BENVOLIO
An if he hear thee, thou wilt anger him.   23
MERCUTIO
This cannot anger him. 'Twould anger him
To raise a spirit in his mistress' circle   25
Of some strange nature, letting it there stand   26
Till she had laid it and conjured it down;   27
That were some spite. My invocation   28
Is fair and honest; in his mistress' name
I conjure only but to raise up him.
BENVOLIO
Come, he hath hid himself among these trees
To be consorted with the humorous night.   32
Blind is his love, and best befits the dark.
MERCUTIO
If love be blind, love cannot hit the mark.
Now will he sit under a medlar tree   35
And wish his mistress were that kind of fruit
As maids call medlars when they laugh alone.
O, Romeo, that she were, O, that she were
An open-arse, and thou a poppering pear!   39
Romeo, good night. I'll to my truckle bed;   40
This field bed is too cold for me to sleep.
Come, shall we go?
BENVOLIO   Go, then, for 'tis in vain
To seek him here that means not to be found.
             Exit [*with Mercutio*].

2.2

ROMEO [*coming forward*]
He jests at scars that never felt a wound.   1
    [*A light appears above, as at Juliet's window.*]
But soft, what light through yonder window breaks?
It is the east, and Juliet is the sun.
Arise, fair sun, and kill the envious moon,
Who is already sick and pale with grief

21 demesnes regions (with bawdy suggestion as to what is adjacent to the thighs; bawdy puns on terms of conjuration continue in *raise, spirit*, i.e., "phallus" or "semen," *circle, stand, laid it, raise up*) **23 An if** **25 circle** (1) conjuring circle (2) vagina **26 strange** belonging to another person (with suggestion of a rival possessing Rosaline sexually) **27 laid it** (1) laid the spirit to rest (2) provided sexual satisfaction leading to cessation of erection **28 were** would be. **spite** injury, vexation **32 consorted** associated. **humorous** moist; also, influenced by humor or mood **35, 39 medlar, poppering** (Fruits used as slang terms for the sexual organs, female and male, respectively. The medlar was edible only when partly decayed; the poppering pear, taking its name from *Poperinghe* in Flanders, had a phallic shape; the sound of its name is also suggestive.) **39 open-arse** (A name for the *medlar*, making explicit the sexual metaphor.) **40 truckle bed** a bed on casters to be rolled under a standing bed **2.2. Location: The action, continuous from the previous scene, is now imaginatively transferred to inside Capulet's orchard. A rhymed couplet links the two scenes. Romeo has been hiding from his friends as though concealed by the orchard wall. He speaks at once and then turns to observe Juliet's window, which is probably in the gallery above, rearstage.**
1 s.d. A light appears (Some editors assume that Juliet is visible at line 1.)

3 fair beauty, i.e., Rosaline **4 matched** compared **6 Alike** i.e., equally with Juliet **7 foe supposed** i.e., Juliet, a Capulet; also, his opposite number in the war of love. **complain** offer his love plaint **8 she steal** she must steal. **fearful** threatening **10 use** are accustomed **13 time means** time lends them means **14 Temp'ring extremities** mitigating the hardships. **sweet** sweetness, pleasure **2.1. Location: Verona. Outside of Capulet's walled orchard.**
1 forward i.e., away **2 dull earth** i.e., Romeo's body. **center** i.e., Juliet. (The figure of speech is that of humankind as a microcosm or little world.) **7 conjure** raise him with magical incantation **8 Humors** moods **12 gossip** crony **13 purblind** dim-sighted **14 Young Abraham** i.e., one who is young and yet, like the Biblical Abraham, old; Cupid was paradoxically the youngest and the oldest of the gods **15 King Cophetua** (In an old ballad, the King falls in love with a beggar maid and makes her his queen.) **17 ape** (Used as a term of endearment.)

That thou her maid art far more fair than she.   6
Be not her maid, since she is envious;
Her vestal livery is but sick and green   8
And none but fools do wear it. Cast it off.
                    [*Juliet is visible at her window.*]
It is my lady, O, it is my love.
O, that she knew she were!
She speaks, yet she says nothing. What of that?
Her eye discourses. I will answer it.
I am too bold. 'Tis not to me she speaks.
Two of the fairest stars in all the heaven,
Having some business, do entreat her eyes
To twinkle in their spheres till they return.   17
What if her eyes were there, they in her head?   18
The brightness of her cheek would shame those
     stars
As daylight doth a lamp; her eyes in heaven
Would through the airy region stream so bright   21
That birds would sing and think it were not night.
See how she leans her cheek upon her hand!
O, that I were a glove upon that hand,
That I might touch that cheek!
JULIET   Ay me!
ROMEO   She speaks.
     O, speak again, bright angel, for thou art
     As glorious to this night, being o'er my head,
     As is a wingèd messenger of heaven
     Unto the white-upturnèd wondering eyes   29
     Of mortals that fall back to gaze on him
     When he bestrides the lazy puffing clouds
     And sails upon the bosom of the air.
JULIET [*to herself*]
     O Romeo, Romeo, wherefore art thou Romeo?   33
     Deny thy father and refuse thy name!
     Or, if thou wilt not, be but sworn my love,
     And I'll no longer be a Capulet.
ROMEO [*aside*]
     Shall I hear more, or shall I speak at this?
JULIET
     'Tis but thy name that is my enemy;
     Thou art thyself, though not a Montague.   39
     What's Montague? It is nor hand, nor foot,   40
     Nor arm, nor face, nor any other part
     Belonging to a man. O, be some other name!
     What's in a name? That which we call a rose
     By any other word would smell as sweet;
     So Romeo would, were he not Romeo called,
     Retain that dear perfection which he owes   46
     Without that title. Romeo, doff thy name,   47
     And for thy name, which is no part of thee,   48

Take all myself.
ROMEO   I take thee at thy word!
     Call me but love, and I'll be new baptized;
     Henceforth I never will be Romeo.
JULIET
     What man art thou that, thus bescreened in night,   52
     So stumblest on my counsel?
ROMEO   By a name   53
     I know not how to tell thee who I am.
     My name, dear saint, is hateful to myself,
     Because it is an enemy to thee;
     Had I it written, I would tear the word.
JULIET
     My ears have yet not drunk a hundred words
     Of thy tongue's uttering, yet I know the sound:
     Art thou not Romeo and a Montague?
ROMEO
     Neither, fair maid, if either thee dislike.   61
JULIET
     How camest thou hither, tell me, and wherefore?
     The orchard walls are high and hard to climb,
     And the place death, considering who thou art,
     If any of my kinsmen find thee here.
ROMEO
     With love's light wings did I o'erperch these walls,   66
     For stony limits cannot hold love out,
     And what love can do, that dares love attempt;
     Therefore thy kinsmen are no stop to me.
JULIET
     If they do see thee, they will murder thee.
ROMEO
     Alack, there lies more peril in thine eye
     Than twenty of their swords. Look thou but sweet,
     And I am proof against their enmity.   73
JULIET
     I would not for the world they saw thee here.
ROMEO
     I have night's cloak to hide me from their eyes;
     And but thou love me, let them find me here.   76
     My life were better ended by their hate
     Than death proroguèd, wanting of thy love.   78
JULIET
     By whose direction found'st thou out this place?
ROMEO
     By love, that first did prompt me to inquire.
     He lent me counsel, and I lent him eyes.
     I am no pilot; yet, wert thou as far
     As that vast shore washed with the farthest sea,
     I should adventure for such merchandise.
JULIET
     Thou knowest the mask of night is on my face,
     Else would a maiden blush bepaint my cheek
     For that which thou hast heard me speak tonight.
     Fain would I dwell on form—fain, fain deny   88
     What I have spoke; but farewell compliment!   89

6 maid i.e., votary of Diana, goddess of the moon and patroness of
virgins 8 Her vestal livery the uniform of Diana's chaste votaries.
sick and green (Suggesting the pallor of moonlight, as well as anemia
or *greensickness* [see 3.5.156], to which teenage girls were susceptible.) 17 spheres transparent concentric shells supposed to carry the
heavenly bodies with them in their revolution around the earth
18 there i.e., in the spheres 21 stream shine 29 white-upturnèd
looking upward so that the whites of the eyes are visible 33 wherefore why 39 though not a Montague i.e., even if you were not a
Montague 40 nor hand neither hand 46 owes owns 47 doff cast
off 48 for in exchange for

52 bescreened concealed 53 counsel secret thought 61 thee dislike displeases you 66 o'erperch fly over 73 proof protected
76 but unless 78 proroguèd postponed. wanting of lacking
88 Fain gladly. dwell on form preserve the proper formalities
89 compliment etiquette, convention

Dost thou love me? I know thou wilt say "Ay,"
And I will take thy word. Yet if thou swear'st
Thou mayst prove false. At lovers' perjuries,
They say, Jove laughs. O gentle Romeo,
If thou dost love, pronounce it faithfully.
Or if thou thinkest I am too quickly won,
I'll frown and be perverse and say thee nay,
So thou wilt woo, but else not for the world.   97
In truth, fair Montague, I am too fond,   98
And therefore thou mayst think my havior light.   99
But trust me, gentleman, I'll prove more true
Than those that have more cunning to be strange.   101
I should have been more strange, I must confess,
But that thou overheard'st, ere I was ware,   103
My true-love passion. Therefore pardon me,
And not impute this yielding to light love,
Which the dark night hath so discoverèd.   106

ROMEO
Lady, by yonder blessèd moon I vow,
That tips with silver all these fruit-tree tops—

JULIET
O, swear not by the moon, th' inconstant moon,
That monthly changes in her circled orb,   110
Lest that thy love prove likewise variable.

ROMEO
What shall I swear by?

JULIET   Do not swear at all;
Or, if thou wilt, swear by thy gracious self,
Which is the god of my idolatry,
And I'll believe thee.

ROMEO   If my heart's dear love—

JULIET
Well, do not swear. Although I joy in thee,
I have no joy of this contract tonight.
It is too rash, too unadvised, too sudden,   117
Too like the lightning, which doth cease to be   118
Ere one can say it lightens. Sweet, good night!
This bud of love, by summer's ripening breath,
May prove a beauteous flower when next we meet.
Good night, good night! As sweet repose and rest   123
Come to thy heart as that within my breast!

ROMEO
O, wilt thou leave me so unsatisfied?

JULIET
What satisfaction canst thou have tonight?

ROMEO
Th' exchange of thy love's faithful vow for mine.

JULIET
I gave thee mine before thou didst request it;
And yet I would it were to give again.   129

ROMEO
Wouldst thou withdraw it? For what purpose, love?

JULIET
But to be frank and give it thee again.   131

And yet I wish but for the thing I have.
My bounty is as boundless as the sea,
My love as deep; the more I give to thee,
The more I have, for both are infinite.
                                    [The Nurse calls within.]
I hear some noise within. Dear love, adieu!—
Anon, good Nurse!—Sweet Montague, be true.
Stay but a little; I will come again.   [Exit, above.]

ROMEO
O blessèd, blessèd night! I am afeard,
Being in night, all this is but a dream,
Too flattering-sweet to be substantial.

                    [Enter Juliet, above.]

JULIET
Three words, dear Romeo, and good night indeed.
If that thy bent of love be honorable,   143
Thy purpose marriage, send me word tomorrow,
By one that I'll procure to come to thee,
Where and what time thou wilt perform the rite,
And all my fortunes at thy foot I'll lay
And follow thee my lord throughout the world.

NURSE [within]   Madam!

JULIET
I come, anon.—But if thou meanest not well,
I do beseech thee—

NURSE [within]   Madam!

JULIET   By and by, I come—   151
To cease thy strife and leave me to my grief.   152
Tomorrow will I send.

ROMEO   So thrive my soul—

JULIET   A thousand times good night!   [Exit, above.]

ROMEO
A thousand times the worse, to want thy light.
Love goes toward love as schoolboys from their
    books,
But love from love, toward school with heavy looks.
                                    [He starts to leave.]

            Enter Juliet [above] again.

JULIET
Hist! Romeo, hist! O, for a falconer's voice,
To lure this tassel-gentle back again!   160
Bondage is hoarse and may not speak aloud,   161
Else would I tear the cave where Echo lies   162
And make her airy tongue more hoarse than mine
With repetition of "My Romeo!"

ROMEO
It is my soul that calls upon my name.
How silver-sweet sound lovers' tongues by night,
Like softest music to attending ears!

JULIET
Romeo!

---

97 So as long as, if only. else otherwise 98 fond infatuated
99 havior light behavior frivolous 101 strange reserved, aloof, modest 103 ware aware 106 Which i.e., which yielding. discoverèd
revealed 110 orb i.e., sphere; see above, line 17 117 contract exchanging of vows 118 unadvised unconsidered 123 As may just as
129 were were available 131 frank liberal, bounteous

143 bent purpose, inclination 151 By and by immediately
152 strife striving 160 tassel-gentle tercel gentle, the male of the
goshawk 161 Bondage is hoarse i.e., in confinement one can speak
only in a loud whisper 162 tear pierce (with noise). Echo (In Book
3 of Ovid's Metamorphoses, Echo, rejected by Narcissus, pines away
in lonely caves until only her voice is left.)

ROMEO   My nyas?

JULIET   What o'clock tomorrow   168
Shall I send to thee?

ROMEO   By the hour of nine.

JULIET
I will not fail. 'Tis twenty years till then.—
I have forgot why I did call thee back.

ROMEO
Let me stand here till thou remember it.

JULIET
I shall forget, to have thee still stand there,   173
Remembering how I love thy company.

ROMEO
And I'll still stay, to have thee still forget,
Forgetting any other home but this.

JULIET
'Tis almost morning. I would have thee gone—
And yet no farther than a wanton's bird,   178
That lets it hop a little from his hand,
Like a poor prisoner in his twisted gyves,   180
And with a silken thread plucks it back again,
So loving-jealous of his liberty.   182

ROMEO
I would I were thy bird.

JULIET   Sweet, so would I.
Yet I should kill thee with much cherishing.
Good night, good night! Parting is such sweet
    sorrow
That I shall say good night till it be morrow.
                                      [*Exit, above.*]

ROMEO
Sleep dwell upon thine eyes, peace in thy breast!
Would I were sleep and peace, so sweet to rest!
Hence will I to my ghostly friar's close cell,   189
His help to crave, and my dear hap to tell.   *Exit.* 190

❧

2.3   *Enter Friar [Laurence] alone, with a basket.*

FRIAR LAURENCE
The gray-eyed morn smiles on the frowning night,
Check'ring the eastern clouds with streaks of light,
And fleckled darkness like a drunkard reels   3
From forth day's path and Titan's fiery wheels.   4
Now, ere the sun advance his burning eye,   5
The day to cheer and night's dank dew to dry,
I must up-fill this osier cage of ours   7
With baleful weeds and precious-juicèd flowers.   8
The earth that's nature's mother is her tomb;
What is her burying grave, that is her womb;
And from her womb children of divers kind
We sucking on her natural bosom find,

Many for many virtues excellent,
None but for some, and yet all different.   14
O, mickle is the powerful grace that lies   15
In plants, herbs, stones, and their true qualities.   16
For naught so vile that on the earth doth live   17
But to the earth some special good doth give;
Nor aught so good but, strained from that fair use,   19
Revolts from true birth, stumbling on abuse.
Virtue itself turns vice, being misapplied,
And vice sometime's by action dignified.

        Enter Romeo.

Within the infant rind of this weak flower
Poison hath residence and medicine power:
For this, being smelt, with that part cheers each
    part;   25
Being tasted, stays all senses with the heart.   26
Two such opposèd kings encamp them still   27
In man as well as herbs—grace and rude will;
And where the worser is predominant,
Full soon the canker death eats up that plant.   30

ROMEO
Good morrow, Father.

FRIAR LAURENCE   Benedicite!   31
What early tongue so sweet saluteth me?
Young son, it argues a distempered head   33
So soon to bid good morrow to thy bed.
Care keeps his watch in every old man's eye,
And where care lodges sleep will never lie;
But where unbruisèd youth with unstuffed brain   37
Doth couch his limbs, there golden sleep doth reign.
Therefore thy earliness doth me assure
Thou art uproused with some distemp'rature;
Or if not so, then here I hit it right:
Our Romeo hath not been in bed tonight.

ROMEO
That last is true. The sweeter rest was mine.

FRIAR LAURENCE
God pardon sin! Wast thou with Rosaline?

ROMEO
With Rosaline, my ghostly father? No.
I have forgot that name, and that name's woe.

FRIAR LAURENCE
That's my good son. But where hast thou been,
    then?

ROMEO
I'll tell thee ere thou ask it me again.
I have been feasting with mine enemy,
Where on a sudden one hath wounded me
That's by me wounded. Both our remedies   51
Within thy help and holy physic lies.   52

---

168 nyas eyas, fledgling **173 still** always **178 wanton's** spoiled
child's **180 gyves** fetters **182 his** its **189 ghostly** spiritual. **close**
narrow **190 dear hap** good fortune
2.3. Location: Verona. Near Friar Laurence's cell, perhaps in the
monastery garden.
3 fleckled dappled **4 From forth** out of the way of. **Titan's** (Helios,
the sun god, was a descendant of the race of Titans.) **5 advance**
raise **7 osier cage** willow basket **8 baleful** harmful

14 None but for some there are none that are not useful for something **15 mickle** great. **grace** beneficent virtue **16 true** proper, inherent **17 For naught so vile** for there is nothing so vile **19 strained**
forced, perverted **25 that part** i.e., the odor **26 stays** halts. **with**
together with **27 them still** themselves always **30 canker** cankerworm **31 Benedicite** a blessing on you **33 argues** demonstrates,
provides evidence of. **distempered** disturbed, disordered **37 unstuffed** not overcharged, carefree **51 Both our remedies** the remedy
for both of us **52 physic** medicine, healing property

I bear no hatred, blessèd man, for, lo,
My intercession likewise steads my foe.   54

FRIAR LAURENCE
Be plain, good son, and homely in thy drift.   55
Riddling confession finds but riddling shrift.   56

ROMEO
Then plainly know my heart's dear love is set
On the fair daughter of rich Capulet.
As mine on hers, so hers is set on mine,
And all combined, save what thou must combine
By holy marriage. When and where and how
We met, we wooed, and made exchange of vow
I'll tell thee as we pass; but this I pray,
That thou consent to marry us today.

FRIAR LAURENCE
Holy Saint Francis, what a change is here!
Is Rosaline, that thou didst love so dear,
So soon forsaken? Young men's love then lies
Not truly in their hearts, but in their eyes.
Jesu Maria, what a deal of brine
Hath washed thy sallow cheeks for Rosaline!   70
How much salt water thrown away in waste
To season love, that of it doth not taste!
The sun not yet thy sighs from heaven clears,
Thy old groans yet ringing in mine ancient ears,
Lo, here upon thy cheek the stain doth sit
Of an old tear that is not washed off yet.
If e'er thou wast thyself and these woes thine,
Thou and these woes were all for Rosaline.   77
And art thou changed? Pronounce this sentence
    then: 79
Women may fall, when there's no strength in men.

ROMEO
Thou chid'st me oft for loving Rosaline.   81

FRIAR LAURENCE
For doting, not for loving, pupil mine.

ROMEO
And bad'st me bury love.

FRIAR LAURENCE   Not in a grave
To lay one in, another out to have.   83

ROMEO
I pray thee, chide not. She whom I love now
Doth grace for grace and love for love allow.   86
The other did not so.

FRIAR LAURENCE   O, she knew well
Thy love did read by rote, that could not spell. 88
But come, young waverer, come, go with me,
In one respect I'll thy assistant be;   90
For this alliance may so happy prove
To turn your households' rancor to pure love.   92

ROMEO
O, let us hence! I stand on sudden haste.   93

FRIAR LAURENCE
Wisely and slow. They stumble that run fast.   54

                                    Exeunt.

❖

2.4   *Enter Benvolio and Mercutio.*

MERCUTIO
Where the devil should this Romeo be?   1
Came he not home tonight?   2

BENVOLIO
Not to his father's. I spoke with his man.

MERCUTIO
Why, that same pale hardhearted wench, that
    Rosaline,
Torments him so that he will sure run mad.

BENVOLIO
Tybalt, the kinsman to old Capulet,
Hath sent a letter to his father's house.

MERCUTIO   A challenge, on my life.

BENVOLIO   Romeo will answer it.   9

MERCUTIO   Any man that can write may answer a letter.

BENVOLIO   Nay, he will answer the letter's master, how 11
he dares, being dared.

MERCUTIO   Alas poor Romeo! He is already dead,
stabbed with a white wench's black eye, run through
the ear with a love song, the very pin of his heart cleft 15
with the blind bow-boy's butt shaft. And is he a man 16
to encounter Tybalt?

BENVOLIO   Why, what is Tybalt?

MERCUTIO   More than prince of cats. O, he's the 19
courageous captain of compliments. He fights as you 20
sing prick song, keeps time, distance, and proportion; 21
he rests his minim rests, one, two, and the third in 22
your bosom. The very butcher of a silk button, a 23
duellist, a duellist, a gentleman of the very first house, 24
of the first and second cause. Ah, the immortal 25
passado! The *punto reverso!* The *hay!*   26

BENVOLIO   The what?

MERCUTIO   The pox of such antic, lisping, affecting phan- 28
tasimes, these new tuners of accent! "By Jesu, a very 29
good blade! A very tall man! A very good whore!" 30
Why, is not this a lamentable thing, grandsire, that we 31

2.4. Location: Verona. A street.
1 should can   **2 tonight** last night   **9 answer it** accept the challenge.
(But Mercutio replies with a pun on "write in reply.")   **11 how** as, to
what extent   **15 pin** peg in the center of a target   **16 butt shaft** unbarbed arrow, allotted to children and thus to Cupid   **19 prince of
cats** (The name of the king of cats in *Reynard the Fox* was Tybalt or
Tybert.)   **20 captain of compliments** master of ceremony and dueling
etiquette   **21 prick song** music written out.   **proportion** rhythm
22 minim rests short rests in musical notation   **23 butcher . . . button** i.e., one able to strike a specific button on his adversary's person
24 first house best school of fencing   **25 first and second cause**
causes according to the code of dueling that would oblige one to seek
the satisfaction of one's honor   **26 passado** forward thrust.   **punto reverso** backhanded stroke.   **hay** thrust through. (From the Italian *hai*,
meaning "you have [it].")   **28 The pox of** plague take.   **antic** grotesque   **28–29 phantasimes** coxcombs, fantastically dressed or mannered   **29 new tuners of accent** those who introduce new foreign
words and slang phrases into their speech   **30 tall** valiant   **31 grandsire** i.e., one who disapproves of the new fashion and prefers old
custom

---

54 intercession petition.   **steads** helps   **55 homely** simple   **56 shrift**
absolution   **70 sallow** sickly yellow   **77 wast thyself** i.e., were sincere   **79 sentence** sententious conclusion   **81 chid'st** rebuked
83 bad'st bade   **86 grace** favor, graciousness   **88 did read by rote**
i.e., repeated conventional expressions without understanding them
90 In one respect for one reason (at least)   **92 To** as to   **93 stand on**
am in need of, insist on

should be thus afflicted with these strange flies, these 32
fashionmongers, these pardon-me's, who stand so 33
much on the new form that they cannot sit at ease on 34
the old bench? O, their bones, their bones! 35

Enter Romeo.

BENVOLIO   Here comes Romeo, here comes Romeo.

MERCUTIO   Without his roe, like a dried herring. O 37
flesh, flesh, how art thou fishified! Now is he for the
numbers that Petrarch flowed in. Laura to his lady 39
was but a kitchen wench—marry, she had a better
love to berhyme her—Dido a dowdy, Cleopatra a 41
gypsy, Helen and Hero hildings and harlots, Thisbe a 42
gray eye or so, but not to the purpose. Signor Romeo, 43
bonjour! There's a French salutation to your French 44
slop. You gave us the counterfeit fairly last night. 45

ROMEO   Good morrow to you both. What counterfeit
did I give you?

MERCUTIO   The slip, sir, the slip. Can you not conceive? 48

ROMEO   Pardon, good Mercutio. My business was great,
and in such a case as mine a man may strain courtesy.

MERCUTIO   That's as much as to say, such a case as yours 51
constrains a man to bow in the hams. 52

ROMEO   Meaning, to curtsy. 53

MERCUTIO   Thou hast most kindly hit it. 54

ROMEO   A most courteous exposition.

MERCUTIO   Nay, I am the very pink of courtesy. 56

ROMEO   Pink for flower.

MERCUTIO   Right.

ROMEO   Why then is my pump well flowered. 59

MERCUTIO   Sure wit, follow me this jest now till thou
hast worn out thy pump, that when the single sole of
it is worn, the jest may remain, after the wearing,
solely singular. 63

ROMEO   O single-soled jest, solely singular for the 64
singleness! 65

MERCUTIO   Come between us, good Benvolio. My wits
faints.

32 flies parasites   **33 pardon-me's** i.e., those who affect overly polite manners.   **stand** (1) insist (2) the opposite of *sit,* line 34
34–35 form . . . bench (*Form* means both "fashion" or "code of manners" and "bench.")   **35 bones** French *bon,* "good" (with play on English *bone*)   **37 Without his roe** i.e., looking thin and emaciated, sexually spent. (With a pun on the first syllable of Romeo's name; the remaining syllables, *me-oh,* sound like the expression of a melancholy lover. *Roe* also suggests a female deer or "dear.")
39 numbers verses.   **Laura** the lady to whom the Italian Renaissance poet Petrarch addressed his love poems. (Other romantic heroines are named in the following passage: Dido, Queen of Carthage; Cleopatra; Helen of Troy; Hero, beloved of Leander; and Thisbe, beloved of Pyramus.)   **to** in comparison with   **41 dowdy** homely woman
42 gypsy Egyptian; whore.   **hildings** good-for-nothings   **43 not** i.e., that is not   **44 to** to match   **44–45 French slop** loose trousers of French fashion   **45 fairly** handsomely, effectively   **48 slip** (Counterfeit coins were called "slips.")   **conceive** i.e., get the joke   **51 case** (1) situation (2) physical condition. (Mercutio also bawdily suggests that Romeo has been in a *case,* i.e., the female genitalia.)   **52 bow in the hams** (1) kneel, curtsy (2) show the effects of venereal disease
53 curtsy make obeisance   **54 kindly** naturally; politely   **56 pink** embodied perfection. (But suggesting also the flower called *pink,* the color, and *pinking* of a shoe; see next note.)   **59 pump** shoe.   **well flowered** expertly pinked or perforated in ornamental figures
63 solely singular unique   **64 single-soled** i.e., thin, contemptible
65 singleness feebleness

ROMEO   Switch and spurs, switch and spurs! Or I'll cry 68
a match. 69

MERCUTIO   Nay, if our wits run the wild-goose chase, I 70
am done, for thou hast more of the wild goose in one
of thy wits than, I am sure, I have in my whole five.
Was I with you there for the goose? 73

ROMEO   Thou wast never with me for anything when
thou wast not there for the goose. 75

MERCUTIO   I will bite thee by the ear for that jest. 76

ROMEO   Nay, good goose, bite not.

MERCUTIO   Thy wit is a very bitter sweeting; it is a most 78
sharp sauce. 79

ROMEO   And is it not, then, well served in to a sweet
goose?

MERCUTIO   O, here's a wit of cheveril, that stretches 82
from an inch narrow to an ell broad! 83

ROMEO   I stretch it out for that word "broad," which,
added to the goose, proves thee far and wide a broad 85
goose.

MERCUTIO   Why, is not this better now than groaning
for love? Now art thou sociable, now art thou Romeo;
now art thou what thou art, by art as well as by nature.
For this driveling love is like a great natural that runs 90
lolling up and down to hide his bauble in a hole. 91

BENVOLIO   Stop there, stop there.

MERCUTIO   Thou desirest me to stop in my tale against 93
the hair. 94

BENVOLIO   Thou wouldst else have made thy tale large.

MERCUTIO   O, thou art deceived; I would have made it
short, for I was come to the whole depth of my tale
and meant indeed to occupy the argument no longer.

ROMEO   Here's goodly gear! 99

Enter Nurse and her man [Peter].

A sail, a sail! 100

MERCUTIO   Two, two: a shirt and a smock. 101

NURSE   Peter!

PETER   Anon!

NURSE   My fan, Peter.

MERCUTIO   Good Peter, to hide her face, for her fan's
the fairer face.

NURSE   God gi' good morrow, gentlemen.

68 Switch and spurs i.e., keep up the rapid pace of the hunt (in the game of wits)   **68–69 cry a match** claim the victory   **70 wild-goose chase** a horse race in which the leading rider dares his competitors to follow him wherever he goes   **73 Was . . . goose** did I score a point in calling you a goose   **75 for the goose** (1) behaving like a goose (2) looking for a prostitute   **76 bite . . . ear** i.e., give you an affectionate nibble on the ear. (Said ironically, however, and Romeo parries.)
78 sweeting sweet-flavored variety of apple   **79 sharp sauce** (1) "biting" retort (2) tart sauce, of the sort that should be served with cooked goose (as Romeo points out)   **82 cheveril** kid leather, easily stretched   **83 ell** (forty-five inches)   **85 broad** large, complete; perhaps also wanton   **90 natural** idiot   **91 lolling** with his tongue (or bauble) hanging out.   **bauble** (1) jester's wand (2) phallus   **93 stop in my tale** (1) stop short in my story (2) stuff in my penis   **93–94 against the hair** against the grain, against my wish (with bawdy suggestion of pubic hair. The sexual punning continues in *large* [erect], *short* [detumescent], *come to the depth of my tale, occupy,* etc.)   **99 goodly gear** matter for mockery (with suggestion of "ample sexual apparatus")   **100 A sail** (To Romeo, the Nurse is an imposing galleon in full sail.)   **101 a shirt and a smock** i.e., a man and a woman

MERCUTIO God gi' good e'en, fair gentlewoman.

NURSE Is it good e'en?   109

MERCUTIO 'Tis no less, I tell ye, for the bawdy hand of
the dial is now upon the prick of noon.   111

NURSE Out upon you! What a man are you?   112

ROMEO One, gentlewoman, that God hath made for
himself to mar.   114

NURSE By my troth, it is well said. "For himself to   115
mar," quoth 'a? Gentlemen, can any of you tell me   116
where I may find the young Romeo?

ROMEO I can tell you; but young Romeo will be older
when you have found him than he was when you
sought him. I am the youngest of that name, for fault   120
of a worse.

NURSE You say well.

MERCUTIO Yea, is the worst well? Very well took, i'   123
faith, wisely, wisely.

NURSE If you be he, sir, I desire some confidence   125
with you.

BENVOLIO She will indite him to some supper.   127

MERCUTIO A bawd, a bawd, a bawd! So ho!   128

ROMEO What hast thou found?

MERCUTIO No hare, sir, unless a hare, sir, in a lenten   130
pie, that is something stale and hoar ere it be spent.   131

[He sings.]

An old hare hoar,
And an old hare hoar,
Is very good meat in Lent.
But a hare that is hoar
Is too much for a score,   136
When it hoars ere it be spent.

Romeo, will you come to your father's? We'll to dinner
thither.

ROMEO I will follow you.

MERCUTIO Farewell, ancient lady. Farewell, [singing]
"Lady, lady, lady."   Exeunt [Mercutio and Benvolio].   142

NURSE I pray you, sir, what saucy merchant was this   143
that was so full of his ropery?   144

ROMEO A gentleman, Nurse, that loves to hear himself
talk, and will speak more in a minute than he will
stand to in a month.   147

NURSE An 'a speak anything against me, I'll take him   148
down, an 'a were lustier than he is, and twenty such   149
Jacks; and if I cannot, I'll find those that shall. Scurvy   150
knave! I am none of his flirt-gills. I am none of his   151
skains-mates. [To Peter.] And thou must stand by, too,   152
and suffer every knave to use me at his pleasure!

PETER I saw no man use you at his pleasure. If I had,
my weapon should quickly have been out; I warrant   155
you, I dare draw as soon as another man, if I see
occasion in a good quarrel, and the law on my side.

NURSE Now, afore God, I am so vexed that every part   158
about me quivers. Scurvy knave! Pray you, sir, a   159
word; and as I told you, my young lady bid me inquire you out. What she bid me say, I will keep to
myself. But first let me tell ye, if ye should lead her in
a fool's paradise, as they say, it were a very gross kind
of behavior, as they say. For the gentlewoman is
young; and therefore if you should deal double with
her, truly it were an ill thing to be offered to any gentlewoman, and very weak dealing.   167

ROMEO Nurse, commend me to thy lady and mistress.
I protest unto thee—   169

NURSE Good heart, and i' faith I will tell her as much.
Lord, Lord, she will be a joyful woman.

ROMEO What wilt thou tell her, Nurse? Thou dost not
mark me.   173

NURSE I will tell her, sir, that you do protest, which, as
I take it, is a gentlemanlike offer.

ROMEO Bid her devise
Some means to come to shrift this afternoon,   177
And there she shall at Friar Laurence' cell
Be shrived and married. Here is for thy pains.   179

[He offers money.]

NURSE No, truly, sir, not a penny.

ROMEO Go to, I say you shall.

NURSE
This afternoon, sir? Well, she shall be there.

ROMEO
And stay, good Nurse, behind the abbey wall.
Within this hour my man shall be with thee
And bring thee cords made like a tackled stair,   185
Which to the high topgallant of my joy   186
Must be my convoy in the secret night.   187
Farewell. Be trusty, and I'll quit thy pains.   188
Farewell. Commend me to thy mistress.

[Romeo starts to leave.]

NURSE
Now God in heaven bless thee! Hark you, sir.

ROMEO What sayst thou my dear Nurse?

NURSE
Is your man secret? Did you ne'er hear say,   192

109 Is it good e'en is it afternoon already 111 prick point on the
dial of a clock (with bawdy suggestion) 112 Out upon you (Expression of indignation.) What what kind of 114 mar i.e., disfigure
morally through sin. (Humankind, made in God's image, mars that
image sinfully.) 115 troth faith 116 quoth 'a said he. (A sarcastic
interjection, meaning "forsooth" or "indeed.") 120 fault lack
123 took understood 125 confidence (The Nurse's mistake for
"conference.") 127 indite (Benvolio's deliberate malapropism for
"invite.") 128 So ho (Cry of hunter sighting game.) 130 hare (Slang
word for "prostitute"; similarly, with stale and meat in the following
lines.) 130–131 a lenten pie a pie that should contain no meat, in
observance of Lent 131 hoar moldy (with pun on "whore"; stale
also can mean "whore"). spent consumed 136 for a score for a
reckoning, to pay good money for 142 "Lady, lady, lady" (Refrain
from the ballad Chaste Susanna.) 143 merchant i.e., fellow
144 ropery vulgar humor, knavery 147 stand to perform, abide by
148–149 take him down cut him down to size (with unintended
bawdy suggestion) 150 Jacks knaves

151 flirt-gills loose women 152 skains-mates (Perhaps dagger-
mates, outlaws, or gangster molls.) 155 weapon (With bawdy suggestion, perhaps unrecognized by the speaker, as also in at his pleasure.) 158–159 every part . . . quivers (More bawdy suggestion,
unrecognized by the Nurse.) 167 weak contemptible 169 protest
vow. (Romeo may intend only to protest his good intentions, but the
Nurse seemingly takes the word to mean "propose," as if Romeo is
making a gentlemanlike offer [line 175] of marriage that would ensure
against Juliet's being led into a fool's paradise [line 163]—i.e., being
seduced.) 173 mark attend to 177 shrift confession and absolution
179 shrived absolved 185 tackled stair rope ladder 186 topgallant
highest mast and sail of a ship, the summit 187 convoy conveyance,
means of passage 188 quit reward, requite 192 secret trustworthy

"Two may keep counsel, putting one away"?   193

ROMEO
'Warrant thee, my man's as true as steel.

NURSE   Well, sir, my mistress is the sweetest lady—
Lord, Lord! When 'twas a little prating thing—O,
there is a nobleman in town, one Paris, that would
fain lay knife aboard; but she, good soul, had as lief   198
see a toad, a very toad, as see him. I anger her
sometimes and tell her that Paris is the properer man,   200
but I'll warrant you, when I say so, she looks as pale as
any clout in the versal world. Doth not rosemary and   202
Romeo begin both with a letter?   203

ROMEO   Ay, Nurse, what of that? Both with an R.

NURSE   Ah, mocker! That's the dog's name; R is for   205
the—No; I know it begins with some other letter; and   206
she hath the prettiest sententious of it, of you and   207
rosemary, that it would do you good to hear it.

ROMEO   Commend me to thy lady.

NURSE   Ay, a thousand times. [*Exit Romeo.*] Peter!

PETER   Anon!

NURSE   Before, and apace.   *Exeunt.*   212

❖

2.5   *Enter Juliet.*

JULIET
The clock struck nine when I did send the Nurse;
In half an hour she promised to return.
Perchance she cannot meet him. That's not so.
O, she is lame! Love's heralds should be thoughts,
Which ten times faster glides than the sun's beams
Driving back shadows over louring hills.   6
Therefore do nimble-pinioned doves draw Love,   7
And therefore hath the wind-swift Cupid wings.
Now is the sun upon the highmost hill
Of this day's journey, and from nine till twelve
Is three long hours, yet she is not come.
Had she affections and warm youthful blood,
She would be as swift in motion as a ball;
My words would bandy her to my sweet love,   14
And his to me.
But old folks, many feign as they were dead—   16
Unwieldy, slow, heavy, and pale as lead.

Enter Nurse [and Peter].

O God, she comes!—O honey Nurse, what news?

Hast thou met with him? Send thy man away.

NURSE   Peter, stay at the gate.   [*Exit Peter.*]

JULIET
Now, good sweet Nurse—O Lord, why lookest
thou sad?
Though news be sad, yet tell them merrily;
If good, thou shamest the music of sweet news
By playing it to me with so sour a face.

NURSE
I am aweary. Give me leave awhile.   25
Fie, how my bones ache! What a jaunce have I had!   26

JULIET
I would thou hadst my bones and I thy news.
Nay, come, I pray thee, speak. Good, good Nurse,
speak.

NURSE
Jesu, what haste! Can you not stay awhile?   29
Do you not see that I am out of breath?

JULIET
How art thou out of breath, when thou hast breath
To say to me that thou art out of breath?
The excuse that thou dost make in this delay
Is longer than the tale thou dost excuse.   34
Is thy news good or bad? Answer to that;
Say either, and I'll stay the circumstance.   36
Let me be satisfied: is 't good or bad?

NURSE   Well, you have made a simple choice. You know   38
not how to choose a man. Romeo? No, not he. Though
his face be better than any man's, yet his leg excels all
men's; and for a hand, and a foot, and a body, though
they be not to be talked on, yet they are past compare. 42
He is not the flower of courtesy, but, I'll warrant him,
as gentle as a lamb. Go thy ways, wench. Serve God.
What, have you dined at home?

JULIET
No, no; but all this did I know before.
What says he of our marriage? What of that?

NURSE
Lord, how my head aches! What a head have I!
It beats as it would fall in twenty pieces.
My back o' t'other side—ah, my back, my back!   50
Beshrew your heart for sending me about   51
To catch my death with jauncing up and down!

JULIET
I' faith, I am sorry that thou art not well.
Sweet, sweet, sweet Nurse, tell me, what says my
love?

NURSE
Your love says, like an honest gentleman,
And a courteous, and a kind, and a handsome,
And, I warrant, a virtuous—Where is your mother?

JULIET
Where is my mother? Why, she is within,
Where should she be? How oddly thou repliest!

---

193 keep counsel keep a secret   **198 fain lay knife aboard** like to assert his claim (just as a guest at an inn did by bringing his knife to the dinner table; with sexual suggestion also).   **lief** willingly   **200 properer** handsomer   **202 clout** rag, cloth.   **versal** universal   **203 a letter** one and the same letter   **205 the dog's name** (The letter *R* was thought to resemble the dog's growl.)   **206 No . . . other letter** (The Nurse perhaps thinks that the letter means "arse" and repudiates the association.)   **207 sententious** (The Nurse probably means "sentences," pithy sayings.)   **212 Before, and apace** go before me quickly
2.5. Location: Verona. Outside Capulet's house, perhaps in the orchard or garden.
6 louring dark, threatening   **7 Love** i.e., Venus, whose chariot was drawn by swift-winged doves   **14 bandy** toss to and fro, as in tennis   **16 feign as** act as though

---

25 Give me leave let me alone   **26 jaunce** jouncing, jolting   **29 stay** wait   **34 excuse** i.e., excuse yourself from telling   **36 stay the circumstance** await the details   **38 simple** foolish   **42 be not to be talked on** are beneath mention (especially in refined ladylike company)   **50 o' t'other** on the other   **51 Beshrew** a curse on (used as a mild oath)

"Your love says, like an honest gentleman,   60
'Where is your mother?' "
NURSE   O God's Lady dear!
Are you so hot? Marry, come up, I trow.   62
Is this the poultice for my aching bones?
Henceforward do your messages yourself.
JULIET
Here's such a coil! Come, what says Romeo?   65
NURSE
Have you got leave to go to shrift today?
JULIET   I have.
NURSE
Then hie you hence to Friar Laurence' cell;   68
There stays a husband to make you a wife.
Now comes the wanton blood up in your cheeks;
They'll be in scarlet straight at any news.   71
Hie you to church. I must another way,
To fetch a ladder, by the which your love
Must climb a bird's nest soon when it is dark.   74
I am the drudge, and toil in your delight,
But you shall bear the burden soon at night.
Go. I'll to dinner. Hie you to the cell.
JULIET
Hie to high fortune! Honest Nurse, farewell.
                              Exeunt [*separately*].

♣

2.6   *Enter Friar* [*Laurence*] *and Romeo.*

FRIAR LAURENCE
So smile the heavens upon this holy act   1
That after-hours with sorrow chide us not!
ROMEO
Amen, amen! But come what sorrow can,
It cannot countervail the exchange of joy   4
That one short minute gives me in her sight.
Do thou but close our hands with holy words,   6
Then love-devouring death do what he dare;
It is enough I may but call her mine.
FRIAR LAURENCE
These violent delights have violent ends
And in their triumph die, like fire and powder,   10
Which as they kiss consume. The sweetest honey
Is loathsome in his own deliciousness,   12
And in the taste confounds the appetite.   13
Therefore love moderately. Long love doth so;
Too swift arrives as tardy as too slow.

Enter Juliet.

Here comes the lady. O, so light a foot
Will ne'er wear out the everlasting flint.
A lover may bestride the gossamers   18
That idles in the wanton summer air,   19
And yet not fall, so light is vanity.   20
JULIET
Good even to my ghostly confessor.   21
FRIAR LAURENCE
Romeo shall thank thee, daughter, for us both.   22
JULIET
As much to him, else is his thanks too much.   23
ROMEO
Ah, Juliet, if the measure of thy joy
Be heaped like mine, and that thy skill be more   25
To blazon it, then sweeten with thy breath   26
This neighbor air, and let rich music's tongue
Unfold the imagined happiness that both   28
Receive in either by this dear encounter.   29
JULIET
Conceit, more rich in matter than in words,   30
Brags of his substance, not of ornament.   31
They are but beggars that can count their worth.
But my true love is grown to such excess
I cannot sum up sum of half my wealth.   34
FRIAR LAURENCE
Come, come with me, and we will make short work;
For, by your leaves, you shall not stay alone
Till Holy Church incorporate two in one.   [*Exeunt.*]

♣

3.1   *Enter Mercutio, Benvolio, and men.*

BENVOLIO
I pray thee, good Mercutio, let's retire.
The day is hot, the Capels are abroad,   2
And if we meet we shall not scape a brawl,
For now, these hot days, is the mad blood stirring.
MERCUTIO   Thou art like one of these fellows that when
he enters the confines of a tavern, claps me his sword
upon the table and says, "God send me no need of
thee!" and by the operation of the second cup draws   8
him on the drawer, when indeed there is no need.   9
BENVOLIO   Am I like such a fellow?
MERCUTIO   Come, come, thou art as hot a Jack in thy   11
mood as any in Italy, and as soon moved to be moody,   12
and as soon moody to be moved.   13

---

60 **honest** honorable   62 **hot** impatient.   **Marry, come up** (An expression of impatient reproof.)   65 **coil** turmoil, fuss   68 **hie** hasten   71 **in scarlet straight** i.e., blushing immediately   74 **bird's nest** i.e., Juliet's room. (Continues the association of Juliet as a bird, as at 1.3.3, 2.2.168–182, perhaps suggesting pubic hair. The bawdry is continued in *bear the burden* two lines later.)
2.6. Location: Verona. Friar Laurence's cell.
1 **So . . . heavens** may the heavens so smile   4 **countervail** outweigh, counterbalance   6 **close** join   10 **powder** gunpowder   12 **his** its   13 **confounds** destroys

18 **gossamers** filmy cobwebs   19 **wanton** playful   20 **vanity** transitory human joy   21 **ghostly** spiritual   22 **thank thee** i.e., give a kiss in thanks for your greeting   23 **As . . . much** i.e., then I greet him with a kiss in repayment, lest I be overpaid   25 **that** if   26 **blazon** describe, set forth. (A heraldic term.)   28 **Unfold** make known.   **imagined** i.e., unexpressed   29 **in either** from each other   30–31 **Conceit . . . ornament** true understanding, more enriched by the actual reality (of love) than by mere words, finds more worth in the substance of that reality than in outward show   34 **sum up sum** add up the total
3.1. Location: Verona. A public place.
2 **Capels** Capulets   8–9 **draws . . . drawer** draws his sword against the tapster or waiter   9 **there is no need** i.e., of his sword   11 **as hot a Jack** as hot-tempered a fellow   12 **moody** angry   13 **to be moved** at being provoked

BENVOLIO   And what to?

MERCUTIO   Nay, an there were two such, we should 15
have none shortly, for one would kill the other. Thou!
Why, thou wilt quarrel with a man that hath a hair
more or a hair less in his beard than thou hast. Thou
wilt quarrel with a man for cracking nuts, having no
other reason but because thou hast hazel eyes. What
eye but such an eye would spy out such a quarrel? Thy
head is as full of quarrels as an egg is full of meat, and 22
yet thy head hath been beaten as addle as an egg for 23
quarreling. Thou hast quarreled with a man for coughing in the street, because he hath wakened thy dog
that hath lain asleep in the sun. Didst thou not fall out
with a tailor for wearing his new doublet before East- 27
er? With another, for tying his new shoes with old
ribbon? And yet thou wilt tutor me from quarreling!

BENVOLIO   An I were so apt to quarrel as thou art, any
man should buy the fee simple of my life for an hour 31
and a quarter.   32

MERCUTIO   The fee simple! O simple!   33

Enter Tybalt, Petruchio, and others.

BENVOLIO   By my head, here comes the Capulets.

MERCUTIO   By my heel, I care not.

TYBALT [*to his companions*]
Follow me close, for I will speak to them.—
Gentlemen, good e'en. A word with one of you.

MERCUTIO   And but one word with one of us? Couple it
with something: make it a word and a blow.

TYBALT   You shall find me apt enough to that, sir, an
you will give me occasion.

MERCUTIO   Could you not take some occasion without
giving?

TYBALT   Mercutio, thou consortest with Romeo.   44

MERCUTIO   "Consort"? What, dost thou make us minstrels? An thou make minstrels of us, look to hear
nothing but discords. Here's my fiddlestick; here's 47
that shall make you dance. Zounds, "consort"!   48

BENVOLIO
We talk here in the public haunt of men.
Either withdraw unto some private place,
Or reason coldly of your grievances,   51
Or else depart; here all eyes gaze on us.   52

MERCUTIO
Men's eyes were made to look, and let them gaze.
I will not budge for no man's pleasure, I.

Enter Romeo.

TYBALT
Well, peace be with you, sir. Here comes my man.

MERCUTIO
But I'll be hanged, sir, if he wear your livery.   56

Marry, go before to field, he'll be your follower;   57
Your worship in that sense may call him "man."   58

TYBALT
Romeo, the love I bear thee can afford
No better term than this: thou art a villain. *(spits)*

ROMEO
Tybalt, the reason that I have to love thee
Doth much excuse the appertaining rage   62
To such a greeting. Villain am I none.
Therefore, farewell. I see thou knowest me not.

TYBALT
Boy, this shall not excuse the injuries *hits hand away*
That thou hast done me. Therefore turn and draw.

ROMEO
I do protest I never injured thee, *bleeding*
But love thee better than thou canst devise   68
Till thou shalt know the reason of my love.
And so, good Capulet—which name I tender   70
As dearly as mine own—be satisfied.

MERCUTIO
O calm, dishonorable, vile submission!
Alla stoccado carries it away.   [*He draws.*] 73
Tybalt, you ratcatcher, will you walk?   74

TYBALT   What wouldst thou have with me?

MERCUTIO   Good king of cats, nothing but one of your
nine lives, that I mean to make bold withal, and, as 77
you shall use me hereafter, dry-beat the rest of the 78
eight. Will you pluck your sword out of his pilcher by 79
the ears? Make haste, lest mine be about your ears ere 80
it be out.

TYBALT   I am for you.   [*He draws.*]

ROMEO
Gentle Mercutio, put thy rapier up.

MERCUTIO   Come, sir, your *passado*.   [*They fight.*] 84

ROMEO
Draw, Benvolio, beat down their weapons.
Gentlemen, for shame, forbear this outrage!
Tybalt, Mercutio, the Prince expressly hath
Forbid this bandying in Verona streets.
Hold, Tybalt! Good Mercutio!
            [*Tybalt under Romeo's arm stabs Mercutio.*]
                      Away Tybalt [*with his followers*].

MERCUTIO   I am hurt.   89
A plague o' both your houses! I am sped.   90
Is he gone, and hath nothing?

BENVOLIO   What, art thou hurt?

MERCUTIO
Ay, ay, a scratch, a scratch; marry, 'tis enough.
Where is my page? Go, villain, fetch a surgeon.
                                        [*Exit Page.*]

---

15 **an** if   22 **meat** i.e., edible matter   23 **addle** addled, confused
27 **doublet** man's jacket   31 **fee simple** outright possession
31–32 **an hour . . . quarter** i.e., my life would last no longer in such
circumstances   33 **O simple** O stupid   44 **consortest** keep company
with. (But Mercutio quibbles on its musical sense of "accompany" or
"play together.")   47 **fiddlestick** (Mercutio means his sword.)
48 **that** that which.   **Zounds** by God's (Christ's) wounds   51 **coldly**
calmly   52 **depart** go away separately   56 **livery** servant's costume.
(Mercutio deliberately mistakes Tybalt's phrase *my man* to mean "my
servant.")

57 **field** field where a duel might occur   58 **Your worship** (A title of
honor used here with mock politeness.)   62 **excuse . . . rage** excuse
my not showing the angry reaction appropriate   68 **devise** imagine
70 **tender** value   73 **Alla stoccado** at the thrust (Italian); here, an insulting nickname for Tybalt.   **carries it away** wins the day   74 **ratcatcher** (An allusion to Tybalt as king of cats; see 2.4.19.)   77 **make
bold withal** make free with   78 **dry-beat** beat soundly (without drawing blood)   79 **his pilcher** its scabbard   79–80 **by the ears** by the
handle, or hilt (perhaps suggested by a play on *pilcher* and "pitcher")
84 **passado** forward thrust. (Said derisively.)   89 s.d. **Away Tybalt**
(Some editors assign this as a speech to Petruchio.)   90 **sped**
done for

ROMEO

Courage, man, the hurt cannot be much.

MERCUTIO No, 'tis not so deep as a well, nor so wide as
a church door, but 'tis enough, 'twill serve. Ask for me
tomorrow, and you shall find me a grave man. I am 97
peppered, I warrant, for this world. A plague o' both 98
your houses! Zounds, a dog, a rat, a mouse, a cat, to
scratch a man to death! A braggart, a rogue, a villain,
that fights by the book of arithmetic! Why the devil 101
came you between us? I was hurt under your arm.

ROMEO I thought all for the best.

MERCUTIO

Help me into some house, Benvolio,
Or I shall faint. A plague o' both your houses!
They have made worm's meat of me. I have it,
And soundly too. Your houses!

Exit [supported by Benvolio].

ROMEO

This gentleman, the Prince's near ally, 108
My very friend, hath got this mortal hurt 109
In my behalf; my reputation stained
With Tybalt's slander—Tybalt, that an hour
Hath been my cousin! O sweet Juliet, 112
Thy beauty hath made me effeminate, 113
And in my temper softened valor's steel. 114

Enter Benvolio.

BENVOLIO

O Romeo, Romeo, brave Mercutio is dead!
That gallant spirit hath aspired the clouds,
Which too untimely here did scorn the earth. 116

ROMEO

This day's black fate on more days doth depend; 118
This but begins the woe others must end. 119

[*Enter Tybalt.*]

BENVOLIO

Here comes the furious Tybalt back again.

ROMEO

Alive in triumph, and Mercutio slain!
Away to heaven, respective lenity,
And fire-eyed fury be my conduct now! 122
Now, Tybalt, take the "villain" back again 123
That late thou gavest me, for Mercutio's soul
Is but a little way above our heads,
Staying for thine to keep him company.
Either thou or I, or both, must go with him.

TYBALT

Thou, wretched boy, that didst consort him here,
Shalt with him hence.

ROMEO   This shall determine that.

They fight. Tybalt falls.

BENVOLIO   Romeo, away, begone!
The citizens are up, and Tybalt slain.

Stand not amazed. The Prince will doom thee death 133
If thou art taken. Hence, begone, away!

ROMEO

O, I am fortune's fool!

BENVOLIO   Why dost thou stay? 135

Exit Romeo.

Enter Citizens.

FIRST CITIZEN

Which way ran he that killed Mercutio?
Tybalt, that murderer, which way ran he?

BENVOLIO

There lies that Tybalt.

FIRST CITIZEN   Up, sir, go with me.
I charge thee in the Prince's name, obey.

*Enter Prince [attended], old Montague, Capulet,
their Wives, and all.*

PRINCE

Where are the vile beginners of this fray?

BENVOLIO

O noble Prince, I can discover all 141
The unlucky manage of this fatal brawl. 142
There lies the man, slain by young Romeo,
That slew thy kinsman, brave Mercutio.

CAPULET'S WIFE

Tybalt, my cousin! O my brother's child!
O Prince! O cousin! Husband! O, the blood is spilled
Of my dear kinsman! Prince, as thou art true,
For blood of ours shed blood of Montague.
O cousin, cousin!

PRINCE

Benvolio, who began this bloody fray?

BENVOLIO

Tybalt, here slain, whom Romeo's hand did slay.
Romeo, that spoke him fair, bid him bethink 152
How nice the quarrel was, and urged withal 153
Your high displeasure. All this—utterèd
With gentle breath, calm look, knees humbly
bowed—
Could not take truce with the unruly spleen 156
Of Tybalt deaf to peace, but that he tilts
With piercing steel at bold Mercutio's breast,
Who, all as hot, turns deadly point to point,
And, with a martial scorn, with one hand beats
Cold death aside and with the other sends
It back to Tybalt, whose dexterity
Retorts it. Romeo he cries aloud, 163
"Hold, friends! Friends, part!" and swifter than his
tongue
His agile arm beats down their fatal points,
And twixt them rushes; underneath whose arm
An envious thrust from Tybalt hit the life 167
Of stout Mercutio, and then Tybalt fled; 168
But by and by comes back to Romeo,
Who had but newly entertained revenge, 170

---

97 **grave** (Mercutio thus puns with his last breath.)   98 **peppered** finished, done for   101 **by . . . arithmetic** by the numbers, as in a textbook on fencing (as at 2.4.20–23)   108 **ally** kinsman   109 **very** true   112 **cousin** kinsman   113 **effeminate** weak   114 **temper** disposition (but with a play on the tempering of a steel sword)   116 **aspired** ascended to   118 **on . . . depend** hangs threateningly over more days   119 **others** other days to come   122 **respective lenity** considerate gentleness   123 **conduct** guide

133 **amazed** dazed.   **doom thee death** sentence you to death   135 **fool** dupe   141 **discover** reveal   142 **manage** conduct   152 **fair** civilly.   **bethink** consider   153 **nice** trivial.   **withal** besides   156 **take truce** make peace   163 **Retorts** returns   167 **envious** malicious   168 **stout** brave   170 **entertained** harbored thoughts of

And to 't they go like lightning, for, ere I
Could draw to part them was stout Tybalt slain,
And, as he fell, did Romeo turn and fly.
This is the truth, or let Benvolio die.

CAPULET'S WIFE
He is a kinsman to the Montague.
Affection makes him false; he speaks not true.   176
Some twenty of them fought in this black strife,
And all those twenty could but kill one life.
I beg for justice, which thou, Prince, must give.
Romeo slew Tybalt; Romeo must not live.

PRINCE
Romeo slew him, he slew Mercutio.
Who now the price of his dear blood doth owe?

MONTAGUE
Not Romeo, Prince, he was Mercutio's friend;
His fault concludes but what the law should end,   184
The life of Tybalt.

PRINCE   And for that offense
Immediately we do exile him hence.
I have an interest in your hate's proceeding;
My blood for your rude brawls doth lie a-bleeding;   188
But I'll amerce you with so strong a fine   189
That you shall all repent the loss of mine.
I will be deaf to pleading and excuses;
Nor tears nor prayers shall purchase out abuses.   192
Therefore use none. Let Romeo hence in haste,   193
Else, when he is found, that hour is his last.   194
Bear hence this body and attend our will.   195
Mercy but murders, pardoning those that kill.   196

Exeunt, [some carrying Tybalt's body].

3.2   *Enter Juliet alone.*

JULIET
Gallop apace, you fiery-footed steeds,   1
Towards Phoebus' lodging! Such a wagoner   2
As Phaëthon would whip you to the west   3
And bring in cloudy night immediately.   4
Spread thy close curtain, love-performing night,   5
That runaways' eyes may wink, and Romeo   6
Leap to these arms, untalked of and unseen.
Lovers can see to do their amorous rites

By their own beauties; or, if love be blind,
It best agrees with night. Come, civil night,   10
Thou sober-suited matron all in black,
And learn me how to lose a winning match   12
Played for a pair of stainless maidenhoods.
Hood my unmanned blood, bating in my cheeks,   14
With thy black mantle till strange love grown bold   15
Think true love acted simple modesty.
Come, night. Come, Romeo. Come, thou day in
    night;
For thou wilt lie upon the wings of night
Whiter than new snow upon a raven's back.
Come, gentle night, come, loving, black-browed
    night,
Give me my Romeo, and when I shall die   21
Take him and cut him out in little stars,
And he will make the face of heaven so fine
That all the world will be in love with night
And pay no worship to the garish sun.   25
O, I have bought the mansion of a love
But not possessed it, and though I am sold,
Not yet enjoyed. So tedious is this day
As is the night before some festival
To an impatient child that hath new robes
And may not wear them. O, here comes my nurse,   31

Enter Nurse, with cords.

And she brings news, and every tongue that speaks
But Romeo's name speaks heavenly eloquence.
Now, Nurse, what news? What hast thou there?
    The cords
That Romeo bid thee fetch?

NURSE   Ay, ay, the cords.
                                    [She throws them down.]

JULIET
Ay me, what news? Why dost thou wring thy
    hands?

NURSE
Ah, weraday! He's dead, he's dead, he's dead!   37
We are undone, lady, we are undone!
Alack the day, he's gone, he's killed, he's dead!

JULIET
Can heaven be so envious?

NURSE   Romeo can,   40
Though heaven cannot. O Romeo, Romeo!
Who ever would have thought it? Romeo!

JULIET
What devil art thou that dost torment me thus?
This torture should be roared in dismal hell.
Hath Romeo slain himself? Say thou but "Ay,"
And that bare vowel "I" shall poison more   46

---

176 Affection partiality   **184 concludes but** only finishes   **188 My
blood** i.e., blood of my kinsman. (Here we learn that Mercutio is kin
to the Prince.)   **189 amerce** punish by a fine   **192 Nor tears** neither
tears.   **purchase out abuses** redeem misdeeds   **193 hence** depart
194 Else otherwise   **195 attend our will** be on hand to hear further
judgment   **196 but murders** i.e., encourages murder by excessive
leniency

3.2. Location: Verona. Capulet's house.
1 apace quickly.   **steeds** i.e., the horses of the sun god's chariot
2 Phoebus (Often equated with Helios, the sun god.)   **lodging** i.e., in
the west, below the horizon   **2–4 Such . . . immediately** i.e., one
who is impetuously young, as we are, would understand the need to
make the day as short as possible and would quickly bring it to an
end. (The mythical allusion is sadly ironic, for Phaëthon drove the
chariot of the sun so badly that he had to be destroyed by Zeus.)
5 close enclosing   **6 runaways'** (Refers to the horses of the sun chariot that ran away with Phaëthon?)   **wink** shut

10 civil circumspect, somberly attired   **12 learn** teach   **14 Hood**
cover. (A term in falconry; the hawk's eyes were covered so that it
would not *bate* or beat its wings.)   **unmanned** untamed (in falconry;
with a pun on "unmarried")   **15 strange** diffident   **21 I** (Often
emended to *he,* following the Fourth Quarto, but Juliet may mean that
when she is dead she will share Romeo's beauty with the world. Dying may also hint at sexual climax.)   **25 garish** dazzling   **31 s.d.
cords** ropes (for the ladder)   **37 weraday** welladay, alas   **40 envious**
malicious   **46 "I"** (Pronounced identically with ay.)

Than the death-darting eye of cockatrice.   47
I am not I, if there be such an "Ay,"
Or those eyes shut, that makes thee answer "Ay."   49
If he be slain, say "Ay," or if not, "No."
Brief sounds determine of my weal or woe.   51

NURSE
I saw the wound. I saw it with mine eyes—
God save the mark!—here on his manly breast.   53
A piteous corpse, a bloody piteous corpse;
Pale, pale as ashes, all bedaubed in blood,
All in gore-blood. I swoonèd at the sight.   56

JULIET
O, break, my heart! Poor bankrupt, break at once!
To prison, eyes; ne'er look on liberty!
Vile earth, to earth resign; end motion here,   59
And thou and Romeo press one heavy bier!   60

NURSE
O Tybalt, Tybalt, the best friend I had!
O courteous Tybalt! Honest gentleman!   62
That ever I should live to see thee dead!

JULIET
What storm is this that blows so contrary?
Is Romeo slaughtered, and is Tybalt dead?
My dearest cousin, and my dearer lord?
Then, dreadful trumpet, sound the general doom!   67
For who is living, if those two are gone?

NURSE
Tybalt is gone, and Romeo banishèd;
Romeo that killed him, he is banishèd.

JULIET
O God! Did Romeo's hand shed Tybalt's blood?

NURSE
It did, it did. Alas the day it did!

JULIET
O serpent heart, hid with a flowering face!   73
Did ever dragon keep so fair a cave?   74
Beautiful tyrant! Fiend angelical!
Dove-feathered raven! Wolvish-ravening lamb!
Despisèd substance of divinest show!   77
Just opposite to what thou justly seem'st,   78
A damnèd saint, an honorable villain!
O nature, what hadst thou to do in hell
When thou didst bower the spirit of a fiend   81
In mortal paradise of such sweet flesh?
Was ever book containing such vile matter
So fairly bound? O, that deceit should dwell
In such a gorgeous palace!

NURSE   There's no trust,
No faith, no honesty in men; all perjured,

All forsworn, all naught, all dissemblers.   87
Ah, where's my man? Give me some aqua vitae.   88
These griefs, these woes, these sorrows make me
   old.
Shame come to Romeo!

JULIET   Blistered be thy tongue
For such a wish! He was not born to shame.
Upon his brow shame is ashamed to sit,
For 'tis a throne where honor may be crowned
Sole monarch of the universal earth.
O, what a beast was I to chide at him!

NURSE
Will you speak well of him that killed your cousin?

JULIET
Shall I speak ill of him that is my husband?
Ah, poor my lord, what tongue shall smooth thy
   name   98
When I, thy three-hours wife, have mangled it?
But wherefore, villain, didst thou kill my cousin?
That villain cousin would have killed my husband.
Back, foolish tears, back to your native spring!
Your tributary drops belong to woe,   103
Which you, mistaking, offer up to joy.
My husband lives, that Tybalt would have slain,   105
And Tybalt's dead, that would have slain my
   husband.
All this is comfort. Wherefore weep I then?
Some word there was, worser than Tybalt's death,
That murdered me. I would forget it fain,   109
But O, it presses to my memory
Like damnèd guilty deeds to sinners' minds:
"Tybalt is dead, and Romeo—banishèd."
That "banishèd," that one word "banishèd,"
Hath slain ten thousand Tybalts. Tybalt's death
Was woe enough, if it had ended there;
Or, if sour woe delights in fellowship
And needly will be ranked with other griefs,   117
Why followed not, when she said "Tybalt's dead,"
"Thy father," or "thy mother," nay, or both,
Which modern lamentation might have moved?   120
But with a rearward following Tybalt's death,   121
"Romeo is banishèd"—to speak that word
Is father, mother, Tybalt, Romeo, Juliet,
All slain, all dead. "Romeo is banishèd!"
There is no end, no limit, measure, bound,
In that word's death; no words can that woe sound.   126
Where is my father and my mother, Nurse?

NURSE
Weeping and wailing over Tybalt's corpse.
Will you go to them? I will bring you thither.

JULIET
Wash they his wounds with tears? Mine shall be
   spent,
When theirs are dry, for Romeo's banishment.

---

47 **cockatrice** basilisk, a mythical serpent that could kill by its look
49 **those eyes shut** if Romeo's eyes are shut (in death) 51 **weal** welfare, happiness 53 **God save the mark** (A familiar exclamation of
apology for an indelicacy, originally an oath intended to avert ill
omen.) 56 **gore-blood** clotted blood 59 **Vile earth** i.e., my body.
resign surrender, return 60 **press** weigh down. **bier** litter for carrying corpses 62 **Honest** honorable 67 **trumpet** i.e., the last trumpet.
general doom Day of Judgment 73 **hid with** hidden by. **flowering**
i.e., fair, like that of the serpent in the Garden of Eden 74 **keep** occupy, guard. **cave** i.e., one with treasure in it 77 **show** appearance
78 **Just** precisely (with a play on *justly*, "truly") 81 **bower** give lodging to

---

87 **naught** worthless, evil 88 **aqua vitae** alcoholic spirits 98 **poor
my lord** my poor lord. **smooth thy name** speak your name kindly
103 **Your . . . woe** you should be shed, offered as a tribute, on some
occasion of real woe 105 **that** whom 109 **fain** gladly 117 **needly**
of necessity. **ranked with** accompanied by 120 **modern** ordinary
121 **rearward** rearguard 126 **sound** (1) fathom (2) express

Take up those cords. Poor ropes, you are beguiled,
Both you and I, for Romeo is exiled.
He made you for a highway to my bed,
But I, a maid, die maiden-widowèd.
Come, cords, come, Nurse. I'll to my wedding bed,
And death, not Romeo, take my maidenhead!

NURSE [*taking up the cords*]
Hie to your chamber. I'll find Romeo
To comfort you. I wot well where he is.   139
Hark ye, your Romeo will be here at night.
I'll to him. He is hid at Laurence' cell.

JULIET
O, find him! Give this ring to my true knight,
                                              [*giving a ring*]
And bid him come to take his last farewell.
                                        Exeunt [*separately*].

❧

3.3   *Enter Friar* [*Laurence*].

FRIAR LAURENCE
Romeo, come forth; come forth, thou fearful man.   1
Affliction is enamored of thy parts,   2
And thou art wedded to calamity.

        [*Enter*] *Romeo.*

ROMEO
Father, what news? What is the Prince's doom?   4
What sorrow craves acquaintance at my hand
That I yet know not?

FRIAR LAURENCE   Too familiar
Is my dear son with such sour company.
I bring thee tidings of the Prince's doom.

ROMEO
What less than doomsday is the Prince's doom?   9

FRIAR LAURENCE
A gentler judgment vanished from his lips: 10
Not body's death, but body's banishment.

ROMEO
Ha, banishment? Be merciful, say "death";
For exile hath more terror in his look,
Much more than death. Do not say "banishment."

FRIAR LAURENCE
Here from Verona art thou banishèd.
Be patient, for the world is broad and wide.

ROMEO
There is no world without Verona walls   17
But purgatory, torture, hell itself.
Hence "banishèd" is banished from the world,
And world's exile is death. Then "banishèd"   20
Is death mistermed. Calling death "banishèd,"
Thou cutt'st my head off with a golden ax
And smilest upon the stroke that murders me.

FRIAR LAURENCE
O deadly sin! O rude unthankfulness!
Thy fault our law calls death, but the kind Prince,   25
Taking thy part, hath rushed aside the law   26
And turned that black word "death" to
   "banishment."
This is dear mercy, and thou seest it not.

ROMEO
'Tis torture, and not mercy. Heaven is here
Where Juliet lives, and every cat and dog
And little mouse, every unworthy thing,
Live here in heaven and may look on her,
But Romeo may not. More validity,   33
More honorable state, more courtship lives   34
In carrion flies than Romeo. They may seize
On the white wonder of dear Juliet's hand
And steal immortal blessing from her lips,
Who even in pure and vestal modesty   38
Still blush, as thinking their own kisses sin;   39
But Romeo may not, he is banishèd.
Flies may do this, but I from this must fly.
They are free men, but I am banishèd.
And sayest thou yet that exile is not death?
Hadst thou no poison mixed, no sharp-ground
   knife,
No sudden mean of death, though ne'er so mean,   45
But "banishèd" to kill me? "Banishèd"?
O Friar, the damnèd use that word in hell;
Howling attends it. How hast thou the heart,
Being a divine, a ghostly confessor,
A sin absolver, and my friend professed,
To mangle me with that word "banishèd"?

FRIAR LAURENCE
Thou fond mad man, hear me a little speak.   52

ROMEO
O, thou wilt speak again of banishment.

FRIAR LAURENCE
I'll give thee armor to keep off that word,
Adversity's sweet milk, philosophy,
To comfort thee, though thou art banishèd.

ROMEO
Yet "banishèd"? Hang up philosophy!   57
Unless philosophy can make a Juliet,
Displant a town, reverse a prince's doom,   59
It helps not, it prevails not. Talk no more.

FRIAR LAURENCE
O, then I see that madmen have no ears.

ROMEO
How should they, when that wise men have no
   eyes?

FRIAR LAURENCE
Let me dispute with thee of thy estate.   63

ROMEO
Thou canst not speak of that thou dost not feel.   64

---

139 wot know
3.3. Location: Verona. Friar Laurence's cell.
1 fearful full of fear   **2 parts** qualities   **4 doom** judgment   **9 dooms-day** the Day of Judgment, i.e., end of the world   **10 vanished** issued (into air)   **17 without** outside of   **20 world's exile** exile from the world

25 Thy fault . . . death for your crime, the law demands a death sentence   **26 rushed** thrust   **33 validity** value   **34 courtship** (1) courtliness (2) occasion for wooing   **38 vestal** maidenly   **39 their own kisses** i.e., their touching each other   **45 mean . . . mean** means . . . base   **52 fond** foolish   **57 Yet** still   **59 Displant** uproot   **63 dispute** reason.   **estate** situation   **64 that** that which

Wert thou as young as I, Juliet thy love,
An hour but married, Tybalt murderèd,
Doting like me, and like me banishèd,
Then mightst thou speak, then mightst thou tear thy
   hair,
And fall upon the ground, as I do now,
Taking the measure of an unmade grave.
                    [*He falls upon the ground.*]
                      Knock [*within*].

FRIAR LAURENCE
Arise. One knocks. Good Romeo, hide thyself.
ROMEO
Not I, unless the breath of heartsick groans,
Mistlike, infold me from the search of eyes.   *Knock.*
FRIAR LAURENCE
Hark, how they knock!—Who's there?—Romeo,
   arise.
Thou wilt be taken.—Stay awhile!—Stand up.
                          Knock.
Run to my study.—By and by!—God's will,
What simpleness is this?—I come, I come!   *Knock.* 77
Who knocks so hard? Whence come you? What's
   your will?   [*Going to the door.*]
NURSE [*within*]
Let me come in, and you shall know my errand.
I come from Lady Juliet.
FRIAR LAURENCE   Welcome, then.
               [*He opens the door.*]

    Enter Nurse.

NURSE
O holy Friar, O, tell me, holy Friar,
Where's my lady's lord, where's Romeo?
FRIAR LAURENCE
There on the ground, with his own tears made
   drunk.
NURSE
O, he is even in my mistress' case,   84
Just in her case! O woeful sympathy!   85
Piteous predicament! Even so lies she,
Blubbering and weeping, weeping and
   blubbering.—
Stand up, stand up! Stand, an you be a man.   88
For Juliet's sake, for her sake, rise and stand!
Why should you fall into so deep an O?   90
ROMEO   Nurse!   [*He rises.*]
NURSE
Ah sir, ah sir! Death's the end of all.
ROMEO
Spakest thou of Juliet? How is it with her?
Doth not she think me an old murderer,   94
Now I have stained the childhood of our joy
With blood removed but little from her own?
Where is she? And how doth she? And what says
My concealed lady to our canceled love?   98

NURSE
O, she says nothing, sir, but weeps and weeps,
And now falls on her bed, and then starts up,
And "Tybalt" calls, and then on Romeo cries, 101
And then down falls again.
ROMEO   As if that name,
Shot from the deadly level of a gun,   103
Did murder her, as that name's cursèd hand
Murdered her kinsman. O, tell me, Friar, tell me,
In what vile part of this anatomy
Doth my name lodge? Tell me, that I may sack 107
The hateful mansion.
         [*He draws a weapon, but is restrained.*]
FRIAR LAURENCE   Hold thy desperate hand!
Art thou a man? Thy form cries out thou art;
Thy tears are womanish, thy wild acts denote
The unreasonable fury of a beast.
Unseemly woman in a seeming man,
And ill-beseeming beast in seeming both!
Thou hast amazed me. By my holy order,
I thought thy disposition better tempered. 115
Hast thou slain Tybalt? Wilt thou slay thyself,
And slay thy lady, that in thy life lives,
By doing damnèd hate upon thyself?
Why railest thou on thy birth, the heaven, and
   earth,
Since birth, and heaven, and earth, all three do meet 120
In thee at once, which thou at once wouldst lose?
Fie, fie, thou shamest thy shape, thy love, thy wit, 122
Which, like a usurer, abound'st in all,   123
And usest none in that true use indeed   124
Which should bedeck thy shape, thy love, thy wit.
Thy noble shape is but a form of wax,   126
Digressing from the valor of a man;   127
Thy dear love sworn but hollow perjury,
Killing that love which thou hast vowed to cherish; 129
Thy wit, that ornament to shape and love,
Misshapen in the conduct of them both,   131
Like powder in a skilless soldier's flask   132
Is set afire by thine own ignorance,
And thou dismembered with thine own defense. 134
What, rouse thee, man! Thy Juliet is alive,
For whose dear sake thou wast but lately dead; 136
There art thou happy. Tybalt would kill thee, 137
But thou slewest Tybalt; there art thou happy.
The law that threatened death becomes thy friend
And turns it to exile; there art thou happy.
A pack of blessings light upon thy back,
Happiness courts thee in her best array,
But like a mishavèd and sullen wench   143

---

77 **simpleness** foolishness 84 **even** exactly. **case** situation 85 **woeful sympathy** mutuality of grief 88 **an** if 90 **an O** a fit of groaning. (A sexual meaning, unrecognized by the speaker, is suggested by *rise and stand* in the previous line.) 94 **old** hardened 98 **concealed** secret. **canceled** nullified (by the impending exile)

101 **on Romeo cries** exclaims against Romeo, calls his name 103 **level** aim 107 **sack** destroy 115 **tempered** harmonized, balanced 120 **heaven, and earth** i.e., soul and body 122 **wit** intellect 123 **Which** (you) who. **all** all capabilities 124 **true use** i.e., proper use of your resources, not usury 126 **form of wax** waxwork, mere outer form 127 **Digressing** if it deviates 129 **Killing** if it kills 131 **conduct** guidance 132 **powder** gunpowder. **flask** powder horn 134 **dismembered . . . defense** blown to pieces by that which should defend you, i.e., your *wit*, or intellect 136 **wast . . . dead** i.e., only recently were wishing yourself dead. (See line 70.) 137 **happy** fortunate 143 **mishavèd** misbehaved

Thou pout'st upon thy fortune and thy love.
Take heed, take heed, for such die miserable.
Go, get thee to thy love, as was decreed. 146
Ascend her chamber; hence and comfort her.
But look thou stay not till the watch be set, 148
For then thou canst not pass to Mantua,
Where thou shalt live till we can find a time
To blaze your marriage, reconcile your friends, 151
Beg pardon of the Prince, and call thee back
With twenty hundred thousand times more joy
Than thou went'st forth in lamentation.
Go before, Nurse. Commend me to thy lady,
And bid her hasten all the house to bed,
Which heavy sorrow makes them apt unto.
Romeo is coming.

NURSE
O Lord, I could have stayed here all the night
To hear good counsel. O, what learning is!—
My lord, I'll tell my lady you will come.
ROMEO
Do so, and bid my sweet prepare to chide.
NURSE [giving a ring]
Here, sir, a ring she bid me give you, sir.
Hie you, make haste, for it grows very late.   [Exit.]
ROMEO
How well my comfort is revived by this! 165
FRIAR LAURENCE
Go hence. Good night. And here stands all your
    state: 166
Either be gone before the watch be set,
Or by the break of day disguised from hence.
Sojourn in Mantua. I'll find out your man,
And he shall signify from time to time
Every good hap to you that chances here. 171
Give me thy hand. 'Tis late. Farewell, good night.

ROMEO
But that a joy past joy calls out on me,
It were a grief so brief to part with thee. 174
Farewell.   Exeunt [separately].

❧

3.4 *Enter old Capulet, his Wife, and Paris.*

CAPULET
Things have fall'n out, sir, so unluckily, 1
That we have had no time to move our daughter. 2
Look you, she loved her kinsman Tybalt dearly,
And so did I. Well, we were born to die.
'Tis very late. She'll not come down tonight.
I promise you, but for your company 6
I would have been abed an hour ago.
PARIS
These times of woe afford no times to woo.

Madam, good night. Commend me to your
    daughter.
WIFE 146
I will, and know her mind early tomorrow.
Tonight she's mewed up to her heaviness. 11
CAPULET
Sir Paris, I will make a desperate tender 12
Of my child's love. I think she will be ruled
In all respects by me; nay, more, I doubt it not.
Wife, go you to her ere you go to bed.
Acquaint her here of my son Paris' love,
And bid her, mark you me, on Wednesday next— 17
But soft, what day is this?
PARIS   Monday, my lord.
CAPULET
Monday! Ha, ha! Well, Wednesday is too soon;
O' Thursday let it be. O' Thursday, tell her,
She shall be married to this noble earl.
Will you be ready? Do you like this haste?
We'll keep no great ado—a friend or two;
For hark you, Tybalt being slain so late, 24
It may be thought we held him carelessly, 25
Being our kinsman, if we revel much.
Therefore we'll have some half a dozen friends,
And there an end. But what say you to Thursday?
PARIS
My lord, I would that Thursday were tomorrow.
CAPULET
Well, get you gone. O' Thursday be it, then.
[To his Wife.] Go you to Juliet ere you go to bed;
Prepare her, wife, against this wedding day.— 32
Farewell, my lord.—Light to my chamber, ho!—
Afore me, it is so very late 34
That we may call it early by and by.
Good night.   Exeunt.

❧

3.5 *Enter Romeo and Juliet aloft [at the window].*

JULIET
Wilt thou be gone? It is not yet near day.
It was the nightingale, and not the lark,
That pierced the fearful hollow of thine ear; 3
Nightly she sings on yond pomegranate tree.
Believe me, love, it was the nightingale.
ROMEO
It was the lark, the herald of the morn,
No nightingale. Look, love, what envious streaks
Do lace the severing clouds in yonder east. 8
Night's candles are burnt out, and jocund day 9
Stands tiptoe on the misty mountain tops.

146 decreed arranged earlier **148 the watch be set** guards are posted (at the city gates) **151 blaze** publish, divulge. **friends** relations **165 comfort** happiness **166 here . . . state** your fortune depends on what follows **171 good hap** fortunate event **174 brief** quickly
3.4. Location: Verona. Capulet's house.
1 fall'n out happened **2 move** persuade **6 promise** assure

11 mewed up to cooped up with. (A term from falconry, reminiscent of 2.2.159–168.) **heaviness** sorrow **12 desperate tender** bold offer **17 mark you me** listen to this **24 late** recently **25 held him carelessly** did not regard him highly **32 against** in anticipation of **34 Afore me** i.e., by my life. (A mild oath.)
3.5. Location: Verona. Capulet's orchard with Juliet's chamber window above, and, at lines 68 ff., the interior of Juliet's chamber.
3 fearful apprehensive, anxious **8 severing** separating **9 jocund** cheerful

I must be gone and live, or stay and die.

JULIET

Yond light is not daylight, I know it, I.
It is some meteor that the sun exhaled   13
To be to thee this night a torchbearer
And light thee on thy way to Mantua.
Therefore stay yet. Thou need'st not to be gone.

ROMEO

Let me be ta'en; let me be put to death.
I am content, so thou wilt have it so.   18
I'll say yon gray is not the morning's eye;
'Tis but the pale reflex of Cynthia's brow.   20
Nor that is not the lark whose notes do beat
The vaulty heaven so high above our heads.
I have more care to stay than will to go.   23
Come, death, and welcome! Juliet wills it so.
How is 't, my soul? Let's talk. It is not day.

JULIET

It is, it is. Hie hence, begone, away!   26
It is the lark that sings so out of tune,
Straining harsh discords and unpleasing sharps.   28
Some say the lark makes sweet division;   29
This doth not so, for she divideth us.
Some say the lark and loathèd toad changed eyes;   31
O, now I would they had changed voices too,
Since arm from arm that voice doth us affray,   33
Hunting thee hence with hunt's-up to the day.   34
O, now begone! More light and light it grows.

ROMEO

More light and light, more dark and dark our woes!

Enter Nurse [hastily].

NURSE Madam!
JULIET Nurse?
NURSE

Your lady mother is coming to your chamber.
The day is broke; be wary, look about.   [*Exit.*]

JULIET

Then window, let day in, and let life out.

ROMEO

Farewell, farewell! One kiss, and I'll descend.
          [*They kiss. He climbs down from the window.*]

JULIET

Art thou gone so? Love, lord, ay, husband, friend!   43
I must hear from thee every day in the hour,
For in a minute there are many days.
O, by this count I shall be much in years   46
Ere I again behold my Romeo!

ROMEO [*from below her window*]   Farewell!

I will omit no opportunity
That may convey my greetings, love, to thee.

JULIET

O, think'st thou we shall ever meet again?

ROMEO

I doubt it not, and all these woes shall serve
For sweet discourses in our times to come.

JULIET

O God, I have an ill-divining soul!   54
Methinks I see thee, now thou art so low,
As one dead in the bottom of a tomb.
Either my eyesight fails or thou lookest pale.

ROMEO

And trust me, love, in my eye so do you.
Dry sorrow drinks our blood. Adieu, adieu!   *Exit.* 59

JULIET

O Fortune, Fortune! All men call thee fickle.
If thou art fickle, what dost thou with him
That is renowned for faith? Be fickle, Fortune.
For then, I hope, thou wilt not keep him long,
But send him back.

Enter Mother [Capulet's Wife].

WIFE   Ho, daughter, are you up?

JULIET

Who is 't that calls? It is my lady mother.
Is she not down so late, or up so early?   66
What unaccustomed cause procures her hither?   67
          [*She goeth down from the window.*]

WIFE

Why, how now, Juliet?

JULIET   Madam, I am not well.

WIFE

Evermore weeping for your cousin's death?
What, wilt thou wash him from his grave with tears?
An if thou couldst, thou couldst not make him live;   71
Therefore, have done. Some grief shows much of
          love,
But much of grief shows still some want of wit.   73

JULIET

Yet let me weep for such a feeling loss.   74

WIFE

So shall you feel the loss, but not the friend
Which you weep for.

JULIET   Feeling so the loss,
I cannot choose but ever weep the friend.   77

WIFE

Well, girl, thou weep'st not so much for his death
As that the villain lives which slaughtered him.

---

13 exhaled i.e., has drawn out of the ground. (Meteors were thought to be vapors of luminous gas drawn up by the sun.) **18 so thou** if you **20 reflex** reflection. **Cynthia's** the moon's **23 care** desire, concern **26 Hie hence** hasten away **28 sharps** notes relatively high in pitch and hence discordant **29 division** variations on a melody, made by dividing each note into notes of briefer duration **31 changed** exchanged. (A popular saying, to account for the observation that the lark has very ordinary eyes and the toad remarkable ones.) **33 arm from arm** from one another's arms. **affray** frighten **34 hunt's-up** a song or tune originally designed to awaken huntsmen; later, used also to serenade a newly married couple **43 friend** lover **46 count** method of calculation. **much in years** very old

54 ill-divining prophesying of evil **59 Dry sorrow** (The heat of the body in sorrow and despair was thought to descend into the bowels and dry up the blood.) **66 down** in bed **67 procures** induces to come. (As indicated by the bracketed stage direction, which is from the First Quarto, Juliet, who has appeared until now at her "window" above the stage, evidently descends quickly to the main stage and joins her mother for the remainder of the scene. The stage, which before was to have been imagined as Capulet's orchard, is now Juliet's chamber. Juliet's mother has entered onto the main stage four lines earlier.) **71 An if** if **73 wit** intellect **74 feeling** deeply felt **77 the friend** (Juliet secretly means "my lover," as at line 43, but, of course, her mother hears it as "Tybalt.")

JULIET
What villain, madam?
WIFE   That same villain, Romeo.
JULIET [aside]
Villain and he be many miles asunder.—
God pardon him! I do, with all my heart;
And yet no man like he doth grieve my heart.   83
WIFE
That is because the traitor murderer lives.
JULIET
Ay, madam, from the reach of these my hands.
Would none but I might venge my cousin's death!
WIFE
We will have vengeance for it, fear thou not.
Then weep no more. I'll send to one in Mantua,
Where that same banished runagate doth live,   89
Shall give him such an unaccustomed dram   90
That he shall soon keep Tybalt company.
And then, I hope, thou wilt be satisfied.
JULIET
Indeed, I never shall be satisfied
With Romeo till I behold him—dead—
Is my poor heart so for a kinsman vexed.
Madam, if you could find out but a man
To bear a poison, I would temper it,   97
That Romeo should, upon receipt thereof,
Soon sleep in quiet. O, how my heart abhors
To hear him named, and cannot come to him
To wreak the love I bore my cousin   101
Upon his body that hath slaughtered him!   102
WIFE
Find thou the means, and I'll find such a man.
But now I'll tell thee joyful tidings, girl.
JULIET
And joy comes well in such a needy time.
What are they, beseech your ladyship?
WIFE
Well, well, thou hast a careful father, child,   107
One who, to put thee from thy heaviness,   108
Hath sorted out a sudden day of joy   109
That thou expects not, nor I looked not for.
JULIET
Madam, in happy time, what day is that?
WIFE
Marry, my child, early next Thursday morn,   112
The gallant, young, and noble gentleman,
The County Paris, at Saint Peter's Church
Shall happily make thee there a joyful bride.
JULIET
Now, by Saint Peter's Church, and Peter too,

He shall not make me there a joyful bride!
I wonder at this haste, that I must wed
Ere he that should be husband comes to woo.
I pray you, tell my lord and father, madam,
I will not marry yet, and when I do I swear
It shall be Romeo, whom you know I hate,
Rather than Paris. These are news indeed!
WIFE
Here comes your father. Tell him so yourself,
And see how he will take it at your hands.

Enter Capulet and Nurse.

CAPULET
When the sun sets, the earth doth drizzle dew,
But for the sunset of my brother's son
It rains downright.
How now, a conduit, girl? What, still in tears?   129
Evermore showering? In one little body
Thou counterfeits a bark, a sea, a wind;   131
For still thy eyes, which I may call the sea,
Do ebb and flow with tears; the bark thy body is,
Sailing in this salt flood; the winds, thy sighs,
Who, raging with thy tears, and they with them,
Without a sudden calm, will overset   136
Thy tempest-tossèd body.—How now, wife?
Have you delivered to her our decree?
WIFE
Ay, sir, but she will none, she gives you thanks.   139
I would the fool were married to her grave!
CAPULET
Soft, take me with you, take me with you, wife.   141
How? Will she none? Doth she not give us thanks?
Is she not proud? Doth she not count her blest,   143
Unworthy as she is, that we have wrought   144
So worthy a gentleman to be her bride?   145
JULIET
Not proud you have, but thankful that you have.
Proud can I never be of what I hate,
But thankful even for hate that is meant love.   148
CAPULET
How, how, how, how, chopped logic? What is this?   149
"Proud," and "I thank you," and "I thank you not,"
And yet "not proud"? Mistress minion, you,   151
Thank me no thankings, nor proud me no prouds,
But fettle your fine joints 'gainst Thursday next   153
To go with Paris to Saint Peter's Church,
Or I will drag thee on a hurdle thither.   155
Out, you greensickness carrion! Out, you baggage!   156
You tallow-face!

83 no man like he no man so much as he. grieve (1) anger (2) grieve with longing. (Juliet speaks to her mother throughout in intentional ambiguities, at lines 85, 86, 99, 100–102, etc.) 89 runagate renegade, fugitive 90 Shall who shall. dram dose. (Literally, one-eighth of a fluid ounce.) 97 temper (1) mix, concoct (2) alloy, dilute. (In her intended double meanings about Romeo dead, poisoned, and sleeping in quiet, Juliet is, of course, unaware of an ironic anticipation of how these things will be fulfilled.) 101 wreak (1) avenge (2) bestow 102 his body that the body of him who 107 careful full of care (for you) 108 heaviness sorrow 109 sorted chosen 112 Marry i.e., by the Virgin Mary

129 conduit water pipe, fountain 131 bark sailing vessel 136 Without . . . calm unless they quickly calm themselves 139 will . . . thanks says "no thank you," she'll have no part of it 141 take . . . you let me understand you 143 count her consider herself 144 wrought produced 145 bride bridegroom 148 hate . . . love that which is hateful but which was meant lovingly 149 chopped logic a shallow and sophistical argument, or arguer 151 minion spoiled darling, minx 153 fettle make ready. 'gainst in anticipation of 155 a hurdle a conveyance on which criminals were dragged to execution 156 greensickness (An anemic ailment of young unmarried women; it suggests Juliet's paleness.) baggage good-for-nothing

WIFE [*to Capulet*]   Fie, fie! What, are you mad?   157

JULIET [*kneeling*]

Good father, I beseech you on my knees,

Hear me with patience but to speak a word.

CAPULET

Hang thee, young baggage, disobedient wretch!

I tell thee what: get thee to church o' Thursday

Or never after look me in the face.

Speak not, reply not, do not answer me!

My fingers itch. Wife, we scarce thought us blest

That God had lent us but this only child;

But now I see this one is one too much,

And that we have a curse in having her.

Out on her, hilding!

NURSE   God in heaven bless her!   168

You are to blame, my lord, to rate her so.   169

CAPULET

And why, my Lady Wisdom? Hold your tongue,

Good Prudence. Smatter with your gossips, go.   171

NURSE

I speak no treason.

CAPULET   O, God-i'-good-e'en!   172

NURSE

May not one speak?

CAPULET   Peace, you mumbling fool!

Utter your gravity o'er a gossip's bowl,   174

For here we need it not.

WIFE   You are too hot.

CAPULET   God's bread, it makes me mad!   177

Day, night, hour, tide, time, work, play,   178

Alone, in company, still my care hath been

To have her matched. And having now provided

A gentleman of noble parentage,

Of fair demesnes, youthful, and nobly liened,   182

Stuffed, as they say, with honorable parts,   183

Proportioned as one's thought would wish a man—

And then to have a wretched puling fool,   185

A whining mammet, in her fortune's tender,   186

To answer, "I'll not wed, I cannot love,

I am too young; I pray you, pardon me."

But, an you will not wed, I'll pardon you.   189

Graze where you will, you shall not house with me.

Look to 't, think on 't. I do not use to jest.   191

Thursday is near. Lay hand on heart; advise.   192

An you be mine, I'll give you to my friend;

An you be not, hang, beg, starve, die in the streets,

For, by my soul, I'll ne'er acknowledge thee,

Nor what is mine shall never do thee good.

Trust to 't, bethink you. I'll not be forsworn.   *Exit.* 197

JULIET

Is there no pity sitting in the clouds

That sees into the bottom of my grief?

O sweet my Mother, cast me not away!

Delay this marriage for a month, a week;

Or if you do not, make the bridal bed

In that dim monument where Tybalt lies.

WIFE

Talk not to me, for I'll not speak a word.

Do as thou wilt, for I have done with thee.   *Exit.*

JULIET [*rising*]

O God!—O Nurse, how shall this be prevented?

My husband is on earth, my faith in heaven.   207

How shall that faith return again to earth,   208

Unless that husband send it me from heaven   209

By leaving earth? Comfort me, counsel me.   210

Alack, alack, that heaven should practice stratagems 211

Upon so soft a subject as myself!

What sayst thou? Hast thou not a word of joy?

Some comfort, Nurse.

NURSE   Faith, here it is.

Romeo is banished, and all the world to nothing   215

That he dares ne'er come back to challenge you,   216

Or if he do, it needs must be by stealth.

Then, since the case so stands as now it doth,

I think it best you married with the County.

O, he's a lovely gentleman!

Romeo's a dishclout to him. An eagle, madam,   221

Hath not so green, so quick, so fair an eye   222

As Paris hath. Beshrew my very heart,   223

I think you are happy in this second match,

For it excels your first; or if it did not,

Your first is dead—or 'twere as good he were,

As living here and you no use of him.   227

JULIET   Speak'st thou from thy heart?

NURSE

And from my soul too. Else beshrew them both.

JULIET   Amen!   230

NURSE   What?

JULIET

Well, thou hast comforted me marvelous much.

Go in, and tell my lady I am gone,

Having displeased my father, to Laurence' cell

To make confession and to be absolved.

NURSE

Marry, I will; and this is wisely done.   [*Exit.*]

JULIET

Ancient damnation! O most wicked fiend!   237

Is it more sin to wish me thus forsworn,   238

Or to dispraise my lord with that same tongue

Which she hath praised him with above compare

---

157 **tallow-face** paleface   168 **hilding** jade, baggage   169 **rate** be-rate, scold   171 **Smatter** chatter.   **gossips** gossiping women friends
172 **God-i'-good-e'en** i.e., for God's sake. (Literally, God give you good evening.)   174 **gravity** wisdom. (Said contemptuously.)
177 **God's bread** i.e., by God's (Christ's) Sacrament   178 **tide** season
182 **demesnes** estates.   **liened** descended   183 **parts** qualities
185 **puling** whining   186 **mammet** doll.   **in . . . tender** when an offer of good fortune is made to her   189 **pardon you** i.e., allow you to depart. (Said caustically.)   191 **do not use** am not accustomed
192 **advise** consider carefully   197 **be forsworn** i.e., go back on my word

207 **my faith in heaven** (Juliet refers to her marriage vows.)
208–210 **How . . . leaving earth** i.e., how can I remarry while Romeo is still alive?   211 **practice** scheme, contrive   215 **all . . . nothing** the odds are overwhelming   216 **challenge** lay claim to
221 **dishclout** dishrag   222 **quick** keen   223 **Beshrew** i.e., cursed be. (Also at line 229.)   227 **here** i.e., on earth   230 **Amen** i.e., yes, indeed, *beshrew* ("cursed be") your heart and soul. (But Juliet does not explain this private meaning to the Nurse.)   237 **Ancient damnation** damnable old woman   238 **forsworn** i.e., false to my marriage vows

So many thousand times? Go, counselor,
Thou and my bosom henceforth shall be twain.   242
I'll to the Friar to know his remedy.
If all else fail, myself have power to die.   *Exit.*

❖

4.1   *Enter Friar [Laurence] and County Paris.*

FRIAR LAURENCE
  On Thursday, sir? The time is very short.
PARIS
  My father Capulet will have it so,
  And I am nothing slow to slack his haste.   3
FRIAR LAURENCE
  You say you do not know the lady's mind?
  Uneven is the course. I like it not.
PARIS
  Immoderately she weeps for Tybalt's death,
  And therefore have I little talked of love,
  For Venus smiles not in a house of tears.   8
  Now, sir, her father counts it dangerous
  That she do give her sorrow so much sway,
  And in his wisdom hastes our marriage   11
  To stop the inundation of her tears,
  Which, too much minded by herself alone,   13
  May be put from her by society.   14
  Now do you know the reason of this haste.
FRIAR LAURENCE [*aside*]
  I would I knew not why it should be slowed.—
  Look, sir, here comes the lady toward my cell.

      Enter Juliet.

PARIS
  Happily met, my lady and my wife!
JULIET
  That may be, sir, when I may be a wife.
PARIS
  That "may be" must be, love, on Thursday next.
JULIET
  What must be shall be.
FRIAR LAURENCE   That's a certain text.
PARIS
  Come you to make confession to this father?
JULIET
  To answer that, I should confess to you.
PARIS
  Do not deny to him that you love me.
JULIET
  I will confess to you that I love him.
PARIS
  So will ye, I am sure, that you love me.

JULIET
  If I do so, it will be of more price,   27
  Being spoke behind your back, than to your face.
PARIS
  Poor soul, thy face is much abused with tears.
JULIET
  The tears have got small victory by that,
  For it was bad enough before their spite.   31
PARIS
  Thou wrong'st it more than tears with that report.
JULIET
  That is no slander, sir, which is a truth;
  And what I spake, I spake it to my face.   34
PARIS
  Thy face is mine, and thou hast slandered it.
JULIET
  It may be so, for it is not mine own.—   36
  Are you at leisure, holy Father, now,
  Or shall I come to you at evening Mass?
FRIAR LAURENCE
  My leisure serves me, pensive daughter, now.   39
  My lord, we must entreat the time alone.   40
PARIS
  God shield I should disturb devotion!   41
  Juliet, on Thursday early will I rouse ye.
  Till then, adieu, and keep this holy kiss.   *Exit.*
JULIET
  O, shut the door! And when thou hast done so,
  Come weep with me—past hope, past cure, past
      help!
FRIAR LAURENCE
  Ah, Juliet, I already know thy grief;
  It strains me past the compass of my wits.   47
  I hear thou must, and nothing may prorogue it,   48
  On Thursday next be married to this county.
JULIET
  Tell me not, Friar, that thou hearest of this,
  Unless thou tell me how I may prevent it.
  If in thy wisdom thou canst give no help,
  Do thou but call my resolution wise
  And with this knife I'll help it presently.   54
          [*She shows a knife.*]
  God joined my heart and Romeo's, thou our hands;
  And ere this hand, by thee to Romeo sealed,
  Shall be the label to another deed,   57
  Or my true heart with treacherous revolt
  Turn to another, this shall slay them both.   59
  Therefore, out of thy long-experienced time,   60
  Give me some present counsel, or, behold,
  Twixt my extremes and me this bloody knife   62
  Shall play the umpire, arbitrating that
  Which the commission of thy years and art   64

---

242 bosom secret thoughts.   **twain** separated
4.1. Location: Verona. Friar Laurence's cell.
3 nothing . . . haste not at all reluctant in a way that might slacken his haste   **8 Venus . . . tears** (1) amorousness is not appropriate in a house of mourning (2) the planet Venus does not exert a favorable influence when it is in an inauspicious *house* or constellation of the zodiac   **11 hastes** hurries   **13 minded** thought about   **14 society** companionship

27 more price greater worth   **31 spite** malice   **34 to my face** (1) openly (2) about my face   **36 is not mine own** (1) is beyond my control, does not reveal me truly (2) belongs to Romeo   **39 pensive** sorrowful   **40 entreat . . . alone** ask you to leave us alone   **41 shield** prevent (that)   **47 compass** bounds   **48 may prorogue** can delay   **54 presently** at once   **57 label** strip attached to a deed to carry the seal; hence, confirmation, seal   **59 both** i.e., hand and heart   **60 time** age   **62 extremes** extreme difficulties   **64 commission** authority.   **art** skill

Could to no issue of true honor bring.
Be not so long to speak; I long to die   66
If what thou speak'st speak not of remedy.

FRIAR LAURENCE
Hold, daughter. I do spy a kind of hope,
Which craves as desperate an execution
As that is desperate which we would prevent.
If, rather than to marry County Paris,
Thou hast the strength of will to slay thyself,
Then is it likely thou wilt undertake
A thing like death to chide away this shame,
That cop'st with Death himself to scape from it;   75
And if thou darest, I'll give thee remedy.

JULIET
O, bid me leap, rather than marry Paris,
From off the battlements of any tower,
Or walk in thievish ways, or bid me lurk   79
Where serpents are; chain me with roaring bears,
Or hide me nightly in a charnel house,   81
O'ercovered quite with dead men's rattling bones,
With reeky shanks and yellow chopless skulls;   83
Or bid me go into a new-made grave
And hide me with a dead man in his tomb—
Things that, to hear them told, have made me
    tremble—
And I will do it without fear or doubt,
To live an unstained wife to my sweet love.

FRIAR LAURENCE
Hold, then. Go home, be merry, give consent
To marry Paris. Wednesday is tomorrow.
Tomorrow night look that thou lie alone;
Let not the Nurse lie with thee in thy chamber.
Take thou this vial, being then in bed,
                                    [showing her a vial]
And this distilling liquor drink thou off,   94
When presently through all thy veins shall run
A cold and drowsy humor; for no pulse   96
Shall keep his native progress, but surcease;   97
No warmth, no breath shall testify thou livest;
The roses in thy lips and cheeks shall fade
To wanny ashes, thy eyes' windows fall   100
Like death when he shuts up the day of life;
Each part, deprived of supple government,   102
Shall, stiff and stark and cold, appear like death.
And in this borrowed likeness of shrunk death
Thou shalt continue two-and-forty hours,
And then awake as from a pleasant sleep.
Now, when the bridegroom in the morning comes
To rouse thee from thy bed, there art thou dead.
Then, as the manner of our country is,
In thy best robes uncovered on the bier
Thou shalt be borne to that same ancient vault
Where all the kindred of the Capulets lie.

In the meantime, against thou shalt awake,   113
Shall Romeo by my letters know our drift,   114
And hither shall he come; and he and I
Will watch thy waking, and that very night
Shall Romeo bear thee hence to Mantua.
And this shall free thee from this present shame,
If no inconstant toy nor womanish fear   119
Abate thy valor in the acting it.

JULIET [taking the vial]
Give me, give me! O, tell not me of fear!

FRIAR LAURENCE
Hold, get you gone. Be strong and prosperous   122
In this resolve. I'll send a friar with speed
To Mantua, with my letters to thy lord.

JULIET
Love give me strength, and strength shall help
    afford.   125
Farewell, dear Father!   Exeunt [separately].

                            ❧

4.2   Enter Father Capulet, Mother [Capulet's Wife],
            Nurse, and Servingmen, two or three.

CAPULET
So many guests invite as here are writ.
                            [Exit one or two servingmen.]
Sirrah, go hire me twenty cunning cooks.   2
SERVINGMAN   You shall have none ill, sir, for I'll try if   3
they can lick their fingers.
CAPULET   How canst thou try them so?
SERVINGMAN   Marry, sir, 'tis an ill cook that cannot lick
his own fingers; therefore he that cannot lick his
fingers goes not with me.
CAPULET   Go, begone.   [Exit Servingman.]
We shall be much unfurnished for this time.   10
What, is my daughter gone to Friar Laurence?
NURSE   Ay, forsooth.
CAPULET
Well, he may chance to do some good on her.
A peevish self-willed harlotry it is.   14

            Enter Juliet.

NURSE
See where she comes from shrift with merry look.
CAPULET
How now, my headstrong, where have you been
    gadding?
JULIET
Where I have learned me to repent the sin
Of disobedient opposition
To you and your behests, and am enjoined   19
By holy Laurence to fall prostrate here,   [kneeling]
To beg your pardon. Pardon, I beseech you!
Henceforward I am ever ruled by you.

---

66 so long so slow (with play on *long*, "yearn")   **75 That cop'st** you
who would encounter or negotiate with; or, a thing that would cope.
it i.e., shame   **79 thievish ways** roads frequented by thieves
81 charnel house vault for human bones   **83 reeky** reeking, mal-
odorous.   **chopless** without the lower jaw   **94 distilling** infusing
96 humor fluid   **97 his native** its natural.   **surcease** cease
100 wanny wan, pale   **102 supple government** control of motion

113 against anticipating when   **114 drift** plan   **119 toy** idle fancy
122 prosperous successful   **125 help afford** provide help
4.2. Location: Verona. Capulet's house.
2 cunning skilled   **3 none ill** no bad ones.   **try** test   **10 unfurnished**
unprovided   **14 A peevish . . . is** i.e., she's a silly good-for-nothing
19 behests commands

CAPULET
    Send for the County! Go tell him of this.
    I'll have this knot knit up tomorrow morning.
JULIET
    I met the youthful lord at Laurence' cell
    And gave him what becomèd love I might,   26
    Not stepping o'er the bounds of modesty.
CAPULET
    Why, I am glad on 't. This is well. Stand up.
                                            [Juliet rises.]
    This is as 't should be. Let me see the County;
    Ay, marry, go, I say, and fetch him hither.
    Now, afore God, this reverend holy friar,
    All our whole city is much bound to him.   32
JULIET
    Nurse, will you go with me into my closet   33
    To help me sort such needful ornaments   34
    As you think fit to furnish me tomorrow?
WIFE
    No, not till Thursday. There is time enough.
CAPULET
    Go, Nurse, go with her. We'll to church tomorrow.
                                    Exeunt [Juliet and Nurse].
WIFE
    We shall be short in our provision.
    'Tis now near night.
CAPULET   Tush, I will stir about,
    And all things shall be well, I warrant thee, wife.
    Go thou to Juliet, help to deck up her.
    I'll not to bed tonight. Let me alone.
    I'll play the huswife for this once.—What, ho!—   43
    They are all forth. Well, I will walk myself
    To County Paris, to prepare up him
    Against tomorrow. My heart is wondrous light,
    Since this same wayward girl is so reclaimed.
                                                    Exeunt.

                            ❖

4.3   *Enter Juliet and Nurse.*

JULIET
    Ay, those attires are best. But, gentle Nurse,
    I pray thee, leave me to myself tonight;
    For I have need of many orisons   3
    To move the heavens to smile upon my state,
    Which, well thou knowest, is cross and full of sin.   5

            Enter Mother [Capulet's Wife].

WIFE
    What, are you busy, ho? Need you my help?
JULIET
    No, madam, we have culled such necessaries   7
    As are behooveful for our state tomorrow.   8
    So please you, let me now be left alone,

26 becomèd befitting   **32 bound** indebted   **33 closet** chamber
34 sort choose   **43 huswife** housewife
4.3. Location: Verona. Capulet's house; Juliet's bed, enclosed by bedcurtains, is set up in the discovery space.
3 orisons prayers   **5 cross** perverse   **7 culled** picked out   **8 behoove-**
ful needful.   **state** ceremony

    And let the Nurse this night sit up with you,
    For I am sure you have your hands full all
    In this so sudden business.
WIFE   Good night.
    Get thee to bed and rest, for thou hast need.
            Exeunt [Capulet's Wife and Nurse].
JULIET
    Farewell! God knows when we shall meet again.
    I have a faint cold fear thrills through my veins   15
    That almost freezes up the heat of life.
    I'll call them back again to comfort me.
    Nurse!—What should she do here?
    My dismal scene I needs must act alone.
    Come, vial.   [She takes out the vial.]
    What if this mixture do not work at all?
    Shall I be married then tomorrow morning?
    No, no, this shall forbid it. Lie thou there.
                            [She lays down a dagger.]
    What if it be a poison, which the Friar
    Subtly hath ministered to have me dead,
    Lest in this marriage he should be dishonored
    Because he married me before to Romeo?
    I fear it is; and yet methinks it should not,
    For he hath still been tried a holy man.   29
    How if, when I am laid into the tomb,
    I wake before the time that Romeo
    Come to redeem me? There's a fearful point!
    Shall I not then be stifled in the vault,
    To whose foul mouth no healthsome air breathes in,
    And there die strangled ere my Romeo comes?
    Or, if I live, is it not very like   36
    The horrible conceit of death and night,   37
    Together with the terror of the place—
    As in a vault, an ancient receptacle,   39
    Where for this many hundred years the bones
    Of all my buried ancestors are packed;
    Where bloody Tybalt, yet but green in earth,   42
    Lies festering in his shroud; where, as they say,
    At some hours in the night spirits resort—
    Alack, alack, is it not like that I,
    So early waking, what with loathsome smells,
    And shrieks like mandrakes torn out of the earth,   47
    That living mortals, hearing them, run mad—   48
    O, if I wake, shall I not be distraught,
    Environèd with all these hideous fears,   50
    And madly play with my forefathers' joints,
    And pluck the mangled Tybalt from his shroud,
    And in this rage, with some great kinsman's bone   53
    As with a club dash out my desperate brains?
    O, look! Methinks I see my cousin's ghost
    Seeking out Romeo, that did spit his body   56
    Upon a rapier's point. Stay, Tybalt, stay!   57

15 faint producing faintness.   **thrills** that pierces, shivers   **29 still** always.   **tried** proved   **36 like** likely. (Also at line 45.)   **37 conceit**
idea   **39 As** namely   **42 green** new, freshly   **47 mandrakes** (The root
of the mandragora or mandrake resembled the human form; the plant
was fabled to utter a shriek when torn from the ground.)   **48 That** so
that   **50 fears** objects of fear   **53 rage** madness.   **great** i.e., of an
earlier generation, as in *great*-grandfather   **56 spit** impale   **57 Stay**
stop

Romeo, Romeo, Romeo! Here's drink—I drink to •
thee.   [*She drinks and falls upon her bed, within the
curtains.*]

4.4   *Enter Lady of the House* [*Capulet's Wife*] *and Nurse.*

WIFE
Hold, take these keys, and fetch more spices, Nurse.

NURSE
They call for dates and quinces in the pastry.   2

Enter old Capulet.

CAPULET
Come, stir, stir, stir! The second cock hath crowed.
The curfew bell hath rung; 'tis three o'clock.
Look to the baked meats, good Angelica.
Spare not for cost.   5

NURSE   Go, you cotquean, go,   6
Get you to bed. Faith, you'll be sick tomorrow
For this night's watching.   8

CAPULET
No, not a whit. What, I have watched ere now
All night for lesser cause, and ne'er been sick.

WIFE
Ay, you have been a mouse-hunt in your time,   11
But I will watch you from such watching now.   12

Exeunt Lady and Nurse.

CAPULET   A jealous hood, a jealous hood!   13

Enter three or four [*Servingmen*] *with spits and logs, and baskets.*

Now, fellow, what is there?

FIRST SERVINGMAN
Things for the cook, sir, but I know not what.

CAPULET
Make haste, make haste. [*Exit First Servingman.*]
Sirrah, fetch drier logs.
Call Peter. He will show thee where they are.

SECOND SERVINGMAN
I have a head, sir, that will find out logs   18
And never trouble Peter for the matter.

CAPULET
Mass, and well said. A merry whoreson, ha!   20
Thou shalt be loggerhead. [*Exit Servingman.*] Good
faith, 'tis day.   21
The County will be here with music straight,   22
For so he said he would.   *Play music* [*within*].

4.4. **Location: Scene continues. Juliet's bed remains visible.**
2 pastry room in which pastry was made   **5 baked meats** pies, pastry
6 cotquean i.e., a man who acts the housewife. (Literally, a cottage
housewife.)   **8 watching** being awake   **11 mouse-hunt** i.e., hunter
of women. (Literally, a weasel.)   **12 watch . . . watching** i.e., keep
an eye on you to prevent such nighttime activity (playing on *watching*
in line 8)   **13 A jealous hood** i.e., you wear the cap of jealousy
18 I . . . logs i.e., (1) I have a good head for finding things (2) my
wooden head knows all about logs   **20 Mass** by the Mass.   **whoreson** i.e., fellow. (An abusive term used familiarly.)   **21 loggerhead**
(1) put in charge of getting logs (2) a blockhead   **22 straight** straightway, immediately

I hear him near.
Nurse! Wife! What, ho! What, Nurse, I say!

Enter Nurse.

Go waken Juliet, go and trim her up.
I'll go and chat with Paris. Hie, make haste,
Make haste. The bridegroom he is come already.
Make haste, I say.   [*Exit Capulet.*]

4.5   [*The Nurse goes to the bed.*]

NURSE
Mistress! What, mistress! Juliet! Fast, I warrant her,
she.   1
Why, lamb, why, lady! Fie, you slugabed!
Why, love, I say! Madam! Sweetheart! Why, bride!
What, not a word? You take your pennyworths
now.   4
Sleep for a week; for the next night, I warrant,
The County Paris hath set up his rest   6
That you shall rest but little. God forgive me,
Marry, and amen! How sound is she asleep!
I needs must wake her. Madam, madam, madam!
Ay, let the County take you in your bed;   10
He'll fright you up, i' faith. Will it not be?
[*She opens the bedcurtains.*]
What, dressed, and in your clothes, and down
again?
I must needs wake you. Lady, lady, lady!
Alas, alas! Help, help! My lady's dead!
O, weraday, that ever I was born!   15
Some aqua vitae, ho! My lord! My lady!   16

[*Enter Capulet's Wife.*]

WIFE
What noise is here?

NURSE   O lamentable day!

WIFE
What is the matter?

NURSE   Look, look! O heavy day!   18

WIFE
O me, O me! My child, my only life!
Revive, look up, or I will die with thee!
Help, help! Call help.

Enter Father [*Capulet*].

CAPULET
For shame, bring Juliet forth. Her lord is come.

NURSE
She's dead, deceased. She's dead, alack the day!

WIFE
Alack the day, she's dead, she's dead, she's dead!

4.5. **Location: Scene continues. Juliet's bed remains visible.**
1 Fast fast asleep   **4 pennyworths** small portions (of sleep)   **6 set up
his rest** firmly resolved. (From primero, a card game, where it means
"staked his reserve." The Nurse speaks bawdily.)   **10 take . . . bed**
(1) find you still abed (2) possess you sexually   **15 weraday** wellaway, alas   **16 aqua vitae** strong alcoholic spirits   **18 heavy**
sorrowful

CAPULET
    Ha! Let me see her. Out, alas! She's cold.
    Her blood is settled, and her joints are stiff;   26
    Life and these lips have long been separated.
    Death lies on her like an untimely frost
    Upon the sweetest flower of all the field.
NURSE
    O lamentable day!
WIFE   O woeful time!
CAPULET
    Death, that hath ta'en her hence to make me wail,
    Ties up my tongue and will not let me speak.

        *Enter Friar [Laurence] and the County [Paris,
        with Musicians].*

FRIAR LAURENCE
    Come, is the bride ready to go to church?
CAPULET
    Ready to go, but never to return.
    O son, the night before thy wedding day
    Hath Death lain with thy wife. There she lies,
    Flower as she was, deflowered by him.
    Death is my son-in-law, Death is my heir;
    My daughter he hath wedded. I will die,
    And leave him all; life, living, all is Death's.   40
PARIS
    Have I thought long to see this morning's face,   41
    And doth it give me such a sight as this?
WIFE
    Accurst, unhappy, wretched, hateful day!   43
    Most miserable hour that e'er time saw
    In lasting labor of his pilgrimage!   45
    But one, poor one, one poor and loving child,
    But one thing to rejoice and solace in,
    And cruel Death hath catched it from my sight!   48
NURSE
    O woe! O woeful, woeful, woeful day!
    Most lamentable day, most woeful day
    That ever, ever I did yet behold!
    O day, O day, O day! O hateful day!
    Never was seen so black a day as this.
    O woeful day, O woeful day!
PARIS
    Beguiled, divorcèd, wrongèd, spited, slain!   55
    Most detestable Death, by thee beguiled,
    By cruel, cruel thee quite overthrown!
    O love! O life! Not life, but love in death!
CAPULET
    Despised, distressèd, hated, martyred, killed!
    Uncomfortable time, why cam'st thou now   60
    To murder, murder our solemnity?   61
    O child! O child! My soul, and not my child!

    Dead art thou! Alack, my child is dead,
    And with my child my joys are buried.   64
FRIAR LAURENCE
    Peace, ho, for shame! Confusion's cure lives not   65
    In these confusions. Heaven and yourself
    Had part in this fair maid; now heaven hath all,
    And all the better is it for the maid.
    Your part in her you could not keep from death,   69
    But heaven keeps his part in eternal life.
    The most you sought was her promotion,   71
    For 'twas your heaven she should be advanced;   72
    And weep ye now, seeing she is advanced
    Above the clouds, as high as heaven itself?
    O, in this love, you love your child so ill
    That you run mad, seeing that she is well.
    She's not well married that lives married long,
    But she's best married that dies married young.
    Dry up your tears, and stick your rosemary   79
    On this fair corpse, and, as the custom is,
    And in her best array, bear her to church;
    For though fond nature bids us all lament,   82
    Yet nature's tears are reason's merriment.   83
CAPULET
    All things that we ordainèd festival   84
    Turn from their office to black funeral: 85
    Our instruments to melancholy bells,
    Our wedding cheer to a sad burial feast,
    Our solemn hymns to sullen dirges change,   88
    Our bridal flowers serve for a buried corpse,
    And all things change them to the contrary.   90
FRIAR LAURENCE
    Sir, go you in, and, madam, go with him,
    And go, Sir Paris. Everyone prepare
    To follow this fair corpse unto her grave.
    The heavens do lour upon you for some ill;   94
    Move them no more by crossing their high will.   95
            Exeunt. Manet [Nurse with Musicians].
FIRST MUSICIAN
    Faith, we may put up our pipes and be gone.
NURSE
    Honest good fellows, ah, put up, put up!
    For well you know this is a pitiful case.   [*Exit.*]
FIRST MUSICIAN
    Ay, by my troth, the case may be amended.   99

        Enter Peter.

26 **settled** congealed   40 **living** means of living, property   41–64 (A stage direction in the First Quarto, *"All at once cry out and wring their hands,"* suggests that the mourners are to speak simultaneously.) 41 **thought long** long looked forward to   43 **unhappy** fatal   45 **lasting** unceasing   48 **catched** snatched   55 **Beguiled** cheated   60 **Uncomfortable** comfortless   61 **solemnity** ceremony, festivity

65 **Confusion's** calamity's   69 **Your part** i.e., the mortal part you begot   71 **promotion** social advancement   72 **your heaven** i.e., your idea of the greatest good   79 **rosemary** symbol of immortality and enduring love; therefore used at both funerals and weddings   82 **fond nature** foolish human nature   83 **nature's . . . merriment** that which causes human nature to weep is an occasion of joy to reason   84 **ordainèd festival** intended to be festive   85 **office** function   88 **sullen** mournful   90 **them** themselves   94 **lour** threaten.   **for some ill** on account of some sin   95 **Move** anger.   **s.d. Manet** she remains onstage   99 **case . . . amended** (1) things generally could be much better (2) the instrument case could be repaired   **s.d. Enter Peter** (The Second Quarto has *Enter Will Kemp*, well-known comic actor and member of Shakespeare's company, for whom Shakespeare, or more probably the bookkeeper, evidently intended this role and so named him in the manuscript.)

PETER Musicians, O, musicians, "Heart's ease," 100
"Heart's ease." O, an you will have me live, play
"Heart's ease."

FIRST MUSICIAN Why "Heart's ease"?

PETER O, musicians, because my heart itself plays "My 104
heart is full." O, play me some merry dump to 105
comfort me.

FIRST MUSICIAN Not a dump we! 'Tis no time to play
now.

PETER You will not, then?

FIRST MUSICIAN No.

PETER I will then give it you soundly.

FIRST MUSICIAN What will you give us?

PETER No money, on my faith, but the gleek; I will give 113
you the minstrel. 114

FIRST MUSICIAN Then will I give you the serving-
creature.

PETER Then will I lay the serving-creature's dagger on
your pate. I will carry no crotchets. I'll re you, I'll fa 118
you. Do you note me? 119

FIRST MUSICIAN An you re us and fa us, you note us.

SECOND MUSICIAN Pray you, put up your dagger and
put out your wit. 122

PETER Then have at you with my wit! I will dry-beat 123
you with an iron wit, and put up my iron dagger. Answer me like men:

"When griping griefs the heart doth wound,
And doleful dumps the mind oppress, 126
Then music with her silver sound—" 128
Why "silver sound"? Why "music with her silver
sound"? What say you, Simon Catling? 130

FIRST MUSICIAN Marry, sir, because silver hath a sweet
sound.

PETER Pretty! What say you, Hugh Rebeck? 133

SECOND MUSICIAN I say "silver sound" because musicians sound for silver. 135

PETER Pretty too! What say you, James Soundpost? 136

THIRD MUSICIAN Faith, I know not what to say.

PETER O, I cry you mercy, you are the singer. I will say 138
for you. It is "music with her silver sound" because
musicians have no gold for sounding: 140
"Then music with her silver sound
With speedy help doth lend redress." *Exit.*

FIRST MUSICIAN What a pestilent knave is this same!

SECOND MUSICIAN Hang him, Jack! Come, we'll in here,
tarry for the mourners, and stay dinner. *Exeunt.* 145

❖

5.1 *Enter Romeo.*

ROMEO
If I may trust the flattering truth of sleep, 1
My dreams presage some joyful news at hand.
My bosom's lord sits lightly in his throne, 3
And all this day an unaccustomed spirit
Lifts me above the ground with cheerful thoughts.
I dreamt my lady came and found me dead—
Strange dream, that gives a dead man leave to
think!—
And breathed such life with kisses in my lips
That I revived and was an emperor.
Ah me, how sweet is love itself possessed 10
When but love's shadows are so rich in joy! 11

Enter Romeo's man [Balthasar, booted].

News from Verona! How now, Balthasar,
Dost thou not bring me letters from the Friar?
How doth my lady? Is my father well?
How fares my Juliet? That I ask again,
For nothing can be ill if she be well.

BALTHASAR
Then she is well, and nothing can be ill.
Her body sleeps in Capels' monument,
And her immortal part with angels lives.
I saw her laid low in her kindred's vault,
And presently took post to tell it you. 21
O, pardon me for bringing these ill news,
Since you did leave it for my office, sir. 23

ROMEO
Is it e'en so? Then I defy you, stars!
Thou knowest my lodging. Get me ink and paper,
And hire post-horses. I will hence tonight.

BALTHASAR
I do beseech you, sir, have patience.
Your looks are pale and wild, and do import 28
Some misadventure.

ROMEO   Tush, thou art deceived.
Leave me, and do the thing I bid thee do.
Hast thou no letters to me from the Friar?

BALTHASAR
No, my good lord.

ROMEO   No matter. Get thee gone,
And hire those horses. I'll be with thee straight.
                                        Exit [Balthasar].
Well, Juliet, I will lie with thee tonight.

100, 104–105 **"Heart's ease," "My heart is full"** (Popular ballads.)
105 **dump** mournful tune or dance 113 **gleek** jest, gibe
113–114 **give you the minstrel** insultingly term you a minstrel, i.e.,
vagabond. (The First Musician replies in kind.) 118 **carry no crotchets** (1) endure no whims (2) sing no quarter notes. **re, fa** musical
notes 119 **note** (1) heed (2) set to music 122 **put out** (1) display (2)
extinguish 123 **dry-beat** thrash (without drawing blood) 126–128
"When . . . sound" (From Richard Edwards' song, "In Commendation of Music," published in *The Paradise of Dainty Devices*, 1576.)
130 **Catling** (A catling was a small lute-string made of catgut.)
133 **Rebeck** (A rebeck was a fiddle with three strings.) 135 **sound**
make music 136 **Soundpost** (A soundpost is the pillar or peg that
supports the sounding board of a stringed instrument.) 138 **cry
you mercy** beg your pardon 140 **have . . . sounding** i.e., (1) are
paid only silver for playing (2) have no gold to jingle in their
pockets

145 **stay** await
5.1. Location: Mantua. A street.
1 **flattering** i.e., telling me what I want to believe 3 **bosom's lord**
i.e., heart 10 **itself possessed** actually enjoyed 11 **love's shadows**
dreams of love. **s.d. booted** wearing riding boots—a conventional
stage sign of traveling 21 **presently took post** at once started off with
post-horses 23 **for my office** as my duty 28 **import** signify

Let's see for means. O mischief, thou art swift   35
To enter in the thoughts of desperate men!
I do remember an apothecary—   37
And hereabouts 'a dwells—which late I noted   38
In tattered weeds, with overwhelming brows,   39
Culling of simples. Meager were his looks;   40
Sharp misery had worn him to the bones;
And in his needy shop a tortoise hung,
An alligator stuffed, and other skins
Of ill-shaped fishes; and about his shelves
A beggarly account of empty boxes,   45
Green earthen pots, bladders, and musty seeds,
Remnants of packthread, and old cakes of roses   47
Were thinly scattered to make up a show.
Noting this penury, to myself I said,
"An if a man did need a poison now,   50
Whose sale is present death in Mantua,   51
Here lives a caitiff wretch would sell it him."   52
O, this same thought did but forerun my need,
And this same needy man must sell it me.
As I remember, this should be the house.
Being holiday, the beggar's shop is shut.
What, ho! Apothecary!

    [*Enter Apothecary.*]

APOTHECARY   Who calls so loud?
ROMEO
Come hither, man. I see that thou art poor.
Hold, there is forty ducats. [*He shows gold.*] Let me
    have   59
A dram of poison, such soon-speeding gear   60
As will disperse itself through all the veins
That the life-weary taker may fall dead,
And that the trunk may be discharged of breath   63
As violently as hasty powder fired
Doth hurry from the fatal cannon's womb.
APOTHECARY
Such mortal drugs I have, but Mantua's law   66
Is death to any he that utters them.   67
ROMEO
Art thou so bare and full of wretchedness,
And fearest to die? Famine is in thy cheeks,
Need and oppression starveth in thy eyes,   70
Contempt and beggary hangs upon thy back.
The world is not thy friend, nor the world's law;
The world affords no law to make thee rich.
Then be not poor, but break it, and take this.
APOTHECARY
My poverty but not my will consents.
ROMEO
I pay thy poverty and not thy will.

APOTHECARY [*giving poison*]
Put this in any liquid thing you will
And drink it off, and if you had the strength
Of twenty men it would dispatch you straight.
ROMEO [*giving gold*]
There is thy gold—worse poison to men's souls,
Doing more murder in this loathsome world
Than these poor compounds that thou mayst not
    sell.
I sell thee poison; thou hast sold me none.
Farewell. Buy food, and get thyself in flesh.
                    [*Exit Apothecary.*]
Come, cordial and not poison, go with me   85
To Juliet's grave, for there must I use thee.   *Exit.*

                    ❧

5.2   *Enter Friar John to Friar Laurence.*

FRIAR JOHN
Holy Franciscan friar! Brother, ho!

        Enter [Friar] Laurence.

FRIAR LAURENCE
This same should be the voice of Friar John.
Welcome from Mantua! What says Romeo?
Or if his mind be writ, give me his letter.
FRIAR JOHN
Going to find a barefoot brother out—
One of our order—to associate me   6
Here in this city visiting the sick,
And finding him, the searchers of the town,   8
Suspecting that we both were in a house
Where the infectious pestilence did reign,
Sealed up the doors and would not let us forth,
So that my speed to Mantua there was stayed.   12
FRIAR LAURENCE
Who bare my letter, then, to Romeo?
FRIAR JOHN
I could not send it—here it is again—
Nor get a messenger to bring it thee,
So fearful were they of infection.   [*He gives a letter.*]
FRIAR LAURENCE
Unhappy fortune! By my brotherhood,
The letter was not nice but full of charge,   18
Of dear import, and the neglecting it   19
May do much danger. Friar John, go hence.
Get me an iron crow and bring it straight   21
Unto my cell.
FRIAR JOHN   Brother, I'll go and bring it thee.   *Exit.*
FRIAR LAURENCE
Now must I to the monument alone.
Within this three hours will fair Juliet wake.

---

35 for means by what means   **37 apothecary** druggist   **38 which
. . . noted** whom lately I noticed   **39 weeds** garments.   **overwhelming brows** eyebrows jutting out over his eyes   **40 simples** medicinal
herbs.   **Meager** impoverished   **45 beggarly account** poor array
47 cakes of roses petals pressed into cakes to be used as perfume
50 An if if   **51 present** immediate   **52 caitiff** miserable.   **would** who
would   **59 ducats** gold coins   **60 soon-speeding gear** quickly effective stuff   **63 trunk** body   **66 mortal** deadly   **67 any he** anyone.   **utters** issues, sells   **70 starveth** are revealed by the starving look

85 cordial restorative for the heart
5.2. Location: Verona. Friar Laurence's cell.
6 associate accompany   **8 searchers of the town** town officials
charged with public health (and especially concerned about the *pestilence* or plague)   **12 speed** successful journey, progress.   **stayed**
stopped   **18 nice** trivial.   **charge** importance   **19 dear** precious, urgent   **21 crow** crowbar

She will beshrew me much that Romeo   26
Hath had no notice of these accidents;   27
But I will write again to Mantua,
And keep her at my cell till Romeo come—
Poor living corpse, closed in a dead man's tomb!

Exit.

❧

5.3 *Enter Paris, and his Page [bearing flowers,
perfumed water, and a torch].*

PARIS
Give me thy torch, boy. Hence, and stand aloof.   1
Yet put it out, for I would not be seen.
Under yond yew trees lay thee all along,   3
Holding thy ear close to the hollow ground.
So shall no foot upon the churchyard tread,
Being loose, unfirm, with digging up of graves,   6
But thou shalt hear it. Whistle then to me
As signal that thou hearest something approach.
Give me those flowers. Do as I bid thee. Go.
PAGE *[aside]*
I am almost afraid to stand alone   10
Here in the churchyard, yet I will adventure.
                                    [He retires.]
PARIS *[strewing flowers and perfumed water]*
Sweet flower, with flowers thy bridal bed I strew—
  O woe! Thy canopy is dust and stones—   13
Which with sweet water nightly I will dew,   14
  Or wanting that, with tears distilled by moans.   15
The obsequies that I for thee will keep   16
Nightly shall be to strew thy grave and weep.
                                    Whistle Boy.
The boy gives warning something doth approach.
What cursèd foot wanders this way tonight
To cross my obsequies and true love's rite?   20
What, with a torch? Muffle me, night, awhile.   21
                                    [He retires.]

*Enter Romeo and [Balthasar, with a torch, a
mattock, and a crowbar].*

ROMEO
Give me that mattock and the wrenching iron.   22
                                    [He takes the tools.]
Hold, take this letter. Early in the morning
See thou deliver it to my lord and father.
                                    [He gives a letter and takes a torch.]
Give me the light. Upon thy life I charge thee,
Whate'er thou hearest or seest, stand all aloof
And do not interrupt me in my course.   27

Why I descend into this bed of death
Is partly to behold my lady's face,
But chiefly to take thence from her dead finger
A precious ring—a ring that I must use
In dear employment. Therefore hence, begone.   32
But if thou, jealous, dost return to pry   33
In what I farther shall intend to do,
By heaven, I will tear thee joint by joint
And strew this hungry churchyard with thy limbs.
The time and my intents are savage-wild,
More fierce and more inexorable far
Than empty tigers or the roaring sea.   39
BALTHASAR
I will be gone, sir, and not trouble ye.
ROMEO
So shalt thou show me friendship. Take thou that.
                                    [He gives him money.]
Live, and be prosperous; and farewell, good fellow.
BALTHASAR *[aside]*
For all this same, I'll hide me hereabout.   43
His looks I fear, and his intents I doubt. *[He retires.]* 44
ROMEO
Thou detestable maw, thou womb of death,   45
Gorged with the dearest morsel of the earth,
Thus I enforce thy rotten jaws to open,
And in despite I'll cram thee with more food.   48
                                    [He begins to open the tomb.]
PARIS
This is that banished haughty Montague
That murdered my love's cousin, with which grief
It is supposèd the fair creature died,
And here is come to do some villainous shame
To the dead bodies. I will apprehend him.
                                    [He comes forward.]
Stop thy unhallowed toil, vile Montague!
Can vengeance be pursued further than death?
Condemnèd villain, I do apprehend thee.
Obey and go with me, for thou must die.
ROMEO
I must indeed, and therefore came I hither.
Good gentle youth, tempt not a desperate man.
Fly hence and leave me. Think upon these gone;   60
Let them affright thee. I beseech thee, youth,
Put not another sin upon my head
By urging me to fury. O, begone!
By heaven, I love thee better than myself,
For I come hither armed against myself.
Stay not, begone. Live, and hereafter say
A madman's mercy bid thee run away.
PARIS
I do defy thy conjuration,   68
And apprehend thee for a felon here.
ROMEO
Wilt thou provoke me? Then have at thee, boy!
                                    [They fight.]

26 **beshrew** i.e., reprove 27 **accidents** events
5.3. Location: Verona. A churchyard and the vault or tomb belonging to the Capulets.
1 **aloof** to one side, at a distance 3 **all along** at full length 6 **Being** i.e., the soil being 10 **stand** stay 13 **canopy** covering 14 **sweet** perfumed. **dew** moisten 15 **wanting** lacking 16 **obsequies** ceremonies in memory of the dead 20 **cross** interrupt 21 **Muffle** conceal. s.d. **mattock** pickax 22 **wrenching iron** crowbar 27 **course** intended action

32 **dear employment** important business 33 **jealous** suspicious
39 **empty** hungry 43 **For all this same** all the same 44 **fear** distrust.
doubt suspect 45 **womb** belly 48 **in despite** defiantly 60 **gone** dead 68 **conjuration** warning entreaty

PAGE
O Lord, they fight! I will go call the watch.   [*Exit.*]
PARIS
O, I am slain! [*He falls.*] If thou be merciful,
Open the tomb, lay me with Juliet.   [*He dies.*]
ROMEO
In faith, I will. Let me peruse this face.
Mercutio's kinsman, noble County Paris!
What said my man when my betossèd soul
Did not attend him as we rode? I think
He told me Paris should have married Juliet.   78
Said he not so? Or did I dream it so?
Or am I mad, hearing him talk of Juliet,
To think it was so? O, give me thy hand,
One writ with me in sour misfortune's book.
I'll bury thee in a triumphant grave.
                         [*He opens the tomb.*]
A grave? O, no! A lantern, slaughtered youth,   84
For here lies Juliet, and her beauty makes
This vault a feasting presence full of light.   86
Death, lie thou there, by a dead man interred.
                     [*He lays Paris in the tomb.*]
How oft when men are at the point of death
Have they been merry, which their keepers call   89
A lightening before death! O, how may I   90
Call this a lightening? O my love, my wife!
Death, that hath sucked the honey of thy breath,
Hath had no power yet upon thy beauty.
Thou art not conquered; beauty's ensign yet   94
Is crimson in thy lips and in thy cheeks,
And death's pale flag is not advancèd there.   96
Tybalt, liest thou there in thy bloody sheet?   97
O, what more favor can I do to thee
Than with that hand that cut thy youth in twain
To sunder his that was thine enemy?   100
Forgive me, cousin! Ah, dear Juliet,
Why art thou yet so fair? Shall I believe
That unsubstantial Death is amorous,   103
And that the lean abhorrèd monster keeps
Thee here in dark to be his paramour?
For fear of that I still will stay with thee   106
And never from this palace of dim night
Depart again. Here, here will I remain
With worms that are thy chambermaids. O, here
Will I set up my everlasting rest   110
And shake the yoke of inauspicious stars
From this world-wearied flesh. Eyes, look your last!
Arms, take your last embrace! And, lips, O you
The doors of breath, seal with a righteous kiss
A dateless bargain to engrossing death!   115
                         [*He kisses Juliet.*]

Come, bitter conduct, come, unsavory guide,   116
Thou desperate pilot, now at once run on   117
The dashing rocks thy seasick weary bark!
Here's to my love. [*He drinks.*] O true apothecary!
Thy drugs are quick. Thus with a kiss I die. [*He dies.*]

Enter [at the other end of the churchyard] Friar
[Laurence] with lantern, crow, and spade.

FRIAR LAURENCE
Saint Francis be my speed! How oft tonight   121
Have my old feet stumbled at graves! Who's there?
BALTHASAR
Here's one, a friend, and one that knows you well.
FRIAR LAURENCE
Bliss be upon you. Tell me, good my friend,
What torch is yond that vainly lends his light   125
To grubs and eyeless skulls? As I discern,   126
It burneth in the Capels' monument.
BALTHASAR
It doth so, holy sir, and there's my master,
One that you love.
FRIAR LAURENCE   Who is it?
BALTHASAR   Romeo.
FRIAR LAURENCE
How long hath he been there?
BALTHASAR   Full half an hour.
FRIAR LAURENCE
Go with me to the vault.
BALTHASAR   I dare not, sir.
My master knows not but I am gone hence,
And fearfully did menace me with death
If I did stay to look on his intents.
FRIAR LAURENCE
Stay, then, I'll go alone. Fear comes upon me.
O, much I fear some ill unthrifty thing.   136
BALTHASAR
As I did sleep under this yew tree here
I dreamt my master and another fought,
And that my master slew him.
FRIAR LAURENCE [*advancing to the tomb*]   Romeo!
Alack, alack, what blood is this which stains
The stony entrance of this sepulcher?
What mean these masterless and gory swords
To lie discolored by this place of peace?
                         [*He enters the tomb.*]
Romeo! O, pale! Who else? What, Paris too?
And steeped in blood? Ah, what an unkind hour   145
Is guilty of this lamentable chance!
The lady stirs.   [*Juliet wakes.*]
JULIET
O comfortable Friar, where is my lord?   148
I do remember well where I should be,
And there I am. Where is my Romeo?
                         [*A noise within.*]
FRIAR LAURENCE
I hear some noise. Lady, come from that nest

78 **should have** was to have   84 **lantern** turret room full of windows   86 **feasting presence** reception chamber for feasting   89 **keepers** attendants, jailers   90 **lightening** exhilaration (supposed to occur just before death)   94 **ensign** banner   96 **advancèd** raised   97 **sheet** shroud   100 **his** i.e., my (Romeo's) own   103 **unsubstantial** lacking material existence   106 **still** always   110 **set . . . rest** (See 4.5.6. The meaning is, "make my final determination," with allusion to the idea of repose.)   115 **dateless bargain** everlasting contract. **engrossing** monopolizing, taking all; also, drawing up the contract

116 **conduct** guide (i.e., the poison)   117 **desperate** reckless, despairing   121 **be my speed** prosper me and let me arrive in time   125 **vainly** uselessly   126 **grubs** insect larvae   136 **unthrifty** unfortunate   145 **unkind** unnatural   148 **comfortable** comforting

Of death, contagion, and unnatural sleep.
A greater power than we can contradict
Hath thwarted our intents. Come, come away.
Thy husband in thy bosom there lies dead,
And Paris, too. Come, I'll dispose of thee
Among a sisterhood of holy nuns.
Stay not to question, for the watch is coming.
Come, go, good Juliet. [*A noise again.*] I dare no
   longer stay.   *Exit* [*Friar Laurence*].

JULIET
Go, get thee hence, for I will not away.
What's here? A cup, closed in my true love's hand?
Poison, I see, hath been his timeless end.   162
O churl, drunk all, and left no friendly drop   163
To help me after? I will kiss thy lips;
Haply some poison yet doth hang on them,   165
To make me die with a restorative.   [*She kisses him.*]
Thy lips are warm.

         Enter [*Paris'*] *Boy and Watch* [*at the other end of
         the churchyard*].

FIRST WATCH   Lead, boy. Which way?
JULIET
Yea, noise? Then I'll be brief. O happy dagger!   169
                          [*She takes Romeo's dagger.*]
This is thy sheath. There rust, and let me die.
                          [*She stabs herself and dies.*]
PAGE
This is the place, there where the torch doth burn.
FIRST WATCH
The ground is bloody. Search about the churchyard.
Go, some of you, whoe'er you find attach.   173
                          [*Exeunt some.*]
Pitiful sight! Here lies the County slain,
And Juliet bleeding, warm, and newly dead,
Who here hath lain these two days buried.
Go tell the Prince. Run to the Capulets.
Raise up the Montagues. Some others search.
                          [*Exeunt others.*]
We see the ground whereon these woes do lie,
But the true ground of all these piteous woes   180
We cannot without circumstance descry.   181

         Enter [*some of the Watch, with*] *Romeo's man*
         [*Balthasar*].

SECOND WATCH
Here's Romeo's man. We found him in the
   churchyard.
FIRST WATCH
Hold him in safety till the Prince come hither.   183

         Enter Friar [*Laurence*], *and another Watchman*
         [*with tools*].

THIRD WATCH
Here is a friar, that trembles, sighs, and weeps.

We took this mattock and this spade from him
As he was coming from this churchyard's side.
FIRST WATCH
A great suspicion. Stay the Friar, too.   187

         Enter the Prince [*and attendants*].

PRINCE
What misadventure is so early up
That calls our person from our morning rest?

         Enter Capels [*Capulet and his Wife*].

CAPULET
What should it be that is so shrieked abroad?
CAPULET'S WIFE
O, the people in the street cry "Romeo,"
Some "Juliet," and some "Paris," and all run
With open outcry toward our monument.
PRINCE
What fear is this which startles in our ears?   194
FIRST WATCH
Sovereign, here lies the County Paris slain,
And Romeo dead, and Juliet, dead before,
Warm and new killed.
PRINCE
Search, seek, and know how this foul murder
   comes.   198
FIRST WATCH
Here is a friar, and slaughtered Romeo's man,
With instruments upon them fit to open   200
These dead men's tombs.
CAPULET
O heavens! O wife, look how our daughter bleeds!
This dagger hath mista'en, for lo, his house   203
Is empty on the back of Montague,
And it mis-sheathèd in my daughter's bosom!
CAPULET'S WIFE
O me! This sight of death is as a bell
That warns my old age to a sepulcher.

         Enter Montague.

PRINCE
Come, Montague, for thou art early up
To see thy son and heir more early down.
MONTAGUE
Alas, my liege, my wife is dead tonight;
Grief of my son's exile hath stopped her breath.
What further woe conspires against mine age?
PRINCE   Look, and thou shalt see.
MONTAGUE [*seeing Romeo's body*]
O thou untaught! What manners is in this,   214
To press before thy father to a grave?   215
PRINCE
Seal up the mouth of outrage for a while,   216
Till we can clear these ambiguities
And know their spring, their head, their true
   descent;   218

162 **timeless** (1) untimely (2) everlasting   163 **churl** miser   165 **Haply**
perhaps   169 **happy** opportune   173 **attach** arrest, detain
180 **ground** basis (playing on the literal meaning in line 179)
181 **circumstance** details   183 **in safety** under guard

187 **Stay** detain   194 **startles** cries alarmingly   198 **know** learn
200 **instruments** tools   203 **his house** its scabbard   214 **untaught** ill-
mannered youth. (Said with affectionate irony.)   215 **press** hasten, go
216 **outrage** outcry   218 **spring, head** source

And then will I be general of your woes   219
And lead you even to death. Meantime, forbear,   220
And let mischance be slave to patience.   221
Bring forth the parties of suspicion.   222

FRIAR LAURENCE
I am the greatest, able to do least,
Yet most suspected, as the time and place
Doth make against me, of this direful murder;   225
And here I stand, both to impeach and purge   226
Myself condemnèd and myself excused.   227

PRINCE
Then say at once what thou dost know in this.

FRIAR LAURENCE
I will be brief, for my short date of breath   229
Is not so long as is a tedious tale.
Romeo, there dead, was husband to that Juliet,
And she, there dead, that Romeo's faithful wife.
I married them, and their stol'n marriage day
Was Tybalt's doomsday, whose untimely death
Banished the new-made bridegroom from this city,
For whom, and not for Tybalt, Juliet pined.
You, to remove that siege of grief from her,
Betrothed and would have married her perforce   238
To County Paris. Then comes she to me,
And with wild looks bid me devise some means
To rid her from this second marriage,
Or in my cell there would she kill herself.
Then gave I her—so tutored by my art—
A sleeping potion, which so took effect
As I intended, for it wrought on her   245
The form of death. Meantime I writ to Romeo   246
That he should hither come as this dire night   247
To help to take her from her borrowed grave,
Being the time the potion's force should cease.
But he which bore my letter, Friar John,
Was stayed by accident, and yesternight   251
Returned my letter back. Then all alone
At the prefixèd hour of her waking
Came I to take her from her kindred's vault,
Meaning to keep her closely at my cell   255
Till I conveniently could send to Romeo.
But when I came, some minute ere the time
Of her awakening, here untimely lay
The noble Paris and true Romeo dead.
She wakes, and I entreated her come forth
And bear this work of heaven with patience.
But then a noise did scare me from the tomb,
And she, too desperate, would not go with me,
But, as it seems, did violence on herself.
All this I know, and to the marriage
Her nurse is privy; and if aught in this   266
Miscarried by my fault, let my old life

Be sacrificed some hour before his time   268
Unto the rigor of severest law.

PRINCE
We still have known thee for a holy man.   270
Where's Romeo's man? What can he say to this?

BALTHASAR
I brought my master news of Juliet's death,
And then in post he came from Mantua   273
To this same place, to this same monument.
This letter he early bid me give his father,   275
                              [showing a letter]
And threatened me with death, going in the vault,
If I departed not and left him there.

PRINCE [taking the letter]
Give me the letter. I will look on it.
Where is the County's page, that raised the watch?
Sirrah, what made your master in this place?   280

PAGE
He came with flowers to strew his lady's grave,
And bid me stand aloof, and so I did.
Anon comes one with light to ope the tomb,
And by and by my master drew on him,
And then I ran away to call the watch.

PRINCE
This letter doth make good the Friar's words,
Their course of love, the tidings of her death;
And here he writes that he did buy a poison
Of a poor 'pothecary, and therewithal   289
Came to this vault to die, and lie with Juliet.
Where be these enemies? Capulet, Montague,
See what a scourge is laid upon your hate,
That heaven finds means to kill your joys with love.   293
And I, for winking at your discords, too   294
Have lost a brace of kinsmen. All are punished.   295

CAPULET
O brother Montague, give me thy hand.
This is my daughter's jointure, for no more   297
Can I demand.

MONTAGUE   But I can give thee more,
For I will raise her statue in pure gold,   299
That whiles Verona by that name is known
There shall no figure at such rate be set   301
As that of true and faithful Juliet.

CAPULET
As rich shall Romeo's by his lady's lie;
Poor sacrifices of our enmity!

PRINCE
A glooming peace this morning with it brings;
    The sun, for sorrow, will not show his head.
Go hence to have more talk of these sad things.
    Some shall be pardoned, and some punishèd;
For never was a story of more woe
Than this of Juliet and her Romeo.   [Exeunt.]

---

219 be . . . woes be leader in lamentation   220 even to death (1) in
lamentation for the dead (2) even if I were to die of grief   221 let
. . . patience i.e., let us bear our misfortune patiently   222 of under
225 make conspire, tell   226–227 to . . . excused to accuse myself
of what is to be condemned in me and to exonerate myself where I
ought to be excused   229 date of breath time left to live   238 perforce by compulsion   245 wrought fashioned   246 form appearance   247 as this this very   251 stayed stopped   255 closely secretly   266 privy in on the secret

268 his its   270 still always   273 post haste   275 early early in the
morning   280 made did   289 therewithal i.e., with the poison
293 kill your joys (1) destroy your happiness (2) kill your children.
with by means of   294 winking at shutting my eyes to   295 a brace
of two   297 jointure marriage portion   299 raise (The Second
Quarto reading, raie, is defended by some editors in the sense of "array," make ready.)   301 rate value

Julius Caesar

Julius Caesar stands midway in Shakespeare's dramatic career, at a critical juncture. In some ways, it is an epilogue to his English history plays of the 1590s; in other ways, it introduces the period of the great tragedies. The play evidently was first performed at the new Globe playhouse in the fall of 1599, shortly after *Henry V* (the last of Shakespeare's history plays about medieval England) and around the time of *As You Like It* (one of the last of Shakespeare's happy romantic comedies). It shortly preceded *Hamlet*. It is placed among the tragedies in the Folio of 1623, where it was first published, and is entitled *The Tragedy of Julius Caesar*, but in the table of contents it is listed as *The Life and Death of Julius Caesar* as though it were a history.

Julius Caesar shares with Shakespeare's history plays an absorption in the problems of civil war and popular unrest. Rome, like England, suffers an internal division that is reflected in the perturbed state of the heavens themselves. The commoners, or plebeians, are easily swayed by demagogues. Opportunists prosper in this atmosphere of crisis, although fittingly even they are sometimes undone by their own scheming. Politics seems to require a morality quite apart from that of personal life, posing a tragic dilemma for Brutus, as it did for Richard II or Henry VI. The blending of history and tragedy in *Julius Caesar*, then, is not unlike that found in several English history plays. Rome was a natural subject to which Shakespeare might turn in his continuing depiction of political behavior. Roman culture had recently been elevated to new importance by the classical orientation of the Renaissance. As a model of political organization, it loomed larger in Elizabethan consciousness than it does in ours, because so few other models were available and because Greek culture was less accessible in language and tradition. According to a widely accepted mythology, Elizabethans considered themselves descended from the Romans through another Brutus, the great-grandson of Aeneas.

Yet the differences between Roman and English history are as important as the similarities. Rome's choice during her civil wars lay between a senatorial republican form of government and a strong single ruler. Although the monarchical English might be inclined to be suspicious of republicanism, they had no experience to compare with it—certainly not their various peasants' revolts, such as Jack Cade's

rebellion (in *2 Henry VI*). On the other hand, Roman one-man rule as it flourished under Octavius Caesar lacked the English sanctions of divine right and monarchical primogeniture. Rome was, after all, a pagan culture, and Shakespeare carefully preserves this non-Christian frame of reference. The gods are frequently invoked and appear to respond with prophetic dreams and auguries, but their ultimate intentions are baffling. Human beings strive blindly; the will of the gods is inscrutable. The outcome of *Julius Caesar* is far different from the restoration of providentially ordained order at the end of *Richard III*. Calm is restored and political authority reestablished, but we are by no means sure that a divine morality has been served. Roman history for Shakespeare is history divested of its divine imperatives and located in a distant political setting, making dispassionate appraisal less difficult. In Plutarch's *Lives of the Noble Grecians and Romans*, as translated by Sir Thomas North, Shakespeare discovered a rich opportunity for pursuing the ironies of political life to which he had been increasingly attracted in the English histories. In fact, he was drawn throughout his career to Plutarch: to the portrait of Portia in "The Life of Marcus Brutus," not only for Portia in *Julius Caesar*, but also for Lucrece in *The Rape of Lucrece*, Kate in *1 Henry IV*, and Portia in *The Merchant of Venice*; to "The Life of Theseus" for the Duke of *A Midsummer Night's Dream*; and to various lives for *Julius Caesar*, *Coriolanus*, *Antony and Cleopatra*, and *Timon of Athens*. Freed from the orthodoxies of the Elizabethan world view, Shakespeare turned in the Roman or classical plays toward irony or outright satire (as in *Troilus and Cressida*) and toward the personal tragedy of political dilemma (as in *Coriolanus* and *Julius Caesar*). These are to be the dominant motifs of the Roman or classical plays, as distinguished from both the English histories and the great tragedies of evil, in which politics plays a lesser part *(Hamlet, Othello, King Lear, Macbeth)*.

Julius Caesar is an ambivalent study of civil conflict. As in *Richard II*, the play is structured around two protagonists rather than one. Caesar and Brutus, men of extraordinary abilities and debilitating weaknesses, are more like one another than either would care to admit. This antithetical balance reflects a dual tradition: the medieval view of Dante and of Geoffrey Chaucer, condemning Brutus and Cassius as conspirators, and the Renaissance view of Sir Philip Sidney and Ben Jonson, condemning Caesar as a tyrant. These opposing views still live on in various twentieth-century productions that seek to enlist the play on the side of conservatism or liberalism. In one famous production by Orson Welles, 1937, Caesar was made out to resemble Benito Mussolini, Italy's fascist dictator. This interpretation reflects what the conspirators themselves believe, as they cry "Liberty! Freedom! Tyranny is dead!" but the play itself will not sustain so one-sided a view. Some more recent productions have favored a balance, as in the film version of the early 1950s by John Houseman and Joseph Mankiewicz, in which the major roles are evenly distributed among various well-known actors and actresses—John Gielgud as Cassius, Marlon Brando as Antony, James Mason as Brutus, Louis Calhern as Caesar, Greer Garson as Calpurnia, Deborah Kerr as Portia—instead of allowing one actor to dominate the play. Most recent criticism similarly has abandoned the fruitless debate among the Victorians as to whether Brutus or Caesar is the tragic protagonist, in favor of a multiple perspective.

Caesar is a study in paradox. He is unquestionably a great general, astute in politics, decisive in his judgments, and sharp in his evaluation of men, as, for example, in his distrust of Cassius with his "lean and hungry look" (1.2.194). Yet this mightiest of men, who in Cassius' phrase bestrides the narrow world "like a Colossus" (line 136), is also deaf in one ear, prone to fevers and epilepsy, unable to compete with Cassius by swimming the Tiber fully armed, and afflicted with a sterile marriage. Physical limitations of this sort are common enough, but in Caesar they are constantly juxtaposed with his aspirations to be above mortal weakness. He dies boasting that he is like the "northern star," constant, unique, "Unshaked of motion" (3.1.61–71). He professes to fear nothing and yet is notoriously superstitious. He calmly reflects that "death, a necessary end, / Will come when it will come," and then arrogantly boasts in the next moment that "Danger knows full well / That Caesar is more dangerous than he" (2.2.36–45). As his wife puts it, Caesar's "wisdom is consumed in confidence" (line 49). He willfully betrays his own best instincts and ignores plain warnings through self-deception. He stops a procession to hear a soothsayer and then dismisses the man as "a dreamer" (1.2.24). He commissions his augurers to determine whether he should stay at home on the ides of March and then persuades himself that acting on their advice would be a sign of weakness. Most fatally, he thinks himself above flattery and so is especially vulnerable to it. So wise and powerful a man as this cannot stop the process of his own fate, because his fate and character are interwoven: he is the victim of his own hubris. His insatiable desire for the crown overbalances his judgment; no warnings of the gods can save him. Even his virtues conspire against him, for he regards himself as one who puts public interest ahead of personal affairs and brushes aside the letter of Artemidorus that would have told him of the conspiracy.

Brutus, for all his opposition to Caesar, is also a paradoxical figure. His strengths are quite unlike those of Caesar, but his weaknesses are surprisingly similar. Brutus is a noble Roman from an ancient family whose glory it has been to defend the personal liberties of Rome, the republican tradition. Brutus' virtues are personal virtues. He enjoys an admirable rapport with his courageous and intelligent wife, and is genuinely kind to his servants. In friendship he is trustworthy. He deplores oaths in the conspiracy because his word is his

bond. He finds Caesar's ambition for power distasteful and vulgar; his opposition to Caesar is both idealistic and patrician. Brutus' hubris is a pride of family, and on this score he is vulnerable to flattery. As Cassius reminds him, alluding to Brutus' ancestor Lucius Junius Brutus, who founded the Roman Republic in 509 B.C.: "There was a Brutus once that would have brooked / Th' eternal devil to keep his state in Rome / As easily as a king" (1.2.159–161). Should not Marcus Brutus be the savior of his country from a return to tyranny? Is not he a more fit leader for Rome than Caesar? " 'Brutus' and 'Caesar.' What should be in that 'Caesar'? / Why should that name be sounded more than yours?" (lines 142–143). Cassius' strategy is to present to Brutus numerous testimonials "all tending to the great opinion / That Rome holds of his name" (lines 318–319). Cassius plays the role of tempter here, but the notion he suggests is not new to Brutus.

The parallelism of Brutus' pride and Caesar's ambition is strongly underscored by the way in which these great figures appear to us in two adjoining scenes: 2.1 and 2.2. In these two scenes, the protagonists enter alone during the troubled night, call for a servant, receive the conspirators, and dispute the wise caution of their wives. Both men are predisposed to the temptations that are placed before them. Brutus has often thought of himself as the indispensable man for the preservation of Rome's liberties. Despite his good breeding and coolly rational manner, he is as dominating a personality as Caesar and as hard to move once his mind is made up. Indeed, the conspiracy founders on Brutus' repeated insistence on having his own way. He allows no oaths among the conspirators and will not kill Antony along with Caesar. He permits Antony to speak after him at Caesar's funeral. He vetoes Cicero as a fellow conspirator. In each instance, the other conspirators are unanimously opposed to Brutus' choice but yield to him. Brutus cuts off Cassius' objections before hearing them fully, being accustomed to having his way without dispute. His motives are in part noble and idealistic: Brutus wishes to have the conspirators behave generously and openly, as heroes rather than as henchmen. Yet there is something loftily patrician in his desire to have the fruits of conspiracy without any of the dirty work. His willingness to have Antony speak after him betrays a vain confidence in his own oratory and an unjustified faith in the plebeian mob. Moreover, when Brutus overrides Cassius once more in the decision to fight at Philippi and is proved wrong by the event, no idealistic motive can excuse Brutus' insistence on being obeyed; Cassius is the more experienced soldier. Still, Brutus' fatal limitations as leader of a coup d'état are inseparable from his virtues as a private man. The truth is that such a noble man is, by his very nature, unsuited for the stern exigencies of assassination and civil war. Brutus is strong-minded about his ideals, but he cannot be ruthless. The means and the end of revolution drift further and further apart. He cannot supply his troops at Philippi because he will not forage among the peasants of the countryside and will not countenance among his allies the routine corruptions of an army in time of war, though at the same time that he upbraids Cassius for not sending him gold he does not stop to ask where the gold would come from. Even suicide is distasteful for Brutus, obliging him to embarrass his friends by asking their help. Brutus is too high-minded and genteel a man for the troubled times in which he lives.

The times indeed seem to demand ruthless action of the sort Antony and Octavius are all too ready to provide. The greatest irony of Brutus' fall is that the coup he undertakes for Roman liberty yields only further diminutions of that liberty. The plebeians are not ready for the commonwealth Brutus envisages. From the first, they are portrayed as amiable but "saucy" (even in the opinion of their tribunes, Flavius and Marullus). They adulate Caesar at the expense of their previous idol, Pompey. When Brutus successfully appeals for a moment to their changeable loyalties, they cry "Let him be Caesar," and "Caesar's better parts / Shall be crowned in Brutus" (3.2.51–52). If Brutus were not swayed by this hero-worship, he would have good cause to be disillusioned. To his credit, he is not the demogogue the plebeians take him for and so cannot continue to bend them to his will. Cassius, too, for all his villainlike role as tempter to Brutus, his envious motive, and his Epicurean skepticism, reveals a finer nature as the play progresses. Inspired perhaps by Brutus' philosophic idealism, Cassius turns philosopher also and accepts defeat in a noble but ineffectual cause. Yet even his death is futile; Cassius is misinformed about the fate of his friend Titinius and so stabs himself just when the battle is going well for the conspirators.

The ultimate victors are Antony and Octavius. Antony, whatever finer nature he may possess, becomes under the stress of circumstance a cunning bargainer with the conspirators and a masterful rhetorician who characterizes himself to the plebeians as a "plain blunt man" (3.2.219). In sardonic soliloquy at the end of his funeral oration, he observes, "Now let it work. Mischief, thou art afoot. / Take thou what course thou wilt" (lines 261–262). He is, to be sure, stirred by loyalty to Caesar's memory, but to the end of avenging Caesar's death he is prepared to unleash violence at whatever risk to the state. He regards Lepidus contemptuously as a mere creature under his command. Antony is older than Octavius and teaches the younger man about political realities, but an Elizabethan audience would probably savor the irony that Octavius will subsequently beat Antony at his own game. At Philippi, Octavius' refusal to accept Antony's directions in the battle (5.1.16–20) gives us a glimpse of the peremptory manner for which he is to become famous, like his predecessor. Antony and Octavius together are, in any case, a fearsome pair, matter-of-factly noting down the names of those who must die, including their

own kinsmen. They cut off the bequests left to the populace in Caesar's will, by which Antony had won the hearts of the plebeians (4.1). Many innocent persons are sacrificed in the new reign of terror, including Cicero and the poet unluckily named Cinna. In such deaths, art and civilization yield to expediency. Rationality gives way to frenzied rhetoric and to a struggle for power in which Rome's republican tradition is buried forever. Such is the achievement of Brutus' noble revolution.

Appropriately for such a depiction of ambivalent political strife, Julius Caesar is written chiefly in the oratorical mode. It resembles its near contemporary, Henry V, in devoting so much attention to speeches of public persuasion. The famous orations following Caesar's assassination—one by Brutus in the so-called Laconic style (that is, concise and sententious) and one by Antony in the Asiatic style (that is, more florid, anecdotal, and literary)—are only the most prominent of many public utterances. In the first scene, Marullus rebukes the plebeians for their disloyalty to Pompey and for the moment dissuades them from idolizing Caesar. Decius Brutus changes Caesar's presumably unalterable mind about staying home on the ides of March (2.2). Caesar lectures the Senate on the virtues of constancy. Before Philippi, the contending armies clash with verbal taunts. Antony and Octavius end the play with tributes to the dead Brutus. In less public scenes as well, oratory serves to win Brutus over to the conspirators, to urge unavailingly that Brutus confide in his wife, or to warn the unheeding Caesar of his danger. The decline of the conspirators' cause shows in their descent from rational discourse to private bickering (4.3). The play gives us a range of rhetorical styles, from the deliberative (having to do with careful consideration of choices) to the forensic (analogous to pleading at law, maintaining one side or the other of a given question), to the epideictic (for display, as in set orations). The imagery, suitably public and rhetorical in its function, is of a fixed star in the firmament, a Colossus bestriding the petty world of humans, a tide of fortune in the affairs of humankind, a statue spouting fountains of blood. The city of Rome is a vivid presence in the play, conveyed at times through Elizabethan anachronisms, such as striking clocks, sweaty nightcaps, "towers and windows, yea, ... chimney tops" (1.1.39), but in an eclectic fusion of native and classical traditions wherein anachronisms become functionally purposeful. Style affords us one more way of considering Julius Caesar as a Janus play, looking back to Shakespeare's history plays and forward to his tragedies.

Women are marginalized in Julius Caesar, much as in Shakespeare's English history plays. Portia and Calpurnia are alike, not only in their concern for their husbands' welfare, but also in their inability to do anything to ensure their husbands' safety and prosperity. Fittingly in such an unremittingly patriarchal play, Portia and Calpurnia are noble Roman matrons of the type we also see earlier in *The Rape of Lucrece* or *Titus Andronicus* and later in Octavia *(Antony and Cleopatra)* and Volumnia *(Coriolanus):* unassailably virtuous, descended from patrician stock, and submissive to the essentially male values of unflinching duty and stoical reserve. Portia, daughter of the great Cato of Utica who committed suicide rather than submit to Caesar's tyranny, emulates her father's example by taking her own life rather than outlive her husband's shame in defeat. Calpurnia expounds her prophetic dream of Caesar's bleeding statue (2.2.76–79) only to be rebuked for womanly cowardice. These women do what they can to offer their men an alternative perspective on political ambition—one in which caution and attentiveness to family values stand in opposition to the competitive mores of the male-dominated world—but the women are doomed, like Cassandra (in *Troilus and Cressida*), to see their quiet wisdom ignored or misinterpreted. Most touching of all is the scene of marital mutuality between Portia and Brutus (2.1.234–310), in which we realize that Portia's concern and sympathy for her husband cannot save Brutus from himself.

A structural pattern to be found in *Julius Caesar,* as noted by John Velz (see bibliography), is the replicating action of rise and fall by which the great men of ancient Rome succeed one another. The process antedates the play itself, for Pompey's faded glory mentioned in Act 1 is a reminder—or should be a reminder—that good fortune lasts but a day. We behold Caesar at the point of his greatest triumph and his imminent decline to death. "O mighty Caesar! Dost thou lie so low?" asks Antony when he sees the prostrate body of the once most powerful man alive. "Are all thy conquests, glories, triumphs, spoils, / Shrunk to this little measure?" (3.1.150–152). Brutus and Cassius step forward into prominence only to be supplanted by Antony and Octavius. Antony is unaware, though presumably the audience is aware, that Antony is to fall at the hands of Octavius. The process of incessant change, reinforced by such metaphors as the tide in the affairs of humans (already noted), offering its mocking comment on Caesar's self-comparison to the fixed northern star, is not simply a meaningless descent on the grand staircase of history, for Octavius' *Pax Romana* lies at the end of the cycle from republic to empire. Still, that resting place is beyond the conclusion of this open-ended play. What we see here again and again is a human blindness to history, through which a succession of protagonists repeat one another's errors without intending to do so. Cassius, like Caesar, goes to his death in the face of unpropitious omens that he now partly believes to be true. The eagles that accompanied Cassius and his army to Philippi desert him as the moment of battle approaches. These omens suggest a balance between character and fate, for, though the leaders of Rome have one by one fallen through their own acts and choices, they have also, it seems, fulfilled a prearranged destiny. Brutus, confronted by the Ghost of Caesar and as-

sured that he will see this spirit of Caesar at Philippi, answers resolutely, "Why, I will see thee at Philippi, then" (4.3.288). Defeated in battle, as he sensed he would be, Brutus unwillingly takes his life in disregard of the stoic creed that has governed the conduct of his entire life. Cassius dies on his birthday. *Sic transit gloria mundi.*

Julius Caesar

[Dramatis Personae

JULIUS CAESAR
CALPURNIA, *Caesar's wife*
MARK ANTONY,
OCTAVIUS CAESAR, } *triumvirs after Caesar's death*
LEPIDUS,

MARCUS BRUTUS
PORTIA, *Brutus' wife*
CAIUS CASSIUS,
CASCA,
DECIUS BRUTUS,
CINNA, } *conspirators with Brutus*
METELLUS CIMBER,
TREBONIUS,
CAIUS LIGARIUS,

CICERO,
PUBLIUS, } *senators*
POPILIUS LENA,
FLAVIUS, } *tribunes of the people*
MARULLUS,

SOOTHSAYER
ARTEMIDORUS, *a teacher of rhetoric*
CINNA, *a poet*
Another POET

LUCILIUS,
TITINIUS,
MESSALA,
YOUNG CATO,
VOLUMNIUS,
VARRO, } *officers and soldiers in the army of Brutus and Cassius*
CLAUDIUS,
CLITUS,
DARDANIUS,
LABEO,
FLAVIUS,

PINDARUS, *Cassius' servant*
LUCIUS, } *Brutus' servants*
STRATO,
Caesar's SERVANT
Antony's SERVANT
Octavius' SERVANT

CARPENTER
COBBLER
Five PLEBEIANS
Three SOLDIERS *in Brutus' army*
Two SOLDIERS *in Antony's army*

MESSENGER

GHOST *of Caesar*

Senators, Plebeians, Officers, Soldiers, and Attendants

SCENE: *Rome; the neighborhood of Sardis; the neighborhood of Philippi*]

1.1

Enter Flavius, Marullus, and certain commoners over the stage.

FLAVIUS
Hence! Home, you idle creatures, get you home!
Is this a holiday? What, know you not,
Being mechanical, you ought not walk 3
Upon a laboring day without the sign 4
Of your profession?—Speak, what trade art thou?
CARPENTER Why, sir, a carpenter.
MARULLUS
Where is thy leather apron and thy rule?
What dost thou with thy best apparel on?—
You, sir, what trade are you?
COBBLER Truly, sir, in respect of a fine workman, I am 10
but, as you would say, a cobbler. 11
MARULLUS
But what trade art thou? Answer me directly.
COBBLER A trade, sir, that I hope I may use with a safe
conscience, which is indeed, sir, a mender of bad soles. 14
FLAVIUS
What trade, thou knave? Thou naughty knave, what
trade? 15
COBBLER Nay, I beseech you, sir, be not out with me. 16
Yet if you be out, sir, I can mend you. 17
FLAVIUS
What mean'st thou by that? Mend me, thou saucy
fellow?
COBBLER Why, sir, cobble you. 19
FLAVIUS Thou art a cobbler, art thou?
COBBLER Truly, sir, all that I live by is with the awl. I 21
meddle with no tradesman's matters nor women's 22
matters, but withal I am indeed, sir, a surgeon to old 23
shoes. When they are in great danger, I recover them. 24
As proper men as ever trod upon neat's leather have 25
gone upon my handiwork. 26

1.1. Location: Rome. A street.
3 mechanical of the class of artisans **4 sign** garb and implements
10 in . . . workman (1) as far as skilled work is concerned (2) compared with a skilled worker **11 cobbler** (1) one who works with shoes (2) bungler **14 soles** (with pun on "souls") **15 naughty** good-for-nothing **16–17 out** (1) out of temper (2) having worn-out soles **17 mend** (1) reform (2) repair **19 cobble you** mend your shoes. (The meaning "to pelt with stones" also suggests itself here, though perhaps it was not in general use until later in the seventeenth century.) **21 awl** (Punning on *all*.) **22–23 meddle, women's matters** (With suggestion of having sexual relations.) **23 withal** yet (with pun on *with awl*) **24 recover** (1) resole (2) cure **25 proper** handsome. **as . . . leather** as ever wore shoes. (Proverbial.) **neat's leather** cowhide **26 gone** walked

FLAVIUS
But wherefore art not in thy shop today?
Why dost thou lead these men about the streets?

COBBLER   Truly, sir, to wear out their shoes, to get myself into more work. But indeed, sir, we make holiday
to see Caesar and to rejoice in his triumph.   31

MARULLUS
Wherefore rejoice? What conquest brings he home?
What tributaries follow him to Rome   33
To grace in captive bonds his chariot wheels?
You blocks, you stones, you worse than senseless
    things!   35
O you hard hearts, you cruel men of Rome,
Knew you not Pompey? Many a time and oft   37
Have you climbed up to walls and battlements,   38
To towers and windows, yea, to chimney tops,   39
Your infants in your arms, and there have sat
The livelong day, with patient expectation,
To see great Pompey pass the streets of Rome.   42
And when you saw his chariot but appear,
Have you not made an universal shout,
That Tiber trembled underneath her banks   45
To hear the replication of your sounds   46
Made in her concave shores?   47
And do you now put on your best attire?
And do you now cull out a holiday?   49
And do you now strew flowers in his way
That comes in triumph over Pompey's blood?   51
Begone!
Run to your houses, fall upon your knees,
Pray to the gods to intermit the plague   54
That needs must light on this ingratitude.   55

FLAVIUS
Go, go, good countrymen, and for this fault
Assemble all the poor men of your sort;   57
Draw them to Tiber banks, and weep your tears
Into the channel, till the lowest stream   59
Do kiss the most exalted shores of all.   60
                        Exeunt all the commoners.
See whe'er their basest mettle be not moved.   61
They vanish tongue-tied in their guiltiness.
Go you down that way towards the Capitol;
This way will I. Disrobe the images   64

---

31 triumph triumphal procession. (Caesar had overthrown the sons of
Pompey the Great in Spain at the Battle of Munda, March 17, 45 B.C.
The triumph was held that October.)   **33 tributaries** captives who
will pay ransom (tribute)   **35 senseless** insensible like stone (hence,
stupid)   **37 Pompey** (Caesar had overthrown the great soldier and
onetime triumvir at the Battle of Pharsalus in 48 B.C., and Pompey
fled to Egypt, where he was murdered.)   **38–39 battlements . . .
chimney tops** (The details are appropriate to an Elizabethan city-
scape.)   **42 great** (Alludes to Pompey's epithet, *Magnus*, ''great.'')
pass pass through   **45 Tiber** the Tiber River   **46 replication** echo
47 concave hollowed out, overhanging   **49 cull out** select, pick out
51 Pompey's blood (1) Pompey's offspring (2) the blood of the Pom-
peys   **54 intermit** suspend   **55 needs must** must necessarily   **57 sort**
rank   **59 the lowest stream** the river at its lowest level   **60 kiss** i.e.,
touch.   **most exalted shores** highest banks   **61 See . . . moved** see
how even their ignoble natures can be appealed to.   **whe'er** whether.
mettle (1) temperament (2) substance, *metal*. (*Metal* and *mettle* are
variants of the same word. A *base metal* is one that is easily changed
or *moved*, unlike gold; compare this with 1.2.309.)   **64 images** statues (of Caesar in royal regalia, set up by his followers)

If you do find them decked with ceremonies.   65
MARULLUS   May we do so?
You know it is the Feast of Lupercal.   67

FLAVIUS
It is no matter. Let no images
Be hung with Caesar's trophies. I'll about   69
And drive away the vulgar from the streets;   70
So do you too, where you perceive them thick.
These growing feathers plucked from Caesar's wing
Will make him fly an ordinary pitch,   73
Who else would soar above the view of men   74
And keep us all in servile fearfulness.   *Exeunt.*

1.2   *Enter Caesar, Antony for the course, Calpurnia,
Portia, Decius, Cicero, Brutus, Cassius, Casca, a
Soothsayer; after them, Marullus and Flavius;
[citizens following].*

CAESAR
Calpurnia!
CASCA   Peace, ho! Caesar speaks.
CAESAR   Calpurnia!
CALPURNIA   Here, my lord.
CAESAR
Stand you directly in Antonio's way
When he doth run his course. Antonio!
ANTONY   Caesar, my lord?
CAESAR
Forget not, in your speed, Antonio,
To touch Calpurnia; for our elders say
The barren, touchèd in this holy chase,
Shake off their sterile curse.
ANTONY   I shall remember.   9
When Caesar says ''Do this,'' it is performed.
CAESAR
Set on, and leave no ceremony out.   *[Flourish.]* 11
SOOTHSAYER   Caesar!
CAESAR   Ha? Who calls?
CASCA
Bid every noise be still. Peace yet again!
                          [The music ceases.]
CAESAR
Who is it in the press that calls on me?   15
I hear a tongue shriller than all the music
Cry ''Caesar!'' Speak. Caesar is turned to hear.

---

65 ceremonies ceremonial trappings of state   **67 Feast of Lupercal** a
feast of purification (*Februa*, whence *February*) in honor of Pan, celebrated from ancient times in Rome on February 15 of each year. (Historically, this celebration came some months after Caesar's triumph in
October of 45 B.C. The celebrants, called *Luperci*, raced around the
Palatine Hill and the Circus carrying thongs of goatskin, with which
they struck those who came in their way. Women so lashed were
suppposed to be cured of barrenness; hence Caesar's wish that Antony would strike Calpurnia, 1.2.6–8.)   **69 about** go about the other
way   **70 vulgar** commoners, plebeians   **73 pitch** highest point in
flight. (A term from falconry.)   **74 else** otherwise
**1.2. Location: A public place or street, perhaps as in the previous
scene.**
s.d. for the course i.e., stripped for the race, carrying a goatskin
thong   **9 sterile curse** curse of barrenness   **11 Set on** proceed
15 press throng

SOOTHSAYER
Beware the ides of March.

CAESAR   What man is that?   18

BRUTUS
A soothsayer bids you beware the ides of March.

CAESAR
Set him before me. Let me see his face.

CASSIUS
Fellow, come from the throng. [*The Soothsayer comes
     forward.*] Look upon Caesar.

CAESAR
What sayst thou to me now? Speak once again.

SOOTHSAYER   Beware the ides of March.

CAESAR
He is a dreamer. Let us leave him. Pass.   24
               Sennet. Exeunt. Manent Brutus and Cassius.

CASSIUS
Will you go see the order of the course?   25

BRUTUS   Not I.

CASSIUS   I pray you, do.

BRUTUS
I am not gamesome. I do lack some part   28
Of that quick spirit that is in Antony.   29
Let me not hinder, Cassius, your desires;
I'll leave you.

CASSIUS
Brutus, I do observe you now of late.
I have not from your eyes that gentleness
And show of love as I was wont to have.   34
You bear too stubborn and too strange a hand   35
Over your friend that loves you.

BRUTUS   Cassius,
Be not deceived. If I have veiled my look,   37
I turn the trouble of my countenance
Merely upon myself. Vexèd I am   39
Of late with passions of some difference,   40
Conceptions only proper to myself,   41
Which give some soil, perhaps, to my behaviors.   42
But let not therefore my good friends be grieved—
Among which number, Cassius, be you one—
Nor construe any further my neglect   45
Than that poor Brutus, with himself at war,
Forgets the shows of love to other men.

CASSIUS
Then, Brutus, I have much mistook your passion,
By means whereof this breast of mine hath buried   49
Thoughts of great value, worthy cogitations.   50
Tell me, good Brutus, can you see your face?

BRUTUS
No, Cassius, for the eye sees not itself

But by reflection, by some other things.

CASSIUS   'Tis just.   54
And it is very much lamented, Brutus,
That you have no such mirrors as will turn
Your hidden worthiness into your eye,
That you might see your shadow. I have heard   58
Where many of the best respect in Rome,   59
Except immortal Caesar, speaking of Brutus
And groaning underneath this age's yoke,
Have wished that noble Brutus had his eyes.   62

BRUTUS
Into what dangers would you lead me, Cassius,
That you would have me seek into myself
For that which is not in me?

CASSIUS
Therefore, good Brutus, be prepared to hear;   66
And since you know you cannot see yourself
So well as by reflection, I, your glass,   68
Will modestly discover to yourself   69
That of yourself which you yet know not of.
And be not jealous on me, gentle Brutus.   71
Were I a common laughter, or did use   72
To stale with ordinary oaths my love   73
To every new protester; if you know   74
That I do fawn on men and hug them hard
And after scandal them, or if you know   76
That I profess myself in banqueting   77
To all the rout, then hold me dangerous.   78
                              Flourish, and shout.

BRUTUS
What means this shouting? I do fear the people
Choose Caesar for their king.

CASSIUS   Ay, do you fear it?
Then must I think you would not have it so.

BRUTUS
I would not, Cassius, yet I love him well.
But wherefore do you hold me here so long?
What is it that you would impart to me?
If it be aught toward the general good,
Set honor in one eye and death i' th' other
And I will look on both indifferently;   87
For let the gods so speed me as I love   88
The name of honor more than I fear death.

CASSIUS
I know that virtue to be in you, Brutus,
As well as I do know your outward favor.   91
Well, honor is the subject of my story.
I cannot tell what you and other men
Think of this life; but, for my single self,

---

18 **ides of March** March 15   24 **s.d. Sennet** trumpet call signaling the
arrival or departure of a dignitary.   **Manent** they remain onstage
25 **order of the course** ritual and progress of the race   28 **gamesome**
fond of sports, merry   29 **quick spirit** alacrity   34 **wont** accustomed
35 **stubborn** rough. (The metaphor is from horsemanship.)   **strange**
aloof   37 **veiled my look** i.e., been introverted, seemed less friendly
39 **Merely** entirely   40 **passions of some difference** conflicting emotions   41 **only proper to** relating only to   42 **soil** blemish   45 **construe any further** interpret any other way   49–50 **By . . . value** because of which misunderstanding (my assuming you were displeased
with me) I have kept to myself important thoughts

54 **just** true   58 **shadow** image, reflection   59 **best respect** highest
repute and station   62 **had his eyes** (1) could see things from the perspective of Caesar's critics, or (2) could see better with his own eyes
66 **Therefore** as to that   68 **glass** mirror   69 **modestly discover** reveal
without exaggeration   71 **jealous on** suspicious of.   **gentle** noble
72 **laughter** laughingstock, as at 4.3.114; or perhaps *laugher*, a shallow fellow who laughs at every jest.   **did use** were accustomed
73 **stale** cheapen, make common.   **ordinary** (1) commonplace (2)
customary (3) tavern   74 **protester** one who protests or declares
friendship   76 **after scandal** afterwards slander   77 **profess myself**
make declarations of friendship   78 **rout** mob   87 **indifferently** impartially   88 **speed me** make me prosper   91 **favor** appearance

I had as lief not be as live to be   95
In awe of such a thing as I myself.   96
I was born free as Caesar, so were you;
We both have fed as well, and we can both
Endure the winter's cold as well as he.
For once, upon a raw and gusty day,
The troubled Tiber chafing with her shores,   101
Caesar said to me, "Dar'st thou, Cassius, now
Leap in with me into this angry flood
And swim to yonder point?" Upon the word,
Accoutred as I was, I plungèd in   105
And bade him follow; so indeed he did.
The torrent roared, and we did buffet it
With lusty sinews, throwing it aside   108
And stemming it with hearts of controversy.   109
But ere we could arrive the point proposed,   110
Caesar cried, "Help me, Cassius, or I sink!"
Ay, as Aeneas, our great ancestor,   112
Did from the flames of Troy upon his shoulder
The old Anchises bear, so from the waves of Tiber
Did I the tirèd Caesar. And this man
Is now become a god, and Cassius is
A wretched creature and must bend his body   117
If Caesar carelessly but nod on him.
He had a fever when he was in Spain,
And when the fit was on him I did mark   120
How he did shake. 'Tis true, this god did shake.
His coward lips did from their color fly,   122
And that same eye whose bend doth awe the world   123
Did lose his luster. I did hear him groan.   124
Ay, and that tongue of his that bade the Romans
Mark him and write his speeches in their books,
Alas, it cried, "Give me some drink, Titinius,"
As a sick girl. Ye gods, it doth amaze me
A man of such a feeble temper should   129
So get the start of the majestic world   130
And bear the palm alone.   *Shout. Flourish.*   131
BRUTUS   Another general shout?
I do believe that these applauses are
For some new honors that are heaped on Caesar.
CASSIUS
Why, man, he doth bestride the narrow world   135
Like a Colossus, and we petty men   136
Walk under his huge legs and peep about
To find ourselves dishonorable graves.   138
Men at some time are masters of their fates.
The fault, dear Brutus, is not in our stars,

But in ourselves, that we are underlings.
"Brutus" and "Caesar." What should be in that
   "Caesar"?
Why should that name be sounded more than
   yours?   143
Write them together, yours is as fair a name;
Sound them, it doth become the mouth as well;
Weigh them, it is as heavy; conjure with 'em,
"Brutus" will start a spirit as soon as "Caesar."   147
Now, in the names of all the gods at once,
Upon what meat doth this our Caesar feed   149
That he is grown so great? Age, thou art shamed!
Rome, thou hast lost the breed of noble bloods!   151
When went there by an age since the great flood   152
But it was famed with more than with one man?   153
When could they say, till now, that talked of Rome,
That her wide walks encompassed but one man?
Now is it Rome indeed, and room enough,   156
When there is in it but one only man.
O, you and I have heard our fathers say
There was a Brutus once that would have brooked   159
Th' eternal devil to keep his state in Rome   160
As easily as a king.   161
BRUTUS
That you do love me, I am nothing jealous.   162
What you would work me to, I have some aim.   163
How I have thought of this and of these times
I shall recount hereafter. For this present,   165
I would not, so with love I might entreat you,   166
Be any further moved. What you have said   167
I will consider; what you have to say
I will with patience hear, and find a time
Both meet to hear and answer such high things.   170
Till then, my noble friend, chew upon this:
Brutus had rather be a villager
Than to repute himself a son of Rome
Under these hard conditions as this time
Is like to lay upon us.
CASSIUS   I am glad that my weak words
Have struck but thus much show of fire from
   Brutus.

                    Enter Caesar and his train.

BRUTUS
The games are done, and Caesar is returning.
CASSIUS
As they pass by, pluck Casca by the sleeve,
And he will, after his sour fashion, tell you
What hath proceeded worthy note today.

---

95 as lief not be just as soon not exist   **96 such . . . myself** i.e., a fellow mortal   **101 chafing with** raging against   **105 Accoutred** fully dressed in armor   **108 lusty sinews** vigorous might. (Literally, tendons.)   **109 stemming** making headway against.   **hearts of controversy** hearts fired up by rivalry   **110 arrive** arrive at   **112 Aeneas** hero of Virgil's *Aeneid*, the legendary founder of Rome (hence *our great ancestor*), who bore his aged father Anchises out of burning Troy as it was falling to the Greeks   **117 bend his body** bow   **120 mark** notice   **122 color** (1) i.e., normal healthy hue (2) military colors, flag. (The lips are personified as deserters.)   **123 bend** glance, gaze   **124 his** its   **129 temper** constitution   **130 get the start of** outstrip   **131 palm** victor's prize   **135 bestride** straddle   **136 Colossus** (A 100-foot-high bronze statue of Helios, the sun god, one of the seven wonders of the ancient world, was commonly supposed to have stood astride the entrance to the harbor of Rhodes.)   **138 dishonorable graves** the ignoble deaths of slaves

143 be sounded (1) be spoken and celebrated (2) resound   **147 start** raise   **149 meat** food   **151 the breed . . . bloods** the bloodline of men of noble stock and valiant spirit   **152 flood** i.e., the classical analogue of Noah's flood, in which all humanity was destroyed except for Deucalion and his wife Pyrrha   **153 famed with** famous for   **156 Rome, room** (Pronounced alike.)   **159 Brutus** i.e., Lucius Junius Brutus, who expelled the Tarquins and founded the Roman republic (c. 509 B.C.).   **brooked** tolerated   **160 eternal** (A common substitution for "infernal"? Compare the Yankee adjective "'tarnal.")   **keep his state** set up his throne   **161 As . . . king** as readily as he would tolerate a king   **162 nothing jealous** not at all doubtful   **163 work** persuade.   **aim** inkling and intention   **165 present** present moment   **166 so . . . you** if I might entreat you in the name of friendship   **167 moved** urged   **170 meet** fitting

BRUTUS
I will do so. But look you, Cassius,
The angry spot doth glow on Caesar's brow,
And all the rest look like a chidden train.   184
Calpurnia's cheek is pale, and Cicero
Looks with such ferret and such fiery eyes   186
As we have seen him in the Capitol,
Being crossed in conference by some senators.   188

CASSIUS
Casca will tell us what the matter is.

CAESAR   Antonio!

ANTONY   Caesar?

CAESAR
Let me have men about me that are fat,
Sleek-headed men, and such as sleep o' nights.
Yond Cassius has a lean and hungry look.
He thinks too much. Such men are dangerous.

ANTONY
Fear him not, Caesar, he's not dangerous.
He is a noble Roman, and well given.   197

CAESAR
Would he were fatter! But I fear him not.
Yet if my name were liable to fear,
I do not know the man I should avoid
So soon as that spare Cassius. He reads much,
He is a great observer, and he looks
Quite through the deeds of men. He loves no plays,   203
As thou dost, Antony; he hears no music.   204
Seldom he smiles, and smiles in such a sort   205
As if he mocked himself and scorned his spirit
That could be moved to smile at anything.
Such men as he be never at heart's ease
Whiles they behold a greater than themselves,
And therefore are they very dangerous.
I rather tell thee what is to be feared
Than what I fear, for always I am Caesar.
Come on my right hand, for this ear is deaf,
And tell me truly what thou think'st of him.
            Sennet. Exeunt Caesar and his train. [Casca remains
                        with Brutus and Cassius.]

CASCA   You pulled me by the cloak. Would you speak   215
with me?

BRUTUS
Ay, Casca. Tell us what hath chanced today,   217
That Caesar looks so sad.   218

CASCA   Why, you were with him, were you not?

BRUTUS
I should not then ask Casca what had chanced.

CASCA   Why, there was a crown offered him; and, being
offered him, he put it by with the back of his hand, 222
thus, and then the people fell a-shouting.

BRUTUS   What was the second noise for?

CASCA   Why, for that too.

CASSIUS
They shouted thrice. What was the last cry for?

CASCA   Why, for that too.

BRUTUS   Was the crown offered him thrice?

CASCA   Ay, marry, was 't, and he put it by thrice, every 229
time gentler than other, and at every putting-by mine
honest neighbors shouted.   231

CASSIUS   Who offered him the crown?

CASCA   Why, Antony.

BRUTUS
Tell us the manner of it, gentle Casca.   234

CASCA   I can as well be hanged as tell the manner of it.
It was mere foolery; I did not mark it. I saw Mark Antony offer him a crown—yet 'twas not a crown neither, 'twas one of these coronets—and, as I told you, 238
he put it by once; but for all that, to my thinking, he
would fain have had it. Then he offered it to him again; 240
then he put it by again; but to my thinking he was
very loath to lay his fingers off it. And then he offered
it the third time. He put it the third time by, and still 243
as he refused it the rabblement hooted and clapped 244
their chapped hands, and threw up their sweaty night- 245
caps, and uttered such a deal of stinking breath be- 246
cause Caesar refused the crown that it had almost
choked Caesar, for he swooned and fell down at it.
And for mine own part I durst not laugh for fear of
opening my lips and receiving the bad air.

CASSIUS
But soft, I pray you. What, did Caesar swoon?   251

CASCA   He fell down in the marketplace, and foamed at
mouth, and was speechless.

BRUTUS
'Tis very like. He hath the falling sickness.   254

CASSIUS
No, Caesar hath it not, but you and I,
And honest Casca, we have the falling sickness.

CASCA   I know not what you mean by that, but I am
sure Caesar fell down. If the tag-rag people did not 258
clap him and hiss him, according as he pleased and
displeased them, as they use to do the players in the 260
theater, I am no true man.   261

BRUTUS
What said he when he came unto himself?

CASCA   Marry, before he fell down, when he perceived
the common herd was glad he refused the crown, he
plucked me ope his doublet and offered them his throat 265
to cut. An I had been a man of any occupation, if I 266
would not have taken him at a word, I would I might
go to hell among the rogues. And so he fell. When he
came to himself again, he said if he had done or said
anything amiss, he desired their worships to think it

---

184 chidden scolded, rebuked.   **train** retinue   **186 ferret** ferretlike,
i.e., small and red   **188 crossed in conference** opposed in debate
197 given disposed   **203 through** i.e., into the motives of   **204 hears
no music** (Regarded as a sign of a morose and treacherous character.)
205 sort manner   **215 cloak** (Elizabethan costume; see also *sleeve*,
line 179, and *doublet*, line 265. The Roman toga was sleeveless.)
217 chanced happened   **218 sad** serious   **222 by** aside

229 marry i.e., indeed. (Originally, "by the Virgin Mary.")   **231 honest** worthy. (Said contemptuously.)   **234 gentle** noble   **238 coronets**
chaplets, garlands   **240 fain** gladly   **243–244 still as** whenever
245–246 nightcaps (Scornful allusion to the *pilleus*, a felt cap worn
by the plebeians on festival days.)   **251 soft** i.e., wait a minute
254 like likely.   **falling sickness** epilepsy. (But Cassius takes it to
mean "falling into servitude.")   **258 tag-rag** ragtag, riffraff   **260 use**
are accustomed   **261 true** honest   **265 plucked me ope** pulled
open. (*Me* is used colloquially.)   **doublet** Elizabethan upper garment,
like a jacket   **266 An** if.   **man . . . occupation** (1) working man (2)
man of action

was his infirmity. Three or four wenches where I stood cried, "Alas, good soul!" and forgave him with all their hearts. But there's no heed to be taken of them; if Caesar had stabbed their mothers they would 274 have done no less.

BRUTUS
And after that, he came thus sad away?   276

CASCA   Ay.

CASSIUS   Did Cicero say anything?

CASCA   Ay, he spoke Greek.

CASSIUS   To what effect?

CASCA   Nay, an I tell you that, I'll ne'er look you i' the face again. But those that understood him smiled at one another and shook their heads; but, for mine own part, it was Greek to me. I could tell you more news too. Marullus and Flavius, for pulling scarves off Cae- 285 sar's images, are put to silence. Fare you well. There 286 was more foolery yet, if I could remember it.

CASSIUS   Will you sup with me tonight, Casca?

CASCA   No, I am promised forth.   289

CASSIUS   Will you dine with me tomorrow?

CASCA   Ay, if I be alive, and your mind hold, and your dinner worth the eating.

CASSIUS   Good. I will expect you.

CASCA   Do so. Farewell both.   *Exit.*

BRUTUS
What a blunt fellow is this grown to be!
He was quick mettle when he went to school.   296

CASSIUS
So is he now in execution
Of any bold or noble enterprise,
However he puts on this tardy form.   299
This rudeness is a sauce to his good wit,   300
Which gives men stomach to digest his words   301
With better appetite.

BRUTUS
And so it is. For this time I will leave you.
Tomorrow, if you please to speak with me,
I will come home to you; or, if you will,
Come home to me, and I will wait for you.

CASSIUS
I will do so. Till then, think of the world.   307
                                                         Exit Brutus.
Well, Brutus, thou art noble. Yet I see
Thy honorable mettle may be wrought   309
From that it is disposed. Therefore it is meet   310
That noble minds keep ever with their likes;

For who so firm that cannot be seduced?
Caesar doth bear me hard, but he loves Brutus.   313
If I were Brutus now, and he were Cassius,
He should not humor me. I will this night   315
In several hands in at his windows throw,   316
As if they came from several citizens,
Writings, all tending to the great opinion   318
That Rome holds of his name, wherein obscurely
Caesar's ambition shall be glancèd at.   320
And after this let Caesar seat him sure,   321
For we will shake him, or worse days endure.   *Exit.*

1.3   *Thunder and lightning. Enter, [meeting,] Casca [with his sword drawn] and Cicero.*

CICERO
Good even, Casca. Brought you Caesar home?   1
Why are you breathless? And why stare you so?

CASCA
Are not you moved, when all the sway of earth   3
Shakes like a thing unfirm? O Cicero,
I have seen tempests when the scolding winds
Have rived the knotty oaks, and I have seen   6
Th' ambitious ocean swell and rage and foam
To be exalted with the threatening clouds;   8
But never till tonight, never till now,
Did I go through a tempest dropping fire.
Either there is a civil strife in heaven,
Or else the world, too saucy with the gods,   12
Incenses them to send destruction.

CICERO
Why, saw you anything more wonderful?   14

CASCA
A common slave—you know him well by sight—
Held up his left hand, which did flame and burn
Like twenty torches joined, and yet his hand,
Not sensible of fire, remained unscorched.   18
Besides—I ha' not since put up my sword—   19
Against the Capitol I met a lion,   20
Who glazed upon me and went surly by   21
Without annoying me. And there were drawn   22
Upon a heap a hundred ghastly women,   23
Transformèd with their fear, who swore they saw
Men all in fire walk up and down the streets.
And yesterday the bird of night did sit   26

---

274 **stabbed** (With bawdy implication.)   276 **sad** somberly
285 **scarves** decorations, festoons   286 **put to silence** dismissed from office. (So reported in Plutarch.)   289 **promised forth** engaged to dine out   296 **quick mettle** of a lively temperament   299 **However** however much.   **tardy form** appearance of sluggishness   300 **rudeness** rough manner.   **wit** intellect   301 **stomach** appetite, inclination   307 **the world** i.e., the state of the world   309 **mettle** (As often, the word combines the senses of *mettle*, "temperament," and *metal*, "substance." The latter meaning continues here in the chemical metaphor of metal that is *wrought* or transmuted. As *honorable mettle* [or *noble metal*], gold cannot be transmuted into base substances, and yet Cassius proposes to do just that with Brutus. Compare this with 1.1.61.)   309–310 **wrought . . . disposed** turned away from its natural disposition   310 **meet** fitting

313 **bear me hard** bear me a grudge. (A metaphor from horsemanship.)   315 **He** i.e., Brutus.   **humor** cajole. Cassius may be saying (1) if he, Brutus, were in my shoes, he wouldn't sway me as I sway him; or (2) he wouldn't be so smug in his behavior toward me as he is now. Or he may mean (3) if I were in Brutus' shoes, Caesar wouldn't cajole me so.   316 **several hands** different handwriting   318 **tending to** concerning; confirming   320 **glancèd** hinted   321 **seat him sure** seat himself securely in power (i.e., watch out)
1.3. Location: A street.
1 **Brought** escorted   3 **sway** established order   6 **rived** split   8 **exalted with** raised to the level of   12 **saucy** insolent   14 **more** else.   **wonderful** wondrous   18 **Not sensible of** not feeling   19 **put up** sheathed   20 **Against** opposite or near   21 **glazed** stared glassily   22 **annoying** harming   22–23 **drawn . . . heap** huddled together   23 **ghastly** pallid   26 **bird of night** owl, a bird of evil omen

Even at noonday upon the marketplace,
Hooting and shrieking. When these prodigies   28
Do so conjointly meet, let not men say,   29
"These are their reasons, they are natural,"
For I believe they are portentous things
Unto the climate that they point upon.   32

CICERO
Indeed, it is a strange-disposèd time.
But men may construe things after their fashion,   34
Clean from the purpose of the things themselves.   35
Comes Caesar to the Capitol tomorrow?

CASCA
He doth; for he did bid Antonio
Send word to you he would be there tomorrow.

CICERO
Good night then, Casca. This disturbèd sky
Is not to walk in.

CASCA   Farewell, Cicero.   *Exit Cicero.*

        Enter Cassius.

CASSIUS
Who's there?

CASCA   A Roman.

CASSIUS   Casca, by your voice.

CASCA
Your ear is good. Cassius, what night is this!   42

CASSIUS
A very pleasing night to honest men.

CASCA
Who ever knew the heavens menace so?

CASSIUS
Those that have known the earth so full of faults.
For my part, I have walked about the streets,
Submitting me unto the perilous night,
And thus unbracèd, Casca, as you see,   48
Have bared my bosom to the thunder-stone;   49
And when the cross blue lightning seemed to open   50
The breast of heaven, I did present myself
Even in the aim and very flash of it.   52

CASCA
But wherefore did you so much tempt the heavens?
It is the part of men to fear and tremble   54
When the most mighty gods by tokens send   55
Such dreadful heralds to astonish us.   56

CASSIUS
You are dull, Casca, and those sparks of life
That should be in a Roman you do want,   58
Or else you use not. You look pale, and gaze,
And put on fear, and cast yourself in wonder,   60
To see the strange impatience of the heavens.
But if you would consider the true cause
Why all these fires, why all these gliding ghosts,

Why birds and beasts from quality and kind,   64
Why old men, fools, and children calculate,   65
Why all these things change from their ordinance,   66
Their natures, and preformèd faculties,   67
To monstrous quality—why, you shall find   68
That heaven hath infused them with these spirits
To make them instruments of fear and warning
Unto some monstrous state.   71
Now could I, Casca, name to thee a man
Most like this dreadful night,
That thunders, lightens, opens graves, and roars
As doth the lion in the Capitol—
A man no mightier than thyself or me
In personal action, yet prodigious grown   77
And fearful, as these strange eruptions are.   78

CASCA
'Tis Caesar that you mean, is it not, Cassius?

CASSIUS
Let it be who it is. For Romans now
Have thews and limbs like to their ancestors;   81
But, woe the while, our fathers' minds are dead,   82
And we are governed with our mothers' spirits.
Our yoke and sufferance show us womanish.   84

CASCA
Indeed, they say the senators tomorrow
Mean to establish Caesar as a king,
And he shall wear his crown by sea and land
In every place save here in Italy.

CASSIUS
I know where I will wear this dagger then;
Cassius from bondage will deliver Cassius.
Therein, ye gods, you make the weak most strong;   91
Therein, ye gods, you tyrants do defeat.
Nor stony tower, nor walls of beaten brass,   93
Nor airless dungeon, nor strong links of iron,
Can be retentive to the strength of spirit;   95
But life, being weary of these worldly bars,   96
Never lacks power to dismiss itself.
If I know this, know all the world besides,   98
That part of tyranny that I do bear
I can shake off at pleasure.   *Thunder still.*

CASCA   So can I.
So every bondman in his own hand bears
The power to cancel his captivity.

CASSIUS
And why should Caesar be a tyrant then?
Poor man, I know he would not be a wolf
But that he sees the Romans are but sheep;
He were no lion, were not Romans hinds.   106

64 from . . . kind (behaving) contrary to their true nature **65 old men** dotards. **calculate** prophesy **66 ordinance** established nature **67 preformèd** innate, congenital **68 monstrous** unnatural **71 Unto . . . state** pointing to some commonwealth or state of affairs that is out of the natural order **77 prodigious** ominous **78 fearful** inspiring fear **81 thews** sinews, muscles **82 woe the while** alas for the age **84 yoke and sufferance** patience under the yoke **91 Therein** i.e., in the ability to commit suicide **93 Nor** neither **95 be . . . spirit** confine a resolute spirit **96 bars** (1) prison bars (2) burdens (such as tyranny) **98 know . . . besides** let the rest of the world know **106 were** would be. **hinds** (1) female of the red deer (2) servants, menials

28 prodigies abnormalities, wonders **29 conjointly meet** coincide **32 climate** region **34 construe** interpret. **after their fashion** in their own way **35 Clean . . . purpose** contrary to the actual import or meaning **42 what night** what a night **48 unbracèd** with doublet unfastened **49 thunder-stone** thunderbolt **50 cross** forked, jagged **52 Even in the aim** at the exact place at which it was aimed **54 part** appropriate role **55 tokens** signs **56 astonish** stun **58 want** lack **60 put on** adopt, show signs of. **in wonder** into a state of wonder

Those that with haste will make a mighty fire
Begin it with weak straws. What trash is Rome,
What rubbish and what offal, when it serves 109
For the base matter to illuminate 110
So vile a thing as Caesar! But, O grief,
Where hast thou led me? I perhaps speak this
Before a willing bondman; then I know
My answer must be made. But I am armed, 114
And dangers are to me indifferent. 115

CASCA
You speak to Casca, and to such a man
That is no fleering telltale. Hold. My hand. 117
Be factious for redress of all these griefs, 118
And I will set this foot of mine as far
As who goes farthest.   [They shake hands.]

CASSIUS   There's a bargain made. 120
Now know you, Casca, I have moved already 121
Some certain of the noblest-minded Romans
To undergo with me an enterprise
Of honorable-dangerous consequence;
And I do know by this they stay for me 125
In Pompey's porch. For now, this fearful night, 126
There is no stir or walking in the streets,
And the complexion of the element 128
In favor 's like the work we have in hand, 129
Most bloody, fiery, and most terrible.

Enter Cinna.

CASCA
Stand close awhile, for here comes one in haste. 131
CASSIUS
'Tis Cinna; I do know him by his gait.
He is a friend.—Cinna, where haste you so?
CINNA
To find out you. Who's that? Metellus Cimber?
CASSIUS
No, it is Casca, one incorporate 135
To our attempts. Am I not stayed for, Cinna?
CINNA
I am glad on 't. What a fearful night is this! 137
There's two or three of us have seen strange sights.
CASSIUS Am I not stayed for? Tell me.
CINNA
Yes, you are. O Cassius, if you could
But win the noble Brutus to our party—
CASSIUS
Be you content. Good Cinna, take this paper, 142
[giving papers]

And look you lay it in the praetor's chair, 143
Where Brutus may but find it. And throw this 144
In at his window. Set this up with wax
Upon old Brutus' statue. All this done, 146
Repair to Pompey's porch, where you shall find us. 147
Is Decius Brutus and Trebonius there?
CINNA
All but Metellus Cimber, and he's gone
To seek you at your house. Well, I will hie, 150
And so bestow these papers as you bade me.
CASSIUS
That done, repair to Pompey's theater.   *Exit Cinna.*
Come, Casca, you and I will yet ere day
See Brutus at his house. Three parts of him 154
Is ours already, and the man entire
Upon the next encounter yields him ours.
CASCA
O, he sits high in all the people's hearts;
And that which would appear offense in us,
His countenance, like richest alchemy, 159
Will change to virtue and to worthiness. 160
CASSIUS
Him and his worth, and our great need of him,
You have right well conceited. Let us go, 162
For it is after midnight, and ere day
We will awake him and be sure of him.   *Exeunt.*

❖

2.1   *Enter Brutus in his orchard.*

BRUTUS What, Lucius, ho!—
I cannot by the progress of the stars
Give guess how near to day.—Lucius, I say!—
I would it were my fault to sleep so soundly.—
When, Lucius, when? Awake, I say! What, Lucius! 5

Enter Lucius.

LUCIUS Called you, my lord?
BRUTUS
Get me a taper in my study, Lucius. 7
When it is lighted, come and call me here.
LUCIUS I will, my lord.   *Exit.*
BRUTUS
It must be by his death. And for my part
I know no personal cause to spurn at him, 11
But for the general. He would be crowned. 12

109 **offal** rubbish, wood shavings 110 **matter** i.e., fuel 114 **My answer . . . made** I will have to answer (to Caesar) for what I have said. **armed** (1) provided with weapons (2) morally fortified 115 **indifferent** unimportant 117 **fleering** fawning; scornful. **Hold. My hand** enough; here is my hand 118 **factious** active as a partisan. **griefs** grievances 120 **who** whoever 121 **moved** urged 125 **by this** by this time. **stay** wait 126 **Pompey's porch** the colonnade of Pompey's great open theater, dedicated in 55 B.C. (Caesar was assassinated there, though Shakespeare has the assassination take place in the Capitol [i.e., the Senate chamber].) 128 **element** sky 129 **favor 's** appearance is 131 **close** concealed, still 135 **incorporate** admitted as a member 137 **on 't** of it 142 **Be you content** set your mind at rest

143 **praetor's chair** official seat of a praetor, Roman magistrate ranking next below the consul. (Brutus was praetor, one of sixteen.) 144 **Where . . . it** where Brutus cannot help finding it 146 **old Brutus** (Lucius Junius Brutus; Brutus was reputed to be his descendant.) 147 **Repair** proceed (also in line 152) 150 **hie** go quickly 154 **parts** i.e., quarters 159 **countenance** (1) support, approval (2) honorable appearance. **alchemy** pseudoscience, the chief object of which was the transmutation of other metals into gold 160 **virtue** (In addition to its literal meaning, a technical term for what the alchemists hoped to attain.) 162 **conceited** (1) conceived, grasped (2) expressed in a figure

2.1. Location: Rome. Brutus' orchard, or garden.
5 **When** (An exclamation of impatience.) 7 **Get me** put. **taper** candle 11 **spurn** kick 12 **general** general cause, common good

How that might change his nature, there's the
    question.
It is the bright day that brings forth the adder,
And that craves wary walking. Crown him that,   15
And then I grant we put a sting in him
That at his will he may do danger with.
Th' abuse of greatness is when it disjoins
Remorse from power. And to speak truth of Caesar, 19
I have not known when his affections swayed   20
More than his reason. But 'tis a common proof   21
That lowliness is young ambition's ladder,   22
Whereto the climber-upward turns his face;
But when he once attains the upmost round   24
He then unto the ladder turns his back,
Looks in the clouds, scorning the base degrees   26
By which he did ascend. So Caesar may.
Then, lest he may, prevent. And since the quarrel
Will bear no color for the thing he is,   29
Fashion it thus: that what he is, augmented,   30
Would run to these and these extremities.
And therefore think him as a serpent's egg
Which, hatched, would, as his kind, grow
    mischievous;   33
And kill him in the shell.

        Enter Lucius.

LUCIUS
The taper burneth in your closet, sir.   35
Searching the window for a flint, I found
This paper, thus sealed up, and I am sure
It did not lie there when I went to bed.
                            Gives him the letter.
BRUTUS
Get you to bed again. It is not day.
Is not tomorrow, boy, the ides of March?   40
LUCIUS   I know not, sir.
BRUTUS
Look in the calendar and bring me word.
LUCIUS   I will, sir.   *Exit.*
BRUTUS
The exhalations whizzing in the air   44
Give so much light that I may read by them.
                    Opens the letter and reads.
"Brutus, thou sleep'st. Awake, and see thyself!
Shall Rome, et cetera? Speak, strike, redress!"
"Brutus, thou sleep'st. Awake!"
Such instigations have been often dropped
Where I have took them up.
"Shall Rome, et cetera?" Thus must I piece it out:
Shall Rome stand under one man's awe? What,
    Rome?
My ancestors did from the streets of Rome
The Tarquin drive, when he was called a king.

"Speak, strike, redress!" Am I entreated
To speak and strike? O Rome, I make thee promise,
If the redress will follow, thou receivest   57
Thy full petition at the hand of Brutus.

        Enter Lucius.

LUCIUS   Sir, March is wasted fifteen days.
                            Knock within.
BRUTUS
'Tis good. Go to the gate; somebody knocks.
                            [Exit Lucius.]
Since Cassius first did whet me against Caesar,   61
I have not slept.
Between the acting of a dreadful thing
And the first motion, all the interim is   64
Like a phantasma or a hideous dream.   65
The genius and the mortal instruments   66
Are then in council; and the state of man,   67
Like to a little kingdom, suffers then
The nature of an insurrection.

        Enter Lucius.

LUCIUS
Sir, 'tis your brother Cassius at the door,   70
Who doth desire to see you.
BRUTUS   Is he alone?
LUCIUS
No, sir. There are more with him.
BRUTUS   Do you know them?
LUCIUS
No, sir. Their hats are plucked about their ears,
And half their faces buried in their cloaks,
That by no means I may discover them   75
By any mark of favor.
BRUTUS   Let 'em enter.   *[Exit Lucius.]* 76
They are the faction. O conspiracy,
Sham'st thou to show thy dangerous brow by night,
When evils are most free? O, then by day   79
Where wilt thou find a cavern dark enough
To mask thy monstrous visage? Seek none,
    conspiracy!
Hide it in smiles and affability;
For if thou put thy native semblance on,
Not Erebus itself were dim enough   84
To hide thee from prevention.   85

        *Enter the conspirators, Cassius, Casca, Decius,
        Cinna, Metellus [Cimber], and Trebonius.*

CASSIUS
I think we are too bold upon your rest.   86

---

57 **If . . . follow** i.e., if striking Caesar will lead to the reform of grievances   **61 whet** incite   **64 motion** proposal or impulse   **65 phantasma** hallucination   **66–67 The genius . . . council** the immortal part of humanity, the rational soul, deliberates or debates violently with the lower or moral faculties, the physical and passionate side   **67 state of man** i.e., humanity as a microcosm, a tiny kingdom   **70 brother** i.e., brother-in-law. (Cassius had married a sister of Brutus.)   **75 discover** identify   **76 favor** appearance   **79 free** free to roam at will   **84 Erebus** region of darkness between earth and Hades   **85 prevention** detection and being forestalled   **86 upon** in intruding upon

15 **craves** requires.   **that** i.e., king, emperor   **19 Remorse** mercy, compassion   **20 affections** passions.   **swayed** ruled   **21 proof** experience   **22 lowliness** pretended humbleness   **24 round** rung   **26 base degrees** (1) lower rungs (2) persons of lower social station   **29 Will . . . is** can carry no appearance of justice so far as his conduct to date is concerned   **30 Fashion it** put the matter   **33 as his kind** according to its nature.   **mischievous** harmful   **35 closet** private chamber, study   **40 ides** fifteenth day   **44 exhalations** meteors

Good morrow, Brutus. Do we trouble you?
BRUTUS
I have been up this hour, awake all night.
Know I these men that come along with you?
CASSIUS
Yes, every man of them, and no man here
But honors you; and every one doth wish
You had but that opinion of yourself
Which every noble Roman bears of you.
This is Trebonius.
BRUTUS   He is welcome hither.
CASSIUS
This, Decius Brutus.
BRUTUS   He is welcome too.
CASSIUS
This, Casca; this, Cinna; and this, Metellus Cimber.
BRUTUS   They are all welcome.
What watchful cares do interpose themselves   98
Betwixt your eyes and night?
CASSIUS   Shall I entreat a word?
                    They [Brutus and Cassius] whisper.
DECIUS
Here lies the east. Doth not the day break here?   101
CASCA   No.
CINNA
O, pardon, sir, it doth; and yon gray lines
That fret the clouds are messengers of day.   104
CASCA
You shall confess that you are both deceived.   105
Here, as I point my sword, the sun arises,
Which is a great way growing on the south,   107
Weighing the youthful season of the year.   108
Some two months hence, up higher toward the
     north
He first presents his fire; and the high east   110
Stands, as the Capitol, directly here.
BRUTUS [*coming forward*]
Give me your hands all over, one by one.   112
CASSIUS
And let us swear our resolution.
BRUTUS
No, not an oath. If not the face of men,   114
The sufferance of our souls, the time's abuse—   115
If these be motives weak, break off betimes,   116
And every man hence to his idle bed;   117
So let high-sighted tyranny range on   118
Till each man drop by lottery. But if these,   119
As I am sure they do, bear fire enough
To kindle cowards and to steel with valor   121

The melting spirits of women, then, countrymen,
What need we any spur but our own cause
To prick us to redress? What other bond   124
Than secret Romans that have spoke the word   125
And will not palter? And what other oath   126
Than honesty to honesty engaged   127
That this shall be or we will fall for it?
Swear priests and cowards and men cautelous,   129
Old feeble carrions, and such suffering souls   130
That welcome wrongs; unto bad causes swear   131
Such creatures as men doubt. But do not stain   132
The even virtue of our enterprise,   133
Nor th' insuppressive mettle of our spirits,   134
To think that or our cause or our performance   135
Did need an oath, when every drop of blood
That every Roman bears—and nobly bears—
Is guilty of a several bastardy   138
If he do break the smallest particle
Of any promise that hath passed from him.
CASSIUS
But what of Cicero? Shall we sound him?   141
I think he will stand very strong with us.
CASCA
Let us not leave him out.
CINNA   No, by no means.
METELLUS
O, let us have him, for his silver hairs
Will purchase us a good opinion   145
And buy men's voices to commend our deeds.
It shall be said his judgment ruled our hands;
Our youths and wildness shall no whit appear,
But all be buried in his gravity.
BRUTUS
O, name him not. Let us not break with him,   150
For he will never follow anything
That other men begin.
CASSIUS   Then leave him out.
CASCA   Indeed he is not fit.
DECIUS
Shall no man else be touched but only Caesar?
CASSIUS
Decius, well urged. I think it is not meet   156
Mark Antony, so well beloved of Caesar,
Should outlive Caesar. We shall find of him   158
A shrewd contriver; and you know his means,   159
If he improve them, may well stretch so far   160
As to annoy us all. Which to prevent,   161

98 **watchful cares** worries preventing sleep   101 **Here** (Decius points eastward.)   104 **fret** mark with interlacing lines   105 **deceived** mistaken   107 **growing** encroaching   108 **Weighing** considering, in consequence of   110 **high** due   112 **all over** one and all   114 **face of men** i.e., grave look of all concerned persons in the state   115 **sufferance** state of suffering.   **the time's abuse** corruptions of the present day   116 **betimes** at once   117 **idle** (1) unused (2) in which men are idle   118 **high-sighted** upward-gazing (compare with 2.1.26); or haughty, looking down from on high   119 **by lottery** i.e., as the capricious tyrant chances to pick on him.   **these** i.e., these injustices just cited   121 **cowards** even cowards

124 **prick** spur   125 **Than . . . word** than the word of Romans who, having given their word of honor, will remain secret   126 **palter** use trickery   127 **honesty** personal honor   129 **Swear** make swear. **cautelous** deceitful; cautious   130 **carrions** men who resemble corpses. **suffering** long-suffering   131 **welcome wrongs** submit supinely to tyranny   132 **Such . . . doubt** contemptible persons one cannot trust   133 **even** steadfast, consistent   134 **insuppressive** indomitable   135 **or . . . or** either . . . or   138 **guilty . . . bastardy** individually guilty of an act that shows it is not true Roman blood   141 **sound him** find out his feelings   145 **purchase** procure (playing on the financial sense of *silver*, line 144)   150 **break with** confide in   156 **meet** fitting   158 **of** in   159 **shrewd** malicious; artful   160 **improve** exploit, make good use of   161 **annoy** injure

Let Antony and Caesar fall together.
BRUTUS
  Our course will seem too bloody, Caius Cassius,
  To cut the head off and then hack the limbs,
  Like wrath in death and envy afterwards;   165
  For Antony is but a limb of Caesar.
  Let's be sacrificers, but not butchers, Caius.
  We all stand up against the spirit of Caesar,
  And in the spirit of men there is no blood.
  O, that we then could come by Caesar's spirit   170
  And not dismember Caesar! But, alas,
  Caesar must bleed for it. And, gentle friends,   172
  Let's kill him boldly, but not wrathfully;
  Let's carve him as a dish fit for the gods,
  Not hew him as a carcass fit for hounds.
  And let our hearts, as subtle masters do,
  Stir up their servants to an act of rage   177
  And after seem to chide 'em. This shall make
  Our purpose necessary, and not envious;   179
  Which so appearing to the common eyes,
  We shall be called purgers, not murderers.   181
  And for Mark Antony, think not of him;
  For he can do no more than Caesar's arm
  When Caesar's head is off.
CASSIUS   Yet I fear him,
  For in the engrafted love he bears to Caesar—   185
BRUTUS
  Alas, good Cassius, do not think of him.
  If he love Caesar, all that he can do
  Is to himself—take thought and die for Caesar.   188
  And that were much he should, for he is given   189
  To sports, to wildness, and much company.
TREBONIUS
  There is no fear in him. Let him not die,   191
  For he will live, and laugh at this hereafter.   192
                      Clock strikes.
BRUTUS
  Peace! Count the clock.
CASSIUS   The clock hath stricken three.
TREBONIUS
  'Tis time to part.
CASSIUS   But it is doubtful yet
  Whether Caesar will come forth today or no;
  For he is superstitious grown of late,
  Quite from the main opinion he held once   197
  Of fantasy, of dreams, and ceremonies.   198
  It may be these apparent prodigies,   199
  The unaccustomed terror of this night,
  And the persuasion of his augurers

May hold him from the Capitol today.
DECIUS
  Never fear that. If he be so resolved,
  I can o'ersway him; for he loves to hear
  That unicorns may be betrayed with trees,   205
  And bears with glasses, elephants with holes,   206
  Lions with toils, and men with flatterers;   207
  But when I tell him he hates flatterers,
  He says he does, being then most flattered.
  Let me work;
  For I can give his humor the true bent,   211
  And I will bring him to the Capitol.
CASSIUS
  Nay, we will all of us be there to fetch him.
BRUTUS
  By the eighth hour. Is that the uttermost?   214
CINNA
  Be that the uttermost, and fail not then.
METELLUS
  Caius Ligarius doth bear Caesar hard,   216
  Who rated him for speaking well of Pompey.   217
  I wonder none of you have thought of him.
BRUTUS
  Now, good Metellus, go along by him.   219
  He loves me well, and I have given him reasons;   220
  Send him but hither, and I'll fashion him.   221
CASSIUS
  The morning comes upon 's. We'll leave you,
    Brutus.
  And, friends, disperse yourselves; but all remember
  What you have said, and show yourselves true
    Romans.
BRUTUS
  Good gentlemen, look fresh and merrily;
  Let not our looks put on our purposes,   226
  But bear it as our Roman actors do,
  With untired spirits and formal constancy.   228
  And so good morrow to you every one.   229
                Exeunt. Manet Brutus.
  Boy! Lucius!—Fast asleep? It is no matter.   230
  Enjoy the honey-heavy dew of slumber.
  Thou hast no figures nor no fantasies   232
  Which busy care draws in the brains of men;   233
  Therefore thou sleep'st so sound.

    Enter Portia.

PORTIA   Brutus, my lord!

---

165 envy malice   **170 come by** get hold of   **172 gentle** noble
177 their servants i.e., our hands   **179 envious** malicious
181 purgers those who heal by bleeding the patient   **185 engrafted**
firmly implanted   **188 take thought** give way to melancholy
189 much he should more than is to be expected of him, hence unlikely; or, eminently desirable   **191 no fear** nothing to fear   **192 s.d.
Clock strikes** (An anachronism much commented upon; the mechanical clock was not invented until c. 1300.)   **197 from the main** contrary to the strong and basic   **198 fantasy** imaginings.   **ceremonies**
omens drawn from the performance of some rite   **199 apparent** manifest, both visible and obvious

205 unicorns . . . trees i.e., by having the unicorn imprison itself by
driving its horn into a tree as it charges at the hunter   **206 glasses**
mirrors (enabling the hunter to approach the bear while it dazzles itself in the mirror).   **holes** pitfalls   **207 toils** nets, snares   **211 humor**
disposition.   **true bent** right direction   **214 uttermost** latest
216 bear Caesar hard bear a grudge toward Caesar. (A metaphor from
horsemanship.)   **217 rated** rebuked   **219 by him** by way of his house
220 reasons i.e., for having affection for me   **221 fashion** shape (to
our purposes)   **226 put on** display, wear in open view   **228 formal
constancy** steadfast appearance, decorum   **229 s.d. Manet** he remains onstage   **230 Lucius** (Brutus calls to his servant, who is evidently within, asleep, after having admitted the conspirators at line
85; later, at line 310, he is still within when Brutus calls to him.)
232 figures imaginings   **233 care** anxiety

BRUTUS
Portia, what mean you? Wherefore rise you now?
It is not for your health thus to commit
Your weak condition to the raw cold morning.

PORTIA
Nor for yours neither. You've ungently, Brutus,   238
Stole from my bed. And yesternight, at supper,
You suddenly arose, and walked about
Musing and sighing, with your arms across,   241
And when I asked you what the matter was,
You stared upon me with ungentle looks.
I urged you further; then you scratched your head
And too impatiently stamped with your foot.
Yet I insisted, yet you answered not,   246
But with an angry wafture of your hand   247
Gave sign for me to leave you. So I did,
Fearing to strengthen that impatience
Which seemed too much enkindled, and withal   250
Hoping it was but an effect of humor,   251
Which sometimes hath his hour with every man.   252
It will not let you eat, nor talk, nor sleep,
And could it work so much upon your shape
As it hath much prevailed on your condition,   255
I should not know you Brutus. Dear my lord,   256
Make me acquainted with your cause of grief.

BRUTUS
I am not well in health, and that is all.

PORTIA
Brutus is wise, and were he not in health
He would embrace the means to come by it.

BRUTUS
Why, so I do. Good Portia, go to bed.   261

PORTIA
Is Brutus sick? And is it physical   262
To walk unbracèd and suck up the humors   263
Of the dank morning? What, is Brutus sick,
And will he steal out of his wholesome bed
To dare the vile contagion of the night,
And tempt the rheumy and unpurgèd air   267
To add unto his sickness? No, my Brutus,
You have some sick offense within your mind,   269
Which by the right and virtue of my place
I ought to know of. [*She kneels.*] And upon my knees
I charm you, by my once-commended beauty,   272
By all your vows of love, and that great vow
Which did incorporate and make us one,
That you unfold to me, your self, your half,
Why you are heavy, and what men tonight   276
Have had resort to you; for here have been   277
Some six or seven, who did hide their faces

Even from darkness.

BRUTUS   Kneel not, gentle Portia.
[*He raises her.*]

PORTIA
I should not need if you were gentle Brutus.
Within the bond of marriage, tell me, Brutus,
Is it excepted I should know no secrets   282
That appertain to you? Am I your self
But as it were in sort or limitation,   284
To keep with you at meals, comfort your bed,   285
And talk to you sometimes? Dwell I but in the
   suburbs   286
Of your good pleasure? If it be no more,
Portia is Brutus' harlot, not his wife.

BRUTUS
You are my true and honorable wife,
As dear to me as are the ruddy drops
That visit my sad heart.

PORTIA
If this were true, then should I know this secret.
I grant I am a woman, but withal   293
A woman that Lord Brutus took to wife.
I grant I am a woman, but withal
A woman well reputed, Cato's daughter.   296
Think you I am no stronger than my sex,
Being so fathered and so husbanded?
Tell me your counsels, I will not disclose 'em.   299
I have made strong proof of my constancy,
Giving myself a voluntary wound
Here, in the thigh. Can I bear that with patience,
And not my husband's secrets?

BRUTUS   O ye gods,
Render me worthy of this noble wife!
Knock [*within*].
Hark, hark, one knocks. Portia, go in awhile,
And by and by thy bosom shall partake
The secrets of my heart.
All my engagements I will construe to thee,   308
All the charactery of my sad brows.   309
Leave me with haste. (*Exit Portia.*) Lucius, who's
   that knocks?

Enter Lucius and [*Caius*] *Ligarius* [*wearing a
   kerchief*].

LUCIUS
Here is a sick man that would speak with you.   311

BRUTUS
Caius Ligarius, that Metellus spake of.
Boy, stand aside. [*Exit Lucius.*] Caius Ligarius, how?   313

---

238 ungently discourteously, unkindly **241 across** folded. (A sign of melancholy.) **246 Yet . . . yet** still . . . still **247 wafture** waving **250 withal** moreover **251 humor** imbalance of temperament **252 his** its **255 condition** inner state of mind **256 know you** recognize you as **261 so I do** (Said with a double meaning not perceived by Portia: I seek through Caesar's death the means to better the health of the state.) **262 physical** healthful **263 unbracèd** with loosened clothing. **humors** damps, mists **267 rheumy** damp. **unpurgèd** not purified of excessive moisture (by the sun) **269 sick offense** harmful disturbance **272 charm** conjure, entreat **276 heavy** sad **277 had resort to** visited

282 excepted made an exception that **284 in . . . limitation** only up to a point. (A legal phrase.) **285 keep** stay, be **286 suburbs** periphery. (In Elizabethan London, prostitutes frequented the suburbs.) **293 withal** in addition **296 Cato's daughter** (Cato the Younger of Utica was famous for his integrity; he sided with Pompey against Caesar in 48 B.C. and later killed himself rather than submit to Caesar's tyranny. He was Brutus' uncle as well as his father-in-law.) **299 counsels** secrets **308 construe** explain fully **309 charactery** handwriting, i.e., what is figured there **311 sick man** (In Elizabethan medicine, not Roman, a poultice was often applied to the forehead of a patient and wrapped in a handkerchief; hence the kerchief in line 316.) **313 how** i.e., how are you

LIGARIUS
Vouchsafe good morrow from a feeble tongue.   314
BRUTUS
O, what a time have you chose out, brave Caius,   315
To wear a kerchief! Would you were not sick!
LIGARIUS
I am not sick, if Brutus have in hand
Any exploit worthy the name of honor.
BRUTUS
Such an exploit have I in hand, Ligarius,
Had you a healthful ear to hear of it.
LIGARIUS
By all the gods that Romans bow before,
I here discard my sickness! Soul of Rome!
                                    [He throws off his kerchief.]
Brave son, derived from honorable loins!
Thou like an exorcist hast conjured up   324
My mortifièd spirit. Now bid me run,   325
And I will strive with things impossible,
Yea, get the better of them. What's to do?
BRUTUS
A piece of work that will make sick men whole.   328
LIGARIUS
But are not some whole that we must make sick?
BRUTUS
That must we also. What it is, my Caius,
I shall unfold to thee as we are going
To whom it must be done.
LIGARIUS   Set on your foot,   332
And with a heart new-fired I follow you
To do I know not what; but it sufficeth
That Brutus leads me on.   *Thunder.*
BRUTUS   Follow me, then.   *Exeunt.*

❧

2.2   *Thunder and lightning. Enter Julius Caesar, in his
nightgown.*

CAESAR
Nor heaven nor earth have been at peace tonight.   1
Thrice hath Calpurnia in her sleep cried out,
"Help, ho, they murder Caesar!"—Who's within?

            Enter a Servant.

SERVANT   My lord?
CAESAR
Go bid the priests do present sacrifice   5
And bring me their opinions of success.   6
SERVANT   I will, my lord.   *Exit.*

            Enter Calpurnia.

CALPURNIA
What mean you, Caesar? Think you to walk forth?
You shall not stir out of your house today.
CAESAR
Caesar shall forth. The things that threatened me   10
Ne'er looked but on my back. When they shall see
The face of Caesar, they are vanishèd.
CALPURNIA
Caesar, I never stood on ceremonies,   13
Yet now they fright me. There is one within,
Besides the things that we have heard and seen,
Recounts most horrid sights seen by the watch.   16
A lioness hath whelpèd in the streets,   17
And graves have yawned and yielded up their dead.   18
Fierce fiery warriors fight upon the clouds   19
In ranks and squadrons and right form of war,   20
Which drizzled blood upon the Capitol.
The noise of battle hurtled in the air;   22
Horses did neigh, and dying men did groan,
And ghosts did shriek and squeal about the streets.
O Caesar, these things are beyond all use,   25
And I do fear them.
CAESAR   What can be avoided
Whose end is purposed by the mighty gods?
Yet Caesar shall go forth; for these predictions
Are to the world in general as to Caesar.   29
CALPURNIA
When beggars die there are no comets seen;
The heavens themselves blaze forth the death of
    princes.   31
CAESAR
Cowards die many times before their deaths;
The valiant never taste of death but once.
Of all the wonders that I yet have heard,
It seems to me most strange that men should fear,
Seeing that death, a necessary end,
Will come when it will come.

            Enter a Servant.

                        What say the augurers?
SERVANT
They would not have you to stir forth today.
Plucking the entrails of an offering forth,
They could not find a heart within the beast.
CAESAR
The gods do this in shame of cowardice.
Caesar should be a beast without a heart
If he should stay at home today for fear.
No, Caesar shall not. Danger knows full well
That Caesar is more dangerous than he.
We are two lions littered in one day,
And I the elder and more terrible;
And Caesar shall go forth.
CALPURNIA   Alas, my lord,

---

314 **Vouchsafe** deign (to accept)   315 **brave** noble   324 **exorcist**
conjurer   325 **mortifièd** deadened   328 **whole** healthy, i.e., free of
the disease of tyranny   332 **To whom** i.e., to him to whom
2.2. Location: Caesar's house.
s.d. nightgown housecoat   1 **Nor** neither   5 **present** immediate.
sacrifice examination of the entrails of sacrificed animals for omens
6 **success** the result, what will follow

10 **forth** go forth   13 **stood on ceremonies** attached importance to
omens   16 **watch** (An anachronism, since there was no *watch*, or
"body of night watchmen," in Caesar's Rome.)   17 **whelpèd** given
birth   18 **yawned** gaped   19 **fight** did fight   20 **right form** regular
formation   22 **hurtled** clashed   25 **use** normal experience   29 **Are
to** are as applicable to   31 **blaze forth** proclaim (in a blaze of light)

Your wisdom is consumed in confidence.   49
Do not go forth today! Call it my fear
That keeps you in the house, and not your own.
We'll send Mark Antony to the Senate House,
And he shall say you are not well today.
Let me, upon my knee, prevail in this.   [*She kneels.*]

CAESAR
Mark Antony shall say I am not well,
And for thy humor I will stay at home.   56
                    [*He raises her.*]

Enter Decius.

Here's Decius Brutus. He shall tell them so.

DECIUS
Caesar, all hail! Good morrow, worthy Caesar.
I come to fetch you to the Senate House.

CAESAR
And you are come in very happy time   60
To bear my greeting to the senators
And tell them that I will not come today.
Cannot is false, and that I dare not, falser;
I will not come today. Tell them so, Decius.

CALPURNIA
Say he is sick.

CAESAR   Shall Caesar send a lie?
Have I in conquest stretched mine arm so far
To be afeard to tell graybeards the truth?
Decius, go tell them Caesar will not come.

DECIUS
Most mighty Caesar, let me know some cause,
Lest I be laughed at when I tell them so.

CAESAR
The cause is in my will: I will not come.
That is enough to satisfy the Senate.
But for your private satisfaction,
Because I love you, I will let you know.
Calpurnia here, my wife, stays me at home.   75
She dreamt tonight she saw my statue,   76
Which like a fountain with an hundred spouts
Did run pure blood; and many lusty Romans   78
Came smiling and did bathe their hands in it.
And these does she apply for warnings and portents   80
Of evils imminent, and on her knee
Hath begged that I will stay at home today.

DECIUS
This dream is all amiss interpreted;
It was a vision fair and fortunate.
Your statue spouting blood in many pipes,
In which so many smiling Romans bathed,
Signifies that from you great Rome shall suck
Reviving blood, and that great men shall press   88
For tinctures, stains, relics, and cognizance.   89
This by Calpurnia's dream is signified.

CAESAR
And this way have you well expounded it.

DECIUS
I have, when you have heard what I can say;
And know it now. The Senate have concluded
To give this day a crown to mighty Caesar.
If you shall send them word you will not come,
Their minds may change. Besides, it were a mock   96
Apt to be rendered for someone to say   97
"Break up the Senate till another time
When Caesar's wife shall meet with better dreams."
If Caesar hide himself, shall they not whisper
"Lo, Caesar is afraid"?
Pardon me, Caesar, for my dear dear love
To your proceeding bids me tell you this,   103
And reason to my love is liable.   104

CAESAR
How foolish do your fears seem now, Calpurnia!
I am ashamèd I did yield to them.
Give me my robe, for I will go.

Enter Brutus, Ligarius, Metellus, Casca,
Trebonius, Cinna, and Publius.

And look where Publius is come to fetch me.

PUBLIUS
Good morrow, Caesar.

CAESAR   Welcome, Publius.
What, Brutus, are you stirred so early too?
Good morrow, Casca. Caius Ligarius,
Caesar was ne'er so much your enemy
As that same ague which hath made you lean.   113
What is 't o'clock?

BRUTUS   Caesar, 'tis strucken eight.

CAESAR
I thank you for your pains and courtesy.

Enter Antony.

See, Antony, that revels long o' nights,
Is notwithstanding up. Good morrow, Antony.

ANTONY   So to most noble Caesar.

CAESAR [*to a Servant*]   Bid them prepare within.   119
                  [*Exit Servant.*]

I am to blame to be thus waited for.
Now, Cinna. Now, Metellus. What, Trebonius,
I have an hour's talk in store for you;
Remember that you call on me today.
Be near me, that I may remember you.

TREBONIUS
Caesar, I will. [*Aside.*] And so near will I be
That your best friends shall wish I had been further.

CAESAR
Good friends, go in and taste some wine with me,
And we, like friends, will straightway go together.

---

49 consumed in confidence destroyed by overconfidence   **56 humor** whim   **60 happy** opportune   **75 stays** detains   **76 tonight** last night   **78 lusty** lively, merry   **80 apply for** interpret as   **88 press** crowd around   **89 tinctures** handkerchiefs dipped in the blood of martyrs, with healing powers; or colors in a coat of arms. (*Tinctures, stains,* and *relics* are all venerated properties, as though Caesar were a saint.) **cognizance** heraldic emblems worn by a nobleman's followers

96–97 mock . . . rendered sarcastic remark apt to be made   **103 proceeding** advancement   **104 reason . . . liable** my reason or sense of propriety is overruled by my affection   **113 ague** fever   **119 prepare within** i.e., set out wine in the other room and prepare to leave. (Perhaps addressed to the servant who entered at line 37, or to Calpurnia.) The ritual drinking of wine is a pledge of friendship that should preclude violence; see lines 127–128.

BRUTUS [aside]
  That every like is not the same, O Caesar,   129
  The heart of Brutus earns to think upon!   Exeunt. 130

❖

2.3 *Enter Artemidorus [reading a paper].*

ARTEMIDORUS "Caesar, beware of Brutus; take heed of
Cassius; come not near Casca; have an eye to Cinna;
trust not Trebonius; mark well Metellus Cimber; Decius Brutus loves thee not; thou hast wronged Caius
Ligarius. There is but one mind in all these men, and
it is bent against Caesar. If thou beest not immortal, 6
look about you. Security gives way to conspiracy. The 7
mighty gods defend thee! Thy lover,   8
                                  Artemidorus."

  Here will I stand till Caesar pass along,
  And as a suitor will I give him this.   11
  My heart laments that virtue cannot live
  Out of the teeth of emulation.   13
  If thou read this, O Caesar, thou mayest live;
  If not, the Fates with traitors do contrive.   Exit. 15

❖

2.4 *Enter Portia and Lucius.*

PORTIA
  I prithee, boy, run to the Senate House.
  Stay not to answer me, but get thee gone.—
  Why dost thou stay?
LUCIUS   To know my errand, madam.
PORTIA
  I would have had thee there and here again
  Ere I can tell thee what thou shouldst do there.
  [Aside.] O constancy, be strong upon my side;   6
  Set a huge mountain 'tween my heart and tongue!
  I have a man's mind, but a woman's might.
  How hard it is for women to keep counsel!—   9
  Art thou here yet?
LUCIUS   Madam, what should I do?
  Run to the Capitol, and nothing else?
  And so return to you, and nothing else?
PORTIA
  Yes, bring me word, boy, if thy lord look well,
  For he went sickly forth; and take good note   14
  What Caesar doth, what suitors press to him.
  Hark, boy, what noise is that?
LUCIUS   I hear none, madam.
PORTIA   Prithee, listen well.
  I heard a bustling rumor, like a fray,   19

  And the wind brings it from the Capitol.
LUCIUS   Sooth, madam, I hear nothing.   21

    Enter the Soothsayer.

PORTIA
  Come hither, fellow. Which way hast thou been?
SOOTHSAYER   At mine own house, good lady.
PORTIA
  What is 't o'clock?
SOOTHSAYER   About the ninth hour, lady.   24
PORTIA
  Is Caesar yet gone to the Capitol?
SOOTHSAYER
  Madam, not yet. I go to take my stand,
  To see him pass on to the Capitol.
PORTIA
  Thou hast some suit to Caesar, hast thou not?
SOOTHSAYER
  That I have, lady, if it will please Caesar
  To be so good to Caesar as to hear me:
  I shall beseech him to befriend himself.
PORTIA
  Why, know'st thou any harms intended towards
    him?
SOOTHSAYER
  None that I know will be, much that I fear may
    chance.
  Good morrow to you. Here the street is narrow.
  The throng that follows Caesar at the heels,
  Of senators, of praetors, common suitors,   36
  Will crowd a feeble man almost to death.
  I'll get me to a place more void, and there   38
  Speak to great Caesar as he comes along.   Exit.
PORTIA
  I must go in. Ay me, how weak a thing
  The heart of woman is! O Brutus,
  The heavens speed thee in thine enterprise!
  Sure, the boy heard me.—Brutus hath a suit
  That Caesar will not grant.—O, I grow faint.—
  Run, Lucius, and commend me to my lord;
  Say I am merry. Come to me again   46
  And bring me word what he doth say to thee.
                          Exeunt [separately].

❖

3.1 *Flourish. Enter Caesar, Brutus, Cassius, Casca,*
        Decius, Metellus [Cimber], Trebonius, Cinna,
        Antony, Lepidus, Artemidorus, Publius, [Popilius
        Lena], and the Soothsayer; [others following].

CAESAR [to the Soothsayer]   The ides of March are come.
SOOTHSAYER   Ay, Caesar, but not gone.
ARTEMIDORUS   Hail, Caesar! Read this schedule.   3

129 **That . . . same** i.e., that not all those who behave "like friends"
(line 128) are actually so. (Proverbial.)   **130 earns** grieves
2.3. Location: A street near the Capitol.
6 bent directed   **7 Security** overconfidence.   **gives way** opens a path
8 lover friend   **11 as a suitor** as if I were a petitioner   **13 Out . . .**
emulation beyond the bite of grudging envy   **15 contrive** conspire
2.4. Location: Before the house of Brutus.
6 constancy resolution   **9 counsel** a secret   **14 take good note** observe closely   **19 bustling rumor** confused sound

21 Sooth truly   **24 the ninth hour** i.e., 9 A.M. (In Roman reckoning,
the ninth hour would be 3 P.M.)   **36 praetors** judges   **38 void** empty,
uncrowded   **46 merry** in good spirits. (Not "mirthful.")
**3.1. Location: Before the Capitol, and, following line 12, within the
Capitol.**
s.d. others following (Citizens may be present, though not certainly
so; see lines 83 and 93–94.)   **3 schedule** document

DECIUS
Trebonius doth desire you to o'erread,
At your best leisure, this his humble suit.
ARTEMIDORUS
O Caesar, read mine first, for mine's a suit
That touches Caesar nearer. Read it, great Caesar.
CAESAR
What touches us ourself shall be last served.
ARTEMIDORUS
Delay not, Caesar, read it instantly.
CAESAR
What, is the fellow mad?
PUBLIUS   Sirrah, give place.   10
CASSIUS
What, urge you your petitions in the street?
Come to the Capitol.

[Caesar goes to the Capitol and takes his place, the
rest following.]

POPILIUS [to Cassius]
I wish your enterprise today may thrive.
CASSIUS   What enterprise, Popilius?
POPILIUS [to Cassius]   Fare you well.
                           [He advances to Caesar.]
BRUTUS   What said Popilius Lena?
CASSIUS
He wished today our enterprise might thrive.
I fear our purpose is discoverèd.
BRUTUS
Look how he makes to Caesar. Mark him.   19
                  [Popilius speaks apart to Caesar.]
CASSIUS
Casca, be sudden, for we fear prevention.   20
Brutus, what shall be done? If this be known,
Cassius or Caesar never shall turn back,   22
For I will slay myself.
BRUTUS   Cassius, be constant.   23
Popilius Lena speaks not of our purposes;
For look, he smiles, and Caesar doth not change. 25
CASSIUS
Trebonius knows his time, for look you, Brutus,
He draws Mark Antony out of the way.
                  [Exit Trebonius with Antony.]
DECIUS
Where is Metellus Cimber? Let him go
And presently prefer his suit to Caesar.   29
BRUTUS
He is addressed. Press near and second him.   30
CINNA
Casca, you are the first that rears your hand.
                  [They press near Caesar.]
CAESAR
Are we all ready? What is now amiss
That Caesar and his Senate must redress?

METELLUS [kneeling]
Most high, most mighty, and most puissant Caesar,
Metellus Cimber throws before thy seat
An humble heart—
CAESAR   I must prevent thee, Cimber.   36
These couchings and these lowly courtesies   37
Might fire the blood of ordinary men,   38
And turn preordinance and first decree   39
Into the law of children. Be not fond   40
To think that Caesar bears such rebel blood   41
That will be thawed from the true quality   42
With that which melteth fools—I mean, sweet
   words,
Low-crookèd curtsies, and base spaniel fawning. 44
Thy brother by decree is banishèd.
If thou dost bend and pray and fawn for him,   46
I spurn thee like a cur out of my way.   47
Know, Caesar doth not wrong, nor without cause
Will he be satisfied.
METELLUS
Is there no voice more worthy than my own
To sound more sweetly in great Caesar's ear
For the repealing of my banished brother?   52
BRUTUS [kneeling]
I kiss thy hand, but not in flattery, Caesar,
Desiring thee that Publius Cimber may
Have an immediate freedom of repeal.   55
CAESAR
What, Brutus?
CASSIUS [kneeling]   Pardon, Caesar! Caesar, pardon!
As low as to thy foot doth Cassius fall,
To beg enfranchisement for Publius Cimber.   58
CAESAR
I could be well moved, if I were as you;
If I could pray to move, prayers would move me. 60
But I am constant as the northern star,   61
Of whose true-fixed and resting quality   62
There is no fellow in the firmament.   63
The skies are painted with unnumbered sparks;
They are all fire and every one doth shine;
But there's but one in all doth hold his place.
So in the world: 'tis furnished well with men,
And men are flesh and blood, and apprehensive;   68
Yet in the number I do know but one
That unassailable holds on his rank,   70
Unshaked of motion. And that I am he,   71
Let me a little show it even in this—
That I was constant Cimber should be banished,

36 prevent forestall   37 couchings, lowly courtesies submissive bows
38 fire the blood of incite   39 preordinance . . . decree a ruling already made   40 law of children i.e., laws to be changed as children
change rules in their games.   fond so foolish as   41 rebel i.e., rebellious against the law and against his own firm nature   42 true
quality proper firmness and stability. (The metaphor is from alchemy.)
44 Low-crookèd curtsies obsequious bows   46 bend bow   47 spurn
kick   52 repealing recall   55 freedom of repeal permission to return
58 enfranchisement liberation (from the decree of banishment)
60 pray to move make petition (as you do)   61 northern star polestar
62 true-fixed firmly fixed, unmovable.   resting unchanging   63 fellow equal   68 apprehensive capable of perception   70 rank place in
line or file, position   71 Unshaked of motion (1) unswayed by petitions (2) with perfect steadiness

10 Sirrah fellow. (A form of address to a social inferior.)   place way
19 makes to advances toward   20 sudden quick.   prevention being
forestalled   22 turn back i.e., return alive   23 constant resolute
25 change change expression   29 presently prefer immediately
present   30 addressed ready

And constant do remain to keep him so.

CINNA [*kneeling*]
O Caesar—

CAESAR   Hence! Wilt thou lift up Olympus?   75

DECIUS [*kneeling*]
Great Caesar—

CAESAR   Doth not Brutus bootless kneel?   76

CASCA   Speak, hands, for me!
                    They stab Caesar, [Casca first, Brutus last].

CAESAR   Et tu, Brutè? Then fall, Caesar!   *Dies.* 78

CINNA
Liberty! Freedom! Tyranny is dead!
Run hence, proclaim, cry it about the streets.

CASSIUS
Some to the common pulpits, and cry out   81
"Liberty, freedom, and enfranchisement!"

BRUTUS
People and senators, be not affrighted.
Fly not; stand still. Ambition's debt is paid.   84

CASCA
Go to the pulpit, Brutus.

DECIUS   And Cassius too.

BRUTUS   Where's Publius?   86

CINNA
Here, quite confounded with this mutiny.   87

METELLUS
Stand fast together, lest some friend of Caesar's
Should chance—

BRUTUS
Talk not of standing. Publius, good cheer.   90
There is no harm intended to your person,
Nor to no Roman else. So tell them, Publius.

CASSIUS
And leave us, Publius, lest that the people,
Rushing on us, should do your age some mischief.

BRUTUS
Do so, and let no man abide this deed   95
But we the doers.   [*Exeunt all but the conspirators.*]

            Enter Trebonius.

CASSIUS
Where is Antony?

TREBONIUS   Fled to his house amazed.
Men, wives, and children stare, cry out, and run
As it were doomsday.

BRUTUS   Fates, we will know your pleasures. 99
That we shall die, we know; 'tis but the time,
And drawing days out, that men stand upon.   101

CASCA
Why, he that cuts off twenty years of life
Cuts off so many years of fearing death.

BRUTUS
Grant that, and then is death a benefit.
So are we Caesar's friends, that have abridged

His time of fearing death. Stoop, Romans, stoop,
And let us bathe our hands in Caesar's blood
Up to the elbows and besmear our swords.
Then walk we forth even to the marketplace,   109
And, waving our red weapons o'er our heads,
Let's all cry "Peace, freedom, and liberty!"

CASSIUS
Stoop, then, and wash. [*They bathe their hands and
    weapons.*] How many ages hence
Shall this our lofty scene be acted over
In states unborn and accents yet unknown!   114

BRUTUS
How many times shall Caesar bleed in sport,   115
That now on Pompey's basis lies along   116
No worthier than the dust!

CASSIUS   So oft as that shall be,
So often shall the knot of us be called   119
The men that gave their country liberty.

DECIUS
What, shall we forth?

CASSIUS   Ay, every man away.
Brutus shall lead, and we will grace his heels   122
With the most boldest and best hearts of Rome.

            Enter a Servant.

BRUTUS
Soft, who comes here? A friend of Antony's.

SERVANT [*kneeling*]
Thus, Brutus, did my master bid me kneel;
Thus did Mark Antony bid me fall down,
And, being prostrate, thus he bade me say:
"Brutus is noble, wise, valiant, and honest;   128
Caesar was mighty, bold, royal, and loving.
Say I love Brutus and I honor him;
Say I feared Caesar, honored him, and loved him.
If Brutus will vouchsafe that Antony   132
May safely come to him and be resolved   133
How Caesar hath deserved to lie in death,
Mark Antony shall not love Caesar dead
So well as Brutus living, but will follow
The fortunes and affairs of noble Brutus
Thorough the hazards of this untrod state   138
With all true faith." So says my master Antony.

BRUTUS
Thy master is a wise and valiant Roman;
I never thought him worse.
Tell him, so please him come unto this place,   142
He shall be satisfied and, by my honor,
Depart untouched.

SERVANT   I'll fetch him presently.   144
                              Exit Servant.

BRUTUS
I know that we shall have him well to friend.   145

---

75 Olympus mountain dwelling of the Greek gods **76 bootless** in vain **78 Et tu, Brutè** even thou, Brutus **81 common pulpits** public platforms or rostra **84 Ambition's debt** what Caesar's ambition deserved **86 Publius** (An old senator, too confused to flee.) **87 mutiny** uprising **90 standing** making a stand **95 abide** (1) suffer the consequences of (2) remain here with **99 As** as if **101 drawing . . . upon** prolonging their lives, that men attach importance to

109 the marketplace i.e., the Forum **114 accents** languages **115 in sport** for entertainment **116 Pompey's basis** pedestal of Pompey's statue. **along** prostrate, at full length **119 knot** group **122 grace** do honor to (by following closely) **128 honest** honorable **132 vouchsafe** allow **133 be resolved** receive an explanation **138 Thorough** through. **untrod state** still unexplored state of affairs **142 so** if it should **144 presently** immediately **145 to friend** for a friend

CASSIUS
I wish we may. But yet have I a mind
That fears him much, and my misgiving still   147
Falls shrewdly to the purpose.   148

Enter Antony.

BRUTUS
But here comes Antony.—Welcome, Mark Antony.

ANTONY
O mighty Caesar! Dost thou lie so low?
Are all thy conquests, glories, triumphs, spoils,
Shrunk to this little measure? Fare thee well.—
I know not, gentlemen, what you intend,
Who else must be let blood, who else is rank;   154
If I myself, there is no hour so fit
As Caesar's death's hour, nor no instrument
Of half that worth as those your swords, made rich
With the most noble blood of all this world.
I do beseech ye, if you bear me hard,   159
Now, whilst your purpled hands do reek and
    smoke,   160
Fulfill your pleasure. Live a thousand years,   161
I shall not find myself so apt to die;   162
No place will please me so, no means of death,
As here by Caesar, and by you cut off,
The choice and master spirits of this age.

BRUTUS
O Antony! Beg not your death of us.
Though now we must appear bloody and cruel,
As by our hands and this our present act
You see we do, yet see you but our hands
And this the bleeding business they have done.
Our hearts you see not. They are pitiful;   171
And pity to the general wrong of Rome—
As fire drives out fire, so pity pity—   173
Hath done this deed on Caesar. For your part,
To you our swords have leaden points, Mark
    Antony.   175
Our arms in strength of malice, and our hearts   176
Of brothers' temper, do receive you in   177
With all kind love, good thoughts, and reverence.

CASSIUS
Your voice shall be as strong as any man's   179
In the disposing of new dignities.   180

BRUTUS
Only be patient till we have appeased
The multitude, beside themselves with fear,
And then we will deliver you the cause   183
Why I, that did love Caesar when I struck him,
Have thus proceeded.

ANTONY   I doubt not of your wisdom.
Let each man render me his bloody hand.
    [*He shakes hands with the conspirators.*]
First, Marcus Brutus, will I shake with you;
Next, Caius Cassius, do I take your hand;
Now, Decius Brutus, yours; now yours, Metellus;
Yours, Cinna; and, my valiant Casca, yours;
Though last, not least in love, yours, good
    Trebonius.
Gentlemen all—alas, what shall I say?
My credit now stands on such slippery ground   193
That one of two bad ways you must conceit me,   194
Either a coward or a flatterer.
That I did love thee, Caesar, O, 'tis true!
If then thy spirit look upon us now,
Shall it not grieve thee dearer than thy death   198
To see thy Antony making his peace,
Shaking the bloody fingers of thy foes—
Most noble!—in the presence of thy corpse?
Had I as many eyes as thou hast wounds,
Weeping as fast as they stream forth thy blood,
It would become me better than to close   204
In terms of friendship with thine enemies.
Pardon me, Julius! Here wast thou bayed, brave
    hart,   206
Here didst thou fall, and here thy hunters stand,
Signed in thy spoil and crimsoned in thy lethe.   208
O world, thou wast the forest to this hart,
And this indeed, O world, the heart of thee!
How like a deer, strucken by many princes,
Dost thou here lie!

CASSIUS
Mark Antony—

ANTONY   Pardon me, Caius Cassius.
The enemies of Caesar shall say this;   214
Then in a friend it is cold modesty.   215

CASSIUS
I blame you not for praising Caesar so,
But what compact mean you to have with us?   217
Will you be pricked in number of our friends,   218
Or shall we on and not depend on you?

ANTONY
Therefore I took your hands, but was indeed
Swayed from the point by looking down on Caesar.
Friends am I with you all, and love you all,
Upon this hope, that you shall give me reasons
Why and wherein Caesar was dangerous.

BRUTUS
Or else were this a savage spectacle.   225
Our reasons are so full of good regard   226
That were you, Antony, the son of Caesar,

---

147 fears distrusts   **147–148 my misgiving . . . purpose** such misgiving on my part always or generally falls ominously close to the mark   **154 let blood** bled (a medical term), i.e., killed.   **rank** diseased and in need of bleeding (with suggestion of "overgrown, too powerful")   **159 bear me hard** bear ill will to me   **160 purpled** bloody.   **reek** steam   **161 Live** if I should live   **162 apt** ready   **171 pitiful** full of pity   **173 pity pity** i.e., pity for the general wrong of Rome has driven out pity for Caesar   **175 leaden** i.e., blunt   **176–177 Our . . . temper** i.e., both our arms, though seeming strong in enmity, and our hearts, full of brotherly feeling   **179 voice** vote, authority   **180 dignities** offices of state   **183 deliver** report to

193 credit credibility   **194 conceit** think, judge   **198 dearer** more deeply   **204 close** come to an agreement   **206 bayed** brought to bay.   **hart** stag (with pun on *heart*)   **208 Signed . . . spoil** marked with the tokens of your slaughter. (The *spoil* in hunting is the cutting up of the quarry and distribution of reward to the hounds.)   **lethe** river of oblivion in the underworld, here associated with death and blood (perhaps fused with Cocytus, river of blood in the underworld)   **214 The enemies** even the enemies   **215 cold modesty** sober moderation   **217 compact** agreement   **218 pricked** marked down   **225 else were this** otherwise this would be   **226 regard** account, consideration

You should be satisfied.

ANTONY   That's all I seek,
And am moreover suitor that I may
Produce his body to the marketplace,   230
And in the pulpit, as becomes a friend,   231
Speak in the order of his funeral.   232

BRUTUS
You shall, Mark Antony.

CASSIUS   Brutus, a word with you.
[*Aside to Brutus.*] You know not what you do. Do
      not consent
That Antony speak in his funeral.
Know you how much the people may be moved
By that which he will utter?

BRUTUS [*aside to Cassius*]   By your pardon:
I will myself into the pulpit first
And show the reason of our Caesar's death.
What Antony shall speak, I will protest   240
He speaks by leave and by permission,
And that we are contented Caesar shall
Have all true rites and lawful ceremonies.
It shall advantage more than do us wrong.

CASSIUS [*aside to Brutus*]
I know not what may fall. I like it not.   245

BRUTUS
Mark Antony, here, take you Caesar's body.
You shall not in your funeral speech blame us,
But speak all good you can devise of Caesar,
And say you do 't by our permission.
Else shall you not have any hand at all
About his funeral. And you shall speak
In the same pulpit whereto I am going,
After my speech is ended.

ANTONY   Be it so.
I do desire no more.

BRUTUS
Prepare the body then, and follow us.   255
                              Exeunt. Manet Antony.

ANTONY
O, pardon me, thou bleeding piece of earth,
That I am meek and gentle with these butchers!
Thou art the ruins of the noblest man
That ever livèd in the tide of times.   259
Woe to the hand that shed this costly blood!   260
Over thy wounds now do I prophesy—
Which, like dumb mouths, do ope their ruby lips
To beg the voice and utterance of my tongue—
A curse shall light upon the limbs of men;
Domestic fury and fierce civil strife
Shall cumber all the parts of Italy;   266
Blood and destruction shall be so in use
And dreadful objects so familiar   268
That mothers shall but smile when they behold
Their infants quartered with the hands of war,   270

All pity choked with custom of fell deeds;   271
And Caesar's spirit, ranging for revenge,   272
With Ate by his side come hot from hell,   273
Shall in these confines with a monarch's voice   274
Cry havoc and let slip the dogs of war,   275
That this foul deed shall smell above the earth   276
With carrion men, groaning for burial.

              Enter Octavius' Servant.

You serve Octavius Caesar, do you not?

SERVANT   I do, Mark Antony.

ANTONY
Caesar did write for him to come to Rome.

SERVANT
He did receive his letters, and is coming,
And bid me say to you by word of mouth—
O Caesar!—   [*Seeing the body.*]

ANTONY
Thy heart is big. Get thee apart and weep.   284
Passion, I see, is catching, for mine eyes,   285
Seeing those beads of sorrow stand in thine,
Began to water. Is thy master coming?

SERVANT
He lies tonight within seven leagues of Rome.   288

ANTONY
Post back with speed and tell him what hath
      chanced.   289
Here is a mourning Rome, a dangerous Rome,
No Rome of safety for Octavius yet;   291
Hie hence and tell him so. Yet stay awhile;   292
Thou shalt not back till I have borne this corpse
Into the marketplace. There shall I try,   294
In my oration, how the people take
The cruel issue of these bloody men,   296
According to the which thou shalt discourse   297
To young Octavius of the state of things.   298
Lend me your hand.   *Exeunt [with Caesar's body].*

                         ❖

3.2   *Enter Brutus and [presently] goes into the pulpit,
          and Cassius, with the Plebeians.*

PLEBEIANS
We will be satisfied! Let us be satisfied!   1

BRUTUS
Then follow me, and give me audience, friends.
Cassius, go you into the other street
And part the numbers.   4

---

230 **Produce** bring forth   231 **pulpit** public platform   232 **order** ceremony   240 **protest** announce, insist   245 **fall** befall, happen
255 s.d. **Manet** he remains onstage   259 **tide of times** course of all
history   260 **costly** (1) valuable (2) fraught with dire consequences
266 **cumber** entangle   268 **objects** sights   270 **quartered** cut to
pieces

271 **custom . . . deeds** the familiarity of cruel deeds   272 **ranging**
roaming up and down in search of prey   273 **Ate** goddess of discord
and moral chaos   274 **confines** regions   275 **Cry havoc** give the signal for sack, pillage, and slaughter.   **let slip** unleash   276 **That** so
that   284 **big** swollen with grief   285 **Passion** sorrow   288 **lies**
lodges.   **seven leagues** about twenty miles   289 **chanced** happened
291 **Rome** (With pun on "room," as at 1.2.156.)   292 **Hie** hasten
294 **try** test   296 **cruel issue** outcome of the cruelty   297 **the which**
the outcome of which   298 **young Octavius** (He was eighteen in
March of 44 B.C.)
3.2. Location: The Forum.
1 **be satisfied** have an explanation   4 **part** divide

Those that will hear me speak, let 'em stay here;
Those that will follow Cassius, go with him;
And public reasons shall be renderèd
Of Caesar's death.
FIRST PLEBEIAN   I will hear Brutus speak.
SECOND PLEBEIAN
I will hear Cassius, and compare their reasons
When severally we hear them renderèd.   10
[*Exit Cassius, with some of the Plebeians.*]
THIRD PLEBEIAN
The noble Brutus is ascended. Silence!
BRUTUS   Be patient till the last.
Romans, countrymen, and lovers, hear me for my 13
cause, and be silent that you may hear. Believe me for
mine honor, and have respect to mine honor, that you
may believe. Censure me in your wisdom, and awake 16
your senses, that you may the better judge. If there be 17
any in this assembly, any dear friend of Caesar's, to
him I say that Brutus' love to Caesar was no less than
his. If then that friend demand why Brutus rose
against Caesar, this is my answer: not that I loved Caesar less, but that I loved Rome more. Had you rather
Caesar were living and die all slaves, than that Caesar
were dead, to live all free men? As Caesar loved me, I
weep for him; as he was fortunate, I rejoice at it; as he
was valiant, I honor him; but, as he was ambitious, I
slew him. There is tears for his love; joy for his fortune; honor for his valor; and death for his ambition.
Who is here so base that would be a bondman? If any,
speak, for him have I offended. Who is here so rude 30
that would not be a Roman? If any, speak, for him
have I offended. Who is here so vile that will not love
his country? If any, speak, for him have I offended. I
pause for a reply.
ALL   None, Brutus, none!
BRUTUS   Then none have I offended. I have done no
more to Caesar than you shall do to Brutus. The ques- 37
tion of his death is enrolled in the Capitol, his glory 38
not extenuated wherein he was worthy, nor his 39
offenses enforced for which he suffered death. 40

*Enter Mark Antony [and others] with Caesar's
body.*

Here comes his body, mourned by Mark Antony, who,
though he had no hand in his death, shall receive the
benefit of his dying, a place in the commonwealth, as
which of you shall not? With this I depart, that, as I
slew my best lover for the good of Rome, I have the 45
same dagger for myself when it shall please my country to need my death.
ALL   Live, Brutus, live, live!   [*Brutus comes down.*]
FIRST PLEBEIAN
Bring him with triumph home unto his house.

SECOND PLEBEIAN
Give him a statue with his ancestors.   50
THIRD PLEBEIAN
Let him be Caesar.
FOURTH PLEBEIAN   Caesar's better parts
Shall be crowned in Brutus.
FIRST PLEBEIAN
We'll bring him to his house with shouts and
clamors.
BRUTUS
My countrymen—
SECOND PLEBEIAN   Peace, silence! Brutus speaks.
FIRST PLEBEIAN   Peace, ho!
BRUTUS
Good countrymen, let me depart alone,
And, for my sake, stay here with Antony.
Do grace to Caesar's corpse, and grace his speech   58
Tending to Caesar's glories, which Mark Antony,   59
By our permission, is allowed to make.
I do entreat you, not a man depart,
Save I alone, till Antony have spoke.   *Exit.*
FIRST PLEBEIAN
Stay, ho, and let us hear Mark Antony.
THIRD PLEBEIAN
Let him go up into the public chair.
We'll hear him. Noble Antony, go up.
ANTONY
For Brutus' sake I am beholding to you.   66
[*He goes into the pulpit.*]
FOURTH PLEBEIAN   What does he say of Brutus?
THIRD PLEBEIAN   He says, for Brutus' sake
He finds himself beholding to us all.
FOURTH PLEBEIAN
'Twere best he speak no harm of Brutus here.
FIRST PLEBEIAN
This Caesar was a tyrant.
THIRD PLEBEIAN   Nay, that's certain.
We are blest that Rome is rid of him.
SECOND PLEBEIAN
Peace! Let us hear what Antony can say.
ANTONY
You gentle Romans—
ALL   Peace, ho! Let us hear him.
ANTONY
Friends, Romans, countrymen, lend me your ears. 75
I come to bury Caesar, not to praise him.
The evil that men do lives after them;
The good is oft interrèd with their bones.
So let it be with Caesar. The noble Brutus
Hath told you Caesar was ambitious.
If it were so, it was a grievous fault,
And grievously hath Caesar answered it.   82

---

10 **severally** separately   13 **lovers** friends. (This speech by Brutus is in what Plutarch calls the Lacedemonian or Spartan style, brief and sententious. Its content is original with Shakespeare.)   16 **Censure** judge   17 **senses** intellectual powers   30 **rude** barbarous   37 **shall** i.e., should, if I were to do as Caesar did   37–38 **The question . . . enrolled** the considerations that necessitated his death are recorded   39 **extenuated** minimized   40 **enforced** exaggerated, insisted upon   45 **lover** friend

50 **s.p. Second Plebeian** (Not the same person who exited at line 10; the numbering here refers to those who stay to hear Brutus.)   58 **Do grace** show respect.   **grace his speech** i.e., listen courteously to Antony's speech   59 **Tending to** relating to, dealing with   66 **beholding** beholden   75 **Friends** (This speech by Antony is thought to illustrate the Asiatic or "florid" style of speaking. In it Shakespeare gathers various hints from Plutarch, Appian, and Dion, but the speech is Shakespeare's invention.)   82 **answered** paid the penalty for

Here, under leave of Brutus and the rest—
For Brutus is an honorable man,
So are they all, all honorable men—
Come I to speak in Caesar's funeral.
He was my friend, faithful and just to me;
But Brutus says he was ambitious,
And Brutus is an honorable man.
He hath brought many captives home to Rome,
Whose ransoms did the general coffers fill.
Did this in Caesar seem ambitious?
When that the poor have cried, Caesar hath wept;
Ambition should be made of sterner stuff.
Yet Brutus says he was ambitious,
And Brutus is an honorable man.
You all did see that on the Lupercal   97
I thrice presented him a kingly crown,
Which he did thrice refuse. Was this ambition?
Yet Brutus says he was ambitious,
And sure he is an honorable man.
I speak not to disprove what Brutus spoke,
But here I am to speak what I do know.
You all did love him once, not without cause.
What cause withholds you then to mourn for him?
O judgment! Thou art fled to brutish beasts,
And men have lost their reason. Bear with me;
My heart is in the coffin there with Caesar,
And I must pause till it come back to me.

FIRST PLEBEIAN
Methinks there is much reason in his sayings.

SECOND PLEBEIAN
If thou consider rightly of the matter,
Caesar has had great wrong.

THIRD PLEBEIAN   Has he, masters?
I fear there will a worse come in his place.

FOURTH PLEBEIAN
Marked ye his words? He would not take the
    crown,
Therefore 'tis certain he was not ambitious.

FIRST PLEBEIAN
If it be found so, some will dear abide it.   116

SECOND PLEBEIAN
Poor soul, his eyes are red as fire with weeping.

THIRD PLEBEIAN
There's not a nobler man in Rome than Antony.

FOURTH PLEBEIAN
Now mark him. He begins again to speak.

ANTONY
But yesterday the word of Caesar might
Have stood against the world. Now lies he there,
And none so poor to do him reverence.   122
O masters! If I were disposed to stir
Your hearts and minds to mutiny and rage,   124
I should do Brutus wrong, and Cassius wrong,
Who, you all know, are honorable men.
I will not do them wrong; I rather choose

To wrong the dead, to wrong myself and you,
Than I will wrong such honorable men.
But here's a parchment with the seal of Caesar.
I found it in his closet; 'tis his will.   131
[He shows the will.]
Let but the commons hear this testament—   132
Which, pardon me, I do not mean to read—
And they would go and kiss dead Caesar's wounds
And dip their napkins in his sacred blood,   135
Yea, beg a hair of him for memory,
And dying, mention it within their wills,
Bequeathing it as a rich legacy
Unto their issue.

FOURTH PLEBEIAN
We'll hear the will! Read it, Mark Antony.

ALL
The will, the will! We will hear Caesar's will.

ANTONY
Have patience, gentle friends: I must not read it.
It is not meet you know how Caesar loved you.   143
You are not wood, you are not stones, but men;
And being men, hearing the will of Caesar,
It will inflame you, it will make you mad.
'Tis good you know not that you are his heirs,
For if you should, O, what would come of it?

FOURTH PLEBEIAN
Read the will! We'll hear it, Antony.
You shall read us the will, Caesar's will.

ANTONY
Will you be patient? Will you stay awhile?
I have o'ershot myself to tell you of it.   152
I fear I wrong the honorable men
Whose daggers have stabbed Caesar; I do fear it.

FOURTH PLEBEIAN
They were traitors. "Honorable men"!

ALL   The will! The testament!

SECOND PLEBEIAN
They were villains, murderers. The will! Read the
    will!

ANTONY
You will compel me then to read the will?
Then make a ring about the corpse of Caesar
And let me show you him that made the will.
Shall I descend? And will you give me leave?

ALL   Come down.

SECOND PLEBEIAN   Descend.

THIRD PLEBEIAN   You shall have leave.
[Antony comes down. They gather around Caesar.]

FOURTH PLEBEIAN   A ring; stand round.

FIRST PLEBEIAN
Stand from the hearse. Stand from the body.   166

SECOND PLEBEIAN
Room for Antony, most noble Antony!

ANTONY
Nay, press not so upon me. Stand far off.   168

ALL   Stand back! Room! Bear back!

---

83 **under leave** by permission **97 Lupercal** (See 1.1.67 and note.)
116 dear abide it pay a heavy penalty for it **122 none . . . rever-**
ence i.e., no one, not even the lowliest person, is below Caesar in
fortune now, making obeisance to him **124 mutiny** riot, tumult

131 closet private chamber **132 commons** common people
135 napkins handkerchiefs **143 meet** fitting that **152 o'ershot my-**
self gone further than I should **166 hearse** bier **168 far** farther

ANTONY

If you have tears, prepare to shed them now.
You all do know this mantle. I remember   171
The first time ever Caesar put it on;
'Twas on a summer's evening in his tent,
That day he overcame the Nervii.   174
Look, in this place ran Cassius' dagger through.
See what a rent the envious Casca made.   176
Through this the well-belovèd Brutus stabbed,
And as he plucked his cursèd steel away,
Mark how the blood of Caesar followed it,
As rushing out of doors to be resolved   180
If Brutus so unkindly knocked or no;   181
For Brutus, as you know, was Caesar's angel.   182
Judge, O you gods, how dearly Caesar loved him!
This was the most unkindest cut of all;   184
For when the noble Caesar saw him stab,
Ingratitude, more strong than traitors' arms,
Quite vanquished him. Then burst his mighty heart,
And in his mantle muffling up his face,
Even at the base of Pompey's statue,
Which all the while ran blood, great Caesar fell.
O, what a fall was there, my countrymen!
Then I, and you, and all of us fell down,
Whilst bloody treason flourished over us.   193
O, now you weep, and I perceive you feel
The dint of pity. These are gracious drops.   195
Kind souls, what weep you when you but behold   196
Our Caesar's vesture wounded? Look you here,   197
Here is himself, marred as you see with traitors.
                                   [*He lifts Caesar's mantle.*]

FIRST PLEBEIAN   O piteous spectacle!
SECOND PLEBEIAN   O noble Caesar!
THIRD PLEBEIAN   O woeful day!
FOURTH PLEBEIAN   O traitors, villains!
FIRST PLEBEIAN   O most bloody sight!
SECOND PLEBEIAN   We will be revenged.
ALL   Revenge! About! Seek! Burn! Fire! Kill! Slay! Let   205
not a traitor live!
ANTONY   Stay, countrymen.
FIRST PLEBEIAN   Peace there! Hear the noble Antony.
SECOND PLEBEIAN   We'll hear him, we'll follow him,
we'll die with him!
ANTONY

Good friends, sweet friends, let me not stir you up
To such a sudden flood of mutiny.
They that have done this deed are honorable.
What private griefs they have, alas, I know not,   214
That made them do it. They are wise and honorable,
And will no doubt with reasons answer you.

171 **mantle** cloak, toga   174 **the Nervii** the Belgian tribe whose defeat in 57 B.C. is described in Caesar's *Gallic Wars*, 2.15–28
176 **rent** tear, hole   **envious** malicious, spiteful   180 **be resolved** learn for certain   181 **unkindly** cruelly and unnaturally   182 **angel** i.e., daimon or genius, second self   184 **unkindest** (1) most cruel (2) most unnatural. (The double superlative was grammatically acceptable in Shakespeare's day.)   193 **flourished** (1) triumphed insolently (2) brandished its sword   195 **dint** impression   196 **what** why, or how much   197 **vesture** clothing   205 **About** to work   214 **griefs** grievances

I come not, friends, to steal away your hearts.
I am no orator, as Brutus is,
But, as you know me all, a plain blunt man
That love my friend, and that they know full well
That gave me public leave to speak of him.   221
For I have neither wit, nor words, nor worth,   222
Action, nor utterance, nor the power of speech   223
To stir men's blood. I only speak right on.
I tell you that which you yourselves do know,
Show you sweet Caesar's wounds, poor poor dumb
   mouths,
And bid them speak for me. But were I Brutus,
And Brutus Antony, there were an Antony
Would ruffle up your spirits and put a tongue   229
In every wound of Caesar that should move
The stones of Rome to rise and mutiny.
ALL
We'll mutiny!
FIRST PLEBEIAN   We'll burn the house of Brutus!
THIRD PLEBEIAN
Away, then! Come, seek the conspirators.
ANTONY
Yet hear me, countrymen. Yet hear me speak.
ALL
Peace, ho! Hear Antony, most noble Antony!
ANTONY
Why, friends, you go to do you know not what.
Wherein hath Caesar thus deserved your loves?
Alas, you know not. I must tell you then:
You have forgot the will I told you of.
ALL
Most true. The will! Let's stay and hear the will.
ANTONY
Here is the will, and under Caesar's seal.
To every Roman citizen he gives,
To every several man, seventy-five drachmas.   243
SECOND PLEBEIAN
Most noble Caesar! We'll revenge his death.
THIRD PLEBEIAN
O royal Caesar!
ANTONY   Hear me with patience.
ALL   Peace, ho!
ANTONY
Moreover, he hath left you all his walks,
His private arbors, and new-planted orchards,   249
On this side Tiber; he hath left them you,
And to your heirs forever—common pleasures,   251
To walk abroad and recreate yourselves.
Here was a Caesar! When comes such another?
FIRST PLEBEIAN
Never, never! Come, away, away!
We'll burn his body in the holy place
And with the brands fire the traitors' houses.

221 **public leave** permission to speak publicly   222 **wit** understanding, intelligence.   **worth** stature, authority   223 **Action** gesture.   **utterance** good delivery   229 **ruffle up** stir to anger   243 **several** individual.   **drachmas** coins. (This is a substantial bequest.)
249 **orchards** gardens   251 **common pleasures** public pleasure gardens (in which)

Take up the body.

SECOND PLEBEIAN   Go fetch fire!

THIRD PLEBEIAN   Pluck down benches!

FOURTH PLEBEIAN   Pluck down forms, windows, any- 259
thing!   *Exeunt Plebeians [with the body].*

ANTONY

Now let it work. Mischief, thou art afoot.
Take thou what course thou wilt.

Enter [Octavius'] Servant.

                    How now, fellow?

SERVANT

Sir, Octavius is already come to Rome.

ANTONY   Where is he?

SERVANT

He and Lepidus are at Caesar's house.

ANTONY

And thither will I straight to visit him.   266
He comes upon a wish. Fortune is merry,   267
And in this mood will give us anything.

SERVANT

I heard him say Brutus and Cassius
Are rid like madmen through the gates of Rome.   270

ANTONY

Belike they had some notice of the people,   271
How I had moved them. Bring me to Octavius.
                                        Exeunt.

❖

3.3   *Enter Cinna the poet, and after him the Plebeians.*

CINNA

I dreamt tonight that I did feast with Caesar,   1
And things unluckily charge my fantasy.   2
I have no will to wander forth of doors,
Yet something leads me forth.

FIRST PLEBEIAN   What is your name?

SECOND PLEBEIAN   Whither are you going?

THIRD PLEBEIAN   Where do you dwell?

FOURTH PLEBEIAN   Are you a married man or a
bachelor?

SECOND PLEBEIAN   Answer every man directly.

FIRST PLEBEIAN   Ay, and briefly.

FOURTH PLEBEIAN   Ay, and wisely.

THIRD PLEBEIAN   Ay, and truly, you were best.   13

CINNA   What is my name? Whither am I going? Where
do I dwell? Am I a married man or a bachelor? Then
to answer every man directly and briefly, wisely and
truly: wisely I say, I am a bachelor.

SECOND PLEBEIAN   That's as much as to say they are
fools that marry. You'll bear me a bang for that, I fear. 19
Proceed directly.   20

CINNA   Directly, I am going to Caesar's funeral.   21

FIRST PLEBEIAN   As a friend or an enemy?

CINNA   As a friend.

SECOND PLEBEIAN   That matter is answered directly.

FOURTH PLEBEIAN   For your dwelling—briefly.

CINNA   Briefly, I dwell by the Capitol.

THIRD PLEBEIAN   Your name, sir, truly.

CINNA   Truly, my name is Cinna.

FIRST PLEBEIAN   Tear him to pieces! He's a conspirator!

CINNA   I am Cinna the poet, I am Cinna the poet!

FOURTH PLEBEIAN   Tear him for his bad verses, tear him
for his bad verses!

CINNA   I am not Cinna the conspirator.

FOURTH PLEBEIAN   It is no matter, his name's Cinna.
Pluck but his name out of his heart, and turn him 35
going.   36

THIRD PLEBEIAN   Tear him, tear him! Come, brands, ho,
firebrands! To Brutus', to Cassius'; burn all! Some to
Decius' house, and some to Casca's; some to Ligarius'.
Away, go!

Exeunt all the Plebeians, [dragging off Cinna].

❖

4.1   *Enter Antony [with a list], Octavius, and Lepidus.*

ANTONY

These many, then, shall die. Their names are
pricked.   1

OCTAVIUS

Your brother too must die. Consent you, Lepidus?

LEPIDUS

I do consent—

OCTAVIUS   Prick him down, Antony.

LEPIDUS

Upon condition Publius shall not live,
Who is your sister's son, Mark Antony.

ANTONY

He shall not live. Look, with a spot I damn him.   6
But Lepidus, go you to Caesar's house.
Fetch the will hither, and we shall determine   8
How to cut off some charge in legacies.   9

LEPIDUS   What, shall I find you here?

OCTAVIUS   Or here or at the Capitol.   *Exit Lepidus.* 11

ANTONY

This is a slight, unmeritable man,   12
Meet to be sent on errands. Is it fit,
The threefold world divided, he should stand   14
One of the three to share it?

---

21 Directly (1) straight there (2) at once   **35–36 turn him going** send
him packing

4.1. Location: Rome. A table is perhaps set out.

1 pricked marked down on a list (appropriate to the use of the stylus
on waxen tablets or of a pin on paper)   **6 spot** mark (on the list).
damn condemn   **8–9 determine . . . legacies** find a way to reduce
the outlay of Caesar's estate, by altering the will   **11 Or** either
12 slight, unmeritable insignificant and undeserving   **14 threefold**
i.e., including Europe, Africa, and Asia. The triumvirate assigned
Gaul to Antony, Spain to Lepidus, and Africa, Sardinia, and Sicily to
Octavius.

---

259 forms benches.   **windows** i.e., shutters   **266 straight** straightway, at once   **267 upon a wish** just when wanted.   **merry** i.e., favorably disposed   **270 Are rid** have ridden   **271 Belike** likely
enough.   **of** about; or, from

3.3. Location: A street.

1 tonight last night   **2 unluckily . . . fantasy** oppress my imagination
with foreboding   **13 you were best** it would be best for you   **19 bear
. . . bang** get a beating from me   **20 directly** without evasion

OCTAVIUS   So you thought him,
And took his voice who should be pricked to die   16
In our black sentence and proscription.   17
ANTONY
Octavius, I have seen more days than you;
And though we lay these honors on this man
To ease ourselves of divers slanderous loads,   20
He shall but bear them as the ass bears gold,
To groan and sweat under the business,
Either led or driven as we point the way;
And having brought our treasure where we will,
Then take we down his load, and turn him off,
Like to the empty ass, to shake his ears   26
And graze in commons.
OCTAVIUS   You may do your will;   27
But he's a tried and valiant soldier.
ANTONY
So is my horse, Octavius, and for that
I do appoint him store of provender.   30
It is a creature that I teach to fight,
To wind, to stop, to run directly on,   32
His corporal motion governed by my spirit.   33
And in some taste is Lepidus but so.   34
He must be taught, and trained, and bid go forth—
A barren-spirited fellow, one that feeds
On objects, arts, and imitations,   37
Which, out of use and staled by other men,   38
Begin his fashion. Do not talk of him   39
But as a property. And now, Octavius,   40
Listen great things. Brutus and Cassius   41
Are levying powers. We must straight make head.   42
Therefore let our alliance be combined,   43
Our best friends made, our means stretched;   44
And let us presently go sit in council   45
How covert matters may be best disclosed   46
And open perils surest answerèd.   47
OCTAVIUS
Let us do so, for we are at the stake   48
And bayed about with many enemies;   49
And some that smile have in their hearts, I fear,
Millions of mischiefs.   *Exeunt.*   51

♣

16 **took his voice** acceded to his opinion (i.e., about Publius)
17 **black sentence** death sentence. **proscription** (Proscription
branded a man as an outlaw, confiscated his property, offered a reward for his murder, and prohibited his sons and grandsons from
holding public office.) **20 divers . . . loads** some of the burdensome
accusations that will be leveled against us **26 empty** unloaded
27 commons public pasture **30 appoint** assign, provide **32 wind**
turn. (Horse trainer's term.) **33 corporal** bodily **34 taste** degree,
sense **37 On . . . imitations** on curiosities, artificial things, and the
following of fashion—copied things merely, taken up secondhand
38 staled made common or cheap **39 Begin his fashion** are for him
the ultimate in fashion **40 property** tool **41 Listen** hear **42 powers** armies. **straight make head** immediately raise an army **43 let
. . . combined** let us work as one **44 made** mustered, made certain.
stretched used to fullest advantage, extended to the utmost **45 presently** at once **46 How . . . disclosed** (to determine) how hidden
dangers may best be discovered **47 surest answerèd** most safely met
48 at the stake i.e., like a bear in the sport of bearbaiting **49 bayed
about** surrounded as by baying dogs **51 mischiefs** harms, evils

4.2   *Drum. Enter Brutus, Lucilius, [Lucius,] and the
army. Titinius and Pindarus meet them.*

BRUTUS   Stand, ho!   1
LUCILIUS   Give the word, ho, and stand!   2
BRUTUS
What now, Lucilius, is Cassius near?
LUCILIUS
He is at hand, and Pindarus is come
To do you salutation from his master.
BRUTUS
He greets me well. Your master, Pindarus,   6
In his own change, or by ill officers,   7
Hath given me some worthy cause to wish
Things done, undone; but if he be at hand
I shall be satisfied.
PINDARUS   I do not doubt   10
But that my noble master will appear
Such as he is, full of regard and honor.   12
BRUTUS
He is not doubted.— A word, Lucilius.
            [*Brutus and Lucilius speak apart.*]
How he received you let me be resolved.   14
LUCILIUS
With courtesy and with respect enough,
But not with such familiar instances   16
Nor with such free and friendly conference   17
As he hath used of old.
BRUTUS   Thou hast described
A hot friend cooling. Ever note, Lucilius:
When love begins to sicken and decay
It useth an enforcèd ceremony.   21
There are no tricks in plain and simple faith.
But hollow men, like horses hot at hand,   23
Make gallant show and promise of their mettle;   24
               Low march within.
But when they should endure the bloody spur,
They fall their crests and like deceitful jades   26
Sink in the trial. Comes his army on?   27
LUCILIUS
They mean this night in Sardis to be quartered.   28
The greater part, the horse in general,   29
Are come with Cassius.

        Enter Cassius and his powers.

BRUTUS   Hark, he is arrived.
March gently on to meet him.   31
CASSIUS   Stand, ho!

4.2. Location: Camp near Sardis, in Asia Minor. Before Brutus' tent.
1–2 Stand . . . stand halt! Pass the word **6 He . . . well** his greetings are welcome **7 In . . . officers** whether from an alteration in his
feelings toward me or through the acts of unworthy subordinates
10 be satisfied have things explained to my satisfaction **12 full . . .
honor** deserving all respect and honor **14 resolved** informed, put out
of doubt **16 familiar instances** proofs of intimate friendship **17 conference** conversation **21 enforcèd** constrained **23 hollow** insincere.
hot at hand restless and full of spirit when held in, at the start
24 mettle spirit **26 fall their crests** lower their necks (literally, the
ridge or mane of the neck), hang their heads. **jades** worthless horses
27 Sink give way, fail **28 Sardis** (The capital city of Lydia in Asia Minor.) **29 the horse in general** all the cavalry **31 gently** mildly, not
hostilely

BRUTUS   Stand, ho! Speak the word along.

FIRST SOLDIER   Stand!

SECOND SOLDIER   Stand!

THIRD SOLDIER   Stand!

CASSIUS
Most noble brother, you have done me wrong.

BRUTUS
Judge me, you gods! Wrong I mine enemies?
And if not so, how should I wrong a brother?

CASSIUS
Brutus, this sober form of yours hides wrongs;   40
And when you do them—

BRUTUS   Cassius, be content;   41
Speak your griefs softly. I do know you well.   42
Before the eyes of both our armies here,
Which should perceive nothing but love from us,
Let us not wrangle. Bid them move away.
Then in my tent, Cassius, enlarge your griefs,   46
And I will give you audience.

CASSIUS   Pindarus,
Bid our commanders lead their charges off   48
A little from this ground.

BRUTUS
Lucius, do you the like, and let no man
Come to our tent till we have done our conference.
Let Lucilius and Titinius guard our door.   52
            Exeunt. Manent Brutus and Cassius.
     [*Lucilius and Titinius stand guard at the door.*]

4.3

CASSIUS
That you have wronged me doth appear in this:
You have condemned and noted Lucius Pella   2
For taking bribes here of the Sardians,
Wherein my letters, praying on his side,   4
Because I knew the man, was slighted off.   5

BRUTUS
You wronged yourself to write in such a case.

CASSIUS
In such a time as this it is not meet   7
That every nice offense should bear his comment.   8

BRUTUS
Let me tell you, Cassius, you yourself
Are much condemned to have an itching palm,   10
To sell and mart your offices for gold   11

To undeservers.

CASSIUS   I an itching palm?
You know that you are Brutus that speaks this,
Or, by the gods, this speech were else your last.   14

BRUTUS
The name of Cassius honors this corruption,   15
And chastisement doth therefore hide his head.   16

CASSIUS   Chastisement?

BRUTUS
Remember March, the ides of March remember.
Did not great Julius bleed for justice' sake?
What villain touched his body that did stab   20
And not for justice? What, shall one of us,   21
That struck the foremost man of all this world
But for supporting robbers, shall we now   23
Contaminate our fingers with base bribes,
And sell the mighty space of our large honors   25
For so much trash as may be graspèd thus?   26
I had rather be a dog and bay the moon   27
Than such a Roman.

CASSIUS   Brutus, bait not me.   28
I'll not endure it. You forget yourself
To hedge me in. I am a soldier, I,   30
Older in practice, abler than yourself
To make conditions.   32

BRUTUS   Go to! You are not, Cassius.

CASSIUS   I am.

BRUTUS   I say you are not.

CASSIUS
Urge me no more; I shall forget myself.   36
Have mind upon your health. Tempt me no farther.   37

BRUTUS   Away, slight man!   38

CASSIUS
Is 't possible?

BRUTUS   Hear me, for I will speak.
Must I give way and room to your rash choler?   40
Shall I be frighted when a madman stares?   41

CASSIUS
O ye gods, ye gods! Must I endure all this?

BRUTUS
All this? Ay, more. Fret till your proud heart break.
Go show your slaves how choleric you are
And make your bondmen tremble. Must I budge?   45
Must I observe you? Must I stand and crouch   46

---

40 sober form dignified manner, appearance   **41 be content** keep calm   **42 griefs** grievances.   **I . . . well** i.e., we've known one another long and can proceed calmly   **46 enlarge** speak freely   **48 charges** troops   **52 Lucilius** (The Folio reads *Lucius* here and *Lucilius* in line 50, but, when Shakespeare interpolated a passage in the next scene at lines 124–166, he evidently intended to have Lucilius guarding the door.)

4.3. Location: The scene is continuous. Brutus and Cassius remain onstage, which now represents the interior of Brutus' tent.   **2 noted** publicly disgraced.   **Lucius Pella** a Roman praetor in Sardis   **4 letters** i.e., letter   **5 slighted off** slightingly dismissed   **7 meet** fitting   **8 nice** trivial.   **bear his comment** be made the object of criticism.   **his** its   **10 condemned to have** accused of having   **11 mart** traffic in

14 else otherwise   **15 honors** lends the appearance of honor to, countenances   **16 chastisement . . . head** i.e., the chastisement lying in my authority is slow to act, as though ashamed. (Brutus cannot punish Cassius because of their friendship and family connection.)   **20–21 What . . . justice** which of us was villain enough to stab for any cause other than justice?   **23 But** only.   **robbers** (According to Plutarch, Caesar "was a favorer and suborner of all of them that did rob and spoil by his countenance and authority.")   **25 the mighty . . . honors** the greatness of our honorable reputations and the high offices we have power to confer   **26 trash** i.e., money (despised in Brutus' stoic philosophy)   **27 bay** howl at   **28 bait** harass   **30 hedge me in** crowd me, limit my authority   **32 make conditions** i.e., manage affairs, make decisions about Lucius Pella and other officers   **36 Urge** provoke   **37 Tempt** provoke   **38 slight** insignificant   **40 way and room** free course and scope.   **choler** wrathful temperament   **41 stares** looks wildly at me   **45 bondmen** (Probably not distinguished from "slaves" in line 44.)   **budge** flinch   **46 observe** pay reverence to.   **crouch** bow, cringe

Under your testy humor? By the gods,   47
You shall digest the venom of your spleen   48
Though it do split you; for, from this day forth,
I'll use you for my mirth, yea, for my laughter,
When you are waspish.
CASSIUS   Is it come to this?   51
BRUTUS
You say you are a better soldier.
Let it appear so; make your vaunting true,   53
And it shall please me well. For mine own part,
I shall be glad to learn of noble men.   55
CASSIUS
You wrong me every way! You wrong me, Brutus.
I said an elder soldier, not a better.
Did I say "better"?
BRUTUS   If you did, I care not.
CASSIUS
When Caesar lived he durst not thus have moved
  me.   59
BRUTUS
Peace, peace! You durst not so have tempted him.   60
CASSIUS   I durst not?
BRUTUS   No.
CASSIUS
What, durst not tempt him?
BRUTUS   For your life you durst not.
CASSIUS
Do not presume too much upon my love.
I may do that I shall be sorry for.
BRUTUS
You have done that you should be sorry for.
There is no terror, Cassius, in your threats,
For I am armed so strong in honesty
That they pass by me as the idle wind,   69
Which I respect not. I did send to you   70
For certain sums of gold, which you denied me;
For I can raise no money by vile means.   72
By heaven, I had rather coin my heart
And drop my blood for drachmas than to wring
From the hard hands of peasants their vile trash
By any indirection. I did send   76
To you for gold to pay my legions,
Which you denied me. Was that done like Cassius?
Should I have answered Caius Cassius so?
When Marcus Brutus grows so covetous
To lock such rascal counters from his friends,   81
Be ready, gods, with all your thunderbolts;
Dash him to pieces!
CASSIUS   I denied you not.
BRUTUS
You did.

CASSIUS   I did not. He was but a fool
That brought my answer back. Brutus hath rived my
  heart.   85
A friend should bear his friend's infirmities,
But Brutus makes mine greater than they are.
BRUTUS
I do not, till you practice them on me.
CASSIUS
You love me not.
BRUTUS   I do not like your faults.
CASSIUS
A friendly eye could never see such faults.
BRUTUS
A flatterer's would not, though they do appear
As huge as high Olympus.
CASSIUS
Come, Antony, and young Octavius, come,
Revenge yourselves alone on Cassius;
For Cassius is aweary of the world,
Hated by one he loves, braved by his brother,   96
Checked like a bondman, all his faults observed,   97
Set in a notebook, learned and conned by rote   98
To cast into my teeth. O, I could weep
My spirit from mine eyes! There is my dagger,
                    [offering his unsheathed dagger]
And here my naked breast; within, a heart
Dearer than Pluto's mine, richer than gold.   102
If that thou be'st a Roman, take it forth.
I, that denied thee gold, will give my heart.   104
Strike, as thou didst at Caesar; for I know,
When thou didst hate him worst, thou loved'st him
  better
Than ever thou loved'st Cassius.
BRUTUS   Sheathe your dagger.
Be angry when you will, it shall have scope;   108
Do what you will, dishonor shall be humor.   109
O Cassius, you are yokèd with a lamb   110
That carries anger as the flint bears fire,
Who, much enforcèd, shows a hasty spark   112
And straight is cold again.
CASSIUS   Hath Cassius lived   113
To be but mirth and laughter to his Brutus
When grief and blood ill-tempered vexeth him?   115
BRUTUS
When I spoke that, I was ill-tempered too.
CASSIUS
Do you confess so much? Give me your hand.
BRUTUS
And my heart too.   [They embrace.]
CASSIUS   O Brutus!
BRUTUS   What's the matter?

---

47 **humor** temperament   48 **digest** swallow.   **spleen** i.e., irascibility
51 **waspish** hotheaded   53 **vaunting** boasting   55 **learn of noble men**
learn of the existence of noble men, or learn from those who have
proved themselves noble   59 **moved** angered   60 **tempted** provoked
69 **idle** insubstantial; insignificant   70 **respect not** pay no attention to
72 **can raise no money** i.e., refuse to raise money   76 **indirection** devious or unjust means   81 **rascal counters** i.e., paltry sums. (*Counters*
were uncurrent coins used by shopkeepers as tokens in making
reckonings.)

85 **rived** cleft, split   96 **braved** defied   97 **Checked** rebuked
98 **conned by rote** memorized   102 **Dearer** more laden with wealth.
Pluto god of the underworld (fused with Plutus, god of riches)
104 **that denied** i.e., who you insist denied   108 **scope** free rein
109 **dishonor . . . humor** i.e., I'll regard your corruption or your flaring temper as something to be humored   110 **yokèd with** allied with
(i.e., Brutus compares himself to the lamb)   112 **enforcèd** provoked,
struck upon   113 **straight** at once   115 **blood ill-tempered** disposition imbalanced by the humors of the body

CASSIUS
Have not you love enough to bear with me,
When that rash humor which my mother gave me   120
Makes me forgetful?
BRUTUS   Yes, Cassius, and from henceforth,
When you are overearnest with your Brutus,
He'll think your mother chides, and leave you so.   123

*Enter a Poet [followed by Lucilius and Titinius,
who have been standing guard at the door].*

POET
Let me go in to see the generals!
There is some grudge between 'em; 'tis not meet
They be alone.
LUCILIUS   You shall not come to them.
POET   Nothing but death shall stay me.
CASSIUS   How now? What's the matter?
POET
For shame, you generals! What do you mean?
Love and be friends, as two such men should be;
For I have seen more years, I'm sure, than ye.
CASSIUS
Ha, ha, how vilely doth this cynic rhyme!   132
BRUTUS
Get you hence, sirrah. Saucy fellow, hence!
CASSIUS
Bear with him, Brutus. 'Tis his fashion.
BRUTUS
I'll know his humor when he knows his time.   135
What should the wars do with these jigging fools?   136
Companion, hence!
CASSIUS   Away, away, begone!   *Exit Poet.* 137
BRUTUS
Lucilius and Titinius, bid the commanders
Prepare to lodge their companies tonight.
CASSIUS
And come yourselves, and bring Messala with you
Immediately to us.   *[Exeunt Lucilius and Titinius.]*
BRUTUS *[to Lucius within]*   Lucius, a bowl of wine.
CASSIUS
I did not think you could have been so angry.
BRUTUS
O Cassius, I am sick of many griefs.
CASSIUS
Of your philosophy you make no use
If you give place to accidental evils.   145
BRUTUS
No man bears sorrow better. Portia is dead.
CASSIUS   Ha? Portia?
BRUTUS   She is dead.
CASSIUS
How scaped I killing when I crossed you so?   149

O insupportable and touching loss!   150
Upon what sickness?
BRUTUS   Impatient of my absence,   151
And grief that young Octavius with Mark Antony
Have made themselves so strong—for with her
death   153
That tidings came—with this she fell distract
And, her attendants absent, swallowed fire.   155
CASSIUS
And died so?
BRUTUS   Even so.
CASSIUS   O ye immortal gods!

Enter Boy [Lucius] with wine and tapers.

BRUTUS
Speak no more of her.—Give me a bowl of wine.—
In this I bury all unkindness, Cassius.   *Drinks.*
CASSIUS
My heart is thirsty for that noble pledge.
Fill, Lucius, till the wine o'erswell the cup;
I cannot drink too much of Brutus' love.   161
                   [He drinks. Exit Lucius.]

Enter Titinius and Messala.

BRUTUS
Come in, Titinius. Welcome, good Messala.
Now sit we close about this taper here
And call in question our necessities.   *[They sit.]* 164
CASSIUS
Portia, art thou gone?
BRUTUS   No more, I pray you.
Messala, I have here receivèd letters
That young Octavius and Mark Antony
Come down upon us with a mighty power,   168
Bending their expedition toward Philippi.   169
                      [He shows letters.]
MESSALA
Myself have letters of the selfsame tenor.
BRUTUS   With what addition?
MESSALA
That by proscription and bills of outlawry   172
Octavius, Antony, and Lepidus
Have put to death an hundred senators.
BRUTUS
Therein our letters do not well agree;
Mine speak of seventy senators that died
By their proscriptions, Cicero being one.
CASSIUS
Cicero one?
MESSALA   Cicero is dead,
And by that order of proscription.

---

120 **that rash humor** i.e., choler, anger   123 **leave you so** let it go at that   132 **cynic** i.e., rude fellow; also one claiming to be a Cynic philosopher, hence outspoken   135 **I'll . . . time** I'll indulge his eccentric behavior when he knows the proper time for it   136 **jigging** rhyming in jerky doggerel   137 **Companion** fellow   145 **place** way. **accidental evils** misfortunes caused by chance (which should be a matter of indifference to a philosopher like Brutus)   149 **scaped I killing** did I escape being killed

150 **touching** grievous   151 **Impatient of** unable to endure   153 **her death** i.e., news of her death   155 **swallowed fire** (According to Plutarch, as translated by Thomas North, Portia "took hot burning coals and cast them in her mouth, and kept her mouth so close that she choked herself.")   161 **s.d. Titinius** (Lucilius does not return with Titinius, as he was ordered to do at lines 140–141, probably because he was not in Shakespeare's original version of this scene.)   164 **call in question** examine, discuss   168 **power** army   169 **Bending** directing. **expedition** rapid march; military power   172 **proscription** (See the note at 4.1.17.)

Had you your letters from your wife, my lord?   180

BRUTUS   No, Messala.

MESSALA

Nor nothing in your letters writ of her?   182

BRUTUS

Nothing, Messala.

MESSALA   That, methinks, is strange.

BRUTUS

Why ask you? Hear you aught of her in yours?

MESSALA   No, my lord.

BRUTUS

Now, as you are a Roman, tell me true.

MESSALA

Then like a Roman bear the truth I tell,

For certain she is dead, and by strange manner.

BRUTUS

Why, farewell, Portia. We must die, Messala.

With meditating that she must die once,   190

I have the patience to endure it now.

MESSALA

Even so great men great losses should endure.   192

CASSIUS

I have as much of this in art as you,   193

But yet my nature could not bear it so.   194

BRUTUS

Well, to our work alive. What do you think   195

Of marching to Philippi presently?

CASSIUS

I do not think it good.

BRUTUS   Your reason?

CASSIUS   This it is:

'Tis better that the enemy seek us.

So shall he waste his means, weary his soldiers,

Doing himself offense, whilst we, lying still,   200

Are full of rest, defense, and nimbleness.

BRUTUS

Good reasons must of force give place to better.   202

The people twixt Philippi and this ground

Do stand but in a forced affection,

For they have grudged us contribution.

The enemy, marching along by them,

By them shall make a fuller number up,

Come on refreshed, new-added, and encouraged;   208

From which advantage shall we cut him off

If at Philippi we do face him there,

These people at our back.

CASSIUS   Hear me, good brother—   211

BRUTUS

Under your pardon. You must note besides   212

That we have tried the utmost of our friends;

Our legions are brim full, our cause is ripe.

The enemy increaseth every day;

We, at the height, are ready to decline.

There is a tide in the affairs of men

Which, taken at the flood, leads on to fortune;

Omitted, all the voyage of their life   219

Is bound in shallows and in miseries.   220

On such a full sea are we now afloat,

And we must take the current when it serves

Or lose our ventures.

CASSIUS   Then, with your will, go on.   223

We'll along ourselves and meet them at Philippi.   224

BRUTUS

The deep of night is crept upon our talk,

And nature must obey necessity,

Which we will niggard with a little rest.   227

There is no more to say.

CASSIUS   No more. Good night.

Early tomorrow will we rise and hence.   229

BRUTUS

Lucius! (*Enter Lucius.*) My gown. [*Exit Lucius.*]

Farewell, good Messala.   230

Good night, Titinius. Noble, noble Cassius,

Good night and good repose.

CASSIUS   O my dear brother!

This was an ill beginning of the night.

Never come such division 'tween our souls!

Let it not, Brutus.

Enter Lucius with the gown.

BRUTUS   Everything is well.

CASSIUS   Good night, my lord.

BRUTUS   Good night, good brother.

TITINIUS, MESSALA   Good night, Lord Brutus.

BRUTUS   Farewell, everyone.

                    Exeunt [all but Brutus and Lucius].

Give me the gown. Where is thy instrument?   241

LUCIUS

Here in the tent.

BRUTUS   What, thou speak'st drowsily?

Poor knave, I blame thee not; thou art o'erwatched.   243

Call Claudius and some other of my men;

I'll have them sleep on cushions in my tent.

LUCIUS   Varro and Claudius!

Enter Varro and Claudius.

VARRO   Calls my lord?

BRUTUS

I pray you, sirs, lie in my tent and sleep.

It may be I shall raise you by and by   249

180–194 **Had . . . so** (This passage is sometimes regarded as contradictory to lines 142–165 and redundant. Perhaps it is the original account of Portia's death, and lines 142–165 are part of a later interpolation, but it is also possible that both are intended, the first being Brutus' intimate revelation of the news to his friend and the second being Brutus' recovery of his stoic reserve now on display for Messala and Titinius.)   182 **nothing . . . her** nothing written about her in the letters you've received   190 **once** at some time   192 **Even so** in just such a way   193 **art** i.e., the acquired theoretical wisdom of stoical fortitude (as contrasted with the gifts of *nature* in line 194)   195 **alive** concerning us who are alive and dealing with present and future realities   200 **offense** harm   202 **of force** necessarily   208 **new-added** reinforced   211 **These . . . back** i.e., with the people our enemy would otherwise recruit being instead in territory we control

212 **Under your pardon** i.e., excuse me, let me continue   219 **Omitted** neglected, missed   220 **bound in** confined to   223 **ventures** investments (of enterprise at sea).   **with your will** as you wish   224 **along** go along   227 **niggard** stint (by sleeping only briefly)   229 **hence** depart   230 **gown** housecoat   241 **instrument** i.e., perhaps a lute or cithern   243 **knave** boy.   **o'erwatched** tired from lack of sleep   249 **raise** rouse

On business to my brother Cassius.

VARRO
So please you, we will stand and watch your
    pleasure.   251

BRUTUS
I will not have it so. Lie down, good sirs.
It may be I shall otherwise bethink me.   253
            [*Varro and Claudius lie down.*]
Look, Lucius, here's the book I sought for so;
I put it in the pocket of my gown.

LUCIUS
I was sure your lordship did not give it me.

BRUTUS
Bear with me, good boy, I am much forgetful.
Canst thou hold up thy heavy eyes awhile
And touch thy instrument a strain or two?   259

LUCIUS
Ay, my lord, an 't please you.

BRUTUS   It does, my boy.   260
I trouble thee too much, but thou art willing.

LUCIUS   It is my duty, sir.

BRUTUS
I should not urge thy duty past thy might;
I know young bloods look for a time of rest.   264

LUCIUS   I have slept, my lord, already.

BRUTUS
It was well done, and thou shalt sleep again;
I will not hold thee long. If I do live,
I will be good to thee.
                Music, and a song. [*Lucius falls asleep.*]
This is a sleepy tune. O murderous slumber,   269
Layest thou thy leaden mace upon my boy,   270
That plays thee music? Gentle knave, good night;
I will not do thee so much wrong to wake thee.
If thou dost nod, thou break'st thy instrument;
I'll take it from thee. And, good boy, good night.
                        [*He removes Lucius' instrument,
                                 and begins to read.*]
Let me see, let me see; is not the leaf turned down
Where I left reading? Here it is, I think.

        Enter the Ghost of Caesar.

How ill this taper burns! Ha! Who comes here?   277
I think it is the weakness of mine eyes
That shapes this monstrous apparition.
It comes upon me.—Art thou any thing?   280
Art thou some god, some angel, or some devil,
That mak'st my blood cold and my hair to stare?   282
Speak to me what thou art.

GHOST
Thy evil spirit, Brutus.

BRUTUS   Why com'st thou?

GHOST
To tell thee thou shalt see me at Philippi.

BRUTUS   Well; then I shall see thee again?

GHOST   Ay, at Philippi.

BRUTUS
Why, I will see thee at Philippi, then.   [*Exit Ghost.*]
Now I have taken heart, thou vanishest.
Ill spirit, I would hold more talk with thee.—
Boy, Lucius! Varro! Claudius! Sirs, awake!
Claudius!

LUCIUS   The strings, my lord, are false.   292

BRUTUS
He thinks he still is at his instrument.
Lucius, awake!

LUCIUS   My lord?

BRUTUS
Didst thou dream, Lucius, that thou so criedst out?

LUCIUS
My lord, I do not know that I did cry.

BRUTUS
Yes, that thou didst. Didst thou see anything?

LUCIUS   Nothing, my lord.

BRUTUS
Sleep again, Lucius. Sirrah Claudius!
[*To Varro.*] Fellow thou, awake!

VARRO   My lord?

CLAUDIUS   My lord?
                                         [*They get up.*]

BRUTUS
Why did you so cry out, sirs, in your sleep?

VARRO, CLAUDIUS
Did we, my lord?

BRUTUS   Ay. Saw you anything?

VARRO
No, my lord, I saw nothing.

CLAUDIUS   Nor I, my lord.

BRUTUS
Go and commend me to my brother Cassius.   305
Bid him set on his powers betimes before,   306
And we will follow.

VARRO, CLAUDIUS   It shall be done, my lord.
                                              Exeunt.

                            ❖

5.1   *Enter Octavius, Antony, and their army.*

OCTAVIUS
Now, Antony, our hopes are answerèd.
You said the enemy would not come down,
But keep the hills and upper regions.   3
It proves not so. Their battles are at hand;   4
They mean to warn us at Philippi here,   5
Answering before we do demand of them.

251 **watch your pleasure** wakefully await your commands   253 **otherwise bethink me** change my mind   259 **touch** i.e., play on.   **strain**
tune, musical phrase   260 **an 't** if it   264 **young bloods** youthful constitutions   269 **murderous** producing the likeness of death
270 **leaden mace** heavy staff of office (used by a sheriff to touch the
shoulder of one being placed under arrest)   277 **How . . . burns** (It is
part of the machinery of apparitions that lights burn low and blue.)
280 **upon** toward   282 **stare** stand on end

292 **false** out of tune   305 **commend me** deliver my greetings
306 **set . . . before** march away with his troops early in the morning,
before me
5.1. Location: The plains of Philippi, in Macedonia.
3 **keep** remain in   4 **battles** armies   5 **warn** challenge

ANTONY
Tut, I am in their bosoms, and I know   7
Wherefore they do it. They could be content
To visit other places, and come down   9
With fearful bravery, thinking by this face   10
To fasten in our thoughts that they have courage;   11
But 'tis not so.   12

Enter a Messenger.

MESSENGER   Prepare you, generals.
The enemy comes on in gallant show.
Their bloody sign of battle is hung out,   14
And something to be done immediately.   15
ANTONY
Octavius, lead your battle softly on   16
Upon the left hand of the even field.
OCTAVIUS
Upon the right hand, I. Keep thou the left.
ANTONY
Why do you cross me in this exigent?   19
OCTAVIUS
I do not cross you, but I will do so.   *March.*   20

Drum. Enter Brutus, Cassius, and their army;
[Lucilius, Titinius, Messala, and others].

BRUTUS   They stand and would have parley.
CASSIUS
Stand fast, Titinius. We must out and talk.   22
OCTAVIUS
Mark Antony, shall we give sign of battle?
ANTONY
No, Caesar, we will answer on their charge.   24
Make forth. The generals would have some words.   25
OCTAVIUS [*to his officers*]   Stir not until the signal.
[*The two sides advance toward one another.*]
BRUTUS
Words before blows. Is it so, countrymen?
OCTAVIUS
Not that we love words better, as you do.
BRUTUS
Good words are better than bad strokes, Octavius.
ANTONY
In your bad strokes, Brutus, you give good words.   30
Witness the hole you made in Caesar's heart,
Crying "Long live! Hail, Caesar!"
CASSIUS   Antony,
The posture of your blows are yet unknown;   33

But for your words, they rob the Hybla bees,   34
And leave them honeyless.
ANTONY   Not stingless too?
BRUTUS   O, yes, and soundless too.
For you have stolen their buzzing, Antony,
And very wisely threat before you sting.   39
ANTONY
Villains! You did not so when your vile daggers   40
Hacked one another in the sides of Caesar.
You showed your teeth like apes, and fawned like
hounds,   42
And bowed like bondmen, kissing Caesar's feet,
Whilst damnèd Casca, like a cur, behind,
Struck Caesar on the neck. O you flatterers!
CASSIUS
Flatterers? Now, Brutus, thank yourself!
This tongue had not offended so today
If Cassius might have ruled.   48
OCTAVIUS
Come, come, the cause. If arguing make us sweat,   49
The proof of it will turn to redder drops.   50
Look,   [*He draws.*]
I draw a sword against conspirators.
When think you that the sword goes up again?   53
Never, till Caesar's three-and-thirty wounds   54
Be well avenged, or till another Caesar   55
Have added slaughter to the sword of traitors.   56
BRUTUS
Caesar, thou canst not die by traitors' hands,   57
Unless thou bring'st them with thee.
OCTAVIUS   So I hope.   58
I was not born to die on Brutus' sword.   59
BRUTUS
O, if thou wert the noblest of thy strain,   60
Young man, thou couldst not die more honorable.
CASSIUS
A peevish schoolboy, worthless of such honor,   62
Joined with a masker and a reveler!   63
ANTONY
Old Cassius still.
OCTAVIUS   Come, Antony, away!—
Defiance, traitors, hurl we in your teeth.
If you dare fight today, come to the field;
If not, when you have stomachs.   67
Exeunt Octavius, Antony, and army.

7 bosoms secret councils   **9 visit other places** i.e., be elsewhere. **come** they come   **10 fearful bravery** (1) awesome ostentation (2) a show of bravery to conceal their fear.   **face** pretense (of courage)   **11 fasten** fix the idea   **12 'tis not so** (1) their plan cannot deceive us (2) they have no courage   **14 bloody sign** red flag or crimson coat of arms as battle signal   **15 to be** is to be   **16 softly** warily, with restraint   **19 cross** contradict.   **exigent** critical moment   **20 cross you** contradict you perversely.   **do so** do as I said   **22 out** go out   **24 answer on their charge** respond when they attack   **25 Make forth** march forward   **30 In . . . words** i.e., as you deliver cruel blows, Brutus, you use deceiving flattery. (Antony deliberately changes Brutus' *Good words* in line 29, ''bravely spoken words,'' into a negative meaning.)   **33 The posture . . . are** how you will strike your blows is

34 for as for.   **Hybla** a mountain and a town in ancient Sicily, famous for honey   **39 very wisely** (Said ironically; Brutus suggests that Antony is all bluster and no action.)   **threat** threaten   **40 so** i.e., give warning   **42 showed your teeth** i.e., in smiles   **48 ruled** prevailed (in urging that Antony be killed)   **49 the cause** to our business   **50 proof** trial   **53 up** in its sheath   **54 three-and-thirty** (Plutarch has it three-and-twenty.)   **55 another Caesar** i.e., myself, Octavius   **56 Have . . . to** has also been slaughtered by   **57–59 Caesar . . . sword** (Brutus says that, if there are any traitors on the battlefield, they will perforce be in Octavius' army; Octavius twists Brutus' taunt by pretending that Brutus meant Octavius could not die on Brutus' sword.)   **60 if** even if.   **strain** lineage   **62 peevish** silly, childish.   **schoolboy** (Octavius was eighteen at the time of Caesar's assassination.)   **worthless** unworthy   **63 a masker . . . reveler** i.e., Antony, noted for his dissipation   **67 stomachs** appetites (for fighting), courage

CASSIUS
  Why, now, blow wind, swell billow and swim bark! 68
  The storm is up, and all is on the hazard. 69
BRUTUS
  Ho, Lucilius! Hark, a word with you.
LUCILIUS (*stands forth*) My lord?
                    [*Brutus and Lucilius converse apart.*]
CASSIUS Messala!
MESSALA (*stands forth*) What says my general?
CASSIUS Messala,
  This is my birthday; as this very day 75
  Was Cassius born. Give me thy hand, Messala.
  Be thou my witness that against my will,
  As Pompey was, am I compelled to set 78
  Upon one battle all our liberties.
  You know that I held Epicurus strong 80
  And his opinion. Now I change my mind
  And partly credit things that do presage. 82
  Coming from Sardis, on our former ensign 83
  Two mighty eagles fell, and there they perched, 84
  Gorging and feeding from our soldiers' hands,
  Who to Philippi here consorted us. 86
  This morning are they fled away and gone,
  And in their steads do ravens, crows, and kites 88
  Fly o'er our heads and downward look on us
  As we were sickly prey. Their shadows seem 90
  A canopy most fatal, under which 91
  Our army lies, ready to give up the ghost.
MESSALA
  Believe not so.
CASSIUS   I but believe it partly, 93
  For I am fresh of spirit and resolved
  To meet all perils very constantly. 95
BRUTUS
  Even so, Lucilius.   [*He rejoins Cassius.*]
CASSIUS   Now, most noble Brutus, 96
  The gods today stand friendly, that we may, 97
  Lovers in peace, lead on our days to age! 98
  But since the affairs of men rest still incertain, 99
  Let's reason with the worst that may befall. 100
  If we do lose this battle, then is this
  The very last time we shall speak together.
  What are you then determinèd to do?
BRUTUS
  Even by the rule of that philosophy

  By which I did blame Cato for the death 105
  Which he did give himself—I know not how,
  But I do find it cowardly and vile,
  For fear of what might fall, so to prevent 108
  The time of life—arming myself with patience 109
  To stay the providence of some high powers 110
  That govern us below.
CASSIUS   Then, if we lose this battle,
  You are contented to be led in triumph
  Thorough the streets of Rome? 113
BRUTUS
  No, Cassius, no. Think not, thou noble Roman,
  That ever Brutus will go bound to Rome;
  He bears too great a mind. But this same day
  Must end that work the ides of March begun.
  And whether we shall meet again I know not;
  Therefore our everlasting farewell take.
  Forever and forever farewell, Cassius!
  If we do meet again, why, we shall smile;
  If not, why then this parting was well made.
CASSIUS
  Forever and forever farewell, Brutus!
  If we do meet again, we'll smile indeed;
  If not, 'tis true this parting was well made.
BRUTUS
  Why, then, lead on. O, that a man might know
  The end of this day's business ere it come!
  But it sufficeth that the day will end,
  And then the end is known.—Come, ho, away!
                            Exeunt.

5.2   *Alarum. Enter Brutus and Messala.*

BRUTUS
  Ride, ride, Messala, ride, and give these bills 1
  Unto the legions on the other side. 2
                  [*He hands him written orders.*]
                            Loud alarum.
  Let them set on at once; for I perceive 3
  But cold demeanor in Octavio's wing, 4
  And sudden push gives them the overthrow.
  Ride, ride, Messala! Let them all come down. 6
                        Exeunt [*separately*].

68 billow wave **69 on the hazard** at stake **75 as** on **78 Pompey** (The reference is to the battle of Pharsalus, where Pompey was persuaded to fight Caesar against his own judgment.) **set** stake **80 Epicurus** Greek philosopher (341–270 B.C.) who, because he held the gods to be indifferent to human affairs, spurned belief in omens or superstitions **82 presage** foretell events **83 former ensign** foremost standard, the legion's *aquila*, a tall standard surmounted by the image of an eagle **84 fell** swooped down **86 Who** which. **consorted** accompanied **88 kites** scavenger birds (also raptors) **90 As** as if **91 fatal** presaging death **93 but** only **95 constantly** resolutely **96 Even so, Lucilius** (This phrase marks the end of Brutus' private conversation apart with Lucilius.) **97 The gods may** the gods may **98 Lovers** friends **99 still** always **100 reason** reckon

105 Cato i.e., Marcus Porcius Cato, Brutus' father-in-law, who killed himself to avoid submission to Caesar in 46 B.C. (See 2.1.296 and note.) Brutus' condemnation of Cato's suicide out of fear of failure can perhaps be reconciled with lines 114–117 below and with Brutus' own later suicide (5.5.50), since on that occasion Brutus is responding to certain defeat and disgrace. The seeming contradiction may also be owing to an ambiguity in North's Plutarch. **108 fall** befall. **prevent** anticipate the end, cut short **109 time** term, end **110 stay** await **113 Thorough** through
5.2. Location: The plains of Philippi. The field of battle.
s.d. Alarum (This is seemingly an anticipatory stage direction; the battle actually begins with the *Loud alarum* at line 2. An *alarum* is offstage sounds, signifying a battle.) **1 bills** orders **2 side** wing (i.e., Cassius' wing) **3 set on** attack **4 cold demeanor** faintheartedness **6 come down** i.e., from the hills where they have been awaiting the battle; see 5.1.2–3.

5.3   *Alarums. Enter Cassius [carrying a standard], and*
         Titinius.

CASSIUS
    O, look, Titinius, look, the villains fly!   1
    Myself have to mine own turned enemy.   2
    This ensign here of mine was turning back;   3
    I slew the coward and did take it from him.   4
TITINIUS
    O Cassius, Brutus gave the word too early,
    Who, having some advantage on Octavius,
    Took it too eagerly. His soldiers fell to spoil,   7
    Whilst we by Antony are all enclosed.   8

         Enter Pindarus.

PINDARUS
    Fly further off, my lord, fly further off!
    Mark Antony is in your tents, my lord.
    Fly therefore, noble Cassius, fly far off.
CASSIUS
    This hill is far enough. Look, look, Titinius:
    Are those my tents where I perceive the fire?
TITINIUS
    They are, my lord.
CASSIUS   Titinius, if thou lovest me,
    Mount thou my horse, and hide thy spurs in him
    Till he have brought thee up to yonder troops
    And here again, that I may rest assured
    Whether yond troops are friend or enemy.
TITINIUS
    I will be here again even with a thought.   *Exit.* 19
CASSIUS
    Go, Pindarus, get higher on that hill.
    My sight was ever thick. Regard Titinius,   21
    And tell me what thou not'st about the field.   22
                          [*Pindarus goes up.*]
    This day I breathèd first. Time is come round,   23
    And where I did begin, there shall I end.
    My life is run his compass.—Sirrah, what news?   25
PINDARUS (*above*) O my lord!
CASSIUS   What news?
PINDARUS [*above*]
    Titinius is enclosèd round about
    With horsemen, that make to him on the spur,   29
    Yet he spurs on. Now they are almost on him.
    Now, Titinius! Now some light. O, he   31
    Lights too. He's ta'en. (*Shout.*) And hark! They
        shout for joy.
CASSIUS   Come down, behold no more.
    O coward that I am, to live so long

5.3. Location: The field of battle still.
1 the villains i.e., my own troops   **2 mine own** my own men   **3 en-**
sign bearer of the standard. (A legion's *aquila*, or "eagle standard,"
had great moral significance and needed to be guarded.)   **4 it** i.e.,
the standard   **7 spoil** looting   **8 enclosed** surrounded   **19 even . . .**
thought as quick as thought   **21 thick** imperfect, dim.   **Regard** observe   **22 s.d. Pindarus goes up** (Pindarus may exit and ascend behind the scenes to the gallery; at line 35, he does *enter* in order to return.)   **23 I breathèd first** i.e., it is my birthday   **25 his compass** its
circuit, circle (as drawn by a geometer's compass)   **29 make . . .**
spur approach him riding rapidly   **31 light** alight, dismount

To see my best friend ta'en before my face!

         Enter Pindarus [from above].

    Come hither, sirrah.
    In Parthia did I take thee prisoner,   37
    And then I swore thee, saving of thy life,   38
    That whatsoever I did bid thee do
    Thou shouldst attempt it. Come now, keep thine
        oath;
    Now be a freeman, and with this good sword,
    That ran through Caesar's bowels, search this
        bosom.   42
    Stand not to answer. Here, take thou the hilts,   43
    And when my face is covered, as 'tis now,
    Guide thou the sword. [*Pindarus does so.*] Caesar,
        thou art revenged,
    Even with the sword that killed thee.   [*He dies.*]
PINDARUS
    So, I am free, yet would not so have been,   47
    Durst I have done my will. O Cassius!   48
    Far from this country Pindarus shall run,
    Where never Roman shall take note of him.   [*Exit.*]

         Enter Titinius [wearing a garland of laurel] and
         Messala.

MESSALA
    It is but change, Titinius; for Octavius   51
    Is overthrown by noble Brutus' power,
    As Cassius' legions are by Antony.
TITINIUS
    These tidings will well comfort Cassius.
MESSALA
    Where did you leave him?
TITINIUS   All disconsolate,
    With Pindarus his bondman, on this hill.
MESSALA
    Is not that he that lies upon the ground?
TITINIUS
    He lies not like the living. O my heart!
MESSALA
    Is not that he?
TITINIUS   No, this was he, Messala,
    But Cassius is no more. O setting sun,
    As in thy red rays thou dost sink to night,   61
    So in his red blood Cassius' day is set.
    The sun of Rome is set. Our day is gone;   63
    Clouds, dews, and dangers come; our deeds are
        done.
    Mistrust of my success hath done this deed.   65
MESSALA
    Mistrust of good success hath done this deed.
    O hateful Error, Melancholy's child,   67
    Why dost thou show to the apt thoughts of men   68

37 Parthia (What is now northern Iran.)   **38 swore . . . of** made you
swear, when I spared   **42 search** probe, penetrate   **43 Stand** delay.
hilts i.e., sword hilt   **47 so** in this manner   **48 Durst** dared
51 change exchange of advantage, quid pro quo   **61 to** toward
63 sun (with pun on *son*)   **65 Mistrust** i.e., Cassius' doubt   **67 Mel-**
ancholy's child i.e., mistaken fantasy, bred of a melancholic temperament   **68 apt** impressionable

The things that are not? O Error, soon conceived,
Thou never com'st unto a happy birth,
But kill'st the mother that engendered thee.   71

TITINIUS
What, Pindarus! Where art thou, Pindarus?

MESSALA
Seek him, Titinius, whilst I go to meet
The noble Brutus, thrusting this report
Into his ears. I may say "thrusting" it,
For piercing steel and darts envenomèd   76
Shall be as welcome to the ears of Brutus
As tidings of this sight.

TITINIUS   Hie you, Messala,   78
And I will seek for Pindarus the while.
                                      [*Exit Messala.*]
Why didst thou send me forth, brave Cassius?
Did I not meet thy friends? And did not they
Put on my brows this wreath of victory
And bid me give it thee? Didst thou not hear their
    shouts?
Alas, thou hast misconstrued everything.
But, hold thee, take this garland on thy brow.   85
        [*He places the garland on Cassius' brow.*]
Thy Brutus bid me give it thee, and I
Will do his bidding. Brutus, come apace   87
And see how I regarded Caius Cassius.
By your leave, gods! This is a Roman's part.
Come, Cassius' sword, and find Titinius' heart.
                        [*He stabs himself and*] dies.

        Alarum. Enter Brutus, Messala, young Cato,
        Strato, Volumnius, and Lucilius, [Labeo, and
        Flavius].

BRUTUS
Where, where, Messala, doth his body lie?
MESSALA
Lo, yonder, and Titinius mourning it.
BRUTUS
Titinius' face is upward.
CATO   He is slain.
BRUTUS
O Julius Caesar, thou art mighty yet!
Thy spirit walks abroad and turns our swords
In our own proper entrails.   *Low alarums.*
CATO   Brave Titinius!   96
Look whe'er he have not crowned dead Cassius.   97
BRUTUS
Are yet two Romans living such as these?
The last of all the Romans, fare thee well!
It is impossible that ever Rome
Should breed thy fellow. Friends, I owe more tears
To this dead man than you shall see me pay.—
I shall find time, Cassius, I shall find time.—
Come, therefore, and to Thasos send his body.   104
His funerals shall not be in our camp,

Lest it discomfort us. Lucilius, come,   106
And come, young Cato, let us to the field.
Labeo and Flavius, set our battles on.   108
'Tis three o'clock, and, Romans, yet ere night
We shall try fortune in a second fight.
                        Exeunt [with the bodies].

5.4   *Alarum. Enter Brutus, Messala, [young] Cato,*
           Lucilius, and Flavius.

BRUTUS
Yet, countrymen, O, yet hold up your heads!
        [*Exit, followed by Messala and Flavius.*]
CATO
What bastard doth not? Who will go with me?   2
I will proclaim my name about the field:
I am the son of Marcus Cato, ho!
A foe to tyrants, and my country's friend.
I am the son of Marcus Cato, ho!

        Enter soldiers, and fight.

LUCILIUS
And I am Brutus, Marcus Brutus I!
Brutus, my country's friend! Know me for Brutus!
        [*Young Cato is slain by Antony's men.*]
O young and noble Cato, art thou down?
Why, now thou diest as bravely as Titinius,
And mayst be honored, being Cato's son.
FIRST SOLDIER [*capturing Lucilius*]
Yield, or thou diest.
LUCILIUS [*offering money*] Only I yield to die.   12
There is so much that thou wilt kill me straight;   13
Kill Brutus, and be honored in his death.
FIRST SOLDIER
We must not. A noble prisoner!
SECOND SOLDIER
Room, ho! Tell Antony, Brutus is ta'en.

        Enter Antony.

FIRST SOLDIER
I'll tell the news. Here comes the General.—
Brutus is ta'en, Brutus is ta'en, my lord.
ANTONY   Where is he?
LUCILIUS
Safe, Antony, Brutus is safe enough.
I dare assure thee that no enemy
Shall ever take alive the noble Brutus.
The gods defend him from so great a shame!
When you do find him, or alive or dead,   24
He will be found like Brutus, like himself.
ANTONY [*to First Soldier*]
This is not Brutus, friend, but, I assure you,
A prize no less in worth. Keep this man safe;
Give him all kindness. I had rather have

71 the mother i.e., the melancholy person who too readily believes
the worst **76 darts** spears **78 Hie** hasten **85 hold thee** wait
87 apace quickly **96 own proper** very own **97 whe'er** whether
104 Thasos an island off the coast of Thrace, near Philippi

106 discomfort us discourage our troops **108 battles** armies
5.4. Location: Scene continues at the field of battle.
2 What . . . not who is so base that he would not do so? **12 Only
. . . die** I surrender only to die immediately **13 There . . . straight**
i.e., here is money if you will kill me at once **24 or alive** either alive

Such men my friends than enemies.—Go on,
And see whe'er Brutus be alive or dead;   30
And bring us word unto Octavius' tent
How everything is chanced.   32
                    Exeunt [separately, some bearing Cato's body].

5.5   *Enter Brutus, Dardanius, Clitus, Strato, and
           Volumnius.*

BRUTUS
Come, poor remains of friends, rest on this rock.
                                        [*He sits.*]
CLITUS
Statilius showed the torchlight, but, my lord,   2
He came not back. He is or ta'en or slain.   3
BRUTUS
Sit thee down, Clitus. Slaying is the word.
It is a deed in fashion. Hark thee, Clitus.
                                [He whispers.]
CLITUS
What, I, my lord? No, not for all the world.
BRUTUS
Peace then. No words.
CLITUS   I'll rather kill myself.
BRUTUS
Hark thee, Dardanius.   [*He whispers.*]
DARDANIUS   Shall I do such a deed?
       [*Dardanius and Clitus move away from Brutus.*]
CLITUS   O Dardanius!
DARDANIUS   O Clitus!
CLITUS
What ill request did Brutus make to thee?
DARDANIUS
To kill him, Clitus. Look, he meditates.
CLITUS
Now is that noble vessel full of grief,
That it runs over even at his eyes.
BRUTUS
Come hither, good Volumnius. List a word.   15
VOLUMNIUS
What says my lord?
BRUTUS   Why, this, Volumnius:
The ghost of Caesar hath appeared to me
Two several times by night—at Sardis once,   18
And this last night here in Philippi fields.
I know my hour is come.
VOLUMNIUS   Not so, my lord.
BRUTUS
Nay, I am sure it is, Volumnius.
Thou seest the world, Volumnius, how it goes;
Our enemies have beat us to the pit.   *Low alarums.* 23

It is more worthy to leap in ourselves
Than tarry till they push us. Good Volumnius,
Thou know'st that we two went to school together.
Even for that, our love of old, I prithee,   27
Hold thou my sword hilts whilst I run on it.   28
VOLUMNIUS
That's not an office for a friend, my lord.   29
                                        Alarum still.
CLITUS
Fly, fly, my lord! There is no tarrying here.
BRUTUS
Farewell to you, and you, and you, Volumnius.
Strato, thou hast been all this while asleep;
Farewell to thee too, Strato. Countrymen,
My heart doth joy that yet in all my life
I found no man but he was true to me.
I shall have glory by this losing day
More than Octavius and Mark Antony
By this vile conquest shall attain unto.   38
So fare you well at once, for Brutus' tongue   39
Hath almost ended his life's history.
Night hangs upon mine eyes; my bones would rest,
That have but labored to attain this hour.   42
              Alarum. Cry within, "Fly, fly, fly!"
CLITUS
Fly, my lord, fly!
BRUTUS   Hence, I will follow.
       [*Exeunt Clitus, Dardanius, and Volumnius.*]
I prithee, Strato, stay thou by thy lord.
Thou art a fellow of a good respect;   45
Thy life hath had some smatch of honor in it.   46
Hold then my sword, and turn away thy face,
While I do run upon it. Wilt thou, Strato?
STRATO
Give me your hand first. Fare you well, my lord.
BRUTUS
Farewell, good Strato. [*He runs on his sword.*]
   Caesar, now be still.
I killed not thee with half so good a will.   *Dies.* 51

       *Alarum. Retreat. Enter Antony, Octavius;
       Messala, Lucilius [as prisoners]; and the army.*

OCTAVIUS   What man is that?
MESSALA
My master's man. Strato, where is thy master?
STRATO
Free from the bondage you are in, Messala.
The conquerors can but make a fire of him,
For Brutus only overcame himself,   56
And no man else hath honor by his death.
LUCILIUS
So Brutus should be found. I thank thee, Brutus,
That thou hast proved Lucilius' saying true.   59

---

30 **whe'er** whether   32 **is chanced** has fallen out
5.5. Location: The field of battle still.
2–3 **Statilius . . . slain** (According to Plutarch, a scout named Statilius has gone through the enemy lines to reconnoitre and to hold up a
torch if all is well at Cassius' camp; he signals back but is then captured and slain.)   3 **or ta'en** either taken   15 **List** listen to   18 **several** separate   23 **beat** driven.   **pit** trap for wild animals; also, a
grave

27 **that, our love** that friendship of ours   28 **hilts** i.e., hilt   29 **office**
duty   38 **vile** paltry   39 **at once** all together, or without further ado
42 **That . . . hour** i.e., all their striving has been toward this moment
of death   45 **respect** reputation   46 **some smatch** some flavor, a
touch   51 **s.d. Retreat** signal to retire   56 **Brutus . . . himself** only
Brutus conquered Brutus   59 **saying** (See 5.4.21–25.)

OCTAVIUS
  All that served Brutus, I will entertain them.   60
  Fellow, wilt thou bestow thy time with me?
STRATO
  Ay, if Messala will prefer me to you.   62
OCTAVIUS Do so, good Messala.
MESSALA How died my master, Strato?
STRATO
  I held the sword, and he did run on it.
MESSALA
  Octavius, then take him to follow thee,   66
  That did the latest service to my master.   67
ANTONY
  This was the noblest Roman of them all.
  All the conspirators save only he
  Did that they did in envy of great Caesar;   70
  He only in a general honest thought
  And common good to all made one of them.
  His life was gentle, and the elements   73
  So mixed in him that Nature might stand up
  And say to all the world, "This was a man!"
OCTAVIUS
  According to his virtue let us use him,
  With all respect and rites of burial.
  Within my tent his bones tonight shall lie,
  Most like a soldier, ordered honorably.   79
  So call the field to rest, and let's away   80
  To part the glories of this happy day.   81
               Exeunt omnes [with Brutus' body].

60 entertain take into service **62 prefer** recommend **66 follow** serve **67 latest** last **70 that** what. **envy of** malice toward **73 gentle** noble. **elements** (Humankind as a microcosm is made up of earth, air, fire, and water, formed into the four humors of phlegm, blood, yellow bile [or choler], and black bile [or melancholy], whose qualities were mingled in Brutus in due proportions.) **79 ordered** treated, arranged for **80 field** army in the field **81 part** share. **s.d. omnes** all

Hamlet, Prince of Denmark

A recurring motif in *Hamlet* is of a seemingly healthy exterior concealing an interior sickness. Mere pretense of virtue, as Hamlet warns his mother, "will but skin and film the ulcerous place, / Whiles rank corruption, mining all within, / Infects unseen" (3.4.154–156). Polonius confesses, when he is about to use his daughter as a decoy for Hamlet, that "with devotion's visage / And pious action we do sugar o'er / The devil himself"; and his observation elicits a more anguished mea culpa from Claudius in an aside: "How smart a lash that speech doth give my conscience! / The harlot's cheek, beautied with plastering art, / Is not more ugly to the thing that helps it / Than is my deed to my most painted word" (3.1.47–54).

This motif of concealed evil and disease continually reminds us that, in both a specific and a broader sense, "Something is rotten in the state of Denmark" (1.4.90). The specific source of contamination is a poison: the poison with which Claudius has killed Hamlet's father, the poison in the players' enactment of "The Murder of Gonzago," and the two poisons (envenomed sword and poisoned drink) with which Claudius and Laertes plot to rid themselves of young Hamlet. More generally, the poison is an evil nature seeking to destroy humanity's better nature, as in the archetypal murder of Abel by Cain. "O, my offense is rank, it smells to heaven," laments Claudius, "It hath the primal eldest curse upon 't, / A brother's murder" (3.3.36–38). To Hamlet, and perhaps to us as well, Hamlet's father and Claudius typify what is best and worst in humanity; one is the sun-god Hyperion and the other, a satyr. Claudius is a "serpent" and a "mildewed ear, / Blasting his wholesome brother" (1.5.40; 3.4.65–66). Many a person, in Hamlet's view, is tragically destined to behold his or her better qualities corrupted by "some vicious mole of nature" over which the individual seems to have no control. "His virtues else, be they as pure as grace, / As infinite as man may undergo, / Shall in the general censure take corruption / From that particular fault." The "dram of evil" pollutes "all the noble substance" (1.4.24–37). Thus, poison spreads outward to infect the whole individual, just as bad individuals can infect an entire court or nation.

Hamlet, his mind attuned to philosophical matters, is keenly and poetically aware of humanity's fallen condition. He is, moreover, a shrewd observer of the Danish court, familiar with its ways and at the same time newly returned from abroad, looking at Denmark with a stranger's eyes. What particularly darkens his view of humanity, however, is not the general fact of corrupted human nature but rather Hamlet's knowledge of a dreadful secret. Even before he learns of his father's murder, Hamlet senses that there is something more deeply amiss than his mother's overhasty marriage to her deceased husband's brother. This is serious enough, to be sure, for it violates a taboo (parallel to the marriage of a widower to his deceased wife's sister, long regarded as incestuous by the English) and is thus understandably referred to as "incest" by Hamlet and his father's ghost. The appalling spectacle of Gertrude's "wicked speed, to post / With such dexterity to incestuous sheets" (1.2.156–157) overwhelms Hamlet with revulsion at carnal appetite and intensifies the emotional crisis any son would go through when forced to contemplate his father's death and his mother's remarriage. Still, the Ghost's revelation is of something far worse, something Hamlet has subconsciously feared and suspected. "O my prophetic soul! My uncle!" (1.5.42). Now Hamlet believes he has confirming evidence for his intuition that the world itself is "an unweeded garden / That grows to seed. Things rank and gross in nature / Possess it merely" (1.2.135–137).

Something is indeed rotten in the state of Denmark. The monarch on whom the health and safety of the kingdom depend is a murderer. Yet few persons know his secret: Hamlet, Horatio only belatedly, Claudius himself, and ourselves as audience. Many ironies and misunderstandings within the play cannot be understood without a proper awareness of this gap between Hamlet's knowledge and most others' ignorance of the murder. For, according to their own lights, Polonius and the rest behave as courtiers normally behave, obeying and flattering a king whom they acknowledge as their legitimate ruler. Hamlet, for his part, is so obsessed with the secret murder that he overreacts to those around him, rejecting overtures of friendship and becoming embittered, callous, brutal, and even violent. His antisocial behavior gives the others good reason to fear him as a menace to the state. Nevertheless, we share with Hamlet a knowledge of the truth and know that he is right, whereas the others are at best unhappily deceived by their own blind complicity in evil.

Rosencrantz and Guildenstern, for instance, are boyhood friends of Hamlet but are now dependent on the favor of King Claudius. Despite their seeming concern for their one-time comrade and Hamlet's initial pleasure in receiving them, they are faceless courtiers whose very names, like their personalities, are virtually interchangeable. "Thanks, Rosencrantz and gentle Guildenstern," says the King, and "Thanks, Guildenstern and gentle Rosencrantz," echoes the

Queen (2.2.33–34). They cannot understand why Hamlet increasingly mocks their overtures of friendship, whereas Hamlet cannot stomach their subservience to the King. The secret murder divides Hamlet from them, since only he knows of it. As the confrontation between Hamlet and Claudius grows more deadly, Rosencrantz and Guildenstern, not knowing the true cause, can only interpret Hamlet's behavior as dangerous madness. The wild display he puts on during the performance of "The Murder of Gonzago" and then the killing of Polonius are evidence of a treasonous threat to the crown, eliciting from them staunch assertions of the divine right of kings. "Most holy and religious fear it is / To keep those many many bodies safe / That live and feed upon Your Majesty," professes Guildenstern, and Rosencrantz reiterates the theme: "The cess of majesty / Dies not alone, but like a gulf doth draw / What's near it with it" (3.3.8–17). These sentiments of Elizabethan orthodoxy, similar to ones frequently heard in Shakespeare's history plays, are here undercut by a devastating irony, since they are spoken unwittingly in defense of a murderer. This irony pursues Rosencrantz and Guildenstern to their graves, for they are killed performing what they see as their duty to convey Hamlet safely to England. They are as ignorant of Claudius' secret orders for the murder of Hamlet in England as they are of Claudius' real reason for wishing to be rid of his stepson. That Hamlet should ingeniously remove the secret commission from Rosencrantz and Guildenstern's packet and substitute an order for their execution is ironically fitting, even though they are guiltless of having plotted Hamlet's death. "Why, man, they did make love to this employment," says Hamlet to Horatio. "They are not near my conscience. Their defeat / Does by their own insinuation grow" (5.2.57–59). They have condemned themselves, in Hamlet's eyes, by interceding officiously in deadly affairs of which they had no comprehension. Hamlet's judgment of them is harsh, and he himself appears hardened and pitiless in his role as agent in their deaths, but he is right that they have courted their own destiny.

Polonius, too, dies for meddling. It seems an unfair fate, since he wishes no physical harm to Hamlet and is only trying to ingratiate himself with Claudius. Yet Polonius' complicity in jaded court politics is deeper than his fatuous parental sententiousness might lead one to suppose. His famous advice to his son, often quoted out of context as though it were wise counsel, is, in fact, a worldly gospel of self-interest and concern for appearances. Like his son, Laertes, he cynically presumes that Hamlet's affection for Ophelia cannot be serious, since princes are not free to marry ladies of the court; accordingly, Polonius obliges his daughter to return the love letters she so cherishes. Polonius' spies are everywhere, seeking to entrap Polonius' own son in fleshly sin or to discover symptoms of Hamlet's presumed lovesickness. Polonius may cut a ridiculous figure as a prattling busybody, but he is wily and even menacing in his in-

tent. He has actually helped Claudius to the throne and is an essential instrument of royal policy. His ineffectuality and ignorance of the murder do not really excuse his guilty involvement.

Ophelia is more innocent than her father and brother, and more truly affectionate toward Hamlet. She earns our sympathy because she is caught between the conflicting wills of the men who are supremely important to her—her lover, her father, and her brother. Obedient by instinct and training to patriarchal instruction, she is unprepared to cope with divided authority and so takes refuge in passivity. Nevertheless, her pitiable story suggests that weak-willed acquiescence is poisoned by the evil to which it surrenders. However passively, Ophelia becomes an instrument through which Claudius attempts to spy on Hamlet. She is much like Gertrude, for the Queen has yielded to Claudius' importunity without ever knowing fully what awful price Claudius has paid for her and for the throne. The resemblance between Ophelia and Gertrude confirms Hamlet's tendency to generalize about feminine weakness—"frailty, thy name is woman" (1.2.146)—and prompts his misogynistic outburst against Ophelia when he concludes she, too, is spying on him. His rejection of love and friendship (except for Horatio's) seems paranoid in character and yet is at least partially justified by the fact that so many of the court are in fact conspiring to learn what he is up to.

Their oversimplification of his dilemma and their facile analyses vex Hamlet as much as their meddling. When they presume to diagnose his malady, the courtiers actually reveal more about themselves than about Hamlet—something we as readers and viewers might well bear in mind. Rosencrantz and Guildenstern think in political terms, reflecting their own ambitious natures, and Hamlet takes mordant delight in leading them on. "Sir, I lack advancement," he mockingly answers Rosencrantz's questioning as to the cause of his distemper. Rosencrantz is immediately taken in: "How can that be, when you have the voice of the King himself for your succession in Denmark?" (3.2.338–341). Actually, Hamlet does hold a grudge against Claudius for having "Popped in between th' election and my hopes" (5.2.65), using the Danish custom of "election" by the chief lords of the realm to deprive young Hamlet of the succession that would normally have been his. Nevertheless, it is a gross oversimplification to suppose that political frustration is the key to Hamlet's sorrow, and to speculate thus is presumptuous. "Why, look you now, how unworthy a thing you would make of me!" Hamlet protests to Rosencrantz and Guildenstern. "You would play upon me, you would seem to know my stops, you would pluck out the heart of my mystery" (3.2.362–365). An even worse offender in the distortion of complex truth is Polonius, whose facile diagnosis of lovesickness appears to have been inspired by recollections of Polonius' own far-off youth. ("Truly in my youth I suffered much extremity for love, very near this,"

2.2.189–191). Polonius' fatuous complacency in his own powers of analysis—"If circumstances lead me, I will find / Where truth is hid, though it were hid indeed / Within the center" (2.2.157–159)—reads like a parody of Hamlet's struggle to discover what is true and what is not.

Thus, although Hamlet may seem to react with excessive bitterness toward those who are set to watch over him, the corruption he decries in Denmark is both real and universal. "The time is out of joint," he laments. "O cursèd spite / That ever I was born to set it right!" (1.5.197–198). How is he to proceed in setting things right? Ever since the nineteenth century, it has been fashionable to discover reasons for Hamlet's delaying his revenge. The basic Romantic approach is to find a defect, or tragic flaw, in Hamlet himself. In Coleridge's words, Hamlet suffers from "an overbalance in the contemplative faculty" and is "one who vacillates from sensibility and procrastinates from thought, and loses the power of action in the energy of resolve." More recent psychological critics, such as Freud's disciple Ernest Jones, still seek answers to the Romantics' question by explaining Hamlet's failure of will. In Jones' interpretation, Hamlet is the victim of an Oedipal trauma: he has longed unconsciously to possess his mother and for that very reason cannot bring himself to punish the hated uncle who has supplanted him in his incestuous and forbidden desire. Such interpretations suggest, among other things, that Hamlet continues to serve as a mirror in which analysts who would pluck out the heart of his mystery see an image of their own concerns—just as Rosencrantz and Guildenstern read politics, and Polonius' lovesickness, into Hamlet's distress.

We can ask, however, not only whether the explanations for Hamlet's supposed delay are valid but also whether the question they seek to answer is itself valid. Is the delay unnecessary or excessive? The question did not even arise until the nineteenth century. Earlier audiences were evidently satisfied that Hamlet must test the Ghost's credibility, since apparitions can tell half-truths to deceive people, and that, once Hamlet has confirmed the Ghost's word, he proceeds as resolutely as his canny adversary allows. More recent criticism, perhaps reflecting a modern absorption in existentialist philosophy, has proposed that Hamlet's dilemma is a matter, not of personal failure, but of the absurdity of action itself in a corrupt world. Does what Hamlet is asked to do make any sense, given the bestial nature of humanity and the impossibility of knowing what is right? In part, it is a matter of style: Claudius' Denmark is crassly vulgar, and to combat this vulgarity on its own terms seems to require the sort of bad histrionics Hamlet derides in actors who mouth their lines or tear a passion to tatters. Hamlet's dilemma of action can best be studied in the play by comparing him with various characters who are obliged to act in situations similar to his own and who respond in meaningfully different ways.

Three young men—Hamlet, Laertes, and Fortinbras—are called upon to avenge their fathers' violent deaths.

Ophelia, too, has lost a father by violent means, and her madness and death are another kind of reaction to such a loss. The responses of Laertes and Fortinbras offer rich parallels to Hamlet, in both cases implying the futility of positive and forceful action. Laertes thinks he has received an unambiguous mandate to take revenge, since Hamlet has undoubtedly slain Polonius and helped to deprive Ophelia of her sanity. Accordingly, Laertes comes back to Denmark in a fury, stirring the rabble with his demagoguery and spouting Senecan rant about dismissing conscience "to the profoundest pit" in his quest for vengeance (4.5.135). When Claudius asks what Laertes would do to Hamlet "To show yourself in deed your father's son / More than in words," Laertes fires back: "To cut his throat i' the church" (4.7.126–127). This resolution is understandable. The pity is, however, that Laertes has only superficially identified the murderer in the case. He is too easily deceived by Claudius, because he has jumped to easy and fallacious conclusions, and so is doomed to become a pawn in Claudius' sly maneuverings. Too late he sees his error and must die for it, begging and receiving Hamlet's forgiveness. Before we accuse Hamlet of thinking too deliberately before acting, we must consider that Laertes does not think enough.

Fortinbras of Norway, as his name implies ("strong in arms"), is one who believes in decisive action. At the beginning of the play, we learn that his father has been slain in battle by old Hamlet and that Fortinbras has collected an army to win back by force the territory fairly won by the Danes in that encounter. Like Hamlet, young Fortinbras does not succeed his father to the throne but must now contend with an uncle-king. When this uncle, at Claudius' instigation, forbids Fortinbras to march against the Danes and rewards him for his restraint with a huge annual income and a commission to fight the Poles instead, Fortinbras sagaciously welcomes the new opportunity. He pockets the money, marches against Poland, and waits for occasion to deliver Denmark as well into his hands. Clearly this is more of a success story than that of Laertes, and Hamlet does, after all, give his blessing to the "election" of Fortinbras to the Danish throne. Fortinbras is the man of the hour, the representative of a restored political stability. Yet Hamlet's admiration for this man on horseback is qualified by a profound reservation. The spectacle of Fortinbras marching against Poland "to gain a little patch of ground / That hath in it no profit but the name" prompts Hamlet to berate himself for inaction, but he cannot ignore the absurdity of the effort. "Two thousand souls and twenty thousand ducats / Will not debate the question of this straw." The soldiers will risk their very lives "Even for an eggshell" (4.4.19–54). It is only one step from this view of the vanity of ambitious striving to the speculation that great Caesar or Alexander, dead and turned to dust, may one day produce the loam or clay with which to stop the bunghole of a beer barrel. Fortinbras epitomizes the ongoing political order after Hamlet's death, but is that order of any consequence to us after we have imagined with Hamlet the futility of most human endeavor?

To ask such a question is to seek passive or self-abnegating answers to the riddle of life, and Hamlet is attuned to such inquiries. Even before he learns of his father's murder, he contemplates suicide, wishing "that the Everlasting had not fixed / His canon 'gainst self-slaughter" (1.2.131–132). As with the alternative of action, other characters serve as foils to Hamlet, revealing both the attractions and perils of withdrawal. Ophelia is destroyed by meekly acquiescing in others' desires. Whether she commits suicide is uncertain, but the very possibility reminds us that Hamlet has twice considered and reluctantly rejected this despairing path as forbidden by Christian teaching—the second such occasion being his "To be, or not to be" soliloquy in 3.1. He has also playacted at the madness to which Ophelia succumbs. Gertrude identifies herself with Ophelia and like her has surrendered her will to male aggressiveness. We suspect she knows little of the actual murder (see 3.4.31) but dares not think how deeply she may be implicated. Although her death is evidently not a suicide (see 5.2.291–297), it is passive and expiatory.

A more attractive alternative to decisive action for Hamlet is acting in the theater, and he is full of exuberant advice to the visiting players. The play they perform before Claudius at Hamlet's request and with some lines added by him—a play consciously archaic in style—offers to the Danish court a kind of heightened reflection of itself, a homiletic artifact, rendering in conventional terms the taut anxieties and terrors of murder for the sake of noble passion. Structurally, the play within the play becomes not an escape for Hamlet into inaction but rather the point on which the whole drama pivots and the scene in which contemplation of past events is largely replaced with stirrings toward action. When Lucianus in the Mousetrap play turns out to be nephew rather than brother to the dead king, the audience finds itself face to face, not with history, but with prophecy. We are not surprised when, in his conversations with the players, Hamlet openly professes his admiration for the way in which art holds "the mirror up to nature, to show virtue her own feature, scorn her own image, and the very age and body of the time his form and pressure" (3.2.22–24). Hamlet admires the dramatist's ability to transmute raw human feeling into tragic art, depicting and ordering reality as Shakespeare's play of Hamlet does for us. Yet playacting can also be, Hamlet recognizes, a self-indulgent escape for him, a way of unpacking his heart with words and of verbalizing his situation without doing something to remedy it. Acting and talking remind him too much of Polonius, who was an actor in his youth and who continues to be, like Hamlet, an inveterate punster.

Of the passive responses in the play, the stoicism of Horatio is by far the most attractive to Hamlet. "More an antique Roman than a Dane" (5.2.343), Horatio is, as Hamlet praises him, immune to flattering or to opportunities for cheap self-advancement. He is "As one, in suffering all, that suffers nothing, / A man that Fortune's buffets and rewards / Hast ta'en with equal thanks" (3.2.65–67). Such a person has a sure defense against the worst that life can offer. Hamlet can trust and love Horatio as he can no one else. Yet even here there are limits, for Horatio's skeptical and Roman philosophy cuts him off from a Christian and metaphysical overview. "There are more things in heaven and earth, Horatio, / Than are dreamt of in your philosophy" (1.5.175–176). After they have beheld together the skulls of Yorick's graveyard, Horatio seemingly does not share with Hamlet the exulting Christian perception that, although human life is indeed vain, Providence will reveal a pattern transcending human sorrow.

Hamlet's path must lie somewhere between the rash suddenness of Laertes or the canny resoluteness of Fortinbras on the one hand, and the passivity of Ophelia or Gertrude and the stoic resignation of Horatio on the other. At first he alternates between action and inaction, finding neither satisfactory. The Ghost has commanded Hamlet to revenge but has not explained how this is to be done; indeed, Gertrude is to be left passively to heaven and her conscience. If this method will suffice for her (and Christian wisdom taught that such a purgation was as thorough as it was sure), why not for Claudius? If Claudius must be killed, should it be while he is at his sin rather than at his prayers? The play is full of questions, stemming chiefly from the enigmatic commands of the Ghost. "Say, why is this? Wherefore? What should we do?" (1.4.57). Hamlet is not incapable of action. He shows unusual strength and cunning on the pirate ship, in his duel with Laertes ("I shall win at the odds"; 5.2.209–210), and especially in his slaying of Polonius—an action hardly characterized by "thinking too precisely on th' event" (4.4.42). Here is forthright action of the sort Laertes espouses. Yet, when the corpse behind his mother's arras turns out to be Polonius rather than Claudius, Hamlet concludes from the mistake that he has offended heaven. Even if Polonius deserves what he got, Hamlet believes he has made himself into a cruel "scourge" of Providence who must himself suffer retribution as well as deal it out. Swift action has not accomplished what the Ghost commanded.

The Ghost does not appear to speak for Providence in any case. His message is of revenge, a pagan concept deeply embedded in most societies but at odds with Christian teaching. His wish that Claudius be sent to hell and that Gertrude be more gently treated might, in fact, be the judgment of an impartial deity but here comes wrapped in the passionate involvement of a murdered man's restless spirit. This is not to say that Hamlet is being tempted to perform a damnable act, as he fears is possible, but that the Ghost's command cannot readily be reconciled with a complex and balanced view of justice. If Hamlet were to spring on Claudius in the fullness of his vice and cut his throat, we would pronounce Hamlet a murderer. What Hamlet believes he has learned instead is that he must become the instrument of Providence according to *its* plans, not his own. After his return from England, he senses triumphantly that all will be for the best if he allows an unseen power to decide the time and place for his final act. Under these conditions, rash action will be right. "Rashly, / And praised be rashness for it—let us know / Our indiscretion sometimes serves us well / When our deep plots do pall, and that should learn us / There's a divinity that shapes our ends, / Rough-hew them how we will" (5.2.6–11). Passivity, too, is now a proper course, for Hamlet puts himself wholly at the disposal of Providence. What had seemed so impossible when Hamlet tried to formulate his own design proves elementary once he trusts to a divine justice in which he now firmly believes. Rashness and passivity are perfectly fused. Hamlet is revenged without having to commit premeditated murder and is relieved of his painful existence without having to commit suicide.

The circumstances of *Hamlet's* catastrophe do indeed seem to accomplish all that Hamlet desires, by a route so circuitous that no one could ever have foreseen or devised it. Polonius' death, as it turns out, was instrumental after all, for it led to Laertes' angry return to Denmark and the challenge to a duel. Every seemingly unrelated event has its place; "There is special providence in the fall of a sparrow" (5.2.217–218). Repeatedly, the characters stress the role of seeming accident leading to just retribution. Even Horatio, for whom the events of the play suggest a pattern of randomness and violence, of "accidental judgments" and "casual slaughters," can see at last, "in this upshot, purposes mistook / Fall'n on th' inventors' heads" (5.2.384–387). In a similar vein, Laertes confesses himself "a woodcock to mine own springe" (line 309). As Hamlet had said earlier, of Rosencrantz and Guildenstern, " 'tis the sport to have the enginer / Hoist with his own petard" (3.4.213–214). Thus, too, Claudius' poisoned cup, intended for Hamlet, kills the Queen for whom Claudius had done such evil in order to acquire her and the throne. The destiny of evil in this play is to overreach itself.

In its final resolution, *Hamlet* incorporates a broader conception of justice than its revenge formula seemed at first to make possible. Yet, in its origins, *Hamlet* is a revenge story, and these traditions have left some residual savagery in the play. In the *Historia Danica* of Saxo Grammaticus, 1180–1208, and in the rather free translation of Saxo into French by François de Belleforest, *Histoires Tragiques* (1576), Hamlet is cunning and bloodily resolute throughout. He kills an eavesdropper without a qualm during the interview with his mother and exchanges letters on his way to England with characteristic shrewdness. Ultimately, he returns to Denmark, sets fire to his uncle's hall, slays its courtly inhabitants, and claims his rightful throne from a grateful people. The Ghost, absent in this account, may well have been supplied by Thomas Kyd, author of *The Spanish Tragedy* (c.

1587) and seemingly of a lost *Hamlet* play in existence by 1589. *The Spanish Tragedy* bears many resemblances to our *Hamlet* and suggests what the lost *Hamlet* may well have contained: a sensational murder, a Senecan Ghost demanding revenge, the avenger hampered by court intrigue, his resort to a feigned madness, and his difficulty in authenticating the ghostly vision. A German version of *Hamlet*, called *Der bestrafte Brudermord* (1710), based seemingly on the older *Hamlet*, includes such details as the play within the play, the sparing of the King at his prayers in order to damn his soul, Ophelia's madness, the fencing match with poisoned swords and poisoned drink, and the final catastrophe of vengeance and death. Similarly, the early pirated First Quarto of *Hamlet* (1603) offers some passages seemingly based on the older play by Kyd.

Although this evidence suggests that Shakespeare received most of the material for the plot intact, his transformation of that material was nonetheless immeasurable. To be sure, Kyd's *The Spanish Tragedy* contains many rhetorical passages on the inadequacy of human justice, but the overall effect is still sensational and the outcome is a triumph for the pagan spirit of revenge. So, too, with the many revenge plays of the 1590s and 1600s that Kyd's dramatic genius had inspired, including Shakespeare's own *Titus Andronicus* (c. 1589–1592). *Hamlet*, written in about 1599–1601 (it is not mentioned by Frances Meres in his *Palladis Tamia: Wit's Treasury*, in 1598, and was entered in the Stationers' Register, the official record book of the London Company of Stationers [booksellers and printers], in 1602), is unparalleled in its philosophical richness. Its ending is truly cathartic, for Hamlet dies, not as a bloodied avenger, but as one who has affirmed the tragic dignity of the human race. His courage and faith, maintained in the face of great odds, atone for the dismal corruption in which Denmark has festered. His resolutely honest inquiries have taken him beyond the revulsion and doubt that express so eloquently, among other matters, the fearful response of Shakespeare's own generation to a seeming breakdown of established political, theological, and cosmological beliefs. Hamlet finally perceives that "if it be not now, yet it will come," and that "The readiness is all" (5.2.219–220). This discovery, this revelation of necessity and meaning in Hamlet's great reversal of fortune, enables him to confront the tragic circumstance of his life with understanding and heroism and to demonstrate the triumph of the human spirit even in the moment of his catastrophe.

Such an assertion of the individual will does not lessen the tragic waste with which *Hamlet* ends. Hamlet is dead, and the great promise of his life is forever lost. Few others have survived. Justice has seemingly been fulfilled in the deaths of Claudius, Gertrude, Rosencrantz and Guildenstern, Polonius, Laertes, and perhaps even Ophelia, but in a wild and extravagant way, as though Justice herself, more vengeful than providential, were unceasingly hungry for victims.

Hamlet, the minister of that justice, has likewise grown indifferent to the spilling of blood, even if he submits himself at last to the will of a force he recognizes as providential. Denmark faces the kind of political uncertainty with which the play began. However much Hamlet may admire Fortinbras' resolution, the prince of Norway seems an alien choice for Denmark—even an ironic one. Horatio sees so little point in outliving the catastrophe of this play that he would choose death, were it not that he must draw his breath in pain to ensure that Hamlet's story is truly told. Still, that truth has been rescued from oblivion. Amid the ruin of the final scene, we share the artist's vision, through which we struggle to interpret and give order to the tragedy that proves inseparable from human existence.

Hamlet, Prince of Denmark

[*Dramatis Personae*

GHOST *of Hamlet, the former King of Denmark*
CLAUDIUS, *King of Denmark, the former King's brother*
GERTRUDE, *Queen of Denmark, widow of the former King and now wife of Claudius*
HAMLET, *Prince of Denmark, son of the late King and of Gertrude*

POLONIUS, *councillor to the King*
LAERTES, *his son*
OPHELIA, *his daughter*
REYNALDO, *his servant*

HORATIO, *Hamlet's friend and fellow student*

VOLTIMAND,
CORNELIUS,
ROSENCRANTZ,
GUILDENSTERN, } *members of the Danish court*
OSRIC,
A GENTLEMAN,
A LORD,

BERNARDO,
FRANCISCO, } *officers and soldiers on watch*
MARCELLUS,

FORTINBRAS, *Prince of Norway*
CAPTAIN *in his army*

Three or Four PLAYERS, *taking the roles of* PROLOGUE, PLAYER KING, PLAYER QUEEN, *and* LUCIANUS
Two MESSENGERS
FIRST SAILOR
Two CLOWNS, *a gravedigger and his companion*
PRIEST
FIRST AMBASSADOR *from England*

Lords, Soldiers, Attendants, Guards, other Players, Followers of Laertes, other Sailors, another Ambassador or Ambassadors from England

SCENE: *Denmark*]

1.1   *Enter Bernardo and Francisco, two sentinels,*
[meeting].

BERNARDO   Who's there?

FRANCISCO
Nay, answer me. Stand and unfold yourself.   2

BERNARDO   Long live the King!

FRANCISCO   Bernardo?

BERNARDO   He.

FRANCISCO
You come most carefully upon your hour.

BERNARDO
'Tis now struck twelve. Get thee to bed, Francisco.

FRANCISCO
For this relief much thanks. 'Tis bitter cold,
And I am sick at heart.

BERNARDO   Have you had quiet guard?

FRANCISCO   Not a mouse stirring.

BERNARDO   Well, good night.
If you do meet Horatio and Marcellus,
The rivals of my watch, bid them make haste.   14

Enter Horatio and Marcellus.

FRANCISCO
I think I hear them.—Stand, ho! Who is there?

HORATIO   Friends to this ground.   16

MARCELLUS   And liegemen to the Dane.   17

FRANCISCO   Give you good night.   18

MARCELLUS
O, farewell, honest soldier. Who hath relieved you?

FRANCISCO
Bernardo hath my place. Give you good night.
Exit Francisco.

MARCELLUS   Holla! Bernardo!

BERNARDO   Say, what, is Horatio there?

HORATIO   A piece of him.

BERNARDO
Welcome, Horatio. Welcome, good Marcellus.

HORATIO
What, has this thing appeared again tonight?

BERNARDO   I have seen nothing.

MARCELLUS
Horatio says 'tis but our fantasy,   27
And will not let belief take hold of him
Touching this dreaded sight twice seen of us.
Therefore I have entreated him along   30
With us to watch the minutes of this night,   31
That if again this apparition come
He may approve our eyes and speak to it.   33

HORATIO
Tush, tush, 'twill not appear.

BERNARDO   Sit down awhile,
And let us once again assail your ears,

That are so fortified against our story,
What we have two nights seen.

HORATIO   Well, sit we down,   37
And let us hear Bernardo speak of this.

BERNARDO   Last night of all,   39
When yond same star that's westward from the pole   40
Had made his course t' illume that part of heaven   41
Where now it burns, Marcellus and myself,
The bell then beating one—

Enter Ghost.

MARCELLUS
Peace, break thee off! Look where it comes again!

BERNARDO
In the same figure like the King that's dead.

MARCELLUS
Thou art a scholar. Speak to it, Horatio.   46

BERNARDO
Looks 'a not like the King? Mark it, Horatio.   47

HORATIO
Most like. It harrows me with fear and wonder.

BERNARDO
It would be spoke to.

MARCELLUS   Speak to it, Horatio.   49

HORATIO
What art thou that usurp'st this time of night,   50
Together with that fair and warlike form
In which the majesty of buried Denmark   52
Did sometime march? By heaven, I charge thee,
speak!   53

MARCELLUS
It is offended.

BERNARDO   See, it stalks away.

HORATIO
Stay! Speak, speak! I charge thee, speak!   *Exit Ghost.*

MARCELLUS   'Tis gone and will not answer.

BERNARDO
How now, Horatio? You tremble and look pale.
Is not this something more than fantasy?
What think you on 't?   59

HORATIO
Before my God, I might not this believe
Without the sensible and true avouch   61
Of mine own eyes.

MARCELLUS   Is it not like the King?

HORATIO   As thou art to thyself.
Such was the very armor he had on
When he the ambitious Norway combated.   65
So frowned he once when, in an angry parle,   66
He smote the sledded Polacks on the ice.   67
'Tis strange.

1.1 Location: Elsinore castle. A guard platform.
2 me (Francisco emphasizes that *he* is the sentry currently on watch.)
unfold yourself reveal your identity   **14 rivals** partners   **16 ground**
country, land   **17 liegemen to the Dane** men sworn to serve the Danish king   **18 Give** i.e., may God give   **27 fantasy** imagination
30 along to come along   **31 watch** keep watch during   **33 approve**
corroborate

37 What with what   **39 Last . . . all** i.e., this *very* last night. (Emphatic.)   **40 pole** polestar, north star   **41 his** its.   **illume** illuminate
46 scholar one learned enough to know how to question a ghost
properly   **47 'a** he   **49 It . . . to** (It was commonly believed that a
ghost could not speak until spoken to.)   **50 usurp'st** wrongfully takes
over   **52 buried Denmark** the buried King of Denmark   **53 sometime**
formerly   **59 on 't** of it   **61 sensible** confirmed by the senses.
avouch warrant, evidence   **65 Norway** King of Norway   **66 parle**
parley   **67 sledded** traveling on sleds.   **Polacks** Poles

MARCELLUS

   Thus twice before, and jump at this dead hour,   69
   With martial stalk hath he gone by our watch.   70

HORATIO

   In what particular thought to work I know not,   71
   But in the gross and scope of mine opinion   72
   This bodes some strange eruption to our state.

MARCELLUS

   Good now, sit down, and tell me, he that knows,   74
   Why this same strict and most observant watch
   So nightly toils the subject of the land,   76
   And why such daily cast of brazen cannon   77
   And foreign mart for implements of war,   78
   Why such impress of shipwrights, whose sore task   79
   Does not divide the Sunday from the week.
   What might be toward, that this sweaty haste   81
   Doth make the night joint-laborer with the day?
   Who is 't that can inform me?

HORATIO   That can I;

   At least, the whisper goes so. Our last king,
   Whose image even but now appeared to us,
   Was, as you know, by Fortinbras of Norway,
   Thereto pricked on by a most emulate pride,   87
   Dared to the combat; in which our valiant Hamlet—
   For so this side of our known world esteemed him— 89
   Did slay this Fortinbras; who by a sealed compact   90
   Well ratified by law and heraldry
   Did forfeit, with his life, all those his lands
   Which he stood seized of, to the conqueror;   93
   Against the which a moiety competent   94
   Was gagèd by our king, which had returned   95
   To the inheritance of Fortinbras   96
   Had he been vanquisher, as, by the same cov'nant   97
   And carriage of the article designed,   98
   His fell to Hamlet. Now, sir, young Fortinbras,
   Of unimprovèd mettle hot and full,   100
   Hath in the skirts of Norway here and there   101
   Sharked up a list of lawless resolutes   102
   For food and diet to some enterprise   103
   That hath a stomach in 't, which is no other—   104
   As it doth well appear unto our state—
   But to recover of us, by strong hand
   And terms compulsatory, those foresaid lands

So by his father lost. And this, I take it,
Is the main motive of our preparations,
The source of this our watch, and the chief head   110
Of this posthaste and rummage in the land.   111

BERNARDO

   I think it be no other but e'en so.
   Well may it sort that this portentous figure   113
   Comes armèd through our watch so like the King
   That was and is the question of these wars.   115

HORATIO

   A mote it is to trouble the mind's eye.   116
   In the most high and palmy state of Rome,   117
   A little ere the mightiest Julius fell,
   The graves stood tenantless, and the sheeted dead   119
   Did squeak and gibber in the Roman streets;
   As stars with trains of fire and dews of blood,   121
   Disasters in the sun; and the moist star   122
   Upon whose influence Neptune's empire stands   123
   Was sick almost to doomsday with eclipse.   124
   And even the like precurse of feared events,   125
   As harbingers preceding still the fates   126
   And prologue to the omen coming on,   127
   Have heaven and earth together demonstrated
   Unto our climatures and countrymen.   129

         Enter Ghost.

But soft, behold! Lo, where it comes again!   130
I'll cross it, though it blast me. (*It spreads his arms.*)
   Stay, illusion!   131
If thou hast any sound or use of voice,
Speak to me!
If there be any good thing to be done
That may to thee do ease and grace to me,
Speak to me!
If thou art privy to thy country's fate,   137
Which, happily, foreknowing may avoid,   138
O, speak!
Or if thou hast uphoarded in thy life
Extorted treasure in the womb of earth,
For which, they say, you spirits oft walk in death,
Speak of it! (*The cock crows.*) Stay and speak!—
   Stop it, Marcellus.

MARCELLUS

   Shall I strike at it with my partisan?   144

HORATIO   Do, if it will not stand.   [*They strike at it.*]

BERNARDO   'Tis here!

HORATIO   'Tis here!   [*Exit Ghost.*]

---

69 jump exactly   **70 stalk** stride   **71 to work** i.e., to collect my thoughts and try to understand this   **72 gross and scope** general drift **74 Good now** (An expression denoting entreaty or expostulation.) **76 toils** causes to toil.   **subject** subjects   **77 cast** casting   **78 mart** buying and selling   **79 impress** impressment, conscription   **81 toward** in preparation   **87 Thereto . . . pride** (Refers to old Fortinbras, not the Danish King.)   **pricked on** incited.   **emulate** emulous, ambitious   **89 this . . . world** i.e., all Europe, the Western world **90 sealed** certified, confirmed   **93 seized** possessed   **94 Against the** in return for.   **moiety competent** corresponding portion   **95 gagèd** engaged, pledged.   **had returned** would have passed   **96 inheritance** possession   **97 cov'nant** i.e., the *sealed compact* of line 90   **98 carriage . . . designed** carrying out of the article or clause drawn up to cover the point   **100 unimprovèd mettle** untried, undisciplined spirits **101 skirts** outlying regions, outskirts   **102 Sharked up** gathered up, as a shark takes fish.   **list** i.e., troop.   **resolutes** desperadoes   **103 For food and diet** i.e., they are to serve as *food*, or "means," *to some enterprise*; also they serve in return for the rations they get   **104 stomach** (1) a spirit of daring (2) an appetite that is fed by the *lawless resolutes*

110 head source   **111 rummage** bustle, commotion   **113 sort** suit **115 question** focus of contention   **116 mote** speck of dust **117 palmy** flourishing   **119 sheeted** shrouded   **121 As** (This abrupt transition suggests that matter is possibly omitted between lines 120 and 121.)   **trains** trails   **122 Disasters** unfavorable signs or aspects. **moist star** i.e., moon, governing tides   **123 Neptune** god of the sea. **stands** depends   **124 sick . . . doomsday** (See Matthew 24:29 and Revelation 6:12.)   **125 precurse** heralding, foreshadowing   **126 harbingers** forerunners.   **still** continually   **127 omen** calamitous event **129 climatures** regions   **130 soft** i.e., enough, break off   **131 cross** stand in its path, confront.   **blast** wither, strike with a curse.   **s.d. his** its   **137 privy to** in on the secret of   **138 happily** haply, perchance **144 partisan** long-handled spear

MARCELLUS 'Tis gone.
We do it wrong, being so majestical,
To offer it the show of violence,
For it is as the air invulnerable,
And our vain blows malicious mockery.

BERNARDO
It was about to speak when the cock crew.

HORATIO
And then it started like a guilty thing
Upon a fearful summons. I have heard
The cock, that is the trumpet to the morn,   156
Doth with his lofty and shrill-sounding throat
Awake the god of day, and at his warning,
Whether in sea or fire, in earth or air,
Th' extravagant and erring spirit hies   160
To his confine; and of the truth herein
This present object made probation.   162

MARCELLUS
It faded on the crowing of the cock.
Some say that ever 'gainst that season comes   164
Wherein our Savior's birth is celebrated,
This bird of dawning singeth all night long,
And then, they say, no spirit dare stir abroad;
The nights are wholesome, then no planets strike,   168
No fairy takes, nor witch hath power to charm,   169
So hallowed and so gracious is that time.   170

HORATIO
So have I heard and do in part believe it.
But, look, the morn in russet mantle clad
Walks o'er the dew of yon high eastward hill.
Break we our watch up, and by my advice
Let us impart what we have seen tonight
Unto young Hamlet; for upon my life,
This spirit, dumb to us, will speak to him.
Do you consent we shall acquaint him with it,
As needful in our loves, fitting our duty?

MARCELLUS
Let's do 't, I pray, and I this morning know
Where we shall find him most conveniently.
                                          Exeunt.

❖

1.2 *Flourish. Enter Claudius, King of Denmark,*
Gertrude the Queen, [the] Council, as Polonius
and his son Laertes, Hamlet, cum aliis [including
Voltimand and Cornelius].

KING
Though yet of Hamlet our dear brother's death   1
The memory be green, and that it us befitted
To bear our hearts in grief and our whole kingdom
To be contracted in one brow of woe,
Yet so far hath discretion fought with nature

That we with wisest sorrow think on him
Together with remembrance of ourselves.
Therefore our sometime sister, now our queen,   8
Th' imperial jointress to this warlike state,   9
Have we, as 'twere with a defeated joy—
With an auspicious and a dropping eye,   11
With mirth in funeral and with dirge in marriage,
In equal scale weighing delight and dole—   13
Taken to wife. Nor have we herein barred
Your better wisdoms, which have freely gone
With this affair along. For all, our thanks.
Now follows that you know young Fortinbras,   17
Holding a weak supposal of our worth,   18
Or thinking by our late dear brother's death
Our state to be disjoint and out of frame,
Co-leaguèd with this dream of his advantage,   21
He hath not failed to pester us with message
Importing the surrender of those lands   23
Lost by his father, with all bonds of law,   24
To our most valiant brother. So much for him.
Now for ourself and for this time of meeting.
Thus much the business is: we have here writ
To Norway, uncle of young Fortinbras—
Who, impotent and bed-rid, scarcely hears   29
Of this his nephew's purpose—to suppress
His further gait herein, in that the levies,   31
The lists, and full proportions are all made   32
Out of his subject; and we here dispatch   33
You, good Cornelius, and you, Voltimand,
For bearers of this greeting to old Norway,
Giving to you no further personal power
To business with the King more than the scope
Of these dilated articles allow.   [*He gives a paper.*] 38
Farewell, and let your haste commend your duty.   39

CORNELIUS, VOLTIMAND
In that, and all things, will we show our duty.

KING
We doubt it nothing. Heartily farewell.   41
                    [*Exeunt Voltimand and Cornelius.*]
And now, Laertes, what's the news with you?
You told us of some suit; what is 't, Laertes?
You cannot speak of reason to the Dane   44
And lose your voice. What wouldst thou beg,
    Laertes,   45
That shall not be my offer, not thy asking?
The head is not more native to the heart,   47
The hand more instrumental to the mouth,   48
Than is the throne of Denmark to thy father.

---

156 trumpet trumpeter **160 extravagant and erring** wandering beyond bounds. (The words have similar meaning.) **hies** hastens **162 probation** proof **164 'gainst** just before **168 strike** destroy by evil influence **169 takes** bewitches **170 gracious** full of grace
1.2. Location: The castle.
s.d. as i.e., such as, including. **cum aliis** with others **1 our** my. (The royal "we"; also in the following lines.)

8 sometime former **9 jointress** woman possessing property with her husband **11 With . . . eye** with one eye smiling and the other weeping **13 dole** grief **17 that you know** what you know already, that; or, that you be informed as follows **18 weak supposal** low estimate **21 Co-leaguèd with** joined to, allied with. **dream . . . advantage** illusory hope of having the advantage. (His only ally is this hope.) **23 Importing** pertaining to **24 bonds** contracts **29 impotent** helpless **31 His** i.e., Fortinbras'. **gait** proceeding **31–33 in that . . . subject** since the levying of troops and supplies is drawn entirely from the King of Norway's own subjects **38 dilated** set out at length **39 let . . . duty** let your swift obeying of orders, rather than mere words, express your dutifulness **41 nothing** not at all **44 the Dane** the Danish king **45 lose your voice** waste your speech **47 native** closely connected, related **48 instrumental** serviceable

What wouldst thou have, Laertes?

LAERTES   My dread lord,
Your leave and favor to return to France,   51
From whence though willingly I came to Denmark
To show my duty in your coronation,
Yet now I must confess, that duty done,
My thoughts and wishes bend again toward France
And bow them to your gracious leave and pardon.   56

KING
Have you your father's leave? What says Polonius?

POLONIUS
H'ath, my lord, wrung from me my slow leave   58
By laborsome petition, and at last
Upon his will I sealed my hard consent.   60
I do beseech you, give him leave to go.

KING
Take thy fair hour, Laertes. Time be thine,   62
And thy best graces spend it at thy will!   63
But now, my cousin Hamlet, and my son—   64

HAMLET
A little more than kin, and less than kind.   65

KING
How is it that the clouds still hang on you?

HAMLET
Not so, my lord. I am too much in the sun.   67

QUEEN
Good Hamlet, cast thy nighted color off,   68
And let thine eye look like a friend on Denmark.   69
Do not forever with thy vailèd lids   70
Seek for thy noble father in the dust.
Thou know'st 'tis common, all that lives must die,   72
Passing through nature to eternity.

HAMLET
Ay, madam, it is common.

QUEEN   If it be,
Why seems it so particular with thee?   75

HAMLET
Seems, madam? Nay, it is. I know not "seems."
'Tis not alone my inky cloak, good Mother,
Nor customary suits of solemn black,   78
Nor windy suspiration of forced breath,   79
No, nor the fruitful river in the eye,   80
Nor the dejected havior of the visage,   81
Together with all forms, moods, shapes of grief,   82

That can denote me truly. These indeed seem,
For they are actions that a man might play.
But I have that within which passes show;
These but the trappings and the suits of woe.

KING
'Tis sweet and commendable in your nature, Hamlet,
To give these mourning duties to your father.
But you must know your father lost a father,
That father lost, lost his, and the survivor bound
In filial obligation for some term
To do obsequious sorrow. But to persever   92
In obstinate condolement is a course   93
Of impious stubbornness. 'Tis unmanly grief.
It shows a will most incorrect to heaven,
A heart unfortified, a mind impatient,   96
An understanding simple and unschooled.   97
For what we know must be and is as common
As any the most vulgar thing to sense,   99
Why should we in our peevish opposition
Take it to heart? Fie, 'tis a fault to heaven,
A fault against the dead, a fault to nature,
To reason most absurd, whose common theme
Is death of fathers, and who still hath cried,   104
From the first corpse till he that died today,   105
"This must be so." We pray you, throw to earth
This unprevailing woe and think of us   107
As of a father; for let the world take note,
You are the most immediate to our throne,   109
And with no less nobility of love
Than that which dearest father bears his son
Do I impart toward you. For your intent   112
In going back to school in Wittenberg,   113
It is most retrograde to our desire,   114
And we beseech you bend you to remain   115
Here in the cheer and comfort of our eye,
Our chiefest courtier, cousin, and our son.

QUEEN
Let not thy mother lose her prayers, Hamlet.
I pray thee, stay with us, go not to Wittenberg.

HAMLET
I shall in all my best obey you, madam.   120

KING
Why, 'tis a loving and a fair reply.
Be as ourself in Denmark. Madam, come.
This gentle and unforced accord of Hamlet
Sits smiling to my heart, in grace whereof   124
No jocund health that Denmark drinks today   125
But the great cannon to the clouds shall tell,
And the King's rouse the heaven shall bruit again,   127

---

51 leave and favor kind permission **56 bow . . . pardon** entreatingly make a deep bow, asking your permission to depart **58 H'ath** he has **60 sealed** (as if sealing a legal document). **hard** reluctant **62 Take thy fair hour** enjoy your time of youth **63 And . . . will** and may your finest qualities guide the way you choose to spend your time **64 cousin** any kin not of the immediate family **65 A little . . . kind** i.e., closer than an ordinary nephew (since I am stepson), and yet more separated in natural feeling (with pun on *kind* meaning "affectionate" and "natural," "lawful." This line is often read as an aside, but it need not be. The King chooses perhaps not to respond to Hamlet's cryptic and bitter remark.) **67 the sun** i.e., the sunshine of the King's royal favor (with pun on *son*) **68 nighted color** (1) mourning garments of black (2) dark melancholy **69 Denmark** the King of Denmark **70 vailèd lids** lowered eyes **72 common** of universal occurrence. (But Hamlet plays on the sense of "vulgar" in line 74.) **75 particular** personal **78 customary** (1) socially conventional (2) habitual with me **79 suspiration** sighing **80 fruitful** abundant **81 havior** expression **82 moods** outward expression of feeling

92 obsequious suited to obsequies or funerals. **persever** persevere **93 condolement** sorrowing **96 unfortified** i.e., against adversity **97 simple** ignorant **99 As . . . sense** as the most ordinary experience **104 still** always **105 the first corpse** (Abel's) **107 unprevailing** unavailing, useless **109 most immediate** next in succession **112 impart toward** i.e., bestow my affection on. **For** as for **113 to school** i.e., to your studies. **Wittenberg** famous German university founded in 1502 **114 retrograde** contrary **115 bend you** incline yourself **120 in all my best** to the best of my ability **124 to** i.e., at. **grace** thanksgiving **125 jocund** merry **127 rouse** drinking of a draft of liquor. **bruit again** loudly echo

Respeaking earthly thunder. Come away. 128
Flourish. Exeunt all but Hamlet.

HAMLET
O, that this too too sullied flesh would melt, 129
Thaw, and resolve itself into a dew!
Or that the Everlasting had not fixed
His canon 'gainst self-slaughter! O God, God, 132
How weary, stale, flat, and unprofitable
Seem to me all the uses of this world! 134
Fie on 't, ah fie! 'Tis an unweeded garden
That grows to seed. Things rank and gross in nature
Possess it merely. That it should come to this! 137
But two months dead—nay, not so much, not two.
So excellent a king, that was to this 139
Hyperion to a satyr, so loving to my mother 140
That he might not beteem the winds of heaven 141
Visit her face too roughly. Heaven and earth,
Must I remember? Why, she would hang on him
As if increase of appetite had grown
By what it fed on, and yet within a month—
Let me not think on 't; frailty, thy name is
    woman!—
A little month, or ere those shoes were old 147
With which she followed my poor father's body,
Like Niobe, all tears, why she, even she— 149
O God, a beast, that wants discourse of reason, 150
Would have mourned longer—married with my
    uncle,
My father's brother, but no more like my father
Than I to Hercules. Within a month,
Ere yet the salt of most unrighteous tears
Had left the flushing in her gallèd eyes, 155
She married. O, most wicked speed, to post 156
With such dexterity to incestuous sheets! 157
It is not, nor it cannot come to good.
But break, my heart, for I must hold my tongue.

Enter Horatio, Marcellus, and Bernardo.

HORATIO
Hail to your lordship!
HAMLET   I am glad to see you well.
Horatio!—or I do forget myself.
HORATIO
The same, my lord, and your poor servant ever.
HAMLET
Sir, my good friend; I'll change that name with you. 163

128 **thunder** i.e., of trumpet and kettledrum, sounded when the King drinks; see 1.4.8–12 129 **sullied** defiled. (The early quartos read *sallied;* the Folio, *solid.*) 132 **canon** law 134 **all the uses** the whole routine 137 **merely** completely 139 **to** in comparison to 140 **Hyperion** Titan sun-god, father of Helios. **satyr** a lecherous creature of classical mythology, half-human but with a goat's legs, tail, ears, and horns 141 **beteem** allow 147 **or ere** even before 149 **Niobe** Tantalus' daughter, Queen of Thebes, who boasted that she had more sons and daughters than Leto; for this, Apollo and Artemis, children of Leto, slew her fourteen children. She was turned by Zeus into a stone that continually dropped tears. 150 **wants . . . reason** lacks the faculty of reason 155 **gallèd** irritated, inflamed 156 **post** hasten 157 **incestuous** (In Shakespeare's day, the marriage of a man like Claudius to his deceased brother's wife was considered incestuous.) 163 **change that name** i.e., give and receive reciprocally the name of "friend" (rather than talk of "servant")

And what make you from Wittenberg, Horatio? 164
Marcellus.
MARCELLUS   My good lord.
HAMLET
I am very glad to see you. [*To Bernardo.*] Good even,
    sir.—
But what in faith make you from Wittenberg?
HORATIO
A truant disposition, good my lord.
HAMLET
I would not hear your enemy say so,
Nor shall you do my ear that violence
To make it truster of your own report
Against yourself. I know you are no truant.
But what is your affair in Elsinore?
We'll teach you to drink deep ere you depart.
HORATIO
My lord, I came to see your father's funeral.
HAMLET
I prithee, do not mock me, fellow student;
I think it was to see my mother's wedding.
HORATIO
Indeed, my lord, it followed hard upon. 179
HAMLET
Thrift, thrift, Horatio! The funeral baked meats 180
Did coldly furnish forth the marriage tables. 181
Would I had met my dearest foe in heaven 182
Or ever I had seen that day, Horatio! 183
My father!—Methinks I see my father.
HORATIO
Where, my lord?
HAMLET   In my mind's eye, Horatio.
HORATIO
I saw him once. 'A was a goodly king. 186
HAMLET
'A was a man. Take him for all in all,
I shall not look upon his like again.
HORATIO
My lord, I think I saw him yesternight.
HAMLET   Saw? Who?
HORATIO   My lord, the King your father.
HAMLET   The King my father?
HORATIO
Season your admiration for a while 193
With an attent ear till I may deliver, 194
Upon the witness of these gentlemen,
This marvel to you.
HAMLET   For God's love, let me hear!
HORATIO
Two nights together had these gentlemen,
Marcellus and Bernardo, on their watch,
In the dead waste and middle of the night, 199
Been thus encountered. A figure like your father,
Armèd at point exactly, cap-à-pie, 201

164 **make you from** are you doing away from 179 **hard** close 180 **baked meats** meat pies 181 **coldly** i.e., as cold leftovers 182 **dearest** closest (and therefore deadliest) 183 **Or ever** before 186 **'A** he 193 **Season your admiration** restrain your astonishment 194 **attent** attentive 199 **dead waste** desolate stillness 201 **at point** correctly in every detail. **cap-à-pie** from head to foot

Appears before them, and with solemn march
Goes slow and stately by them. Thrice he walked
By their oppressed and fear-surprisèd eyes
Within his truncheon's length, whilst they, distilled   205
Almost to jelly with the act of fear,   206
Stand dumb and speak not to him. This to me
In dreadful secrecy impart they did,   208
And I with them the third night kept the watch,
Where, as they had delivered, both in time,
Form of the thing, each word made true and good,
The apparition comes. I knew your father;
These hands are not more like.

HAMLET   But where was this?

MARCELLUS
My lord, upon the platform where we watch.

HAMLET
Did you not speak to it?

HORATIO   My lord, I did,
But answer made it none. Yet once methought
It lifted up its head and did address   217
Itself to motion, like as it would speak;   218
But even then the morning cock crew loud,   219
And at the sound it shrunk in haste away
And vanished from our sight.

HAMLET   'Tis very strange.

HORATIO
As I do live, my honored lord, 'tis true,
And we did think it writ down in our duty
To let you know of it.

HAMLET
Indeed, indeed, sirs. But this troubles me.
Hold you the watch tonight?

ALL   We do, my lord.

HAMLET   Armed, say you?

ALL   Armed, my lord.

HAMLET   From top to toe?

ALL   My lord, from head to foot.

HAMLET   Then saw you not his face?

HORATIO
O, yes, my lord, he wore his beaver up.   232

HAMLET   What looked he, frowningly?   233

HORATIO
A countenance more in sorrow than in anger.

HAMLET   Pale or red?

HORATIO   Nay, very pale.

HAMLET   And fixed his eyes upon you?

HORATIO   Most constantly.

HAMLET   I would I had been there.

HORATIO   It would have much amazed you.

HAMLET   Very like, very like. Stayed it long?

HORATIO
While one with moderate haste might tell a hundred.   242

MARCELLUS, BERNARDO   Longer, longer.

HORATIO   Not when I saw 't.

HAMLET   His beard was grizzled—no?   245

HORATIO
It was, as I have seen it in his life,
A sable silvered.

HAMLET   I will watch tonight.   247
Perchance 'twill walk again.

HORATIO   I warrant it will.   248

HAMLET
If it assume my noble father's person,
I'll speak to it though hell itself should gape
And bid me hold my peace. I pray you all,
If you have hitherto concealed this sight,
Let it be tenable in your silence still,   253
And whatsoever else shall hap tonight,
Give it an understanding but no tongue.
I will requite your loves. So, fare you well.
Upon the platform twixt eleven and twelve
I'll visit you.

ALL   Our duty to your honor.

HAMLET
Your loves, as mine to you. Farewell.
                              Exeunt [all but Hamlet].
My father's spirit in arms! All is not well.
I doubt some foul play. Would the night were come!   261
Till then sit still, my soul. Foul deeds will rise,
Though all the earth o'erwhelm them, to men's eyes.
                                        Exit.

❧

1.3   *Enter Laertes and Ophelia, his sister.*

LAERTES
My necessaries are embarked. Farewell.
And, sister, as the winds give benefit
And convoy is assistant, do not sleep   3
But let me hear from you.

OPHELIA   Do you doubt that?

LAERTES
For Hamlet, and the trifling of his favor,
Hold it a fashion and a toy in blood,   6
A violet in the youth of primy nature,   7
Forward, not permanent, sweet, not lasting,   8
The perfume and suppliance of a minute—   9
No more.

OPHELIA   No more but so?

LAERTES   Think it no more.
For nature crescent does not grow alone   11
In thews and bulk, but as this temple waxes   12
The inward service of the mind and soul
Grows wide withal. Perhaps he loves you now,   14
And now no soil nor cautel doth besmirch   15
The virtue of his will; but you must fear,   16

---

247 **sable silvered** black mixed with white   248 **warrant** assure you
253 **tenable** held   261 **doubt** suspect
1.3. Location: Polonius' chambers.
3 **convoy is assistant** means of conveyance are available   6 **toy in
blood** passing amorous fancy   7 **primy** in its prime, springtime
8 **Forward** precocious   9 **suppliance** supply, filler   11 **crescent** growing, waxing   12 **thews** bodily strength.   **temple** i.e., body
14 **Grows wide withal** grows along with it   15 **soil** blemish.   **cautel**
deceit   16 **will** desire

---

205 **truncheon** officer's staff.   **distilled** dissolved   206 **act** action, operation   208 **dreadful** full of dread   217–218 **did . . . speak** began
to move as though it were about to speak   219 **even then** at that very
instant   232 **beaver** visor on the helmet   233 **What** how   242 **tell**
count   245 **grizzled** gray

His greatness weighed, his will is not his own.   17
For he himself is subject to his birth.
He may not, as unvalued persons do,
Carve for himself, for on his choice depends   20
The safety and health of this whole state,
And therefore must his choice be circumscribed
Unto the voice and yielding of that body   23
Whereof he is the head. Then if he says he
    loves you,
It fits your wisdom so far to believe it
As he in his particular act and place   26
May give his saying deed, which is no further
Than the main voice of Denmark goes withal.   28
Then weigh what loss your honor may sustain
If with too credent ear you list his songs,   30
Or lose your heart, or your chaste treasure open
To his unmastered importunity.
Fear it, Ophelia, fear it, my dear sister,
And keep you in the rear of your affection,   34
Out of the shot and danger of desire.
The chariest maid is prodigal enough   36
If she unmask her beauty to the moon.   37
Virtue itself scapes not calumnious strokes.
The canker galls the infants of the spring   39
Too oft before their buttons be disclosed,   40
And in the morn and liquid dew of youth   41
Contagious blastments are most imminent.   42
Be wary then; best safety lies in fear.
Youth to itself rebels, though none else near.   44

OPHELIA
I shall the effect of this good lesson keep
As watchman to my heart. But, good my brother,
Do not, as some ungracious pastors do,   47
Show me the steep and thorny way to heaven,
Whiles like a puffed and reckless libertine   49
Himself the primrose path of dalliance treads,
And recks not his own rede.

    Enter Polonius.

LAERTES   O, fear me not.   51
I stay too long. But here my father comes.
A double blessing is a double grace;   53
Occasion smiles upon a second leave.   54

POLONIUS
Yet here, Laertes? Aboard, aboard, for shame!
The wind sits in the shoulder of your sail,

And you are stayed for. There—my blessing with
    thee!
And these few precepts in thy memory
Look thou character. Give thy thoughts no tongue,   59
Nor any unproportioned thought his act.   60
Be thou familiar, but by no means vulgar.   61
Those friends thou hast, and their adoption tried,   62
Grapple them unto thy soul with hoops of steel,
But do not dull thy palm with entertainment   64
Of each new-hatched, unfledged courage. Beware   65
Of entrance to a quarrel, but being in,
Bear 't that th' opposèd may beware of thee.   67
Give every man thy ear, but few thy voice;
Take each man's censure, but reserve thy judgment.   69
Costly thy habit as thy purse can buy,   70
But not expressed in fancy; rich, not gaudy,   71
For the apparel oft proclaims the man,
And they in France of the best rank and station
Are of a most select and generous chief in that.   74
Neither a borrower nor a lender be,
For loan oft loses both itself and friend,
And borrowing dulleth edge of husbandry.   77
This above all: to thine own self be true,
And it must follow, as the night the day,
Thou canst not then be false to any man.
Farewell. My blessing season this in thee!   81

LAERTES
Most humbly do I take my leave, my lord.

POLONIUS
The time invests you. Go, your servants tend.   83

LAERTES
Farewell, Ophelia, and remember well
What I have said to you.

OPHELIA   'Tis in my memory locked,
And you yourself shall keep the key of it.

LAERTES   Farewell.   *Exit Laertes.*

POLONIUS
What is 't, Ophelia, he hath said to you?

OPHELIA
So please you, something touching the Lord Hamlet.

POLONIUS   Marry, well bethought.   91
'Tis told me he hath very oft of late
Given private time to you, and you yourself
Have of your audience been most free and bounteous.
If it be so—as so 'tis put on me,   95
And that in way of caution—I must tell you
You do not understand yourself so clearly
As it behooves my daughter and your honor.   98
What is between you? Give me up the truth.

---

17 **His greatness weighed** if you take into account his high position 20 **Carve** i.e., choose 23 **voice and yielding** assent, approval 26 **in . . . place** in his particular restricted circumstances 28 **main voice** general assent. **withal** along with 30 **credent** credulous. **list** listen to 34 **keep . . . affection** don't advance as far as your affection might lead you. (A military metaphor.) 36 **chariest** most scrupulously modest 37 **If she unmask** if she does no more than show her beauty. **moon** (Symbol of chastity.) 39 **canker galls** cankerworm destroys 40 **buttons** buds. **disclosed** opened 41 **liquid dew** i.e., time when dew is fresh and bright 42 **blastments** blights 44 **Youth . . . rebels** youth is inherently rebellious 47 **ungracious** ungodly 49 **puffed** bloated, or swollen with pride 51 **recks** heeds. **rede** counsel. **fear me not** don't worry on my account 53 **double** (Laertes has already bid his father good-bye.) 54 **Occasion . . . leave** happy is the circumstance that provides a second leave-taking. (The goddess Occasion, or Opportunity, smiles.)

59 **Look** be sure that. **character** inscribe 60 **unproportioned** badly calculated, intemperate. **his** its 61 **familiar** sociable. **vulgar** common 62 **and their adoption tried** and also their suitability for adoption as friends having been tested 64 **dull thy palm** i.e., shake hands so often as to make the gesture meaningless 65 **courage** young man of spirit 67 **Bear 't that** manage it so that 69 **censure** opinion, judgment 70 **habit** clothing 71 **fancy** excessive ornament, decadent fashion 74 **Are . . . that** are of a most refined and well-bred preeminence in choosing what to wear 77 **husbandry** thrift 81 **season** mature 83 **invests** besieges, presses upon. **tend** attend, wait 91 **Marry** i.e., by the Virgin Mary. (A mild oath.) 95 **put on** impressed on, told to 98 **behooves** befits

OPHELIA
He hath, my lord, of late made many tenders   100
Of his affection to me.

POLONIUS
Affection? Pooh! You speak like a green girl,
Unsifted in such perilous circumstance.   103
Do you believe his tenders, as you call them?

OPHELIA
I do not know, my lord, what I should think.

POLONIUS
Marry, I will teach you. Think yourself a baby
That you have ta'en these tenders for true pay
Which are not sterling. Tender yourself more dearly,   108
Or—not to crack the wind of the poor phrase,   109
Running it thus—you'll tender me a fool.   110

OPHELIA
My lord, he hath importuned me with love
In honorable fashion.

POLONIUS
Ay, fashion you may call it. Go to, go to.   113

OPHELIA
And hath given countenance to his speech, my lord,   114
With almost all the holy vows of heaven.

POLONIUS
Ay, springes to catch woodcocks. I do know,   116
When the blood burns, how prodigal the soul   117
Lends the tongue vows. These blazes, daughter,
Giving more light than heat, extinct in both
Even in their promise as it is a-making,   120
You must not take for fire. From this time
Be something scanter of your maiden presence.   122
Set your entreatments at a higher rate   123
Than a command to parle. For Lord Hamlet,   124
Believe so much in him that he is young,   125
And with a larger tether may he walk
Than may be given you. In few, Ophelia,   127
Do not believe his vows, for they are brokers,   128
Not of that dye which their investments show,   129
But mere implorators of unholy suits,   130
Breathing like sanctified and pious bawds,   131
The better to beguile. This is for all: 132
I would not, in plain terms, from this time forth
Have you so slander any moment leisure   134
As to give words or talk with the Lord Hamlet.

Look to 't, I charge you. Come your ways.   136
OPHELIA   I shall obey, my lord.   *Exeunt.*

❦

1.4   *Enter Hamlet, Horatio, and Marcellus.*

HAMLET
The air bites shrewdly; it is very cold.   1
HORATIO
It is a nipping and an eager air.   2
HAMLET
What hour now?
HORATIO   I think it lacks of twelve.   3
MARCELLUS
No, it is struck.
HORATIO   Indeed? I heard it not.
It then draws near the season   5
Wherein the spirit held his wont to walk.   6
A flourish of trumpets, and two pieces go off [within].
What does this mean, my lord?
HAMLET
The King doth wake tonight and takes his rouse,   8
Keeps wassail, and the swaggering upspring reels;   9
And as he drains his drafts of Rhenish down,   10
The kettledrum and trumpet thus bray out
The triumph of his pledge.
HORATIO   Is it a custom?   12
HAMLET   Ay, marry, is 't,
But to my mind, though I am native here
And to the manner born, it is a custom   15
More honored in the breach than the observance.   16
This heavy-headed revel east and west   17
Makes us traduced and taxed of other nations.   18
They clepe us drunkards, and with swinish phrase   19
Soil our addition; and indeed it takes   20
From our achievements, though performed at height,   21
The pith and marrow of our attribute.   22
So, oft it chances in particular men,
That for some vicious mole of nature in them,   24
As in their birth—wherein they are not guilty,
Since nature cannot choose his origin—   26
By their o'ergrowth of some complexion,   27
Oft breaking down the pales and forts of reason,   28

---

100 tenders offers   **103 Unsifted** i.e., untried   **108 sterling** legal currency.   **Tender** hold, look after, offer   **109 crack the wind** i.e., run it until it is broken-winded   **110 tender me a fool** (1) show yourself to me as a fool (2) show me up as a fool (3) present me with a grandchild. (*Fool* was a term of endearment for a child.)   **113 fashion** mere form, pretense.   **Go to** (An expression of impatience.)   **114 countenance** credit, confirmation   **116 springes** snares.   **woodcocks** birds easily caught; here used to connote gullibility   **117 prodigal** prodigally   **120 it** i.e., the promise   **122 something** somewhat   **123 entreatments** negotiations for surrender. (A military term.)   **124 parle** discuss terms with the enemy. (Polonius urges his daughter, in the metaphor of military language, not to meet with Hamlet and consider giving in to him merely because he requests an interview.)   **125 so . . . him** this much concerning him   **127 In few** briefly   **128 brokers** go-betweens, procurers   **129 dye** color or sort.   **investments** clothes. (The vows are not what they seem.)   **130 mere implorators** out and out solicitors   **131 Breathing** speaking   **132 for all** once for all, in sum   **134 slander** abuse, misuse.   **moment** moment's

136 Come your ways come along
1.4. Location: The guard platform.
1 shrewdly keenly, sharply   **2 eager** biting   **3 lacks of** is just short of   **5 season** time   **6 held his wont** was accustomed.   **s.d. pieces** i.e., of ordnance, cannon   **8 wake** stay awake and hold revel.   **takes his rouse** carouses   **9 wassail** carousal.   **upspring** wild German dance.   **reels** dances   **10 Rhenish** Rhine wine   **12 The triumph . . . pledge** i.e., his feat in draining the wine in a single draft   **15 manner** custom (of drinking)   **16 More . . . observance** better neglected than followed   **17 east and west** i.e., everywhere   **18 taxed of** censured by   **19 clepe** call.   **with swinish phrase** i.e., by calling us swine   **20 addition** reputation   **21 at height** outstandingly   **22 The pith . . . attribute** the essence of the reputation that others attribute to us   **24 for** on account of.   **mole of nature** natural blemish in one's constitution   **26 his** its   **27 their o'ergrowth . . . complexion** the excessive growth in individuals of some natural trait   **28 pales** palings, fences (as of a fortification)

Or by some habit that too much o'erleavens   29
The form of plausive manners, that these men,   30
Carrying, I say, the stamp of one defect,
Being nature's livery or fortune's star,   32
His virtues else, be they as pure as grace,   33
As infinite as man may undergo,   34
Shall in the general censure take corruption   35
From that particular fault. The dram of evil   36
Doth all the noble substance often dout   37
To his own scandal.

Enter Ghost.

HORATIO   Look, my lord, it comes!   38
HAMLET
Angels and ministers of grace defend us!   39
Be thou a spirit of health or goblin damned,   40
Bring with thee airs from heaven or blasts from hell,   41
Be thy intents wicked or charitable,   42
Thou com'st in such a questionable shape   43
That I will speak to thee. I'll call thee Hamlet,
King, father, royal Dane. O, answer me!
Let me not burst in ignorance, but tell
Why thy canonized bones, hearsèd in death,   47
Have burst their cerements; why the sepulcher   48
Wherein we saw thee quietly inurned   49
Hath oped his ponderous and marble jaws
To cast thee up again. What may this mean,
That thou, dead corpse, again in complete steel,   52
Revisits thus the glimpses of the moon,   53
Making night hideous, and we fools of nature   54
So horridly to shake our disposition   55
With thoughts beyond the reaches of our souls?
Say, why is this? Wherefore? What should we do?
[The Ghost] beckons [Hamlet].

HORATIO
It beckons you to go away with it,
As if it some impartment did desire   59
To you alone.
MARCELLUS   Look with what courteous action
It wafts you to a more removèd ground.
But do not go with it.
HORATIO   No, by no means.
HAMLET
It will not speak. Then I will follow it.
HORATIO
Do not, my lord!

HAMLET   Why, what should be the fear?
I do not set my life at a pin's fee,   65
And for my soul, what can it do to that,
Being a thing immortal as itself?
It waves me forth again. I'll follow it.
HORATIO
What if it tempt you toward the flood, my lord,   69
Or to the dreadful summit of the cliff
That beetles o'er his base into the sea,   71
And there assume some other horrible form
Which might deprive your sovereignty of reason   73
And draw you into madness? Think of it.
The very place puts toys of desperation,   75
Without more motive, into every brain
That looks so many fathoms to the sea
And hears it roar beneath.
HAMLET
It wafts me still.—Go on, I'll follow thee.
MARCELLUS
You shall not go, my lord.   *[They try to stop him.]*
HAMLET   Hold off your hands!
HORATIO
Be ruled. You shall not go.
HAMLET   My fate cries out,   81
And makes each petty artery in this body   82
As hardy as the Nemean lion's nerve.   83
Still am I called. Unhand me, gentlemen.
By heaven, I'll make a ghost of him that lets me!   85
I say, away!—Go on, I'll follow thee.
Exeunt Ghost and Hamlet.
HORATIO
He waxes desperate with imagination.
MARCELLUS
Let's follow. 'Tis not fit thus to obey him.
HORATIO
Have after. To what issue will this come?   89
MARCELLUS
Something is rotten in the state of Denmark.
HORATIO
Heaven will direct it.
MARCELLUS   Nay, let's follow him. *Exeunt.* 91

1.5   *Enter Ghost and Hamlet.*

HAMLET
Whither wilt thou lead me? Speak. I'll go no further.
GHOST
Mark me.
HAMLET   I will.
GHOST   My hour is almost come,

---

29 o'erleavens induces a change throughout (as yeast works in dough)
30 plausive pleasing   **32 nature's livery** sign of one's servitude to nature.   **fortune's star** the destiny that chance brings   **33 His virtues else** i.e., the other qualities of *these men* (line 30)   **34 may undergo** can sustain   **35 general censure** general opinion that people have of him   **36–38 The dram . . . scandal** i.e., the small drop of evil blots out or works against the noble substance of the whole and brings it into disrepute. To *dout* is to blot out. (A famous crux.)   **39 ministers of grace** messengers of God   **40 Be thou** whether you are.   **spirit of health** good angel   **41 Bring** whether you bring   **42 Be thy intents** whether your intentions are   **43 questionable** inviting question   **47 canonized** buried according to the canons of the church.   **hearsèd** coffined   **48 cerements** grave clothes   **49 inurned** entombed   **52 complete steel** full armor   **53 glimpses of the moon** pale and uncertain moonlight   **54 fools of nature** mere men, limited to natural knowledge and subject to nature   **55 So . . . disposition** to distress our mental composure so violently   **59 impartment** communication

65 fee value   **69 flood** sea   **71 beetles o'er** overhangs threateningly (like bushy eyebrows).   **his** its   **73 deprive . . . reason** take away the rule of reason over your mind   **75 toys of desperation** fancies of desperate acts, i.e., suicide   **81 My fate cries out** my destiny summons me   **82 petty** weak.   **artery** (through which the vital spirits were thought to have been conveyed)   **83 Nemean lion** one of the monsters slain by Hercules in his twelve labors.   **nerve** sinew   **85 lets** hinders   **89 Have after** let's go after him.   **issue** outcome   **91 it** i.e., the outcome
1.5. Location: The battlements of the castle.

When I to sulfurous and tormenting flames
Must render up myself.

HAMLET   Alas, poor ghost!

GHOST
Pity me not, but lend thy serious hearing
To what I shall unfold.

HAMLET   Speak. I am bound to hear.   7

GHOST
So art thou to revenge, when thou shalt hear.

HAMLET   What?

GHOST   I am thy father's spirit,
Doomed for a certain term to walk the night,
And for the day confined to fast in fires,   12
Till the foul crimes done in my days of nature   13
Are burnt and purged away. But that I am forbid   14
To tell the secrets of my prison house,
I could a tale unfold whose lightest word
Would harrow up thy soul, freeze thy young blood,   17
Make thy two eyes like stars start from their spheres,   18
Thy knotted and combinèd locks to part,   19
And each particular hair to stand on end
Like quills upon the fretful porcupine.
But this eternal blazon must not be
To ears of flesh and blood. List, list, O, list!   22
If thou didst ever thy dear father love—

HAMLET   O God!

GHOST
Revenge his foul and most unnatural murder.

HAMLET   Murder?

GHOST
Murder most foul, as in the best it is,   28
But this most foul, strange, and unnatural.

HAMLET
Haste me to know 't, that I, with wings as swift
As meditation or the thoughts of love,
May sweep to my revenge.

slow process

GHOST   I find thee apt;
And duller shouldst thou be than the fat weed   33
That roots itself in ease on Lethe wharf,   34
Wouldst thou not stir in this. Now, Hamlet, hear.
'Tis given out that, sleeping in my orchard,   36
A serpent stung me. So the whole ear of Denmark
Is by a forgèd process of my death   38
Rankly abused. But know, thou noble youth,   39
The serpent that did sting thy father's life
Now wears his crown.

HAMLET   O, my prophetic soul! My uncle!

GHOST
Ay, that incestuous, that adulterate beast,   43
With witchcraft of his wit, with traitorous gifts—   44

O wicked wit and gifts, that have the power
So to seduce!—won to his shameful lust
The will of my most seeming-virtuous queen.
O Hamlet, what a falling off was there!
From me, whose love was of that dignity
That it went hand in hand even with the vow   50
I made to her in marriage, and to decline
Upon a wretch whose natural gifts were poor
To those of mine!   53
But virtue, as it never will be moved,   54
Though lewdness court it in a shape of heaven,   55
So lust, though to a radiant angel linked,
Will sate itself in a celestial bed   57
And prey on garbage.
But soft, methinks I scent the morning air.
Brief let me be. Sleeping within my orchard,
My custom always of the afternoon,
Upon my secure hour thy uncle stole,   62
With juice of cursèd hebona in a vial,   63
And in the porches of my ears did pour   64
The leprous distillment, whose effect   65
Holds such an enmity with blood of man
That swift as quicksilver it courses through
The natural gates and alleys of the body,
And with a sudden vigor it doth posset   69
And curd, like eager droppings into milk,   70
The thin and wholesome blood. So did it mine,
And a most instant tetter barked about,   72
Most lazar-like, with vile and loathsome crust,   73
All my smooth body.
Thus was I, sleeping, by a brother's hand
Of life, of crown, of queen at once dispatched,   76
Cut off even in the blossoms of my sin,
Unhouseled, disappointed, unaneled,   78
No reckoning made, but sent to my account   79
With all my imperfections on my head.
O, horrible! O, horrible, most horrible!
If thou hast nature in thee, bear it not.   82
Let not the royal bed of Denmark be
A couch for luxury and damnèd incest.   84
But, howsoever thou pursues this act,
Taint not thy mind nor let thy soul contrive
Against thy mother aught. Leave her to heaven
And to those thorns that in her bosom lodge,
To prick and sting her. Fare thee well at once.
The glowworm shows the matin to be near,   90
And 'gins to pale his uneffectual fire.   91
Adieu, adieu, adieu! Remember me.   [*Exit.*]

---

50 even with the vow with the very vow   **53 To** compared to
54 virtue, as it as virtue   **55 shape of heaven** heavenly form   **57 sate
. . . bed** cease to find sexual pleasure in a virtuously lawful marriage
62 secure confident, unsuspicious   **63 hebona** a poison. (The word
seems to be a form of *ebony*, though it is thought perhaps to be related to *henbane*, a poison, or to *ebenus*, "yew.")   **64 porches of my
ears** ears as a porch or entrance of the body   **65 leprous distillment**
distillation causing leprosylike disfigurement   **69 posset** coagulate,
curdle   **70 eager** sour, acid   **72 tetter** eruption of scabs.   **barked**
covered with a rough covering, like bark on a tree   **73 lazar-like**
leperlike   **76 dispatched** suddenly deprived   **78 Unhouseled** without
having received the Sacrament.   **disappointed** unready (spiritually) for
the last journey.   **unaneled** without having received extreme unction
79 reckoning settling of accounts   **82 nature** i.e., the promptings of a
son   **84 luxury** lechery   **90 matin** morning   **91 his** its

---

7 bound (1) ready (2) obligated by duty and fate. (The Ghost, in line
8, answers in the second sense.)   **12 fast** do penance by fasting
13 crimes sins.   **of nature** as a mortal   **14 But that** were it not that
17 harrow up lacerate, tear   **18 spheres** i.e., eye-sockets, here compared to the orbits or transparent revolving spheres in which, according to Ptolemaic astronomy, the heavenly bodies were fixed
19 knotted . . . locks hair neatly arranged and confined   **22 eternal
blazon** revelation of the secrets of eternity   **28 in the best** even at
best   **33 shouldst thou be** you would have to be.   **fat** torpid, lethargic   **34 Lethe** the river of forgetfulness in Hades   **36 orchard** garden
38 forgèd process falsified account   **39 abused** deceived   **43 adulterate** adulterous   **44 gifts** (1) talents (2) presents

HAMLET
O all you host of heaven! O earth! What else?
And shall I couple hell? O, fie! Hold, hold, my heart,   94
And you, my sinews, grow not instant old,   95
But bear me stiffly up. Remember thee?
Ay, thou poor ghost, whiles memory holds a seat
In this distracted globe. Remember thee?   98
Yea, from the table of my memory   99
I'll wipe away all trivial fond records,   100
All saws of books, all forms, all pressures past   101
That youth and observation copied there,
And thy commandment all alone shall live
Within the book and volume of my brain,
Unmixed with baser matter. Yes, by heaven!
O most pernicious woman!
O villain, villain, smiling, damnèd villain!
My tables—meet it is I set it down   108
That one may smile, and smile, and be a villain.
At least I am sure it may be so in Denmark.
                                          [Writing.]
So, uncle, there you are. Now to my word: 111
It is "Adieu, adieu! Remember me."
I have sworn 't.

          Enter Horatio and Marcellus.

HORATIO   My lord, my lord!
MARCELLUS   Lord Hamlet!
HORATIO   Heavens secure him!   116
HAMLET   So be it.
MARCELLUS   Hilo, ho, ho, my lord!
HAMLET   Hillo, ho, ho, boy! Come, bird, come.   119
MARCELLUS   How is 't, my noble lord?
HORATIO   What news, my lord?
HAMLET   O, wonderful!
HORATIO   Good my lord, tell it.
HAMLET   No, you will reveal it.
HORATIO   Not I, my lord, by heaven.
MARCELLUS   Nor I, my lord.
HAMLET
How say you, then, would heart of man once think
     it?   127
But you'll be secret?
HORATIO, MARCELLUS Ay, by heaven, my lord.
HAMLET
There's never a villain dwelling in all Denmark
But he's an arrant knave.   130
HORATIO
There needs no ghost, my lord, come from the grave
To tell us this.
HAMLET   Why, right, you are in the right.
And so, without more circumstance at all,   133
I hold it fit that we shake hands and part,

You as your business and desire shall point you—
For every man hath business and desire,
Such as it is—and for my own poor part,
Look you, I'll go pray.
HORATIO
These are but wild and whirling words, my lord.
HAMLET
I am sorry they offend you, heartily;
Yes, faith, heartily.
HORATIO   There's no offense, my lord.
HAMLET
Yes, by Saint Patrick, but there is, Horatio,   142
And much offense too. Touching this vision here,   143
It is an honest ghost, that let me tell you.   144
For your desire to know what is between us,
O'ermaster 't as you may. And now, good friends,
As you are friends, scholars, and soldiers,
Give me one poor request.
HORATIO   What is 't, my lord? We will.
HAMLET
Never make known what you have seen tonight.
HORATIO, MARCELLUS   My lord, we will not.
HAMLET   Nay, but swear 't.
HORATIO   In faith, my lord, not I.   153
MARCELLUS   Nor I, my lord, in faith.
HAMLET   Upon my sword.   [He holds out his sword.] 155
MARCELLUS   We have sworn, my lord, already.   156
HAMLET   Indeed, upon my sword, indeed.
GHOST (cries under the stage) Swear.
HAMLET
Ha, ha, boy, sayst thou so? Art thou there,
     truepenny?   159
Come on, you hear this fellow in the cellarage.
Consent to swear.
HORATIO   Propose the oath, my lord.
HAMLET
Never to speak of this that you have seen,
Swear by my sword.
GHOST [beneath] Swear.   [They swear.] 164
HAMLET
Hic et ubique? Then we'll shift our ground.   165
                              [He moves to another spot.]
Come hither, gentlemen,
And lay your hands again upon my sword.
Swear by my sword
Never to speak of this that you have heard.
GHOST [beneath] Swear by his sword.   [They swear.]
HAMLET
Well said, old mole. Canst work i' th' earth so fast?

94 couple add. Hold hold together 95 instant instantly 98 globe
(1) head (2) world 99 table tablet, slate 100 fond foolish
101 saws wise sayings. forms shapes or images copied onto the
slate; general ideas. pressures impressions stamped 108 tables
writing tablets. meet it is it is fitting 111 there you are i.e., there,
I've written that down against you 116 secure him keep him safe
119 Hillo . . . come (A falconer's call to a hawk in air. Hamlet
mocks the hallooing as though it were a part of hawking.) 127 once
ever 130 arrant thoroughgoing 133 circumstance ceremony,
elaboration

142 Saint Patrick (The keeper of Purgatory and patron saint of all
blunders and confusion.) 143 offense (Hamlet deliberately changes
Horatio's "no offense taken" to "an offense against all decency.")
144 an honest ghost i.e., a real ghost and not an evil spirit 153 In
faith . . . I i.e., I swear not to tell what I have seen. (Horatio is not
refusing to swear.) 155 sword i.e., the hilt in the form of a cross
156 We . . . already i.e., we swore in faith 159 truepenny honest
old fellow 164 s.d. They swear (Seemingly they swear here, and at
lines 170 and 190, as they lay their hands on Hamlet's sword. Triple
oaths would have particular force; these three oaths deal with what
they have seen, what they have heard, and what they promise about
Hamlet's antic disposition.) 165 Hic et ubique here and everywhere.
(Latin.)

A worthy pioner!—Once more remove, good friends. 172
[*He moves again.*]

HORATIO
O day and night, but this is wondrous strange!

HAMLET
And therefore as a stranger give it welcome. 174
There are more things in heaven and earth, Horatio,
Than are dreamt of in your philosophy. 176
But come;
Here, as before, never, so help you mercy, 178
How strange or odd soe'er I bear myself—
As I perchance hereafter shall think meet
To put an antic disposition on— 181
That you, at such times seeing me, never shall,
With arms encumbered thus, or this headshake, 183
Or by pronouncing of some doubtful phrase
As "Well, we know," or "We could, an if we
would," 185
Or "If we list to speak," or "There be, an if they
might," 186
Or such ambiguous giving out, to note 187
That you know aught of me—this do swear, 188
So grace and mercy at your most need help you.

GHOST [*beneath*]   Swear.   [*They swear.*]

HAMLET
Rest, rest, perturbèd spirit! So, gentlemen,
With all my love I do commend me to you;
And what so poor a man as Hamlet is 192
May do t' express his love and friending to you,
God willing, shall not lack. Let us go in together, 194
And still your fingers on your lips, I pray. 195
The time is out of joint. O cursèd spite 196
That ever I was born to set it right! 197

[*They wait for him to leave first.*]
Nay, come, let's go together.   *Exeunt.* 199

❖

2.1   *Enter old Polonius with his man* [*Reynaldo*].

POLONIUS
Give him this money and these notes, Reynaldo.
[*He gives money and papers.*]

REYNALDO   I will, my lord.

POLONIUS
You shall do marvelous wisely, good Reynaldo, 3

Before you visit him, to make inquire 4
Of his behavior.

REYNALDO   My lord, I did intend it.

POLONIUS
Marry, well said, very well said. Look you, sir,
Inquire me first what Danskers are in Paris, 7
And how, and who, what means, and where they
keep, 8
What company, at what expense; and finding
By this encompassment and drift of question 10
That they do know my son, come you more nearer 11
Than your particular demands will touch it. 12
Take you, as 'twere, some distant knowledge of him, 13
As thus, "I know his father and his friends,
And in part him." Do you mark this, Reynaldo?

REYNALDO   Ay, very well, my lord.

POLONIUS
"And in part him, but," you may say, "not well.
But if 't be he I mean, he's very wild,
Addicted so and so," and there put on him 19
What forgeries you please—marry, none so rank 20
As may dishonor him, take heed of that,
But, sir, such wanton, wild, and usual slips 22
As are companions noted and most known
To youth and liberty.

REYNALDO   As gaming, my lord.

POLONIUS   Ay, or drinking, fencing, swearing,
Quarreling, drabbing—you may go so far. 27

REYNALDO   My lord, that would dishonor him.

POLONIUS
Faith, no, as you may season it in the charge. 29
You must not put another scandal on him
That he is open to incontinency; 31
That's not my meaning. But breathe his faults so
quaintly 32
That they may seem the taints of liberty, 33
The flash and outbreak of a fiery mind,
A savageness in unreclaimèd blood, 35
Of general assault. 36

REYNALDO   But, my good lord—

POLONIUS
Wherefore should you do this?

REYNALDO   Ay, my lord, I would know that.

POLONIUS   Marry, sir, here's my drift,
And I believe it is a fetch of warrant. 41
You laying these slight sullies on my son,
As 'twere a thing a little soiled wi' the working, 43
Mark you,
Your party in converse, him you would sound, 45

---

172 **pioner** foot soldier assigned to dig tunnels and excavations
174 **as a stranger** i.e., needing your hospitality   176 **your philosophy**
this subject called "natural philosophy" or "science" that people talk
about   178 **so help you mercy** as you hope for God's mercy when
you are judged   181 **antic** fantastic   183 **encumbered** folded
185 **an if** if   186 **list** wished.   **There . . . might** i.e., there are people here (we, in fact) who could tell news if we were at liberty to do
so   187 **giving out** intimation.   **note** draw attention to the fact
188 **aught** i.e., something secret   192 **do . . . you** entrust myself to
you   194 **friending** friendliness   195 **lack** be lacking   196 **still** always   197 **The time** the state of affairs.   **spite** i.e., the spite of Fortune   199 **let's go together** (Probably they wait for him to leave first,
but he refuses this ceremoniousness.)
2.1. Location: Polonius' chambers.
3 marvelous marvelously

4 **inquire** inquiry   7 **Danskers** Danes   8 **what means** what wealth
(they have).   **keep** dwell   10 **encompassment** roundabout talking.
drift gradual approach or course   11–12 **come . . . it** you will find
out more this way than by asking pointed questions (*particular demands*)   13 **Take you** assume, pretend   19 **put on** impute to
20 **forgeries** invented tales.   **rank** gross   22 **wanton** sportive, unrestrained   27 **drabbing** whoring   29 **season** temper, soften   31 **incontinency** habitual sexual excess   32 **quaintly** artfully, subtly
33 **taints of liberty** faults resulting from free living   35–36 **A savageness . . . assault** a wildness in untamed youth that assails all indiscriminately   41 **fetch of warrant** legitimate trick   43 **soiled wi' the
working** soiled by handling while it is being made, i.e., by involvement in the ways of the world   45 **converse** conversation.   **sound**
i.e., sound out

Having ever seen in the prenominate crimes   46
The youth you breathe of guilty, be assured   47
He closes with you in this consequence: 48
"Good sir," or so, or "friend," or "gentleman,"
According to the phrase or the addition   50
Of man and country.

REYNALDO   Very good, my lord.

POLONIUS   And then, sir, does 'a this—'a does—what
was I about to say? By the Mass, I was about to say
something. Where did I leave?

REYNALDO   At "closes in the consequence."

POLONIUS

At "closes in the consequence," ay, marry.
He closes thus: "I know the gentleman,
I saw him yesterday," or "th' other day,"
Or then, or then, with such or such, "and as you
    say,
There was 'a gaming," "there o'ertook in 's rouse,"   60
"There falling out at tennis," or perchance   61
"I saw him enter such a house of sale,"
Videlicet a brothel, or so forth. See you now,   63
Your bait of falsehood takes this carp of truth;   64
And thus do we of wisdom and of reach,   65
With windlasses and with assays of bias,   66
By indirections find directions out.   67
So by my former lecture and advice
Shall you my son. You have me, have you not?   69

REYNALDO
My lord, I have.

POLONIUS   God b'wi' ye; fare ye well.   70

REYNALDO   Good my lord.

POLONIUS

Observe his inclination in yourself.   72

REYNALDO   I shall, my lord.

POLONIUS   And let him ply his music.

REYNALDO   Well, my lord.

POLONIUS

Farewell.   *Exit Reynaldo.*

        Enter Ophelia.

        How now, Ophelia, what's the matter?

OPHELIA
O my lord, my lord, I have been so affrighted!

POLONIUS   With what, i' the name of God?

OPHELIA
My lord, as I was sewing in my closet,   79
Lord Hamlet, with his doublet all unbraced,   80
No hat upon his head, his stockings fouled,
Ungartered, and down-gyvèd to his ankle,   82

Pale as his shirt, his knees knocking each other,
And with a look so piteous in purport   84
As if he had been loosèd out of hell
To speak of horrors—he comes before me.

POLONIUS
Mad for thy love?

OPHELIA   My lord, I do not know,
But truly I do fear it.

POLONIUS   What said he?

OPHELIA
He took me by the wrist and held me hard.
Then goes he to the length of all his arm,
And, with his other hand thus o'er his brow
He falls to such perusal of my face
As 'a would draw it. Long stayed he so.   93
At last, a little shaking of mine arm
And thrice his head thus waving up and down,
He raised a sigh so piteous and profound
As it did seem to shatter all his bulk   97
And end his being. That done, he lets me go,
And with his head over his shoulder turned
He seemed to find his way without his eyes,
For out o' doors he went without their helps,
And to the last bended their light on me.

POLONIUS
Come, go with me. I will go seek the King.
This is the very ecstasy of love,   104
Whose violent property fordoes itself   105
And leads the will to desperate undertakings
As oft as any passion under heaven
That does afflict our natures. I am sorry.
What, have you given him any hard words of late?

OPHELIA
No, my good lord, but as you did command
I did repel his letters and denied
His access to me.

POLONIUS   That hath made him mad.
I am sorry that with better heed and judgment
I had not quoted him. I feared he did but trifle   114
And meant to wrack thee. But beshrew my jealousy!   115
By heaven, it is as proper to our age   116
To cast beyond ourselves in our opinions   117
As it is common for the younger sort
To lack discretion. Come, go we to the King.
This must be known, which, being kept close, might
    move   120
More grief to hide than hate to utter love.   121
Come.   *Exeunt.*

                    ♣

46 **Having ever** if he has ever. **prenominate crimes** before-mentioned offenses 47 **breathe** speak 48 **closes . . . consequence** takes you into his confidence in some fashion, as follows 50 **addition** title 60 **o'ertook in 's rouse** overcome by drink 61 **falling out** quarreling 63 **Videlicet** namely 64 **carp** a fish 65 **reach** capacity, ability 66 **windlasses** i.e., circuitous paths. (Literally, circuits made to head off the game in hunting.) **assays of bias** attempts through indirection (like the curving path of the bowling ball, which is biased or weighted to one side) 67 **directions** i.e., the way things really are 69 **have** understand 70 **b' wi'** be with 72 **in yourself** in your own person (as well as by asking questions) 79 **closet** private chamber 80 **doublet** close-fitting jacket. **unbraced** unfastened 82 **down-gyvèd** fallen to the ankles (like gyves or fetters)

84 **in purport** in what it expressed 93 **As** as if (also in line 97) 97 **bulk** body 104 **ecstasy** madness 105 **property** nature. **fordoes** destroys 114 **quoted** observed 115 **wrack** ruin, seduce. **beshrew my jealousy** a plague upon my suspicious nature 116 **proper . . . age** characteristic of us (old) men 117 **cast beyond** overshoot, miscalculate. (A metaphor from hunting.) 120 **known** made known (to the King). **close** secret 120–121 **might . . . love** i.e., might cause more grief (because of what Hamlet might do) by hiding the knowledge of Hamlet's strange behavior to Ophelia than unpleasantness by telling it

2.2   *Flourish. Enter King and Queen, Rosencrantz,*
and Guildenstern [with others].

KING
Welcome, dear Rosencrantz and Guildenstern.
Moreover that we much did long to see you,   2
The need we have to use you did provoke
Our hasty sending. Something have you heard
Of Hamlet's transformation—so call it,
Sith nor th' exterior nor the inward man   6
Resembles that it was. What it should be,   7
More than his father's death, that thus hath put him
So much from th' understanding of himself,
I cannot dream of. I entreat you both
That, being of so young days brought up with him,   11
And sith so neighbored to his youth and havior,   12
That you vouchsafe your rest here in our court   13
Some little time, so by your companies
To draw him on to pleasures, and to gather
So much as from occasion you may glean,   16
Whether aught to us unknown afflicts him thus
That, opened, lies within our remedy.   18
QUEEN
Good gentlemen, he hath much talked of you,
And sure I am two men there is not living
To whom he more adheres. If it will please you
To show us so much gentry and good will
As to expend your time with us awhile   22
For the supply and profit of our hope,
Your visitation shall receive such thanks   24
As fits a king's remembrance.
ROSENCRANTZ   Both Your Majesties   26
Might, by the sovereign power you have of us,   27
Put your dread pleasures more into command   28
Than to entreaty.
GUILDENSTERN   But we both obey,
And here give up ourselves in the full bent   30
To lay our service freely at your feet,
To be commanded.
KING
Thanks, Rosencrantz and gentle Guildenstern.
QUEEN
Thanks, Guildenstern and gentle Rosencrantz.
And I beseech you instantly to visit
My too much changèd son. Go, some of you,
And bring these gentlemen where Hamlet is.
GUILDENSTERN
Heavens make our presence and our practices   38
Pleasant and helpful to him!
QUEEN   Ay, amen!

Exeunt Rosencrantz and Guildenstern [with some
attendants].
Enter Polonius.

POLONIUS
Th' ambassadors from Norway, my good lord,
Are joyfully returned.
KING
Thou still hast been the father of good news.   42
POLONIUS
Have I, my lord? I assure my good liege
I hold my duty, as I hold my soul,   44
Both to my God and to my gracious king;
And I do think, or else this brain of mine
Hunts not the trail of policy so sure   47
As it hath used to do, that I have found
The very cause of Hamlet's lunacy.
KING
O, speak of that! That do I long to hear.
POLONIUS
Give first admittance to th' ambassadors.
My news shall be the fruit to that great feast.   52
KING
Thyself do grace to them and bring them in.   53
                    [*Exit Polonius.*]
He tells me, my dear Gertrude, he hath found
The head and source of all your son's distemper.
QUEEN
I doubt it is no other but the main,   56
His father's death and our o'erhasty marriage.

Enter Ambassadors [Voltimand and Cornelius,
with Polonius].

KING
Well, we shall sift him.—Welcome, my good
    friends!   58
Say, Voltimand, what from our brother Norway?   59
VOLTIMAND
Most fair return of greetings and desires.   60
Upon our first, he sent out to suppress   61
His nephew's levies, which to him appeared
To be a preparation 'gainst the Polack,
But, better looked into, he truly found
It was against Your Highness. Whereat grieved
That so his sickness, age, and impotence   66
Was falsely borne in hand, sends out arrests   67
On Fortinbras, which he, in brief, obeys,
Receives rebuke from Norway, and in fine   69
Makes vow before his uncle never more
To give th' assay of arms against Your Majesty.   71
Whereon old Norway, overcome with joy,
Gives him three thousand crowns in annual fee
And his commission to employ those soldiers,

2.2. Location: The castle.
2 Moreover that besides the fact that   **6 Sith nor** since neither
7 that what   **11 of . . . days** from such early youth   **12 And sith so**
neighbored to and since you are (or, and since that time you are) inti-
mately acquainted with.   **havior** demeanor   **13 vouchsafe your rest**
please to stay   **16 occasion** opportunity   **18 opened** being revealed
22 gentry courtesy   **24 supply . . . hope** aid and furtherance of what
we hope for   **26 As fits . . . remembrance** as would be a fitting gift
of a king who rewards true service   **27 of** over   **28 dread** inspiring
awe   **30 in . . . bent** to the utmost degree of our capacity. (An archery metaphor.)   **38 practices** doings

42 still always   **44 hold** maintain.   **as** as firmly as   **47 policy** sagacity   **52 fruit** dessert   **53 grace** honor (punning on *grace* said before a
feast, line 52)   **56 doubt** fear, suspect.   **main** chief point, principal
concern   **58 sift him** question Polonius closely   **59 brother** fellow
king   **60 desires** good wishes   **61 Upon our first** at our first words
on the business   **66 impotence** helplessness   **67 borne in hand** deluded, taken advantage of.   **arrests** orders to desist   **69 in fine** in
conclusion   **71 give th' assay** make trial of strength, challenge

So levied as before, against the Polack,
With an entreaty, herein further shown,
                              [*giving a paper*]
That it might please you to give quiet pass
Through your dominions for this enterprise
On such regards of safety and allowance   79
As therein are set down.
KING   It likes us well,   80
And at our more considered time we'll read,   81
Answer, and think upon this business.
Meantime we thank you for your well-took labor.
Go to your rest; at night we'll feast together.
Most welcome home!   *Exeunt Ambassadors.*
POLONIUS   This business is well ended.
My liege, and madam, to expostulate   86
What majesty should be, what duty is,
Why day is day, night night, and time is time,
Were nothing but to waste night, day, and time.
Therefore, since brevity is the soul of wit,   90
And tediousness the limbs and outward flourishes,
I will be brief. Your noble son is mad.
Mad call I it, for, to define true madness,
What is 't but to be nothing else but mad?
But let that go.
QUEEN   More matter, with less art.
POLONIUS
Madam, I swear I use no art at all.
That he's mad, 'tis true; 'tis true 'tis pity,
And pity 'tis 'tis true—a foolish figure,   98
But farewell it, for I will use no art.
Mad let us grant him, then, and now remains
That we find out the cause of this effect,
Or rather say, the cause of this defect,
For this effect defective comes by cause.   103
Thus it remains, and the remainder thus.
Perpend.   105
I have a daughter—have while she is mine—
Who, in her duty and obedience, mark,
Hath given me this. Now gather and surmise.   108
[*He reads the letter.*] "To the celestial and my soul's
idol, the most beautified Ophelia"—
That's an ill phrase, a vile phrase; "beautified" is a
vile phrase. But you shall hear. Thus: [*He reads.*]
"In her excellent white bosom, these, etc."   113
QUEEN   Came this from Hamlet to her?
POLONIUS
Good madam, stay awhile, I will be faithful.   115
                              [*He reads.*]
     "Doubt thou the stars are fire,
       Doubt that the sun doth move,
     Doubt truth to be a liar,
       But never doubt I love.   118

O dear Ophelia, I am ill at these numbers. I have not 120
art to reckon my groans. But that I love thee best, O 121
most best, believe it. Adieu.
          Thine evermore, most dear lady, whilst this
               machine is to him, Hamlet."   124
This in obedience hath my daughter shown me,
And, more above, hath his solicitings,   126
As they fell out by time, by means, and place,   127
All given to mine ear.
KING   But how hath she   128
Received his love?
POLONIUS   What do you think of me?
KING
As of a man faithful and honorable.
POLONIUS
I would fain prove so. But what might you think,   131
When I had seen this hot love on the wing—
As I perceived it, I must tell you that,
Before my daughter told me—what might you,
Or my dear Majesty your queen here, think,
If I had played the desk or table book,   136
Or given my heart a winking, mute and dumb,   137
Or looked upon this love with idle sight?   138
What might you think? No, I went round to work,   139
And my young mistress thus I did bespeak: 140
"Lord Hamlet is a prince out of thy star;   141
This must not be." And then I prescripts gave her, 142
That she should lock herself from his resort,   143
Admit no messengers, receive no tokens.
Which done, she took the fruits of my advice;
And he, repellèd—a short tale to make—
Fell into a sadness, then into a fast,
Thence to a watch, thence into a weakness,   148
Thence to a lightness, and by this declension   149
Into the madness wherein now he raves,
And all we mourn for.
KING [*to the Queen*]   Do you think 'tis this? 151
QUEEN   It may be, very like.
POLONIUS
Hath there been such a time—I would fain know
     that—
That I have positively said "'Tis so,"
When it proved otherwise?
KING   Not that I know.
POLONIUS
Take this from this, if this be otherwise.   156
If circumstances lead me, I will find

79 On . . . allowance i.e., with such considerations for the safety of Denmark and permission for Fortinbras   **80 likes** pleases   **81 considered** suitable for deliberation   **86 expostulate** expound, inquire into   **90 wit** sense or judgment   **98 figure** figure of speech   **103 For . . . cause** i.e., for this defective behavior, this madness, has a cause   **105 Perpend** consider   **108 gather and surmise** draw your own conclusions   **113 In . . . bosom** (The letter is poetically addressed to her heart.)   **these** i.e., the letter   **115 stay** wait.   **faithful** i.e., in reading the letter accurately   **118 Doubt** suspect

120 ill . . . numbers unskilled at writing verses   **121 reckon** (1) count (2) number metrically, scan   **124 machine** i.e., body   **126 more above** moreover   **127 fell out** occurred.   **by** according to   **128 given . . . ear** i.e., told me about   **131 fain** gladly   **136 played . . . table book** i.e., remained shut up, concealing the information   **137 given . . . winking** closed the eyes of my heart to this   **138 with idle sight** complacently or incomprehendingly   **139 round** roundly, plainly   **140 bespeak** address   **141 out of thy star** above your sphere, position   **142 prescripts** orders   **143 his resort** his visits   **148 watch** state of sleeplessness   **149 lightness** lightheadedness.   **declension** decline; deterioration (with a pun on the grammatical sense)   **151 all we** all of us, or, into everything that we   **156 Take this from this** (The actor probably gestures, indicating that he means his head from his shoulders, or his staff of office or chain from his hands or neck, or something similar.)

Where truth is hid, though it were hid indeed
Within the center.

KING   How may we try it further?   159

POLONIUS
You know sometimes he walks four hours together
Here in the lobby.

QUEEN   So he does indeed.

POLONIUS
At such a time I'll loose my daughter to him.   162
Be you and I behind an arras then.   163
Mark the encounter. If he love her not
And be not from his reason fall'n thereon,   165
Let me be no assistant for a state,
But keep a farm and carters.

KING   We will try it.   167

Enter Hamlet [reading on a book].

QUEEN
But look where sadly the poor wretch comes reading.   168

POLONIUS
Away, I do beseech you both, away.
I'll board him presently. O, give me leave.   170
       Exeunt King and Queen [with attendants].
How does my good Lord Hamlet?

HAMLET   Well, God-a-mercy.   172

POLONIUS   Do you know me, my lord?

HAMLET   Excellent well. You are a fishmonger.   174

POLONIUS   Not I, my lord.

HAMLET   Then I would you were so honest a man.

POLONIUS   Honest, my lord?

HAMLET   Ay, sir. To be honest, as this world goes, is to be one man picked out of ten thousand.

POLONIUS   That's very true, my lord.

HAMLET   For if the sun breed maggots in a dead dog, being a good kissing carrion—Have you a daughter?   182

POLONIUS   I have, my lord.

HAMLET   Let her not walk i' the sun. Conception is a   184 blessing, but as your daughter may conceive, friend, look to 't.

POLONIUS *[aside]*   How say you by that? Still harping on my daughter. Yet he knew me not at first; 'a said   188 I was a fishmonger. 'A is far gone. And truly in my youth I suffered much extremity for love, very near this. I'll speak to him again.—What do you read, my lord?

HAMLET   Words, words, words.

POLONIUS   What is the matter, my lord?   194

HAMLET   Between who?

POLONIUS   I mean, the matter that you read, my lord.

HAMLET   Slanders, sir; for the satirical rogue says here that old men have gray beards, that their faces are wrinkled, their eyes purging thick amber and plum-tree   199 gum, and that they have a plentiful lack of wit, to-   200 gether with most weak hams. All which, sir, though I most powerfully and potently believe, yet I hold it not honesty to have it thus set down, for yourself, sir, shall   203 grow old as I am, if like a crab you could go backward.   204

POLONIUS *[aside]*   Though this be madness, yet there is method in 't.—Will you walk out of the air, my lord?   206

HAMLET   Into my grave.

POLONIUS   Indeed, that's out of the air. *[Aside.]* How pregnant sometimes his replies are! A happiness that   209 often madness hits on, which reason and sanity could not so prosperously be delivered of. I will leave him   211 and suddenly contrive the means of meeting between   212 him and my daughter.—My honorable lord, I will most humbly take my leave of you.

HAMLET   You cannot, sir, take from me anything that I will more willingly part withal—except my life, except   216 my life, except my life.

Enter Guildenstern and Rosencrantz.

POLONIUS   Fare you well, my lord.

HAMLET   These tedious old fools!   219

POLONIUS   You go to seek the Lord Hamlet. There he is.

ROSENCRANTZ *[to Polonius]*   God save you, sir!
                        [Exit Polonius.]

GUILDENSTERN   My honored lord!

ROSENCRANTZ   My most dear lord!

HAMLET   My excellent good friends! How dost thou, Guildenstern? Ah, Rosencrantz! Good lads, how do you both?

ROSENCRANTZ
As the indifferent children of the earth.   227

GUILDENSTERN
Happy in that we are not overhappy.
On Fortune's cap we are not the very button.

HAMLET   Nor the soles of her shoe?

ROSENCRANTZ   Neither, my lord.

HAMLET   Then you live about her waist, or in the middle of her favors?   233

GUILDENSTERN   Faith, her privates we.   234

HAMLET   In the secret parts of Fortune? O, most true, she is a strumpet. What news?   236

ROSENCRANTZ   None, my lord, but the world's grown honest.

HAMLET   Then is doomsday near. But your news is not true. Let me question more in particular. What have

---

159 center middle point of the earth (which is also the center of the Ptolemaic universe). **try** test, judge **162 loose** (as one might release an animal that is being mated) **163 arras** hanging, tapestry **165 thereon** on that account **167 carters** wagon drivers **168 sadly** seriously **170 board** accost. **presently** at once. **give me leave** i.e., excuse me, leave me alone. (Said to those he hurries offstage, including the King and Queen.) **172 God-a-mercy** God have mercy, i.e., thank you **174 fishmonger** fish merchant **182 a good kissing carrion** i.e., a good piece of flesh for kissing, or for the sun to kiss **184 i' the sun** in public (with additional implication of the sunshine of princely favors). **Conception** (1) understanding (2) pregnancy **188 'a** he **194 matter** substance. (But Hamlet plays on the sense of "basis for a dispute.")

199 purging discharging. **amber** i.e., resin, like the resinous *plum-tree gum* **200 wit** understanding **203 honesty** decency, decorum **204 old** as old **206 out of the air** (The open air was considered dangerous for sick people.) **209 pregnant** quick-witted, full of meaning. **happiness** felicity of expression **211 prosperously** successfully **212 suddenly** immediately **216 withal** with **219 old fools** i.e., old men like Polonius **227 indifferent** ordinary, at neither extreme of fortune or misfortune **233 favors** i.e., sexual favors **234 her privates we** i.e., (1) we are sexually intimate with Fortune, the fickle goddess who bestows her favors indiscriminately (2) we are her private citizens **236 strumpet** prostitute. (A common epithet for indiscriminate Fortune; see line 493.)

you, my good friends, deserved at the hands of
Fortune that she sends you to prison hither?

GUILDENSTERN   Prison, my lord?

HAMLET   Denmark's a prison.

ROSENCRANTZ   Then is the world one.

HAMLET   A goodly one, in which there are many
confines, wards, and dungeons, Denmark being one 247
o' the worst.

ROSENCRANTZ   We think not so, my lord.

HAMLET   Why then 'tis none to you, for there is nothing
either good or bad but thinking makes it so. To me it
is a prison.

ROSENCRANTZ   Why then, your ambition makes it one.
'Tis too narrow for your mind.

HAMLET   O God, I could be bounded in a nutshell and
count myself a king of infinite space, were it not that
I have bad dreams.

GUILDENSTERN   Which dreams indeed are ambition, for
the very substance of the ambitious is merely the 259
shadow of a dream.

HAMLET   A dream itself is but a shadow.

ROSENCRANTZ   Truly, and I hold ambition of so airy
and light a quality that it is but a shadow's shadow.

HAMLET   Then are our beggars bodies, and our mon- 264
archs and outstretched heroes the beggars' shadows. 265
Shall we to the court? For, by my fay, I cannot reason. 266

ROSENCRANTZ, GUILDENSTERN   We'll wait upon you. 267

HAMLET   No such matter. I will not sort you with the 268
rest of my servants, for, to speak to you like an honest
man, I am most dreadfully attended. But, in the 270
beaten way of friendship, what make you at Elsinore? 271

ROSENCRANTZ   To visit you, my lord, no other occasion.

HAMLET   Beggar that I am, I am even poor in thanks;
but I thank you, and sure, dear friends, my thanks are
too dear a halfpenny. Were you not sent for? Is it your 275
own inclining? Is it a free visitation? Come, come, deal 276
justly with me. Come, come. Nay, speak.

GUILDENSTERN   What should we say, my lord?

HAMLET   Anything but to the purpose. You were sent 279
for, and there is a kind of confession in your looks
which your modesties have not craft enough to color. 281
I know the good King and Queen have sent for you.

ROSENCRANTZ   To what end, my lord?

HAMLET   That you must teach me. But let me conjure 284
you, by the rights of our fellowship, by the conso- 285
nancy of our youth, by the obligation of our ever-pre- 286

served love, and by what more dear a better proposer 287
could charge you withal, be even and direct with me 288
whether you were sent for or no.

ROSENCRANTZ [aside to Guildenstern]   What say you?

HAMLET [aside]   Nay, then, I have an eye of you.—If 291
you love me, hold not off. 292

GUILDENSTERN   My lord, we were sent for.

HAMLET   I will tell you why; so shall my anticipation 294
prevent your discovery, and your secrecy to the King 295
and Queen molt no feather. I have of late—but 296
wherefore I know not—lost all my mirth, forgone all
custom of exercises; and indeed it goes so heavily with
my disposition that this goodly frame, the earth,
seems to me a sterile promontory; this most excellent
canopy, the air, look you, this brave o'erhanging 301
firmament, this majestical roof fretted with golden 302
fire, why, it appeareth nothing to me but a foul and
pestilent congregation of vapors. What a piece of work 304
is a man! How noble in reason, how infinite in faculties,
in form and moving how express and admirable, in 306
action how like an angel, in apprehension how like a 307
god! The beauty of the world, the paragon of animals!
And yet, to me, what is this quintessence of dust? 309
Man delights not me—no, nor woman neither,
though by your smiling you seem to say so.

ROSENCRANTZ   My lord, there was no such stuff in my
thoughts.

HAMLET   Why did you laugh, then, when I said man
delights not me?

ROSENCRANTZ   To think, my lord, if you delight not in
man, what Lenten entertainment the players shall 317
receive from you. We coted them on the way, and 318
hither are they coming to offer you service.

HAMLET   He that plays the king shall be welcome; His
Majesty shall have tribute of me. The adventurous 321
knight shall use his foil and target, the lover shall not 322
sigh gratis, the humorous man shall end his part in 323
peace, the clown shall make those laugh whose lungs 324
are tickle o' the sear, and the lady shall say her mind 325
freely, or the blank verse shall halt for 't. What players 326
are they?

ROSENCRANTZ   Even those you were wont to take such
delight in, the tragedians of the city. 329

HAMLET   How chances it they travel? Their residence, 330

---

247 **confines** places of confinement.   **wards** cells   259 **the very . . . ambitious** that seemingly very substantial thing that the ambitious pursue   264 **bodies** i.e., solid substances rather than shadows (since beggars are not ambitious)   265 **outstretched** (1) far-reaching in their ambition (2) elongated as shadows   266 **fay** faith   267 **wait upon** accompany, attend. (But Hamlet uses the phrase in the sense of providing menial service.)   268 **sort** class, categorize   270 **dreadfully attended** waited upon in slovenly fashion   271 **beaten way** familiar path, tried-and-true course.   **make** do   275 **too dear a halfpenny** (1) too expensive at even a halfpenny, i.e., of little worth (2) too expensive *by* a halfpenny in return for worthless kindness   276 **free** voluntary   279 **Anything but to the purpose** anything except a straightforward answer. (Said ironically.)   281 **modesties** sense of shame.   **color** disguise   284 **conjure** adjure, entreat   285–286 **the consonancy of our youth** our closeness in our younger days

287 **better** more skillful   288 **charge** urge.   **even** straight, honest   291 **of** on   292 **hold not off** don't hold back   294–295 **so . . . discovery** in that way my saying it first will spare you from revealing the truth   296 **molt no feather** i.e., not diminish in the least   301 **brave** splendid   302 **fretted** adorned (with fretwork, as in a vaulted ceiling)   304 **congregation** mass.   **piece of work** masterpiece   306 **express** well-framed, exact, expressive   307 **apprehension** power of comprehending   309 **quintessence** the fifth essence of ancient philosophy, beyond earth, water, air, and fire, supposed to be the substance of the heavenly bodies and to be latent in all things   317 **Lenten entertainment** meager reception (appropriate to Lent)   318 **coted** overtook and passed by   321 **tribute** (1) applause (2) homage paid in money.   **of** from   322 **foil and target** sword and shield   323 **gratis** for nothing.   **humorous man** eccentric character, dominated by one trait or "humor"   323–324 **in peace** i.e., with full license   325 **tickle o' the sear** easy on the trigger, ready to laugh easily. (A *sear* is part of a gunlock.)   326 **halt** limp   329 **tragedians** actors   330 **residence** remaining in their usual place, i.e., in the city

both in reputation and profit, was better both ways.

ROSENCRANTZ I think their inhibition comes by the 332
means of the late innovation.   333

HAMLET Do they hold the same estimation they did
when I was in the city? Are they so followed?

ROSENCRANTZ No, indeed are they not.

HAMLET How comes it? Do they grow rusty?   337

ROSENCRANTZ Nay, their endeavor keeps in the wonted 338
pace. But there is, sir, an aerie of children, little eyases, 339
that cry out on the top of question and are most tyran- 340
nically clapped for 't. These are now the fashion, and 341
so berattle the common stages—so they call them— 342
that many wearing rapiers are afraid of goose quills 343
and dare scarce come thither.

HAMLET What, are they children? Who maintains 'em?
How are they escoted? Will they pursue the quality no 346
longer than they can sing? Will they not say after- 347
wards, if they should grow themselves to common 348
players—as it is most like, if their means are no 349
better—their writers do them wrong to make them 350
exclaim against their own succession?   351

ROSENCRANTZ Faith, there has been much to-do on 352
both sides, and the nation holds it no sin to tar them to 353
controversy. There was for a while no money bid for 354
argument unless the poet and the player went to cuffs 355
in the question.   356

HAMLET Is 't possible?

GUILDENSTERN O, there has been much throwing
about of brains.

HAMLET Do the boys carry it away?   360

ROSENCRANTZ Ay, that they do, my lord—Hercules 361
and his load too.   362

HAMLET It is not very strange; for my uncle is King of
Denmark, and those that would make mouths at him 364
while my father lived give twenty, forty, fifty, a
hundred ducats apiece for his picture in little. 'Sblood, 366

there is something in this more than natural, if philos- 367
ophy could find it out.   368

A flourish [of trumpets within].

GUILDENSTERN There are the players.

HAMLET Gentlemen, you are welcome to Elsinore. Your
hands, come then. Th' appurtenance of welcome is 371
fashion and ceremony. Let me comply with you in this 372
garb, lest my extent to the players, which, I tell you, 373
must show fairly outwards, should more appear like 374
entertainment than yours. You are welcome. But my 375
uncle-father and aunt-mother are deceived.

GUILDENSTERN In what, my dear lord?

HAMLET I am but mad north-north-west. When the 378
wind is southerly I know a hawk from a handsaw. 379

Enter Polonius.

POLONIUS Well be with you, gentlemen!

HAMLET Hark you, Guildenstern, and you too; at each
ear a hearer. That great baby you see there is not yet
out of his swaddling clouts.   383

ROSENCRANTZ Haply he is the second time come to 384
them, for they say an old man is twice a child.

HAMLET I will prophesy he comes to tell me of the
players. Mark it.—You say right, sir, o' Monday
morning, 'twas then indeed.

POLONIUS My lord, I have news to tell you.

HAMLET My lord, I have news to tell you. When Ros- 390
cius was an actor in Rome—   391

POLONIUS The actors are come hither, my lord.

HAMLET Buzz, buzz!   393

POLONIUS Upon my honor—

HAMLET Then came each actor on his ass.

POLONIUS The best actors in the world, either for
tragedy, comedy, history, pastoral, pastoral-comical,
historical-pastoral, tragical-historical, tragical-comical-
historical-pastoral, scene individable, or poem unlim- 399
ited. Seneca cannot be too heavy, nor Plautus too 400
light. For the law of writ and the liberty, these are the 401
only men.

HAMLET O Jephthah, judge of Israel, what a treasure 403
hadst thou!

POLONIUS What a treasure had he, my lord?

---

332 inhibition formal prohibition (from acting plays in the city)
333 late recent. **innovation** i.e., the new fashion in satirical plays
performed by boy actors in the "private" theaters; or possibly a political uprising; or the strict limitations set on the theaters in London in
1600 **337–362 How . . . load too** (The passage, omitted from the
early quartos, alludes to the so-called War of the Theaters, 1599–
1602, the rivalry between the children's companies and the adult actors.) **338 keeps** continues. **wonted** usual **339 aerie** nest. **eyases**
young hawks **340 cry . . . question** speak shrilly, dominating the
controversy (in decrying the public theaters) **340–341 tyrannically**
outrageously **342 berattle** berate, clamor against. **common stages**
public theaters **343 many wearing rapiers** i.e., many men of fashion, afraid to patronize the common players for fear of being satirized
by the poets writing for the boy actors. **goose quills** i.e., pens of sat-
irists **346 escoted** maintained. **quality** (acting) profession
346–347 no longer . . . sing i.e., only until their voices change
348 common regular, adult **349 like** likely **349–350 if . . . better**
if they find no better way to support themselves **351 succession** i.e.,
future careers **352 to-do** ado **353 tar** set on (as dogs) **354–
356 There . . . question** i.e., for a while, no money was offered by
the acting companies to playwrights for the plot to a play unless the
satirical poets who wrote for the boys and the adult actors came to
blows in the play itself **360 carry it away** i.e., win the day **361–
362 Hercules . . . load** (Thought to be an allusion to the sign of the
Globe Theatre, which was Hercules bearing the world on his shoulders.) **364 mouths** faces **366 ducats** gold coins. **in little** in miniature. **'Sblood** by God's (Christ's) blood

367–368 philosophy i.e., scientific inquiry **371 appurtenance**
proper accompaniment **372 comply** observe the formalities of courtesy **373 garb** i.e., manner. **my extent** that which I extend, i.e.,
my polite behavior **374 show fairly outwards** show every evidence
of cordiality **375 entertainment** a (warm) reception **378 north-
north-west** just off true north, only partly **379 hawk, handsaw** i.e.,
two very different things, though also perhaps meaning a mattock (or
hack) and a carpenter's cutting tool, respectively; also birds, with a
play on *hernshaw*, or heron **383 swaddling clouts** cloths in which
to wrap a newborn baby **384 Haply** perhaps **390–391 Roscius** a
famous Roman actor who died in 62 B.C. **393 Buzz** (An interjection
used to denote stale news.) **399 scene individable** a play observing
the unity of place; or perhaps one that is unclassifiable, or performed
without intermission **399–400 poem unlimited** a play disregarding
the unities of time and place; one that is all-inclusive **400 Seneca**
writer of Latin tragedies. **Plautus** writer of Latin comedy **401 law
. . . liberty** dramatic composition both according to the rules and disregarding the rules. **these** i.e., the actors **403 Jephthah . . . Israel**
(Jephthah had to sacrifice his daughter; see Judges 11. Hamlet goes
on to quote from a ballad on the theme.)

HAMLET   Why,
   "One fair daughter, and no more,
   The which he lovèd passing well."   408
POLONIUS [aside]   Still on my daughter.
HAMLET   Am I not i' the right, old Jephthah?
POLONIUS   If you call me Jephthah, my lord, I have a
  daughter that I love passing well.
HAMLET   Nay, that follows not.
POLONIUS   What follows then, my lord?
HAMLET   Why,
   "As by lot, God wot,"   416
and then, you know,
   "It came to pass, as most like it was"—   418
the first row of the pious chanson will show you more,   419
for look where my abridgement comes.   420

Enter the Players.

You are welcome, masters; welcome, all. I am glad to
see thee well. Welcome, good friends. O, old friend!
Why, thy face is valanced since I saw thee last. Com'st   423
thou to beard me in Denmark? What, my young lady   424
and mistress! By 'r Lady, your ladyship is nearer to   425
heaven than when I saw you last, by the altitude of a
chopine. Pray God your voice, like a piece of uncur-   427
rent gold, be not cracked within the ring. Masters, you   428
are all welcome. We'll e'en to 't like French falconers,   429
fly at anything we see. We'll have a speech straight.   430
Come, give us a taste of your quality. Come, a   431
passionate speech.
FIRST PLAYER   What speech, my good lord?
HAMLET   I heard thee speak me a speech once, but it
was never acted, or if it was, not above once, for the
play, I remember, pleased not the million; 'twas cav-   436
iar to the general. But it was—as I received it, and   437
others, whose judgments in such matters cried in the   438
top of mine—an excellent play, well digested in the   439
scenes, set down with as much modesty as cunning. I   440
remember one said there were no sallets in the lines to   441
make the matter savory, nor no matter in the phrase
that might indict the author of affectation, but called it 443
an honest method, as wholesome as sweet, and by very
much more handsome than fine. One speech in 't I   445
chiefly loved: 'twas Aeneas' tale to Dido, and there-

about of it especially when he speaks of Priam's   447
slaughter. If it live in your memory, begin at this line: 448
let me see, let me see—
   "The rugged Pyrrhus, like th' Hyrcanian beast"—   450
'Tis not so. It begins with Pyrrhus:
   "The rugged Pyrrhus, he whose sable arms,   452
Black as his purpose, did the night resemble
When he lay couchèd in the ominous horse,   454
Hath now this dread and black complexion smeared
With heraldry more dismal. Head to foot   456
Now is he total gules, horridly tricked   457
With blood of fathers, mothers, daughters, sons,
Baked and impasted with the parching streets,   459
That lend a tyrannous and a damnèd light   460
To their lord's murder. Roasted in wrath and fire,   461
And thus o'ersizèd with coagulate gore,   462
With eyes like carbuncles, the hellish Pyrrhus   463
Old grandsire Priam seeks."
So proceed you.
POLONIUS   'Fore God, my lord, well spoken, with good
accent and good discretion.
FIRST PLAYER   "Anon he finds him
Striking too short at Greeks. His antique sword,   469
Rebellious to his arm, lies where it falls,
Repugnant to command. Unequal matched,   471
Pyrrhus at Priam drives, in rage strikes wide,
But with the whiff and wind of his fell sword   473
Th' unnervèd father falls. Then senseless Ilium,   474
Seeming to feel this blow, with flaming top
Stoops to his base, and with a hideous crash   476
Takes prisoner Pyrrhus' ear. For, lo! His sword,
Which was declining on the milky head   478
Of reverend Priam, seemed i' th' air to stick.
So as a painted tyrant Pyrrhus stood,   480
And, like a neutral to his will and matter,   481
Did nothing.
But as we often see against some storm   483
A silence in the heavens, the rack stand still,   484
The bold winds speechless, and the orb below   485

---

408 passing surpassingly **416 lot** chance. **wot** knows **418 like**
likely, probable **419 row** stanza. **chanson** ballad, song **420 my
abridgment** something that cuts short my conversation; also, a diversion **423 valanced** fringed (with a beard) **424 beard** confront,
challenge (with obvious pun). **young lady** i.e., boy playing women's
parts **425 By 'r Lady** by Our Lady **427 chopine** thick-soled shoe of
Italian fashion **427–428 uncurrent** not passable as lawful coinage
428 cracked . . . ring i.e., changed from adolescent to male voice,
no longer suitable for women's roles. (Coins featured rings enclosing
the sovereign's head; if the coin was cracked within this ring, it was
unfit for currency.) **429 e'en to 't** go at it **430 straight** at once
431 quality professional skill **436–437 caviar to the general** caviar
to the multitude, i.e., a choice dish too elegant for coarse tastes
438–439 cried in the top of i.e., spoke with greater authority than
439 digested arranged, ordered **440 modesty** moderation, restraint.
cunning skill **441 sallets** i.e., something savory, spicy improprieties
443 indict convict **445 handsome** well-proportioned. **fine** elaborately ornamented, showy

447–448 Priam's slaughter the slaying of the ruler of Troy, when the
Greeks finally took the city **450 Pyrrhus** a Greek hero in the Trojan
War, also known as Neoptolemus, son of Achilles—another avenging
son. **Hyrcanian beast** i.e., tiger. (On the death of Priam, see Virgil,
Aeneid, 2.506 ff.; compare the whole speech with Marlowe's *Dido
Queen of Carthage,* 2.1.214 ff. On the *Hyrcanian* tiger, see *Aeneid,*
4.366–367. Hyrcania is on the Caspian Sea.) **452 rugged** shaggy,
savage. **sable** black (for reasons of camouflage during the episode of
the Trojan horse) **454 couchèd** concealed. **ominous horse** fateful
Trojan horse, by which the Greeks gained access to Troy **456 dismal**
ill-omened **457 total gules** entirely red. (A heraldic term.) **tricked**
spotted and smeared. (Heraldic.) **459 impasted** crusted, like a thick
paste. **with . . . streets** by the parching heat of the streets (because
of the fires everywhere) **460 tyrannous** cruel **461 their lord's** i.e.,
Priam's **462 o'ersizèd** covered as with size or glue **463 carbuncles**
large fiery-red precious stones thought to emit their own light
469 antique ancient, long-used **471 Repugnant** disobedient, resistant
473 fell cruel **474 unnervèd** strengthless. **senseless Ilium** inanimate
citadel of Troy **476 his** its **478 declining** descending. **milky**
white-haired **480 painted** i.e., painted in a picture **481 like . . .
matter** i.e., as though suspended between his intention and its fulfillment **483 against** just before **484 rack** mass of clouds **485 orb**
globe, earth

As hush as death, anon the dreadful thunder
Doth rend the region, so, after Pyrrhus' pause,   487
A rousèd vengeance sets him new a-work,
And never did the Cyclops' hammers fall   489
On Mars's armor forged for proof eterne   490
With less remorse than Pyrrhus' bleeding sword   491
Now falls on Priam.
Out, out, thou strumpet Fortune! All you gods
In general synod take away her power!   494
Break all the spokes and fellies from her wheel,   495
And bowl the round nave down the hill of heaven   496
As low as to the fiends!"
POLONIUS   This is too long.
HAMLET   It shall to the barber's with your beard.—Pri-
thee, say on. He's for a jig or a tale of bawdry, or he   500
sleeps. Say on; come to Hecuba.   501
FIRST PLAYER
"But who, ah woe! had seen the moblèd queen"—   502
HAMLET   "The moblèd queen?"
POLONIUS   That's good. "Moblèd queen" is good.
FIRST PLAYER
"Run barefoot up and down, threat'ning the flames   505
With bisson rheum, a clout upon that head   506
Where late the diadem stood, and, for a robe,   507
About her lank and all o'erteemèd loins   508
A blanket, in the alarm of fear caught up—
Who this had seen, with tongue in venom steeped,
'Gainst Fortune's state would treason have
pronounced.   511
But if the gods themselves did see her then
When she saw Pyrrhus make malicious sport
In mincing with his sword her husband's limbs,
The instant burst of clamor that she made,
Unless things mortal move them not at all,
Would have made milch the burning eyes of heaven,   517
And passion in the gods."   518
POLONIUS   Look whe'er he has not turned his color and   519
has tears in 's eyes. Prithee, no more.
HAMLET   'Tis well; I'll have thee speak out the rest of
this soon.—Good my lord, will you see the players well
bestowed? Do you hear, let them be well used, for they   523
are the abstract and brief chronicles of the time. After   524
your death you were better have a bad epitaph than
their ill report while you live.
POLONIUS   My lord, I will use them according to their
desert.

HAMLET   God's bodikin, man, much better. Use every   529
man after his desert, and who shall scape whipping?
Use them after your own honor and dignity. The less   531
they deserve, the more merit is in your bounty. Take
them in.
POLONIUS   Come, sirs.   [Exit.]
HAMLET   Follow him, friends. We'll hear a play tomorrow. [As they start to leave, Hamlet detains the First
Player.] Dost thou hear me, old friend? Can you play
The Murder of Gonzago?
FIRST PLAYER   Ay, my lord.
HAMLET   We'll ha 't tomorrow night. You could, for a   540
need, study a speech of some dozen or sixteen lines   541
which I would set down and insert in 't, could you
not?
FIRST PLAYER   Ay, my lord.
HAMLET   Very well. Follow that lord, and look you mock
him not. (Exeunt Players.) My good friends, I'll leave
you till night. You are welcome to Elsinore.
ROSENCRANTZ   Good my lord!
                    Exeunt [Rosencrantz and Guildenstern].
HAMLET
Ay, so, goodbye to you.—Now I am alone.
O, what a rogue and peasant slave am I!
Is it not monstrous that this player here,
But in a fiction, in a dream of passion,   552
Could force his soul so to his own conceit   553
That from her working all his visage wanned,   554
Tears in his eyes, distraction in his aspect,   555
A broken voice, and his whole function suiting   556
With forms to his conceit? And all for nothing!   557
For Hecuba!
What's Hecuba to him, or he to Hecuba,
That he should weep for her? What would he do
Had he the motive and the cue for passion
That I have? He would drown the stage with tears
And cleave the general ear with horrid speech,   563
Make mad the guilty and appall the free,   564
Confound the ignorant, and amaze indeed   565
The very faculties of eyes and ears. Yet I,
A dull and muddy-mettled rascal, peak   567
Like John-a-dreams, unpregnant of my cause,   568
And can say nothing—no, not for a king
Upon whose property and most dear life   570
A damned defeat was made. Am I a coward?   571

---

487 **region** sky   489 **Cyclops** giant armor makers in the smithy of
Vulcan   490 **proof eterne** eternal resistance to assault   491 **remorse**
pity   494 **synod** assembly   495 **fellies** pieces of wood forming the
rim of a wheel   496 **nave** hub.   **hill of heaven** Mount Olympus
500 **jig** comic song and dance often given at the end of a play
501 **Hecuba** wife of Priam   502 **who . . . had** anyone who had (also
in line 510).   **moblèd** muffled   505 **threat'ning the flames** i.e.,
weeping hard enough to dampen the flames   506 **bisson rheum**
blinding tears.   **clout** cloth   507 **late** lately   508 **all o'erteemèd** utterly worn out with bearing children   511 **state** rule, managing.
pronounced proclaimed   517 **milch** milky, moist with tears.   **burning eyes of heaven** i.e., heavenly bodies   518 **passion** overpowering
emotion   519 **whe'er** whether   523 **bestowed** lodged   524 **abstract**
summary account

529 **God's bodikin** by God's (Christ's) little body, *bodykin*. (Not to be
confused with *bodkin*, "dagger.")   531 **after** according to   540 **ha 't**
have it   541 **study** memorize   552 **But** merely   553 **force . . . conceit** bring his innermost being so entirely into accord with his conception (of the role)   554 **from her working** as a result of, or in response
to, his soul's activity.   **wanned** grew pale   555 **aspect** look, glance
556–557 **his whole . . . conceit** all his bodily powers responding
with actions to suit his thought   563 **the general ear** everyone's ear.
horrid horrible   564 **appall** (Literally, make pale.)   **free** innocent
565 **Confound the ignorant** i.e., dumbfound those who know nothing
of the crime that has been committed.   **amaze** stun   567 **muddy-
mettled** dull-spirited.   **peak** mope, pine   568 **John-a-dreams** a
sleepy, dreaming idler.   **unpregnant of** not quickened by   570 **property** i.e., the crown; also character, quality   571 **damned defeat**
damnable act of destruction

Who calls me villain? Breaks my pate across?   572
Plucks off my beard and blows it in my face?
Tweaks me by the nose? Gives me the lie i' the
    throat   574
As deep as to the lungs? Who does me this?
Ha, 'swounds, I should take it; for it cannot be   576
But I am pigeon-livered and lack gall   577
To make oppression bitter, or ere this   578
I should ha' fatted all the region kites   579
With this slave's offal. Bloody, bawdy villain!   580
Remorseless, treacherous, lecherous, kindless villain!   581
O, vengeance!
Why, what an ass am I! This is most brave,   583
That I, the son of a dear father murdered,
Prompted to my revenge by heaven and hell,
Must like a whore unpack my heart with words
And fall a-cursing, like a very drab,   587
A scullion! Fie upon 't, foh! About, my brains!   588
Hum, I have heard
That guilty creatures sitting at a play
Have by the very cunning of the scene   591
Been struck so to the soul that presently   592
They have proclaimed their malefactions;
For murder, though it have no tongue, will speak
With most miraculous organ. I'll have these players
Play something like the murder of my father
Before mine uncle. I'll observe his looks;
I'll tent him to the quick. If 'a do blench,   598
I know my course. The spirit that I have seen
May be the devil, and the devil hath power
T' assume a pleasing shape; yea, and perhaps,
Out of my weakness and my melancholy,
As he is very potent with such spirits,   603
Abuses me to damn me. I'll have grounds   604
More relative than this. The play's the thing   605
Wherein I'll catch the conscience of the King.   *Exit.*

❖

3.1   *Enter King, Queen, Polonius, Ophelia,*
       Rosencrantz, Guildenstern, lords.

KING
And can you by no drift of conference   1
Get from him why he puts on this confusion,
Grating so harshly all his days of quiet
With turbulent and dangerous lunacy?

ROSENCRANTZ
He does confess he feels himself distracted,
But from what cause 'a will by no means speak.
GUILDENSTERN
Nor do we find him forward to be sounded,   7
But with a crafty madness keeps aloof
When we would bring him on to some confession
Of his true state.
QUEEN   Did he receive you well?
ROSENCRANTZ   Most like a gentleman.
GUILDENSTERN
But with much forcing of his disposition.   12
ROSENCRANTZ
Niggard of question, but of our demands   13
Most free in his reply.
QUEEN   Did you assay him   14
To any pastime?
ROSENCRANTZ
Madam, it so fell out that certain players
We o'erraught on the way. Of these we told him,   17
And there did seem in him a kind of joy
To hear of it. They are here about the court,
And, as I think, they have already order
This night to play before him.
POLONIUS   'Tis most true,
And he beseeched me to entreat Your Majesties
To hear and see the matter.
KING
With all my heart, and it doth much content me
To hear him so inclined.
Good gentlemen, give him a further edge   26
And drive his purpose into these delights.
ROSENCRANTZ
We shall, my lord.
         Exeunt Rosencrantz and Guildenstern.
KING   Sweet Gertrude, leave us too,
For we have closely sent for Hamlet hither,   29
That he, as 'twere by accident, may here
Affront Ophelia.   31
Her father and myself, lawful espials,   32
Will so bestow ourselves that seeing, unseen,
We may of their encounter frankly judge,
And gather by him, as he is behaved,
If 't be th' affliction of his love or no
That thus he suffers for.
QUEEN   I shall obey you.
And for your part, Ophelia, I do wish
That your good beauties be the happy cause
Of Hamlet's wildness. So shall I hope your virtues
Will bring him to his wonted way again,   41
To both your honors.
OPHELIA   Madam, I wish it may.
                [Exit Queen.]
POLONIUS
Ophelia, walk you here.—Gracious, so please you,   43

---

572 pate head   **574 Gives . . . throat** calls me an out-and-out liar
576 'swounds by his (Christ's) wounds   **577 pigeon-livered** (The pigeon or dove was popularly supposed to be mild because it secreted no gall.)   **578 bitter** i.e., bitter to me   **579 region kites** kites (birds of prey) of the air   **580 offal** entrails   **581 Remorseless** pitiless.   **kindless** unnatural   **583 brave** fine, admirable. (Said ironically.)   **587 drab** whore   **588 scullion** menial kitchen servant (apt to be foulmouthed).   **About** about it, to work   **591 cunning** art, skill.   **scene** dramatic presentation   **592 presently** at once   **598 tent** probe.   **the quick** the tender part of a wound, the core.   **blench** quail, flinch   **603 spirits** humors (of melancholy)   **604 Abuses** deludes   **605 relative** cogent, pertinent
3.1. Location: The castle.
1 drift of conference directing of conversation

7 forward willing.   **sounded** questioned   **12 disposition** inclination
13 Niggard stingy.   **question** conversation   **14 assay** try to win
17 o'erraught overtook   **26 edge** incitement   **29 closely** privately
31 Affront confront, meet   **32 espials** spies   **41 wonted** accustomed
43 Gracious Your Grace (i.e., the King)

We will bestow ourselves. [*To Ophelia.*] Read on this
   book,   [*giving her a book*] 44
That show of such an exercise may color   45
Your loneliness. We are oft to blame in this—   46
'Tis too much proved—that with devotion's visage   47
And pious action we do sugar o'er
The devil himself.
KING [*aside*]   O, 'tis too true!
How smart a lash that speech doth give my
   conscience!
The harlot's cheek, beautied with plastering art,
Is not more ugly to the thing that helps it   53
Than is my deed to my most painted word.
O heavy burden!
POLONIUS
I hear him coming. Let's withdraw, my lord.   56

     [*The King and Polonius withdraw.*]

    Enter Hamlet. [*Ophelia pretends to read a book.*]

HAMLET
To be, or not to be, that is the question:
Whether 'tis nobler in the mind to suffer
The slings and arrows of outrageous fortune,   59
Or to take arms against a sea of troubles
And by opposing end them. To die, to sleep—
No more—and by a sleep to say we end
The heartache and the thousand natural shocks
That flesh is heir to. 'Tis a consummation
Devoutly to be wished. To die, to sleep;
To sleep, perchance to dream. Ay, there's the rub,   66
For in that sleep of death what dreams may come,
When we have shuffled off this mortal coil,   68
Must give us pause. There's the respect   69
That makes calamity of so long life.   70
For who would bear the whips and scorns of time,
Th' oppressor's wrong, the proud man's contumely,   72
The pangs of disprized love, the law's delay,   73
The insolence of office, and the spurns   74
That patient merit of th' unworthy takes,   75
When he himself might his quietus make   76
With a bare bodkin? Who would fardels bear,   77
To grunt and sweat under a weary life,
But that the dread of something after death,
The undiscovered country from whose bourn   80
No traveler returns, puzzles the will,
And makes us rather bear those ills we have
Than fly to others that we know not of?

Thus conscience does make cowards of us all;
And thus the native hue of resolution   85
Is sicklied o'er with the pale cast of thought,   86
And enterprises of great pitch and moment   87
With this regard their currents turn awry   88
And lose the name of action.—Soft you now,   89
The fair Ophelia. Nymph, in thy orisons   90
Be all my sins remembered.
OPHELIA   Good my lord,
How does your honor for this many a day?
HAMLET
I humbly thank you; well, well, well.
OPHELIA
My lord, I have remembrances of yours,
That I have longèd long to redeliver.
I pray you, now receive them.   [*She offers tokens.*]
HAMLET
No, not I, I never gave you aught.
OPHELIA
My honored lord, you know right well you did,
And with them words of so sweet breath composed
As made the things more rich. Their perfume lost,
Take these again, for to the noble mind
Rich gifts wax poor when givers prove unkind.
There, my lord.   [*She gives tokens.*]
HAMLET   Ha, ha! Are you honest?   104
OPHELIA   My lord?
HAMLET   Are you fair?   106
OPHELIA   What means your lordship?
HAMLET   That if you be honest and fair, your honesty 108
  should admit no discourse to your beauty.   109
OPHELIA   Could beauty, my lord, have better com- 110
merce than with honesty?   111
HAMLET   Ay, truly, for the power of beauty will sooner
transform honesty from what it is to a bawd than the
force of honesty can translate beauty into his likeness. 114
This was sometime a paradox, but now the time gives 115
it proof. I did love you once.
OPHELIA   Indeed, my lord, you made me believe so.
HAMLET   You should not have believed me, for virtue
cannot so inoculate our old stock but we shall relish of 119
it. I loved you not.   120
OPHELIA   I was the more deceived.
HAMLET   Get thee to a nunnery. Why wouldst thou be a 122
breeder of sinners? I am myself indifferent honest, but 123
yet I could accuse me of such things that it were better
my mother had not borne me: I am very proud,
revengeful, ambitious, with more offenses at my beck 126

---

44 **bestow** conceal   45 **exercise** religious exercise. (The book she
reads is one of devotion.)   **color** give a plausible appearance to
46 **loneliness** being alone   47 **too much proved** too often shown to
be true, too often practiced   53 to compared to: **the thing** i.e., the
cosmetic   56 **s.d. withdraw** (The King and Polonius may retire behind
an arras. The stage directions specify that they ''enter'' again near the
end of the scene.)   59 **slings** missiles   66 **rub** (Literally, an obstacle
in the game of bowls.)   68 **shuffled** sloughed, cast.   **coil** turmoil
69 **respect** consideration   70 **of . . . life** so long-lived, something we
willingly endure for so long (also suggesting that long life is itself a calamity)   72 **contumely** insolent abuse   73 **disprized** unvalued
74 **office** officialdom.   **spurns** insults   75 **of . . . takes** receives from
unworthy persons   76 **quietus** acquitance; here, death   77 **a bare
bodkin** a mere dagger, unsheathed.   **fardels** burdens   80 **bourn**
frontier, boundary

85 **native hue** natural color, complexion   86 **cast** tinge, shade of
color   87 **pitch** height (as of a falcon's flight).   **moment** importance
88 **regard** respect, consideration.   **currents** courses   89 **Soft you** i.e.,
wait a minute, gently   90 **orisons** prayers   104 **honest** (1) truthful (2)
chaste   106 **fair** (1) beautiful (2) just, honorable   108 **your honesty**
your chastity   109 **discourse to** familiar dealings with   110–
111 **commerce** dealings, intercourse   114 **his** its   115 **sometime** formerly.   **a paradox** a view opposite to commonly held opinion.   **the
time** the present age   119 **inoculate** graft, be engrafted to
119–120 **but . . . it** that we do not still have about us a taste of the
old stock, retain our sinfulness   122 **nunnery** convent (with possibly an awareness that the word was also used derisively to denote a
brothel)   123 **indifferent honest** reasonably virtuous   126 **beck**
command

than I have thoughts to put them in, imagination to give them shape, or time to act them in. What should such fellows as I do crawling between earth and heaven? We are arrant knaves all; believe none of us. Go thy ways to a nunnery. Where's your father?

OPHELIA   At home, my lord.

HAMLET   Let the doors be shut upon him, that he may play the fool nowhere but in 's own house. Farewell.

OPHELIA   O, help him, you sweet heavens!

HAMLET   If thou dost marry, I'll give thee this plague for thy dowry: be thou as chaste as ice, as pure as snow, thou shalt not escape calumny. Get thee to a nunnery, farewell. Or, if thou wilt needs marry, marry a fool, for wise men know well enough what monsters you 140 make of them. To a nunnery, go, and quickly too. Farewell.

OPHELIA   Heavenly powers, restore him!

HAMLET   I have heard of your paintings too, well enough. God hath given you one face, and you make yourselves another. You jig, you amble, and you 146 lisp, you nickname God's creatures, and make your 147 wantonness your ignorance. Go to, I'll no more on 't; 148 it hath made me mad. I say we will have no more marriage. Those that are married already—all but one—shall live. The rest shall keep as they are. To a nunnery, go.   *Exit.*

OPHELIA
O, what a noble mind is here o'erthrown!
The courtier's, soldier's, scholar's, eye, tongue, sword,
Th' expectancy and rose of the fair state,   155
The glass of fashion and the mold of form,   156
Th' observed of all observers, quite, quite down!   157
And I, of ladies most deject and wretched,
That sucked the honey of his music vows,   159
Now see that noble and most sovereign reason
Like sweet bells jangled out of tune and harsh,
That unmatched form and feature of blown youth   162
Blasted with ecstasy. O, woe is me,   163
T' have seen what I have seen, see what I see!

Enter King and Polonius.

KING
Love? His affections do not that way tend;   165
Nor what he spake, though it lacked form a little,
Was not like madness. There's something in his soul
O'er which his melancholy sits on brood,   168
And I do doubt the hatch and the disclose   169
Will be some danger; which for to prevent,

I have in quick determination
Thus set it down: he shall with speed to England   172
For the demand of our neglected tribute.   173
Haply the seas and countries different
With variable objects shall expel   175
This something-settled matter in his heart,   176
Whereon his brains still beating puts him thus   177
From fashion of himself. What think you on 't?   178

POLONIUS
It shall do well. But yet do I believe
The origin and commencement of his grief
Sprung from neglected love.—How now, Ophelia?
You need not tell us what Lord Hamlet said;
We heard it all.—My lord, do as you please,
But, if you hold it fit, after the play
Let his queen-mother all alone entreat him   185
To show his grief. Let her be round with him;   186
And I'll be placed, so please you, in the ear
Of all their conference. If she find him not,   188
To England send him, or confine him where
Your wisdom best shall think.

KING   It shall be so.
Madness in great ones must not unwatched go.
                                        Exeunt.

3.2   *Enter Hamlet and three of the Players.*

HAMLET   Speak the speech, I pray you, as I pronounced it to you, trippingly on the tongue. But if you mouth it, as many of our players do, I had as lief the town crier 3 spoke my lines. Nor do not saw the air too much with your hand, thus, but use all gently; for in the very torrent, tempest, and, as I may say, whirlwind of your passion, you must acquire and beget a temperance that may give it smoothness. O, it offends me to the soul to hear a robustious periwig-pated fellow tear a 9 passion to tatters, to very rags, to split the ears of the groundlings, who for the most part are capable of 11 nothing but inexplicable dumb shows and noise. I 12 would have such a fellow whipped for o'erdoing Ter- 13 magant. It out-Herods Herod. Pray you, avoid it.   14

FIRST PLAYER   I warrant your honor.

HAMLET   Be not too tame neither, but let your own discretion be your tutor. Suit the action to the word,

---

140 monsters (An illusion to the horns of a cuckold.) **you** i.e., you women   **146 jig** dance.   **amble** move coyly   **147 you nickname** . . . **creatures** i.e., you give trendy names to things in place of their God-given names   **147–148 make . . . ignorance** i.e., excuse your affectation on the grounds of pretended ignorance   **148 on 't** of it **155 expectancy** hope.   **rose** ornament   **156 The glass** . . . **form** the mirror of true self-fashioning and the pattern of courtly behavior **157 Th' observed . . . observers** i.e., the center of attention and honor in the court   **159 music** musical, sweetly uttered   **162 blown** blooming   **163 Blasted** withered.   **ecstasy** madness   **165 affections** emotions, feelings   **168 sits on brood** sits like a bird on a nest, about to *hatch* mischief (line 169)   **169 doubt** fear.   **disclose** disclosure, hatching

172 set it down resolved   **173 For . . . of** to demand   **175 variable objects** various sights and surroundings to divert him   **176 This something . . . heart** the strange matter settled in his heart   **177 still** continually   **178 From . . . himself** out of his natural manner **185 queen-mother** queen and mother   **186 round** blunt   **188 find him not** fails to discover what is troubling him
3.2. Location: The castle.
3 our players players nowadays.   **I had as lief** I would just as soon **9 robustious** violent, boisterous.   **periwig-pated** wearing a wig **11 groundlings** spectators who paid least and stood in the yard of the theater.   **capable of** able to understand   **12 dumb shows** mimed performances, often used before Shakespeare's time to precede a play or each act   **13–14 Termagant** a supposed deity of the Mohammedans, not found in any English medieval play but elsewhere portrayed as violent and blustering   **14 Herod** Herod of Jewry. (A character in *The Slaughter of the Innocents* and other cycle plays. The part was played with great noise and fury.)

the word to the action, with this special observance,
that you o'erstep not the modesty of nature. For 19
anything so o'erdone is from the purpose of playing, 20
whose end, both at the first and now, was and is to
hold as 't were the mirror up to nature, to show virtue
her feature, scorn her own image, and the very age 23
and body of the time his form and pressure. Now this 24
overdone or come tardy off, though it makes the 25
unskillful laugh, cannot but make the judicious grieve, 26
the censure of the which one must in your allowance 27
o'erweigh a whole theater of others. O, there be players that I have seen play, and heard others praise, and
that highly, not to speak it profanely, that, neither 30
having th' accent of Christians nor the gait of Chris- 31
tian, pagan, nor man, have so strutted and bellowed 32
that I have thought some of nature's journeymen had 33
made men and not made them well, they imitated
humanity so abominably.   35

FIRST PLAYER I hope we have reformed that indifferently 36
with us, sir.

HAMLET   O, reform it altogether. And let those that play
your clowns speak no more than is set down for them;
for there be of them that will themselves laugh, to set 40
on some quantity of barren spectators to laugh too, 41
though in the meantime some necessary question of
the play be then to be considered. That's villainous,
and shows a most pitiful ambition in the fool that uses
it. Go make you ready.   [Exeunt Players.]

Enter Polonius, Guildenstern, and Rosencrantz.

How now, my lord, will the King hear this piece of
work?

POLONIUS   And the Queen too, and that presently.   48

HAMLET   Bid the players make haste.   [Exit Polonius.]
Will you two help to hasten them?

ROSENCRANTZ
Ay, my lord.   *Exeunt they two.*

HAMLET   What ho, Horatio!

Enter Horatio.

HORATIO   Here, sweet lord, at your service.

HAMLET
Horatio, thou art e'en as just a man
As e'er my conversation coped withal.   54

HORATIO
O, my dear lord—

HAMLET   Nay, do not think I flatter,

For what advancement may I hope from thee
That no revenue hast but thy good spirits
To feed and clothe thee? Why should the poor be
flattered?
No, let the candied tongue lick absurd pomp,   59
And crook the pregnant hinges of the knee   60
Where thrift may follow fawning. Dost thou hear?   61
Since my dear soul was mistress of her choice
And could of men distinguish her election,   63
Sh' hath sealed thee for herself, for thou hast been   64
As one, in suffering all, that suffers nothing,
A man that Fortune's buffets and rewards
Hast ta'en with equal thanks; and blest are those
Whose blood and judgment are so well commeddled 68
That they are not a pipe for Fortune's finger
To sound what stop she please. Give me that man   70
That is not passion's slave, and I will wear him
In my heart's core, ay, in my heart of heart,
As I do thee.—Something too much of this.—
There is a play tonight before the King.
One scene of it comes near the circumstance
Which I have told thee of my father's death.
I prithee, when thou seest that act afoot,
Even with the very comment of thy soul   78
Observe my uncle. If his occulted guilt   79
Do not itself unkennel in one speech,   80
It is a damnèd ghost that we have seen,   81
And my imaginations are as foul
As Vulcan's stithy. Give him heedful note,   83
For I mine eyes will rivet to his face,
And after we will both our judgments join
In censure of his seeming.

HORATIO   Well, my lord.   86
If 'a steal aught the whilst this play is playing   87
And scape detecting, I will pay the theft.

          [Flourish.] Enter trumpets and kettledrums, King,
          Queen, Polonius, Ophelia, [Rosencrantz,
          Guildenstern, and other lords, with guards
          carrying torches].

HAMLET   They are coming to the play. I must be idle. 89
Get you a place.   [The King, Queen, and courtiers sit.]

KING   How fares our cousin Hamlet?   91

HAMLET   Excellent, i' faith, of the chameleon's dish: I eat 92
the air, promise-crammed. You cannot feed capons so. 93

19 **modesty** restraint, moderation   20 **from** contrary to   23 **scorn**
i.e., something foolish and deserving of scorn   23–24 **the very . . .
time** i.e., the present state of affairs   24 **his** its.   **pressure** stamp, impressed character   25 **come tardy off** inadequately done   25–26 **the
unskillful** those lacking in judgment   27 **the censure . . . one** the
judgment of even one of whom.   **your allowance** your scale of values   30 **not . . . profanely** (Hamlet anticipates his idea in lines
33–34 that some men were not made by God at all.)   31 **Christians**
i.e., ordinary decent folk   32 **nor man** i.e., nor any human being at
all   33 **journeymen** laborers who are not yet masters in their trade
35 **abominably** (Shakespeare's usual spelling, *abhominably*, suggests a
literal though etymologically incorrect meaning, "removed from human nature.")   36 **indifferently** tolerably   40 **of them** some among
them   41 **barren** i.e., of wit   48 **presently** at once   54 **my . . .
withal** my dealings encountered

59 **candied** sugared, flattering   60 **pregnant** compliant   61 **thrift**
profit   63 **could . . . election** could make distinguishing choices
among persons   64 **sealed thee** (Literally, as one would seal a legal
document to mark possession.)   68 **blood** passion.   **commeddled**
commingled   70 **stop** hole in a wind instrument for controlling the
sound   78 **very . . . soul** your most penetrating observation and consideration   79 **occulted** hidden   80 **unkennel** (As one would say of a
fox driven from its lair.)   81 **damnèd** in league with Satan   83 **stithy**
smithy, place of stiths (anvils)   86 **censure of his seeming** judgment
of his appearance or behavior   87 **If 'a steal aught** if he gets away
with anything   89 **idle** (1) unoccupied (2) mad   91 **cousin** i.e., close
relative   92 **chameleon's dish** (Chameleons were supposed to feed on
air. Hamlet deliberately misinterprets the King's *fares* as "feeds." By
his phrase *eat the air* he also plays on the idea of feeding himself with
the promise of succession, of being the *heir*.)   93 **capons** roosters castrated and *crammed* with feed to make them succulent

KING   I have nothing with this answer, Hamlet. These 94
words are not mine. 95

HAMLET   No, nor mine now. [*To Polonius.*] My lord, you 96
played once i' th' university, you say?

POLONIUS   That did I, my lord, and was accounted a
good actor.

HAMLET   What did you enact?

POLONIUS   I did enact Julius Caesar. I was killed i' the
Capitol; Brutus killed me.

HAMLET   It was a brute part of him to kill so capital a 103
calf there.—Be the players ready? 104

ROSENCRANTZ   Ay, my lord. They stay upon your 105
patience.

QUEEN   Come hither, my dear Hamlet, sit by me.

HAMLET   No, good Mother, here's metal more attractive. 108

POLONIUS [*to the King*]   O, ho, do you mark that?

HAMLET   Lady, shall I lie in your lap?

[*Lying down at Ophelia's feet.*]

OPHELIA   No, my lord.

HAMLET   I mean, my head upon your lap?

OPHELIA   Ay, my lord.

HAMLET   Do you think I meant country matters? 114

OPHELIA   I think nothing, my lord.

HAMLET   That's a fair thought to lie between maids'
legs.

OPHELIA   What is, my lord?

HAMLET   Nothing. 119

OPHELIA   You are merry, my lord.

HAMLET   Who, I?

OPHELIA   Ay, my lord.

HAMLET   O God, your only jig maker. What should a 123
man do but be merry? For look you how cheerfully my
mother looks, and my father died within 's two hours. 125

OPHELIA   Nay, 'tis twice two months, my lord.

HAMLET   So long? Nay then, let the devil wear black, for
I'll have a suit of sables. O heavens! Die two months 128
ago, and not forgotten yet? Then there's hope a great
man's memory may outlive his life half a year. But, by
'r Lady, 'a must build churches, then, or else shall 'a
suffer not thinking on, with the hobbyhorse, whose 132
epitaph is "For O, for O, the hobbyhorse is forgot." 133

94 have . . . with make nothing of, or gain nothing from   **95 are not
mine** do not respond to what I asked   **96 nor mine now** (Once spoken, words are proverbially no longer the speaker's own—and hence
should be uttered warily.)   **103 brute** (The Latin meaning of *brutus*,
"stupid," was often used punningly with the name Brutus.)   **part** (1)
deed (2) role   **104 calf** fool   **105 stay upon** await   **108 metal** substance that is *attractive*, i.e., magnetic, but with suggestion also of
mettle, "disposition"   **114 country matters** sexual intercourse (making a bawdy pun on the first syllable of *country*)   **119 Nothing** the
figure zero or naught, suggesting the female sexual anatomy. (*Thing*
not infrequently has a bawdy connotation of male or female anatomy,
and the reference here could be male.)   **123 only jig maker** very best
composer of jigs, i.e., pointless merriment. (Hamlet replies sardonically to Ophelia's observation that he is merry by saying, "If you're
looking for someone who is really merry, you've come to the right
person.")   **125 within 's** within this (i.e., these)   **128 suit of sables**
garments trimmed with the fur of the sable and hence suited for a
wealthy person, not a mourner (but with a pun on *sable*, "black,"
ironically suggesting mourning once again)   **132 suffer . . . on** undergo oblivion   **133 For . . . forgot** (Verse of a song occurring also
in *Love's Labor's Lost*, 3.1.27–28. The hobbyhorse was a character
made up to resemble a horse and rider, appearing in the morris dance
and such May-game sports. This song laments the disappearance of
such customs under pressure from the Puritans.)

The trumpets sound. Dumb show follows.

*Enter a King and a Queen [very lovingly]; the
Queen embracing him, and he her. [She kneels,
and makes show of protestation unto him.] He
takes her up, and declines his head upon her neck.
He lies him down upon a bank of flowers. She,
seeing him asleep, leaves him. Anon comes in
another man, takes off his crown, kisses it, pours
poison in the sleeper's ears, and leaves him. The
Queen returns, finds the King dead, makes
passionate action. The Poisoner with some three or
four come in again, seem to condole with her. The
dead body is carried away. The Poisoner woos the
Queen with gifts; she seems harsh awhile, but in
the end accepts love.*

[*Exeunt players.*]

OPHELIA   What means this, my lord?

HAMLET   Marry, this' miching mallico; it means mis- 135
chief.

OPHELIA   Belike this show imports the argument of the 137
play.

Enter Prologue.

HAMLET   We shall know by this fellow. The players cannot keep counsel; they'll tell all. 140

OPHELIA   Will 'a tell us what this show meant?

HAMLET   Ay, or any show that you will show him. Be 142
not you ashamed to show, he'll not shame to tell you 143
what it means.

OPHELIA   You are naught, you are naught. I'll mark the 145
play.

PROLOGUE
For us, and for our tragedy,
Here stooping to your clemency,
We beg your hearing patiently. [*Exit.*] 148

HAMLET   Is this a prologue, or the posy of a ring? 150

OPHELIA   'Tis brief, my lord.

HAMLET   As woman's love.

Enter [two Players as] King and Queen.

PLAYER KING
Full thirty times hath Phoebus' cart gone round 153
Neptune's salt wash and Tellus' orbèd ground, 154
And thirty dozen moons with borrowed sheen 155
About the world have times twelve thirties been,
Since love our hearts and Hymen did our hands 157
Unite commutual in most sacred bands. 158

PLAYER QUEEN
So many journeys may the sun and moon
Make us again count o'er ere love be done!
But, woe is me, you are so sick of late,

135 this' miching mallico this is sneaking mischief   **137 Belike** probably.   **argument** plot   **140 counsel** secret   **142–143 Be not you** provided you are not   **145 naught** indecent. (Ophelia is reacting to
Hamlet's pointed remarks about not being ashamed to show all.)
148 stooping bowing   **150 posy . . . ring** brief motto in verse inscribed in a ring   **153 Phoebus' cart** the sun-god's chariot, making its
yearly cycle   **154 salt wash** the sea.   **Tellus** goddess of the earth, of
the *orbèd ground*   **155 borrowed** i.e., reflected   **157 Hymen** god of
matrimony   **158 commutual** mutually.   **bands** bonds

So far from cheer and from your former state,
That I distrust you. Yet, though I distrust,   163
Discomfort you, my lord, it nothing must.   164
For women's fear and love hold quantity;   165
In neither aught, or in extremity.   166
Now, what my love is, proof hath made you know,   167
And as my love is sized, my fear is so.   168
Where love is great, the littlest doubts are fear;
Where little fears grow great, great love grows there.

PLAYER KING
Faith, I must leave thee, love, and shortly too;
My operant powers their functions leave to do.   172
And thou shalt live in this fair world behind,   173
Honored, beloved; and haply one as kind
For husband shalt thou—

PLAYER QUEEN   O, confound the rest!
Such love must needs be treason in my breast.
In second husband let me be accurst!
None wed the second but who killed the first.   178

HAMLET   Wormwood, wormwood.   179

PLAYER QUEEN
The instances that second marriage move   180
Are base respects of thrift, but none of love.   181
A second time I kill my husband dead
When second husband kisses me in bed.

PLAYER KING
I do believe you think what now you speak,
But what we do determine oft we break.
Purpose is but the slave to memory,   186
Of violent birth, but poor validity,   187
Which now, like fruit unripe, sticks on the tree,   188
But fall unshaken when they mellow be.
Most necessary 'tis that we forget   190
To pay ourselves what to ourselves is debt.   191
What to ourselves in passion we propose,
The passion ending, doth the purpose lose.
The violence of either grief or joy
Their own enactures with themselves destroy.   195
Where joy most revels, grief doth most lament;   196
Grief joys, joy grieves, on slender accident.   197
This world is not for aye, nor 'tis not strange   198
That even our loves should with our fortunes
   change;
For 'tis a question left us yet to prove,
Whether love lead fortune, or else fortune love.

The great man down, you mark his favorite flies;   202
The poor advanced makes friends of enemies.   203
And hitherto doth love on fortune tend;   204
For who not needs shall never lack a friend,   205
And who in want a hollow friend doth try   206
Directly seasons him his enemy.   207
But, orderly to end where I begun,
Our wills and fates do so contrary run   209
That our devices still are overthrown;   210
Our thoughts are ours, their ends none of our own.   211
So think thou wilt no second husband wed,
But die thy thoughts when thy first lord is dead.

PLAYER QUEEN
Nor earth to me give food, nor heaven light,   214
Sport and repose lock from me day and night,   215
To desperation turn my trust and hope,
An anchor's cheer in prison be my scope!   217
Each opposite that blanks the face of joy   218
Meet what I would have well and it destroy!   219
Both here and hence pursue me lasting strife   220
If, once a widow, ever I be wife!

HAMLET   If she should break it now!

PLAYER KING
'Tis deeply sworn. Sweet, leave me here awhile;
My spirits grow dull, and fain I would beguile   224
The tedious day with sleep.

PLAYER QUEEN   Sleep rock thy brain,
And never come mischance between us twain!

   [He sleeps.] Exit [Player Queen].

HAMLET   Madam, how like you this play?

QUEEN   The lady doth protest too much, methinks.   228

HAMLET   O, but she'll keep her word.

KING   Have you heard the argument? Is there no   230
offense in 't?   231

HAMLET   No, no, they do but jest, poison in jest. No of-   232
fense i' the world.   233

KING   What do you call the play?

HAMLET   The Mousetrap. Marry, how? Tropically.   235
This play is the image of a murder done in Vienna.
Gonzago is the Duke's name, his wife, Baptista. You   237
shall see anon. 'Tis a knavish piece of work, but what
of that? Your Majesty, and we that have free souls, it   239

163 distrust am anxious about   164 Discomfort distress.   nothing
not at all   165 hold quantity keep proportion with one another
166 In . . . extremity i.e., women fear and love either too little or
too much, but the two, fear and love, are equal in either case
167 proof experience   168 sized in size   172 operant powers vital
functions.   leave to do cease to perform   173 behind after I have
gone   178 None i.e., let no woman.   but who except the one who
179 Wormwood i.e., how bitter. (Literally, a bitter-tasting plant.)
180 instances motives.   move motivate   181 base . . . thrift ignoble
considerations of material prosperity   186 Purpose . . . memory our
good intentions are subject to forgetfulness   187 validity strength, durability   188 Which i.e., purpose   190–191 Most . . . debt it's inevitable that in time we forget the obligations we have imposed on ourselves   195 enactures fulfillments   196–197 Where . . . accident
the capacity for extreme joy and grief go together, and often one extreme is instantly changed into its opposite on the slightest provocation   198 aye ever

202 down fallen in fortune   203 The poor . . . enemies when one of
humble station is promoted, you see his enemies suddenly becoming
his friends   204 hitherto up to this point in the argument, or, to this
extent.   tend attend   205 who not needs he who is not in need (of
wealth)   206 who in want he who, being in need.   try test (his generosity)   207 seasons him ripens him into   209 Our . . . run what
we want and what we get go so contrarily   210 devices still intentions continually   211 ends results   214 Nor let neither   215 Sport
. . . night may day deny me its pastimes and night its repose
217 anchor's cheer anchorite's or hermit's fare.   my scope the extent
of my happiness   218–219 Each . . . destroy may every adverse
thing that causes the face of joy to turn pale meet and destroy everything that I desire to see prosper.   blanks causes to blanch or grow
pale   220 hence in the life hereafter   224 spirits vital spirits
228 doth . . . much makes too many promises and protestations
230 argument plot   231–233 offense . . . offense cause for objection . . . actual injury, crime   232 jest make believe   235 Tropically
figuratively. (The First Quarto reading, trapically, suggests a pun on
trap in Mousetrap.)   237 Duke's i.e., King's. (A slip that may be due
to Shakespeare's possible source, the alleged murder of the Duke of
Urbino by Luigi Gonzaga in 1538.)   239 free guiltless

touches us not. Let the galled jade wince, our withers 240
are unwrung. 241

Enter Lucianus.

This is one Lucianus, nephew to the King.

OPHELIA   You are as good as a chorus, my lord. 243

HAMLET   I could interpret between you and your love, 244
if I could see the puppets dallying. 245

OPHELIA   You are keen, my lord, you are keen. 246

HAMLET   It would cost you a groaning to take off mine
edge.

OPHELIA   Still better, and worse. 249

HAMLET   So you mis-take your husbands. Begin, mur- 250
derer; leave thy damnable faces and begin. Come, the
croaking raven doth bellow for revenge.

LUCIANUS

Thoughts black, hands apt, drugs fit, and time
agreeing,
Confederate season, else no creature seeing, 254
Thou mixture rank, of midnight weeds collected,
With Hecate's ban thrice blasted, thrice infected, 256
Thy natural magic and dire property 257
On wholesome life usurp immediately.

[He pours the poison into the sleeper's ear.]

HAMLET   'A poisons him i' the garden for his estate. His 259
name's Gonzago. The story is extant, and written in
very choice Italian. You shall see anon how the
murderer gets the love of Gonzago's wife.

[Claudius rises.]

OPHELIA   The King rises.

HAMLET   What, frighted with false fire? 264

QUEEN   How fares my lord?

POLONIUS   Give o'er the play.

KING   Give me some light. Away!

POLONIUS   Lights, lights, lights!

Exeunt all but Hamlet and Horatio.

HAMLET

"Why, let the strucken deer go weep, 269
The hart ungallèd play. 270
For some must watch, while some must sleep; 271
Thus runs the world away." 272

Would not this, sir, and a forest of feathers—if the 273
rest of my fortunes turn Turk with me—with two 274
Provincial roses on my razed shoes, get me a fellow- 275
ship in a cry of players? 276

HORATIO   Half a share.

HAMLET   A whole one, I.
"For thou dost know, O Damon dear, 279
This realm dismantled was 280
Of Jove himself, and now reigns here 281
A very, very—pajock." 282

HORATIO   You might have rhymed.

HAMLET   O good Horatio, I'll take the ghost's word for
a thousand pound. Didst perceive?

HORATIO   Very well, my lord.

HAMLET   Upon the talk of the poisoning?

HORATIO   I did very well note him.

Enter Rosencrantz and Guildenstern.

HAMLET   Aha! Come, some music! Come, the re- 289
corders. 290
"For if the King like not the comedy,
Why then, belike, he likes it not, perdy." 292
Come, some music.

GUILDENSTERN   Good my lord, vouchsafe me a word
with you.

HAMLET   Sir, a whole history.

GUILDENSTERN   The King, sir—

HAMLET   Ay, sir, what of him?

GUILDENSTERN   Is in his retirement marvelous dis- 299
tempered. 300

HAMLET   With drink, sir?

GUILDENSTERN   No, my lord, with choler. 302

HAMLET   Your wisdom should show itself more richer
to signify this to the doctor, for for me to put him to his
purgation would perhaps plunge him into more 305
choler.

GUILDENSTERN   Good my lord, put your discourse into
some frame and start not so wildly from my affair. 308

HAMLET   I am tame, sir. Pronounce.

GUILDENSTERN   The Queen, your mother, in most great
affliction of spirit, hath sent me to you.

---

240 galled jade horse whose hide is rubbed by saddle or harness.
withers the part between the horse's shoulder blades   **241 unwrung**
not rubbed sore   **243 chorus** (In many Elizabethan plays, the forthcoming action was explained by an actor known as the "chorus"; at a
puppet show, the actor who spoke the dialogue was known as an "interpreter," as indicated by the lines following.)   **244 interpret** (1)
ventriloquize the dialogue, as in puppet show (2) act as pander
245 puppets dallying (With suggestion of sexual play, continued in
keen, "sexually aroused," *groaning*, "moaning in pregnancy," and
edge, "sexual desire" or "impetuosity.")   **246 keen** sharp, bitter
249 Still . . . worse more keen, always *bettering* what other people
say with witty wordplay, but at the same time more offensive   **250 So**
even thus (in marriage).   **mis-take** take falseheartedly and cheat on.
(The marriage vows say "for better, for worse.")   **254 Confederate**
season the time and occasion conspiring (to assist the murderer).
else otherwise.   **seeing** seeing me   **256 Hecate's ban** the curse of
Hecate, the goddess of witchcraft   **257 dire property** baleful quality
259 estate i.e., the kingship.   **His** i.e., the King's   **264 false fire** the
blank discharge of a gun loaded with powder but no shot
269–272 Why . . . away (Probably from an old ballad, with allusion
to the popular belief that a wounded deer retires to weep and die;
compare with *As You Like It*, 2.1.33–66.)   **270 ungallèd** unafflicted
271 watch remain awake   **272 Thus . . . away** thus the world goes

273 this i.e., the play.   **feathers** (Allusion to the plumes that Elizabethan actors were fond of wearing.)   **274 turn Turk with** turn renegade against, go back on   **275 Provincial roses** rosettes of ribbon,
named for roses grown in a part of France.   **razed** with ornamental
slashing   **275–276 fellowship . . . players** partnership in a theatrical
company   **276 cry** pack (of hounds)   **279 Damon** the friend of Pythias, as Horatio is friend of Hamlet; or, a traditional pastoral name
280–282 This realm . . . pajock i.e., Jove, representing divine authority and justice, has abandoned this realm to its own devices, leaving in his stead only a peacock or vain pretender to virtue (though the
rhyme-word expected in place of *pajock* or "peacock" suggests that
the realm is now ruled over by an "ass").   **280 dismantled** stripped,
divested   **289–290 recorders** wind instruments of the flute kind
292 perdy (A corruption of the French *par dieu*, "by God.")
299 retirement withdrawal to his chambers   **299–300 distempered**
out of humor. (But Hamlet deliberately plays on the wider application
to any illness of mind or body, as in lines 335–336, especially to
drunkenness.)   **302 choler** anger. (But Hamlet takes the word in its
more basic humoral sense of "bilious disorder.")   **305 purgation**
(Hamlet hints at something going beyond medical treatment to bloodletting and the extraction of confession.)   **308 frame** order.   **start** shy
or jump away (like a horse; the opposite of *tame* in line 309)

HAMLET   You are welcome.

GUILDENSTERN   Nay, good my lord, this courtesy is not of the right breed. If it shall please you to make me a 314 wholesome answer, I will do your mother's command- ment; if not, your pardon and my return shall be the 316 end of my business.

HAMLET   Sir, I cannot.

ROSENCRANTZ   What, my lord?

HAMLET   Make you a wholesome answer; my wit's dis- eased. But, sir, such answer as I can make, you shall command, or rather, as you say, my mother. Therefore no more, but to the matter. My mother, you say—

ROSENCRANTZ   Then thus she says: your behavior hath struck her into amazement and admiration.   325

HAMLET   O wonderful son, that can so stonish a mother! But is there no sequel at the heels of this mother's ad- miration? Impart.

ROSENCRANTZ   She desires to speak with you in her closet ere you go to bed.   330

HAMLET   We shall obey, were she ten times our mother. Have you any further trade with us?

ROSENCRANTZ   My lord, you once did love me.

HAMLET   And do still, by these pickers and stealers.   334

ROSENCRANTZ   Good my lord, what is your cause of distemper? You do surely bar the door upon your own liberty if you deny your griefs to your friend.   337

HAMLET   Sir, I lack advancement.

ROSENCRANTZ   How can that be, when you have the voice of the King himself for your succession in Denmark?

HAMLET   Ay, sir, but "While the grass grows"—the 342 proverb is something musty.   343

Enter the Players with recorders.

O, the recorders. Let me see one. [*He takes a recorder.*] To withdraw with you: why do you go about to recover 345 the wind of me, as if you would drive me into a toil? 346

GUILDENSTERN   O, my lord, if my duty be too bold, my 347 love is too unmannerly.   348

HAMLET   I do not well understand that. Will you play 349 upon this pipe?

GUILDENSTERN   My lord, I cannot.

HAMLET   I pray you.

GUILDENSTERN   Believe me, I cannot.

HAMLET   I do beseech you.

GUILDENSTERN   I know no touch of it, my lord.

HAMLET   It is as easy as lying. Govern these ventages 356

with your fingers and thumb, give it breath with your mouth, and it will discourse most eloquent music. Look you, these are the stops.

GUILDENSTERN   But these cannot I command to any utterance of harmony. I have not the skill.

HAMLET   Why, look you now, how unworthy a thing you make of me! You would play upon me, you would seem to know my stops, you would pluck out the heart of my mystery, you would sound me from my lowest 365 note to the top of my compass, and there is much 366 music, excellent voice, in this little organ, yet cannot 367 you make it speak. 'Sblood, do you think I am easier to be played on than a pipe? Call me what instrument you will, though you can fret me, you cannot play 370 upon me.

Enter Polonius.

God bless you, sir!

POLONIUS   My lord, the Queen would speak with you, and presently.   374

HAMLET   Do you see yonder cloud that's almost in shape of a camel?

POLONIUS   By the Mass and 'tis, like a camel indeed.

HAMLET   Methinks it is like a weasel.

POLONIUS   It is backed like a weasel.

HAMLET   Or like a whale.

POLONIUS   Very like a whale.

HAMLET   Then I will come to my mother by and by. 382 [*Aside.*] They fool me to the top of my bent.—I will 383 come by and by.

POLONIUS   I will say so.   [*Exit.*]

HAMLET   "By and by" is easily said. Leave me, friends.
                                      [*Exeunt all but Hamlet.*]
'Tis now the very witching time of night,   387
When churchyards yawn and hell itself breathes out
Contagion to this world. Now could I drink hot
   blood
And do such bitter business as the day
Would quake to look on. Soft, now to my mother.
O heart, lose not thy nature! Let not ever   392
The soul of Nero enter this firm bosom.   393
Let me be cruel, not unnatural;
I will speak daggers to her, but use none.
My tongue and soul in this be hypocrites:
How in my words soever she be shent,   397
To give them seals never my soul consent!   *Exit.* 398

❖

---

314 breed (1) kind (2) breeding, manners   **316 pardon** permission to depart   **325 admiration** bewilderment   **330 closet** private chamber **334 pickers and stealers** i.e., hands. (So called from the catechism, "to keep my hands from picking and stealing.")   **337 liberty** i.e., be- ing freed from *distemper*, line 336; but perhaps with a veiled threat as well.   **deny** refuse to share   **342 While . . . grows** (The rest of the proverb is "the silly horse starves"; Hamlet may not live long enough to succeed to the kingdom.)   **343 something** somewhat.   **s.d. Players** actors   **345 withdraw** speak privately   **345–346 recover the wind** get to the windward side (thus driving the game into the *toil,* or "net") **346 toil** snare   **347–348 if . . . unmannerly** if I am using an un- mannerly boldness, it is my love that occasions it   **349 I . . . that** i.e., I don't understand how genuine love can be unmannerly **356 ventages** finger-holes or *stops* (line 359) of the recorder

365 sound (1) fathom (2) produce sound in   **366 compass** range (of voice)   **367 organ** musical instrument   **370 fret** irritate (with a quib- ble on *fret,* meaning the piece of wood, gut, or metal that regulates the fingering on an instrument)   **374 presently** at once   **382 by and by** quite soon   **383 fool me** trifle with me, humor my fooling.   **top of my bent** limit of my ability or endurance. (Literally, the extent to which a bow may be bent.)   **387 witching time** time when spells are cast and evil is abroad   **392 nature** natural feeling   **393 Nero** mur- derer of his mother, Agrippina   **397 How . . . soever** however much by my words.   **shent** rebuked   **398 give them seals** i.e., confirm them with deeds

3.3   *Enter King, Rosencrantz, and Guildenstern.*

KING
I like him not, nor stands it safe with us   1
To let his madness range. Therefore prepare you.
I your commission will forthwith dispatch,   3
And he to England shall along with you.
The terms of our estate may not endure   5
Hazard so near 's as doth hourly grow
Out of his brows.
GUILDENSTERN   We will ourselves provide.   7
Most holy and religious fear it is   8
To keep those many many bodies safe
That live and feed upon Your Majesty.

ROSENCRANTZ
The single and peculiar life is bound   11
With all the strength and armor of the mind
To keep itself from noyance, but much more   13
That spirit upon whose weal depends and rests
The lives of many. The cess of majesty   15
Dies not alone, but like a gulf doth draw   16
What's near it with it; or it is a massy wheel   17
Fixed on the summit of the highest mount,
To whose huge spokes ten thousand lesser things
Are mortised and adjoined, which, when it falls,   20
Each small annexment, petty consequence,   21
Attends the boisterous ruin. Never alone   22
Did the King sigh, but with a general groan.

KING
Arm you, I pray you, to this speedy voyage,   24
For we will fetters put about this fear,
Which now goes too free-footed.
ROSENCRANTZ   We will haste us.

Exeunt gentlemen [Rosencrantz and Guildenstern].

Enter Polonius.

POLONIUS
My lord, he's going to his mother's closet.
Behind the arras I'll convey myself   28
To hear the process. I'll warrant she'll tax him home,   29
And, as you said—and wisely was it said—
'Tis meet that some more audience than a mother,   31
Since nature makes them partial, should o'erhear
The speech, of vantage. Fare you well, my liege.   33
I'll call upon you ere you go to bed

And tell you what I know.
KING   Thanks, dear my lord.
                          Exit [Polonius].
O, my offense is rank! It smells to heaven.
It hath the primal eldest curse upon 't,   37
A brother's murder. Pray can I not,
Though inclination be as sharp as will;   39
My stronger guilt defeats my strong intent,
And like a man to double business bound   41
I stand in pause where I shall first begin,
And both neglect. What if this cursèd hand
Were thicker than itself with brother's blood,
Is there not rain enough in the sweet heavens
To wash it white as snow? Whereto serves mercy   46
But to confront the visage of offense?   47
And what's in prayer but this twofold force,
To be forestallèd ere we come to fall,   49
Or pardoned being down? Then I'll look up.
My fault is past. But O, what form of prayer
Can serve my turn? "Forgive me my foul murder"?
That cannot be, since I am still possessed
Of those effects for which I did the murder:
My crown, mine own ambition, and my queen.
May one be pardoned and retain th' offense?   56
In the corrupted currents of this world   57
Offense's gilded hand may shove by justice,   58
And oft 'tis seen the wicked prize itself   59
Buys out the law. But 'tis not so above.
There is no shuffling, there the action lies   61
In his true nature, and we ourselves compelled,   62
Even to the teeth and forehead of our faults,   63
To give in evidence. What then? What rests?   64
Try what repentance can. What can it not?
Yet what can it, when one cannot repent?
O wretched state, O bosom black as death,
O limèd soul that, struggling to be free,   68
Art more engaged! Help, angels! Make assay.   69
Bow, stubborn knees, and heart with strings of steel,
Be soft as sinews of the newborn babe!
All may be well.   *[He kneels.]*

Enter Hamlet.

HAMLET
Now might I do it pat, now 'a is a-praying;   73
And now I'll do 't. *[He draws his sword.]* And so 'a
    goes to heaven,

3.3. Location: The castle.
1 him i.e., his behavior   **3 dispatch** prepare, cause to be drawn up
5 terms of our estate circumstances of my royal position   **7 Out of his brows** i.e., from his brain, in the form of plots and threats   **8 religious fear** sacred concern   **11 single and peculiar** individual and private   **13 noyance** harm   **15 cess** decease, cessation   **16 gulf** whirlpool   **17 massy** massive   **20 mortised** fastened (as with a fitted joint). **when it falls** i.e., when it descends, like the wheel of Fortune, bringing a king down with it   **21 Each . . . consequence** i.e., every hanger-on and unimportant person or thing connected with the King   **22 Attends** participates in   **24 Arm** prepare   **28 arras** screen of tapestry placed around the walls of household apartments. (On the Elizabethan stage, the arras was presumably over a door or discovery space in the tiring-house facade.)   **29 process** proceedings. **tax him home** reprove him severely   **31 meet** fitting   **33 of vantage** from an advantageous place, or, in addition

37 the primal eldest curse the curse of Cain, the first murderer; he killed his brother Abel   **39 Though . . . will** though my desire is as strong as my determination   **41 bound** (1) destined (2) obliged. (The King wants to repent and still enjoy what he has gained.)   **46–47 Whereto . . . offense** what function does mercy serve other than to meet sin face to face?   **49 forestallèd** prevented (from sinning)   **56 th' offense** the thing for which one offended   **57 currents** courses   **58 gilded hand** hand offering gold as a bribe. **shove by** thrust aside   **59 wicked prize** prize won by wickedness   **61 There** i.e., in heaven. **shuffling** escape by trickery. **the action lies** the accusation is made manifest. (A legal metaphor.)   **62 his** its   **63 to the teeth and forehead** face to face, concealing nothing   **64 give in** provide. **rests** remains   **68 limèd** caught as with birdlime, a sticky substance used to ensnare birds   **69 engaged** entangled. **assay** trial. (Said to himself.)   **73 pat** opportunely

And so am I revenged. That would be scanned: 75
A villain kills my father, and for that,
I, his sole son, do this same villain send
To heaven.
Why, this is hire and salary, not revenge.
'A took my father grossly, full of bread,   80
With all his crimes broad blown, as flush as May;   81
And how his audit stands who knows save heaven?   82
But in our circumstance and course of thought   83
'Tis heavy with him. And am I then revenged,
To take him in the purging of his soul,
When he is fit and seasoned for his passage?   86
No!
Up, sword, and know thou a more horrid hent.   88
            [*He puts up his sword.*]
When he is drunk asleep, or in his rage,   89
Or in th' incestuous pleasure of his bed,
At game, a-swearing, or about some act   91
That has no relish of salvation in 't—   92
Then trip him, that his heels may kick at heaven,
And that his soul may be as damned and black
As hell, whereto it goes. My mother stays.   95
This physic but prolongs thy sickly days.   *Exit.* 96

KING
My words fly up, my thoughts remain below.
Words without thoughts never to heaven go.   *Exit.*

❖

3.4   *Enter [Queen] Gertrude and Polonius.*

POLONIUS
'A will come straight. Look you lay home to him.   1
Tell him his pranks have been too broad to bear
   with,   2
And that Your Grace hath screened and stood
   between
Much heat and him. I'll shroud me even here.   4
Pray you, be round with him.   5
HAMLET (*within*)   Mother, Mother, Mother!
QUEEN   I'll warrant you, fear me not.
Withdraw, I hear him coming.
         [*Polonius hides behind the arras.*]

Enter Hamlet.

HAMLET   Now, Mother, what's the matter?
QUEEN
Hamlet, thou hast thy father much offended.   10
HAMLET
Mother, you have my father much offended.
QUEEN
Come, come, you answer with an idle tongue.   12
HAMLET
Go, go, you question with a wicked tongue.
QUEEN
Why, how now, Hamlet?
HAMLET   What's the matter now?
QUEEN
Have you forgot me?
HAMLET   No, by the rood, not so: 15
You are the Queen, your husband's brother's wife,
And—would it were not so!—you are my mother.
QUEEN
Nay, then, I'll set those to you that can speak.   18
HAMLET
Come, come, and sit you down; you shall not
   budge.
You go not till I set you up a glass
Where you may see the inmost part of you.
QUEEN
What wilt thou do? Thou wilt not murder me?
Help, ho!
POLONIUS [*behind the arras*]   What ho! Help!
HAMLET [*drawing*]
How now? A rat? Dead for a ducat, dead!   25
       [*He thrusts his rapier through the arras.*]
POLONIUS [*behind the arras*]
O, I am slain!   [*He falls and dies.*]
QUEEN   O me, what hast thou done?
HAMLET   Nay, I know not. Is it the King?
QUEEN
O, what a rash and bloody deed is this!
HAMLET
A bloody deed—almost as bad, good Mother,
As kill a king, and marry with his brother.
QUEEN
As kill a king!
HAMLET   Ay, lady, it was my word.
    [*He parts the arras and discovers Polonius.*]
Thou wretched, rash, intruding fool, farewell!
I took thee for thy better. Take thy fortune.
Thou find'st to be too busy is some danger.—   34
Leave wringing of your hands. Peace, sit you down,
And let me wring your heart, for so I shall,
If it be made of penetrable stuff,
If damnèd custom have not brazed it so   38
That it be proof and bulwark against sense.   39
QUEEN
What have I done, that thou dar'st wag thy tongue

---

75 **would be scanned** needs to be looked into, or, would be interpreted as follows   80 **grossly, full of bread** i.e., enjoying his worldly pleasures rather than fasting. (See Ezekiel 16:49.)   81 **crimes broad blown** sins in full bloom.   **flush** vigorous   82 **audit** account.   **save** except for   83 **in . . . thought** as we see it from our mortal perspective   86 **seasoned** matured, readied   88 **know . . . hent** await to be grasped by me on a more horrid occasion.   **hent** act of seizing   89 **drunk . . . rage** dead drunk, or in a fit of sexual passion   91 **game** gambling   92 **relish** trace, savor   95 **stays** awaits (me)   96 **physic** purging (by prayer); or, Hamlet's postponement of the killing
3.4. Location: The Queen's private chamber.
1 **lay home** thrust to the heart, reprove him soundly   2 **broad** unrestrained   4 **Much heat** i.e., the King's anger.   **shroud** conceal (with ironic fitness to Polonius' imminent death. The word is only in the First Quarto; the Second Quarto and the Folio read "silence.")   5 **round** blunt

10 **thy father** i.e., your stepfather, Claudius   12 **idle** foolish   15 **forgot me** i.e., forgotten that I am your mother.   **rood** cross of Christ   18 **speak** i.e., to someone so rude   25 **Dead for a ducat** i.e., I bet a ducat he's dead; or, a ducat is his life's fee   34 **busy** nosey   38 **damnèd custom** habitual wickedness.   **brazed** brazened, hardened   39 **proof** armor.   **sense** feeling

In noise so rude against me?
HAMLET   Such an act
That blurs the grace and blush of modesty,
Calls virtue hypocrite, takes off the rose
From the fair forehead of an innocent love
And sets a blister there, makes marriage vows   45
As false as dicers' oaths. O, such a deed
As from the body of contraction plucks   47
The very soul, and sweet religion makes   48
A rhapsody of words. Heaven's face does glow   49
O'er this solidity and compound mass   50
With tristful visage, as against the doom,   51
Is thought-sick at the act.
QUEEN   Ay me, what act,   52
That roars so loud and thunders in the index?   53
HAMLET [showing her two likenesses]
Look here upon this picture, and on this,
The counterfeit presentment of two brothers.   55
See what a grace was seated on this brow:
Hyperion's curls, the front of Jove himself,   57
An eye like Mars to threaten and command,   58
A station like the herald Mercury   59
New-lighted on a heaven-kissing hill—   60
A combination and a form indeed
Where every god did seem to set his seal   62
To give the world assurance of a man.
This was your husband. Look you now what
     follows:
Here is your husband, like a mildewed ear,   65
Blasting his wholesome brother. Have you eyes?   66
Could you on this fair mountain leave to feed   67
And batten on this moor? Ha, have you eyes?   68
You cannot call it love, for at your age
The heyday in the blood is tame, it's humble,   70
And waits upon the judgment, and what judgment
Would step from this to this? Sense, sure, you have, 72
Else could you not have motion, but sure that sense
Is apoplexed, for madness would not err,   74
Nor sense to ecstasy was ne'er so thralled,
But it reserved some quantity of choice   76
To serve in such a difference. What devil was 't 77

That thus hath cozened you at hoodman-blind?   78
Eyes without feeling, feeling without sight,
Ears without hands or eyes, smelling sans all,   80
Or but a sickly part of one true sense
Could not so mope. O shame, where is thy blush?   82
Rebellious hell,
If thou canst mutine in a matron's bones,   84
To flaming youth let virtue be as wax   85
And melt in her own fire. Proclaim no shame   86
When the compulsive ardor gives the charge,   87
Since frost itself as actively doth burn,   88
And reason panders will.   89
QUEEN   O Hamlet, speak no more!
Thou turn'st mine eyes into my very soul,
And there I see such black and grainèd spots   92
As will not leave their tinct.
HAMLET   Nay, but to live   93
In the rank sweat of an enseamèd bed,   94
Stewed in corruption, honeying and making love   95
Over the nasty sty!
QUEEN   O, speak to me no more!
These words like daggers enter in my ears.
No more, sweet Hamlet!
HAMLET   A murderer and a villain,
A slave that is not twentieth part the tithe   100
Of your precedent lord, a vice of kings,   101
A cutpurse of the empire and the rule,
That from a shelf the precious diadem stole
And put it in his pocket!
QUEEN   No more!

     Enter Ghost [in his nightgown].

HAMLET   A king of shreds and patches—   106
Save me, and hover o'er me with your wings,
You heavenly guards! What would your gracious
     figure?
QUEEN   Alas, he's mad!
HAMLET
Do you not come your tardy son to chide,
That, lapsed in time and passion, lets go by   111
Th' important acting of your dread command?   112
O, say!
GHOST
Do not forget. This visitation
Is but to whet thy almost blunted purpose.

45 **sets a blister** i.e., brands as a harlot 47 **contraction** the marriage contract 48 **sweet religion makes** i.e., makes marriage vows 49 **rhapsody** senseless string 49–52 **Heaven's . . . act** heaven's face blushes at this solid world compounded of the various elements, with sorrowful face as though the day of doom were near, and is sick with horror at the deed (i.e., Gertrude's marriage) 53 **index** table of contents, prelude or preface 55 **counterfeit presentment** portrayed representation 57 **Hyperion's** the sun-god's. **front** brow 58 **Mars** god of war 59 **station** manner of standing. **Mercury** winged messenger of the gods 60 **New-lighted** newly alighted 62 **set his seal** i.e., affix his approval 65 **ear** i.e., of grain 66 **Blasting** blighting 67 **leave** cease 68 **batten** gorge. **moor** barren or marshy ground (suggesting also "dark-skinned") 70 **heyday** state of excitement. **blood** passion 72 **Sense** perception through the five senses (the functions of the middle or sensible soul) 74 **apoplexed** paralyzed. (Hamlet goes on to explain that, without such a paralysis of will, mere madness would not so err, nor would the five senses so enthrall themselves to *ecstasy* or lunacy; even such deranged states of mind would be able to make the obvious choice between Hamlet Senior and Claudius.) **err** so err 76 **But** but that 77 **To . . . difference** to help in making a choice between two such men

78 **cozened** cheated. **hoodman-blind** blindman's buff. (In this game, says Hamlet, the devil must have pushed Claudius toward Gertrude while she was blindfolded.) 80 **sans** without 82 **mope** be dazed, act aimlessly 84 **mutine** incite mutiny 85–86 **be as wax . . . fire** melt like a candle or stick of sealing wax held over the candle flame 86–89 **Proclaim . . . will** call it no shameful business when the compelling ardor of youth delivers the attack, i.e., commits lechery, since the *frost* of advanced age burns with as active a fire of lust and reason perverts itself by fomenting lust rather than restraining it 92 **grainèd** dyed in grain, indelible 93 **leave their tinct** surrender their color 94 **enseamèd** saturated in the grease and filth of passionate lovemaking 95 **Stewed** soaked, bathed (with a suggestion of "stew," brothel) 100 **tithe** tenth part 101 **precedent lord** former husband. **vice** buffoon. (A reference to the Vice of the morality plays.) 106 **shreds and patches** i.e., motley, the traditional costume of the clown or fool 111 **lapsed** delaying 112 **important** importunate, urgent

But look, amazement on thy mother sits.   116
O, step between her and her fighting soul!
Conceit in weakest bodies strongest works.   118
Speak to her, Hamlet.
HAMLET   How is it with you, lady?
QUEEN   Alas, how is 't with you,
That you do bend your eye on vacancy,
And with th' incorporal air do hold discourse?   122
Forth at your eyes your spirits wildly peep,
And, as the sleeping soldiers in th' alarm,   124
Your bedded hair, like life in excrements,   125
Start up and stand on end. O gentle son,
Upon the heat and flame of thy distemper   127
Sprinkle cool patience. Whereon do you look?
HAMLET
On him, on him! Look you how pale he glares!
His form and cause conjoined, preaching to stones,   130
Would make them capable.—Do not look upon me,   131
Lest with this piteous action you convert   132
My stern effects. Then what I have to do   133
Will want true color—tears perchance for blood.   134
QUEEN   To whom do you speak this?
HAMLET   Do you see nothing there?
QUEEN
Nothing at all, yet all that is I see.
HAMLET   Nor did you nothing hear?
QUEEN   No, nothing but ourselves.
HAMLET
Why, look you there, look how it steals away!
My father, in his habit as he lived!   141
Look where he goes even now out at the portal!
                                             Exit Ghost.
QUEEN
This is the very coinage of your brain.   143
This bodiless creation ecstasy   144
Is very cunning in.   145
HAMLET   Ecstasy?
My pulse as yours doth temperately keep time,
And makes as healthful music. It is not madness
That I have uttered. Bring me to the test,
And I the matter will reword, which madness   150
Would gambol from. Mother, for love of grace,   151
Lay not that flattering unction to your soul   152
That not your trespass but my madness speaks.
It will but skin and film the ulcerous place,   154
Whiles rank corruption, mining all within,   155

Infects unseen. Confess yourself to heaven,
Repent what's past, avoid what is to come,
And do not spread the compost on the weeds   158
To make them ranker. Forgive me this my virtue;   159
For in the fatness of these pursy times   160
Virtue itself of vice must pardon beg,
Yea, curb and woo for leave to do him good.   162
QUEEN
O Hamlet, thou hast cleft my heart in twain.
HAMLET
O, throw away the worser part of it,
And live the purer with the other half.
Good night. But go not to my uncle's bed;
Assume a virtue, if you have it not.
That monster, custom, who all sense doth eat,   168
Of habits devil, is angel yet in this,   169
That to the use of actions fair and good
He likewise gives a frock or livery   171
That aptly is put on. Refrain tonight,   172
And that shall lend a kind of easiness
To the next abstinence; the next more easy;
For use almost can change the stamp of nature,   175
And either . . . the devil, or throw him out   176
With wondrous potency. Once more, good night;
And when you are desirous to be blest,   178
I'll blessing beg of you. For this same lord,   179
                                  [pointing to Polonius]
I do repent; but heaven hath pleased it so
To punish me with this, and this with me,
That I must be their scourge and minister.   182
I will bestow him, and will answer well   183
The death I gave him. So, again, good night.
I must be cruel only to be kind.
This bad begins, and worse remains behind.   186
One word more, good lady.
QUEEN   What shall I do?
HAMLET
Not this by no means that I bid you do:
Let the bloat king tempt you again to bed,   189
Pinch wanton on your cheek, call you his mouse,   190
And let him, for a pair of reechy kisses,   191
Or paddling in your neck with his damned fingers,   192

116 amazement distraction   118 Conceit imagination   122 incorporal immaterial   124 as . . . alarm like soldiers called out of sleep by an alarum   125 bedded laid flat.   like life in excrements i.e., as though hair, an outgrowth of the body, had a life of its own. (Hair was thought to be lifeless because it lacks sensation, and so its standing on end would be unnatural and ominous.)   127 distemper disorder   130 His . . . conjoined his appearance joined to his cause for speaking   131 capable receptive   132–133 convert . . . effects divert me from my stern duty   134 want . . . blood lack plausibility so that (with a play on the normal sense of color) I shall shed colorless tears instead of blood   141 habit clothes.   as as when   143 very mere   144–145 This . . . in madness is skillful in creating this kind of hallucination   150 reword repeat word for word   151 gambol skip away   152 unction ointment   154 skin grow a skin for   155 mining working under the surface

158 compost manure   159 this my virtue my virtuous talk in reproving you   160 fatness grossness.   pursy flabby, out of shape   162 curb bow, bend the knee.   leave permission   168 who . . . eat which consumes all proper or natural feeling, all sensibility   169 Of habits devil devil-like in prompting evil habits   171 livery an outer appearance, a customary garb (and hence a predisposition easily assumed in time of stress)   172 aptly readily   175 use habit.   the stamp of nature our inborn traits   176 And either (A defective line, usually emended by inserting the word master after either, following the Fourth Quarto and early editors.)   178–179 when . . . you i.e., when you are ready to be penitent and seek God's blessing, I will ask your blessing as a dutiful son should   182 their scourge and minister i.e., agent of heavenly retribution. (By scourge, Hamlet also suggests that he himself will eventually suffer punishment in the process of fulfilling heaven's will.)   183 bestow stow, dispose of.   answer account or pay for   186 This i.e., the killing of Polonius.   behind to come   189 bloat bloated   190 Pinch wanton i.e., leave his love pinches on your cheeks, branding you as wanton   191 reechy dirty, filthy   192 paddling fingering amorously

Make you to ravel all this matter out   193
That I essentially am not in madness,
But mad in craft. 'Twere good you let him know,   195
For who that's but a queen, fair, sober, wise,
Would from a paddock, from a bat, a gib,   197
Such dear concernings hide? Who would do so?   198
No, in despite of sense and secrecy,   199
Unpeg the basket on the house's top,   200
Let the birds fly, and like the famous ape,   201
To try conclusions, in the basket creep   202
And break your own neck down.   203

QUEEN
Be thou assured, if words be made of breath,
And breath of life, I have no life to breathe
What thou hast said to me.

HAMLET
I must to England. You know that?

QUEEN   Alack,
I had forgot. 'Tis so concluded on.

HAMLET
There's letters sealed, and my two schoolfellows,
Whom I will trust as I will adders fanged,
They bear the mandate; they must sweep my way   211
And marshal me to knavery. Let it work.   212
For 'tis the sport to have the enginer   213
Hoist with his own petard, and 't shall go hard   214
But I will delve one yard below their mines   215
And blow them at the moon. O, 'tis most sweet
When in one line two crafts directly meet.   217
This man shall set me packing.   218
I'll lug the guts into the neighbor room.
Mother, good night indeed. This counselor
Is now most still, most secret, and most grave,
Who was in life a foolish prating knave.—
Come, sir, to draw toward an end with you.—   223
Good night, Mother.
       Exeunt [separately, Hamlet dragging in Polonius].

❧

193 **ravel . . . out** unravel, disclose 195 **in craft** by cunning. **good** (Said sarcastically; also the following eight lines.) 197 **paddock** toad. **gib** tomcat 198 **dear concernings** important affairs 199 **sense and secrecy** secrecy that common sense requires 200 **Unpeg the basket** open the cage, i.e., let out the secret 201 **famous ape** (In a story now lost.) 202 **try conclusions** test the outcome (in which the ape apparently enters a cage from which birds have been released and then tries to fly out of the cage as they have done, falling to its death) 203 **down** in the fall; utterly 211–212 **sweep . . . knavery** sweep a path before me and conduct me to some *knavery* or treachery prepared for me 212 **work** proceed 213 **enginer** maker of military contrivances 214 **Hoist with** blown up by. **petard** an explosive used to blow in a door or make a breach 214–215 **'t shall . . . will** unless luck is against me, I will 215 **mines** tunnels used in warfare to undermine the enemy's emplacements; Hamlet will countermine by going under their mines 217 **in one line** i.e., mines and countermines on a collision course, or the countermines directly below the mines. **crafts** acts of guile, plots 218 **set me packing** set me to making schemes, and set me to lugging (him), and, also, send me off in a hurry 223 **draw . . . end** finish up (with a pun on *draw*, "pull")

4.1   *Enter King and Queen, with Rosencrantz and Guildenstern.*

KING
There's matter in these sighs, these profound
       heaves.   1
You must translate; 'tis fit we understand them.
Where is your son?

QUEEN
Bestow this place on us a little while.
                    [*Exeunt Rosencrantz and Guildenstern.*]
Ah, mine own lord, what have I seen tonight!

KING
What, Gertrude? How does Hamlet?

QUEEN
Mad as the sea and wind when both contend
Which is the mightier. In his lawless fit,
Behind the arras hearing something stir,
Whips out his rapier, cries, "A rat, a rat!"
And in this brainish apprehension kills   11
The unseen good old man.

KING   O heavy deed!   12
It had been so with us, had we been there.   13
His liberty is full of threats to all—
To you yourself, to us, to everyone.
Alas, how shall this bloody deed be answered?   16
It will be laid to us, whose providence   17
Should have kept short, restrained, and out of haunt 18
This mad young man. But so much was our love,
We would not understand what was most fit,
But, like the owner of a foul disease,
To keep it from divulging, let it feed   22
Even on the pith of life. Where is he gone?

QUEEN
To draw apart the body he hath killed,
O'er whom his very madness, like some ore   25
Among a mineral of metals base,   26
Shows itself pure: 'a weeps for what is done.

KING   O Gertrude, come away!
The sun no sooner shall the mountains touch
But we will ship him hence, and this vile deed
We must with all our majesty and skill
Both countenance and excuse.—Ho, Guildenstern!   32

Enter Rosencrantz and Guildenstern.

Friends both, go join you with some further aid.
Hamlet in madness hath Polonius slain,

4.1. Location: The castle.
s.d. Enter . . . Queen (Some editors argue that Gertrude never exits in 3.4 and that the scene is continuous here, as suggested in the Folio, but the Second Quarto marks an entrance for her and at line 35 Claudius speaks of Gertrude's *closet* as though it were elsewhere. A short time has elapsed, during which the King has become aware of her highly wrought emotional state.) **1 matter** significance. **heaves** heavy sighs **11 brainish apprehension** headstrong conception **12 heavy** grievous **13 us** i.e., me. (The royal "we"; also in line 15.) **16 answered** explained **17 providence** foresight **18 short** i.e., on a short tether. **out of haunt** secluded **22 divulging** becoming evident **25 ore** vein of gold **26 mineral** mine **32 countenance** put the best face on

And from his mother's closet hath he dragged him.
Go seek him out, speak fair, and bring the body
Into the chapel. I pray you, haste in this.
                    [*Exeunt Rosencrantz and Guildenstern.*]
Come, Gertrude, we'll call up our wisest friends
And let them know both what we mean to do
And what's untimely done   40
Whose whisper o'er the world's diameter,   41
As level as the cannon to his blank,   42
Transports his poisoned shot, may miss our name
And hit the woundless air. O, come away!   44
My soul is full of discord and dismay.   *Exeunt.*

❖

4.2   *Enter Hamlet.*

HAMLET   Safely stowed.
ROSENCRANTZ, GUILDENSTERN (*within*)   Hamlet! Lord
    Hamlet!
HAMLET   But soft, what noise? Who calls on Hamlet? O,
    here they come.

    Enter Rosencrantz and Guildenstern.

ROSENCRANTZ
    What have you done, my lord, with the dead body?
HAMLET
    Compounded it with dust, whereto 'tis kin.
ROSENCRANTZ
    Tell us where 'tis, that we may take it thence
    And bear it to the chapel.
HAMLET   Do not believe it.
ROSENCRANTZ   Believe what?
HAMLET   That I can keep your counsel and not mine   12
    own. Besides, to be demanded of a sponge, what rep-   13
    lication should be made by the son of a king?   14
ROSENCRANTZ   Take you me for a sponge, my lord?
HAMLET   Ay, sir, that soaks up the King's countenance,   16
    his rewards, his authorities. But such officers do the   17
    King best service in the end. He keeps them, like an
    ape, an apple, in the corner of his jaw, first mouthed
    to be last swallowed. When he needs what you have
    gleaned, it is but squeezing you, and, sponge, you
    shall be dry again.
ROSENCRANTZ   I understand you not, my lord.
HAMLET   I am glad of it. A knavish speech sleeps in a   24
    foolish ear.
ROSENCRANTZ   My lord, you must tell us where the
    body is and go with us to the King.

HAMLET   The body is with the King, but the King is not   28
    with the body. The King is a thing—   29
GUILDENSTERN   A thing, my lord?
HAMLET   Of nothing. Bring me to him. Hide fox, and all   31
    after!   *Exeunt* [*running*]. 32

❖

4.3   *Enter King, and two or three.*

KING
    I have sent to seek him, and to find the body.
    How dangerous is it that this man goes loose!
    Yet must not we put the strong law on him.
    He's loved of the distracted multitude,   4
    Who like not in their judgment, but their eyes,   5
    And where 'tis so, th' offender's scourge is weighed,   6
    But never the offense. To bear all smooth and even,   7
    This sudden sending him away must seem
    Deliberate pause. Diseases desperate grown   9
    By desperate appliance are relieved,   10
    Or not at all.

    Enter Rosencrantz, [*Guildenstern,*]
    and all the rest.

                    How now, what hath befall'n?
ROSENCRANTZ
    Where the dead body is bestowed, my lord,
    We cannot get from him.
KING   But where is he?
ROSENCRANTZ
    Without, my lord; guarded, to know your pleasure.
KING
    Bring him before us.
ROSENCRANTZ   Ho! Bring in the lord.

    They enter [*with Hamlet*].

KING   Now, Hamlet, where's Polonius?
HAMLET   At supper.
KING   At supper? Where?
HAMLET   Not where he eats, but where 'a is eaten. A
    certain convocation of politic worms are e'en at him. 20

---

40 And . . . done (A defective line; conjectures as to the missing
words include *So, haply, slander* [Capell and others]; *For, haply, slander* [Theobald and others]; and *So envious slander* [Jenkins].)   41 diameter extent from side to side   42 As level with as direct aim.   his
blank its target at point-blank range   44 woundless invulnerable
4.2. Location: The castle.
12–13 That . . . own i.e., that I can follow your advice (by telling
where the body is) and still keep my own secret   13 demanded of
questioned by   13–14 replication reply   16 countenance favor
17 authorities delegated power, influence   24 sleeps in has no
meaning to

28–29 The . . . body (Perhaps alludes to the legal commonplace of
"the king's two bodies," which drew a distinction between the sacred
office of kingship and the particular mortal who possessed it at any
given time. Hence, although Claudius' body is necessarily a part of
him, true kingship is not contained in it. Similarly, Claudius will have
Polonius' body when it is found, but there is no kingship in this business either.)   31 Of nothing (1) of no account (2) lacking the essence
of kingship, as in lines 28–29 and note   31–32 Hide . . . after (An
old signal cry in the game of hide-and-seek, suggesting that Hamlet
now runs away from them.)
4.3. Location: The castle.
4 of by.   distracted fickle, unstable   5 Who . . . eyes who choose
not by judgment but by appearance   6 scourge punishment. (Literally, blow with a whip.)   weighed sympathetically considered   7 To
. . . even to manage the business in an unprovocative way   9 Deliberate pause carefully considered action   10 appliance remedies
20 politic worms crafty worms (suited to a master spy like Polonius).
e'en even now

Your worm is your only emperor for diet. We fat all 21
creatures else to fat us, and we fat ourselves for maggots. Your fat king and your lean beggar is but
variable service—two dishes, but to one table. That's 24
the end.

KING   Alas, alas!

HAMLET   A man may fish with the worm that hath eat 27
of a king, and eat of the fish that hath fed of that
worm.

KING   What dost thou mean by this?

HAMLET   Nothing but to show you how a king may go
a progress through the guts of a beggar. 32

KING   Where is Polonius?

HAMLET   In heaven. Send thither to see. If your messenger find him not there, seek him i' th' other place yourself. But if indeed you find him not within this month,
you shall nose him as you go up the stairs into the
lobby.

KING [to some attendants]   Go seek him there.

HAMLET   'A will stay till you come. [Exeunt attendants.]

KING
Hamlet, this deed, for thine especial safety—
Which we do tender, as we dearly grieve 42
For that which thou hast done—must send thee
    hence
With fiery quickness. Therefore prepare thyself.
The bark is ready, and the wind at help, 45
Th' associates tend, and everything is bent 46
For England.

HAMLET   For England!

KING   Ay, Hamlet.

HAMLET   Good.

KING
So is it, if thou knew'st our purposes.

HAMLET   I see a cherub that sees them. But come, for 52
England! Farewell, dear mother.

KING   Thy loving father, Hamlet.

HAMLET   My mother. Father and mother is man and
wife, man and wife is one flesh, and so, my mother.
Come, for England!   Exit.

KING
Follow him at foot; tempt him with speed aboard. 58
Delay it not. I'll have him hence tonight.
Away! For everything is sealed and done
That else leans on th' affair. Pray you, make haste. 61
            [Exeunt all but the King.]
And, England, if my love thou hold'st at aught— 62
As my great power thereof may give thee sense, 63
Since yet thy cicatrice looks raw and red 64

After the Danish sword, and thy free awe 65
Pays homage to us—thou mayst not coldly set 66
Our sovereign process, which imports at full, 67
By letters congruing to that effect, 68
The present death of Hamlet. Do it, England, 69
For like the hectic in my blood he rages, 70
And thou must cure me. Till I know 'tis done,
Howe'er my haps, my joys were ne'er begun.   Exit. 72

4.4   Enter Fortinbras with his army over the stage.

FORTINBRAS
Go, Captain, from me greet the Danish king.
Tell him that by his license Fortinbras
Craves the conveyance of a promised march 3
Over his kingdom. You know the rendezvous.
If that His Majesty would aught with us,
We shall express our duty in his eye; 6
And let him know so.

CAPTAIN   I will do 't, my lord.

FORTINBRAS   Go softly on.   [Exeunt all but the Captain.] 9

Enter Hamlet, Rosencrantz, [Guildenstern,] etc.

HAMLET   Good sir, whose powers are these? 10

CAPTAIN   They are of Norway, sir.

HAMLET   How purposed, sir, I pray you?

CAPTAIN   Against some part of Poland.

HAMLET   Who commands them, sir?

CAPTAIN
The nephew to old Norway, Fortinbras.

HAMLET
Goes it against the main of Poland, sir, 16
Or for some frontier?

CAPTAIN
Truly to speak, and with no addition, 18
We go to gain a little patch of ground
That hath in it no profit but the name.
To pay five ducats, five, I would not farm it; 21
Nor will it yield to Norway or the Pole
A ranker rate, should it be sold in fee. 23

HAMLET
Why, then the Polack never will defend it.

CAPTAIN
Yes, it is already garrisoned.

HAMLET
Two thousand souls and twenty thousand ducats
Will not debate the question of this straw. 27
This is th' impostume of much wealth and peace, 28
That inward breaks, and shows no cause without

21 Your worm your average worm. Compare your fat king and your
lean beggar in line 23.)   diet food, eating (with a punning reference
to the Diet of Worms, a famous convocation held in 1521)   24 variable service different courses of a single meal   27 eat eaten. (Pronounced et.)   32 progress royal journey of state   42 tender regard,
hold dear.   dearly intensely   45 bark sailing vessel   46 tend wait.
bent in readiness   52 cherub (Cherubim are angels of knowledge.
Hamlet hints that both he and heaven are onto Claudius' tricks.)
58 at foot close behind, at heel   61 leans on bears upon, is related to
62 England i.e., King of England.   at aught at any value   63 As . . .
sense for so my great power may give you a just appreciation of the
importance of valuing my love   64 cicatrice scar

65 free awe voluntary show of respect   66 coldly set regard with indifference   67 process command.   imports at full conveys specific
directions for   68 congruing agreeing   69 present immediate
70 hectic persistent fever   72 haps fortunes
4.4 Location: The coast of Denmark.
2 license permission   3 the conveyance of escort during   6 duty respect.   eye presence   9 softly slowly, circumspectly   10 powers
forces   16 main main part   18 addition exaggeration   21 To pay
i.e., for a yearly rental of.   farm it take a lease of it   23 ranker
higher.   in fee fee simple, outright   27 debate . . . straw settle this
trifling matter   28 impostume abscess

Why the man dies. I humbly thank you, sir.
CAPTAIN
  God b' wi' you, sir.   [*Exit.*]
ROSENCRANTZ   Will 't please you go, my lord?
HAMLET
  I'll be with you straight. Go a little before.
                            [*Exeunt all except Hamlet.*]
  How all occasions do inform against me   33
  And spur my dull revenge! What is a man,
  If his chief good and market of his time   35
  Be but to sleep and feed? A beast, no more.
  Sure he that made us with such large discourse,   37
  Looking before and after, gave us not   38
  That capability and godlike reason
  To fust in us unused. Now, whether it be   40
  Bestial oblivion, or some craven scruple   41
  Of thinking too precisely on th' event—   42
  A thought which, quartered, hath but one part
      wisdom
  And ever three parts coward—I do not know
  Why yet I live to say "This thing's to do,"
  Sith I have cause, and will, and strength, and means 46
  To do 't. Examples gross as earth exhort me: 47
  Witness this army of such mass and charge,   48
  Led by a delicate and tender prince,   49
  Whose spirit with divine ambition puffed
  Makes mouths at the invisible event,   51
  Exposing what is mortal and unsure
  To all that fortune, death, and danger dare,   53
  Even for an eggshell. Rightly to be great   54
  Is not to stir without great argument,   55
  But greatly to find quarrel in a straw   56
  When honor's at the stake. How stand I, then,   57
  That have a father killed, a mother stained,
  Excitements of my reason and my blood,   59
  And let all sleep, while to my shame I see
  The imminent death of twenty thousand men
  That for a fantasy and trick of fame   62
  Go to their graves like beds, fight for a plot   63
  Whereon the numbers cannot try the cause,   64
  Which is not tomb enough and continent   65
  To hide the slain? O, from this time forth
  My thoughts be bloody or be nothing worth!   *Exit.*

♣

33 **inform against** denounce, betray; take shape against   35 **market of** profit of, compensation for   37 **discourse** power of reasoning   38 **Looking before and after** able to review past events and anticipate the future   40 **fust** grow moldy   41 **oblivion** forgetfulness.   **craven** cowardly   42 **precisely** scrupulously.   **event** outcome   46 **Sith** since   47 **gross** obvious   48 **charge** expense   49 **delicate and tender** of fine and youthful qualities   51 **Makes mouths** makes scornful faces.   **invisible event** unforeseeable outcome   53 **dare** could do (to him)   54–57 **Rightly . . . stake** true greatness does not normally consist of rushing into action over some trivial provocation; however, when one's honor is involved, even a trifling insult requires that one respond greatly (?)   **at the stake** (A metaphor from gambling or bear-baiting.)   59 **Excitements** of promptings by   62 **fantasy** fanciful caprice, illusion.   **trick** trifle, deceit   63 **plot** plot of ground   64 **Whereon . . . cause** on which there is insufficient room for the soldiers needed to engage in a military contest   65 **continent** receptacle, container

---

4.5 *Enter Horatio, [Queen] Gertrude, and a Gentleman.*

QUEEN
  I will not speak with her.
GENTLEMAN   She is importunate,
  Indeed distract. Her mood will needs be pitied.   2
QUEEN   What would she have?
GENTLEMAN
  She speaks much of her father, says she hears
  There's tricks i' the world, and hems, and beats her
      heart,   5
  Spurns enviously at straws, speaks things in doubt 6
  That carry but half sense. Her speech is nothing,
  Yet the unshapèd use of it doth move   8
  The hearers to collection; they yawn at it,   9
  And botch the words up fit to their own thoughts,   10
  Which, as her winks and nods and gestures yield
      them,   11
  Indeed would make one think there might be
      thought,   12
  Though nothing sure, yet much unhappily.   13
HORATIO
  'Twere good she were spoken with, for she may
      strew
  Dangerous conjectures in ill-breeding minds.   15
QUEEN   Let her come in.   [*Exit Gentleman.*]
  [*Aside.*] To my sick soul, as sin's true nature is,
  Each toy seems prologue to some great amiss.   18
  So full of artless jealousy is guilt,   19
  It spills itself in fearing to be spilt.   20

        Enter Ophelia [distracted].

OPHELIA
  Where is the beauteous majesty of Denmark?
QUEEN   How now, Ophelia?
OPHELIA (*she sings*)
  "How should I your true love know
      From another one?
  By his cockle hat and staff,   25
      And his sandal shoon."   26
QUEEN   Alas, sweet lady, what imports this song?
OPHELIA   Say you? Nay, pray you, mark.
  "He is dead and gone, lady,   (*Song.*)
      He is dead and gone;
  At his head a grass-green turf,
      At his heels a stone."
  O, ho!

4.5. Location: The castle.
2 **distract** distracted   5 **tricks** deceptions.   **hems** makes "hmm" sounds.   **heart** i.e., breast   6 **Spurns . . . straws** kicks spitefully, takes offense at trifles.   **in doubt** obscurely   8 **unshapèd use** incoherent manner   9 **collection** inference, a guess at some sort of meaning.   **yawn** gape, wonder; grasp. (The Folio reading, *aim*, is possible.)   10 **botch** patch   11 **Which** which words.   **yield** deliver, represent   12 **thought** intended   13 **unhappily** unpleasantly near the truth, shrewdly   15 **ill-breeding** prone to suspect the worst and to make mischief   18 **toy** trifle.   **amiss** calamity   19–20 **So . . . spilt** guilt is so full of suspicion that it unskillfully betrays itself in fearing betrayal   20 s.d. **Enter Ophelia** (In the First Quarto, Ophelia enters, "playing on a lute, and her hair down, singing.")   25 **cockle hat** hat with cockle-shell stuck in it as a sign that the wearer had been a pilgrim to the shrine of Saint James of Compostella in Spain   26 **shoon** shoes

QUEEN   Nay, but Ophelia—
OPHELIA   Pray you, mark.
[*Sings.*] "White his shroud as the mountain snow"—

Enter King.

QUEEN   Alas, look here, my lord.
OPHELIA
    "Larded with sweet flowers;   (*Song.*)   38
    Which bewept to the ground did not go
    With true-love showers."   40
KING   How do you, pretty lady?
OPHELIA   Well, God 'ild you! They say the owl was a   42
baker's daughter. Lord, we know what we are, but
know not what we may be. God be at your table!
KING   Conceit upon her father.   45
OPHELIA   Pray let's have no words of this; but when
they ask you what it means, say you this:
    "Tomorrow is Saint Valentine's day,   (*Song.*)
    All in the morning betime,   49
    And I a maid at your window,
    To be your Valentine.
    Then up he rose, and donned his clothes,
    And dupped the chamber door,   53
    Let in the maid, that out a maid
    Never departed more."
KING   Pretty Ophelia—
OPHELIA   Indeed, la, without an oath, I'll make an end
on 't:
    [*Sings.*] "By Gis and by Saint Charity,   59
    Alack, and fie for shame!
    Young men will do 't, if they come to 't;
    By Cock, they are to blame.   62
    Quoth she, 'Before you tumbled me,
    You promised me to wed.' "
He answers:
    " 'So would I ha' done, by yonder sun,
    An thou hadst not come to my bed.' "   67
KING   How long hath she been thus?
OPHELIA   I hope all will be well. We must be patient,
but I cannot choose but weep to think they would lay
him i' the cold ground. My brother shall know of it.
And so I thank you for your good counsel. Come, my
coach! Good night, ladies, good night, sweet ladies,
good night, good night.   [*Exit.*]
KING [*to Horatio*]
Follow her close. Give her good watch, I pray you.
                   [*Exit Horatio.*]
O, this is the poison of deep grief; it springs
All from her father's death—and now behold!
O Gertrude, Gertrude,
When sorrows come, they come not single spies,
But in battalions. First, her father slain;   79
Next, your son gone, and he most violent author

Of his own just remove; the people muddied,   82
Thick and unwholesome in their thoughts and
   whispers
For good Polonius' death—and we have done but
   greenly,   84
In hugger-mugger to inter him; poor Ophelia   85
Divided from herself and her fair judgment,
Without the which we are pictures or mere beasts;
Last, and as much containing as all these,   88
Her brother is in secret come from France,
Feeds on this wonder, keeps himself in clouds,   90
And wants not buzzers to infect his ear   91
With pestilent speeches of his father's death,
Wherein necessity, of matter beggared,   93
Will nothing stick our person to arraign   94
In ear and ear. O my dear Gertrude, this,   95
Like to a murdering piece, in many places   96
Gives me superfluous death.   *A noise within.*   97
QUEEN   Alack, what noise is this?
KING   Attend!   99
Where is my Switzers? Let them guard the door.   100

Enter a Messenger.

What is the matter?
MESSENGER   Save yourself, my lord!
The ocean, overpeering of his list,   102
Eats not the flats with more impetuous haste   103
Than young Laertes, in a riotous head,   104
O'erbears your officers. The rabble call him lord,
And, as the world were now but to begin,   106
Antiquity forgot, custom not known,
The ratifiers and props of every word,   108
They cry, "Choose we! Laertes shall be king!"
Caps, hands, and tongues applaud it to the clouds, 110
"Laertes shall be king, Laertes king!"
QUEEN
How cheerfully on the false trail they cry!
                A noise within.
O, this is counter, you false Danish dogs!   113

Enter Laertes with others.

KING   The doors are broke.
LAERTES
Where is this King?—Sirs, stand you all without.

---

38 Larded decorated   **40 showers** i.e., tears   **42 God 'ild** God yield
or reward.   **owl** (Refers to a legend about a baker's daughter who
was turned into an owl for being ungenerous when Jesus begged a
loaf of bread.)   **45 Conceit** brooding   **49 betime** early   **53 dupped**
did up, opened   **59 Gis** Jesus   **62 Cock** (A perversion of "God" in
oaths; here also with a quibble on the slang word for penis.)   **67 An**
if   **79 spies** scouts sent in advance of the main force

82 remove removal.   **muddied** stirred up, confused   **84 greenly** in an
inexperienced way, foolishly   **85 hugger-mugger** secret haste   **88 as
much containing** as full of serious matter   **90 Feeds . . . clouds**
feeds his resentment or shocked grievance, holds himself inscrutable
and aloof amid all this rumor   **91 wants** lacks.   **buzzers** gossipers,
informers   **93 necessity** i.e., the need to invent some plausible explanation.   **of matter beggared** unprovided with facts   **94–95 Will . . .
ear** will not hesitate to accuse my (royal) person in everybody's ears
96 murdering piece cannon loaded so as to scatter its shot   **97 Gives
. . . death** kills me over and over   **99 Attend** i.e., guard me
100 Switzers Swiss guards, mercenaries   **102 overpeering of his list**
overflowing its shore, boundary   **103 flats** i.e., flatlands near shore.
impetuous violent (perhaps also with the meaning of *impiteous* [*impitious*, Q2], "pitiless")   **104 head** insurrection   **106 as** as if   **108 The
ratifiers . . . word** i.e., *antiquity* (or tradition) and *custom* ought to
confirm (*ratify*) and underprop our every word or promise   **110 Caps**
(The caps are thrown in the air.)   **113 counter** (A hunting term,
meaning to follow the trail in a direction opposite to that which the
game has taken.)

ALL　No, let's come in.

LAERTES　I pray you, give me leave.

ALL　We will, we will.

LAERTES
I thank you. Keep the door. [*Exeunt followers.*] O thou
　vile king,
Give me my father!

QUEEN [*restraining him*]　Calmly, good Laertes.

LAERTES
That drop of blood that's calm proclaims me bastard,
Cries cuckold to my father, brands the harlot
Even here, between the chaste unsmirchèd brow　　123
Of my true mother.

KING　　　　　　　What is the cause, Laertes,
That thy rebellion looks so giantlike?
Let him go, Gertrude. Do not fear our person.　　126
There's such divinity doth hedge a king　　127
That treason can but peep to what it would,　　128
Acts little of his will. Tell me, Laertes,　　129
Why thou art thus incensed. Let him go, Gertrude.
Speak, man.

LAERTES　　Where is my father?

KING　　　　　　　　　Dead.

QUEEN
But not by him.

KING　　　　　Let him demand his fill.

LAERTES
How came he dead? I'll not be juggled with.　　133
To hell, allegiance! Vows, to the blackest devil!
Conscience and grace, to the profoundest pit!
I dare damnation. To this point I stand,　　136
That both the worlds I give to negligence,　　137
Let come what comes, only I'll be revenged
Most throughly for my father.　　139

KING　Who shall stay you?

LAERTES　My will, not all the world's.　　141
And for my means, I'll husband them so well　　142
They shall go far with little.

KING　　　　　　　Good Laertes,
If you desire to know the certainty
Of your dear father, is 't writ in your revenge
That, swoopstake, you will draw both friend and
　foe,　　146
Winner and loser?

LAERTES　None but his enemies.

KING　Will you know them, then?

LAERTES
To his good friends thus wide I'll ope my arms,
And like the kind life-rendering pelican　　151

Repast them with my blood.

KING　　　　　　Why, now you speak　　152
Like a good child and a true gentleman.
That I am guiltless of your father's death,
And am most sensibly in grief for it,　　155
It shall as level to your judgment 'pear　　156
As day does to your eye.　　　*A noise within.*

LAERTES
How now, what noise is that?

　　　Enter Ophelia.

KING　　　　　　Let her come in.

LAERTES
O heat, dry up my brains! Tears seven times salt
Burn out the sense and virtue of mine eye!　　160
By heaven, thy madness shall be paid with weight　　161
Till our scale turn the beam. O rose of May!　　162
Dear maid, kind sister, sweet Ophelia!
O heavens, is 't possible a young maid's wits
Should be as mortal as an old man's life?
Nature is fine in love, and where 'tis fine　　166
It sends some precious instance of itself　　167
After the thing it loves.　　168

OPHELIA
　"They bore him barefaced on the bier,　　(*Song.*)
　　Hey non nonny, nonny, hey nonny,
　　And in his grave rained many a tear—"
Fare you well, my dove!

LAERTES
Hadst thou thy wits and didst persuade revenge,　　173
It could not move thus.

OPHELIA　You must sing "A-down a-down," and you　175
"call him a-down-a." O, how the wheel becomes it! It　176
is the false steward that stole his master's daughter.　177

LAERTES　This nothing's more than matter.　　178

OPHELIA　There's rosemary, that's for remembrance;　179
pray you, love, remember. And there is pansies; that's　180
for thoughts.

LAERTES　A document in madness, thoughts and re-　182
membrance fitted.

OPHELIA　There's fennel for you, and columbines.　184
There's rue for you, and here's some for me; we may　185
call it herb of grace o' Sundays. You must wear your
rue with a difference. There's a daisy. I would give　187

123 **between** in the middle of　126 **fear our** fear for my　127 **hedge**
protect, as with a surrounding barrier　128 **can . . . would** can only
peep furtively, as through a barrier, at what it would intend
129 **Acts . . . will** (but) performs little of what it intends　133 **juggled
with** cheated, deceived　136 **To . . . stand** I am resolved in this
137 **both . . . negligence** i.e., both this world and the next are of no
consequence to me　139 **throughly** thoroughly　141 **My will . . .
world's** I'll stop (*stay*) when my will is accomplished, not for anyone
else's.　142 **for** as for　146 **swoopstake** i.e., indiscriminately. (Literally, taking all stakes on the gambling table at once. *Draw* is also a
gambling term, meaning "take from.")　151 **pelican** (Refers to the
belief that the female pelican fed its young with its own blood.)

152 **Repast** feed　155 **sensibly** feelingly　156 **level** plain　160 **virtue**
faculty, power　161 **paid with weight** repaid, avenged equally or
more　162 **beam** crossbar of a balance　166 **fine in** refined by
167 **instance** token　168 **After . . . loves** i.e., into the grave, along
with Polonius　173 **persuade** argue cogently for　175–176 **You . . .
a-down-a** (Ophelia assigns the singing of refrains, like her own "Hey
non nonny," to others present.)　176 **wheel** spinning wheel as accompaniment to the song, or refrain　177 **false steward** (The story is
unknown.)　178 **This . . . matter** this seeming nonsense is more eloquent than sane utterance　179 **rosemary** (Used as a symbol of remembrance both at weddings and at funerals.)　180 **pansies** (Emblems of love and courtship; perhaps from French *pensées*,
"thoughts.")　182 **document** instruction, lesson　184 **fennel** (Emblem
of flattery.)　**columbines** (Emblems of unchastity or ingratitude.)
185 **rue** (Emblem of repentance—a signification that is evident in its
popular name, *herb of grace*.)　187 **with a difference** (A device used
in heraldry to distinguish one family from another on the coat of
arms, here suggesting that Ophelia and the others have different
causes of sorrow and repentance; perhaps with a play on *rue* in
the sense of "ruth," "pity.")　**daisy** (Emblem of dissembling,
faithlessness.)

you some violets, but they withered all when my   188
father died. They say 'a made a good end—
[*Sings.*] "For bonny sweet Robin is all my joy."

LAERTES
Thought and affliction, passion, hell itself,   191
She turns to favor and to prettiness.   192

OPHELIA
"And will 'a not come again?   (*Song.*)
And will 'a not come again?
   No, no, he is dead.
   Go to thy deathbed,
He never will come again.

"His beard was as white as snow,
All flaxen was his poll.
   He is gone, he is gone,   199
   And we cast away moan.
God ha' mercy on his soul!"
And of all Christian souls, I pray God. God b' wi' you.
           [*Exit, followed by Gertrude.*]

LAERTES   Do you see this, O God?

KING
Laertes, I must commune with your grief,
Or you deny me right. Go but apart,
Make choice of whom your wisest friends you will,   207
And they shall hear and judge twixt you and me.
If by direct or by collateral hand   209
They find us touched, we will our kingdom give,   210
Our crown, our life, and all that we call ours
To you in satisfaction; but if not,
Be you content to lend your patience to us,
And we shall jointly labor with your soul
To give it due content.   Let this be so.

LAERTES
His means of death, his obscure funeral—
No trophy, sword, nor hatchment o'er his bones,   217
No noble rite, nor formal ostentation—   218
Cry to be heard, as 'twere from heaven to earth,
That I must call 't in question.

KING   So you shall,   220
And where th' offense is, let the great ax fall.
I pray you, go with me.   *Exeunt.*

❖

4.6   *Enter Horatio and others.*

HORATIO
What are they that would speak with me?
GENTLEMAN   Seafaring men, sir. They say they have
letters for you.
HORATIO   Let them come in.   [*Exit Gentleman.*]
I do not know from what part of the world

I should be greeted, if not from Lord Hamlet.

    Enter Sailors.

FIRST SAILOR   God bless you, sir.
HORATIO   Let him bless thee too.
FIRST SAILOR   'A shall, sir, an 't please him. There's a   9
letter for you, sir—it came from th' ambassador that   10
was bound for England—if your name be Horatio, as
I am let to know it is.   [*He gives a letter.*]
HORATIO [*reads*]   "Horatio, when thou shalt have over-   13
looked this, give these fellows some means to the King;   14
they have letters for him. Ere we were two days old at
sea, a pirate of very warlike appointment gave us   16
chase. Finding ourselves too slow of sail, we put on a
compelled valor, and in the grapple I boarded them.
On the instant they got clear of our ship, so I alone
became their prisoner. They have dealt with me like
thieves of mercy, but they knew what they did: I am to   21
do a good turn for them. Let the King have the letters
I have sent, and repair thou to me with as much speed   23
as thou wouldest fly death. I have words to speak in
thine ear will make thee dumb, yet are they much too
light for the bore of the matter. These good fellows will   26
bring thee where I am. Rosencrantz and Guildenstern
hold their course for England. Of them I have much to
tell thee. Farewell.
        He that thou knowest thine, Hamlet."
Come, I will give you way for these your letters,   31
And do 't the speedier that you may direct me
To him from whom you brought them.   *Exeunt.*

4.7   *Enter King and Laertes.*

KING
Now must your conscience my acquittance seal,   1
And you must put me in your heart for friend,
Sith you have heard, and with a knowing ear,   3
That he which hath your noble father slain
Pursued my life.

LAERTES   It well appears. But tell me
Why you proceeded not against these feats   6
So crimeful and so capital in nature,   7
   As by your safety, greatness, wisdom, all things
   else,
You mainly were stirred up.   9

KING   O, for two special reasons,
Which may to you perhaps seem much unsinewed,   11
But yet to me they're strong. The Queen his mother
Lives almost by his looks, and for myself—
My virtue or my plague, be it either which—

She is so conjunctive to my life and soul　　　　15
That, as the star moves not but in his sphere,　　16
I could not but by her. The other motive
Why to a public count I might not go　　　　18
Is the great love the general gender bear him,　　19
Who, dipping all his faults in their affection,
Work like the spring that turneth wood to stone,　21
Convert his gyves to graces, so that my arrows,　22
Too slightly timbered for so loud a wind,　　23
Would have reverted to my bow again　　　24
But not where I had aimed them.

LAERTES
And so have I a noble father lost,
A sister driven into desperate terms,　　　27
Whose worth, if praises may go back again,　　28
Stood challenger on mount of all the age　　29
For her perfections. But my revenge will come.

KING
Break not your sleeps for that. You must not think
That we are made of stuff so flat and dull
That we can let our beard be shook with danger
And think it pastime. You shortly shall hear more.
I loved your father, and we love ourself;
And that, I hope, will teach you to imagine—

Enter a Messenger with letters.

How now? What news?
MESSENGER　　　　　Letters, my lord, from Hamlet:
This to Your Majesty, this to the Queen.
　　　　　　　　　　　[He gives letters.]
KING　From Hamlet? Who brought them?
MESSENGER
Sailors, my lord, they say. I saw them not.
They were given me by Claudio. He received them
Of him that brought them.
KING　　　　　Laertes, you shall hear them.—
Leave us.　　　　　　　　　*[Exit Messenger.]*
[He reads.] "High and mighty, you shall know I am set
naked on your kingdom. Tomorrow shall I beg leave　45
to see your kingly eyes, when I shall, first asking your
pardon, thereunto recount the occasion of my sudden　47
and more strange return.　　　　　　Hamlet."
What should this mean? Are all the rest come back?
Or is it some abuse, and no such thing?　　50
LAERTES
Know you the hand?
KING　　　　　　'Tis Hamlet's character. "Naked!"　51
And in a postscript here he says "alone."

Can you devise me?　　　　　　　　　53
LAERTES
I am lost in it, my lord. But let him come.
It warms the very sickness in my heart
That I shall live and tell him to his teeth,
"Thus didst thou."
KING　　　　　If it be so, Laertes—　　57
As how should it be so? How otherwise?—　58
Will you be ruled by me?
LAERTES　　　　　　Ay, my lord,
So you will not o'errule me to a peace.　　60
KING
To thine own peace. If he be now returned,
As checking at his voyage, and that he means　62
No more to undertake it, I will work him
To an exploit, now ripe in my device,　　64
Under the which he shall not choose but fall;
And for his death no wind of blame shall breathe,
But even his mother shall uncharge the practice　67
And call it accident.
LAERTES　　　　　My lord, I will be ruled,
The rather if you could devise it so
That I might be the organ.
KING　　　　　　It falls right.　　70
You have been talked of since your travel much,
And that in Hamlet's hearing, for a quality
Wherein they say you shine. Your sum of parts　73
Did not together pluck such envy from him
As did that one, and that, in my regard,
Of the unworthiest siege.　　　　　76
LAERTES　What part is that, my lord?
KING
A very ribbon in the cap of youth,
Yet needful too, for youth no less becomes　79
The light and careless livery that it wears
Than settled age his sables and his weeds　81
Importing health and graveness. Two months since　82
Here was a gentleman of Normandy.
I have seen myself, and served against, the French,
And they can well on horseback, but this gallant　85
Had witchcraft in 't; he grew unto his seat,
And to such wondrous doing brought his horse
As had he been incorpsed and demi-natured　88
With the brave beast. So far he topped my thought　89
That I in forgery of shapes and tricks　90
Come short of what he did.
LAERTES　　　　　A Norman was 't?

---

15 conjunctive closely united. (An astronomical metaphor.)　**16 his** its.　**sphere** one of the hollow spheres in which, according to Ptolemaic astronomy, the planets were supposed to move　**18 count** account, reckoning, indictment　**19 general gender** common people　**21 Work** operate, act.　**spring** i.e., a spring with such a concentration of lime that it coats a piece of wood with limestone, in effect gilding and petrifying it　**22 gyves** fetters (which, gilded by the people's praise, would look like badges of honor)　**23 slightly timbered** light.　**loud** (suggesting public outcry on Hamlet's behalf)　**24 reverted** returned　**27 terms** state, condition　**28 go back** i.e., recall what she was　**29 on mount** set up on high　**45 naked** destitute, unarmed, without following　**47 pardon** permission　**50 abuse** deceit.　**no such thing** not what it appears　**51 character** handwriting

53 devise explain to　**57 Thus didst thou** i.e., here's for what you did to my father　**58 As . . . otherwise** how can this (Hamlet's return) be true? Yet how otherwise than true (since we have the evidence of his letter)?　**60 So** provided that　**62 checking at** i.e., turning aside from (like a falcon leaving the quarry to fly at a chance bird).　**that** if　**64 device** devising, invention　**67 uncharge the practice** acquit the stratagem of being a plot　**70 organ** agent, instrument　**73 Your . . . parts** i.e., all your other virtues　**76 unworthiest siege** least important rank　**79 no less becomes** is no less suited by　**81 his sables** its rich robes furred with sable.　**weeds** garments　**82 Importing . . . graveness** signifying a concern for health and dignified prosperity; also, giving an impression of comfortable prosperity　**85 can well** are skilled　**88 As . . . demi-natured** as if he had been of one body and nearly of one nature (like the centaur)　**89 topped** surpassed　**90 forgery** imagining

KING   A Norman.
LAERTES
Upon my life, Lamord.
KING   The very same.
LAERTES
I know him well. He is the brooch indeed   94
And gem of all the nation.
KING   He made confession of you,   96
And gave you such a masterly report
For art and exercise in your defense,   98
And for your rapier most especial,
That he cried out 'twould be a sight indeed
If one could match you. Th' escrimers of their
    nation,   101
He swore, had neither motion, guard, nor eye
If you opposed them. Sir, this report of his
Did Hamlet so envenom with his envy
That he could nothing do but wish and beg
Your sudden coming o'er, to play with you.   106
Now, out of this—
LAERTES   What out of this, my lord?
KING
Laertes, was your father dear to you?
Or are you like the painting of a sorrow,
A face without a heart?
LAERTES   Why ask you this?
KING
Not that I think you did not love your father,
But that I know love is begun by time,   112
And that I see, in passages of proof,   113
Time qualifies the spark and fire of it.   114
There lives within the very flame of love
A kind of wick or snuff that will abate it,   116
And nothing is at a like goodness still,   117
For goodness, growing to a pleurisy,   118
Dies in his own too much. That we would do,   119
We should do when we would; for this "would"
    changes
And hath abatements and delays as many   121
As there are tongues, are hands, are accidents,   122
And then this "should" is like a spendthrift sigh, 123
That hurts by easing. But, to the quick o' th' ulcer: 124
Hamlet comes back. What would you undertake
To show yourself in deed your father's son
More than in words?
LAERTES   To cut his throat i' the church.

KING
No place, indeed, should murder sanctuarize;   128
Revenge should have no bounds. But good Laertes,
Will you do this, keep close within your chamber. 130
Hamlet returned shall know you are come home.
We'll put on those shall praise your excellence   132
And set a double varnish on the fame
The Frenchman gave you, bring you in fine
    together,   134
And wager on your heads. He, being remiss,   135
Most generous, and free from all contriving,   136
Will not peruse the foils, so that with ease,
Or with a little shuffling, you may choose
A sword unbated, and in a pass of practice   139
Requite him for your father.
LAERTES   I will do 't,
And for that purpose I'll anoint my sword.
I bought an unction of a mountebank   142
So mortal that, but dip a knife in it,
Where it draws blood no cataplasm so rare,   144
Collected from all simples that have virtue   145
Under the moon, can save the thing from death   146
That is but scratched withal. I'll touch my point
With this contagion, that if I gall him slightly, 148
It may be death.
KING   Let's further think of this,
Weigh what convenience both of time and means
May fit us to our shape. If this should fail,   151
And that our drift look through our bad
    performance,   152
'Twere better not assayed. Therefore this project
Should have a back or second, that might hold
If this did blast in proof. Soft, let me see.   155
We'll make a solemn wager on your cunnings—   156
I ha 't!
When in your motion you are hot and dry—
As make your bouts more violent to that end—   159
And that he calls for drink, I'll have prepared him
A chalice for the nonce, whereon but sipping,   161
If he by chance escape your venomed stuck,   162
Our purpose may hold there. [*A cry within.*] But
    stay, what noise?

Enter Queen.

QUEEN
One woe doth tread upon another's heel,

94 **brooch** ornament   96 **confession** testimonial, admission of superiority   98 **For . . . defense** with respect to your skill and practice with your weapon   101 **escrimers** fencers   106 **sudden** immediate.   **play** fence   112 **begun by time** i.e., created by the right circumstance and hence subject to change   113 **passages of proof** actual instances that prove it   114 **qualifies** weakens, moderates   116 **snuff** the charred part of a candlewick   117 **nothing . . . still** nothing remains at a constant level of perfection   118 **pleurisy** excess, plethora. (Literally, a chest inflammation.)   119 **in . . . much** of its own excess.   **That** that which   121 **abatements** diminutions   122 **As . . . accidents** as there are tongues to dissuade, hands to prevent, and chance events to intervene   123 **spendthrift sigh** (An allusion to the belief that sighs draw blood from the heart.)   124 **hurts by easing** i.e., costs the heart blood and wastes precious opportunity even while it affords emotional relief.   **quick o' th' ulcer** i.e., heart of the matter

128 **sanctuarize** protect from punishment. (Alludes to the right of sanctuary with which certain religious places were invested.)   130 **Will you do this** if you wish to do this   132 **put on those shall** arrange for some to   134 **in fine** finally   135 **remiss** negligently unsuspicious   136 **generous** noble-minded   139 **unbated** not blunted, having no button.   **pass of practice** treacherous thrust   142 **unction** ointment.   **mountebank** quack doctor   144 **cataplasm** plaster or poultice   145 **simples** herbs.   **virtue** potency   146 **Under the moon** i.e., anywhere (with reference perhaps to the belief that herbs gathered at night had a special power)   148 **gall** graze, wound   151 **shape** part we propose to act   152 **drift . . . performance** intention should be made visible by our bungling   155 **blast in proof** burst in the test (like a cannon)   156 **cunnings** respective skills   159 **As** i.e., and you should   161 **nonce** occasion   162 **stuck** thrust. (From *stoccado*, a fencing term.)

So fast they follow. Your sister's drowned, Laertes.

LAERTES   Drowned! O, where?

QUEEN
There is a willow grows askant the brook,   167
That shows his hoar leaves in the glassy stream;   168
Therewith fantastic garlands did she make
Of crowflowers, nettles, daisies, and long purples,   170
That liberal shepherds give a grosser name,   171
But our cold maids do dead men's fingers call them.   172
There on the pendent boughs her crownet weeds   173
Clamb'ring to hang, an envious sliver broke,   174
When down her weedy trophies and herself   175
Fell in the weeping brook. Her clothes spread wide,
And mermaidlike awhile they bore her up,
Which time she chanted snatches of old lauds,   178
As one incapable of her own distress,   179
Or like a creature native and endued   180
Unto that element. But long it could not be
Till that her garments, heavy with their drink,
Pulled the poor wretch from her melodious lay
To muddy death.

LAERTES   Alas, then she is drowned?

QUEEN   Drowned, drowned.

LAERTES
Too much of water hast thou, poor Ophelia,
And therefore I forbid my tears. But yet
It is our trick; nature her custom holds,   188
Let shame say what it will. [*He weeps.*] When these
   are gone,   189
The woman will be out. Adieu, my lord.   190
I have a speech of fire that fain would blaze,
But that this folly douts it.   *Exit.*

KING   Let's follow, Gertrude.   192
How much I had to do to calm his rage!
Now fear I this will give it start again;
Therefore let's follow.   *Exeunt.*

❧

5.1   *Enter two Clowns [with spades and mattocks].*

FIRST CLOWN   Is she to be buried in Christian burial,
when she willfully seeks her own salvation?   2

SECOND CLOWN   I tell thee she is; therefore make her

grave straight. The crowner hath sat on her, and finds   4
it Christian burial.   5

FIRST CLOWN   How can that be, unless she drowned
herself in her own defense?

SECOND CLOWN   Why, 'tis found so.   8

FIRST CLOWN   It must be *se offendendo*, it cannot be else. 9
For here lies the point: if I drown myself wittingly,
it argues an act, and an act hath three branches—it is
to act, to do, and to perform. Argal, she drowned her-   12
self wittingly.

SECOND CLOWN   Nay, but hear you, goodman delver—   14

FIRST CLOWN   Give me leave. Here lies the water; good.
Here stands the man; good. If the man go to this
water and drown himself, it is, will he, nill he, he   17
goes, mark you that. But if the water come to him and
drown him, he drowns not himself. Argal, he that is
not guilty of his own death shortens not his own life.

SECOND CLOWN   But is this law?

FIRST CLOWN   Ay, marry, is 't—crowner's quest law.   22

SECOND CLOWN   Will you ha' the truth on 't? If this had
not been a gentlewoman, she should have been
buried out o' Christian burial.

FIRST CLOWN   Why, there thou sayst. And the more   26
pity that great folk should have countenance in this   27
world to drown or hang themselves, more than their
even-Christian. Come, my spade. There is no ancient   29
gentlemen but gardeners, ditchers, and grave makers.
They hold up Adam's profession.   31

SECOND CLOWN   Was he a gentleman?

FIRST CLOWN   'A was the first that ever bore arms.   33

SECOND CLOWN   Why, he had none.

FIRST CLOWN   What, art a heathen? How dost thou
understand the Scripture? The Scripture says Adam
digged. Could he dig without arms? I'll put another   37
question to thee. If thou answerest me not to the
purpose, confess thyself—   39

SECOND CLOWN   Go to.

FIRST CLOWN   What is he that builds stronger than
either the mason, the shipwright, or the carpenter?

SECOND CLOWN   The gallows maker, for that frame   43
outlives a thousand tenants.

FIRST CLOWN   I like thy wit well, in good faith. The
gallows does well. But how does it well? It does well to 46
those that do ill. Now thou dost ill to say the gallows

---

167 **askant** aslant   168 **hoar leaves** white or gray undersides of the
leaves   170 **long purples** early purple orchids   171 **liberal** free-spoken.   **a grosser name** (The testicle-resembling tubers of the orchid,
which also in some cases resemble *dead men's fingers*, have earned
various slang names such as "dogstones" and "cullions.")   172 **cold**
chaste   173 **pendent** overhanging.   **crownet** made into a chaplet or
coronet   174 **envious sliver** malicious branch   175 **weedy** i.e., of
plants   178 **lauds** hymns   179 **incapable of** lacking capacity to apprehend   180 **endued** adapted by nature   188 **It is our trick** i.e.,
weeping is our natural way (when sad)   189–190 **When . . . out**
when my tears are all shed, the woman in me will be expended, satisfied   192 **douts** extinguishes. (The Second Quarto reads "drowns.")
5.1. Location: A churchyard.
s.d. Clowns rustics   2 **salvation** (A blunder for "damnation," or perhaps a suggestion that Ophelia was taking her own shortcut to
heaven.)

4 **straight** straightway, immediately. (But with a pun on *strait*, "narrow.")   **crowner** coroner.   **sat on her** conducted an inquest on her
case   4–5 **finds it** gives his official verdict that her means of death
was consistent with   8 **found so** determined so in the coroner's verdict   9 **se offendendo** (A comic mistake for *se defendendo*, a term
used in verdicts of justifiable homicide.)   12 **Argal** (Corruption of
ergo, "therefore.")   14 **goodman** (An honorific title often used with
the name of a profession or craft.)   17 **will he, nill he** whether he
will or no, willy-nilly   22 **quest** inquest   26 **there thou sayst** i.e.,
that's right   27 **countenance** privilege   29 **even-Christian** fellow
Christians.   **ancient** going back to ancient times   31 **hold up** maintain   33 **bore arms** (To be entitled to bear a coat of arms would make
Adam a gentleman, but as one who bore a spade, our common ancestor was an ordinary delver in the earth.)   37 **arms** i.e., the arms of
the body   39 **confess thyself** (The saying continues, "and be
hanged.")   43 **frame** (1) gallows (2) structure   46 **does well** (1) is an
apt answer (2) does a good turn

is built stronger than the church. Argal, the gallows may do well to thee. To 't again, come.

SECOND CLOWN   "Who builds stronger than a mason, a shipwright, or a carpenter?"

FIRST CLOWN   Ay, tell me that, and unyoke.   52

SECOND CLOWN   Marry, now I can tell.

FIRST CLOWN   To 't.

SECOND CLOWN   Mass, I cannot tell.   55

Enter Hamlet and Horatio [at a distance].

FIRST CLOWN   Cudgel thy brains no more about it, for your dull ass will not mend his pace with beating; and when you are asked this question next, say "a grave maker." The houses he makes lasts till doomsday. Go get thee in and fetch me a stoup of liquor.   60

[Exit Second Clown. First Clown digs.]
Song.

"In youth, when I did love, did love,   61
   Methought it was very sweet,
To contract—O—the time for—a—my behove,   63
   O, methought there—a—was nothing—a—
     meet."   64

HAMLET   Has this fellow no feeling of his business, 'a   65 sings in grave-making?

HORATIO   Custom hath made it in him a property of   67 easiness.   68

HAMLET   'Tis e'en so. The hand of little employment hath the daintier sense.   70

FIRST CLOWN   *Song.*

"But age with his stealing steps
   Hath clawed me in his clutch,
And hath shipped me into the land,   73
   As if I had never been such."

[He throws up a skull.]

HAMLET   That skull had a tongue in it and could sing once. How the knave jowls it to the ground, as if   76 'twere Cain's jawbone, that did the first murder! This might be the pate of a politician, which this ass now   78 o'erreaches, one that would circumvent God, might   79 it not?

HORATIO   It might, my lord.

HAMLET   Or of a courtier, which could say, "Good morrow, sweet lord! How dost thou, sweet lord?" This might be my Lord Such-a-one, that praised my Lord Such-a-one's horse when 'a meant to beg it, might it not?

HORATIO   Ay, my lord.

HAMLET   Why, e'en so, and now my Lady Worm's, chapless, and knocked about the mazard with a sex-   89 ton's spade. Here's fine revolution, an we had the trick   90 to see 't. Did these bones cost no more the breeding   91 but to play at loggets with them? Mine ache to think   92 on 't.

FIRST CLOWN   *Song.*

"A pickax and a spade, a spade,
   For and a shrouding sheet;   95
O, a pit of clay for to be made
   For such a guest is meet."

[He throws up another skull.]

HAMLET   There's another. Why may not that be the skull of a lawyer? Where be his quiddities now, his quilli-   99 ties, his cases, his tenures, and his tricks? Why does   100 he suffer this mad knave now to knock him about the sconce with a dirty shovel, and will not tell him of his   102 action of battery? Hum, this fellow might be in 's time   103 a great buyer of land, with his statutes, his recogni-   104 zances, his fines, his double vouchers, his recoveries.   105 Is this the fine of his fines and the recovery of his   106 recoveries, to have his fine pate full of fine dirt? Will   107 his vouchers vouch him no more of his purchases, and double ones too, than the length and breadth of a pair of indentures? The very conveyances of his lands   110 will scarcely lie in this box, and must th' inheritor   111 himself have no more, ha?

HORATIO   Not a jot more, my lord.

HAMLET   Is not parchment made of sheepskins?

HORATIO   Ay, my lord, and of calves' skins too.

HAMLET   They are sheep and calves which seek out as-   116 surance in that. I will speak to this fellow.—Whose   117 grave's this, sirrah?   118

FIRST CLOWN   Mine, sir.

[Sings.] "O, pit of clay for to be made
     For such a guest is meet."

HAMLET   I think it be thine, indeed, for thou liest in 't.

FIRST CLOWN   You lie out on 't, sir, and therefore 'tis not yours. For my part, I do not lie in 't, yet it is mine.

---

52 unyoke i.e., after this great effort, you may unharness the team of your wits   **55 Mass** by the Mass   **60 stoup** two-quart measure   **61 In . . . love** (This and the two following stanzas, with nonsensical variations, are from a poem attributed to Lord Vaux and printed in *Tottel's Miscellany*, 1557. The O and a [for "ah"] seemingly are the grunts of the digger.)   **63 To contract** i.e., to shorten the time for my own advantage. (Perhaps he means to *prolong* it.)   **64 meet** suitable, i.e., more suitable   **65 'a** that he   **67–68 property of easiness** something he can do easily and indifferently   **70 daintier sense** more delicate sense of feeling   **73 into the land** i.e., toward my grave (?) (But note the lack of rhyme in *steps, land*.)   **76 jowls** dashes (with a pun on *jowl*, "jawbone")   **78 politician** schemer, plotter   **79 o'er-reaches** circumvents, gets the better of (with a quibble on the literal sense)

89 chapless having no lower jaw.   **mazard** i.e., head. (Literally, a drinking vessel.)   **90 revolution** turn of Fortune's wheel, change.   **an** if   **90–91 trick to see** knack of seeing   **91–92 cost . . . but** involve so little expense and care in upbringing that we may   **92 loggets** a game in which pieces of hard wood shaped like Indian clubs or bowling pins are thrown to lie as near as possible to a stake   **95 For and** and moreover   **99 quiddities** subtleties, quibbles. (From Latin *quid*, "a thing.")   **99–100 quillities** verbal niceties, subtle distinctions. (Variation of *quiddities*.)   **100 tenures** the holding of a piece of property or office, or the conditions or period of such holding   **102 sconce** head   **103 action of battery** lawsuit about physical assault   **104–105 statutes, recognizances** legal documents guaranteeing a debt by attaching land and property   **105 fines, recoveries** ways of converting entailed estates into "fee simple" or freehold.   **double** signed by two signatories.   **vouchers** guarantees of the legality of a title to real estate   **106–107 fine of his fines . . . fine pate . . . fine dirt** end of his legal maneuvers . . . elegant head . . . minutely sifted dirt   **110 pair of indentures** legal document drawn up in duplicate on a single sheet and then cut apart on a zigzag line so that each pair was uniquely matched. (Hamlet may refer to two rows of teeth or dentures.)   **conveyances** deeds   **111 box** (1) deed box (2) coffin. ("Skull" has been suggested.)   **inheritor** possessor, owner   **116–117 assurance in that** safety in legal parchments   **118 sirrah** (A term of address to inferiors.)

HAMLET   Thou dost lie in 't, to be in 't and say it is thine. 'Tis for the dead, not for the quick; therefore 126 thou liest.

FIRST CLOWN   'Tis a quick lie, sir; 'twill away again from me to you.

HAMLET   What man dost thou dig it for?

FIRST CLOWN   For no man, sir.

HAMLET   What woman, then?

FIRST CLOWN   For none, neither.

HAMLET   Who is to be buried in 't?

FIRST CLOWN   One that was a woman, sir, but, rest her soul, she's dead.

HAMLET   How absolute the knave is! We must speak by 137 the card, or equivocation will undo us. By the Lord, 138 Horatio, this three years I have took note of it: the age 139 is grown so picked that the toe of the peasant comes so 140 near the heel of the courtier, he galls his kibe.—How 141 long hast thou been grave maker?

FIRST CLOWN   Of all the days i' the year, I came to 't that day that our last king Hamlet overcame Fortinbras.

HAMLET   How long is that since?

FIRST CLOWN   Cannot you tell that? Every fool can tell that. It was that very day that young Hamlet was born—he that is mad and sent into England.

HAMLET   Ay, marry, why was he sent into England?

FIRST CLOWN   Why, because 'a was mad. 'A shall recover his wits there, or if 'a do not, 'tis no great matter there.

HAMLET   Why?

FIRST CLOWN   'Twill not be seen in him there. There the men are as mad as he.

HAMLET   How came he mad?

FIRST CLOWN   Very strangely, they say.

HAMLET   How strangely?

FIRST CLOWN   Faith, e'en with losing his wits.

HAMLET   Upon what ground? 160

FIRST CLOWN   Why, here in Denmark. I have been sexton here, man and boy, thirty years.

HAMLET   How long will a man lie i' th' earth ere he rot?

FIRST CLOWN   Faith, if 'a be not rotten before 'a die—as we have many pocky corpses nowadays, that will 165 scarce hold the laying in—'a will last you some eight 166 year or nine year. A tanner will last you nine year.

HAMLET   Why he more than another?

FIRST CLOWN   Why, sir, his hide is so tanned with his trade that 'a will keep out water a great while, and your water is a sore decayer of your whoreson dead 171 body. [*He picks up a skull.*] Here's a skull now hath lien you i' th' earth three-and-twenty years. 173

HAMLET   Whose was it?

FIRST CLOWN   A whoreson mad fellow's it was. Whose do you think it was?

HAMLET   Nay, I know not.

FIRST CLOWN   A pestilence on him for a mad rogue! 'A poured a flagon of Rhenish on my head once. This 179 same skull, sir, was, sir, Yorick's skull, the King's jester.

HAMLET   This?

FIRST CLOWN   E'en that.

HAMLET   Let me see. [*He takes the skull.*] Alas, poor Yorick! I knew him, Horatio, a fellow of infinite jest, of most excellent fancy. He hath bore me on his back a 185 thousand times, and now how abhorred in my imagination it is! My gorge rises at it. Here hung those 187 lips that I have kissed I know not how oft. Where be your gibes now? Your gambols, your songs, your flashes of merriment that were wont to set the table on 190 a roar? Not one now, to mock your own grinning? 191 Quite chopfallen? Now get you to my lady's chamber 192 and tell her, let her paint an inch thick, to this favor 193 she must come. Make her laugh at that. Prithee, Horatio, tell me one thing.

HORATIO   What's that, my lord?

HAMLET   Dost thou think Alexander looked o' this fashion i' th' earth?

HORATIO   E'en so.

HAMLET   And smelt so? Pah! [*He throws down the skull.*]

HORATIO   E'en so, my lord.

HAMLET   To what base uses we may return, Horatio! Why may not imagination trace the noble dust of Alexander till 'a find it stopping a bunghole? 204

HORATIO   'Twere to consider too curiously to consid- 205 er so.

HAMLET   No, faith, not a jot, but to follow him thither with modesty enough, and likelihood to lead it. As 208 thus: Alexander died, Alexander was buried, Alexander returneth to dust, the dust is earth, of earth we make loam, and why of that loam whereto he was 211 converted might they not stop a beer barrel?
Imperious Caesar, dead and turned to clay, 213
Might stop a hole to keep the wind away.
O, that that earth which kept the world in awe
Should patch a wall t' expel the winter's flaw! 216

Enter King, Queen, Laertes, and the corpse [*of Ophelia, in procession, with Priest, lords, etc.*].

But soft, but soft awhile! Here comes the King, 217
The Queen, the courtiers. Who is this they follow?
And with such maimèd rites? This doth betoken 219
The corpse they follow did with desperate hand

126 **quick** living   137 **absolute** strict, precise   137–138 **by the card** i.e., with precision. (Literally, by the mariner's compass-card, on which the points of the compass were marked.)   138 **equivocation** ambiguity in the use of terms   139 **took** taken   140 **picked** refined, fastidious   141 **galls his kibe** chafes the courtier's chilblain   160 **ground** cause. (But, in the next line, the gravedigger takes the word in the sense of "land," "country.")   165 **pocky** rotten, diseased. (Literally, with the pox, or syphilis.)   166 **hold the laying in** hold together long enough to be interred.   **last you** last. (*You* is used colloquially here and in the following lines.)   171 **sore** i.e., terrible, great.   **whoreson** i.e., vile, scurvy   173 **lien you** lain. (See the note at line 166.)

179 **Rhenish** Rhine wine   185 **bore** borne   187 **My gorge rises** i.e., I feel nauseated   190 **were wont** used   191 **mock your own grinning** mock at the way your skull seems to be grinning (just as you used to mock at yourself and those who grinned at you)   192 **chopfallen** (1) lacking the lower jaw (2) dejected   193 **favor** aspect, appearance   204 **bunghole** hole for filling or emptying a cask   205 **curiously** minutely   208 **modesty** plausible moderation   211 **loam** mortar consisting chiefly of moistened clay and straw   213 **Imperious** imperial   216 **flaw** gust of wind   217 **soft** i.e., wait, be careful   219 **maimèd** mutilated, incomplete

Fordo its own life. 'Twas of some estate.   221
Couch we awhile and mark.   222

[He and Horatio conceal themselves.
Ophelia's body is taken to the grave.]

LAERTES   What ceremony else?

HAMLET *[to Horatio]*
That is Laertes, a very noble youth. Mark.

LAERTES   What ceremony else?

PRIEST
Her obsequies have been as far enlarged
As we have warranty. Her death was doubtful,   227
And but that great command o'ersways the order   228
She should in ground unsanctified been lodged   229
Till the last trumpet. For charitable prayers,   230
Shards, flints, and pebbles should be thrown on her.   231
Yet here she is allowed her virgin crants,   232
Her maiden strewments, and the bringing home   233
Of bell and burial.   234

LAERTES
Must there no more be done?

PRIEST   No more be done.
We should profane the service of the dead
To sing a requiem and such rest to her   237
As to peace-parted souls.

LAERTES   Lay her i' th' earth,   238
And from her fair and unpolluted flesh
May violets spring! I tell thee, churlish priest,   240
A ministering angel shall my sister be
When thou liest howling.

HAMLET *[to Horatio]*   What, the fair Ophelia!   242

QUEEN *[scattering flowers]* Sweets to the sweet! Farewell.
I hoped thou shouldst have been my Hamlet's wife.
I thought thy bride-bed to have decked, sweet maid,
And not t' have strewed thy grave.

LAERTES   O, treble woe
Fall ten times treble on that cursèd head
Whose wicked deed thy most ingenious sense   248
Deprived thee of! Hold off the earth awhile,
Till I have caught her once more in mine arms.

[He leaps into the grave and embraces Ophelia.]
Now pile your dust upon the quick and dead,
Till of this flat a mountain you have made
T' o'ertop old Pelion or the skyish head   253
Of blue Olympus.

HAMLET *[coming forward]*   What is he whose grief   254
Bears such an emphasis, whose phrase of sorrow   255

Conjures the wandering stars and makes them
stand   256
Like wonder-wounded hearers? This is I,   257
Hamlet the Dane.   258

LAERTES *[grappling with him]*   The devil take thy soul! 259

HAMLET   Thou pray'st not well.
I prithee, take thy fingers from my throat,
For though I am not splenitive and rash,   262
Yet have I in me something dangerous,
Which let thy wisdom fear. Hold off thy hand.

KING   Pluck them asunder.

QUEEN   Hamlet, Hamlet!

ALL   Gentlemen!

HORATIO   Good my lord, be quiet.

[Hamlet and Laertes are parted.]

HAMLET
Why, I will fight with him upon this theme
Until my eyelids will no longer wag.   270

QUEEN   O my son, what theme?

HAMLET
I loved Ophelia. Forty thousand brothers
Could not with all their quantity of love
Make up my sum. What wilt thou do for her?

KING   O, he is mad, Laertes.

QUEEN   For love of God, forbear him.   276

HAMLET
'Swounds, show me what thou'lt do.   277
Woo't weep? Woo't fight? Woo't fast? Woo't tear
thyself?   278
Woo't drink up eisel? Eat a crocodile?   279
I'll do 't. Dost come here to whine?
To outface me with leaping in her grave?
Be buried quick with her, and so will I.   282
And if thou prate of mountains, let them throw
Millions of acres on us, till our ground,
Singeing his pate against the burning zone,   285
Make Ossa like a wart! Nay, an thou'lt mouth,   286
I'll rant as well as thou.

QUEEN   This is mere madness,   287
And thus awhile the fit will work on him;
Anon, as patient as the female dove
When that her golden couplets are disclosed,   290

221 Fordo destroy.   **estate** rank   **222 Couch we** let's hide, lie low
227 warranty i.e., ecclesiastical authority   **228 great . . . order** orders from on high overrule the prescribed procedures   **229 She should . . . lodged** she should have been buried in unsanctified ground   **230 For** in place of   **231 Shards** broken bits of pottery
232 crants garlands betokening maidenhood   **233 strewments** flowers strewn on a coffin   **233–234 bringing . . . burial** laying the body to rest, to the sound of the bell   **237 such rest** i.e., to pray for such rest
238 peace-parted souls those who have died at peace with God
240 violets (See 4.5.188 and note.)   **242 howling** i.e., in hell
248 ingenious sense a mind that is quick, alert, of fine qualities
253–254 Pelion, Olympus sacred mountains in the north of Thessaly; see also *Ossa*, below, at line 286   **255 emphasis** i.e., rhetorical and florid emphasis. (*Phrase* has a similar rhetorical connotation.)

256 wandering stars planets   **257 wonder-wounded** struck with amazement   **258 the Dane** (This title normally signifies the King; see 1.1.17 and note.)   **259 s.d. grappling with him** The testimony of the First Quarto that *"Hamlet leaps in after Laertes"* and the "Elegy on Burbage" ("Oft have I seen him leap into the grave") seem to indicate one way in which this fight was staged; however, the difficulty of fitting two contenders and Ophelia's body into a confined space (probably the trapdoor) suggests to many editors the alternative, that Laertes jumps out of the grave to attack Hamlet.)   **262 splenitive** quick-tempered   **270 wag** move. (A fluttering eyelid is a conventional sign that life has not yet gone.)   **276 forbear him** leave him alone
277 'Swounds by His (Christ's) wounds   **278 Woo't** wilt thou
279 drink up drink deeply.   **eisel** vinegar.   **crocodile** (Crocodiles were tough and dangerous, and were supposed to shed hypocritical tears.)   **282 quick** alive   **285 his pate** its head, i.e., top.   **burning zone** zone in the celestial sphere containing the sun's orbit, between the tropics of Cancer and Capricorn   **286 Ossa** another mountain in Thessaly. (In their war against the Olympian gods, the giants attempted to heap Ossa on Pelion to scale Olympus.)   **an** if.   **mouth** i.e., rant   **287 mere** utter   **290 golden couplets** two baby pigeons, covered with yellow down.   **disclosed** hatched

His silence will sit drooping.

HAMLET   Hear you, sir.
What is the reason that you use me thus?
I loved you ever. But it is no matter.
Let Hercules himself do what he may,   294
The cat will mew, and dog will have his day.   295

                     Exit Hamlet.

KING
I pray thee, good Horatio, wait upon him.

               [Exit] Horatio.

[*To Laertes.*] Strengthen your patience in our last
   night's speech;   297
We'll put the matter to the present push.—   298
Good Gertrude, set some watch over your son.—
This grave shall have a living monument.   300
An hour of quiet shortly shall we see;   301
Till then, in patience our proceeding be.   *Exeunt.*

❦

5.2   *Enter Hamlet and Horatio.*

HAMLET
So much for this, sir; now shall you see the other.   1
You do remember all the circumstance?

HORATIO   Remember it, my lord!

HAMLET
Sir, in my heart there was a kind of fighting
That would not let me sleep. Methought I lay
Worse than the mutines in the bilboes. Rashly,   6
And praised be rashness for it—let us know   7
Our indiscretion sometimes serves us well   8
When our deep plots do pall, and that should
   learn us   9
There's a divinity that shapes our ends,
Rough-hew them how we will—

HORATIO   That is most certain.   11

HAMLET   Up from my cabin,
My sea-gown scarfed about me, in the dark   13
Groped I to find out them, had my desire,   14
Fingered their packet, and in fine withdrew   15
To mine own room again, making so bold,
My fears forgetting manners, to unseal
Their grand commission; where I found, Horatio—
Ah, royal knavery!—an exact command,
Larded with many several sorts of reasons   20

Importing Denmark's health and England's too,   21
With, ho! such bugs and goblins in my life,   22
That on the supervise, no leisure bated,   23
No, not to stay the grinding of the ax,   24
My head should be struck off.

HORATIO   Is 't possible?

HAMLET [*giving a document*]
Here's the commission. Read it at more leisure.
But wilt thou hear now how I did proceed?

HORATIO   I beseech you.

HAMLET
Being thus benetted round with villainies—
Ere I could make a prologue to my brains,   30
They had begun the play—I sat me down,   31
Devised a new commission, wrote it fair.   32
I once did hold it, as our statists do,   33
A baseness to write fair, and labored much   34
How to forget that learning, but, sir, now
It did me yeoman's service. Wilt thou know   36
Th' effect of what I wrote?

HORATIO   Ay, good my lord.   37

HAMLET
An earnest conjuration from the King,   38
As England was his faithful tributary,
As love between them like the palm might flourish,   40
As peace should still her wheaten garland wear   41
And stand a comma 'tween their amities,   42
And many suchlike "as"es of great charge,   43
That on the view and knowing of these contents,
Without debatement further more or less,
He should those bearers put to sudden death,
Not shriving time allowed.

HORATIO   How was this sealed?   47

HAMLET
Why, even in that was heaven ordinant.   48
I had my father's signet in my purse,   49
Which was the model of that Danish seal;   50
Folded the writ up in the form of th' other,   51
Subscribed it, gave 't th' impression, placed it safely,   52
The changeling never known. Now, the next day   53
Was our sea fight, and what to this was sequent   54
Thou knowest already.

HORATIO
So Guildenstern and Rosencrantz go to 't.

294–295 Let . . . day i.e., (1) even Hercules couldn't stop Laertes' theatrical rant (2) I, too, will have my turn; i.e., despite any blustering attempts at interference, every person will sooner or later do what he or she must do   **297 in** i.e., by recalling   **298 present push** immediate test   **300 living** lasting. (For Laertes' private understanding, Claudius also hints that Hamlet's death will serve as such a monument.) **301 hour of quiet** time free of conflict
5.2. Location: The castle.
1 see the other hear the other news   **6 mutines** mutineers. **bilboes** shackles. **Rashly** on impulse. (This adverb goes with lines 12 ff.)
7 know acknowledge   **8 indiscretion** lack of foresight and judgment (not an indiscreet act)   **9 pall** fail, falter, go stale. **learn** teach
11 Rough-hew shape roughly   **13 sea-gown** seaman's coat. **scarfed** loosely wrapped   **14 them** i.e., Rosencrantz and Guildenstern
15 Fingered pilfered, pinched. **in fine** finally, in conclusion
20 Larded garnished. **several** different

21 Importing relating to   **22 bugs** bugbears, hobgoblins. **in my life** i.e., to be feared if I were allowed to live   **23 supervise** reading. **leisure bated** delay allowed   **24 stay** await   **30–31 Ere . . . play** before I could consciously turn my brain to the matter, it had started working on a plan   **32 fair** in a clear hand   **33 statists** statesmen
34 baseness i.e., lower-class trait   **36 yeoman's** i.e., substantial, faithful, loyal   **37 effect** purport   **38 conjuration** entreaty   **40 palm** (An image of health; see Psalm 92:12.)   **41 still** always. **wheaten garland** (Symbolic of fruitful agriculture, of peace and plenty.)
42 comma (Indicating continuity, link.)   **43 "as"es** (1) the "whereases" of a formal document (2) asses. **charge** (1) import (2) burden (appropriate to asses)   **47 shriving time** time for confession and absolution   **48 ordinant** directing   **49 signet** small seal   **50 model** replica
51 writ writing   **52 Subscribed** signed (with forged signature). **impression** i.e., with a wax seal   **53 changeling** i.e., substituted letter. (Literally, a fairy child substituted for a human one.)   **54 was sequent** followed

HAMLET
Why, man, they did make love to this employment.
They are not near my conscience. Their defeat 58
Does by their own insinuation grow. 59
'Tis dangerous when the baser nature comes 60
Between the pass and fell incensèd points 61
Of mighty opposites.
HORATIO   Why, what a king is this! 62
HAMLET
Does it not, think thee, stand me now upon— 63
He that hath killed my king and whored my mother,
Popped in between th' election and my hopes, 65
Thrown out his angle for my proper life, 66
And with such cozenage—is 't not perfect
   conscience 67
To quit him with this arm? And is 't not to be
   damned 68
To let this canker of our nature come 69
In further evil? 70
HORATIO
It must be shortly known to him from England
What is the issue of the business there.
HAMLET
It will be short. The interim is mine,
And a man's life's no more than to say "one."
But I am very sorry, good Horatio,
That to Laertes I forgot myself,
For by the image of my cause I see
The portraiture of his. I'll court his favors.
But, sure, the bravery of his grief did put me
Into a tow'ring passion.
HORATIO   Peace, who comes here?

          Enter a Courtier [Osric].

OSRIC Your lordship is right welcome back to Denmark.
HAMLET I humbly thank you, sir. [To Horatio.] Dost
   know this water fly?
HORATIO No, my good lord.
HAMLET Thy state is the more gracious, for 'tis a vice to
   know him. He hath much land, and fertile. Let a beast 86
   be lord of beasts, and his crib shall stand at the King's 87
   mess. 'Tis a chuff, but, as I say, spacious in the 88
   possession of dirt.
OSRIC Sweet lord, if your lordship were at leisure, I
   should impart a thing to you from His Majesty.
HAMLET I will receive it, sir, with all diligence of spirit.
   Put your bonnet to his right use; 'tis for the head. 93

OSRIC I thank your lordship, it is very hot.
HAMLET No, believe me, 'tis very cold. The wind is
   northerly.
OSRIC It is indifferent cold, my lord, indeed. 97
HAMLET But yet methinks it is very sultry and hot for
   my complexion. 99
OSRIC Exceedingly, my lord. It is very sultry, as
   'twere—I cannot tell how. My lord, His Majesty bade
   me signify to you that 'a has laid a great wager on your
   head. Sir, this is the matter—
HAMLET I beseech you, remember.
        [Hamlet moves him to put on his hat.]
OSRIC Nay, good my lord; for my ease, in good faith. 105
   Sir, here is newly come to court Laertes—believe me,
   an absolute gentleman, full of most excellent differ- 107
   ences, of very soft society and great showing. Indeed, 108
   to speak feelingly of him, he is the card or calendar of 109
   gentry, for you shall find in him the continent of what 110
   part a gentleman would see. 111
HAMLET Sir, his definement suffers no perdition in 112
   you, though I know to divide him inventorially would 113
   dozy th' arithmetic of memory, and yet but yaw 114
   neither in respect of his quick sail. But, in the verity of 115
   extolment, I take him to be a soul of great article, and 116
   his infusion of such dearth and rareness as, to make 117
   true diction of him, his semblable is his mirror and 118
   who else would trace him his umbrage, nothing 119
   more.
OSRIC Your lordship speaks most infallibly of him.
HAMLET The concernancy, sir? Why do we wrap the 122
   gentleman in our more rawer breath? 123
OSRIC Sir?
HORATIO Is 't not possible to understand in another 125
   tongue? You will do 't, sir, really. 126
HAMLET What imports the nomination of this gentle- 127
   man?
OSRIC Of Laertes?

58 defeat destruction 59 insinuation intrusive intervention, sticking their noses in my business 60 baser of lower social station 61 pass thrust. fell fierce 62 opposites antagonists 63 stand me now upon become incumbent on me now 65 election (The Danish monarch was "elected" by a small number of high-ranking electors.) 66 angle fishhook. proper very 67 cozenage trickery 68 quit requite, pay back 69 canker ulcer 69–70 come In grow into 74 a man's . . . "one" one's whole life occupies such a short time, only as long as it takes to count to 1 79 bravery bravado 86–88 Let . . . mess i.e., if a man, no matter how beastlike, is as rich in livestock and possessions as Osric, he may eat at the King's table 87 crib manger 88 chuff boor, churl. (The Second Quarto spelling, chough, is a variant spelling that also suggests the meaning here of "chattering jackdaw.") 93 bonnet any kind of cap or hat. his its

97 indifferent somewhat 99 complexion temperament 105 for my ease (A conventional reply declining the invitation to put his hat back on.) 107 absolute perfect 107–108 differences special qualities 108 soft society agreeable manners. great showing distinguished appearance 109 feelingly with just perception. card chart, map. calendar guide 110 gentry good breeding 110–111 the continent . . . see one who contains in him all the qualities a gentleman would like to see. (A continent is that which contains.) 112 definement definition. (Hamlet proceeds to mock Osric by throwing his lofty diction back at him.) perdition loss, diminution 113 you your description. divide him inventorially enumerate his graces 114 dozy dizzy. yaw swing unsteadily off course. (Said of a ship.) 115 neither for all that. in respect of in comparison with 115–116 in . . . extolment in true praise (of him) 116 of great article one with many articles in his inventory 117 infusion essence, character infused into him by nature. dearth and rareness rarity 117–118 make true diction speak truly 118 semblable only true likeness 119 who . . . trace any other person who would wish to follow. umbrage shadow 122 concernancy import, relevance 123 rawer breath unrefined speech that can only come short in praising him 125–126 to understand . . . tongue i.e., for you, Osric, to understand when someone else speaks your language. (Horatio twits Osric for not being able to understand the kind of flowery speech he himself uses, when Hamlet speaks in such a vein. Alternatively, all this could be said to Hamlet.) 126 You will do 't i.e., you can if you try, or, you may well have to try (to speak plainly) 127 nomination naming

HORATIO [to Hamlet]   His purse is empty already; all 's golden words are spent.

HAMLET   Of him, sir.

OSRIC   I know you are not ignorant—

HAMLET   I would you did, sir. Yet in faith if you did, it would not much approve me. Well, sir?　135

OSRIC   You are not ignorant of what excellence Laertes is—

HAMLET   I dare not confess that, lest I should compare 138 with him in excellence. But to know a man well were 139 to know himself.　140

OSRIC   I mean, sir, for his weapon; but in the imputa- 141 tion laid on him by them, in his meed he's unfellowed. 142

HAMLET   What's his weapon?

OSRIC   Rapier and dagger.

HAMLET   That's two of his weapons—but well.　145

OSRIC   The King, sir, hath wagered with him six Barbary horses, against the which he has impawned, as I take 147 it, six French rapiers and poniards, with their assigns, 148 as girdle, hangers, and so. Three of the carriages, in 149 faith, are very dear to fancy, very responsive to the 150 hilts, most delicate carriages, and of very liberal con- 151 ceit.　152

HAMLET   What call you the carriages?

HORATIO [to Hamlet]   I knew you must be edified by the margent ere you had done.　155

OSRIC   The carriages, sir, are the hangers.

HAMLET   The phrase would be more germane to the matter if we could carry a cannon by our sides; I would it might be hangers till then. But, on: six Barbary horses against six French swords, their assigns, and three lib- eral-conceited carriages; that's the French bet against the Danish. Why is this impawned, as you call it?

OSRIC   The King, sir, hath laid, sir, that in a dozen 163 passes between yourself and him, he shall not exceed 164 you three hits. He hath laid on twelve for nine, and it would come to immediate trial, if your lordship would vouchsafe the answer.　167

HAMLET   How if I answer no?

OSRIC   I mean, my lord, the opposition of your person in trial.

HAMLET   Sir, I will walk here in the hall. If it please His Majesty, it is the breathing time of day with me. Let 172

the foils be brought, the gentleman willing, and the King hold his purpose, I will win for him an I can; if not, I will gain nothing but my shame and the odd hits.

OSRIC   Shall I deliver you so?　177

HAMLET   To this effect, sir—after what flourish your nature will.

OSRIC   I commend my duty to your lordship.　180

HAMLET   Yours, yours. [Exit Osric.] 'A does well to commend it himself; there are no tongues else for 's 182 turn.　183

HORATIO   This lapwing runs away with the shell on his 184 head.

HAMLET   'A did comply with his dug before 'a sucked 186 it. Thus has he—and many more of the same breed that I know the drossy age dotes on—only got the 188 tune of the time and, out of an habit of encounter, a 189 kind of yeasty collection, which carries them through 190 and through the most fanned and winnowed opin- 191 ions; and do but blow them to their trial, the bubbles 192 are out.　193

Enter a Lord.

LORD   My lord, His Majesty commended him to you by young Osric, who brings back to him that you attend him in the hall. He sends to know if your pleasure hold to play with Laertes, or that you will take longer 197 time.

HAMLET   I am constant to my purposes; they follow the King's pleasure. If his fitness speaks, mine is ready; 200 now or whensoever, provided I be so able as now.

LORD   The King and Queen and all are coming down.

HAMLET   In happy time.　203

LORD   The Queen desires you to use some gentle enter- 204 tainment to Laertes before you fall to play.　205

HAMLET   She well instructs me.　　　　　[Exit Lord.]

HORATIO   You will lose, my lord.

HAMLET   I do not think so. Since he went into France, I have been in continual practice; I shall win at the odds. But thou wouldst not think how ill all's here about my heart; but it is no matter.

HORATIO   Nay, good my lord—

135 **approve** commend   138–140 **I dare . . . himself** I dare not boast of knowing Laertes' excellence lest I seem to imply a compara- ble excellence in myself. Certainly, to know another person well, one must know oneself.   141 **for** i.e., with   141–142 **imputation . . . them** reputation given him by others   142 **meed** merit.   **unfellowed** unmatched   145 **but well** but never mind   147 **he** i.e., Laertes.   **im- pawned** staked, wagered   148 **poniards** daggers.   **assigns** appurte- nances   149 **hangers** straps on the sword belt (*girdle*), from which the sword hung.   **and so** and so on.   **carriages** (An affected way of say- ing *hangers*; literally, gun carriages.)   150 **dear to fancy** delightful to the fancy.   **responsive** corresponding closely, matching or well ad- justed   151 **delicate** (i.e., in workmanship)   151–152 **liberal conceit** elaborate design   155 **margent** margin of a book, place for explana- tory notes   163 **laid** wagered   164 **passes** bouts. (The odds of the betting are hard to explain. Possibly the King bets that Hamlet will win at least five out of twelve, at which point Laertes raises the odds against himself by betting he will win nine.)   167 **vouchsafe the an- swer** be so good as to accept the challenge. (Hamlet deliberately takes the phrase in its literal sense of replying.)   172 **breathing time** exercise period.   **Let** i.e., if

177 **deliver you** report what you say   180 **commend** commit to your favor. (A conventional salutation, but Hamlet wryly uses a more literal meaning, "recommend," "praise," in line 182.)   182–183 **for 's turn** for his purposes, i.e., to do it for him   184 **lapwing** (A prover- bial type of youthful forwardness. Also, a bird that draws intruders away from its nest and was thought to run about with its head in the shell when newly hatched; a seeming reference to Osric's hat.) 186 **comply . . . dug** observe ceremonious formality toward his nurse's or mother's teat   188 **drossy** laden with scum and impurities, frivolous   189 **tune** temper, mood, manner of speech.   **an habit of encounter** a demeanor in conversing (with courtiers of his own kind) 190 **yeasty** frothy.   **collection** i.e., of current phrases   190–192 **car- ries . . . opinions** sustains them right through the scrutiny of persons whose opinions are select and refined. (Literally, like grain separated from its chaff. Osric is both the chaff and the bubbly froth on the sur- face of the liquor that is soon blown away.)   192 **and do** yet do 192–193 **blow . . . out** test them by merely blowing on them, and their bubbles burst   197 **that** if   200 **If . . . ready** if he declares his readiness, my convenience waits on his   203 **In happy time** (A phrase of courtesy indicating that the time is convenient.)   204– 205 **entertainment** greeting

HAMLET   It is but foolery, but it is such a kind of gain-   213
giving as would perhaps trouble a woman.   214

HORATIO   If your mind dislike anything, obey it. I will
forestall their repair hither and say you are not fit.   216

HAMLET   Not a whit, we defy augury. There is special
providence in the fall of a sparrow. If it be now, 'tis
not to come; if it be not to come, it will be now; if it
be not now; yet it will come. The readiness is all. Since   220
no man of aught he leaves knows, what is 't to leave   221
betimes? Let be.   222

*A table prepared. [Enter] trumpets, drums, and
officers with cushions; King, Queen, [Osric,] and
all the state; foils, daggers, [and wine borne in;]
and Laertes.*

KING
Come, Hamlet, come and take this hand from me.
[The King puts Laertes' hand into Hamlet's.]

HAMLET *[to Laertes]*
Give me your pardon, sir. I have done you wrong,
But pardon 't as you are a gentleman.
This presence knows,   226
And you must needs have heard, how I am
punished   227
With a sore distraction. What I have done
That might your nature, honor, and exception   229
Roughly awake, I here proclaim was madness.
Was 't Hamlet wronged Laertes? Never Hamlet.
If Hamlet from himself be ta'en away,
And when he's not himself does wrong Laertes,
Then Hamlet does it not, Hamlet denies it.
Who does it, then? His madness. If 't be so,
Hamlet is of the faction that is wronged;   236
His madness is poor Hamlet's enemy.
Sir, in this audience
Let my disclaiming from a purposed evil
Free me so far in your most generous thoughts
That I have shot my arrow o'er the house   241
And hurt my brother.

LAERTES   I am satisfied in nature,   242
Whose motive in this case should stir me most   243
To my revenge. But in my terms of honor
I stand aloof, and will no reconcilement
Till by some elder masters of known honor
I have a voice and precedent of peace   247
To keep my name ungored. But till that time   248
I do receive your offered love like love,
And will not wrong it.

HAMLET   I embrace it freely,
And will this brothers' wager frankly play.—   251
Give us the foils. Come on.

LAERTES   Come, one for me.

HAMLET
I'll be your foil, Laertes. In mine ignorance   253
Your skill shall, like a star i' the darkest night,
Stick fiery off indeed.

LAERTES   You mock me, sir.   255

HAMLET   No, by this hand.

KING
Give them the foils, young Osric. Cousin Hamlet,
You know the wager?

HAMLET   Very well, my lord.
Your Grace has laid the odds o' the weaker side.   259

KING
I do not fear it; I have seen you both.
But since he is bettered, we have therefore odds.   261

LAERTES
This is too heavy. Let me see another.
[He exchanges his foil for another.]

HAMLET
This likes me well. These foils have all a length?   263
[They prepare to play.]

OSRIC   Ay, my good lord.

KING
Set me the stoups of wine upon that table.
If Hamlet give the first or second hit,
Or quit in answer of the third exchange,   267
Let all the battlements their ordnance fire.
The King shall drink to Hamlet's better breath,   269
And in the cup an union shall he throw   270
Richer than that which four successive kings
In Denmark's crown have worn. Give me the cups,
And let the kettle to the trumpet speak,   273
The trumpet to the cannoneer without,
The cannons to the heavens, the heaven to earth,
"Now the King drinks to Hamlet." Come, begin.
Trumpets the while.
And you, the judges, bear a wary eye.

HAMLET   Come on, sir.

LAERTES Come, my lord. *[They play. Hamlet scores a hit.]*

HAMLET   One.

LAERTES   No.

HAMLET   Judgment.

OSRIC   A hit, a very palpable hit.
*Drum, trumpets, and shot. Flourish.
A piece goes off.*

LAERTES   Well, again.

KING
Stay, give me drink. Hamlet, this pearl is thine.
*[He drinks, and throws a pearl in
Hamlet's cup.]*
Here's to thy health. Give him the cup.

HAMLET
I'll play this bout first. Set it by awhile.

213–214 gaingiving misgiving   **216 repair** coming   **220–222 Since
. . . Let be** since no one has knowledge of what he is leaving behind,
what does an early death matter after all? Enough; don't struggle
against it.   **226 presence** royal assembly   **227 punished** afflicted
229 exception disapproval   **236 faction** party   **241 That I have** as if I
had   **242 in nature** as to my personal feelings   **243 motive**
prompting   **247 voice** authoritative pronouncement.   **of peace** for
reconciliation   **248 name ungored** reputation unwounded
251 frankly without ill feeling or the burden of rancor

253 foil thin metal background which sets a jewel off (with pun on
the blunted rapier for fencing)   **255 Stick fiery off** stand out brilliantly   **259 laid the odds o'** bet on, backed   **261 is bettered** has
improved; is the odds-on favorite. (Laertes' handicap is the "three
hits" specified in line 165.)   **263 likes me** pleases me   **267 Or . . .
exchange** i.e., or requites Laertes in the third bout for having won the
first two   **269 better breath** improved vigor   **270 union** pearl. (So
called, according to Pliny's *Natural History*, 9, because pearls are
unique, never identical.)   **273 kettle** kettledrum

Come. [*They play.*] Another hit; what say you?

LAERTES   A touch, a touch, I do confess 't.

KING

Our son shall win.

QUEEN   He's fat and scant of breath.   289

Here, Hamlet, take my napkin, rub thy brows.   290

The Queen carouses to thy fortune, Hamlet.   291

HAMLET   Good madam!

KING   Gertrude, do not drink.

QUEEN

I will, my lord, I pray you pardon me.   [*She drinks.*]

KING [*aside*]

It is the poisoned cup. It is too late.

HAMLET

I dare not drink yet, madam; by and by.

QUEEN   Come, let me wipe thy face.

LAERTES [*to King*]

My lord, I'll hit him now.

KING   I do not think 't.

LAERTES [*aside*]

And yet it is almost against my conscience.

HAMLET

Come, for the third, Laertes. You do but dally.

I pray you, pass with your best violence;   301

I am afeard you make a wanton of me.   302

LAERTES   Say you so? Come on.   [*They play.*]

OSRIC   Nothing neither way.

LAERTES

Have at you now!   305

[*Laertes wounds Hamlet; then, in scuffling,*
they change rapiers, and Hamlet wounds Laertes.]

KING   Part them! They are incensed.

HAMLET

Nay, come, again.   [*The Queen falls.*]

OSRIC   Look to the Queen there, ho!

HORATIO

They bleed on both sides. How is it, my lord?

OSRIC   How is 't, Laertes?

LAERTES

Why, as a woodcock to mine own springe, Osric;   309

I am justly killed with mine own treachery.

HAMLET

How does the Queen?

KING   She swoons to see them bleed.

QUEEN

No, no, the drink, the drink—O my dear Hamlet—

The drink, the drink! I am poisoned.   [*She dies.*]

HAMLET

O villainy! Ho, let the door be locked!

Treachery! Seek it out.   [*Laertes falls. Exit Osric.*]

LAERTES

It is here, Hamlet. Hamlet, thou art slain.

No med'cine in the world can do thee good;

In thee there is not half an hour's life.

The treacherous instrument is in thy hand,

Unbated and envenomed. The foul practice   320

Hath turned itself on me. Lo, here I lie,

Never to rise again. Thy mother's poisoned.

I can no more. The King, the King's to blame.

HAMLET

The point envenomed too? Then, venom, to thy

work.   [*He stabs the King.*]

ALL   Treason! Treason!

KING

O, yet defend me, friends! I am but hurt.

HAMLET [*forcing the King to drink*]

Here, thou incestuous, murderous, damnèd Dane,

Drink off this potion. Is thy union here?   328

Follow my mother.   [*The King dies.*]

LAERTES   He is justly served.

It is a poison tempered by himself.   330

Exchange forgiveness with me, noble Hamlet.

Mine and my father's death come not upon thee,

Nor thine on me!   [*He dies.*]

HAMLET

Heaven make thee free of it! I follow thee.

I am dead, Horatio. Wretched Queen, adieu!

You that look pale and tremble at this chance,   336

That are but mutes or audience to this act,   337

Had I but time—as this fell sergeant, Death,   338

Is strict in his arrest—O, I could tell you—   339

But let it be. Horatio, I am dead;

Thou livest. Report me and my cause aright

To the unsatisfied.

HORATIO   Never believe it.

I am more an antique Roman than a Dane.   343

Here's yet some liquor left.

[*He attempts to drink from the poisoned cup.*
Hamlet prevents him.]

HAMLET   As thou'rt a man,

Give me the cup! Let go! By heaven, I'll ha 't.

O God, Horatio, what a wounded name,

Things standing thus unknown, shall I leave

behind me!

If thou didst ever hold me in thy heart,

Absent thee from felicity awhile,

And in this harsh world draw thy breath in pain

To tell my story.   *A march afar off* [*and a volley within*].

What warlike noise is this?

Enter Osric.

OSRIC

Young Fortinbras, with conquest come from Poland,

To th' ambassadors of England gives

This warlike volley.

---

289 fat not physically fit, out of training **290 napkin** handkerchief
291 carouses drinks a toast **301 pass** thrust **302 make . . . me**
i.e., treat me like a spoiled child, trifle with me **305 s.d. in scuffling,**
they change rapiers (This stage direction occurs in the Folio. According to a widespread stage tradition, Hamlet receives a scratch, realizes that Laertes' sword is unbated, and accordingly forces an exchange.) **309 woodcock** a bird, a type of stupidity or as a decoy.
springe trap, snare

320 Unbated not blunted with a button. **practice** plot **328 union**
pearl. (See line 270; with grim puns on the word's other meanings:
marriage, shared death.) **330 tempered** mixed **336 chance** mischance **337 mutes** silent observers. (Literally, actors with nonspeaking parts.) **338 fell** cruel. **sergeant** sheriff's officer **339 strict** (1)
severely just (2) unavoidable. **arrest** (1) taking into custody (2) stopping my speech **343 Roman** (Suicide was an honorable choice for
many Romans as an alternative to a dishonorable life.)

HAMLET   O, I die, Horatio!
The potent poison quite o'ercrows my spirit.   355
I cannot live to hear the news from England,
But I do prophesy th' election lights
On Fortinbras. He has my dying voice.   358
So tell him, with th' occurrents more and less   359
Which have solicited—the rest is silence.   [He dies.] 360
HORATIO
Now cracks a noble heart. Good night, sweet prince,
And flights of angels sing thee to thy rest!
                                [March within.]
Why does the drum come hither?

        Enter Fortinbras, with the [English] Ambassadors
        [with drum, colors, and attendants].

FORTINBRAS
Where is this sight?
HORATIO   What is it you would see?
If aught of woe or wonder, cease your search.
FORTINBRAS
This quarry cries on havoc. O proud Death,   366
What feast is toward in thine eternal cell,   367
That thou so many princes at a shot
So bloodily hast struck?
FIRST AMBASSADOR   The sight is dismal,
And our affairs from England come too late.
The ears are senseless that should give us hearing,
To tell him his commandment is fulfilled,
That Rosencrantz and Guildenstern are dead.
Where should we have our thanks?
HORATIO   Not from his mouth,   374
Had it th' ability of life to thank you.
He never gave commandment for their death.
But since, so jump upon this bloody question,   377
You from the Polack wars, and you from England,
Are here arrived, give order that these bodies
High on a stage be placèd to the view,   380
And let me speak to th' yet unknowing world
How these things came about. So shall you hear
Of carnal, bloody, and unnatural acts,
Of accidental judgments, casual slaughters,   384
Of deaths put on by cunning and forced cause,   385
And, in this upshot, purposes mistook
Fall'n on th' inventors' heads. All this can I
Truly deliver.
FORTINBRAS   Let us haste to hear it,
And call the noblest to the audience.
For me, with sorrow I embrace my fortune.
I have some rights of memory in this kingdom,   391

Which now to claim my vantage doth invite me.   392
HORATIO
Of that I shall have also cause to speak,
And from his mouth whose voice will draw on
  more.   394
But let this same be presently performed,   395
Even while men's minds are wild, lest more
  mischance
On plots and errors happen.
FORTINBRAS   Let four captains   397
Bear Hamlet, like a soldier, to the stage,
For he was likely, had he been put on,   399
To have proved most royal; and for his passage,   400
The soldiers' music and the rite of war
Speak loudly for him.   402
Take up the bodies. Such a sight as this
Becomes the field, but here shows much amiss.   404
Go bid the soldiers shoot.
        Exeunt [marching, bearing off the dead bodies;
                a peal of ordnance is shot off].

392 **vantage** favorable opportunity 394 **voice . . . more** vote will influence still others 395 **presently** immediately 397 **On** on the basis of; on top of 399 **put on** i.e., invested in royal office and so put to the test 400 **passage** i.e., from life to death 402 **Speak** (let them) speak 404 **Becomes the field** suits the field of battle

355 **o'ercrows** triumphs over (like the winner in a cockfight) 358 **voice** vote 359 **occurrents** events, incidents 360 **solicited** moved, urged. (Hamlet doesn't finish saying what the events have prompted—presumably, his acts of vengeance, or his reporting of those events to Fortinbras.) 366 **quarry** heap of dead. **cries on havoc** proclaims a general slaughter 367 **feast** i.e., Death feasting on those who have fallen. **toward** in preparation 374 **his** i.e., Claudius' 377 **jump** precisely, immediately. **question** dispute, affair 380 **stage** platform 384 **judgments** retributions. **casual** occurring by chance 385 **put on** instigated. **forced cause** contrivance 391 **of memory** traditional, remembered, unforgotten

Othello, the Moor of Venice

Othello differs in several respects from the other three major Shakespearean tragedies with which it is usually ranked. Written seemingly about the time of its performance at court by the King's men (Shakespeare's acting company) on November 1, 1604, after *Hamlet* (c. 1599–1601) and before *King Lear* (1605-1606) and *Macbeth* (c. 1606–1607), *Othello* shares with these other plays a fascination with evil in its most virulent and universal aspect. These plays study the devastating effects of ambitious pride, ingratitude, wrath, jealousy, and vengeful hate—the deadly sins of the spirit—with only a passing interest in the political strife to which Shakespeare's Roman or classical tragedies are generally devoted. Of the four, *Othello* is the most concentrated upon one particular evil. The action concerns sexual jealousy, and, although human sinfulness is such that jealousy ceaselessly touches on other forms of depravity, the center of interest always returns in *Othello* to the destruction of a love through jealousy. *Othello* is a tragic portrait of a marriage. The protagonist is not a king or a prince, as in the tragedies already mentioned, but a general recently married. There are no supernatural visitations, as in *Hamlet* and *Macbeth*. Ideas of divine justice, while essential to *Othello*'s portrayal of a battle between good and evil for the allegiance of the protagonist, do not encompass the wide sweep of *King Lear*, nor do we find here the same broad indictment of humanity. Social order is not seriously shaken by Othello's tragedy. The fair-minded Duke of Venice remains firmly in control, and his deputy Lodovico oversees a just conclusion on Cyprus.

By the same token, *Othello* does not offer the remorseless questioning about humanity's relationship to the cosmos that we find in *King Lear, Hamlet,* and *Macbeth*. The battle of good and evil is, of course, cosmic, but in *Othello* that battle is realized through a taut narrative of jealousy and murder. Its poetic images are accordingly focused to a large extent on the natural world. One cluster of images is domestic and animal, having to do with goats, monkeys, wolves, baboons, guinea hens, wildcats, spiders, flies, asses, dogs, copulating horses and sheep, serpents, and toads; other images, more wide-ranging in scope, include green-eyed monsters, devils, blackness, poisons, money purses, tarnished jewels, music untuned, and light extinguished. The story is immediate and direct, retaining the sensational atmosphere of its Italian prose source by Giovanni Baptista Giraldi Cinthio, in his *Hecatommithi* of 1565 (translated into French in 1584). Events move even more swiftly than in Cinthio's work, for Shakespeare has compressed the story into two or three nights and days (albeit with an intervening sea journey and with an elastic use of stage time to allow for the maturing of long-term plans, as when we learn that Iago has begged Emilia "a hundred times" to steal Desdemona's handkerchief, 3.3.308, or that Iago has accused Cassio of making love to Desdemona "A thousand times," 5.2.219). *Othello* does not have a fully developed double plot, as in *King Lear,* or a comparatively large group of characters serving as foils to the protagonist, as in *Hamlet*. *Othello*'s cast is small, and the plot is concentrated to an unusual degree on Othello, Desdemona, and Iago. What *Othello* may lose in breadth it gains in dramatic intensity.

Daringly, Shakespeare opens this tragedy of love, not with a direct and sympathetic portrayal of the lovers themselves, but with a scene of vicious insinuation about their marriage. The images employed by Iago to describe the coupling of Othello and Desdemona are revoltingly animalistic, sodomistic. "Even now, now, very now, an old black ram / Is tupping your white ewe," he taunts Desdemona's father, Brabantio. (Tupping is a word used specifically for the copulating of sheep.) "You'll have your daughter covered with a Barbary horse; you'll have your nephews neigh to you"; "your daughter and the Moor are now making the beast with two backs"; "the devil will make a grandsire of you" (1.1.90–93, 113–120). This degraded view reduces the marriage to one of utter carnality, with repeated emphasis on the word "gross": Desdemona has yielded "to the gross clasps of a lascivious Moor" and has made "a gross revolt" against her family and society (lines 129, 137). Iago's second theme, one that is habitual with him, is money. "What ho, Brabantio! Thieves, thieves, thieves! / Look to your house, your daughter, and your bags" (lines 81–82). The implication is of a sinister bond between thievery in sex and thievery in gold. Sex and money are both commodities to be protected by watchful fathers against libidinous and opportunistic children.

We as audience make plentiful allowance for Iago's bias in all this, since he has admitted to Roderigo his knavery and resentment of Othello. Even so, the carnal vision of love we confront is calculatedly disturbing, because it seems so equated with a pejorative image of blackness. Othello is unquestionably a black man, referred to disparagingly by his detractors as the "thick-lips," with a "sooty bosom" (1.1.68; 1.2.71); Elizabethan usage applied the term "Moor" to Africans without attempting to distinguish between Arabian and Negroid peoples. From the ugly start of the play, Othello and Desdemona have to prove the worth of their love in the face of preset attitudes against miscegenation. Brabantio takes refuge in the thought that Othello must have bewitched Desdemona. His basic assumption—one to be echoed later by Iago and by Othello himself—is that miscegenation is unnatural by definition. In confronting and accusing Othello, he repeatedly appeals "to all things of sense" (that is, to common sense) and asks if it is not "gross in sense" (self-evident) that Othello has practiced magic on her, since nothing else could prompt human nature so to leave its natural path. "For nature so preposterously to err, / Being not deficient, blind, or lame of sense, / Sans witchcraft could not" (1.2.65, 73; 1.3.64–66). We as audience can perceive the racial bias in Brabantio's view and can recognize also in him the type of imperious father who conventionally opposes romantic love. It is sadly ironic that he should now prefer Roderigo as a son-in-law, evidently concluding that any white Venetian would be preferable to the prince of blacks. Still, Brabantio has been hospitable to the Moor and trusting of his daughter. He is a sorrowful rather than ridiculous figure, and the charge he levels at the married pair, however much it is based on a priori assumptions of what is "natural" in human behavior, remains to be answered.

After all, we find ourselves wondering, what did attract Othello and Desdemona to one another? Even though he certainly did not use witchcraft, may Othello not have employed a subtler kind of enchantment in the exotic character of his travels among "the Cannibals that each other eat, / The Anthropophagi, and men whose heads / Do grow beneath their shoulders" (1.3.145–147)? These "passing strange" events fascinate Desdemona as they do everyone, including the Duke of Venice ("I think this tale would win my daughter too"). Othello has not practiced unfairly on her—"This only is the witchcraft I have used" (lines 162, 171–173). Yet may he not represent for Desdemona a radical novelty, being a man at once less devious and more mysterious than the dissolute Venetian swaggerers, such as Roderigo and the "wealthy curlèd darlings of our nation" (1.2.69), who follow her about? Was her deceiving of her father by means of the elopement a protest, an escape from conventionality? Why has she been attracted to a man so much older than herself? For his part, Othello gives the impression of being inexperienced with women, at least of Desdemona's rank and complexion, and is both intrigued and flattered by her attentions. "She loved me for the dangers I had passed, / And I loved her that she did pity them" (1.3.169–170). Desdemona fulfills a place in Othello's view of himself. Does she also represent status for him in Venetian society, where he has been employed as a military commander but treated nonetheless as something of an alien?

These subtle but impertinent ways of doubting the motivations of Othello and Desdemona are thrust upon us by the play's opening and are later crucial to Iago's strategy of breeding mistrust. Just as importantly, however, these insinuations are refuted by Othello and especially by Desdemona. Whatever others may think, she never gives the slightest indication of regarding her husband as different or exotic because he is black and old. In fact, the images of blackness and age are significantly reversed during the play's early scenes. Othello has already embraced the Christian faith, much as Elizabethan Englishmen hoped would happen with innocent natives dwelling in heathen lands. His first appearance onstage, when he confronts a party of torch-bearing men coming to arrest him and bids his followers sheathe their swords (1.2.60), is perhaps reminiscent of Christ's arrest in the Garden of Gethsemane; if so, it suggests a fleeting comparison between Othello and the Christian God whose charity and forbearance he seeks to emulate. Othello's blackness may be used in part as an emblem of fallen humanity, but so are we all fallen. His age similarly strengthens our impression of his wisdom, restraint, and leadership. Any suggestions of comic sexual infidelity in the marriage of an old man and an attractive young bride are confuted by what we see in Desdemona's chaste yet sensual regard for the good man she has chosen.

Desdemona is devoted to Othello, admiring, and faithful. We believe her when she says that she does not even know what it means to be unfaithful; the word *whore* is not in her vocabulary. She is defenseless against the charges brought against her, because she does not even comprehend them and cannot believe that anyone would imagine such things. Her love, both erotic and chaste, is of that transcendent wholesomeness common to several late Shakespearean heroines, such as Cordelia in *King Lear* and Hermione in *The Winter's Tale*. Her "preferring" Othello to her father, like Cordelia's placing her duty to a husband before that to a father, is not ungrateful but natural and proper. And Othello, however much he may regard Desdemona in terms of his own identity (he calls her "my fair warrior"), does cherish Desdemona as she deserves. "I cannot speak enough of this content," he exclaims when he rejoins her on Cyprus. "It stops me here; it is too much of joy" (2.1.181, 196–197). The passionate intensity of his love prepares the way for his tragedy; he speaks more truly than he knows in saying, "when I love thee not, / Chaos is come again" (3.3.99–100). Iago speaks truly also when he observes that Othello "Is of a constant, loving, noble nature" (2.1.290). Othello's tragedy is not that he is easily duped, but that his strong faith can be destroyed at such terrible cost. Othello never forgets how much he is losing. The threat to his love is not an initial lack of his being happily married, but rather the insidious assumption that Desdemona cannot love him because such a love is unnatural. The fear of being unlovable exists in Othello's mind, but the human instrument of this vicious gospel is Iago.

Iago belongs to a select group of villains in Shakespeare who, while plausibly motivated in human terms, also take delight in evil for its own sake: Aaron the Moor in *Titus Andronicus*, Richard III, Don John in *Much Ado About Nothing*, Iago, Edmund in *King Lear*. They are not, like Macbeth or like Claudius in *Hamlet*, men driven by ambition to commit crimes they clearly recognize to be wrong. Although Edmund does belatedly try to make amends, these villains are essentially conscienceless, sinister, and amused by their own cunning. They are related to one another by a stage metaphor of personified evil derived from the Vice of the morality play, whose typical role is to win the Mankind figure away from virtue and to corrupt him with worldly enticements. Like that engaging tempter, Shakespeare's villains in these plays take the audience into their confidence, boast in soliloquy of their cleverness, exult in the triumph of evil, and improvise plans with daring and resourcefulness. They are all superb actors, deceiving virtually every character onstage until late in the action with their protean and hypocritical display. They take pleasure in this "sport" and amaze us by their virtuosity. The role is paradoxically comic in its use of ingenious and resourceful deception—the grim and ironic comedy of vice. We know that we are to condemn morally even while we applaud the skill.

This theatrical tradition of the Vice may best explain a puzzling feature of Iago, noted long ago and memorably phrased by Samuel Taylor Coleridge as "the motive hunting of a motiveless malignity." To be sure, Iago does offer plausible motives for what he does. Despite his resemblance to the morality Vice, he is no allegorized abstraction but an ensign in the army, a junior field officer who hates being outranked by a theoretician or staff officer. As an old-school professional, he also resents that he has not been promoted on the basis of seniority, the "old gradation" (1.1.38). Even his efforts at using influence with Othello have come to naught, and Iago can scarcely be blamed for supposing that Cassio's friendship with Othello has won him special favor. Thus, Iago has reason to plot against Cassio as well as Othello. Nevertheless a further dimension is needed to explain Iago's gloating, his utter lack of moral reflection, his concentration on destroying Desdemona (who has not wronged Iago), his absorption in ingenious methods of plotting, his finesse and style. Hatred precedes any plausible motive in Iago and ultimately does not depend on psychological causality. Probably the tradition of the stage Machiavel (another type of gloating villain based on stereotyped attitudes toward the heretical political ideas of Niccolò Machiavelli), as in Marlowe's *The Jew of Malta*, contributes to the portraiture; this tradition was readily assimilated with that of the Vice.

Iago's machinations yield him both "sport" and "profit" (1.3.387); that is, he enjoys his evildoing, although he is also driven by a motive. This Vice-like behavior in human garb creates a restless sense of a dark metaphysical reality lying behind his visible exterior. Even his stated motives do not always make sense. When in an outburst of hatred he soliloquizes that "I hate the Moor; / And it is thought abroad that

twixt my sheets / He's done my office," Iago goes on to concede the unlikelihood of this charge. "I know not if 't be true; / But I, for mere suspicion in that kind, / Will do as if for surety" (lines 387–391). The charge is so absurd, in fact, that we have to look into Iago himself for the origin of this jealous paranoia. The answer may be partly emblematic: as the embodiment and genius of sexual jealousy, Iago suffers with ironic appropriateness from the evil he preaches, and without external cause. Emilia understands that jealousy is not a rational affliction but a self-induced disease of the mind. Jealous persons, she tells Desdemona, "are not ever jealous for the cause, / But jealous for they're jealous. It is a monster / Begot upon itself, born on itself" (3.4.161–163). Iago's own testimonial bears this out, for his jealousy is at once wholly irrational and agonizingly self-destructive. "I do suspect the lusty Moor / Hath leaped into my seat, the thought whereof / Doth, like a poisonous mineral, gnaw my innards" (2.1.296–298). In light of this nightmare, we can see that even his seemingly plausible resentment of Cassio's promotion is jealous envy. The "daily beauty" in Cassio's life makes Iago feel "ugly" by comparison (5.1.19–20), engendering in Iago a profound sense of lack of worth from which he can temporarily find relief only by reducing Othello and others to his own miserable condition. He is adept at provoking self-hatred in others because he suffers from it himself. His declaration to Othello that "I am your own forever" (3.3.495) is, of course, cynical, but it also signals the extent to which Iago has succeeded in wooing Othello away from Desdemona and Cassio into a murderous union between two women-hating men. The Iago who thus dedicates himself as partner in the fulfillment of Othello's homicidal fantasies is, we learn, capable of fantasizing a bizarre amorous encounter between himself and Cassio (lines 429–441).

Othello comes at last to regard Iago as a "demi-devil" who has tempted Othello to damn himself "beneath all depth in hell"; Lodovico speaks of Iago in the closing lines of the play as a "hellish villain" (5.2.142, 309, 379); and Iago himself boasts that "When devils will the blackest sins put on, / They do suggest at first with heavenly shows, / As I do now" (2.3.345–347). Iago thus bears some affinity to both Vice and the devil, suggesting his relationship both to Othello's inner temptation and to a preexistent evil force in the universe itself. Conversely, Desdemona is in Emilia's words an "angel," purely chaste; "So come my soul to bliss as I speak true" (5.2.134, 259). When Desdemona lands on Cyprus, she is greeted in words that echo the *Ave Maria*: "Hail to thee, lady! And the grace of heaven . . . Enwheel thee round" (2.1.87–89). These images introduce metaphorically a conflict of good and evil in which Othello, typical of fallen humanity, has chosen evil and destroyed the good at the prompting of a diabolical counselor. Again we see the heritage of the morality play, especially of the later morality play in which the Mankind figure was sometimes damned rather than saved. Even so, to allegorize *Othello* is to obscure and misread its clash of human passion. In fact, we see that the impulse to reduce human complexity to simplistic moral absolutes is a fatal weakness in Othello; by insisting on viewing Desdemona as a type or abstraction, he loses sight of her wonderful humanity. The theological issue of salvation or damnation is not relevant in dramatic terms; the play is not a homily on the dangers of jealousy. The metaphysical dimensions of a homiletic tradition are transmuted into human drama. Acknowledging these limitations, we can notwithstanding see a spiritual analogy in Iago's devil-like method of undoing his victims.

His trick resembles that of the similarly mischief-making Don John in *Much Ado About Nothing*: an optical illusion by which the blameless heroine is impugned as an adulteress. The concealed Othello must watch Cassio boasting of sexual triumphs and believe he is talking about Desdemona. Like the devil, Iago is given power over people's frail senses, especially the eyes. He can create illusions to induce Othello to see what Iago wants him to see, as Don John does with Claudio, but Othello's acceptance of the lie must be his own responsibility, a failure of his corrupted will. Iago practices on Othello with an a priori logic used before on Brabantio and Roderigo, urging the proneness of all mortals to sin and the unnaturalness of a black-white marriage. All women have appetites; Desdemona is a woman; hence, Desdemona has appetites. "The wine she drinks is made of grapes," he scoffs to Roderigo. "If she had been blessed, she would never have loved the Moor" (2.1.253–255). She is a Venetian, and "In Venice they do let God see the pranks / They dare not show their husbands" (3.3.216–217). Therefore, she, too, is a hypocrite; "She did deceive her father" (line 220). Most of all, it stands to reason that she must long for a man of her own race. Iago succeeds in getting Othello to concur: "And yet, how nature erring from itself—" (line 243). This proposition that Nature teaches all persons, including Desdemona, to seek a harmonious matching of "clime, complexion, and degree" strikes a responsive chord in Othello, since he knows that he is black and alien. "Haply, for I am black / And have not those soft parts of conversation / That chamberers have." Then, too, he is sensitive that he is considerably older than she, "declined / Into the vale of years" (lines 246, 279–282), "the young affects / In me defunct" (1.3.266–267). And so, if one must conclude from the preceding that Desdemona will seek a lover, the only question is who. "This granted—as it is a most pregnant and unforced position—who stands so eminent in the degree of this fortune as Cassio does?" (2.1.237–239). Once Othello has accepted this syllogistic sequence of proofs, specious not through any lapse in logic but because the axiomatic assumptions about human nature are degraded and do not apply to Desdemona, Othello has arrived at an unshakable conclusion to which all subsequent evidence must be applied. "Villain, be sure thou prove my love

a whore," he commissions Iago (3.3.375). Desdemona's innocent pleading for Cassio only makes things look worse. Cassio's reputed muttering while asleep, like the handkerchief seen in his possession or his giddy talk about his mistress Bianca, "speaks against her [Desdemona] with the other proofs" (line 456).

How has Othello fallen so far in so short a time? His bliss with Desdemona as they are rejoined on Cyprus knows no limit. These two persons represent married love at its very best, erotic and spiritual, she enhancing his manliness, he cherishing her beauty and virtue. His blackness and age are positive images in him, despite earlier insinuations to the contrary. He is a man of public worthiness, of command, of self-assurance. Desdemona is the most domestic of Shakespeare's tragic heroines, even while she is also representative of so much that is transcendent. Husband and wife are bound happily in one of Shakespeare's few detailed portraits of serious commitment in marriage. Othello initially has the wisdom to know that Desdemona's feminine attractiveness ought not to be threatening to him: he need not be jealous because she is beautiful, "free of speech," and loves dancing and music, since "Where virtue is, these are more virtuous." Nor does he see any reason at first to fear her "revolt" simply because he is black and older than his wife; "she had eyes, and chose me" (3.3.197–203). Othello's self-assurance through the love he perceives in Desdemona is the strongest sign of his happiness in marriage.

What then gives way? We look at Iago for one important insight, but ultimately the cause must be in Othello himself. Arthur Kirsch has argued persuasively (in *Shakespeare and the Experience of Love*, 1981) that Othello's most grave failing is an insufficient regard for himself. It is in part an inability to counter the effects on him of a culture that regards him as an outsider; he is at last persuaded to see himself with the eyes of Venice, not just of Iago, but of Brabantio (who gladly entertains Othello until he has the presumption to elope with Brabantio's white daughter) and others. The resulting destruction of self-regard is devastating. Othello's jealousy stems from a profound suspicion that others cannot love him because he does not deem himself lovable.

Othello has loved Desdemona as an extention of himself, and, in his moments of greatest contentedness, his marriage is sustained by an idealized vision of himself serving as the object of his exalted romantic passion. When he destroys Desdemona, as he realizes with a terrible clarity, Othello destroys himself; the act is a prelude to his actual suicide. Iago's means of temptation, then, is to persuade Othello to regard himself with the eyes of Venice, to accept the view that Othello is himself alien and that any woman who loves him does so perversely. In Othello's tainted state of mind, Desdemona's very sexuality becomes an unbearable threat to him, her warmth and devotion a "proof" of disloyalty. Othello's most tortured speeches (3.4.57–77, 4.2.49–66) reveal the extent to which he equates the seemingly betraying woman, whom he has so depended on for happiness, with his own mother, who gave Othello's father a handkerchief and threatened him with loss of her love if he should lose it. Othello has briefly learned and then forgotten the precious art of harmonizing erotic passion and spiritual love, and, as these two great aims of love are driven apart in him, he comes to loathe and fear the sexuality that puts him so much in mind of his physical frailty and dependence on woman. The horror and pity of *Othello* rests, above all, in the spectacle of a love that was once so whole and noble made filthy by self-hatred. The tragic flaw thus lies in Othello's maleness, in his fear of betrayal by the innocent woman he loves, and his apparent need to degrade her for the very thing he finds desirable in her—a tendency so common among men that Freud, in the early twentieth century, could declare it to be "the most prevalent form of degradation in erotic life" (in Freud's *Sammlung*, volume 4).

The increasing surrender of Othello's judgment to passion can be measured in three successive trial scenes in the play: the entirely fair trial of Othello himself by the Venetian Senate concerning the elopement, Othello's trial of Cassio for drinking and rioting (when, ominously, Othello's "blood begins my safer guides to rule," 2.3.199), and finally the prejudged sentencing of Desdemona without providing her any opportunity to defend herself. In a corollary decline, Othello falls from the Christian compassion of the opening scenes (he customarily confesses to heaven "the vices of my blood," 1.3.125) to the pagan savagery of his vengeful and ritualistic execution of his wife. "My heart is turned to stone" (4.1.182–183), he vows, and at the play's end he grievingly characterizes himself as a "base Indian" who "threw a pearl away / Richer than all his tribe" (5.2.357–358). Iago knows that he must persuade Othello to sentence and to execute Desdemona himself, for only by active commitment to evil will Othello damn himself. In nothing does Iago so resemble the devil as in his wish to see Othello destroy the innocence and goodness on which his happiness depends.

The fate of some of the lesser characters echoes that of Othello, for Iago's evil intent is to "enmesh them all" (2.3.356). Cassio, in particular, is, like Othello, an attractive man with a single, vulnerable weakness—in his case, a fleshly appetite for wine and women. For him, alternately idolizing and depreciating women as he does, the gap between spiritual and sensual love remains vast, but he is essentially good-natured and trustworthy. His seemingly genial flaws lead to disaster, because they put him at the mercy of a remorseless enemy. Iago is, with fitting irony, the apostle of absolute self-control: "Our bodies are our gardens, to the which our wills are gardeners" (1.3.323–324). Thus, Cassio's tragedy is anything but a straightforward homily on the virtues of temperance. Similarly, Bianca is undone, not through any simple cause-and-effect punishment of her sexual conduct—she is, after all, fond of Cassio and loyal to him, even if he will not marry her—but because Iago is able

to turn appearances against her. With his usual appeal to a priori logic, he builds a case that she and Cassio are in cahoots: "I do suspect this trash / To be a party in this injury . . . This is the fruits of whoring" (5.1.86–87, 118). Roderigo is another of Iago's victims, a contemptible one, led by the nose because he, too, has surrendered reason to passion. Emilia cannot escape Iago's evil influence and steals the handkerchief for him, despite knowing its value for Desdemona. Flaws are magnified into disasters by a remorseless evil intelligence. Men and women both must be ceaselessly circumspect; a good reputation is sooner lost than recovered. Emilia is a conventionally decent enough woman—she jests to Desdemona that she would be faithless in marriage only for a very high price—and yet her one small compromise with her conscience contributes to the murder of her mistress. Like Othello, she offers atonement too late, by denouncing her husband in a gesture of defiance toward male authority that says much about the tragic consequences of male mistrust of women. Desdemona is the only person in the play too good to be struck down through some inner flaw, which may explain why Iago is so intent on destroying her along with Othello and Cassio.

As a tragic hero, Othello obtains self-knowledge at a terrible price. He knows finally that what he has destroyed was ineffably good. The discovery is too late for him to make amends, and he dies by his own hand as atonement. The deaths of Othello and Desdemona are, in their separate ways, equally devastating: he is in part the victim of racism, though he nobly refuses to deny his own culpability, and she is the victim of sexism, lapsing sadly into the stereotypical role of passive and silent sufferer that the Venetian world expects of women. Despite the loss, however, Othello's reaffirmation of faith in Desdemona's goodness undoes what the devil-like Iago had most hoped to achieve: the separation of Othello from his loving trust in one who is good. In this important sense, Othello's self-knowledge is cathartic and a compensation for the terrible price he has paid. The very existence of a person as good as Desdemona gives the lie to Iago's creed that everyone has his or her price. She is the sacrificial victim who must die for Othello's loss of faith and, by dying, rekindle that faith. ("My life upon her faith!" Othello prophetically affirms, in response to her father's warning that she may deceive [1.3.297].) She cannot restore him to himself, for self-hatred has done its ugly work, but she is the means by which he understands at last the chimerical and wantonly destructive nature of his jealousy. His greatness appears in his acknowledgment of this truth and in the heroic struggle with which he has confronted an inner darkness we all share.

Othello, the Moor of Venice

The Names of the Actors

OTHELLO, *the Moor*
BRABANTIO, *[a senator,] father to Desdemona*
CASSIO, *an honorable lieutenant [to Othello]*
IAGO, *[Othello's ancient,] a villain*
RODERIGO, *a gulled gentleman*
DUKE OF VENICE
SENATORS *[of Venice]*
MONTANO, *Governor of Cyprus*
GENTLEMEN *of Cyprus*
LODOVICO *and* GRATIANO, *[kinsmen to Brabantio,] two noble Venetians*
SAILORS
CLOWN

DESDEMONA, *[daughter to Brabantio and] wife to Othello*
EMILIA, *wife to Iago*
BIANCA, *a courtesan [and mistress to Cassio]*

[A MESSENGER
A HERALD
A MUSICIAN

Servants, Attendants, Officers, Senators, Musicians, Gentlemen

SCENE: *Venice; a seaport in Cyprus]*

1.1   *Enter Roderigo and Iago.*

RODERIGO
  Tush, never tell me! I take it much unkindly   1
  That thou, Iago, who hast had my purse
  As if the strings were thine, shouldst know of this.   3
IAGO   'Sblood, but you'll not hear me.   4
  If ever I did dream of such a matter,
  Abhor me.
RODERIGO
  Thou toldst me thou didst hold him in thy hate.
IAGO   Despise me
  If I do not. Three great ones of the city,
  In personal suit to make me his lieutenant,
  Off-capped to him; and by the faith of man,   11

  I know my price, I am worth no worse a place.
  But he, as loving his own pride and purposes,
  Evades them with a bombast circumstance   14
  Horribly stuffed with epithets of war,   15
  And, in conclusion,
  Nonsuits my mediators. For, "Certes," says he,   17
  "I have already chose my officer."
  And what was he?
  Forsooth, a great arithmetician,   20
  One Michael Cassio, a Florentine,
  A fellow almost damned in a fair wife,   22
  That never set a squadron in the field
  Nor the division of a battle knows   24
  More than a spinster—unless the bookish theoric,   25
  Wherein the togaed consuls can propose   26
  As masterly as he. Mere prattle without practice
  Is all his soldiership. But he, sir, had th' election;
  And I, of whom his eyes had seen the proof   29
  At Rhodes, at Cyprus, and on other grounds
  Christened and heathen, must be beleed and calmed   31
  By debitor and creditor. This countercaster,   32
  He, in good time, must his lieutenant be,   33
  And I—God bless the mark!—his Moorship's
      ancient.   34
RODERIGO
  By heaven, I rather would have been his hangman.   35
IAGO
  Why, there's no remedy. 'Tis the curse of service;
  Preferment goes by letter and affection,   37
  And not by old gradation, where each second   38
  Stood heir to th' first. Now, sir, be judge yourself
  Whether I in any just term am affined   40
  To love the Moor.
RODERIGO   I would not follow him then.
IAGO   O sir, content you.   43
  I follow him to serve my turn upon him.
  We cannot all be masters, nor all masters
  Cannot be truly followed. You shall mark   46
  Many a duteous and knee-crooking knave
  That, doting on his own obsequious bondage,
  Wears out his time, much like his master's ass,

1.1. Location: Venice. A street.
1 never tell me (An expression of incredulity, like "tell me another one.") **3 this** i.e., Desdemona's elopement **4 'Sblood** by His (Christ's) blood **11 him** i.e., Othello

14 bombast circumstance wordy evasion. (*Bombast* is cotton padding.) **15 epithets of war** military expressions **17 Nonsuits** rejects the petition of. **Certes** certainly **20 arithmetician** i.e., a man whose military knowledge is merely theoretical, based on books of tactics **22 A . . . wife** (Cassio does not seem to be married, but his counterpart in Shakespeare's source does have a woman in his house. See also 4.1.131.) **24 division of a battle** disposition of a military unit **25 a spinster** i.e., a housewife, one whose regular occupation is spinning. **theoric** theory **26 togaed** wearing the toga. **consuls** counselors, senators. **propose** discuss **29 his** i.e., Othello's **31 Christened** Christian. **beleed and calmed** left to leeward without wind, becalmed. (A sailing metaphor.) **32 debitor and creditor** (A name for a system of bookkeeping, here used as a contemptuous nickname for Cassio.) **countercaster** bookkeeper, one who tallies with *counters*, or "metal disks." (Said contemptuously.) **33 in good time** opportunely, i.e., forsooth **34 God bless the mark** (Perhaps originally a formula to ward off evil; here an expression of impatience.) **ancient** standard-bearer, ensign **35 his hangman** the executioner of him **37 Preferment** promotion. **letter and affection** personal influence and favoritism **38 old gradation** step-by-step seniority, the traditional way **40 term** respect. **affined** bound **43 content you** don't you worry about that **46 truly** faithfully

For naught but provender, and when he's old,
cashiered.   50
Whip me such honest knaves. Others there are   51
Who, trimmed in forms and visages of duty,   52
Keep yet their hearts attending on themselves,
And, throwing but shows of service on their lords,
Do well thrive by them, and when they have lined
their coats,   55
Do themselves homage. These fellows have some
soul,   56
And such a one do I profess myself. For, sir,
It is as sure as you are Roderigo,
Were I the Moor I would not be Iago.   59
In following him, I follow but myself—
Heaven is my judge, not I for love and duty,
But seeming so for my peculiar end.   62
For when my outward action doth demonstrate
The native act and figure of my heart   64
In compliment extern, 'tis not long after   65
But I will wear my heart upon my sleeve
For daws to peck at. I am not what I am.   67

RODERIGO
What a full fortune does the thick-lips owe   68
If he can carry 't thus!

IAGO   Call up her father.   69
Rouse him, make after him, poison his delight,
Proclaim him in the streets; incense her kinsmen,
And, though he in a fertile climate dwell,   72
Plague him with flies. Though that his joy be joy, 73
Yet throw such changes of vexation on 't   74
As it may lose some color.   75

RODERIGO
Here is her father's house. I'll call aloud.

IAGO
Do, with like timorous accent and dire yell   77
As when, by night and negligence, the fire   78
Is spied in populous cities.

RODERIGO
What ho, Brabantio! Signor Brabantio, ho!

IAGO
Awake! What ho, Brabantio! Thieves, thieves,
thieves!
Look to your house, your daughter, and your bags!

Thieves, thieves!   83

        Brabantio [enters] above [at a window].

BRABANTIO
What is the reason of this terrible summons?
What is the matter there?   85

RODERIGO
Signor, is all your family within?

IAGO
Are your doors locked?

BRABANTIO   Why, wherefore ask you this?

IAGO
Zounds, sir, you're robbed. For shame, put on your
gown!   88
Your heart is burst; you have lost half your soul.
Even now, now, very now, an old black ram
Is tupping your white ewe. Arise, arise!   91
Awake the snorting citizens with the bell,   92
Or else the devil will make a grandsire of you.   93
Arise, I say!

BRABANTIO   What, have you lost your wits?

RODERIGO
Most reverend signor, do you know my voice?

BRABANTIO   Not I. What are you?

RODERIGO   My name is Roderigo.

BRABANTIO   The worser welcome.
I have charged thee not to haunt about my doors.
In honest plainness thou hast heard me say
My daughter is not for thee; and now, in madness,
Being full of supper and distempering drafts,   102
Upon malicious bravery dost thou come   103
To start my quiet.   104

RODERIGO
Sir, sir, sir—

BRABANTIO   But thou must needs be sure
My spirits and my place have in their power   106
To make this bitter to thee.

RODERIGO   Patience, good sir.

BRABANTIO
What tell'st thou me of robbing? This is Venice;
My house is not a grange.

RODERIGO   Most grave Brabantio,   109
In simple and pure soul I come to you.   110

IAGO   Zounds, sir, you are one of those that will not
serve God if the devil bid you. Because we come to do
you service and you think we are ruffians, you'll have
your daughter covered with a Barbary horse; you'll 114
have your nephews neigh to you; you'll have coursers 115
for cousins and jennets for germans.   116

---

50 cashiered dismissed from service   **51 Whip me** whip, as far as I'm
concerned   **52 trimmed . . . duty** dressed up in the mere form and
show of dutifulness   **55 lined their coats** i.e., stuffed their purses
56 Do themselves homage i.e., attend to self-interest solely   **59 Were
. . . Iago** i.e., if I were able to assume command, I certainly would
not choose to remain a subordinate, or, I would keep a suspicious
eye on a flattering subordinate   **62 peculiar** particular, personal
64 native innate.   **figure** shape, intent   **65 compliment extern** outward show (conforming in this case to the inner workings and intention of the heart)   **67 daws** small crowlike birds, proverbially stupid
and avaricious.   **I am not what I am** i.e., I am not one who wears
his heart on his sleeve   **68 full** swelling.   **thick-lips** (Elizabethans often applied the term "Moor" to Negroes.)   **owe** own   **69 carry 't
thus** carry this off   **72–73 though . . . flies** though he seems prosperous and happy now, vex him with misery   **73 Though . . . be joy** although he seems fortunate and happy. (Repeats the idea of line 72.)
74 changes of vexation vexing changes   **75 As it may** that may
cause it to.   **some color** some of its fresh gloss   **77 timorous** frightening   **78 and negligence** i.e., by negligence

83 s.d. at a window (This stage direction, from the Quarto, probably
calls for an appearance on the gallery above and rearstage.)   **85 the
matter** your business   **88 Zounds** by His (Christ's) wounds   **91 tupping** covering, copulating with. (Said of sheep.)   **92 snorting** snoring
93 the devil (The devil was conventionally pictured as black.)
102 distempering intoxicating   **103 Upon malicious bravery** with
hostile intent to defy me   **104 start** startle, disrupt   **106 My spirits
and my place** my temperament and my authority of office.   **have in**
have it in   **109 grange** isolated country house   **110 simple** sincere
114 Barbary from northern Africa (and hence associated with Othello)
115 nephews i.e., grandsons.   **coursers** powerful horses   **116 cousins** kinsmen.   **jennets** small Spanish horses.   **germans** near relatives

BRABANTIO   What profane wretch art thou?

IAGO   I am one, sir, that comes to tell you your daughter and the Moor are now making the beast with two backs.

BRABANTIO
Thou art a villain.

IAGO   You are—a senator.   121

BRABANTIO
This thou shalt answer. I know thee, Roderigo.   122

RODERIGO
Sir, I will answer anything. But I beseech you,
If 't be your pleasure and most wise consent—   124
As partly I find it is—that your fair daughter,
At this odd-even and dull watch o' the night,   126
Transported with no worse nor better guard   127
But with a knave of common hire, a gondolier,   128
To the gross clasps of a lascivious Moor—
If this be known to you and your allowance   130
We then have done you bold and saucy wrongs.   131
But if you know not this, my manners tell me
We have your wrong rebuke. Do not believe
That, from the sense of all civility,   134
I thus would play and trifle with your reverence.   135
Your daughter, if you have not given her leave,
I say again, hath made a gross revolt,
Tying her duty, beauty, wit, and fortunes   138
In an extravagant and wheeling stranger   139
Of here and everywhere. Straight satisfy yourself.   140
If she be in her chamber or your house,
Let loose on me the justice of the state
For thus deluding you.

BRABANTIO   Strike on the tinder, ho!   144
Give me a taper! Call up all my people!
This accident is not unlike my dream.   146
Belief of it oppresses me already.
Light, I say, light!   Exit [above].

IAGO   Farewell, for I must leave you.
It seems not meet nor wholesome to my place   149
To be produced—as, if I stay, I shall—   150
Against the Moor. For I do know the state,
However this may gall him with some check,   152
Cannot with safety cast him, for he's embarked   153
With such loud reason to the Cyprus wars,   154
Which even now stands in act, that, for their souls,   155

Another of his fathom they have none   156
To lead their business; in which regard,   157
Though I do hate him as I do hell pains,
Yet for necessity of present life   159
I must show out a flag and sign of love,
Which is indeed but sign. That you shall surely find him,
Lead to the Sagittary the raisèd search,   162
And there will I be with him. So farewell.   Exit. 163

*Enter [below] Brabantio [in his nightgown] with
servants and torches.*

BRABANTIO
It is too true an evil. Gone she is;
And what's to come of my despisèd time   165
Is naught but bitterness. Now, Roderigo,
Where didst thou see her?—O unhappy girl!—
With the Moor, sayst thou?—Who would be a father!—
How didst thou know 'twas she?—O, she deceives me
Past thought!—What said she to you?—Get more tapers.
Raise all my kindred.—Are they married, think you?

RODERIGO   Truly, I think they are.

BRABANTIO
O heaven! How got she out? O treason of the blood!
Fathers, from hence trust not your daughters' minds
By what you see them act. Is there not charms   175
By which the property of youth and maidhood   176
May be abused? Have you not read, Roderigo,   177
Of some such thing?

RODERIGO   Yes, sir, I have indeed.

BRABANTIO
Call up my brother.—O, would you had had her!—
Some one way, some another.—Do you know
Where we may apprehend her and the Moor?

RODERIGO
I think I can discover him, if you please   182
To get good guard and go along with me.

BRABANTIO
Pray you, lead on. At every house I'll call;
I may command at most.—Get weapons, ho!   185
And raise some special officers of night.—
On, good Roderigo. I will deserve your pains.   187
                                        Exeunt.

❧

121 **a senator** (Said with mock politeness, as though the word itself were an insult.) 122 **answer** be held accountable for 124 **wise** well-informed 126 **odd-even** between one day and the next, i.e., about midnight 127 **with** by 128 **But with a knave** than by a low fellow, a servant 130 **allowance** permission 131 **saucy** insolent 134 **from** contrary to. **civility** good manners, decency 135 **your reverence** the respect due to you 138 **wit** intelligence 139 **extravagant** expatriate, wandering far from home. **wheeling** roving about, vagabond. **stranger** foreigner 140 **Straight** straightway 144 **tinder** charred linen ignited by a spark from flint and steel, used to light torches or *tapers* (lines 145, 170) 146 **accident** occurrence, event 149 **meet** fitting. **place** position (as ensign) 150 **produced** produced (as a witness) 152 **gall** rub; oppress. **check** rebuke 153 **cast** dismiss. **embarked** engaged 154 **loud reason** unanimous shout of confirmation (in the Senate) 155 **stands in act** are going on. **for their souls** to save themselves

156 **fathom** i.e., ability, depth of experience 157 **in which regard** out of regard for which 159 **life** livelihood 162 **Sagittary** (An inn or house where Othello and Desdemona are staying, named for its sign of Sagittarius, or Centaur.) **raisèd search** search party roused out of sleep 163 **s.d. nightgown** dressing gown. (This costuming is specified in the Quarto text.) 165 **time** i.e., remainder of life 175 **charms** spells 176 **property** special quality, nature 177 **abused** deceived 182 **discover** reveal, uncover 185 **command** demand assistance 187 **deserve** show gratitude for

1.2   *Enter Othello, Iago, attendants with torches.*

IAGO
Though in the trade of war I have slain men,
Yet do I hold it very stuff o' the conscience   2
To do no contrived murder. I lack iniquity   3
Sometimes to do me service. Nine or ten times
I had thought t' have yerked him here under the
    ribs.   5

OTHELLO
'Tis better as it is.

IAGO   Nay, but he prated,
And spoke such scurvy and provoking terms
Against your honor
That, with the little godliness I have,
I did full hard forbear him. But, I pray you, sir,   10
Are you fast married? Be assured of this,
That the magnifico is much beloved,   12
And hath in his effect a voice potential   13
As double as the Duke's. He will divorce you,
Or put upon you what restraint or grievance
The law, with all his might to enforce it on,
Will give him cable.

OTHELLO   Let him do his spite.   17
My services which I have done the seigniory   18
Shall out-tongue his complaints. 'Tis yet to know—   19
Which, when I know that boasting is an honor,
I shall promulgate—I fetch my life and being
From men of royal siege, and my demerits   22
May speak unbonneted to as proud a fortune   23
As this that I have reached. For know, Iago,
But that I love the gentle Desdemona,
I would not my unhousèd free condition   26
Put into circumscription and confine   27
For the sea's worth. But look, what lights come
    yond?   28

Enter Cassio [and certain officers] with torches.

IAGO
Those are the raisèd father and his friends.
You were best go in.

OTHELLO   Not I. I must be found.
My parts, my title, and my perfect soul   31
Shall manifest me rightly. Is it they?

IAGO   By Janus, I think no.   33

OTHELLO
The servants of the Duke? And my lieutenant?
The goodness of the night upon you, friends!
What is the news?

CASSIO   The Duke does greet you, General,
And he requires your haste-post-haste appearance
Even on the instant.

OTHELLO   What is the matter, think you?   38

CASSIO
Something from Cyprus, as I may divine.   39
It is a business of some heat. The galleys   40
Have sent a dozen sequent messengers   41
This very night at one another's heels,
And many of the consuls, raised and met,   43
Are at the Duke's already. You have been hotly
    called for;
When, being not at your lodging to be found,
The Senate hath sent about three several quests   46
To search you out.

OTHELLO   'Tis well I am found by you.
I will but spend a word here in the house
And go with you.   [*Exit.*]

CASSIO   Ancient, what makes he here?   49

IAGO
Faith, he tonight hath boarded a land carrack.   50
If it prove lawful prize, he's made forever.   51

CASSIO
I do not understand.

IAGO   He's married.

CASSIO   To who?

[Enter Othello.]

IAGO
Marry, to—Come, Captain, will you go?   53

OTHELLO   Have with you.   54

CASSIO
Here comes another troop to seek for you.   55

*Enter Brabantio, Roderigo, with officers and
torches.*

IAGO
It is Brabantio. General, be advised.   56
He comes to bad intent.

OTHELLO   Holla! Stand there!

RODERIGO
Signor, it is the Moor.

BRABANTIO   Down with him, thief!
                    [*They draw on both sides.*]

1.2. **Location:** Venice. Another street, before Othello's lodgings.
2 very stuff essence, basic material (continuing the metaphor of *trade*
from line 1)   **3 contrived** premeditated   **5 yerked** stabbed.   **him** i.e.,
Roderigo   **10 I . . . him** I restrained myself with great difficulty from
assaulting him   **12 magnifico** Venetian grandee, i.e., Brabantio
13 in his effect at his command.   **potential** powerful   **17 cable** i.e.,
scope   **18 seigniory** Venetian government   **19 yet to know** not yet
widely known   **22 siege** i.e., rank. (Literally, a seat used by a person
of distinction.)   **demerits** deserts   **23 unbonneted** without removing
the hat, i.e., on equal terms (? Or "with hat off," "in all due modesty.")   **26 unhoused** unconfined, undomesticated   **27 circumscription and confine** restriction and confinement   **28 the sea's worth** all
the riches at the bottom of the sea.   **s.d. officers** (The Quarto text
calls for "Cassio with lights, officers with torches.")   **31 My . . . soul**
my natural gifts, my position or reputation, and my unflawed
conscience

33 Janus Roman two-faced god of beginnings   **38 matter** business
39 divine guess   **40 heat** urgency   **41 sequent** successive   **43 consuls** senators   **46 about** all over the city.   **several** separate
49 makes does   **50 boarded** gone aboard and seized as an act of piracy (with sexual suggestion).   **carrack** large merchant ship   **51 prize**
booty   **53 Marry** (An oath, originally "by the Virgin Mary"; here used
with wordplay on *married*.)   **54 Have with you** i.e., let's go   **55 s.d.
officers and torches** (The Quarto text calls for "others with lights and
weapons.")   **56 be advised** be on your guard

IAGO
You, Roderigo! Come, sir, I am for you.

OTHELLO
Keep up your bright swords, for the dew will rust
   them.   60
Good signor, you shall more command with years
Than with your weapons.

BRABANTIO
O thou foul thief, where hast thou stowed my
   daughter?
Damned as thou art, thou hast enchanted her!
For I'll refer me to all things of sense,   65
If she in chains of magic were not bound
Whether a maid so tender, fair, and happy,
So opposite to marriage that she shunned
The wealthy curlèd darlings of our nation,
Would ever have, t' incur a general mock,
Run from her guardage to the sooty bosom   71
Of such a thing as thou—to fear, not to delight.
Judge me the world if 'tis not gross in sense   73
That thou hast practiced on her with foul charms,
Abused her delicate youth with drugs or minerals   75
That weakens motion. I'll have 't disputed on;   76
'Tis probable and palpable to thinking.
I therefore apprehend and do attach thee   78
For an abuser of the world, a practicer
Of arts inhibited and out of warrant.—   80
Lay hold upon him! If he do resist,
Subdue him at his peril.

OTHELLO   Hold your hands,
Both you of my inclining and the rest.   83
Were it my cue to fight, I should have known it
Without a prompter.—Whither will you that I go
To answer this your charge?

BRABANTIO   To prison, till fit time
Of law and course of direct session   88
Call thee to answer.

OTHELLO   What if I do obey?
How may the Duke be therewith satisfied,
Whose messengers are here about my side
Upon some present business of the state
To bring me to him?

OFFICER   'Tis true, most worthy signor.
The Duke's in council, and your noble self,
I am sure, is sent for.

BRABANTIO   How? The Duke in council?
In this time of the night? Bring him away.   96
Mine's not an idle cause. The Duke himself,   97
Or any of my brothers of the state,
Cannot but feel this wrong as 'twere their own;

For if such actions may have passage free,   100
Bondslaves and pagans shall our statesmen be.
                         Exeunt.

1.3   *Enter Duke [and] Senators [and sit at a table, with
lights], and Officers. [The Duke and Senators
are reading dispatches.]*

DUKE
There is no composition in these news   1
That gives them credit.

FIRST SENATOR   Indeed, they are disproportioned.   3
My letters say a hundred and seven galleys.

DUKE
And mine, a hundred forty.

SECOND SENATOR   And mine, two hundred.
But though they jump not on a just account—   6
As in these cases, where the aim reports   7
'Tis oft with difference—yet do they all confirm
A Turkish fleet, and bearing up to Cyprus.

DUKE
Nay, it is possible enough to judgment.
I do not so secure me in the error   11
But the main article I do approve   12
In fearful sense.

SAILOR *(within)*   What ho, what ho, what ho!

              Enter Sailor.

OFFICER   A messenger from the galleys.

DUKE   Now, what's the business?

SAILOR
The Turkish preparation makes for Rhodes.   16
So was I bid report here to the state
By Signor Angelo.

DUKE
How say you by this change?

FIRST SENATOR   This cannot be   19
By no assay of reason. 'Tis a pageant   20
To keep us in false gaze. When we consider   21
Th' importance of Cyprus to the Turk,
And let ourselves again but understand
That, as it more concerns the Turk than Rhodes,
So may he with more facile question bear it,   25
For that it stands not in such warlike brace,   26
But altogether lacks th' abilities   27

---

60 Keep up keep in the sheath **65 refer me** submit my case. **things
of sense** commonsense understandings, or, creatures possessing common sense **71 her guardage** my guardianship of her **73 gross in
sense** obvious **75 minerals** i.e., poisons **76 weakens motion** impair
the vital faculties. **disputed on** argued in court by professional counsel, debated by experts **78 attach** arrest **80 arts inhibited** prohibited
arts, black magic. **out of warrant** illegal **83 inclining** following,
party **88 course of direct session** regular or specially convened legal
proceedings **96 away** right along **97 idle** trifling

100 have passage free are allowed to go unchecked
1.3. Location: Venice. A council chamber.
s.d. Enter . . . Officers (The Quarto text calls for the Duke and senators to "sit at a table with lights and attendants.") **1 composition**
consistency **3 disproportioned** inconsistent **6 jump** agree. **just exact** **7 the aim** conjecture **11–12 I do not . . . approve** I do not
take such (false) comfort in the discrepancies that I fail to perceive the
main point, i.e., that the Turkish fleet is threatening **16 preparation**
fleet prepared for battle **19 by** about **20 assay** test. **pageant** mere
show **21 in false gaze** looking the wrong way **25 So may . . . it** so
also he (the Turk) can more easily capture it (Cyprus) **26 For that**
since. **brace** state of defense **27 abilities** means of self-defense

That Rhodes is dressed in—if we make thought of
 this,   28
We must not think the Turk is so unskillful   29
To leave that latest which concerns him first,   30
Neglecting an attempt of ease and gain
To wake and wage a danger profitless.   32
DUKE
 Nay, in all confidence, he's not for Rhodes.
OFFICER   Here is more news.

Enter a Messenger.

MESSENGER
 The Ottomites, reverend and gracious,
Steering with due course toward the isle of Rhodes,
Have there injointed them with an after fleet.   37
FIRST SENATOR
 Ay, so I thought. How many, as you guess?
MESSENGER
 Of thirty sail; and now they do restem   39
Their backward course, bearing with frank
 appearance   40
Their purposes toward Cyprus. Signor Montano,
Your trusty and most valiant servitor,   42
With his free duty recommends you thus,   43
And prays you to believe him.
DUKE   'Tis certain then for Cyprus.
Marcus Luccicos, is not he in town?
FIRST SENATOR   He's now in Florence.
DUKE
 Write from us to him, post-post-haste. Dispatch.
FIRST SENATOR
 Here comes Brabantio and the valiant Moor.

*Enter Brabantio, Othello, Cassio, Iago, Roderigo,
 and officers.*

DUKE
 Valiant Othello, we must straight employ you   50
Against the general enemy Ottoman.   51
 [*To Brabantio.*] I did not see you; welcome, gentle
 signor.   52
We lacked your counsel and your help tonight.
BRABANTIO
 So did I yours. Good Your Grace, pardon me;
Neither my place nor aught I heard of business   55
Hath raised me from my bed, nor doth the general
 care
Take hold on me, for my particular grief   57
Is of so floodgate and o'erbearing nature   58
That it engluts and swallows other sorrows   59

And it is still itself.
DUKE   Why, what's the matter?   60
BRABANTIO
 My daughter! O, my daughter!
DUKE AND SENATORS   Dead?
BRABANTIO   Ay, to me.
 She is abused, stol'n from me, and corrupted   62
By spells and medicines bought of mountebanks;
For nature so preposterously to err,
Being not deficient, blind, or lame of sense,   65
Sans witchcraft could not.   66
DUKE
 Whoe'er he be that in this foul proceeding
Hath thus beguiled your daughter of herself,
And you of her, the bloody book of law
You shall yourself read in the bitter letter
After your own sense—yea, though our proper son   71
Stood in your action.
BRABANTIO   Humbly I thank Your Grace.   72
 Here is the man, this Moor, whom now it seems
Your special mandate for the state affairs
Hath hither brought.
ALL   We are very sorry for 't.
DUKE [*to Othello*]
 What, in your own part, can you say to this?
BRABANTIO   Nothing, but this is so.
OTHELLO
 Most potent, grave, and reverend signors,
My very noble and approved good masters: 79
That I have ta'en away this old man's daughter,
It is most true; true, I have married her.
The very head and front of my offending   82
Hath this extent, no more. Rude am I in my speech, 83
And little blessed with the soft phrase of peace;
For since these arms of mine had seven years' pith, 85
Till now some nine moons wasted, they have used   86
Their dearest action in the tented field;   87
And little of this great world can I speak
More than pertains to feats of broils and battle,
And therefore little shall I grace my cause
In speaking for myself. Yet, by your gracious
 patience,
I will a round unvarnished tale deliver   92
Of my whole course of love—what drugs, what
 charms,
What conjuration, and what mighty magic,
For such proceeding I am charged withal,   95
I won his daughter.
BRABANTIO   A maiden never bold;

---

28 dressed in equipped with   **29 unskillful** deficient in judgment
30 latest last   **32 wake** stir up.   **wage** risk   **37 injointed them** joined
themselves.   **after** second, following   **39–40 restem . . . course** retrace their original course   **40 frank appearance** undisguised intent
42 servitor officer under your command   **43 free duty** freely given
and loyal service.   **recommends** commends himself and reports to
50 straight straightway   **51 general enemy** universal enemy to all
Christendom   **52 gentle** noble   **55 place** official position   **57 particular** personal   **58 floodgate** i.e., overwhelming (as when floodgates
are opened)   **59 engluts** engulfs

60 is still itself remains undiminished   **62 abused** deceived
65 deficient defective.   **lame of sense** deficient in sensory perception
66 Sans without   **71 After . . . sense** according to your own interpretation.   **our proper** my own   **72 Stood . . . action** were under your
accusation   **79 approved** proved, esteemed   **82 head and front**
height and breadth, entire extent   **83 Rude** unpolished   **85 since
. . . pith** i.e., since I was seven.   **pith** strength, vigor   **86 Till . . .
wasted** until some nine months ago (since when Othello has evidently
not been on active duty, but in Venice)   **87 dearest** most valuable
92 round plain   **95 withal** with

Of spirit so still and quiet that her motion   97
Blushed at herself; and she, in spite of nature,   98
Of years, of country, credit, everything,   99
To fall in love with what she feared to look on!
It is a judgment maimed and most imperfect
That will confess perfection so could err   102
Against all rules of nature, and must be driven
To find out practices of cunning hell   104
Why this should be. I therefore vouch again   105
That with some mixtures powerful o'er the blood,   106
Or with some dram conjured to this effect,   107
He wrought upon her.
DUKE   To vouch this is no proof,
Without more wider and more overt test   109
Than these thin habits and poor likelihoods   110
Of modern seeming do prefer against him.   111
FIRST SENATOR   But Othello, speak.
Did you by indirect and forcèd courses   113
Subdue and poison this young maid's affections?
Or came it by request and such fair question   115
As soul to soul affordeth?
OTHELLO   I do beseech you,
Send for the lady to the Sagittary
And let her speak of me before her father.
If you do find me foul in her report,
The trust, the office I do hold of you
Not only take away, but let your sentence
Even fall upon my life.
DUKE   Fetch Desdemona hither.
OTHELLO
Ancient, conduct them. You best know the place.
                        [*Exeunt Iago and attendants.*]
And, till she come, as truly as to heaven
I do confess the vices of my blood,   125
So justly to your grave ears I'll present   126
How I did thrive in this fair lady's love,
And she in mine.
DUKE   Say it, Othello.
OTHELLO
Her father loved me, oft invited me,
Still questioned me the story of my life   131
From year to year—the battles, sieges, fortunes
That I have passed.
I ran it through, even from my boyish days
To th' very moment that he bade me tell it,
Wherein I spoke of most disastrous chances,
Of moving accidents by flood and field,   137
Of hairbreadth scapes i' th' imminent deadly breach,   138

Of being taken by the insolent foe
And sold to slavery, of my redemption thence,
And portance in my travels' history,   141
Wherein of antres vast and deserts idle,   142
Rough quarries, rocks, and hills whose heads touch
  heaven,   143
It was my hint to speak—such was my process—   144
And of the Cannibals that each other eat,
The Anthropophagi, and men whose heads   146
Do grow beneath their shoulders. These things to
  hear
Would Desdemona seriously incline;
But still the house affairs would draw her thence,
Which ever as she could with haste dispatch
She'd come again, and with a greedy ear
Devour up my discourse. Which I, observing,
Took once a pliant hour, and found good means   153
To draw from her a prayer of earnest heart
That I would all my pilgrimage dilate,   155
Whereof by parcels she had something heard,   156
But not intentively. I did consent,   157
And often did beguile her of her tears,
When I did speak of some distressful stroke
That my youth suffered. My story being done,
She gave me for my pains a world of sighs.
She swore, in faith, 'twas strange, 'twas passing
  strange,   162
'Twas pitiful, 'twas wondrous pitiful.
She wished she had not heard it, yet she wished
That heaven had made her such a man. She
  thanked me,   165
And bade me, if I had a friend that loved her,
I should but teach him how to tell my story,
And that would woo her. Upon this hint I spake.   168
She loved me for the dangers I had passed,
And I loved her that she did pity them.
This only is the witchcraft I have used.
Here comes the lady. Let her witness it.

Enter Desdemona, Iago, [and] attendants.

DUKE
I think this tale would win my daughter too.
Good Brabantio,
Take up this mangled matter at the best.   175
Men do their broken weapons rather use
Than their bare hands.
BRABANTIO   I pray you, hear her speak.
If she confess that she was half the wooer,
Destruction on my head if my bad blame
Light on the man!—Come hither, gentle mistress.
Do you perceive in all this noble company

97–98 her . . . herself i.e., she blushed easily at herself. (*Motion* can suggest the impulse of the soul or of the emotions, or physical movement.)   **99 years** i.e., difference in age.   **credit** virtuous reputation   **102 confess** concede (that)   **104 practices** plots   **105 vouch** assert   **106 blood** passions   **107 dram . . . effect** dose made by magical spells to have this effect   **109 more wider** fuller.   **test** testimony   **110 habits** garments, i.e., appearances.   **poor likelihoods** weak inferences   **111 modern seeming** commonplace assumption.   **prefer** bring forth   **113 forcèd courses** means used against her will   **115 question** conversation   **125 blood** passions, human nature   **126 justly** truthfully, accurately   **131 Still** continually   **137 moving accidents** stirring happenings   **138 imminent . . . breach** death-threatening gaps made in a fortification

141 portance conduct   **142 antres** caverns.   **idle** barren, desolate   **143 Rough quarries** rugged rock formations   **144 hint** occasion, opportunity   **146 Anthropophagi** man-eaters. (A term from Pliny's *Natural History*.)   **153 pliant** well-suiting   **155 dilate** relate in detail   **156 by parcels** piecemeal   **157 intentively** with full attention, continuously   **162 passing** exceedingly   **165 made her** created her to be   **168 hint** opportunity. (Othello does not mean that she was dropping hints.)   **175 Take . . . best** make the best of a bad bargain

Where most you owe obedience?

DESDEMONA   My noble Father,
I do perceive here a divided duty.
To you I am bound for life and education;   184
My life and education both do learn me   185
How to respect you. You are the lord of duty;   186
I am hitherto your daughter. But here's my
    husband,
And so much duty as my mother showed
To you, preferring you before her father,
So much I challenge that I may profess   190
Due to the Moor my lord.

BRABANTIO   God be with you! I have done.
Please it Your Grace, on to the state affairs.
I had rather to adopt a child than get it.   194
Come hither, Moor.   [*He joins the hands of Othello
                                    and Desdemona.*]
I here do give thee that with all my heart   196
Which, but thou hast already, with all my heart   197
I would keep from thee.—For your sake, jewel,   198
I am glad at soul I have no other child,
For thy escape would teach me tyranny,   200
To hang clogs on them.—I have done, my lord.   201

DUKE
Let me speak like yourself, and lay a sentence   202
Which, as a grece or step, may help these lovers   203
Into your favor.
When remedies are past, the griefs are ended   205
By seeing the worst, which late on hopes depended.   206
To mourn a mischief that is past and gone   207
Is the next way to draw new mischief on.   208
What cannot be preserved when fortune takes,   209
Patience her injury a mockery makes.   210
The robbed that smiles steals something from the
    thief;
He robs himself that spends a bootless grief.   212

BRABANTIO
So let the Turk of Cyprus us beguile,
We lose it not, so long as we can smile.
He bears the sentence well that nothing bears   215
But the free comfort which from thence he hears,   216
But he bears both the sentence and the sorrow   217
That, to pay grief, must of poor patience borrow.   218

These sentences, to sugar or to gall,   219
Being strong on both sides, are equivocal.   220
But words are words. I never yet did hear
That the bruised heart was piercèd through the ear.   222
I humbly beseech you, proceed to th' affairs of state.

DUKE   The Turk with a most mighty preparation makes
for Cyprus. Othello, the fortitude of the place is best   225
known to you; and though we have there a substitute   226
of most allowed sufficiency, yet opinion, a sovereign   227
mistress of effects, throws a more safer voice on you.   228
You must therefore be content to slubber the gloss of   229
your new fortunes with this more stubborn and   230
boisterous expedition.

OTHELLO
The tyrant custom, most grave senators,
Hath made the flinty and steel couch of war
My thrice-driven bed of down. I do agnize   234
A natural and prompt alacrity
I find in hardness, and do undertake   236
These present wars against the Ottomites.
Most humbly therefore bending to your state,   238
I crave fit disposition for my wife,
Due reference of place and exhibition,   240
With such accommodation and besort   241
As levels with her breeding.   242

DUKE
Why, at her father's.

BRABANTIO   I will not have it so.

OTHELLO
Nor I.

DESDEMONA   Nor I. I would not there reside,
To put my father in impatient thoughts
By being in his eye. Most gracious Duke,
To my unfolding lend your prosperous ear,   247
And let me find a charter in your voice,   248
T' assist my simpleness.

DUKE   What would you, Desdemona?

DESDEMONA
That I did love the Moor to live with him,
My downright violence and storm of fortunes   252
May trumpet to the world. My heart's subdued   253
Even to the very quality of my lord.   254
I saw Othello's visage in his mind,
And to his honors and his valiant parts   256

184 **education** upbringing   185 **learn** teach   186 **of duty** to whom
duty is due   190 **challenge** claim   194 **get** beget   196 **with all my
heart** wherein my whole affection has been engaged   197 **with all
my heart** willingly, gladly   198 **For your sake** on your account
200 **escape** elopement   201 **clogs** (Literally, blocks of wood fastened
to the legs of criminals or convicts to inhibit escape.)   202 **like yourself** i.e., as you would, in your proper temper.   **lay a sentence** apply
a maxim   203 **grece** step   205 **remedies** hopes of remedy
206 **which . . . depended** which griefs were sustained until recently
by hopeful anticipation   207 **mischief** misfortune, injury   208 **next**
nearest   209 **What** whatever   210 **Patience . . . makes** patience
laughs at the injury inflicted by fortune (and thus eases the pain)
212 **spends a bootless grief** indulges in unavailing grief
215–218 **He bears . . . borrow** a person well bears out your maxim
who can enjoy its platitudinous comfort, free of all genuine sorrow,
but anyone whose grief bankrupts his poor patience is left with your
saying and his sorrow, too. (*Bears the sentence* also plays on the
meaning, "receives judicial sentence.")

219–220 **These . . . equivocal** these fine maxims are equivocal, either sweet or bitter in their application   222 **piercèd . . . ear** i.e.,
surgically lanced and cured by mere words of advice   225 **fortitude**
strength   226 **substitute** deputy   227 **allowed** acknowledged   227–
228 **opinion . . . on you** general opinion, an important determiner of
affairs, chooses you as the best man   229 **slubber** soil, sully
230 **stubborn** harsh, rough   234 **thrice-driven** thrice sifted, winnowed.   **agnize** know in myself, acknowledge   236 **hardness** hardship   238 **bending . . . state** bowing or kneeling to your authority
240 **reference . . . exhibition** provision of appropriate place to live
and allowance of money   241 **accommodation** suitable provision.
besort attendance   242 **levels** equals, suits.   **breeding** social position, upbringing   247 **unfolding** explanation, proposal.   **prosperous**
propitious   248 **charter** privilege, authorization   252 **My . . . fortunes** my plain and total breach of social custom, taking my future by
storm and disrupting my whole life   253–254 **My heart's . . . lord**
my heart is brought wholly into accord with Othello's virtues; I love
him for his virtues   256 **parts** qualities

Did I my soul and fortunes consecrate.
So that, dear lords, if I be left behind
A moth of peace, and he go to the war,   259
The rites for why I love him are bereft me,   260
And I a heavy interim shall support
By his dear absence. Let me go with him.   262
OTHELLO   Let her have your voice.   263
Vouch with me, heaven, I therefor beg it not
To please the palate of my appetite,
Nor to comply with heat—the young affects   266
In me defunct—and proper satisfaction,   267
But to be free and bounteous to her mind.   268
And heaven defend your good souls that you think   269
I will your serious and great business scant
When she is with me. No, when light-winged toys
Of feathered Cupid seel with wanton dullness   272
My speculative and officed instruments,   273
That my disports corrupt and taint my business,   274
Let huswives make a skillet of my helm,
And all indign and base adversities   276
Make head against my estimation!   277
DUKE
Be it as you shall privately determine,
Either for her stay or going. Th' affair cries haste,
And speed must answer it.
A SENATOR   You must away tonight.
DESDEMONA
Tonight, my lord?
DUKE   This night.
OTHELLO   With all my heart.
DUKE
At nine i' the morning here we'll meet again.
Othello, leave some officer behind,
And he shall our commission bring to you,
With such things else of quality and respect   285
As doth import you.
OTHELLO   So please Your Grace, my ancient;   286
A man he is of honesty and trust.
To his conveyance I assign my wife,
With what else needful Your Good Grace shall think
To be sent after me.
DUKE   Let it be so.
Good night to everyone. [To Brabantio.] And, noble
   signor,
If virtue no delighted beauty lack,   292
Your son-in-law is far more fair than black.
FIRST SENATOR
Adieu, brave Moor. Use Desdemona well.

BRABANTIO
Look to her, Moor, if thou hast eyes to see.
She has deceived her father, and may thee.
         Exeunt [Duke, Brabantio, Cassio, Senators, and
                                              officers].
OTHELLO
My life upon her faith! Honest Iago,
My Desdemona must I leave to thee.
I prithee, let thy wife attend on her,
And bring them after in the best advantage.   300
Come, Desdemona. I have but an hour
Of love, of worldly matters and direction,   302
To spend with thee. We must obey the time.   303
                          Exit [with Desdemona].
RODERIGO   Iago—
IAGO   What sayst thou, noble heart?
RODERIGO   What will I do, think'st thou?
IAGO   Why, go to bed and sleep.
RODERIGO   I will incontinently drown myself.   308
IAGO   If thou dost, I shall never love thee after. Why,
   thou silly gentleman?
RODERIGO   It is silliness to live when to live is torment;
   and then have we a prescription to die when death is   312
   our physician.
IAGO   O villainous! I have looked upon the world for   314
   four times seven years, and, since I could distinguish
   betwixt a benefit and an injury, I never found man
   that knew how to love himself. Ere I would say I
   would drown myself for the love of a guinea hen, I   318
   would change my humanity with a baboon.
RODERIGO   What should I do? I confess it is my shame
   to be so fond, but it is not in my virtue to amend it.   321
IAGO   Virtue? A fig! 'Tis in ourselves that we are thus or   322
   thus. Our bodies are our gardens, to the which our
   wills are gardeners; so that if we will plant nettles or
   sow lettuce, set hyssop and weed up thyme, supply it   325
   with one gender of herbs or distract it with many,   326
   either to have it sterile with idleness or manured with   327
   industry—why, the power and corrigible authority of   328
   this lies in our wills. If the beam of our lives had not   329
   one scale of reason to poise another of sensuality, the   330
   blood and baseness of our natures would conduct us   331
   to most preposterous conclusions. But we have reason
   to cool our raging motions, our carnal stings, our   333
   unbitted lusts, whereof I take this that you call love to   334
   be a sect or scion.   335
RODERIGO   It cannot be.
IAGO   It is merely a lust of the blood and a permission

---

259 moth i.e., one who consumes merely   **260 rites** rites of love
(with a suggestion, too, of "rights," sharing)   **262 dear** (1) heartfelt (2)
costly   **263 voice** consent   **266 heat** sexual passion.   **young affects**
passions of youth, desires   **267 proper** personal   **268 free** generous
269 defend forbid.   **think** should think   **272 seel** i.e., make blind (as
in falconry, by sewing up the eyes of the hawk during training)
273 speculative . . . instruments eyes and other faculties used in the
performance of duty   **274 That** so that.   **disports** sexual pastimes.
taint impair   **276 indign** unworthy, shameful   **277 Make head** raise
an army.   **estimation** reputation   **285 of quality and respect** of importance and relevance   **286 import** concern   **292 delighted** capable
of delighting

300 in . . . advantage at the most favorable opportunity   **302 direction** instructions   **303 the time** the urgency of the present crisis
308 incontinently immediately, without self-restraint   **312 prescription** (1) right based on long-established custom (2) doctor's prescription   **314 villainous** i.e., what perfect nonsense   **318 guinea hen** (A
slang term for a prostitute.)   **321 fond** infatuated.   **virtue** strength,
nature   **322 fig** (To give a fig is to thrust the thumb between the first
and second fingers in a vulgar and insulting gesture.)   **325 hyssop** a
herb of the mint family   **326 gender** kind.   **distract it with** divide it
among   **327 idleness** want of cultivation   **328 corrigible authority**
power to correct   **329 beam** balance   **330 poise** counterbalance
331 blood natural passions   **333 motions** appetites   **334 unbitted** unbridled, uncontrolled   **335 sect or scion** cutting or offshoot

of the will. Come, be a man. Drown thyself? Drown cats and blind puppies. I have professed me thy friend, and I confess me knit to thy deserving with cables of perdurable toughness. I could never better stead thee 341 than now. Put money in thy purse. Follow thou the wars; defeat thy favor with an usurped beard. I say, 343 put money in thy purse. It cannot be long that Desdemona should continue her love to the Moor—put money in thy purse—nor he his to her. It was a violent commencement in her, and thou shalt see an answerable sequestration—put but money in thy purse. 347 These Moors are changeable in their wills—fill thy 348 purse with money. The food that to him now is as 349 luscious as locusts shall be to him shortly as bitter as 351 coloquintida. She must change for youth; when she is 352 sated with his body, she will find the error of her choice. She must have change, she must. Therefore put money in thy purse. If thou wilt needs damn thyself, do it a more delicate way than drowning. Make 356 all the money thou canst. If sanctimony and a frail vow 357 betwixt an erring barbarian and a supersubtle Vene- 358 tian be not too hard for my wits and all the tribe of hell, thou shalt enjoy her. Therefore make money. A pox of drowning thyself! It is clean out of the way. 361 Seek thou rather to be hanged in compassing thy joy 362 than to be drowned and go without her.

RODERIGO Wilt thou be fast to my hopes if I depend on 364 the issue? 365

IAGO Thou art sure of me. Go, make money. I have told thee often, and I retell thee again and again, I hate the Moor. My cause is hearted; thine hath no less rea- 368 son. Let us be conjunctive in our revenge against him. 369 If thou canst cuckold him, thou dost thyself a pleasure, me a sport. There are many events in the womb of time which will be delivered. Traverse, go, provide thy 372 money. We will have more of this tomorrow. Adieu.

RODERIGO Where shall we meet i' the morning?

IAGO At my lodging.

RODERIGO I'll be with thee betimes. [He starts to leave.] 376

IAGO Go to, farewell.—Do you hear, Roderigo?

RODERIGO What say you?

IAGO No more of drowning, do you hear?

RODERIGO I am changed.

IAGO Go to, farewell. Put money enough in your purse.

RODERIGO I'll sell all my land.   Exit.

IAGO
Thus do I ever make my fool my purse;
For I mine own gained knowledge should profane

If I would time expend with such a snipe   386
But for my sport and profit. I hate the Moor;
And it is thought abroad that twixt my sheets   388
He's done my office. I know not if 't be true;   389
But I, for mere suspicion in that kind,
Will do as if for surety. He holds me well;   391
The better shall my purpose work on him.
Cassio's a proper man. Let me see now: 393
To get his place and to plume up my will   394
In double knavery—How, how?—Let's see:
After some time, to abuse Othello's ear   396
That he is too familiar with his wife.   397
He hath a person and a smooth dispose   398
To be suspected, framed to make women false.
The Moor is of a free and open nature,   400
That thinks men honest that but seem to be so,
And will as tenderly be led by the nose   402
As asses are.
I have 't. It is engendered. Hell and night
Must bring this monstrous birth to the world's light.
                                                [Exit.]

❖

2.1   *Enter Montano and two Gentlemen.*

MONTANO
What from the cape can you discern at sea?

FIRST GENTLEMAN
Nothing at all. It is a high-wrought flood.   2
I cannot, twixt the heaven and the main,   3
Descry a sail.

MONTANO
Methinks the wind hath spoke aloud at land;
A fuller blast ne'er shook our battlements.
If it hath ruffianed so upon the sea,   7
What ribs of oak, when mountains melt on them,   8
Can hold the mortise? What shall we hear of this?   9

SECOND GENTLEMAN
A segregation of the Turkish fleet.   10
For do but stand upon the foaming shore,
The chidden billow seems to pelt the clouds;   12
The wind-shaked surge, with high and monstrous
    mane,   13
Seems to cast water on the burning Bear   14

341 **perdurable** very durable. **stead** assist 343 **defeat thy favor** disguise your face. **usurped** (The suggestion is that Roderigo is not man enough to have a beard of his own.) 347–348 **an answerable sequestration** a corresponding separation or estrangement 349 **wills** carnal appetites 351 **locusts** fruit of the carob tree (see Matthew 3:4), or perhaps honeysuckle 352 **coloquintida** colocynth or bitter apple, a purgative 356 **Make** raise, collect 357 **sanctimony** sacred ceremony 358 **erring** wandering, vagabond, unsteady 361 **clean . . . way** entirely unsuitable as a course of action 362 **compassing** encompassing, embracing 364 **fast** true 365 **issue** (successful) outcome 368 **hearted** fixed in the heart, heartfelt 369 **conjunctive** united 372 **Traverse** (A military marching term.) 376 **betimes** early

386 **snipe** woodcock, i.e., fool 388 **it is thought abroad** it is rumored 389 **my office** i.e., my sexual function as husband 391 **do . . . surety** act as if on certain knowledge. **holds me well** regards me favorably 393 **proper** handsome 394 **plume up** put a feather in the cap of, i.e., glorify, gratify 396 **abuse** deceive 397 **he** i.e., Cassio 398 **dispose** disposition 400 **free** frank, generous. **open** unsuspicious 402 **tenderly** readily
2.1. Location: A seaport in Cyprus. An open place near the quay.
2 **high-wrought flood** very agitated sea 3 **main** ocean (also at line 41) 7 **ruffianed** raged 8 **mountains** i.e., of water 9 **hold the mortise** hold their joints together. (A *mortise* is the socket hollowed out in fitting timbers.) 10 **segregation** dispersal 12 **chidden** i.e., rebuked, repelled (by the shore), and thus shot into the air 13 **monstrous mane** (The surf is like the mane of a wild beast.) 14 **the burning Bear** i.e., the constellation Ursa Minor or the Little Bear, which includes the polestar (and hence regarded as the *guards of th' ever-fixèd pole* in the next line; sometimes the term *guards* is applied to the two "pointers" of the Big Bear or Dipper, which may be intended here.)

And quench the guards of th' ever-fixèd pole.
I never did like molestation view   16
On the enchafèd flood.   17
MONTANO   If that the Turkish fleet   18
Be not ensheltered and embayed, they are drowned;   19
It is impossible to bear it out.   20

Enter a [Third] Gentleman.

THIRD GENTLEMAN   News, lads! Our wars are done.
The desperate tempest hath so banged the Turks
That their designment halts. A noble ship of Venice   23
Hath seen a grievous wreck and sufferance   24
On most part of their fleet.
MONTANO   How? Is this true?
THIRD GENTLEMAN   The ship is here put in,
A Veronesa; Michael Cassio,   28
Lieutenant to the warlike Moor Othello,
Is come on shore; the Moor himself at sea,
And is in full commission here for Cyprus.
MONTANO
I am glad on 't. 'Tis a worthy governor.
THIRD GENTLEMAN
But this same Cassio, though he speak of comfort
Touching the Turkish loss, yet he looks sadly   34
And prays the Moor be safe, for they were parted
With foul and violent tempest.
MONTANO   Pray heaven he be,
For I have served him, and the man commands
Like a full soldier. Let's to the seaside, ho!   38
As well to see the vessel that's come in
As to throw out our eyes for brave Othello,
Even till we make the main and th' aerial blue   41
An indistinct regard.
THIRD GENTLEMAN   Come, let's do so,   42
For every minute is expectancy   43
Of more arrivance.   44

Enter Cassio.

CASSIO
Thanks, you the valiant of this warlike isle,
That so approve the Moor! O, let the heavens   46
Give him defense against the elements,
For I have lost him on a dangerous sea.
MONTANO   Is he well shipped?
CASSIO
His bark is stoutly timbered, and his pilot
Of very expert and approved allowance;   51
Therefore my hopes, not surfeited to death,   52

Stand in bold cure.
             [*A cry*] *within:* "A sail, a sail, a sail!"   53
CASSIO   What noise?
A GENTLEMAN
The town is empty. On the brow o' the sea   55
Stand ranks of people, and they cry "A sail!"
CASSIO
My hopes do shape him for the governor.   57
                                      [*A shot within.*]
SECOND GENTLEMAN
They do discharge their shot of courtesy;   58
Our friends at least.
CASSIO   I pray you, sir, go forth,
And give us truth who 'tis that is arrived.
SECOND GENTLEMAN   I shall.   *Exit.*
MONTANO
But, good Lieutenant, is your general wived?
CASSIO
Most fortunately. He hath achieved a maid
That paragons description and wild fame,   64
One that excels the quirks of blazoning pens,   65
And in th' essential vesture of creation   66
Does tire the enginer.

Enter [Second] Gentleman.

                    How now? Who has put in?   67
SECOND GENTLEMAN
'Tis one Iago, ancient to the General.
CASSIO
He's had most favorable and happy speed.
Tempests themselves, high seas, and howling
    winds,
The guttered rocks and congregated sands—   71
Traitors ensteeped to clog the guiltless keel—   72
As having sense of beauty, do omit   73
Their mortal natures, letting go safely by   74
The divine Desdemona.
MONTANO   What is she?
CASSIO
She that I spake of, our great captain's captain,
Left in the conduct of the bold Iago,
Whose footing here anticipates our thoughts   78
A sennight's speed. Great Jove, Othello guard,   79
And swell his sail with thine own powerful breath,
That he may bless this bay with his tall ship,   81
Make love's quick pants in Desdemona's arms,
Give renewed fire to our extinct spirits,

---

16 **like molestation** comparable disturbance   17 **enchafèd** angry
18 **If that** if   19 **embayed** sheltered by a bay   20 **bear it out** survive,
weather the storm   23 **designment** design, enterprise.   **halts** is lame
24 **wreck** shipwreck.   **sufferance** damage, disaster   28 **Veronesa** i.e.,
fitted out in Verona for Venetian service, or possibly *Verennessa* (the
Folio spelling), i.e., *verrinessa*, a cutter (from *verrinare*, "to cut
through")   34 **sadly** gravely   38 **full** perfect   41 **the main . . . blue**
the sea and the sky   42 **An indistinct regard** indistinguishable in our
view   43 **is expectancy** gives expectation   44 **arrivance** arrival
46 **approve** admire, honor   51 **approved allowance** tested reputation
52 **surfeited to death** i.e., overextended, worn thin through repeated
application or delayed fulfillment

53 **in bold cure** in strong hopes of fulfillment   55 **brow o' the sea**
cliff-edge   57 **My . . . for** I hope it is   58 **discharge . . . courtesy**
fire a salute in token of respect and courtesy   64 **paragons** surpasses.
wild fame extravagant report   65 **quirks** witty conceits.   **blazoning**
setting forth as though in heraldic language   66–67 **in . . . enginer**
in her real, God-given, beauty, (she) defeats any attempt to praise her.
enginer engineer, i.e., poet, one who devises.   s.d. **Second Gentleman** (So identified in the Quarto text here and in lines 58, 61, 68,
and 96; the Folio calls him a gentleman.)   67 **put in** i.e., to harbor
71 **guttered** jagged, trenched   72 **ensteeped** lying under water
73 **As** as if.   **omit** forbear to exercise   74 **mortal** deadly   78 **footing**
landing   79 **sennight's** week's   81 **tall** splendid, gallant

And bring all Cyprus comfort!

Enter Desdemona, Iago, Roderigo, and Emilia.

O, behold,
The riches of the ship is come on shore!
You men of Cyprus, let her have your knees.
            [*The gentlemen make curtsy to Desdemona.*]
Hail to thee, lady! And the grace of heaven
Before, behind thee, and on every hand
Enwheel thee round!

DESDEMONA   I thank you, valiant Cassio.
What tidings can you tell me of my lord?

CASSIO
He is not yet arrived, nor know I aught
But that he's well and will be shortly here.

DESDEMONA
O, but I fear—How lost you company?

CASSIO
The great contention of the sea and skies
Parted our fellowship.
                    (*Within*) "A sail, a sail!" [*A shot.*]
                But hark. A sail!

SECOND GENTLEMAN
They give their greeting to the citadel.
This likewise is a friend.

CASSIO   See for the news.
                    [*Exit Second Gentleman.*]
Good Ancient, you are welcome. [*Kissing Emilia.*]
    Welcome, mistress.
Let it not gall your patience, good Iago,
That I extend my manners; 'tis my breeding   100
That gives me this bold show of courtesy.

IAGO
Sir, would she give you so much of her lips
As of her tongue she oft bestows on me,
You would have enough.

DESDEMONA   Alas, she has no speech!   105

IAGO   In faith, too much.
I find it still, when I have list to sleep.   107
Marry, before your ladyship, I grant,
She puts her tongue a little in her heart
And chides with thinking.

EMILIA   You have little cause to say so.   110

IAGO
Come on, come on. You are pictures out of doors,   111
Bells in your parlors, wildcats in your kitchens,   112
Saints in your injuries, devils being offended,   113
Players in your huswifery, and huswives in your
    beds.   114

DESDEMONA   O, fie upon thee, slanderer!

IAGO
Nay, it is true, or else I am a Turk.   116
You rise to play, and go to bed to work.

EMILIA
You shall not write my praise.

IAGO   No, let me not.

DESDEMONA
What wouldst write of me, if thou shouldst praise
    me?

IAGO
O gentle lady, do not put me to 't,
For I am nothing if not critical.   121

DESDEMONA
Come on, essay.—There's one gone to the harbor?   122

IAGO   Ay, madam.

DESDEMONA
I am not merry, but I do beguile
The thing I am by seeming otherwise.   125
Come, how wouldst thou praise me?

IAGO
I am about it, but indeed my invention
Comes from my pate as birdlime does from frieze—   128
It plucks out brains and all. But my Muse labors,   129
And thus she is delivered:
If she be fair and wise, fairness and wit,
The one's for use, the other useth it.   132

DESDEMONA
Well praised! How if she be black and witty?   133

IAGO
If she be black, and thereto have a wit,
She'll find a white that shall her blackness fit.   135

DESDEMONA
Worse and worse.

EMILIA   How if fair and foolish?

IAGO
She never yet was foolish that was fair,
For even her folly helped her to an heir.   138

DESDEMONA   These are old fond paradoxes to make fools 139
    laugh i' th' alehouse. What miserable praise hast thou
    for her that's foul and foolish?   141

IAGO
There's none so foul and foolish thereunto,   142
But does foul pranks which fair and wise ones do.   143

DESDEMONA O heavy ignorance! Thou praisest the worst
    best. But what praise couldst thou bestow on a deserv-
    ing woman indeed, one that, in the authority of her mer-
    it, did justly put on the vouch of very malice itself? 147

---

100 extend give scope to. **breeding** training in the niceties of etiquette **105 she has no speech** i.e., she's not a chatterbox, as you allege **107 still** always. **list** desire **110 with thinking** i.e., in her
thoughts only **111 pictures out of doors** i.e., silent and well-behaved in public **112 Bells** i.e., jangling, noisy, and brazen. **in your
kitchens** i.e., in domestic affairs. (Ladies would not do the cooking.)
113 Saints martyrs **114 Players** idlers, triflers, or deceivers. **huswifery** housekeeping. **huswives** hussies (i.e., women are "busy" in
bed, or unduly thrifty in dispensing sexual favors)

116 a Turk an infidel, not to be believed **121 critical** censorious
122 essay try **125 The thing I am** i.e., my anxious self **128 birdlime** sticky substance used to catch small birds. **frieze** coarse
woolen cloth **129 labors** (1) exerts herself (2) prepares to deliver a
child (with a following pun on *delivered* in line 130) **132 The one's
. . . it** i.e., her cleverness will make use of her beauty **133 black**
dark-complexioned, brunette **135 a white** a fair person (with wordplay on "wight," a person). **fit** (with sexual suggestion of mating)
138 folly (with added meaning of "lechery, wantonness"). **to an
heir** i.e., to bear a child **139 fond** foolish **141 foul** ugly
142 thereunto in addition **143 foul** sluttish **147 put . . . vouch**
compel the approval

IAGO
  She that was ever fair, and never proud,
  Had tongue at will, and yet was never loud,
  Never lacked gold and yet went never gay,   150
  Fled from her wish, and yet said, "Now I may," 151
  She that being angered, her revenge being nigh,
  Bade her wrong stay and her displeasure fly,   153
  She that in wisdom never was so frail
  To change the cod's head for the salmon's tail, 155
  She that could think and ne'er disclose her mind,
  See suitors following and not look behind,
  She was a wight, if ever such wight were—
DESDEMONA To do what?
IAGO
  To suckle fools and chronicle small beer.   160
DESDEMONA O most lame and impotent conclusion! Do
not learn of him, Emilia, though he be thy husband.
How say you, Cassio? Is he not a most profane and 163
liberal counselor?   164
CASSIO He speaks home, madam. You may relish him 165
more in the soldier than in the scholar.   166

        [Cassio and Desdemona stand together,
                conversing intimately.]

IAGO *[aside]* He takes her by the palm. Ay, well said, 167
whisper. With as little a web as this will I ensnare as
great a fly as Cassio. Ay, smile upon her, do; I will
gyve thee in thine own courtship. You say true; 'tis so, 170
indeed. If such tricks as these strip you out of your
lieutenantry, it had been better you had not kissed
your three fingers so oft, which now again you are
most apt to play the sir in. Very good; well kissed! An 174
excellent courtesy! 'Tis so, indeed. Yet again your fingers to your lips? Would they were clyster pipes for 176
your sake! *[Trumpet within.]* The Moor! I know his
trumpet.
CASSIO 'Tis truly so.
DESDEMONA Let's meet him and receive him.
CASSIO Lo, where he comes!

        Enter Othello and attendants.

OTHELLO
  O my fair warrior!
DESDEMONA   My dear Othello!
OTHELLO
  It gives me wonder great as my content
  To see you here before me. O my soul's joy,
  If after every tempest come such calms,
  May the winds blow till they have wakened death,

  And let the laboring bark climb hills of seas
  Olympus-high, and duck again as low
  As hell's from heaven! If it were now to die,
  'Twere now to be most happy, for I fear
  My soul hath her content so absolute
  That not another comfort like to this
  Succeeds in unknown fate.
DESDEMONA   The heavens forbid 192
  But that our loves and comforts should increase
  Even as our days do grow!
OTHELLO Amen to that, sweet powers!
  I cannot speak enough of this content.
  It stops me here; it is too much of joy.
  And this, and this, the greatest discords be 198
                   [They kiss]
  That e'er our hearts shall make!
IAGO *[aside]* O, you are well tuned now!
  But I'll set down the pegs that make this music, 201
  As honest as I am.   202
OTHELLO Come, let us to the castle.
  News, friends! Our wars are done, the Turks are
    drowned.
  How does my old acquaintance of this isle?—
  Honey, you shall be well desired in Cyprus; 206
  I have found great love amongst them. O my sweet,
  I prattle out of fashion, and I dote 208
  In mine own comforts.—I prithee, good Iago,
  Go to the bay and disembark my coffers. 210
  Bring thou the master to the citadel; 211
  He is a good one, and his worthiness
  Does challenge much respect.—Come,
    Desdemona.—   213
  Once more, well met at Cyprus!

        Exeunt Othello and Desdemona [and all
                but Iago and Roderigo].

IAGO *[to an attendant]* Do thou meet me presently at
the harbor. *[To Roderigo.]* Come hither. If thou be'st
valiant—as, they say, base men being in love have 217
then a nobility in their natures more than is native to
them—list me. The Lieutenant tonight watches on 219
the court of guard. First, I must tell thee this: 220
Desdemona is directly in love with him.
RODERIGO With him? Why, 'tis not possible.
IAGO Lay thy finger thus, and let thy soul be instructed. 223
Mark me with what violence she first loved the Moor,
but for bragging and telling her fantastical lies. To love 225
him still for prating? Let not thy discreet heart think it.
Her eye must be fed; and what delight shall she have
to look on the devil? When the blood is made dull with
the act of sport, there should be, again to inflame it 229
and to give satiety a fresh appetite, loveliness in favor, 230

150 gay extravagantly clothed **151 Fled . . . may** avoided temptation where the choice was hers **153 Bade . . . stay** i.e., resolved to
put up with her injury patiently **155 To . . . tail** i.e., to exchange a
lackluster husband for a sexy lover (?) (*Cod's head* is slang for "penis," and *tail,* for "pudendum.") **160 suckle fools** breastfeed babies.
chronicle small beer i.e., keep petty household accounts, keep track
of trivial matters **163 profane** irreverent, ribald **164 liberal** licentious, free-spoken **165 home** right to the target. (A term from fencing.) **relish** appreciate **166 in** in the character of **167 well said**
well done **170 gyve** fetter, shackle. **courtship** courtesy, show of
courtly manners. **You say true** i.e., that's right, go ahead **174 the
sir** i.e., the fine gentleman **176 clyster pipes** tubes used for enemas
and douches

192 Succeeds . . . fate i.e., can follow in the unknown future
198 s.d. They kiss (The direction is from the Quarto.) **201 set down**
loosen (and hence untune the instrument) **202 As . . . I am** for all
my supposed honesty **206 desired** welcomed **208 out of fashion**
irrelevantly, incoherently (?) **210 coffers** chests, baggage **211 master** ship's captain **213 challenge** lay claim to, deserve **217 base
men** even lowly born men **219 list** listen to **220 court of guard**
guardhouse. (Cassio is in charge of the watch.) **223 thus** i.e., on
your lips **225 but** only **229 the act of sport** sex **230 favor**
appearance

sympathy in years, manners, and beauties—all which ²³¹
the Moor is defective in. Now, for want of these
required conveniences, her delicate tenderness will ²³³
find itself abused, begin to heave the gorge, disrelish ²³⁴
and abhor the Moor. Very nature will instruct her in it ²³⁵
and compel her to some second choice. Now, sir, this
granted—as it is a most pregnant and unforced ²³⁷
position—who stands so eminent in the degree of this ²³⁸
fortune as Cassio does? A knave very voluble, no ²³⁹
further conscionable than in putting on the mere form ²⁴⁰
of civil and humane seeming for the better compass- ²⁴¹
ing of his salt and most hidden loose affection. Why, ²⁴²
none, why, none. A slipper and subtle knave, a finder ²⁴³
out of occasions, that has an eye can stamp and ²⁴⁴
counterfeit advantages, though true advantage never ²⁴⁵
present itself; a devilish knave. Besides, the knave is
handsome, young, and hath all those requisites in him
that folly and green minds look after. A pestilent ²⁴⁸
complete knave, and the woman hath found him ²⁴⁹
already.

RODERIGO   I cannot believe that in her. She's full of
most blessed condition. ²⁵²

IAGO   Blessed fig's end! The wine she drinks is made of ²⁵³
grapes. If she had been blessed, she would never have
loved the Moor. Blessed pudding! Didst thou not see ²⁵⁵
her paddle with the palm of his hand? Didst not mark
that?

RODERIGO   Yes, that I did; but that was but courtesy.

IAGO   Lechery, by this hand. An index and obscure pro- ²⁵⁹
logue to the history of lust and foul thoughts. They
met so near with their lips that their breaths embraced
together. Villainous thoughts, Roderigo! When these
mutualities so marshal the way, hard at hand comes ²⁶³
the master and main exercise, th' incorporate conclu- ²⁶⁴
sion. Pish! But, sir, be you ruled by me. I have brought
you from Venice. Watch you tonight; for the com- ²⁶⁶
mand, I'll lay 't upon you. Cassio knows you not. I'll ²⁶⁷
not be far from you. Do you find some occasion to
anger Cassio, either by speaking too loud, or tainting ²⁶⁹
his discipline, or from what other course you please,
which the time shall more favorably minister. ²⁷¹

RODERIGO   Well.

IAGO   Sir, he's rash and very sudden in choler, and hap- ²⁷³
ly may strike at you. Provoke him that he may, for ²⁷⁴

even out of that will I cause these of Cyprus to mutiny, ²⁷⁵
whose qualification shall come into no true taste again ²⁷⁶
but by the displanting of Cassio. So shall you have a
shorter journey to your desires by the means I shall
then have to prefer them, and the impediment most ²⁷⁹
profitably removed, without the which there were no
expectation of our prosperity.

RODERIGO   I will do this, if you can bring it to any
opportunity.

IAGO   I warrant thee. Meet me by and by at the citadel. ²⁸⁴
I must fetch his necessaries ashore. Farewell.

RODERIGO   Adieu.   *Exit.*

IAGO
That Cassio loves her, I do well believe 't;
That she loves him, 'tis apt and of great credit.   ²⁸⁸
The Moor, howbeit that I endure him not,
Is of a constant, loving, noble nature,
And I dare think he'll prove to Desdemona
A most dear husband. Now, I do love her too,
Not out of absolute lust—though peradventure
I stand accountant for as great a sin—   ²⁹⁴
But partly led to diet my revenge   ²⁹⁵
For that I do suspect the lusty Moor
Hath leaped into my seat, the thought whereof
Doth, like a poisonous mineral, gnaw my innards;
And nothing can or shall content my soul
Till I am evened with him, wife for wife,
Or failing so, yet that I put the Moor
At least into a jealousy so strong
That judgment cannot cure. Which thing to do,
If this poor trash of Venice, whom I trace   ³⁰⁴
For his quick hunting, stand the putting on,   ³⁰⁵
I'll have our Michael Cassio on the hip,   ³⁰⁶
Abuse him to the Moor in the rank garb—   ³⁰⁷
For I fear Cassio with my nightcap too—   ³⁰⁸
Make the Moor thank me, love me, and reward me
For making him egregiously an ass
And practicing upon his peace and quiet   ³¹¹
Even to madness. 'Tis here, but yet confused.
Knavery's plain face is never seen till used.   *Exit.*

❖

2.2   *Enter Othello's Herald with a proclamation.*

HERALD   It is Othello's pleasure, our noble and valiant
general, that, upon certain tidings now arrived, importing the mere perdition of the Turkish fleet, every ³

231 **sympathy** correspondence, similarity   233 **required conveniences**
things conducive to sexual compatibility   234 **abused** cheated, revolted.   **heave the gorge** experience nausea   235 **Very nature** her
very instincts   237 **pregnant** evident, cogent   238 **in . . . of** as next
in line for   239 **voluble** facile, glib   240 **conscionable** conscientious, conscience-bound   241 **humane** polite, courteous   242 **salt** licentious.   **affection** passion   243 **slipper** slippery   244 **an eye can
stamp** an eye that can coin, create   245 **advantages** favorable opportunities   248 **folly** wantonness.   **green** immature   249 **found him**
sized him up, perceived his intent   252 **condition** disposition
253 **fig's end** (See 1.3.322 for the vulgar gesture of the fig.)
255 **pudding** sausage   259 **index** table of contents.   **obscure** (i.e.,
the *lust and foul thoughts*, line 260, are secret, hidden from view)
263 **mutualities** exchanges, intimacies.   **hard at hand** closely following   264 **incorporate** carnal   266 **Watch you** stand watch
266–267 **for the command . . . you** I'll arrange for you to be appointed, given orders   269 **tainting** disparaging   271 **minister** provide   273 **choler** wrath   273–274 **haply** perhaps

275 **mutiny** riot   276 **qualification** appeasement.   **true taste** i.e., acceptable state   279 **prefer** advance   284 **warrant** assure.   **by and by**
immediately   288 **apt** probable.   **credit** credibility   294 **accountant**
accountable   295 **diet** feed   304 **trace** i.e., train, or follow (?), or
perhaps *trash,* a hunting term, meaning to put weights on a hunting
dog in order to slow him down   305 **For** to make more eager.   **stand
. . . on** respond properly when I incite him to quarrel   306 **on the
hip** at my mercy, where I can throw him. (A wrestling term.)
307 **Abuse** slander.   **rank garb** coarse manner, gross fashion
308 **with my nightcap** i.e., as a rival in my bed, as one who gives me
cuckold's horns   311 **practicing upon** plotting against
2.2. Location: Cyprus. A street.
3 **mere perdition** complete destruction

man put himself into triumph: some to dance, some to 4
make bonfires, each man to what sport and revels his
addiction leads him. For, besides these beneficial 6
news, it is the celebration of his nuptial. So much was
his pleasure should be proclaimed. All offices are open, 8
and there is full liberty of feasting from this present
hour of five till the bell have told eleven. Heaven bless
the isle of Cyprus and our noble general Othello!

Exit.

❖

2.3   *Enter Othello, Desdemona, Cassio, and
attendants.*

OTHELLO
Good Michael, look you to the guard tonight.
Let's teach ourselves that honorable stop   2
Not to outsport discretion.   3
CASSIO
Iago hath direction what to do,
But notwithstanding, with my personal eye
Will I look to 't.
OTHELLO   Iago is most honest.
Michael, good night. Tomorrow with your earliest 7
Let me have speech with you. [*To Desdemona.*]
   Come, my dear love,
The purchase made, the fruits are to ensue;   9
That profit's yet to come 'tween me and you.—   10
Good night.
            Exit [*Othello, with Desdemona and attendants*].

         Enter Iago.

CASSIO   Welcome, Iago. We must to the watch.
IAGO   Not this hour, Lieutenant; 'tis not yet ten o' the 13
clock. Our general cast us thus early for the love of his 14
Desdemona; who let us not therefore blame. He hath 15
not yet made wanton the night with her, and she is
sport for Jove.
CASSIO   She's a most exquisite lady.
IAGO   And, I'll warrant her, full of game.
CASSIO   Indeed, she's a most fresh and delicate creature.
IAGO   What an eye she has! Methinks it sounds a parley 21
to provocation.
CASSIO   An inviting eye, and yet methinks right modest.
IAGO   And when she speaks, is it not an alarum to love? 24
CASSIO   She is indeed perfection.
IAGO   Well, happiness to their sheets! Come, Lieutenant,
I have a stoup of wine, and here without are a brace of 27

Cyprus gallants that would fain have a measure to the 28
health of black Othello.
CASSIO   Not tonight, good Iago. I have very poor and
unhappy brains for drinking. I could well wish courtesy would invent some other custom of entertainment.
IAGO   O, they are our friends. But one cup! I'll drink for 34
you.   35
CASSIO   I have drunk but one cup tonight, and that was
craftily qualified too, and behold what innovation it 37
makes here. I am unfortunate in the infirmity and 38
dare not task my weakness with any more.
IAGO   What, man? 'Tis a night of revels. The gallants
desire it.
CASSIO   Where are they?
IAGO   Here at the door. I pray you, call them in.
CASSIO   I'll do 't, but it dislikes me.   *Exit.* 44
IAGO
If I can fasten but one cup upon him,
With that which he hath drunk tonight already,
He'll be as full of quarrel and offense   47
As my young mistress' dog. Now, my sick fool
   Roderigo,
Whom love hath turned almost the wrong side out,
To Desdemona hath tonight caroused   50
Potations pottle-deep; and he's to watch.   51
Three lads of Cyprus—noble swelling spirits,   52
That hold their honors in a wary distance,   53
The very elements of this warlike isle—   54
Have I tonight flustered with flowing cups,
And they watch too. Now, 'mongst this flock of
   drunkards   56
Am I to put our Cassio in some action
That may offend the isle.—But here they come.

         *Enter Cassio, Montano, and gentlemen; [servants
         following with wine].*

If consequence do but approve my dream,   59
My boat sails freely both with wind and stream. 60
CASSIO   'Fore God, they have given me a rouse already. 61
MONTANO   Good faith, a little one; not past a pint, as I
am a soldier.
IAGO   Some wine, ho!

[*He sings.*] "And let me the cannikin clink, clink, 65
            And let me the cannikin clink.
               A soldier's a man,
               O, man's life's but a span;   68
            Why, then, let a soldier drink."

---

4 **triumph** public celebration   6 **addiction** inclination   8 **offices**
rooms where food and drink are kept
2.3. Location: Cyprus. The citadel.
2 **stop** restraint   3 **outsport** celebrate beyond the bounds of   7 **with
your earliest** at your earliest convenience   9–10 **The purchase . . .
you** i.e., though married, we haven't yet consummated our love
13 **Not this hour** not for an hour yet   14 **cast** dismissed   15 **who**
i.e., Othello   21 **sounds a parley** calls for a conference, issues an invitation   24 **alarum** signal calling men to arms (continuing the military metaphor of *parley*, line 21)   27 **stoup** measure of liquor, two
quarts.   **without** outside.   **brace** pair

28 **fain have a measure** gladly drink a toast   34–35 **for you** in your
place. (Iago will do the steady drinking to keep the gallants company
while Cassio has only one cup.)   37 **qualified** diluted.   **innovation**
disturbance, insurrection   38 **here** i.e., in my head   44 **it dislikes me**
i.e., I'm reluctant   47 **offense** readiness to take offense   50 **caroused**
drunk off   51 **pottle-deep** to the bottom of the tankard.   **watch** stand
watch   52 **swelling** proud   53 **hold . . . distance** i.e., are extremely
sensitive of their honor   54 **very elements** typical sort   56 **watch** are
members of the guard   59 **If . . . dream** if subsequent events will
only substantiate my scheme   60 **stream** current   61 **rouse** full draft
of liquor   65 **cannikin** small drinking vessel   68 **span** brief span of
time. (Compare Psalm 39:5 as rendered in the Book of Common
Prayer: "Thou hast made my days as it were a span long.")

Some wine, boys!

CASSIO   'Fore God, an excellent song.

IAGO   I learned it in England, where indeed they are
most potent in potting. Your Dane, your German, and 73
your swag-bellied Hollander—drink, ho!—are nothing to your English.

CASSIO   Is your Englishman so exquisite in his drinking?

IAGO   Why, he drinks you, with facility, your Dane 77
dead drunk; he sweats not to overthrow your Almain; 78
he gives your Hollander a vomit ere the next pottle can
be filled.

CASSIO   To the health of our general!

MONTANO   I am for it, Lieutenant, and I'll do you justice. 82

IAGO   O sweet England! [*He sings.*]

"King Stephen was and-a worthy peer,
   His breeches cost him but a crown;
He held them sixpence all too dear,
   With that he called the tailor lown.   87

He was a wight of high renown,
   And thou art but of low degree.
'Tis pride that pulls the country down;   90
   Then take thy auld cloak about thee."   91

Some wine, ho!

CASSIO   'Fore God, this is a more exquisite song than
the other.

IAGO   Will you hear 't again?

CASSIO   No, for I hold him to be unworthy of his place
that does those things. Well, God's above all; and
there be souls must be saved, and there be souls must
not be saved.

IAGO   It's true, good Lieutenant.

CASSIO   For mine own part—no offense to the General,
nor any man of quality—I hope to be saved.   102

IAGO   And so do I too, Lieutenant.

CASSIO   Ay, but, by your leave, not before me; the lieutenant is to be saved before the ancient. Let's have no
more of this; let's to our affairs.—God forgive us our
sins!—Gentlemen, let's look to our business. Do not
think, gentlemen, I am drunk. This is my ancient; this
is my right hand, and this is my left. I am not drunk
now. I can stand well enough, and speak well enough.

GENTLEMEN   Excellent well.

CASSIO   Why, very well then; you must not think then
that I am drunk.   *Exit.*

MONTANO

To th' platform, masters. Come, let's set the watch. 114
                       [*Exeunt Gentlemen.*]

IAGO

You see this fellow that is gone before.
He's a soldier fit to stand by Caesar
And give direction; and do but see his vice.

'Tis to his virtue a just equinox,   118
The one as long as th' other. 'Tis pity of him.
I fear the trust Othello puts him in,
On some odd time of his infirmity,
Will shake this island.

MONTANO   But is he often thus?

IAGO
'Tis evermore the prologue to his sleep.
He'll watch the horologe a double set,   124
If drink rock not his cradle.

MONTANO   It were well
The General were put in mind of it.
Perhaps he sees it not, or his good nature
Prizes the virtue that appears in Cassio
And looks not on his evils. Is not this true?

Enter Roderigo.

IAGO [*aside to him*]   How now, Roderigo?
I pray you, after the Lieutenant; go.   [*Exit Roderigo.*]

MONTANO
And 'tis great pity that the noble Moor
Should hazard such a place as his own second   133
With one of an engraffed infirmity.   134
It were an honest action to say so
To the Moor.

IAGO   Not I, for this fair island.
I do love Cassio well and would do much
To cure him of this evil.   [*Cry within:* "Help! Help!"]
                       But, hark! What noise?   138

Enter Cassio, pursuing Roderigo.

CASSIO   Zounds, you rogue! You rascal!

MONTANO   What's the matter, Lieutenant?

CASSIO   A knave teach me my duty? I'll beat the knave
into a twiggen bottle.   142

RODERIGO   Beat me?

CASSIO   Dost thou prate, rogue?   [*He strikes Roderigo.*]

MONTANO   Nay, good Lieutenant. [*Restraining him.*] I
pray you, sir, hold your hand.

CASSIO   Let me go, sir, or I'll knock you o'er the
mazard.   148

MONTANO   Come, come, you're drunk.

CASSIO   Drunk?   [*They fight.*]

IAGO [*aside to Roderigo*]
Away, I say. Go out and cry a mutiny.   151
                       [*Exit Roderigo.*]
Nay, good Lieutenant—God's will, gentlemen—
Help, ho!—Lieutenant—sir—Montano—sir—
Help, masters!—Here's a goodly watch indeed!   154
                       [*A bell rings.*]

---

73 potting drinking **77 drinks you** drinks. **your Dane** your typical
Dane **78 sweats not** i.e., need not exert himself. **Almain** German
82 I'll . . . justice i.e., I'll drink as much as you **87 lown** lout, rascal **90 pride** i.e., extravagance in dress **91 auld** old **102 quality**
rank **114 set the watch** mount the guard

118 just equinox exact counterpart. (*Equinox* is an equal length of
days and nights.) **124 watch . . . set** stay awake twice around the
clock or *horologe* **133–134 hazard . . . With** risk giving such an
important position as his second in command to **134 engraffed** engrafted, inveterate **138 s.d. pursuing** (The Quarto text reads, "driving
in.") **142 twiggen** wicker-covered. (Cassio vows to assail Roderigo
until his skin resembles wickerwork or until he has driven Roderigo
through the holes in a wickerwork.) **148 mazard** i.e., head. (Literally, a drinking vessel.) **151 mutiny** riot **154 masters** sirs. **s.d. A
bell rings** (This direction is from the Quarto, as are *Exit Roderigo* at
line 131, *They fight* at line 150, and *with weapons* at line 157.)

Who's that which rings the bell?—Diablo, ho!   155
The town will rise. God's will, Lieutenant, hold!   156
You'll be ashamed forever.

Enter Othello and attendants [with weapons].

OTHELLO
What is the matter here?
MONTANO   Zounds, I bleed still.
I am hurt to th' death. He dies! *[He thrusts at Cassio.]*
OTHELLO   Hold, for your lives!
IAGO
Hold, ho! Lieutenant—sir—Montano—gentlemen—
Have you forgot all sense of place and duty?
Hold! The General speaks to you. Hold, for shame!
OTHELLO
Why, how now, ho! From whence ariseth this?
Are we turned Turks, and to ourselves do that   164
Which heaven hath forbid the Ottomites?   165
For Christian shame, put by this barbarous brawl!
He that stirs next to carve for his own rage   167
Holds his soul light; he dies upon his motion.   168
Silence that dreadful bell. It frights the isle
From her propriety. What is the matter, masters?   170
Honest Iago, that looks dead with grieving,
Speak. Who began this? On thy love, I charge thee.
IAGO
I do not know. Friends all but now, even now,
In quarter and in terms like bride and groom   174
Devesting them for bed; and then, but now—   175
As if some planet had unwitted men—
Swords out, and tilting one at others' breasts
In opposition bloody. I cannot speak   178
Any beginning to this peevish odds;   179
And would in action glorious I had lost
Those legs that brought me to a part of it!
OTHELLO
How comes it, Michael, you are thus forgot?   182
CASSIO
I pray you, pardon me. I cannot speak.
OTHELLO
Worthy Montano, you were wont be civil;   184
The gravity and stillness of your youth   185
The world hath noted, and your name is great
In mouths of wisest censure. What's the matter   187
That you unlace your reputation thus   188
And spend your rich opinion for the name   189
Of a night-brawler? Give me answer to it.
MONTANO
Worthy Othello, I am hurt to danger.

Your officer, Iago, can inform you—
While I spare speech, which something now offends
    me—   193
Of all that I do know; nor know I aught
By me that's said or done amiss this night,
Unless self-charity be sometimes a vice,
And to defend ourselves it be a sin
When violence assails us.
OTHELLO   Now, by heaven,
My blood begins my safer guides to rule,   199
And passion, having my best judgment collied,   200
Essays to lead the way. Zounds, if I stir,   201
Or do but lift this arm, the best of you
Shall sink in my rebuke. Give me to know
How this foul rout began, who set it on;   204
And he that is approved in this offense,   205
Though he had twinned with me, both at a birth,
Shall lose me. What? In a town of war   207
Yet wild, the people's hearts brim full of fear,
To manage private and domestic quarrel?   209
In night, and on the court and guard of safety?   210
'Tis monstrous. Iago, who began 't?
MONTANO *[to Iago]*
If partially affined, or leagued in office,   212
Thou dost deliver more or less than truth,
Thou art no soldier.
IAGO   Touch me not so near.
I had rather have this tongue cut from my mouth
Than it should do offense to Michael Cassio;
Yet, I persuade myself, to speak the truth
Shall nothing wrong him. Thus it is, General.
Montano and myself being in speech,
There comes a fellow crying out for help,
And Cassio following him with determined sword
To execute upon him. Sir, this gentleman   222
                            [indicating Montano]
Steps in to Cassio and entreats his pause.   223
Myself the crying fellow did pursue,
Lest by his clamor—as it so fell out—
The town might fall in fright. He, swift of foot,
Outran my purpose, and I returned, the rather   227
For that I heard the clink and fall of swords
And Cassio high in oath, which till tonight
I ne'er might say before. When I came back—
For this was brief—I found them close together
At blow and thrust, even as again they were
When you yourself did part them.
More of this matter cannot I report.
But men are men; the best sometimes forget.   235
Though Cassio did some little wrong to him,
As men in rage strike those that wish them best, 237

155 Diablo the devil   156 rise grow riotous   164–165 to ourselves . . . Ottomites inflict on ourselves the harm that heaven has prevented the Turks from doing (by destroying their fleet)   167 carve for i.e., indulge, satisfy with his sword   168 Holds . . . light i.e., places little value on his life.   upon his motion if he moves   170 propriety proper state or condition   174 In quarter in friendly conduct, within bounds.   in terms on good terms   175 Devesting them undressing themselves   178 speak explain   179 peevish odds childish quarrel   182 are thus forgot have forgotten yourself thus   184 wont be accustomed to be   185 stillness sobriety   187 censure judgment   188 unlace undo, lay open (as one might loose the strings of a purse containing reputation)   189 opinion reputation

193 something somewhat.   offends pains   199 blood passion (of anger).   guides i.e., reason   200 collied darkened   201 Essays undertakes   204 rout riot   205 approved in found guilty of   207 town of town garrisoned for   209 manage undertake   210 on . . . safety at the main guardhouse or headquarters and on watch   212 partially affined made partial by some personal relationship.   leagued in office in league as fellow officers   222 execute give effect to (his anger)   223 his pause him to stop   227 rather sooner   235 forget forget themselves   237 those . . . best i.e., even those who are well disposed

Yet surely Cassio, I believe, received
From him that fled some strange indignity,
Which patience could not pass.

OTHELLO   I know, Iago,   240
Thy honesty and love doth mince this matter,
Making it light to Cassio. Cassio, I love thee,
But nevermore be officer of mine.

Enter Desdemona, attended.

Look if my gentle love be not raised up.
I'll make thee an example.

DESDEMONA
What is the matter, dear?

OTHELLO   All's well now, sweeting;
Come away to bed. [*To Montano.*] Sir, for your hurts,
Myself will be your surgeon.—Lead him off.   248
                              [*Montano is led off.*]
Iago, look with care about the town
And silence those whom this vile brawl distracted.
Come, Desdemona. 'Tis the soldiers' life
To have their balmy slumbers waked with strife.
                    Exit [with all but Iago and Cassio].

IAGO   What, are you hurt, Lieutenant?

CASSIO   Ay, past all surgery.

IAGO   Marry, God forbid!

CASSIO   Reputation, reputation, reputation! O, I have
lost my reputation! I have lost the immortal part of
myself, and what remains is bestial. My reputation,
Iago, my reputation!

IAGO   As I am an honest man, I thought you had
received some bodily wound; there is more sense in
that than in reputation. Reputation is an idle and most
false imposition, oft got without merit and lost with-   263
out deserving. You have lost no reputation at all,
unless you repute yourself such a loser. What, man,
there are more ways to recover the General again. You   266
are but now cast in his mood—a punishment more in   267
policy than in malice, even so as one would beat his   268
offenseless dog to affright an imperious lion. Sue to   269
him again and he's yours.

CASSIO   I will rather sue to be despised than to deceive
so good a commander with so slight, so drunken, and   272
so indiscreet an officer. Drunk? And speak parrot?   273
And squabble? Swagger? Swear? And discourse fustian with one's own shadow? O thou invisible spirit
of wine, if thou hast no name to be known by, let us
call thee devil!

IAGO   What was he that you followed with your sword?
What had he done to you?

CASSIO   I know not.

IAGO   Is 't possible?

CASSIO   I remember a mass of things, but nothing

distinctly; a quarrel, but nothing wherefore. O God,   283
that men should put an enemy in their mouths to steal
away their brains! That we should, with joy, pleasance, revel, and applause transform ourselves into   286
beasts!

IAGO   Why, but you are now well enough. How came
you thus recovered?

CASSIO   It hath pleased the devil drunkenness to give
place to the devil wrath. One unperfectness shows me
another, to make me frankly despise myself.

IAGO   Come, you are too severe a moraler. As the time,   293
the place, and the condition of this country stands, I
could heartily wish this had not befallen; but since it is
as it is, mend it for your own good.

CASSIO   I will ask him for my place again; he shall tell
me I am a drunkard. Had I as many mouths as Hydra,   298
such an answer would stop them all. To be now a
sensible man, by and by a fool, and presently a beast!
O, strange! Every inordinate cup is unblessed, and the
ingredient is a devil.

IAGO   Come, come, good wine is a good familiar
creature, if it be well used. Exclaim no more against it.
And, good Lieutenant, I think you think I love you.

CASSIO   I have well approved it, sir. I drunk!   306

IAGO   You or any man living may be drunk at a time,   307
man. I'll tell you what you shall do. Our general's wife
is now the general—I may say so in this respect, for   309
that he hath devoted and given up himself to the   310
contemplation, mark, and denotement of her parts   311
and graces. Confess yourself freely to her; importune
her help to put you in your place again. She is of so
free, so kind, so apt, so blessed a disposition, she   314
holds it a vice in her goodness not to do more than she
is requested. This broken joint between you and her
husband entreat her to splinter; and, my fortunes   317
against any lay worth naming, this crack of your love   318
shall grow stronger than it was before.

CASSIO   You advise me well.

IAGO   I protest, in the sincerity of love and honest   321
kindness.

CASSIO   I think it freely; and betimes in the morning I   323
will beseech the virtuous Desdemona to undertake for
me. I am desperate of my fortunes if they check me   325
here.

IAGO   You are in the right. Good night, Lieutenant. I
must to the watch.

CASSIO   Good night, honest Iago.   *Exit Cassio.*

IAGO
And what's he then that says I play the villain,
When this advice is free I give, and honest,   331

240 **pass** pass over, overlook   248 **be your surgeon** i.e., make sure you receive medical attention   263 **false imposition** thing artificially imposed and of no real value   266 **recover** regain favor with   267 **cast in his mood** dismissed in a moment of anger   267–268 **in policy** done for expediency's sake and as a public gesture   268–269 **would . . . lion** i.e., would make an example of a minor offender in order to deter more important and dangerous offenders   269 **Sue** petition   272 **slight** worthless   273 **speak parrot** talk nonsense, rant. (*Discourse fustian*, lines 274–275, has much the same meaning.)

283 **wherefore** why   286 **applause** desire for applause   293 **moraler** moralizer   298 **Hydra** the Lernaean Hydra, a monster with many heads and the ability to grow two heads when one was cut off, slain by Hercules as the second of his twelve labors   306 **approved** proved   307 **at a time** at one time or another   309–310 **in . . . that** in view of this fact, that   311 **mark, and denotement** (Both words mean "observation.")   **parts** qualities   314 **free** generous   317 **splinter** bind with splints   318 **lay** stake, wager   321 **protest** insist, declare   323 **freely** unreservedly   325 **check** repulse   331 **free** (1) free from guile (2) freely given

Probal to thinking, and indeed the course   332
To win the Moor again? For 'tis most easy
Th' inclining Desdemona to subdue   334
In any honest suit; she's framed as fruitful   335
As the free elements. And then for her   336
To win the Moor—were 't to renounce his baptism,
All seals and symbols of redeemèd sin—
His soul is so enfettered to her love
That she may make, unmake, do what she list,
Even as her appetite shall play the god   341
With his weak function. How am I then a villain,   342
To counsel Cassio to this parallel course   343
Directly to his good? Divinity of hell!   344
When devils will the blackest sins put on,   345
They do suggest at first with heavenly shows,   346
As I do now. For whiles this honest fool
Plies Desdemona to repair his fortune,
And she for him pleads strongly to the Moor,
I'll pour this pestilence into his ear,
That she repeals him for her body's lust;   351
And by how much she strives to do him good,
She shall undo her credit with the Moor.
So will I turn her virtue into pitch,   354
And out of her own goodness make the net
That shall enmesh them all.

                    Enter Roderigo.

                              How now, Roderigo?
RODERIGO   I do follow here in the chase, not like a
hound that hunts, but one that fills up the cry. My   358
money is almost spent; I have been tonight exceed-
ingly well cudgeled; and I think the issue will be I shall
have so much experience for my pains, and so,   361
with no money at all and a little more wit, return again
to Venice.
IAGO
How poor are they that have not patience!
What wound did ever heal but by degrees?
Thou know'st we work by wit, and not by
    witchcraft,
And wit depends on dilatory time.
Does 't not go well? Cassio hath beaten thee,
And thou, by that small hurt, hast cashiered Cassio. 369
Though other things grow fair against the sun,   370
Yet fruits that blossom first will first be ripe.   371
Content thyself awhile. By the Mass, 'tis morning!
Pleasure and action make the hours seem short.

Retire thee; go where thou art billeted.
Away, I say! Thou shalt know more hereafter.
Nay, get thee gone.   *Exit Roderigo.*
                    Two things are to be done.
My wife must move for Cassio to her mistress;   377
I'll set her on;
Myself the while to draw the Moor apart
And bring him jump when he may Cassio find   380
Soliciting his wife. Ay, that's the way.
Dull not device by coldness and delay.   *Exit.* 382

                         ❖

3.1   *Enter Cassio [and] Musicians.*

CASSIO
Masters, play here—I will content your pains—   1
Something that's brief, and bid "Good morrow,
    General."   [*They play.*]
                [*Enter*] *Clown.*

CLOWN   Why, masters, have your instruments been in
Naples, that they speak i' the nose thus?   4
A MUSICIAN   How, sir, how?
CLOWN   Are these, I pray you, wind instruments?
A MUSICIAN   Ay, marry, are they, sir.
CLOWN   O, thereby hangs a tail.
A MUSICIAN   Whereby hangs a tale, sir?
CLOWN   Marry, sir, by many a wind instrument that I   10
know. But, masters, here's money for you. [*He gives
money.*] And the General so likes your music that he
desires you, for love's sake, to make no more noise   13
with it.
A MUSICIAN   Well, sir, we will not.
CLOWN   If you have any music that may not be heard,   16
to 't again; but, as they say, to hear music the General
does not greatly care.
A MUSICIAN   We have none such, sir.
CLOWN   Then put up your pipes in your bag, for I'll   20
away. Go, vanish into air, away!   *Exeunt Musicians.* 21
CASSIO   Dost thou hear, mine honest friend?
CLOWN   No, I hear not your honest friend; I hear you.
CASSIO   Prithee, keep up thy quillets. There's a poor   24
piece of gold for thee. [*He gives money.*] If the gentlewoman that attends the General's wife be stirring, tell
her there's one Cassio entreats her a little favor of   27
speech. Wilt thou do this?   28

---

332 Probal probable, reasonable   **334 inclining** favorably disposed.
subdue persuade   **335 framed as fruitful** created as generous
336 free elements i.e., earth, air, fire, and water, unrestrained and
spontaneous   **341 her appetite** her desire, or, perhaps, his desire for
her   **342 function** exercise of faculties (weakened by his fondness for
her)   **343 parallel** corresponding to these facts and to his best interests   **344 Divinity of hell** inverted theology of hell (which seduces the
soul to its damnation)   **345 put on** further, instigate   **346 suggest**
tempt   **351 repeals him** attempts to get him restored   **354 pitch** i.e.,
(1) foul blackness (2) a snaring substance   **358 fills up the cry** merely
takes part as one of the pack   **361 so much** just so much and no
more   **369 cashiered** dismissed from service   **370–371 Though . . .
ripe** i.e., plans that are well prepared and set expeditiously in motion
will soonest ripen into success

377 move plead   **380 jump** precisely   **382 device** plot.   **coldness**
lack of zeal
3.1. Location: Before the chamber of Othello and Desdemona.
1 content your pains reward your efforts   **4 speak i' the nose** (1)
sound nasal (2) sound like one whose nose has been attacked by
syphilis. (Naples was popularly supposed to have a high incidence of
venereal disease.)   **10 wind instrument** (With a joke on flatulence.
The *tail*, line 8, that hangs nearby the *wind instrument* suggests the
penis.)   **13 for love's sake** (1) out of friendship and affection (2) for
the sake of lovemaking in Othello's marriage   **16 may not** cannot
20–21 I'll away (Possibly a misprint, or a snatch of song?)   **24 keep
up** do not bring out, do not use.   **quillets** quibbles, puns   **27–28 a
little . . . speech** the favor of a brief talk

CLOWN   She is stirring, sir. If she will stir hither, I shall   29
seem to notify unto her.   30

CASSIO
Do, good my friend.   *Exit Clown.*

Enter Iago.

In happy time, Iago.   31

IAGO   You have not been abed, then?

CASSIO   Why, no. The day had broke
Before we parted. I have made bold, Iago,
To send in to your wife. My suit to her
Is that she will to virtuous Desdemona
Procure me some access.

IAGO   I'll send her to you presently;
And I'll devise a means to draw the Moor
Out of the way, that your converse and business
May be more free.

CASSIO
I humbly thank you for 't.   *Exit [Iago].*
I never knew
A Florentine more kind and honest.   43

Enter Emilia.

EMILIA
Good morrow, good Lieutenant. I am sorry
For your displeasure; but all will sure be well.   45
The General and his wife are talking of it,
And she speaks for you stoutly. The Moor replies   47
That he you hurt is of great fame in Cyprus   48
And great affinity, and that in wholesome wisdom   49
He might not but refuse you; but he protests he
loves you   50
And needs no other suitor but his likings
To take the safest occasion by the front   52
To bring you in again.

CASSIO   Yet I beseech you,
If you think fit, or that it may be done,
Give me advantage of some brief discourse
With Desdemon alone.

EMILIA   Pray you, come in.
I will bestow you where you shall have time
To speak your bosom freely.   58

CASSIO   I am much bound to you.   *[Exeunt.]*

❧

3.2   *Enter Othello, Iago, and Gentlemen.*

OTHELLO *[giving letters]*
These letters give, Iago, to the pilot,
And by him do my duties to the Senate.   2
That done, I will be walking on the works;   3

Repair there to me.
IAGO   Well, my good lord, I'll do 't.   4
OTHELLO
This fortification, gentlemen, shall we see 't?
GENTLEMEN   We'll wait upon your lordship.   *Exeunt.*   6

❧

3.3   *Enter Desdemona, Cassio, and Emilia.*

DESDEMONA
Be thou assured, good Cassio, I will do
All my abilities in thy behalf.
EMILIA
Good madam, do. I warrant it grieves my husband
As if the cause were his.
DESDEMONA
O, that's an honest fellow. Do not doubt, Cassio,
But I will have my lord and you again
As friendly as you were.
CASSIO   Bounteous madam,
Whatever shall become of Michael Cassio,
He's never anything but your true servant.
DESDEMONA
I know 't. I thank you. You do love my lord;
You have known him long, and be you well assured
He shall in strangeness stand no farther off   12
Than in a politic distance.
CASSIO   Ay, but, lady,   13
That policy may either last so long,
Or feed upon such nice and waterish diet,   15
Or breed itself so out of circumstance,   16
That, I being absent and my place supplied,   17
My general will forget my love and service.
DESDEMONA
Do not doubt that. Before Emilia here   19
I give thee warrant of thy place. Assure thee,   20
If I do vow a friendship I'll perform it
To the last article. My lord shall never rest.
I'll watch him tame and talk him out of patience;   23
His bed shall seem a school, his board a shrift;   24
I'll intermingle everything he does
With Cassio's suit. Therefore be merry, Cassio,
For thy solicitor shall rather die   27
Than give thy cause away.   28

Enter Othello and Iago [at a distance].

EMILIA   Madam, here comes my lord.
CASSIO   Madam, I'll take my leave.
DESDEMONA   Why, stay, and hear me speak.

---

29 stir bestir herself (with a play on *stirring*, "rousing herself from rest") **30 seem** deem it good, think fit **31 In happy time** i.e., well met **43 Florentine** i.e., even a fellow Florentine. (Iago is a Venetian; Cassio is a Florentine.) **45 displeasure** fall from favor **47 stoutly** spiritedly **48 fame** reputation, importance **49 affinity** kindred, family connection **50 protests** insists **52 occasion . . . front** opportunity by the forelock **58 bosom** inmost thoughts
3.2. Location: The citadel.
2 do my duties convey my respects **3 works** breastworks, fortifications

4 Repair return, come **6 wait upon** attend
3.3. Location: The garden of the citadel.
12 strangeness aloofness **13 politic** required by wise policy **15 Or . . . diet** or sustain itself at length upon such trivial and meager technicalities **16 breed . . . circumstance** continually renew itself so out of chance events, or yield so few chances for my being pardoned **17 supplied** filled by another person **19 doubt** fear **20 warrant** guarantee **23 watch him tame** tame him by keeping him from sleeping. (A term from falconry.) **out of patience** past his endurance **24 board** dining table. **shrift** confessional **27 solicitor** advocate **28 away** up

CASSIO
    Madam, not now. I am very ill at ease,
    Unfit for mine own purposes.
DESDEMONA   Well, do your discretion.   *Exit Cassio.* 34
IAGO   Ha? I like not that.
OTHELLO   What dost thou say?
IAGO
    Nothing, my lord; or if—I know not what.
OTHELLO
    Was not that Cassio parted from my wife?
IAGO
    Cassio, my lord? No, sure, I cannot think it,
    That he would steal away so guiltylike,
    Seeing you coming.
OTHELLO   I do believe 'twas he.
DESDEMONA   How now, my lord?
    I have been talking with a suitor here,
    A man that languishes in your displeasure.
OTHELLO   Who is 't you mean?
DESDEMONA
    Why, your lieutenant, Cassio. Good my lord,
    If I have any grace or power to move you,
    His present reconciliation take;   49
    For if he be not one that truly loves you,
    That errs in ignorance and not in cunning,   51
    I have no judgment in an honest face.
    I prithee, call him back.
OTHELLO   Went he hence now?
DESDEMONA   Yes, faith, so humbled
    That he hath left part of his grief with me
    To suffer with him. Good love, call him back.
OTHELLO
    Not now, sweet Desdemon. Some other time.
DESDEMONA   But shall 't be shortly?
OTHELLO   The sooner, sweet, for you.
DESDEMONA   Shall 't be tonight at supper?
OTHELLO   No, not tonight.
DESDEMONA   Tomorrow dinner, then?   63
OTHELLO   I shall not dine at home.
    I meet the captains at the citadel.
DESDEMONA
    Why, then, tomorrow night, or Tuesday morn,
    On Tuesday noon, or night, on Wednesday morn.
    I prithee, name the time, but let it not
    Exceed three days. In faith, he's penitent;
    And yet his trespass, in our common reason—   70
    Save that, they say, the wars must make example   71
    Out of her best—is not almost a fault   72
    T' incur a private check. When shall he come?   73
    Tell me, Othello. I wonder in my soul
    What you would ask me that I should deny,
    Or stand so mammering on. What? Michael Cassio,   76

That came a-wooing with you, and so many a time,
    When I have spoke of you dispraisingly,
    Hath ta'en your part—to have so much to do
    To bring him in! By 'r Lady, I could do much—   80
OTHELLO
    Prithee, no more. Let him come when he will;
    I will deny thee nothing.
DESDEMONA   Why, this is not a boon.
    'Tis as I should entreat you wear your gloves,
    Or feed on nourishing dishes, or keep you warm,
    Or sue to you to do a peculiar profit   86
    To your own person. Nay, when I have a suit
    Wherein I mean to touch your love indeed,   88
    It shall be full of poise and difficult weight,   89
    And fearful to be granted.
OTHELLO   I will deny thee nothing.
    Whereon, I do beseech thee, grant me this,   92
    To leave me but a little to myself.
DESDEMONA
    Shall I deny you? No. Farewell, my lord.
OTHELLO
    Farewell, my Desdemona. I'll come to thee straight.   95
DESDEMONA
    Emilia, come.—Be as your fancies teach you;   96
    Whate'er you be, I am obedient.   *Exit [with Emilia].*
OTHELLO
    Excellent wretch! Perdition catch my soul   98
    But I do love thee! And when I love thee not,   99
    Chaos is come again.   100
IAGO   My noble lord—
OTHELLO   What dost thou say, Iago?
IAGO
    Did Michael Cassio, when you wooed my lady,
    Know of your love?
OTHELLO
    He did, from first to last. Why dost thou ask?
IAGO
    But for a satisfaction of my thought;
    No further harm.
OTHELLO   Why of thy thought, Iago?
IAGO
    I did not think he had been acquainted with her.
OTHELLO
    O, yes, and went between us very oft.
IAGO   Indeed?
OTHELLO
    Indeed? Ay, indeed. Discern'st thou aught in that?
    Is he not honest?
IAGO   Honest, my lord?
OTHELLO   Honest. Ay, honest.
IAGO   My lord, for aught I know.
OTHELLO   What dost thou think?

---

34 do your discretion act according to your own discretion   **49 His . . . take** let him be reconciled to you right away   **51 in cunning** wittingly   **63 dinner** (The noontime meal.)   **70 common reason** everyday judgments   **71–72 Save . . . best** were it not that, as the saying goes, military discipline requires making an example of the very best men. (*Her* refers to *wars* as a singular concept.)   **72 not almost** scarcely   **73 a private check** even a private reprimand   **76 mammering on** wavering about

80 bring him in restore him to favor   **86 peculiar** particular, personal   **88 touch** test   **89 poise** weight, heaviness; or equipoise, delicate balance involving hard choice   **92 Whereon** in return for which   **95 straight** straightway   **96 fancies** inclinations   **98 wretch** (A term of affectionate endearment.)   **99–100 And . . . again** i.e., my love for you will last forever, until the end of time when chaos will return. (But with an unconscious, ironic suggestion that, if anything should induce Othello to cease loving Desdemona, the result would be chaos.)

IAGO   Think, my lord?
OTHELLO
"Think, my lord?" By heaven, thou echo'st me,
As if there were some monster in thy thought
Too hideous to be shown. Thou dost mean
    something.
I heard thee say even now, thou lik'st not that,
When Cassio left my wife. What didst not like?
And when I told thee he was of my counsel   123
In my whole course of wooing, thou criedst
    "Indeed?"
And didst contract and purse thy brow together   125
As if thou then hadst shut up in thy brain
Some horrible conceit. If thou dost love me,   127
Show me thy thought.
IAGO   My lord, you know I love you.
OTHELLO   I think thou dost;
And, for I know thou'rt full of love and honesty,   131
And weigh'st thy words before thou giv'st them
    breath,
Therefore these stops of thine fright me the more;   133
For such things in a false disloyal knave
Are tricks of custom, but in a man that's just   135
They're close dilations, working from the heart   136
That passion cannot rule.
IAGO   For Michael Cassio,   137
I dare be sworn I think that he is honest.
OTHELLO
I think so too.
IAGO   Men should be what they seem;
Or those that be not, would they might seem none!   140
OTHELLO
Certain, men should be what they seem.
IAGO
Why, then, I think Cassio's an honest man.
OTHELLO   Nay, yet there's more in this.
I prithee, speak to me as to thy thinkings,
As thou dost ruminate, and give thy worst of
    thoughts
The worst of words.
IAGO   Good my lord, pardon me.
Though I am bound to every act of duty,
I am not bound to that all slaves are free to.   148
Utter my thoughts? Why, say they are vile and false,
As where's that palace whereinto foul things
Sometimes intrude not? Who has that breast so pure
But some uncleanly apprehensions
Keep leets and law days, and in sessions sit   153
With meditations lawful?   154

OTHELLO
Thou dost conspire against thy friend, Iago,   155
If thou but think'st him wronged and mak'st his ear
A stranger to thy thoughts
IAGO   I do beseech you,
Though I perchance am vicious in my guess—   158
As I confess it is my nature's plague
To spy into abuses, and oft my jealousy   160
Shapes faults that are not—that your wisdom then,   161
From one that so imperfectly conceits,   162
Would take no notice, nor build yourself a trouble
Out of his scattering and unsure observance.   164
It were not for your quiet nor your good,
Nor for my manhood, honesty, and wisdom,
To let you know my thoughts.
OTHELLO   What dost thou mean?
IAGO
Good name in man and woman, dear my lord,
Is the immediate jewel of their souls.   169
Who steals my purse steals trash; 'tis something,
    nothing;
'Twas mine, 'tis his, and has been slave to
    thousands;
But he that filches from me my good name
Robs me of that which not enriches him
And makes me poor indeed.
OTHELLO   By heaven, I'll know thy thoughts.
IAGO
You cannot, if my heart were in your hand,   176
Nor shall not, whilst 'tis in my custody.
OTHELLO   Ha?
IAGO   O, beware, my lord, of jealousy.
It is the green-eyed monster which doth mock   179
The meat it feeds on. That cuckold lives in bliss   180
Who, certain of his fate, loves not his wronger;   181
But O, what damnèd minutes tells he o'er   182
Who dotes, yet doubts, suspects, yet fondly loves!
OTHELLO   O misery!
IAGO
Poor and content is rich, and rich enough,   185
But riches fineless is as poor as winter   186
To him that ever fears he shall be poor.
Good God, the souls of all my tribe defend
From jealousy!
OTHELLO   Why, why is this?
Think'st thou I'd make a life of jealousy,
To follow still the changes of the moon   192
With fresh suspicions? No! To be once in doubt   193

123 of my counsel in my confidence   **125 purse** knit   **127 conceit** fancy   **131 for** because   **133 stops** pauses   **135 of custom** customary   **136 close dilations** secret or involuntary expressions or delays **137 That passion cannot rule** i.e., that are too passionately strong to be restrained (referring to the workings), or, that cannot rule its own passions (referring to the heart).   **For** as for   **140 none** i.e., not to be men, or not seem to be honest   **148 that** that which.   **free to** free with respect to   **153 Keep leets and law days** i.e., hold court, set up their authority in one's heart. (*Leets* are a kind of manor court; *law days* are the days courts sit in session, or those sessions.)   **154 With** along with.   **lawful** innocent

155 thy friend i.e., Othello   **158 vicious** wrong   **160 jealousy** suspicious nature   **161 then** on that account   **162 one** i.e., myself, Iago. **conceits** judges, conjectures   **164 scattering** random   **169 immediate** essential, most precious   **176 if** even if   **179–180 doth mock . . . on** mocks and torments the heart of its victim, the man who suffers jealousy   **181 his wronger** i.e., his faithless wife. (The unsuspecting cuckold is spared the misery of loving his wife only to discover she is cheating on him.)   **182 tells** counts   **185 Poor . . . enough** to be content with what little one has is the greatest wealth of all. (Proverbial.)   **186 fineless** boundless   **192–193 To follow . . . suspicions** to be constantly imagining new causes for suspicion, changing incessantly like the moon

Is once to be resolved. Exchange me for a goat   194
When I shall turn the business of my soul
To such exsufflicate and blown surmises   196
Matching thy inference. 'Tis not to make me jealous   197
To say my wife is fair, feeds well, loves company,
Is free of speech, sings, plays, and dances well;
Where virtue is, these are more virtuous.
Nor from mine own weak merits will I draw
The smallest fear or doubt of her revolt,   202
For she had eyes, and chose me. No, Iago,
I'll see before I doubt; when I doubt, prove;
And on the proof, there is no more but this—
Away at once with love or jealousy.

IAGO
I am glad of this, for now I shall have reason
To show the love and duty that I bear you
With franker spirit. Therefore, as I am bound,
Receive it from me. I speak not yet of proof.
Look to your wife; observe her well with Cassio.
Wear your eyes thus, not jealous nor secure.   212
I would not have your free and noble nature,
Out of self-bounty, be abused. Look to 't.   214
I know our country disposition well;
In Venice they do let God see the pranks
They dare not show their husbands; their best
    conscience
Is not to leave 't undone, but keep 't unknown.

OTHELLO   Dost thou say so?

IAGO
She did deceive her father, marrying you;
And when she seemed to shake and fear your looks,
She loved them most.

OTHELLO   And so she did.

IAGO   Why, go to, then!   222
She that, so young, could give out such a seeming,   223
To seel her father's eyes up close as oak,   224
He thought 'twas witchcraft! But I am much to
    blame.
I humbly do beseech you of your pardon
For too much loving you.

OTHELLO   I am bound to thee forever.   228

IAGO
I see this hath a little dashed your spirits.

OTHELLO
Not a jot, not a jot.

IAGO   I' faith, I fear it has.
I hope you will consider what is spoke
Comes from my love. But I do see you're moved.
I am to pray you not to strain my speech

To grosser issues nor to larger reach   234
Than to suspicion.

OTHELLO   I will not.

IAGO   Should you do so, my lord,
My speech should fall into such vile success   238
Which my thoughts aimed not. Cassio's my worthy
    friend.
My lord, I see you're moved.

OTHELLO   No, not much moved.
I do not think but Desdemona's honest.   241

IAGO
Long live she so! And long live you to think so!

OTHELLO
And yet, how nature erring from itself—

IAGO
Ay, there's the point! As—to be bold with you—
Not to affect many proposèd matches   245
Of her own clime, complexion, and degree,   246
Whereto we see in all things nature tends—
Foh! One may smell in such a will most rank,   248
Foul disproportion, thoughts unnatural.   249
But pardon me. I do not in position   250
Distinctly speak of her, though I may fear
Her will, recoiling to her better judgment,   252
May fall to match you with her country forms   253
And happily repent.

OTHELLO   Farewell, farewell!   254
If more thou dost perceive, let me know more.
Set on thy wife to observe. Leave me, Iago.

IAGO [going]   My lord, I take my leave.

OTHELLO
Why did I marry? This honest creature doubtless
Sees and knows more, much more, than he unfolds.

IAGO [returning]
My Lord, I would I might entreat your honor
To scan this thing no farther. Leave it to time.   261
Although 'tis fit that Cassio have his place—
For, sure, he fills it up with great ability—
Yet, if you please to hold him off awhile,
You shall by that perceive him and his means.   265
Note if your lady strain his entertainment   266
With any strong or vehement importunity;
Much will be seen in that. In the meantime,
Let me be thought too busy in my fears—   269
As worthy cause I have to fear I am—
And hold her free, I do beseech your honor.   271

OTHELLO   Fear not my government.   272

IAGO   I once more take my leave.   *Exit.*

---

194 once once and for all.   **resolved** free of doubt, having settled the matter   **196 exsufflicate and blown** inflated and blown up, rumored about, or, spat out and flyblown, hence, loathsome, disgusting   **197 inference** description or allegation   **202 doubt . . . revolt** fear of her unfaithfulness   **212 not** neither.   **secure** free from uncertainty   **214 self-bounty** inherent or natural goodness and generosity.   **abused** deceived   **222 go to** (An expression of impatience.)   **223 seeming** false appearance   **224 seel** blind. (A term from falconry.)   **oak** (A close-grained wood.)   **228 bound** indebted (but perhaps with ironic sense of "tied")

234 issues significances.   **reach** meaning, scope   **238 success** effect, result   **241 honest** chaste   **245 affect** prefer, desire   **246 clime . . . degree** country, color, and social position   **248 will** sensuality, appetite   **249 disproportion** abnormality   **250 position** argument, proposition   **252 recoiling** reverting.   **better** i.e., more natural and reconsidered   **253 fall . . . forms** undertake to compare you with Venetian norms of handsomeness   **254 happily repent** haply repent her marriage   **261 scan** scrutinize   **265 his means** the method he uses (to regain his post)   **266 strain his entertainment** urge his reinstatement   **269 busy** interfering   **271 hold her free** regard her as innocent   **272 government** self-control, conduct

OTHELLO
This fellow's of exceeding honesty,
And knows all qualities, with a learnèd spirit,   275
Of human dealings. If I do prove her haggard,   276
Though that her jesses were my dear heartstrings,   277
I'd whistle her off and let her down the wind   278
To prey at fortune. Haply, for I am black   279
And have not those soft parts of conversation   280
That chamberers have, or for I am declined   281
Into the vale of years—yet that's not much—
She's gone. I am abused, and my relief   283
Must be to loathe her. O curse of marriage,
That we can call these delicate creatures ours
And not their appetites! I had rather be a toad
And live upon the vapor of a dungeon
Than keep a corner in the thing I love
For others' uses. Yet, 'tis the plague of great ones;
Prerogatived are they less than the base.   290
'Tis destiny unshunnable, like death.
Even then this forkèd plague is fated to us   292
When we do quicken. Look where she comes.   293

Enter Desdemona and Emilia.

If she be false, O, then heaven mocks itself!
I'll not believe 't.
DESDEMONA   How now, my dear Othello?
Your dinner, and the generous islanders   296
By you invited, do attend your presence.   297
OTHELLO
I am to blame.
DESDEMONA   Why do you speak so faintly?
Are you not well?
OTHELLO
I have a pain upon my forehead here.
DESDEMONA
Faith, that's with watching. 'Twill away again.   301
                    [*She offers her handkerchief.*]
Let me but bind it hard, within this hour
It will be well.
OTHELLO   Your napkin is too little.   303
Let it alone. Come, I'll go in with you.   304
          [*He puts the handkerchief from him, and it drops.*]
DESDEMONA
I am very sorry that you are not well.
                              Exit [*with Othello*].

275 **qualities** natures, types   276 **haggard** wild (like a wild female hawk)   277 **jesses** straps fastened around the legs of a trained hawk   278 **I'd . . . wind** i.e., I'd let her go forever. (To release a hawk downwind was to invite it not to return.)   279 **prey at fortune** fend for herself in the wild.   **Haply, for** perhaps because   280 **soft . . . conversation** pleasing graces of social behavior   281 **chamberers** gallants   283 **abused** deceived   290 **Prerogatived** privileged (to have honest wives).   **the base** ordinary citizens. (Socially prominent men are especially prone to the unavoidable destiny of being cuckolded and to the public shame that goes with it.)   292 **forkèd** (An allusion to the horns of the cuckold.)   293 **quicken** receive life. (*Quicken* may also mean to swarm with maggots as the body festers, as in 4.2.69, in which case lines 292–293 suggest that *even then*, in death, we are cuckolded by *forkèd* worms.)   296 **generous** noble   297 **attend** await   301 **watching** too little sleep   303 **napkin** handkerchief   304 **Let it alone** i.e., never mind

EMILIA [*picking up the handkerchief*]
I am glad I have found this napkin.
This was her first remembrance from the Moor.
My wayward husband hath a hundred times   308
Wooed me to steal it, but she so loves the token—
For he conjured her she should ever keep it—
That she reserves it evermore about her
To kiss and talk to. I'll have the work ta'en out,   312
And give 't Iago. What he will do with it
Heaven knows, not I;
I nothing but to please his fantasy.   315

Enter Iago.

IAGO
How now? What do you here alone?
EMILIA
Do not you chide. I have a thing for you.
IAGO
You have a thing for me? It is a common thing—   318
EMILIA   Ha?
IAGO   To have a foolish wife.
EMILIA
O, is that all? What will you give me now
For that same handkerchief?
IAGO   What handkerchief?
EMILIA   What handkerchief?
Why, that the Moor first gave to Desdemona;
That which so often you did bid me steal.
IAGO   Hast stolen it from her?
EMILIA
No, faith. She let it drop by negligence,
And to th' advantage I, being here, took 't up.   329
Look, here 'tis.
IAGO   A good wench! Give it me.
EMILIA
What will you do with 't, that you have been so earnest
To have me filch it?
IAGO [*snatching it*]   Why, what is that to you?
EMILIA
If it be not for some purpose of import,
Give 't me again. Poor lady, she'll run mad
When she shall lack it.
IAGO   Be not acknown on 't.   335
I have use for it. Go, leave me.   *Exit Emilia*.
I will in Cassio's lodging lose this napkin   337
And let him find it. Trifles light as air
Are to the jealous confirmations strong
As proofs of Holy Writ. This may do something.
The Moor already changes with my poison.
Dangerous conceits are in their natures poisons,   342

308 **wayward** capricious   312 **work ta'en out** design of the embroidery copied   315 **fantasy** whim   318 **common thing** (With bawdy suggestion; *common* suggests coarseness and availability to all comers, and *thing* is a slang term for the pudendum.)   329 **to th' advantage** taking the opportunity   335 **lack** miss.   **Be . . . on 't** do not confess knowledge of it   337 **lose** (The Folio spelling, *loose*, is a normal spelling for "lose," but it may also contain the idea of "let go," "release.")   342 **conceits** fancies, ideas

Which at the first are scarce found to distaste,   343
But with a little act upon the blood   344
Burn like the mines of sulfur.

     Enter Othello.

                         I did say so.
Look where he comes! Not poppy nor mandragora   346
Nor all the drowsy syrups of the world
Shall ever medicine thee to that sweet sleep
Which thou owedst yesterday.

OTHELLO   Ha, ha, false to me?   349

IAGO
   Why, how now, General? No more of that.

OTHELLO
   Avaunt! Begone! Thou hast set me on the rack.
   I swear 'tis better to be much abused
   Than but to know 't a little.

IAGO   How now, my lord?

OTHELLO
   What sense had I of her stolen hours of lust?
   I saw 't not, thought it not, it harmed not me.
   I slept the next night well, fed well, was free and
     merry;   356
   I found not Cassio's kisses on her lips.
   He that is robbed, not wanting what is stolen,   358
   Let him not know 't and he's not robbed at all.

IAGO   I am sorry to hear this.

OTHELLO
   I had been happy if the general camp,
   Pioners and all, had tasted her sweet body,   362
   So I had nothing known. O, now, forever   363
   Farewell the tranquil mind! Farewell content!
   Farewell the plumèd troops and the big wars   365
   That makes ambition virtue! O, farewell!
   Farewell the neighing steed and the shrill trump,
   The spirit-stirring drum, th' ear-piercing fife,
   The royal banner, and all quality,   369
   Pride, pomp, and circumstance of glorious war!   370
   And O, you mortal engines, whose rude throats   371
   Th' immortal Jove's dread clamors counterfeit,   372
   Farewell! Othello's occupation's gone.

IAGO   Is 't possible, my lord?

OTHELLO
   Villain, be sure thou prove my love a whore!
   Be sure of it. Give me the ocular proof,
   Or, by the worth of mine eternal soul,
   Thou hadst been better have been born a dog
   Than answer my waked wrath!

IAGO   Is 't come to this?

OTHELLO
   Make me to see 't, or at the least so prove it
   That the probation bear no hinge nor loop   381
   To hang a doubt on, or woe upon thy life!

IAGO   My noble lord—

OTHELLO
   If thou dost slander her and torture me,
   Never pray more; abandon all remorse;   385
   On horror's head horrors accumulate;   386
   Do deeds to make heaven weep, all earth amazed;   387
   For nothing canst thou to damnation add
   Greater than that.

IAGO   O grace! O heaven forgive me!
   Are you a man? Have you a soul or sense?
   God b' wi' you; take mine office. O wretched fool,   391
   That lov'st to make thine honesty a vice!   392
   O monstrous world! Take note, take note, O world,
   To be direct and honest is not safe.
   I thank you for this profit, and from hence   395
   I'll love no friend, sith love breeds such offense.   396

OTHELLO   Nay, stay. Thou shouldst be honest.   397

IAGO
   I should be wise, for honesty's a fool
   And loses that it works for.

OTHELLO   By the world,   399
   I think my wife be honest and think she is not;
   I think that thou art just and think thou art not.
   I'll have some proof. My name, that was as fresh
   As Dian's visage, is now begrimed and black   403
   As mine own face. If there be cords, or knives,
   Poison, or fire, or suffocating streams,
   I'll not endure it. Would I were satisfied!

IAGO
   I see, sir, you are eaten up with passion.
   I do repent me that I put it to you.
   You would be satisfied?

OTHELLO   Would? Nay, and I will.

IAGO
   And may; but how? How satisfied, my lord?
   Would you, the supervisor, grossly gape on?   411
   Behold her topped?

OTHELLO   Death and damnation! O!

IAGO
   It were a tedious difficulty, I think,
   To bring them to that prospect. Damn them then,   414
   If ever mortal eyes do see them bolster   415
   More than their own. What then? How then?   416
   What shall I say? Where's satisfaction?
   It is impossible you should see this,
   Were they as prime as goats, as hot as monkeys,   419
   As salt as wolves in pride, and fools as gross   420
   As ignorance made drunk. But yet I say,

---

343 distaste be distasteful   **344 act** action, working   **346 mandragora** an opiate made of the mandrake root   **349 thou owedst** you did own   **356 free** carefree   **358 wanting** missing   **362 Pioners** diggers of mines, the lowest grade of soldiers   **363 So** provided   **365 big** stately   **369 quality** character, essential nature   **370 Pride** rich display. **circumstance** pageantry   **371 mortal engines** i.e., cannon. (*Mortal* means "deadly.")   **372 Jove's dread clamors** i.e., thunder **381 probation** proof

385 remorse pity, penitent hope for salvation   **386 horrors accumulate** add still more horrors   **387 amazed** confounded with horror **391 O wretched fool** (Iago addresses himself as a fool for having carried honesty too far.)   **392 vice** failing, something overdone **395 profit** profitable instruction. **hence** henceforth   **396 sith** since. **offense** i.e., harm to the one who offers help and friendship **397 Thou shouldst be** it appears that you are. (But Iago replies in the sense of "ought to be.")   **399 that** what   **403 Dian** Diana, goddess of the moon and of chastity   **411 supervisor** onlooker   **414 Damn them then** i.e., they would have to be really incorrigible   **415 bolster** go to bed together, share a bolster   **416 More** other. **own** own eyes **419 prime** lustful   **420 salt** wanton, sensual. **pride** heat

OTHELLO, THE MOOR OF VENICE: 3.4 **1147**

If imputation and strong circumstances 422
Which lead directly to the door of truth
Will give you satisfaction, you might have 't.

OTHELLO
Give me a living reason she's disloyal.

IAGO I do not like the office.
But sith I am entered in this cause so far, 427
Pricked to 't by foolish honesty and love, 428
I will go on. I lay with Cassio lately,
And being troubled with a raging tooth
I could not sleep. There are a kind of men
So loose of soul that in their sleeps will mutter
Their affairs. One of this kind is Cassio.
In sleep I heard him say, "Sweet Desdemona,
Let us be wary, let us hide our loves!"
And then, sir, would he grip and wring my hand,
Cry "O sweet creature!", then kiss me hard,
As if he plucked up kisses by the roots
That grew upon my lips; then laid his leg
Over my thigh, and sighed, and kissed, and then
Cried, "Cursèd fate that gave thee to the Moor!"

OTHELLO
O monstrous! Monstrous!

IAGO   Nay, this was but his dream.

OTHELLO
But this denoted a foregone conclusion. 443
'Tis a shrewd doubt, though it be but a dream. 444

IAGO
And this may help to thicken other proofs
That do demonstrate thinly.

OTHELLO   I'll tear her all to pieces.

IAGO
Nay, but be wise. Yet we see nothing done;
She may be honest yet. Tell me but this:
Have you not sometimes seen a handkerchief
Spotted with strawberries in your wife's hand? 450

OTHELLO
I gave her such a one. 'Twas my first gift.

IAGO
I know not that; but such a handkerchief—
I am sure it was your wife's—did I today
See Cassio wipe his beard with.

OTHELLO   If it be that—

IAGO
If it be that, or any that was hers,
It speaks against her with the other proofs.

OTHELLO
O, that the slave had forty thousand lives! 457
One is too poor, too weak for my revenge.
Now do I see 'tis true. Look here, Iago,
All my fond love thus do I blow to heaven. 460
'Tis gone.
Arise, black vengeance, from the hollow hell!
Yield up, O love, thy crown and hearted throne 463

To tyrannous hate! Swell, bosom, with thy freight, 464
For 'tis of aspics' tongues! 465

IAGO Yet be content. 466

OTHELLO O, blood, blood, blood!

IAGO
Patience, I say. Your mind perhaps may change.

OTHELLO
Never, Iago. Like to the Pontic Sea, 469
Whose icy current and compulsive course
Ne'er feels retiring ebb, but keeps due on
To the Propontic and the Hellespont, 472
Even so my bloody thoughts with violent pace
Shall ne'er look back, ne'er ebb to humble love,
Till that a capable and wide revenge 475
Swallow them up. Now, by yond marble heaven, 476
[Kneeling] In the due reverence of a sacred vow
I here engage my words.

IAGO   Do not rise yet.
[He kneels.] Witness, you ever-burning lights above, 479
You elements that clip us round about, 480
Witness that here Iago doth give up
The execution of his wit, hands, heart, 482
To wronged Othello's service. Let him command,
And to obey shall be in me remorse, 484
What bloody business ever.   [They rise.]

OTHELLO   I greet thy love, 485
Not with vain thanks, but with acceptance
    bounteous,
And will upon the instant put thee to 't. 487
Within these three days let me hear thee say
That Cassio's not alive.

IAGO   My friend is dead;
'Tis done at your request. But let her live.

OTHELLO
Damn her, lewd minx! O, damn her, damn her! 491
Come, go with me apart. I will withdraw
To furnish me with some swift means of death
For the fair devil. Now art thou my lieutenant.

IAGO I am your own forever.   Exeunt.

❧

3.4 *Enter Desdemona, Emilia, and Clown.*

DESDEMONA Do you know, sirrah, where Lieutenant 1
    Cassio lies? 2

CLOWN I dare not say he lies anywhere.

DESDEMONA Why, man?

CLOWN He's a soldier, and for me to say a soldier lies,
    'tis stabbing.

422 **imputation . . . circumstances** strong circumstantial evidence
427 **sith** since 428 **Pricked** spurred 443 **foregone conclusion** concluded experience or action 444 **shrewd doubt** suspicious circumstance 450 **Spotted with strawberries** embroidered with a strawberry pattern 457 **the slave** i.e., Cassio 460 **fond** foolish (but also suggesting "affectionate") 463 **hearted** fixed in the heart

464 **freight** burden 465 **aspics'** venomous serpents' 466 **content** calm 469 **Pontic Sea** Black Sea 472 **Propontic** Sea of Marmora, between the Black Sea and the Aegean. **Hellespont** Dardanelles, straits where the Sea of Marmora joins with the Aegean 475 **capable** ample, comprehensive 476 **marble** i.e., gleaming like marble and unrelenting 479 **s.d. He kneels** (In the Quarto text, Iago kneels here after Othello has knelt at line 477.) 480 **clip** encompass 482 **execution** exercise, action. **wit** mind 484 **remorse** pity (for Othello's wrongs) 485 **ever** soever 487 **to 't** to the proof 491 **minx** wanton
3.4. **Location: Before the citadel.**
1 **sirrah** (A form of address to an inferior.) 2 **lies** lodges. (But the Clown makes the obvious pun.)

DESDEMONA   Go to. Where lodges he?

CLOWN   To tell you where he lodges is to tell you where
I lie.

DESDEMONA   Can anything be made of this?

CLOWN   I know not where he lodges, and for me to devise a lodging and say he lies here, or he lies there,
were to lie in mine own throat.   13

DESDEMONA   Can you inquire him out, and be edified
by report?

CLOWN   I will catechize the world for him; that is, make
questions, and by them answer.

DESDEMONA   Seek him, bid him come hither. Tell him I
have moved my lord on his behalf and hope all will be   19
well.

CLOWN   To do this is within the compass of man's wit,
and therefore I will attempt the doing it.   *Exit Clown.*

DESDEMONA
Where should I lose that handkerchief, Emilia?

EMILIA   I know not, madam.

DESDEMONA
Believe me, I had rather have lost my purse
Full of crusadoes; and but my noble Moor   26
Is true of mind and made of no such baseness
As jealous creatures are, it were enough
To put him to ill thinking.

EMILIA   Is he not jealous?

DESDEMONA
Who, he? I think the sun where he was born
Drew all such humors from him.

EMILIA   Look where he comes. 31

Enter Othello.

DESDEMONA
I will not leave him now till Cassio
Be called to him.—How is 't with you, my lord?

OTHELLO
Well, my good lady. [*Aside.*] O, hardness to
dissemble!—
How do you, Desdemona?

DESDEMONA   Well, my good lord.

OTHELLO
Give me your hand. [*She gives her hand.*] This hand is
moist, my lady.

DESDEMONA
It yet hath felt no age nor known no sorrow.

OTHELLO
This argues fruitfulness and liberal heart.   38
Hot, hot, and moist. This hand of yours requires
A sequester from liberty, fasting and prayer,   40
Much castigation, exercise devout;   41
For here's a young and sweating devil here
That commonly rebels. 'Tis a good hand,
A frank one.

DESDEMONA   You may indeed say so,   44
For 'twas that hand that gave away my heart.

OTHELLO
A liberal hand. The hearts of old gave hands,   46
But our new heraldry is hands, not hearts.   47

DESDEMONA
I cannot speak of this. Come now, your promise.

OTHELLO   What promise, chuck?   49

DESDEMONA
I have sent to bid Cassio come speak with you.

OTHELLO
I have a salt and sorry rheum offends me;   51
Lend me thy handkerchief.

DESDEMONA   Here, my lord.   [*She offers a handkerchief.*]

OTHELLO
That which I gave you.

DESDEMONA   I have it not about me.

OTHELLO   Not?

DESDEMONA   No, faith, my lord.

OTHELLO
That's a fault. That handkerchief
Did an Egyptian to my mother give.
She was a charmer, and could almost read   59
The thoughts of people. She told her, while she
kept it
'Twould make her amiable and subdue my father   61
Entirely to her love, but if she lost it
Or made a gift of it, my father's eye
Should hold her loathèd and his spirits should hunt
After new fancies. She, dying, gave it me,   65
And bid me, when my fate would have me wived,
To give it her. I did so; and take heed on 't;   67
Make it a darling like your precious eye.
To lose 't or give 't away were such perdition   69
As nothing else could match.

DESDEMONA   Is 't possible?

OTHELLO
'Tis true. There's magic in the web of it.   71
A sibyl, that had numbered in the world
The sun to course two hundred compasses,   73
In her prophetic fury sewed the work;   74
The worms were hallowed that did breed the silk,
And it was dyed in mummy which the skillful   76
Conserved of maidens' hearts.

DESDEMONA   I' faith! Is 't true?   77

OTHELLO
Most veritable. Therefore look to 't well.

DESDEMONA
Then would to God that I had never seen 't!

---

13 lie . . . throat (1) lie egregiously and deliberately (2) use the windpipe to speak a lie   **19 moved** petitioned   **26 crusadoes** Portuguese
gold coins   **31 humors** (Refers to the four bodily fluids thought to determine temperament.)   **38 argues** gives evidence of.   **fruitfulness**
generosity, amorousness, and fecundity.   **liberal** generous and sexually free   **40 sequester** separation, sequestration   **41 castigation**
corrective discipline.   **exercise devout** i.e., prayer, religious meditation, etc.

44 frank generous, open (with sexual suggestion)   **46 The hearts . . .
hands** i.e., in former times, people would give their hearts when they
gave their hands to something   **47 But . . . hearts** i.e., in our decadent times, the joining of hands is no longer a badge to signify the
giving of hearts   **49 chuck** (A term of endearment.)   **51 salt . . .
rheum** distressful head cold or watering of the eyes   **59 charmer** sorceress   **61 amiable** desirable   **65 fancies** loves   **67 her** i.e., to my
wife   **69 perdition** loss   **71 web** fabric, weaving   **73 compasses** annual circlings. (The *sibyl*, or prophetess, was two hundred years old.)
74 prophetic fury frenzy of prophetic inspiration.   **work** embroidered
pattern   **76 mummy** medicinal or magical preparation drained from
mummified bodies   **77 Conserved of** prepared or preserved out of

OTHELLO   Ha? Wherefore?

DESDEMONA

Why do you speak so startingly and rash?   81

OTHELLO

Is 't lost? Is 't gone? Speak, is 't out o' the way?   82

DESDEMONA   Heaven bless us!

OTHELLO   Say you?

DESDEMONA

It is not lost; but what an if it were?   85

OTHELLO   How?

DESDEMONA

I say it is not lost.

OTHELLO   Fetch 't, let me see 't.

DESDEMONA

Why, so I can, sir, but I will not now.

This is a trick to put me from my suit.

Pray you, let Cassio be received again.

OTHELLO

Fetch me the handkerchief! My mind misgives.

DESDEMONA   Come, come,

You'll never meet a more sufficient man.   93

OTHELLO

The handkerchief!

DESDEMONA   I pray, talk me of Cassio.   94

OTHELLO

The handkerchief!

DESDEMONA   A man that all his time   95

Hath founded his good fortunes on your love,

Shared dangers with you—

OTHELLO   The handkerchief!

DESDEMONA   I' faith, you are to blame.

OTHELLO   Zounds!   *Exit Othello.*

EMILIA   Is not this man jealous?

DESDEMONA   I ne'er saw this before.

Sure, there's some wonder in this handkerchief.

I am most unhappy in the loss of it.

EMILIA

'Tis not a year or two shows us a man.   105

They are all but stomachs, and we all but food;   106

They eat us hungerly, and when they are full   107

They belch us.

              Enter Iago and Cassio.

                    Look you, Cassio and my husband.

IAGO [*to Cassio*]

There is no other way; 'tis she must do 't.

And, lo, the happiness! Go and importune her.   110

DESDEMONA

How now, good Cassio? What's the news with you?

CASSIO

Madam, my former suit. I do beseech you

That by your virtuous means I may again   113

Exist and be a member of his love

Whom I, with all the office of my heart,   115

Entirely honor. I would not be delayed.

If my offense be of such mortal kind   117

That nor my service past, nor present sorrows,   118

Nor purposed merit in futurity

Can ransom me into his love again,

But to know so must be my benefit;   121

So shall I clothe me in a forced content,

And shut myself up in some other course,   123

To fortune's alms.

DESDEMONA   Alas, thrice-gentle Cassio,   124

My advocation is not now in tune.   125

My lord is not my lord; nor should I know him,

Were he in favor as in humor altered.   127

So help me every spirit sanctified

As I have spoken for you all my best

And stood within the blank of his displeasure   130

For my free speech! You must awhile be patient.

What I can do I will, and more I will

Than for myself I dare. Let that suffice you.

IAGO

Is my lord angry?

EMILIA   He went hence but now,

And certainly in strange unquietness.

IAGO

Can he be angry? I have seen the cannon

When it hath blown his ranks into the air,

And like the devil from his very arm

Puffed his own brother—and is he angry?

Something of moment then. I will go meet him.   140

There's matter in 't indeed, if he be angry.

DESDEMONA

I prithee, do so.   *Exit [Iago].*

                    Something, sure, of state,   142

Either from Venice, or some unhatched practice   143

Made demonstrable here in Cyprus to him,

Hath puddled his clear spirit; and in such cases   145

Men's natures wrangle with inferior things,

Though great ones are their object. 'Tis even so;

For let our finger ache, and it indues   148

Our other, healthful members even to a sense

Of pain. Nay, we must think men are not gods,

Nor of them look for such observancy   151

As fits the bridal. Beshrew me much, Emilia,   152

I was, unhandsome warrior as I am,   153

Arraigning his unkindness with my soul;   154

But now I find I had suborned the witness,   155

---

115 office loyal service **117 mortal** fatal **118 nor . . . nor** neither
. . . nor **121 But . . . benefit** merely to know that my case is hopeless will have to content me (and will be better than uncertainty)
123 shut . . . in confine myself to **124 To fortune's alms** throwing
myself on the mercy of fortune **125 advocation** advocacy **127 favor** appearance. **humor** mood **130 within the blank** within point-
blank range. (The *blank* is the center of the target.) **140 of moment**
of immediate importance, momentous **142 of state** concerning state
affairs **143 unhatched practice** as yet unexecuted or undiscovered
plot **145 puddled** muddied **148 indues** brings to the same condition **151 observancy** attentiveness **152 bridal** wedding (when a
bridegroom is newly attentive to his bride). **Beshrew me** (A mild
oath.) **153 unhandsome** insufficient, unskillful **154 with** before the
bar of **155 suborned the witness** induced the witness to give false
testimony

---

81 startingly and rash disjointedly and impetuously, excitedly **82 out
o' the way** lost, misplaced **85 an if** if **93 sufficient** able, complete
94 talk talk to **95 all his time** throughout his career **105 'Tis . . .
man** i.e., you can't really know a man even in a year or two of experience (?), or, real men come along seldom (?) **106 but** nothing but
107 hungerly hungrily **110 the happiness** in happy time, fortunately
met **113 virtuous** efficacious

And he's indicted falsely.

EMILIA   Pray heaven it be
State matters, as you think, and no conception
Nor no jealous toy concerning you.   158

DESDEMONA
Alas the day! I never gave him cause.

EMILIA
But jealous souls will not be answered so;
They are not ever jealous for the cause,
But jealous for they're jealous. It is a monster   162
Begot upon itself, born on itself.   163

DESDEMONA
Heaven keep that monster from Othello's mind!

EMILIA   Lady, amen.

DESDEMONA
I will go seek him. Cassio, walk hereabout.
If I do find him fit, I'll move your suit
And seek to effect it to my uttermost.

CASSIO
I humbly thank your ladyship.
                              Exit [Desdemona with Emilia].

            Enter Bianca.

BIANCA
Save you, friend Cassio!

CASSIO   What make you from home?   170
How is 't with you, my most fair Bianca?
I' faith, sweet love, I was coming to your house.

BIANCA
And I was going to your lodging, Cassio.
What, keep a week away? Seven days and nights?
Eightscore-eight hours? And lovers' absent hours   175
More tedious than the dial eightscore times?   176
O weary reckoning!

CASSIO   Pardon me, Bianca.
I have this while with leaden thoughts been pressed;
But I shall, in a more continuate time,   179
Strike off this score of absence. Sweet Bianca,   180
            [giving her Desdemona's handkerchief]
Take me this work out.

BIANCA   O Cassio, whence came this?   181
This is some token from a newer friend.   182
To the felt absence now I feel a cause.
Is 't come to this? Well, well.

CASSIO   Go to, woman!
Throw your vile guesses in the devil's teeth,
From whence you have them. You are jealous now
That this is from some mistress, some remembrance.
No, by my faith, Bianca.

BIANCA   Why, whose is it?

CASSIO
I know not, neither. I found it in my chamber.
I like the work well. Ere it be demanded—   190

As like enough it will—I would have it copied.   191
Take it and do 't, and leave me for this time.

BIANCA   Leave you? Wherefore?

CASSIO
I do attend here on the General,
And think it no addition, nor my wish,   195
To have him see me womaned.

BIANCA   Why, I pray you?

CASSIO   Not that I love you not.

BIANCA   But that you do not love me.
I pray you, bring me on the way a little,   200
And say if I shall see you soon at night.

CASSIO
'Tis but a little way that I can bring you,
For I attend here; but I'll see you soon.

BIANCA
'Tis very good. I must be circumstanced.   204
                              Exeunt omnes.

                              ❖

4.1   Enter Othello and Iago.

IAGO
Will you think so?

OTHELLO   Think so, Iago?

IAGO   What,
To kiss in private?

OTHELLO   An unauthorized kiss!

IAGO
Or to be naked with her friend in bed
An hour or more, not meaning any harm?

OTHELLO
Naked in bed, Iago, and not mean harm?
It is hypocrisy against the devil.
They that mean virtuously and yet do so,
The devil their virtue tempts, and they tempt
      heaven.

IAGO
If they do nothing, 'tis a venial slip.   9
But if I give my wife a handkerchief—

OTHELLO   What then?

IAGO
Why then, 'tis hers, my lord, and being hers,
She may, I think, bestow 't on any man.

OTHELLO
She is protectress of her honor too.
May she give that?

IAGO
Her honor is an essence that's not seen;
They have it very oft that have it not.   17
But, for the handkerchief—

OTHELLO
By heaven, I would most gladly have forgot it.
Thou saidst—O, it comes o'er my memory

---

158 **toy** fancy   162 **for** because   163 **Begot upon itself** generated solely from itself   170 **Save** God save.   **make** do   175 **Eightscore-eight** one hundred sixty-eight, the number of hours in a week   176 **the dial** a complete revolution of the clock   179 **continuate** uninterrupted   180 **Strike . . . score** settle this account   181 **Take . . . out** copy this embroidery for me   182 **friend** mistress   190 **demanded** inquired for

191 **like** likely   195 **addition** i.e., addition to my reputation   200 **bring** accompany   204 **be circumstanced** be governed by circumstance, yield to your conditions
4.1. Location: Before the citadel.
9 **venial** pardonable   17 **They have it** i.e., they enjoy a reputation for it

As doth the raven o'er the infectious house,   21
Boding to all—he had my handkerchief.

IAGO
Ay, what of that?

OTHELLO   That's not so good now.

IAGO   What
If I had said I had seen him do you wrong?
Or heard him say—as knaves be such abroad,   25
Who having, by their own importunate suit,
Or voluntary dotage of some mistress,   27
Convinèd or supplied them, cannot choose   28
But they must blab—

OTHELLO   Hath he said anything?

IAGO
He hath, my lord; but, be you well assured,
No more than he'll unswear.

OTHELLO   What hath he said?

IAGO
Faith, that he did—I know not what he did.

OTHELLO   What? What?

IAGO
Lie—

OTHELLO   With her?

IAGO   With her, on her; what you will.

OTHELLO   Lie with her? Lie on her? We say "lie on her"
when they belie her. Lie with her? Zounds, that's ful-   36
some.—Handkerchief—confessions—handkerchief!   37
—To confess and be hanged for his labor—first to be   38
hanged and then to confess.—I tremble at it. Nature   39
would not invest herself in such shadowing passion   40
without some instruction. It is not words that shakes   41
me thus. Pish! Noses, ears, and lips.—Is 't pos-
sible?—Confess—handkerchief!—O devil!

                                    Falls in a trance.

IAGO   Work on,
My medicine, work! Thus credulous fools are
  caught,
And many worthy and chaste dames even thus,
All guiltless, meet reproach.—What, ho! My lord!
My lord, I say! Othello!

            Enter Cassio.

                        How now, Cassio?

CASSIO   What's the matter?

IAGO
My lord is fall'n into an epilepsy.
This is his second fit. He had one yesterday.

CASSIO
Rub him about the temples.

IAGO   No, forbear.
The lethargy must have his quiet course.   53
If not, he foams at mouth, and by and by
Breaks out to savage madness. Look, he stirs.
Do you withdraw yourself a little while.
He will recover straight. When he is gone,
I would on great occasion speak with you.   58

                                    [*Exit Cassio.*]
How is it, General? Have you not hurt your head?

OTHELLO
Dost thou mock me?

IAGO   I mock you not, by heaven.   60
Would you would bear your fortune like a man!

OTHELLO
A hornèd man's a monster and a beast.

IAGO
There's many a beast then in a populous city,
And many a civil monster.   64

OTHELLO   Did he confess it?

IAGO   Good sir, be a man.
Think every bearded fellow that's but yoked   67
May draw with you. There's millions now alive   68
That nightly lie in those unproper beds   69
Which they dare swear peculiar. Your case is better.   70
O, 'tis the spite of hell, the fiend's arch-mock,
To lip a wanton in a secure couch   72
And to suppose her chaste! No, let me know,
And knowing what I am, I know what she shall be.   74

OTHELLO   O, thou art wise. 'Tis certain.

IAGO   Stand you awhile apart;
Confine yourself but in a patient list.   77
Whilst you were here o'erwhelmèd with your
  grief—
A passion most unsuiting such a man—
Cassio came hither. I shifted him away,   80
And laid good 'scuse upon your ecstasy,   81
Bade him anon return and here speak with me,
The which he promised. Do but encave yourself   83
And mark the fleers, the gibes, and notable scorns   84
That dwell in every region of his face;
For I will make him tell the tale anew,
Where, how, how oft, how long ago, and when
He hath and is again to cope your wife.   88
I say, but mark his gesture. Marry, patience!
Or I shall say you're all-in-all in spleen,   90
And nothing of a man.

OTHELLO   Dost thou hear, Iago?
I will be found most cunning in my patience;

---

21 raven . . . house (Allusion to the belief that the raven hovered over a house of sickness or infection, such as one visited by the plague.) **25 abroad** around about **27 voluntary dotage** willing infatuation **28 Convincèd or supplied** seduced or sexually gratified **36 belie** slander **36–37 fulsome** foul **38–39 first . . . to confess** (Othello reverses the proverbial *confess and be hanged*; Cassio is to be given no time to confess before he dies.) **39–41 Nature . . . instruction** i.e., without some foundation in fact, nature would not have dressed herself in such an overwhelming passion that comes over me now and fills my mind with images, or in such a lifelike fantasy as Cassio had in his dream of lying with Desdemona **41 words** mere words

53 lethargy coma. **his** its **58 on great occasion** on a matter of great importance **60 mock me** (Othello takes Iago's question about hurting his head to be a mocking reference to the cuckold's horns.) **64 civil** i.e., dwelling in a city **67 yoked** (1) married (2) put into the yoke of infamy and cuckoldry **68 draw with you** pull as you do, like oxen who are yoked, i.e., share your fate as cuckold **69 unproper** not exclusively their own **70 peculiar** private, their own. **better** i.e., because you know the truth **72 lip** kiss. **secure** free from suspicion **74 what I am** i.e., a cuckold. **she shall be** will happen to her **77 in . . . list** within the bounds of patience **80 shifted him away** used a dodge to get rid of him **81 ecstasy** trance **83 encave** conceal **84 fleers** sneers. **notable** obvious **88 cope** encounter with, have sex with **90 all-in-all in spleen** utterly governed by passionate impulses

But—dost thou hear?—most bloody.
IAGO   That's not amiss;
But yet keep time in all. Will you withdraw?   94
                              [*Othello stands apart.*]
Now will I question Cassio of Bianca,
A huswife that by selling her desires   96
Buys herself bread and clothes. It is a creature
That dotes on Cassio—as 'tis the strumpet's plague
To beguile many and be beguiled by one.
He, when he hears of her, cannot restrain   100
From the excess of laughter. Here he comes.

          Enter Cassio.

As he shall smile, Othello shall go mad;
And his unbookish jealousy must conster   103
Poor Cassio's smiles, gestures, and light behaviors
Quite in the wrong.—How do you now,
      Lieutenant?
CASSIO
The worser that you give me the addition   106
Whose want even kills me.   107
IAGO
Ply Desdemona well and you are sure on 't.
[*Speaking lower.*] Now, if this suit lay in Bianca's
      power,
How quickly should you speed!
CASSIO [*laughing*]   Alas, poor caitiff!   111
OTHELLO [*aside*]   Look how he laughs already!
IAGO
I never knew a woman love man so.
CASSIO
Alas, poor rogue! I think, i' faith, she loves me.
OTHELLO
Now he denies it faintly, and laughs it out.
IAGO
Do you hear, Cassio?
OTHELLO   Now he importunes him
To tell it o'er. Go to! Well said, well said.   117
IAGO
She gives it out that you shall marry her.
Do you intend it?
CASSIO   Ha, ha, ha!
OTHELLO
Do you triumph, Roman? Do you triumph?   121
CASSIO   I marry her? What? A customer? Prithee, bear 122
some charity to my wit; do not think it so unwhole- 123
some. Ha, ha, ha!
OTHELLO   So, so, so, so! They laugh that win.   125
IAGO   Faith, the cry goes that you shall marry her. 126
CASSIO   Prithee, say true.
IAGO   I am a very villain else.   128
OTHELLO   Have you scored me? Well.   129

CASSIO   This is the monkey's own giving out. She is
persuaded I will marry her out of her own love and
flattery, not out of my promise.   132
OTHELLO   Iago beckons me. Now he begins the story. 133
CASSIO   She was here even now; she haunts me in every
place. I was the other day talking on the seabank with 135
certain Venetians, and thither comes the bauble, and, 136
by this hand, she falls me thus about my neck—   137
                              [*He embraces Iago.*]
OTHELLO   Crying, "O dear Cassio!" as it were; his gesture imports it.
CASSIO   So hangs and lolls and weeps upon me, so
shakes and pulls me. Ha, ha, ha!
OTHELLO   Now he tells how she plucked him to my
chamber. O, I see that nose of yours, but not that dog 143
I shall throw it to.   144
CASSIO   Well, I must leave her company.
IAGO   Before me, look where she comes.   146

          Enter Bianca [with Othello's handkerchief].

CASSIO   'Tis such another fitchew! Marry, a perfumed 147
one.—What do you mean by this haunting of me?
BIANCA   Let the devil and his dam haunt you! What did 149
you mean by that same handkerchief you gave me
even now? I was a fine fool to take it. I must take out
the work? A likely piece of work, that you should find 152
it in your chamber and know not who left it there!
This is some minx's token, and I must take out the
work? There; give it your hobbyhorse. [*She gives him 155
the handkerchief.*] Wheresoever you had it, I'll take out
no work on 't.
CASSIO   How now, my sweet Bianca? How now? How
now?
OTHELLO   By heaven, that should be my handkerchief! 159
BIANCA   If you'll come to supper tonight, you may; if
you will not, come when you are next prepared for. 161
                                          Exit.
IAGO   After her, after her.
CASSIO   Faith, I must. She'll rail in the streets else.
IAGO   Will you sup there?
CASSIO   Faith, I intend so.
IAGO   Well, I may chance to see you, for I would very
fain speak with you.
CASSIO   Prithee, come. Will you?
IAGO   Go to. Say no more.   [*Exit Cassio.*] 169
OTHELLO [*advancing*]   How shall I murder him, Iago?
IAGO   Did you perceive how he laughed at his vice?
OTHELLO   O, Iago!
IAGO   And did you see the handkerchief?
OTHELLO   Was that mine?
IAGO   Yours, by this hand. And to see how he prizes

94 keep time keep yourself steady (as in music)   96 huswife hussy
100 restrain refrain   103 unbookish uninstructed.   conster construe
106 addition title   107 Whose want the lack of which   111 caitiff
wretch   117 Go to (An expression of remonstrance.)   Well said well
done   121 Roman (The Romans were noted for their *triumphs* or triumphal processions.)   122 customer i.e., prostitute   122–123 bear
. . . wit be more charitable to my judgment   125 They . . . win i.e.,
they that laugh last laugh best   126 cry rumor   128 I . . . else call
me a complete rogue if I'm not telling the truth   129 scored me
scored off me, beaten me, made up my reckoning, branded me

132 flattery self-flattery, self-deception   133 beckons signals
135 seabank seashore   136 bauble plaything   137 by this hand I
make my vow   143–144 not . . . to (Othello imagines himself cutting off Cassio's nose and throwing it to a dog.)   146 Before me i.e.,
on my soul   147 'Tis . . . fitchew what a polecat she is! Just like all
the others.   fitchew (Polecats were often compared with prostitutes
because of their rank smell and presumed lechery.)   149 dam mother
152 A likely . . . work a fine story   155 hobbyhorse harlot
159 should be must be   161 when . . . for when I'm ready for you
(i.e., never)   169 Go to (An expression of remonstrance.)

the foolish woman your wife! She gave it him, and he hath given it his whore.

OTHELLO   I would have him nine years a-killing. A fine woman! A fair woman! A sweet woman!

IAGO   Nay, you must forget that.

OTHELLO   Ay, let her rot and perish, and be damned tonight, for she shall not live. No, my heart is turned to stone; I strike it, and it hurts my hand. O, the world hath not a sweeter creature! She might lie by an emperor's side and command him tasks.

IAGO   Nay, that's not your way.   186

OTHELLO   Hang her! I do but say what she is. So delicate with her needle! An admirable musician! O, she will sing the savageness out of a bear. Of so high and plenteous wit and invention!   190

IAGO   She's the worse for all this.

OTHELLO   O, a thousand, a thousand times! And then, of so gentle a condition!   193

IAGO   Ay, too gentle.   194

OTHELLO   Nay, that's certain. But yet the pity of it, Iago! O, Iago, the pity of it, Iago!

IAGO   If you are so fond over her iniquity, give her patent to offend, for if it touch not you it comes near nobody.   197

OTHELLO   I will chop her into messes. Cuckold me?   199

IAGO   O, 'tis foul in her.

OTHELLO   With mine officer?

IAGO   That's fouler.

OTHELLO   Get me some poison, Iago, this night. I'll not expostulate with her, lest her body and beauty unprovide my mind again. This night, Iago.   204 205

IAGO   Do it not with poison. Strangle her in her bed, even the bed she hath contaminated.

OTHELLO Good, good! The justice of it pleases. Very good.

IAGO   And for Cassio, let me be his undertaker. You shall hear more by midnight.   209

OTHELLO   Excellent good. [*A trumpet within.*] What trumpet is that same?

IAGO   I warrant, something from Venice.

Enter Lodovico, Desdemona, and attendants.

'Tis Lodovico. This comes from the Duke.
See, your wife's with him.

LODOVICO   God save you, worthy General!

OTHELLO   With all my heart, sir.   215

LODOVICO [*giving him a letter*]
The Duke and the senators of Venice greet you.

OTHELLO   I kiss the instrument of their pleasures.
           [*He opens the letter, and reads.*]

DESDEMONA   And what's the news, good cousin Lodovico?

IAGO   I am very glad to see you, signor.
Welcome to Cyprus.

LODOVICO   I thank you. How does Lieutenant Cassio?

IAGO   Lives, sir.

DESDEMONA   Cousin, there's fall'n between him and my lord
An unkind breach; but you shall make all well.   224

OTHELLO   Are you sure of that?

DESDEMONA   My lord?

OTHELLO [*reads*]   "This fail you not to do, as you will—"

LODOVICO   He did not call; he's busy in the paper.
Is there division twixt my lord and Cassio?

DESDEMONA   A most unhappy one. I would do much
T' atone them, for the love I bear to Cassio.   231

OTHELLO   Fire and brimstone!

DESDEMONA   My lord?

OTHELLO   Are you wise?

DESDEMONA   What, is he angry?

LODOVICO   Maybe the letter moved him;
For, as I think, they do command him home,
Deputing Cassio in his government.   237

DESDEMONA   By my troth, I am glad on 't.   238

OTHELLO   Indeed?

DESDEMONA   My lord?

OTHELLO   I am glad to see you mad.   241

DESDEMONA   Why, sweet Othello—

OTHELLO [*striking her*]   Devil!

DESDEMONA   I have not deserved this.

LODOVICO   My lord, this would not be believed in Venice,
Though I should swear I saw 't. 'Tis very much.   246
Make her amends; she weeps.

OTHELLO   O devil, devil!
If that the earth could teem with woman's tears,   248
Each drop she falls would prove a crocodile.   249
Out of my sight!

DESDEMONA   I will not stay to offend you. [*Going.*]

LODOVICO   Truly, an obedient lady.
I do beseech your lordship, call her back.

OTHELLO   Mistress!

DESDEMONA [*returning*]   My lord?

OTHELLO   What would you with her, sir?   255

LODOVICO   Who, I, my lord?

OTHELLO   Ay, you did wish that I would make her turn.
Sir, she can turn, and turn, and yet go on
And turn again; and she can weep, sir, weep;

---

186 **your way** i.e., the way you should think of her   190 **invention** imagination   193 **gentle a condition** wellborn and well-bred   194 **gentle** generous, yielding (to other men)   197 **fond** foolish. **patent** license   199 **messes** portions of meat, i.e., bits   204–205 **unprovide** weaken, render unfit   209 **be his undertaker** undertake to dispatch him   215 **With all my heart** i.e., I thank you most heartily

224 **unkind** unnatural, contrary to their natures; hurtful   231 **atone** reconcile   237 **government** office   238 **on 't** of it   241 **I am . . . mad** i.e., I am glad to see that you are insane enough to rejoice in Cassio's promotion (? Othello bitterly plays on Desdemona's *I am glad.*)   246 **very much** too much, outrageous   248 **teem** breed, be impregnated   249 **falls** lets fall. **crocodile** (Crocodiles were supposed to weep hypocritical tears for their victims.)   255 **What . . . sir** (Othello implies that Desdemona is pliant and will do a *turn*, lines 257–259, for any man.)

And she's obedient, as you say, obedient,   260
Very obedient.—Proceed you in your tears.—
Concerning this, sir—O well-painted passion!—   262
I am commanded home.—Get you away;
I'll send for you anon.—Sir, I obey the mandate
And will return to Venice.—Hence, avaunt!
                                        [*Exit Desdemona.*]
Cassio shall have my place. And, sir, tonight
I do entreat that we may sup together.
You are welcome, sir, to Cyprus.—Goats and
   monkeys!   *Exit.* 268

LODOVICO
Is this the noble Moor whom our full Senate
Call all in all sufficient? Is this the nature
Whom passion could not shake? Whose solid virtue
The shot of accident nor dart of chance
Could neither graze nor pierce?
IAGO   He is much changed.
LODOVICO
Are his wits safe? Is he not light of brain?
IAGO
He's that he is. I may not breathe my censure   275
What he might be. If what he might he is not,   276
I would to heaven he were!
LODOVICO   What, strike his wife?   277
IAGO
Faith, that was not so well; yet would I knew
That stroke would prove the worst!
LODOVICO   Is it his use?   279
Or did the letters work upon his blood   280
And new-create his fault?
IAGO   Alas, alas!
It is not honesty in me to speak
What I have seen and known. You shall observe
   him,
And his own courses will denote him so   284
That I may save my speech. Do but go after,
And mark how he continues.
LODOVICO
I am sorry that I am deceived in him.   *Exeunt.*

❖

4.2   *Enter Othello and Emilia.*

OTHELLO   You have seen nothing then?
EMILIA
Nor ever heard, nor ever did suspect.
OTHELLO
Yes, you have seen Cassio and she together.
EMILIA
But then I saw no harm, and then I heard
Each syllable that breath made up between them.

OTHELLO   What, did they never whisper?
EMILIA   Never, my lord.
OTHELLO   Nor send you out o' the way?
EMILIA   Never.
OTHELLO
To fetch her fan, her gloves, her mask, nor nothing?
EMILIA   Never, my lord.
OTHELLO   That's strange.
EMILIA
I durst, my lord, to wager she is honest,
Lay down my soul at stake. If you think other,   14
Remove your thought; it doth abuse your bosom.   15
If any wretch have put this in your head,
Let heaven requite it with the serpent's curse!   17
For if she be not honest, chaste, and true,
There's no man happy; the purest of their wives
Is foul as slander.
OTHELLO   Bid her come hither. Go.
                                   Exit Emilia.
She says enough; yet she's a simple bawd   21
That cannot say as much. This is a subtle whore,   22
A closet lock and key of villainous secrets.   23
And yet she'll kneel and pray; I have seen her do 't.

   Enter Desdemona and Emilia.

DESDEMONA   My lord, what is your will?
OTHELLO   Pray you, chuck, come hither.
DESDEMONA
What is your pleasure?
OTHELLO   Let me see your eyes.
Look in my face.
DESDEMONA   What horrible fancy's this?
OTHELLO [*to Emilia*]   Some of your function, mistress. 29
Leave procreants alone and shut the door;   30
Cough or cry "hem" if anybody come.
Your mystery, your mystery! Nay, dispatch.   32
                                   Exit Emilia.
DESDEMONA [*kneeling*]
Upon my knees, what doth your speech import?
I understand a fury in your words,
But not the words.
OTHELLO
Why, what art thou?
DESDEMONA   Your wife, my lord, your true
And loyal wife.
OTHELLO   Come, swear it, damn thyself,
Lest, being like one of heaven, the devils themselves   38
Should fear to seize thee. Therefore be double
   damned:
Swear thou art honest.
DESDEMONA   Heaven doth truly know it.

260 obedient (With much the same sexual connotation as *turn* in lines 257–259.)   **262 passion** i.e., grief   **268 Goats and monkeys** (See 3.3.419.)   **275–277 I may . . . were** i.e., I dare not venture an opinion as to whether he's of unsound mind, as you suggest, but, if he isn't, then it might be better to wish he were in fact insane, since only that could excuse his wild behavior   **279 use** custom   **280 blood** passions   **284 courses will denote** actions will reveal   **4.2. Location: The citadel.**

14 at stake as the wager   **15 abuse your bosom** deceive you   **17 the serpent's curse** the curse pronounced by God on the serpent for deceiving Eve, just as some man has done to Othello and Desdemona. (See Genesis 3:14.)   **21–22 she's . . . much** i.e., any procuress or go-between who couldn't make up as plausible a story as Emilia's would have to be pretty stupid   **22 This** i.e., Desdemona   **23 closet lock and key** i.e., concealer   **29 Some . . . function** i.e., practice your chosen profession, that of bawd (by guarding the door)   **30 procreants** mating couples   **32 mystery** trade, occupation   **38 being . . . heaven** looking like an angel

OTHELLO
Heaven truly knows that thou art false as hell.
DESDEMONA
To whom, my lord? With whom? How am I false?
OTHELLO [weeping]
Ah, Desdemon! Away, away, away!
DESDEMONA
Alas the heavy day! Why do you weep?
Am I the motive of these tears, my lord?   45
If haply you my father do suspect
An instrument of this your calling back,
Lay not your blame on me. If you have lost him,
I have lost him too.
OTHELLO   Had it pleased heaven
To try me with affliction, had they rained   50
All kinds of sores and shames on my bare head,
Steeped me in poverty to the very lips,
Given to captivity me and my utmost hopes,
I should have found in some place of my soul
A drop of patience. But, alas, to make me
A fixèd figure for the time of scorn   56
To point his slow and moving finger at!   57
Yet could I bear that too, well, very well.
But there where I have garnered up my heart,   59
Where either I must live or bear no life,
The fountain from the which my current runs   61
Or else dries up—to be discarded thence!
Or keep it as a cistern for foul toads   63
To knot and gender in! Turn thy complexion there, 64
Patience, thou young and rose-lipped cherubin—   65
Ay, there look grim as hell!   66
DESDEMONA
I hope my noble lord esteems me honest.   67
OTHELLO
O, ay, as summer flies are in the shambles,   68
That quicken even with blowing. O thou weed,   69
Who art so lovely fair and smell'st so sweet
That the sense aches at thee, would thou hadst ne'er
    been born!
DESDEMONA
Alas, what ignorant sin have I committed?   72
OTHELLO
Was this fair paper, this most goodly book,
Made to write "whore" upon? What committed?
Committed? O thou public commoner!   75
I should make very forges of my cheeks,
That would to cinders burn up modesty,
Did I but speak thy deeds. What committed?

Heaven stops the nose at it and the moon winks;   79
The bawdy wind, that kisses all it meets,   80
Is hushed within the hollow mine of earth   81
And will not hear 't. What committed?
Impudent strumpet!
DESDEMONA   By heaven, you do me wrong.
OTHELLO
Are not you a strumpet?
DESDEMONA   No, as I am a Christian.
If to preserve this vessel for my lord   86
From any other foul unlawful touch
Be not to be a strumpet, I am none.
OTHELLO   What, not a whore?
DESDEMONA   No, as I shall be saved.
OTHELLO   Is 't possible?
DESDEMONA
O, heaven forgive us!
OTHELLO   I cry you mercy, then.   92
I took you for that cunning whore of Venice
That married with Othello. [Calling out.] You,
    mistress,
That have the office opposite to Saint Peter
And keep the gate of hell!

        Enter Emilia.

                              You, you, ay, you!
We have done our course. There's money for your
    pains.   [He gives money.] 97
I pray you, turn the key and keep our counsel. *Exit.*
EMILIA
Alas, what does this gentleman conceive?   99
How do you, madam? How do you, my good lady?
DESDEMONA   Faith, half asleep.   101
EMILIA
Good madam, what's the matter with my lord?
DESDEMONA   With who?
EMILIA   Why, with my lord, madam.
DESDEMONA
Who is thy lord?
EMILIA   He that is yours, sweet lady.
DESDEMONA
I have none. Do not talk to me, Emilia.
I cannot weep, nor answers have I none
But what should go by water. Prithee, tonight   108
Lay on my bed my wedding sheets, remember;
And call thy husband hither.
EMILIA   Here's a change indeed!   *Exit.*
DESDEMONA
'Tis meet I should be used so, very meet.   112
How have I been behaved, that he might stick   113
The small'st opinion on my least misuse?   114

        Enter Iago and Emilia.

45 motive cause   **50 they** i.e., heavenly powers   **56 time of scorn** i.e., scornful world   **57 his** its.   **slow and moving finger** i.e., hour hand of the clock, moving so slowly it seems hardly to move at all. (Othello envisages himself as being eternally pointed at by the scornful world as the numbers on a clock are pointed at by the hour hand.)   **59 garnered** stored   **61 fountain** spring   **63 cistern** cesspool   **64 knot** couple.   **gender** engender.   **Turn . . . there** change your color, grow pale, at such a sight   **65–66 Patience . . . hell** (Even Patience, that rose-lipped cherub, will look grim and pale at this spectacle.)   **67 honest** chaste   **68 shambles** slaughterhouse   **69 quicken** come to life.   **with blowing** i.e., with the puffing up of something rotten in which maggots are breeding   **72 ignorant sin** sin in ignorance   **75 commoner** prostitute

79 winks closes her eyes. (The moon symbolizes chastity.)   **80 bawdy** kissing one and all   **81 mine** cave (where the winds were thought to dwell)   **86 vessel** body   **92 cry you mercy** beg your pardon   **97 course** business (with an indecent suggestion of "trick," turn at sex)   **99 conceive** suppose, think   **101 half asleep** i.e., dazed   **108 go by water** be expressed by tears   **112 meet** fitting   **113 stick** attach   **114 opinion** censure.   **least misuse** slightest misconduct

IAGO
What is your pleasure, madam? How is 't with you?
DESDEMONA
I cannot tell. Those that do teach young babes
Do it with gentle means and easy tasks.
He might have chid me so, for, in good faith,
I am a child to chiding.
IAGO   What is the matter, lady?
EMILIA
Alas, Iago, my lord hath so bewhored her,
Thrown such despite and heavy terms upon her,
That true hearts cannot bear it.
DESDEMONA   Am I that name, Iago?
IAGO   What name, fair lady?
DESDEMONA
Such as she said my lord did say I was.
EMILIA
He called her whore. A beggar in his drink
Could not have laid such terms upon his callet.   128
IAGO   Why did he so?
DESDEMONA [weeping]
I do not know. I am sure I am none such.
IAGO   Do not weep, do not weep. Alas the day!
EMILIA
Hath she forsook so many noble matches,
Her father and her country and her friends,
To be called whore? Would it not make one weep?
DESDEMONA
It is my wretched fortune.
IAGO   Beshrew him for 't!   135
How comes this trick upon him?
DESDEMONA   Nay, heaven doth know. 136
EMILIA
I will be hanged if some eternal villain,   137
Some busy and insinuating rogue,   138
Some cogging, cozening slave, to get some office,   139
Have not devised this slander. I will be hanged else.
IAGO
Fie, there is no such man. It is impossible.
DESDEMONA
If any such there be, heaven pardon him!
EMILIA
A halter pardon him! And hell gnaw his bones!   143
Why should he call her whore? Who keeps her
    company?
What place? What time? What form? What
    likelihood?   145
The Moor's abused by some most villainous knave,
Some base notorious knave, some scurvy fellow.
O heaven, that such companions thou'dst unfold,   148
And put in every honest hand a whip
To lash the rascals naked through the world
Even from the east to th' west!
IAGO   Speak within door.   151

EMILIA
O, fie upon them! Some such squire he was   152
That turned your wit the seamy side without   153
And made you to suspect me with the Moor.
IAGO
You are a fool. Go to.
DESDEMONA   Alas, Iago,   155
What shall I do to win my lord again?
Good friend, go to him; for, by this light of heaven,
I know not how I lost him. Here I kneel. [She kneels.]
If e'er my will did trespass 'gainst his love,
Either in discourse of thought or actual deed,   160
Or that mine eyes, mine ears, or any sense   161
Delighted them in any other form;   162
Or that I do not yet, and ever did,   163
And ever will—though he do shake me off
To beggarly divorcement—love him dearly,
Comfort forswear me! Unkindness may do much,   166
And his unkindness may defeat my life,   167
But never taint my love. I cannot say "whore."
It does abhor me now I speak the word;   169
To do the act that might the addition earn   170
Not the world's mass of vanity could make me.   171
                                          [She rises.]
IAGO
I pray you, be content. 'Tis but his humor.   172
The business of the state does him offense,
And he does chide with you.
DESDEMONA   If 'twere no other—
IAGO   It is but so, I warrant.   [Trumpets within.]
Hark, how these instruments summon you to
    supper!
The messengers of Venice stays the meat.   178
Go in, and weep not. All things shall be well.
                         Exeunt Desdemona and Emilia.

            Enter Roderigo.

How now, Roderigo?
RODERIGO I do not find that thou deal'st justly with me.
IAGO   What in the contrary?
RODERIGO Every day thou daff'st me with some de-   183
vice, Iago, and rather, as it seems to me now, keep'st 184
from me all conveniency than suppliest me with the 185
least advantage of hope. I will indeed no longer   186
endure it, nor am I yet persuaded to put up in peace 187
what already I have foolishly suffered.
IAGO   Will you hear me, Roderigo?
RODERIGO Faith, I have heard too much, for your words
and performances are no kin together.
IAGO   You charge me most unjustly.
RODERIGO With naught but truth. I have wasted myself

---

128 callet whore 135 Beshrew curse 136 trick strange behavior,
delusion 137 eternal inveterate 138 insinuating ingratiating, fawning, wheedling 139 cogging cheating. cozening defrauding
143 halter hangman's noose 145 form appearance, circumstance
148 that would that. companions fellows. unfold expose
151 within door i.e., not so loud

152 squire fellow 153 seamy side without wrong side out 155 Go
to i.e., that's enough 160 discourse of thought process of thinking
161 that if. (Also in line 163.) 162 Delighted them took delight
163 yet still 166 Comfort forswear may heavenly comfort forsake
167 defeat destroy 169 abhor (1) fill me with abhorrence (2) make
me whorelike 170 addition title 171 vanity showy splendor
172 humor mood 178 stays the meat are waiting to dine 183 thou
daff'st me you put me off 183–184 device excuse, trick 185 conveniency advantage, opportunity 186 advantage increase 187 put
up submit to, tolerate

out of my means. The jewels you have had from me to
deliver Desdemona would half have corrupted a vo- 195
tarist. You have told me she hath received them and 196
returned me expectations and comforts of sudden re- 197
spect and acquaintance, but I find none.   198

IAGO   Well, go to, very well.

RODERIGO   "Very well"! "Go to"! I cannot go to, man, 200
nor 'tis not very well. By this hand, I think it is scurvy,
and begin to find myself fopped in it.   202

IAGO   Very well.

RODERIGO   I tell you 'tis not very well. I will make myself 204
known to Desdemona. If she will return me my jewels,
I will give over my suit and repent my unlawful solicitation; if not, assure yourself I will seek satisfaction 207
of you.

IAGO   You have said now?   209

RODERIGO   Ay, and said nothing but what I protest
intendment of doing.   211

IAGO   Why, now I see there's mettle in thee, and even
from this instant do build on thee a better opinion
than ever before. Give me thy hand, Roderigo. Thou
hast taken against me a most just exception; but yet I
protest I have dealt most directly in thy affair.

RODERIGO   It hath not appeared.

IAGO   I grant indeed it hath not appeared, and your
suspicion is not without wit and judgment. But,
Roderigo, if thou hast that in thee indeed which I have
greater reason to believe now than ever—I mean
purpose, courage, and valor—this night show it. If
thou the next night following enjoy not Desdemona,
take me from this world with treachery and devise
engines for my life.   225

RODERIGO   Well, what is it? Is it within reason and
compass?

IAGO   Sir, there is especial commission come from
Venice to depute Cassio in Othello's place.

RODERIGO   Is that true? Why, then Othello and Desdemona return again to Venice.

IAGO   O, no; he goes into Mauritania and takes away
with him the fair Desdemona, unless his abode be
lingered here by some accident; wherein none can be
so determinate as the removing of Cassio.   235

RODERIGO   How do you mean, removing of him?

IAGO   Why, by making him uncapable of Othello's
place—knocking out his brains.

RODERIGO   And that you would have me to do?

IAGO   Ay, if you dare do yourself a profit and a right.
He sups tonight with a harlotry, and thither will I go to 241
him. He knows not yet of his honorable fortune. If
you will watch his going thence, which I will fashion
to fall out between twelve and one, you may take him 244

at your pleasure. I will be near to second your attempt,
and he shall fall between us. Come, stand not amazed
at it, but go along with me. I will show you such a
necessity in his death that you shall think yourself
bound to put it on him. It is now high suppertime, 249
and the night grows to waste. About it.   250

RODERIGO   I will hear further reason for this.

IAGO   And you shall be satisfied.   *Exeunt.*

❖

4.3   *Enter Othello, Lodovico, Desdemona, Emilia, and
attendants.*

LODOVICO
I do beseech you, sir, trouble yourself no further.

OTHELLO
O, pardon me; 'twill do me good to walk.

LODOVICO
Madam, good night. I humbly thank your ladyship.

DESDEMONA
Your honor is most welcome.

OTHELLO   Will you walk, sir?
O, Desdemona!

DESDEMONA   My lord?

OTHELLO   Get you to bed on th' instant. I will be returned forthwith. Dismiss your attendant there. Look
't be done.

DESDEMONA   I will, my lord.
                Exit [Othello, with Lodovico and attendants].

EMILIA   How goes it now? He looks gentler than he did.

DESDEMONA
He says he will return incontinent,   12
And hath commanded me to go to bed,
And bid me to dismiss you.

EMILIA   Dismiss me?

DESDEMONA
It was his bidding. Therefore, good Emilia,
Give me my nightly wearing, and adieu.
We must not now displease him.

EMILIA   I would you had never seen him!

DESDEMONA
So would not I. My love doth so approve him
That even his stubbornness, his checks, his
    frowns—   21
Prithee, unpin me—have grace and favor in them.
            [Emilia prepares Desdemona for bed.]

EMILIA   I have laid those sheets you bade me on the
bed.

DESDEMONA
All's one. Good faith, how foolish are our minds!   25
If I do die before thee, prithee shroud me
In one of these same sheets.

EMILIA   Come, come, you talk.   27

195 deliver deliver to   **195–196 votarist** nun   **197–198 sudden respect** immediate consideration   **200 I cannot go to** (Roderigo
changes Iago's *go to,* an expression urging patience, to *I cannot go to,*
"I have no opportunity for success in wooing.")   **202 fopped** fooled,
duped   **204 not very well** (Roderigo changes Iago's *very well,* "all
right, then," to *not very well,* "not at all good.")   **207 satisfaction** repayment. (The term normally means settling of accounts in a duel.)
209 You . . . now have you finished?   **211 intendment** intention
225 engines for plots against   **235 determinate** conclusive   **241 harlotry** slut   **244 fall out** occur

249 high fully   **250 grows to waste** wastes away
4.3. Location: The citadel.
12 incontinent immediately   **21 stubbornness** roughness.   **checks**
rebukes   **25 All's one** all right. It doesn't really matter   **27 talk** i.e.,
prattle

DESDEMONA
   My mother had a maid called Barbary.
   She was in love, and he she loved proved mad   29
   And did forsake her. She had a song of "Willow."
   An old thing 'twas, but it expressed her fortune,
   And she died singing it. That song tonight
   Will not go from my mind; I have much to do   33
   But to go hang my head all at one side   34
   And sing it like poor Barbary. Prithee, dispatch.

EMILIA   Shall I go fetch your nightgown?   36

DESDEMONA   No, unpin me here.
   This Lodovico is a proper man.   38

EMILIA   A very handsome man.

DESDEMONA   He speaks well.

EMILIA   I know a lady in Venice would have walked
barefoot to Palestine for a touch of his nether lip.

DESDEMONA [singing]
     "The poor soul sat sighing by a sycamore tree,
       Sing all a green willow;   44
     Her hand on her bosom, her head on her knee,
       Sing willow, willow, willow.
     The fresh streams ran by her and murmured
       her moans;
       Sing willow, willow, willow;
     Her salt tears fell from her, and softened the
       stones—"
   Lay by these.
   [Singing.] "Sing willow, willow, willow—"
   Prithee, hie thee. He'll come anon.   52
   [Singing.] "Sing all a green willow must be my
       garland.
     Let nobody blame him; his scorn I approve—"
   Nay, that's not next.—Hark! Who is 't that knocks?

EMILIA   It's the wind.

DESDEMONA [singing]
     "I called my love false love; but what said he
       then?
       Sing willow, willow, willow;
     If I court more women, you'll couch with more
       men."
   So, get thee gone. Good night. Mine eyes do itch;
   Doth that bode weeping?

EMILIA   'Tis neither here nor there.

DESDEMONA
   I have heard it said so. O, these men, these men!
   Dost thou in conscience think—tell me, Emilia—
   That there be women do abuse their husbands   64
   In such gross kind?

EMILIA   There be some such, no question.

DESDEMONA
   Wouldst thou do such a deed for all the world?

EMILIA
   Why, would not you?

DESDEMONA   No, by this heavenly light!

EMILIA
   Nor I neither by this heavenly light;
   I might do 't as well i' the dark.

DESDEMONA
   Wouldst thou do such a deed for all the world?

EMILIA
   The world's a huge thing. It is a great price
   For a small vice.

DESDEMONA
   Good troth, I think thou wouldst not.

EMILIA   By my troth, I think I should, and undo 't when
I had done. Marry, I would not do such a thing for a
joint ring, nor for measures of lawn, nor for gowns,   76
petticoats, nor caps, nor any petty exhibition. But for   77
all the whole world! Uds pity, who would not make   78
her husband a cuckold to make him a monarch? I
should venture purgatory for 't.

DESDEMONA
   Beshrew me if I would do such a wrong
   For the whole world.

EMILIA   Why, the wrong is but a wrong i' the world, and
having the world for your labor, 'tis a wrong in your
own world, and you might quickly make it right.

DESDEMONA
   I do not think there is any such woman.

EMILIA   Yes, a dozen, and as many
   To th' vantage as would store the world they played
     for.   88
   But I do think it is their husbands' faults
   If wives do fall. Say that they slack their duties   90
   And pour our treasures into foreign laps,   91
   Or else break out in peevish jealousies,
   Throwing restraint upon us? Or say they strike us,   93
   Or scant our former having in despite?   94
   Why, we have galls, and though we have some
     grace,   95
   Yet have we some revenge. Let husbands know
   Their wives have sense like them. They see, and
     smell,   97
   And have their palates both for sweet and sour,
   As husbands have. What is it that they do
   When they change us for others? Is it sport?   100
   I think it is. And doth affection breed it?   101
   I think it doth. Is 't frailty that thus errs?
   It is so, too. And have not we affections,
   Desires for sport, and frailty, as men have?
   Then let them use us well; else let them know,
   The ills we do, their ills instruct us so.

DESDEMONA
   Good night, good night. God me such uses send   107

---

29 **mad** wild, i.e., faithless 33–34 **I . . . hang** I can scarcely keep myself from hanging 36 **nightgown** dressing gown 38 **proper** handsome 44 **willow** (A conventional emblem of disappointed love.) 52 **hie thee** hurry. **anon** right away 64 **abuse** deceive

76 **joint ring** a ring made in separate halves. **lawn** fine linen 77 **exhibition** gift 78 **Uds** God's 88 **To th' vantage** in addition, to boot. **store** populate. **played** (1) gambled (2) sported sexually 90 **duties** marital duties 91 **pour . . . laps** i.e., are unfaithful, give what is rightfully ours (semen) to other women 93 **Throwing . . . us** i.e., jealously restricting our freedom to see other men 94 **scant . . . despite** reduce our allowance to spite us 95 **have galls** i.e., are capable of resenting injury and insult 97 **sense** physical sense 100 **sport** sexual pastime 101 **affection** passion 107 **uses** habit, practice

Not to pick bad from bad, but by bad mend!   108
                                        Exeunt.

❖

5.1   *Enter Iago and Roderigo.*

IAGO
Here stand behind this bulk. Straight will he come.   1
Wear thy good rapier bare, and put it home.   2
Quick, quick! Fear nothing. I'll be at thy elbow.
It makes us or it mars us. Think on that,
And fix most firm thy resolution.

RODERIGO
Be near at hand. I may miscarry in 't.

IAGO
Here, at thy hand. Be bold, and take thy stand.
          [Iago stands aside. Roderigo conceals himself.]

RODERIGO
I have no great devotion to the deed;
And yet he hath given me satisfying reasons.
'Tis but a man gone. Forth, my sword! He dies.
                              [He draws.]

IAGO
I have rubbed this young quat almost to the sense,   11
And he grows angry. Now, whether he kill Cassio
Or Cassio him, or each do kill the other,
Every way makes my gain. Live Roderigo,   14
He calls me to a restitution large
Of gold and jewels that I bobbed from him   16
As gifts to Desdemona.
It must not be. If Cassio do remain,
He hath a daily beauty in his life
That makes me ugly; and besides, the Moor
May unfold me to him; there stand I in much peril.   21
No, he must die. Be 't so. I hear him coming.

          Enter Cassio.

RODERIGO *[coming forth]*
I know his gait, 'tis he.—Villain, thou diest!
                              [He attacks Cassio.]

CASSIO
That thrust had been mine enemy indeed,
But that my coat is better than thou know'st.   25
I will make proof of thine.
          [He draws, and wounds Roderigo.]

RODERIGO   O, I am slain!   *[He falls.]* 26

          [Iago, from behind, wounds Cassio
          in the leg, and exit.]

CASSIO
I am maimed forever. Help, ho! Murder! Murder!

          Enter Othello.

OTHELLO
The voice of Cassio! Iago keeps his word.
RODERIGO   O, villain that I am!
OTHELLO   It is even so.
CASSIO   O, help, ho! Light! A surgeon!
OTHELLO
'Tis he. O brave Iago, honest and just,
That hast such noble sense of thy friend's wrong!
Thou teachest me. Minion, your dear lies dead,   34
And your unblest fate hies. Strumpet, I come.   35
Forth of my heart those charms, thine eyes, are
   blotted;   36
Thy bed, lust-stained, shall with lust's blood be
   spotted.   *Exit Othello.*

          Enter Lodovico and Gratiano.

CASSIO
What ho! No watch? No passage? Murder! Murder!   38
GRATIANO
'Tis some mischance. The voice is very direful.
CASSIO   O, help!
LODOVICO   Hark!
RODERIGO   O wretched villain!
LODOVICO
Two or three groan. 'Tis heavy night;   43
These may be counterfeits. Let's think 't unsafe
To come in to the cry without more help.   45
          [They remain near the entrance.]

RODERIGO
Nobody come? Then shall I bleed to death.

          Enter Iago [in his shirtsleeves, with a light].

LODOVICO   Hark!
GRATIANO
Here's one comes in his shirt, with light and
   weapons.
IAGO
Who's there? Whose noise is this that cries on
   murder?   49
LODOVICO
We do not know.
IAGO   Did not you hear a cry?
CASSIO
Here, here! For heaven's sake, help me!
IAGO   What's the matter?
          [He moves toward Cassio.]

GRATIANO *[to Lodovico]*
This is Othello's ancient, as I take it.
LODOVICO *[to Gratiano]*
The same indeed, a very valiant fellow.

---

108 Not . . . mend i.e., not to learn bad conduct from others' badness (as Emilia has suggested women learn from men), but to mend my ways by perceiving what badness is, making spiritual benefit out of evil and adversity
5.1. Location: A street in Cyprus.
1 bulk framework projecting from the front of a shop   **2 bare** unsheathed   **11 quat** pimple, pustule.   **to the sense** to the quick
14 Live Roderigo if Roderigo lives   **16 bobbed** swindled   **21 unfold** expose   **25 coat** (Possibly a garment of mail under the outer clothing, or simply a tougher coat than Roderigo expected.)   **26 proof** a test

34 Minion hussy (i.e., Desdemona)   **35 hies** hastens on   **36 Forth of** from out   **38 passage** people passing by   **43 heavy** thick, dark   **45 come in to** approach   **49 cries on** cries out

IAGO [*to Cassio*]
What are you here that cry so grievously?   54

CASSIO
Iago? O, I am spoiled, undone by villains!   55
Give me some help.

IAGO
O me, Lieutenant! What villains have done this?

CASSIO
I think that one of them is hereabout,
And cannot make away.

IAGO   O treacherous villains!   59
[*To Lodovico and Gratiano.*] What are you there? Come
in, and give some help.   [*They advance.*]

RODERIGO   O, help me there!

CASSIO
That's one of them.

IAGO   O murderous slave! O villain!
[*He stabs Roderigo.*]

RODERIGO
O damned Iago! O inhuman dog!

IAGO
Kill men i' the dark?—Where be these bloody
thieves?—
How silent is this town!—Ho! Murder, murder!—
[*To Lodovico and Gratiano.*] What may you be? Are
you of good or evil?

LODOVICO   As you shall prove us, praise us.   67

IAGO   Signor Lodovico?

LODOVICO   He, sir.

IAGO
I cry you mercy. Here's Cassio hurt by villains.   70

GRATIANO   Cassio?

IAGO   How is 't, brother?

CASSIO   My leg is cut in two.

IAGO   Marry, heaven forbid!
Light, gentlemen! I'll bind it with my shirt.
[*He hands them the light, and tends to Cassio's
wound.*]

Enter Bianca.

BIANCA
What is the matter, ho? Who is 't that cried?

IAGO   Who is 't that cried?

BIANCA   O my dear Cassio!
My sweet Cassio! O Cassio, Cassio, Cassio!

IAGO
O notable strumpet! Cassio, may you suspect
Who they should be that have thus mangled you?

CASSIO   No.

GRATIANO
I am sorry to find you thus. I have been to seek you.

IAGO
Lend me a garter. [*He applies a tourniquet.*] So.—O,
for a chair,   83
To bear him easily hence!

BIANCA
Alas, he faints! O Cassio, Cassio, Cassio!

IAGO
Gentlemen all, I do suspect this trash
To be a party in this injury.—
Patience awhile, good Cassio.—Come, come;
Lend me a light. [*He shines the light on Roderigo.*]
Know we this face or no?
Alas, my friend and my dear countryman
Roderigo! No.—Yes, sure.—O heaven! Roderigo!

GRATIANO   What, of Venice?

IAGO   Even he, sir. Did you know him?

GRATIANO   Know him? Ay.

IAGO
Signor Gratiano? I cry your gentle pardon.   95
These bloody accidents must excuse my manners   96
That so neglected you.

GRATIANO   I am glad to see you.

IAGO
How do you, Cassio? O, a chair, a chair!

GRATIANO   Roderigo!

IAGO
He, he, 'tis he. [*A litter is brought in.*] O, that's well
said; the chair.   100
Some good man bear him carefully from hence;
I'll fetch the General's surgeon. [*To Bianca.*] For you,
mistress,
Save you your labor.—He that lies slain here,
Cassio,   103
Was my dear friend. What malice was between you?   104

CASSIO
None in the world, nor do I know the man.

IAGO [*to Bianca*]
What, look you pale?—O, bear him out o' th' air.   106
[*Cassio and Roderigo are borne off.*]
Stay you, good gentlemen.—Look you pale,
mistress?—   107
Do you perceive the gastness of her eye?—   108
Nay, if you stare, we shall hear more anon.—   109
Behold her well; I pray you, look upon her.
Do you see, gentlemen? Nay, guiltiness
Will speak, though tongues were out of use.

[*Enter Emilia.*]

EMILIA
'Las, what's the matter? What's the matter, husand?

IAGO
Cassio hath here been set on in the dark
By Roderigo and fellows that are scaped.
He's almost slain, and Roderigo dead.

EMILIA
Alas, good gentleman! Alas, good Cassio!

IAGO
This is the fruits of whoring. Prithee, Emilia,
Go know of Cassio where he supped tonight.   119

54 What who (also at lines 60 and 66) **55 spoiled** ruined, done for
59 make get **67 praise** appraise **70 I cry you mercy** I beg your pardon **83 chair** litter

95 gentle noble **96 accidents** sudden events **100 well said** well done **103 Save . . . labor** i.e., never you mind tending Cassio **104 malice** enmity **106 bear . . . air** (Fresh air was thought to be dangerous for a wound.) **107 Stay you** (Lodovico and Gratiano are evidently about to leave.) **108 gastness** terror **109 stare** (Iago pretends to interpret Bianca's wild looks as an involuntary confession of guilt.) **119 know** learn

[*To Bianca.*] What, do you shake at that?

BIANCA
He supped at my house, but I therefore shake not.

IAGO
O, did he so? I charge you go with me.

EMILIA   O, fie upon thee, strumpet!

BIANCA
I am no strumpet, but of life as honest   124
As you that thus abuse me.

EMILIA   As I? Faugh! Fie upon thee!

IAGO
Kind gentlemen, let's go see poor Cassio dressed.—   127
Come, mistress, you must tell 's another tale.
Emilia, run you to the citadel
And tell my lord and lady what hath happened.—
Will you go on afore? [*Aside.*] This is the night
That either makes me or fordoes me quite.   *Exeunt.* 132

❖

5.2   *Enter Othello [with a light], and Desdemona in her bed.*

OTHELLO
It is the cause, it is the cause, my soul.
Let me not name it to you, you chaste stars!   1
It is the cause. Yet I'll not shed her blood,
Nor scar that whiter skin of hers than snow,
And smooth as monumental alabaster.   5
Yet she must die, else she'll betray more men.
Put out the light, and then put out the light.   7
If I quench thee, thou flaming minister,   8
I can again thy former light restore,
Should I repent me; but once put out thy light,   10
Thou cunning'st pattern of excelling nature,   11
I know not where is that Promethean heat   12
That can thy light relume. When I have plucked thy
    rose,   13
I cannot give it vital growth again;
It needs must wither. I'll smell thee on the tree.
            [*He kisses her.*]
O balmy breath, that dost almost persuade
Justice to break her sword! One more, one more.
Be thus when thou art dead, and I will kill thee,
And love thee after. One more, and that's the last.
            [*He kisses her.*]
So sweet was ne'er so fatal. I must weep,
But they are cruel tears. This sorrow's heavenly;   21

It strikes where it doth love. She wakes.   22

DESDEMONA   Who's there? Othello?

OTHELLO   Ay, Desdemona.

DESDEMONA   Will you come to bed, my lord?

OTHELLO   Have you prayed tonight, Desdemon?

DESDEMONA   Ay, my lord.

OTHELLO
If you bethink yourself of any crime   28
Unreconciled as yet to heaven and grace,
Solicit for it straight.   30

DESDEMONA
Alack, my lord, what may you mean by that?

OTHELLO
Well, do it, and be brief. I will walk by.
I would not kill thy unprepared spirit.
No, heaven forfend! I would not kill thy soul.   34

DESDEMONA
Talk you of killing?

OTHELLO   Ay, I do.

DESDEMONA   Then heaven
Have mercy on me!

OTHELLO   Amen, with all my heart!

DESDEMONA
If you say so, I hope you will not kill me.

OTHELLO   Humh!

DESDEMONA
And yet I fear you; for you're fatal then
When your eyes roll so. Why I should fear I know
    not,
Since guiltiness I know not; but yet I feel I fear.

OTHELLO
Think on thy sins.

DESDEMONA   They are loves I bear to you.   42

OTHELLO   Ay, and for that thou diest.

DESDEMONA
That death's unnatural that kills for loving.
Alas, why gnaw you so your nether lip?
Some bloody passion shakes your very frame.
These are portents; but yet I hope, I hope,
They do not point on me.   48

OTHELLO   Peace, and be still!

DESDEMONA   I will so. What's the matter?

OTHELLO
That handkerchief which I so loved and gave thee
Thou gav'st to Cassio.

DESDEMONA   No, by my life and soul!
Send for the man and ask him.

OTHELLO
Sweet soul, take heed, take heed of perjury.
Thou art on thy deathbed.

DESDEMONA
Ay, but not yet to die.

OTHELLO   Yes, presently.   56
Therefore confess thee freely of thy sin;

---

124 **honest** chaste 127 **Cassio dressed** Cassio's wounds dressed
132 **fordoes** undoes, ruins
5.2. Location: A bedchamber in the citadel.
s.d. in her bed (Either the curtains are drawn back to reveal the bed in a recessed area backstage, or the bed is "thrust out" onstage as the scene begins.) 1 **cause** i.e., cause of justice, the offense itself, which Othello must correct as an agent of justice 5 **monumental** i.e., used in making tombs and funeral monuments 7 **the light . . . light** the torch or lamp . . . Desdemona's life 8 **flaming minister** torch or lamp that serves me 10 **repent me** change my mind 11 **Thou . . . pattern** you skillfully wrought perfect example 12 **Promethean heat** divine fire. (Alluding to the theft of fire from heaven by Prometheus.) 13 **relume** rekindle 21 **cruel** unrelenting

22 **It . . . love** (Compare Hebrews 12:6: "For whom the Lord loveth he chasteneth.") 28 **crime** sin 30 **Solicit** petition, pray. **straight** immediately 34 **forfend** forbid 42 **They are . . . you** i.e., if I sinned, it was in loving you more than my father or more than God 48 **point on** point at, predict what is to happen to 56 **presently** immediately

For to deny each article with oath
Cannot remove nor choke the strong conception   59
That I do groan withal. Thou art to die.   60

DESDEMONA
Then Lord have mercy on me!

OTHELLO   I say, amen.

DESDEMONA
And have you mercy too! I never did
Offend you in my life; never loved Cassio   63
But with such general warranty of heaven   64
As I might love. I never gave him token.

OTHELLO
By heaven, I saw my handkerchief in 's hand.
O perjured woman! Thou dost stone my heart,   67
And makes me call what I intend to do
A murder, which I thought a sacrifice.
I saw the handkerchief.

DESDEMONA   He found it, then.
I never gave it him. Send for him hither;
Let him confess a truth.

OTHELLO   He hath confessed.

DESDEMONA   What, my lord?

OTHELLO
That he hath used thee.

DESDEMONA   How? Unlawfully?

OTHELLO   Ay.

DESDEMONA
He will not say so.

OTHELLO   No, his mouth is stopped;
Honest Iago hath ta'en order for 't.   76

DESDEMONA
O, my fear interprets. What, is he dead?

OTHELLO
Had all his hairs been lives, my great revenge
Had stomach for them all.

DESDEMONA
Alas, he is betrayed and I undone!   [She weeps.]

OTHELLO
Out, strumpet! Weep'st thou for him to my face?

DESDEMONA
O, banish me, my lord, but kill me not!

OTHELLO   Down, strumpet!

DESDEMONA
Kill me tomorrow; let me live tonight!

OTHELLO   Nay, if you strive—

DESDEMONA
But half an hour!

OTHELLO   Being done, there is no pause.   86

DESDEMONA
But while I say one prayer!

OTHELLO   It is too late.
                                        Smothers her.

EMILIA (at the door)
My lord, my lord! What, ho! My lord, my lord!

OTHELLO
What noise is this? Not dead? Not yet quite dead?
I that am cruel am yet merciful;
I would not have thee linger in thy pain.
                              [He dispatches her.]
So, so.

EMILIA (within) What, ho! My lord, my lord!

OTHELLO   Who's there?

EMILIA [within]
O, good my lord, I would speak a word with you!

OTHELLO
Yes, 'tis Emilia.—By and by.—She's dead.
'Tis like she comes to speak of Cassio's death.—   95
The noise was here. Ha! No more moving?   96
Still as the grave. Shall she come in? Were 't
   good?—
I think she stirs again. No. What's best to do?
If she come in, she'll sure speak to my wife.
My wife! My wife! What wife? I have no wife.
O, insupportable! O heavy hour!
Methinks it should be now a huge eclipse
Of sun and moon, and that th' affrighted globe
Should yawn at alteration.

EMILIA [within]   I do beseech you   104
That I may speak with you, O, good my lord!

OTHELLO
I had forgot thee. O, come in, Emilia.—
Soft, by and by. Let me the curtains draw.—   107
      [He closes the bed-curtains and opens the door.]
Where art thou?

            Enter Emilia.

                  What's the matter with thee now?

EMILIA
O, my good lord, yonder's foul murders done!

OTHELLO   What, now?

EMILIA   But now, my lord.

OTHELLO
It is the very error of the moon;   112
She comes more nearer earth than she was wont,
And makes men mad.

EMILIA
Cassio, my lord, hath killed a young Venetian
Called Roderigo.

OTHELLO   Roderigo killed?
And Cassio killed?

EMILIA   No, Cassio is not killed.

OTHELLO
Not Cassio killed? Then murder's out of tune,
And sweet revenge grows harsh.

DESDEMONA   O, falsely, falsely murdered!

EMILIA   O Lord, what cry is that?

OTHELLO   That? What?

---

59 **conception** (1) belief in your guilt (2) plan in my mind   60 **groan withal** (1) groan at in sorrow (2) as in giving birth   63 **Offend** wrong   64 **warranty** sanction   67 **stone** turn to stone, harden   76 **ta'en order** taken measures   86 **Being done** i.e., since justice has begun its relentless course

95 **like** likely that   96 **here** (The Folio's *high* is possible, suggesting that the commotion of the attack on Cassio was loud.)   104 **yawn** gape in amazement, i.e., move in an earthquake. (According to Pliny, earthquakes often happen during eclipses.)   **at alteration** at these cataclysmic events in nature, well suited to express the horror of Desdemona's death   107 **Soft** wait a minute   112 **error** aberration, irregularity

EMILIA
Out and alas, that was my lady's voice.   123
                              [*She opens the bed-curtains.*]
Help, help, ho, help! O lady, speak again!
Sweet Desdemona! O sweet mistress, speak!
DESDEMONA   A guiltless death I die.
EMILIA   O, who hath done this deed?
DESDEMONA   Nobody; I myself. Farewell.
Commend me to my kind lord. O, farewell! [*She dies.*]
OTHELLO
Why, how should she be murdered?
EMILIA   Alas, who knows?
OTHELLO
You heard her say herself it was not I.
EMILIA
She said so. I must needs report the truth.
OTHELLO
She's like a liar gone to burning hell!
'Twas I that killed her.
EMILIA   O, the more angel she,
And you the blacker devil!
OTHELLO
She turned to folly, and she was a whore.   136
EMILIA
Thou dost belie her, and thou art a devil.   137
OTHELLO   She was false as water.
EMILIA   Thou art rash as fire to say
That she was false. O, she was heavenly true!
OTHELLO
Cassio did top her. Ask thy husband else.   141
O, I were damned beneath all depth in hell
But that I did proceed upon just grounds
To this extremity. Thy husband knew it all.
EMILIA   My husband?
OTHELLO   Thy husband.
EMILIA   That she was false to wedlock?
OTHELLO
Ay, with Cassio. Nay, had she been true,
If heaven would make me such another world
Of one entire and perfect chrysolite,   150
I'd not have sold her for it.
EMILIA   My husband?
OTHELLO
Ay, 'twas he that told me on her first.
An honest man he is, and hates the slime
That sticks on filthy deeds.
EMILIA   My husband?
OTHELLO
What needs this iterance, woman? I say thy
  husband.   157
EMILIA
O mistress, villainy hath made mocks with love!   158
My husband say she was false?
OTHELLO   He, woman;
I say thy husband. Dost understand the word?
My friend, thy husband, honest, honest Iago.

EMILIA
If he say so, may his pernicious soul
Rot half a grain a day! He lies to th' heart.
She was too fond of her most filthy bargain.
OTHELLO   Ha?   [*He draws.*]
EMILIA   Do thy worst!
This deed of thine is no more worthy heaven
Than thou wast worthy her.
OTHELLO   Peace, you were best.   168
EMILIA
Thou hast not half that power to do me harm
As I have to be hurt. O gull! O dolt!   170
As ignorant as dirt! Thou hast done a deed—
I care not for thy sword; I'll make thee known,
Though I lost twenty lives.—Help! Help, ho, help!
The Moor hath killed my mistress! Murder, murder!

       Enter Montano, Gratiano, and Iago.

MONTANO
What is the matter? How now, General?
EMILIA
O, are you come, Iago? You have done well,
That men must lay their murders on your neck.
GRATIANO   What is the matter?
EMILIA [*to Iago*]
Disprove this villain, if thou be'st a man.
He says thou toldst him that his wife was false.
I know thou didst not; thou'rt not such a villain.
Speak, for my heart is full.
IAGO
I told him what I thought, and told no more
Than what he found himself was apt and true.   184
EMILIA
But did you ever tell him she was false?
IAGO   I did.
EMILIA
You told a lie, an odious, damnèd lie!
Upon my soul, a lie, a wicked lie.
She false with Cassio? Did you say with Cassio?
IAGO
With Cassio, mistress. Go to, charm your tongue.   190
EMILIA
I will not charm my tongue; I am bound to speak.
My mistress here lies murdered in her bed—
ALL   O heavens forfend!
EMILIA
And your reports have set the murder on.
OTHELLO
Nay, stare not, masters. It is true indeed.
GRATIANO   'Tis a strange truth.
MONTANO
O monstrous act!
EMILIA   Villainy, villainy, villainy!
I think upon 't—I think I smell 't! O villainy!
I thought so then—I'll kill myself for grief—   199
O villainy, villainy!

---

123 **Out** (A cry of dismay, intensifying *alas*.)   136 **folly** i.e., wantonness, fleshly sin   137 **belie** slander   141 **else** i.e., if you don't believe me   150 **chrysolite** precious topaz   157 **iterance** iteration, repetition   158 **made mocks with** derided, made sport of

168 **you were best** it would be best for you   170 **to be hurt** i.e., to endure hurt. **gull** dupe   184 **apt** plausible   190 **charm** keep silent (as though by a magic spell)   199 **then** (Perhaps at 3.3.331–332 and 4.2.137–154.)

IAGO
What, are you mad? I charge you, get you home.
EMILIA
Good gentlemen, let me have leave to speak.
'Tis proper I obey him, but not now.
Perchance, Iago, I will ne'er go home.
OTHELLO
O! O! O!   [*Othello falls on the bed.*]
EMILIA   Nay, lay thee down and roar,   205
For thou hast killed the sweetest innocent
That e'er did lift up eye.
OTHELLO [*rising*]   O, she was foul!   207
I scarce did know you, uncle. There lies your niece,
Whose breath indeed these hands have newly
     stopped.
I know this act shows horrible and grim.   210
GRATIANO
Poor Desdemon! I am glad thy father's dead.
Thy match was mortal to him, and pure grief
Shore his old thread in twain. Did he live now,   213
This sight would make him do a desperate turn,   214
Yea, curse his better angel from his side,
And fall to reprobance.   216
OTHELLO
'Tis pitiful. But yet Iago knows
That she with Cassio hath the act of shame
A thousand times committed. Cassio confessed it;
And she did gratify his amorous works   220
With that recognizance and pledge of love   221
Which I first gave her. I saw it in his hand;
It was a handkerchief, an antique token
My father gave my mother.
EMILIA   O God! O heavenly God!
IAGO
Zounds, hold your peace.
EMILIA   'Twill out, 'twill out! I peace?
No, I will speak as liberal as the north.   227
Let heaven and men and devils, let them all,
All, all, cry shame against me, yet I'll speak.
IAGO
Be wise, and get you home.
EMILIA   I will not.
     [*Iago threatens Emilia.*]
GRATIANO   Fie,
Your sword upon a woman?
EMILIA
O thou dull Moor! That handkerchief thou speak'st of
I found by fortune and did give my husband;
For often, with a solemn earnestness,
More than indeed belonged to such a trifle,   235
He begged of me to steal 't.
IAGO   Villainous whore!

EMILIA
She give it Cassio? No, alas! I found it,
And I did give 't my husband.
IAGO   Filth, thou liest!
EMILIA
By heaven, I do not, I do not, gentlemen.
O murderous coxcomb! What should such a fool   240
Do with so good a wife?
OTHELLO   Are there no stones in heaven   242
But what serves for the thunder?—Precious villain!   243
     [*He runs at Iago; Montano disarms Othello. Iago,*
         from behind, stabs Emilia.]
GRATIANO
The woman falls! Sure he hath killed his wife.
EMILIA
Ay, ay. O, lay me by my mistress' side.
     [*Exit Iago.*]
GRATIANO   He's gone, but his wife's killed.
MONTANO
'Tis a notorious villain. Take you this weapon,
Which I have here recovered from the Moor.
Come, guard the door without. Let him not pass,
But kill him rather. I'll after that same villain,
For 'tis a damnèd slave.
     Exit [*with all but Othello and Emilia,*
         who has been laid by Desdemona's side].
OTHELLO   I am not valiant neither,
But every puny whipster gets my sword.   253
But why should honor outlive honesty?   254
Let it go all.
EMILIA   What did thy song bode, lady?
Hark, canst thou hear me? I will play the swan,
And die in music. [*She sings.*] "Willow, willow,
     willow."
Moor, she was chaste. She loved thee, cruel Moor.
So come my soul to bliss as I speak true.
So speaking as I think, alas, I die.   [*She dies.*]
OTHELLO
I have another weapon in this chamber;
It was a sword of Spain, the ice-brook's temper—   262
O, here it is. [*He finds a sword.*] Uncle, I must come
     forth.
GRATIANO [*within*]
If thou attempt it, it will cost thee dear.
Thou hast no weapon, and perforce must suffer.
OTHELLO
Look in upon me then and speak with me,
Or, naked as I am, I will assault thee.   267

     [*Enter Gratiano.*]

GRATIANO
What is the matter?

205 s.d. Othello . . . bed (This direction is from the Quarto, as also *He kisses her* at line 19 and *She dies* at line 129.)   **207 lift up eye** i.e., lift her eyes to heaven   **210 shows** looks   **213 Shore . . . thread** sheared the thread of his old age (as Atropos, one of the three Fates, was thought to do)   **214 turn** deed   **216 reprobance** damnation, i.e., suicide   **220 gratify** reward   **221 recognizance** token   **227 liberal as the north** freely as the north wind (blows)   **235 belonged** was appropriate

240 coxcomb fool. (Addressed to Othello.)   **242 stones** bolts, such as those used for thunderbolts   **243 Precious** i.e., arrant, utter.   **s.d. He . . . Emilia** (The Quarto text reads, "The Moor runs at Iago. Iago kills his wife." The Quarto also specifies the exit of Iago at line 245 and the death of Emilia at line 260.)   **253 whipster** contemptible fellow (one who is always ready to whip out his sword)   **254 honor** i.e., the bravery for which one enjoys a soldier's reputation. **honesty** true integrity   **262 the icebrook's temper** tempered in ice-cold water   **267 naked** unarmed

OTHELLO   Behold, I have a weapon;
A better never did itself sustain
Upon a soldier's thigh. I have seen the day
That, with this little arm and this good sword,
I have made my way through more impediments
Than twenty times your stop. But O, vain boast!   273
Who can control his fate? 'Tis not so now.
Be not afraid, though you do see me weaponed;
Here is my journey's end, here is my butt   276
And very seamark of my utmost sail.   277
                         [*Gratiano steps back.*]
Do you go back dismayed? 'Tis a lost fear;   278
Man but a rush against Othello's breast   279
And he retires. Where should Othello go?
                    [*He turns to Desdemona.*]
Now, how dost thou look now? O ill-starred wench!
Pale as thy smock! When we shall meet at compt,   282
This look of thine will hurl my soul from heaven,
And fiends will snatch at it. Cold, cold, my girl?
Even like thy chastity. O cursèd, cursèd slave!   285
Whip me, ye devils,
From the possession of this heavenly sight!
Blow me about in winds! Roast me in sulfur!
Wash me in steep-down gulfs of liquid fire!
O Desdemon! Dead, Desdemon! Dead! O! O!   290

Enter Lodovico, Cassio [*carried in a litter*],
Montano, and Iago [*prisoner*], *with officers.*

LODOVICO
Where is this rash and most unfortunate man?
OTHELLO
That's he that was Othello. Here I am.
LODOVICO
Where is that viper? Bring the villain forth.
                         [*Iago is led forward.*]
OTHELLO
I look down towards his feet; but that's a fable.   294
If that thou be'st a devil, I cannot kill thee.
                         [*He wounds Iago.*]
LODOVICO
Wrench his sword from him.   [*Othello is disarmed.*]
IAGO   I bleed, sir, but not killed.
OTHELLO
I am not sorry neither. I'd have thee live,
For in my sense 'tis happiness to die.   298
LODOVICO
O thou Othello, that was once so good,
Fall'n in the practice of a cursèd slave,   300
What shall be said to thee?
OTHELLO   Why, anything.
An honorable murderer, if you will,
For naught I did in hate, but all in honor.

LODOVICO
This wretch hath part confessed his villainy.
Did you and he consent in Cassio's death?   305
OTHELLO   Ay.
CASSIO
Dear General, I never gave you cause.
OTHELLO
I do believe it, and I ask your pardon.
Will you, I pray, demand that demi-devil
Why he hath thus ensnared my soul and body?
IAGO
Demand me nothing. What you know, you know.
From this time forth I never will speak word.
LODOVICO   What, not to pray?
GRATIANO   Torments will ope your lips.   314
OTHELLO   Well, thou dost best.
LODOVICO
Sir, you shall understand what hath befall'n,
Which, as I think, you know not. Here is a letter
Found in the pocket of the slain Roderigo;
And here another. [*He produces letters.*] The one of
    them imports
The death of Cassio, to be undertook
By Roderigo.
OTHELLO
O villain!
CASSIO   Most heathenish and most gross!   322
LODOVICO [*showing another paper*]
Now here's another discontented paper   323
Found in his pocket too. And this, it seems,
Roderigo meant t' have sent this damnèd villain;
But that belike Iago in the interim   326
Came in and satisfied him.   327
OTHELLO   O thou pernicious caitiff!—
How came you, Cassio, by that handkerchief
That was my wife's?
CASSIO   I found it in my chamber;
And he himself confessed but even now
That there he dropped it for a special purpose
Which wrought to his desire.
OTHELLO   O fool, fool, fool!   333
CASSIO
There is besides in Roderigo's letter
How he upbraids Iago, that he made him
Brave me upon the watch, whereon it came   336
That I was cast; and even but now he spake,   337
After long seeming dead, Iago hurt him,
Iago set him on.
LODOVICO [*to Othello*]
You must forsake this room and go with us.
Your power and your command is taken off,   341
And Cassio rules in Cyprus. For this slave,
If there be any cunning cruelty

---

273 stop power (to stop)   **276 butt** goal, limit. (An archery term.)
277 seamark beacon (marking his destination or limit)   **278 lost**
wasted, unneeded   **279 Man . . . rush** wield no more than a reed
282 compt account, judgment day   **285 slave** i.e., Othello himself
290 s.d. in a litter (The Quarto specifies that Cassio is "in a chair.")
294 towards his feet i.e., to see if they are cloven, as the devil's are
fabled to be   **298 in my sense** to one who feels as I do   **300 in the
practice** through the plotting, into the snare.   **slave** villain

305 consent agree   **314 Torments** torture   **322 gross** monstrous
323 discontented full of discontent   **326 belike** most likely
327 Came . . . him interposed and gave him satisfactory explanation
333 wrought . . . desire worked out as he wished, fitted in with his
plan   **336 Brave** defy.   **whereon it came** whereof it came about
337 cast dismissed   **341 taken off** taken away

That can torment him much and hold him long,   344
It shall be his. You shall close prisoner rest   345
Till that the nature of your fault be known
To the Venetian state.—Come, bring away.

OTHELLO
Soft you; a word or two before you go.   348
I have done the state some service, and they know 't.
No more of that. I pray you, in your letters,
When you shall these unlucky deeds relate,   351
Speak of me as I am; nothing extenuate,
Nor set down aught in malice. Then must you speak
Of one that loved not wisely but too well;
Of one not easily jealous but, being wrought,   355
Perplexed in the extreme; of one whose hand,   356
Like the base Indian, threw a pearl away   357
Richer than all his tribe; of one whose subdued
    eyes,   358
Albeit unusèd to the melting mood,
Drops tears as fast as the Arabian trees
Their medicinable gum. Set you down this;   361
And say besides that in Aleppo once,
Where a malignant and a turbaned Turk
Beat a Venetian and traduced the state,
I took by th' throat the circumcisèd dog
And smote him, thus.   [He stabs himself.] 366
LODOVICO   O bloody period!   367
GRATIANO   All that is spoke is marred.
OTHELLO
I kissed thee ere I killed thee. No way but this,
Killing myself, to die upon a kiss.
                    [He kisses Desdemona and] dies.

CASSIO
This did I fear, but thought he had no weapon;
For he was great of heart.
LODOVICO [to Iago]   O Spartan dog,   372
More fell than anguish, hunger, or the sea!   373
Look on the tragic loading of this bed.
This is thy work. The object poisons sight;
Let it be hid. Gratiano, keep the house,   376
                    [The bed curtains are drawn]
And seize upon the fortunes of the Moor,   377
For they succeed on you. [To Cassio.] To you, Lord
    Governor,   378
Remains the censure of this hellish villain,   379
The time, the place, the torture. O, enforce it!
Myself will straight aboard, and to the state
This heavy act with heavy heart relate.   Exeunt.

344 hold him long keep him alive a long time (during his torture)
345 rest remain   **348 Soft you** one moment   **351 unlucky** unfortunate   **355 wrought** worked upon, worked into a frenzy   **356 Perplexed** distraught   **357 Indian** (This reading from the Quarto pictures
an ignorant savage who cannot recognize the value of a precious
jewel. The Folio reading, *Iudean* or *Judean*, i.e., infidel or disbeliever,
may refer to Herod, who slew Miriamne in a fit of jealousy, or to Judas Iscariot, the betrayer of Christ.)   **358 subdued** i.e., overcome by
grief   **361 gum** i.e., myrrh   **366 s.d. He stabs himself** (This direction is in the Quarto text.)   **367 period** termination, conclusion
372 Spartan dog (Spartan dogs were noted for their savagery and silence.)   **373 fell** cruel   **376 Let it be hid** i.e., draw the bed curtains.
(No stage direction specifies that the dead are to be carried offstage at
the end of the play.)   **keep** remain in   **377 seize upon** take legal
possession of   **378 succeed on** pass as though by inheritance to
379 censure sentencing

King Lear

In *King Lear*, Shakespeare pushes to its limit the hypothesis of a malign or at least indifferent universe in which human life is meaningless and brutal. Few plays other than *Hamlet* and *Macbeth* approach *King Lear* in evoking the wretchedness of human existence, and even they cannot match the devastating spectacle of the Earl of Gloucester blinded or Cordelia dead in Lear's arms. The responses of the chief characters are correspondingly searing. "Is man no more than this?" rages Lear. "Unaccommodated man is no more but such a poor, bare, forked animal as thou art" (3.4.101–107). Life he calls a "great stage of fools," an endless torment: "the first time that we smell the air / We wawl and cry" (4.6.179–183). Gloucester's despair takes the form of accusing the gods of gleeful malice toward humanity: "As flies to wanton boys are we to th' gods; / They kill us for their sport" (4.1.36–37). Gloucester's ministering son Edgar can offer him no greater consolation than stoic resolve: "Men must endure / Their going hence, even as their coming hither; / Ripeness is all" (5.2.9–11). These statements need not be read as choric expressions of meaning for the play as a whole, but they do attest to the depth of suffering. In no other Shakespearean play does injustice appear to triumph so ferociously, for so long, and with such impunity. Will the heavens countenance this reign of injustice on earth? Retribution is late in coming and is not certainly the work of the heavens themselves. For, at the last, we must confront the wanton death of the innocent Cordelia—a death no longer willed even by the villain who arranged her execution. "Is this the promised end?" (5.3.268) asks the Earl of Kent, stressing the unparalleled horror of the catastrophe.

Throughout its earlier history, the ancient story of King Lear had always ended happily. In the popular folktale of Cinderella, to which the legend of Lear's daughters bears a significant resemblance, the youngest and virtuous daughter triumphs over her two older wicked sisters and is married to her princely wooer. Geoffrey of Monmouth's *Historia Regum Britanniae* (c. 1136), the earliest known version of the Lear story, records that, after Lear is overthrown by his sons-in-law (more than by his daughters), he is restored to his throne by the intervention of the French King and is allowed to enjoy his kingdom and Cordelia's love until his natural death. (Cordelia, as his successor, is later dethroned and murdered by her wicked nephews, but that is another story.) Sixteenth-century Tudor versions of the Lear story with which Shakespeare was familiar—John Higgins' account in *The First Part of the Mirror for Magistrates* (1574), Raphael Holinshed's *Chronicles* (1587), Edmund Spenser's *The Faerie Queene*, 2.10.27–32, and a play called *The True Chronicle History of King Leir* (by 1594, published 1605)—all retain the happy ending. The tragic pattern may have been suggested instead by Shakespeare's probable source for the Gloucester-Edgar-Edmund plot, Sir Philip Sidney's *Arcadia*, 2.10, in which the Paphlagonian King is the victim of filial ingratitude and deceit.

Yet even Shakespeare's authority was not sufficient to put down the craving for a happy resolution. Nahum Tate's adaptation (1681), which banished the Fool as indecorous for a tragedy and united Edgar and Cordelia in marriage, placing Lear once again on his throne, held the English stage for about 150 years. David Garrick restored some of Shakespeare's lines, and Edmund Kean restored the tragic ending, but it was not until 1838 that *King Lear* was again performed more or less as the dramatist wrote it. One of Shakespeare's editors, Dr. Samuel Johnson, evidently spoke for most eighteenth-century audiences when he confessed that he could not bring himself to read Shakespeare's text. Cordelia's slaughter violated that age's longing for "poetic justice." Her death implied a wanton universe and so counseled philosophic despair. Today, Shakespeare's relentless honesty and refusal to accept easy answers convince us that he was right to defy the conventions of his source, though no doubt we, too, distort the play to conform with our supposed toughness of vision. For all its unforgettable excellence and persuasiveness, Peter Brook's film version of *King Lear* (1970) is avowedly modern in perspective and employs rearrangements and cuts not wholly unlike those of Tate, though opposite in their thrust.

Shakespeare evidently wrote *King Lear* some time before it was performed at court in December of 1606, probably in 1605 and certainly no earlier than 1603–1604; Edgar's speeches as Tom o' Bedlam contain references to Samuel Harsnett's *Declaration of Egregious Popish Impostures*, which was registered for publication in March of 1603. Thus, *King Lear* was probably written between *Othello* (c. 1603–1604) and *Macbeth* (c. 1606–1607), when Shakespeare was at the height of his literary power in the writing of tragedies.

When we look at the play in formal terms, we are apt to be struck first by its complex double plot. Nowhere else in Shakespearean tragedy do we find anything approaching the rich orchestration of the double plotting in *King Lear*. The links and parallels between the two plots are established on a narrative level early in the play and continue to the end. King Lear misjudges his children and disinherits his loving daughter Cordelia in favor of her duplicitous sisters, whereas Gloucester falls prey to Edmund's deceptions and disinherits his loyal son Edgar; Lear is turned out into the storm by his false daughters, while Gloucester is branded as a traitor by Edmund and deprived of his eyesight; Lear in his madness realizes his fault against Cordelia, while the blind Gloucester "sees" at last the truth about Edgar; and both fathers are cared for by their loving children and are belatedly reconciled to them, but they die brokenhearted. As recent criticism has noted, these narrative parallels are not especially significant in themselves; we are moved, not by the mere repetition of events, but by the enlargement of tragic vision that results from the counterpointing of two such actions. When we see juxtaposed to each other two scenes of trial, Lear's mad arraignment of the absent Goneril and Regan and then the cruel imposition of the mere "form of justice" on the pinioned Gloucester (3.6 and 3.7), we begin to measure the extent to which justice and injustice are inverted by cruelty. When at last the two old men come together, during the storm scenes and especially at Dover, the sad comfort they derive from sharing the wreckage of their lives calls forth piercing eloquence against the stench of mortality. The sight is "most pitiful in the meanest wretch, / Past speaking of in a king" (4.6.204–205).

The play's double structure suggests another duality central to *King Lear:* an opposition of parable and realism, in which "divided and distinguished worlds" are bound together for instructive contrast. (These terms are Maynard Mack's, in his *King Lear in Our Time,* 1965.) To a remarkable degree, this play derives its story from folklore and legend, with many of the wondrous and implausible circumstances of popular romance. A prose rendition might almost begin, "Once upon a time there was a king who had three daughters. . . ." Yet Shakespeare arouses romantic expectation only to crush it by aborting the conventional happy ending, setting up a dramatic tension between an idealized world of make-believe and the actual world of disappointed hopes. We are aware of artifice and convention, and yet are deeply moved by the "truth" of suffering, love, and hatred. The characters pull us two ways at once; we regard them as types with universalized characteristics—a king and father, his cruel daughters, his loving daughter, and the like—and yet we scrutinize them for psychological motivation because they seem so real and individual.

This duality appears in both the central and the secondary characters. The King of France is in part a hero out of romance, who makes selfless choices and rescues the heroine Cordelia from her distress; yet his motive must also be appraised in the context of a bitter struggle for power. Why does he leave the English court "in choler," and why does he return to England with an army? Is it only to aid his wife and her beleaguered father, or is he negotiating for military advantage? Certainly, a French invasion of England on behalf of Lear complicates the issues of loyalty for the well-meaning Duke of Albany (and perhaps as well for an English Renaissance audience, with its habitual mistrust of the

French). The dual focus of the play invites conflicting interpretation. Similarly, Edgar is presented to us on the one hand as the traduced victim in a starkly pessimistic story, dominated by his rationalistic brother, Edmund, who scoffs at religion and undertakes to manipulate those around him for personal gain; on the other hand, Edgar's story grows increasingly improbable as he undertakes a series of disguises and emerges finally as an anonymous champion of chivalry, challenging his brother in the lists like a knight-errant out of Arthurian romance. Edgar's motives are hard to follow. Is he the hero of a fabulous story whose disguises and contriving of illusions for his father are simply part of that storytelling tradition, or is he, in more realistic terms, a man whose disguises are a defensive mask and whose elaborate contrivances defeat themselves? Edmund, his brother, is no less complex. Onstage today he is usually interpreted as smooth and plausible, well-motivated by his father's condescending attitude and by the arbitrariness of the law that has excluded him from legitimacy and inheritance. Yet parable elevates Edmund into something monstrous. He becomes an embodiment of gleeful villainy, like Iago in *Othello,* malignantly evil simply because the evil that is in the universe must find a human form through which to express itself. Edmund's belated attempt to do some good adds to our difficulties in appraising his character, but the restless power of the dual conception supplies a vitality not to be found in pure fable or in realistic literature.

What we see then in Edmund and in others is the union of the universal and the particular, making *King Lear* at once parable and compellingly real. The parable or folktale element is prominent at the beginning of the play and focuses attention on the archetypal situations with which the story is concerned: rivalry between siblings, fear of parental rejection, and, at the same time, parental fear of children's callousness. The "unrealistic" contrast between Cordelia and her wicked sisters, or between Edgar and Edmund, is something we accept as a convention of storytelling, because it expresses vividly the psychic truth of rivalry between brothers and sisters. We identify with Cordelia and Edgar as virtuous children whose worth is misjudged, and who are losing to wicked siblings the contest for parental approval. (In folklore, the rejecting parent is usually a stepparent, which signifies our conviction that he or she is not a true parent at all.) Similarly, we accept as a meaningful convention of storytelling the equally "unrealistic" device by which Lear tests the love of his daughters. Like any parent, he wishes to be loved and appreciated in response to the kindnesses he has performed. The tension between fathers and their marriageable daughters is a recurrent pattern in Shakespeare's late plays, as in *Othello* (in which Brabantio accuses Desdemona of deceiving and deserting him), in *Pericles, Cymbeline,* and *The Winter's Tale,* and in *The Tempest,* in which the pattern is best resolved. In *King Lear,* Shakespeare explores the inherently explosive situation of an imperious father who, having provided for his children and having grown old, assumes he has a right to expect that those children will express their love and gratitude by looking after him.

The difficulty is that the parable of Lear and his children presents two contrasting viewpoints—that of the unappreciated child and that of the unwanted aging parent. Tragic misunderstanding is inevitable, and it outweighs the question of assessing blame. From Lear's point of view, Cordelia's silence is a truculent scanting of obedience. What he has devised is, after all, only a prearranged formality, with Cordelia to receive the richest third of England. Cannot such a ceremony be answered with the conventional hyperbole of courtly language, to which the King's ear is attuned? Don't parents have a right to be verbally reassured of their children's love? How can children be so laconic about such a precious matter? For her part, however, Cordelia senses that Lear is demanding love as payment for his parental kindliness, quid pro quo. Genuine love ought rather to be selfless, as the King of France tells the Duke of Burgundy: "Love's not love / When it is mingled with regards that stands / Aloof from th' entire point" (1.1.242–244). Is Cordelia being asked to prefer Lear before her own husband-to-be? Is this the price she must pay for her upbringing? Lear's ego seems fully capable of demanding this sacrifice from his daughters, especially from his favorite, Cordelia; he has given them his whole kingdom, now let them care for him as befits his royal rank and patriarchal role. The "second childishness" of his old age brings with it a self-centered longing to monopolize the lives of his children and to be a child again. Besides, as king, Lear has long grown accustomed to flattery and absolute obedience. Goneril and Regan are content to flatter and promise obedience, knowing they will turn him out once he has relinquished his authority. Cordelia refuses to lie in this fashion, but she also will not yield to Lear's implicit request for her undivided affection. Part of her must be loyal to her own husband and her children, in the natural cycle of the generations. "When I shall wed, / That lord whose hand must take my plight shall carry / Half my love with him, half my care and duty" (1.1.100–102). Marriage will not prevent her from obeying, loving, and honoring her father as is fit but will establish for her a new priority. To Lear, as to other fathers contemplating a daughter's marriage in late Shakespearean plays, this savors of desertion.

Lear is sadly deficient in self-knowledge. As Regan dryly observes, "he hath ever but slenderly known himself" (1.1.296–297) and has grown ever more changeable and imperious with age. By dividing his kingdom in three, ostensibly so that "future strife / May be prevented now" (lines 44–45), he instead sets in motion a civil war and French invasion. His intention of putting aside his regal authority while still retaining 'The name and all th' addition to a king" (line 136) perhaps betrays a lack of comprehension of the realities of power, although Lear may also have plausible political reasons for what he does, in view of the restive ambitions of the Dukes of Cornwall, Albany, and Burgundy. In any case, he welcomes poisoned flattery but interprets well-intended criticism, whether from Cordelia or Kent, as treason. These failures in no sense justify what Lear's ungrateful children do to him; as he later says, just before going mad, "I am a man / More sinned against than sinning" (3.2.59–60). His failures are, however, tokens of his worldly insolence, for which he must fall. The process is a painful one, but, since it brings self-discovery, it is not without its compensations. Indeed, a central paradox of the play is that by no other way could Lear have learned what human suffering and need are all about.

Lear's Fool is instrumental in elucidating this paradox. The Fool offers Lear advice in palatable form as mere foolery or entertainment and thus obtains a hearing when Kent and Cordelia have been angrily dismissed. Beneath his seemingly innocent jibes, however, are plain warnings of the looming disaster Lear blindly refuses to acknowledge. The Fool knows, as indeed any fool could tell, that Goneril and Regan are remorseless and unnatural. The real fool, therefore, is Lear himself, for having placed himself in their power. In a paradox familiar to Renaissance audiences—as in Erasmus' *In Praise of Folly*, Cervantes' *Don Quixote*, and Shakespeare's own earlier *As You Like It* and *Twelfth Night*—folly and wisdom exchange places. By a similar inversion of logic, the Fool offers his coxcomb to the Earl of Kent for siding with Lear in his exile, "for taking one's part that's out of favor" (1.4.97). Worldly wisdom suggests that we serve those whose fortunes are on the rise, as the obsequious and servile Oswald does. Indeed, the sinister progress of the first half of the play seems to confirm the Fool's contention that kindness and love are a sure way to exile and poverty. "Let go thy hold when a great wheel runs down a hill lest it break thy neck with following; but the great one that goes upward, let him draw thee after" (2.4.70–73). Yet the Fool resolves to ignore his own sardonic advice; "I would have none but knaves follow it, since a fool gives it" (lines 74–75). Beneath his mocking, the Fool expresses the deeper truth that it is better to be a "fool" and suffer than to win on the cynical world's terms. The greatest fools truly are those who prosper through cruelty and become hardened in sin. As the Fool puts it, deriving a seemingly contrary lesson from Lear's rejection of Cordelia: "Why, this fellow has banished two on 's daughters and did the third a blessing against his will" (1.4.99–101).

These inversions find a parallel in Christian teaching, although the play is nominally pagan in setting. (The lack of explicit Christian reference may be in part the result of a parliamentary order in 1606 banning references to "God" onstage as blasphemous.) Christianity does not hold a monopoly on the idea that one must lose the world in order to win a better world, but its expressions of that idea were plentifully available to Shakespeare: "Blessed are the meek, for they shall inherit the earth" (the Sermon on the Mount); "Go and sell that thou hast, and give to the poor, and thou shalt have treasure in heaven" (Matthew 19:21); "He hath put down the mighty from their seats, and exalted them of low degree" (Luke 1:52). Cordelia's vision of genuine love is of this exalted spiritual order. She is, as the King of France extols her, "most rich being poor, / Most choice, forsaken, and most loved, despised" (1.1.254–255). This is the sense in which Lear has bestowed on her an unintended blessing, by exiling her from a worldly prosperity that is inherently pernicious. Now, with poetic fitness, Lear must learn the same lesson himself. He does so, paradoxically, at the very moment he goes mad, parting ways with the conventional truths of the corrupted world. "My wits begin to turn," he says (3.2.67), and then speaks his first kind words to the Fool, who is his companion in the storm. Lear senses companionship with a fellow mortal who is cold and outcast as he is. In his madness, he perceives both the worth of this insight and the need for suffering to attain it: "The art of our necessities is strange, / And can make vile things precious" (lines 70–71). Misery teaches Lear things he never could know as king about other "Poor naked wretches" who "bide the pelting of this pitiless storm." How are such poor persons to be fed and clothed? "O, I have ta'en / Too little care of this! Take physic, pomp; / Expose thyself to feel what wretches feel, / That thou mayst shake the superflux to them / And show the heavens more just" (3.4.28–36). This vision of perfect justice is visionary and utopian, utterly mad, in fact, but it is also spiritual wisdom dearly bought.

Gloucester learns a similar truth and expresses it in much the same way. Like Lear, he has driven into exile a virtuous child and has placed himself in the power of the wicked. Enlightenment comes only through suffering. Just as Lear achieves spiritual wisdom when he goes mad, Gloucester achieves spiritual vision when he is physically blinded. His eyes having been ground out by the heel of Cornwall's boot, Gloucester asks for Edmund only to learn that Edmund has betrayed him in return for siding with Lear in the approaching civil war. Gloucester's response, however, is not to accuse Edmund of treachery but to beg forgiveness of the wronged Edgar. No longer does Gloucester need eyes to see this truth: "I stumbled when I saw." Although the discovery is shattering, Gloucester perceives, as does Lear, that adversity is paradoxically of some benefit, since prosperity had previously caused him to be so spiritually blind. "Full oft 'tis seen / Our means secure us, and our mere defects / Prove our commodities" (4.1.19–21). And this realization leads him, as it does Lear, to express a longing for utopian social justice in which arrogant men will be humbled and the poor raised up by redistributed wealth. "Heavens, deal so still! / Let the superfluous and lust-dieted man, / That slaves your ordinance, that will not see / Because he does not feel, feel your pow'r quickly! / So distribution should undo excess / And each man have enough" (lines 65–70).

To say that Lear and Gloucester learn something precious is not, however, to deny that they are also devastated and broken by their savage humiliation. Indeed, Gloucester is driven to a despairing attempt at suicide, and Lear remains obsessed with the rotten stench of his own mortality, "bound / Upon a wheel of fire" (4.7.47–48). Every decent value that we like to associate with civilization is grotesquely inverted during the storm scenes. Justice, for example, is portrayed in two sharply contrasting scenes: the mere "form of justice" by which Cornwall condemns Gloucester for treason (3.7.26) and the earnestly playacted trial by which the mad Lear arraigns Goneril and Regan of filial ingratitude (3.6). The appearance and the reality of justice have exchanged places, as have folly and wisdom or blindness and seeing. The trial of Gloucester is outwardly correct, for Cornwall possesses the legal authority to try his subjects and at least goes through the motions of interrogating his prisoner. The outcome is, however, cruelly predetermined. In the playacting trial concurrently taking place in a wretched hovel, the outward appearance of justice is pathetically absurd. Here, justice on earth is personified by a madman (Lear), Edgar disguised as another madman (Tom o' Bedlam), and a Fool, of whom the latter two are addressed by Lear as "Thou robèd man of justice" and "thou, his yokefellow of equity" (lines 36–37). They are caught up in a pastime of illusion, using a footstool to represent Lear's ungrateful daughters. Yet true justice is here and not inside the manor house.

Similar contrasts invert the values of loyalty, obedience, and family bonds. Edmund becomes, in the language of the villains, the "loyal" son whose loyalty is demonstrated by turning on his own "traitorous" father. Cornwall becomes a new father to Edmund ("thou shalt find a dearer father in my love," 3.5.25–26). Conversely, a servant who tries to restrain Cornwall from blinding Gloucester is, in Regan's eyes, monstrously insubordinate. "A peasant stand up thus?" (3.7.83). Personal and sexual relationships betray signs of the universal malaise. The explicitly sexual ties in the play, notably those of Goneril, Regan, and Edmund, are grossly carnal and lead to jealousy and murder, while in Cordelia's wifely role the sensual is underplayed. The relationships we cherish—those of Cordelia, Kent, the Fool, and Gloucester to King Lear, and Edgar to Gloucester—are filial or are characterized by loyal service, both of which are pointedly nonsexual. Nowhere do we find an embodiment of love that is both sensual and spiritual, as in Desdemona in *Othello* or Hermione in *The Winter's Tale*. The Fool's and Tom o' Bedlam's (i.e., Edgar's) gibes about codpieces and plackets (3.2.27–40, 3.4.96) anticipate Lear's towering indictment of carnality, in which his fear of woman's insatiable appetite and his revulsion at her body "Down from the waist" ("there is the sulfurous pit, burning, scalding, stench, consumption.

Fie, fie, fie! Pah, pah!") combine with a destructive self-hatred (4.6.124–130).

All these inversions and polarizations are subsumed in the inversion of the word "natural." Edmund is the "natural" son of Gloucester, meaning literally that he is illegitimate. Figuratively, he therefore represents a violation of traditional moral order. In appearance he is smooth and plausible, but in reality he is an archdeceiver like the Vice in a morality play, a superb actor who boasts to the audience in soliloquy of his protean villainy. "Nature" is Edmund's goddess, and by this he means something like a naturalistic universe in which the race goes to the swiftest and in which conscience, morality, and religion are empty myths. Whereas Lear invokes Nature as a goddess who will punish ungrateful daughters and defend rejected fathers (1.4.274–288) and whereas Gloucester believes in a cosmic correspondence between eclipses of the moon or sun and mutinous discords among people (1.2.106–117), Edmund scoffs at all such metaphysical speculations. He spurns, in other words, the Boethian conception of a divine harmony uniting the cosmos and humankind, with humankind at the center of the universe. As a rationalist, Edmund echoes Jacobean disruptions of the older world order in politics and religion as well as in science. He is Machiavellian, an atheist, and Epicurean—everything inimical to traditional Elizabethan ideals of order. To him, "natural" means precisely what Lear and Gloucester call "unnatural."

His creed provides the play with its supreme test. Which definition of "natural" is true? Does heaven exist, and will it let Edmund and the other villainous persons get away with their evil? The question is frequently asked, but the answers are ambiguous. "If you do love old men," Lear implores the gods, "if your sweet sway / Allow obedience, if you yourselves are old, / Make it your cause" (2.4.191–193). His exhortations mount into frenzied rant, until finally the heavens do send down a terrible storm—on Lear himself. Witnesses agree that the absence of divine order in the universe would have the gravest consequences. "If that the heavens do not their visible spirits / Send quickly down to tame these vile offenses," says Albany of Lear's ordeal, "It will come, / Humanity must perforce prey on itself, / Like monsters of the deep" (4.2.47–51). And Cornwall's servants (in a passage missing from the Folio text) have perceived earlier the dire implications of their masters' evil deeds. "I'll never care what wickedness I do, / If this man come to good," says one, and his fellow agrees: "If she [Regan] live long, / And in the end meet the old course of death, / Women will all turn monsters" (3.7.102–105). Yet these servants do, in fact, obey their own best instincts, turning on Cornwall and ministering to Gloucester despite danger to themselves. Similarly, Albany abandons his mild attempts to conciliate his domineering wife and instead uses his power for good. Cordelia's ability to forgive and cherish her father, and Edgar's comparable ministering to Gloucester, give the lie to

Edmund's "natural" or amoral view of humanity; a few people, at least, are capable of charity, even when it does not serve their own material self-interest. Conversely, the play suggests that villainy will at last destroy itself, and not simply because the gods are just; Albany's hopeful insistence that "This shows you are above, / You justicers" (4.2.79–80) may be a little more than wishful thinking, to be undercut by some fresh disaster, but at least the insatiable ambitions of Edmund, Goneril, Regan, Cornwall, and Oswald do lead to their violent deaths. Edmund's belated attempt to save the life of Cordelia, though unsuccessful, suggests that this intelligent villain has at last begun to understand the great flaw in his naturalistic creed and to see that, like Goneril and Regan, he has been consumed by his own lust.

Even with such reassurances that villainy will eventually undo itself, the devastation at the end of King Lear is so appalling that our questions about justice remain finally unanswered. To ask the question "Who must pay for Lear's self-knowledge?" is to remind ourselves that women must often die in Shakespeare's tragedies so that men may learn, and to perceive even further that, in the absurdist world of Lear, the Cartesian logic of cause and effect and poetic justice simply will not account for all that we long to understand. As Roland Barthes well expresses the matter in an essay on Racine, "tragedy is only a means of reclaiming human unhappiness, of subsuming it, thus justifying it under the form of necessity, or wisdom, or purification." Tragedy cannot explain away the death of Cordelia and the heartbreak of her father. The last tableau is a vision of doomsday, with Cordelia strangled, Lear broken and dying, and the "gored state" in such disarray that we cannot be sure what restoration can occur. The very question of political order is dwarfed by the enormity of the personal disaster of Lear and Cordelia. No one wishes longer life for the King: "He hates him / That would upon the rack of this tough world / Stretch him out longer." He is dead; "The wonder is he hath endured so long" (5.3.319–326). Lear's view of life's terrible corruption, pronounced in his madness, seems confirmed in his end. Perhaps the only way in which this tragedy can reclaim so much unhappiness is to suggest that, given the incurable badness of the world, we can at least choose whether to attempt to be like Cordelia and Edgar (knowing what the price may be for such courage) or to settle for being our worst selves, like Edmund, Goneril, and Regan. Overwhelmed as we are by the testimonial before us of humankind's vicious capacity for self-destruction, we are stirred nonetheless by the ability of some men and women to confront their fearful destiny with probity and stoic renunciation, adhering to what they believe to be good and expecting Fortune to give them absolutely nothing. The power of love, though learned too late to avert catastrophe, is at last discovered in its very defeat.

King Lear

[*Dramatis Personae*

KING LEAR
GONERIL,
REGAN, } *Lear's daughters*
CORDELIA
DUKE OF ALBANY, *Goneril's husband*
DUKE OF CORNWALL, *Regan's husband*
KING OF FRANCE, *Cordelia's suitor and husband*
DUKE OF BURGUNDY, *suitor to Cordelia*

EARL OF KENT, *later disguised as Caius*
EARL OF GLOUCESTER
EDGAR, *Gloucester's son and heir, later disguised as poor Tom*
EDMUND, *Gloucester's bastard son*

OSWALD, *Goneril's steward*
A KNIGHT *serving King Lear*
Lear's FOOL
CURAN, *in Gloucester's household*
GENTLEMEN
Three SERVANTS
OLD MAN, *a tenant of Gloucester*
Three MESSENGERS
DOCTOR *attending Cordelia*
Two CAPTAINS
HERALD

Knights, Gentlemen, Attendants, Servants, Officers, Soldiers, Trumpeters

SCENE: *Britain*]

1.1   *Enter Kent, Gloucester, and Edmund.*

KENT   I thought the King had more affected the Duke of 1
Albany than Cornwall. 2
GLOUCESTER   It did always seem so to us; but now in
the division of the kingdom it appears not which of
the dukes he values most, for equalities are so weighed 5
that curiosity in neither can make choice of either's 6
moiety. 7
KENT   Is not this your son, my lord?
GLOUCESTER   His breeding, sir, hath been at my charge. 9
I have so often blushed to acknowledge him that now
I am brazed to 't. 11

1.1. Location: King Lear's palace.
1 more affected better liked   **2 Albany** i.e., Scotland   **5–7 equalities
. . . moiety** the shares balance so equally that close scrutiny cannot
find advantage in either's portion   **9 breeding** raising, care.   **charge**
expense   **11 brazed** hardened

KENT   I cannot conceive you. 12
GLOUCESTER   Sir, this young fellow's mother could;
whereupon she grew round-wombed and had indeed,
sir, a son for her cradle ere she had a husband
for her bed. Do you smell a fault? 16
KENT   I cannot wish the fault undone, the issue of it 17
being so proper. 18
GLOUCESTER   But I have a son, sir, by order of law, some 19
year elder than this, who yet is no dearer in my ac- 20
count. Though this knave came something saucily to 21
the world before he was sent for, yet was his mother
fair, there was good sport at his making, and the
whoreson must be acknowledged.—Do you know this 24
noble gentleman, Edmund?
EDMUND   No, my lord.
GLOUCESTER   My lord of Kent. Remember him hereafter as my honorable friend.
EDMUND   My services to your lordship. 29
KENT   I must love you, and sue to know you better. 30
EDMUND   Sir, I shall study deserving. 31
GLOUCESTER   He hath been out nine years, and away 32
he shall again. The King is coming. 33

*Sennet. Enter [one bearing a coronet, then] King
Lear, Cornwall, Albany, Goneril, Regan, Cordelia,
and attendants.*

LEAR
Attend the lords of France and Burgundy,
Gloucester. 34
GLOUCESTER   I shall, my liege.   *Exit.*
LEAR
Meantime we shall express our darker purpose. 36
Give me the map there. [*He takes a map.*] Know that
we have divided
In three our kingdom; and 'tis our fast intent 38
To shake all cares and business from our age,
Conferring them on younger strengths while we
Unburdened crawl toward death. Our son of
Cornwall,
And you, our no less loving son of Albany,
We have this hour a constant will to publish 43
Our daughters' several dowers, that future strife 44
May be prevented now. The princes, France and
Burgundy,
Great rivals in our youngest daughter's love,

12 conceive understand. (But Gloucester puns in the sense of "become pregnant.")   **16 fault** (1) sin (2) loss of scent by the hounds
17 issue (1) result (2) offspring   **18 proper** (1) excellent (2) handsome
19 by order of law legitimate   **19–20 some year** about a year   **20–
21 account** estimation   **21 knave** young fellow (not said disapprov-
ingly, though the word is ironic).   **something** somewhat   **24 whoreson** low fellow; suggesting bastardy, but (like *knave* above) used with
affectionate condescension   **29 services** duty   **30 sue** petition, beg
31 study deserving strive to be worthy (of your esteem)   **32 out** i.e.,
abroad, absent   **33 s.d. Sennet** trumpet signal heralding a procession.
one . . . then (This direction is from the Quarto. The *coronet* is perhaps intended for Cordelia or her betrothed. A coronet signifies nobility below the rank of king.)   **34 Attend** i.e., wait on them ceremoni-
ally, usher them into our presence   **36 we, our** (The royal plural; also
in lines 37–44, etc.)   **darker purpose** undeclared intention   **38 fast**
firm   **43 constant . . . publish** firm resolve to proclaim   **44 several**
individual

Long in our court have made their amorous sojourn
And here are to be answered. Tell me, my
  daughters—
Since now we will divest us both of rule,
Interest of territory, cares of state—   50
Which of you shall we say doth love us most,
That we our largest bounty may extend
Where nature doth with merit challenge? Goneril,   53
Our eldest born, speak first.

GONERIL
Sir, I love you more than words can wield the
  matter,
Dearer than eyesight, space, and liberty,   56
Beyond what can be valued, rich or rare,
No less than life, with grace, health, beauty, honor;
As much as child e'er loved, or father found;   59
A love that makes breath poor and speech unable.   60
Beyond all manner of so much I love you.

CORDELIA [aside]
What shall Cordelia speak? Love and be silent.

LEAR [indicating on map]
Of all these bounds, even from this line to this,
With shadowy forests and with champains riched,   64
With plenteous rivers and wide-skirted meads,   65
We make thee lady. To thine and Albany's issue
Be this perpetual.—What says our second daughter,
Our dearest Regan, wife of Cornwall? Speak.

REGAN
I am made of that self mettle as my sister,   69
And prize me at her worth. In my true heart   70
I find she names my very deed of love;   71
Only she comes too short, that I profess   72
Myself an enemy to all other joys
Which the most precious square of sense possesses,   74
And find I am alone felicitate   75
In your dear Highness' love.

CORDELIA [aside]   Then poor Cordelia!
And yet not so, since I am sure my love's
More ponderous than my tongue.   78

LEAR
To thee and thine hereditary ever
Remain this ample third of our fair kingdom,
No less in space, validity, and pleasure   81
Than that conferred on Goneril.—Now, our joy,
Although our last and least, to whose young love   83
The vines of France and milk of Burgundy   84

Strive to be interested, what can you say to draw   85
A third more opulent than your sisters'? Speak.

CORDELIA   Nothing, my lord.

LEAR   Nothing?

CORDELIA   Nothing.

LEAR
Nothing will come of nothing. Speak again.

CORDELIA
Unhappy that I am, I cannot heave
My heart into my mouth. I love Your Majesty
According to my bond, no more nor less.   93

LEAR
How, how, Cordelia? Mend your speech a little,
Lest you may mar your fortunes.

CORDELIA   Good my lord,
You have begot me, bred me, loved me. I
Return those duties back as are right fit,   97
Obey you, love you, and most honor you.
Why have my sisters husbands if they say
They love you all? Haply, when I shall wed,   100
That lord whose hand must take my plight shall
  carry   101
Half my love with him, half my care and duty.
Sure I shall never marry like my sisters,
To love my father all.

LEAR
But goes thy heart with this?

CORDELIA   Ay, my good lord.

LEAR   So young, and so untender?

CORDELIA   So young, my lord, and true.

LEAR
Let it be so! Thy truth then be thy dower!
For, by the sacred radiance of the sun,
The mysteries of Hecate and the night,   110
By all the operation of the orbs   111
From whom we do exist and cease to be,   112
Here I disclaim all my paternal care,
Propinquity, and property of blood,   114
And as a stranger to my heart and me
Hold thee from this forever. The barbarous Scythian, 116
Or he that makes his generation messes 117
To gorge his appetite, shall to my bosom
Be as well neighbored, pitied, and relieved
As thou my sometime daughter.

KENT   Good my liege—   120

LEAR   Peace, Kent!
Come not between the dragon and his wrath.
I loved her most, and thought to set my rest   123

---

50 Interest of right or title to, possession of   **53 Where . . . challenge** where both natural affection and merit claim it as due
56 space freedom from confinement   **59 found** i.e., found himself to be loved   **60 breath** voice, speech.   **unable** incompetent, inadequate   **64 shadowy** shady.   **champains riched** fertile plains
65 wide-skirted meads extensive, spread out meadows   **69 self** same.
mettle spirit, temperament. (But with the meaning also of *metal*, "substance," continued in the metaphor of *prize* and *worth*, line 70.)
70 prize . . . worth value myself as her equal (in love for you). (*Prize* suggests "price.")   **71 names . . . love** describes my love in action
72 that in that   **74 most . . . possesses** most delicate test of my sensibility, most delicately sensitive part of my nature, can enjoy   **75 felicitate** made happy   **78 ponderous** weighty   **81 validity** value.
pleasure pleasing features   **83 least** youngest   **84 vines** vineyards.
milk pastures (?)

85 be interested be affiliated, establish a claim, be admitted as to a privilege.   **draw** win   **93 bond** filial obligation   **97 right fit** proper and fitting   **100 all** exclusively, and with all of themselves.   **Haply** perhaps, with luck   **101 plight** pledge in marriage   **110 mysteries** secret rites.   **Hecate** goddess of witchcraft and the moon   **111 operation** influence.   **orbs** planets and stars   **112 From whom** under whose influence   **114 Propinquity . . . blood** close kinship
116 this this time forth.   **Scythian** (Scythians were famous in antiquity for savagery.)   **117 makes . . . messes** makes meals of his children or parents   **120 sometime** former   **123 set my rest** rely wholly. (A phrase from a game of cards, meaning "to stake all.")

On her kind nursery. [*To Cordelia.*] Hence, and avoid
   my sight!—   124
So be my grave my peace, as here I give   125
Her father's heart from her. Call France. Who stirs?   126
Call Burgundy. [*Exit one.*] Cornwall and Albany,
With my two daughters' dowers digest the third.   128
Let pride, which she calls plainness, marry her.   129
I do invest you jointly with my power,
Preeminence, and all the large effects   131
That troop with majesty. Ourself by monthly course,   132
With reservation of an hundred knights   133
By you to be sustained, shall our abode
Make with you by due turns. Only we shall retain
The name and all th' addition to a king.   136
The sway, revenue, execution of the rest,   137
Belovèd sons, be yours, which to confirm,
This coronet part between you.

KENT   Royal Lear,   139
   Whom I have ever honored as my king,
   Loved as my father, as my master followed,
   As my great patron thought on in my prayers—

LEAR
   The bow is bent and drawn. Make from the shaft.   143

KENT
   Let it fall rather, though the fork invade   144
   The region of my heart. Be Kent unmannerly
   When Lear is mad. What wouldst thou do, old man?
   Think'st thou that duty shall have dread to speak
   When power to flattery bows?
   To plainness honor's bound   149
   When majesty falls to folly. Reserve thy state,   150
   And in thy best consideration check   151
   This hideous rashness. Answer my life my
      judgment,   152
   Thy youngest daughter does not love thee least,
   Nor are those emptyhearted whose low sounds
   Reverb no hollowness.

   LEAR   Kent, on thy life, no more.   155

KENT
   My life I never held but as a pawn   156
   To wage against thine enemies, nor fear to lose it,   157
   Thy safety being motive.

   LEAR   Out of my sight!   158

KENT
   See better, Lear, and let me still remain   159
   The true blank of thine eye.   160
LEAR   Now, by Apollo—
KENT   Now, by Apollo, King,
   Thou swear'st thy gods in vain.
LEAR   O, vassal! Miscreant!   164
                  [*Laying his hand on his sword.*]
ALBANY, CORNWALL   Dear sir, forbear.
KENT
   Kill thy physician, and the fee bestow
   Upon the foul disease. Revoke thy gift,
   Or whilst I can vent clamor from my throat
   I'll tell thee thou dost evil.
LEAR
   Hear me, recreant, on thine allegiance hear me!   170
   That thou hast sought to make us break our vows,   171
   Which we durst never yet, and with strained pride   172
   To come betwixt our sentence and our power,   173
   Which nor our nature nor our place can bear,   174
   Our potency made good, take thy reward.   175
   Five days we do allot thee for provision
   To shield thee from disasters of the world,
   And on the sixth to turn thy hated back
   Upon our kingdom. If on the tenth day following
   Thy banished trunk be found in our dominions,   180
   The moment is thy death. Away! By Jupiter,
   This shall not be revoked.
KENT
   Fare thee well, King. Sith thus thou wilt appear,   183
   Freedom lives hence and banishment is here.
   [*To Cordelia.*] The gods to their dear shelter take
      thee, maid,
   That justly think'st and hast most rightly said!
   [*To Regan and Goneril.*] And your large speeches may
      your deeds approve,   187
   That good effects may spring from words of love.
   Thus Kent, O princes, bids you all adieu.
   He'll shape his old course in a country new.   *Exit.* 190

      *Flourish. Enter Gloucester, with France and
      Burgundy; attendants.*

GLOUCESTER
   Here's France and Burgundy, my noble lord.
LEAR   My lord of Burgundy,
   We first address toward you, who with this king   193
   Hath rivaled for our daughter. What in the least   194

---

124 nursery nursing, care.   **avoid** leave   **125 So . . . peace, as** as I hope to rest peacefully in my grave   **126 Who stirs?** i.e., somebody do something; don't just stand there   **128 digest** assimilate, incorporate   **129 Let . . . her** let her pride be her dowry and get her a husband   **131 effects** outward shows   **132 troop with** accompany, serve.   **Ourself** (The royal "we.")   **133 With reservation of** reserving to myself the right to be attended by   **136 addition** honors and prerogatives   **137 sway** sovereign authority   **139 coronet** (Perhaps Lear gestures toward this coronet that was to have symbolized Cordelia's dowry and marriage, hands it to his sons-in-law, or actually attempts to divide it.)   **143 Make from** get out of the way of   **144 fall** strike.   **fork** barbed head of an arrow   **149 To . . . bound** loyalty demands frankness   **150 Reserve thy state** retain your royal authority   **151 in . . . consideration** with wise deliberation.   **check** restrain, withhold   **152 Answer . . . judgment** I wager my life on my judgment that   **155 Reverb no hollowness** do not reverberate like a hollow drum, insincerely   **156 held** regarded.   **pawn** weakest chess piece   **157 wage** wager, hazard in warfare   **158 motive** that which prompts me to act

159 still always   **160 The true . . . eye** i.e., the means to enable you to see better. (*Blank* means "the white center of the target," or, more probably, "the true direct aim," as in "point-blank," traveling in a straight line.)   **164 vassal** i.e., wretch.   **Miscreant** (Literally, infidel; hence, villain, rascal.)   **170 recreant** traitor   **171 That** in that, since   **172 strained** excessive   **173 To . . . power** i.e., to block my power to command and judge   **174 Which . . . place** which neither my temperament nor my office as king   **175 Our . . . good** my power enacted, demonstrated   **180 trunk** body   **183 Sith** since   **187 your . . . approve** may your deeds confirm your speeches with their vast claims   **190 shape . . . course** follow his traditional plainspoken ways.   **s.d. Flourish** trumpet fanfare used for the entrance or exit of important persons   **193 address** address myself   **194 rivaled** competed.   **in the least** at the lowest

Will you require in present dower with her
Or cease your quest of love?

BURGUNDY   Most royal Majesty,
I crave no more than hath Your Highness offered,
Nor will you tender less.

LEAR   Right noble Burgundy,   198
When she was dear to us we did hold her so,   199
But now her price is fallen. Sir, there she stands.
If aught within that little-seeming substance,   201
Or all of it, with our displeasure pieced,   202
And nothing more, may fitly like Your Grace,   203
She's there, and she is yours.

BURGUNDY   I know no answer.

LEAR
Will you, with those infirmities she owes,   205
Unfriended, new-adopted to our hate,
Dowered with our curse and strangered with our
  oath,   207
Take her, or leave her?

BURGUNDY   Pardon me, royal sir.
Election makes not up in such conditions.   209

LEAR
Then leave her, sir, for by the power that made me,
I tell you all her wealth. [To France.] For you, great
  King,   211
I would not from your love make such a stray   212
To match you where I hate; therefore beseech you   213
T' avert your liking a more worthier way   214
Than on a wretch whom Nature is ashamed
Almost t' acknowledge hers.

FRANCE   This is most strange,
That she whom even but now was your best object,
The argument of your praise, balm of your age,   218
The best, the dearest, should in this trice of time   219
Commit a thing so monstrous to dismantle   220
So many folds of favor. Sure her offense
Must be of such unnatural degree
That monsters it, or your forevouched affection   223
Fall into taint, which to believe of her   224
Must be a faith that reason without miracle
Should never plant in me.   226

CORDELIA   I yet beseech Your Majesty—
If for I want that glib and oily art   228
To speak and purpose not, since what I well intend   229
I'll do 't before I speak—that you make known
It is no vicious blot, murder, or foulness,
No unchaste action or dishonored step

That hath deprived me of your grace and favor,
But even for want of that for which I am richer: 234
A still-soliciting eye and such a tongue   235
That I am glad I have not, though not to have it
Hath lost me in your liking.

LEAR   Better thou
Hadst not been born than not t' have pleased me
  better.

FRANCE
Is it but this? A tardiness in nature
Which often leaves the history unspoke   240
That it intends to do? My lord of Burgundy,
What say you to the lady? Love's not love
When it is mingled with regards that stands   243
Aloof from th' entire point. Will you have her?   244
She is herself a dowry.

BURGUNDY   Royal King,
Give but that portion which yourself proposed,
And here I take Cordelia by the hand,
Duchess of Burgundy.

LEAR
Nothing. I have sworn. I am firm.

BURGUNDY [to Cordelia]
I am sorry, then, you have so lost a father
That you must lose a husband.

CORDELIA   Peace be with Burgundy!
Since that respects of fortune are his love,   252
I shall not be his wife.

FRANCE
Fairest Cordelia, that art most rich being poor,
Most choice, forsaken, and most loved, despised,
Thee and thy virtues here I seize upon,
Be it lawful I take up what's cast away.   257
                                    [He takes her hand.]
Gods, gods! 'Tis strange that from their cold'st
  neglect   258
My love should kindle to inflamed respect.—   259
Thy dowerless daughter, King, thrown to my chance,   260
Is queen of us, of ours, and our fair France.
Not all the dukes of waterish Burgundy   262
Can buy this unprized precious maid of me.—   263
Bid them farewell, Cordelia, though unkind.   264
Thou losest here, a better where to find.   265

LEAR
Thou hast her, France. Let her be thine, for we
Have no such daughter, nor shall ever see
That face of hers again. Therefore begone   268
Without our grace, our love, our benison.   269

198 tender offer   199 so i.e., *dear*, beloved and valued at a high
price.   201 little-seeming substance one who seems substantial but
whose substance is, in fact, little, or, one who refuses to flatter
202 pieced added, joined   203 like please   205 owes owns
207 strangered with made a stranger by   209 Election . . . conditions no choice is possible under such conditions   211 tell you (1)
inform you of (2) enumerate for you.   For as for   212 make such a
stray stray so far   213 To as to.   beseech I beseech   214 avert your
liking turn your affections   218 argument theme   219 trice moment
220 to as to   223 monsters it makes it monstrous   223–224 or . . .
taint or else the affection for her you have hitherto affirmed (forevouched) must fall into suspicion (taint), or, before (ere, *or*) your hith-
erto-proclaimed affection could have fallen into decay   224 which
i.e., that her offense is monstrous   226 Should could   228 for I want
because I lack   229 purpose not not intend to do what I say

234 for which for want of which   235 still-soliciting ever begging
240 leaves . . . unspoke does not speak aloud the action   243–
244 regards . . . point irrelevant considerations   252 Since that
since.   respects of fortune concern for wealth and position   257 Be
it lawful if it be lawful that   258 from . . . neglect i.e., because the
gods seem to have deserted Cordelia   259 inflamed respect ardent affection   260 chance lot   262 waterish (1) well-watered with rivers (2)
feeble, watery   263 unprized not appreciated (with perhaps a sense
also of "priceless")   264 though unkind though they have behaved
unnaturally   265 here this place.   where place elsewhere   268–
269 Therefore . . . benison (Said perhaps to Cordelia and to the King
of France.)   benison blessing

Come, noble Burgundy.

Flourish. Exeunt [all but France, Goneril, Regan, and Cordelia].

FRANCE   Bid farewell to your sisters.

CORDELIA
Ye jewels of our father, with washed eyes   272
Cordelia leaves you. I know you what you are,
And like a sister am most loath to call   274
Your faults as they are named. Love well our father.   275
To your professèd bosoms I commit him.   276
But yet, alas, stood I within his grace,
I would prefer him to a better place.   278
So, farewell to you both.

REGAN
Prescribe not us our duty.

GONERIL   Let your study
Be to content your lord, who hath received you
At Fortune's alms. You have obedience scanted,   282
And well are worth the want that you have wanted.   283

CORDELIA
Time shall unfold what plighted cunning hides;   284
Who covers faults, at last shame them derides.   285
Well may you prosper!

FRANCE   Come, my fair Cordelia.

Exeunt France and Cordelia.

GONERIL   Sister, it is not little I have to say of what most nearly appertains to us both. I think our father will hence tonight.

REGAN   That's most certain, and with you; next month with us.

GONERIL   You see how full of changes his age is; the observation we have made of it hath not been little. He always loved our sister most, and with what poor judgment he hath now cast her off appears too grossly.   295

REGAN   'Tis the infirmity of his age. Yet he hath ever but slenderly known himself.

GONERIL   The best and soundest of his time hath been   298 but rash. Then must we look from his age to receive   299 not alone the imperfections of long-ingraffed condi-   300 tion, but therewithal the unruly waywardness that in-   301 firm and choleric years bring with them.

REGAN   Such unconstant starts are we like to have from   303 him as this of Kent's banishment.

GONERIL   There is further compliment of leave-taking   305 between France and him. Pray you, let us hit together.   306 If our father carry authority with such disposition as   307 he bears, this last surrender of his will but offend us.   308

REGAN   We shall further think of it.

GONERIL   We must do something, and i' the heat.   310

Exeunt.

❖

1.2   *Enter Bastard [Edmund, with a letter].*

EDMUND
Thou, Nature, art my goddess; to thy law   1
My services are bound. Wherefore should I
Stand in the plague of custom and permit   3
The curiosity of nations to deprive me,   4
For that I am some twelve or fourteen moonshines   5
Lag of a brother? Why bastard? Wherefore base?   6
When my dimensions are as well compact,   7
My mind as generous, and my shape as true,   8
As honest madam's issue? Why brand they us   9
With base? With baseness? Bastardy? Base, base?
Who in the lusty stealth of nature take   11
More composition and fierce quality   12
Than doth within a dull, stale, tirèd bed
Go to th' creating a whole tribe of fops   14
Got 'tween asleep and wake? Well, then,   15
Legitimate Edgar, I must have your land.
Our father's love is to the bastard Edmund
As to th' legitimate. Fine word, "legitimate"!
Well, my legitimate, if this letter speed   19
And my invention thrive, Edmund the base   20
Shall top th' legitimate. I grow, I prosper.
Now, gods, stand up for bastards!

Enter Gloucester.

GLOUCESTER
Kent banished thus? And France in choler parted?
And the King gone tonight? Prescribed his power,   24
Confined to exhibition? All this done   25
Upon the gad? Edmund, how now? What news?   26

EDMUND   So please your lordship, none.

[Putting up the letter.]

GLOUCESTER   Why so earnestly seek you to put up that letter?

EDMUND   I know no news, my lord.

GLOUCESTER   What paper were you reading?

EDMUND   Nothing, my lord.

GLOUCESTER   No? What needed then that terrible dis-   33 patch of it into your pocket? The quality of nothing   34 hath not such need to hide itself. Let's see. Come, if it be nothing I shall not need spectacles.

EDMUND   I beseech you, sir, pardon me. It is a letter
from my brother, that I have not all o'erread; and for 38
so much as I have perused, I find it not fit for your
o'erlooking.   40

GLOUCESTER   Give me the letter, sir.

EDMUND   I shall offend either to detain or give it. The
contents, as in part I understand them, are to blame. 43

GLOUCESTER   Let's see, let's see.

[Edmund gives the letter.]

EDMUND   I hope for my brother's justification he wrote
this but as an essay or taste of my virtue.   46

GLOUCESTER (*reads*) "This policy and reverence of age 47
makes the world bitter to the best of our times, keeps 48
our fortunes from us till our oldness cannot relish
them. I begin to find an idle and fond bondage in the 50
oppression of aged tyranny, who sways not as it hath 51
power but as it is suffered. Come to me, that of this I 52
may speak more. If our father would sleep till I waked
him, you should enjoy half his revenue forever and live
the beloved of your brother,   Edgar."
Hum! Conspiracy! "Sleep till I waked him, you should
enjoy half his revenue." My son Edgar! Had he
a hand to write this? A heart and brain to breed it
in? When came you to this? Who brought it?   59

EDMUND   It was not brought me, my lord; there's the
cunning of it. I found it thrown in at the casement of 61
my closet.   62

GLOUCESTER   You know the character to be your 63
brother's?

EDMUND   If the matter were good, my lord, I durst 65
swear it were his; but in respect of that I would fain 66
think it were not.

GLOUCESTER   It is his.

EDMUND   It is his hand, my lord, but I hope his heart is
not in the contents.

GLOUCESTER   Has he never before sounded you in this
business?

EDMUND   Never, my lord. But I have heard him oft
maintain it to be fit that, sons at perfect age and fathers 74
declined, the father should be as ward to the son, and 75
the son manage his revenue.

GLOUCESTER   O villain, villain! His very opinion in the 77
letter! Abhorred villain! Unnatural, detested, brutish 78
villain! Worse than brutish! Go, sirrah, seek him. I'll 79
apprehend him. Abominable villain! Where is he?

EDMUND   I do not well know, my lord. If it shall please
you to suspend your indignation against my brother
till you can derive from him better testimony of his
intent, you should run a certain course; where, if you 84

violently proceed against him, mistaking his purpose,
it would make a great gap in your own honor and
shake in pieces the heart of his obedience. I dare pawn 87
down my life for him that he hath writ this to feel my 88
affection to your honor, and to no other pretense of 89
danger.   90

GLOUCESTER   Think you so?

EDMUND   If your honor judge it meet, I will place you 92
where you shall hear us confer of this, and by an 93
auricular assurance have your satisfaction, and that 94
without any further delay than this very evening.

GLOUCESTER   He cannot be such a monster—

EDMUND   Nor is not, sure.

GLOUCESTER   To his father, that so tenderly and entirely loves him. Heaven and earth! Edmund, seek
him out; wind me into him, I pray you. Frame the 100
business after your own wisdom. I would unstate 101
myself to be in a due resolution.   102

EDMUND   I will seek him, sir, presently, convey the 103
business as I shall find means, and acquaint you
withal.   105

GLOUCESTER   These late eclipses in the sun and moon 106
portend no good to us. Though the wisdom of nature 107
can reason it thus and thus, yet nature finds itself
scourged by the sequent effects. Love cools, friend- 109
ship falls off, brothers divide; in cities, mutinies; in
countries, discord; in palaces, treason; and the bond
cracked twixt son and father. This villain of mine
comes under the prediction; there's son against father.
The King falls from bias of nature; there's father 114
against child. We have seen the best of our time.
Machinations, hollowness, treachery, and all ruinous
disorders follow us disquietly to our graves. Find out
this villain, Edmund; it shall lose thee nothing. Do it 118
carefully. And the noble and truehearted Kent banished! His offense, honesty! 'Tis strange.   *Exit.*

EDMUND   This is the excellent foppery of the world, that 121
when we are sick in fortune—often the surfeits of our 122
own behavior—we make guilty of our disasters the 123
sun, the moon, and stars, as if we were villains on 124
necessity, fools by heavenly compulsion, knaves,
thieves, and treachers by spherical predominance, 126
drunkards, liars, and adulterers by an enforced obedience of planetary influence, and all that we are evil
in, by a divine thrusting on. An admirable evasion of 129
whoremaster man, to lay his goatish disposition on 130

---

38 for as for   **40 o'erlooking** perusal   **43 to blame** (The Folio reading, *too blame*, "too blameworthy to be shown," may be correct.)
46 essay or taste assay, test   **47 policy and reverence of** policy of
reverencing   **48 the best . . . times** the best years of our lives, i.e.,
our youth   **50 idle** useless.   **fond** foolish   **51 who sways** which
rules   **52 suffered** permitted (by the young, who could seize power if
they wished)   **59 to this** upon this (letter)   **61 casement** window
62 closet private room   **63 character** handwriting   **65 matter** contents   **66 in . . . that** considering what the contents are.   **fain** gladly
74 fit fitting, appropriate.   **perfect age** full maturity   **75 declined**
having become feeble   **77 villain** vile wretch, diabolical schemer
78 Abhorred abhorrent.   **detested** hated and hateful   **79 sirrah**
(Form of address used to inferiors or children.)   **84 run a certain
course** proceed with safety and certainty.   **where** whereas

87–88 pawn down stake   **88 feel** feel out   **89–90 pretense of danger** dangerous purpose   **92 meet** fitting, proper   **93–94 by an . . .
satisfaction** satisfy yourself as to the truth by what you hear
100 wind me into him insinuate yourself into his confidence. (*Me* is
used colloquially.)   **Frame** arrange   **101 after your own wisdom** as
you think best   **101–102 unstate . . . resolution** give up anything
and everything to know the truth, have my doubts resolved
103 presently immediately.   **convey** manage   **105 withal** therewith
106 late recent   **107 the wisdom of nature** natural science   **109 sequent effects** i.e., devastating consequences   **114 bias of nature** natural inclination   **118 lose thee nothing** i.e., earn you a reward
121 foppery foolishness   **122–123 surfeits . . . behavior** consequences of our own overindulgence   **124 on** by   **126 treachers** traitors.   **spherical predominance** astrological determinism, because a
certain planet was ascendant at the hour of our birth   **129 divine** supernatural   **130 goatish** lecherous   **130–131 on the charge** to the responsibility

the charge of a star! My father compounded with my 131
mother under the Dragon's tail and my nativity was 132
under Ursa Major, so that it follows I am rough and 133
lecherous. Fut, I should have been that I am, had the 134
maidenliest star in the firmament twinkled on my
bastardizing. Edgar—

Enter Edgar.

and pat he comes like the catastrophe of the old 137
comedy. My cue is villainous melancholy, with a sigh
like Tom o' Bedlam.—O, these eclipses do portend 139
these divisions! Fa, sol, la, mi.   140

EDGAR   How now, brother Edmund, what serious
contemplation are you in?

EDMUND   I am thinking, brother, of a prediction I read
this other day, what should follow these eclipses.   144

EDGAR   Do you busy yourself with that?

EDMUND   I promise you, the effects he writes of succeed 146
unhappily, as of unnaturalness between the child and 147
the parent, death, dearth, dissolutions of ancient amities, divisions in state, menaces and maledictions
against king and nobles, needless diffidences, banish- 150
ment of friends, dissipation of cohorts, nuptial 151
breaches, and I know not what.

EDGAR   How long have you been a sectary astronom- 153
ical?   154

EDMUND   Come, come, when saw you my father last?

EDGAR   The night gone by.

EDMUND   Spake you with him?

EDGAR   Ay, two hours together.

EDMUND   Parted you in good terms? Found you no
displeasure in him by word nor countenance?   160

EDGAR   None at all.

EDMUND   Bethink yourself wherein you may have offended him, and at my entreaty forbear his presence 163
until some little time hath qualified the heat of his 164
displeasure, which at this instant so rageth in him that
with the mischief of your person it would scarcely 166
allay.   167

EDGAR   Some villain hath done me wrong.

EDMUND   That's my fear. I pray you, have a continent 169
forbearance till the speed of his rage goes slower; and, 170
as I say, retire with me to my lodging, from whence I
will fitly bring you to hear my lord speak. Pray ye, go! 172
There's my key. [*He gives a key.*] If you do stir abroad,
go armed.

EDGAR   Armed, brother?

EDMUND   Brother, I advise you to the best. I am no honest man if there be any good meaning toward you. I 177
have told you what I have seen and heard, but faintly, 178
nothing like the image and horror of it. Pray you, 179
away.

EDGAR   Shall I hear from you anon?

EDMUND
I do serve you in this business.   *Exit* [*Edgar*].
A credulous father and a brother noble,
Whose nature is so far from doing harms
That he suspects none; on whose foolish honesty
My practices ride easy. I see the business.   186
Let me, if not by birth, have lands by wit.   187
All with me's meet that I can fashion fit.   *Exit.* 188

1.3   *Enter Goneril, and* [*Oswald, her*] *steward.*

GONERIL   Did my father strike my gentleman for chiding of his fool?

OSWALD   Ay, madam.

GONERIL
By day and night he wrongs me! Every hour
He flashes into one gross crime or other   5
That sets us all at odds. I'll not endure it.
His knights grow riotous, and himself upbraids us
On every trifle. When he returns from hunting
I will not speak with him. Say I am sick.
If you come slack of former services   10
You shall do well; the fault of it I'll answer.   11
                                                       [*Horns within.*]

OSWALD   He's coming, madam. I hear him.

GONERIL
Put on what weary negligence you please,
You and your fellows. I'd have it come to question.   14
If he distaste it, let him to my sister,   15
Whose mind and mine, I know, in that are one,
Not to be overruled. Idle old man,   17
That still would manage those authorities   18
That he hath given away! Now, by my life,
Old fools are babes again, and must be used
With checks as flatteries, when they are seen
    abused.   21
Remember what I have said.

OSWALD   Well, madam.

GONERIL
And let his knights have colder looks among you.
What grows of it, no matter. Advise your fellows so.

131–132 **compounded . . . Dragon's tail** had sex with my mother
under the constellation Draco   133 **Ursa Major** the big bear   134 **Fut**
i.e., 'sfoot, by Christ's foot.   **that** what   137 **pat** on cue.   **catastrophe** conclusion, resolution (of a play)   139 **Tom o' Bedlam** a lunatic
patient of Bethlehem Hospital in London turned out to beg for his
bread   140 **divisions** social and family conflicts (but with a musical
sense also of florid variations on a theme, thus prompting Edmund's
singing)   144 **this other day** the other day   146 **promise** assure
146–147 **succeed unhappily** follow unluckily   150 **needless diffidences** groundless distrust of others   151 **dissipation of cohorts**
breaking up of military companies, large-scale desertions   153–
154 **sectary astronomical** believer in astrology   160 **countenance** demeanor   163 **forbear his presence** avoid meeting him   164 **qualified**
moderated   166 **with . . . person** with the harmful effect of your
presence; or, even if there were injury done to you   167 **allay** be allayed   169–170 **have . . . forbearance** keep a wary distance
172 **fitly** at a fit time

177 **meaning** intention   178 **but faintly** only with a faint impression
179 **image and horror** horrid reality   186 **practices** plots.   **the business** i.e., how my plots should proceed   187 **wit** intelligence
188 **meet** justifiable.   **fit** to my purpose
1.3. Location: The Duke of Albany's palace.
5 **crime** offense   10 **come slack** fall short   11 **answer** be answerable
for   14 **come to question** be made an issue   15 **distaste** dislike
17 **Idle** foolish   18 **manage those authorities** exercise those prerogatives   21 **With . . . abused** with rebukes instead of flattery, when
they (old men) are seen to be deceived by, or too apt to take advantage of, flatteries

I would breed from hence occasions, and I shall,   26
That I may speak. I'll write straight to my sister   27
To hold my very course. Prepare for dinner. *Exeunt.*

1.4   *Enter Kent [disguised].*

KENT
If but as well I other accents borrow   1
That can my speech diffuse, my good intent   2
May carry through itself to that full issue   3
For which I razed my likeness. Now, banished Kent,   4
If thou canst serve where thou dost stand
condemned,
So may it come thy master, whom thou lov'st,   6
Shall find thee full of labors.

*Horns within. Enter Lear, [Knights,] and
attendants.*

LEAR   Let me not stay a jot for dinner. Go get it ready.   8
[*Exit an Attendant.*] How now, what art thou?   9
KENT   A man, sir.
LEAR   What dost thou profess? What wouldst thou with   11
us?
KENT   I do profess to be no less than I seem: to serve
him truly that will put me in trust, to love him that is
honest, to converse with him that is wise and says   15
little, to fear judgment, to fight when I cannot choose,   16
and to eat no fish.   17
LEAR   What art thou?
KENT   A very honest-hearted fellow, and as poor as the
King.
LEAR   If thou be'st as poor for a subject as he's for a
king, thou'rt poor enough. What wouldst thou?
KENT   Service.
LEAR   Who wouldst thou serve?
KENT   You.
LEAR   Dost thou know me, fellow?
KENT   No, sir, but you have that in your countenance   27
which I would fain call master.
LEAR   What's that?
KENT   Authority.
LEAR   What services canst do?
KENT   I can keep honest counsel, ride, run, mar a curi-   32
ous tale in telling it, and deliver a plain message   33
bluntly. That which ordinary men are fit for I am
qualified in, and the best of me is diligence.

LEAR   How old art thou?
KENT   Not so young, sir, to love a woman for singing,   37
nor so old to dote on her for anything. I have years on
my back forty-eight.
LEAR   Follow me; thou shalt serve me. If I like thee no
worse after dinner, I will not part from thee yet.
Dinner, ho, dinner! Where's my knave, my fool? Go
you and call my fool hither.   [*Exit one.*]

Enter steward [Oswald].

You! You, sirrah, where's my daughter?
OSWALD   So please you—   *Exit.*
LEAR   What says the fellow there? Call the clodpoll back.   46
[*Exit a Knight.*] Where's my fool, ho? I think the
world's asleep.

[*Enter Knight.*]

How now? Where's that mongrel?
KNIGHT   He says, my lord, your daughter is not well.
LEAR   Why came not the slave back to me when I called
him?
KNIGHT   Sir, he answered me in the roundest manner,   53
he would not.
LEAR   He would not?
KNIGHT   My lord, I know not what the matter is, but to
my judgment Your Highness is not entertained with
that ceremonious affection as you were wont. There's
a great abatement of kindness appears as well in the
general dependents as in the Duke himself also and   60
your daughter.
LEAR   Ha? Sayst thou so?
KNIGHT   I beseech you, pardon me, my lord, if I be
mistaken, for my duty cannot be silent when I think
Your Highness wronged.
LEAR   Thou but rememberest me of mine own concep-   66
tion. I have perceived a most faint neglect of late,   67
which I have rather blamed as mine own jealous   68
curiosity than as a very pretense and purpose of   69
unkindness. I will look further into 't. But where's my
fool? I have not seen him this two days.   71
KNIGHT   Since my young lady's going into France, sir,
the Fool hath much pined away.
LEAR   No more of that. I have noted it well. Go you and
tell my daughter I would speak with her. [*Exit one.*]
Go you call hither my fool.   [*Exit one.*]

Enter steward [Oswald].

O, you, sir, you, come you hither, sir. Who am I, sir?
OSWALD   My lady's father.
LEAR   "My lady's father"? My lord's knave! You whore-
son dog, you slave, you cur!
OSWALD   I am none of these, my lord, I beseech your
pardon.
LEAR   Do you bandy looks with me, you rascal?   83
[*He strikes Oswald.*]

26–27 I would . . . speak I wish to create from these incidents the
opportunity to speak out   **27 straight** immediately
**1.4. Location: The Duke of Albany's palace still. The sense of time is
virtually continuous.**
1 as well i.e., as well as I have disguised myself by means of costume
2 diffuse render confused or indistinct   **3 carry . . . issue** succeed to
that perfect result   **4 razed my likeness** scraped off my beard, erased
my outward appearance   **6 come** come to pass that   **8 stay** wait
9 s.d. Attendant (This attendant may be a knight; certainly the one
who speaks at line 50 is a knight.)   **11 What . . . profess** what is
your special calling? (But Kent puns in his answer on *profess* meaning
to "claim.")   **15 honest** honorable.   **converse** associate   **16 judgment** i.e., God's judgment.   **choose** i.e., choose but to fight   **17 eat
no fish** i.e., eat a manly diet (?), be a good Protestant (?)   **27 countenance** face and bearing   **32 keep honest counsel** respect confidences
32–33 curious ornate, elaborate

37 to love as to love   **46 clodpoll** blockhead   **53 roundest** bluntest
60 general dependents servants generally   **66 rememberest** remind
66–67 conception idea, thought   **67 faint** halfhearted   **68–69 jealous curiosity** overscrupulous regard for matters of etiquette   **69 very
pretense** true intention   **71 this** these   **83 bandy** volley, exchange (as
in tennis)

OSWALD   I'll not be strucken, my lord.   84
KENT   Nor tripped neither, you base football player.   85
                        [*He trips up Oswald's heels.*]
LEAR   I thank thee, fellow. Thou serv'st me, and I'll love
thee.
KENT   Come, sir, arise, away! I'll teach you differences. 88
Away, away! If you will measure your lubber's length 89
again, tarry; but away! Go to. Have you wisdom? So.   90
                        [*He pushes Oswald out.*]
LEAR   Now, my friendly knave, I thank thee. There's
earnest of thy service.   [*He gives Kent money.*] 92

          Enter Fool.

FOOL   Let me hire him too. Here's my coxcomb.   93
                        [*Offering Kent his cap.*]
LEAR   How now, my pretty knave, how dost thou?
FOOL   [*to Kent*] Sirrah, you were best take my coxcomb. 95
KENT   Why, Fool?
FOOL   Why? For taking one's part that's out of favor.
Nay, an thou canst not smile as the wind sits, thou'lt 98
catch cold shortly. There, take my coxcomb. Why, this 99
fellow has banished two on 's daughters and did the   100
third a blessing against his will. If thou follow him, thou 101
must needs wear my coxcomb.—How now, nuncle? 102
Would I had two coxcombs and two daughters.
LEAR   Why, my boy?
FOOL   If I gave them all my living, I'd keep my   105
coxcombs myself. There's mine; beg another of thy 106
daughters.
LEAR   Take heed, sirrah—the whip.
FOOL   Truth's a dog must to kennel. He must be
whipped out, when the Lady Brach may stand by the 110
fire and stink.
LEAR   A pestilent gall to me!   112
FOOL   Sirrah, I'll teach thee a speech.
LEAR   Do.
FOOL   Mark it, nuncle:
          Have more than thou showest,   116
          Speak less than thou knowest,
          Lend less than thou owest,   118
          Ride more than thou goest,   119
          Learn more than thou trowest,   120

          Set less than thou throwest;   121
          Leave thy drink and thy whore,
          And keep in-a-door,   123
          And thou shalt have more   124
          Than two tens to a score.   125
KENT   This is nothing, Fool.
FOOL   Then 'tis like the breath of an unfee'd lawyer; you 127
gave me nothing for 't. Can you make no use of noth-
ing, nuncle?
LEAR   Why, no, boy. Nothing can be made out of
nothing.
FOOL   [*to Kent*] Prithee, tell him; so much the rent of his 132
land comes to. He will not believe a fool.
LEAR   A bitter fool!   134
FOOL   Dost know the difference, my boy, between a
bitter fool and a sweet one?
LEAR   No, lad. Teach me.
FOOL
          That lord that counseled thee
               To give away thy land,
          Come place him here by me;
               Do thou for him stand.   141
          The sweet and bitter fool
               Will presently appear: 143
          The one in motley here,   144
               The other found out there.   145
LEAR   Dost thou call me fool, boy?
FOOL   All thy other titles thou hast given away; that
thou wast born with.
KENT   This is not altogether fool, my lord.
FOOL   No, faith, lords and great men will not let me; if 150
I had a monopoly out, they would have part on 't. And 151
ladies too, they will not let me have all the fool to my-
self; they'll be snatching. Nuncle, give me an egg and 153
I'll give thee two crowns.
LEAR   What two crowns shall they be?
FOOL   Why, after I have cut the egg i' the middle and eat 156
up the meat, the two crowns of the egg. When thou 157
clovest thy crown i' the middle and gav'st away both
parts, thou bor'st thine ass on thy back o'er the dirt. 159
Thou hadst little wit in thy bald crown when thou
gav'st thy golden one away. If I speak like myself in 161
this, let him be whipped that first finds it so.   162

---

84 **strucken** struck   85 **football** (A raucous street game played by the lower classes.)   88 **differences** distinctions in rank   89–90 **If . . . again** i.e., if you want to be laid out flat again, you clumsy ox   90 **Have you wisdom** i.e., are you smart enough to make a quick retreat?   92 **earnest** partial advance payment   93 **coxcomb** fool's cap, crested with a red comb   95 **you were best** you had better   98 **an . . . sits** i.e., if you can't play along with those in power   99 **catch cold** i.e., find yourself out in the cold   100 **banished** (i.e., paradoxically, by giving Goneril and Regan his kingdom, Lear has lost them, given them power over him.)   **on 's** of his   101 **blessing** i.e., bestowing Cordelia on France and saving her from the curse of insolent prosperity   102 **nuncle** (Contraction of ''mine uncle,'' the Fool's way of addressing Lear.)   105 **living** property   105–106 **keep my coxcombs** (as proof of my folly)   106 **another** (Lear's folly deserves two coxcombs.)   110 **Brach** hound bitch (here suggesting flattery)   112 **gall** irritation, bitterness—literally, a painful swelling, or bile. (Lear is stung by the Fool's gibe because it is so true.)   116 **Have . . . showest** don't display your wealth ostentatiously   118 **owest** own   119 **goest** i.e., on foot. (Travel prudently on horseback, not afoot.)   120 **Learn** i.e., listen to.   **trowest** believe

121 **Set . . . throwest** don't stake everything on a single throw   123 **in-a-door** indoors, at home   124–125 **shalt . . . score** i.e., will do better than break even (since a *score* equals two tens, or twenty)   127 **breath** speech, counsel   132 **rent** (Lear has no land, hence no rent.)   134 **bitter** satirical   141 **for him stand** impersonate him   143 **presently** immediately   144 **motley** the parti-colored dress of the professional fool. (The Fool identifies himself as the sweet fool, Lear as the bitter fool who counseled himself to give away his kingdom.)   145 **found out there** discovered there. (The Fool points at Lear.)   150 **No . . . let me** i.e., great persons at court will not let me monopolize folly; I am not *altogether* a *score* in the sense of being ''all the fool there is''   151 **a monopoly out** a corner on the market. (The granting of monopolies was a common abuse under King James and Queen Elizabeth.)   **on 't** of it   153 **snatching** seizing their share; perhaps snatching at the Fool's phallic bauble or crotch   156 **eat** eaten, et   157 **the meat** the edible part   159 **bor'st . . . dirt** i.e., bore the ass instead of letting the ass bear you   161 **like myself** i.e., like a fool   162 **whipped** i.e., as a fool.   **finds it so** discovers from his experience that it is true (as Lear is now discovering)

[*Sings.*] "Fools had ne'er less grace in a year,   163
 For wise men are grown foppish   164
And know not how their wits to wear,   165
 Their manners are so apish."

LEAR When were you wont to be so full of songs, sirrah?

FOOL I have used it, nuncle, e'er since thou mad'st thy 169 daughters thy mothers; for when thou gav'st them the rod and putt'st down thine own breeches,
[*Sings*] "Then they for sudden joy did weep,
 And I for sorrow sung,
That such a king should play bo-peep   174
 And go the fools among."
Prithee, nuncle, keep a schoolmaster that can teach thy fool to lie. I would fain learn to lie.

LEAR An you lie, sirrah, we'll have you whipped.   178

FOOL I marvel what kin thou and thy daughters are. They'll have me whipped for speaking true, thou'lt have me whipped for lying, and sometimes I am whipped for holding my peace. I had rather be any kind o' thing than a fool. And yet I would not be thee, nuncle. Thou hast pared thy wit o' both sides and left nothing i' the middle. Here comes one o' the parings.

Enter Goneril.

LEAR
How now, daughter? What makes that frontlet on?   186
You are too much of late i' the frown.

FOOL Thou wast a pretty fellow when thou hadst no need to care for her frowning; now thou art an O with-   189 out a figure. I am better than thou art now; I am a fool,   190 thou art nothing. [*To Goneril.*] Yes, forsooth, I will hold my tongue; so your face bids me, though you say nothing.
 Mum, mum,
 He that keeps nor crust nor crumb,   195
 Weary of all, shall want some.   196
[*Pointing to Lear.*] That's a shelled peascod.   197

GONERIL
Not only, sir, this your all-licensed fool,   198
But other of your insolent retinue
Do hourly carp and quarrel, breaking forth   200
In rank and not-to-be-endurèd riots. Sir,   201
I had thought by making this well known unto you
To have found a safe redress, but now grow fearful,   203
By what yourself too late have spoke and done,   204
That you protect this course and put it on   205
By your allowance; which if you should, the fault   206

Would not scape censure, nor the redresses sleep   207
Which in the tender of a wholesome weal   208
Might in their working do you that offense,
Which else were shame, that then necessity   210
Will call discreet proceeding.   211

FOOL For you know, nuncle,
 "The hedge sparrow fed the cuckoo so long   213
 That it had its head bit off by its young."   214
So, out went the candle, and we were left darkling.   215

LEAR Are you our daughter?

GONERIL
I would you would make use of your good wisdom,
Whereof I know you are fraught, and put away   218
These dispositions which of late transport you   219
From what you rightly are.

FOOL May not an ass know when the cart draws the   221 horse? Whoop, Jug! I love thee.   222

LEAR
Does any here know me? This is not Lear.
Does Lear walk thus, speak thus? Where are his eyes?
Either his notion weakens, his discernings   225
Are lethargied—Ha! Waking? 'Tis not so.   226
Who is it that can tell me who I am?

FOOL Lear's shadow.

LEAR
I would learn that; for, by the marks of sovereignty,   229
Knowledge, and reason, I should be false persuaded   230
I had daughters.   231

FOOL Which they will make an obedient father.   232

LEAR Your name, fair gentlewoman?

GONERIL
This admiration, sir, is much o' the savor   234
Of other your new pranks. I do beseech you   235
To understand my purposes aright.
As you are old and reverend, should be wise.   237
Here do you keep a hundred knights and squires,
Men so disordered, so debauched and bold   239
That this our court, infected with their manners,
Shows like a riotous inn. Epicurism and lust   241
Makes it more like a tavern or a brothel
Than a gracèd palace. The shame itself doth speak   243

163 Fools . . . year fools have never enjoyed less favor; i.e., they are made obsolete by the folly of supposed wise men   **164 foppish** foolish, vain   **165 wear** use   **169 used** practiced   **174 bo-peep** (A child's game.)   **178 An** if   **186 makes** is doing.   **frontlet** a band worn on the forehead; here, frown   **189–190 O without a figure** zero, cipher of no value unless preceded by a digit   **195–196 He . . . some** i.e., that person who, having grown weary of his possessions, gives all away, will find himself in need of part of what is gone   **195 nor . . . nor** neither . . . nor   **196 want** lack   **197 shelled peascod** shelled pea pod, empty of its contents   **198 all-licensed** allowed to speak or act as he pleases   **200 carp** find fault   **201 rank** gross, excessive   **203 safe** certain   **204 too late** all too recently   **205 put it on** encourage it   **206 allowance** approval

207 redresses sleep punishments (for the riotous conduct of Lear's attendants) lie dormant   **208 tender . . . weal** care for preservation of the peace of the state   **210 else were** in other circumstances would be regarded as.   **then necessity** the necessity of the times   **211 discreet** prudent   **213 cuckoo** a bird that lays its eggs in other birds' nests   **214 its young** i.e., the young cuckoo   **215 darkling** in the dark   **218 fraught** freighted, laden   **219 dispositions** states of mind, moods   **221–222 May . . . horse** i.e., may not even a fool see that matters are backwards when a daughter lectures her father?   **222 Jug** i.e., Joan. (The origin of this phrase is uncertain.)   **225 notion** intellectual power   **225–226 discernings Are lethargied** faculties are asleep   **226 Waking** i.e., am I really awake?   **229 that** i.e., who I am.   **marks of sovereignty** outward and visible evidence of being king   **230–231 I should . . . daughters** i.e., all these outward signs of sanity and status would seem to suggest (falsely) that I am the king who had obedient daughters   **232 Which** whom   **234 admiration** (guise of) wonderment   **235 other** other of   **237 should** i.e., you should   **239 disordered** disorderly.   **debauched** (1) led away from proper service and allegiance (2) depraved.   **bold** impudent   **241 Shows** appears.   **Epicurism** excess, hedonism   **243 gracèd** honorable, graced by a royal presence

For instant remedy. Be then desired,   244
By her that else will take the thing she begs,
A little to disquantity your train,   246
And the remainders that shall still depend   247
To be such men as may besort your age,   248
Which know themselves and you.
LEAR   Darkness and devils!
Saddle my horses! Call my train together! [*Exit one.*]
Degenerate bastard, I'll not trouble thee.
Yet have I left a daughter.
GONERIL
You strike my people, and your disordered rabble
Make servants of their betters.

Enter Albany.

LEAR
Woe, that too late repents!—O, sir, are you come?   255
Is it your will? Speak, sir.—Prepare my horses.
                                        [*Exit one.*]
Ingratitude, thou marble-hearted fiend,
More hideous when thou show'st thee in a child
Than the sea monster!
ALBANY   Pray, sir, be patient.
LEAR [*to Goneril*]   Detested kite, thou liest!   261
My train are men of choice and rarest parts,   262
That all particulars of duty know
And in the most exact regard support   264
The worships of their name. O most small fault,   265
How ugly didst thou in Cordelia show!
Which, like an engine, wrenched my frame of nature   267
From the fixed place, drew from my heart all love,
And added to the gall. O Lear, Lear, Lear!
Beat at this gate [*striking his head*] that let thy folly in
And thy dear judgment out! Go, go, my people.   271
                              [*Exeunt some.*]
ALBANY
My lord, I am guiltless as I am ignorant
Of what hath moved you.
LEAR   It may be so, my lord.
Hear, Nature, hear! Dear goddess, hear!
Suspend thy purpose if thou didst intend
To make this creature fruitful!
Into her womb convey sterility;
Dry up in her the organs of increase,
And from her derogate body never spring   279
A babe to honor her! If she must teem,   280
Create her child of spleen, that it may live   281
And be a thwart disnatured torment to her!   282
Let it stamp wrinkles in her brow of youth,
With cadent tears fret channels in her cheeks,   284

Turn all her mother's pains and benefits   285
To laughter and contempt, that she may feel
How sharper than a serpent's tooth it is
To have a thankless child! Away, away!
        Exit [*with Kent and the rest of Lear's followers*].
ALBANY
Now, gods that we adore, whereof comes this?
GONERIL
Never afflict yourself to know more of it,
But let his disposition have that scope   291
As dotage gives it.   292

        Enter Lear.

LEAR
What, fifty of my followers at a clap?
Within a fortnight?
ALBANY   What's the matter, sir?
LEAR
I'll tell thee. [*To Goneril.*] Life and death! I am
   ashamed
That thou hast power to shake my manhood thus,
That these hot tears, which break from me perforce,
Should make thee worth them. Blasts and fogs upon
   thee!   298
Th' untented woundings of a father's curse   299
Pierce every sense about thee! Old fond eyes,   300
Beweep this cause again, I'll pluck ye out   301
And cast you, with the waters that you loose,   302
To temper clay. Yea, is 't come to this?   303
Ha! Let it be so. I have another daughter,
Who, I am sure, is kind and comfortable.   305
When she shall hear this of thee, with her nails
She'll flay thy wolvish visage. Thou shalt find
That I'll resume the shape which thou dost think
I have cast off forever.   *Exit.*
GONERIL   Do you mark that?   309
ALBANY
I cannot be so partial, Goneril,
To the great love I bear you—   311
GONERIL
Pray you, content.—What, Oswald, ho!
[*To the Fool.*] You, sir, more knave than fool, after
   your master.
FOOL   Nuncle Lear, nuncle Lear! Tarry, take the Fool 314
   with thee.   315
        A fox, when one has caught her,
        And such a daughter
        Should sure to the slaughter,   318
        If my cap would buy a halter.
        So the Fool follows after.   *Exit.*

---

244 **desired** requested   246 **disquantity your train** diminish the number of your attendants   247 **the remainders . . . depend** those who remain to attend you   248 **besort** befit   255 **Woe, that** woe to the person who   261 **kite** bird of prey   262 **parts** qualities   264 **in . . . regard** with close attention to detail   265 **worships** honors, reputations   267 **engine** powerful mechanical contrivance, able to wrench Lear's *frame of nature* or natural self from his *fixed place* or foundation, like a building being torn from its foundation   271 **dear** precious   279 **derogate** debased   280 **teem** increase the species   281 **of spleen** consisting only of malice   282 **thwart disnatured** obstinate, perverse, and unnatural, unfilial   284 **cadent** falling.   **fret** wear

285 **benefits** kind offerings   291 **disposition** humor, mood   292 **As which**   298 **Should . . . them** should seem to suggest that you are worth a king's tears.   **Blasts and fogs** infectious blights and disease-bearing fogs   299 **untented** too deep to be probed and cleansed   300 **fond** foolish   301 **Beweep** if you weep for   302 **loose** let loose   303 **temper** soften, bring to a proper consistency for use. (Lear will throw away his tears on a lowly object.)   305 **comfortable** willing to comfort   309 **Do . . . that** i.e., did you hear his threat to resume royal power?   311 **To** because of   314–315 **take . . . thee** (1) take me with you (2) take the name ''fool'' with you. (A stock phrase of taunting farewell.)   318 **Should sure** should certainly be sent

GONERIL
 This man hath had good counsel. A hundred
  knights?
 'Tis politic and safe to let him keep   322
 At point a hundred knights—yes, that on every
  dream,   323
 Each buzz, each fancy, each complaint, dislike,   324
 He may enguard his dotage with their powers
 And hold our lives in mercy.—Oswald, I say!   326
ALBANY Well, you may fear too far.   327
GONERIL Safer than trust too far.
 Let me still take away the harms I fear,   329
 Not fear still to be taken. I know his heart.   330
 What he hath uttered I have writ my sister.
 If she sustain him and his hundred knights
 When I have showed th' unfitness—

  Enter steward [Oswald].

                              How now, Oswald?
 What, have you writ that letter to my sister?
OSWALD Ay, madam.
GONERIL
 Take you some company and away to horse.
 Inform her full of my particular fear,
 And thereto add such reasons of your own
 As may compact it more. Get you gone,   339
 And hasten your return. [*Exit Oswald.*] No, no, my
  lord,
 This milky gentleness and course of yours   341
 Though I condemn not, yet, under pardon,   342
 You're much more attasked for want of wisdom   343
 Than praised for harmful mildness.   344
ALBANY
 How far your eyes may pierce I cannot tell.   345
 Striving to better, oft we mar what's well.
GONERIL Nay, then—
ALBANY Well, well, th' event.   *Exeunt.* 348

                    ❧

1.5 *Enter Lear, Kent [disguised as Caius], and Fool.*

LEAR [*giving a letter to Kent*] Go you before to Gloucester 1
 with these letters. Acquaint my daughter no further 2
 with anything you know than comes from her demand 3
 out of the letter. If your diligence be not speedy, I shall 4
 be there afore you.
KENT I will not sleep, my lord, till I have delivered your
 letter.   *Exit.*

FOOL If a man's brains were in 's heels, were 't not in
 danger of kibes?   9
LEAR Ay, boy.
FOOL Then, I prithee, be merry. Thy wit shall not go
 slipshod.   12
LEAR Ha, ha, ha!
FOOL Shalt see thy other daughter will use thee kindly, 14
 for though she's as like this as a crab's like an apple, 15
 yet I can tell what I can tell.
LEAR What canst tell, boy?
FOOL She will taste as like this as a crab does to a crab.
 Thou canst tell why one's nose stands i' the middle
 on 's face?   20
LEAR No.
FOOL Why, to keep one's eyes of either side 's nose,   22
 that what a man cannot smell out he may spy into.
LEAR I did her wrong.   24
FOOL Canst tell how an oyster makes his shell?
LEAR No.
FOOL Nor I neither. But I can tell why a snail has a
 house.
LEAR Why?
FOOL Why, to put 's head in, not to give it away to his
 daughters and leave his horns without a case.   31
LEAR I will forget my nature. So kind a father!—Be my   32
 horses ready?
FOOL Thy asses are gone about 'em. The reason why   34
 the seven stars are no more than seven is a pretty   35
 reason.
LEAR Because they are not eight.
FOOL Yes, indeed. Thou wouldst make a good fool.
LEAR To take 't again perforce! Monster ingratitude!   39
FOOL If thou wert my fool, nuncle, I'd have thee beaten
 for being old before thy time.
LEAR How's that?
FOOL Thou shouldst not have been old till thou hadst
 been wise.
LEAR
 O, let me not be mad, not mad, sweet heaven!
 Keep me in temper; I would not be mad!

  [*Enter Gentleman.*]

 How now, are the horses ready?
GENTLEMAN Ready, my lord.
LEAR Come, boy.   [*Exeunt Lear and Gentleman.*]
FOOL
 She that's a maid now, and laughs at my departure,

---

322 politic prudent. (Said ironically.)   **323 At point** under arms.
dream i.e., imagined wrong   **324 buzz** idle rumor   **326 in mercy** at
his mercy   **327 fear too far** overestimate the danger   **329 still take
away** always remove   **330 Not . . . taken** rather than dwell continually in the fear of being overtaken (by the *harms*)   **339 compact** confirm   **341 milky . . . course** effeminate and gentle way   **342 under
pardon** if you'll excuse my saying so   **343 attasked** taken to task for,
blamed   **344 harmful mildness** mildness that causes harm
345 pierce i.e., see into matters   **348 th' event** i.e., time will show
1.5. Location: Before Albany's palace.
1 Gloucester i.e., the place in Gloucestershire   **2 these letters** this
letter   **3 demand** inquiry   **4 out of** prompted by

9 kibes chilblains   **12 slipshod** in slippers, worn because of chilblains. (There are no brains, says the Fool, in the heels of one who is
on his way to visit Regan.)   **14 Shalt** thou shalt.   **kindly** (1) according
to filial nature. (Said ironically.) (2) according to her own nature
15 crab crab apple   **20 on 's** of his   **22 of either side 's** on either
side of his   **24 her** i.e., Cordelia   **31 horns** (Suggests cuckold's
horns, as though Lear were figuratively not the father of Goneril and
Regan.)   **32 forget my nature** (Compare this with 1.4.227: "Who is it
that can tell me who I am?" Lear can no longer recognize the kind,
beloved father he thought himself to be.)   **34 Thy . . . 'em** i.e., your
servants (who labor like asses) have gone about readying the horses
35 seven stars Pleiades   **39 To take . . . perforce** i.e., to think that
Goneril would forcibly take back again the privileges guaranteed to
me. (Some editors suggest, less persuasively, that Lear is meditating
an armed restoration of his monarchy.)

Shall not be a maid long, unless things be cut
shorter.   *Exit.* 51

❧

2.1   *Enter Bastard [Edmund] and Curan, severally.*

EDMUND   Save thee, Curan.   1
CURAN   And you, sir. I have been with your father and
given him notice that the Duke of Cornwall and Regan
his duchess will be here with him this night.
EDMUND   How comes that?
CURAN   Nay, I know not. You have heard of the news
abroad—I mean the whispered ones, for they are yet 7
but ear-kissing arguments?   8
EDMUND   Not I. Pray you, what are they?
CURAN   Have you heard of no likely wars toward twixt 10
the Dukes of Cornwall and Albany?
EDMUND   Not a word.
CURAN   You may do, then, in time. Fare you well, sir.
                                                  Exit.

EDMUND
The Duke be here tonight? The better! Best!   14
This weaves itself perforce into my business.
My father hath set guard to take my brother,
And I have one thing, of a queasy question,   17
Which I must act. Briefness and fortune, work!—   18
Brother, a word. Descend. Brother, I say!

    Enter Edgar.

My father watches. O sir, fly this place!
Intelligence is given where you are hid.
You have now the good advantage of the night.
Have you not spoken 'gainst the Duke of Cornwall?
He's coming hither, now, i' the night, i' the haste, 24
And Regan with him. Have you nothing said
Upon his party 'gainst the Duke of Albany?   26
Advise yourself.
EDGAR   I am sure on 't, not a word.   27
EDMUND
I hear my father coming. Pardon me;
In cunning I must draw my sword upon you.
Draw. Seem to defend yourself. Now, quit you
    well.—   [*They draw.*] 30
Yield! Come before my father!—Light, ho, here!—   31
Fly, brother.—Torches, torches!—So, farewell.   32
                                          Exit Edgar.

Some blood drawn on me would beget opinion   33
Of my more fierce endeavor. I have seen drunkards 34
Do more than this in sport. [*He wounds himself in the
    arm.*] Father, Father!
Stop, stop! No help?

    Enter Gloucester, and servants with torches.

GLOUCESTER   Now, Edmund, where's the villain?
EDMUND
Here stood he in the dark, his sharp sword out,
Mumbling of wicked charms, conjuring the moon
To stand 's auspicious mistress.
GLOUCESTER   But where is he?   39
EDMUND
Look, sir, I bleed.
GLOUCESTER   Where is the villain, Edmund?
EDMUND
Fled this way, sir. When by no means he could—
GLOUCESTER
Pursue him, ho! Go after. [*Exeunt some servants.*] By
    no means what?
EDMUND
Persuade me to the murder of your lordship,
But that I told him the revenging gods   44
'Gainst parricides did all the thunder bend,   45
Spoke with how manifold and strong a bond
The child was bound to th' father; sir, in fine,   47
Seeing how loathly opposite I stood   48
To his unnatural purpose, in fell motion   49
With his preparèd sword he charges home   50
My unprovided body, latched mine arm;   51
And when he saw my best alarumed spirits,   52
Bold in the quarrel's right, roused to th' encounter, 53
Or whether gasted by the noise I made,   54
Full suddenly he fled.
GLOUCESTER   Let him fly far.   55
Not in this land shall he remain uncaught;
And found—dispatch. The noble Duke my master,   57
My worthy arch and patron, comes tonight.   58
By his authority I will proclaim it
That he which finds him shall deserve our thanks,
Bringing the murderous coward to the stake;   61
He that conceals him, death.
EDMUND
When I dissuaded him from his intent
And found him pight to do it, with curst speech   64
I threatened to discover him. He replied,   65
"Thou unpossessing bastard, dost thou think,   66

---

51 things i.e., penises. **cut shorter** (A bawdy joke addressed to the
audience.)
2.1. Location: The Earl of Gloucester's house.
s.d. severally separately **1 Save** God save **7 ones** i.e., the news, regarded as plural **8 ear-kissing arguments** lightly whispered topics
10 toward impending **14 The better! Best** so much the better; in
fact, the best that could happen **17 queasy question** matter not for
queasy stomachs **18 Briefness and fortune** expeditious dispatch and
good luck **24 i' the haste** in great haste **26 Upon his party 'gainst**
i.e., (too zealously) on Cornwall's behalf, or, (too critically) on the
subject of his antagonism toward. (It would be dangerous to speak on
either side.) **27 Advise yourself** think it over carefully. **on 't** of it
30 quit you defend, acquit yourself **31–32 Yield . . . farewell** (Edmund speaks loudly as though trying to arrest Edgar, calls for others to
help, and privately bids Edgar to flee.)

33–34 beget . . . endeavor create an impression of my having fought
fiercely **39 stand 's** stand his, act as his **44 that** when **45 bend**
aim **47 in fine** in conclusion **48 loathly opposite** loathingly opposed **49 fell motion** deadly thrust **50 preparèd** unsheathed and
ready. **home** to the very heart **51 unprovided** unprotected.
latched nicked, lanced **52 best alarumed** thoroughly aroused to action, as by a trumpet **53 quarrel's right** justice of the cause
54 gasted frightened **55 Let him fly far** i.e., any fleeing, no matter
how far, will be in vain **57 dispatch** i.e., that will be the end for
him **58 arch and patron** chief patron **61 to the stake** i.e., to reckoning **64 pight** determined. **curst** angry **65 discover** expose
66 unpossessing unable to inherit, beggarly

If I would stand against thee, would the reposal 67
Of any trust, virtue, or worth in thee
Make thy words faithed? No. What I should deny— 69
As this I would, ay, though thou didst produce
My very character—I'd turn it all 71
To thy suggestion, plot, and damnèd practice; 72
And thou must make a dullard of the world 73
If they not thought the profits of my death 74
Were very pregnant and potential spirits 75
To make thee seek it."

GLOUCESTER   O strange and fastened villain! 76
Would he deny his letter, said he?
I never got him.   _Tucket within._ 78
Hark, the Duke's trumpets! I know not why he
 comes.
All ports I'll bar; the villain shall not scape. 80
The Duke must grant me that. Besides, his picture
I will send far and near, that all the kingdom
May have due note of him; and of my land,
Loyal and natural boy, I'll work the means 84
To make thee capable. 85

   Enter Cornwall, Regan, and attendants.

CORNWALL
How now, my noble friend? Since I came hither,
Which I can call but now, I have heard strange
 news.
REGAN
If it be true, all vengeance comes too short
Which can pursue th' offender. How dost, my lord?
GLOUCESTER
O madam, my old heart is cracked, it's cracked!
REGAN
What, did my father's godson seek your life?
He whom my father named? Your Edgar?
GLOUCESTER
O, lady, lady, shame would have it hid!
REGAN
Was he not companion with the riotous knights
That tended upon my father?
GLOUCESTER
I know not, madam. 'Tis too bad, too bad.
EDMUND
Yes, madam, he was of that consort. 97
REGAN
No marvel, then, though he were ill affected. 98
'Tis they have put him on the old man's death, 99
To have th' expense and spoil of his revenues. 100
I have this present evening from my sister

Been well informed of them, and with such cautions
That if they come to sojourn at my house
I'll not be there.
CORNWALL   Nor I, assure thee, Regan.
Edmund, I hear that you have shown your father
A childlike office.
EDMUND   It was my duty, sir. 106
GLOUCESTER [_to Cornwall_]
He did bewray his practice, and received 107
This hurt you see striving to apprehend him. 108
CORNWALL Is he pursued?
GLOUCESTER Ay, my good lord.
CORNWALL
If he be taken, he shall never more
Be feared of doing harm. Make your own purpose, 112
How in my strength you please. For you, Edmund, 113
Whose virtue and obedience doth this instant
So much commend itself, you shall be ours.
Natures of such deep trust we shall much need;
You we first seize on.
EDMUND   I shall serve you, sir,
Truly, however else. 118
GLOUCESTER For him I thank Your Grace.
CORNWALL
You know not why we came to visit you—
REGAN
—Thus out of season, threading dark-eyed night:
Occasions, noble Gloucester, of some poise, 122
Wherein we must have use of your advice.
Our father he hath writ, so hath our sister,
Of differences, which I least thought it fit 125
To answer from our home. The several messengers 126
From hence attend dispatch. Our good old friend, 127
Lay comforts to your bosom, and bestow
Your needful counsel to our businesses, 129
Which craves the instant use. 130
GLOUCESTER I serve you, madam.
Your Graces are right welcome. _Flourish. Exeunt._

2.2 _Enter Kent [disguised as Caius] and steward_
   [Oswald], severally.

OSWALD Good dawning to thee, friend. Art of this 1
house?
KENT Ay.
OSWALD Where may we set our horses?
KENT I' the mire.

---

67 reposal placing **69 faithed** believed. **What** that which, whatever **71 character** written testimony, handwriting. **turn** attribute **72 suggestion** instigation. **practice** plot **73 make . . . world** think everyone idiotic **74 not thought** did not think. **of my death** that you would gain through my death **75 pregnant . . . spirits** fertile and potent tempters **76 strange** unnatural. **fastened** hardened **78 got** begot. **s.d. Tucket** series of notes on the trumpet, here indicating Cornwall's arrival **80 ports** seaports, or gateways **84 natural** (1) prompted by natural feelings of loyalty and affection (2) bastard **85 capable** legally able to become the inheritor **97 consort** crew **98 though** if. **ill affected** ill-disposed, disloyal **99 put him on** incited him to **100 expense and spoil** squandering

106 childlike filial **107 bewray his practice** expose his (Edgar's) plot **108 apprehend** arrest **112–113 Make . . . please** form your plans, making free use of my authority and resources **113 For** as for **118 however else** i.e., whether capably or not **122 poise** weight **125 differences** quarrels. **which** i.e., which letters **126 from our home** while still at our palace in Cornwall **127 attend dispatch** wait to be dispatched **129 needful** necessary **130 the instant use** immediate attention

2.2 Location: Before Gloucester's house.
s.d. severally at separate doors **1 dawning** (It is not yet day.)

OSWALD Prithee, if thou lov'st me, tell me. 6

KENT I love thee not.

OSWALD Why then, I care not for thee. 8

KENT If I had thee in Lipsbury pinfold, I would make 9
thee care for me. 10

OSWALD Why dost thou use me thus? I know thee not. 11

KENT Fellow, I know thee. 12

OSWALD What dost thou know me for?

KENT A knave, a rascal, an eater of broken meats; 14
a base, proud, shallow, beggarly, three-suited, 15
hundred-pound, filthy worsted-stocking knave; a 16
lily-livered, action-taking, whoreson, glass-gazing, 17
superserviceable, finical rogue; one-trunk-inheriting 18
slave; one that wouldst be a bawd in way of good ser- 19
vice, and art nothing but the composition of a knave, 20
beggar, coward, pander, and the son and heir of a
mongrel bitch; one whom I will beat into clamorous
whining if thou deny'st the least syllable of thy addi- 23
tion. 24

OSWALD Why, what a monstrous fellow art thou thus
to rail on one that is neither known of thee nor knows
thee!

KENT What a brazen-faced varlet art thou to deny thou
knowest me! Is it two days since I tripped up thy heels
and beat thee before the King? Draw, you rogue, for
though it be night, yet the moon shines. I'll make a
sop o' the moonshine of you, you whoreson, cullionly 32
barbermonger. Draw! [He brandishes his sword.] 33

OSWALD Away! I have nothing to do with thee.

KENT Draw, you rascal! You come with letters against
the King, and take Vanity the puppet's part against 36
the royalty of her father. Draw, you rogue, or I'll so
carbonado your shanks—draw, you rascal! Come 38
your ways. 39

OSWALD Help, ho! Murder! Help!

KENT Strike, you slave! Stand, rogue, stand, you neat 41
slave, strike! [He beats him.]

OSWALD Help, ho! Murder! Murder!

6 if thou lov'st me i.e., if you bear good will toward me. (But Kent
deliberately takes the phrase in its literal, not courtly, sense.)
8–10 care not for . . . care for do not like . . . have an anxious regard for **9 in Lipsbury pinfold** i.e., within the pinfold of the lips, between my teeth. (A *pinfold* is a pound for stray animals.)
11–12 know thee not . . . know thee am unacquainted with you
. . . can see through you **14 broken meats** scraps of food (such as
were passed out to the most lowly) **15 three-suited** (Three suits a
year were allowed to servants.) **16 hundred-pound** (Possible allusion
to the fee paid by some parvenus to be knighted by James I.) **worsted-stocking** i.e., too poor and menial to wear silk stockings **17 lily-
livered** cowardly (the liver being pale through lack of blood). **action-
taking** settling quarrels by resort to law instead of arms, cowardly.
glass-gazing fond of looking in the mirror **18 superserviceable** officious. **finical** foppish, fastidious. **one-trunk-inheriting** possessing
effects sufficient for one trunk only **19–20 bawd . . . service** i.e.,
pimp or pander as a way of providing whatever is wanted **20 composition** compound **23–24 thy addition** the titles I've given you
32 sop o' the moonshine something so perforated that it will soak up
moonshine as a sop (floating piece of toast) soaks up liquor **32–
33 cullionly barbermonger** base frequenter of barber shops, fop. (*Cullion* originally meant "testicle.") **36 Vanity . . . part** i.e., the part of
Goneril (here personified as a character in a morality play) **38 carbonado** cut crosswise, like meat for broiling **38–39 Come your
ways** come on **41 neat** (1) foppish (2) calflike. (*Neat* means "horned
cattle.")

*Enter Bastard [Edmund, with his rapier drawn],
Cornwall, Regan, Gloucester, servants.*

EDMUND How now, what's the matter? Part! 44

KENT With you, goodman boy, an you please! Come, 45
I'll flesh ye. Come on, young master. 46

GLOUCESTER Weapons? Arms? What's the matter here?

CORNWALL Keep peace, upon your lives! [*Kent and
Oswald are parted.*] He dies that strikes again. What is
the matter?

REGAN The messengers from our sister and the King.

CORNWALL What's your difference? Speak. 52

OSWALD I am scarce in breath, my lord.

KENT No marvel, you have so bestirred your valor.
You cowardly rascal, nature disclaims in thee. A tailor 55
made thee.

CORNWALL Thou art a strange fellow. A tailor make a
man?

KENT A tailor, sir. A stonecutter or a painter could not
have made him so ill, though they had been but two
years o' the trade.

CORNWALL Speak yet, how grew your quarrel?

OSWALD This ancient ruffian, sir, whose life I have
spared at suit of his gray beard—

KENT Thou whoreson zed! Thou unnecessary letter!— 65
My lord, if you'll give me leave, I will tread this un- 66
bolted villain into mortar and daub the wall of a jakes 67
with him. —Spare my gray beard, you wagtail? 68

CORNWALL Peace, sirrah!
You beastly knave, know you no reverence?

KENT
Yes, sir, but anger hath a privilege.

CORNWALL Why art thou angry?

KENT
That such a slave as this should wear a sword,
Who wears no honesty. Such smiling rogues as
these,
Like rats, oft bite the holy cords atwain 75
Which are too intrinse t' unloose; smooth every
passion 76
That in the natures of their lords rebel,
Bring oil to fire, snow to their colder moods, 78
Renege, affirm, and turn their halcyon beaks 79
With every gale and vary of their masters, 80
Knowing naught, like dogs, but following.—
A plague upon your epileptic visage! 82
Smile you my speeches, as I were a fool? 83

44 matter i.e., trouble. (But Kent takes the meaning "cause for quarrel.") **45 With you** I'll fight with you; my quarrel is with you.
goodman boy (A contemptuous epithet, a title of mock respect, addressed seemingly to Edmund.) **an** if **46 flesh** initiate into combat
52 difference quarrel **55 disclaims in** disowns **65 zed** the letter *z*,
regarded as unnecessary and often not included in dictionaries of the
time **66–67 unbolted** unsifted; hence, coarse **67 daub** plaster.
jakes privy **68 wagtail** bird wagging its tail feathers in pert obsequiousness **75 holy cords** sacred bonds of affection and order
76 intrinse intrinsicate, tightly knotted. **smooth** flatter, humor
78 Bring oil to fire i.e., flattering servants fuel the flame of their masters' angry passions **79 Renege** deny. **halcyon beaks** (The halcyon
or kingfisher, if hung up, would supposedly turn its beak into the
wind.) **80 gale and vary** variation in the wind **82 epileptic** i.e.,
trembling and pale with fright and distorted with a grin **83 Smile you**
do you smile at. **as** as if

Goose, an I had you upon Sarum plain,   84
I'd drive ye cackling home to Camelot.   85
CORNWALL What, art thou mad, old fellow?
GLOUCESTER How fell you out? Say that.
KENT
No contraries hold more antipathy
Than I and such a knave.
CORNWALL
Why dost thou call him knave? What is his fault?
KENT His countenance likes me not.   91
CORNWALL
No more, perchance, does mine, nor his, nor hers.
KENT
Sir, 'tis my occupation to be plain:
I have seen better faces in my time
Than stands on any shoulder that I see
Before me at this instant.
CORNWALL   This is some fellow
Who, having been praised for bluntness, doth affect   97
A saucy roughness, and constrains the garb   98
Quite from his nature. He cannot flatter, he;   99
An honest mind and plain, he must speak truth!
An they will take 't, so; if not, he's plain.   101
These kind of knaves I know, which in this
    plainness
Harbor more craft and more corrupter ends
Than twenty silly-ducking observants   104
That stretch their duties nicely.   105
KENT
Sir, in good faith, in sincere verity,   106
Under th' allowance of your great aspect,   107
Whose influence, like the wreath of radiant fire   108
On flickering Phoebus' front—
CORNWALL   What mean'st by this? 109
KENT To go out of my dialect, which you discommend
so much. I know, sir, I am no flatterer. He that be- 111
guiled you in a plain accent was a plain knave, which 112
for my part I will not be, though I should win your 113
displeasure to entreat me to 't.   114
CORNWALL What was th' offense you gave him?

OSWALD I never gave him any.
It pleased the King his master very late   117
To strike at me, upon his misconstruction;   118
When he, compact, and flattering his displeasure, 119
Tripped me behind; being down, insulted, railed,   120
And put upon him such a deal of man   121
That worthied him, got praises of the King   122
For him attempting who was self-subdued;   123
And, in the fleshment of this dread exploit,   124
Drew on me here again.
KENT None of these rogues and cowards   126
But Ajax is their fool.
CORNWALL   Fetch forth the stocks! 127
You stubborn, ancient knave, you reverend braggart, 128
We'll teach you.
KENT   Sir, I am too old to learn.
Call not your stocks for me. I serve the King,
On whose employment I was sent to you.
You shall do small respect, show too bold malice
Against the grace and person of my master,   133
Stocking his messenger.
CORNWALL
Fetch forth the stocks! As I have life and honor,
There shall he sit till noon.
REGAN
Till noon? Till night, my lord, and all night too.
KENT
Why, madam, if I were your father's dog
You should not use me so.   139
REGAN Sir, being his knave, I will.   140
CORNWALL
This is a fellow of the selfsame color   141
Our sister speaks of.—Come, bring away the stocks! 142
                                    Stocks brought out.
GLOUCESTER
Let me beseech Your Grace not to do so.
His fault is much, and the good King his master
Will check him for 't. Your purposed low correction 145
Is such as basest and contemned'st wretches   146
For pilferings and most common trespasses
Are punished with. The King must take it ill
That he, so slightly valued in his messenger,
Should have him thus restrained.
CORNWALL   I'll answer that. 150
REGAN
My sister may receive it much more worse
To have her gentleman abused, assaulted,

84–85 Goose . . . Camelot (The reference is obscure, but the general
sense is that Kent scorns Oswald as a cackling goose.) an if. Sarum
Salisbury. Camelot legendary seat of King Arthur and his Round Table, said to have been at Cadbury and at Winchester, and hence in
the general vicinity of Salisbury and Gloucester 91 likes pleases
97 affect adopt the style of 98–99 constrains . . . nature i.e., distorts plainness to the point of caricature, away from its true purpose
101 An . . . plain if people will take his rudeness, fine; if not, his excuse is that he speaks plain truth 104 silly-ducking observants foolishly bowing, obsequious attendants 105 stretch . . . nicely exert
themselves in their courtly duties punctiliously 106 Sir, in good
faith, etc. (Kent assumes the wordy mannerisms of courtly flattery.)
107 allowance approval. aspect (1) countenance (2) astrological position 108 influence astrological power 109 Phoebus' front i.e., the
sun's forehead 111–112 He . . . accent i.e., the man who used
plain speech to you craftily (see lines 102–105) and thereby taught
you to suspect plain speakers of being deceitful 112–114 which
. . . me to 't i.e., I will no longer use plain speech, despite the incentive of incurring your displeasure by doing so. (Kent prefers to displease Cornwall, since Cornwall is pleased only by flatterers, and
Kent has assumed until now that plain speech was the best way to offend, but he now argues mockingly that he can no longer speak
plainly, since his honest utterance will be interpreted as duplicity.)

117 late recently 118 upon his misconstruction as a result of the
King's misunderstanding (me) 119 he i.e., Kent. compact joined,
united with the King. flattering his displeasure gratifying the King's
anger (at me) 120 being down, insulted i.e., when I was down, he
exulted over me 121 put . . . man acted like such a hero 122 worthied won a reputation for 123 For . . . self-subdued for assailing
one (i.e., myself) who chose not to resist 124 fleshment excitement
resulting from a first success. dread exploit (Said ironically.)
126–127 None . . . fool i.e., you never find any rogues and cowards
of this sort who do not outdo the blustering Ajax in their boasting
128 reverend (because old) 133 grace sovereignty, royal grace
139 should would 140 being since you are 141 color complexion,
character 142 away along 145 check rebuke, correct 146 contemned'st most despised 150 answer be answerable for

For following her affairs. Put in his legs.
                         [*Kent is put in the stocks.*]
Come, my good lord, away.
                         Exeunt [all but Gloucester and Kent].

GLOUCESTER
I am sorry for thee, friend. 'Tis the Duke's pleasure,
Whose disposition, all the world well knows,
Will not be rubbed nor stopped. I'll entreat for thee.   157

KENT
Pray, do not, sir. I have watched and traveled hard.   158
Some time I shall sleep out; the rest I'll whistle.
A good man's fortune may grow out at heels.   160
Give you good morrow!   161

GLOUCESTER
The Duke's to blame in this. 'Twill be ill taken.   *Exit.*

KENT
Good King, that must approve the common saw,   163
Thou out of heaven's benediction com'st
To the warm sun!   [*He takes out a letter.*]
Approach, thou beacon to this under globe,   166
That by thy comfortable beams I may   167
Peruse this letter. Nothing almost sees miracles   168
But misery. I know 'tis from Cordelia,   169
Who hath most fortunately been informed
Of my obscurèd course, and shall find time   171
From this enormous state, seeking to give   172
Losses their remedies. All weary and o'erwatched,   173
Take vantage, heavy eyes, not to behold   174
This shameful lodging.   175
Fortune, good night. Smile once more; turn thy
    wheel!   [*He sleeps.*]   176

2.3   *Enter Edgar.*

EDGAR   I heard myself proclaimed,
And by the happy hollow of a tree   2
Escaped the hunt. No port is free, no place   3
That guard and most unusual vigilance   4

Does not attend my taking. Whiles I may scape   5
I will preserve myself, and am bethought   6
To take the basest and most poorest shape
That ever penury, in contempt of man,   8
Brought near to beast. My face I'll grime with filth,
Blanket my loins, elf all my hairs in knots,   10
And with presented nakedness outface   11
The winds and persecutions of the sky.
The country gives me proof and precedent   13
Of Bedlam beggars who with roaring voices   14
Strike in their numbed and mortifièd arms   15
Pins, wooden pricks, nails, sprigs of rosemary;   16
And with this horrible object, from low farms,   17
Poor pelting villages, sheepcotes, and mills,   18
Sometimes with lunatic bans, sometimes with
    prayers,   19
Enforce their charity. Poor Turlygod! Poor Tom!   20
That's something yet. Edgar I nothing am.   *Exit.* 21

2.4   *Enter Lear, Fool, and Gentleman.*

LEAR
'Tis strange that they should so depart from home
And not send back my messenger.

GENTLEMAN   As I learned,
The night before there was no purpose in them
Of this remove.

KENT   Hail to thee, noble master!   4

LEAR   Ha?
Mak'st thou this shame thy pastime?

KENT   No, my lord.

FOOL   Ha, ha, he wears cruel garters. Horses are tied by 7
the heads, dogs and bears by the neck, monkeys by
the loins, and men by the legs. When a man's over- 9
lusty at legs, then he wears wooden netherstocks.   10

LEAR
What's he that hath so much thy place mistook
To set thee here?

KENT   It is both he and she: 12
Your son and daughter.

LEAR   No.

KENT   Yes.

LEAR   No, I say.

KENT   I say yea.

157 rubbed hindered, obstructed. (A term from bowls.) **158 watched** gone sleepless **160 A . . . heels** i.e., even good men suffer decline in fortune at times. (To be out at heels is literally to be threadbare, coming through one's stockings.) **161 Give you** i.e., God give you **163 approve** prove true. **saw** proverb (i.e., "To run out of God's blessing into the warm sun," meaning "to go from better to worse," from a state of bliss into the pitiless world. Kent sees Lear as heading for trouble.) **166 beacon . . . globe** i.e., the sun (?). (Some editors believe that Kent means the moon, since it is night at lines 31 and 176, but he probably is saying that he hopes for daylight soon in order that he can read the letter from Cordelia.) **167 comfortable** useful, aiding **168–169 Nothing . . . misery** scarcely anything can make one appreciate miracles like being in a state of misery; to the miserable, any relief seems miraculous **171 obscurèd** disguised **171–173 and . . . remedies** (This seemingly incoherent passage may be textually corrupt or may be meant to represent fragments from the letter Kent is reading.) **172 From . . . state** i.e., to provide relief from this monstrous state of affairs, this enormity (?) **173 Losses** reversals of fortune. **o'erwatched** exhausted with staying awake **174 vantage** advantage (of sleep) **175 lodging** i.e., the stocks **176 wheel** (Since Kent is at the bottom of Fortune's wheel, any turning will improve his situation.) **2.3. Location: Scene continues. Kent is dozing in the stocks. 2 happy** luckily found **3 port** (See 2.1.80 and note.) **4 That** in which

5 attend my taking lie in wait to capture me **6 bethought** resolved **8 in . . . man** in order to show how contemptible humankind is **10 elf** tangle into elflocks **11 presented** exposed to view, displayed **13 proof** example **14 Bedlam** (See the note to 1.2.139.) **15 Strike** stick. **mortified** deadened **16 wooden pricks** skewers **17 object** spectacle. **low** lowly **18 pelting** paltry **19 bans** curses **20 Enforce their charity** manage to beg something. **Poor . . . Tom** (Edgar practices the begging role he is about to adopt. Beggars were known as "poor Toms.") **Turlygod** (Meaning unknown.) **21 That's something yet** there's some kind of existence still for me as poor Tom. **Edgar . . . am** as Edgar, I'm done for. (Suggesting also, "I am Edgar no longer.") **2.4. Location: Scene continues before Gloucester's house. Kent still dozing in the stocks. 4 remove** change of residence **7 cruel** (1) unkind (2) crewel (compare the Quarto spelling, *crewell*), a thin yarn of which garters were made **9–10 overlusty at legs** given to running away **10 netherstocks** stockings **12 To** as to

LEAR   No, no, they would not.
KENT   Yes, they have.
LEAR   By Jupiter, I swear no.
KENT
   By Juno, I swear ay.
LEAR   They durst not do 't!
   They could not, would not do 't. 'Tis worse than
      murder
   To do upon respect such violent outrage.   23
   Resolve me with all modest haste which way   24
   Thou mightst deserve, or they impose, this usage,
   Coming from us.
KENT   My lord, when at their home   26
   I did commend Your Highness' letters to them,   27
   Ere I was risen from the place that showed   28
   My duty kneeling, came there a reeking post,   29
   Stewed in his haste, half breathless, panting forth   30
   From Goneril his mistress salutations;
   Delivered letters, spite of intermission,   32
   Which presently they read; on whose contents   33
   They summoned up their meiny, straight took horse,   34
   Commanded me to follow and attend
   The leisure of their answer, gave me cold looks;
   And meeting here the other messenger,
   Whose welcome, I perceived, had poisoned mine—
   Being the very fellow which of late
   Displayed so saucily against Your Highness—   40
   Having more man than wit about me, drew.   41
   He raised the house with loud and coward cries.
   Your son and daughter found this trespass worth
   The shame which here it suffers.
FOOL   Winter's not gone yet if the wild geese fly that   45
way.   46
      Fathers that wear rags
         Do make their children blind,   48
      But fathers that bear bags   49
         Shall see their children kind.
      Fortune, that arrant whore,
      Ne'er turns the key to the poor.   52
   But, for all this, thou shalt have as many dolors for thy 53
   daughters as thou canst tell in a year.   54
LEAR
   O, how this mother swells up toward my heart!   55
   Hysterica passio, down, thou climbing sorrow!   56

   Thy element's below.—Where is this daughter?   57
KENT   With the Earl, sir, here within.
LEAR   Follow me not. Stay here.   Exit.
GENTLEMAN
   Made you no more offense but what you speak of?
KENT   None.
   How chance the King comes with so small a
      number?   62
FOOL   An thou hadst been set i' the stocks for that ques- 63
tion, thou'dst well deserved it.
KENT   Why, Fool?
FOOL   We'll set thee to school to an ant to teach thee   66
there's no laboring i' the winter. All that follow their   67
noses are led by their eyes but blind men, and there's   68
not a nose among twenty but can smell him that's   69
stinking. Let go thy hold when a great wheel runs   70
down a hill lest it break thy neck with following; but
the great one that goes upward, let him draw thee after. When a wise man gives thee better counsel, give
me mine again. I would have none but knaves follow
it, since a fool gives it.
      That sir which serves and seeks for gain,
         And follows but for form,
      Will pack when it begins to rain   78
         And leave thee in the storm.
      But I will tarry; the fool will stay,
         And let the wise man fly.
      The knave turns fool that runs away;   82
         The fool no knave, pardie.   83

      Enter Lear and Gloucester.

KENT   Where learned you this, Fool?
FOOL   Not i' the stocks, fool.
LEAR
   Deny to speak with me? They are sick? They are
      weary?
   They have traveled all the night? Mere fetches,   87
   The images of revolt and flying off.   88
   Fetch me a better answer.
GLOUCESTER   My dear lord,
   You know the fiery quality of the Duke,
   How unremovable and fixed he is
   In his own course.
LEAR
   Vengeance! Plague! Death! Confusion!   93
   Fiery? What quality? Why, Gloucester, Gloucester,
   I'd speak with the Duke of Cornwall and his wife.
GLOUCESTER
   Well, my good lord, I have informed them so.

---

23 upon respect i.e., against my officers (who deserve respect)
24 Resolve enlighten.   modest moderate   26 their home (Kent and
Oswald went first to Cornwall's palace after leaving Albany's palace.)
27 commend deliver   28–29 from . . . kneeling from the kneeling
posture that showed my duty   29 reeking steaming (with heat of
travel)   30 Stewed i.e., thoroughly heated, soaked   32 spite of intermission in disregard of interrupting me, or, in spite of the interruptions caused by his being out of breath   33 presently instantly.   on
on the basis of   34 meiny retinue of servants, household   40 Displayed so saucily behaved so insolently   41 man manhood, courage.
wit discretion, sense   45–46 Winter's . . . way i.e., the signs still
point to continued and worsening fortune; the wild geese are still flying south   48 blind i.e., indifferent to their father's needs   49 bags
i.e., of gold   52 turns the key opens the door   53 dolors griefs (with
pun on "dollars," English word for an Austrian or Spanish coin).   for
(1) on account of (2) in exchange for   54 tell (1) relate (2) count
55, 56 mother, Hysterica passio i.e., hysteria, giving the sensation of
choking or suffocating

---

57 element's proper place is. (Hysteria, from the Greek *hystera*,
womb, was thought to be produced by vapors ascending from the
uterus or abdomen.)   62 chance chances it   63 An if   66–67 We'll
. . . winter i.e., just as the ant knows not to labor in the winter, the
wise man knows not to labor for one whose fortunes are fallen
67–70 All . . . stinking i.e., one who is out of favor can be easily
detected (he smells of misfortune) and so is easily avoided by
timeservers   78 pack be off   82 The knave . . . away i.e., deserting
one's master is the greatest folly   83 pardie *par Dieu* (French), "by
God"   87 fetches pretexts, dodges   88 images signs.   flying off desertion   93 Confusion destruction

LEAR
Informed them? Dost thou understand me, man?

GLOUCESTER   Ay, my good lord.

LEAR
The King would speak with Cornwall. The dear
    father
Would with his daughter speak, commands, tends
    service.   100
Are they informed of this? My breath and blood!   101
Fiery? The fiery Duke? Tell the hot Duke that—
No, but not yet. Maybe he is not well.
Infirmity doth still neglect all office   104
Whereto our health is bound; we are not ourselves   105
When nature, being oppressed, commands the mind
To suffer with the body. I'll forbear,
And am fallen out with my more headier will,   108
To take the indisposed and sickly fit   109
For the sound man. [Looking at Kent.] Death on my
    state! Wherefore   110
Should he sit here? This act persuades me
That this remotion of the Duke and her   112
Is practice only. Give me my servant forth.   113
Go tell the Duke and 's wife I'd speak with them,
Now, presently. Bid them come forth and hear me,   115
Or at their chamber door I'll beat the drum
Till it cry sleep to death.   117

GLOUCESTER   I would have all well betwixt you.   Exit.

LEAR
O me, my heart, my rising heart! But down!

FOOL   Cry to it, nuncle, as the cockney did to the eels   120
when she put 'em i' the paste alive. She knapped 'em   121
o' the coxcombs with a stick and cried, "Down, wan-   122
tons, down!" 'Twas her brother that, in pure kindness   123
to his horse, buttered his hay.   124

Enter Cornwall, Regan, Gloucester, [and]
servants.

LEAR   Good morrow to you both.

CORNWALL   Hail to Your Grace!

Kent here set at liberty.

REGAN   I am glad to see Your Highness.

LEAR
Regan, I think you are. I know what reason
I have to think so. If thou shouldst not be glad,
I would divorce me from thy mother's tomb,   130

Sepulch'ring an adultress. [To Kent.] O, are you free?   131
Some other time for that.—Belovèd Regan,
Thy sister's naught. O Regan, she hath tied   133
Sharp-toothed unkindness, like a vulture, here.
    [He lays his hand on his heart.]
I can scarce speak to thee. Thou'lt not believe
With how depraved a quality—O Regan!   136

REGAN
I pray you, sir, take patience. I have hope   137
You less know how to value her desert   138
Than she to scant her duty.

LEAR   Say? How is that?   139

REGAN
I cannot think my sister in the least
Would fail her obligation. If, sir, perchance
She have restrained the riots of your followers,
'Tis on such ground and to such wholesome end
As clears her from all blame.

LEAR   My curses on her!

REGAN   O, sir, you are old;
Nature in you stands on the very verge   147
Of his confine. You should be ruled and led   148
By some discretion that discerns your state   149
Better than you yourself. Therefore, I pray you,
That to our sister you do make return.
Say you have wronged her.

LEAR   Ask her forgiveness?
Do you but mark how this becomes the house: 153
[Kneeling] "Dear daughter, I confess that I am old;
Age is unnecessary. On my knees I beg   155
That you'll vouchsafe me raiment, bed, and food."

REGAN
Good sir, no more. These are unsightly tricks.
Return you to my sister.

LEAR [rising]   Never, Regan.
She hath abated me of half my train,   159
Looked black upon me, struck me with her tongue
Most serpentlike upon the very heart.
All the stored vengeances of heaven fall
On her ingrateful top! Strike her young bones,   163
You taking airs, with lameness!

CORNWALL   Fie, sir, fie!   164

LEAR
You nimble lightnings, dart your blinding flames
Into her scornful eyes! Infect her beauty,
You fen-sucked fogs drawn by the powerful sun   167
To fall and blister!   168

100 tends attends, waits for 101 My . . . blood i.e., by my very life.
(An oath.) 104 still always 104–105 all . . . bound all duties
which in good health we are bound to perform 108–109 am . . .
take now disapprove of my more impetuous will in having rashly
taken 110 Death on my state may death come to my royal authority. (An oath with ironic appropriateness.) 112 remotion removal, in-
accessibility 113 practice deception. forth out of the stocks
115 presently at once 117 cry sleep to death i.e., put an end to
sleep by the noise 120 cockney i.e., a Londoner, ignorant of ways
of cooking eels 121 paste pastry pie. knapped rapped 122 coxcombs heads 122–123 wantons playful creatures, sexy rogues. (A
term of affectionate abuse.) 123–124 'Twas . . . hay (Another city
ignorance; the act is well intended, but horses do not like greasy hay.
As with Lear, good intentions are not enough.) brother i.e., fellow
creature, foolishly tenderhearted in the same way 130 divorce me
from i.e., refuse to be buried beside

131 Sepulch'ring i.e., since it would surely contain the dead body of
133 naught wicked 136 quality disposition 137–139 I have . . .
duty I trust this is more a matter of your undervaluing her merit than
of her falling slack in her duty to you 139 Say? come again? 147–
148 Nature . . . confine i.e., your life has almost completed its allotted scope 149 discretion discreet person. discerns your state understands your dependent situation and aged condition (with an ironic
reminder that state also means "royal power") 153 becomes the
house suits domestic decorum, is suited to the family or household
and its dutiful relationships. (Said with bitter irony.) 155 Age is unnecessary old people are useless 159 abated deprived 163 ingrateful top ungrateful head 164 taking infectious 167 fen-sucked (It
was supposed that the sun sucked up poisons from fens or marshes.)
168 To fall and blister to fall upon her and blister her beauty

REGAN
O the blest gods! So will you wish on me
When the rash mood is on.

LEAR
No, Regan, thou shalt never have my curse.
Thy tender-hafted nature shall not give   172
Thee o'er to harshness. Her eyes are fierce, but thine
Do comfort and not burn. 'Tis not in thee
To grudge my pleasures, to cut off my train,
To bandy hasty words, to scant my sizes,   176
And, in conclusion, to oppose the bolt   177
Against my coming in. Thou better know'st
The offices of nature, bond of childhood,   179
Effects of courtesy, dues of gratitude.   180
Thy half o' the kingdom hast thou not forgot,
Wherein I thee endowed.

REGAN   Good sir, to the purpose.   182

LEAR
Who put my man i' the stocks?   *Tucket within.*

CORNWALL   What trumpet's that?

REGAN
I know 't—my sister's. This approves her letter,   184
That she would soon be here.

          Enter steward [Oswald].

                    Is your lady come?

LEAR
This is a slave, whose easy-borrowed pride   186
Dwells in the fickle grace of her he follows.   187
Out, varlet, from my sight!

CORNWALL   What means Your Grace?   188

LEAR
Who stocked my servant? Regan, I have good hope
Thou didst not know on 't.

          Enter Goneril.

                    Who comes here? O heavens,
If you do love old men, if your sweet sway
Allow obedience, if you yourselves are old,   192
Make it your cause; send down, and take my part!
[*To Goneril.*] Art not ashamed to look upon this
     beard?   [*Goneril and Regan join hands.*] 194
O Regan, will you take her by the hand?

GONERIL
Why not by th' hand, sir? How have I offended?
All's not offense that indiscretion finds   197
And dotage terms so.

LEAR   O sides, you are too tough!   198
Will you yet hold?—How came my man i' the stocks?

CORNWALL
I set him there, sir; but his own disorders
Deserved much less advancement.

LEAR   You? Did you?   201

REGAN
I pray you, Father, being weak, seem so.   202
If till the expiration of your month
You will return and sojourn with my sister,
Dismissing half your train, come then to me.
I am now from home, and out of that provision
Which shall be needful for your entertainment.   207

LEAR
Return to her? And fifty men dismissed?
No! Rather I abjure all roofs, and choose
To wage against the enmity o' th' air,   210
To be a comrade with the wolf and owl—
Necessity's sharp pinch. Return with her?
Why, the hot-blooded France, that dowerless took   213
Our youngest born—I could as well be brought
To knee his throne and, squirelike, pension beg   215
To keep base life afoot. Return with her?
Persuade me rather to be slave and sumpter   217
To this detested groom.   [*He points to Oswald.*]

GONERIL   At your choice, sir.

LEAR
I prithee, daughter, do not make me mad.
I will not trouble thee, my child. Farewell.
We'll no more meet, no more see one another.
But yet thou art my flesh, my blood, my daughter—
Or rather a disease that's in my flesh,
Which I must needs call mine. Thou art a boil,
A plague-sore, or embossèd carbuncle   225
In my corrupted blood. But I'll not chide thee;
Let shame come when it will, I do not call it.   227
I do not bid the thunder-bearer shoot,   228
Nor tell tales of thee to high-judging Jove.   229
Mend when thou canst; be better at thy leisure.
I can be patient. I can stay with Regan,
I and my hundred knights.

REGAN   Not altogether so.
I looked not for you yet, nor am provided   234
For your fit welcome. Give ear, sir, to my sister;
For those that mingle reason with your passion   236
Must be content to think you old, and so—   237
But she knows what she does.

LEAR   Is this well spoken?

REGAN
I dare avouch it, sir. What, fifty followers?   239
Is it not well? What should you need of more?
Yea, or so many, sith that both charge and danger   241
Speak 'gainst so great a number? How in one house

---

172 tender-hafted set in a tender *haft,* i.e., "handle" or "frame";
moved by a tender feeling, gently disposed   **176 bandy** volley, exchange.   **scant my sizes** diminish my allowances   **177 oppose the
bolt** lock the door   **179 offices of nature** natural duties.   **bond of
childhood** filial obligations due to parents   **180 Effects** actions, manifestations   **182 purpose** point   **184 approves** confirms   **186 easy-
borrowed** i.e., acquired with little effort at deserving and with weak
commitment   **187 grace** favor   **188 varlet** worthless fellow   **192 Allow** approve, sanction   **194 beard** (A sign of age and presumed entitlement to respect.)   **197 indiscretion finds** poor judgment deems to
be so   **198 sides** i.e., sides of the chest (stretched by the swelling
heart)

201 much less advancement far less honor, i.e., far worse treatment
202 seem so i.e., don't act as if you were strong   **207 entertainment**
proper reception   **210 wage** wage war   **213 hot-blooded** choleric.
(Compare this with 1.2.23.)   **215 knee** fall on my knees before
217 sumpter packhorse; hence, drudge   **225 embossèd** swollen, tu-
mid   **227 call** summon   **228 the thunder-bearer** i.e., Jove
229 high-judging judging from on high   **234 looked not for** did not
expect   **236 mingle . . . passion** consider your passionate behavior
with the cold eye of reason   **237 Must . . . to** must inevitably
239 avouch vouch for   **241 sith that** since.   **charge** expense

Should many people under two commands
Hold amity? 'Tis hard, almost impossible.

GONERIL
Why might not you, my lord, receive attendance
From those that she calls servants, or from mine?

REGAN
Why not, my lord? If then they chanced to slack ye,   247
We could control them. If you will come to me—   248
For now I spy a danger—I entreat you
To bring but five-and-twenty. To no more
Will I give place or notice.   251

LEAR
I gave you all—

REGAN   And in good time you gave it.

LEAR
Made you my guardians, my depositaries,   253
But kept a reservation to be followed   254
With such a number. What, must I come to you
With five-and-twenty? Regan, said you so?

REGAN
And speak 't again, my lord. No more with me.

LEAR
Those wicked creatures yet do look well-favored   258
When others are more wicked; not being the worst
Stands in some rank of praise. [To Goneril.] I'll go
     with thee.   260
Thy fifty yet doth double five-and-twenty,
And thou art twice her love.

GONERIL   Hear me, my lord:
What need you five-and-twenty, ten, or five,
To follow in a house where twice so many   264
Have a command to tend you?

REGAN   What need one?

LEAR
O, reason not the need! Our basest beggars   266
Are in the poorest thing superfluous.   267
Allow not nature more than nature needs,   268
Man's life is cheap as beast's. Thou art a lady;
If only to go warm were gorgeous,   270
Why, nature needs not what thou gorgeous wear'st,   271
Which scarcely keeps thee warm. But, for true
     need—   272
You heavens, give me that patience, patience I need!
You see me here, you gods, a poor old man,
As full of grief as age, wretched in both.
If it be you that stirs these daughters' hearts
Against their father, fool me not so much   277
To bear it tamely; touch me with noble anger,   278
And let not women's weapons, water drops,

Stain my man's cheeks. No, you unnatural hags,
I will have such revenges on you both
That all the world shall—I will do such things—
What they are yet I know not, but they shall be
The terrors of the earth. You think I'll weep;
No, I'll not weep.   Storm and tempest.
I have full cause of weeping; but this heart
Shall break into a hundred thousand flaws   287
Or ere I'll weep. O Fool, I shall go mad!   288
          Exeunt [Lear, Gloucester, Kent, Gentleman,
                                              and Fool].

CORNWALL
Let us withdraw. 'Twill be a storm.

REGAN
This house is little. The old man and 's people
Cannot be well bestowed.   291

GONERIL
'Tis his own blame hath put himself from rest,   292
And must needs taste his folly.   293

REGAN
For his particular, I'll receive him gladly,   294
But not one follower.

GONERIL
So am I purposed. Where is my Lord of Gloucester?

CORNWALL
Followed the old man forth.

          Enter Gloucester.

                         He is returned.

GLOUCESTER
The King is in high rage.

CORNWALL   Whither is he going?

GLOUCESTER
He calls to horse, but will I know not whither.

CORNWALL
'Tis best to give him way. He leads himself.   300

GONERIL [to Gloucester]
My lord, entreat him by no means to stay.

GLOUCESTER
Alack, the night comes on, and the bleak winds
Do sorely ruffle. For many miles about   303
There's scarce a bush.

REGAN   O, sir, to willful men
The injuries that they themselves procure
Must be their schoolmasters. Shut up your doors.
He is attended with a desperate train,
And what they may incense him to, being apt   308
To have his ear abused, wisdom bids fear.   309

CORNWALL
Shut up your doors, my lord; 'tis a wild night.
My Regan counsels well. Come out o' the storm.
                                              Exeunt.

                         ❧

3.1

Storm still. Enter Kent [disguised as Caius] and a Gentleman, severally.

KENT   Who's there, besides foul weather?

GENTLEMAN
One minded like the weather, most unquietly.

KENT   I know you. Where's the King?

GENTLEMAN
Contending with the fretful elements;
Bids the wind blow the earth into the sea
Or swell the curlèd waters 'bove the main,   6
That things might change or cease; tears his white
    hair,   7
Which the impetuous blasts with eyeless rage
Catch in their fury and make nothing of;   9
Strives in his little world of man to outstorm   10
The to-and-fro-conflicting wind and rain.
This night, wherein the cub-drawn bear would
    couch,   12
The lion and the belly-pinchèd wolf
Keep their fur dry, unbonneted he runs
And bids what will take all.

KENT   But who is with him?   15

GENTLEMAN
None but the Fool, who labors to outjest   16
His heart-struck injuries.

KENT   Sir, I do know you,   17
And dare upon the warrant of my note   18
Commend a dear thing to you. There is division,   19
Although as yet the face of it is covered
With mutual cunning, twixt Albany and Cornwall;
Who have—as who have not, that their great stars   22
Throned and set high?—servants, who seem no less,   23
Which are to France the spies and speculations   24
Intelligent of our state. What hath been seen,   25
Either in snuffs and packings of the Dukes,   26
Or the hard rein which both of them hath borne
Against the old kind King, or something deeper,
Whereof perchance these are but furnishings—   29
But true it is, from France there comes a power   30
Into this scattered kingdom, who already,   31
Wise in our negligence, have secret feet   32
In some of our best ports and are at point   33
To show their open banner. Now to you:
If on my credit you dare build so far   35
To make your speed to Dover, you shall find

Some that will thank you, making just report   37
Of how unnatural and bemadding sorrow
The King hath cause to plain.   39
I am a gentleman of blood and breeding,
And from some knowledge and assurance offer
This office to you.   42

GENTLEMAN
I will talk further with you.

KENT   No, do not.
For confirmation that I am much more
Than my outwall, open this purse and take   45
What it contains. [*He gives a purse and a ring.*] If you
    shall see Cordelia—
As fear not but you shall—show her this ring,
And she will tell you who that fellow is   48
That yet you do not know. Fie on this storm!
I will go seek the King.

GENTLEMAN
Give me your hand. Have you no more to say?

KENT
Few words, but, to effect, more than all yet: 52
That when we have found the King—in which your
    pain   53
That way, I'll this—he that first lights on him   54
Holla the other.   *Exeunt [separately].*

❦

3.2

Storm still. Enter Lear and Fool.

LEAR
Blow, winds, and crack your cheeks! Rage, blow!
You cataracts and hurricanoes, spout   2
Till you have drenched our steeples, drowned the
    cocks!   3
You sulfurous and thought-executing fires,   4
Vaunt-couriers of oak-cleaving thunderbolts,   5
Singe my white head! And thou, all-shaking
    thunder,
Strike flat the thick rotundity o' the world!
Crack nature's molds, all germens spill at once   8
That makes ingrateful man!

FOOL   O nuncle, court holy water in a dry house is bet-   10
ter than this rainwater out o' door. Good nuncle, in,
ask thy daughters blessing. Here's a night pities   12
neither wise men nor fools.

LEAR
Rumble thy bellyful! Spit, fire! Spout, rain!
Nor rain, wind, thunder, fire are my daughters.

3.1. **Location: An open place in Gloucestershire.**
s.d. severally at separate doors   **6 main** mainland   **7 things** all things
9 make nothing of treat disrespectfully   **10 little world of man** i.e.,
microcosm, which is an epitome of the macrocosm or universe
12 cub-drawn famished, with udders sucked dry (and hence ravenous).   **couch** lie close in its den   **15 bids . . . all** (A cry of desperate
defiance; "take all" is the cry of a gambler in staking his last.)
16 outjest exorcise or relieve by jesting   **17 heart-struck injuries** injuries that strike to the very heart   **18 upon . . . note** on the strength of
what I know (about you)   **19 Commend . . . thing** entrust a precious
undertaking   **22 that** whom.   **stars** destinies   **23 no less** i.e., no
other than servants   **24 speculations** scouts, spies   **25 Intelligent of**
supplying intelligence pertinent to   **26 snuffs** quarrels.   **packings** intrigues   **29 furnishings** outward shows   **30 power** army   **31 scattered** divided   **32 Wise in** taking advantage of.   **feet** footholds
33 at point ready   **35 credit** trustworthiness.   **so far** so far as

37 making just report for making an accurate report   **39 plain** complain   **42 office** assignment   **45 outwall** exterior appearance   **48 fellow**, Kent   **52 to effect** in their consequences   **53–54 in which
. . . this** in which task, you search in that direction while I go this
way
3.2. **Location: An open place, as before.**
2 hurricanoes waterspouts   **3 drenched** drowned.   **cocks** weather-
cocks   **4 thought-executing** acting with the quickness of thought.
fires i.e., lightning   **5 Vaunt-couriers** forerunners   **8 nature's molds**
the molds in which nature makes all life.   **germens** germs, seeds.
spill destroy   **10 court holy water** flattery   **12 ask . . . blessing** (For
Lear to do so would be to acknowledge their authority.)

I tax not you, you elements, with unkindness;   16
I never gave you kingdom, called you children.
You owe me no subscription. Then let fall   18
Your horrible pleasure. Here I stand your slave,
A poor, infirm, weak, and despised old man.
But yet I call you servile ministers,   21
That will with two pernicious daughters join
Your high-engendered battles 'gainst a head   23
So old and white as this. O, ho! 'Tis foul!
FOOL   He that has a house to put 's head in has a good
headpiece.   26
          The codpiece that will house   27
            Before the head has any,   28
          The head and he shall louse;   29
            So beggars marry many.   30
          The man that makes his toe   31
            What he his heart should make   32
          Shall of a corn cry woe,   33
            And turn his sleep to wake.   34
For there was never yet fair woman but she made 35
mouths in a glass.   36
LEAR
No, I will be the pattern of all patience;
I will say nothing.

             Enter Kent, [disguised as Caius].

KENT   Who's there?
FOOL   Marry, here's grace and a codpiece; that's a wise 40
man and a fool.
KENT
Alas, sir, are you here? Things that love night
Love not such nights as these. The wrathful skies
Gallow the very wanderers of the dark   44
And make them keep their caves. Since I was man,   45
Such sheets of fire, such bursts of horrid thunder,
Such groans of roaring wind and rain I never
Remember to have heard. Man's nature cannot carry 48
Th' affliction nor the fear.
LEAR   Let the great gods,   49
That keep this dreadful pother o'er our heads,   50
Find out their enemies now. Tremble, thou wretch,   51
That hast within thee undivulgèd crimes
Unwhipped of justice! Hide thee, thou bloody hand,   53
Thou perjured, and thou simular of virtue   54

That art incestuous! Caitiff, to pieces shake,   55
That under covert and convenient seeming   56
Has practiced on man's life! Close pent-up guilts,   57
Rive your concealing continents and cry   58
These dreadful summoners grace! I am a man   59
More sinned against than sinning.
KENT   Alack, bareheaded?
Gracious my lord, hard by here is a hovel;
Some friendship will it lend you 'gainst the tempest.
Repose you there while I to this hard house—
More harder than the stones whereof 'tis raised,
Which even but now, demanding after you,   65
Denied me to come in—return and force
Their scanted courtesy.
LEAR   My wits begin to turn.   67
Come on, my boy. How dost, my boy? Art cold?
I am cold myself.—Where is this straw, my fellow?
The art of our necessities is strange,
And can make vile things precious. Come, your
    hovel.—
Poor fool and knave, I have one part in my heart
That's sorry yet for thee.
FOOL [*sings*]
          "He that has and a little tiny wit,   74
            With heigh-ho, the wind and the rain,
          Must make content with his fortunes fit,
            Though the rain it raineth every day."   77
LEAR
True, boy.—Come, bring us to this hovel.
                              Exit [with Kent].
FOOL   This is a brave night to cool a courtesan. I'll speak 79
a prophecy ere I go:

When priests are more in word than matter;   81
When brewers mar their malt with water;   82
When nobles are their tailors' tutors,   83
No heretics burned but wenches' suitors,   84
Then shall the realm of Albion   85
Come to great confusion.

When every case in law is right,   87
No squire in debt, nor no poor knight;
When slanders do not live in tongues,
Nor cutpurses come not to throngs;

---

16 tax accuse. **with** of **18 subscription** allegiance **21 ministers**
agents **23 high-engendered battles** battalions engendered in the
heavens **26 headpiece** (1) helmetlike covering for the head (2) head
for common sense **27–34 The codpiece . . . wake** i.e., a man who
houses his genitals in a sexual embrace before he provides a roof for
his head can expect the lice-infested penury of a penniless marriage;
and one who cherishes an ignoble part of his body above what is noble (as Lear has done with his daughters) can expect misery and
wakeful tossing from that very part he has so foolishly favored. **codpiece** covering for the genitals worn by men with their close-fitting
hose; here, representing the genitals themselves **35–36 made . . .
glass** practiced making attractive faces in a mirror **40 Marry** (An
oath, originally "by the Virgin Mary.") **grace** royal grace. **codpiece**
(Often prominent in the Fool's costume.) **44 Gallow** i.e., gally,
frighten. **wanderers of the dark** nocturnal wild beasts **45 keep** occupy, remain inside **48 carry** endure **49 affliction** physical affliction **50 pother** hubbub, turmoil **51 Find . . . now** i.e., expose
criminals (by the criminals' terrified response to this storm) **53 of** by
54 perjured perjurer. **simular** pretender

55 Caitiff wretch **56 seeming** hypocrisy **57 practiced on** plotted
against. **Close** secret **58 Rive . . . continents** split open the covering that contains you **58–59 cry . . . grace** pray for mercy at the
hands of these officers of divine justice. (*Summoners* are the police officers of an ecclesiastical court.) **65 Which** i.e., the occupants of
which. **demanding I** inquiring **67 scanted** stinted **74–77 He . . .
day** (Derived from the popular song that Feste sings in *Twelfth Night,*
5.1.389 ff.) **79 This . . . courtesan** i.e., this wretched night might
put courtesans off from streetwalking (?) **brave** fine **81 more . . .
matter** better as talkers about virtue than as practitioners of it. (This
and the next three lines satirize the present state of affairs.) **82 mar**
adulterate **83 are . . . tutors** can instruct their own tailors about
fashion **84 No . . . suitors** when heresy is a matter, not of religious
faith, but of perjured lovers (whose burning is not at the stake but in
catching venereal disease) **85 realm of Albion** kingdom of England.
(The Fool is parodying a pseudo-Chaucerian prophetic verse.)
87 right just. (This and the next five lines offer a utopian vision of justice and charity that will never be realized in this corrupted world.)

When usurers tell their gold i' the field,   91
And bawds and whores do churches build,
Then comes the time, who lives to see 't,
That going shall be used with feet.   94

This prophecy Merlin shall make, for I live before his 95
time.   *Exit.*

❧

3.3   *Enter Gloucester and Edmund [with lights].*

GLOUCESTER   Alack, alack, Edmund, I like not this unnatural dealing. When I desired their leave that I might
pity him, they took from me the use of mine own 3
house, charged me on pain of perpetual displeasure
neither to speak of him, entreat for him, or any way
sustain him.

EDMUND
Most savage and unnatural!

GLOUCESTER   Go to; say you nothing. There is division 8
between the Dukes, and a worse matter than that. I
have received a letter this night; 'tis dangerous to be
spoken; I have locked the letter in my closet. These in- 11
juries the King now bears will be revenged home; 12
there is part of a power already footed. We must in- 13
cline to the King. I will look him and privily relieve 14
him. Go you and maintain talk with the Duke, that
my charity be not of him perceived. If he ask for me, 16
I am ill and gone to bed. If I die for 't, as no less is
threatened me, the King my old master must be relieved. There is strange things toward, Edmund. Pray 19
you, be careful.   *Exit.*

EDMUND
This courtesy forbid thee shall the Duke   21
Instantly know, and of that letter too.
This seems a fair deserving, and must draw me   23
That which my father loses—no less than all.
The younger rises when the old doth fall.   *Exit.*

❧

3.4   *Enter Lear, Kent [disguised as Caius], and Fool.*

KENT
Here is the place, my lord. Good my lord, enter.
The tyranny of the open night's too rough
For nature to endure.   *Storm still.*
LEAR   Let me alone.   3

KENT
Good my lord, enter here.
LEAR   Wilt break my heart?   4
KENT
I had rather break mine own. Good my lord, enter.
LEAR
Thou think'st 'tis much that this contentious storm
Invades us to the skin. So 'tis to thee,
But where the greater malady is fixed   8
The lesser is scarce felt. Thou'dst shun a bear,
But if thy flight lay toward the roaring sea
Thou'dst meet the bear i' the mouth. When the
     mind's free,   11
The body's delicate. This tempest in my mind   12
Doth from my senses take all feeling else
Save what beats there. Filial ingratitude!
Is it not as this mouth should tear this hand   15
For lifting food to 't? But I will punish home.   16
No, I will weep no more. In such a night
To shut me out? Pour on; I will endure.
In such a night as this? O Regan, Goneril,
Your old kind father, whose frank heart gave all—   20
O, that way madness lies; let me shun that!
No more of that.
KENT   Good my lord, enter here.
LEAR
Prithee, go in thyself; seek thine own ease.
This tempest will not give me leave to ponder   24
On things would hurt me more. But I'll go in.   25
[*To the Fool.*] In, boy; go first. You houseless
     poverty—
Nay, get thee in. I'll pray, and then I'll sleep.
                                            Exit [Fool into the hovel].
Poor naked wretches, wheresoe'er you are,
That bide the pelting of this pitiless storm,   29
How shall your houseless heads and unfed sides,   30
Your looped and windowed raggedness, defend you 31
From seasons such as these? O, I have ta'en
Too little care of this! Take physic, pomp;   33
Expose thyself to feel what wretches feel,
That thou mayst shake the superflux to them   35
And show the heavens more just.
EDGAR [*within*]   Fathom and half, fathom and half! 37
Poor Tom!

                         Enter Fool [from the hovel].

FOOL   Come not in here, nuncle; here's a spirit. Help
me, help me!

---

91 tell count.   **i' the field** i.e., openly, without fear   **94 going . . .
feet** walking will be done on foot   **95 Merlin** (A great wizard of the
court of King Arthur, who came after Lear.)
3.3. Location: Gloucester's house.
3 pity be merciful to, relieve   **8 Go to** i.e., no more of that
11 closet private chamber   **12 home** thoroughly   **13 power** armed
force.   **footed** landed   **13–14 incline to** side with   **14 look** look for
16 of by   **19 toward** impending   **21 courtesy forbid thee** kindess (to
Lear) which you were forbidden to show   **23 fair deserving** meritorious action
3.4. Location: An open place. Before a hovel.
3 nature human nature

4 break my heart i.e., cause me anguish by relieving my physical
wants and thus forcing me to confront again my *greater malady* (line
8)   **8 fixed** lodged, implanted   **11 i' the mouth** i.e., head-on.   **free**
free of anxiety   **12 The body's delicate** i.e., the body's importunate
needs can assert themselves   **15 as** as if   **16 home** fully   **20 frank**
liberal   **24 will . . . leave** i.e., keeps me too preoccupied   **25 things
would** things (such as filial ingratitude) that would   **29 bide** endure
30 unfed sides i.e., lean ribs   **31 looped and windowed** full of openings like windows and loopholes   **33 Take physic, pomp** cure yourself, O distempered great ones   **35 superflux** superfluity (with suggestion of *flux,* "bodily discharge," introduced by *physic,* "purgative," in
line 33)   **37 Fathom and half** (A sailor's cry while taking soundings,
hence appropriate to a deluge.)

KENT   Give me thy hand. Who's there?

FOOL   A spirit, a spirit! He says his name's poor Tom.

KENT

What art thou that dost grumble there i' the straw?   43
Come forth.

Enter Edgar [disguised as a madman].

EDGAR   Away! The foul fiend follows me! Through the   45
sharp hawthorn blows the cold wind. Hum! Go to thy   46
bed and warm thee.

LEAR   Didst thou give all to thy daughters? And art
thou come to this?

EDGAR   Who gives anything to poor Tom? Whom the
foul fiend hath led through fire and through flame,
through ford and whirlpool, o'er bog and quagmire;
that hath laid knives under his pillow and halters in   53
his pew, set ratsbane by his porridge, made him   54
proud of heart to ride on a bay trotting horse over   55
four-inched bridges to course his own shadow for a   56
traitor. Bless thy five wits! Tom's a-cold. O, do de,   57
do de, do de. Bless thee from whirlwinds, star-blast-   58
ing, and taking! Do poor Tom some charity, whom the   59
foul fiend vexes. There could I have him now—and   60
there—and there again—and there.   *Storm still.*

LEAR

Has his daughters brought him to this pass?—   62
Couldst thou save nothing? Wouldst thou give 'em
all?

FOOL   Nay, he reserved a blanket, else we had been all   64
shamed.

LEAR

Now, all the plagues that in the pendulous air   66
Hang fated o'er men's faults light on thy daughters!   67

KENT   He hath no daughters, sir.

LEAR

Death, traitor! Nothing could have subdued nature
To such a lowness but his unkind daughters.
Is it the fashion that discarded fathers
Should have thus little mercy on their flesh?   72
Judicious punishment! 'Twas this flesh begot   73
Those pelican daughters.   74

EDGAR   Pillicock sat on Pillicock Hill. Alow, alow, loo,   75
loo!

FOOL   This cold night will turn us all to fools and madmen.

EDGAR   Take heed o' the foul fiend. Obey thy parents;
keep thy word's justice; swear not; commit not with   80
man's sworn spouse; set not thy sweet heart on proud
array. Tom's a-cold.

LEAR   What hast thou been?

EDGAR   A servingman, proud in heart and mind, that   84
curled my hair, wore gloves in my cap, served the lust   85
of my mistress' heart, and did the act of darkness with
her; swore as many oaths as I spake words, and broke
them in the sweet face of heaven. One that slept in the
contriving of lust and waked to do it. Wine loved I
deeply, dice dearly, and in woman out-paramoured   90
the Turk. False of heart, light of ear, bloody of hand;   91
hog in sloth, fox in stealth, wolf in greediness, dog in
madness, lion in prey. Let not the creaking of shoes   93
nor the rustling of silks betray thy poor heart to
woman. Keep thy foot out of brothels, thy hand out of
plackets, thy pen from lenders' books, and defy the   96
foul fiend. Still through the hawthorn blows the cold
wind; says suum, mun, nonny. Dolphin my boy, boy,   98
sessa! Let him trot by.   *Storm still.*   99

LEAR   Thou wert better in a grave than to answer with
thy uncovered body this extremity of the skies. Is man
no more than this? Consider him well. Thou ow'st the   102
worm no silk, the beast no hide, the sheep no wool,
the cat no perfume. Ha! Here's three on 's are sophis-   104
ticated. Thou art the thing itself; unaccommodated   105
man is no more but such a poor, bare, forked animal
as thou art. Off, off, you lendings! Come, unbutton
here.   *[Tearing off his clothes.]*

FOOL   Prithee, nuncle, be contented; 'tis a naughty night   109
to swim in. Now a little fire in a wild field were like   110
an old lecher's heart—a small spark, all the rest on 's   111
body cold.

Enter Gloucester, with a torch.

Look, here comes a walking fire.

EDGAR   This is the foul fiend Flibbertigibbet! He begins   114
at curfew and walks till the first cock; he gives the web   115
and the pin, squinnies the eye and makes the harelip,   116
mildews the white wheat, and hurts the poor creature   117
of earth.

---

43 **grumble** utter inarticulate sounds   45 **Away** keep away   45–
46 **Through . . . wind** (Possibly a line from a ballad.)   53–54 **knives,
halters, ratsbane** (These are means to commit suicide and hence be
damned.)   54 **pew** gallery, place (?)   **ratsbane** rat poison.   **porridge**
soup   55–56 **over four-inched bridges** i.e., taking mad risks on narrow bridges with the devil's assistance   56 **course** chase.   **for** as
57 **five wits** either the five senses, or common wit, imagination, fantasy, estimation, and memory   58–59 **star-blasting** being blighted by
influence of the stars   59 **taking** infection, evil influence, enchantment   60 **There** (Perhaps he slaps at lice and other vermin as if they
were devils.)   62 **pass** miserable plight   64 **reserved a blanket** kept a
wrap (for his nakedness)   66 **pendulous** suspended, overhanging
67 **fated** having the power of fate   72 **have . . . flesh** i.e., punish
themselves, as Edgar has done (probably with pins and thorns stuck in
his flesh)   73 **Judicious** appropriate to the crime   74 **pelican** greedy.
(Young pelicans supposedly smote their parents and fed on the blood
of their mothers' breasts.)   75 **Pillicock** (From an old rhyme, suggested by the sound of *pelican. Pillicock* in nursery rhyme seems to
have been a euphemism for penis; *Pillicock Hill,* for the Mount of
Venus.)

80 **justice** integrity.   **commit not** i.e., do not commit adultery.
(Edgar's mad catechism contains fragments of the Ten Commandments.)   84 **servingman** either a ''servant'' in the language of courtly
love or an ambitious servant in a household   85 **gloves** i.e., my mistress's favors   90–91 **out-paramoured the Turk** outdid the Sultan in
keeping mistresses   91 **light of ear** credulous in believing malicious
talk   93 **prey** preying   96 **plackets** slits in skirts or petticoats.   **thy
pen . . . books** i.e., do not sign a contract for a loan   98 **suum . . .
nonny** (Imitative of the wind?)   **Dolphin my boy** (A slang phrase or
bit of song?)   99 **sessa** i.e., away, cease (?)   102 **ow'st** have borrowed from   104 **cat** civet cat   104–105 **sophisticated** clad in the
trappings of civilized life; adulterated   105 **unaccommodated** unfurnished with the trappings of civilization   109 **naughty** bad   110 **wild**
barren, uncultivated   111 **on 's** of his   114 **Flibbertigibbet** (A devil
from Elizabethan folklore whose name appears in Samuel Harsnett's
Declaration of Egregious Popish Impostures, 1603, and elsewhere.)
115 **first cock** midnight   115–116 **web and the pin** cataract of the
eye   116 **squinnies** causes to squint   117 **white** ripening

Swithold footed thrice the 'old;   119
He met the nightmare and her ninefold;   120
   Bid her alight,
   And her troth plight,
And aroint thee, witch, aroint thee!   123
KENT   How fares Your Grace?
LEAR   What's he?
KENT   Who's there? What is 't you seek?
GLOUCESTER   What are you there? Your names?
EDGAR   Poor Tom, that eats the swimming frog, the
toad, the tadpole, the wall newt and the water; that in   129
the fury of his heart, when the foul fiend rages, eats
cow dung for salads, swallows the old rat and the
ditch-dog, drinks the green mantle of the standing   132
pool; who is whipped from tithing to tithing and   133
stock-punished and imprisoned; who hath had three   134
suits to his back, six shirts to his body,   135
   Horse to ride, and weapon to wear;
   But mice and rats and such small deer   137
Have been Tom's food for seven long year.
Beware my follower. Peace, Smulkin! Peace, thou fiend!   139
GLOUCESTER
What, hath Your Grace no better company?
EDGAR   The Prince of Darkness is a gentleman. Modo   141
he's called, and Mahu.   142
GLOUCESTER
Our flesh and blood, my lord, is grown so vile   143
That it doth hate what gets it.   144
EDGAR   Poor Tom's a-cold.
GLOUCESTER
Go in with me. My duty cannot suffer   146
T' obey in all your daughters' hard commands.
Though their injunction be to bar my doors
And let this tyrannous night take hold upon you,
Yet have I ventured to come seek you out
And bring you where both fire and food is ready.
LEAR
First let me talk with this philosopher.
[*To Edgar.*] What is the cause of thunder?
KENT   Good my lord,
Take his offer. Go into the house.
LEAR
I'll talk a word with this same learnèd Theban.   155
[*To Edgar.*] What is your study?   156

EDGAR   How to prevent the fiend, and to kill vermin.   157
LEAR   Let me ask you one word in private.
                 [*Lear and Edgar talk apart.*]
KENT [*to Gloucester*]
Importune him once more to go, my lord.
His wits begin t' unsettle.
GLOUCESTER   Canst thou blame him?
                        Storm still.
His daughters seek his death. Ah, that good Kent!
He said it would be thus, poor banished man.
Thou sayest the King grows mad; I'll tell thee, friend,
I am almost mad myself. I had a son,
Now outlawed from my blood; he sought my life   165
But lately, very late. I loved him, friend,
No father his son dearer. True to tell thee,
The grief hath crazed my wits. What a night 's
   this!—
I do beseech Your Grace—
LEAR   O, cry you mercy, sir.   170
[*To Edgar.*] Noble philosopher, your company.
EDGAR   Tom's a-cold.
GLOUCESTER [*to Edgar*]
In, fellow, there, in th' hovel. Keep thee warm.
LEAR [*starting toward the hovel*]
Come, let's in all.
KENT   This way, my lord.
LEAR   With him!
I will keep still with my philosopher.
KENT [*to Gloucester*]
Good my lord, soothe him. Let him take the fellow.   176
GLOUCESTER [*to Kent*]   Take him you on.   177
KENT [*to Edgar*]
Sirrah, come on. Go along with us.
LEAR   Come, good Athenian.   179
GLOUCESTER   No words, no words! Hush.
EDGAR
Child Rowland to the dark tower came;   181
His word was still, "Fie, foh, and fum,   182
I smell the blood of a British man."   *Exeunt.* 183

               ❖

3.5   *Enter Cornwall and Edmund* [*with a letter*].

CORNWALL   I will have my revenge ere I depart his
  house.
EDMUND   How, my lord, I may be censured, that nature   3
  thus gives way to loyalty, something fears me to   4
  think of.
CORNWALL   I now perceive it was not altogether your

---

119 Swithold Saint Withold, an Anglo-Saxon exorcist, who here provides defense against the *nightmare,* or demon thought to afflict sleepers, by commanding the nightmare to *alight,* i.e., stop riding over the sleeper, and *plight* her *troth,* i.e., vow true faith, promise to do no harm. (Or, an error for *Swithin.*) **footed . . . 'old** thrice traversed the wold (tract of hilly upland) **120 ninefold** nine offspring (with possible pun on *fold, foal*) **123 aroint thee** begone **129 water** i.e., water newt **132 ditch-dog** i.e., dead dog in a ditch. **mantle** scum. **standing** stagnant **133 tithing to tithing** i.e., one ward or parish to another **134 stock-punished** placed in the stocks **134–135 three suits** (Like the menial servant at 2.2.15.) **137 deer** animals **139 follower** familiar, attendant devil **139, 141,142 Smulkin, Modo, Mahu** (Shakespeare found these Elizabethan devils in Samuel Harsnett's *Declaration.*) **143–144 Our . . . gets it** (1) life is so wretched that it cries out against having been born (2) our children hate their parents. **gets** begets **146 suffer** permit me **155 Theban** i.e., one deeply versed in "philosophy" or natural science **156 study** special competence

157 prevent thwart **165 outlawed . . . blood** disowned, disinherited, and legally outlawed **170 cry you mercy** I beg your pardon **176 soothe** humor **177 Take . . . on** i.e., go on ahead with Edgar **179 Athenian** i.e., philosopher **181 Child Rowland,** etc. (Probably a fragment of a ballad about the hero of the Charlemagne legends. A *child* is a candidate for knighthood.) **182 word** watchword. **still** always **182–183 Fie . . . man** (This is essentially what the Giant says in "Jack, the Giant Killer.")

3.5 Location: Gloucester's house.

3 censured judged. **nature** attachment to family **4 something fears** somewhat frightens

brother's evil disposition made him seek his death, 7
but a provoking merit set awork by a reprovable 8
badness in himself. 9

EDMUND   How malicious is my fortune, that I must 10
repent to be just! This is the letter he spoke of, which 11
approves him an intelligent party to the advantages 12
of France. O heavens! That this treason were not, or
not I the detector!

CORNWALL   Go with me to the Duchess.

EDMUND   If the matter of this paper be certain, you have
mighty business in hand.

CORNWALL   True or false, it hath made thee Earl of
Gloucester. Seek out where thy father is, that he may
be ready for our apprehension. 20

EDMUND [aside]   If I find him comforting the King, it 21
will stuff his suspicion more fully.—I will persevere 22
in my course of loyalty, though the conflict be sore
between that and my blood. 24

CORNWALL   I will lay trust upon thee, and thou shalt
find a dearer father in my love.   Exeunt.

3.6   *Enter Kent [disguised as Caius] and Gloucester.*

GLOUCESTER   Here is better than the open air; take it
thankfully. I will piece out the comfort with what 2
addition I can. I will not be long from you.

KENT   All the power of his wits have given way to his
impatience. The gods reward your kindness! 5
                              Exit [Gloucester].

Enter Lear, Edgar [as poor Tom], and Fool.

EDGAR   Frateretto calls me, and tells me Nero is an 6
angler in the lake of darkness. Pray, innocent, and 7
beware the foul fiend.

FOOL   Prithee, nuncle, tell me whether a madman be a
gentleman or a yeoman? 10

LEAR   A king, a king!

FOOL   No, he's a yeoman that has a gentleman to his
son; for he's a mad yeoman that sees his son a
gentleman before him.

LEAR
To have a thousand with red burning spits
Come hizzing in upon 'em— 16

EDGAR   The foul fiend bites my back. 17

FOOL   He's mad that trusts in the tameness of a wolf, a 18
horse's health, a boy's love, or a whore's oath. 19

LEAR
It shall be done; I will arraign them straight. 20
[To Edgar.] Come, sit thou here, most learnèd
justicer. 21
[To the Fool.] Thou, sapient sir, sit here. Now, you
she-foxes!

EDGAR   Look where he stands and glares! Want'st thou 23
eyes at trial, madam? 24
[Sings.] "Come o'er the burn, Bessy, to me—" 25

FOOL [sings]
      Her boat hath a leak,
      And she must not speak
Why she dares not come over to thee.

EDGAR   The foul fiend haunts poor Tom in the voice of
a nightingale. Hoppedance cries in Tom's belly for two 30
white herring. Croak not, black angel; I have no food 31
for thee.

KENT
How do you, sir? Stand you not so amazed. 33
Will you lie down and rest upon the cushions?

LEAR
I'll see their trial first. Bring in their evidence. 35
[To Edgar.] Thou robèd man of justice, take thy
place; 36
[To the Fool.] And thou, his yokefellow of equity, 37
Bench by his side. [To Kent.] You are o' the
commission; 38
Sit you, too.   [They sit.]

EDGAR   Let us deal justly.   [He sings.]
      Sleepest or wakest thou, jolly shepherd?
      Thy sheep be in the corn; 42
      And for one blast of thy minikin mouth, 43
      Thy sheep shall take no harm. 44

---

7 his i.e., his father's   **8–9 a provoking . . . himself** i.e., the badness of Gloucester which deserved punishment, set awork by an evil propensity in Edgar himself   **10–11 How . . . just** i.e., how cruel of fate to oblige me to be upright and loyal by betraying my own father, which breaks my heart   **12 approves** proves. **an intelligent . . . advantages** a spy in the service   **20 apprehension** arrest   **21 him** i.e., Gloucester. **comforting** offering aid and comfort to, helping   **22 his suspicion** the suspicion of Gloucester   **24 blood** family loyalty, filial instincts

3.6. Location: Within a building on Gloucester's estate, near or adjoining his house, or part of the house itself. See 3.4.146–154. Cushions are provided, and stools.

2 piece eke   **5 impatience** rage, inability to endure more   **6 Frateretto** (Another of the fiends from Harsnett.)   **6–7 Nero is an angler** (Chaucer's "Monk's Tale," lines 2474–2475, tells how Nero fished in the Tiber with nets of gold thread; in Rabelais, 2.30, Nero is described as a hurdy-gurdy player and Trajan an angler for frogs in the underworld.)   **7 innocent** simpleton, fool (i.e., the Fool)   **10 yeoman** property owner below the rank of gentleman. (The Fool's bitter jest in lines 12–14 is that such a man might go mad to see his son advanced over him.)

16 hizzing hissing. (Lear imagines his wicked daughters suffering torments in hell or being attacked by enemies.)   **17 bites** (i.e., in the shape of a louse)   **18–19 tameness . . . health** (Wolves are untamable, and horses are prone to disease.)   **20 arraign them** (Lear now imagines the trial of his cruel daughters.)   **21 justicer** judge, justice   **23 he** (Probably one of Edgar's devils, or, Lear.)   **23–24 Want'st . . . trial** do you lack spectators at your trial? or, can't you see who's looking at you?   **25 Come . . . me** (First line of a ballad by William Birche, 1558. A *burn* is a brook. The Fool makes a ribald reply, in which the *leaky boat* suggests her easy virtue or perhaps her menstrual period.)   **30 nightingale** (Edgar pretends to take the Fool's singing for that of a fiend disguised as a nightingale.) **Hoppedance** (Harsnett mentions "Hoberdidance.")   **31 white** unsmoked (contrasted with *black angel*, a demon). **Croak** (Refers to the rumbling in Edgar's stomach, denoting hunger.)   **33 amazed** bewildered   **35 their evidence** the witnesses against them   **36 robèd man** i.e., Edgar, with his blanket   **37 yokefellow of equity** partner in the law   **38 Bench** take your place on the bench. **o' the commission** one commissioned to be a justice   **42 corn** grainfield   **43–44 And . . . harm** (This may mean that, if the shepherd recalls his sheep by piping to them before they consume the grainfield, they will not be put in the pound.)   **43 minikin** dainty, pretty

Purr the cat is gray.　　　　　　　　　　　　　　45

LEAR　Arraign her first; 'tis Goneril, I here take my oath
before this honorable assembly, kicked the poor King　47
her father.

FOOL　Come hither, mistress. Is your name Goneril?

LEAR　She cannot deny it.

FOOL　Cry you mercy, I took you for a joint stool.　　51

LEAR

And here's another, whose warped looks proclaim
What store her heart is made on. Stop her there!　　53
Arms, arms, sword, fire! Corruption in the place!　　54
False justicer, why hast thou let her scape?

EDGAR　Bless thy five wits!

KENT

O, pity! Sir, where is the patience now
That you so oft have boasted to retain?

EDGAR [aside]

My tears begin to take his part so much
They mar my counterfeiting.

LEAR　The little dogs and all,
Tray, Blanch, and Sweetheart, see, they bark at me.

EDGAR　Tom will throw his head at them. Avaunt, you　63
curs!

Be thy mouth or black or white,　　　　　　　　65
Tooth that poisons if it bite,
Mastiff, greyhound, mongrel grim,
Hound or spaniel, brach or lym,　　　　　　　　68
Bobtail tike or trundle-tail,　　　　　　　　　　69
Tom will make him weep and wail;
For, with throwing thus my head,
Dogs leapt the hatch, and all are fled.　　　　　72
Do de, de, de. Sessa! Come, march to wakes and fairs　73
and market towns. Poor Tom, thy horn is dry.　　74

LEAR　Then let them anatomize Regan; see what breeds　75
about her heart. Is there any cause in nature that makes
these hard hearts? [To Edgar.] You, sir, I entertain　77
for one of my hundred; only I do not like the fashion of
your garments. You will say they are Persian; but let　79
them be changed.

KENT

Now, good my lord, lie here and rest awhile.

LEAR [lying on cushions] Make no noise, make no
noise. Draw the curtains. So, so. We'll go to supper　83
i' the morning.
　　　　　　　　　　　　　　　　[He sleeps.]

FOOL　And I'll go to bed at noon.

Enter Gloucester.

GLOUCESTER

Come hither, friend. Where is the King my master?

KENT

Here, sir, but trouble him not; his wits are gone.

GLOUCESTER

Good friend, I prithee, take him in thy arms.
I have o'erheard a plot of death upon him.　　　　89
There is a litter ready; lay him in 't
And drive toward Dover, friend, where thou shalt
　meet
Both welcome and protection. Take up thy master.
If thou shouldst dally half an hour, his life,
With thine and all that offer to defend him,
Stand in assurèd loss. Take up, take up,　　　　95
And follow me, that will to some provision　　　　96
Give thee quick conduct.

KENT　　　　　　　　　Oppressèd nature sleeps.　97
This rest might yet have balmed thy broken sinews,　98
Which, if convenience will not allow,　　　　　　99
Stand in hard cure. [To the Fool.] Come, help to
　bear thy master.　　　　　　　　　　　　　100
Thou must not stay behind.　　　　[They pick up Lear.]

GLOUCESTER　　　　　　　　　　Come, come, away!
　　　　　　　　　　　　　　　Exeunt [all but Edgar].

EDGAR

When we our betters see bearing our woes,　　　102
We scarcely think our miseries our foes.　　　　103
Who alone suffers suffers most i' the mind,　　　104
Leaving free things and happy shows behind;　　105
But then the mind much sufferance doth o'erskip　106
When grief hath mates, and bearing fellowship.　107
How light and portable my pain seems now,　　108
When that which makes me bend makes the King
　bow—
He childed as I fathered. Tom, away!　　　　　110
Mark the high noises, and thyself bewray　　　111
When false opinion, whose wrong thoughts defile
　thee,
In thy just proof repeals and reconciles thee.　　113
What will hap more tonight, safe scape the King!　114
Lurk, lurk.　　　　　　　　　　　　　　[Exit.]

❧

---

45 Purr the cat (A devil or familiar from Harsnett; see the note for 3.4.114. *Purr* may be the sound the familiar makes.)　**47 kicked** who kicked　**51 joint stool** low stool made by a joiner, or maker of furniture with joined parts. (Proverbially, the phrase "I took . . . stool" meant "I beg your pardon for failing to notice you." The reference is also presumably to a real stool onstage.)　**53 store** material.　**on** of　**54 Corruption in the place** i.e., there is iniquity or bribery in this court　**63 throw his head at** i.e., threaten　**65 or black** either black　**68 brach** hound bitch.　**lym** bloodhound　**69 Bobtail tike** short-tailed, small cur.　**trundle-tail** long-tailed dog　**72 hatch** lower half of a divided door　**73 Sessa** i.e., away, cease (?)　**wakes** (Here, parish festivals.)　**74 horn** i.e., horn bottle, used by beggars to beg for drinks　**75 anatomize** dissect　**77 entertain** take into my service　**79 Persian** (Lear madly asks if Edgar's wretched blanket is a rich Persian fabric.)　**83 curtains** bed curtains. (They presumably exist only in Lear's mad imagination.)

89 upon against　**95 Stand . . . loss** will assuredly be lost　**96 provision** supplies, or, means of providing for safety　**97 conduct** guidance　**98 balmed** cured, healed.　**sinews** nerves　**99 convenience** circumstances　**100 Stand . . . cure** will be hard to cure　**102 our woes** woes like ours　**103 We . . . foes** we almost forget our own miseries (since we see how human suffering afflicts even the great)　**104–105 Who . . . behind** when we think of our own misfortunes as unique, we suffer the mental anguish of reflecting on all the carefree joys and happy scenes that were once ours　**106 sufferance** suffering　**107 bearing fellowship** tribulation (has) company　**108 portable** bearable, endurable　**110 He . . . fathered** i.e., he suffering cruelty from his children as I from my father　**111 Mark . . . noises** i.e., observe what is being said about those in high places or about great events.　**bewray** reveal　**113 In . . . thee** upon your being proved innocent recalls you and restores you to favor　**114 What . . . King** whatever else happens tonight, may the King escape safely

3.7   *Enter Cornwall, Regan, Goneril, Bastard*
      [Edmund], and Servants.

CORNWALL *[to Goneril]* Post speedily to my lord your hus- 1
band; show him this letter. *[He gives a letter.]* The army
of France is landed.—Seek out the traitor Gloucester.
                              [Exeunt some Servants.]
REGAN   Hang him instantly.
GONERIL   Pluck out his eyes.
CORNWALL   Leave him to my displeasure. Edmund,
keep you our sister company. The revenges we are 7
bound to take upon your traitorous father are not fit 8
for your beholding. Advise the Duke, where you are 9
going, to a most festinate preparation; we are bound 10
to the like. Our posts shall be swift and intelligent 11
betwixt us. Farewell, dear sister; farewell, my lord of 12
Gloucester.   13

      Enter steward [Oswald].

How now? Where's the King?
OSWALD
My lord of Gloucester hath conveyed him hence.
Some five- or six-and-thirty of his knights,   16
Hot questrists after him, met him at gate,   17
Who, with some other of the lord's dependents,   18
Are gone with him toward Dover, where they boast
To have well-armèd friends.
CORNWALL Get horses for your mistress. *[Exit Oswald.]*
GONERIL   Farewell, sweet lord, and sister.
CORNWALL
Edmund, farewell.   *Exeunt [Goneril and Edmund].*
            Go seek the traitor Gloucester.
Pinion him like a thief; bring him before us.
                              [Exeunt Servants.]
Though well we may not pass upon his life   25
Without the form of justice, yet our power
Shall do a court'sy to our wrath, which men   27
May blame but not control.

      Enter Gloucester, and Servants [leading him].

            Who's there? The traitor?
REGAN   Ingrateful fox! 'Tis he.
CORNWALL   Bind fast his corky arms.   30
GLOUCESTER
What means Your Graces? Good my friends,
      consider
You are my guests. Do me no foul play, friends.
CORNWALL
Bind him, I say.   *[Servants bind him.]*
REGAN   Hard, hard. O filthy traitor!

GLOUCESTER
Unmerciful lady as you are, I'm none.
CORNWALL
To this chair bind him.—Villain, thou shalt find—
                  [Regan plucks Gloucester's beard.]
GLOUCESTER
By the kind gods, 'tis most ignobly done
To pluck me by the beard.
REGAN
So white, and such a traitor?
GLOUCESTER   Naughty lady,   38
These hairs which thou dost ravish from my chin
Will quicken and accuse thee. I am your host.   40
With robbers' hands my hospitable favors   41
You should not ruffle thus. What will you do?   42
CORNWALL
Come, sir, what letters had you late from France?   43
REGAN
Be simple-answered, for we know the truth.   44
CORNWALL
And what confederacy have you with the traitors
Late footed in the kingdom?
REGAN   To whose hands   46
You have sent the lunatic King. Speak.
GLOUCESTER
I have a letter guessingly set down,   48
Which came from one that's of a neutral heart,
And not from one opposed.
CORNWALL   Cunning.
REGAN   And false.
CORNWALL   Where hast thou sent the King?
GLOUCESTER   To Dover.
REGAN
Wherefore to Dover? Wast thou not charged at
      peril—   55
CORNWALL
Wherefore to Dover? Let him answer that.
GLOUCESTER
I am tied to th' stake, and I must stand the course. 57
REGAN   Wherefore to Dover?
GLOUCESTER
Because I would not see thy cruel nails
Pluck out his poor old eyes, nor thy fierce sister
In his anointed flesh rash boarish fangs.   61
The sea, with such a storm as his bare head
In hell-black night endured, would have buoyed up   63
And quenched the stellèd fires;   64
Yet, poor old heart, he help the heavens to rain.   65

---

1 **Post speedily** hurry   **7 sister** i.e., sister-in-law, Goneril   **8 bound**
intending; obliged   **9 the Duke** i.e., Albany   **10 festinate** hasty.   **are**
bound intend, are committed   **11 posts** messengers.   **intelligent** serviceable in bearing information, knowledgeable   **12–13 my . . .**
Gloucester i.e., Edmund, the recipient now of his father's forfeited estate and title. (Two lines later, Oswald uses the same title to refer to
Edmund's father.)   **16 his** Lear's   **17 questrists after him** searchers for
Lear   **18 the lord's** i.e., Gloucester's   **25 pass upon his life** pass the
death sentence upon him   **27 do a court'sy** i.e., bow before, yield
precedence   **30 corky** withered with age

38 white i.e., white-haired, venerable.   **Naughty** wicked
40 quicken come to life   **41 my hospitable favors** the features of me,
your host   **42 ruffle** tear or snatch at, treat with such violence
43 late lately   **44 simple-answered** straightforward in your answers
46 footed landed   **48 guessingly set down** which was tentatively
stated   **55 charged at peril** commanded on peril of your life   **57 tied**
to th' stake i.e., like a bear to be baited with dogs.   **the course** the
dogs' attack   **61 anointed** consecrated with holy oil.   **rash** slash sideways with   **63–64 would . . . fires** would have swelled high
enough, like a wave-lifted buoy, to quench the stars. (The storm was
monstrous in its scope and in its assault on order.)   **stellèd** starry, or
fixed   **65 holp** helped

If wolves had at thy gate howled that dern time,   66
Thou shouldst have said, "Good porter, turn the
    key."   67
All cruels else subscribe. But I shall see   68
The wingèd Vengeance overtake such children.   69

CORNWALL
See 't shalt thou never. Fellows, hold the chair.
Upon these eyes of thine I'll set my foot.

GLOUCESTER
He that will think to live till he be old,   72
Give me some help!
    [Servants hold the chair as Cornwall grinds
    out one of Gloucester's eyes with his boot.]
        O cruel! O you gods!

REGAN
One side will mock another. Th' other too.

CORNWALL
If you see Vengeance—

FIRST SERVANT   Hold your hand, my lord!
I have served you ever since I was a child;
But better service have I never done you
Than now to bid you hold.

REGAN   How now, you dog?

FIRST SERVANT [to Regan]
If you did wear a beard upon your chin,
I'd shake it on this quarrel.—What do you mean?   80

CORNWALL   My villain?   [He draws his sword.]   81

FIRST SERVANT [drawing]
Nay, then, come on, and take the chance of anger.   82
    [They fight. Cornwall is wounded.]

REGAN [to another Servant]
Give me thy sword. A peasant stand up thus?   83
    [She takes a sword and runs at him behind.]

FIRST SERVANT
O, I am slain! My lord, you have one eye left
To see some mischief on him. O!   [He dies.]   85

CORNWALL
Lest it see more, prevent it. Out, vile jelly!
    [He puts out Gloucester's other eye.]
Where is thy luster now?

GLOUCESTER
All dark and comfortless. Where's my son Edmund?
Edmund, enkindle all the sparks of nature   89
To quit this horrid act.

REGAN   Out, treacherous villain!   90
Thou call'st on him that hates thee. It was he
That made the overture of thy treasons to us,   92
Who is too good to pity thee.

GLOUCESTER
O my follies! Then Edgar was abused.   94
Kind gods, forgive me that, and prosper him!

REGAN
Go thrust him out at gates and let him smell
His way to Dover. Exit [a Servant] with Gloucester.
    How is 't, my lord? How look you?   97

CORNWALL
I have received a hurt. Follow me, lady.—
Turn out that eyeless villain. Throw this slave
Upon the dunghill.—Regan, I bleed apace.
Untimely comes this hurt. Give me your arm.
    Exeunt [Cornwall, supported by Regan].

SECOND SERVANT
I'll never care what wickedness I do,
If this man come to good.

THIRD SERVANT   If she live long,
And in the end meet the old course of death,   104
Women will all turn monsters.

SECOND SERVANT
Let's follow the old Earl, and get the Bedlam
To lead him where he would. His roguish madness   107
Allows itself to anything.   108

THIRD SERVANT
Go thou. I'll fetch some flax and whites of eggs
To apply to his bleeding face. Now, heaven help
    him!   Exeunt [with the body].   110

❦

4.1   Enter Edgar [as poor Tom].

EDGAR
Yet better thus, and known to be contemned,   1
Than still contemned and flattered. To be worst,   2
The lowest and most dejected thing of fortune,   3
Stands still in esperance, lives not in fear.   4
The lamentable change is from the best;   5
The worst returns to laughter. Welcome, then,   6
Thou unsubstantial air that I embrace!
The wretch that thou hast blown unto the worst
Owes nothing to thy blasts.

    Enter Gloucester, and an Old Man [leading him].

            But who comes here?   9
My father, poorly led? World, world, O world!
But that thy strange mutations make us hate thee,   11
Life would not yield to age.   12

66 dern dire, dread   67 turn the key i.e., let them in   68 All . . .
subscribe all other cruel creatures would show forgiveness except
you; this cruelty is unparalleled   69 The wingèd Vengeance the swift
vengeance of the avenging angel of divine wrath   72 will think hopes
80 I'd . . . quarrel i.e., I'd pull your beard in vehement defiance in
this cause.   What do you mean i.e., what are you thinking of, what
do you think you're doing? (Said perhaps to Cornwall.)   81 villain
servant, bondman. (Cornwall's question implies, "How dare you do
such a thing?")   82 the chance of anger the risks of an angry encounter   83 s.d. She . . . behind (This stage direction appears in the
Quarto.)   85 mischief injury   89 nature i.e., filial love   90 quit requite.   Out (An exclamation of anger or impatience.)   92 overture
disclosure

94 abused wronged   97 How look you how is it with you?   104 old
customary, natural   107–108 His . . . anything i.e., his being a
madman and derelict allows him to do anything   110 s.d. Exeunt (At
some point after lines 99–100, the body of the slain First Servant
must be removed.)
4.1. Location: An open place.
1 Yet better thus i.e., it is better to be a beggar.   known know what
it is.   contemned despised   2 contemned and flattered despised behind your back and flattered to your face   3 dejected . . . of debased
or humbled by   4 esperance hope.   fear i.e., of something worse
happening   5–6 The lamentable . . . laughter any change from the
best is grievous, just as any change from the worst is bound to be for
the better   9 Owes nothing can pay no more, is free of obligation
11–12 But . . . age if it were not for your hateful inconstancy, we
would never be reconciled to old age and death

OLD MAN
O, my good lord, I have been your tenant
And your father's tenant these fourscore years.
GLOUCESTER
Away, get thee away! Good friend, begone.
Thy comforts can do me no good at all;   16
Thee they may hurt.
OLD MAN   You cannot see your way.
GLOUCESTER
I have no way and therefore want no eyes;
I stumbled when I saw. Full oft 'tis seen
Our means secure us, and our mere defects   20
Prove our commodities. O dear son Edgar,   21
The food of thy abusèd father's wrath!   22
Might I but live to see thee in my touch,   23
I'd say I had eyes again!
OLD MAN   How now? Who's there?
EDGAR [aside]
O gods! Who is 't can say, "I am at the worst"?
I am worse than e'er I was.
OLD MAN   'Tis poor mad Tom.
EDGAR [aside]
And worse I may be yet. The worst is not   27
So long as we can say, "This is the worst."   28
OLD MAN
Fellow, where goest?
GLOUCESTER   Is it a beggar-man?
OLD MAN   Madman and beggar too.
GLOUCESTER
He has some reason, else he could not beg.   31
I' the last night's storm I such a fellow saw,
Which made me think a man a worm. My son
Came then into my mind, and yet my mind
Was then scarce friends with him. I have heard
    more since.
As flies to wanton boys are we to th' gods;   36
They kill us for their sport.
EDGAR [aside]   How should this be?   37
Bad is the trade that must play fool to sorrow,   38
Ang'ring itself and others.—Bless thee, master!   39
GLOUCESTER
Is that the naked fellow?
OLD MAN   Ay, my lord.
GLOUCESTER
Then, prithee, get thee gone. If for my sake
Thou wilt o'ertake us hence a mile or twain   42
I' the way toward Dover, do it for ancient love,   43

And bring some covering for this naked soul,
Which I'll entreat to lead me.
OLD MAN   Alack, sir, he is mad.
GLOUCESTER
'Tis the time's plague, when madmen lead the blind. 46
Do as I bid thee, or rather do thy pleasure;
Above the rest, begone.   48
OLD MAN
I'll bring him the best 'parel that I have,
Come on 't what will.   Exit.
GLOUCESTER   Sirrah, naked fellow—   50
EDGAR
Poor Tom's a-cold. [Aside.] I cannot daub it further. 51
GLOUCESTER   Come hither, fellow.
EDGAR [aside]
And yet I must.—Bless thy sweet eyes, they bleed.
GLOUCESTER   Know'st thou the way to Dover?
EDGAR   Both stile and gate, horseway and footpath.
Poor Tom hath been scared out of his good wits. Bless
thee, good man's son, from the foul fiend! Five fiends
have been in poor Tom at once: of lust, as Obidicut; 58
Hobbididance, prince of dumbness; Mahu, of steal-   59
ing; Modo, of murder; Flibbertigibbet, of mopping   60
and mowing, who since possesses chambermaids and 61
waiting women. So, bless thee, master!
GLOUCESTER [giving a purse]
Here, take this purse, thou whom the heavens'
    plagues
Have humbled to all strokes. That I am wretched   64
Makes thee the happier. Heavens, deal so still!
Let the superfluous and lust-dieted man,   66
That slaves your ordinance, that will not see   67
Because he does not feel, feel your pow'r quickly!   68
So distribution should undo excess
And each man have enough. Dost thou know
    Dover?
EDGAR   Ay, master.
GLOUCESTER
There is a cliff, whose high and bending head   72
Looks fearfully in the confinèd deep.   73
Bring me but to the very brim of it
And I'll repair the misery thou dost bear
With something rich about me. From that place
I shall no leading need.
EDGAR   Give me thy arm.
Poor Tom shall lead thee.   Exeunt.

❖

16 comforts kindnesses   20 Our means secure us our prosperity
makes us overconfident.   mere defects sheer afflictions   21 commodities benefits   22 The . . . wrath on whom thy deceived father's
wrath fed, the object of his anger   23 in i.e., by means of
27–28 The worst . . . worst so long as we can speak and act and
delude ourselves with false hopes, our fortunes can, in fact, grow
worse   31 reason power of reason   36 wanton playful   37 How . . .
be i.e., how can he have suffered so much, changed so much?
38 Bad . . . sorrow i.e., it's a bad business to have to play the fool to
my sorrowing father   39 Ang'ring offending, distressing   42 o'ertake
us catch up to us (after you have found clothing for Tom o' Bedlam)
43 ancient love i.e., the mutually trusting relationship of master and
tenant that Gloucester and the Old Man have long enjoyed

46 'Tis the time's plague i.e., it well expresses the spreading sickness
of our present state   48 the rest all   50 on 't of it   51 daub it further
i.e., keep up this pretense   58–60 Obidicut . . . Flibbertigibbet
(Fiends borrowed, as before in 3.4.114 and 139–142, from Harsnett.)
60–61 mopping and mowing making grimaces and mouths   61 since
since that time   64 Have . . . strokes have brought so low as to be
prepared to accept every blow of Fortune   66 superfluous immoderate, gluttonous.   lust-dieted feeding luxuriously   67 slaves your ordinance makes the laws of heaven his slaves   68 feel feel sympathy or
fellow feeling; suffer   72 bending overhanging   73 in . . . deep i.e.,
into the sea below, which is confined by its shores

4.2   *Enter Goneril [and] Bastard [Edmund].*

GONERIL
Welcome, my lord. I marvel our mild husband   1
Not met us on the way.

        [Enter] steward [Oswald].

                  Now, where's your master?   2

OSWALD
Madam, within, but never man so changed.
I told him of the army that was landed;
He smiled at it. I told him you were coming;
His answer was "The worse." Of Gloucester's
    treachery
And of the loyal service of his son
When I informed him, then he called me sot   8
And told me I had turned the wrong side out.
What most he should dislike seems pleasant to him;
What like, offensive.

GONERIL *[to Edmund]*   Then shall you go no further.
It is the cowish terror of his spirit,   11
That dares not undertake. He'll not feel wrongs   12
Which tie him to an answer. Our wishes on the way   13
May prove effects. Back, Edmund, to my brother;   14
Hasten his musters and conduct his powers.   15
I must change names at home and give the distaff   16
Into my husband's hands. This trusty servant   17
Shall pass between us. Ere long you are like to hear, 19
If you dare venture in your own behalf,
A mistress's command. Wear this; spare speech.   21
                [She gives him a favor.]
Decline your head. *[She kisses him.]* This kiss, if it durst
    speak,
Would stretch thy spirits up into the air.
Conceive, and fare thee well.   24

EDMUND
Yours in the ranks of death.   *Exit.*

GONERIL   My most dear Gloucester!
O, the difference of man and man!
To thee a woman's services are due;
My fool usurps my body.   28

OSWALD   Madam, here comes my lord.   *[Exit.]* 29

    Enter Albany.

GONERIL
I have been worth the whistling.

ALBANY   O Goneril,   30
You are not worth the dust which the rude wind
Blows in your face. I fear your disposition;   32
That nature which contemns its origin   33
Cannot be bordered certain in itself.   34
She that herself will sliver and disbranch   35
From her material sap perforce must wither   36
And come to deadly use.   37

GONERIL   No more. The text is foolish.   38

ALBANY
Wisdom and goodness to the vile seem vile;
Filths savor but themselves. What have you done?   40
Tigers, not daughters, what have you performed?
A father, and a gracious agèd man,
Whose reverence even the head-lugged bear would
    lick,
                              43
Most barbarous, most degenerate, have you
    madded.
                              44
Could my good brother suffer you to do it?   45
A man, a prince, by him so benefited?
If that the heavens do not their visible spirits   47
Send quickly down to tame these vile offenses,
It will come,
Humanity must perforce prey on itself,
Like monsters of the deep.

GONERIL   Milk-livered man,   51
That bear'st a cheek for blows, a head for wrongs,
Who hast not in thy brows an eye discerning   53
Thine honor from thy suffering, that not know'st   54
Fools do those villains pity who are punished   55
Ere they have done their mischief. Where's thy
    drum?
                              56
France spreads his banners in our noiseless land,   57
With plumèd helm thy state begins to threat,   58
Whilst thou, a moral fool, sits still and cries,   59
"Alack, why does he so?"

ALBANY   See thyself, devil!   60
Proper deformity shows not in the fiend   61

4.2. Location: **Before the Duke of Albany's palace.**
1 Welcome (Goneril, who has just arrived home from Gloucestershire escorted by Edmund, bids him brief welcome before he must return.)
2 Not met has not met   **8 sot** fool   **12 cowish** cowardly   **13 undertake** venture   **13–14 He'll . . . answer** he will ignore insults that, if he took notice, would oblige him to respond, to fight   **14–15 Our . . . effects** the hopes we discussed on our journey here (presumably concerning the supplanting of Albany by Edmund) may come to pass   **15 brother** i.e., brother-in-law, Cornwall   **16 musters** assembling of troops.   **powers** armed forces   **17 change names** i.e., exchange the roles of master and mistress of the household, and exchange the insignia of man and woman: the sword and the *distaff*.   **distaff** spinning staff, symbolizing the wife's role   **19 like** likely   **21 mistress's** (With sexual double meaning.)   **24 Conceive** understand, take my meaning (with sexual double entendre, continuing from *stretch thy spirits* in the previous line and continued in *death*, line 25, and a *woman's services*, line 27)   **28 My fool . . . body** i.e., my husband claims possession of me but is unfitted to do so   **29 s.d. Exit** (Oswald could exit later with Goneril, at line 88.)

30 worth the whistling i.e., worth the attentions of men. (Alludes to the proverb, "it is a poor dog that is not worth the whistling.")
32 fear your disposition mistrust your nature   **33 contemns** despises   **34 bordered certain** safely restrained, kept within bounds   **35 sliver** tear off   **36 material sap** nourishing substance, the stock from which she grew   **37 to deadly use** to destruction, like firewood   **38 The text** i.e., on which you have been preaching   **40 savor but themselves** hunger only for that which is filthy   **43 head-lugged** dragged by the head (or by the ring in its nose) and infuriated   **44 madded** driven mad   **45 brother** brother-in-law (Cornwall)   **47 visible** made visible   **51 Milk-livered** white-livered, cowardly   **53–54 discerning . . . suffering** able to tell the difference between an insult to your honor and something you should tolerate   **55 Fools** i.e., only fools. (Goneril goes on to say that only fools are so tenderhearted as to worry about injustices to potential troublemakers, like Lear and Gloucester, instead of applauding measures taken to insure order.)   **56 thy drum** i.e., your military preparations   **57 noiseless** peaceful, having none of the bustle of war   **58 thy state . . . threat** (France) begins to threaten your kingdom   **59 moral** moralizing   **60 why does he so** i.e., why does the King of France invade England?   **61 Proper deformity** i.e., the deformity appropriate to the fiend. (Such deformity seems even uglier in a woman's features than in a fiend's, since it is appropriate in a fiend's.)

So horrid as in woman.

GONERIL   O vain fool!

ALBANY
Thou changèd and self-covered thing, for shame,   63
Bemonster not thy feature. Were 't my fitness   64
To let these hands obey my blood,   65
They are apt enough to dislocate and tear   66
Thy flesh and bones. Howe'er thou art a fiend,   67
A woman's shape doth shield thee.   68

GONERIL   Marry, your manhood! Mew!   69

Enter a Messenger.

ALBANY   What news?

MESSENGER
O, my good lord, the Duke of Cornwall's dead,
Slain by his servant, going to put out
The other eye of Gloucester.

ALBANY   Gloucester's eyes!

MESSENGER
A servant that he bred, thrilled with remorse,   74
Opposed against the act, bending his sword   75
To his great master, who, thereat enraged,   76
Flew on him and amongst them felled him dead,   77
But not without that harmful stroke which since
Hath plucked him after.

ALBANY   This shows you are above,   79
You justicers, that these our nether crimes   80
So speedily can venge! But, O poor Gloucester!
Lost he his other eye?

MESSENGER   Both, both, my lord.—
This letter, madam, craves a speedy answer;
'Tis from your sister.   [*He gives her a letter.*]

GONERIL [*aside*]   One way I like this well;   84
But being widow, and my Gloucester with her,
May all the building in my fancy pluck   86
Upon my hateful life. Another way   87
The news is not so tart.—I'll read, and answer.   88
                                    [*Exit.*]

ALBANY
Where was his son when they did take his eyes?

MESSENGER
Come with my lady hither.

ALBANY   He is not here.

MESSENGER
No, my good lord. I met him back again.   91

63 changèd transformed. self-covered having the true nature concealed 64 Bemonster . . . feature do not, however evil you are,
take on the outward form of a monster or a fiend. my fitness suitable for me 65 blood passion 66 apt ready 67 Howe'er . . . fiend
however much you may be a fiend in reality 68 shield (Since I, a
gentleman, cannot lay violent hands on a lady.) 69 Mew (An exclamation of disgust, a derisive catcall: You speak of manhood in shielding me as a woman. Some manhood!) 74 bred kept in his household. thrilled with remorse deeply moved with pity 75 Opposed
opposed himself 75–76 bending . . . To directing his sword against
77 amongst them together with the others (?) in their midst (?) out of
their number (?) 79 after along (to death) 80 justicers (heavenly)
judges. nether i.e., committed here below, on earth 84 One way
i.e., because Edmund is now Duke of Gloucester, and Cornwall, a
dangerous rival for the throne, is dead 86–87 May . . . life i.e.,
may pull down my imagined happiness (of possessing the entire kingdom with Edmund) and make hateful my life 88 tart bitter, sour
91 back going back

ALBANY   Knows he the wickedness?

MESSENGER
Ay, my good lord. 'Twas he informed against him,
And quit the house on purpose that their
    punishment
Might have the freer course.

ALBANY   Gloucester, I live
To thank thee for the love thou show'dst the King
And to revenge thine eyes.—Come hither, friend.
Tell me what more thou know'st.   *Exeunt.*

4.3   *Enter Kent [disguised] and a Gentleman.*

KENT   Why the King of France is so suddenly gone back
know you no reason?

GENTLEMAN   Something he left imperfect in the state,   3
which since his coming forth is thought of, which im-   4
ports to the kingdom so much fear and danger that his   5
personal return was most required and necessary.

KENT
Who hath he left behind him general?

GENTLEMAN
The Marshal of France, Monsieur la Far.

KENT   Did your letters pierce the Queen to any demonstration of grief?

GENTLEMAN
Ay, sir. She took them, read them in my presence,
And now and then an ample tear trilled down   12
Her delicate cheek. It seemed she was a queen
Over her passion, who, most rebel-like,   14
Sought to be king o'er her.

KENT   O, then it moved her?

GENTLEMAN
Not to a rage. Patience and sorrow strove
Who should express her goodliest. You have seen   17
Sunshine and rain at once. Her smiles and tears
Were like a better way; those happy smilets   19
That played on her ripe lip seemed not to know
What guests were in her eyes, which parted thence   21
As pearls from diamonds dropped. In brief,
Sorrow would be a rarity most beloved   23
If all could so become it.   24

KENT   Made she no verbal question?   25

GENTLEMAN
Faith, once or twice she heaved the name of "father" 26
Pantingly forth, as if it pressed her heart;
Cried, "Sisters, sisters! Shame of ladies, sisters!
Kent! Father! Sisters! What, i' the storm, i' the night?
Let pity not be believed!" There she shook   30
The holy water from her heavenly eyes,

4.3. Location: The French camp near Dover.
3 imperfect in the state unsettled in state affairs 4–5 imports portends 12 trilled trickled 14 passion, who emotion, which 17 Who
. . . goodliest which of the two could make her appear more lovely
19 like a better way better than that, though similar 21 which i.e.,
which *guests* or tears 23 a rarity i.e., a precious thing, like a jewel
24 If . . . it i.e., if all persons were as attractive in sorrow as she
25 verbal i.e., as distinguished from her tears and looks 26 heaved
breathed out with difficulty 30 believed i.e., believed to be extant

And, clamor-moistened, then away she started   32
To deal with grief alone.
KENT   It is the stars,
The stars above us, govern our conditions,   34
Else one self mate and make could not beget   35
Such different issues. You spoke not with her since? 36
GENTLEMAN   No.
KENT
Was this before the King returned?
GENTLEMAN   No, since.   38
KENT
Well, sir, the poor distressèd Lear's i' the town,
Who sometimes in his better tune remembers   40
What we are come about, and by no means
Will yield to see his daughter.
GENTLEMAN   Why, good sir?
KENT
A sovereign shame so elbows him—his own
unkindness   43
That stripped her from his benediction, turned her   44
To foreign casualties, gave her dear rights   45
To his dog-hearted daughters—these things sting
His mind so venomously that burning shame
Detains him from Cordelia.
GENTLEMAN   Alack, poor gentleman!
KENT
Of Albany's and Cornwall's powers you heard not?   50
GENTLEMAN   'Tis so. They are afoot.   51
KENT
Well, sir, I'll bring you to our master Lear
And leave you to attend him. Some dear cause   53
Will in concealment wrap me up awhile.
When I am known aright, you shall not grieve   55
Lending me this acquaintance. I pray you, go   56
Along with me.   Exeunt.

❧

4.4   *Enter, with drum and colors, Cordelia, Doctor,*
         and soldiers.

CORDELIA
Alack, 'tis he! Why, he was met even now
As mad as the vexed sea, singing aloud,
Crowned with rank fumiter and furrow weeds,   3
With hardocks, hemlock, nettles, cuckooflowers,   4
Darnel, and all the idle weeds that grow   5
In our sustaining corn. A century send forth!   6

Search every acre in the high-grown field
And bring him to our eye. [*Exit a soldier or soldiers.*]
   What can man's wisdom   8
In the restoring his bereavèd sense?
He that helps him take all my outward worth.   10
DOCTOR   There is means, madam.
Our foster nurse of nature is repose,
The which he lacks. That to provoke in him   13
Are many simples operative, whose power   14
Will close the eye of anguish.
CORDELIA   All blest secrets,
All you unpublished virtues of the earth,   16
Spring with my tears! Be aidant and remediate   17
In the good man's distress! Seek, seek for him,
Lest his ungoverned rage dissolve the life   19
That wants the means to lead it.

Enter Messenger.

MESSENGER   News, madam.   20
The British powers are marching hitherward.   21
CORDELIA
'Tis known before. Our preparation stands
In expectation of them. O dear Father,
It is thy business that I go about;
Therefore great France
My mourning and importuned tears hath pitied.   26
No blown ambition doth our arms incite,   27
But love, dear love, and our aged father's right.
Soon may I hear and see him!   *Exeunt.*

❧

4.5   *Enter Regan and steward [Oswald].*

REGAN   But are my brother's powers set forth?   1
OSWALD   Ay, madam.
REGAN   Himself in person there?
OSWALD   Madam, with much ado.   4
Your sister is the better soldier.
REGAN
Lord Edmund spake not with your lord at home?
OSWALD   No, madam.
REGAN
What might import my sister's letters to him?   8
OSWALD   I know not, lady.
REGAN
Faith, he is posted hence on serious matter.   10
It was great ignorance, Gloucester's eyes being out, 11
To let him live. Where he arrives he moves
All hearts against us. Edmund, I think, is gone,
In pity of his misery, to dispatch

32 clamor-moistened i.e., her outcry of grief assuaged by tears.
started i.e., went   **34 conditions** characters   **35 Else . . . make** otherwise, one couple (husband and wife)   **36 issues** offspring   **38 the
King** the King of France   **40 better tune** more composed state
43 sovereign overruling.   **elbows him** i.e., prods his memory, jostles
him, thrusts him back   **44 turned her** turned her out   **45 foreign casualties** chances of fortune abroad   **50 powers** troops, armies
51 afoot on the march   **53 dear cause** important purpose   **55–
56 grieve . . . acquaintance** regret having made my acquaintance
4.4. Location: The French camp.
3 fumiter i.e., fumitory, a weed or herb   **4 hardocks** i.e., burdocks or
hoardocks, white-leaved (?) (Identity uncertain.)   **5 Darnel** (A weed of
the grass kind.)   **idle** worthless   **6 sustaining** giving sustenance.
corn grain.   **century** troop of one hundred men

8 What . . . wisdom i.e., what can medical knowledge accomplish
10 outward material   **13 That to provoke** to induce that   **14 simples**
medicinal plants.   **operative** effective   **16 unpublished virtues** little-
known benign herbs   **17 Spring** grow.   **aidant and remediate** helpful
and remedial   **19 rage** frenzy   **20 wants** lacks.   **means** i.e., his reason   **21 powers** armies   **26 importuned** importunate   **27 blown**
puffed up with pride
4.5. Location; Gloucester's house.
1 my brother's powers i.e., Albany's forces   **4 with much ado** after
much fuss and persuasion   **8 import** bear as its purport, express
10 is posted has hurried   **11 ignorance** error, folly

His nighted life; moreover to descry   15
The strength o' th' enemy.

OSWALD
I must needs after him, madam, with my letter.

REGAN
Our troops set forth tomorrow. Stay with us;
The ways are dangerous.

OSWALD   I may not, madam.
My lady charged my duty in this business.   20

REGAN
Why should she write to Edmund? Might not you
Transport her purposes by word? Belike   22
Something—I know not what. I'll love thee much;
Let me unseal the letter.

OSWALD   Madam, I had rather—

REGAN
I know your lady does not love her husband,
I am sure of that; and at her late being here   26
She gave strange oeillades and most speaking looks   27
To noble Edmund. I know you are of her bosom.   28

OSWALD   I, madam?

REGAN
I speak in understanding; y' are, I know 't.   30
Therefore I do advise you, take this note: 31
My lord is dead; Edmund and I have talked,   32
And more convenient is he for my hand   33
Than for your lady's. You may gather more.   34
If you do find him, pray you, give him this;   35
And when your mistress hears thus much from you,   36
I pray, desire her call her wisdom to her.   37
So, fare you well.
If you do chance to hear of that blind traitor,
Preferment falls on him that cuts him off.   40

OSWALD
Would I could meet him, madam! I should show
What party I do follow.

REGAN   Fare thee well.
                              Exeunt [*separately*].

❧

4.6 *Enter Gloucester, and Edgar* [*in peasant's clothes,*
        leading his father].

GLOUCESTER
When shall I come to th' top of that same hill?   1

EDGAR
You do climb up it now. Look how we labor.

---

15 nighted benighted, blinded **20 charged my duty** laid great stress on my obedience **22 Belike** it may be **26 late** recently **27 oeillades** amorous glances **28 of her bosom** in her confidence **30 y' are** you are **31 take this note** take note of this **32 have talked** have come to an understanding **33 convenient** fitting **34 gather more** infer what I am trying to suggest **35 this** i.e., this information, or a love token, or possibly a letter (though only one letter, Goneril's, is found on his dead body at 4.6.262) **36 thus much** what I have told you **37 call . . . to her** recall her to her senses **40 Preferment** advancement
4.6. Location: Open place near Dover.
1 that same hill i.e., the cliff we talked about (4.1.72–74)

GLOUCESTER
Methinks the ground is even.

EDGAR   Horrible steep.
Hark, do you hear the sea?

GLOUCESTER   No, truly.

EDGAR
Why, then, your other senses grow imperfect
By your eyes' anguish.

GLOUCESTER   So may it be, indeed.
Methinks thy voice is altered, and thou speak'st
In better phrase and matter than thou didst.

EDGAR
You're much deceived. In nothing am I changed
But in my garments.

GLOUCESTER   Methinks you're better spoken.

EDGAR
Come on, sir, here's the place. Stand still. How
  fearful
And dizzy 'tis to cast one's eyes so low!
The crows and choughs that wing the midway air   13
Show scarce so gross as beetles. Halfway down   14
Hangs one that gathers samphire—dreadful trade!   15
Methinks he seems no bigger than his head.
The fishermen that walk upon the beach
Appear like mice, and yond tall anchoring bark
Diminished to her cock; her cock, a buoy   19
Almost too small for sight. The murmuring surge,
That on th' unnumbered idle pebble chafes,   21
Cannot be heard so high. I'll look no more,
Lest my brain turn, and the deficient sight   23
Topple down headlong.

GLOUCESTER   Set me where you stand.   24

EDGAR
Give me your hand. You are now within a foot
Of th' extreme verge. For all beneath the moon
Would I not leap upright.

GLOUCESTER   Let go my hand.   27
Here, friend, 's another purse; in it a jewel
Well worth a poor man's taking. [*He gives a purse*].
  Fairies and gods   29
Prosper it with thee! Go thou further off.   30
Bid me farewell, and let me hear thee going.

EDGAR [*moving away*]
Now fare ye well, good sir.

GLOUCESTER   With all my heart.

EDGAR [*aside*]
Why I do trifle thus with his despair
Is done to cure it.

GLOUCESTER [*kneeling*]   O you mighty gods!
This world I do renounce, and in your sights
Shake patiently my great affliction off.

---

13 choughs jackdaws. **midway** halfway down **14 gross** large
15 samphire (A herb used in pickling.) **19 Diminished . . . cock** reduced to the size of her cockboat, small ship's boat **21 unnumbered idle pebble** innumerable, randomly shifting, pebbles **23–24 the deficient sight Topple** my failing sight topple me **27 upright** i.e., up and down, much less forward **29–30 Fairies . . . thee** may the fairies and gods cause this to multiply in your possession

If I could bear it longer, and not fall
To quarrel with your great opposeless wills,   38
My snuff and loathèd part of nature should   39
Burn itself out. If Edgar live, O, bless him!
Now, fellow, fare thee well.   *[He falls forward.]*

EDGAR   Gone, sir. Farewell.—
And yet I know not how conceit may rob   42
The treasury of life, when life itself
Yields to the theft. Had he been where he thought,   44
By this had thought been past. Alive or dead?—
Ho, you, sir! Friend! Hear you, sir! Speak!—
Thus might he pass indeed; yet he revives.—   47
What are you, sir?

GLOUCESTER   Away, and let me die.   48

EDGAR
Hadst thou been aught but gossamer, feathers, air,
So many fathom down precipitating,
Thou'dst shivered like an egg; but thou dost
     breathe,
Hast heavy substance, bleed'st not, speak'st, art
     sound.   52
Ten masts at each make not the altitude   53
Which thou hast perpendicularly fell.
Thy life's a miracle. Speak yet again.

GLOUCESTER   But have I fallen or no?

EDGAR
From the dread summit of this chalky bourn.   57
Look up aheight; the shrill-gorged lark so far   58
Cannot be seen or heard. Do but look up.

GLOUCESTER   Alack, I have no eyes.
Is wretchedness deprived that benefit
To end itself by death? 'Twas yet some comfort
When misery could beguile the tyrant's rage   63
And frustrate his proud will.

EDGAR   Give me your arm.
                                        [He lifts him up.]
Up—so. How is 't? Feel you your legs? You stand.

GLOUCESTER
Too well, too well.

EDGAR   This is above all strangeness.
Upon the crown o' the cliff what thing was that
Which parted from you?

GLOUCESTER   A poor unfortunate beggar.

EDGAR
As I stood here below, methought his eyes
Were two full moons; he had a thousand noses,
Horns whelked and waved like the enridgèd sea.   71
It was some fiend. Therefore, thou happy father,   72
Think that the clearest gods, who make them honors   73

Of men's impossibilities, have preserved thee.   74

GLOUCESTER
I do remember now. Henceforth I'll bear
Affliction till it do cry out itself   76
"Enough, enough," and die. That thing you
     speak of,   77
I took it for a man; often 'twould say
"The fiend, the fiend." He led me to that place.

EDGAR
Bear free and patient thoughts.

     *Enter Lear [mad, fantastically dressed with wild
     flowers].*

                                        But who comes here?   80
The safer sense will ne'er accommodate   81
His master thus.   82

LEAR   No, they cannot touch me for coining. I am the   83
King himself.

EDGAR   O thou side-piercing sight!   85

LEAR   Nature's above art in that respect. There's your   86
press money. That fellow handles his bow like a crow-   87
keeper. Draw me a clothier's yard. Look, look, a   88
mouse! Peace, peace; this piece of toasted cheese will
do 't. There's my gauntlet; I'll prove it on a giant. Bring   90
up the brown bills. O, well flown, bird! I' the clout, i'   91
the clout—hewgh! Give the word.   92

EDGAR   Sweet marjoram.   93

LEAR   Pass.

GLOUCESTER   I know that voice.

LEAR   Ha! Goneril with a white beard? They flattered
me like a dog and told me I had white hairs in my   97
beard ere the black ones were there. To say ay and   98
no to everything that I said ay and no to was   99
no good divinity. When the rain came to wet me   100
once and the wind to make me chatter, when the
thunder would not peace at my bidding, there I found   102
'em, there I smelt 'em out. Go to, they are not men o'   103

38 To quarrel with into rebellion against. **opposeless** irresistible
39 snuff i.e., useless residue. (Literally, the smoking wick of a candle.) **of nature** i.e., of my life   **42 conceit** imagination   **44 Yields**
consents   **47 pass** die   **48 What** who. (Edgar now speaks in a new
voice, differing from that of "poor Tom" and also from the "altered"
voice he used at the start of this scene; see lines 7–10.)   **52 heavy
substance** the substance of the flesh   **53 at each** end to end
57 bourn limit, boundary (i.e., the edge of the sea)   **58 aheight** on
high.   **shrill-gorged** shrill-throated   **63 beguile** outwit   **71 whelked**
twisted, convoluted.   **enridgèd** furrowed (by the wind)   **72 happy father** lucky old man   **73 clearest** purest, most righteous

73–74 who . . . impossibilities who win our awe and reverence by
doing things impossible to men   **76–77 till . . . die** i.e., until affliction itself has had enough, or until I die   **80 free** i.e., free from despair   **81–82 The safer . . . thus** i.e., a person in his right senses
would never dress himself in such a fashion.   **His master** the owner
of the *safer sense* or sane mind. (*His* means "its.")   **83 touch** arrest,
prosecute.   **coining** minting coins. (A royal prerogative; the King
wants money for his imaginary soldiers, lines 86–87.)   **85 side-piercing** heartrending (with a suggestion also of Christ's suffering on the
cross)   **86 Nature's . . . respect** i.e., a born king is superior to anything art (or counterfeiting) can produce (?)   **87 press money** enlist-
ment bonus   **87–88 crowkeeper** laborer hired to scare away the
crows   **88 Draw . . . yard** i.e., draw your bow to the full length of
the arrow, a cloth-yard long.   **me** for me   **90 do 't** i.e., capture the
mouse, an imagined enemy.   **gauntlet** armored glove thrown down
as a challenge.   **prove it on** maintain it against   **91 brown bills** soldiers carrying pikes (painted brown), or the pikes themselves.   **well
flown, bird** (Lear uses the language of hawking to describe the flight
of an arrow.)   **clout** target, bull's-eye   **92 hewgh** (The arrow's
noise.)   **word** password   **93 Sweet marjoram** (A herb used to cure
madness.)   **97 like a dog** as a dog fawns   **97–98 had . . . beard**
i.e., had wisdom   **98–100 To . . . divinity** i.e., to agree flatteringly
with everything I said was not good theology, since the Bible teaches
us to "let your yea be yea and your nay, nay" (James 5:12; see also
Matthew 5:37 and 2 Cor. 1:18)   **102–103 found 'em** found them
out   **103 Go to** (An expression of impatience.)

their words. They told me I was everything. 'Tis a lie;
I am not ague-proof.   105

GLOUCESTER

The trick of that voice I do well remember.   106
Is 't not the King?

LEAR   Ay, every inch a king.
When I do stare, see how the subject quakes.
I pardon that man's life. What was thy cause?   109
Adultery?
Thou shalt not die. Die for adultery? No.
The wren goes to 't, and the small gilded fly
Does lecher in my sight.
Let copulation thrive; for Gloucester's bastard son
Was kinder to his father than my daughters
Got 'tween the lawful sheets.
To 't, luxury, pell-mell, for I lack soldiers.   117
Behold yond simpering dame,
Whose face between her forks presages snow,   119
That minces virtue and does shake the head   120
To hear of pleasure's name;   121
The fitchew nor the soilèd horse goes to 't   122
With a more riotous appetite.
Down from the waist they're centaurs,   124
Though women all above.
But to the girdle do the gods inherit;   126
Beneath is all the fiends'.
There's hell, there's darkness, there is the sulfurous pit,
burning, scalding, stench, consumption. Fie, fie, fie!
Pah, pah! Give me an ounce of civet, good apothecary,   130
sweeten my imagination. There's money for thee.

GLOUCESTER   O, let me kiss that hand!

LEAR   Let me wipe it first; it smells of mortality.

GLOUCESTER

O ruined piece of nature! This great world   134
Shall so wear out to naught. Dost thou know me?   135

LEAR   I remember thine eyes well enough. Dost thou
squinny at me? No, do thy worst, blind Cupid; I'll not   137
love. Read thou this challenge. Mark but the penning
of it.

GLOUCESTER

Were all thy letters suns, I could not see.

EDGAR [aside]

I would not take this from report. It is,   141
And my heart breaks at it.

LEAR   Read.

GLOUCESTER   What, with the case of eyes?   144

LEAR   Oho, are you there with me? No eyes in your   145

head, nor no money in your purse? Your eyes are in a
heavy case, your purse in a light, yet you see how this   147
world goes.

GLOUCESTER   I see it feelingly.   149

LEAR   What, art mad? A man may see how this world
goes with no eyes. Look with thine ears. See how
yond justice rails upon yond simple thief. Hark in   152
thine ear: change places and, handy-dandy, which is   153
the justice, which is the thief? Thou hast seen a
farmer's dog bark at a beggar?

GLOUCESTER   Ay, sir.

LEAR   And the creature run from the cur? There thou   157
mightst behold the great image of authority: a dog's   158
obeyed in office.   159
Thou rascal beadle, hold thy bloody hand!   160
Why dost thou lash that whore? Strip thine own
  back;
Thou hotly lusts to use her in that kind   162
For which thou whipp'st her. The usurer hangs the
  cozener.   163
Through tattered clothes small vices do appear;
Robes and furred gowns hide all. Plate sin with gold,   165
And the strong lance of justice hurtless breaks;   166
Arm it in rags, a pygmy's straw does pierce it.
None does offend, none, I say, none. I'll able 'em.   168
Take that of me, my friend, who have the power   169
To seal th' accuser's lips. Get thee glass eyes,   170
And like a scurvy politician seem
To see the things thou dost not. Now, now, now,
  now!
Pull off my boots. Harder, harder! So.

EDGAR [aside]

O, matter and impertinency mixed,   174
Reason in madness!

LEAR

If thou wilt weep my fortunes, take my eyes.
I know thee well enough; thy name is Gloucester.
Thou must be patient. We came crying hither.
Thou know'st the first time that we smell the air
We wawl and cry. I will preach to thee. Mark.

GLOUCESTER   Alack, alack the day!

LEAR

When we are born, we cry that we are come
To this great stage of fools.—This' a good block.   183
It were a delicate stratagem to shoe   184

---

105 ague-proof immune against illness (literally, fever)   **106 trick** peculiar characteristic   **109 cause** offense   **117 luxury** lechery
119 Whose . . . snow whose frosty countenance seems to suggest frigidity between her legs   **120 minces** affects, mimics   **121 of pleasure's name** the very name of pleasure   **122 The fitchew** neither the polecat.   **soilèd horse** horse turned out to grass, well-fed and hence wanton   **124 centaurs** fabulous creatures with the head, trunk, and arms of a man joined to the body and legs of a horse   **126 But** only. **girdle** waist.   **inherit** possess   **130 civet** musk perfume   **134 piece** masterpiece.   **This great world** i.e., the macrocosm, of which humanity, the masterpiece of nature, is the microcosm   **135 so** similarly **137 squinny** squint   **141 take** believe, credit.   **It is** it is taking place, incredibly enough   **144 case** mere sockets   **145 are . . . me** is that your meaning, the point you are making?

147 heavy case sad plight (with pun on *case* in line 144)   **149 feelingly** (1) by touch (2) keenly, painfully   **152 simple** of humble station **153 handy-dandy** take your choice of hands (as in a well-known child's game)   **157 creature** poor fellow   **158–159 a dog's . . . office** i.e., even currish power commands submission   **160 beadle** parish officer, responsible for giving whippings   **162 kind** way   **163 The usurer** i.e., a judge guilty of lending money at usurious rates.   **cozener** petty cheater   **165 Plate** arm in plate armor   **166 hurtless breaks** splinters harmlessly   **168 able** give warrant to   **169 that** i.e., a guarantee of immunity   **170 glass eyes** (With glass eyes, possibly spectacles, Gloucester could pretend to see or understand what he does not comprehend, like a vile *politician* governing through opportunism and trickery, hiding his blindness behind his glass eyes.) **174 matter and impertinency** sense and nonsense   **183 This'** this is. **block** felt hat (?) (Lear may refer to the weeds strewn in his hair, which he removes as though doffing a hat before preaching a sermon.)   **184 delicate** subtle

A troop of horse with felt. I'll put 't in proof,   185
And when I have stol'n upon these son-in-laws,
Then, kill, kill, kill, kill, kill, kill!

Enter a Gentleman [with attendants].

GENTLEMAN
O, here he is. Lay hand upon him.—Sir,
Your most dear daughter—
LEAR
No rescue? What, a prisoner? I am even
The natural fool of fortune. Use me well;   191
You shall have ransom. Let me have surgeons;
I am cut to th' brains.
GENTLEMAN   You shall have anything.   193
LEAR   No seconds? All myself?   194
Why, this would make a man of salt   195
To use his eyes for garden waterpots,
Ay, and laying autumn's dust.
I will die bravely, like a smug bridegroom. What?   198
I will be jovial. Come, come, I am a king,
Masters, know you that?
GENTLEMAN
You are a royal one, and we obey you.
LEAR   Then there's life in 't. Come, an you get it, you 202
shall get it by running. Sa, sa, sa, sa.   203

Exit [running, followed by attendants].

GENTLEMAN
A sight most pitiful in the meanest wretch,
Past speaking of in a king! Thou hast one daughter
Who redeems nature from the general curse   206
Which twain have brought her to.
EDGAR   Hail, gentle sir.   208
GENTLEMAN   Sir, speed you. What's your will?   209
EDGAR
Do you hear aught, sir, of a battle toward?   210
GENTLEMAN
Most sure and vulgar. Everyone hears that   211
Which can distinguish sound.
EDGAR   But, by your favor,   212
How near's the other army?
GENTLEMAN
Near and on speedy foot. The main descry   214
Stands on the hourly thought.   215
EDGAR   I thank you, sir; that's all.
GENTLEMAN
Though that the Queen on special cause is here,   217
Her army is moved on.
EDGAR   I thank you, sir.

Exit [Gentleman].

GLOUCESTER
You ever-gentle gods, take my breath from me;
Let not my worser spirit tempt me again   220
To die before you please!
EDGAR   Well pray you, father.   222
GLOUCESTER   Now, good sir, what are you?   223
EDGAR
A most poor man, made tame to fortune's blows,   224
Who, by the art of known and feeling sorrows,   225
Am pregnant to good pity. Give me your hand.   226
I'll lead you to some biding.   *[He offers his arm.]*
GLOUCESTER   Hearty thanks.   227
The bounty and the benison of heaven   228
To boot, and boot!

Enter steward [Oswald].

OSWALD   A proclaimed prize! Most happy!   229
                              [He draws his sword.]
That eyeless head of thine was first framed flesh   230
To raise my fortunes. Thou old unhappy traitor,
Briefly thyself remember. The sword is out   232
That must destroy thee.
GLOUCESTER   Now let thy friendly hand   233
Put strength enough to 't.   *[Edgar intervenes.]*
OSWALD   Wherefore, bold peasant,
Durst thou support a published traitor? Hence,   235
Lest that th' infection of his fortune take   236
Like hold on thee. Let go his arm.   237
EDGAR   'Chill not let go, zir, without vurther 'cagion.   238
OSWALD   Let go, slave, or thou diest!
EDGAR   Good gentleman, go your gait, and let poor volk 240
pass. An 'chud ha' bin zwaggered out of my life, 241
'twould not ha' bin zo long as 'tis by a vortnight. Nay, 242
come not near the old man; keep out, 'che vor ye, or 243
Ise try whether your costard or my ballow be the 244
harder. 'Chill be plain with you.
OSWALD   Out, dunghill!
EDGAR   'Chill pick your teeth, zir. Come, no matter vor
your foins. *[They fight. Edgar fells him with his cudgel.]* 248
OSWALD
Slave, thou hast slain me. Villain, take my purse.   249
If ever thou wilt thrive, bury my body
And give the letters which thou find'st about me   251

185 **felt** i.e., padding to deaden the sound of the footfall. **in proof** to the test 191 **natural fool** born plaything 193 **cut** wounded 194 **seconds** supporters 195 **of salt** of salt tears 198 **bravely** (1) courageously (2) splendidly attired. **smug** trimly dressed. (*Bridegroom* continues the punning sexual suggestion of *die bravely*, "have sex successfully.") 202 **life** i.e., hope still. **an** if 203 **Sa . . . sa** (A hunting cry.) 206 **general curse** fallen condition of the human race 208 **gentle** noble 209 **speed** Godspeed 210 **toward** imminent 211 **vulgar** in everyone's mouth, generally known 212 **Which** who 214–215 **The main . . . thought** the full view of the main body is expected any hour now 217 **on special cause** for a special reason, i.e., to minister to Lear

220 **worser spirit** bad angel, or ill thoughts 222 **father** (A term of respect to older men, as also in lines 72, 259, and 290, though with ironic double meaning throughout the scene.) 223 **what** who. (Again, Edgar alters his voice to personate a new stranger assisting Gloucester. See line 48, above, and note.) 224 **tame** submissive 225 **known** personally experienced. **feeling** heartfelt, deep 226 **pregnant** prone 227 **biding** abode 228–229 **The bounty . . . and boot** in addition to my thanks, I wish you the bounty and blessings of heaven 229 **proclaimed prize** one with a price on his head. **happy** fortunate 230 **framed flesh** born 232 **thyself remember** i.e., confess your sins 233 **friendly** i.e., welcome, since I desire death 235 **published** proclaimed 236 **Lest that** lest 237 **Like** similar 238 **'Chill** I will. (Literally, a contraction of *Ich will*. Edgar adopts Somerset dialect, a stage convention regularly used for peasants.) **vurther 'cagion** further occasion 240 **go your gait** go your own way 241 **An 'chud** if I could. **zwaggered** swaggered, bluffed 242 **'twould . . . vortnight** it (my life) wouldn't have lasted as long as it has 243 **'che vor ye** I warrant you 244 **Ise** I shall. **costard** head. (Literally, an apple.) **ballow** cudgel 248 **foins** thrusts 249 **Villain** serf 251 **letters** letter. **about me** upon my person

To Edmund, Earl of Gloucester. Seek him out
Upon the English party. O, untimely death!   253
Death!   [*He dies.*]

EDGAR
I know thee well: a serviceable villain,   255
As duteous to the vices of thy mistress
As badness would desire.

GLOUCESTER   What, is he dead?

EDGAR   Sit you down, father. Rest you.[*Gloucester sits.*]
Let's see these pockets; the letters that he speaks of
May be my friends. He's dead; I am only sorry
He had no other deathsman. Let us see.   262
                          [*He finds a letter and opens it.*]
Leave, gentle wax, and, manners, blame us not.   263
To know our enemies' minds we rip their hearts;
Their papers is more lawful.   (*Reads the letter.*)
   "Let our reciprocal vows be remembered. You have
many opportunities to cut him off; if your will want 267
not, time and place will be fruitfully offered. There is 268
nothing done if he return the conqueror. Then am I 269
the prisoner, and his bed my jail, from the loathed
warmth whereof deliver me and supply the place for 271
your labor.   272
Your—wife, so I would say— affectionate servant,
    and for you her own for venture,   Goneril." 274
O indistinguished space of woman's will!   275
A plot upon her virtuous husband's life,
And the exchange my brother! Here in the sands
Thee I'll rake up, the post unsanctified   278
Of murderous lechers; and in the mature time   279
With this ungracious paper strike the sight   280
Of the death-practiced Duke. For him 'tis well   281
That of thy death and business I can tell.
                          [*Exit with the body.*]

GLOUCESTER
The King is mad. How stiff is my vile sense,   283
That I stand up and have ingenious feeling   284
Of my huge sorrows! Better I were distract;   285
So should my thoughts be severed from my griefs,
And woes by wrong imaginations lose   287
The knowledge of themselves.   *Drum afar off.*

         [*Enter Edgar.*]

EDGAR   Give me your hand.
Far off, methinks, I hear the beaten drum.

Come, father, I'll bestow you with a friend.   290
         Exeunt, [Edgar leading his father].

                    ❖

4.7   *Enter Cordelia, Kent [dressed still in his disguise
          costume, and Doctor].*

CORDELIA
O thou good Kent, how shall I live and work
To match thy goodness? My life will be too short,
And every measure fail me.   3

KENT
To be acknowledged, madam, is o'erpaid.
All my reports go with the modest truth,   5
Nor more nor clipped, but so.

CORDELIA   Be better suited.   6
These weeds are memories of those worser hours;   7
I prithee, put them off.

KENT   Pardon, dear madam;
Yet to be known shortens my made intent.   9
My boon I make it that you know me not   10
Till time and I think meet.   11

CORDELIA
Then be 't so, my good lord. [*To the Doctor.*] How
    does the King?

DOCTOR   Madam, sleeps still.

CORDELIA   O you kind gods,
Cure this great breach in his abusèd nature!
Th' untuned and jarring senses, O, wind up   16
Of this child-changèd father!   17

DOCTOR   So please Your Majesty
That we may wake the King? He hath slept long.

CORDELIA
Be governed by your knowledge, and proceed
I' the sway of your own will.—Is he arrayed?   21

         *Enter Lear in a chair carried by servants, [attended
          by a Gentleman].*

GENTLEMAN
Ay, madam. In the heaviness of sleep
We put fresh garments on him.

DOCTOR
Be by, good madam, when we do awake him.
I doubt not of his temperance.

CORDELIA   Very well.   [*Music.*] 25

---

253 Upon on. **party** side   **255 serviceable** officious   **262 deaths-man** executioner   **263 Leave** by your leave.   **wax** wax seal on the letter   **267–268 want not** is not lacking   **268 fruitfully** plentifully and with results   **268–269 There is nothing done** i.e., we will have accomplished nothing   **271–272 for your labor** (1) as recompense for your efforts (2) as a place for your amorous labors   **274 and for . . . venture** and one ready to venture her own fortunes for your sake   **275 indistinguished . . . will** limitless and incalculable range of woman's appetite   **278 rake up** cover up.   **post unsanctified** unholy messenger   **279 in . . . time** when the time is ripe   **280 ungracious** wicked.   **strike** blast   **281 death-practiced** whose death is plotted   **283 stiff** obstinate.   **sense** consciousness, sane mental powers   **284 ingenious** conscious. (Gloucester laments that he remains sane and hence fully conscious of his troubles, unlike Lear.)   **285 distract** distracted, crazy   **287 wrong imaginations** delusions

290 bestow lodge. (At the scene's end, Edgar leads off Gloucester; presumably, here or at line 282, he must also dispose of Oswald's body in the trapdoor or by lugging it offstage.)
4.7. Location: The French camp.
3 every . . . me every attempt (to match your goodness) will fall short   **5 All my reports go** let all reports (of my service as Caius to Lear) conform   **6 Nor . . . clipped** i.e., neither more nor less.   **suited** dressed   **7 weeds** garments.   **memories** remembrances   **9 Yet . . . intent** to reveal my true identity now would alter my carefully made plan   **10 My . . . it** the favor I seek is.   **know** acknowledge   **11 meet** appropriate   **16 wind up** tune (as by winding the slackened string of an instrument)   **17 child-changèd** changed (in mind) by children's cruelty   **21 I' the sway** under the direction   **25 temperance** self-control, calm behavior

DOCTOR
Please you, draw near.—Louder the music there!
CORDELIA [*kissing him*]
O my dear Father! Restoration hang
Thy medicine on my lips, and let this kiss
Repair those violent harms that my two sisters
Have in thy reverence made!
KENT   Kind and dear princess!
CORDELIA
Had you not been their father, these white flakes   31
Did challenge pity of them. Was this a face   32
To be opposed against the warring winds?
To stand against the deep dread-bolted thunder   34
In the most terrible and nimble stroke
Of quick cross lightning? To watch—poor perdu!—   36
With this thin helm? Mine enemy's dog,   37
Though he had bit me, should have stood that night
Against my fire; and wast thou fain, poor Father,   39
To hovel thee with swine and rogues forlorn   40
In short and musty straw? Alack, alack!   41
'Tis wonder that thy life and wits at once
Had not concluded all.—He wakes! Speak to him.   43
DOCTOR   Madam, do you; 'tis fittest.
CORDELIA
How does my royal lord? How fares Your Majesty?
LEAR
You do me wrong to take me out o' the grave.
Thou art a soul in bliss; but I am bound
Upon a wheel of fire, that mine own tears   48
Do scald like molten lead.
CORDELIA   Sir, do you know me?
LEAR
You are a spirit, I know. Where did you die?
CORDELIA   Still, still, far wide!   51
DOCTOR
He's scarce awake. Let him alone awhile.
LEAR
Where have I been? Where am I? Fair daylight?
I am mightily abused. I should ev'n die with pity   54
To see another thus. I know not what to say.   55
I will not swear these are my hands. Let's see;
I feel this pinprick. Would I were assured
Of my condition!
CORDELIA [*kneeling*]   O, look upon me, sir,
And hold your hands in benediction o'er me.
                                    [*He attempts to kneel.*]
No, sir, you must not kneel.
LEAR   Pray, do not mock me.
I am a very foolish fond old man,   61

Fourscore and upward, not an hour more nor less;
And, to deal plainly,
I fear I am not in my perfect mind.
Methinks I should know you, and know this man,
Yet I am doubtful; for I am mainly ignorant   66
What place this is, and all the skill I have
Remembers not these garments, nor I know not
Where I did lodge last night. Do not laugh at me,
For, as I am a man, I think this lady
To be my child Cordelia.
CORDELIA [*weeping*]   And so I am, I am.
LEAR
Be your tears wet? Yes, faith. I pray, weep not.
If you have poison for me I will drink it.
I know you do not love me, for your sisters
Have, as I do remember, done me wrong.
You have some cause, they have not.
CORDELIA   No cause, no cause.
LEAR   Am I in France?
KENT   In your own kingdom, sir.
LEAR   Do not abuse me.   81
DOCTOR
Be comforted, good madam. The great rage,   82
You see, is killed in him, and yet it is danger
To make him even o'er the time he has lost.   84
Desire him to go in. Trouble him no more
Till further settling.   86
CORDELIA   Will 't please Your Highness walk?   87
LEAR   You must bear with me.
Pray you now, forget and forgive.
I am old and foolish.
                    Exeunt [all but Kent and Gentleman].
GENTLEMAN   Holds it true, sir, that the Duke of Corn- 91
wall was so slain?
KENT   Most certain, sir.
GENTLEMAN   Who is conductor of his people?   94
KENT   As 'tis said, the bastard son of Gloucester.
GENTLEMAN   They say Edgar, his banished son, is with
the Earl of Kent in Germany.
KENT   Report is changeable. 'Tis time to look about; the 98
powers of the kingdom approach apace.   99
GENTLEMAN   The arbitrament is like to be bloody. Fare 100
you well, sir.   [*Exit.*]
KENT
My point and period will be throughly wrought,   102
Or well or ill, as this day's battle's fought.   *Exit.* 103

❖

31 **Had you** even if you had.   **flakes** locks of hair   32 **Did challenge**
would have demanded   34 **deep** bass-voiced.   **dread-bolted** furnished with the dreadful thunderbolt   36 **cross** zigzag.   **watch** stay
awake (like a sentry on duty).   **perdu** lost one; a sentinel placed in a
position of peculiar danger   37 **helm** helmet, i.e., his scanty hair
39 **Against** before, in front of.   **fain** glad, constrained   40 **rogues forlorn** abandoned vagabonds   41 **short** broken up and hence uncomfortable   43 **concluded all** come to an end altogether   48 **wheel of
fire** (A hellish torment for the eternally damned.)   **that** so that
51 **wide** wide of the mark, wandering   54 **abused** confused, deluded
55 **thus** i.e., thus confused, bewildered   61 **fond** foolish

66 **mainly** perfectly   81 **abuse** deceive. (Or perhaps Lear feels hurt by
the reminder of his having divided the kingdom.)   82 **rage** frenzy
84 **even o'er** fill in, go over in his mind   86 **settling** composing of his
mind   87 **walk** withdraw   91 **Holds it true** is it still held to be true
94 **conductor** leader, general   98 **look about** be wary   99 **powers of
the kingdom** British armies (marching against the French invaders)
100 **arbitrament** decision by arms, decisive encounter   102 **My . . .
wrought** i.e., the conclusion of my destiny (literally, the full stop at
the end of my life's sentence) will be thoroughly brought about
103 **Or** either.   **as** according as

5.1   *Enter, with drum and colors, Edmund, Regan,*
Gentlemen, and soldiers.

EDMUND [*to a Gentleman*]
Know of the Duke if his last purpose hold,   1
Or whether since he is advised by aught   2
To change the course. He's full of alteration   3
And self-reproving. Bring his constant pleasure.   4
                                    [*Exit Gentleman.*]
REGAN
Our sister's man is certainly miscarried.   5
EDMUND
'Tis to be doubted, madam.
REGAN   Now, sweet lord,   6
You know the goodness I intend upon you.   7
Tell me, but truly—but then speak the truth—
Do you not love my sister?
EDMUND   In honored love.   9
REGAN
But have you never found my brother's way
To the forfended place?   11
EDMUND   That thought abuses you.   12
REGAN
I am doubtful that you have been conjunct   13
And bosomed with her, as far as we call hers.   14
EDMUND   No, by mine honor, madam.
REGAN
I never shall endure her. Dear my lord,
Be not familiar with her.   17
EDMUND
Fear me not.—She and the Duke her husband!   18

Enter, with drum and colors, Albany, Goneril,
[and] soldiers.

GONERIL [*aside*]
I had rather lose the battle than that sister
Should loosen him and me.
ALBANY
Our very loving sister, well bemet.   21
Sir, this I heard: the King is come to his daughter,
With others whom the rigor of our state   23
Forced to cry out. Where I could not be honest,   24
I never yet was valiant. For this business,   25
It touches us as France invades our land,   26
Not bolds the King, with others whom, I fear,   27
Most just and heavy causes make oppose.   28
EDMUND   Sir, you speak nobly.

REGAN   Why is this reasoned?   30
GONERIL
Combine together 'gainst the enemy;
For these domestic and particular broils   32
Are not the question here.
ALBANY   Let's then determine
With th' ancient of war on our proceeding.   34
EDMUND
I shall attend you presently at your tent.   35
REGAN   Sister, you'll go with us?
GONERIL   No.
REGAN
'Tis most convenient. Pray, go with us.   38
GONERIL [*aside*]
Oho, I know the riddle.—I will go.   39

[As they are going out,] enter Edgar [disguised].

EDGAR [*to Albany*]
If e'er Your Grace had speech with man so poor,
Hear me one word.
ALBANY [*to the others*]   I'll overtake you.
                                    Exeunt both the armies.
                                        Speak.
EDGAR [*giving a letter*]
Before you fight the battle, ope this letter.   42
If you have victory, let the trumpet sound   43
For him that brought it. Wretched though I seem,
I can produce a champion that will prove   45
What is avouchèd there. If you miscarry,   46
Your business of the world hath so an end,
And machination ceases. Fortune love you!   48
ALBANY   Stay till I have read the letter.
EDGAR   I was forbid it.
When time shall serve, let but the herald cry
And I'll appear again.   *Exit [Edgar].*
ALBANY
Why, fare thee well. I will o'erlook thy paper.   53

Enter Edmund.

EDMUND
The enemy's in view. Draw up your powers.
                                    [*He offers Albany a paper.*]
Here is the guess of their true strength and forces   55
By diligent discovery, but your haste   56
Is now urged on you.
ALBANY   We will greet the time.   *Exit.* 57
EDMUND
To both these sisters have I sworn my love,
Each jealous of the other as the stung   59

5.1. Location: The British camp near Dover.
1 Know inquire. **last purpose hold** most recent intention (to fight) remains firm **2 since** since then. **advised by aught** persuaded by any consideration **3 alteration** vacillation **4 constant pleasure** settled decision **5 man** i.e., Oswald. **miscarried** lost, perished **6 doubted** feared **7 intend** intend to confer **9 honored** honorable **11 forfended** forbidden (by the commandment against adultery) **12 abuses** degrades, wrongs **13–14 I am . . . hers** I fear that you have been sexually intimate with her **17 familiar** intimate **18 Fear me not** don't worry about me on that score **21 bemet** met **23 rigor of our state** harshness of our rule **24 Where** in a case where. **honest** honorable **25 For** as for **26 touches us as** concerns us insofar as **27–28 Not . . . oppose** not because France encourages the King and others who, I fear, are driven into opposition by just and weighty grievances. **bolds** emboldens by offering encouragement and support

30 Why . . . reasoned i.e., why are we arguing about reasons for fighting, instead of fighting? **32 particular broils** private quarrels **34 ancient of war** veteran officers **35 presently** at once **38 convenient** proper, befitting **39 know the riddle** i.e., understand the reason for Regan's enigmatic demand that Goneril accompany her, which is that Regan wants to keep Goneril from Edmund **42 this letter** i.e., Goneril's letter to Edmund found on Oswald's body **43 sound** sound a summons **45 prove** i.e., in trial by combat **46 avouchèd** maintained. **miscarry** perish, come to destruction **48 machination** plotting (against your life) **53 o'erlook** peruse **55 guess** estimate **56 discovery** reconnoitering **57 greet the time** meet the occasion **59 jealous** suspicious

Are of the adder. Which of them shall I take?
Both? One? Or neither? Neither can be enjoyed
If both remain alive. To take the widow
Exasperates, makes mad her sister Goneril,
And hardly shall I carry out my side,   64
Her husband being alive. Now then, we'll use
His countenance for the battle, which being done,   66
Let her who would be rid of him devise
His speedy taking off. As for the mercy   68
Which he intends to Lear and to Cordelia,
The battle done and they within our power,
Shall never see his pardon, for my state   71
Stands on me to defend, not to debate.   72
                                                              Exit.

❧

5.2   *Alarum within. Enter, with drum and colors, Lear,*
          Cordelia, and soldiers, over the stage; and exeunt.

          Enter Edgar and Gloucester.

EDGAR
Here, father, take the shadow of this tree   1
For your good host. Pray that the right may thrive.   2
If ever I return to you again,
I'll bring you comfort.
GLOUCESTER   Grace go with you, sir!   4
                                               Exit [Edgar].

          Alarum and retreat within. Enter Edgar.

EDGAR
Away, old man! Give me thy hand. Away!
King Lear hath lost, he and his daughter ta'en.
Give me thy hand. Come on.
GLOUCESTER
No further, sir. A man may rot even here.
EDGAR
What, in ill thoughts again? Men must endure
Their going hence, even as their coming hither;
Ripeness is all. Come on.
GLOUCESTER   And that's true too.   11
                                               Exeunt.

❧

5.3   *Enter, in conquest, with drum and colors, Edmund;*
          Lear and Cordelia, as prisoners; soldiers, Captain.

EDMUND
Some officers take them away. Good guard,   1

Until their greater pleasures first be known   2
That are to censure them.
CORDELIA [*to Lear*]   We are not the first   3
Who with best meaning have incurred the worst.   4
For thee, oppressèd King, I am cast down;
Myself could else outfrown false Fortune's frown.
Shall we not see these daughters and these sisters?   7
LEAR
No, no, no, no! Come, let's away to prison.
We two alone will sing like birds i' the cage.
When thou dost ask me blessing, I'll kneel down
And ask of thee forgiveness. So we'll live,
And pray, and sing, and tell old tales, and laugh
At gilded butterflies, and hear poor rogues   13
Talk of court news; and we'll talk with them too—
Who loses and who wins; who's in, who's out—
And take upon 's the mystery of things,   16
As if we were God's spies; and we'll wear out,   17
In a walled prison, packs and sects of great ones,   18
That ebb and flow by th' moon.
EDMUND   Take them away.   19
LEAR
Upon such sacrifices, my Cordelia,
The gods themselves throw incense. Have I caught
    thee?   21
He that parts us shall bring a brand from heaven   22
And fire us hence like foxes. Wipe thine eyes;   23
The goodyears shall devour them, flesh and fell,   24
Ere they shall make us weep. We'll see 'em starved
    first.
Come.   *Exit [with Cordelia, guarded].*
EDMUND   Come hither, Captain. Hark.
Take thou this note. [*He gives a paper.*] Go follow
    them to prison.
One step I have advanced thee; if thou dost
As this instructs thee, thou dost make thy way
To noble fortunes. Know thou this: that men
Are as the time is. To be tender-minded
Does not become a sword. Thy great employment   33
Will not bear question; either say thou'lt do 't   34
Or thrive by other means.
CAPTAIN   I'll do 't, my lord.
EDMUND
About it, and write "happy" when th' hast done.   36

---

64 carry out my side fulfill my ambition and satisfy her (Goneril)
66 countenance backing, authority of his name   **68 taking off** killing
71 Shall they shall   **71–72 my state . . . debate** my position depends upon maintenance by forceful action, not by talk
5.2. Location: The battlefield.
s.d. Alarum trumpet call to arms   **1 father** i.e., reverend old man
2 host shelterer   **4 s.d. retreat** trumpet signal for withdrawal
11 Ripeness (Humans shouldn't die before their time, just as fruit doesn't fall until it's ripe.)
5.3. Location: The British camp.
1 Good guard guard them well

2 their greater pleasures the wishes of those in command   **3 censure** judge   **4 meaning** intentions   **7 Shall . . . sisters** i.e., aren't we even allowed to speak to Goneril and Regan before they order to prison their own father and sister?   **13 gilded butterflies** i.e., gaily dressed courtiers and other ephemeral types, or perhaps actual butterflies
16 take upon 's assume the burden of, or profess to understand
17 God's spies i.e., detached observers surveying the deeds of humanity from an eternal vantage point.   **wear out** outlast   **18–19 packs . . . moon** i.e., followers and cliques attached to persons of high station, whose fortunes change erratically and constantly
21 throw incense participate as celebrants   **22–23 He . . . foxes** i.e., anyone seeking to part us will have to employ a heavenly firebrand to drive us out of our prison refuge, as foxes are driven out of their holes by fire and smoke. (Suggests that only death will part them.)   **24 goodyears** (Apparently a word connoting evil or conceivably the passage of time.)   **flesh and fell** flesh and skin, completely
33 become a sword i.e., suit a warrior   **34 bear question** admit of discussion   **36 write "happy"** call yourself fortunate.   **th'** thou

Mark, I say, instantly, and carry it so   37
As I have set it down.
CAPTAIN
I cannot draw a cart, nor eat dried oats;
If it be man's work, I'll do 't.   Exit Captain.

*Flourish. Enter Albany, Goneril, Regan, [another
Captain, and] soldiers.*

ALBANY
Sir, you have showed today your valiant strain,
And fortune led you well. You have the captives
Who were the opposites of this day's strife;   43
I do require them of you, so to use them
As we shall find their merits and our safety
May equally determine.
EDMUND   Sir, I thought it fit
To send the old and miserable King
To some retention and appointed guard,   49
Whose age had charms in it, whose title more,   50
To pluck the common bosom on his side   51
And turn our impressed lances in our eyes   52
Which do command them. With him I sent the
    Queen,   53
My reason all the same; and they are ready
Tomorrow, or at further space, t' appear   55
Where you shall hold your session. At this time
We sweat and bleed; the friend hath lost his friend,
And the best quarrels in the heat are cursed   58
By those that feel their sharpness.   59
The question of Cordelia and her father
Requires a fitter place.
ALBANY   Sir, by your patience,
I hold you but a subject of this war,   62
Not as a brother.
REGAN   That's as we list to grace him.   63
Methinks our pleasure might have been demanded   64
Ere you had spoke so far. He led our powers,
Bore the commission of my place and person,
The which immediacy may well stand up   67
And call itself your brother.
GONERIL   Not so hot!
In his own grace he doth exalt himself
More than in your addition.
REGAN   In my rights,   70
By me invested, he compeers the best.   71
GONERIL
That were the most if he should husband you.   72

REGAN
Jesters do oft prove prophets.
GONERIL   Holla, holla!   73
That eye that told you so looked but asquint.   74
REGAN
Lady, I am not well, else I should answer
From a full-flowing stomach. [*To Edmund.*] General,   76
Take thou my soldiers, prisoners, patrimony;   77
Dispose of them, of me; the walls is thine.   78
Witness the world that I create thee here
My lord and master.
GONERIL   Mean you to enjoy him?
ALBANY
The let-alone lies not in your good will.   81
EDMUND
Nor in thine, lord.
ALBANY   Half-blooded fellow, yes.   82
REGAN [*to Edmund*]
Let the drum strike and prove my title thine.   83
ALBANY
Stay yet; hear reason. Edmund, I arrest thee
On capital treason; and, in thy attaint   85
This gilded serpent. [*Pointing to Goneril.*] For your
    claim, fair sister,
I bar it in the interest of my wife;
'Tis she is subcontracted to this lord,
And I, her husband, contradict your banns.   89
If you will marry, make your loves to me;
My lady is bespoke.
GONERIL   An interlude!   91
ALBANY
Thou art armed, Gloucester. Let the trumpet sound.
If none appear to prove upon thy person
Thy heinous, manifest, and many treasons,
There is my pledge. [*He throws down a glove.*] I'll
    make it on thy heart,   95
Ere I taste bread, thou art in nothing less   96
Than I have here proclaimed thee.
REGAN   Sick, O, sick!
GONERIL [*aside*]   If not, I'll ne'er trust medicine.   99
EDMUND [*throwing down a glove*]
There's my exchange. What in the world he is   100
That names me traitor, villain-like he lies.
Call by the trumpet. He that dares approach,
On him, on you—who not?—I will maintain
My truth and honor firmly.

---

37 carry it carry it out **43 opposites** enemies **49 retention** confinement **50 Whose** i.e., the King's. **whose title more** and whose title as king is even more of a magic spell **51 common bosom** affection of the multitude **52–53 turn . . . them** i.e., turn against us the weapons of those very troops whom we impressed into service **53 Which** of us who **55 space** interval of time **58–59 And . . . sharpness** and even the best of causes, at this moment when the passions of battle have not cooled, are viewed with hatred by those who have suffered the painful consequences. (Edmund pretends to worry that Lear and Cordelia would not receive a fair trial.) **62 subject of** subordinate in **63 list** please **64 pleasure** wish. **demanded** asked about **67 immediacy** nearness of connection **70 your addition** the titles you confer **71 compeers** is equal with **72 That . . . most** that investiture would be most complete

73 prove turn out to be **74 asquint** (Jealousy proverbially makes the eye look *asquint*, "furtively, suspiciously.") **76 full-flowing stomach** full tide of angry rejoinder **77 patrimony** inheritance **78 the walls is thine** i.e., the citadel of my heart and body surrenders completely to you **81 let-alone** preventing, denying **82 Half-blooded** only partly of noble blood, bastard **83 Let . . . strike** i.e., to announce our banns (?) **85 in thy attaint** i.e., as partner in your corruption and as one who has (unwittingly) provided the *attaint* or impeachment against you **89 banns** public announcement of a proposed marriage **91 An interlude** a play; i.e., you are being melodramatic, or, what a farce this is **95 make** prove **96 in nothing less** in no respect less guilty **99 medicine** i.e., poison **100 What** whoever

ALBANY
  A herald, ho!
EDMUND   A herald, ho, a herald!

    Enter a Herald.

ALBANY
  Trust to thy single virtue; for thy soldiers,   106
  All levied in my name, have in my name
  Took their discharge.
REGAN   My sickness grows upon me.
ALBANY
  She is not well. Convey her to my tent.
              [Exit Regan, supported.]
  Come hither, herald. Let the trumpet sound,
  And read out this.   *[He gives a paper.]*
CAPTAIN Sound, trumpet!   *A trumpet sounds.*
HERALD *(reads)* "If any man of quality or degree within 113
  the lists of the army will maintain upon Edmund, sup-
  posed Earl of Gloucester, that he is a manifold traitor,
  let him appear by the third sound of the trumpet. He
  is bold in his defense."
EDMUND Sound!   *First trumpet.*
HERALD Again!   *Second trumpet.*
HERALD Again!   *Third trumpet.*
            Trumpet answers within.

    Enter Edgar, armed, [with a trumpeter before
    him].

ALBANY
  Ask him his purposes, why he appears
  Upon this call o' the trumpet.
HERALD   What are you?   122
  Your name, your quality, and why you answer
  This present summons?
EDGAR   Know my name is lost,
  By treason's tooth bare-gnawn and canker-bit. 125
  Yet am I noble as the adversary
  I come to cope.
ALBANY   Which is that adversary? 127
EDGAR
  What's he that speaks for Edmund, Earl of
    Gloucester?
EDMUND
  Himself. What sayst thou to him?
EDGAR   Draw thy sword,
  That, if my speech offend a noble heart,
  Thy arm may do thee justice. Here is mine.
             [He draws his sword.]
  Behold, it is the privilege of mine honors,   132
  My oath, and my profession. I protest,   133
  Maugre thy strength, place, youth, and eminence, 134
  Despite thy victor sword and fire-new fortune, 135
  Thy valor, and thy heart, thou art a traitor— 136
  False to thy gods, thy brother, and thy father,

  Conspirant 'gainst this high-illustrious prince,
  And from th' extremest upward of thy head 139
  To the descent and dust below thy foot 140
  A most toad-spotted traitor. Say thou no, 141
  This sword, this arm, and my best spirits are bent 142
  To prove upon thy heart, whereto I speak,
  Thou liest.
EDMUND   In wisdom I should ask thy name. 144
  But since thy outside looks so fair and warlike,
  And that thy tongue some say of breeding breathes, 146
  What safe and nicely I might well delay 147
  By rule of knighthood, I disdain and spurn. 148
  Back do I toss those treasons to thy head, 149
  With the hell-hated lie o'erwhelm thy heart, 150
  Which—for they yet glance by and scarcely bruise— 151
  This sword of mine shall give them instant way, 152
  Where they shall rest forever. Trumpets, speak! 153
      [He draws.] Alarums. Fight. [Edmund falls.]
ALBANY *[to Edgar]*
  Save him, save him!
GONERIL   This is practice, Gloucester. 154
  By th' law of arms thou wast not bound to answer
  An unknown opposite. Thou art not vanquished,
  But cozened and beguiled.
ALBANY   Shut your mouth, dame, 157
  Or with this paper shall I stopple it.—Hold, sir.— 158
  [To Goneril.] Thou worse than any name, read thine
    own evil.   *[He shows her the letter.]*
  No tearing, lady; I perceive you know it.
GONERIL
  Say if I do, the laws are mine, not thine.
  Who can arraign me for 't?
ALBANY   Most monstrous! O!
  Know'st thou this paper?
GONERIL   Ask me not what I know.
                  Exit.
ALBANY
  Go after her. She's desperate; govern her. 164
              [Exit a soldier.]
EDMUND
  What you have charged me with, that have I done,
  And more, much more. The time will bring it out.
  'Tis past, and so am I. But what art thou
  That hast this fortune on me? If thou'rt noble, 168

---

106 single virtue unaided prowess **113 degree** rank **122 What** who
125 canker-bit eaten as by the caterpillar **127 cope** encounter
132 of mine honors i.e., of my knighthood **133 profession** i.e.,
knighthood **134 Maugre** in spite of **135 victor** victorious.
fire-new newly minted **136 heart** courage

139 upward top **140 descent** lowest extreme **141 toad-spotted** venomous, or having spots of infamy. **Say thou** if you say **142 bent**
prepared **144 wisdom** prudence **146 say** smack, taste, indication
147 safe and nicely prudently and punctiliously **148 I . . . spurn**
i.e., I disdain to insist on my right to refuse combat with one of lower
rank **149 treasons . . . head** i.e., accusations of treason in your
teeth **150 hell-hated** hated as hell is hated **151 Which . . . bruise**
i.e., which charges of treason—since as yet they merely glance off
your armor and do no harm **152 give . . . way** provide them an immediate pathway (to your heart) **153 Where . . . forever** i.e., my
victory in trial by combat will prove forever that the charges of treason apply to you **154 Save** spare. (Albany wishes to spare Edmund's
life so that he may confess and be found guilty.) **practice** trickery, or
(said sardonically), astute management **157 cozened** tricked
158 stopple stop up. **Hold, sir** (Perhaps addressed to Edgar; see line
154 and note.) **164 govern** restrain **168 fortune on** victory over

I do forgive thee.

EDGAR   Let's exchange charity.   169
I am no less in blood than thou art, Edmund;
If more, the more th' hast wronged me.   171
My name is Edgar, and thy father's son.
The gods are just, and of our pleasant vices   173
Make instruments to plague us.
The dark and vicious place where thee he got   175
Cost him his eyes.

EDMUND   Th' hast spoken right. 'Tis true.
The wheel is come full circle; I am here.   177

ALBANY [to Edgar]
Methought thy very gait did prophesy
A royal nobleness. I must embrace thee.
                                          [They embrace.]
Let sorrow split my heart if ever I
Did hate thee or thy father!

EDGAR   Worthy prince, I know 't.

ALBANY   Where have you hid yourself?
How have you known the miseries of your father?

EDGAR
By nursing them, my lord. List a brief tale,   185
And when 'tis told, O, that my heart would burst!
The bloody proclamation to escape   187
That followed me so near—O, our lives' sweetness,
That we the pain of death would hourly die
Rather than die at once!—taught me to shift
Into a madman's rags, t' assume a semblance
That very dogs disdained; and in this habit
Met I my father with his bleeding rings,   193
Their precious stones new lost; became his guide,
Led him, begged for him, saved him from despair;
Never—O fault!—revealed myself unto him   196
Until some half hour past, when I was armed.
Not sure, though hoping, of this good success,   198
I asked his blessing, and from first to last
Told him our pilgrimage. But his flawed heart—   200
Alack, too weak the conflict to support—
Twixt two extremes of passion, joy and grief,
Burst smilingly.

EDMUND   This speech of yours hath moved me,
And shall perchance do good. But speak you on;
You look as you had something more to say.

ALBANY
If there be more, more woeful, hold it in,
For I am almost ready to dissolve,   207
Hearing of this.

EDGAR   This would have seemed a period   208
To such as love not sorrow; but another,   209
To amplify too much, would make much more   210
And top extremity. Whilst I   211

Was big in clamor, came there in a man   212
Who, having seen me in my worst estate,
Shunned my abhorred society; but then, finding
Who 'twas that so endured, with his strong arms
He fastened on my neck and bellowed out
As he'd burst heaven, threw him on my father,   217
Told the most piteous tale of Lear and him
That ever ear received, which in recounting
His grief grew puissant, and the strings of life   220
Began to crack. Twice then the trumpets sounded,
And there I left him tranced.

ALBANY   But who was this?   222

EDGAR
Kent, sir, the banished Kent, who in disguise
Followed his enemy king and did him service   224
Improper for a slave.

        Enter a Gentleman [with a bloody knife].

GENTLEMAN
Help, help, O, help!

EDGAR   What kind of help?

ALBANY   Speak, man.

EDGAR
What means this bloody knife?

GENTLEMAN   'Tis hot, it smokes.   227
It came even from the heart of—O, she's dead!

ALBANY   Who dead? Speak, man.

GENTLEMAN
Your lady, sir, your lady! And her sister
By her is poisoned; she confesses it.

EDMUND
I was contracted to them both. All three
Now marry in an instant.

EDGAR   Here comes Kent.

        Enter Kent.

ALBANY
Produce the bodies, be they alive or dead.
                                    [Exit Gentleman.]
This judgment of the heavens, that makes us
    tremble,
Touches us not with pity.—O, is this he?
[To Kent.] The time will not allow the compliment   237
Which very manners urges.

KENT   I am come   238
To bid my king and master aye good night.   239
Is he not here?

ALBANY   Great thing of us forgot!
Speak, Edmund, where's the King? And where's
    Cordelia?
            Goneril's and Regan's bodies [are] brought out.
Seest thou this object, Kent?   242

---

169 **charity** forgiveness (for Edmund's wickedness toward Edgar and Edgar's having slain Edmund)   171 **th'** thou   173 **pleasant** pleasurable   175 **got** begot   177 **wheel** i.e., wheel of fortune. **here** i.e., at its bottom   185 **List** listen to   187 **The . . . escape** in order to escape the death-threatening proclamation   193 **rings** sockets   196 **fault** mistake   198 **success** outcome   200 **flawed** cracked   207 **dissolve** i.e., in tears   208 **a period** the limit   209 **love not** are not in love with   209–211 **but . . . extremity** i.e., but another sorrowful circumstance, adding to what is already too much, would increase it and exceed the limit

212 **big in clamor** loud in my lamenting   217 **As** as if. **threw . . . father** threw himself on my father's body   220 **His** i.e., Kent's. **puissant** powerful. **strings of life** heartstrings   222 **tranced** entranced, senseless   224 **his enemy king** i.e., the king who had rejected and banished him   227 **smokes** steams   237 **compliment** ceremony   238 **very manners urges** mere decency requires   239 **aye good night** farewell forever. (Kent believes he himself is near death, his heartstrings having begun to crack.)   242 **object** sight

KENT   Alack, why thus?

EDMUND   Yet Edmund was beloved.
  The one the other poisoned for my sake
  And after slew herself.

ALBANY   Even so. Cover their faces.

EDMUND
  I pant for life. Some good I mean to do,
  Despite of mine own nature. Quickly send—
  Be brief in it—to th' castle, for my writ
  Is on the life of Lear and on Cordelia.
  Nay, send in time.

ALBANY   Run, run, O, run!

EDGAR
  To who, my lord? Who has the office? Send   253
  Thy token of reprieve.

EDMUND   Well thought on. Take my sword. The captain!
  Give it the Captain.

EDGAR   Haste thee, for thy life.
              [Exit one with Edmund's sword.]

EDMUND
  He hath commission from thy wife and me
  To hang Cordelia in the prison and
  To lay the blame upon her own despair,
  That she fordid herself.   260

ALBANY
  The gods defend her! Bear him hence awhile.
                        [Edmund is borne off.]

      Enter Lear, with Cordelia in his arms; [Captain].

LEAR
  Howl, howl, howl! O, you are men of stones!
  Had I your tongues and eyes, I'd use them so
  That heaven's vault should crack. She's gone forever.
  I know when one is dead and when one lives;
  She's dead as earth. Lend me a looking glass;
  If that her breath will mist or stain the stone,   267
  Why, then she lives.

KENT   Is this the promised end?   268

EDGAR
  Or image of that horror?

ALBANY   Fall and cease!   269

LEAR
  This feather stirs; she lives! If it be so,
  It is a chance which does redeem all sorrows
  That ever I have felt.

KENT [kneeling]   O my good master!

LEAR
  Prithee, away.

EDGAR   'Tis noble Kent, your friend.

LEAR
  A plague upon you, murderers, traitors all!
  I might have saved her; now she's gone forever!
  Cordelia, Cordelia! Stay a little. Ha?
  What is 't thou sayst? Her voice was ever soft,
  Gentle, and low, an excellent thing in woman.

  I killed the slave that was a-hanging thee.

CAPTAIN   244
  'Tis true, my lords, he did.

LEAR   Did I not, fellow?
  I have seen the day, with my good biting falchion   281
  I would have made them skip. I am old now,
  And these same crosses spoil me.—Who are you?   283
  Mine eyes are not o' the best; I'll tell you straight. 284

KENT
  If Fortune brag of two she loved and hated,   285
  One of them we behold.

LEAR
  This is a dull sight. Are you not Kent?

KENT   The same,   287
  Your servant Kent. Where is your servant Caius?   288

LEAR
  He's a good fellow, I can tell you that;
  He'll strike, and quickly too. He's dead and rotten.

KENT
  No, my good lord, I am the very man—

LEAR   I'll see that straight.   292

KENT
  That from your first of difference and decay   293
  Have followed your sad steps—

LEAR   You are welcome hither.

KENT
  Nor no man else. All's cheerless, dark, and deadly. 295
  Your eldest daughters have fordone themselves,   296
  And desperately are dead.

LEAR   Ay, so I think.   297

ALBANY
  He knows not what he says, and vain is it
  That we present us to him.

EDGAR   Very bootless.   299

          Enter a Messenger.

MESSENGER   Edmund is dead, my lord.

ALBANY   That's but a trifle here.
  You lords and noble friends, know our intent:
  What comfort to this great decay may come   303
  Shall be applied. For us, we will resign,   304
  During the life of this old majesty,
  To him our absolute power; [to Edgar and Kent] you,
    to your rights,
  With boot and such addition as your honors   307
  Have more than merited. All friends shall taste
  The wages of their virtue, and all foes

---

244 Yet despite everything   253 office commission   260 fordid destroyed   267 stone crystal or polished stone of which the mirror is made   268 promised end i.e., Last Judgment   269 image representation.   Fall and cease i.e., let heavens fall and all things cease

281 falchion light sword   283 crosses spoil me adversities take away my strength   284 I'll . . . straight I'll recognize you in a moment   285 two i.e., Lear and a hypothetical individual whose misfortunes are without parallel.   loved and hated i.e., first raised and then lowered   287 This . . . sight i.e., my vision is clouding, or, this is a dismal spectacle   288 Caius (Kent's disguise name)   292 see that straight attend to that in a moment, or, comprehend that soon   293 first of difference beginning of your quarrel (with Cordelia).   decay decline of fortune   295 Nor . . . else no, not I nor anyone else, or, I am the very man (line 291), him and no one else   296 fordone destroyed   297 desperately in despair   299 bootless in vain   303 What . . . come i.e., whatever means of comforting this ruined king may present themselves   304 For as for   307 boot advantage, good measure.   addition titles, further distinctions

The cup of their deservings.—O, see, see!

LEAR

And my poor fool is hanged! No, no, no life?   311
Why should a dog, a horse, a rat have life,
And thou no breath at all? Thou'lt come no more,
Never, never, never, never, never!
Pray you, undo this button. Thank you, sir.
Do you see this? Look on her, look, her lips,
Look there, look there!   *He dies.*

EDGAR   He faints. My lord, my lord!

KENT

Break, heart, I prithee, break!

EDGAR   Look up, my lord.

KENT

Vex not his ghost. O, let him pass! He hates him   319
That would upon the rack of this tough world   320
Stretch him out longer.

EDGAR   He is gone indeed.

KENT

The wonder is he hath endured so long.
He but usurped his life.

ALBANY

Bear them from hence. Our present business
Is general woe. [*To Kent and Edgar.*] Friends of my
    soul, you twain
Rule in this realm, and the gored state sustain.

KENT

I have a journey, sir, shortly to go.   327
My master calls me; I must not say no.

EDGAR

The weight of this sad time we must obey;
Speak what we feel, not what we ought to say.
The oldest hath borne most; we that are young
Shall never see so much nor live so long.   332

                      Exeunt, with a dead march.

311 poor fool i.e., Cordelia. (*Fool* is here a term of endearment.)
319 ghost departing spirit   **320 rack** torture rack (with suggestion, in
the Folio and Quarto spelling *wracke*, of shipwreck, disaster)
327 journey i.e., to another world   **332 s.d. Exeunt** (Presumably the
dead bodies are borne out in procession.)

Macbeth

Macbeth is seemingly the last of four great Shakespearean tragedies—Hamlet (c. 1599–1601), Othello (c. 1603–1604), King Lear (1605–1606), and Macbeth (c. 1606–1607)—that examine the dimensions of spiritual evil, as distinguished from the political strife of Roman tragedies such as Julius Caesar, Antony and Cleopatra, and Coriolanus. Whether or not Shakespeare intended Macbeth as a culmination of a series of tragedies on evil, the play does offer a particularly terse and gloomy view of humanity's encounter with the powers of darkness. Macbeth, more consciously than any other of Shakespeare's major tragic protagonists, has to face the temptation of committing what he knows to be a monstrous crime. Like Doctor Faustus in Christopher Marlowe's play, The Tragedy of Doctor Faustus (c. 1588–1592), and to a lesser extent like Adam in John Milton's Paradise Lost (1667), Macbeth understands the reasons for resisting evil and yet goes ahead with his disastrous plan. His awareness and sensitivity to moral issues, together with his conscious choice of evil, produce an unnerving account of human failure, all the more distressing because Macbeth is so representatively human. He seems to possess freedom of will and accepts personal responsibility for his fate, and yet his tragic doom seems unavoidable. Nor is there eventual salvation to be hoped for, as there is in Paradise Lost, since Macbeth's crime is too heinous and his heart too hardened. He is more like Doctor Faustus—damned and in despair.

To an extent not found in the other tragedies, the issue is stated in terms of salvation versus damnation. Macbeth knows before he acts that King Duncan's virtues "Will plead like angels, trumpet-tongued, against / The deep damnation of his taking-off" (1.7.19–20). After the murder, he is equally aware that he has "Put rancors in the vessel of my peace . . . and mine eternal jewel / Given to the common enemy of man" (3.1.68–70). His enemies later describe him as a devil and a "hellhound" (5.8.3). He, like Marlowe's Doctor Faustus before him, has knowingly sold his soul for gain. And, although as a mortal he still has time to repent his crimes, horrible as they are, Macbeth cannot find the words to be penitent. "Wherefore could not I pronounce 'Amen'?" he implores his wife after they have committed the murder. "I had most need of blessing, and 'Amen' / Stuck in my throat" (2.2.35–37). Macbeth's own answer seems to be that he has committed himself so inexorably to evil that he cannot turn back. Sentence has been pronounced:

"Glamis hath murdered sleep, and therefore Cawdor / Shall sleep no more; Macbeth shall sleep no more" (lines 46–47).

Macbeth is not a conventional morality play (even less so than Doctor Faustus) and is not concerned primarily with preaching against sinfulness or demonstrating that Macbeth is finally damned for what he does. A tradition of moral and religious drama has been transformed into an intensely human study of the psychological effects of evil on a particular man and, to a lesser extent, on his wife. That moral tradition nevertheless provides as its legacy a perspective on the operation of evil in human affairs. A perverse ambition seemingly inborn in Macbeth himself is abetted by dark forces dwelling in the universe, waiting to catch him off guard. Among Shakespeare's tragedies, indeed, Macbeth is remarkable for its focus on evil in the protagonist and on his relationship to the sinister forces tempting him. In no other Shakespearean play is the audience asked to identify to such an extent with the evildoer himself. Richard III also focuses on an evil protagonist, but in that play the spectators are distanced by the character's gloating and are not partakers in the introspective soliloquies of a man confronting his own ambition. Macbeth is more representatively human. If he betrays an inclination toward brutality, he also humanely attempts to resist that urge. We witness and struggle to understand his downfall through two phases: the spiritual struggle before he actually commits the crime and the despairing aftermath, with its vain quest for security through continued violence. Evil is thus presented in two aspects: first as an insidious suggestion leading Macbeth on toward an illusory promise of gain and then as a frenzied addiction to the hated thing by which he is possessed.

In the first phase, before the commission of the crime, we wonder to what extent the powers of darkness are a determining factor in what Macbeth does. Can he avoid the fate the witches proclaim? Evidently, he and Lady Macbeth have previously considered murdering Duncan; the witches appear after the thought, not before. Lady Macbeth reminds her wavering husband that he was the first to "break this enterprise" to her, on some previous occasion when "Nor time nor place / Did then adhere, and yet you would make both" (1.7.49–53). Elizabethans would probably understand that evil spirits such as witches appear when summoned, whether by our conscious or unconscious minds. Macbeth is ripe for their insinuations: a mind free of taint would see no sinister invitation in their prophecy of greatness to come. And, in a saner moment, Macbeth knows that his restless desire to interfere with destiny is arrogant and useless. "If chance will have me king, why, chance may crown me / Without my stir" (1.3.145–146). Banquo, his companion, serves as his dramatic opposite by consistently displaying a more stoical attitude toward the witches. "Speak then to me," he addresses them, "who neither beg nor fear / Your favors nor your hate" (lines 60–61). Like Horatio in Hamlet, Banquo strongly resists the blandishments of fortune as well as its buffets, though not without an agonizing night of moral struggle. Indeed, promises of success are often more ruinous than setbacks—as in the seemingly paradoxical instance of the farmer, cited by Macbeth's porter, who "hanged himself on th' expectation of plenty" (2.3.4–5). It is by showing Macbeth that he is two-thirds of his way to the throne that the witches tempt him to seize the last third at whatever cost. "Glamis, and Thane of Cawdor! / The greatest is behind" (1.3.116–117).

Banquo comprehends the nature of temptation. "To win us to our harm," he observes, "The instruments of darkness tell us truths, / Win us with honest trifles, to betray 's / In deepest consequence" (1.3.123–126). The devil can speak true, and his strategy is to invite us into a trap we help prepare. Without our active consent in evil (as Othello also learns), we cannot fall. Yet in what sense are the witches trifling with Macbeth or prevaricating? When they address him as one "that shalt be king hereafter" (line 50), they are stating a certainty, for they can "look into the seeds of time / And say which grain will grow and which will not," as Banquo says (lines 58–59). They know that Banquo will be "Lesser than Macbeth, and greater, / Not so happy, yet much happier" (lines 65–66), since Banquo will beget a race of kings and Macbeth will not. How then do they know that Macbeth will be king? If we consider the hypothetical question, what if Macbeth does *not* murder Duncan, we can gain some understanding of the relationship between character and fate; for the only valid answer is that the question remains hypothetical—Macbeth *does* kill Duncan, the witches are right in their prediction. It is idle to speculate that Providence would have found another way to make Macbeth king, for the witches' prophecy is self-fulfilling in the very way they foresee. Character is fate; they know Macbeth's fatal weakness and know they can "enkindle" him to seize the crown by laying irresistible temptations before him. This does not mean that they determine his choice but, rather, that Macbeth's choice is predictable and therefore unvoidable, even though not preordained. He has free choice, but that choice will, in fact, go only one way—as with Adam and Eve in Milton's *Paradise Lost* and in the medieval tradition from which this poem was derived.

Although the powers of evil cannot determine Macbeth's choice, they can influence the external conditions affecting that choice. By a series of apparently circumstantial events, well timed in their effect, they can repeatedly assail him just when he is about to rally to the call of conscience. The witches, armed with supernatural knowledge, inform Macbeth of his new title shortly before the King's ambassadors confirm that he is to be the Thane of Cawdor. Duncan chooses this night to lodge under Macbeth's roof. And, just when Macbeth resolves to abandon even this unparalleled opportunity, his wife intervenes on the side of the witches. Macbeth commits the murder in part to keep his word to her and to prove he is no coward (like Donwald, the slayer of

King Duff in one of Shakespeare's chief sources, Raphael Holinshed's *Chronicles*). Not only the opportunities presented to Macbeth, but also the obstacles put in his way are cannily timed to overwhelm his conscience. When King Duncan announces that his son Malcolm is now Prince of Cumberland and official heir to the throne (1.4.36–42), the unintended threat deflects Macbeth's mood from one of gratitude and acceptance to one of hostility. These are mitigating circumstances that affect our judgment of Macbeth, and, even though they cannot excuse him, they certainly increase our sympathetic identification.

We are moved, too, by the poetic intensity of Macbeth's moral vision. His soliloquies are memorable as poetry, not merely because Shakespeare wrote them, but because Macbeth is sensitive and aware. The horror, indeed, of his crime is that his cultivated self is revolted by what he cannot prevent himself from doing. He understands with a terrible clarity, not only the moral wrong of what he is about to do, but also the inescapably destructive consequences for himself. He is as reluctant as we to see the crime committed, and yet he goes to it with a sad and rational deliberateness rather than in a self-blinding fury. For Macbeth, there is no seeming loss of perspective, and yet there is total alienation of the act from his moral consciousness. The arguments for and against murdering Duncan, as Macbeth pictures them in his acutely visual imagination, when weighed, are overwhelmingly opposed to the deed. Duncan is his king and his guest, deserving Macbeth's duty and hospitality. The King is virtuous and able. He has shown every favor to Macbeth, thereby removing any sane motive for striving after further promotion. All human history shows that murders of this sort "return / To plague th' inventor" (1.7.9–10), that is, provide only guilt and punishment rather than satisfaction. Finally, judgment in "the life to come" includes the prospect of eternal torment. On the other side of the argument is nothing but Macbeth's "Vaulting ambition, which o'erleaps itself" (line 27)—a perverse refusal to be content with his present good fortune because there is more that beckons. Who could weigh the issues so dispassionately and still choose the wrong? Yet the failure is, in fact, predictable; Macbeth is presented to us as typically human, both in his understanding and in his perverse ambition.

Macbeth's clarity of moral imagination is contrasted with his wife's imperceptiveness. He is always seeing visions or hearing voices—a dagger in the air, the ghost of Banquo, a voice crying "Sleep no more!"—and she is always denying them. "The sleeping and the dead / Are but as pictures," she insists. He knows that "all great Neptune's ocean" cannot wash the blood from his hands; "No, this my hand will rather / The multitudinous seas incarnadine, / Making the green one red." To Lady Macbeth, contrastingly, "A little water clears us of this deed. / How easy is it, then!" (2.2.57–72). Macbeth knows that the murder of Duncan is but the beginning: "We have scorched the snake, not killed it."

Lady Macbeth would prefer to believe that "What's done is done" (3.2.14–15). Ironically, it is she, finally, who must endure visions of the most agonizing sort, sleepwalking in her madness and trying to rub away the "damned spot" that before seemed so easy to remove. "All the perfumes of Arabia will not sweeten this little hand," she laments (5.1.34–51). This relationship between Macbeth and Lady Macbeth owes much to traditional contrasts between male and female principles. As in the pairing of Adam and Eve, the man is putatively the more rational of the two but knowingly shares his wife's sin through fondness for her. She has failed to foresee the long-range consequences of sinful ambition and so becomes a temptress to her husband. The fall of man and woman into the bondage of sin takes place in an incongruous atmosphere of domestic intimacy and mutual concern; Lady Macbeth is motivated by ambition for her husband in much the same way that he sins to win her approbation.

The fatal disharmony flawing this domestic accord is conveyed through images of sexual inversion. Lady Macbeth prepares for her ordeal with the incantation, "Come, you spirits / That tend on mortal thoughts, unsex me here . . . Come to my woman's breasts / And take my milk for gall" (1.5.40–48). When she accuses her husband of unmanly cowardice and vows she would dash out the brains of her own infant for such effeminacy as he has displayed, he extols her with "Bring forth men-children only! / For thy undaunted mettle should compose / Nothing but males" (1.7.73–75). She takes the initiative, devising and then carrying out the plan to drug Duncan's chamber-guards with wine. This assumption of the dominant male role by the woman might well remind Elizabethan spectators of numerous biblical, medieval, and classical parallels deploring the ascendancy of passion over reason: Eve choosing for Adam, Noah's wife taking command of the ark, the Wife of Bath dominating her husbands, Venus emasculating Mars, and others.

In *Macbeth*, sexual inversion also allies Lady Macbeth with the witches or weird sisters, the bearded women. Their unnaturalness betokens disorder in nature, for they can sail in a sieve and "look not like th' inhabitants o' th' earth / And yet are on 't" (1.3.41–42). Characteristically, they speak in paradoxes: "When the battle's lost and won," "Fair is foul, and foul is fair" (1.1.4,11). Shakespeare probably drew on numerous sources to depict the witches: Holinshed's *Chronicles* (in which he conflated two accounts, one of Duncan and Macbeth, and the other of King Duff slain by Donwald with the help of his wife), King James' writings on witchcraft, Samuel Harsnett's *Declaration of Egregious Popish Impostures* (used also for *King Lear*), and the accounts of the Scottish witch trials published around 1590. In the last, particularly, Shakespeare could have found mention of witches raising storms and sailing in sieves to endanger vessels at sea, performing threefold rituals blaspheming

the Trinity, and brewing witches' broth. Holinshed's *Chronicles* refer to the weird sisters as "goddesses of destiny," associating them with the three fates, Clotho, Lachesis, and Atropos, who spin, pull, and cut the thread of life. In *Macbeth*, the weird sisters' power to control fortune is curtailed, and they are portrayed as witches according to popular contemporary understanding, rather than as goddesses of destiny; nonetheless, witches were thought to be servants of the devil (Banquo wonders if the devil can speak true in their utterances, 1.3.107), and through them Macbeth has made an ominous pact with evil itself. His visit to their seething cauldron in 4.1 brings him to the witches' masters, those unknown powers that know his very thought and who tempt him with those equivocations of which Banquo has warned Macbeth. The popularity of witchlore tempted Shakespeare's acting company to expand the witches' scenes with spectacles of song and dance; even the Folio text we have evidently contains interpolations derived in part from Thomas Middleton's *The Witch* (see especially 3.5 and part of 4.1, containing mention of Middleton's songs "Come away" and "Black spirits"). Nevertheless, Shakespeare's original theme of a disharmony in nature remains clearly visible.

The disharmonies of gender relations in *Macbeth* suggest another disturbing dimension of this tragedy. The play is filled with what Janet Adelman (in *Cannibals, Witches, and Divorce*, edited by Marjorie Garber, 1985) aptly calls fantasies of maternal power. Macbeth, like many males, attempts to cope with his imaginings of a destructive maternal power and his fantasies of escape into a world fashioned and controlled solely by himself. Initially, he submits to his wife's idea of manliness and commits murder in order to win her approval, destroying in the process a fatherly figure whose manhood is nonetheless ambivalently presented to us: Duncan is to be sure a nurturing father-king, but he is also too soft and trusting for his own good. Macbeth chooses to side with his masculinized wife against the gentler side of human nature, lauding her as a woman who should "Bring forth men-children only," since her "undaunted mettle should compose / Nothing but males" (1.7.73–75), but, in the longer term, Macbeth finds himself desiccated by his own vulnerability to this all-male mother. He turns unsuccessfully to the witches for the power he needs to make him author of himself; in the process of attempting to make himself wholly "masculine," he manages instead to strip away from himself "honor, love, obedience, troops of friends," and all the graces that should "accompany old age" (5.3.24–25). His nemesis is appropriately one who was not, in the normal sense, "of woman born," since Macduff "was from his mother's womb / Untimely ripped" (5.8.13–16). Macduff represents, in other words, the self-creating and invulnerable masculinity that Macbeth cannot fashion for himself. The ending of the play is distressingly absolute in its consolidation of male power—a reestablishment of control that seems necessary in view of the virulence of the maternal power the play has dared to unleash.

Patterns of imagery throughout the play point similarly to disorders in nature and in human relationships. The murder of Duncan, like that of Caesar in *Julius Caesar*, is accompanied by signs of the heavens' anger. Various observers report that chimneys blow down during the unruly night, that owls clamor and attack falcons, that the earth shakes, and that Duncan's horses devour each other. (Some of these portents are from Holinshed.) Banquo's ghost returns from the dead to haunt his murderer, prompting Macbeth to speak in metaphors of charnel houses and graves that send back their dead and of birds of prey that devour the corpses. The drunken porter who opens the gate to Macduff and Lennox after the murder (2.3) invokes images of judgment and everlasting bonfire, through which the scene takes on the semblance of hell gate and the Harrowing of Hell. Owls appear repeatedly in the imagery, along with other creatures associated with nighttime and horror: wolves, serpents, scorpions, bats, toads, beetles, crows, rooks. Darkness itself assumes tangible and menacing shapes of hidden stars or extinguished candles, a thick blanket shrouded "in the dunnest smoke of hell" (1.5.51), an entombment of the earth in place of "living light" (2.4.10), a scarf to hoodwink the eye of "pitiful day" (3.2.50), and a bloody and invisible hand to tear to pieces the lives of the virtuous. Sleep is transformed from "great nature's second course" and a "nourisher" of life that "knits up the raveled sleave of care" (2.2.41–44) into "death's counterfeit" (2.3.77) and a living hell for Lady Macbeth. Life becomes sterile for Macbeth, a denial of harvest, the lees or dregs of the wine and "the sere, the yellow leaf" (5.3.23). In a theatrical metaphor, life becomes for him unreal, "a walking shadow, a poor player / That struts and frets his hour upon the stage / And then is heard no more" (5.5.24–26). This theme of empty illusion carries over into the recurring image of borrowed or ill-fitting garments that belie the wearer. Macbeth is an actor, a hypocrite, whose "False face must hide what the false heart doth know" (1.7.83) and who must "Look like th' innocent flower, / But be the serpent under 't" (1.5.65–66). Even the show of grief is an assumed mask whereby evildoers deceive the virtuous, so much so that Malcolm, Donalbain, and Macduff learn to conceal their true feelings rather than be thought to "show an unfelt sorrow" (2.3.138).

Blood is not only a literal sign of disorder but an emblem of Macbeth's remorseless butchery, a "damned spot" on the conscience, and a promise of divine vengeance: "It will have blood, they say; blood will have blood" (3.4.123). The emphasis on corrupted blood also suggests disease, in which Macbeth's tyranny is a sickness to his country as well as to himself. Scotland bleeds (4.3.32), needing a physician; Macduff and his allies call themselves "the med'cine of the sickly weal" (5.2.27). Lady Macbeth's disease is incurable, something spiritually corrupt wherein "the patient / Must

minister to himself" (5.3.47–48). Conversely, the English King Edward is renowned for his divine gift of curing what was called the king's evil, or scrofula. These images are generally paternalistic in their invocation of kings and fathers who heal and unite.

Throughout, the defenders of righteousness are associated with positive images of natural order and with patriarchal control. Duncan rewards his subjects by saying, "I have begun to plant thee, and will labor / To make thee full of growing" (1.4.28–29). His arrival at Inverness Castle is heralded by signs of summer, sweet air, and "the temple-haunting martlet" (1.6.4). He is a fatherly figure, so much so that even Lady Macbeth balks at an act so like patricide. Macduff, too, is a father and husband whose family is butchered. The forest of Birnam marching to confront Macbeth, although rationally explainable as a device of camouflage for Macduff's army, is emblematic of the natural order itself rising up against the monstrosity of Macbeth's crimes. Banquo is, above all, a patriarchal figure, ancestor of the royal line governing Scotland and England at the time the play was written. These harmonies are to an extent restorative. Even the witches' riddling prophecies, "th' equivocation of the fiend" (5.5.43), luring Macbeth into further atrocities with the vain promise of security, anticipate a just retribution.

Nonetheless, the play's vision of evil shakes us deeply. Scotland's peace has been violated, so much so that "to do harm / Is often laudable, to do good sometimes / Accounted dangerous folly" (4.2.76–78). Macduff has been forced to deny his proper manly role of protecting his wife and family; Lady Macduff and her son, along with young Siward, have had to pay with their innocent lives the terrible price of Scotland's tyranny. In his frenzied attempt to prevent the fulfillment of the prophecy about Banquo's lineage inheriting the kingdom, Macbeth has, like King Herod, slaughtered much of the younger generation on whom the future depends. We can only hope that the stability to which Scotland returns after his death will be lasting. Banquo's line is to rule eventually and to produce a line of kings reaching down to the royal occupant to whom Shakespeare will present his play, but, when *Macbeth* ends, it is Malcolm who is king. The killing of a traitor (Macbeth) and the placing of his head on a pole replicate the play's beginning in the treason and beheading of the Thane of Cawdor—a gentleman on whom Duncan built "An absolute trust" (1.4.14). Most troublingly, the humanly representative nature of Macbeth's crime leaves us with little assurance that we could resist his temptation. The most that can be said is that wise and good persons such as Banquo and Macduff have learned to know the evil in themselves and to resist it as nobly as they can.

Macbeth

[*Dramatis Personae*

DUNCAN, *King of Scotland*
MALCOLM } *his sons*
DONALBAIN

MACBETH, *Thane of Glamis, later of Cawdor, later King of Scotland*
LADY MACBETH

BANQUO, *a thane of Scotland*
FLEANCE, *his son*
MACDUFF, *Thane of Fife*
LADY MACDUFF
SON *of Macduff and Lady Macduff*

LENNOX
ROSS
MENTEITH } *thanes and noblemen of Scotland*
ANGUS
CAITHNESS

SIWARD, *Earl of Northumberland*
YOUNG SIWARD, *his son*
SEYTON, *an officer attending Macbeth*
Another LORD
ENGLISH DOCTOR
SCOTTISH DOCTOR
GENTLEWOMAN *attending Lady Macbeth*
CAPTAIN *serving Duncan*
PORTER
OLD MAN
Three MURDERERS *of Banquo*
FIRST MURDERER *at Macduff's castle*
MESSENGER *to Lady Macbeth*
MESSENGER *to Lady Macduff*
SERVANT *to Macbeth*
SERVANT *to Lady Macbeth*
Three WITCHES *or* WEIRD SISTERS
HECATE
Three APPARITIONS

Lords, Gentlemen, Officers, Soldiers, Murderers, and Attendants

SCENE: *Scotland; England*]

1.1 *Thunder and lightning. Enter three Witches.*

FIRST WITCH
When shall we three meet again?
In thunder, lightning, or in rain?

1.1. Location: An open place.

SECOND WITCH
When the hurlyburly's done,
When the battle's lost and won. 3
THIRD WITCH
That will be ere the set of sun.
FIRST WITCH
Where the place?
SECOND WITCH   Upon the heath.
THIRD WITCH
There to meet with Macbeth.
FIRST WITCH   I come, Grimalkin! 8
SECOND WITCH   Paddock calls. 9
THIRD WITCH   Anon. 10
ALL
Fair is foul, and foul is fair.
Hover through the fog and filthy air.   *Exeunt.*

❧

1.2   *Alarum within. Enter King* [*Duncan*], *Malcolm, Donalbain, Lennox, with attendants, meeting a bleeding Captain.*

DUNCAN
What bloody man is that? He can report,
As seemeth by his plight, of the revolt
The newest state.
MALCOLM   This is the sergeant 3
Who like a good and hardy soldier fought
'Gainst my captivity. Hail, brave friend!
Say to the King the knowledge of the broil 6
As thou didst leave it.
CAPTAIN   Doubtful it stood,
As two spent swimmers that do cling together 8
And choke their art. The merciless Macdonwald— 9
Worthy to be a rebel, for to that 10
The multiplying villainies of nature 11
Do swarm upon him—from the Western Isles 12
Of kerns and gallowglasses is supplied; 13
And Fortune, on his damnèd quarrel smiling, 14
Showed like a rebel's whore. But all's too weak; 15
For brave Macbeth—well he deserves that name— 16
Disdaining Fortune, with his brandished steel,
Which smoked with bloody execution,
Like valor's minion carved out his passage 19
Till he faced the slave, 20

3 hurlyburly tumult **8 Grimalkin** i.e., gray cat, name of the witch's familiar—a demon or evil spirit supposed to answer a witch's call and to allow him or her to perform black magic **9 Paddock** toad; also a familiar **10 Anon** at once, right away
1.2. Location: A camp near Forres.
s.d. Alarum trumpet call to arms **3 newest state** latest news. **sergeant** i.e., staff officer. (There may be no inconsistency with his rank of "captain" in the stage direction and speech prefixes in the Folio.)
6 broil battle **8 spent** tired out **9 choke their art** render their skill in swimming useless **10 to that** as if to that end or purpose
11–12 The multiplying . . . him ever increasing numbers of villainous rebels (or perhaps villainous qualities) swarm about him like vermin **12 Western Isles** islands to the west of Scotland—the Hebrides and perhaps Ireland **13 Of kerns** with light-armed Irish foot soldiers. **gallowglasses** horsemen armed with axes **14 quarrel** cause
15 Showed appeared **16 name** i.e., "brave" **19 minion** darling
20 the slave i.e., Macdonwald

Which ne'er shook hands nor bade farewell to him 21
Till he unseamed him from the nave to th' chops, 22
And fixed his head upon our battlements.

DUNCAN
O valiant cousin, worthy gentleman! 24

CAPTAIN
As whence the sun 'gins his reflection 25
Shipwrecking storms and direful thunders break,
So from that spring whence comfort seemed to come
Discomfort swells. Mark, King of Scotland, mark.
No sooner justice had, with valor armed,
Compelled these skipping kerns to trust their heels 30
But the Norweyan lord, surveying vantage, 31
With furbished arms and new supplies of men,
Began a fresh assault.

DUNCAN
Dismayed not this our captains, Macbeth and
   Banquo?

CAPTAIN
Yes, as sparrows eagles, or the hare the lion.
If I say sooth, I must report they were 36
As cannons overcharged with double cracks, 37
So they doubly redoubled strokes upon the foe,
Except they meant to bathe in reeking wounds 39
Or memorize another Golgotha, 40
I cannot tell.
But I am faint. My gashes cry for help.

DUNCAN
So well thy words become thee as thy wounds;
They smack of honor both.—Go get him surgeons.
                          [*Exit Captain, attended.*]

               Enter Ross and Angus.

Who comes here?

MALCOLM   The worthy Thane of Ross. 45

LENNOX What a haste looks through his eyes!
So should he look that seems to speak things
   strange. 47

ROSS God save the King!

DUNCAN Whence cam'st thou, worthy thane?

ROSS From Fife, great King,
Where the Norweyan banners flout the sky 51
And fan our people cold. 52
Norway himself, with terrible numbers, 53
Assisted by that most disloyal traitor,
The Thane of Cawdor, began a dismal conflict, 55
Till that Bellona's bridegroom, lapped in proof, 56

Confronted him with self-comparisons, 57
Point against point, rebellious arm 'gainst arm,
Curbing his lavish spirit; and to conclude,
The victory fell on us.

DUNCAN   Great happiness!

ROSS   That now
Sweno, the Norways' king, craves composition; 62
Nor would we deign him burial of his men
Till he disbursèd at Saint Colme's Inch 64
Ten thousand dollars to our general use. 65

DUNCAN
No more that Thane of Cawdor shall deceive
Our bosom interest. Go pronounce his present
   death, 67
And with his former title greet Macbeth.

ROSS   I'll see it done.

DUNCAN
What he hath lost noble Macbeth hath won.
                                    Exeunt.

                        ❖

1.3   *Thunder. Enter the three Witches.*

FIRST WITCH Where hast thou been, sister?

SECOND WITCH Killing swine.

THIRD WITCH Sister, where thou?

FIRST WITCH
A sailor's wife had chestnuts in her lap,
And munched, and munched, and munched. "Give
   me," quoth I.
"Aroint thee, witch!" the rump-fed runnion cries. 6
Her husband's to Aleppo gone, master o' the *Tiger*; 7
But in a sieve I'll thither sail,
And like a rat without a tail 9
I'll do, I'll do, and I'll do. 10

SECOND WITCH
I'll give thee a wind.

FIRST WITCH
Thou'rt kind.

THIRD WITCH
And I another.

FIRST WITCH
I myself have all the other, 14
And the very ports they blow, 15
All the quarters that they know
I' the shipman's card. 17
I'll drain him dry as hay.

---

21 Which who, i.e., Macbeth. **ne'er . . . to him** proffered no polite salutation or farewell, acted without ceremony **22 nave** navel. **chops** jaws **24 cousin** kinsman **25 As whence** just as from the place where. **'gins his reflection** begins its turning back (from its southward progression during winter) **30 skipping** (1) lightly armed, quick at maneuvering (2) skittish **31 surveying vantage** seeing an opportunity **36 say sooth** tell the truth **37 cracks** charges of explosive **39 Except** unless **40 memorize** make memorable or famous. **Golgotha** "place of a skull," where Christ was crucified. (Mark 15:22.) **45 Thane** Scottish title of honor, roughly equivalent to "Earl" **47 seems to** seems about to **51 flout** mock, insult **52 fan . . . cold** fan cold fear into our troops **53 Norway** the King of Norway. **terrible numbers** terrifying numbers of troops **55 dismal** ominous **56 Till . . . proof** i.e., until Macbeth, clad in well-tested armor. (Bellona was the Roman goddess of war.)

57 him i.e., the King of Norway. **self-comparisons** i.e., matching counterthrusts **62 Norways'** Norwegians'. **composition** agreement, treaty of peace **64 Saint Colme's Inch** Inchcolm, the Isle of St. Columba in the Firth of Forth **65 dollars** Spanish or Dutch coins **67 Our** (The royal "we.") **bosom** close and affectionate. **present** immediate

1.3. Location: A heath near Forres.

6 Aroint thee begone. **rump-fed** fed on refuse, or fat-rumped. **runnion** mangy creature, scabby woman **7 Tiger** (A ship's name.) **9–10 like . . . do** (Suggestive of the witches' deformity and sexual insatiability. Witches were thought to seduce men sexually.) **do** (1) act (2) perform sexually **14 other** others **15 And . . . blow** (The witches can prevent a ship from entering port by causing the winds to blow from land.) **17 shipman's card** compass card

Sleep shall neither night nor day
Hang upon his penthouse lid.   20
He shall live a man forbid.   21
Weary sev'nnights nine times nine   22
Shall he dwindle, peak, and pine.   23
Though his bark cannot be lost,
Yet it shall be tempest-tossed.
Look what I have.

SECOND WITCH   Show me, show me.

FIRST WITCH
Here I have a pilot's thumb,
Wrecked as homeward he did come.   *Drum within.*

THIRD WITCH
A drum, a drum!
Macbeth doth come.

ALL [*dancing in a circle*]
The Weird Sisters, hand in hand,   32
Posters of the sea and land,   33
Thus do go about, about,
Thrice to thine, and thrice to mine,
And thrice again, to make up nine.
Peace! The charm's wound up.

        Enter Macbeth and Banquo.

MACBETH
So foul and fair a day I have not seen.

BANQUO
How far is 't called to Forres?—What are these,   39
So withered and so wild in their attire,
That look not like th' inhabitants o' th' earth
And yet are on 't?—Live you? Or are you aught
That man may question? You seem to understand me
By each at once her chappy finger laying   44
Upon her skinny lips. You should be women,
And yet your beards forbid me to interpret
That you are so.

MACBETH   Speak, if you can. What are you?

FIRST WITCH
All hail, Macbeth! Hail to thee, Thane of Glamis!

SECOND WITCH
All hail, Macbeth! Hail to thee, Thane of Cawdor!

THIRD WITCH
All hail, Macbeth, that shalt be king hereafter!

BANQUO
Good sir, why do you start and seem to fear
Things that do sound so fair?—I' the name of truth,
Are ye fantastical or that indeed   53
Which outwardly ye show? My noble partner   54
You greet with present grace and great prediction   55
Of noble having and of royal hope,
That he seems rapt withal. To me you speak not.   57
If you can look into the seeds of time

And say which grain will grow and which will not,
Speak then to me, who neither beg nor fear   60
Your favors nor your hate.   61

FIRST WITCH   Hail!
SECOND WITCH   Hail!
THIRD WITCH   Hail!

FIRST WITCH
Lesser than Macbeth, and greater.

SECOND WITCH
Not so happy, yet much happier.   66

THIRD WITCH
Thou shalt get kings, though thou be none.   67
So all hail, Macbeth and Banquo!

FIRST WITCH
Banquo and Macbeth, all hail!

MACBETH
Stay, you imperfect speakers, tell me more!   70
By Sinel's death I know I am Thane of Glamis;   71
But how of Cawdor? The Thane of Cawdor lives
A prosperous gentleman; and to be king
Stands not within the prospect of belief,
No more than to be Cawdor. Say from whence   75
You owe this strange intelligence, or why   76
Upon this blasted heath you stop our way   77
With such prophetic greeting? Speak, I charge you.
                                        Witches vanish.

BANQUO
The earth hath bubbles, as the water has,
And these are of them. Whither are they vanished?

MACBETH
Into the air; and what seemed corporal melted,   81
As breath into the wind. Would they had stayed!

BANQUO
Were such things here as we do speak about?
Or have we eaten on the insane root   84
That takes the reason prisoner?

MACBETH
Your children shall be kings.

BANQUO   You shall be king.

MACBETH
And Thane of Cawdor too. Went it not so?

BANQUO
To th' selfsame tune and words.—Who's here?

        Enter Ross and Angus.

ROSS
The King hath happily received, Macbeth,
The news of thy success; and when he reads   90
Thy personal venture in the rebels' fight,   91
His wonders and his praises do contend   92
Which should be thine or his. Silenced with that,   93

---

20 penthouse lid i.e., eyelid (which projects out over the eye like a
penthouse or slope-roofed structure) **21 forbid** accursed **22 sev'n-
nights** weeks **23 peak** grow peaked or thin **32 Weird Sisters**
women connected with fate or destiny; also women having a mysterious or unearthly, uncanny appearance **33 Posters of** swift travelers
over **39 is 't called** is it said to be **44 chappy** chapped **53 fantastical** creatures of fantasy or imagination **54 show** appear **55 grace**
honor **57 rapt withal** carried out of himself, distracted by these predictions. **withal** with it, by it

60–61 beg . . . hate beg your favors nor fear your hate **66 happy**
fortunate **67 get** beget **70 imperfect** cryptic **71 Sinel's** (Sinel was
Macbeth's father.) **75–76 Say . . . intelligence** say from what
source you have this unusual information **77 blasted** blighted
81 corporal bodily **84 on** of. **insane root** root causing insanity; variously identified **90 reads** i.e., considers **91 Thy . . . fight** your endangering yourself in fighting the rebels; or (reading *fight* as *sight*)
your endangering yourself before the very eyes of the rebels
92–93 His . . . that i.e., your wondrous deeds so outdo any praise
he could offer that he is silenced

In viewing o'er the rest o' the selfsame day
He finds thee in the stout Norweyan ranks,
Nothing afeard of what thyself didst make,   96
Strange images of death. As thick as tale   97
Came post with post, and every one did bear   98
Thy praises in his kingdom's great defense,
And poured them down before him.
ANGUS   We are sent
To give thee from our royal master thanks,
Only to herald thee into his sight,
Not pay thee.
ROSS
And, for an earnest of a greater honor,   104
He bade me, from him, call thee Thane of Cawdor;
In which addition, hail, most worthy thane,   106
For it is thine.
BANQUO   What, can the devil speak true?
MACBETH
The Thane of Cawdor lives. Why do you dress me
In borrowed robes?
ANGUS   Who was the thane lives yet,   109
But under heavy judgment bears that life
Which he deserves to lose. Whether he was
combined   111
With those of Norway, or did line the rebel   112
With hidden help and vantage, or that with both
He labored in his country's wrack, I know not;   114
But treasons capital, confessed and proved,   115
Have overthrown him.
MACBETH [aside]   Glamis, and Thane of Cawdor!
The greatest is behind. [To Ross and Angus.] Thanks
for your pains.   117
[Aside to Banquo.] Do you not hope your children
shall be kings
When those that gave the Thane of Cawdor to me
Promised no less to them?
BANQUO [to Macbeth]   That, trusted home,   120
Might yet enkindle you unto the crown,
Besides the Thane of Cawdor. But 'tis strange;
And oftentimes to win us to our harm
The instruments of darkness tell us truths,   124
Win us with honest trifles, to betray 's
In deepest consequence.—   126
Cousins, a word, I pray you.   127
            [He converses apart with Ross and Angus.]
MACBETH [aside]   Two truths are told,
As happy prologues to the swelling act   129
Of the imperial theme.—I thank you, gentlemen.
[Aside.] This supernatural soliciting   131
Cannot be ill, cannot be good. If ill,
Why hath it given me earnest of success

Commencing in a truth? I am Thane of Cawdor.
If good, why do I yield to that suggestion
Whose horrid image doth unfix my hair   136
And make my seated heart knock at my ribs,
Against the use of nature? Present fears   138
Are less than horrible imaginings.
My thought, whose murder yet is but fantastical,   140
Shakes so my single state of man   141
That function is smothered in surmise,   142
And nothing is but what is not.   143
BANQUO   Look how our partner's rapt.
MACBETH [aside]
If chance will have me king, why, chance may
crown me
Without my stir.
BANQUO   New honors come upon him,   146
Like our strange garments, cleave not to their mold 147
But with the aid of use.
MACBETH [aside]   Come what come may,   148
Time and the hour runs through the roughest day.   149
BANQUO
Worthy Macbeth, we stay upon your leisure.   150
MACBETH
Give me your favor. My dull brain was wrought   151
With things forgotten. Kind gentlemen, your pains
Are registered where every day I turn   153
The leaf to read them. Let us toward the King.
[Aside to Banquo.] Think upon what hath chanced,
and at more time,   155
The interim having weighed it, let us speak
Our free hearts each to other.   157
BANQUO [to Macbeth]   Very gladly.
MACBETH [to Banquo]   Till then, enough.—Come, friends.
                                        Exeunt.

❧

1.4   *Flourish. Enter King [Duncan], Lennox, Malcolm,*
          Donalbain, and attendants.

DUNCAN
Is execution done on Cawdor? Are not
Those in commission yet returned?
MALCOLM   My liege,   2
They are not yet come back. But I have spoke
With one that saw him die, who did report
That very frankly he confessed his treasons,

96 **Nothing** not at all   97–98 **As . . . with post** as fast as could be told, i.e., counted, came messenger after messenger (unless the text should be amended to "As thick as hail")   104 **earnest** token payment   106 **addition** title   109 **Who** he who   111 **combined** confederate   112 **line** reinforce.   **the rebel** i.e., Macdonwald   114 **in . . . wrack** to bring about his country's ruin   115 **capital** deserving death   117 **behind** to come   120 **home** all the way   124 **darkness** (Indicates the demonic beyond the witches.)   126 **In deepest consequence** in the profoundly important sequel   127 **Cousins** i.e., fellow lords   129 **swelling act** stately drama   131 **soliciting** tempting

136 **horrid** literally, "bristling," like Macbeth's hair   138 **use** custom. **fears** things feared   140 **whose** in which.   **but fantastical** merely imagined   141 **single . . . man** weak human condition   142 **function** normal power of action.   **surmise** speculation, imaginings   143 **nothing . . . not** only unreal imaginings have (for me) any reality   146 **stir** bestirring (myself).   **come** i.e., which have come   147–148 **cleave . . . use** do not take the shape of the wearer until often worn. (Macbeth is often connected in the text with clothes that don't really fit him.)   149 **Time . . . day** i.e., what must happen will happen one way or another   150 **stay** wait   151 **favor** pardon. **wrought** shaped, preoccupied   153 **registered** recorded (in my memory)   155 **at more time** at a time of greater leisure   157 **Our free hearts** our hearts freely
1.4. Location: Forres. The palace.
2 **in commission** having warrant (to see to the execution of Cawdor)

Implored Your Highness' pardon, and set forth
A deep repentance. Nothing in his life
Became him like the leaving it. He died
As one that had been studied in his death   9
To throw away the dearest thing he owed   10
As 'twere a careless trifle.

DUNCAN   There's no art   11
To find the mind's construction in the face.
He was a gentleman on whom I built
An absolute trust.

Enter Macbeth, Banquo, Ross, and Angus.

                                   O worthiest cousin!
The sin of my ingratitude even now
Was heavy on me. Thou art so far before   16
That swiftest wing of recompense is slow
To overtake thee. Would thou hadst less deserved,
That the proportion both of thanks and payment   19
Might have been mine! Only I have left to say,   20
More is thy due than more than all can pay.

MACBETH
The service and the loyalty I owe,
In doing it, pays itself. Your Highness' part
Is to receive our duties; and our duties
Are to your throne and state children and servants, 25
Which do but what they should by doing every-
   thing
Safe toward your love and honor.

DUNCAN   Welcome hither!   27
I have begun to plant thee, and will labor
To make thee full of growing. Noble Banquo,
That hast no less deserved, nor must be known
No less to have done so, let me infold thee
And hold thee to my heart.

BANQUO   There if I grow,
The harvest is your own.

DUNCAN   My plenteous joys,
Wanton in fullness, seek to hide themselves   34
In drops of sorrow.—Sons, kinsmen, thanes,
And you whose places are the nearest, know
We will establish our estate upon   37
Our eldest, Malcolm, whom we name hereafter
The Prince of Cumberland; which honor must   39
Not unaccompanied invest him only,   40
But signs of nobleness, like stars, shall shine
On all deservers.—From hence to Inverness,   42
And bind us further to you.   43

MACBETH
The rest is labor which is not used for you.   44
I'll be myself the harbinger and make joyful   45
The hearing of my wife with your approach;
So humbly take my leave.

DUNCAN   My worthy Cawdor!

MACBETH *[aside]*
The Prince of Cumberland! That is a step
On which I must fall down or else o'erleap,
For in my way it lies. Stars, hide your fires;   50
Let not light see my black and deep desires.
The eye wink at the hand; yet let that be   52
Which the eye fears, when it is done, to see.   *Exit.*

DUNCAN
True, worthy Banquo. He is full so valiant,   54
And in his commendations I am fed;   55
It is a banquet to me. Let's after him,
Whose care is gone before to bid us welcome.
It is a peerless kinsman.   *Flourish. Exeunt.*

❧

1.5   *Enter Macbeth's Wife, alone, with a letter.*

LADY MACBETH *[reads]* "They met me in the day of success; and I have learned by the perfect'st report they 2
have more in them than mortal knowledge. When I
burnt in desire to question them further, they made
themselves air, into which they vanished. Whiles I
stood rapt in the wonder of it came missives from the 6
King, who all-hailed me 'Thane of Cawdor,' by which
title, before, these Weird Sisters saluted me, and referred me to the coming on of time with 'Hail, king
that shalt be!' This have I thought good to deliver thee, 10
my dearest partner of greatness, that thou mightst not
lose the dues of rejoicing by being ignorant of what
greatness is promised thee. Lay it to thy heart, and
farewell."
Glamis thou art, and Cawdor, and shalt be
What thou art promised. Yet do I fear thy nature;   16
It is too full o' the milk of human kindness
To catch the nearest way. Thou wouldst be great,
Art not without ambition, but without
The illness should attend it. What thou wouldst
   highly,   20
That wouldst thou holily; wouldst not play false,
And yet wouldst wrongly win. Thou'dst have, great
   Glamis,

[marginal handwritten note] feminine

That which cries "Thus thou must do," if thou have
    it,   23
And that which rather thou dost fear to do   24
Than wishest should be undone. Hie thee hither,   25
That I may pour my spirits in thine ear
And chastise with the valor of my tongue
All that impedes thee from the golden round   28
Which fate and metaphysical aid doth seem   29
To have thee crowned withal.

> *Enter [a servant as] Messenger.*

                               What is your tidings? 30

MESSENGER
The King comes here tonight.
LADY MACBETH   Thou'rt mad to say it!
Is not thy master with him, who, were 't so,
Would have informed for preparation?   33
MESSENGER
So please you, it is true. Our thane is coming.
One of my fellows had the speed of him,   35
Who, almost dead for breath, had scarcely more
Than would make up his message.
LADY MACBETH   Give him tending; 37
He brings great news.   *Exit Messenger.*
                    The raven himself is hoarse
That croaks the fatal entrance of Duncan
Under my battlements. Come, you spirits
That tend on mortal thoughts, unsex me here   41
And fill me from the crown to the toe top-full
Of direst cruelty! Make thick my blood;
Stop up th' access and passage to remorse,   44
That no compunctious visitings of nature   45
Shake my fell purpose, nor keep peace between   46
Th' effect and it! Come to my woman's breasts   47
And take my milk for gall, you murdering ministers, 48
Wherever in your sightless substances   49
You wait on nature's mischief! Come, thick night,   50
And pall thee in the dunnest smoke of hell,   51
That my keen knife see not the wound it makes,
Nor heaven peep through the blanket of the dark
To cry "Hold, hold!"

> *Enter Macbeth.*

                  Great Glamis! Worthy Cawdor!
Greater than both by the all-hail hereafter!
Thy letters have transported me beyond   56

This ignorant present, and I feel now
The future in the instant.
MACBETH   My dearest love,
Duncan comes here tonight.
LADY MACBETH   And when goes hence?
MACBETH
Tomorrow, as he purposes.
LADY MACBETH   O, never
Shall sun that morrow see!
Your face, my thane, is as a book where men
May read strange matters. To beguile the time,   63
Look like the time; bear welcome in your eye,   64
Your hand, your tongue. Look like th' innocent
    flower,
But be the serpent under 't. He that's coming
Must be provided for; and you shall put
This night's great business into my dispatch,   68
Which shall to all our nights and days to come
Give solely sovereign sway and masterdom.
MACBETH
We will speak further.
LADY MACBETH   Only look up clear. 71
To alter favor ever is to fear.   72
Leave all the rest to me.   *Exeunt.*

✽

1.6   *Hautboys and torches. Enter King [Duncan],*
        Malcolm, Donalbain, Banquo, Lennox, Macduff,
        Ross, Angus, and attendants.

DUNCAN
This castle hath a pleasant seat. The air   1
Nimbly and sweetly recommends itself
Unto our gentle senses.
BANQUO   This guest of summer, 3
The temple-haunting martlet, does approve   4
By his loved mansionry that the heaven's breath   5
Smells wooingly here. No jutty, frieze,   6
Buttress, nor coign of vantage but this bird   7
Hath made his pendent bed and procreant cradle.   8
Where they most breed and haunt, I have observed
The air is delicate.

> *Enter Lady [Macbeth].*

DUNCAN   See, see, our honored hostess!
The love that follows us sometimes is our trouble,   11
Which still we thank as love. Herein I teach you   12

How you shall bid God 'ild us for your pains, 13
And thank us for your trouble.

LADY MACBETH   All our service
In every point twice done, and then done double,
Were poor and single business to contend 16
Against those honors deep and broad wherewith 17
Your Majesty loads our house. For those of old, 18
And the late dignities heaped up to them, 19
We rest your hermits.

DUNCAN   Where's the Thane of Cawdor? 20
We coursed him at the heels, and had a purpose 21
To be his purveyor; but he rides well, 22
And his great love, sharp as his spur, hath holp him 23
To his home before us. Fair and noble hostess,
We are your guest tonight.

LADY MACBETH   Your servants ever 25
Have theirs, themselves, and what is theirs in compt 26
To make their audit at Your Highness' pleasure, 27
Still to return your own.

DUNCAN   Give me your hand. 28
Conduct me to mine host. We love him highly, 29
And shall continue our graces towards him.
By your leave, hostess.   *Exeunt.*

❖

1.7 *Hautboys. Torches. Enter a sewer, and divers
servants with dishes and service, [and pass] over
the stage. Then enter Macbeth.*

MACBETH
If it were done when 'tis done, then 'twere well
It were done quickly. If th' assassination
Could trammel up the consequence, and catch 3
With his surcease success—that but this blow 4
Might be the be-all and the end-all!—here, 5
But here, upon this bank and shoal of time,
We'd jump the life to come. But in these cases 7
We still have judgment here, that we but teach 8
Bloody instructions, which, being taught, return 9

13 bid . . . pains ask God to reward me for the trouble I'm giving
you. (This is said in the same gently jocose spirit as lines 11–12.)
'ild yield, repay   **16 single** small, inconsiderable   **16–17 contend
Against** vie with   **18 those of old** i.e., honors formerly bestowed on
us   **19 late** recent.   **to** besides, in addition to   **20 rest** remain.   **hermits** i.e., those who will pray for you like hermits or beadsmen
21 coursed followed (as in a hunt)   **22 purveyor** an officer sent ahead
to provide for entertainment; here, forerunner   **23 holp** helped
25–28 Your . . . own those who serve you hold their own servants,
themselves, and all their possessions in trust from you, and can render
an account whenever you wish, ready always to render back to you
what is yours. (A feudal concept of obligation.)   **29 We** (The royal
"we.")
1.7. Location: Macbeth's castle; an inner courtyard.
s.d. sewer chief waiter, butler   **3 trammel . . . consequence** entangle
as in a net and prevent the consequences that follow any action
4 his surcease cessation (of the assassination and of Duncan's life).
success what succeeds, follows. (If only the assassination itself were
the end of the matter.)   **that but** so that only   **5 here** in this world
7 jump risk. (But imaging the physical act is characteristic of Macbeth; compare this with line 27.)   **8 still have judgment** are invariably punished.   **that** in that   **9 instructions** lessons

To plague th' inventor. This evenhanded justice
Commends th' ingredience of our poisoned chalice 11
To our own lips. He's here in double trust:
First, as I am his kinsman and his subject,
Strong both against the deed; then, as his host,
Who should against his murderer shut the door,
Not bear the knife myself. Besides, this Duncan
Hath borne his faculties so meek, hath been 17
So clear in his great office, that his virtues 18
Will plead like angels, trumpet-tongued, against
The deep damnation of his taking-off; 20
And Pity, like a naked newborn babe
Striding the blast, or heaven's cherubin, horsed 22
Upon the sightless couriers of the air, 23
Shall blow the horrid deed in every eye,
That tears shall drown the wind. I have no spur 25
To prick the sides of my intent, but only
Vaulting ambition, which o'erleaps itself
And falls on th' other— 28

Enter Lady [Macbeth].

How now, what news?

LADY MACBETH
He has almost supped. Why have you left the
chamber?

MACBETH
Hath he asked for me?

LADY MACBETH   Know you not he has?

MACBETH
We will proceed no further in this business.
He hath honored me of late, and I have bought 33
Golden opinions from all sorts of people,
Which would be worn now in their newest gloss, 35
Not cast aside so soon.

LADY MACBETH   Was the hope drunk
Wherein you dressed yourself? Hath it slept since?
And wakes it now, to look so green and pale 38
At what it did so freely? From this time
Such I account thy love. Art thou afeard
To be the same in thine own act and valor
As thou art in desire? Wouldst thou have that
Which thou esteem'st the ornament of life, 43
And live a coward in thine own esteem,
Letting "I dare not" wait upon "I would," 45
Like the poor cat i' th' adage?

MACBETH   Prithee, peace! 46
I dare do all that may become a man;
Who dares do more is none.

LADY MACBETH   What beast was 't, then,

11 Commends presents.   **ingredience** contents of a mixture   **17 faculties** powers of office   **18 clear** free of taint   **20 taking-off** murder
22 Striding bestriding.   **blast** tempest (of compassionate horror)
23 sightless couriers invisible steeds or runners, i.e., the winds
25 shall drown the wind i.e., will be as heavy as a downpour of rain
and thereby still the wind   **28 other** other side. (The image is of a
horseman vaulting into his saddle and ignominiously falling on the
opposite side.)   **33 bought** acquired (by bravery in battle)   **35 would**
ought to, should   **38 green** sickly   **43 the ornament of life** i.e., the
crown   **45 wait upon** accompany, always follow   **46 adage** (i.e.,
"The cat would eat fish but she will not wet her feet")

That made you break this enterprise to me?   49
When you durst do it, then you were a man;
And, to be more than what you were, you would
Be so much more the man. Nor time nor place
Did then adhere, and yet you would make both.   53
They have made themselves, and that their
    fitness now   54
Does unmake you. I have given suck, and know
How tender 'tis to love the babe that milks me;
I would, while it was smiling in my face,
Have plucked my nipple from his boneless gums
And dashed the brains out, had I so sworn as you
Have done to this.
MACBETH   If we should fail?
LADY MACBETH   We fail?
But screw your courage to the sticking place   61
And we'll not fail. When Duncan is asleep—
Whereto the rather shall his day's hard journey
Soundly invite him—his two chamberlains   64
Will I with wine and wassail so convince   65
That memory, the warder of the brain,   66
Shall be a fume, and the receipt of reason   67
A limbeck only. When in swinish sleep   68
Their drenchèd natures lies as in a death,
What cannot you and I perform upon
Th' unguarded Duncan? What not put upon
His spongy officers, who shall bear the guilt   72
Of our great quell?
MACBETH   Bring forth men-children only!   73
For thy undaunted mettle should compose   74
Nothing but males. Will it not be received,   75
When we have marked with blood those sleepy two
Of his own chamber and used their very daggers,
That they have done 't?
LADY MACBETH   Who dares receive it other,   78
As we shall make our griefs and clamor roar   79
Upon his death?
MACBETH   I am settled, and bend up   80
Each corporal agent to this terrible feat.   81
Away, and mock the time with fairest show.   82
False face must hide what the false heart doth
    know.   *Exeunt.*

❖

2.1   *Enter Banquo, and Fleance, with a torch before him.*
BANQUO   How goes the night, boy?
FLEANCE
The moon is down. I have not heard the clock.
BANQUO
And she goes down at twelve.
FLEANCE   I take 't, 'tis later, sir.
BANQUO
Hold, take my sword. [*He gives him his sword.*]
    There's husbandry in heaven;   4
Their candles are all out. Take thee that too.
        [*He gives him his belt and dagger.*]
A heavy summons lies like lead upon me,   6
And yet I would not sleep. Merciful powers,   7
Restrain in me the cursèd thoughts that nature
Gives way to in repose!

    Enter Macbeth, and a Servant with a torch.

Give me my sword. Who's there? [*He takes his sword.*]
MACBETH   A friend.
BANQUO
What, sir, not yet at rest? The King's abed.
He hath been in unusual pleasure,
And sent forth great largess to your offices.   14
This diamond he greets your wife withal,
By the name of most kind hostess, and shut up   16
In measureless content.   [*He gives a diamond.*]
MACBETH   Being unprepared,   17
Our will became the servant to defect,   18
Which else should free have wrought.   19
BANQUO   All's well.
I dreamt last night of the three Weird Sisters.
To you they have showed some truth.
MACBETH   I think not of them.
Yet, when we can entreat an hour to serve,
We would spend it in some words upon that
    business,
If you would grant the time.
BANQUO   At your kind'st leisure.
MACBETH
If you shall cleave to my consent when 'tis,   26
It shall make honor for you.
BANQUO   So I lose none   27
In seeking to augment it, but still keep
My bosom franchised and allegiance clear,   29

49 break broach   53 adhere agree, suit.   would wanted to   54 that their fitness that very suitability of time and place   61 But only.   the sticking place the notch into which is fitted the string of a crossbow cranked taut for shooting   64 chamberlains attendants on the bedchamber   65 wassail carousal, drink.   convince overpower   66–68 warder . . . only (The brain was thought to be divided into three ventricles: imagination in front, memory at the back, and between them the seat of reason. The fumes of wine, arising from the stomach, would deaden memory and judgment.)   67 receipt receptacle, ventricle   68 limbeck device for distilling liquids   72 spongy soaked, drunken   73 quell murder   74 mettle (the same word as metal): substance, temperament   75 received i.e., as truth   78 other otherwise   79 As inasmuch as   80–81 bend . . . agent strain every muscle   82 mock deceive

2.1. Location: Inner courtyard of Macbeth's castle. Time is virtually continuous from the previous scene.
s.d. torch (This may mean "torchbearer," although it does not at line 9 s.d.)   4 husbandry economy   6 summons i.e., to sleep   7 would not am reluctant to (owing to my uneasy fears).   powers order of angels deputed by God to resist demons   14 largess gifts, gratuities.   offices quarters used for the household work   16–17 shut up In concluded what he had to say with expressions of, or, perhaps, he professes himself enclosed in   18 Our . . . defect our good will (to entertain the King handsomely) was limited by our meager means (at such short notice)   19 free freely, unrestrainedly   26 cleave . . . 'tis give me your support, adhere to my view, when the time comes   27 So provided   29 franchised free (from guilt).   clear unstained

I shall be counseled.
MACBETH   Good repose the while!   30
BANQUO   Thanks, sir. The like to you.

Exit Banquo [with Fleance].

MACBETH *[to Servant]*
Go bid thy mistress, when my drink is ready,   32
She strike upon the bell. Get thee to bed.

Exit [Servant].

Is this a dagger which I see before me,
The handle toward my hand? Come, let me clutch
  thee.
I have thee not, and yet I see thee still.
Art thou not, fatal vision, sensible   37
To feeling as to sight? Or art thou but
A dagger of the mind, a false creation,
Proceeding from the heat-oppressèd brain?   40
I see thee yet, in form as palpable
As this which now I draw.   *[He draws a dagger.]*
Thou marshall'st me the way that I was going,   43
And such an instrument I was to use.
Mine eyes are made the fools o' th' other senses,   45
Or else worth all the rest. I see thee still,   46
And on thy blade and dudgeon gouts of blood,   47
Which was not so before. There's no such thing.
It is the bloody business which informs   49
Thus to mine eyes. Now o'er the one half world
Nature seems dead, and wicked dreams abuse   51
The curtained sleep. Witchcraft celebrates   52
Pale Hecate's offerings, and withered Murder,   53
Alarumed by his sentinel, the wolf,   54
Whose howl's his watch, thus with his stealthy
  pace,   55
With Tarquin's ravishing strides, towards his design   56
Moves like a ghost. Thou sure and firm-set earth,
Hear not my steps which way they walk, for fear
Thy very stones prate of my whereabouts
And take the present horror from the time   60
Which now suits with it. Whiles I threat, he lives;   61
Words to the heat of deeds too cold breath gives.   62

A bell rings.

I go, and it is done. The bell invites me.

---

30 counseled receptive to suggestion   **32 drink** i.e., posset or bedtime drink of hot spiced milk curdled with ale or wine, as also in
2.2.6   **37 fatal** ominous.   **sensible** perceivable by the senses
40 heat-oppressèd fevered   **43 Thou . . . going** you seem to guide
me toward the destiny I intended, toward Duncan's chambers
45–46 Mine . . . rest i.e., either this is a fantasy, deceiving me with
what my eyes seem to see, or else it is a true vision expressing something that is beyond ordinary sensory experience   **47 dudgeon** hilt of
a dagger.   **gouts** drops   **49 informs** creates forms or impressions
51 abuse deceive   **52 curtained** (1) veiled by bed curtains (2)
screened from rationality and consciousness   **53 Pale Hecate's offerings** sacrificial offerings to Hecate, the goddess of night and witchcraft. (She is *pale* because she is identified with the pale moon.)
54 Alarumed given the signal to action   **55 watch** watchword, or cry
like the hourly call of the night watchman   **56 Tarquin's** (Tarquin was
a Roman tyrant who ravished Lucrece.)   **60–61 And take . . . with it**
and thus echo and augment the horror which is so suited to this evil
hour, or, usurp the present horror by breaking the silence   **62 Words
. . . gives** words give only lifeless expression to live deeds, are no
substitute for deeds

Hear it not, Duncan, for it is a knell
That summons thee to heaven or to hell.   *Exit.*

2.2   *Enter Lady [Macbeth].*

LADY MACBETH
That which hath made them drunk hath made me
  bold;
What hath quenched them hath given me fire. Hark!
  Peace!
It was the owl that shrieked, the fatal bellman,   3
Which gives the stern'st good-night. He is about it.   4
The doors are open; and the surfeited grooms   5
Do mock their charge with snores. I have drugged
  their possets,   6
That death and nature do contend about them
Whether they live or die.
MACBETH *[within]*   Who's there? What, ho!
LADY MACBETH
Alack, I am afraid they have awaked,
And 'tis not done. Th' attempt and not the deed
Confounds us. Hark! I laid their daggers ready;   11
He could not miss 'em. Had he not resembled
My father as he slept, I had done 't.

Enter Macbeth, [bearing bloody daggers].

My husband!
MACBETH
I have done the deed. Didst thou not hear a noise?
LADY MACBETH
I heard the owl scream and the crickets cry.   16
Did not you speak?
MACBETH   When?
LADY MACBETH   Now.
MACBETH   As I descended?
LADY MACBETH   Ay.
MACBETH   Hark! Who lies i' the second chamber?
LADY MACBETH   Donalbain.
MACBETH *[looking at his hands]*   This is a sorry sight.
LADY MACBETH
A foolish thought, to say a sorry sight.
MACBETH
There's one did laugh in 's sleep, and one cried
  "Murder!"
That they did wake each other. I stood and heard
  them.
But they did say their prayers, and addressed them   28
Again to sleep.
LADY MACBETH   There are two lodged together.   29

2.2. Location: Scene continues.
3 bellman one who rings a bell to announce a death or to mark the
hours of the night   **4 stern'st good-night** i.e., notice to condemned
criminals that they are to be executed in the morning   **5 grooms** servants   **6 mock their charge** make a mockery of their guard duty.
possets hot bedtime drinks (as in 2.1.32)   **11 Confounds** ruins
16 owl, crickets (The sounds of both could be ominous and prophetic
of death.)   **28 addressed them** settled themselves   **29 two** i.e., Malcolm and Donalbain

MACBETH
One cried "God bless us!" and "Amen!" the other,
As they had seen me with these hangman's hands.   31
List'ning their fear, I could not say "Amen"
When they did say "God bless us!"

LADY MACBETH   Consider it not so deeply.

MACBETH
But wherefore could not I pronounce "Amen"?
I had most need of blessing, and "Amen"
Stuck in my throat.

LADY MACBETH   These deeds must not be thought 37
After these ways; so, it will make us mad.   38

MACBETH
Methought I heard a voice cry "Sleep no more!
Macbeth does murder sleep," the innocent sleep,
Sleep that knits up the raveled sleave of care,   41
The death of each day's life, sore labor's bath,   42
Balm of hurt minds, great nature's second course,   43
Chief nourisher in life's feast—

LADY MACBETH   What do you mean?

MACBETH
Still it cried "Sleep no more!" to all the house;
"Glamis hath murdered sleep, and therefore Cawdor
Shall sleep no more; Macbeth shall sleep no more."

LADY MACBETH
Who was it that thus cried? Why, worthy thane,
You do unbend your noble strength to think   49
So brainsickly of things. Go get some water
And wash this filthy witness from your hand.   51
Why did you bring these daggers from the place?
They must lie there. Go, carry them and smear
The sleepy grooms with blood.

MACBETH   I'll go no more.
I am afraid to think what I have done;
Look on 't again I dare not.

LADY MACBETH   Infirm of purpose!
Give me the daggers. The sleeping and the dead
Are but as pictures. 'Tis the eye of childhood
That fears a painted devil. If he do bleed,
I'll gild the faces of the grooms withal,   60
For it must seem their guilt.

            [She takes the daggers, and] exit. Knock within.

MACBETH   Whence is that knocking?
How is 't with me, when every noise appalls me?
What hands are here? Ha! They pluck out mine
    eyes.
Will all great Neptune's ocean wash this blood
Clean from my hand? No, this my hand will rather
The multitudinous seas incarnadine,   66
Making the green one red.   67

31 As as if. hangman's hands bloody hands (because the hangman would draw and quarter the condemned, and also executed with an ax) 37 thought thought about 38 so if we do so 41 raveled sleave tangled skein 42 bath i.e., to relieve the soreness 43 second course (Ordinary feasts had two courses, of which the second was the chief nourisher; here, sleep is seen as following eating in a restorative process.) 49 unbend slacken (as one would a bow; contrast with "bend up" in 1.7.80) 51 witness evidence 60 gild smear, coat, as if with a thin layer of gold. (Gold was ordinarily spoken of as red.) 66 multitudinous both multiform and teeming. incarnadine make red 67 one red one all-pervading red

Enter Lady [Macbeth].

LADY MACBETH
My hands are of your color, but I shame
To wear a heart so white. (Knock.) I hear a knocking
At the south entry. Retire we to our chamber.
A little water clears us of this deed.
How easy is it, then! Your constancy   72
Hath left you unattended. (Knock.) Hark! More
    knocking.   73
Get on your nightgown, lest occasion call us   74
And show us to be watchers. Be not lost   75
So poorly in your thoughts.   76

MACBETH
To know my deed, 'twere best not know myself.   77
                                                Knock.
Wake Duncan with thy knocking! I would thou
    couldst!   Exeunt.

2.3   Knocking within. Enter a Porter.

PORTER   Here's a knocking indeed! If a man were porter
of hell gate, he should have old turning the key.   2
(Knock.) Knock, knock, knock! Who's there, i' the
name of Beelzebub? Here's a farmer that hanged   4
himself on th' expectation of plenty. Come in time!   5
Have napkins enough about you; here you'll sweat for   6
't (Knock.) Knock, knock! Who's there, in th' other
devil's name? Faith, here's an equivocator, that could   8
swear in both the scales against either scale, who
committed treason enough for God's sake, yet could
not equivocate to heaven. O, come in, equivocator.
(Knock.) Knock, knock, knock! Who's there? Faith,
here's an English tailor come hither for stealing out of
a French hose. Come in, tailor. Here you may roast   14
your goose. (Knock.) Knock, knock! Never at quiet!   15
What are you? But this place is too cold for hell. I'll
devil-porter it no further. I had thought to have let in

72–73 Your . . . unattended your firmness has deserted you 74 nightgown dressing gown 75 watchers those who have remained awake 76 poorly dejectedly 77 To . . . myself i.e., it were better to be lost in my thoughts than to have consciousness of my deed; if I am to live with myself, I will have to shut this out or be no longer the person I was
2.3. Location: Scene continues. The knocking at the door has already been heard in 2.2. It is not necessary to assume literally, however, that Macbeth and Lady Macbeth have been talking near the south entry (2.2.70) where the knocking is heard.
2 old plenty of 4 Beelzebub a devil 4–5 Here's . . . plenty i.e., here's a farmer who has hoarded in anticipation of a scarcity and will be justly punished by a crop surplus and low prices 5 Come in time i.e., you have come in good time 6 napkins handkerchiefs (to mop up the sweat) 8 equivocator (This is regarded by many editors as an allusion to the trial of the Jesuit Henry Garnet for treason in the spring of 1606 and to the doctrine of equivocation said to have been presented in his defense; according to this doctrine, a lie was not a lie if the utterer had in his mind a different meaning in which the utterance was true.) 14 French hose very narrow breeches of the sort that would easily reveal the tailor's attempt to skimp on the cloth supplied him for their manufacture—as he evidently had done with impunity when the French style ran to loose-fitting breeches 14–15 roast your goose heat your tailor's smoothing iron (with an obvious pun on the sense, "cook your goose")

some of all professions that go the primrose way to th'
everlasting bonfire. (*Knock.*) Anon, anon! [*He opens the
gate.*] I pray you, remember the porter.

Enter Macduff and Lennox.

MACDUFF
Was it so late, friend, ere you went to bed,
That you do lie so late?

PORTER   Faith, sir, we were carousing till the second 23
cock; and drink, sir, is a great provoker of three things. 24

MACDUFF   What three things does drink especially
provoke?

PORTER   Marry, sir, nose-painting, sleep, and urine. 27
Lechery, sir, it provokes and unprovokes: it provokes
the desire but it takes away the performance. Therefore much drink may be said to be an equivocator
with lechery: it makes him and it mars him; it sets him
on and it takes him off; it persuades him and disheartens him, makes him stand to and not stand to; 33
in conclusion, equivocates him in a sleep and, giving 34
him the lie, leaves him.   35

MACDUFF   I believe drink gave thee the lie last night. 36

PORTER   That it did, sir, i' the very throat on me. But I 37
requited him for his lie, and, I think, being too strong
for him, though he took up my legs sometimes, yet I 39
made a shift to cast him.   40

MACDUFF   Is thy master stirring?

Enter Macbeth.

Our knocking has awaked him. Here he comes.
                                              [*Exit Porter.*]

LENNOX
Good morrow, noble sir.

MACBETH   Good morrow, both.

MACDUFF
Is the King stirring, worthy thane?

MACBETH   Not yet.

MACDUFF
He did command me to call timely on him.   45
I have almost slipped the hour.

MACBETH   I'll bring you to him.   46

MACDUFF
I know this is a joyful trouble to you,
But yet 'tis one.

MACBETH
The labor we delight in physics pain.   49

23–24 second cock i.e., 3 A.M., when the cock was thought to crow
a second time   **27 Marry** (Originally, an oath, "by the Virgin Mary.")
nose-painting i.e., reddening of the nose through drink   **33 makes
. . . stand to** stimulates him sexually but without sexual capability
34 equivocates . . . sleep (1) lulls him asleep (2) gives him an erotic
experience in dream only   **34–35 giving him the lie** (1) deceiving
him (2) laying him out flat   **35 leaves him** (1) dissipates as intoxication (2) is passed off as urine   **36 gave thee the lie** (1) called you a
liar (2) made you unable to stand and put you to sleep   **37 i' the . . .
me** i.e., insulting me with a deliberate lie that requires a duel (with a
pun on the literal sense).   **on of   39 took up my legs** lifted me as a
wrestler would (with a suggestion of the drunkard's unsteadiness on
his legs and perhaps also of lifting the leg as a dog might to urinate)
40 made a shift managed.   **cast** (1) throw, as in wrestling (2) vomit
45 timely betimes, early   **46 slipped** let slip   **49 physics pain** i.e.,
cures that labor of its troublesome aspect

This is the door.

MACDUFF   I'll make so bold to call,
For 'tis my limited service.   *Exit Macduff.* 51

LENNOX   Goes the King hence today?

MACBETH   He does; he did appoint so.

LENNOX
The night has been unruly. Where we lay,
Our chimneys were blown down, and, as they say,
Lamentings heard i' th' air, strange screams of
   death,
And prophesying with accents terrible   57
Of dire combustion and confused events   58
New hatched to the woeful time. The obscure bird   59
Clamored the livelong night. Some say the earth
Was feverous and did shake.

MACBETH   'Twas a rough night.

LENNOX
My young remembrance cannot parallel
A fellow to it.

Enter Macduff.

MACDUFF   O, horror, horror, horror!
Tongue nor heart cannot conceive nor name thee!

MACBETH AND LENNOX   What's the matter?

MACDUFF
Confusion now hath made his masterpiece!   66
Most sacrilegious murder hath broke ope
The Lord's anointed temple and stole thence
The life o' the building!

MACBETH   What is 't you say? The life?

LENNOX   Mean you His Majesty?

MACDUFF
Approach the chamber and destroy your sight
With a new Gorgon. Do not bid me speak;   73
See, and then speak yourselves.

                              Exeunt Macbeth and Lennox.
                                           Awake, awake!
Ring the alarum bell. Murder and treason!
Banquo and Donalbain, Malcolm, awake!
Shake off this downy sleep, death's counterfeit,
And look on death itself! Up, up, and see
The great doom's image! Malcolm, Banquo,   79
As from your graves rise up and walk like sprites   80
To countenance this horror! Ring the bell. *Bell rings.* 81

Enter Lady [*Macbeth*].

LADY MACBETH   What's the business,
That such a hideous trumpet calls to parley   83
The sleepers of the house? Speak, speak!

MACDUFF   O gentle lady,
'Tis not for you to hear what I can speak.

---

51 limited appointed   **57 accents terrible** terrifying utterances
58 combustion tumult   **59 New . . . time** newly born to accompany
the woeful nature of the time.   **obscure bird** owl, the bird of darkness
66 Confusion destruction   **73 Gorgon** one of three monsters with hideous faces (Medusa was a Gorgon), whose look turned the beholders
to stone   **79 great doom's image** replica of Doomsday   **80 As . . .
rise up** (At the Last Judgment, the dead will rise from their graves to
be judged.)   **sprites** souls, ghosts   **81 countenance** (1) be in keeping
with (2) behold   **83 trumpet** (Another metaphorical suggestion of the
Last Judgment; the *trumpet* here is the shouting and the bell.)

The repetition in a woman's ear   87
Would murder as it fell.

Enter Banquo.

                              O Banquo, Banquo,
Our royal master's murdered!
LADY MACBETH   Woe, alas!
What, in our house?
BANQUO   Too cruel anywhere.
Dear Duff, I prithee, contradict thyself
And say it is not so.

Enter Macbeth, Lennox, and Ross.

MACBETH
Had I but died an hour before this chance   93
I had lived a blessèd time; for from this instant
There's nothing serious in mortality.   95
All is but toys. Renown and grace is dead;   96
The wine of life is drawn, and the mere lees   97
Is left this vault to brag of.   98

Enter Malcolm and Donalbain.

DONALBAIN
What is amiss?
MACBETH   You are, and do not know 't.
The spring, the head, the fountain of your blood
Is stopped, the very source of it is stopped.
MACDUFF
Your royal father's murdered.
MALCOLM   O, by whom?
LENNOX
Those of his chamber, as it seemed, had done 't.
Their hands and faces were all badged with blood;   104
So were their daggers, which unwiped we found
Upon their pillows. They stared and were distracted;
No man's life was to be trusted with them.
MACBETH
O, yet I do repent me of my fury,
That I did kill them.
MACDUFF   Wherefore did you so?
MACBETH
Who can be wise, amazed, temp'rate and furious,   110
Loyal and neutral, in a moment? No man.
Th' expedition of my violent love   112
Outran the pauser, reason. Here lay Duncan,
His silver skin laced with his golden blood,   114
And his gashed stabs looked like a breach in nature 115
For ruin's wasteful entrance; there the murderers, 116
Steeped in the colors of their trade, their daggers
Unmannerly breeched with gore. Who could refrain   118
That had a heart to love, and in that heart

Courage to make 's love known?
LADY MACBETH [*fainting*]   Help me hence, ho! 120
MACDUFF
Look to the lady.
MALCOLM [*aside to Donalbain*]
                    Why do we hold our tongues,
That most may claim this argument for ours?   122
DONALBAIN [*aside to Malcolm*]
What should be spoken here, where our fate,
Hid in an auger hole, may rush and seize us?   124
Let's away. Our tears are not yet brewed.
MALCOLM [*aside to Donalbain*]
Nor our strong sorrow upon the foot of motion.   126
BANQUO   Look to the lady.

              [*Lady Macbeth is helped out.*]
And when we have our naked frailties hid,   128
That suffer in exposure, let us meet
And question this most bloody piece of work   130
To know it further. Fears and scruples shake us.   131
In the great hand of God I stand, and thence   132
Against the undivulged pretense I fight   133
Of treasonous malice.
MACDUFF   And so do I.
ALL   So all.   134
MACBETH
Let's briefly put on manly readiness   135
And meet i' the hall together.
ALL   Well contented.
              Exeunt [all but Malcolm and Donalbain].
MALCOLM
What will you do? Let's not consort with them.   137
To show an unfelt sorrow is an office
Which the false man does easy. I'll to England.   139
DONALBAIN
To Ireland, I. Our separated fortune
Shall keep us both the safer. Where we are,
There's daggers in men's smiles; the nea'er in blood, 142
The nearer bloody.
MALCOLM   This murderous shaft that's shot 143
Hath not yet lighted, and our safest way   144
Is to avoid the aim. Therefore to horse,
And let us not be dainty of leave-taking,   146
But shift away. There's warrant in that theft   147
Which steals itself when there's no mercy left.
                                        Exeunt.

❧

120 **make 's love known** make manifest his love   **122 argument**
topic, business   **124 in an auger hole** i.e., in some hiding place, in
ambush   **126 upon . . . motion** yet in motion, ready to act   **128 our
naked frailties hid** clothed our poor, shivering bodies (which remind
us of our human frailty)   **130 question** discuss   **131 scruples** doubts,
suspicions   **132–134 thence . . . malice** with God's help, I will fight
against the as-yet-unknown purpose that prompted this treason
133 pretense design   **134 malice** enmity   **135 briefly** quickly.
manly readiness men's clothing and resolute purpose   **137 consort**
keep company, associate   **139 easy** easily   **142–143 the nea'er
. . . bloody** the closer the kinship, the greater the danger of being
murdered   **144 lighted** alighted, descended   **146 dainty of** particular
about   **147 shift away** disappear by stealth.   **warrant** justification

87 **repetition** recital, report   **93 chance** occurrence (the murder of
Duncan)   **95 serious in mortality** worthwhile in mortal life   **96 toys**
trifles   **97 lees** dregs   **98 vault** (1) wine-vault (2) earth, with its
vaulted sky   **104 badged** marked, as with a badge or emblem
110 amazed bewildered   **112 expedition** haste   **114 golden** (See the
note for 2.2.60.)   **115 breach in nature** gap in the defenses of life. (A
metaphor of military siege.)   **116 wasteful** destructive   **118 breeched
with gore** covered (as with breeches) to the hilts with gore

2.4

Enter Ross with an Old Man.

OLD MAN
Threescore and ten I can remember well,
Within the volume of which time I have seen
Hours dreadful and things strange, but this sore
  night
Hath trifled former knowings.   3

ROSS   Ha, good father,   4
Thou seest the heavens, as troubled with man's act,   5
Threatens his bloody stage. By th' clock 'tis day,   6
And yet dark night strangles the traveling lamp.   7
Is 't night's predominance or the day's shame   8
That darkness does the face of earth entomb
When living light should kiss it?

OLD MAN   'Tis unnatural,
Even like the deed that's done. On Tuesday last
A falcon, towering in her pride of place,   12
Was by a mousing owl hawked at and killed.   13

ROSS
And Duncan's horses—a thing most strange and
  certain—
Beauteous and swift, the minions of their race,   15
Turned wild in nature, broke their stalls, flung out,
Contending 'gainst obedience, as they would   17
Make war with mankind.

OLD MAN   'Tis said they eat each other. 18

ROSS
They did so, to th' amazement of mine eyes
That looked upon 't.

        Enter Macduff.

                Here comes the good Macduff.—
How goes the world, sir, now?

MACDUFF   Why, see you not?

ROSS
Is 't known who did this more than bloody deed?

MACDUFF
Those that Macbeth hath slain.

ROSS   Alas the day,
What good could they pretend?

MACDUFF   They were suborned.   24
Malcolm and Donalbain, the King's two sons,
Are stol'n away and fled, which puts upon them
Suspicion of the deed.

ROSS   'Gainst nature still!
Thriftless ambition, that will ravin up   28
Thine own life's means! Then 'tis most like   29
The sovereignty will fall upon Macbeth.

MACDUFF
He is already named and gone to Scone   31
To be invested.

ROSS   Where is Duncan's body?

MACDUFF   Carried to Colmekill,   33
The sacred storehouse of his predecessors
And guardian of their bones.

ROSS   Will you to Scone?

MACDUFF
No, cousin, I'll to Fife.

ROSS   Well, I will thither.   36

MACDUFF
Well, may you see things well done there. Adieu,
Lest our old robes sit easier than our new!

ROSS Farewell, father.

OLD MAN
God's benison go with you, and with those   40
That would make good of bad, and friends of foes!

                              Exeunt omnes.

                        ❧

3.1

Enter Banquo.

BANQUO
Thou hast it now—King, Cawdor, Glamis, all
As the weird women promised, and I fear
Thou played'st most foully for 't. Yet it was said
It should not stand in thy posterity,   4
But that myself should be the root and father
Of many kings. If there come truth from them—
As upon thee, Macbeth, their speeches shine—   7
Why, by the verities on thee made good,
May they not be my oracles as well
And set me up in hope? But hush, no more.   10

    Sennet sounded. Enter Macbeth as King, Lady
    [Macbeth], Lennox, Ross, lords, and attendants.

MACBETH
Here's our chief guest.

LADY MACBETH   If he had been forgotten,
It had been as a gap in our great feast
And all-thing unbecoming.   13

MACBETH
Tonight we hold a solemn supper, sir,   14
And I'll request your presence.

BANQUO   Let Your Highness
Command upon me, to the which my duties   16
Are with a most indissoluble tie
Forever knit.

MACBETH Ride you this afternoon?

BANQUO Ay, my good lord.

2.4. Location: Outside Macbeth's castle of Inverness.
3 sore dreadful, grievous **4 trifled former knowings** made trivial all
former experiences. **father** old man **5–6 heavens, act, stage** (A
theatrical metaphor; the *heavens* refer to the decorated roof over the
stage.) **7 traveling lamp** i.e., sun **8 predominance** ascendancy, superior influence (as of a heavenly body) **12 towering** circling higher
and higher. (A term in falconry.) **place** pitch, highest point in the falcon's flight **13 mousing** i.e., ordinarily preying on mice **15 minions**
darlings **17 as** as if **18 eat** ate. (Pronounced "et.") **24 What . . .**
pretend i.e., what could they hope to gain by it? **pretend** intend.
suborned bribed, hired **28 Thriftless** wasteful. **ravin up** devour ravenously **29 like** likely

31 named chosen. (See the note for 1.4.50.) **Scone** ancient royal
city of Scotland near Perth **33 Colmekill** Icolmkill, i.e., Cell of St.
Columba, the barren islet of Iona in the Western Islands, a sacred
spot where the kings were buried; here, called a *storehouse* **36 Fife**
(Of which Macduff is Thane.) **40 benison** blessing
3.1. Location: Forres. The palace.
4 stand stay, remain **7 shine** are brilliantly manifest **10 s.d. Sennet**
trumpet call **13 all-thing** in every way **14 solemn** ceremonious
16 Command lay your command

MACBETH
We should have else desired your good advice,
Which still hath been both grave and prosperous,   22
In this day's council; but we'll take tomorrow.
Is 't far you ride?

BANQUO
As far, my lord, as will fill up the time
Twixt this and supper. Go not my horse the better,   26
I must become a borrower of the night
For a dark hour or twain.

MACBETH   Fail not our feast.
BANQUO   My lord, I will not.

MACBETH
We hear our bloody cousins are bestowed   31
In England and in Ireland, not confessing
Their cruel parricide, filling their hearers
With strange invention. But of that tomorrow,   34
When therewithal we shall have cause of state   35
Craving us jointly. Hie you to horse. Adieu,   36
Till you return at night. Goes Fleance with you?

BANQUO
Ay, my good lord. Our time does call upon 's.

MACBETH
I wish your horses swift and sure of foot,
And so I do commend you to their backs.   40
Farewell.   *Exit Banquo.*
Let every man be master of his time
Till seven at night. To make society
The sweeter welcome, we will keep ourself   44
Till suppertime alone. While then, God be with you!   45
        Exeunt Lords [and all but Macbeth and a Servant].
Sirrah, a word with you. Attend those men   46
Our pleasure?

SERVANT
They are, my lord, without the palace gate.

MACBETH
Bring them before us.   *Exit Servant.*
                        To be thus is nothing,   49
But to be safely thus.—Our fears in Banquo   50
Stick deep, and in his royalty of nature   51
Reigns that which would be feared. 'Tis much he
    dares;   52
And to that dauntless temper of his mind   53
He hath a wisdom that doth guide his valor
To act in safety. There is none but he
Whose being I do fear; and under him
My genius is rebuked, as it is said   57
Mark Antony's was by Caesar. He chid the sisters   58
When first they put the name of king upon me,
And bade them speak to him. Then, prophetlike,

They hailed him father to a line of kings.
Upon my head they placed a fruitless crown
And put a barren scepter in my grip,
Thence to be wrenched with an unlineal hand,   64
No son of mine succeeding. If 't be so,
For Banquo's issue have I filed my mind;   66
For them the gracious Duncan have I murdered,
Put rancors in the vessel of my peace   68
Only for them, and mine eternal jewel   69
Given to the common enemy of man   70
To make them kings, the seeds of Banquo kings.
Rather than so, come fate into the list,   72
And champion me to th' utterance!—Who's there?   73

        Enter Servant and two Murderers.

Now go to the door, and stay there till we call.
                                Exit Servant.
Was it not yesterday we spoke together?

MURDERERS
It was, so please Your Highness.

MACBETH   Well then, now
Have you considered of my speeches? Know
That it was he in the times past which held you
So under fortune, which you thought had been   79
Our innocent self. This I made good to you
In our last conference, passed in probation with you   81
How you were borne in hand, how crossed, the
    instruments,   82
Who wrought with them, and all things else that
    might
To half a soul and to a notion crazed   84
Say, "Thus did Banquo."

FIRST MURDERER   You made it known to us.

MACBETH
I did so, and went further, which is now
Our point of second meeting. Do you find
Your patience so predominant in your nature
That you can let this go? Are you so gospeled   89
To pray for this good man and for his issue,
Whose heavy hand hath bowed you to the grave
And beggared yours forever?

FIRST MURDERER   We are men, my liege.   92

MACBETH
Ay, in the catalogue ye go for men,   93
As hounds and greyhounds, mongrels, spaniels,
    curs,
Shoughs, water-rugs, and demi-wolves are clept   95
All by the name of dogs. The valued file   96

---

22 still always. **grave** weighty. **prosperous** profitable   **26 Go . . . better** unless my horse makes better time than I expect   **31 bestowed** lodged   **34 invention** falsehood (i.e., that Macbeth was the murderer)   **35–36 cause . . . jointly** questions of state occupying our joint attention   **40 commend** commit, entrust   **44 we . . . ourself** I will keep to myself   **45 While** till   **46 Sirrah** (A form of address to a social inferior.)   **49 thus** i.e., king   **50 But un-less. in** concerning   **51 royalty of nature** natural kingly bearing   **52 would be** deserves to be   **53 to** added to   **57 My genius is rebuked** my guardian spirit is daunted or abashed   **58 Caesar** Octavius Caesar

64 with by.   **unlineal** not of lineal descent from me   **66 filed** defiled   **68 rancors** malignant enemies (here visualized as a poison added to a vessel full of wholesome drink)   **69 eternal jewel** i.e., soul   **70 common . . . man** i.e., devil   **72 list** lists, place of combat   **73 champion me** fight with me in single combat.   **to th' utterance** to the last extremity (French, *à l'outrance*)   **79 under fortune** down in your fortunes   **81 passed in probation** went over the proof   **82 borne in hand** deceived by false promises.   **crossed** thwarted.   **instruments** agents   **84 To half a soul** even to a half-wit.   **notion** mind   **89 gospeled** imbued with the gospel spirit   **92 yours** your family   **93 go for** pass for, are entered for   **95 Shoughs** a kind of shaggy dog.   **water-rugs** long-haired water dogs.   **demi-wolves** a cross breed with the wolf.   **clept** called   **96 valued file** list classified according to value

Distinguishes the swift, the slow, the subtle,
The housekeeper, the hunter, every one   98
According to the gift which bounteous nature
Hath in him closed, whereby he does receive   100
Particular addition from the bill   101
That writes them all alike; and so of men.   102
Now, if you have a station in the file,   103
Not i' the worst rank of manhood, say 't,
And I will put that business in your bosoms
Whose execution takes your enemy off,   106
Grapples you to the heart and love of us,
Who wear our health but sickly in his life,   108
Which in his death were perfect.

SECOND MURDERER   I am one, my liege,
Whom the vile blows and buffets of the world
Hath so incensed that I am reckless what
I do to spite the world.

FIRST MURDERER   And I another,
So weary with disasters, tugged with fortune,   113
That I would set my life on any chance   114
To mend it or be rid on 't.

MACBETH   Both of you
Know Banquo was your enemy.

BOTH MURDERERS   True, my lord.

MACBETH
So is he mine, and in such bloody distance   117
That every minute of his being thrusts   118
Against my near'st of life. And though I could   119
With barefaced power sweep him from my sight   120
And bid my will avouch it, yet I must not,   121
For certain friends that are both his and mine,   122
Whose loves I may not drop, but wail his fall   123
Who I myself struck down. And thence it is   124
That I to your assistance do make love,   125
Masking the business from the common eye
For sundry weighty reasons.

SECOND MURDERER   We shall, my lord,
Perform what you command us.

FIRST MURDERER   Though our lives—

MACBETH
Your spirits shine through you. Within this hour at
    most   129
I will advise you where to plant yourselves,   130
Acquaint you with the perfect spy o' the time,   131
The moment on 't, for 't must be done tonight,   132

And something from the palace; always thought   133
That I require a clearness. And with him—   134
To leave no rubs nor botches in the work—   135
Fleance his son, that keeps him company,
Whose absence is no less material to me
Than is his father's, must embrace the fate
Of that dark hour. Resolve yourselves apart;   139
I'll come to you anon.

BOTH MURDERERS   We are resolved, my lord.

MACBETH
I'll call upon you straight. Abide within.
                              Exeunt [*Murderers*].
It is concluded. Banquo, thy soul's flight,
If it find heaven, must find it out tonight.   [*Exit.*]

❖

3.2   *Enter Macbeth's Lady and a Servant.*

LADY MACBETH   Is Banquo gone from court?

SERVANT
Ay, madam, but returns again tonight.

LADY MACBETH
Say to the King I would attend his leisure
For a few words.

SERVANT   Madam, I will.   *Exit.*

LADY MACBETH   Naught's had, all's spent,
Where our desire is got without content.   7
'Tis safer to be that which we destroy
Than by destruction dwell in doubtful joy.   9

Enter Macbeth.

How now, my lord? Why do you keep alone,
Of sorriest fancies your companions making,   11
Using those thoughts which should indeed have
    died   12
With them they think on? Things without all
    remedy   13
Should be without regard. What's done is done.   14

MACBETH
We have scorched the snake, not killed it.   15
She'll close and be herself, whilst our poor malice   16
Remains in danger of her former tooth.   17
But let the frame of things disjoint, both the worlds
    suffer,   18
Ere we will eat our meal in fear and sleep
In the affliction of these terrible dreams
That shake us nightly. Better be with the dead,

98 housekeeper watchdog **100 in him closed** enclosed in him, set in him like a jewel **101–102 Particular . . . alike** particular qualification apart from the catalog that lists them all indiscriminately **103 file** military row, as in "rank and file"; see *rank* in line 104 **106 Whose execution** the doing of which **108 in his life** while he lives **113 tugged with** pulled about by (as in wrestling) **114 set** risk, stake **117 distance** (1) hostility, enmity (2) interval of distance between fencers **118 thrusts** (as in fencing) **119 near'st of life** most vital part, the heart **120 With barefaced power** by open use of my supreme royal authority **121 And . . . avouch it** and use my mere wish as my justification **122 For** because of, for the sake of **123 wail** i.e., I must lament **124 Who** whom **125 to . . . make love** woo your aid **129 Your . . . you** i.e., enough; I can see your determination in your faces **130 advise** instruct **131–132 with . . . on 't** with full and precise instructions as to when it is to be done. **spy** espial, observation

133 something from some distance removed from. **thought** being borne in mind **134 clearness** freedom from suspicion **135 rubs** defects, rough spots **139 Resolve yourselves apart** make up your minds in private conference
3.2. Location: The palace.
7 content contentedness **9 Than . . . joy** than by destroying achieve only an apprehensive joy **11 sorriest** most despicable or wretched **12 Using** keeping company with, entertaining **13 without** beyond **14 without regard** not pondered upon **15 scorched** slashed, cut **16 close** heal, close up again. **poor malice** feeble hostility **17 her former tooth** her fang, just as before **18 let . . . suffer** let the universe itself fall apart, both heaven and earth perish

Whom we, to gain our peace, have sent to peace,   22
Than on the torture of the mind to lie   23
In restless ecstasy. Duncan is in his grave;   24
After life's fitful fever he sleeps well.
Treason has done his worst; nor steel, nor poison,   26
Malice domestic, foreign levy, nothing   27
Can touch him further.
LADY MACBETH   Come on,
Gentle my lord, sleek o'er your rugged looks.   30
Be bright and jovial among your guests tonight.
MACBETH
So shall I, love, and so, I pray, be you.
Let your remembrance apply to Banquo;   33
Present him eminence, both with eye and tongue—   34
Unsafe the while, that we   35
Must lave our honors in these flattering streams   36
And make our faces vizards to our hearts,   37
Disguising what they are.
LADY MACBETH   You must leave this.
MACBETH
O, full of scorpions is my mind, dear wife!
Thou know'st that Banquo and his Fleance lives.
LADY MACBETH
But in them nature's copy's not eterne.   41
MACBETH
There's comfort yet; they are assailable.   42
Then be thou jocund. Ere the bat hath flown
His cloistered flight, ere to black Hecate's summons   44
The shard-borne beetle with his drowsy hums   45
Hath rung night's yawning peal, there shall be done   46
A deed of dreadful note.
LADY MACBETH   What's to be done?
MACBETH
Be innocent of the knowledge, dearest chuck,   48
Till thou applaud the deed. Come, seeling night,   49
Scarf up the tender eye of pitiful day,   50
And with thy bloody and invisible hand
Cancel and tear to pieces that great bond   52
Which keeps me pale! Light thickens,   53

And the crow makes wing to th' rooky wood;   54
Good things of day begin to droop and drowse,
Whiles night's black agents to their preys do rouse.   56
Thou marvel'st at my words, but hold thee still.
Things bad begun make strong themselves by ill.
So, prithee, go with me.   *Exeunt.*

3.3   *Enter three Murderers.*

FIRST MURDERER
But who did bid thee join with us?
THIRD MURDERER   Macbeth.
SECOND MURDERER *[to the First Murderer]*
He needs not our mistrust, since he delivers   2
Our offices and what we have to do   3
To the direction just.
FIRST MURDERER   Then stand with us.   4
The west yet glimmers with some streaks of day.
Now spurs the lated traveler apace   6
To gain the timely inn, and near approaches   7
The subject of our watch.
THIRD MURDERER   Hark, I hear horses.
BANQUO (*within*) Give us a light there, ho!
SECOND MURDERER   Then 'tis he. The rest
That are within the note of expectation   12
Already are i' the court.
FIRST MURDERER   His horses go about.   14
THIRD MURDERER
Almost a mile; but he does usually—
So all men do—from hence to th' palace gate
Make it their walk.

Enter Banquo and Fleance, with a torch.

SECOND MURDERER   A light, a light!
THIRD MURDERER   'Tis he.
FIRST MURDERER   Stand to 't.
BANQUO   It will be rain tonight.
FIRST MURDERER   Let it come down!

[*They attack Banquo.*]

BANQUO
O, treachery! Fly, good Fleance, fly, fly, fly!
Thou mayst revenge.—O slave!

[*He dies. Fleance escapes.*]

THIRD MURDERER
Who did strike out the light?
FIRST MURDERER   Was 't not the way?   25
THIRD MURDERER
There's but one down; the son is fled.

---

22 to gain . . . to peace to gain contentedness through satisfied ambition, have sent to eternal rest **23 torture** rack **24 ecstasy** frenzy **26 nor steel** neither steel **27 Malice domestic** civil war. **foreign levy** the levying of troops abroad (against Scotland) **30 Gentle . . . looks** my noble lord, smooth over your rough looks **33 Let . . . apply** remember to pay special attention **34 eminence** favor **35–36 Unsafe . . . streams** i.e., we are unsafe at present and so must put on a show of flattering cordiality to make our reputation look clean, or, we are unsafe so long as we must flatter thus. (*Lave* means "wash.") **37 vizards** masks **41 nature's copy** lease of life (i.e., by copyhold or lease subject to cancellation); also, the individual human being made from nature's mold. **eterne** perpetual **42 There's** i.e., in that thought there is **44 cloistered** i.e., in and among buildings. **Hecate** goddess of night and witchcraft, as in 2.1.53 **45 shard-borne** borne on shards, or horny wing cases, or, *shard-born,* bred in cow-droppings (shards) **46 yawning** drowsy **48 chuck** (A term of endearment.) **49 seeling** eye-closing. (Night is pictured here as a falconer sewing up the eyes of day lest it should struggle against the deed that is to be done.) **50 Scarf up** blindfold. **pitiful** compassionate **52 bond** i.e., bond by which Banquo and Fleance hold their lives from nature, or moral law against murder, or bond of prophecy **53 pale** pallid from fear (with a suggestion perhaps of *paled,* "fenced in"). **thickens** grows opaque and dim

54 crow rook. **rooky** full of rooks **56 to . . . rouse** bestir themselves to hunt their prey
3.3. Location: A park near the palace.
2–3 He . . . offices we need not mistrust this man, since he states exactly our duties (as told us by Macbeth) **4 To** according to. **just** exactly. (That is, one can tell he comes from Macbeth, since he has instructions identical to ours.) **6 lated** belated **7 timely** arrived at in good time **12 within . . . expectation** in the list of those expected **14 go about** i.e., can be heard as servants take them to the stables (while Banquo and Fleance, provided with a torch, walk from the palace gate to the castle) **25 way** i.e., thing to do

SECOND MURDERER
You have lost best half of our affair.

FIRST MURDERER
Well, let's away and say how much is done.   28
                                          Exeunt.

❧

3.4 *Banquet prepared. Enter Macbeth, Lady
       [Macbeth], Ross, Lennox, Lords, and attendants.*

MACBETH
You know your own degrees; sit down. At first   1
And last, the hearty welcome.   [*They sit.*]
LORDS   Thanks to Your Majesty. 2
MACBETH
Ourself will mingle with society   3
And play the humble host.
Our hostess keeps her state, but in best time   5
We will require her welcome.   6
LADY MACBETH
Pronounce it for me, sir, to all our friends,
For my heart speaks they are welcome.

    Enter First Murderer [to the door].

MACBETH
See, they encounter thee with their hearts' thanks.   9
Both sides are even. Here I'll sit i' the midst.   10
Be large in mirth; anon we'll drink a measure   11
The table round. [*He goes to the Murderer.*]
    There's blood upon thy face.
MURDERER 'Tis Banquo's, then.
MACBETH
'Tis better thee without than he within.   14
Is he dispatched?
MURDERER
My lord, his throat is cut. That I did for him.
MACBETH Thou art the best o' the cutthroats.
Yet he's good that did the like for Fleance;
If thou didst it, thou art the nonpareil.   19
MURDERER Most royal sir, Fleance is scaped.
MACBETH
Then comes my fit again. I had else been perfect,
Whole as the marble, founded as the rock,   22
As broad and general as the casing air.   23
But now I am cabined, cribbed, confined, bound in   24
To saucy doubts and fears. But Banquo's safe?   25

28 s.d. Exeunt (Presumably, the murderers drag the body of Banquo offstage as they go.)
3.4. Location: A room of state in the palace.
1 degrees ranks (as a determinant of seating) **1–2 At . . . last** once for all **3 mingle with society** i.e., leave the chair of state and circulate among the guests **5 keeps her state** remains in her canopied chair of state. **in best time** when it is most appropriate **6 require her welcome** call upon her to give the welcome **9 encounter** respond to **10 even** full, with equal numbers on both sides **11 large** liberal, free. **measure** i.e., cup filled to the brim for a toast **14 'Tis . . . within** it is better for you to have his blood on you than he to have it within him **19 the nonpareil** without equal **22 founded** firmly established **23 broad and general** unconfined. **casing** encasing, enveloping **24 cribbed** shut in **25 saucy** sharp, impudent, importunate

MURDERER
Ay, my good lord. Safe in a ditch he bides,
With twenty trenchèd gashes on his head,
The least a death to nature.
MACBETH   Thanks for that.
There the grown serpent lies; the worm that's fled   29
Hath nature that in time will venom breed,
No teeth for th' present. Get thee gone. Tomorrow
We'll hear ourselves again.   *Exit Murderer.*
LADY MACBETH   My royal lord,   32
You do not give the cheer. The feast is sold   33
That is not often vouched, while 'tis a-making,   34
'Tis given with welcome. To feed were best at home; 35
From thence, the sauce to meat is ceremony;   36
Meeting were bare without it.   37

    *Enter the Ghost of Banquo, and sits in Macbeth's
    place.*

MACBETH   Sweet remembrancer!
Now, good digestion wait on appetite,   38
And health on both!
LENNOX   May 't please Your Highness sit?
MACBETH
Here had we now our country's honor roofed   40
Were the graced person of our Banquo present,
Who may I rather challenge for unkindness   42
Than pity for mischance.
ROSS   His absence, sir,
Lays blame upon his promise. Please 't Your
    Highness
To grace us with your royal company?
MACBETH [*seeing his place occupied*]
The table's full.
LENNOX   Here is a place reserved, sir.
MACBETH Where?
LENNOX
Here, my good lord. What is 't that moves Your
    Highness?
MACBETH
Which of you have done this?
LORDS   What, my good lord?
MACBETH
Thou canst not say I did it. Never shake
Thy gory locks at me.
ROSS
Gentlemen, rise. His Highness is not well.
                              [*They start to rise.*]
LADY MACBETH
Sit, worthy friends. My lord is often thus,
And hath been from his youth. Pray you, keep seat.

29 worm small serpent **32 hear ourselves** confer **33 give the cheer** welcome your guests **33–35 is sold . . . welcome** seems grudgingly given, as if in return for money, unless it is often accompanied with assurances of welcome while it is in progress **35 To feed . . . home** mere eating is best done at home, dining in company. **meat** food **36 From thence** away from home **37 Meeting were bare** gatherings of friends would be unadorned **38 wait on** attend **40 roofed** under one roof **42 Who may I** whom I hope I may. **challenge for** reprove for

The fit is momentary; upon a thought   55
He will again be well. If much you note him
You shall offend him and extend his passion.   57
Feed, and regard him not.—[*She confers apart with
Macbeth.*] Are you a man?

MACBETH
Ay, and a bold one, that dare look on that
Which might appall the devil.

LADY MACBETH   O, proper stuff!   60
This is the very painting of your fear.
This is the air-drawn dagger which, you said,   62
Led you to Duncan. O, these flaws and starts,   63
Impostors to true fear, would well become   64
A woman's story at a winter's fire,
Authorized by her grandam. Shame itself!   66
Why do you make such faces? When all's done,
You look but on a stool.

MACBETH   Prithee, see there!
Behold, look! Lo, how say you?
Why, what care I? If thou canst nod, speak too.
If charnel houses and our graves must send   71
Those that we bury back, our monuments   72
Shall be the maws of kites.   [*Exit Ghost.*] 73

LADY MACBETH   What, quite unmanned in folly?

MACBETH
If I stand here, I saw him.

LADY MACBETH   Fie, for shame!

MACBETH
Blood hath been shed ere now, i' th' olden time,
Ere humane statute purged the gentle weal;   77
Ay, and since too, murders have been performed
Too terrible for the ear. The time has been
That, when the brains were out, the man would die,
And there an end; but now they rise again
With twenty mortal murders on their crowns,   82
And push us from our stools. This is more strange   83
Than such a murder is.

LADY MACBETH   My worthy lord,
Your noble friends do lack you.

MACBETH   I do forget.
Do not muse at me, my most worthy friends;
I have a strange infirmity, which is nothing
To those that know me. Come, love and health
   to all!
Then I'll sit down. Give me some wine. Fill full.
                        [*He is given wine.*]

        Enter Ghost.

I drink to the general joy o' th' whole table,
And to our dear friend Banquo, whom we miss.
Would he were here! To all, and him, we thirst,   92
And all to all.

LORDS   Our duties and the pledge.   93
                        [*They drink.*]

MACBETH [*seeing the Ghost*]
Avaunt, and quit my sight! Let the earth hide thee!
Thy bones are marrowless, thy blood is cold;
Thou hast no speculation in those eyes   96
Which thou dost glare with!

LADY MACBETH   Think of this, good peers,
But as a thing of custom. 'Tis no other;
Only it spoils the pleasure of the time.

MACBETH   What man dare, I dare.
Approach thou like the rugged Russian bear,
The armed rhinoceros, or th' Hyrcan tiger;   102
Take any shape but that, and my firm nerves   103
Shall never tremble. Or be alive again
And dare me to the desert with thy sword.   105
If trembling I inhabit then, protest me   106
The baby of a girl. Hence, horrible shadow!   107
Unreal mockery, hence! [*Exit Ghost.*] Why, so;
   being gone,
I am a man again. Pray you, sit still.

LADY MACBETH
You have displaced the mirth, broke the good
   meeting
With most admired disorder.

MACBETH   Can such things be,   111
And overcome us like a summer's cloud,   112
Without our special wonder? You make me strange   113
Even to the disposition that I owe,   114
When now I think you can behold such sights
And keep the natural ruby of your cheeks
When mine is blanched with fear.

ROSS   What sights, my lord?

LADY MACBETH
I pray you, speak not. He grows worse and worse;
Question enrages him. At once, good night.   119
Stand not upon the order of your going,   120
But go at once.

LENNOX   Good night, and better health   121
Attend His Majesty!

LADY MACBETH   A kind good night to all!
                Exeunt Lords [and attendants].

MACBETH
It will have blood, they say; blood will have blood.

55 upon a thought in a moment   57 offend him make him worse.
extend prolong   60 O, proper stuff O nonsense   62 air-drawn made
of thin air, or floating disembodied in space   63 flaws gusts, outbursts   64 to compared with.   become befit   66 Authorized by told
on the authority of   71 charnel houses depositories for bones or bodies   72–73 our . . . kites i.e., we will have to leave the unburied
bodies to scavenging birds of prey   77 Ere . . . weal before the institution of law cleansed the commonwealth of violence and made it
gentle.   humane (This spelling, interchangeable with human, carries
both meanings: "appertaining to humankind" and "befitting humanity.")   82 mortal murders deadly wounds.   crowns heads   83 push
. . . stools usurp our places at feasts (with a suggestion of usurpation
of the throne)

92 thirst desire to drink   93 all to all all good wishes to all, or, let all
drink to everyone else.   Our . . . pledge in drinking the toast you
just proposed, we offer our homage   96 speculation power of sight
102 armed armor-plated.   Hyrcan of Hyrcania, in ancient times a region near the Caspian Sea   103 nerves sinews   105 the desert some
solitary place   106 If . . . then i.e., if then I tremble.   protest proclaim   107 The baby of a girl a baby girl, or, girl's doll   111 admired wondered at.   disorder lack of self-control   112 overcome
come over   113–114 You make . . . owe you cause me to feel I do
not know my own nature (which I had presumed to be that of a brave
man)   119 Question talk.   At once to you all; now   120 Stand . . .
going i.e., do not take the time to leave in ceremonious order of rank,
as you entered   121 at once all together and now

Stones have been known to move, and trees to
   speak;   124
Augurs and understood relations have   125
By maggotpies and choughs and rooks brought
   forth   126
The secret'st man of blood. What is the night?   127

LADY MACBETH
Almost at odds with morning, which is which.

MACBETH
How sayst thou, that Macduff denies his person   129
At our great bidding?

LADY MACBETH   Did you send to him, sir?

MACBETH
I hear it by the way; but I will send.   131
There's not a one of them but in his house
I keep a servant fee'd. I will tomorrow—   133
And betimes I will—to the Weird Sisters.   134
More shall they speak, for now I am bent to know   135
By the worst means the worst. For mine own good
All causes shall give way. I am in blood   137
Stepped in so far that, should I wade no more,   138
Returning were as tedious as go o'er.   139
Strange things I have in head, that will to hand,
Which must be acted ere they may be scanned.   141

LADY MACBETH
You lack the season of all natures, sleep.   142

MACBETH
Come, we'll to sleep. My strange and self-abuse   143
Is the initiate fear that wants hard use.   144
We are yet but young in deed.   *Exeunt.*

❧

3.5   *Thunder. Enter the three Witches, meeting Hecate.*

FIRST WITCH
Why, how now, Hecate? You look angerly.   1

HECATE
Have I not reason, beldams as you are?   2
Saucy and overbold, how did you dare
To trade and traffic with Macbeth
In riddles and affairs of death,
And I, the mistress of your charms,
The close contriver of all harms,   7
Was never called to bear my part

Or show the glory of our art?
And, which is worse, all you have done
Hath been but for a wayward son,
Spiteful and wrathful, who, as others do,
Loves for his own ends, not for you.
But make amends now. Get you gone,
And at the pit of Acheron   15
Meet me i' the morning. Thither he
Will come to know his destiny.
Your vessels and your spells provide,
Your charms and everything beside.
I am for th' air. This night I'll spend
Unto a dismal and a fatal end.   21
Great business must be wrought ere noon.
Upon the corner of the moon
There hangs a vaporous drop profound;   24
I'll catch it ere it come to ground,
And that, distilled by magic sleights,
Shall raise such artificial sprites   27
As by the strength of their illusion
Shall draw him on to his confusion.   29
He shall spurn fate, scorn death, and bear
His hopes 'bove wisdom, grace, and fear.
And you all know, security   32
Is mortals' chiefest enemy.   *Music and a song.*
Hark! I am called. My little spirit, see,
Sits in a foggy cloud and stays for me.   *[Exit.]* 35
     Sing within, "Come away, come away," etc.

FIRST WITCH
Come, let's make haste. She'll soon be back again.
                                 Exeunt.

❧

3.6   *Enter Lennox and another Lord.*

LENNOX
My former speeches have but hit your thoughts,   1
Which can interpret farther. Only I say   2
Things have been strangely borne. The gracious
   Duncan   3
Was pitied of Macbeth; marry, he was dead.   4
And the right valiant Banquo walked too late,
Whom you may say, if 't please you, Fleance killed,
For Fleance fled. Men must not walk too late.
Who cannot want the thought how monstrous   8
It was for Malcolm and for Donalbain
To kill their gracious father? Damnèd fact!   10
How it did grieve Macbeth! Did he not straight   11

---

124 **Stones . . . speak** i.e., even inanimate nature speaks in such a way as to reveal the unnatural act of murder 125 **Augurs** prophecies. **understood relations** reports able to be interpreted or understood, or the hidden ties that link the parts of nature to one another 126 **By . . . choughs** by means of magpies and jackdaws. **brought forth** revealed 127 **man of blood** murderer. **the night** i.e., the time of night 129 **How sayst thou** what do you say to the fact 131 **by the way** indirectly 133 **fee'd** i.e., paid to spy 134 **betimes** (1) early (2) while there is still time 135 **bent** determined 137 **All causes** all other considerations 138 **should . . . more** even if I were to wade no farther 139 **were** would be. **go** going 141 **acted . . . scanned** put into performance even before there is time to scrutinize them 142 **season** preservative 143 **strange and self-abuse** strange self-delusion 144 **initiate fear** fear experienced by a novice. **wants hard use** lacks toughening experience
3.5. Location: A heath. (This scene is probably by another author.)
1 angerly angrily, angry **2 beldams** hags **7 close** secret

15 **Acheron** the river of sorrows in Hades; here, hell itself 21 **dismal** disastrous, ill-omened 24 **profound** i.e., heavily pendent, ready to drop off 27 **artificial sprites** spirits produced by magical arts 29 **confusion** ruin 32 **security** overconfidence 35 **s.d. Come away** etc. (The song occurs in Thomas Middleton's *The Witch*.)
3.6. Location: Somewhere in Scotland.
1–2 My . . . farther what I've just said has coincided with your own thought. I needn't say more; you can surmise the rest 3 **borne** carried on 4 **of** by. **marry . . . dead** i.e., to be sure, this pity occurred after Duncan died, not before 8 **cannot . . . thought** can help thinking 10 **fact** deed, crime 11 **straight** straightway, at once

In pious rage the two delinquents tear   12
That were the slaves of drink and thralls of sleep?   13
Was not that nobly done? Ay, and wisely too;
For 'twould have angered any heart alive
To hear the men deny 't. So that I say
He has borne all things well; and I do think   17
That had he Duncan's sons under his key—
As, an 't please heaven, he shall not—they should
    find   19
What 'twere to kill a father. So should Fleance.
But peace! For from broad words, and 'cause he
    failed   21
His presence at the tyrant's feast, I hear   22
Macduff lives in disgrace. Sir, can you tell
Where he bestows himself?
LORD   The son of Duncan,   24
From whom this tyrant holds the due of birth,   25
Lives in the English court, and is received
Of the most pious Edward with such grace   27
That the malevolence of fortune nothing
Takes from his high respect. Thither Macduff   29
Is gone to pray the holy king, upon his aid,   30
To wake Northumberland and warlike Siward,   31
That by the help of these—with Him above
To ratify the work—we may again
Give to our tables meat, sleep to our nights,   34
Free from our feasts and banquets bloody knives,   35
Do faithful homage, and receive free honors—   36
All which we pine for now. And this report
Hath so exasperate the King that he   38
Prepares for some attempt of war.
LENNOX   Sent he to Macduff?
LORD
He did; and with an absolute "Sir, not I,"   41
The cloudy messenger turns me his back   42
And hums, as who should say, "You'll rue the time   43
That clogs me with this answer."
LENNOX   And that well might   44
Advise him to a caution, t' hold what distance   45
His wisdom can provide. Some holy angel   46
Fly to the court of England and unfold
His message ere he come, that a swift blessing

May soon return to this our suffering country   49
Under a hand accursed!   50
LORD   I'll send my prayers with him.   *Exeunt.*

❦

4.1   [*A cauldron.*] *Thunder. Enter the three Witches.*

FIRST WITCH
Thrice the brinded cat hath mewed.   1
SECOND WITCH
Thrice, and once the hedgepig whined.   2
THIRD WITCH
Harpier cries. 'Tis time, 'tis time!   3
FIRST WITCH
Round about the cauldron go;
In the poisoned entrails throw.
Toad, that under cold stone
Days and nights has thirty-one   7
Sweltered venom, sleeping got,   8
Boil thou first i' the charmèd pot.
ALL [*as they dance round the cauldron*]
Double, double, toil and trouble;
Fire burn, and cauldron bubble.
SECOND WITCH
Fillet of a fenny snake,   12
In the cauldron boil and bake;
Eye of newt and toe of frog,
Wool of bat and tongue of dog,
Adder's fork and blindworm's sting,   16
Lizard's leg and owlet's wing,
For a charm of powerful trouble,
Like a hell-broth boil and bubble.
ALL
Double, double, toil and trouble;
Fire burn, and cauldron bubble.
THIRD WITCH
Scale of dragon, tooth of wolf,
Witches' mummy, maw and gulf   23
Of the ravined salt-sea shark,   24
Root of hemlock digged i' the dark,
Liver of blaspheming Jew,
Gall of goat, and slips of yew   27
Slivered in the moon's eclipse,   28
Nose of Turk and Tartar's lips,
Finger of birth-strangled babe

12 pious holy, loyal, sonlike **13 thralls** slaves **17 borne all things well** managed everything cleverly **19 an 't** if it. **should** would be sure to **21 from broad words** on account of plain speech **22 His presence** i.e., to be present **24 bestows himself** is quartered, has taken refuge **25 holds . . . birth** withholds the birthright (i.e., the Scottish crown) **27 Of** by. **Edward** Edward the Confessor, King of England **29 his high respect** the high respect paid to him. (Being out of fortune has not lessened the dignity with which Malcolm is received in England.) **30 upon his aid** in aid of Malcolm **31 wake Northumberland** rouse the people of Northumberland **34 meat** food **35 Free . . . banquets** free our feasts and banquets from **36 free** freely bestowed, or, pertaining to freemen **38 exasperate the King** exasperated Macbeth **41 with . . . I** i.e., when Macduff answered the messenger curtly with a refusal **42 cloudy** louring, scowling. **turns me** i.e., turns. (*Me* is used colloquially for emphasis.) **43 hums . . . say** says "umph!" as if to say **44 clogs** encumbers, loads **45–46 Advise . . . provide** warn him (Macduff) to keep what safe distance he can (from Macbeth)

49–50 suffering country Under country suffering under
4.1. Location: A cavern (see 3.5.15). In the middle, a boiling cauldron (provided presumably by means of the trapdoor; see 4.1.106. The trapdoor must also be used in this scene for the apparitions.)
1 brinded marked by streaks (as by fire), brindled **2 hedgepig** hedgehog **3 Harpier** (The name of a familiar spirit; probably derived from *harpy*.) **cries** i.e., gives the signal to begin **7–8 Days . . . got** for thirty-one days and nights has exuded venom formed during sleep **12 Fillet** slice. **fenny** inhabiting fens or swamps **16 fork** forked tongue. **blindworm** slowworm, a harmless burrowing lizard **23 mummy** mummified flesh made into a magical potion. **maw and gulf** gullet and stomach **24 ravined** ravenous, or glutted with prey (?) **27 Gall** the secretion of the liver, bile. **slips** cuttings for grafting or planting. **yew** (A tree often planted in churchyards and associated with mourning.) **28 Slivered** broken off (as a branch)

Ditch-delivered by a drab,   31
Make the gruel thick and slab.   32
Add thereto a tiger's chaudron   33
For th' ingredience of our cauldron.   34

ALL
Double, double, toil and trouble;
Fire burn, and cauldron bubble.

SECOND WITCH
Cool it with a baboon's blood,
Then the charm is firm and good.   38

Enter Hecate to the other three Witches.

HECATE
O, well done! I commend your pains,   39
And everyone shall share i' the gains.
And now about the cauldron sing
Like elves and fairies in a ring,
Enchanting all that you put in.   43
                    Music and a song: "Black spirits," etc.
                                               [*Exit Hecate.*]

SECOND WITCH
By the pricking of my thumbs,
Something wicked this way comes.
         Open, locks,
         Whoever knocks!

Enter Macbeth.

MACBETH
How now, you secret, black, and midnight hags?   48
What is 't you do?
ALL   A deed without a name.
MACBETH
I conjure you, by that which you profess,
Howe'er you come to know it, answer me.
Though you untie the winds and let them fight
Against the churches, though the yeasty waves   53
Confound and swallow navigation up,   54
Though bladed corn be lodged and trees blown
   down,   55
Though castles topple on their warders' heads,
Though palaces and pyramids do slope   57
Their heads to their foundations, though the
   treasure
Of nature's germens tumble all together,   59
Even till destruction sicken, answer me   60
To what I ask you.
FIRST WITCH   Speak.
SECOND WITCH   Demand.
THIRD WITCH   We'll answer.

FIRST WITCH   31
Say if thou'dst rather hear it from our mouths
Or from our masters?
MACBETH   Call 'em. Let me see 'em.
FIRST WITCH
Pour in sow's blood, that hath eaten
Her nine farrow; grease that's sweaten   65
From the murderer's gibbet throw   66
Into the flame.
ALL   Come high or low,   67
Thyself and office deftly show!   68

Thunder. First Apparition, an armed Head.

MACBETH
Tell me, thou unknown power—
FIRST WITCH   He knows thy thought.
Hear his speech, but say thou naught.
FIRST APPARITION
Macbeth! Macbeth! Macbeth! Beware Macduff,
Beware the Thane of Fife. Dismiss me. Enough.   72
                                          He descends.
MACBETH
Whate'er thou art, for thy good caution, thanks;
Thou hast harped my fear aright. But one word
   more—   74
FIRST WITCH
He will not be commanded. Here's another,
More potent than the first.   76

Thunder. Second Apparition, a bloody Child.

SECOND APPARITION   Macbeth! Macbeth! Macbeth!
MACBETH   Had I three ears, I'd hear thee.
SECOND APPARITION
Be bloody, bold, and resolute; laugh to scorn
The power of man, for none of woman born
Shall harm Macbeth.   *Descends.*
MACBETH
Then live, Macduff; what need I fear of thee?
But yet I'll make assurance double sure,
And take a bond of fate. Thou shalt not live,   84
That I may tell pale-hearted fear it lies,
And sleep in spite of thunder.   86

*Thunder. Third Apparition, a Child crowned, with
a tree in his hand.*

                              What is this
That rises like the issue of a king   87

31 **Ditch . . . drab** born in a ditch of a harlot   32 **slab** viscous
33 **chaudron** entrails   34 **ingredience** contents of a mixture   38 **s.d.
other** (Said because Hecate is a witch, too, not because more witches
enter.)   **39–43 O . . . in** (These lines are universally regarded as
non-Shakespearean.)   43 **s.d. Black spirits etc.** (This song is found in
Middleton's *The Witch*.)   48 **black** i.e., dealing in black magic
53 **yeasty** foamy   54 **Confound** destroy   55 **bladed corn** grain that is
enclosed in the blade, not yet in full ear.   **lodged** thrown down, laid
flat   57 **slope** bend   59 **nature's germens** seed or elements from
which all nature operates   60 **sicken** be surfeited, grow faint with
horror and nausea at its own excess

65 **nine farrow** litter of nine.   **sweaten** sweated   66 **gibbet** gallows
67 **high or low** of the upper or lower air, from under the earth or in
hell; or, of whatever rank   68 **office** function.   **s.d. armed Head**
(Perhaps symbolizes the head of Macbeth cut off by Macduff and presented by him to Malcolm, or else the head of Macduff, armed in rebellion against Macbeth.)   72 **s.d. He descends** (i.e., by means of
the trapdoor)   74 **harped** hit, touched (as in touching a harp to make
it sound)   76 **s.d. bloody Child** (Symbolizes Macduff untimely ripped
from his mother's womb; see 5.8.15–16.)   84 **take a bond of** get a
guarantee from (i.e., by killing Macduff, to make doubly sure he can
do no harm)   86 **s.d. Child . . . hand** (Symbolizes Malcolm, the royal
child; the tree anticipates the cutting of boughs in Birnam Wood,
5.4.)   87 **like** in the likeness of

And wears upon his baby brow the round   88
And top of sovereignty?
ALL   Listen, but speak not to 't.   89
THIRD APPARITION
Be lion-mettled, proud, and take no care
Who chafes, who frets, or where conspirers are.
Macbeth shall never vanquished be until
Great Birnam Wood to high Dunsinane Hill
Shall come against him.   *Descends.*
MACBETH   That will never be.
Who can impress the forest, bid the tree   95
Unfix his earthbound root? Sweet bodements, good!   96
Rebellious dead, rise never till the wood   97
Of Birnam rise, and our high-placed Macbeth
Shall live the lease of nature, pay his breath   99
To time and mortal custom. Yet my heart   100
Throbs to know one thing. Tell me, if your art
Can tell so much: shall Banquo's issue ever
Reign in this kingdom?
ALL   Seek to know no more.
MACBETH
I will be satisfied. Deny me this,
And an eternal curse fall on you! Let me know.
                  [The cauldron descends.] Hautboys.
Why sinks that cauldron? And what noise is this?   106
FIRST WITCH   Show!
SECOND WITCH   Show!
THIRD WITCH   Show!
ALL
Show his eyes, and grieve his heart;
Come like shadows, so depart!   111

        A show of eight Kings and Banquo last; [the eighth
        King] with a glass in his hand.

MACBETH
Thou art too like the spirit of Banquo. Down!
Thy crown does sear mine eyeballs. And thy hair,
Thou other gold-bound brow, is like the first.   114
A third is like the former. Filthy hags,
Why do you show me this? A fourth? Start, eyes!   116
What, will the line stretch out to th' crack of doom?   117
Another yet? A seventh? I'll see no more.
And yet the eighth appears, who bears a glass
Which shows me many more; and some I see
That twofold balls and treble scepters carry.   121
Horrible sight! Now I see 'tis true,
For the blood-boltered Banquo smiles upon me   123

And points at them for his. *[The apparitions vanish.]*
    What, is this so?   124
FIRST WITCH
Ay, sir, all this is so. But why   125
Stands Macbeth thus amazedly?   126
Come, sisters, cheer we up his sprites   127
And show the best of our delights.
I'll charm the air to give a sound,
While you perform your antic round,   130
That this great king may kindly say
Our duties did his welcome pay.   132
        Music. The Witches dance, and vanish.
MACBETH
Where are they? Gone? Let this pernicious hour
Stand aye accursèd in the calendar!
Come in, without there!

        Enter Lennox.

LENNOX   What's Your Grace's will?
MACBETH
Saw you the Weird Sisters?
LENNOX   No, my lord.
MACBETH
Came they not by you?
LENNOX   No, indeed, my lord.
MACBETH
Infected be the air whereon they ride,
And damned all those that trust them! I did hear
The galloping of horse. Who was 't came by?   140
LENNOX
'Tis two or three, my lord, that bring you word
Macduff is fled to England.
MACBETH   Fled to England!
LENNOX
Ay, my good lord.
MACBETH *[aside]*
Time, thou anticipat'st my dread exploits.   144
The flighty purpose never is o'ertook   145
Unless the deed go with it. From this moment   146
The very firstlings of my heart shall be   147
The firstlings of my hand. And even now,   148
To crown my thoughts with acts, be it thought and
    done:
The castle of Macduff I will surprise,   150
Seize upon Fife, give to th' edge o' the sword
His wife, his babes, and all unfortunate souls
That trace him in his line. No boasting like a fool;   153
This deed I'll do before this purpose cool.

88–89 round And top crown   **95 impress** press into service, like soldiers   **96 bodements** prophecies   **97 Rebellious dead** i.e., Banquo
and his lineage (?)   **99 lease of nature** natural period, full life span
100 mortal custom death, the common lot of humanity   **106 noise**
music   **111 s.d. eight Kings** (Banquo was the supposed ancestor of
the Stuart dynasty, ending in King James VI of Scotland and James I of
England, the *eighth King* here.)   **glass** (magic) mirror (also in line
119)   **114 other** i.e., second   **116 Start** bulge from their sockets
117 th' crack of doom the thunder-peal of Doomsday at the end of
time   **121 twofold balls** (A probable reference to the double coronation of James at Scone and Westminster, as King of England and Scotland.)   **treble scepters** (Probably refers to James' assumed title as
King of Great Britain, France, and Ireland.)   **123 blood-boltered** having his hair matted with blood

124 for his as his descendants   **125–132 Ay . . . pay** (These lines
are assumed to have been written by someone other than
Shakespeare.)   **126 amazedly** stunned   **127 sprites** spirits   **130 antic
round** grotesque dance in a circle   **132 pay** repay   **140 horse** horses
144 thou anticipat'st you forestall (since, by allowing time to pass
without my acting, I have lost an opportunity)   **145 flighty** fleeting
146 Unless . . . it unless the execution of the deed accompanies the
conception of it immediately   **147–148 The very . . . hand** the firstborn promptings of my heart will be the purposes I will first act upon
150 surprise seize without warning   **153 trace . . . line** follow him in
the line of inheritance

But no more sights!—Where are these gentlemen?
Come, bring me where they are.   *Exeunt.*

❖

4.2   *Enter Macduff's Wife, her Son, and Ross.*

LADY MACDUFF
    What had he done to make him fly the land?
ROSS
    You must have patience, madam.
LADY MACDUFF   He had none.
    His flight was madness. When our actions do not,   3
    Our fears do make us traitors.
ROSS   You know not   4
    Whether it was his wisdom or his fear.
LADY MACDUFF
    Wisdom? To leave his wife, to leave his babes,
    His mansion, and his titles in a place   7
    From whence himself does fly? He loves us not,
    He wants the natural touch; for the poor wren,   9
    The most diminutive of birds, will fight,
    Her young ones in her nest, against the owl.   11
    All is the fear and nothing is the love,
    As little is the wisdom, where the flight
    So runs against all reason.
ROSS   My dearest coz,   14
    I pray you, school yourself. But, for your husband,   15
    He is noble, wise, judicious, and best knows
    The fits o' the season. I dare not speak much further,   17
    But cruel are the times when we are traitors   18
    And do not know ourselves, when we hold rumor   19
    From what we fear, yet know not what we fear,   20
    But float upon a wild and violent sea
    Each way and none. I take my leave of you;   22
    Shall not be long but I'll be here again.   23
    Things at the worst will cease, or else climb upward
    To what they were before.—My pretty cousin,
    Blessing upon you!
LADY MACDUFF
    Fathered he is, and yet he's fatherless.
ROSS
    I am so much a fool, should I stay longer
    It would be my disgrace and your discomfort.   29
    I take my leave at once.   *Exit Ross.*

LADY MACDUFF   Sirrah, your father's dead;   31
    And what will you do now? How will you live?
SON
    As birds do, Mother.
LADY MACDUFF   What, with worms and flies?
SON
    With what I get, I mean; and so do they.
LADY MACDUFF   Poor bird! Thou'dst never fear
    The net nor lime, the pitfall nor the gin.   36
SON
    Why should I, Mother? Poor birds they are not
        set for.   37
    My father is not dead, for all your saying.
LADY MACDUFF
    Yes, he is dead. How wilt thou do for a father?
SON   Nay, how will you do for a husband?
LADY MACDUFF   Why, I can buy me twenty at any
    market.
SON   Then you'll buy 'em to sell again.
LADY MACDUFF   Thou speak'st with all thy wit,
    And yet, i' faith, with wit enough for thee.
SON   Was my father a traitor, Mother?
LADY MACDUFF   Ay, that he was.
SON   What is a traitor?
LADY MACDUFF   Why, one that swears and lies.   49
SON   And be all traitors that do so?
LADY MACDUFF
    Every one that does so is a traitor,
    And must be hanged.
SON
    And must they all be hanged that swear and lie?
LADY MACDUFF   Every one.
SON   Who must hang them?
LADY MACDUFF   Why, the honest men.
SON   Then the liars and swearers are fools, for there are
    liars and swearers enough to beat the honest men and
    hang up them.
LADY MACDUFF   Now, God help thee, poor monkey!
    But how wilt thou do for a father?
SON   If he were dead, you'd weep for him; if you would
    not, it were a good sign that I should quickly have a
    new father.
LADY MACDUFF   Poor prattler, how thou talk'st!

        Enter a Messenger.

MESSENGER
    Bless you, fair dame! I am not to you known,
    Though in your state of honor I am perfect.   67
    I doubt some danger does approach you nearly.   68
    If you will take a homely man's advice,   69
    Be not found here. Hence with your little ones!
    To fright you thus, methinks, I am too savage;

4.2. Location: Fife. Macduff's castle.
3–4 When . . . traitors even when we have committed no treasonous act, our fearful responses make us look guilty (since fleeing to the English court is in itself treasonous)   **7 titles** possessions to which he has title   **9 wants . . . touch** lacks the natural instinct (to protect one's family)   **11 Her . . . nest** when her young ones are in the nest   **14 coz** kinswoman   **15 school** control.   **for** as for   **17 fits o' the season** violent convulsions of the time   **18–19 are traitors . . . ourselves** are accused of treason without recognizing ourselves as such, or are alienated from one another by a climate of fear and suspected treason   **19–20 hold . . . From what we fear** believe every fearful rumor on the basis of what we fear   **22 Each . . . none** being tossed this way and that without any real progress   **23 Shall** it shall.   **but** before   **29 It . . . discomfort** I should disgrace my manhood by weeping and cause you distress

31 Sirrah (Here, an affectionate form of address to a child.)   **36 lime** birdlime (a sticky substance put on branches to snare birds).   **gin** snare   **37 Poor . . . for** i.e., traps are not set for *poor* birds, as you call me   **49 swears and lies** swears an oath and breaks it (though the boy may understand *swears* to mean ''uses profanity'')   **67 in . . . honor** with your honorable state.   **perfect** perfectly acquainted   **68 doubt** fear   **69 homely** plain

To do worse to you were fell cruelty,   72
Which is too nigh your person. Heaven preserve
  you!   73
I dare abide no longer.   *Exit Messenger.*

LADY MACDUFF   Whither should I fly?
I have done no harm. But I remember now
I am in this earthly world, where to do harm
Is often laudable, to do good sometimes
Accounted dangerous folly. Why then, alas,
Do I put up that womanly defense
To say I have done no harm?

          Enter Murderers.

          What are these faces?
FIRST MURDERER   Where is your husband?
LADY MACDUFF
I hope in no place so unsanctified
Where such as thou mayst find him.
FIRST MURDERER   He's a traitor.
SON
Thou liest, thou shag-haired villain!
FIRST MURDERER   What, you egg?
          [*He stabs him.*]
Young fry of treachery!
SON   He has killed me, Mother.   85
Run away, I pray you!   [*He dies.*]
          Exit [*Lady Macduff*] *crying "Murder!"*
          [*followed by the Murderers with the Son's body*].

          ❧

4.3   *Enter Malcolm and Macduff.*

MALCOLM
Let us seek out some desolate shade, and there
Weep our sad bosoms empty.
MACDUFF   Let us rather
Hold fast the mortal sword, and like good men   3
Bestride our downfall'n birthdom. Each new morn   4
New widows howl, new orphans cry, new sorrows
Strike heaven on the face, that it resounds   6
As if it felt with Scotland and yelled out   7
Like syllable of dolor.
MALCOLM   What I believe, I'll wail;   8
What know, believe; and what I can redress,   9
As I shall find the time to friend, I will.   10
What you have spoke it may be so, perchance.
This tyrant, whose sole name blisters our tongues,   12
Was once thought honest. You have loved him well;

He hath not touched you yet. I am young; but
  something   14
You may deserve of him through me, and wisdom   15
To offer up a weak, poor, innocent lamb
T' appease an angry god.
MACDUFF   I am not treacherous.
MALCOLM   But Macbeth is.
A good and virtuous nature may recoil   20
In an imperial charge. But I shall crave your pardon.   21
That which you are my thoughts cannot transpose;   22
Angels are bright still, though the brightest fell.   23
Though all things foul would wear the brows of
  grace,   24
Yet grace must still look so.
MACDUFF   I have lost my hopes.   25
MALCOLM
Perchance even there where I did find my doubts.   26
Why in that rawness left you wife and child,   27
Those precious motives, those strong knots of love,   28
Without leave-taking? I pray you,
Let not my jealousies be your dishonors,   30
But mine own safeties. You may be rightly just,   31
Whatever I shall think.
MACDUFF   Bleed, bleed, poor country!
Great tyranny, lay thou thy basis sure,   33
For goodness dare not check thee; wear thou thy
  wrongs,   34
The title is affeered! Fare thee well, lord.   35
I would not be the villain that thou think'st
For the whole space that's in the tyrant's grasp,
And the rich East to boot.
MALCOLM   Be not offended.   38
I speak not as in absolute fear of you.   39
I think our country sinks beneath the yoke;
It weeps, it bleeds, and each new day a gash
Is added to her wounds. I think withal   42
There would be hands uplifted in my right;   43
And here from gracious England have I offer   44

14 He . . . yet i.e., the fact that Macbeth hasn't hurt you yet makes me suspicious of your loyalties.   **young** i.e., inexperienced   **14–15 something . . . me** i.e., you may win favor with Macbeth by delivering me to him   **15 wisdom** i.e., it would be worldly-wise   **20 recoil** give way, fall back (as in the firing of a gun)   **21 In . . . charge** under pressure from royal command. (*Charge* puns on the idea of a quantity of powder and shot for a gun, as in *recoil*.)   **22 That . . . transpose** my suspicious thoughts cannot change you from what you are, cannot make you evil   **23 the brightest** i.e., Lucifer   **24–25 Though . . . so** even though evil puts on the appearance of good so often as to cast that appearance into deep suspicion, yet goodness must go on looking and acting like itself   **25 hopes** i.e., hopes of persuading Malcolm to lead the cause against Macbeth   **26 Perchance even there** i.e., perhaps in that same mistrustful frame of mind.   **doubts** i.e., fears such as that Macduff may covertly be on Macbeth's side   **27 rawness** unprotected condition. (Malcolm suggests that Macduff's leaving his family unprotected could be construed as more evidence of his not having anything to fear from Macbeth.)   **28 motives** persons inspiring you to cherish and protect them; incentives to offer strong protection   **30–31 Let . . . safeties** may it be true that my suspicions of your lack of honor are founded only in my own wariness   **33 basis** foundation   **34 check** rebuke, call to account.   **wear . . . wrongs** continue to enjoy your wrongfully gained powers   **35 affeered** confirmed, certified   **38 to boot** in addition   **39 absolute fear** complete mistrust   **42 withal** in addition   **43 right** cause   **44 England** i.e., the King of England

72 To do worse i.e., actually to harm you.   **fell** savage   **73 Which . . . person** i.e., which savage cruelty is all too near at hand   **85 fry** spawn, progeny
4.3. Location: England. Before King Edward the Confessor's palace.
3 mortal deadly   **4 Bestride** stand over in defense.   **birthdom** native land   **6 that it resounds** so that it echoes   **7–8 As . . . dolor** as if heaven, feeling itself the blow delivered to Scotland, cried out with a similar cry of pain   **8–9 What . . . believe** i.e., what I believe to be amiss in Scotland I will grieve for, and anything I am certain to be true I will believe. (But one must be cautious in these duplicitous times.)   **10 to friend** opportune, congenial   **12 sole** mere

Of goodly thousands. But, for all this,
When I shall tread upon the tyrant's head,
Or wear it on my sword, yet my poor country
Shall have more vices than it had before,
More suffer, and more sundry ways than ever,   49
By him that shall succeed.

MACDUFF   What should he be?   50

MALCOLM
It is myself I mean, in whom I know
All the particulars of vice so grafted   52
That, when they shall be opened, black Macbeth   53
Will seem as pure as snow, and the poor state
Esteem him as a lamb, being compared
With my confineless harms.

MACDUFF   Not in the legions   56
Of horrid hell can come a devil more damned
In evils to top Macbeth.

MALCOLM   I grant him bloody,   58
Luxurious, avaricious, false, deceitful,   59
Sudden, malicious, smacking of every sin   60
That has a name. But there's no bottom, none,
In my voluptuousness. Your wives, your daughters,
Your matrons, and your maids could not fill up
The cistern of my lust, and my desire
All continent impediments would o'erbear   65
That did oppose my will. Better Macbeth   66
Than such an one to reign.

MACDUFF   Boundless intemperance
In nature is a tyranny; it hath been   68
Th' untimely emptying of the happy throne
And fall of many kings. But fear not yet   70
To take upon you what is yours. You may
Convey your pleasures in a spacious plenty,   72
And yet seem cold; the time you may so hoodwink.   73
We have willing dames enough. There cannot be
That vulture in you to devour so many
As will to greatness dedicate themselves,
Finding it so inclined.

MALCOLM   With this there grows
In my most ill-composed affection such   78
A stanchless avarice that, were I king,   79
I should cut off the nobles for their lands,
Desire his jewels and this other's house,   81
And my more-having would be as a sauce
To make me hunger more, that I should forge   83
Quarrels unjust against the good and loyal,
Destroying them for wealth.

MACDUFF   This avarice
Sticks deeper, grows with more pernicious root

Than summer-seeming lust, and it hath been   87
The sword of our slain kings. Yet do not fear;   88
Scotland hath foisons to fill up your will   89
Of your mere own. All these are portable,   90
With other graces weighed.   91

MALCOLM
But I have none. The king-becoming graces,
As justice, verity, temperance, stableness,
Bounty, perseverance, mercy, lowliness,   94
Devotion, patience, courage, fortitude,
I have no relish of them, but abound   96
In the division of each several crime,   97
Acting it many ways. Nay, had I power, I should
Pour the sweet milk of concord into hell,
Uproar the universal peace, confound   100
All unity on earth.

MACDUFF   O Scotland, Scotland!

MALCOLM
If such a one be fit to govern, speak.
I am as I have spoken.

MACDUFF   Fit to govern?
No, not to live. O nation miserable,
With an untitled tyrant bloody-sceptered,   105
When shalt thou see thy wholesome days again,
Since that the truest issue of thy throne
By his own interdiction stands accurst   108
And does blaspheme his breed? Thy royal father   109
Was a most sainted king; the queen that bore thee,
Oft'ner upon her knees than on her feet,
Died every day she lived. Fare thee well.   112
These evils thou repeat'st upon thyself
Hath banished me from Scotland. O my breast,   114
Thy hope ends here!

MALCOLM   Macduff, this noble passion,
Child of integrity, hath from my soul   116
Wiped the black scruples, reconciled my thoughts
To thy good truth and honor. Devilish Macbeth
By many of these trains hath sought to win me   119
Into his power, and modest wisdom plucks me   120
From overcredulous haste. But God above
Deal between thee and me! For even now
I put myself to thy direction and
Unspeak mine own detraction, here abjure   124
The taints and blames I laid upon myself
For strangers to my nature. I am yet   126
Unknown to woman, never was forsworn,   127
Scarcely have coveted what was mine own,
At no time broke my faith, would not betray

---

49 more sundry in more various   50 What . . . be? whom could you
possibly mean?   52 grafted (1) engrafted, indissolubly mixed (2)
grafted like a plant that will then *open* or unfold   53 opened unfolded (like a bud)   56 my confineless harms the boundless injuries I
shall inflict   58 top surpass   59 Luxurious lecherous   60 Sudden violent, passionate   65 continent (1) chaste (2) restraining, containing
66 will lust (also in line 89)   68 nature human nature   70 yet nevertheless   72 Convey manage with secrecy   73 cold chaste.   the time
. . . hoodwink you may thus deceive the age.   hoodwink blindfold
78 ill-composed affection evil disposition   79 stanchless insatiable
81 his one man's.   this other's another's   83 that so that

87 summer-seeming appropriate to youth (and lessening in later years)
88 sword i.e., cause of overthrow   89 foisons resources, plenty
90 Of . . . own out of your own royal estates alone.   portable bearable   91 weighed counterbalanced   94 lowliness humility   96 relish
flavor or trace   97 division subdivisions, various possible forms.
several separate   100 Uproar throw into an uproar   105 untitled
lacking rightful title, usurping   108 interdiction debarring of self
109 does blaspheme his breed defames his breeding, i.e., is a disgrace to his royal lineage   112 Died . . . lived lived a life of daily
mortification   114 breast heart   116 Child of integrity a product of
your integrity of spirit   119 trains plots, artifices   120 modest . . .
me wise prudence holds me back   124 mine own detraction my detraction of myself   126 For as   127 Unknown to woman a virgin

The devil to his fellow, and delight
No less in truth than life. My first false speaking
Was this upon myself. What I am truly   132
Is thine and my poor country's to command—
Whither indeed, before thy here-approach,
Old Siward with ten thousand warlike men,
Already at a point, was setting forth.   136
Now we'll together; and the chance of goodness   137
Be like our warranted quarrel!—Why are you silent?   138

MACDUFF
Such welcome and unwelcome things at once
'Tis hard to reconcile.

Enter a Doctor.

MALCOLM
Well, more anon.—Comes the King forth, I pray
    you?

DOCTOR
Ay, sir. There are a crew of wretched souls
That stay his cure. Their malady convinces   143
The great essay of art; but at his touch—   144
Such sanctity hath heaven given his hand—
They presently amend.

MALCOLM   I thank you, Doctor.   146

Exit [Doctor].

MACDUFF
What's the disease he means?

MALCOLM   'Tis called the evil.   147
A most miraculous work in this good king,
Which often, since my here-remain in England,   149
I have seen him do. How he solicits heaven   150
Himself best knows; but strangely-visited people,   151
All swoll'n and ulcerous, pitiful to the eye,
The mere despair of surgery, he cures,   153
Hanging a golden stamp about their necks   154
Put on with holy prayers; and 'tis spoken,
To the succeeding royalty he leaves   156
The healing benediction. With this strange virtue   157
He hath a heavenly gift of prophecy,
And sundry blessings hang about his throne
That speak him full of grace.

Enter Ross.

MACDUFF   See who comes here.

MALCOLM
My countryman, but yet I know him not.   161

MACDUFF
My ever-gentle cousin, welcome hither.   162

MALCOLM
I know him now. Good God betimes remove   163

The means that makes us strangers!

ROSS   Sir, amen.

MACDUFF
Stands Scotland where it did?

ROSS   Alas, poor country,
Almost afraid to know itself. It cannot
Be called our mother, but our grave; where nothing   167
But who knows nothing is once seen to smile;   168
Where sighs and groans and shrieks that rend the
    air
Are made, not marked; where violent sorrow seems   170
A modern ecstasy. The dead man's knell   171
Is there scarce asked for who, and good men's lives
Expire before the flowers in their caps,   173
Dying or ere they sicken.

MACDUFF   O, relation   174
Too nice, and yet too true!

MALCOLM   What's the newest grief?   175

ROSS
That of an hour's age doth hiss the speaker;   176
Each minute teems a new one.

MACDUFF   How does my wife?   177

ROSS
Why, well.

MACDUFF   And all my children?

ROSS   Well too.   178

MACDUFF
The tyrant has not battered at their peace?

ROSS
No, they were well at peace when I did leave 'em.

MACDUFF
Be not a niggard of your speech. How goes 't?

ROSS
When I came hither to transport the tidings
Which I have heavily borne, there ran a rumor   183
Of many worthy fellows that were out,   184
Which was to my belief witnessed the rather   185
For that I saw the tyrant's power afoot.   186
Now is the time of help. [*To Malcolm.*] Your eye in
    Scotland
Would create soldiers, make our women fight,
To doff their dire distresses.

MALCOLM   Be 't their comfort   189
We are coming thither. Gracious England hath   190
Lent us good Siward and ten thousand men;
An older and a better soldier none   192
That Christendom gives out.

ROSS   Would I could answer   193

132 **upon** against   136 **at a point** prepared   137–138 **the chance
. . . quarrel** may the chance of success be proportionate to the justice
of our cause   143 **stay** wait for.   **convinces** conquers   144 **essay of
art** efforts of medical skill   146 **presently** immediately   147 **evil** i.e.,
scrofula, supposedly cured by the royal touch; James I claimed this
power   149 **here-remain** stay   150 **solicits** prevails by prayer with
151 **strangely-visited** afflicted by strange diseases   153 **mere** utter
154 **stamp** minted coin   156–157 **To . . . benediction** to his royal
successors he bequeathes this healing blessedness   157 **virtue** healing
power   161 **My countryman** (So identified by his dress.)   **know** recognize   162 **gentle** noble   163 **betimes** speedily

167–168 **nothing But who** nobody except a person who   168 **once**
ever   170 **marked** noticed (because they are so common)   171 **modern ecstasy** commonplace emotion   173 **flowers** (Often worn in Elizabethan caps.)   174 **or ere they sicken** before they have had time to
fall ill.   **relation** report   175 **nice** minutely accurate, elaborately
phrased   176 **hiss** cause to be hissed (for repeating stale news)
177 **teems** teems with, yields   178 **well** (Ross quibbles, in his reluctance to tell the bad news, on the saying that "the dead are well,"
i.e., at rest.)   183 **heavily** sadly   184 **Of . . . out** i.e., that many
worthy Scots had taken up arms in rebellion against tyranny
185 **witnessed the rather** made the more believable   186 **For that** because, in that.   **power** army   189 **doff** put off, get rid of   190 **Gracious England** i.e., Edward the Confessor   192 **none** there is none
193 **gives out** tells of, proclaims

This comfort with the like! But I have words
That would be howled out in the desert air, 195
Where hearing should not latch them.

MACDUFF   What concern they? 196
The general cause? Or is it a fee-grief 197
Due to some single breast?

ROSS   No mind that's honest 198
But in it shares some woe, though the main part
Pertains to you alone.

MACDUFF   If it be mine,
Keep it not from me; quickly let me have it.

ROSS
Let not your ears despise my tongue forever,
Which shall possess them with the heaviest sound 203
That ever yet they heard.

MACDUFF   Hum! I guess at it.

ROSS
Your castle is surprised, your wife and babes
Savagely slaughtered. To relate the manner
Were, on the quarry of these murdered deer, 207
To add the death of you.

MALCOLM   Merciful heaven!
What, man, ne'er pull your hat upon your brows; 209
Give sorrow words. The grief that does not speak
Whispers the o'erfraught heart and bids it break. 211

MACDUFF
My children too?

ROSS   Wife, children, servants, all
That could be found.

MACDUFF   And I must be from thence! 213
My wife killed too?

ROSS   I have said.

MALCOLM   Be comforted.
Let's make us medicines of our great revenge
To cure this deadly grief.

MACDUFF
He has no children. All my pretty ones? 217
Did you say all? O hell-kite! All?
What, all my pretty chickens and their dam
At one fell swoop? 220

MALCOLM Dispute it like a man. 221

MACDUFF I shall do so;
But I must also feel it as a man.
I cannot but remember such things were,
That were most precious to me. Did heaven look on
And would not take their part? Sinful Macduff,
They were all struck for thee! Naught that I am, 227
Not for their own demerits, but for mine,

Fell slaughter on their souls. Heaven rest them now!

MALCOLM
Be this the whetstone of your sword. Let grief
Convert to anger; blunt not the heart, enrage it. 231

MACDUFF
O, I could play the woman with mine eyes
And braggart with my tongue! But, gentle heavens,
Cut short all intermission. Front to front 234
Bring thou this fiend of Scotland and myself;
Within my sword's length set him. If he scape, 236
Heaven forgive him too!

MALCOLM   This tune goes manly. 237
Come, go we to the King. Our power is ready; 238
Our lack is nothing but our leave. Macbeth 239
Is ripe for shaking, and the powers above
Put on their instruments. Receive what cheer
you may. 241
The night is long that never finds the day.   *Exeunt.*

❧

5.1 *Enter a Doctor of Physic and a Waiting-
Gentlewoman.*

DOCTOR I have two nights watched with you, but can
perceive no truth in your report. When was it she last
walked?

GENTLEWOMAN Since His Majesty went into the field, I
have seen her rise from her bed, throw her nightgown
upon her, unlock her closet, take forth paper, fold it, 5
write upon 't, read it, afterwards seal it, and again
return to bed; yet all this while in a most fast sleep.

DOCTOR A great perturbation in nature, to receive at
once the benefit of sleep and do the effects of 9
watching! In this slumbery agitation, besides her 10
walking and other actual performances, what, at any
time, have you heard her say?

GENTLEWOMAN That, sir, which I will not report after her.

DOCTOR You may to me, and 'tis most meet you should. 15

GENTLEWOMAN Neither to you nor anyone, having no
witness to confirm my speech.

Enter Lady [Macbeth], with a taper.

Lo you, here she comes! This is her very guise, and,
upon my life, fast asleep. Observe her. Stand close. 19
                              [They stand aside.]

DOCTOR How came she by that light?

GENTLEWOMAN Why, it stood by her. She has light by
her continually. 'Tis her command.

DOCTOR   You see her eyes are open.

GENTLEWOMAN   Ay, but their sense are shut.

DOCTOR   What is it she does now? Look how she rubs her hands.

GENTLEWOMAN   It is an accustomed action with her to seem thus washing her hands. I have known her continue in this a quarter of an hour.

LADY MACBETH   Yet here's a spot.

DOCTOR   Hark, she speaks. I will set down what comes from her, to satisfy my remembrance the more 32 strongly.

LADY MACBETH   Out, damned spot! Out, I say! One—two—why then, 'tis time to do 't. Hell is murky.—Fie, my lord, fie, a soldier, and afeard? What need we fear who knows it, when none can call our power to account? Yet who would have thought the old man to have had so much blood in him?

DOCTOR   Do you mark that?

LADY MACBETH   The Thane of Fife had a wife. Where is she now?—What, will these hands ne'er be clean?—No more o' that, my lord, no more o' that; you mar all with this starting. 44

DOCTOR   Go to, go to. You have known what you 45 should not.

GENTLEWOMAN   She has spoke what she should not, I am sure of that. Heaven knows what she has known.

LADY MACBETH   Here's the smell of the blood still. All the perfumes of Arabia will not sweeten this little hand. O, o, o!

DOCTOR   What a sigh is there! The heart is sorely 52 charged. 53

GENTLEWOMAN   I would not have such a heart in my bosom for the dignity of the whole body. 55

DOCTOR   Well, well, well.

GENTLEWOMAN   Pray God it be, sir. 57

DOCTOR   This disease is beyond my practice. Yet I have known those which have walked in their sleep who have died holily in their beds.

LADY MACBETH   Wash your hands, put on your night-gown; look not so pale! I tell you yet again, Banquo's buried. He cannot come out on 's grave. 63

DOCTOR   Even so?

LADY MACBETH   To bed, to bed! There's knocking at the gate. Come, come, come, come, give me your hand. What's done cannot be undone. To bed, to bed, to bed!   *Exit Lady.*

DOCTOR   Will she go now to bed?

GENTLEWOMAN   Directly.

DOCTOR
Foul whisperings are abroad. Unnatural deeds
Do breed unnatural troubles. Infected minds
To their deaf pillows will discharge their secrets.
More needs she the divine than the physician.
God, God forgive us all! Look after her;

Remove from her the means of all annoyance, 76
And still keep eyes upon her. So, good night. 77
My mind she has mated, and amazed my sight. 78
I think, but dare not speak.

GENTLEWOMAN   Good night, good Doctor.
                                          Exeunt.

❖

5.2   *Drum and colors. Enter Menteith, Caithness, Angus, Lennox, [and] soldiers.*

MENTEITH
The English power is near, led on by Malcolm,
His uncle Siward, and the good Macduff.
Revenges burn in them, for their dear causes 3
Would to the bleeding and the grim alarm 4
Excite the mortified man.

ANGUS   Near Birnam Wood 5
Shall we well meet them; that way are they coming. 6

CAITHNESS
Who knows if Donalbain be with his brother?

LENNOX
For certain, sir, he is not. I have a file 8
Of all the gentry. There is Siward's son,
And many unrough youths that even now 10
Protest their first of manhood.

MENTEITH   What does the tyrant? 11

CAITHNESS
Great Dunsinane he strongly fortifies.
Some say he's mad, others that lesser hate him
Do call it valiant fury; but for certain
He cannot buckle his distempered cause 15
Within the belt of rule.

ANGUS   Now does he feel
His secret murders sticking on his hands;
Now minutely revolts upbraid his faith-breach. 18
Those he commands move only in command, 19
Nothing in love. Now does he feel his title
Hang loose about him, like a giant's robe
Upon a dwarfish thief.

MENTEITH   Who then shall blame
His pestered senses to recoil and start, 23
When all that is within him does condemn
Itself for being there?

CAITHNESS   Well, march we on
To give obedience where 'tis truly owed.
Meet we the med'cine of the sickly weal, 27

32 **satisfy** confirm, support   44 **this starting** these startled movements   45 **Go to** (An exclamation of reproof, directed at Lady Macbeth.)   52–53 **sorely charged** heavily burdened   55 **dignity** worth, value   57 **Pray . . . sir** pray God it will turn out well, as you say, sir (playing on the Doctor's "*Well, well*," i.e., "dear, dear")   63 **on 's** of his

76 **annoyance** i.e., harming herself   77 **still** constantly   78 **mated** bewildered, stupefied
5.2. Location: The country near Dunsinane.
3–5 **their . . . man** their grievous wrongs would awaken even the dead to answer the bloody and grim call to battle   6 **well** no doubt   8 **file** list, roster   10 **unrough** beardless   11 **Protest** assert publicly   15 **distempered** disease-swollen, dropsical   18 **minutely** every minute.   **upbraid** censure.   **faith-breach** violation of all trust and sacred vows   19 **in command** under orders   23 **pestered** troubled, tormented   27 **Meet we . . . weal** i.e., let us join forces with Malcolm, the physician of our sick land

And with him pour we in our country's purge   28
Each drop of us.
LENNOX   Or so much as it needs   29
To dew the sovereign flower and drown the weeds.   30
Make we our march towards Birnam.

Exeunt, marching.

♣

5.3   *Enter Macbeth, Doctor, and attendants.*

MACBETH
Bring me no more reports. Let them fly all!   1
Till Birnam Wood remove to Dunsinane,
I cannot taint with fear. What's the boy Malcolm?   3
Was he not born of woman? The spirits that know
All mortal consequences have pronounced me thus: 5
"Fear not, Macbeth. No man that's born of woman
Shall e'er have power upon thee." Then fly, false
    thanes,
And mingle with the English epicures!   8
The mind I sway by and the heart I bear   9
Shall never sag with doubt nor shake with fear.

Enter Servant.

The devil damn thee black, thou cream-faced loon!   11
Where gott'st thou that goose look?
SERVANT
There is ten thousand—
MACBETH   Geese, villain?
SERVANT   Soldiers, sir.
MACBETH
Go prick thy face and over-red thy fear,   14
Thou lily-livered boy. What soldiers, patch?   15
Death of thy soul! Those linen cheeks of thine   16
Are counselors to fear. What soldiers, whey-face?   17
SERVANT   The English force, so please you.
MACBETH
Take thy face hence. [*Exit Servant.*] Seyton!—I am
    sick at heart
When I behold—Seyton, I say!—This push   20
Will cheer me ever, or disseat me now.   21
I have lived long enough. My way of life   22
Is fall'n into the sere, the yellow leaf,   23

And that which should accompany old age,
As honor, love, obedience, troops of friends,   25
I must not look to have, but in their stead
Curses, not loud but deep, mouth-honor, breath
Which the poor heart would fain deny and dare not.
Seyton!

Enter Seyton.

SEYTON
What's your gracious pleasure?
MACBETH   What news more?
SEYTON
All is confirmed, my lord, which was reported.
MACBETH
I'll fight till from my bones my flesh be hacked.
Give me my armor.
SEYTON   'Tis not needed yet.
MACBETH   I'll put it on.
Send out more horses. Skirr the country round.   36
Hang those that talk of fear. Give me mine armor.
How does your patient, Doctor?
DOCTOR   Not so sick, my lord,
As she is troubled with thick-coming fancies
That keep her from her rest.
MACBETH   Cure her of that.
Canst thou not minister to a mind diseased,
Pluck from the memory a rooted sorrow,
Raze out the written troubles of the brain,   44
And with some sweet oblivious antidote   45
Cleanse the stuffed bosom of that perilous stuff
Which weighs upon the heart?
DOCTOR   Therein the patient
Must minister to himself.
MACBETH
Throw physic to the dogs! I'll none of it.   49
Come, put mine armor on. Give me my staff.   50
                      [*Attendants arm him.*]
Seyton, send out. Doctor, the thanes fly from me.—
Come, sir, dispatch.—If thou couldst, Doctor, cast   52
The water of my land, find her disease,   53
And purge it to a sound and pristine health,
I would applaud thee to the very echo,
That should applaud again.—Pull 't off, I say.—   56
What rhubarb, senna, or what purgative drug   57
Would scour these English hence? Hear'st thou of
    them?   58
DOCTOR
Ay, my good lord. Your royal preparation
Makes us hear something.
MACBETH   Bring it after me.—   60
I will not be afraid of death and bane,

28–29 pour . . . of us i.e., let us shed all our blood as a bloodletting or *purge* of our country **30 dew** bedew, water. **sovereign** (1) royal (2) medically efficacious
5.3. Location: Dunsinane. Macbeth's castle.
1 them i.e., the thanes. **fly** desert **3 taint with** become imbued or infected with, weakened by **5 mortal consequences** what befalls humanity **8 English epicures** luxury-loving Englishmen (as seen from the Scottish point of view) **9 sway** rule myself **11 loon** stupid fellow **14 Go prick . . . fear** i.e., go prick or pinch your pale cheeks to bring some color into them. (The servant's blood has all retired into his lower abdomen on account of his fear, so that he is very pale and there is no blood in his liver, where his courage should have resided—hence, *lily-livered*, line 15.) **15 patch** domestic fool **16 of** thy on your **17 Are . . . fear** i.e., teach others to fear **20 behold** (Macbeth does not finish this thought.) **push** effort, crisis **21 cheer** (with a suggestion of "chair"). **disseat** dethrone **22 way** course **23 sere** dry and withered

25 As such as **36 Skirr** scour **44 Raze** (suggesting also *race*, "erase, obliterate"). **written troubles of** troubles written on **45 oblivious** causing forgetfulness **49 physic** medicine **50 staff** lance or baton of office **52 dispatch** hurry **52–53 cast The water** diagnose disease by the inspection of urine **56 Pull 't off** (Refers to some part of the armor not properly put on.) **57 senna** a purgative drug **58 scour** purge, cleanse, rid **60 it** i.e., the armor not yet put on Macbeth

Till Birnam Forest come to Dunsinane.
                                        Exeunt [all but the Doctor].

DOCTOR
    Were I from Dunsinane away and clear,
    Profit again should hardly draw me here.   [*Exit.*]

✤

5.4

*Drum and colors. Enter Malcolm, Siward,
Macduff, Siward's Son, Menteith, Caithness,
Angus, [Lennox, Ross,] and soldiers, marching.*

MALCOLM
    Cousins, I hope the days are near at hand
    That chambers will be safe.
MENTEITH   We doubt it nothing.   2
SIWARD
    What wood is this before us?
MENTEITH   The wood of Birnam.
MALCOLM
    Let every soldier hew him down a bough
    And bear 't before him. Thereby shall we shadow
    The numbers of our host and make discovery   6
    Err in report of us.
SOLDIERS   It shall be done.
SIWARD
    We learn no other but the confident tyrant   8
    Keeps still in Dunsinane and will endure   9
    Our setting down before 't.
MALCOLM   'Tis his main hope;   10
    For where there is advantage to be given,   11
    Both more and less have given him the revolt,   12
    And none serve with him but constrainèd things
    Whose hearts are absent too.
MACDUFF   Let our just censures   14
    Attend the true event, and put we on   15
    Industrious soldiership.
SIWARD   The time approaches
    That will with due decision make us know
    What we shall say we have and what we owe.   18
    Thoughts speculative their unsure hopes relate,   19
    But certain issue strokes must arbitrate—   20
    Towards which advance the war.   *Exeunt, marching.* 21

✤

5.5

*Enter Macbeth, Seyton, and soldiers, with drum
and colors.*

MACBETH
    Hang out our banners on the outward walls.
    The cry is still, "They come!" Our castle's strength
    Will laugh a siege to scorn. Here let them lie
    Till famine and the ague eat them up.
    Were they not forced with those that should be ours, 5
    We might have met them dareful, beard to beard, 6
    And beat them backward home.
                        A cry within of women.
                        What is that noise?
SEYTON
    It is the cry of women, my good lord.
                        [*He goes to the door.*]
MACBETH
    I have almost forgot the taste of fears.
    The time has been my senses would have cooled   10
    To hear a night-shriek, and my fell of hair   11
    Would at a dismal treatise rouse and stir   12
    As life were in 't. I have supped full with horrors;   13
    Direness, familiar to my slaughterous thoughts,
    Cannot once start me.

            [*Seyton returns.*]

                        Wherefore was that cry?   15
SEYTON   The Queen, my lord, is dead.
MACBETH   She should have died hereafter;   17
    There would have been a time for such a word.
    Tomorrow, and tomorrow, and tomorrow   19
    Creeps in this petty pace from day to day   20
    To the last syllable of recorded time,
    And all our yesterdays have lighted fools   22
    The way to dusty death. Out, out, brief candle!   23
    Life's but a walking shadow, a poor player
    That struts and frets his hour upon the stage
    And then is heard no more. It is a tale
    Told by an idiot, full of sound and fury,
    Signifying nothing.   28

            Enter a Messenger.

    Thou com'st to use thy tongue; thy story quickly.
MESSENGER   Gracious my lord,
    I should report that which I say I saw,
    But know not how to do 't.
MACBETH   Well, say, sir.

5.4. Location: Country near Birnam Wood.
2 chambers . . . safe i.e., we may sleep safely in our bedchambers.
nothing not at all **6 discovery** scouting reports **8 no other but** no
other news but that **9 Keeps** remains. **endure** allow, not attempt to
prevent **10 setting down before** laying siege to **11 advantage** opportunity (i.e., in military operations outside Macbeth's castle in
which it is possible for would-be deserters to slip away; in a siege, his
forces will be more confined to the castle and under his watchful eye)
12 more and less high and low **14–15 Let . . . event** let us postpone judgment about these uncertain matters until we've achieved
our goal **18 What . . . owe** what we only claim to have, as distinguished from what we actually have (or perhaps what we owe as
duty). **owe** own **19–20 Thoughts . . . arbitrate** speculating can
only convey our sense of hope; blows must decide the actual outcome **21 war** army

5.5. Location: Dunsinane. Macbeth's castle.
5 forced reinforced **6 dareful** boldly, in open battle **10 cooled** felt
the chill of terror **11 my fell of hair** the hair of my scalp **12 dismal
treatise** sinister story **13 As** as if **15 start me** make me start
17 She . . . hereafter she would have died someday, or, she should
have died at some more appropriate time, freed from the relentless
pressures of the moment **19–28 Tomorrow . . . nothing** (For biblical echoes in this speech, see Psalms 18:28, 22:15, 90:9; Job 8:9,
14:1–2, 18:6.) **20 this** at this **22 lighted** (The metaphor is of a candle used to light one to bed, just as life is a brief transit for wretched
mortals to their deathbeds.) **23 dusty** (Since life, made out of dust,
returns to dust.)

MESSENGER
As I did stand my watch upon the hill,
I looked toward Birnam, and anon, methought,
The wood began to move.
MACBETH   Liar and slave!
MESSENGER
Let me endure your wrath if 't be not so.
Within this three mile may you see it coming;
I say, a moving grove.
MACBETH   If thou speak'st false,
Upon the next tree shall thou hang alive
Till famine cling thee. If thy speech be sooth,   40
I care not if thou dost for me as much.
I pull in resolution, and begin   42
To doubt th' equivocation of the fiend
That lies like truth. "Fear not, till Birnam Wood
Do come to Dunsinane," and now a wood
Comes toward Dunsinane. Arm, arm, and out!
If this which he avouches does appear,
There is nor flying hence nor tarrying here.
I 'gin to be aweary of the sun,
And wish th' estate o' the world were now undone.   50
Ring the alarum bell! Blow wind, come wrack,   51
At least we'll die with harness on our back.   Exeunt. 52

❖

5.6   *Drum and colors. Enter Malcolm, Siward,*
         Macduff, and their army, with boughs.

MALCOLM
Now near enough. Your leafy screens throw down,
And show like those you are. You, worthy uncle,   2
Shall with my cousin, your right noble son,
Lead our first battle. Worthy Macduff and we   4
Shall take upon 's what else remains to do,
According to our order.
SIWARD   Fare you well.   6
Do we but find the tyrant's power tonight,   7
Let us be beaten, if we cannot fight.
MACDUFF
Make all our trumpets speak! Give them all breath,
Those clamorous harbingers of blood and death.   10
                              Exeunt. Alarums continued.

5.7   *Enter Macbeth.*

MACBETH
They have tied me to a stake. I cannot fly,

But bearlike I must fight the course. What's he   2
That was not born of woman? Such a one
Am I to fear, or none.

        Enter young Siward.

YOUNG SIWARD   What is thy name?
MACBETH   Thou'lt be afraid to hear it.
YOUNG SIWARD
No, though thou call'st thyself a hotter name
Than any is in hell.
MACBETH   My name's Macbeth.
YOUNG SIWARD
The devil himself could not pronounce a title
More hateful to mine ear.
MACBETH   No, nor more fearful.
YOUNG SIWARD
Thou liest, abhorrèd tyrant! With my sword
I'll prove the lie thou speak'st.
                Fight, and young Siward slain.
MACBETH   Thou wast born of woman. 12
But swords I smile at, weapons laugh to scorn,
Brandished by man that's of a woman born.   *Exit.*

        Alarums. Enter Macduff.

MACDUFF
That way the noise is. Tyrant, show thy face!
If thou be'st slain, and with no stroke of mine,
My wife and children's ghosts will haunt me still.
I cannot strike at wretched kerns, whose arms   18
Are hired to bear their staves. Either thou, Macbeth,   19
Or else my sword with an unbattered edge
I sheathe again undeeded. There thou shouldst be;   21
By this great clatter one of greatest note
Seems bruited. Let me find him, Fortune,   23
And more I beg not.   *Exit. Alarums.*

        Enter Malcolm and Siward.

SIWARD
This way, my lord. The castle's gently rendered: 25
The tyrant's people on both sides do fight,
The noble thanes do bravely in the war,
The day almost itself professes yours,   28
And little is to do.
MALCOLM   We have met with foes

40 **cling** cause to shrivel.   **sooth** truth   42 **pull in resolution** can no
longer give free rein to my self-confident determination   50 **estate**
settled order   51 **wrack** ruin   52 **harness** armor
5.6. Location: Dunsinane. Before Macbeth's castle.
2 **show** appear.   **uncle** i.e., Siward   4 **battle** battalion   6 **order**
plan of battle   7 **Do we** if we do.   **power** army   10 **harbingers** forerunners
5.7. Location: Before Macbeth's castle; the battle action is continuous here.

2 **course** bout or round of bearbaiting, in which the bear was tied to a
stake and dogs were set upon him   **12 s.d. young Siward slain** (In
some unspecified way, young Siward's body must be removed from
the stage; his own father enters at line 24 and perceives nothing
amiss, and in 5.8.38 young Siward is reported *missing* in action. Perhaps Macbeth drags off the body, or perhaps it is removed by soldiers
during the alarums.)   **18 kerns** (Properly, Irish foot soldiers; here, applied contemptuously to the rank and file.)   **19 staves** spears.   **Either
thou** i.e., either I find you   **21 undeeded** having seen no action.
shouldst be ought to be (judging by the noise)   **23 bruited** announced
25 gently rendered surrendered without fighting   **28 professes** declares itself

That strike beside us.

SIWARD   Enter, sir, the castle.   30
                                 Exeunt. Alarum.

5.8   *Enter Macbeth.*

MACBETH
Why should I play the Roman fool and die   1
On mine own sword? Whiles I see lives, the gashes   2
Do better upon them.

      Enter Macduff.

MACDUFF   Turn, hellhound, turn!

MACBETH
Of all men else I have avoided thee.
But get thee back! My soul is too much charged
With blood of thine already.

MACDUFF   I have no words;
My voice is in my sword, thou bloodier villain
Than terms can give thee out!   *Fight. Alarum.*

MACBETH   Thou losest labor.   8
As easy mayst thou the intrenchant air   9
With thy keen sword impress as make me bleed.   10
Let fall thy blade on vulnerable crests;
I bear a charmèd life, which must not yield
To one of woman born.

MACDUFF   Despair thy charm,   13
And let the angel whom thou still hast served   14
Tell thee, Macduff was from his mother's womb
Untimely ripped.   16

MACBETH
Accursèd be that tongue that tells me so,
For it hath cowed my better part of man!   18
And be these juggling fiends no more believed   19
That palter with us in a double sense,   20
That keep the word of promise to our ear
And break it to our hope. I'll not fight with thee.

MACDUFF   Then yield thee, coward,
And live to be the show and gaze o' the time!   24
We'll have thee, as our rarer monsters are,
Painted upon a pole, and underwrit,   26
"Here may you see the tyrant."

MACBETH   I will not yield
To kiss the ground before young Malcolm's feet
And to be baited with the rabble's curse.
Though Birnam Wood be come to Dunsinane,
And thou opposed, being of no woman born,

Yet I will try the last. Before my body   32
I throw my warlike shield. Lay on, Macduff,
And damned be him that first cries, "Hold, enough!" 34
                    Exeunt, fighting. Alarums.

     Enter fighting, and Macbeth slain. [Exit Macduff
     with Macbeth's body.] Retreat, and flourish. Enter,
     with drum and colors, Malcolm, Siward, Ross,
     thanes, and soldiers.

MALCOLM
I would the friends we miss were safe arrived.

SIWARD
Some must go off; and yet, by these I see   36
So great a day as this is cheaply bought.

MALCOLM
Macduff is missing, and your noble son.

ROSS
Your son, my lord, has paid a soldier's debt.
He only lived but till he was a man,
The which no sooner had his prowess confirmed
In the unshrinking station where he fought,   42
But like a man he died.

SIWARD   Then he is dead?

ROSS
Ay, and brought off the field. Your cause of sorrow
Must not be measured by his worth, for then
It hath no end.

SIWARD   Had he his hurts before?

ROSS
Ay, on the front.

SIWARD   Why then, God's soldier be he!
Had I as many sons as I have hairs
I would not wish them to a fairer death.
And so, his knell is knolled.

MALCOLM   He's worth more sorrow,
And that I'll spend for him.

SIWARD   He's worth no more.
They say he parted well and paid his score,   52
And so, God be with him! Here comes newer
comfort.

     Enter Macduff, with Macbeth's head.

MACDUFF
Hail, King! For so thou art. Behold where stands   54
Th' usurper's cursèd head. The time is free.   55
I see thee compassed with thy kingdom's pearl,   56
That speak my salutation in their minds,

---

30 **strike beside us** fight on our side, or miss us deliberately
**5.8. Location: Before Macbeth's castle, as the battle continues; after
line 34, within the castle.**
1 **Roman fool** i.e., suicide, like Brutus, Mark Antony, and others
2 **Whiles . . . lives** i.e., as long as I see any enemy living   8 **give
thee out** name you, describe you   9 **intrenchant** that cannot be cut,
indivisible   10 **impress** make an impression on   13 **Despair** despair
of   14 **angel** evil angel, Macbeth's genius.   **still** always   16 **Untimely** prematurely, i.e., by Caesarian delivery   18 **better . . . man**
i.e., courage   19 **juggling** deceiving   20 **palter . . . sense** equivocate
with us   24 **gaze o' the time** spectacle or sideshow of the age
26 **Painted . . . pole** i.e., painted on a board or cloth and suspended
on a pole

32 **the last** i.e., my last resort: my own strength and resolution
34 **s.d. Retreat** a trumpet call ordering an end to the fighting.   **Enter,
with drum and colors, etc.** (The remainder of the play is perhaps
imagined as taking place in Macbeth's castle and could be marked as
a separate scene. In Shakespeare's theater, however, the shift is so
nonrepresentational and without scenic alteration that the action is
virtually continuous.)   36 **go off** die.   **by these** to judge by these (assembled)   42 **unshrinking station** post from which he did not shrink
52 **parted** departed, died.   **score** reckoning   54 **stands** i.e., on a
pole   55 **free** released from tyranny   56 **compassed . . . pearl** surrounded by the nobles of your kingdom (literally, the pearls encircling
a crown)

Whose voices I desire aloud with mine:
Hail, King of Scotland!
ALL   Hail, King of Scotland!   *Flourish.*
MALCOLM
We shall not spend a large expense of time
Before we reckon with your several loves   62
And make us even with you. My thanes and kinsmen,   63
Henceforth be earls, the first that ever Scotland
In such an honor named. What's more to do
Which would be planted newly with the time,   66
As calling home our exiled friends abroad
That fled the snares of watchful tyranny,
Producing forth the cruel ministers   69
Of this dead butcher and his fiendlike queen—
Who, as 'tis thought, by self and violent hands   71
Took off her life—this, and what needful else
That calls upon us, by the grace of Grace
We will perform in measure, time, and place.
So, thanks to all at once and to each one,
Whom we invite to see us crowned at Scone.
                             Flourish. Exeunt omnes.

---

62 reckon come to a reckoning.   **several** individual   **63 make . . .
you** i.e., repay your worthiness   **66 would . . . time** should be established at the commencement of this new era   **69 Producing forth**
bringing forward to trial.   **ministers** agents   **71 self and violent** her
own violent

Timon
of
Athens

Timon of Athens is Shakespeare's most relentless study in misanthropy. It expresses, with *King Lear*, a moral outrage at human depravity but refuses to soften anger with compassionate tears. The protagonist learns little other than bitterness from his encounters with avarice and ingratitude. In its mordant vision of human folly, *Timon of Athens* resembles a number of other Roman or classical plays. As in *Julius Caesar, Titus Andronicus, Coriolanus,* and *Troilus and Cressida,* the dominant mood is one of futility. Political conflicts end in stalemate or a victory for opportunists; the populace and their leaders are fickle and craven; private virtues of noble men must yield to crass considerations of statecraft. Banishment or self-exile is too often the reward of those who have given their lives to public service. Shakespeare's misanthropic vision in *Timon of Athens* is, then, integral to his portrayal of humanity's political and social nature in the ancient classical world. This is a world to which Shakespeare turned often during his writing career, especially during the period from about 1599 to 1608. As a group, the Roman and classical plays tend to differ from the great tragedies of evil written during this same period *(Hamlet, Othello, King Lear, Macbeth)* in that the classical plays focus on a sardonic and dispiriting view of life's tragic absurdity. Even in *Antony and Cleopatra,* in which Shakespeare offers us an ennobling dream of greatness to offset the worldly failure of his protagonists, the arena of human conflict remains pitiless and disillusioning. *Timon of Athens* offers no compensatory vision; it is bleak to the end and unwavering in its denial.

Timon of Athens appears to have been written between 1605 and 1608 and is often grouped with *King Lear* (c. 1605) on grounds of stylistic and thematic similarity. For its chief source, it uses Thomas North's translation of Plutarch's *Lives of the Noble Grecians and Romans,* a source also for *Julius Caesar, Antony and Cleopatra, Coriolanus,* and parts of other plays. *Timon of Athens* also makes use, through intermediary versions, of the dialogue called *Timon,* or *The Misanthrope,* by the Greek satirist Lucian. The play may not have been produced; the text, not printed until the 1623 Folio, appears to have been taken from the author's unfinished manuscript, with contradictory uncan-

celed lines (see Timon's will, 5.4.70–73), unresolved discrepancies as to the amount of money Timon gives or requests, and passages of half-versified prose. Whatever the exact date and circumstance of composition, the play certainly belongs to the period of Shakespeare's most unsparing portrayal of human villainy and corruption.

Like *Troilus and Cressida, Timon of Athens* defies the conventional categories of tragedy, comedy, and history. Generically, the play stands chiefly between tragedy and satire in its preoccupation with dying and sterility. The play portrays a tragic fall from greatness, and presents us with a tragic hero who learns through suffering, but the learning is less about the hero himself than about the failings of humanity. The vision is thus primarily satiric rather than cathartic in its exposure of an unfeeling society. Satire prompts a comic response; we are invited to laugh sardonically at the hypocrisies of Timon's fair-weather friends. The play is also a history, drawn from historical sources, as its Folio title, *The Life of Timon of Athens,* suggests. We ought to see or read it with the expectations not simply of tragedy but also of satire and ironic history.

As a genre, in fact, the play most resembles those works that the Painter and the Poet wish to offer Timon himself: a "moral painting" and a "satire against the softness of prosperity" (1.1.95 and 5.1.32–33). Such a deliberately old-fashioned genre recalls the medieval morality plays and the "hybrid" morality plays of the 1570s and 1580s, like Thomas Lupton's *All for Money* (c. 1577) or Thomas Lodge and Robert Greene's *A Looking Glass for London and England* (1587–1591), which inveigh against usury and the neglect of military heroes. John Marston's later quasi-morality, *Histriomastix* (c. 1599), proclaims the decline of civilization through worldly insolence. Ben Jonson's *Volpone* (1605–1606), though "comical" rather than "tragical" in its satire, similarly castigates human greed. The *Parnassus* trilogy (1598–1603), a series of three mordantly satirical plays written to be acted by students at Cambridge, indulges in a massive venting of spleen against a philistine culture. Satire against governmental policies and politicians led to reprisals in the form of prohibitions, imprisonments, and book burning. *Timon of Athens,* though not topically controversial in this sense, follows a tradition of social satire derived from both English and classical models. Like most satire of the 1600s, both dramatic and nondramatic, it is crabbed in style, features a railing protagonist, and denounces through exaggerated caricature an ugly array of types representing a broad social spectrum. Choice of the satiric morality play as a generic model accords well with the play's acerbic view of decadence and "softness."

Human greed, with which *Timon of Athens* is so occupied, lends itself readily to satiric treatment. Avarice does not ordinarily seem terrifying at first, like the spiritual sins of envy or prideful ambition as portrayed in *Othello* and *Macbeth;* instead, it is disgusting, ludicrous, and incredibly tenacious. Avarice is, after all, one of the Deadly Sins and is often referred to in medieval commentary as the pivotal Sin, the *radix malorum,* or root of all evils. Although less vivid in its manifestation than pride or envy, greed is insidious and all-embracing. We see its corrupting effects in Timon's friends. Those who sponge off him and then desert him are quick to return when he is rumored to have found gold in his exile. Greed is also self-deceiving and hypocritical. Many are the excuses offered for failing to come to Timon's aid: one friend rates Timon as a bad credit risk, another happens to be short of ready cash at the moment, a third insists that Timon's generosity to him wasn't as great as people suppose, and so on. No wonder Timon feels he must devise for such hypocrites a suitable comeuppance, consisting of a farewell banquet in which their crass expectations are rewarded with a mocking litany of curses and a dinner of water and stones.

Appropriately for this satirical depiction of human greed, the characters are virtually all types or social abstractions in a generic portrayal of avarice. Several represent the crafts and professions and are abstractly labeled as such: the Poet, the Painter, the Jeweler, the Merchant. Others are "flattering lords" or "false friends" or "thieves." Seldom in Shakespeare do we find so many characters without proper names. They are depersonalized, and we are distanced from them. Apemantus is another type, a "churlish philosopher," recognizable in all his appearances by this one feature; we learn little about him other than that he professes to scoff at worldliness with a scabrous wit, derived in part from legends about Diogenes the Cynic philosopher and other devotees of an extravagantly simple mode of life. Abstraction of this sort is close to allegory, especially an allegory of social malaise. Timon himself becomes a type in his conversion to misanthropy, "infected," as Apemantus says, by "A poor unmanly melancholy sprung / From change of fortune" (4.3.204–206). Apemantus' remark appeals to a view of personality as governed by "humors" or dominant traits, such as melancholy or irascibility, which are generated by imbalance in the body of the four "humors": blood, phlegm, bile, and black bile. Images of disease, of cannibalism, and of gold, prominent throughout the play, are often derived from such "humorous" imbalances. The imagery also associates character types, as in Jonson's *Volpone,* with various beasts: the lion, the fox, the ass, the wolf, the bear, and, most of all, the dog.

By means of such techniques, Shakespeare portrays those whom Timon comes to despise with a seemingly intentional one-sidedness; the caricatures of avarice are vivid and amusing, with little allowance for subtlety or change. The plot, too, is, by Shakespeare's standard, unusually lacking in complication: Timon discovers the ingratitude and graspingness of his fellow humans and retires from a world he can no longer tolerate, breathing upon it his dying curse. The dramatic tension of this uneventful story lies instead in Timon's

own tortured spiritual saga, in the painful process of realization, in the revulsion, the refusal to compromise, the spurning even of honest friendship, the bitter renunciation and longing for oblivion. Alcibiades, too, is a complex character, offering as he does the alternatives of vengeful action against an ungrateful world or of successful conciliation; the debate between Alcibiades and Timon is an essential part of Timon's working toward total rejection of hope. The true drama is thus inner, and is increasingly contrasted with a static and superficial society toward which we are asked to feel revulsion.

There are no villains in *Timon of Athens,* though there are plenty of weak and foolish people. What is depressing about greed, in fact, is its insidious normality. Those who desert Timon have many prudent arguments on their side. After all, his original generosity is excessive and reckless. If his friends take advantage of him, they can at least say they have tried to warn him. Even a fool can see what lies in store. Much of Timon's wealth goes into drunken and gluttonous debauchery, into "feasts, pomps, and vainglories" (1.2.247–248). Timon does not know how to use prosperity wisely, and even his loyal servants deplore the "riot" (2.2.3). He is deaf to the friendly counsel of his steward, Flavius. For one who is so open-handed, Timon is surprisingly churlish with his creditors. And is he not presumptuous to assume that his friends will come to his aid when such vast sums are needed? Are they to be blamed for not emulating his prodigal decline into poverty? Clearly, Timon expects too much. We readily though sadly perceive, as do all Timon's friends, that commerce is a god worshiped by all; need he be so shocked at this? As bystanders, we share with Timon's choric servants the certainty that his large requests for help will be refused. And yet, no matter how stupid or blind Timon may be, the desertion of him is still monstrous. Timon differs from us chiefly in being an idealist, in expecting that people will repay kindness with gratitude. We know, as do Timon's sympathetic servants, that most people are not like that.

Timon thus tears himself apart in a rage at what we consider the way of the world. We find his misanthropy intemperate, and yet we cannot help being moved by his sweeping indictment of human pettiness and inhumanity. Timon's furor carries him beyond satire. He is, like Lear, all the more clear-sighted for being near to madness. Wisdom and folly exchange places, as Apemantus' friend the Fool has already pointed out (2.2.99–120). In Timon's nearly mad vision, beggars and lords are interchangeable, distinguished only by wealth and position. Love of gold, he sees, inverts everything decent in human life, making "Black white, foul fair, wrong right, / Base noble, old young, coward valiant" (4.3.29–30). Thieves and whores are at least more honest than their counterparts in everyday life, the respectable citizens of Athens and their wives, and so Timon mockingly rewards the thieves and insults the hypocrites. Yet Timon also inveighs furiously against women and all sexuality in a way that suggests feelings of betrayal. Though women occupy virtually no place in Timon's life, he himself has sought to displace women by serving as the generous source of comfort for all his friends—a self-created and narcissistic role that is destined to collapse into self-hatred and dread of all human feeling. His curse embraces the cosmos as well as humanity, inverting all semblance of hierarchical order: obedience must turn to rebellion, fidelity to incontinence, virginity to lasciviousness. "Degrees, observances, customs, and laws" must "Decline to your confounding contraries" (4.1.19–20). Clothing and cosmetics must be stripped away, as in *King Lear,* so that human monstrosity may be revealed for what it truly is.

Three persons, Apemantus, Alcibiades, and Flavius, serve as chief foils to Timon in his estrangement from humanity. Apemantus the Cynic, who first taught Timon to rail at greed, now counsels him to find stoic contentment in renunciation of desire or, conversely, to thrive as a flatterer by preying on those who have undone him (4.3.200–234). Alcibiades, the military commander banished by an ungrateful Athenian Senate for presuming to beg the life of one who had rashly shed blood in a quarrel, offers Timon the example of revenge against his enemies; subsequently, he offers Athens the olive branch with the sword, making "war breed peace" (5.4.83), in an accommodating move that is important for the conclusion of the play and its final mitigating tone. Timon, although resembling both men as railer and as victim of ingratitude, rejects their counsels as too politic, too worldly. His stand is unflinching, absolute, so lacking in compromise that his sole choice can be to curse, die, and hope for oblivion. Only Flavius, his steward, offers brief consolation. Flavius comes to him, like Kent to King Lear, offering love and service in exile. Flavius even speaks in paradoxes reminiscent of *King Lear,* calling Timon "My dearest lord, blest to be most accurst, / Rich only to be wretched" (4.2.43–44). These are precious words, showing that humanity is not utterly irredeemable. Still, this consolation is evidently too late to offset the nightmarish truth that Timon has learned. Timon experiences little of the compassionate love that comes to Lear in his madness, but he at least faces the bleakness of human existence with unbending honesty.

Timon of Athens

The Actors' Names

TIMON OF ATHENS
LUCIUS *and* LUCULLUS, } *two flattering lords*
SEMPRONIUS, *another flattering lord*
VENTIDIUS, *one of Timon's false friends*
APEMANTUS, *a churlish philosopher*
ALCIBIADES, *an Athenian captain*
[PHRYNIA, TIMANDRA,] *mistresses of Alcibiades*
AN OLD ATHENIAN]
Certain SENATORS [*and* LORDS]
[FLAVIUS, *steward to Timon*]
POET, PAINTER, JEWELER, [*and*] MERCHANT
FLAMINIUS, *one of Timon's servants*
[LUCILIUS, *another*]
SERVILIUS, *another*
CAPHIS,
PHILOTUS' [SERVANT],
TITUS' [SERVANT],
HORTENSIUS' [SERVANT],
[ISIDORE'S SERVANT,
Two of] VARRO'S [SERVANTS],
} *several servants to usurers* [*Timon's creditors*]
[A PAGE
A FOOL
Three STRANGERS
Two MESSENGERS]
Certain THIEVES [*or* BANDITTI]
CUPID [*and*] *certain* MASKERS [*as Amazons*]

With divers other Servants and Attendants, [*other Lords, Officers, Soldiers*]

[SCENE: *Athens, and the neighboring woods*]

1.1   *Enter Poet, Painter, Jeweler, and Merchant, at several doors.* [*The Poet and Painter form one group, the Jeweler and Merchant another.*]

POET   Good day, sir.
PAINTER   I am glad you're well.
POET
    I have not seen you long. How goes the world?   3

1.1. Location: Athens. Timon's house.
s.d. **several** separate   **3 long** for a long time.   **How . . . world** i.e., how are you doing? (But the Painter quibbles on the literal sense.)

PAINTER
It wears, sir, as it grows.

POET   Ay, that's well known.   4
But what particular rarity? What strange,   5
Which manifold record not matches? See,   6
Magic of bounty, all these spirits thy power   7
Hath conjured to attend! I know the merchant.

PAINTER
I know them both. Th' other's a jeweler.

MERCHANT [to the Jeweler]
O, 'tis a worthy lord!

JEWELER   Nay, that's most fixed.   10

MERCHANT
A most incomparable man, breathed, as it were,   11
To an untirable and continuate goodness.   12
He passes.   13

JEWELER   I have a jewel here—

MERCHANT
O, pray, let's see 't. For the Lord Timon, sir?

JEWELER
If he will touch the estimate. But for that—   16

POET [reciting to himself]
"When we for recompense have praised the vile,
It stains the glory in that happy verse   18
Which aptly sings the good."

MERCHANT [looking at the jewel]   'Tis a good form.   19

JEWELER   And rich. Here is a water, look ye.   20

PAINTER [to the Poet]
You are rapt, sir, in some work, some dedication   21
To the great lord.

POET   A thing slipped idly from me.   22
Our poesy is as a gum which oozes   23
From whence 'tis nourished. The fire i' the flint   24
Shows not till it be struck; our gentle flame
Provokes itself and like the current flies   26
Each bound it chafes. What have you there?   27

PAINTER
A picture, sir. When comes your book forth?

POET
Upon the heels of my presentment, sir.   29
Let's see your piece.   [He examines the painting.]

PAINTER   'Tis a good piece.

POET
So 'tis. This comes off well and excellent.

PAINTER
Indifferent.

POET   Admirable! How this grace   33
Speaks his own standing! What a mental power   34
This eye shoots forth! How big imagination   35
Moves in this lip! To th' dumbness of the gesture   36
One might interpret.   37

PAINTER
It is a pretty mocking of the life.   38
Here is a touch; is 't good?

POET   I will say of it,
It tutors nature. Artificial strife   40
Lives in these touches, livelier than life.

Enter certain Senators.

PAINTER   How this lord is followed!

POET
The senators of Athens. Happy man!

PAINTER   Look, more!
[The Senators pass over the stage, and exeunt.]

POET
You see this confluence, this great flood of visitors.
[He shows his poem.]
I have in this rough work shaped out a man
Whom this beneath world doth embrace and hug   47
With amplest entertainment. My free drift   48
Halts not particularly, but moves itself   49
In a wide sea of tax. No leveled malice   50
Infects one comma in the course I hold,   51
But flies an eagle flight, bold and forth on,   52
Leaving no tract behind.   53

PAINTER   How shall I understand you?   54

POET   I will unbolt to you.   55
You see how all conditions, how all minds,   56
As well of glib and slippery creatures as
Of grave and austere quality, tender down   58
Their services to Lord Timon. His large fortune,
Upon his good and gracious nature hanging,   60
Subdues and properties to his love and tendance   61
All sorts of hearts; yea, from the glass-faced flatterer   62

---

4 **wears** decays. **grows** ages 5 **rarity** unusual occurrence. **strange** strange event 6 **Which . . . matches** which all recorded history cannot equal 7 **Magic of bounty** the remarkable attractive power of generosity. **spirits** i.e., beings, persons (spoken of as if they were spirits conjured by magic) 10 **worthy lord** i.e., Timon. **fixed** certain 11 **breathed** inspired, or, trained through exercise 12 **untirable** inexhaustible. **continuate** habitual 13 **passes** surpasses 16 **touch the estimate** offer or meet the price 18 **happy** felicitous, matching truthful praise to a worthy object 19 **form** shape, appearance. (Refers to the jewel.) 20 **water** luster 21 **dedication** (Such works were regularly dedicated to great nobles.) 22 **idly** casually 23–24 **Our . . . nourished** the poetry we write oozes from us like gummy sap from the tree that nourishes it 24 **The fire i' the flint** (Flint, struck against a stone, yields a spark, and so may seem to have fire latent in it.) 26 **Provokes itself** is self-generating 26–27 **flies . . . chafes** seeks escape from the riverbanks that confine it 29 **Upon . . . presentment** as soon as I have presented it (to Lord Timon, in hopes of obtaining his patronage)

33 **Indifferent** not bad, so-so. **this grace** i.e., of the person in the picture 34 **Speaks . . . standing** conveys the dignity of its subject 35 **big** largely 36–37 **To . . . interpret** one might easily supply words to express this silent gesture 38 **mocking** mirroring 40 **Artificial strife** the striving of art to surpass nature 47 **beneath** sublunar, beneath the moon 48 **entertainment** welcome. **drift** design 49 **Halts not particularly** doesn't concern itself with criticizing anyone individually 50 **tax** censure. (The Poet enunciates a familiar classical theory of satire.) **leveled** aimed, as a gun is aimed at a particular object 51 **comma** i.e., detail 52 **forth on** straight on 53 **tract** track, trace 54 **How . . . you** what do you mean? 55 **unbolt** unlock, disclose 56 **conditions** ranks, temperaments 58 **quality** nature. **tender down** tender, offer 60 **hanging** providing attractive adornment, like rich clothes. (But the Poet also unconsciously implies the hard truth that good nature counts for little without a large fortune to attend it.) 61 **properties** appropriates. **love and tendance** loving and being in attendance on him 62 **glass-faced** reflecting superficially the tastes and whims of his patron

To Apemantus, that few things loves better
Than to abhor himself—even he drops down
The knee before him and returns in peace   65
Most rich in Timon's nod.   66

PAINTER I saw them speak together.

POET
Sir, I have upon a high and pleasant hill
Feigned Fortune to be throned. The base o' the mount 69
Is ranked with all deserts, all kind of natures, 70
That labor on the bosom of this sphere   71
To propagate their states. Amongst them all   72
Whose eyes are on this sovereign lady fixed,
One do I personate of Lord Timon's frame,   74
Whom Fortune with her ivory hand wafts to her,   75
Whose present grace to present slaves and servants 76
Translates his rivals.

PAINTER   ʼTis conceived to scope.   77
This throne, this Fortune, and this hill, methinks,
With one man beckoned from the rest below,
Bowing his head against the steepy mount   80
To climb his happiness, would be well expressed   81
In our condition.

POET   Nay, sir, but hear me on.   82
All those which were his fellows but of late—
Some better than his value—on the moment   84
Follow his strides, his lobbies fill with tendance, 85
Rain sacrificial whisperings in his ear,   86
Make sacred even his stirrup, and through him   87
Drink the free air.

PAINTER   Ay, marry, what of these?   88

POET
When Fortune in her shift and change of mood
Spurns down her late beloved, all his dependents,   90
Which labored after him to the mountain's top
Even on their knees and hands, let him slip down,
Not one accompanying his declining foot.

PAINTER ʼTis common.
A thousand moral paintings I can show   95
That shall demonstrate these quick blows of
    Fortune's
More pregnantly than words. Yet you do well
To show Lord Timon that mean eyes have seen   98

The foot above the head.   99

*Trumpets sound. Enter Lord Timon, addressing
himself courteously to every suitor; [a Messenger
from Ventidius talking with him; Lucilius and
other servants following].*

TIMON Imprisoned is he, say you?

MESSENGER
Ay, my good lord. Five talents is his debt,   101
His means most short, his creditors most strait.   102
Your honorable letter he desires   103
To those have shut him up, which failing   104
Periods his comfort.

TIMON   Noble Ventidius! Well,   105
I am not of that feather to shake off   106
My friend when he must need me. I do know him   107
A gentleman that well deserves a help,
Which he shall have. I'll pay the debt and free him.

MESSENGER Your lordship ever binds him.   110

TIMON
Commend me to him. I will send his ransom;
And being enfranchised, bid him come to me.   112
ʼTis not enough to help the feeble up,
But to support him after. Fare you well.   114

MESSENGER All happiness to your honor!   *Exit.*

Enter an Old Athenian.

OLD ATHENIAN
Lord Timon, hear me speak.

TIMON   Freely, good father.   116

OLD ATHENIAN
Thou hast a servant named Lucilius.

TIMON I have so. What of him?

OLD ATHENIAN
Most noble Timon, call the man before thee.

TIMON
Attends he here or no? Lucilius!

LUCILIUS Here, at your lordship's service.

OLD ATHENIAN
This fellow here, Lord Timon, this thy creature,   122
By night frequents my house. I am a man
That from my first have been inclined to thrift,
And my estate deserves an heir more raised   125
Than one which holds a trencher.

TIMON   Well, what further? 126

OLD ATHENIAN
One only daughter have I, no kin else

---

65 **returns** departs 66 **in Timon's nod** for having been acknowledged by Timon 69 **Feigned** imagined, supposed 70 **ranked . . . deserts** filled with persons of all degrees of merit standing in ranks 71 **this sphere** i.e., the earth 72 **propagate** enlarge. **states** fortunes 74 **personate** represent. **frame** mold, nature 75 **ivory** white. **wafts** beckons, waves 76–77 **Whose . . . rivals** whose (Fortune's) present gracious favor transforms his (Timon's) rivals immediately into slaves and servants 77 **to scope** to the purpose, in correct proportion 80 **Bowing his head** i.e., bending forward with the effort. **steepy** steep 81 **his happiness** to his good fortune 81–82 **would . . . condition** would find a striking parallel in the human condition 82 **hear me on** hear me speak further 84 **better . . . value** of more worth, and worth more, than he. **on the moment** immediately 85 **his lobbies . . . tendance** fill the anterooms of his house with their attentive presence 86 **sacrificial whisperings** whispers of sacrifices made in his honor, or whispers offered with reverential deference as a sacrifice is offered 87 **stirrup** i.e., as they help him to his horse 87–88 **through . . . air** seem to breathe the free air only through his bounty 88 **marry** (A mild oath, originally "By Mary.") 90 **Spurns down** kicks or thrusts down 95 **moral paintings** paintings pointing out a moral 98 **mean eyes** even the eyes of persons of low degree

99 **The foot . . . head** i.e., highest fortune tumbling headlong downward by the turn of Fortune's wheel, or, the foot of Fortune poised over the head of the once-prosperous man 101 **talents** units of money today worth $2,000 or more. (But Shakespeare was evidently uncertain about the *talent's* value as he wrote this play. *Talents* is also a biblical term; see, for example, Matthew 2:14–29.) 102 **short** limited. **strait** severe, exacting 103 **Your . . . letter** a letter from your honor 104 **those** those who 104–105 **which failing Periods** the lack of which puts an end to 106 **feather** i.e., disposition (as in "birds of a feather") 107 **know him** know him to be 110 **binds him** i.e., to grateful obligation 112 **enfranchised** set free 114 **But** i.e., but one must continue 116 **Freely** readily, gladly. **father** (Respectful term of address to an old man.) 122 **creature** dependent, hanger-on 125 **more raised** of higher social position 126 **holds a trencher** i.e., serves at table, handling wooden dishes

On whom I may confer what I have got.   128
The maid is fair, o' the youngest for a bride,   129
And I have bred her at my dearest cost   130
In qualities of the best. This man of thine
Attempts her love. I prithee, noble lord,   132
Join with me to forbid him her resort;   133
Myself have spoke in vain.

TIMON   The man is honest.

OLD ATHENIAN   Therefore he will be, Timon.   136
His honesty rewards him in itself;
It must not bear my daughter.   138

TIMON   Does she love him?

OLD ATHENIAN   She is young and apt.   140
Our own precedent passions do instruct us   141
What levity's in youth.

TIMON [to Lucilius]   Love you the maid?

LUCILIUS
Ay, my good lord, and she accepts of it.   143

OLD ATHENIAN
If in her marriage my consent is missing,
I call the gods to witness, I will choose
Mine heir from forth the beggars of the world
And dispossess her all.   147

TIMON   How shall she be endowed   148
If she be mated with an equal husband?   149

OLD ATHENIAN
Three talents on the present; in future, all.   150

TIMON
This gentleman of mine hath served me long;
To build his fortune I will strain a little,
For 'tis a bond in men. Give him thy daughter.   153
What you bestow, in him I'll counterpoise,   154
And make him weigh with her.

OLD ATHENIAN   Most noble lord,   155
Pawn me to this your honor, she is his.   156

TIMON
My hand to thee; mine honor on my promise.

LUCILIUS
Humbly I thank your lordship. Never may
That state or fortune fall into my keeping   159
Which is not owed to you!   160

              Exeunt [Lucilius and Old Athenian].

POET [presenting his poem]
Vouchsafe my labor, and long live your lordship!   161

TIMON
I thank you; you shall hear from me anon.   162

Go not away.—What have you there, my friend?

PAINTER
A piece of painting, which I do beseech   164
Your lordship to accept.   [He presents his painting.]

TIMON   Painting is welcome.
The painting is almost the natural man;   166
For since dishonor traffics with man's nature,   167
He is but outside; these penciled figures are   168
Even such as they give out. I like your work,   169
And you shall find I like it. Wait attendance   170
Till you hear further from me.

PAINTER   The gods preserve ye!

TIMON
Well fare you, gentleman. Give me your hand;
We must needs dine together.—Sir, your jewel   173
Hath suffered under praise.

JEWELER   What, my lord, dispraise?   174

TIMON
A mere satiety of commendations.   175
If I should pay you for 't as 'tis extolled,
It would unclew me quite.

JEWELER   My lord, 'tis rated   177
As those which sell would give; but you well know   178
Things of like value differing in the owners
Are prizèd by their masters. Believe 't, dear lord,   180
You mend the jewel by the wearing it.

              [He presents a jewel.]

TIMON   Well mocked.   182

MERCHANT
No, my good lord, he speaks the common tongue   183
Which all men speak with him.

              Enter Apemantus.

TIMON   Look who comes here. Will you be chid?   185

JEWELER   We'll bear, with your lordship.   186

MERCHANT   He'll spare none.

TIMON
Good morrow to thee, gentle Apemantus!

APEMANTUS
Till I be gentle, stay thou for thy good morrow—   189
When thou art Timon's dog, and these knaves
honest.   190

TIMON
Why dost thou call them knaves? Thou know'st
them not.

164 piece example, specimen   166 the natural man humanity as it
truly is, not what it pretends to be   167 traffics deals (improperly)
168 He is but outside i.e., humanity becomes a mere outward appearance, hypocritical.   penciled painted   169 Even . . . out exactly
what they profess to be   170 Wait remain in   173 needs necessarily,
of course   174 suffered under praise been overwhelmed by praise.
(But the Jeweler misunderstands as "suffered underpraise.")
175 mere utter   177 unclew unwind, i.e., ruin   178 As . . . give at
a price which merchants would pay, i.e., at cost   180 prizèd . . .
masters valued as their owners are respected. (The gem will increase
in value because Timon will wear it.)   182 Well mocked a well-
turned bit of flattery, well counterfeited   183 common tongue general
opinion   185 Will you be chid are you prepared to be scolded?
186 We'll . . lordship i.e., we'll put up with it if your lordship can
189–190 Till . . . honest i.e., you must wait for my "good morrow"
until I have become free of satirical sharpness and until men are free
of the faults I criticize, something as likely to happen as Timon changing places with his dog

128 got acquired   129 o' the . . . bride just of marriageable age
130 bred . . . cost brought her up at great expense   132 Attempts
tries to win   133 her resort access to her   136 Therefore he will be
i.e., his honorable nature (honesty) will show itself in his honoring my
wishes, or, his conduct will be honorable (and chaste) if we forbid
him to see my daughter   138 bear my daughter carry off my daughter
into the bargain   140 apt easily wooed, impressionable   141 precedent former (when we were young)   143 accepts of accepts   147 all
wholly   148 How . . . endowed what dowry will she be given
149 an equal husband one of equal estate   150 on the present immediately   153 bond obligation.   in among   154 counterpoise match,
counterbalance   155 weigh with her be equal to her in estate
156 Pawn . . . honor if you'll pledge your word of honor to do as
you have said   159 That i.e., any   160 owed to you acknowledged
to be from you   161 Vouchsafe deign to accept   162 anon shortly

APEMANTUS   Are they not Athenians?

TIMON   Yes.

APEMANTUS   Then I repent not.   194

JEWELER   You know me, Apemantus?

APEMANTUS   Thou know'st I do. I called thee by thy   196
name.   197

TIMON   Thou art proud, Apemantus.

APEMANTUS   Of nothing so much as that I am not like
Timon.

TIMON   Whither art going?

APEMANTUS   To knock out an honest Athenian's brains.

TIMON   That's a deed thou'lt die for.

APEMANTUS   Right, if doing nothing be death by the law.   204

TIMON   How lik'st thou this picture, Apemantus?

APEMANTUS   The best, for the innocence.   206

TIMON   Wrought he not well that painted it?

APEMANTUS   He wrought better that made the painter,
and yet he's but a filthy piece of work.   210

PAINTER   You're a dog.

APEMANTUS   Thy mother's of my generation. What's   211
she, if I be a dog?   212

TIMON   Wilt dine with me, Apemantus?

APEMANTUS   No. I eat not lords.   214

TIMON   An thou shouldst, thou'dst anger ladies.   215

APEMANTUS   O, they eat lords. So they come by great   216
bellies.   217

TIMON   That's a lascivious apprehension.   218

APEMANTUS   So thou apprehend'st it. Take it for thy labor.   219

TIMON   How dost thou like this jewel, Apemantus?

APEMANTUS   Not so well as plain dealing, which will
not cost a man a doit.   222

TIMON   What dost thou think 'tis worth?

APEMANTUS   Not worth my thinking.—How now,
poet?

POET   How now, philosopher?

APEMANTUS   Thou liest.

POET   Art not one?

APEMANTUS   Yes.

POET   Then I lie not.

APEMANTUS   Art not a poet?

POET   Yes.

APEMANTUS   Then thou liest. Look in thy last work,   233
where thou hast feigned him a worthy fellow.   234

POET   That's not feigned. He is so.

194 repent not don't regret what I said   196–197 thy name i.e.,
knave   204 doing nothing i.e., since there are no honest Athenians, I
will be doing nothing.   death by the law subject to the death penalty. (Athenians have no brains; therefore, to knock out their brains is
to do nothing.)   206 innocence innocuous character, inability to do
harm (as real life can)   210 dog (Cynic is derived from the Greek for
"dog.")   211 generation species   211–212 What's she i.e., isn't she
a bitch   214 eat not lords do not consume the substance of great
men. (But, in his next speech, Apemantus gives the phrase a sexual
meaning.)   215 An if   216 eat (1) take into their bellies (sexually) (2)
consume the substance of.   come by acquire   216–217 great bellies
(1) pregnant wombs (2) bellies plump from eating   218 apprehension
(1) interpretation (2) seizure, grasp (with a bawdy suggestion in the
idea of seizing physically)   219 So . . . labor that's your interpretation, not mine. You can keep it for your pains. (With a pun on labor,
"giving birth.")   222 doit half a farthing, coin of slight value
233 Then thou liest (because poets are supposed to feign)   234 him
i.e., Timon

APEMANTUS   Yes, he is worthy of thee, and to pay thee
for thy labor. He that loves to be flattered is worthy o'
the flatterer. Heavens, that I were a lord!

TIMON   What wouldst do then, Apemantus?

APEMANTUS   E'en as Apemantus does now: hate a lord
with my heart.

TIMON   What, thyself?

APEMANTUS   Ay.

TIMON   Wherefore?

APEMANTUS   That I had no angry wit to be a lord.—Art   245
not thou a merchant?

MERCHANT   Ay, Apemantus.

APEMANTUS   Traffic confound thee, if the gods will not!   248

MERCHANT   If traffic do it, the gods do it.

APEMANTUS   Traffic's thy god, and thy god confound
thee!

Trumpet sounds. Enter a Messenger.

TIMON   What trumpet's that?

MESSENGER
'Tis Alcibiades and some twenty horse,   253
All of companionship.   254

TIMON
Pray, entertain them; give them guide to us.   255
                                   [*Exeunt some attendants.*]
[*To his guests.*] You must needs dine with me. Go
not you hence
Till I have thanked you.—When dinner's done,
Show me this piece.—I am joyful of your sights.   258

Enter Alcibiades, with the rest.

Most welcome, sir!

APEMANTUS   So, so, there! Aches contract   259
And starve your supple joints! That there should be   260
Small love amongst these sweet knaves, and all
This courtesy! The strain of man's bred out   262
Into baboon and monkey.

ALCIBIADES
Sir, you have saved my longing, and I feed   264
Most hungerly on your sight.

TIMON   Right welcome, sir!   265
Ere we depart, we'll share a bounteous time   266
In different pleasures. Pray you, let us in.   267
                              Exeunt [all except Apemantus].

Enter two Lords.

FIRST LORD   What time o' day is 't, Apemantus?

APEMANTUS   Time to be honest.

FIRST LORD   That time serves still.   270

245 That . . . lord i.e., that I had no more sense than to wish to become a lord and thus forfeit the angry wit that only an independent
philosopher can enjoy   248 Traffic confound may business or trade
ruin   253 horse horsemen   254 of companionship companions with
one another   255 entertain them show them hospitality.   give them
guide show them in   258 of your sights to see you   259 So, so,
there well, well, look at that (i.e., at all the bowing and scraping)
260 starve destroy   262 strain race, stock.   bred out degenerated
264 saved anticipated and thus prevented   265 hungerly on your
sight hungrily on the sight of you   266 depart part company
267 different various.   in enter   270 still always

APEMANTUS   The most accursèd thou, that still omitt'st it. 271

SECOND LORD   Thou art going to Lord Timon's feast?

APEMANTUS   Ay, to see meat fill knaves and wine heat fools.

SECOND LORD   Fare thee well, fare thee well.

APEMANTUS   Thou art a fool to bid me farewell twice.

SECOND LORD   Why, Apemantus?

APEMANTUS   Shouldst have kept one to thyself, for I mean to give thee none.

FIRST LORD   Hang thyself!

APEMANTUS   No, I will do nothing at thy bidding. Make thy requests to thy friend.

SECOND LORD   Away, unpeaceable dog, or I'll spurn 283 thee hence!

APEMANTUS   I will fly, like a dog, the heels o' the ass. 285

[Exit.]

FIRST LORD
He's opposite to humanity. Come, shall we in   286
And taste Lord Timon's bounty? He outgoes   287
The very heart of kindness.   288

SECOND LORD
He pours it out. Plutus, the god of gold,
Is but his steward. No meed but he repays   290
Sevenfold above itself; no gift to him
But breeds the giver a return exceeding
All use of quittance.

FIRST LORD   The noblest mind he carries   293
That ever governed man.

SECOND LORD
Long may he live in fortunes! Shall we in?

FIRST LORD   I'll keep you company.   *Exeunt.*

❖

1.2   *Hautboys playing loud music. A great banquet served in, [Flavius and others attending]; and then enter Lord Timon, the states, the Athenian Lords, [Alcibiades, and] Ventidius (which Timon redeemed from prison). Then comes, dropping after all, Apemantus, discontentedly, like himself.*

VENTIDIUS   Most honored Timon,
It hath pleased the gods to remember my father's age
And call him to long peace.   3
He is gone happy and has left me rich.   4
Then, as in grateful virtue I am bound
To your free heart, I do return those talents,   6
Doubled with thanks and service, from whose help
I derived liberty.   *[He offers money.]*

TIMON   O, by no means,
Honest Ventidius. You mistake my love.

I gave it freely ever, and there's none
Can truly say he gives if he receives.   12
If our betters play at that game, we must not dare   13
To imitate them. Faults that are rich are fair.   14

VENTIDIUS   A noble spirit!
[They all stand ceremoniously looking on Timon.]

TIMON
Nay, my lords, ceremony was but devised at first
To set a gloss on faint deeds, hollow welcomes,   17
Recanting goodness, sorry ere 'tis shown;   18
But where there is true friendship, there needs none.   19
Pray, sit. More welcome are ye to my fortunes
Than my fortunes to me.   *[They sit.]*

FIRST LORD
My lord, we always have confessed it.   22

APEMANTUS
Ho, ho, confessed it? Hanged it, have you not?   23

TIMON
O, Apemantus, you are welcome.

APEMANTUS   No,
You shall not make me welcome.
I come to have thee thrust me out of doors.   26

TIMON
Fie, thou'rt a churl. You've got a humor there   27
Does not become a man; 'tis much to blame.   28
They say, my lords, *Ira furor brevis est*, but yond 29
man is ever angry. Go, let him have a table by himself,
for he does neither affect company nor is he fit for 't, 31
indeed.

APEMANTUS   Let me stay at thine apperil, Timon. I come 33
to observe; I give thee warning on 't.

TIMON   I take no heed of thee. Thou'rt an Athenian,
therefore welcome. I myself would have no power;   36
prithee, let my meat make thee silent.   37

APEMANTUS   I scorn thy meat; 'twould choke me, for I 38
should ne'er flatter thee. O you gods, what a number 39
of men eats Timon, and he sees 'em not! It grieves me
to see so many dip their meat in one man's blood; and 41
all the madness is, he cheers them up, too.   42
I wonder men dare trust themselves with men.

---

271 most i.e., more. **omitt'st** fail to take advantage of   **283 unpeaceable** quarrelsome, incessantly barking.   **spurn** kick   **285 fly** flee   **286 opposite to** (1) antagonistic to (2) the reverse of   **287 outgoes** surpasses   **288 heart** essence   **290 meed** merit, or, gift   **293 use of quittance** usual rates of repayment with interest
1.2. Location: A banqueting room in Timon's house.
s.d. Hautboys oboelike instruments.   **states** i.e., rulers of the state, senators.   **dropping** i.e., "dropping in," arriving casually.   **like himself** not in finery   **3 long peace** eternal rest   **4 gone** died   **6 free** generous

12 gives . . . receives (Compare with Acts 20:35: "It is more blessed to give than to receive.")   **13 at that game** i.e., at taking in wealth while seeming to be generous   **13–14 dare To imitate** i.e., offend the gods by imitating   **14 that are rich** i.e., in those who are rich.   **fair** i.e., excused by their wealth   **17 set a gloss on** give a speciously fair appearance to   **18 Recanting goodness** generosity that takes back what it has offered   **19 there needs none** there is no need for ceremony   **22 confessed it** acknowledged the truth of what you say   **23 Hanged it** i.e., killed it instead. (Apemantus replies with a jesting allusion to the saying, "Confess and be hanged.")   **26 have thee thrust** provoke you into thrusting   **27 churl** surly person.   **humor** disposition   **28 Does** that does   **29 Ira furor brevis est** wrath is a brief madness (Horace's *Epistles*, 1.2.62)   **31 affect** (1) like (2) seek, aim at   **33 thine apperil** your peril, risk   **36 would . . . power** do not wish the power (to silence you)   **37 meat** food   **38–39 'twould . . . thee** (Apemantus implies that Timon's food is to reward flatterers; Apemantus, being none, would choke on it.)   **41 one man's blood** (Possible allusion to the Last Supper; the *fellow* in lines 46–49, who shares food and drink only to betray his host, is like Judas.)   **42 all . . . too** the most mad aspect of his behavior is that he encourages them

Methinks they should invite them without knives; 44
Good for their meat, and safer for their lives. 45
There's much example for 't. The fellow that sits next
him, now parts bread with him, pledges the breath of 47
him in a divided draft, is the readiest man to kill 48
him. 'T has been proved. If I were a huge man, I 49
should fear to drink at meals,
Lest they should spy my windpipe's dangerous
notes. 51
Great men should drink with harness on their throats. 52
TIMON [*toasting a Lord who drinks to him*]
My lord, in heart! And let the health go round. 53
SECOND LORD
Let it flow this way, my good lord. 54
APEMANTUS   Flow this way? A brave fellow! He keeps 55
his tides well. Those healths will make thee and thy 56
state look ill, Timon. 57
Here's that which is too weak to be a sinner: 58
Honest water, which ne'er left man i' the mire. 59
This and my food are equals; there's no odds. 60
Feasts are too proud to give thanks to the gods. 61

Apemantus' grace.

Immortal gods, I crave no pelf. 62
I pray for no man but myself.
Grant I may never prove so fond 64
To trust man on his oath or bond, 65
Or a harlot for her weeping,
Or a dog that seems a-sleeping,
Or a keeper with my freedom, 68
Or my friends, if I should need 'em.
Amen. So fall to 't. 70
Rich men sin, and I eat root. [*He eats and drinks.*]
Much good dich thy good heart, Apemantus! 72
TIMON   Captain Alcibiades, your heart's in the field 73
now.
ALCIBIADES   My heart is ever at your service, my lord.
TIMON   You had rather be at a breakfast of enemies 76
than a dinner of friends. 77
ALCIBIADES   So they were bleeding new, my lord, 78
there's no meat like 'em. I could wish my best friend
at such a feast.

APEMANTUS   Would all those flatterers were thine enemies then, that then thou mightst kill 'em—and bid
me to 'em! 83
FIRST LORD Might we but have that happiness, my lord,
that you would once use our hearts, whereby we 85
might express some part of our zeals, we should think 86
ourselves forever perfect. 87
TIMON   O, no doubt, my good friends, but the gods
themselves have provided that I shall have much help
from you. How had you been my friends else? Why
have you that charitable title from thousands, did not 91
you chiefly belong to my heart? I have told more of 92
you to myself than you can with modesty speak in 93
your own behalf; and thus far I confirm you. O you 94
gods, think I, what need we have any friends if we 95
should ne'er have need of 'em? They were the most
needless creatures living, should we ne'er have use for 97
'em, and would most resemble sweet instruments 98
hung up in cases, that keeps their sounds to themselves. Why, I have often wished myself poorer, that I
might come nearer to you. We are born to do benefits;
and what better or properer can we call our own than 102
the riches of our friends? O, what a precious comfort
'tis to have so many, like brothers, commanding one 104
another's fortunes! O, joy's e'en made away ere 't can 105
be born! Mine eyes cannot hold out water, methinks. 106
To forget their faults, I drink to you. 107
                    [*He weeps, and drinks a toast.*]
APEMANTUS   Thou weep'st to make them drink, Timon. 108
SECOND LORD [*to Timon*]
Joy had the like conception in our eyes,
And at that instant like a babe sprung up. 110
APEMANTUS
Ho, ho! I laugh to think that babe a bastard. 111
THIRD LORD [*to Timon*]
I promise you, my lord, you moved me much. 112
APEMANTUS   Much!   *Sound tucket* [*within*]. 113
TIMON
What means that trump?

Enter Servant.

                                   How now? 114
SERVANT   Please you, my lord, there are certain ladies
most desirous of admittance.
TIMON   Ladies? What are their wills?

---

44 without knives (Refers to the Renaissance custom of guests bringing their own knives.)   **45 Good . . . meat** i.e., without knives, the
guests would eat less food   **47 parts** shares.   **pledges the breath** i.e.,
drinks to the health   **48 a divided draft** a cup that they share   **49 'T
has been proved** there are precedents for it. (Compare with line 143.)
huge great in rank and wealth   **51 windpipe's . . . notes** indications
on my throat of where my windpipe is (and hence where it might be
slit) as the head is thrown back. (The *windpipe* also suggests a bagpipe capable of *notes* or musical sounds.)   **52 harness** armor   **53 in
heart** heartily.   **health** toast, and the cup   **54 flow** circulate
55 brave fine, foppish. (Said ironically.)   **56 tides** times, seasons
(with quibbling reference to *flow* of tides; Apemantus comments sardonically that the Second Lord is making sure that he will get plenty
to drink.)   **57 state** (1) physical condition (2) fortune, estate   **58 a
sinner** an incentive to sin   **59 i' the mire** i.e., in trouble   **60 there's
no odds** there's nothing to choose between them   **61 Feasts** i.e., givers and partakers of fine feasts   **62 pelf** property, possessions
64 fond foolish   **65 To** as to   **68 keeper** jailer   **70 fall to 't** i.e., begin to eat   **72 dich** may it do. (Originally a contraction of "d' it ye"
in the phrase "much good do it you.")   **73 field** battlefield   **76 of**
consisting of   **77 of** among   **78 So** provided that

83 to 'em i.e., to eat them   **85 use our hearts** make trial of our love
86 zeals love   **87 forever perfect** completely happy   **91 charitable
title** beloved name.   **from** from among   **92 told** (1) recited (2)
counted   **92–93 of you** i.e., concerning your deservings
94 confirm you endorse your claim (to be my worthy friends)
95 what why   **97 needless** useless   **98 instruments** musical instruments   **102 properer** more fittingly   **104 commanding** having at their
disposal   **105 made away** destroyed, i.e., turned to tears   **106 born**
i.e., expressed   **107 To . . . faults** i.e., to mask my weakness in giving way to tears   **108 Thou . . . drink** i.e., you ought to weep at the
way your absurd sentimentalizing is just giving them an excuse to
drink up your substance   **110 sprung up** (1) leaped from the womb
(2) welled up like a spring of tears   **111 bastard** i.e., illegitimate,
without genuine source. (Refers to the guests' tears.)   **112 promise** assure   **113 Much** (An expression of contemptuous disbelief; playing on
much in the previous line.)   **s.d. tucket** trumpet call   **114 trump**
trumpet blast

SERVANT   There comes with them a forerunner, my
lord, which bears that office to signify their pleasures.   119

TIMON   I pray, let them be admitted.   [*Exit Servant.*]

Enter Cupid.

CUPID

Hail to thee, worthy Timon, and to all
That of his bounties taste! The five best senses
Acknowledge thee their patron, and come freely
To gratulate thy plenteous bosom. Th' ear,   124
Taste, touch, and smell, pleased from thy table rise;
They only now come but to feast thine eyes.   126

TIMON

They're welcome all. Let 'em have kind admittance.
Music, make their welcome!

[*Cupid summons the maskers.*]

FIRST LORD

You see, my lord, how ample you're beloved.   129

[*Music.*] *Enter a masque of Ladies* [*as*] *Amazons,
with lutes in their hands, dancing and playing.*

APEMANTUS   Hoyday!   130
What a sweep of vanity comes this way!
They dance? They are madwomen.
Like madness is the glory of this life   133
As this pomp shows to a little oil and root.   134
We make ourselves fools to disport ourselves   135
And spend our flatteries to drink those men   136
Upon whose age we void it up again   137
With poisonous spite and envy.   138
Who lives that's not depravèd or depraves?   139
Who dies that bears not one spurn to their graves   140
Of their friends' gift?   141
I should fear those that dance before me now
Would one day stamp upon me. 'T has been done;
Men shut their doors against a setting sun.   144

*The Lords rise from table, with much adoring of
Timon; and to show their loves each singles out an
Amazon, and all dance, men with women, a lofty
strain or two to the hautboys, and cease.*

TIMON

You have done our pleasures much grace, fair ladies,
Set a fair fashion on our entertainment,   146
Which was not half so beautiful and kind.   147
You have added worth unto 't and luster,
And entertained me with mine own device.   149

I am to thank you for 't.   150

FIRST LADY

My lord, you take us even at the best.   151

APEMANTUS   Faith, for the worst is filthy and would not   152
hold taking, I doubt me.   153

TIMON

Ladies, there is an idle banquet attends you;   154
Please you to dispose yourselves.   155

ALL LADIES   Most thankfully, my lord.

Exeunt [*Cupid and Ladies*].

TIMON   Flavius!

FLAVIUS

My lord?

TIMON   The little casket bring me hither.

FLAVIUS   Yes, my lord. [*Aside.*] More jewels yet?
There is no crossing him in 's humor;   160
Else I should tell him well, i' faith I should,   161
When all's spent, he'd be crossed then, an he could.   162
'Tis pity bounty had not eyes behind,   163
That man might ne'er be wretched for his mind.   164

Exit.

FIRST LORD   Where be our men?

SERVANT   Here, my lord, in readiness.

SECOND LORD

Our horses!

Enter Flavius [*with the casket*].

TIMON   O my friends, I have one word
To say to you. Look you, my good lord,
I must entreat you honor me so much   169
As to advance this jewel; accept it and wear it,   170
Kind my lord.   [*He offers a jewel.*]   171

FIRST LORD

I am so far already in your gifts—   172

ALL   So are we all.

Enter a Servant.

SERVANT

My lord, there are certain nobles of the Senate
Newly alighted and come to visit you.

TIMON

They are fairly welcome.   [*Exit Servant.*]

FLAVIUS   I beseech your honor,   176
Vouchsafe me a word; it does concern you near.   177

TIMON

Near? Why then, another time I'll hear thee.
I prithee, let's be provided to show them
entertainment.

---

119 which who. **office** function. **pleasures** wishes **124 gratulate**
greet, salute. **plenteous bosom** generous heart **126 They** i.e., the
maskers. **only now come but** come only **129 ample** amply
130 Hoyday (Exclamation denoting surprise; a variety of "heyday.")
133 Like similar, equal. **glory** vainglory **134 As . . . root** i.e., in
the same way as this splendid feast appears when compared with the
bare necessities of life **135 disport** entertain **136–138 And . . .
envy** and lavish our flatteries in drinking the healths of those upon
whom, when they are old, we cast up our surfeit in poisonous spite
and malice **139 depravèd** vilified, slandered. **depraves** slanders
140 spurn injury, insult **141 gift** giving **144 s.d. adoring of** paying
homage to **146 Set . . . on** given grace and elegance to **147 was
not** i.e., before your arrival was not. **kind** gracious **149 with . . .
device** (The masque appears to have been designed by Timon to surprise his guests, or, he acknowledges that it was designed especially
for him.)

150 am to am under obligation to **151 take . . . best** i.e., praise us
most generously **152 for the worst** i.e., since the worst part of you.
(An obscene suggestion.) **152–153 would . . . taking** i.e., (1) would
not warrant notice (2) is too rotten with venereal disease **153 doubt
me** fear **154 idle** trifling, slight **155 dispose yourselves** take your
places **160 humor** frame of mind **161 well** plainly **162 crossed** (1)
wishing to have his debts canceled (2) thwarted (as in line 160). **an**
if **163 bounty** generosity. **had not eyes behind** i.e., is not able to
be more cautious **164 for his mind** on account of his generous inclinations **169 you honor** you to honor **170 advance** make more worthy, i.e., by possessing it **171 Kind my lord** my kind lord **172 in
your gifts** indebted to you for your gifts **176 fairly** sincerely
177 near closely

FLAVIUS [*aside*]   I scarce know how.

Enter another Servant.

SECOND SERVANT
May it please your honor, Lord Lucius,
Out of his free love, hath presented to you
Four milk-white horses trapped in silver.   183
TIMON
I shall accept them fairly. Let the presents   184
Be worthily entertained.   [*Exit Servant.*]

Enter a third Servant.

                              How now? What news?   185
THIRD SERVANT   Please you, my lord, that honorable
gentleman, Lord Lucullus, entreats your company to-
morrow to hunt with him and has sent your honor
two brace of greyhounds.   189
TIMON
I'll hunt with him; and let them be received,
Not without fair reward.   [*Exit Servant.*]
FLAVIUS [*aside*]   What will this come to?
He commands us to provide, and give great gifts,
And all out of an empty coffer;
Nor will he know his purse, or yield me this,   194
To show him what a beggar his heart is,
Being of no power to make his wishes good.   196
His promises fly so beyond his state   197
That what he speaks is all in debt; he owes
For every word. He is so kind that he now
Pays interest for 't; his land's put to their books.   200
Well, would I were gently put out of office
Before I were forced out!
Happier is he that has no friend to feed
Than such that do e'en enemies exceed.   204
I bleed inwardly for my lord.   *Exit.*
TIMON [*to the Lords*]   You do yourselves
Much wrong, you bate too much of your own
    merits.—   206
Here, my lord, a trifle of our love.   [*He offers a gift.*]
SECOND LORD
With more than common thanks I will receive it.
THIRD LORD   O, he's the very soul of bounty!
TIMON   And now I remember, my lord, you gave good   210
words the other day of a bay courser I rode on. 'Tis   211
yours because you liked it.
THIRD LORD
O, I beseech you, pardon me, my lord, in that.   213
TIMON
You may take my word, my lord: I know no man

Can justly praise but what he does affect.   215
I weigh my friends' affection with mine own.   216
I'll tell you true, I'll call to you.   217
ALL LORDS   O, none so welcome.
TIMON
I take all and your several visitations   219
So kind to heart, 'tis not enough to give.   220
Methinks I could deal kingdoms to my friends
And ne'er be weary. Alcibiades,
Thou art a soldier, therefore seldom rich.
It comes in charity to thee; for all thy living   224
Is 'mongst the dead, and all the lands thou hast
Lie in a pitched field.   226
ALCIBIADES   Ay, defiled land, my lord.   227
FIRST LORD   We are so virtuously bound—
TIMON   And so am I to you.
SECOND LORD   So infinitely endeared—   230
TIMON   All to you. [*To servants.*] Lights, more lights!   231
FIRST LORD
The best of happiness, honor, and fortunes
Keep with you, Lord Timon!   233
TIMON   Ready for his friends.   234
                Exeunt lords [and all but Apemantus and Timon].
APEMANTUS   What a coil's here!   235
Serving of becks and jutting-out of bums!   236
I doubt whether their legs be worth the sums   237
That are given for 'em. Friendship's full of dregs.
Methinks false hearts should never have sound legs.   239
Thus honest fools lay out their wealth on curtsies.   240
TIMON
Now, Apemantus, if thou wert not sullen,
I would be good to thee.
APEMANTUS   No, I'll nothing; for if I should be bribed
too, there would be none left to rail upon thee, and
then thou wouldst sin the faster. Thou giv'st so long,
Timon, I fear me thou wilt give away thyself in paper   246
shortly. What needs these feasts, pomps, and vain-   247
glories?
TIMON   Nay, an you begin to rail on society once, I am   249
sworn not to give regard to you. Farewell, and come   250
with better music.   *Exit.*
APEMANTUS   So.
Thou wilt not hear me now; thou shalt not then.   253
I'll lock thy heaven from thee.   254

183 **trapped in silver** in silver-mounted trappings   184 **fairly** graciously   185 **Be worthily entertained** be given the reception they deserve   189 **brace** pair   194 **purse** financial situation.   **yield me this**
grant me opportunity   196 **Being of** i.e., the desires of his heart having   197 **state** estate   200 **put . . . books** mortgaged to those whom
he has befriended with gifts   204 **Than . . . exceed** i.e., than he that
feeds so-called "friends" who, by consuming his wealth, outdo his
enemies in ruining him   206 **bate . . . of** belittle too much
210–211 **gave good words** spoke favorably   211 **bay courser** dark
brown horse with black mane and tail   213 **pardon . . . that** i.e.,
forgive my declining the offer; my mentioning the horse was not
meant as a hint

215 **but . . . affect** a thing unless he likes and desires it   216 **weigh
. . . with** give equal weight to . . . as compared with   217 **call to**
call on, or, perhaps, appeal to in time of need   219 **all . . . several**
your joint and individual   220 **kind** kindly.   **'tis . . . give** there isn't
enough wealth in my possession to match my wish to be generous
224 **It . . . thee** i.e., giving to you is an act of real charity.   **living** (1)
existence (2) property, wealth   226 **pitched field** battlefield
227 **defiled** (1) with a quibble on *pitched*; compare with Ecclesiasticus 13:1: "He that toucheth pitch shall be defiled" (2) arrayed with
files or rows of soldiers   230 **endeared** obligated   231 **All to you**
i.e., the obligation is entirely mine, or, all mine is yours   233 **Keep**
dwell, remain   234 **Ready for** ready to assist   235 **coil** fuss
236 **Serving of becks** bowing   237 **legs** (1) limbs (2) bows, curtsies
239 **sound legs** i.e., healthy legs able to make deceptively flattering
bows   240 **curtsies** (1) bows (2) courtesies   246 **I fear me** I fear.
paper bonds, promises to pay   247 **What needs** what necessity is
there for   249 **an . . . once** if once you begin   250 **give regard to**
take notice of   253 **thou shalt not then** you won't have the opportunity later   254 **thy heaven** i.e., my saving advice

O, that men's ears should be
To counsel deaf, but not to flattery!   *Exit.*

❧

2.1   *Enter a Senator [with papers in his hand].*

SENATOR
    And late, five thousand. To Varro and to Isidore   1
    He owes nine nine thousand, besides my former sum,
    Which makes it five-and-twenty. Still in motion   3
    Of raging waste? It cannot hold; it will not.   4
    If I want gold, steal but a beggar's dog   5
    And give it Timon, why, the dog coins gold.
    If I would sell my horse and buy twenty more
    Better than he, why, give my horse to Timon—
    Ask nothing, give it him—it foals me straight,   9
    And able horses. No porter at his gate,   10
    But rather one that smiles and still invites   11
    All that pass by. It cannot hold. No reason   12
    Can sound his state in safety.—Caphis, ho!   13
    Caphis, I say!

        Enter Caphis.

CAPHIS   Here, sir. What is your pleasure?
SENATOR
    Get on your cloak and haste you to Lord Timon.
    Importune him for my moneys. Be not ceased   16
    With slight denial, nor then silenced when   17
    "Commend me to your master" and the cap   18
    Plays in the right hand, thus, but tell him   19
    My uses cry to me; I must serve my turn   20
    Out of mine own. His days and times are past,   21
    And my reliances on his fracted dates   22
    Have smit my credit. I love and honor him,   23
    But must not break my back to heal his finger.
    Immediate are my needs, and my relief
    Must not be tossed and turned to me in words,   26
    But find supply immediate. Get you gone.
    Put on a most importunate aspect,
    A visage of demand, for I do fear
    When every feather sticks in his own wing   30
    Lord Timon will be left a naked gull,   31
    Which flashes now a phoenix. Get you gone.   32

CAPHIS   I go, sir.
SENATOR [*giving him bonds*]
    Ay, go, sir. Take the bonds along with you
    And have the dates in compt.
CAPHIS   I will, sir.
SENATOR   Go.   *Exeunt.* 35

❧

2.2   *Enter steward [Flavius] with many bills in his hand.*

FLAVIUS
    No care, no stop! So senseless of expense
    That he will neither know how to maintain it   2
    Nor cease his flow of riot, takes no account   3
    How things go from him nor resumes no care   4
    Of what is to continue. Never mind   5
    Was to be so unwise to be so kind.   6
    What shall be done? He will not hear till feel.   7
    I must be round with him, now he comes from
        hunting.   8
    Fie, fie, fie, fie!

        *Enter Caphis [and the Servants of] Isidore and
        Varro.*

CAPHIS
    Good even, Varro. What, you come for money?   10
VARRO'S SERVANT   Is 't not your business too?
CAPHIS   It is. And yours too, Isidore?
ISIDORE'S SERVANT   It is so.
CAPHIS   Would we were all discharged!   14
VARRO'S SERVANT   I fear it.   15
CAPHIS   Here comes the lord.

        Enter Timon and his train [with Alcibiades].

TIMON
    So soon as dinner's done we'll forth again,   17
    My Alcibiades.—With me? What is your will?
CAPHIS [*presenting a bill*]
    My lord, here is a note of certain dues.   19
TIMON   Dues? Whence are you?
CAPHIS   Of Athens here, my lord.
TIMON   Go to my steward.
CAPHIS
    Please it your lordship, he hath put me off
    To the succession of new days this month.   24
    My master is awaked by great occasion   25
    To call upon his own, and humbly prays you   26
    That with your other noble parts you'll suit   27

2.1. Location: Athens. A Senator's house.
1 late lately **3–4 Still . . . waste** perpetually and ceaselessly squandering **4 hold** hold out, last (also in line 12) **5 steal but** I need only steal **9 foals me straight** at once yields me foals, i.e., more horses (as gifts) **10 And able horses** i.e., and what's more, they are full-grown horses, not literally foals. **porter** one who sternly denies entrance **11 still** constantly **12 reason** rational inquiry **13 sound . . . safety** by sounding the depth of Timon's financial position find it to be safe **16 ceased** silenced, put off **17 slight** negligent, offhand **17–19 when . . . thus** i.e., when he offers fair greetings and flattering gestures in lieu of real payment **20 uses** needs **20–21 I must . . . own** I must address my own necessities with my own money **21 days and times** i.e., dates for repayment of his loans **22 fracted** broken (by failure to meet payments on notes due) **23 smit** smitten, hurt **26 tossed and turned** i.e., bandied back, as in tennis **30 When . . . wing** i.e., when everything is in the hands of its rightful possessor **31 gull** (1) unfledged bird (2) dupe **32 Which flashes now** who now showily displays himself as. **phoenix** mythical bird, one of a kind, i.e., rare and precious creature

35 in compt reckoned
2.2. Location: Athens. Before Timon's house.
2 know learn **3 riot** uncontrolled reveling **4–5 resumes . . . continue** makes no provision for continuing **5–6 Never . . . kind** never was there a mind so unwise in being so kind, so determined to be stupidly generous **7 till feel** until he suffers feelingly **8 round** plain-spoken. **now** now that **10 Good even** (A greeting used any time after noon.) **14 discharged** paid **15 fear it** i.e., am apprehensive about our being paid **17 forth** go forth **19 dues** debts **24 To . . . month** from one day to another all month **25 awaked** roused, driven **26 his own** i.e., that which he has lent you **27 with . . . parts** in conformity to your other noble qualities

In giving him his right.

TIMON   Mine honest friend,
I prithee but repair to me next morning.   29

CAPHIS
Nay, good my lord—

TIMON   Contain thyself, good friend.

VARRO'S SERVANT
One Varro's servant, my good lord—

ISIDORE'S SERVANT
From Isidore; he humbly prays your speedy
payment.

CAPHIS
If you did know, my lord, my master's wants—

VARRO'S SERVANT
'Twas due on forfeiture, my lord, six weeks and
past.   34

ISIDORE'S SERVANT
Your steward puts me off, my lord, and I
Am sent expressly to your lordship.

TIMON   Give me breath.—   37
I do beseech you, good my lords, keep on;   38
I'll wait upon you instantly.
                        [*Exeunt Alcibiades and Lords.*]
                        [*To Flavius.*] Come hither. Pray you,   39
How goes the world, that I am thus encountered
With clamorous demands of broken bonds
And the detention of long-since-due debts   42
Against my honor?

FLAVIUS   Please you, gentlemen,   43
The time is unagreeable to this business.
Your importunacy cease till after dinner,   45
That I may make his lordship understand   46
Wherefore you are not paid.

TIMON   Do so, my friends.—   47
See them well entertained.   [*Exit.*]
FLAVIUS   Pray, draw near.   *Exit.* 48

Enter Apemantus and Fool.

CAPHIS   Stay, stay, here comes the Fool with Apemantus. Let's ha' some sport with 'em.   50

VARRO'S SERVANT   Hang him! He'll abuse us.   51

ISIDORE'S SERVANT   A plague upon him, dog!

VARRO'S SERVANT   How dost, Fool?

APEMANTUS   Dost dialogue with thy shadow?   54

VARRO'S SERVANT   I speak not to thee.

APEMANTUS   No, 'tis to thyself. [*To the Fool.*] Come away. 56

ISIDORE'S SERVANT [*to Varro's Servant*]   There's the fool 57
hangs on your back already.   58

APEMANTUS   No, thou stand'st single; thou'rt not on 59
him yet.   60

CAPHIS [*to Isidore's Servant*]   Where's the fool now?   61

APEMANTUS   He last asked the question. Poor rogues 62
and usurers' men, bawds between gold and want!   63

ALL THE SERVANTS   What are we, Apemantus?

APEMANTUS   Asses.

ALL THE SERVANTS   Why?

APEMANTUS   That you ask me what you are, and do not
know yourselves. Speak to 'em, Fool.

FOOL   How do you, gentlemen?

ALL THE SERVANTS   Gramercies, good Fool. How does 70
your mistress?

FOOL   She's e'en setting on water to scald such chickens 72
as you are. Would we could see you at Corinth!   73

APEMANTUS   Good! Gramercy.

Enter Page.

FOOL   Look you, here comes my mistress' page.

PAGE [*to the Fool*]   Why, how now, captain? What do
you in this wise company?—How dost thou,
Apemantus?

APEMANTUS   Would I had a rod in my mouth, that I 79
might answer thee profitably.   80

PAGE   Prithee, Apemantus, read me the superscription 81
of these letters. I know not which is which.
                        [*He shows two letters.*]

APEMANTUS   Canst not read?

PAGE   No.

APEMANTUS   There will little learning die then that day
thou art hanged. This is to Lord Timon, this to
Alcibiades. Go, thou wast born a bastard and thou'lt
die a bawd.

PAGE   Thou wast whelped a dog, and thou shalt famish 89
a dog's death. Answer not; I am gone.   *Exit.*

APEMANTUS   E'en so thou outrunn'st grace. Fool, I will 91
go with you to Lord Timon's.

FOOL   Will you leave me there?

APEMANTUS   If Timon stay at home.—You three serve 94
three usurers?

ALL THE SERVANTS   Ay. Would they served us!   96

APEMANTUS   So would I—as good a trick as ever
hangman served thief.

---

29 but repair only come   **34 on forfeiture** on penalty of forfeiting the
security for it if not paid on the date prescribed   **37 breath** breathing
space, time to breathe   **38 keep on** go ahead without me   **39 wait
. . . instantly** be with you in a moment   **42 the detention** the charge
of withholding payment   **43 Against my honor** contrary to my honorable reputation   **45 importunacy** persistent demands   **46 That** so that
47 Wherefore why   **48 entertained** received, treated.   **draw near**
come this way. (Said to Timon, or possibly to the creditors' servants,
who, however, decide to remain.)   **50 ha'** have   **51 abuse** vilify
54 shadow mirror image (reflecting your own folly)   **56 'tis to thyself**
i.e., you (Varro's servant) speak to yourself when you say "fool"
57–58 There's . . . already i.e., you (Varro's servant) have been labeled fool already. (See line 56.)

59–60 No . . . yet i.e., no, you (Isidore's servant), a fool, are standing by yourself; you're not on the back of Varro's servant yet
61 Where's . . . now i.e., whose back is labeled fool now? (implying
that it is the turn of Isidore's servant to wear that label)   **62 He** he
who (i.e., Caphis, who has now been called a fool like the others)
63 bawds . . . want middlemen who, like panders, bring together
usurers and needy men   **70 Gramercies** many thanks   **72 e'en . . .
water** just putting water on the fire.   **scald such chickens** (Allusion to
the sweating-tub treatment for venereal disease, which causes loss of
hair, just as a chicken loses its feathers through scalding. The Fool
also implies that they are fools deserving to be plucked.)   **73 Corinth**
a city noted for its brothels; hence, a brothel or the district for such
houses   **79 rod** stick (to use for a beating)   **80 profitably** to your
profit (by teaching you a lesson)   **81 superscription** address
89 whelped born.   **famish** die   **91 E'en so** precisely so.   **thou outrunn'st grace** you run away from profitable teaching and God's grace
94 If . . . home i.e., while Timon remains at home, a fool is there.
You three do you three   **96 Would . . . us** would that they looked
after us adequately. (But Apemantus deliberately misunderstands
serve, answering, "It would serve you right to be hanged.")

FOOL   Are you three usurers' men?

ALL THE SERVANTS   Ay, Fool.

FOOL   I think no usurer but has a fool to his servant; my 101
mistress is one, and I am her fool. When men come to 102
borrow of your masters, they approach sadly and go
away merry, but they enter my mistress' house
merrily and go away sadly. The reason of this?

VARRO'S SERVANT   I could render one.   106

APEMANTUS   Do it then, that we may account thee a
whoremaster and a knave; which notwithstanding,
thou shalt be no less esteemed.   109

VARRO'S SERVANT   What is a whoremaster, Fool?

FOOL   A fool in good clothes, and something like thee.
'Tis a spirit; sometimes 't appears like a lord, some- 112
times like a lawyer, sometimes like a philosopher,
with two stones more than 's artificial one. He is very 114
often like a knight; and generally, in all shapes that
man goes up and down in from fourscore to thirteen,
this spirit walks in.

VARRO'S SERVANT   Thou art not altogether a fool.

FOOL   Nor thou altogether a wise man. As much
foolery as I have, so much wit thou lack'st.

APEMANTUS   That answer might have become Apeman- 121
tus.

ALL THE SERVANTS   Aside, aside! Here comes Lord Timon.

[They stand aside.]

Enter Timon and steward [Flavius].

APEMANTUS   Come with me, Fool, come.

FOOL   I do not always follow lover, elder brother, and 125
woman; sometimes the philosopher.   126

[Exeunt Apemantus and Fool.]

FLAVIUS *[to Servants]*
Pray you, walk near. I'll speak with you anon.   127

Exeunt [Servants].

TIMON
You make me marvel wherefore ere this time
Had you not fully laid my state before me,   129
That I might so have rated my expense   130
As I had leave of means.

FLAVIUS   You would not hear me.   131
At many leisures I proposed—

TIMON   Go to!   132
Perchance some single vantages you took,   133

When my indisposition put you back,
And that unaptness made your minister   135
Thus to excuse yourself.

FLAVIUS   O my good lord,   136
At many times I brought in my accounts,
Laid them before you. You would throw them off
And say you found them in mine honesty.   139
When for some trifling present you have bid me
Return so much, I have shook my head and wept;   141
Yea, 'gainst th' authority of manners prayed you   142
To hold your hand more close. I did endure
Not seldom nor no slight checks when I have   144
Prompted you in the ebb of your estate   145
And your great flow of debts. My lovèd lord,
Though you hear now too late, yet now's a time;   147
The greatest of your having lacks a half   148
To pay your present debts.

TIMON   Let all my land be sold.

FLAVIUS
'Tis all engaged, some forfeited and gone,   151
And what remains will hardly stop the mouth   152
Of present dues. The future comes apace;   153
What shall defend the interim? And at length
How goes our reckoning?

TIMON
To Lacedaemon did my land extend.   156

FLAVIUS
O my good lord, the world is but a word.
Were it all yours to give it in a breath,
How quickly were it gone!

TIMON   You tell me true.

FLAVIUS
If you suspect my husbandry of falsehood,   160
Call me before th' exactest auditors
And set me on the proof. So the gods bless me,   162
When all our offices have been oppressed   163
With riotous feeders, when our vaults have wept   164
With drunken spilth of wine, when every room   165
Hath blazed with lights and brayed with minstrelsy,
I have retired me to a wasteful cock   167
And set mine eyes at flow.

TIMON   Prithee, no more.

FLAVIUS
Heavens, have I said, the bounty of this lord!
How many prodigal bits have slaves and peasants   170

101–102 my mistress is one (A bawd is a kind of usurer from whom customers "borrow" pleasure at great personal expense.)   106 one (Implies that the Fool's mistress's house is a bawdy house, where men come merrily but leave diseased and poorer.)   109 no less esteemed i.e., no less esteemed than at present, since these professions are highly regarded in Athens and since a usurer's servant is universally despised   112 spirit i.e., one that can assume various shapes   114 stones testicles.   than 's than his, the philosopher's.   artificial one i.e., the philosopher's stone, supposed to change other metals into gold   121 become been fitted for   125–126 lover . . . woman i.e., various sorts of persons proverbially connected with folly; an elder brother is the oldest son, one who will inherit property and hence might be unwisely generous   127 walk near remain nearby   129 fully . . . state completely detailed my financial position   130 rated i.e., estimated and regulated   131 As . . . means as my means permitted   132 leisures times when you were free.   proposed conferred, conversed.   Go to (An exclamation of impatience.)   133 single vantages occasional opportunities

135–136 that . . . yourself i.e., my disinclination to listen on those occasions served as your excuse thereafter for remaining silent. (Made your minister means "became your agent or means.")   139 found . . . honesty i.e., found warrant for believing the books properly kept in knowing me to be honest   141 Return so much give as in repayment a large gift   142 'gainst . . . manners contrary to what good manners dictated   144 checks rebukes   145 in in regard to   147 yet . . . time i.e., late as it is, it is necessary that you be made acquainted with it   148 The greatest . . . having your total wealth at a most optimistic reckoning   151 engaged mortgaged   152–153 stop . . . Of satisfy   153 dues debts.   apace quickly   156 Lacedaemon Sparta   160 husbandry management, stewardship   162 set . . . proof put me to the test   163 offices rooms, especially the kitchen and pantries   164 vaults wine cellars   165 spilth spilling   167 retired . . . cock withdrawn to sit beside the wastefully flowing faucet of a barrel   170 prodigal bits wasteful morsels

This night englutted! Who is not Timon's?   171
What heart, head, sword, force, means, but is Lord
    Timon's?   172
Great Timon, noble, worthy, royal Timon!
Ah, when the means are gone that buy this praise,
The breath is gone whereof this praise is made.
Feast-won, fast-lost; one cloud of winter showers,   176
These flies are couched.   [*He weeps.*]

TIMON   Come, sermon me no further.   177
No villainous bounty yet hath passed my heart;   178
Unwisely, not ignobly, have I given.
Why dost thou weep? Canst thou the conscience
    lack   180
To think I shall lack friends? Secure thy heart.   181
If I would broach the vessels of my love   182
And try the argument of hearts by borrowing,   183
Men and men's fortunes could I frankly use   184
As I can bid thee speak.

FLAVIUS   Assurance bless your thoughts!   186

TIMON
And in some sort these wants of mine are crowned,   187
That I account them blessings; for by these   188
Shall I try friends. You shall perceive how you   189
Mistake my fortunes; I am wealthy in my friends.—
Within there! Flaminius! Servilius!

Enter three servants [Flaminius, Servilius, and
another].

SERVANTS   My lord? My lord?

TIMON   I will dispatch you severally: [*to Servilius*] you   193
to Lord Lucius; [*to Flaminius*] to Lord Lucullus you—
I hunted with his honor today; [*to the other*] you to
Sempronius. Commend me to their loves, and, I am
proud, say, that my occasions have found time to use   197
'em toward a supply of money. Let the request be fifty   198
talents.

FLAMINIUS   As you have said, my lord.
                    [*Exeunt Servants.*]

FLAVIUS [*aside*]   Lord Lucius and Lucullus? Humh!

TIMON   Go you, sir, to the senators,
Of whom, even to the state's best health, I have   203
Deserved this hearing. Bid 'em send o' th' instant   204
A thousand talents to me.

FLAVIUS   I have been bold—
For that I knew it the most general way—   206

To them to use your signet and your name,   207
But they do shake their heads, and I am here
No richer in return.

TIMON   Is 't true? Can 't be?

FLAVIUS
They answer, in a joint and corporate voice,   210
That now they are at fall, want treasure, cannot   211
Do what they would, are sorry; you are honorable,
But yet they could have wished—they know not—
Something hath been amiss—a noble nature
May catch a wrench—would all were well—'tis pity.   215
And so, intending other serious matters,   216
After distasteful looks and these hard fractions,   217
With certain half-caps and cold-moving nods   218
They froze me into silence.

TIMON   You gods, reward them!
Prithee, man, look cheerly. These old fellows   220
Have their ingratitude in them hereditary.
Their blood is caked, 'tis cold, it seldom flows;   222
'Tis lack of kindly warmth they are not kind;   223
And nature, as it grows again toward earth,   224
Is fashioned for the journey, dull and heavy.
Go to Ventidius. Prithee, be not sad.
Thou art true and honest—ingeniously I speak—   227
No blame belongs to thee. Ventidius lately
Buried his father, by whose death he's stepped
Into a great estate. When he was poor,   230
Imprisoned, and in scarcity of friends,   231
I cleared him with five talents. Greet him from me.   232
Bid him suppose some good necessity   233
Touches his friend, which craves to be remembered   234
With those five talents. That had, give 't these
    fellows   235
To whom 'tis instant due. Ne'er speak or think
That Timon's fortunes 'mong his friends can sink.

FLAVIUS   I would I could not think it.
That thought is bounty's foe;   239
Being free itself, it thinks all others so.   *Exeunt.* 240

❖

171 **is not** i.e., does not profess himself to be   172 **means** financial resources   176 **fast-lost** (1) lost in time of fast (2) lost quickly and for good   177 **are couched** hide themselves (to avoid Timon's requests for help). **sermon** lecture   178 **villainous bounty** generosity that I am ashamed of   180 **conscience** faith, or judgment   181 **Secure** set at ease   182 **broach** tap, open. **my love** the love others have for me   183 **try . . . hearts** test protestations of love   184 **frankly** as freely.   186 **Assurance . . . thoughts** may your hopes prove well founded   187 **sort** manner, sense. **crowned** given a special dignity   188 **That** so that   189 **try** test   193 **severally** separately   197 **occasions** needs. **time** opportunity   198 **toward** for   203 **to . . . health** i.e., for my services in behalf of the state's welfare. (Compare with 4.3.93–96, where Alcibiades refers to Timon's sword and fortune offered in the defense of Athens.)   204 **o' th' instant** at once   206 **For that** because. **general** comprehensive, or customary (?)

207 **signet** signet ring and seal, token of authority   210 **corporate** united   211 **at fall** at low ebb. **want** lack   215 **catch a wrench** accidentally be wrenched away from its true bent   216 **intending** turning their attention to, or pretending (?)   217 **hard fractions** harsh broken sentences   218 **half-caps** i.e., salutations halfheartedly given. **cold-moving** chilling   220 **cheerly** cheerful   222 **caked** congealed   223 **'Tis . . . kind** it is lack of natural warmth that makes them not generous (with pun on *kind,* "natural," "of humankind")   224 **earth** i.e., the grave   227 **ingeniously** frankly   230–232 **When he was poor,** etc. (These lines echo Matthew 25:34–37 where Jesus discusses the Last Judgment.)   231 **scarcity** need   232 **cleared** freed   233 **good** genuine   234–235 **which . . . talents** which necessity of mine calls out for the return of those five talents as demonstration of his remembering my generosity   235 **That had** when you have that. **these fellows** to these fellows   239 **That . . . foe** i.e., the naive assumption that friends will remain true in hard times is the fatal weakness, and perhaps the undoing, of the bounteous impulse   240 **free** generous

3.1   [*Enter*] *Flaminius, waiting to speak with a lord,* [*Lucullus,*] *from his master. Enter a Servant to him.*

LUCULLUS' SERVANT   I have told my lord of you. He is coming down to you.

FLAMINIUS   I thank you, sir.

Enter Lucullus.

LUCULLUS' SERVANT   Here's my lord.

LUCULLUS [*aside*]   One of Lord Timon's men? A gift, I warrant. Why, this hits right; I dreamt of a silver basin 6 and ewer tonight.—Flaminius, honest Flaminius, you 7 are very respectively welcome, sir. [*To Servant.*] Fill me 8 some wine. [*Exit Servant.*] And how does that honorable, complete, free-hearted gentleman of Athens, thy 10 very bountiful good lord and master?

FLAMINIUS   His health is well, sir.

LUCULLUS   I am right glad that his health is well, sir. And what hast thou there under thy cloak, pretty Flaminius?

FLAMINIUS   Faith, nothing but an empty box, sir, which, in my lord's behalf, I come to entreat your honor to supply; who, having great and instant 18 occasion to use fifty talents, hath sent to your lordship 19 to furnish him, nothing doubting your present assis- 20 tance therein.

LUCULLUS   La, la, la la! "Nothing doubting," says he? Alas, good lord! A noble gentleman 'tis, if he would 23 not keep so good a house. Many a time and often I ha' 24 dined with him and told him on 't, and come again to 25 supper to him of purpose to have him spend less, and 26 yet he would embrace no counsel, take no warning by 27 my coming. Every man has his fault, and honesty is 28 his. I ha' told him on 't, but I could ne'er get him from 't. 30

Enter Servant, with wine.

SERVANT   Please your lordship, here is the wine.

LUCULLUS   Flaminius, I have noted thee always wise. Here's to thee.   [*He offers a toast.*]

FLAMINIUS   Your lordship speaks your pleasure. 34

LUCULLUS   I have observed thee always for a towardly 35 prompt spirit—give thee thy due—and one that 36 knows what belongs to reason; and canst use the time 37 well, if the time use thee well. Good parts in thee! [*To Servant.*] Get you gone, sirrah. [*Exit Servant.*] Draw nearer, honest Flaminius. Thy lord's a bountiful gentleman; but thou art wise, and thou know'st well

enough, although thou com'st to me, that this is no time to lend money, especially upon bare friendship, 43 without security. Here's three solidares for thee. [*He 44 gives a tip.*] Good boy, wink at me, and say thou 45 sawst me not. Fare thee well.

FLAMINIUS
Is 't possible the world should so much differ,   47
And we alive that lived? Fly, damnèd baseness,   48
To him that worships thee! [*He throws the money back.*]

LUCULLUS   Ha? Now I see thou art a fool, and fit for thy master.   *Exit Lucullus.*

FLAMINIUS
May these add to the number that may scald thee!   52
Let molten coin be thy damnation,   53
Thou disease of a friend and not himself!   54
Has friendship such a faint and milky heart
It turns in less than two nights? O you gods!   56
I feel my master's passion. This slave   57
Unto his honor has my lord's meat in him.   58
Why should it thrive and turn to nutriment
When he is turned to poison?   60
O, may diseases only work upon 't!   61
And, when he's sick to death, let not that part of nature
Which my lord paid for be of any power
To expel sickness, but prolong his hour!   *Exit.*

❖

3.2   *Enter Lucius, with three Strangers.*

LUCIUS   Who, the Lord Timon? He is my very good friend and an honorable gentleman.

FIRST STRANGER   We know him for no less, though we 3 are but strangers to him. But I can tell you one thing, my lord, and which I hear from common rumors: now 5 Lord Timon's happy hours are done and past, and his estate shrinks from him.

LUCIUS   Fie, no, do not believe it! He cannot want for 8 money.

SECOND STRANGER   But believe you this, my lord, that not long ago one of his men was with the Lord Lucullus to borrow so many talents, nay, urged extremely 12 for 't, and showed what necessity belonged to 't, and 13 yet was denied.

3.1. Location: Athens. Lucullus' house.
6 hits right accords perfectly   **7 ewer** pitcher.   **tonight** last night
8 respectively respectfully   **10 complete** accomplished   **18 supply** fill
18–19 instant occasion urgent need   **20 nothing** not at all.   **present** immediate   **23 'tis** he is   **24 keep . . . house** be so lavish in his entertaining   **25 on 't** of it   **26 of** on.   **have him** persuade him to
27 by from   **28 honesty** liberality   **30 from 't** away from it   **34 Your . . . pleasure** it pleases your lordship to say so   **35–36 towardly prompt** quick to meet another's thoughts, well-disposed
37–38 canst . . . thee well can make the most of an opportunity when it presents itself   **38 parts** qualities

43 bare mere   **44 solidares** small coins. (A term invented by Shakespeare, evidently.)   **45 wink** shut the eyes   **47–48 so . . . lived** i.e., change so much in our lifetime   **52 scald** i.e., roast in hell
53 Let . . . damnation i.e., may you be punished in hell by having molten metal poured down your throat   **54 Thou . . . himself** you who are no true friend at all but only a diseased resemblance   **56 It turns** that it sours like milk (with quibble on the idea of *turn* as in "turncoat")   **57 feel . . . passion** i.e., feel angry on my master's behalf, share his anger and his suffering   **57–58 slave Unto his honor** person slavishly devoted to his own dignity. (Said ironically.)
58 meat i.e., food of a feast   **60 When . . . poison** when his behavior is so poisonous   **61 work upon 't** thrive upon it, *my lord's meat in him*

3.2. Location: Athens. A public place.
3 for no less to be no less than you say   **5 which** one which   **8 want for** lack   **12 urged extremely** begged insistently   **13 what . . . to 't** how necessary it was

LUCIUS   How?   15
SECOND STRANGER   I tell you, denied, my lord.
LUCIUS   What a strange case was that! Now, before the
  gods, I am ashamed on 't. Denied that honorable
  man? There was very little honor showed in 't. For my
  own part, I must needs confess, I have received some
  small kindnesses from him, as money, plate, jewels,
  and suchlike trifles, nothing comparing to his; yet had   22
  he mistook him and sent to me, I should ne'er have   23
  denied his occasion so many talents.   24

            Enter Servilius.

SERVILIUS   See, by good hap, yonder's my lord. I have   25
  sweat to see his honor. [*To Lucius.*] My honored lord—   26
LUCIUS   Servilius? You are kindly met, sir. Fare thee
  well. Commend me to thy honorable virtuous lord,
  my very exquisite friend.   [*He starts to go.*] 29
SERVILIUS   May it please your honor, my lord hath
  sent—
LUCIUS   Ha? What has he sent? I am so much endeared   32
  to that lord; he's ever sending. How shall I thank him,
  think'st thou? And what has he sent now?
SERVILIUS   He's only sent his present occasion now, my
  lord, requesting your lordship to supply his instant   36
  use with so many talents.   37
LUCIUS
  I know his lordship is but merry with me;
  He cannot want fifty—five hundred—talents.   39
SERVILIUS
  But in the meantime he wants less, my lord.
  If his occasion were not virtuous,   41
  I should not urge it half so faithfully.
LUCIUS
  Dost thou speak seriously, Servilius?
SERVILIUS   Upon my soul, 'tis true, sir.
LUCIUS   What a wicked beast was I to disfurnish myself   45
  against such a good time, when I might ha' shown   46
  myself honorable! How unluckily it happened that I   47
  should purchase the day before for a little part, and   48
  undo a great deal of honor! Servilius, now before the   49
  gods, I am not able to do—the more beast, I say—I
  was sending to use Lord Timon myself, these gentle-   51
  men can witness; but I would not for the wealth of   52
  Athens I had done 't now. Commend me bountifully
  to his good lordship, and I hope his honor will con-   54
  ceive the fairest of me, because I have no power to be   55
  kind. And tell him this from me: I count it one of my

greatest afflictions, say, that I cannot pleasure such an 57
  honorable gentleman. Good Servilius, will you be-
  friend me so far as to use mine own words to him?
SERVILIUS   Yes, sir, I shall.
LUCIUS   I'll look you out a good turn, Servilius.   61
                                          Exit Servilius.
  True, as you said, Timon is shrunk indeed;   62
  And he that's once denied will hardly speed.   63
                                                    Exit.
FIRST STRANGER   Do you observe this, Hostilius?
SECOND STRANGER   Ay, too well.
FIRST STRANGER   Why, this is the world's soul,   66
  And just of the same piece   67
  Is every flatterer's sport. Who can call him his friend 68
  That dips in the same dish? For, in my knowing,   69
  Timon has been this lord's father   70
  And kept his credit with his purse,   71
  Supported his estate; nay, Timon's money
  Has paid his men their wages. He ne'er drinks
  But Timon's silver treads upon his lip.   74
  And yet—O, see the monstrousness of man
  When he looks out in an ungrateful shape!—   76
  He does deny him, in respect of his,   77
  What charitable men afford to beggars.
THIRD STRANGER
  Religion groans at it.
FIRST STRANGER   For mine own part,
  I never tasted Timon in my life,   80
  Nor came any of his bounties over me   81
  To mark me for his friend; yet I protest,
  For his right noble mind, illustrious virtue,   83
  And honorable carriage,   84
  Had his necessity made use of me,
  I would have put my wealth into donation   86
  And the best half should have returned to him,
  So much I love his heart. But I perceive
  Men must learn now with pity to dispense,
  For policy sits above conscience.   *Exeunt.* 90

                        ❧

3.3   *Enter a third Servant [of Timon's] with
          Sempronius, another of Timon's friends.*

SEMPRONIUS
  Must he needs trouble me in 't? Hum! 'Bove all
  others?

---

15 How? what's that you say? **22 his** i.e., Lucullus' receiving of generosity **23 mistook . . . me** i.e., mistakenly sent to me, who owe him less **24 occasion** need (as also in line 35) **25 hap** fortune **25–26 I have sweat** i.e., I have been hurrying **29 exquisite** sought after, extraordinary **32 endeared** obliged **36–37 supply . . . use** provide for his immediate need **39 He cannot . . . talents** (Probably an indication of Shakespeare's uncertainty over the value of this currency; see also *so many* above in lines 12, 24, and 37.) **41 were not virtuous** were due to a fault instead of a virtue, i.e., generosity **45–46 disfurnish . . . time** leave myself unprepared for such an excellent opportunity **47–49 that I . . . honor** i.e., that I just yesterday laid out a sum of money in a small investment and thus made it impossible now to acquire a great honor by helping Timon **51 use** borrow from **52 would not** could not bring myself to wish **54–55 conceive the fairest** think the best **55 because** i.e., even though

57 pleasure satisfy, please **61 look you out** seek occasion to do you **62 shrunk** brought low **63 speed** prosper **66 soul** real essence, vital principle **67 just . . . piece** exactly the same, cut from the same piece of cloth **68 sport** plaything, diversion **69 dips . . . dish** (Alludes to Judas' betrayal of Christ; see Matthew 26:23.) **in my knowing** to my knowledge **70 father** i.e., patron **71 kept his** i.e., maintained Lucius'. **his purse** i.e., Timon's wealth **74 treads** presses **76 looks out** appears **77 He . . . his** i.e., Lucius denies Timon an amount that equals, in relation to Lucius' total wealth **80 tasted Timon** i.e., sampled Timon's liberality **81 Nor . . . me** nor did any of his generosities light on me **83 For** because of **84 carriage** conduct **86 put . . . donation** made a gift of my wealth **90 policy** self-interest

3.3. Location: Athens. Sempronius' house.

He might have tried Lord Lucius or Lucullus;
And now Ventidius is wealthy too,
Whom he redeemed from prison. All these
Owe their estates unto him.

SERVANT My lord,
They have all been touched and found base metal,   7
For they have all denied him.

SEMPRONIUS How? Have they denied him?
Has Ventidius and Lucullus denied him?
And does he send to me? Three? Humh!
It shows but little love or judgment in him.
Must I be his last refuge? His friends, like
   physicians,
Thrive, give him over. Must I take th' cure upon me?   14
He's much disgraced me in 't. I'm angry at him,
That might have known my place. I see no sense
   for 't   16
But his occasions might have wooed me first;   17
For, in my conscience, I was the first man   18
That e'er receivèd gift from him.
And does he think so backwardly of me now   20
That I'll requite it last? No!   21
So it may prove an argument of laughter   22
To th' rest, and I 'mongst lords be thought a fool.
I'd rather than the worth of thrice the sum
He'd sent to me first, but for my mind's sake;   25
I'd such a courage to do him good. But now return,   26
And with their faint reply this answer join:
Who bates mine honor shall not know my coin.   28
                                                    Exit.

SERVANT Excellent! Your lordship's a goodly villain.   29
The devil knew not what he did when he made man
politic; he crossed himself by 't, and I cannot think but   31
in the end the villainies of man will set him clear.   32
How fairly this lord strives to appear foul! Takes vir-   33
tuous copies to be wicked, like those that under hot   34
ardent zeal would set whole realms on fire.   35
Of such a nature is his politic love.
This was my lord's best hope; now all are fled,
Save only the gods. Now his friends are dead,   38
Doors that were ne'er acquainted with their wards   39
Many a bounteous year must be employed   40
Now to guard sure their master.   41

And this is all a liberal course allows: 42
Who cannot keep his wealth must keep his house.   43
                                                    Exit.

�֍

3.4 *Enter [two of] Varro's Men, meeting [Titus'
        Servant and] others, all [being servants of]
        Timon's creditors, to wait for his coming out. Then
        enter Lucius' [Servant] and Hortensius' [Servant].*

VARRO'S FIRST SERVANT
Well met. Good morrow, Titus and Hortensius.
TITUS' SERVANT
The like to you, kind Varro.
HORTENSIUS' SERVANT   Lucius!
What, do we meet together?
LUCIUS' SERVANT   Ay, and I think
One business does command us all;
For mine is money.
TITUS' SERVANT   So is theirs and ours.

        Enter Philotus' [Servant].

LUCIUS' SERVANT
And Sir Philotus too!
PHILOTUS' SERVANT   Good day at once.   6
LUCIUS' SERVANT Welcome, good brother.
What do you think the hour?
PHILOTUS' SERVANT   Laboring for nine.   8
LUCIUS' SERVANT
So much?
PHILOTUS' SERVANT Is not my lord seen yet?
LUCIUS' SERVANT   Not yet.   9
PHILOTUS' SERVANT
I wonder on 't. He was wont to shine at seven.   10
LUCIUS' SERVANT
Ay, but the days are waxed shorter with him.   11
You must consider that a prodigal course
Is like the sun's,
But not, like his, recoverable. I fear   14
'Tis deepest winter in Lord Timon's purse;
That is, one may reach deep enough and yet
Find little.
PHILOTUS' SERVANT I am of your fear for that.   17
TITUS' SERVANT
I'll show you how t' observe a strange event.   18
Your lord sends now for money?
HORTENSIUS' SERVANT   Most true, he does.
TITUS' SERVANT
And he wears jewels now of Timon's gift,
For which I wait for money.   21
HORTENSIUS' SERVANT It is against my heart.   22

---

7 **touched** (Metaphor derived from testing metals with a touchstone to
see if they are gold.)   **14 Thrive . . . over** i.e., thrive on his wealth,
but now give him up as beyond help   **16 That . . . place** who should
have acknowledged my position (among his friends).   **sense** reason
17 But his occasions but that he, in his need   **18 in my conscience** to
my knowledge   **20 think . . . me** (1) think I am so backward (2) think
of me last   **21 requite** repay   **22 argument of** subject for   **25 but
. . . sake** if only in recognition of my good feeling toward him
26 courage desire   **28 Who bates** whoever abates, detracts from
29 goodly proper. (Said ironically.)   **31 politic** cunning.   **crossed**
foiled (by making man his rival in treachery)   **32 set him clear** i.e.,
make even the devil look innocent   **33 How fairly** with what a plausible appearance of virtue   **33–35 Takes . . . fire** how this lord appears to model himself on the virtuous only for wicked purposes, like
religious bigots who for zealous purposes would burn down whole
kingdoms   **38 Now** now that.   **dead** dead to him, alienated
39 wards bolts, locks   **40 Many** for many   **41 guard sure** i.e., protect
from arrest for debt

42 liberal generous   **43 keep . . . keep** preserve . . . stay inside
3.4. Location: Athens. Timon's house.
6 at once to one and all   **8 Laboring for** moving toward   **9 much**
i.e., late   **10 was . . . shine** used to be up   **11 are waxed** have
grown   **14 But . . . recoverable** i.e., the sun will return from its wintry path, but Timon cannot recover (since his funds are not *recoverable*)   **17 am of** share   **18 observe** i.e., analyze   **21 For . . . money**
i.e., while I wait for the money used to buy those jewels   **22 heart**
wish, feeling

LUCIUS' SERVANT   Mark how strange it shows:
Timon in this should pay more than he owes,
And e'en as if your lord should wear rich jewels   25
And send for money for 'em.   26
HORTENSIUS' SERVANT
I'm weary of this charge, the gods can witness.   27
I know my lord hath spent of Timon's wealth,
And now ingratitude makes it worse than stealth.   29
VARRO'S FIRST SERVANT
Yes, mine's three thousand crowns. What's yours?
LUCIUS' SERVANT   Five thousand, mine.
VARRO'S FIRST SERVANT
'Tis much deep, and it should seem by th' sum   32
Your master's confidence was above mine,   33
Else surely his had equaled.   34

Enter Flaminius.

TITUS' SERVANT   One of Lord Timon's men.
LUCIUS' SERVANT   Flaminius? Sir, a word. Pray, is my
lord ready to come forth?
FLAMINIUS   No, indeed, he is not.
TITUS' SERVANT We attend his lordship. Pray signify so   39
much.
FLAMINIUS   I need not tell him that. He knows you are
too diligent.   [*Exit.*]   41

Enter steward [Flavius] in a cloak, muffled.

LUCIUS' SERVANT
Ha! Is not that his steward muffled so?
He goes away in a cloud. Call him, call him.   43
TITUS' SERVANT [*to Flavius*]   Do you hear, sir?
VARRO'S SECOND SERVANT [*to Flavius*] By your leave, sir.
FLAVIUS
What do ye ask of me, my friend?
TITUS' SERVANT
We wait for certain money here, sir.
FLAVIUS   Ay,   47
If money were as certain as your waiting,
'Twere sure enough.
Why then preferred you not your sums and bills   50
When your false masters eat of my lord's meat?   51
Then they could smile and fawn upon his debts,
And take down th' interest into their gluttonous
maws.   53
You do yourselves but wrong to stir me up.   54
Let me pass quietly.
Believe 't, my lord and I have made an end;   56
I have no more to reckon, he to spend.   57

LUCIUS' SERVANT   Ay, but this answer will not serve.   58
FLAVIUS
If 'twill not serve, 'tis not so base as you,
For you serve knaves.   [*Exit.*]
VARRO'S FIRST SERVANT How? What does his cashiered   61
worship mutter?
VARRO'S SECOND SERVANT   No matter what; he's poor,
and that's revenge enough. Who can speak broader   64
than he that has no house to put his head in? Such   65
may rail against great buildings.   66

Enter Servilius.

TITUS' SERVANT   O, here's Servilius. Now we shall
know some answer.
SERVILIUS   If I might beseech you, gentlemen, to repair   69
some other hour, I should derive much from 't. For   70
take 't of my soul, my lord leans wondrously to discon-   71
tent. His comfortable temper has forsook him; he's   72
much out of health and keeps his chamber.   73
LUCIUS' SERVANT
Many do keep their chambers are not sick,   74
And if it be so far beyond his health,   75
Methinks he should the sooner pay his debts
And make a clear way to the gods.
SERVILIUS   Good gods!   77
TITUS' SERVANT
We cannot take this for an answer, sir.
FLAMINIUS (*within*) Servilius, help! My lord, my lord!

Enter Timon, in a rage.

TIMON
What, are my doors opposed against my passage?
Have I been ever free, and must my house
Be my retentive enemy, my jail?   82
The place which I have feasted, does it now,
Like all mankind, show me an iron heart?
LUCIUS' SERVANT   Put in now, Titus.   85
TITUS' SERVANT   My lord, here is my bill.
LUCIUS' SERVANT   Here's mine.
HORTENSIUS' SERVANT   And mine, my lord.
BOTH VARRO'S SERVANTS   And ours, my lord.
PHILOTUS' SERVANT   All our bills.
TIMON
Knock me down with 'em! Cleave me to the girdle!   91
LUCIUS' SERVANT   Alas, my lord—
TIMON   Cut my heart in sums!   93
TITUS' SERVANT   Mine, fifty talents.

25–26 e'en . . . for 'em i.e., it's just as though your master should both wear the jewels Timon gave him and simultaneously demand the money that paid for those jewels **27 charge** commission **29 stealth** theft **32 much deep** very great **33 mine** my master's **34 his had equaled** i.e., my master's loan would have equaled in amount your master's **39 attend** are waiting for **41 diligent** i.e., officious **43 in a cloud** (1) muffled (2) in a state of gloom and ignominy **47 certain** certain sums of. (But Flavius puns bitterly in the next line on the sense of "reliable," "predictable.") **50 preferred** presented **51 eat** ate. (Pronounced *et*.) **53 th' interest** i.e., the food and drink they consumed as though it were interest on the loans. **maws** stomachs. (A term used of animals.) **54 do yourselves but** only do yourselves **56 made an end** severed our relationship **57 reckon** keep account of

58 serve do. (But Flavius punningly replies in the sense of "act as servant.") **61 How?** what's this? **cashiered** dismissed. (*His cashiered worship* is offered sardonically as if it were a title of dignity.) **64 broader** (1) more freely (2) more in the open, abroad **65–66 Such . . . buildings** i.e., a man who is houseless and out of service, like Flavius, has nothing to lose and can inveigh against injustice and inequality **69 repair** return **70 derive** benefit **71 take 't . . . soul** i.e., believe I speak sincerely **72 comfortable temper** cheerful disposition **73 keeps** stays in **74 are** who are **75 if . . . health** if his condition is so far from good health **77 make . . . gods** i.e., pay all his debts to smooth his way to heaven. **Good gods** (1) the gods are good (2) good god **82 retentive** confining **85 Put in** i.e., make your claim **91 Knock, Cleave** (Timon puns on *bills* as weapons.) **girdle** belt **93 in sums** into sums of money

TIMON   Tell out my blood!   95

LUCIUS' SERVANT   Five thousand crowns, my lord.

TIMON
Five thousand drops pays that. What yours?
And yours?

VARRO'S FIRST SERVANT   My lord—

VARRO'S SECOND SERVANT   My lord—

TIMON
Tear me, take me, and the gods fall upon you!   100

Exit Timon.

HORTENSIUS' SERVANT   Faith, I perceive our masters
may throw their caps at their money. These debts 102
may well be called desperate ones, for a madman owes 103
'em.   *Exeunt.*

Enter Timon [and Flavius].

TIMON
They have e'en put my breath from me, the slaves.   105
Creditors? Devils!

FLAVIUS   My dear lord—

TIMON   What if it should be so?   108

FLAVIUS   My lord—

TIMON
I'll have it so. My steward!

FLAVIUS   Here, my lord.

TIMON
So fitly? Go, bid all my friends again,   111
Lucius, Lucullus, and Sempronius—all.
I'll once more feast the rascals.

FLAVIUS   O my lord,
You only speak from your distracted soul;
There's not so much left to furnish out   115
A moderate table.

TIMON   Be it not in thy care. Go,   117
I charge thee, invite them all. Let in the tide
Of knaves once more. My cook and I'll provide.

Exeunt.

❦

3.5

*Enter three Senators at one door, Alcibiades
meeting them, with attendants.*

FIRST SENATOR [*to another Senator*]
My lord, you have my voice to 't.   1
The fault's bloody;   2
'Tis necessary he should die.
Nothing emboldens sin so much as mercy.

SECOND SENATOR   Most true. The law shall bruise 'em. 5

ALCIBIADES
Honor, health, and compassion to the Senate!   6

FIRST SENATOR   Now, Captain?

ALCIBIADES
I am an humble suitor to your virtues;
For pity is the virtue of the law,   9
And none but tyrants use it cruelly.
It pleases time and fortune to lie heavy   11
Upon a friend of mine, who in hot blood   12
Hath stepped into the law, which is past depth   13
To those that without heed do plunge into 't.   14
He is a man, setting his fate aside,   15
Of comely virtues;
Nor did he soil the fact with cowardice—   17
An honor in him which buys out his fault—   18
But with a noble fury and fair spirit,
Seeing his reputation touched to death,   20
He did oppose his foe;
And with such sober and unnoted passion   22
He did behave his anger, ere 'twas spent,   23
As if he had but proved an argument.   24

FIRST SENATOR
You undergo too strict a paradox,   25
Striving to make an ugly deed look fair.
Your words have took such pains as if they labored
To bring manslaughter into form and set quarreling 28
Upon the head of valor—which indeed   29
Is valor misbegot, and came into the world
When sects and factions were newly born.
He's truly valiant that can wisely suffer
The worst that man can breathe,   33
And make his wrongs his outsides,   34
To wear them like his raiment, carelessly,   35
And ne'er prefer his injuries to his heart,   36
To bring it into danger.
If wrongs be evils and enforce us kill,   38
What folly 'tis to hazard life for ill!   39

ALCIBIADES
My lord—

FIRST SENATOR   You cannot make gross sins look clear. 40
To revenge is no valor, but to bear.   41

ALCIBIADES
My lords, then, under favor, pardon me   42
If I speak like a captain.

---

95 Tell out count out by the drop   **100 the gods fall upon you** i.e.,
may the gods attack you as with an army   **102 throw . . . at** i.e.,
give up hope of recovering   **103 desperate** (1) unlikely to be recovered (2) resulting from desperate madness   **105 e'en . . . me** left me
breathless   **108 What . . . so?** i.e., what is there to do in that case?
(Timon has evidently thought of the mock banquet he will serve in
3.6.)   **111 fitly** conveniently   **115 furnish out** supply   **117 Be . . .
care** don't you worry about it
3.5. Location: Athens. The Senate House.
1 voice to 't vote in favor of it (the death sentence under consideration)   **2 fault's bloody** crime involved bloodshed   **5 'em** i.e., all
such offenders

6 compassion to the Senate i.e., may the Senate have compassion
9 virtue chief merit, essence   **11–12 lie . . . Upon** oppress
13 stepped into incurred the penalties of   **13–14 past depth To** over
the heads of   **15 setting . . . aside** setting aside his ill-fated action
17 fact deed   **18 buys out** redeems   **20 touched to death** fatally
threatened   **22 unnoted** so well under control as to be unobservable
23 behave control   **24 but . . . argument** only been testing a philosophical proposition   **25 undergo** undertake.   **strict** strained
28 bring . . . form make manslaughter appear respectable, or according to legal form   **28–29 set . . . of** make quarreling the highest kind
of, or subdivision of   **29 which** i.e., quarreling, duelling   **33 breathe**
speak (as also in line 61)   **34 make . . . outsides** treat the wrongs he
receives as merely external circumstance   **35 raiment** clothing.
carelessly without taking offense   **36 prefer** present, promote to the
dignity of being taken to heart   **38 kill** to kill   **39 'tis** this is, i.e., this
code that obliges one to repay evil with violence.   **for ill** in a bad
cause   **40 clear** innocent   **41 to bear** i.e., bearing insults calmly is
true valor   **42 under favor** by your leave

Why do fond men expose themselves to battle,   44
And not endure all threats? Sleep upon 't,   45
And let the foes quietly cut their throats
Without repugnancy? If there be   47
Such valor in the bearing, what make we   48
Abroad? Why then, women are more valiant   49
That stay at home, if bearing carry it,   50
And the ass more captain than the lion, the felon
Loaden with irons wiser than the judge,   52
If wisdom be in suffering. O my lords,
As you are great, be pitifully good.   54
Who cannot condemn rashness in cold blood?
To kill, I grant, is sin's extremest gust,   56
But in defense, by mercy, 'tis most just.   57
To be in anger is impiety,
But who is man that is not angry?   59
Weigh but the crime with this.

SECOND SENATOR   You breathe in vain.

ALCIBIADES   In vain? His service done
   At Lacedaemon and Byzantium
   Were a sufficient briber for his life.

FIRST SENATOR   What's that?

ALCIBIADES
Why, I say, my lords, he's done fair service   66
And slain in fight many of your enemies.
How full of valor did he bear himself
In the last conflict, and made plenteous wounds!

SECOND SENATOR
He has made too much plenty with 'em.   70
He's a sworn rioter; he has a sin that often   71
Drowns him and takes his valor prisoner.
If there were no foes, that were enough   73
To overcome him. In that beastly fury
He has been known to commit outrages
And cherish factions. 'Tis inferred to us   76
His days are foul and his drink dangerous.

FIRST SENATOR
He dies.

ALCIBIADES   Hard fate! He might have died in war.
My lords, if not for any parts in him—   79
Though his right arm might purchase his own time   80
And be in debt to none—yet, more to move you,
Take my deserts to his and join 'em both;   82
And, for I know your reverend ages love   83

Security, I'll pawn my victories, all   84
My honors, to you, upon his good returns.   85
If by this crime he owes the law his life,
Why, let the war receive 't in valiant gore,   87
For law is strict, and war is nothing more.

FIRST SENATOR
We are for law. He dies; urge it no more,
On height of our displeasure. Friend or brother,   90
He forfeits his own blood that spills another.   91

ALCIBIADES
Must it be so? It must not be. My lords,
I do beseech you, know me.

SECOND SENATOR   How?

ALCIBIADES   Call me to your remembrances.

THIRD SENATOR   What?

ALCIBIADES
I cannot think but your age has forgot me.   97
It could not else be I should prove so base   98
To sue and be denied such common grace.   99
My wounds ache at you.

FIRST SENATOR   Do you dare our anger?
'Tis in few words, but spacious in effect: 101
We banish thee forever.

ALCIBIADES   Banish me?
Banish your dotage, banish usury,
That makes the Senate ugly.

FIRST SENATOR
If after two days' shine Athens contain thee,
Attend our weightier judgment.   106
And, not to swell our spirit,   107
He shall be executed presently.   *Exeunt [Senators].* 108

ALCIBIADES
Now the gods keep you old enough   109
That you may live
Only in bone, that none may look on you!—   111
I'm worse than mad. I have kept back their foes,
While they have told their money and let out   113
Their coin upon large interest, I myself
Rich only in large hurts. All those for this?   115
Is this the balsam that the usuring Senate   116
Pours into captains' wounds? Banishment!
It comes not ill; I hate not to be banished.   118
It is a cause worthy my spleen and fury,   119
That I may strike at Athens. I'll cheer up
My discontented troops and lay for hearts.   121

---

44 fond foolish   **45 Sleep upon 't** i.e., why do they not disregard it   **47 repugnancy** resistance   **48 the bearing** i.e., putting up with insults.   **make** do   **49 Abroad** away from home   **50 bearing** putting up with insults (with a pun on "childbearing" and perhaps on "supporting the man in sexual intercourse").   **carry it** wins the day   **52 Loaden with irons** weighed down with shackles   **54 pitifully good** good by showing mercy   **56 sin's extremest gust** the relish of extremest sin. (*Gust* means "outburst, indulgence.")   **57 defense** self-defense.   **by mercy** by a merciful interpretation of law   **59 not** i.e., never   **66 fair** excellent   **70 has made . . . 'em** i.e., has dealt them out too generously and has traded on his soldierly reputation as an excuse for an excess of riotous pleasure (playing on *plenty, plenteous*)   **71 sworn rioter** inveterate debauchee.   **a sin** i.e., drunkenness   **73 If** even if.   **foes** accusers   **76 cherish factions** encourage dissension and conspiracy.   **inferred** alleged   **79 parts** admirable traits   **80 his right . . . time** i.e., his ability in war should obtain his freedom and let him live out his natural life   **82 to** in addition to   **83 for** because

84 Security (1) safety (2) collateral for a loan (using a financial metaphor found also in *purchase, pawn, good returns*, etc.)   **85 upon . . . returns** as a pledge that he will make a good return on your investment in him, i.e., fight bravely in war   **87 let . . . gore** i.e., let him pay his debt by bleeding as a soldier   **90 On . . . our** on pain of our highest   **91 another** i.e., another's   **97 your age has** you, in your advanced age, have   **98 else be** otherwise be (that).   **prove** i.e., be considered   **99 To sue** as to plead for   **101 spacious in effect** of great import (with quibble on the spacious world to which Alcibiades is banished)   **106 Attend . . . judgment** expect our more severe sentence   **107 spirit** anger   **108 presently** immediately   **109 keep . . . enough** preserve you to such an old age   **111 Only . . . you** i.e., mere skeletons, forgotten or avoided by everyone   **113 told** reckoned.   **let** lent   **115 hurts** injuries   **116 balsam** balm, medicine   **118 It . . . ill** it is not such a bad thing after all   **119 worthy** worthy of   **121 lay for hearts** endeavor to win their affection

'Tis honor with most lands to be at odds.   122
Soldiers should brook as little wrongs as gods. *Exit.* 123

❖

3.6 [*Music. Tables and seats set out; servants
attending.*] *Enter divers friends* [*of Timon*] *at
several doors.*

FIRST LORD The good time of day to you, sir.
SECOND LORD I also wish it to you. I think this honorable lord did but try us this other day. 3
FIRST LORD Upon that were my thoughts tiring when 4
we encountered. I hope it is not so low with him as he 5
made it seem in the trial of his several friends.
SECOND LORD It should not be, by the persuasion of 7
his new feasting.
FIRST LORD I should think so. He hath sent me an earnest inviting, which many my near occasions did urge 10
me to put off; but he hath conjured me beyond them, 11
and I must needs appear. 12
SECOND LORD In like manner was I in debt to my im- 13
portunate business, but he would not hear my excuse.
I am sorry, when he sent to borrow of me, that my
provision was out. 16
FIRST LORD I am sick of that grief too, as I understand 17
how all things go. 18
SECOND LORD Every man here's so. What would he
have borrowed of you?
FIRST LORD A thousand pieces. 21
SECOND LORD A thousand pieces?
FIRST LORD What of you?
SECOND LORD He sent to me, sir—Here he comes.

Enter Timon and attendants. [*Music plays.*]

TIMON With all my heart, gentlemen both! And how
fare you?
FIRST LORD Ever at the best, hearing well of your lordship.
SECOND LORD The swallow follows not summer more
willing than we your lordship.
TIMON [*aside*] Nor more willingly leaves winter, such
summer birds are men.—Gentlemen, our dinner
will not recompense this long stay. Feast your ears 33
with the music awhile, if they will fare so harshly o' 34
the trumpet's sound. We shall to 't presently.

FIRST LORD I hope it remains not unkindly with your
lordship that I returned you an empty messenger.
TIMON O, sir, let it not trouble you.
SECOND LORD My noble lord—
TIMON Ah, my good friend, what cheer?
                                    The banquet brought in.
SECOND LORD My most honorable lord, I am e'en sick 41
of shame that when your lordship this other day sent
to me I was so unfortunate a beggar. 43
TIMON Think not on 't, sir.
SECOND LORD If you had sent but two hours before—
TIMON Let it not cumber your better remembrance.— 46
Come, bring in all together.
SECOND LORD All covered dishes! 48
FIRST LORD Royal cheer, I warrant you.
THIRD LORD Doubt not that, if money and the season
can yield it.
FIRST LORD How do you? What's the news?
THIRD LORD Alcibiades is banished. Hear you of it?
FIRST AND SECOND LORDS Alcibiades banished?
THIRD LORD 'Tis so, be sure of it.
FIRST LORD How? How?
SECOND LORD I pray you, upon what? 57
TIMON My worthy friends, will you draw near?
THIRD LORD I'll tell you more anon. Here's a noble
feast toward. 60
SECOND LORD This is the old man still. 61
THIRD LORD Will 't hold? Will 't hold? 62
SECOND LORD It does; but time will—and so— 63
THIRD LORD I do conceive. 64
TIMON Each man to his stool, with that spur as he 65
would to the lip of his mistress. Your diet shall be in 66
all places alike. Make not a city feast of it, to let the 67
meat cool ere we can agree upon the first place; sit, sit. 68
[*They sit.*] The gods require our thanks.

    You great benefactors, sprinkle our society with
thankfulness. For your own gifts, make yourselves
praised; but reserve still to give, lest your deities be 72
despised. Lend to each man enough, that one need not
lend to another; for, were your godheads to borrow of
men, men would forsake the gods. Make the meat be
beloved more than the man that gives it. Let no assembly of twenty be without a score of villains. If there sit
twelve women at the table, let a dozen of them be—as
they are. The rest of your fees, O gods—the senators 79
of Athens, together with the common tag of people— 80
what is amiss in them, you gods, make suitable for

---

122 'Tis . . . odds it's honorable to be at variance with a country (and
its political leaders) in most instances **123 brook . . . gods** endure
insults as little as the gods do
3.6. Location: Athens. A banqueting room in Timon's house.
s.d. several separate **3 did but try** was only testing us **4 tiring** preying, feeding, i.e., busily engaged **5 encountered** met. **it is . . . him**
his financial situation is not so desperate **7 persuasion** evidence
10 inviting invitation. **many . . . occasions** my many urgent necessities or business **11 conjured . . . them** summoned me so urgently as
to overcome my previous commitments **12 needs** necessarily **13 in
debt to** obligated to **16 provision was out** resources were exhausted
17–18 as . . . go particularly as I now understand the state of affairs.
(Perhaps hinting at Timon's seeming ability to entertain lavishly
again.) **21 pieces** i.e., gold coins **33 stay** delay **34 they . . . o'**
they (your ears) will deign to feast on such rough fare as

41 e'en quite **43 so . . . beggar** so unfortunate as to be out of ready
reserves **46 cumber . . . remembrance** trouble your happier
thoughts, memories **48 covered** (Implies particularly elegant fare.)
57 what what ground **60 toward** imminent **61 old man still** man
we once knew **62 hold** last **63 will** i.e., will tell **64 conceive** understand **65 that spur** the same eagerness **66 diet** food **66–67 in
. . . alike** the same wherever you sit to eat **67 city feast** formal occasion, with seating by rank **68 first place** place of honor **72 reserve still** always hold back something **79 fees** i.e., what is held in
fee from you, your gifts or benefactions (?) or, those who hold their
lives in fee from you (?) **80 tag** rabble

destruction. For these my present friends, as they are 82
to me nothing, so in nothing bless them, and to nothing are they welcome.

Uncover, dogs, and lap!
        [*The dishes are uncovered and seen to contain
                        warm water and stones.*]
SOME SPEAK What does his lordship mean?
SOME OTHERS I know not.
TIMON
May you a better feast never behold,
You knot of mouth-friends! Smoke and lukewarm
        water   89
Is your perfection. This is Timon's last,   90
Who, stuck and spangled with your flatteries,   91
Washes it off and sprinkles in your faces
Your reeking villainy.
                [*He throws the water in their faces.*]
                        Live loathed and long,
Most smiling, smooth, detested parasites,
Courteous destroyers, affable wolves, meek bears,
You fools of fortune, trencher-friends, time's flies,   96
Cap-and-knee slaves, vapors, and minute-jacks!   97
Of man and beast the infinite malady   98
Crust you quite o'er! What, dost thou go?
Soft! Take thy physic first! Thou too, and thou!   100
Stay, I will lend thee money, borrow none.
                [*He assaults them and drives them out.*]
What, all in motion? Henceforth be no feast
Whereat a villain's not a welcome guest.
Burn, house! Sink, Athens! Henceforth hated be
Of Timon, man, and all humanity!   *Exit.* 105

        Enter the Senators, with other Lords, [*returning*].

FIRST LORD How now, my lords?
SECOND LORD Know you the quality of Lord Timon's 107
        fury?
THIRD LORD Push! Did you see my cap?   109
FOURTH LORD I have lost my gown.
FIRST LORD He's but a mad lord, and naught but hu- 111
        mors sways him. He gave me a jewel th' other day, 112
        and now he has beat it out of my hat. Did you see my
        jewel?   [*They search for their belongings.*]
THIRD LORD Did you see my cap?
SECOND LORD Here 'tis.
FOURTH LORD Here lies my gown.
FIRST LORD Let's make no stay.
SECOND LORD
        Lord Timon's mad.

82 For as for 89 knot company, crowd. mouth-friends friends in
words only. Smoke i.e., steam, "hot air" 90 Is your perfection
suits you perfectly 91 stuck and spangled bespattered and decorated
96 fools toadies, and, in the long run, dupes. trencher-friends
friends only while being fed. time's flies fair-weather insects
97 Cap-and-knee slaves men obsequious with their caps and curtsies.
vapors substanceless creatures. minute-jacks mannikins that strike a
bell on the outside of a clock; hence, timeservers 98 Of . . . malady
may every loathsome disease known to humanity 100 Soft i.e., wait a minute. physic medicine 105 Of by
107 quality original nature, occasion 109 Push pshaw 111—
112 humors caprice, an imbalance in his physiological humors

THIRD LORD   I feel 't upon my bones.
FOURTH LORD
One day he gives us diamonds, next day stones.
                        Exeunt the Senators [*etc.*].

4.1   *Enter Timon.*

TIMON
Let me look back upon thee. O thou wall
That girdles in those wolves, dive in the earth
And fence not Athens! Matrons, turn incontinent!   3
Obedience fail in children! Slaves and fools,   4
Pluck the grave wrinkled Senate from the bench
And minister in their steads! To general filths   6
Convert o' th' instant, green virginity!   7
Do 't in your parents' eyes. Bankrupts, hold fast;
Rather than render back, out with your knives
And cut your trusters' throats! Bound servants, steal! 10
Large-handed robbers your grave masters are,   11
And pill by law. Maid, to thy master's bed!   12
Thy mistress is o' the brothel. Son of sixteen,
Pluck the lined crutch from thy old limping sire;   14
With it beat out his brains! Piety and fear,   15
Religion to the gods, peace, justice, truth,   16
Domestic awe, night rest, and neighborhood,   17
Instruction, manners, mysteries, and trades,   18
Degrees, observances, customs, and laws,   19
Decline to your confounding contraries,   20
And yet confusion live! Plagues, incident to men,   21
Your potent and infectious fevers heap
On Athens, ripe for stroke! Thou cold sciatica,   23
Cripple our senators, that their limbs may halt   24
As lamely as their manners! Lust and liberty   25
Creep in the minds and marrows of our youth,   26
That 'gainst the stream of virtue they may strive   27
And drown themselves in riot! Itches, blains,   28
Sow all th' Athenian bosoms, and their crop   29
Be general leprosy! Breath infect breath,
That their society, as their friendship, may   31
Be merely poison! Nothing I'll bear from thee   32
But nakedness, thou detestable town!
                [*He strips off his garments.*]
Take thou that too, with multiplying bans!   34
Timon will to the woods, where he shall find

4.1. Location: Outside the walls of Athens.
3 fence (1) enclose (2) defend. incontinent lascivious 4 Obedience
fail let obedience fail 6 general filths common prostitutes 7 green
young 10 trusters' creditors'. Bound indentured 11 Large-handed
rapacious 12 pill by law plunder by legal means. to go to
14 lined stuffed, padded 15 fear religious awe 16 Religion to veneration of 17 Domestic awe respect for the seniors of a household.
neighborhood neighborliness 18 mysteries crafts 19 Degrees established ranks of society 20 confounding contraries opposites that reduce all to chaos 21 yet i.e., henceforth still let 23 cold chilling,
or caused by chill. sciatica nerve pain in hip and leg 24 halt limp
25 liberty licentiousness 26 marrows soft tissues filling the cavities
of bone (thought of as the source of vitality and strength) 27 stream
current 28 riot dissoluteness. blains blisters 29 Sow fall like seed
in 31 society associating with one another 32 merely entirely
34 bans curses

Th' unkindest beast more kinder than mankind.   36
The gods confound—hear me, you good gods all—
Th' Athenians both within and out that wall!
And grant, as Timon grows, his hate may grow
To the whole race of mankind, high and low!
Amen.   *Exit.*

❖

4.2   *Enter steward [Flavius], with two or three*
Servants.

FIRST SERVANT
Hear you, Master Steward, where's our master?
Are we undone, cast off, nothing remaining?
FLAVIUS
Alack, my fellows, what should I say to you?
Let me be recorded by the righteous gods,   4
I am as poor as you.
FIRST SERVANT   Such a house broke?
So noble a master fall'n? All gone, and not
One friend to take his fortune by the arm   7
And go along with him?
SECOND SERVANT   As we do turn our backs
From our companion thrown into his grave,
So his familiars to his buried fortunes   11
Slink all away, leave their false vows with him
Like empty purses picked; and his poor self,
A dedicated beggar to the air,   14
With his disease of all-shunned poverty,
Walks, like contempt, alone. More of our fellows.   16

Enter other Servants.

FLAVIUS
All broken implements of a ruined house.
THIRD SERVANT
Yet do our hearts wear Timon's livery;   18
That see I by our faces. We are fellows still,
Serving alike in sorrow. Leaked is our bark,   20
And we, poor mates, stand on the dying deck,   21
Hearing the surges threat. We must all part   22
Into this sea of air.
FLAVIUS   Good fellows all,
The latest of my wealth I'll share amongst you.   24
Wherever we shall meet, for Timon's sake,
Let's yet be fellows. Let's shake our heads and say,   26
As 'twere a knell unto our master's fortunes,   27

"We have seen better days." Let each take some.
[*He gives them money.*]
Nay, put out all your hands. Not one word more.   29
Thus part we rich in sorrow, parting poor.
[*Servants*] *embrace, and part several ways.*
O, the fierce wretchedness that glory brings us!
Who would not wish to be from wealth exempt,
Since riches point to misery and contempt?   33
Who would be so mocked with glory, or to live
But in a dream of friendship,
To have his pomp and all what state compounds   36
But only painted, like his varnished friends?   37
Poor honest lord, brought low by his own heart,
Undone by goodness! Strange, unusual blood,   39
When man's worst sin is he does too much good!
Who then dares to be half so kind again?
For bounty, that makes gods, do still mar men.   42
My dearest lord, blest to be most accurst,   43
Rich only to be wretched, thy great fortunes
Are made thy chief afflictions. Alas, kind lord!
He's flung in rage from this ingrateful seat   46
Of monstrous friends,
Nor has he with him to supply his life,   48
Or that which can command it.   49
I'll follow and inquire him out.
I'll ever serve his mind with my best will;   51
Whilst I have gold, I'll be his steward still.   *Exit.*

❖

4.3   *Enter Timon, in the woods [with a spade].*

TIMON
O blessèd breeding sun, draw from the earth
Rotten humidity; below thy sister's orb   2
Infect the air! Twinned brothers of one womb,
Whose procreation, residence, and birth
Scarce is dividant, touch them with several fortunes, 5
The greater scorns the lesser. Not nature,   6
To whom all sores lay siege, can bear great fortune   7
But by contempt of nature.   8
Raise me this beggar, and deny 't that lord;   9
The senator shall bear contempt hereditary,   10
The beggar native honor.   11

---

36 unkindest (1) cruellest (2) most unnatural, turning against kin and kind. (*Kinder* continues the wordplay.)
4.2. Location: Athens. Timon's house.
4 be recorded by say in the hearing of   **7 his fortune** i.e., Timon in his misfortune. (The dialogue here fulfills the allegorical scene of fallen fortune imagined by the Poet in 1.1.68–93.)   **11 his familiars . . . fortunes** those close to him when he was fortunate, now perceiving his ruin   **14 dedicated . . . air** beggar having nothing and nowhere to go   **16 like contempt** as if he were contemptibility itself   **18 livery** uniform worn by male household servants (here used metaphorically)   **20 bark** sailing vessel   **21 mates** (1) fellows (2) mates of a vessel.   **dying** i.e., sinking   **22 surges** waves   **24 latest** last remnant   **26 yet** still.   **shake our heads** (in sorrow)   **27 knell** tolling of a bell, announcing a death or other misfortune

29 put out all all put out   **33 point to** tend to   **36 what state compounds** that which constitutes dignity and splendor   **37 But only** nothing more than   **39 blood** nature   **42 bounty . . . men** i.e., generosity, a godlike attribute, brings mere mortals to ruin. (Bounteousness can be a kind of hubris.)   **43 to be** only to be   **46 flung** rushed off   **48 Nor . . . life** nor has he anything to maintain himself with   **49 that . . . it** i.e., money   **51 serve his mind** execute his wishes
4.3. Location: Woods and cave, near the seashore; in front of Timon's cave.
2 Rotten humidity rot-causing damp.   **thy sister's** i.e., the moon's   **5 dividant** separate, distinguishable.   **touch** if you test.   **several** different   **6 The** and the result is that the   **6–8 Not . . . nature** i.e., human nature, which suffers so many afflictions, cannot experience good fortune without scorning fellow creatures who are less fortunate   **9 Raise me** raise. (*Me* is a colloquial usage meaning something like "believe me.")   **10 bear contempt hereditary** be treated with contempt as though he were born low   **11 native honor** (will be treated with) honor as though born great

It is the pasture lards the brother's sides,   12
The want that makes him lean. Who dares, who
  dares   13
In purity of manhood stand upright
And say "This man's a flatterer"? If one be,
So are they all, for every grece of fortune   16
Is smoothed by that below. The learnèd pate   17
Ducks to the golden fool. All's obliquy;   18
There's nothing level in our cursèd natures   19
But direct villainy. Therefore, be abhorred
All feasts, societies, and throngs of men!
His semblable, yea, himself, Timon disdains.   22
Destruction fang mankind! Earth, yield me roots!   23
                                  [He digs.]
Who seeks for better of thee, sauce his palate   24
With thy most operant poison! [He finds gold.] What
  is here?   25
Gold? Yellow, glittering, precious gold?
No, gods, I am no idle votarist.   27
Roots, you clear heavens! Thus much of this will
  make   28
Black white, foul fair, wrong right,
Base noble, old young, coward valiant.
Ha, you gods! Why this? What this, you gods?
  Why, this
Will lug your priests and servants from your sides,
Pluck stout men's pillows from below their heads.   33
This yellow slave
Will knit and break religions, bless th' accurst,   35
Make the hoar leprosy adored, place thieves   36
And give them title, knee, and approbation   37
With senators on the bench. This is it
That makes the wappened widow wed again;   39
She whom the spital house and ulcerous sores   40
Would cast the gorge at, this embalms and spices   41
To th' April day again. Come, damnèd earth,   42
Thou common whore of mankind, that puts odds   43
Among the rout of nations, I will make thee   44
Do thy right nature. (March afar off.) Ha? A drum?   45
  Thou'rt quick,

But yet I'll bury thee. Thou'lt go, strong thief,   46
When gouty keepers of thee cannot stand.
                             [He buries the gold.]
Nay, stay thou out for earnest.   [He keeps some gold.] 48

*Enter Alcibiades, with drum and fife, in warlike
manner, and Phrynia and Timandra.*

ALCIBIADES   What art thou there? Speak.
TIMON
  A beast, as thou art. The canker gnaw thy heart   50
  For showing me again the eyes of man!
ALCIBIADES
  What is thy name? Is man so hateful to thee
  That art thyself a man?
TIMON
  I am Misanthropos and hate mankind.   54
  For thy part, I do wish thou wert a dog,   55
  That I might love thee something.
ALCIBIADES   I know thee well,   56
  But in thy fortunes am unlearned and strange.   57
TIMON
  I know thee too; and more than that I know thee
  I not desire to know. Follow thy drum;   59
  With man's blood paint the ground gules, gules.   60
  Religious canons, civil laws, are cruel;   61
  Then what should war be? This fell whore of thine   62
  Hath in her more destruction than thy sword,
  For all her cherubin look.
PHRYNIA   Thy lips rot off!   64
TIMON
  I will not kiss thee; then the rot returns
  To thine own lips again.
ALCIBIADES
  How came the noble Timon to this change?
TIMON
  As the moon does, by wanting light to give.   68
  But then renew I could not, like the moon;   69
  There were no suns to borrow of.   70
ALCIBIADES Noble Timon, what friendship may I do thee?
TIMON None, but to maintain my opinion.
ALCIBIADES What is it, Timon?
TIMON Promise me friendship, but perform none. If 74
  thou wilt not promise, the gods plague thee, for thou 75
  art a man! If thou dost perform, confound thee, for 76
  thou art a man!   77
ALCIBIADES
  I have heard in some sort of thy miseries.
TIMON
  Thou sawst them when I had prosperity.

12–13 It is . . . lean i.e., it is the inheritance and possessing of pasture that makes one brother fat, the lack (want) that makes him, the younger brother, lean. (The Folio reads *leave* for *lean,* which could mean that the younger brother has to leave in search of riches elsewhere.)   lards that fattens.   want lack (of good pasture)   16 grece step   17 smoothed assiduously prepared.   pate head   18 Ducks bows obsequiously.   golden rich.   All's obliquy i.e., all's deviating from the right   19 level direct. (The contrary to *obliquy.*)   22 His semblable i.e., his own kind, his own image   23 fang seize   24 Who whoever.   sauce stimulate, tickle   25 operant active, potent   27 no idle votarist no trifler in my vows (of leading a spare existence)   28 clear pure.   this i.e., the gold   33 Pluck . . . heads i.e., expedite the death of healthy men by pulling the pillows from beneath their heads as they sleep (supposedly a way of throttling them)   35 knit . . . religions knit men together in religious harmony and then break that harmony apart   36 hoar white-skinned.   place give recognized status and high office to   37 knee the bended deferential knee   39 makes enables.   wappened worn out   40 spital house house for the diseased (compare with "hospital")   41 cast the gorge vomit   41–42 this . . . again i.e., money enables the diseased old woman to embalm herself with wealth to look April-like and marriageable   42 damnèd earth i.e., gold   43–44 puts . . . nations causes strife among various peoples   45 Do . . . nature i.e., cause strife, according to your true nature.   quick (1) swift to act (2) alive

46 go be able to walk   48 for earnest as an installment or pledge.   s.d. drum and fife i.e., soldiers playing drum and fife   50 The canker may a spreading ulcer   54 Misanthropos hater of mankind   55 For thy part as for you   56 something somewhat, a little   57 unlearned and strange uninformed and ignorant   59 not desire do not desire   60 gules (Heraldic name for "red.")   61 canons rules, laws   62 fell deadly   64 cherubin angelic.   Thy lips may thy lips   68 wanting lacking   69 renew become new again (with a quibble on the idea of renewing a loan)   70 suns (punning on *sons,* i.e., "men")   74–77 If . . . a man i.e., may the gods plague you for being a man whether you perform your promises or don't even make promises

ALCIBIADES
    I see them now. Then was a blessèd time.

TIMON
    As thine is now, held with a brace of harlots.   81

TIMANDRA
    Is this th' Athenian minion whom the world   82
    Voiced so regardfully?

TIMON   Art thou Timandra?

TIMANDRA   Yes.   83

TIMON
    Be a whore still. They love thee not that use thee;
    Give them diseases, leaving with thee their lust.   85
    Make use of thy salt hours. Season the slaves   86
    For tubs and baths; bring down rose-cheeked youth   87
    To the tub-fast and the diet.

TIMANDRA   Hang thee, monster!

ALCIBIADES
    Pardon him, sweet Timandra, for his wits
    Are drowned and lost in his calamities.—
    I have but little gold of late, brave Timon,
    The want whereof doth daily make revolt   92
    In my penurious band. I have heard and grieved   93
    How cursèd Athens, mindless of thy worth,
    Forgetting thy great deeds, when neighbor states,
    But for thy sword and fortune, trod upon them—   96

TIMON
    I prithee, beat thy drum and get thee gone.

ALCIBIADES
    I am thy friend and pity thee, dear Timon.

TIMON
    How dost thou pity him whom thou dost trouble?
    I had rather be alone.

ALCIBIADES
    Why, fare thee well. Here is some gold for thee.
                                        [He offers gold.]

TIMON   Keep it. I cannot eat it.

ALCIBIADES
    When I have laid proud Athens on a heap—

TIMON
    Warr'st thou 'gainst Athens?

ALCIBIADES   Ay, Timon, and have cause.

TIMON
    The gods confound them all in thy conquest,   105
    And thee after, when thou hast conquered!

ALCIBIADES   Why me, Timon?

TIMON   That by killing of villains   108
    Thou wast born to conquer my country.   109

Put up thy gold. Go on—here's gold—go on.
                                    [He offers gold.]
    Be as a planetary plague, when Jove   111
    Will o'er some high-viced city hang his poison   112
    In the sick air. Let not thy sword skip one.
    Pity not honored age for his white beard;
    He is an usurer. Strike me the counterfeit matron;   115
    It is her habit only that is honest,   116
    Herself's a bawd. Let not the virgin's cheek
    Make soft thy trenchant sword; for those milk paps,   118
    That through the window bars bore at men's eyes,   119
    Are not within the leaf of pity writ,   120
    But set them down horrible traitors. Spare not the
        babe,   121
    Whose dimpled smiles from fools exhaust their
        mercy;   122
    Think it a bastard, whom the oracle
    Hath doubtfully pronounced thy throat shall cut,   124
    And mince it sans remorse. Swear against objects;   125
    Put armor on thine ears and on thine eyes,
    Whose proof nor yells of mothers, maids, nor babes,   127
    Nor sight of priests in holy vestments bleeding,
    Shall pierce a jot. There's gold to pay thy soldiers.
    Make large confusion; and, thy fury spent,   130
    Confounded be thyself! Speak not, begone.

ALCIBIADES
    Hast thou gold yet? I'll take the gold thou givest me,
    Not all thy counsel.   [He takes gold.]

TIMON
    Dost thou or dost thou not, heaven's curse upon
        thee!   134

PHRYNIA AND TIMANDRA
    Give us some gold, good Timon. Hast thou more?

TIMON
    Enough to make a whore forswear her trade,
    And to make whores, a bawd. Hold up, you sluts,   137
    Your aprons mountant. [He throws gold into their
        aprons.] You are not oathable,   138
    Although I know you'll swear—terribly swear
    Into strong shudders and to heavenly agues—   140
    Th' immortal gods that hear you. Spare your oaths;
    I'll trust to your conditions. Be whores still;   142
    And he whose pious breath seeks to convert you,

---

81 brace pair (with a quibble on the meaning "clamp," one that holds Alcibiades in its grip)   **82 Athenian minion** darling of Athens   **83 Voiced** spoke of.   **regardfully** respectfully   **85 leaving** while they are leaving   **86 salt** lecherous.   **Season the slaves** i.e., pickle and spice the villains as if preparing them for the pickling tub; make them ready   **87 tubs and baths** (Allusion to the treatments for venereal diseases, as also in *tub-fast* and *diet* in the next line.)   **92 want** lack.   **make revolt** provoke mutiny   **93 penurious** poverty-stricken   **96 But . . . fortune** (A suggestion of Timon's history as a great military leader, for which Athens ought to be grateful.)   **trod** would have trodden   **105 confound** destroy   **108–109 That . . . country** (Timon evidently applauds the deed but not the doer. His words are obscure, and the text may be corrupt.)

111 planetary plague (Allusion to the belief in the malignant influence of planets.)   **112 high-viced** extremely vicious   **115 Strike me** i.e., strike.   **counterfeit** pretending respectability   **116 habit** costume, outward appearance.   **honest** chaste   **118 trenchant** sharp.   **milk paps** nipples   **119 window bars** i.e., latticework of her bodice (?)   **120 Are . . . writ** are not written down on the list of those to whom pity is to be shown   **121 traitors** i.e., betrayers of men   **122 exhaust** draw forth   **124 doubtfully** ambiguously.   **thy . . . cut** will cut your throat. (However, the phrase can also be ambiguously reversed.)   **125 mince** slash, cut in small pieces.   **sans** without.   **Swear against objects** bind yourself by oath against objections (to your cruelty)   **127 Whose proof** the tested strength of which armor.   **nor yells** neither the yells   **130 large confusion** wholesale destruction   **134 Dost . . . not** whether you do or not   **137 to . . . bawd** i.e., to make a bawd retire from turning women into whores   **138 mountant** (A heraldic coinage, with sexual suggestion of raising up for erotic purposes; see also *erection* in line 166.)   **oathable** to be believed on your oath   **140 strong** violent.   **agues** feverish shivers   **142 your conditions** what you are, your characters

Be strong in whore, allure him, burn him up.   144
Let your close fire predominate his smoke,   145
And be no turncoats. Yet may your pains six
    months   146
Be quite contrary. And thatch your poor thin roofs   147
With burdens of the dead—some that were hanged,   148
No matter; wear them, betray with them. Whore
    still;   149
Paint till a horse may mire upon your face.   150
A pox of wrinkles!
PHRYNIA AND TIMANDRA   Well, more gold. What then?   151
Believe 't that we'll do anything for gold.
TIMON   Consumptions sow   153
In hollow bones of man; strike their sharp shins,
And mar men's spurring. Crack the lawyer's voice,   155
That he may never more false title plead,
Nor sound his quillets shrilly. Hoar the flamen,   157
That scolds against the quality of flesh   158
And not believes himself. Down with the nose,   159
Down with it flat; take the bridge quite away
Of him that, his particular to foresee,   161
Smells from the general weal. Make curled-pate
    ruffians bald,   162
And let the unscarred braggarts of the war
Derive some pain from you. Plague all,
That your activity may defeat and quell
The source of all erection. There's more gold.   166
                              [He gives gold.]
Do you damn others, and let this damn you,
And ditches grave you all!   168
PHRYNIA AND TIMANDRA
    More counsel with more money, bounteous Timon.
TIMON
    More whore, more mischief first. I have given you
        earnest.   170
ALCIBIADES
    Strike up the drum towards Athens. Farewell,
        Timon.

If I thrive well, I'll visit thee again.
TIMON
    If I hope well, I'll never see thee more.   173
ALCIBIADES   I never did thee harm.
TIMON
    Yes, thou spok'st well of me.
ALCIBIADES   Call'st thou that harm?
TIMON
    Men daily find it. Get thee away, and take   176
Thy beagles with thee.
ALCIBIADES   We but offend him. Strike!   177
                    [Drum beats.] Exeunt [Alcibiades,
                         Phrynia, and Timandra].
TIMON
    That nature, being sick of man's unkindness,   178
Should yet be hungry! [He digs.] Common mother,
    thou   179
Whose womb unmeasurable and infinite breast
Teems and feeds all, whose selfsame mettle   181
Whereof thy proud child, arrogant man, is puffed   182
Engenders the black toad and adder blue,
The gilded newt and eyeless venomed worm,   184
With all th' abhorred births below crisp heaven
Whereon Hyperion's quickening fire doth shine: 186
Yield him who all thy human sons do hate,   187
From forth thy plenteous bosom, one poor root!
Ensear thy fertile and conceptious womb;   189
Let it no more bring out ingrateful man!
Go great with tigers, dragons, wolves, and bears;   191
Teem with new monsters, whom thy upward face   192
Hath to the marbled mansion all above   193
Never presented! [He finds a root.] O, a root! Dear
    thanks!—
Dry up thy marrows, vines, and plow-torn leas,   195
Whereof ingrateful man with liquorish drafts   196
And morsels unctuous greases his pure mind,   197
That from it all consideration slips—   198

            Enter Apemantus.

More man? Plague, plague!
APEMANTUS
    I was directed hither. Men report
Thou dost affect my manners and dost use them.   201
TIMON
    'Tis, then, because thou dost not keep a dog,

---

144 Be . . . whore be resolute in whoring.   burn him up (1) inflame
him with desire (2) infect him with venereal disease   145 Let . . .
smoke i.e., let your secret and disease-carrying passion overcome his
pious rhetoric   146 be no turncoats i.e., don't betray your profession
of whoring; whore still   146–147 Yet . . . contrary i.e., may you
suffer intense pain or alteration six months later (?) (Perhaps six
months is simply an arbitrary figure or alludes to the gestation period
for early symptoms of syphilis.)   147–148 thatch . . . dead i.e.,
cover your balding heads (caused by venereal disease) with wigs
made of the hair of corpses   149 betray with them i.e., use these
wigs to create false beauty to betray more men   150 mire upon bog
down in. (Timon sardonically urges so thick a cosmetic covering that
even a horse would become mired.)   151 A pox of wrinkles i.e.,
may you be plagued with wrinkles   153 Consumptions sow plant
wasting diseases such as syphilis. (Addressed to Phrynia and Timandra.)   155 spurring i.e., riding (here used as a sexual metaphor)
157 quillets quibbles.   Hoar the flamen whiten (with venereal disease or leprosy) the priest (with a pun on hoar, "whore")   158 quality of flesh fleshly desire   159 And . . . himself i.e., and doesn't
practice what he preaches.   Down . . . nose (An effect of syphilis.)
161 his . . . foresee in order to look out for his own interests
162 Smells . . . weal (1) loses the scent of the common good (2)
stinks above the common crowd.   curled-pate curly-headed
166 erection (1) advancement (2) sexual erection   168 grave enclose
in the grave (with a pun on "ditches" and "damming" continued
from line 167)   170 whore whoring.   mischief destruction.   earnest
earnest money, token payment

---

173 If I hope well if my hopes are realized   176 find it i.e., find it
harmful to be spoken well of   177 beagles i.e., beagle hounds, fawning followers—the prostitutes   178 That to think that.   sick of sickened by, surfeited with   179 Common mother i.e., the earth
181 Teems abundantly bears offspring.   mettle spirit, essence (with a
pun on metal; the words were virtually interchangeable)
182 Whereof with which   184 gilded iridescent.   eyeless venomed
worm the blindworm (wrongly supposed poisonous, as were the toad
and the newt)   186 Hyperion's i.e., the sun's.   quickening life-giving
187 who . . . hate who hates all your human offspring   189 Ensear
dry up.   conceptious fertile   191 Go great be pregnant   192 upward
upturned   193 the marbled . . . above i.e., the heavens   195 marrows i.e., marrow in the earth's bones, denoting her fecundity.
plow-torn leas plowed-up pastureland   196 liquorish drafts sweet, alcoholic drinks   197 unctuous fatty, oily.   greases his pure mind
makes greasy and vile his once-pure mind   198 That so that.   consideration reflection, rationality; regard for others or for things other
than sensual   201 affect put on

Whom I would imitate. Consumption catch thee! 203
APEMANTUS
This is in thee a nature but infected, 204
A poor unmanly melancholy sprung
From change of fortune. Why this spade? This
  place?
This slavelike habit and these looks of care? 207
Thy flatterers yet wear silk, drink wine, lie soft,
Hug their diseased perfumes, and have forgot 209
That ever Timon was. Shame not these woods
By putting on the cunning of a carper. 211
Be thou a flatterer now and seek to thrive
By that which has undone thee. Hinge thy knee,
And let his very breath whom thou'lt observe 214
Blow off thy cap. Praise his most vicious strain 215
And call it excellent. Thou wast told thus. 216
Thou gav'st thine ears, like tapsters that bade
  welcome, 217
To knaves and all approachers. 'Tis most just
That thou turn rascal; hadst thou wealth again,
Rascals should have 't. Do not assume my likeness.
TIMON
Were I like thee, I'd throw away myself.
APEMANTUS
Thou hast cast away thyself, being like thyself—
A madman so long, now a fool. What, think'st 223
That the bleak air, thy boisterous chamberlain, 224
Will put thy shirt on warm? Will these mossed trees, 225
That have outlived the eagle, page thy heels 226
And skip when thou point'st out? Will the cold
  brook, 227
Candied with ice, caudle thy morning taste 228
To cure thy o'ernight's surfeit? Call the creatures
Whose naked natures live in all the spite 230
Of wreakful heaven, whose bare unhousèd trunks, 231
To the conflicting elements exposed,
Answer mere nature; bid them flatter thee. 233
O, thou shalt find—
TIMON   A fool of thee. Depart. 234
APEMANTUS
I love thee better now than e'er I did.
TIMON
I hate thee worse.
APEMANTUS   Why?
TIMON   Thou flatter'st misery.
APEMANTUS
I flatter not, but say thou art a caitiff. 237

TIMON Why dost thou seek me out?
APEMANTUS   To vex thee.
TIMON
Always a villain's office or a fool's.
Dost please thyself in 't?
APEMANTUS   Ay.
TIMON   What, a knave too? 241
APEMANTUS
If thou didst put this sour cold habit on 242
To castigate thy pride, 'twere well, but thou 243
Dost it enforcedly. Thou'dst courtier be again
Wert thou not beggar. Willing misery 245
Outlives incertain pomp, is crowned before: 246
The one is filling still, never complete, 247
The other at high wish. Best state, contentless, 248
Hath a distracted and most wretched being, 249
Worse than the worst, content. 250
Thou shouldst desire to die, being miserable.
TIMON
Not by his breath that is more miserable. 252
Thou art a slave whom Fortune's tender arm
With favor never clasped but bred a dog. 254
Hadst thou, like us from our first swathe, proceeded 255
The sweet degrees that this brief world affords
To such as may the passive drudges of it 257
Freely command, thou wouldst have plunged thyself 258
In general riot, melted down thy youth 259
In different beds of lust, and never learned 260
The icy precepts of respect, but followed
The sugared game before thee. But myself— 262
Who had the world as my confectionary, 263
The mouths, the tongues, the eyes, and hearts
  of men
At duty, more than I could frame employment, 265
That numberless upon me stuck, as leaves 266
Do on the oak, have with one winter's brush 267
Fell from their boughs and left me open, bare 268
For every storm that blows—I to bear this, 269
That never knew but better, is some burden. 270
Thy nature did commence in sufferance; time 271
Hath made thee hard in 't. Why shouldst thou hate
  men? 272

241 **a knave too** i.e., a fool and a villain to boot (since it is villainous to take pleasure in vexing others) 242 **habit** disposition 243 **'twere well** it would be a commendable thing 245–246 **Willing . . . before** willingly accepted poverty outlasts the life of insecure ceremony and wealth, and is sooner crowned with spiritual reward 247 **The one** i.e., incertain pomp. **is filling still** is never satisfied 248 **at high wish** at the height of contentment 248–250 **Best . . . content** being at the height of prosperity without contentment means a wretched existence, worse than being at the bottom of prosperity with contentment 252 **Not . . . miserable** not when he who speaks (Apemantus) is more wretched than I 254 **but bred** i.e., but whom Fortune bred 255 **swathe** swaddling clothes. **proceeded** passed through (like a student taking an academic degree) 257–258 **To such . . . command** i.e., to those who have the world and its sycophants at command 259 **riot** debauchery 260 **different** various 262 **sugared game** sweet-tasting quarry 263 **my confectionary** maker of sweetmeats just for me; a place where such sweetmeats are stored 265 **At duty** subservient to my wishes. **frame** provide with 266 **stuck** having stuck 267 **winter's brush** gust of wintry wind 268 **Fell** fallen. **open** exposed 269 **I . . . this** that I should bear this 270 **That . . . better** who have known only better fortune 271 **sufferance** suffering, poverty 272 **hard in 't** hardened to it

203 **would** would prefer to. **Consumption catch thee** may a wasting illness lay hold on you 204 **but infected** i.e., not inborn and philosophical but induced by misery and hence shallow 207 **habit** garment 209 **perfumes** perfumed mistresses 211 **putting . . . carper** assuming the manner and profession of a fault-finding cynic 214 **observe** bow obsequiously before 215 **strain** quality 216 **Thou . . . thus** i.e., you were spoken to flatteringly in exactly this manner 217 **ears** i.e., attention. **like . . . welcome** i.e., like barkeeps who welcome all comers indiscriminately 223–225 **think'st . . . warm** (Alludes to the practice of having a servant warm one's garment by the fire.) 226 **page thy heels** follow at your heels like a page 227 **skip . . . out** jump to fulfill your command 228 **Candied** encrusted, as if with sugar. **caudle . . . taste** i.e., provide you with a caudle, a hot spiced drink 230 **in** exposed to 231 **wreakful** vengeful. **trunks** i.e., bodies 233 **Answer** cope with, contend with. **mere** stark, unrelieved 234 **of** in 237 **caitiff** wretch

They never flattered thee. What hast thou given?
If thou wilt curse, thy father, that poor rag,   274
Must be thy subject, who in spite put stuff   275
To some she-beggar and compounded thee   276
Poor rogue hereditary. Hence, begone!   277
If thou hadst not been born the worst of men,   278
Thou hadst been a knave and flatterer.

APEMANTUS
Art thou proud yet?

TIMON   Ay, that I am not thee.   280

APEMANTUS   I, that I was no prodigal.

TIMON   I, that I am one now.
Were all the wealth I have shut up in thee,   283
I'd give thee leave to hang it. Get thee gone.   284
That the whole life of Athens were in this!   285
Thus would I eat it.   [He eats a root.]

APEMANTUS [offering food]   Here, I will mend thy feast.

TIMON
First mend my company: take away thyself.

APEMANTUS
So I shall mend mine own by th' lack of thine.

TIMON
'Tis not well mended so; it is but botched.   289
If not, I would it were.   290

APEMANTUS   What wouldst thou have to Athens?   291

TIMON
Thee thither in a whirlwind. If thou wilt,
Tell them there I have gold. Look, so I have.
                                        [He shows his gold.]

APEMANTUS
Here is no use for gold.

TIMON   The best and truest,
For here it sleeps and does no hirèd harm.

APEMANTUS   Where liest anights, Timon?   296

TIMON   Under that's above me. Where feed'st thou   297
adays, Apemantus?   298

APEMANTUS   Where my stomach finds meat; or, rather,
where I eat it.

TIMON   Would poison were obedient and knew my
mind!

APEMANTUS   Where wouldst thou send it?

TIMON   To sauce thy dishes.   304

APEMANTUS   The middle of humanity thou never knew-
est, but the extremity of both ends. When thou wast
in thy gilt and thy perfume, they mocked thee for too   307
much curiosity; in thy rags thou know'st none, but art   308

despised for the contrary. There's a medlar for thee.   309
Eat it.   [He gives a fruit.]

TIMON   On what I hate I feed not.

APEMANTUS   Dost hate a medlar?

TIMON   Ay, though it look like thee.   313

APEMANTUS   An thou'dst hated meddlers sooner, thou   314
shouldst have loved thyself better now. What man
didst thou ever know unthrift that was beloved after   316
his means?   317

TIMON   Who, without those means thou talk'st of, didst
thou ever know beloved?

APEMANTUS   Myself.

TIMON   I understand thee: thou hadst some means to   321
keep a dog.   322

APEMANTUS   What things in the world canst thou
nearest compare to thy flatterers?

TIMON   Women nearest. But men—men are the things
themselves. What wouldst thou do with the world,
Apemantus, if it lay in thy power?

APEMANTUS   Give it the beasts, to be rid of the men.

TIMON   Wouldst thou have thyself fall in the confusion 329
of men and remain a beast with the beasts?   330

APEMANTUS   Ay, Timon.

TIMON   A beastly ambition, which the gods grant thee
t' attain to! If thou wert the lion, the fox would beguile
thee. If thou wert the lamb, the fox would eat thee. If
thou wert the fox, the lion would suspect thee when
peradventure thou wert accused by the ass. If thou   336
wert the ass, thy dullness would torment thee, and still 337
thou livedst but as a breakfast to the wolf. If thou wert 338
the wolf, thy greediness would afflict thee, and oft
thou shouldst hazard thy life for thy dinner. Wert thou
the unicorn, pride and wrath would confound thee   341
and make thine own self the conquest of thy fury. Wert
thou a bear, thou wouldst be killed by the horse. Wert
thou a horse, thou wouldst be seized by the leopard.
Wert thou a leopard, thou wert germane to the lion,   345
and the spots of thy kindred were jurors on thy life; all 346
thy safety were remotion and thy defense absence.   347
What beast couldst thou be, that were not subject to a
beast? And what a beast art thou already, that seest
not thy loss in transformation!   350

---

309 medlar fruit like a small brown-skinned apple, eaten when nearly decayed; used here, as often, for the sake of a quibble on *meddler*, one given to sexual promiscuity   **313 like thee** i.e., in a state of decay, or, as one who meddles   **314 An thou'dst** if thou hadst.   **meddlers** busybodies (with sexual meaning also)   **316 unthrift** to be unthrifty   **316–317 after his means** (1) after his wealth was gone (2) according to his means   **321–322 thou . . . dog** i.e., even in your poverty you were able to keep a dog, and it loved you (since all creatures love only in return for favors)   **329–330 in . . . men** i.e., in the destruction of mankind you've just wished for   **336 peradventure** by chance   **337 still** continually   **338 livedst** wouldst live   **341 unicorn** (A legendary creature, supposedly caught by being goaded into charging a tree and embedding its horn in the tree trunk.)   **345 germane** akin, related   **346 the spots . . . life** i.e., the crimes of those closely related to you would bring down a sentence of death upon you (with a pun on *spots*, meaning "leopard's spots" and "stains, crimes")   **346–347 all . . . remotion** your only safety would consist in your constantly going from place to place   **350 in transformation** in being changed into a beast

---

274 rag i.e., wretch   **275 in spite** out of malice   **275–276 put stuff To** fornicated with   **276 compounded** begot   **277 hereditary** by right of inheritance   **278 worst** lowest in station   **280 yet** still   **283 shut up** contained   **284 hang it** i.e., hang yourself   **285 That** I wish that   **289 botched** badly mended (since you remain in your own company)   **290 If . . . were** i.e., even if you don't think things are made worse by having yourself for a companion, I wish you did (since I'd prefer to see you unhappy), or, even if it's only a botched job, I'd still prefer to see you get away from here, or, if my company isn't to be mended by your absence, I can only wish it were   **291 What . . . have** what would you have me convey. (But Timon caustically jests in a more literal sense of the phrase.)   **296 anights** at night   **297 that's** that which is   **298 adays** by day   **304 sauce** flavor   **307 gilt** fine trappings   **308 curiosity** fastidiousness, refinement

APEMANTUS If thou couldst please me with speaking to 351
me, thou mightst have hit upon it here. The common- 352
wealth of Athens is become a forest of beasts.

TIMON How, has the ass broke the wall, that thou art 354
out of the city?

APEMANTUS Yonder comes a poet and a painter. The 356
plague of company light upon thee! I will fear to catch
it, and give way. When I know not what else to do, I'll 358
see thee again.

TIMON When there is nothing living but thee, thou
shalt be welcome. I had rather be a beggar's dog than
Apemantus.

APEMANTUS
Thou art the cap of all the fools alive.   363

TIMON
Would thou wert clean enough to spit upon!

APEMANTUS
A plague on thee! Thou art too bad to curse.

TIMON
All villains that do stand by thee are pure.   366

APEMANTUS
There is no leprosy but what thou speak'st.

TIMON If I name thee.
I'd beat thee, but I should infect my hands.

APEMANTUS
I would my tongue could rot them off!

TIMON
Away, thou issue of a mangy dog!   371
Choler does kill me that thou art alive;
I swoon to see thee.

APEMANTUS
Would thou wouldst burst!

TIMON   Away, thou tedious rogue!
I am sorry I shall lose a stone by thee.
                  [He throws a stone at Apemantus.]

APEMANTUS Beast!

TIMON Slave!

APEMANTUS Toad!

TIMON Rogue, rogue, rogue!
I am sick of this false world, and will love naught
But even the mere necessities upon 't.   381
Then, Timon, presently prepare thy grave.   382
Lie where the light foam of the sea may beat
Thy gravestone daily. Make thine epitaph,
That death in me at others' lives may laugh.   385
[To the gold.] O thou sweet king-killer and dear
divorce
Twixt natural son and sire! Thou bright defiler   387
Of Hymen's purest bed! Thou valiant Mars!   388
Thou ever young, fresh, loved, and delicate wooer,

Whose blush doth thaw the consecrated snow   390
That lies on Dian's lap! Thou visible god,   391
That solderest close impossibilities   392
And mak'st them kiss; that speak'st with every
tongue
To every purpose! O thou touch of hearts!   394
Think thy slave, man, rebels, and by thy virtue   395
Set them into confounding odds, that beasts   396
May have the world in empire!

APEMANTUS   Would 'twere so!
But not till I am dead. I'll say thou'st gold;   398
Thou wilt be thronged to shortly.

TIMON   Thronged to?

APEMANTUS   Ay.

TIMON
Thy back, I prithee.

APEMANTUS   Live, and love thy misery.   400

TIMON
Long live so, and so die! I am quit.   401

              Enter the Banditti.

APEMANTUS
More things like men! Eat, Timon, and abhor them. 402
                              Exit Apemantus.

FIRST BANDIT Where should he have this gold? It is 403
some poor fragment, some slender ort of his remain- 404
der. The mere want of gold and the falling-from of his 405
friends drove him into this melancholy.

SECOND BANDIT It is noised he hath a mass of treasure. 407

THIRD BANDIT Let us make the assay upon him. If he 408
care not for 't, he will supply us easily. If he covetously 409
reserve it, how shall 's get it?   410

SECOND BANDIT True, for he bears it not about him.
'Tis hid.

FIRST BANDIT Is not this he?

BANDITTI Where?

SECOND BANDIT 'Tis his description.

THIRD BANDIT He. I know him.

BANDITTI [*coming forward*] Save thee, Timon.   417

TIMON Now, thieves?

BANDITTI
Soldiers, not thieves.

TIMON   Both, too, and women's sons.   419

BANDITTI
We are not thieves, but men that much do want.   420

TIMON
Your greatest want is, you want much of meat.   421

390 **blush** i.e., reddish glow of gold 391 **Dian** Diana, goddess of the hunt and patroness of chastity 392 **That . . . impossibilities** you who solder tightly together things apparently incapable of being united 394 **touch** touchstone 395 **virtue** power 396 **Set . . . odds** set men in self-destroying conflict with one another 398 **thou'st** thou hast 400 **Thy back** i.e., show me your back 401 **quit** rid (of Apemantus) 402 **them** i.e., the bandits 403 **should he have** can he have obtained 404 **ort** fragment 405 **mere** utter 407 **noised** rumored 408 **assay** trial, test (as one would test gold ore for its content) 409 **for 't** for the gold 410 **shall 's** shall we 417 **Save** God save 419 **Both, too** you are both 420 **much do want** are greatly in need. (But Timon answers as if they meant "want too much.") 421 **Your . . . meat** your main need arises from the fact that you crave such rich food (as Timon goes on to explain)

351–352 **If . . . here** if it were possible for anything you say to please me, what you've just said (comparing men with beasts) would be pleasing 354 **How** what is this 356 **Yonder . . . painter** (In fact, they do not appear until 5.1; this line may give evidence of an incompletely revised manuscript.) 358 **give way** (I will) retire 363 **cap** acme, summit (with wordplay on "fool's cap") 366 **that . . . thee** compared to you 371 **issue** offspring 381 **But even** except 382 **presently** immediately 385 **That** in order that. **in** through 387 **natural** truly begotten (not illegitimate) 388 **Hymen** god of marriage. **Mars** i.e., as the adulterous lover of Venus

Why should you want? Behold, the earth hath roots;
Within this mile break forth a hundred springs;
The oaks bear mast, the briers scarlet hips.   424
The bounteous huswife Nature on each bush
Lays her full mess before you. What? Why want?   426

FIRST BANDIT
We cannot live on grass, on berries, water,
As beasts and birds and fishes.

TIMON
Nor on the beasts themselves, the birds and fishes;
You must eat men. Yet thanks I must you con   430
That you are thieves professed, that you work not
In holier shapes; for there is boundless theft
In limited professions. [*He gives gold.*] Rascal thieves, 433
Here's gold. Go, suck the subtle blood o' the grape   434
Till the high fever seethe your blood to froth,   435
And so scape hanging. Trust not the physician;   436
His antidotes are poison, and he slays
More than you rob. Take wealth and lives together.   438
Do villainy, do, since you protest to do 't,   439
Like workmen. I'll example you with thievery.   440
The sun's a thief, and with his great attraction   441
Robs the vast sea. The moon's an arrant thief,   442
And her pale fire she snatches from the sun.
The sea's a thief, whose liquid surge resolves   444
The moon into salt tears. The earth's a thief,
That feeds and breeds by a composture stol'n   446
From general excrement. Each thing's a thief.
The laws, your curb and whip, in their rough power 448
Has unchecked theft. Love not yourselves. Away!   449
Rob one another. There's more gold. Cut throats.
All that you meet are thieves. To Athens go,
Break open shops; nothing can you steal
But thieves do lose it. Steal less for this I give you,   453
And gold confound you howsoe'er! Amen.   454

THIRD BANDIT   He's almost charmed me from my pro- 455
fession by persuading me to it.

FIRST BANDIT   'Tis in the malice of mankind that he   457
thus advises us, not to have us thrive in our mystery. 458

SECOND BANDIT   I'll believe him as an enemy, and give 459
over my trade.

FIRST BANDIT   Let us first see peace in Athens. There is 461
no time so miserable but a man may be true.   462

Exeunt Thieves.

Enter the steward [Flavius] to Timon.

FLAVIUS   O you gods!
Is yond despised and ruinous man my lord?   464
Full of decay and failing? O monument   465
And wonder of good deeds evilly bestowed!   466
What an alteration of honor has desp'rate want
made!
What viler thing upon the earth than friends,
Who can bring noblest minds to basest ends!   469
How rarely does it meet with this time's guise,   470
When man was wished to love his enemies!   471
Grant I may ever love, and rather woo
Those that would mischief me than those that do!— 473
He's caught me in his eye. I will present   474
My honest grief unto him, and as my lord
Still serve him with my life.—My dearest master!

TIMON
Away! What art thou?

FLAVIUS   Have you forgot me, sir?

TIMON
Why dost ask that? I have forgot all men.
Then, if thou grant'st thou'rt a man, I have forgot
thee.

FLAVIUS   An honest poor servant of yours.

TIMON   Then I know thee not.
I never had honest man about me, I; all
I kept were knaves, to serve in meat to villains.   483

FLAVIUS   The gods are witness,
Ne'er did poor steward wear a truer grief
For his undone lord than mine eyes for you.

[*He weeps.*]

TIMON
What, dost thou weep? Come nearer, then, I love
thee
Because thou art a woman and disclaim'st
Flinty mankind, whose eyes do never give   489
But thorough lust and laughter. Pity's sleeping.   490
Strange times, that weep with laughing, not with
weeping!

FLAVIUS
I beg of you to know me, good my lord,
T' accept my grief, and whilst this poor wealth lasts

---

424 **mast** acorns.   **hips** fruit of the rosebush   426 **mess** food, meal
430 **thanks . . . con** I must offer you thanks   433 **limited** regulated,
legalized (with a play on *boundless*, line 432, as the opposite of *limited*)   434 **subtle** (1) delicate (2) treacherous in its influence
435 **high fever** (induced by intoxication).   **seethe** boil   436 **scape
hanging** i.e., avoid execution by dying of excess drinking, using a
natural substance   438 **Take . . . together** i.e., murder your robbery
victims   439 **protest** openly profess   440 **example you with** give you
instances of   441 **attraction** power to draw up   442 **arrant** notorious
444 **resolves** melts, dissolves. (Alludes to the belief that the moon
draws moisture from the air and deposits it in the sea, thus creating
the effect of tides.)   446 **composture** compost, manure
448–449 **The laws . . . theft** the laws, which restrain and punish
you, provide opportunity for unlimited abuse to those who administer
them   453 **But . . . it** i.e., without robbing from persons who are
themselves thieves   453–454 **Steal . . . howsoe'er** if you steal less
because of my giving you this gold, may gold destroy you no matter
what happens   455 **charmed** dissuaded (as if by means of enchantment)   457 **the malice of** i.e., his hating of   458 **mystery** trade
459 **as** as I would. (One can learn even from an enemy.)

461–462 **Let . . . true** i.e., let's not rush into reformation, at least
not until there is peace in Athens; besides, there will always be time
to repent   464 **ruinous** brought to ruin   465 **failing** downfall   465–
466 **monument . . . wonder** astonishing memorial   466 **evilly bestowed** wrongly bestowed on the wicked   469 **bring . . . ends** reduce even the noblest-minded (like Timon) to wretchedness
470–471 **How . . . enemies** i.e., how perfectly does the commandment to love one's enemies suit this degenerate age (since one's supposed friends are the ones who do greatest harm)   473 **Those . . . do**
i.e., those who openly profess themselves to be my enemies rather
than those who, professing friendship, actually do the greater harm
474 **caught . . . eye** seen me   483 **serve in meat** serve food
489 **Flinty** hardhearted.   **give** give forth tears   490 **But thorough**
except through

To entertain me as your steward still.   494

                     [He offers money.]

TIMON   Had I a steward

So true, so just, and now so comfortable?   496

It almost turns my dangerous nature mild.   497

Let me behold thy face. Surely, this man

Was born of woman.

Forgive my general and exceptless rashness,   500

You perpetual-sober gods! I do proclaim   501

One honest man—mistake me not, but one;   502

No more, I pray—and he's a steward.

How fain would I have hated all mankind,   504

And thou redeem'st thyself! But all, save thee,

I fell with curses.   506

Methinks thou art more honest now than wise,

For by oppressing and betraying me

Thou mightst have sooner got another service;   509

For many so arrive at second masters

Upon their first lord's neck. But tell me true—   511

For I must ever doubt, though ne'er so sure—   512

Is not thy kindness subtle, covetous,

A usuring kindness, and, as rich men deal gifts,

Expecting in return twenty for one?

FLAVIUS

No, my most worthy master, in whose breast

Doubt and suspect, alas, are placed too late.   517

You should have feared false times when you did

    feast.   518

Suspect still comes where an estate is least.   519

That which I show, heaven knows, is merely love,   520

Duty, and zeal to your unmatchèd mind,

Care of your food and living; and believe it,   522

My most honored lord,

For any benefit that points to me,   524

Either in hope or present, I'd exchange   525

For this one wish: that you had power and wealth

To requite me by making rich yourself.   527

TIMON

Look thee, 'tis so. Thou singly honest man,   528

Here, take. *[He offers gold.]* The gods out of my

    misery

Has sent thee treasure. Go, live rich and happy,

But thus conditioned: thou shalt build from men,   531

Hate all, curse all, show charity to none,

But let the famished flesh slide from the bone

Ere thou relieve the beggar. Give to dogs

What thou deniest to men. Let prisons swallow 'em,

Debts wither 'em to nothing. Be men like blasted

    woods,   536

And may diseases lick up their false bloods!

And so farewell and thrive.

FLAVIUS   O, let me stay

And comfort you, my master.

TIMON   If thou hat'st curses,

Stay not; fly, whilst thou art blest and free.

Ne'er see thou man, and let me ne'er see thee.

         Exit [Flavius; Timon retires to his cave].

5.1

Enter Poet and Painter. [Timon enters at some point to watch them from his cave.]

PAINTER   As I took note of the place, it cannot be far where he abides.

POET   What's to be thought of him? Does the rumor hold for true that he's so full of gold?

PAINTER   Certain. Alcibiades reports it. Phrynia and Timandra had gold of him. He likewise enriched poor straggling soldiers with great quantity. 'Tis said he gave unto his steward a mighty sum.

POET   Then this breaking of his has been but a try for 9 his friends?

PAINTER   Nothing else. You shall see him a palm in Ath- 11 ens again, and flourish with the highest. Therefore 'tis not amiss we tender our loves to him in this supposed 13 distress of his. It will show honestly in us and is very 14 likely to load our purposes with what they travail for, 15 if it be a just and true report that goes of his having. 16

POET   What have you now to present unto him?

PAINTER   Nothing at this time but my visitation. Only I will promise him an excellent piece.

POET   I must serve him so too, tell him of an intent 20 that's coming toward him.   21

PAINTER   Good as the best. Promising is the very air o' 22 the time; it opens the eyes of expectation. Performance is ever the duller for his act, and but in the plainer 24 and simpler kind of people the deed of saying is quite 25 out of use. To promise is most courtly and fashionable. 26 Performance is a kind of will or testament which 27 argues a great sickness in his judgment that makes it.

    Enter Timon from his cave.

TIMON *[aside]*   Excellent workman! Thou canst not paint a man so bad as is thyself.

---

494 entertain receive, employ **496 comfortable** comforting **497 dangerous** savage **500 exceptless** making no exception **501 perpetual-sober** eternally grave and sedate **502 but** only **504 fain** gladly **506 fell** cut down **509 service** position **511 Upon . . . neck** by stepping on the bowed neck of their former master **512 though . . . sure** however persuasive the evidence **517 suspect** suspicion **518 feast** entertain lavishly **519 Suspect . . . least** wariness inevitably arrives (too late) when one's fortunes are ruined **520 merely** purely **522 Care . . . living** concern for your having food and maintenance **524 For** as for. **points to me** appears in prospect for me **525 in hope** in the future **527 requite** repay **528 singly** (1) uniquely (2) earnestly **531 thus conditioned** upon this condition. **from** away from

536 Be men let men be. **blasted** withered
5.1. Location: The woods. Before Timon's cave. The scene is virtually continuous; Timon may well remain visible to the audience.
9 breaking bankruptcy. **try** test **11 a palm** a dignitary (probably referring to Psalm 92:12: "The righteous man shall flourish like a palm") **13 we tender** that we should offer **14 show honestly** appear to be seemly or worthy **15 load our purposes** i.e., crown our efforts. **travail** labor **16 goes of his having** is current about his wealth **20 intent** project **21 coming toward** intended for **22 Good as the best** i.e., that's perfect. **air** style **24 for his act** for its being completed. **but in** except among **25 deed of saying** actions fulfilling words or promises **26 use** fashion **27 a kind . . . testament** i.e., a desperate attempt to settle accounts, as if one were about to die

POET   I am thinking what I shall say I have provided for 31
him. It must be a personating of himself, a satire 32
against the softness of prosperity, with a discovery of 33
the infinite flatteries that follow youth and opulency.

TIMON *[aside]*   Must thou needs stand for a villain in 35
thine own work? Wilt thou whip thine own faults in 36
other men? Do so, I have gold for thee.

POET   Nay, let's seek him.
Then do we sin against our own estate   39
When we may profit meet and come too late.   40

PAINTER   True.
When the day serves, before black-cornered night,   42
Find what thou want'st by free and offered light.   43
Come.

TIMON *[aside]*
I'll meet you at the turn. What a god's gold,   45
That he is worshiped in a baser temple   46
Than where swine feed!
'Tis thou that rigg'st the bark and plow'st the foam,   48
Settlest admirèd reverence in a slave.   49
To thee be worship, and thy saints for aye   50
Be crowned with plagues, that thee alone obey!   51
Fit I meet them.   *[He comes forward.]* 52

POET   Hail, worthy Timon!

PAINTER   Our late noble master!

TIMON
Have I once lived to see two honest men?   55

POET   Sir,
Having often of your open bounty tasted,
Hearing you were retired, your friends fall'n off,   58
Whose thankless natures—O abhorrèd spirits!
Not all the whips of heaven are large enough—
What, to you,
Whose starlike nobleness gave life and influence   62
To their whole being? I am rapt, and cannot cover   63
The monstrous bulk of this ingratitude
With any size of words.   65

TIMON
Let it go naked; men may see 't the better.   66
You that are honest, by being what you are
Make them best seen and known.

PAINTER   He and myself   68
Have traveled in the great show'r of your gifts   69

And sweetly felt it.

TIMON   Ay, you are honest men.

PAINTER
We are hither come to offer you our service.

TIMON
Most honest men! Why, how shall I requite you?
Can you eat roots and drink cold water? No.

BOTH
What we can do we'll do to do you service.

TIMON
You're honest men. You've heard that I have gold;
I am sure you have. Speak truth; you're honest men.

PAINTER
So it is said, my noble lord, but therefor   77
Came not my friend nor I.

TIMON
Good honest men! *[To the Painter.]* Thou draw'st a
counterfeit   79
Best in all Athens. Thou'rt indeed the best;
Thou counterfeit'st most lively.

PAINTER   So-so, my lord.   81

TIMON
E'en so, sir, as I say. *[To the Poet.]* And for thy
fiction,   82
Why, thy verse swells with stuff so fine and smooth   83
That thou art even natural in thine art.   84
But for all this, my honest-natured friends,
I must needs say you have a little fault.
Marry, 'tis not monstrous in you, neither wish I   87
You take much pains to mend.

BOTH   Beseech your honor   88
To make it known to us.

TIMON   You'll take it ill.

BOTH   Most thankfully, my lord.

TIMON   Will you, indeed?

BOTH   Doubt it not, worthy lord.

TIMON
There's never a one of you but trusts a knave   93
That mightily deceives you.

BOTH   Do we, my lord?

TIMON
Ay, and you hear him cog, see him dissemble,   95
Know his gross patchery, love him, feed him,   96
Keep in your bosom; yet remain assured   97
That he's a made-up villain.   98

PAINTER   I know none such, my lord.

POET   Nor I.

TIMON
Look you, I love you well. I'll give you gold;
Rid me these villains from your companies,   100

---

31 provided planned   **32 personating of himself** representation of his
case   **33 discovery** disclosure   **35 needs** necessarily.   **stand for**
serve as a model for   **36 in** in your portrayal of   **39 estate** worldly
well-being   **40 may profit meet** have a chance to make a profit
42 black-cornered night night which darkens as in corners   **43 free
and offered light** the light of day, freely offered to all   **45 at the turn**
i.e., trick for trick in a cheating game   **46 a baser temple** i.e., the human body   **48 rigg'st the bark** sets the ship's sail   **49 Settlest . . .
slave** engenders in the servile worshiper a wondering awe of money
or of his master   **50–51 thy saints . . . obey** may your saints (i.e.,
members of your sect) who obey you only, be eternally crowned with
plagues   **52 Fit** it is fit that   **55 once** actually   **58 were retired** had
withdrawn.   **fall'n off** estranged   **62 Whose . . . influence** i.e.,
whose nobility of character was of such power as to influence men's
destinies. (An astrological metaphor.)   **63 rapt** i.e., overwhelmed
65 size (1) quantity (2) covering glue applied by painters   **66 naked**
(Timon plays on *bulk*, line 64, in the sense of "trunk or body.")
68 them i.e., the ungrateful men you condemn, or, ungrateful acts
69 traveled walked (with a suggestion also of "worked, travailed," as
one would labor for a patron)

77 therefor for that reason   **79 counterfeit** picture, likeness (with
quibble on the idea of "fraudulent imitation")   **81 So-so** passably
82 fiction any creative writing; here, poetry (with connotation of "lying")   **83 swells . . . smooth** (1) is elegantly styled and adorned (2) is
a vainglorious concoction of specious fabrication   **84 thou . . . thine
art** (1) your art is a triumph of natural verisimilitude and has become
second nature to you (2) you're a born fool and a liar in your art
87 monstrous unnatural   **88 mend** mend your ways   **93 There's . . .
but** i.e., each of you   **95 cog** cheat   **96 patchery** knavery   **97 Keep**
keep him   **98 made-up** utter, complete   **100 Rid me** if you'll rid

Hang them or stab them, drown them in a draft,   101
Confound them by some course, and come to me,   102
I'll give you gold enough.
BOTH   Name them, my lord, let's know them.
TIMON
You that way and you this, but two in company;   105
Each man apart, all single and alone,   106
Yet an archvillain keeps him company.   107
[*To one.*] If where thou art two villains shall not be,   108
Come not near him. [*To the other.*] If thou wouldst
    not reside   109
But where one villain is, then him abandon.—
Hence, pack! There's gold. You came for gold, ye
    slaves.   111
[*To one.*] You have work for me; there's payment.
    Hence!   112
[*To the other.*] You are an alchemist; make gold of
    that.   113
Out, rascal dogs!
                    Exeunt [Poet and Painter, beaten out by Timon,
                                    who retires to his cave].

                    Enter steward [Flavius] and two Senators.

FLAVIUS
It is in vain that you would speak with Timon;
For he is set so only to himself   116
That nothing but himself which looks like man
Is friendly with him.
FIRST SENATOR   Bring us to his cave.   118
It is our part and promise to th' Athenians   119
To speak with Timon.
SECOND SENATOR   At all times alike
Men are not still the same. 'Twas time and griefs   121
That framed him thus. Time with his fairer hand
Offering the fortunes of his former days,
The former man may make him. Bring us to him,   124
And chance it as it may.
FLAVIUS   Here is his cave.—   125
Peace and content be here! Lord Timon! Timon!
Look out, and speak to friends. Th' Athenians,
By two of their most reverend Senate, greet thee.
Speak to them, noble Timon.

                    Enter Timon out of his cave.

TIMON
Thou sun that comforts, burn! Speak and be hanged!
For each true word a blister, and each false   131
Be as a cauterizing to the root o' the tongue,

Consuming it with speaking!
FIRST SENATOR   Worthy Timon—   133
TIMON
Of none but such as you, and you of Timon.   134
FIRST SENATOR
The senators of Athens greet thee, Timon.
TIMON
I thank them, and would send them back the
    plague,
Could I but catch it for them.
FIRST SENATOR   O, forget
What we are sorry for ourselves in thee.   138
The senators with one consent of love   139
Entreat thee back to Athens, who have thought
On special dignities which vacant lie
For thy best use and wearing.
SECOND SENATOR   They confess
Toward thee forgetfulness too general gross;   143
Which now the public body, which doth seldom   144
Play the recanter, feeling in itself   145
A lack of Timon's aid, hath sense withal   146
Of its own fail, restraining aid to Timon,   147
And send forth us to make their sorrowed render,   148
Together with a recompense more fruitful
Than their offense can weigh down by the dram—   150
Ay, even such heaps and sums of love and wealth
As shall to thee blot out what wrongs were theirs   152
And write in thee the figures of their love,   153
Ever to read them thine.
TIMON   You witch me in it,   154
Surprise me to the very brink of tears.
Lend me a fool's heart and a woman's eyes,
And I'll beweep these comforts, worthy senators.   157
FIRST SENATOR
Therefore, so please thee to return with us,   158
And of our Athens, thine and ours, to take
The captainship, thou shalt be met with thanks,
Allowed with absolute power, and thy good name   161
Live with authority. So soon we shall drive back   162
Of Alcibiades th' approaches wild,   163
Who, like a boar too savage, doth root up
His country's peace.
SECOND SENATOR   And shakes his threatening sword
Against the walls of Athens.
FIRST SENATOR   Therefore, Timon—

---

133 Worthy noble. (But Timon deliberately mistakes the meaning as "deserving.") **134 Of . . . Timon** i.e., we are worthy of nothing better than being punished by one another **138 What . . . thee** those wrongs that we regret having done you **139 consent** unanimous voice **143 general gross** evident to everyone **144 public body** state **145 Play the recanter** i.e., change its mind and apologize **146 Timon's aid** aid to Timon. (But suggesting also "aid to be given by Timon to Athens.") **withal** in addition **147 fail** failing. **restraining** in withholding **148 sorrowed** sorrowful. **render** rendering, i.e., of their apologies **150 can . . . dram** can outweigh under the most scrupulous measurement **152 theirs** of their making **153 figures** (1) representations (2) numbers written in a ledger **154 Ever . . . thine** i.e., to provide a perpetual record of the Athenians' love for you. **witch** bewitch **157 beweep these comforts** weep gratefully at these comforting tidings **158 so** if it **161 Allowed** vested **162 Live with** continue to exercise, be alive with **163 Of . . . wild** the savage attacks of Alcibiades

---

101 draft privy, cesspool **102 Confound** destroy. **course** means **105–107 You . . . him company** (Timon riddlingly suggests that, if the two of them stand apart from one another with no one else around, each has an *archvillain*—himself—to keep him company.) **108 shall not be** are not to be **109 him** i.e., the other one **111 pack** be off **112 there's payment** i.e., here's a beating or a thrown stone **113 alchemist** i.e., one who transmutes nature into poetry and art, as the alchemist is supposed to transmute base metals into gold. **that** i.e., a beating or a thrown stone **116 set . . . himself** so self-absorbed **118 friendly with** congenial to **119 our . . . promise** the part we have promised to undertake **121 still** always **124 The former . . . him** may turn him into his former self **125 chance it** let it happen **131 each false** may each false word

TIMON
Well, sir, I will; therefore, I will, sir; thus:
If Alcibiades kill my countrymen,
Let Alcibiades know this of Timon,
That Timon cares not. But if he sack fair Athens
And take our goodly agèd men by th' beards,
Giving our holy virgins to the stain   172
Of contumelious, beastly, mad-brained war,   173
Then let him know, and tell him Timon speaks it
In pity of our agèd and our youth,
I cannot choose but tell him that I care not,
And let him take 't at worst—for their knives care
  not,   177
While you have throats to answer. For myself,   178
There's not a whittle in th' unruly camp   179
But I do prize it at my love before   180
The reverend'st throat in Athens. So I leave you
To the protection of the prosperous gods,   182
As thieves to keepers.
FLAVIUS [to Senators]   Stay not; all's in vain.   183
TIMON
Why, I was writing of my epitaph;
It will be seen tomorrow. My long sickness
Of health and living now begins to mend,
And nothing brings me all things. Go, live still;   187
Be Alcibiades your plague, you his,
And last so long enough!
FIRST SENATOR   We speak in vain.   189
TIMON
But yet I love my country and am not
One that rejoices in the common wrack,   191
As common bruit doth put it.   192
FIRST SENATOR   That's well spoke.
TIMON
Commend me to my loving countrymen—
FIRST SENATOR
These words become your lips as they pass through
  them.   194
SECOND SENATOR
And enter in our ears like great triumphers   195
In their applauding gates.
TIMON   Commend me to them,   196
And tell them that, to ease them of their griefs,
Their fears of hostile strokes, their aches, losses,
Their pangs of love, with other incident throes   199
That nature's fragile vessel doth sustain   200
In life's uncertain voyage, I will some kindness do
  them:

I'll teach them to prevent wild Alcibiades' wrath.   202
FIRST SENATOR [to the Second Senator]
I like this well. He will return again.
TIMON
I have a tree, which grows here in my close,   204
That mine own use invites me to cut down,   205
And shortly must I fell it. Tell my friends,
Tell Athens, in the sequence of degree   207
From high to low throughout, that whoso please
To stop affliction, let him take his haste,
Come hither ere my tree hath felt the ax,
And hang himself. I pray you, do my greeting.
FLAVIUS [to Senators]
Trouble him no further. Thus you still shall find him.
TIMON
Come not to me again. But say to Athens,
Timon hath made his everlasting mansion   214
Upon the beachèd verge of the salt flood,   215
Who once a day with his embossèd froth   216
The turbulent surge shall cover. Thither come,
And let my gravestone be your oracle.   218
Lips, let four words go by and language end!   219
What is amiss, plague and infection mend!
Graves only be men's works and death their gain!
Sun, hide thy beams! Timon hath done his reign.
                       Exit Timon [into his cave].
FIRST SENATOR
His discontents are unremovably
Coupled to nature.   224
SECOND SENATOR
Our hope in him is dead. Let us return
And strain what other means is left unto us
In our dear peril.
FIRST SENATOR   It requires swift foot.   *Exeunt.* 227

✧

5.2   *Enter two other Senators, with a Messenger.*

THIRD SENATOR
Thou hast painfully discovered. Are his files   1
As full as thy report?
MESSENGER   I have spoke the least.   2
Besides, his expedition promises   3
Present approach.   4

---

172 stain pollution **173 contumelious** insolent **177 take 't at worst**
put the worst possible construction on what I say, or, do the worst destruction possible. **their** of Alcibiades' troops **178 answer** suffer the
consequences **179 whittle** small clasp-knife **180 at** in. **before**
above **182 prosperous** auspicious, favorable **183 As . . . keepers**
as I would leave thieves to the mercy of their hardhearted jailers
187 nothing oblivion, death **189 last . . . enough** remain in that
state as long as possible **191 wrack** destruction **192 bruit** rumor
194 become grace, do credit to **195 triumphers** those coming in triumph **196 applauding gates** i.e., gates crowded with applauding citizens **199 incident throes** naturally occurring agonies **200 nature's
. . . vessel** i.e., the body

202 prevent frustrate, forestall (with a quibble on "anticipate")
204 close enclosure **205 use** need **207 in . . . degree** in order of
social rank **214 everlasting mansion** i.e., grave **215 verge . . .
flood** boundary or margin of the sea. (See 5.4.66.) **216 Who** whom
or which, i.e., Timon or his grave, his *everlasting mansion* (line 214),
both of which the foaming tide will cover daily. **his** its. **embossèd**
foaming (like a hunted animal, foaming at the mouth) **218 oracle**
source of wisdom **219 four words** i.e., few words **224 Coupled to
nature** integrally part of him **227 dear** costly, dire. **foot** i.e., action
5.2. Location: Before the walls of Athens.
1 painfully discovered revealed unsettling news, or, reconnoitered
with painstaking effort. **files** military ranks **2 spoke the least** given
the lowest estimate **3 expedition** speed **4 Present** immediate

FOURTH SENATOR

We stand much hazard if they bring not Timon.   5

MESSENGER

I met a courier, one mine ancient friend,   6

Whom, though in general part we were opposed,   7

Yet our old love made a particular force   8

And made us speak like friends. This man was
riding

From Alcibiades to Timon's cave

With letters of entreaty which imported   11

His fellowship i' the cause against your city,   12

In part for his sake moved.

Enter the other Senators [from Timon].

THIRD SENATOR   Here come our brothers.   13

FIRST SENATOR

No talk of Timon; nothing of him expect.

The enemies' drum is heard, and fearful scouring   15

Doth choke the air with dust. In, and prepare.   16

Ours is the fall, I fear, our foe's the snare.   *Exeunt.*   17

❧

5.3   *Enter a Soldier in the woods, seeking Timon.*

SOLDIER

By all description this should be the place.

Who's here? Speak, ho! No answer? What is this?
               [He finds a rude tomb.]

"Timon is dead, who hath outstretched his span.   3

Some beast read this; there does not live a man."   4

Dead, sure, and this his grave. What's on this tomb

I cannot read. The character I'll take with wax.   6

               [He makes a wax impression.]

Our captain hath in every figure skill,   7

An aged interpreter, though young in days.   8

Before proud Athens he's set down by this,   9

Whose fall the mark of his ambition is.   *Exit.*   10

❧

5.4   *Trumpets sound. Enter Alcibiades with his powers
before Athens.*

ALCIBIADES

Sound to this coward and lascivious town   1

Our terrible approach.   *Sounds a parley.*   2

The Senators appear on the walls.

Till now you have gone on and filled the time

With all licentious measure, making your wills   4

The scope of justice. Till now myself and such   5

As slept within the shadow of your power   6

Have wandered with our traversed arms and
breathed   7

Our sufferance vainly. Now the time is flush,   8

When crouching marrow in the bearer strong   9

Cries of itself, "No more!" Now breathless wrong   10

Shall sit and pant in your great chairs of ease,

And pursy insolence shall break his wind   12

With fear and horrid flight.

FIRST SENATOR   Noble and young,   13

When thy first griefs were but a mere conceit,   14

Ere thou hadst power or we had cause of fear,

We sent to thee, to give thy rages balm,

To wipe out our ingratitude with loves   17

Above their quantity.

SECOND SENATOR   So did we woo   18

Transformèd Timon to our city's love

By humble message and by promised means.   20

We were not all unkind, nor all deserve

The common stroke of war.

FIRST SENATOR   These walls of ours   22

Were not erected by their hands from whom

You have received your grief; nor are they such

That these great tow'rs, trophies, and schools
should fall   25

For private faults in them.

SECOND SENATOR   Nor are they living   26

Who were the motives that you first went out.   27

Shame, that they wanted cunning, in excess   28

Hath broke their hearts. March, noble lord,

---

5 stand much hazard are at great risk.   **they** i.e., the senators who
were sent to Timon   **6 one mine ancient friend** a friend of mine of
long standing   **7 Whom** on whom.   **in general part** on public issues
8 made . . . force exerted a strong personal influence   **11 imported**
(1) concerned, had to do with (2) importuned   **12 fellowship** partnership   **13 In . . . moved** undertaken or initiated partly on his (Timon's)
behalf   **15 scouring** hurrying along, aggressive movement   **16 In** let
us go in   **17 Ours . . . snare** our part, I fear, is to fall, our foe's part
is to set the trap
5.3. Location: The woods. Seemingly near Timon's cave but also at
the edge of the sea; see 5.1.214–217 and 5.4.66. A rude tomb is
seen.
3 outstretched his span stretched out his span of life to its limit
4 Some . . . man i.e., whoever reads this will be a beast, since all
men are beasts   **6 I cannot read** (Suggests there is another inscription
in another language, perhaps Latin, or that this scene shows signs of
incomplete revision and hence apparent inconsistency.)   **The . . .
wax** I'll take an impression of the inscription in wax   **7 every figure**
all kinds of writing   **8 aged** experienced   **9 Before . . . this** by this
time he has laid siege to proud Athens   **10 Whose fall** the fall of
which.   **mark** goal

5.4. Location: Before the walls of Athens. Appearances *on the walls*
are presumably located in the gallery, above, to the rear of the stage.
s.d. powers armed forces   **1 Sound** proclaim   **2 terrible** terrifying.
s.d. parley trumpet call to a negotiation   **4 all licentious measure** every kind of licentious behavior   **4–5 making . . . justice** equating
justice with your wills   **6 slept** within, dwelled   **7 traversed arms** weapons transverse or crossed. (A term in military drill.)   **7–8 breathed
Our sufferance** voiced our sufferings   **8 flush** at flood, ripe
9 crouching marrow latent resolution and might   **10 of itself** of its
own accord.   **breathless wrong** wrongdoers (i.e., you senators) who
are frightened into breathlessness   **12 pursy** short-winded.   **break his
wind** pant for breath (perhaps suggesting also to void air from the
bowels in fright)   **13 horrid** terrified   **14 griefs** grievances.   **conceit**
fancy, imagined scheme of action   **17–18 loves . . . quantity** offers
of friendship exceeding the quantity of your grievances   **20 means**
terms, wealth   **22 common** indiscriminate   **25 trophies** monuments.
schools public buildings   **26 private** personal.   **them** i.e., those from
whom you have received your injuries   **27 motives . . . out** instiga-
tors that prompted your banishment   **28 Shame . . . excess** i.e., an
excess of shame for their lack of cunning in statecraft

Into our city with thy banners spread.
By decimation and a tithèd death—   31
If thy revenges hunger for that food
Which nature loathes—take thou the destined tenth,
And by the hazard of the spotted die   34
Let die the spotted.
FIRST SENATOR   All have not offended.   35
For those that were, it is not square to take   36
On those that are, revenge. Crimes, like lands,   37
Are not inherited. Then, dear countryman,   38
Bring in thy ranks, but leave without thy rage.   39
Spare thy Athenian cradle and those kin   40
Which in the bluster of thy wrath must fall
With those that have offended. Like a shepherd
Approach the fold and cull th' infected forth,   43
But kill not all together.
SECOND SENATOR   What thou wilt,
Thou rather shalt enforce it with thy smile
Than hew to 't with thy sword.
FIRST SENATOR   Set but thy foot
Against our rampired gates and they shall ope,   47
So thou wilt send thy gentle heart before   48
To say thou'lt enter friendly.
SECOND SENATOR   Throw thy glove,   49
Or any token of thine honor else,   50
That thou wilt use the wars as thy redress
And not as our confusion, all thy powers   52
Shall make their harbor in our town till we   53
Have sealed thy full desire.
ALCIBIADES [throwing a glove] Then there's my glove.   54
Descend, and open your unchargèd ports.   55
Those enemies of Timon's and mine own
Whom you yourselves shall set out for reproof   57
Fall, and no more; and, to atone your fears   58
With my more noble meaning, not a man   59
Shall pass his quarter or offend the stream   60
Of regular justice in your city's bounds   61
But shall be remedied to your public laws   62
At heaviest answer.
BOTH   'Tis most nobly spoken.   63
ALCIBIADES   Descend, and keep your words.   64
          [The Senators descend, and open the gates.]

     Enter [Soldier as] a messenger [with a wax tablet].

SOLDIER
My noble general, Timon is dead,
Entombed upon the very hem o' the sea;   66
And on his gravestone this insculpture, which   67
With wax I brought away, whose soft impression
Interprets for my poor ignorance.
ALCIBIADES (reads the epitaph)
"Here lies a wretched corpse, of wretched soul bereft. 70
Seek not my name. A plague consume you wicked
     caitiffs left!   71
Here lie I, Timon, who, alive, all living men did
     hate.
Pass by and curse thy fill, but pass and stay not
     here thy gait."   73
These well express in thee thy latter spirits.   74
Though thou abhorredst in us our human griefs,
Scornedst our brains' flow and those our droplets
     which   76
From niggard nature fall, yet rich conceit   77
Taught thee to make vast Neptune weep for aye   78
On thy low grave, on faults forgiven. Dead
Is noble Timon, of whose memory
Hereafter more. Bring me into your city,
And I will use the olive with my sword,   82
Make war breed peace, make peace stint war, make
     each   83
Prescribe to other as each other's leech.   84
Let our drums strike.   [Drums.] Exeunt.

66 hem i.e., edge, shore 67 insculpture inscription 70–73 Here
. . . gait (Of these two inscriptions, both found in Plutarch,
Shakespeare would presumably have deleted one, since they contradict one another.) 71 caitiffs wretches 73 gait journey 74 latter
spirits recent sentiments 76 brains' flow i.e., tears 77 niggard nature parsimonious human nature (unable to produce quantities of
tears to compete with the sea). conceit imagination, fancy 78 Neptune the god of the sea in Roman mythology. aye ever 82 olive,
sword (Symbols of peace and war.) 83 stint stop 84 leech physician. (War can cure the decadent softness of a prolonged peacetime;
peace can cure war's violence.)

31 decimation, tithèd death selection of every tenth to die. (The two
phrases mean the same thing.) 34 die (Singular of dice; with a play
on the verb die.) 35 the spotted the corrupt, wicked (with a play on
the spots on the dice) 36 were were living then (and did you offense). square just 37 are are now alive 37–38 like . . . inherited are not inherited, as lands are 39 without outside 40 thy Athenian cradle Athens, your birthplace 43 cull . . . forth pick out the
tainted 47 rampired barricaded. ope open 48 So if only
49 Throw if you will throw 50 token pledge 52 confusion overthrow. powers armed forces 53 make their harbor find safe lodging 54 sealed satisfied, ratified 55 unchargèd ports unattacked
gates 57 set out for reproof pick out for punishment 58 atone appease, make "at one" 59 man i.e., soldier of mine 60 pass his
quarter leave his assigned duty area 60–61 offend . . . justice violate the norms set by established law 62 But . . . remedied without
being remanded 63 At heaviest answer to receive severest punishment 64 s.d. open the gates (Presumably, the gates are a door in the
tiring-house facade representing here the walls of Athens; the gallery
above is on the walls.)

Antony and Cleopatra

Shakespeare probably wrote *Antony and Cleopatra* in 1606 or 1607; it was registered for publication on May 20, 1608, and apparently influenced a revision of Samuel Daniel's *Cleopatra* that was published "newly altered" in 1607. *Antony and Cleopatra* was thus roughly contemporary with *King Lear* and *Macbeth*. Yet the contrast between those two tragedies and *Antony and Cleopatra* is immense. Unlike *Macbeth*, with its taut focus on a murderer and his wife, *Antony and Cleopatra* moves back and forth across the Mediterranean in its epic survey of characters and events, bringing together the fates of Pompey, Octavius Caesar, Octavia, and Lepidus with those of the protagonists. *King Lear* gives proper names to fourteen characters, *Macbeth* to eighteen, *Antony and Cleopatra* to thirty-one. The Roman play requires no less than forty-two separate scenes, of which most occur in what modern editors label Acts 3 and 4, although no play is less suited to the classical rigors of five-act structure, and these divisions are not found in the reliable Folio text of 1623. Indeed, it is as though Shakespeare resolved at the height of his career to show that he could dispense entirely with the classical "rules," which had never taken serious hold of the English popular stage in any case. The flouting of the unities is so extreme that John Dryden, in his *All for Love or The World Well Lost* (1678), undertook not so much to revise Shakespeare as to start afresh on the same subject. Dryden's play is restricted to the last few hours of the protagonists' lives, at Cleopatra's tomb in Alexandria, with a severely limited cast of characters and much of the narrative revealed through recollection. Although a substantial achievement in its own right, *All for Love* surely reveals that Shakespeare knew what he was doing, for Dryden has excised a good deal of the panorama, the excitement, and the "infinite variety" (2.2.246).

Shakespeare departs also from the somber tone of his tragedies of evil. He creates, instead, a world that bears affinities to the ambivalent conflicts of the other Roman plays, to the varying humorous perspectives of the comedies, and to the imaginative reconstructions of the late romances. As protagonists, Antony and Cleopatra lack tragic stature, or so it first appears: she is a tawny gypsy temptress and he a "strumpet's fool," a once-great general now bound in "strong Egyptian fetters" and lost in "dotage" (1.1.13; 1.2.122–123). Several scenes, especially those set in Egypt, are comic and delightfully bawdy: Charmian learning her fortune from the soothsayer, Cleopatra practicing her charms in vain to keep Antony from leaving Egypt or raunchily daydreaming of being Antony's horse "to bear the weight of Antony" (1.5.22), Cleopatra flying into a magnificent rage at the news of Antony's marriage to Octavia and then consoling herself with catty reflections on Octavia's reported low voice and shortness of stature ("I think so, Charmian. Dull of tongue, and dwarfish," 3.3.17). In its comic texture, the play somewhat resembles *Romeo and Juliet,* an earlier play about a younger pair of lovers, although there the bawdry is used chiefly to characterize the lovers' companions and confidants, whereas in *Antony and Cleopatra* it is central to our vision of Cleopatra especially. In any case, the later play is a tragedy about lovers who, despite their quarrels and uncertainties and betrayals of self, are reconciled in a vision of the greatness of their love. In its depiction of two contrasting worlds, also, *Antony and Cleopatra* recalls the movement of several earlier comedies from the realistic world of political conniving to a dreamworld of the romantic and the unexpected. We can endorse neither world fully in *Antony and Cleopatra,* and, accordingly, the vision of life presented is often ambivalent and ironic as much as it is tragic. The contrast of values separating Egypt and Rome underscores the paradox of humanity's quest for seemingly irreconcilable goals. The ending is neither a triumph nor a defeat for the lovers but something of both. If Antony and Cleopatra seem in one way too small to be tragic protagonists, in another way they seem too large, creating imaginative visions of themselves and their union that escape the realm of tragedy altogether. Our attention is focused less on the way in which the protagonists come to understand some meaningful relationship between their character and the fate required of them by a tragic universe than on the almost comic way in which the absurdities of Roman worldly striving and Egyptian dissipation are transfigured in the world of the imagination.

The Roman point of view opens the play and never entirely loses its force. At first, it may seem superior to that of Egypt. Demetrius and Philo, who invite us to view the play's first encounter between Antony and Cleopatra (1.1) from the perspective of the professional Roman soldier, lament the decline of Antony into Circean enslavement. Their tragic concept is of the Fall of Princes, all the more soberly edifying because of the height from which Antony has toppled. "You shall see in him / The triple pillar of the world transformed / Into a strumpet's fool" (1.1.11–13). Egypt is enchanting but clearly enervating—a bizarre assemblage of soothsayers, eunuchs, and waiting-gentlewomen who wish to be "married to three kings in a forenoon and widow them all" (1.2.28–29). Their mirth is all bawdry, tinged with practices, such as transvestism, that Roman custom views as licentious. The prevailing images are of procreation in various shapes, sleep (mandragora, Lethe), the oriental opulence of Cleopatra's barge (a golden poop, purple sails, silver oars, divers-colored fans), Epicurean feasting, and drinking. As Enobarbus says, "Mine, and most of our fortunes tonight, shall be—drunk to bed" (1.2.47–48).

Antony, for all his reckless defiance of Rome, agrees in his more reflective moments with what Demetrius and Philo have said. "A Roman thought hath struck him," Cleopatra observantly remarks, and Antony has indeed determined that "I must from this enchanting queen break off" (1.2.88, 135). His later return to Cleopatra is at least in part a surrender, a betrayal of his marriage vows to Octavia and his political assurances to Caesar. In the ensuing battles, Antony submits himself dangerously to Cleopatra's governance, and this inversion of dominance in sexual roles, as conventionally understood by the Roman patriarchal world, is emblematic of a deeper disorder within Antony. As Enobarbus concludes bitterly, Antony "would make his will / Lord of his reason" and so has subverted his "judgment" (3.13.3–4, 37) to passion.

From the beginning, Cleopatra has sought dominance over Antony in the war of the sexes. When Antony first came to her on the River Cydnus, we learn, he was so overcome in all his senses that he was "barbered ten times o'er" (2.2.234). Cleopatra boasts that she "angled" for Antony on many occasions, catching him the way fishermen "betray" fish, and that, when she had "drunk him to his bed," she "put my tires and mantles on him, whilst / I wore his sword Philippan" (2.5.10–23). Caesar, affronted by such transvestite debauchery, charges that Antony "is not more manlike / Than Cleopatra, nor the queen of Ptolemy / More womanly than he" (1.4.5–7). During the battle scenes, Antony's followers complain that "Photinus, an eunuch" (probably Mardian), and Cleopatra's maids manage the war: "So our leader's led, / And we are women's men" (3.7.14–15, 70–71). Antony confesses too late that they were right. He becomes a "doting mallard," one whose heart is "tied by th' strings" to Cleopatra's rudder when her ships retreat in the first naval engagement (3.10.20, 3.11.56). In the mythic images used to raise their relationship to heroic proportions, Antony is like Mars to Cleopatra's Venus (1.5.19), both in a positive and a negative sense. The image has positive connotations of the way in which, as Milton puts it, the "two great sexes animate the world," the masterful soldier and his attractive consort complementing one another in a right relationship of martial prowess and beauty, bravery and love, reason and will; however, to the Renaissance, the myth of Mars and Venus could also be read in a destructive sense, as an adulterous relationship in which reason is subverted to appetite. In another mythic comparison, Antony is like Hercules, not in his prime, but with the shirt of Nessus on his back—a poisoned shirt given to Hercules by his wife in a mistaken hope of thereby assuring his love for her (4.12.43). Antony's sol-

diers understandably believe that the god Hercules has deserted his reputed descendant and onetime champion (4.3.21–22).

Despite Antony's shameful violation of manhood, honor, attention to duty, self-knowledge, and all that Rome stands for, however, the end of his story is anything but a one-sided endorsement for the Roman point of view. The actual Rome, disfigured by political conniving, falls far short of the ideal. Antony has a point when he protests that "Kingdoms are clay" (1.1.37). Alliances are unstable and are governed by mere political expediency. At first, Antony's wife Fulvia and his brother Lucius have fought one another until forced to unite against the greater threat of Octavius Caesar. Similarly, Antony and Caesar come together only because Pompey has become dangerously powerful at sea and has won the favor of the fickle mob, "Our slippery people" (1.2.192). This detente is not meant to last. As Enobarbus bluntly puts it, "if you borrow one another's love for the instant, you may, when you hear no more words of Pompey, return it again" (2.2.109–111). Enobarbus is rebuked for his unstatesmanlike tone, but no one denies the validity of what he says. In this cynical negotiation, Octavia is a pawn between husband and brother, shabbily treated by both. Caesar coldly bargains away the happiness of the one person of whom he protests that "no brother / Did ever love so dearly" (2.2.159–160). Antony, although hating false promises and resolving to be loyal to Octavia, knows within himself that it won't work. To make matters worse for the fair-minded Antony, he has received great favors from Pompey that he must now uncharitably repudiate in the interests of politics. Pompey does not miss the opportunity to remind Antony of his ingratitude, but the prevailing mood is not so much of bitterness as of ironic futility. Old friendships must be sacrificed; no one seems wholly to blame, and no one can stop the game. Pompey is as much in the wrong as anyone and as powerless. Despite his idealistic hope of rescuing Rome from political infighting, he has had to ally himself with pirates who offer him sinister temptations. He could be "lord of all the world" (2.7.62) if he would only murder on occasion, but Pompey is destined to be trapped between lofty ends and ignoble means. Lepidus is still another dismaying victim of political callousness, used condescendingly by Caesar and permitted to drink himself into oblivion, until he is cashiered on a trumped-up charge and imprisoned for life.

Octavius Caesar embodies most of all the ironic limits of political ambition. He has avoided enslavement to passion at the very real cost of enslaving himself to his public career as general, triumvir, and future emperor. His ideal warrior is one who, driven by military necessity, would "drink / The stale [urine] of horses and the gilded puddle / Which beasts would cough at" (1.4.62–64). As a general, he is Antony's opposite in every way. He attacks only when he has the advantage and places those who have deserted Antony in his own front lines so "That Antony may seem to spend his fury

/ Upon himself" (4.6.10–11). He controls his supplies cannily, believing it a "waste" to feast his army (4.1.17). He, of course, declines Antony's offers of single combat. Antony meantime recklessly accepts Caesar's challenge to fight at sea, feasts debauchingly in one "gaudy night" after another (3.13.186), and generously refuses to blame or penalize those who leave him. His sending Enobarbus' belongings after him into Caesar's camp convinces that honest soldier he has made a fatal error, for, however imprudent Antony's chivalry may be, it is unquestionably noble and greathearted. Caesar is a superb general and political genius, but he is also a military automaton, a logistical reckoner, a Machiavellian pragmatist. In his personal life, he is no less austere and puritanical. He deplores loosening his tongue with alcohol. About women, he is deeply cynical, believing that "want will perjure / The ne'er-touched vestal" (3.12.30–31). Between him and Cleopatra, there is a profound antipathy, based in part on his revulsion at her earlier affair with his namesake and adoptive father, Julius Caesar (3.6.6). Cleopatra may entertain briefly the notion of trying to seduce this new Caesar (3.13.46 ff.), for like Charmian she loves long life "better than figs"(1.2.34), but, if so, she soon discovers that she and Caesar are not compatible. All that he represents she must instead grandly repudiate, choosing death and the fantasy of an eternity with Antony as her way to "call great Caesar ass / Unpolicied" (5.2.307–308).

Cleopatra is a "lass unparalleled" (5.2.316), whose greatness is elusive and all the more enthralling because it is so mysterious. She rises above her counterpart in Shakespeare's source, Plutarch's Lives of the Noble Grecians and Romans, in which she is an impressive queenly woman but still essentially a temptress causing the lamentable fall of the hero. Shakespeare's Cleopatra is that but is also something indefinable that can be gotten at only through paradox. Her very character is the essence of contradiction: she knows how "to chide, to laugh, / To weep" (1.1.51–52), to be sullen or violent, like a skillful actor keeping Antony continually off guard. Dispassionately examined, she is a woman no longer young who abuses messengers like an oriental despot, who sends Antony a false report of her death out of fear for her own safety, who will not risk leaving her monument even when Antony lies outside mortally wounded, and who lies about her wealth when captured by Caesar (what is she planning to do with that wealth, anyway?). We cannot be sure that she would not have "packed cards with Caesar" (4.14.19) if she had found him susceptible to her charms. Yet we are not invited to see her dispassionately. Her charm is eternal, and so are the myths surrounding that charm. Observers evoking her splendor do not describe her person directly but, rather, her effects and surroundings: Enobarbus says simply that "For her own person, / It beggared all description" and goes on to catalogue her cloth-of-gold pavilion and her mermaidlike attendants. Most of all, she is a paradox: she makes defect perfection, age can

not wither her, and "vilest things / Become themselves in her, that the holy priests / Bless her when she is riggish" (2.2.207–250). She is both a whore and the Lucretian Venus; both sluttish and holy.

Inspired by Cleopatra, Antony shows himself ready to break down conventional barriers between the sexes and to explore new emotional territory by giving up part of his self-protective masculinity. Antony's embracing of an attractive but sexually dangerous woman is all the more remarkable in a play that follows the harrowing depictions of sexual conflict in Hamlet, Othello, and Lear and the degrading portrait of erotic enslavement in the "Dark Lady" sonnets, for here the relationship of the lovers, though doomed, is also triumphant. Shakespeare takes a look at something like middle-age crisis, conceding freely how ridiculous the male appears to himself and to others in his compulsive tendency to polarize women into saints and whores. Yet Shakespeare also explores ways in which the man and the woman attempt to become increasingly like each other, enabling the man to participate in a vision of union with the feminine principle of generative, erotic, fertile, life-giving vitality, and enabling the woman to join her "husband" in the noble resolve of a Roman suicide.

In Cleopatra, "fancy" exceeds "nature"; the fertility of her Egypt overflows the measure, exceeding the sterility of Rome as her own imaginative fertility exceeds reality itself. When she protests that she will not go to Rome to behold herself in a wretched play and thus see "Some squeaking Cleopatra boy my greatness / I' the posture of a whore" (5.2.220–221), we realize that Shakespeare is calling attention to his own art as well, pointing out how Elizabethan boy actors on a bare stage can transform reality into a dream that we believe. Cleopatra's mystery is like that of poetry itself. The "real" world pales into insignificance of a "little O, the earth," something "No better than a sty," full of illusory shadows that "mock our eyes with air" (5.2.80, 4.15.64, 4.14.7); and Caesar's triumph vanishes with it. In its place, Antony and Cleopatra raise up a vision of themselves as lovers who, through art, have indeed become eternal. Together they will overpicture Venus and Mars, and will be so renowned that "Dido and her Aeneas shall want troops, / And all the haunt be ours" (4.14.53–54). They are virtually husband and wife—"Husband, I come!" exclaims Cleopatra just before she dies (5.2.287)—united at last in a re-creative vision almost appropriate to comedy; and in their marriage they find a kind of redemption for the defeat that history can inflict. Antony is no longer dying Hercules but the god of Cleopatra's dream whose "legs bestrid the ocean; his reared arm / Crested the world; his voice was propertied / As all the tunèd spheres" (lines 81–83). Through Cleopatra's vision, we realize how all the characteristics that made Antony at once so noble and so sure to fall before Caesar—his generosity amounting to imprudence, his spontaneity, his impatience with the ordinary, his staking his all on love when he hears of Cleopatra's supposed death—have not deserted him. His death serves to reaffirm the magnificence of the very qualities that have brought him down. His essential nobility is confirmed, even if it must be defined in non-Roman ways. He and Cleopatra share the "immortal longings" for which she goes willingly to her death, dressed in her "best attires" like a queen (lines 281, 228), for neither lover will accept anything less than greatness.

Antony and Cleopatra

[*Dramatis Personae*

MARK ANTONY,
OCTAVIUS CAESAR, } *triumvirs*
LEPIDUS,

CLEOPATRA,
CHARMIAN,
IRAS,
ALEXAS,
MARDIAN, *a eunuch,*
DIOMEDES,
SELEUCUS, *Cleopatra's treasurer,* } *Cleopatra's attendants*

OCTAVIA, *sister of Octavius Caesar and wife of Antony*

DEMETRIUS,
PHILO,
DOMITIUS ENOBARBUS,
VENTIDIUS,
SILIUS,
EROS,
CANIDIUS,
SCARUS,
DERCETUS, } *Antony's friends and followers*
A SCHOOLMASTER, *Antony's* AMBASSADOR *to Caesar*

MAECENAS,
AGRIPPA,
TAURUS,
THIDIAS,
DOLABELLA,
GALLUS,
PROCULEIUS, } *Octavius Caesar's friends and followers*

SEXTUS POMPEIUS *or* POMPEY
MENAS,
MENECRATES, } *Pompey's friends*
VARRIUS,

MESSENGERS *to Antony, Octavius, Caesar, and Cleopatra*
A SOOTHSAYER
Two SERVANTS *of Pompey*
SERVANTS *of Antony and Cleopatra*
A BOY
SOLDIERS, SENTRIES, GUARDSMEN *of Antony and Octavius Caesar*
A CAPTAIN *in Antony's army*
An EGYPTIAN

A CLOWN *with figs*

Ladies attending Cleopatra, Eunuchs, Servants, Soldiers, Captains, Officers, silent named characters
(Rannius, Lucillius, Lamprius)

SCENE: *In several parts of the Roman Empire*]

1.1   *Enter Demetrius and Philo.*

PHILO
Nay, but this dotage of our general's   1
O'erflows the measure. Those his goodly eyes,   2
That o'er the files and musters of the war   3
Have glowed like plated Mars, now bend, now turn 4
The office and devotion of their view   5
Upon a tawny front. His captain's heart,   6
Which in the scuffles of great fights hath burst
The buckles on his breast, reneges all temper   8
And is become the bellows and the fan
To cool a gypsy's lust.

*Flourish. Enter Antony, Cleopatra, her ladies, the
train, with eunuchs fanning her.*

                                    Look, where they come.   10
Take but good note, and you shall see in him
The triple pillar of the world transformed   12
Into a strumpet's fool. Behold and see.   13
CLEOPATRA
If it be love indeed, tell me how much.
ANTONY
There's beggary in the love that can be reckoned.   15
CLEOPATRA
I'll set a bourn how far to be beloved.   16
ANTONY
Then must thou needs find out new heaven, new
  earth.   17

Enter a Messenger.

MESSENGER   News, my good lord, from Rome.
ANTONY   Grates me! The sum.   19
CLEOPATRA   Nay, hear them, Antony.   20

Fulvia perchance is angry, or who knows   21
If the scarce-bearded Caesar have not sent   22
His powerful mandate to you, "Do this, or this;
Take in that kingdom, and enfranchise that;   24
Perform 't, or else we damn thee."   25
ANTONY   How, my love?   26
CLEOPATRA   Perchance? Nay, and most like.   27
You must not stay here longer; your dismission   28
Is come from Caesar. Therefore hear it, Antony.
Where's Fulvia's process? Caesar's, I would say.
  Both?   30
Call in the messengers. As I am Egypt's queen,
Thou blushest, Antony, and that blood of thine
Is Caesar's homager; else so thy cheek pays shame 33
When shrill-tongued Fulvia scolds. The messengers!
ANTONY
Let Rome in Tiber melt and the wide arch
Of the ranged empire fall! Here is my space.   36
Kingdoms are clay; our dungy earth alike   37
Feeds beast as man. The nobleness of life
Is to do thus; when such a mutual pair   39
And such a twain can do 't, in which I bind,   40
On pain of punishment, the world to weet   41
We stand up peerless.
CLEOPATRA   Excellent falsehood!
Why did he marry Fulvia, and not love her?   43
I'll seem the fool I am not. Antony   44
Will be himself.
ANTONY   But stirred by Cleopatra.   45
Now, for the love of Love and her soft hours,
Let's not confound the time with conference harsh.   47
There's not a minute of our lives should stretch   48
Without some pleasure now. What sport tonight?
CLEOPATRA
Hear the ambassadors.
ANTONY   Fie, wrangling queen!
Whom everything becomes—to chide, to laugh,
To weep; whose every passion fully strives
To make itself, in thee, fair and admired!
No messenger but thine; and all alone
Tonight we'll wander through the streets and note
The qualities of people. Come, my queen,
Last night you did desire it.—Speak not to us.
Exeunt [Antony and Cleopatra] with the train.

1.1. Location: Alexandria. Cleopatra's palace.
1 dotage foolish affection, sometimes associated with old age
2 O'erflows the measure exceeds moderation, exceeds the means of
measuring it   **3 files and musters** orderly formations   **4 plated**
clothed in armor   **5 office** function   **6 tawny front** dark face. (Literally, forehead.)   **8 reneges** renounces.   **temper** moderation   **10 gypsy's** (Gypsies were widely believed to have come from Egypt, to enjoy
magical powers, and to be lustful and cunning.)   **s.d. Flourish** trumpet fanfare announcing the arrival or departure of an important person.   **train** retinue   **12 triple** one of three. (Alludes to the triumvirate
of Antony, Lepidus, and Octavius Caesar; also to tripartite division of
the world into Asia, Africa, and Europe.)   **13 fool** plaything
15 There's . . . reckoned i.e., love that can be quantified is paltry;
ours is infinite   **16 bourn** boundary, limit   **17 Then . . . earth** i.e.,
only in some new universe could you find a limit to my love. (The
language echoes Revelation 21:1 and other biblical passages.)
19 Grates me it annoys me.   **The sum** i.e., be brief   **20 them** i.e.,
the news

21 Fulvia Antony's wife   **22 scarce-bearded Caesar** (Octavius Caesar
was twenty-three in 40 B.C., at the time of the play's opening. Antony was forty-three.)   **24 Take in** conquer.   **enfranchise** set free
25 damn condemn to death   **26 How** i.e., what's that you say?
27 Perchance (Cleopatra reconsiders what she has said in line 21.)
like likely   **28 dismission** order to depart   **30 process** writ to appear
in court   **33 homager** vassal, one who does homage.   **else so** or
else.   **thy cheek pays shame** your blushing pays the tribute of shame
36 ranged ordered, or possibly, extended   **37 dungy** composed of
dung   **39 thus** (May indicate an embrace, or Antony may refer more
generally to their way of life.)   **40 bind** obligate   **41 pain** penalty.
weet know, acknowledge   **43 and not** if he did not   **44 I'll . . . not**
i.e., I'll pretend to be gullible and believe him, though I know better
45 be himself i.e., be the Roman Antony, the fool and deceiver he
always is, etc.   **stirred** (1) prompted to noble deeds (2) moved to
folly (3) sexually stirred   **47 confound** ruin, waste.   **conference** conversation   **48 should** that should.   **stretch** (Suggests that time can be
stretched or extended.)

DEMETRIUS
Is Caesar with Antonius prized so slight?   58

PHILO
Sir, sometimes when he is not Antony
He comes too short of that great property   60
Which still should go with Antony.

DEMETRIUS   I am full sorry   61
That he approves the common liar, who   62
Thus speaks of him at Rome; but I will hope
Of better deeds tomorrow. Rest you happy!   *Exeunt.*   64

♣

1.2 *Enter Enobarbus, Lamprius, a Soothsayer,
Rannius, Lucillius, Charmian, Iras, Mardian the
eunuch, and Alexas.*

CHARMIAN   Lord Alexas, sweet Alexas, most anything
Alexas, almost most absolute Alexas, where's the   2
soothsayer that you praised so to the Queen? O, that
I knew this husband, which, you say, must charge his   4
horns with garlands!   5

ALEXAS   Soothsayer!

SOOTHSAYER   Your will?

CHARMIAN
Is this the man?—Is 't you, sir, that know things?

SOOTHSAYER
In nature's infinite book of secrecy
A little I can read.

ALEXAS [*to Charmian*]   Show him your hand.

ENOBARBUS [*to servants within*]
Bring in the banquet quickly; wine enough   12
Cleopatra's health to drink.

CHARMIAN [*giving her hand to the Soothsayer*]   Good sir,
give me good fortune.

SOOTHSAYER   I make not, but foresee.

CHARMIAN   Pray, then, foresee me one.

SOOTHSAYER
You shall be yet far fairer than you are.

CHARMIAN   He means in flesh.   19

IRAS   No, you shall paint when you are old.   20

CHARMIAN   Wrinkles forbid!

ALEXAS   Vex not his prescience. Be attentive.

CHARMIAN   Hush!

SOOTHSAYER
You shall be more beloving than beloved.

CHARMIAN   I had rather heat my liver with drinking.   25

ALEXAS   Nay, hear him.

CHARMIAN   Good now, some excellent fortune! Let me   27
be married to three kings in a forenoon and widow
them all. Let me have a child at fifty, to whom Herod   29
of Jewry may do homage. Find me to marry me with   30
Octavius Caesar, and companion me with my mis-   31
tress.

SOOTHSAYER
You shall outlive the lady whom you serve.

CHARMIAN   O, excellent! I love long life better than figs.   34

SOOTHSAYER
You have seen and proved a fairer former fortune   35
Than that which is to approach.

CHARMIAN   Then belike my children shall have no   37
names. Prithee, how many boys and wenches must I   38
have?

SOOTHSAYER
If every of your wishes had a womb,
And fertile every wish, a million.

CHARMIAN   Out, fool! I forgive thee for a witch.   42

ALEXAS   You think none but your sheets are privy to   43
your wishes.

CHARMIAN   Nay, come, tell Iras hers.

ALEXAS   We'll know all our fortunes.

ENOBARBUS   Mine, and most of our fortunes tonight,
shall be—drunk to bed.

IRAS [*giving her hand to the Soothsayer*]   There's a palm
presages chastity, if nothing else.

CHARMIAN   E'en as the o'erflowing Nilus presageth   51
famine.   52

IRAS   Go, you wild bedfellow, you cannot soothsay.   53

CHARMIAN   Nay, if an oily palm be not a fruitful prog-   54
nostication, I cannot scratch mine ear. Prithee, tell her   55
but a workaday fortune.   56

SOOTHSAYER   Your fortunes are alike.

IRAS   But how, but how? Give me particulars.

SOOTHSAYER   I have said.   59

IRAS   Am I not an inch of fortune better than she?

CHARMIAN   Well, if you were but an inch of fortune bet-   61
ter than I, where would you choose it?   63

IRAS   Not in my husband's nose.   63

CHARMIAN   Our worser thoughts heavens mend! Al-   64
exas—come, his fortune, his fortune! O, let him marry
a woman that cannot go, sweet Isis, I beseech thee,   66
and let her die too, and give him a worse, and let

---

58 prized valued   **60 property** quality, distinction   **61 still** always
62 approves corroborates   **64 Of** for
1.2. Location: Alexandria. Cleopatra's palace.
s.d. Lamprius etc. (Lamprius may possibly be the soothsayer, but Rannius and Lucillius have no speaking parts here and do not appear
again in the play. Mardian is mute here but does speak in later
scenes.)   **2 absolute** perfect   **4–5 must . . . garlands** i.e., must decorate his cuckold's horns with a garland of flowers, like a sacrificial
beast. (Cuckolded men were derisively thought of as growing horns,
as a badge of their infamy.)   **12 banquet** light repast, dessert   **19 in
flesh** i.e., by putting on weight   **20 paint** i.e., use makeup   **25 heat
. . . drinking** i.e., heat my liver with wine rather than with unrequited love. (The liver was believed to be the seat of sexual desire.)

27 Good now come on, now   **29–30 Herod of Jewry** i.e., even the
blustering tyrant who massacred the children of Judea   **30 Find** i.e.,
find in my palm   **31 companion me with** give me equal fortune with
34 better than figs (Probably a proverbial expression; with genital
suggestion.)   **35 proved** experienced   **37 belike** probably
37–38 have no names be illegitimate   **38 wenches** girls   **42 Out
. . . witch** (Charmian jokingly says that, since soothsayers, like fools,
are allowed to speak freely without penalty, she will not charge him
with the crime of wizardry.)   **43 privy to** in on the secret of   **51–
52 E'en . . . famine** (Charmian speaks ironically; the overflowing Nile
presaged abundance. See 2.7.17–23.)   **53 wild** wanton   **54 oily
palm** sweaty or moist palm (indicating a sensual disposition)   **54–
55 fruitful prognostication** omen of fertility   **56 workaday** ordinary
59 I have said I have no more to say   **61, 63 inch, nose** (With suggestion that Iras would prefer her husband to be sexually well
endowed.)   **64 Our . . . mend** (Charmian pretends to be shocked:
may heaven improve our dirty minds!)   **66 cannot go** (1) is lame (2)
cannot make love satisfactorily or cannot bear children.   **Isis** Egyptian
goddess usually identified with fertility and the moon

worse follow worse till the worst of all follow him
laughing to his grave, fiftyfold a cuckold! Good Isis,
hear me this prayer, though thou deny me a matter of 70
more weight; good Isis, I beseech thee!

IRAS   Amen, dear goddess, hear that prayer of the people! For, as it is a heart-breaking to see a handsome
man loose-wived, so it is a deadly sorrow to behold a 74
foul knave uncuckolded. Therefore, dear Isis, keep de- 75
corum, and fortune him accordingly!   76

CHARMIAN   Amen.

ALEXAS   Lo now, if it lay in their hands to make me a
cuckold, they would make themselves whores but 79
they'd do 't.   80

Enter Cleopatra.

ENOBARBUS
Hush! Here comes Antony.

CHARMIAN   Not he. The Queen.

CLEOPATRA   Saw you my lord?

ENOBARBUS   No, lady.

CLEOPATRA   Was he not here?

CHARMIAN   No, madam.

CLEOPATRA
He was disposed to mirth, but on the sudden   87
A Roman thought hath struck him. Enobarbus!

ENOBARBUS   Madam?

CLEOPATRA
Seek him and bring him hither. Where's Alexas?

ALEXAS
Here at your service.—My lord approaches.

Enter Antony with a Messenger.

CLEOPATRA
We will not look upon him. Go with us.
        Exeunt [all but Antony and the Messenger.]

FIRST MESSENGER
Fulvia thy wife first came into the field.   93

ANTONY Against my brother Lucius?

FIRST MESSENGER   Ay.
But soon that war had end, and the time's state   96
Made friends of them, jointing their force 'gainst
    Caesar,   97
Whose better issue in the war from Italy   98
Upon the first encounter drave them.   99

ANTONY Well, what worst?

FIRST MESSENGER
The nature of bad news infects the teller.   101

ANTONY
When it concerns the fool or coward. On.
Things that are past are done with me. 'Tis thus:
Who tells me true, though in his tale lie death,

I hear him as he flattered.

FIRST MESSENGER   Labienus—   105
This is stiff news—hath with his Parthian force
Extended Asia; from Euphrates   107
His conquering banner shook, from Syria
To Lydia and to Ionia,
Whilst—

ANTONY   Antony, thou wouldst say.

FIRST MESSENGER   O, my lord!

ANTONY
Speak to me home; mince not the general tongue. 111
Name Cleopatra as she is called in Rome;
Rail thou in Fulvia's phrase, and taunt my faults 113
With such full license as both truth and malice
Have power to utter. O, then we bring forth weeds
When our quick minds lie still, and our ills told us 116
Is as our earing. Fare thee well awhile.   117

FIRST MESSENGER   At your noble pleasure.
                Exit [First] Messenger.

Enter another Messenger

ANTONY
From Sicyon, ho, the news! Speak there.

SECOND MESSENGER
The man from Sicyon—is there such an one?   120

THIRD MESSENGER [*at the door*]
He stays upon your will.

ANTONY   Let him appear.—   121
        [Exeunt Second and Third Messengers.]
These strong Egyptian fetters I must break,
Or lose myself in dotage.

Enter another Messenger, with a letter.

                What are you?

FOURTH MESSENGER   Fulvia thy wife is dead.

ANTONY   Where died she?

FOURTH MESSENGER   In Sicyon.
Her length of sickness, with what else more serious
Importeth thee to know, this bears. [*He gives a letter.*]

ANTONY   Forbear me.   128
        [Exit Fourth Messenger.]
There's a great spirit gone! Thus did I desire it.
What our contempts doth often hurl from us
We wish it ours again. The present pleasure,

---

70 hear me hear (on my behalf) **74 loose-wived** with an unfaithful
wife **75 foul** ugly **75–76 keep decorum** deal suitably with the case
76 fortune him grant him fortune **79–80 they . . . do 't** i.e., they
would stop at nothing, even becoming whores, to cuckold me **87 on
the sudden** suddenly **93 field** battlefield **96 time's state** circumstances prevailing at the moment **97 jointing** uniting **98 better
issue** success **98–99 from . . . them** drove them from Italy upon
the very first encounter **101 infects the teller** i.e., makes the teller
seem bad

105 as as if. **Labienus** (Brutus and Cassius [see *Julius Caesar*] had
sent Quintus Labienus to Orodes, King of Parthia, to seek aid against
Antony and Octavius Caesar; with a force thus obtained, he is now
overrunning the Roman provinces in the Middle East.) **107 Extended**
seized upon. (A legal phrase.) **111 Speak . . . tongue** speak bluntly;
don't minimize the common report **113 phrase** manner of speech
116 quick alive, inventive **116–117 our ills . . . earing** hearing our
faults told to us improves us, as plowing (*earing*) improves land by
rooting out the weeds **120 The man from Sicyon** (The messenger
who has just entered, not being from Sicyon, realizes in some confusion that Antony wants to hear the news from Sicyon. This second
messenger therefore calls out to ask if the messenger from Sicyon is to
be found. Another messenger at the door replies that such a man is
indeed waiting, and in a moment that messenger from Sicyon enters
with his report. Some editors change the second and third messengers
into attendants.) *Sicyon* is an ancient city in Greece, where Antony
left Fulvia. **121 stays upon** awaits **128 Importeth** concerns. **Forbear** leave

By revolution lowering, does become 132
The opposite of itself. She's good, being gone;
The hand could pluck her back that shoved her on. 134
I must from this enchanting queen break off. 135
Ten thousand harms more than the ills I know
My idleness doth hatch.—How now, Enobarbus!

Enter Enobarbus.

ENOBARBUS   What's your pleasure, sir?

ANTONY   I must with haste from hence.

ENOBARBUS   Why, then, we kill all our women. We see how mortal an unkindness is to them; if they suffer our departure, death's the word.

ANTONY   I must be gone.

ENOBARBUS   Under a compelling occasion, let women die. It were pity to cast them away for nothing, though between them and a great cause they should be esteemed nothing. Cleopatra, catching but the least noise 147 of this, dies instantly; I have seen her die twenty times 148 upon far poorer moment. I do think there is mettle in 149 death, which commits some loving act upon her, she hath such a celerity in dying.

ANTONY   She is cunning past man's thought.

ENOBARBUS   Alack, sir, no, her passions are made of nothing but the finest part of pure love. We cannot call her winds and waters sighs and tears; they are greater 155 storms and tempests than almanacs can report. This cannot be cunning in her; if it be, she makes a shower of rain as well as Jove.

ANTONY   Would I had never seen her!

ENOBARBUS   O, sir, you had then left unseen a wonderful piece of work, which not to have been blessed withal would have discredited your travel.

ANTONY   Fulvia is dead.

ENOBARBUS   Sir?

ANTONY   Fulvia is dead.

ENOBARBUS   Fulvia?

ANTONY   Dead.

ENOBARBUS   Why, sir, give the gods a thankful sacrifice. When it pleaseth their deities to take the wife of a man from him, it shows to man the tailors of the earth; 170 comforting therein, that when old robes are worn out, there are members to make new. If there were no more 172 women but Fulvia, then had you indeed a cut, and the case to be lamented. This grief is crowned with consolation; your old smock brings forth a new petticoat, and indeed the tears live in an onion that should water 176 this sorrow. 177

ANTONY
The business she hath broachèd in the state 178
Cannot endure my absence.

ENOBARBUS   And the business you have broached here cannot be without you, especially that of Cleopatra's, which wholly depends on your abode. 182

ANTONY
No more light answers. Let our officers 183
Have notice what we purpose. I shall break 184
The cause of our expedience to the Queen 185
And get her leave to part. For not alone 186
The death of Fulvia, with more urgent touches, 187
Do strongly speak to us, but the letters too
Of many our contriving friends in Rome 189
Petition us at home. Sextus Pompeius 190
Hath given the dare to Caesar and commands
The empire of the sea. Our slippery people, 192
Whose love is never linked to the deserver
Till his deserts are past, begin to throw 194
Pompey the Great and all his dignities 195
Upon his son, who—high in name and power,
Higher than both in blood and life—stands up 197
For the main soldier; whose quality, going on, 198
The sides o' the world may danger. Much is
breeding, 199
Which, like the courser's hair, hath yet but life, 200
And not a serpent's poison. Say our pleasure, 201
To such whose place is under us, requires 202
Our quick remove from hence. 203

ENOBARBUS   I shall do 't.   [*Exeunt separately.*]

❖

1.3   *Enter Cleopatra, Charmian, Alexas, and Iras.*

CLEOPATRA
Where is he?

CHARMIAN   I did not see him since. 1

CLEOPATRA [*to Alexas*]
See where he is, who's with him, what he does.
I did not send you. If you find him sad, 3
Say I am dancing; if in mirth, report

---

132 By revolution lowering losing value by the revolution of Fortune's wheel and the changing of our opinions   **134 could** would be willing to   **135 enchanting** having the power of a witch   **147 noise** hint, rumor   **148 dies** (with sexual suggestion of achieving orgasm) **149 poorer moment** lesser cause. **mettle** i.e., sexual vigor **155 sighs** i.e., mere sighs   **170 the tailors** (Just as tailors fashion a new garment, widowed men can comfort themselves with new sexual partners.)   **172 members** (The word has a bawdy suggestion, pursued in lines 173–174 and 180 in *cut, case, business,* and *broached; cut* and *case* suggest the female sexual organs; *broached* suggests something that is stabbed, pricked, opened.)   **176–177 the tears . . . sorrow** i.e., only an onion could produce tears on this occasion of Fulvia's death

178 broachèd opened up. (But see the note for line 172.)   **182 abode** staying   **183 light** frivolous, indelicate   **184 break** i.e., break the news of   **185 expedience** haste   **186 leave** consent   **187 urgent touches** pressing matters   **189 Of . . . friends** from many friends working in our interest   **190 at home** i.e., to come home.   **Sextus Pompeius** son of Pompey the Great, who, though outlawed, had been able to exploit the division between Antony and Octavius and thereby gain command of Sicily and the sea; he appears in Act 2   **192 slippery** fickle   **194 throw** bestow   **195 Pompey the Great** i.e., the title and honored status of "Pompey the Great"   **197 blood and life** mettle and vitality   **197–198 stands . . . soldier** is achieving position as, or claims to be, the leading military leader   **198 quality** character and position.   **going on** i.e., if this keeps on   **199 The sides . . . danger** may endanger the frame of the world   **200 like . . . hair** (Allusion to the popular belief that a horsehair put into water would turn to a snake.)   **201–203 Say . . . hence** tell those who serve me that my wish is to depart quickly

1.3. Location: Alexandria. Cleopatra's palace.
1 since lately   **3 I did . . . you** i.e., do not let him know I sent you. **sad** serious

That I am sudden sick. Quick, and return.   5
                              [*Exit Alexas.*]
CHARMIAN
  Madam, methinks, if you did love him dearly,
  You do not hold the method to enforce   7
  The like from him.
CLEOPATRA   What should I do I do not? 8
CHARMIAN
  In each thing give him way. Cross him in nothing.
CLEOPATRA
  Thou teachest like a fool: the way to lose him.
CHARMIAN
  Tempt him not so too far. I wish, forbear;   11
  In time we hate that which we often fear.

    Enter Antony.

  But here comes Antony.
CLEOPATRA   I am sick and sullen.   13
ANTONY
  I am sorry to give breathing to my purpose—   14
CLEOPATRA
  Help me away, dear Charmian! I shall fall.
  It cannot be thus long; the sides of nature   16
  Will not sustain it.
ANTONY   Now, my dearest queen—
CLEOPATRA
  Pray you, stand farther from me.
ANTONY   What's the matter? 18
CLEOPATRA
  I know by that same eye there's some good news.
  What, says the married woman you may go?   20
  Would she had never given you leave to come!
  Let her not say 'tis I that keep you here.
  I have no power upon you; hers you are.
ANTONY
  The gods best know—
CLEOPATRA   O, never was there queen
  So mightily betrayed! Yet at the first
  I saw the treasons planted.
ANTONY   Cleopatra—
CLEOPATRA
  Why should I think you can be mine, and true—
  Though you in swearing shake the thronèd gods—
  Who have been false to Fulvia? Riotous madness,   29
  To be entangled with those mouth-made vows,   30
  Which break themselves in swearing!
ANTONY   Most sweet queen— 31
CLEOPATRA
  Nay, pray you, seek no color for your going,   32
  But bid farewell and go. When you sued staying,   33
  Then was the time for words. No going then.

Eternity was in our lips and eyes,   35
Bliss in our brows' bent; none our parts so poor   36
But was a race of heaven. They are so still,   37
Or thou, the greatest soldier of the world,
Art turned the greatest liar.
ANTONY   How now, lady?
CLEOPATRA
  I would I had thy inches. Thou shouldst know   40
  There were a heart in Egypt.
ANTONY   Hear me, Queen: 41
  The strong necessity of time commands
  Our services awhile, but my full heart
  Remains in use with you. Our Italy   44
  Shines o'er with civil swords; Sextus Pompeius   45
  Makes his approaches to the port of Rome;
  Equality of two domestic powers   47
  Breed scrupulous faction; the hated, grown to
    strength,   48
  Are newly grown to love; the condemned Pompey,   49
  Rich in his father's honor, creeps apace   50
  Into the hearts of such as have not thrived
  Upon the present state, whose numbers threaten;   52
  And quietness, grown sick of rest, would purge   53
  By any desperate change. My more particular,   54
  And that which most with you should safe my
    going,   55
  Is Fulvia's death.
CLEOPATRA
  Though age from folly could not give me freedom,
  It does from childishness. Can Fulvia die?
ANTONY   She's dead, my queen.   [*He offers letters.*]
  Look here, and at thy sovereign leisure read
  The garboils she awaked, at the last, best,   61
  See when and where she died.
CLEOPATRA   O most false love!
  Where be the sacred vials thou shouldst fill   63
  With sorrowful water? Now I see, I see,
  In Fulvia's death how mine received shall be.
ANTONY
  Quarrel no more, but be prepared to know

5 **sudden** suddenly taken   7 **hold the method** follow the right course   8 **I do not** that I am not doing   11 **Tempt** try.   **I wish** I wish you would   13 **sullen** depressed, melancholy   14 **breathing** utterance   16 **It . . . long** i.e., I can't last long at this rate.   **sides of nature** i.e., human body, frame   18 **stand farther from me** i.e., give me air   20 **the married woman** i.e., Fulvia   29 **Who** you who.   **Riotous madness** i.e., what folly on my part   30 **mouth-made** i.e., insincerely spoken   31 **in swearing** even while they are being sworn   32 **color** pretext   33 **sued staying** begged to stay

35 **our** i.e., my. (The royal plural.)   36 **bent** arch, curve.   **none . . . poor** none of my features, however poor   37 **race of heaven** of heavenly origin, or, possibly, of the flavor of heaven   40 **inches** (1) height (2) manly strength (with perhaps a bawdy suggestion. Cleopatra is saying she'd fight him if he were a man but, being a woman, will take his "inches" of sexual potency.)   41 **a heart in Egypt** i.e., a mighty courage in the Queen of Egypt   44 **in use with you** for your use   45 **Shines o'er** glitters everywhere.   **civil swords** i.e., weapons of civil war   47 **Equality . . . powers** i.e., the equal splitting of domestic power between two, Caesar and Antony   48 **scrupulous** carping, concerned with trifles   48–49 **the hated . . . love** those (like Pompey) who were out of favor, being now strong, have recently come back into popular favor   49–50 **Pompey . . . honor** i.e., Sextus Pompeius, richly inheriting the honor once accorded Pompey the Great   50 **creeps apace** quickly insinuates himself   52 **state** government (i.e., of the triumvirate).   **whose** i.e., those supporting Pompey   53 **purge** cleanse or purify itself to be rid of sickness. (Peace, long continued, seems diseased and requires the purging effect of war.)   54 **particular** personal concern   55 **safe** make safe   61 **garboils** disturbances, commotions.   **best** i.e., best of all   63 **sacred vials** (Alludes to the supposed Roman custom of putting bottles filled with tears in the tombs of the departed.)

The purposes I bear, which are or cease   67
As you shall give th' advice. By the fire   68
That quickens Nilus' slime, I go from hence   69
Thy soldier, servant, making peace or war
As thou affects.

CLEOPATRA   Cut my lace, Charmian, come!   71
But let it be; I am quickly ill, and well,
So Antony loves.

ANTONY   My precious queen, forbear,   73
And give true evidence to his love which stands   74
An honorable trial.

CLEOPATRA   So Fulvia told me.   75
I prithee, turn aside and weep for her;
Then bid adieu to me, and say the tears
Belong to Egypt. Good now, play one scene   78
Of excellent dissembling, and let it look
Like perfect honor.

ANTONY   You'll heat my blood. No more.   80

CLEOPATRA
You can do better yet; but this is meetly.   81

ANTONY
Now, by my sword—

CLEOPATRA   And target. Still he mends.   82
But this is not the best. Look, prithee, Charmian,
How this Herculean Roman does become   84
The carriage of his chafe.   85

ANTONY   I'll leave you, lady.

CLEOPATRA   Courteous lord, one word.
Sir, you and I must part, but that's not it;
Sir, you and I have loved, but there's not it;
That you know well. Something it is I would—   90
O, my oblivion is a very Antony,   91
And I am all forgotten.

ANTONY   But that your royalty   92
Holds idleness your subject, I should take you   93
For idleness itself.

CLEOPATRA   'Tis sweating labor   94
To bear such idleness so near the heart   95
As Cleopatra this. But sir, forgive me,
Since my becomings kill me when they do not   97

Eye well to you. Your honor calls you hence;   98
Therefore be deaf to my unpitied folly,
And all the gods go with you! Upon your sword
Sit laurel victory, and smooth success   101
Be strewed before your feet!

ANTONY   Let us go. Come;
Our separation so abides and flies   103
That thou, residing here, goes yet with me,
And I, hence fleeting, here remain with thee.
Away!   Exeunt.

❧

1.4   *Enter Octavius [Caesar], reading a letter, Lepidus, and their train.*

CAESAR
You may see, Lepidus, and henceforth know,
It is not Caesar's natural vice to hate
Our great competitor. From Alexandria   3
This is the news: he fishes, drinks, and wastes
The lamps of night in revel; is not more manlike
Than Cleopatra, nor the queen of Ptolemy   6
More womanly than he; hardly gave audience, or   7
Vouchsafed to think he had partners. You shall find
  there
A man who is the abstract of all faults   9
That all men follow.

LEPIDUS   I must not think there are
Evils enough to darken all his goodness.
His faults in him seem as the spots of heaven,   12
More fiery by night's blackness, hereditary
Rather than purchased, what he cannot change   14
Than what he chooses.

CAESAR
You are too indulgent. Let's grant it is not   16
Amiss to tumble on the bed of Ptolemy,
To give a kingdom for a mirth, to sit   18
And keep the turn of tippling with a slave,   19
To reel the streets at noon, and stand the buffet   20
With knaves that smells of sweat. Say this becomes
  him—
As his composure must be rare indeed   22
Whom these things cannot blemish—yet must
  Antony
No way excuse his foils when we do bear   24
So great weight in his lightness. If he filled   25
His vacancy with his voluptuousness,   26

67 **which are** which will proceed   68 **fire** i.e., sun   69 **quickens** brings to life.   **Nilus' slime** the mud left by the overflow of the Nile
71 **thou affects** you desire.   **lace** cord or laces fastening the bodice. (Cleopatra pretends she is fainting.)   73 **So** provided that, or, possibly, "in the same way, with changes as sudden as my own"   74 **evidence** witness (?)   **stands** will sustain   75 **told** has taught (by her example of being quickly forgotten by Antony)   78 **Belong to Egypt** are shed for the Queen of Egypt.   **Good now** (An expression of entreaty.)
80 **heat my blood** i.e., anger me   81 **meetly** i.e., fairly well acted
82 **target** shield.   **mends** improves (in his "scene / Of excellent dissembling")   84–85 **How . . . chafe** i.e., how Antony, who claims descent from Hercules, plays the role of his enraged ancestor well. (Hercules had become a stock figure of the enraged hero or tyrant.)
chafe rage   90 **would** wished to say   91 **my . . . Antony** my forgetful memory is like Antony (who is now leaving and thus forgetting me)   92 **I . . . forgotten** (1) I have forgotten what I was going to say (2) I am entirely forgotten (by Antony)   92–94 **But . . . itself** since you are a queen, your frivolousness must be your subject (i.e., ruled by you); otherwise, I'd think you were frivolousness itself   94–95 (*Sweating, labor,* and *bear* are all associated with pregnancy.)
95 **such idleness** such apparently trifling banter   97 **my becomings** those qualities that become me (i.e., are attractive in me or are suitable to my present position); perhaps also, the various roles that I become

98 **Eye** appear   101 **laurel** wreathed with laurel   103 **so abides and flies** mingles remaining and going in such a paradoxical fashion
1.4. Location: Rome.
3 **competitor** partner (with a suggestion also of "rival")   6 **Ptolemy** (Cleopatra's royal brother, to whom she had been married according to Egyptian custom.)   7 **gave audience** i.e., received messengers
9 **abstract** epitome   12 **seem as** are made conspicuous like.   **spots** i.e., stars   14 **purchased** acquired   16 **Let's grant** even if we were to grant   18 **mirth** jest, diversion   19 **keep . . . of** take turns   20 **stand the buffet** exchange blows   22 **As his composure** considering that a man's composition or temperament   24 **foils** blemishes
24–25 **when . . . lightness** when we have to carry the heavy burden imposed by his levity   26 **His vacancy** his leisure time

Full surfeits and the dryness of his bones 27
Call on him for 't. But to confound such time 28
That drums him from his sport and speaks as loud 29
As his own state and ours, 'tis to be chid 30
As we rate boys who, being mature in knowledge, 31
Pawn their experience to their present pleasure 32
And so rebel to judgment.

Enter a Messenger.

LEPIDUS   Here's more news. 33
FIRST MESSENGER
Thy biddings have been done, and every hour,
Most noble Caesar, shalt thou have report
How 'tis abroad. Pompey is strong at sea,
And it appears he is beloved of those 37
That only have feared Caesar. To the ports 38
The discontents repair, and men's reports 39
Give him much wronged.   [*Exit.*]
CAESAR   I should have known no less. 40
It hath been taught us from the primal state 41
That he which is was wished until he were; 42
And the ebbed man, ne'er loved till ne'er worth
   love, 43
Comes deared by being lacked. This common body, 44
Like to a vagabond flag upon the stream, 45
Goes to and back, lackeying the varying tide 46
To rot itself with motion.

[*Enter a Second Messenger.*]

SECOND MESSENGER   Caesar, I bring thee word
Menecrates and Menas, famous pirates, 49
Makes the sea serve them, which they ear and
   wound 50
With keels of every kind. Many hot inroads
They make in Italy. The borders maritime 52
Lack blood to think on 't, and flush youth revolt. 53
No vessel can peep forth but 'tis as soon
Taken as seen; for Pompey's name strikes more 55
Than could his war resisted.   [*Exit.*]
CAESAR   Antony, 56

Leave thy lascivious wassails. When thou once 57
Was beaten from Modena, where thou slew'st
Hirtius and Pansa, consuls, at thy heel
Did famine follow, whom thou fought'st against, 60
Though daintily brought up, with patience more
Than savages could suffer. Thou didst drink 62
The stale of horses and the gilded puddle 63
Which beasts would cough at. Thy palate then did
   deign 64
The roughest berry on the rudest hedge.
Yea, like the stag, when snow the pasture sheets, 66
The barks of trees thou browsèd. On the Alps 67
It is reported thou didst eat strange flesh,
Which some did die to look on. And all this—
It wounds thine honor that I speak it now—
Was borne so like a soldier that thy cheek
So much as lanked not. 72
LEPIDUS   'Tis pity of him. 73
CAESAR   Let his shames quickly
Drive him to Rome. 'Tis time we twain
Did show ourselves i' the field, and to that end
Assemble we immediate council. Pompey
Thrives in our idleness.
LEPIDUS   Tomorrow, Caesar,
I shall be furnished to inform you rightly
Both what by sea and land I can be able 80
To front this present time.
CAESAR   Till which encounter 81
It is my business too. Farewell.
LEPIDUS
Farewell, my lord. What you shall know meantime
Of stirs abroad, I shall beseech you, sir, 84
To let me be partaker.
CAESAR
Doubt not, sir, I knew it for my bond. 86
          Exeunt [*separately*].

❖

1.5   *Enter Cleopatra, Charmian, Iras, and Mardian.*

CLEOPATRA   Charmian!
CHARMIAN   Madam?
CLEOPATRA
Ha, ha! Give me to drink mandragora. 3
CHARMIAN   Why, madam?
CLEOPATRA
That I might sleep out this great gap of time
My Antony is away.
CHARMIAN   You think of him too much.
CLEOPATRA
O, 'tis treason!
CHARMIAN   Madam, I trust not so.

27–28 Full . . . for 't i.e., the physical disabilities resulting from such voluptuousness (such as venereal disease) would call him to account and would be adequate punishment   **28 confound** ruin, waste   **29 drums** summons (as by a military drum).   **sport** amorous pastime   **29–30 speaks . . . ours** i.e., summons him urgently in view of his political position and ours as well   **30 chid** chided, reprimanded   **31 rate** berate.   **mature in knowledge** old enough to know what their duty is   **32 Pawn . . . pleasure** risk for the sake of immediate gratification what experience tells them will be ultimately painful   **33 to judgment** against better judgment   **37 of** by   **38 That . . . Caesar** i.e., that have obeyed Caesar only through fear   **39 discontents** discontented. (See 1.3.48–52.)   **40 Give him** represent him as   **41 from . . . state** since the first government, or, possibly, since the earliest state of being   **42 That . . . were** that the man in power was desired (by the populace) until he obtained power   **43 ebbed** decayed in fortune.   **ne'er loved . . . love** not loved until he was unworthy of love, i.e., until he lost power   **44 Comes deared** becomes loved, gains value in people's eyes.   **common body** populace   **45 vagabond** (1) drifting (2) rascally.   **flag** iris   **46 lackeying** following in servile fashion, like a lackey   **49 famous** notorious   **50 ear** plow   **52 borders maritime** coastal territories   **53 Lack blood** turn pale.   **flush** vigorous; flushed, ruddy (contrasted with those who *Lack blood*)   **55–56 strikes . . . resisted** inflicts more damage than his forces could against our resistance

57 wassails carousals   **60 whom** i.e., famine   **62 suffer** display in suffering   **63 stale** urine.   **gilded** covered with iridescent slime   **64 deign** not disdain   **66 sheets** covers   **67 browsèd** fed upon   **72 lanked** became thin   **73 of** about   **80 be able** be capable of mustering   **81 front** confront, deal with   **84 stirs** events   **86 knew** already knew.   **bond** duty, obligation
1.5. Location: Egypt. Cleopatra's palace.
3 mandragora juice of the mandrake (a narcotic)

CLEOPATRA
Thou, eunuch Mardian!

MARDIAN   What's Your Highness' pleasure?

CLEOPATRA
Not now to hear thee sing. I take no pleasure
In aught an eunuch has. 'Tis well for thee   11
That, being unseminared, thy freer thoughts   12
May not fly forth of Egypt. Hast thou affections?   13

MARDIAN   Yes, gracious madam.

CLEOPATRA   Indeed?   15

MARDIAN
Not in deed, madam, for I can do nothing   16
But what indeed is honest to be done.   17
Yet have I fierce affections, and think
What Venus did with Mars.

CLEOPATRA   O Charmian,
Where think'st thou he is now? Stands he or sits he?
Or does he walk? Or is he on his horse?
O happy horse, to bear the weight of Antony!
Do bravely, horse, for wott'st thou whom thou
     mov'st?   23
The demi-Atlas of this earth, the arm   24
And burgonet of men. He's speaking now,   25
Or murmuring, "Where's my serpent of old Nile?"
For so he calls me. Now I feed myself
With most delicious poison. Think on me,   28
That am with Phoebus' amorous pinches black   29
And wrinkled deep in time. Broad-fronted Caesar,   30
When thou wast here above the ground, I was
A morsel for a monarch. And great Pompey   32
Would stand and make his eyes grow in my brow;   33
There would he anchor his aspect, and die   34
With looking on his life.   35

Enter Alexas.

ALEXAS   Sovereign of Egypt, hail!

CLEOPATRA
How much unlike art thou Mark Antony!
Yet, coming from him, that great medicine hath   38
With his tinct gilded thee.   39
How goes it with my brave Mark Antony?   40

ALEXAS   Last thing he did, dear Queen,
He kissed—the last of many doubled kisses—
This orient pearl. [*He gives a pearl.*] His speech sticks
     in my heart.   43

CLEOPATRA
Mine ear must pluck it thence.

ALEXAS   "Good friend," quoth he,
"Say the firm Roman to great Egypt sends   45
This treasure of an oyster; at whose foot,
To mend the petty present, I will piece   47
Her opulent throne with kingdoms. All the East,
Say thou, shall call her mistress." So he nodded,
And soberly did mount an arm-gaunt steed,   50
Who neighed so high that what I would have spoke
Was beastly dumbed by him.   52

CLEOPATRA   What, was he sad, or merry?

ALEXAS
Like to the time o' the year between the extremes
Of hot and cold, he was nor sad nor merry.   55

CLEOPATRA
O well-divided disposition! Note him,   56
Note him, good Charmian, 'tis the man; but
     note him.   57
He was not sad, for he would shine on those   58
That make their looks by his; he was not merry,   59
Which seemed to tell them his remembrance lay
In Egypt with his joy; but between both.
O heavenly mingle! Be'st thou sad or merry,
The violence of either thee becomes,   63
So does it no man else.—Mett'st thou my posts?   64

ALEXAS
Ay, madam, twenty several messengers.   65
Why do you send so thick?

CLEOPATRA   Who's born that day   66
When I forget to send to Antony
Shall die a beggar. Ink and paper, Charmian.
Welcome, my good Alexas. Did I, Charmian,
Ever love Caesar so?

CHARMIAN   O, that brave Caesar!

CLEOPATRA
Be choked with such another emphasis!   71
Say, "the brave Antony."

CHARMIAN   The valiant Caesar!

CLEOPATRA
By Isis, I will give thee bloody teeth
If thou with Caesar paragon again   74
My man of men.

CHARMIAN   By your most gracious pardon,
I sing but after you.

---

11 aught (With bawdy suggestion.)   **12 unseminared** castrated **13 fly forth of Egypt** i.e., (1) try to leave as Antony has done (2) scatter sperm in some woman other than the Queen of Egypt. **affections** passions **15–16 Indeed? / Not in deed** (Mardian punningly takes the *deed* of *indeed* to mean "physical act.") **16 do** (with suggestion of sexual intercourse) **17 honest** chaste **23 Do** (with sexual suggestion, as in line 16.) **wott'st thou** do you know **24 demi-Atlas** one who (together with Caesar) supports the weight of the whole world, as Atlas did. (Cleopatra disregards Lepidus as a triumvir.) **arm** strong right arm or weapon **25 burgonet** light helmet or steel cap, i.e., protector **28–30 Think . . . time** (Cleopatra reflects on her ability to attract Antony, given the fact that she is dark-skinned [as from the amorous pinches of her lover, the sun] and increasingly wrinkled with age.) **29 Phoebus'** the sun's **30 Broad-fronted** with broad forehead. **Caesar** i.e., Julius Caesar **32 great Pompey** Gnaeus Pompey, oldest son of Pompey the Great. (Shakespeare may conflate the two.) **33 make . . . brow** i.e., rivet his eyes on my face **34 aspect** look, gaze. **die** i.e., suffer the extremity of love (and with suggestion of orgasm, as at 1.2.148) **35 his life** that which he lived for **38 great medicine** supposed substance by which alchemists hoped to turn all baser metals into gold **39 his tinct** its alchemical potency; also, its color **40 brave** splendid

43 orient shining, bright. (The best pearls were from the East or Orient.) **45 firm** constant, true. **Egypt** the Queen of Egypt **47 piece** augment **50 arm-gaunt** made trim and hard by warlike service, or, possibly, gaunt of limb, or hungry for battle **52 dumbed** drowned out, made inaudible **55 nor sad** neither sad **56 well-divided disposition** well-balanced temperament **57 the man** i.e., perfectly characteristic of him. **but** do but, only **58 would** wished to **59 make . . . his** model their appearance on his look, or, are dependent on his appearance for their moods **63 thee becomes** is becoming to you **64 posts** messengers **65 several** separate, distinct (also in line 80) **66 Who's** anyone who is **71 emphasis** emphatic expression **74 paragon** match or compare

CLEOPATRA   My salad days,
When I was green in judgment, cold in blood,   77
To say as I said then. But, come, away,
Get me ink and paper.
He shall have every day a several greeting,
Or I'll unpeople Egypt.   *Exeunt.* 81

❧

2.1   *Enter Pompey, Menecrates, and Menas, in warlike
manner.*

POMPEY
If the great gods be just, they shall assist
The deeds of justest men.
MENAS   Know, worthy Pompey,   2
That what they do delay they not deny.   3
POMPEY
Whiles we are suitors to their throne, decays   4
The thing we sue for.
MENAS   We, ignorant of ourselves,   5
Beg often our own harms, which the wise powers
Deny us for our good; so find we profit
By losing of our prayers.
POMPEY   I shall do well.
The people love me, and the sea is mine;
My powers are crescent, and my auguring hope   10
Says it will come to th' full. Mark Antony   11
In Egypt sits at dinner, and will make
No wars without doors. Caesar gets money where   13
He loses hearts. Lepidus flatters both,
Of both is flattered; but he neither loves,   15
Nor either cares for him.
MENAS   Caesar and Lepidus
Are in the field. A mighty strength they carry.   17
POMPEY
Where have you this? 'Tis false.
MENAS   From Silvius, sir.
POMPEY
He dreams. I know they are in Rome together
Looking for Antony. But all the charms of love,   20
Salt Cleopatra, soften thy waned lip!   21
Let witchcraft joined with beauty, lust with both,
Tie up the libertine in a field of feasts,   23
Keep his brain fuming. Epicurean cooks,   24
Sharpen with cloyless sauce his appetite,   25

That sleep and feeding may prorogue his honor   26
Even till a Lethe'd dullness—
            Enter Varrius.

                            How now, Varrius?   27
VARRIUS
This is most certain that I shall deliver: 28
Mark Antony is every hour in Rome
Expected. Since he went from Egypt 'tis
A space for further travel.   31
POMPEY   I could have given less matter   32
A better ear. Menas, I did not think
This amorous surfeiter would have donned his helm   34
For such a petty war. His soldiership
Is twice the other twain. But let us rear   36
The higher our opinion, that our stirring   37
Can from the lap of Egypt's widow pluck   38
The ne'er-lust-wearied Antony.
MENAS   I cannot hope   39
Caesar and Antony shall well greet together.   40
His wife that's dead did trespasses to Caesar;   41
His brother warred upon him, although, I think,   42
Not moved by Antony.
POMPEY   I know not, Menas,   43
How lesser enmities may give way to greater.
Were 't not that we stand up against them all,
'Twere pregnant they should square between
    themselves,   46
For they have entertainèd cause enough   47
To draw their swords. But how the fear of us
May cement their divisions and bind up
The petty difference, we yet not know.
Be 't as our gods will have 't! It only stands   51
Our lives upon to use our strongest hands.   52
Come, Menas.   *Exeunt.*

❧

2.2   *Enter Enobarbus and Lepidus.*

LEPIDUS
Good Enobarbus, 'tis a worthy deed,
And shall become you well, to entreat your captain
To soft and gentle speech.
ENOBARBUS   I shall entreat him
To answer like himself. If Caesar move him,   4
Let Antony look over Caesar's head   5

---

77 green immature **81 Or . . . Egypt** i.e., or if not, it will be because I have used up all my subjects as messengers
2.1. Location: Pompey's camp, probably at Messina, Sicily.
2 Menas (The Folio assigns the speeches in this scene to "Mene.";
some could be for Menecrates, but Pompey ignores him entirely at
lines 43–52, and Menecrates never reappears in the play.) **3 not
deny** i.e., do not necessarily deny **4–5 Whiles . . . for** while we
are praying, that for which we pray is being destroyed **10 powers**
armed forces. **crescent** on the increase. **auguring** prophesying
11 it i.e., my, Pompey's, powers or fortune (seen as a crescent moon,
becoming full) **13 without doors** outdoors, i.e., in the battlefield,
rather than in the bedroom **15 Of** by. **neither loves** loves neither
17 A . . . carry they command a mighty army **20 Looking for** awaiting. **charms** spells **21 Salt** lustful. **waned** faded, withered **23 Tie
. . . feasts** i.e., tether him like an animal in a rich pasture **24 Epicurean** i.e., let epicurean **25 cloyless** which will not satiate

26 prorogue defer the operation of **27 Lethe'd** oblivious. (From the
river of the underworld whose waters cause forgetfulness in those who
drink.) **28 deliver** report **31 space . . . travel** time enough for an
even longer journey **32 less** less important **34 helm** helmet
36 rear raise **37 opinion** i.e., of ourselves **38 Egypt's widow** i.e.,
Cleopatra, widow of the young King Ptolemy **39 hope** expect
40 well greet greet one another kindly **41 did trespasses to** wronged
42 brother i.e., Lucius Antonius. (See 1.2.94 ff.) **43 moved** provoked, incited **46 pregnant** clear, obvious. **square** quarrel **47 entertainèd** maintained **51–52 It . . . hands** our very lives depend
upon our using our greatest strength
**2.2. Location: Rome. Furniture is put out on which Antony and Cae-
sar are to sit.**
4 like himself i.e., in a way befitting his greatness. **move him** i.e., to
anger **5 look . . . head** i.e., condescend to Caesar as a smaller man

And speak as loud as Mars. By Jupiter,
Were I the wearer of Antonio's beard,
I would not shave 't today.   8
LEPIDUS
'Tis not a time for private stomaching.
ENOBARBUS   Every time   9
Serves for the matter that is then born in 't.
LEPIDUS
But small to greater matters must give way.
ENOBARBUS
Not if the small come first.
LEPIDUS   Your speech is passion;
But pray you stir no embers up. Here comes   13
The noble Antony.

            Enter Antony and Ventidius [in conversation].

ENOBARBUS   And yonder, Caesar.

            *Enter Caesar, Maecenas, and Agrippa, [also in
            conversation, by another door].*

ANTONY
If we compose well here, to Parthia.   15
Hark, Ventidius.   [*They confer apart.*]
CAESAR
I do not know, Maecenas, ask Agrippa.
LEPIDUS   Noble friends,
That which combined us was most great, and let not
A leaner action rend us. What's amiss,   20
May it be gently heard. When we debate
Our trivial difference loud, we do commit
Murder in healing wounds. Then, noble partners,   23
The rather for I earnestly beseech,   24
Touch you the sourest points with sweetest terms,
Nor curstness grow to th' matter.
ANTONY   'Tis spoken well.   26
Were we before our armies, and to fight,   27
I should do thus.   *Flourish.*
CAESAR   Welcome to Rome.
ANTONY   Thank you.
CAESAR   Sit.
ANTONY   Sit, sir.
CAESAR   Nay, then.   [*They sit.*]
ANTONY
I learn you take things ill which are not so,
Or being, concern you not.
CAESAR   I must be laughed at   35
If, or for nothing or a little, I   36
Should say myself offended, and with you
Chiefly i' the world; more laughed at that I should   38
Once name you derogately, when to sound your
    name   39

8 **I . . . shave 't** i.e., I would continue to wear it and thereby dare
Caesar to pluck it (in a symbolic gesture for starting a fight)   **9 private
stomaching** personal resentment   **13 embers** i.e., old quarrels
15 compose come to an agreement   **20 leaner** lesser, more trivial.
rend divide.   **What's** whatever is   **23 healing** i.e., attempting to heal
24 The rather for all the more because   **26 Nor . . . grow** nor let ill
humor be added   **27 to** about to   **35 being** being so, i.e., even if
they are amiss   **36 or . . . or** either . . . or   **38 i' the world** of all
people   **39 Once** under any circumstances.   **derogately** disparagingly   **39–40 when . . . concerned me** i.e., if, as you say, it were
none of my business

It not concerned me.   40
ANTONY
My being in Egypt, Caesar, what was 't to you?
CAESAR
No more than my residing here at Rome
Might be to you in Egypt. Yet if you there
Did practice on my state, your being in Egypt   44
Might be my question.
ANTONY   How intend you "practiced"? 45
CAESAR
You may be pleased to catch at mine intent   46
By what did here befall me. Your wife and brother
Made wars upon me, and their contestation
Was theme for you. You were the word of war.   49
ANTONY
You do mistake your business. My brother never
Did urge me in his act. I did inquire it,   51
And have my learning from some true reports   52
That drew their swords with you. Did he not rather   53
Discredit my authority with yours,   54
And make the wars alike against my stomach,   55
Having alike your cause? Of this my letters   56
Before did satisfy you. If you'll patch a quarrel,   57
As matter whole you have to make it with,   58
It must not be with this.
CAESAR   You praise yourself   59
By laying defects of judgment to me, but
You patched up your excuses.
ANTONY   Not so, not so.
I know you could not lack—I am certain on 't—   62
Very necessity of this thought, that I,   63
Your partner in the cause 'gainst which he fought,   64
Could not with graceful eyes attend those wars   65
Which fronted mine own peace. As for my wife,   66
I would you had her spirit in such another.   67
The third o' the world is yours, which with a snaffle   68
You may pace easy, but not such a wife.   69
ENOBARBUS   Would we had all such wives, that the men
    might go to wars with the women!
ANTONY
So much uncurbable, her garboils, Caesar,   72
Made out of her impatience—which not wanted   73
Shrewdness of policy too—I grieving grant   74
Did you too much disquiet. For that you must   75

44 practice on my state plot against my position   **45 question** business.   **How intend you** what do you mean   **46 catch at** infer
49 Was . . . war provided you with a theme, had you for its theme
(or perhaps, operated in your behalf); your name was the watchword,
i.e., the central cause, of that conflict   **51 urge . . . act** claim that he
was fighting in my behalf.   **inquire** inquire into   **52 reports** reporters
53 drew . . . you i.e., fought in your army   **54 Discredit** injure.
with along with   **55 stomach** i.e., desire   **56 Having . . . cause** i.e.,
I having just as much reason as you to deplore Lucius' action
57–59 If . . . this if you insist on manufacturing a quarrel out of
shreds and patches, even though you have substantial material to
make it with, you've chosen a weak matter to use   **62–63 I know
. . . thought** I'm certain you must have known   **64 he** i.e., Lucius
65 with . . . attend regard favorably   **66 fronted** confronted, opposed   **67 her . . . another** i.e., a wife such as she was   **68 snaffle**
bridle bit   **69 pace** put through its paces, manage   **72–75 So . . .
disquiet** I unhappily concede that her unmanageable commotions,
caused by her impatience but not lacking in keenness of stratagem,
did too much to disquiet you, Caesar

But say I could not help it.

CAESAR   I wrote to you   76
When rioting in Alexandria; you   77
Did pocket up my letters and with taunts
Did gibe my missive out of audience.

ANTONY   Sir,   79
He fell upon me ere admitted, then.   80
Three kings I had newly feasted, and did want   81
Of what I was i' the morning. But next day   82
I told him of myself, which was as much   83
As to have asked him pardon. Let this fellow
Be nothing of our strife; if we contend,   85
Out of our question wipe him.

CAESAR   You have broken   86
The article of your oath, which you shall never   87
Have tongue to charge me with.

LEPIDUS   Soft, Caesar!   89

ANTONY   No, Lepidus, let him speak.
The honor is sacred which he talks on now,
Supposing that I lacked it. But, on, Caesar: 92
The article of my oath—

CAESAR
To lend me arms and aid when I required them,   94
The which you both denied.

ANTONY   Neglected, rather;
And then when poisoned hours had bound me up
From mine own knowledge. As nearly as I may   97
I'll play the penitent to you, but mine honesty   98
Shall not make poor my greatness, nor my power   99
Work without it. Truth is that Fulvia,   100
To have me out of Egypt, made wars here,
For which myself, the ignorant motive, do   102
So far ask pardon as befits mine honor
To stoop in such a case.

LEPIDUS   'Tis noble spoken.   104

MAECENAS
If it might please you to enforce no further
The griefs between ye; to forget them quite   106
Were to remember that the present need
Speaks to atone you.

LEPIDUS   Worthily spoken, Maecenas.   108

ENOBARBUS   Or, if you borrow one another's love for the
instant, you may, when you hear no more words of
Pompey, return it again. You shall have time to wrangle in when you have nothing else to do.

ANTONY
Thou art a soldier only. Speak no more.

ENOBARBUS   That truth should be silent I had almost
forgot.

ANTONY
You wrong this presence. Therefore speak no more.   116

ENOBARBUS   Go to, then; your considerate stone.   117

CAESAR
I do not much dislike the matter, but
The manner of his speech; for 't cannot be
We shall remain in friendship, our conditions   120
So differing in their acts. Yet, if I knew
What hoop should hold us staunch, from edge to
    edge   122
O' the world I would pursue it.

AGRIPPA   Give me leave, Caesar.

CAESAR   Speak, Agrippa.

AGRIPPA
Thou hast a sister by the mother's side,
Admired Octavia. Great Mark Antony
Is now a widower.

CAESAR   Say not so, Agrippa.
If Cleopatra heard you, your reproof
Were well deserved of rashness.   130

ANTONY
I am not married, Caesar. Let me hear
Agrippa further speak.

AGRIPPA
To hold you in perpetual amity,
To make you brothers, and to knit your hearts
With an unslipping knot, take Antony
Octavia to his wife, whose beauty claims
No worse a husband than the best of men,
Whose virtue and whose general graces speak   138
That which none else can utter. By this marriage   139
All little jealousies, which now seem great,   140
And all great fears, which now import their dangers,   141
Would then be nothing. Truths would be tales,   142
Where now half tales be truths. Her love to both   143
Would each to other and all loves to both
Draw after her. Pardon what I have spoke,
For 'tis a studied, not a present thought,
By duty ruminated.

ANTONY   Will Caesar speak?

CAESAR
Not till he hears how Antony is touched   148
With what is spoke already.   149

ANTONY   What power is in Agrippa
If I would say, "Agrippa, be it so,"
To make this good?

CAESAR   The power of Caesar and
His power unto Octavia.

ANTONY   May I never   153
To this good purpose, that so fairly shows,   154

---

76 But only   **77 When** while you were   **79 gibe** taunt.   **missive** messenger.   **out of audience** out of your presence   **80 fell** burst in   **81–82 did want . . . morning** was not at my best as I had been earlier in the day   **83 of myself** i.e., of my having had a lot to drink   **85 Be nothing of** have nothing to do with   **86 question** contention   **87 article** terms   **89 Soft** gently, go easy   **92 Supposing** if we supposed   **94 required** requested   **97 From . . . knowledge** from knowing myself   **98–100 mine . . . it** my honesty (in admitting my overindulgence) will not go so far as to dishonor my greatness, nor, conversely, will my great power function without honesty   **102 motive** moving or inciting cause   **104 noble** nobly   **106 griefs** grievances   **108 atone** reconcile

116 presence company   **117 Go to, then** i.e., all right, all right.   **your considerate stone** i.e., I shall continue to think (consider) but be as silent as a stone   **120 conditions** temperaments, dispositions   **122 hoop** barrel hoop.   **staunch** firm, watertight   **130 of rashness** because of your rashness (in overlooking Cleopatra's claim to Antony)   **138–139 graces . . . utter** i.e., virtues speak for themselves in a way that no one else can do justice to or rival   **140 jealousies** misunderstandings, suspicions   **141 import** carry with them   **142–143 Truths . . . truths** true reports (no matter how distressing) would then be discounted as mere rumors, whereas at present half-true reports are taken for the whole truth   **148–149 touched With** affected by   **153 unto** over   **154 so fairly shows** looks so promising

Dream of impediment! Let me have thy hand
Further this act of grace, and from this hour   156
The heart of brothers govern in our loves
And sway our great designs!
CAESAR   There's my hand.
                              [*They clasp hands.*]
A sister I bequeath you whom no brother
Did ever love so dearly. Let her live
To join our kingdoms and our hearts; and never   161
Fly off our loves again!
LEPIDUS   Happily, amen!   162
ANTONY
I did not think to draw my sword 'gainst Pompey,
For he hath laid strange courtesies and great   164
Of late upon me. I must thank him only,   165
Lest my remembrance suffer ill report;   166
At heel of that, defy him.
LEPIDUS   Time calls upon 's.   167
Of us must Pompey presently be sought,   168
Or else he seeks out us.
ANTONY   Where lies he?
CAESAR
About the mount Misena.
ANTONY   What is his strength   171
By land?
CAESAR   Great and increasing; but by sea
He is an absolute master.
ANTONY   So is the fame.   173
Would we had spoke together! Haste we for it.   174
Yet, ere we put ourselves in arms, dispatch we
The business we have talked of.
CAESAR   With most gladness,   176
And do invite you to my sister's view,   177
Whither straight I'll lead you.   178
ANTONY
Let us, Lepidus, not lack your company.
LEPIDUS
Noble Antony, not sickness should detain me.   180
            Flourish. Exeunt. Manent Enobarbus, Agrippa,
                                      Maecenas.
MAECENAS   Welcome from Egypt, sir.
ENOBARBUS   Half the heart of Caesar, worthy Maecenas! 182
My honorable friend, Agrippa!
AGRIPPA   Good Enobarbus!
MAECENAS   We have cause to be glad that matters are so
well digested. You stayed well by 't in Egypt.   186
ENOBARBUS   Ay, sir, we did sleep day out of counte- 187
nance and made the night light with drinking.   188

MAECENAS   Eight wild boars roasted whole at a breakfast, and but twelve persons there; is this true?
ENOBARBUS   This was but as a fly by an eagle. We had 191
much more monstrous matter of feast, which worthily
deserved noting.
MAECENAS   She's a most triumphant lady, if report be 194
square to her.   195
ENOBARBUS   When she first met Mark Antony, she
pursed up his heart upon the river of Cydnus.   197
AGRIPPA   There she appeared indeed, or my reporter de- 198
vised well for her.   199
ENOBARBUS   I will tell you.
The barge she sat in, like a burnished throne   201
Burnt on the water. The poop was beaten gold;   202
Purple the sails, and so perfumèd that
The winds were lovesick with them. The oars were
   silver,
Which to the tune of flutes kept stroke, and made
The water which they beat to follow faster,
As amorous of their strokes. For her own person,   207
It beggared all description: she did lie
In her pavilion—cloth-of-gold of tissue—   209
O'erpicturing that Venus where we see
The fancy outwork nature. On each side her   211
Stood pretty dimpled boys, like smiling Cupids,
With divers-colored fans, whose wind did seem   213
To glow the delicate cheeks which they did cool,   214
And what they undid did.
AGRIPPA   O, rare for Antony!
ENOBARBUS
Her gentlewomen, like the Nereides,   216
So many mermaids, tended her i' th' eyes   217
And made their bends adornings. At the helm   218
A seeming mermaid steers. The silken tackle
Swell with the touches of those flower-soft hands,
That yarely frame the office. From the barge   221
A strange invisible perfume hits the sense
Of the adjacent wharfs. The city cast   223
Her people out upon her; and Antony,
Enthroned i' the marketplace, did sit alone,
Whistling to th' air, which, but for vacancy,   226
Had gone to gaze on Cleopatra too,
And made a gap in nature.
AGRIPPA   Rare Egyptian!
ENOBARBUS
Upon her landing, Antony sent to her,
Invited her to supper. She replied
It should be better he became her guest,
Which she entreated. Our courteous Antony,
Whom ne'er the word of "No" woman heard speak,

156 **Further** i.e., in furtherance of   161–162 **never . . . again** may
our amity never desert us again   164 **strange** remarkable   165 **only**
at least   166 **remembrance** readiness to remember or acknowledge
favors done   167 **At heel of that** immediately after   168 **Of** by.   **presently** at once   171 **Misena** i.e., Misenum, in southern Italy (not in
Sicily, where 2.1 perhaps takes place)   173 **So is the fame** so it is reported   174 **Would . . . together** i.e., would the negotiations with
Pompey were already over (?)   176 **most** the greatest   177 **to my sister's view** to see my sister   178 **straight** straightway   180 **s.d. Manent** they remain onstage   182 **Half the heart** i.e., one of Caesar's
two closest advisers, along with Agrippa, or, simply, a very close
friend of Caesar's   186 **digested** disposed.   **stayed well by 't** kept at
it   187–188 **we . . . countenance** we insulted day by sleeping right
through it   188 **light** giddy and debauched (with play on the commoner meaning of "bright")

191 **by** beside, compared with   194 **triumphant** magnificent
195 **square** just   197 **pursed up** pocketed up, put in her purse   198–
199 **devised** invented   201 **burnished** lustrous, shiny   202 **poop** a
short deck built over the main deck at the stern of the vessel   207 **As**
as if.   **For** as for   209 **cloth-of-gold of tissue** cloth made of gold
thread and silk woven together   211 **fancy** imagination   213 **divers-
colored** multicolored   214 **glow** cause to glow   216 **Nereides** sea
nymphs   217 **So many** i.e., as if they were so many.   **i' th' eyes** in
her sight, watching and obeying her every look (?)   218 **made . . .
adornings** made their graceful bowings beautiful, as in a work of art
221 **yarely frame** nimbly perform.   **office** task   223 **wharfs** banks
226 **but for vacancy** except that it would have created a vacuum

Being barbered ten times o'er, goes to the feast,
And for his ordinary pays his heart 235
For what his eyes eat only.

AGRIPPA   Royal wench! 236
She made great Caesar lay his sword to bed; 237
He plowed her, and she cropped.

ENOBARBUS   I saw her once 238
Hop forty paces through the public street,
And having lost her breath, she spoke and panted,
That she did make defect perfection, 241
And, breathless, power breathe forth.

MAECENAS
Now Antony must leave her utterly.

ENOBARBUS Never. He will not.
Age cannot wither her, nor custom stale 245
Her infinite variety. Other women cloy
The appetites they feed, but she makes hungry
Where most she satisfies; for vilest things
Become themselves in her, that the holy priests 249
Bless her when she is riggish. 250

MAECENAS
If beauty, wisdom, modesty can settle
The heart of Antony, Octavia is
A blessèd lottery to him.

AGRIPPA   Let us go. 253
Good Enobarbus, make yourself my guest
Whilst you abide here.

ENOBARBUS   Humbly, sir, I thank you.
Exeunt.

❖

2.3 *Enter Antony, Caesar, Octavia between them.*

ANTONY
The world and my great office will sometimes
Divide me from your bosom.

OCTAVIA   All which time
Before the gods my knee shall bow my prayers
To them for you.

ANTONY   Good night, sir. My Octavia,
Read not my blemishes in the world's report. 5
I have not kept my square, but that to come 6
Shall all be done by th' rule. Good night, dear lady.
Good night, sir.

CAESAR Good night.   *Exit [with Octavia].*

Enter Soothsayer.

ANTONY
Now, sirrah: you do wish yourself in Egypt? 10

SOOTHSAYER Would I had never come from thence,
nor you thither! 12

ANTONY If you can, your reason?

SOOTHSAYER I see it in in my motion, have it not in my 14
tongue; but yet hie you to Egypt again. 15

ANTONY
Say to me, whose fortunes shall rise higher,
Caesar's or mine?

SOOTHSAYER Caesar's.
Therefore, O Antony, stay not by his side.
Thy daemon—that thy spirit which keeps thee—is 20
Noble, courageous, high unmatchable, 21
Where Caesar's is not; but near him thy angel 22
Becomes afeard, as being o'erpowered. Therefore
Make space enough between you.

ANTONY   Speak this no more.

SOOTHSAYER
To none but thee; no more but when to thee. 25
If thou dost play with him at any game,
Thou art sure to lose; and of that natural luck 27
He beats thee 'gainst the odds. Thy luster thickens 28
When he shines by. I say again, thy spirit 29
Is all afraid to govern thee near him;
But, he away, 'tis noble.

ANTONY   Get thee gone.
Say to Ventidius I would speak with him.
Exit [Soothsayer].
He shall to Parthia.—Be it art or hap, 33
He hath spoken true. The very dice obey him,
And in our sports my better cunning faints 35
Under his chance. If we draw lots, he speeds; 36
His cocks do win the battle still of mine 37
When it is all to naught, and his quails ever 38
Beat mine, inhooped, at odds. I will to Egypt; 39
And though I make this marriage for my peace,
I' th' East my pleasure lies.

Enter Ventidius.

                O, come, Ventidius.
You must to Parthia. Your commission's ready;
Follow me, and receive 't.   *Exeunt.*

❖

2.4 *Enter Lepidus, Maecenas, and Agrippa.*

LEPIDUS
Trouble yourselves no further. Pray you, hasten
Your generals after.

AGRIPPA   Sir, Mark Antony 2
Will e'en but kiss Octavia, and we'll follow. 3

235 ordinary meal, supper (such as one might obtain at a public table in a tavern) **236 eat** ate. (Pronounced *et*.) **237 Caesar** i.e., Julius Caesar, by whom Cleopatra had a son named Caesarion **238 cropped** bore fruit (a son) **241 That** so that **245 custom** repeated experience. **stale** make stale **249 Become themselves** are becoming, attractive. **that** so that **250 riggish** lustful **253 lottery** prize, gift of fortune
2.3. Location: Rome.
5 Read interpret. **in** according to **6 kept my square** kept to a straight course (as guided by a carpenter's square; with pun on *rule*, "ruler" in next line). **that** that which is **10 sirrah** (A form of address to a social inferior.)

12 thither to that place **14 in my motion** intuitively, by inward prompting **15 hie** hasten **20 daemon** guardian spirit. **that thy spirit** that spirit of yours. **keeps** protects **21 high unmatchable** unmatchable in the extreme **22 not** absent **25 no more but when** only when **27 of** by **28 thickens** grows dim **29 by** nearby **33 art or hap** skill or luck **35 cunning** skill **36 chance** luck. **speeds** wins **37 still** always. **of** from **38 When . . . naught** when the odds are everything to nothing (in my favor) **39 inhooped** (The birds were enclosed in hoops to make them fight.) **at odds** against the odds
2.4. Location: Rome.
2 Your generals after after your generals **3 e'en but** only, just

LEPIDUS
Till I shall see you in your soldier's dress,   4
Which will become you both, farewell.
MAECENAS   We shall,   5
As I conceive the journey, be at th' Mount   6
Before you, Lepidus.
LEPIDUS   Your way is shorter;
My purposes do draw me much about.   8
You'll win two days upon me.
MAECENAS, AGRIPPA   Sir, good success!
LEPIDUS   Farewell.   Exeunt.

❧

2.5   Enter Cleopatra, Charmian, Iras, and Alexas.

CLEOPATRA
Give me some music; music, moody food   1
Of us that trade in love.
ALL   The music, ho!

Enter Mardian the eunuch.

CLEOPATRA
Let it alone. Let's to billiards. Come, Charmian.
CHARMIAN
My arm is sore. Best play with Mardian.
CLEOPATRA
As well a woman with an eunuch played
As with a woman. Come, you'll play with me, sir?
MARDIAN   As well as I can, madam.
CLEOPATRA
And when good will is showed, though 't come too
    short,   8
The actor may plead pardon. I'll none now.   9
Give me mine angle; we'll to the river. There,   10
My music playing far off, I will betray
Tawny-finned fishes. My bended hook shall pierce
Their slimy jaws, and as I draw them up
I'll think them every one an Antony,
And say, "Aha! You're caught."
CHARMIAN   'Twas merry when
You wagered on your angling, when your diver
Did hang a salt fish on his hook, which he   17
With fervency drew up.
CLEOPATRA   That time—O times!—   18
I laughed him out of patience; and that night
I laughed him into patience. And next morn,
Ere the ninth hour, I drunk him to his bed,   21
Then put my tires and mantles on him, whilst   22

I wore his sword Philippan.

Enter a Messenger.

                    O, from Italy!   23
Ram thou thy fruitful tidings in mine ears,
That long time have been barren.
MESSENGER   Madam, madam—
CLEOPATRA
Antonio's dead! If thou say so, villain,
Thou kill'st thy mistress; but well and free,
If thou so yield him, there is gold, and here   28
My bluest veins to kiss—a hand that kings
Have lipped, and trembled kissing.
            [She offers him gold, and her hand to kiss.]
MESSENGER   First, madam, he is well.
CLEOPATRA
Why, there's more gold. But, sirrah, mark, we use
To say the dead are well. Bring it to that,   33
The gold I give thee will I melt and pour
Down thy ill-uttering throat.
MESSENGER   Good madam, hear me.
CLEOPATRA   Well, go to, I will.   37
But there's no goodness in thy face, if Antony
Be free and healthful—so tart a favor   39
To trumpet such good tidings! If not well,
Thou shouldst come like a Fury crowned with
    snakes,   41
Not like a formal man.
MESSENGER   Will 't please you hear me?   42
CLEOPATRA
I have a mind to strike thee ere thou speak'st.
Yet, if thou say Antony lives, is well,
Or friends with Caesar, or not captive to him,
I'll set thee in a shower of gold and hail
Rich pearls upon thee.
MESSENGER   Madam, he's well.
CLEOPATRA   Well said.
MESSENGER
And friends with Caesar.
CLEOPATRA   Thou'rt an honest man.   48
MESSENGER
Caesar and he are greater friends than ever.
CLEOPATRA
Make thee a fortune from me.
MESSENGER   But yet, madam—
CLEOPATRA
I do not like "But yet"; it does allay   51
The good precedence. Fie upon "But yet"!   52
"But yet" is as a jailer to bring forth
Some monstrous malefactor. Prithee, friend,
Pour out the pack of matter to mine ear,   55

---

4 dress garb, apparel   **5 become** suit   **6 conceive** understand.   **th' Mount** i.e., Mount Misenum   **8 about** roundabout
2.5. Location: Alexandria. Cleopatra's palace.
1 moody melancholy   **8 too short** (A bawdy joke on Mardian's being castrated; *will* suggests "sexual desire"; *come* suggests "reach orgasm.")   **9 I'll none now** i.e., I won't play billiards after all   **10 angle** rod and line   **17 salt** dried, preserved in salt   **18 With fervency** excitedly   **21 ninth hour** i.e., 9 A.M.   **drunk** drank   **22 tires** headdresses, or perhaps attire.   **mantles** garments

23 Philippan (Named for Antony's victory over Brutus and Cassius at Philippi.)   **28 yield** (1) grant (2) report   **33 well** i.e., well out of it, in heaven.   **Bring it to that** if that is your meaning   **37 go to** i.e., all right, then. (Said remonstratingly.)   **39 tart a favor** sour a face   **41 Fury** avenging goddess of classical mythology   **42 like . . . man** in ordinary human form   **48 honest** worthy   **51–52 allay . . . precedence** annul the good news that preceded it   **55 pack of matter** entire contents (as of a peddler's pack)

The good and bad together. He's friends with
  Caesar,
In state of health, thou sayst, and, thou sayst, free.
MESSENGER
  Free, madam? No, I made no such report.
  He's bound unto Octavia.
CLEOPATRA   For what good turn?   59
MESSENGER
  For the best turn i' the bed.
CLEOPATRA   I am pale, Charmian.
MESSENGER
  Madam, he's married to Octavia.
CLEOPATRA
  The most infectious pestilence upon thee!
                                        Strikes him down.
MESSENGER
  Good madam, patience.
CLEOPATRA   What say you?   *Strikes him.*
                                              Hence,
  Horrible villain, or I'll spurn thine eyes   64
  Like balls before me! I'll unhair thy head!   65
                                She hales him up and down.
  Thou shalt be whipped with wire and stewed in
    brine,
  Smarting in lingering pickle!
MESSENGER   Gracious madam,   67
  I that do bring the news made not the match.
CLEOPATRA
  Say 'tis not so, a province I will give thee
  And make thy fortunes proud. The blow thou hadst
  Shall make thy peace for moving me to rage,   71
  And I will boot thee with what gift besides   72
  Thy modesty can beg.
MESSENGER   He's married, madam.   73
CLEOPATRA
  Rogue, thou hast lived too long!   *Draw a knife.*
MESSENGER   Nay then, I'll run.
  What mean you, madam? I have made no fault. *Exit.*
CHARMIAN
  Good madam, keep yourself within yourself.   76
  The man is innocent.
CLEOPATRA
  Some innocents scape not the thunderbolt.
  Melt Egypt into Nile, and kindly creatures
  Turn all to serpents! Call the slave again.   79
  Though I am mad, I will not bite him. Call!   81
CHARMIAN
  He is afeard to come.
CLEOPATRA   I will not hurt him.
                                [The Messenger is sent for.]
  These hands do lack nobility, that they strike

A meaner than myself, since I myself   84
Have given myself the cause.

                    Enter the Messenger again.

                            Come hither, sir.   85
Though it be honest, it is never good
To bring bad news. Give to a gracious message
An host of tongues, but let ill tidings tell   88
Themselves when they be felt.   89
MESSENGER   I have done my duty.
CLEOPATRA   Is he married?
  I cannot hate thee worser than I do
  If thou again say "Yes."
MESSENGER   He's married, madam.
CLEOPATRA
  The gods confound thee! Dost thou hold there still?   94
MESSENGER
  Should I lie, madam?
CLEOPATRA   O, I would thou didst,
  So half my Egypt were submerged and made   96
  A cistern for scaled snakes! Go, get thee hence.   97
  Hadst thou Narcissus in thy face, to me   98
  Thou wouldst appear most ugly. He is married?
MESSENGER
  I crave Your Highness' pardon.
CLEOPATRA   He is married?
MESSENGER
  Take no offense that I would not offend you.   101
  To punish me for what you make me do
  Seems much unequal. He's married to Octavia.   103
CLEOPATRA
  O, that his fault should make a knave of thee,   104
  That art not what thou'rt sure of! Get thee hence.   105
  The merchandise which thou hast brought from
    Rome
  Are all too dear for me. Lie they upon thy hand,   107
  And be undone by 'em!   *[Exit Messenger.]*
CHARMIAN   Good Your Highness, patience. 108
CLEOPATRA
  In praising Antony, I have dispraised Caesar.
CHARMIAN   Many times, madam.
CLEOPATRA
  I am paid for 't now. Lead me from hence;
  I faint. O Iras, Charmian! 'Tis no matter.
  Go to the fellow, good Alexas. Bid him
  Report the feature of Octavia: her years,

---

59 **turn** favor, purpose. (But the Messenger replies in the sense of "feat, bout," with sexual suggestion.) 64 **spurn** kick 65 **s.d. hales** drags 67 **pickle** pickling solution 71 **make thy peace** compensate, mollify me 72 **boot thee with** give you into the bargain, or, make amends with. **what** whatever 73 **Thy modesty** one of your modest expectations 76 **keep . . . yourself** i.e., control yourself 79 **kindly** endowed with innately good qualities 81 **mad** (1) angry (2) insane, and so apt to bite

84 **A meaner** one of lower social station 84–85 **since . . . cause** since I am the one I ought to blame 85 **the cause** i.e., by loving Antony 88 **host** multitude 89 **when . . . felt** i.e., when they occur; let bad tidings announce themselves 94 **confound** destroy. **hold there still** stick to your story 96 **So** even if 97 **cistern** tank. **scaled** scaly 98 **Narcissus** beautiful youth of Greek mythology who fell in love with his own reflected image 101 **Take . . . offend you** don't be offended that I hesitate to offend you (by telling bad news), or, don't interpret as offense what is not meant to offend 103 **much unequal** most unjust 104–105 **O, that . . . sure of** i.e., it's too bad that Antony's fault puts you in the wrong, you who shouldn't be equated with the bad news you report as true 107 **dear** (1) expensive (2) emotionally precious 107–108 **Lie . . . by 'em** may they remain in your possession unsold, and may you be bankrupt, financially ruined (i.e., may you never profit from your bad tidings)

Her inclination. Let him not leave out   115
The color of her hair. Bring me word quickly.
                                        [*Exit Alexas.*]
Let him forever go!—Let him not, Charmian.   117
Though he be painted one way like a Gorgon,   118
The other way's a Mars. [*To Mardian.*] Bid you
    Alexas   119
Bring me word how tall she is.—Pity me, Charmian,
But do not speak to me. Lead me to my chamber.
                                        Exeunt.

❧

2.6   *Flourish. Enter Pompey [and] Menas at one door,*
           with drum and trumpet; at another, Caesar,
           Lepidus, Antony, Enobarbus, Maecenas, Agrippa,
           with soldiers marching.

POMPEY
    Your hostages I have, so have you mine,
    And we shall talk before we fight.
CAESAR   Most meet   2
    That first we come to words; and therefore have we
    Our written purposes before us sent,   4
    Which if thou hast considered, let us know
    If 'twill tie up thy discontented sword   6
    And carry back to Sicily much tall youth   7
    That else must perish here.
POMPEY   To you all three,
    The senators alone of this great world,   9
    Chief factors for the gods: I do not know   10
    Wherefore my father should revengers want,   11
    Having a son and friends, since Julius Caesar,   12
    Who at Philippi the good Brutus ghosted,   13
    There saw you laboring for him. What was 't   14
    That moved pale Cassius to conspire? And what
    Made th' all-honored, honest Roman Brutus,   16
    With the armed rest, courtiers of beauteous
        freedom,   17
    To drench the Capitol, but that they would   18
    Have one man but a man? And that is it   19

115 inclination disposition   **117 him** i.e., Antony   **118–119 Though
. . . Mars** (Alludes to a type of picture known as a perspective, which
shows different objects when looked at from different angles of vision.)   **a Gorgon** a female monster with serpents in her hair; her head
was capable of turning to stone anything that met her gaze
**2.6. Location: Near Misenum, in southern Italy near modern Naples.
(But 2.1 perhaps took place in Messina, Sicily.)**
2 meet fitting   **4 purposes** propositions   **6 tie . . . sword** i.e., satisfy
your concerns and allow you to forgo a fight   **7 tall** brave   **9 senators alone** i.e., sole rulers of the empire (and those who have thus
supplanted the Senate)   **10 factors** agents   **10–14 I do . . . for him**
(Julius Caesar defeated Pompey's father, Pompey the Great, and was
subsequently assassinated by Brutus and Cassius, among others. Caesar's ghost appeared to Brutus at Philippi, where the combined forces
of Antony, Octavius, and Lepidus defeated Brutus and Cassius. [See
Julius Caesar.] Since Antony, Octavius, and Lepidus thus defeated the
avengers of Pompey the Great's death, Pompey the Great's sons and
friends should become his avengers by continuing to war on Antony,
Octavius, and Lepidus.)   **11 want** lack   **13 ghosted** haunted
16 honest honorable   **17 the armed rest** i.e., the rest of those who
were armed.   **courtiers** wooers, those who serve freedom only
18 drench bathe in blood   **19 Have . . . a man** (The republican conspirators acted to keep Julius Caesar from accepting the crown.)

Hath made me rig my navy, at whose burden
The angered ocean foams, with which I meant
To scourge th' ingratitude that despiteful Rome   22
Cast on my noble father.
CAESAR   Take your time.   23
ANTONY
    Thou canst not fear us, Pompey, with thy sails;   24
    We'll speak with thee at sea. At land thou know'st   25
    How much we do o'ercount thee.
POMPEY   At land indeed   26
    Thou dost o'ercount me of my father's house;
    But since the cuckoo builds not for himself,   28
    Remain in 't as thou mayst.
LEPIDUS   Be pleased to tell us—   29
    For this is from the present—how you take   30
    The offers we have sent you.
CAESAR   There's the point.
ANTONY
    Which do not be entreated to, but weigh   32
    What it is worth embraced.
CAESAR   And what may follow,   33
    To try a larger fortune.
POMPEY   You have made me offer   34
    Of Sicily, Sardinia; and I must
    Rid all the sea of pirates; then, to send   36
    Measures of wheat to Rome. This 'greed upon,
    To part with unhacked edges and bear back   38
    Our targes undinted.
CAESAR, ANTONY, LEPIDUS   That's our offer.
POMPEY   Know then   39
    I came before you here a man prepared
    To take this offer, but Mark Antony
    Put me to some impatience. Though I lose
    The praise of it by telling, you must know,   43
    When Caesar and your brother were at blows,
    Your mother came to Sicily and did find
    Her welcome friendly.
ANTONY   I have heard it, Pompey,
    And am well studied for a liberal thanks   47
    Which I do owe you.
POMPEY   Let me have your hand.
                                    [*They shake hands.*]
    I did not think, sir, to have met you here.
ANTONY
    The beds i' th' East are soft; and thanks to you,
    That called me timelier than my purpose hither,   51

22 despiteful cruel, malicious   **23 Take your time** i.e., say your fill,
go on   **24 fear** frighten   **25 speak with** confront   **26 o'ercount** out-
number. (But Pompey's use of the word in the next line implies that
Antony has cheated him. Plutarch informs us that Antony bought the
elder Pompey's house at auction and later refused to pay for it.)
28 cuckoo a bird that builds no nest for itself but lays its eggs in other
birds' nests. (Perhaps suggests also that Antony is a cuckold maker.)
29 as thou mayst as long as you can, or, since you can   **30 from the
present** digressing from the business at hand.   **take** i.e., respond to
32 do . . . to i.e., do not accept merely because we ask   **33 embraced** if accepted by you   **34 To . . . fortune** i.e., if you decide to
risk war with the triumvirs, or, if you join with us to share a greater
fortune   **36 to send** I am to send   **38 To part** we are to part company.   **edges** swords   **39 targes** shields   **43 praise of** credit for
47 well studied for well prepared to deliver   **51 timelier** earlier

For I have gained by 't.
CAESAR   Since I saw you last
There's a change upon you.
POMPEY   Well, I know not
What counts harsh Fortune casts upon my face,   54
But in my bosom shall she never come
To make my heart her vassal.
LEPIDUS   Well met here.
POMPEY
I hope so, Lepidus. Thus we are agreed.
I crave our composition may be written   58
And sealed between us.
CAESAR   That's the next to do.   59
POMPEY
We'll feast each other ere we part, and let's
Draw lots who shall begin.
ANTONY   That will I, Pompey.   61
POMPEY
No, Antony, take the lot. But, first or last,   62
Your fine Egyptian cookery shall have
The fame. I have heard that Julius Caesar
Grew fat with feasting there.
ANTONY   You have heard much.
POMPEY   I have fair meanings, sir.   67
ANTONY   And fair words to them.   68
POMPEY   Then so much have I heard.   69
And I have heard Apollodorus carried—   70
ENOBARBUS
No more of that. He did so.
POMPEY   What, I pray you?   71
ENOBARBUS
A certain queen to Caesar in a mattress.   72
POMPEY
I know thee now. How far'st thou, soldier?
ENOBARBUS   Well,
And well am like to do, for I perceive
Four feasts are toward.
POMPEY   Let me shake thy hand.   75
                    [They shake hands.]
I never hated thee. I have seen thee fight
When I have envied thy behavior.
ENOBARBUS   Sir,
I never loved you much, but I ha' praised ye
When you have well deserved ten times as much
As I have said you did.
POMPEY   Enjoy thy plainness;   80
It nothing ill becomes thee.   81
Aboard my galley I invite you all.

Will you lead, lords?
CAESAR, ANTONY, LEPIDUS   Show 's the way, sir.
POMPEY   Come.   83
              Exeunt. Manent Enobarbus and Menas.
MENAS [*aside*] Thy father, Pompey, would ne'er have
made this treaty.—You and I have known, sir.   85
ENOBARBUS   At sea, I think.
MENAS   We have, sir.
ENOBARBUS   You have done well by water.
MENAS   And you by land.
ENOBARBUS   I will praise any man that will praise me,
though it cannot be denied what I have done by land.
MENAS   Nor what I have done by water.
ENOBARBUS   Yes, something you can deny for your own
safety: you have been a great thief by sea.
MENAS   And you by land.
ENOBARBUS   There I deny my land service. But give me 96
your hand, Menas. [*They shake hands.*] If our eyes had
authority, here they might take two thieves kissing. 98
MENAS   All men's faces are true, whatsoe'er their hands
are.
ENOBARBUS   But there is never a fair woman has a true 101
face.
MENAS   No slander; they steal hearts.   103
ENOBARBUS   We came hither to fight with you.
MENAS For my part, I am sorry it is turned to a drinking. 105
Pompey doth this day laugh away his fortune.
ENOBARBUS   If he do, sure he cannot weep 't back
again.
MENAS   You've said, sir. We looked not for Mark 109
Antony here. Pray you, is he married to Cleopatra?
ENOBARBUS   Caesar's sister is called Octavia.
MENAS   True, sir. She was the wife of Caius Marcellus.
ENOBARBUS   But she is now the wife of Marcus Anto-
nius.
MENAS   Pray ye, sir?   115
ENOBARBUS   'Tis true.
MENAS   Then is Caesar and he forever knit together.
ENOBARBUS   If I were bound to divine of this unity, I 118
would not prophesy so.
MENAS   I think the policy of that purpose made more in 120
the marriage than the love of the parties.
ENOBARBUS   I think so too. But you shall find the band
that seems to tie their friendship together will be the
very strangler of their amity. Octavia is of a holy, cold,
and still conversation.   125
MENAS   Who would not have his wife so?
ENOBARBUS   Not he that himself is not so, which is
Mark Antony. He will to his Egyptian dish again.
Then shall the sighs of Octavia blow the fire up in
Caesar, and, as I said before, that which is the strength

54 counts tally marks. (From the practice of casting accounts or reckonings by means of marks or notches on tallies.)   casts calculates
58 composition agreement   59 sealed between us stamped with the
official seal of each co-signer   61 That will I i.e., I will begin
62 take the lot draw lots with the rest of us, accept the results of the
lottery.   first or last whether you win the lottery to go first or last
67 fair i.e., friendly   68 fair i.e., well-chosen   69 Then . . . heard
i.e., I am not implying more about Antony in Egypt than my words
honestly mean   70–72 Apollodorus . . . mattress (Alludes to a tale
told by Plutarch according to which Cleopatra had herself rolled up in
a mattress and carried secretly by Apollodorus to meet Julius Caesar.)
75 toward coming up   80 Enjoy thy plainness give free rein to your
bluntness   81 nothing . . . thee suits you not at all badly

83 s.d. Manent they remain onstage   85 known known each other
96 There in respect to that   98 authority i.e., to make arrests, like a
constable.   take arrest.   two thieves kissing (1) our two thieving
hands shaking (2) two thieves greeting each other   101 true honest
(because women use cosmetic art to conceal defects)   103 No slander i.e., you speak true (since women in their own way are thieves,
stealing men's affections)   105 a drinking an occasion for drinking
109 You've said i.e., you've spoken truly   115 Pray ye are you in
earnest   118 divine of prophesy about   120 made more played more
of a role   125 conversation demeanor

of their amity shall prove the immediate author of their variance. Antony will use his affection where it is; he married but his occasion here. 131 132 133

MENAS   And thus it may be. Come, sir, will you aboard? I have a health for you. 135

ENOBARBUS   I shall take it, sir. We have used our throats in Egypt.

MENAS   Come, let's away.   *Exeunt.*

❖

2.7   *Music plays. Enter two or three Servants with a banquet.*

FIRST SERVANT   Here they'll be, man. Some o' their plants are ill-rooted already; the least wind i' the world will blow them down. 2

SECOND SERVANT   Lepidus is high-colored. 4

FIRST SERVANT   They have made him drink alms drink. 5

SECOND SERVANT   As they pinch one another by the disposition, he cries out, "No more," reconciles them to his entreaty, and himself to the drink. 6 7 8

FIRST SERVANT   But it raises the greater war between him and his discretion.

SECOND SERVANT   Why, this it is to have a name in great men's fellowship. I had as lief have a reed that will do me no service as a partisan I could not heave. 11 12 13

FIRST SERVANT   To be called into a huge sphere, and not to be seen to move in 't, are the holes where eyes should be, which pitifully disaster the cheeks. 14 15 16

> *A sennet sounded. Enter Caesar, Antony,*
> *Pompey, Lepidus, Agrippa, Maecenas, Enobarbus,*
> *Menas, with other captains [and a Boy].*

ANTONY
Thus do they, sir: they take the flow o' the Nile   17
By certain scales i' the pyramid. They know   18
By the height, the lowness, or the mean if dearth   19
Or foison follow. The higher Nilus swells   20
The more it promises; as it ebbs, the seedsman

Upon the slime and ooze scatters his grain,
And shortly comes to harvest.

LEPIDUS   You've strange serpents there.

ANTONY   Ay, Lepidus.

LEPIDUS   Your serpent of Egypt is bred now of your mud by the operation of your sun; so is your crocodile. 26

ANTONY   They are so.

POMPEY   Sit—and some wine. A health to Lepidus!   29
                            [*They sit and drink.*]

LEPIDUS   I am not so well as I should be, but I'll ne'er out. 30 31

ENOBARBUS   Not till you have slept; I fear me you'll be in till then. 33

LEPIDUS   Nay, certainly, I have heard the Ptolemies' pyramises are very goodly things; without contradiction I have heard that. 35

MENAS [*aside to Pompey*]   Pompey, a word.

POMPEY [*to Menas*]   Say in mine ear. What is 't?

MENAS (*whispers in 's ear*)
Forsake thy seat, I do beseech thee, captain,
And hear me speak a word.

POMPEY [*to Menas*]
Forbear me till anon.—This wine for Lepidus!   41

LEPIDUS   What manner o' thing is your crocodile?

ANTONY   It is shaped, sir, like itself, and it is as broad as it hath breadth. It is just so high as it is, and moves with its own organs. It lives by that which nourisheth it, and, the elements once out of it, it transmigrates. 46

LEPIDUS   What color is it of?

ANTONY   Of its own color too.

LEPIDUS   'Tis a strange serpent.

ANTONY   'Tis so. And the tears of it are wet. 50

CAESAR   Will this description satisfy him?

ANTONY   With the health that Pompey gives him, else he is a very epicure. [*Menas whispers again.*] 53

POMPEY [*aside to Menas*]
Go hang, sir, hang! Tell me of that? Away!
Do as I bid you.—Where's this cup I called for?

MENAS [*aside to Pompey*]
If for the sake of merit thou wilt hear me, 56
Rise from thy stool.

POMPEY [*to Menas*]   I think thou'rt mad. [*He rises, and they walk aside.*] The matter?

MENAS
I have ever held my cap off to thy fortunes. 58

POMPEY
Thou hast served me with much faith. What's else to say?— 59

131–132 author . . . variance cause of their falling out   132–133 use . . . it is i.e., satisfy his passion in Egypt   133 his occasion what his interests demanded   135 health toast
2.7. Location: On board Pompey's galley, off Misenum in southern Italy. A table and stools are brought on.
s.d. banquet a course of the feast, probably dessert   2 plants soles of the feet (with pun on usual sense)   4 high-colored flushed   5 alms drink drink given or taken in charity (?), i.e., to further the business of reconciliation (as indicated in the following speech)   6–7 pinch . . . disposition chafe one another, fall to bickering as prompted by their contrasting temperaments. (Lepidus stops them but has to join them in fresh rounds of drink.)   8 his entreaty i.e., that they stop quarreling   11 a name a name only   12 had as lief would just as soon   13 partisan long-bladed spear. (Here, metaphorically, too large a weapon for Lepidus to wield.)   14–16 To . . . cheeks to be summoned by fortune to greatness and yet not be able to fulfill the role greatly is like having eye sockets with no eyes in them, a defect that will disfigure (*disaster*) the cheeks. (The underlying image is of a heavenly body that cannot move properly in its sphere, causing *disaster*, meaning both disfigurement and the evil effects of unfavorable aspect of a planet.)   16 s.d. sennet trumpet call signaling the approach of a procession   17 sir (Usually thought to refer to Caesar, but the matter is uncertain.)   take measure   18 scales graduated markings   19 mean middle   20 foison plenty

26 Your serpent i.e., this serpent that people talk about. (The colloquial indefinite *your*.)   29 health toast. (Lepidus is obliged to drink up every time a toast is proposed to him.)   30–31 I'll ne'er out i.e., I'll never refuse a toast, never quit   33 in (1) in drink, in your cups (2) indoors. (Enobarbus quibbles on *in* as the antithesis of *out* in line 31.)   35 pyramises (Lepidus' drunken error for *pyramides*, plural of *pyramis* or *pyramid*.)   41 Forbear leave.   till anon for a moment   46 elements vital elements   50 tears (Alludes to the ancient belief that the crocodile wept insincere "crocodile tears" over its victim before devouring it.)   53 epicure (1) glutton (2) atheist. (The Epicureans did not believe in an afterlife.)   56 merit i.e., my merits as a loyal follower, or, the merit of my ideas   58 held . . . off i.e., been a respectful and faithful servant   59 faith faithfulness

Be jolly, lords.

ANTONY   These quicksands, Lepidus,
Keep off them, for you sink.

[Menas and Pompey speak aside.]

MENAS
Wilt thou be lord of all the world?

POMPEY   What sayst thou?

MENAS
Wilt thou be lord of the whole world? That's twice.

POMPEY
How should that be?

MENAS   But entertain it,   64
And, though thou think me poor, I am the man
Will give thee all the world.

POMPEY   Hast thou drunk well?

MENAS
No, Pompey, I have kept me from the cup.
Thou art, if thou dar'st be, the earthly Jove.
Whate'er the ocean pales or sky inclips   69
Is thine, if thou wilt ha 't.

POMPEY   Show me which way.

MENAS
These three world-sharers, these competitors,   71
Are in thy vessel. Let me cut the cable,
And, when we are put off, fall to their throats.   73
All there is thine.

POMPEY   Ah, this thou shouldst have done
And not have spoke on 't! In me 'tis villainy;   75
In thee 't had been good service. Thou must know,   76
'Tis not my profit that does lead mine honor;
Mine honor, it. Repent that e'er thy tongue   78
Hath so betrayed thine act. Being done unknown,   79
I should have found it afterwards well done,
But must condemn it now. Desist, and drink.

[He returns to the feast.]

MENAS *[aside]*   For this,
I'll never follow thy palled fortunes more.   83
Who seeks and will not take when once 'tis offered   84
Shall never find it more.

POMPEY   This health to Lepidus!

ANTONY
Bear him ashore. I'll pledge it for him, Pompey.   86

ENOBARBUS
Here's to thee, Menas!   *[They drink.]*

MENAS   Enobarbus, welcome!

POMPEY   Fill till the cup be hid.

ENOBARBUS   There's a strong fellow, Menas.

[Pointing to one who carries off Lepidus.]

MENAS   Why?

ENOBARBUS   'A bears the third part of the world, man; 91
seest not?

MENAS
The third part, then, is drunk. Would it were all,
That it might go on wheels!   94

ENOBARBUS   Drink thou; increase the reels.   95

MENAS   Come.

POMPEY
This is not yet an Alexandrian feast.

ANTONY
It ripens towards it. Strike the vessels, ho!   98
Here's to Caesar!

CAESAR   I could well forbear 't.
It's monstrous labor when I wash my brain
And it grows fouler.

ANTONY   Be a child o' the time.

CAESAR   Possess it, I'll make answer.   102
But I had rather fast from all four days   103
Than drink so much in one.

ENOBARBUS *[to Antony]*   Ha, my brave emperor!   104
Shall we dance now the Egyptian Bacchanals   105
And celebrate our drink?   106

POMPEY   Let's ha 't, good soldier.

ANTONY   Come, let's all take hands
Till that the conquering wine hath steeped our sense 109
In soft and delicate Lethe.

ENOBARBUS   All take hands.   110
Make battery to our ears with the loud music,   111
The while I'll place you; then the boy shall sing.
The holding every man shall bear as loud   113
As his strong sides can volley.   114

Music plays. Enobarbus places them hand in hand.

The Song.

BOY *[sings]*
Come, thou monarch of the vine,
Plumpy Bacchus with pink eyne!   116
In thy fats our cares be drowned,   117
With thy grapes our hairs be crowned.

ALL   Cup us till the world go round,   119
Cup us till the world go round!

CAESAR
What would you more? Pompey, good night.—
Good brother,
Let me request you off. Our graver business   122
Frowns at this levity. Gentle lords, let's part;
You see we have burnt our cheeks. Strong Enobarb   124
Is weaker than the wine, and mine own tongue
Splits what it speaks. The wild disguise hath almost 126

---

64 **But entertain it** only accept the possibility   69 **pales** impales, fences in.   **inclips** embraces   71 **competitors** partners (with secondary sense of "rivals")   73 **are put off** have put to sea   75 **on 't** of it   76 **Thou must know** I must inform you that   78 **Mine honor, it** i.e., my honor comes before my personal profit.   **Repent** regret   79 **unknown** i.e., without my knowledge   83 **palled** decayed, darkened   84 **Who** he who   86 **pledge** it i.e., drink the toast (since Lepidus is too far gone to drink)   91 **'A** he

94 **go on wheels** go fast or easily. (Proverbial.)   95 **reels** (1) revels (2) reeling and whirling of drunkenness   98 **Strike the vessels** broach or tap the casks   102 **Possess it** drink it off.   **make answer** drink in return (? Or Caesar may be saying, "My answer is, 'Be master of the time.' ")   103 **all** all nourishment   104 **brave** splendid   105 **Bacchanals** drunken dance to Bacchus, god of wine   106 **celebrate** consecrate with observances   109 **Till that** until   110 **Lethe** i.e., forgetfulness. (Literally, the river of oblivion in Hades.)   111 **Make battery to** assault   113 **holding** refrain.   **bear** carry, sing   114 **volley** sing in return, answering the stanza with the refrain   116 **pink eyne** (i.e., eyes half-shut, from drinking)   117 **fats** vats, vessels   119 **Cup** intoxicate   122 **off** to come away   124 **we . . . cheeks** our complexions are flushed with drinking   126 **disguise** (1) masque (2) drunkenness as a disguise

Anticked us all. What needs more words? Good
   night.   127
Good Antony, your hand.
POMPEY   I'll try you on the shore.   128
ANTONY
And shall, sir. Give 's your hand.
POMPEY   O Antony,
You have my father's house. But what? We are
   friends.
Come down into the boat.
ENOBARBUS   Take heed you fall not.
             [*Exeunt all but Enobarbus and Menas.*]
Menas, I'll not on shore.
MENAS   No, to my cabin.
These drums, these trumpets, flutes! What!
Let Neptune hear we bid a loud farewell
To these great fellows. Sound and be hanged,
   sound out!   *Sound a flourish, with drums.*
ENOBARBUS   Hoo! says 'a. There's my cap.
                 [*He flings it in the air.*]
MENAS   Hoo! Noble captain, come.   *Exeunt.*

❦

3.1   *Enter Ventidius as it were in triumph [with Silius,
and other Romans, officers, and soldiers], the dead
body of Pacorus borne before him.*

VENTIDIUS
Now, darting Parthia, art thou struck, and now   1
Pleased fortune does of Marcus Crassus' death   2
Make me revenger. Bear the King's son's body
Before our army. Thy Pacorus, Orodes,   4
Pays this for Marcus Crassus.
SILIUS   Noble Ventidius,
Whilst yet with Parthian blood thy sword is warm,
The fugitive Parthians follow. Spur through Media,   7
Mesopotamia, and the shelters whither
The routed fly. So thy grand captain, Antony,
Shall set thee on triumphant chariots and   10
Put garlands on thy head.
VENTIDIUS   O Silius, Silius,
I have done enough. A lower place, note well,   12
May make too great an act. For learn this, Silius:
Better to leave undone than by our deed
Acquire too high a fame when him we serve's away.
Caesar and Antony have ever won
More in their officer than person. Sossius,   17

One of my place in Syria, his lieutenant,   18
For quick accumulation of renown,
Which he achieved by th' minute, lost his favor.   20
Who does i' the wars more than his captain can   21
Becomes his captain's captain; and ambition,
The soldier's virtue, rather makes choice of loss   23
Than gain which darkens him.   24
I could do more to do Antonius good,
But 'twould offend him, and in his offense   26
Should my performance perish.
SILIUS   Thou hast, Ventidius, that   28
Without the which a soldier and his sword   29
Grants scarce distinction. Thou wilt write to Antony? 30
VENTIDIUS
I'll humbly signify what in his name,
That magical word of war, we have effected: 32
How with his banners and his well-paid ranks
The ne'er-yet-beaten horse of Parthia   34
We have jaded out o' the field.
SILIUS   Where is he now?   35
VENTIDIUS
He purposeth to Athens, whither, with what haste
The weight we must convey with 's will permit,   37
We shall appear before him.—On, there. Pass along!
                         Exeunt.

❦

3.2   *Enter Agrippa at one door, Enobarbus at another.*

AGRIPPA   What, are the brothers parted?   1
ENOBARBUS
They have dispatched with Pompey; he is gone.   2
The other three are sealing. Octavia weeps   3
To part from Rome; Caesar is sad; and Lepidus,   4
Since Pompey's feast, as Menas says, is troubled
With the greensickness.
AGRIPPA   'Tis a noble Lepidus.   6
ENOBARBUS
A very fine one. O, how he loves Caesar!   7
AGRIPPA
Nay, but how dearly he adores Mark Antony!
ENOBARBUS
Caesar? Why, he's the Jupiter of men.
AGRIPPA
What's Antony? The god of Jupiter.

---

127 Anticked us (1) made dancers of us in a masque (2) made buffoons or fools of us   **128 try you** i.e., take you on in a drinking
contest
3.1. Location: The Middle East.
1 darting (The Parthians were famous for archery and for the Parthian
dart which they discharged as they fled.)   **Parthia** i.e., Orodes, King
of Parthia   **2 Crassus' death** (Crassus, member of the first triumvirate
with Pompey the Great and Julius Caesar, was overthrown and treacherously murdered by Orodes in 53 B.C.)   **4 Pacorus, Orodes** (Pacorus
was the son of Orodes.)   **7 The . . . follow** follow the fleeing
Parthians   **10 triumphant** triumphal   **12 A lower place** i.e., one of
lower rank   **17 More . . . person** more through the actions of their
lieutenants than by their own efforts

18 of my place of the same rank as I.   **his lieutenant** i.e., the commanding officer acting for Antony   **20 by th' minute** minute by
minute, continually   **21 Who** he who   **23 makes choice of** chooses
24 which darkens him achieved at the expense of darkening his reputation   **26 offense** taking offense   **28–30 that . . . distinction** i.e.,
discretion, without the which a soldier can scarcely be distinguished
from the sword he uses   **30 Grants scarce** scarcely admits of
32 word of war watchword.   **effected** achieved   **34 horse** cavalry
35 jaded driven exhausted like jades, inferior horses   **37 with 's**
with us
3.2. Location: Rome.
1 brothers brothers-in-law.   **parted** departed   **2 dispatched** concluded the business   **3 sealing** affixing seals to their agreements, settling matters   **4 sad** sober   **6 greensickness** a kind of anemia supposed to affect young women, especially those afflicted with love-
longing. (Used ironically here to refer to Lepidus' hangover and to his
love for Antony and Caesar.)   **7 fine** *Lepidus* in Latin means "fine,"
"elegant."

ENOBARBUS
  Spake you of Caesar? How, the nonpareil!

AGRIPPA
  O Antony, O thou Arabian bird!   12

ENOBARBUS
  Would you praise Caesar, say "Caesar"; go no
    further.

AGRIPPA
  Indeed, he plied them both with excellent praises.

ENOBARBUS
  But he loves Caesar best; yet he loves Antony.
  Hoo! Hearts, tongues, figures, scribes, bards, poets,
    cannot   16
  Think, speak, cast, write, sing, number, hoo!   17
  His love to Antony. But as for Caesar,
  Kneel down, kneel down, and wonder.

AGRIPPA   Both he loves.

ENOBARBUS
  They are his shards, and he their beetle. [*Trumpets
    within.*] So;   20
  This is to horse. Adieu, noble Agrippa.   21

AGRIPPA
  Good fortune, worthy soldier, and farewell.

          Enter Caesar, Antony, Lepidus, and Octavia.

ANTONY   No further, sir.   23

CAESAR
  You take from me a great part of myself;
  Use me well in 't.—Sister, prove such a wife
  As my thoughts make thee, and as my farthest bond 26
  Shall pass on thy approof.—Most noble Antony,   27
  Let not the piece of virtue, which is set   28
  Betwixt us as the cement of our love
  To keep it builded, be the ram to batter
  The fortress of it; for better might we
  Have loved without this mean, if on both parts   32
  This be not cherished.

ANTONY   Make me not offended
  In your distrust.

CAESAR   I have said.

ANTONY   You shall not find,   34
  Though you be therein curious, the least cause   35
  For what you seem to fear. So the gods keep you,
  And make the hearts of Romans serve your ends!
  We will here part.

CAESAR
  Farewell, my dearest sister, fare thee well.
  The elements be kind to thee, and make
  Thy spirits all of comfort! Fare thee well.

OCTAVIA [*weeping*]   My noble brother!

ANTONY
  The April's in her eyes; it is love's spring,
  And these the showers to bring it on.—Be cheerful.

OCTAVIA [*to Caesar*]
  Sir, look well to my husband's house; and—   45

CAESAR
  What, Octavia?

OCTAVIA   I'll tell you in your ear.
                          [*She whispers to Caesar.*]

ANTONY
  Her tongue will not obey her heart, nor can   47
  Her heart inform her tongue—the swan's down
    feather,   48
  That stands upon the swell at full of tide,   49
  And neither way inclines.   50

ENOBARBUS [*aside to Agrippa*]   Will Caesar weep?

AGRIPPA [*aside to Enobarbus*]   He has a cloud in 's face.

ENOBARBUS [*aside to Agrippa*]
  He were the worse for that, were he a horse;   53
  So is he, being a man.

AGRIPPA [*aside to Enobarbus*]   Why, Enobarbus,
  When Antony found Julius Caesar dead,
  He cried almost to roaring; and he wept
  When at Philippi he found Brutus slain.

ENOBARBUS [*aside to Agrippa*]
  That year indeed he was troubled with a rheum.   58
  What willingly he did confound he wailed,   59
  Believe 't, till I wept too.

CAESAR   No, sweet Octavia,
  You shall hear from me still. The time shall not   61
  Outgo my thinking on you.

ANTONY   Come, sir, come,   62
  I'll wrestle with you in my strength of love.
  Look, here I have you [*embracing him*]; thus I let
    you go,
  And give you to the gods.

CAESAR   Adieu. Be happy!

LEPIDUS
  Let all the number of the stars give light
  To thy fair way!

CAESAR   Farewell, farewell!   *Kisses Octavia.*

ANTONY   Farewell!
          Trumpets sound. Exeunt [in separate groups].

                              ❖

3.3   *Enter Cleopatra, Charmian, Iras, and Alexas.*

CLEOPATRA
  Where is the fellow?

---

12 **Arabian bird** i.e., the fabled phoenix. (Only one existed at a time; it re-created itself by arising from its ashes.) 16 **figures** figures of speech 17 **cast** calculate. **number** write verses 20 **shards** patches of dung, or, perhaps, wings or wing-cases, i.e., protectors, patrons 21 **This is to horse** i.e., the trumpet call gives the signal to depart 23 **No further** i.e., you need not go on urging your point, or, you need accompany me no further 26–27 **as . . . approof** such that my utmost bond shall be justified in certifying what you will prove to be 28 **piece** masterpiece 32 **mean** intermediary, or means 34 **In** by. **I have said** i.e., I stand by what I've said 35 **curious** overly inquisitive or touchy

45 **husband's house** i.e., Antony's house, as at 2.7.130, though Octavia is also a widow; see 3.3.29 47–50 **Her . . . inclines** i.e., her conflicting emotions make her unable to speak aloud, like a swan's down feather floating at full tide, moving neither up nor down stream 53 **He . . . horse** (Alludes to the belief that a horse without any light coloring on its face was apt to be bad-tempered.) 58 **rheum** i.e., running at the eyes. (Said of any discharge of secretion from the head.) 59 **confound** destroy. **wailed** bewailed 61 **still** regularly 61–62 **The time . . . you** time itself will not outlast my thinking of you

3.3. Location: Alexandria. Cleopatra's palace.

ALEXAS   Half afeard to come.
CLEOPATRA
Go to, go to.

Enter the Messenger as before.

Come hither, sir.
ALEXAS   Good Majesty,   2
Herod of Jewry dare not look upon you   3
But when you are well pleased.
CLEOPATRA   That Herod's head
I'll have; but how, when Antony is gone,
Through whom I might command it?—Come thou
    near.
MESSENGER   Most gracious Majesty!
CLEOPATRA   Didst thou behold Octavia?
MESSENGER
Ay, dread Queen.
CLEOPATRA   Where?
MESSENGER   Madam, in Rome.
I looked her in the face, and saw her led
Between her brother and Mark Antony.
CLEOPATRA
Is she as tall as me?
MESSENGER   She is not, madam.
CLEOPATRA
Didst hear her speak? Is she shrill-tongued or low?
MESSENGER
Madam, I heard her speak. She is low-voiced.
CLEOPATRA
That's not so good. He cannot like her long.   15
CHARMIAN
Like her! O Isis, 'tis impossible.
CLEOPATRA
I think so, Charmian. Dull of tongue, and
    dwarfish.—
What majesty is in her gait? Remember,
If e'er thou looked'st on majesty.
MESSENGER   She creeps:
Her motion and her station are as one.   20
She shows a body rather than a life,   21
A statue than a breather.
CLEOPATRA   Is this certain?   22
MESSENGER
Or I have no observance.
CHARMIAN   Three in Egypt   23
Cannot make better note.
CLEOPATRA   He's very knowing,   24
I do perceive 't. There's nothing in her yet.
The fellow has good judgment.
CHARMIAN   Excellent.
CLEOPATRA   Guess at her years, I prithee.
MESSENGER   Madam,
She was a widow—

CLEOPATRA   Widow? Charmian, hark.
MESSENGER   And I do think she's thirty.
CLEOPATRA
Bear'st thou her face in mind? Is 't long or round?
MESSENGER   Round, even to faultiness.
CLEOPATRA
For the most part, too, they are foolish that are so.—
Her hair, what color?
MESSENGER   Brown, madam; and her forehead
As low as she would wish it.   36
CLEOPATRA [*giving money*]   There's gold for thee.
Thou must not take my former sharpness ill.
I will employ thee back again; I find thee   39
Most fit for business. Go make thee ready;
Our letters are prepared.   [*Exit Messenger.*]
CHARMIAN   A proper man.   41
CLEOPATRA
Indeed, he is so. I repent me much
That so I harried him. Why, methinks, by him,   43
This creature's no such thing.
CHARMIAN   Nothing, madam.   44
CLEOPATRA
The man hath seen some majesty, and should know.
CHARMIAN
Hath he seen majesty? Isis else defend,   46
And serving you so long!   47
CLEOPATRA
I have one thing more to ask him yet, good
    Charmian—
But 'tis no matter; thou shalt bring him to me
Where I will write. All may be well enough.
CHARMIAN   I warrant you, madam.   *Exeunt.* 51

3.4   *Enter Antony and Octavia.*

ANTONY
Nay, nay, Octavia, not only that—
That were excusable, that and thousands more
Of semblable import—but he hath waged   3
New wars 'gainst Pompey; made his will, and
    read it   4
To public ear;
Spoke scantly of me; when perforce he could not   6
But pay me terms of honor, cold and sickly
He vented them, most narrow measure lent me;   8
When the best hint was given him, he not took 't,   9
Or did it from his teeth.
OCTAVIA   O my good lord,   10

2 **Go to** (An expression of impatience.)   3 **Herod of Jewry** i.e., even
the famous tyrant who slaughtered the children. (See 1.2.29–30.)
15 **not so good** i.e., not so good for her   20 **Her . . . one** i.e., she
moves with so little animation that it's all the same whether she's
moving or standing   21 **shows** appears as   22 **breather** living being
23–24 **Three . . . note** there are not three people in Egypt who are
better observers

36 **As . . . it** i.e., such that she wouldn't wish it to be any lower. (A
colloquial way of suggesting she is ugly; high foreheads were thought
more beautiful.)   39 **employ . . . again** send you back with a message   41 **proper** good   43 **harried** maltreated.   **by** according to
44 **no such thing** nothing much   46 **else defend** forbid that it be otherwise. (An interjection.)   47 **serving** i.e., he having served   51 **warrant** assure
3.4. Location: Athens.
3 **semblable** similar   4 **read it** (to win the populace by showing them
what benefits they might expect from him)   6 **scantly** slightingly
8 **vented** gave vent to, expressed.   **narrow measure lent me** gave me
small credit   9 **hint** occasion (to praise Antony)   10 **from his teeth**
i.e., between clenched teeth, not from the heart

Believe not all, or, if you must believe,
Stomach not all. A more unhappy lady,   12
If this division chance, ne'er stood between,   13
Praying for both parts.
The good gods will mock me presently   15
When I shall pray, "O, bless my lord and husband!"
Undo that prayer by crying out as loud,   17
"O, bless my brother!" Husband win, win brother,
Prays and destroys the prayer; no midway
Twixt these extremes at all.
ANTONY   Gentle Octavia,
Let your best love draw to that point which seeks   21
Best to preserve it. If I lose mine honor,   22
I lose myself; better I were not yours
Than yours so branchless. But, as you requested,   24
Yourself shall go between 's. The meantime, lady,   25
I'll raise the preparation of a war   26
Shall stain your brother. Make your soonest haste;   27
So your desires are yours.
OCTAVIA   Thanks to my lord.   28
The Jove of power make me, most weak, most
     weak,
Your reconciler! Wars twixt you twain would be
As if the world should cleave, and that slain men   31
Should solder up the rift.   32
ANTONY
When it appears to you where this begins,   33
Turn your displeasure that way, for our faults   34
Can never be so equal that your love   35
Can equally move with them. Provide your going;   36
Choose your own company and command what cost
Your heart has mind to.   *Exeunt.*

❧

3.5   *Enter Enobarbus and Eros, [meeting].*

ENOBARBUS   How now, friend Eros?
EROS   There's strange news come, sir.
ENOBARBUS   What, man?
EROS   Caesar and Lepidus have made wars upon Pompey.
ENOBARBUS   This is old. What is the success?   6
EROS   Caesar, having made use of him in the wars   7
'gainst Pompey, presently denied him rivality, would   8
not let him partake in the glory of the action; and, not

resting here, accuses him of letters he had formerly   10
wrote to Pompey; upon his own appeal seizes him.   11
So the poor third is up, till death enlarge his confine. 12
ENOBARBUS
Then, world, thou hast a pair of chops, no more;   13
And throw between them all the food thou hast,
They'll grind the one the other. Where's Antony?   15
EROS
He's walking in the garden—thus, and spurns   16
The rush that lies before him; cries, "Fool Lepidus!" 17
And threats the throat of that his officer   18
That murdered Pompey.
ENOBARBUS   Our great navy's rigged.   19
EROS
For Italy and Caesar. More, Domitius: 20
My lord desires you presently. My news   21
I might have told hereafter.
ENOBARBUS   'Twill be naught,
But let it be. Bring me to Antony.
EROS   Come, sir. *Exeunt.*

❧

3.6   *Enter Agrippa, Maecenas, and Caesar.*

CAESAR
Contemning Rome, he has done all this and more   1
In Alexandria. Here's the manner of 't:
I' the marketplace, on a tribunal silvered,   3
Cleopatra and himself in chairs of gold
Were publicly enthroned. At the feet sat
Caesarion, whom they call my father's son,   6
And all the unlawful issue that their lust
Since then hath made between them. Unto her
He gave the stablishment of Egypt, made her   9
Of lower Syria, Cyprus, Lydia,
Absolute queen.
MAECENAS   This in the public eye?
CAESAR
I' the common showplace, where they exercise.   12
His sons he there proclaimed the kings of kings:
Great Media, Parthia, and Armenia
He gave to Alexander; to Ptolemy he assigned
Syria, Cilicia, and Phoenicia. She

---

12 Stomach resent **13 chance** occur **15 presently** immediately
17 Undo i.e., and then undo, or, I shall undo **21–22 Let . . . it** let
your warmest love be given to that one of us who seeks to preserve it
(your love) best **24 branchless** pruned (of honor) **25 The meantime**
in the meantime **26–27 I'll . . . brother** I'll raise an army that will
deprive your brother of his luster **28 So . . . yours** i.e., thus you
have obtained your desire (to go). (Or, *so* may mean "as long as.")
31 cleave split **32 Should** would be needed to **33 where this begins** who started this quarrel **34 our** i.e., Caesar's and mine
34–36 our faults . . . them i.e., you will have to judge between our
faults and choose **36 Provide** make arrangements for
3.5. Location: Athens.
6 success outcome, result **7 him** i.e., Lepidus **8 presently** immediately. **rivality** rights of a partner. (Caesar and Lepidus have newly
gone to war against Pompey and have defeated him.)

10 resting here stopping with this insult **11 his own appeal** Caesar's
own accusation **12 up** shut up (in prison). **enlarge his confine** set
him free **13 pair of chops** two jaws. **no more** no more than one
pair, no third partner **15 They'll . . . other** the jaws will still grind
against each other, grind each other down **16 thus** (Eros imitates
Antony's angry walk.) **spurns** kicks **17 rush** strewn rushes
18 threats the throat i.e., threatens the life. **that his officer** that officer of his (Antony's) **19 Pompey** (After his defeat by Caesar and
Lepidus, Pompey was murdered—perhaps, according to history, on
Antony's orders, but here Antony blames his officer for killing Pompey, because he might have been a useful ally against Caesar.)
20 More I have more to say **21 presently** immediately
3.6. Location: Rome.
1 Contemning disdaining **3 tribunal** seat of state, dais **6 my father's**
i.e., Julius Caesar's. (Julius Caesar had adopted his grandnephew Octavius as his son.) **9 stablishment** settled possession **12 exercise** indulge in vulgar entertainments and sports, or, possibly, perform ceremonial functions

In th' habiliments of the goddess Isis   17
That day appeared, and oft before gave audience,
As 'tis reported, so.   19
MAECENAS   Let Rome be thus informed.
AGRIPPA
Who, queasy with his insolence already,   21
Will their good thoughts call from him.   22
CAESAR
The people knows it, and have now received
His accusations.
AGRIPPA   Who does he accuse?
CAESAR
Caesar, and that, having in Sicily
Sextus Pompeius spoiled, we had not rated him   26
His part o' th' isle. Then does he say he lent me   27
Some shipping, unrestored. Lastly, he frets   28
That Lepidus of the triumvirate   29
Should be deposed, and, being, that we detain   30
All his revenue.
AGRIPPA   Sir, this should be answered.
CAESAR
'Tis done already, and the messenger gone.
I have told him Lepidus was grown too cruel,
That he his high authority abused
And did deserve his change. For what I have
    conquered,   35
I grant him part; but then in his Armenia,
And other of his conquered kingdoms, I
Demand the like.
MAECENAS   He'll never yield to that.
CAESAR
Nor must not then be yielded to in this.

Enter Octavia with her train.

OCTAVIA
Hail, Caesar, and my lord! Hail, most dear Caesar!
CAESAR
That ever I should call thee castaway!
OCTAVIA
You have not called me so, nor have you cause.
CAESAR
Why have you stol'n upon us thus? You come not
Like Caesar's sister. The wife of Antony
Should have an army for an usher and
The neighs of horse to tell of her approach   46
Long ere she did appear. The trees by th' way   47
Should have borne men, and expectation fainted,
Longing for what it had not. Nay, the dust
Should have ascended to the roof of heaven,
Raised by your populous troops. But you are come
A market maid to Rome, and have prevented   52

The ostentation of our love, which, left unshown,   53
Is often left unloved. We should have met you   54
By sea and land, supplying every stage   55
With an augmented greeting.
OCTAVIA   Good my lord,
To come thus was I not constrained, but did it
On my free will. My lord, Mark Antony,
Hearing that you prepared for war, acquainted
My grievèd ear withal, whereon I begged
His pardon for return.
CAESAR   Which soon he granted,   61
Being an obstruct 'tween his lust and him.   62
OCTAVIA
Do not say so, my lord.
CAESAR   I have eyes upon him,
And his affairs come to me on the wind.
Where is he now?
OCTAVIA   My lord, in Athens.
CAESAR
No, my most wrongèd sister. Cleopatra
Hath nodded him to her. He hath given his empire
Up to a whore; who now are levying   69
The kings o' th' earth for war. He hath assembled
Bocchus, the King of Libya; Archelaus,
Of Cappadocia; Philadelphos, King
Of Paphlagonia; the Thracian king, Adallas;
King Manchus of Arabia; King of Pont;
Herod of Jewry; Mithridates, King
Of Comagene; Polemon and Amyntas,
The Kings of Mede and Lycaonia,
With a more larger list of scepters.   78
OCTAVIA   Ay me, most wretched,
That have my heart parted betwixt two friends
That does afflict each other!
CAESAR   Welcome hither.
Your letters did withhold our breaking forth   82
Till we perceived both how you were wrong led
And we in negligent danger. Cheer your heart.   84
Be you not troubled with the time, which drives   85
O'er your content these strong necessities,   86
But let determined things to destiny   87
Hold unbewailed their way. Welcome to Rome,   88
Nothing more dear to me. You are abused   89
Beyond the mark of thought, and the high gods,   90

---

53 ostentation ceremonial display   **53–54 which . . . unloved** i.e., a love that is not given proper outward display often remains unexercised and dwindles into neglect. (Also, Caesar wants the display of love to be seen publicly.)   **55 stage** stage of your journey   **61 pardon** permission   **62 Being . . . him** i.e., since your return to Rome removed the obstacle between him and the gratification of his desires   **69 who** i.e., and they   **78 a more larger** an even longer   **82 withhold** restrain.   **breaking forth** attacking   **84 negligent danger** danger through negligence   **85 the time** the present state of affairs   **85–86 drives . . . necessities** drives these strong necessities over your happiness as a team of animals might drive a chariot, trampling your happiness underfoot   **87–88 let . . . way** allow inevitable events to go unbewailed to their destined conclusion   **89 Nothing . . . me** i.e., you who are more dear to me than anything   **90 mark** reach   **90–92 the high . . . you** i.e., the high gods (here a single concept) make us and those that love you their ministers of justice in your cause

---

17 habiliments attire   **19 so** i.e., dressed as Isis, the Egyptian goddess of the moon and fertility   **21 queasy** nauseated, "fed up." (Refers to the Roman people.)   **22 call** withdraw   **26 spoiled** despoiled, plundered.   **rated him** allotted to Antony   **27 th' isle** i.e., Sicily   **28 unrestored** i.e., that I did not return to him   **29 of** from   **30 being** having been deposed   **35 For** as for   **46 horse** horses   **47 by** along   **52 prevented** forestalled (by your too-early arrival)

To do you justice, makes his ministers 91
Of us and those that love you. Best of comfort, 92
And ever welcome to us.
AGRIPPA Welcome, lady.
MAECENAS Welcome, dear madam.
Each heart in Rome does love and pity you.
Only th' adulterous Antony, most large 97
In his abominations, turns you off 98
And gives his potent regiment to a trull 99
That noises it against us.
OCTAVIA   Is it so, sir? 100
CAESAR
Most certain. Sister, welcome. Pray you
Be ever known to patience. My dear'st sister! *Exeunt.* 102

❖

3.7   *Enter Cleopatra and Enobarbus.*

CLEOPATRA
I will be even with thee, doubt it not.
ENOBARBUS But why, why, why?
CLEOPATRA
Thou hast forspoke my being in these wars, 3
And sayst it is not fit.
ENOBARBUS   Well, is it, is it? 4
CLEOPATRA
If not denounced against us, why should not we 5
Be there in person?
ENOBARBUS [*aside*]   Well, I could reply.
If we should serve with horse and mares together, 7
The horse were merely lost; the mares would bear 8
A soldier and his horse.
CLEOPATRA   What is 't you say?
ENOBARBUS
Your presence needs must puzzle Antony, 10
Take from his heart, take from his brain, from 's time
What should not then be spared. He is already
Traduced for levity, and 'tis said in Rome 13
That Photinus, an eunuch, and your maids 14
Manage this war.
CLEOPATRA   Sink Rome, and their tongues rot
That speak against us! A charge we bear i' the war, 16
And as the president of my kingdom will
Appear there for a man. Speak not against it. 18

I will not stay behind.

Enter Antony and Canidius.

ENOBARBUS   Nay, I have done.
Here comes the Emperor.
ANTONY   Is it not strange, Canidius,
That from Tarentum and Brundusium
He could so quickly cut the Ionian sea 22
And take in Toryne?—You have heard on 't, sweet? 23
CLEOPATRA
Celerity is never more admired 24
Than by the negligent.
ANTONY ,   A good rebuke,
Which might have well becomed the best of men, 26
To taunt at slackness. Canidius, we
Will fight with him by sea.
CLEOPATRA   By sea, what else?
CANIDIUS Why will my lord do so?
ANTONY For that he dares us to 't. 30
ENOBARBUS
So hath my lord dared him to single fight.
CANIDIUS
Ay, and to wage this battle at Pharsalia,
Where Caesar fought with Pompey. But these offers,
Which serve not for his vantage, he shakes off,
And so should you.
ENOBARBUS   Your ships are not well manned;
Your mariners are muleteers, reapers, people 36
Engrossed by swift impress. In Caesar's fleet 37
Are those that often have 'gainst Pompey fought;
Their ships are yare, yours heavy. No disgrace 39
Shall fall you for refusing him at sea, 40
Being prepared for land.
ANTONY   By sea, by sea.
ENOBARBUS
Most worthy sir, you therein throw away
The absolute soldiership you have by land,
Distract your army, which doth most consist 44
Of war-marked footmen, leave unexecuted 45
Your own renownèd knowledge, quite forgo
The way which promises assurance, and
Give up yourself merely to chance and hazard 48
From firm security.
ANTONY   I'll fight at sea.
CLEOPATRA
I have sixty sails, Caesar none better.
ANTONY
Our overplus of shipping will we burn,
And with the rest full-manned, from th' head of
Actium 52

97 **large** unrestrained 98 **turns you off** rejects you 99 **regiment**
government, rule. **trull** prostitute 100 **noises it** is clamorous
102 **known to patience** patient
**3.7. Location: Near Actium, on the northwestern coast of Greece.
Antony's camp.**
3 **forspoke** spoken against 4 **fit** appropriate 5 **If . . . us** i.e., even if
the war were not declared against me (which it is) 7, 8 **horse** stal-
lions 8 **merely** utterly 10 **puzzle** bewilder 13 **Traduced** criticized,
censured 14 **an eunuch** (Probably Mardian. In North's Plutarch, Caesar complains that "Mardian the eunuch, Photinus, and Iras . . . and
Charmian . . . ruled the affairs of Antonius' empire." But Photinus
[or Pothinus] was a eunuch, too.) 16 **charge** responsibility, cost
18 **for** in the capacity of

22 **Ionian** (Often applied to the Aegean, but here the Adriatic. Tarentum and Brundusium or Brundisium are in the "heel" of Italy, across
the Adriatic from Actium and Toryne.) 23 **take in** conquer 24 **Celerity** swiftness. **admired** wondered at 26 **becomed** become, suited
30 **For that** because 36 **muleteers** mule-drivers, peasants 37 **Engrossed** collected wholesale. **impress** impressment, conscription
39 **yare** quick, maneuverable 40 **fall** befall 44 **Distract** divide, divert, confuse the purpose of. **most** for the most part 45 **footmen**
foot soldiers. **unexecuted** unused 48 **merely** entirely 52 **head**
promontory

Beat th' approaching Caesar. But if we fail,
We then can do 't at land.

Enter a Messenger.

           Thy business?

MESSENGER
The news is true, my lord; he is descried.   55
Caesar has taken Toryne.
ANTONY
Can he be there in person? 'Tis impossible;
Strange that his power should be. Canidius,   58
Our nineteen legions thou shalt hold by land,
And our twelve thousand horse. We'll to our ship.
Away, my Thetis!

Enter a Soldier.

           How now, worthy soldier?   61

SOLDIER
O noble Emperor, do not fight by sea;
Trust not to rotten planks. Do you misdoubt
This sword and these my wounds? Let th' Egyptians
And the Phoenicians go a-ducking; we   65
Have used to conquer standing on the earth   66
And fighting foot to foot.
ANTONY   Well, well, away!
Exeunt Antony, Cleopatra, and Enobarbus.
SOLDIER
By Hercules, I think I am i' the right.
CANIDIUS
Soldier, thou art; but his whole action grows   69
Not in the power on 't. So our leader's led,   70
And we are women's men.
SOLDIER   You keep by land   71
The legions and the horse whole, do you not?   72
CANIDIUS
Marcus Octavius, Marcus Justeius,
Publicola, and Caelius are for sea;
But we keep whole by land. This speed of Caesar's
Carries beyond belief.   76
SOLDIER   While he was yet in Rome
His power went out in such distractions as   78
Beguiled all spies.
CANIDIUS   Who's his lieutenant, hear you?
SOLDIER
They say, one Taurus.
CANIDIUS   Well I know the man.

Enter a Messenger.

MESSENGER   The Emperor calls Canidius.

CANIDIUS
With news the time's in labor, and throws forth   82
Each minute some.   *Exeunt.* 83

❧

3.8 *Enter Caesar [and Taurus] with his army, marching.*

CAESAR   Taurus!
TAURUS   My lord?
CAESAR
Strike not by land; keep whole. Provoke not battle
Till we have done at sea. Do not exceed
The prescript of this scroll. [*He gives a scroll.*] Our
    fortune lies   5
Upon this jump.   *Exeunt.* 6

3.9 *Enter Antony and Enobarbus.*

ANTONY
Set we our squadrons on yond side o' the hill,
In eye of Caesar's battle, from which place   2
We may the number of the ships behold
And so proceed accordingly.   *Exeunt.*

3.10 *Canidius marcheth with his land army one way over the stage, and Taurus, the lieutenant of Caesar, the other way. After their going in is heard the noise of a sea fight.*

Alarum. Enter Enobarbus.

ENOBARBUS
Naught, naught, all naught! I can behold no longer.   1
Th' *Antoniad*, the Egyptian admiral,   2
With all their sixty, fly and turn the rudder.
To see 't mine eyes are blasted.

Enter Scarus.

SCARUS   Gods and goddesses,
All the whole synod of them!
ENOBARBUS   What's thy passion?   5
SCARUS
The greater cantle of the world is lost   6
With very ignorance; we have kissed away   7

82–83 With news . . . some more news is born each minute.
throws forth gives birth
3.8. Location: A field near Actium, as before.
5 prescript orders   **6 jump** chance, hazard
3.9. Location: A field near Actium, as before.
2 eye sight.   **battle** battle line
3.10. Location: A field near Actium, as before.
1 Naught i.e., all has come to naught   **2 admiral** flagship   **5 synod** assembly.   **What's** what is the cause of   **6 cantle** corner; hence, piece or part   **7 With very ignorance** through utter stupidity

55 he is descried he has been sighted   **58 his power** i.e., his army, let alone himself   **61 Thetis** sea goddess, the mother of Achilles   **65 go a-ducking** (1) get drenched (2) cringe   **66 Have used** are accustomed.   **standing on the earth** (1) fighting on land (2) standing upright, not *ducking*, or "cringing"   **69–70 his . . . on 't** his whole strategy has been developed without regard to where his power really lies   **71 men** servingmen   **72 horse** cavalry.   **whole** undivided, held in reserve   **76 Carries** surpasses (like an arrow in archery)   **78 distractions** detachments, divisions

Kingdoms and provinces.
ENOBARBUS   How appears the fight?
SCARUS
On our side like the tokened pestilence,   9
Where death is sure. Yon ribaudred nag of Egypt—   10
Whom leprosy o'ertake!—i' the midst o' the fight,
When vantage like a pair of twins appeared   12
Both as the same, or rather ours the elder,   13
The breeze upon her, like a cow in June,   14
Hoists sails and flies.
ENOBARBUS   That I beheld.
Mine eyes did sicken at the sight, and could not
Endure a further view.
SCARUS   She once being loofed,   18
The noble ruin of her magic, Antony,   19
Claps on his sea wing and, like a doting mallard,   20
Leaving the fight in height, flies after her.   21
I never saw an action of such shame.
Experience, manhood, honor, ne'er before
Did violate so itself.
ENOBARBUS   Alack, alack!

Enter Canidius.

CANIDIUS
Our fortune on the sea is out of breath,
And sinks most lamentably. Had our general
Been what he knew himself, it had gone well.
O, he has given example for our flight
Most grossly by his own!
ENOBARBUS
Ay, are you thereabouts? Why then, good night
  indeed.   30
CANIDIUS
Toward Peloponnesus are they fled.   31
SCARUS
'Tis easy to 't, and there I will attend   32
What further comes.
CANIDIUS   To Caesar will I render   33
My legions and my horse. Six kings already   34
Show me the way of yielding.
ENOBARBUS   I'll yet follow
The wounded chance of Antony, though my reason   36
Sits in the wind against me.   [*Exeunt separately.*] 37

❦

3.11   *Enter Antony with attendants.*

ANTONY
Hark! The land bids me tread no more upon 't;
It is ashamed to bear me. Friends, come hither.
I am so lated in the world that I   3
Have lost my way forever. I have a ship
Laden with gold. Take that, divide it; fly,   5
And make your peace with Caesar.
ALL   Fly? Not we.
ANTONY
I have fled myself, and have instructed cowards
To run and show their shoulders. Friends, begone.   8
I have myself resolved upon a course
Which has no need of you. Begone.
My treasure's in the harbor. Take it. O,
I followed that I blush to look upon!   12
My very hairs do mutiny, for the white   13
Reprove the brown for rashness, and they them   14
For fear and doting. Friends, begone. You shall
Have letters from me to some friends that will
Sweep your way for you. Pray you, look not sad,   17
Nor make replies of loathness. Take the hint   18
Which my despair proclaims. Let that be left   19
Which leaves itself. To the seaside straightway!   20
I will possess you of that ship and treasure.
Leave me, I pray, a little. Pray you now,   22
Nay, do so, for indeed I have lost command.   23
Therefore I pray you. I'll see you by and by.   24
          [*Exeunt attendants. Antony*] *sits down.*

Enter Cleopatra led by Charmian, [Iras,] and Eros.

EROS
Nay, gentle madam, to him, comfort him.
IRAS Do, most dear Queen.
CHARMIAN Do; why, what else?
CLEOPATRA Let me sit down. O Juno!
ANTONY No, no, no, no, no.
EROS See you here, sir?
ANTONY O fie, fie, fie!
CHARMIAN Madam!
IRAS Madam, O good Empress!
EROS Sir, sir!
ANTONY
Yes, my lord, yes. He at Philippi kept   35
His sword e'en like a dancer, while I struck   36

---

9 tokened pestilence (Certain red spots appeared on the bodies of the plague-smitten, called tokens.)   **10 ribaudred** foul, obscene   **12–13 When . . . same** i.e., when the advantage was equal on either side   **13 elder** i.e., more advanced, more likely to inherit   **14 breeze** (1) gadfly (2) light wind   **18 loofed** luffed, with ship's head brought close to the wind (with a pun on *aloofed*, "becoming distant")   **19 ruin** object ruined by   **20 Claps . . . sea wing** i.e., hoists sail, preparing for flight like a water bird.   **mallard** drake   **21 in** at its   **30 thereabouts** i.e., of that mind, thinking of desertion.   **good night indeed** i.e., it's all over   **31 Peloponnesus** southern Greece (from which Antony then crosses the Mediterranean to Egypt)   **32 to 't** to get to it.   **attend** await   **33 render** surrender   **34 horse** cavalry   **36 wounded chance** broken fortunes   **37 Sits . . . me** i.e., is on my downwind side, tracking me and hunting me down

3.11. Location: Historically, events such as dispatching the Schoolmaster to Caesar took place in Egypt; however, the dramatic impression of this scene is that it occurs soon after the battle.
3 lated belated, like a traveler still journeying when night falls   **5 fly** flee   **8 shoulders** i.e., backs   **12 that** that which   **13 mutiny** contend among themselves   **14 they them** i.e., the brown hairs reprove the white   **17 Sweep your way** clear your way (to Caesar)   **18 loathness** unwillingness.   **hint** opportunity   **19 that** i.e., Antony and his cause   **20 leaves** is untrue to, deserts   **22 a little** for a moment   **23 lost command** (1) lost command of myself (2) lost command of my troops and my right to command   **24 pray** entreat (as opposed to "command")   **35 Yes . . . yes** (Antony is absorbed in his own bitter thoughts, as also in lines 29 and 31.)   **He** i.e., Octavius.   **kept** kept in its sheath   **36 e'en . . . dancer** i.e., as though for ornament only, in a dance

The lean and wrinkled Cassius, and 'twas I
That the mad Brutus ended. He alone   38
Dealt on lieutenantry, and no practice had   39
In the brave squares of war; yet now—no matter.   40

CLEOPATRA
Ah, stand by.

EROS   The Queen, my lord, the Queen.   41

IRAS
Go to him, madam, speak to him.
He's unqualitied with very shame.   43

CLEOPATRA   Well then, sustain me. O!

EROS
Most noble sir, arise. The Queen approaches.
Her head's declined, and death will seize her but   46
Your comfort makes the rescue.

ANTONY
I have offended reputation,
A most unnoble swerving.

EROS   Sir, the Queen.   49

ANTONY
O, whither hast thou led me, Egypt? See   50
How I convey my shame out of thine eyes   51
By looking back what I have left behind   52
'Stroyed in dishonor.

CLEOPATRA   O my lord, my lord,   53
Forgive my fearful sails! I little thought   54
You would have followed.

ANTONY   Egypt, thou knew'st too well
My heart was to thy rudder tied by th' strings,   56
And thou shouldst tow me after. O'er my spirit
Thy full supremacy thou knew'st, and that
Thy beck might from the bidding of the gods   59
Command me.

CLEOPATRA   O, my pardon!

ANTONY   Now I must   60
To the young man send humble treaties, dodge   61
And palter in the shifts of lowness, who   62
With half the bulk o' the world played as I pleased,
Making and marring fortunes. You did know
How much you were my conqueror, and that
My sword, made weak by my affection, would   66
Obey it on all cause.

CLEOPATRA   Pardon, pardon!   67

ANTONY
Fall not a tear, I say; one of them rates   68

---

38 ended i.e., defeated. (Not *killed*; Brutus and Cassius committed suicide.) **alone** merely   **39 Dealt on lieutenantry** let his subordinates do the fighting   **40 brave squares** splendid squadrons, bodies of troops drawn up in square formation   **41 stand by** (Cleopatra indicates she is about to faint and needs assistance.)   **43 unqualitied** dispossessed of his own nature, i.e., not himself   **46 but** unless   **49 swerving** lapse, transgression   **50–53 See . . . dishonor** i.e., see how I weep, conveying to my eyes the signs of shame that appear in yours, as I look back on the ruin of my fortunes and honor (?)   **54 fearful** frightened   **56 th' strings** (1) the heartstrings (2) towing cable   **59–60 Thy . . . Command me** your mere beckoning would command me away from doing the bidding of the gods themselves   **61 treaties** entreaties, propositions for settlement.   **dodge** shuffle, cringe   **62 palter** use trickery, prevaricate, equivocate.   **shifts of lowness** pitiful evasions used by those lacking power   **66 affection** passion   **67 on all cause** whatever the reason   **68 Fall** let fall.   **rates** equals

---

All that is won and lost. Give me a kiss.   [*They kiss.*]
Even this repays me.—We sent our schoolmaster;   70
Is 'a come back?—Love, I am full of lead.—
Some wine, within there, and our viands! Fortune
   knows   72
We scorn her most when most she offers blows.
                 Exeunt.

❖

3.12   *Enter Caesar, Agrippa, [Thidias,] and Dolabella,*
        with others.

CAESAR
Let him appear that's come from Antony.
Know you him?

DOLABELLA   Caesar, 'tis his schoolmaster—
An argument that he is plucked, when hither   3
He sends so poor a pinion of his wing,   4
Which had superfluous kings for messengers   5
Not many moons gone by.

        Enter Ambassador from Antony.

CAESAR   Approach and speak.

AMBASSADOR
Such as I am, I come from Antony.
I was of late as petty to his ends   8
As is the morn-dew on the myrtle leaf
To his grand sea.

CAESAR   Be 't so. Declare thine office.   10

AMBASSADOR
Lord of his fortunes he salutes thee, and
Requires to live in Egypt; which not granted,   12
He lessens his requests, and to thee sues   13
To let him breathe between the heavens and earth   14
A private man in Athens. This for him.
Next, Cleopatra does confess thy greatness,
Submits her to thy might, and of thee craves
The circle of the Ptolemies for her heirs,   18
Now hazarded to thy grace.

CAESAR   For Antony,   19
I have no ears to his request. The Queen
Of audience nor desire shall fail, so she   21
From Egypt drive her all-disgracèd friend
Or take his life there. This if she perform
She shall not sue unheard. So to them both.   24

AMBASSADOR
Fortune pursue thee!

CAESAR   Bring him through the bands.   25
            [*Exit Ambassador, attended.*]

---

70 Even this this by itself.   **schoolmaster** (Identified in Plutarch as Euphronius, tutor to Antony's children by Cleopatra.)   **72 viands** food
3.12. Location: Egypt. Caesar's camp.
3 An argument an indication   **4 pinion** i.e., pinion-feather, outer feather   **5 Which** who   **8 petty to** insignificant in terms of   **10 To . . . sea** compared to its, the dewdrop's, great source, the sea.   **thine office** your official business   **12 Requires** asks.   **which not granted** and if that request is not granted   **13 sues** petitions   **14 breathe** i.e., live   **18 circle** crown   **19 hazarded . . . grace** dependent on your favor.   **For** as for   **21 Of audience** neither of hearing.   **so** provided that   **24 So** with these terms, go   **25 Bring** escort.   **bands** troops on guard, military lines

[*To Thidias.*] To try thy eloquence now 'tis time.
  Dispatch.
From Antony win Cleopatra. Promise,
And in our name, what she requires; add more,   28
From thine invention, offers. Women are not   29
In their best fortunes strong, but want will perjure   30
The ne'er-touched vestal. Try thy cunning, Thidias.   31
Make thine own edict for thy pains, which we   32
Will answer as a law.
THIDIAS   Caesar, I go.   33
CAESAR
  Observe how Antony becomes his flaw,   34
  And what thou think'st his very action speaks   35
  In every power that moves.
THIDIAS   Caesar, I shall.   *Exeunt.* 36

❖

3.13 *Enter Cleopatra, Enobarbus, Charmian, and Iras.*

CLEOPATRA
  What shall we do, Enobarbus?
ENOBARBUS   Think, and die.   1
CLEOPATRA
  Is Antony or we in fault for this?   2
ENOBARBUS
  Antony only, that would make his will   3
  Lord of his reason. What though you fled
  From that great face of war, whose several ranges   5
  Frighted each other? Why should he follow?
  The itch of his affection should not then   7
  Have nicked his captainship, at such a point,   8
  When half to half the world opposed, he being   9
  The merèd question. 'Twas a shame no less   10
  Than was his loss, to course your flying flags   11
  And leave his navy gazing.
CLEOPATRA   Prithee, peace.

  Enter the Ambassador with Antony.

ANTONY   Is that his answer?
AMBASSADOR   Ay, my lord.
ANTONY
  The Queen shall then have courtesy, so she   15
  Will yield us up.
AMBASSADOR   He says so.
ANTONY   Let her know 't.—
  To the boy Caesar send this grizzled head,

And he will fill thy wishes to the brim
With principalities.
CLEOPATRA   That head, my lord?
ANTONY
  To him again. Tell him he wears the rose
  Of youth upon him, from which the world should
    note
  Something particular. His coin, ships, legions,   22
  May be a coward's, whose ministers would prevail   23
  Under the service of a child as soon
  As i' the command of Caesar. I dare him therefore
  To lay his gay caparisons apart   26
  And answer me declined, sword against sword,   27
  Ourselves alone. I'll write it. Follow me.
              [*Exeunt Antony and Ambassador.*]
ENOBARBUS [*aside*]
  Yes, like enough, high-battled Caesar will   29
  Unstate his happiness and be staged to th' show   30
  Against a sworder! I see men's judgments are   31
  A parcel of their fortunes, and things outward   32
  Do draw the inward quality after them   33
  To suffer all alike. That he should dream,   34
  Knowing all measures, the full Caesar will   35
  Answer his emptiness! Caesar, thou hast subdued   36
  His judgment too.

  Enter a Servant.

SERVANT   A messenger from Caesar.
CLEOPATRA
  What, no more ceremony? See, my women,
  Against the blown rose may they stop their nose   39
  That kneeled unto the buds.—Admit him, sir.
                              [*Exit Servant.*]
ENOBARBUS [*aside*]
  Mine honesty and I begin to square.   41
  The loyalty well held to fools does make   42
  Our faith mere folly; yet he that can endure   43
  To follow with allegiance a fall'n lord
  Does conquer him that did his master conquer   45
  And earns a place i' the story.

  Enter Thidias.

CLEOPATRA   Caesar's will?
THIDIAS
  Hear it apart.
CLEOPATRA   None but friends. Say boldly.   47

---

28 requires asks   **28–29 add . . . offers** add ideas of your own
30 In . . . fortunes even when at the height of their fortune.   **want**
lack, need.   **perjure** cause to break her vows (of chastity)   **31 vestal**
priestess of Vesta, committed to chastity, or, simply, "virgin."   **cunning** skill   **32 Make . . . edict** decree your own reward   **33 answer
as a law** confirm as if it were a law   **34 becomes his flaw** bears his
misfortune and disgrace   **35 speaks** signifies   **36 In . . . moves** in every motion he makes
3.13. Location: Alexandria. Cleopatra's palace.
1 Think i.e., reflect on our grievous situation   **2 we** I   **3 will** desire
(especially sexual)   **5 ranges** ranks, lines (of ships)   **7 affection** sexual
passion   **8 nicked** cut short or damaged (from being nicked), or (from
gaming), got the better of, since a *nick* was a winning throw in a
game of chance.   **point** crisis   **9 half to . . . opposed** the two halves
of the world found themselves in conflict   **10 merèd question** sole
ground of quarrel   **11 course** pursue (as in hunting)   **15 so** provided

22 Something particular some achievement or exploit of his own
23 May be could as well be.   **ministers** agents, subordinates   **26 gay
caparisons** resplendent trappings   **27 answer me declined** meet me as
I am, lowered in fortune and advanced in years   **29 high-battled** provided with or raised up by noble armies   **30 Unstate** depose.   **happiness** good fortune.   **staged to th' show** exhibited publicly, as in a
gladiatorial contest   **31 sworder** one fighting with a sword, a gladiator   **32 A parcel of** of a piece with   **33 quality** nature   **34 To . . .
alike** i.e., so that they deteriorate simultaneously   **35 Knowing all
measures** i.e., having experienced every degree of fortune.   **full** at
full fortune   **36 Answer** (1) meet man to man (2) correspond with
39 blown overblown, starting to decay   **41 honesty** (With meaning
also of "honor.")   **42–43 The . . . folly** a stubborn
loyalty bestowed on fools is folly itself   **45 Does . . . conquer** i.e.,
achieves a moral victory over the very fortune that subdued one's
own master   **47 apart** in private

THIDIAS
So haply are they friends to Antony.   48

ENOBARBUS
He needs as many, sir, as Caesar has,
Or needs not us. If Caesar please, our master   50
Will leap to be his friend. For us, you know   51
Whose he is we are, and that is Caesar's.

THIDIAS   So.   52
Thus then, thou most renowned: Caesar entreats
Not to consider in what case thou stand'st   54
Further than he is Caesar.

CLEOPATRA   Go on: right royal.   55

THIDIAS
He knows that you embrace not Antony
As you did love, but as you feared him.

CLEOPATRA   O!

THIDIAS
The scars upon your honor therefore he
Does pity as constrainèd blemishes,   59
Not as deserved.

CLEOPATRA   He is a god and knows
What is most right. Mine honor was not yielded,   61
But conquered merely.

ENOBARBUS [aside]   To be sure of that,   62
I will ask Antony. Sir, sir, thou art so leaky
That we must leave thee to thy sinking, for
Thy dearest quit thee.   Exit Enobarbus.

THIDIAS   Shall I say to Caesar
What you require of him? For he partly begs   66
To be desired to give. It much would please him
That of his fortunes you should make a staff
To lean upon; but it would warm his spirits
To hear from me you had left Antony
And put yourself under his shroud,   71
The universal landlord.

CLEOPATRA   What's your name?

THIDIAS
My name is Thidias.

CLEOPATRA   Most kind messenger,
Say to great Caesar this in deputation: 74
I kiss his conquering hand. Tell him I am prompt   75
To lay my crown at 's feet, and there to kneel
Till from his all-obeying breath I hear   77
The doom of Egypt.

THIDIAS   'Tis your noblest course.   78
Wisdom and fortune combating together,   79
If that the former dare but what it can,   80

No chance may shake it. Give me grace to lay   81
My duty on your hand.   [He kisses her hand.]

CLEOPATRA   Your Caesar's father oft,   83
When he hath mused of taking kingdoms in,   84
Bestowed his lips on that unworthy place,
As it rained kisses.

Enter Antony and Enobarbus.

ANTONY   Favors? By Jove that thunders!   86
What art thou, fellow?

THIDIAS   One that but performs
The bidding of the fullest man, and worthiest   88
To have command obeyed.

ENOBARBUS [aside]   You will be whipped.

ANTONY [calling for Servants]
Approach, there!—Ah, you kite!—Now, gods and
   devils!   90
Authority melts from me of late. When I cried
   "Ho!",
Like boys unto a muss kings would start forth   92
And cry, "Your will?"—Have you no ears? I am
Antony yet.

Enter a Servant [followed by others].

          Take hence this jack and whip him.   94

ENOBARBUS [aside]
'Tis better playing with a lion's whelp   95
Than with an old one dying.

ANTONY   Moon and stars!
Whip him. Were 't twenty of the greatest tributaries   97
That do acknowledge Caesar, should I find them
So saucy with the hand of she here—what's her
   name
Since she was Cleopatra? Whip him, fellows,
Till like a boy you see him cringe his face   101
And whine aloud for mercy. Take him hence.

THIDIAS
Mark Antony—

ANTONY   Tug him away! Being whipped,
Bring him again. This jack of Caesar's shall
Bear us an errand to him.
           Exeunt [Servants] with Thidias.
[To Cleopatra.] You were half blasted ere I knew you.
   Ha?   106
Have I my pillow left unpressed in Rome,
Forborne the getting of a lawful race,   108
And by a gem of women, to be abused   109
By one that looks on feeders?   110

CLEOPATRA   Good my lord—

---

48 **haply** perhaps 50 **Or . . . us** i.e., or else he doesn't need even us, his case being hopeless 51 **For** as for 52 **Whose . . . Caesar's** i.e., we are Antony's friends, and he is Caesar's, so that we, too, are Caesar's 54–55 **Not . . . Caesar** i.e., not to worry about your situation other than to consider that you are dealing with Caesar, the embodiment of magnanimity 55 **right royal** i.e., that is very magnanimous 59 **constrainèd** forced upon you 61 **right** true 62 **merely** utterly 66 **require** ask. **partly** i.e., as commensurate with his dignity 71 **shroud** shelter (with suggestion too of a burial cloth) 74 **in deputation** by you as deputy 75 **prompt** ready 77 **all-obeying** obeyed by all 78 **The doom of Egypt** i.e., my fate 79–81 **Wisdom . . . shake it** i.e., if, when fortune afflicts the wise, they dare to do only what they know they can do (thus accepting the inevitable), no ill fortune can harm them. (If you submit to the fortunate Caesar, you will be all right.)

83 **Your Caesar's father** i.e., Julius Caesar, actually Octavius' great-uncle. (See note at 3.6.6.) 84 **mused . . . in** thought about conquering kingdoms 86 **As** as if. **Favors** (Cleopatra is bestowing special marks of favor on Thidias.) 88 **fullest** most fortunate, best 90 **kite** a rapacious bird of prey that feeds on ignoble objects, and a slang word for "whore." (Said of Cleopatra.) 92 **muss** game in which small objects are thrown down to be scrambled for 94 **jack** fellow. (Contemptuous.) 95 **whelp** cub 97 **tributaries** rulers who paid tribute (to Rome) 101 **cringe** contract in pain 106 **blasted** withered, blighted 108 **getting** begetting. **lawful** legitimate 109 **abused** deceived, betrayed 110 **feeders** servants

ANTONY   You have been a boggler ever.   112
But when we in our viciousness grow hard—
O misery on 't!—the wise gods seel our eyes,   114
In our own filth drop our clear judgments, make us
Adore our errors, laugh at 's while we strut
To our confusion.
CLEOPATRA   O, is 't come to this?   117
ANTONY
I found you as a morsel cold upon
Dead Caesar's trencher; nay, you were a fragment   119
Of Gnaeus Pompey's, besides what hotter hours,   120
Unregistered in vulgar fame, you have   121
Luxuriously picked out. For I am sure,   122
Though you can guess what temperance should be,
You know not what it is.
CLEOPATRA   Wherefore is this?   124
ANTONY
To let a fellow that will take rewards
And say "God quit you!" be familiar with   126
My playfellow, your hand, this kingly seal
And plighter of high hearts! O, that I were   128
Upon the hill of Basan, to outroar   129
The hornèd herd! For I have savage cause,   130
And to proclaim it civilly were like
A haltered neck which does the hangman thank
For being yare about him.

Enter a Servant with Thidias.

    Is he whipped?   133
SERVANT   Soundly, my lord.
ANTONY   Cried he? And begged 'a pardon?
SERVANT   He did ask favor.
ANTONY [*to Thidias*]
If that thy father live, let him repent
Thou wast not made his daughter; and be thou sorry
To follow Caesar in his triumph, since
Thou hast been whipped for following him.
   Henceforth
The white hand of a lady fever thee;   141
Shake thou to look on 't. Get thee back to Caesar.
Tell him thy entertainment. Look thou say   143
He makes me angry with him; for he seems
Proud and disdainful, harping on what I am,
Not what he knew I was. He makes me angry,
And at this time most easy 'tis to do 't,
When my good stars, that were my former guides,
Have empty left their orbs and shot their fires   149
Into th' abysm of hell. If he mislike   150

My speech and what is done, tell him he has
Hipparchus, my enfranchèd bondman, whom   152
He may at pleasure whip, or hang, or torture,
As he shall like, to quit me. Urge it thou.   154
Hence with thy stripes, begone!
    Exit [*Servant with*] *Thidias.*
CLEOPATRA   Have you done yet?
ANTONY
Alack, our terrene moon is now eclipsed,   156
And it portends alone the fall of Antony.
CLEOPATRA   I must stay his time.   158
ANTONY
To flatter Caesar, would you mingle eyes
With one that ties his points?
CLEOPATRA   Not know me yet?   160
ANTONY
Coldhearted toward me?
CLEOPATRA   Ah, dear, if I be so,
From my cold heart let heaven engender hail,
And poison it in the source, and the first stone
Drop in my neck; as it determines, so   164
Dissolve my life! The next Caesarion smite,
Till by degrees the memory of my womb,   166
Together with my brave Egyptians all,   167
By the discandying of this pelleted storm   168
Lie graveless till the flies and gnats of Nile
Have buried them for prey!
ANTONY   I am satisfied.   170
Caesar sits down in Alexandria, where   171
I will oppose his fate. Our force by land   172
Hath nobly held; our severed navy too
Have knit again, and fleet, threat'ning most sealike.   174
Where hast thou been, my heart? Dost thou hear,
   lady?   175
If from the field I shall return once more
To kiss these lips, I will appear in blood;   177
I and my sword will earn our chronicle.   178
There's hope in 't yet.
CLEOPATRA   That's my brave lord!
ANTONY
I will be treble-sinewed, hearted, breathed,   181
And fight maliciously. For when mine hours   182
Were nice and lucky, men did ransom lives   183
Of me for jests; but now I'll set my teeth   184

---

112 **boggler** waverer, shifty person. (Often used of shying horses.) 114 **seel** blind. (A term in falconry for sewing shut the eyes of wild hawks in order to tame them.) 117 **confusion** destruction 119 **trencher** wooden plate. **fragment** leftover 120 **Gnaeus Pompey's** (See 1.5.32 and note.) 121 **vulgar fame** common gossip 122 **Luxuriously** lustfully 124 **Wherefore is this** i.e., what brought this on? 126 **quit** reward. (*God quit you* is said obsequiously to acknowledge a tip.) 128 **plighter** pledger 129–130 **hill of Basan . . . The hornèd herd** (Allusion to the strong bulls of Bashan, Psalms 22:12 and 68:15. Antony imagines himself as the greatest horned beast, i.e., cuckold, of that herd.) 133 **yare** deft, quick 141 **fever thee** make you shiver 143 **entertainment** reception. **Look** be sure that 149 **orbs** spheres 150 **abysm** abyss

152 **Hipparchus** (According to Plutarch, the man was a deserter to Caesar's side.) **enfranchèd** enfranchised, freed 154 **quit** requite, pay back 156 **terrene moon** (Antony considers Cleopatra his earthly [*terrene*] moon; her eclipse dooms him.) 158 **stay his time** i.e., be patient until his fury has subsided 160 **his** Caesar's. **points** laces by which articles of clothing were secured 164 **neck** throat or head. **determines** comes to an end, dissolves (see line 168) 166 **memory of my womb** i.e., my offspring 167 **brave** splendid (also in line 180) 168 **discandying** melting. **pelleted** falling in pellets 170 **for prey** i.e., by eating them 171 **sits down in** lays siege to 172 **oppose his fate** confront his (seemingly irresistible) fortune 174 **fleet** float 175 **heart** courage 177 **in blood** (1) bloody from battle (2) fullspirited 178 **chronicle** place in history 181 **hearted** treble-hearted. **breathed** treble-breathed 182 **maliciously** violently, fiercely 183 **nice** delicate, fastidious, able to appreciate chivalrous niceties 183–184 **men . . . jests** i.e., I allowed enemies to be ransomed for trifles or as a magnanimous gesture

And send to darkness all that stop me. Come,   185
Let's have one other gaudy night. Call to me   186
All my sad captains. Fill our bowls once more;
Let's mock the midnight bell.
CLEOPATRA   It is my birthday.
I had thought t' have held it poor; but since my lord   189
Is Antony again, I will be Cleopatra.
ANTONY   We will yet do well.
CLEOPATRA [to attendants]
Call all his noble captains to my lord.
ANTONY
Do so. We'll speak to them, and tonight I'll force
The wine peep through their scars. Come on, my
    queen,
There's sap in 't yet. The next time I do fight   195
I'll make Death love me, for I will contend   196
Even with his pestilent scythe.   197
                           Exeunt [all but Enobarbus].

ENOBARBUS
Now he'll outstare the lightning. To be furious   198
Is to be frighted out of fear, and in that mood
The dove will peck the estridge; and I see still   200
A diminution in our captain's brain
Restores his heart. When valor preys on reason,   202
It eats the sword it fights with. I will seek   203
Some way to leave him.   Exit.

❖

4.1   Enter Caesar, Agrippa, and Maecenas, with his
          army, Caesar reading a letter.

CAESAR
He calls me boy, and chides as he had power   1
To beat me out of Egypt. My messenger
He hath whipped with rods, dares me to personal
    combat,
Caesar to Antony. Let the old ruffian know
I have many other ways to die, meantime
Laugh at his challenge.   6
MAECENAS   Caesar must think,
When one so great begins to rage, he's hunted   8
Even to falling. Give him no breath, but now   9
Make boot of his distraction. Never anger   10
Made good guard for itself.
CAESAR   Let our best heads   11
Know that tomorrow the last of many battles
We mean to fight. Within our files there are,   13

Of those that served Mark Antony but late,   14
Enough to fetch him in. See it done,   15
And feast the army; we have store to do 't,   16
And they have earned the waste. Poor Antony!   17
                                          Exeunt.

❖

4.2   Enter Antony, Cleopatra, Enobarbus, Charmian,
          Iras, Alexas, with others.

ANTONY
He will not fight with me, Domitius?
ENOBARBUS   No.
ANTONY   Why should he not?
ENOBARBUS
He thinks, being twenty times of better fortune,
He is twenty men to one.
ANTONY   Tomorrow, soldier,
By sea and land I'll fight. Or I will live   6
Or bathe my dying honor in the blood
Shall make it live again. Woo't thou fight well?   8
ENOBARBUS
I'll strike, and cry, "Take all."
ANTONY   Well said. Come on!   9
Call forth my household servants. Let's tonight   10

        Enter three or four servitors.

Be bounteous at our meal.—Give me thy hand.
Thou hast been rightly honest—so hast thou—   12
Thou—and thou—and thou. You have served me
    well,
And kings have been your fellows.
CLEOPATRA [aside to Enobarbus]   What means this? 14
ENOBARBUS [aside to Cleopatra]
'Tis one of those odd tricks which sorrow shoots
Out of the mind.
ANTONY   And thou art honest too.
I wish I could be made so many men,   17
And all of you clapped up together in   18
An Antony, that I might do you service
So good as you have done.
ALL   The gods forbid!
ANTONY
Well, my good fellows, wait on me tonight:
Scant not my cups, and make as much of me   22
As when mine empire was your fellow too,   23
And suffered my command.
CLEOPATRA [aside to Enobarbus] What does he mean?   24
ENOBARBUS [aside to Cleopatra]
To make his followers weep.
ANTONY   Tend me tonight;

185 **to darkness** i.e., to death, the underworld   186 **gaudy** festive
189 **held it poor** celebrated it simply   195 **sap in 't** i.e., life in our
enterprise   196–197 **I will . . . scythe** i.e., I will outdo even Death
himself and his scythe of *pestilence* or plague. (The contest will be
one of loving emulation, as between two gods.)   198 **outstare** stare
down.   **furious** frenzied   200 **estridge** ostrich, or, a kind of hawk.
still constantly   202–203 **When . . . with** when valor turns to unreasonable fury, it destroys the very quality of reasonableness that valor
depends on in battle
4.1. Location: Before Alexandria. Caesar's camp.
1 **as** if   6 **Laugh** i.e., let him know I laugh   8 **rage** rave   9 **breath**
breathing space   10 **boot** advantage.   **distraction** frenzy   11 **best
heads** commanding officers   13 **files** (As in "rank and file.")

14 **late** lately   15 **fetch him in** surround, capture him   16 **store** provisions   17 **waste** lavish expenditure
4.2. Location: Alexandria. Cleopatra's palace.
6 **Or** either   8 **Shall** that shall.   **Woo't** wilt   9 **strike . . . Take all** (1)
fight to the finish, crying, "Winner take all" (2) strike sail and surrender   10 **s.d. servitors** attendants   12 **honest** true, loyal   14 **fellows**
i.e., fellow servants of me   17 **made . . . men** divided into as many
men as you are   18 **clapped up** combined   22 **Scant not my cups**
i.e., provide generously   23 **fellow** i.e., fellow servant   24 **suffered**
acknowledged, submitted to

May be it is the period of your duty.   26
Haply you shall not see me more, or if,   27
A mangled shadow. Perchance tomorrow   28
You'll serve another master. I look on you
As one that takes his leave. Mine honest friends,
I turn you not away, but, like a master
Married to your good service, stay till death.
Tend me tonight two hours, I ask no more,
And the gods yield you for 't!
ENOBARBUS   What mean you, sir,   34
To give them this discomfort? Look, they weep,
And I, an ass, am onion-eyed. For shame,
Transform us not to women.
ANTONY   Ho, ho, ho!
Now the witch take me if I meant it thus!   38
Grace grow where those drops fall! My hearty
    friends,   39
You take me in too dolorous a sense,
For I spake to you for your comfort, did desire you
To burn this night with torches. Know, my hearts,   42
I hope well of tomorrow, and will lead you
Where rather I'll expect victorious life
Than death and honor. Let's to supper, come,
And drown consideration.   *Exeunt.* 46

♣

4.3   *Enter a company of Soldiers.*

FIRST SOLDIER
Brother, good night. Tomorrow is the day.
SECOND SOLDIER
It will determine one way. Fare you well.   2
Heard you of nothing strange about the streets?   3
FIRST SOLDIER   Nothing. What news?
SECOND SOLDIER
Belike 'tis but a rumor. Good night to you.   5
FIRST SOLDIER   Well, sir, good night.

          They meet other Soldiers.

SECOND SOLDIER   Soldiers, have careful watch.
THIRD SOLDIER   And you. Good night, good night.
          They place themselves in every corner of the stage.
SECOND SOLDIER   Here we. And if tomorrow   9
Our navy thrive, I have an absolute hope
Our landmen will stand up.
FIRST SOLDIER   'Tis a brave army, and full of purpose.   12
          Music of the hautboys is under the stage.
SECOND SOLDIER   Peace! What noise?
FIRST SOLDIER   List, list!   14
SECOND SOLDIER   Hark!

FIRST SOLDIER   Music i' th' air.
THIRD SOLDIER   Under the earth.
FOURTH SOLDIER   It signs well, does it not?   18
THIRD SOLDIER   No.
FIRST SOLDIER   Peace, I say! What should this mean?
SECOND SOLDIER
'Tis the god Hercules, whom Antony loved,
Now leaves him.
FIRST SOLDIER   Walk; let's see if other watchmen
Do hear what we do.
          [They advance toward their fellow watchmen.]
SECOND SOLDIER   How now, masters?
ALL [*speak together*]   How now? How now? Do you
hear this?
FIRST SOLDIER   Ay. Is 't not strange?
THIRD SOLDIER   Do you hear, masters? Do you hear?   28
FIRST SOLDIER
Follow the noise so far as we have quarter;   29
Let's see how it will give off.   30
ALL   Content. 'Tis strange.   *Exeunt.*

♣

4.4   *Enter Antony and Cleopatra, with [Charmian and]
          others [attending].*

ANTONY
Eros! Mine armor, Eros!
CLEOPATRA   Sleep a little.
ANTONY
No, my chuck. Eros, come, mine armor, Eros!   2

          Enter Eros [with armor].

Come, good fellow, put thine iron on.   3
If fortune be not ours today, it is
Because we brave her. Come.
CLEOPATRA   Nay, I'll help too.   5
What's this for?   *[She helps to arm him.]*
ANTONY   Ah, let be, let be! Thou art
The armorer of my heart. False, false; this, this.   7
CLEOPATRA
Sooth, la, I'll help. Thus it must be.
ANTONY   Well, well,   8
We shall thrive now. Seest thou, my good fellow?
Go, put on thy defenses.
EROS   Briefly, sir.   10
CLEOPATRA
Is not this buckled well?
ANTONY   Rarely, rarely.   11
He that unbuckles this, till we do please   12
To doff 't for our repose, shall hear a storm.   13

---

26 period end   **27 Haply** perhaps.   **if** i.e., if you do   **28 shadow**
ghost   **34 yield** reward   **38 the witch take me** may I be bewitched
39 Grace grow (1) may rue or herb of grace grow (2) may gracious
fortune flourish.   **hearty** loving   **42 burn . . . torches** i.e., revel
through the night   **46 consideration** thinking, brooding
4.3. Location: Alexandria. Before the palace.
2 determine one way be decided, come to an end one way or the
other   **3 about** in   **5 Belike** probably   **9 Here we** here's our station
12 brave splendid, gallant.   **s.d. hautboys** oboelike instruments
14 List listen

18 signs well is a good sign   **28 masters** i.e., sirs   **29 as we have**
quarter as our watch post extends   **30 give off** cease
4.4. Location: Alexandria. The palace.
2 chuck (A term of endearment.)   **3 thine iron** i.e., my armor that
you have there. (Or perhaps he is telling Eros to arm.)   **5 brave** defy
7 False you're putting it on wrong   **8 Sooth** in truth   **10 defenses** armor.   **Briefly** in a moment   **11 Rarely** excellently   **12–13 He . . .**
storm i.e., anyone who attempts to burst my armor in the fight, before I choose myself to unarm and rest, will be greeted by a storm of
blows   **13 doff 't** take it off

Thou fumblest, Eros, and my queen's a squire   14
More tight at this than thou. Dispatch. O love,   15
That thou couldst see my wars today, and knew'st   16
The royal occupation! Thou shouldst see   17
A workman in 't.

Enter an armed Soldier.

     Good morrow to thee. Welcome.   18
Thou look'st like him that knows a warlike charge.   19
To business that we love we rise betimes   20
And go to 't with delight.
SOLDIER   A thousand, sir,
Early though 't be, have on their riveted trim   22
And at the port expect you. *Shout. Trumpets flourish.* 23

Enter Captains and soldiers.

CAPTAIN
The morn is fair. Good morrow, General.
ALL
Good morrow, General.
ANTONY   'Tis well blown, lads.   25
This morning, like the spirit of a youth
That means to be of note, begins betimes.
So, so. Come, give me that. This way. Well said.   28
Fare thee well, dame. Whate'er becomes of me,
This is a soldier's kiss. [*He kisses her.*] Rebukable,
And worthy shameful check it were, to stand   31
On more mechanic compliment. I'll leave thee   32
Now like a man of steel. —You that will fight,
Follow me close. I'll bring you to 't. Adieu.
     Exeunt [Antony, Eros, Captains, and soldiers].
CHARMIAN
Please you, retire to your chamber?
CLEOPATRA   Lead me.
He goes forth gallantly. That he and Caesar might
Determine this great war in single fight!
Then Antony—but now—Well, on.   *Exeunt.*

❧

4.5 *Trumpets sound. Enter Antony and Eros; [a Soldier meeting them].*

SOLDIER
The gods make this a happy day to Antony!   1
ANTONY
Would thou and those thy scars had once prevailed   2
To make me fight at land!
SOLDIER   Hadst thou done so,
The kings that have revolted, and the soldier   4

That has this morning left thee, would have still
Followed thy heels.
ANTONY   Who's gone this morning?
SOLDIER   Who?
One ever near thee. Call for Enobarbus,
He shall not hear thee, or from Caesar's camp
Say, "I am none of thine."
ANTONY   What sayest thou?
SOLDIER   Sir,
He is with Caesar.
EROS   Sir, his chests and treasure
He has not with him.
ANTONY   Is he gone?
SOLDIER   Most certain.
ANTONY
Go, Eros, send his treasure after. Do it.
Detain no jot, I charge thee. Write to him—
I will subscribe—gentle adieus and greetings.   14
Say that I wish he never find more cause
To change a master. O, my fortunes have
Corrupted honest men! Dispatch.—Enobarbus!   17
     Exeunt.

❧

4.6 *Flourish. Enter Agrippa, Caesar, with Enobarbus, and Dolabella.*

CAESAR
Go forth, Agrippa, and begin the fight.
Our will is Antony be took alive;
Make it so known.
AGRIPPA   Caesar, I shall.   [*Exit.*]
CAESAR
The time of universal peace is near.   5
Prove this a prosperous day, the three-nooked
    world   6
Shall bear the olive freely.

Enter a Messenger.

MESSENGER   Antony   7
Is come into the field.
CAESAR   Go charge Agrippa   8
Plant those that have revolted in the van,   9
That Antony may seem to spend his fury
Upon himself.   *Exeunt [all but Enobarbus].*
ENOBARBUS
Alexas did revolt and went to Jewry on   12
Affairs of Antony, there did dissuade   13
Great Herod to incline himself to Caesar
And leave his master Antony. For this pains,

14 squire officer charged with attendance on a knight or noble **15 tight** deft, skillful. **Dispatch** finish up **16–17 knew'st . . . occupation** (would that) you knew how to appreciate fully the royal art of warfare **18 workman** craftsman, professional **19 charge** duty, responsibility **20 betimes** early **22 riveted trim** i.e., armor riveted into place **23 port** gate **25 'Tis well blown** i.e., the morning begins well, or, refers to trumpets in line 23 s.d. **28 said** done **31 check** reproof **31–32 stand . . . compliment** insist on vulgar and routine ceremonies of leavetaking
4.5. Location: Before Alexandria. Antony's camp.
1 happy fortunate **2 once** formerly **4 revolted** deserted

14 subscribe sign **17 Dispatch** make haste, get on with it
4.6. Location: Before Alexandria. Caesar's camp.
5 The . . . near (The Renaissance identified Octavius Caesar, or the Emperor Augustus as he was subsequently titled, with this *Pax Romana*, peace under the Roman Empire.) **6 Prove this** if this prove to be. **three-nooked** three-cornered. (Refers to Asia, Europe, and Africa.) **7 bear** (1) bring forth (2) wear as a triumphal garland. **olive** symbol of peace **8 charge Agrippa** order Agrippa to **9 van** vanguard, front lines **12 Jewry** Judaea **13 dissuade** i.e., from following Antony

Caesar hath hanged him. Canidius and the rest
That fell away have entertainment but   17
No honorable trust. I have done ill,
Of which I do accuse myself so sorely   19
That I will joy no more.

Enter a Soldier of Caesar's.

SOLDIER   Enobarbus, Antony
Hath after thee sent all thy treasure, with
His bounty overplus. The messenger   22
Came on my guard, and at thy tent is now   23
Unloading of his mules.
ENOBARBUS   I give it you.
SOLDIER   Mock not, Enobarbus,
I tell you true. Best you safed the bringer   27
Out of the host. I must attend mine office,   28
Or would have done 't myself. Your emperor
Continues still a Jove.   *Exit.*

ENOBARBUS
I am alone the villain of the earth,   31
And feel I am so most. O Antony,   32
Thou mine of bounty, how wouldst thou have paid   33
My better service, when my turpitude
Thou dost so crown with gold! This blows my heart.   35
If swift thought break it not, a swifter mean   36
Shall outstrike thought; but thought will do 't, I feel.   37
I fight against thee? No, I will go seek
Some ditch wherein to die. The foul'st best fits
My latter part of life.   *Exit.*

❖

4.7   *Alarum. Drums and trumpets. Enter Agrippa*
      [and others].

AGRIPPA
Retire! We have engaged ourselves too far.   1
Caesar himself has work, and our oppression   2
Exceeds what we expected.   *Exeunt.* 3

Alarums. Enter Antony, and Scarus wounded.

SCARUS
O my brave Emperor, this is fought indeed!
Had we done so at first, we had droven them home 5
With clouts about their heads.
ANTONY   Thou bleed'st apace.   6
SCARUS
I had a wound here that was like a T,

But now 'tis made an H.   *[Sound retreat] far off.*
ANTONY   They do retire.   8
SCARUS
We'll beat 'em into bench holes. I have yet   9
Room for six scotches more.   10

Enter Eros.

EROS
They are beaten, sir, and our advantage serves   11
For a fair victory.
SCARUS   Let us score their backs   12
And snatch 'em up, as we take hares, behind!
'Tis sport to maul a runner.
ANTONY   I will reward thee   14
Once for thy spritely comfort and tenfold
For thy good valor. Come thee on.
SCARUS   I'll halt after.   *Exeunt.* 17

4.8   *Alarum. Enter Antony again in a march; Scarus,*
      with others.

ANTONY
We have beat him to his camp. Run one before   1
And let the Queen know of our gests. [*Exit a Soldier.*]
   Tomorrow,   2
Before the sun shall see 's, we'll spill the blood
That has today escaped. I thank you all,
For doughty-handed are you, and have fought   5
Not as you served the cause, but as 't had been   6
Each man's like mine; you have shown all Hectors.   7
Enter the city, clip your wives, your friends,   8
Tell them your feats, whilst they with joyful tears
Wash the congealment from your wounds and kiss
The honored gashes whole.

Enter Cleopatra [attended].

                   [*To Scarus.*] Give me thy hand;
To this great fairy I'll commend thy acts,   12
Make her thanks bless thee. [*To Cleopatra.*] O thou
   day o' the world,   13
Chain mine armed neck; leap thou, attire and all,   14
Through proof of harness to my heart, and there   15
Ride on the pants triumphing!   [*They embrace.*]
CLEOPATRA   Lord of lords,   16
O infinite virtue, com'st thou smiling from   17

---

17 entertainment employment, maintenance   **19 sorely** heavily
22 overplus in addition   **23 on my guard** while I was standing guard
27 Best you safed you would do well to provide safe-
conduct for   **28 host** army.   **attend mine office** see to my duties
31 alone the the only, the greatest   **32 And . . . most** and am the
one who feels it most   **33 mine** i.e., abundant store   **35 blows**
causes to swell to the bursting point   **36 mean** i.e., suicide
37 thought melancholy.   **do 't** i.e., break my heart
4.7. Location: Field of battle between the camps.
1 Retire retreat   **2 has work** is hard pressed.   **our oppression** the
heavy attacks against us   **3 s.d. Exeunt** (The cleared stage technically
marks a new scene, although the alarums provide a sense of continuous action.)   **5 droven** driven   **6 clouts** (1) bandages (2) blows and
knocks

8 H i.e., the bottom of the T has been cut across to make an H lying
on its side. (There is a pun on *ache*, pronounced *aitch*.)   **9 bench
holes** the holes of privies, i.e., any desperate place to hide
10 scotches cuts   **11–12 our . . . victory** i.e., we are in such a favorable position that a complete victory seems in prospect   **12 score**
mark by cuts from a whip   **14 a runner** i.e., one in retreat   **17 halt**
limp
4.8. Location: Before Alexandria. The action is virtually continuous.
1 beat driven.   **Run one** let someone run   **2 gests** deeds   **5 doughty-
handed** valiant   **6 as . . . as 't** as if . . . as if it.   **the cause** merely
the general cause   **7 shown** shown yourselves   **8 clip** embrace
12 fairy enchantress, dispenser of good fortune   **13 thou day o' the
world** (Antony means that she lights up his world.)   **14 Chain . . .
neck** hang around my neck in an embrace like a medal on a chain
15 proof of harness proof-armor, tested armor   **16 pants** heartbeats
17 virtue valor

The world's great snare uncaught?

ANTONY   My nightingale,
We have beat them to their beds. What, girl, though
    gray
Do something mingle with our younger brown, yet
    ha' we   20
A brain that nourishes our nerves and can   21
Get goal for goal of youth. Behold this man;   22
Commend unto his lips thy favoring hand.—   23
Kiss it, my warrior. [*Scarus kisses Cleopatra's hand.*] He
    hath fought today
As if a god, in hate of mankind, had
Destroyed in such a shape.

CLEOPATRA   I'll give thee, friend,
An armor all of gold; it was a king's.

ANTONY
He has deserved it, were it carbuncled   28
Like holy Phoebus' car. Give me thy hand.   29
Through Alexandria make a jolly march;
Bear our hacked targets like the men that owe them. 31
Had our great palace the capacity
To camp this host, we all would sup together   33
And drink carouses to the next day's fate,   34
Which promises royal peril. Trumpeters,   35
With brazen din blast you the city's ear;
Make mingle with our rattling taborins,   37
That heaven and earth may strike their sounds
    together,   38
Applauding our approach. [*Trumpets sound.*] *Exeunt.*

❧

4.9   *Enter a Sentry and his company. Enobarbus
          follows.*

SENTRY
If we be not relieved within this hour,
We must return to th' court of guard. The night   2
Is shiny, and they say we shall embattle   3
By the second hour i' the morn.

FIRST WATCH   This last day was a shrewd one to 's. 5

ENOBARBUS   O, bear me witness, night—

SECOND WATCH   What man is this?

FIRST WATCH   Stand close, and list him.   8
                              [*They stand aside.*]

ENOBARBUS
Be witness to me, O thou blessèd moon,
When men revolted shall upon record   10

Bear hateful memory: poor Enobarbus did
Before thy face repent.

SENTRY   Enobarbus?

SECOND WATCH   Peace! Hark further.

ENOBARBUS
O sovereign mistress of true melancholy,   15
The poisonous damp of night disponge upon me,   16
That life, a very rebel to my will,
May hang no longer on me. Throw my heart
Against the flint and hardness of my fault,
Which, being dried with grief, will break to powder 20
And finish all foul thoughts. O Antony,
Nobler than my revolt is infamous,
Forgive me in thine own particular,   23
But let the world rank me in register   24
A master-leaver and a fugitive.   25
O Antony! O Antony!   [*He dies.*]

FIRST WATCH   Let's speak to him.

SENTRY
Let's hear him, for the things he speaks
May concern Caesar.

SECOND WATCH   Let's do so. But he sleeps.

SENTRY
Swoons rather, for so bad a prayer as his
Was never yet for sleep.

FIRST WATCH   Go we to him.   31
                        [*They approach Enobarbus.*]

SECOND WATCH   Awake, sir, awake. Speak to us.

FIRST WATCH   Hear you, sir?

SENTRY   The hand of death hath raught him.   34
                              Drums afar off.
Hark, the drums demurely wake the sleepers.   35
Let us bear him to the court of guard;
He is of note. Our hour is fully out.   37

SECOND WATCH
Come on, then. He may recover yet.
                        Exeunt [*with the body*].

❧

4.10   *Enter Antony and Scarus, with their army.*

ANTONY
Their preparation is today by sea;
We please them not by land.

SCARUS   For both, my lord.

ANTONY
I would they'd fight i' the fire or i' th' air;   3

---

20 something somewhat   **21 nerves** sinews, tendons   **22 Get . . . of**
i.e., stay competitively equal with.   **this man** i.e., Scarus   **23 Com-**
mend entrust, commit   **28 carbuncled** set with jewels   **29 Phoebus'**
car the chariot of the sun   **31 targets** shields.   **like** as becomes.
owe own   **33 camp this host** accommodate this army   **34 carouses**
toasts   **35 royal peril** i.e., war, the sport of monarchs   **37 taborins**
drums   **38 That . . . together** i.e., the heavens are to echo the loud
noise of the drums, augmenting the acclaim
4.9. Location: Caesar's camp.
2 court of guard guardroom   **3 shiny** bright, moonlit.   **embattle** fall
in for the combat   **5 shrewd** unlucky   **8 close** concealed.   **list** listen
to   **10 revolted** who have broken their allegiance.   **upon record** in
the record of history

15 mistress . . . melancholy i.e., the moon, so addressed because of
her supposed influence in causing lunacy   **16 disponge** pour down
(as from a squeezed sponge)   **20 Which** i.e., the heart.   **dried with**
grief (Elizabethans thought that the spirits of a man in Enobarbus' state
of mind would descend into his bowels, leaving his heart dry.)   **23 in**
. . . particular in your own person   **24 rank me in register** put me
down in its records   **25 master-leaver** (1) one who deserts his master
(2) nonpareil of deserters.   **fugitive** deserter   **31 for** a prelude to
34 raught reached   **35 demurely** with subdued sound   **37 of note** of
rank
4.10. Location: The field of battle.
3 fire, air (Comprising the four elements, along with earth and water
where Antony is already prepared.)

We'd fight there too. But this it is: our foot   4
Upon the hills adjoining to the city
Shall stay with us—order for sea is given;   6
They have put forth the haven—   7
Where their appointment we may best discover   8
And look on their endeavor.   *Exeunt.*

4.11 *Enter Caesar and his army.*

CAESAR
But being charged, we will be still by land,   1
Which, as I take 't, we shall; for his best force   2
Is forth to man his galleys. To the vales,   3
And hold our best advantage.   *Exeunt.* 4

4.12 *Enter Antony and Scarus.*

ANTONY
Yet they are not joined. Where yond pine does
   stand,
I shall discover all. I'll bring thee word
Straight how 'tis like to go.   *Exit.*
         Alarum afar off, as at a sea fight.
SCARUS   Swallows have built   3
In Cleopatra's sails their nests. The augurers   4
Say they know not, they cannot tell, look grimly,
And dare not speak their knowledge. Antony
Is valiant, and dejected, and by starts
His fretted fortunes give him hope and fear   8
Of what he has, and has not.

     Enter Antony.

ANTONY   All is lost!
This foul Egyptian hath betrayèd me.
My fleet hath yielded to the foe, and yonder
They cast their caps up and carouse together
Like friends long lost. Triple-turned whore! 'Tis thou 13
Hast sold me to this novice, and my heart
Makes only wars on thee. Bid them all fly;   15
For when I am revenged upon my charm,   16
I have done all. Bid them all fly. Begone!
                 [Exit Scarus.]
O sun, thy uprise shall I see no more.
Fortune and Antony part here; even here
Do we shake hands. All come to this? The hearts   20

That spanieled me at heels, to whom I gave   21
Their wishes, do discandy, melt their sweets   22
On blossoming Caesar; and this pine is barked   23
That overtopped them all. Betrayed I am.
O, this false soul of Egypt! This grave charm,   25
Whose eye becked forth my wars and called them
   home,   26
Whose bosom was my crownet, my chief end,   27
Like a right gypsy hath at fast and loose   28
Beguiled me to the very heart of loss.   29
What, Eros, Eros!

     Enter Cleopatra.

            Ah, thou spell! Avaunt!   30
CLEOPATRA
Why is my lord enraged against his love?
ANTONY
Vanish, or I shall give thee thy deserving
And blemish Caesar's triumph. Let him take thee   33
And hoist thee up to the shouting plebeians!
Follow his chariot, like the greatest spot   35
Of all thy sex; most monsterlike be shown   36
For poor'st diminutives, for dolts, and let   37
Patient Octavia plow thy visage up
With her preparèd nails!   *Exit Cleopatra.*
           'Tis well thou'rt gone,
If it be well to live; but better 'twere
Thou fell'st into my fury, for one death   41
Might have prevented many. Eros, ho!   42
The shirt of Nessus is upon me. Teach me,   43
Alcides, thou mine ancestor, thy rage.   44
Let me lodge Lichas on the horns o' the moon,   45
And with those hands, that grasped the heaviest
   club,
Subdue my worthiest self. The witch shall die.
To the young Roman boy she hath sold me, and I
   fall
Under this plot. She dies for 't. Eros, ho!   *Exit.*

❧

4 foot foot soldiers **6 for sea** to fight at sea **7 forth** forth from
8 appointment disposition of forces, equipment. **discover** descry
4.11. Location: The field of battle.
1 But being unless we are. **still** inactive **2 we shall** i.e., we will be
left undisturbed **3 Is forth** has gone forth. **vales** valleys **4 hold**
. . . advantage take the most advantageous position
4.12. Location: The field of battle at first, though by scene's end the
action appears to be located in Alexandria.
3 Straight immediately. **like** likely **4 augurers** augurs, soothsayers
8 fretted worn away, vexed, checkered **13 Triple-turned** three times
faithless (to Julius Caesar, Gnaeus Pompey, and now Antony)
15 Makes . . . thee wages war on you alone **16 charm** practicer of
charms or spells **20 shake hands** i.e., in parting. **hearts** good
fellows

21 spanieled fawned upon like a spaniel **22 Their wishes** whatever
they wished. **discandy** melt, dissolve **23 this pine** i.e., Antony.
barked stripped of its bark and thus killed **25 This grave charm** i.e.,
this sorceress who has fatal spells **26 becked** beckoned **27 crownet**
coronet. **end** aim. (Cleopatra's love was the crown of Antony's
achievements and the reward of his labors.) **28 right** veritable. **fast**
and loose a cheating game in which the victim bets that he can make
fast a knot in an ingeniously coiled rope, whereupon the knot is
pulled loose **29 loss** ruin **30 spell** enchantment, spell
maker (?). **Avaunt** begone **33 blemish Caesar's triumph** i.e., mutilate you and thereby frustrate Caesar's plan to display you in his triumphal procession into Rome **35 spot** blemish, disgrace **36 shown**
exhibited **37 diminutives** underlings, i.e., the populace **41 Thou**
fell'st into you had fallen a victim to **42 many** i.e., many shameful
experiences (?), or, many other killings through Antony's rage (?)
43–45 Nessus, Alcides, Lichas (When Hercules or *Alcides* had fatally
wounded the centaur *Nessus* for trying to rape Hercules' wife Deianira, Nessus vengefully gave his blood-soaked shirt to Deianira as a
supposed love charm for her husband. The poison gave Hercules such
agony that he cast his page *Lichas* into the air.)

4.13   *Enter Cleopatra, Charmian, Iras, [and] Mardian.*

CLEOPATRA
    Help me, my women! O, he's more mad
    Than Telamon for his shield; the boar of Thessaly   2
    Was never so embossed.
CHARMIAN   To the monument!   3
    There lock yourself and send him word you are
        dead.
    The soul and body rive not more in parting   5
    Than greatness going off.
CLEOPATRA   To the monument!   6
    Mardian, go tell him I have slain myself.
    Say that the last I spoke was "Antony,"   8
    And word it, prithee, piteously. Hence, Mardian,
    And bring me how he takes my death. To th'
        monument!   *Exeunt.*

❖

4.14   *Enter Antony and Eros.*

ANTONY
    Eros, thou yet behold'st me?
EROS   Ay, noble lord.
ANTONY
    Sometimes we see a cloud that's dragonish,   2
    A vapor sometimes like a bear or lion,
    A towered citadel, a pendant rock,   4
    A forkèd mountain, or blue promontory
    With trees upon 't that nod unto the world
    And mock our eyes with air. Thou hast seen these
        signs;
    They are black vesper's pageants.
EROS   Ay, my lord.   8
ANTONY
    That which is now a horse, even with a thought
    The rack dislimns and makes it indistinct   10
    As water is in water.
EROS   It does, my lord.
ANTONY
    My good knave Eros, now thy captain is   12
    Even such a body. Here I am Antony,
    Yet cannot hold this visible shape, my knave.
    I made these wars for Egypt, and the Queen,
    Whose heart I thought I had, for she had mine—
    Which whilst it was mine had annexed unto 't

    A million more, now lost—she, Eros, has
    Packed cards with Caesar and false-played my glory   19
    Unto an enemy's triumph.   20
    Nay, weep not, gentle Eros. There is left us
    Ourselves to end ourselves.

        Enter Mardian.

                              O, thy vile lady!
    She has robbed me of my sword.
MARDIAN   No, Antony,   23
    My mistress loved thee, and her fortunes mingled
    With thine entirely.
ANTONY   Hence, saucy eunuch, peace!   25
    She hath betrayed me and shall die the death.   26
MARDIAN
    Death of one person can be paid but once,   27
    And that she has discharged. What thou wouldst do   28
    Is done unto thy hand. The last she spake   29
    Was, "Antony, most noble Antony!"
    Then in the midst a tearing groan did break
    The name of Antony; it was divided   32
    Between her heart and lips. She rendered life   33
    Thy name so buried in her.
ANTONY   Dead, then?
MARDIAN   Dead.   34
ANTONY
    Unarm, Eros. The long day's task is done,
    And we must sleep. [*To Mardian.*] That thou
        depart'st hence safe
    Does pay thy labor richly; go.   *Exit Mardian.*
                    Off, pluck off! [*Eros unarms him.*]
    The sevenfold shield of Ajax cannot keep   38
    The battery from my heart. O, cleave, my sides!   39
    Heart, once be stronger than thy continent;   40
    Crack thy frail case! Apace, Eros, apace.   41
    No more a soldier. Bruisèd pieces, go;
    You have been nobly borne.—From me awhile.   43
                              Exit Eros.
    I will o'ertake thee, Cleopatra, and
    Weep for my pardon. So it must be, for now
    All length is torture; since the torch is out,   46
    Lie down, and stray no farther. Now all labor
    Mars what it does; yea, very force entangles   48
    Itself with strength. Seal then, and all is done.   49
    Eros!—I come, my queen.—Eros!—Stay for me.   50

4.13. Location: Alexandria. This scene appears to follow scene 12 closely. The sense of location is very fluid, and it is not clear where the end of scene 12 takes place.
2 Telamon Ajax Telamon, who after the capture of Troy went mad and slew himself when he was not awarded the shield and armor of Achilles. **the boar of Thessaly** the boar sent by Diana or Artemis to ravage the fields of Calydon, slain by Meleager **3 embossed** foaming at the mouth from rage and exhaustion. **monument** tomb built in anticipation of Cleopatra's death **5 rive** split, sever **6 going off** i.e., bidding farewell to its glory **8 last** last word
4.14. Location: Alexandria. (See location of scene 13; again, the sense of time is immediate and the place is fluid.)
2 dragonish shaped like a dragon **4 pendant** overhanging **8 black vesper's pageants** i.e., shows heralding the approach of night **10 rack** floating vapor or cloud. **dislimns** effaces **12 knave** boy

19 Packed cards i.e., stacked the deck. **false-played** falsely played away **20 triumph** (1) victory (2) trump card **23 sword** i.e., prowess as a soldier, masculinity **25 saucy** insolent **26 die the death** be put to death **27 of** by **28 discharged** paid **29 unto thy hand** for you, without your having to lift a finger **32–33 it . . . lips** i.e., she groaned out half of Antony's name and then died with the unspoken part in her heart only **33–34 rendered . . . in her** gave back to Nature a life she no longer desired, with your name thus buried in her heart **38 sevenfold** with seven thicknesses (The shield of Ajax was of brass reinforced with seven thicknesses of oxhide.) **39 battery** battering, bombardment. **cleave** split **40 thy continent** that which contains you **41 Apace** quickly **43 From** go from **46 length** prolongation of life. **the torch** i.e., the life of Cleopatra **48 very force** any resolute action **49 with strength** i.e., with its own strength. **Seal** finish the business (as in sealing a letter) **50 Eros** (The meaning of Eros' name, erotic love, is especially apt here.)

Where souls do couch on flowers, we'll hand in
   hand,   51
And with our sprightly port make the ghosts gaze.   52
Dido and her Aeneas shall want troops,   53
And all the haunt be ours.—Come, Eros, Eros!   54

Enter Eros.

EROS
What would my lord?

ANTONY   Since Cleopatra died   55
I have lived in such dishonor that the gods
Detest my baseness. I, that with my sword
Quartered the world, and o'er green Neptune's back   58
With ships made cities, condemn myself to lack   59
The courage of a woman—less noble mind
Than she which by her death our Caesar tells
"I am conqueror of myself." Thou art sworn, Eros,
That when the exigent should come which now   63
Is come indeed, when I should see behind me
Th' inevitable prosecution of   65
Disgrace and horror, that on my command
Thou then wouldst kill me. Do 't. The time is come.
Thou strik'st not me, 'tis Caesar thou defeat'st.
Put color in thy cheek.

EROS   The gods withhold me!   69
Shall I do that which all the Parthian darts,
Though enemy, lost aim and could not?

ANTONY   Eros,
Wouldst thou be windowed in great Rome and see   72
Thy master thus with pleached arms, bending down   73
His corrigible neck, his face subdued   74
To penetrative shame, whilst the wheeled seat   75
Of fortunate Caesar, drawn before him, branded   76
His baseness that ensued?

EROS   I would not see 't.   77

ANTONY
Come, then, for with a wound I must be cured.
Draw that thy honest sword, which thou hast worn   79
Most useful for thy country.

EROS   O, sir, pardon me!   80

ANTONY
When I did make thee free, swor'st thou not then
To do this when I bade thee? Do it at once,

---

51 **couch** lie (here, in the Elysian fields)   52 **sprightly** (1) high-spirited
(2) spiritlike, ghostly.   **port** bearing   53 **Dido . . . troops** i.e., Antony and Cleopatra will be the most distinguished lovers in the Elysian
fields, outshining even the Queen of Carthage and her famous lover.
(In the *Aeneid*, Aeneas deserts Dido in order to found Rome, putting
public good ahead of private passion as Antony does not. Dido scorns
Aeneas when they meet in the underworld; Antony here imagines
himself and Cleopatra in the Elysian fields.)   **want troops** lack followers   54 **all . . . ours** i.e., we shall be the objects of everyone's attention   55 **would my lord** does my lord desire   58 **Quartered** cut into
quarters, divided and conquered.   **o'er . . . back** i.e., on the sea
59 **With . . . cities** i.e., assembled flotillas as dense and populous as
cities.   **to lack** for lacking   63 **exigent** exigency, time of compelling
need   65 **prosecution** pursuit   69 **The gods withhold me** i.e., God
forbid   72 **windowed** placed as in a window   73 **pleached** folded or
bound   74 **corrigible** submissive to correction   75 **penetrative** penetrating.   **wheeled seat** chariot   76–77 **branded . . . ensued** stigmatized, as by a brand, the shame of him that followed   79 **honest** honorable   80 **pardon me** excuse me from doing this

Or thy precedent services are all   83
But accidents unpurposed. Draw, and come.   84

EROS
Turn from me then that noble countenance
Wherein the worship of the whole world lies.   86

ANTONY   Lo thee!   [*He turns away.*]

EROS [*drawing his sword*]
My sword is drawn.

ANTONY   Then let it do at once
That thing why thou hast drawn it.

EROS   My dear master,
My captain, and my emperor, let me say,
Before I strike this bloody stroke, farewell.

ANTONY   'Tis said, man, and farewell.

EROS
Farewell, great chief. Shall I strike now?

ANTONY   Now, Eros.

EROS (*kills himself*)
Why, there then! Thus I do escape the sorrow
Of Antony's death.   [*He dies.*]

ANTONY   Thrice nobler than myself!
Thou teachest me, O valiant Eros, what
I should, and thou couldst not. My queen and Eros   97
Have by their brave instruction got upon me   98
A nobleness in record. But I will be   99
A bridegroom in my death, and run into 't
As to a lover's bed. Come, then, and Eros,
Thy master dies thy scholar. To do thus
I learned of thee.   [*He falls on his sword.*]
           How, not dead? Not dead?
The guard, ho! O, dispatch me!   104

Enter [Dercetus and others of] a Guard.

FIRST GUARD   What's the noise?

ANTONY   I have done my work ill, friends.
O, make an end of what I have begun!

SECOND GUARD   The star is fallen.

FIRST GUARD   And time is at his period.   109

ALL   Alas, and woe!

ANTONY   Let him that loves me strike me dead.

FIRST GUARD   Not I.

SECOND GUARD   Nor I.

THIRD GUARD   Nor anyone.   *Exeunt [Guard].*

DERCETUS
Thy death and fortunes bid thy followers fly.
This sword but shown to Caesar, with this tidings,
Shall enter me with him. [*He takes up Antony's sword.*]   117

Enter Diomedes.

DIOMEDES   Where's Antony?

DERCETUS   There, Diomed, there.

DIOMEDES
Lives he? Wilt thou not answer, man? [*Exit Dercetus.*]

---

83 **precedent** former   84 **accidents unpurposed** events leading to no
purpose   86 **worship** honor, worth   97 **I should . . . not** I should
have done for myself and you couldn't do for me   98–99 **got . . .
record** won a noble place in history before I have   104 **dispatch** finish   109 **his period** its end   117 **enter . . . him** admit me to his service, put me in his good graces

ANTONY
Art thou there, Diomed? Draw thy sword and
  give me
Sufficing strokes for death.
DIOMEDES   Most absolute lord,   122
My mistress Cleopatra sent me to thee.
ANTONY
When did she send thee?
DIOMEDES   Now, my lord.
ANTONY   Where is she?
DIOMEDES
Locked in her monument. She had a prophesying
  fear
Of what hath come to pass. For when she saw—
Which never shall be found—you did suspect 127
She had disposed with Caesar, and that your rage 128
Would not be purged, she sent you word she was
  dead;
But, fearing since how it might work, hath sent
Me to proclaim the truth, and I am come,
I dread, too late.
ANTONY
Too late, good Diomed. Call my guard, I prithee.
DIOMEDES
What ho, the Emperor's guard! The guard, what ho!
Come, your lord calls.

       Enter four or five of the Guard of Antony.

ANTONY
Bear me, good friends, where Cleopatra bides. 136
'Tis the last service that I shall command you.
FIRST GUARD
Woe, woe are we, sir, you may not live to wear 138
All your true followers out.
ALL   Most heavy day! 139
ANTONY
Nay, good my fellows, do not please sharp fate
To grace it with your sorrows. Bid that welcome 141
Which comes to punish us, and we punish it,
Seeming to bear it lightly. Take me up.
I have led you oft; carry me now, good friends,
And have my thanks for all.
      Exeunt, bearing Antony [and Eros].

              ❖

4.15 *Enter Cleopatra and her maids aloft, with*
      Charmian and Iras.

CLEOPATRA
O Charmian, I will never go from hence.
CHARMIAN
Be comforted, dear madam.
CLEOPATRA   No, I will not.
All strange and terrible events are welcome,

But comforts we despise. Our size of sorrow,
Proportioned to our cause, must be as great
As that which makes it.
      Enter [below] Diomedes.
           How now? Is he dead?
DIOMEDES
His death's upon him, but not dead.
Look out o' th' other side your monument;
His guard have brought him thither.
     Enter [below] Antony, and the Guard
     [bearing him].
CLEOPATRA   O sun,
Burn the great sphere thou mov'st in; darkling stand 11
The varying shore o' the world! O Antony,
Antony, Antony! Help, Charmian, help, Iras, help!
Help, friends below! Let's draw him hither.
ANTONY   Peace!
Not Caesar's valor hath o'erthrown Antony,
But Antony's hath triumphed on itself.
CLEOPATRA
So it should be, that none but Antony
Should conquer Antony; but woe 'tis so!
ANTONY
I am dying, Egypt, dying. Only
I here importune death awhile, until 20
Of many thousand kisses the poor last
I lay upon thy lips.
CLEOPATRA   I dare not, dear— 22
Dear my lord, pardon—I dare not,
Lest I be taken. Not th' imperious show 24
Of the full-fortuned Caesar ever shall
Be brooched with me. If knife, drugs, serpents, have 26
Edge, sting, or operation, I am safe. 27
Your wife Octavia, with her modest eyes
And still conclusion, shall acquire no honor 29
Demuring upon me. But come, come, Antony— 30
Help me, my women—we must draw thee up.
Assist, good friends.
ANTONY   O, quick, or I am gone.
      [They begin lifting.]
CLEOPATRA
Here's sport indeed! How heavy weighs my lord!
Our strength is all gone into heaviness, 34
That makes the weight. Had I great Juno's power,
The strong-winged Mercury should fetch thee up
And set thee by Jove's side. Yet come a little;
Wishers were ever fools. O, come, come, come! 38
     They heave Antony aloft to Cleopatra.
And welcome, welcome! Die when thou hast lived; 39

---

122 Suffering sufficient **127 found** found true **128 disposed with** come to terms with **136 bides** abides, dwells **138–139 live . . . out** i.e., outlive those that serve you **141 To grace** by gracing or honoring
4.15. Location: Alexandria. Cleopatra's monument.
s.d. aloft in the gallery above the main stage

11 sphere concentric sphere in which, according to Ptolemaic astronomy, the sun moved about the earth as did the planets and stars. **darkling** in darkness **20 importune** i.e., beg a delay of **22 I dare not** i.e., I dare not come down **24 imperious show** imperial triumphal procession **26 brooched** adorned (as with a brooch) **27 operation** power, efficacy **29 still conclusion** silent judgment **30 Demuring** looking demurely **34 heaviness** (1) sadness (2) weight
38 Wishers . . . fools i.e., when we wish for unattainable things we fool ourselves **39 Die . . . lived** i.e., live a little longer before dying

Quicken with kissing. Had my lips that power,   40
Thus would I wear them out.   [*She kisses him.*]
ALL   A heavy sight!   42
ANTONY   I am dying, Egypt, dying.
Give me some wine, and let me speak a little.
CLEOPATRA
No, let me speak, and let me rail so high
That the false huswife Fortune break her wheel,   46
Provoked by my offense.
ANTONY   One word, sweet Queen: 47
Of Caesar seek your honor, with your safety. O!   48
CLEOPATRA
They do not go together.
ANTONY   Gentle, hear me.
None about Caesar trust but Proculeius.
CLEOPATRA
My resolution and my hands I'll trust,
None about Caesar.
ANTONY
The miserable change now at my end
Lament nor sorrow at, but please your thoughts   54
In feeding them with those my former fortunes,
Wherein I lived the greatest prince o' the world,
The noblest; and do now not basely die,
Not cowardly put off my helmet to
My countryman—a Roman by a Roman
Valiantly vanquished. Now my spirit is going;
I can no more.
CLEOPATRA   Noblest of men, woo't die?   61
Hast thou no care of me? Shall I abide
In this dull world, which in thy absence is
No better than a sty? [*Antony dies.*] O, see, my
     women,
The crown o' th' earth doth melt. My lord!
O, withered is the garland of the war;
The soldier's pole is fall'n! Young boys and girls   67
Are level now with men. The odds is gone,   68
And there is nothing left remarkable
Beneath the visiting moon.   [*She faints.*]
CHARMIAN   O, quietness, lady!
IRAS   She's dead too, our sovereign.
CHARMIAN   Lady!
IRAS   Madam!
CHARMIAN   O madam, madam, madam!
IRAS   Royal Egypt, Empress!   [*Cleopatra stirs.*]
CHARMIAN   Peace, peace, Iras.
CLEOPATRA
No more but e'en a woman, and commanded
By such poor passion as the maid that milks
And does the meanest chares. It were for me   80
To throw my scepter at the injurious gods,
To tell them that this world did equal theirs
Till they had stol'n our jewel. All's but naught;

---

40 **Quicken** revive   42 **heavy** doleful   46 **false** treacherous.   **huswife**
hussy, wanton   47 **offense** offensive speech   48 **Of** from   54 **Lament**
i.e., neither lament   61 **woo't** wilt thou   67 **pole** polestar or battle
standard (probably with a suggestion of a sexual potency now withered and fallen through death)   68 **The odds is gone** the distinction
between great and small has disappeared   80 **chares** chores, drudgery.   **were** would be fitting

---

Patience is sottish, and impatience does   84
Become a dog that's mad. Then is it sin   85
To rush into the secret house of death
Ere death dare come to us? How do you, women?
What, what, good cheer! Why, how now,
     Charmian?
My noble girls! Ah, women, women! Look,
Our lamp is spent, it's out. Good sirs, take heart.   90
We'll bury him; and then, what's brave, what's
     noble,   91
Let's do 't after the high Roman fashion
And make death proud to take us. Come, away.
This case of that huge spirit now is cold.
Ah, women, women! Come. We have no friend
But resolution, and the briefest end.   96
     Exeunt, [those above] bearing off Antony's body.

                                   ❧

5.1   *Enter Caesar, Agrippa, Dolabella, Maecenas,*
          [Gallus, Proculeius,] with his council of war.

CAESAR
Go to him, Dolabella, bid him yield;
Being so frustrate, tell him, he mocks
The pauses that he makes.   2
DOLABELLA   Caesar, I shall.   [*Exit.*] 3

     Enter Dercetus, with the sword of Antony.

CAESAR
Wherefore is that? And what art thou that dar'st
Appear thus to us?
DERCETUS   I am called Dercetus.
Mark Antony I served, who best was worthy
Best to be served. Whilst he stood up and spoke
He was my master, and I wore my life
To spend upon his haters. If thou please   9
To take me to thee, as I was to him
I'll be to Caesar; if thou pleasest not,
I yield thee up my life.
CAESAR   What is 't thou sayst?
DERCETUS
I say, O Caesar, Antony is dead.
CAESAR
The breaking of so great a thing should make   14
A greater crack. The round world   15
Should have shook lions into civil streets   16
And citizens to their dens. The death of Antony   17
Is not a single doom; in the name lay   18

84–85 Patience . . . mad i.e., patience is for fools, and impatience is
for the mad; both are useless here   **90 Good sirs** (Addressed to the
women.)   **91 brave** fine   **96 briefest** swiftest
5.1. Location: Alexandria. Caesar's camp.
2 frustrate helpless, baffled   **2–3 mocks . . . makes** makes himself
ridiculous by his delays   **9 spend** expend   **14 breaking**
(1) destruction (2) disclosure   **15 crack** (1) cracking apart (2) loud report   **16 civil** city   **17 their** i.e., the lions', or else, the citizens scurry
to safety indoors, in their own "dens." (In either case, nature is inverted in a kind of disorder that earlier accompanied the death of
Julius Caesar.)   **18 Is . . . doom** i.e., signifies the death and destruction of much more than a single man

A moiety of the world.

DERCETUS   He is dead, Caesar,   19
Not by a public minister of justice,
Nor by a hirèd knife; but that self hand   21
Which writ his honor in the acts it did
Hath, with the courage which the heart did lend it,
Splitted the heart. This is his sword.
                    [*He offers the sword.*]
I robbed his wound of it. Behold it stained
With his most noble blood.

CAESAR   Look you sad, friends?
The gods rebuke me, but it is tidings   27
To wash the eyes of kings.

AGRIPPA   And strange it is   28
That nature must compel us to lament
Our most persisted deeds.

MAECENAS   His taints and honors   30
Waged equal with him.

AGRIPPA   A rarer spirit never   31
Did steer humanity; but you gods will give us   32
Some faults to make us men. Caesar is touched.

MAECENAS
When such a spacious mirror's set before him,
He needs must see himself.

CAESAR   O Antony,
I have followed thee to this; but we do launch 36
Diseases in our bodies. I must perforce   37
Have shown to thee such a declining day,   38
Or look on thine; we could not stall together   39
In the whole world. But yet let me lament
With tears as sovereign as the blood of hearts 41
That thou, my brother, my competitor   42
In top of all design, my mate in empire,   43
Friend and companion in the front of war,   44
The arm of mine own body, and the heart   45
Where mine his thoughts did kindle—that our stars, 46
Unreconciliable, should divide   47
Our equalness to this. Hear me, good friends—   48

                    Enter an Egyptian.

But I will tell you at some meeter season.   49
The business of this man looks out of him;   50
We'll hear him what he says.—Whence are you?   51

EGYPTIAN
A poor Egyptian yet, the Queen my mistress,   52
Confined in all she has, her monument,
Of thy intents desires instruction,
That she preparedly may frame herself   55
To th' way she's forced to.

CAESAR   Bid her have good heart.
She soon shall know of us, by some of ours,   57
How honorable and how kindly we
Determine for her; for Caesar cannot live
To be ungentle.

EGYPTIAN   So the gods preserve thee!   *Exit.*

CAESAR
Come hither, Proculeius. Go and say
We purpose her no shame. Give her what comforts 62
The quality of her passion shall require,   63
Lest, in her greatness, by some mortal stroke   64
She do defeat us; for her life in Rome   65
Would be eternal in our triumph. Go,   66
And with your speediest bring us what she says 67
And how you find of her.

PROCULEIUS   Caesar, I shall.   68
                    Exit Proculeius.

CAESAR
Gallus, go you along. [*Exit Gallus.*] Where's
    Dolabella,
To second Proculeius?

ALL   Dolabella!

CAESAR
Let him alone, for I remember now   71
How he's employed. He shall in time be ready.
Go with me to my tent, where you shall see
How hardly I was drawn into this war,   74
How calm and gentle I proceeded still   75
In all my writings. Go with me and see   76
What I can show in this.   *Exeunt.*

❖

5.2   *Enter Cleopatra, Charmian, Iras, and Mardian.*

CLEOPATRA
My desolation does begin to make
A better life. 'Tis paltry to be Caesar;   2
Not being Fortune, he's but Fortune's knave,   3
A minister of her will. And it is great

---

19 moiety half   **21 self** same   **27–28 The gods . . . kings** (Caesar supposes that the gods rebuke him for unmanly tears but excuses himself by reflecting that these tidings would make kings weep.)   **30 persisted** persistently desired or pursued   **31 Waged equal with** battled equally in   **32 steer humanity** govern any individual.   **will give** insist on giving   **36 followed** pursued   **36–37 but . . . bodies** i.e., I have hurt you to cure myself, as men lance diseases in their own bodies   **37 perforce** necessarily   **38 shown to thee** i.e., suffered myself at your hands   **39 stall** dwell   **41 as sovereign . . . hearts** as precious or efficacious as hearts' blood   **42 competitor** associate, partner (and rival)   **43 In . . . design** at the head of every grand enterprise   **44 front** forehead, face   **45–46 the heart . . . kindle** i.e., (Antony was) the brave heart where my heart kindled its *(his)* thoughts of courage   **47–48 should . . . this** should divide our equal partnership to this extreme   **49 meeter season** more suitable time   **50 looks . . . him** reveals itself in his expression   **51 Whence are you** where do you come from?

52 A . . . yet i.e., (I come from) Egyptian Cleopatra, still reduced in circumstance (and awaiting your will), or, I am a poor Egyptian still, though subject to Rome's authority   **55 frame herself** shape her course of action   **57 ours** my people   **62 purpose** intend   **63 passion** grief   **64 greatness** greatness of spirit   **65 life in Rome** presence in Rome alive   **66 eternal in our triumph** an eternal glory in our triumphal procession   **67 with your speediest** as quickly as you can   **68 of** concerning   **71 Let him alone** don't bother about him now   **74 hardly** reluctantly   **75 still** always   **76 writings** i.e., letters to Antony

5.2. Location: Alexandria. Cleopatra's monument.
2 better i.e., rising above the vicissitudes of fortune   **3 knave** servant

To do that thing that ends all other deeds, 5
Which shackles accidents and bolts up change, 6
Which sleeps and never palates more the dung, 7
The beggar's nurse and Caesar's. 8

Enter [to the gates of the monument] Proculeius.

PROCULEIUS
Caesar sends greeting to the Queen of Egypt,
And bids thee study on what fair demands 10
Thou mean'st to have him grant thee.
CLEOPATRA   What's thy name?
PROCULEIUS
My name is Proculeius.
CLEOPATRA   Antony
Did tell me of you, bade me trust you; but
I do not greatly care to be deceived, 14
That have no use for trusting. If your master 15
Would have a queen his beggar, you must tell him
That majesty, to keep decorum, must
No less beg than a kingdom. If he please
To give me conquered Egypt for my son,
He gives me so much of mine own as I 20
Will kneel to him with thanks.
PROCULEIUS   Be of good cheer;
You're fall'n into a princely hand. Fear nothing.
Make your full reference freely to my lord, 23
Who is so full of grace that it flows over
On all that need. Let me report to him
Your sweet dependency, and you shall find 26
A conqueror that will pray in aid for kindness 27
Where he for grace is kneeled to.
CLEOPATRA   Pray you, tell him
I am his fortune's vassal, and I send him 29
The greatness he has got. I hourly learn 30
A doctrine of obedience, and would gladly
Look him i' the face.
PROCULEIUS   This I'll report, dear lady.
Have comfort, for I know your plight is pitied
Of him that caused it. 34

[Roman soldiers enter from
behind Cleopatra and take her prisoner.]
You see how easily she may be surprised.
[To the soldiers.] Guard her till Caesar come.
IRAS   Royal Queen!
CHARMIAN
O Cleopatra! Thou art taken, Queen.
CLEOPATRA *[drawing a dagger]*
Quick, quick, good hands.

5–8 To do . . . Caesar's i.e., to commit suicide, which subdues accident and change and by which we sleep in death, relishing no more
the dungy earth that sustains both Caesar and the beggar. (*Bolts up*
means "fetters" or "locks up.") 10 study on consider carefully
14 do . . . to be am wary of being 15 That since I 20 as that
23 Make . . . reference refer your case 26 dependency submissiveness 27 pray in aid beg your assistance. (A legal term meaning "to
call in the assistance of an outside person.") for kindness i.e., in
thinking of ways to be kind 29–30 I send . . . got i.e., I acknowledge his superiority over all he has won, including myself 34 Of by.
s.d. Roman soldiers (Perhaps led by Gallus; see 5.1.69. Possibly some
speech for him has been omitted.)

PROCULEIUS   Hold, worthy lady, hold!
[He disarms her.]
Do not yourself such wrong, who are in this
Relieved, but not betrayed.
CLEOPATRA   What, of death too, 40
That rids our dogs of languish?
PROCULEIUS   Cleopatra, 41
Do not abuse my master's bounty by 42
Th' undoing of yourself. Let the world see
His nobleness well acted, which your death 44
Will never let come forth.
CLEOPATRA   Where art thou, Death? 45
Come hither, come! Come, come, and take a queen
Worth many babes and beggars!
PROCULEIUS   O, temperance, lady! 47
CLEOPATRA
Sir, I will eat no meat, I'll not drink, sir;
If idle talk will once be necessary, 49
I'll not sleep, neither. This mortal house I'll ruin,
Do Caesar what he can. Know, sir, that I
Will not wait pinioned at your master's court, 52
Nor once be chastised with the sober eye
Of dull Octavia. Shall they hoist me up
And show me to the shouting varletry 55
Of censuring Rome? Rather a ditch in Egypt
Be gentle grave unto me! Rather on Nilus' mud
Lay me stark nak'd and let the waterflies
Blow me into abhorring! Rather make 59
My country's high pyramides my gibbet 60
And hang me up in chains!
PROCULEIUS   You do extend
These thoughts of horror further than you shall
Find cause in Caesar.

Enter Dolabella.

DOLABELLA   Proculeius,
What thou hast done thy master Caesar knows,
And he hath sent for thee. For the Queen, 65
I'll take her to my guard.
PROCULEIUS   So, Dolabella,
It shall content me best. Be gentle to her.
[To Cleopatra.] To Caesar I will speak what you shall
please, 68
If you'll employ me to him.
CLEOPATRA   Say I would die.
Exit Proculeius [with soldiers].
DOLABELLA
Most noble Empress, you have heard of me?

40 Relieved rescued. of death too i.e., (1) am I *relieved* or deprived
even of death (2) am I *betrayed* even of the right to die 41 our dogs
even our dogs. languish lingering disease 42 bounty generosity
44 acted accomplished 45 let come forth allow to be displayed
47 babes and beggars i.e., those whom death takes easily and often,
those to whom "relief" is often given 49 If . . . necessary even if
on occasion I must resort to idle talk (to keep myself awake) 52 wait
attend, as a slave. pinioned like a bird with clipped wings, unable
to fly 55 varletry rabble 59 Blow . . . abhorring cause me to swell
abhorrently with maggots, or, deposit their eggs on me until I become
abhorrent 60 gibbet gallows 65 For as for 68 what whatever

CLEOPATRA
I cannot tell.
DOLABELLA   Assuredly you know me.
CLEOPATRA
No matter, sir, what I have heard or known.
You laugh when boys or women tell their dreams;
Is 't not your trick?
DOLABELLA   I understand not, madam.   74
CLEOPATRA
I dreamt there was an emperor Antony.
O, such another sleep, that I might see
But such another man!
DOLABELLA   If it might please ye—
CLEOPATRA
His face was as the heavens, and therein stuck   78
A sun and moon, which kept their course and
    lighted
The little O, the earth.
DOLABELLA   Most sovereign creature—
CLEOPATRA
His legs bestrid the ocean; his reared arm   81
Crested the world; his voice was propertied   82
As all the tunèd spheres, and that to friends;   83
But when he meant to quail and shake the orb,   84
He was as rattling thunder. For his bounty,   85
There was no winter in 't; an autumn 'twas
That grew the more by reaping. His delights   87
Were dolphinlike; they showed his back above   88
The element they lived in. In his livery   89
Walked crowns and crownets; realms and islands
    were   90
As plates dropped from his pocket.
DOLABELLA   Cleopatra—   91
CLEOPATRA
Think you there was or might be such a man
As this I dreamt of?
DOLABELLA   Gentle madam, no.
CLEOPATRA
You lie, up to the hearing of the gods.
But if there be nor ever were one such,   95
It's past the size of dreaming. Nature wants stuff   96
To vie strange forms with fancy; yet t' imagine   97
An Antony were nature's piece 'gainst fancy,   98
Condemning shadows quite.
DOLABELLA   Hear me, good madam: 99

74 trick manner, way   78 stuck were set   81 bestrid straddled
82 Crested formed a crest for; surmounted (like a raised arm in heraldry)   82–83 propertied . . . friends endowed with qualities which,
when he spoke to friends, recalled the harmony of the heavenly bodies in their spheres   84 quail make quail, overawe.   orb world
85 For as for   87–89 His . . . in i.e., the delight he enjoyed and
gave to others was sustained both by his great capacity for immersion
in the life he led and by his capacity to rise above that life, just as a
dolphin rises out of the element in which it lives, the sea   89–90 In
. . . crownets i.e., among his retainers (those who would wear his
livery) were kings and princes   91 plates coins   95 nor ever were or
if there never existed   96 It's . . . dreaming no dream can come up
to it, my image of him   96–97 Nature . . . fancy nature lacks material to equal the remarkable forms produced by fancy or imagination
97–99 yet . . . quite i.e., yet an Antony such as I have pictured forth
would himself be a work of nature, in fact would be nature's masterpiece in the competition with the imagination

Your loss is as yourself, great; and you bear it
As answering to the weight. Would I might never   101
O'ertake pursued success but I do feel,   102
By the rebound of yours, a grief that smites   103
My very heart at root.
CLEOPATRA   I thank you, sir.
Know you what Caesar means to do with me?
DOLABELLA
I am loath to tell you what I would you knew.
CLEOPATRA
Nay, pray you, sir.
DOLABELLA   Though he be honorable—
CLEOPATRA   He'll lead me, then, in triumph.
DOLABELLA   Madam, he will, I know 't.   Flourish.

Enter Proculeius, Caesar, Gallus, Maecenas, and
others of his train.

ALL   Make way there! Caesar!
CAESAR   Which is the Queen of Egypt?
DOLABELLA   It is the Emperor, madam.
Cleopatra kneels.
CAESAR   Arise, you shall not kneel. I pray you, rise.
Rise, Egypt.
CLEOPATRA [rising]   Sir, the gods will have it thus;
My master and my lord I must obey.
CAESAR   Take to you no hard thoughts.   116
The record of what injuries you did us,
Though written in our flesh, we shall remember
As things but done by chance.
CLEOPATRA   Sole sir o' the world,   119
I cannot project mine own cause so well   120
To make it clear, but do confess I have   121
Been laden with like frailties which before
Have often shamed our sex.
CAESAR   Cleopatra, know
We will extenuate rather than enforce.   124
If you apply yourself to our intents,   125
Which towards you are most gentle, you shall find
A benefit in this change; but if you seek
To lay on me a cruelty by taking   128
Antony's course, you shall bereave yourself   129
Of my good purposes and put your children
To that destruction which I'll guard them from
If thereon you rely. I'll take my leave.
CLEOPATRA
And may, through all the world! 'Tis yours, and we,   133
Your scutcheons and your signs of conquest, shall   134
Hang in what place you please. Here, my good lord.   135
[She gives him a scroll.]

101 As . . . weight commensurate with the weightiness of the loss
101–102 Would . . . do i.e., may I never succeed at what I desire if
I do not   103 rebound reflection   116 Take . . . thoughts don't torment yourself with reproaches   119 sir master   120 project set forth
121 clear free of blame   124 enforce lay stress upon and punish (the
faults)   125 If . . . intents if you comply with my plans   128 lay
. . . cruelty force me to be cruel   129 bereave rob   133 And may
i.e., (1) you may leave when you choose (2) you may have your will
in anything   134 scutcheons shields showing armorial bearings;
hence, shields hung up as monuments of victory   135 Hang (1) be
hung up or displayed as your trophies (2) be hanged as your captives

CAESAR
You shall advise me in all for Cleopatra.   136
CLEOPATRA
This is the brief of money, plate, and jewels   137
I am possessed of. 'Tis exactly valued,
Not petty things admitted. Where's Seleucus?   139

    [*Enter Seleucus.*]

SELEUCUS   Here, madam.
CLEOPATRA
This is my treasurer. Let him speak, my lord,
Upon his peril, that I have reserved
To myself nothing. Speak the truth, Seleucus.
SELEUCUS
Madam, I had rather seal my lips
Than to my peril speak that which is not.
CLEOPATRA   What have I kept back?
SELEUCUS
Enough to purchase what you have made known.
CAESAR
Nay, blush not, Cleopatra. I approve
Your wisdom in the deed.
CLEOPATRA   See, Caesar! O, behold
How pomp is followed! Mine will now be yours,   150
And, should we shift estates, yours would be mine. 151
The ingratitude of this Seleucus does
Even make me wild.—O slave, of no more trust
Than love that's hired! [*Seleucus retreats from her.*]
    What, goest thou back? Thou shalt   154
Go back, I warrant thee! But I'll catch thine eyes,
Though they had wings. Slave, soulless villain, dog!
O rarely base!
CAESAR   Good Queen, let us entreat you.   157
CLEOPATRA
O Caesar, what a wounding shame is this,
That thou vouchsafing here to visit me,   159
Doing the honor of thy lordliness
To one so meek, that mine own servant should
Parcel the sum of my disgraces by   162
Addition of his envy! Say, good Caesar,   163
That I some lady trifles have reserved,   164
Immoment toys, things of such dignity   165
As we greet modern friends withal, and say   166
Some nobler token I have kept apart
For Livia and Octavia, to induce   168
Their mediation; must I be unfolded   169
With one that I have bred? The gods! It smites me   170
Beneath the fall I have. [*To Seleucus.*] Prithee, go
    hence,
Or I shall show the cinders of my spirits   172

Through th' ashes of my chance. Wert thou a man,   173
Thou wouldst have mercy on me.
CAESAR   Forbear, Seleucus.   [*Exit Seleucus.*] 175
CLEOPATRA
Be it known that we, the greatest, are misthought   176
For things that others do; and when we fall
We answer others' merits in our name,   178
Are therefore to be pitied.
CAESAR   Cleopatra,
Not what you have reserved nor what acknowledged
Put we i' the roll of conquest. Still be 't yours;
Bestow it at your pleasure, and believe   182
Caesar's no merchant, to make prize with you   183
Of things that merchants sold. Therefore be cheered.
Make not your thoughts your prisons. No, dear
    Queen,   185
For we intend so to dispose you as   186
Yourself shall give us counsel. Feed and sleep.
Our care and pity is so much upon you
That we remain your friend; and so adieu.
CLEOPATRA
My master, and my lord!
CAESAR   Not so. Adieu.
    Flourish. Exeunt Caesar and his train.
CLEOPATRA
He words me, girls, he words me, that I should not   191
Be noble to myself. But hark thee, Charmian.   192
            [*She whispers to Charmian.*]
IRAS
Finish, good lady. The bright day is done,
And we are for the dark.
CLEOPATRA [*to Charmian*]   Hie thee again.   194
I have spoke already, and it is provided;   195
Go put it to the haste.
CHARMIAN   Madam, I will.

    Enter Dolabella.

DOLABELLA
Where's the Queen?
CHARMIAN   Behold, sir.   [*Exit.*]
CLEOPATRA   Dolabella!
DOLABELLA
Madam, as thereto sworn by your command,
Which my love makes religion to obey,   199
I tell you this: Caesar through Syria
Intends his journey, and within three days
You with your children will he send before.
Make your best use of this. I have performed
Your pleasure and my promise.
CLEOPATRA   Dolabella,
I shall remain your debtor.

---

136 in all for Cleopatra i.e., in all matters pertaining to yourself
137 brief list   **139 Not . . . admitted** petty things omitted
150 pomp is followed noble and royal persons are served.   **Mine** my
followers   **151 shift estates** reverse fortunes, exchange places
154 hired paid for   **157 rarely** exceptionally   **159 vouchsafing** deigning to come   **162 Parcel** particularize   **163 envy** malice   **164 lady**
ladylike, feminine   **165 Immoment toys** trifles of no moment or importance   **166 modern** common.   **withal** with   **168 Livia** Octavius
Caesar's wife   **169–170 unfolded With** exposed by   **170 one that I
have bred** one of my household   **172 cinders** smoldering hot coals

173 chance (fallen) fortune   **175 Forbear** withdraw   **176 misthought**
misjudged   **178 We . . . name** we are accountable for the deeds of
others done in our name   **182 Bestow** use   **183 make prize** haggle
185 Make . . . prisons i.e., don't imprison yourself in your thoughts
by misconceiving of your situation   **186 dispose** dispose of   **191–
192 words . . . myself** tries to deceive me with mere words to keep
me from suicide   **194 Hie thee again** return quickly   **195 spoke**
given orders (for the means of suicide)   **199 makes religion** i.e., absolutely binds me

DOLABELLA   I your servant.
Adieu, good Queen. I must attend on Caesar.
CLEOPATRA
Farewell, and thanks.   *Exit [Dolabella].*
                    Now, Iras, what think'st thou?
Thou an Egyptian puppet shall be shown
In Rome as well as I. Mechanic slaves   209
With greasy aprons, rules, and hammers shall   210
Uplift us to the view. In their thick breaths,
Rank of gross diet, shall we be enclouded   212
And forced to drink their vapor.
IRAS   The gods forbid!   213
CLEOPATRA
Nay, 'tis most certain, Iras. Saucy lictors   214
Will catch at us like strumpets, and scald rhymers   215
Ballad us out o' tune. The quick comedians   216
Extemporally will stage us and present   217
Our Alexandrian revels; Antony
Shall be brought drunken forth, and I shall see
Some squeaking Cleopatra boy my greatness   220
I' the posture of a whore.
IRAS   O the good gods!
CLEOPATRA   Nay, that's certain.
IRAS
I'll never see 't! For I am sure my nails
Are stronger than mine eyes.
CLEOPATRA   Why, that's the way
To fool their preparation and to conquer
Their most absurd intents.

Enter Charmian.

                    Now, Charmian!
Show me, my women, like a queen. Go fetch   227
My best attires. I am again for Cydnus,
To meet Mark Antony. Sirrah Iras, go—   229
Now, noble Charmian, we'll dispatch indeed—   230
And when thou hast done this chare I'll give thee
    leave   231
To play till doomsday. Bring our crown and all.   232
                    [Exit Iras.] A noise within.
Wherefore's this noise?

Enter a Guardsman.

GUARDSMAN   Here is a rural fellow
That will not be denied Your Highness' presence.
He brings you figs.
CLEOPATRA
Let him come in.   *Exit Guardsman.*
                    What poor an instrument   236
May do a noble deed! He brings me liberty.

My resolution's placed, and I have nothing   238
Of woman in me. Now from head to foot
I am marble-constant; now the fleeting moon   240
No planet is of mine.

Enter Guardsman, and Clown [bringing in a basket].

GUARDSMAN   This is the man.   241
CLEOPATRA   Avoid, and leave him.   *Exit Guardsman.*   242
Hast thou the pretty worm of Nilus there,   243
That kills and pains not?
CLOWN   Truly, I have him, but I would not be the party
    that should desire you to touch him, for his biting is
    immortal. Those that do die of it do seldom or never   247
    recover.
CLEOPATRA   Remember'st thou any that have died on 't?
CLOWN   Very many, men and women too. I heard of   250
    one of them no longer than yesterday—a very honest
    woman, but something given to lie, as a woman   252
    should not do but in the way of honesty—how she
    died of the biting of it, what pain she felt. Truly, she
    makes a very good report o' the worm. But he that will
    believe all that they say shall never be saved by half
    that they do. But this is most falliable, the worm's an   257
    odd worm.
CLEOPATRA   Get thee hence, farewell.
CLOWN   I wish you all joy of the worm.
                    [He sets down his basket.]
CLEOPATRA   Farewell.
CLOWN   You must think this, look you, that the worm
    will do his kind.   263
CLEOPATRA   Ay, ay; farewell.
CLOWN   Look you, the worm is not to be trusted but in
    the keeping of wise people, for indeed there is no
    goodness in the worm.
CLEOPATRA   Take thou no care; it shall be heeded.   268
CLOWN   Very good. Give it nothing, I pray you, for it is
    not worth the feeding.
CLEOPATRA   Will it eat me?
CLOWN   You must not think I am so simple but I know
    the devil himself will not eat a woman. I know that a
    woman is a dish for the gods, if the devil dress her   274
    not. But truly, these same whoreson devils do the   275
    gods great harm in their women, for in every ten that
    they make, the devils mar five.
CLEOPATRA   Well, get thee gone. Farewell.
CLOWN   Yes, forsooth. I wish you joy o' the worm.
                    Exit.

[Enter Iras with royal attire.]

209 Mechanic slaves common laborers   **210 rules** straight-edged measuring sticks   **212 Rank . . . diet** reeking of coarse food   **213 drink** drink in, breathe deeply   **214 lictors** minor officials in attendance on Roman magistrates   **215 scald** scurvy   **216 Ballad us** sing ballads about us.   **quick** quick-witted   **217 Extemporally** in improvised performance   **220 boy** (Allusion to the practice of having women's parts acted by boys on the Elizabethan stage.)   **227 Show** display   **229 Sirrah** (Compare *sirs*, addressed to the women, in 4.15.90.)   **230 dispatch** (1) finish (2) hasten   **231 chare** task, chore   **232 s.d. Exit Iras** (It is possible that Charmian leaves, too.)   **236 What** how

238 placed fixed   **240 fleeting** inconstant, changing   **241 s.d. Clown** rustic   **242 Avoid** withdraw   **243 worm** snake, serpent (but elsewhere in this scene with the added connotation of "the male sexual organ" and "earthworm")   **247 immortal** (Blunder for "mortal.")   **250 heard of** heard from   **252 to lie** (with sexual second meaning hinted at also in *honest*, i.e., "chaste," *die*, i.e., "reach orgasm," and *worm*)   **257 falliable** (Blunder for "infallible.")   **263 his kind** its natural function   **268 Take thou no care** don't worry   **274 dress** prepare, as in cooking (with a suggestion also of dressing in alluring clothes)   **275 whoreson** i.e., rascally, abominable. (A slang expression.)

CLEOPATRA
  Give me my robe. Put on my crown. I have
  Immortal longings in me. Now no more   281
  The juice of Egypt's grape shall moist this lip.
                                    [*The women dress her.*]
  Yare, yare, good Iras; quick. Methinks I hear   283
  Antony call; I see him rouse himself
  To praise my noble act. I hear him mock
  The luck of Caesar, which the gods give men
  To excuse their after wrath. Husband, I come!   287
  Now to that name my courage prove my title!   288
  I am fire and air; my other elements   289
  I give to baser life. So, have you done?
  Come then, and take the last warmth of my lips.
  Farewell, kind Charmian. Iras, long farewell.
                      [*She kisses them. Iras falls and dies.*]
  Have I the aspic in my lips? Dost fall?   293
  If thou and nature can so gently part,
  The stroke of death is as a lover's pinch,
  Which hurts, and is desired. Dost thou lie still?
  If thus thou vanishest, thou tell'st the world
  It is not worth leave-taking.   298
CHARMIAN
  Dissolve, thick cloud, and rain, that I may say
  The gods themselves do weep!
CLEOPATRA   This proves me base.
  If she first meet the curlèd Antony,   301
  He'll make demand of her, and spend that kiss   302
  Which is my heaven to have. [*To an asp.*] Come,
    thou mortal wretch,   303
  With thy sharp teeth this knot intrinsicate   304
  Of life at once untie. Poor venomous fool,
  Be angry, and dispatch. O, couldst thou speak,
  That I might hear thee call great Caesar ass
  Unpolicied!
CHARMIAN   O eastern star!
CLEOPATRA   Peace, peace!   308
  Dost thou not see my baby at my breast,
  That sucks the nurse asleep?
CHARMIAN   O, break! O, break!
CLEOPATRA
  As sweet as balm, as soft as air, as gentle—
  O Antony!—Nay, I will take thee too.
                      [*Applying another asp to her arm.*]
  What should I stay—   *Dies.* 313
CHARMIAN
  In this wild world? So, fare thee well.   314
  Now boast thee, Death, in thy possession lies

---

281 Immortal longings longings for immortality   **283 Yare** quick
287 their after wrath i.e., the wrath of the gods visited on those who
have been insolent in their good fortune   **288 to . . . title** may my
courage prove my right to call myself Antony's wife   **289 other elements** i.e., earth and water, the heavier elements   **293 aspic** asp
298 is . . . leave-taking does not deserve a ceremonious farewell
301 curlèd with curled hair   **302 make demand** (1) ask questions (2)
ask pleasure.   **spend that kiss** expend his desire on her   **303 mortal**
deadly.   **wretch** (An affectionate term of abuse, like *fool* in line 305.)
304 intrinsicate intricate   **308 Unpolicied** outwitted.   **eastern star**
i.e., Venus, the morning star   **313 What** why   **314 wild** savage.
(Sometimes emended to *vild*, "vile.")

  A lass unparalleled. Downy windows, close;   316
  And golden Phoebus never be beheld
  Of eyes again so royal! Your crown's awry;   318
  I'll mend it, and then play—   319
              Enter the Guard, rustling in.

FIRST GUARD
  Where's the Queen?
CHARMIAN   Speak softly. Wake her not.
FIRST GUARD
  Caesar hath sent—
CHARMIAN   Too slow a messenger.
                      [*She applies an asp to herself.*]
  O, come apace, dispatch! I partly feel thee.
FIRST GUARD
  Approach, ho! All's not well. Caesar's beguiled.   323
SECOND GUARD
  There's Dolabella sent from Caesar. Call him.
                                    [*Exit a guard.*]
FIRST GUARD
  What work is here, Charmian? Is this well done?
CHARMIAN
  It is well done, and fitting for a princess
  Descended of so many royal kings.
  Ah, soldier!   *Charmian dies.*

              Enter Dolabella.

DOLABELLA
  How goes it here?
SECOND GUARD   All dead.
DOLABELLA   Caesar, thy thoughts
  Touch their effects in this. Thyself art coming   330
  To see performed the dreaded act which thou
  So sought'st to hinder.

              Enter Caesar and all his train, marching.

ALL   A way there, a way for Caesar!   333
DOLABELLA
  O sir, you are too sure an augurer;
  That you did fear is done.
CAESAR   Bravest at the last,   335
  She leveled at our purposes and, being royal,   336
  Took her own way. The manner of their deaths?
  I do not see them bleed.
DOLABELLA   Who was last with them?
FIRST GUARD
  A simple countryman, that brought her figs.   339
  This was his basket.
CAESAR   Poisoned, then.
FIRST GUARD   O Caesar,
  This Charmian lived but now; she stood and spake.
  I found her trimming up the diadem
  On her dead mistress; tremblingly she stood,
  And on the sudden dropped.
CAESAR   O, noble weakness!
  If they had swallowed poison, 'twould appear

---

316 Downy windows i.e., soft eyelids   **318 Of** by   **319 mend** fix,
straighten   **323 beguiled** cheated, tricked   **330 Touch their effects**
meet with realization   **333 A way** make a path   **335 That** that which
336 leveled at aimed at, guessed   **339 simple** humbly born

By external swelling; but she looks like sleep,   346
As she would catch another Antony   347
In her strong toil of grace.
DOLABELLA   Here on her breast 348
There is a vent of blood and something blown;   349
The like is on her arm.
FIRST GUARD
This is an aspic's trail, and these fig leaves
Have slime upon them, such as th' aspic leaves
Upon the caves of Nile.
CAESAR   Most probable
That so she died; for her physician tells me
She hath pursued conclusions infinite   355
Of easy ways to die. Take up her bed,
And bear her women from the monument.
She shall be buried by her Antony.
No grave upon the earth shall clip in it   359
A pair so famous. High events as these
Strike those that make them; and their story is   361
No less in pity than his glory which   362
Brought them to be lamented. Our army shall   363
In solemn show attend this funeral,
And then to Rome. Come, Dolabella, see
High order in this great solemnity.   366
                    Exeunt omnes, [bearing the dead bodies].

346 like sleep as if asleep   **347 As** as if   **348 toil** net   **349 vent** discharge.   **blown** deposited, or, swollen   **355 conclusions** experiments
359 clip embrace, clasp   **361 Strike . . . them** touch with sorrow
those who brought about these deeds   **361–363 their story . . . lamented** the story of these famous lovers is no less pitiable than the
fame of him who brought them low is glorious   **366 s.d. omnes** all

Coriolanus

Coriolanus may be Shakespeare's last tragedy. Even though external evidence is scarce as to its actual date, the style suggests a time around 1608. If so, Shakespeare's final statement on humanity's tragic destiny is disillusioned, wry, almost anticlimactic, in the vein of his Roman and classical tragedies rather than of his great tragedies of evil *(Hamlet, Othello, King Lear, Macbeth)*. Shakespeare based *Coriolanus* on Plutarch's *Lives of the Noble Grecians and Romans,* in the translation by Sir Thomas North. As in the presumably earlier Plutarchan plays, *Julius Caesar, Timon of Athens,* and *Antony and Cleopatra,* and in the non-Plutarchan *Titus Andronicus* and *Troilus and Cressida,* Shakespeare's ancient political world is one of constant upheaval. In the clash of ideologies, the plebeian mob turns giddily from one idol to the next, and strong men rise briefly, only to be supplanted by a rival. The result of unceasing change is political stalemate. The great men of the ancient world seem fascinatingly alive to us, but they also seem blind to their own limitations, fatally proud, and hemmed in by circumstance. Their virtues and their defects are inseparable and indeed often identical, for private virtues serve these tragic heroes poorly in the amoral and pitiless arena of politics. Their natures cannot easily be moved from a predilection for catastrophe, and so their downfall proceeds inexorably from what Aristotle, writing of Greek tragedy, termed a flaw, or hamartia, in their characters. The ending, ironic rather than cathartic in its effect, leaves us with an impression of tragic waste.

Coriolanus admirably captures this conflict dividing personal nobility from political reality. The play returns to a political problem that has been studied before in *Julius Caesar:* the rivalry in ancient Rome between republican and absolutist forms of government. *Coriolanus,* although written later than *Julius Caesar,* analyzes an earlier period of Roman history. In *Coriolanus,* we witness the birth of republicanism in its distinctively Roman form, a blend of aristocratic and democratic elements; in *Julius Caesar,* we see the demise of this delicately balanced regime. Shakespeare views both events with ironic detachment.

Republicanism was potentially a matter of controversy on the Jacobean stage, insofar as spectators might draw analogies between it and parliamentary efforts to curb the power of the English throne. The differences are real, of course, especially in *Julius Caesar,* in which Caesar's claim to abso-

lute rule has no sanction of divine right and Brutus' republicanism is ineffably genteel rather than populist. *Coriolanus,* however, hits closer to home. Here the plebeians are profoundly dissatisfied with aristocratic rule. Popular unrest over famine and high prices leads to rioting and the expression of democratic sentiments such as were heard and feared by the authorities in England. Riots over scarcity of grain occurred in Northamptonshire, Warwickshire, and Leicestershire during the summer of 1607. King James I, who had come to the throne in 1603, adopted a hostile stance toward Puritan efforts to democratize Church government and of corresponding challenges in Parliament on behalf of the common law. From the vantage point of ancient Rome, distant in time and place, *Coriolanus* appraises the conflict in terms that bear no precise relation to Jacobean England but yet have a timeless relevance. Without taking sides, the play dwells on the ambiguity of the struggle and on the indecisive, self-defeating results ironically achieved by both parties.

As in *Julius Caesar,* men on both sides are passionately sincere but driven to shortsighted extremism. The tribunes insist on behalf of the mob that the people's voice is to be the ultimate law of Rome. Coriolanus, in angry response, sees the mob and its elected tribunes as the enemies of hierarchical prerogative, threatening the very existence of the state. Which view is correct? Is the people's voice a brave force of resistance against aristocratic hauteur and class privilege, as exemplified by Coriolanus, or is the tribunes' program a grab for power by demagogues willing to risk anarchy and to weaken Rome's military might? Shakespeare seems to offer no unequivocal answer. Like Plutarch, he explores the weaknesses and strengths of both parties. He uses a dramatic structure, as in *Julius Caesar,* of sustained ambiguity. If any conclusion emerges, it is that violent political struggle leads only to an undoing of those civilized institutions that persons of moderation, caught in the middle, strive vainly to preserve.

The citizens play a dominant role in *Coriolanus.* The action begins, as in *Julius Caesar,* with a mob scene, setting a tone of ominous instability. The mob is too easily swayed. Lacking any consistent political philosophy of its own, it will follow whatever charismatic orator catches its fancy. It despises Coriolanus one moment and adulates him the next. Its own members agree that the mob is a "many-headed multitude," directionless and irresponsible (2.3.10–17). Other characters besides Coriolanus protest the offensive stench of the crowd, "stinking" breaths, "reechy" necks, "stinking greasy caps," and unclean teeth (2.1.208,235; 4.6.138). The Roman citizens are a "herd," "apron-men," "garlic eaters," curs, hares, foxes, geese, a "cockle of rebellion, insolence, sedition" (3.1.35,73; 4.6.101–103). This deliberately repulsive portrayal merely intensifies what is true in the other Roman plays and in the English history plays as well. Nowhere in Shakespeare does mob action lead to anything constructive or even politically acceptable. At the same time, the mob does not bear chief responsibility for disaster either, in *Coriolanus* or elsewhere in Shakespeare. Individually, its members are good-natured, slow to be aroused, quick to forget injury, too credulous indeed for their own good. In *Coriolanus,* they have to be prompted again and again by the tribunes to press forward with their resentment. Many citizens, left to themselves, are wise and patient. They are a neutral force, dangerous only when whipped up to collective frenzy by demagogic persuasion.

Much blame would seem to fall then on the tribunes, and indeed even the more moderate patricians, such as Menenius, are deeply mistrustful of Junius Brutus and Sicinius Velutus. These tribunes are willing to risk mob violence to achieve their ends, especially when they urge the "rabble of plebeians" to "bustle about Coriolanus" (3.1.183–188). Ignoring Menenius' pleas that "This is the way to kindle, not to quench," and that "Confusion's near" (lines 193, 200), the tribunes deliberately goad Coriolanus to anger. Their strategy is to foment clamor, and "with a din confused / Enforce the present execution," shouting down reason with hysteria (3.3.21–22). They carefully stage each confrontation with Coriolanus, rehearsing the citizens in what they are to do, cannily timing their provocations. They talk like conspirators. Shakespeare's audience, accustomed to governmental warnings against mob violence, would probably have understood the menace posed by the tribunes and would have savored the irony that Rome is weakened rather than strengthened by their machinations.

Still, Shakespeare's portrayal of the tribunes is remarkably sympathetic. They honestly fear that Coriolanus seeks "one sole throne, without assistance" (4.6.34), and that as consul he will do everything he can to suppress the people's liberties. This is no idle fear; Coriolanus' own friends merely counsel him to attack the tribunes after he has achieved power, not before. Although the tribunes do arouse the people to actions they would not otherwise take, the tribunes believe they are doing so in the people's best interests, providing leadership for a constituency that has hitherto lacked a voice. They believe in a government "by the consent of all" that can hold aristocratic insolence in check through the "lawful censure" of the common people. "What is the city but the people?" (3.1.202–204; 3.3.50). Moreover, they are not revolutionaries by temperament and do abandon mob tactics once they have made their point. Their achievements mock them when Rome proves defenseless against the return of Coriolanus, but even here they can argue with some reason that Rome would have achieved peace had it not been for Coriolanus' lawless vengeance.

Perhaps, then, Coriolanus must bear the responsibility for provoking democratic extremism through his contempt of the citizenry. From his first appearance, he antagonizes us, as well as the populace, with his curt, insulting manner. He addresses the people as "dissentious rogues," itching with scabby diseases, and dismisses them as "curs" who are "beneath abhorring" (1.1.163–167). His hatred amounts to revulsion, and we fear he is all too ready to employ his sword on "thousands of these quartered slaves" (line 198). When denied the consulship by the tribunes, in fact, he draws his sword in the marketplace, relishing the opportunity for a military solution. His tendency to forget names betrays a coldness. Although he professes not to speak merely in anger, he is too easily baited by the tribunes and too quick to speak his mind. Even those who admire his virtues concede that "to seem to affect the malice and displeasure of the people is as bad as that which he dislikes, to flatter them for their love" (2.2.21–23). Coriolanus is glad to hear of the impending Volscian attack on Rome, for he prefers war to peace and sees conscription as a way of channeling revolutionary energies against an outward foe. He professes love of his country, but, because his attachment is to an exclusively patrician order, he is ready to turn traitor against a Rome that gives a political voice to the plebeians he so abhors.

Nevertheless, the portrayal of Coriolanus, as of the tribunes, is delicately balanced. We admire Coriolanus' hatred of hypocrisy. He is scrupulously honest, refusing all spoils of war except those to which his fellow soldiers are entitled. Despite his pride in family and name, he genuinely dislikes to hear himself praised. Though he disdains to lead cowardly citizen-soldiers and shines most in single deeds of valor rather than in generalship, he is inspiring and even popular among valiant soldiers like himself. He is generous in praising the achievements of his colleagues. Even in matters of state, he shows resoluteness and integrity. He has a consistent political philosophy, bolstered by Menenius' comparison of the state to a body in which the members must harmoniously interact (1.1.94 ff). Jacobean spectators would recognize in this analogy the orthodox appeal to order and degree they heard regularly from pulpit and throne, even though they might also recognize that it is being self-interestedly applied by one who enjoys the perquisites of noble birth. Coriolanus, at any rate, firmly believes that the established prerogatives of the aristocracy are Rome's only safe bulwark against chaos. By granting power to the tribunes, in his view, the Senate has sealed its doom. He sees the people as their own worst enemies, insatiable and irrational in their demands, unable to comprehend the subtleties of government, instinctively envious of their betters. Such base mortals require subjection to their masters, though they cannot be expected to realize this themselves. Coriolanus knows that his views are out of fashion and that the current trend is to appease popular demands with compromise, but he can see no end to the compromises that will be needed once the tribunes have established their prerogatives. He prefers a battle to the death and welcomes the danger to himself. If his courage and consistency are "too absolute," if he is "too noble for the world" (3.2.41;

3.1.261), he would prefer to believe that the fault lies in that world rather than in him.

Between the extremes of democratic and aristocratic rule, the middle position of compromise offers many attractions. Menenius sanely desires to see "On both sides more respect" and pleads with those who would be "truly your country's friend" to "temperately proceed to what you would / Thus violently redress" (3.1.184; 222–224). Although his sympathies are patrician, he acknowledges the tribunes' power as a political reality which must be dealt with. He finds fault with Coriolanus for not having "temporized" (4.6.17). Menenius is a bluff, honest fellow who directs our sympathies, like the equally outspoken Enobarbus in *Antony and Cleopatra*. Yet compromise always has its ridiculous aspect. Menenius increasingly assumes the self-contradictory and sardonically amusing role of the appeaser, like York of *Richard II*, urging actions that are repugnant to him personally. His seemingly sage advice to the plebeians in his fable of the belly is in part at least a rhetorical strategy calculated to quiet plebeian restiveness without addressing their real demands. At the last, after having denounced the tribunes for betraying Rome, Menenius must go as their ambassador to beg mercy of Coriolanus. When Aufidius' guardsmen scoff at him for having been turned away by Coriolanus, Menenius is beyond caring for their taunts. He does, in fact, hold to a consistent principle—the survival of his beloved city at whatever cost to his pride. He and Rome pragmatically blunder through, though not without loss of dignity.

Coriolanus' mother, Volumnia, is caught in an even more ironic dilemma. She, of course, shares her son's aristocratic pride, having taught him a code of death before dishonor. The emotional bond between mother and son is extraordinarily, even distressingly, close. Emotionally, it takes the place of Coriolanus' bloodless marriage to the chaste and retiring Virgilia. Volumnia, in fact, speaks of Coriolanus metaphorically as her husband and of his warlike prowess as a vicarious substitute for "the embracements of his bed" (1.3.4–5). Throughout, Coriolanus' deeds of war are love offerings to his mother. Every citizen of Rome knows that whatever Coriolanus has done for his country he also did "to please his mother" (1.1.37). Yet, because Volumnia has not been a properly nourishing mother, Coriolanus is poised between two irreconcilable cravings: to please a mother whose demands can never be satisfied and to fashion an identity that is entirely self-made. He needs her approval but also wishes to be beholden to no one, least of all to her. His rigid masculinity in war, we realize, is in part an attempt to escape from his sense of vulnerability to his mother and to the plebeians whom he must beg for votes—indeed, to Rome itself, the city that has banished him like a rejecting mother and that he finally cannot bring himself to destroy. Coriolanus cannot separate himself from his mother; even his soldiership collapses into an attempt to please her.

The conflict reaches its crisis when Volumnia's oppressive demands take the form of insisting that her son achieve fame not only in war but also in politics. Here she must, like Menenius, encourage the compromise and "policy" that they all hate. She and Menenius stage Coriolanus' public appearances with as much care as the tribunes rehearse their plebeians. They "prompt" Coriolanus to "perform a part" for which he has no aptitude (3.2.108–111); as he later says, capitulating to his mother for the last time, "Like a dull actor now, / I have forgot my part, and I am out" (5.3.40–41). This integrity has its admirable side but brings disaster to Volumnia's plans. She is defeated by the very pride she has engendered in him, and he is defeated by her overriding ambition for him. To win her praise, he must put away his true disposition, becoming effeminate and emasculated like a "harlot" or "an eunuch" (3.2.114–116). To satisfy her quest for fame, he must give up his attack on Rome, perjure himself to Aufidius, and die a condemned traitor to the Volscian state. Volumnia's crushing and engulfing love for her son proves ironically fatal to everything they have cherished.

Coriolanus' relationship to Aufidius is one of love as well as hate, and it, too, poses a fatal conflict. Despite their rivalry to the death, these two military heroes are singularly attracted to one another. Coriolanus confesses "I sin in envying his nobility," and considers Aufidius "a lion / That I am proud to hunt" (1.1.231–237). Coriolanus' fate is to love his enemy and hate his birthplace. Aufidius, in turn, greets Coriolanus with more joy "Than when I first my wedded mistress saw / Bestride my threshold" (4.5.122–123). Yet Aufidius has always resented Coriolanus' superiority in battle and has planned to overcome him by fair means or foul. In their brief military alliance, Coriolanus proves too attractive a rival, overshadowing the achievements of Aufidius. For these reasons, Aufidius secretly exults in Coriolanus' fatal dilemma, since the Volscian general prefers vengeance to victory over Rome. In a final disillusioning scene, he stages one more public outcry against Coriolanus, goading him into a proud rage, and then with his fellow conspirators ingloriously performs an execution "whereat valor will weep" (5.6.139). Aufidius' virtues, like those of Coriolanus, have been betrayed by his worst instincts. Throughout, the Volscians have been cunning enemies, lying in wait for Rome to tear herself apart. The laws governing the relations between states are brutally competitive, characterized by the "slippery turns" (4.4.12) of fortune that ironically bring together former enemies as allies and then turn them against one another. In this world of sudden reversals, Coriolanus' last act is something he could never have foreseen: saving the Roman state and its tribunes from a destruction he himself had wished on it. As Coriolanus wryly observes of his own destiny (5.3.184–185), "The gods look down, and this unnatural scene / They laugh at."

Coriolanus

[*Dramatis Personae*

CAIUS MARCIUS, *afterward* CAIUS MARCIUS CORIOLANUS

TITUS LARTIUS,⎱ *Roman generals*
COMINIUS, ⎰
MENENIUS AGRIPPA, *friend of Coriolanus*
SICINIUS VELUTUS,⎱ *Roman tribunes*
JUNIUS BRUTUS, ⎰
NICANOR, *a Roman traitor*
Two Roman PATRICIANS
Two Roman SENATORS
An AEDILE
Two Roman OFFICERS
A Roman LIEUTENANT
Roman SOLDIERS
A Roman HERALD
Seven Roman CITIZENS
MESSENGERS

VOLUMNIA, *Coriolanus' mother*
VIRGILIA, *Coriolanus' wife*
Young MARCIUS, *son of Coriolanus and Virgilia*
VALERIA, *friend of Virgilia*
A GENTLEWOMAN, *attending Virgilia*

TULLUS AUFIDIUS, *Volscian general*
Two SENATORS *of Corioles*
Three Volscian LORDS
A Volscian LIEUTENANT
A Volscian SOLDIER
Three CONSPIRATORS
ADRIAN, *a Volscian*
A CITIZEN *of Antium*
Two Volscian WATCHMEN
Three SERVINGMEN *of Aufidius*

Roman and Volscian Senators, Patricians, Aediles, Lictors, Captains, Soldiers, Citizens, Messengers, Servingmen, an Usher attending Valeria, and Attendants

SCENE: *Rome and the neighborhood; Corioles and the neighborhood; Antium*]

1.1

Enter a company of mutinous Citizens, with staves, clubs, and other weapons.

FIRST CITIZEN Before we proceed any further, hear me speak.
ALL Speak, speak.

1.1. Location: Rome. A street

FIRST CITIZEN You are all resolved rather to die than to famish? 5
ALL Resolved, resolved.
FIRST CITIZEN First, you know Caius Marcius is chief enemy to the people.
ALL We know 't, we know 't.
FIRST CITIZEN Let us kill him, and we'll have corn at 10
our own price. Is 't a verdict? 11
ALL No more talking on 't. Let it be done. Away, away! 12
SECOND CITIZEN One word, good citizens.
FIRST CITIZEN We are accounted poor citizens, the patricians good. What authority surfeits on would relieve 15
us. If they would yield us but the superfluity while it 16
were wholesome, we might guess they relieved us hu- 17
manely. But they think we are too dear. The leanness 18
that afflicts us, the object of our misery, is as an inven- 19
tory to particularize their abundance. Our sufferance is 20
a gain to them. Let us revenge this with our pikes ere 21
we become rakes; for the gods know I speak this in 22
hunger for bread, not in thirst for revenge.
SECOND CITIZEN Would you proceed especially against Caius Marcius?
ALL Against him first. He's a very dog to the common- 26
alty. 27
SECOND CITIZEN Consider you what services he has done for his country?
FIRST CITIZEN Very well, and could be content to give him good report for 't, but that he pays himself with being proud.
SECOND CITIZEN Nay, but speak not maliciously.
FIRST CITIZEN I say unto you, what he hath done fa- 34
mously he did it to that end. Though soft-conscienced 35
men can be content to say it was for his country, he
did it to please his mother and to be partly proud, 37
which he is, even to the altitude of his virtue. 38
SECOND CITIZEN What he cannot help in his nature you account a vice in him. You must in no way say he is covetous.
FIRST CITIZEN If I must not, I need not be barren of ac- 42
cusations. He hath faults, with surplus, to tire in repe- 43
tition. (*Shouts within.*) What shouts are these? The 44
other side o' the city is risen. Why stay we prating 45
here? To the Capitol! 46
ALL Come, come.

5 famish starve **10 corn** grain, such as wheat or barley **11 Is 't a verdict** are we agreed? **12 on 't** of it, about it **15 good** i.e., noble, well-to-do. **authority** those in authority, the nobility **16 but the superfluity** merely the excess **17 wholesome** good to eat **17–18 humanely** out of common humanity **18 too dear** costing more than we are worth (but also, paradoxically, *a gain*; see line 21) **19 object** spectacle **19–20 is as . . . abundance** serves as a catalogue or inventory to point out in detail (by means of contrast) how rich they are **20 sufferance** suffering **21 pikes** spears, lances; pitchforks (playing on *rakes*, line 22) **22 rakes** i.e., as lean as rakes **26 a very dog** i.e., inhumanly cruel **26–27 commonalty** common people **34–35 famously** achieving fame **35 to that end** i.e., in order to become famous. **soft-conscienced** weak-minded, lacking real conviction **37 to be partly proud** partly out of pride **38 even . . . virtue** i.e., he is as proud as he is brave **42 If** even if **43–44 to tire in repetition** to tire out the speaker in reporting them **45 prating** talking idly **46 Capitol** Temple of Jupiter on Capitoline Hill; used here to stand for the Senate building

FIRST CITIZEN   Soft, who comes here?   48

Enter Menenius Agrippa.

SECOND CITIZEN   Worthy Menenius Agrippa, one that
hath always loved the people.

FIRST CITIZEN   He's one honest enough. Would all the
rest were so!

MENENIUS
What work's, my countrymen, in hand? Where go
   you
With bats and clubs? The matter? Speak, I pray you. 54

FIRST CITIZEN   Our business is not unknown to the
Senate. They have had inkling this fortnight what we
intend to do, which now we'll show 'em in deeds.
They say poor suitors have strong breaths; they shall 58
know we have strong arms too.

MENENIUS
Why, masters, my good friends, mine honest
   neighbors,   60
Will you undo yourselves?   61

FIRST CITIZEN
We cannot, sir. We are undone already.

MENENIUS
I tell you, friends, most charitable care
Have the patricians of you. For your wants,   64
Your suffering in this dearth, you may as well   65
Strike at the heaven with your staves as lift them
Against the Roman state, whose course will on   67
The way it takes, cracking ten thousand curbs   68
Of more strong link asunder than can ever
Appear in your impediment. For the dearth,   70
The gods, not the patricians, make it, and
Your knees to them, not arms, must help. Alack,   72
You are transported by calamity   73
Thither where more attends you, and you slander   74
The helms o' the state, who care for you like fathers,   75
When you curse them as enemies.

FIRST CITIZEN   Care for us? True indeed! They ne'er
cared for us yet. Suffer us to famish, and their storehouses crammed with grain; make edicts for usury to 79
support usurers; repeal daily any wholesome act established against the rich; and provide more piercing 81
statutes daily to chain up and restrain the poor. If the
wars eat us not up, they will; and there's all the love
they bear us.

MENENIUS   Either you must
Confess yourselves wondrous malicious,
Or be accused of folly. I shall tell you
A pretty tale. It may be you have heard it,
But, since it serves my purpose, I will venture

To stale 't a little more.   90

FIRST CITIZEN   Well, I'll hear it, sir; yet you must not
think to fob off our disgrace with a tale. But, an 't 92
please you, deliver.   93

MENENIUS
There was a time when all the body's members
Rebelled against the belly, thus accused it:
That only like a gulf it did remain   96
I' the midst o' the body, idle and unactive,
Still cupboarding the viand, never bearing   98
Like labor with the rest, where th' other instruments 99
Did see and hear, devise, instruct, walk, feel,   100
And, mutually participate, did minister   101
Unto the appetite and affection common   102
Of the whole body. The belly answered—

FIRST CITIZEN   Well, sir, what answer made the belly?

MENENIUS
Sir, I shall tell you. With a kind of smile,
Which ne'er came from the lungs, but even thus—   106
For, look you, I may make the belly smile
As well as speak—it tauntingly replied
To th' discontented members, the mutinous parts
That envied his receipt; even so most fitly   110
As you malign our senators for that   111
They are not such as you.

FIRST CITIZEN   Your belly's answer—What?
The kingly-crownèd head, the vigilant eye,
The counselor heart, the arm our soldier,
Our steed the leg, the tongue our trumpeter,
With other muniments and petty helps   117
In this our fabric, if that they—

MENENIUS   What then?   118
'Fore me, this fellow speaks! What then? What then? 119

FIRST CITIZEN
Should by the cormorant belly be restrained,   120
Who is the sink o' the body—

MENENIUS   Well, what then?   121

FIRST CITIZEN
The former agents, if they did complain,   122
What could the belly answer?

MENENIUS   I will tell you.
If you'll bestow a small—of what you have little—   124
Patience awhile, you'st hear the belly's answer.   125

FIRST CITIZEN
You're long about it.

MENENIUS   Note me this, good friend;
Your most grave belly was deliberate,   127
Not rash like his accusers, and thus answered:

90 stale 't make it stale by repeating it   **92 fob . . . disgrace** set aside by a trick our feeling of suffering hardship.   **an 't** if it   **93 deliver** tell your tale   **96 gulf** open pit, whirlpool   **98 Still . . . viand** always stowing away the food   **99 Like** equal.   **where** whereas.   **instruments** organs   **100 devise** deliberate, think   **101 participate** participating, taking part   **102 affection** inclination   **106 lungs** i.e., supposed organ of laughter   **110 his receipt** what it received.   **fitly** fittingly, justly. (Said ironically.)   **111 for that** because   **117 muniments** furnishings, or defenses   **118 fabric** body formed by the conjunction of various parts.   **if that** if   **119 'Fore me** (An oath.)   **120 cormorant** ravenous, rapacious (like the voracious seabird known by that name)   **121 sink** cesspool   **122 former** just-named   **124 small** small quantity   **125 you'st** you shall   **127 Your** i.e., this

48 Soft stay, stop   **54 bats** cudgels   **58 suitors** petitioners.   **strong** strong-smelling (with a play in the next line on *strong*, "mighty")   **60 masters** i.e., good sirs. (A term appropriate to ordinary citizens.)   **61 undo** ruin   **64 For** as for (also in line 70)   **65 dearth** famine   **67 on** continue on   **68 curbs** restraints. (A term from horsemanship; the curb is attached to the bit.)   **70 in your impediment** in any hindrance you may be able to offer   **72 knees** i.e., prayers (with a play on *arms* as parts of the body and as weapons)   **73 transported** carried away   **74 attends** awaits   **75 helms** helmsmen   **79 for** permitting   **81 piercing** severe

"True is it, my incorporate friends," quoth he,   129
"That I receive the general food at first   130
Which you do live upon; and fit it is,
Because I am the storehouse and the shop   132
Of the whole body. But, if you do remember,
I send it through the rivers of your blood
Even to the court, the heart, to the seat o' the brain;   135
And, through the cranks and offices of man,   136
The strongest nerves and small inferior veins   137
From me receive that natural competency   138
Whereby they live. And though that all at once"—
You, my good friends, this says the belly, mark
    me—

FIRST CITIZEN
Ay, sir, well, well.

MENENIUS   "Though all at once cannot
See what I do deliver out to each,
Yet I can make my audit up, that all   143
From me do back receive the flour of all,   144
And leave me but the bran." What say you to 't?   145

FIRST CITIZEN
It was an answer. How apply you this?

MENENIUS
The senators of Rome are this good belly,
And you the mutinous members. For examine
Their counsels and their cares, digest things rightly   149
Touching the weal o' the common, you shall find   150
No public benefit which you receive
But it proceeds or comes from them to you
And no way from yourselves. What do you think,
You, the great toe of this assembly?

FIRST CITIZEN   I the great toe? Why the great toe?

MENENIUS
For that, being one o' the lowest, basest, poorest,
Of this most wise rebellion, thou goest foremost.
Thou rascal, that art worst in blood to run,   158
Lead'st first to win some vantage.   159
But make you ready your stiff bats and clubs.   160
Rome and her rats are at the point of battle;
The one side must have bale.

            Enter Caius Marcius.

                        Hail, noble Marcius!   162

MARCIUS
Thanks.—What's the matter, you dissentious rogues,   163

That, rubbing the poor itch of your opinion,
Make yourselves scabs?

FIRST CITIZEN   We have ever your good word.   165

MARCIUS
He that will give good words to thee will flatter   166
Beneath abhorring. What would you have, you curs,   167
That like nor peace nor war? The one affrights you,   168
The other makes you proud. He that trusts to you,   169
Where he should find you lions, finds you hares;
Where foxes, geese. You are no surer, no,   171
Than is the coal of fire upon the ice,   172
Or hailstone in the sun. Your virtue is   173
To make him worthy whose offense subdues him,   174
And curse that justice did it. Who deserves
    greatness   175
Deserves your hate; and your affections are   176
A sick man's appetite, who desires most that
Which would increase his evil. He that depends   178
Upon your favors swims with fins of lead
And hews down oaks with rushes. Hang ye!
    Trust ye?   180
With every minute you do change a mind
And call him noble that was now your hate,   182
Him vile that was your garland. What's the matter,   183
That in these several places of the city   184
You cry against the noble Senate, who,
Under the gods, keep you in awe, which else   186
Would feed on one another?—What's their seeking?   187

MENENIUS
For corn at their own rates, whereof, they say,   188
The city is well stored.

MARCIUS   Hang 'em! They say?
They'll sit by th' fire and presume to know
What's done i' the Capitol, who's like to rise,   191
Who thrives and who declines; side factions and
    give out   192
Conjectural marriages, making parties strong   193
And feebling such as stand not in their liking   194
Below their cobbled shoes. They say there's grain
    enough?   195
Would the nobility lay aside their ruth   196
And let me use my sword, I'd make a quarry   197

---

129 **incorporate** belonging to one body   130 **the general food** the
food for everyone   132 **shop** workshop   135 **to the court . . . brain**
i.e., to the heart, which is the court and vital center, and to the brain,
which is the throne   136 **cranks** winding passages.   **offices** service
rooms of a household; kitchen, etc.   137 **nerves** sinews   138 **natural
competency** sufficiency for the purposes of nature   143 **audit** balance
sheet   144 **the flour** i.e., the nourishing part (with a play on the
flower, "the pick"; spelled *Flowre* in the Folio)   145 **bran** chaff
149 **digest** analyze, interpret (with a play on the gastronomic sense)
150 **weal o' the common** public welfare   158 **rascal** lean deer not
worth the hunting. (Hence the modern meaning. The term is here
seemingly applied to a hunting dog.)   **in blood** in vigor, condition. (A
hunting term.)   159 **Lead'st . . . vantage** you lead the pack to gain
some personal advantage   160 **stiff bats** sturdy cudgels   162 **The one
. . . bale** one side or the other must get the worst of it, receive injury
163 **dissentious** rebellious

165 **scabs** (1) scurvy fellows, rascals (2) sores.   **ever** always
166 **give good words to** praise   167 **abhorring** contempt   168 **nor
. . . nor** neither . . . nor.   **The one** i.e., war   169 **The other** i.e.,
peace.   **proud** arrogant and demanding   171 **no surer** no more reliable   172–173 **Than . . . sun** than a pan of burning coals set down
on solid ice or hailstones lying in the warming sun (both ineffectual
and short-lived)   173 **virtue** unusual distinction. (Said sardonically.)
174–175 **To make . . . it** to glorify that person whose wrongdoing
subjects him to punishment and to curse the justice that punishes him
175 **Who deserves** whoever has a right to   176 **Deserves** acquires,
incurs.   **affections** desires, propensities   178 **evil** malady
180 **rushes** slender reeds   182 **now** just now   183 **garland** object of
highest honor and praise   184 **several** different, various   186 **which
else** who otherwise   187 **seeking** demand   188 **corn** grain.   **rates**
prices   191 **like** likely   192 **side** take sides with.   **give out** report
193 **marriages** i.e., political alliances.   **making parties strong** asserting certain parties to be strong, giving support to them   194 **feebling**
declaring to be weak   195 **Below . . . shoes** i.e., beneath their feet.
cobbled mended   196 **Would the nobility** if only the nobility would.
ruth tenderheartedness   197 **quarry** heap of slain deer

With thousands of these quartered slaves as high 198
As I could pick my lance.

MENENIUS
Nay, these are almost thoroughly persuaded,
For though abundantly they lack discretion,
Yet are they passing cowardly. But I beseech you, 202
What says the other troop?

MARCIUS They are dissolved. Hang 'em!
They said they were an-hungry; sighed forth
    proverbs, 205
That hunger broke stone walls, that dogs must eat, 206
That meat was made for mouths, that the gods
    sent not 207
Corn for the rich men only. With these shreds 208
They vented their complainings, which being
    answered 209
And a petition granted them—a strange one,
To break the heart of generosity 211
And make bold power look pale—they threw their
    caps
As they would hang them on the horns o' the
    moon, 213
Shouting their emulation.

MENENIUS   What is granted them? 214

MARCIUS
Five tribunes to defend their vulgar wisdoms, 215
Of their own choice. One's Junius Brutus,
Sicinius Velutus, and I know not—'Sdeath! 217
The rabble should have first unroofed the city
Ere so prevailed with me. It will in time
Win upon power and throw forth greater themes 220
For insurrection's arguing. 221

MENENIUS This is strange.

MARCIUS Go get you home, you fragments! 223

Enter a Messenger, hastily.

MESSENGER
Where's Caius Marcius?

MARCIUS   Here. What's the matter?

MESSENGER
The news is, sir, the Volsces are in arms.

MARCIUS
I am glad on 't. Then we shall ha' means to vent 226
Our musty superfluity.—See, our best elders. 227

*Enter Sicinius Velutus, Junius Brutus, Cominius,
Titus Lartius, with other Senators.*

FIRST SENATOR
Marcius, 'tis true that you have lately told us: 228

The Volsces are in arms. 198

MARCIUS   They have a leader, 199
Tullus Aufidius, that will put you to 't. 230
I sin in envying his nobility,
And were I anything but what I am
I would wish me only he.

COMINIUS   You have fought together? 233

MARCIUS
Were half to half the world by the ears and he 234
Upon my party, I'd revolt, to make 235
Only my wars with him. He is a lion 236
That I am proud to hunt.

FIRST SENATOR   Then, worthy Marcius, 207
Attend upon Cominius to these wars. 238

COMINIUS
It is your former promise.

MARCIUS   Sir, it is, 209
And I am constant. Titus Lartius, thou 240
Shalt see me once more strike at Tullus' face.
What, art thou stiff? Stand'st out?

LARTIUS   No, Caius Marcius, 242
I'll lean upon one crutch and fight with t'other
Ere stay behind this business.

MENENIUS   O, true bred!

FIRST SENATOR
Your company to th' Capitol, where, I know, 245
Our greatest friends attend us.

LARTIUS *[to Cominius]*   Lead you on. 217
[To Marcius.] Follow Cominius. We must follow you;
Right worthy you priority.

COMINIUS   Noble Marcius! 248

FIRST SENATOR *[to the Citizens]* 221
Hence to your homes, begone!

MARCIUS   Nay, let them follow. 223
The Volsces have much corn; take these rats thither
To gnaw their garners.—Worshipful mutineers, 251
Your valor puts well forth. Pray follow. 252

Exeunt. Citizens steal away.
Manent Sicinius and Brutus.

SICINIUS
Was ever man so proud as is this Marcius?

BRUTUS He has no equal.

SICINIUS
When we were chosen tribunes for the people—

BRUTUS
Marked you his lip and eyes?

SICINIUS   Nay, but his taunts.

BRUTUS
Being moved, he will not spare to gird the gods. 257

198 **quartered** cut into quarters, slaughtered like criminals 199 **pick** pitch 202 **passing** exceedingly 205 **an-hungry** hungry. (The prefix *an* is an archaic intensifier.) 206 **dogs** i.e., even dogs 207 **meat** food 208 **shreds** bits, scraps (of wisdom) 209 **vented** discharged, excreted 211 **generosity** the nobles 213 **As** as if 214 **emulation** rivalry of one another in shouting, or, envy of superiors 215 **tribunes** official representatives of the people's interests 217 **'Sdeath** i.e., by God's death. (An oath.) 220 **Win upon** gain advantage over 221 **For insurrection's arguing** to be urged by uprisings 223 **fragments** scraps. (A term of contempt.) 226 **on 't** of it. **vent** discharge, excrete 227 **musty superfluity** moldy excess 228 **that** what

230 **to 't** i.e., to the test 233 **together** against one another 234 **by the ears** at variance (with the other half) 235 **Upon my party** on my side 236 **with** against 238 **Attend upon** serve under 240 **constant** true to my promise 242 **stiff** resistant, reluctant. (But Lartius answers as though the word had meant "stiff with age.") **Stand'st out** do you refuse to engage? 245 **Your company** let me request your company 248 **Right . . . priority** you well deserve to take precedence 251 **garners** granaries, storehouses. **Worshipful mutineers** worthy mutineers. (Said with mock politeness.) 252 **puts well forth** begins to bud, shows a fair promise. (Said ironically.) **s.d. Manent** they remain onstage 257 **moved** angered. **spare to gird** refrain from scoffing at

SICINIUS   Bemock the modest moon.   258

BRUTUS
The present wars devour him! He is grown   259
Too proud to be so valiant.

SICINIUS   Such a nature,   260
Tickled with good success, disdains the shadow   261
Which he treads on at noon. But I do wonder
His insolence can brook to be commanded   263
Under Cominius.

BRUTUS   Fame, at the which he aims,   264
In whom already he's well graced, cannot   265
Better be held nor more attained than by
A place below the first; for what miscarries   267
Shall be the general's fault, though he perform
To th' utmost of a man, and giddy censure   269
Will then cry out of Marcius, "O, if he
Had borne the business!"

SICINIUS   Besides, if things go well,
Opinion that so sticks on Marcius shall   272
Of his demerits rob Cominius.

BRUTUS   Come.   273
Half all Cominius' honors are to Marcius,   274
Though Marcius earned them not, and all his faults   275
To Marcius shall be honors, though indeed   276
In aught he merit not.

SICINIUS   Let's hence and hear   277
How the dispatch is made, and in what fashion,   278
More than his singularity, he goes   279
Upon this present action.

BRUTUS   Let's along.   *Exeunt.*   280

❖

1.2   *Enter Tullus Aufidius with Senators of Corioles.*

FIRST SENATOR
So, your opinion is, Aufidius,
That they of Rome are entered in our counsels   2
And know how we proceed.

AUFIDIUS   Is it not yours?
What ever have been thought on in this state   4
That could be brought to bodily act ere Rome
Had circumvention? 'Tis not four days gone   6
Since I heard thence. These are the words—I think   7
I have the letter here. Yes, here it is. [*Finding a letter.*]

---

258 **modest** i.e., as representing Diana, goddess of chastity   259 **The present** i.e., may the present   260 **to be** of being. (Or, Brutus may mean that Marcius' excessive pride makes his valor dangerous.)
261 **Tickled with** flattered by, greatly excited by   263 **brook** endure
263–264 **be commanded Under** be under the command of
265 **whom** which   267 **miscarries** goes wrong   269 **giddy censure** thoughtless popular opinion   272 **Opinion . . . on** the fine reputation that adheres so to   273 **demerits** merits, deserts   274 **are to** belong to   275–277 **all his . . . merit not** all Cominius' failings will redound to Marcius' honor, even though Marcius doesn't deserve it
277 **aught** anything   278 **dispatch** execution of the business
279 **More . . . singularity** i.e., with even more than his usual share of arrogance and idiosyncrasy   280 **along** go, go join
1.2. Location: Corioles (or Corioli), southeast of Rome.
2 **entered in** acquainted with   4 **What** what things   6 **circumvention** i.e., warning enabling them to circumvent.   **gone** ago   7 **thence** from there

---

[*He reads.*] "They have pressed a power, but it is not known   9
Whether for east or west. The dearth is great,   10
The people mutinous; and, it is rumored,
Cominius, Marcius your old enemy,
Who is of Rome worse hated than of you,   13
And Titus Lartius, a most valiant Roman,
These three lead on this preparation
Whither 'tis bent. Most likely 'tis for you.   16
Consider of it."

FIRST SENATOR   Our army's in the field.
We never yet made doubt but Rome was ready
To answer us.

AUFIDIUS   Nor did you think it folly
To keep your great pretenses veiled till when   20
They needs must show themselves, which in the
hatching,   21
It seemed, appeared to Rome. By the discovery   22
We shall be shortened in our aim, which was   23
To take in many towns ere almost Rome   24
Should know we were afoot.

SECOND SENATOR   Noble Aufidius,
Take your commission; hie you to your bands.   26
Let us alone to guard Corioles.
If they set down before 's, for the remove   28
Bring up your army; but I think you'll find
They've not prepared for us.

AUFIDIUS   O, doubt not that;   30
I speak from certainties. Nay, more,
Some parcels of their power are forth already,   32
And only hitherward. I leave your honors.   33
If we and Caius Marcius chance to meet,
'Tis sworn between us we shall ever strike   35
Till one can do no more.

ALL   The gods assist you!

AUFIDIUS   And keep your honors safe!

FIRST SENATOR   Farewell.

SECOND SENATOR   Farewell.

ALL   Farewell.   *Exeunt omnes.*   41

❖

1.3   *Enter Volumnia and Virgilia, mother and wife to Marcius. They set them down on two low stools and sew.*

VOLUMNIA   I pray you, daughter, sing, or express yourself in a more comfortable sort. If my son were   2

---

9 **pressed a power** raised an army   10 **dearth** famine   13 **of** by
16 **Whither 'tis bent** against whatever destination it is intended for
20 **pretenses** intentions   21 **needs** necessarily   22 **appeared** became evident.   **discovery** disclosure   23 **be shortened in** fall short of
24 **take in** capture.   **ere almost** even before   26 **hie** hasten.   **bands** companies of soldiers   28 **set down before 's** lay siege to us.   **remove** raising of the siege   30 **prepared for us** i.e., laid plans to besiege us   32 **parcels** parts.   **forth** marching forward   33 **only hitherward** i.e., marching toward this place and this alone.   **your honors** i.e., you. (Plural and honorific.)   35 **ever strike** keep on exchanging blows   41 **s.d. omnes** all
1.3. Location: Rome. Marcius' house, which may be (as indicated in Plutarch) his mother's house; see 2.1.194.
2 **comfortable sort** cheerful manner

my husband, I should freelier rejoice in that absence 3
wherein he won honor than in the embracements of
his bed where he would show most love. When yet
he was but tender-bodied and the only son of my 6
womb, when youth with comeliness plucked all gaze 7
his way, when for a day of kings' entreaties a mother 8
should not sell him an hour from her beholding, I, con- 9
sidering how honor would become such a person— 10
that it was no better than picturelike to hang by the
wall, if renown made it not stir—was pleased to let 12
him seek danger where he was like to find fame. To a 13
cruel war I sent him, from whence he returned, his
brows bound with oak. I tell thee, daughter, I sprang 15
not more in joy at first hearing he was a man-child than
now in first seeing he had proved himself a man. 17

VIRGILIA   But had he died in the business, madam,
how then?

VOLUMNIA   Then his good report should have been my
son; I therein would have found issue. Hear me pro- 21
fess sincerely: had I a dozen sons, each in my love alike
and none less dear than thine and my good Marcius,
I had rather had eleven die nobly for their country
than one voluptuously surfeit out of action. 25

Enter a Gentlewoman.

GENTLEWOMAN   Madam, the Lady Valeria is come to
visit you.

VIRGILIA
Beseech you, give me leave to retire myself. 28

VOLUMNIA   Indeed, you shall not.
Methinks I hear hither your husband's drum, 30
See him pluck Aufidius down by th' hair; 31
As children from a bear, the Volsces shunning him. 32
Methinks I see him stamp thus, and call thus: 33
"Come on, you cowards! You were got in fear, 34
Though you were born in Rome." His bloody brow
With his mailed hand then wiping, forth he goes 36
Like to a harvestman that's tasked to mow 37
Or all or lose his hire. 38

VIRGILIA
His bloody brow? O Jupiter, no blood!

VOLUMNIA
Away, you fool! It more becomes a man
Than gilt his trophy. The breasts of Hecuba, 41

When she did suckle Hector, looked not lovelier
Than Hector's forehead when it spit forth blood
At Grecian sword, contemning.—Tell Valeria 44
We are fit to bid her welcome.   *Exit Gentlewoman.* 45

VIRGILIA
Heavens bless my lord from fell Aufidius! 46

VOLUMNIA
He'll beat Aufidius' head below his knee
And tread upon his neck. 48

Enter Valeria, with an usher and a Gentlewoman.

VALERIA   My ladies both, good day to you.

VOLUMNIA   Sweet madam!

VIRGILIA   I am glad to see your ladyship.

VALERIA   How do you both? You are manifest house- 52
keepers. What are you sewing here? A fine spot, in 53
good faith. How does your little son?

VIRGILIA   I thank your ladyship; well, good madam.

VOLUMNIA   He had rather see the swords and hear a
drum than look upon his schoolmaster.

VALERIA   O' my word, the father's son. I'll swear 'tis a 58
very pretty boy. O' my troth, I looked upon him o'
Wednesday half an hour together. H'as such a con- 60
firmed countenance! I saw him run after a gilded but- 61
terfly, and when he caught it, he let it go again, and
after it again, and over and over he comes and up 63
again, catched it again. Or whether his fall enraged 64
him, or how 'twas, he did so set his teeth and tear 65
it! O, I warrant, how he mammocked it! 66

VOLUMNIA   One on 's father's moods. 67

VALERIA   Indeed, la, 'tis a noble child.

VIRGILIA   A crack, madam. 69

VALERIA   Come, lay aside your stitchery. I must have
you play the idle huswife with me this afternoon. 71

VIRGILIA   No, good madam, I will not out of doors. 72

VALERIA   Not out of doors?

VOLUMNIA   She shall, she shall.

VIRGILIA   Indeed, no, by your patience. I'll not over the 75
threshold till my lord return from the wars.

VALERIA   Fie, you confine yourself most unreasonably.
Come, you must go visit the good lady that lies in. 78

VIRGILIA   I will wish her speedy strength and visit her
with my prayers, but I cannot go thither.

VOLUMNIA   Why, I pray you?

VIRGILIA   'Tis not to save labor, nor that I want love. 82

VALERIA   You would be another Penelope. Yet they 83
say all the yarn she spun in Ulysses' absence did but

---

3 **freelier** more readily   6 **tender-bodied** i.e., young   7 **comeliness** beauty.   **all gaze** the gaze of all   8 **for** even for   9 **should . . . beholding** i.e., would not let her son out of her sight even for an hour at any price   10 **such a person** such a fine figure of a youth   12 **renown made it not stir** desire for fame did not stir it to action   13 **like** likely   15 **bound with oak** i.e., as a badge to signify that he had saved the life of a Roman citizen. (The *cruel war* was that against the Latins and Tarquin the Proud; see 2.1.148–149 and note.)   17 **now** i.e., then, when he returned from war   21 **issue** offspring   25 **voluptuously surfeit** live extravagantly for pleasure   28 **retire myself** go in   30 **hither** coming this way, or from here   31 **See** i.e., methinks I see   32 **As . . . him** (methinks I see) the Volsces avoiding him as children flee from a bear   33 **stamp thus** (Volumnia gestures.)   **call** i.e., exhort his own troops   34 **got** begotten   36 **mailed** protected by mail, armored   37 **tasked** set the task   38 **Or** either.   **hire** wages   41 **Than . . . trophy** i.e., than a thin layer of gold adorns his monument.   **Hecuba** Queen of Troy, mother of Hector and many other sons

44 **contemning** scorning the Grecian sword, as if spitting on it   45 **fit** ready   46 **bless** protect.   **fell** cruel   48 **s.d. an usher** a lady's male attendant   52–53 **manifest housekeepers** clearly being stay-at-homes today   53 **sewing** embroidering.   **spot** pattern, figure   58 **O'** on   60 **H'as** he has   60–61 **confirmed** resolute   61 **gilded** brilliantly colored   63 **over and over** head over heels   64 **Or whether** whether   65 **set** clench   66 **mammocked** tore into fragments   67 **on 's** of his   69 **crack** pert little fellow   71 **huswife** housewife   72 **out** go out   75 **over** step over   78 **lies in** is expecting a child   82 **want** am deficient in   83 **You would be** i.e., one might take you for.   **Penelope** faithful wife of Ulysses in Homer's *Odyssey*, who delayed her suitors by insisting she must finish the weaving which she then unraveled every night

fill Ithaca full of moths. Come, I would your cambric 85
were sensible as your finger, that you might leave 86
pricking it for pity. Come, you shall go with us.

VIRGILIA   No, good madam, pardon me; indeed, I will
not forth.

VALERIA   In truth, la, go with me, and I'll tell you
excellent news of your husband.

VIRGILIA   O, good madam, there can be none yet.

VALERIA   Verily, I do not jest with you. There came
news from him last night.

VIRGILIA   Indeed, madam?

VALERIA   In earnest, it's true; I heard a senator speak it.
Thus it is: the Volsces have an army forth, against
whom Cominius the general is gone with one part of
our Roman power. Your lord and Titus Lartius are set
down before their city Corioles. They nothing doubt 100
prevailing, and to make it brief wars. This is true, on 101
mine honor, and so, I pray, go with us.

VIRGILIA   Give me excuse, good madam. I will obey
you in everything hereafter.

VOLUMNIA   Let her alone, lady. As she is now, she will
but disease our better mirth. 106

VALERIA   In troth, I think she would. Fare you well, 107
then. Come, good sweet lady. Prithee, Virgilia, turn
thy solemness out o' door and go along with us.

VIRGILIA   No, at a word, madam. Indeed, I must not. I 110
wish you much mirth.

VALERIA   Well, then, farewell.   *Exeunt ladies.*

❧

1.4   *Enter Marcius, Titus Lartius, with drum and
colors, with captains and soldiers, as before the city
[of] Corioles. To them a Messenger.*

MARCIUS
Yonder comes news. A wager they have met.

LARTIUS
My horse to yours, no.

MARCIUS   'Tis done.

LARTIUS   Agreed.   2

MARCIUS *[to the Messenger]*
Say, has our general met the enemy?

MESSENGER
They lie in view, but have not spoke as yet.   4

LARTIUS
So, the good horse is mine.

MARCIUS   I'll buy him of you.   5

LARTIUS
No, I'll nor sell nor give him. Lend you him I will   6

For half a hundred years.—Summon the town.   7

MARCIUS   How far off lie these armies?

MESSENGER   Within this mile and half.

MARCIUS
Then shall we hear their 'larum and they ours.   10
Now, Mars, I prithee, make us quick in work,   11
That we with smoking swords may march from
hence   12
To help our fielded friends! Come, blow thy blast.   13

*They sound a parley. Enter two Senators, with
others, on the walls of Corioles.*

Tullus Aufidius, is he within your walls?

FIRST SENATOR
No, nor a man that fears you less than he: 15
That's lesser than a little. (*Drum afar off.*) Hark! Our
drums   16
Are bringing forth our youth. We'll break our walls   17
Rather than they shall pound us up. Our gates,   18
Which yet seem shut, we have but pinned with
rushes;   19
They'll open of themselves. (*Alarum far off.*) Hark
you, far off!
There is Aufidius. List what work he makes   21
Amongst your cloven army.
                    [*Exeunt Volscians from the walls.*]
MARCIUS   O, they are at it!   22

LARTIUS
Their noise be our instruction. Ladders, ho!   23

Enter the army of the Volsces [from the city].

MARCIUS
They fear us not, but issue forth their city.   24
Now put your shields before your hearts, and fight
With hearts more proof than shields. Advance,
brave Titus!   26
They do disdain us much beyond our thoughts,   27
Which makes me sweat with wrath. Come on, my
fellows!
He that retires, I'll take him for a Volsce,
And he shall feel mine edge.   30

*Alarum. The Romans are beat back to their
trenches [and thus exeunt].
Enter Marcius, cursing, [with Soldiers].*

MARCIUS
All the contagion of the south light on you,   31

85 moths (1) insects eating the cloth (2) idle courtiers parasitically consuming her wealth. **would** wish. **cambric** fine white linen **86 sensible** sensitive. **leave** cease **100–101 nothing doubt prevailing** have no doubt at all that they will prevail **106 disease . . . mirth** trouble our mirth, which would be greater without her **107 troth** truth, faith **110 at a word** once for all
1.4. Location: Before Corioles.
2 My horse . . . no i.e., I'll bet my horse against yours that they, Cominius' Roman force and the Volscian army under Aufidius, one and one half miles away, have not met in battle **4 in view** i.e., in view of one another. **spoke** i.e., encountered **5 of** (back) from **6 nor sell** neither sell

7 Summon i.e., summon by trumpet, to parley **10 'larum** call to arms **11 Mars** Roman god of war **12 smoking** steaming **13 fielded** in the field of battle. **s.d. on the walls** i.e., in the gallery backstage. (Throughout this scene, the tiring-house facade represents the *walls* of Corioles, and a door in that facade represents the *gates*.) **15 that fears** i.e., but fears. (Since Aufidius doesn't fear Marcius at all, they are all accordingly fearless.) **16 lesser than a little** virtually not at all **17 break** break out of **18 pound us up** shut us up as in a pound **19 rushes** hollow-stemmed reeds **21 List** listen to **22 cloven** split in two, divided, cut to pieces **23 Their** let their. **our instruction** a lesson to us, an example to us **24 issue forth** rush out of **26 proof** impenetrable **27 beyond our thoughts** more than we thought possible **30 edge** sword edge **31 south** south wind (as a supposed source of contagion)

You shames of Rome! You herd of—Boils and
    plagues
Plaster you o'er, that you may be abhorred   33
Farther than seen, and one infect another   34
Against the wind a mile! You souls of geese,   35
That bear the shapes of men, how have you run
From slaves that apes would beat! Pluto and hell!   37
All hurt behind! Backs red, and faces pale   38
With flight and agued fear! Mend and charge home,   39
Or, by the fires of heaven, I'll leave the foe
And make my wars on you. Look to 't. Come on!
If you'll stand fast, we'll beat them to their wives,
As they us to our trenches. Follow 's!

> *Another alarum; [the Volsces fly back into the
> city,] and Marcius follows them to [the] gates.*

So, now the gates are ope. Now prove good
    seconds!   44
'Tis for the followers fortune widens them,   45
Not for the fliers. Mark me, and do the like.   46

> *Enter the gates and is shut in.*

FIRST SOLDIER   Foolhardiness. Not I.
SECOND SOLDIER   Nor I.
FIRST SOLDIER   See, they have shut him in.
ALL   To th' pot, I warrant him.   50

> *Alarum continues.*

> *Enter Titus Lartius.*

LARTIUS
    What is become of Marcius?
ALL   Slain, sir, doubtless.
FIRST SOLDIER
    Following the fliers at the very heels,
    With them he enters, who upon the sudden
    Clapped to their gates. He is himself alone,   54
    To answer all the city.
LARTIUS   O noble fellow!   55
    Who sensibly outdares his senseless sword,   56
    And, when it bows, stand'st up. Thou art left,
        Marcius.   57
    A carbuncle entire, as big as thou art,   58
    Were not so rich a jewel. Thou wast a soldier
    Even to Cato's wish, not fierce and terrible   60
    Only in strokes, but, with thy grim looks and
    The thunderlike percussion of thy sounds,
    Thou mad'st thine enemies shake, as if the world
    Were feverous and did tremble.

> *Enter Marcius, bleeding, [from the city], assaulted
> by the enemy.*

FIRST SOLDIER   Look, sir.
LARTIUS   O, 'tis Marcius!
    Let's fetch him off, or make remain alike.   67

> *They fight, and all enter the city.*

1.5   *Enter certain Romans, with spoils.*

FIRST ROMAN   This will I carry to Rome.
SECOND ROMAN   And I this.
THIRD ROMAN   A murrain on 't! I took this for silver.   3

> *Alarum continues still afar off.*

> *Enter Marcius and Titus [Lartius] with a trumpet.*
> *Exeunt [Romans with spoils].*

MARCIUS
    See here these movers that do prize their hours   4
    At a cracked drachma! Cushions, leaden spoons,   5
    Irons of a doit, doublets that hangmen would   6
    Bury with those that wore them, these base slaves,   7
    Ere yet the fight be done, pack up. Down with them!
    And hark, what noise the General makes! To him!   9
    There is the man of my soul's hate, Aufidius,
    Piercing our Romans. Then, valiant Titus, take
    Convenient numbers to make good the city,   12
    Whilst I, with those that have the spirit, will haste
    To help Cominius.
LARTIUS   Worthy sir, thou bleed'st.
    Thy exercise hath been too violent
    For a second course of fight.
MARCIUS   Sir, praise me not.   16
    My work hath yet not warmed me. Fare you well.
    The blood I drop is rather physical   18
    Than dangerous to me. To Aufidius thus
    I will appear, and fight.
LARTIUS   Now the fair goddess Fortune
    Fall deep in love with thee, and her great charms   22
    Misguide thy opposers' swords! Bold gentleman,
    Prosperity be thy page!
MARCIUS   Thy friend no less   24
    Than those she placeth highest! So, farewell.   25

33–34 **abhorred . . . seen** loathed (because of your foul smell) before
you are even seen   35 **Against . . . mile** so greatly that it will carry a
mile against the wind   37 **Pluto** Roman god of the underworld
38 **hurt behind** wounded in the back (i.e., in cowardly fashion)
39 **agued** trembling as though with an ague or fever.   **Mend** (1) do
better, reform your battle ranks (2) recover from fever.   **home** to the
heart of the enemy's defenses   44 **seconds** supporters   45 **followers**
pursuers   46 **the fliers** those pursued   50 **To th' pot** to the cooking
pot (i.e., to certain destruction)   54 **Clapped to** shut   55 **answer**
stand up to, confront   56–57 **Who . . . up** who, though sensitive to
pain, dares more than his insensible sword; it might bend to fear, he
would not   57 **left** left alone (in the city); unique   58 **carbuncle** brilliant, red gemstone.   **entire** flawless   60 **Cato** Marcus Cato the Censor (234–149 B.C.), celebrated in Plutarch as a staunch soldier and
exponent of Roman ethics

67 **fetch him off** rescue him.   **make remain alike** remain to share
his fate
1.5. Location: The siege of Corioles continues.
s.d. Enter i.e., enter from the city, through the stage door in the facade; see 1.4.13 s.d. note. Also at line 3 s.d.   **3 murrain** plague.
s.d. trumpet trumpeter   **4 movers** active persons. (Here used ironically.)   **prize their hours** value their time   **5 drachma** small Greek
coin   **6 Irons of a doit** weapons worth a coin of small value.   **dou-**
blets tight-fitting coats, usually quilted and decorated   **6–7 hangmen**
. . . them i.e., hangmen, entitled to the clothes of persons they put to
death, would not have these   **9 the General** i.e., Cominius, fighting
Aufidius nearby   **12 make good** hold, secure   **16 course** bout, engagement. (Perhaps suggesting also *course*, as in a banquet.)   **praise**
me not (Coriolanus answers ironically, as though Laertius were praising him for bleeding instead of cautioning him.)   **18 physical** healthful. (Through bloodletting, a standard treatment.)   **22 charms** spells
24 Prosperity be thy page i.e., may success attend on you.   **Thy . . .**
less i.e., may prosperity be no less your friend   **25 those** i.e., to
those

LARTIUS   Thou worthiest Marcius!   [*Exit Marcius.*]
Go sound thy trumpet in the marketplace.
Call thither all the officers o' the town,
Where they shall know our mind. Away!   *Exeunt.*

❧

1.6   *Enter Cominius, as it were in retire, with soldiers.*

COMINIUS
Breathe you, my friends. Well fought! We are
  come off   1
Like Romans, neither foolish in our stands   2
Nor cowardly in retire. Believe me, sirs,
We shall be charged again. Whiles we have struck, 4
By interims and conveying gusts we have heard   5
The charges of our friends. The Roman gods   6
Lead their successes as we wish our own,   7
That both our powers, with smiling fronts
  encount'ring,   8
May give you thankful sacrifice!

            Enter a Messenger.

                    Thy news?

MESSENGER
The citizens of Corioles have issued   10
And given to Lartius and to Marcius battle.
I saw our party to their trenches driven,
And then I came away.
COMINIUS   Though thou speakest truth,
Methinks thou speak'st not well. How long is 't
  since?
MESSENGER   Above an hour, my lord.
COMINIUS
'Tis not a mile; briefly we heard their drums.   16
How couldst thou in a mile confound an hour   17
And bring thy news so late?
MESSENGER   Spies of the Volsces   18
Held me in chase, that I was forced to wheel   19
Three or four miles about; else had I, sir,   20
Half an hour since brought my report.   [*Exit.*]

            Enter Marcius, [bloody].

COMINIUS   Who's yonder,   21
That does appear as he were flayed? O gods!   22
He has the stamp of Marcius, and I have   23
Before-time seen him thus.
MARCIUS   Come I too late?   24

COMINIUS
The shepherd knows not thunder from a tabor   25
More than I know the sound of Marcius' tongue
From every meaner man.
MARCIUS   Come I too late?   27
COMINIUS
Ay, if you come not in the blood of others,   28
But mantled in your own.
MARCIUS   O, let me clip ye   29
In arms as sound as when I wooed, in heart
As merry as when our nuptial day was done,
And tapers burnt to bedward!   [*They embrace.*] 32
COMINIUS
Flower of warriors, how is 't with Titus Lartius?
MARCIUS
As with a man busied about decrees: 34
Condemning some to death, and some to exile;
Ransoming him, or pitying, threat'ning th' other; 36
Holding Corioles in the name of Rome,
Even like a fawning greyhound in the leash,
To let him slip at will.
COMINIUS   Where is that slave   39
Which told me they had beat you to your trenches?
Where is he? Call him hither.
MARCIUS   Let him alone;
He did inform the truth. But for our gentlemen,   42
The common file—a plague! Tribunes for them!—   43
The mouse ne'er shunned the cat as they did budge 44
From rascals worse than they.
COMINIUS   But how prevailed you?
MARCIUS
Will the time serve to tell? I do not think.
Where is the enemy? Are you lords o' the field?
If not, why cease you till you are so?
COMINIUS
Marcius, we have at disadvantage fought
And did retire to win our purpose.   50
MARCIUS
How lies their battle? Know you on which side   51
They have placed their men of trust?
COMINIUS   As I guess, Marcius,
Their bands i' the vaward are the Antiates,   53
Of their best trust; o'er them Aufidius,   54
Their very heart of hope.
MARCIUS   I do beseech you,   55
By all the battles wherein we have fought,
By th' blood we have shed together, by th' vows we
  have made

1.6. **Location:** Near the camp of Cominius. The fighting near Corioles, heard until now at a short distance, is at a lull.
s.d. in retire disengaged from the fighting (also in line 3)   **1 Breathe you** catch your breath.   **are come off** have left the field of battle   **2 foolish** foolhardy   **4 struck** fought, been striking blows   **5 By . . . gusts** at intervals and borne to us on the wind   **6 friends** i.e., the besiegers of Corioles.   **The Roman** may the Roman   **7 their successes** the fortunes of our friends (i.e., Laertius and Marcius)   **8 powers** armies.   **fronts** (1) foreheads, brows (2) front lines   **10 issued** issued forth   **16 briefly** a short time ago (and at short distance)   **17 confound** consume   **18 Spies** scouts   **19 that** so that   **19–20 wheel . . . about** make a detour of three or four miles   **20 else** otherwise   **21 since** ago   **22 as** as if   **23 stamp** bearing, form   **24 Before-time** formerly

25 **knows** distinguishes (also in line 26).   **tabor** small drum   27 **meaner** less noble   28–29 **Ay . . . own** i.e., if you yourself are bleeding all that blood, you are presumably too weak to help, but if it is enemies' blood, you are in time to shed more   29 **clip** embrace   32 **tapers . . . bedward** i.e., candles burned low, indicating the approach of bedtime or showing the way to bed   34 **busied about decrees** busy with judicial decisions   36 **Ransoming . . . th' other** releasing one man for ransom money, mercifully releasing another without ransom, threatening still another   39 **let him slip** unleash him   42 **inform** report.   **gentlemen** (Said sarcastically of the ordinary soldiers.)   43 **common file** ordinary soldiers, plebeians   44 **budge** flinch   50 **to . . . purpose** i.e., to regroup   51 **battle** army, battle line   53 **bands** troops.   **vaward** vanguard.   **Antiates** inhabitants of Antium   54 **Of . . . trust** their most trustworthy   55 **Their . . . hope** the leader on whom their hopes depend

To endure friends, that you directly set me 58
Against Aufidius and his Antiates,
And that you not delay the present, but, 60
Filling the air with swords advanced and darts, 61
We prove this very hour.
COMINIUS　　　　　　　　Though I could wish 62
You were conducted to a gentle bath
And balms applied to you, yet dare I never 64
Deny your asking. Take your choice of those
That best can aid your action.
MARCIUS　　　　　　　　　　Those are they
That most are willing. If any such be here—
As it were sin to doubt—that love this painting 68
Wherein you see me smeared; if any fear
Lesser his person than an ill report; 70
If any think brave death outweighs bad life,
And that his country's dearer than himself,
Let him alone, or so many so minded, 73
Wave thus [*waving his sword*] to express his
disposition,
And follow Marcius.
　　　　They all shout and wave their swords,
　　　take him up in their arms, and cast up their caps.
O, me alone! Make you a sword of me? 76
If these shows be not outward, which of you 77
But is four Volsces? None of you but is 78
Able to bear against the great Aufidius
A shield as hard as his. A certain number,
Though thanks to all, must I select from all;
The rest shall bear the business in some other fight,
As cause will be obeyed. Please you to march, 83
And I shall quickly draw out my command, 84
Which men are best inclined.
COMINIUS　　　　　　　　March on, my fellows.
Make good this ostentation, and you shall 86
Divide in all with us.　　　　　　*Exeunt.* 87

❖

1.7　*Titus Lartius, having set a guard upon Corioles,*
going with drum and trumpet toward Cominius
and Caius Marcius, enters [from the city] with a
Lieutenant, other soldiers, and a scout.

LARTIUS
So, let the ports be guarded. Keep your duties 1
As I have set them down. If I do send, dispatch
Those centuries to our aid; the rest will serve 3

For a short holding. If we lose the field, 4
We cannot keep the town.
LIEUTENANT　　　　　Fear not our care, sir. 5
LARTIUS　Hence, and shut your gates upon 's. 6
[*To the scout.*] Our guider, come; to th' Roman camp
conduct us.
　　　Exeunt [separately, the Lieutenant returning
　　　　　　　　　　　　　　into the city].

1.8　*Alarum as in battle. Enter Marcius and Aufidius*
at several doors.

MARCIUS
I'll fight with none but thee, for I do hate thee
Worse than a promise-breaker.
AUFIDIUS　　　　　　　We hate alike.
Not Afric owns a serpent I abhor 3
More than thy fame and envy. Fix thy foot. 4
MARCIUS
Let the first budger die the other's slave, 5
And the gods doom him after!
AUFIDIUS
If I fly, Marcius, hollo me like a hare. 7
MARCIUS　Within these three hours, Tullus,
Alone I fought in your Corioles' walls,
And made what work I pleased. 'Tis not my blood
Wherein thou seest me masked. For thy revenge
Wrench up thy power to th' highest.
AUFIDIUS　　　　　　Wert thou the Hector 12
That was the whip of your bragged progeny, 13
Thou shouldst not scape me here.　*Here they fight,*
　　　and certain Volsces come in the aid of Aufidius.
　　　Marcius fights till they be driven in breathless.
Officious, and not valiant, you have shamed me 15
In your condemnèd seconds.　　[*Exeunt.*] 16

1.9　*Flourish. Alarum. A retreat is sounded. Enter, at*
one door, Cominius with the Romans; at another
door Marcius, with his arm in a scarf.

COMINIUS
If I should tell thee o'er this thy day's work, 1
Thou 't not believe thy deeds. But I'll report it 2

58 endure continue.　**directly** (1) at once (2) face to face　**60 not delay the present** do not delay now　**61 advanced** raised.　**darts** lances　**62 prove** try the fortunes of　**64 balms** healing ointments　**68 painting** i.e., blood　**70 Lesser . . . report** less for his safety than for his reputation　**73 Let him alone** let that individual by himself.　**or so many** or as many as are　**76 O . . . of me** do you make a sword of me alone, choose me as your weapon? (Some editors assign this line to the soldiers.)　**77 outward** external, deceptive　**78 But is** is not the equal of　**83 As . . . obeyed** as necessity shall require　**84 draw out my command** pick out my chosen troop　**86 ostentation** show of zeal　**87 Divide** share
1.7. Location: Before the gates of Corioles. The military action near Corioles continues.
1 ports gates　**3 centuries** companies of a hundred

4 short holding i.e., brief occupation of the city　**5 Fear not** don't worry about　**6 Hence** get a move on
1.8. Location: A field of battle near the Roman camp. The military action near Corioles continues.
s.d. several separate　**3 Not . . . serpent** there is no serpent in Africa　**4 fame and envy** hated reputation.　**Fix thy foot** i.e., stand and fight　**5 budger** one who flinches　**7 hollo** cry in pursuit of　**12 Wrench up** strain, wrest, pull　**13 the whip . . . progeny** the scourge of his enemies among your boasted (Trojan) ancestors. (Alludes to the supposed descent of the Romans from the Trojans via Aeneas.)　**15 Officious** meddling, offering unwanted help　**16 condemnèd seconds** futile and despised efforts at assistance
1.9. Location: Scene continues. The Roman camp. The military action near Corioles continues.
s.d. retreat trumpet signal to call off pursuit.　**scarf** sling　**1 If . . . work** if I should recount to you this day's work of yours　**2 Thou 't** thou wouldst

Where senators shall mingle tears with smiles,
Where great patricians shall attend and shrug,   4
I' th' end admire; where ladies shall be frighted   5
And, gladly quaked, hear more; where the dull
  tribunes,   6
That with the fusty plebeians hate thine honors,   7
Shall say against their hearts, "We thank the gods   8
Our Rome hath such a soldier."
Yet cam'st thou to a morsel of this feast,   10
Having fully dined before.

*Enter Titus [Lartius] with his power, from the
pursuit.*

LARTIUS   O General,   11
Here is the steed, we the caparison.   12
Hadst thou beheld—

MARCIUS   Pray now, no more. My mother,
Who has a charter to extol her blood,   14
When she does praise me grieves me. I have done
As you have done—that's what I can;
Induced as you have been—that's for my country.
He that has but effected his good will   18
Hath overta'en mine act.

COMINIUS   You shall not be   19
The grave of your deserving. Rome must know   20
The value of her own. 'Twere a concealment
Worse than a theft, no less than a traducement,   22
To hide your doings and to silence that
Which, to the spire and top of praises vouched,   24
Would seem but modest. Therefore, I beseech you—   25
In sign of what you are, not to reward   26
What you have done—before our army hear me.

MARCIUS
I have some wounds upon me, and they smart
To hear themselves remembered.

COMINIUS   Should they not,   29
Well might they fester 'gainst ingratitude   30
And tent themselves with death. Of all the horses,   31
Whereof we have ta'en good and good store, of all   32
The treasure in this field achieved and city,
We render you the tenth, to be ta'en forth   34
Before the common distribution
At your only choice.

MARCIUS   I thank you, General,   36

But cannot make my heart consent to take
A bribe to pay my sword. I do refuse it,
And stand upon my common part with those   39
That have beheld the doing.   *A long flourish.*   40
              They all cry "Marcius! Marcius!",
                cast up their caps and lances.
                Cominius and Lartius stand bare.
May these same instruments, which you profane,
Never sound more! When drums and trumpets shall
I' the field prove flatterers, let courts and cities be
Made all of false-faced soothing! When steel grows   44
Soft as the parasite's silk, let him be made   45
An overture for th' wars. No more, I say!   46
For that I have not washed my nose that bled,   47
Or foiled some debile wretch—which without note   48
Here's many else have done—you shout me forth   49
In acclamations hyperbolical,   50
As if I loved my little should be dieted   51
In praises sauced with lies.

COMINIUS   Too modest are you,   52
More cruel to your good report than grateful
To us that give you truly. By your patience,   54
If 'gainst yourself you be incensed, we'll put you,
Like one that means his proper harm, in manacles,   56
Then reason safely with you. Therefore be it known,
As to us, to all the world, that Caius Marcius
Wears this war's garland, in token of the which   59
My noble steed, known to the camp, I give him,
With all his trim belonging; and from this time,   61
For what he did before Corioles, call him,
With all th' applause and clamor of the host,
Caius Marcius Coriolanus! Bear
Th' addition nobly ever!   65
              Flourish. Trumpets sound, and drums.

ALL   Caius Marcius Coriolanus!
CORIOLANUS   I will go wash,
And when my face is fair you shall perceive   68
Whether I blush or no. Howbeit, I thank you.   69
I mean to stride your steed, and at all times   70
To undercrest your good addition   71
To th' fairness of my power.

COMINIUS   So, to our tent,   72
Where, ere we do repose us, we will write
To Rome of our success. You, Titus Lartius,
Must to Corioles back. Send us to Rome

---

4 attend listen. **shrug** i.e., indicate incredulity **5 admire** marvel
6 gladly quaked glad to be frightened. **dull** sullen **7 fusty** moldy,
ill-smelling **8 against their hearts** unwillingly **10–11 Yet cam'st
. . . before** i.e., this battle was just a small skirmish in comparison
with the major battle you had already fought. **of** in **11 s.d. power**
army **12 steed** i.e., Marcius. **caparison** mere trappings of a steed
14 charter . . . blood right to praise her child **18 He** anyone. **effected** manifested in action **19 overta'en** surpassed **19–20 You
. . . deserving** you shall not conceal your merit (by your modesty)
22 traducement calumny, slander **24 to . . . vouched** proclaimed in
the highest possible terms of praise **25 modest** moderate, barely sufficient (in relation to all you did) **26 sign** token merely **29 not** i.e.,
not hear themselves praised. (A smarting, open wound is less likely to
fester.) **30 'gainst** i.e., being infected by **31 tent . . . death** i.e.,
find no remedy short of death. (To *tent* a wound is to probe and keep
it open with a rolled bandage, to prevent festering.) **32 good and
good store** excellent ones and plenty of them **34 the tenth** one tenth
36 At . . . choice exactly as you choose

39 stand . . . part insist on having only my regular share **40 beheld
the doing** seen the action. **s.d. bare** bareheaded **44 Made . . .
soothing** given over utterly to hypocritical flattery **44–46 When . . .
wars** i.e., when steel armor grows soft with peace, like the silks of
flatterers, let it (this softened steel) be made an overture to war, an invitation to invasion by foreign enemies (? Various emendations proposed.) **47 For that** because **48 foiled** have overthrown. **debile**
weak. **note** notice taken **49 else** others **49–50 shout . . . hyperbolical** proclaim my merits in public with exaggerated praise **51 my
little** that the little I have done. **dieted** fed **52 In** on, by. **sauced**
seasoned **54 give** report **56 means . . . harm** intends to injure himself **59 garland** (An emblem of victory.) **61 his trim belonging** the
equipment that goes with him **65 addition** title **68 fair** clean
69 Howbeit nevertheless **70 stride** bestride **71 undercrest** adopt
and support, bear up (as a heraldic crest) **72 fairness of my power**
best of my ability

The best, with whom we may articulate
For their own good and ours.   76

LARTIUS   I shall, my lord.

CORIOLANUS
The gods begin to mock me. I, that now
Refused most princely gifts, am bound to beg   79
Of my lord general.

COMINIUS   Take 't, 'tis yours. What is 't?   80

CORIOLANUS
I sometime lay here in Corioles   81
At a poor man's house; he used me kindly.   82
He cried to me; I saw him prisoner;   83
But then Aufidius was within my view,
And wrath o'erwhelmed my pity. I request you
To give my poor host freedom.

COMINIUS   O, well begged!
Were he the butcher of my son, he should
Be free as is the wind. Deliver him, Titus.   88

LARTIUS
Marcius, his name?

CORIOLANUS   By Jupiter, forgot!
I am weary; yea, my memory is tired.
Have we no wine here?

COMINIUS   Go we to our tent.
The blood upon your visage dries; 'tis time
It should be looked to. Come.

A flourish. Cornets. Exeunt.

❖

1.10 *Enter Tullus Aufidius, bloody, with two or three*
Soldiers.

AUFIDIUS   The town is ta'en.

A SOLDIER
'Twill be delivered back on good condition.   2

AUFIDIUS   Condition?
I would I were a Roman, for I cannot,
Being a Volsce, be that I am. Condition?   5
What good condition can a treaty find   6
I' the part that is at mercy? Five times, Marcius,   7
I have fought with thee; so often hast thou beat me,   8
And wouldst do so, I think, should we encounter
As often as we eat. By th' elements,
If e'er again I meet him beard to beard,
He's mine or I am his. Mine emulation   12
Hath not that honor in 't it had; for where   13
I thought to crush him in an equal force,   14
True sword to sword, I'll potch at him some way   15

Or wrath or craft may get him.

A SOLDIER   He's the devil.   16

AUFIDIUS
Bolder, though not so subtle. My valor's poisoned
With only suffering stain by him; for him   18
Shall fly out of itself. Nor sleep nor sanctuary,   19
Being naked, sick, nor fane nor Capitol,   20
The prayers of priests nor times of sacrifice,   21
Embarquements all of fury, shall lift up   22
Their rotten privilege and custom 'gainst   23
My hate to Marcius. Where I find him, were it   24
At home, upon my brother's guard, even there,   25
Against the hospitable canon, would I   26
Wash my fierce hand in 's heart. Go you to th' city;
Learn how 'tis held, and what they are that must   28
Be hostages for Rome.

A SOLDIER   Will not you go?   29

AUFIDIUS
I am attended at the cyprus grove. I pray you—   30
'Tis south the city mills—bring me word thither   31
How the world goes, that to the pace of it   32
I may spur on my journey.

A SOLDIER   I shall, sir.

[Exeunt separately.]

❖

2.1 *Enter Menenius with the two tribunes of the*
people, Sicinius and Brutus.

MENENIUS   The augurer tells me we shall have news   1
tonight.

BRUTUS   Good or bad?

MENENIUS   Not according to the prayer of the people,   4
for they love not Marcius.

SICINIUS   Nature teaches beasts to know their friends.   6

MENENIUS   Pray you, who does the wolf love?

SICINIUS   The lamb.

MENENIUS   Ay, to devour him, as the hungry plebeians
would the noble Marcius.

---

76 best i.e., best in blood among the Volscians.   **articulate** come to
terms (about the return of Corioles to the Volscians)   **79 bound**
obliged   **80 Of** from   **81 sometime lay** once lodged   **82 used** treated
83 cried cried out (at the time of the battle just ended)   **88 Deliver**
release
1.10. Location: Outside of Corioles, after the battle.
2 condition terms   **5 be . . . am** i.e., be honorable, proud   **6 good
condition** state of well-being (with a play on "favorable terms," as in
line 2)   **7 I' . . . mercy** for the side that lies at the mercy of the winner   **8 so** just so   **12 emulation** rivalry   **13 where** whereas   **14 in an
equal force** on equal terms   **15 potch** thrust

16 Or . . . craft in which either wrath or craftiness   **18 stain** disgrace, eclipse   **19 Shall . . . itself** (my valor) shall deviate from its
own natural course   **19–24 Nor . . . Marcius** i.e., neither his being
asleep nor protected by sanctuary, nor any other circumstances that
would normally ensure Marcius' safety, will protect him from me next
time. (*Sanctuary* provides immunity from law or attack to those who
take refuge in a church or temple.)   **20 naked** unarmed.   **fane** temple, shrine   **22 Embarquements** embargoes, restraints   **23 rotten** corrupt, worn out.   **privilege and custom** traditional immunity   **25 At
home** in my own house.   **upon** under.   **guard** protection   **26 hospitable canon** law of hospitality   **28–29 what . . . Rome** i.e., who
they are that are to be taken to Rome as hostages during the negotiations about the return of Corioles to the Volscians; see 1.9.76   **30 attended** waited for   **31 south** south of.   **mills** i.e., grain mills   **32 to
the pace of it** in accordance with the speed of events
**2.1. Location: Rome. The ovation prepared for Coriolanus is proba-
bly to be imagined as beginning outside the city and moving toward
the Capitol (see line 203).**
1 augurer auger, Roman religious figure charged with reading signs to
predict the future   **4 Not . . . people** not what the people would
wish   **6 beasts** i.e., even beasts

BRUTUS   He's a lamb indeed, that baas like a bear.   11

MENENIUS   He's a bear indeed, that lives like a lamb. 12
You two are old men; tell me one thing that I shall
ask you.

BOTH   Well, sir?

MENENIUS   In what enormity is Marcius poor in, that 16
you two have not in abundance?

BRUTUS   He's poor in no one fault, but stored with all. 18

SICINIUS   Especially in pride.

BRUTUS   And topping all others in boasting.

MENENIUS   This is strange now. Do you two know how
you are censured here in the city, I mean of us o' the 22
right-hand file? Do you?   23

BOTH   Why, how are we censured?

MENENIUS   Because you talk of pride now—will you
not be angry?

BOTH   Well, well, sir, well?

MENENIUS   Why, 'tis no great matter; for a very little 28
thief of occasion will rob you of a great deal of 29
patience. Give your dispositions the reins and be 30
angry at your pleasures—at the least, if you take it as
a pleasure to you in being so. You blame Marcius for
being proud?

BRUTUS   We do it not alone, sir.

MENENIUS   I know you can do very little alone, for your
helps are many, or else your actions would grow
wondrous single. Your abilities are too infantlike for 37
doing much alone. You talk of pride. O, that you
could turn your eyes toward the napes of your necks 39
and make but an interior survey of your good selves!
O, that you could!

BOTH   What then, sir?

MENENIUS   Why, then you should discover a brace of 43
unmeriting, proud, violent, testy magistrates, alias 44
fools, as any in Rome.

SICINIUS   Menenius, you are known well enough too.

MENENIUS   I am known to be a humorous patrician, and 47
one that loves a cup of hot wine with not a drop of
allaying Tiber in 't; said to be something imperfect in 49
favoring the first complaint, hasty and tinderlike 50
upon too trivial motion; one that converses more with 51
the buttock of the night than with the forehead of the 52
morning. What I think I utter, and spend my malice in 53
my breath. Meeting two such wealsmen as you are— 54
I cannot call you Lycurguses—if the drink you give 55

me touch my palate adversely, I make a crooked face 56
at it. I cannot say your worships have delivered the 57
matter well, when I find the ass in compound with the 58
major part of your syllables; and though I must be con- 59
tent to bear with those that say you are reverend grave
men, yet they lie deadly that tell you you have good 61
faces. If you see this in the map of my microcosm, 62
follows it that I am known well enough too? What 63
harm can your bisson conspectuities glean out of this 64
character, if I be known well enough too?   65

BRUTUS   Come, sir, come, we know you well enough.

MENENIUS   You know neither me, yourselves, nor anything. You are ambitious for poor knaves' caps and 68
legs. You wear out a good wholesome forenoon in 69
hearing a cause between an orange-wife and a faucet- 70
seller, and then rejourn the controversy of threepence 71
to a second day of audience. When you are hearing a 72
matter between party and party, if you chance to be 73
pinched with the colic, you make faces like mummers, 74
set up the bloody flag against all patience, and, in roar- 75
ing for a chamber pot, dismiss the controversy bleed- 76
ing, the more entangled by your hearing. All the peace 77
you make in their cause is calling both the parties 78
knaves. You are a pair of strange ones.   79

BRUTUS   Come, come, you are well understood to be a 80
perfecter giber for the table than a necessary bencher 81
in the Capitol.   82

MENENIUS   Our very priests must become mockers if
they shall encounter such ridiculous subjects as you 84
are. When you speak best unto the purpose, it is not 85
worth the wagging of your beards, and your beards
deserve not so honorable a grave as to stuff a botcher's 87
cushion or to be entombed in an ass's packsaddle.
Yet you must be saying Marcius is proud; who, in a 89
cheap estimation, is worth all your predecessors since 90
Deucalion, though peradventure some of the best of 91
'em were hereditary hangmen. Good e'en to your wor- 92

56 make . . . face i.e., show displeasure   **57 delivered** reported
58–59 I find . . . syllables i.e., I find asininity in nearly everything
you say (with a pun on *ass in compound*, meaning legal phrases end-
ing in -*as*, like *whereas*)   **61 deadly** excessively   **62 this** i.e., all that I
have freely admitted.   **the map of my microcosm** my face, or chart
of my little world (as opposed to the macrocosm or great world)
63 known . . . too (Menenius mocks their phrase, line 46, and its implication that they "see through" him.)   **64 bisson conspectuities**
blind faculty of sight   **65 character** character sketch   **68–69 caps
and legs** doffing caps and making obeisances to indicate respect
69 wholesome forenoon morning that might be put to better use
70 cause law case.   **orange-wife** woman who sells oranges and other
fruit   **70–71 faucet-seller** one who sells taps for drawing liquor from
barrels   **71 rejourn** adjourn, postpone.   **of** about   **72 audience** hearing   **73 party and party** the two parties in a dispute   **74 pinched
with the colic** afflicted with griping pains in the belly.   **mummers**
masqueraders, performers in dumb shows   **75 set . . . flag** i.e., declare violent war   **76–77 bleeding** unhealed, unsettled   **77–
79 peace . . . knaves** (Perhaps a reference to the song "Hold thy
peace, thou knave"; see *Twelfth Night*, 2.3.63–70.)   **80–82 a perfecter . . . Capitol** i.e., better at dinner-table jesting than at sitting in
the Senate as a counselor   **84 subjects** (1) topics (2) citizens
85 When i.e., even when   **87 botcher** one who patches old clothes
or boots   **89–90 in a cheap estimation** even at the lowest estimation
of his worth   **91 Deucalion** the Noah of classical story, survivor of a
great flood.   **peradventure** perhaps   **92 hereditary hangmen** men
serving as executioners (a very ignoble occupation) generation after
generation.   **Good e'en** good evening (used for any time after noon)

11–12 He's a lamb . . . a lamb i.e., Some lamb! Have you heard
his growl?—How can you accuse him of being a bear when he acts
so unthreateningly?   **16 enormity** wickedness   **18 stored** well
stocked   **22 censured** judged   **23 right-hand file** i.e., party of aristocrats (who took the honorable right-hand position in battle)   **28–30 a
very . . . patience** any slight pretext will rob you of your patience
37 single poor, feeble   **39 turn . . . necks** i.e., turn your gaze in order to see within   **43 brace** pair   **44 testy** headstrong   **47 humorous**
whimsical, governed by humors   **49 allaying Tiber** water used to dilute   **49–50 something . . . complaint** somewhat at fault for deciding in favor of the complainant before hearing the other side of the
case   **50 tinderlike** quick-tempered   **51 motion** cause   **51–53 one
. . . morning** one who is better acquainted with the late hours of the
night than with the early hours of the morning   **53 spend** expend
54 breath words.   **wealsmen** statesmen   **55 Lycurguses** (Said ironically; Lycurgus was the famous Spartan lawgiver.)   **55–56 drink you
give me** (With a suggestion also of "things you tell me.")

ships. More of your conversation would infect my 93
brain, being the herdsmen of the beastly plebeians. I 94
will be bold to take my leave of you.

Brutus and Sicinius [stand] aside.

Enter Volumnia, Virgilia, and Valeria.

How now, my as fair as noble ladies—and the moon, 96
were she earthly, no nobler—whither do you follow 97
your eyes so fast? 98

VOLUMNIA   Honorable Menenius, my boy Marcius approaches. For the love of Juno, let's go. 100

MENENIUS   Ha? Marcius coming home?

VOLUMNIA   Ay, worthy Menenius, and with most pros- 102
perous approbation. 103

MENENIUS   Take my cap, Jupiter, and I thank thee. [*He
tosses his cap.*] Hoo! Marcius coming home?

VALERIA, VIRGILIA   Nay, 'tis true.

VOLUMNIA   Look, here's a letter from him. [*Showing a
letter.*] The state hath another, his wife another, and I
think there's one at home for you.

MENENIUS   I will make my very house reel tonight. A
letter for me?

VIRGILIA   Yes, certain, there's a letter for you; I saw 't.

MENENIUS   A letter for me! It gives me an estate of seven 113
years' health, in which time I will make a lip at the 114
physician. The most sovereign prescription in Galen 115
is but empiricutic and, to this preservative, of no bet- 116
ter report than a horse drench. Is he not wounded? He 117
was wont to come home wounded. 118

VIRGILIA   O, no, no, no.

VOLUMNIA   O, he is wounded, I thank the gods for 't.

MENENIUS   So do I too, if it be not too much. Brings 'a 121
victory in his pocket, the wounds become him.

VOLUMNIA   On 's brows, Menenius. He comes the 123
third time home with the oaken garland.

MENENIUS   Has he disciplined Aufidius soundly? 125

VOLUMNIA   Titus Lartius writes they fought together,
but Aufidius got off.

MENENIUS   And 'twas time for him too, I'll warrant him
that. An he had stayed by him, I would not have been 129
so fidiused for all the chests in Corioles and the gold 130
that's in them. Is the Senate possessed of this? 131

VOLUMNIA   Good ladies, let's go.—Yes, yes, yes; the
Senate has letters from the General, wherein he gives
my son the whole name of the war. He hath in this 134
action outdone his former deeds doubly.

VALERIA   In troth, there's wondrous things spoke of 136
him.

MENENIUS   Wondrous? Ay, I warrant you, and not
without his true purchasing. 139

VIRGILIA   The gods grant them true!

VOLUMNIA   True? Pow waw. 141

MENENIUS   True? I'll be sworn they are true. Where is
he wounded? [*To the tribunes.*] God save your good
worships! Marcius is coming home. He has more
cause to be proud.—Where is he wounded?

VOLUMNIA   I' the shoulder and i' the left arm. There will
be large cicatrices to show the people, when he shall 147
stand for his place. He received in the repulse of 148
Tarquin seven hurts i' the body. 149

MENENIUS   One i' the neck and two i' the thigh—there's
nine that I know.

VOLUMNIA   He had, before this last expedition, twenty-
five wounds upon him.

MENENIUS   Now it's twenty-seven. Every gash was an
enemy's grave. (*A shout and flourish.*) Hark, the trumpets.

VOLUMNIA   These are the ushers of Marcius. Before him
he carries noise, and behind him he leaves tears.
Death, that dark spirit, in 's nervy arm doth lie, 159
Which, being advanced, declines, and then men die. 160

*A sennet. Trumpets sound. Enter Cominius the
general, and Titus Lartius; between them,
Coriolanus, crowned with an oaken garland; with
captains and soldiers, and a Herald.*

HERALD
Know, Rome, that all alone Marcius did fight
Within Corioles gates, where he hath won,
With fame, a name to Caius Marcius; these 163
In honor follows "Coriolanus."
Welcome to Rome, renownèd Coriolanus!

Sound flourish.

ALL
Welcome to Rome, renownèd Coriolanus!

CORIOLANUS
No more of this. It does offend my heart.
Pray now, no more.

COMINIUS   Look, sir, your mother.

CORIOLANUS   O,
You have, I know, petitioned all the gods
For my prosperity!   *Kneels.*

VOLUMNIA   Nay, my good soldier, up, 170
My gentle Marcius, worthy Caius, and
By deed-achieving honor newly named— 172
What is it? Coriolanus must I call thee?—
But, O, thy wife!

CORIOLANUS [*rising*]   My gracious silence, hail!
Wouldst thou have laughed had I come coffined
home,

93 **conversation** society   94 **being** you being   96 **the moon** i.e., Diana, goddess of chastity   97–98 **whither . . . fast** where are you going so eagerly in hopes of some sight?   100 **Juno** wife of Jupiter and
Queen of the gods   102–103 **prosperous approbation** success and
acclaim   113 **estate** (1) endowment (2) condition   114 **make a lip**
make a contemptuous face, mock   115 **sovereign** efficacious.   **Galen**
Greek physician and authority on medicine (born considerably after
the time of Coriolanus)   116 **empiricutic** quacklike.   **to** compared to
117 **report** reputation, standing.   **horse drench** dose of medicine for
horses   118 **wont** accustomed   121 **Brings 'a** if he brings   123 **On 's
brows** i.e., the *victory is on his brows* (in the form of a garland) rather
than *in his pocket*, as Menenius suggests. (Said as a pleasantry.)
125 **disciplined** beaten   129 **An** if   130 **fidiused** (Menenius' coined
word, meaning "treated as Aufidius deserves, beaten.")   131 **possessed** informed   134 **name** credit, reputation   136 **troth** truth, faith

139 **his true purchasing** deserving on his part   141 **Pow waw** i.e.,
pish   147 **cicatrices** scars   148 **stand for his place** i.e., seek the consulship   148–149 **repulse of Tarquin** (Plutarch reports that Marcius
fought his first battle against King Tarquin the Proud in about 496 B.C.
on the occasion of Tarquin's last attempt to regain the kingdom; see
1.3.13–15 and note, and 2.2.88 ff.)   159 **in 's** in his.   **nervy** sinewy
160 **advanced** raised.   **declines** descends.   **s.d. A sennet** a trumpet
call accompanying an entrance   163 **With** in addition to.   **to** added
to   170 **prosperity** success   172 **deed-achieving** achieved by deeds

That weep'st to see me triumph? Ah, my dear,
Such eyes the widows in Corioles wear,
And mothers that lack sons.

MENENIUS   Now, the gods crown thee!

CORIOLANUS [to Menenius]
And live you yet? [To Valeria.] O my sweet lady,
    pardon.

VOLUMNIA
I know not where to turn. O, welcome home!
[To Cominius.] And welcome, General! And you're
    welcome all.

MENENIUS
A hundred thousand welcomes! I could weep
And I could laugh; I am light and heavy. Welcome.   183
A curse begin at very root on 's heart   184
That is not glad to see thee! You are three
That Rome should dote on; yet, by the faith of men,
We have some old crab trees here at home that
    will not   187
Be grafted to your relish. Yet welcome, warriors!   188
We call a nettle but a nettle, and   189
The faults of fools but folly.   190

COMINIUS   Ever right.

CORIOLANUS   Menenius ever, ever.   192

HERALD
Give way there, and go on!

CORIOLANUS [to Volumnia and Virgilia]
                        Your hand, and yours.
Ere in our own house I do shade my head,   194
The good patricians must be visited,
From whom I have received not only greetings,
But with them change of honors.

VOLUMNIA   I have lived   197
To see inherited my very wishes   198
And the buildings of my fancy. Only   199
There's one thing wanting, which I doubt not but   200
Our Rome will cast upon thee.

CORIOLANUS   Know, good Mother,   201
I had rather be their servant in my way
Than sway with them in theirs.

COMINIUS   On, to the Capitol!   203
   Flourish. Cornets. Exeunt in state, as before.
                Brutus and Sicinius [come forward].

BRUTUS
All tongues speak of him, and the bleared sights   204
Are spectacled to see him. Your prattling nurse   205
Into a rapture lets her baby cry   206
While she chats him. The kitchen malkin pins   207

Her richest lockram 'bout her reechy neck,   208
Clamb'ring the walls to eye him. Stalls, bulks,
    windows   209
Are smothered up, leads filled and ridges horsed   210
With variable complexions, all agreeing   211
In earnestness to see him. Seld-shown flamens   212
Do press among the popular throngs and puff   213
To win a vulgar station. Our veiled dames   214
Commit the war of white and damask in   215
Their nicely-gauded cheeks to th' wanton spoil   216
Of Phoebus' burning kisses—such a pother   217
As if that whatsoever god who leads him   218
Were slyly crept into his human powers   219
And gave him graceful posture.

SICINIUS   On the sudden   220
I warrant him consul.

BRUTUS   Then our office may,
During his power, go sleep.   222

SICINIUS
He cannot temperately transport his honors   223
From where he should begin and end, but will   224
Lose those he hath won.

BRUTUS   In that there's comfort.

SICINIUS   Doubt not   225
The commoners, for whom we stand, but they   226
Upon their ancient malice will forget   227
With the least cause these his new honors—which   228
That he will give them make I as little question   229
As he is proud to do 't.

BRUTUS   I heard him swear,   230
Were he to stand for consul, never would he
Appear i' the marketplace nor on him put
The napless vesture of humility,   233
Nor, showing, as the manner is, his wounds
To th' people, beg their stinking breaths.

SICINIUS   'Tis right. 235

BRUTUS
It was his word. O, he would miss it rather   236
Than carry it but by the suit of the gentry to him   237
And the desire of the nobles.

SICINIUS   I wish no better
Than have him hold that purpose and to put it

183 **light and heavy** merry and sad   184 **on 's** of his   187 **old crab trees** old crab apple trees, i.e., sour-natured old men (such as the tribunes)   188 **grafted to your relish** implanted with a liking for you (something that would sweeten their sourness)   189–190 **We . . . folly** i.e., some unpleasant and foolish things cannot be changed and must be acknowledged for what they are   192 **Menenius ever** same old Menenius   194 **shade** rest   197 **change of honors** promotion, fresh honors   198 **inherited** realized, possessed   199 **fancy** imagination   200 **wanting** lacking   201 **cast upon** offer   203 **sway with** rule over   204–205 **bleared . . . spectacled** people with dimmed vision put on spectacles   205 **Your prattling nurse** the typical chattering nurse, the kind of nurse people talk about, your average nurse   206 **rapture** fit   207 **chats him** i.e., gossips about Coriolanus.   **malkin** untidy servantmaid

208 **lockram** coarse linen fabric.   **reechy** dirty, filthy   209 **Clamb'ring** climbing.   **Stalls** benches in front of shops displaying wares.   **bulks** structures projecting from the front of a shop   210 **leads** leaded roofs   210–211 **ridges . . . complexions** the roof-ridges bestridden by people of all sorts   211 **agreeing** alike   212 **Seld-shown flamens** priests (of ancient Rome) who rarely appear in public   213 **popular** plebeian, vulgar.   **puff** pant, exert themselves   214 **vulgar station** place in the crowd   215 **damask** red or pink, like the damask rose   216 **nicely-gauded** daintily adorned or made up.   **wanton spoil** (1) ravages (2) amorous despoiling   217 **Phoebus'** i.e., the sun's.   **pother** hubbub   218 **him** i.e., Coriolanus   219 **his human powers** i.e., Coriolanus' body   220 **posture** bearing.   **On the sudden** suddenly   222 **power** term of authority   223 **temperately transport** carry in a temperate and self-controlled way   224 **and end** i.e., to a proper conclusion   225–227 **Doubt not . . . forget** do not doubt that the commoners, whom we represent, will, because of their long-standing hostility, forget   228 **With . . . cause** upon the slightest provocation.   **which** i.e., which provocation   229 **make . . . question** I have as little doubt   230 **As** as that   233 **napless vesture** threadbare garment   235 **breaths** i.e., voices, votes   236 **miss it** i.e., go without the consulship   237 **carry it but** win it otherwise than

In execution.

BRUTUS 'Tis most like he will. 240

SICINIUS
It shall be to him then as our good wills, 241
A sure destruction.

BRUTUS So it must fall out
To him, or our authority's for an end. 243
We must suggest the people in what hatred 244
He still hath held them; that to 's power he would 245
Have made them mules, silenced their pleaders, and 246
Dispropertied their freedoms, holding them 247
In human action and capacity
Of no more soul nor fitness for the world
Than camels in their war, who have their provand 250
Only for bearing burdens, and sore blows
For sinking under them.

SICINIUS This—as you say, suggested
At some time when his soaring insolence
Shall touch the people, which time shall not want 254
If he be put upon 't, and that's as easy 255
As to set dogs on sheep—will be his fire 256
To kindle their dry stubble; and their blaze 257
Shall darken him forever.

Enter a Messenger.

BRUTUS What's the matter? 258

MESSENGER
You are sent for to the Capitol. 'Tis thought
That Marcius shall be consul. I have seen
The dumb men throng to see him, and the blind
To hear him speak. Matrons flung gloves,
Ladies and maids their scarves and handkerchiefs,
Upon him as he passed. The nobles bended
As to Jove's statue, and the commons made
A shower and thunder with their caps and shouts.
I never saw the like.

BRUTUS Let's to the Capitol,
And carry with us ears and eyes for the time, 268
But hearts for the event.

SICINIUS Have with you. *Exeunt.* 269

♣

2.2 *Enter two Officers, to lay cushions, as it were in
the Capitol.*

FIRST OFFICER Come, come, they are almost here. How
many stand for consulships?

SECOND OFFICER Three, they say; but 'tis thought of 3
everyone Coriolanus will carry it.

FIRST OFFICER That's a brave fellow, but he's vengeance 5
proud and loves not the common people.

SECOND OFFICER Faith, there hath been many great men
that have flattered the people who ne'er loved them; 8
and there be many that they have loved, they know 9
not wherefore; so that, if they love they know not 10
why, they hate upon no better a ground. Therefore,
for Coriolanus neither to care whether they love or
hate him manifests the true knowledge he has in their 13
disposition, and out of his noble carelessness lets them 14
plainly see 't.

FIRST OFFICER If he did not care whether he had their
love or no, he waved indifferently twixt doing them 17
neither good nor harm; but he seeks their hate with
greater devotion than they can render it him, and
leaves nothing undone that may fully discover him 20
their opposite. Now, to seem to affect the malice and 21
displeasure of the people is as bad as that which he
dislikes, to flatter them for their love.

SECOND OFFICER He hath deserved worthily of his coun- 24
try, and his ascent is not by such easy degrees as those 25
who, having been supple and courteous to the people,
bonneted, without any further deed to have them at 27
all into their estimation and report. But he hath so 28
planted his honors in their eyes and his actions in
their hearts that for their tongues to be silent and not
confess so much were a kind of ingrateful injury. To
report otherwise were a malice that, giving itself the 32
lie, would pluck reproof and rebuke from every ear 33
that heard it.

FIRST OFFICER No more of him; he's a worthy man.
Make way, they are coming. 36

*A sennet. Enter the patricians and the tribunes of
the people, lictors before them; Coriolanus,
Menenius, Cominius the consul. Sicinius and
Brutus take their places by themselves. Coriolanus
stands.*

MENENIUS
Having determined of the Volsces and 37
To send for Titus Lartius, it remains,
As the main point of this our after-meeting, 39
To gratify his noble service that 40
Hath thus stood for his country. Therefore
please you, 41
Most reverend and grave elders, to desire

3 of by 5 brave excellent. vengeance terribly 8 who i.e., the people. them i.e., the great men 9 they the people 10 wherefore
why 13 in of 14 noble carelessness patrician indifference to public
opinion 17 waved indifferently would waver impartially 20–
21 discover . . . opposite reveal him to be their adversary 21 affect
seek out, desire 24 deserved worthily of justifiably merited much
from 25 degrees steps 27 bonneted took their hats off. have them
gain their way 28 estimation and report esteem and good opinion
32–33 giving . . . lie manifesting its own falsehood 36 s.d. lictors
officials attendant upon Roman magistrates 37 determined of i.e.,
reached a decision concerning (the terms for returning Corioles, etc.)
39 after-meeting follow-up meeting 40 gratify reward, requite
41 stood for fought for, defended

240 like likely 241 as . . . wills as our interest demands 243 for an
end doomed 244 suggest insinuate to 245 still always. to 's
power to the extent of his power 246 mules i.e., beasts of burden.
pleaders i.e., the tribunes 247 Dispropertied dispossessed, deprived
(them) of 250 provand provender, food 254 want be lacking
255 put upon 't urged, incited to it 256 his fire i.e., the spark that
kindles his hatred 257 To kindle . . . stubble (Coriolanus' fiery
wrath will, in turn, kindle the inflammable emotions of the plebeians.)
258 darken eclipse, deprive of authority or renown 268 time present
situation 269 hearts . . . event i.e., deeper desires and purposes for
what is to follow. Have with you I'm with you, let's go
2.2. Location: Rome. The Capitol.

The present consul and last general   43
In our well-found successes to report   44
A little of that worthy work performed
By Caius Marcius Coriolanus, whom
We met here both to thank and to remember
With honors like himself.   [*Coriolanus sits.*]

FIRST SENATOR   Speak, good Cominius.   48
Leave nothing out for length, and make us think
Rather our state's defective for requital   50
Than we to stretch it out. [*To the tribunes.*] Masters o'
    the people,   51
We do request your kindest ears and, after,   52
Your loving motion toward the common body   53
To yield what passes here.

SICINIUS   We are convented   54
Upon a pleasing treaty, and have hearts   55
Inclinable to honor and advance
The theme of our assembly.

BRUTUS   Which the rather   57
We shall be blest to do if he remember   58
A kinder value of the people than   59
He hath hereto prized them at.

MENENIUS   That's off, that's off!   60
I would you rather had been silent. Please you
To hear Cominius speak?

BRUTUS   Most willingly;
But yet my caution was more pertinent   63
Than the rebuke you give it.

MENENIUS   He loves your people;
But tie him not to be their bedfellow.   65
Worthy Cominius, speak.
            Coriolanus rises and offers to go away.
                                Nay, keep your place.   66

FIRST SENATOR
Sit, Coriolanus. Never shame to hear
What you have nobly done.

CORIOLANUS   Your honors' pardon.
I had rather have my wounds to heal again
Than hear say how I got them.

BRUTUS   Sir, I hope
My words disbenched you not?

CORIOLANUS   No, sir. Yet oft,   71
When blows have made me stay, I fled from words.
You soothed not, therefore hurt not. But your
    people,   73
I love them as they weigh—

MENENIUS   Pray now, sit down.   74

CORIOLANUS
I had rather have one scratch my head i' the sun   75
When the alarum were struck than idly sit   76
To hear my nothings monstered.   *Exit Coriolanus.*

MENENIUS   Masters of the people,   77
Your multiplying spawn how can he flatter—   78
That's thousand to one good one—when you
    now see   79
He had rather venture all his limbs for honor   80
Than one on 's ears to hear it?—Proceed, Cominius. 81

COMINIUS
I shall lack voice. The deeds of Coriolanus
Should not be uttered feebly. It is held
That valor is the chiefest virtue and
Most dignifies the haver; if it be,
The man I speak of cannot in the world
Be singly counterpoised. At sixteen years,   87
When Tarquin made a head for Rome, he fought   88
Beyond the mark of others. Our then dictator,   89
Whom with all praise I point at, saw him fight,   90
When with his Amazonian chin he drove   91
The bristled lips before him. He bestrid   92
An o'erpressed Roman, and i' the Consul's view   93
Slew three opposers. Tarquin's self he met,
And struck him on his knee. In that day's feats,   95
When he might act the woman in the scene,   96
He proved best man i' the field, and for his meed   97
Was brow-bound with the oak. His pupil age   98
Man-entered thus, he waxèd like a sea,   99
And in the brunt of seventeen battles since   100
He lurched all swords of the garland. For this last, 101
Before and in Corioles, let me say,
I cannot speak him home. He stopped the fliers,   103
And by his rare example made the coward   104
Turn terror into sport. As weeds before
A vessel under sail, so men obeyed
And fell below his stem. His sword, death's stamp, 107
Where it did mark, it took; from face to foot   108
He was a thing of blood, whose every motion

---

43 last late, recent **44 well-found** fortunately met with, found to be good **48 like himself** i.e., worthy of his greatness **50–51 Rather . . . out** that our state lacks means to reward adequately rather than that we are defective in intention to extend what reward we have at our disposal **52 after** in addition to that **53 loving . . . body** friendly intervention with the common people **54 yield** assent to, grant. **passes** is voted. **convented** summoned, convened **55 Upon** in order to consider. **treaty** proposal **57 theme** business. **rather** sooner **58 blest** happy **59 kinder value** more favorable estimation **60 off** jarring, not pertinent **63 pertinent** appropriate **65 tie** oblige **66 s.d. offers** starts **71 disbenched you not** did not make you leave your seat **73 soothed** flattered **74 as they weigh** according to their deserts

75–76 have . . . struck i.e., engage in idle pleasure when the battle signal is sounded. **alarum** call to arms **77 monstered** made into unnatural marvels **78 multiplying spawn** fast-breeding commoners **79 That's . . . one** in which there are a thousand bad ones to one good one, or, a thousand bad ones contrasted to the noble Coriolanus **80 venture** risk **81 on 's** of his. **it** i.e., praise of his honor **87 singly counterpoised** equaled by any other individual **88 made . . . for** raised a force to attack (and reconquer) **89 mark** ability, reach. **dictator** leader constitutionally given absolute authority to deal with a specific emergency, such as a war **90 point at** i.e., refer to. (The unnamed dictator of those earlier times, probably Aulus Posthumus Regillensis, is not present.) **91 Amazonian** i.e., beardless (like the female warriors, the Amazons) **92 bristled lips** i.e., bearded warriors. **bestrid** stood over in battle, protected **93 o'erpressed** overwhelmed **95 on** to **96 he . . . scene** i.e., he was young enough not to have been blamed for cowardice (with an allusion to boys playing women's roles in the theater) **97 meed** reward **98 brow-bound** i.e., presented with a garland as an emblem of victory **99 Man-entered** initiated into manhood **100 brunt** violence, shock **101 lurched** robbed, cheated. **For** as for **103 speak him home** praise him adequately. **the fliers** those who tried to flee the battle **104 the coward** even the coward **107 stem** main timber of the prow of a ship. **stamp** tool for imprinting a design or pattern **108 took** made an impression, slew

Was timed with dying cries. Alone he entered 110
The mortal gate o' the city, which he painted 111
With shunless destiny; aidless came off, 112
And with a sudden reinforcement struck 113
Corioles like a planet. Now all's his, 114
When by and by the din of war 'gan pierce 115
His ready sense; then straight his doubled spirit 116
Requickened what in flesh was fatigate, 117
And to the battle came he, where he did
Run reeking o'er the lives of men as if 119
'Twere a perpetual spoil; and till we called 120
Both field and city ours, he never stood 121
To ease his breast with panting.

MENENIUS   Worthy man!

FIRST SENATOR
He cannot but with measure fit the honors
Which we devise him. 123

COMINIUS   Our spoils he kicked at, 124
And looked upon things precious as they were 125
The common muck of the world. He covets less
Than misery itself would give, rewards 127
His deeds with doing them, and is content 128
To spend the time to end it.

MENENIUS   He's right noble. 129
Let him be called for.

FIRST SENATOR   Call Coriolanus.

OFFICER   He doth appear.

Enter Coriolanus.

MENENIUS
The Senate, Coriolanus, are well pleased
To make thee consul.

CORIOLANUS   I do owe them still 134
My life and services.

MENENIUS   It then remains
That you do speak to the people.

CORIOLANUS   I do beseech you,
Let me o'erleap that custom, for I cannot
Put on the gown, stand naked, and entreat them 138
For my wounds' sake to give their suffrage. Please
    you
That I may pass this doing.

SICINIUS   Sir, the people 140

Must have their voices; neither will they bate 141
One jot of ceremony.

MENENIUS [*to Coriolanus*] Put them not to 't. 142
Pray you, go fit you to the custom and
Take to you, as your predecessors have,
Your honor with your form.

CORIOLANUS   It is a part 145
That I shall blush in acting, and might well
Be taken from the people.

BRUTUS [*to Sicinius*]   Mark you that?

CORIOLANUS
To brag unto them, "Thus I did, and thus!"
Show them th' unaching scars which I should hide,
As if I had received them for the hire 150
Of their breath only!

MENENIUS   Do not stand upon 't.— 151
We recommend to you, tribunes of the people, 152
Our purpose to them, and to our noble consul 153
Wish we all joy and honor.

SENATORS
To Coriolanus come all joy and honor! 155

Flourish cornets. Then exeunt. Manent Sicinius
and Brutus.

BRUTUS
You see how he intends to use the people.

SICINIUS
May they perceive 's intent! He will require them 157
As if he did contemn what he requested 158
Should be in them to give.

BRUTUS   Come, we'll inform them 159
Of our proceedings here. On the marketplace 160
I know they do attend us.   [*Exeunt.*] 161

❖

2.3   *Enter seven or eight Citizens.*

FIRST CITIZEN Once, if he do require our voices, we 1
ought not to deny him.

SECOND CITIZEN We may, sir, if we will.

THIRD CITIZEN We have power in ourselves to do it,
but it is a power that we have no power to do; for if he 5
show us his wounds and tell us his deeds, we are to
put our tongues into those wounds and speak for 7
them; so, if he tell us his noble deeds, we must also tell
him our noble acceptance of them. Ingratitude is
monstrous, and for the multitude to be ingrateful were
to make a monster of the multitude; of the which we,
being members, should bring ourselves to be monstrous members.

---

110 **Was timed** kept time, was accompanied 111 **mortal** deadly.
which (Refers to the *city*.) **painted** i.e., stained 112 **shunless destiny** i.e., the blood of those who could not escape their doom
113 **reinforcement** fresh assault 114 **like a planet** (Refers to the
power of striking or blasting, believed in astrology to belong to the
planets.) 114–115 **Now . . . When** no sooner was everything his
than 115 **'gan** began to 116 **ready sense** i.e., alert sense of hearing. **straight** at once. **doubled** renewed, twice what it was before
117 **Requickened** revivified. **fatigate** fatigued 119 **reeking** steaming
(with enemies' blood) 120 **perpetual spoil** endless slaughter
121 **stood** stopped 123 **He . . . fit** he can't help but measure up to
124 **devise** devise for. **kicked at** spurned 125 **as** as if 127 **misery**
poverty 127–128 **rewards . . . doing them** finds reward for his actions in the satisfaction that comes from having acted well
128–129 **is content . . . end it** is satisfied to be repaid for his time
spent with the pleasure of having spent his time thus 134 **still** ever
138 **naked** exposed 140 **pass** disregard, omit

141 **voices** votes. **bate** abate, do without 142 **Put . . . to 't** i.e., do
not force the issue 145 **with your form** with the ceremony that custom prescribes to you 150 **hire** wages 151 **breath** i.e., votes.
stand upon 't make a point of it 152 **recommend** commit, consign
153 **purpose to** proposal regarding 155 **s.d. Manent** they remain onstage 157 **require** ask, solicit 158 **contemn** scorn (that) 159 **in
them** theirs 160 **On** in 161 **attend** wait for
2.3. Location: Rome. The Forum, or marketplace.
1 **Once** once and for all 5 **no power to do** i.e., no moral right to exercise 7 **put . . . wounds** i.e., let the wounds inspire our tongues

FIRST CITIZEN   And to make us no better thought of, a 14
little help will serve; for once we stood up about the 15
corn, he himself stuck not to call us the many-headed 16
multitude.

THIRD CITIZEN We have been called so of many; not that 18
our heads are some brown, some black, some abram, 19
some bald, but that our wits are so diversely colored;
and truly I think if all our wits were to issue out of one
skull, they would fly east, west, north, south, and their
consent of one direct way should be at once to all the 23
points o' the compass.

SECOND CITIZEN   Think you so? Which way do you
judge my wit would fly?

THIRD CITIZEN   Nay, your wit will not so soon out as 27
another man's will; 'tis strongly wedged up in a blockhead. But if it were at liberty, 'twould, sure, south- 29
ward. 30

SECOND CITIZEN   Why that way?

THIRD CITIZEN   To lose itself in a fog where, being three
parts melted away with rotten dews, the fourth would 33
return for conscience' sake, to help to get thee a wife.

SECOND CITIZEN You are never without your tricks. You 35
may, you may. 36

THIRD CITIZEN   Are you all resolved to give your
voices? But that's no matter, the greater part carries it. 38
I say, if he would incline to the people, there was 39
never a worthier man.

Enter Coriolanus in a gown of humility, with
Menenius.

Here he comes, and in the gown of humility. Mark his
behavior. We are not to stay all together, but to come
by him where he stands by ones, by twos, and by
threes. He's to make his requests by particulars, 44
wherein every one of us has a single honor in giving him 45
our own voices with our own tongues. Therefore follow me, and I'll direct you how you shall go by him. 47

ALL   Content, content.   [*Exeunt Citizens.*]

MENENIUS
O sir, you are not right. Have you not known
The worthiest men have done 't?

CORIOLANUS   What must I say?
"I pray, sir"—Plague upon 't! I cannot bring
My tongue to such a pace. "Look, sir, my wounds!
I got them in my country's service, when
Some certain of your brethren roared and ran
From th' noise of our own drums."

MENENIUS   O me, the gods!
You must not speak of that. You must desire them
To think upon you.

CORIOLANUS   Think upon me? Hang 'em! 57

I would they would forget me, like the virtues 58
Which our divines lose by 'em.

MENENIUS   You'll mar all. 59
I'll leave you. Pray you speak to 'em, I pray you,
In wholesome manner.   *Exit.*

Enter three of the Citizens.

CORIOLANUS   Bid them wash their faces 61
And keep their teeth clean. So, here comes a
brace.— 62
You know the cause, sir, of my standing here.

THIRD CITIZEN
We do, sir. Tell us what hath brought you to 't.

CORIOLANUS   Mine own desert.

SECOND CITIZEN   Your own desert?

CORIOLANUS   Ay, but not mine own desire.

THIRD CITIZEN   How, not your own desire?

CORIOLANUS   No, sir, 'twas never my desire yet to
trouble the poor with begging.

THIRD CITIZEN   You must think, if we give you anything, we hope to gain by you.

CORIOLANUS   Well then, I pray, your price o' the con- 73
sulship?

FIRST CITIZEN   The price is to ask it kindly.

CORIOLANUS   Kindly, sir, I pray, let me ha 't. I have
wounds to show you, which shall be yours in 77
private.—Your good voice, sir. What say you?

SECOND CITIZEN   You shall ha 't, worthy sir.

CORIOLANUS   A match, sir. There's in all two worthy 80
voices begged. I have your alms. Adieu.

THIRD CITIZEN   But this is something odd. 82

SECOND CITIZEN   An 'twere to give again—but 'tis no 83
matter.   *Exeunt [the three Citizens].*

Enter two other Citizens.

CORIOLANUS   Pray you now, if it may stand with the 85
tune of your voices that I may be consul, I have here
the customary gown.

FOURTH CITIZEN   You have deserved nobly of your
country, and you have not deserved nobly.

CORIOLANUS   Your enigma? 90

FOURTH CITIZEN   You have been a scourge to her 91
enemies; you have been a rod to her friends. You have 92
not indeed loved the common people.

CORIOLANUS You should account me the more virtuous
that I have not been common in my love. I will, sir, 95
flatter my sworn brother, the people, to earn a dearer 96
estimation of them; 'tis a condition they account gen- 97
tle. And since the wisdom of their choice is rather to 98

14–15 a little . . . serve a small amount of effort on our part will suffice   **15 once** when   **16 stuck not** did not hesitate   **18 of** by.   **that**
because   **19 abram** auburn   **23 consent of** agreement upon   **27 out**
go out   **29–30 southward** (The south wind was believed to bring
pestilence.)   **33 rotten** unwholesome   **35–36 You may** i.e., go on,
say what you like   **38 greater part** majority   **39 incline to** sympathize with   **44 by particulars** to individuals, one by one   **45 single**
separate, individual   **47 go by** appear before   **57 think upon** think
kindly of

58 I would I wish   **59 divines** priests.   **lose by 'em** vainly seek to instill in them (by preaching)   **61 wholesome** calculated to do good.
(But Coriolanus answers sarcastically to the sense of "healthful.")
62 brace pair. (Used contemptuously here.)   **73 o' the** for the
77 yours available for your inspection   **80 match** deal, bargain
82 something somewhat   **83 An 'twere** if it were   **85 stand with** be
consistent with   **90 enigma** riddle   **91 scourge** instrument of punishment   **92 rod** stick or whip used to inflict punishment   **95 common**
vulgar, promiscuous (playing on *common* in line 93)   **96 sworn**
brother one of two friends bound by oath to each other   **96–**
97 dearer . . . them higher esteem on their part   **97–98 'tis . . .**
gentle i.e., they think it genteel to be flattered by an aristocrat and
view flattery as noble

have my hat than my heart, I will practice the insin- 99
uating nod and be off to them most counterfeitly. That 100
is, sir, I will counterfeit the bewitchment of some pop- 101
ular man and give it bountiful to the desirers. There- 102
fore, beseech you I may be consul.

FIFTH CITIZEN We hope to find you our friend, and
therefore give you our voices heartily.

FOURTH CITIZEN You have received many wounds for
your country.

CORIOLANUS I will not seal your knowledge with show- 108
ing them. I will make much of your voices and so
trouble you no farther.

BOTH CITIZENS The gods give you joy, sir, heartily!
[Exeunt Citizens.]

CORIOLANUS Most sweet voices!
Better it is to die, better to starve,
Than crave the hire which first we do deserve. 114
Why in this woolvish toge should I stand here 115
To beg of Hob and Dick that does appear 116
Their needless vouches? Custom calls me to 't. 117
What custom wills, in all things should we do 't, 118
The dust on antique time would lie unswept 119
And mountainous error be too highly heaped
For truth to o'erpeer. Rather than fool it so, 121
Let the high office and the honor go
To one that would do thus. I am half through; 123
The one part suffered, the other will I do.

Enter three Citizens more.

Here come more voices.— 125
Your voices! For your voices I have fought;
Watched for your voices; for your voices bear 127
Of wounds two dozen odd. Battles thrice six
I have seen and heard of; for your voices have 129
Done many things, some less, some more. Your
voices!
Indeed, I would be consul.

SIXTH CITIZEN He has done nobly, and cannot go
without any honest man's voice.

SEVENTH CITIZEN Therefore let him be consul. The gods
give him joy, and make him good friend to the
people!

ALL Amen, amen. God save thee, noble Consul!
[Exeunt Citizens.]

CORIOLANUS Worthy voices!

Enter Menenius, with Brutus and Sicinius.

MENENIUS
You have stood your limitation, and the tribunes 139
Endue you with the people's voice. Remains 140
That, in th' official marks invested, you 141
Anon do meet the Senate.

CORIOLANUS   Is this done? 142

SICINIUS
The custom of request you have discharged. 143
The people do admit you, and are summoned
To meet anon, upon your approbation. 145

CORIOLANUS
Where? At the Senate House?

SICINIUS   There, Coriolanus.

CORIOLANUS
May I change these garments?

SICINIUS   You may, sir.

CORIOLANUS
That I'll straight do and, knowing myself again,
Repair to the Senate House. 149

MENENIUS
I'll keep you company.—Will you along?

BRUTUS
We stay here for the people.

SICINIUS   Fare you well.
Exeunt Coriolanus and Menenius.
He has it now, and by his looks methinks
'Tis warm at 's heart.

BRUTUS   With a proud heart he wore
His humble weeds. Will you dismiss the people?

Enter the Plebeians.

SICINIUS
How now, my masters, have you chose this man?

FIRST CITIZEN He has our voices, sir.

BRUTUS
We pray the gods he may deserve your loves.

SECOND CITIZEN
Amen, sir. To my poor unworthy notice, 158
He mocked us when he begged our voices.

THIRD CITIZEN
Certainly he flouted us downright.

FIRST CITIZEN
No, 'tis his kind of speech. He did not mock us.

SECOND CITIZEN
Not one amongst us, save yourself, but says
He used us scornfully. He should have showed us
His marks of merit, wounds received for 's country.

SICINIUS Why, so he did, I am sure.

ALL No, no. No man saw 'em.

THIRD CITIZEN
He said he had wounds, which he could show in
private,
And with his hat, thus waving it in scorn,
"I would be consul," says he. "Agèd custom,

99 my hat i.e., my hat in my hand as a gesture of courtesy **99–100 insinuating** ingratiating **100 be off** doff my hat. **counterfeitly** hypocritically **101 bewitchment** sorcery, bewitching powers **101–102 popular man** demagogue **102 bountiful** bountifully **108 seal** confirm **114 crave . . . deserve** beg the reward or wages we have already earned **115 woolvish toge** wolf's toga (making me look like a wolf in sheep's clothing) **116 Hob and Dick** (Typical names for rustics.) **that does appear** who make their appearance **117 needless vouches** unnecessary confirmations of approval. (To Coriolanus, only the Senate's appointment is necessary.) **118 in . . . do 't** if we should obey custom indiscriminately **119 antique time** old-fashioned traditions **121 o'erpeer** overtop, be visible over or be able to see over. **fool it so** be so foolhardy (as to challenge ancient custom in its huge accumulation of error) **123 do thus** i.e., go through with this meaningless ritual **125 voices** votes **127 Watched** kept watch (in camp) **129 heard of** heard, i.e., been present at

139 limitation allotted time **140 Endue** endow. **Remains** it remains **141 official marks** insignia of office. **invested** dressed **142 Anon** immediately **143 custom of request** i.e., custom of asking the people's voices. **discharged** performed **145 upon your approbation** to confirm your having been elected **149 Repair** go **158 notice** observation

But by your voices, will not so permit me;
Your voices therefore." When we granted that,
Here was "I thank you for your voices. Thank you.
Your most sweet voices! Now you have left your
    voices,
I have no further with you." Was not this mockery? 174

SICINIUS
Why either were you ignorant to see 't,   175
Or, seeing it, of such childish friendliness
To yield your voices?

BRUTUS   Could you not have told him
As you were lessoned? When he had no power,   178
But was a petty servant to the state,
He was your enemy, ever spake against   180
Your liberties and the charters that you bear   181
I' the body of the weal; and now, arriving   182
A place of potency and sway o' the state,
If he should still malignantly remain
Fast foe to the plebii, your voices might   185
Be curses to yourselves. You should have said
That as his worthy deeds did claim no less
Than what he stood for, so his gracious nature   188
Would think upon you for your voices and   189
Translate his malice towards you into love,   190
Standing your friendly lord.

SICINIUS   Thus to have said,   191
As you were fore-advised, had touched his spirit   192
And tried his inclination; from him plucked
Either his gracious promise, which you might,
As cause had called you up, have held him to;   195
Or else it would have galled his surly nature,   196
Which easily endures not article   197
Tying him to aught. So putting him to rage,
You should have ta'en th' advantage of his choler   199
And passed him unelected.

BRUTUS   Did you perceive
He did solicit you in free contempt   201
When he did need your loves, and do you think
That his contempt shall not be bruising to you
When he hath power to crush? Why, had your
    bodies
No heart among you? Or had you tongues to cry   205
Against the rectorship of judgment?

SICINIUS   Have you   206
Ere now denied the asker? And now   207
Again, of him that did not ask but mock,   208

Bestow your sued-for tongues?

THIRD CITIZEN   He's not confirmed.
We may deny him yet.

SECOND CITIZEN   And will deny him.
I'll have five hundred voices of that sound.

FIRST CITIZEN
I twice five hundred, and their friends to piece 'em. 212

BRUTUS
Get you hence instantly, and tell those friends
They have chose a consul that will from them take
Their liberties, make them of no more voice
Than dogs that are as often beat for barking
As therefor kept to do so.

SICINIUS   Let them assemble,   217
And on a safer judgment all revoke   218
Your ignorant election. Enforce his pride   219
And his old hate unto you. Besides, forget not   220
With what contempt he wore the humble weed,   221
How in his suit he scorned you; but your loves,   222
Thinking upon his services, took from you
Th' apprehension of his present portance,   224
Which most gibingly, ungravely, he did fashion   225
After the inveterate hate he bears you.

BRUTUS   Lay   226
A fault on us, your tribunes, that we labored,   227
No impediment between, but that you must   228
Cast your election on him.

SICINIUS   Say you chose him
More after our commandment than as guided
By your own true affections, and that your minds,
Preoccupied with what you rather must do
Than what you should, made you against the grain   233
To voice him consul. Lay the fault on us.

BRUTUS
Ay, spare us not. Say we read lectures to you,
How youngly he began to serve his country,   236
How long continued, and what stock he springs of,
The noble house o' the Marcians, from whence
    came
That Ancus Marcius, Numa's daughter's son,   239
Who after great Hostilius here was king;
Of the same house Publius and Quintus were,
That our best water brought by conduits hither;   242
. . . .   243
And nobly namèd so, twice being censor,   244

---

174 **further with** further use for   175 **ignorant** too dull   178 **lessoned**
instructed   180 **ever** always   181 **charters** privileges   182 **body of
the weal** commonwealth.   **arriving** attaining   185 **plebii** plebeians
188 **what . . . for** the office he was seeking   189 **Would think upon**
should esteem   190 **Translate** transform   191 **Standing . . . lord** i.e.,
acting on your behalf   192 **had touched** would have tested (as gold
and silver were tested with the touchstone)   195 **cause** occasion.
called you up aroused you (during his consulship)   196 **galled** irritated, rubbed sore   197 **article** stipulated condition   199 **choler** anger   201 **free** frank   205 **heart** i.e., as a seat of courage and wisdom.   **to cry** only to rebel   206 **rectorship of judgment** guidance of
common sense   206–207 **Have . . . asker** haven't you on previous
occasions denied one asking for your support?   208 **of** upon

212 **piece** add to, reinforce   217 **therefor** for that purpose   218 **safer**
sounder   219 **Enforce** lay stress upon   220 **forget not** don't forget to
mention   221 **weed** garment   222 **suit** petition (with a pun on "garment")   224 **apprehension** perceiving, comprehending.   **portance**
behavior   225 **gibingly** jeeringly.   **ungravely** not seriously   226 **After** in accord with   227 **A fault** the blame   228 **No impediment between** allowing nothing to stand in the way   233 **against the grain**
i.e., against your natural inclination   236 **youngly** early (in his life)
239 **Numa** legendary successor of Romulus as King of Rome; Tullus
Hostilius (line 240) was traditionally the third king; Ancus Martius, the
fourth   242 **conduits** aqueducts   243 (A line is evidently missing
here. From Plutarch, editors guess that the line may have read something like "And Censorinus, that was so surnamed.")   244 **censor** Roman magistrate charged also with the supervision of the census

Was his great ancestor.

SICINIUS   One thus descended,
That hath besides well in his person wrought   246
To be set high in place, we did commend
To your remembrances; but you have found,
Scaling his present bearing with his past,   249
That he's your fixèd enemy, and revoke
Your sudden approbation.

BRUTUS   Say you ne'er had done 't— 251
Harp on that still—but by our putting on.   252
And presently, when you have drawn your number, 253
Repair to th' Capitol.

ALL   We will so. Almost all 254
Repent in their election.   *Exeunt Plebeians.*

BRUTUS   Let them go on.   255
This mutiny were better put in hazard   256
Than stay, past doubt, for greater.   257
If, as his nature is, he fall in rage
With their refusal, both observe and answer   259
The vantage of his anger.

SICINIUS   To th' Capitol, come. 260
We will be there before the stream o' the people;
And this shall seem, as partly 'tis, their own,
Which we have goaded onward.   *Exeunt.*

❖

3.1   *Cornets. Enter Coriolanus, Menenius, all the
gentry, Cominius, Titus Lartius, and other
Senators.*

CORIOLANUS
Tullus Aufidius then had made new head?   1

LARTIUS
He had, my lord; and that it was which caused
Our swifter composition.   3

CORIOLANUS
So then the Volsces stand but as at first,
Ready, when time shall prompt them, to make road 5
Upon 's again.

COMINIUS   They are worn, Lord Consul, so,   6
That we shall hardly in our ages see   7
Their banners wave again.

CORIOLANUS [*to Lartius*]   Saw you Aufidius?

LARTIUS
On safeguard he came to me, and did curse   9
Against the Volsces for they had so vilely   10

Yielded the town. He is retired to Antium.   11

CORIOLANUS
Spoke he of me?

LARTIUS   He did, my lord.

CORIOLANUS   How? What?

LARTIUS
How often he had met you, sword to sword;
That of all things upon the earth he hated
Your person most; that he would pawn his fortunes
To hopeless restitution, so he might   16
Be called your vanquisher.

CORIOLANUS   At Antium lives he?

LARTIUS   At Antium.

CORIOLANUS
I wish I had a cause to seek him there,
To oppose his hatred fully. Welcome home.

Enter Sicinius and Brutus.

Behold, these are the tribunes of the people,
The tongues o' the common mouth. I do despise
   them,
For they do prank them in authority   24
Against all noble sufferance.   25

SICINIUS [*advancing*]   Pass no further.

CORIOLANUS   Ha? What is that?

BRUTUS
It will be dangerous to go on. No further.

CORIOLANUS   What makes this change?

MENENIUS   The matter?

COMINIUS
Hath he not passed the noble and the common?   31

BRUTUS
Cominius, no.

CORIOLANUS   Have I had children's voices?

FIRST SENATOR
Tribunes, give way. He shall to the marketplace.

BRUTUS
The people are incensed against him.

SICINIUS   Stop,
Or all will fall in broil.

CORIOLANUS   Are these your herd?   35
Must these have voices, that can yield them now   36
And straight disclaim their tongues? What are your
   offices?   37
You being their mouths, why rule you not their
   teeth?
Have you not set them on?

MENENIUS   Be calm, be calm.

CORIOLANUS
It is a purposed thing, and grows by plot,   40
To curb the will of the nobility.

---

246 That . . . wrought who in addition has well deserved by his own actions   **249 Scaling** estimating, weighing   **251 sudden** hasty   **252 putting on** urging   **253 presently** immediately.   **drawn your number** assembled your supporters   **254 Repair** go, proceed   **255 in** of   **256 put in hazard** risked   **257 Than . . . greater** than wait for the chance of a greater uprising that would certainly occur   **259–260 answer The vantage** take advantage of
3.1. Location: Rome. A street. The procession is on its way to the marketplace; see line 33.
1 made new head raised another army   **3 composition** coming to terms (about the return of Corioles to the Volscians)   **5 road** inroad, attack   **6 worn** i.e., militarily weakened   **7 ages** lifetimes   **9 On safeguard** under safe-conduct   **10 for** because

11 is retired has returned   **16 To . . . restitution** beyond hope of recovery.   **so** provided that   **24 prank them** dress themselves up   **25 Against . . . sufferance** beyond the power of nobility to tolerate   **31 passed . . . common** been approved by the nobility and the common people   **35 broil** tumult   **36 yield** grant, bestow.   **now** one instant   **37 straight** immediately afterward.   **offices** duties   **40 purposed** prearranged

Suffer 't, and live with such as cannot rule   42
Nor ever will be ruled.
BRUTUS   Call 't not a plot.
The people cry you mocked them; and of late,   44
When corn was given them gratis, you repined,   45
Scandaled the suppliants for the people, called them   46
Timepleasers, flatterers, foes to nobleness.
CORIOLANUS
Why, this was known before.
BRUTUS   Not to them all.
CORIOLANUS
Have you informed them sithence?
BRUTUS   How? I inform them? 49
COMINIUS
You are like to do such business.   50
BRUTUS
Not unlike, each way, to better yours.   51
CORIOLANUS
Why then should I be consul? By yond clouds,
Let me deserve so ill as you, and make me
Your fellow tribune.
SICINIUS   You show too much of that   54
For which the people stir. If you will pass   55
To where you are bound, you must inquire
    your way,   56
Which you are out of, with a gentler spirit,   57
Or never be so noble as a consul,
Nor yoke with him for tribune.
MENENIUS   Let's be calm.   59
COMINIUS
The people are abused, set on. This paltering   60
Becomes not Rome, nor has Coriolanus   61
Deserved this so dishonored rub, laid falsely   62
I' the plain way of his merit.
CORIOLANUS   Tell me of corn?   63
This was my speech, and I will speak 't again.
MENENIUS Not now, not now.
FIRST SENATOR   Not in this heat, sir, now.
CORIOLANUS Now, as I live, I will.
My nobler friends, I crave their pardons. For   68
The mutable, rank-scented meiny, let them   69
Regard me as I do not flatter, and   70
Therein behold themselves. I say again,   71
In soothing them, we nourish 'gainst our Senate
The cockle of rebellion, insolence, sedition,   73
Which we ourselves have plowed for, sowed, and
    scattered

By mingling them with us, the honored number,   75
Who lack not virtue, no, nor power, but that
Which they have given to beggars.
MENENIUS   Well, no more.
FIRST SENATOR
No more words, we beseech you.
CORIOLANUS   How? No more?
As for my country I have shed my blood,
Not fearing outward force, so shall my lungs
Coin words till their decay against those measles   81
Which we disdain should tetter us, yet sought   82
The very way to catch them.
BRUTUS   You speak o' the people 83
As if you were a god to punish, not
A man of their infirmity.
SICINIUS   'Twere well   85
We let the people know 't.
MENENIUS   What, what? His choler?
CORIOLANUS Choler?
Were I as patient as the midnight sleep,
By Jove, 'twould be my mind.
SICINIUS   It is a mind   89
That shall remain a poison where it is,
Not poison any further.
CORIOLANUS   "Shall remain"?
Hear you this Triton of the minnows? Mark you   92
His absolute "shall"?
COMINIUS   'Twas from the canon.
CORIOLANUS   "Shall"? 93
O good but most unwise patricians! Why,
You grave but reckless senators, have you thus
Given Hydra here to choose an officer,   96
That with his peremptory "shall," being but   97
The horn and noise o' the monster's, wants not spirit 98
To say he'll turn your current in a ditch   99
And make your channel his? If he have power,   100
Then vail your ignorance; if none, awake   101
Your dangerous lenity. If you are learned,   102
Be not as common fools; if you are not,
Let them have cushions by you. You are plebeians   104
If they be senators; and they are no less   105
When, both your voices blended, the great'st taste   106
Most palates theirs. They choose their magistrate,   107
And such a one as he, who puts his "shall,"

---

42 live i.e., you will have to live 44 of late lately 45 repined expressed regret 46 Scandaled defamed 49 sithence since 50 like likely 51 Not . . . yours not unlikely to prove, in any case, a better way (of providing for the welfare of the state) than yours 54 that i.e., that quality 55 stir are aroused, angry 55–56 If . . . bound i.e., if you wish to get to the marketplace and attain the consulship 57 are out of have strayed from 59 yoke be joined. (Sicinius insults Coriolanus by treating his sarcastic offer to be a tribune, lines 52–54, as though it were serious.) 60 abused deceived. set on incited. paltering equivocation, ruse 61 Becomes not is not appropriate or suitably dignified for 62 dishonored dishonoring. rub obstacle (as in the game of bowls). laid falsely treacherously placed 63 plain way clear path (as in bowls) 68–71 For . . . themselves as for the changeable, foul-smelling multitude, let them see themselves in the unflattering truth I show to them 73 cockle weed

75 honored honorable 81 till their decay i.e., until my lungs are no more. measles loathsome disease spots 82 tetter infect with tetter (skin eruption). sought have sought 83 catch (As one would catch a disease.) 85 of their infirmity sharing their human imperfections 89 mind opinion 92 Triton of the minnows i.e., god of the little fish. (Triton was Neptune's son and trumpeter.) 93 from the canon i.e., out of order, exceeding the authority granted the tribunes 96 Given permitted. Hydra many-headed monster slain by Hercules; here, the mob 97 his peremptory "shall" his use of the command form of the verb (shall) 98 horn and noise noisy horn. (See allusion to Triton above.) wants lacks 99 turn divert. current stream (of power). in into 100 make your channel his i.e., preempt for himself your channel of authority 101 vail your ignorance bow down to him in your ignorant yielding 101–102 awake . . . lenity arouse yourselves from your dangerous mildness 102 learned wise 104 cushions i.e., seats in the Senate 105–107 and . . . theirs and they are to all intents and purposes senators if, when their voices are mingled with yours, the resulting action savors of them more than of you

His popular "shall," against a graver bench   109
Than ever frowned in Greece. By Jove himself,   110
It makes the consuls base! And my soul aches
To know, when two authorities are up,   112
Neither supreme, how soon confusion   113
May enter twixt the gap of both and take   114
The one by th' other.

COMINIUS   Well, on to th' marketplace.   115

CORIOLANUS
Whoever gave that counsel to give forth
The corn o' the storehouse gratis, as 'twas used   117
Sometime in Greece—

MENENIUS   Well, well, no more of that.   118

CORIOLANUS
Though there the people had more absolute power,
I say they nourished disobedience, fed
The ruin of the state.

BRUTUS   Why shall the people give
One that speaks thus their voice?

CORIOLANUS   I'll give my reasons,
More worthier than their voices. They know the
    corn
Was not our recompense, resting well assured   124
They ne'er did service for 't. Being pressed to
    the war,   125
Even when the navel of the state was touched,   126
They would not thread the gates. This kind of service 127
Did not deserve corn gratis. Being i' the war,
Their mutinies and revolts, wherein they showed
Most valor, spoke not for them. Th' accusation   130
Which they have often made against the Senate,
All cause unborn, could never be the native   132
Of our so frank donation. Well, what then?   133
How shall this bosom multiplied digest   134
The Senate's courtesy? Let deeds express
What's like to be their words: "We did request it;   136
We are the greater poll, and in true fear   137
They gave us our demands." Thus we debase
The nature of our seats and make the rabble
Call our cares fears, which will in time   140
Break ope the locks o' the Senate and bring in
The crows to peck the eagles.

MENENIUS   Come, enough.

BRUTUS
Enough, with overmeasure.

CORIOLANUS   No, take more!
What may be sworn by, both divine and human,   144

Seal what I end withal! This double worship—   145
Where one part does disdain with cause, the other
Insult without all reason, where gentry, title,
    wisdom   147
Cannot conclude but by the yea and no   148
Of general ignorance—it must omit   149
Real necessities, and give way the while   150
To unstable slightness. Purpose so barred, it follows 151
Nothing is done to purpose. Therefore, beseech
    you—   152
You that will be less fearful than discreet,   153
That love the fundamental part of state   154
More than you doubt the change on 't, that prefer 155
A noble life before a long, and wish
To jump a body with a dangerous physic   157
That's sure of death without it—at once pluck out
The multitudinous tongue; let them not lick   159
The sweet which is their poison. Your dishonor   160
Mangles true judgment and bereaves the state   161
Of that integrity which should become 't,   162
Not having the power to do the good it would
For th' ill which doth control 't.

BRUTUS   He's said enough.   164

SICINIUS
He's spoken like a traitor and shall answer   165
As traitors do.

CORIOLANUS   Thou wretch, despite o'erwhelm thee!   166
What should the people do with these bald tribunes, 167
On whom depending, their obedience fails
To th' greater bench? In a rebellion,   169
When what's not meet, but what must be, was law, 170
Then were they chosen. In a better hour,
Let what is meet be said it must be meet,   172
And throw their power i' the dust.

BRUTUS   Manifest treason!

SICINIUS   This a consul? No!

BRUTUS
The aediles, ho!

Enter an Aedile.

Let him be apprehended.   176

109 **popular** on behalf of the populace. **graver bench** more august
deliberative body 110 **frowned** looked austere in judgment.
Greece (Famous for its law-giving institutions.) 112 **up** established,
in action 113 **confusion** chaos 114 **gap of both** space between the
two. **take** destroy 115 **by** by means of 117 **used** practiced, customary 118 **Sometime** formerly 124 **our recompense** reward from
us 125 **pressed** conscripted, enlisted 126 **navel** vital center.
touched threatened 127 **thread** pass through 130 **spoke not** did not
speak well 132 **All cause unborn** unjustifiably. **native** natural
source or origin 133 **frank** freely granted and generous 134 **bosom
multiplied** multiple stomach. **digest** i.e., consider, regard (with also
the literal sense of eating the grain) 136 **like** likely 137 **greater poll**
majority, greater number of heads 140 **cares** concern (for them and
for the state). **which** i.e., which insubordination 144 **What** (may)
whatever

145 **Seal** confirm. **withal** with. **double worship** divided authority
147 **Insult** behave insolently. **without** beyond. **gentry** noble birth
148 **conclude** come to a final decision 149 **general** popular, common. **omit** neglect 150 **the while** in the meanwhile 151 **slightness**
vacillation, trifling. **Purpose so barred** sound policy and planning
being thus obstructed 152 **purpose** any effect 153 **less . . . discreet**
actuated less by fear than by foresight 154–155 **That . . . on 't** i.e.,
that love the essentials of our government more than you fear changes
in it (such as getting rid of the tribunes) 157 **jump** risk (treating).
physic cure 159 **The multitudinous tongue** the voice of the multitude, i.e., the tribunes 160 **sweet . . . poison** i.e., power which in
their hands will undo them as well as Rome. **dishonor** present dishonorable state 161 **bereaves** deprives 162 **become 't** adorn it
164 **For** because of. **ill** i.e., tribunal, popular power. **control** overmaster 165 **answer** answer for it 166 **despite** scorn 167 **bald**
petty, barren (literally and figuratively) 169 **greater bench** i.e., senators collectively 170 **When . . . was law** when "might makes right"
prevailed 172 **Let . . . be meet** i.e., let us openly say that what is
right is what should be done 176 **aediles** officers attached to the
tribunes

SICINIUS
   Go, call the people [*Exit Aedile*], in whose name
      myself
   Attach thee as a traitorous innovator,   178
   A foe to th' public weal. Obey, I charge thee,   179
   And follow to thine answer.
CORIOLANUS   Hence, old goat!   180
ALL PATRICIANS
   We'll surety him.
COMINIUS [*to Sicinius*]   Aged sir, hands off.   181
CORIOLANUS [*to Sicinius*]
   Hence, rotten thing! Or I shall shake thy bones
   Out of thy garments.
SICINIUS   Help, ye citizens!

      Enter a rabble of plebeians, with the aediles.

MENENIUS   On both sides more respect.   184
SICINIUS
   Here's he that would take from you all your power.
BRUTUS   Seize him, aediles!
ALL PLEBEIANS   Down with him! Down with him!
SECOND SENATOR   Weapons, weapons, weapons!
                        They all bustle about Coriolanus.
ALL
   Tribunes!—Patricians!—Citizens!—What, ho!—
   Sicinius!—Brutus!—Coriolanus!—Citizens!—
   Peace, peace, peace!—Stay, hold, peace!
MENENIUS
   What is about to be? I am out of breath.
   Confusion's near; I cannot speak. You, tribunes
   To th' people! Coriolanus, patience!
   Speak, good Sicinius.
SICINIUS   Hear me, people. Peace!
ALL PLEBEIANS
   Let's hear our tribune. Peace! Speak, speak, speak.
SICINIUS
   You are at point to lose your liberties.   197
   Marcius would have all from you—Marcius,   198
   Whom late you have named for consul.
MENENIUS   Fie, fie, fie!   199
   This is the way to kindle, not to quench.
FIRST SENATOR
   To unbuild the city and to lay all flat.
SICINIUS
   What is the city but the people?
ALL PLEBEIANS   True,
   The people are the city.
BRUTUS
   By the consent of all, we were established
   The people's magistrates.
ALL PLEBEIANS   You so remain.
MENENIUS   And so are like to do.   207
COMINIUS
   That is the way to lay the city flat,
   To bring the roof to the foundation,

   And bury all which yet distinctly ranges   210
   In heaps and piles of ruin.
SICINIUS   This deserves death.   211
BRUTUS
   Or let us stand to our authority   212
   Or let us lose it. We do here pronounce,
   Upon the part o' the people, in whose power   214
   We were elected theirs, Marcius is worthy
   Of present death.
SICINIUS   Therefore lay hold of him!   216
   Bear him to th' rock Tarpeian, and from thence   217
   Into destruction cast him.
BRUTUS   Aediles, seize him!
ALL PLEBEIANS
   Yield, Marcius, yield!
MENENIUS   Hear me one word.
   Beseech you, tribunes, hear me but a word.
AEDILES   Peace, peace!
MENENIUS [*to the tribunes*]
   Be that you seem, truly your country's friend,   222
   And temperately proceed to what you would
   Thus violently redress.
BRUTUS   Sir, those cold ways,
   That seem like prudent helps, are very poisonous   225
   Where the disease is violent.—Lay hands upon him
   And bear him to the rock.
                        Coriolanus draws his sword.
CORIOLANUS   No, I'll die here.
   There's some among you have beheld me fighting.
   Come, try upon yourselves what you have seen me.
MENENIUS
   Down with that sword! Tribunes, withdraw awhile.
BRUTUS
   Lay hands upon him.
MENENIUS   Help Marcius, help!
   You that be noble, help him, young and old!
ALL PLEBEIANS   Down with him, down with him!   233
                In this mutiny, the tribunes, the aediles,
                        and the people are beat in.
MENENIUS [*to Coriolanus*]
   Go, get you to your house. Begone, away!
   All will be naught else.
SECOND SENATOR   Get you gone.
CORIOLANUS   Stand fast!   235
   We have as many friends as enemies.
MENENIUS
   Shall it be put to that?
FIRST SENATOR   The gods forbid!
   I prithee, noble friend, home to thy house;
   Leave us to cure this cause.   239
MENENIUS   For 'tis a sore upon us
   You cannot tent yourself. Begone, beseech you.   241

---

178 Attach arrest. **innovator** revolutionary **179 weal** welfare **180 answer** defense, answer to a charge **181 surety** go bail for **184 more** let there be more **197 at point to lose** on the verge of losing **198 Marcius** (Sicinius pointedly omits the title "Coriolanus.") **199 late** recently **207 like** likely

210 distinctly ranges stretches out in proper order **211 This** i.e., Coriolanus' defiance of the tribunes **212 Or** either. **stand to** maintain **214 Upon the part o'** on behalf of. **in** by **216 present** immediate **217 rock Tarpeian** famous precipice on the Capitoline Hill in ancient Rome from which persons condemned for offenses against the state were thrown down **222 that** what **225 helps** remedies **233 s.d. beat in** i.e., driven offstage **235 naught else** ruined otherwise **239 cause** disease **241 tent** treat (by probing a wound), cure

COMINIUS Come, sir, along with us.

CORIOLANUS
I would they were barbarians, as they are,
Though in Rome littered; not Romans, as they
    are not,
Though calved i' the porch o' the Capitol.

MENENIUS   Begone!
Put not your worthy rage into your tongue.
One time will owe another.

CORIOLANUS   On fair ground   247
I could beat forty of them.

MENENIUS   I could myself
Take up a brace o' the best of them; yea, the two
    tribunes.   249

COMINIUS
But now 'tis odds beyond arithmetic,   250
And manhood is called foolery when it stands   251
Against a falling fabric. Will you hence   252
Before the tag return, whose rage doth rend   253
Like interrupted waters and o'erbear   254
What they are used to bear?

MENENIUS   Pray you, begone.   255
I'll try whether my old wit be in request   256
With those that have but little. This must be patched   257
With cloth of any color.   258

COMINIUS   Nay, come away.
        Exeunt Coriolanus and Cominius [with others].

A PATRICIAN This man has marred his fortune.

MENENIUS
His nature is too noble for the world.
He would not flatter Neptune for his trident   262
Or Jove for 's power to thunder. His heart's his
    mouth.   263
What his breast forges, that his tongue must vent,   264
And, being angry, does forget that ever
He heard the name of death.   *A noise within.*
                        Here's goodly work!

A PATRICIAN I would they were abed!

MENENIUS
I would they were in Tiber! What the vengeance!
Could he not speak 'em fair?

        Enter Brutus and Sicinius, with the rabble again.

SICINIUS   Where is this viper   269
That would depopulate the city and
Be every man himself?

MENENIUS   You worthy tribunes—

SICINIUS
He shall be thrown down the Tarpeian rock
With rigorous hands. He hath resisted law,   273

And therefore law shall scorn him further trial   274
Than the severity of the public power
Which he so sets at naught.

FIRST CITIZEN   He shall well know   276
The noble tribunes are the people's mouths,
And we their hands.

ALL PLEBEIANS He shall, sure on 't.   279

MENENIUS   Sir, sir—

SICINIUS   Peace!

MENENIUS
Do not cry havoc, where you should but hunt   282
With modest warrant.

SICINIUS   Sir, how comes 't that you   283
Have holp to make this rescue?

MENENIUS   Hear me speak.   284
As I do know the Consul's worthiness,
So can I name his faults.

SICINIUS   Consul? What consul?

MENENIUS   The Consul Coriolanus.

BRUTUS   He consul?

ALL PLEBEIANS   No, no, no, no, no.

MENENIUS
If, by the tribunes' leave and yours, good people,   291
I may be heard, I would crave a word or two,
The which shall turn you to no further harm
Than so much loss of time.

SICINIUS   Speak briefly then,
For we are peremptory to dispatch   295
This viperous traitor. To eject him hence   296
Were but one danger, and to keep him here
Our certain death; therefore it is decreed
He dies tonight.

MENENIUS   Now the good gods forbid
That our renownèd Rome, whose gratitude
Towards her deservèd children is enrolled   301
In Jove's own book, like an unnatural dam   302
Should now eat up her own!

SICINIUS
He's a disease that must be cut away.

MENENIUS
O, he's a limb that has but a disease—
Mortal to cut it off; to cure it easy.   306
What has he done to Rome that's worthy death?
Killing our enemies, the blood he hath lost—
Which I dare vouch is more than that he hath
By many an ounce—he dropped it for his country;
And what is left, to lose it by his country   311
Were to us all that do 't and suffer it
A brand to th' end o' th' world.

SICINIUS   This is clean kam.   313

BRUTUS
Merely awry. When he did love his country,   314

---

247 **One . . . another** another time will pay for this **249 Take up**
take on. **brace** pair **250 'tis . . . arithmetic** i.e., we are thoroughly
outnumbered **251 manhood** manliness. **foolery** folly **252 fabric**
building. **hence** leave **253 tag** rabble **254 interrupted waters**
waves breaking over their banks. **o'erbear** overwhelm **255 bear**
submit to **256 try** test. **request** demand **257–258 patched . . .
color** i.e., mended in any way possible **262 trident** three-pronged
spear, the symbol of Neptune, classical god of the sea **263 His . . .
mouth** i.e., what he feels is exactly what he speaks **264 vent** express
269 'em fair to them courteously **273 rigorous** severe

274 **scorn** refuse. **further** any further **276 sets at naught** views as
worthless **279 sure on 't** be sure of it **282 cry havoc** give the order
for general slaughter **283 modest warrant** limited license **284 holp**
helped. **make this rescue** (*Make rescue* is a technical legal term for
the forcible removal of a prisoner from custody.) **291 leave** permission **295 peremptory** determined **296 eject him hence** exile him
301 deservèd deserving **302 dam** mother **306 Mortal** fatal
311 by at the hands of **313 brand** i.e., brand of infamy, stigma.
clean kam quite perverse, wrong **314 Merely** completely

It honored him.

SICINIUS   The service of the foot,
Being once gangrened, is not then respected
For what before it was.

BRUTUS   We'll hear no more.
Pursue him to his house and pluck him thence,
Lest his infection, being of catching nature,   319
Spread further.

MENENIUS   One word more, one word.
This tiger-footed rage, when it shall find
The harm of unscanned swiftness, will too late   323
Tie leaden pounds to 's heels. Proceed by process,   324
Lest parties—as he is beloved—break out   325
And sack great Rome with Romans.

BRUTUS   If it were so—   326
SICINIUS   What do ye talk?   327
Have we not had a taste of his obedience?
Our aediles smote? Ourselves resisted? Come.

MENENIUS
Consider this: he has been bred i' the wars
Since 'a could draw a sword, and is ill schooled   331
In bolted language; meal and bran together   332
He throws without distinction. Give me leave;
I'll go to him and undertake to bring him
Where he shall answer, by a lawful form,   335
In peace, to his utmost peril.

FIRST SENATOR   Noble tribunes,   336
It is the humane way. The other course
Will prove too bloody, and the end of it
Unknown to the beginning.

SICINIUS   Noble Menenius,
Be you then as the people's officer.—
Masters, lay down your weapons.

BRUTUS   Go not home.
SICINIUS
Meet on the marketplace.—We'll attend you there,   342
Where, if you bring not Marcius, we'll proceed
In our first way.

MENENIUS   I'll bring him to you.
[To the Senators.] Let me desire your company. He
    must come,
Or what is worst will follow.

FIRST SENATOR   Pray you, let's to him.   347
                              Exeunt omnes.

❧

3.2   Enter Coriolanus, with Nobles.

CORIOLANUS
Let them pull all about mine ears, present me   1
Death on the wheel or at wild horses' heels,   2

319 **of catching nature** infectious   323 **unscanned** unconsidered
324 **pounds** weights.   **to 's** to its.   **process** legal method   325 **par-**
ties factions   326 **with** by means of   327 **What** why   331 **'a** he
332 **bolted** sifted, refined.   **meal and bran** flour and husks   335–
336 **answer . . . peril** stand trial peacefully even though his life is at
stake   342 **attend** await   347 **s.d. omnes** all
3.2. Location: Rome. Coriolanus' house.
1 **pull . . . ears** pull everything down on top of me, crush me.
present me i.e., sentence me to   2 **wheel** instrument of torture and
death by which the victim's limbs were broken

Or pile ten hills on the Tarpeian rock,
That the precipitation might down stretch   4
Below the beam of sight, yet will I still   5
Be thus to them.

A PATRICIAN   You do the nobler.
CORIOLANUS   I muse my mother   8
Does not approve me further, who was wont   9
To call them woolen vassals, things created   10
To buy and sell with groats, to show bare heads   11
In congregations, to yawn, be still, and wonder   12
When one but of my ordinance stood up   13
To speak of peace or war.

        Enter Volumnia.

                         I talk of you.
Why did you wish me milder? Would you have me
False to my nature? Rather say I play
The man I am.

VOLUMNIA   O, sir, sir, sir,
I would have had you put your power well on   18
Before you had worn it out.

CORIOLANUS   Let go.   20
VOLUMNIA
You might have been enough the man you are
With striving less to be so. Lesser had been
The thwartings of your dispositions if
You had not showed them how ye were disposed
Ere they lacked power to cross you.

CORIOLANUS   Let them hang!   25
VOLUMNIA   Ay, and burn too.

        Enter Menenius with the Senators.

MENENIUS
Come, come, you have been too rough, something
    too rough;   27
You must return and mend it.

FIRST SENATOR   There's no remedy,
Unless, by not so doing, our good city
Cleave in the midst and perish.

VOLUMNIA   Pray be counseled.   30
I have a heart as little apt as yours,   31
But yet a brain that leads my use of anger
To better vantage.

MENENIUS   Well said, noble woman!
Before he should thus stoop to th' herd, but that   34
The violent fit o' the time craves it as physic   35
For the whole state, I would put mine armor on,
Which I can scarcely bear.

CORIOLANUS   What must I do?

4 **precipitation** precipitousness   5 **beam** range   8 **muse** wonder that
9 **further** to a greater degree.   **was wont** used   10 **woolen** coarsely
clad   11 **To . . . groats** i.e., to be nothing more than petty traders.
groats fourpenny pieces   12 **congregations** assemblies.   **yawn** i.e.,
gape with amazement   13 **ordinance** rank   18 **I would . . . well on**
I would have preferred that you had learned to achieve and use your
authority well   20 **Let go** enough   25 **Ere . . . you** before they lost
their power to thwart you. (As consul, Coriolanus would be beyond
their control.)   27 **something** somewhat   30 **Cleave in the midst** split
down the middle   31 **apt** compliant   34 **but** were it not   35 **fit** (1)
convulsion (2) fever.   **craves** demands.   **physic** medicine

MENENIUS
Return to th' tribunes.

CORIOLANUS   Well, what then? What then?

MENENIUS   Repent what you have spoke.

CORIOLANUS
For them? I cannot do it to the gods.
Must I then do 't to them?

VOLUMNIA   You are too absolute,   41
Though therein you can never be too noble,   42
But when extremities speak. I have heard you say   43
Honor and policy, like unsevered friends,   44
I' the war do grow together. Grant that, and tell me
In peace what each of them by th' other lose
That they combine not there.

CORIOLANUS   Tush, tush!

MENENIUS   A good demand.

VOLUMNIA
If it be honor in your wars to seem
The same you are not, which for your best ends
You adopt your policy, how is it less or worse   50
That it shall hold companionship in peace
With honor as in war, since that to both
It stands in like request?

CORIOLANUS   Why force you this?   53

VOLUMNIA
Because that now it lies you on to speak   54
To th' people, not by your own instruction,   55
Nor by th' matter which your heart prompts you,
But with such words that are but roted in   57
Your tongue, though but bastards and syllables
Of no allowance to your bosom's truth.   59
Now, this no more dishonors you at all
Than to take in a town with gentle words,   61
Which else would put you to your fortune and   62
The hazard of much blood.
I would dissemble with my nature where   64
My fortunes and my friends at stake required
I should do so in honor. I am in this   66
Your wife, your son, these senators, the nobles;   67
And you will rather show our general louts   68
How you can frown, than spend a fawn upon 'em   69
For the inheritance of their loves and safeguard   70
Of what that want might ruin.

MENENIUS   Noble lady!—   71
Come, go with us; speak fair. You may salve so,   72
Not what is dangerous present, but the loss   73

Of what is past.

VOLUMNIA   I prithee now, my son,   74
Go to them, with this bonnet in thy hand,   75
And thus far having stretched it—here be with
them—   76
Thy knee bussing the stones—for in such business   77
Action is eloquence, and the eyes of th' ignorant
More learnèd than the ears—waving thy head,   79
Which often thus correcting thy stout heart,   80
Now humble as the ripest mulberry   81
That will not hold the handling. Or say to them   82
Thou art their soldier, and being bred in broils   83
Hast not the soft way which, thou dost confess,
Were fit for thee to use as they to claim,   85
In asking their good loves; but thou wilt frame   86
Thyself, forsooth, hereafter theirs, so far   87
As thou hast power and person.

MENENIUS   This but done   88
Even as she speaks, why, their hearts were yours;   89
For they have pardons, being asked, as free   90
As words to little purpose.

VOLUMNIA   Prithee now,
Go, and be ruled; although I know thou hadst rather
Follow thine enemy in a fiery gulf   93
Than flatter him in a bower.

Enter Cominius.

                    Here is Cominius.   94

COMINIUS
I have been i' the marketplace; and, sir, 'tis fit   95
You make strong party, or defend yourself   96
By calmness or by absence. All's in anger.

MENENIUS
Only fair speech.

COMINIUS   I think 'twill serve, if he
Can thereto frame his spirit.

VOLUMNIA   He must, and will.
Prithee, now, say you will, and go about it.

CORIOLANUS
Must I go show them my unbarbed sconce? Must I   101
With my base tongue give to my noble heart
A lie that it must bear? Well, I will do 't.
Yet, were there but this single plot to lose,   104
This mold of Marcius, they to dust should grind it   105
And throw 't against the wind. To th' marketplace!
You have put me now to such a part which never

41 absolute uncompromising **42–43 therein . . . speak** i.e., being uncompromising in your nobility is a fine thing, except when the situation is critically extreme **44 policy** the proper consideration of stratagem and craft. **unsevered** inseparable **50 adopt** adopt as **53 It . . . request** it is equally needed. **force** urge **54 lies you on** is your duty **55 instruction** i.e., conviction, inner prompting **57 are but roted in** have been learned merely by rote in **59 Of . . . to** unacknowledged by **61 take in** capture **62 else . . . fortune** otherwise would force you to take your chance (in battle) **64 dissemble . . . nature** pretend to be other than I was **66 in honor** in compliance with the requirements of honor **66–67 I am . . . wife** in this I represent your wife **68 will rather** willfully prefer to. **general** common, vulgar **69 fawn** flattering appeal **70 inheritance** obtaining **71 that want** i.e., the lack of their loves **72 salve** remedy **73–74 Not . . . past** not only the present danger but what has been lost already

75 bonnet cap **76 And . . . them** i.e., and go to them holding your hat out thus—do it this way for them. (She gestures.) **77 bussing** kissing **79 learnèd** i.e., receptive. **waving** bowing up and down **80 Which** (Referring perhaps to *thy head;* sometimes emended to *with* or *while.*) **correcting** chastising. **stout** proud **81–82 Now . . . handling** i.e., now is as soft and malleable as overripe fruit. (Or *humble* may mean "abase, let droop.") **82 hold** bear, tolerate **83 broils** battles **85 fit** as fit. **as they** as for them **86 In asking** in your asking for. **frame** conform **87 theirs** to suit their wish **87–88 so far . . . person** to the full extent of your ability and authority **89 Even as** precisely in the manner. **were** will be, would be **90 as free** i.e., which they will grant as freely **93 in** into **94 bower** arbor, orchard **95 fit** appropriate **96 make strong party** support your side strongly, or gather a strong faction around you **101 unbarbed sconce** unhelmeted head **104 this single plot** this piece of earth only (i.e., my own person) **105 mold** (1) bodily form (2) earth

I shall discharge to th' life.

COMINIUS   Come, come, we'll prompt you. 108

VOLUMNIA
I prithee now, sweet son, as thou hast said
My praises made thee first a soldier, so,
To have my praise for this, perform a part
Thou hast not done before.

CORIOLANUS   Well, I must do 't.
Away, my disposition, and possess me
Some harlot's spirit! My throat of war be turned,   114
Which choirèd with my drum, into a pipe   115
Small as an eunuch or the virgin voice   116
That babies lulls asleep! The smiles of knaves   117
Tent in my cheeks, and schoolboys' tears take up   118
The glasses of my sight! A beggar's tongue   119
Make motion through my lips, and my armed knees,
Who bowed but in my stirrup, bend like his
That hath received an alms! I will not do 't,   122
Lest I surcease to honor mine own truth   123
And by my body's action teach my mind
A most inherent baseness.

VOLUMNIA   At thy choice, then.   125
To beg of thee, it is my more dishonor
Than thou of them. Come all to ruin. Let   127
Thy mother rather feel thy pride than fear   128
Thy dangerous stoutness, for I mock at death   129
With as big heart as thou. Do as thou list.   130
Thy valiantness was mine, thou suck'st it from me,
But owe thy pride thyself.

CORIOLANUS   Pray, be content.   132
Mother, I am going to the marketplace.
Chide me no more. I'll mountebank their loves,   134
Cog their hearts from them, and come home beloved 135
Of all the trades in Rome. Look, I am going.
Commend me to my wife. I'll return consul,
Or never trust to what my tongue can do
I' the way of flattery further.

VOLUMNIA   Do your will.
                                  Exit Volumnia.

COMINIUS
Away! The tribunes do attend you. Arm yourself   140
To answer mildly; for they are prepared
With accusations, as I hear, more strong
Than are upon you yet.

CORIOLANUS
The word is "mildly." Pray you, let us go.   144
Let them accuse me by invention; I   145

Will answer in mine honor.

MENENIUS   Ay, but mildly.   146

CORIOLANUS
Well, mildly be it then. Mildly!   *Exeunt.*

❧

3.3   *Enter Sicinius and Brutus.*

BRUTUS
In this point charge him home, that he affects   1
Tyrannical power. If he evade us there,
Enforce him with his envy to the people,   3
And that the spoil got on the Antiates   4
Was ne'er distributed.

        Enter an Aedile.

                          What, will he come?   5

AEDILE   He's coming.

BRUTUS   How accompanied?

AEDILE
With old Menenius, and those senators
That always favored him.

SICINIUS   Have you a catalogue
Of all the voices that we have procured
Set down by th' poll?

AEDILE   I have; 'tis ready.   11

SICINIUS
Have you collected them by tribes?

AEDILE   I have.   12

SICINIUS
Assemble presently the people hither;   13
And when they hear me say "It shall be so
I' the right and strength o' the commons," be it either
For death, for fine, or banishment, then let them,
If I say "Fine," cry "Fine!", if "Death," cry "Death!",
Insisting on the old prerogative   18
And power i' the truth o' the cause.

AEDILE   I shall inform them. 19

BRUTUS
And when such time they have begun to cry,   20
Let them not cease, but with a din confused
Enforce the present execution   22
Of what we chance to sentence.

AEDILE   Very well.

SICINIUS
Make them be strong, and ready for this hint
When we shall hap to give 't them.

BRUTUS   Go about it.   25
                                  [Exit Aedile.]

---

108 **discharge to th' life** perform convincingly   114 **harlot's** (1) rascal's (2) whore's.   **throat of war** i.e., soldier's voice   115 **choirèd** harmonized, sang in tune   116 **Small** high-pitched   117 **babies lulls** lulls babies or dolls   118 **Tent** lodge, set up camp.   **take up** fill up, occupy   119 **The glasses of my sight** my eyeballs   122 **an alms** a gift of charity   123 **surcease** cease   125 **inherent** irremovable, fixed   127–129 **Let . . . stoutness** let me rather suffer the worst your pride can do for us than go on living in fear of your dangerous obstinacy; I'm not going to beg any longer   130 **big heart** noble courage.   **list** please   132 **owe** own   134 **mountebank** win over as with the tricks of a quack medicine salesman   135 **Cog** cheat, beguile   140 **attend** await.   **Arm** prepare   144 **word** watchword   145 **accuse . . . invention** invent charges against me to their heart's desire

146 **in** in accordance with
3.3. Location: Rome. The Forum or marketplace.
1 **charge him home** press home your charges.   **affects** aspires to
3 **Enforce . . . to** urge against him his inveterate malice toward
4 **spoil got on** property taken from   5 **s.d. Aedile** (See note at 3.1.176.)   11 **by th' poll** by individual names, by head count
12 **tribes** divisions of the Roman populace   13 **presently** immediately
18 **old prerogative** traditional privilege or position   19 **truth** justice.
cause case   20 **cry** cry out, shout   22 **Enforce** insist upon.   **present execution** immediate performance   25 **hap** happen

Put him to choler straight. He hath been used   26
Ever to conquer and to have his worth   27
Of contradiction. Being once chafed, he cannot   28
Be reined again to temperance; then he speaks
What's in his heart, and that is there which looks   30
With us to break his neck.   31

Enter Coriolanus, Menenius, and Cominius, with
others [Senators and patricians].

SICINIUS   Well, here he comes.
MENENIUS   Calmly, I do beseech you.
CORIOLANUS
Ay, as an hostler, that for th' poorest piece   34
Will bear the knave by th' volume.—Th' honored
gods   35
Keep Rome in safety and the chairs of justice
Supplied with worthy men! Plant love among 's!
Throng our large temples with the shows of peace,   38
And not our streets with war!
FIRST SENATOR   Amen, amen.
MENENIUS   A noble wish.

Enter the Aedile, with the plebeians.

SICINIUS   Draw near, ye people.
AEDILE
List to your tribunes. Audience! Peace, I say!   43
CORIOLANUS   First, hear me speak.
BOTH TRIBUNES   Well, say.—Peace, ho!
CORIOLANUS
Shall I be charged no further than this present?   46
Must all determine here?
SICINIUS   I do demand   47
If you submit you to the people's voices,   48
Allow their officers, and are content   49
To suffer lawful censure for such faults   50
As shall be proved upon you?
CORIOLANUS   I am content.
MENENIUS
Lo, citizens, he says he is content.
The warlike service he has done, consider. Think
Upon the wounds his body bears, which show
Like graves i' the holy churchyard.
CORIOLANUS   Scratches with briers,
Scars to move laughter only.
MENENIUS   Consider further,
That when he speaks not like a citizen,
You find him like a soldier. Do not take

His rougher accents for malicious sounds,
But, as I say, such as become a soldier
Rather than envy you.
COMINIUS   Well, well, no more.   61
CORIOLANUS   What is the matter
That, being passed for consul with full voice,
I am so dishonored that the very hour
You take it off again?
SICINIUS   Answer to us.   66
CORIOLANUS   Say, then. 'Tis true, I ought so.   67
SICINIUS
We charge you that you have contrived to take
From Rome all seasoned office and to wind   69
Yourself into a power tyrannical,
For which you are a traitor to the people.
CORIOLANUS
How? Traitor?
MENENIUS   Nay, temperately! Your promise.
CORIOLANUS
The fires i' the lowest hell fold in the people!   73
Call me their traitor? Thou injurious tribune!   74
Within thine eyes sat twenty thousand deaths,   75
In thy hands clutched as many millions, in   76
Thy lying tongue both numbers, I would say   77
"Thou liest" unto thee with a voice as free
As I do pray the gods.
SICINIUS   Mark you this, people?
ALL PLEBEIANS   To the rock, to the rock with him!
SICINIUS   Peace!
We need not put new matter to his charge.   83
What you have seen him do and heard him speak,
Beating your officers, cursing yourselves,
Opposing laws with strokes, and here defying   86
Those whose great power must try him—even this,
So criminal and in such capital kind,   88
Deserves th' extremest death.
BRUTUS   But since he hath
Served well for Rome—
CORIOLANUS   What do you prate of service?   90
BRUTUS   I talk of that that know it.
CORIOLANUS   You?
MENENIUS
Is this the promise that you made your mother?
COMINIUS   Know, I pray you—
CORIOLANUS   I'll know no further.
Let them pronounce the steep Tarpeian death,
Vagabond exile, flaying, pent to linger   97
But with a grain a day, I would not buy   98
Their mercy at the price of one fair word,
Nor check my courage for what they can give,   100

26 **choler** anger. **straight** straightway. **used** accustomed 27 **Ever** always. **worth** i.e., full quota or portion 28 **contradiction** prerogative of answering back. (Coriolanus is accustomed to giving as good as he gets.) 30 **looks** promises, tends 31 **With us** from our point of view, with our assistance 34 **hostler** caretaker of horses. **piece** coin, piece of money 35 **bear . . . by th' volume** endure being called knave, or being condescended to by a knave, to any extent or any number of times. **Th' honored** may the honored 38 **Throng our large temples** let our large temples be crowded. **shows** ceremonies 43 **List** listen. **Audience** listen, give heed 46 **this present** this present occasion, the matter in hand 47 **determine** come to an end, be concluded. **demand** ask 48 **If** whether 49 **Allow** acknowledge the authority of 50 **censure** judgment

61 **Rather . . . you** rather than such as show malice toward you 66 **Answer to us** i.e., we'll do the asking, not you 67 **so** to do so 69 **seasoned** established. **wind** insinuate 73 **fold in** enclose, encircle 74 **their traitor** a traitor to them. **injurious** insulting 75–77 **Within . . . numbers** (Understand "although" before each of the three clauses.) 83 **put new matter** add new particulars 86 **strokes** blows 88 **capital** death-deserving 90 **prate** talk idly 97–98 **pent . . . day** imprisoned to starve with but a small particle of food a day 100 **check** restrain

To have 't with saying "Good morrow."
SICINIUS   For that he has,   101
As much as in him lies, from time to time   102
Envied against the people, seeking means   103
To pluck away their power, as now at last   104
Given hostile strokes, and that not in the presence   105
Of dreaded justice, but on the ministers
That doth distribute it; in the name o' the people
And in the power of us the tribunes, we,
Ev'n from this instant, banish him our city,
In peril of precipitation   110
From off the rock Tarpeian, never more
To enter our Rome gates. I' the people's name,
I say it shall be so.
ALL PLEBEIANS
It shall be so, it shall be so! Let him away!
He's banished, and it shall be so!
COMINIUS
Hear me, my masters, and my common friends—
SICINIUS
He's sentenced. No more hearing.
COMINIUS   Let me speak.
I have been consul, and can show for Rome
Her enemies' marks upon me. I do love
My country's good with a respect more tender,   120
More holy and profound, than mine own life,
My dear wife's estimate, her womb's increase,   122
And treasure of my loins. Then if I would
Speak that—
SICINIUS   We know your drift. Speak what?
BRUTUS
There's no more to be said, but he is banished   126
As enemy to the people and his country.
It shall be so.
ALL PLEBEIANS   It shall be so, it shall be so!
CORIOLANUS
You common cry of curs, whose breath I hate   130
As reek o' the rotten fens, whose loves I prize   131
As the dead carcasses of unburied men
That do corrupt my air, I banish you!
And here remain with your uncertainty!   134
Let every feeble rumor shake your hearts!
Your enemies, with nodding of their plumes,   136
Fan you into despair! Have the power still   137
To banish your defenders, till at length
Your ignorance—which finds not till it feels,   139
Making but reservation of yourselves,   140
Still your own foes—deliver you   141
As most abated captives to some nation   142

That won you without blows! Despising
For you the city, thus I turn my back.   144
There is a world elsewhere.
                                 Exeunt Coriolanus, Cominius,
                        [Menenius, Senators, and patricians].
AEDILE   The people's enemy is gone, is gone!
ALL PLEBEIANS
Our enemy is banished! He is gone! Hoo! Hoo!
                       They all shout and throw up their caps.
SICINIUS
Go see him out at gates, and follow him,
As he hath followed you, with all despite;   149
Give him deserved vexation. Let a guard   150
Attend us through the city.
ALL PLEBEIANS
Come, come, let's see him out at gates! Come.
The gods preserve our noble tribunes! Come.
                                                Exeunt.

❖

4.1   *Enter Coriolanus, Volumnia, Virgilia, Menenius,*
           Cominius, with the young nobility of Rome.

CORIOLANUS
Come, leave your tears. A brief farewell. The beast   1
With many heads butts me away. Nay, Mother,
Where is your ancient courage? You were used   3
To say extremities was the trier of spirits;   4
That common chances common men could bear;
That when the sea was calm all boats alike
Showed mastership in floating; fortune's blows   7
When most struck home, being gentle wounded
   craves   8
A noble cunning. You were used to load me   9
With precepts that would make invincible
The heart that conned them.   11
VIRGILIA
O heavens! O heavens!
CORIOLANUS   Nay, I prithee, woman—
VOLUMNIA
Now the red pestilence strike all trades in Rome,   13
And occupations perish!
CORIOLANUS   What, what, what!   14
I shall be loved when I am lacked. Nay, Mother,   15
Resume that spirit when you were wont to say,   16
If you had been the wife of Hercules,
Six of his labors you'd have done and saved   18
Your husband so much sweat. Cominius,

---

101 To have 't with saying if I might have it merely by saying.   **For that** because   **102 in him lies** he could   **103 Envied against** showed malice toward   **104 as** i.e., and inasmuch as (he has)   **105 not** not merely   **110 precipitation** being thrown   **120 respect** regard, feeling   **122 estimate** reputation   **126 but** but that   **130 cry** pack   **131 reek** vapor   **134 remain** may you remain.   **uncertainty** inconstancy, fickleness; also, insecurity (as explained in the following lines)   **136 Your** may your.   **with** merely with   **137 Have** may you have   **139 finds . . . feels** learns only through experience   **140 Making . . . yourselves** seeking only to preserve yourselves, or, excepting no one but yourselves from banishment   **141 Still your own foes** always your own worst enemies   **142 abated** humbled

144 For because of   **149 despite** disdain, contempt   **150 vexation** torment
4.1. Location: Rome, near the gates of the city (see line 47).
1 leave cease, leave off   **3 ancient** former.   **used** accustomed   **4 extremities** crisis   **7–9 fortune's . . . cunning** i.e., when fortune strikes her hardest blows, to bear one's afflictions like a true gentleman requires great wisdom and nobility   **11 conned** studied, memorized   **13 red pestilence** (Red spots presaged death to those stricken with the plague.)   **14 occupations** trades, handicrafts   **15 lacked** missed   **16 wont** accustomed   **18 Six of his labors** i.e., half of the twelve labors of Hercules

Droop not. Adieu. Farewell, my wife, my mother.
I'll do well yet. Thou old and true Menenius,
Thy tears are salter than a younger man's,
And venomous to thine eyes.—My sometime
   general,   23
I have seen thee stern, and thou hast oft beheld
Heart-hardening spectacles; tell these sad women
'Tis fond to wail inevitable strokes   26
As 'tis to laugh at 'em. My Mother, you wot well   27
My hazards still have been your solace, and—   28
Believe 't not lightly—though I go alone,
Like to a lonely dragon that his fen   30
Makes feared and talked of more than seen, your son
Will or exceed the common or be caught   32
With cautelous baits and practice.
VOLUMNIA   My first son,   33
Whither wilt thou go? Take good Cominius
With thee awhile. Determine on some course
More than a wild exposure to each chance   36
That starts i' the way before thee.
VIRGILIA   O the gods!   37
COMINIUS
I'll follow thee a month, devise with thee   38
Where thou shalt rest, that thou mayst hear of us
And we of thee; so if the time thrust forth
A cause for thy repeal, we shall not send   41
O'er the vast world to seek a single man,
And lose advantage, which doth ever cool   43
I' th' absence of the needer.
CORIOLANUS   Fare ye well.   44
Thou hast years upon thee, and thou art too full
Of the wars' surfeits to go rove with one   46
That's yet unbruised. Bring me but out at gate. 47
Come, my sweet wife, my dearest Mother, and
My friends of noble touch; when I am forth, 49
Bid me farewell, and smile. I pray you, come.
While I remain above the ground, you shall
Hear from me still, and never of me aught
But what is like me formerly.
MENENIUS   That's worthily
As any ear can hear. Come, let's not weep.
If I could shake off but one seven years
From these old arms and legs, by the good gods,
I'd with thee every foot.
CORIOLANUS   Give me thy hand.
Come.   *Exeunt.*

❖

4.2   *Enter the two tribunes, Sicinius and Brutus, with
the Aedile.*

SICINIUS [*to the Aedile*]
Bid them all home. He's gone, and we'll no further. 1
The nobility are vexed, whom we see have sided
In his behalf.
BRUTUS   Now we have shown our power,
Let us seem humbler after it is done
Than when it was a-doing.
SICINIUS   Bid them home.
Say their great enemy is gone, and they
Stand in their ancient strength.
BRUTUS   Dismiss them home. 7
                      [*Exit Aedile.*]
Here comes his mother.

     Enter Volumnia, Virgilia, and Menenius.

SICINIUS   Let's not meet her.
BRUTUS   Why?
SICINIUS   They say she's mad.
BRUTUS
They have ta'en note of us. Keep on your way.
                  [*They start to leave.*]
VOLUMNIA
O, you're well met. Th' hoarded plague o' the gods 13
Requite your love!
MENENIUS   Peace, peace! Be not so loud. 14
VOLUMNIA
If that I could for weeping, you should hear—
Nay, and you shall hear some. Will you be gone?
VIRGILIA
You shall stay too. I would I had the power 17
To say so to my husband.
SICINIUS   Are you mankind? 18
VOLUMNIA
Ay, fool, is that a shame?—Note but this fool.— 19
Was not a man my father? Hadst thou foxship 20
To banish him that struck more blows for Rome
Than thou hast spoken words?
SICINIUS   O blessèd heavens!
VOLUMNIA
More noble blows than ever thou wise words,
And for Rome's good. I'll tell thee what—yet go.
Nay, but thou shalt stay too. I would my son 25
Were in Arabia, and thy tribe before him, 26
His good sword in his hand.
SICINIUS   What then?
VIRGILIA   What then?
He'd make an end of thy posterity. 28

---

23 **sometime** former. (Said to Cominius.) 26 **fond** foolish 27 **wot**
know 28 **still** always 30 **fen** lurking place, marsh 32 **or . . . common** either exceed the ordinary deeds of men 33 **cautelous** crafty,
deceitful. **practice** treacherous methods 36 **exposure** exposure (of
yourself) 37 **starts** breaks from cover, darts across your path 38 **follow** go with 41 **repeal** recall from banishment 43 **advantage** the
opportune moment 44 **the needer** the person who needs to seize the
moment 46 **wars' surfeits** wearing effects of military service
47 **Bring** conduct 49 **noble touch** approved nobility. (From the use
of the touchstone with precious metal.)

4.2. Location: Rome. A street.
1 **home** go home 7 **ancient** former 13 **hoarded** stored up 14 **Requite** repay 17 **You shall stay too** (Sometimes read as if addressed to
the second of the two tribunes, but it may mean ''you shall too stay,''
i.e., whether you want to or not. See line 25.) 18 **mankind** masculine (i.e., railing like a man), or, infuriated. (Volumnia responds as
though it meant ''of the human race.'') 19 **Note but this fool** (The
line could read, ''Note but this, fool,'' addressed to Sicinius.)
20 **foxship** craftiness 25 **would** wish 26 **Arabia** i.e., a deserted
spot, with no place to hide. **tribe** family, fraternity, set 28 **posterity**
descendants

VOLUMNIA Bastards and all.
 Good man, the wounds that he does bear for Rome!
MENENIUS Come, come, peace.
SICINIUS
 I would he had continued to his country
 As he began, and not unknit himself   33
 The noble knot he made.
BRUTUS   I would he had.   34
VOLUMNIA
 "I would he had"? 'Twas you incensed the rabble—
 Cats, that can judge as fitly of his worth   36
 As I can of those mysteries which heaven
 Will not have earth to know!
BRUTUS
 Pray, let's go.
VOLUMNIA   Now, pray, sir, get you gone.
 You have done a brave deed. Ere you go, hear this:
 As far as doth the Capitol exceed
 The meanest house in Rome, so far my son—   42
 This lady's husband here, this, do you see?—
 Whom you have banished, does exceed you all.
BRUTUS
 Well, well, we'll leave you.
SICINIUS   Why stay we to be baited   45
 With one that wants her wits?   *Exeunt tribunes.*
VOLUMNIA   Take my prayers with you.   46
 I would the gods had nothing else to do
 But to confirm my curses! Could I meet 'em   48
 But once a day, it would unclog my heart   49
 Of what lies heavy to 't.
MENENIUS   You have told them home,   50
 And, by my troth, you have cause. You'll sup with
  me?   51
VOLUMNIA
 Anger's my meat. I sup upon myself,
 And so shall starve with feeding. *[To Virgilia.]*
  Come, let's go.
 Leave this faint puling and lament as I do,   54
 In anger, Juno-like. Come, come, come.   55
MENENIUS Fie, fie, fie!   *Exeunt.*

❖

4.3 *Enter [Nicanor,] a Roman, and [Adrian,] a
        Volsce.*

ROMAN I know you well, sir, and you know me. Your
 name, I think, is Adrian.
VOLSCE It is so, sir. Truly, I have forgot you.
ROMAN I am a Roman; and my services are, as you are,
 against 'em. Know you me yet?   5
VOLSCE Nicanor, no?

ROMAN The same, sir.
VOLSCE You had more beard when I last saw you, but
 your favor is well approved by your tongue. What's the   9
 news in Rome? I have a note from the Volscian state   10
 to find you out there. You have well saved me a day's
 journey.
ROMAN There hath been in Rome strange insurrections:
 the people against the senators, patricians, and nobles.
VOLSCE Hath been? Is it ended, then? Our state thinks
 not so. They are in a most warlike preparation, and
 hope to come upon them in the heat of their division.
ROMAN The main blaze of it is past, but a small thing
 would make it flame again; for the nobles receive so to
 heart the banishment of that worthy Coriolanus that
 they are in a ripe aptness to take all power from the
 people and to pluck from them their tribunes forever.
 This lies glowing, I can tell you, and is almost mature   23
 for the violent breaking out.
VOLSCE Coriolanus banished?
ROMAN Banished, sir.
VOLSCE You will be welcome with this intelligence,
 Nicanor.
ROMAN The day serves well for them now. I have heard   29
 it said the fittest time to corrupt a man's wife is when
 she's fallen out with her husband. Your noble Tullus
 Aufidius will appear well in these wars, his great
 opposer Coriolanus being now in no request of his   33
 country.
VOLSCE He cannot choose. I am most fortunate thus   35
 accidentally to encounter you. You have ended my
 business, and I will merrily accompany you home.
ROMAN I shall, between this and supper, tell you most   38
 strange things from Rome, all tending to the good of
 their adversaries. Have you an army ready, say you?
VOLSCE A most royal one: the centurions and their   41
 charges, distinctly billeted, already in th' entertain-   42
 ment, and to be on foot at an hour's warning.   43
ROMAN I am joyful to hear of their readiness, and am
 the man, I think, that shall set them in present action.   45
 So, sir, heartily well met, and most glad of your
 company.
VOLSCE You take my part from me, sir; I have the most   48
 cause to be glad of yours.
ROMAN Well, let us go together.   *Exeunt.*

❖

4.4 *Enter Coriolanus in mean apparel, disguised and
        muffled.*

CORIOLANUS
 A goodly city is this Antium. City,

9 **your . . . tongue** your face and appearance are well confirmed by
your voice   10 **note** instruction   23 **glowing** smoldering   29 **them**
i.e., the Volsces   33 **in no request of** unvalued by   35 **choose** do
otherwise (than appear well)   38 **this** this present time   41 **centurions**
officers each in command of a hundred men or "century"   41–
42 **their charges** the men under their command   42 **distinctly billeted**
separately enrolled   42–43 **in th' entertainment** mobilized, on the
payroll   45 **present** immediate   48 **my part** i.e., the words I should
say
4.4. Location: Antium. Before Aufidius' house.

33–34 **unknit . . . made** i.e., untied the knot of service and gratitude
binding him and Rome together   36 **Cats** (A term of contempt.)
42 **meanest** poorest   45–46 **baited With** harassed by   48 **'em** i.e.,
the tribunes   49 **unclog** unburden   50 **to 't** upon it.   **told them
home** berated them thoroughly   51 **sup** dine   54 **puling** whimpering
55 **Juno-like** resembling Juno, chief goddess of the Romans (whose
unforgiving anger is mentioned by Virgil in *Aeneid* 1.4)
4.3. Location: A road between Rome and Antium.
5 **against 'em** i.e., on behalf of the Volsces against Rome

'Tis I that made thy widows. Many an heir
Of these fair edifices 'fore my wars
Have I heard groan and drop. Then know me not,   3
Lest that thy wives with spits and boys with stones
In puny battle slay me.

Enter a Citizen.

                              Save you, sir.   6
CITIZEN
   And you.
CORIOLANUS   Direct me, if it be your will,
   Where great Aufidius lies. Is he in Antium?   8
CITIZEN
   He is, and feasts the nobles of the state
   At his house this night.
CORIOLANUS   Which is his house, beseech you?
CITIZEN
   This here before you.
CORIOLANUS   Thank you, sir. Farewell.
                                   Exit Citizen.
O world, thy slippery turns! Friends now fast sworn,   12
Whose double bosoms seems to wear one heart,
Whose hours, whose bed, whose meal and exercise
Are still together, who twin, as 'twere, in love   15
Unseparable, shall within this hour,   16
On a dissension of a doit, break out   17
To bitterest enmity; so fellest foes,   18
Whose passions and whose plots have broke their
   sleep   19
To take the one the other, by some chance,   20
Some trick not worth an egg, shall grow dear friends   21
And interjoin their issues. So with me: 22
My birthplace hate I, and my love's upon
This enemy town. I'll enter. If he slay me,
He does fair justice; if he give me way,   25
I'll do his country service.   *Exit.*

4.5
Music plays. Enter a Servingman.

FIRST SERVINGMAN   Wine, wine, wine! What service is
here? I think our fellows are asleep.   [*Exit.*]   2

Enter another Servingman.

SECOND SERVINGMAN   Where's Cotus? My master calls
for him. Cotus!   *Exit.*

Enter Coriolanus.

CORIOLANUS
A goodly house. The feast smells well, but I

---

3 **'fore my wars** in the face of my onslaught   6 **puny** petty.   **Save**
God save   8 **lies** dwells   12 **slippery turns** fickle shifts of fortune.
fast firmly   15 **still** ever   16 **this hour** an hour   17 **dissension of a
doit** i.e., paltry dispute. (A *doit* is a small coin.)   18 **so** similarly.
fellest fiercest   19–20 **Whose . . . other** whose passions and whose
plotting to undo each other have kept them awake at night   21 **trick**
trifle   22 **issues** children (by marriage?); fortunes (?)   25 **give me way**
accede to my request
4.5. Location: Antium. The house of Aufidius. The sense of time here
is virtually continuous; the stage is imaginatively transformed from
the outside to the inside of Aufidius' house.
2 **fellows** fellow servants

Appear not like a guest.

Enter the First Servingman.

FIRST SERVINGMAN   What would you have, friend?
Whence are you? Here's no place for you. Pray go to   8
the door.   *Exit.*   9
CORIOLANUS
I have deserved no better entertainment
In being Coriolanus.   10

Enter Second Servingman.

SECOND SERVINGMAN   Whence are you, sir? Has the
porter his eyes in his head, that he gives entrance
to such companions? Pray, get you out.   14
CORIOLANUS   Away!
SECOND SERVINGMAN   Away? Get you away.
CORIOLANUS   Now thou'rt troublesome.
SECOND SERVINGMAN   Are you so brave? I'll have you   18
talked with anon.   19

*Enter Third Servingman. The First, [entering,]
meets him.*

THIRD SERVINGMAN   What fellow's this?
FIRST SERVINGMAN   A strange one as ever I looked on.
I cannot get him out o' the house. Prithee, call my
master to him.
THIRD SERVINGMAN   What have you to do here, fellow?
Pray you, avoid the house.   25
CORIOLANUS   Let me but stand. I will not hurt your
hearth.
THIRD SERVINGMAN   What are you?
CORIOLANUS   A gentleman.
THIRD SERVINGMAN   A marvelous poor one.
CORIOLANUS   True, so I am.
THIRD SERVINGMAN   Pray you, poor gentleman, take
up some other station; here's no place for you. Pray   33
you, avoid. Come.
CORIOLANUS   Follow your function, go, and batten on   35
cold bits.   *Pushes him away from him.*
THIRD SERVINGMAN   What, you will not?—Prithee, tell
my master what a strange guest he has here.
SECOND SERVINGMAN   And I shall.
                            Exit Second Servingman.
THIRD SERVINGMAN   Where dwell'st thou?
CORIOLANUS   Under the canopy.   41
THIRD SERVINGMAN   Under the canopy?
CORIOLANUS   Ay.
THIRD SERVINGMAN   Where's that?
CORIOLANUS   I' the city of kites and crows.   45
THIRD SERVINGMAN   I' the city of kites and crows?
What an ass it is! Then thou dwell'st with daws too?   47
CORIOLANUS   No, I serve not thy master.

---

8 **Whence** from where   8–9 **go to the door** get out   10 **entertainment** reception   14 **companions** rascals, base persons   18 **brave** insolent   19 **anon** immediately   25 **avoid** leave   33 **station** place to
stand (with a play on the idea of a gentleman's "station" or rank)
35 **Follow your function** go back to your ordinary business.   **batten**
grow fat   41 **canopy** i.e., of heaven (with ironic suggestion of a canopied royal throne)   45 **kites and crows** i.e., scavengers and birds of
prey   47 **daws** jackdaws. (Conventional emblems of foolishness.)

THIRD SERVINGMAN How, sir? Do you meddle with 49
my master?

CORIOLANUS Ay, 'tis an honester service than to meddle
with thy mistress. Thou prat'st and prat'st. Serve with
thy trencher. Hence! 53
           Beats him away. [Exit Third Servingman.]

    Enter Aufidius with the [Second] Servingman.

AUFIDIUS Where is this fellow?

SECOND SERVINGMAN Here, sir. I'd have beaten him
like a dog, but for disturbing the lords within. 56
           [He and First Servingman stand aside.]

AUFIDIUS
Whence com'st thou? What wouldst thou? Thy
  name?
Why speak'st not? Speak, man. What's thy name?

CORIOLANUS [*unmuffling*] If, Tullus,
Not yet thou know'st me, and, seeing me, dost not
Think me for the man I am, necessity
Commands me name myself.

AUFIDIUS   What is thy name?

CORIOLANUS
A name unmusical to the Volscians' ears,
And harsh in sound to thine.

AUFIDIUS   Say, what's thy name?
Thou hast a grim appearance, and thy face
Bears a command in 't; though thy tackle's torn, 66
Thou show'st a noble vessel. What's thy name? 67

CORIOLANUS
Prepare thy brow to frown. Know'st thou me yet?

AUFIDIUS I know thee not. Thy name?

CORIOLANUS
My name is Caius Marcius, who hath done
To thee particularly and to all the Volsces 71
Great hurt and mischief; thereto witness may 72
My surname, Coriolanus. The painful service, 73
The extreme dangers, and the drops of blood
Shed for my thankless country are requited
But with that surname—a good memory, 76
And witness of the malice and displeasure
Which thou shouldst bear me. Only that name
  remains.
The cruelty and envy of the people,
Permitted by our dastard nobles, who
Have all forsook me, hath devoured the rest,
And suffered me by th' voice of slaves to be
Whooped out of Rome. Now this extremity 83
Hath brought me to thy hearth; not out of hope—
Mistake me not—to save my life, for if
I had feared death, of all the men i' the world
I would have 'voided thee, but in mere spite, 87
To be full quit of those my banishers, 88

Stand I before thee here. Then if thou hast
A heart of wreak in thee, that wilt revenge 90
Thine own particular wrongs and stop those maims 91
Of shame seen through thy country, speed thee
  straight 92
And make my misery serve thy turn. So use it
That my revengeful services may prove
As benefits to thee, for I will fight
Against my cankered country with the spleen 96
Of all the under fiends. But if so be 97
Thou dar'st not this, and that to prove more fortunes 98
Thou'rt tired, then, in a word, I also am
Longer to live most weary, and present
My throat to thee and to thy ancient malice; 101
Which not to cut would show thee but a fool,
Since I have ever followed thee with hate,
Drawn tuns of blood out of thy country's breast, 104
And cannot live but to thy shame, unless
It be to do thee service.

AUFIDIUS   O Marcius, Marcius!
Each word thou hast spoke hath weeded from my
  heart
A root of ancient envy. If Jupiter 108
Should from yond cloud speak divine things
And say '"Tis true," I'd not believe them more
Than thee, all-noble Marcius. Let me twine
Mine arms about that body, whereagainst
My grainèd ash an hundred times hath broke 113
And scarred the moon with splinters. [*They embrace.*]
  Here I clip 114
The anvil of my sword, and do contest 115
As hotly and as nobly with thy love
As ever in ambitious strength I did
Contend against thy valor. Know thou first,
I loved the maid I married; never man
Sighed truer breath. But that I see thee here,
Thou noble thing, more dances my rapt heart 121
Than when I first my wedded mistress saw
Bestride my threshold. Why, thou Mars, I tell thee 123
We have a power on foot, and I had purpose 124
Once more to hew thy target from thy brawn, 125
Or lose mine arm for 't. Thou hast beat me out 126
Twelve several times, and I have nightly since 127
Dreamt of encounters twixt thyself and me—
We have been down together in my sleep, 129
Unbuckling helms, fisting each other's throat— 130
And waked half dead with nothing. Worthy Marcius, 131
Had we no other quarrel else to Rome but that

90 **wreak** vengeance 91 **stop** close up 91–92 **maims Of shame** dishonoring injuries 92 **through** throughout. **speed** hasten. **straight** straightway 96 **cankered** infected with evils (as from the action of the cankerworm) 97 **under fiends** fiends of the underworld 98 **prove more fortunes** try your fortunes further 101 **ancient** longstanding 104 **tuns** large barrels 108 **envy** malice 113 **grainèd ash** spear with long-grained ashen shaft 114 **clip** embrace 115 **anvil** i.e., Coriolanus, on whom Aufidius' sword has beaten as on an anvil 121 **dances** makes to dance. **rapt** enraptured 123 **Bestride** step across 124 **power on foot** force in the field 125 **hew** cut, strike. **target** shield. **brawn** i.e., muscular arm 126 **out** thoroughly 127 **several** distinct 129 **down together** fighting on the ground. **sleep** i.e., dreams 130 **helms** helmets. **fisting** clutching 131 **waked** (I have) awakened

49 **meddle** concern yourself with. (But Coriolanus answers in the sense of "have sexual intercourse with.") 53 **trencher** wooden plate 56 **but for** except for (fear of) 66 **a command** authority. **tackle** rigging of a ship (i.e., Coriolanus' clothing) 67 **show'st** appear to be. **vessel** (1) ship (2) body containing the soul 71 **particularly** personally 72 **mischief** injury 73 **painful** arduous 76 **memory** reminder 83 **Whooped** driven with hoots 87 **mere** utter 88 **full quit of** fully even with

Thou art thence banished, we would muster all   133
From twelve to seventy and, pouring war   134
Into the bowels of ungrateful Rome,
Like a bold flood o'erbear 't. O, come, go in,   136
And take our friendly senators by the hands,
Who now are here, taking their leaves of me,
Who am prepared against your territories,   139
Though not for Rome itself.

CORIOLANUS   You bless me, gods!

AUFIDIUS
Therefore, most absolute sir, if thou wilt have   141
The leading of thine own revenges, take
Th' one half of my commission; and set down—   143
As best thou art experienced, since thou know'st
Thy country's strength and weakness—thine own
   ways,
Whether to knock against the gates of Rome
Or rudely visit them in parts remote
To fright them ere destroy. But come in.
Let me commend thee first to those that shall   149
Say yea to thy desires. A thousand welcomes!
And more a friend than e'er an enemy;
Yet, Marcius, that was much. Your hand. Most
   welcome!   *Exeunt [Coriolanus and Aufidius].*
            Two of the Servingmen [come forward].

FIRST SERVINGMAN   Here's a strange alteration!

SECOND SERVINGMAN   By my hand, I had thought to
have strucken him with a cudgel; and yet my mind
gave me his clothes made a false report of him.   156

FIRST SERVINGMAN   What an arm he has! He turned me
about with his finger and his thumb as one would
set up a top.   159

SECOND SERVINGMAN Nay, I knew by his face that there
was something in him. He had, sir, a kind of face,
methought—I cannot tell how to term it.

FIRST SERVINGMAN   He had so, looking as it were—
Would I were hanged but I thought there was more   164
in him than I could think.

SECOND SERVINGMAN   So did I, I'll be sworn. He is
simply the rarest man i' the world.   167

FIRST SERVINGMAN   I think he is. But a greater soldier
than he you wot on.   169

SECOND SERVINGMAN   Who, my master?

FIRST SERVINGMAN   Nay, it's no matter for that.   171

SECOND SERVINGMAN   Worth six on him.   172

FIRST SERVINGMAN   Nay, not so neither. But I take him   173
to be the greater soldier.

SECOND SERVINGMAN   Faith, look you, one cannot tell
how to say that. For the defense of a town our general
is excellent.

FIRST SERVINGMAN   Ay, and for an assault too.   133

         Enter the Third Servingman.

THIRD SERVINGMAN   O slaves, I can tell you news—   136
news, you rascals!

FIRST AND SECOND SERVINGMEN   What, what, what?
Let's partake.

THIRD SERVINGMAN   I would not be a Roman, of all
nations; I had as lief be a condemned man.   184

FIRST AND SECOND SERVINGMEN   Wherefore? Wherefore?   185

THIRD SERVINGMAN   Why, here's he that was wont to   186
thwack our general, Caius Marcius.

FIRST SERVINGMAN Why do you say "thwack our general"?

THIRD SERVINGMAN I do not say "thwack our general,"
but he was always good enough for him.

SECOND SERVINGMAN   Come, we are fellows and
friends. He was ever too hard for him; I have heard
him say so himself.

FIRST SERVINGMAN   He was too hard for him, directly
to say the truth on 't, before Corioles; he scotched him   195
and notched him like a carbonado.   196

SECOND SERVINGMAN   An he had been cannibally   197
given, he might have boiled and eaten him too.

FIRST SERVINGMAN   But, more of thy news.

THIRD SERVINGMAN Why, he is so made on here within   200
as if he were son and heir to Mars; set at upper end o'   201
the table; no question asked him by any of the senators but they stand bald before him. Our general him-   203
self makes a mistress of him, sanctifies himself   204
with 's hand, and turns up the white o' the eye to his   205
discourse. But the bottom of the news is, our general is   206
cut i' the middle and but one half of what he was
yesterday, for the other has half by the entreaty and
grant of the whole table. He'll go, he says, and sowl   209
the porter of Rome gates by th' ears. He will mow all
down before him, and leave his passage polled.   211

SECOND SERVINGMAN   And he's as like to do 't as any
man I can imagine.

THIRD SERVINGMAN Do 't? He will do 't! For look you, sir,
he has as many friends as enemies; which friends, sir,
as it were, durst not, look you, sir, show themselves,
as we term it, his friends whilst he's in directitude.   217

FIRST SERVINGMAN   Directitude? What's that?

THIRD SERVINGMAN But when they shall see, sir, his crest
up again, and the man in blood, they will out of their   220
burrows like coneys after rain, and revel all with him.   221

FIRST SERVINGMAN   But when goes this forward?

THIRD SERVINGMAN   Tomorrow, today, presently. You   223
shall have the drum struck up this afternoon. 'Tis,

---

133 **muster all** enlist everyone   134 **twelve** i.e., aged twelve
136 **o'erbear 't** overflow, surge over, beat down Rome   139 **am prepared** i.e., have forces ready to move   141 **absolute** perfect
143 **commission** command.   **set down** determine upon   149 **commend** present   156 **gave** told   159 **set up** set going   164 **but I
thought** if I didn't think   167 **rarest** most remarkable   169 **you wot
on** you know of, know who I mean—i.e., Aufidius   171 **Nay . . .
that** i.e., never mind about names   172 **on** of   173 **him** i.e., Aufidius. (Some commentators argue that *him* is Coriolanus; the servingmen tend to contradict themselves in their newfound admiration for
Coriolanus and their loyalty toward their own general.)

184 **as lief** as soon   185 **Wherefore** why   186 **was wont** used
195 **on 't** of it.   **scotched** scored, gashed   196 **carbonado** meat
scored across for broiling   197 **An** if   200 **made on** made much of
201 **at upper end** i.e., at the place of honor   203 **but unless.**   **bald**
bareheaded   204–205 **sanctifies . . . hand** touches his (Coriolanus')
hand as though it were a holy relic   206 **bottom** last item, gist
209 **sowl** drag   211 **polled** stripped (as one would strip branches or
foliage)   217 **directitude** (A blunder for something like *discretitude* or
discredit.)   220 **in blood** in full vigor. (Usually said of hounds.)   **will
out** will come out   221 **coneys** rabbits   223 **presently** immediately

as it were, a parcel of their feast, and to be executed 225
ere they wipe their lips.

SECOND SERVINGMAN Why, then we shall have a stirring 227
world again. This peace is nothing but to rust iron,
increase tailors, and breed ballad makers.

FIRST SERVINGMAN Let me have war, say I. It exceeds
peace as far as day does night. It's spritely walking,
audible, and full of vent. Peace is a very apoplexy, 232
lethargy; mulled, deaf, sleepy, insensible; a getter of 233
more bastard children than war's a destroyer of men.

SECOND SERVINGMAN 'Tis so. And as wars in some
sort may be said to be a ravisher, so it cannot be
denied but peace is a great maker of cuckolds.

FIRST SERVINGMAN Ay, and it makes men hate one
another.

THIRD SERVINGMAN Reason: because they then less need
one another. The wars for my money! I hope to see
Romans as cheap as Volscians.—They are rising, 242
they are rising.

FIRST AND SECOND SERVINGMEN In, in, in, in!

Exeunt.

❧

4.6   *Enter the two tribunes, Sicinius and Brutus.*

SICINIUS
We hear not of him, neither need we fear him.
His remedies are tame: the present peace   2
And quietness of the people, which before
Were in wild hurry. Here do we make his friends   4
Blush that the world goes well, who rather had,
Though they themselves did suffer by 't, behold
Dissentious numbers pestering streets than see   7
Our tradesmen singing in their shops and going
About their functions friendly.

BRUTUS
We stood to 't in good time.

Enter Menenius.

                                        Is this Menenius?   10

SICINIUS
'Tis he, 'tis he. O, he is grown most kind
Of late.—Hail, sir!

MENENIUS   Hail to you both!

SICINIUS
Your Coriolanus is not much missed
But with his friends. The commonwealth doth
   stand,   14
And so would do were he more angry at it.   15

---

225 **parcel** part   227 **stirring** active   232 **audible** keen of hearing, or,
heard as it makes its cry. (War is here seen as a hunting animal.)   **full
of vent** full of activity and vitality, quick to pick up the scent.   **apoplexy** paralysis   233 **mulled** insipid, drowsy.   **getter** begetter
242 **rising** i.e., rising from table
4.6. Location: Rome. A public place.
2 **His . . . tame** (Sicinius argues that the quietness of the populace affords no opportunity for those who hope to foment further trouble and
thereby bring about Coriolanus' return.)   4 **hurry** commotion   7 **pestering** crowding, blocking   10 **stood to 't** i.e., stood up against Coriolanus   14 **But with** except among   15 **were** even were

---

MENENIUS
All's well, and might have been much better if
He could have temporized.   17

SICINIUS   Where is he, hear you?

MENENIUS   Nay, I hear nothing.
His mother and his wife hear nothing from him.

Enter three or four Citizens.

ALL CITIZENS
The gods preserve you both!

SICINIUS   Good e'en, our neighbors.

BRUTUS
Good e'en to you all, good e'en to you all.

FIRST CITIZEN
Ourselves, our wives, and children, on our knees
Are bound to pray for you both.

SICINIUS   Live and thrive!

BRUTUS
Farewell, kind neighbors. We wished Coriolanus
Had loved you as we did.

ALL CITIZENS   Now the gods keep you!

BOTH TRIBUNES   Farewell, farewell.   *Exeunt Citizens.*

SICINIUS
This is a happier and more comely time   28
Than when these fellows ran about the streets
Crying confusion.

BRUTUS   Caius Marcius was
A worthy officer i' the war, but insolent,
O'ercome with pride, ambitious, past all thinking
Self-loving.

SICINIUS
And affecting one sole throne, without assistance.   34

MENENIUS   I think not so.

SICINIUS
We should by this, to all our lamentation,   36
If he had gone forth consul, found it so.   37

BRUTUS
The gods have well prevented it, and Rome
Sits safe and still without him.

Enter an Aedile.

AEDILE   Worthy tribunes,
There is a slave, whom we have put in prison,
Reports the Volsces with two several powers   41
Are entered in the Roman territories,
And with the deepest malice of the war
Destroy what lies before 'em.

MENENIUS   'Tis Aufidius,
Who, hearing of our Marcius' banishment,
Thrusts forth his horns again into the world,   46
Which were inshelled when Marcius stood for Rome,   47
And durst not once peep out.

SICINIUS   Come, what talk you of Marcius?   49

---

17 **temporized** compromised   28 **comely** gracious   34 **affecting . . .
throne** desiring to rule alone.   **assistance** any help whatsoever, partnership (in rule)   36 **should** should have.   **this** this time   37 **found
have found**   41 **several powers** separate armed forces   46 **Thrusts
. . . again** (i.e., like a snail)   47 **inshelled** i.e., drawn in the shell like
a snail's horns.   **stood** fought   49 **what** why

BRUTUS
Go see this rumorer whipped. It cannot be
The Volsces dare break with us.

MENENIUS   Cannot be?   51
We have record that very well it can,
And three examples of the like hath been
Within my age. But reason with the fellow   54
Before you punish him, where he heard this,
Lest you shall chance to whip your information   56
And beat the messenger who bids beware
Of what is to be dreaded.

SICINIUS   Tell not me.
I know this cannot be.

BRUTUS   Not possible.

Enter a Messenger.

MESSENGER
The nobles in great earnestness are going
All to the Senate House. Some news is come
That turns their countenances.

SICINIUS   'Tis this slave—   62
Go whip him 'fore the people's eyes—his raising,   63
Nothing but his report.

MESSENGER   Yes, worthy sir,
The slave's report is seconded, and more,   65
More fearful, is delivered.

SICINIUS   What more fearful?   66

MESSENGER
It is spoke freely out of many mouths—
How probable I do not know—that Marcius,
Joined with Aufidius, leads a power 'gainst Rome,
And vows revenge as spacious as between   70
The young'st and oldest thing.

SICINIUS   This is most likely!   71

BRUTUS
Raised only that the weaker sort may wish   72
Good Marcius home again.

SICINIUS   The very trick on 't.   74

MENENIUS   This is unlikely.
He and Aufidius can no more atone   76
Than violent'st contrariety.   77

Enter [a Second] Messenger.

SECOND MESSENGER
You are sent for to the Senate.
A fearful army, led by Caius Marcius   79
Associated with Aufidius, rages
Upon our territories, and have already
O'erborne their way, consumed with fire, and took   82
What lay before them.

Enter Cominius.

COMINIUS   O, you have made good work!

MENENIUS   What news? What news?

COMINIUS
You have holp to ravish your own daughters and   86
To melt the city leads upon your pates,   87
To see your wives dishonored to your noses—   88

MENENIUS   What's the news? What's the news?

COMINIUS
Your temples burnèd in their cement, and   90
Your franchises, whereon you stood, confined   91
Into an auger's bore.

MENENIUS   Pray now, your news?—   92
You have made fair work, I fear me.—Pray, your
news?
If Marcius should be joined wi' the Volscians—

COMINIUS   If?
He is their god. He leads them like a thing
Made by some other deity than Nature,
That shapes man better; and they follow him
Against us brats with no less confidence   98
Than boys pursuing summer butterflies
Or butchers killing flies.

MENENIUS   You have made good work,
You and your apron-men, you that stood so much   101
Upon the voice of occupation and   102
The breath of garlic eaters!

COMINIUS   He'll shake your Rome about your ears.

MENENIUS
As Hercules did shake down mellow fruit.   105
You have made fair work!

BRUTUS   But is this true, sir?

COMINIUS   Ay, and you'll look pale
Before you find it other. All the regions   109
Do smilingly revolt, and who resists   110
Are mocked for valiant ignorance   111
And perish constant fools. Who is 't can blame him? 112
Your enemies and his find something in him.   113

MENENIUS   We are all undone, unless
The noble man have mercy.

COMINIUS   Who shall ask it?
The tribunes cannot do 't for shame; the people
Deserve such pity of him as the wolf
Does of the shepherds. For his best friends, if they 118
Should say "Be good to Rome," they charged him
even   119
As those should do that had deserved his hate   120
And therein showed like enemies.

MENENIUS   'Tis true.   121

---

51 break break their treaty   **54 age** lifetime   **56 information** source of information   **62 turns** changes   **62–63 slave . . . his raising** slave's incitement, for which let him be publicly whipped   **65 seconded** confirmed   **66 delivered** reported   **70–71 as spacious . . . thing** comprehensive enough to embrace every living person **72 Raised** invented, stirred up. (See *raising*, line 63 above.)   **74 trick on 't** stratagem of it   **76 atone** come to a reconciliation   **77 violent'st contrariety** most extreme opposites   **79 fearful** frightening   **82 O'erborne their way** carried all before them

86 holp helped   **87 leads** roofs of lead.   **pates** heads   **88 to** before **90 in their cement** i.e., to their foundations   **91 franchises** political rights.   **stood** insisted   **92 auger's bore** hole drilled by an auger, i.e., narrow space   **98 brats** mere children   **101 apron-men** artisans (who wore aprons)   **102 voice of occupation** votes of the laboring men **105 Hercules . . . fruit** (Hercules' eleventh labor was to carry off the golden apples of the Hesperides.)   **109 other** otherwise   **110 smilingly** gladly.   **who** whoever   **111 valiant ignorance** foolish valor **112 constant** loyal   **113 Your . . . him** i.e., both your enemies, the patricians, and his enemies, the Volscians, find cause to ally themselves with him, or, all find him irresistible   **118 For** as for **119–121 they charged . . . enemies** they would be urging him with the same language that those who deserved his hate (the tribunes and plebeians) would use and in that respect would be behaving as his enemies would behave   **121 showed** would appear

If he were putting to my house the brand   122
That should consume it, I have not the face
To say "Beseech you, cease." You have made fair
    hands,   124
You and your crafts! You have crafted fair!

COMINIUS   You have brought 125
A trembling upon Rome, such as was never
S' incapable of help.

BOTH TRIBUNES   Say not we brought it. 127

MENENIUS
How? Was 't we? We loved him, but, like beasts
And cowardly nobles, gave way unto your clusters, 129
Who did hoot him out o' the city.

COMINIUS   But I fear
They'll roar him in again. Tullus Aufidius,   131
The second name of men, obeys his points   132
As if he were his officer. Desperation
Is all the policy, strength, and defense
That Rome can make against them.

Enter a troop of Citizens.

MENENIUS   Here come the clusters.—
And is Audifius with him? You are they
That made the air unwholesome when you cast
Your stinking greasy caps in hooting at
Coriolanus' exile. Now he's coming,
And not a hair upon a soldier's head
Which will not prove a whip. As many coxcombs   141
As you threw caps up will he tumble down,
And pay you for your voices. 'Tis no matter;
If he could burn us all into one coal,   144
We have deserved it.

ALL CITIZENS   Faith, we hear fearful news.

FIRST CITIZEN   For mine own part,
When I said, banish him, I said, 'twas pity.

SECOND CITIZEN   And so did I.

THIRD CITIZEN   And so did I; and, to say the truth, so
did very many of us. That we did, we did for the best; 151
and though we willingly consented to his banishment,
yet it was against our will.

COMINIUS   You're goodly things, you voices!

MENENIUS   You have made good work,
You and your cry!—Shall 's to the Capitol?   156

COMINIUS   O, ay, what else?
                Exeunt both [Cominius and Menenius].

SICINIUS
Go, masters, get you home, be not dismayed.
These are a side that would be glad to have   159
This true which they so seem to fear. Go home,
And show no sign of fear.

FIRST CITIZEN   The gods be good to us! Come, masters,

let 's home. I ever said we were i' the wrong when we
banished him.

SECOND CITIZEN   So did we all. But, come, let 's home.
                        Exeunt Citizens.

BRUTUS   I do not like this news.

SICINIUS   Nor I.

BRUTUS
Let 's to the Capitol. Would half my wealth   168
Would buy this for a lie!

SICINIUS   Pray, let 's go.   169
                        Exeunt tribunes.

❖

4.7   *Enter Aufidius with his Lieutenant.*

AUFIDIUS   Do they still fly to the Roman?

LIEUTENANT
I do not know what witchcraft's in him, but
Your soldiers use him as the grace 'fore meat,
Their talk at table, and their thanks at end;
And you are darkened in this action, sir,   5
Even by your own.

AUFIDIUS   I cannot help it now,   6
Unless by using means I lame the foot   7
Of our design. He bears himself more proudlier,
Even to my person, than I thought he would
When first I did embrace him. Yet his nature
In that's no changeling, and I must excuse   11
What cannot be amended.

LIEUTENANT   Yet I wish, sir—
I mean for your particular—you had not   13
Joined in commission with him, but either
Have borne the action of yourself or else   15
To him had left it solely.

AUFIDIUS
I understand thee well, and be thou sure,
When he shall come to his account, he knows not   18
What I can urge against him. Although it seems—   19
And so he thinks, and is no less apparent
To th' vulgar eye—that he bears all things fairly   21
And shows good husbandry for the Volscian state,   22
Fights dragonlike, and does achieve as soon   23
As draw his sword, yet he hath left undone   24
That which shall break his neck or hazard mine
Whene'er we come to our account.

LIEUTENANT
Sir, I beseech you, think you he'll carry Rome?   27

168–169 Would . . . lie I would give half of my fortune if this could
be proven a lie
4.7. Location: A camp, at a small distance from Rome.
5 you . . . action your glory is dimmed in this undertaking **6 your
own** i.e., your followers, or, your own action (in making Coriolanus
your fellow general) **7 means** remedies **11 changeling** i.e., fickle
thing **13 for your particular** regarding your self-interest **15 Have
. . . yourself** had led the campaign yourself **18 account** judgment
19 urge against him accuse him of **21 vulgar** common. **bears** carries out **22 husbandry for** management on behalf of **23 achieve** accomplish his goals **24 As draw** as he does draw **27 carry** capture

---

122 brand torch **124 made fair hands** done fine work. (Said ironically.) **125 crafted fair** (1) cleverly advanced the interests of the
crafts or occupations (2) shown your expert craft or cunning **127 S'**
so **129 clusters** mobs **131 roar . . . again** i.e., roar with pain when
he returns **132 second . . . men** second greatest name among men.
his points Coriolanus' instructions **141 coxcombs** i.e., fools' heads
144 into one coal into one cindery mass **151 That** what **156 cry**
pack. **Shall 's** shall we go **159 side** party, faction

AUFIDIUS
All places yields to him ere he sits down,   28
And the nobility of Rome are his;
The senators and patricians love him too. The
    tribunes are no soldiers, and their people
Will be as rash in the repeal as hasty   32
To expel him thence. I think he'll be to Rome
As is the osprey to the fish, who takes it   34
By sovereignty of nature. First he was
A noble servant to them, but he could not
Carry his honors even. Whether 'twas pride,   37
Which out of daily fortune ever taints   38
The happy man; whether defect of judgment,   39
To fail in the disposing of those chances   40
Which he was lord of; or whether nature,   41
Not to be other than one thing, not moving   42
From th' casque to th' cushion, but commanding
    peace   43
Even with the same austerity and garb   44
As he controlled the war; but one of these—
As he hath spices of them all—not all,   46
For I dare so far free him—made him feared,   47
So hated, and so banished. But he has a merit   48
To choke it in the utterance. So our virtues   49
Lie in th' interpretation of the time;   50
And power, unto itself most commendable,   51
Hath not a tomb so evident as a chair   52
T' extol what it hath done.   53
One fire drives out one fire; one nail, one nail;
Rights by rights falter, strengths by strengths do fail.   55
Come, let 's away. When, Caius, Rome is thine,
Thou art poor'st of all; then shortly art thou mine.
                        Exeunt.

❖

5.1   *Enter Menenius, Cominius; Sicinius, Brutus, the*
      two tribunes; with others.

MENENIUS
No, I'll not go. You hear what he hath said   1

28 **sits down** besieges   32 **repeal** recall from exile   34 **osprey** fish
hawk, said to have had the power to fascinate fishes so by its kingly
sovereignty (line 35) that they would turn belly up and allow themselves to be taken without a struggle   37 **Carry . . . even** bear his
honors temperately   38–39 **out of . . . man** as a result of continuous
success always corrupts the fortunate man   40 **disposing** clever using
41 **whether nature** whether it was his nature   42 **Not . . . thing** i.e.,
always rigidly the same, in peace as in war   43 **casque** helmet (as
symbolic of the warrior).   **cushion** i.e., seat for a senator   44 **austerity and garb** austere behavior   46 **spices** tastes, traces.   **not all** not
all in full measure   47 **free** free from blame   48 **So . . . banished** because he was feared he was hated, and because he was hated he was
banished   48–49 **he . . . utterance** i.e., his merit is of the perverse
sort that undoes the praise it should receive; it *chokes* itself by its very
utterance. (Also interpreted as meaning, "He has so many counterbal-
ancing good points that the words stick in my throat.")   50 **the time**
i.e., our contemporaries   51–53 **power . . . done** i.e., power, however worthy in itself, is quickly forgotten even while it is being com-
memorated from the public rostrum   55 **by rights falter** i.e., are
made to seem less by other rights. (The point is that great deeds,
eclipsed by the subsequent deeds of others, are soon forgotten.)
5.1. Location: Rome. A public place.
1 he i.e., Cominius

Which was sometime his general, who loved him   2
In a most dear particular. He called me father;
But what o' that? Go you that banished him;
A mile before his tent fall down and knee   5
The way into his mercy. Nay, if he coyed   6
To hear Cominius speak, I'll keep at home.
COMINIUS
He would not seem to know me.
MENENIUS   Do you hear?   8
COMINIUS
Yet one time he did call me by my name.
I urged our old acquaintance, and the drops
That we have bled together. "Coriolanus"
He would not answer to; forbade all names.
He was a kind of nothing, titleless,
Till he had forged himself a name o' the fire
Of burning Rome.
MENENIUS   Why, so; you have made good work!
A pair of tribunes that have wracked for Rome   16
To make coals cheap! A noble memory!   17
COMINIUS
I minded him how royal 'twas to pardon   18
When it was less expected. He replied,
It was a bare petition of a state   20
To one whom they had punished.
MENENIUS   Very well.
Could he say less?
COMINIUS
I offered to awaken his regard   23
For 's private friends. His answer to me was,   24
He could not stay to pick them in a pile   25
Of noisome musty chaff. He said 'twas folly,   26
For one poor grain or two, to leave unburnt
And still to nose th' offense.   28
MENENIUS   For one poor grain or two!
I am one of those! His mother, wife, his child,
And this brave fellow too, we are the grains;
You are the musty chaff, and you are smelt
Above the moon. We must be burnt for you.
SICINIUS
Nay, pray, be patient. If you refuse your aid
In this so-never-needed help, yet do not   35
Upbraid 's with our distress. But sure, if you   36
Would be your country's pleader, your good tongue,
More than the instant army we can make,   38
Might stop our countryman.
MENENIUS   No, I'll not meddle.
SICINIUS
Pray you, go to him.

2 **Which** who.   **sometime** formerly   3 **In . . . particular** with warmest personal affection.   **He** i.e., Coriolanus   5 **knee** crawl on your
knees (like penitents approaching shrines)   6 **coyed** showed reluctance, disdained   8 **would not seem** pretended not   16 **wracked for**
brought ruin to (with a play on "striven for")   17 **coals** charcoal
(which will be cheap because Rome will be burnt to cinders; see
4.6.144).   **memory** memorial   18 **minded** reminded   20 **bare** barefaced, paltry   23 **offered** attempted   24 **For 's private** for his personal   25 **stay . . . them** take time to pick them out   26 **noisome**
evil-smelling   28 **nose th' offense** smell the offensive stuff   35 **In
. . . help** in this strait where help is needed as never before   36 **sure**
certainly   38 **instant army** army we can raise at this instant

MENENIUS   What should I do?

BRUTUS

Only make trial what your love can do
For Rome, towards Marcius.

MENENIUS

Well, and say that Marcius return me,   43
As Cominius is returned, unheard—what then?
But as a discontented friend, grief-shot   45
With his unkindness? Say 't be so?

SICINIUS   Yet your good will
Must have that thanks from Rome after the measure   48
As you intended well.

MENENIUS   I'll undertake 't.   49
I think he'll hear me. Yet, to bite his lip   50
And hum at good Cominius much unhearts me.   51
He was not taken well; he had not dined.   52
The veins unfilled, our blood is cold, and then
We pout upon the morning, are unapt   54
To give or to forgive; but when we have stuffed
These pipes and these conveyances of our blood   56
With wine and feeding, we have suppler souls
Than in our priestlike fasts. Therefore I'll watch him
Till he be dieted to my request,   59
And then I'll set upon him.

BRUTUS

You know the very road into his kindness,
And cannot lose your way.

MENENIUS   Good faith, I'll prove him, 62
Speed how it will. I shall ere long have knowledge 63
Of my success.   Exit.

COMINIUS   He'll never hear him.

SICINIUS   Not?   64

COMINIUS

I tell you, he does sit in gold, his eye   65
Red as 'twould burn Rome; and his injury   66
The jailer to his pity. I kneeled before him;
'Twas very faintly he said "Rise"; dismissed me   68
Thus, with his speechless hand. What he would do
He sent in writing after me; what he would not,   70
Bound with an oath to yield to his conditions;   71
So that all hope is vain
Unless his noble mother and his wife,   73
Who, as I hear, mean to solicit him
For mercy to his country. Therefore, let 's hence
And with our fair entreaties haste them on.   Exeunt.

43 say that i.e., what if   **45 But as** i.e., what if he send me back only as.   **grief-shot** grief-stricken   **48–49 after . . . As** in proportion that   **50 to bite his lip** (An expression of anger, like humming in line 51; see below, 5.4.21.)   **51 unhearts** disheartens, discourages   **52 taken well** approached at the right time   **54 pout upon** are out of temper with   **56 conveyances** channels   **59 dieted to** fed properly so as to be in a mood for   **62 prove** attempt   **63 Speed** turn out, succeed   **64 success** outcome   **65 in gold** in a golden chair   **66 Red** i.e., with anger; also the color normally used to describe gold.   **his injury** his sense of having been wronged   **68 faintly** coldly, indifferently   **70–71 what . . . conditions** i.e., what terrible actions he would not take against Rome if we bound ourselves under oath to agree to his terms. (See 5.3.14.) Or Cominius may mean that Coriolanus is bound by his own oath not to relent.   **73 Unless** if it were not for; except for

5.2   *Enter Menenius to the Watch, or Guard.*

FIRST WATCH   Stay! Whence are you?   1
SECOND WATCH   Stand, and go back.   2

MENENIUS

You guard like men; 'tis well. But, by your leave,
I am an officer of state, and come
To speak with Coriolanus.

FIRST WATCH   From whence?

MENENIUS   From Rome.

FIRST WATCH

You may not pass; you must return. Our general
Will no more hear from thence.

SECOND WATCH

You'll see your Rome embraced with fire before
You'll speak with Coriolanus.

MENENIUS   Good my friends,
If you have heard your general talk of Rome
And of his friends there, it is lots to blanks   13
My name hath touched your ears. It is Menenius.

FIRST WATCH

Be it so; go back. The virtue of your name   15
Is not here passable.

MENENIUS   I tell thee, fellow,   16
Thy general is my lover. I have been   17
The book of his good acts, whence men have read
His fame unparalleled happily amplified;   19
For I have ever verified my friends—   20
Of whom he's chief—with all the size that verity   21
Would without lapsing suffer. Nay, sometimes,   22
Like to a bowl upon a subtle ground,   23
I have tumbled past the throw, and in his praise   24
Have almost stamped the leasing. Therefore, fellow,   25
I must have leave to pass.   26

FIRST WATCH   Faith, sir, if you had told as many lies in 27
his behalf as you have uttered words in your own, you
should not pass here; no, though it were as virtuous   29
to lie as to live chastely. Therefore go back.   30

MENENIUS   Prithee, fellow, remember my name is
Menenius, always factionary on the party of your   32
general.

SECOND WATCH   Howsoever you have been his liar, as
you say you have, I am one that, telling true under   35
him, must say you cannot pass. Therefore go back.   36

MENENIUS   Has he dined, canst thou tell? For I would
not speak with him till after dinner.

FIRST WATCH   You are a Roman, are you?

5.2. Location: The Volscian camp before Rome.
1 Whence are you where are you from?   **2 Stand** stop   **13 lots to blanks** prize-winning tickets compared to valueless ones (i.e., all the world to nothing)   **15 virtue** strength   **16 passable** current (like a coin), and able to provide passage   **17 lover** friend   **19 happily** aptly, felicitously, or, *haply,* perhaps   **20 verified** testified to the worth of   **21 size** amplification.   **verity** truth   **22 lapsing** erring, distorting.   **suffer** allow   **23 bowl** ball used in bowls.   **subtle** deceptively irregular   **24 tumbled . . . throw** overshot the mark   **25 stamped the leasing** given the stamp of truth to lying (i.e., overstated praise of him)   **26 leave** permission   **27 if** even if   **29 though** even if   **30 chastely** honestly (but with a sexual quibble, taking *lie* in a sexual sense)   **32 factionary** active as a partisan   **35–36 telling . . . him** telling the truth in his service

MENENIUS   I am, as thy general is.

FIRST WATCH   Then you should hate Rome, as he does.
Can you, when you have pushed out your gates the 42
very defender of them, and, in a violent popular ig- 43
norance, given your enemy your shield, think to front 44
his revenges with the easy groans of old women, the 45
virginal palms of your daughters, or with the palsied 46
intercession of such a decayed dotant as you seem to 47
be? Can you think to blow out the intended fire your
city is ready to flame in with such weak breath as
this? No, you are deceived; therefore, back to Rome
and prepare for your execution. You are condemned;
our general has sworn you out of reprieve and pardon. 52

MENENIUS   Sirrah, if thy captain knew I were here, he 53
would use me with estimation. 54

FIRST WATCH   Come, my captain knows you not.

MENENIUS   I mean thy general.

FIRST WATCH   My general cares not for you. Back, I say,
go, lest I let forth your half-pint of blood. Back! That's
the utmost of your having. Back! 59

MENENIUS   Nay, but, fellow, fellow—

Enter Coriolanus with Aufidius.

CORIOLANUS   What's the matter?

MENENIUS   Now, you companion, I'll say an errand for 62
you. You shall know now that I am in estimation; you 63
shall perceive that a Jack guardant cannot office me 64
from my son Coriolanus. Guess but by my entertain- 65
ment with him if thou stand'st not i' the state of hang- 66
ing or of some death more long in spectatorship and 67
crueller in suffering; behold now presently, and 68
swoon for what's to come upon thee. [*To Coriolanus.*]
The glorious gods sit in hourly synod about thy partic- 70
ular prosperity and love thee no worse than thy old
father Menenius does! O my son, my son! Thou art
preparing fire for us; look thee, here's water to quench 73
it. I was hardly moved to come to thee; but being as- 74
sured none but myself could move thee, I have been
blown out of our gates with sighs, and conjure thee
to pardon Rome and thy petitionary countrymen. The 77
good gods assuage thy wrath, and turn the dregs of it
upon this varlet here—this, who, like a block, hath 79
denied my access to thee.

CORIOLANUS   Away!

MENENIUS   How? Away?

CORIOLANUS
Wife, mother, child, I know not. My affairs

Are servanted to others. Though I owe 84
My revenge properly, my remission lies 85
In Volscian breasts. That we have been familiar, 86
Ingrate forgetfulness shall poison rather 87
Than pity note how much. Therefore, begone. 88
Mine ears against your suits are stronger than
Your gates against my force. Yet, for I loved thee, 90
Take this along; I writ it for thy sake, [*giving a letter*]
And would have sent it. Another word, Menenius,
I will not hear thee speak.—This man, Aufidius,
Was my beloved in Rome; yet thou behold'st!

AUFIDIUS   You keep a constant temper. 95

Exeunt. Manent the Guard and Menenius.

FIRST WATCH   Now, sir, is your name Menenius?

SECOND WATCH   'Tis a spell, you see, of much power.
You know the way home again.

FIRST WATCH   Do you hear how we are shent for keep- 99
ing your greatness back?

SECOND WATCH   What cause, do you think, I have to
swoon?

MENENIUS   I neither care for the world nor your general.
For such things as you, I can scarce think there's any, 104
you're so slight. He that hath a will to die by himself 105
fears it not from another. Let your general do his
worst. For you, be that you are, long; and your misery 107
increase with your age! I say to you, as I was said to,
Away! *Exit.*

FIRST WATCH   A noble fellow, I warrant him.

SECOND WATCH   The worthy fellow is our general. He's
the rock, the oak not to be wind-shaken. *Exit Watch.*

❖

5.3   *Enter Coriolanus and Aufidius [with Volscian
soldiers. Coriolanus and Aufidius sit.]*

CORIOLANUS
We will before the walls of Rome tomorrow
Set down our host. My partner in this action, 2
You must report to th' Volscian lords how plainly 3
I have borne this business.

AUFIDIUS   Only their ends 4
You have respected, stopped your ears against
The general suit of Rome, never admitted
A private whisper, no, not with such friends
That thought them sure of you.

CORIOLANUS   This last old man,
Whom with a cracked heart I have sent to Rome,

---

42 **out** out at; out of   43–44 **violent popular ignorance** folly of mob
violence   44 **shield** defender, i.e., Coriolanus.   **front** meet   45 **easy
groans** i.e., groans that are easily provoked   46 **virginal . . . daughters** uplifted hands of your virgin daughters   47 **dotant** dotard, old
fool   52 **out of** beyond the reach of   53 **Sirrah** (Term of address to
inferiors.)   54 **use** treat.   **estimation** esteem   59 **the utmost of your
having** all you are going to get   62 **companion** fellow.   **say an errand** deliver a message   63 **in estimation** well regarded   64 **Jack
guardant** knave on guard duty.   **office** officiously keep   65–66 **entertainment with** reception by   66 **stand'st . . . state** are not at risk
67 **spectatorship** watching   68 **presently** immediately   70 **synod**
council, assembly   73 **water** i.e., tears   74 **hardly moved** with difficulty persuaded   77 **petitionary** suppliant, petitioning   79 **block** (1)
impediment (2) blockhead

84 **servanted** subjected.   **owe** own, possess   85 **properly** as my own.
remission power to forgive   86–88 **That . . . much** i.e., though we
have been close, I will allow ungrateful forgetfulness (prompted by
Rome's ingratitude) to poison the memory of our friendship rather
than allow my pity to recall how much we meant to each other
90 **for** because   95 **constant temper** firm mind.   **s.d. Manent** they remain onstage   99 **shent** rebuked   104 **For** as for (also in line 107)
105 **slight** insignificant.   **by himself** by his own hand   107 **that** what.
long through a long (and tedious) lifetime
5.3. Location: The Volscian camp, as in scene 2. The tent of Coriolanus.
2 **Set down our host** lay siege with our army   3 **plainly** openly
4 **their ends** i.e., the Volscians' purposes

Loved me above the measure of a father,
Nay, godded me indeed. Their latest refuge   11
Was to send him, for whose old love I have—
Though I showed sourly to him—once more offered   13
The first conditions, which they did refuse
And cannot now accept. To grace him only   15
That thought he could do more, a very little   16
I have yielded to. Fresh embassies and suits,   17
Nor from the state nor private friends, hereafter   18
Will I lend ear to. (*Shout within.*) Ha? What shout is
    this?
Shall I be tempted to infringe my vow
In the same time 'tis made? I will not.

    Enter Virgilia, Volumnia, Valeria, young
    Marcius, with attendants.

My wife comes foremost; then the honored mold   22
Wherein this trunk was framed, and in her hand   23
The grandchild to her blood. But, out, affection!
All bond and privilege of nature, break!   25
Let it be virtuous to be obstinate. [*The women bow.*] 26
What is that curtsy worth? Or those doves' eyes,   27
Which can make gods forsworn? I melt, and am not
Of stronger earth than others. My mother bows,
As if Olympus to a molehill should
In supplication nod, and my young boy
Hath an aspect of intercession which   32
Great Nature cries "Deny not." Let the Volsces   33
Plow Rome and harrow Italy, I'll never
Be such a gosling to obey instinct, but stand   35
As if a man were author of himself
And knew no other kin.
VIRGILIA   My lord and husband!
CORIOLANUS
These eyes are not the same I wore in Rome.   38
VIRGILIA
The sorrow that delivers us thus changed   39
Makes you think so.
CORIOLANUS   Like a dull actor now,   40
I have forgot my part, and I am out,   41
Even to a full disgrace. Best of my flesh,
Forgive my tyranny, but do not say   43
For that, "Forgive our Romans." O, a kiss
Long as my exile, sweet as my revenge!   [*They kiss.*]
Now, by the jealous queen of heaven, that kiss   46
I carried from thee, dear, and my true lip
Hath virgined it e'er since. You gods! I prate,   48

And the most noble mother of the world
Leave unsaluted. Sink, my knee, i' the earth. *Kneels.*
Of thy deep duty more impression show   51
Than that of common sons.
VOLUMNIA   O, stand up blest!
                             [*He rises.*]
Whilst with no softer cushion than the flint
I kneel before thee, and unproperly   54
Show duty, as mistaken all this while
Between the child and parent.   [*She kneels.*]
CORIOLANUS   What's this?
Your knees to me? To your corrected son?   57
                          [*He raises her.*]
Then let the pebbles on the hungry beach   58
Fillip the stars! Then let the mutinous winds   59
Strike the proud cedars 'gainst the fiery sun,   60
Murdering impossibility, to make   61
What cannot be slight work.
VOLUMNIA   Thou art my warrior;   62
I holp to frame thee. Do you know this lady?   63
CORIOLANUS
The noble sister of Publicola,
The moon of Rome, chaste as the icicle   65
That's curded by the frost from purest snow   66
And hangs on Dian's temple—dear Valeria!
VOLUMNIA [*indicating young Marcius*]
This is a poor epitome of yours,   68
Which by th' interpretation of full time   69
May show like all yourself.
CORIOLANUS [*to his son*]   The god of soldiers, 70
With the consent of supreme Jove, inform   71
Thy thoughts with nobleness, that thou mayst prove
To shame unvulnerable, and stick i' the wars   73
Like a great seamark, standing every flaw   74
And saving those that eye thee!
VOLUMNIA [*to young Marcius*]   Your knee, sirrah. 75
                    [*Young Marcius kneels.*]
CORIOLANUS   That's my brave boy!
VOLUMNIA
Even he, your wife, this lady, and myself
Are suitors to you.
CORIOLANUS   I beseech you, peace.
Or, if you'd ask, remember this before:
The thing I have forsworn to grant may never   80
Be held by you denials. Do not bid me   81

---

11 godded deified.   **latest refuge** last resource   **13 showed** acted
15 grace gratify   **16–17 a very . . . yielded to** I have conceded a little, but almost nothing   **18 Nor** neither   **22 mold** form, body (of my
mother)   **23 this trunk** my body   **25 bond . . . nature** natural ties
and claims of love   **26 obstinate** hard-hearted   **27 curtsy** (1) bow (2)
courtesy.   **doves' eyes** i.e., beautiful and seductive eyes. (See Song of
Solomon 1:15.)   **32 aspect of intercession** pleading look   **33 Let**
even should   **35 gosling** baby goose (i.e., foolish, inexperienced person).   **to** as to   **38–40 These . . . so** (Coriolanus says, "I see differently now that I am not in Rome." Virgilia replies, taking his words
literally, "Our sorrow has so changed us that you cannot recognize
us.")   **delivers** presents   **41 I am out** I have forgotten my lines, I am
at a loss for words   **43 tyranny** cruelty   **46 jealous . . . heaven** i.e.,
Juno, patroness of marriage   **48 virgined it** remained untouched.
prate talk idly

51 more impression a deeper mark   **54 unproperly** unfittingly, violating due propriety   **57 corrected** chastised (by her ironic rebuke)
58 hungry unfertile, barren   **59 Fillip** strike   **60 Strike . . . sun** uproot huge cedar trees and throw them against the sun   **61 Murdering**
negating the very concept of   **62 What . . . slight work** an easy task
of what cannot be, is impossible   **63 holp** helped   **65 moon of Rome**
(Allusion to Diana, goddess of chastity and associated with the
moon.)   **66 curded** congealed   **68 epitome** abridgement   **69 by . . .
time** when time shall have revealed and fulfilled all. (Time will expand the *epitome*, giving *interpretation* to its full meaning.)   **70 show**
look.   **The god of soldiers** i.e., Mars   **71 inform** inspire   **73 To
shame unvulnerable** incapable of shameful deeds.   **stick** stand out
74 seamark reference object used by mariners in navigating.   **standing** withstanding.   **flaw** gust of wind   **75 eye thee** i.e., guide themselves by you, use you as a *seamark*   **80–81 The thing . . . denials**
i.e., it would be unjust to regard me as refusing to grant what I have
sworn not to grant and hence no longer have the power of granting

Dismiss my soldiers or capitulate   82
Again with Rome's mechanics. Tell me not   83
Wherein I seem unnatural; desire not
T' allay my rages and revenges with
Your colder reasons.

VOLUMNIA   O, no more, no more!
You have said you will not grant us anything;
For we have nothing else to ask but that
Which you deny already. Yet we will ask,
That, if you fail in our request, the blame   90
May hang upon your hardness. Therefore hear us.

CORIOLANUS
Aufidius, and you Volsces, mark; for we'll
Hear naught from Rome in private. [*He sits.*] Your
  request?

VOLUMNIA
Should we be silent and not speak, our raiment   94
And state of bodies would bewray what life   95
We have led since thy exile. Think with thyself   96
How more unfortunate than all living women
Are we come hither; since that thy sight, which
  should   98
Make our eyes flow with joy, hearts dance with
  comforts,
Constrains them weep and shake with fear and
  sorrow,
Making the mother, wife, and child to see
The son, the husband, and the father tearing
His country's bowels out. And to poor we
Thine enmity's most capital. Thou barr'st us   104
Our prayers to the gods, which is a comfort
That all but we enjoy; for how can we,
Alas, how can we for our country pray,
Whereto we are bound, together with thy victory,
Whereto we are bound? Alack, or we must lose   109
The country, our dear nurse, or else thy person,
Our comfort in the country. We must find
An evident calamity, though we had   112
Our wish, which side should win; for either thou   113
Must as a foreign recreant be led   114
With manacles through our streets, or else
Triumphantly tread on thy country's ruin,
And bear the palm for having bravely shed   117
Thy wife and children's blood. For myself, son,
I purpose not to wait on fortune till   119
These wars determine. If I cannot persuade thee   120
Rather to show a noble grace to both parts   121
Than seek the end of one, thou shalt no sooner
March to assault thy country than to tread—
Trust to 't, thou shalt not—on thy mother's womb   124
That brought thee to this world.

VIRGILIA   Ay, and mine,

That brought you forth this boy to keep your name
Living to time.

YOUNG MARCIUS 'A shall not tread on me;   127
I'll run away till I am bigger, but then I'll fight.

CORIOLANUS
Not of a woman's tenderness to be   129
Requires nor child nor woman's face to see.   130
I have sat too long.   [*He rises.*]

VOLUMNIA   Nay, go not from us thus.   131
If it were so that our request did tend
To save the Romans, thereby to destroy
The Volsces whom you serve, you might
  condemn us
As poisonous of your honor. No, our suit
Is that you reconcile them, while the Volsces   136
May say, "This mercy we have showed," the Ro-
  mans,
"This we received," and each in either side   138
Give the all-hail to thee and cry, "Be blest   139
For making up this peace!" Thou know'st, great son,
The end of war's uncertain, but this certain,
That, if thou conquer Rome, the benefit
Which thou shalt thereby reap is such a name
Whose repetition will be dogged with curses,
Whose chronicle thus writ: "The man was noble,
But with his last attempt he wiped it out,   146
Destroyed his country, and his name remains
To th' ensuing age abhorred." Speak to me, son.
Thou hast affected the fine strains of honor,   149
To imitate the graces of the gods,
To tear with thunder the wide cheeks o' the air,   151
And yet to charge thy sulfur with a bolt   152
That should but rive an oak. Why dost not speak?   153
Think'st thou it honorable for a nobleman
Still to remember wrongs? Daughter, speak you;   155
He cares not for your weeping. Speak thou, boy;   156
Perhaps thy childishness will move him more
Than can our reasons. There's no man in the world
More bound to 's mother, yet here he lets me prate   159
Like one i' the stocks.—Thou hast never in thy life   160
Showed thy dear mother any courtesy,
When she, poor hen, fond of no second brood,   162
Has clucked thee to the wars and safely home,   163
Loaden with honor. Say my request's unjust,
And spurn me back; but if it be not so,
Thou art not honest, and the gods will plague thee   166
That thou restrain'st from me the duty which   167

---

82 capitulate come to terms   **83 mechanics** tradesmen   **90 fail in** do
not grant   **94 Should we** even if we should.   **raiment** clothes
95 state of the condition of our.   **bewray** reveal   **96 Think with thyself** reflect   **98 thy sight** the sight of you   **104 capital** fatal   **109 or**
either   **112 evident** certain   **113 which** whichever   **114 recreant**
traitor   **117 palm** i.e., emblem of victory   **119 purpose** propose
120 determine come to an end, settle matters   **121 grace** favor,
mercy.   **parts** sides   **124 Trust . . . not** (Read this parenthetical
phrase after *sooner* in line 122.)

127 'A he   **129–130 Not . . . see** if a man is not to yield to a womanly tenderness, he must not look upon any child's or woman's face
131 sat i.e., stayed here listening   **136 while** so that at the same time
138 each everyone.   **in** on   **139 all-hail** general acclaim   **146 attempt** undertaking.   **it** i.e., his nobility   **149 affected** sought, cherished   **151 cheeks** (On Renaissance maps, the winds were often portrayed as issuing from the cheeks of Aeolus, Greek god of the winds.)
152 charge load.   **sulfur** lightning.   **bolt** thunderbolt   **153 but rive
an oak** i.e., do no undeserved harm to men; Coriolanus wishes to be,
like Jupiter, mighty but wise in his use of power   **155 Still** always
156 cares not for is unmoved by   **159–160 prate . . . stocks** i.e.,
talk uselessly like a prisoner who has been publicly humiliated
162 When whereas.   **fond** desirous   **163 clucked** marshaled as a hen
her brood   **166 honest** honorable, just   **167 thou restrain'st** you
withhold

To a mother's part belongs.—He turns away.
Down, ladies! Let us shame him with our knees.
To his surname Coriolanus 'longs more pride   170
Than pity to our prayers. Down! [*They kneel.*]
    An end;
This is the last. So we will home to Rome,   172
And die among our neighbors.—Nay, behold 's!
This boy, that cannot tell what he would have,   174
But kneels and holds up hands for fellowship,   175
Does reason our petition with more strength   176
Than thou hast to deny 't.—Come, let us go.
    [*They rise.*]
This fellow had a Volscian to his mother;   178
His wife is in Corioles, and his child   179
Like him by chance.—Yet give us our dispatch.   180
I am hushed until our city be afire,
And then I'll speak a little.
    [*He*] *holds her by the hand, silent.*
CORIOLANUS   O Mother, Mother!
What have you done? Behold, the heavens do ope,
The gods look down, and this unnatural scene
They laugh at. O my Mother, Mother! O!
You have won a happy victory to Rome;
But for your son—believe it, O, believe it!—
Most dangerously you have with him prevailed,
If not most mortal to him. But let it come.—   189
Aufidius, though I cannot make true wars,   190
I'll frame convenient peace. Now, good Aufidius,   191
Were you in my stead, would you have heard
A mother less? Or granted less, Aufidius?
AUFIDIUS
I was moved withal.
CORIOLANUS   I dare be sworn you were.   194
And, sir, it is no little thing to make
Mine eyes to sweat compassion. But, good sir,   196
What peace you'll make, advise me. For my part,
I'll not to Rome. I'll back with you; and pray you,   198
Stand to me in this cause.—O Mother! Wife!   199
AUFIDIUS [*aside*]
I am glad thou hast set thy mercy and thy honor
At difference in thee. Out of that I'll work
Myself a former fortune.
    [*The ladies make signs to Coriolanus.*]
CORIOLANUS [*to the ladies*]   Ay, by and by;   202
But we will drink together; and you shall bear
A better witness back than words, which we,   204
On like conditions, will have countersealed.   205
Come, enter with us. Ladies, you deserve
To have a temple built you. All the swords

In Italy, and her confederate arms,   208
Could not have made this peace.   *Exeunt.*

5.4   *Enter Menenius and Sicinius.*

MENENIUS   See you yond coign o' the Capitol, yond cor-   1
nerstone?
SICINIUS   Why, what of that?
MENENIUS   If it be possible for you to displace it with
your little finger, there is some hope the ladies of
Rome, especially his mother, may prevail with him.
But I say there is no hope in 't; our throats are
sentenced, and stay upon execution.   8
SICINIUS   Is 't possible that so short a time can alter the
condition of a man?   10
MENENIUS   There is difference between a grub and a
butterfly, yet your butterfly was a grub. This Marcius
is grown from man to dragon. He has wings; he's
more than a creeping thing.
SICINIUS   He loved his mother dearly.
MENENIUS   So did he me; and he no more remembers
his mother now than an eight-year-old horse. The tartness of his face sours ripe grapes. When he walks, he
moves like an engine, and the ground shrinks before   19
his treading. He is able to pierce a corslet with his eye,   20
talks like a knell, and his hum is a battery. He sits in   21
his state as a thing made for Alexander. What he bids   22
be done is finished with his bidding. He wants noth-   23
ing of a god but eternity and a heaven to throne in.   24
SICINIUS   Yes, mercy, if you report him truly.   25
MENENIUS   I paint him in the character. Mark what   26
mercy his mother shall bring from him. There is no
more mercy in him than there is milk in a male tiger;
that shall our poor city find. And all this is long of you.   29
SICINIUS   The gods be good unto us!
MENENIUS   No, in such a case the gods will not be good
unto us. When we banished him, we respected not
them; and, he returning to break our necks, they respect not us.

    Enter a Messenger.

MESSENGER
Sir, if you'd save your life, fly to your house!
The plebeians have got your fellow tribune
And hale him up and down, all swearing, if
The Roman ladies bring not comfort home,   37
They'll give him death by inches.

    Enter another Messenger.

---

170 **'longs** belongs   172 **will home** will go home   174 **This boy** i.e.,
Coriolanus' son.   **cannot . . . have** does not understand what he is
asking for   175 **for fellowship** merely to keep us company   176 **reason** argue for   178 **to** for   179 **his child** this boy, supposed his son
180 **dispatch** dismissal, leave to go   189 **mortal** fatally   190 **true**
i.e., as I vowed to do   191 **convenient** fitting, proper   194 **withal** by
it   196 **sweat compassion** i.e., weep with pity   198 **back** go back
199 **Stand to** stand by   202 **former fortune** fortune great as formerly
204 **better witness** i.e., formal document of peace   205 **On . . .
countersealed** having agreed to the same conditions, will both have
sealed and guaranteed

208 **her confederate arms** the weapons of her allies
5.4. Location: Rome. A public place.
1 **coign** corner   8 **stay upon** await   10 **condition** nature   19 **engine**
heavy instrument of war, such as a battering ram   20 **corslet** body armor   21 **a knell** the tolling of a bell announcing a death.   **hum** (An
expression of anger.)   **battery** assault by artillery   22 **state** chair of
state.   **as . . . Alexander** as though he were a statue of Alexander the
Great (who lived after Coriolanus)   23 **finished . . . bidding** i.e., as
good as done once he orders it   23–24 **wants nothing** lacks no attribute   24 **throne** be enthroned   25 **mercy** i.e., he lacks mercy
26 **in the character** to the life   29 **long of** owing to   37 **hale** drag

SICINIUS   What's the news? 39

SECOND MESSENGER
Good news, good news! The ladies have prevailed,
The Volscians are dislodged, and Marcius gone. 41
A merrier day did never yet greet Rome,
No, not th' expulsion of the Tarquins. 43

SICINIUS
Friend, art thou certain this is true?
Is 't most certain?

SECOND MESSENGER
As certain as I know the sun is fire.
Where have you lurked, that you make doubt of it?
Ne'er through an arch so hurried the blown tide 48
As the recomforted through the gates. Why,
   hark you! 49
        Trumpets, hautboys, drums beat, all together.
The trumpets, sackbuts, psalteries, and fifes, 50
Tabors and cymbals, and the shouting Romans, 51
Make the sun dance. Hark you! *A shout within.*

MENENIUS   This is good news.
I will go meet the ladies. This Volumnia
Is worth of consuls, senators, patricians,
A city full; of tribunes, such as you,
A sea and land full. You have prayed well today.
This morning for ten thousand of your throats
I'd not have given a doit. Hark, how they joy! 58
        Sound still, with the shouts.

SICINIUS
First, the gods bless you for your tidings!
Next, accept my thankfulness.

SECOND MESSENGER
Sir, we have all great cause to give great thanks.

SICINIUS   They are near the city?

SECOND MESSENGER   Almost at point to enter. 63

SICINIUS   We'll meet them, and help the joy. *Exeunt.*

5.5   *Enter two Senators with ladies [Volumnia, Virgilia,
        Valeria] passing over the stage, with other lords.*

FIRST SENATOR
Behold our patroness, the life of Rome!
Call all your tribes together, praise the gods,
And make triumphant fires! Strew flowers before
   them!
Unshout the noise that banished Marcius; 4
Repeal him with the welcome of his mother. 5
Cry, "Welcome, ladies, welcome!"

ALL   Welcome, ladies, welcome!
        A flourish with drums and trumpets. [Exeunt.]

❖

5.6   *Enter Tullus Aufidius, with attendants.*

AUFIDIUS
Go tell the lords o' the city I am here.
Deliver them this paper. [*He gives a paper.*] Having
   read it,
Bid them repair to the marketplace, where I, 3
Even in theirs and in the commons' ears,
Will vouch the truth of it. Him I accuse 5
The city ports by this hath entered and 6
Intends t' appear before the people, hoping
To purge himself with words. Dispatch.
        [*Exeunt attendants.*]

*Enter three or four Conspirators of Aufidius'
faction.*

                                          Most welcome!

FIRST CONSPIRATOR
How is it with our general?

AUFIDIUS   Even so
As with a man by his own alms empoisoned
And with his charity slain.

SECOND CONSPIRATOR   Most noble sir, 11
If you do hold the same intent wherein
You wished us parties, we'll deliver you 13
Of your great danger.

AUFIDIUS   Sir, I cannot tell. 14
We must proceed as we do find the people.

THIRD CONSPIRATOR
The people will remain uncertain whilst
Twixt you there's difference, but the fall of either 17
Makes the survivor heir of all.

AUFIDIUS   I know it,
And my pretext to strike at him admits 19
A good construction. I raised him, and I pawned 20
Mine honor for his truth; who, being so heightened, 21
He watered his new plants with dews of flattery, 22
Seducing so my friends; and to this end
He bowed his nature, never known before
But to be rough, unswayable, and free. 25

THIRD CONSPIRATOR   Sir, his stoutness 26
When he did stand for consul, which he lost
By lack of stooping—

AUFIDIUS   That I would have spoke of. 28
Being banished for 't, he came unto my hearth,
Presented to my knife his throat. I took him,

---

39 **death by inches** slow and lingering death 41 **dislodged** gone from
their camp 43 **th' expulsion of the Tarquins** i.e., the expulsion of
Rome's last kings and beginning of the Republic 48 **arch** i.e., arch
of a bridge, such as London Bridge. **blown** swollen, driven by the
wind 49 **s.d., hautboys** oboelike instruments 50 **sackbuts** early
trombones. **psalteries** stringed instruments played by plucking the
strings 51 **Tabors** small drums 58 **doit** very small coin 63 **at point**
ready
5.5. **Location: Rome. A street near the gate, seemingly continuous
from the previous scene; the time is virtually continuous.**
4 **Unshout** recall, or, cancel by more shouting 5 **Repeal** recall

5.6. **Location: Corioles. A Volscian city. (Plutarch sets this action in
Antium, Aufidius' "native town" [in line 49], but in line 94 and following, the place is Corioles.)**
3 **repair** go 5 **vouch** affirm. **Him** he whom 6 **ports** gates. **by this**
by this time 11 **with his** by his own 13 **parties** as allies, partners
14 **Of** from 17 **difference** disagreement 19 **pretext** intention, motive 20 **construction** interpretation. **pawned** pledged 21 **truth** loyalty. **heightened** raised to power 22 **He . . . flattery** i.e., he bestowed flattering honors on those who now depended on him for
patronage 25 **free** plainspoken 26 **stoutness** obstinacy 28 **That
. . . of** I was about to mention that

Made him joint servant with me, gave him way 31
In all his own desires; nay, let him choose
Out of my files, his projects to accomplish, 33
My best and freshest men; served his designments 34
In mine own person; holp to reap the fame
Which he did end all his; and took some pride 36
To do myself this wrong—till at the last
I seemed his follower, not partner, and
He waged me with his countenance, as if 39
I had been mercenary.
FIRST CONSPIRATOR   So he did, my lord. 40
The army marveled at it, and, in the last, 41
When he had carried Rome and that we looked 42
For no less spoil than glory—
AUFIDIUS   There was it 43
For which my sinews shall be stretched upon him. 44
At a few drops of women's rheum, which are 45
As cheap as lies, he sold the blood and labor
Of our great action. Therefore shall he die,
And I'll renew me in his fall. But hark! 48

Drums and trumpets sounds,
with great shouts of the people.

FIRST CONSPIRATOR
Your native town you entered like a post, 49
And had no welcomes home; but he returns,
Splitting the air with noise.
SECOND CONSPIRATOR   And patient fools,
Whose children he hath slain, their base throats tear
With giving him glory.
THIRD CONSPIRATOR   Therefore, at your vantage, 53
Ere he express himself or move the people
With what he would say, let him feel your sword,
Which we will second. When he lies along, 56
After your way his tale pronounced shall bury 57
His reasons with his body.
AUFIDIUS   Say no more. 58
Here come the lords.

Enter the Lords of the city.

ALL LORDS
You are most welcome home.
AUFIDIUS   I have not deserved it.
But, worthy lords, have you with heed perused 61
What I have written to you?
ALL LORDS   We have.
FIRST LORD   And grieve to hear 't.
What faults he made before the last, I think 65
Might have found easy fines; but there to end 66
Where he was to begin, and give away 67

The benefit of our levies, answering us 68
With our own charge, making a treaty where 69
There was a yielding—this admits no excuse. 70
AUFIDIUS   He approaches. You shall hear him.

Enter Coriolanus, marching with drum and colors;
the commoners being with him.

CORIOLANUS
Hail, lords! I am returned your soldier,
No more infected with my country's love 73
Than when I parted hence, but still subsisting 74
Under your great command. You are to know
That prosperously I have attempted, and 76
With bloody passage led your wars even to
The gates of Rome. Our spoils we have brought
  home
Doth more than counterpoise a full third part 79
The charges of the action. We have made peace 80
With no less honor to the Antiates
Than shame to th' Romans; and we here deliver,
Subscribed by th' consuls and patricians, 83
Together with the seal o' the Senate, what
We have compounded on.   [*He offers a document.*] 85
AUFIDIUS   Read it not, noble lords,
But tell the traitor, in the highest degree
He hath abused your powers.
CORIOLANUS   "Traitor"? How now?
AUFIDIUS   Ay, traitor, Marcius.
CORIOLANUS   "Marcius"?
AUFIDIUS
Ay, Marcius, Caius Marcius. Dost thou think
I'll grace thee with that robbery, thy stol'n name
Coriolanus, in Corioles?
You lords and heads o' the state, perfidiously
He has betrayed your business and given up,
For certain drops of salt, your city Rome— 97
I say your city—to his wife and mother,
Breaking his oath and resolution like
A twist of rotten silk, never admitting 100
Counsel o' the war, but at his nurse's tears 101
He whined and roared away your victory,
That pages blushed at him and men of heart 103
Looked wondering each at other.
CORIOLANUS   Hear'st thou, Mars?
AUFIDIUS   Name not the god, thou boy of tears!
CORIOLANUS   Ha?
AUFIDIUS   No more. 107
CORIOLANUS
Measureless liar, thou hast made my heart

---

31 joint servant partner   **33 files** ranks, troops   **34 designments** designs, enterprises   **36 end all his** gather in as all his own   **39 waged** remunerated.   **countenance** patronage, favor   **40 mercenary** a hired soldier   **41 last** end   **42 had carried** had virtually overcome, or, might have overcome   **43 There was it** that was the thing   **44 my . . . upon** I shall exert all my strength against   **45 rheum** i.e., tears   **48 renew me** restore my reputation   **49 post** messenger   **53 at your vantage** seizing your opportune moment   **56 along** prostrate   **57 After . . . pronounced** your own version of the story   **58 reasons** justifications   **61 with heed** carefully   **65 made** committed   **66 easy fines** light penalties   **66–67 there . . . begin** to give up right at the threshold of his potentially greatest victory

68 levies expenses incurred in raising an army   **68–69 answering . . . charge** rewarding us with our own expenses, or, answering our protests with the claim that he acted with the authority we had given him in charge   **70 yielding** surrender   **73 infected with** influenced by (but with the suggestion of contamination)   **74 hence** i.e., from Antium.   **subsisting** continuing   **76 prosperously . . . attempted** my warlike enterprise has been prosperous   **79 Doth . . . part** outweigh by a full third   **80 charges** costs   **83 Subscribed** signed   **85 compounded** agreed   **97 certain . . . salt** some particular tears (i.e., those of Volumnia and Virgilia)   **100 twist** twisted thread   **100– 101 admitting . . . war** taking counsel from other officers   **103 heart** courage   **107 No more** i.e., no more than a boy

Too great for what contains it. "Boy"? O slave!
Pardon me, lords, 'tis the first time that ever
I was forced to scold. Your judgments, my grave
    lords,
Must give this cur the lie; and his own notion—   112
Who wears my stripes impressed upon him, that
Must bear my beating to his grave—shall join
To thrust the lie unto him.

FIRST LORD   Peace, both, and hear me speak.

CORIOLANUS
Cut me to pieces, Volsces. Men and lads,
Stain all your edges on me. "Boy"? False hound!   118
If you have writ your annals true, 'tis there   119
That, like an eagle in a dovecote, I   120
Fluttered your Volscians in Corioles.
Alone I did it. "Boy"!

AUFIDIUS   Why, noble lords,
Will you be put in mind of his blind fortune,   123
Which was your shame, by this unholy braggart,
'Fore your own eyes and ears?

ALL CONSPIRATORS   Let him die for 't.

ALL PEOPLE   Tear him to pieces!—Do it presently!— 126
He killed my son!—My daughter!—He killed my
cousin Marcus!—He killed my father!

SECOND LORD   Peace, ho! No outrage! Peace!
The man is noble, and his fame folds in   130
This orb o' the earth. His last offenses to us
Shall have judicious hearing. Stand, Aufidius,   132
And trouble not the peace.

CORIOLANUS   O, that I had him,
With six Aufidiuses, or more, his tribe,
To use my lawful sword!

AUFIDIUS   Insolent villain!

ALL CONSPIRATORS   Kill, kill, kill, kill, kill him!
        Draw the Conspirators, and kill Marcius,
                who falls. Aufidius stands on him.

LORDS   Hold, hold, hold, hold!

AUFIDIUS
My noble masters, hear me speak.

FIRST LORD   O Tullus!

SECOND LORD
Thou hast done a deed whereat valor will weep.   139

THIRD LORD
Tread not upon him, masters. All be quiet;
Put up your swords.

AUFIDIUS
My lords, when you shall know—as in this rage,
Provoked by him, you cannot—the great danger
Which this man's life did owe you, you'll rejoice   144
That he is thus cut off. Please it your honors
To call me to your Senate, I'll deliver   146
Myself your loyal servant, or endure

Your heaviest censure.   109

FIRST LORD   Bear from hence his body,
And mourn you for him. Let him be regarded
As the most noble corpse that ever herald
Did follow to his urn.

SECOND LORD   His own impatience   151
Takes from Aufidius a great part of blame.
Let's make the best of it.

AUFIDIUS   My rage is gone,
And I am struck with sorrow. Take him up.
Help, three o' the chiefest soldiers; I'll be one.   155
Beat thou the drum that it speak mournfully;
Trail your steel pikes. Though in this city he   157
Hath widowed and unchilded many a one,
Which to this hour bewail the injury,
Yet he shall have a noble memory.   160
Assist.   *Exeunt, bearing the body of Marcius.*
                    A dead march sounded.

151 impatience rage   155 be one i.e., be the fourth   157 Trail . . .
pikes carry your lances reversed with the point trailing along the
ground (as a sign of mourning)   160 memory memorial

109 Too . . . it swollen with rage so that my breast cannot contain it
112 notion understanding, sense of the truth   118 edges swords
119 there recorded there   120 dovecote pigeon house   123 blind
fortune gift of Fortune, the blind goddess; mere good luck   126 presently immediately   130 folds in overspreads, enwraps   132 judicious
judicial.   Stand stop   139 whereat at which   144 did owe you had
for you, held in store for you   146 deliver show, demonstrate

The Romances

Pericles

Cymbeline

The Winter's Tale

The Tempest

The Two Noble Kinsmen

Pericles

Pericles is a deceptively simple play. Although it was popular in its own time and in recent years has proved to be successful and deeply moving onstage, the play may seem naive and trivial on the printed page. Its apparent lack of "depth" seems especially striking when we compare it with its contemporaries, *King Lear, Macbeth, Timon of Athens,* and *Antony and Cleopatra.* It purports to be the work of a medieval poet, John Gower, who, as presenter, or chorus, apologizes to his sophisticated Jacobean audience ("born in these latter times / When wit's more ripe") for the "lame feet of my rhyme" and the quaintness of his ditty (1.0.11–12; 4.0.48). The narrative offers a series of sea voyages, separations, hairbreadth escapes, and reunions. Thrilling circumstances abound: Pericles fleeing the wrath of Antiochus; his wife, Thaisa, giving birth to their daughter, Marina, on board ship in the midst of a gigantic storm; and Marina later being rescued by pirates from a would-be murderer only to be sold by her new captors to a house of prostitution. Time leaps forward from Pericles' own youth to that of his daughter. The action takes place in remote lands, shifting constantly back and forth among six eastern Mediterranean localities: Antioch, Tyre, Tarsus, Pentapolis, Ephesus, and Mytilene. Conventional devices of plot include the expounding of riddles, the discovery of incest at court, the exposure of infants to the hostile elements, the miraculous restoration of life after seeming death, the appearance of the gods in a vision, and recognition of long-lost loved ones by means of signs or tokens.

These are the attributes of popular romance, a distinctly old-fashioned genre in 1606–1608 when *Pericles* was apparently written. Robert Greene had composed prose romances of this sort in the 1580s and early 1590s, including *Pandosto,* Shakespeare's source for *The Winter's Tale.* Sir Philip Sidney's *Arcadia* had endowed romance with noble eloquence and literary fashionableness, but that, too, was in the late 1580s. (The name Pericles may well owe something to the *Arcadia's* Pyrocles, though Shakespeare may also have been attracted to the Pericles of fifth-century Athens and to the mellifluous quality of the name.) One source for *Pericles* itself, a prose history of Apollonius of Tyre by Laurence Twine, was registered for publication in 1576, although no edition exists before that of 1594 or 1595. Earlier accounts of Apollonius (as the hero was originally named), going back to Greek romance, include a ninth-century *His-toria Apollonii Regis Tyri,* Godfrey of Viterbo's *Pantheon* (c. 1186), John Gower's *Confessio Amantis* (c. 1383–1393), and the *Gesta Romanorum.* Why did Shakespeare's company refurbish such an outmoded romantic story in 1606–1608?

The puzzle is aggravated by questions of authorship and textual reliability. The editors of the First Folio did not include *Pericles* in the canon of Shakespeare's plays. Perhaps they experienced copyright difficulties or could not lay their hands on the playbook, but it is also possible they either suspected or knew that Shakespeare was not the sole author. Printed editions were available to them: the First Quarto of 1609 and the subsequent quartos of 1609, 1611, and 1619, each based on the preceding edition. The First Quarto was, however, a bad text with occasional glaring contradictions. In 1.2, for example, Pericles' lords wish him a safe journey when no one has yet spoken of his departure, and Helicanus rebukes these same lords for flattery even though they have not said anything remotely sycophantic. Other scenes present similar difficulties, especially in the first two acts. The characters do not always seem consistent: Cleon is condemned in Act 5 for having tried to murder Marina, even though our earlier impression of him is of a man who is genuinely horrified at his wife's villainy. He weakly bends to the will of Dionyza but is no murderer. Such inconsistencies and errors, and the naiveté of the whole, have generally led to three hypotheses: that Shakespeare worked with a collaborator such as Thomas Heywood or George Wilkins, that he revised an older play and left the first two acts pretty much as they were, or that he wrote the entire play, which was then "pirated" by two unemployed actors whose portions differed markedly in accuracy.

To complicate matters still further, a prose version of the story called *The Painful Adventures of Pericles* by George Wilkins appeared in 1608, purporting to be "the true History of the Play of Pericles," that is, to be a prose account of a dramatic performance. This redaction is indeed close at times to the play we have, but at other times it departs widely. The departures of the later work are sometimes explained with the hypothesis that Wilkins based his account on an older play, to which Wilkins might have contributed himself; another and more current opinion favors the notion that Wilkins took what he needed from the play we have, borrowing also from Twine's prose version or from his own imagination. Apparently, then, *Pericles* was such a popular stage success that it inspired Wilkins' *Painful Adventures* in 1608, a new reprint in 1607 of Twine's *Pattern of Painful Adventures* on which the play itself had been partly based, and a botched surreptitious quarto edition of the play in 1609. Shakespeare's sole authorship must remain in doubt, although the incongruities, especially in the first two acts, are sometimes explained as the result of faulty memorial reporting and compositorial error. Onstage, to be sure, even the first two acts make fine dramatic sense, establishing motifs and situations that are essential to the rest of the play, so that the overall impression in the theater is of cohesion.

The naiveté of *Pericles* is probably deliberate. Its romantic motifs continue on into that group of plays known generally as the late romances: *Cymbeline* (c. 1608–1610), *The Winter's Tale* (c. 1609–1611), and *The Tempest* (c. 1610–1611). Nor are these motifs entirely new in *Pericles:* the "problem" comedies *All's Well That Ends Well* and *Measure for Measure* use a tragicomic structure in which miraculous cures or providential interventions triumph over the semblance of death. *Pericles* occupies an integral place, then, in the development of Shakespearean comedy during the period of his great tragedies. To that development, it offers a new emphasis on the simplicity of folk legend. Of the four late romances, *Pericles,* the earliest, is also the nearest in tone to the romances of the 1580s. The play seems to have constituted a revival of that old genre and was so immensely popular that it did much to establish the vogue of tragicomedy exploited by Beaumont and Fletcher.

The Chorus, old Gower, gives to the episodic materials of the play a unified point of view. He speaks with the authority of one who has told the story before, even though his *Confessio Amantis* (c. 1383–1393) was probably not Shakespeare's immediate source. Gower adopts a kind of Chaucerian persona, appealing to "what mine authors say" (1.0.20) and apologizing for his rude simplicity. Like the Chorus of *Henry V,* he repeatedly urges his auditors to transcend the limitations of his naive art, using the power of imagination to bridge gaps in time and to suppose the stage a storm-tossed ship or the city of Antioch. His appearances divide the action into seven episodic segments, surely a more authentic structure than the five "acts" conventionally employed by later editions. He offers moral appraisals of his various characters, often before we have had a chance to see them, contrasting the good with the bad. Most important, he presides as a sort of benign deity over the changing fortunes of his characters, assuring us that as narrator he will not allow the virtuous to come to grief or the wicked to escape punishment. He thus paces our expectations and provides a comic reassurance appropriate to romance. He promises to "show you those in trouble's reign, / Losing a mite, a mountain gain." To the virtuous, he will ultimately give his "benison." Under his direction, the vacillations of fortune take on a predictable rhythm, whereby the rewards of virtuous conduct may be delayed but cannot eventually fail. Pericles, he tells us, will suffer adversity "Till fortune, tired with doing bad, / Threw him ashore, to give him glad" (2.0.7–38). This pattern is repeated several times.

The characters often remind us of characters from a fairy story, outwardly stereotyped and one-dimensional, divided for the most part into contrasting types of villainy and virtue, and yet suggesting beneath their conventional surfaces the conflicts in family relationships that are essential to the fairy story. Incest is a recurrent motif, from its most blunt and evil

manifestation in the court of Antiochus to more subtle inversions and variations in the relationships of Simonides and his daughter Thaisa, and, most centrally, of Pericles and his daughter Marina. The interest in fathers and daughters, and in the difficulties fathers have in coming to terms with their daughters' marrying other men, continues to fascinate Shakespeare from *Othello* and *King Lear* into all of his late romances. The mystery of incest is stated in terms of a riddle at the start of *Pericles,* and the moving dramatic conclusion in which the hero is reunited at last with his daughter seems to represent at some level a resolution of conflict between father and daughter. Pericles and Marina have "found" each other and themselves, literally in the narrative sense and also in some deeper psychic and spiritual way.

The characters expressing this and other conflicts are repeatedly paired opposite to one another as contrasting foils, illustrating a type of human depravity and its ideal opposite. One such contrast is that of tyranny and true monarchy. For example, both Antiochus and Simonides seem to welcome the various suitors who flock to their courts, seeking the hand in marriage of the two kings' daughters. Antiochus does so deceitfully, however, since he is his daughter's incestuous lover. Pericles learns in Antioch the danger of perceiving too much about the private affairs of a suspicious and vengeful tyrant. Simonides is, on the other hand, a true prince, beloved by even the simplest of his subjects, generous, lacking in envy, courteous to strangers, and more impressed with inner substance than with outward show. He approves of Pericles as a son-in-law, though (like Prospero in *The Tempest*) he imposes artificial restraints on the lovers to make their eventual triumph of love seem all the more sweet. Antiochus and his daughter are eventually shriveled up by a fire from heaven, whereas Simonides and Thaisa earn the just rewards of gracious hospitality. Another opposing pair of characters, Thaliard and Helicanus, are conventionally typed as false and true courtiers. Thaliard, ordered by Antiochus to murder Pericles, is evasive and self-serving; Helicanus, when offered the opportunity to supplant Pericles as ruler of Tyre, loyally awaits his master's return.

Pericles is apparently conceived in these same conventional terms as a prince of chivalry, young, brave, admirable both as a romantic wooer and as a resolute adventurer. His visit to the city of Tarsus, which has recently been toppled from wealth to poverty, shows him practicing the generosity that befits his lofty rank and innately noble qualities. Even when fortune strips him of his finery, his princely bearing is evident to discerning observers like King Simonides and Thaisa. Pericles thus differs outwardly from the flawed tragicomic protagonists more often found in the late romances, such as Posthumus in *Cymbeline* and Leontes in *The Winter's Tale,* who bring grief upon themselves and must suffer agonizing contrition before gaining an unexpected second chance. Pericles seems to be virtually without fault, a hero of romance rather than of tragedy. His soliloquies and eloquent speeches are not darkly introspective and psychological, like Leontes'. Although he grieves in sackcloth and ashes, he does so for undeserved misfortune rather than for his own follies. The play accordingly has little to say about humanity's perverse instinct for self-destruction. Yet critics have been unable to agree as to whether Pericles is simply a good man buffeted by misfortune or a man somehow perplexed by inner conflict. Are there unresolved wishes in his relationships to Thaisa and Marina that link him to the manifestly flawed protagonists of *Cymbeline* and *The Winter's Tale,* and, more explicitly, to Antiochus and his daughter in this play? What is it that causes his excessive despair in his grief and his withdrawal into absolute silence? On the surface, his story is one of undeserved misfortune, leading at last to happy reunion and an end of his trials. He learns a more affirmative and patient response from his courageous daughter Marina, whereupon his trials have run their necessary course. Even his learning such a lesson is of less importance than the sublime sense of mystery and joy that accompanies his reunion with Marina.

In several ways, Marina is a typical heroine of Shakespeare's late romances. Her name, like that of Perdita in *The Winter's Tale,* signifies loss and recovery. Marina is the gift of the sea, that mysterious power of fortune in *Pericles* that takes with one hand even while it gives with the other. Just as the sea tosses Pericles on the coast of Pentapolis and then returns to him the suit of armor in which he will joust for the love of fair Thaisa, so in another storm at sea Thaisa apparently dies giving birth to Marina. The child is a "fresh new seafarer" on the troubled voyage of life (3.1.41). The sea parts her from her mother and father and leads to the misunderstandings whereby Marina is supposed dead, but the sea also eventually deposits Pericles on the coast of Mytilene, where he finds his long-lost daughter. Like Perdita, Marina is associated with flowers and with Tellus, a divinity of the earth. The inscription on her monument, when she is thought dead, speaks of elemental strife between the sea and the shore caused by her death, in which the angry sea gods "Make raging battery upon shores of flint" (4.4.39–43). She is a princess from folk legend, like Snow White or like Imogen in *Cymbeline,* who must flee the envious wrath of a witchlike stepmother and queen. Her true mother, Thaisa, another princess in a folktale, is washed ashore in a treasure-filled chest, smelling sweetly and betokening some miraculous change of fortune.

Most important, Marina is one who can preach conversion to the sinful and cure distempered souls. She recovers her husband-to-be, Lysimachus, from the brothels of Mytilene, and even converts pimps and prostitutes by her innocent faith. As one with a strange power to bring new life to dead hope, she resembles a number of mysterious artist-figures and magicians in the late romances (or, earlier, in *All's Well That Ends Well*). One such is Cerimon, who restores life to Thaisa. Like him, or like Paulina in *The Win-*

ter's Tale, whose devices are "lawful" though seemingly magical, Marina offers cures that can be rationally explained and yet appear to be miraculous. To Pericles, her ministrations seem "the rarest dream that e'er dull sleep / Did mock sad fools withal" (5.1.166–167). Yet what she has taught him, by her own example, is simple patience; she has suffered even more than he but nevertheless knows how to endure, how to "look / Like Patience gazing on kings' graves and smiling / Extremity out of act" (lines 140–142). Marina has the power to renew her father and restore him to life, perhaps because she represents the way in which the dangerous sexuality of women can be legitimated: she dwells for a time in a house of prostitution and is eminently desirable by men, and yet at the same time is so pure that she can teach men the way to control their own libidinousness. She is thus whore and saint in one person, able to refute the low premise about the carnality of the human condition that Pericles elsewhere finds so threatening. In his recovery of Marina and in his glad disposing of her as the bride of Lysimachus, Pericles at last comes to terms with the incestuous bond between father and daughter that had posed itself so menacingly for him in the court of King Antiochus.

Through Marina's ministrations, Pericles is reunited with his wife as well. Here, too, the narrative suggests a successful resolution of guilt after long years of inner conflict. Pericles is obliged to throw his wife's body overboard in a storm after she has died in childbirth. The fault is not his, since the sailors insist that the storm cannot be abated until the ship is cleared of the dead (3.1.47–49), but the emotional burden of loss is incalculable. Thaisa's miraculous recovery makes possible an eventual reunion that coincides with the rediscovery of the daughter. Viewed in these terms, the tale is one in which a husband finds it possible to love again a wife he threw away from him long ago. As in *The Winter's Tale,* where King Leontes causes the death of his queen at the time of her childbearing and then regains her after years of penance, the husband learns again, late in life, to cherish a long-lost wife who has aged and whom he is now able to love in spite of that aging. In *Pericles,* the husband's guilt is not manifest, nor is his wife's sexuality an open threat to him in her youthful childbearing vitality, and yet the narrative itself of separation and reunion resembles a slow and difficult coming to terms with the emotional demands of marriage. Perhaps it is significant in some way that Shakespeare lived apart from his family most of his working life and that when he wrote his late romances he was about to retire from London to Stratford.

Whatever the psychological dimension of the story of Pericles, his daughter, and his wife, old Gower as Chorus searches for meaning in simpler, pious terms. Gower wishes us to understand finally why Providence has allowed so much misfortune to afflict the virtuous: only by such testing can humanity learn to conquer time and death. Time will always remain "the king of men; / He's both their parent and he is their grave, / And gives them what he will, not what they crave" (2.3.47–49). Nevertheless, Providence can turn the accidents of time and fortune to good purpose for those who are Joblike in their patient faith. Even pirates unknowingly take part in a divine plan, rescuing Marina from the clutches of the evil Dionyza. As Gower puts it, those who are "assailed with fortune fierce and keen" are also "Led on by heaven, and crowned with joy at last" (5.3.89–91). To Pericles, such a delayed reward is ample compensation for his sorrows, almost indeed an unbearable joy. "No more, you gods!" he movingly pleads. "Your present kindness / Makes my past miseries sports" (lines 41–42).

Pericles

[*Dramatis Personae*

GOWER, *as Presenter or Chorus*

ANTIOCHUS, *King of Antioch*
DAUGHTER *of Antiochus*
THALIARD, *a lord of Antioch*
MESSENGER *to Antiochus*

PERICLES, *Prince of Tyre*
THAISA, *his wife, daughter of Simonides*
MARINA, *their daughter*
HELICANUS,⎫ *two lords of Tyre*
ESCANES, ⎭
Three other LORDS *of Tyre*

CLEON, *Governor of Tarsus*
DIONYZA, *his wife*
LEONINE, *a murderer*
A LORD *of Tarsus*

SIMONIDES, *King of Pentapolis*
Three FISHERMEN *of Pentapolis*
Five KNIGHTS *who compete for Thaisa's hand*
Three LORDS *of Pentapolis*
A MARSHAL

LYCHORIDA, *Marina's nurse*
MASTER *of a ship*
A SAILOR *of the ship*

CERIMON, *a lord of Ephesus*
PHILEMON, *his servant*
Two GENTLEMEN *of Ephesus*
Two SERVANTS *of Ephesus*

Three PIRATES

LYSIMACHUS, *Governor of Mytilene*
PANDER, ⎫ *three bawds, or dealers*
BAWD, *his wife,* ⎬ *in prostitution*
BOLT, *their man,* ⎭
Two GENTLEMEN *of Mytilene*

SAILOR *of Tyre*
SAILOR *of Mytilene*
GENTLEMAN *of Tyre*
LORD *of Mytilene*

DIANA, *goddess of chastity*

Lords, Ladies, Gentlemen, Attendants, Servants, Messengers, young Ladies accompanying Marina, Vestal Virgins, inhabitants of Ephesus

SCENE: *In various eastern Mediterranean countries*]

1. Chorus

Enter Gower [before the palace of Antioch, on the walls of which can be seen a row of impaled heads].

GOWER

To sing a song that old was sung,	1
From ashes ancient Gower is come,	2
Assuming man's infirmities	3
To glad your ear and please your eyes.	
It hath been sung at festivals,	
On ember eves and holy-ales;	6
And lords and ladies in their lives	
Have read it for restoratives.	8
The purchase is to make men glorious,	9
Et bonum quo antiquius, eo melius.	10
If you, born in these latter times	
When wit's more ripe, accept my rhymes,	12
And that to hear an old man sing	13
May to your wishes pleasure bring,	
I life would wish, and that I might	
Waste it for you, like taper light.	16
This Antioch, then. Antiochus the Great	17
Built up this city for his chiefest seat,	
The fairest in all Syria—	
I tell you what mine authors say.	20
This king unto him took a peer,	21
Who died and left a female heir,	
So buxom, blithe, and full of face	23
As heaven had lent her all his grace;	24
With whom the father liking took	25
And her to incest did provoke.	
Bad child, worse father, to entice his own	
To evil should be done by none!	28
But custom what they did begin	29
Was with long use account'd no sin.	
The beauty of this sinful dame	
Made many princes thither frame	32
To seek her as a bedfellow,	
In marriage pleasures playfellow;	
Which to prevent he made a law,	
To keep her still, and men in awe,	36
That whoso asked her for his wife,	
His riddle told not, lost his life.	38

So for her many a wight did die,   39
As yon grim looks do testify.
        [He points to the heads of the unsuccessful
                      suitors, displayed on the walls.]
What now ensues, to the judgment of your eye
I give my cause, who best can justify.   *Exit.* 42

1.1   *Enter Antiochus, Prince Pericles, and followers.*

ANTIOCHUS
Young Prince of Tyre, you have at large received   1
The danger of the task you undertake.
PERICLES
I have, Antiochus, and with a soul
Emboldened with the glory of her praise
Think death no hazard in this enterprise.
ANTIOCHUS   Music!
Bring in our daughter, clothèd like a bride
For th' embracements even of Jove himself,
At whose conception, till Lucina reigned,   9
Nature this dowry gave: to glad her presence,   10
The senate house of planets all did sit   11
To knit in her their best perfections.   12

      [Music.] Enter Antiochus' Daughter.

PERICLES
See where she comes, appareled like the spring,
Graces her subjects, and her thoughts the king   14
Of every virtue gives renown to men!   15
Her face the book of praises, where is read   16
Nothing but curious pleasures, as from thence   17
Sorrow were ever razed, and testy wrath   18
Could never be her mild companion.   19
You gods that made me man, and sway in love,   20
That have inflamed desire in my breast
To taste the fruit of yon celestial tree
Or die in the adventure, be my helps,   23
As I am son and servant to your will,   24
To compass such a boundless happiness!   25
ANTIOCHUS   Prince Pericles—
PERICLES
That would be son to great Antiochus.
ANTIOCHUS
Before thee stands this fair Hesperides,   28

1.0. (Gower is seen to be standing before the palace of Antioch, where scene 1 will take place.)
1 old of old   **2 ancient Gower** the fourteenth-century poet John Gower, who related the adventures of Apollonius of Tyre (of which *Pericles* is a version) in his *Confessio Amantis*   **3 Assuming man's infirmities** taking on a mortal body   **6 ember eves** evenings before the ember days—the periodic fast days which coincide with the four changes of the seasons.   **holy-ales** i.e., church ales or festivals   **8 for restoratives** for its nourishing or healing properties   **9 purchase** profit.   **glorious** renowned, lustrous   **10 Et . . . melius** a good thing is better for being older. (Latin.)   **12 wit's more ripe** wisdom is more seasoned   **13 And that** i.e., and if   **16 Waste** spend.   **like taper light** i.e., like a candle that consumes itself in giving illumination   **17 This** i.e., this is   **20 authors** authorities   **21 peer** consort   **23 buxom** cheerful, lively.   **full of face** beautiful and round of face   **24 As** as if.   **his** its   **25 liking** a lustful desire   **28 should** that should   **29 custom** continued practice (of)   **32 frame** direct their steps   **36 still** always, forever.   **and men** and to keep men   **38 His riddle told not** if he left his (Antiochus') riddle unsolved

39 wight person   **42 I . . . justify** i.e., I submit my case, my story, to those who can best render a favorable verdict (the audience) or possibly to the actors who can best justify the truth of it
1.1. Location: Antioch. The palace, as before.
1 at large received heard in detail   **9 At . . . reigned** i.e., from her conception until her birth. (Lucina was goddess of childbirth in her capacity as goddess of light.)   **10–12 Nature . . . perfections** i.e., Nature bestowed on her, to make her presence gladsome, a favorable aspect of all the planets so that all perfect qualities would be combined in her   **14 Graces her subjects** with graces for her subjects. (She commands every graceful quality and virtue known to humanity.)   **15 gives** that gives   **16 book of praises** collection of praiseworthy qualities   **17 curious** exquisite.   **as** as if   **18 ever razed** forever scraped away or erased   **19 her mild companion** companion of her mildness   **20 sway** rule   **23 adventure** attempt   **24 As** as surely as   **25 compass** encompass   **28 Hesperides** (Correctly speaking, nymphs who guarded Juno's golden fruit. The name was frequently applied to the garden where these fruits grew. Here it applies to the Princess, beyond price but dangerous to seek.)

With golden fruit, but dangerous to be touched,
For deathlike dragons here affright thee hard.   30
Her face, like heaven, enticeth thee to view
Her countless glory, which desert must gain;   32
And which, without desert, because thine eye   33
Presumes to reach, all the whole heap must die.   34
Yon sometime famous princes, like thyself,   35
            [*pointing to the heads on the walls*]
Drawn by report, adventurous by desire,   36
Tell thee with speechless tongues and semblance
    pale   37
That without covering, save yon field of stars,
Here they stand martyrs slain in Cupid's wars,
And with dead cheeks advise thee to desist
For going on death's net, whom none resist.   41

PERICLES
Antiochus, I thank thee, who hath taught
My frail mortality to know itself,
And by those fearful objects to prepare
This body, like to them, to what I must;   45
For death remembered should be like a mirror,   46
Who tells us life's but breath, to trust it error.
I'll make my will then, and, as sick men do,
Who know the world, see heaven, but, feeling woe,   49
Grip not at earthly joys as erst they did,   50
So I bequeath a happy peace to you
And all good men, as every prince should do;
My riches to the earth from whence they came,
[*To the Princess*] But my unspotted fire of love to you.
Thus ready for the way of life or death,
I wait the sharpest blow, Antiochus.

ANTIOCHUS
Scorning advice, read the conclusion, then;   57
Which read and not expounded, 'tis decreed,
As these before thee, thou thyself shalt bleed.

DAUGHTER
Of all 'sayed yet, mayst thou prove prosperous!   60
Of all 'sayed yet, I wish thee happiness!   61

PERICLES
Like a bold champion, I assume the lists,   62
Nor ask advice of any other thought
But faithfulness and courage.   [*He reads*] *the riddle.*
    I am no viper, yet I feed   65
    On mother's flesh which did me breed.   66
    I sought a husband, in which labor
    I found that kindness in a father.   68
    He's father, son, and husband mild;
    I mother, wife, and yet his child.

How they may be, and yet in two,   71
    As you will live, resolve it you.
[*Aside.*] Sharp physic is the last! But, O you powers   73
That gives heaven countless eyes to view men's acts,   74
Why cloud they not their sights perpetually
If this be true which makes me pale to read it?
Fair glass of light, I loved you, and could still,   77
Were not this glorious casket stored with ill.
But I must tell you now my thoughts revolt,
For he's no man on whom perfections wait   80
That, knowing sin within, will touch the gate.
You are a fair viol, and your sense the strings   82
Who, fingered to make man his lawful music,
Would draw heaven down and all the gods to
    hearken,
But, being played upon before your time,
Hell only danceth at so harsh a chime.   86
Good sooth, I care not for you.   87

ANTIOCHUS
Prince Pericles, touch not, upon thy life,   88
For that's an article within our law
As dangerous as the rest. Your time's expired.
Either expound now, or receive your sentence.

PERICLES   Great King,
Few love to hear the sins they love to act;
'Twould braid yourself too near for me to tell it.   94
Who has a book of all that monarchs do,   95
He's more secure to keep it shut than shown.
For vice repeated is like the wandering wind,   97
Blows dust in others' eyes to spread itself;   98
And yet the end of all is bought thus dear,   99
The breath is gone, and the sore eyes see clear   100
To stop the air would hurt them. The blind mole
    casts   101
Copped hills towards heaven to tell the earth is
    thronged   102
By man's oppression, and the poor worm doth die
    for 't.   103
Kings are earth's gods; in vice their law's their will;
And if Jove stray, who dares say Jove doth ill?
It is enough you know; and it is fit,   106
What being more known grows worse, to smother it. 107
All love the womb that their first being bred;
Then give my tongue like leave to love my head.   109

---

30 **deathlike dragons** (Alludes to the dragon that guarded the garden of the Hesperides.)   32 **countless glory** innumerable starlike beauties 33–34 **And . . . reach** i.e., and if you presume to aspire to her without deserving   34 **heap** i.e., body of Pericles   35 **sometime** once, formerly   36 **adventurous by desire** made rash by passion   37 **semblance** outward aspect   41 **For going on** from entering   45 **must** must someday be   46 **remembered** called to mind   49 **Who . . . woe** i.e., who, weary of this world's miseries and seeing the imminence of heavenly bliss   50 **Grip** clutch.   **erst** formerly   57 **conclusion** problem, riddle   60, 61 **'sayed** who have assayed, attempted 62 **champion** combatant.   **assume the lists** i.e., undertake the combat, enter the tournament ground   65–66 **I am . . . breed** (Vipers at birth were thought to gnaw their way through their mother's sides, thus killing the mother.)   68 **kindness** (1) affection (2) kinship

71 **two** i.e., two people   73 **Sharp . . . last** i.e., this last condition—to stake my life on solving this riddle—is bitter medicine. **powers** celestial beings who control destiny   74 **eyes** i.e., the stars 77 **glass of light** mirror or glass vessel that is ambiguously radiant and of light virtue (i.e., the Princess, fair in appearance only)   80 **on . . . wait** with perfections as his attendants   82 **sense** senses   86 **only** alone   87 **Good sooth** in truth   88 **touch not** (Antiochus evidently believes Pericles is about to touch the Princess' hand or some such forbidden thing.)   94 **braid . . . near** upbraid you too directly 95 **Who** he who   97 **repeated** talked about   98 **Blows . . . itself** i.e., which in spreading itself blows dust in offenders' eyes   99 **thus dear** at this high price   100–101 **The breath . . . them** i.e., the speaker has wasted his breath, whereas the offenders can see well enough, despite the irritating dust, to stop the breath of those who have attempted to indict them   102 **Copped** peaked.   **to tell** to tell that. **thronged** beset   103 **worm** i.e., creature. (The image is of a lowly creature like Pericles who dares to sound a warning against tyranny only at peril to himself.)   106 **you know** i.e., that you know that I know your riddle   107 **What . . . it** to cover up a deed that is only worsened by revelation   109 **like leave** similar permission

ANTIOCHUS [*aside*]
Heaven, that I had thy head! He has found the
   meaning.
But I will gloze with him.—Young Prince of Tyre,   111
Though by the tenor of our strict edict,
Your exposition misinterpreting,   113
We might proceed to cancel of your days,   114
Yet hope, succeeding from so fair a tree   115
As your fair self, doth tune us otherwise.   116
Forty days longer we do respite you,
If by which time our secret be undone,   118
This mercy shows we'll joy in such a son.
And until then your entertain shall be   120
As doth befit our honor and your worth.   121
                              [*Exeunt.*] *Manet Pericles solus.*

PERICLES
How courtesy would seem to cover sin,   122
When what is done is like an hypocrite,
The which is good in nothing but in sight!   124
If it be true that I interpret false,
Then were it certain you were not so bad
As with foul incest to abuse your soul;
Where now you're both a father and a son
By your untimely claspings with your child,
Which pleasures fits a husband, not a father,
And she an eater of her mother's flesh
By the defiling of her parent's bed;
And both like serpents are, who, though they feed
On sweetest flowers, yet they poison breed.
Antioch, farewell, for wisdom sees those men   135
Blush not in actions blacker than the night
Will 'schew no course to keep them from the light.   137
One sin, I know, another doth provoke;
Murder's as near to lust as flame to smoke.   139
Poison and treason are the hands of sin,
Ay, and the targets, to put off the shame.   141
Then, lest my life be cropped to keep you clear,   142
By flight I'll shun the danger which I fear.   *Exit.*

Enter Antiochus.

ANTIOCHUS   He hath found the meaning,
For which we mean to have his head.
He must not live to trumpet forth my infamy,
Nor tell the world Antiochus doth sin
In such a loathèd manner;
And therefore instantly this prince must die,
For by his fall my honor must keep high.—
Who attends us there?

Enter Thaliard.

THALIARD   Doth Your Highness call?
ANTIOCHUS
Thaliard, you are of our chamber, Thaliard,   153
And our mind partakes her private actions   154
To your secrecy; and for your faithfulness
We will advance you, Thaliard. Behold.
                      [*He gives poison and money.*]
Here's poison and here's gold. We hate the Prince
Of Tyre, and thou must kill him. It fits thee not
To ask the reason why: because we bid it.
Say, is it done?
THALIARD   My lord, 'tis done.
ANTIOCHUS   Enough.

Enter a Messenger.

Let your breath cool yourself, telling your haste.   161
MESSENGER   My lord, Prince Pericles is fled.   [*Exit.*]
ANTIOCHUS [*to Thaliard*]   As thou wilt live, fly after,
and like an arrow shot from a well-experienced archer
hits the mark his eye doth level at, so thou never re-   165
turn unless thou say Prince Pericles is dead.
THALIARD   My lord, if I can get him within my pistol's
length, I'll make him sure enough. So farewell to Your   168
Highness.
ANTIOCHUS
Thaliard, adieu! [*Exit Thaliard.*] Till Pericles be dead,
My heart can lend no succor to my head.   [*Exit.*]

1.2   *Enter Pericles with his Lords.*

PERICLES
Let none disturb us. [*The Lords stay at the door.*]
   Why should this change of thoughts,   1
The sad companion, dull-eyed melancholy,
Be my so used a guest as not an hour   3
In the day's glorious walk or peaceful night,   4
The tomb where grief should sleep, can breed me
   quiet?
Here pleasures court mine eyes, and mine eyes
   shun them,
And danger, which I feared, is at Antioch,
Whose arm seems far too short to hit me here.
Yet neither pleasure's art can joy my spirits,
Nor yet the other's distance comfort me.
Then it is thus: the passions of the mind,
That have their first conception by misdread,   12
Have after-nourishment and life by care;   13
And what was first but fear what might be done
Grows elder now, and cares it be not done.   15
And so with me: the great Antiochus,

111 **gloze** talk smoothly and speciously   113 **Your . . . misinterpreting** since your exposition interprets wrongly   114 **to cancel of** to cancellation of   115 **Yet . . . tree** yet hope (or fear) of your answering correctly, issuing from so fair a royal stock   116 **tune us** adjust or alter my intention. (*Us* is the royal "we.")   118 **undone** unraveled, solved   120 **entertain** entertainment, reception   121 **s.d. Manet** he remains onstage.   **solus** alone   122 **would seem** speciously endeavors   124 **sight** appearance   135 **sees those men** sees that those men who   137 **'schew** eschew, or, possibly, *shew,* "shy away from." **keep . . . light** i.e., keep their guilty actions hidden   139 **Murder's . . . lust** (A sentious truism of the time.)   141 **targets** shields.   **put off** deflect   142 **cropped** harvested, cut down.   **clear** free from accusation

153 **of our chamber** my chamberlain   154 **partakes** imparts   161 **Let . . . haste** cool your hot haste with the breath of your explanation for it   165 **level** aim   168 **length** range.   **sure** harmless (i.e., dead)
1.2. Location: Tyre. The palace.
1 **us** i.e., me.   **change of thoughts** altered disposition of mind
3 **used** familiar.   **as that**   4 **walk** i.e., traversing of the sun   12 **misdread** fear   13 **care** anxiety   15 **cares** takes care, is anxious

'Gainst whom I am too little to contend,
Since he's so great can make his will his act,   18
Will think me speaking, though I swear to silence;
Nor boots it me to say I honor him,   20
If he suspect I may dishonor him.
And what may make him blush in being known,   22
He'll stop the course by which it might be known.
With hostile forces he'll o'erspread the land,
And with th' ostent of war will look so huge   25
Amazement shall drive courage from the state,   26
Our men be vanquished ere they do resist,
And subjects punished that ne'er thought offense;
Which care of them, not pity of myself—
Who am no more but as the tops of trees
Which fence the roots they grow by, and defend
  them—   31
Makes both my body pine and soul to languish,
And punish that before that he would punish.   33

Enter [Helicanus and] all the Lords to Pericles.

FIRST LORD
Joy and all comfort in your sacred breast!
SECOND LORD
And keep your mind, till you return to us,   35
Peaceful and comfortable!
HELICANUS
Peace, peace, and give experience tongue.   37
They do abuse the King that flatter him.
For flattery is the bellows blows up sin;   39
The thing the which is flattered, but a spark   40
To which that blast gives heat and stronger glowing;   41
Whereas reproof, obedient and in order,
Fits kings as they are men, for they may err.
When Signor Sooth here does proclaim peace,   44
He flatters you, makes war upon your life.
Prince, pardon me, or strike me, if you please;
I cannot be much lower than my knees.   [*He kneels.*]
PERICLES
All leave us else; but let your cares o'erlook   48
What shipping and what lading's in our haven,   49
And then return to us. [*Exeunt Lords.*] Helicanus,
Thou hast moved us. What seest thou in our looks?   51
HELICANUS   An angry brow, dread lord.

PERICLES
If there be such a dart in princes' frowns,
How durst thy tongue move anger to our face?
HELICANUS
How dares the plants look up to heaven,
From whence they have their nourishment?
PERICLES
Thou knowest I have power to take thy life from
  thee.
HELICANUS   I have ground the ax myself;
Do you but strike the blow.
PERICLES
Rise, prithee, rise. [*He rises.*] Sit down. Thou art no
  flatterer,
I thank thee for 't, and heaven forbid
That kings should let their ears hear their faults hid!   62
Fit counselor and servant for a prince,
Who by thy wisdom makes a prince thy servant,
What wouldst thou have me do?
HELICANUS   To bear with patience such griefs
As you yourself do lay upon yourself.
PERICLES
Thou speak'st like a physician, Helicanus,
That ministers a potion unto me
That thou wouldst tremble to receive thyself.
Attend me, then: I went to Antioch,   71
Where, as thou know'st, against the face of death
I sought the purchase of a glorious beauty   73
From whence an issue I might propagate,
Are arms to princes and bring joys to subjects.   75
Her face was to mine eye beyond all wonder;
The rest—hark in thine ear—as black as incest,
Which by my knowledge found, the sinful father
Seemed not to strike, but smooth. But thou know'st
  this,   79
'Tis time to fear when tyrants seem to kiss.
Which fear so grew in me, I hither fled
Under the covering of a careful night,   82
Who seemed my good protector, and, being here,
Bethought me what was past, what might succeed.   84
I knew him tyrannous, and tyrants' fears
Decrease not, but grow faster than the years;
And should he doubt—as doubt no doubt he
  doth—   87
That I should open to the listening air   88
How many worthy princes' bloods were shed
To keep his bed of blackness unlaid ope,   90
To lop that doubt he'll fill this land with arms   91
And make pretense of wrong that I have done him;
When all for mine—if I may call 't—offense   93
Must feel war's blow, who spares not innocence;   94
Which love to all, of which thyself art one,

---

18 so great can so powerful that he can   **20 boots** avails   **22 in being known** if it were to become known   **25 ostent** display
26 Amazement (that) frenzy, consternation   **31 fence** shield, shelter
33 punish . . . he he punishes me beforehand (through fear) whom he (Antiochus)   **35 till you return to us** (Here, the lords of Tyre appear to know of Pericles' departure. In the next scene, we find that he left *unlicensed of their loves,* i.e., without their knowledge. The prose narratives that recount the same story state that his departure was accomplished secretly. This is one of the several inconsistencies of this rather garbled text.)   **37 give experience tongue** let the experienced speak   **39 blows up** that inflames, heats   **40 the which** which
41 blast i.e., flattering speech. (In Wilkins' *Painful Adventures,* this scene is more clearly presented: Helicanus upbraids Pericles for his bad humor and then justifies such plain talk as preferable to flattery.)
44 When while.   **Signor Sooth** Sir Flattery, one who flatters. (Though, puzzlingly, no one in this scene has, in fact, flattered Pericles; see the note for line 41.)   **48 else** i.e., except Helicanus.   **cares** watchfulness.   **o'erlook** supervise   **49 lading's** cargo is   **51 moved** angered

62 hear . . . hid hear words that gloss over their faults   **71 Attend** listen to   **73 purchase** acquisition   **75 Are** which are, or, such as are. (The antecedent is in the plural idea of *issue,* i.e., sons.)   **arms** weapons, defense   **79 Seemed** pretended.   **smooth** gloss over, conciliate
82 careful protecting   **84 succeed** follow   **87 he doubt** he suspect
88 open reveal   **90 unlaid ope** unrevealed   **91 lop that doubt** cut off that fear   **93 all . . . offense** all (my subjects) for my offense—if I may call it offense   **94 who** which, i.e., war

Who now reprov'st me for 't—   96
HELICANUS   Alas, sir!
PERICLES
Drew sleep out of mine eyes, blood from my cheeks,
Musings into my mind, with thousand doubts
How I might stop this tempest ere it came;
And finding little comfort to relieve them,
I thought it princely charity to grieve for them.
HELICANUS
Well, my lord, since you have given me leave to
    speak,
Freely will I speak. Antiochus you fear,
And justly too, I think, you fear the tyrant,
Who either by public war or private treason
Will take away your life.
Therefore, my lord, go travel for a while,
Till that his rage and anger be forgot,
Or till the Destinies do cut his thread of life.
Your rule direct to any; if to me,   111
Day serves not light more faithful than I'll be.
PERICLES   I do not doubt thy faith;
But should he wrong my liberties in my absence?   114
HELICANUS
We'll mingle our bloods together in the earth,   115
From whence we had our being and our birth.
PERICLES
Tyre, I now look from thee, then, and to Tarsus
Intend my travel, where I'll hear from thee,
And by whose letters I'll dispose myself.   118
The care I had and have of subjects' good
On thee I lay, whose wisdom's strength can bear it.
I'll take thy word for faith, not ask thine oath.
Who shuns not to break one will sure crack both.   123
But in our orbs we'll live so round and safe   124
That time of both this truth shall ne'er convince: 125
Thou showed'st a subject's shine, I a true prince'.   126
                                              Exeunt.

                          ❧

1.3   *Enter Thaliard solus.*

THALIARD   So, this is Tyre, and this the court. Here
    must I kill King Pericles; and if I do it not, I am sure to
    be hanged at home. 'Tis dangerous. Well, I perceive he   3
    was a wise fellow and had good discretion that, being
    bid to ask what he would of the King, desired he might
    know none of his secrets. Now do I see he had some   6
    reason for 't; for if a king bid a man be a villain, he's

bound by the indenture of his oath to be one. Husht!   8
Here comes the lords of Tyre.

            Enter Helicanus [and] Escanes, with other Lords
            [of Tyre. Thaliard stands aside.]

HELICANUS
You shall not need, my fellow peers of Tyre,
Further to question me of your king's departure.
His sealed commission left in trust with me   12
Does speak sufficiently he's gone to travel.
THALIARD [*aside*]   How? The King gone?
HELICANUS
If further yet you will be satisfied
Why, as it were, unlicensed of your loves   16
He would depart, I'll give some light unto you.
Being at Antioch—
THALIARD [*aside*]   What from Antioch?
HELICANUS
Royal Antiochus—on what cause I know not—
Took some displeasure at him, at least he judged so;
And doubting lest he had erred or sinned,   21
To show his sorrow, he'd correct himself;   22
So puts himself unto the shipman's toil,   23
With whom each minute threatens life or death.
THALIARD [*aside*]   Well, I perceive
I shall not be hanged now, although I would;   26
But since he's gone, the King's ears it must please
He scaped the land, to perish at the seas.
I'll present myself.—Peace to the lords of Tyre!
HELICANUS
Lord Thaliard from Antiochus is welcome.
THALIARD   From him I come
With message unto princely Pericles;
But since my landing I have understood
Your lord has betaken himself to unknown travels;
Now message must return from whence it came.   35
HELICANUS
We have no reason to desire it,   36
Commended to our master, not to us.   37
Yet ere you shall depart, this we desire,
As friends to Antioch, we may feast in Tyre.
                                              Exeunt.

                          ❧

1.4   *Enter Cleon, the Governor of Tarsus, with*
            [Dionyza] his wife, and others.

CLEON
My Dionyza, shall we rest us here
And, by relating tales of others' griefs,
See if 'twill teach us to forget our own?

---

96 **now** just now   111 **direct** delegate   114 **should he** what if he
(Antiochus) should.   **liberties** royal rights and prerogatives, and those
of my subjects   115 **mingle . . . earth** i.e., die fighting him   118 **Intend** direct, purpose   123 **Who** he who   124 **orbs** orbits, spheres.
round with probity (but punning on the idea of circularity in *round*. A
line appears to be lost here, rhyming with *safe*.)   125 **time . . . convince** time will never confute this truth regarding us two   126 **shine**
brightness, honor (as of true gold).   **prince'** prince's
1.3. Location: Tyre. The palace.
3–6 he . . . secrets (So the poet Philippides asked of Lysimachus;
mentioned by Plutarch and Barnabe Riche.)

8 **indenture** terms by which a servant is bound to his master
12 **sealed** bearing the royal seal   16 **unlicensed . . . loves** without
your loving assent. (Compare with the note for 1.2.35.)   21 **doubting
lest** fearing that   22 **he'd correct himself** he wished to impose a penalty on himself   23 **toil** travail, hence dangers   26 **although I would**
even if I wished to be   35 **message** my message   36 **desire it** i.e.,
wish to know the message's contents   37 **Commended** directed
as it is
1.4. Location: Tarsus. The Governor's house.

DIONYZA

That were to blow at fire in hope to quench it,
For who digs hills because they do aspire   5
Throws down one mountain to cast up a higher.
O my distressed lord, even such our griefs are;
Here they are but felt, and seen with mischief's
    eyes,   8
But like to groves, being topped, they higher rise.   9

CLEON   O Dionyza,

Who wanteth food and will not say he wants it,   11
Or can conceal his hunger till he famish?   12
Our tongues and sorrows do sound deep our woes   13
Into the air; our eyes do weep till lungs
Fetch breath that may proclaim them louder, that,   15
If heaven slumber while their creatures want,   16
They may awake their helps to comfort them.   17
I'll then discourse our woes, felt several years,
And, wanting breath to speak, help me with tears.   19

DIONYZA   I'll do my best, sir.

CLEON

This Tarsus, o'er which I have the government,   21
A city on whom Plenty held full hand,   22
For Riches strewed herself even in her streets;   23
Whose towers bore heads so high they kissed the
    clouds,
And strangers ne'er beheld but wondered at;
Whose men and dames so jetted and adorned,   26
Like one another's glass to trim them by;   27
Their tables were stored full, to glad the sight,
And not so much to feed on as delight;
All poverty was scorned, and pride so great,
The name of help grew odious to repeat.   31

DIONYZA   O, 'tis too true.

CLEON

But see what heaven can do by this our change: 33
These mouths who but of late earth, sea, and air
Were all too little to content and please,
Although they gave their creatures in abundance,
As houses are defiled for want of use,   37
They are now starved for want of exercise.
Those palates who, not yet two summers younger,
Must have inventions to delight the taste,   40

Would now be glad of bread and beg for it.
Those mothers who, to nuzzle up their babes,   42
Thought naught too curious, are ready now   43
To eat those little darlings whom they loved.
So sharp are hunger's teeth that man and wife
Draw lots who first shall die to lengthen life.   46
Here stands a lord and there a lady weeping;
Here many sink, yet those which see them fall
Have scarce strength left to give them burial.
Is not this true?

DIONYZA

Our cheeks and hollow eyes do witness it.

CLEON

O, let those cities that of Plenty's cup
And her prosperities so largely taste,
With their superfluous riots, hear these tears!   54
The misery of Tarsus may be theirs.

Enter a Lord.

LORD   Where's the Lord Governor?

CLEON   Here.

Speak out thy sorrows which thou bring'st in haste,
For comfort is too far for us to expect.

LORD

We have descried, upon our neighboring shore,
A portly sail of ships make hitherward.   61

CLEON   I thought as much.

One sorrow never comes but brings an heir
That may succeed as his inheritor,
And so in ours. Some neighboring nation,
Taking advantage of our misery,
Hath stuffed these hollow vessels with their power   67
To beat us down, the which are down already,
And make a conquest of unhappy men,
Whereas no glory's got to overcome.   70

LORD

That's the least fear, for by the semblance   71
Of their white flags displayed they bring us peace,
And come to us as favorers, not as foes.

CLEON

Thou speak'st like him 's untutored to repeat: 74
Who makes the fairest show means most deceit.   75
But bring they what they will and what they can,
What need we fear?
Our ground's the lowest, and we are halfway there.   78
Go tell their general we attend him here,
To know for what he comes and whence he comes
And what he craves.

LORD   I go, my lord.   [*Exit.*]

5 **who digs** whoever digs up, removes. **aspire** mount up 8 **Here
. . . eyes** i.e., our misfortunes seem bad enough in our present downcast state. **mischief's** calamity's 9 **topped** cut back. (If we inquire
into our present misfortunes, they will only grow worse.) 11 **wanteth**
lacks 12 **famish** starve to death 13 **sound deep** sound forth solemnly (with suggestion of plumbing unfathomable depths) 15 **them**
i.e., *woes* (line 13) 16 **their creatures** living beings, dependent on
heaven's mercy 17 **They . . . helps** i.e., mortals may awaken the assistance of the heavens 19 **wanting** i.e., when I lack. **help me** i.e.,
you help me 21 **This Tarsus** this is Tarsus 22 **on whom . . . hand**
over which Plenty poured her gifts generously 23 **Riches** (A singular
concept, probably derived from the French *richesse*, equivalent to
"plenty"; the image is that of the cornucopia being held aloft over the
city.) **her** i.e., the city's 26 **jetted** strutted. **adorned** adorned
themselves 27 **glass . . . by** mirror by which to adorn themselves,
or, to mirror each other's finery 31 **The name . . . repeat** i.e., that it
became odious even to mention the very possibility of asking for help
33 **see . . . change** see by our change in fortune what heaven can do
37 **for want** through lack 40 **Must have inventions** insisted on
novelties

42 **nuzzle up** nurture 43 **naught too curious** nothing too choice (for
their babes) 46 **lengthen life** i.e., provide food for the other to can-
nibalize 54 **superfluous riots** prodigal living. **tears** i.e., sounds of
weeping 61 **A portly . . . hitherward** a stately fleet of ships sails toward us 67 **power** force of armed men 70 **Whereas . . . overcome**
a conquest that brings no glory 71 **the least fear** i.e., something not
to be feared in the least 74 **him 's . . . repeat** one who has never
been taught to recite (the following maxim) and is therefore unaware
of its truth 75 **Who** he who 78 **Our . . . lowest** i.e., one who's already down on the ground can fall no lower. (Proverbial.)

CLEON
Welcome is peace, if he on peace consist;   83
If wars, we are unable to resist.

Enter Pericles with attendants.

PERICLES
Lord Governor, for so we hear you are,
Let not our ships and number of our men
Be like a beacon fired t' amaze your eyes.   87
We have heard your miseries as far as Tyre
And seen the desolation of your streets;
Nor come we to add sorrow to your tears,
But to relieve them of their heavy load;
And these our ships, you happily may think   92
Are like the Trojan horse was stuffed within   93
With bloody veins expecting overthrow,   94
Are stored with corn to make your needy bread   95
And give them life whom hunger starved half dead.
ALL [*kneeling*]   The gods of Greece protect you!
And we'll pray for you.
PERICLES   Arise, I pray you, rise.
We do not look for reverence but for love,
And harborage for ourself, our ships, and men.
CLEON [*rising*]
The which when any shall not gratify,   102
Or pay you with unthankfulness in thought,
Be it our wives, our children, or ourselves,
The curse of heaven and men succeed their evils!   105
Till when—the which I hope shall ne'er be seen—
Your Grace is welcome to our town and us.
PERICLES
Which welcome we'll accept, feast here awhile,
Until our stars that frown lend us a smile.   *Exeunt.*

❖

2. Chorus

Enter Gower.

GOWER
Here have you seen a mighty king
His child, iwis, to incest bring;   2
A better prince and benign lord,   3
That will prove awful both in deed and word.   4
Be quiet then, as men should be,
Till he hath passed necessity.   6
I'll show you those in trouble's reign,   7
Losing a mite, a mountain gain.
The good in conversation,   9

To whom I give my benison,   10
Is still at Tarsus, where each man
Thinks all is writ he spoken can;   12
And, to remember what he does,   13
Build his statue to make him glorious.
But tidings to the contrary   15
Are brought your eyes. What need speak I?

Dumb Show.

*Enter at one door Pericles talking with Cleon, all
the train with them. Enter at another door a
Gentleman, with a letter to Pericles; Pericles shows
the letter to Cleon; Pericles gives the Messenger a
reward, and knights him. Exit Pericles at one door,
and Cleon at another.*

Good Helicane, that stayed at home—
Not to eat honey like a drone
From others' labors, for though he strive   19
To killen bad, keep good alive,
And to fulfill his prince' desire—
Sends word of all that haps in Tyre:
How Thaliard came full bent with sin   23
And hid intent to murder him,   24
And that in Tarsus was not best
Longer for him to make his rest.
He, doing so, put forth to seas,   27
Where when men been there's seldom ease;   28
For now the wind begins to blow;
Thunder above and deeps below
Makes such unquiet that the ship
Should house him safe is wrecked and split,   32
And he, good prince, having all lost,
By waves from coast to coast is tossed.
All perishen of man, of pelf,   35
Ne aught escapend but himself;   36
Till fortune, tired with doing bad,
Threw him ashore, to give him glad.   38
And here he comes. What shall be next,
Pardon old Gower—this 'longs the text.   [*Exit.*] 40

2.1   *Enter Pericles, wet.*

PERICLES
Yet cease your ire, you angry stars of heaven!
Wind, rain, and thunder, remember earthly man   2
Is but a substance that must yield to you,
And I, as fits my nature, do obey you.

83 **on peace consist** is resolved on peace **87 amaze** terrify **92 you happily** which you perchance **93 was** which was **94 bloody veins** i.e., bloodthirsty Greek warriors. **expecting overthrow** i.e., in anticipation of the overthrow of Troy. (Or the phrase perhaps modifies *you* in line 92.) **95 corn** grain. **your needy bread** desperately needed bread, or, bread for your needy people **102 gratify** show gratitude for or toward **105 succeed** follow as a consequence of
2.0.
2 **iwis** certainly 3 **A better prince** i.e., and you have also seen a better prince, Pericles 4 **awful** deserving of awe, respect 6 **necessity** those hardships imposed by fate 7 **those** i.e., those who 9 **The good in conversation** the good man (Pericles) in matters of conduct

10 **benison** blessing 12 **writ** holy writ. **he spoken can** that he (Pericles) speaks. (A deliberately medieval expression, as also in *killen, been, perishen,* and *Ne aught escapend,* lines 20, 28, 35, and 36.) 13 **remember** commemorate 15 **to the contrary** adverse 19 **for** (Difficult to explain as the text stands; some editors emend to "forth," and others omit it.) 23 **bent with** intent upon 24 **hid** hidden 27 **so** i.e., as advised 28 **been** are 32 **Should** that should 35 **pelf** goods, property 36 **Ne aught escapend** nothing escaping 38 **glad** gladness 40 **'longs the text** belongs to the text of the play proper. (Or Gower may be saying that his speech is already long enough or too long.)
2.1. Location: Pentapolis. The seaside.
2 **remember** remember that

Alas, the seas hath cast me on the rocks,
Washed me from shore to shore, and left me breath
Nothing to think on but ensuing death.
Let it suffice the greatness of your powers
To have bereft a prince of all his fortunes,
And, having thrown him from your watery grave,
Here to have death in peace is all he'll crave.

Enter three Fishermen.

FIRST FISHERMAN What, ho, Pilch! 12
SECOND FISHERMAN Ha, come and bring away the nets! 13
FIRST FISHERMAN What, Patchbreech, I say! 14
THIRD FISHERMAN What say you, master?
FIRST FISHERMAN Look how thou stirr'st now! Come 16
away, or I'll fetch th' with a wanion. 17
THIRD FISHERMAN Faith, master, I am thinking of the
poor men that were cast away before us even now. 19
FIRST FISHERMAN Alas, poor souls, it grieved my heart
to hear what pitiful cries they made to us to help them,
when, welladay, we could scarce help ourselves. 22
THIRD FISHERMAN Nay, master, said not I as much
when I saw the porpoise how he bounced and tum- 24
bled? They say they're half fish, half flesh. A plague
on them, they ne'er come but I look to be washed. 26
Master, I marvel how the fishes live in the sea.
FIRST FISHERMAN Why, as men do aland: the great 28
ones eat up the little ones. I can compare our rich misers to nothing so fitly as to a whale: 'a plays and tum- 30
bles, driving the poor fry before him, and at last devours them all at a mouthful. Such whales have I heard 32
on o' the land, who never leave gaping till they swal- 33
lowed the whole parish, church, steeple, bells, and all.
PERICLES [*aside*] A pretty moral.
THIRD FISHERMAN But, master, if I had been the sexton,
I would have been that day in the belfry.
SECOND FISHERMAN Why, man?
THIRD FISHERMAN Because he should have swallowed
me too, and when I had been in his belly I would
have kept such a jangling of the bells that he should
never have left till he cast bells, steeple, church, and 42
parish up again. But if the good King Simonides were
of my mind—
PERICLES [*aside*] Simonides?
THIRD FISHERMAN We would purge the land of these
drones that rob the bee of her honey.
PERICLES [*aside*]
How from the finny subject of the sea 48
These fishers tell the infirmities of men,
And from their watery empire recollect 50
All that may men approve or men detect!— 51

Peace be at your labor, honest fishermen. 52
SECOND FISHERMAN "Honest," good fellow? What's that? 53
If it be a day fits you, search out of the calendar, and 54
nobody look after it. 55
PERICLES
May see the sea hath cast upon your coast— 56
SECOND FISHERMAN What a drunken knave was the
sea to cast thee in our way! 58
PERICLES
A man whom both the waters and the wind,
In that vast tennis court, hath made the ball
For them to play upon, entreats you pity him.
He asks of you that never used to beg. 62
FIRST FISHERMAN No, friend, cannot you beg? Here's
them in our country of Greece gets more with begging
than we can do with working.
SECOND FISHERMAN Canst thou catch any fishes, then?
PERICLES I never practiced it.
SECOND FISHERMAN Nay then, thou wilt starve, sure,
for here's nothing to be got nowadays unless thou
canst fish for 't. 70
PERICLES
What I have been I have forgot to know,
But what I am, want teaches me to think on:
A man thronged up with cold. My veins are chill, 73
And have no more of life than may suffice
To give my tongue that heat to ask your help—
Which if you shall refuse, when I am dead,
For that I am a man, pray you see me buried. 77
FIRST FISHERMAN Die, quotha? Now gods forbid 't, an I 78
have a gown here! Come, put it on, keep thee warm.
[*He gives a garment; Pericles puts it on.*] Now, afore me, a 80
handsome fellow! Come, thou shalt go home, and
we'll have flesh for holidays, fish for fasting days, and
moreo'er puddings and flapjacks, and thou shalt be 83
welcome.
PERICLES I thank you, sir.
SECOND FISHERMAN Hark you, my friend. You said
you could not beg?
PERICLES I did but crave. 88
SECOND FISHERMAN But crave? Then I'll turn craver
too, and so I shall scape whipping. 90
PERICLES Why, are your beggars whipped, then?
SECOND FISHERMAN O, not all, my friend, not all; for if
all your beggars were whipped, I would wish no better
office than to be beadle. But, master, I'll go draw up 94
the net. [*Exit with Third Fisherman.*]

52–55 Peace . . . after it (Most commentators think something has been lost here, perhaps a line in which Pericles bids the fishermen good day; if so, the Second Fisherman's reply could mean, "if the day fits your wretched condition, scratch it out of the calendar and let no one miss it.") 56 May you may 58 cast (punning on *vomit*, as suggested by *drunken;* see line 42) 62 used made it a practice 70 fish for 't i.e., obtain it by sly means and insinuation 73 thronged up overwhelmed 77 For that because 78 quotha says he. an if, so long as 80 afore me (A mild oath.) 83 puddings sausages 88 crave request 90 scape whipping i.e., escape the punishment for begging (as required by Elizabethan law. The Second Fisherman jokes that crave is only a polite term for *beg*.) 94 beadle parish official responsible for administering corporal punishment (who would be busy and well paid if all those who beg under the pretext of seeking favor at court were to be whipped as beggars)

12, 14 Pilch, Patchbreech (Names derived from the clothes they presumably wear; *Pilch,* "a leather garment.") 13 bring away bring here, bring along 16 Look . . . now i.e., get a move on 17 fetch th' deal you a blow. wanion vengeance 19 before us before our eyes 22 welladay alas 24 porpoise (These actions of porpoises were recognized prognostications of stormy weather.) 26 washed i.e., wetted by a storm 28 aland on the land 30 'a he 32–33 heard on heard of 42 cast vomited 48 subject i.e., residents, citizens 50 recollect gather up 51 may . . . detect may commend men or expose them

PERICLES [*aside*]
How well this honest mirth becomes their labor!   96

FIRST FISHERMAN   Hark you, sir, do you know where
ye are?

PERICLES   Not well.

FIRST FISHERMAN   Why, I'll tell you. This is called
Pentapolis, and our king the good Simonides.

PERICLES   "The good Simonides" do you call him?

FIRST FISHERMAN   Ay, sir, and he deserves so to be
called for his peaceable reign and good government.

PERICLES   He is a happy king, since he gains from his
subjects the name of "good" by his government. How
far is his court distant from this shore?

FIRST FISHERMAN   Marry, sir, half a day's journey. And   108
I'll tell you, he hath a fair daughter, and tomorrow is
her birthday; and there are princes and knights come
from all parts of the world to joust and tourney for her   111
love.

PERICLES   Were my fortunes equal to my desires, I could
wish to make one there.   114

FIRST FISHERMAN   O, sir, things must be as they may;
and what a man cannot get, he may lawfully deal for
his wife's soul.   117

*Enter the two [other] Fishermen, drawing up a
net.*

SECOND FISHERMAN   Help, master, help! Here's a fish
hangs in the net like a poor man's right in the law;
'twill hardly come out. Ha! Bots on 't, 'tis come at last,   120
and 'tis turned to a rusty armor.

[*He hauls in Pericles' armor.*]

PERICLES
An armor, friends? I pray you, let me see it.
Thanks, Fortune, yet that after all thy crosses   123
Thou givest me somewhat to repair myself;
And though it was mine own, part of my heritage,   125
Which my dead father did bequeath to me
With this strict charge, even as he left his life:
"Keep it, my Pericles; it hath been a shield
Twixt me and death," and pointed to this brace;   129
"For that it saved me, keep it. In like necessity—   130
The which the gods protect thee from!—may 't
defend thee."
It kept where I kept, I so dearly loved it,   132
Till the rough seas, that spares not any man,
Took it in rage, though calmed have given 't again.
I thank thee for 't. My shipwreck now's no ill,
Since I have here my father gave in his will.   136

FIRST FISHERMAN   What mean you, sir?

PERICLES
To beg of you, kind friends, this coat of worth,   138
For it was sometime target to a king;   139

I know it by this mark. He loved me dearly,
And for his sake I wish the having of it,
And that you'd guide me to your sovereign's court,
Where with it I may appear a gentleman.
And if that ever my low fortune's better,
I'll pay your bounties; till then rest your debtor.   145

FIRST FISHERMAN   Why, wilt thou tourney for the lady?

PERICLES
I'll show the virtue I have borne in arms.   147

FIRST FISHERMAN   Why, d' ye take it, and the gods give
thee good on 't!   [*Pericles puts it on.*]   149

SECOND FISHERMAN   Ay, but hark you, my friend, 'twas
we that made up this garment through the rough
seams of the waters. There are certain condolements,   152
certain vails. I hope, sir, if you thrive, you'll remember   153
from whence you had them.   154

PERICLES   Believe 't, I will.
By your furtherance I am clothed in steel,
And spite of all the rapture of the sea   157
This jewel holds his building on my arm.   158
Unto thy value I will mount myself   159
Upon a courser, whose delightful steps   160
Shall make the gazer joy to see him tread.
Only, my friend, I yet am unprovided
Of a pair of bases.   163

SECOND FISHERMAN   We'll sure provide. Thou shalt have
my best gown to make thee a pair; and I'll bring thee
to the court myself.

PERICLES
Then honor be but equal to my will,
This day I'll rise, or else add ill to ill.   [*Exeunt.*]

❖

2.2   *Enter [King] Simonides, with attendance, and
Thaisa, [and take their places].*

SIMONIDES
Are the knights ready to begin the triumph?   1

FIRST LORD   They are, my liege,
And stay your coming to present themselves.   3

SIMONIDES
Return them we are ready; and our daughter,   4
In honor of whose birth these triumphs are,
Sits here like Beauty's child, whom Nature gat   6
For men to see and, seeing, wonder at.   [*Exit one.*]

---

96 becomes suits   **108 Marry** (A mild oath, originally "by the Virgin
Mary.")   **111 tourney** take part in a tournament   **114 make one** be
among those   **117 his wife's soul** (A difficult line; the text may be imperfect here.)   **120 Bots on 't** i.e., plague take it. (*Bots* is a disease of
horses.)   **123 crosses** thwartings, misfortunes   **125 And though** even
though   **129 brace** mailed arm protector   **130 For that** because.
like similar   **132 kept** lodged   **136 my father** what my father
138 coat i.e., armor, coat of mail   **139 target** shield, i.e., protector

145 pay repay.   **bounties** acts of generosity.   **rest** I will remain
147 virtue bravery, knightly qualities   **149 on 't** of it, from it
152 seams (The metaphor is from tailoring, as if the furrowed waves
of the sea were seams.)   **condolements** (Probably confused with or
derived from "dole.")   **153 vails** (1) perquisites, tips (2) tailors' remnants of cloth   **154 them** i.e., the pieces of armor   **157 rapture** plundering   **158 holds his building** occupies its proper place (and will
provide a means to buy a horse)   **159 thy** i.e., the jewel's
160 courser spirited horse   **163 bases** pleated skirts attached to the
doublet and reaching from the waist to the knee, worn under the armor by a mounted knight
2.2. Location: Pentapolis. A public way leading to the lists. A pavilion by the side of it for the reception of the King, Princess, Lords,
etc.
1 triumph tournament, festive spectacle   **3 stay** await   **4 Return** reply
to   **6 gat** begot

THAISA
It pleaseth you, my royal father, to express
My commendations great, whose merit's less.
SIMONIDES
It's fit it should be so, for princes are   10
A model which heaven makes like to itself.
As jewels lose their glory if neglected,
So princes their renowns if not respected.
'Tis now your honor, daughter, to entertain   14
The labor of each knight in his device.   15
THAISA
Which, to preserve mine honor, I'll perform.

*The First Knight passes by [and his Squire presents
his shield to the Princess].*

SIMONIDES
Who is the first that doth prefer himself?   17
THAISA
A knight of Sparta, my renownèd father,
And the device he bears upon his shield
Is a black Ethiop reaching at the sun;
The word, *Lux tua vita mihi.*   21
SIMONIDES
He loves you well that holds his life of you.
                    The Second Knight [passes by].
Who is the second that presents himself?
THAISA
A prince of Macedon, my royal father,
And the device he bears upon his shield
Is an armed knight that's conquered by a lady;
The motto thus, in Spanish, *Piùe per dolcezza che per
    forza.*   *Third Knight [passes by].*   27
SIMONIDES
And what's the third?
THAISA   The third of Antioch,
And his device, a wreath of chivalry;   29
The word, *Me pompae provexit apex.*   30
                    Fourth Knight [passes by].
SIMONIDES   What is the fourth?
THAISA
A burning torch that's turnèd upside down;
The word, *Quod me alit, me extinguit.*   33
SIMONIDES
Which shows that beauty hath his power and will, 34
Which can as well inflame as it can kill.
                    Fifth Knight [passes by].
THAISA
The fifth, an hand environèd with clouds,
Holding out gold that's by the touchstone tried; 37
The motto thus, *Sic spectanda fides.*   38

*Sixth Knight, [Pericles, passes by;
he himself presents his device to Thaisa].*

SIMONIDES   And what's
The sixth and last, the which the knight himself
With such a graceful courtesy delivered?
THAISA
He seems to be a stranger; but his present is   42
A withered branch, that's only green at top;
The motto, *In hac spe vivo.*   44
SIMONIDES   A pretty moral;
From the dejected state wherein he is,
He hopes by you his fortunes yet may flourish.
FIRST LORD
He had need mean better than his outward show   48
Can any way speak in his just commend,   49
For by his rusty outside he appears
To have practiced more the whipstock than the
    lance.   51
SECOND LORD
He well may be a stranger, for he comes
To an honored triumph strangely furnished.   53
THIRD LORD
And on set purpose let his armor rust
Until this day, to scour it in the dust.   55
SIMONIDES
Opinion's but a fool, that makes us scan   56
The outward habit by the inward man.   57
But stay, the knights are coming.
We will withdraw into the gallery.   [*Exeunt.*] 59
                    *Great shouts [within], and all cry
                    "The mean knight!"*

❧

2.3   [*A banquet prepared.*] *Enter the King [Simonides,
Thaisa, Marshal, Ladies, Lords, attendants], and
Knights from tilting, [in armor].*

SIMONIDES   Knights,
To say you're welcome were superfluous.
To place upon the volume of your deeds,
As in a title page, your worth in arms
Were more than you expect or more than's fit,
Since every worth in show commends itself.   6
Prepare for mirth, for mirth becomes a feast.   7
You are princes and my guests.
THAISA [*to Pericles*]   But you my knight and guest, 9
To whom this wreath of victory I give,

---

10 princes persons, both male and female, of royal rank **14 honor**
i.e., honorable duty. **entertain** receive, review **15 device** emblem
with motto on the knights' shields **17 prefer** present **21 word**
motto. **Lux . . . mihi** your light is my life. (Latin; also at lines 30,
33, 38, 44.) **27 Piùe . . . forza** more by gentleness than by force.
(Italian, not Spanish.) **29 wreath of chivalry** twisted band joining the
crest to the knight's helmet **30 Me . . . apex** the highest summit of
honor has led me on **33 Quod . . . extinguit** who feeds my flame
puts out my light **34 his** its **37 touchstone** black quartz, used to test
gold for purity **38 Sic spectanda fides** thus is faith to be tried

42 present presented device **44 In . . . vivo** in this hope I live **48–
49 He . . . commend** he'd certainly better have some nobler meaning, more than his present wretched outward appearance can in any
way speak to commend him. **commend** commendation **51 whipstock** handle of a whip (which he would use to drive workhorses)
53 strangely (The witticism plays on *strangely,* "oddly," and *stranger,*
"a visitor from a foreign land.") **55 scour** (The joke is that he will
polish his rusty armor by falling off his horse in the dust.) **56 Opinion** judgment of a person's worth in terms of mere reputation
56–57 scan . . . man i.e., interpret the inner person by his mere exterior. (The construction is inverted and probably corrupt.) **59 s.d.
mean** humble, undistinguished in appearance
2.3. Location: Pentapolis. The palace.
6 in show by being revealed through deeds **7 becomes** suits **9 you**
you are

And crown you king of this day's happiness.
                    [*She crowns Pericles with a wreath.*]
PERICLES
'Tis more by fortune, lady, than by merit.
SIMONIDES
Call it by what you will, the day is yours,
And here, I hope, is none that envies it.
In framing an artist, art hath thus decreed: 15
To make some good but others to exceed;
And you are her labored scholar.—Come, queen o'
    the feast—   17
For, daughter, so you are—here take your place.
[*To the Marshal.*] Marshal, the rest, as they deserve
    their grace.   19
KNIGHTS
We are honored much by good Simonides.
                            [*They take their places.*]
SIMONIDES
Your presence glads our days. Honor we love,
For who hates honor hates the gods above.   22
MARSHAL [*to Pericles*]   Sir, yonder is your place.
PERICLES   Some other is more fit.
FIRST KNIGHT
Contend not, sir, for we are gentlemen
Have neither in our hearts nor outward eyes   26
Envied the great, nor shall the low despise.
PERICLES   You are right courteous knights.
SIMONIDES   Sit, sir, sit.   [*They sit.*]
[*Aside.*] By Jove, I wonder, that is king of thoughts,   30
These cates resist me, he not thought upon.   31
THAISA [*aside*]
By Juno, that is queen of marriage,
All viands that I eat do seem unsavory,
Wishing him my meat. [*To Simonides.*] Sure he's a
    gallant gentleman.
SIMONIDES [*to Thaisa*]
He's but a country gentleman.
He's done no more than other knights have done;
He's broken a staff or so. So let it pass.   37
THAISA [*aside*]
To me he seems like diamond to glass.   38
PERICLES [*aside*]
Yon king's to me like to my father's picture,
Which tells me in that glory once he was—   40
Had princes sit like stars about his throne,
And he the sun for them to reverence.
None that beheld him but, like lesser lights,
Did vail their crowns to his supremacy;   44
Where now his son's like a glowworm in the night,   45
The which hath fire in darkness, none in light.

Whereby I see that Time's the king of men;
He's both their parent and he is their grave,
And gives them what he will, not what they crave.
SIMONIDES   What, are you merry, knights?
KNIGHTS
Who can be other in this royal presence?
SIMONIDES
Here, with a cup that's stored unto the brim—
As you do love, fill to your mistress' lips—   53
We drink this health to you.   [*He drinks a toast.*]
KNIGHTS   We thank Your Grace.
SIMONIDES   Yet pause awhile.
Yon knight doth sit too melancholy,
As if the entertainment in our court
Had not a show might countervail his worth.   58
Note it not you, Thaisa?
THAISA   What is 't to me, my father?
SIMONIDES   O, attend, my daughter. Princes in this
Should live like gods above, who freely give
To everyone that come to honor them;
And princes not doing so are like to gnats,
Which make a sound but, killed, are wondered at.   65
Therefore to make his entrance more sweet,
Here, say we drink this standing-bowl of wine
    to him.   [*He drinks a toast.*] 67
THAISA
Alas, my father, it befits not me
Unto a stranger knight to be so bold.
He may my proffer take for an offense,
Since men take women's gifts for impudence.
SIMONIDES   How?
Do as I bid you, or you'll move me else.   73
THAISA [*aside*]
Now, by the gods, he could not please me better.
SIMONIDES
And furthermore tell him we desire to know of him
Of whence he is, his name and parentage.
THAISA [*going to Pericles*]
The King my father, sir, has drunk to you—
PERICLES   I thank him.
THAISA
Wishing it so much blood unto your life.   79
PERICLES
I thank both him and you, and pledge him freely.   80
THAISA
And further, he desires to know of you
Of whence you are, your name and parentage.
PERICLES
A gentleman of Tyre, my name Pericles,
My education been in arts and arms;   84
Who, looking for adventures in the world,
Was by the rough seas reft of ships and men,   86

---

15 framing making   **17 her labored scholar** the one on whom art has bestowed the most pains   **19 the rest** i.e., place the rest of the company.   **grace** favor   **22 who** he who   **26 Have** who have.   **outward eyes** i.e., eyes that see outward   **30–31 By Jove . . . upon** by Jove, who rules over human thoughts, I marvel that these delicacies do not seem appealing to me, since I would rather be thinking about him (Pericles)   **37 broken a staff** (Shattering the lance became the aim in sixteenth-century tilting matches.)   **38 to** compared with   **40 that** similar, like   **44 vail** lower, remove submissively   **45 glowworm in the night** i.e., a glowworm, best seen at night, but paled by the light of day (as the next line makes clear)

53 fill . . . lips i.e., each knight is to drink a full cup to his mistress   **58 might countervail** that could equal   **65 are wondered at** i.e., cause amazement at the loud noise such small insects could make while living   **67 standing-bowl** drinking vessel that stands on feet or on stem and base   **73 move** anger   **79 Wishing . . . life** (Wine was thought to replenish the blood.)   **80 pledge him** drink his health (in a return toast)   **84 been** has been.   **arts and arms** liberal education and military training   **86 reft** bereft

And after shipwreck driven upon this shore.
THAISA [*returning to the King*]
  He thanks Your Grace; names himself Pericles,
  A gentleman of Tyre,
  Who only by misfortune of the seas,
  Bereft of ships and men, cast on this shore.   91
SIMONIDES
  Now, by the gods, I pity his misfortune
  And will awake him from his melancholy.—
  Come, gentlemen, we sit too long on trifles
  And waste the time which looks for other revels.
  Even in your armors, as you are addressed,   96
  Will well become a soldier's dance.   97
  I will not have excuse with saying this: 98
  Loud music is too harsh for ladies' heads,   99
  Since they love men in arms as well as beds.   100
                                            They dance.
  So this was well asked, 'twas so well performed.   101
  Come, sir,   [*presenting Thaisa to Pericles*]
  Here's a lady that wants breathing too.   103
  And I have heard you knights of Tyre
  Are excellent in making ladies trip,   105
  And that their measures are as excellent.   106
PERICLES
  In those that practice them they are, my lord.
SIMONIDES
  O, that's as much as you would be denied   108
  Of your fair courtesy.   *They dance.*
                  Unclasp, unclasp!   109
  Thanks, gentlemen, to all; all have done well,
  [*To Pericles*] But you the best.—Pages and lights, to
      conduct
  These knights unto their several lodgings! [*To
      Pericles.*] Yours, sir,
  We have given order to be next our own.
PERICLES   I am at Your Grace's pleasure.
SIMONIDES
  Princes, it is too late to talk of love,
  And that's the mark I know you level at.   116
  Therefore each one betake him to his rest.
  Tomorrow all for speeding do their best.   [*Exeunt.*]   118

❧

2.4   *Enter Helicanus and Escanes.*

HELICANUS   No, Escanes, know this of me,
  Antiochus from incest lived not free;
  For which, the most high gods not minding longer   3

To withhold the vengeance that they had in store
Due to this heinous capital offense,
Even in the height and pride of all his glory,
When he was seated in a chariot of
An inestimable value, and his daughter with him,
A fire from heaven came and shriveled up
Those bodies even to loathing; for they so stunk
That all those eyes adored them ere their fall   11
Scorn now their hand should give them burial.
ESCANES
  'Twas very strange.
HELICANUS   And yet but justice, for though
  This king were great, his greatness was no guard
  To bar heaven's shaft, but sin had his reward.   15
ESCANES   'Tis very true.

        Enter two or three Lords.

FIRST LORD
  See, not a man in private conference
  Or council has respect with him but he.   18
SECOND LORD
  It shall no longer grieve without reproof.   19
THIRD LORD
  And curst be he that will not second it.
FIRST LORD
  Follow me, then.—Lord Helicane, a word.
HELICANUS
  With me? And welcome. Happy day, my lords.
FIRST LORD
  Know that our griefs are risen to the top,   23
  And now at length they overflow their banks.
HELICANUS
  Your griefs? For what? Wrong not your prince you
      love.
FIRST LORD
  Wrong not yourself, then, noble Helicane;
  But if the Prince do live, let us salute him,
  Or know what ground's made happy by his breath.   28
  If in the world he live, we'll seek him out;
  If in his grave he rest, we'll find him there,
  And be resolved he lives to govern us,   31
  Or dead, give 's cause to mourn his funeral
  And leave us to our free election.
SECOND LORD
  Whose death's indeed the strongest in our censure;   34
  And knowing this kingdom is without a head—
  Like goodly buildings left without a roof   36
  Soon fall to ruin—your noble self,
  That best know how to rule and how to reign,
  We thus submit unto, our sovereign.
ALL   Live, noble Helicane!
HELICANUS
  Try honor's cause; forbear your suffrages.   41

91 **cast** was cast   96 **addressed** accoutered   97 **Will** you will
98 **have . . . this** allow any excuses to what I say   99 **Loud music**
i.e., noise of armor (?) (The next line punningly suggests a play on
men in arms and partners in bed.)   100 s.d. **They dance** (Dancing in
armor gave courtly dancers opportunity to display strength and
swordsmanship.)   101 **So . . . asked** just as this was well worth suggesting   103 **breathing** exercise   105 **trip** dance lightly (with a suggestion of "go astray")   106 **measures** stately, formal dances (with
suggestion of "stratagems in wooing")   108–109 **that's . . . courtesy**
that's the equivalent of your denial of your accomplishment out of politeness   116 **level** aim   118 **speeding** succeeding (as wooers)
2.4. Location: Tyre. The Governor's house.
3 minding intending

11 **adored** that adored   15 **his** its   18 **respect** influence.   **he** i.e., Escanes   19 **grieve without reproof** cause grievance without (our) protest   23 **griefs** grievances (also in line 25)   28 **ground** i.e., country.
breath i.e., presence   31 **resolved** satisfied, assured   34 **Whose . . .
censure** and indeed his death is the likeliest probability in our judgment   36 **Like** as   41 **Try . . . suffrages** i.e., follow the honorable
course; refrain from choosing me in your *free election* (line 33)

If that you love Prince Pericles, forbear.   42
Take I your wish, I leap into the seas,   43
Where's hourly trouble for a minute's ease.
A twelvemonth longer let me entreat you
To forbear the absence of your king,   46
If in which time expired he not return,
I shall with agèd patience bear your yoke.
But if I cannot win you to this love,   49
Go search like nobles, like noble subjects,
And in your search spend your adventurous worth;   51
Whom if you find, and win unto return,   52
You shall like diamonds sit about his crown.

FIRST LORD
To wisdom he's a fool that will not yield;
And since Lord Helicane enjoineth us,
We with our travels will endeavor.   56

HELICANUS
Then you love us, we you, and we'll clasp hands.
When peers thus knit, a kingdom ever stands.
[Exeunt.]

❖

2.5 *Enter the King [Simonides] reading of a letter, at
one door; the Knights meet him.*

FIRST KNIGHT
Good morrow to the good Simonides.
SIMONIDES
Knights, from my daughter this I let you know,
That for this twelvemonth she'll not undertake
A married life.
Her reason to herself is only known,
Which from her by no means can I get.
SECOND KNIGHT
May we not get access to her, my lord?
SIMONIDES
Faith, by no means. She hath so strictly tied
Her to her chamber that 'tis impossible.
One twelve moons more she'll wear Diana's livery.   10
This by the eye of Cynthia hath she vowed,   11
And on her virgin honor will not break it.
THIRD KNIGHT
Loath to bid farewell, we take our leaves.
[Exeunt Knights.]
SIMONIDES So,
They are well dispatched. Now to my daughter's
   letter.
She tells me here she'll wed the stranger knight,
Or never more to view nor day nor light.   17
'Tis well, mistress. Your choice agrees with mine;
I like that well. Nay, how absolute she's in 't,   19
· Not minding whether I dislike or no!

Well, I do commend her choice
And will no longer have it be delayed.
Soft, here he comes. I must dissemble it.

Enter Pericles.

PERICLES
All fortune to the good Simonides!
SIMONIDES
To you as much! Sir, I am beholding to you   25
For your sweet music this last night. I do
Protest my ears were never better fed
With such delightful pleasing harmony.
PERICLES
It is Your Grace's pleasure to commend,
Not my desert.
SIMONIDES   Sir, you are music's master.
PERICLES
The worst of all her scholars, my good lord.
SIMONIDES Let me ask you one thing:
What do you think of my daughter, sir?
PERICLES A most virtuous princess.
SIMONIDES And she is fair too, is she not?
PERICLES
As a fair day in summer, wondrous fair.
SIMONIDES
Sir, my daughter thinks very well of you,
Ay, so well that you must be her master,
And she will be your scholar. Therefore look to it.
PERICLES
I am unworthy for her schoolmaster.
SIMONIDES
She thinks not so. Peruse this writing else.   41
[He gives a letter.]
PERICLES [aside]   What's here?
A letter, that she loves the knight of Tyre!
'Tis the King's subtlety to have my life.—   44
O, seek not to entrap me, gracious lord,
A stranger and distressèd gentleman,
That never aimed so high to love your daughter,   47
But bent all offices to honor her.   48
SIMONIDES
Thou hast bewitched my daughter, and thou art
A villain.
PERICLES By the gods, I have not!
Never did thought of mine levy offense,   52
Nor never did my actions yet commence
A deed might gain her love or your displeasure.   54
SIMONIDES
Traitor, thou liest!
PERICLES   Traitor?
SIMONIDES   Ay, traitor.
PERICLES
Even in his throat—unless it be the King—
That calls me traitor, I return the lie.
SIMONIDES [aside]
Now, by the gods, I do applaud his courage.

---

42 **If that** if   43 **Take . . . wish** if I should act on your wish   46 **forbear** put up with   49 **love** act of loyal devotion   51 **spend . . .
worth** use up your noble adventurous spirits   52 **win unto return** persuade him to return   56 **endeavor** i.e., try to find him
2.5. Location: Pentapolis. The palace.
10 **wear Diana's livery** continue to serve Diana, goddess of chastity
11 **Cynthia** the moon goddess, equated with Diana   17 **nor day nor**
either day or. (A double negative.)   19 **absolute** unconditional,
positive

25 **beholding** beholden   41 **else** i.e., if you don't believe me
44 **subtlety** trick   47 **to** as to   48 **bent all offices** devoted all my service   52 **levy** raise, collect, receive, or, perhaps, *level*, aim at (?)
54 **might** that might

PERICLES
My actions are as noble as my thoughts,
That never relished of a base descent.   60
I came unto your court for honor's cause,
And not to be a rebel to her state;   62
And he that otherwise accounts of me,
This sword shall prove he's honor's enemy.

SIMONIDES   No?
Here comes my daughter. She can witness it.

Enter Thaisa.

PERICLES
Then, as you are as virtuous as fair,
Resolve your angry father if my tongue   68
Did e'er solicit, or my hand subscribe
To any syllable that made love to you.

THAISA
Why, sir, say if you had, who takes offense
At that would make me glad?   72

SIMONIDES
Yea, mistress, are you so peremptory?   73
(*Aside.*) I am glad on 't with all my heart.—
I'll tame you; I'll bring you in subjection!
Will you, not having my consent,
Bestow your love and your affections
Upon a stranger? (*Aside.*) Who, for aught I know,
May be, nor can I think the contrary,
As great in blood as I myself.—
Therefore hear you, mistress: either frame   81
Your will to mine—and you, sir, hear you—
Either be ruled by me, or I'll make you—
Man and wife.
Nay, come, your hands and lips must seal it too.
And being joined, I'll thus your hopes destroy;
And for further grief—God give you joy!
What, are you both pleased?

THAISA   Yes, if you love me, sir.

PERICLES
Even as my life my blood that fosters it.   90

SIMONIDES   What, are you both agreed?

BOTH   Yes, if 't please Your Majesty.

SIMONIDES
It pleaseth me so well that I will see you wed,
And then, with what haste you can, get you to bed.
                                          Exeunt.

❖

3. Chorus

Enter Gower.

GOWER
Now sleep yslakèd hath the rout;   1
No din but snores the house about,
Made louder by the o'erfed breast

Of this most pompous marriage feast.   4
The cat, with eyne of burning coal,   5
Now couches 'fore the mouse's hole,
And crickets sing at the oven's mouth,
Are the blither for their drouth.   8
Hymen hath brought the bride to bed,   9
Where, by the loss of maidenhead,
A babe is molded. Be attent,   11
And time that is so briefly spent
With your fine fancies quaintly eche.   13
What's dumb in show I'll plain with speech.   14

[Dumb Show.]

*Enter Pericles and Simonides, at one door, with
attendants. A Messenger meets them, kneels, and
gives Pericles a letter. Pericles shows it Simonides;
the Lords kneel to him [Pericles]. Then enter
Thaisa with child, with Lychorida, a nurse. The
King shows her the letter; she rejoices. She and
Pericles take leave of her father, and depart [with
Lychorida and their attendants. Then exeunt
Simonides and the rest.]*

By many a dern and painful perch   15
Of Pericles the careful search,
By the four opposing coigns   17
Which the world together joins,
Is made with all due diligence
That horse and sail and high expense
Can stead the quest. At last from Tyre,   21
Fame answering the most strange inquire,   22
To th' court of King Simonides
Are letters brought, the tenor these:
Antiochus and his daughter dead,
The men of Tyrus on the head
Of Helicanus would set on
The crown of Tyre, but he will none.
The mutiny he there hastes t' appease;
Says to 'em, if King Pericles
Come not home in twice six moons,
He, obedient to their dooms,   32
Will take the crown. The sum of this,
Brought hither to Pentapolis,
Y-ravishèd the regions round,   35
And everyone with claps can sound,   36
"Our heir apparent is a king!
Who dreamt, who thought of such a thing?"
Brief, he must hence depart to Tyre.   39
His queen, with child, makes her desire—
Which who shall cross?—along to go.
Omit we all their dole and woe.   42
Lychorida, her nurse, she takes,
And so to sea. Their vessel shakes

---

60 **relished of** showed any trace of   62 **her** i.e., honor's   68 **Resolve** satisfy, explain to   72 **that** that which   73 **peremptory** willfully determined   81 **frame** accommodate, shape   90 **my life** i.e., my life loves
3.0.
1 **yslakèd . . . rout** has laid to rest the whole assembly

4 **pompous** ceremonial, splendid   5 **eyne** eyes   8 **Are . . . drouth** (and) are the happier for their dryness   9 **Hymen** god of marriage
11 **attent** attentive   13 **quaintly eche** cleverly eke out   14 **plain** make plain   15 **many . . . perch** many a dreary and laborious measure of distance, many a weary mile   17 **opposing coigns** opposite corners, compass points   21 **stead** assist   22 **Fame . . . inquire** rumor answering inquiry into the most remote areas   32 **dooms** judgments
35 **Y-ravishèd** delighted   36 **can sound** began to proclaim   39 **Brief** in short   42 **dole** sorrow (of leave-taking)

On Neptune's billow; half the flood   45
Hath their keel cut. But Fortune's mood   46
Varies again; the grizzled North   47
Disgorges such a tempest forth
That, as a duck for life that dives,
So up and down the poor ship drives.
The lady shrieks, and well-a-near   51
Does fall in travail with her fear;   52
And what ensues in this fell storm   53
Shall for itself itself perform.
I nill relate; action may   55
Conveniently the rest convey,
Which might not what by me is told.   57
In your imagination hold   58
This stage the ship, upon whose deck
The sea-tossed Pericles appears to speak.   [*Exit.*] 60

3.1 *Enter Pericles, a-shipboard.*

PERICLES
Thou god of this great vast, rebuke these surges,   1
Which wash both heaven and hell! And thou that
   hast   2
Upon the winds command, bind them in brass,
Having called them from the deep! O, still
Thy deafening, dreadful thunders; gently quench   5
Thy nimble, sulfurous flashes!—O, how, Lychorida,
How does my queen?—Thou stormest venomously;
Wilt thou spit all thyself? The seaman's whistle   8
Is as a whisper in the ears of death,   9
Unheard.—Lychorida!—Lucina, O   10
Divinest patroness and midwife gentle
To those that cry by night, convey thy deity
Aboard our dancing boat; make swift the pangs
Of my queen's travails!

Enter Lychorida [with an infant].

                    Now, Lychorida!

LYCHORIDA
Here is a thing too young for such a place,
Who, if it had conceit, would die, as I   16
Am like to do. Take in your arms this piece   17
Of your dead queen.

PERICLES   How? How, Lychorida?

LYCHORIDA
Patience, good sir. Do not assist the storm.   19
Here's all that is left living of your queen,

A little daughter. For the sake of it,
Be manly and take comfort.   [*She gives him the child.*]
PERICLES   O you gods!
Why do you make us love your goodly gifts
And snatch them straight away? We here below
Recall not what we give, and therein may   25
Use honor with you.
LYCHORIDA   Patience, good sir,   26
Even for this charge.
PERICLES   Now, mild may be thy life!   27
For a more blustrous birth had never babe.
Quiet and gentle thy conditions! For   29
Thou art the rudeliest welcome to this world   30
That ever was prince's child. Happy what follows!
Thou hast as chiding a nativity   32
As fire, air, water, earth, and heaven can make
To herald thee from the womb. Poor inch of nature!   34
Even at the first thy loss is more than can   35
Thy portage quit, with all thou canst find here.   36
Now the good gods throw their best eyes upon 't!   37

Enter two Sailors, [one the ship's Master].

MASTER What courage, sir? God save you!
PERICLES
Courage enough. I do not fear the flaw;   39
It hath done to me the worst. Yet for the love
Of this poor infant, this fresh new seafarer,
I would it would be quiet.
MASTER Slack the bowlines there!—Thou wilt not, wilt   43
   thou? Blow, and split thyself.   44
SAILOR But sea room, an the brine and cloudy billow   45
   kiss the moon, I care not.   ·
MASTER Sir, your queen must overboard. The sea
   works high, the wind is loud, and will not lie till the 48
   ship be cleared of the dead.
PERICLES That's your superstition.
MASTER Pardon us, sir. With us at sea it hath been still 51
   observed, and we are strong in custom. Therefore
   briefly yield 'er, for she must overboard straight.   53
PERICLES As you think meet. Most wretched queen!
LYCHORIDA Here she lies, sir.   55

45–46 **half . . . cut** i.e., their vessel has completed half the voyage
47 **grizzled** gray, grizzly. **North** north wind 51 **well-a-near** alas
52 **travail** labor 53 **fell** fierce 55 **nill** will not 57 **Which . . . told**
which action could not dramatize easily the story I've just told
58 **hold** suppose 60 **appears to speak** appears and speaks
3.1. Location: A ship at sea.
1 **Thou god** i.e., Neptune. **vast** expanse (of sea) 2 **thou** i.e., Aeolus, god of the winds 5 **Thy** i.e., Jupiter, god of thunder 8 **spit** i.e.,
expel violently, give violent utterance, or, perhaps, *split*, as in line 44
9–10 **Is . . . Unheard** is no more audible than a whisper in the ears
of a dead person 10 **Lucina** goddess of childbirth (as in 1.1.9)
16 **conceit** understanding (of its precarious position) 17 **like** likely
19 **assist** i.e., with your sighs and tears

25 **Recall** take back. **therein** in that respect 26 **Use . . . you** i.e.,
make use of honor in remonstrance against you gods, or, vie with you
gods in honor 27 **for this charge** for the sake of this infant, this responsibility 29 **conditions** circumstances 30 **the rudeliest welcome**
the most rudely welcomed 32 **chiding** clamorous 34 **Poor inch of
nature** (This half-line is from Wilkins' *Painful Adventures.*)
35–36 **Even . . . here** your loss at birth (of your mother) exceeds
anything that your life can offer by way of compensation. (*Portage* is
the cargo one has aboard at the start of a voyage, i.e., one's natural
endowments.) **quit** requite 37 **best eyes** most auspicious looks
39 **flaw** gust, squall 43–44 **Thou wilt . . . thyself** (Addressed to the
storm.) 45 **But sea room** so long as we have room enough to maneuver without being driven on the rocks. **an** even if. **cloudy billow** waves breaking into misty spray, high as the clouds 48 **lie** subside 51 **still** always 53 **briefly** quickly. **straight** straightway (also
in line 59) 55 **Here she lies** (Perhaps Lychorida reveals Thaisa's body
by drawing the curtains of a "discovery space" rearstage, or possibly
the sailors have brought the Queen's body onstage, but it may be that
Pericles apostrophizes her in her absence in lines 56–64. Line 55
could mean, "Here is what is left of the Queen; here is her
daughter.")

PERICLES
A terrible childbed hast thou had, my dear;
No light, no fire. Th' unfriendly elements
Forgot thee utterly, nor have I time
To give thee hallowed to thy grave, but straight
Must cast thee, scarcely coffined, in the ooze;   60
Where, for a monument upon thy bones,   61
And aye-remaining lamps, the belching whale   62
And humming water must o'erwhelm thy corpse,
Lying with simple shells. O Lychorida,
Bid Nestor bring me spices, ink and paper,
My casket and my jewels; and bid Nicander
Bring me the satin coffin. Lay the babe   67
Upon the pillow. Hie thee, whiles I say   68
A priestly farewell to her. Suddenly, woman.   69
                              [*Exit Lychorida.*]
SAILOR   Sir, we have a chest beneath the hatches,
caulked and bitumed ready.   71
PERICLES
I thank thee. Mariner, say what coast is this?
MASTER   We are near Tarsus.
PERICLES   Thither, gentle mariner,
Alter thy course for Tyre. When canst thou reach it?   75
MASTER   By break of day, if the wind cease.
PERICLES   O, make for Tarsus!
There will I visit Cleon, for the babe
Cannot hold out to Tyrus. There I'll leave it
At careful nursing. Go thy ways, good mariner.   80
I'll bring the body presently.   *Exeunt.*   81

❧

3.2   *Enter Lord Cerimon, with a Servant [and one or
more other persons who have suffered from the
storm].*

CERIMON   Philemon, ho!

Enter Philemon.

PHILEMON   Doth my lord call?
CERIMON
Get fire and meat for these poor men.   3
                              [*Exit Philemon.*]
'T has been a turbulent and stormy night.
SERVANT
I have been in many, but such a night as this
Till now I ne'er endured.
CERIMON [*to Servant*]
Your master will be dead ere you return;   7

There's nothing can be ministered to nature   8
That can recover him. [*To another.*] Give this to the
pothecary,   9
And tell me how it works.   [*Exeunt all but Cerimon.*]

Enter two Gentlemen.

FIRST GENTLEMAN   Good morrow.
SECOND GENTLEMAN   Good morrow to your lordship.
CERIMON
Gentlemen, why do you stir so early?
FIRST GENTLEMAN   Sir,
Our lodgings, standing bleak upon the sea,   15
Shook as the earth did quake;   16
The very principals did seem to rend   17
And all to topple. Pure surprise and fear   18
Made me to quit the house.
SECOND GENTLEMAN
That is the cause we trouble you so early;
'Tis not our husbandry.   21
CERIMON   O, you say well.
FIRST GENTLEMAN
But I much marvel that your lordship, having
Rich tire about you, should at these early hours   24
Shake off the golden slumber of repose.
'Tis most strange
Nature should be so conversant with pain,   27
Being thereto not compelled.
CERIMON   I hold it ever   28
Virtue and cunning were endowments greater   29
Than nobleness and riches. Careless heirs
May the two latter darken and expend,   31
But immortality attends the former,
Making a man a god. 'Tis known I ever
Have studied physic, through which secret art,   34
By turning o'er authorities, I have,   35
Together with my practice, made familiar
To me and to my aid the blest infusions   37
That dwells in vegetives, in metals, stones;   38
And can speak of the disturbances
That nature works, and of her cures; which doth
give me
A more content in course of true delight   41
Than to be thirsty after tottering honor,   42
Or tie my pleasure up in silken bags   43
To please the fool and death.   44

60 **ooze** muddy ocean bed   61 **for** in place of   62 **aye-remaining**
ever burning.   **belching** blowing, spouting   67 **coffin** coffer   68 **Hie
thee** hasten   69 **Suddenly** quickly.   **s.d. Exit Lychorida** (Evidently she
takes the babe with her.)   71 **bitumed** caulked with pitch   75 **Alter
. . . Tyre** change your course, which has been for Tyre   80 **Go thy
ways** i.e., about it   81 **presently** immediately.   **s.d. Exeunt** (If Thaisa's body was brought onstage before line 55, it must presumably be
carried off now.)
3.2. **Location: Ephesus. Cerimon's house.**
3 **meat** food   7 **Your master** i.e., one of those who have suffered in
the storm and have been brought to Cerimon for help

8 **can . . . nature** that can be administered in aid of nature   9 **recover** restore.   **pothecary** druggist   15 **bleak upon** exposed to   16 **as**
as if   17 **principals** main timbers of houses.   **rend** come apart
18 **all to topple** quite to topple, or, *to-topple*, topple completely.
Pure sheer   21 **husbandry** industrious habits, zeal for rising early
24 **tire** furnishings   27 **pain** toil   28 **hold it ever** have always believed that   29 **cunning** knowledge, skill   31 **May . . . expend** may
sully the gloss of nobility and squander riches   34 **physic** medicine
35 **turning o'er authorities** turning the pages of learned texts   37 **my
aid** i.e., the medical assistance I provide, or, perhaps, my assistant
Philemon.   **infusions** medicinal properties, substances to be administered   38 **vegetives** herbs, plants   41 **more** greater.   **course** pursuit
42 **tottering honor** wavering, unstable reputation   43 **tie . . . bags**
confine my pleasures to the hoarding of silken moneybags   44 **the
fool** anyone who is fool enough to trust in wealth.   **death** (since all
wealth ends in death)

SECOND GENTLEMAN
Your honor has through Ephesus poured forth
Your charity, and hundreds call themselves
Your creatures, who by you have been restored;   47
And not your knowledge, your personal pain, but
    even   48
Your purse, still open, hath built Lord Cerimon   49
Such strong renown as time shall never—   50

Enter two or three [Servants] with a chest.

FIRST SERVANT
So, lift there.
CERIMON   What's that?
FIRST SERVANT   Sir, even now
Did the sea toss up upon our shore this chest.
'Tis of some wreck.
CERIMON   Set 't down. Let's look upon 't.
SECOND GENTLEMAN
'Tis like a coffin, sir.
CERIMON   Whate'er it be,
'Tis wondrous heavy. Wrench it open straight.
If the sea's stomach be o'ercharged with gold,
'Tis a good constraint of fortune it belches upon us.   57
SECOND GENTLEMAN
'Tis so, my lord.
CERIMON   How close 'tis caulked and bitumed!
Did the sea cast it up?
FIRST SERVANT
I never saw so huge a billow, sir,
As tossed it upon shore.
CERIMON   Wrench it open.
Soft! It smells most sweetly in my sense.   62
SECOND GENTLEMAN   A delicate odor.
CERIMON
As ever hit my nostril. So, up with it.
                              [*They open the chest.*]
O you most potent gods! What's here? A corpse?
SECOND GENTLEMAN   Most strange!
CERIMON
Shrouded in cloth of state, balmed and entreasured   67
With full bags of spices! A passport too!   68
Apollo, perfect me in the characters!   69
                              [*He reads from a scroll.*]
    "Here I give to understand,
    If e'er this coffin drives aland,
    I, King Pericles, have lost
    This queen, worth all our mundane cost.   73
    Who finds her, give her burying;   74
    She was the daughter of a king.
    Besides this treasure for a fee,
    The gods requite his charity!"

If thou livest, Pericles, thou hast a heart
That even cracks for woe! This chanced tonight.   79
SECOND GENTLEMAN
Most likely, sir.
CERIMON   Nay, certainly tonight,
For look how fresh she looks. They were too rough   81
That threw her in the sea. Make a fire within.
Fetch hither all my boxes in my closet.
                              [*Exit a Servant.*]
Death may usurp on nature many hours,
And yet the fire of life kindle again
The o'erpressed spirits. I heard of an Egyptian
That had nine hours lain dead,
Who was by good appliance recovered.

Enter one with [boxes,] napkins, and fire.

Well said, well said! The fire and cloths.   89
The rough and woeful music that we have,   90
Cause it to sound, beseech you.
The vial once more. How thou stirr'st, thou block!   92
The music there! [*Music.*] I pray you, give her air.
Gentlemen, this queen will live. Nature awakes;
A warmth breathes out of her. She hath not been
Entranced above five hours. See how she 'gins   96
To blow into life's flower again!
FIRST GENTLEMAN   The heavens,   97
Through you, increase our wonder and sets up
Your fame forever.
CERIMON   She is alive! Behold,
Her eyelids, cases to those heavenly jewels
Which Pericles hath lost, begin to part
Their fringes of bright gold. The diamonds
Of a most praisèd water doth appear,   103
To make the world twice rich.—Live, and make
Us weep to hear your fate, fair creature,
Rare as you seem to be.   *She moves.*
THAISA   O dear Diana,
Where am I? Where's my lord? What world is this?
SECOND GENTLEMAN   Is not this strange?
FIRST GENTLEMAN   Most rare.
CERIMON   Hush, my gentle neighbors!
Lend me your hands. To the next chamber bear her.
Get linen. Now this matter must be looked to,   112
For her relapse is mortal. Come, come!   113
And Aesculapius guide us!   114
                    They carry her away. Exeunt omnes.

47 Your creatures i.e., people dependent for their very lives on your restoratives 48 not not only. pain labor 49 still always 50 s.d. two or three (One of these may well be Philemon or at least the same actor; also at line 88.) 57 constraint of act controlled by, compulsion of 62 Soft gently, wait a minute 67 cloth of state fabric fit for royalty; literally, a canopy for a chair of state. balmed anointed. entreasured laid up like valuables in a treasury 68 passport document identifying the bearer 69 Apollo god of eloquence and of medicine. perfect . . . characters enable me to read the writing 73 mundane cost worldly wealth 74 Who whoever

79 chanced tonight happened last night 81 rough i.e., hasty 89 Well said well done 90 rough discordant. (Cerimon may be apologizing for the only music he can provide at short notice.) 92 vial (The Quarto text reads Violl, appropriate perhaps to the music just ordered, but it could mean a vial of medicine.) How thou stirr'st i.e., how slow you are 96 Entranced unconscious 97 blow bloom 103 water luster and clearness. (Used about precious stones.) 112 Now right now 113 is mortal would be fatal 114 Aesculapius god of healing

3.3   *Enter Pericles at Tarsus, with Cleon and Dionyza*
        [and Lychorida with Marina in her arms].

PERICLES
  Most honored Cleon, I must needs be gone.
  My twelve months are expired, and Tyrus stands   2
  In a litigious peace. You and your lady   3
  Take from my heart all thankfulness! The gods   4
  Make up the rest upon you!   5

CLEON
  Your shakes of fortune, though they haunt you
      mortally,   6
  Yet glance full wonderingly on us.   7

DIONYZA
  O, your sweet queen! That the strict fates had
      pleased
  You had brought her hither, to have blessed mine
      eyes with her!

PERICLES
  We cannot but obey the powers above us.
  Could I rage and roar as doth the sea
  She lies in, yet the end must be as 'tis.
  My gentle babe Marina,
  Whom, for she was born at sea, I have named so, 14
  Here I charge your charity withal,   15
  Leaving her the infant of your care,
  Beseeching you to give her princely training,
  That she may be mannered as she is born.   18

CLEON   Fear not, my lord, but think
  Your Grace, that fed my country with your corn,
  For which the people's prayers still fall upon you,
  Must in your child be thought on. If neglection 22
  Should therein make me vile, the common body,   23
  By you relieved, would force me to my duty.
  But if to that my nature need a spur,
  The gods revenge it upon me and mine
  To the end of generation!

PERICLES   I believe you.   27
  Your honor and your goodness teach me to 't   28
  Without your vows. Till she be married, madam,
  By bright Diana, whom we honor, all
  Unscissored shall this hair of mine remain,
  Though I show ill in 't. So I take my leave.   32
  Good madam, make me blessèd in your care   33
  In bringing up my child.

DIONYZA   I have one myself,
  Who shall not be more dear to my respect   35

Than yours, my lord.

PERICLES   Madam, my thanks and prayers.

CLEON
  We'll bring Your Grace e'en to the edge o' the shore,
  Then give you up to the masked Neptune and   38
  The gentlest winds of heaven.

PERICLES
  I will embrace your offer.—Come, dearest
      madam.—
  O, no tears, Lychorida, no tears.
  Look to your little mistress, on whose grace   42
  You may depend hereafter.—Come, my lord.
                                    [Exeunt.]

❖

3.4   *Enter Cerimon and Thaisa.*

CERIMON
  Madam, this letter and some certain jewels
  Lay with you in your coffer, which are
  At your command. Know you the character?   3
                        [He shows her the letter.]

THAISA
  It is my lord's. That I was shipped at sea
  I well remember, even on my eaning time;   5
  But whether there delivered, by the holy gods,   6
  I cannot rightly say. But since King Pericles,
  My wedded lord, I ne'er shall see again,
  A vestal livery will I take me to,   9
  And never more have joy.

CERIMON
  Madam, if this you purpose as ye speak,
  Diana's temple is not distant far,
  Where you may abide till your date expire.   13
  Moreover, if you please, a niece of mine
  Shall there attend you.

THAISA
  My recompense is thanks, that's all;
  Yet my good will is great, though the gift small.
                                    Exeunt.

❖

4. Chorus

Enter Gower.

GOWER
  Imagine Pericles arrived at Tyre,
  Welcomed and settled to his own desire.   2
  His woeful queen we leave at Ephesus,
  Unto Diana there 's a votaress.   4
  Now to Marina bend your mind,
  Whom our fast-growing scene must find

3.3. Location: Tarsus. Cleon's (the Governor's) house.
2 twelve months (Pericles was given a year to return to Tyre; see
3.0.30–33.)   **3 litigious** disturbed by disputes (especially legal)
4 Take receive   **4–5 The gods . . . you** may the gods requite your
goodness as fully as it deserves (of which my gratitude can supply
only part).   **upon** to   **6–7 Your . . . on us** your violent shocks of
fortune, though they prey upon you with deadly intent, fill us, too,
with amazement and sorrow   **14 for** since   **15 charge** burden.
withal with   **18 mannered . . . born** taught manners and graces to
accord with her high birth   **22 neglection** neglect   **23 common body**
common people   **27 of generation** i.e., of my descendants, or, until
all procreation ceases   **28 to 't** to do so   **32 show ill** look unattractive. (The Quarto's *show will* could mean ''display willfulness.'')
33 blessèd in your care fortunate in having the care you provide
35 to my respect in my regard

38 masked i.e., deceivingly calm   **42 grace** favor
3.4. Location: Ephesus. Cerimon's house.
3 character handwriting   **5 eaning time** time of delivery   **6 whether
there delivered** whether I gave birth there   **9 A vestal livery** garments
of chastity, nun's habit   **13 date** term of life
4.0.
2 to in accordance with   **4 there 's** there as, or there (she) is

At Tarsus, and by Cleon trained
In music, letters, who hath gained
Of education all the grace,
Which makes her both the heart and place   10
Of general wonder. But, alack,   11
That monster Envy, oft the wrack   12
Of earnèd praise, Marina's life
Seeks to take off by treason's knife.   14
And in this kind hath our Cleon   15
One daughter, and a wench full grown,
Even ripe for marriage rite. This maid
Hight Philoten, and it is said   18
For certain in our story, she
Would ever with Marina be.
Be 't when she weaved the sleided silk   21
With fingers long, small, white as milk;   22
Or when she would with sharp needle wound
The cambric, which she made more sound   24
By hurting it; or when to the lute
She sung, and made the night bird mute,   26
That still records with moan; or when   27
She would with rich and constant pen   28
Vail to her mistress Dian; still   29
This Philoten contends in skill
With absolute Marina. So   31
With the dove of Paphos might the crow   32
Vie feathers white. Marina gets   33
All praises, which are paid as debts,   34
And not as given. This so darks   35
In Philoten all graceful marks
That Cleon's wife, with envy rare,   37
A present murder does prepare   38
For good Marina, that her daughter
Might stand peerless by this slaughter.   40
The sooner her vile thoughts to stead,   41
Lychorida, our nurse, is dead;
And cursèd Dionyza hath
The pregnant instrument of wrath   44
Prest for this blow. The unborn event   45
I do commend to your content;   46
Only I carry wingèd Time
Post on the lame feet of my rhyme,   48
Which never could I so convey
Unless your thoughts went on my way.
Dionyza does appear,
With Leonine, a murderer.   *Exit.*

10–11 both . . . wonder the focal point of the admiration of all
12 wrack ruin, destruction 14 treason's treachery's 15 kind manner
18 Hight is called 21 sleided divided into filaments 22 small slender 24 cambric a fine white linen 26 night bird nightingale with its sad song (*moan,* line 27) 27 still records with moan incessantly tells her story in plaintive song 28 constant fixedly loyal. pen (Used in writing hymns of praise.) 29 Vail do homage 31 absolute free from any imperfection 31–33 So . . . white with equal ill success might the crow attempt to outdo the white plumage of Venus' doves 32 Paphos city sacred to Venus 34 as debts as owed to her 35 given i.e., gratuitous gifts, compliments. darks darkens, obscures 37 rare keen 38 present immediate 40 by by means of 41 stead assist 44 pregnant willing, ready 45 Prest prepared. event outcome 46 content pleasure (in watching) 48 Post swiftly

4.1 *Enter Dionyza with Leonine.*

DIONYZA
Thy oath remember. Thou hast sworn to do 't.
'Tis but a blow, which never shall be known.
Thou canst not do a thing in the world so soon
To yield thee so much profit. Let not conscience,   4
Which is but cold, inflaming love i' thy bosom,   5
Inflame too nicely; nor let pity, which   6
Even women have cast off, melt thee, but be
A soldier to thy purpose.
LEONINE   I will do 't;
But yet she is a goodly creature.
DIONYZA
The fitter, then, the gods should have her.
Here she comes, weeping for her only nurse's
    death.   11
Thou art resolved?
LEONINE   I am resolved.

Enter Marina, with a basket of flowers.

MARINA
No, I will rob Tellus of her weed   14
To strew thy green with flowers. The yellows, blues,   15
The purple violets, and marigolds
Shall as a carpet hang upon thy grave
While summer days doth last. Ay me, poor maid,
Born in a tempest when my mother died,
This world to me is a lasting storm
Whirring me from my friends.   21
DIONYZA
How now, Marina? Why do you keep alone?   22
How chance my daughter is not with you?   23
Do not consume your blood with sorrowing;   24
Have you a nurse of me. Lord, how your favor's   25
Changed with this unprofitable woe!
Come, give me your flowers. On the sea margent   27
Walk with Leonine; the air is quick there,   28
And it pierces and sharpens the stomach.   29
Come, Leonine, take her by the arm, walk with her.
MARINA   No, I pray you,
I'll not bereave you of your servant.
DIONYZA   Come, come,
I love the King your father and yourself
With more than foreign heart. We every day   35
Expect him here. When he shall come and find
Our paragon to all reports thus blasted,   37
He will repent the breadth of his great voyage,

4.1. Location: Tarsus. An open place near the seashore.
4–6 Let not . . . nicely do not let conscience, thus far unawakened, inflame your heart with love of goodness and scruples. too nicely overscrupulously 11 only nurse's i.e., Lychorida's. (*Only* means "one and only.") 14 Tellus goddess of the earth. weed garment (here, flowers) 15 green i.e., grass-covered grave 21 Whirring whirling, blowing 22 keep remain 23 How chance how does it happen that 24 with sorrowing i.e., with sighs, thought to cost the heart its blood 25 Have . . . me i.e., take me as your nurse. favor face, appearance 27 margent margin, shore 28 quick fresh, invigorating 29 stomach appetite 35 more . . . heart i.e., as though we were related by blood 37 Our . . . blasted the person whom all regard as a paragon of beauty thus withered

Blame both my lord and me that we have taken
No care to your best courses. Go, I pray you,   40
Walk, and be cheerful once again. Reserve   41
That excellent complexion which did steal
The eyes of young and old. Care not for me;   43
I can go home alone.
MARINA   Well, I will go,
  But yet I have no desire to it.
DIONYZA
  Come, come, I know 'tis good for you.
  Walk half an hour, Leonine, at the least.
  Remember what I have said.
LEONINE   I warrant you, madam.   48
DIONYZA
  I'll leave you, my sweet lady, for a while.
  Pray walk softly; do not heat your blood.   50
  What, I must have a care of you.
MARINA   My thanks, sweet madam.   [Exit Dionyza.]
  Is this wind westerly that blows?
LEONINE   Southwest.
MARINA
  When I was born, the wind was north.
LEONINE   Was 't so?
MARINA
  My father, as Nurse says, did never fear,
  But cried "Good seamen!" to the sailors,
  Galling his kingly hands, haling ropes,   57
  And, clasping to the mast, endured a sea
  That almost burst the deck.
LEONINE   When was this?
MARINA   When I was born.
  Never was waves nor wind more violent;
  And from the ladder-tackle washes off   63
  A canvas-climber. "Ha!" says one, "wolt out?"   64
  And with a dropping industry they skip   65
  From stem to stern. The boatswain whistles, and
  The master calls and trebles their confusion.
LEONINE   Come, say your prayers.
MARINA   What mean you?
LEONINE
  If you require a little space for prayer,
  I grant it. Pray, but be not tedious, for   71
  The gods are quick of ear, and I am sworn
  To do my work with haste.
MARINA   Why will you kill me?
LEONINE   To satisfy my lady.
MARINA   Why would she have me killed?
  Now, as I can remember, by my troth,   77
  I never did her hurt in all my life.
  I never spake bad word nor did ill turn
  To any living creature. Believe me, la,

I never killed a mouse nor hurt a fly.
I trod upon a worm against my will,
But I wept for 't. How have I offended,
Wherein my death might yield her any profit,
Or my life imply her any danger?
LEONINE   My commission
  Is not to reason of the deed, but do 't.
MARINA
  You will not do 't for all the world, I hope.
  You are well favored, and your looks foreshow   89
  You have a gentle heart. I saw you lately,
  When you caught hurt in parting two that fought;   91
  Good sooth, it showed well in you. Do so now.   92
  Your lady seeks my life; come you between
  And save poor me, the weaker.
LEONINE   I am sworn,
  And will dispatch.   [He seizes her.]

        Enter Pirates.

FIRST PIRATE   Hold, villain!   [Leonine runs away.]
SECOND PIRATE   A prize, a prize!
THIRD PIRATE   Half-part, mates, half-part. Come, let's 98
  have her aboard suddenly.   99
                Exeunt [Pirates with Marina].

        Enter Leonine.

LEONINE
  These roguing thieves serve the great pirate Valdes,   100
  And they have seized Marina. Let her go.
  There's no hope she will return. I'll swear she's dead
  And thrown into the sea. But I'll see further;
  Perhaps they will but please themselves upon her,
  Not carry her aboard. If she remain,
  Whom they have ravished must by me be slain. Exit.

                ❖

4.2   Enter the three bawds [Pander, Bawd, and Bolt].

PANDER   Bolt!
BOLT   Sir?
PANDER   Search the market narrowly. Mytilene is full of 3
  gallants. We lost too much money this mart by being   4
  too wenchless.
BAWD   We were never so much out of creatures. We   6
  have but poor three, and they can do no more than
  they can do; and they with continual action are even
  as good as rotten.   9
PANDER   Therefore let's have fresh ones, whate'er we
  pay for them. If there be not a conscience to be used in 11
  every trade, we shall never prosper.

40 courses interests   41 Reserve preserve, show once more   43 Care
not for me don't concern yourself about me   48 warrant promise
50 softly gently, slowly   57 Galling chafing, blistering.   haling hauling on   63 ladder-tackle rope ladder in the ship's rigging   64 wolt
out so you want to get out. (Addressed perhaps as a cruel jest to the
canvas-climber or sailor in the rigging who is washed overboard.)
65 with . . . industry dripping wet as they labor   71 tedious long-
winded   77 as as far as

89 well favored pleasant-looking.   foreshow proclaim   91 caught
hurt received an injury   92 sooth truth   98 Half-part shares   99 suddenly immediately   100 roguing roving about like rogues
4.2. Location: Mytilene, on the island of Lesbos. A brothel.
s.d. bawds (Used for either sex to mean dealers in prostitution.)   Bolt
(The name phallically suggests a shaft, projectile, or arrow.)   3 narrowly carefully   4 this mart at the last market time   6 creatures i.e.,
prostitutes   9 rotten i.e., with venereal disease   11 If . . . used i.e.,
if one does not conscientiously offer good quality

BAWD   Thou sayst true. 'Tis not our bringing up of poor 13
bastards—as, I think, I have brought up some 14
eleven—

BOLT   Ay, to eleven, and brought them down again. 16
But shall I search the market?

BAWD   What else, man? The stuff we have, a strong 18
wind will blow it to pieces, they are so pitifully
sodden. 20

PANDER   Thou sayest true. There's two unwholesome, 21
o' conscience. The poor Transylvanian is dead that lay 22
with the little baggage. 23

BOLT   Ay, she quickly pooped him. She made him 24
roast meat for worms. But I'll go search the market.
Exit.

PANDER   Three or four thousand chequins were as 26
pretty a proportion to live quietly, and so give over. 27

BAWD   Why to give over, I pray you? Is it a shame to get 28
when we are old?

PANDER   O, our credit comes not in like the commodity, 30
nor the commodity wages not with the danger. There- 31
fore, if in our youths we could pick up some pretty
estate, 'twere not amiss to keep our door hatched. Be- 33
sides, the sore terms we stand upon with the gods will
be strong with us for giving o'er. 35

BAWD   Come, other sorts offend as well as we. 36

PANDER   As well as we? Ay, and better too; we offend
worse. Neither is our profession any trade; it's no
calling. But here comes Bolt.

Enter Bolt with the Pirates and Marina.

BOLT   Come your ways, my masters. You say she's a 40
virgin?

FIRST PIRATE   O, sir, we doubt it not.

BOLT   Master, I have gone through for this piece you 43
see. If you like her, so; if not, I have lost my earnest. 44

BAWD   Bolt, has she any qualities?

BOLT   She has a good face, speaks well, and has excel- 47
lent good clothes. There's no farther necessity of qualities can make her be refused. 48

13–14 'Tis . . . bastards i.e., raising bastard children doesn't bring us
enough wealth. (As Bolt points out, the children are raised only to be
introduced into prostitution.)   16 to eleven to the age of eleven.
brought . . . again i.e., lowered them into debauchery (with a pun
on going to bed with customers)   18 stuff goods   20 sodden boiled
(by being treated in the sweating tub for venereal disease)   21 unwholesome who are diseased   22 o' on my   23 baggage whore
24 pooped him i.e., did for him, by infecting him with venereal disease   26 chequins gold coins   27 proportion to portion or fortune on
which.   give over give up business   28 get earn money   30 credit
reputation.   comes not in like doesn't accumulate as readily as.
commodity profit   31 wages not does not keep pace   33 keep . . .
hatched keep the lower half-door (the hatch) closed, i.e., closed to
customers   35 strong strong inducement   36 sorts kinds of people.
as well as we in addition to ourselves. (But Pander, in reply, puns on
well as opposed to *worse*. Pandering is worse than other offenses because it is more carnal and because, as an occupation, it is a profession only in the sense of amorous avowals rather than of true vocation; it *trades* in flesh but is not an honest *trade*.)   40 Come your
ways come along.   my masters i.e., my good sirs, good fellows
43 gone through made a deal.   piece piece of flesh, girl   44 so well
and good.   earnest earnest money, down payment   47–48 necessity
of qualities requisite accomplishments   48 can i.e., the lack of which
can

BAWD   What's her price, Bolt?

BOLT   I cannot be bated one doit of a thousand pieces. 50

PANDER   Well, follow me, my masters; you shall have
your money presently. Wife, take her in. Instruct her 52
what she has to do, that she may not be raw in her 53
entertainment.   [*Exeunt Pander and Pirates.*] 54

BAWD   Bolt, take you the marks of her, the color of her
hair, complexion, height, her age, with warrant of her
virginity, and cry, "He that will give most shall have
her first." Such a maidenhead were no cheap thing, if
men were as they have been. Get this done as I
command you.

BOLT   Performance shall follow.   *Exit.*

MARINA
Alack that Leonine was so slack, so slow!
He should have struck, not spoke; or that these
    pirates,
Not enough barbarous, had not o'erboard
    thrown me
For to seek my mother!

BAWD   Why lament you, pretty one?

MARINA   That I am pretty.

BAWD   Come, the gods have done their part in you.

MARINA   I accuse them not.

BAWD   You are light into my hands, where you are like 70
to live. 71

MARINA   The more my fault, 72
To scape his hands where I was like to die.

BAWD   Ay, and you shall live in pleasure.

MARINA   No.

BAWD   Yes, indeed shall you, and taste gentlemen of all
fashions. You shall fare well; you shall have the dif- 77
ference of all complexions. What do you stop your ears? 78

MARINA   Are you a woman?

BAWD   What would you have me be, an I be not a 80
woman?

MARINA   An honest woman, or not a woman. 82

BAWD   Marry, whip the gosling! I think I shall have 83
something to do with you. Come, you're a young fool- 84
ish sapling and must be bowed as I would have you.

MARINA   The gods defend me!

BAWD   If it please the gods to defend you by men, then 87
men must comfort you, men must feed you, men must
stir you up. Bolt's returned.

[*Enter Bolt.*]

Now, sir, hast thou cried her through the market? 90

BOLT   I have cried her almost to the number of her 91
hairs; I have drawn her picture with my voice. 92

50 be bated get the price lowered (? Or perhaps *I* should read *It*.)
doit small coin.   of less than   52 presently immediately   53 raw inexperienced   54 entertainment reception of customers   70 are light
have chanced to light (with a pun on becoming a *light* or immoral
woman).   like likely   71 live remain   72 fault misfortune   77–
78 difference variety.   78 complexions appearances and temperaments.   What why   80 an if   82 honest chaste   83 whip the gosling
i.e., the devil take this goose of a girl   84 something to do i.e., my
hands full   87 by men by means of men   90 cried proclaimed, advertised   91–92 almost . . . hairs almost to the point of numbering
the hairs of her head

BAWD   And, I prithee, tell me how dost thou find the inclination of the people, especially of the younger sort?

BOLT   Faith, they listened to me as they would have hearkened to their father's testament. There was a 97 Spaniard's mouth watered an he went to bed to her 98 very description.

BAWD   We shall have him here tomorrow with his best ruff on. 101

BOLT   Tonight, tonight. But, mistress, do you know the French knight that cowers i' the hams? 103

BAWD   Who, Monsieur Verolles? 104

BOLT   Ay, he. He offered to cut a caper at the procla- 105 mation, but he made a groan at it, and swore he would see her tomorrow.

BAWD   Well, well, as for him, he brought his disease 108 hither; here he does but repair it. I know he will come 109 in our shadow, to scatter his crowns in the sun. 110

BOLT   Well, if we had of every nation a traveler, we should lodge them with this sign. 112

BAWD   [*to Marina*] Pray you, come hither awhile. You have fortunes coming upon you. Mark me: you must seem to do that fearfully which you commit willingly, despise profit where you have most gain. To weep 116 that you live as ye do makes pity in your lovers; sel- dom but that pity begets you a good opinion, and that opinion a mere profit. 119

MARINA   I understand you not.

BOLT   O, take her home, mistress, take her home! 121 These blushes of hers must be quenched with some present practice.

BAWD   Thou sayest true, i' faith, so they must, for your 124 bride goes to that with shame which is her way to go 125 with warrant. 126

BOLT   Faith, some do and some do not. But, mistress, if I have bargained for the joint— 128

BAWD   Thou mayst cut a morsel off the spit. 129

BOLT   I may so.

BAWD   Who should deny it?—Come, young one, I like the manner of your garments well.

BOLT   Ay, by my faith, they shall not be changed 133 yet. 134

BAWD   Bolt, spend thou that in the town. [*She gives money.*] Report what a sojourner we have; you'll lose nothing by custom. When nature framed this piece, 137 she meant thee a good turn; therefore say what a para- 138 gon she is, and thou hast the harvest out of thine own report.

BOLT   I warrant you, mistress, thunder shall not so awake the beds of eels as my giving out her beauty 142 stirs up the lewdly inclined. I'll bring home some tonight. [*Exit.*]

BAWD   Come your ways. Follow me. 145

MARINA
   If fires be hot, knives sharp, or waters deep,
   Untied I still my virgin knot will keep.
   Diana aid my purpose! 148

BAWD   What have we to do with Diana? Pray you, will you go with us? *Exeunt.*

❧

4.3   *Enter Cleon and Dionyza.*

DIONYZA
   Why, are you foolish? Can it be undone?
CLEON
   O Dionyza, such a piece of slaughter
   The sun and moon ne'er looked upon!
DIONYZA
   I think you'll turn a child again.
CLEON
   Were I chief lord of all this spacious world,
   I'd give it to undo the deed. A lady   6
   Much less in blood than virtue, yet a princess
   To equal any single crown o' th' earth
   I' the justice of compare! O villain Leonine!   9
   Whom thou hast poisoned too.
   If thou hadst drunk to him, 't had been a kindness 11
   Becoming well thy fact. What canst thou say   12
   When noble Pericles shall demand his child?
DIONYZA
   That she is dead. Nurses are not the Fates;
   To foster is not ever to preserve.   15
   She died at night; I'll say so. Who can cross it,   16

97 **testament** will   98 **an** as if   101 **ruff** (The large starched collars worn by Spanish gentlemen were a matter of jest to the English.)
103 **cowers i' the hams** i.e., crouches, showing a weakness typical of venereal disease   104 **Verolles** (From the French *vérole*, "pox," "syphilis.")   105 **offered** tried, made as if to.   **cut a caper** leap up and click his heels together   108–109 **brought . . . hither** was al- ready diseased when he came. (Syphilis was popularly known in Eng- land as "the French disease.")   109 **repair** (1) return with (2) mend, renew   110 **in our shadow** i.e., under our roof.   **crowns in the sun** i.e., gold coins, known as "crowns of the sun," with perhaps the sug- gestion of squandering gold on bright beauty. (A French crown also plays on the idea of a bald head resulting from venereal disease.)
112 **lodge . . . sign** i.e., attract them to lodge here by means of Mari- na's picture, metaphorically hung out as though it were a shop sign
116 **despise** and must seem to despise   119 **mere** utter, absolute
121 **take her home** talk plainly, i.e., be direct with her, or, take her inside   124–125 **your bride** even your ordinary bride   125 **that** i.e., first sex   126 **with warrant** with lawful sanction   128 **joint** roast of meat   129 **off the spit** while it is still roasting on the spit, be- fore it is served up to customers. (Bolt is bargaining for the right to take Marina's chastity.)

133–134 **they shall . . . yet** (Marina's clothes proclaim her to be a wellborn virgin; she does not wear a prostitute's distinctive dress.)
137 **by custom** by increasing our trade (since you'll get a commis- sion).   **piece** (1) masterpiece (2) piece of woman's flesh, as in line 43
138 **a good turn** (1) a favor (2) an occasion for sex, a *piece* in the sex- ual sense   142 **beds of eels** (Seager, *Natural History*, p. 98, quotes *Hortus Sanitatus*: the eel "is disturbed by the sound of thunder." Used here with possible bawdy connotation; eels are often associated with the penis.)   145 **Come your ways** come along   148 **Diana** goddess of chastity, as in 2.5.10
4.3. Location: Tarsus. Cleon's (the Governor's) house.
6 **lady** i.e., Marina   9 **I' . . . compare** if justly compared   11 **drunk to him** i.e., drunk his health from the poisoned cup. (If Dionyza had poisoned herself, it would have befitted her crime.)   12 **Becoming . . . fact** suitably gracing what you have done   15 **To . . . preserve** i.e., one can foster life, but one cannot preserve it forever; that is in the hands of the Fates   16 **cross** contradict

Unless you play the impious innocent   17
And, for an honest attribute, cry out,   18
"She died by foul play"?
CLEON   O, go to. Well, well,   19
Of all the faults beneath the heavens, the gods
Do like this worst.
DIONYZA   Be one of those that thinks
The petty wrens of Tarsus will fly hence
And open this to Pericles. I do shame   23
To think of what a noble strain you are,
And of how coward a spirit.
CLEON   To such proceeding
Whoever but his approbation added,   26
Though not his prime consent, he did not flow   27
From honorable courses.
DIONYZA   Be it so, then.   28
Yet none does know but you how she came dead,
Nor none can know, Leonine being gone.
She did distain my child and stood between   31
Her and her fortunes. None would look on her,
But cast their gazes on Marina's face,
Whilst ours was blurted at and held a malkin   34
Not worth the time of day. It pierced me through;
And though you call my course unnatural,   36
You not your child well loving, yet I find   37
It greets me as an enterprise of kindness   38
Performed to your sole daughter.
CLEON   Heavens forgive it!
DIONYZA   And as for Pericles,
What should he say? We wept after her hearse,
And yet we mourn. Her monument   43
Is almost finished, and her epitaphs
In glittering golden characters express
A general praise to her and care in us
At whose expense 'tis done.
CLEON   Thou art like the harpy,   47
Which, to betray, dost, with thine angel's face,
Seize with thine eagle's talons.
DIONYZA
You're like one that superstitiously   50
Do swear to th' gods that winter kills the flies.   51
But yet I know you'll do as I advise.   [Exeunt.]

♣

17 play . . . innocent impiously play the innocent. (*Impious* suggests
"undutiful to me, your wife.") 18 attribute reputation 19 go to (A
term of reproach or anger.) 23 open reveal. (In ancient times, birds
were thought to reveal murders.) 26 but merely 27 prime original,
previous 27–28 he . . . courses would be to show that such a person did not come from noble tributary streambeds, i.e., lacked noble
origins 31 distain tarnish by comparison 34 blurted at scorned (by
means of a derisive noise made with the lips). malkin slut
36–38 And though . . . kindness and though you, who do not know
how to love your daughter properly, call my course unnatural, my
deed strikes me as an enterprise of natural affection 43 yet still
47 harpy monstrous bird with the face and torso of a woman 50–
51 You're . . . flies i.e., you blame the death of flies on winter, thus
exculpating yourself before the gods, or, perhaps, you are one of
those milquetoasts who piously exclaim against death, despite its being such a natural thing. (Dionyza accuses her husband of superstitiously and hypocritically washing his hands of the dirty business by
which his own daughter has been helped; see lines 36–39.)

4.4   [*Enter Gower, before the monument of Marina at Tarsus.*]

GOWER
Thus time we waste and long leagues make short,   1
Sail seas in cockles, have and wish but for 't,   2
Making to take your imagination   3
From bourn to bourn, region to region.   4
By you being pardoned, we commit no crime
To use one language in each several clime   6
Where our scenes seem to live. I do beseech you
To learn of me, who stand i' the gaps to teach you,   8
The stages of our story. Pericles
Is now again thwarting the wayward seas,   10
Attended on by many a lord and knight,
To see his daughter, all his life's delight.
Old Helicanus goes along. Behind
Is left to govern, if you bear in mind,
Old Escanes, whom Helicanus late   15
Advanced in time to great and high estate.
Well-sailing ships and bounteous winds have
    brought
This King to Tarsus—think his pilot thought;   18
So with his steerage shall your thoughts grow on—   19
To fetch his daughter home, who first is gone.   20
Like motes and shadows see them move awhile;   21
Your ears unto your eyes I'll reconcile.   22

[*Dumb Show.*]

*Enter Pericles at one door with all his train, Cleon
and Dionyza at the other. Cleon shows Pericles the
tomb, whereat Pericles makes lamentation, puts on
sackcloth, and in a mighty passion departs.* [*Then
exeunt Cleon and Dionyza.*]

See how belief may suffer by foul show!   23
This borrowed passion stands for true-owed woe;   24
And Pericles, in sorrow all devoured,
With sighs shot through and biggest tears
    o'ershowered,
Leaves Tarsus and again embarks. He swears

4.4. Location: Tarsus.
s.d. the monument of Marina (Perhaps Gower reveals this monument
by drawing a curtain hung before the "discovery space" here, or perhaps Cleon draws back the curtain at line 22 s.d.) 1 waste i.e., pass
quickly over 2 cockles scallop shells, or, small boats. (Supernatural
creatures sometimes sail in this fashion. Gower is alluding to the
imaginary crossing of the seas between scenes of the play.) have
. . . for 't have something if we but wish it 3 Making . . . imagination causing your imagination to be taken, by means of our fiction,
or, proceeding by means of taking your imagination 4 bourn frontier
6 several clime different region 8 stand i' the gaps bridge the gaps
(of time and space between scenes) 10 thwarting crossing. wayward unruly, hostile 15 late recently 18 think . . . thought imagine that he is being piloted by our swift thoughts as we accompany
him 19 his steerage the steering of his ship. grow on proceed
20 first already 21 motes specks in a beam of light. shadows (with
a suggestion of the ever changing images created by actors) 22 s.d.
passion grief 23 suffer by foul show be abused by dissembling
24 This borrowed . . . woe i.e., this feigned lamentation of Dionyza
and Cleon is substituted for genuine and deserved woe, or, this grief
simulated by the actor of Pericles stands for genuine sorrow, as contrasted with the feigning of Dionyza and Cleon

Never to wash his face nor cut his hairs;
He puts on sackcloth, and to sea. He bears   29
A tempest, which his mortal vessel tears,   30
And yet he rides it out. Now please you wit   31
The epitaph is for Marina writ   32
By wicked Dionyza.
       [He reads the inscription on Marina's monument.]
  "The fairest, sweetest, and best lies here,
  Who withered in her spring of year.
  She was of Tyrus the King's daughter,
  On whom foul death hath made this slaughter.
Marina was she called and at her birth,
Thetis, being proud, swallowed some part o' th'
    earth.   39
Therefore the earth, fearing to be o'erflowed,
Hath Thetis' birth-child on the heavens bestowed;
Wherefore she does, and swears she'll never stint,   42
Make raging battery upon shores of flint."   43

No visor does become black villainy
So well as soft and tender flattery.
Let Pericles believe his daughter's dead
And bear his courses to be orderèd   47
By Lady Fortune, while our scene must play   48
His daughter's woe and heavy welladay   49
In her unholy service. Patience, then,   50
And think you now are all in Mytilene.   *Exit.*

4.5 *Enter [from the brothel] two Gentlemen.*

FIRST GENTLEMAN Did you ever hear the like?
SECOND GENTLEMAN No, nor never shall do in such a
place as this, she being once gone.
FIRST GENTLEMAN But to have divinity preached there!
Did you ever dream of such a thing?
SECOND GENTLEMAN No, no. Come, I am for no more
bawdy houses. Shall 's go hear the vestals sing?   7
FIRST GENTLEMAN I'll do anything now that is virtuous,
but I am out of the road of rutting forever.   *Exeunt.* 9

4.6 *Enter three bawds [Pander, Bawd, and Bolt].*

PANDER Well, I had rather than twice the worth of her
she had ne'er come here.

BAWD Fie, fie upon her! She's able to freeze the god
Priapus and undo a whole generation. We must ei-   4
ther get her ravished or be rid of her. When she
should do for clients her fitment and do me the kind-   6
ness of our profession, she has me her quirks, her reasons, her master reasons, her prayers, her knees, that
she would make a puritan of the devil if he should
cheapen a kiss of her.   10
BOLT Faith, I must ravish her, or she'll disfurnish us   11
of all our cavalleria and make our swearers priests.   12
PANDER Now, the pox upon her greensickness for me!   13
BAWD Faith, there's no way to be rid on 't but by the   14
way to the pox. Here comes the Lord Lysimachus dis-   15
guised.
BOLT We should have both lord and loon, if the pee-   17
vish baggage would but give way to customers.   18

    Enter Lysimachus.

LYSIMACHUS How now? How a dozen of virginities?   19
BAWD Now, the gods to-bless your honor!   20
BOLT I am glad to see your honor in good health.
LYSIMACHUS You may so; 'tis the better for you that
your resorters stand upon sound legs. How now?   23
Wholesome iniquity have you, that a man may deal   24
withal and defy the surgeon?   25
BAWD We have here one, sir, if she would—but there
never came her like in Mytilene.
LYSIMACHUS If she'd do the deeds of darkness, thou
wouldst say.
BAWD Your honor knows what 'tis to say well enough.   30
LYSIMACHUS Well, call forth, call forth. *[Exit Pander.]*
BOLT For flesh and blood, sir, white and red, you shall
see a rose; and she were a rose indeed, if she had
but—   34
LYSIMACHUS What, prithee?
BOLT O, sir, I can be modest.
LYSIMACHUS That dignifies the renown of a bawd no   37
less than it gives a good report to a number to be   38
chaste.   39

    [Enter Pander with Marina.]

BAWD Here comes that which grows to the stalk;
never plucked yet, I can assure you. Is she not a fair
creature?

---

29 He bears i.e., he bears within him **30 his mortal vessel tears** afflicts with anguish his human body, racks his frame **31 wit** know
32 is that is **39 Thetis** a sea nymph, often confused (as here) with
Tethys, a Titaness and consort of Oceanus. **swallowed . . . earth**
(The fanciful image is that of the oceans rejoicing over Marina's birth
at sea with such destructive flood tides that the earth resolves to be
rid of Marina by sending her to heaven; it is in angry reprisal that the
sea continues to beat against the shore.) **42 she** i.e., Thetis. **stint**
cease **43 Make . . . flint** continuously beats upon rocky shores
47–48 bear . . . Fortune direct his passage as Fortune orders
49 welladay wellaway, lamentation **50 In her unholy service** i.e., in
the brothel
4.5. Location: Mytilene. The brothel.
7 Shall 's shall we. **vestals** virgins consecrated to tend the sacred altar **9 rutting** sexual indulgence
4.6. Location: The brothel, as before.

4 Priapus god of fertility and lechery. **undo . . . generation** (1) prevent the engendering of the next generation (2) prevent the pleasures
of the present generation **6 fitment** sexual duty. **do me** do. (Me is
an emphatic marker; see also has me in the next line.) **10 cheapen**
bargain for **11 disfurnish** deprive **12 cavalleria** cavaliers. **our
swearers** our sworn (i.e., faithful) customers, or, our profane customers (?) **13 greensickness** i.e., moody obstinacy or squeamishness,
like that caused by anemia in young women. **for me** as far as I'm
concerned **14 on 't** of it, of this difficulty **15 pox** syphilis. (In line
13, *pox* is used in an oath, i.e., "the plague upon her.") **17 loon**
low fellow, person of low birth **17–18 peevish** perverse, stubborn
19 How a what price for **20 to-bless** bless completely **23 your resorters** those who resort to your place, customers **24 Wholesome iniquity** healthy prostitutes **25 withal** with. **surgeon** barber-surgeon
(to treat syphilis) **30 what 'tis to say** what I'm trying to say **34 but**
(To catch the sexual innuendo of this remark, compare the completed
phrase, "No roses without prickles.") **37–39 That . . . chaste** i.e.,
modesty in speech gives good reputation to a bawd, as well as attest-
ing to the chastity of many women who deserve no such reputation

LYSIMACHUS   Faith, she would serve after a long voyage 43
at sea. Well, there's for you. [*He gives money.*] Leave us. 44

BAWD   I beseech your honor, give me leave a word, and 45
I'll have done presently. 46

LYSIMACHUS   I beseech you, do.

BAWD [*aside to Marina*]   First, I would have you note 48
this is an honorable man.

MARINA   I desire to find him so, that I may worthily
note him. 51

BAWD   Next, he's the Governor of this country, and a
man whom I am bound to. 53

MARINA   If he govern the country, you are bound to 54
him indeed, but how honorable he is in that, I know
not.

BAWD   Pray you, without any more virginal fencing,
will you use him kindly? He will line your apron with
gold.

MARINA   What he will do graciously, I will thankfully
receive.

LYSIMACHUS   Ha' you done?

BAWD   My lord, she's not paced yet. You must take 63
some pains to work her to your manage.—Come, we 64
will leave his honor and her together. Go thy ways.

[*Exeunt Bawd, Pander, and Bolt.*]

LYSIMACHUS   Now, pretty one, how long have you
been at this trade?

MARINA   What trade, sir?

LYSIMACHUS   Why, I cannot name 't but I shall offend. 69

MARINA   I cannot be offended with my trade. Please
you to name it.

LYSIMACHUS   How long have you been of this profession?

MARINA   E'er since I can remember.

LYSIMACHUS   Did you go to 't so young? Were you a 75
gamester at five, or at seven? 76

MARINA   Earlier too, sir, if now I be one.

LYSIMACHUS   Why, the house you dwell in proclaims
you to be a creature of sale.

MARINA   Do you know this house to be a place of such 80
resort, and will come into 't? I hear say you're of hon- 81
orable parts and are the Governor of this place. 82

LYSIMACHUS   Why, hath your principal made known
unto you who I am?

MARINA   Who is my principal?

LYSIMACHUS   Why, your herbwoman, she that sets
seeds and roots of shame and iniquity. O, you have
heard something of my power, and so stand aloof for
more serious wooing. But I protest to thee, pretty one,
my authority shall not see thee, or else look friendly 90
upon thee. Come, bring me to some private place.
Come, come.

43–44 she . . . sea i.e., she is just the thing for a man who is sexually ravenous   45 a word i.e., to say a few words in private to her   46 have done presently be done in a moment   48, 51 note (1) observe (2) set down as having a certain character, in this case a good character   53, 54 bound (1) obligated (2) subject   63, 64 paced, manage (Terms used in training horses.)   69 but . . . offend without offending   75 go to 't i.e., practice sexual acts   76 gamester wanton woman   80–81 of such resort to be visited for such a purpose   82 parts qualities   90 my authority . . . thee i.e., I'll wink at your offenses, not enforce the laws against prostitutes

MARINA
If you were born to honor, show it now;
If put upon you, make the judgment good 94
That thought you worthy of it.

LYSIMACHUS
How's this? How's this? Some more. Be sage.

MARINA   For me,
That am a maid, though most ungentle fortune
Have placed me in this sty, where, since I came,
Diseases have been sold dearer than physic— 99
That the gods
Would set me free from this unhallowed place,
Though they did change me to the meanest bird 102
That flies i' the purer air!

LYSIMACHUS   I did not think
Thou couldst have spoke so well, ne'er dreamt thou
couldst.
Had I brought hither a corrupted mind,
Thy speech had altered it. Hold, here's gold for thee. 106
Persevere in that clear way thou goest, 107
And the gods strengthen thee!   [*He gives gold.*]

MARINA   The good gods preserve you!

LYSIMACHUS   For me, be you thoughten 110
That I came with no ill intent, for to me
The very doors and windows savor vilely.
Fare thee well. Thou art a piece of virtue, and
I doubt not but thy training hath been noble.
Hold, here's more gold for thee.   [*He gives gold.*]
A curse upon him, die he like a thief,
That robs thee of thy goodness! If thou dost
Hear from me, it shall be for thy good.

[*Enter Bolt.*]

BOLT   I beseech your honor, one piece for me.

LYSIMACHUS   Avaunt, thou damnèd doorkeeper!
Your house, but for this virgin that doth prop it,
Would sink and overwhelm you. Away!   [*Exit.*]

BOLT   How's this? We must take another course with
you. If your peevish chastity, which is not worth a
breakfast in the cheapest country under the cope, shall 125
undo a whole household, let me be gelded like a spaniel. Come your ways.

MARINA   Whither would you have me?

BOLT   I must have your maidenhead taken off, or the
common hangman shall execute it. Come your ways.
We'll have no more gentlemen driven away. Come
your ways, I say.

Enter Bawd [and Pander].

BAWD   How now, what's the matter?

BOLT   Worse and worse, mistress. She has here spoken
holy words to the Lord Lysimachus.

BAWD   O, abominable!

BOLT   She makes our profession as it were to stink afore
the face of the gods.

94 If put upon you i.e., if your high position was conferred after birth, not through inheritance   99 physic medicine   102 meanest lowest   106 had would have   107 clear virtuous   110 be you thoughten assure yourself   125 cope firmament

BAWD   Marry, hang her up forever!

BOLT   The nobleman would have dealt with her like a   140
nobleman, and she sent him away as cold as a snow-   141
ball, saying his prayers too.

BAWD   Bolt, take her away. Use her at thy pleasure.
Crack the glass of her virginity and make the rest
malleable.

BOLT   An if she were a thornier piece of ground than   146
she is, she shall be plowed.

MARINA   Hark, hark, you gods!

BAWD   She conjures. Away with her! Would she had
never come within my doors!—Marry, hang you!—
She's born to undo us.—Will you not go the way of
women-kind? Marry, come up, my dish of chastity   152
with rosemary and bays!   [Exeunt Bawd and Pander.]   153

BOLT   Come, mistress, come your ways with me.

MARINA   Whither wilt thou have me?

BOLT   To take from you the jewel you hold so dear.

MARINA   Prithee, tell me one thing first.

BOLT   Come now, your one thing.   158

MARINA
What canst thou wish thine enemy to be?   159

BOLT   Why, I could wish him to be my master, or   160
rather, my mistress.   161

MARINA
Neither of these are so bad as thou art,
Since they do better thee in their command.   163
Thou hold'st a place for which the pained'st fiend   164
Of hell would not in reputation change.
Thou art the damnèd doorkeeper to every
Coistrel that comes inquiring for his Tib.   167
To the choleric fisting of every rogue   168
Thy ear is liable; thy food is such
As hath been belched on by infected lungs.

BOLT   What would you have me do? Go to the wars,
would you, where a man may serve seven years for   172
the loss of a leg and have not money enough in the
end to buy him a wooden one?

MARINA
Do anything but this thou doest. Empty
Old receptacles, or common shores, of filth;   176
Serve by indenture to the common hangman.   177
Any of these ways are yet better than this;
For what thou professest, a baboon, could he speak,   179
Would own a name too dear. That the gods   180

Would safely deliver me from this place!
Here, here's gold for thee.   [She gives gold.]
If that thy master would gain by me,
Proclaim that I can sing, weave, sew, and dance,
With other virtues, which I'll keep from boast,   185
And will undertake all these to teach.
I doubt not but this populous city will
Yield many scholars.   188

BOLT   But can you teach all this you speak of?

MARINA
Prove that I cannot, take me home again   190
And prostitute me to the basest groom   191
That doth frequent your house.

BOLT   Well, I will see what I can do for thee. If I can
place thee, I will.

MARINA   But amongst honest women.

BOLT   Faith, my acquaintance lies little amongst them.
But since my master and mistress hath bought you,
there's no going but by their consent. Therefore I will
make them acquainted with your purpose, and I
doubt not but I shall find them tractable enough.
Come, I'll do for thee what I can. Come your ways.
                                                    Exeunt.

❧

5. Chorus

Enter Gower.

GOWER
Marina thus the brothel scapes and chances
    Into an honest house, our story says.
She sings like one immortal, and she dances
    As goddesslike to her admirèd lays.   4
Deep clerks she dumbs, and with her neele
    composes   5
    Nature's own shape, of bud, bird, branch, or
    berry,
That even her art sisters the natural roses;   7
    Her inkle, silk, twin with the rubied cherry,   8
That pupils lacks she none of noble race,
    Who pour their bounty on her, and her gain
She gives the cursèd bawd. Here we her place,
    And to her father turn our thoughts again,
Where we left him, on the sea. We there him lost,
    Where, driven before the winds, he is arrived
Here where his daughter dwells; and on this coast
    Suppose him now at anchor. The city strived   16
God Neptune's annual feast to keep, from whence
    Lysimachus our Tyrian ship espies,
His banners sable, trimmed with rich expense,   19
    And to him in his barge with fervor hies.   20

140–141 like a nobleman i.e., as a nobleman would have done, using her and rewarding her   146 An if even if   152 Marry, come up
i.e., hoity-toity   153 rosemary and bays (Customary garnishes for certain foods; the Bawd means that Marina's chastity is beyond the ordinary; she is a fancy dish.)   158 thing (Bolt plays on Marina's *one
thing* [line 157] in a lewd sense, referring to her sexual anatomy.)
159 What . . . to be i.e., what is the worst possible evil you could
wish upon your enemy?   160–161 my master . . . mistress i.e., like
my master in wickedness, or, even more, like my mistress   163 do
. . . command i.e., have the advantage of being in command over
you. (A servant who does the actual dirty work is especially damnable.)   164 pained'st most tormented   167 Coistrel knave.   Tib common woman   168 choleric fisting angry blows   172 would you
would you have me.   for i.e., to end up with   176 shores sewers,
or, garbage dumps at the water's edge   177 by indenture i.e., as an
apprentice   179 what thou professest your profession   180 own . . .
dear consider himself and his reputation too good for that

185 virtues accomplishments   188 scholars pupils   190 Prove if you
find   191 groom menial
5.0.
4 lays songs   5 Deep . . . dumbs she silences profound scholars.
neele needle   7 That . . . art so that even her skill, let alone herself,
sisters equals in appearance   8 inkle linen thread or yarn.   twin with
resemble closely   16 strived outdid itself   19, 20 His, him its, it
19 sable black

In your supposing once more put your sight; 21
   Of heavy Pericles think this his bark, 22
Where what is done in action, more, if might, 23
   Shall be discovered. Please you, sit and hark. *Exit.* 24

5.1   *Enter Helicanus. To him two Sailors, [one
belonging to the Tyrian vessel, the other to a barge
of Mytilene that is evidently alongside, out of
view].*

TYRIAN SAILOR [*to the Sailor of Mytilene*]
  Where is Lord Helicanus? He can resolve you. 1
  O, here he is.
  Sir, there is a barge put off from Mytilene,
  And in it is Lysimachus the Governor,
  Who craves to come aboard. What is your will?
HELICANUS
  That he have his. Call up some gentlemen.
TYRIAN SAILOR   Ho, gentlemen! My lord calls.

Enter two or three Gentlemen.

FIRST GENTLEMAN   Doth your lordship call?
HELICANUS   Gentlemen,
  There is some of worth would come aboard. 10
  I pray, greet him fairly. 11
           *[The Gentlemen and the two Sailors
              go to greet Lysimachus.]*

Enter [as from the barge] Lysimachus, [escorted].

TYRIAN SAILOR [*to Lysimachus*]   Sir,
  This is the man that can, in aught you would, 13
  Resolve you.
LYSIMACHUS
  Hail, reverend sir! The gods preserve you!
HELICANUS   And you, to outlive the age I am,
  And die as I would do.
LYSIMACHUS   You wish me well. 17
  Being on shore, honoring of Neptune's triumphs, 18
  Seeing this goodly vessel ride before us,
  I made to it, to know of whence you are.
HELICANUS   First, what is your place? 21
LYSIMACHUS
  I am the Governor of this place you lie before. 22
HELICANUS   Sir,
  Our vessel is of Tyre, in it the King,
  A man who for this three months hath not spoken
  To anyone, nor taken sustenance
  But to prorogue his grief. 27

LYSIMACHUS
  Upon what ground is his distemperature? 28
HELICANUS
  'Twould be too tedious to repeat,
  But the main grief springs from the loss
  Of a belovèd daughter and a wife.
LYSIMACHUS   May we not see him?
HELICANUS   You may,
  But bootless is your sight. He will not speak 34
  To any.
LYSIMACHUS   Yet let me obtain my wish.
HELICANUS
  Behold him. [*Pericles is discovered to view, in rough
    clothing and with long hair and beard.*] This was
    a goodly person,
  Till the disaster that, one mortal night, 38
  Drove him to this.
LYSIMACHUS
  Sir King, all hail! The gods preserve you!
  Hail, royal sir!
HELICANUS
  It is in vain. He will not speak to you.
FIRST LORD   Sir,
  We have a maid in Mytilene, I durst wager,
  Would win some words of him.
LYSIMACHUS   'Tis well bethought.
  She questionless, with her sweet harmony
  And other chosen attractions, would allure, 47
  And make a battery through his deafened ports, 48
  Which now are midway stopped. 49
  She is all happy as the fairest of all 50
  And, with her fellow maids, is now upon
  The leafy shelter that abuts against
  The island's side.   [*He signals to the Lord, who goes
                  off to bring Marina.*]
HELICANUS
  Sure, all effectless; yet nothing we'll omit 54
  That bears recovery's name. But since your kindness 55
  We have stretched thus far, let us beseech you
  That for our gold we may provision have,
  Wherein we are not destitute for want,
  But weary for the staleness.
LYSIMACHUS   O, sir, a courtesy 59
  Which if we should deny, the most just gods
  For every graft would send a caterpillar, 61
  And so inflict our province. Yet once more 62
  Let me entreat to know at large the cause 63
  Of your king's sorrow.
HELICANUS
  Sit, sir, I will recount it to you.—
  But, see, I am prevented. 66

---

21 In . . . sight visualize again in your imagination **22 heavy** sorrowful **23 action** stage action. **more, if might** i.e., and we would show more if it were possible **24 discovered** revealed, shown
5.1. Location: On board Pericles' ship, off Mytilene. A pavilion for Pericles is provided onstage, with a curtain before it, perhaps by means of a "discovery space"; Pericles, reclining within, is "discovered" at line 37 by the drawing back of the curtain.
1 resolve answer, satisfy **10 some of worth** some nobleman (who) **11 fairly** courteously **13 in aught you would** in whatever you wish to know **17 as I would do** i.e., at the end of a long and honorable life **18 honoring . . . triumphs** celebrating a festival in honor of Neptune **21 place** office **22 lie** lie at anchor **27 prorogue** prolong

28 Upon . . . distemperature what is the cause of his disturbance of mind? **34 bootless** fruitless **38 mortal** fatal **47 chosen** choice **48 make . . . ports** i.e., force an entrance through his deafened sense of hearing **49 midway stopped** shut so that communications get only halfway through **50 all happy** completely fortunate (in having such beauty) **54 effectless** useless **55 bears recovery's name** deserves the name of cure **59 for** because of **61 graft** scion, shoot, grafted plant **62 inflict** afflict **63 at large** in detail **66 prevented** forestalled

[*Enter, as though from the barge, Lord, with Marina, and a young lady.*]

LYSIMACHUS
O, here's the lady that I sent for.—
Welcome, fair one!—Is 't not a goodly presence?   68
HELICANUS   She's a gallant lady.   69
LYSIMACHUS
She's such a one that, were I well assured
Came of a gentle kind and noble stock,   71
I'd wish no better choice, and think me rarely
      wed.—   72
Fair one, all goodness that consists in bounty   73
Expect even here, where is a kingly patient;
If that thy prosperous and artificial feat   75
Can draw him but to answer thee in aught,
Thy sacred physic shall receive such pay   77
As thy desires can wish.
MARINA   Sir, I will use
My utmost skill in his recovery, provided
That none but I and my companion maid
Be suffered to come near him.
LYSIMACHUS   Come, let us leave her; 81
And the gods make her prosperous!   82
      [*They stand aside.*] *The song* [*by Marina*].
LYSIMACHUS [*advancing*]
Marked he your music?
MARINA   No, nor looked on us.
LYSIMACHUS [*to Helicanus*]   See, she will speak to him.
MARINA [*to Pericles*]   Hail, sir! My lord, lend ear.
PERICLES   Hum, ha!   [*He pushes her away.*]
MARINA
I am a maid, my lord, that ne'er before
Invited eyes, but have been gazèd on   88
Like a comet. She speaks,   89
My lord, that maybe hath endured a grief
Might equal yours, if both were justly weighed.
Though wayward fortune did malign my state,   92
My derivation was from ancestors
Who stood equivalent with mighty kings;
But time hath rooted out my parentage,
And to the world and awkward casualties   96
Bound me in servitude. [*Aside.*] I will desist;
But there is something glows upon my cheek,
And whispers in mine ear, "Go not till he speak."
PERICLES
My fortunes—parentage—good parentage—
To equal mine!—Was it not thus? What say you?
MARINA
I said, my lord, if you did know my parentage,
You would not do me violence.

PERICLES
I do think so. Pray you, turn your eyes upon me.   104
You're like something that—What countrywoman?
Here of these shores?
MARINA   No, nor of any shores.
Yet I was mortally brought forth, and am   107
No other than I appear.
PERICLES
I am great with woe and shall deliver weeping.   109
My dearest wife was like this maid, and such a one
My daughter might have been. My queen's square
      brows;
Her stature to an inch; as wandlike straight;
As silver-voiced; her eyes as jewel-like
And cased as richly; in pace another Juno;   114
Who starves the ears she feeds, and makes them
      hungry
The more she gives them speech.—Where do you
      live?
MARINA
Where I am but a stranger. From the deck
You may discern the place.
PERICLES
Where were you bred? And how achieved you these
Endowments which you make more rich to owe?   120
MARINA
If I should tell my history, it would seem
Like lies disdained in the reporting.
PERICLES   Prithee, speak.   122
Falseness cannot come from thee, for thou lookest
Modest as Justice, and thou seemest a palace
For the crowned Truth to dwell in. I will believe thee
And make my senses credit thy relation   126
To points that seem impossible, for thou lookest
Like one I loved indeed. What were thy friends?   128
Didst thou not say, when I did push thee back—
Which was when I perceived thee—that thou cam'st
From good descending?
MARINA   So indeed I did.   131
PERICLES
Report thy parentage. I think thou saidst
Thou hadst been tossed from wrong to injury,
And that thou thought'st thy griefs might equal
      mine,
If both were opened.
MARINA   Some such thing   135
I said, and said no more but what my thoughts
Did warrant me was likely.
PERICLES   Tell thy story.
If thine, considered, prove the thousand part   138
Of my endurance, thou art a man, and I   139
Have suffered like a girl. Yet thou dost look

68 Is 't . . . presence? is not her demeanor good?   69 gallant splendid (said of either sex)   71 gentle kind noble kindred   72 rarely excellently   73 all . . . bounty (In the Quarto, which reads *beauty* for *bounty,* this phrase could mean: You, Marina, possessed of all good that beauty can contain.)   75 prosperous producing favorable results. artificial skillful   77 physic medicine   81 suffered permitted   82 s.d. The song (Not given in the Quarto.)   88 Invited eyes asked to be looked at   88–89 gazèd . . . comet i.e., stared at in astonishment   92 wayward contrary.   did . . . state has dealt malignantly with my condition   96 awkward casualties adverse misfortunes

104 I do think so I agree   107 mortally humanly   109 great (1) pregnant (2) heavy.   deliver (1) give birth (2) speak   114 cased enclosed, framed.   pace gait, carriage   120 to owe by possessing   122 in the reporting even as I spoke them   126 credit believe.   relation account   128 friends relatives   131 descending descent   135 opened revealed   138 thousand thousandth   139 my endurance what I have endured

Like Patience gazing on kings' graves and smiling 141
Extremity out of act. What were thy friends? 142
How lost thou them? Thy name, my most kind
    virgin?
Recount, I do beseech thee. Come, sit by me.
MARINA [*sitting*]   My name is Marina.
PERICLES   O, I am mocked,
And thou by some incensèd god sent hither 147
To make the world to laugh at me.
MARINA   Patience, good sir, or here I'll cease.
PERICLES
Nay, I'll be patient. Thou little know'st how thou
Dost startle me to call thyself Marina.
MARINA   The name
Was given me by one that had some power:
My father, and a king.
PERICLES   How, a king's daughter?
And called Marina?
MARINA   You said you would believe me;
But, not to be a troubler of your peace,
I will end here.
PERICLES   But are you flesh and blood?
Have you a working pulse, and are no fairy? 158
Motion? Well, speak on. Where were you born? 159
And wherefore called Marina?
MARINA   Called Marina
For I was born at sea.
PERICLES   At sea! What mother? 161
MARINA
My mother was the daughter of a king,
Who died the minute I was born,
As my good nurse Lychorida hath oft
Delivered weeping.
PERICLES   O, stop there a little! 165
This is the rarest dream that e'er dull sleep
Did mock sad fools withal. This cannot be 167
My daughter—buried!—Well, where were you
    bred?
I'll hear you more, to th' bottom of your story,
And never interrupt you.
MARINA
You scorn. Believe me, 'twere best I did give o'er. 171
PERICLES
I will believe you by the syllable 172
Of what you shall deliver. Yet give me leave:
How came you in these parts? Where were you
    bred?
MARINA
The King my father did in Tarsus leave me,
Till cruel Cleon, with his wicked wife,
Did seek to murder me; and having wooed
A villain to attempt it, who having drawn to 't, 178
A crew of pirates came and rescued me,

Brought me to Mytilene. But, good sir,
Whither will you have me? Why do you weep? It
    may be 181
You think me an impostor. No, good faith,
I am the daughter to King Pericles,
If good King Pericles be. 184
PERICLES   Ho, Helicanus!
HELICANUS   Calls my lord?
PERICLES
Thou art a grave and noble counselor,
Most wise in general. Tell me, if thou canst,
What this maid is, or what is like to be, 189
That thus hath made me weep?
HELICANUS   I know not,
But here's the regent, sir, of Mytilene
Speaks nobly of her.
LYSIMACHUS   She never would tell 192
Her parentage; being demanded that,
She would sit still and weep.
PERICLES
O Helicanus, strike me, honored sir,
Give me a gash, put me to present pain, 196
Lest this great sea of joys rushing upon me
O'erbear the shores of my mortality, 198
And drown me with their sweetness.—O, come
    hither,
Thou that begett'st him that did thee beget, 200
Thou that wast born at sea, buried at Tarsus,
And found at sea again!—O Helicanus,
Down on thy knees! Thank the holy gods as loud 203
As thunder threatens us. This is Marina.— 204
What was thy mother's name? Tell me but that,
For truth can never be confirmed enough,
Though doubts did ever sleep. 207
MARINA
First, sir, I pray, what is your title?
PERICLES
I am Pericles of Tyre. But tell me now
My drowned queen's name, as in the rest you said
Thou hast been godlike perfect, the heir of
    kingdoms, 211
And another life to Pericles thy father. 212
MARINA
Is it no more to be your daughter than 213
To say my mother's name was Thaisa?
Thaisa was my mother, who did end
The minute I began.
PERICLES
Now, blessing on thee! Rise, thou'rt my child.—

141 **gazing on kings' graves** i.e., viewing with equanimity the evidence that all human greatness ends in death   141–142 **smiling . . . act** disarming with a smile the worst that fortune can do   147 **sent** are sent   158 **working** beating   159 **Motion** i.e., have you motion   161 **For** because   165 **Delivered** recited, told (also in line 173)   167 **withal** with   171 **give o'er** cease   172 **by the syllable** i.e., to the letter   178 **drawn** drawn his sword

181 **Whither . . . me** where are you leading me in this interrogation?   184 **be** live   189 **what . . . to be** who she might be   192 **Speaks** who speaks   196 **present** immediate   198 **O'erbear . . . mortality** overwhelm the boundaries of my life   200 **Thou . . . beget** i.e., you who renew the life of your own father   203–204 **as loud . . . us** i.e., with hosannas as loud as the thunder with which the gods threaten us   207 **Though . . . sleep** i.e., even though all doubts were laid to rest forever   211 **godlike perfect** all-knowing like a god.   **the heir** i.e., if you can do this, you will show yourself to be the heir   212 **another life** i.e., the bringer of a new life   213 **Is it no more** is nothing more required

Give me fresh garments.—Mine own Helicanus,   218
She is not dead at Tarsus, as she should have been,   219
By savage Cleon. She shall tell thee all,   220
When thou shalt kneel, and justify in knowledge   221
She is thy very princess.—Who is this?

HELICANUS
Sir, 'tis the Governor of Mytilene,
Who, hearing of your melancholy state,
Did come to see you.

PERICLES [to Lysimachus]   I embrace you.
Give me my robes. I am wild in my beholding.   227
                              [He is freshly attired.]
O heavens bless my girl! But, hark, what music?
Tell Helicanus, my Marina, tell him
O'er, point by point, for yet he seems to doubt,   230
How sure you are my daughter. But, what music?   231

HELICANUS   My lord, I hear none.

PERICLES   None?
The music of the spheres! List, my Marina.   233

LYSIMACHUS
It is not good to cross him. Give him way.

PERICLES   Rarest sounds! Do ye not hear?

LYSIMACHUS
Music, my lord? I hear.

PERICLES   Most heavenly music!   236
It nips me unto listening, and thick slumber   237
Hangs upon mine eyes. Let me rest.   [He sleeps.]

LYSIMACHUS
A pillow for his head. So, leave him all.
Well, my companion friends,
If this but answer to my just belief,   241
I'll well remember you.   [Exeunt all but Pericles.] 242

Diana [appears to Pericles as in a vision].

DIANA
My temple stands in Ephesus. Hie thee thither
And do upon mine altar sacrifice.
There, when my maiden priests are met together
Before the people all,
Reveal how thou at sea didst lose thy wife.
To mourn thy crosses, with thy daughter's, call   248
And give them repetition to the life.   249
Or perform my bidding, or thou livest in woe;   250
Do 't, and happy, by my silver bow!

Awake, and tell thy dream.   [She disappears.]

PERICLES
Celestial Dian, goddess argentine,   253
I will obey thee. Helicanus!

[Enter Helicanus, Lysimachus, and Marina.]

HELICANUS   Sir?

PERICLES
My purpose was for Tarsus, there to strike
The inhospitable Cleon, but I am
For other service first. Toward Ephesus
Turn our blown sails; eftsoons I'll tell thee why.   258
[To Lysimachus.] Shall we refresh us, sir, upon your
    shore
And give you gold for such provision
As our intents will need?

LYSIMACHUS   Sir,
With all my heart; and, when you come ashore,
I have another suit.

PERICLES   You shall prevail,
Were it to woo my daughter, for it seems
You have been noble towards her.

LYSIMACHUS   Sir, lend me your arm.

PERICLES   Come, my Marina.   *Exeunt.*

❧

5.2   *[Enter Gower, before the temple of Diana of
          Ephesus; Thaisa standing near the altar, as high
          priestess; a number of virgins on each side;
          Cerimon and other inhabitants of Ephesus
          attending.]*

GOWER
Now our sands are almost run;
More a little, and then dumb.   2
This my last boon give me,
For such kindness must relieve me:
That you aptly will suppose   5
What pageantry, what feats, what shows,
What minstrelsy, and pretty din
The regent made in Mytilin
To greet the King. So he thrived   9
That he is promised to be wived
To fair Marina, but in no wise
Till he had done his sacrifice   12
As Dian bade; whereto being bound,   13
The interim, pray you, all confound.   14
In feathered briefness sails are filled,   15
And wishes fall out as they're willed.
At Ephesus the temple see,
Our King and all his company.

---

218 Mine own Helicanus (Perhaps this should read "Mine own, Helicanus!"—i.e., she is my own daughter.)   **219 should have been** was
thought to be, or, was intended to have been   **220 By** at the hands of
221 When whereupon.   **justify in knowledge** assure yourself (that)
227 wild . . . beholding elated and delirious in everything I see, or,
possibly, unkempt, savage in appearance   **230 doubt** (or perhaps
dote, be in a daze; the Quarto reads *doat*)   **231 sure** certainly
233 music of the spheres celestial harmony, supposedly produced by
the ordered movements of the heavenly bodies. (Whether the music is
to be heard in the theater is not clear.)   **236 I hear** (Lysimachus may
hear music or may say this to humor Pericles and *give him way* [line
234]. Editors sometimes regard the word *music* in line 236 as a stage
direction or assign *I hear* to Pericles.)   **237 nips me** arrests my attention   **241 but . . . belief** only turns out as I expect it to   **242 remember** reward.   **s.d. Diana appears** (Perhaps she descends from the
heavens and reascends at line 252.)   **248 crosses** misfortunes.   **call**
lift your voice   **249 give . . . life** repeat them point for point
250 Or either

253 argentine silvery in appearance (as appropriate to the moon goddess)   **258 blown** inflated by the wind and blown great distances.
eftsoons shortly, later on
5.2. Location: The temple of Diana at Ephesus.
s.d. before the temple (Perhaps Gower reveals this scene, by means
of a curtain, at line 17.)   **2 More . . . dumb** a little more of the story,
and then I shall be silent   **5 aptly** readily   **9 So he thrived** he (Lysimachus) fared so well   **12 he** i.e., Pericles   **13 bade** commanded
14 confound do away with, omit   **15 feathered** winged

That he can hither come so soon
Is by your fancies' thankful doom.   [*Exit.*] 20

5.3   [*Enter Pericles, with his train; Lysimachus,*
         Helicanus, Marina, and a lady.]

PERICLES
Hail, Dian! To perform thy just command,   1
I here confess myself the King of Tyre,
Who, frighted from my country, did wed
At Pentapolis the fair Thaisa.
At sea in childbed died she, but brought forth
A maid child called Marina, who, O goddess,   6
Wears yet thy silver livery. She at Tarsus   7
Was nursed with Cleon, who at fourteen years   8
He sought to murder; but her better stars
Brought her to Mytilene, 'gainst whose shore
Riding, her fortunes brought the maid aboard us,   11
Where, by her own most clear remembrance, she
Made known herself my daughter.
THAISA   Voice and favor!   13
You are, you are—O royal Pericles!   [*She faints.*]
PERICLES
What means the nun? She dies! Help, gentlemen!
CERIMON   Noble sir,
If you have told Diana's altar true,
This is your wife.
PERICLES   Reverend appearer, no;   18
I threw her overboard with these very arms.
CERIMON
Upon this coast, I warrant you.
PERICLES   'Tis most certain.
CERIMON
Look to the lady; O, she's but overjoyed.
Early one blustering morn this lady was
Thrown upon this shore. I oped the coffin,
Found there rich jewels, recovered her, and
   placed her   24
Here in Diana's temple.
PERICLES   May we see them?
CERIMON
Great sir, they shall be brought you to my house,
Whither I invite you. Look, Thaisa is
Recovered.
THAISA [*rising*]   O, let me look!
If he be none of mine, my sanctity   30
Will to my sense bend no licentious ear,   31
But curb it, spite of seeing. O, my lord,   32

Are you not Pericles? Like him you spake,
Like him you are. Did you not name a tempest,
A birth, and death?
PERICLES   The voice of dead Thaisa!
THAISA
That Thaisa am I, supposèd dead
And drowned.
PERICLES
Immortal Dian!
THAISA   Now I know you better.
When we with tears parted Pentapolis,   39
The King my father gave you such a ring.   40
                    [*She points to his ring.*]
PERICLES
This, this! No more, you gods! Your present
   kindness
Makes my past miseries sports. You shall do well   42
That on the touching of her lips I may   43
Melt and no more be seen.—O, come, be buried
A second time within these arms!   [*They embrace.*]
MARINA [*kneeling*]   My heart
Leaps to be gone into my mother's bosom.
PERICLES
Look who kneels here! Flesh of thy flesh, Thaisa,
Thy burden at the sea, and called Marina
For she was yielded there.
THAISA   Blest, and mine own!   49
                         [*They embrace.*]
HELICANUS
Hail, madam, and my queen!
THAISA   I know you not.
PERICLES
You have heard me say, when I did fly from Tyre
I left behind an ancient substitute.
Can you remember what I called the man?
I have named him oft.
THAISA   'Twas Helicanus then.
PERICLES   Still confirmation!
Embrace him, dear Thaisa, this is he. [*They embrace.*]
Now do I long to hear how you were found,
How possibly preserved, and who to thank,   59
Besides the gods, for this great miracle.
THAISA
Lord Cerimon, my lord; this man,
Through whom the gods have shown their power,
   that can
From first to last resolve you.
PERICLES   Reverend sir,   63
The gods can have no mortal officer   64
More like a god than you. Will you deliver   65
How this dead queen re-lives?
CERIMON   I will, my lord.

---

20 **Is . . . doom** is thanks to the consent (and willing participation) of
your imaginations
5.3. Location: Scene continues; the temple, as before.
1 **just** exact   6 **maid child** baby girl   7 **Wears . . . livery** i.e., is still
a virgin   8 **with Cleon** under Cleon's care   11 **Riding** (we) riding at
anchor   13 **favor** face, appearance   18 **Reverend appearer** you who
appear reverend   24 **recovered** revived   30–32 **If . . . seeing** if he is
not my husband, my holy way of life will lend no credence to my
physical sense of sight and my sensual inclination but will curb my
longings (for marriage, my lost life of domestic pleasure), despite what
I see before me

39 **parted** departed from   40 s.d. **She points to his ring** (Possibly Pericles included this ring among the jewels he laid in Thaisa's casket, or,
more probably, she may recognize it on his finger now.)   42 **sports**
mere amusements   43 **That** if. (If the gods so willed, Pericles would
happily die at this moment of reunion.)   49 **For** because.   **yielded**
brought forth, born   59 **possibly** by what possible means   63 **resolve**
you satisfy your curiosity   64 **mortal officer** human agent   65 **deliver**
recount

Beseech you, first go with me to my house,
Where shall be shown you all was found with her,   68
How she came placed here in the temple,
No needful thing omitted.

PERICLES

Pure Dian, I bless thee for thy vision, and   71
Will offer night oblations to thee. Thaisa,   72
This prince, the fair betrothèd of your daughter,
Shall marry her at Pentapolis. And now
This ornament   75
Makes me look dismal will I clip to form;   76
And what this fourteen years no razor touched,
To grace thy marriage day, I'll beautify.

THAISA

Lord Cerimon hath letters of good credit, sir,   79
My father's dead.

PERICLES

Heavens make a star of him! Yet there, my queen,   81
We'll celebrate their nuptials, and ourselves
Will in that kingdom spend our following days.
Our son and daughter shall in Tyrus reign.
Lord Cerimon, we do our longing stay   85
To hear the rest untold. Sir, lead 's the way.   86

[*Exeunt.*]

[*Enter Gower.*]

GOWER

In Antiochus and his daughter you have heard
Of monstrous lust the due and just reward.
In Pericles, his queen, and daughter seen,
Although assailed with fortune fierce and keen,
Virtue preserved from fell destruction's blast,   91
Led on by heaven, and crowned with joy at last.
In Helicanus may you well descry
A figure of truth, of faith, of loyalty.
In reverend Cerimon there well appears
The worth that learnèd charity aye wears.
For wicked Cleon and his wife, when fame   97
Had spread his cursèd deed to the honored name   98
Of Pericles, to rage the city turn,   99
That him and his they in his palace burn;   100
The gods for murder seemèd so content
To punish—although not done, but meant.   102
So, on your patience evermore attending,
New joy wait on you! Here our play has ending.

[*Exit.*]

68 **all was** all that was   71 **thy vision** appearing to me in a vision
72 **night oblations** nightly sacrifices, evening prayers   75 **ornament**
i.e., hair and beard   76 **Makes** which makes.   **to form** to proper
shape   79 **of good credit** trustworthy   81 **there** i.e., in Pentapolis
85 **do . . . stay** merely postpone the completion of our desires
86 **untold** that is not yet told   91 **fell** cruel   97 **fame** report; common
talk   98 **his . . . deed to** i.e., the deed done by him and his family,
especially Dionyza, against   99 **turn** did turn   100 **That** so that.   **his**
his family, notably Dionyza   102 **although . . . meant** i.e., even
though the crime was only intended and not actually carried out

Cymbeline

The genre of *Cymbeline* can be suggested by such critical terms as romance, tragicomedy, and the comedy of forgiveness. As in *Pericles, The Winter's Tale,* and other late plays, Shakespeare turns to the improbable fictions of romance: a stepmother-queen skilled in the use of poisons and envious of her fair and virtuous stepdaughter (as in *Snow White*), lost sons recognized by the inevitable birthmark, the reunion of many persons long separated by exile and wandering, the intervention of the gods by means of a riddling and inane prophecy. These are the distinguishing features of English romance in the 1580s, a titillating vogue exploited by Robert Greene and other professional writers of the period. From two romantic plays of the 1580s—*Sir Clyomon and Sir Clamydes* and *The Rare Triumphs of Love and Fortune*—Shakespeare may, in fact, have drawn source material. Why did he turn to such old-fashioned models in 1608–1610? The choice has puzzled many critics and has prompted them to speak condescendingly of Shakespeare's dotage or to assign parts of the play (notably the descent of Jupiter) to some other dramatist.

Shakespeare nevertheless courted the improbabilities, even the deliberate absurdities, of romance with a serious artistic purpose. In part, he was responding to a new literary fashion, evident especially in the private theaters, for a tragicomedy of refined sensibility—a literary fashion that produced Francis Beaumont and John Fletcher's *Philaster*. This play of about 1609 features, like *Cymbeline*, a rapidly moving and ingeniously woven plot of separation and reunion, a king's daughter betrothed by her father to a churl and then wrongly accused of infidelity, a young maiden in male disguise, and other comparable details. Whether *Cymbeline* preceded or followed *Philaster* is a matter that is difficult to determine, since *Cymbeline* can be dated only approximately as from 1608–1610 on grounds of style; in any case, Shakespeare's fascination with romance goes back at least to *All's Well That Ends Well* (c. 1601–1604) and *Pericles* (c. 1606–1608). His experiments in the genre must be viewed as innovative and unique. Despite the affinities to Fletcherian tragicomedy, Shakespeare never indulges in the cloying sensationalism, the exaggerated heightening of exotic emotion, and (except in *The Winter's Tale*) the trickery of concealing essential information from the audience, such as we find in works of Beaumont and Fletcher. Shakespeare's interest in romantic improbability is related to the serious motif of redemption, of an unexpected and undeserved second chance for erring humanity.

The tragic possibilities are manifold. Cymbeline, like Lear (another king from British legendary history in Raphael Holinshed's *Chronicles*, 1578), tyrannically repulses a virtuous daughter and rewards the vicious members of his family, with predictably unhappy consequences. Posthumus Leonatus, like Othello, commands the death of his beloved mistress because he believes a groundless but cunningly presented accusation of her infidelity; finally, concluding that he has destroyed the only person capable of giving order to his life, he despairingly longs for death. Whereas in a similar situation Lear and Othello suffer the tragic consequences of their choice, Cymbeline and Posthumus are spared. Some benign force, integral to the world of this play, prevents fallible mortals from pursuing their misguided intentions to the point of irreversible injury. Posthumus relies for his vengeance on the virtuous Pisanio, who cannot bring himself to slay Imogen. The Queen's box of "poison," given ultimately to Imogen by the well-meaning but duped Pisanio, is only a sleeping potion concocted by that kindly manipulator behind the scenes, Doctor Cornelius. These fortunate avoidances of disaster recall other such narrow escapes in *Much Ado About Nothing, All's Well That Ends Well,* and *Measure for Measure.* They also anticipate similar events in *The Winter's Tale.*

Because *Cymbeline* begins with dilemmas like those of *King Lear* and *Othello*, the prevailing tone is at first serious. (The editors of the 1623 First Folio printed the play among the tragedies.) The King's behavior toward Imogen and her virtuous but nonaristocratic husband, Posthumus, is tyrannical. Disinterested observers condemn the wicked Queen's dominance over Cymbeline and laugh privately at the Queen's cowardly and ridiculous son Cloten. A good man like Belarius suffers lifelong banishment from the envious court and spends his exile dwelling in caves. Many conventional features of romantic narrative—wandering and return, loss and rediscovery, apparent death and rebirth—are set in motion by the need to escape from a court dominated by the wicked Queen. One by one, honest persons of the play—Posthumus, Imogen, Pisanio—leave society in disfavor to be reunited in the wild landscape of Belarius and his foster sons. Italy is no better a place than the English court. Its evil genius is Iachimo, apostle of animal appetite, duplicity, and cynical indifference to human values.

Despite the prevailing tragic mood at first, there are promises of brighter prospects. Posthumus' birth is attended by wondrous circumstances that would appear to single him out for an extraordinary career. In the first scene, moreover, we learn that the King's only two sons were stolen from their nursery in their infancy—an obvious hint that they will turn up sooner or later. Cloten, too, strikes us as a ludicrous suitor for Imogen, the type of buffoonish rival appropriate to a love comedy. Because he is witless, superficial, and preoccupied with clothes, he deserves to be exposed and ridiculed. Even his death is grotesquely comic. He acts as a foil or caricature to Posthumus, in whose clothes he is erroneously taken by Imogen to be her dead husband; the outward resemblance of the two men suggests to us that Posthumus has not been unlike Cloten when he has suspected Imogen of betraying him and has vowed revenge. Cloten's death signals an end to Posthumus' disposition to be fooled by appearances.

The initial somber mood, with its threat of tragic outcome, is further lightened by the juxtaposition of sorrow and hope. When Arviragus and Guiderius mourn the "death" of Imogen with an exquisite song on the vanity of human striving, we respond to the appropriateness of the sentiment and yet qualify our sorrow with our consoling knowledge that she has really taken a sleeping potion. Similarly, when Posthumus jests eloquently about death with his jailer and prepares to find his only freedom in surcease, we cannot ignore Jupiter's assurance of eventual redress. As in *Measure for Measure*, suffering and regret are framed in the benign context of a providential design that the audience alone can fully appreciate.

Tragicomedy threatens and consoles at the same time. The chief source of anxiety is Posthumus' renunciation of Imogen. The sensationalism of the plot derives in part from the use of the "wager" motif found in several Italianate *novelle*, such as the ninth tale of the second day in Giovanni Boccaccio's *Decameron*. The psychological portrait of Posthumus' wavering and fall, like that of Othello or Leontes, is intense and ugly, fraught with grotesque images of sexual coupling. As with Othello and Leontes, Posthumus is threatened by his wife's sexuality and is unable to respond securely to her offered love that is appropriately sensual and spiritual. He is comfortable only when he thinks of her as sexually restrained even in her marriage bed, praying forbearance of her husband with "A pudency so rosy the sweet view on 't / Might well have warmed old Saturn" (2.5.11–12). He is aroused by virginal unresponsiveness but repelled by too great a responsiveness. Such unbalanced expectations leave him prone to insinuations that women practice deception. Once Imogen has been made to appear carnal to him, she becomes monstrous and insatiable in his imagination. He conjures up the imagined sexual triumph of Iachimo in animalistic terms: "Perchance he spoke not, but, / Like a full-acorned boar, a German one, / Cried 'O!' and mounted" (lines 15–17). Like Othello, he insists on being proved a cuckold; once he has experienced jealousy, he can expect only one conclusion. He longs "to tear her limbmeal," and like Lear he would violently destroy "The woman's part in me" (2.4.150; 2.5.20).

Posthumus suffers from dark fantasies about women such as we find elsewhere in Shakespeare. Because he regards women as male property, he is all too ready to engage in a contest with other males "in praise of our country mistresses" and to boast that Imogen is (in the terms of the contest) "more fair, virtuous, wise, chaste, constant, qualified, and less attemptable" than any other lady alive (1.4.57–61). The results are predictably disastrous, as they were earlier in Shakespeare's *The Rape of Lucrece*. By engaging in the objectification of women, Posthumus betrays his emotional kinship to Iachimo, who takes advantage of his concealment in Imogen's bedchamber to catalogue in clinical detail her physical charms along with the furniture of the room itself (2.2). Posthumus' misogynistic outburst against women as "half-workers" in the act of generation (2.5.1 ff.) reveals his fear of betrayal by all women (including his own mother) and hence his own helpless vulnerability to what he supposes to be women's lying, flattering, deceiving, "Lust and rank thoughts," revenges, "Nice longing, slanders, mutability, / All faults that have a name, nay, that hell knows" (lines 22–27). This male phobia is deeply sculpted in the male world of *Cymbeline*, for we see it also in Cloten's warped desire to possess Imogen and in Cymbeline's troubled patriarchal relations with his daughter and his domineering wife. In Posthumus, this typically male perversity threatens disaster and demands either a tragic ending or the contrived happy ending of tragicomedy. His failure places a special burden on Imogen to endure his frailty and to redeem it; only through her can Posthumus receive a second chance. Meantime, his failure has raised a familiarly Shakespearean question about his responsibility for his fall. How could he have avoided accusing Imogen falsely?

Powerful forces militate against Posthumus. Iachimo is a plausible villain, in the vein of Don John (*Much Ado About Nothing*), Iago (*Othello*), and Edmund (*King Lear*). Like them, he plots to arouse envy and dissension in others, by means of appearances falsely presented to the senses. We can readily understand him in human terms as a quarrelsome and lecherous man, and yet his sinister delight in mischief also suggests a more all-encompassing and diabolical evil. His contention is that every woman has her price (and every man, too). When he discovers in Imogen a wholesomeness that will not yield to his insinuations, he seeks to destroy her as a dangerous refutation of his low premise about human nature. He states the confrontation between them in cosmic terms: "Though this a heavenly angel, hell is here" (2.2.50). He does not, to be sure, boast gleefully to the audience or dominate the play as Iago does; moreover, he himself experiences the beneficent change brought about by the play's happy ending and speaks in praise of Imogen's virtue. As befits a tragicomedy, he is more sinister than potent, almost at times a travesty of a tragic villain. Nevertheless, in his scenes of villainy, his function is that of a diabolical tempter working through humanity's frail senses. His use of the ring as evidence recalls the handkerchief in *Othello*. Iachimo creates a minutely circumstantial inference of Imogen's transgression and lets Posthumus' inclination to believe the worst do the rest.

Like Othello, then, Posthumus must bear the blame for his loss of faith. The tempter can prevail upon his senses, but humanity's own wavering heart chooses evil. Trustworthy observers perceive Posthumus' fallacy and indicate the correct response; as Philario says, "This is not strong enough to be believed / Of one persuaded well of" (2.4.134–135). True faith urges that, being what she is, Imogen could not do the thing alleged. She is, like Helena and Desdemona before her, a virtuous woman who responds to her undeserved tribulations with forbearance (though even her patience has a limit, and she, too, is capable of overreacting and misjudging). She overbalances male faithlessness with her forgiveness. Her perseverance in virtue confounds Iachimo's thesis and rescues Posthumus from his worst self. Iachimo and she are spiritual contestants for the allegiance of Posthumus' faith. She triumphs, not through Posthumus' choice (which is for evil), but through her own unassailable goodness. Belatedly, too, Posthumus makes the amends that are necessary if we are to accept him as the restored hero. He forgives Imogen even before he knows of her innocence, seeks death as an atonement, and moves by degrees through sin to regret, confession of guilt, and penance. His peasant costume in Act 5 signals the resignation of worldly desire he must achieve to be worthy of an almost miraculous second chance. As fallen man, he can never truly deserve that mercy, but he can strive at least to atone for what he has done.

The story of King Cymbeline's long-lost sons is similarly tragicomic and is even more explicitly indebted to the conventions of romance with its motifs of banishment, wandering, and eventual recognition and reunion. The sylvan setting of this romantic narrative lends to the second half of the play a primal vigor and mystery (as also in *The Winter's Tale*). Arviragus and Guiderius remind us of medieval legends about Parzival; that is, like Parzival, they are young princes raised in a wilderness, lacking courtly training and yet possessing an "invisible instinct" (4.2.179) that prompts them to assert their royal blood. Ignoring their stepfather's warnings about the ingratitude and decadence of the courtly society he has abandoned, the princes long to prove themselves in deeds of chivalry. They are a rejuvenating force in this play, bringing together the ideals of medieval knighthood and the unsullied strength of their sylvan world. Cloten, that effete semblance of a courtier and their foil in every respect, is appropriately killed by these agents of "divine Nature" (line 172). They cherish Imogen as one of their own and grieve for her seeming death with the vivid immediacy of those who have lived with nature. Her seeming death and reawakening is for them something like the restorative cycle of the seasons, bringing a renewal of natural vigor that nicely complements the spiritual grace she embodies for Posthumus. Her name to them is appropriately "Fidele." Old Belarius' reconciliation with Cymbeline signals an end to political injustice, still another consequence of humanity's fallen condition for which grace must be provided.

The story of the war between Britain and Rome, derived in part from Holinshed's *Chronicles,* contributes also to the process of spiritual rebirth. The war sets in motion a series of apparently unrelated events, including the return to Britain of Posthumus and Iachimo, without which the play's happy conclusion would be impossible. Although the war itself is destructive and is supported chiefly by Cloten and the Queen (whose patriotic speeches show us just how hollow a thing patriotism can be), the war does lead ultimately to new life for Britain, as well as for the romantic lovers. Sudden turns in the battle, especially when an old man and two boys defend a narrow lane against an army, are seen as marvels directed by some higher power. In the benign aftermath of peace, the King, no longer misled by evil counselors, finds reconciliation with his daughter and her husband, as well as with Rome. The final scene, in which the seeming accidents of fortune are unraveled, is a structural tour de force of comic discovery.

The three main plots of *Cymbeline*—of Posthumus and Imogen, of the King's lost sons, and of the war between Britain and Rome—may seem outwardly unconnected with one another. Certainly, the play ranges over a wide geographical space and introduces a host of characters, many of whom never meet until the final scene. Yet the three plots are unified by being structurally like one another. In each, we perceive a pattern of fall from innocence, followed by conflict and eventual redemption. Posthumus is tempted into a loss of faith and attempted murder, from which he recovers through penance. The saga of the King's sons provides a secular equivalent in its story of estrangement, mistaken identity, and eventual recovery of loss. Politically, Britain is alienated from Rome through the machinations of the Queen only to rediscover after many years a new harmony. The plots impinge on one another in ways that seem contrived (as, for example, when the accidents of war finally bring together Imogen, Posthumus, and Iachimo in the presence of Cymbeline), and yet we understand at last that the contrivance is providential and benign, intended to test humanity and then reward those who have persevered or at least have found true contrition.

Despite the symmetries of structure among the various plots of *Cymbeline*, the play manages to keep us constantly off balance. Its tragicomic pattern of innocence, conflict, and eventual redemption is repeatedly disturbed by the odd juxtapositions of imperial Rome, Renaissance Rome, and prehistoric Britain contrived from chronicle, romance, and pastoral. The play yields weird moments, such as Imogen's awakening near Milford Haven to find herself next to Cloten's headless body and to mistake it for Posthumus' body (4.2.294–335), or Jupiter's descent to earth on the back of an eagle (5.4.92 ff.). The play's denouement relies on the unraveling of an absurdly infantile riddle. The final accommodation of Britain into the Roman empire may add topical complexity by casting oblique glances in the direction of King James I of England and his dream of assuming a central role in the forging of a pacified Europe. Generically, the play is a deliberate mingling of history and romance, however successfully it may attempt to harmonize these genres; formally, it opts for instability through the intrusion of the comic into the serious. An implicit relationship between the psychosexual in the private realm and the political in the public realm is everywhere apparent and yet elusive.

Through such boldly experimental means, Shakespeare creates his dramatic world of accident and design, of odd juxtapositions and symmetry. The dramatist chooses by experimental and outrageous means to bring together disparate elements and to flaunt the lack of a perfectly smooth resolution, even while suggesting an overall sense of purpose and harmony that human witnesses can only imperfectly comprehend. Jupiter becomes the spokesman for a providential view in his role as *deus ex machina*—literally illustrating that term, since he "descends" from the stage roof by means of some mechanical device. The scene of this divine intervention (5.4) is so blatantly unrealistic that, as we have seen, many critics have wished to exonerate Shakespeare of having written it, but this very unreality is the key to the play's ending. Jupiter places the human suffering of the play in a larger perspective: "Whom best I love I cross, to make my gift, / The more delayed, delighted. Be content" (5.4.101–102). In the tragicomic view, suffering is the manifestation of a design engineered and supervised by a loving deity to test and strengthen humankind. Understood as such, the test affirms Imogen's strength, shows Posthumus a reason to cherish what he would otherwise destroy, and even reclaims the evil agent by whom the test had been put in operation. As Caius Lucius insists to the long-suffering Fidele, "Some falls are means the happier to arise" (4.2.406).

Cymbeline

[Dramatis Personae

CYMBELINE, *King of Britain*
QUEEN, *wife of Cymbeline*
CLOTEN, *her son by a former husband*
IMOGEN, *daughter of Cymbeline by a former queen*
POSTHUMUS LEONATUS, *a gentleman, Imogen's husband*
BELARIUS, *a banished lord, disguised as Morgan*
GUIDERIUS, } *sons of Cymbeline, disguised*
ARVIRAGUS, } *as Polydore and Cadwal, supposed sons of Morgan*

PISANIO, *servant of Posthumus*
CORNELIUS, *a physician*
Two LORDS *attending Cloten*
Two GENTLEMEN *of Cymbeline's court*
HELEN, *a lady attending Imogen*
Another LADY *attending Imogen, or possibly the same*
A LADY *attending the Queen*
A British LORD
Two British CAPTAINS
Two JAILERS
Two MESSENGERS

PHILARIO, *friend of Posthumus,* } *Italians*
IACHIMO, *friend of Philario,* }
A FRENCHMAN, *friend of Philario*

CAIUS LUCIUS, *general of the Roman forces*
Two Roman SENATORS
A TRIBUNE
A Roman CAPTAIN
Philharmonus, *a* SOOTHSAYER

JUPITER
The Ghost of SICILIUS *Leonatus, father of Posthumus*
The Ghost of Leonatus' MOTHER
The Ghosts of Leonatus' two BROTHERS

Lords, Ladies, Attendants, Musicians attending Cloten, a Dutchman, a Spaniard, Senators, Tribunes, Captains, and Soldiers

SCENE: *Britain; Italy*]

1.1   *Enter two Gentlemen.*

FIRST GENTLEMAN
You do not meet a man but frowns. Our bloods   1
No more obey the heavens than our courtiers'   2
Still seem as does the King's.
SECOND GENTLEMAN   But what's the matter?   3
FIRST GENTLEMAN
His daughter, and the heir of 's kingdom, whom
He purposed to his wife's sole son—a widow   5
That late he married—hath referred herself   6
Unto a poor but worthy gentleman. She's wedded,
Her husband banished, she imprisoned. All
Is outward sorrow, though I think the King   9
Be touched at very heart.
SECOND GENTLEMAN   None but the King?
FIRST GENTLEMAN
He that hath lost her, too. So is the Queen,   11
That most desired the match. But not a courtier,
Although they wear their faces to the bent   13
Of the King's looks, hath a heart that is not
Glad at the thing they scowl at.
SECOND GENTLEMAN   And why so?
FIRST GENTLEMAN
He that hath missed the Princess is a thing
Too bad for bad report, and he that hath her—
I mean, that married her, alack, good man!
And therefore banished—is a creature such
As, to seek through the regions of the earth
For one his like, there would be something failing   21
In him that should compare. I do not think   22
So fair an outward and such stuff within   23
Endows a man but he.
SECOND GENTLEMAN   You speak him far.   24
FIRST GENTLEMAN
I do extend him, sir, within himself,   25
Crush him together rather than unfold   26
His measure duly.
SECOND GENTLEMAN What's his name and birth?   27
FIRST GENTLEMAN
I cannot delve him to the root. His father   28
Was called Sicilius, who did join his honor   29
Against the Romans with Cassibelan,   30
But had his titles by Tenantius, whom   31

1.1. Location: Britain. At the court of King Cymbeline.
1–3 Our . . . King's the constitutions and dispositions of us mortals
are not more obedient to the influence of the heavenly bodies than
our courtiers' demeanors and looks follow those of the King   **5 purposed to** intended for   **6 late** lately.   **referred** given (in marriage)
9 outward mere pretense of (as explained in lines 12–22)   **11 He
. . . her** i.e., Cloten, the Queen's son, Imogen's unsuccessful wooer
(also in line 16)   **13 bent** inclination   **21 his like** like him   **22 him
. . . compare** anyone chosen for comparison   **23 stuff** (1) substance
(2) fabric (as the imagery of lines 26–27 further suggests)   **24 speak
him far** go far in praising him   **25 I . . . himself** I expand his virtues
within the limits of what he actually is   **26–27 unfold . . . duly** disclose his dimensions to the degree that he merits   **28 delve . . . root**
i.e., account fully for his lineage   **29 join his honor** give his honorable assistance in arms   **30 Cassibelan** Cymbeline's uncle; see 3.1.5.
(According to Holinshed, Cassibelan was Cymbeline's great-uncle, being younger brother and successor to King Lud.)   **31 Tenantius** Cymbeline's father, son of King Lud. (In Holinshed, Tenantius is Cassibelan's nephew.)

He served with glory and admired success,
So gained the sur-addition Leonatus;   33
And had, besides this gentleman in question,
Two other sons, who in the wars o' the time
Died with their swords in hand; for which their
   father,
Then old and fond of issue, took such sorrow   37
That he quit being, and his gentle lady,   38
Big of this gentleman our theme, deceased   39
As he was born. The King he takes the babe   40
To his protection, calls him Posthumus Leonatus,
Breeds him and makes him of his bedchamber,   42
Puts to him all the learnings that his time   43
Could make him the receiver of, which he took,
As we do air, fast as 'twas ministered,
And in 's spring became a harvest, lived in court— 46
Which rare it is to do—most praised, most loved,
A sample to the youngest, to th' more mature   48
A glass that feated them, and to the graver   49
A child that guided dotards. To his mistress,   50
For whom he now is banished, her own price   51
Proclaims how she esteemed him; and his virtue
By her election may be truly read   53
What kind of man he is.
SECOND GENTLEMAN   I honor him
Even out of your report. But pray you, tell me,   55
Is she sole child to the King?
FIRST GENTLEMAN   His only child.
He had two sons; if this be worth your hearing,
Mark it: The eldest of them at three years old,
I' the swaddling-clothes the other, from their nursery
Were stol'n, and to this hour no guess in knowledge 60
Which way they went.
SECOND GENTLEMAN   How long is this ago?
FIRST GENTLEMAN   Some twenty years.
SECOND GENTLEMAN
That a king's children should be so conveyed,   64
So slackly guarded, and the search so slow
That could not trace them!
FIRST GENTLEMAN   Howso'er 'tis strange,
Or that the negligence may well be laughed at,
Yet is it true, sir.
SECOND GENTLEMAN   I do well believe you.
FIRST GENTLEMAN
We must forbear. Here comes the gentleman,   69
The Queen, and Princess.   *Exeunt.*

---

33 sur-addition additional title, surname.   **Leonatus** lion-born
37 fond of issue devoted to his children and despairing of having
more   **38 quit being** left existence, died.   **gentle** noble   **39 Big . . .
theme** pregnant with this Posthumus we are talking about   **40 King
he** i.e., King   **42 Breeds** raises, educates.   **of his bedchamber** one of
his intimate retinue   **43 Puts to** sets before.   **time** time of life, age
46 in 's . . . harvest i.e., in his youth became ripe in learning
48 sample example   **49 A glass . . . them** a mirror that reflected their
best features, one that offered him as a model for their best selves
49–50 to . . . dotards i.e., to older courtiers he offered wise example as if a child were to instruct doddering old men   **50 To** as for, or,
in the eyes of   **51 her own price** the price she willingly paid (of her
father's hostility)   **53 election** choice (of him)   **55 out of** judging by
60 guess in knowledge credible conjecture   **64 conveyed** carried off
69 forbear stop talking and withdraw

Enter the Queen, Posthumus, and Imogen.

QUEEN
No, be assured you shall not find me, daughter,
After the slander of most stepmothers,   72
Evil-eyed unto you. You're my prisoner, but
Your jailer shall deliver you the keys
That lock up your restraint. For you, Posthumus,   75
So soon as I can win th' offended King
I will be known your advocate. Marry, yet   77
The fire of rage is in him, and 'twere good
You leaned unto his sentence with what patience   79
Your wisdom may inform you.

POSTHUMUS   Please Your Highness, 80
I will from hence today.

QUEEN   You know the peril.
I'll fetch a turn about the garden, pitying
The pangs of barred affections, though the King
Hath charged you should not speak together.   *Exit.*

IMOGEN   O
Dissembling courtesy! How fine this tyrant
Can tickle where she wounds! My dearest husband,
I something fear my father's wrath, but nothing—   87
Always reserved my holy duty—what   88
His rage can do on me. You must be gone,
And I shall here abide the hourly shot
Of angry eyes, not comforted to live   91
But that there is this jewel in the world
That I may see again.

POSTHUMUS   My queen, my mistress!
O lady, weep no more, lest I give cause   94
To be suspected of more tenderness   95
Than doth become a man. I will remain   96
The loyal'st husband that did e'er plight troth.
My residence in Rome at one Philario's,   98
Who to my father was a friend, to me
Known but by letter; thither write, my queen,
And with mine eyes I'll drink the words you send,
Though ink be made of gall.

Enter Queen.

QUEEN   Be brief, I pray you.
If the King come, I shall incur I know not
How much of his displeasure. [*Aside.*] Yet I'll
    move him
To walk this way. I never do him wrong   105
But he does buy my injuries, to be friends,   106
Pays dear for my offenses.   [*Exit.*] 107

POSTHUMUS [*to Imogen*]   Should we be taking leave
As long a term as yet we have to live,

The loathness to depart would grow. Adieu!

IMOGEN   Nay, stay a little!
Were you but riding forth to air yourself,   112
Such parting were too petty. Look here, love:
This diamond was my mother's. Take it, heart,
But keep it till you woo another wife   115
When Imogen is dead.

[*She gives a ring, or puts it on his finger.*]

POSTHUMUS   How, how? Another?
You gentle gods, give me but this I have,
And cere up my embracements from a next   118
With bonds of death! Remain, remain thou here   119
While sense can keep it on. And, sweetest, fairest, 120
As I my poor self did exchange for you   121
To your so infinite loss, so in our trifles   122
I still win of you. For my sake wear this.   123
It is a manacle of love; I'll place it
Upon this fairest prisoner.

[*He puts a bracelet upon her arm.*]

IMOGEN   O the gods!
When shall we see again?

Enter Cymbeline and lords.

POSTHUMUS   Alack, the King!   126

CYMBELINE [*to Posthumus*]
Thou basest thing, avoid hence, from my sight!   127
If after this command thou freight the court   128
With thy unworthiness, thou diest. Away!
Thou'rt poison to my blood.

POSTHUMUS   The gods protect you,
And bless the good remainders of the court!   131
I am gone.   *Exit.*

IMOGEN   There cannot be a pinch in death   132
More sharp than this is.

CYMBELINE   O disloyal thing,
That shouldst repair my youth, thou heap'st   134
A year's age on me.

IMOGEN   I beseech you, sir,   135
Harm not yourself with your vexation.
I am senseless of your wrath; a touch more rare   137
Subdues all pangs, all fears.

CYMBELINE   Past grace? Obedience?

IMOGEN
Past hope and in despair; that way past grace.   139

CYMBELINE
That mightst have had the sole son of my queen!

---

72 **After the slander** according to what is slanderously told   75 **your restraint** your prison   77 **Marry** i.e., indeed. (Originally, "by the Virgin Mary.")   79 **leaned unto** deferred to   80 **inform** instill in   87 **something** somewhat.   **nothing** not in the least   88 **Always . . . duty** although never forgetting my sacred duty to him. (Though dutiful and even fearful, Imogen will not let her father's rage alter her determination.)   91 **comforted to live** finding comfort in life   94–96 **lest . . . man** i.e., lest I, too, shed tears, which would be unmanly in me   98 **Rome** i.e., Rome is   105–107 **I . . . offenses** whenever I wrong him, he interprets those injuries as kindnesses and submits to them in order to remain on good terms

112 **air yourself** take some fresh air   115 **But** only   118 **cere up** wrap in cerecloth or waxed cloth used for wrapping a dead body; perhaps with a play on sealing a document with wax (see *bonds* in the next line)   119 **Remain** (The ring will remind him of Imogen always.)   120 **sense** sensory feeling.   **it** (Said of the ring.)   121 **exchange** (In their wedding vows, they have given themselves to each other.)   122 **trifles** i.e., love tokens   123 **still** always   126 **see** see each other   127 **avoid hence** begone   128 **freight** burden   131 **remainders of** those who remain at   132 **pinch** pang   134 **repair** restore   134–135 **thou . . . on me** you've added a year to my age   137 **senseless of** insensible to.   **a touch** a feeling (of love for Posthumus and pain at his banishment)   139 **despair . . . grace** (Imogen puns bitterly on *grace*, by which the King meant "gracious dutifulness"; in her religious metaphor, to despair is to be beyond God's grace.)

IMOGEN
  O blessèd, that I might not! I chose an eagle   141
  And did avoid a puttock.   142

CYMBELINE
  Thou took'st a beggar, wouldst have made my
    throne
  A seat for baseness.

IMOGEN   No, I rather added
  A luster to it.

CYMBELINE   O thou vile one!

IMOGEN   Sir,
  It is your fault that I have loved Posthumus.
  You bred him as my playfellow, and he is
  A man worth any woman, overbuys me   148
  Almost the sum he pays.

CYMBELINE   What, art thou mad?   149

IMOGEN
  Almost, sir. Heaven restore me! Would I were
  A neatherd's daughter, and my Leonatus   151
  Our neighbor shepherd's son!

        Enter Queen.

CYMBELINE   Thou foolish thing!—
  [*To the Queen.*] They were again together. You have
    done
  Not after our command. Away with her
  And pen her up.

QUEEN   Beseech your patience.—Peace,   155
  Dear lady daughter, peace!—Sweet sovereign,
  Leave us to ourselves, and make yourself some
    comfort
  Out of your best advice.

CYMBELINE   Nay, let her languish   158
  A drop of blood a day, and, being aged,   159
  Die of this folly!   *Exit [with lords].*

QUEEN   Fie, you must give way.   160

        Enter Pisanio.

  Here is your servant.—How now, sir? What news?

PISANIO
  My lord your son drew on my master.

QUEEN   Ha?   162
  No harm, I trust, is done?

PISANIO   There might have been,
  But that my master rather played than fought
  And had no help of anger. They were parted   165
  By gentlemen at hand.

QUEEN   I am very glad on 't.   166

IMOGEN
  Your son's my father's friend; he takes his part   167
  To draw upon an exile. O, brave sir!   168
  I would they were in Afric both together,   169
  Myself by with a needle, that I might prick
  The goer-back.—Why came you from your master?

PISANIO
  On his command. He would not suffer me
  To bring him to the haven, left these notes
  Of what commands I should be subject to
  When 't pleased you to employ me.

QUEEN [*to Imogen*]   This hath been
  Your faithful servant. I dare lay mine honor   176
  He will remain so.

PISANIO   I humbly thank Your Highness.

QUEEN [*to Imogen*]   Pray, walk awhile.   179

IMOGEN [*to Pisanio*]   About some half hour hence,
  Pray you, speak with me. You shall at least
  Go see my lord aboard. For this time leave me.

                                        Exeunt.

                        ❖

1.2   *Enter Cloten and two Lords.*

FIRST LORD   Sir, I would advise you to shift a shirt. The   1
  violence of action hath made you reek as a sacrifice.
  Where air comes out, air comes in; there's none
  abroad so wholesome as that you vent.   4

CLOTEN   If my shirt were bloody, then to shift it. Have   5
  I hurt him?

SECOND LORD [*aside*]   No, faith, not so much as his   7
  patience.   8

FIRST LORD   Hurt him? His body's a passable carcass if   9
  he be not hurt. It is a thoroughfare for steel if it be not 10
  hurt.

SECOND LORD [*aside*]   His steel was in debt; it went o'   12
  the backside the town.   13

CLOTEN   The villain would not stand me.   14

SECOND LORD [*aside*]   No, but he fled forward still,   15
  toward your face.

FIRST LORD   Stand you? You have land enough of your
  own, but he added to your having, gave you some   18
  ground.   19

---

141 blessèd (Imogen continues the religious paradox: she is *blessèd* in her love, though *past grace*, or damned, in terms of the King's favor.) **142 puttock** kite, bird of prey **148–149 overbuys . . . pays** pays more for me than I am worth by almost as much as the price he pays (which is his banishment) **149 mad** insane. (But Imogen uses the word to mean "mad with grief"; compare with her pun on *grace* in line 139.) **151 neatherd's** cowherd's **155 Beseech** I beseech **158 best advice** most mature reflection.   **languish** pine away **159 drop of blood** (Each sigh was supposed to deprive the heart of a drop of blood.) **160 Fie . . . way** (Said to the departing King as a way of pretending, for Imogen's benefit, the Queen's concern for her.) **162 My . . . master** i.e., Cloten drew his sword on Posthumus **165 had . . . anger** was not whetted on by anger **166 on 't** of it

167 takes his part sides with the King, or, plays the role one would expect of him   **168 To draw** in drawing   **169 in Afric** i.e., in some deserted spot   **176 lay wager**   **179 walk awhile** i.e., walk with me awhile

1.2. Location: Britain. At the court of Cymbeline, as before. The time is virtually continuous; Cloten still sweats from his duel (1.1.162).
1 shift change   **4 abroad** outside you. (The First Lord flatteringly suggests that the outside air is not as wholesome as that of Cloten's own sweet body, as though the outside air were the cause of the odor of perspiration, but the effect of *reek* and *vent* is to inform us at any rate that the odor is rank.)   **5 then to shift it** in that case, I would change it   **7–8 his patience** (Posthumus' patience has been sorely tried by this encounter, but little else.)   **9 passable** (1) penetrable (2) tolerably good   **9–10 if . . . hurt** i.e., I don't know what you mean by "hurt" otherwise   **12–13 His . . . town** i.e., Cloten's rapier avoided the fight in a cowardly fashion, as a debtor hides in back streets (with an antithetical play on *backside / thoroughfare*)   **14 stand me** stand up to me   **15 still** continually   **18–19 gave . . . ground** fell back before your advance (with pun on literal meaning)

SECOND LORD [*aside*] As many inches as you have ₂₀
   oceans. Puppies! ₂₁

CLOTEN I would they had not come between us.

SECOND LORD [*aside*] So would I, till you had measured how long a fool you were upon the ground.

CLOTEN And that she should love this fellow and refuse me!

SECOND LORD [*aside*] If it be a sin to make a true election, she is damned. ₂₈

FIRST LORD Sir, as I told you always, her beauty and her brain go not together. She's a good sign, but I have ₃₀ seen small reflection of her wit. ₃₁

SECOND LORD [*aside*] She shines not upon fools, lest the reflection should hurt her. ₃₃

CLOTEN Come, I'll to my chamber. Would there had been some hurt done!

SECOND LORD [*aside*] I wish not so, unless it had been the fall of an ass, which is no great hurt.

CLOTEN You'll go with us? ₃₈

FIRST LORD I'll attend your lordship.

CLOTEN Nay, come, let's go together.

SECOND LORD Well, my lord.   *Exeunt.*

❧

1.3   *Enter Imogen and Pisanio.*

IMOGEN
   I would thou grew'st unto the shores o' the haven
   And questionedst every sail. If he should write
   And I not have it, 'twere a paper lost ₃
   As offered mercy is. What was the last ₄
   That he spake to thee?

PISANIO   It was his queen, his queen!

IMOGEN
   Then waved his handkerchief?

PISANIO   And kissed it, madam.

IMOGEN
   Senseless linen, happier therein than I! ₇
   And that was all?

PISANIO   No, madam; for so long
   As he could make me with this eye or ear
   Distinguish him from others, he did keep
   The deck, with glove, or hat, or handkerchief
   Still waving, as the fits and stirs of 's mind
   Could best express how slow his soul sailed on,
   How swift his ship.

IMOGEN   Thou shouldst have made him

As little as a crow, or less, ere left ₁₅
   To after-eye him.

PISANIO   Madam, so I did. ₁₆

IMOGEN
   I would have broke mine eyestrings, cracked them, but ₁₇
   To look upon him till the diminution
   Of space had pointed him sharp as my needle—
   Nay, followed him till he had melted from
   The smallness of a gnat to air, and then
   Have turned mine eye and wept. But, good Pisanio,
   When shall we hear from him?

PISANIO   Be assured, madam,
   With his next vantage. ₂₄

IMOGEN
   I did not take my leave of him, but had
   Most pretty things to say. Ere I could tell him
   How I would think on him at certain hours
   Such thoughts and such; or I could make him swear
   The shes of Italy should not betray
   Mine interest and his honor; or have charged him
   At the sixth hour of morn, at noon, at midnight
   T' encounter me with orisons, for then ₃₂
   I am in heaven for him; or ere I could ₃₃
   Give him that parting kiss which I had set
   Betwixt two charming words, comes in my father, ₃₅
   And like the tyrannous breathing of the north ₃₆
   Shakes all our buds from growing.

      Enter a Lady.

LADY   The Queen, madam,
   Desires Your Highness' company.

IMOGEN
   Those things I bid you do, get them dispatched. ₃₉
   I will attend the Queen.

PISANIO   Madam, I shall.   *Exeunt.*

❧

1.4   *Enter Philario, Iachimo, a Frenchman, a
            Dutchman, and a Spaniard.*

IACHIMO Believe it, sir, I have seen him in Britain. He was then of a crescent note, expected to prove so ₂ worthy as since he hath been allowed the name of. But ₃ I could then have looked on him without the help of admiration, though the catalogue of his endowments ₅ had been tabled by his side and I to peruse him by ₆ items.

20–21 As . . . oceans i.e., none **21 Puppies** arrogant, vain cubs
28 election choice. (With a pun on the theological meaning.) **30 go not together** do not match. **sign** semblance, appearance **31 wit** intelligence **33 reflection** (The Second Lord plays on *reflection*, "shining," in line 31, suggesting here that, if Imogen were to show favor to fools, it would *reflect on*, or bring reproach on, her character.)
38 You'll . . . us (Addressed to the Second Lord or to both.)
1.3. Location: Britain. At the court of Cymbeline.
3–4 'twere . . . is i.e., the loss of such a letter would be as unfortunate as a pardon offered but failing to arrive before the execution, or as God's mercy similarly having no effect **7 Senseless** without feeling

15–16 ere . . . him before you left off following him with your gaze
17 eyestrings the muscles, nerves, or tendons of the eye, thought to break or crack at loss of sight. **but** merely **24 next vantage** first opportunity **32 encounter** join. **orisons** prayers **33 in heaven** i.e., praying **35 charming** having magical potency (to protect Posthumus from evil) **36 north** north wind **39 bid** bade, ordered
1.4. Location: Rome. Philario's house. Perhaps a feast is in progress; see 5.5.157.
2 crescent note growing reputation of importance **3 allowed the name of** granted to have the reputation for **5 admiration** wonder. (Iachimo insists he was not dazzled by Posthumus.) **6 tabled** set down in a list

PHILARIO   You speak of him when he was less furnished than now he is with that which makes him both with- 9 out and within. 10

FRENCHMAN   I have seen him in France. We had very many there could behold the sun with as firm eyes 12 as he.

IACHIMO   This matter of marrying his king's daughter, wherein he must be weighed rather by her value than his own, words him, I doubt not, a great deal from the 16 matter. 17

FRENCHMAN   And then his banishment.

IACHIMO   Ay, and the approbation of those that weep 19 this lamentable divorce under her colors are wonder- 20 fully to extend him, be it but to fortify her judgment, 21 which else an easy battery might lay flat for taking a 22 beggar without less quality. But how comes it he is to 23 sojourn with you? How creeps acquaintance? 24

PHILARIO   His father and I were soldiers together, to whom I have been often bound for no less than my life.

Enter Posthumus.

Here comes the Briton. Let him be so entertained amongst you as suits, with gentlemen of your know- 29 ing, to a stranger of his quality.—I beseech you all, be 30 better known to this gentleman, whom I commend to you as a noble friend of mine. How worthy he is I will leave to appear hereafter rather than story him in his 33 own hearing.

FRENCHMAN   Sir, we have known together in Orleans. 35

POSTHUMUS   Since when I have been debtor to you for courtesies which I will be ever to pay and yet pay still. 37

FRENCHMAN   Sir, you o'errate my poor kindness. I was glad I did atone my countryman and you. It had been 39 pity you should have been put together with so mortal 40 a purpose as then each bore, upon importance of so 41 slight and trivial a nature.

POSTHUMUS   By your pardon, sir, I was then a young traveler; rather shunned to go even with what I heard 44 than in my every action to be guided by others' experiences. But upon my mended judgment—if I 46 offend not to say it is mended—my quarrel was not altogether slight.

FRENCHMAN   Faith, yes, to be put to the arbitrament of 49 swords, and by such two that would by all likelihood have confounded one the other or have fallen both. 51

IACHIMO   Can we, with manners, ask what was the difference? 53

FRENCHMAN   Safely, I think; 'twas a contention in public, which may without contradiction suffer the 55 report. It was much like an argument that fell out last 56 night, where each of us fell in praise of our country 57 mistresses, this gentleman at that time vouching—and 58 upon warrant of bloody affirmation—his to be more 59 fair, virtuous, wise, chaste, constant, qualified, and less 60 attemptable than any the rarest of our ladies in France. 61

IACHIMO   That lady is not now living, or this gentle- man's opinion by this worn out. 63

POSTHUMUS   She holds her virtue still, and I my mind. 64

IACHIMO   You must not so far prefer her 'fore ours of 65 Italy.

POSTHUMUS   Being so far provoked as I was in France, I would abate her nothing, though I profess myself 68 her adorer, not her friend. 69

IACHIMO   As fair and as good—a kind of hand-in-hand 70 comparison—had been something too fair and too 71 good for any lady in Britain. If she went before others 72 I have seen, as that diamond of yours outlusters many 73 I have beheld, I could not but believe she excelled many. But I have not seen the most precious diamond that is, nor you the lady.

POSTHUMUS   I praised her as I rated her. So do I my stone.

IACHIMO   What do you esteem it at?

POSTHUMUS   More than the world enjoys. 80

IACHIMO   Either your unparagoned mistress is dead, or 81 she's outprized by a trifle. 82

POSTHUMUS   You are mistaken. The one may be sold or 84 given, or if there were wealth enough for the purchase 84 or merit for the gift. The other is not a thing for sale, and only the gift of the gods. 86

IACHIMO   Which the gods have given you?

POSTHUMUS   Which, by their graces, I will keep.

IACHIMO   You may wear her in title yours; but you 89 know strange fowl light upon neighboring ponds. 90

9–10 makes . . . within establishes him as regards both his fortune and his character   **12 behold the sun** i.e., like an eagle, a royal bird supposedly able to stare at the sun unblinkingly   **16–17 words . . . matter** causes him to be described in accounts that go beyond the truth   **19 weep** weep for   **20 divorce** i.e., separation through banishment.   **under her colors** i.e., in Imogen's party, carrying her banner   **20–21 are . . . extend him** seek by all means possible to praise him beyond his merit   **22–23 which . . . quality** i.e., which judgment of hers would otherwise be vulnerable to attack for having chosen a beggar lacking the qualities they ascribe to him   **24 How creeps acquaintance** how has he crept into your favor?   **29–30 knowing** knowledge of affairs, *savoir faire*   **30 stranger** foreigner.   **quality** rank   **33 story** give an account of   **35 known together** been acquainted   **37 which . . . still** which I will always be indebted to you for, even if I go on paying forever   **39 atone** set at one, reconcile   **40 put together** set opposite one another in a duel.   **mortal** deadly   **41 importance** matter, occasion   **44 shunned to go even** declined to agree   **46 upon** even upon.   **mended** improved

49 arbitrament arbitration   **51 confounded** destroyed   **53 difference** quarrel   **55–56 without . . . report** without objection be reported or told.   **suffer** permit, tolerate   **57–58 our country mistresses** the lady each of us loves in his native land   **59 bloody affirmation** affirming the truth in a duel   **60 qualified** having fine qualities   **61 attemptable** open to attempts on her virtue.   **any the rarest** any of the finest   **63 by this** by now   **64 mind** opinion   **65 prefer her** advance her claims   **68 would abate her nothing** would not lower my estimate of her in the slightest   **68–69 though . . . friend** even though I should (as at that time, in France) profess myself to be her adorer or wor- shiper in the ''courtly'' sense, not her accepted lover   **70–71 hand- in-hand comparison** comparison claiming equality only, not superior- ity   **71 had** would have   **72 went before** excelled   **73 diamond** i.e., the ring Imogen gave Posthumus   **80 the world enjoys** anything in the world   **81–82 Either . . . trifle** (In that case, jests Iachimo, you must love your jewel more than her, for if she is alive she is ''in the world.'')   **84 or if** if either   **86 only . . . gods** the gift of the gods alone   **89 wear . . . yours** possess her in name, claim title to her   **90 strange . . . ponds** i.e., claiming possession doesn't prevent strangers from infiltrating one's private domain

Your ring may be stolen too. So your brace of unpriz- 91
able estimations, the one is but frail and the other ca- 92
sual. A cunning thief or a that-way-accomplished cour- 93
tier would hazard the winning both of first and last.

POSTHUMUS Your Italy contains none so accomplished a
courtier to convince the honor of my mistress, if, in 96
the holding or loss of that, you term her frail. I do
nothing doubt you have store of thieves; notwith- 98
standing, I fear not my ring. 99

PHILARIO Let us leave here, gentlemen. 100

POSTHUMUS Sir, with all my heart. This worthy signor,
I thank him, makes no stranger of me; we are familiar 102
at first. 103

IACHIMO With five times so much conversation I
should get ground of your fair mistress, make her go 105
back even to the yielding, had I admittance and 106
opportunity to friend. 107

POSTHUMUS No, no.

IACHIMO I dare thereupon pawn the moiety of my estate 109
to your ring, which in my opinion o'ervalues it some- 110
thing. But I make my wager rather against your confi- 111
dence than her reputation, and, to bar your offense 112
herein too, I durst attempt it against any lady in the
world.

POSTHUMUS You are a great deal abused in too bold a 115
persuasion, and I doubt not you sustain what you're 116
worthy of by your attempt.

IACHIMO What's that?

POSTHUMUS A repulse—though your attempt, as you
call it, deserve more: a punishment too.

PHILARIO Gentlemen, enough of this. It came in too
suddenly; let it die as it was born, and, I pray you, be
better acquainted.

IACHIMO Would I had put my estate and my neighbor's 124
on th' approbation of what I have spoke! 125

POSTHUMUS What lady would you choose to assail?

IACHIMO Yours, whom in constancy you think stands
so safe. I will lay you ten thousand ducats to your ring 128
that, commend me to the court where your lady is, 129
with no more advantage than the opportunity of a
second conference, and I will bring from thence that
honor of hers which you imagine so reserved. 132

POSTHUMUS I will wage against your gold, gold to it. 133
My ring I hold dear as my finger; 'tis part of it.

IACHIMO You are a friend, and therein the wiser. If you 135
buy ladies' flesh at a million a dram, you cannot
preserve it from tainting. But I see you have some
religion in you, that you fear. 138

POSTHUMUS This is but a custom in your tongue. You
bear a graver purpose, I hope.

IACHIMO I am the master of my speeches and would
undergo what's spoken, I swear. 142

POSTHUMUS Will you? I shall but lend my diamond till
your return. Let there be covenants drawn between 's.
My mistress exceeds in goodness the hugeness of your
unworthy thinking. I dare you to this match; here's
my ring.   [*He wagers his ring.*] 147

PHILARIO I will have it no lay. 148

IACHIMO By the gods, it is one. If I bring you no
sufficient testimony that I have enjoyed the dearest
bodily part of your mistress, my ten thousand ducats
are yours; so is your diamond too. If I come off and
leave her in such honor as you have trust in, she your
jewel, this your jewel, and my gold are yours—
provided I have your commendation for my more free 155
entertainment. 156

POSTHUMUS I embrace these conditions. Let us have
articles betwixt us. Only, thus far you shall answer: if
you make your voyage upon her and give me directly 159
to understand you have prevailed, I am no further your 160
enemy; she is not worth our debate. If she remain un-
seduced, you not making it appear otherwise, for your
ill opinion and th' assault you have made to her chastity you shall answer me with your sword.

IACHIMO Your hand; a covenant. [*They shake hands.*]
We will have these things set down by lawful counsel,
and straight away for Britain, lest the bargain should
catch cold and starve. I will fetch my gold and have 168
our two wagers recorded.

POSTHUMUS Agreed.   [*Exeunt Posthumus and Iachimo.*]

FRENCHMAN Will this hold, think you?

PHILARIO Signor Iachimo will not from it. Pray let us 172
follow 'em.   *Exeunt.*

❖

1.5   *Enter Queen, Ladies, and Cornelius.*

QUEEN
Whiles yet the dew's on ground, gather those
    flowers.
Make haste. Who has the note of them?

A LADY   I, madam.   2

---

91 ring (Often, as here, symbolic of a chastity that can be lost.) **91–92 your . . . estimations** of the pair of objects (lady and ring) that you esteem beyond value **92–93 casual** susceptible to accident (such as theft) **93 that-way-accomplished** i.e., accomplished in seducing women **96 to convince** as to overcome **98 nothing** not at all. **store** plenty **99 fear not** fear not for **100 leave** leave off, cease **102–103 familiar at first** on familiar terms right from the start **105 get ground** gain the advantage **105–106 go back** succumb, give way. (The metaphor is from fencing, with sexual suggestion.) **107 to friend** to assist me **109 moiety** half **110–111 something** somewhat **112 bar your offense** avoid offending you individually **115–116 abused . . . persuasion** deceived by too bold an opinion **116 sustain** will sustain, receive **124 put** wagered **125 approbation** attestation, confirmation **128 lay** wager **129 commend me** provide me a letter of introduction **132 reserved** kept safe **133 wage** lay as a wager. **to it** in equal amount

135 You . . . wiser i.e., you know her too well, being her lover, to bet your ring on her **138 that** since. **fear** (1) experience "the fear of the Lord" that is the beginning of true wisdom (2) are fearful **142 undergo** undertake **147 s.d. wagers his ring** (Possibly Posthumus hands the ring to Iachimo or to Philario as official of the wager, or perhaps he still keeps it himself; see 2.4.108.) **148 I . . . lay** I will not let it be a wager **155 commendation** introduction (to Imogen) **155–156 free entertainment** ready welcome **159 directly** straight-forwardly, unequivocally **160 you** that you **168 starve** die (through second thoughts and cooling of resolve) **172 from it** depart from it
1.5. Location: Britain. At the court of Cymbeline.
2 note list

QUEEN Dispatch.   *Exeunt Ladies.*
Now, Master Doctor, have you brought those drugs?
CORNELIUS
Pleaseth Your Highness, ay. Here they are, madam. 5
                              [*He presents a small box.*]
But I beseech Your Grace, without offense—
My conscience bids me ask—wherefore you have 7
Commanded of me these most poisonous
    compounds,
Which are the movers of a languishing death,
But though slow, deadly?
QUEEN   I wonder, Doctor,
Thou ask'st me such a question. Have I not been
Thy pupil long? Hast thou not learned me how 12
To make perfumes? Distill? Preserve? Yea, so
That our great king himself doth woo me oft
For my confections? Having thus far proceeded— 15
Unless thou think'st me devilish—is 't not meet
That I did amplify my judgment in 17
Other conclusions? I will try the forces 18
Of these thy compounds on such creatures as
We count not worth the hanging—but none
    human—
To try the vigor of them and apply 21
Allayments to their act, and by them gather 22
Their several virtues and effects.
CORNELIUS   Your Highness 23
Shall from this practice but make hard your heart. 24
Besides, the seeing these effects will be
Both noisome and infectious.
QUEEN   O, content thee. 26

              Enter Pisanio.

[*Aside.*] Here comes a flattering rascal; upon him
Will I first work. He's for his master, 28
And enemy to my son.—How now, Pisanio?—
Doctor, your service for this time is ended;
Take your own way.
CORNELIUS [*aside*]   I do suspect you, madam, 31
But you shall do no harm.
QUEEN [*to Pisanio*]   Hark thee, a word.
CORNELIUS [*aside*]
I do not like her. She doth think she has
Strange lingering poisons. I do know her spirit
And will not trust one of her malice with
A drug of such damned nature. Those she has
Will stupefy and dull the sense awhile,
Which first, perchance, she'll prove on cats and
    dogs, 38
Then afterward up higher; but there is
No danger in what show of death it makes

More than the locking-up the spirits a time,
To be more fresh, reviving. She is fooled
With a most false effect, and I the truer 43
So to be false with her.
QUEEN   No further service, Doctor,
Until I send for thee.
CORNELIUS   I humbly take my leave.   *Exit.*
QUEEN   [*to Pisanio*]
Weeps she still, sayst thou? Dost thou think in time
She will not quench, and let instructions enter 49
Where folly now possesses? Do thou work.
When thou shalt bring me word she loves my son,
I'll tell thee on the instant thou art then
As great as is thy master; greater, for
His fortunes all lie speechless, and his name
Is at last gasp. Return he cannot, nor
Continue where he is. To shift his being 56
Is to exchange one misery with another,
And every day that comes comes to decay 58
A day's work in him. What shalt thou expect 59
To be depender on a thing that leans, 60
Who cannot be new built, nor has no friends,
So much as but to prop him? [*The Queen drops the
    box: Pisanio takes it up.*] Thou tak'st up
Thou know'st not what; but take it for thy labor.
It is a thing I made, which hath the King
Five times redeemed from death. I do not know
What is more cordial. Nay, I prithee, take it; 66
It is an earnest of a farther good 67
That I mean to thee. Tell thy mistress how
The case stands with her; do 't as from thyself. 69
Think what a chance thou changest on, but think 70
Thou hast thy mistress still—to boot, my son, 71
Who shall take notice of thee. I'll move the King 72
To any shape of thy preferment such 73
As thou'lt desire; and then myself, I chiefly,
That set thee on to this desert, am bound 75
To load thy merit richly. Call my women.
Think on my words.   *Exit Pisanio.*
              A sly and constant knave,
Not to be shaked; the agent for his master, 78
And the remembrancer of her to hold 79
The handfast to her lord. I have given him that 80
Which, if he take, shall quite unpeople her 81
Of liegers for her sweet, and which she after, 82

---

5 **Pleaseth** may it please. **s.d. He presents a small box** (Perhaps Cornelius hesitates before actually giving it to her; she may snatch it from him.) 7 **wherefore** why 12 **learned** taught 15 **confections** compounds (of drugs) 17 **did** i.e., should 18 **conclusions** experiments. **try** test 21–23 **To try . . . effects** to test their efficacy and apply antidotes to their action, and by these experiments determine their various operative powers and effects 24 **but** only 26 **noisome** noxious, foul-smelling. **content thee** do not trouble yourself 28 **He's for** i.e., he's an agent for 31 **Take your own way** be off, go about your business 38 **prove** test

43 **truer** more honest 49 **quench** become cool. **instructions** good counsel 56 **shift his being** change his abode 58–59 **And . . . him** i.e., and every new day that arrives means the undoing of a day's fruitful endeavor as far as he's concerned 59 **What . . . expect** what can you expect for yourself 60 **leans** is about to fall 66 **cordial** restorative (literally, to the heart) 67 **earnest** first payment 69 **as from thyself** as if from your own advice 70 **Think . . . on** think what an improvement in your fortunes you come upon in this change of service 71 **Thou . . . still** i.e., you will have Imogen as your patroness still, as the wife of Cloten, your new lord. **to boot** and besides her (you will have) 72 **take notice of thee** look out for you, offer advancement to you 73 **preferment** advancement 75 **That . . . desert** who urged you to take this action for which you will be rewarded 78 **shaked** shaken (in his loyalty) 79 **remembrancer of her** one who reminds her 80 **handfast** marriage contract 81–82 **shall . . . sweet** will thoroughly deprive her of the services of any ambassadors to her sweet Posthumus

Except she bend her humor, shall be assured   83
To taste of too.

Enter Pisanio, and Ladies [with flowers].

    So, so. Well done, well done.
The violets, cowslips, and the primroses
Bear to my closet. Fare thee well, Pisanio;   86
Think on my words.   *Exeunt Queen and Ladies.*

PISANIO And shall do.
But when to my good lord I prove untrue,
I'll choke myself. There's all I'll do for you.   *Exit.*

    ❧

1.6 *Enter Imogen alone.*

IMOGEN
A father cruel and a stepdame false,
A foolish suitor to a wedded lady
That hath her husband banished. O, that husband!   3
My supreme crown of grief, and those repeated   4
Vexations of it! Had I been thief-stol'n,
As my two brothers, happy! But most miserable
Is the desire that's glorious. Blest be those,   7
How mean soe'er, that have their honest wills,   8
Which seasons comfort.—Who may this be? Fie!   9

Enter Pisanio and Iachimo.

PISANIO
Madam, a noble gentleman of Rome,
Comes from my lord with letters.
IACHIMO   Change you, madam;   11
The worthy Leonatus is in safety
And greets Your Highness dearly.
        [He presents a letter.]
IMOGEN   Thanks, good sir.
You're kindly welcome.   *[She reads.]*
IACHIMO *[aside]*
All of her that is out of door most rich!
If she be furnished with a mind so rare,   15
She is alone th' Arabian bird, and I   17
Have lost the wager. Boldness be my friend!
Arm me, audacity, from head to foot!
Or, like the Parthian, I shall flying fight—   20
Rather, directly fly.
IMOGEN *(reads)* "He is one of the noblest note, to   22
whose kindnesses I am most infinitely tied. Reflect   23
upon him accordingly, as you value your trust—
        Leonatus."

So far I read aloud.
But even the very middle of my heart
Is warmed by th' rest and takes it thankfully.
You are as welcome, worthy sir, as I
Have words to bid you, and shall find it so
In all that I can do.
IACHIMO   Thanks, fairest lady.
What, are men mad? Hath nature given them eyes
To see this vaulted arch and the rich crop   33
Of sea and land, which can distinguish twixt   34
The fiery orbs above and the twinned stones   35
Upon th' unnumbered beach, and can we not   36
Partition make with spectacles so precious   37
Twixt fair and foul?
IMOGEN   What makes your admiration?   38
IACHIMO
It cannot be i' th' eye, for apes and monkeys
Twixt two such shes would chatter this way and   40
Contemn with mows the other; nor i' the judgment,   41
For idiots in this case of favor would   42
Be wisely definite; nor i' th' appetite: 43
Sluttery, to such neat excellence opposed,   44
Should make desire vomit emptiness,   45
Not so allured to feed.   46
IMOGEN
What is the matter, trow?
IACHIMO   The cloyèd will—   47
That satiate yet unsatisfied desire, that tub   48
Both filled and running—ravening first the lamb,   49
Longs after for the garbage.
IMOGEN   What, dear sir,
Thus raps you? Are you well?   51
IACHIMO
Thanks, madam, well. *[To Pisanio.]* Beseech you, sir,
Desire my man's abode where I did leave him.   53
He's strange and peevish.
PISANIO   I was going, sir,   54
To give him welcome.   *Exit.*
IMOGEN
Continues well my lord? His health, beseech you?
IACHIMO Well, madam.
IMOGEN
Is he disposed to mirth? I hope he is.
IACHIMO
Exceeding pleasant; none a stranger there   59
So merry and so gamesome. He is called

83 Except . . . humor unless she changes her mind (about not accepting Cloten) **86 closet** private chamber
1.6. Location: Britain. At the court.
3 That . . . banished whose husband is banished **4 repeated** already enumerated **7 the desire that's glorious** i.e., the ungratified yearning of a person in high station **8 mean** lowly. **honest wills** simple desires **9 seasons** adds relish to **11 Comes** who comes. **letters** i.e., (probably) a letter. **Change you** i.e., cheer up, don't be sad, or, *Change you, madam?* i.e., does your expression change at news of letters from Rome? **15 out of door** external **17 Arabian bird** i.e., phoenix, therefore unique **20 Parthian** (The Parthians were proverbial in ancient times for discharging a flight of arrows as they fled.) **22 note** reputation **23 Reflect** bestow favor

33 vaulted arch sky. **crop** harvest, produce **34–35 distinguish . . . stones** distinguish star from star and stone from stone. **twinned** exactly alike **36 unnumbered** numberless **37 Partition** distinction. **with . . . precious** i.e., with organs of vision so acutely sensitive **38 admiration** wonder **40 chatter this way** indicate approval of Imogen **41 Contemn** show scorn toward. **mows** grimaces, wry faces **42 in . . . favor** in question concerning a face of such grace and beauty **43 Be wisely definite** choose wisely **44–46 Sluttery . . . feed** sluttishness itself, confronted with such pure excellence, would void its own empty desire, not being tempted to feed its lust on Imogen **47 trow** do you think. **will** lustful appetite **48 satiate** glutted, *cloyèd*, as in line 47. (The perverted sexual appetite is at once glutted and insatiable.) **49 running** emptying itself. **ravening** devouring greedily **51 raps** transports, makes rapt **53 Desire . . . abode** bid my servant remain **54 strange and peevish** a stranger and easily upset **59 none a stranger** no other foreigner

The Briton reveler.
IMOGEN   When he was here
He did incline to sadness, and ofttimes   62
Not knowing why.
IACHIMO   I never saw him sad.
There is a Frenchman his companion, one
An eminent monsieur that, it seems, much loves
A Gallian girl at home. He furnaces   66
The thick sighs from him, whiles the jolly Briton— 67
Your lord, I mean—laughs from 's free lungs,
    cries "O,   68
Can my sides hold, to think that man, who knows
By history, report, or his own proof   70
What woman is, yea, what she cannot choose
But must be, will 's free hours languish   72
For assurèd bondage?"
IMOGEN   Will my lord say so?   73
IACHIMO
Ay, madam, with his eyes in flood with laughter.
It is a recreation to be by
And hear him mock the Frenchman. But heavens
    know
Some men are much to blame.
IMOGEN   Not he, I hope.
IACHIMO
Not he; but yet heaven's bounty towards him might 78
Be used more thankfully. In himself, 'tis much;   79
In you, which I account his, beyond all talents. 80
Whilst I am bound to wonder, I am bound
To pity too.
IMOGEN   What do you pity, sir?
IACHIMO
Two creatures heartily.
IMOGEN   Am I one, sir?
You look on me. What wrack discern you in me   84
Deserves your pity?
IACHIMO   Lamentable! What,   85
To hide me from the radiant sun, and solace   86
I' the dungeon by a snuff?
IMOGEN   I pray you, sir,   87
Deliver with more openness your answers
To my demands. Why do you pity me?   89
IACHIMO   That others do—
I was about to say—enjoy your—But
It is an office of the gods to venge it,   92
Not mine to speak on 't.
IMOGEN   You do seem to know   93
Something of me, or what concerns me. Pray you—

Since doubting things go ill often hurts more   95
Than to be sure they do; for certainties
Either are past remedies, or, timely knowing,   97
The remedy then born—discover to me   98
What both you spur and stop.
IACHIMO   Had I this cheek   99
To bathe my lips upon; this hand, whose touch,
Whose every touch, would force the feeler's soul
To th' oath of loyalty; this object, which
Takes prisoner the wild motion of mine eye,
Fixing it only here; should I, damned then,
Slaver with lips as common as the stairs
That mount the Capitol; join grips with hands   106
Made hard with hourly falsehood—falsehood as   107
With labor; then by-peeping in an eye   108
Base and illustrous as the smoky light   109
That's fed with stinking tallow; it were fit
That all the plagues of hell should at one time
Encounter such revolt.
IMOGEN   My lord, I fear,   112
Has forgot Britain.
IACHIMO   And himself. Not I,   113
Inclined to this intelligence, pronounce   114
The beggary of his change, but 'tis your graces 115
That from my mutest conscience to my tongue   116
Charms this report out.
IMOGEN   Let me hear no more.
IACHIMO
O dearest soul, your cause doth strike my heart
With pity that doth make me sick. A lady
So fair, and fastened to an empery   120
Would make the great'st king double—to be
    partnered   121
With tomboys hired with that self exhibition   122
Which your own coffers yield; with diseased
    ventures   123
That play with all infirmities for gold   124
Which rottenness can lend nature; such boiled stuff 125
As well might poison poison! Be revenged,
Or she that bore you was no queen, and you
Recoil from your great stock.   128
IMOGEN   Revenged?
How should I be revenged? If this be true—

62 **sadness** seriousness   66 **Gallian** Gallic, French.   **furnaces** gives forth like a furnace   67 **thick** coming thick and fast   68 **from 's free lungs** i.e., without restraint, heartily   70 **proof** experience   72 **will 's** will his.   **free** (1) independent (2) licentious. (Sexual insinuation occurs throughout Iachimo's speech, in *merry, gamesome, reveler, jolly*, etc.)   **languish** give up to languishing   73 **assurèd** (1) certain (2) betrothed   78 **bounty** generosity (in bestowing on him his own qualities and Imogen)   79 **In . . . much** i.e., as for his own qualities, heaven has been generous   80 **In you** i.e., as for heaven's generosity in giving him you.   **beyond all talents** i.e., that goes far beyond his own heaven-given endowments, or beyond computation (playing on *talents* as coins)   84 **wrack** ruin   85 **Deserves** that deserves   86 **hide me** i.e., hide.   **solace** take delight   87 **snuff** smoking candlewick   89 **demands** inquiries   92 **office** function   93 **on 't** of it

95 **doubting** fearing (that)   97 **timely knowing** if one knows in time   98 **then born** i.e., is then born.   **discover** reveal   99 **What . . . stop** i.e., what you simultaneously urge toward disclosure and then conceal, as if spurring and then reining in a horse   106 **grips** claspings   107–108 **as With labor** as much as if they had been made hard by actual labor   108 **by-peeping** giving sidelong glances   109 **illustrous** not lustrous   112 **Encounter** meet (with punishment).   **revolt** inconstancy   113–114 **Not . . . pronounce** not through any inclination to disclose this information do I report   115 **The beggary of his change** his change to baseness   116 **mutest conscience** most silent inner knowledge   120 **empery** empire (i.e., her graces and possessions)   121 **Would** that would.   **double** as having twice the majesty and power   121–122 **partnered With** put on a level with, made to share rights with   122 **tomboys** wantons.   **self exhibition** very allowance (of money)   123–125 **with diseased . . . nature** with diseased prostitutes who, for gold, play around with all the infirmities that rottenness (venereal disease) can lend to human nature. (*Lend*, because we can be said only to "borrow" infirmities until we die. *Ventures* suggests both commerce and risk.)   125 **boiled stuff** i.e., women treated by "sweating" for venereal disease   128 **Recoil** fall away, degenerate

As I have such a heart that both mine ears   131
Must not in haste abuse—if it be true,   132
How should I be revenged?
IACHIMO   Should he make me
Live like Diana's priest betwixt cold sheets   134
Whiles he is vaulting variable ramps,   135
In your despite, upon your purse? Revenge it.   136
I dedicate myself to your sweet pleasure,
More noble than that runagate to your bed,   138
And will continue fast to your affection,   139
Still close as sure.
IMOGEN [calling]   What, ho, Pisanio!   140
IACHIMO
Let me my service tender on your lips.
IMOGEN
Away! I do condemn mine ears that have
So long attended thee. If thou wert honorable,   143
Thou wouldst have told this tale for virtue, not
For such an end thou seek'st—as base as strange.   145
Thou wrong'st a gentleman who is as far
From thy report as thou from honor, and
Solicits here a lady that disdains   148
Thee and the devil alike.—What ho, Pisanio!—
The King my father shall be made acquainted
Of thy assault. If he shall think it fit   151
A saucy stranger in his court to mart   152
As in a Romish stew and to expound   153
His beastly mind to us, he hath a court
He little cares for and a daughter who
He not respects at all.—What, ho, Pisanio!
IACHIMO
O happy Leonatus! I may say
The credit that thy lady hath of thee   158
Deserves thy trust, and thy most perfect goodness
Her assured credit.—Blessèd live you long,   160
A lady to the worthiest sir that ever
Country called his, and you his mistress, only   162
For the most worthiest fit! Give me your pardon.   163
I have spoke this to know if your affiance   164
Were deeply rooted, and shall make your lord
That which he is new o'er; and he is one   166
The truest mannered, such a holy witch   167
That he enchants societies into him.   168
Half all men's hearts are his.
IMOGEN   You make amends.   169

IACHIMO   131
He sits 'mongst men like a descended god.
He hath a kind of honor sets him off   171
More than a mortal seeming. Be not angry,   172
Most mighty Princess, that I have adventured
To try your taking of a false report, which hath
Honored with confirmation your great judgment
In the election of a sir so rare,   176
Which you know cannot err. The love I bear him   177
Made me to fan you thus, but the gods made you,   178
Unlike all others, chaffless. Pray, your pardon.   179
IMOGEN
All's well, sir. Take my power i' the court for yours.
IACHIMO
My humble thanks. I had almost forgot
T' entreat Your Grace but in a small request,
And yet of moment too, for it concerns   183
Your lord, myself, and other noble friends
Are partners in the business.
IMOGEN   Pray, what is 't?   185
IACHIMO
Some dozen Romans of us and your lord—
The best feather of our wing—have mingled sums   187
To buy a present for the Emperor;
Which I, the factor for the rest, have done   189
In France. 'Tis plate of rare device, and jewels   190
Of rich and exquisite form, their values great,
And I am something curious, being strange,   192
To have them in safe stowage. May it please you
To take them in protection?
IMOGEN   Willingly;
And pawn mine honor for their safety. Since
My lord hath interest in them, I will keep them   196
In my bedchamber.
IACHIMO   They are in a trunk,
Attended by my men. I will make bold
To send them to you, only for this night;
I must aboard tomorrow.
IMOGEN   O, no, no.
IACHIMO
Yes, I beseech, or I shall short my word   201
By lengthening my return. From Gallia   202
I crossed the seas on purpose and on promise   203
To see Your Grace.
IMOGEN   I thank you for your pains.
But not away tomorrow!
IACHIMO   O, I must, madam.
Therefore I shall beseech you, if you please
To greet your lord with writing, do 't tonight.
I have outstood my time, which is material   208

---

131 As i.e., I say "if," since   **132 Must . . . abuse** must not overhastily wrong (by being too credulous)   **134 Diana's priest** i.e., priestess devoted to the goddess of chastity   **135 vaulting . . . ramps** mounting various prostitutes   **136 In your despite** in contempt of you. **upon your purse** spending your money   **138 runagate** renegade **139 fast** firm   **140 Still close** always secret   **143 attended** listened to **145 strange** adventitious, opposite to the purported virtue you claim to act for   **148 Solicits** solicitest   **151 fit** fit that   **152 to mart** should bargain   **153 Romish stew** Roman house of prostitution   **158 credit . . . of** faith . . . in   **160 Her assured credit** deserves her faith in you, Leonatus   **162 called his** called its own   **163 fit** match **164 affiance** fidelity   **166 new o'er** refreshed and renewed, made over again   **166–167 one . . . mannered** uniquely, above all others honorably disposed   **167 witch** charmer, fascinating person   **168 societies into him** whole groups of people to his circle (with a play on the idea of a magic circle)   **169 Half . . . his** all men give him half their hearts

171 sets that sets   **172 More . . . seeming** beyond the appearance of ordinary mortals, or, as if seeming to be more than mortal   **176 election** choice   **177 Which** who   **178 fan** test. (A metaphor from winnowing of grain.)   **179 chaffless** without chaff, i.e., perfect   **183 moment** importance   **185 Are** who are   **187 The best . . . wing** i.e., the choicest spirit of our company   **189 factor** agent   **190 plate** ware plated with precious metal.   **jewels** pieces of jewelry **192 something curious** somewhat anxious.   **strange** a foreigner **196 interest** share   **201 short** fall short of   **202 Gallia** Gaul, France **203 on promise** i.e., because I promised Posthumus   **208 outstood** outstayed

To th' tender of our present.
IMOGEN   I will write.   209
Send your trunk to me; it shall safe be kept
And truly yielded you. You're very welcome. *Exeunt.* 211

❧

2.1   *Enter Cloten and the two Lords.*

CLOTEN   Was there ever man had such luck? When I
kissed the jack upon an upcast, to be hit away! I had 2
a hundred pound on 't. And then a whoreson jacka- 3
napes must take me up for swearing, as if I borrowed 4
mine oaths of him and might not spend them at my
pleasure.
FIRST LORD   What got he by that? You have broke his 7
pate with your bowl.   8
SECOND LORD [*aside*]   If his wit had been like him that
broke it, it would have run all out.   10
CLOTEN   When a gentleman is disposed to swear, it is
not for any standers-by to curtail his oaths, ha? 12
SECOND LORD   No, my lord; [*aside*] nor crop the ears of
them.
CLOTEN   Whoreson dog! I gave him satisfaction? Would 15
he had been one of my rank!   16
SECOND LORD [*aside*]   To have smelled like a fool.
CLOTEN   I am not vexed more at anything in the earth. A 18
pox on 't! I had rather not be so noble as I am. They 19
dare not fight with me because of the Queen my
mother. Every jack-slave hath his bellyful of fighting, 21
and I must go up and down like a cock that nobody 22
can match.   23
SECOND LORD [*aside*]   You are cock and capon too, and 24
you crow, cock, with your comb on.   25
CLOTEN   Sayest thou?   26
SECOND LORD   It is not fit your lordship should under- 27
take every companion that you give offense to.   28

209 tender of our present offering of our gift   **211 truly yielded you**
duly returned to you
2.1. Location: Britain. At the court.
2 kissed the jack touched and lay near the small bowl used as target
in the game of bowls.   **upcast** i.e., crucial throw in the game of
bowls   **3–4 whoreson jackanapes** wretched ape, coxcomb   **4 take
me up** take me to task   **7–8 broke his pate** i.e., ruptured the skin
with a superficial head wound.   (But the Second Lord jokes as though
a *broken* head would allow brains to run out.)   **10 run all out** i.e.,
because Cloten's brains are watery. (The image is also suggestive of
exhausting and of running away.)   **12 curtail** shorten, as one might
bob the tail (and sometimes the ears) of a curtal dog; hence, *crop the
ears* (of the *oaths*) in the next speech   **15 gave** was to give. (To *give
satisfaction* is to accept a challenge to a duel from one who feels himself insulted—something that Cloten professes himself unwilling to do
because the opponent is of lower social rank, though Cloten's real
motive appears to have been cowardice.)   **16 rank** social class. (But
the Second Lord takes it in the sense of "rankness of smell.")
18–19 A pox on 't i.e., a plague on it   **21 jack-slave** lowborn fellow
22–23 like a cock . . . match (Like the champion cock in cockfight-
ing, complains Cloten, I am unchallenged because all are socially unequal to me.)   **24 capon** castrated rooster (used quibblingly for
cap-on, i.e., with fool's cap or coxcomb)   **25 with your comb on**
(There is a play here on "coxcomb" and "cock's comb.")   **26 Sayest
thou** what do you say?   **27–28 undertake** engage with, give satisfaction to   **28 companion** fellow.   **give offense to** attack or insult in
the code of dueling. (But the speaker also suggests that Cloten gives
offense to virtually everyone by being who he is. The insinuation is
present in line 31 as well: no one but your lordship is so adept at giving offense.)

CLOTEN   No, I know that, but it is fit I should commit 29
offense to my inferiors.   30
SECOND LORD   Ay, it is fit for your lordship only.
CLOTEN   Why, so I say.
FIRST LORD   Did you hear of a stranger that's come to
court tonight?   34
CLOTEN   A stranger, and I not know on 't?
SECOND LORD [*aside*]   He's a strange fellow himself,
and knows it not.
FIRST LORD   There's an Italian come, and, 'tis thought,
one of Leonatus' friends.
CLOTEN   Leonatus? A banished rascal; and he's another,
whatsoever he be. Who told you of this stranger?
FIRST LORD   One of your lordship's pages.
CLOTEN   Is it fit I went to look upon him? Is there no
derogation in 't?   44
SECOND LORD   You cannot derogate, my lord.   45
CLOTEN   Not easily, I think.
SECOND LORD [*aside*]   You are a fool granted; therefore 47
your issues, being foolish, do not derogate.   48
CLOTEN   Come, I'll go see this Italian. What I have lost
today at bowls I'll win tonight of him. Come, go.
SECOND LORD   I'll attend your lordship.
                            Exeunt [*Cloten and First Lord*].
That such a crafty devil as is his mother
Should yield the world this ass! A woman that
Bears all down with her brain, and this her son 54
Cannot take two from twenty, for his heart,   55
And leave eighteen. Alas, poor Princess,
Thou divine Imogen, what thou endur'st,
Betwixt a father by thy stepdame governed,
A mother hourly coining plots, a wooer
More hateful than the foul expulsion is
Of thy dear husband, than that horrid act
Of the divorce he'd make! The heavens hold firm
The walls of thy dear honor, keep unshaked
That temple, thy fair mind, that thou mayst stand
T' enjoy thy banished lord and this great land! *Exit.*

❧

2.2   *Enter Imogen in her bed, and a lady* [*Helen,
attending. A trunk is brought on.*]

IMOGEN
Who's there? My woman Helen?
HELEN   Please you, madam.

29–30 commit offense to attack, initiate action against (with unintended sense of "defecate upon")   **34 tonight** last night   **44 derogation** action unbecoming my position   **45 cannot derogate** (1) cannot
do anything undignified (2) have no dignity to lose   **47 a fool granted**
(1) admitted by everyone to be a fool (2) given the formal title of fool
48 issues offspring, i.e., deeds, actions   **54 Bears all down** carries all
before her, triumphs over everyone   **55 for his heart** for the life of
him
2.2 Location: Britain. Imogen's bedchamber in Cymbeline's palace.
s.d. in her bed (On the Elizabethan stage, a curtain presumably would
be withdrawn from a recessed area backstage, revealing a bed and
trunk within. Alternatively, a bed could be "thrust out" at this point
and the trunk carried on containing Iachimo, unless he uses the trapdoor or other such device. Imogen has a book; a lighted candle is
provided.)

IMOGEN

What hour is it?

HELEN   Almost midnight, madam.

IMOGEN

I have read three hours then. Mine eyes are weak.

[She gives her the book.]

Fold down the leaf where I have left. To bed.

Take not away the taper; leave it burning.

And if thou canst awake by four o' the clock,

I prithee, call me. Sleep hath seized me wholly.

[Exit lady, Helen, leaving the book beside the bed.]

To your protection I commend me, gods.

From fairies and the tempters of the night

Guard me, beseech ye.   9

Sleeps. Iachimo [comes] from the trunk.

IACHIMO

The crickets sing, and man's o'erlabored sense

Repairs itself by rest. Our Tarquin thus   12

Did softly press the rushes ere he wakened   13

The chastity he wounded. Cytherea,   14

How bravely thou becom'st thy bed, fresh lily,   15

And whiter than the sheets! That I might touch!

But kiss, one kiss! Rubies unparagoned,

How dearly they do 't! 'Tis her breathing that   18

Perfumes the chamber thus. The flame o' the taper

Bows toward her and would underpeep her lids

To see th' enclosèd lights, now canopied

Under these windows, white and azure-laced   22

With blue of heaven's own tinct. But my design— 23

To note the chamber. I will write all down.

[He writes.]

Such and such pictures; there the window; such

Th' adornment of her bed; the arras, figures,   26

Why, such and such; and the contents o' the story. 27

Ah, but some natural notes about her body   28

Above ten thousand meaner movables   29

Would testify t' enrich mine inventory.

O sleep, thou ape of death, lie dull upon her,   31

And be her sense but as a monument   32

Thus in a chapel lying! Come off, come off;

[taking off her bracelet]

As slippery as the Gordian knot was hard!   34

'Tis mine; and this will witness outwardly,

As strongly as the conscience does within,   36

To th' madding of her lord. On her left breast   37

A mole cinque-spotted, like the crimson drops   38

I' the bottom of a cowslip. Here's a voucher

Stronger than ever law could make. This secret

Will force him think I have picked the lock and ta'en

The treasure of her honor. No more. To what end?

Why should I write this down that's riveted,

Screwed to my memory? She hath been reading late

The tale of Tereus; here the leaf's turned down   45

Where Philomel gave up. I have enough.

To th' trunk again, and shut the spring of it.

Swift, swift, you dragons of the night, that dawning

May bare the raven's eye! I lodge in fear;   49

Though this a heavenly angel, hell is here.

Clock strikes.

One, two, three. Time, time!   51

[He goes into the trunk.] Exeunt.

❖

2.3   *Enter Cloten and Lords.*

FIRST LORD   Your lordship is the most patient man in

loss, the most coldest that ever turned up ace.   2

CLOTEN   It would make any man cold to lose.   3

FIRST LORD   But not every man patient after the noble

temper of your lordship. You are most hot and furious

when you win.

CLOTEN   Winning will put any man into courage. If I

could get this foolish Imogen, I should have gold

enough. It's almost morning, is 't not?

FIRST LORD   Day, my lord.

CLOTEN   I would this music would come. I am advised

to give her music o' mornings; they say it will pene- 12

trate.   13

Enter Musicians.

Come on, tune. If you can penetrate her with your

fingering, so; we'll try with tongue too. If none will   15

do, let her remain, but I'll never give o'er. First, a very

excellent good-conceited thing; after, a wonderful   17

sweet air, with admirable rich words to it—and then 18

let her consider.   *[Music plays.]*

Song.

MUSICIAN *[sings]*

Hark, hark, the lark at heaven's gate sings,

And Phoebus 'gins arise,   21

His steeds to water at those springs

On chalicèd flowers that lies;

9 **fairies** i.e., evil spirits   12 **Our Tarquin** the Roman Sextus Tarquinius, who raped Lucrece   13 **press the rushes** (Elizabethan floors were strewn with rushes or reeds.)   14 **Cytherea** Venus   15 **bravely** handsomely   18 **do 't** i.e., kiss each other   22 **windows** i.e., eyelids   23 **tinct** color, hue   26 **arras** hangings of tapestry.   **figures** carvings   27 **story** room (?), or, subject set forth in embroidery on the tapestry (?)   28 **notes** marks   29 **meaner movables** less important furnishings   31 **ape** i.e., imitator.   **dull** heavy   32 **be . . . monument** let her be as insensible as a horizontal effigy on a tomb   34 **slippery** easy to slip off.   **Gordian knot** (According to prophecy, whoever untied the knot binding the yoke to the pole of the chariot of Gordius, peasant King of Phrygia, should be king of all Asia. Alexander severed the knot with his sword.)   36 **conscience** consciousness, internal conviction   37 **madding** maddening   38 **cinque-spotted** with five spots

45 **Tereus** mythical king of Thrace, who raped Philomela, sister of his wife, Procne. (He had Philomela's tongue cut out so that she could not tell the story, but she wove it into a tapestry.)   49 **raven's eye** (The raven was supposed to wake at early dawn.)   51 s.d. **Exeunt** (Presumably the bed, and trunk with Iachimo inside, are carried offstage, unless Iachimo exits by a trapdoor or other means as a way of reentering the "trunk.")

2.3. **Location:** Britain. Adjoining Imogen's apartments. **The sense of time is nearly continuous, since it is early morn.**

2 **most coldest** coolest, most deliberate.   **turned up ace** made the losing throw of one at dice (with a pun on *ass*)   3 **cold** gloomy, dispirited   12–13 **penetrate** affect the feelings (with suggestion of penetrating her sexually; continued in *fingering* and *tongue*, line 15. See also lines 72, 77, and notes.)   15 **so** it is well   17 **good-conceited** imaginatively invented   18 **air** accompanied song for single voice   21 **Phoebus** i.e., the sun-god with his chariot and horses

And winking marybuds begin   24
  To ope their golden eyes.
With everything that pretty is,
  My lady sweet, arise,
    Arise, arise!

CLOTEN   So, get you gone. If this penetrate, I will con- 29
sider your music the better; if it do not, it is a vice in 30
her ears, which horsehairs and calves' guts, nor the 31
voice of unpaved eunuch to boot, can never amend. 32
                              [Exeunt Musicians.]

          Enter Cymbeline and Queen.

SECOND LORD   Here comes the King.
CLOTEN   I am glad I was up so late, for that's the reason
I was up so early. He cannot choose but take this ser-
vice I have done fatherly.—Good morrow to Your 36
Majesty, and to my gracious mother.
CYMBELINE
Attend you here the door of our stern daughter?
Will she not forth?
CLOTEN   I have assailed her with musics, but she vouch-
safes no notice.
CYMBELINE
The exile of her minion is too new;   42
She hath not yet forgot him. Some more time   43
Must wear the print of his remembrance on 't,   44
And then she's yours.
QUEEN   You are most bound to th' King,
Who lets go by no vantages that may   46
Prefer you to his daughter. Frame yourself   47
To orderly solicits, and be friended   48
With aptness of the season; make denials   49
Increase your services; so seem as if
You were inspired to do those duties which
You tender to her; that you in all obey her,
Save when command to your dismission tends,   53
And therein you are senseless.   54
CLOTEN   Senseless? Not so.

          [Enter a Messenger.]

MESSENGER
So like you, sir, ambassadors from Rome;   56
The one is Caius Lucius.
CYMBELINE   A worthy fellow,   57
Albeit he comes on angry purpose now;
But that's no fault of his. We must receive him
According to the honor of his sender;

And towards himself, his goodness forespent on us, 61
We must extend our notice. Our dear son,   62
When you have given good morning to your
  mistress,
Attend the Queen and us. We shall have need
T' employ you towards this Roman. Come, our
  queen.   Exeunt [all but Cloten].
CLOTEN
If she be up, I'll speak with her; if not,
Let her lie still and dream.—By your leave, ho!—
I know her women are about her. What
If I do line one of their hands? 'Tis gold   69
Which buys admittance—oft it doth—yea, and
  makes
Diana's rangers false themselves, yield up   71
Their deer to th' stand o' th' stealer; and 'tis gold 72
Which makes the true man killed and saves the thief, 73
Nay, sometimes hangs both thief and true man.
  What   74
Can it not do and undo? I will make
One of her women lawyer to me, for   76
I yet not understand the case myself.—   77
By your leave.   Knocks.

          Enter a Lady.

LADY
Who's there that knocks?
CLOTEN   A gentleman.
LADY   No more?
CLOTEN
Yes, and a gentlewoman's son.
LADY [aside]   That's more
Than some, whose tailors are as dear as yours,   81
Can justly boast of.—What's your lordship's
  pleasure?
CLOTEN
Your lady's person. Is she ready?
LADY   Ay,   83
[Aside] To keep her chamber.
CLOTEN   There is gold for you;
Sell me your good report.   [He offers money.] 85
LADY
How? My good name? Or to report of you
What I shall think is good?—The Princess!   87
                              [Exit Lady.]

          Enter Imogen.

24 winking marybuds closed buds of marigolds, as though with closed eyes   29–30 consider reward (?) value (?)   31 horsehairs and calves' guts i.e., bow hair and fiddle strings   32 unpaved unstoned, castrated   36 fatherly as a father would receive it, graciously and thankfully   42 minion darling   43–44 more . . . on 't more time must elapse, erasing the image of him on the memory   46 vantages favorable occasions   47 Prefer recommend.   Frame conform, prepare   48 solicits solicitings, importunings   48–49 be . . . season make timely use of your best opportunity   49 denials i.e., Imogen's refusals   53 dismission dismissal, rejection   54 senseless insensible (to her commands; however, Cloten understands the word as meaning "stupid")   56 So like you if you please   57 The one one of them, the chief

61 his goodness forespent (because of) his goodness previously bestowed   62 extend our notice show special attentiveness   69 line i.e., with gold   71 rangers gamekeepers, i.e., nymphs (vowed to chastity).   false forswear   72 deer (With a familiar pun on "dear," i.e., dear selves.)   stand (1) station of huntsman waiting for game (2) erection   73–74 Which . . . true man (Gold can corrupt justice, but it also tempts all sorts to commit crimes.)   true honest   76 lawyer to advocate for   77 understand the case know how to conduct my suit (with bawdy pun on stand again, line 72, and on case, meaning "vagina," as well as a legal case requiring a lawyer)   81 dear costly. (The Lady jests that expensive clothes are no guarantee of gentility.)   83 person (1) presence (2) body.   ready dressed. (But the Lady quibbles in another sense of "prepared, inclined.")   85 Sell . . . report i.e., speak favorably on my behalf. (But the Lady quibbles on report in the sense of "reputation, good name.")   87 What . . . good what seems good to me to report (favorable or unfavorable)

CLOTEN
Good morrow, fairest. Sister, your sweet hand.

IMOGEN
Good morrow, sir. You lay out too much pains
For purchasing but trouble. The thanks I give
Is telling you that I am poor of thanks
And scarce can spare them.

CLOTEN   Still, I swear I love you.

IMOGEN
If you but said so, 'twere as deep with me.   93
If you swear still, your recompense is still   94
That I regard it not.

CLOTEN   This is no answer.

IMOGEN
But that you shall not say I yield being silent,   96
I would not speak. I pray you, spare me. Faith,
I shall unfold equal discourtesy   98
To your best kindness. One of your great knowing   99
Should learn, being taught, forbearance.

CLOTEN
To leave you in your madness, 'twere my sin.
I will not.

IMOGEN
Fools are not mad folks.

CLOTEN   Do you call me fool?   103

IMOGEN   As I am mad, I do.   104
If you'll be patient, I'll no more be mad;
That cures us both. I am much sorry, sir,
You put me to forget a lady's manners
By being so verbal; and learn now for all   108
That I, which know my heart, do here pronounce,   109
By th' very truth of it, I care not for you,
And am so near the lack of charity
To accuse myself I hate you—which I had rather   112
You felt than make 't my boast.

CLOTEN   You sin against   113
Obedience, which you owe your father. For   114
The contract you pretend with that base wretch,   115
One bred of alms and fostered with cold dishes,
With scraps o' the court, it is no contract, none.
And though it be allowed in meaner parties—   118
Yet who than he more mean?—to knit their souls,

On whom there is no more dependency   120
But brats and beggary, in self-figured knot,   121
Yet you are curbed from that enlargement by   122
The consequence o' the crown, and must not foil   123
The precious note of it with a base slave,   124
A hilding for a livery, a squire's cloth,   125
A pantler—not so eminent.

IMOGEN   Profane fellow!   126
Wert thou the son of Jupiter and no more
But what thou art besides, thou wert too base
To be his groom. Thou wert dignified enough,   129
Even to the point of envy, if 'twere made   130
Comparative for your virtues, to be styled   131
The underhangman of his kingdom, and hated
For being preferred so well.

CLOTEN   The south fog rot him!   133

IMOGEN
He never can meet more mischance than come
To be but named of thee. His meanest garment   135
That ever hath but clipped his body is dearer   136
In my respect than all the hairs above thee,   137
Were they all made such men.—How now, Pisanio!

Enter Pisanio.

CLOTEN   "His garment!" Now the devil—

IMOGEN
To Dorothy my woman hie thee presently.   140

CLOTEN
"His garment!"

IMOGEN   I am sprited with a fool,   141
Frighted, and angered worse. Go bid my woman
Search for a jewel that too casually
Hath left mine arm. It was thy master's. 'Shrew me   144
If I would lose it for a revenue
Of any king's in Europe. I do think
I saw 't this morning; confident I am
Last night 'twas on mine arm; I kissed it.
I hope it be not gone to tell my lord
That I kiss aught but he.

PISANIO   'Twill not be lost.

IMOGEN
I hope so. Go and search.   [*Exit Pisanio.*]

CLOTEN   You have abused me.
"His meanest garment!"

IMOGEN   Ay, I said so, sir.
If you will make 't an action, call witness to 't.   153

---

93 deep binding, efficacious. (Imogen's point is that Cloten's oath adds nothing to his unwelcome protestation of love.) **94 still** constantly. (Imogen puns on Cloten's *Still*, "nonetheless," in line 92.) **96 But . . . silent** if it were not for the fact that you might interpret my silence as giving consent **98 unfold equal discourtesy** display discourtesy equal **99 knowing** knowledge, discernment. (Said with tactful irony.) **103 Fools . . . folks** i.e., I may be a fool to refuse you or to waste time talking with you, but that doesn't make me mad (?), or, if I'm mad, as you say, at least I'm not a fool like you (?) **104 As I am mad** insofar as I am mad (and you, after all, were the one who said I was mad) **108 By . . . verbal** (If the phrase refers to Cloten, the meaning of *verbal* is "verbose"; if it refers to Imogen, "plainspoken.") **for all** once and for all **109 which** who **111 so . . . charity** so nearly lacking in Christian charity as **112 To accuse . . . you** as to be obliged to accuse myself of hating you **113 felt** i.e., perceived without your having to say it **114 For** as for **115 pretend** allege falsely as your pretext **118 meaner parties** persons of lower social rank, who, says Cloten, are allowed to choose in marriage because the only consequence is their own child-burdened poverty

120 On whom from whose marriage. **dependency** consequence
121 But i.e., than. **self-figured** self-contracted **122 enlargement** liberty, freedom of action **123 consequence** succession, all that follows as a result of your being heir to the throne. **foil** defile, foul
124 note distinction **125 hilding for a livery** good-for-nothing fellow fit only for wearing a servant's uniform. **cloth** dress, livery
126 pantler pantry-servant. **not** not even **129 his** i.e., Posthumus'.
wert dignified would be elevated in dignity **130–131 if . . . virtues** i.e., if you both were given positions corresponding to your innate qualities **133 preferred** advanced. **south fog** (The south wind was supposed to be laden with poisonous vapors and diseases.) **135 of** by **136 clipped** embraced **137 respect** regard. **above thee** on your head **140 hie thee presently** go at once **141 sprited with** haunted by **144 'Shrew me** beshrew me. (A mild oath.) **153 action** action at law

CLOTEN
I will inform your father.
IMOGEN   Your mother too.
She's my good lady and will conceive, I hope,   155
But the worst of me. So, I leave you, sir,
To th' worst of discontent.   *Exit.*
CLOTEN   I'll be revenged.
"His meanest garment!" Well.   *Exit.*

♣

2.4   *Enter Posthumus and Philario.*

POSTHUMUS
Fear it not, sir. I would I were so sure
To win the King as I am bold her honor   2
Will remain hers.
PHILARIO   What means do you make to him?   3
POSTHUMUS
Not any, but abide the change of time,
Quake in the present winter's state, and wish
That warmer days would come. In these feared
    hopes   6
I barely gratify your love; they failing,   7
I must die much your debtor.
PHILARIO
Your very goodness and your company
O'erpays all I can do. By this, your king   10
Hath heard of great Augustus; Caius Lucius   11
Will do 's commission throughly. And I think   12
He'll grant the tribute, send th' arrearages,   13
Or look upon our Romans, whose remembrance   14
Is yet fresh in their grief.
POSTHUMUS   I do believe,   15
Statist though I am none, nor like to be,   16
That this will prove a war; and you shall hear
The legions now in Gallia sooner landed
In our not-fearing Britain than have tidings
Of any penny tribute paid. Our countrymen
Are men more ordered than when Julius Caesar   21
Smiled at their lack of skill but found their courage
Worthy his frowning at. Their discipline,   23
Now mingled with their courages, will make known
To their approvers they are people such   25
That mend upon the world.

Enter Iachimo.

PHILARIO   See! Iachimo!   26

---

155 good lady i.e., patroness. (Said ironically.)   **conceive** believe,
think.   **hope** (Continues the irony, though it can also mean "expect.")
2.4. Location: Rome. Philario's house.
2 bold confident   **3 means** overtures.   **him** i.e., the King   **6 feared**
mixed with fear   **7 gratify** repay   **10 this** this time   **11 of** from
12 do 's do his.   **throughly** thoroughly   **13 He'll** i.e., Cymbeline
will.   **arrearages** arrears, parts of the tribute due but unpaid   **14 Or**
(1) or else, or (2) before (he will).   **look upon** face   **15 their** i.e., the
Britons', or, caused by the Romans. (The Britons have painful remembrances of the Romans as fighters.)   **16 Statist** statesman.   **like** likely
21 more ordered better disciplined and governed   **23 frowning** i.e.,
in stern military resolve, not disapproval   **25 their approvers** those
who test their courage   **26 mend . . . world** surpass other peoples,
improve on very Nature

POSTHUMUS
The swiftest harts have posted you by land,   27
And winds of all the corners kissed your sails,   28
To make your vessel nimble.
PHILARIO   Welcome, sir.
POSTHUMUS
I hope the briefness of your answer made   30
The speediness of your return.
IACHIMO   Your lady
Is one of the fairest that I have looked upon.
POSTHUMUS
And therewithal the best, or let her beauty
Look through a casement to allure false hearts   34
And be false with them.
IACHIMO   Here are letters for you.
                    [*He gives a letter or letters.*]
POSTHUMUS
Their tenor good, I trust.
IACHIMO   'Tis very like.   36
PHILARIO
Was Caius Lucius in the Briton court
When you were there?
IACHIMO   He was expected then,
But not approached.
POSTHUMUS   All is well yet.   40
Sparkles this stone as it was wont, or is 't not
Too dull for your good wearing? [*Indicating the ring.*]
IACHIMO   If I have lost it,   42
I should have lost the worth of it in gold.
I'll make a journey twice as far t' enjoy
A second night of such sweet shortness which
Was mine in Britain, for the ring is won.
POSTHUMUS
The stone's too hard to come by.
IACHIMO   Not a whit,
Your lady being so easy.
POSTHUMUS   Make not, sir,
Your loss your sport. I hope you know that we
Must not continue friends.
IACHIMO   Good sir, we must,
If you keep covenant. Had I not brought
The knowledge of your mistress home, I grant   52
We were to question farther; but I now   53
Profess myself the winner of her honor,
Together with your ring, and not the wronger
Of her or you, having proceeded but
By both your wills.
POSTHUMUS   If you can make 't apparent
That you have tasted her in bed, my hand

---

27 harts i.e., horses as swift as deer. (Proverbially swift runners.)
posted sped   **28 of all the corners** from every corner   **30 hope** expect.   **your answer** the answer you were given   **34 Look through a
casement** (As a whore might show herself to attract customers. The
casement here is her body or perhaps her laced bodice.)   **36 like**
likely   **40 All is well yet** (Posthumus is evidently reassured by what
he has read of the letter.)   **42 s.d. Indicating the ring** (The ring possibly is in the custody of Philario as official of the wager; although Posthumus appears to have it himself at line 108, he may then take it
from Philario and give it to Iachimo.)   **52 knowledge** i.e., carnal
knowledge   **53 question** dispute, i.e., settle matters by a duel

And ring is yours; if not, the foul opinion
You had of her pure honor gains or loses   60
Your sword or mine, or masterless leaves both   61
To who shall find them.

IACHIMO   Sir, my circumstances,   62
Being so near the truth as I will make them,
Must first induce you to believe; whose strength
I will confirm with oath, which I doubt not
You'll give me leave to spare when you shall find   66
You need it not.

POSTHUMUS   Proceed.

IACHIMO   First, her bedchamber—
Where, I confess, I slept not, but profess
Had that was well worth watching—it was hanged   69
With tapestry of silk and silver; the story
Proud Cleopatra when she met her Roman,
And Cydnus swelled above the banks, or for   72
The press of boats or pride. A piece of work
So bravely done, so rich, that it did strive   74
In workmanship and value, which I wondered   75
Could be so rarely and exactly wrought,
Since the true life on 't was—

POSTHUMUS   This is true;   77
And this you might have heard of here, by me
Or by some other.

IACHIMO   More particulars
Must justify my knowledge.

POSTHUMUS   So they must,   80
Or do your honor injury.

IACHIMO   The chimney
Is south the chamber, and the chimneypiece   82
Chaste Dian bathing. Never saw I figures   83
So likely to report themselves. The cutter   84
Was as another nature, dumb; outwent her,   85
Motion and breath left out.

POSTHUMUS   This is a thing   86
Which you might from relation likewise reap,   87
Being, as it is, much spoke of.

IACHIMO   The roof o' the chamber
With golden cherubins is fretted. Her andirons—   89
I had forgot them—were two winking Cupids   90
Of silver, each on one foot standing, nicely
Depending on their brands.

POSTHUMUS   This is her honor!   92

Let it be granted you have seen all this—and praise
Be given to your remembrance—the description   94
Of what is in her chamber nothing saves   95
The wager you have laid.

IACHIMO   Then, if you can
Be pale, I beg but leave to air this jewel. See!
                    [He shows the bracelet.]
And now 'tis up again. It must be married   98
To that your diamond; I'll keep them.

POSTHUMUS   Jove!
Once more let me behold it. Is it that
Which I left with her?

IACHIMO   Sir—I thank her—that.
She stripped it from her arm; I see her yet;
Her pretty action did outsell her gift,   103
And yet enriched it too. She gave it me
And said she prized it once.

POSTHUMUS   Maybe she plucked it off
To send it me.

IACHIMO   She writes so to you, doth she?

POSTHUMUS
O, no, no, no! 'Tis true. Here, take this too.
                    [He gives the ring.]
It is a basilisk unto mine eye,   109
Kills me to look on 't. Let there be no honor
Where there is beauty, truth where semblance, love
Where there's another man. The vows of women   112
Of no more bondage be to where they are made   113
Than they are to their virtues, which is nothing.
O, above measure false!

PHILARIO   Have patience, sir,
And take your ring again; 'tis not yet won.
It may be probable she lost it; or   117
Who knows if one her women, being corrupted,   118
Hath stolen it from her?

POSTHUMUS   Very true,
And so, I hope, he came by 't. Back my ring!
                    [He takes back the ring.]
Render to me some corporal sign about her
More evident than this; for this was stolen.   123

IACHIMO
By Jupiter, I had it from her arm.

POSTHUMUS
Hark you, he swears; by Jupiter he swears.
'Tis true—nay, keep the ring—'tis true. I am sure
She would not lose it. Her attendants are
All sworn and honorable. They induced to steal it?
And by a stranger? No, he hath enjoyed her.
The cognizance of her incontinency   130
Is this. She hath bought the name of whore thus
    dearly.

60–61 gains . . . mine i.e., means that we must fight a duel
62 who whoever. **circumstances** detailed observations **66 spare**
leave out. **watching** remaining awake (for) **69 that** that which.
72 Cydnus a river in Cilicia, or modern-day southern Turkey, the
scene of the meeting of Antony and Cleopatra. (See *Antony and
Cleopatra*, 2.2.196–236.) **or for** either because of **74 bravely**
handsomely **74–75 it did . . . value** it was a question whether the
workmanship or the intrinsic value contained in the material was the
greater **77 on 't** of it **80 justify** confirm **82 chimneypiece** sculptured mantelpiece **83 Dian** Diana, goddess of chastity **84 So . . .
themselves** so like what they purported to represent, speaking likenesses **84–85 cutter . . . dumb** sculptor rivaled nature in creative
power, giving mute eloquence to his creation. **her** i.e., nature
86 left out excepted **87 relation** hearsay, secondhand **89 fretted**
adorned with carved or embossed work in decorative patterns
90 winking i.e., blind **92 Depending** leaning. **brands** tall hymeneal
torches, against which the Cupids lean. **This . . . honor** i.e., is this
what you can allege to impugn her honor? (Said sarcastically.)

94 remembrance ability to remember **95 nothing** not at all
98 up put up, pocketed **103 outsell** exceed in value **109 basilisk**
fabulous serpent or dragon whose look was fatal **112 The vows** i.e.,
let the vows **113 bondage** obligation. **where** i.e., the men to
whom **117 probable** provable **118 one her** one of her **123 evident** conclusive **130 cognizance** mark or token by which a thing is
recognized, as a servant is identified by his livery and identifying
mark

There, take thy hire, and all the fiends of hell   132
Divide themselves between you!
  [*He gives the ring again.*]
PHILARIO   Sir, be patient.   133
This is not strong enough to be believed
Of one persuaded well of.
POSTHUMUS   Never talk on 't.   135
She hath been colted by him.
IACHIMO   If you seek   136
For further satisfying, under her breast—
Worthy the pressing—lies a mole, right proud
Of that most delicate lodging. By my life,
I kissed it, and it gave me present hunger
To feed again, though full. You do remember
This stain upon her?
POSTHUMUS   Ay, and it doth confirm
Another stain, as big as hell can hold,
Were there no more but it.
IACHIMO   Will you hear more?
POSTHUMUS
Spare your arithmetic! Never count the turns.   145
Once, and a million!
IACHIMO   I'll be sworn—
POSTHUMUS   No swearing.   146
If you will swear you have not done 't, you lie,
And I will kill thee if thou dost deny
Thou'st made me cuckold.
IACHIMO   I'll deny nothing.
POSTHUMUS
O, that I had her here, to tear her limbmeal!   150
I will go there and do 't, i' the court, before
Her father. I'll do something—   *Exit.*   152
PHILARIO   Quite beside
The government of patience! You have won.
Let's follow him and pervert the present wrath   154
He hath against himself.
IACHIMO   With all my heart. *Exeunt.*

2.5   *Enter Posthumus.*

POSTHUMUS
Is there no way for men to be, but women   1
Must be half-workers? We are all bastards,   2
And that most venerable man which I
Did call my father was I know not where
When I was stamped. Some coiner with his tools   5
Made me a counterfeit; yet my mother seemed

The Dian of that time. So doth my wife   7
The nonpareil of this. O, vengeance, vengeance!   8
Me of my lawful pleasure she restrained
And prayed me oft forbearance; did it with
A pudency so rosy the sweet view on 't   11
Might well have warmed old Saturn, that I
    thought her   12
As chaste as unsunned snow. O, all the devils!
This yellow Iachimo, in an hour, was 't not?   14
Or less? At first? Perchance he spoke not, but,   15
Like a full-acorned boar, a German one,   16
Cried "O!" and mounted; found no opposition
But what he looked for should oppose and she   18
Should from encounter guard. Could I find out
The woman's part in me! For there's no motion   20
That tends to vice in man but I affirm
It is the woman's part. Be it lying, note it,
The woman's; flattering, hers; deceiving, hers;
Lust and rank thoughts, hers, hers; revenges, hers;
Ambitions, covetings, change of prides, disdain,   25
Nice longing, slanders, mutability,   26
All faults that have a name, nay, that hell knows,
Why, hers, in part or all, but rather all.
For even to vice
They are not constant, but are changing still   30
One vice but of a minute old for one
Not half so old as that. I'll write against them,   32
Detest them, curse them. Yet 'tis greater skill   33
In a true hate to pray they have their will;
The very devils cannot plague them better.   *Exit.*

❖

3.1   *Enter in state, Cymbeline, Queen, Cloten, and lords at one door, and at another, Caius Lucius and attendants.*

CYMBELINE
Now say, what would Augustus Caesar with us?
LUCIUS
When Julius Caesar, whose remembrance yet   2
Lives in men's eyes, and will to ears and tongues   3
Be theme and hearing ever, was in this Britain   4
And conquered it, Cassibelan, thine uncle—
Famous in Caesar's praises no whit less
Than in his feats deserving it—for him
And his succession granted Rome a tribute,

132–133 all . . . you i.e., may you and Imogen suffer equal torments
in hell   135 persuaded well of well thought of.   on 't of it
136 colted enjoyed sexually   145 turns (with a bitter suggestion of
"tricks," sexual encounters with a customer)   146 Once, and a million i.e., what does it matter if once or a million times; it's all the
same   150 limbmeal limb from limb   152 beside beyond   154 pervert divert
2.5. Location: Philario's house, as before. The scene may be virtually
continuous.
1 be exist   2 half-workers partners, collaborators   5 stamped (The
image of procreation as an act of coinage by the father occurs often in
Shakespeare.)   tools (With bitter suggestion of the male sexual
organ.)

7 Dian Diana, goddess of chastity   8 nonpareil one that has no
equal.   this this time   11 pudency modesty.   rosy blushing (that).
on 't of it   12 Saturn father of Jupiter, associated with old age
14 yellow sallow   15 At first right at first   16 full-acorned full of
acorns, favorite food of boars. (In German, *eichel*, "acorn," also
means "penis" because of its glanslike shape.)   18 But . . . oppose
i.e., except for the pleasant physical friction or barrier (the hymen) he
expected in entering. (Imogen is no longer a virgin, being married,
but the hymen still symbolizes what she should *guard* from *encounter*,
line 19.)   20 part (With bitter sexual suggestion.)   motion impulse
25 change of prides varying vanities (in dress, etc.)   26 Nice fastidious, wanton.   mutability inconstancy   30 still continuously
32 write against denounce   33 skill reason
3.1. Location: Britain. At the court of Cymbeline.
2–4 whose . . . ever i.e., our eyes still bear witness to Caesar's great
accomplishments, which poets and historians will immortalize

Yearly three thousand pounds, which by thee lately
Is left untendered.
QUEEN   And, to kill the marvel,   10
Shall be so ever.
CLOTEN   There be many Caesars
Ere such another Julius. Britain's a world
By itself, and we will nothing pay
For wearing our own noses.
QUEEN   That opportunity   14
Which then they had to take from 's, to resume   15
We have again. Remember, sir, my liege,   16
The kings your ancestors, together with
The natural bravery of your isle, which stands
As Neptune's park, ribbed and palèd in   19
With rocks unscalable and roaring waters,
With sands that will not bear your enemies' boats,
But suck them up to th' topmast. A kind of con-
quest
Caesar made here, but made not here his brag
Of "Came and saw and overcame." With shame—
The first that ever touched him—he was carried
From off our coast, twice beaten; and his shipping,
Poor ignorant baubles, on our terrible seas   27
Like eggshells moved upon their surges, cracked   28
As easily 'gainst our rocks. For joy whereof
The famed Cassibelan, who was once at point—   30
O giglot fortune!—to master Caesar's sword,   31
Made Lud's Town with rejoicing fires bright   32
And Britons strut with courage.
CLOTEN   Come, there's no more tribute to be paid. Our
kingdom is stronger than it was at that time; and, as I
said, there is no more such Caesars. Other of them may
have crooked noses, but to owe such straight arms,   37
none.
CYMBELINE   Son, let your mother end.   39
CLOTEN   We have yet many among us can grip as hard 40
as Cassibelan. I do not say I am one; but I have a hand.
Why tribute? Why should we pay tribute? If Caesar
can hide the sun from us with a blanket, or put the
moon in his pocket, we will pay him tribute for light;
else, sir, no more tribute, pray you now.
CYMBELINE [*to Lucius*]   You must know,
Till the injurious Romans did extort   47
This tribute from us, we were free. Caesar's
ambition,
Which swelled so much that it did almost stretch
The sides o' the world, against all color here   50

Did put the yoke upon 's, which to shake off
Becomes a warlike people, whom we reckon
Ourselves to be. We do say then to Caesar,
Our ancestor was that Mulmutius which
Ordained our laws, whose use the sword of Caesar   55
Hath too much mangled, whose repair and franchise   56
Shall, by the power we hold, be our good deed,
Though Rome be therefore angry. Mulmutius made
  our laws,
Who was the first of Britain which did put
His brows within a golden crown and called
Himself a king.
LUCIUS   I am sorry, Cymbeline,
That I am to pronounce Augustus Caesar—
Caesar, that hath more kings his servants than
Thyself domestic officers—thine enemy.
Receive it from me, then: war and confusion   65
In Caesar's name pronounce I 'gainst thee. Look
For fury not to be resisted. Thus defied,   67
I thank thee for myself.
CYMBELINE   Thou art welcome, Caius.   68
Thy Caesar knighted me; my youth I spent
Much under him. Of him I gathered honor,
Which he to seek of me again perforce   71
Behooves me keep at utterance. I am perfect   72
That the Pannonians and Dalmatians for   73
Their liberties are now in arms, a precedent
Which not to read would show the Britons cold.   75
So Caesar shall not find them.
LUCIUS   Let proof speak.   76
CLOTEN   His Majesty bids you welcome. Make pastime
with us a day or two, or longer. If you seek us after-
wards in other terms, you shall find us in our saltwater
girdle. If you beat us out of it, it is yours; if you fall in
the adventure, our crows shall fare the better for you,
and there's an end.
LUCIUS   So, sir.
CYMBELINE
I know your master's pleasure and he mine.
All the remain is "Welcome!"   *Exeunt.* 85

3.2   *Enter Pisanio, reading of a letter.*

PISANIO
How? Of adultery? Wherefore write you not
What monster's her accuser? Leonatus,
O master, what a strange infection
Is fall'n into thy ear! What false Italian,
As poisonous-tongued as handed, hath prevailed   5

---

10 kill the marvel end the surprise (by making nonpayment a regular
practice)   **14 our own noses** i.e., British, not Roman, noses. (See
Cloten's gibe at the Romans' *crooked noses* in line 37.)   **15–16 to
resume . . . again** we now have the opportunity to take it back
19 ribbed enclosed.   **palèd** fenced   **27 ignorant** silly, unskilled.
baubles trifles   **28 their surges** the waves of the sea   **30 Cassibelan**
(The incident referred to is recorded of Nennius, brother of Cassibelan, in Holinshed.)   **30–31 at point . . . to master** on the point . . .
of mastering   **31 giglot** lewd, wanton   **32 Lud's Town** London (supposedly named after King Lud, Cymbeline's grandfather)   **37 owe**
own.   **straight** i.e., strong   **39 end** finish speaking   **40 can grip**
who can grasp (a sword)   **47 injurious** insolent   **50 against all color**
in defiance of all rightful claim. (*Color*, "arguable ground or claim,"
may also pun on *yoke*, "collar," in the next line.)

55 whose use the exercise of which laws   **56 whose . . . franchise**
the repair and free exercise of which laws   **65 confusion** discomfiture, destruction   **67 Thus defied** you having been thus defied
68 thank . . . myself thank you personally for this welcome   **71 he
to seek** his seeking it   **72 keep at utterance** to defend to the last extremity. (From the French *à outrance.*)   **perfect** well aware   **73 for**
defend   **75 cold** lacking spirit   **76 proof** experiment, trial (by way of
combat)   **85 All the remain** all that remains (to be said)
3.2. Location: Britain. At the court of Cymbeline.
s.d. reading of reading   **5 As . . . handed** as skilled in slander as in
the art of secret poisoning (for which the Italians were notorious)

On thy too ready hearing? Disloyal? No.
She's punished for her truth and undergoes,   7
More goddesslike than wifelike, such assaults
As would take in some virtue. O my master,   9
Thy mind to her is now as low as were   10
Thy fortunes. How? That I should murder her,
Upon the love and truth and vows which I   12
Have made to thy command? I, her? Her blood?
If it be so to do good service, never
Let me be counted serviceable. How look I,
That I should seem to lack humanity
So much as this fact comes to? [*He reads.*] "Do 't.
    The letter   17
That I have sent her, by her own command
Shall give thee opportunity." O damned paper,
Black as the ink that's on thee! Senseless bauble,   20
Art thou a fedarie for this act, and look'st   21
So virginlike without? Lo, here she comes.

                Enter Imogen.

I am ignorant in what I am commanded.   23
IMOGEN   How now, Pisanio?
PISANIO
    Madam, here is a letter from my lord.
IMOGEN [*taking the letter*]
    Who, thy lord that is my lord, Leonatus?
    O, learned indeed were that astronomer   27
    That knew the stars as I his characters;   28
    He'd lay the future open. You good gods,
    Let what is here contained relish of love,   30
    Of my lord's health, of his content—yet not   31
    That we two are asunder; let that grieve him.
    Some griefs are med'cinable; that is one of them,   33
    For it doth physic love—of his content   34
    All but in that! Good wax, thy leave. [*She breaks the*
        seal.] Blest be
    You bees that make these locks of counsel! Lovers   36
    And men in dangerous bonds pray not alike;   37
    Though forfeiters you cast in prison, yet   38
    You clasp young Cupid's tables. Good news, gods!   39
        [*She reads.*] "Justice and your father's wrath, should
    he take me in his dominion, could not be so cruel to me   41
    as you, O the dearest of creatures, would even renew   42
    me with your eyes. Take notice that I am in Cambria,   43
    at Milford Haven. What your own love will out of this
    advise you, follow. So he wishes you all happiness

that remains loyal to his vow, and your increasing in   46
love.   Leonatus Posthumus."   47
O, for a horse with wings! Hear'st thou, Pisanio?
He is at Milford Haven. Read, and tell me
How far 'tis thither. If one of mean affairs   50
May plod it in a week, why may not I
Glide thither in a day? Then, true Pisanio,
Who long'st like me to see thy lord, who long'st—
O, let me bate—but not like me, yet long'st,   54
But in a fainter kind—O, not like me,
For mine's beyond beyond; say, and speak thick—   56
Love's counselor should fill the bores of hearing,   57
To th' smothering of the sense—how far it is   58
To this same blessèd Milford. And by th' way   59
Tell me how Wales was made so happy as
T' inherit such a haven. But first of all,   61
How we may steal from hence, and for the gap
That we shall make in time from our hence-going
And our return, to excuse. But first, how get hence?
Why should excuse be born or ere begot?   65
We'll talk of that hereafter. Prithee, speak,
How many score of miles may we well ride
Twixt hour and hour?
PISANIO   One score twixt sun and sun,   68
Madam, 's enough for you—and too much too.   69
IMOGEN
    Why, one that rode to 's execution, man,
    Could never go so slow. I have heard of riding
        wagers   71
    Where horses have been nimbler than the sands
    That run i' the clock's behalf. But this is fool'ry.   73
    Go bid my woman feign a sickness, say
    She'll home to her father; and provide me presently   75
    A riding suit no costlier than would fit
    A franklin's huswife.
PISANIO   Madam, you're best consider.   77
IMOGEN
    I see before me, man. Nor here, nor here,   78
    Nor what ensues, but have a fog in them   79
    That I cannot look through. Away, I prithee!

---

7 truth fidelity. **undergoes** i.e., withstands **9 take in** cause to yield **10 to her** compared to hers **12 Upon** on the basis of **17 fact** deed **20 Senseless bauble** trifle incapable of feeling **21 fedarie** accomplice **23 am ignorant in** will pretend not to know **27 astronomer** astrologer **28 characters** handwriting (with a suggestion, too, of astrological symbols) **30 relish** taste **31 not** i.e., not content **33 med'cinable** curative, health-giving **34 physic** make healthy, strong **36 locks of counsel** waxen seals enclosing confidential matters **36–39 Lovers . . . tables** people in love don't address the same prayers to you waxmaking bees as do men at risk of penalties for contracts they've signed; your beeswax, used to seal documents, puts forfeiters of contracts in prison, whereas you bees seal with wax the writing tablets or love letters used in the affairs of Cupid **41 take** apprehend **42 as** but that. (The letter, however, is studiously ambiguous and suggests also that no one can be so cruel as she.) **43 Cambria** Wales

46 that remains loyal more ambiguity: (1) you who remain loyal (2) on condition that you remain loyal **46–47 your increasing in love** (he wishes) your advancement and prosperity in love; suggesting, too, he wishes your love for your husband were greater **50 mean affairs** ordinary business **54 bate** reduce in amount, modify **56 beyond beyond** i.e., even greater than something already great. **thick** many words quickly **57 the bores of hearing** the ears **58 To . . . sense** to the point of overwhelming the sense of hearing **59 by th' way** as we go **61 T' inherit** to come to possess **65 Why . . . begot** i.e., why worry about how to excuse our absence before we've figured how to get away? **68 Twixt hour and hour** in an hour. **One . . . and sun** twenty miles a day **69 too much too** i.e., even that would exhaust you (but suggesting also that she will arrive too soon at her fatal destiny. Her answer unconsciously picks up the irony.) **71 riding** racing **73 i' . . . behalf** i.e., doing the service of a clock, in an hourglass **75 She'll . . . father** (The waiting woman's pretended emergency will justify her asking for a riding habit that Imogen can then use.) **77 franklin's** yeoman's. (A franklin was a farmer who owned his own land but was not of noble birth.) **you're best** you had better **78 before me** immediately in front of me. **Nor . . . here** (She gestures: not to this side, not to that.) **79 ensues** happens later. (Imogen can only look directly ahead to Milford Haven, nowhere else and not beyond.)

Do as I bid thee. There's no more to say.
Accessible is none but Milford way.

Exeunt [separately].

❖

3.3   *Enter [from the cave] Belarius; Guiderius, and Arviragus [following].*

BELARIUS
A goodly day not to keep house with such   1
Whose roof's as low as ours. Stoop, boys; this gate
Instructs you how t' adore the heavens and
    bows you   3
To a morning's holy office. The gates of monarchs   4
Are arched so high that giants may jet through   5
And keep their impious turbans on, without
Good morrow to the sun.—Hail, thou fair heaven!
We house i' the rock, yet use thee not so hardly   8
As prouder livers do.
GUIDERIUS   Hail, heaven!   9
ARVIRAGUS   Hail, heaven!
BELARIUS
Now for our mountain sport. Up to yond hill;
Your legs are young. I'll tread these flats. Consider,
When you above perceive me like a crow,   12
That it is place which lessens and sets off,   13
And you may then revolve what tales I have
    told you   14
Of courts, of princes, of the tricks in war.
This service is not service, so being done,   16
But being so allowed. To apprehend thus   17
Draws us a profit from all things we see;
And often, to our comfort, shall we find
The sharded beetle in a safer hold   20
Than is the full-winged eagle. O, this life
Is nobler than attending for a check,   22
Richer than doing nothing for a bauble,   23
Prouder than rustling in unpaid-for silk;   24
Such gain the cap of him that makes him fine, 25
Yet keeps his book uncrossed. No life to ours. 26
GUIDERIUS
Out of your proof you speak. We poor unfledged   27
Have never winged from view o' the nest, nor
    know not

What air's from home. Haply this life is best,   29
If quiet life be best, sweeter to you
That have a sharper known, well corresponding
With your stiff age; but unto us it is
A cell of ignorance, traveling abed,   33
A prison for a debtor that not dares
To stride a limit.
ARVIRAGUS   What should we speak of   35
When we are old as you? When we shall hear
The rain and wind beat dark December, how,   37
In this our pinching cave, shall we discourse   38
The freezing hours away? We have seen nothing.
We are beastly: subtle as the fox for prey,
Like warlike as the wolf for what we eat.   41
Our valor is to chase what flies. Our cage   42
We make a choir, as doth the prisoned bird,
And sing our bondage freely.
BELARIUS   How you speak!   44
Did you but know the city's usuries
And felt them knowingly; the art o' the court,
As hard to leave as keep, whose top to climb   47
Is certain falling, or so slippery that
The fear's as bad as falling; the toil o' the war,   49
A pain that only seems to seek out danger   50
I' the name of fame and honor, which dies i' the
    search
And hath as oft a slanderous epitaph
As record of fair act; nay, many times
Doth ill deserve by doing well; what's worse,   54
Must curtsy at the censure. O boys, this story
The world may read in me. My body's marked
With Roman swords, and my report was once   57
First with the best of note. Cymbeline loved me,   58
And when a soldier was the theme, my name
Was not far off. Then was I as a tree
Whose boughs did bend with fruit. But in one night,   61
A storm, or robbery, call it what you will,
Shook down my mellow hangings, nay, my leaves,   63
And left me bare to weather.
GUIDERIUS   Uncertain favor!
BELARIUS
My fault being nothing—as I have told you oft—
But that two villains, whose false oaths prevailed
Before my perfect honor, swore to Cymbeline
I was confederate with the Romans. So
Followed my banishment, and this twenty years
This rock and these demesnes have been my world,   70
Where I have lived at honest freedom, paid   71
More pious debts to heaven than in all

3.3. Location: Wales. Before the cave of Belarius.
1 keep house stay at home   **3 bows you** makes you bow   **4 holy office** i.e., morning prayer   **5 jet** strut   **8 use . . . hardly** treat you not so badly, do not offend heaven as much (with a play on the idea of *rock* and *hard*)   **9 prouder livers** those who live more proudly and magnificently   **12 like a crow** appearing through distance as small as a crow   **13 place** position. **sets off** enhances   **14 revolve** ponder   **16–17 This . . . allowed** i.e., any act of service at court is valued not for itself, but is valued by the lord as proof of his greatness in acknowledging or accepting such tokens of submission   **20 sharded** living in dung, or, covered with the sheaths of insects' wings. **hold** stronghold   **22 attending . . . check** doing service (at court) only to be rewarded with a rebuke   **23 bauble** trifle   **24 unpaid-for** for which the wearer is in debt to his tailor   **25 Such . . . fine** such finery wins the respectful greeting of him who dresses elegantly, or of his tailor   **26 keeps . . . uncrossed** does nothing to cancel his record of debts. **to** compared to   **27 proof** experience

29 What . . . home what things are like away from home. **Haply** perhaps   **33 abed** i.e., in imagination only, in dreams   **35 stride a limit** overpass a bound (where he will be liable for arrest)   **37 beat dark December** beat down, as befitting dark December   **38 pinching** nippingly cold, or, confining   **41 Like** alike, equally   **42 flies** flees   **44 freely** (Said ironically: their only freedom is to sing of their bondage.)   **47 keep** dwell in   **49 the toil o' the war** i.e., did you but know the toil of war   **50 pain** labor   **54 deserve** earn   **57 report** reputation   **58 the best of note** persons of the highest distinction   **61 Whose . . . fruit** laden with rewards, the harvest of my efforts   **63 hangings** hanging fruit   **70 demesnes** domains, regions   **71 at honest freedom** (Compare the phrases "at peace," "at liberty.")

The fore-end of my time. But up to th' mountains!   73
This is not hunters' language. He that strikes
The venison first shall be the lord o' the feast;
To him the other two shall minister,
And we will fear no poison, which attends   77
In place of greater state. I'll meet you in the valleys.
                    Exeunt [Guiderius and Arviragus].
How hard it is to hide the sparks of nature!
These boys know little they are sons to th' King,
Nor Cymbeline dreams that they are alive.
They think they are mine; and though trained up
    thus meanly
I' the cave wherein they bow, their thoughts do hit
The roofs of palaces, and nature prompts them
In simple and low things to prince it much   85
Beyond the trick of others. This Polydore,   86
The heir of Cymbeline and Britain, who
The King his father called Guiderius—Jove!
When on my three-foot stool I sit and tell
The warlike feats I have done, his spirits fly out
Into my story; say, "Thus mine enemy fell,
And thus I set my foot on 's neck," even then
The princely blood flows in his cheek, he sweats,
Strains his young nerves, and puts himself in
    posture   94
That acts my words. The younger brother, Cadwal,
Once Arviragus, in as like a figure   96
Strikes life into my speech and shows much more   97
His own conceiving. [*Sounds of hunting are heard.*]
    Hark, the game is roused!—   98
O Cymbeline, heaven and my conscience knows
Thou didst unjustly banish me; whereon,
At three and two years old, I stole these babes,
Thinking to bar thee of succession as
Thou refts me of my lands. Euriphile,   103
Thou wast their nurse; they took thee for their
    mother,
And every day do honor to her grave.   105
Myself, Belarius, that am Morgan called,
They take for natural father.—The game is up.   107
                                    Exit.

❧

3.4   *Enter Pisanio and Imogen.*

IMOGEN
Thou toldst me, when we came from horse, the
    place   1
Was near at hand. Ne'er longed my mother so
To see me first as I have now. Pisanio, man,   3

Where is Posthumus? What is in thy mind
That makes thee stare thus? Wherefore breaks that
    sigh
From th' inward of thee? One but painted thus
Would be interpreted a thing perplexed   7
Beyond self-explication. Put thyself   8
Into a havior of less fear, ere wildness   9
Vanquish my staider senses. What's the matter?   10
                    [*He offers her a letter.*]
Why tender'st thou that paper to me with   11
A look untender? If 't be summer news,
Smile to 't before; if winterly, thou need'st
But keep that countenance still. My husband's hand?
That drug-damned Italy hath outcrafted him,   15
And he's at some hard point. Speak, man. Thy
    tongue   16
May take off some extremity, which to read   17
Would be even mortal to me.
PISANIO   Please you, read,
And you shall find me, wretched man, a thing
The most disdained of fortune.
IMOGEN (*reads*)   "Thy mistress, Pisanio, hath played the
    strumpet in my bed, the testimonies whereof lies
    bleeding in me. I speak not out of weak surmises but
    from proof as strong as my grief and as certain as I
    expect my revenge. That part thou, Pisanio, must act
    for me, if thy faith be not tainted with the breach of
    hers. Let thine own hands take away her life. I shall
    give thee opportunity at Milford Haven—she hath
    my letter for the purpose—where, if thou fear to strike
    and to make me certain it is done, thou art the pander
    to her dishonor and equally to me disloyal."
PISANIO
What shall I need to draw my sword? The paper
Hath cut her throat already. No, 'tis slander,
Whose edge is sharper than the sword, whose
    tongue
Outvenoms all the worms of Nile, whose breath   35
Rides on the posting winds and doth belie   36
All corners of the world. Kings, queens, and states,   37
Maids, matrons, nay, the secrets of the grave
This viperous slander enters.—What cheer, madam?
IMOGEN
False to his bed? What is it to be false?
To lie in watch there and to think on him?   41
To weep twixt clock and clock? If sleep charge
    nature,   42
To break it with a fearful dream of him   43
And cry myself awake? That's false to 's bed, is it?

73 **fore-end** earlier part   77 **attends** is present, renders service
85 **prince it** play the prince   86 **trick** manner   94 **nerves** sinews
96 **in . . . figure** acting his part equally well   97–98 **shows . . .
conceiving** i.e., adds to my story his own conception   103 **Thou refts
you** have bereft, deprived   105 **her** (Belarius shifts easily from apos-
trophizing the dead Euriphile to speaking about her.)   107 **up** roused.
(Belarius hears a hunting cry.)
3.4. Location: Wales. Country near Milford Haven.
1 **came from horse** dismounted   3 **have** i.e., have longing to see
Posthumus

7 **perplexed** distressed   8 **Beyond self-explication** beyond the ability
to express his condition   9 **havior of less fear** less fearsome behavior
9–10 **ere . . . senses** before frenzy and panic overcome my calm
11 **tender'st** offerest (with a play on *untender* in the next line)
15 **drug-damned** condemned for its drugs and poisons.   **outcrafted
him** outwitted him, overcome him by craft   16 **hard point** dangerous
crisis   17 **take . . . extremity** reduce somewhat the shock
35 **worms** serpents   36 **posting** hastening.   **belie** spread lies throughout   37 **states** statesmen   41 **in watch** awake   42 **twixt . . . clock**
from hour to hour.   **charge nature** i.e., overcome wakefulness
43 **fearful dream of him** fearful dream about his safety

PISANIO   Alas, good lady!

IMOGEN

I false? Thy conscience witness! Iachimo,   46
Thou didst accuse him of incontinency.
Thou then lookedst like a villain; now methinks
Thy favor's good enough. Some jay of Italy,   49
Whose mother was her painting, hath betrayed him.   50
Poor I am stale, a garment out of fashion,   51
And, for I am richer than to hang by the walls,   52
I must be ripped. To pieces with me! O,   53
Men's vows are women's traitors! All good seeming,
By thy revolt, O husband, shall be thought   55
Put on for villainy; not born where 't grows,   56
But worn a bait for ladies.

PISANIO   Good madam, hear me.

IMOGEN

True honest men being heard like false Aeneas   58
Were in his time thought false, and Sinon's weeping   59
Did scandal many a holy tear, took pity   60
From most true wretchedness. So thou, Posthumus,   61
Wilt lay the leaven on all proper men;   62
Goodly and gallant shall be false and perjured   63
From thy great fail.—Come, fellow, be thou honest;   64
Do thou thy master's bidding. When thou
    seest him,
A little witness my obedience. Look,   66
        [drawing her sword and offering it to him]
I draw the sword myself. Take it, and hit
The innocent mansion of my love, my heart.
Fear not; 'tis empty of all things but grief.
Thy master is not there, who was indeed
The riches of it. Do his bidding; strike.
Thou mayst be valiant in a better cause,   72
But now thou seem'st a coward.

PISANIO [rejecting the sword]   Hence, vile instrument!
Thou shalt not damn my hand.

IMOGEN   Why, I must die;
And if I do not by thy hand, thou art
No servant of thy master's. Against self-slaughter
There is a prohibition so divine
That cravens my weak hand. Come, here's my heart.   78

Something's afore 't. Soft, soft! We'll no defense;   79
Obedient as the scabbard. What is here?   80
        [She takes letters from her bodice.]
The scriptures of the loyal Leonatus,   81
All turned to heresy? Away, away,
Corrupters of my faith! [She throws away the letters.]
    You shall no more
Be stomachers to my heart. Thus may poor fools   84
Believe false teachers. Though those that are
    betrayed   85
Do feel the treason sharply, yet the traitor
Stands in worse case of woe. And thou, Posthumus,   87
That didst set up   88
My disobedience 'gainst the King my father
And make me put into contempt the suits
Of princely fellows, shalt hereafter find   91
It is no act of common passage, but   92
A strain of rareness; and I grieve myself   93
To think, when thou shalt be disedged by her   94
That now thou tirest on, how thy memory   95
Will then be panged by me.—Prithee, dispatch.   96
The lamb entreats the butcher. Where's thy knife?
Thou art too slow to do thy master's bidding
When I desire it too.

PISANIO   O gracious lady,
Since I received command to do this business
I have not slept one wink.

IMOGEN   Do 't, and to bed then.

PISANIO
I'll wake mine eyeballs blind first.

IMOGEN   Wherefore then   102
Didst undertake it? Why hast thou abused
So many miles with a pretense? This place?
Mine action and thine own? Our horses' labor?
The time inviting thee? The perturbed court,
For my being absent, whereunto I never
Purpose return? Why hast thou gone so far,
To be unbent when thou hast ta'en thy stand,   109
Th' elected deer before thee?

PISANIO   But to win time   110
To lose so bad employment, in the which   111
I have considered of a course. Good lady,
Hear me with a patience.

IMOGEN   Talk thy tongue weary. Speak.
I have heard I am a strumpet, and mine ear,
Therein false struck, can take no greater wound,   115

46 **Thy conscience witness** let your conscience bear me witness. (She apostrophizes Posthumus.)   49 **favor's** countenance is.   **jay** i.e., flashy or light woman   50 **Whose . . . painting** i.e., who owed her beauty to cosmetics   51 **stale** no longer fresh (but with bitter suggestion of "harlot")   52 **for . . . than** because I am too fine.   **to hang by the walls** i.e., like discarded clothing or armor   53 **ripped** torn apart (1) in murder (2) like rich garments unsewn to recover the cloth   55 **revolt** inconstancy   56 **born** i.e., innate   58 **being heard like** when they were heard to speak like.   **Aeneas** (Thought of as the pattern of faithless love because of his desertion of Dido.)   59 **Were . . . false** i.e., were mistrusted because of Aeneas' deceptive speech, which was indeed false; his smooth falsehood cast doubt even on perfectly honest professions of love.   **Sinon** Greek who by his guile persuaded the Trojans to introduce within the walls of Troy the wooden horse filled with armed men   60 **scandal** bring scandal to, discredit   60–61 **took pity From** prevented the bestowing of well-deserved pity upon   62 **lay . . . men** take credit away from all well-deserving and honorable men (just as sour *leaven* or fermenting dough causes more dough to ferment and spoil).   **proper** honest   63 **be** i.e., be thought   64 **fail** fault, offense.   **honest** loyal to your vow of obedience. (Said with bitter irony.)   66 **A little witness** testify somewhat to   72 **Thou mayst be** maybe you are   78 **cravens** makes cowardly

79 **Something's** i.e., Posthumus' letter is.   **Soft** i.e., wait a minute   80 **Obedient** i.e., as willing to receive the sword   81 **scriptures** writings, letters (with a play on "Holy Scriptures")   84 **stomachers** ornamental coverings for the breast   85 **false teachers** i.e., those who teach heresy   87 **Stands . . . woe** i.e., risks the penalty of damnation   88 **set up** incite, encourage   91 **princely fellows** fellow princes   92–93 **It . . . rareness** that my choice (of you) was no act of a common sort but a rare trait   94 **disedged** surfeited, having the edge of appetite taken off   95 **thou tirest on** you tear or devour ravenously (as a bird of prey)   96 **panged** pained, tortured   102 **wake . . . blind** remain awake until I can no longer see   109 **To be unbent** to unbend your bow again (and thus refuse to shoot).   **stand** place from which to shoot game   110 **elected** chosen.   **But** only   111 **which** i.e., which time   115 **take** receive

Nor tent to bottom that. But speak.
PISANIO   Then, madam, 116
I thought you would not back again.
IMOGEN   Most like, 117
Bringing me here to kill me.
PISANIO   Not so, neither.
But if I were as wise as honest, then 119
My purpose would prove well. It cannot be 120
But that my master is abused. Some villain, 121
Ay, and singular in his art, hath done 122
You both this cursèd injury.
IMOGEN
Some Roman courtesan.
PISANIO   No, on my life.
I'll give but notice you are dead, and send him
Some bloody sign of it, for 'tis commanded
I should do so. You shall be missed at court,
And that will well confirm it.
IMOGEN   Why, good fellow,
What shall I do the while? Where bide? How live?
Or in my life what comfort, when I am
Dead to my husband?
PISANIO   If you'll back to th' court—
IMOGEN
No court, no father, nor no more ado
With that harsh, noble, simple nothing,
That Cloten, whose love suit hath been to me
As fearful as a siege.
PISANIO   If not at court,
Then not in Britain must you bide.
IMOGEN   Where, then?
Hath Britain all the sun that shines? Day, night,
Are they not but in Britain? I' the world's volume 138
Our Britain seems as of it but not in 't, 139
In a great pool a swan's nest. Prithee, think
There's livers out of Britain.
PISANIO   I am most glad 141
You think of other place. Th' ambassador,
Lucius the Roman, comes to Milford Haven
Tomorrow. Now, if you could wear a mind 144
Dark as your fortune is, and but disguise 145
That which, t' appear itself, must not yet be 146
But by self-danger, you should tread a course
Pretty and full of view; yea, haply near 148
The residence of Posthumus, so nigh at least
That, though his actions were not visible, yet
Report should render him hourly to your ear
As truly as he moves.
IMOGEN   O, for such means!

Though peril to my modesty, not death on 't, 153
I would adventure.
PISANIO   Well, then, here's the point.
You must forget to be a woman, change
Command into obedience; fear and niceness— 156
The handmaids of all women, or, more truly,
Woman its pretty self—into a waggish courage; 158
Ready in gibes, quick-answered, saucy, and
As quarrelous as the weasel. Nay, you must 160
Forget that rarest treasure of your cheek,
Exposing it—but O, the harder heart! 162
Alack, no remedy—to the greedy touch
Of common-kissing Titan, and forget 164
Your laborsome and dainty trims, wherein 165
You made great Juno angry.
IMOGEN   Nay, be brief. 166
I see into thy end and am almost
A man already.
PISANIO   First, make yourself but like one.
Forethinking this, I have already fit— 169
'Tis in my cloak bag—doublet, hat, hose, all
That answer to them. Would you in their serving, 171
And with what imitation you can borrow
From youth of such a season, 'fore noble Lucius 173
Present yourself, desire his service, tell him 174
Wherein you're happy—which will make him
    know, 175
If that his head have ear in music—doubtless 176
With joy he will embrace you, for he's honorable 177
And, doubling that, most holy. Your means abroad, 178
You have me, rich, and I will never fail 179
Beginning nor supplyment. [*He gives her a cloak bag.*]
IMOGEN   Thou art all the comfort 180
The gods will diet me with. Prithee, away.
There's more to be considered, but we'll even 182
All that good time will give us. This attempt
I am soldier to, and will abide it with 184
A prince's courage. Away, I prithee.
PISANIO
Well, madam, we must take a short farewell, 186
Lest, being missed, I be suspected of

116 tent . . . that probe that wound to the bottom **117 back** go back (to court). **like** likely **119–120 But . . . well** (Pisanio hopes the plan he is going to propose will be as clever as he is honest in intent.) **121 abused** deceived **122 singular** unexcelled **138 but** except **139 as . . . in 't** i.e., as part of it but a small and relatively insignificant part, on the periphery, like a page torn out of a volume **141 livers** persons living **144 wear a mind** choose an intention, play a part **145 Dark** obscure **146 That** i.e., the fact that you are a woman. **appear itself** reveal itself for what it truly is **148 Pretty . . . view** advantageous and promising, affording a fair prospect. **haply** perhaps (with a suggestion also of "happily, fortunately")

153 Though . . . on 't as long as the risk to my modesty would not be fatal to it **156 Command** i.e., as befitting one of royal birth. (Imogen will be disguising her royal birth and assuming the guise of one who must obey orders.) **niceness** fastidiousness, reserve **158 waggish** roguish, masculine **160 quarrelous** quarrelsome **162 harder** too hard. (Pisanio is either reproaching his own cruelty in speaking so, or that of Posthumus, or possibly suggesting that Imogen must harden her heart.) **164 common-kissing** kissing everybody and everything. **Titan** god of the sun **165 laborsome . . . trims** elaborate and dainty apparel **166 angry** i.e., jealous **169 Forethinking** anticipating. **fit** ready **171 answer to** go along with. **Would you** if you would. **in their serving** assisted by them **173 of . . . season** i.e., of such an age as you will represent **174 his service** employment in his service **175 happy** gifted, skillful. **make him know** convince him **176 If . . . music** i.e., if he has an ear for music, since he then cannot fail to appreciate your voice **177 embrace you** take you in (to his service) **178 Your means abroad** as for your financial means while you are abroad **179 rich** adequately supplied with funds **180 supplyment** continuation of supply **182 even** keep pace with, profit by **184 soldier to** enlisted in, courageously prepared for. **abide it** sustain it, stick with it **186 short** hasty

Your carriage from the court. My noble mistress,   188
Here is a box; I had it from the Queen.
                                        [*He gives a box.*]
What's in 't is precious. If you are sick at sea
Or stomach-qualmed at land, a dram of this
Will drive away distemper. To some shade,   192
And fit you to your manhood. May the gods
Direct you to the best!
IMOGEN   Amen. I thank thee.
                                        Exeunt [*separately*].

❧

3.5   *Enter Cymbeline, Queen, Cloten, Lucius,*
          [*Attendants,*] *and Lords.*

CYMBELINE
  Thus far, and so farewell.
LUCIUS   Thanks, royal sir.   1
  My emperor hath wrote I must from hence;   2
  And am right sorry that I must report ye
  My master's enemy.
CYMBELINE   Our subjects, sir,
  Will not endure his yoke, and for ourself
  To show less sovereignty than they must needs
  Appear unkinglike.
LUCIUS   So, sir. I desire of you   7
  A conduct overland to Milford Haven.   8
  Madam, all joy befall Your Grace, and you!   9
CYMBELINE
  My lords, you are appointed for that office;   10
  The due of honor in no point omit.
  So farewell, noble Lucius.
LUCIUS [*to Cloten*]   Your hand, my lord.
CLOTEN
  Receive it friendly; but from this time forth
  I wear it as your enemy.
LUCIUS   Sir, the event   14
  Is yet to name the winner. Fare you well.
CYMBELINE
  Leave not the worthy Lucius, good my lords,
  Till he have crossed the Severn. Happiness!
                                        Exeunt Lucius etc.
QUEEN
  He goes hence frowning, but it honors us
  That we have given him cause.
CLOTEN   'Tis all the better;
  Your valiant Britons have their wishes in it.
CYMBELINE
  Lucius hath wrote already to the Emperor
  How it goes here. It fits us therefore ripely   22
  Our chariots and our horsemen be in readiness.

The powers that he already hath in Gallia   24
Will soon be drawn to head, from whence he moves 25
His war for Britain.
QUEEN   'Tis not sleepy business,
  But must be looked to speedily and strongly.
CYMBELINE
  Our expectation that it would be thus
  Hath made us forward. But, my gentle queen,   29
  Where is our daughter? She hath not appeared
  Before the Roman, nor to us hath tendered
  The duty of the day. She looks us like   32
  A thing more made of malice than of duty.
  We have noted it.—Call her before us, for
  We have been too slight in sufferance.
                                        [*Exit an Attendant.*]
QUEEN   Royal sir,   35
  Since the exile of Posthumus, most retired
  Hath her life been; the cure whereof, my lord,
  'Tis time must do. Beseech Your Majesty,
  Forbear sharp speeches to her. She's a lady
  So tender of rebukes that words are strokes
  And strokes death to her.

          Enter [*Attendant as*] *a messenger.*

CYMBELINE   Where is she, sir? How
  Can her contempt be answered?
ATTENDANT   Please you, sir,   42
  Her chambers are all locked, and there's no answer
  That will be given to the loud'st of noise we make.
QUEEN
  My lord, when last I went to visit her,
  She prayed me to excuse her keeping close,   46
  Whereto constrained by her infirmity
  She should that duty leave unpaid to you   48
  Which daily she was bound to proffer. This
  She wished me to make known, but our great court 50
  Made me to blame in memory.
CYMBELINE   Her doors locked?
  Not seen of late? Grant, heavens, that which I fear
  Prove false!   *Exit.*
QUEEN   Son, I say, follow the King.
CLOTEN
  That man of hers, Pisanio, her old servant,
  I have not seen these two days.
QUEEN   Go, look after.
                                        Exit [*Cloten*].
  Pisanio, thou that stand'st so for Posthumus!   56
  He hath a drug of mine; I pray his absence
  Proceed by swallowing that, for he believes   58
  It is a thing most precious. But for her,
  Where is she gone? Haply despair hath seized her,
  Or, winged with fervor of her love, she's flown
  To her desired Posthumus. Gone she is

---

188 Your carriage having removed you   **192 distemper** illness.
shade secluded and protected spot
3.5. Location: At the court of Cymbeline.
1 Thus far thus far we can escort you   **2 wrote** written (also in line
21)   **7 So** i.e., very good. (A polite way of closing the discussion.)
8 conduct safe-conduct, escort   **9 and you** (Possibly addressed to
Cloten, or, more probably, to the King. Lucius bids farewell to Cloten
in line 12.)   **10 office** duty (as escorts of Lucius)   **14 event** outcome
22 fits befits.   **ripely** speedily

24 powers armed forces   **25 drawn to head** brought together, assembled   **29 forward** well prepared   **32 looks us** seems to us (?) looks at
us (?)   **35 slight in sufferance** permissive   **42 answered** accounted for
46 close in private   **48 She . . . leave** she found herself obliged to
leave that duty   **50 great court** important courtly business   **56 thou
that stand'st so** you who stand up so for, look out for the interests of
58 by from

To death or to dishonor, and my end   63
Can make good use of either. She being down,
I have the placing of the British crown.

Enter Cloten.

How now, my son?
CLOTEN   'Tis certain she is fled.
Go in and cheer the King. He rages; none
Dare come about him.
QUEEN   All the better. May
This night forestall him of the coming day!   69
                              Exit Queen.

CLOTEN
I love and hate her. For she's fair and royal,   70
And that she hath all courtly parts more exquisite   71
Than lady, ladies, woman—from every one   72
The best she hath, and she, of all compounded,   73
Outsells them all—I love her therefore. But   74
Disdaining me and throwing favors on   75
The low Posthumus slanders so her judgment   76
That what's else rare is choked; and in that point   77
I will conclude to hate her, nay, indeed,
To be revenged upon her. For when fools
Shall—

Enter Pisanio. [He attempts to avoid Cloten.]

Who is here? What, are you packing, sirrah?   80
Come hither. Ah, you precious pander! Villain,
Where is thy lady? In a word, or else
Thou art straightway with the fiends.
                    [He threatens him with his sword.]
PISANIO   O, good my lord!
CLOTEN
Where is thy lady? Or, by Jupiter,
I will not ask again. Close villain,   85
I'll have this secret from thy heart or rip
Thy heart to find it. Is she with Posthumus,
From whose so many weights of baseness cannot   88
A dram of worth be drawn?
PISANIO   Alas, my lord,   89
How can she be with him? When was she missed?
He is in Rome.
CLOTEN   Where is she, sir? Come nearer.   91
No farther halting. Satisfy me home   92
What is become of her.
PISANIO
O, my all-worthy lord!
CLOTEN   All-worthy villain!
Discover where thy mistress is at once,   95
At the next word. No more of "worthy lord"!

Speak, or thy silence on the instant is
Thy condemnation and thy death.
PISANIO   Then, sir,
This paper is the history of my knowledge
Touching her flight.   *[He presents a letter.]*
CLOTEN   Let's see 't. I will pursue her
Even to Augustus' throne.
PISANIO *[aside]*   Or this or perish.   101
She's far enough, and what he learns by this
May prove his travel, not her danger.
CLOTEN *[reading]*   Hum!
PISANIO *[aside]*
I'll write to my lord she's dead. O Imogen,
Safe mayst thou wander, safe return again!
CLOTEN   Sirrah, is this letter true?
PISANIO   Sir, as I think.
CLOTEN   It is Posthumus' hand, I know 't. Sirrah, if thou
wouldst not be a villain, but do me true service, un- 109
dergo those employments wherein I should have   110
cause to use thee with a serious industry—that is,   111
what villainy soe'er I bid thee do, to perform it directly
and truly—I would think thee an honest man. Thou
shouldst neither want my means for thy relief nor my
voice for thy preferment.   115
PISANIO   Well, my good lord.
CLOTEN   Wilt thou serve me? For since patiently and
constantly thou hast stuck to the bare fortune of that
beggar Posthumus, thou canst not, in the course of
gratitude, but be a diligent follower of mine. Wilt thou
serve me?
PISANIO   Sir, I will.
CLOTEN   Give me thy hand; here's my purse. *[He gives* 123
money.] Hast any of thy late master's garments in thy 124
possession?
PISANIO   I have, my lord, at my lodging the same suit
he wore when he took leave of my lady and mistress.
CLOTEN   The first service thou dost me, fetch that suit
hither. Let it be thy first service. Go.
PISANIO   I shall, my lord.   *Exit.*
CLOTEN   Meet thee at Milford Haven!—I forgot to ask
him one thing; I'll remember 't anon.—Even there,
thou villain Posthumus, will I kill thee. I would these
garments were come. She said upon a time—the bitterness of it I now belch from my heart—that she held
the very garment of Posthumus in more respect than   136
my noble and natural person, together with the adornment of my qualities. With that suit upon my back
will I ravish her; first kill him, and in her eyes. There
shall she see my valor, which will then be a torment to
her contempt. He on the ground, my speech of insult- 141
ment ended on his dead body, and when my lust hath 142
dined—which, as I say, to vex her I will execute in the
clothes that she so praised—to the court I'll knock her
back, foot her home again. She hath despised me re- 145

---

63 end intent   **69 forestall** deprive (i.e., bring about his death)
70 For because   **71 that** because.   **parts** endowments, graces
72 Than lady, ladies, woman than any lady, or all ladies, or indeed
womankind   **72–73 from . . . she hath** she has the best qualities of
each   **74 Outsells** outvalues, excels   **75 Disdaining** her disdaining
76 slanders discredits   **77 rare** excellent   **80 packing** plotting.   **sirrah** (Form of address to a social inferior; also in lines 106 and 108.)
85 Close secretive   **88–89 From . . . drawn** from whom not even a
tiny amount of worthiness can be extracted, so heavy is the prepon-
derance of baseness   **91 Come nearer** answer more to the point
92 home completely   **95 Discover** disclose

101 Or either   **109–110 undergo** undertake   **111 industry** assiduity
115 preferment advancement   **123 purse** (Cloten is not giving Pisanio
salary but making him his purse bearer.)   **124 late** recent. (Not
"dead.")   **136 more respect** higher regard   **141–142 insultment**
contemptuous triumph   **145 foot** kick

joicingly, and I'll be merry in my revenge.

        Enter Pisanio [with the clothes].

Be those the garments?

PISANIO   Ay, my noble lord.

CLOTEN   How long is 't since she went to Milford
Haven?

PISANIO   She can scarce be there yet.

CLOTEN   Bring this apparel to my chamber; that is the
second thing that I have commanded thee. The third
is that thou wilt be a voluntary mute to my design. Be   154
but duteous, and true preferment shall tender itself to
thee. My revenge is now at Milford. Would I had
wings to follow it! Come, and be true.   *Exit.*

PISANIO

Thou bidd'st me to my loss; for true to thee
Were to prove false, which I will never be,
To him that is most true. To Milford go,
And find not her whom thou pursuest. Flow, flow,
You heavenly blessings, on her! This fool's speed   162
Be crossed with slowness; labor be his meed!   *Exit.* 163

3.6   *Enter Imogen alone [in boy's clothes].*

IMOGEN

I see a man's life is a tedious one.
I have tired myself, and for two nights together   2
Have made the ground my bed. I should be sick
But that my resolution helps me. Milford,
When from the mountain top Pisanio showed thee,
Thou wast within a ken. O Jove, I think   6
Foundations fly the wretched—such, I mean,   7
Where they should be relieved. Two beggars told me
I could not miss my way. Will poor folks lie,
That have afflictions on them, knowing 'tis
A punishment or trial? Yes; no wonder,   11
When rich ones scarce tell true. To lapse in fullness   12
Is sorer than to lie for need, and falsehood   13
Is worse in kings than beggars. My dear lord!
Thou art one o' the false ones. Now I think on thee,
My hunger's gone; but even before I was   16
At point to sink for food. [*She sees the cave.*] But what
is this?   17
Here is a path to 't. 'Tis some savage hold.   18
I were best not call; I dare not call. Yet famine,
Ere clean it o'erthrow nature, makes it valiant.   20
Plenty and peace breeds cowards; hardness ever   21
Of hardiness is mother.—Ho! Who's here?   22

If anything that's civil, speak; if savage,   23
Take or lend. Ho!—No answer? Then I'll enter.   24
Best draw my sword; an if mine enemy   25
But fear the sword like me, he'll scarcely look on 't.
Such a foe, good heavens!   27

        [She draws her sword, and]
               exit [into the cave].

    Enter Belarius, Guiderius, and Arviragus.

BELARIUS

You, Polydore, have proved best woodman and   28
Are master of the feast. Cadwal and I
Will play the cook and servant; 'tis our match.   30
The sweat of industry would dry and die   31
But for the end it works to. Come, our stomachs   32
Will make what's homely savory; weariness   33
Can snore upon the flint, when resty sloth   34
Finds the down pillow hard. Now peace be here,
Poor house, that keep'st thyself!

GUIDERIUS   I am throughly weary. 36

ARVIRAGUS

I am weak with toil, yet strong in appetite.

GUIDERIUS

There is cold meat i' the cave. We'll browse on that   38
Whilst what we have killed be cooked.

BELARIUS [*looking into the cave*]   Stay, come not in.
But that it eats our victuals, I should think
Here were a fairy.

GUIDERIUS   What's the matter, sir?

BELARIUS

By Jupiter, an angel! Or, if not,
An earthly paragon! Behold divineness
No elder than a boy!

        Enter Imogen.

IMOGEN   Good masters, harm me not.   45
Before I entered here, I called, and thought
To have begged or bought what I have took. Good
troth,   47
I have stol'n naught, nor would not, though I had
found
Gold strewed i' the floor. Here's money for my
meat.   *[She offers money.]*
I would have left it on the board so soon
As I had made my meal, and parted
With prayers for the provider.

GUIDERIUS   Money, youth?

ARVIRAGUS

All gold and silver rather turn to dirt,   53
As 'tis no better reckoned but of those   54
Who worship dirty gods.

---

154 **Be** if you be   162 **This fool's** may this fool's   163 **crossed**
thwarted.   **meed** reward
3.6. Location: Wales. Before the cave of Belarius.
2 **tired** (1) exhausted (2) attired   6 **within a ken** within sight
7 **Foundations** (1) fixed places (2) charitable institutions.   **fly the
wretched** i.e., are never there when most needed   11 **trial** test of virtue. (Poverty may be a Job-like affliction visited on those God wishes
to test, in which case lying is dangerously sinful.)   12 **lapse in fullness** lie and commit other sins in a state of prosperity   13 **sorer**
worse, more wicked   16 **but even before** just now   17 **for** for lack of
18 **hold** stronghold, fastness   20 **clean** altogether   21 **hardness** hardship   22 **Of hardiness is mother** breeds courage

23 **civil** civilized   24 **Take or lend** rob me (or something worse), or
give me food   25 **Best** it were best to.   **an if** if   27 **Such . . . heavens** may the heavens grant me a foe as timid as myself   28 **woodman**
woodsman, huntsman   30 **match** agreement, bargain   31–32 **The
sweat . . . works to** human labor would dry up and cease if it were
not for the desired end   33 **homely** plain   34 **resty** sluggish, indolent
36 **keep'st thyself** i.e., is untended, empty.   **throughly** thoroughly
38 **browse** nibble   45 **masters** i.e., sirs. (Addressed to ordinary folk.)
47 **Good troth** in truth   53 **All gold** i.e., let all gold   54 **but of**
except by

IMOGEN   I see you're angry.
Know, if you kill me for my fault, I should
Have died had I not made it.
BELARIUS   Whither bound?   57
IMOGEN   To Milford Haven.
BELARIUS   What's your name?
IMOGEN
    Fidele, sir. I have a kinsman who
    Is bound for Italy. He embarked at Milford,   61
    To whom being going, almost spent with hunger,
    I am fall'n in this offense.
BELARIUS   Prithee, fair youth,   63
    Think us no churls, nor measure our good minds
    By this rude place we live in. Well encountered!
    'Tis almost night. You shall have better cheer
    Ere you depart, and thanks to stay and eat it.
    Boys, bid him welcome.
GUIDERIUS   Were you a woman, youth,
    I should woo hard but be your groom in honesty,   69
    Ay, bid for you as I do buy.   70
ARVIRAGUS [to Guiderius]   I'll make 't my comfort
    He is a man; I'll love him as my brother.
    [To Imogen.] And such a welcome as I'd give to him   73
    After long absence, such is yours. Most welcome!
    Be sprightly, for you fall 'mongst friends.
IMOGEN   'Mongst friends,   75
    If brothers. [Aside.] Would it had been so that they   76
    Had been my father's sons! Then had my prize   77
    Been less, and so more equal ballasting   78
    To thee, Posthumus.
BELARIUS   He wrings at some distress.   79
GUIDERIUS
    Would I could free 't!
ARVIRAGUS   Or I; whate'er it be,
    What pain it cost, what danger! Gods!
BELARIUS   Hark, boys.   81
                  [He whispers to them.]
IMOGEN [to herself]   Great men
    That had a court no bigger than this cave,
    That did attend themselves and had the virtue   84
    Which their own conscience sealed them, laying by   85
    That nothing-gift of differing multitudes,   86
    Could not outpeer these twain. Pardon me, gods!   87
    I'd change my sex to be companion with them,
    Since Leonatus's false.
BELARIUS   It shall be so.   89
    Boys, we'll go dress our hunt. Fair youth, come in.   90

57 made committed   **61 embarked** was to have embarked   **63 in** into **69 but be** i.e., but I'd be, before I should fail to be   **70 Ay, bid . . . buy** i.e., yes, I would bid for you as one who would seek to buy you **73 him** i.e., such a brother   **75–76 'Mongst . . . brothers** i.e., certainly I am among friends, if the three of us are to be like brothers **77 prize** (1) value, since I would not then be heir to the throne (2) *prize* in the nautical sense of a captured sea vessel   **78 ballasting** cargo of a sea vessel giving it stability   **79 wrings** writhes   **81 What pain it cost** whatever pain it would cost me, or, what pain it must have cost (to Imogen)   **84–86 That . . . multitudes** who had no one to attend them but themselves and no moral excellence to boast of other than what their own self-knowledge could swear to, disregarding the valueless gift of adulation from the fickle populace   **87 outpeer** excel   **89 It shall be so** (Belarius finishes his conversation apart with Arviragus and Guiderius.)   **90 hunt** game taken in the hunt

Discourse is heavy, fasting; when we have supped,
We'll mannerly demand thee of thy story,
So far as thou wilt speak it.
GUIDERIUS   Pray draw near.
ARVIRAGUS
    The night to th' owl and morn to th' lark less
       welcome.
IMOGEN   Thanks, sir.
ARVIRAGUS   I pray, draw near.   *Exeunt.*

3.7   *Enter two Roman Senators and Tribunes.*

FIRST SENATOR
    This is the tenor of the Emperor's writ:
    That since the common men are now in action
    'Gainst the Pannonians and Dalmatians,
    And that the legions now in Gallia are
    Full weak to undertake our wars against
    The fall'n-off Britons, that we do incite   6
    The gentry to this business. He creates
    Lucius proconsul, and to you the tribunes,
    For this immediate levy, he commends   9
    His absolute commission. Long live Caesar!   10
A TRIBUNE
    Is Lucius general of the forces?
SECOND SENATOR   Ay.
A TRIBUNE
    Remaining now in Gallia?
FIRST SENATOR   With those legions
    Which I have spoke of, whereunto your levy
    Must be supplyant. The words of your commission   14
    Will tie you to the numbers and the time   15
    Of their dispatch.
A TRIBUNE   We will discharge our duty.
                           Exeunt.

4.1   *Enter Cloten alone, [dressed in Posthumus' garments].*

CLOTEN   I am near to the place where they should meet, if Pisanio have mapped it truly. How fit his garments   2 serve me! Why should his mistress, who was made by him that made the tailor, not be fit too? The rather—saving reverence of the word—for 'tis said a   5 woman's fitness comes by fits. Therein I must play the   6 workman. I dare speak it to myself, for it is not vainglory for a man and his glass to confer in his own chamber—I mean, the lines of my body are as well drawn as his; no less young, more strong, not beneath

3.7. Location: Rome. A public place, perhaps the Senate House.
6 fall'n-off revolted   **9 commends** entrusts   **10 absolute commission** unlimited authority   **14 supplyant** reinforcing, auxiliary   **15 tie you to** specify for you
4.1. Location: Wales. Near the cave of Belarius.
2 his Posthumus'   **5 saving reverence** asking pardon (i.e., for the indecent punning on *fitness* and *fit*.)   **for** because   **6 fitness** sexual inclination.   **fits** fits and starts

him in fortunes, beyond him in the advantage of the 11
time, above him in birth, alike conversant in general 12
services, and more remarkable in single oppositions. 13
Yet this imperceiverant thing loves him in my despite. 14
What mortality is! Posthumus, thy head, which now is 15
growing upon thy shoulders, shall within this hour be
off, thy mistress enforced, thy garments cut to pieces
before her face; and all this done, spurn her home to her
father, who may haply be a little angry for my so rough 19
usage; but my mother, having power of his testiness, 20
shall turn all into my commendations. My horse is tied
up safe. Out, sword, and to a sore purpose! [*He draws.*] 22
Fortune put them into my hand! This is the very description of their meeting place, and the fellow dares
not deceive me.   [*Exit.*]

4.2 *Enter Belarius, Guiderius, Arviragus, and Imogen*
from the cave.

BELARIUS [*to Imogen*]
 You are not well. Remain here in the cave;
 We'll come to you after hunting.
ARVIRAGUS [*to Imogen*]   Brother, stay here.
 Are we not brothers?
IMOGEN   So man and man should be,   3
 But clay and clay differs in dignity,   4
 Whose dust is both alike. I am very sick.   5
GUIDERIUS [*to Arviragus and Belarius*]
 Go you to hunting. I'll abide with him.
IMOGEN
 So sick I am not, yet I am not well;   7
 But not so citizen a wanton as   8
 To seem to die ere sick. So please you, leave me;   9
 Stick to your journal course. The breach of custom   10
 Is breach of all. I am ill, but your being by me
 Cannot amend me; society is no comfort
 To one not sociable. I am not very sick,
 Since I can reason of it. Pray you, trust me here—   14
 I'll rob none but myself—and let me die,   15
 Stealing so poorly.
GUIDERIUS   I love thee—I have spoke it—   16
 How much the quantity, the weight as much,   17

 As I do love my father.
BELARIUS   What? How? How?
ARVIRAGUS
 If it be sin to say so, sir, I yoke me   19
 In my good brother's fault. I know not why
 I love this youth; and I have heard you say
 Love's reason's without reason. The bier at door,
 And a demand who is 't shall die, I'd say
 "My father, not this youth."
BELARIUS [*aside*]   O noble strain!   24
 O worthiness of nature! Breed of greatness!
 Cowards father cowards and base things sire base;
 Nature hath meal and bran, contempt and grace.   27
 I'm not their father; yet who this should be   28
 Doth miracle itself, loved before me.   29
 [*Aloud.*] 'Tis the ninth hour o' the morn.
ARVIRAGUS   Brother, farewell.
IMOGEN
 I wish ye sport.
ARVIRAGUS You health. [*To Belarius.*] So please you, sir.   31
IMOGEN [*aside*]
 These are kind creatures. Gods, what lies I have
      heard!
 Our courtiers say all's savage but at court.
 Experience, O, thou disprov'st report!
 Th' imperious seas breeds monsters; for the dish,   35
 Poor tributary rivers as sweet fish.   36
 I am sick still, heartsick. Pisanio,
 I'll now taste of thy drug.   [*She swallows some.*]
GUIDERIUS   I could not stir him.   38
 He said he was gentle, but unfortunate;   39
 Dishonestly afflicted, but yet honest.   40
ARVIRAGUS
 Thus did he answer me, yet said hereafter
 I might know more.
BELARIUS   To th' field, to th' field!—
 We'll leave you for this time. Go in and rest.
ARVIRAGUS
 We'll not be long away.
BELARIUS   Pray be not sick,
 For you must be our huswife.
IMOGEN   Well or ill,
 I am bound to you.   Exit [*to the cave*].
BELARIUS   And shalt be ever.   47
 This youth, howe'er distressed, appears he hath had   48
 Good ancestors.
ARVIRAGUS   How angel-like he sings!

11–12 the advantage of the time superiority in social opportunity
12–13 alike . . . services equally versed in military matters **13 single oppositions** single combat **14 imperceiverant** dull of perception
15 What mortality is what a thing life is **19 haply** perchance
20 power of control over **22 sore** grievous
**4.2. Location: Before the cave of Belarius. The scene may be virtu-
ally continuous.**
3–5 So . . . alike i.e., we are brothers, as all humans should be, being made out of the same dust, though social distinctions impose their
artificial differences. **clay and clay** different persons. **dignity** social
position, rank. **dust** (of which we are made and to which we return)
7 So sick I am not I am not that sick **8–9 not . . . sick** i.e., not
such a namby-pamby as to suffer imaginary agonies without really being sick at all **10 journal** daily **14 reason of** talk sensibly about,
without raving feverishly **15–16 I'll . . . poorly** (Imogen's witticism
is that, since she will only be robbing herself of their company, not
taking their food as in 3.6, only she should pay the penalty of loneliness for such a petty "crime.") **17 How . . . as much** just as much
in quantity and weight

19 yoke me join company **24 strain** inherited disposition **27 meal
. . . grace** grain and husks, the worthy and the contemptible
28–29 who . . . before me it is miraculous that this youth, whoever
he is, should be loved in preference to me **31 You** i.e., I wish you.
So please you at your service **35 imperious** imperial, as contrasted
with *tributary* **36 as sweet fish** i.e., breed as sweet fish (for eating) as
can be found anywhere. (In other words, goodness can be found in
unpretentious surroundings, not only at the monstrous court.) **38 stir
him** persuade him to tell about himself **39 gentle** wellborn **40 Dishonestly afflicted** afflicted by adverse and ignominious fortune
47 bound obligated. (But Belarius answers in the sense of "bound by
affection.") **48 he hath had** i.e., to have had

GUIDERIUS
But his neat cookery! He cut our roots in characters 50
And sauced our broths as Juno had been sick 51
And he her dieter.

ARVIRAGUS   Nobly he yokes
A smiling with a sigh, as if the sigh
Was that it was for not being such a smile; 54
The smile mocking the sigh, that it would fly
From so divine a temple to commix
With winds that sailors rail at.

GUIDERIUS   I do note 57
That grief and patience, rooted in him both,
Mingle their spurs together.

ARVIRAGUS   Grow, patience, 59
And let the stinking elder, grief, untwine 60
His perishing root with the increasing vine! 61

BELARIUS
It is great morning. Come, away!—Who's there? 62

Enter Cloten, [not seeing them at first].

CLOTEN
I cannot find those runagates. That villain 63
Hath mocked me. I am faint.

BELARIUS   "Those runagates"?
Means he not us? I partly know him. 'Tis 65
Cloten, the son o' the Queen. I fear some ambush.
I saw him not these many years, and yet 67
I know 'tis he. We are held as outlaws. Hence! 68

GUIDERIUS
He is but one. You and my brother search
What companies are near. Pray you, away. 70
Let me alone with him.

                    [Exeunt Belarius and Arviragus.]

CLOTEN   Soft, what are you 71
That fly me thus? Some villain mountaineers?
I have heard of such. What slave art thou?

GUIDERIUS   A thing
More slavish did I ne'er than answering
A slave without a knock.

CLOTEN   Thou art a robber, 75
A lawbreaker, a villain. Yield thee, thief.

GUIDERIUS
To who? To thee? What art thou? Have not I
An arm as big as thine? A heart as big?
Thy words, I grant, are bigger, for I wear not
My dagger in my mouth. Say what thou art,
Why I should yield to thee.

CLOTEN   Thou villain base,
Know'st me not by my clothes? 82

GUIDERIUS   No, nor thy tailor, rascal,

Who is thy grandfather. He made those clothes, 84
Which, as it seems, make thee.

CLOTEN   Thou precious varlet, 85
My tailor made them not.

GUIDERIUS   Hence, then, and thank
The man that gave them thee. Thou art some fool;
I am loath to beat thee.

CLOTEN   Thou injurious thief, 88
Hear but my name, and tremble.

GUIDERIUS   What's thy name?

CLOTEN   Cloten, thou villain.

GUIDERIUS
Cloten, thou double villain, be thy name,
I cannot tremble at it. Were it Toad, or Adder,
    Spider,
'Twould move me sooner.

CLOTEN   To thy further fear,
Nay, to thy mere confusion, thou shalt know 94
I am son to th' Queen.

GUIDERIUS   I am sorry for 't; not seeming
So worthy as thy birth.

CLOTEN   Art not afeard?

GUIDERIUS
Those that I reverence, those I fear—the wise. 97
At fools I laugh, not fear them.

CLOTEN   Die the death! 98
When I have slain thee with my proper hand, 99
I'll follow those that even now fled hence
And on the gates of Lud's Town set your heads.
Yield, rustic mountaineer!   *Fight, and exeunt.*

Enter Belarius and Arviragus.

BELARIUS   No company's abroad?

ARVIRAGUS
None in the world. You did mistake him, sure.

BELARIUS
I cannot tell. Long is it since I saw him,
But time hath nothing blurred those lines of favor 106
Which then he wore. The snatches in his voice 107
And burst of speaking were as his. I am absolute 108
'Twas very Cloten.

ARVIRAGUS   In this place we left them. 109
I wish my brother make good time with him, 110
You say he is so fell.

BELARIUS   Being scarce made up, 111
I mean to man, he had not apprehension 112
Of roaring terrors; for defect of judgment 113
Is oft the cause of fear.

Enter Guiderius [with Cloten's head].

                    But see, thy brother. 114

50 **characters** letters, designs 51 **as** as if 54 **that** what 57 **winds**
. . . at i.e., the rude wind, so infinitely rougher than the sigh
59 **spurs** roots 59–61 **Grow . . . vine** (Arviragus expresses a wish
that patience may increase in Fidele and thereby cure his grief.)
60 **elder** elder tree (on which Judas is supposed to have hanged himself). **untwine** cease to twine 61 **perishing** baleful. **with . . . vine**
(1) with patience (2) as patience increases 62 **great morning** broad
day 63 **runagates** renegades, runaways 65 **partly** slightly 67 **saw**
have seen 68 **held** regarded 70 **companies** companions 71 **Let**
. . . him leave me alone to deal with him. **Soft** i.e., wait a minute
75 **without a knock** without giving him a blow 82 **Know'st . . .**
clothes (Cloten is dressed as one from the court.)

84–85 **grandfather . . . thee** (A jest on the proverbial idea that the
tailor, or several tailors, make the man.) 85 **precious varlet** arrant
rascal 88 **injurious** insulting, malicious 94 **mere confusion** utter
ruin 97 **fear** regard with awe 98 **Die the death** (A solemn pronouncement of the sentence of death.) 99 **proper** own 106 **nothing**
not at all. **lines of favor** facial lines 107 **snatches** hesitations
108 **absolute** positive 109 **very Cloten** Cloten himself 110 **make**
good time acquit himself well 111 **fell** fierce 111–114 **Being . . .**
fear i.e., even when he was a boy, Guiderius was unafraid of anything, not suffering from fears that are often irrational (?) (Editors
sometimes refer the passage to Cloten, and emend *defect* to *th' effect*
or *cause* to *cease*.)

GUIDERIUS

This Cloten was a fool, an empty purse;
There was no money in 't. Not Hercules
Could have knocked out his brains, for he had none.
Yet I not doing this, the fool had borne   118
My head as I do his.

BELARIUS   What hast thou done?

GUIDERIUS

I am perfect what: cut off one Cloten's head,   120
Son to the Queen, after his own report,   121
Who called me traitor, mountaineer, and swore
With his own single hand he'd take us in,   123
Displace our heads where—thanks, ye gods!—they
    grow,   124
And set them on Lud's Town.

BELARIUS   We are all undone.

GUIDERIUS

Why, worthy Father, what have we to lose
But that he swore to take, our lives? The law   127
Protects not us. Then why should we be tender   128
To let an arrogant piece of flesh threat us,
Play judge and executioner all himself,
For we do fear the law? What company   131
Discover you abroad?

BELARIUS   No single soul
Can we set eye on; but in all safe reason
He must have some attendants. Though his humor   134
Was nothing but mutation—ay, and that   135
From one bad thing to worse—not frenzy,
Not absolute madness could so far have raved
To bring him here alone. Although perhaps
It may be heard at court that such as we
Cave here, hunt here, are outlaws, and in time
May make some stronger head, the which he
    hearing—   141
As it is like him—might break out and swear   142
He'd fetch us in, yet is 't not probable   143
To come alone, either he so undertaking   144
Or they so suffering. Then on good ground we fear,   145
If we do fear this body hath a tail
More perilous than the head.

ARVIRAGUS   Let ordinance   147
Come as the gods foresay it. Howsoe'er,
My brother hath done well.

BELARIUS   I had no mind   149
To hunt this day. The boy Fidele's sickness
Did make my way long forth.

GUIDERIUS   With his own sword,   151
Which he did wave against my throat, I have ta'en
His head from him. I'll throw 't into the creek
Behind our rock, and let it to the sea
And tell the fishes he's the Queen's son, Cloten.

That's all I reck.   Exit.

BELARIUS   I fear 'twill be revenged.   156
Would, Polydore, thou hadst not done 't, though
    valor
Becomes thee well enough.

ARVIRAGUS   Would I had done 't,
So the revenge alone pursued me! Polydore,   159
I love thee brotherly, but envy much
Thou hast robbed me of this deed. I would revenges   161
That possible strength might meet would seek us
    through   162
And put us to our answer.

BELARIUS   Well, 'tis done.   163
We'll hunt no more today, nor seek for danger
Where there's no profit. I prithee, to our rock.
You and Fidele play the cooks. I'll stay
Till hasty Polydore return, and bring him   167
To dinner presently.

ARVIRAGUS   Poor sick Fidele!
I'll willingly to him. To gain his color   169
I'd let a parish of such Clotens blood,   170
And praise myself for charity.   Exit [into the cave].

BELARIUS   O thou goddess,
Thou divine Nature, how thyself thou blazon'st   172
In these two princely boys! They are as gentle
As zephyrs blowing below the violet,
Not wagging his sweet head; and yet as rough,
Their royal blood enchafed, as the rud'st wind   176
That by the top doth take the mountain pine
And make him stoop to the vale. 'Tis wonder
That an invisible instinct should frame them   179
To royalty unlearned, honor untaught,
Civility not seen from other, valor   181
That wildly grows in them but yields a crop   182
As if it had been sowed. Yet still it's strange
What Cloten's being here to us portends,
Or what his death will bring us.

Enter Guiderius.

GUIDERIUS   Where's my brother?
I have sent Cloten's clodpoll down the stream   186
In embassy to his mother. His body's hostage   187
For his return.   Solemn music.

BELARIUS   My ingenious instrument!   188
Hark, Polydore, it sounds. But what occasion
Hath Cadwal now to give it motion? Hark!

GUIDERIUS

Is he at home?

---

118 Yet . . . this yet if I had not done this.   had would have
120 perfect well aware   121 after according to   123 take us in
overcome us   124 where from where   127 that that which   128 tender quick, keen   131 For because   134 humor disposition   135 mutation changeability   141 make assemble.   head armed force
142 break out burst out (in speech)   143 fetch us in capture us
144 To come that he would come   145 suffering permitting   147 ordinance what is ordained   149 mind inclination   151 make . . .
forth make my wanderings (from the cave) seem long.   his i.e.,
Cloten's

156 reck care   159 So so that.   pursued would have pursued
161 Thou that thou   161–163 I would . . . answer I wish that such
revenges as it were possible for human strength to take on would seek
us thoroughly and put us to the test, force us to respond   167 hasty
rash   169 gain his color restore the color (to his cheeks)   170 let
. . . blood drain the blood from a parish full of such Clotens
172 how . . . blazon'st how you proudly display yourself   176 enchafed being heated (with anger).   rud'st roughest   179 frame
shape, direct   181 not seen from other not learned by observing it in
some other person   182 wildly grows grows wild   186 clodpoll
blockhead, head (with a play on Cloten's name)   187 body's body is.
hostage (Guiderius' grim joke is that, since the head has been sent as
ambassador in a parley between warring sides, the body will be held
as hostage to ensure the safe return of the "ambassador.")   188 ingenious skillfully made (?)

BELARIUS   He went hence even now.
GUIDERIUS
What does he mean? Since death of my dear'st
    mother
It did not speak before. All solemn things   193
Should answer solemn accidents. The matter?   194
Triumphs for nothing and lamenting toys   195
Is jollity for apes and grief for boys.
Is Cadwal mad?

Enter Arviragus, with Imogen, [as] dead, bearing
her in his arms.

BELARIUS   Look, here he comes,
And brings the dire occasion in his arms
Of what we blame him for.
ARVIRAGUS   The bird is dead
That we have made so much on. I had rather   200
Have skipped from sixteen years of age to sixty,
To have turned my leaping-time into a crutch,   202
Than have seen this.
GUIDERIUS   O sweetest, fairest lily!
My brother wears thee not the one half so well   204
As when thou grew'st thyself.
BELARIUS   O Melancholy,   205
Who ever yet could sound thy bottom, find   206
The ooze to show what coast thy sluggish crare   207
Might eas'liest harbor in?—Thou blessèd thing,   208
Jove knows what man thou mightst have made;
    but I,   209
Thou diedst, a most rare boy, of melancholy.
How found you him?
ARVIRAGUS   Stark, as you see,   211
Thus smiling, as some fly had tickled slumber,   212
Not as death's dart being laughed at; his right cheek   213
Reposing on a cushion.
GUIDERIUS   Where?
ARVIRAGUS   O' the floor,
His arms thus leagued. I thought he slept, and put   215
My clouted brogues from off my feet, whose
    rudeness   216
Answered my steps too loud.
GUIDERIUS   Why, he but sleeps.
If he be gone, he'll make his grave a bed;
With female fairies will his tomb be haunted,
And worms will not come to thee.
ARVIRAGUS   With fairest flowers 220
Whilst summer lasts and I live here, Fidele,
I'll sweeten thy sad grave. Thou shalt not lack

The flower that's like thy face, pale primrose, nor
The azured harebell, like thy veins, no, nor   224
The leaf of eglantine, whom, not to slander,   225
Outsweetened not thy breath. The ruddock would   226
With charitable bill—O bill sore shaming
Those rich-left heirs that let their fathers lie
Without a monument!—bring thee all this,
Yea, and furred moss besides, when flowers are
    none,
To winter-ground thy corpse.
GUIDERIUS   Prithee, have done,   231
And do not play in wenchlike words with that   232
Which is so serious. Let us bury him
And not protract with admiration what   234
Is now due debt. To the grave!
ARVIRAGUS   Say, where shall 's lay him? 235
GUIDERIUS
By good Euriphile, our mother.
ARVIRAGUS   Be 't so.
And let us, Polydore, though now our voices
Have got the mannish crack, sing him to th' ground,
As once to our mother; use like note and words,   239
Save that "Euriphile" must be "Fidele."
GUIDERIUS   Cadwal,
I cannot sing. I'll weep, and word it with thee;
For notes of sorrow out of tune are worse
Than priests and fanes that lie.
ARVIRAGUS   We'll speak it, then.   244
BELARIUS
Great griefs, I see, med'cine the less, for Cloten
Is quite forgot. He was a queen's son, boys,
And, though he came our enemy, remember
He was paid for that. Though mean and mighty,   248
    rotting
Together, have one dust, yet reverence,   249
That angel of the world, doth make distinction   250
Of place 'tween high and low. Our foe was princely,
And though you took his life as being our foe,
Yet bury him as a prince.
GUIDERIUS   Pray you, fetch him hither.
Thersites' body is as good as Ajax'   255
When neither are alive.
ARVIRAGUS   If you'll go fetch him,
We'll say our song the whilst. Brother, begin.
         [Exit Belarius.]
GUIDERIUS
Nay, Cadwal, we must lay his head to th' east.   258

193 did not speak has not sounded   **194 answer** correspond to. **ac-cidents** events   **195 lamenting toys** grief over trifles (such as Cloten's death)   **200 on** of   **202 leaping-time** time of energetic youth **204–205 My . . . thyself** i.e., it is not even half so beautiful a sight to see you carried by my brother, as though he were wearing a lily, as when you lived and grew   **206 sound thy bottom** measure your depth   **207 what coast** what kind of coast. (Who can ever know where Melancholy will lodge, says Belarius, when she afflicts even so fair a youth as this? They all conclude that "Fidele" died of melancholy.)   **crare** skiff, small boat   **208 thing** i.e., Fidele   **209 but I** i.e., but I know that   **211 Stark** stiff   **212 as** as if   **213 Not as . . . laughed at** not as though laughing at death's dart (which Belarius believes Fidele to be doing)   **215 leagued** folded   **216 clouted brogues** hobnailed boots   **220 to thee** (Addressed to Imogen.)

224 like thy veins i.e., blue   **225 eglantine** i.e., the sweetbrier rose **225–226 whom . . . breath** it is no slander to the eglantine to say that its fragrance was not sweeter than your breath   **226 ruddock** robin redbreast. (According to fable, the robin would cover graves with flowers and moss, thus showing more tenderness and reverence than forgetful humans.)   **231 winter-ground** cover so as to protect from frost. **have done** stop   **232 wenchlike** womanish   **234 admira-tion** wonder   **235 due debt** i.e., a ceremonial obligation (of burial) that must be paid now. **shall 's** shall we   **239 like** similar **244 fanes** temples   **248 mean** those lowly born   **249–250 rever-ence . . . world** (Reverence, or respectful respect for rank, presides over the world like an *angel* or attendant spirit.)   **255 Thersites' . . . Ajax'** (Thersites was the base scoffer in the *Iliad*; Ajax, a Greek hero.) **258 lay . . . east** (Opposite to the Christian custom and hence sugges-tive here of pre-Christian worship.)

My father hath a reason for 't.
ARVIRAGUS   'Tis true.
GUIDERIUS
Come on, then, and remove him.
    [*They lay out Imogen with her head to the east.*]
ARVIRAGUS   So. Begin.
              Song.
GUIDERIUS
   Fear no more the heat o' the sun,
     Nor the furious winter's rages;
   Thou thy worldly task hast done,
     Home art gone, and ta'en thy wages.
   Golden lads and girls all must,
   As chimney sweepers, come to dust.
ARVIRAGUS
   Fear no more the frown o' the great;
     Thou art past the tyrant's stroke.
   Care no more to clothe and eat;
     To thee the reed is as the oak.   270
   The scepter, learning, physic, must   271
   All follow this and come to dust.
GUIDERIUS
   Fear no more the lightning flash,
ARVIRAGUS
     Nor th' all-dreaded thunderstone.   274
GUIDERIUS
   Fear not slander, censure rash;
ARVIRAGUS
     Thou hast finished joy and moan.
BOTH
   All lovers young, all lovers must
   Consign to thee and come to dust.   278
GUIDERIUS
   No exorciser harm thee!   279
ARVIRAGUS
   Nor no witchcraft charm thee!
GUIDERIUS
   Ghost unlaid forbear thee!   281
ARVIRAGUS
   Nothing ill come near thee!
BOTH
   Quiet consummation have,   283
   And renownèd be thy grave!

   Enter Belarius, with the [headless] body of Cloten.

GUIDERIUS
We have done our obsequies. Come, lay him down.
    [*Cloten is laid next to Imogen.*]
BELARIUS
Here's a few flowers, but 'bout midnight, more.
    [*They strew flowers.*]
The herbs that have on them cold dew o' the night

Are strewings fitt'st for graves. Upon their faces.   288
You were as flowers, now withered; even so
These herblets shall, which we upon you strew.
Come on, away; apart upon our knees.
The ground that gave them first has them again.
Their pleasures here are past, so is their pain.
   Exeunt [Belarius, Guiderius, and Arviragus].
IMOGEN (*awakes*)
Yes, sir, to Milford Haven. Which is the way?
I thank you. By yond bush? Pray, how far thither?
Ods pittikins! Can it be six mile yet?   296
I have gone all night. Faith, I'll lie down and sleep.   297
But soft, no bedfellow? [*She sees or touches Cloten's
   body.*] O gods and goddesses!
These flowers are like the pleasures of the world,
This bloody man the care on 't. I hope I dream,   300
For so I thought I was a cave keeper   301
And cook to honest creatures. But 'tis not so.
'Twas but a bolt of nothing, shot at nothing,   303
Which the brain makes of fumes. Our very eyes   304
Are sometimes like our judgments, blind. Good faith,
I tremble still with fear; but if there be
Yet left in heaven as small a drop of pity
As a wren's eye, feared gods, a part of it!   308
The dream's here still. Even when I wake, it is
Without me, as within me; not imagined, felt.   310
A headless man? The garments of Posthumus?
I know the shape of 's leg; this is his hand,
His foot Mercurial, his Martial thigh,   313
The brawns of Hercules; but his Jovial face—   314
Murder in heaven? How? 'Tis gone. Pisanio,
All curses madded Hecuba gave the Greeks,   316
And mine to boot, be darted on thee! Thou,
Conspired with that irregulous devil, Cloten,   318
Hath here cut off my lord. To write and read   319
Be henceforth treacherous! Damned Pisanio
Hath with his forgèd letters—damned Pisanio—
From this most bravest vessel of the world
Struck the maintop! O Posthumus! Alas,   323
Where is thy head? Where's that? Ay me, where's
   that?
Pisanio might have killed thee at the heart
And left this head on. How should this be? Pisanio?
'Tis he and Cloten. Malice and lucre in them   327

270 **reed, oak** (Contrasting symbols of a fragility that survives by being flexible and a mightiness often overthrown. Fidele is past caring for the lesson contained in this contrast.) 271 **physic** medical learning 274 **thunderstone** (The supposed solid body accompanying a stroke of lightning.) 278 **Consign to** co-sign with, share a similar fate with, submit to the same terms with 279 **exorciser** conjurer 281 **unlaid** not laid to rest 283 **consummation** end, death

288 **Upon their faces** i.e., strew flowers on the dead persons' faces or perhaps on the front of their bodies. (Since Cloten is headless. The line may be corrupt.) 296 **Ods pittikins** God's pity. (A diminutive oath.) 297 **gone** walked 300 **the care on 't** i.e., is like the troubles of this world 301 **For so** for in just the same way. (Since my thought of dwelling in a cave has proved to be a dream, may this awful sight prove one, too.) **cave keeper** one who dwells in a cave 303 **bolt** arrow 304 **fumes** vapors engendered of humors which, according to current theory, rose up into the brain and, by affecting imagination in the forechamber of the brain, caused dreams 308 **wren's eye** i.e., a very small eye, rendering a small teardrop. **a part** i.e., give me a part 310 **Without me** outside of me, externally real and not just imagined (within) 313 **Mercurial** nimble and swift like the foot of Mercury. **Martial** powerful for war like that of Mars 314 **brawns** muscles. **Jovial** Jove-like 316 **madded** maddened. **Hecuba** wife of Priam, King of Troy 318 **Conspired** conspiring. **irregulous** lawless 319 **Hath** hast 323 **maintop** top of mainmast, i.e., head 327 **lucre** greed

Have laid this woe here. O, 'tis pregnant, pregnant!   328
The drug he gave me, which he said was precious
And cordial to me, have I not found it   330
Murd'rous to th' senses? That confirms it home.   331
This is Pisanio's deed, and Cloten.—O!   332
Give color to my pale cheek with thy blood,   333
That we the horrider may seem to those
Which chance to find us. O, my lord, my lord!

                                 [*She falls on the body.*]

          Enter Lucius, Captains, and a Soothsayer.

CAPTAIN
To them the legions garrisoned in Gallia,   336
After your will, have crossed the sea, attending   337
You here at Milford Haven with your ships.
They are in readiness.
LUCIUS   But what from Rome?
CAPTAIN
The Senate hath stirred up the confiners   340
And gentlemen of Italy, most willing spirits,
That promise noble service, and they come
Under the conduct of bold Iachimo,
Siena's brother.
LUCIUS   When expect you them?   344
CAPTAIN
With the next benefit o' the wind.
LUCIUS   This forwardness
Makes our hopes fair. Command our present
     numbers
Be mustered; bid the captains look to 't.—Now, sir,
What have you dreamed of late of this war's
     purpose?   348
SOOTHSAYER
Last night the very gods showed me a vision—
I fast and prayed for their intelligence—thus:
  350
I saw Jove's bird, the Roman eagle, winged
From the spongy south to this part of the west,   352
There vanished in the sunbeams, which portends—
Unless my sins abuse my divination—   354
Success to th' Roman host.
LUCIUS   Dream often so,
And never false. [*He sees Cloten and Imogen.*] Soft, ho,
     what trunk is here
Without his top? The ruin speaks that sometime
It was a worthy building. How? A page?
Or dead or sleeping on him? But dead rather;   359
For nature doth abhor to make his bed
With the defunct, or sleep upon the dead.
Let's see the boy's face.
CAPTAIN   He's alive, my lord.
LUCIUS
He'll then instruct us of this body.—Young one,
Inform us of thy fortunes, for it seems

They crave to be demanded. Who is this
Thou mak'st thy bloody pillow? Or who was he
That, otherwise than noble nature did,   367
Hath altered that good picture? What's thy interest
In this sad wrack? How came 't? Who is 't?   369
What art thou?
IMOGEN   I am nothing; or if not,
Nothing to be were better. This was my master,
A very valiant Briton and a good,
That here by mountaineers lies slain. Alas,
There is no more such masters. I may wander
From east to occident, cry out for service,
Try many, all good, serve truly, never
Find such another master.
LUCIUS   'Lack, good youth!
Thou mov'st no less with thy complaining than   378
Thy master in bleeding. Say his name, good friend.
IMOGEN
Richard du Champ. [*Aside.*] If I do lie and do
No harm by it, though the gods hear, I hope
They'll pardon it.—Say you, sir?
LUCIUS   Thy name?
IMOGEN   Fidele, sir.
LUCIUS
Thou dost approve thyself the very same;   383
Thy name well fits thy faith, thy faith thy name.
Wilt take thy chance with me? I will not say
Thou shalt be so well mastered, but be sure
No less beloved. The Roman Emperor's letters
Sent by a consul to me should not sooner
Than thine own worth prefer thee. Go with me.   389
IMOGEN
I'll follow, sir. But first, an 't please the gods,   390
I'll hide my master from the flies as deep
As these poor pickaxes can dig; and when   392
With wild-wood leaves and weeds I ha' strewed his
     grave
And on it said a century of prayers,   394
Such as I can, twice o'er, I'll weep and sigh,
And leaving so his service, follow you,
So please you entertain me.
LUCIUS   Ay, good youth,   397
And rather father thee than master thee.—
My friends,
The boy hath taught us manly duties. Let us
Find out the prettiest daisied plot we can
And make him with our pikes and partisans   402
A grave. Come, arm him. Boy, he's preferred   403
By thee to us, and he shall be interred
As soldiers can. Be cheerful; wipe thine eyes.
Some falls are means the happier to arise.
                 Exeunt, [*bearing Cloten's body*].

4.3 *Enter Cymbeline, Lords, [Attendants,] and
Pisanio.*

CYMBELINE
Again, and bring me word how 'tis with her.
                              [*Exit an Attendant.*]
A fever with the absence of her son,   2
A madness, of which her life's in danger. Heavens,
How deeply you at once do touch me! Imogen,   4
The great part of my comfort, gone; my queen
Upon a desperate bed, and in a time
When fearful wars point at me; her son gone,
So needful for this present! It strikes me past
The hope of comfort.—But for thee, fellow,
Who needs must know of her departure and
Dost seem so ignorant, we'll enforce it from thee   11
By a sharp torture.
PISANIO   Sir, my life is yours;
I humbly set it at your will. But for my mistress,   13
I nothing know where she remains, why gone,
Nor when she purposes return. Beseech Your
    Highness,
Hold me your loyal servant.
A LORD   Good my liege,   16
The day that she was missing he was here.
I dare be bound he's true and shall perform
All parts of his subjection loyally. For Cloten,   19
There wants no diligence in seeking him,   20
And will no doubt be found.
CYMBELINE   The time is troublesome.   21
[*To Pisanio.*] We'll slip you for a season, but our
    jealousy   22
Does yet depend.
A LORD   So please Your Majesty,   23
The Roman legions, all from Gallia drawn,
Are landed on your coast with a supply
Of Roman gentlemen by the Senate sent.
CYMBELINE
Now for the counsel of my son and queen!
I am amazed with matter.
A LORD   Good my liege,   28
Your preparation can affront no less   29
Than what you hear of. Come more, for more you're
    ready.   30
The want is but to put those powers in motion   31
That long to move.
CYMBELINE   I thank you. Let's withdraw,
And meet the time as it seeks us. We fear not
What can from Italy annoy us, but   34

We grieve at chances here. Away!   35
                              Exeunt [all but Pisanio].
PISANIO
I heard no letter from my master since
I wrote him Imogen was slain. 'Tis strange.
Nor hear I from my mistress, who did promise
To yield me often tidings. Neither know I
What is betid to Cloten, but remain   40
Perplexed in all. The heavens still must work.
Wherein I am false I am honest; not true, to be true.
These present wars shall find I love my country,
Even to the note o' the King, or I'll fall in them.   44
All other doubts, by time let them be cleared;   45
Fortune brings in some boats that are not steered.
                                              Exit.

❧

4.4 *Enter Belarius, Guiderius, and Arviragus.*

GUIDERIUS
The noise is round about us.
BELARIUS   Let us from it.
ARVIRAGUS
What pleasure, sir, find we in life, to lock it
From action and adventure?
GUIDERIUS   Nay, what hope
Have we in hiding us? This way the Romans   4
Must or for Britons slay us or receive us   5
For barbarous and unnatural revolts   6
During their use, and slay us after.
BELARIUS   Sons,   7
We'll higher to the mountains, there secure us.
To the King's party there's no going. Newness
Of Cloten's death—we being not known, not
    mustered
Among the bands—may drive us to a render   11
Where we have lived, and so extort from 's that
Which we have done, whose answer would be
    death   13
Drawn on with torture.
GUIDERIUS   This is, sir, a doubt   14
In such a time nothing becoming you   15
Nor satisfying us.
ARVIRAGUS   It is not likely
That when they hear the Roman horses neigh,
Behold their quartered fires, have both their eyes   18
And ears so cloyed importantly as now,   19
That they will waste their time upon our note,   20

4.3. Location: Britain. At the court of Cymbeline.
2 with brought on by   **4 touch** wound, afflict   **11 seem** pretend
to be   **13 for** as for (also in line 19)   **16 Hold** regard   **19 subjection**
duty as a subject   **20 wants** is lacking   **21 will** he will.   **troublesome**
filled with deep troubles   **22 slip you** let you go.   **jealousy** suspicion   **23 depend** impend, threaten   **28 amazed with matter** confused and overwhelmed by the pressure of affairs   **29 preparation**
military force already mustered   **29–30 affront . . . Than** confront in
combat as large (an army) as   **30 Come more** if more (enemy) come
31 want is but sole thing needed is.   **powers** armed forces   **34 annoy** injure

35 chances accidents (the Queen's illness, etc.)   **40 is betid** has happened   **44 Even . . . King** to the extent of attracting the favorable notice of the King (for my bravery)   **45 let them** i.e., let us pray that
they
4.4. Location: Wales. Before the cave of Belarius.
4 This way i.e., if we take such a course of conduct   **5 Must or** must
either   **6 revolts** deserters, rebels   **7 During their use** as long as they
find us useful   **11 bands** army rolls.   **render** rendering of an account,
relation   **13 answer** consequence   **14 Drawn on with** brought about
and lengthened by   **15 nothing** not at all   **18 quartered fires** camp-
fires   **19 cloyed importantly** filled with urgent business   **20 upon our
note** in observing us

To know from whence we are.
BELARIUS   O, I am known
Of many in the army. Many years,
Though Cloten then but young, you see, not
    wore him
From my remembrance. And besides, the King
Hath not deserved my service nor your loves,
Who find in my exile the want of breeding,   26
The certainty of this hard life, aye hopeless   27
To have the courtesy your cradle promised,   28
But to be still hot summer's tanlings and   29
The shrinking slaves of winter.
GUIDERIUS   Than be so,   30
Better to cease to be. Pray, sir, to th' army.
I and my brother are not known; yourself
So out of thought, and thereto so o'ergrown,   33
Cannot be questioned.
ARVIRAGUS   By this sun that shines,
I'll thither. What thing is 't that I never   35
Did see man die, scarce ever looked on blood
But that of coward hares, hot goats, and venison!   37
Never bestrid a horse, save one that had
A rider like myself, who ne'er wore rowel   39
Nor iron on his heel! I am ashamed
To look upon the holy sun, to have
The benefit of his blest beams, remaining
So long a poor unknown.
GUIDERIUS   By heavens, I'll go.
If you will bless me, sir, and give me leave,
I'll take the better care, but if you will not,   45
The hazard therefore due fall on me by   46
The hands of Romans!
ARVIRAGUS   So say I. Amen.
BELARIUS
No reason I, since of your lives you set
So slight a valuation, should reserve
My cracked one to more care. Have with you, boys! 50
If in your country wars you chance to die,   51
That is my bed too, lads, and there I'll lie.
Lead, lead. [*Aside.*] The time seems long; their blood
    thinks scorn
Till it fly out and show them princes born.   *Exeunt.*

❧

5.1   *Enter Posthumus alone [in Italian dress, with a
bloody handkerchief].*

POSTHUMUS
Yea, bloody cloth, I'll keep thee, for I wished

Thou shouldst be colored thus. You married ones,
If each of you should take this course, how many
Must murder wives much better than themselves
For wrying but a little! O Pisanio!   5
Every good servant does not all commands;
No bond but to do just ones. Gods, if you   7
Should have ta'en vengeance on my faults, I never   8
Had lived to put on this; so had you saved   9
The noble Imogen to repent, and struck
Me, wretch, more worth your vengeance. But alack,
You snatch some hence for little faults; that's love, 12
To have them fall no more; you some permit   13
To second ills with ills, each elder worse,   14
And make them dread it, to the doers' thrift.   15
But Imogen is your own. Do your best wills,
And make me blest to obey! I am brought hither
Among th' Italian gentry, and to fight
Against my lady's kingdom. 'Tis enough
That, Britain, I have killed thy mistress; peace,
I'll give no wound to thee. Therefore, good heavens,
Hear patiently my purpose: I'll disrobe me
Of these Italian weeds and suit myself   23
As does a Briton peasant; so I'll fight
Against the part I come with; so I'll die   25
For thee, O Imogen, even for whom my life
Is every breath a death; and thus, unknown,   27
Pitied nor hated, to the face of peril   28
Myself I'll dedicate. Let me make men know
More valor in me than my habits show.   30
Gods, put the strength o' the Leonati in me!
To shame the guise o' the world, I will begin 32
The fashion: less without and more within.   *Exit.* 33

5.2   *Enter Lucius, Iachimo, and the Roman army at
one door, and the Briton army at another,
Leonatus Posthumus following like a poor soldier.
They march over and go out. Then enter again, in
skirmish, Iachimo and Posthumus; he vanquisheth
and disarmeth Iachimo, and then leaves him.*

IACHIMO
The heaviness and guilt within my bosom
Takes off my manhood. I have belied a lady,
The princess of this country, and the air on 't   3
Revengingly enfeebles me; or could this carl,   4
A very drudge of nature's, have subdued me
In my profession? Knighthoods and honors borne
As I wear mine are titles but of scorn.

26–28 **Who . . . promised** you who find in exile with me a lack of
proper education and hardship from which there is no escape, without hope of ever achieving the cultivated existence promised you by
your gentle birth (as sons of a onetime courtier and soldier) 29 **But**
i.e., but destined instead. **tanlings** those tanned by the sun
30 **shrinking** i.e., shrinking from the cold and cowering in servitude
33 **thereto** in addition. **o'ergrown** i.e., with hair and beard
35 **What thing** i.e., what a disgraceful thing 37 **hot** lecherous
39 **rowel** wheel of a spur 45 **take the better care** proceed with better prospects of success 46 **hazard therefore due** danger resulting
from disobedience and lack of parental blessing 50 **cracked** i.e.,
with age. **Have with you** come on, then 51 **country** country's
5.1. Location: Britain. An open place.

5 **wrying** swerving from the right course 7 **bond but** obligation except 8 **Should have** had, as you should have 9 **put on** incite, encourage (?) burden myself with (?) 12–13 **that's . . . more** that is a
loving act, since it makes them sin no more 14 **second** follow up.
elder subsequent (sin) 15 **make . . . thrift** i.e., make those evildoers
repent their deeds, to their ultimate spiritual profit 23 **suit** clothe
25 **part** party, side 27 **Is . . . death** i.e., is like dying again and
again, every instant, from painful remorse 28 **Pitied** neither pitied
30 **habits** clothes 32 **guise** custom 33 **The fashion: less without** the
fashion of relying less on outward show
**5.2. Location: Britain. Field of battle. The scene is probably continu-
ous with the previous.**
s.d. poor of low rank and poorly outfitted 3 **on 't** of it 4 **or** otherwise. **carl** churl, peasant

If that thy gentry, Britain, go before   8
This lout as he exceeds our lords, the odds
Is that we scarce are men and you are gods.   *Exit.*

> The battle continues; the Britons fly; Cymbeline is
> taken. Then enter, to his rescue, Belarius,
> Guiderius, and Arviragus.

BELARIUS
Stand, stand! We have th' advantage of the ground;
The lane is guarded. Nothing routs us but
The villainy of our fears.
GUIDERIUS, ARVIRAGUS   Stand, stand, and fight!

> Enter Posthumus, and seconds the Britons. They
> rescue Cymbeline, and exeunt. Then enter Lucius,
> Iachimo, and Imogen.

LUCIUS
Away, boy, from the troops, and save thyself!
For friends kill friends, and the disorder's such
As war were hoodwinked.
IACHIMO   'Tis their fresh supplies.   16
LUCIUS
It is a day turned strangely. Or betimes   17
Let's reinforce, or fly.   *Exeunt.*

5.3
> *Enter Posthumus [dressed as a British peasant
> still], and a Briton Lord.*

LORD
Cam'st thou from where they made the stand?
POSTHUMUS   I did,
Though you, it seems, come from the fliers?
LORD   I did.
POSTHUMUS
No blame be to you, sir, for all was lost,
But that the heavens fought. The King himself   4
Of his wings destitute, the army broken,   5
And but the backs of Britons seen, all flying
Through a strait lane; the enemy fullhearted,   7
Lolling the tongue with slaughtering, having work   8
More plentiful than tools to do 't, struck down
Some mortally, some slightly touched, some falling   10
Merely through fear, that the strait pass was dammed
With dead men hurt behind, and cowards living   12
To die with lengthened shame.
LORD   Where was this lane?   13
POSTHUMUS
Close by the battle, ditched, and walled with turf;
Which gave advantage to an ancient soldier,
An honest one, I warrant, who deserved   16
So long a breeding as his white beard came to,   17

In doing this for 's country. Athwart the lane,
He, with two striplings—lads more like to run   19
The country base than to commit such slaughter,   20
With faces fit for masks, or rather fairer   21
Than those for preservation cased or shame—   22
Made good the passage, cried to those that fled,   23
"Our Britain's harts die flying, not our men.
To darkness fleet souls that fly backwards. Stand!   25
Or we are Romans and will give you that   26
Like beasts which you shun beastly, and may save   27
But to look back in frown. Stand, stand!" These
  three,   28
Three thousand confident, in act as many—
For three performers are the file when all   30
The rest do nothing—with this word "Stand, stand,"
Accommodated by the place, more charming   32
With their own nobleness, which could have turned   33
A distaff to a lance, gilded pale looks,   34
Part shame, part spirit renewed, that some, turned
  coward   35
But by example—O, a sin in war,   36
Damned in the first beginners!—'gan to look   37
The way that they did and to grin like lions   38
Upon the pikes o' the hunters. Then began   39
A stop i' the chaser, a retire, anon   40
A rout, confusion thick. Forthwith they fly   41
Chickens, the way which they stooped eagles; slaves, 42
The strides they victors made. And now our
  cowards,   43
Like fragments in hard voyages, became   44
The life o' the need. Having found the back door
  open   45
Of the unguarded hearts, heavens, how they
  wound!
Some slain before, some dying, some their friends   47
O'erborne i' the former wave, ten chased by one,   48

---

8 go before excel **16 As** as if. **hoodwinked** blindfolded. (War swings his weapons blindly, without looking to see who is struck.) **17 Or betimes** either swiftly

5.3. Location: The field of battle, as before.
4 But that if it had not been for the fact that **5 wings** flanks of the army **7 strait** narrow. **fullhearted** full of courage and confidence **8 Lolling** letting hang out **10 touched** wounded **12 behind** from the rear (while running away) **13 lengthened** lingering (for the rest of their lives) **16 honest** worthy **17 breeding** life, support. (His long white beard betokens the length of years that he deserves to be honored.)

19 like likely **20 base** prisoner's base, a game in which rapid running is the means to victory **21 fit for masks** delicate enough to deserve sheltering from the elements **22 those . . . shame** ladies' faces masked (*cased*) either for protection against the elements or for modesty **23 Made good** secured **25 darkness** i.e., ignominy, hell. **fleet** hasten **26 we are Romans** i.e., we three will act like Romans. **that** i.e., death blows **27 Like beasts** as if to beasts. **beastly** like cowards. **save** prevent **28 But . . . frown** only by looking back in defiance, only if you turn and defy the enemy **30 file** i.e., entire force (as in "rank and file") **32 Accommodated** provided with advantage. **more charming** and, more important, working their spell on others as if by magic (thus persuading them to turn and fight) **33 With** by the example of **34 A distaff to a lance** i.e., a housewife into a soldier. **gilded** imparted a flush of color to **35 Part . . . renewed** (moved them so that) shame revived some, courage others **35–36 turned . . . example** having been converted into cowards only by imitation **37 first beginners** i.e., those who first set an example of cowardice. **'gan** began **38 they** i.e., Belarius and his two "sons." **grin** bare the teeth **39 Upon** directly against, face to face with **40 stop i' the chaser** stopping of those who had been the pursuers, i.e., the Romans. **retire** retreat **41 Forthwith** immediately **42 Chickens** i.e., like chickens. **the way . . . eagles** along the very path that just before they had swooped down upon like eagles **42–43 slaves . . . made** retracing, like slaves, the steps they had taken as victors **44 fragments** scraps, fragments of food, something to fall back on as a last resort **45 The life o' the need** vital support in time of necessity. **back door** i.e., vulnerable soft spot of the Romans **47–48 Some . . . by one** i.e., some who were given up for dead or dying, and some comrades overwhelmed in the previous Roman assault who had yielded by the tens to each Roman soldier

Are now each one the slaughterman of twenty.
Those that would die or ere resist are grown   50
The mortal bugs o' the field.

LORD   This was strange chance: 51
A narrow lane, an old man, and two boys!

POSTHUMUS
Nay, do not wonder at it. You are made
Rather to wonder at the things you hear
Than to work any. Will you rhyme upon 't   55
And vent it for a mockery? Here is one: 56
"Two boys, an old man twice a boy, a lane,   57
Preserved the Britons, was the Romans' bane."

LORD
Nay, be not angry, sir.

POSTHUMUS   'Lack, to what end?   59
Who dares not stand his foe, I'll be his friend;   60
For if he'll do as he is made to do,   61
I know he'll quickly fly my friendship too.   62
You have put me into rhyme.

LORD   Farewell. You're angry.
                                                Exit.

POSTHUMUS
Still going? This is a lord! O noble misery,   64
To be i' the field, and ask "What news?" of me!
Today how many would have given their honors
To have saved their carcasses! Took heel to do 't,
And yet died too! I, in mine own woe charmed,   68
Could not find Death where I did hear him groan,
Nor feel him where he struck. Being an ugly
    monster,
'Tis strange he hides him in fresh cups, soft beds,
Sweet words, or hath more ministers than we
That draw his knives i' the war. Well, I will find him;
For being now a favorer to the Briton,   74
                      [removing his British garb]
No more a Briton, I have resumed again   75
The part I came in. Fight I will no more,   76
But yield me to the veriest hind that shall   77
Once touch my shoulder. Great the slaughter is   78
Here made by th' Roman; great the answer be   79
Britons must take. For me, my ransom's death.
On either side I come to spend my breath,   81
Which neither here I'll keep nor bear again,
But end it by some means for Imogen.

50 **would die** previously were ready to die.   **or ere** rather than
51 **mortal bugs** deadly bugbears, terrors   55 **work any** perform any
such wonders yourself. (Said reproachfully.)   55–56 **Will . . . one**
i.e., would you like to compose rhymes on this event in ballad fashion and thus make a mockery of it with your cheap exploitation? Here
is a sample.   **vent** air, circulate   57 **twice a boy** in his second childhood   59 **'Lack** alack.   **to what end** why should I be angry?
60–62 Who . . . too i.e., I can put up with the friendship of any
coward (like myself), for, if he is true to his colors, he'll run away
and thus rid me of his company.   **Who** whoever.   **stand** stand
against.   **made** inclined   64 **going** fleeing—even from me.   **noble
misery** miserable specimen of the nobility   68 **charmed** made invulnerable as if by a spell   74 **being . . . favorer to** i.e., since Death
now favors, or, although I have given my support until now   75 **No
. . . Briton** I remaining no longer a Briton   76 **The part . . . in** i.e.,
my Roman guise (in which my capture and execution seem assured)
77 **hind** peasant   78 **touch my shoulder** i.e., place me under arrest
79 **answer be** retaliation is that   81 **spend my breath** give up my life

---

Enter two [British] Captains and soldiers.

FIRST CAPTAIN
Great Jupiter be praised! Lucius is taken.
'Tis thought the old man and his sons were angels.

SECOND CAPTAIN
There was a fourth man, in a silly habit,   86
That gave th' affront with them.

FIRST CAPTAIN   So 'tis reported,   87
But none of 'em can be found.—Stand! Who's
    there?

POSTHUMUS   A Roman,
Who had not now been drooping here if seconds   90
Had answered him.

SECOND CAPTAIN   Lay hands on him; a dog!   91
A leg of Rome shall not return to tell   92
What crows have pecked them here. He brags his
    service
As if he were of note. Bring him to th' King.

*Enter Cymbeline, Belarius, Guiderius, Arviragus,
Pisanio, [soldiers, attendants,] and Roman
captives. The Captains present Posthumus to
Cymbeline, who delivers him over to a Jailer.
                                    [Then exeunt.]*

5.4   *Enter Posthumus [in chains] and [two] Jailer[s].*

FIRST JAILER
You shall not now be stol'n; you have locks
    upon you.
So graze as you find pasture.

SECOND JAILER   Ay, or a stomach.   2
                              [Exeunt Jailers.]

POSTHUMUS
Most welcome, bondage! For thou art a way,
I think, to liberty. Yet am I better
Than one that's sick o' the gout, since he had rather
Groan so in perpetuity than be cured
By th' sure physician, Death, who is the key
T' unbar these locks. My conscience, thou art fettered
More than my shanks and wrists. You good gods,
    give me
The penitent instrument to pick that bolt,   10
Then, free forever! Is 't enough I am sorry?
So children temporal fathers do appease;
Gods are more full of mercy. Must I repent,   13

86 **silly** simple, rustic   87 **affront** attack   90 **drooping** languishing.
seconds supporters   91 **answered him** followed his lead, or answered his call for help   92 **leg** i.e., one of the lower extremities, one
who does the walking (and the running away)
5.4. Location: A British prison or stockade. Possibly the scene is continuous; see the next note.
s.d. Enter (The scene may be continuous, with Posthumus and the
jailers remaining onstage, though the Folio does mark an entrance for
Posthumus and one jailer, and the scene does appear to call for manacles [lines 9, 191]. On the unlocalized Elizabethan stage, the change
of scene is achieved chiefly by the actors and their dialogue.)
2 graze . . . pasture i.e., like a horse, fettered by one leg   10 **penitent . . . bolt** i.e., penitence to unlock the fetters encumbering my
conscience and to find the death I seek   13 **Must I** if I must

I cannot do it better than in gyves,   14
Desired more than constrained. To satisfy,   15
If of my freedom 'tis the main part, take   16
No stricter render of me than my all.   17
I know you are more clement than vile men,
Who of their broken debtors take a third,   19
A sixth, a tenth, letting them thrive again
On their abatement. That's not my desire.   21
For Imogen's dear life take mine; and though
'Tis not so dear, yet 'tis a life; you coined it.   23
'Tween man and man they weigh not every stamp;   24
Though light, take pieces for the figure's sake;   25
You rather mine, being yours. And so, great powers,   26
If you will take this audit, take this life   27
And cancel these cold bonds. O Imogen!   28
I'll speak to thee in silence.   [*He sleeps.*]

> *Solemn music. Enter, as in an apparition, Sicilius
> Leonatus, father to Posthumus, an old man, attired
> like a warrior; leading in his hand an ancient
> matron, his wife, and mother to Posthumus, with
> music before them. Then, after other music, follows
> the two young Leonati, brothers to Posthumus,
> with wounds as they died in the wars. They circle
> Posthumus round, as he lies sleeping.*

SICILIUS
No more, thou Thunder-master, show   30
    Thy spite on mortal flies.   31
With Mars fall out, with Juno chide,
    That thy adulteries   33
        Rates and revenges.   34
Hath my poor boy done aught but well,
    Whose face I never saw?
I died whilst in the womb he stayed
    Attending nature's law;   38
Whose father then—as men report   39
    Thou orphans' father art—   40
Thou shouldst have been, and shielded him
    From this earth-vexing smart.   42

MOTHER
Lucina lent not me her aid,   43
    But took me in my throes,
That from me was Posthumus ripped,
    Came crying 'mongst his foes,
        A thing of pity!

SICILIUS
Great nature, like his ancestry,   48
    Molded the stuff so fair   49
That he deserved the praise o' the world
    As great Sicilius' heir.

FIRST BROTHER
When once he was mature for man,   52
    In Britain where was he   53
That could stand up his parallel,
    Or fruitful object be
In eye of Imogen, that best
    Could deem his dignity?   57

MOTHER
With marriage wherefore was he mocked,
    To be exiled and thrown
From Leonati seat, and cast
    From her his dearest one,
        Sweet Imogen?

SICILIUS
Why did you suffer Iachimo,
    Slight thing of Italy,   64
To taint his nobler heart and brain
    With needless jealousy,
And to become the geck and scorn   67
    O' th' other's villainy?

SECOND BROTHER
For this from stiller seats we came,   69
    Our parents and us twain,
That striking in our country's cause   71
    Fell bravely and were slain,
Our fealty and Tenantius' right   73
    With honor to maintain.

FIRST BROTHER
Like hardiment Posthumus hath   75
    To Cymbeline performed.
Then, Jupiter, thou king of gods,
    Why hast thou thus adjourned   78
The graces for his merits due,
    Being all to dolors turned?

SICILIUS
Thy crystal window ope; look out.
    No longer exercise
Upon a valiant race thy harsh
    And potent injuries.

MOTHER
Since, Jupiter, our son is good,
    Take off his miseries.

SICILIUS
Peep through thy marble mansion. Help,
    Or we poor ghosts will cry
To th' shining synod of the rest   89
    Against thy deity.

---

14 gyves fetters   **15 constrained** forced (upon me).   **satisfy** make atonement   **16 If . . . part** i.e., if such atonement is essential to freeing my conscience   **17 stricter render** sterner repayment   **19 broken** bankrupt   **21 abatement** diminished principal   **23 so dear** as valuable as hers   **24 'Tween . . . stamp** in commercial transactions, men don't weigh every coin exactly   **25 Though . . . sake** even if some coins may be under the exact weight, men accept them for the sake of the image stamped thereon, i.e., the image of the king   **26 You . . . yours** i.e., you should all the more readily take my life, even though I am a light (worthless) coin, since I am stamped in your image   **27 take this audit** accept this accounting   **28 bonds** (1) fetters, both literal and figurative (2) legal contracts   **30 Thunder-master** i.e., Jupiter   **31 mortal flies** i.e., petty creatures, mere humans   **33 That** who (i.e., Juno)   **34 Rates** scolds   **38 Attending nature's law** i.e., awaiting the completion of his term in the womb   **39–40 Whose father . . . art** (Psalm 68:5 praises God as "A father of the fatherless.")   **42 earth-vexing smart** suffering to which all life is prone   **43 Lucina** goddess of childbirth

48 like acting in concert with, or, taking the part of   **49 stuff** substance   **52 mature for man** grown to manhood   **53 he** any man   **57 deem** judge   **64 Slight** worthless   **67 geck** dupe   **69 stiller seats** quieter abodes (i.e., the Elysian Fields)   **71 That** who   **73 Tenantius'** Cymbeline's father's   **75 Like hardiment** similar bold exploits   **78 adjourned** deferred   **89 synod of the rest** assembly of the gods

BROTHERS
Help, Jupiter, or we appeal,
And from thy justice fly.

*Jupiter descends in thunder and lightning, sitting
upon an eagle. He throws a thunderbolt. The
ghosts fall on their knees.*

JUPITER
No more, you petty spirits of region low,
Offend our hearing. Hush! How dare you ghosts
Accuse the Thunderer, whose bolt, you know,
Sky-planted, batters all rebelling coasts?   96
Poor shadows of Elysium, hence, and rest
Upon your never-withering banks of flowers.
Be not with mortal accidents oppressed.   99
No care of yours it is; you know 'tis ours.
Whom best I love I cross, to make my gift,
The more delayed, delighted. Be content.   102
Your low-laid son our godhead will uplift.
His comforts thrive, his trials well are spent.   104
Our Jovial star reigned at his birth, and in   105
Our temple was he married. Rise, and fade.   106
He shall be lord of Lady Imogen,
And happier much by his affliction made.
This tablet lay upon his breast, wherein
Our pleasure his full fortune doth confine.   110
                                    [*He delivers a tablet.*]
And so away! No farther with your din
Express impatience, lest you stir up mine.
Mount, eagle, to my palace crystalline.   *Ascends.*
SICILIUS
He came in thunder; his celestial breath
Was sulfurous to smell. The holy eagle
Stooped, as to foot us. His ascension is   116
More sweet than our blest fields. His royal bird   117
Prunes the immortal wing and cloys his beak,   118
As when his god is pleased.
ALL   Thanks, Jupiter!
SICILIUS
The marble pavement closes; he is entered   120
His radiant roof. Away! And, to be blest,
Let us with care perform his great behest.
                          [*The ghosts place the tablet on
                          Posthumus' breast, and*] *vanish.*
POSTHUMUS [*waking*]
Sleep, thou hast been a grandsire and begot
A father to me; and thou hast created
A mother and two brothers. But, O scorn,   125
Gone! They went hence so soon as they were born.
And so I am awake. Poor wretches that depend
On greatness' favor dream as I have done,

Wake and find nothing. But, alas, I swerve!   129
                          [*He sees the tablet.*]
Many dream not to find, neither deserve,   130
And yet are steeped in favors; so am I,
That have this golden chance and know not why.
What fairies haunt this ground? A book? O rare one!   133
Be not, as is our fangled world, a garment   134
Nobler than that it covers! Let thy effects
So follow, to be most unlike our courtiers,   136
As good as promise.
      (*Reads.*) "Whenas a lion's whelp shall, to himself 138
unknown, without seeking find and be embraced by
a piece of tender air; and when from a stately cedar
shall be lopped branches which, being dead many
years, shall after revive, be jointed to the old stock, and
freshly grow; then shall Posthumus end his miseries,
Britain be fortunate and flourish in peace and plenty."
'Tis still a dream, or else such stuff as madmen
Tongue and brain not; either both or nothing,   146
Or senseless speaking or a speaking such   147
As sense cannot untie. Be what it is,   148
The action of my life is like it, which
I'll keep, if but for sympathy.   150

            Enter [*First*] *Jailer.*

FIRST JAILER   Come, sir, are you ready for death?
POSTHUMUS   Overroasted rather; ready long ago.
FIRST JAILER   Hanging is the word, sir. If you be ready   153
for that, you are well cooked.
POSTHUMUS   So, if I prove a good repast to the spectators, the dish pays the shot.   156
FIRST JAILER   A heavy reckoning for you, sir. But the
comfort is, you shall be called to no more payments,
fear no more tavern bills, which are often the sadness   159
of parting as the procuring of mirth. You come in faint
for want of meat, depart reeling with too much drink;
sorry that you have paid too much, and sorry that you
are paid too much; purse and brain both empty; the   163
brain the heavier for being too light, the purse too   164
light, being drawn of heaviness. Of this contradiction   165
you shall now be quit. O, the charity of a penny cord!   166
It sums up thousands in a trice. You have no true   167
debitor and creditor but it; of what's past, is, and to 168
come, the discharge. Your neck, sir, is pen, book, and   169
counters; so the acquittance follows.   170

---

96 Sky-planted growing out of the sky   **99 accidents** events   **102 de-**
lighted (the more) delighted in   **104 spent** ended   **105 Jovial star** the
planet Jupiter, the happiest of all planets to be born under   **106 fade**
vanish   **110 confine** precisely state   **116 Stooped** swooped down.
as as if.   **foot** seize (in his talons)   **116–117 His . . . fields** his ascent gives a favorable aspect and a sweet odor surpassing that of the
Elysian Fields   **118 Prunes** preens.   **cloys** claws, strokes with the
claw   **120 marble pavement** heavens (above the Elizabethan stage;
compare with *marble mansion* in line 87)   **125 scorn** mockery

129 swerve mistake, go astray   **130 to find** of finding   **133 book** i.e.,
the tablet or scroll.   **rare** excellent   **134 fangled** characterized by
fripperies or gaudiness   **136** to so as to   **138 Whenas** when
146 Tongue speak.   **brain** understand.   **either both** either of the two
(a dream, or madness) (?)   **147 Or** either.   **senseless speaking** (as in
madness)   **147–148 speaking . . . cannot untie** (as in a dream).
sense reason   **150 sympathy** i.e., resemblance (between my life and
this mystery)   **153 Hanging** (1) hanging up like cooking meat (2) being hanged as a criminal   **156 the dish . . . shot** (1) the food is worth
the tavern reckoning (2) my death settles my account   **159 often** as
often   **163 are paid** are subdued (by excessive drink)   **164 heavier**
heavier with sleep   **165 drawn** tapped, emptied   **166 charity** benevolent action, one that settles all debts   **167 sums up** (1) totals up a
reckoning (2) collects, summarizes.   **trice** (1) instant (2) tricing up,
hauling up by a rope   **168 debitor and creditor** account book
169 discharge (1) payment of debt (2) disburdening, release, as in
death   **170 counters** metal disks used for calculating.   **acquittance**
(1) discharge of an account (2) deliverance

POSTHUMUS I am merrier to die than thou art to live.
FIRST JAILER Indeed, sir, he that sleeps feels not the
toothache. But a man that were to sleep your sleep, 173
and a hangman to help him to bed, I think he would
change places with his officer; for, look you, sir, you 175
know not which way you shall go.   176
POSTHUMUS Yes, indeed do I, fellow.
FIRST JAILER Your death has eyes in 's head then; I
have not seen him so pictured. You must either be 179
directed by some that take upon them to know, or to 180
take upon yourself that which I am sure you do not
know, or jump the after-inquiry on your own peril. 182
And how you shall speed in your journey's end, I 183
think you'll never return to tell one.
POSTHUMUS I tell thee, fellow, there are none want eyes 185
to direct them the way I am going but such as wink 186
and will not use them.
FIRST JAILER What an infinite mock is this, that a man
should have the best use of eyes to see the way of
blindness! I am sure hanging's the way of winking. 190

Enter a Messenger.

MESSENGER Knock off his manacles. Bring your prisoner to the King.
POSTHUMUS Thou bring'st good news. I am called to
be made free.   [*He is freed from his irons.*] 194
FIRST JAILER I'll be hanged then.   195
POSTHUMUS Thou shalt be then freer than a jailer; no
bolts for the dead.   *Exeunt [all but the First Jailer].*
FIRST JAILER Unless a man would marry a gallows and
beget young gibbets, I never saw one so prone. Yet, 199
on my conscience, there are verier knaves desire to 200
live, for all he be a Roman; and there be some of them 201
too that die against their wills. So should I, if I were 202
one. I would we were all of one mind, and one mind 203
good. O, there were desolation of jailers and gal- 204
lowses! I speak against my present profit, but my wish 205
hath a preferment in 't.   [*Exit.*] 206

❖

173 **a man that were to** if there were a man who was destined to
175 **officer** i.e., the hangman 176 **which . . . go** i.e., to heaven or
hell; but Posthumus answers in the sense of knowing that death will
release all sorrows 179 **so pictured** (The traditional death's-head is
an eyeless skull.) 180 **take upon them** undertake, profess
182 **jump** finesse 183 **speed** succeed 185 **none want** none who
lack 186 **wink** close the eyes 190 **hanging's . . . winking** hanging
will close up the eyes 194 **made free** i.e., executed and thereby
freed from existence 195 **I'll be hanged then** (The jailer is using a
conventional expression, like "I'll be damned if that's so," but Posthumus replies that he means *free* in a spiritual sense.) 199 **prone**
ready, eager 200–203 **there . . . were one** i.e., he's not such a
bad fellow, even if he is a Roman; worse men than he desire to live
when they're to be executed, as I would in such a plight. (Romans
were supposed to be stoical in the face of death.) 204–205 **there
. . . gallowses** i.e., if all men were good, there would be no work left
for jailers and gallows 206 **a preferment** i.e., a preference for us all
to live in a better world (with a hope that this pious wish may stand
me in good stead at my day of reckoning and thus "prefer" me to
bliss). Possibly, the jailer thinks of more worldly promotion to a better
office.

5.5
Enter Cymbeline, Belarius, Guiderius, Arviragus,
Pisanio, [officers, attendants,] and lords.

CYMBELINE
Stand by my side, you whom the gods have made
Preservers of my throne. Woe is my heart
That the poor soldier that so richly fought,
Whose rags shamed gilded arms, whose naked
    breast
Stepped before targes of proof, cannot be found. 5
He shall be happy that can find him, if
Our grace can make him so.
BELARIUS   I never saw   7
Such noble fury in so poor a thing,
Such precious deeds in one that promised naught
But beggary and poor looks.
CYMBELINE   No tidings of him?
PISANIO
He hath been searched among the dead and living,
But no trace of him.
CYMBELINE   To my grief, I am
The heir of his reward, [*to Belarius, Guiderius, and*
    Arviragus] which I will add
To you, the liver, heart, and brain of Britain,   14
By whom I grant she lives. 'Tis now the time
To ask of whence you are. Report it.
BELARIUS   Sir,
In Cambria are we born, and gentlemen.
Further to boast were neither true nor modest,
Unless I add we are honest.
CYMBELINE   Bow your knees.
                        [*They kneel.*]
Arise my knights o' the battle. I create you   20
Companions to our person and will fit you
With dignities becoming your estates. [*They rise.*] 22

Enter Cornelius and Ladies.

There's business in these faces. Why so sadly
Greet you our victory? You look like Romans,
And not o' the court of Britain.
CORNELIUS   Hail, great King!
To sour your happiness, I must report
The Queen is dead.
CYMBELINE   Who worse than a physician   27
Would this report become? But I consider   28
By med'cine life may be prolonged, yet death
Will seize the doctor too. How ended she?
CORNELIUS
With horror, madly dying, like her life,
Which, being cruel to the world, concluded
Most cruel to herself. What she confessed
I will report, so please you. These her women
Can trip me, if I err, who with wet cheeks   35

5.5. Location: Britain. The camp of King Cymbeline.
5 targes of proof shields hardened to withstand tests **7 grace** favor
14 liver, heart, and brain i.e., heart and soul **20 knights o' the battle** knights created on the battlefield **22 estates** i.e., new status **27–
28 Who . . . become** i.e., a report of death does not speak well for
the doctor, of all people **35 trip** refute, contradict

Were present when she finished.
CYMBELINE   Prithee, say.
CORNELIUS
First, she confessed she never loved you, only
Affected greatness got by you, not you;   38
Married your royalty, was wife to your place,
Abhorred your person.
CYMBELINE   She alone knew this;
And, but she spoke it dying, I would not   41
Believe her lips in opening it. Proceed.   42
CORNELIUS
Your daughter, whom she bore in hand to love   43
With such integrity, she did confess
Was as a scorpion to her sight, whose life,
But that her flight prevented it, she had   46
Ta'en off by poison.
CYMBELINE   O most delicate fiend!   47
Who is 't can read a woman? Is there more?
CORNELIUS
More, sir, and worse. She did confess she had
For you a mortal mineral which, being took,   50
Should by the minute feed on life and, ling'ring, 51
By inches waste you. In which time she purposed,
By watching, weeping, tendance, kissing, to   53
O'ercome you with her show and, in fine,   54
When she had fitted you with her craft, to work   55
Her son into th' adoption of the crown;   56
But, failing of her end by his strange absence,
Grew shameless desperate; opened, in despite   58
Of heaven and men, her purposes; repented   59
The evils she hatched were not effected; so
Despairing died.
CYMBELINE   Heard you all this, her women?
LADIES   We did, so please Your Highness.
CYMBELINE   Mine eyes
Were not in fault, for she was beautiful;
Mine ears, that heard her flattery; nor my heart, 65
That thought her like her seeming. It had been
vicious   66
To have mistrusted her. Yet, O my daughter,
That it was folly in me thou mayst say,
And prove it in thy feeling. Heaven mend all!   69

*Enter Lucius, Iachimo, [the Soothsayer,] and other
Roman prisoners, [guarded; Posthumus] Leonatus
behind, and Imogen [disguised as Fidele].*

Thou com'st not, Caius, now for tribute. That
The Britons have rased out, though with the loss   71
Of many a bold one, whose kinsmen have made suit

That their good souls may be appeased with
slaughter
Of you their captives, which ourself have granted.
So think of your estate.   75
LUCIUS
Consider, sir, the chance of war. The day
Was yours by accident. Had it gone with us,
We should not, when the blood was cool, have
threatened
Our prisoners with the sword. But since the gods
Will have it thus, that nothing but our lives
May be called ransom, let it come. Sufficeth
A Roman with a Roman's heart can suffer.
Augustus lives to think on 't; and so much   83
For my peculiar care. This one thing only   84
I will entreat: my boy, a Briton born,
Let him be ransomed. Never master had
A page so kind, so duteous, diligent,
So tender over his occasions, true,   88
So feat, so nurselike. Let his virtue join   89
With my request, which I'll make bold Your
Highness   90
Cannot deny. He hath done no Briton harm,
Though he have served a Roman. Save him, sir,
And spare no blood besides.
CYMBELINE   I have surely seen him;   93
His favor is familiar to me. Boy,   94
Thou hast looked thyself into my grace   95
And art mine own. I know not why, wherefore,
To say "Live, boy." Ne'er thank thy master. Live, 97
And ask of Cymbeline what boon thou wilt,   98
Fitting my bounty and thy state, I'll give it,
Yea, though thou do demand a prisoner,
The noblest ta'en.
IMOGEN   I humbly thank Your Highness.
LUCIUS
I do not bid thee beg my life, good lad,
And yet I know thou wilt.
IMOGEN   No, no, alack,
There's other work in hand. I see a thing   104
Bitter to me as death. Your life, good master,
Must shuffle for itself.
LUCIUS   The boy disdains me,
He leaves me, scorns me. Briefly die their joys   107
That place them on the truth of girls and boys.   108
Why stands he so perplexed?   [She studies Iachimo.]
CYMBELINE   What wouldst thou, boy? 109
I love thee more and more. Think more and more
What's best to ask. Know'st him thou look'st on?
Speak,
Wilt have him live? Is he thy kin? Thy friend?

38 Affected desired   41 but were it not that   42 opening revealing
43 bore in hand pretended   46 had would have   47 Ta'en off ended.
delicate subtle   50 mortal mineral deadly poison   51 by the minute
minute by minute   53 tendance attentiveness   54 in fine in conclusion   55 fitted you shaped you to her wish   56 adoption right of an
adopted heir   58 opened revealed   59 repented regretted   65 Mine
. . . flattery i.e., my ears were not at fault, that heard her fine
speeches (which we now know to have been flattery)   66 had been
vicious would have been wrong   69 in thy feeling by feeling it, by
what you have suffered. (Cymbeline apostrophizes the absent Imogen,
who then ironically enters in disguise.)   71 rased out erased

75 estate spiritual estate (in preparation for your death)   83 think on
't i.e., consider what revenge to take   84 my peculiar care my concern for myself   88 tender over his occasions solicitous of his master's needs   89 feat adroit, neat   90 make bold venture   93 And
even if (you)   94 favor face   95 looked . . . grace won my favor by
your appearance   97 Ne'er thank thy master i.e., don't attribute your
being saved to his request   98 ask if you ask   104 thing i.e., the ring
on Iachimo's finger   107–108 Briefly . . . That swiftly die the joys of
those who   108 truth fidelity   109 perplexed distressed

IMOGEN
  He is a Roman, no more kin to me
  Than I to Your Highness; who, being born your
    vassal,   114
  Am something nearer.
CYMBELINE   Wherefore ey'st him so?   115
IMOGEN
  I'll tell you, sir, in private, if you please
  To give me hearing.
CYMBELINE   Ay, with all my heart,
  And lend my best attention. What's thy name?
IMOGEN
  Fidele, sir.
CYMBELINE Thou'rt my good youth, my page;
  I'll be thy master. Walk with me; speak freely.
          [*Cymbeline and Imogen converse apart.*]
BELARIUS [*to Arviragus and Guiderius*]
  Is not this boy revived from death?
ARVIRAGUS One sand another   122
  Not more resembles that sweet rosy lad   123
  Who died, and was Fidele. What think you?   124
GUIDERIUS The same dead thing alive.
BELARIUS
  Peace, peace! See further. He eyes us not; forbear.
  Creatures may be alike. Were 't he, I am sure
  He would have spoke to us.
GUIDERIUS   But we saw him dead.
BELARIUS
  Be silent; let's see further.
PISANIO [*aside*]   It is my mistress.
  Since she is living, let the time run on   130
  To good or bad. [*Cymbeline and Imogen come forward.*]
CYMBELINE   Come, stand thou by our side.   131
  Make thy demand aloud. [*To Iachimo.*] Sir, step you
    forth;
  Give answer to this boy, and do it freely,   133
  Or, by our greatness and the grace of it,   134
  Which is our honor, bitter torture shall
  Winnow the truth from falsehood.—On, speak
    to him.
IMOGEN
  My boon is that this gentleman may render   137
  Of whom he had this ring.
        [*She points to the ring Iachimo wears.*]
POSTHUMUS [*aside*]   What's that to him?
CYMBELINE [*to Iachimo*]
  That diamond upon your finger, say
  How came it yours?
IACHIMO
  Thou'lt torture me to leave unspoken that   141
  Which, to be spoke, would torture thee.
CYMBELINE   How? Me?

IACHIMO
  I am glad to be constrained to utter that
  Which torments me to conceal. By villainy
  I got this ring. 'Twas Leonatus' jewel,
  Whom thou didst banish; and—which more may
    grieve thee,
  As it doth me—a nobler sir ne'er lived
  Twixt sky and ground. Wilt thou hear more, my
    lord?
CYMBELINE
  All that belongs to this.
IACHIMO   That paragon, thy daughter,
  For whom my heart drops blood and my false spirits 150
  Quail to remember—Give me leave; I faint.
CYMBELINE
  My daughter? What of her? Renew thy strength.
  I had rather thou shouldst live while nature will   153
  Than die ere I hear more. Strive, man, and speak.
IACHIMO
  Upon a time—unhappy was the clock
  That struck the hour!—it was in Rome—accurst
  The mansion where!—'twas at a feast—O, would
  Our viands had been poisoned, or at least
  Those which I heaved to head!—the good
    Posthumus—   159
  What should I say? He was too good to be
  Where ill men were, and was the best of all
  Amongst the rar'st of good ones—sitting sadly,
  Hearing us praise our loves of Italy   163
  For beauty that made barren the swelled boast   164
  Of him that best could speak; for feature, laming   165
  The shrine of Venus or straight-pight Minerva,   166
  Postures beyond brief nature; for condition,   167
  A shop of all the qualities that man   168
  Loves woman for, besides that hook of wiving,   169
  Fairness which strikes the eye—
CYMBELINE   I stand on fire.
  Come to the matter.
IACHIMO   All too soon I shall,
  Unless thou wouldst grieve quickly. This Posthumus,
  Most like a noble lord in love and one
  That had a royal lover, took his hint,   174
  And not dispraising whom we praised—therein
  He was as calm as virtue—he began
  His mistress' picture; which by his tongue being
    made,
  And then a mind put in 't, either our brags   178
  Were cracked of kitchen trulls, or his description 179

---

114 who i.e., I, Fidele **115 something** somewhat **122–124 One
. . . died** one grain of sand does not resemble another more than this
youth resembles the sweet rose-cheeked lad who died **130–131 let
. . . bad** i.e., let come what must come **133 freely** without reserve
134 the grace of that which adorns **137 render** give account
141 to leave for leaving, if I leave. (You'll torture me to force me to
talk, says Iachimo, whereas what I have to say will torture you.)

150 and and whom **153 live . . . will** continue to live as long as nature permits (with your death sentence forgiven) **159 heaved to head**
raised to my lips **163–168 Hearing . . . shop** hearing us offer high-
flown praise of our Italian mistresses for beauty that made lame and
impotent even the exaggerated boast of our most eloquent speaker,
for figures that made even the image of Venus in her temple or
stately, straight-backed Minerva seem crippled by comparison—so
beyond the transient workmanship of nature were the carriages we ascribed to our mistresses—and for qualities of mind and character that
constituted a virtual storehouse **169 hook of wiving** bait for marriage
174 hint occasion **178 put in 't** inserted into the picture
179 cracked of kitchen trulls boastfully offered in praise of kitchen
maids

Proved us unspeaking sots.
CYMBELINE   Nay, nay, to th' purpose. 180
IACHIMO
Your daughter's chastity—there it begins.
He spake of her as Dian had hot dreams   182
And she alone were cold; whereat I, wretch,
Made scruple of his praise and wagered with him   184
Pieces of gold 'gainst this which then he wore
Upon his honored finger, to attain
In suit the place of 's bed and win this ring   187
By hers and mine adultery. He, true knight,
No lesser of her honor confident
Than I did truly find her, stakes this ring;
And would so, had it been a carbuncle   191
Of Phoebus' wheel, and might so safely, had it   192
Been all the worth of 's car. Away to Britain   193
Post I in this design. Well may you, sir,   194
Remember me at court, where I was taught
Of your chaste daughter the wide difference   196
Twixt amorous and villainous. Being thus quenched
Of hope, not longing, mine Italian brain   198
'Gan in your duller Britain operate   199
Most vilely; for my vantage, excellent.   200
And, to be brief, my practice so prevailed   201
That I returned with simular proof enough   202
To make the noble Leonatus mad
By wounding his belief in her renown   204
With tokens thus and thus; averring notes   205
Of chamber hanging, pictures, this her bracelet—   206
                              [showing the bracelet]
Oh cunning, how I got it!—nay, some marks
Of secret on her person, that he could not
But think her bond of chastity quite cracked,
I having ta'en the forfeit. Whereupon—   210
Methinks, I see him now—
POSTHUMUS [advancing]   Ay, so thou dost,
Italian fiend! Ay me, most credulous fool,
Egregious murderer, thief, anything
That's due to all the villains past, in being,
To come! O, give me cord, or knife, or poison,
Some upright justicer! Thou, King, send out   216
For torturers ingenious! It is I
That all th' abhorred things o' th' earth amend   218
By being worse than they. I am Posthumus,
That killed thy daughter—villain-like, I lie—
That caused a lesser villain than myself,
A sacrilegious thief, to do 't. The temple
Of virtue was she, yea, and she herself.   223

Spit, and throw stones, cast mire upon me, set
The dogs o' the street to bay me! Every villain
Be called Posthumus Leonatus, and
Be "villainy" less than 'twas! O Imogen!   227
My queen, my life, my wife! O Imogen,
Imogen, Imogen!
IMOGEN   Peace, my lord. Hear, hear—
POSTHUMUS
Shall 's have a play of this? Thou scornful page,   230
There lie thy part.   [He strikes her; she falls.]
PISANIO   O, gentlemen, help!   231
                            [He goes to her assistance.]
Mine and your mistress! O my lord Posthumus,
You ne'er killed Imogen till now. Help, help!
Mine honored lady!
CYMBELINE   Does the world go round?   234
POSTHUMUS
How comes these staggers on me?
PISANIO   Wake, my mistress! 235
CYMBELINE
If this be so, the gods do mean to strike me
To death with mortal joy.
PISANIO   How fares my mistress?
IMOGEN   O, get thee from my sight!
Thou gav'st me poison. Dangerous fellow, hence!
Breathe not where princes are.
CYMBELINE   The tune of Imogen!   241
PISANIO   Lady,
The gods throw stones of sulfur on me if   243
That box I gave you was not thought by me
A precious thing. I had it from the Queen.
CYMBELINE
New matter still?
IMOGEN   It poisoned me.
CORNELIUS   O gods!
I left out one thing which the Queen confessed,
[To Pisanio] Which must approve thee honest. "If
Pisanio   248
Have," said she, "given his mistress that confection   249
Which I gave him for cordial, she is served
As I would serve a rat."
CYMBELINE   What's this, Cornelius?
CORNELIUS
The Queen, sir, very oft importuned me
To temper poisons for her, still pretending   253
The satisfaction of her knowledge only
In killing creatures vile, as cats and dogs,
Of no esteem. I, dreading that her purpose
Was of more danger, did compound for her
A certain stuff which, being ta'en, would cease   258
The present power of life, but in short time
All offices of nature should again

---

180 unspeaking sots inarticulate blockheads unable to describe our mistresses adequately   **182 as** as if   **184 Made scruple** expressed doubts   **187 In suit** by urging my suit   **191 would so** would have done so   **192 Phoebus' wheel** i.e., the wheel of the sun-god's chariot   **193 's car** his chariot   **194 Post** hasten   **196 Of** by   **198 not longing** though not of my desire   **199 duller** i.e., slower-minded (supposedly caused by the northern climate)   **200 vantage** profit   **201 practice** scheming   **202 simular** simulated, or, pretended, plausible   **204 renown** good name   **205 averring** avouching, citing   **206 hanging** hangings   **210 the forfeit** i.e., what was forfeited by the breaking of her bond of chaste loyalty   **216 justicer** judge   **218 That . . . amend** who make all loathsome things seem better in comparison   **223 she herself** i.e., Virtue herself

227 Be . . . 'twas let the name "villainy" signify something less heinous than it used to   **230 Shall 's** shall we   **231 There lie thy part** your part is to lie there on the ground   **234 Does . . . round** i.e., is the ground turning under my feet? (An expression of dizziness.)   **235 staggers** dizziness, bewilderment   **241 tune** accent, voice   **243 stones of sulfur** thunderbolts   **248 approve** prove   **249 confection** composition of drugs   **253 temper** mix   **258 cease** cause to cease

Do their due functions.—Have you ta'en of it?
IMOGEN
Most like I did, for I was dead.
BELARIUS [*to Guiderius and Arviragus*]   My boys,   262
There was our error.
GUIDERIUS   This is, sure, Fidele.
IMOGEN [*to Posthumus*]
Why did you throw your wedded lady from you?
[*She embraces him.*]
Think that you are upon a rock, and now   265
Throw me again.   [*They embrace.*]
POSTHUMUS   Hang there like fruit, my soul,
Till the tree die!
CYMBELINE   How now, my flesh, my child?
What, mak'st thou me a dullard in this act?   268
Wilt thou not speak to me?
IMOGEN [*kneeling*]   Your blessing, sir.
BELARIUS [*to Guiderius and Arviragus*]
Though you did love this youth, I blame ye not;
You had a motive for 't.
CYMBELINE   My tears that fall
Prove holy water on thee! Imogen,
Thy mother's dead.
IMOGEN [*rising*]   I am sorry for 't, my lord.
CYMBELINE
O, she was naught; and long of her it was   274
That we meet here so strangely. But her son
Is gone, we know not how nor where.
PISANIO   My lord,
Now fear is from me, I'll speak truth. Lord Cloten,
Upon my lady's missing, came to me
With his sword drawn, foamed at the mouth, and
swore
If I discovered not which way she was gone   280
It was my instant death. By accident
I had a feignèd letter of my master's   282
Then in my pocket, which directed him
To seek her on the mountains near to Milford;
Where, in a frenzy, in my master's garments,
Which he enforced from me, away he posts
With unchaste purpose and with oath to violate
My lady's honor. What became of him
I further know not.
GUIDERIUS   Let me end the story:
I slew him there.
CYMBELINE   Marry, the gods forfend!   290
I would not thy good deeds should from my lips   291
Pluck a hard sentence. Prithee, valiant youth,
Deny 't again.   293
GUIDERIUS   I have spoke it, and I did it.
CYMBELINE   He was a prince.

GUIDERIUS
A most incivil one. The wrongs he did me
Were nothing princelike, for he did provoke me
With language that would make me spurn the sea
If it could so roar to me. I cut off 's head,
And am right glad he is not standing here
To tell this tale of mine.
CYMBELINE   I am sorrow for thee.   301
By thine own tongue thou art condemned and must
Endure our law. Thou'rt dead.
IMOGEN   That headless man
I thought had been my lord.
CYMBELINE   Bind the offender,
And take him from our presence.
[*Guards start to bind Guiderius.*]
BELARIUS   Stay, sir King.
This man is better than the man he slew,
As well descended as thyself, and hath
More of thee merited than a band of Clotens
Had ever scar for. [*To the Guard.*] Let his arms alone;   309
They were not born for bondage.
CYMBELINE   Why, old soldier,
Wilt thou undo the worth thou art unpaid for
By tasting of our wrath? How of descent
As good as we?
ARVIRAGUS   In that he spake too far.
CYMBELINE [*to Belarius*]
And thou shalt die for 't.
BELARIUS   We will die all three
But I will prove that two on 's are as good   315
As I have given out him. My sons, I must   316
For mine own part unfold a dangerous speech,   317
Though, haply, well for you.
ARVIRAGUS   Your danger's ours.
GUIDERIUS
And our good his.
BELARIUS   Have at it then, by leave.   319
Thou hadst, great King, a subject who
Was called Belarius.
CYMBELINE   What of him? He is
A banished traitor.
BELARIUS   He it is that hath
Assumed this age; indeed a banished man,   323
I know not how a traitor.
CYMBELINE   Take him hence!
The whole world shall not save him.
BELARIUS   Not too hot.
First pay me for the nursing of thy sons,
And let it be confiscate all so soon
As I have received it.
CYMBELINE   Nursing of my sons?
BELARIUS
I am too blunt and saucy. Here's my knee. [*He kneels.*]

262 like likely   **265 a rock** i.e., solid ground (?) (Some editors conjecture *lock*, "a wrestling embrace.")   **268 mak'st . . . dullard** do you treat me like a dolt (by leaving me out)   **274 naught** wicked.   **long of** on account of   **280 discovered** disclosed   **282 feignèd** (Pisanio would not have wished to show Cloten the real letter, since it ordered Pisanio to kill Imogen.)   **290 forfend** forbid   **291 thy good deeds** i.e., that you, who fought so valiantly against the Romans   **293 again** i.e., in speaking again and denying what you've just said

301 tell . . . mine i.e., tell of cutting off my head.   **sorrow** sorry   **309 Had ever scar for** ever merited by their battle scars   **315 But I will** if I do not.   **on 's** of us   **316 given out** reported   **317 For . . . speech** unfold a speech that is dangerous for me   **319 And our good his** i.e., and whatever fortune comes to us we share with him, Belarius. (Said perhaps to the King or Arviragus.)   **Have . . . leave** here goes, with your permission   **323 Assumed** reached, attained

Ere I arise, I will prefer my sons; 330
Then spare not the old father. Mighty sir,
These two young gentlemen, that call me father
And think they are my sons, are none of mine;
They are the issue of your loins, my liege,
And blood of your begetting.
CYMBELINE   How? My issue?
BELARIUS
So sure as you your father's. I, old Morgan,
Am that Belarius whom you sometime banished.
Your pleasure was my mere offense, my
    punishment 338
Itself, and all my treason; that I suffered 339
Was all the harm I did. These gentle princes— 340
For such and so they are—these twenty years 341
Have I trained up; those arts they have as I
Could put into them. My breeding was, sir, as
Your Highness knows. Their nurse, Euriphile,
Whom for the theft I wedded, stole these children
Upon my banishment. I moved her to 't,
Having received the punishment before
For that which I did then. Beaten for loyalty 348
Excited me to treason. Their dear loss,
The more of you 'twas felt, the more it shaped 350
Unto my end of stealing them. But, gracious sir, 351
Here are your sons again, and I must lose
Two of the sweet'st companions in the world.
The benediction of these covering heavens
Fall on their heads like dew! For they are worthy
To inlay heaven with stars.
CYMBELINE   Thou weep'st and speak'st. 356
The service that you three have done is more 357
Unlike than this thou tell'st. I lost my children; 358
If these be they, I know not how to wish
A pair of worthier sons.
BELARIUS [rising]   Be pleased awhile. 360
This gentleman, whom I call Polydore,
Most worthy prince, as yours, is true Guiderius;
This gentleman, my Cadwal, Arviragus,
Your younger princely son. He, sir, was lapped 364
In a most curious mantle, wrought by th' hand 365
Of his queen mother, which for more probation 366
I can with ease produce.
CYMBELINE   Guiderius had
Upon his neck a mole, a sanguine star; 368
It was a mark of wonder.
BELARIUS   This is he, 369
Who hath upon him still that natural stamp.

It was wise nature's end in the donation 371
To be his evidence now.
CYMBELINE   O, what, am I 372
A mother to the birth of three? Ne'er mother 373
Rejoiced deliverance more. Blest pray you be, 374
That, after this strange starting from your orbs, 375
You may reign in them now! O Imogen, 376
Thou hast lost by this a kingdom.
IMOGEN   No, my lord,
I have got two worlds by 't. O my gentle brothers,
Have we thus met? O, never say hereafter
But I am truest speaker. You called me brother,
When I was but your sister; I you brothers,
When ye were so indeed.
CYMBELINE   Did you e'er meet?
ARVIRAGUS
Ay, my good lord.
GUIDERIUS   And at first meeting loved;
Continued so until we thought he died.
CORNELIUS
By the Queen's dram she swallowed.
CYMBELINE   O rare instinct!
When shall I hear all through? This fierce
    abridgement 386
Hath to it circumstantial branches, which 387
Distinction should be rich in. Where, how lived you? 388
And when came you to serve our Roman captive?
How parted with your brothers? How first met
    them?
Why fled you from the court? And whither? These,
And your three motives to the battle, with 392
I know not how much more, should be demanded,
And all the other by-dependencies 394
From chance to chance; but nor the time nor place 395
Will serve our long interrogatories. See,
Posthumus anchors upon Imogen,
And she, like harmless lightning, throws her eye
On him, her brothers, me, her master, hitting 399
Each object with a joy; the counterchange 400
Is severally in all. Let's quit this ground 401
And smoke the temple with our sacrifices. 402
[To Belarius.] Thou art my brother; so we'll hold thee
    ever.
IMOGEN [to Belarius]
You are my father too, and did relieve me 404
To see this gracious season.
CYMBELINE   All o'erjoyed, 405
Save these in bonds. Let them be joyful too,

330 **prefer** promote   338–340 **Your . . . did** your displeasure toward me was all the offense I committed; so, too, my punishment and my supposed treason were the creation of your royal whim; what I suffered was the extent of my wrongdoing   340 **gentle** nobly born   341 **such and so** i.e., both princes and gentle   348 **Beaten** being beaten   350 **of** by   350–351 **shaped . . . of** fitted my purpose in   356 **To . . . stars** to be inlaid in heaven, like stars   356–358 **Thou . . . tell'st** i.e., your weeping seems a testimony of the truth of what you speak, and your story is, in any event, more credible—strange though it seems—than the brave service you three did in battle.   **Unlike** incredible   360 **Be pleased awhile** i.e., be so kind as to listen a while longer   364 **lapped** enfolded   365 **curious** exquisitely made   366 **probation** proof   368 **sanguine** bloodred   369 **of wonder** to be wondered at

371 **end in the donation** aim in giving it to him   372 **his evidence** evidence of his identity   373–374 **Ne'er . . . more** never did deliverance (in childbed) more rejoice a mother   375 **starting . . . orbs** shooting from your orbits, i.e., leaving your places at court   376 **reign** i.e., both as royal persons and as planets with influence   386 **fierce abridgment** drastically compressed account   387–388 **circumstantial . . . in** details and ramifications to be distinguished in all their abundance   392 **your three motives** the motives of you three   394 **by-dependencies** attendant circumstances   395 **chance to chance** event to event.   **nor the** neither the   399 **her master** i.e., Lucius   400–401 **the counterchange . . . all** the exchange (of happy glances) involves each of us to everyone else   402 **smoke** fill with incense   404 **relieve** bring rescue and deliverance to, as to a besieged town   405 **To see** so that I might see

For they shall taste our comfort.

IMOGEN [*to Lucius*]   My good master,
    I will yet do you service.

LUCIUS   Happy be you!

CYMBELINE
    The forlorn soldier, that so nobly fought,   409
    He would have well becomed this place and graced   410
    The thankings of a king.

POSTHUMUS   I am, sir,
    The soldier that did company these three
    In poor beseeming; 'twas a fitment for   413
    The purpose I then followed. That I was he,
    Speak, Iachimo. I had you down and might
    Have made you finish.

IACHIMO [*kneeling*]   I am down again;   416
    But now my heavy conscience sinks my knee,   417
    As then your force did. Take that life, beseech you,
    Which I so often owe; but your ring first;   419
    And here the bracelet of the truest princess
    That ever swore her faith.   [*He gives ring and bracelet.*]

POSTHUMUS   Kneel not to me.
    The power that I have on you is to spare you;
    The malice towards you to forgive you. Live,
    And deal with others better.   [*Iachimo rises.*]

CYMBELINE   Nobly doomed!   424
    We'll learn our freeness of a son-in-law;   425
    Pardon's the word to all.

ARVIRAGUS [*to Posthumus*] You holp us, sir,   426
    As you did mean indeed to be our brother;   427
    Joyed are we that you are.

POSTHUMUS
    Your servant, princes. [*To Lucius.*] Good my lord of
      Rome,
    Call forth your soothsayer. As I slept, methought
    Great Jupiter, upon his eagle backed,
    Appeared to me, with other spritely shows   432
    Of mine own kindred. When I waked, I found
    This label on my bosom [*showing tablet*], whose
      containing   434
    Is so from sense in hardness that I can   435
    Make no collection of it. Let him show   436
    His skill in the construction.

LUCIUS   Philharmonus!   437

SOOTHSAYER
    Here, my good lord.

LUCIUS   Read, and declare the meaning.

SOOTHSAYER (*reads*) "Whenas a lion's whelp shall, to
    himself unknown, without seeking find and be em-
    braced by a piece of tender air; and when from a stately
    cedar shall be lopped branches which, being dead
    many years, shall after revive, be jointed to the old
    stock and freshly grow; then shall Posthumus end his

miseries, Britain be fortunate and flourish in peace
    and plenty."
    Thou, Leonatus, art the lion's whelp;
    The fit and apt construction of thy name,
    Being Leo-natus, doth import so much.   449
    [*To Cymbeline.*] The piece of tender air, thy virtuous
      daughter,
    Which we call *"mollis aer,"* and *"mollis aer"*   451
    We term it *"mulier"*; which *"mulier"* I divine
    Is this most constant wife; who, even now,   453
    Answering the letter of the oracle,   [*to Posthumus*] 454
    Unknown to you, unsought, were clipped about   455
    With this most tender air.

CYMBELINE   This hath some seeming.   456

SOOTHSAYER
    The lofty cedar, royal Cymbeline,
    Personates thee, and thy lopped branches point
    Thy two sons forth; who, by Belarius stol'n,
    For many years thought dead, are now revived,
    To the majestic cedar joined, whose issue
    Promises Britain peace and plenty.

CYMBELINE   Well,
    My peace we will begin. And, Caius Lucius,
    Although the victor, we submit to Caesar
    And to the Roman empire, promising
    To pay our wonted tribute, from the which
    We were dissuaded by our wicked queen,
    Whom heavens in justice both on her and hers   468
    Have laid most heavy hand.

SOOTHSAYER
    The fingers of the powers above do tune
    The harmony of this peace. The vision
    Which I made known to Lucius ere the stroke
    Of this yet scarce-cold battle at this instant
    Is full accomplished; for the Roman eagle,
    From south to west on wing soaring aloft,
    Lessened herself, and in the beams o' the sun   476
    So vanished; which foreshowed our princely eagle,   477
    Th' imperial Caesar, should again unite
    His favor with the radiant Cymbeline,
    Which shines here in the west.

CYMBELINE   Laud we the gods,   480
    And let our crooked smokes climb to their nostrils   481
    From our blest altars. Publish we this peace
    To all our subjects. Set we forward. Let
    A Roman and a British ensign wave
    Friendly together. So through Lud's Town march,
    And in the temple of great Jupiter
    Our peace we'll ratify, seal it with feasts.
    Set on there! Never was a war did cease,   488
    Ere bloody hands were washed, with such a peace.   489

                          Exeunt.

---

409 forlorn missing, or, poorly dressed   **410 graced** adorned **413 beseeming** appearance.   **fitment** makeshift disguise   **416 made you finish** put an end to you   **417 sinks** causes to sink   **419 often** many times over   **424 doomed** decreed, judged   **425 freeness** liberality, generosity   **426 holp** helped   **427 As** as if   **432 spritely** ghostly, in the form of spirits.   **shows** appearances   **434 label** tablet, paper   **434–435 whose . . . hardness** whose meaning is so remote from sense in its difficulty   **436 collection of** inference or deduction from   **437 construction** construing of it

449 Leo-natus one born of the lion   **451 mollis aer** tender air. (A fanciful derivation of Latin *mulier*, "woman.")   **453 who** (Perhaps referring to Posthumus, but the grammar is loose and the point of reference may shift after line 454.)   **454 Answering** corresponding with **455 were clipped about** i.e., you were embraced   **456 seeming** plausibility   **468 Whom** on whom.   **hers** i.e., Cloten   **476 Lessened herself** i.e., grew smaller to sight   **477 foreshowed** foreshowed that **480 Laud** praise   **481 crooked** curling, twining   **488 Set on there** forward march.   **was a war** was there a war that   **489 Ere . . . washed** before hands were washed in blood or free of blood

The Winter's Tale

The Winter's Tale (c. 1609–1611), with its almost symmetrical division into two halves of bleak tragedy and comic romance, illustrates perhaps more clearly than any other Shakespearean play the genre of tragicomedy. To be sure, all the late romances feature journeys of separation, apparent deaths, and tearful reconciliations. Marina and Thaisa in *Pericles,* Imogen in *Cymbeline,* and Ferdinand in *The Tempest,* all supposed irrecoverably lost, are brought back to life by apparently miraculous devices. Of the four late romances, however, *The Winter's Tale* uses the most formal structure to evoke the antithesis of tragedy and romance. It is sharply divided into contrasting halves by a gap of sixteen years. The tragic first half takes place almost entirely in Sicilia, whereas the action of the second half is limited for the most part to Bohemia. At the court of Sicilia, we see tyrannical jealousy producing a spiritual climate of "winter / In storm perpetual"; in Bohemia, we witness a pastoral landscape and a sheepshearing evoking "the sweet o' the year," "When daffodils begin to peer" (3.2.212–213; 4.3.1–3). Paradoxically, the contrast between the two halves is intensified by parallels between the two: both begin with Camillo onstage and proceed to scenes of confrontation and jealousy in which, ironically, the innocent cause of jealousy in the first half, Polixenes, becomes the jealous tyrant of the second half. The mirroring reminds us of the cyclical nature of time and the hope it brings of renewal as we move from tragedy to romantic comedy.

Although this motif of a renewing journey from jaded court to idealized countryside reminds us of *As You Like It* and other early comedies, we sense in the late romances and especially in *The Winter's Tale* a new preoccupation with humanity's tragic folly. The vision of human depravity is world-weary and pessimistic, as though infected by the gloomy spirit of the great tragedies. And because humanity is so bent on destroying itself, the restoration is at once more urgently needed and more miraculous than in the "festive" world of early comedy. Renewal is mythically associated with the seasonal cycle from winter to summer.

King Leontes' tragedy seems at first irreversible and terrifying, like that of Shakespeare's greatest tragic protagonists. He suffers from irrational jealousy, as does Othello, and attempts to destroy the person on whom all his happiness depends. As with Othello, his jealousy stems from a characteristically male fear of inadequacy and rejection. Unlike Othello, however, Leontes needs no diabolical tempter such as Iago to poison his mind against Queen Hermione. Leontes is undone by his own fantasies. No differences in race or age can explain Leontes' fears of estrangement from Hermione. She is not imprudent in her conduct, like her counterpart in Robert Greene's *Pandosto* (1588), the prose romance from which Shakespeare drew his narrative. Although Hermione is graciously fond of Leontes' dear friend Polixenes and urges him to stay longer in Sicilia, she does so only with a hospitable warmth demanded by the occasion and encouraged by her husband. In every way, then, Shakespeare strips away from Leontes the motive and the occasion for plausible doubting of his wife. All observers in the Sicilian court are incredulous and shocked at the King's accusations. Even so, Leontes is neither an unsympathetic nor an unbelievable character. Like Othello, Leontes cherishes his wife and perceives with a horrifying intensity what a fearful cost they both must pay for his suspicions. Not only his marriage, but also his lifelong friendship with Polixenes, his sense of pride in his children, and his enjoyment of his subjects' warm regard, all must be sacrificed to a single overwhelming compulsion.

Whatever may be the psychological cause of this obsession, it manifests itself as a revulsion against all sexual behavior. Like mad Lear, Leontes imagines lechery to be the unavoidable fact of the cosmos and of the human condition, the lowest common denominator to which all persons (including Hermione) must stoop. He is persuaded that "It is a bawdy planet," in which cuckolded man has "his pond fished by his next neighbor, by / Sir Smile, his neighbor" (1.2.195–201). Leontes' tortured soliloquies are laden with sexual images, of unattended "gates" letting in and out the enemy "With bag and baggage," and of a "dagger" that must be "muzzled / Lest it should bite its master" (lines 197, 206, 156–157). As in *King Lear,* order is inverted to disorder, sanity to madness, legitimacy to illegitimacy. Sexual misconduct is emblematic of a universal malaise: "Why, then the world and all that's in 't is nothing, / The covering sky is nothing, Bohemia nothing, / My wife is nothing" (lines 292–294). Other characters, too, see the trial of Hermione as a testing of humanity's worth: if Hermione proves false, Antigonus promises, he will treat his own wife as a stable horse and will "geld" his three daughters (2.1.148). Prevailing images are of spiders, venom, infection, sterility, and the "dungy earth" (line 158).

Cosmic order is never really challenged, however, even though the human suffering is very real and the injustice to women especially apparent. Leontes' fantasies of universal disorder are chimerical. His wife is, in fact, chaste, Polixenes true, and the King's courtiers loyal. Camillo refuses to carry out Leontes' order to murder Polixenes, not only because he knows murder to be wrong, but also because history offers not one example of a man "that had struck anointed kings / And flourished after" (1.2.357–358). The cosmos of this play is one in which crimes are invariably and swiftly punished. The Delphic oracle vindicates Hermione and gives Leontes stern warning. When Leontes persists in his madness, his son Mamillius' death follows as an immediate consequence. As Leontes at once perceives, "Apollo's angry, and the heavens themselves / Do strike at my injustice" (3.2.146–147). Leontes paradoxically welcomes the lengthy contrition he must undergo, for it confirms a pattern in the universe of just cause and effect. Although as tragic protagonist he has discovered the truth about Hermione moments too late and so must pay richly for his error, Leontes has at least recovered faith in Hermione's transcendent goodness. His nightmare now over, he accepts and embraces suffering as a necessary atonement.

The transition to romance is therefore anticipated to an extent by the play's first half, even though the tone of the last two acts is strikingly different. The old Shepherd signals a momentous change when he speaks to his son of a cataclysmic storm and a ravenous bear set in opposition to the miraculous discovery of a child: "Now bless thyself. Thou mett'st with things dying, I with things newborn" (3.3.110–111). Time comes onstage as Chorus, like Gower in *Pericles,* to remind us of the conscious artifice of the dramatist. He can "o'erthrow law" and carry us over sixteen years as if we had merely dreamed out the interim (4.1). Shakespeare flaunts the improbability of his story by giving Bohemia a seacoast (much to the distress of Ben Jonson) and by bringing onstage either a live bear or an actor costumed as one ("*Exit, pursued by a bear*"; 3.3.57 s.d.). The narrative uses many typical devices of romance: a babe abandoned to the elements, a princess brought up by shepherds, a prince disguised as a swain, a sea voyage, and a recognition scene. Love is threatened, not by the internal psychic obstacle of jealousy, but by the external obstacles of parental opposition and a seeming disparity of social rank between the lovers. Comedy easily finds solutions for such difficulties by the unraveling of illusion. This comic world also properly includes clownish shepherds, coy shepherdesses, and Autolycus, the roguish peddler, whose machinations contribute in an unforeseen manner to the working out of the love plot. Autolycus is in many ways the presiding genius of the play's second half, as dominant a character as Leontes in the first half and one whose delightful function is to do good "against my will" (5.2.125). In this paradox of knavery converted surprisingly to benign ends, we see how the comic providence of Shakespeare's tragicomic world makes use of the most implausible and outrageous happenings in pursuit of its own inscrutable design.

The conventional romantic ending is infused, however, with a sadness and a mystery that take the play well beyond what is usual in comedy. Mamillius and Antigonus are really dead, and that irredeemable fact is not forgotten in the play's final happy moments. Hermione, although vindicated by the gods, has suffered public shame, the death of one child, separation from her other child, and prolonged isolation from her husband; like Imogen in *Cymbeline,* she has had to endure the consequences of male frailty and thereby redeem her husband through her suffering. Her husband, having thrown her aside, must, like Pericles, rediscover and learn to cherish the woman he once chose who now has aged; he must reconfirm his marriage to her, even as he learns to accept the marriage of his daughter to a younger man. All of these crucial turnings hinge upon Shakespeare's most notable departure from his source, Greene's *Pandosto:* Hermione is brought back to life. All observers regard this event, and the rediscovery of Perdita, as grossly implausible, "so like an old tale that the verity of it is in strong suspicion" (5.2.29–30). The play's very title, *The Winter's Tale,* reinforces this sense of naive improbability. Why does Shakespeare stress this riddling paradox of an unbelievable reality, and why does he deliberately mislead his audience into believing that Hermione has, in fact, died (3.3.15–45), using a kind of theatrical trickery found in no other Shakespearean play? The answer may well be that, in Paulina's words, we must awake our faith, accepting a narrative of death and return to life that cannot ultimately be comprehended by reason. On the rational level, we are told that Hermione has been kept in hiding for sixteen years, in order to fulfill the condition of the oracle that Leontes is to live without an heir (and hence without a wife) until Perdita is found. Such an explanation seems psychologically incomprehensible, however, for it demands that Hermione live in extended isolation and that Paulina serve as the King's conscience for such a long period of time without any way for them to know when their suffering will end. Instead, we are drawn toward an emblematic interpretation, bearing in mind that it is more an evocative hint than a complete truth. Throughout the play, Hermione has been repeatedly associated with "Grace" and with the goddess Proserpina, whose return from the underworld, after "Three crabbèd months had soured themselves to death" (1.2.102), signals the coming of spring. Perdita, also associated with Proserpina (4.4.116), is welcomed by her father "As is the spring to th' earth" (5.1.152). The emphasis on the bond of father and daughter, so characteristic of Shakespeare's late plays and especially his romances, goes importantly beyond the patriarchalism of Shakespeare's earlier history plays in its exploration of family relationships. Paulina has a similarly emblematic role, that of Conscience, patiently guiding the King to a divinely appointed renewal of his joy. Paulina speaks of herself as an artist figure, like Prospero in *The Tempest,* performing wonders of illusion, though she rejects the assistance of wicked powers. These emblematic hints do not rob the story of its human drama, but they do lend a transcendent significance to Leontes' bittersweet story of sinful error, affliction, and an unexpected second happiness.

The Winter's Tale

The Names of the Actors

LEONTES, *King of Sicilia*
MAMILLIUS, *young prince of Sicilia*
CAMILLO,
ANTIGONUS,
CLEOMENES, } *four Lords of Sicilia*
DION,

HERMIONE, *Queen to Leontes*
PERDITA, *daughter to Leontes and Hermione*
PAULINA, *wife to Antigonus*
EMILIA, *a lady [attending on Hermione]*

POLIXENES, *King of Bohemia*
FLORIZEL, *Prince of Bohemia*
ARCHIDAMUS, *a lord of Bohemia*
Old SHEPHERD, *reputed father of Perdita*
CLOWN, *his son*
AUTOLYCUS, *a rogue*

[MOPSA,
[DORCAS,] } *Shepherdesses.*]

[A MARINER
A JAILER
Two LADIES *attending Hermione*
Two SERVANTS *attending Leontes*
One or more LORDS *attending Leontes*
An OFFICER *of the court*
A GENTLEMAN *attending Leontes*
Three GENTLEMEN *of the court of Sicilia*
A SERVANT *of the Old Shepherd*

TIME, *as Chorus*]

Other Lords and Gentlemen, [Ladies, Officers,] and
Servants; Shepherds and Shepherdesses; [Twelve
Countrymen disguised as Satyrs]

[SCENE: *Sicilia, and Bohemia.*]

1.1   *Enter Camillo and Archidamus.*

ARCHIDAMUS   If you shall chance, Camillo, to visit Bohemia on the like occasion whereon my services are
now on foot, you shall see, as I have said, great
difference betwixt our Bohemia and your Sicilia.

1.1 Location: Sicilia. The court of Leontes.

CAMILLO   I think this coming summer the King of Sicilia
means to pay Bohemia the visitation which he justly 6
owes him.
ARCHIDAMUS   Wherein our entertainment shall shame 8
us, we will be justified in our loves; for indeed— 9
CAMILLO   Beseech you—
ARCHIDAMUS   Verily, I speak it in the freedom of my 11
knowledge. We cannot with such magnificence—in 12
so rare—I know not what to say. We will give you
sleepy drinks, that your senses, unintelligent of our 14
insufficience, may, though they cannot praise us, as
little accuse us.
CAMILLO   You pay a great deal too dear for what's
given freely.
ARCHIDAMUS   Believe me, I speak as my understanding
instructs me and as mine honesty puts it to utterance.
CAMILLO   Sicilia cannot show himself overkind to Bo- 21
hemia. They were trained together in their childhoods, 22
and there rooted betwixt them then such an affection
which cannot choose but branch now. Since their 24
more mature dignities and royal necessities made
separation of their society, their encounters, though 26
not personal, hath been royally attorneyed with 27
interchange of gifts, letters, loving embassies, that
they have seemed to be together though absent,
shook hands as over a vast, and embraced as it were 30
from the ends of opposed winds. The heavens con- 31
tinue their loves!
ARCHIDAMUS   I think there is not in the world either
malice or matter to alter it. You have an unspeakable
comfort of your young prince Mamillius. It is a 35
gentleman of the greatest promise that ever came into
my note. 37
CAMILLO   I very well agree with you in the hopes of
him. It is a gallant child, one that indeed physics the 39
subject, makes old hearts fresh. They that went on 40
crutches ere he was born desire yet their life to see him
a man.
ARCHIDAMUS   Would they else be content to die?
CAMILLO   Yes, if there were no other excuse why they
should desire to live.
ARCHIDAMUS   If the King had no son, they would desire 46
to live on crutches till he had one.   *Exeunt.* 47

6 Bohemia the King of Bohemia (also at lines 21–22)   **8–9 Wherein
. . . loves** in whatever way our attempts to entertain you will shame
us by falling short of your entertainment of us, we will make up for by
our affection.   **justified** absolved, as of spiritual sin, by faith or love
11–12 in . . . knowledge as my knowledge entitles me to speak
14 sleepy sleep-inducing.   **unintelligent** unaware   **21 Sicilia** the King
of Sicilia   **22 trained** (1) educated (2) managed horticulturally to grow
a particular way   **24 branch** put forth new growth, flourish (also perhaps with opposite and unconscious suggestion of "divide")   **26 their
society** their being together   **27 personal** in person.   **attorneyed** carried out by deputy   **30 vast** boundless space   **31 ends . . . winds**
i.e., opposite ends of the earth.   **The heavens** may the heavens
35 of in the person of   **37 note** observation   **39–40 physics the subject** acts as a medicine to the nation   **46–47 If . . . one** (While applauding the subjects' loyalty to their king, Archidamus also jokes that
most people will look for an excuse to live longer.)

1.2
Enter Leontes, Hermione, Mamillius, Polixenes, Camillo.

POLIXENES
Nine changes of the watery star hath been   1
The shepherd's note since we have left our throne   2
Without a burden. Time as long again   3
Would be filled up, my brother, with our thanks,
And yet we should for perpetuity   5
Go hence in debt. And therefore, like a cipher,   6
Yet standing in rich place, I multiply   7
With one "We thank you" many thousands more
That go before it.

LEONTES   Stay your thanks awhile
And pay them when you part.

POLIXENES   Sir, that's tomorrow.
I am questioned by my fears of what may chance   11
Or breed upon our absence, that may blow   12
No sneaping winds at home to make us say   13
"This is put forth too truly." Besides, I have stayed   14
To tire your royalty.

LEONTES   We are tougher, brother,
Than you can put us to 't.

POLIXENES   No longer stay.   16

LEONTES
One sev'nnight longer.

POLIXENES   Very sooth, tomorrow.   17

LEONTES
We'll part the time between 's, then, and in that   18
I'll no gainsaying.

POLIXENES   Press me not, beseech you, so.   19
There is no tongue that moves, none, none i' the
    world
So soon as yours could win me. So it should now,
Were there necessity in your request, although
'Twere needful I denied it. My affairs
Do even drag me homeward, which to hinder
Were in your love a whip to me, my stay   25
To you a charge and trouble. To save both,   26
Farewell, our brother.

LEONTES   Tongue-tied, our Queen? Speak you.

HERMIONE
I had thought, sir, to have held my peace until
You had drawn oaths from him not to stay. You, sir,
Charge him too coldly. Tell him you are sure
All in Bohemia's well; this satisfaction   31
The bygone day proclaimed. Say this to him,   32

He's beat from his best ward.

LEONTES   Well said, Hermione.   33

HERMIONE
To tell he longs to see his son were strong.   34
But let him say so then, and let him go.
But let him swear so and he shall not stay;   36
We'll thwack him hence with distaffs.
[*To Polixenes.*] Yet of your royal presence I'll
    adventure   38
The borrow of a week. When at Bohemia   39
You take my lord, I'll give him my commission   40
To let him there a month behind the gest   41
Prefixed for 's parting.—Yet, good deed, Leontes,   42
I love thee not a jar o' the clock behind   43
What lady she her lord.—You'll stay?

POLIXENES   No, madam.   44

HERMIONE
Nay, but you will?

POLIXENES   I may not, verily.

HERMIONE   Verily?
You put me off with limber vows; but I,   47
Though you would seek t' unsphere the stars with
    oaths,
Should yet say, "Sir, no going." Verily,
You shall not go. A lady's "verily" is
As potent as a lord's. Will you go yet?
Force me to keep you as a prisoner,
Not like a guest: so you shall pay your fees   53
When you depart, and save your thanks. How
    say you?
My prisoner or my guest? By your dread "verily,"
One of them you shall be.

POLIXENES   Your guest, then, madam.
To be your prisoner should import offending,   57
Which is for me less easy to commit
Than you to punish.

HERMIONE   Not your jailer, then,
But your kind hostess. Come, I'll question you
Of my lord's tricks and yours when you were boys.
You were pretty lordings then?

POLIXENES   We were, fair Queen,
Two lads that thought there was no more behind   63
But such a day tomorrow as today,
And to be boy eternal.

HERMIONE   Was not my lord
The verier wag o' the two?   66

POLIXENES
We were as twinned lambs that did frisk i' the sun
And bleat the one at th' other. What we changed   68
Was innocence for innocence; we knew not

1.2. Location: The same.
1 watery star moon   **2 note** observation.   **we** i.e., I. (The royal "we.")   **3 burden** i.e., occupant   **5 for perpetuity** forever   **6–7 like . . . place** like a zero at the end of a number, increasing its value by powers of ten, though of itself without value   **11–14 I am . . . truly** I am anxious about what may happen in my absence, especially a stirring up of envy and backbiting that would cause me to say my fears were all too plausible   **16 Than . . . to 't** than anything you can do to try me   **17 sev'nnight** sevennight, week.   **Very sooth** truly   **18 part the time** split the difference, i.e., divide a week in two   **19 I'll no gainsaying** I will take no refusal   **25 Were . . . whip** would be a punishment to me, though done through love   **26 charge** expense, burden   **31–32 this . . . proclaimed** yesterday brought news to satisfy on that score (that all is well in Bohemia)   **32 Say** if you say

33 ward defensive posture. (A fencing term.)   **34 tell** tell us that.   **strong** a strong argument   **36 he shall not stay** i.e., we wouldn't let him stay even if he wanted to   **38 adventure** risk (because, as she explains, she'll undertake to repay each week with a month)   **39 borrow** borrowing   **40 take** capture; receive   **41 let him** let him stay.   **gest** time allotted for a halt in a royal progress or journey   **42 good deed** i.e., in truth   **43 jar** tick   **44 What lady she** any lady   **47 limber** limp   **53 fees** payments often demanded by jailers of prisoners at the time of their release   **57 import offending** imply my having offended   **63 behind** still to come   **66 The verier wag** truly the more mischievous   **68 changed** exchanged

The doctrine of ill-doing, nor dreamed
That any did. Had we pursued that life,
And our weak spirits ne'er been higher reared
With stronger blood, we should have answered
    heaven   73
Boldly "Not guilty," the imposition cleared   74
Hereditary ours.
HERMIONE   By this we gather   75
You have tripped since.
POLIXENES   O my most sacred lady,
Temptations have since then been born to 's, for
In those unfledged days was my wife a girl;   78
Your precious self had then not crossed the eyes
Of my young playfellow.
HERMIONE   Grace to boot!   80
Of this make no conclusion, lest you say   81
Your queen and I are devils. Yet go on.
Th' offenses we have made you do we'll answer,
If you first sinned with us, and that with us   84
You did continue fault, and that you slipped not   85
With any but with us.
LEONTES   Is he won yet?   86
HERMIONE
He'll stay, my lord.
LEONTES   At my request he would not.
Hermione, my dearest, thou never spok'st
To better purpose.
HERMIONE   Never?
LEONTES   Never but once.
HERMIONE
What? Have I twice said well? When was 't before?
I prithee, tell me. Cram 's with praise and make 's
As fat as tame things. One good deed dying
    tongueless   92
Slaughters a thousand waiting upon that.   93
Our praises are our wages. You may ride 's
With one soft kiss a thousand furlongs ere
With spur we heat an acre. But to the goal: 96
My last good deed was to entreat his stay.
What was my first? It has an elder sister,
Or I mistake you. O, would her name were Grace!
But once before I spoke to the purpose. When?
Nay, let me have 't; I long.
LEONTES   Why, that was when
Three crabbèd months had soured themselves to
    death
Ere I could make thee open thy white hand
And clap thyself my love. Then didst thou utter,   104

"I am yours forever."
HERMIONE   'Tis grace indeed.
Why, lo you now, I have spoke to the purpose twice:
The one forever earned a royal husband,
Th' other for some while a friend.
            [*She gives her hand to Polixenes.*]
LEONTES [*aside*]   Too hot, too hot!
To mingle friendship far is mingling bloods.   109
I have *tremor cordis* on me. My heart dances,   110
But not for joy, not joy. This entertainment   111
May a free face put on, derive a liberty   112
From heartiness, from bounty, fertile bosom,   113
And well become the agent. 'T may, I grant.   114
But to be paddling palms and pinching fingers,
As now they are, and making practiced smiles
As in a looking glass, and then to sigh, as 'twere
The mort o' the deer; O, that is entertainment   118
My bosom likes not, nor my brows.—Mamillius,   119
Art thou my boy?
MAMILLIUS   Ay, my good lord.
LEONTES   I' fecks,   120
Why, that's my bawcock. What, hast smutched thy
    nose?   121
They say it is a copy out of mine. Come, captain,
We must be neat; not neat, but cleanly, captain.   123
And yet the steer, the heifer, and the calf
Are all called neat.—Still virginaling   125
Upon his palm?—How now, you wanton calf?   126
Art thou my calf?
MAMILLIUS   Yes, if you will, my lord.
LEONTES
Thou want'st a rough pash and the shoots that I
    have   128
To be full like me. Yet they say we are   129
Almost as like as eggs. Women say so,
That will say anything. But were they false
As o'erdyed blacks, as wind, as waters, false   132
As dice are to be wished by one that fixes   133
No bourn twixt his and mine, yet were it true   134
To say this boy were like me. Come, sir page,
Look on me with your welkin eye. Sweet villain!   136

---

73 stronger blood i.e., mature sexual passions **74–75 the imposition . . . ours** i.e., excepting of course the original sin that is the condition of all mortals, or, perhaps, being freed from original sin itself (if
we had continued in that pure state) **78 unfledged** not yet feathered,
i.e., immature **80 Grace to boot** i.e., Heaven help me **81 Of . . .
conclusion** don't follow your implied line of reasoning to its logical
conclusion **84 that** if (also in line 85) **85 fault** offense **86 Is he
won yet** (Leontes has been out of hearing for much of their conversation.) **92 tongueless** unpraised, unsung **93 Slaughters . . . that** i.e.,
will inhibit many other good deeds that would have been inspired by
that praise **96 heat** traverse as in a race. **to the goal** to come to the
point **104 clap** clasp hands, plight troth

109 mingling bloods (Sexual intercourse was thought to produce a
mingling of bloods.) **110 tremor cordis** fluttering of the heart
111 entertainment i.e., of Polixenes by Hermione **112 free face** innocent appearance **113 fertile bosom** i.e., generous affection
114 well . . . agent do credit to the doer **118 mort** note sounded on
a horn at the death of the hunted deer **119 brows** (Alludes to cuckolds' horns, the supposed badge of men whose wives are unfaithful.)
120 I' fecks in faith **121 bawcock** i.e., fine fellow. (French *beau
coq*.) **123 not . . . cleanly** (Leontes changes the word because *neat*
also means "cattle" and hence reminds him of cuckolds' horns.)
125 virginaling touching hands, as in playing on the virginals, a
keyed instrument **126 wanton** frisky **128 Thou want'st** you lack.
rough pash shaggy head. **shoots** horns. (Another allusion to cuckolds' horns.) **129 full** fully **132 o'erdyed blacks** black garments that
have been weakened by too much dye or that have been dyed over
another color (thereby betraying a falseness in the mourner)
133–134 one . . . mine i.e., one who, setting no boundary between
his possessions and mine, intends to cheat me at dice **136 welkin**
sky-blue

Most dear'st! My collop! Can thy dam?—
   may 't be?—   137
Affection, thy intention stabs the center.   138
Thou dost make possible things not so held,   139
Communicat'st with dreams—how can this be?—   140
With what's unreal thou coactive art,   141
And fellow'st nothing. Then 'tis very credent   142
Thou mayst cojoin with something; and thou dost,   143
And that beyond commission, and I find it,   144
And that to the infection of my brains
And hardening of my brows.

POLIXENES   What means Sicilia?   146
HERMIONE
  He something seems unsettled.
POLIXENES   How, my lord?   147
  What cheer? How is 't with you, best brother?
HERMIONE   You look
  As if you held a brow of much distraction.
  Are you moved, my lord?
LEONTES   No, in good earnest.   150
How sometimes nature will betray its folly,   151
Its tenderness, and make itself a pastime   152
To harder bosoms! Looking on the lines   153
Of my boy's face, methought I did recoil   154
Twenty-three years, and saw myself unbreeched,   155
In my green velvet coat, my dagger muzzled   156
Lest it should bite its master and so prove,
As ornaments oft do, too dangerous.
How like, methought, I then was to this kernel,
This squash, this gentleman.—Mine honest friend,   160
Will you take eggs for money?   161
MAMILLIUS   No, my lord, I'll fight.
LEONTES
  You will? Why, happy man be 's dole!—My brother,   163
  Are you so fond of your young prince as we
  Do seem to be of ours?
POLIXENES   If at home, sir,
He's all my exercise, my mirth, my matter,   166
Now my sworn friend and then mine enemy,
My parasite, my soldier, statesman, all.
He makes a July's day short as December,
And with his varying childness cures in me   170

Thoughts that would thick my blood.
LEONTES   So stands this squire   171
Officed with me. We two will walk, my lord,   172
And leave you to your graver steps. Hermione,
How thou lov'st us, show in our brother's welcome.   174
Let what is dear in Sicily be cheap.   175
Next to thyself and my young rover, he's
Apparent to my heart.
HERMIONE   If you would seek us,   177
We are yours i' the garden. Shall 's attend you there? 178
LEONTES
  To your own bents dispose you. You'll be found,   179
  Be you beneath the sky. [_Aside._] I am angling now,
Though you perceive me not how I give line.   181
Go to, go to!   182
How she holds up the neb, the bill to him,   183
And arms her with the boldness of a wife   184
To her allowing husband!

          [_Exeunt Polixenes and Hermione._]
          Gone already!   185
Inch thick, knee-deep, o'er head and ears a
  forked one!—   186
Go play, boy, play. Thy mother plays, and I   187
Play too, but so disgraced a part, whose issue   188
Will hiss me to my grave. Contempt and clamor
Will be my knell. Go play, boy, play. There have
  been,
Or I am much deceived, cuckolds ere now;
And many a man there is, even at this present,
Now while I speak this, holds his wife by th' arm,
That little thinks she has been sluiced in 's absence 194
And his pond fished by his next neighbor, by
Sir Smile, his neighbor. Nay, there's comfort in 't
Whiles other men have gates and those gates
  opened,   197
As mine, against their will. Should all despair
That have revolted wives, the tenth of mankind   199
Would hang themselves. Physic for 't there's none.   200
It is a bawdy planet, that will strike   201
Where 'tis predominant; and 'tis powerful, think it,   202

---

137 collop small piece of meat; i.e., of my own flesh.   **dam** mother
138–143 Affection . . . something Strong passion, your intense
power pierces to the very center, the soul. You make possible things
normally considered fantastic, partaking as you do of the nature of
dreams. How can this be? You collaborate with unreality and imagined fantasies. It's all the likelier, then, that such imaginings may also
fasten on a real object.   **146 What
means Sicilia** i.e., why is the King of Sicilia looking so distracted?
147 something somewhat   **150 moved** angry   **151 nature** i.e., affectionate feeling between parent and child   **152 pastime** occasion for
amusement   **153 To harder bosoms** for persons who are less tenderhearted   **154 methought** it seemed to me.   **recoil** i.e., go back in
memory   **155 unbreeched** not yet wearing breeches   **156 muzzled**
i.e., sheathed. (With phallic suggestion.)   **160 squash** unripe
peascod or pea pod.   **honest** worthy   **161 take eggs for money** i.e.,
be imposed upon, taken advantage of, cheated. (Proverbial.)
163 happy . . . dole may good fortune be his lot. (Proverbial.)
166 matter concern   **170 childness** childlike ways

171 thick my blood (Melancholy thoughts were supposed to thicken
the blood.)   **172 Officed** placed in particular function
174–175 How . . . cheap (A hidden second meaning in these lines
may be intentional: show just how much you love me by the way you
encourage Polixenes' attentions and thereby cheapen the most precious thing in Sicily.)   **177 Apparent** heir apparent (perhaps with a
suggestion too of "evident, revealed")   **178 Shall 's** shall we   **179 To
. . . dispose you** act according to your inclinations (with more bitter
double meaning, continued in _You'll be found,_ i.e., found out)
181 give line pay out line (to let the fish hook itself well)   **182 Go to**
(An expression of remonstrance.)   **183 neb** beak, i.e., nose, mouth
184 arms her with assumes   **185 allowing** approving   **186 forked**
horned   **187 play** play games.   **plays** i.e., in a sexual liaison
188 Play play a role.   **issue** outcome (with a pun on the sense of
"offspring" and "theatrical exit")   **194 sluiced** drawn off, as by a
sluice. (The water in his pond, so to speak, has been drawn off by a
cheating neighbor.)   **197 gates** sluice gates, suggestive of the wife's
chastity that has been opened and robbed   **199 revolted** unfaithful
200 Physic medicine   **201 It . . . planet** i.e., this unchastity is like
the planet Venus.   **strike** blast, destroy by a malign influence
202 predominant in the ascendant. (Said of a planet.)   **think it** be assured of this

From east, west, north, and south. Be it concluded,
No barricado for a belly. Know 't,   204
It will let in and out the enemy
With bag and baggage. Many thousand on 's   206
Have the disease and feel 't not.—How now, boy?

MAMILLIUS
I am like you, they say.

LEONTES   Why, that's some comfort.
What, Camillo there?

CAMILLO [coming forward] Ay, my good lord.

LEONTES
Go play, Mamillius; thou'rt an honest man.
                                   [Exit Mamillius.]
Camillo, this great sir will yet stay longer.

CAMILLO
You had much ado to make his anchor hold.
When you cast out, it still came home.

LEONTES   Didst note it?   213

CAMILLO
He would not stay at your petitions, made
His business more material.

LEONTES   Didst perceive it?   215
[Aside.] They're here with me already, whispering,
   rounding,   216
"Sicilia is a so-forth." 'Tis far gone   217
When I shall gust it last.—How came 't, Camillo,   218
That he did stay?

CAMILLO   At the good Queen's entreaty.

LEONTES
"At the Queen's" be 't. "Good" should be pertinent,   220
But so it is, it is not. Was this taken   221
By any understanding pate but thine?
For thy conceit is soaking, will draw in   223
More than the common blocks. Not noted, is 't,   224
But of the finer natures? By some severals   225
Of headpiece extraordinary? Lower messes   226
Perchance are to this business purblind? Say.   227

CAMILLO
Business, my lord? I think most understand
Bohemia stays here longer.

LEONTES
Ha?

CAMILLO   Stays here longer.

LEONTES   Ay, but why?

CAMILLO
To satisfy Your Highness and the entreaties
Of our most gracious mistress.

LEONTES   Satisfy?   232

Th' entreaties of your mistress? Satisfy?
Let that suffice. I have trusted thee, Camillo,
With all the nearest things to my heart, as well   235
My chamber councils, wherein, priestlike, thou   236
Hast cleansed my bosom. I from thee departed
Thy penitent reformed. But we have been
Deceived in thy integrity, deceived
In that which seems so.

CAMILLO   Be it forbid, my lord!   240

LEONTES
To bide upon 't, thou art not honest; or,   241
If thou inclin'st that way, thou art a coward,   242
Which hoxes honesty behind, restraining   243
From course required; or else thou must be counted   244
A servant grafted in my serious trust   245
And therein negligent; or else a fool
That seest a game played home, the rich stake
   drawn,   247
And tak'st it all for jest.

CAMILLO   My gracious lord,
I may be negligent, foolish, and fearful;
In every one of these no man is free,
But that his negligence, his folly, fear,
Among the infinite doings of the world
Sometimes puts forth. In your affairs, my lord,   253
If ever I were willful-negligent,
It was my folly; if industriously   255
I played the fool, it was my negligence,   256
Not weighing well the end; if ever fearful
To do a thing where I the issue doubted,   258
Whereof the execution did cry out   259
Against the nonperformance, 'twas a fear   260
Which oft infects the wisest. These, my lord,
Are such allowed infirmities that honesty   262
Is never free of. But, beseech Your Grace,
Be plainer with me. Let me know my trespass
By its own visage. If I then deny it,   265
'Tis none of mine.

LEONTES   Ha' not you seen, Camillo—
But that's past doubt; you have, or your eyeglass   267
Is thicker than a cuckold's horn—or heard—   268
For to a vision so apparent, rumor   269
Cannot be mute—or thought—for cogitation

204 barricado barricade. Know 't be certain of this 206 bag and
baggage (With sexual suggestion, as earlier in dagger [line 156],
sluiced, gates, let in and out, etc.) on 's of us 213 still came home
always came back to the ship, failed to hold 215 material important
216 They're . . . already people are already onto my situation.
rounding whispering, gossiping 217 a so-forth a so-and-so, a you-
know-what 218 gust taste, i.e., hear of 220 pertinent i.e., appropriately applied 221 so it is as things stand. taken perceived
223 conceit understanding. soaking i.e., very receptive 224 blocks
blockheads 225 But . . . natures except by those of rarefied intellect. severals individuals 226 Lower messes those who sit lower at
table, i.e., inferior persons 227 purblind totally blind 232 Satisfy
(Leontes takes the word in a sexual sense.)

235 as well as well as with 236 chamber councils private affairs
240 Be it forbid i.e., God forbid I should do such a thing 241 To
bide upon 't (1) to dwell on this matter still further, or (2) for you to
insist thus on your integrity. or either 242 inclin'st that way i.e.,
prefer being honest under ordinary circumstances 243 Which i.e.,
which cowardice. hoxes hamstrings 244 From course required
i.e., from the direction honest inquiry must take to find the truth
245 grafted . . . trust taken into my complete confidence. (Grafted
means "deeply embedded," like a graft.) 247 home i.e., for keeps,
in earnest. (With perhaps a sexual double meaning, continued in rich
stake drawn.) drawn won 253 puts forth shows itself 255 industriously willfully 256 played the fool i.e., took some matter lightly
258 the issue doubted feared the outcome 259–260 Whereof . . .
nonperformance in which the completion of the task showed how
wrong I was in being reluctant to undertake it 262 allowed acknowledged. that as 265 visage face, i.e., plain appearance 267 eyeglass lens of the eye 268 cuckold's horn (A thin sheet of horn can be
seen through like a lens, though a cuckold's horn is another matter.)
269 to a vision so apparent about something so plainly visible

Resides not in that man that does not think—   271
My wife is slippery? If thou wilt confess,
Or else be impudently negative   273
To have nor eyes nor ears nor thought, then say   274
My wife's a hobbyhorse, deserves a name   275
As rank as any flax-wench that puts to   276
Before her trothplight. Say 't and justify 't.   277

CAMILLO
I would not be a stander-by to hear
My sovereign mistress clouded so without
My present vengeance taken. 'Shrew my heart,   280
You never spoke what did become you less
Than this, which to reiterate were sin   282
As deep as that, though true.

LEONTES   Is whispering nothing?   283
Is leaning cheek to cheek? Is meeting noses?
Kissing with inside lip? Stopping the career   285
Of laughter with a sigh—a note infallible
Of breaking honesty? Horsing foot on foot?   287
Skulking in corners? Wishing clocks more swift,
Hours minutes, noon midnight? And all eyes   289
Blind with the pin and web but theirs, theirs only,   290
That would unseen be wicked? Is this nothing?
Why, then the world and all that's in 't is nothing,
The covering sky is nothing, Bohemia nothing,
My wife is nothing, nor nothing have these
    nothings,
If this be nothing.

CAMILLO   Good my lord, be cured
Of this diseased opinion, and betimes,   296
For 'tis most dangerous.

LEONTES   Say it be, 'tis true.   297

CAMILLO
No, no, my lord.

LEONTES   It is. You lie, you lie!
I say thou liest, Camillo, and I hate thee,
Pronounce thee a gross lout, a mindless slave,
Or else a hovering temporizer, that   301
Canst with thine eyes at once see good and evil,
Inclining to them both. Were my wife's liver
Infected as her life, she would not live   304
The running of one glass.

CAMILLO   Who does infect her?   305

LEONTES
Why, he that wears her like her medal, hanging   306

About his neck, Bohemia—who, if I
Had servants true about me, that bare eyes   308
To see alike mine honor as their profits,
Their own particular thrifts, they would do that   310
Which should undo more doing. Ay, and thou,   311
His cupbearer—whom I from meaner form   312
Have benched and reared to worship, who mayst
    see   313
Plainly as heaven sees earth and earth sees heaven
How I am galled—mightst bespice a cup   315
To give mine enemy a lasting wink,   316
Which draft to me were cordial.

CAMILLO   Sir, my lord,   317
I could do this, and that with no rash potion,   318
But with a lingering dram that should not work
Maliciously like poison. But I cannot   320
Believe this crack to be in my dread mistress,   321
So sovereignly being honorable.   322
I have loved thee—

LEONTES   Make that thy question, and go rot!   323
Dost think I am so muddy, so unsettled,   324
To appoint myself in this vexation, sully   325
The purity and whiteness of my sheets—
Which to preserve is sleep, which being spotted
Is goads, thorns, nettles, tails of wasps—
Give scandal to the blood o' the Prince my son,
Who I do think is mine and love as mine,
Without ripe moving to 't? Would I do this?   331
Could man so blench?

CAMILLO   I must believe you, sir.   332
I do, and will fetch off Bohemia for 't;   333
Provided that, when he's removed, Your Highness
Will take again your queen as yours at first,
Even for your son's sake, and thereby for sealing   336
The injury of tongues in courts and kingdoms
Known and allied to yours.

LEONTES   Thou dost advise me
Even so as I mine own course have set down.
I'll give no blemish to her honor, none.

CAMILLO   My lord,
Go then, and with a countenance as clear
As friendship wears at feasts, keep with Bohemia   343
And with your queen. I am his cupbearer.
If from me he have wholesome beverage,
Account me not your servant.

LEONTES   This is all.
Do 't and thou hast the one half of my heart;

271 **think** i.e., think so   273–274 **Or . . . eyes** the only possible alternative to which is to insist impudently that you have neither eyes   275 **hobbyhorse** wanton woman   276 **flax-wench** common slut. **puts to** engages in sex   277 **justify** affirm   280 **present** immediate. **'Shrew** beshrew, curse   282–283 **which . . . true** i.e., to repeat which accusation would be to sin as deeply as her supposed adultery or your sinfulness in thus accusing her, even if it were true (which it isn't)   285 **career** full gallop   287 **honesty** chastity. **Horsing foot on foot** placing one's foot on that of another person and then moving the feet up and down together   289 **Hours minutes** wishing hours were minutes   290 **pin and web** cataract of the eye. (The lovers wish to think themselves unobserved.)   296 **betimes** quickly   297 **Say it be** i.e., even if it is dangerous   301 **hovering** wavering   304 **Infected as her life** as full of disease as is her moral conduct   305 **glass** hourglass   306 **like her medal** like a miniature portrait of her, worn in a locket

308 **bare** bore, had   310 **thrifts** gains   311 **undo** prevent   312 **meaner form** humbler station   313 **benched** placed on the bench of authority.   **worship** dignity, honor   315 **galled** rubbed, chafed   316 **lasting wink** everlasting closing of the eyes (in death)   317 **were cordial** would be restorative   318 **rash** quick-acting (and therefore easily detected)   320 **Maliciously** virulently   321 **crack** flaw. **dread** worthy of awe   322 **sovereignly** supremely   323 **Make . . . rot** i.e., if you're going to question my accusations, may you rot in hell   324 **muddy** muddle-headed   325 **To . . . vexation** to give myself this vexation   331 **ripe** ample, urgent   332 **blench** swerve (from sensible conduct)   333 **fetch off** do away with, or, with deliberate ambiguity, rescue (as also in *removed* in the next line)   336 **for sealing** for the sake of silencing. (Some editors prefer *forsealing*, sealing up tight.)   343 **keep** remain in company

Do 't not, thou splitt'st thine own.
CAMILLO   I'll do 't, my lord.
LEONTES
I will seem friendly, as thou hast advised me.   *Exit.*
CAMILLO
O miserable lady! But, for me,
What case stand I in? I must be the poisoner
Of good Polixenes, and my ground to do 't
Is the obedience to a master, one
Who in rebellion with himself will have
All that are his so too. To do this deed,   355
Promotion follows. If I could find example   356
Of thousands that had struck anointed kings
And flourished after, I'd not do 't; but since   358
Nor brass, nor stone, nor parchment bears not one,   359
Let villainy itself forswear 't. I must
Forsake the court. To do 't or no is certain   361
To me a breakneck. Happy star reign now!   362
Here comes Bohemia.

Enter Polixenes.

POLIXENES [*to himself*]   This is strange. Methinks
My favor here begins to warp. Not speak?—   364
Good day, Camillo.
CAMILLO   Hail, most royal sir!
POLIXENES
What is the news i' the court?
CAMILLO   None rare, my lord.   366
POLIXENES
The King hath on him such a countenance
As he had lost some province and a region   368
Loved as he loves himself. Even now I met him
With customary compliment, when he,
Wafting his eyes to th' contrary and falling   371
A lip of much contempt, speeds from me, and
So leaves me to consider what is breeding   373
That changeth thus his manners.
CAMILLO   I dare not know, my lord.
POLIXENES
How, dare not? Do not? Do you know, and dare not?   376
Be intelligent to me. 'Tis thereabouts,   377
For to yourself what you do know you must,   378
And cannot say you dare not. Good Camillo,   379
Your changed complexions are to me a mirror
Which shows me mine changed too; for I must be   381
A party in this alteration, finding   382

Myself thus altered with 't.
CAMILLO   There is a sickness
Which puts some of us in distemper, but
I cannot name the disease; and it is caught
Of you that yet are well.
POLIXENES   How? Caught of me?   386
Make me not sighted like the basilisk.   387
I have looked on thousands who have sped the
better   388
By my regard, but killed none so. Camillo,   389
As you are certainly a gentleman, thereto   390
Clerklike experienced, which no less adorns   391
Our gentry than our parents' noble names,   392
In whose success we are gentle, I beseech you,   393
If you know aught which does behoove my
knowledge
Thereof to be informed, imprison 't not
In ignorant concealment.
CAMILLO   I may not answer.   396
POLIXENES
A sickness caught of me, and yet I well?
I must be answered. Dost thou hear, Camillo?
I conjure thee, by all the parts of man   399
Which honor does acknowledge, whereof the least   400
Is not this suit of mine, that thou declare   401
What incidency thou dost guess of harm   402
Is creeping toward me; how far off, how near;
Which way to be prevented, if to be;   404
If not, how best to bear it.
CAMILLO   Sir, I will tell you,
Since I am charged in honor and by him
That I think honorable. Therefore mark my counsel,
Which must be even as swiftly followed as
I mean to utter it, or both yourself and me
Cry lost, and so good night!
POLIXENES   On, good Camillo.   410
CAMILLO
I am appointed him to murder you.   411
POLIXENES
By whom, Camillo?
CAMILLO   By the King.
POLIXENES   For what?
CAMILLO
He thinks, nay, with all confidence he swears,
As he had seen 't or been an instrument
To vice you to 't, that you have touched his queen   415
Forbiddenly.
POLIXENES   O, then my best blood turn
To an infected jelly, and my name

---

355 **All . . . too** i.e., all his followers like him in rebelling against the best in themselves and in obeying his worst self. **To do** if I do 356 **If** even if 358–359 **but . . . one** i.e., but since recorded history shows no instances of persons who have killed a king and prospered afterwards 361 **To do 't or no** i.e., either to kill Polixenes or not to kill him 362 **breakneck** destruction, ruin. **Happy** propitious, favorable 364 **warp** change, shrivel, grow askew (as wood warps). **Not speak** (Leontes has just passed by Polixenes without speaking.) 366 **rare** noteworthy 368 **As** as if 371 **Wafting . . . contrary** averting his eyes. **falling** letting fall 373 **breeding** hatching 376 **Do not** i.e., or do you mean you don't know? 377 **intelligent** intelligible. **'Tis thereabouts** it must be something of this sort, i.e., that you know and dare not tell 378–379 **For . . . dare not** i.e., for in your heart, whatever it is you know, you must in fact know, and can't claim it's a matter of not daring to know 381–382 **for . . . alteration** i.e., for my looks must have changed, too, reflecting this change in my position

386 **Of** from 387 **sighted** provided with a gaze. **basilisk** a fabled serpent whose gaze was fatal 388 **sped** prospered 389 **regard** look 390 **thereto** in addition to which 391 **Clerklike experienced** i.e., a cultivated and educated person 392 **gentry** gentlemanlike condition 393 **whose success** succession from whom. **gentle** wellborn 396 **ignorant concealment** concealment that would keep me ignorant or that would proceed from pretended ignorance on your part 399 **parts** obligations 400–401 **whereof . . . not** not the least of which is (to answer) 402 **incidency** likelihood 404 **if to be** if it can be (prevented) 410 **good night** i.e., this is the end 411 **him** by him (Leontes); or, the one 415 **vice** force, as with a carpenter's tool, or, impel, tempt. (The *Vice* was a tempter in the morality play.)

Be yoked with his that did betray the Best!   418
Turn then my freshest reputation to
A savor that may strike the dullest nostril   420
Where I arrive, and my approach be shunned,
Nay, hated too, worse than the great'st infection
That e'er was heard or read!

CAMILLO   Swear his thought over   423
By each particular star in heaven and
By all their influences, you may as well
Forbid the sea for to obey the moon   426
As or by oath remove or counsel shake   427
The fabric of his folly, whose foundation   428
Is piled upon his faith and will continue   429
The standing of his body.

POLIXENES   How should this grow?   430

CAMILLO
I know not. But I am sure 'tis safer to
Avoid what's grown than question how 'tis born.
If therefore you dare trust my honesty,
That lies enclosèd in this trunk which you   434
Shall bear along impawned, away tonight!   435
Your followers I will whisper to the business,   436
And will by twos and threes at several posterns   437
Clear them o' the city. For myself, I'll put
My fortunes to your service, which are here
By this discovery lost. Be not uncertain,   440
For, by the honor of my parents, I
Have uttered truth, which if you seek to prove,   442
I dare not stand by; nor shall you be safer   443
Than one condemned by the King's own mouth,
  thereon
His execution sworn.

POLIXENES   I do believe thee;
I saw his heart in 's face. Give me thy hand.
Be pilot to me, and thy places shall   447
Still neighbor mine. My ships are ready, and   448
My people did expect my hence departure
Two days ago. This jealousy
Is for a precious creature. As she's rare,
Must it be great; and as his person's mighty,
Must it be violent; and as he does conceive
He is dishonored by a man which ever
Professed to him, why, his revenges must   455
In that be made more bitter. Fear o'ershades me.
Good expedition be my friend, and comfort   457
The gracious Queen, part of his theme, but nothing   458
Of his ill-ta'en suspicion! Come, Camillo,   459

I will respect thee as a father if
Thou bear'st my life off. Hence! Let us avoid.   461

CAMILLO
It is in mine authority to command
The keys of all the posterns. Please Your Highness
To take the urgent hour. Come, sir, away.   *Exeunt.*

2.1   *Enter Hermione, Mamillius, [and] Ladies.*

HERMIONE
Take the boy to you. He so troubles me,
'Tis past enduring.

FIRST LADY [*taking Mamillius from the Queen*]
                              Come, my gracious lord,
Shall I be your playfellow?

MAMILLIUS
No, I'll none of you.

FIRST LADY   Why, my sweet lord?   4

MAMILLIUS
You'll kiss me hard and speak to me as if
I were a baby still.—I love you better.

SECOND LADY
And why so, my lord?

MAMILLIUS   Not for because   7
Your brows are blacker; yet black brows, they say,
Become some women best, so that there be not   9
Too much hair there, but in a semicircle,
Or a half-moon made with a pen.

SECOND LADY   Who taught' this?   11

MAMILLIUS
I learned it out of women's faces. Pray now,
What color are your eyebrows?

FIRST LADY   Blue, my lord.

MAMILLIUS
Nay, that's a mock. I have seen a lady's nose
That has been blue, but not her eyebrows.

FIRST LADY   Hark ye,
The Queen your mother rounds apace. We shall
Present our services to a fine new prince
One of these days, and then you'd wanton with us,   18
If we would have you.

SECOND LADY   She is spread of late
Into a goodly bulk. Good time encounter her!   20

HERMIONE [*calling to her women*]
What wisdom stirs amongst you?—Come, sir, now
I am for you again. Pray you, sit by us   22
And tell 's a tale.

MAMILLIUS   Merry or sad shall 't be?

HERMIONE   As merry as you will.

MAMILLIUS
A sad tale's best for winter. I have one
Of sprites and goblins.

HERMIONE   Let's have that, good sir.
Come on, sit down. Come on, and do your best

418 his . . . Best the name of him (Judas) who betrayed Christ
420 savor stench   423 Swear . . . over i.e., even if you should deny
his suspicion with oaths   426 for to to   427 or . . . or either . . . or
428 fabric edifice   428–430 whose . . . body the foundation of
which is built upon an unshaken conviction and which will last as
long as his body exists   430 standing life, existence.   How . . .
grow i.e., how could this suspicion have arisen?   434 trunk body
(with a suggestion too of a traveling trunk)   435 impawned i.e., as a
pledge of good faith   436 whisper to secretly inform of and urge
437 posterns rear gates   440 discovery revelation, disclosure
442 prove test   443 stand by affirm publicly; stay   447–448 thy
. . . mine your official position will always be near to me   455 Professed openly professed friendship   457–459 Good . . . suspicion
may good speed befriend me, and may my quick departure ease the
predicament of the gracious Queen, who is the object of the King's
suspicions but who is guiltless of them

461 bear'st my life off can get me out of this alive.   avoid depart
2.1. Location: Sicilia. The royal court.
4 none of you have nothing to do with you   7 for because because
9 so provided   11 taught' taught you   18 wanton sport, play
20 Good . . . her may she have a happy issue   22 for you ready
for you

To fright me with your sprites. You're powerful at it.

MAMILLIUS
There was a man—

HERMIONE   Nay, come sit down, then on.
                          [*Mamillius sits.*]

MAMILLIUS
Dwelt by a churchyard. I will tell it softly;
Yond crickets shall not hear it.   31

HERMIONE
Come on, then, and give 't me in mine ear.
                    [*They converse privately.*]

[*Enter*] Leontes, Antigonus, Lords, [*and others*].

LEONTES
Was he met there? His train? Camillo with him?

A LORD
Behind the tuft of pines I met them. Never
Saw I men scour so on their way. I eyed them   35
Even to their ships.

LEONTES   How blest am I
In my just censure, in my true opinion!   37
Alack, for lesser knowledge! How accurst   38
In being so blest! There may be in the cup   39
A spider steeped, and one may drink, depart,   40
And yet partake no venom, for his knowledge
Is not infected; but if one present
Th' abhorred ingredient to his eye, make known
How he hath drunk, he cracks his gorge, his sides,   44
With violent hefts. I have drunk, and seen the
   spider.   45
Camillo was his help in this, his pander.
There is a plot against my life, my crown.
All's true that is mistrusted. That false villain   48
Whom I employed was pre-employed by him.
He has discovered my design, and I   50
Remain a pinched thing, yea, a very trick   51
For them to play at will. How came the posterns   52
So easily open?

A LORD   By his great authority,
Which often hath no less prevailed than so
On your command.

LEONTES   I know 't too well.
[*To Hermione.*] Give me the boy. I am glad you did
   not nurse him.
Though he does bear some signs of me, yet you
Have too much blood in him.

HERMIONE   What is this? Sport?   59

LEONTES [*to a Lord*]
Bear the boy hence; he shall not come about her.
Away with him! And let her sport herself
With that she's big with, [*to Hermione*] for 'tis
   Polixenes

31 **crickets** i.e., the court ladies, tittering and laughing 35 **scour**
scurry 37 **censure** judgment 38 **Alack . . . knowledge** would that
there were less for me to know 39 **blest** i.e., with knowledge (that
causes unhappiness) 40 **A spider** (The superstition referred to here is
that the drinker is not poisoned by the spider in the cup unless he
knows the spider to be there.) 44 **gorge** throat 45 **hefts** heavings,
retchings 48 **mistrusted** suspected 50 **discovered** disclosed
51 **pinched** tortured, ridiculous. **trick** plaything 52 **play** play with
59 **Sport** a joke

Has made thee swell thus.   [*Mamillius is led out.*]

HERMIONE   But I'd say he had not,   63
And I'll be sworn you would believe my saying,
Howe'er you lean to the nayward.

LEONTES   You, my lords,   65
Look on her, mark her well. Be but about
To say "She is a goodly lady," and   67
The justice of your hearts will thereto add
"'Tis pity she's not honest, honorable."   69
Praise her but for this her without-door form,   70
Which on my faith deserves high speech, and
   straight   71
The shrug, the hum or ha, these petty brands   72
That calumny doth use—O, I am out,   73
That mercy does, for calumny will sear   74
Virtue itself—these shrugs, these hums and ha's,
When you have said she's goodly, come between   76
Ere you can say she's honest. But be 't known,
From him that has most cause to grieve it should be,
She's an adulteress.

HERMIONE   Should a villain say so,
The most replenished villain in the world,   80
He were as much more villain. You, my lord,   81
Do but mistake.

LEONTES   You have mistook, my lady, 82
Polixenes for Leontes. O thou thing!
Which I'll not call a creature of thy place,   84
Lest barbarism, making me the precedent,
Should a like language use to all degrees   86
And mannerly distinguishment leave out   87
Betwixt the prince and beggar. I have said
She's an adulteress; I have said with whom.
More, she's a traitor, and Camillo is
A fedarie with her, and one that knows   91
What she should shame to know herself   92
But with her most vile principal, that she's   93
A bed-swerver, even as bad as those   94
That vulgars give bold'st titles, ay, and privy   95
To this their late escape.

HERMIONE   No, by my life,
Privy to none of this. How will this grieve you,
When you shall come to clearer knowledge, that
You thus have published me! Gentle my lord,   99
You scarce can right me throughly then to say   100

63 **I'd** I need only 65 **nayward** negative, opposite 67 **goodly**
attractive 69 **honest** chaste 70 **without-door** outward, external
71 **straight** straightway, at once 72 **brands** i.e., signs, stigmas
73 **out** wrong, in error 74 **does** uses. (Leontes' point is that no
one commits calumny by suggesting with a shrug that Hermione is
unchaste; calumny attacks *virtue itself*, whereas Hermione has
only the false appearance of virtue.) 76 **come between** interrupt
80 **replenished** complete 81 **He . . . villain** his saying so would
double his villainy 82 **mistook** taken wrongly (playing bitterly on
mistake, "misapprehend") 84 **Which . . . place** (The King will not
desecrate Hermione's exalted rank by calling her what she really is.)
86 **degrees** social ranks 87 **mannerly distinguishment** polite distinctions 91 **fedarie** confederate 92–93 **to know . . . principal** to
acknowledge privately even with her contemptible partner 94 **bed-
swerver** adulteress 95 **vulgars . . . titles** common people call
by the rudest names. **privy** in on the secret 99 **published** proclaimed. **Gentle my** my noble 100 **throughly** thoroughly. **to say**
by saying

You did mistake.

LEONTES   No. If I mistake
In those foundations which I build upon,
The center is not big enough to bear   103
A schoolboy's top.—Away with her to prison!
He who shall speak for her is afar off guilty   105
But that he speaks.

HERMIONE   There's some ill planet reigns. 106
I must be patient till the heavens look
With an aspect more favorable. Good my lords,
I am not prone to weeping, as our sex
Commonly are, the want of which vain dew
Perchance shall dry your pities; but I have
That honorable grief lodged here which burns
Worse than tears drown. Beseech you all, my lords,
With thoughts so qualified as your charities   114
Shall best instruct you, measure me; and so   115
The King's will be performed!

LEONTES   Shall I be heard?   116

HERMIONE
Who is 't that goes with me? Beseech Your Highness
My women may be with me, for you see
My plight requires it.—Do not weep, good fools;   119
There is no cause. When you shall know your
    mistress
Has deserved prison, then abound in tears
As I come out. This action I now go on   122
Is for my better grace.—Adieu, my lord.   123
I never wished to see you sorry; now
I trust I shall. My women, come, you have leave.

LEONTES   Go, do our bidding. Hence!
                        [Exit Queen, guarded, with Ladies.]

A LORD
Beseech Your Highness, call the Queen again.

ANTIGONUS
Be certain what you do, sir, lest your justice
Prove violence, in the which three great ones suffer:
Yourself, your queen, your son.

A LORD   For her, my lord,
I dare my life lay down and will do 't, sir,
Please you t' accept it, that the Queen is spotless
I' th' eyes of heaven and to you—I mean
In this which you accuse her.

ANTIGONUS   If it prove
She's otherwise, I'll keep my stables where   135
I lodge my wife. I'll go in couples with her;   136
Than when I feel and see her no farther trust her.   137
For every inch of woman in the world,
Ay, every dram of woman's flesh is false,
If she be.

LEONTES   Hold your peaces.

A LORD   Good my lord—   140

ANTIGONUS
It is for you we speak, not for ourselves.
You are abused, and by some putter-on   142
That will be damned for 't. Would I knew the
    villain;
I would land-damn him. Be she honor-flawed,   144
I have three daughters—the eldest is eleven,
The second and the third, nine and some five—   146
If this prove true, they'll pay for 't. By mine honor,
I'll geld 'em all! Fourteen they shall not see
To bring false generations. They are co-heirs,   149
And I had rather glib myself than they   150
Should not produce fair issue.

LEONTES   Cease, no more!   151
You smell this business with a sense as cold
As is a dead man's nose; but I do see 't and feel 't
As you feel doing thus, and see withal   154
The instruments that feel.

ANTIGONUS   If it be so,   155
We need no grave to bury honesty;
There's not a grain of it the face to sweeten
Of the whole dungy earth.

LEONTES   What? Lack I credit?   158

A LORD
I had rather you did lack than I, my lord,
Upon this ground; and more it would content me   160
To have her honor true than your suspicion,
Be blamed for 't how you might.

LEONTES   Why, what need we   162
Commune with you of this, but rather follow
Our forceful instigation? Our prerogative   164
Calls not your counsels, but our natural goodness   165
Imparts this; which if you—or stupefied   166
Or seeming so in skill—cannot or will not   167
Relish a truth like us, inform yourselves   168
We need no more of your advice. The matter,
The loss, the gain, the ordering on 't, is all   170
Properly ours.

ANTIGONUS   And I wish, my liege,
You had only in your silent judgment tried it,
Without more overture.

LEONTES   How could that be?   173
Either thou art most ignorant by age,   174
Or thou wert born a fool. Camillo's flight,
Added to their familiarity—

103 **center** earth   105 **afar off** indirectly   106 **But . . . speaks**
merely by speaking   114 **qualified** tempered   115 **measure** judge
116 **heard** i.e., obeyed   119 **fools** (Here, a term of endearment.)
122 **come out** am released from prison   122–123 **The action . . .
grace** what I now must undergo will ultimately make me seem more
gracious in others' eyes and ennoble me by suffering   135–136 **I'll
. . . wife** (If Hermione is an adulteress, says Antigonus, then all
women are no better than animals, to be penned up and guarded suspiciously.)   136 **in couples** i.e., like two hounds leashed together and
hence inseparable   137 **Than . . . her** trust her no further than I can
feel her next to me and actually see her

140 **she** i.e., Hermione   142 **abused** deceived.   **putter-on** instigator
144 **land-damn** lambaste (? Meaning uncertain.)   146 **some** about
149 **bring false generations** have illegitimate children.   **They are co-
heirs** i.e., they will share my inheritance (since I have no son to inherit all)   150 **glib** castrate, geld   151 **fair** legitimate   154 **thus** (Leontes presumably grasps Antigonus by the arm or pinches him or
tweaks his nose.)   **withal** in addition   155 **instruments** i.e., Leontes'
fingers   158 **credit** credibility   160 **Upon this ground** in this matter
162 **we** I. (The royal "we.")   164 **instigation** incentive
164–166 **Our prerogative . . . this** my royal prerogative is under no
obligation to consult you, but rather out of natural generosity I inform
you of the matter   166 **or** either   167 **Or . . . skill** or pretending to
be stupefied out of cunning   168 **Relish** savor, appreciate   170 **on 't**
of it   173 **overture** public disclosure   174 **by age** through the folly of
old age

Which was as gross as ever touched conjecture,   177
That lacked sight only, naught for approbation   178
But only seeing, all other circumstances
Made up to th' deed—doth push on this
    proceeding.   180
Yet, for a greater confirmation—
For in an act of this importance 'twere
Most piteous to be wild—I have dispatched in post   183
To sacred Delphos, to Apollo's temple,   184
Cleomenes and Dion, whom you know
Of stuffed sufficiency. Now from the oracle   186
They will bring all, whose spiritual counsel had   187
Shall stop or spur me. Have I done well?

A LORD   Well done, my lord.

LEONTES
Though I am satisfied, and need no more
Than what I know, yet shall the oracle
Give rest to the minds of others, such as he   192
Whose ignorant credulity will not
Come up to th' truth. So have we thought it good   194
From our free person she should be confined,   195
Lest that the treachery of the two fled hence   196
Be left her to perform. Come, follow us.
We are to speak in public, for this business
Will raise us all.

ANTIGONUS [aside]   To laughter, as I take it,   199
If the good truth were known.   Exeunt.

❖

2.2
   Enter Paulina, a Gentleman, [and attendants].

PAULINA
The keeper of the prison, call to him.
Let him have knowledge who I am. [*Gentleman goes*
   to the door.] Good lady,   2
No court in Europe is too good for thee;
What dost thou then in prison?

      [*Enter*] *Jailer.*

                Now, good sir,
You know me, do you not?

JAILER   For a worthy lady
And one who much I honor.

PAULINA   Pray you then,
Conduct me to the Queen.

JAILER   I may not, madam.
To the contrary I have express commandment.

PAULINA
Here's ado, to lock up honesty and honor from

Th' access of gentle visitors! Is 't lawful, pray you,
To see her women? Any of them? Emilia?

JAILER   So please you, madam,
To put apart these your attendants, I   13
Shall bring Emilia forth.

PAULINA   I pray now, call her.—
Withdraw yourselves.
      [*Gentleman and attendants withdraw.*]

JAILER   And, madam,
I must be present at your conference.

PAULINA   Well, be 't so, prithee.   [*Exit Jailer.*]
Here's such ado, to make no stain a stain
As passes coloring.

    [*Enter Jailer, with*] *Emilia.*

                Dear gentlewoman,   20
How fares our gracious lady?

EMILIA
As well as one so great and so forlorn
May hold together. On her frights and griefs—   23
Which never tender lady hath borne greater—   24
She is something before her time delivered.   25

PAULINA
A boy?

EMILIA   A daughter, and a goodly babe,
Lusty and like to live. The Queen receives   27
Much comfort in 't, says, "My poor prisoner,
I am innocent as you."

PAULINA   I dare be sworn.
These dangerous unsafe lunes i' the King, beshrew
   them!   30
He must be told on 't, and he shall. The office   31
Becomes a woman best; I'll take 't upon me.   32
If I prove honeymouthed, let my tongue blister   33
And never to my red-looked anger be   34
The trumpet any more. Pray you, Emilia,
Commend my best obedience to the Queen.   36
If she dares trust me with her little babe,
I'll show 't the King and undertake to be
Her advocate to th' loud'st. We do not know   39
How he may soften at the sight o' the child.
The silence often of pure innocence
Persuades when speaking fails.

EMILIA   Most worthy madam,
Your honor and your goodness is so evident
That your free undertaking cannot miss   44
A thriving issue. There is no lady living   45
So meet for this great errand. Please your ladyship   46
To visit the next room, I'll presently   47
Acquaint the Queen of your most noble offer,
Who but today hammered of this design,   49

---

177 as gross . . . conjecture as palpably evident as any conjecture ever touched upon and verified **178 approbation** proof **180 Made up** added up. **push on** urge onward **183 wild** rash. **post** haste **184 Delphos** (See note at 3.1.2.) **186 Of stuffed sufficiency** abundantly qualified and trustworthy **187 all** the whole truth. **had** having been obtained **192 he** any person (such as Antigonus) **194 Come up to** face **195 From** away from. **free** accessible **196 treachery** i.e., suspected plot to murder Leontes (see line 47) **199 raise** rouse
2.2. Location: Sicilia. A prison.
2 Good lady (Addressed to the absent Hermione.)

13 put apart dismiss **20 passes coloring** surpasses any justification, passes all excuse (with a pun on *stain*, "coloring," in the previous line) **23 On** in consequence of **24 Which** than which **25 something** somewhat (also in line 55) **27 Lusty** vigorous. **like** likely **30 lunes** fits of lunacy **31 on 't** of it **32 Becomes** suits **33 blister** (It was popularly supposed that lying blistered the tongue.) **34 red-looked** red-faced **36 Commend** deliver **39 to th' loud'st** as loudly as I can **44 free** generous **45 thriving issue** successful outcome **46 meet** suited. **Please** if it please **47 presently** at once **49 hammered of** formulated, conceived

But durst not tempt a minister of honor   50
Lest she should be denied.

PAULINA   Tell her, Emilia,
I'll use that tongue I have. If wit flow from 't   52
As boldness from my bosom, let 't not be doubted
I shall do good.

EMILIA   Now be you blest for it!
I'll to the Queen.—Please you, come something
    nearer.   55

JAILER
Madam, if 't please the Queen to send the babe,
I know not what I shall incur to pass it,   57
Having no warrant.

PAULINA   You need not fear it, sir.
This child was prisoner to the womb and is
By law and process of great Nature thence
Freed and enfranchised, not a party to
The anger of the King nor guilty of,
If any be, the trespass of the Queen.   63

JAILER   I do believe it.

PAULINA
Do not you fear. Upon mine honor, I
Will stand betwixt you and danger.   *Exeunt.*

✿

2.3   *Enter Leontes.*

LEONTES
Nor night nor day, no rest! It is but weakness
To bear the matter thus, mere weakness. If
The cause were not in being—part o' the cause,   3
She th' adulteress, for the harlot King   4
Is quite beyond mine arm, out of the blank   5
And level of my brain, plot-proof, but she   6
I can hook to me—say that she were gone,   7
Given to the fire, a moiety of my rest   8
Might come to me again.—Who's there?

    [Enter a] Servant.

SERVANT   My lord?
LEONTES   How does the boy?
SERVANT
He took good rest tonight; 'tis hoped   11
His sickness is discharged.

LEONTES   To see his nobleness!
Conceiving the dishonor of his mother,   13
He straight declined, drooped, took it deeply,
Fastened and fixed the shame on 't in himself,   15
Threw off his spirit, his appetite, his sleep,

And downright languished.—Leave me solely. Go,   17
See how he fares. [*Exit Servant.*] Fie, fie! No
    thought of him.   18
The very thought of my revenges that way
Recoil upon me—in himself too mighty,
And in his parties, his alliance. Let him be,
Until a time may serve. For present vengeance,
Take it on her. Camillo and Polixenes
Laugh at me, make their pastime at my sorrow.
They should not laugh if I could reach them, nor
Shall she, within my power.

    *Enter Paulina [with a baby]; Antigonus and Lords
    [and a Servant, trying to hold her back].*

A LORD   You must not enter.
PAULINA
Nay, rather, good my lords, be second to me.   27
Fear you his tyrannous passion more, alas,
Than the Queen's life? A gracious innocent soul,
More free than he is jealous.

ANTIGONUS   That's enough.   30
SERVANT
Madam, he hath not slept tonight, commanded
None should come at him.

PAULINA   Not so hot, good sir.
I come to bring him sleep. 'Tis such as you,
That creep like shadows by him and do sigh
At each his needless heavings, such as you   35
Nourish the cause of his awaking. I   36
Do come with words as medicinal as true,
Honest as either, to purge him of that humor   38
That presses him from sleep.

LEONTES   What noise there, ho?
PAULINA
No noise, my lord, but needful conference
About some gossips for Your Highness.

LEONTES   How?   41
Away with that audacious lady! Antigonus,
I charged thee that she should not come about me.
I knew she would.

ANTIGONUS   I told her so, my lord,
On your displeasure's peril and on mine,
She should not visit you.

LEONTES   What, canst not rule her?
PAULINA
From all dishonesty he can. In this,
Unless he take the course that you have done—
Commit me for committing honor—trust it,   49
He shall not rule me.

ANTIGONUS   La you now, you hear!   50
When she will take the rein I let her run,
But she'll not stumble.

PAULINA   Good my liege, I come—
And, I beseech you hear me, who professes
Myself your loyal servant, your physician,

---

50 tempt solicit (to serve as ambassador in such a case) **52 wit** wisdom **55 come . . . nearer** i.e., come into the next room (as in lines 46–47) **57 to pass it** if I let it pass **63 If any be** if there be any guilt

2.3. Location: Sicilia. The royal court.
3 not in being dead **4 harlot** lewd. (Originally applied to either sex.) **5–6 out . . . level** beyond the range. (Archery terms: *blank* is the center of the target or the close range needed for a direct shot at it, as in "point-blank"; *level* is the action of aiming.) **7 hook** (as with grappling hooks) **8 Given to the fire** burned at the stake (as a traitor conspiring against the King). **moiety** portion **11 tonight** last night **13 Conceiving** grasping the enormity of **15 on 't** of it

17 solely alone **18 him** i.e., Polixenes **27 be second to** aid, second **30 free** innocent **35 heavings** sighs or groans **36 awaking** inability to sleep **38 humor** distemper **41 gossips** godparents for the baby at its baptism **49 Commit** i.e., to prison **50 La . . . hear** i.e., there now, you hear how she will go on talking

Your most obedient counselor, yet that dares
Less appear so in comforting your evils   56
Than such as most seem yours—I say, I come   57
From your good queen.

LEONTES   Good queen?

PAULINA
Good queen, my lord, good queen, I say good
    queen,
And would by combat make her good, so were I   61
A man, the worst about you.

LEONTES   Force her hence.   62

PAULINA
Let him that makes but trifles of his eyes
First hand me. On mine own accord I'll off,
But first I'll do my errand. The good Queen,
For she is good, hath brought you forth a
    daughter—
Here 'tis—commends it to your blessing.
                            [*She lays down the baby.*]

LEONTES   Out!
A mankind witch! Hence with her, out o' door!   68
A most intelligencing bawd!

PAULINA   Not so.   69
I am as ignorant in that as you
In so entitling me, and no less honest
Than you are mad; which is enough, I'll warrant,
As this world goes, to pass for honest.

LEONTES   Traitors!
Will you not push her out? [*To Antigonus.*] Give her
    the bastard.
Thou dotard, thou art woman-tired, unroosted   75
By thy Dame Partlet here. Take up the bastard!   76
Take 't up, I say. Give 't to thy crone.

PAULINA [*to Antigonus*]   Forever
Unvenerable be thy hands if thou
Tak'st up the Princess by that forcèd baseness   79
Which he has put upon 't!

LEONTES   He dreads his wife.

PAULINA
So I would you did. Then 'twere past all doubt
You'd call your children yours.

LEONTES   A nest of traitors!

ANTIGONUS
I am none, by this good light.

PAULINA   Nor I, nor any   83
But one that's here, and that's himself; for he
The sacred honor of himself, his queen's,
His hopeful son's, his babe's, betrays to slander,

Whose sting is sharper than the sword's; and will
    not—
For, as the case now stands, it is a curse   88
He cannot be compelled to 't—once remove   89
The root of his opinion, which is rotten   90
As ever oak or stone was sound.

LEONTES   A callet   91
Of boundless tongue, who late hath beat her
    husband
And now baits me! This brat is none of mine;   93
It is the issue of Polixenes.
Hence with it, and together with the dam
Commit them to the fire!

PAULINA   It is yours;
And, might we lay th' old proverb to your charge,
So like you, 'tis the worse. Behold, my lords,   98
Although the print be little, the whole matter
And copy of the father—eye, nose, lip,
The trick of 's frown, his forehead, nay, the valley,   101
The pretty dimples of his chin and cheek, his smiles,
The very mold and frame of hand, nail, finger.
And thou, good goddess Nature, which hast made it
So like to him that got it, if thou hast   105
The ordering of the mind too, 'mongst all colors
No yellow in 't, lest she suspect, as he does,   107
Her children not her husband's!

LEONTES   A gross hag!
And, lozel, thou art worthy to be hanged,   109
That wilt not stay her tongue.

ANTIGONUS   Hang all the husbands   110
That cannot do that feat, you'll leave yourself
Hardly one subject.

LEONTES   Once more, take her hence.

PAULINA
A most unworthy and unnatural lord
Can do no more.

LEONTES   I'll ha' thee burnt.

PAULINA   I care not.
It is an heretic that makes the fire,   115
Not she which burns in 't. I'll not call you tyrant;   116
But this most cruel usage of your queen,
Not able to produce more accusation   118
Than your own weak-hinged fancy, something
    savors
Of tyranny and will ignoble make you,

56–57 in comforting . . . yours when it comes to encouraging your evil courses than those flatterers who seem to be your most loyal servants **61 by combat** by trial by combat. **make** prove **62 worst** least manly, or, lowest in rank **68 mankind** masculine, behaving like a man **69 intelligencing bawd** acting as go-between and spy (for the Queen and Polixenes) **75 woman-tired** henpecked. (From *tire* in falconry, meaning "tear with the beak.") **unroosted** driven from perch **76 Partlet** or Pertilote, a common name for a hen (as in *Reynard the Fox* and in Chaucer's "Nun's Priest's Tale") **79 by that forcèd baseness** under that wrongfully imposed name of bastard **83 by this good light** by the light of day, or, by my eyesight. (A common oath.)

88–90 as . . . opinion i.e., since he is King, it's a shame he can't be compelled to change his deeply rooted opinion **91 callet** scold **93 baits** (With a pun on *beat* in the previous line, pronounced "bate.") **98 So . . . worse** he's so like you that he fares the worse for it **101 trick** characteristic expression. **valley** indentation between nose and lip (?) **105 got** begot **107 No yellow** let there be no yellow, i.e., the color of jealousy. (A chaste woman could hardly expect that her own children are illegitimate, but Paulina may be hyperbolically ridiculing Leontes' suspicions.) **109 lozel** worthless person, scoundrel. (Addressed to Antigonus.) **110 stay** restrain **115–116 It is . . . in 't** i.e., in burning me, you who would be making or building the fire are the heretic, not me (since loss of faith in innocence is a kind of heresy), or, you can burn a woman if you like, but it's a heretic's fire only if she is, in fact, a heretic **118 Not able** you not being able

Yea, scandalous to the world.
LEONTES [*to Antigonus*]   On your allegiance,
  Out of the chamber with her! Were I a tyrant,
  Where were her life? She durst not call me so   123
  If she did know me one. Away with her!
PAULINA
  I pray you, do not push me; I'll be gone.
  Look to your babe, my lord; 'tis yours. Jove send her
  A better guiding spirit!—What needs these hands?   127
  You that are thus so tender o'er his follies
  Will never do him good, not one of you.
  So, so. Farewell, we are gone.   *Exit.*
LEONTES [*to Antigonus*]
  Thou, traitor, hast set on thy wife to this.
  My child? Away with 't! Even thou, that hast
  A heart so tender o'er it, take it hence
  And see it instantly consumed with fire;
  Even thou and none but thou. Take it up straight.
  Within this hour bring me word 'tis done,
  And by good testimony, or I'll seize thy life,
  With what thou else call'st thine. If thou refuse
  And wilt encounter with my wrath, say so;
  The bastard brains with these my proper hands   140
  Shall I dash out. Go, take it to the fire,
  For thou sett'st on thy wife.
ANTIGONUS   I did not, sir.
  These lords, my noble fellows, if they please,
  Can clear me in 't.
LORDS   We can. My royal liege,
  He is not guilty of her coming hither.
LEONTES   You're liars all.
A LORD
  Beseech Your Highness, give us better credit.   147
  We have always truly served you, and beseech'   148
  So to esteem of us; and on our knees we beg,
  As recompense of our dear services   150
  Past and to come, that you do change this purpose,
  Which being so horrible, so bloody, must
  Lead on to some foul issue. We all kneel.
LEONTES
  I am a feather for each wind that blows.
  Shall I live on to see this bastard kneel
  And call me father? Better burn it now
  Than curse it then. But be it; let it live.
  It shall not neither. [*To Antigonus.*] You, sir, come
    you hither,
  You that have been so tenderly officious
  With Lady Margery, your midwife there,   160
  To save this bastard's life—for 'tis a bastard,
  So sure as this beard's gray. What will you
    adventure   162
  To save this brat's life?
ANTIGONUS   Anything, my lord,

That my ability may undergo
And nobleness impose. At least thus much:
I'll pawn the little blood which I have left
To save the innocent—anything possible.
LEONTES [*holding his sword*]
  It shall be possible. Swear by this sword
  Thou wilt perform my bidding.
ANTIGONUS [*his hand on the hilt*]   I will, my lord.
LEONTES
  Mark and perform it, seest thou; for the fail   170
  Of any point in 't shall not only be
  Death to thyself but to thy lewd-tongued wife,
  Whom for this time we pardon. We enjoin thee,
  As thou art liege man to us, that thou carry
  This female bastard hence, and that thou bear it
  To some remote and desert place quite out
  Of our dominions, and that there thou leave it,
  Without more mercy, to its own protection
  And favor of the climate. As by strange fortune
  It came to us, I do in justice charge thee,
  On thy soul's peril and thy body's torture,
  That thou commend it strangely to some place   182
  Where chance may nurse or end it. Take it up.
ANTIGONUS [*taking up the baby*]
  I swear to do this, though a present death
  Had been more merciful. Come on, poor babe.
  Some powerful spirit instruct the kites and ravens
  To be thy nurses! Wolves and bears, they say,
  Casting their savageness aside, have done
  Like offices of pity. Sir, be prosperous
  In more than this deed does require!—And blessing 190
  Against this cruelty fight on thy side,
  Poor thing, condemned to loss!   *Exit* [*with the baby*].
LEONTES   No, I'll not rear   192
  Another's issue.

        Enter a Servant.

SERVANT   Please Your Highness, posts   193
  From those you sent to th' oracle are come
  An hour since. Cleomenes and Dion,
  Being well arrived from Delphos, are both landed,
  Hasting to th' court.
A LORD   So please you, sir, their speed
  Hath been beyond account.
LEONTES   Twenty-three days   198
  They have been absent. 'Tis good speed, foretells
  The great Apollo suddenly will have   200
  The truth of this appear. Prepare you, lords.
  Summon a session, that we may arraign   202
  Our most disloyal lady; for, as she hath
  Been publicly accused, so shall she have
  A just and open trial. While she lives

---

123 Where . . . life how could she escape execution at my command?   **127 What . . . hands** what need is there to push me?
140 proper own   **147 credit** belief   **148 beseech'** beseech you
150 dear loyal, heartfelt   **160 Margery** (A derisive term, evidently equivalent to *Partlet* in line 76.)   **162 this beard's** (Probably Antigonus'.)

170 seest thou i.e., do you hear.   **fail** failure   **182 commend . . . place** commit it to some foreign place, or, as a stranger   **190 more** i.e., more ways, more extent.   **require** deserve   **192 loss** destruction
193 posts messengers   **198 beyond account** unprecedented, or, beyond explanation   **200 suddenly** at once   **202 session** trial

My heart will be a burden to me. Leave me,
And think upon my bidding.   *Exeunt [separately]*.

3.1   *Enter Cleomenes and Dion.*

CLEOMENES
The climate's delicate, the air most sweet,
Fertile the isle, the temple much surpassing   2
The common praise it bears.
DION   I shall report,
For most it caught me, the celestial habits—   4
Methinks I so should term them—and the
    reverence
Of the grave wearers. O, the sacrifice!
How ceremonious, solemn, and unearthly
It was i' th' offering!
CLEOMENES   But of all, the burst
And the ear-deafening voice o' th' oracle,
Kin to Jove's thunder, so surprised my sense   10
That I was nothing.
DION   If th' event o' the journey   11
Prove as successful to the Queen—O, be 't so!—
As it hath been to us rare, pleasant, speedy,
The time is worth the use on 't.
CLEOMENES   Great Apollo   14
Turn all to th' best! These proclamations,
So forcing faults upon Hermione,
I little like.
DION   The violent carriage of it   17
Will clear or end the business. When the oracle,
Thus by Apollo's great divine sealed up,   19
Shall the contents discover, something rare   20
Even then will rush to knowledge. Go. Fresh horses!
And gracious be the issue!   *Exeunt.*

3.2   *Enter Leontes, Lords, [and] Officers.*

LEONTES
This sessions, to our great grief we pronounce,
Even pushes 'gainst our heart: the party tried
The daughter of a king, our wife, and one
Of us too much beloved. Let us be cleared   4
Of being tyrannous, since we so openly
Proceed in justice, which shall have due course
Even to the guilt or the purgation.   7
Produce the prisoner.

OFFICER
It is His Highness' pleasure that the Queen
Appear in person here in court. Silence!

    *[Enter] Hermione, as to her trial, [Paulina, and]
    Ladies.*

LEONTES   Read the indictment.
OFFICER *[reads]* "Hermione, Queen to the worthy
Leontes, King of Sicilia, thou art here accused and ar-
raigned of high treason, in committing adultery with
Polixenes, King of Bohemia, and conspiring with
Camillo to take away the life of our sovereign lord the
King, thy royal husband; the pretense whereof being   17
by circumstances partly laid open, thou, Hermione,
contrary to the faith and allegiance of a true subject,
didst counsel and aid them, for their better safety, to
fly away by night."
HERMIONE
Since what I am to say must be but that
Which contradicts my accusation, and
The testimony on my part no other
But what comes from myself, it shall scarce boot me   25
To say "not guilty." Mine integrity,
Being counted falsehood, shall, as I express it,
Be so received. But thus: if powers divine
Behold our human actions, as they do,
I doubt not then but innocence shall make
False accusation blush and tyranny
Tremble at patience. You, my lord, best know,
Who least will seem to do so, my past life
Hath been as continent, as chaste, as true,
As I am now unhappy; which is more
Than history can pattern, though devised   36
And played to take spectators. For behold me—   37
A fellow of the royal bed, which owe   38
A moiety of the throne, a great king's daughter,   39
The mother to a hopeful prince—here standing
To prate and talk for life and honor 'fore
Who please to come and hear. For life, I prize it   42
As I weigh grief, which I would spare. For honor,   43
'Tis a derivative from me to mine,   44
And only that I stand for. I appeal   45
To your own conscience, sir, before Polixenes   46
Came to your court, how I was in your grace,
How merited to be so; since he came,
With what encounter so uncurrent I   49
Have strained t' appear thus; if one jot beyond   50
The bound of honor, or in act or will
That way inclining, hardened be the hearts
Of all that hear me, and my near'st of kin
Cry fie upon my grave!
LEONTES   I ne'er heard yet

3.1. Location: Sicilia. On the way to Leontes' court.
2 isle (Shakespeare follows Greene's *Pandosto* in fictitiously placing
Delphi on an island. Delphi, sometimes known as Delphos [see
2.1.184, 2.3.196, and 3.2.126], was often confused with Delos, the
island birthplace of Apollo and location also of an oracle.)   **4 habits**
vestments   **10 surprised** overwhelmed   **11 event** outcome   **14 is
worth . . . on 't** has been well employed   **17 carriage** execution,
management   **19 great divine** chief priest   **20 discover** reveal
3.2. Location: Sicilia. A place of justice, probably at court.
4 Of us by me   **7 purgation** clearing from the accusation

17 pretense purpose, design   **25 boot** avail   **36 history** story, drama.
pattern show a similar example for   **37 take** please, charm
38 which owe who owns   **39 moiety** share   **42 Who please** whoever
chooses   **42–45 For . . . stand for** as for life, I value it as I value
grief, and would as willingly do without; as for honor, it is transmitted
from me to my descendants, and that only I make a stand for
46 conscience consideration, inward knowledge   **49–50 With . . .
thus** (I ask) by what behavior so out of the ordinary I have transgressed so that I appear thus (in disgrace and on trial)

That any of these bolder vices wanted   55
Less impudence to gainsay what they did   56
Than to perform it first.
HERMIONE   That's true enough,
Though 'tis a saying, sir, not due to me.   58
LEONTES
You will not own it.
HERMIONE   More than mistress of   59
Which comes to me in name of fault, I must not   60
At all acknowledge. For Polixenes,   61
With whom I am accused, I do confess
I loved him as in honor he required;   63
With such a kind of love as might become
A lady like me; with a love even such,
So, and no other, as yourself commanded;
Which not to have done I think had been in me
Both disobedience and ingratitude
To you and toward your friend, whose love had
    spoke,   69
Even since it could speak, from an infant, freely   70
That it was yours. Now, for conspiracy,   71
I know not how it tastes, though it be dished   72
For me to try how. All I know of it
Is that Camillo was an honest man;
And why he left your court, the gods themselves,
Wotting no more than I, are ignorant.   76
LEONTES
You knew of his departure, as you know
What you have underta'en to do in 's absence.
HERMIONE   Sir,
You speak a language that I understand not.
My life stands in the level of your dreams,   81
Which I'll lay down.
LEONTES   Your actions are my dreams.   82
You had a bastard by Polixenes,
And I but dreamed it. As you were past all shame—
Those of your fact are so—so past all truth,   85
Which to deny concerns more than avails; for as   86
Thy brat hath been cast out, like to itself,   87
No father owning it—which is indeed
More criminal in thee than it—so thou
Shalt feel our justice, in whose easiest passage   90
Look for no less than death.
HERMIONE   Sir, spare your threats.   91
The bug which you would fright me with I seek.   92

To me can life be no commodity.   93
The crown and comfort of my life, your favor,
I do give lost, for I do feel it gone,   95
But know not how it went. My second joy
And firstfruits of my body, from his presence
I am barred, like one infectious. My third comfort,
Starred most unluckily, is from my breast,   99
The innocent milk in its most innocent mouth,
Haled out to murder; myself on every post   101
Proclaimed a strumpet; with immodest hatred   102
The childbed privilege denied, which longs   103
To women of all fashion; lastly, hurried   104
Here to this place, i' th' open air, before
I have got strength of limit. Now, my liege,   106
Tell me what blessings I have here alive
That I should fear to die? Therefore proceed.
But yet hear this; mistake me not. No life,   109
I prize it not a straw. But for mine honor,
Which I would free, if I shall be condemned
Upon surmises, all proofs sleeping else
But what your jealousies awake, I tell you
'Tis rigor and not law. Your honors all,   114
I do refer me to the oracle.
Apollo be my judge!
A LORD   This your request
Is altogether just. Therefore bring forth,
And in Apollo's name, his oracle.
                    [*Exeunt certain Officers.*]
HERMIONE
The Emperor of Russia was my father.
O, that he were alive and here beholding
His daughter's trial! That he did but see
The flatness of my misery, yet with eyes   122
Of pity, not revenge!

[*Enter Officers, with*] Cleomenes [*and*] Dion.

OFFICER [*holding a sword*]
You here shall swear upon this sword of justice
That you, Cleomenes and Dion, have
Been both at Delphos, and from thence have
    brought
This sealed-up oracle, by the hand delivered
Of great Apollo's priest, and that since then
You have not dared to break the holy seal
Nor read the secrets in 't.
CLEOMENES, DION   All this we swear.
LEONTES
Break up the seals and read.   131
OFFICER [*reads*]   "Hermione is chaste, Polixenes blameless, Camillo a true subject, Leontes a jealous tyrant, his innocent babe truly begotten, and the King shall live without an heir if that which is lost be not found."

55–56 **wanted Less** were more lacking in   58 **due** applicable
59–61 **More . . . acknowledge** I will not acknowledge that I am answerable for more than what may be called ordinary human faults. (Hermione insists she is not guilty of the *bolder vices* of line 55.)
61 **For** as for   63 **required** deserved   69–71 **your friend . . . yours** i.e., Polixenes, who professed love for you from earliest childhood (as you for him)   71 **for** as for   72 **dished** served up   76 **Wotting** supposing they know   81 **level** aim, range   82 **Which** i.e., my life.
Your . . . dreams i.e., you have performed what I have fantasized, and what you have done preys on my mind   85 **Those of your fact** all those who do what you did   86 **concerns . . . avails** may seem an understandable concern on your part but will not help
87 **like to itself** as an outcast, fatherless brat ought to be   90–91 **in whose . . . death** i.e., which will impose the death sentence at least, perhaps torture also   92 **bug** bugbear, bogey, imaginary object of terror

93 **commodity** asset   95 **give** reckon as, or give up for   99 **Starred most unluckily** born under a most unlucky star   101 **post** posting place for public notices   102 **immodest** immoderate   103 **longs belongs**, i.e., is fitting   104 **all fashion** every rank   106 **got . . . limit** i.e., regained my strength after having borne a child   109 **No life** i.e., I do not ask for life   114 **rigor** tyranny   122 **flatness** absoluteness   131 **up** open

LORDS
Now blessèd be the great Apollo!

HERMIONE   Praised!

LEONTES
Hast thou read truth?

OFFICER   Ay, my lord, even so
As it is here set down.

LEONTES
There is no truth at all i' th' oracle.
The sessions shall proceed. This is mere falsehood.

[Enter a Servant.]

SERVANT
My lord the King, the King!

LEONTES   What is the business?

SERVANT
O sir, I shall be hated to report it!   143
The Prince your son, with mere conceit and fear   144
Of the Queen's speed, is gone.

LEONTES   How? Gone?

SERVANT   Is dead.   145

LEONTES
Apollo's angry, and the heavens themselves
Do strike at my injustice. *[Hermione swoons.]* How
    now there?

PAULINA
This news is mortal to the Queen. Look down
And see what death is doing.

LEONTES   Take her hence.
Her heart is but o'ercharged; she will recover.
I have too much believed mine own suspicion.
Beseech you, tenderly apply to her
Some remedies for life.
          [Exeunt Paulina and Ladies, with Hermione.]
                              Apollo, pardon
My great profaneness 'gainst thine oracle!
I'll reconcile me to Polixenes,
New woo my queen, recall the good Camillo,
Whom I proclaim a man of truth, of mercy;
For, being transported by my jealousies
To bloody thoughts and to revenge, I chose
Camillo for the minister to poison
My friend Polixenes; which had been done,
But that the good mind of Camillo tardied   162
My swift command, though I with death and with
Reward did threaten and encourage him,
Not doing it and being done. He, most humane   165
And filled with honor, to my kingly guest
Unclasped my practice, quit his fortunes here,   167
Which you knew great, and to the hazard
Of all incertainties himself commended,   169
No richer than his honor. How he glisters   170
Through my rust! And how his piety

143 to report for reporting   **144 conceit and fear** i.e., anxious concern   **145 speed** fate, fortune   **162 tardied** delayed   **165 Not . . . done** i.e., death if he did not do it and reward if he did   **167 Unclasped my practice** disclosed my plot   **169 himself commended** entrusted himself   **170 No richer than** with no riches except.   **glisters** shines

Does my deeds make the blacker!

[Enter Paulina.]

PAULINA   Woe the while!
O, cut my lace, lest my heart, cracking it,   173
Break too!

A LORD   What fit is this, good lady?

PAULINA
What studied torments, tyrant, hast for me?
What wheels, racks, fires? What flaying, boiling
In leads or oils? What old or newer torture
Must I receive, whose every word deserves
To taste of thy most worst? Thy tyranny,
Together working with thy jealousies—
Fancies too weak for boys, too green and idle   181
For girls of nine—O, think what they have done,
And then run mad indeed, stark mad! For all
Thy bygone fooleries were but spices of it.   184
That thou betrayedst Polixenes, 'twas nothing;
That did but show thee, of a fool, inconstant   186
And damnable ingrateful. Nor was 't much
Thou wouldst have poisoned good Camillo's honor,
To have him kill a king—poor trespasses,   189
More monstrous standing by; whereof I reckon   190
The casting forth to crows thy baby daughter
To be or none or little, though a devil   192
Would have shed water out of fire ere done 't.   193
Nor is 't directly laid to thee, the death
Of the young Prince, whose honorable thoughts,
Thoughts high for one so tender, cleft the heart   196
That could conceive a gross and foolish sire   197
Blemished his gracious dam. This is not, no,
Laid to thy answer. But the last—O lords,
When I have said, cry woe! The Queen, the Queen,   200
The sweet'st, dear'st creature's dead, and vengeance
    for 't
Not dropped down yet.

A LORD   The higher powers forbid!

PAULINA
I say she's dead. I'll swear 't. If word nor oath
Prevail not, go and see. If you can bring
Tincture or luster in her lip, her eye,
Heat outwardly or breath within, I'll serve you
As I would do the gods. But, O thou tyrant!
Do not repent these things, for they are heavier
Than all thy woes can stir. Therefore betake thee   209
To nothing but despair. A thousand knees
Ten thousand years together, naked, fasting,
Upon a barren mountain, and still winter   212
In storm perpetual, could not move the gods
To look that way thou wert.

LEONTES   Go on, go on.   214

173 my lace the lace of my stays   **181 idle** foolish   **184 spices** foretastes, samples   **186 of a fool, inconstant** i.e., being a fool naturally and then inconstant into the bargain   **189 To have** by having.   **poor slight**   **190 More . . . by** when more monstrous sins are at hand for comparison   **192 or none** either none   **193 shed . . . fire** wept from his fiery eyes or while surrounded by hellfire   **196 tender** young   **197 conceive** apprehend that   **200 said** finished speaking   **209 woes can stir** penance can remove   **212 still** always   **214 To look . . . wert** to regard you

Thou canst not speak too much. I have deserved
All tongues to talk their bitt'rest.

A LORD [*to Paulina*]   Say no more.
Howe'er the business goes, you have made fault
I' the boldness of your speech.

PAULINA   I am sorry for 't.
All faults I make, when I shall come to know them,   219
I do repent. Alas, I have showed too much
The rashness of a woman! He is touched
To th' noble heart. What's gone and what's past
help
Should be past grief.—Do not receive affliction   223
At my petition. I beseech you, rather   224
Let me be punished, that have minded you   225
Of what you should forget. Now, good my liege,
Sir, royal sir, forgive a foolish woman.
The love I bore your queen—lo, fool again!
I'll speak of her no more, nor of your children;
I'll not remember you of my own lord,   230
Who is lost too. Take your patience to you,   231
And I'll say nothing.

LEONTES   Thou didst speak but well
When most the truth, which I receive much better
Than to be pitied of thee. Prithee, bring me
To the dead bodies of my queen and son.
One grave shall be for both. Upon them shall
The causes of their death appear, unto
Our shame perpetual. Once a day I'll visit
The chapel where they lie, and tears shed there
Shall be my recreation. So long as nature
Will bear up with this exercise, so long
I daily vow to use it. Come and lead me
To these sorrows.   *Exeunt.*

❋

3.3   *Enter Antigonus [and] a Mariner, [with a] babe.*

ANTIGONUS
Thou art perfect then, our ship hath touched upon   1
The deserts of Bohemia?

MARINER   Ay, my lord, and fear   2
We have landed in ill time. The skies look grimly
And threaten present blusters. In my conscience,   4
The heavens with that we have in hand are angry
And frown upon 's.

ANTIGONUS
Their sacred wills be done! Go, get aboard;
Look to thy bark. I'll not be long before
I call upon thee.

MARINER   Make your best haste, and go not
Too far i' the land. 'Tis like to be loud weather.   10

Besides, this place is famous for the creatures
Of prey that keep upon 't.

ANTIGONUS   Go thou away.   12
I'll follow instantly.

MARINER   I am glad at heart
To be so rid o' the business.   [*Exit.*]

ANTIGONUS   Come, poor babe.
I have heard, but not believed, the spirits o' the dead
May walk again. If such thing be, thy mother
Appeared to me last night, for ne'er was dream
So like a waking. To me comes a creature,
Sometimes her head on one side, some another;   19
I never saw a vessel of like sorrow,
So filled and so becoming. In pure white robes,   21
Like very sanctity, she did approach
My cabin where I lay, thrice bowed before me,
And, gasping to begin some speech, her eyes
Became two spouts. The fury spent, anon
Did this break from her: "Good Antigonus,
Since fate, against thy better disposition,
Hath made thy person for the thrower-out
Of my poor babe, according to thine oath,
Places remote enough are in Bohemia;
There weep and leave it crying. And, for the babe   31
Is counted lost forever, Perdita,   32
I prithee, call 't. For this ungentle business   33
Put on thee by my lord, thou ne'er shalt see
Thy wife Paulina more." And so, with shrieks,
She melted into air. Affrighted much,
I did in time collect myself and thought
This was so and no slumber. Dreams are toys;   38
Yet for this once, yea, superstitiously,
I will be squared by this. I do believe   40
Hermione hath suffered death, and that
Apollo would, this being indeed the issue
Of King Polixenes, it should here be laid,
Either for life or death, upon the earth
Of its right father. Blossom, speed thee well!
                           [*He lays down the baby.*]
There lie, and there thy character; there these,   46
        [*He places a box and a fardel beside the baby.*]
Which may, if fortune please, both breed thee,
   pretty,   47
And still rest thine. [*Thunder.*] The storm begins.
   Poor wretch,   48
That for thy mother's fault art thus exposed
To loss and what may follow! Weep I cannot,   50

---

219 I make that I make   **223–224 Do . . . petition** do not afflict
yourself with remorse at my urging   **225 minded you** put you in mind
230 remember remind   **231 Take . . . you** arm yourself with patience
3.3. Location: Bohemia. The seacoast.
1 perfect certain   **2 deserts of Bohemia** i.e., deserted region on the
coast. (Shakespeare follows Greene's *Pandosto* in giving Bohemia a
seacoast.)   **4 present** immediate.   **conscience** opinion   **10 like**
likely.   **loud** stormy

12 keep upon 't inhabit it   **19 some another** sometimes the other
21 So . . . becoming i.e., so filled with sorrow and able to bear it so
gracefully   **31 for** because   **32 Perdita** i.e., the lost one   **33 ungentle** ignoble   **38 toys** trifles   **40 squared** directed in my course
46 thy character the written account of you (i.e., the one that subsequently will serve to identify Perdita).   **these** i.e., the gold and jewels
found by the Shepherd, also later used to identify her.   **s.d. box,
fardel** (The box, containing gold and jewels, is later produced by the
old Shepherd and the Clown; see 4.4.758–759. They also have a
fardel, or "bundle," consisting evidently of the bearing cloth
[3.3.112] and/or mantle [5.2.34] in which the babe was found.)
47 breed thee keep you, pay for your support.   **pretty** pretty one
48 And still rest thine i.e., and still provide a heritage with what is
unspent   **50 To loss** to being lost.   **Weep I cannot** i.e., I cannot
weep as the Queen instructed me (line 31)

But my heart bleeds; and most accurst am I
To be by oath enjoined to this. Farewell!
The day frowns more and more. Thou'rt like to have
A lullaby too rough. I never saw
The heavens so dim by day. A savage clamor!
Well may I get aboard! This is the chase.
I am gone forever.   *Exit, pursued by a bear.*

                [Enter a] Shepherd.

SHEPHERD   I would there were no age between ten and
three-and-twenty, or that youth would sleep out the
rest, for there is nothing in the between but getting
wenches with child, wronging the ancientry, stealing, 61
fighting—Hark you now, would any but these boiled 62
brains of nineteen and two-and-twenty hunt this 63
weather? They have scared away two of my best sheep,
which I fear the wolf will sooner find than the master.
If anywhere I have them, 'tis by the seaside, browsing
of ivy. Good luck, an 't be thy will! [*Seeing the child.*] 67
What have we here? Mercy on 's, a bairn, a very pretty 68
bairn! A boy or a child, I wonder? A pretty one, a very 69
pretty one. Sure some scape. Though I am not bookish, 70
yet I can read waiting-gentlewoman in the scape.
This has been some stair-work, some trunk-work, 72
some behind-door-work. They were warmer that got 73
this than the poor thing is here. I'll take it up for pity.
Yet I'll tarry till my son come; he hallooed but even
now.—Whoa, ho, hoa!   76

                Enter Clown.

CLOWN   Hilloa, loa!
SHEPHERD   What, art so near? If thou'lt see a thing to
talk on when thou art dead and rotten, come hither.
What ail'st thou, man?
CLOWN   I have seen two such sights, by sea and by
land! But I am not to say it is a sea, for it is now the sky;
betwixt the firmament and it you cannot thrust a
bodkin's point.   84
SHEPHERD   Why, boy, how is it?
CLOWN   I would you did but see how it chafes, how it
rages, how it takes up the shore! But that's not to the 87
point. O, the most piteous cry of the poor souls! Sometimes to see 'em, and not to see 'em; now the ship
boring the moon with her mainmast, and anon swallowed with yeast and froth, as you'd thrust a cork into 91
a hogshead. And then for the land service, to see how 92
the bear tore out his shoulder bone; how he cried to
me for help and said his name was Antigonus, a nobleman. But to make an end of the ship: to see how

the sea flapdragoned it! But first, how the poor souls 96
roared and the sea mocked them, and how the poor
gentleman roared and the bear mocked him, both
roaring louder than the sea or weather.
SHEPHERD   Name of mercy, when was this, boy?
CLOWN   Now, now. I have not winked since I saw these 101
sights. The men are not yet cold under water, nor the
bear half dined on the gentleman. He's at it now.
SHEPHERD   Would I had been by, to have helped the
old man!
CLOWN   I would you had been by the ship side, to have
helped her. There your charity would have lacked
footing.   108
SHEPHERD   Heavy matters, heavy matters! But look thee
here, boy. Now bless thyself. Thou mett'st with things
dying, I with things newborn. Here's a sight for thee;
look thee, a bearing cloth for a squire's child! Look 112
thee here; take up, take up, boy. Open 't. So, let's see.
It was told me I should be rich by the fairies. This is
some changeling. Open 't. What's within, boy?   115

                [The Clown opens the box.]

CLOWN   You're a made old man. If the sins of your
youth are forgiven you, you're well to live. Gold, all 117
gold!
SHEPHERD   This is fairy gold, boy, and 'twill prove so.
Up with 't, keep it close. Home, home, the next way. 120
We are lucky, boy, and to be so still requires nothing 121
but secrecy. Let my sheep go. Come, good boy, the 122
next way home.
CLOWN   Go you the next way with your findings. I'll go
see if the bear be gone from the gentleman, and how
much he hath eaten. They are never curst but when 126
they are hungry. If there be any of him left, I'll bury it.
SHEPHERD   That's a good deed. If thou mayest discern
by that which is left of him what he is, fetch me to the
sight of him.
CLOWN   Marry, will I; and you shall help to put him i' 131
the ground.
SHEPHERD   'Tis a lucky day, boy, and we'll do good
deeds on 't.   *Exeunt.*

                              ❖

4.1   *Enter Time, the Chorus.*

TIME
    I, that please some, try all, both joy and terror   1
    Of good and bad, that makes and unfolds error,   2

---

61 ancientry old people   **62–63 boiled brains** addlepated youths
67 Good . . . will i.e., may God grant me good luck in finding my
sheep   **68 bairn** child   **69 child** i.e., female infant   **70 scape** sexual
escapade   **72–73 stair-work . . . behind-door-work** i.e., sexual liai-
sons under or behind the stairs or using a room or a trunk for concealment   **73 got** begot   **76 s.d. Clown** country fellow, rustic
84 bodkin's needle's. (A *bodkin* can also be a dagger, awl, etc.)
87 takes up (1) contends with, rebukes (2) swallows   **91 yeast** foam
92 hogshead large barrel. (The image is of a cork swimming in a turbulent expanse of frothing liquid.)   **land service** (1) dish of food
served on land (2) military service on land (as distinguished from naval service); here, the doings on land

96 flapdragoned swallowed as one would a flapdragon, i.e., a raisin
or the like swallowed out of burning brandy in the game of snapdragon   **101 winked** closed my eyes   **108 footing** (1) foothold (2)
establishment of a charitable foundation, one that would provide
charity (line 107)   **112 bearing cloth** rich cloth or mantle in which a
child was carried to its baptism   **115 changeling** child left or taken by
fairies   **117 well to live** well-to-do   **120 close** secret.   **next** nearest
121–122 to be . . . secrecy (To talk about fairy gifts would be to insure bad luck.)   **still** on a continuing basis   **126 curst** mean, fierce
131 Marry i.e., indeed. (Originally an oath, "by the Virgin Mary.")
4.1.
1 try test   **2 that . . . error** i.e., I who make error, thus bringing joy
to the bad and terror to the good, and then at last unfold or disclose
error, thus bringing joy to the good and terror to the bad

Now take upon me, in the name of Time,
To use my wings. Impute it not a crime
To me or my swift passage, that I slide
O'er sixteen years and leave the growth untried   6
Of that wide gap, since it is in my power
To o'erthrow law and in one self-born hour   8
To plant and o'erwhelm custom. Let me pass
The same I am ere ancient'st order was   10
Or what is now received. I witness to   11
The times that brought them in; so shall I do   12
To th' freshest things now reigning, and make stale
The glistering of this present, as my tale   14
Now seems to it. Your patience this allowing,   15
I turn my glass and give my scene such growing   16
As you had slept between. Leontes leaving—   17
Th' effects of his fond jealousies so grieving   18
That he shuts up himself—imagine me,
Gentle spectators, that I now may be
In fair Bohemia. And remember well
I mentioned a son o' the King's, which Florizel
I now name to you; and with speed so pace   23
To speak of Perdita, now grown in grace
Equal with wondering. What of her ensues   25
I list not prophesy; but let Time's news   26
Be known when 'tis brought forth. A shepherd's
    daughter,
And what to her adheres, which follows after,   28
Is th' argument of Time. Of this allow,   29
If ever you have spent time worse ere now;
If never, yet that Time himself doth say   31
He wishes earnestly you never may.   *Exit.*

4.2   *Enter Polixenes and Camillo.*

POLIXENES   I pray thee, good Camillo, be no more
importunate. 'Tis a sickness denying thee anything, a
death to grant this.
CAMILLO   It is fifteen years since I saw my country.
Though I have for the most part been aired abroad, I   5
desire to lay my bones there. Besides, the penitent
King, my master, hath sent for me, to whose feeling   7
sorrows I might be some allay—or I o'erween to think   8
so—which is another spur to my departure.

POLIXENES   As thou lov'st me, Camillo, wipe not out the
rest of thy services by leaving me now. The need I
have of thee thine own goodness hath made. Better
not to have had thee than thus to want thee. Thou,   13
having made me businesses which none without thee
can sufficiently manage, must either stay to execute
them thyself or take away with thee the very services
thou hast done; which if I have not enough
considered—as too much I cannot—to be more thank-   18
ful to thee shall be my study, and my profit therein the
heaping friendships. Of that fatal country, Sicilia,   20
prithee, speak no more, whose very naming punishes
me with the remembrance of that penitent, as thou
call'st him, and reconciled King, my brother, whose
loss of his most precious queen and children are even
now to be afresh lamented. Say to me, when sawst
thou the Prince Florizel, my son? Kings are no less
unhappy, their issue not being gracious, than they are 27
in losing them when they have approved their virtues. 28
CAMILLO   Sir, it is three days since I saw the Prince.
What his happier affairs may be are to me unknown;
but I have missingly noted he is of late much retired 31
from court and is less frequent to his princely exercises 32
than formerly he hath appeared.
POLIXENES   I have considered so much, Camillo, and   34
with some care, so far that I have eyes under my ser-   35
vice which look upon his removedness; from whom I   36
have this intelligence, that he is seldom from the   37
house of a most homely shepherd—a man, they say,   38
that from very nothing, and beyond the imagination
of his neighbors, is grown into an unspeakable estate. 40
CAMILLO   I have heard, sir, of such a man, who hath a
daughter of most rare note. The report of her is   42
extended more than can be thought to begin from
such a cottage.
POLIXENES   That's likewise part of my intelligence; but,
I fear, the angle that plucks our son thither. Thou shalt 46
accompany us to the place, where we will, not appearing what we are, have some question with the shep-   48
herd; from whose simplicity I think it not uneasy to   49
get the cause of my son's resort thither. Prithee, be my
present partner in this business, and lay aside the
thoughts of Sicilia.
CAMILLO   I willingly obey your command.
POLIXENES   My best Camillo! We must disguise ourselves.   *Exit* [*with Camillo*].

❧

6 **growth untried** developments unexplored   8 **law** any established
order (including the rule of the unity of time in a dramatic performance, normally limiting the action to twenty-four hours).   **self-born**
selfsame, or born of myself (since hours are the creations of Time)
10–11 ere . . . received i.e., from the beginning of time to the
present   **12 them** i.e., law and custom   **14 glistering** glistening freshness   **15 seems to it** seems (stale) when compared with the present
16 glass hourglass   **17 As** as if.   **Leontes leaving** leaving behind Leontes for the moment   **18 Th' effects . . . grieving** so grieving at the
effects of his foolish jealousies   **23 pace** proceed   **25 Equal with
wondering** as great as the wonder people feel in seeing her   **26 list
not** do not care to   **28 to her adheres** concerns her   **29 argument**
subject of the story   **31 yet that** i.e., yet allow that
4.2. Location: Bohemia. The court of Polixenes.
5 been aired abroad lived abroad   **7 feeling** heartfelt   **8 allay** means
of abatement.   **o'erween** am presumptuous enough

13 want lack   **18 considered** i.e., rewarded   **20 heaping friendships**
heaping up of (your) kind services and our mutual affection   **27 their
. . . gracious** if their children behave ungraciously   **28 approved**
proved   **31 missingly** being aware that he is missing   **32 frequent to**
devoted to   **34 so much** i.e., all that you say   **35–36 eyes . . . removedness** spies who keep an eye on him in his absence   **37 intelligence** news.   **from** away from   **38 homely** simple   **40 unspeakable**
beyond description   **42 note** distinction   **46 angle** baited fishhook.
our (The royal "we"; also in *us*, line 47.)   **48 question** talk   **49 uneasy** difficult

4.3   *Enter Autolycus, singing.*

AUTOLYCUS

When daffodils begin to peer,   1
   With heigh, the doxy over the dale!   2
Why, then comes in the sweet o' the year,
   For the red blood reigns in the winter's pale.   4

The white sheet bleaching on the hedge,
   With heigh, the sweet birds, O, how they
      sing!
Doth set my pugging tooth on edge,   7
   For a quart of ale is a dish for a king.   8

The lark, that tirralirra chants,
   With heigh, with heigh, the thrush and the
      jay!
Are summer songs for me and my aunts,   11
   While we lie tumbling in the hay.

I have served Prince Florizel and in my time wore
three-pile, but now I am out of service.   14

But shall I go mourn for that, my dear?   15
   The pale moon shines by night,
And when I wander here and there,   17
   I then do most go right.   18

If tinkers may have leave to live,   19
   And bear the sow-skin budget,   20
Then my account I well may give,   21
   And in the stocks avouch it.   22

My traffic is sheets; when the kite builds, look to lesser 23
linen. My father named me Autolycus, who, being, as   24
I am, littered under Mercury, was likewise a snap-   25
per-up of unconsidered trifles. With die and drab I   26
purchased this caparison, and my revenue is the silly   27
cheat. Gallows and knock are too powerful on the   28
highway; beating and hanging are terrors to me. For   29

the life to come, I sleep out the thought of it. A prize, 30
a prize!

Enter Clown.

CLOWN   Let me see: every 'leven wether tods; every tod   32
   yields pound and odd shilling; fifteen hundred shorn,
   what comes the wool to?
AUTOLYCUS [*aside*]   If the springe hold, the cock's mine. 35
CLOWN   I cannot do 't without counters. Let me see;   36
   what am I to buy for our sheepshearing feast? Three
   pound of sugar, five pound of currants, rice—what
   will this sister of mine do with rice? But my father hath
   made her mistress of the feast, and she lays it on. She
   hath made me four-and-twenty nosegays for the shear-   41
   ers—three-man-song men all, and very good ones;   42
   but they are most of them means and basses, but one   43
   Puritan amongst them, and he sings psalms to horn-   44
   pipes. I must have saffron to color the warden pies;   45
   mace; dates?—none, that's out of my note; nutmegs,   46
   seven; a race or two of ginger, but that I may beg; four 47
   pound of prunes, and as many of raisins o' the sun.   48
AUTOLYCUS   O, that ever I was born! [*He grovels on the
   ground.*]
CLOWN   I' the name of me!   50
AUTOLYCUS   O, help me, help me! Pluck but off these
   rags, and then death, death!
CLOWN   Alack, poor soul! Thou hast need of more rags
   to lay on thee, rather than have these off.
AUTOLYCUS   O sir, the loathsomeness of them offend
   me more than the stripes I have received, which are
   mighty ones and millions.
CLOWN   Alas, poor man! A million of beating may come
   to a great matter.
AUTOLYCUS   I am robbed, sir, and beaten; my money
   and apparel ta'en from me, and these detestable things
   put upon me.
CLOWN   What, by a horseman or a footman?   63
AUTOLYCUS   A footman, sweet sir, a footman.
CLOWN   Indeed, he should be a footman by the gar-
   ments he has left with thee. If this be a horseman's
   coat, it hath seen very hot service. Lend me thy hand;
   I'll help thee. Come, lend me thy hand. [*He helps him
   up.*]
AUTOLYCUS   O, good sir, tenderly. O!
CLOWN   Alas, poor soul!
AUTOLYCUS   O, good sir, softly, good sir! I fear, sir, my
   shoulder blade is out.

4.3. Location: Bohemia. A road near the Shepherd's cottage.
1 peer peep out, appear   **2 doxy** beggar's wench   **4 pale** (1) paleness
(2) domain, region of authority. (The image is of red blood restoring
vitality to a pale complexion.)   **7 set . . . on edge** i.e., whets the appetite of my thieving tooth, my taste for thieving. (To *pug* is to "pull,
tug.")   **8 quart of ale** (To be paid for perhaps with profits from theft
of sheets.)   **11 aunts** i.e., whores   **14 three-pile** velvet having very
rich pile or nap   **15 for that** i.e., for being out of service   **17 wander**
(i.e., as a thief)   **18 most go right** i.e., live the life that is meant for
me   **19 live** i.e., practice their trade   **20 budget** tool bag   **21 my account** an account of myself   **22 in . . . avouch it** i.e., affirm that I
am a tinker if I find myself sitting in the stocks, where vagabonds often end up. (Autolycus passes himself off as a tinker to mask his real
calling of thief.)   **23 kite** (The kite, a bird of prey, was supposed to
carry off small pieces of linen with which to construct its nest,
whereas Autolycus makes off with larger linen or sheets hung out to
dry.)   **24 Autolycus** (Like his namesake, Ulysses' grandfather, the son
of Mercury, this Autolycus is an expert thief.)   **who** (Refers ambiguously to Autolycus and "My father"; see next note.)   **25 littered under Mercury** (1) sired by Mercury, the god of thieves (2) born when
the planet Mercury was in the ascendant   **26 unconsidered** left unattended, not worth thinking about   **26–28 With . . . cheat** i.e., gambling and whoring have brought me to the wearing of these tattered
rags, and my source of income is petty trickery used to cheat simpletons   **28 Gallows and knock** hanging and being beaten (the hazards
of being a highwayman)   **29 For** as for

30 sleep . . . it i.e., don't give a thought to punishment in the next
world.   **prize** booty   **32 every . . . tods** every eleven sheep yield a
tod, i.e., a bulk of wool weighing twenty-eight pounds   **35 springe**
snare.   **cock** woodcock. (A proverbially stupid bird.)   **36 counters**
metal disks used in reckoning   **41 made me** made. (*Me* is used colloquially.)   **42 three-man-song men** singers of songs for three male
voices: bass, tenor, and treble   **43 means** tenors   **43–45 but . . .
hornpipes** i.e., except for one Puritan, who is a treble but who sings
psalms even to merry dance tunes. (The Puritans were often laughed
at for their pious singing.)   **45 warden** made of the warden pear
46 out of my note not on my list   **47 race** root   **48 o' the sun** dried
in the sun   **50 I' the name of me** (An unusual and perhaps comic
oath.)   **63 horseman** highwayman.   **footman** footpad. (As the Clown
observes in line 65, a common robber on foot would have poorer
clothes than a mounted highwayman.)

CLOWN   How now? Canst stand?

AUTOLYCUS [*picking his pocket*]   Softly, dear sir; good sir, softly. You ha' done me a charitable office.

CLOWN [*reaching for his purse*]   Dost lack any money? I 76 have a little money for thee. 77

AUTOLYCUS   No, good sweet sir; no, I beseech you, sir. I have a kinsman not past three quarters of a mile hence, unto whom I was going; I shall there have money or anything I want. Offer me no money, I pray you. That kills my heart.

CLOWN   What manner of fellow was he that robbed you?

AUTOLYCUS   A fellow, sir, that I have known to go about with troll-my-dames. I knew him once a servant of the 85 Prince. I cannot tell, good sir, for which of his virtues it was, but he was certainly whipped out of the court.

CLOWN   His vices, you would say. There's no virtue whipped out of the court. They cherish it to make it stay there; and yet it will no more but abide. 90

AUTOLYCUS   Vices, I would say, sir. I know this man well. He hath been since an ape bearer, then a process 92 server, a bailiff. Then he compassed a motion of 93 the Prodigal Son and married a tinker's wife within a mile where my land and living lies, and, having flown 95 over many knavish professions, he settled only in rogue. Some call him Autolycus.

CLOWN   Out upon him! Prig, for my life, prig! He 98 haunts wakes, fairs, and bearbaitings. 99

AUTOLYCUS   Very true, sir. He, sir, he. That's the rogue that put me into this apparel.

CLOWN   Not a more cowardly rogue in all Bohemia. If you had but looked big and spit at him, he'd have run.

AUTOLYCUS   I must confess to you, sir, I am no fighter. I am false of heart that way, and that he knew, I 106 warrant him.

CLOWN   How do you now?

AUTOLYCUS   Sweet sir, much better than I was. I can stand and walk. I will even take my leave of you and pace softly towards my kinsman's. 111

CLOWN   Shall I bring thee on the way? 112

AUTOLYCUS   No, good-faced sir, no, sweet sir.

CLOWN   Then fare thee well. I must go buy spices for our sheepshearing. *Exit.*

AUTOLYCUS   Prosper you, sweet sir! Your purse is not 116 hot enough to purchase your spice. I'll be with you at 117 your sheepshearing too. If I make not this cheat bring 118 out another, and the shearers prove sheep, let me be 119 unrolled and my name put in the book of virtue! 120

Song.

Jog on, jog on, the footpath way,
    And merrily hent the stile-a; 122
A merry heart goes all the day,
    Your sad tires in a mile-a. *Exit.*

4.4   *Enter Florizel [in shepherd's garb, and] Perdita [in holiday attire].*

FLORIZEL
These your unusual weeds to each part of you 1
Does give a life; no shepherdess, but Flora 2
Peering in April's front. This your sheepshearing 3
Is as a meeting of the petty gods, 4
And you the queen on 't.

PERDITA   Sir, my gracious lord,
To chide at your extremes it not becomes me. 6
O, pardon that I name them! Your high self,
The gracious mark o' the land, you have obscured 8
With a swain's wearing, and me, poor lowly maid, 9
Most goddesslike pranked up. But that our feasts 10
In every mess have folly, and the feeders 11
Digest it with a custom, I should blush 12
To see you so attired, swoon, I think,
To show myself a glass.

FLORIZEL   I bless the time 14
When my good falcon made her flight across
Thy father's ground.

PERDITA   Now Jove afford you cause!
To me the difference forges dread; your greatness 17
Hath not been used to fear. Even now I tremble
To think your father by some accident
Should pass this way as you did. O, the Fates!
How would he look to see his work, so noble,
Vilely bound up? What would he say? Or how 22
Should I, in these my borrowed flaunts, behold 23
The sternness of his presence?

FLORIZEL   Apprehend
Nothing but jollity. The gods themselves,
Humbling their deities to love, have taken

76–77 **I have . . . thee** (The Clown reaches for his money and might have discovered the robbery if Autolycus had not quickly begged him not to bother.)   85 **troll-my-dames** or troll-madams (from the French *trou-madame*), a game in which the object was to *troll* balls through arches set on a board. (Autolycus uses the word to suggest women who *troll* or saunter about.)   90 **no more but abide** make only a temporary or unwilling stay   92 **ape bearer** one who carries a monkey about for exhibition   92–93 **process server** sheriff's officer who serves processes or summonses   93 **compassed a motion** got possession of or devised a puppet show   95 **living** property   98 **Prig** thief   99 **wakes** village festivals   106 **false** cowardly   111 **softly** slowly   112 **bring . . . way** go part of the way with you   116 **Prosper . . . sir** (Said to the departing Clown.)   116–117 **Your . . . spice** i.e., you'll find but a cold purse to pay for your hot spices; an empty purse is a cold one. (Said after the Clown's departure.)

118–119 **cheat bring out** swindle lead to   120 **unrolled** taken off the roll (of rogues and vagabonds)   122 **hent** take hold of (as a means of leaping over)

4.4. Location: Bohemia. The Shepherd's cottage. (See lines 181–182, 187, etc.)
1 **unusual weeds** special, holiday attire   2 **Flora** goddess of flowers
3 **Peering . . . front** peeping forth in early April, or, in April's countenance or garb   4 **petty** minor   6 **extremes** extravagant statements
8 **mark o' the land** one who is noted and used as a model by everyone   9 **wearing** garb   10 **pranked up** bedecked.   **But that** were it not that   11 **In every mess** at every table, in each group or course of dishes   12 **Digest** swallow, i.e., accept.   **with a custom** from habit
14 **To show . . . glass** if I were to see myself in a mirror   17 **difference** i.e., of rank.   **forges** i.e., creates   22 **bound up** i.e., covered in lowly outer garments. (The metaphor is from bookbinding.)
23 **flaunts** finery

The shapes of beasts upon them. Jupiter   27
Became a bull, and bellowed; the green Neptune   28
A ram, and bleated; and the fire-robed god,   29
Golden Apollo, a poor humble swain,   30
As I seem now. Their transformations
Were never for a piece of beauty rarer,
Nor in a way so chaste, since my desires   33
Run not before mine honor, nor my lusts
Burn hotter than my faith.
PERDITA   O, but sir,
Your resolution cannot hold when 'tis
Opposed, as it must be, by th' power of the King.
One of these two must be necessities,
Which then will speak: that you must change this
    purpose
Or I my life.
FLORIZEL   Thou dearest Perdita,   40
With these forced thoughts, I prithee, darken not   41
The mirth o' the feast. Or I'll be thine, my fair,   42
Or not my father's. For I cannot be
Mine own, not anything to any, if   44
I be not thine. To this I am most constant,
Though destiny say no. Be merry, gentle!   46
Strangle such thoughts as these with anything   47
That you behold the while. Your guests are coming.   48
Lift up your countenance as it were the day   49
Of celebration of that nuptial which
We two have sworn shall come.
PERDITA   O Lady Fortune,
Stand you auspicious!
FLORIZEL   See, your guests approach.
Address yourself to entertain them sprightly,   53
And let's be red with mirth.

[Enter] Shepherd, Clown; Polixenes, Camillo
[disguised]; Mopsa, Dorcas; servants.

SHEPHERD
Fie, daughter! When my old wife lived, upon
This day she was both pantler, butler, cook,   56
Both dame and servant; welcomed all, served all;   57
Would sing her song and dance her turn; now here,
At upper end o' the table, now i' the middle;
On his shoulder, and his; her face afire   60
With labor, and the thing she took to quench it   61
She would to each one sip. You are retired,   62
As if you were a feasted one and not
The hostess of the meeting. Pray you, bid
These unknown friends to 's welcome, for it is   65

A way to make us better friends, more known.   66
Come, quench your blushes and present yourself
That which you are, mistress o' the feast. Come on,
And bid us welcome to your sheepshearing,
As your good flock shall prosper.
PERDITA [to Polixenes]   Sir, welcome.
It is my father's will I should take on me
The hostess-ship o' the day. [To Camillo.] You're
    welcome, sir.
Give me those flowers there, Dorcas. Reverend sirs,
For you there's rosemary and rue; these keep
Seeming and savor all the winter long.   75
Grace and remembrance be to you both,   76
And welcome to our shearing! [Giving them flowers.]
POLIXENES   Shepherdess—
A fair one are you—well you fit our ages
With flowers of winter.
PERDITA   Sir, the year growing ancient, 79
Not yet on summer's death nor on the birth
Of trembling winter, the fairest flow'rs o' the season
Are our carnations and streaked gillyvors,   82
Which some call nature's bastards. Of that kind   83
Our rustic garden's barren, and I care not
To get slips of them.
POLIXENES   Wherefore, gentle maiden,   85
Do you neglect them?
PERDITA   For I have heard it said   86
There is an art which in their piedness shares   87
With great creating nature.
POLIXENES   Say there be;
Yet nature is made better by no mean   89
But nature makes that mean. So, over that art   90
Which you say adds to nature is an art
That nature makes. You see, sweet maid, we marry
A gentler scion to the wildest stock,   93
And make conceive a bark of baser kind
By bud of nobler race. This is an art
Which does mend nature—change it, rather—but
The art itself is nature.
PERDITA   So it is.
POLIXENES
Then make your garden rich in gillyvors,
And do not call them bastards.
PERDITA   I'll not put
The dibble in earth to set one slip of them,   100
No more than, were I painted, I would wish   101
This youth should say 'twere well, and only
    therefore

27–30 Jupiter . . . swain (Jupiter in the guise of a bull wooed Europa, Neptune disguised as a ram deceived Bisaltis [Ovid, *Metamorphoses*, 6.117], and Apollo took the guise of a humble shepherd to enable Admetus to woo Alcestis.)   33 in a way i.e., pursuing a purpose   40 Or I my life i.e., or I will be threatened with loss of life (as Polixenes indeed threatens at lines 436–443)   41 forced farfetched, unnatural   42 Or either   44 not anything nor I will not be anything   46 gentle i.e., my gentle love   47–48 Strangle . . . while i.e., put down such thoughts by attending to matters at hand   49 as as if   53 Address prepare   56 pantler pantry servant   57 dame mistress of the household   60 On his . . . his at one person's . . . another's   61–62 and . . . sip and she would toast each one with the drink she took to quench the fire of her labor   65 to 's each to his

66 more known better acquainted   75 Seeming outward appearance, color   76 Grace and remembrance divine grace and remembrance after death. (Equated respectively with rue and rosemary.)   79 the year . . . ancient i.e., when autumn arrives   82 gillyvors gillyflowers, a kind of carnation   83 nature's bastards i.e., the result of artificial breeding. (See lines 86–88.)   85 slips cuttings   86 For because   87 art i.e., of crossbreeding.   piedness particolored appearance. (Perdita disclaims the art of crossbreeding, since it infringes on what nature itself does so well.)   89 mean means   90 But unless. (Polixenes' point is that the art of improving on nature is itself natural.)   93 gentler nobler, more cultivated   100 dibble tool for making holes in which to implant seed   101 painted made artificially beautiful by cosmetics

Desire to breed by me. Here's flowers for you:
[*giving them flowers*]
Hot lavender, mints, savory, marjoram, 104
The marigold, that goes to bed wi' the sun
And with him rises weeping. These are flowers
Of middle summer, and I think they are given 107
To men of middle age. You're very welcome.

CAMILLO
I should leave grazing, were I of your flock,
And only live by gazing.

PERDITA   Out, alas!
You'd be so lean that blasts of January
Would blow you through and through. [*To Florizel.*]
Now, my fair'st friend,
I would I had some flow'rs o' the spring that might
Become your time of day; [*to the Shepherdesses*] and
yours, and yours,
That wear upon your virgin branches yet
Your maidenheads growing. O Proserpina, 116
For the flow'rs now that, frighted, thou lett'st fall
From Dis's wagon! Daffodils,
That come before the swallow dares, and take 119
The winds of March with beauty; violets dim,
But sweeter than the lids of Juno's eyes
Or Cytherea's breath; pale primroses, 122
That die unmarried ere they can behold
Bright Phoebus in his strength—a malady 124
Most incident to maids; bold oxlips and 125
The crown imperial; lilies of all kinds, 126
The flower-de-luce being one. O, these I lack 127
To make you garlands of, and my sweet friend, 128
To strew him o'er and o'er!

FLORIZEL   What, like a corpse?

PERDITA
No, like a bank for Love to lie and play on, 130
Not like a corpse; or if, not to be buried, 131
But quick and in mine arms. Come, take your
flowers.   [*Giving flowers.*] 132
Methinks I play as I have seen them do
In Whitsun pastorals. Sure this robe of mine 134
Does change my disposition.

FLORIZEL   What you do
Still betters what is done. When you speak, sweet, 136

I'd have you do it ever. When you sing,
I'd have you buy and sell so, so give alms,
Pray so; and, for the ordering your affairs,
To sing them too. When you do dance, I wish you
A wave o' the sea, that you might ever do
Nothing but that—move still, still so,
And own no other function. Each your doing, 143
So singular in each particular, 144
Crowns what you are doing in the present deeds, 145
That all your acts are queens.

PERDITA   O Doricles, 146
Your praises are too large. But that your youth 147
And the true blood which peeps fairly through 't
Do plainly give you out an unstained shepherd, 149
With wisdom I might fear, my Doricles,
You wooed me the false way.

FLORIZEL   I think you have
As little skill to fear as I have purpose 152
To put you to 't. But come, our dance, I pray.
Your hand, my Perdita. So turtles pair, 154
That never mean to part.

PERDITA   I'll swear for 'em. 155
[*They speak apart.*]

POLIXENES [*to Camillo*]
This is the prettiest lowborn lass that ever
Ran on the greensward. Nothing she does or seems
But smacks of something greater than herself,
Too noble for this place.

CAMILLO   He tells her something
That makes her blood look out. Good sooth, she is 160
The queen of curds and cream.

CLOWN   Come on, strike up!

DORCAS
Mopsa must be your mistress. Marry, garlic, 162
To mend her kissing with!

MOPSA   Now, in good time! 163

CLOWN
Not a word, a word. We stand upon our manners. 164
Come, strike up! 165
[*Music.*] *Here a dance of shepherds and*
shepherdesses.

POLIXENES
Pray, good shepherd, what fair swain is this
Which dances with your daughter?

SHEPHERD
They call him Doricles, and boasts himself 168
To have a worthy feeding; but I have it 169
Upon his own report and I believe it.

---

104 Hot eager, ardent, aromatic (?) (Spices were classified as hot or cold.)   **107 middle summer** (Having no autumn flowers in any case [lines 79–82], since it is too early in the season, Perdita flatters her older guests by giving them flowers appropriate to *middle age.*) **116 Proserpina** daughter of Ceres, stolen away by Pluto (*Dis*) and taken to Hades when, according to Ovid, she was gathering flowers **119 take** charm   **122 Cytherea's** Venus'   **124 Phoebus** the sun-god **124–125 a malady . . . maids** (Young maids, suffering from greensickness, a kind of anemia, are pale like the primrose.)   **126 crown imperial** flower from the Levant, cultivated in English gardens **127 flower-de-luce** fleur-de-lis.   **I lack** (because the season is too late for them)   **128 To . . . friend** to make garlands of them for you (Polixenes and Camillo) and for my sweet friend (Florizel)   **130 like . . . play on** as if one were strewing a bank where Cupid himself might lie in amorous play   **131 or if** or if like a corpse, that is, a living body   **132 quick** alive   **134 Whitsun pastorals** plays (including Robin Hood plays) and English morris dances often performed at Whitsuntide, seven Sundays after Easter. (The part of Maid Marian strikes Perdita as immodest for her usual behavior.)   **136 Still . . . done** always surpasses anything else

143 Each your doing each thing you do and how you do it   **144 singular** unique and peerless   **145 Crowns . . . deeds** makes whatever you are doing at the moment seem supremely wonderful **146 Doricles** (Florizel's disguise name.)   **147 large** lavish.   **But that** were it not that   **149 give you out** proclaim you to be   **152 skill** reason   **154 turtles** turtledoves, as symbols of faithful love   **155 I'll swear for 'em** i.e., I'll be sworn they do   **160 makes . . . out** makes her blush   **162 mistress** i.e., partner in the dance   **163 kissing** i.e., bad breath. (Dorcas jests that even garlic would improve Mopsa's breath.)   **in good time** (An expression of indignation.)   **164 stand upon** set store by   **165 s.d. dance** (Probably a morris dance.) **168 and** i.e., and they say he   **169 feeding** pasturage, lands

He looks like sooth. He says he loves my daughter. 171
I think so too, for never gazed the moon
Upon the water as he'll stand and read,
As 'twere, my daughter's eyes; and, to be plain,
I think there is not half a kiss to choose
Who loves another best.

POLIXENES   She dances featly. 176

SHEPHERD
So she does anything—though I report it
That should be silent. If young Doricles
Do light upon her, she shall bring him that 179
Which he not dreams of.

Enter Servant.

SERVANT O master, if you did but hear the peddler at
the door, you would never dance again after a tabor 182
and pipe; no, the bagpipe could not move you. He
sings several tunes faster than you'll tell money. He 184
utters them as he had eaten ballads and all men's ears 185
grew to his tunes.

CLOWN He could never come better. He shall come in. 187
I love a ballad but even too well, if it be doleful matter 188
merrily set down, or a very pleasant thing indeed and 189
sung lamentably. 190

SERVANT He hath songs for man or woman, of all sizes. 191
No milliner can so fit his customers with gloves. He 192
has the prettiest love songs for maids, so without
bawdry, which is strange, with such delicate burdens 194
of dildos and fadings, "Jump her and thump her"; and 195
where some stretchmouthed rascal would, as it were, 196
mean mischief and break a foul gap into the matter, 197
he makes the maid to answer, "Whoop, do me no
harm, good man"; puts him off, slights him, with
"Whoop, do me no harm, good man."

POLIXENES This is a brave fellow. 201

CLOWN Believe me, thou talkest of an admirable con- 202
ceited fellow. Has he any unbraided wares? 203

SERVANT He hath ribbons of all the colors i' the
rainbow; points more than all the lawyers in Bohemia 205
can learnedly handle, though they come to him by the
gross; inkles, caddisses, cambrics, lawns. Why, he 207
sings 'em over as they were gods or goddesses; you
would think a smock were a she-angel, he so chants to
the sleevehand and the work about the square on 't. 210

CLOWN Prithee, bring him in, and let him approach
singing.

PERDITA Forewarn him that he use no scurrilous words
in 's tunes.   [*The Servant goes to the door.*]

CLOWN You have of these peddlers that have more in 215
them than you'd think, sister.

PERDITA Ay, good brother, or go about to think. 217

Enter Autolycus, singing.

AUTOLYCUS
Lawn as white as driven snow,
Cyprus black as e'er was crow, 219
Gloves as sweet as damask roses, 220
Masks for faces and for noses,
Bugle bracelet, necklace amber, 222
Perfume for a lady's chamber,
Golden coifs and stomachers, 224
For my lads to give their dears,
Pins and poking-sticks of steel, 226
What maids lack from head to heel,
Come buy of me, come. Come buy, come buy.
Buy, lads, or else your lasses cry.
Come buy.

CLOWN If I were not in love with Mopsa, thou shouldst
take no money of me, but being enthralled as I am, it 232
will also be the bondage of certain ribbons and gloves. 233

MOPSA I was promised them against the feast, but they 234
come not too late now.

DORCAS He hath promised you more than that, or 236
there be liars. 237

MOPSA He hath paid you all he promised you. Maybe
he has paid you more, which will shame you to give 239
him again. 240

CLOWN Is there no manners left among maids? Will 241
they wear their plackets where they should bear their 242
faces? Is there not milking time, when you are going to 243
bed, or kilnhole, to whistle of these secrets, but you 214
must be tittle-tattling before all our guests? 'Tis well
they are whispering. Clamor your tongues, and not a 246
word more.

MOPSA I have done. Come, you promised me a tawdry 248
lace and a pair of sweet gloves. 249

CLOWN Have I not told thee how I was cozened by the 250
way and lost all my money?

---

171 **like sooth** truthful 176 **another** the other. **featly** gracefully
179 **light upon** choose 182 **tabor** small drum 184 **tell** count
185 **as** as if (also in line 208) 187 **better** at a better time 188 **but
even too well** all too well 189 **pleasant** merry 190 **lamentably**
mournfully 191 **sizes** sorts 192 **milliner** vendor of fancy ware and
apparel, including gloves, ribbons, and bonnets 194 **burdens** refrains
195 **dildos and fadings** words used as part of the refrains of ballads
(but with bawdy double meaning unperceived by the servant, as also
in *jump her, thump her, do me no harm,* etc.) 196 **stretchmouthed**
widemouthed, foulmouthed 197 **break . . . matter** insert some gross
obscenity into the song, or, act in a suggestive way 201 **brave** excellent 202–203 **admirable conceited** wonderfully witty and clever
203 **unbraided** not shopworn, undamaged 205 **points** (1) laces for
fastening clothes (2) headings in an argument 207 **inkles** linen tapes.
caddisses worsted tape used for garters. **cambrics** fine linen fabrics.
lawns fine sheer linens 210 **sleevehand** wristband. **square on 't**
embroidered bosom or yoke of the garment

215 **You . . . peddlers** you'll find peddlers 217 **go about** intend,
wish. **s.d. Enter Autolycus** (Apparently he is wearing a false beard;
later in this scene, he removes it to impersonate a courtier to the
Clown and Shepherd.) 219 **Cyprus** crepe 220 **sweet** i.e., perfumed
(also in line 249) 222 **Bugle bracelet** bracelet of black glossy beads
224 **coifs** close-fitting caps. **stomachers** embroidered fronts for ladies' dresses 226 **poking-sticks** rods used for ironing and stiffening
the plaits of ruffs 232–233 **it will . . . bondage** it will mean the taking into custody (by means of purchase and tying up into a parcel)
234 **against** in anticipation of, in time for 236–237 **He . . . liars**
i.e., he promised to marry you, too, or else rumor is a liar 239 **paid
you more** i.e., made you pregnant 239–240 **which . . . again** i.e.,
which will shame you by giving birth to his child 241–243 **Will
. . . faces** i.e., will they always be talking and revealing personal secrets? **plackets** slits in petticoats (with bawdy suggestion of the pudendum, as in line 613) 244 **kilnhole** fire hole of a baking oven
(where maids might gossip). **whistle** whisper 246 **Clamor** i.e., silence 248–249 **tawdry lace** cheap and showy lace, or, neckerchief.
(So called from St. Audrey's Fair.) 250 **cozened** cheated

AUTOLYCUS And indeed, sir, there are cozeners abroad;
therefore it behooves men to be wary.

CLOWN Fear not thou, man, thou shalt lose nothing
here.

AUTOLYCUS I hope so, sir, for I have about me many
parcels of charge.   257

CLOWN What hast here? Ballads?

MOPSA Pray now, buy some. I love a ballad in print
alife, for then we are sure they are true.   260

AUTOLYCUS Here's one to a very doleful tune, how a
usurer's wife was brought to bed of twenty moneybags at a burden, and how she longed to eat adders' 263
heads and toads carbonadoed.   264

MOPSA Is it true, think you?

AUTOLYCUS Very true, and but a month old.

DORCAS Bless me from marrying a usurer!   267

AUTOLYCUS Here's the midwife's name to 't, one
Mistress Taleporter, and five or six honest wives that 269
were present. Why should I carry lies abroad?

MOPSA Pray you now, buy it.

CLOWN Come on, lay it by, and let's first see more
ballads. We'll buy the other things anon.

AUTOLYCUS Here's another ballad, of a fish that appeared upon the coast on Wednesday the fourscore of 275
April, forty thousand fathom above water, and sung 276
this ballad against the hard hearts of maids. It was
thought she was a woman and was turned into a cold
fish for she would not exchange flesh with one that
loved her. The ballad is very pitiful and as true.

DORCAS Is it true too, think you?

AUTOLYCUS Five justices' hands at it, and witnesses 282
more than my pack will hold.

CLOWN Lay it by too. Another.

AUTOLYCUS This is a merry ballad, but a very pretty
one.

MOPSA Let's have some merry ones.

AUTOLYCUS Why, this is a passing merry one and goes 288
to the tune of "Two Maids Wooing a Man." There's
scarce a maid westward but she sings it. 'Tis in 290
request, I can tell you.

MOPSA We can both sing it. If thou'lt bear a part, thou
shalt hear; 'tis in three parts.

DORCAS We had the tune on 't a month ago.   294

AUTOLYCUS I can bear my part; you must know 'tis my
occupation. Have at it with you.   296

Song.

AUTOLYCUS
    Get you hence, for I must go
    Where it fits not you to know.
DORCAS
            Whither?
MOPSA
                    O, whither?
DORCAS
                            Whither?

MOPSA
    It becomes thy oath full well,
    Thou to me thy secrets tell.
DORCAS
        Me too. Let me go thither.
MOPSA
    Or thou goest to th' grange or mill.   303
DORCAS
    If to either, thou dost ill.
AUTOLYCUS
        Neither.
DORCAS
                What, neither?
AUTOLYCUS
                        Neither.
DORCAS
    Thou hast sworn my love to be.
MOPSA
    Thou hast sworn it more to me.
        Then whither goest? Say, whither?

CLOWN We'll have this song out anon by ourselves. 309
My father and the gentlemen are in sad talk, and we'll 310
not trouble them. Come, bring away thy pack after
me. Wenches, I'll buy for you both. Peddler, let's have
the first choice. Follow me, girls.
                    [*Exit with Dorcas and Mopsa.*]

AUTOLYCUS And you shall pay well for 'em.
                            [*He follows singing.*]

Song.
    Will you buy any tape,
    Or lace for your cape,
    My dainty duck, my dear-a?
    Any silk, any thread,
    And toys for your head,   319
    Of the new'st and fin'st, fin'st wear-a?
    Come to the peddler;
    Money's a meddler,   322
    That doth utter all men's ware-a.   *Exit.* 323

    [*Enter a Servant.*]

SERVANT Master, there is three carters, three shepherds, three neatherds, three swineherds, that have 325
made themselves all men of hair. They call themselves 326
saultiers, and they have a dance which the wenches say 327
is a gallimaufry of gambols, because they are not in 't; 328
but they themselves are o' the mind, if it be not too
rough for some that know little but bowling, it will 330
please plentifully.

SHEPHERD Away! We'll none on 't. Here has been too
much homely foolery already.—I know, sir, we 333
weary you.

POLIXENES You weary those that refresh us. Pray, let's
see these four threes of herdsmen.

___

257 **parcels of charge** valuable items   260 **alife** dearly   263 **at a burden** in one childbirth   264 **carbonadoed** scored across and grilled
267 **Bless** protect, keep   269 **Taleporter** i.e., talebearer, gossip
275 **fourscore** eightieth (!)   276 **forty thousand fathom** 240,000 feet
282 **hands** signatures   288 **passing** surpassingly   290 **westward** in the
West Country   294 **on 't** of it   296 **Have at it** here goes

303 **Or** either.   **grange** farm   309 **have this song out** finish this song
310 **sad** serious   319 **toys** trifles   322 **meddler** i.e., go-between in
commercial transactions   323 **utter** put on the market   325 **neatherds** cowherds   326 **of hair** dressed in skins   327 **saultiers** leapers
or vaulters (with perhaps a play on *Saltiers* as a blunder for "satyrs")
328 **gallimaufry** jumble   330 **bowling** (A more gentle sport than the
vigorous satyr dancing.)   333 **homely** unpolished

SERVANT   One three of them, by their own report, sir, 337
  hath danced before the King, and not the worst of the
  three but jumps twelve foot and a half by the square. 339
SHEPHERD   Leave your prating. Since these good men 340
  are pleased, let them come in; but quickly now.
SERVANT   Why, they stay at door, sir.
                              [*He goes to the door.*]

            Here a dance of twelve Satyrs.

POLIXENES [*to the Shepherd*]
  O, father, you'll know more of that hereafter. 343
  [*To Camillo.*] Is it not too far gone? 'Tis time to part
    them.
  He's simple and tells much. [*To Florizel.*] How now,
    fair shepherd? 345
  Your heart is full of something that does take
  Your mind from feasting. Sooth, when I was young
  And handed love as you do, I was wont 348
  To load my she with knacks. I would have ransacked
  The peddler's silken treasury and have poured it
  To her acceptance; you have let him go,
  And nothing marted with him. If your lass 352
  Interpretation should abuse and call this 353
  Your lack of love or bounty, you were straited 354
  For a reply, at least if you make a care
  Of happy holding her.
FLORIZEL   Old sir, I know 356
  She prizes not such trifles as these are.
  The gifts she looks from me are packed and locked 358
  Up in my heart, which I have given already,
  But not delivered. [*To Perdita.*] O, hear me breathe
    my life 360
  Before this ancient sir, who, it should seem, 361
  Hath sometime loved! I take thy hand, this hand,
  As soft as dove's down and as white as it,
  Or Ethiopian's tooth, or the fanned snow that's
    bolted 364
  By th' northern blasts twice o'er.   [*He takes her hand.*]
POLIXENES   What follows this?
  How prettily the young swain seems to wash
  The hand was fair before! I have put you out. 367
  But to your protestation; let me hear 368
  What you profess.
FLORIZEL   Do, and be witness to 't.
POLIXENES
  And this my neighbor too?
FLORIZEL   And he, and more
  Than he, and men—the earth, the heavens, and all:

That, were I crowned the most imperial monarch,
Thereof most worthy, were I the fairest youth 373
That ever made eye swerve, had force and
  knowledge 374
More than was ever man's, I would not prize them
Without her love; for her employ them all,
Commend them and condemn them to her service 377
Or to their own perdition.
POLIXENES   Fairly offered. 378
CAMILLO
This shows a sound affection.
SHEPHERD   But, my daughter,
  Say you the like to him?
PERDITA   I cannot speak
  So well, nothing so well; no, nor mean better.
  By th' pattern of mine own thoughts I cut out 382
  The purity of his.
SHEPHERD   Take hands, a bargain! 383
  And, friends unknown, you shall bear witness to 't:
  I give my daughter to him and will make
  Her portion equal his.
FLORIZEL   O, that must be
  I' the virtue of your daughter. One being dead,
  I shall have more than you can dream of yet;
  Enough then for your wonder. But come on: 389
  Contract us 'fore these witnesses.
SHEPHERD   Come, your hand;
  And, daughter, yours.
POLIXENES   Soft, swain, awhile, beseech you. 391
  Have you a father?
FLORIZEL   I have, but what of him?
POLIXENES   Knows he of this?
FLORIZEL   He neither does nor shall.
POLIXENES   Methinks a father
  Is at the nuptial of his son a guest
  That best becomes the table. Pray you, once more,
  Is not your father grown incapable
  Of reasonable affairs? Is he not stupid 400
  With age and altering rheums? Can he speak? Hear? 401
  Know man from man? Dispute his own estate? 402
  Lies he not bedrid, and again does nothing
  But what he did being childish?
FLORIZEL   No, good sir, 404
  He has his health and ampler strength indeed
  Than most have of his age.
POLIXENES   By my white beard,
  You offer him, if this be so, a wrong
  Something unfilial. Reason my son 408

337 three threesome 339 by the square precisely 340 Leave leave
off 343 O . . . hereafter (Polixenes completes the conversation he
has been having with the old Shepherd during the dance. *Father* is a
respectful term of address for older men.) 345 He's simple the old
Shepherd is guileless 348 handed handled, dealt in 352 nothing
marted with have done no business with 353 Interpretation should
abuse should interpret wrongly 354 were straited would be hard-
pressed 356 happy holding her keeping her happy 358 looks looks
for 360 But not delivered i.e., but I have not confirmed it by a solemn vow before witnesses, making binding the contract. breathe my
life i.e., pronounce eternal vows 361 this ancient sir i.e., Polixenes
364 fanned blown. bolted sifted 367 was that was. put you out
interrupted what you were saying 368 to your protestation on with
your public affirmation

373 Thereof most worthy the most worthy of monarchs 374 swerve
turn in my direction (out of awe and respect) 377–378 Commend
. . . perdition either commend them to her service, or, failing that,
condemn them to deserved destruction 382–383 By . . . of his (Perdita uses a metaphor of clothes-making to express her view that Florizel's pure thoughts must be like her own—not patterned on hers but
rather perceived by her to be a model for her own.) 389 Enough
. . . wonder there will be enough then for you to wonder at
391 Soft wait a minute 400 reasonable affairs matters requiring the
use of reason 401 altering rheums weakening catarrhs or other diseases 402 Dispute discuss. estate affairs, condition 404 being
childish when he was a child 408 Something somewhat. Reason
my son it is reasonable that my son. (The disguised Polixenes seems
to be speaking hypothetically, using himself as an example, but of
course the application to Florizel is direct.)

Should choose himself a wife, but as good reason
The father, all whose joy is nothing else
But fair posterity, should hold some counsel   411
In such a business.

FLORIZEL   I yield all this;   412
But for some other reasons, my grave sir,
Which 'tis not fit you know, I not acquaint
My father of this business.

POLIXENES   Let him know 't.

FLORIZEL
He shall not.

POLIXENES   Prithee, let him.

FLORIZEL   No, he must not.

SHEPHERD
Let him, my son. He shall not need to grieve
At knowing of thy choice.

FLORIZEL   Come, come, he must not.
Mark our contract.

POLIXENES   Mark your divorce, young sir,
                                      [discovering himself]
Whom son I dare not call. Thou art too base
To be acknowledged. Thou a scepter's heir,
That thus affects a sheephook?—Thou old traitor,   422
I am sorry that by hanging thee I can
But shorten thy life one week.—And thou, fresh
   piece
Of excellent witchcraft, who of force must know   425
The royal fool thou cop'st with—

SHEPHERD   O, my heart!   426

POLIXENES
I'll have thy beauty scratched with briers and made
More homely than thy state.—For thee, fond boy,   428
If I may ever know thou dost but sigh
That thou no more shalt see this knack—as never   430
I mean thou shalt—we'll bar thee from succession,
Not hold thee of our blood, no, not our kin,
Far than Deucalion off. Mark thou my words.   433
Follow us to the court.—Thou churl, for this time,   434
Though full of our displeasure, yet we free thee
From the dead blow of it.—And you, enchantment,   436
Worthy enough a herdsman—yea, him too,   437
That makes himself, but for our honor therein,   438
Unworthy thee—if ever henceforth thou   439
These rural latches to his entrance open,
Or hoop his body more with thy embraces,
I will devise a death as cruel for thee
As thou art tender to 't.   Exit.

PERDITA   Even here undone!
I was not much afeard; for once or twice
I was about to speak and tell him plainly
The selfsame sun that shines upon his court
Hides not his visage from our cottage, but

Looks on alike. Will 't please you, sir, begone?   448
I told you what would come of this. Beseech you,
Of your own state take care. This dream of mine—
Being now awake, I'll queen it no inch farther,
But milk my ewes and weep.

CAMILLO   Why, how now, father?
Speak ere thou diest.

SHEPHERD   I cannot speak, nor think,   453
Nor dare to know that which I know. [To Florizel.]
   O sir,
You have undone a man of fourscore three,
That thought to fill his grave in quiet, yea,
To die upon the bed my father died,   457
To lie close by his honest bones; but now
Some hangman must put on my shroud and lay me
Where no priest shovels in dust. [To Perdita.] O
   cursed wretch,
That knew'st this was the Prince, and wouldst
   adventure
To mingle faith with him! Undone, undone!   462
If I might die within this hour, I have lived
To die when I desire.   Exit.

FLORIZEL [to Perdita]   Why look you so upon me?
I am but sorry, not afeard; delayed,
But nothing altered. What I was, I am,
More straining on for plucking back, not following   468
My leash unwillingly.

CAMILLO   Gracious my lord,
You know your father's temper. At this time
He will allow no speech, which I do guess
You do not purpose to him; and as hardly
Will he endure your sight as yet, I fear.
Then, till the fury of his highness settle,   474
Come not before him.

FLORIZEL   I not purpose it.
I think Camillo?

CAMILLO   Even he, my lord.

PERDITA
How often have I told you 'twould be thus?
How often said my dignity would last   478
But till 'twere known?

FLORIZEL   It cannot fail but by
The violation of my faith; and then   480
Let nature crush the sides o' th' earth together
And mar the seeds within! Lift up thy looks.   482
From my succession wipe me, Father; I
Am heir to my affection.

CAMILLO   Be advised.   484

FLORIZEL
I am, and by my fancy. If my reason   485

411 **hold some counsel** be consulted   412 **yield** concede   422 **af-fects** desires, shows inclination for   425 **of force** of necessity
426 **thou cop'st** you deal   428 **homely** (1) unattractive (2) humble.
fond foolish   430 **knack** trifle, schemer   433 **Far . . . off** farther off
in kinship than Deucalion (the Noah of classical mythology)
434 **churl** i.e., the Shepherd   436 **dead** deadly.   **enchantment** i.e.,
Perdita   437–439 **him too . . . thee** worthy indeed of him (Florizel)
whose behavior renders him unworthy even of you, if we were to set
aside for the moment the question of the dignity of our royal house

448 **alike** both the same   453 **ere thou diest** before you die of grief
(?) (Although Polixenes has relented of his threat to hang the Shepherd, the Shepherd is gloomily sure it will come to a hanging, lines
459–460.)   457 **died** died on   462 **mingle faith** exchange pledges
468 **More . . . back** i.e., like a hound on the leash, all the more eager to go forward for having been restrained   474 **his highness** his
towering rage (or else *His Highness*, as a title)   478 **my dignity** i.e.,
the new status this marriage would have offered   480 **then** when that
happens   482 **mar the seeds within** i.e., destroy the very sources of
life on earth (since all material life was thought to be derived from
seeds)   484 **affection** passionate love.   **Be advised** think carefully, be
receptive to wise advice   485 **fancy** love

Will thereto be obedient, I have reason;   486
If not, my senses, better pleased with madness,
Do bid it welcome.

CAMILLO   This is desperate, sir.

FLORIZEL
So call it, but it does fulfill my vow;
I needs must think it honesty. Camillo,
Not for Bohemia nor the pomp that may
Be thereat gleaned, for all the sun sees or
The close earth wombs or the profound seas hides   493
In unknown fathoms, will I break my oath
To this my fair beloved. Therefore, I pray you,
As you have ever been my father's honored friend,
When he shall miss me—as, in faith, I mean not
To see him any more—cast your good counsels
Upon his passion. Let myself and fortune   499
Tug for the time to come. This you may know   500
And so deliver: I am put to sea   501
With her who here I cannot hold on shore;   502
And most opportune to our need I have
A vessel rides fast by, but not prepared   504
For this design. What course I mean to hold
Shall nothing benefit your knowledge nor   506
Concern me the reporting.

CAMILLO   O my lord,   507
I would your spirit were easier for advice   508
Or stronger for your need.

FLORIZEL   Hark, Perdita.
[To Camillo.] I'll hear you by and by.
                          [He draws Perdita aside.]

CAMILLO [aside]   He's irremovable,   510
Resolved for flight. Now were I happy if
His going I could frame to serve my turn,   512
Save him from danger, do him love and honor,
Purchase the sight again of dear Sicilia
And that unhappy king, my master, whom
I so much thirst to see.

FLORIZEL   Now, good Camillo,
I am so fraught with curious business that   517
I leave out ceremony.

CAMILLO   Sir, I think   518
You have heard of my poor services i' the love
That I have borne your father?

FLORIZEL   Very nobly
Have you deserved. It is my father's music
To speak your deeds, not little of his care
To have them recompensed as thought on.

CAMILLO   Well, my lord,   523
If you may please to think I love the King
And through him what's nearest to him, which is
Your gracious self, embrace but my direction,

If your more ponderous and settled project   527
May suffer alteration. On mine honor,   528
I'll point you where you shall have such receiving
As shall become your highness, where you may   530
Enjoy your mistress—from the whom I see
There's no disjunction to be made but by,
As heavens forfend, your ruin—marry her,   533
And, with my best endeavors in your absence,   534
Your discontenting father strive to qualify   535
And bring him up to liking.

FLORIZEL   How, Camillo,   536
May this, almost a miracle, be done,
That I may call thee something more than man,
And after that trust to thee?

CAMILLO   Have you thought on   539
A place whereto you'll go?

FLORIZEL   Not any yet.
But as th' unthought-on accident is guilty   541
To what we wildly do, so we profess   542
Ourselves to be the slaves of chance and flies   543
Of every wind that blows.

CAMILLO   Then list to me.
This follows, if you will not change your purpose
But undergo this flight: make for Sicilia,
And there present yourself and your fair princess—
For so I see she must be—'fore Leontes.
She shall be habited as it becomes   549
The partner of your bed. Methinks I see
Leontes opening his free arms and weeping   551
His welcomes forth; asks thee there "Son,
      forgiveness!"
As 'twere i' the father's person; kisses the hands
Of your fresh princess; o'er and o'er divides him   554
Twixt his unkindness and his kindness. Th' one   555
He chides to hell, and bids the other grow
Faster than thought or time.

FLORIZEL   Worthy Camillo,   557
What color for my visitation shall I   558
Hold up before him?

CAMILLO   Sent by the King your father 559
To greet him and to give him comforts. Sir,
The manner of your bearing towards him, with
What you, as from your father, shall deliver—   562
Things known betwixt us three—I'll write you down,
The which shall point you forth at every sitting   564
What you must say, that he shall not perceive

---

486 **have reason** (1) will be reasonable (2) will be sane   493 **wombs** encloses, conceals   499 **passion** anger   500 **Tug** contend   501 **deliver** report   502 **who** whom   504 **rides** that rides at anchor.   **but though**   506–507 **Shall . . . reporting** would not behoove you to know nor me to report   508 **easier for** more open to   510 **irremovable** immovable   512 **frame** shape   517 **curious** demanding care   518 **I leave out ceremony** (Florizel apologizes for whispering with Perdita and failing to observe proper ceremony toward Camillo.)   523 **as thought on** as deservingly as his opinion merits

527 **ponderous** serious and carefully deliberated   528 **suffer** permit   530 **become your highness** suit your royal rank, or, suit Your Highness   533 **forfend** forbid   534 **with** together with   535 **discontenting** discontented, displeased.   **qualify** appease, pacify   536 **bring . . . liking** get him to the point of approval   539 **after** ever after   541–542 **as . . . wildly do** just as the unexpected happening (e.g., of our being discovered by the King) is responsible for what we rashly do at this point   543 **flies** i.e., insignificant insects, blown about by the winds of chance   549 **habited** (richly) dressed   551 **free** generous, noble   554 **fresh** young and beautiful   554–555 **divides . . . kindness** divides his speech between his former unkindness (which he condemns) and his present intention of kindness   557 **Faster** firmer; also, more swiftly   558 **color** excuse, pretext   559 **Hold up before** present to.   **Sent** i.e., say you are sent   562 **deliver** say   564 **point you forth** indicate to you.   **sitting** conference

But that you have your father's bosom there   566
And speak his very heart.
FLORIZEL   I am bound to you.
There is some sap in this.
CAMILLO   A course more promising
Than a wild dedication of yourselves
To unpathed waters, undreamed shores, most certain
To miseries enough; no hope to help you,
But as you shake off one to take another;   572
Nothing so certain as your anchors, who   573
Do their best office if they can but stay you   574
Where you'll be loath to be. Besides, you know   575
Prosperity's the very bond of love,   576
Whose fresh complexion and whose heart together   577
Affliction alters.
PERDITA   One of these is true: 578
I think affliction may subdue the cheek,   579
But not take in the mind.
CAMILLO   Yea, say you so?   580
There shall not at your father's house these seven
years   581
Be born another such.
FLORIZEL   My good Camillo,
She's as forward of her breeding as she is   583
I' the rear 'our birth.   584
CAMILLO   I cannot say 'tis pity
She lacks instructions, for she seems a mistress   585
To most that teach.
PERDITA   Your pardon, sir; for this   586
I'll blush you thanks.
FLORIZEL   My prettiest Perdita!
But O, the thorns we stand upon! Camillo,
Preserver of my father, now of me,
The medicine of our house, how shall we do?
We are not furnished like Bohemia's son,
Nor shall appear in Sicilia.
CAMILLO   My lord,   592
Fear none of this. I think you know my fortunes
Do all lie there. It shall be so my care
To have you royally appointed as if   595
The scene you play were mine. For instance, sir,
That you may know you shall not want, one word.

[They talk aside.]

Enter Autolycus.

AUTOLYCUS Ha, ha, what a fool Honesty is! And Trust,
his sworn brother, a very simple gentleman! I have

sold all my trumpery; not a counterfeit stone, not a
ribbon, glass, pomander, brooch, table book, ballad,   601
knife, tape, glove, shoe tie, bracelet, horn ring, to
keep my pack from fasting. They throng who should   603
buy first, as if my trinkets had been hallowed and   604
brought a benediction to the buyer; by which means
I saw whose purse was best in picture, and what I   606
saw, to my good use I remembered. My clown, who
wants but something to be a reasonable man, grew so   608
in love with the wenches' song that he would not stir
his pettitoes till he had both tune and words, which   610
so drew the rest of the herd to me that all their other
senses stuck in ears. You might have pinched a   612
placket, it was senseless. 'Twas nothing to geld a cod- 613
piece of a purse. I could have filed keys off that hung 614
in chains. No hearing, no feeling, but my sir's song,   615
and admiring the nothing of it. So that in this time of 616
lethargy I picked and cut most of their festival purses;
and had not the old man come in with hubbub
against his daughter and the King's son and scared my
choughs from the chaff, I had not left a purse alive in 620
the whole army.

[Camillo, Florizel, and Perdita come forward.]

CAMILLO
Nay, but my letters, by this means being there
So soon as you arrive, shall clear that doubt.
FLORIZEL
And those that you'll procure from King Leontes—
CAMILLO
Shall satisfy your father.
PERDITA   Happy be you!
All that you speak shows fair.
CAMILLO [seeing Autolycus]   Who have we here?
We'll make an instrument of this, omit
Nothing may give us aid.   628
AUTOLYCUS [aside] If they have overheard me now,
why, hanging.
CAMILLO How now, good fellow? Why shak'st thou so?
Fear not, man, here's no harm intended to thee.
AUTOLYCUS I am a poor fellow, sir.
CAMILLO Why, be so still. Here's nobody will steal that
from thee. Yet for the outside of thy poverty we must   635
make an exchange. Therefore discase thee instantly—   636
thou must think there's a necessity in 't—and change   637
garments with this gentleman. Though the penny-   638
worth on his side be the worst, yet hold thee, there's   639
some boot.   [He gives money.]   640

AUTOLYCUS   I am a poor fellow, sir. [*Aside.*] I know ye
well enough.

CAMILLO   Nay, prithee, dispatch. The gentleman is half   643
flayed already.   644

AUTOLYCUS   Are you in earnest, sir? [*Aside.*] I smell the
trick on 't.

FLORIZEL   Dispatch, I prithee.

AUTOLYCUS   Indeed, I have had earnest, but I cannot   648
with conscience take it.

CAMILLO   Unbuckle, unbuckle.
　　　　　[*Florizel and Autolycus exchange garments.*]
Fortunate mistress—let my prophecy   651
Come home to ye!—you must retire yourself   652
Into some covert. Take your sweetheart's hat   653
And pluck it o'er your brows, muffle your face,
Dismantle you, and, as you can, disliken   655
The truth of your own seeming, that you may—   656
For I do fear eyes over—to shipboard   657
Get undescried.

PERDITA　　　　　　I see the play so lies
That I must bear a part.

CAMILLO　　　　　　　No remedy.—
Have you done there?

FLORIZEL　　　　　　Should I now meet my father,
He would not call me son.

CAMILLO   Nay, you shall have no hat.
　　　　　　　　[*He gives it to Perdita.*]
Come, lady, come. Farewell, my friend.

AUTOLYCUS　　　　　　　Adieu, sir.

FLORIZEL
O Perdita, what have we twain forgot?
Pray you, a word.　　　　[*They speak aside.*]

CAMILLO [*aside*]
What I do next shall be to tell the King
Of this escape and whither they are bound;
Wherein my hope is I shall so prevail
To force him after, in whose company
I shall re-view Sicilia, for whose sight   670
I have a woman's longing.

FLORIZEL　　　　　　Fortune speed us!
Thus we set on, Camillo, to th' seaside.

CAMILLO   The swifter speed the better.
　　　　　　　Exit [*with Florizel and Perdita*]

AUTOLYCUS   I understand the business; I hear it. To
have an open ear, a quick eye, and a nimble hand is
necessary for a cutpurse; a good nose is requisite also,
to smell out work for th' other senses. I see this is the
time that the unjust man doth thrive. What an
exchange had this been without boot! What a boot is   679
here with this exchange! Sure the gods do this year
connive at us, and we may do anything extempore.   681
The Prince himself is about a piece of iniquity, stealing 682

away from his father with his clog at his heels. If I   683
thought it were a piece of honesty to acquaint the King
withal, I would not do 't. I hold it the more knavery to   685
conceal it; and therein am I constant to my profession.

　　　　Enter Clown and Shepherd [*carrying a bundle and
　　　　a box*].

Aside, aside! Here is more matter for a hot brain.
Every lane's end, every shop, church, session, hang-   688
ing, yields a careful man work.　　　[*He stands aside.*]

CLOWN   See, see, what a man you are now! There is no
other way but to tell the King she's a changeling and   691
none of your flesh and blood.

SHEPHERD   Nay, but hear me.

CLOWN   Nay, but hear me.

SHEPHERD   Go to, then.   695

CLOWN   She being none of your flesh and blood, your
flesh and blood has not offended the King, and so
your flesh and blood is not to be punished by him.
Show those things you found about her, those secret
things, all but what she has with her. This being done,
let the law go whistle, I warrant you.

SHEPHERD   I will tell the King all, every word, yea, and
his son's pranks too; who, I may say, is no honest
man, neither to his father nor to me, to go about to   704
make me the King's brother-in-law.

CLOWN   Indeed, brother-in-law was the farthest off you
could have been to him, and then your blood had
been the dearer by I know not how much an ounce.

AUTOLYCUS [*aside*]   Very wisely, puppies!

SHEPHERD   Well, let us to the King. There is that in this
fardel will make him scratch his beard.   711

AUTOLYCUS [*aside*]   I know not what impediment this
complaint may be to the flight of my master.   713

CLOWN   Pray heartily he be at' palace.   714

AUTOLYCUS [*aside*]   Though I am not naturally honest,
I am so sometimes by chance. Let me pocket up my
peddler's excrement. [*He takes off his false beard.*] How 717
now, rustics, whither are you bound?

SHEPHERD   To the palace, an it like your worship.   719

AUTOLYCUS   Your affairs there, what, with whom, the
condition of that fardel, the place of your dwelling,   721
your names, your ages, of what having, breeding, and   722
anything that is fitting to be known, discover.   723

CLOWN   We are but plain fellows, sir.   724

AUTOLYCUS   A lie; you are rough and hairy. Let me have
no lying. It becomes none but tradesmen, and they
often give us soldiers the lie, but we pay them for it   727
with stamped coin, not stabbing steel; therefore they

---

643 **dispatch** hurry (also in line 647)　**644 flayed** skinned, i.e., undressed　**648 earnest** advance payment (playing on *in earnest* in line
645)　**651–652 let . . . to ye** i.e., let my prophecy that you, Perdita,
will be fortunate be fulfilled for you　**653 covert** hidden place
655–656 as you . . . seeming as much as you can, disguise your outward appearance　**657 eyes over** spying eyes　**670 re-view** see again
679 without boot i.e., even without added payment.　**What a boot**
what a profit　**681 connive at** look indulgently at　**682 about**
engaged in

683 **clog** encumbrance (i.e., Perdita)　**685 withal** with it　**688 session**
court session　**691 changeling** child left by the fairies　**695 Go to** go
ahead. (Or, an expression of impatience.)　**704 go about** make it his
object　**711 fardel** bundle　**713 my master** i.e., Florizel. (See
4.3.13.)　**714 at'** at the　**717 excrement** outgrowth of hair, beard
719 an it like if it please　**721 condition** nature　**722 having** property
723 discover reveal　**724 plain** simple. (But Autolycus plays on the
meaning ''smooth.'')　**727 give . . . lie** i.e., cheat us. (But *giving the
lie* also means to accuse a person to his face of lying, an affront
which a soldier would repay with *stabbing steel*.)

do not give us the lie.   729

CLOWN   Your worship had like to have given us one, if 730
you had not taken yourself with the manner.   731

SHEPHERD   Are you a courtier, an 't like you, sir?

AUTOLYCUS   Whether it like me or no, I am a courtier.
Seest thou not the air of the court in these enfoldings? 734
Hath not my gait in it the measure of the court? Re- 735
ceives not thy nose court odor from me? Reflect I not
on thy baseness court contempt? Think'st thou, for 737
that I insinuate to toze from thee thy business, I am 738
therefore no courtier? I am courtier cap-a-pie, and one 739
that will either push on or pluck back thy business
there. Whereupon I command thee to open thy affair. 741

SHEPHERD   My business, sir, is to the King.

AUTOLYCUS   What advocate hast thou to him?

SHEPHERD   I know not, an 't like you.

CLOWN [aside to Shepherd]   "Advocate"'s the court
word for a pheasant. Say you have none.   746

SHEPHERD   None, sir. I have no pheasant, cock nor hen.

AUTOLYCUS [aside]
How blessed are we that are not simple men!
Yet nature might have made me as these are;
Therefore I will not disdain.

CLOWN [to Shepherd]   This cannot be but a great courtier.

SHEPHERD   His garments are rich, but he wears them
not handsomely.

CLOWN   He seems to be the more noble in being fantas- 755
tical. A great man, I'll warrant. I know by the picking 756
on 's teeth.   757

AUTOLYCUS   The fardel there? What's i' the fardel?
Wherefore that box?

SHEPHERD   Sir, there lies such secrets in this fardel and
box which none must know but the King, and which
he shall know within this hour if I may come to the
speech of him.

AUTOLYCUS   Age, thou hast lost thy labor.   764

SHEPHERD   Why, sir?

AUTOLYCUS   The King is not at the palace. He is gone
aboard a new ship to purge melancholy and air
himself; for, if thou be'st capable of things serious, 768
thou must know the King is full of grief.

SHEPHERD   So 'tis said, sir; about his son, that should
have married a shepherd's daughter.

AUTOLYCUS   If that shepherd be not in handfast, let him 772
fly. The curses he shall have, the tortures he shall feel,

will break the back of man, the heart of monster.

CLOWN   Think you so, sir?

AUTOLYCUS   Not he alone shall suffer what wit can make 776
heavy and vengeance bitter, but those that are ger- 777
mane to him, though removed fifty times, shall all 778
come under the hangman—which, though it be great
pity, yet it is necessary. An old sheep-whistling rogue, 780
a ram tender, to offer to have his daughter come into 781
grace? Some say he shall be stoned; but that death is 782
too soft for him, say I. Draw our throne into a sheepcote? All deaths are too few, the sharpest too easy.

CLOWN   Has the old man e'er a son, sir, do you hear,
an 't like you, sir?

AUTOLYCUS   He has a son, who shall be flayed alive; then,
'nointed over with honey, set on the head of a wasp's
nest; then stand till he be three-quarters and a dram 789
dead; then recovered again with aqua vitae or some 790
other hot infusion; then, raw as he is, and in the hottest day prognostication proclaims, shall he be set 792
against a brick wall, the sun looking with a southward
eye upon him, where he is to behold him with flies 794
blown to death. But what talk we of these traitorly ras- 795
cals, whose miseries are to be smiled at, their offenses
being so capital? Tell me, for you seem to be honest
plain men, what you have to the King. Being some- 798
thing gently considered, I'll bring you where he is 799
aboard, tender your persons to his presence, whisper 800
him in your behalfs; and if it be in man besides the
King to effect your suits, here is man shall do it.

CLOWN [to Shepherd]   He seems to be of great authority. Close with him, give him gold; and though au- 804
thority be a stubborn bear, yet he is oft led by the nose
with gold. Show the inside of your purse to the outside of his hand, and no more ado. Remember—
"stoned," and "flayed alive."

SHEPHERD   An 't please you, sir, to undertake the
business for us, here is that gold I have. [He offers
money.] I'll make it as much more and leave this young
man in pawn till I bring it you.

AUTOLYCUS   After I have done what I promised?

SHEPHERD   Ay, sir.

AUTOLYCUS [taking the money]   Well, give me the moiety. 815
[To the Clown.] Are you a party in this business?

CLOWN   In some sort, sir. But, though my case be a piti- 817
ful one, I hope I shall not be flayed out of it.

AUTOLYCUS   O, that's the case of the shepherd's son.
Hang him, he'll be made an example.

CLOWN [to Shepherd]   Comfort, good comfort! We must
to the King and show our strange sights. He must
know 'tis none of your daughter nor my sister; we are
gone else.—Sir, I will give you as much as this old 824

---

729 give (Autolycus punningly observes that, since soldiers pay
tradesmen for their wares, the tradesmen cannot be said to have *given*
the lie, and so a duel is avoided.)   **730 had like** was about
731 taken . . . manner i.e., caught yourself in the act, stopped short.
(The Clown observes that Autolycus has once again avoided the "giving of the lie" and its consequences in a duel by his clever equivocation. Compare with Touchstone in *As You Like It*, 5.4.)   **734 enfoldings** clothes   **735 measure** stately tread   **737–738 for that** because
738 insinuate to toze pry in order to tease, draw out, comb out
739 cap-a-pie from head to foot   **741 open** reveal   **746 pheasant**
(The rustics suppose that Autolycus has asked them what gift they propose to present as a bribe, as one might do to a judge in a court of
law.)   **755–756 fantastical** eccentric   **756–757 picking on 's teeth**
(A stylish affectation in Shakespeare's time.)   **764 Age** old man
768 be'st capable of know anything about   **772 handfast** custody
(with a play on "betrothal")

776 wit ingenuity   **777–778 germane** related   **780 sheep-whistling**
tending sheep by whistling after them   **781 offer** dare   **782 grace** favor   **789 a dram** i.e., a small amount, a fraction   **790 aqua vitae**
brandy   **792 prognostication** forecasting (in the almanac)   **794 he**
i.e., the sun   **795 blown** swollen.   **what** i.e., why   **798 what you
have to** what business you have with   **798–799 Being . . . considered** i.e., (1) being a gentleman of some influence (2) if I receive a
gentlemanly consideration, a bribe   **800 tender your persons** introduce you   **804 Close with him** accept his offer   **815 moiety** half
817 case (1) cause (2) skin   **824 gone else** undone otherwise

man does when the business is performed, and
remain, as he says, your pawn till it be brought you.

AUTOLYCUS   I will trust you. Walk before toward the
seaside; go on the right hand. I will but look upon the   828
hedge and follow you.   829

CLOWN [to Shepherd]   We are blessed in this man, as I
may say, even blessed.

SHEPHERD   Let's before, as he bids us. He was provided
to do us good.   Exeunt [Shepherd and Clown].

AUTOLYCUS   If I had a mind to be honest, I see Fortune
would not suffer me; she drops booties in my mouth.
I am courted now with a double occasion: gold, and a   836
means to do the Prince my master good, which who
knows how that may turn back to my advancement? I   838
will bring these two moles, these blind ones, aboard   839
him. If he think it fit to shore them again and that the   840
complaint they have to the King concerns him noth-   841
ing, let him call me rogue for being so far officious, for   842
I am proof against that title and what shame else   843
belongs to 't. To him will I present them. There may be
matter in it.   [Exit.]

❖

5.1   Enter Leontes, Cleomenes, Dion, Paulina, [and]
servants.

CLEOMENES
Sir, you have done enough, and have performed
A saintlike sorrow. No fault could you make
Which you have not redeemed—indeed, paid down
More penitence than done trespass. At the last,
Do as the heavens have done, forget your evil;
With them forgive yourself.

LEONTES   Whilst I remember
Her and her virtues, I cannot forget
My blemishes in them, and so still think of   8
The wrong I did myself, which was so much
That heirless it hath made my kingdom and
Destroyed the sweet'st companion that e'er man
Bred his hopes out of. True?

PAULINA   Too true, my lord.
If one by one you wedded all the world,
Or from the all that are took something good   14
To make a perfect woman, she you killed
Would be unparalleled.

LEONTES   I think so. Killed?
She I killed? I did so, but thou strik'st me
Sorely to say I did. It is as bitter
Upon thy tongue as in my thought. Now,
good now,   19

Say so but seldom.

CLEOMENES   Not at all, good lady.
You might have spoken a thousand things that
would
Have done the time more benefit and graced
Your kindness better.

PAULINA   You are one of those
Would have him wed again.

DION   If you would not so,
You pity not the state nor the remembrance   25
Of his most sovereign name, consider little   26
What dangers by His Highness' fail of issue   27
May drop upon his kingdom and devour
Incertain lookers-on. What were more holy   29
Than to rejoice the former queen is well?   30
What holier than, for royalty's repair,
For present comfort and for future good,
To bless the bed of majesty again
With a sweet fellow to 't?

PAULINA   There is none worthy,
Respecting her that's gone. Besides, the gods   35
Will have fulfilled their secret purposes;   36
For has not the divine Apollo said,
Is 't not the tenor of his oracle,
That King Leontes shall not have an heir
Till his lost child be found? Which that it shall
Is all as monstrous to our human reason
As my Antigonus to break his grave   42
And come again to me, who, on my life,
Did perish with the infant. 'Tis your counsel   44
My lord should to the heavens be contrary,
Oppose against their wills. [To Leontes.] Care not for
issue.   46
The crown will find an heir. Great Alexander
Left his to th' worthiest; so his successor   48
Was like to be the best.

LEONTES   Good Paulina,
Who hast the memory of Hermione,
I know, in honor, O, that ever I
Had squared me to thy counsel! Then even now   52
I might have looked upon my queen's full eyes,
Have taken treasure from her lips—

PAULINA   And left them
More rich for what they yielded.

LEONTES   Thou speak'st truth.
No more such wives, therefore no wife. One worse,   56
And better used, would make her sainted spirit   57

828–829 **look . . . hedge** i.e., relieve myself   836 **occasion** opportunity   838 **turn back** redound   839–840 **aboard him** i.e., to him
(Prince Florizel) aboard his ship   840 **shore** put ashore
841–842 **nothing** not at all   843 **proof against** invulnerable to
5.1. Location: Sicilia. The royal court.
8 **in them** in thinking of them, or, in comparison with them   14 **the
all that are** all the women that there are   19 **good now** i.e., if you
please

25 **nor the remembrance** i.e., nor give consideration to the perpetua-
tion (through bearing a child and heir)   26 **consider** you consider
27 **fail of issue** failure to produce an heir   29 **Incertain** not knowing
what to think or do (about the royal succession)   30 **well** happy, at
rest (in heaven)   35 **Respecting** in comparison to   36 **Will . . . purposes** are determined to have their secret purposes fulfilled   42 **As** as
for   44 **'Tis your counsel** it's your advice that   46 **Oppose** oppose
himself.   **Care not for** do not be anxious about   48 **Left . . . worthiest** (When Alexander the Great died in 323 B.C., his son Alexander
was yet unborn, necessitating the choice of an heir.)   52 **squared me**
adjusted or regulated myself   56–57 **One . . . used** i.e., if I took a
new, less excellent wife and treated her better   57 **her** i.e.,
Hermione's

Again possess her corpse, and on this stage,   58
Where we're offenders now, appear soul-vexed,
And begin, "Why to me?"
PAULINA   Had she such power,   60
She had just cause.
LEONTES   She had, and would incense me   61
To murder her I married.
PAULINA   I should so.   62
Were I the ghost that walked, I'd bid you mark
Her eye and tell me for what dull part in 't
You chose her. Then I'd shriek, that even your ears
Should rift to hear me, and the words that followed 66
Should be, "Remember mine."
LEONTES   Stars, stars,   67
And all eyes else dead coals! Fear thou no wife;
I'll have no wife, Paulina.
PAULINA   Will you swear
Never to marry but by my free leave?
LEONTES
Never, Paulina, so be blest my spirit!
PAULINA
Then, good my lords, bear witness to his oath.
CLEOMENES
You tempt him overmuch.
PAULINA   Unless another,   73
As like Hermione as is her picture,
Affront his eye.
CLEOMENES   Good madam—
PAULINA   I have done.   75
Yet if my lord will marry—if you will, sir,
No remedy, but you will—give me the office
To choose you a queen. She shall not be so young
As was your former, but she shall be such
As, walked your first queen's ghost, it should take
  joy   80
To see her in your arms.
LEONTES   My true Paulina,
We shall not marry till thou bidd'st us.
PAULINA   That
Shall be when your first queen's again in breath;
Never till then.   84

          Enter a Gentleman.

GENTLEMAN
One that gives out himself Prince Florizel,   85
Son of Polixenes, with his princess—she
The fairest I have yet beheld—desires access
To your high presence.
LEONTES   What with him? He comes not   88
Like to his father's greatness. His approach,   89

So out of circumstance and sudden, tells us   90
'Tis not a visitation framed, but forced   91
By need and accident. What train?
GENTLEMAN   But few,   92
And those but mean.
LEONTES   His princess, say you, with him?   93
GENTLEMAN
Ay, the most peerless piece of earth, I think,
That e'er the sun shone bright on.
PAULINA   O Hermione,
As every present time doth boast itself
Above a better gone, so must thy grave
Give way to what's seen now! [*To the Gentleman.*]
   Sir, you yourself
Have said and writ so, but your writing now
Is colder than that theme. She had not been   102
Nor was not to be equaled—thus your verse   103
Flowed with her beauty once. 'Tis shrewdly ebbed   104
To say you have seen a better.
GENTLEMAN   Pardon, madam.
The one I have almost forgot—your pardon!
The other, when she has obtained your eye,
Will have your tongue too. This is a creature,   106
Would she begin a sect, might quench the zeal
Of all professors else, make proselytes   108
Of who she but bid follow.
PAULINA   How? Not women!   109
GENTLEMAN
Women will love her that she is a woman
More worth than any man; men, that she is
The rarest of all women.
LEONTES   Go, Cleomenes.
Yourself, assisted with your honored friends,
Bring them to our embracement.
                     Exit [*Cleomenes with others*].
                          Still, 'tis strange
He thus should steal upon us.
PAULINA   Had our prince,
Jewel of children, seen this hour, he had paired
Well with this lord. There was not full a month
Between their births.
LEONTES   Prithee, no more, cease. Thou know'st
He dies to me again when talked of. Sure,
When I shall see this gentleman, thy speeches
Will bring me to consider that which may
Unfurnish me of reason. They are come.   123

     Enter Florizel, Perdita, Cleomenes, and others.

Your mother was most true to wedlock, Prince,
For she did print your royal father off,
Conceiving you. Were I but twenty-one,

---

58 **possess her corpse** i.e., return to earth (*this stage*) in Hermione's
human shape   60 **Why to me** i.e., why this offense to me?   61 **had**
would have.   **incense** stir up, incite   62 **should so** would similarly
incite you   66 **rift** rive, split   67 **mine** my eyes.   **Stars** i.e., her eyes
were stars   73 **tempt** bear down on   75 **Affront** confront   80 **walked
. . . ghost** if your first queen's ghost were to walk.   **take joy** be overjoyed   84 s.d. **Enter a Gentleman** (He is called a "Servant" in the
Folio text, but his writing poetry in lines 100–104 is more consistent
with his being a courtier. Any such person at court is a servant of the
king.)   85 **gives out himself** reports himself to be   88 **What** what retinue   89 **Like to** in a manner consistent with

90 **out of circumstance** without ceremony   91 **framed** planned
92 **train** retinue   93 **mean** lowly   102 **that theme** i.e., Hermione, the
subject of your verses   102–103 **She . . . equaled** (Presumably, the
poet wrote "She has not been nor is not to be equaled.")   104 **'Tis
shrewdly ebbed** i.e., you've egregiously gone back on your word
106 **tongue** i.e., approval   108 **professors else** believers in other sects
or deities   109 **Of . . . follow** of all those whom she merely told to
follow her.   **How? Not women!** what do you mean? Surely women
wouldn't become converts   123 **Unfurnish** deprive, divest

Your father's image is so hit in you,   127
His very air, that I should call you brother,
As I did him, and speak of something wildly
By us performed before. Most dearly welcome!
And your fair princess—goddess! O! Alas,
I lost a couple that twixt heaven and earth
Might thus have stood begetting wonder as
You, gracious couple, do. And then I lost—
All mine own folly—the society,
Amity too, of your brave father, whom,   136
Though bearing misery, I desire my life   137
Once more to look on him.
FLORIZEL   By his command   138
Have I here touched Sicilia, and from him
Give you all greetings that a king, at friend,   140
Can send his brother; and but infirmity,   141
Which waits upon worn times, hath something
   seized   142
His wished ability, he had himself   143
The lands and waters twixt your throne and his
Measured to look upon you, whom he loves—   145
He bade me say so—more than all the scepters
And those that bear them living.
LEONTES   O my brother!   147
Good gentleman, the wrongs I have done thee stir
Afresh within me, and these thy offices,   149
So rarely kind, are as interpreters   150
Of my behindhand slackness. Welcome hither,   151
As is the spring to th' earth. And hath he too
Exposed this paragon to th' fearful usage—
At least ungentle—of the dreadful Neptune,
To greet a man not worth her pains, much less
Th' adventure of her person?
FLORIZEL   Good my lord,   156
She came from Libya.
LEONTES   Where the warlike Smalus,
That noble honored lord, is feared and loved?
FLORIZEL
Most royal sir, from thence, from him, whose
   daughter   159
His tears proclaimed his, parting with her. Thence,   160
A prosperous south wind friendly, we have crossed,
To execute the charge my father gave me
For visiting Your Highness. My best train
I have from your Sicilian shores dismissed,
Who for Bohemia bend, to signify   165
Not only my success in Libya, sir,
But my arrival and my wife's in safety
Here where we are.
LEONTES   The blessèd gods
Purge all infection from our air whilst you

Do climate here! You have a holy father,   170
A graceful gentleman, against whose person,   171
So sacred as it is, I have done sin,
For which the heavens, taking angry note,
Have left me issueless; and your father's blest,
As he from heaven merits it, with you,
Worthy his goodness. What might I have been,
Might I a son and daughter now have looked on,
Such goodly things as you?

Enter a Lord.

LORD   Most noble sir,
That which I shall report will bear no credit
Were not the proof so nigh. Please you, great sir,
Bohemia greets you from himself by me;
Desires you to attach his son, who has—   182
His dignity and duty both cast off—   183
Fled from his father, from his hopes, and with
A shepherd's daughter.
LEONTES   Where's Bohemia? Speak.
LORD
Here in your city. I now came from him.
I speak amazedly, and it becomes   187
My marvel and my message. To your court   188
Whiles he was hastening—in the chase, it seems,
Of this fair couple—meets he on the way
The father of this seeming lady and
Her brother, having both their country quitted
With this young prince.
FLORIZEL   Camillo has betrayed me,
Whose honor and whose honesty till now
Endured all weathers.
LORD   Lay 't so to his charge.   195
He's with the King your father.
LEONTES   Who? Camillo?
LORD
Camillo, sir. I spake with him, who now
Has these poor men in question. Never saw I   198
Wretches so quake. They kneel, they kiss the earth,
Forswear themselves as often as they speak.
Bohemia stops his ears and threatens them
With divers deaths in death.
PERDITA   O my poor father!   202
The heaven sets spies upon us, will not have
Our contract celebrated.
LEONTES   You are married?
FLORIZEL
We are not, sir, nor are we like to be.   205
The stars, I see, will kiss the valleys first;
The odds for high and low's alike.
LEONTES   My lord,   207

127 hit exactly reproduced   **136 brave** noble   **137 my life** i.e., to
live long enough   **138 him** (Redundant in modern syntax.)   **140 at
friend** in friendship   **141 but** were it not that   **142 waits . . . times**
attends old age   **142–143 something . . . ability** to some extent
taken away his ability (to travel) as he wishes   **145 Measured** traversed   **147 those . . . living** those living kings who bear scepters
149 offices messages of good will, courteous attentions   **150 rarely**
exceptionally   **150–151 interpreters Of** commentators on   **156 adventure** hazard   **159–160 whose . . . her** whose tears, as he parted
with her, proclaimed her to be his daughter   **165 bend** direct their
course

170 climate dwell, reside (in this clime)   **171 graceful** full of grace,
gracious   **182 attach** arrest   **183 dignity and duty** princely dignity
and filial duty   **187–188 I . . . message** i.e., I speak perplexedly as
befits my perplexity and my astonishing news   **195 Lay . . . charge**
i.e., confront him with it directly   **198 in question** under interrogation   **202 deaths** i.e., tortures   **205 like** likely   **207 The odds . . .
alike** i.e., Fortune is the same for the high and low (?), or perhaps, the
odds of a high roll in dice are the same as those of a low roll—we
are at the mercy of chance—or, the odds of a union of high and
low in marriage are about the same as those of the stars kissing the
valleys

Is this the daughter of a king?

FLORIZEL   She is,
When once she is my wife.

LEONTES
That "once," I see, by your good father's speed
Will come on very slowly. I am sorry,
Most sorry, you have broken from his liking
Where you were tied in duty, and as sorry
Your choice is not so rich in worth as beauty,   214
That you might well enjoy her.

FLORIZEL [to Perdita]   Dear, look up.
Though Fortune, visible an enemy,   216
Should chase us with my father, power no jot   217
Hath she to change our loves.—Beseech you, sir,
Remember since you owed no more to time   219
Than I do now. With thought of such affections, 220
Step forth mine advocate. At your request
My father will grant precious things as trifles.

LEONTES
Would he do so, I'd beg your precious mistress,
Which he counts but a trifle.

PAULINA   Sir, my liege,
Your eye hath too much youth in 't. Not a month
'Fore your queen died, she was more worth such
   gazes
Than what you look on now.

LEONTES   I thought of her
Even in these looks I made. [To Florizel.] But your
   petition
Is yet unanswered. I will to your father.
Your honor not o'erthrown by your desires,   230
I am friend to them and you. Upon which errand
I now go toward him. Therefore follow me,
And mark what way I make. Come, good my lord.   233
                                        Exeunt.

❖

5.2   Enter Autolycus and a Gentleman.

AUTOLYCUS Beseech you, sir, were you present at this
   relation?   2
FIRST GENTLEMAN I was by at the opening of the fardel,
   heard the old shepherd deliver the manner how he   4
   found it; whereupon, after a little amazedness, we
   were all commanded out of the chamber. Only this,
   methought, I heard the shepherd say: he found the
   child.
AUTOLYCUS I would most gladly know the issue of it.
FIRST GENTLEMAN I make a broken delivery of the busi-   10
   ness, but the changes I perceived in the King and Cam-

illo were very notes of admiration. They seemed al-   12
most, with staring on one another, to tear the cases of   13
their eyes. There was speech in their dumbness, lan-   14
guage in their very gesture. They looked as they had   15
heard of a world ransomed, or one destroyed. A notable
passion of wonder appeared in them, but the wisest
beholder, that knew no more but seeing, could not say   18
if th' importance were joy or sorrow; but in the ex-   19
tremity of the one it must needs be.   20

   Enter another Gentleman.

Here comes a gentleman that haply knows more.—   21
The news, Rogero?
SECOND GENTLEMAN Nothing but bonfires. The oracle
   is fulfilled; the King's daughter is found. Such a deal of
   wonder is broken out within this hour that ballad
   makers cannot be able to express it.

   Enter another Gentleman.

Here comes the Lady Paulina's steward. He can deliver
you more.—How goes it now, sir? This news which is
called true is so like an old tale that the verity of it is in
strong suspicion. Has the King found his heir?
THIRD GENTLEMAN Most true, if ever truth were preg-   31
   nant by circumstance. That which you hear you'll   32
   swear you see, there is such unity in the proofs. The
   mantle of Queen Hermione's, her jewel about the neck
   of it, the letters of Antigonus found with it which they
   know to be his character, the majesty of the creature in   36
   resemblance of the mother, the affection of nobleness   37
   which nature shows above her breeding, and many   38
   other evidences proclaim her with all certainty to be
   the King's daughter. Did you see the meeting of the
   two kings?
SECOND GENTLEMAN No.
THIRD GENTLEMAN Then have you lost a sight which
   was to be seen, cannot be spoken of. There might you
   have beheld one joy crown another, so and in such
   manner that it seemed Sorrow wept to take leave of
   them, for their joy waded in tears. There was casting
   up of eyes, holding up of hands, with countenance of   48
   such distraction that they were to be known by
   garment, not by favor. Our king, being ready to leap   50
   out of himself for joy of his found daughter, as if that
   joy were now become a loss, cries, "O, thy mother,
   thy mother!" then asks Bohemia forgiveness; then
   embraces his son-in-law; then again worries he his
   daughter with clipping her; now he thanks the old   55
   shepherd, which stands by like a weather-bitten con-   56
   duit of many kings' reigns. I never heard of such   57

---

214 worth rank 216–217 Though . . . father though Fortune were
to become visible as our enemy and join my father in chasing us
219–220 since . . . now when you were no older than I am now
220 With . . . affections recalling what it was to be in love at that
age 230 Your . . . desires i.e., if your chaste honor has not been
overcome by sexual desire, or, if what you want in this match is compatible with your royal honor 233 way progress
5.2. Location: Sicilia. At court.
2 relation narrative, account 4 deliver report 10 broken disjointed,
fragmented

12 very notes of admiration veritable marks of wonderment, like exclamation marks 13–14 cases of their eyes eyelids 15 as as if
18 no . . . seeing nothing except what he could see 19 importance
import, meaning 20 of the one of one or the other 21 haply perhaps 31–32 pregnant by circumstance made apparent by circumstantial evidence 36 character handwriting 37 affection of natural
disposition to 38 breeding rearing 48 countenance bearing, demeanor 50 favor features 55 clipping embracing 56–57 conduit
fountain (weeping tears) 57 of many i.e., that has stood there during
many

another encounter, which lames report to follow it and
undoes description to do it.   59
SECOND GENTLEMAN   What, pray you, became of Antigonus, that carried hence the child?
THIRD GENTLEMAN Like an old tale still, which will have
matter to rehearse though credit be asleep and not an   63
ear open. He was torn to pieces with a bear. This   64
avouches the shepherd's son, who has not only his   65
innocence, which seems much, to justify him, but a   66
handkerchief and rings of his that Paulina knows.   67
FIRST GENTLEMAN   What became of his bark and his
followers?
THIRD GENTLEMAN   Wrecked the same instant of their
master's death and in the view of the shepherd; so that
all the instruments which aided to expose the child
were even then lost when it was found. But O, the
noble combat that twixt joy and sorrow was fought in
Paulina! She had one eye declined for the loss of her   75
husband, another elevated that the oracle was fulfilled. 76
She lifted the Princess from the earth, and so locks her
in embracing as if she would pin her to her heart, that
she might no more be in danger of losing.   79
FIRST GENTLEMAN   The dignity of this act was worth
the audience of kings and princes, for by such was it
acted.
THIRD GENTLEMAN   One of the prettiest touches of all,
and that which angled for mine eyes—caught the
water, though not the fish—was when, at the relation
of the Queen's death, with the manner how she came
to 't bravely confessed and lamented by the King,
how attentiveness wounded his daughter; till, from   88
one sign of dolor to another, she did, with an "Alas!" I 89
would fain say, bleed tears, for I am sure my heart
wept blood. Who was most marble there changed   91
color; some swooned, all sorrowed. If all the world
could have seen 't, the woe had been universal.
FIRST GENTLEMAN   Are they returned to the court?
THIRD GENTLEMAN   No. The Princess hearing of her
mother's statue, which is in the keeping of Paulina—a
piece many years in doing and now newly performed   97
by that rare Italian master, Julio Romano, who, had he 98
himself eternity and could put breath into his work,
would beguile Nature of her custom, so perfectly he is 100
her ape; he so near to Hermione hath done Hermione 101
that they say one would speak to her and stand in
hope of answer—thither with all greediness of affec- 103
tion are they gone, and there they intend to sup.   104
SECOND GENTLEMAN I thought she had some great mat-

ter there in hand, for she hath privately twice or thrice
a day, ever since the death of Hermione, visited that
removed house. Shall we thither and with our com-   108
pany piece the rejoicing?   109
FIRST GENTLEMAN   Who would be thence that has the
benefit of access? Every wink of an eye some new
grace will be born. Our absence makes us unthrifty to 112
our knowledge. Let's along.   Exeunt [Gentlemen].
AUTOLYCUS   Now, had I not the dash of my former life 114
in me, would preferment drop on my head. I brought
the old man and his son aboard the Prince, told him I
heard them talk of a fardel and I know not what. But
he at that time overfond of the shepherd's daughter—so he then took her to be—who began to be
much seasick, and himself little better, extremity of
weather continuing, this mystery remained undiscovered. But 'tis all one to me, for had I been the finder 122
out of this secret, it would not have relished among 123
my other discredits.

Enter Shepherd and Clown, [dressed in finery].

Here come those I have done good to against my will,
and already appearing in the blossoms of their fortune.
SHEPHERD   Come, boy. I am past more children, but
thy sons and daughters will be all gentlemen born.
CLOWN   You are well met, sir. You denied to fight with
me this other day because I was no gentleman born. 131
See you these clothes? Say you see them not and think
me still no gentleman born. You were best say these
robes are not gentlemen born. Give me the lie, do, and 134
try whether I am not now a gentleman born.
AUTOLYCUS   I know you are now, sir, a gentleman born.
CLOWN   Ay, and have been so any time these four
hours.
SHEPHERD   And so have I, boy.
CLOWN   So you have. But I was a gentleman born before
my father; for the King's son took me by the hand
and called me brother; and then the two kings called
my father brother; and then the Prince my brother and
the Princess my sister called my father father; and so
we wept, and there was the first gentlemanlike tears
that ever we shed.
SHEPHERD   We may live, son, to shed many more.
CLOWN   Ay, or else 'twere hard luck, being in so pre- 148
posterous estate as we are.   149
AUTOLYCUS   I humbly beseech you, sir, to pardon me
all the faults I have committed to your worship, and to
give me your good report to the Prince my master.   152
SHEPHERD   Prithee, son, do; for we must be gentle, now 153
we are gentlemen.
CLOWN   Thou wilt amend thy life?
AUTOLYCUS   Ay, an it like your good worship.   156

59 undoes . . . it beggars description to do justice to it 63 rehearse
relate. credit belief 64 with by 65 avouches confirms, corroborates 66 innocence simplemindedness (such that he would seem unable to invent such a story) 67 his i.e., Antigonus' 75–76 She . . .
fulfilled i.e., she wept and laughed at the same time 79 losing being
lost 88 attentiveness listening to it 89 dolor grief 91 Who . . .
marble even the most hardhearted 97 performed completed
98 Julio Romano Italian painter and sculptor of the sixteenth century,
better known as a painter (and an anachronism in this play) 100 beguile deprive, cheat. custom trade 101 ape imitator
103–104 greediness of affection eagerness born of love 104 sup
i.e., feed their hungry eyes (?) or, perhaps, have a commemorative
banquet (?)

108 removed sequestered 109 piece add to, augment 112 unthrifty
to passing up an opportunity to increase 114 dash touch 122 'tis
all one it's all the same 123 relished tasted well, suited 131 this
other the other 134 Give me the lie accuse me to my face of lying
(an insult that requires a challenge to a duel) 148–149 preposterous
(Blunder for "prosperous.") 152 me on my behalf 153 gentle nobly
generous 156 an it like if it please

CLOWN   Give me thy hand. I will swear to the Prince
thou art as honest a true fellow as any is in Bohemia. 158

SHEPHERD   You may say it, but not swear it.

CLOWN   Not swear it, now I am a gentleman? Let boors 160
and franklins say it; I'll swear it. 161

SHEPHERD   How if it be false, son?

CLOWN   If it be ne'er so false, a true gentleman may
swear it in the behalf of his friend.—And I'll swear to
the Prince thou art a tall fellow of thy hands and that 165
thou wilt not be drunk; but I know thou art no tall
fellow of thy hands and that thou wilt be drunk. But
I'll swear it, and I would thou wouldst be a tall fellow
of thy hands.

AUTOLYCUS   I will prove so, sir, to my power. 170

CLOWN   Ay, by any means prove a tall fellow. If I do not
wonder how thou dar'st venture to be drunk, not
being a tall fellow, trust me not. Hark, the kings and
the princes, our kindred, are going to see the Queen's
picture. Come, follow us. We'll be thy good masters. 175
Exeunt.

❧

5.3   *Enter Leontes, Polixenes, Florizel, Perdita,
Camillo, Paulina, lords, etc.*

LEONTES
O grave and good Paulina, the great comfort
That I have had of thee!

PAULINA   What, sovereign sir,
I did not well, I meant well. All my services
You have paid home. But that you have vouchsafed, 4
With your crowned brother and these your
contracted
Heirs of your kingdoms, my poor house to visit,
It is a surplus of your grace which never
My life may last to answer.

LEONTES   O Paulina,   8
We honor you with trouble. But we came   9
To see the statue of our queen. Your gallery
Have we passed through, not without much content
In many singularities; but we saw not   12
That which my daughter came to look upon,
The statue of her mother.

PAULINA   As she lived peerless,
So her dead likeness, I do well believe,
Excels whatever yet you looked upon
Or hand of man hath done. Therefore I keep it
Lonely, apart. But here it is. Prepare   18
To see the life as lively mocked as ever   19

Still sleep mocked death. Behold, and say 'tis well.   20
[*Paulina draws a curtain, and discovers*]
Hermione [*standing*] *like a statue.*
I like your silence; it the more shows off
Your wonder. But yet speak; first, you, my liege.
Comes it not something near?

LEONTES   Her natural posture!   23
Chide me, dear stone, that I may say indeed
Thou art Hermione; or rather, thou art she
In thy not chiding, for she was as tender
As infancy and grace. But yet, Paulina,
Hermione was not as much wrinkled, nothing   28
So agèd as this seems.

POLIXENES   O, not by much.

PAULINA
So much the more our carver's excellence,
Which lets go by some sixteen years and makes her
As she lived now.

LEONTES   As now she might have done,   32
So much to my good comfort as it is
Now piercing to my soul. O, thus she stood,
Even with such life of majesty—warm life,
As now it coldly stands—when first I wooed her!
I am ashamed. Does not the stone rebuke me
For being more stone than it? O royal piece!   38
There's magic in thy majesty, which has
My evils conjured to remembrance and
From thy admiring daughter took the spirits,   41
Standing like stone with thee.

PERDITA   And give me leave,
And do not say 'tis superstition, that
I kneel and then implore her blessing. Lady,
[*kneeling*]
Dear Queen, that ended when I but began,
Give me that hand of yours to kiss.

PAULINA   O, patience!
The statue is but newly fixed; the color's   47
Not dry.

CAMILLO
My lord, your sorrow was too sore laid on,   49
Which sixteen winters cannot blow away,
So many summers dry. Scarce any joy   51
Did ever so long live; no sorrow
But killed itself much sooner.

POLIXENES   Dear my brother,
Let him that was the cause of this have power   54
To take off so much grief from you as he
Will piece up in himself.

PAULINA   Indeed, my lord,   56
If I had thought the sight of my poor image
Would thus have wrought you—for the stone is
mine—   58

---

158 honest a true worthy an honest   **160 boors** peasants   **161 franklins** farmers owning their own small farms   **165 tall . . . hands** brave
fellow   **170 my power** the best of my ability. (Autolycus slyly promises to use his hands well—in picking pockets.)   **175 picture** i.e.,
likeness, painted statue
5.3. Location: Sicilia. Paulina's house.
4 home fully   **8 last** last long enough.   **answer** repay adequately
9 We . . . trouble i.e., we trouble you with the demands of hospitality, though you are kind enough to call it an honor   **12 singularities**
rarities, curiosities   **18 Lonely** isolated   **19 as lively mocked** as realis-
tically counterfeited

20 Still motionless   **23 something** somewhat   **28 nothing** not at all
32 As she as if she   **38 piece** work of art   **41 admiring** filled with
wonder.   **spirits** vital spirits   **47 fixed** made fast in its color   **49 sore**
heavily   **51 So . . . dry** i.e., and sixteen summers cannot dry up.
(Camillo tells the King that he has imposed too heavy a sorrow on
himself if even sixteen years' time cannot end it.)   **54 him** i.e., myself
(as an innocent cause, but still a cause)   **56 piece up in himself** add
to his own burden   **58 wrought** affected

I'd not have showed it.

LEONTES   Do not draw the curtain.

PAULINA
No longer shall you gaze on 't, lest your fancy
May think anon it moves.

LEONTES   Let be, let be.
Would I were dead but that methinks already—
What was he that did make it? See, my lord,
Would you not deem it breathed? And that those
    veins
Did verily bear blood?

POLIXENES   Masterly done.
The very life seems warm upon her lip.

LEONTES
The fixture of her eye has motion in 't,   67
As we are mocked with art.

PAULINA   I'll draw the curtain.   68
My lord's almost so far transported that
He'll think anon it lives.

LEONTES   O sweet Paulina,
Make me to think so twenty years together!
No settled senses of the world can match   72
The pleasure of that madness. Let 't alone.

PAULINA
I am sorry, sir, I have thus far stirred you; but
I could afflict you farther.

LEONTES   Do, Paulina;
For this affliction has a taste as sweet
As any cordial comfort. Still methinks   77
There is an air comes from her. What fine chisel
Could ever yet cut breath? Let no man mock me,
For I will kiss her.

PAULINA   Good my lord, forbear.
The ruddiness upon her lip is wet;
You'll mar it if you kiss it, stain your own
With oily painting. Shall I draw the curtain?   83

LEONTES
No, not these twenty years.

PERDITA   So long could I
Stand by, a looker on.

PAULINA   Either forbear,   85
Quit presently the chapel, or resolve you   86
For more amazement. If you can behold it,
I'll make the statue move indeed, descend
And take you by the hand. But then you'll think—
Which I protest against—I am assisted
By wicked powers.

LEONTES   What you can make her do
I am content to look on, what to speak
I am content to hear; for 'tis as easy
To make her speak as move.

PAULINA   It is required
You do awake your faith. Then all stand still.
On; those that think it is unlawful business   96

67 The fixture . . . in 't i.e., her eye, though motionless, gives the
appearance of motion 68 As . . . art in such a way that we are
fooled by artistic illusion 72 No settled . . . world no calm mind in
the world 77 cordial restorative, heartwarming 83 painting paint
85 forbear withdraw 86 presently immediately 96 On; those (Often emended to Or those.)

I am about, let them depart.

LEONTES   Proceed.
No foot shall stir.

PAULINA   Music, awake her; strike!   [Music.] 98
'Tis time. Descend. Be stone no more. Approach.
Strike all that look upon with marvel. Come,   100
I'll fill your grave up. Stir, nay, come away,
Bequeath to death your numbness, for from him   102
Dear life redeems you.—You perceive she stirs.
                    [Hermione comes down.]
Start not. Her actions shall be holy as
You hear my spell is lawful. Do not shun her   105
Until you see her die again, for then   106
You kill her double. Nay, present your hand.   107
When she was young you wooed her. Now in age
Is she become the suitor?   [Leontes touches her.]

LEONTES   O, she's warm!
If this be magic, let it be an art
Lawful as eating.

POLIXENES   She embraces him.

CAMILLO   She hangs about his neck.
If she pertain to life, let her speak too.

POLIXENES
Ay, and make it manifest where she has lived,
Or how stol'n from the dead.

PAULINA   That she is living,
Were it but told you, should be hooted at
Like an old tale; but it appears she lives,
Though yet she speak not. Mark a little while.
[To Perdita.] Please you to interpose, fair madam.
    Kneel,   120
And pray your mother's blessing.—Turn, good
    lady;
Our Perdita is found.

HERMIONE   You gods, look down
And from your sacred vials pour your graces
Upon my daughter's head!—Tell me, mine own,
Where hast thou been preserved? Where lived?
    How found
Thy father's court? For thou shalt hear that I,
Knowing by Paulina that the oracle
Gave hope thou wast in being, have preserved
Myself to see the issue.

PAULINA   There's time enough for that,
Lest they desire upon this push to trouble   131
Your joys with like relation. Go together,   132
You precious winners all; your exultation
Partake to everyone. I, an old turtle,   134
Will wing me to some withered bough and there
My mate, that's never to be found again,   136
Lament till I am lost.

LEONTES   O, peace, Paulina!   137

98 strike strike up 100 upon on 102 him i.e., death 105–107 Do
. . . double i.e., if you ever shun her during the rest of her life, you
will kill her again 106 then in that case 107 double a second time
120 madam (Addressed to Perdita as Princess and affianced to be
married.) 131–132 Lest . . . relation lest they insist, at this critical
juncture, on interrupting this moment of joy with your relating of your
story or with their telling what has happened to them 134 Partake to
share with, communicate. turtle turtledove 136–137 My mate
. . . lost grieve for my lost mate until I die

Thou shouldst a husband take by my consent,
As I by thine a wife. This is a match,
And made between 's by vows. Thou hast found
   mine,
But how is to be questioned, for I saw her,
As I thought, dead, and have in vain said many
A prayer upon her grave. I'll not seek far—
For him, I partly know his mind—to find thee   144
An honorable husband. Come, Camillo,
And take her by the hand, whose worth and
   honesty   146
Is richly noted and here justified   147
By us, a pair of kings. Let's from this place.
[*To Hermione.*] What? Look upon my brother. Both
   your pardons,
That e'er I put between your holy looks
My ill suspicion. This' your son-in-law   151
And son unto the King, whom, heavens directing,
Is trothplight to your daughter. Good Paulina,   153
Lead us from hence, where we may leisurely
Each one demand and answer to his part
Performed in this wide gap of time since first
We were dissevered. Hastily lead away.   *Exeunt.*

144 For as for   **146 whose** i.e., Camillo's   **147 richly noted** abundantly acknowledged.   **justified** avouched   **151 This'** this is
153 trothplight betrothed

The Tempest

Shakespeare creates in *The Tempest* a world of the imagination, a place of conflict and ultimately of magical rejuvenation, like the forests of *A Midsummer Night's Dream* and *As You Like It*. The journey to Shakespeare's island is to a realm of art where everything is controlled by the artist-figure. Yet the journey is no escape from reality, for the island shows people what they are, as well as what they ought to be. Even its location juxtaposes the "real" world with an idealized landscape: like Plato's New Atlantis or Thomas More's Utopia, Shakespeare's island is to be found both somewhere and nowhere. On the narrative level, it is located in the Mediterranean Sea. Yet there are overtones of the New World, the Western Hemisphere, where Thomas More had situated his island of Utopia. Ariel fetches dew at Prospero's command from the "Bermudas" (1.2.230). Caliban when prostrate reminds Trinculo of a "dead Indian" (2.2.33) who might be displayed before gullible crowds eager to see such a prodigious creature from across the seas, and Caliban's god, Setebos, was, according to Richard Eden's account of Magellan's circumnavigation of the globe (in *History of Travel*, 1577), worshiped by South American natives. An inspiration for Shakespeare's story (for which no direct literary source is known) may well have been various accounts of the shipwreck in the Bermudas in 1609 of the *Sea Venture*, which was carrying settlers to the new Virginian colony. Shakespeare borrowed details from Sylvester Jourdain's *A Discovery of the Bermudas, Otherwise Called the Isle of Devils*, published in 1610, and from William Strachey's *A True Reportory of the Wreck and Redemption . . . from the Islands of the Bermudas*, which Shakespeare must have seen in manuscript since it was not published until after his death. He wrote the play shortly after reading these works, for *The Tempest* was acted at court in 1611. He may also have known or heard of various accounts of Magellan's circumnavigation of the world in 1519–1522 (including Richard Eden's shortened English version, as part of his *History of Travel*, of an Italian narrative by Antonio Pigafetta), Francis Fletcher's journal of Sir Francis Drake's circumnavigation in 1577–1580, Richard Rich's *News from Virginia* (1610), and still other potential sources of information. Shakespeare's fascination with the Western Hemisphere gave him, not the actual location of his story, which remains Mediterranean, but a state of mind associated with newness and the unfamiliar. From this strange and unknown place, we gain a radical perspective on the old world of European culture. Miranda sees on the island a "new world" in which humankind appears "brave" (5.1.185), and, although her wonder must be tempered by Prospero's rejoinder that "'Tis new to thee" (line 186) and by Aldous Huxley's still more ironic use of her phrase in the title of his satirical novel *Brave New World*, the island endures as a restorative vision. Even though we experience it fleetingly, as in a dream, this nonexistent realm assumes a permanence enjoyed by all great works of art.

Prospero rules autocratically as artist-king and patriarch over this imaginary world, conjuring up trials and visions to test people's intentions and awaken their consciences. To the island come an assortment of persons who, because they require varied ordeals, are separated by Prospero and Ariel into three groups: King Alonso and those accompanying him; Alonso's son, Ferdinand; and Stephano and Trinculo. Prospero's authority over them, though strong, has limits. As Duke of Milan, he was bookishly inattentive to political matters and thus vulnerable to the Machiavellian conniving of his younger brother, Antonio. Only in this world apart, the artist's world, do his powers derived from learning find their proper sphere. Because he cannot control the world beyond his isle, he must wait for "strange, bountiful Fortune, / Now my dear lady" (1.2.179–180) to bring his enemies near his shore. He eschews, moreover, the black arts of diabolism. His is a white magic, devoted ultimately to what he considers moral ends: rescuing Ariel from the spell of the witch Sycorax, curbing the appetite of Caliban, spying on Antonio and Sebastian in the role of Conscience. He sees Fortune's gift of delivering his enemies into his hands as an opportunity for him to forgive and restore them, not be revenged.

Such an assumption of godlike power is close to arrogance, even blasphemy, for Prospero is no god. His chief power, learned from books and exercised through Ariel, is to control the elements so as to create illusion—of separation, of death, of the gods' blessing. Yet, since he is human, even this power is an immense burden and temptation. Prospero has much to learn, like those whom he controls. He must subdue his anger, his self-pity, his readiness to blame others, his domineering over Miranda. He must overcome the vengeful impulse he experiences toward those who have wronged him, and he must conquer the longing any father feels to hold on to his daughter when she is desired by another man. He struggles with these problems through his art, devising games and shows in which his angry self-pity and jealousy are transmuted into playacting scenes of divine warning and forgiveness toward his enemies and watchful parental austerity toward Miranda and Ferdinand. Prospero's responsibilities cause him to behave magisterially and to be resented by the spirits of the isle. His authority is problematic to us because he seems so patriarchal, colonialist, even sexist and racist in his arrogating to himself the right and responsibility to control others in the name of Western and Christian values. Ariel longs to be free of this authority. Perhaps our sympathy for Prospero is greatest when we perceive that he, too, with mixed feelings of genuine relief and melancholy, is ready to lay aside his demanding and self-important role as creative moral intelligence.

Alonso and his court party variously illustrate the unregenerate world left behind in Naples and Milan. We first see them on shipboard, panicky and desperate, their titles and finery mocked by roaring waves. Futile ambition seems destined for a watery demise. Yet death by water in this play is a transfiguration rather than an end, a mystical rebirth, as in the regenerative cycle of the seasons from winter to summer. Ariel suggests as much in his song about a drowned father: "Those are pearls that were his eyes. / Nothing of him that doth fade / But doth suffer a sea change / Into something rich and strange" (1.2.402–405). Still, this miracle is not apparent at first to those who are caught in the illusion of death. As in T. S. Eliot's *The Waste Land,* which repeatedly alludes to *The Tempest,* self-blinded human beings fear a disaster that is ironically the prelude to reawakening.

The illusions created on the island serve to test these imperfect men and to make them reveal their true selves. Only Gonzalo, who long ago aided Prospero and Miranda when they were banished from Milan, responds affirmatively to illusion. He alone notices that his garments and those of his shipwrecked companions have miraculously been left unharmed by the salt water. His ideal commonwealth (2.1.150–171), which Shakespeare drew in part from an essay by Montaigne, postulates a natural goodness in humanity and makes no allowance for the darker propensities of human behavior, but at least Gonzalo's cheerfulness is in refreshing contrast to the jaded sneers of some of his companions. Sebastian and Antonio react to the magic isle, as to Gonzalo's commonwealth, by cynically refusing to believe in miracles. Confident that they are unobserved, they seize the opportunity afforded by Alonso's being asleep to plot a murder and political coup. This attempt is not only despicable but also madly ludicrous, for they are all shipwrecked and no longer have kingdoms over which to quarrel. Even more ironically, Sebastian and Antonio, despite their insolent belief in their self-sufficiency, are being observed. The villains must be taught that an unseen power keeps track of their misdeeds. However presumptuous Prospero may be to assume through Ariel's means the role of godlike observer, he does awaken conscience and prevent murder. The villains may revert to type when returned to their usual habitat, but even they are at least briefly moved to an awareness of the unseen (3.3.21–27). Alonso, more worthy than they, though burdened, too, with sin, responds to his situation with guilt and despair, for he assumes that his son Ferdinand's death is the just punishment of the gods for Alonso's part in the earlier overthrow of Prospero. Alonso must be led, by means of curative illusions, through the purgative experience of contrition to the reward he thinks impossible and undeserved: reunion with his lost son.

Alonso is thus, like Posthumus in *Cymbeline* or Leontes in *The Winter's Tale,* a tragicomic figure—sinful, contrite, forgiven. Alonso's son Ferdinand must also undergo ordeals and visions devised by Prospero to test his worth, but more on the level of romantic comedy. Ferdinand is young, innocent, and hopeful, well-matched to Miranda. From the start, Prospero obviously approves of his prospective son-in-law. Yet even Prospero, needing to prepare himself for a life in which Miranda will no longer be solely his, is not ready to lay aside at least the comic fiction of parental opposition. He invents difficulties, imposes tasks of logbearing (like those assigned Caliban), and issues stern warnings against premarital lust. In the comic mode, parents are expected to cross their children in matters of the heart. Prospero is so convincing in his role of overbearing parent, insisting on absolute unthinking obedience from his daughter, that we remain unsure whether he is truly like that or whether we are meant to sense in his performance a grappling with his own deepest feelings of possessiveness and autocratic authority, tempered finally by his awareness of the arbitrariness of such a role and his readiness to let Miranda decide for herself. As a teacher of youth, moreover, Prospero is convinced by long experience that prizes too easily won are too lightly esteemed. Manifold are the temptations urging Ferdinand to surrender to the natural rhythms of the isle and to fulfill his desire like Caliban. In place of ceremonies conducted in civilized societies by the church, Prospero must create the illusion of ceremony by his art. The marriage of Ferdinand and Miranda accordingly unites the best of both worlds: the natural innocence of the island, which teaches them to avoid the corruptions of civilization at its worst, and the higher law of nature achieved through moral wisdom at its best. To this marriage, the goddesses Iris, Ceres, and Juno bring promises of bounteous harvest, "refreshing showers," celestial harmony, and a springtime brought back to the earth by Proserpina's return from Hades (4.1.79–117). In Ferdinand and Miranda, "nurture" is wedded to "nature." This bond unites spirit and flesh, legitimizing erotic pleasure by incorporating it within Prospero's vision of a cosmic moral order.

At the lowest level of this traditional cosmic and moral framework, in Prospero's view, are Stephano and Trinculo. Their comic scenes juxtapose them with Caliban, for he represents untutored Nature, whereas they represent the unnatural depths to which human beings brought up in civilized society can fall. In this they resemble Sebastian and Antonio, who have learned in supposedly civilized Italy arts of intrigue and political murder. The antics of Stephano and Trinculo burlesque the conduct of their presumed betters, thereby exposing to ridicule the self-deceptions of ambitious men. The clowns desire to exploit the natural wonders of the isle by taking Caliban back to civilization to be shown in carnivals or by plying him with strong drink and whetting his resentment against authority. These plottings are in vain, however, for, like Sebastian and Antonio, the clowns are being watched. The clowns teach Caliban to cry out for "freedom" (2.2.184), by which they mean license to do as one pleases, but are foiled by Ariel as comic nemesis. Because they are degenerate buffoons, Prospero as satirist devises for them an exposure that is appropriately humiliating and satirical.

In contrast with them, Caliban is in many ways a sympathetic character. His sensitivity to natural beauty, as in his descriptions of the "nimble marmoset" or the dreaming music he so often hears (2.2.168; 3.2.137–145), is entirely appropriate to this child of nature. He is, to be sure, the child of a witch and is called many harsh names by Miranda and Prospero, such as "Abhorrèd slave" and "a born devil, on whose nature / Nurture can never stick" (1.2.354; 4.1.188–189). Yet he protests with some justification that the island was his in the first place and that Prospero and Miranda are interlopers. His very existence calls radically into question the value of civilization, which has shown itself capable of limitless depravity. What profit has Caliban derived from learning Prospero's language other than, as he puts it, to "know how to curse" (1.2.367)? With instinctive cunning, he senses that books are his chief enemy and plots to destroy them first in his attempt at rebellion. The unspoiled natural world does indeed offer civilization a unique perspective on itself. In this it resembles Gonzalo's ideal commonwealth, which, no matter how laughably implausible from the cynic's point of view, does at least challenge the very assumptions upon which Western civilization is based.

Radical perspectives of this kind invite consideration of many unsettling questions about exploration, colonialist empire building, and sexual imperialism. The fleeting comparison of Caliban to an American Indian (2.2.33), although ignored in stage productions of the play until the late nineteenth century, suggests a discourse on colonialism in The Tempest that anticipates to a remarkable degree a doleful history of exploitation, of providing rum and guns to the natives, and of taking away land through violent expropriation in the name of bringing civilization and God to the New World. Stephano and Trinculo, pouring wine down Caliban's throat and thus reducing him to a worshiping slave, show exploitation at its worst, but surely the play allows us to wonder also if Prospero's enslavement of Caliban, however high-minded in its claims of preventing disorder and rape, is not tainted by the same imperatives of possession and control. The issue is wonderfully complex. Caliban is a projection of both the naturally depraved savage described in many explorers' accounts and the nobly innocent savage described by Montaigne. By dramatizing the conflict without taking sides, Shakespeare leaves open a debate about the worth of Prospero's endeavor to contain Caliban's oth-

erness and produces an ambivalent result in which the apparent victory of colonialism and censorship does not entirely conceal the contradictory struggle through which those values are imposed. The play's many open-ended questions apply not only to the New World but also, nearer at hand, to Ireland—an island on the margins of Britain that was regarded as both savage and threatening.

The play's discourse also raises issues of class, in that the battle between Prospero and Caliban is one of "master" and "man" (2.2.183); even if Caliban's cry of "freedom" leads him only into further enslavement by Stephano and Trinculo (who are themselves masterless men), the questions of mastery and freedom are not thereby resolved simply in favor of a reimposition of hierarchy. Similarly, Prospero's vision of a harmonious marriage presided over by goddesses of fecundity cannot conceal the extent to which the marriage represents for him a vindication of his own power as father and returning Duke of Milan; Miranda has a crucial role to play in the political alliance that will unite the ruling families of Milan and Naples. Prospero's masque, his ultimate vision of the triumph of civilization, recreates the myth of the rape of a daughter (Proserpina) in such a way as to allay Prospero's own anxiety about the chastity of his daughter. The court marriage celebrated in this play must have taken on a special resonance when The Tempest was performed before King James at Whitehall in November of 1611 and then again at court in 1613 in celebration of the marriage of James' daughter Elizabeth to Frederick, the Elector Palatine.

The play's ending is far from perfectly stable. Antonio never repents, and we cannot be sure what the island will be like once Prospero has disappeared from the scene. Since Prospero's occupation of the island replicates in a sense the process by which he himself was overthrown, we cannot know when the cycle of revolution will ever cease. We cannot even be sure of the extent to which Shakespeare is master of his own colonial debate in The Tempest or, conversely, the extent to which today we should feel ourselves free to relativize, ironize, or in other ways criticize this play for apparent or probable prejudices. Not even a great author like Shakespeare can escape the limits of his own time, any more than we can escape the limits of our own. Perhaps we can nonetheless project ourselves, as spectators and readers, into Shakespeare's attempt to celebrate humanity's highest achievement in the union of the island with the civilized world. Miranda and Ferdinand have bright hopes for the future, even if those hopes must be qualified by Prospero's melancholic observation that the "brave new world" with "such people in 't" is only "new to thee," to those who are young and not yet experienced in the world's vexations. Even Caliban may be at last reconciled to Prospero's insistent idea of a harmony between will and reason, no matter how perilously and delicately achieved. Prospero speaks of Caliban as a "thing of darkness I / Acknowledge mine," and Caliban vows to "be wise hereafter / And seek for grace"

(5.1.278–279, 298–299). Prospero's view is that the natural human within is more contented, better understood, and more truly free when harmonized with reason.

Caliban is a part of humanity; Ariel is not. Ariel can comprehend what compassion and forgiveness would be like, "were I human" (5.1.20), and can take good-natured part in Prospero's designs to castigate or reform his fellow mortals, but Ariel longs to be free in quite another sense from that meant by Caliban. Ariel takes no part in the final integration of human society. This spirit belongs to a magic world of song, music, and illusion that the artist borrows for his use but that exists eternally outside of him. Like the elements of air, earth, fire, and water in which it mysteriously dwells, this spirit is morally neutral but incredibly vital. From it the artist achieves powers of imagination, enabling him to bedim the noontide sun or call forth the dead from their graves. These visions are illusory in the profound sense that all life is illusory, an "insubstantial pageant" melted into thin air (4.1.150–155). Prospero the artist cherishes his own humanity, as a promise of surcease from his labors. Yet the artifact created by the artist endures, existing apart from time and place, as does Ariel: "Then to the elements / Be free, and fare thou well!" (5.1.321–322). No doubt it is a romantic fiction to associate the dramatist Shakespeare with Prospero's farewell to his art, but it is an almost irresistible idea, because we are so moved by the sense of completion and yet humility, the exultation and yet the calm contained in this leave-taking.

The Tempest

Names of the Actors

ALONSO, *King of Naples*
SEBASTIAN, *his brother*
PROSPERO, *the right Duke of Milan*
ANTONIO, *his brother, the usurping Duke of Milan*
FERDINAND, *son to the King of Naples*
GONZALO, *an honest old councillor*
ADRIAN and } *lords*
FRANCISCO,
CALIBAN, *a savage and deformed slave*
TRINCULO, *a jester*
STEPHANO, *a drunken butler*
MASTER *of a ship*
BOATSWAIN
MARINERS

MIRANDA, *daughter to Prospero*

ARIEL, *an airy spirit*
IRIS
CERES,
JUNO, } *[presented by] spirits*
NYMPHS
REAPERS,

[*Other Spirits attending on Prospero*]

THE SCENE: *An uninhabited island*

1.1
A tempestuous noise of thunder and lightning heard. Enter a Shipmaster and a Boatswain.

MASTER Boatswain!
BOATSWAIN Here, Master. What cheer?
MASTER Good, speak to the mariners. Fall to 't yarely, 3
or we run ourselves aground. Bestir, bestir! *Exit.*

Enter Mariners.

BOATSWAIN Heigh, my hearts! Cheerly, cheerly, my
hearts! Yare, yare! Take in the topsail. Tend to the Mas- 6
ter's whistle.—Blow till thou burst thy wind, if room 7
enough! 8

*Enter Alonso, Sebastian, Antonio, Ferdinand,
Gonzalo, and others.*

1.1. Location: On board ship, off the island's coast.
3 Good i.e., it's good you've come, or, my good fellow. **yarely** nimbly **6 Tend** attend **7 Blow** (Addressed to the wind.) **7–8 if room enough** as long as we have sea room enough

ALONSO Good Boatswain, have care. Where's the Mas-
ter? Play the men.   10
BOATSWAIN I pray now, keep below.
ANTONIO Where is the Master, Boatswain?
BOATSWAIN Do you not hear him? You mar our labor.
Keep your cabins! You do assist the storm.   14
GONZALO Nay, good, be patient.   15
BOATSWAIN When the sea is. Hence! What cares these
roarers for the name of king? To cabin! Silence! Trou-   17
ble us not.
GONZALO Good, yet remember whom thou hast
aboard.
BOATSWAIN None that I more love than myself. You are
a councillor; if you can command these elements to
silence and work the peace of the present, we will not   23
hand a rope more. Use your authority. If you cannot,   24
give thanks you have lived so long and make yourself
ready in your cabin for the mischance of the hour, if it
so hap.—Cheerly, good hearts!—Out of our way,   27
I say.   Exit.
GONZALO I have great comfort from this fellow. Methinks he hath no drowning mark upon him; his com-   30
plexion is perfect gallows. Stand fast, good Fate, to his   31
hanging! Make the rope of his destiny our cable, for
our own doth little advantage. If he be not born to be   33
hanged, our case is miserable.   Exeunt [courtiers].   34

        Enter Boatswain.

BOATSWAIN Down with the topmast! Yare! Lower,
lower! Bring her to try wi' the main course. (A cry   36
within.) A plague upon this howling! They are louder
than the weather or our office.   38

        Enter Sebastian, Antonio, and Gonzalo.

Yet again? What do you here? Shall we give o'er and   39
drown? Have you a mind to sink?
SEBASTIAN A pox o' your throat, you bawling, blasphemous, incharitable dog!
BOATSWAIN Work you, then.
ANTONIO Hang, cur! Hang, you whoreson, insolent
noisemaker! We are less afraid to be drowned than
thou art.
GONZALO I'll warrant him for drowning, though the   47
ship were no stronger than a nutshell and as
leaky as an unstanched wench.   49
BOATSWAIN Lay her ahold, ahold! Set her two courses. 50

Off to sea again! Lay her off!

        Enter Mariners, wet.

MARINERS All lost! To prayers, to prayers! All lost!
[The Mariners run about in confusion, exiting at
random.]
BOATSWAIN What, must our mouths be cold?   53
GONZALO
The King and Prince at prayers! Let's assist them,
For our case is as theirs.
SEBASTIAN   I am out of patience.
ANTONIO
We are merely cheated of our lives by drunkards.   56
This wide-chapped rascal! Would thou mightst lie
drowning   57
The washing of ten tides!
GONZALO   He'll be hanged yet,   58
Though every drop of water swear against it
And gape at wid'st to glut him.
(A confused noise within:)   "Mercy on us!"—   60
"We split, we split!"—"Farewell my wife and
children!"—   61
"Farewell, brother!"—"We split, we split, we split!"
[Exit Boatswain.]
ANTONIO Let's all sink wi' the King.
SEBASTIAN Let's take leave of him.
Exit [with Antonio].
GONZALO Now would I give a thousand furlongs of sea
for an acre of barren ground: long heath, brown furze,   66
anything. The wills above be done! But I would fain   67
die a dry death.   Exit.

1.2 Enter Prospero [in his magic cloak] and Miranda.

MIRANDA
If by your art, my dearest father, you have   1
Put the wild waters in this roar, allay them.   2
The sky, it seems, would pour down stinking pitch,
But that the sea, mounting to th' welkin's cheek,   4
Dashes the fire out. O, I have suffered
With those that I saw suffer! A brave vessel,   6
Who had, no doubt, some noble creature in her,
Dashed all to pieces. O, the cry did knock
Against my very heart! Poor souls, they perished.
Had I been any god of power, I would
Have sunk the sea within the earth or ere   11
It should the good ship so have swallowed and

10 Play the men act like men (?) ply, urge the men to exert themselves (?) 14 Keep remain in 15 good good fellow 17 roarers
waves or winds, or both; spoken to as though they were "bullies" or
"blusterers" 23 work . . . present bring calm to our present circumstances 24 hand handle 27 hap happen 30–31 complexion . . .
gallows appearance shows he was born to be hanged (and therefore,
according to the proverb, in no danger of drowning) 33 our . . . advantage our own cable is of little benefit 34 case is miserable circumstances are desperate 36 Bring . . . course sail her close to the
wind by means of the mainsail 38 our office i.e., the noise we make
at our work 39 give o'er give up 47 warrant him for drowning
guarantee that he will never be drowned 49 unstanched insatiable,
loose, unrestrained (suggesting also "incontinent" and "menstrual")
50 ahold ahull, close to the wind. courses sails, i.e., foresail as well
as mainsail, set in an attempt to get the ship back out into open water

53 must . . . cold i.e., must we drown in the cold sea, or, let us heat
up our mouths with liquor 56 merely utterly 57 wide-chapped with
mouth wide open 57–58 lie . . . tides (Pirates were hanged on the
shore and left until three tides had come in.) 60 at wid'st wide
open. glut swallow 61 split break apart 66 heath heather. furze
gorse, a weed growing on wasteland 67 fain rather
1.2. Location: The island, near Prospero's cell. On the Elizabethan
stage, this cell is implicitly at hand throughout the play, although in
some scenes the convention of flexible distance allows us to imagine
characters in other parts of the island.
1 art magic 2 allay pacify 4 welkin's cheek sky's face 6 brave gallant, splendid 11 or ere before

The freighting souls within her.

PROSPERO   Be collected.   13
No more amazement. Tell your piteous heart   14
There's no harm done.

MIRANDA   O, woe the day!

PROSPERO   No harm.
I have done nothing but in care of thee,   16
Of thee, my dear one, thee, my daughter, who
Art ignorant of what thou art, naught knowing
Of whence I am, nor that I am more better   19
Than Prospero, master of a full poor cell,   20
And thy no greater father.

MIRANDA   More to know
Did never meddle with my thoughts.

PROSPERO   'Tis time   22
I should inform thee farther. Lend thy hand
And pluck my magic garment from me. So,
       [*laying down his magic cloak and staff*]
Lie there, my art.—Wipe thou thine eyes. Have
   comfort.
The direful spectacle of the wreck, which touched   26
The very virtue of compassion in thee,   27
I have with such provision in mine art   28
So safely ordered that there is no soul—
No, not so much perdition as an hair   30
Betid to any creature in the vessel   31
Which thou heard'st cry, which thou saw'st sink. Sit
   down,   32
For thou must now know farther.

MIRANDA [*sitting*]   You have often
Begun to tell me what I am, but stopped
And left me to a bootless inquisition,   35
Concluding, "Stay, not yet."

PROSPERO   The hour's now come;
The very minute bids thee ope thine ear.
Obey, and be attentive. Canst thou remember
A time before we came unto this cell?
I do not think thou canst, for then thou wast not
Out three years old.

MIRANDA   Certainly, sir, I can.   41

PROSPERO
By what? By any other house or person?
Of anything the image, tell me, that
Hath kept with thy remembrance.

MIRANDA   'Tis far off,
And rather like a dream than an assurance   45
That my remembrance warrants. Had I not   46
Four or five women once that tended me?

PROSPERO
Thou hadst, and more, Miranda. But how is it
That this lives in thy mind? What seest thou else
In the dark backward and abysm of time?   50

If thou rememberest aught ere thou cam'st here,   51
How thou cam'st here thou mayst.

MIRANDA   But that I do not.

PROSPERO
Twelve year since, Miranda, twelve year since,
Thy father was the Duke of Milan and
A prince of power.

MIRANDA   Sir, are not you my father?

PROSPERO
Thy mother was a piece of virtue, and   56
She said thou wast my daughter; and thy father
Was Duke of Milan, and his only heir
And princess no worse issued.

MIRANDA   O the heavens!   59
What foul play had we, that we came from thence?
Or blessèd was 't we did?

PROSPERO   Both, both, my girl.
By foul play, as thou sayst, were we heaved thence,
But blessedly holp hither.

MIRANDA   O, my heart bleeds   63
To think o' the teen that I have turned you to,   64
Which is from my remembrance! Please you, farther.   65

PROSPERO
My brother and thy uncle, called Antonio—
I pray thee mark me—that a brother should
Be so perfidious!—he whom next thyself   68
Of all the world I loved, and to him put
The manage of my state, as at that time   70
Through all the seigniories it was the first,   71
And Prospero the prime duke, being so reputed   72
In dignity, and for the liberal arts
Without a parallel; those being all my study,
The government I cast upon my brother
And to my state grew stranger, being transported   76
And rapt in secret studies. Thy false uncle—
Dost thou attend me?

MIRANDA   Sir, most heedfully.

PROSPERO
Being once perfected how to grant suits,   79
How to deny them, who t' advance and who
To trash for overtopping, new created   81
The creatures that were mine, I say, or changed 'em,   82
Or else new formed 'em; having both the key   83
Of officer and office, set all hearts i' the state
To what tune pleased his ear, that now he was   85
The ivy which had hid my princely trunk
And sucked my verdure out on 't. Thou
   attend'st not.   87

13 freighting forming the cargo. **collected** calm, composed
14 amazement consternation. **piteous** pitying **16 but** except
19 more better of higher rank **20 full** very **22 meddle** mingle
26 wreck shipwreck **27 virtue** essence **28 provision** foresight
30 perdition loss **31 Betid** happened **32 Which** whom **35 bootless inquisition** profitless inquiry **41 Out** fully **45–46 assurance
. . . warrants** certainty that my memory guarantees **50 backward
. . . time** abyss of the past

51 aught anything **56 piece** masterpiece, exemplar **59 no worse issued** no less nobly born, descended **63 holp** helped **64 teen . . .
to** trouble I've caused you to remember or put you to **65 from** out of
68 next next to **70 manage** management, administration
71 seigniories i.e., city-states of northern Italy **72 prime** first in rank
and importance **76 to . . . stranger** i.e., withdrew from my responsibilities as duke. **transported** carried away **79 perfected** grown
skillful **81 trash** check a hound by tying a cord or weight to its neck.
overtopping running too far ahead of the pack; surmounting, exceeding one's authority **82 creatures** dependents **82–83 or changed
. . . formed 'em** i.e., either changed their loyalties and duties or else
created new ones **83 key** (1) key for unlocking (2) tool for tuning
stringed instruments **85 that** so that **87 verdure** vitality. **on 't** of it

MIRANDA
O, good sir, I do.
PROSPERO   I pray thee, mark me.
I, thus neglecting worldly ends, all dedicated
To closeness and the bettering of my mind   90
With that which, but by being so retired,   91
O'erprized all popular rate, in my false brother   92
Awaked an evil nature; and my trust,
Like a good parent, did beget of him   94
A falsehood in its contrary as great
As my trust was, which had indeed no limit,
A confidence sans bound. He being thus lorded   97
Not only with what my revenue yielded
But what my power might else exact, like one   99
Who, having into truth by telling of it,   100
Made such a sinner of his memory   101
To credit his own lie, he did believe   102
He was indeed the Duke, out o' the substitution   103
And executing th' outward face of royalty   104
With all prerogative. Hence his ambition growing—
Dost thou hear?
MIRANDA   Your tale, sir, would cure deafness.
PROSPERO
To have no screen between this part he played   107
And him he played it for, he needs will be   108
Absolute Milan. Me, poor man, my library   109
Was dukedom large enough. Of temporal royalties   110
He thinks me now incapable; confederates—   111
So dry he was for sway—wi' the King of Naples   112
To give him annual tribute, do him homage,   113
Subject his coronet to his crown, and bend   114
The dukedom yet unbowed—alas, poor Milan!—   115
To most ignoble stooping.
MIRANDA   O the heavens!
PROSPERO
Mark his condition and th' event, then tell me   117
If this might be a brother.
MIRANDA   I should sin
To think but nobly of my grandmother.   119
Good wombs have borne bad sons.
PROSPERO   Now the condition.

90 closeness retirement, seclusion **91–92 but . . . rate** i.e., were it not that its private nature caused me to neglect my public responsibilities, had a value far beyond what public opinion could appreciate, or, simply because it was done in such seclusion, had a value not appreciated by popular opinion **94 good parent** (Alludes to the proverb that good parents often bear bad children; see also line 120.) **of** in **97 sans** without. **lorded** raised to lordship, with power and wealth **99 else** otherwise, additionally **100–102 Who . . . lie** i.e., who, by repeatedly telling the lie (that he was indeed Duke of Milan), made his memory such a confirmed sinner against truth that he began to believe his own lie. **into** unto, against. **To** so as to **103 out o'** as a result of **104 And . . . royalty** and (as a result of) his carrying out all the visible functions of royalty **107–108 To have . . . it for** to have no separation or barrier between his role and himself. (Antonio wanted to act in his own person, not as substitute.) **108 needs will be** insisted on becoming **109 Absolute Milan** unconditional Duke of Milan **110 temporal royalties** practical prerogatives and responsibilities of a sovereign **111 confederates** conspires, allies himself **112 dry** thirsty. **sway** power **113 him** i.e., the King of Naples **114 his . . . his** Antonio's . . . the King of Naples'. **bend** make bow down **115 yet** hitherto **117 condition** pact. **event** outcome **119 but** other than

This King of Naples, being an enemy
To me inveterate, hearkens my brother's suit,   122
Which was that he, in lieu o' the premises   123
Of homage and I know not how much tribute,
Should presently extirpate me and mine   125
Out of the dukedom and confer fair Milan,
With all the honors, on my brother. Whereon,
A treacherous army levied, one midnight
Fated to th' purpose did Antonio open
The gates of Milan, and, i' the dead of darkness,
The ministers for the purpose hurried thence   131
Me and thy crying self.
MIRANDA   Alack, for pity!
I, not remembering how I cried out then,
Will cry it o'er again. It is a hint   134
That wrings mine eyes to 't.
PROSPERO   Hear a little further,   135
And then I'll bring thee to the present business
Which now's upon 's, without the which this story
Were most impertinent.
MIRANDA   Wherefore did they not   138
That hour destroy us?
PROSPERO   Well demanded, wench.   139
My tale provokes that question. Dear, they durst
not,
So dear the love my people bore me, nor set   141
A mark so bloody on the business, but   142
With colors fairer painted their foul ends.   143
In few, they hurried us aboard a bark,   144
Bore us some leagues to sea, where they prepared
A rotten carcass of a butt, not rigged,   146
Nor tackle, sail, nor mast; the very rats   147
Instinctively have quit it. There they hoist us,   148
To cry to th' sea that roared to us, to sigh
To th' winds whose pity, sighing back again,
Did us but loving wrong.
MIRANDA   Alack, what trouble   151
Was I then to you!
PROSPERO   O, a cherubin
Thou wast that did preserve me. Thou didst smile,
Infusèd with a fortitude from heaven,
When I have decked the sea with drops full salt,   155
Under my burden groaned, which raised in me   156
An undergoing stomach, to bear up   157
Against what should ensue.
MIRANDA   How came we ashore?
PROSPERO   By Providence divine.

122 hearkens listens to **123 he** the King of Naples. **in . . . premises** in return for the stipulation **125 presently extirpate** at once remove **131 ministers . . . purpose** agents employed to do this. **thence** from there **134 hint** occasion **135 wrings** (1) constrains (2) wrings tears from **138 impertinent** irrelevant. **Wherefore** why **139 demanded** asked. **wench** (Here a term of endearment.) **141–142 set . . . bloody** i.e., make obvious their murderous intent. (From the practice of marking with the blood of the prey those who have participated in a successful hunt.) **143 fairer** apparently more attractive **144 few** few words. **bark** ship **146 butt** cask, tub **147 Nor tackle** neither rigging **148 quit** abandoned **151 Did . . . wrong** (i.e., the winds pitied Prospero and Miranda, though of necessity they blew them from shore) **155 decked** covered (with salt tears); adorned **156 which** i.e., the smile **157 undergoing stomach** courage to go on

Some food we had, and some fresh water, that
A noble Neapolitan, Gonzalo,
Out of his charity, who being then appointed
Master of this design, did give us, with
Rich garments, linens, stuffs, and necessaries,   165
Which since have steaded much. So, of his
    gentleness,   166
Knowing I loved my books, he furnished me
From mine own library with volumes that
I prize above my dukedom.

MIRANDA   Would I might   169
But ever see that man!

PROSPERO   Now I arise.   170

         [*He puts on his magic cloak.*]

Sit still, and hear the last of our sea sorrow.   171
Here in this island we arrived; and here
Have I, thy schoolmaster, made thee more profit   173
Than other princess' can, that have more time   174
For vainer hours and tutors not so careful.   175

MIRANDA
Heavens thank you for 't! And now, I pray you,
    sir—
For still 'tis beating in my mind—your reason
For raising this sea storm?

PROSPERO   Know thus far forth:
By accident most strange, bountiful Fortune,
Now my dear lady, hath mine enemies
Brought to this shore; and by my prescience   180
I find my zenith doth depend upon
A most auspicious star, whose influence   182
If now I court not, but omit, my fortunes   183
Will ever after droop. Here cease more questions.   184
Thou art inclined to sleep. 'Tis a good dullness,   186
And give it way. I know thou canst not choose.   187

           [*Miranda sleeps.*]

Come away, servant, come! I am ready now.   188
Approach, my Ariel, come.

       Enter Ariel.

ARIEL
All hail, great master, grave sir, hail! I come
To answer thy best pleasure; be 't to fly,
To swim, to dive into the fire, to ride
On the curled clouds, to thy strong bidding task   193
Ariel and all his quality.

PROSPERO   Hast thou, spirit,   194
Performed to point the tempest that I bade thee?   195

ARIEL   To every article.
I boarded the King's ship. Now on the beak,   197

Now in the waist, the deck, in every cabin,   198
I flamed amazement. Sometimes I'd divide   199
And burn in many places; on the topmast,
The yards, and bowsprit would I flame distinctly,   201
Then meet and join. Jove's lightning, the precursors
O' the dreadful thunderclaps, more momentary
And sight-outrunning were not. The fire and cracks   204
Of sulfurous roaring the most mighty Neptune   205
Seem to besiege and make his bold waves tremble,
Yea, his dread trident shake.

PROSPERO   My brave spirit!
Who was so firm, so constant, that this coil   208
Would not infect his reason?

ARIEL   Not a soul
But felt a fever of the mad and played   210
Some tricks of desperation. All but mariners
Plunged in the foaming brine and quit the vessel,
Then all afire with me. The King's son, Ferdinand,
With hair up-staring—then like reeds, not hair—   214
Was the first man that leapt; cried, "Hell is empty,
And all the devils are here!"

PROSPERO   Why, that's my spirit!
But was not this nigh shore?

ARIEL   Close by, my master.

PROSPERO
But are they, Ariel, safe?

ARIEL   Not a hair perished.
On their sustaining garments not a blemish,   219
But fresher than before; and, as thou bad'st me,   220
In troops I have dispersed them 'bout the isle.   221
The King's son have I landed by himself,
Whom I left cooling of the air with sighs   223
In an odd angle of the isle, and sitting,   224
His arms in this sad knot.   [*He folds his arms.*]

PROSPERO   Of the King's ship,   225
The mariners, say how thou hast disposed,
And all the rest o' the fleet.

ARIEL   Safely in harbor
Is the King's ship; in the deep nook, where once   228
Thou called'st me up at midnight to fetch dew   229
From the still-vexed Bermudas, there she's hid;   230
The mariners all under hatches stowed,
Who, with a charm joined to their suffered labor,   232
I have left asleep. And for the rest o' the fleet,
Which I dispersed, they all have met again
And are upon the Mediterranean float   235
Bound sadly home for Naples,

---

165 stuffs supplies   **166 steaded much** been of much use.   **So, of** similarly, out of   **169 Would** I wish   **170 But ever** i.e., someday   **171 sea sorrow** sorrowful adventure at sea   **173 more profit** profit more   **174 princess'** princesses. (Or the word may be *princes*, referring to royal children both male and female.)   **175 vainer** more foolishly spent   **180 my dear lady** (Refers to Fortune, not Miranda.)   **182 zenith** height of fortune. (Astrological term.)   **183 influence** astrological power   **184 omit** ignore   **186 dullness** drowsiness   **187 give it way** let it happen (i.e., don't fight it)   **188 Come away** come   **193 task** make demands upon   **194 quality** (1) fellow spirits (2) abilities   **195 to point** to the smallest detail   **197 beak** prow

198 waist midships.   **deck** poop deck at the stern   **199 flamed amazement** struck terror in the guise of fire, i.e., Saint Elmo's fire   **201 distinctly** in different places   **204 sight-outrunning** swifter than sight.   **were not** could not have been   **205 Neptune** Roman god of the sea   **208 coil** tumult   **210 of the mad** i.e., such as madmen feel   **214 up-staring** standing on end   **219 sustaining garments** garments that buoyed them up in the sea   **220 bad'st** ordered   **221 troops** groups   **223 cooling of** cooling   **224 angle** corner   **225 sad knot** (Folded arms are indicative of melancholy.)   **228 nook** bay   **229 dew** (Collected at midnight for magical purposes; compare with line 324.)   **230 still-vexed Bermudas** ever stormy Bermudas. (Perhaps refers to the then recent Bermuda shipwreck; see play Introduction. The Folio text reads "Bermoothes.")   **232 with . . . labor** by means of a spell added to all the labor they have undergone   **235 float** sea

Supposing that they saw the King's ship wrecked
And his great person perish.

PROSPERO   Ariel, thy charge
Exactly is performed. But there's more work.
What is the time o' the day?

ARIEL   Past the mid season.   240

PROSPERO
At least two glasses. The time twixt six and now   241
Must by us both be spent most preciously.

ARIEL
Is there more toil? Since thou dost give me pains,   243
Let me remember thee what thou hast promised,   244
Which is not yet performed me.

PROSPERO   How now? Moody?
What is 't thou canst demand?

ARIEL   My liberty.

PROSPERO
Before the time be out? No more!

ARIEL   I prithee,
Remember I have done thee worthy service,
Told thee no lies, made thee no mistakings, served
Without or grudge or grumblings. Thou did promise
To bate me a full year.

PROSPERO   Dost thou forget   251
From what a torment I did free thee?

ARIEL   No.

PROSPERO
Thou dost, and think'st it much to tread the ooze
Of the salt deep,
To run upon the sharp wind of the north,
To do me business in the veins o' the earth   256
When it is baked with frost.

ARIEL   I do not, sir.   257

PROSPERO
Thou liest, malignant thing! Hast thou forgot
The foul witch Sycorax, who with age and envy   259
Was grown into a hoop? Hast thou forgot her?   260

ARIEL   No, sir.

PROSPERO
Thou hast. Where was she born? Speak. Tell me.

ARIEL
Sir, in Argier.

PROSPERO   O, was she so? I must   263
Once in a month recount what thou hast been,
Which thou forgett'st. This damned witch Sycorax,
For mischiefs manifold and sorceries terrible
To enter human hearing, from Argier,
Thou know'st, was banished. For one thing she did   268
They would not take her life. Is not this true?

ARIEL   Ay, sir.

PROSPERO
This blue-eyed hag was hither brought with child   271

And here was left by the sailors. Thou, my slave,
As thou report'st thyself, was then her servant;
And, for thou wast a spirit too delicate   274
To act her earthy and abhorred commands,
Refusing her grand hests, she did confine thee,   276
By help of her more potent ministers
And in her most unmitigable rage,
Into a cloven pine, within which rift
Imprisoned thou didst painfully remain
A dozen years; within which space she died
And left thee there, where thou didst vent thy
    groans
As fast as mill wheels strike. Then was this island—   283
Save for the son that she did litter here,   284
A freckled whelp, hag-born—not honored with   285
A human shape.

ARIEL   Yes, Caliban her son.   286

PROSPERO
Dull thing, I say so: he, that Caliban   287
Whom now I keep in service. Thou best know'st
What torment I did find thee in. Thy groans
Did make wolves howl, and penetrate the breasts
Of ever-angry bears. It was a torment
To lay upon the damned, which Sycorax
Could not again undo. It was mine art,
When I arrived and heard thee, that made gape   294
The pine and let thee out.

ARIEL   I thank thee, master.

PROSPERO
If thou more murmur'st, I will rend an oak
And peg thee in his knotty entrails till   297
Thou hast howled away twelve winters.

ARIEL   Pardon, master.
I will be correspondent to command   299
And do my spriting gently.   300

PROSPERO   Do so, and after two days
I will discharge thee.

ARIEL   That's my noble master!
What shall I do? Say what? What shall I do?

PROSPERO
Go make thyself like a nymph o' the sea. Be subject
To no sight but thine and mine, invisible
To every eyeball else. Go take this shape
And hither come in 't. Go, hence with diligence!
                                    Exit [Ariel].
Awake, dear heart, awake! Thou hast slept well.
Awake!

MIRANDA   The strangeness of your story put
Heaviness in me.

PROSPERO   Shake it off. Come on,   310
We'll visit Caliban, my slave, who never
Yields us kind answer.

240 mid season noon   241 glasses hourglasses   243 pains labors
244 remember remind   251 bate remit, deduct   256 do me do for
me. veins veins of minerals, or, underground streams, thought to be
analogous to the veins of the human body   257 baked hardened
259 envy malice   260 grown into a hoop i.e., so bent over with age
as to resemble a hoop   263 Argier Algiers   268 one . . . did (Perhaps a reference to her pregnancy, for which her life would be
spared.)   271 blue-eyed with dark circles under the eyes or with blue
eyelids, implying pregnancy. with child pregnant

274 for because   276 hests commands   283 as mill wheels strike as
the blades of a mill wheel strike the water   284 Save except. litter
give birth to   285 whelp offspring. (Used of animals.) hag-born born
of a female demon   286 Yes . . . son (Ariel is probably concurring
with Prospero's comment about a "freckled whelp," not contradicting
the point about "A human shape.")   287 Dull . . . so i.e., exactly,
that's what I said, you dullard   294 gape open wide   297 his its
299 correspondent responsive, submissive   300 spriting duties as a
spirit. gently willingly, ungrudgingly   310 Heaviness drowsiness

MIRANDA   'Tis a villain, sir,
I do not love to look on.
PROSPERO   But, as 'tis,
We cannot miss him. He does make our fire,   314
Fetch in our wood, and serves in offices   315
That profit us.—What ho! Slave! Caliban!
Thou earth, thou! Speak.
CALIBAN (within)   There's wood enough within.
PROSPERO
Come forth, I say! There's other business for thee.
Come, thou tortoise! When?   319

            Enter Ariel like a water nymph.

Fine apparition! My quaint Ariel,   320
Hark in thine ear.   [*He whispers.*]
ARIEL   My lord, it shall be done.   *Exit.*
PROSPERO
Thou poisonous slave, got by the devil himself   322
Upon thy wicked dam, come forth!   323

            Enter Caliban.

CALIBAN
As wicked dew as e'er my mother brushed   324
With raven's feather from unwholesome fen   325
Drop on you both! A southwest blow on ye   326
And blister you all o'er!
PROSPERO
For this, be sure, tonight thou shalt have cramps,
Side-stitches that shall pen thy breath up. Urchins   329
Shall forth at vast of night that they may work   330
All exercise on thee. Thou shalt be pinched
As thick as honeycomb, each pinch more stinging   332
Than bees that made 'em.
CALIBAN   I must eat my dinner.   333
This island's mine, by Sycorax my mother,
Which thou tak'st from me. When thou cam'st first,
Thou strok'st me and made much of me, wouldst
      give me
Water with berries in 't, and teach me how
To name the bigger light, and how the less,   338
That burn by day and night. And then I loved thee
And showed thee all the qualities o' th' isle,
The fresh springs, brine pits, barren place and
      fertile.
Cursed be I that did so! All the charms   342
Of Sycorax, toads, beetles, bats, light on you!
For I am all the subjects that you have,
Which first was mine own king; and here you
      sty me   345

In this hard rock, whiles you do keep from me
The rest o' th' island.
PROSPERO   Thou most lying slave,
Whom stripes may move, not kindness! I have used
      thee,   348
Filth as thou art, with humane care, and lodged thee 349
In mine own cell, till thou didst seek to violate
The honor of my child.
CALIBAN
Oho, Oho! Would 't had been done!
Thou didst prevent me; I had peopled else   353
This isle with Calibans.
MIRANDA   Abhorrèd slave,   354
Which any print of goodness wilt not take,   355
Being capable of all ill! I pitied thee,
Took pains to make thee speak, taught thee each
      hour
One thing or other. When thou didst not, savage,
Know thine own meaning, but wouldst gabble like
A thing most brutish, I endowed thy purposes   360
With words that made them known. But thy vile
      race,   361
Though thou didst learn, had that in 't which good
      natures
Could not abide to be with; therefore wast thou
Deservedly confined into this rock,
Who hadst deserved more than a prison.   365
CALIBAN
You taught me language, and my profit on 't
Is I know how to curse. The red plague rid you   367
For learning me your language!
PROSPERO   Hagseed, hence!   368
Fetch us in fuel, and be quick, thou'rt best,   369
To answer other business. Shrugg'st thou, malice?   370
If thou neglect'st or dost unwillingly
What I command, I'll rack thee with old cramps,   372
Fill all thy bones with aches, make thee roar   373
That beasts shall tremble at thy din.
CALIBAN   No, pray thee.
[*Aside.*] I must obey. His art is of such power
It would control my dam's god, Setebos,   376
And make a vassal of him.
PROSPERO   So, slave, hence!   377
                                    Exit Caliban.

*Enter Ferdinand; and Ariel, invisible, playing and
singing.* [*Ferdinand does not see Prospero and
Miranda.*]

314 miss do without   **315 offices** functions, duties   **319 When** (An
exclamation of impatience.)   **320 quaint** ingenious   **322 got** begotten, sired   **323 dam** mother. (Used of animals.)   **324 wicked** mischievous, harmful   **325 fen** marsh, bog   **326 southwest** i.e., wind
thought to bring disease   **329 Urchins** hedgehogs; here, suggesting
goblins in the guise of hedgehogs   **330 vast** lengthy, desolate time.
(Malignant spirits were thought to be restricted to the hours of darkness.)   **332 As thick as honeycomb** i.e., all over, with as many
pinches as a honeycomb has cells   **333 'em** i.e., the honeycomb
338 the bigger . . . less i.e., the sun and the moon. (See Genesis
1:16: "God then made two great lights: the greater light to rule the
day, and the less light to rule the night.")   **342 charms** spells
345 sty confine as in a sty

348 stripes lashes   **349 humane** (Not distinguished as a word from
human.)   **353 peopled else** otherwise populated   **354–365 Abhorrèd
. . . prison** (Sometimes assigned by editors to Prospero.)   **355 print**
imprint, impression   **360 purposes** meanings, desires   **361 race** natural disposition; species, nature   **367 red plague** plague characterized by red sores and evacuation of blood.   **rid** destroy   **368 learning** teaching.   **Hagseed** offspring of a female demon   **369 thou'rt
best** you'd be well advised   **370 answer other business** perform
other tasks   **372 old** such as old people suffer, or, plenty of
373 aches (Pronounced "aitches.")   **376 Setebos** (A god of the Patagonians, named in Richard Eden's *History of Travel,* 1577.)   **377 s.d.
Ariel, invisible** (Ariel wears a garment that by convention indicates he
is invisible to the other characters.)

Ariel's Song.

ARIEL

Come unto these yellow sands,
    And then take hands;
Curtsied when you have, and kissed   380
    The wild waves whist;   381
Foot it featly here and there,   382
    And, sweet sprites, bear   383
The burden. Hark, hark!   384
        Burden, dispersedly [*within*]. Bow-wow. 385
    The watchdogs bark.
        [*Burden, dispersedly within.*] Bow-wow.
Hark, hark! I hear
The strain of strutting chanticleer
    Cry Cock-a-diddle-dow.

FERDINAND

Where should this music be? I' th' air or th' earth?
It sounds no more; and sure it waits upon   392
Some god o' th' island. Sitting on a bank,   393
Weeping again the King my father's wreck,
This music crept by me upon the waters,
Allaying both their fury and my passion   396
With its sweet air. Thence I have followed it,   397
Or it hath drawn me rather. But 'tis gone.
No, it begins again.

Ariel's Song.

ARIEL

Full fathom five thy father lies.
    Of his bones are coral made.
Those are pearls that were his eyes.
    Nothing of him that doth fade
But doth suffer a sea change
Into something rich and strange.
Sea nymphs hourly ring his knell.   406
        Burden [*within*]. Ding dong.
Hark, now I hear them, ding dong bell.

FERDINAND

The ditty does remember my drowned father.   409
This is no mortal business, nor no sound
That the earth owes. I hear it now above me.   411

PROSPERO [*to Miranda*]

The fringèd curtains of thine eye advance   412
And say what thou seest yond.

MIRANDA   What is 't? A spirit?
Lord, how it looks about! Believe me, sir,
It carries a brave form. But 'tis a spirit.   415

PROSPERO

No, wench, it eats and sleeps and hath such senses
As we have, such. This gallant which thou seest
Was in the wreck; and, but he's something stained   418

With grief, that's beauty's canker, thou mightst
    call him   419
A goodly person. He hath lost his fellows
And strays about to find 'em.

MIRANDA   I might call him
A thing divine, for nothing natural
I ever saw so noble.

PROSPERO [*aside*]   It goes on, I see,   423
As my soul prompts it.—Spirit, fine spirit, I'll free
    thee
Within two days for this.

FERDINAND [*seeing Miranda*]   Most sure, the goddess
On whom these airs attend!—Vouchsafe my prayer   426
May know if you remain upon this island,   427
And that you will some good instruction give
How I may bear me here. My prime request,   429
Which I do last pronounce, is—O you wonder!—   430
If you be maid or no?

MIRANDA   No wonder, sir,   431
But certainly a maid.

FERDINAND   My language? Heavens!
I am the best of them that speak this speech,   433
Were I but where 'tis spoken.

PROSPERO [*coming forward*]   How? The best?
What wert thou if the King of Naples heard thee?

FERDINAND

A single thing, as I am now, that wonders   436
To hear thee speak of Naples. He does hear me,   437
And that he does I weep. Myself am Naples,   438
Who with mine eyes, never since at ebb, beheld   439
The King my father wrecked.

MIRANDA   Alack, for mercy!

FERDINAND

Yes, faith, and all his lords, the Duke of Milan
And his brave son being twain.

PROSPERO [*aside*]   The Duke of Milan   442
And his more braver daughter could control thee,   443
If now 'twere fit to do 't. At the first sight
They have changed eyes.—Delicate Ariel,   445
I'll set thee free for this. [*To Ferdinand.*] A word,
    good sir.
I fear you have done yourself some wrong. A word!   447

MIRANDA [*aside*]

Why speaks my father so ungently? This
Is the third man that e'er I saw, the first
That e'er I sighed for. Pity move my father
To be inclined my way!

---

380 **Curtsied . . . have** when you have curtsied 380–381 **kissed . . . whist** kissed the waves into silence, or, kissed while the waves are being hushed 382 **Foot it featly** dance nimbly 383 **sprites** spirits 384 **burden** refrain, undersong 385 **s.d. dispersedly** i.e., from all directions, not in unison 392 **waits upon** serves, attends 393 **bank** sandbank 396 **passion** grief 397 **Thence** i.e., from the bank on which I sat 406 **knell** announcement of a death by the tolling of a bell 409 **remember** commemorate 411 **owes** owns 412 **advance** raise 415 **brave** excellent 418 **but** except that. **something stained** somewhat disfigured

419 **canker** cankerworm (feeding on buds and leaves) 423 **It goes on** i.e., my plan works 426 **airs** songs. **Vouchsafe** grant 427 **May know** i.e., that I may know. **remain** dwell 429 **bear me** conduct myself. **prime** chief 430 **wonder** (Miranda's name means "to be wondered at.") 431 **maid or no** i.e., a human maiden as opposed to a goddess or married woman 433 **best** i.e., in birth 436 **single** (1) solitary, being at once King of Naples and myself (2) feeble 437, 438 **Naples** the King of Naples 437 **He does hear me** i.e., the King of Naples does hear my words, for I am King of Naples 438 **And . . . weep** i.e., and I weep at this reminder that my father is seemingly dead, leaving me heir 439 **at ebb** i.e., dry, not weeping 442 **son** (The only reference in the play to a son of Antonio.) 443 **more braver** more splendid. **control** refute 445 **changed eyes** exchanged amorous glances 447 **done . . . wrong** i.e., spoken falsely

FERDINAND   O, if a virgin,
And your affection not gone forth, I'll make you
The Queen of Naples.
PROSPERO   Soft, sir! One word more. ← 3rd wheel
[Aside.] They are both in either's power's; but this
  swift business   454
I must uneasy make, lest too light winning   455
Make the prize light. [To Ferdinand.] One word
  more: I charge thee   456
That thou attend me. Thou dost here usurp   457
The name thou ow'st not, and hast put thyself   458
Upon this island as a spy, to win it
From me, the lord on 't.
FERDINAND   No, as I am a man.   460
MIRANDA
There's nothing ill can dwell in such a temple.
If the ill spirit have so fair a house,
Good things will strive to dwell with 't.
PROSPERO   Follow me.—   463
Speak not you for him; he's a traitor.—Come,
I'll manacle thy neck and feet together.
Seawater shalt thou drink; thy food shall be
The fresh-brook mussels, withered roots, and husks
Wherein the acorn cradled. Follow.
FERDINAND   No!
I will resist such entertainment till   469
Mine enemy has more power.   470
          He draws, and is charmed from moving.
MIRANDA   O dear father,
Make not too rash a trial of him, for   471
He's gentle, and not fearful.
PROSPERO   What, I say,   472
My foot my tutor?—Put thy sword up, traitor,   473
Who mak'st a show but dar'st not strike, thy
  conscience
Is so possessed with guilt. Come, from thy ward,   475
For I can here disarm thee with this stick
And make thy weapon drop. [He brandishes his staff.]
MIRANDA [trying to hinder him] Beseech you, father!
PROSPERO
Hence! Hang not on my garments.
MIRANDA   Sir, have pity!
I'll be his surety.
PROSPERO   Silence! One word more   479
Shall make me chide thee, if not hate thee. What,
An advocate for an impostor? Hush!
Thou think'st there is no more such shapes as he,
Having seen but him and Caliban. Foolish wench,
To the most of men this is a Caliban,   484
And they to him are angels.
MIRANDA   My affections
Are then most humble; I have no ambition

To see a goodlier man.
PROSPERO [to Ferdinand] Come on, obey.
Thy nerves are in their infancy again   488
And have no vigor in them.
FERDINAND   So they are.
My spirits, as in a dream, are all bound up.   490
My father's loss, the weakness which I feel,
The wreck of all my friends, nor this man's threats
To whom I am subdued, are but light to me,   493
Might I but through my prison once a day
Behold this maid. All corners else o' th' earth   495
Let liberty make use of; space enough
Have I in such a prison.
PROSPERO [aside] It works. [To Ferdinand.] Come on.—
Thou hast done well, fine Ariel! [To Ferdinand.]
    Follow me.
[To Ariel.] Hark what thou else shalt do me.
MIRANDA [to Ferdinand]   Be of comfort. 499
My father's of a better nature, sir,
Than he appears by speech. This is unwonted   501
Which now came from him.
PROSPERO [to Ariel]   Thou shalt be as free
As mountain winds; but then exactly do   503
All points of my command.
ARIEL   To th' syllable.
PROSPERO [to Ferdinand]
Come, follow. [To Miranda.] Speak not for him.
                                                  Exeunt.

                          ❖

2.1   *Enter Alonso, Sebastian, Antonio, Gonzalo,*
          Adrian, Francisco, and others.

GONZALO [to Alonso]
Beseech you, sir, be merry. You have cause,
So have we all, of joy, for our escape
Is much beyond our loss. Our hint of woe   3
Is common; every day some sailor's wife,
The masters of some merchant, and the merchant,   5
Have just our theme of woe. But for the miracle,
I mean our preservation, few in millions
Can speak like us. Then wisely, good sir, weigh
Our sorrow with our comfort.
ALONSO   Prithee, peace.   9
SEBASTIAN [aside to Antonio] He receives comfort like
cold porridge.   11
ANTONIO [aside to Sebastian] The visitor will not give 12
him o'er so.   13

454 **both in either's** each in the other's   455 **uneasy** difficult   455–
456 **light . . . light** easy . . . cheap   457 **attend** follow, obey
458 **ow'st** ownest   460 **on 't** of it   463 **strive . . . with 't** i.e., expel
the evil and occupy the *temple*, the body   469 **entertainment** treatment   470 **s.d. charmed** magically prevented   471 **rash** harsh
472 **gentle** wellborn. **fearful** frightening, dangerous, or perhaps,
cowardly   473 **foot** subordinate. (Miranda, the foot, presumes to instruct Prospero, the head.)   475 **ward** defensive posture (in fencing)
479 **surety** guarantee   484 **To** compared to

488 **nerves** sinews   490 **spirits** vital powers   493 **light** unimportant
495 **corners else** other corners, regions   499 **me** for me   501 **unwonted** unusual   503 **then** until then, or, if that is to be so
2.1. Location: Another part of the island.
3 **hint** occasion   5 **masters . . . the merchant** officers of some merchant vessel and the merchant himself, the owner   9 **with** against
11 **porridge** (punningly suggested by *peace,* i.e., "peas" or "pease,"
a common ingredient of porridge)   12 **visitor** one taking nourishment
and comfort to the sick, as Gonzalo is doing   12–13 **give him o'er**
abandon him

SEBASTIAN   Look, he's winding up the watch of his wit; by and by it will strike.

GONZALO [to Alonso]   Sir—

SEBASTIAN [aside to Antonio]   One. Tell.   17

GONZALO   When every grief is entertained   18
That's offered, comes to th' entertainer—   19

SEBASTIAN   A dollar.   20

GONZALO   Dolor comes to him, indeed. You have spoken truer than you purposed.

SEBASTIAN   You have taken it wiselier than I meant you should.

GONZALO [to Alonso]   Therefore, my lord—

ANTONIO   Fie, what a spendthrift is he of his tongue!

ALONSO [to Gonzalo]   I prithee, spare.   27

GONZALO   Well, I have done. But yet—

SEBASTIAN [aside to Antonio]   He will be talking.

ANTONIO [aside to Sebastian]   Which, of he or Adrian,   30
for a good wager, first begins to crow?   31

SEBASTIAN   The old cock.   32

ANTONIO   The cockerel.   33

SEBASTIAN   Done. The wager?

ANTONIO   A laughter.   35

SEBASTIAN   A match!   36

ADRIAN   Though this island seem to be desert—   37

ANTONIO   Ha, ha, ha!

SEBASTIAN   So, you're paid.   39

ADRIAN   Uninhabitable and almost inaccessible—

SEBASTIAN   Yet—

ADRIAN   Yet—

ANTONIO   He could not miss 't.   43

ADRIAN   It must needs be of subtle, tender, and delicate   44
temperance.   45

ANTONIO   Temperance was a delicate wench.   46

SEBASTIAN   Ay, and a subtle, as he most learnedly   47
delivered.   48

ADRIAN   The air breathes upon us here most sweetly.

SEBASTIAN   As if it had lungs, and rotten ones.

ANTONIO   Or as 'twere perfumed by a fen.

GONZALO   Here is everything advantageous to life.

ANTONIO   True, save means to live.   53

SEBASTIAN   Of that there's none, or little.

GONZALO   How lush and lusty the grass looks! How   55
green!

ANTONIO   The ground indeed is tawny.   57

SEBASTIAN   With an eye of green in 't.   58

ANTONIO   He misses not much.

SEBASTIAN   No. He doth but mistake the truth totally.   60

GONZALO   But the rarity of it is—which is indeed
almost beyond credit—

SEBASTIAN   As many vouched rarities are.   63

GONZALO   That our garments, being, as they were,
drenched in the sea, hold notwithstanding their freshness and glosses, being rather new-dyed than stained
with salt water.

ANTONIO   If but one of his pockets could speak, would   68
it not say he lies?

SEBASTIAN   Ay, or very falsely pocket up his report.   70

GONZALO   Methinks our garments are now as fresh as
when we put them on first in Afric, at the marriage of
the King's fair daughter Claribel to the King of Tunis.

SEBASTIAN   'Twas a sweet marriage, and we prosper
well in our return.

ADRIAN   Tunis was never graced before with such a
paragon to their queen.   77

GONZALO   Not since widow Dido's time.   78

ANTONIO [aside to Sebastian]   Widow? A pox o' that!
How came that "widow" in? Widow Dido!

SEBASTIAN   What if he had said "widower Aeneas"
too? Good Lord, how you take it!   82

ADRIAN [to Gonzalo]   "Widow Dido" said you? You make
me study of that. She was of Carthage, not of Tunis.   84

GONZALO   This Tunis, sir, was Carthage.

ADRIAN   Carthage?

GONZALO   I assure you, Carthage.

ANTONIO   His word is more than the miraculous harp.   88

SEBASTIAN   He hath raised the wall, and houses too.

ANTONIO   What impossible matter will he make easy
next?

SEBASTIAN   I think he will carry this island home in his
pocket and give it his son for an apple.

17 Tell keep count 18–19 When . . . entertainer when every sorrow that presents itself is accepted without resistance, there comes to the recipient 20 dollar widely circulated coin, the German thaler and the Spanish piece of eight. (Sebastian puns on entertainer in the sense of innkeeper; to Gonzalo, dollar suggests "dolor," grief.)
27 spare forbear, cease 30–31 Which . . . crow which of the two, Gonzalo or Adrian, do you bet will speak (crow) first? 32 old cock i.e., Gonzalo 33 cockerel i.e., Adrian 35 laughter (1) burst of laughter (2) sitting of eggs. (When Adrian, the cockerel, begins to speak two lines later, Sebastian loses the bet. The Folio speech prefixes in lines 38–39 are here reversed so that Antonio enjoys his laugh as the prize for winning, as in the proverb "He who laughs last laughs best" or "He laughs that wins." The Folio assignment can work in the theater, however, if Sebastian pays for losing with a sardonic laugh of concession.) 36 A match a bargain; agreed
37 desert uninhabited 39 you're paid i.e., you've had your laugh 43 miss 't (1) avoid saying "Yet" (2) miss the island 44 must needs be has to be 45 temperance mildness of climate 46 Temperance a girl's name. delicate (Here it means "given to pleasure, voluptuous"; in line 44, "pleasant." Antonio is evidently suggesting that tender, and delicate temperance sounds like a Puritan phrase, which Antonio then mocks by applying the words to a woman rather than an island. He began this bawdy comparison with a double entendre on inaccessible, line 40.) 47 subtle (Here it means "tricky, sexually crafty"; in line 44, "delicate.") 48 delivered uttered. (Sebastian joins Antonio in baiting the Puritans with his use of the pious cant phrase learnedly delivered.)

53 save except 55 lusty healthy 57 tawny dull brown, yellowish 58 eye tinge, or spot (perhaps with reference to Gonzalo's eye or judgment) 60 but merely 63 vouched rarities allegedly real though strange sights 68 pockets i.e., because they are muddy 70 pocket up i.e., conceal, suppress; often used in the sense of "receive unprotestingly, fail to respond to a challenge." his report (Sebastian's jest is that the evidence of Gonzalo's soggy and sea-stained pockets would confute Gonzalo's speech and his reputation for truth telling.) 77 to for 78 widow Dido Queen of Carthage, deserted by Aeneas. (She was, in fact, a widow when Aeneas, met her, but Antonio may be amused at Gonzalo's prudish use of the term "widow" to describe a woman deserted by her lover.) 82 take understand, respond to, interpret 84 study of think about 88 miraculous harp (Alludes to Amphion's harp, with which he raised the walls of Thebes; Gonzalo has exceeded that deed by recreating ancient Carthage—wall and houses—mistakenly on the site of modern-day Tunis. Some Renaissance commentators believed, like Gonzalo, that the two sites were near each other.)

ANTONIO   And, sowing the kernels of it in the sea, 94
bring forth more islands.

GONZALO   Ay.   96

ANTONIO   Why, in good time.   97

GONZALO [to Alonso]   Sir, we were talking that our 98
garments seem now as fresh as when we were at
Tunis at the marriage of your daughter, who is now
queen.

ANTONIO   And the rarest that e'er came there.   101

SEBASTIAN   Bate, I beseech you, widow Dido.   102

ANTONIO   O, widow Dido? Ay, widow Dido.

GONZALO   Is not, sir, my doublet as fresh as the first 104
day I wore it? I mean, in a sort.   105

ANTONIO   That "sort" was well fished for.   106

GONZALO   When I wore it at your daughter's marriage.

ALONSO
You cram these words into mine ears against
The stomach of my sense. Would I had never   109
Married my daughter there! For, coming thence,   110
My son is lost and, in my rate, she too,   111
Who is so far from Italy removed
I ne'er again shall see her. O thou mine heir
Of Naples and of Milan, what strange fish
Hath made his meal on thee?

FRANCISCO   Sir, he may live.
I saw him beat the surges under him   116
And ride upon their backs. He trod the water,
Whose enmity he flung aside, and breasted
The surge most swoll'n that met him. His bold head
'Bove the contentious waves he kept, and oared
Himself with his good arms in lusty stroke   121
To th' shore, that o'er his wave-worn basis bowed, 122
As stooping to relieve him. I not doubt   123
He came alive to land.

ALONSO   No, no, he's gone.

SEBASTIAN [to Alonso]
Sir, you may thank yourself for this great loss,
That would not bless our Europe with your
daughter,   126
But rather loose her to an African,   127
Where she at least is banished from your eye,   128
Who hath cause to wet the grief on 't.

ALONSO   Prithee, peace.   129

SEBASTIAN
You were kneeled to and importuned otherwise   130
By all of us, and the fair soul herself   131
Weighed between loathness and obedience at   132
Which end o' the beam should bow. We have lost
your son,   133
I fear, forever. Milan and Naples have
More widows in them of this business' making   135
Than we bring men to comfort them.
The fault's your own.

ALONSO   So is the dear'st o' the loss.   138

GONZALO   My lord Sebastian,
The truth you speak doth lack some gentleness
And time to speak it in. You rub the sore   141
When you should bring the plaster.

SEBASTIAN   Very well.   142

ANTONIO   And most chirurgeonly.   143

GONZALO [to Alonso]
It is foul weather in us all, good sir,
When you are cloudy.

SEBASTIAN [to Antonio]   Fowl weather?

ANTONIO [to Sebastian]   Very foul.   145

GONZALO
• Had I plantation of this isle, my lord—   146

ANTONIO [to Sebastian]
He'd sow 't with nettle seed.

SEBASTIAN   Or docks, or mallows.   147

GONZALO
And were the king on 't, what would I do?

SEBASTIAN   Scape being drunk for want of wine.   149

GONZALO
I' the commonwealth I would by contraries   150
Execute all things; for no kind of traffic   151
Would I admit; no name of magistrate;
Letters should not be known; riches, poverty,   153
And use of service, none; contract, succession,   154
Bourn, bound of land, tilth, vineyard, none;   155
No use of metal, corn, or wine, or oil;   156
No occupation; all men idle, all,
And women too, but innocent and pure;
No sovereignty—

SEBASTIAN   Yet he would be king on 't.

---

94 kernels seeds   **96 Ay** (Gonzalo may be reasserting his point about Carthage, or he may be responding ironically to Antonio, who, in turn, answers sarcastically.)   **97 in good time** (An expression of ironical acquiescence or amazement, i.e., "sure, right away.")   **98 talking** saying   **101 rarest** most remarkable, beautiful   **102 Bate** abate, except, leave out. (Sebastian says sardonically, surely you should allow widow Dido to be an exception.)   **104 doublet** close-fitting jacket   **105 in a sort** in a way   **106 sort** (Antonio plays on the idea of drawing lots and on "fishing" for something to say.)   **109 The stomach . . . sense** my appetite for hearing them   **110 Married** given in marriage   **111 rate** estimation, opinion   **116 surges** waves   **121 lusty** vigorous   **122 that . . . bowed** i.e., that projected out over the base of the cliff that had been eroded by the surf, thus seeming to bend down toward the sea.   **his** its   **123 As** as if   **126 That** you who   **127 rather** would rather.   **loose** (1) release, let loose (2) lose   **128 is banished from your eye** is not constantly before your eye to serve as a reproachful reminder of what you have done   **129 Who . . . on 't** i.e., your eye, which has good reason to weep because of this, or, Claribel, who has good reason to weep for it

130 importuned urged, implored   **131–133 the fair . . . bow** Claribel herself was poised uncertainly between unwillingness to marry and obedience to her father as to which end of the scales should sink, which should prevail   **135 of . . . making** on account of this marriage and subsequent shipwreck   **138 dear'st** heaviest, most costly   **141 time** appropriate time   **142 plaster** (A medical application.)   **143 chirurgeonly** like a skilled surgeon. (Antonio mocks Gonzalo's medical analogy of a plaster applied curatively to a wound.)   **145 Fowl** (with a pun on foul, returning to the imagery of lines 30–35)   **146 plantation** colonization (with subsequent wordplay on the literal meaning, "planting.")   **147 docks, mallows** (Weeds used as antidotes for nettle stings.)   **149 Scape** escape.   **want** lack. (Sebastian jokes sarcastically that this hypothetical ruler would be saved from dissipation only by the barrenness of the island.)   **150 by contraries** by what is directly opposite to usual custom   **151 traffic** trade   **153 Letters** learning   **154 use of service** custom of employing servants.   **succession** holding of property by right of inheritance   **155 Bourn . . . tilth** boundaries, property limits, tillage of soil   **156 corn** grain

ANTONIO   The latter end of his commonwealth forgets the beginning.

GONZALO
All things in common nature should produce
Without sweat or endeavor. Treason, felony,
Sword, pike, knife, gun, or need of any engine   164
Would I not have; but nature should bring forth,
Of its own kind, all foison, all abundance,   166
To feed my innocent people.

SEBASTIAN   No marrying 'mong his subjects?

ANTONIO   None, man, all idle—whores and knaves.

GONZALO
I would with such perfection govern, sir,
T' excel the Golden Age.

SEBASTIAN   'Save His Majesty!   171

ANTONIO
Long live Gonzalo!

GONZALO   And—do you mark me, sir?

ALONSO
Prithee, no more. Thou dost talk nothing to me.

GONZALO   I do well believe Your Highness, and did it
to minister occasion to these gentlemen, who are of   175
such sensible and nimble lungs that they always use   176
to laugh at nothing.

ANTONIO   'Twas you we laughed at.

GONZALO   Who in this kind of merry fooling am nothing
to you; so you may continue, and laugh at nothing still.

ANTONIO   What a blow was there given!

SEBASTIAN   An it had not fallen flat-long.   182

GONZALO   You are gentlemen of brave mettle; you   183
would lift the moon out of her sphere if she would   184
continue in it five weeks without changing.

Enter Ariel [invisible] playing solemn music.

SEBASTIAN   We would so, and then go a-batfowling.   186

ANTONIO   Nay, good my lord, be not angry.

GONZALO   No, I warrant you, I will not adventure my   188
discretion so weakly. Will you laugh me asleep? For I   189
am very heavy.   190

ANTONIO   Go sleep, and hear us.   191

[*All sleep except Alonso, Sebastian, and Antonio.*]

ALONSO
What, all so soon asleep? I wish mine eyes

Would, with themselves, shut up my thoughts. I find   193
They are inclined to do so.

SEBASTIAN   Please you, sir,
Do not omit the heavy offer of it.   195
It seldom visits sorrow; when it doth,
It is a comforter.

ANTONIO   We two, my lord,
Will guard your person while you take your rest,
And watch your safety.

ALONSO   Thank you. Wondrous heavy.
[*Alonso sleeps. Exit Ariel.*]

SEBASTIAN
What a strange drowsiness possesses them!

ANTONIO
It is the quality o' the climate.

SEBASTIAN   Why
Doth it not then our eyelids sink? I find not
Myself disposed to sleep.

ANTONIO   Nor I. My spirits are nimble.
They fell together all, as by consent;   204
They dropped, as by a thunderstroke. What might,
Worthy Sebastian, O, what might—? No more.
And yet methinks I see it in thy face,
What thou shouldst be. Th' occasion speaks thee, and   208
My strong imagination sees a crown
Dropping upon thy head.

SEBASTIAN   What, art thou waking?

ANTONIO
Do you not hear me speak?

SEBASTIAN   I do, and surely
It is a sleepy language, and thou speak'st   212
Out of thy sleep. What is it thou didst say?
This is a strange repose, to be asleep
With eyes wide open—standing, speaking, moving—
And yet so fast asleep.

ANTONIO   Noble Sebastian,
Thou lett'st thy fortune sleep—die, rather; wink'st   217
Whiles thou art waking.

SEBASTIAN   Thou dost snore distinctly;   218
There's meaning in thy snores.

ANTONIO
I am more serious than my custom. You
Must be so too if heed me, which to do   221
Trebles thee o'er.

SEBASTIAN   Well, I am standing water.   222

ANTONIO
I'll teach you how to flow.

---

164 **pike** lance. **engine** instrument of warfare 166 **foison** plenty
171 **the Golden Age** the age, according to Hesiod, when Cronus, or Saturn, ruled the world; an age of innocence and abundance. **'Save** God save 175 **minister occasion** furnish opportunity 176 **sensible** sensitive. **use** are accustomed 182 **An** if. **flat-long** with the flat of the sword, i.e., ineffectually. (Compare with "fallen flat.") 183 **mettle** temperament, courage. (The sense of *metal*, indistinguishable as a form from *mettle*, continues the metaphor of the sword.) 184 **sphere** orbit. (Literally, one of the concentric zones occupied by planets in Ptolemaic astronomy.) 186 **a-batfowling** hunting birds at night with lantern and *bat*, or "stick"; also, gulling a simpleton. (Gonzalo is the simpleton, or fowl, and Sebastian will use the moon as his lantern.) 188–189 **adventure . . . weakly** risk my reputation for discretion for so trivial a cause (by getting angry at these sarcastic fellows) 190 **heavy** sleepy 191 **Go . . . us** i.e., get ready for sleep, and we'll do our part by laughing

193 **Would . . . thoughts** would shut off my melancholy brooding when they close themselves in sleep 195 **omit** neglect. **heavy** drowsy 204 **They** the sleepers. **consent** common agreement 208 **occasion speaks thee** opportunity of the moment calls upon you, i.e., proclaims you usurper of Alonso's crown 212 **sleepy** dreamlike, fantastic 217 **wink'st** (you) shut your eyes 218 **distinctly** articulately 221 **if heed** if you heed 222 **Trebles thee o'er** makes you three times as great and rich. **standing water** water that neither ebbs nor flows, at a standstill

SEBASTIAN   Do so. To ebb 223
Hereditary sloth instructs me.
ANTONIO   O, 224
If you but knew how you the purpose cherish 225
Whiles thus you mock it! How, in stripping it, 226
You more invest it! Ebbing men, indeed, 227
Most often do so near the bottom run 228
By their own fear or sloth.
SEBASTIAN   Prithee, say on.
The setting of thine eye and cheek proclaim 230
A matter from thee, and a birth indeed 231
Which throes thee much to yield.
ANTONIO   Thus, sir: 232
Although this lord of weak remembrance, this 233
Who shall be of as little memory
When he is earthed, hath here almost persuaded— 235
For he's a spirit of persuasion, only 236
Professes to persuade—the King his son's alive, 237
'Tis as impossible that he's undrowned
As he that sleeps here swims.
SEBASTIAN   I have no hope
That he's undrowned.
ANTONIO   O, out of that "no hope"
What great hope have you! No hope that way is 241
Another way so high a hope that even
Ambition cannot pierce a wink beyond, 243
But doubt discovery there. Will you grant with me 244
That Ferdinand is drowned?
SEBASTIAN   He's gone.
ANTONIO   Then tell me,
Who's the next heir of Naples?
SEBASTIAN   Claribel.
ANTONIO
She that is Queen of Tunis; she that dwells
Ten leagues beyond man's life; she that from Naples 248
Can have no note, unless the sun were post— 249
The Man i' the Moon's too slow—till newborn chins
Be rough and razorable; she that from whom 251
We all were sea-swallowed, though some cast again, 252

And by that destiny to perform an act
Whereof what's past is prologue, what to come
In yours and my discharge. 255
SEBASTIAN   What stuff is this? How say you?
'Tis true my brother's daughter's Queen of Tunis,
So is she heir of Naples, twixt which regions
There is some space.
ANTONIO   A space whose every cubit 259
Seems to cry out, "How shall that Claribel
Measure us back to Naples? Keep in Tunis, 261
And let Sebastian wake." Say this were death 262
That now hath seized them, why, they were no
 worse
Than now they are. There be that can rule Naples 264
As well as he that sleeps, lords that can prate 265
As amply and unnecessarily
As this Gonzalo. I myself could make 267
A chough of as deep chat. O, that you bore 268
The mind that I do! What a sleep were this
For your advancement! Do you understand me?
SEBASTIAN
Methinks I do.
ANTONIO   And how does your content 271
Tender your own good fortune?
SEBASTIAN   I remember 272
You did supplant your brother Prospero.
ANTONIO   True.
And look how well my garments sit upon me,
Much feater than before. My brother's servants 275
Were then my fellows. Now they are my men.
SEBASTIAN   But, for your conscience?
ANTONIO
Ay, sir, where lies that? If 'twere a kibe, 278
'Twould put me to my slipper; but I feel not 279
This deity in my bosom. Twenty consciences
That stand twixt me and Milan, candied be they 281
And melt ere they molest! Here lies your brother, 282
No better than the earth he lies upon,
If he were that which now he's like—that's dead,
Whom I, with this obedient steel, three inches of it,
Can lay to bed forever; whiles you, doing thus, 286
To the perpetual wink for aye might put 287
This ancient morsel, this Sir Prudence, who
Should not upbraid our course. For all the rest, 289
They'll take suggestion as a cat laps milk; 290
They'll tell the clock to any business that 291
We say befits the hour.

223 ebb recede, decline   **224 Hereditary sloth** natural laziness and the position of younger brother, one who cannot inherit   **225–226 If . . . mock it** if you only knew how much you really enhance the value of ambition even while your words mock your purpose   **226–227 How . . . invest it** i.e., how the more you speak flippantly of ambition, the more you, in effect, affirm it.   **invest** clothe. (Antonio's paradox is that, by skeptically stripping away illusions, Sebastian can see the essence of a situation and the opportunity it presents or that, by disclaiming and deriding his purpose, Sebastian shows how valuable it really is.)   **228 the bottom** i.e., on which unadventurous men may go aground and miss the tide of fortune   **230 setting** set expression (of earnestness)   **231 matter** matter of importance   **232 throes** causes pain, as in giving birth.   **yield** give forth, speak about   **233 this lord** i.e., Gonzalo.   **remembrance** (1) power of remembering (2) being remembered after his death   **235 earthed** buried   **236–237 only . . . persuade** whose whole function (as a privy councillor) is to persuade   **241 that way** i.e., in regard to Ferdinand's being saved   **243–244 Ambition . . . there** ambition itself cannot see any further than that hope (of the crown), is unsure of finding anything to achieve beyond it or even there.   **wink** glimpse   **248 Ten . . . life** i.e., further than the journey of a lifetime   **249 note** news, intimation.   **post** messenger   **251 razorable** ready for shaving.   **from** on our voyage from   **252 cast** were disgorged (with a pun on *casting* of parts for a play)

255 discharge performance   **259 cubit** ancient measure of length of about twenty inches   **261 Measure us** i.e., traverse the cubits, find her way.   **Keep** stay. (Addressed to Claribel.)   **262 wake** i.e., to his good fortune   **264 There be** there are those   **265 prate** speak foolishly   **267–268 I . . . chat** I could teach a jackdaw to talk as wisely, or, be such a garrulous talker myself   **271 content** desire, inclination   **272 Tender** regard, look after   **275 feater** more becomingly, fittingly   **278 kibe** chilblain, here a sore on the heel   **279 put me to** oblige me to wear   **281 Milan** the dukedom of Milan.   **candied** frozen, congealed in crystalline form.   **be they** may they be   **282 molest** interfere   **286 thus** similarly. (The actor makes a stabbing gesture.)   **287 wink** sleep, closing of eyes.   **aye** ever   **289 Should not** would not then be able to   **290 take suggestion** respond to prompting   **291 tell the clock** i.e., agree, answer appropriately, chime

SEBASTIAN   Thy case, dear friend,
  Shall be my precedent. As thou gott'st Milan,
  I'll come by Naples. Draw thy sword. One stroke
  Shall free thee from the tribute which thou payest,   295
  And I the king shall love thee.
ANTONIO   Draw together;
  And when I rear my hand, do you the like
  To fall it on Gonzalo.   [*They draw.*]
SEBASTIAN   O, but one word.   298
                                    [*They talk apart.*]

        Enter Ariel [invisible], with music and song.

ARIEL [*to Gonzalo*]
  My master through his art foresees the danger
  That you, his friend, are in, and sends me forth—
  For else his project dies—to keep them living.
                          Sings in Gonzalo's ear.

      While you here do snoring lie,
      Open-eyed conspiracy
          His time doth take.   304
      If of life you keep a care,
      Shake off slumber, and beware.
          Awake, awake!
ANTONIO   Then let us both be sudden.   308
GONZALO [*waking*] Now, good angels preserve the King!
                                    [*The others wake.*]
ALONSO
  Why, how now, ho, awake? Why are you drawn?
  Wherefore this ghastly looking?
GONZALO   What's the matter?
SEBASTIAN
  Whiles we stood here securing your repose,   312
  Even now, we heard a hollow burst of bellowing
  Like bulls, or rather lions. Did 't not wake you?
  It struck mine ear most terribly.
ALONSO   I heard nothing.
ANTONIO
  O, 'twas a din to fright a monster's ear,
  To make an earthquake! Sure it was the roar
  Of a whole herd of lions.
ALONSO   Heard you this, Gonzalo?
GONZALO
  Upon mine honor, sir, I heard a humming,
  And that a strange one too, which did awake me.
  I shaked you, sir, and cried. As mine eyes opened,   322
  I saw their weapons drawn. There was a noise,
  That's verily. 'Tis best we stand upon our guard,   324
  Or that we quit this place. Let's draw our weapons.
ALONSO
  Lead off this ground, and let's make further search
  For my poor son.
GONZALO   Heavens keep him from these beasts!
  For he is, sure, i' th' island.
ALONSO   Lead away.

ARIEL [*aside*]
  Prospero my lord shall know what I have done.
  So, King, go safely on to seek thy son.
                          Exeunt [separately].

                          ❖

2.2   *Enter Caliban with a burden of wood. A noise of
          thunder heard.*

CALIBAN
  All the infections that the sun sucks up
  From bogs, fens, flats, on Prosper fall, and make
      him   2
  By inchmeal a disease! His spirits hear me,   3
  And yet I needs must curse. But they'll nor pinch, 4
  Fright me with urchin shows, pitch me i' the mire, 5
  Nor lead me, like a firebrand, in the dark   6
  Out of my way, unless he bid 'em. But
  For every trifle are they set upon me,
  Sometimes like apes, that mow and chatter at me   9
  And after bite me; then like hedgehogs, which
  Lie tumbling in my barefoot way and mount
  Their pricks at my footfall. Sometimes am I
  All wound with adders, who with cloven tongues   13
  Do hiss me into madness.

        Enter Trinculo.
                              Lo, now, lo!
  Here comes a spirit of his, and to torment me
  For bringing wood in slowly. I'll fall flat.
  Perchance he will not mind me.   [*He lies down.*] 17
TRINCULO Here's neither bush nor shrub to bear off   18
  any weather at all. And another storm brewing; I hear
  it sing i' the wind. Yond same black cloud, yond huge
  one, looks like a foul bombard that would shed his 21
  liquor. If it should thunder as it did before, I know not
  where to hide my head. Yond same cloud cannot
  choose but fall by pailfuls. [*Seeing Caliban.*] What have
  we here, a man or a fish? Dead or alive? A fish, he
  smells like a fish; a very ancient and fishlike smell; a
  kind of not-of-the-newest Poor John. A strange fish! 27
  Were I in England now, as once I was, and had but
  this fish painted, not a holiday fool there but would 29
  give a piece of silver. There would this monster make 30
  a man. Any strange beast there makes a man. When 31
  they will not give a doit to relieve a lame beggar, they 32
  will lay out ten to see a dead Indian. Legged like a
  man, and his fins like arms! Warm, o' my troth! I do 34
  now let loose my opinion, hold it no longer: this is no 35
  fish, but an islander, that hath lately suffered by a 36

2.2. Location: Another part of the island.
2 flats swamps   **3 By inchmeal** inch by inch   **4 needs must** have to.
nor neither   **5 urchin shows** elvish apparitions shaped like hedgehogs
6 like a firebrand they in the guise of a will-o'-the-wisp   **9 mow**
make faces   **13 wound with** entwined by   **17 mind** notice   **18 bear
off** keep off   **21 foul bombard** dirty leather jug.   **his** its   **27 Poor
John** salted fish, type of poor fare   **29 painted** i.e., painted on a sign
set up outside a booth or tent at a fair   **30–31 make a man** (1) make
one's fortune (2) be indistinguishable from an Englishman   **32 doit**
small coin   **34 o' my troth** by my faith   **35 hold it** hold it in   **36 suffered** i.e., died

---

295 tribute (See 1.2.113–124.)   **298 fall it** let it fall   **304 time** opportunity   **308 sudden** quick   **312 securing** standing guard over
322 cried called out   **324 verily** true

thunderbolt. [*Thunder.*] Alas, the storm is come again!
My best way is to creep under his gaberdine. There is 38
no other shelter hereabout. Misery acquaints a man
with strange bedfellows. I will here shroud till the 40
dregs of the storm be past. 41
                        [*He creeps under Caliban's garment.*]

                Enter Stephano, singing, [*a bottle in his hand*].

STEPHANO
    "I shall no more to sea, to sea,
        Here shall I die ashore—"
This is a very scurvy tune to sing at a man's funeral.
Well, here's my comfort.   *Drinks.*
(*Sings.*)
    "The master, the swabber, the boatswain, and I, 46
        The gunner and his mate,
    Loved Mall, Meg, and Marian, and Margery,
        But none of us cared for Kate.
            For she had a tongue with a tang, 50
            Would cry to a sailor, 'Go hang!'
    She loved not the savor of tar nor of pitch,
    Yet a tailor might scratch her where'er she did
        itch. 53
        Then to sea, boys, and let her go hang!"
This is a scurvy tune too. But here's my comfort.
                                            Drinks.
CALIBAN   Do not torment me! O! 56
STEPHANO   What's the matter? Have we devils here? Do 57
you put tricks upon 's with savages and men of Ind, 58
ha? I have not scaped drowning to be afeard now of
your four legs. For it hath been said, "As proper a man 60
as ever went on four legs cannot make him give 61
ground"; and it shall be said so again while Stephano
breathes at' nostrils. 63
CALIBAN   This spirit torments me! O!
STEPHANO   This is some monster of the isle with four
legs, who hath got, as I take it, an ague. Where the 66
devil should he learn our language? I will give him 67
some relief, if it be but for that. If I can recover him 68
and keep him tame and get to Naples with him, he's
a present for any emperor that ever trod on neat's 70
leather. 71
CALIBAN   Do not torment me, prithee. I'll bring my
wood home faster.
STEPHANO   He's in his fit now and does not talk after 74
the wisest. He shall taste of my bottle. If he have never 75
drunk wine afore, it will go near to remove his fit. If I 76

can recover him and keep him tame, I will not take too 77
much for him. He shall pay for him that hath him, and 78
that soundly.
CALIBAN   Thou dost me yet but little hurt; thou wilt
anon, I know it by thy trembling. Now Prosper works 81
upon thee.
STEPHANO   Come on your ways. Open your mouth. Here
is that which will give language to you, cat. Open your 84
mouth. This will shake your shaking, I can tell you, 85
and that soundly. [*Giving Caliban a drink.*] You cannot
tell who's your friend. Open your chaps again. 87
TRINCULO   I should know that voice. It should be—but
he is drowned, and these are devils. O, defend me!
STEPHANO   Four legs and two voices—a most delicate 90
monster! His forward voice now is to speak well of his
friend; his backward voice is to utter foul speeches and 92
to detract. If all the wine in my bottle will recover him, 93
I will help his ague. Come. [*Giving a drink.*] Amen! I 94
will pour some in thy other mouth.
TRINCULO   Stephano!
STEPHANO   Doth thy other mouth call me? Mercy, 97
mercy! This is a devil, and no monster. I will leave
him. I have no long spoon. 99
TRINCULO   Stephano! If thou beest Stephano, touch me
and speak to me, for I am Trinculo—be not afeard—
thy good friend Trinculo.
STEPHANO   If thou beest Trinculo, come forth. I'll pull
thee by the lesser legs. If any be Trinculo's legs, these
are they. [*Pulling him out.*] Thou art very Trinculo
indeed! How cam'st thou to be the siege of this 106
mooncalf? Can he vent Trinculos? 107
TRINCULO   I took him to be killed with a thunderstroke.
But art thou not drowned, Stephano? I hope now thou
art not drowned. Is the storm overblown? I hid me 110
under the dead mooncalf's gaberdine for fear of the
storm. And art thou living, Stephano? O Stephano,
two Neapolitans scaped!   [*He capers with Stephano.*]
STEPHANO   Prithee, do not turn me about. My stomach
is not constant. 115
CALIBAN
These be fine things, an if they be not spirits. 116
That's a brave god, and bears celestial liquor. 117
I will kneel to him.
STEPHANO   How didst thou scape? How cam'st thou
hither? Swear by this bottle how thou cam'st hither. I

38 gaberdine cloak, loose upper garment   **40 shroud** take shelter
41 dregs i.e., last remains (as in a *bombard* or jug, line 21)
46 swabber crew member whose job is to wash the decks   **50 tang**
sting   **53 tailor . . . itch** (A dig at tailors for their supposed effeminacy and a bawdy suggestion of satisfying a sexual craving.)   **56 Do
. . . me** (Caliban assumes that one of Prospero's spirits has come to
punish him.)   **57 What's the matter** what's going on here?   **58 put
tricks upon 's** trick us with conjuring shows.   **Ind** India   **60 proper**
handsome   **61 four legs** (The conventional phrase would supply *two
legs,* but the creature Stephano thinks he sees has four.)   **63 at'** at the
66 ague fever. (Probably both Caliban and Trinculo are quaking; see
lines 56 and 81.)   **67 should he learn** could he have learned   **68 for
that** i.e., for knowing our language.   **recover** restore   **70–71 neat's
leather** cowhide   **74–75 after the wisest** in the wisest fashion
76 afore before.   **go near to** be in a fair way to

77 recover restore   **77–78 I will . . . much** i.e., no sum can be too
much   **78 He shall . . . hath him** i.e., anyone who wants him will
have to pay dearly for him.   **hath** possesses, receives   **81 anon** presently   **84–85 cat . . . mouth** (Allusion to the proverb "Good liquor
will make a cat speak.")   **87 chaps** jaws   **90 delicate** ingenious
92 backward voice (Trinculo and Caliban are facing in opposite directions. Stephano supposes the monster to have a rear end that can emit
foul speeches or foul-smelling wind at the monster's *other mouth,* line
95.)   **93 If . . . him** even if it takes all the wine in my bottle to cure
him   **94 help** cure   **97 call me** i.e., call me by name, know supernaturally who I am   **99 long spoon** (Allusion to the proverb "He that
sups with the devil has need of a long spoon.")   **106 siege** excrement
107 mooncalf monstrous or misshapen creature (whose deformity is
caused by the malignant influence of the moon).   **vent** excrete, defecate   **110 overblown** blown over   **115 not constant** unsteady
116 an if if   **117 brave** fine, magnificent.   **bears** he carries

escaped upon a butt of sack which the sailors heaved 121
o'erboard—by this bottle, which I made of the bark of 122
a tree with mine own hands since I was cast ashore. 123

CALIBAN [*kneeling*]   I'll swear upon that bottle to be
thy true subject, for the liquor is not earthly.

STEPHANO   Here. Swear then how thou escapedst.

TRINCULO   Swum ashore, man, like a duck. I can swim
like a duck, I'll be sworn.

STEPHANO   Here, kiss the book. Though thou canst 129
swim like a duck, thou art made like a goose.
                                   [*Giving him a drink.*]

TRINCULO   O Stephano, hast any more of this?

STEPHANO   The whole butt, man. My cellar is in a rock
by the seaside, where my wine is hid.—How now,
mooncalf? How does thine ague?

CALIBAN   Hast thou not dropped from heaven?

STEPHANO   Out o' the moon, I do assure thee. I was the
Man i' the Moon when time was.   137

CALIBAN
I have seen thee in her, and I do adore thee.
My mistress showed me thee, and thy dog, and thy
bush.   139

STEPHANO   Come, swear to that. Kiss the book. I will
furnish it anon with new contents. Swear.
                                   [*Giving him a drink.*]

TRINCULO   By this good light, this is a very shallow 142
monster! I afeard of him? A very weak monster! The
Man i' the Moon? A most poor credulous monster!
Well drawn, monster, in good sooth!   145

CALIBAN [*to Stephano*]
I'll show thee every fertile inch o' th' island,
And I will kiss thy foot. I prithee, be my god.

TRINCULO   By this light, a most perfidious and drunken
monster! When 's god's asleep, he'll rob his bottle. 149

CALIBAN
I'll kiss thy foot. I'll swear myself thy subject.

STEPHANO   Come on then. Down, and swear.
                                   [*Caliban kneels.*]

TRINCULO   I shall laugh myself to death at this puppy-
headed monster. A most scurvy monster! I could find
in my heart to beat him—

STEPHANO   Come, kiss.

TRINCULO   But that the poor monster's in drink. An 156
abominable monster!

CALIBAN
I'll show thee the best springs. I'll pluck thee berries.
I'll fish for thee and get thee wood enough.
A plague upon the tyrant that I serve!
I'll bear him no more sticks, but follow thee,
Thou wondrous man.

TRINCULO   A most ridiculous monster, to make a
wonder of a poor drunkard!

CALIBAN
I prithee, let me bring thee where crabs grow,   165
And I with my long nails will dig thee pignuts,   166
Show thee a jay's nest, and instruct thee how
To snare the nimble marmoset. I'll bring thee   168
To clustering filberts, and sometimes I'll get thee
Young scamels from the rock. Wilt thou go with me? 170

STEPHANO   I prithee now, lead the way without any
more talking.—Trinculo, the King and all our company else being drowned, we will inherit here.—   173
Here, bear my bottle.—Fellow Trinculo, we'll fill him
by and by again.

CALIBAN (*sings drunkenly*)
Farewell, master, farewell, farewell!

TRINCULO   A howling monster; a drunken monster!

CALIBAN
No more dams I'll make for fish,
    Nor fetch in firing   179
    At requiring,
Nor scrape trenchering, nor wash dish.   181
    'Ban, 'Ban, Ca–Caliban
    Has a new master. Get a new man!   183
Freedom, high-day! High-day, freedom! Freedom,   184
high-day, freedom!

STEPHANO   O brave monster! Lead the way.   *Exeunt.*

3.1   *Enter Ferdinand, bearing a log.*

FERDINAND
There be some sports are painful, and their labor   1
Delight in them sets off. Some kinds of baseness   2
Are nobly undergone, and most poor matters   3
Point to rich ends. This my mean task   4
Would be as heavy to me as odious, but   5
The mistress which I serve quickens what's dead   6
And makes my labors pleasures. O, she is
Ten times more gentle than her father's crabbed,
And he's composed of harshness. I must remove
Some thousands of these logs and pile them up,
Upon a sore injunction. My sweet mistress   11
Weeps when she sees me work and says such
    baseness

---

121 butt of sack barrel of Canary wine   **122 by this bottle** i.e., I
swear by this bottle   **123 since** after   **129 book** i.e., bottle (but with
ironic reference to the practice of kissing the Bible in swearing an
oath; see *I'll be sworn* in line 128)   **137 when time was** once upon a
time   **139 dog . . . bush** (The Man in the Moon was popularly imagined to have with him a dog and a bush of thorn.)   **142 By . . . light**
by God's light, by this good light from heaven   **145 Well drawn** well
pulled (on the bottle).   **in good sooth** truly, indeed   **149 When . . .
bottle** i.e., Caliban wouldn't even stop at robbing his god of his bottle
if he could catch him asleep   **156 in drink** drunk

165 crabs crab apples, or perhaps crabs   **166 pignuts** earthnuts, edible tuberous roots   **168 marmoset** small monkey   **170 scamels** (Possibly *seamews*, mentioned in Strachey's letter, or shellfish, or perhaps
from *squamelle*, "furnished with little scales." Contemporary French
and Italian travel accounts report that the natives of Patagonia in
South America ate small fish described as *fort scameux* and *squame*.)
173 else in addition, besides ourselves.   **inherit** take possession
179 firing firewood   **181 trenchering** trenchers, wooden plates
183 Get a new man (Addressed to Prospero.)   **184 high-day** holiday
3.1. Location: Before Prospero's cell.
1–2 There . . . sets off some pastimes are laborious, but the pleasure
we get from them compensates for the effort. (Pleasure is *set off* by labor as a jewel is set off by its foil.)   **2 baseness** menial activity   **3 undergone** undertaken.   **most poor** poorest   **4 mean** lowly   **5 but** were
it not that   **6 quickens** gives life to   **11 sore injunction** severe command

Had never like executor. I forget;   13
But these sweet thoughts do even refresh my labors,
Most busy lest when I do it.

Enter Miranda; and Prospero [at a distance,
unseen].

MIRANDA   Alas now, pray you,   15
Work not so hard. I would the lightning had
Burnt up those logs that you are enjoined to pile!   17
Pray, set it down and rest you. When this burns,   18
'Twill weep for having wearied you. My father   19
Is hard at study. Pray now, rest yourself.
He's safe for these three hours.
FERDINAND   O most dear mistress,   21
The sun will set before I shall discharge   22
What I must strive to do.
MIRANDA   If you'll sit down,
I'll bear your logs the while. Pray, give me that.
I'll carry it to the pile.
FERDINAND   No, precious creature,
I had rather crack my sinews, break my back,
Than you should such dishonor undergo
While I sit lazy by.
MIRANDA   It would become me
As well as it does you; and I should do it
With much more ease, for my good will is to it,
And yours it is against.
PROSPERO [*aside*]   Poor worm, thou art infected!
This visitation shows it.
MIRANDA   You look wearily.   32
FERDINAND
No, noble mistress, 'tis fresh morning with me
When you are by at night. I do beseech you—   34
Chiefly that I might set it in my prayers—
What is your name?
MIRANDA   Miranda.—O my father,
I have broke your hest to say so.
FERDINAND   Admired Miranda!   37
Indeed the top of admiration, worth
What's dearest to the world! Full many a lady   39
I have eyed with best regard, and many a time   40
The harmony of their tongues hath into bondage
Brought my too diligent ear. For several virtues   42
Have I liked several women, never any
With so full soul but some defect in her
Did quarrel with the noblest grace she owed   45
And put it to the foil. But you, O you,   46

So perfect and so peerless, are created
Of every creature's best!
MIRANDA   I do not know   48
One of my sex; no woman's face remember,
Save, from my glass, mine own. Nor have I seen
More that I may call men than you, good friend,
And my dear father. How features are abroad   52
I am skilless of; but, by my modesty,   53
The jewel in my dower, I would not wish
Any companion in the world but you;
Nor can imagination form a shape,
Besides yourself, to like of. But I prattle   57
Something too wildly, and my father's precepts   58
I therein do forget.
FERDINAND   I am in my condition   59
A prince, Miranda; I do think, a king—
I would, not so!—and would no more endure   61
This wooden slavery than to suffer   62
The flesh-fly blow my mouth. Hear my soul speak: 63
The very instant that I saw you did
My heart fly to your service, there resides
To make me slave to it, and for your sake
Am I this patient log-man.
MIRANDA   Do you love me?
FERDINAND
O heaven, O earth, bear witness to this sound,
And crown what I profess with kind event   69
If I speak true! If hollowly, invert   70
What best is boded me to mischief! I   71
Beyond all limit of what else i' the world   72
Do love, prize, honor you.
MIRANDA [*weeping*]   I am a fool
To weep at what I am glad of.
PROSPERO [*aside*]   Fair encounter
Of two most rare affections! Heavens rain grace
On that which breeds between 'em!
FERDINAND   Wherefore weep you?
MIRANDA
At mine unworthiness, that dare not offer
What I desire to give, and much less take
What I shall die to want. But this is trifling,   79
And all the more it seeks to hide itself
The bigger bulk it shows. Hence, bashful cunning,   81
And prompt me, plain and holy innocence!
I am your wife, if you will marry me;
If not, I'll die your maid. To be your fellow   84
You may deny me, but I'll be your servant
Whether you will or no.
FERDINAND   My mistress, dearest,   86

13 Had . . . executor i.e., was never before undertaken by so noble
a being. I forget i.e., I forget that I'm supposed to be working, or, I
forget my happiness, oppressed by my labor 15 Most . . . it i.e.,
busy at my labor but with my mind on other things (?) (The line may
be in need of emendation.) 17 enjoined commanded 18 this i.e.,
the log 19 weep i.e., exude resin 21 these the next 22 discharge
complete 32 visitation (1) Miranda's visit to Ferdinand (2) visitation
of the plague, i.e., infection of love 34 by nearby 37 hest command. Admired Miranda (Her names means "to be admired or wondered at.") 39 dearest most treasured 40 best regard thoughtful
and approving attention 42 diligent attentive. several various (also
in line 43) 45 owed owned 46 put . . . foil (1) overthrew it (as in
wrestling) (2) served as a *foil*, or "contrast," to set it off

48 Of out of 52 How . . . abroad what people look like in other
places 53 skilless ignorant. modesty virginity 57 like of be
pleased with, be fond of 58 Something somewhat 59 condition
rank 61 would wish (it were) 62 wooden slavery being compelled
to carry wood 63 flesh-fly insect that deposits its eggs in dead flesh.
blow befoul with fly eggs 69 kind event favorable outcome
70 hollowly insincerely, falsely. invert turn 71 boded in store for.
mischief harm 72 what whatever 79 die (Probably with an unconscious sexual meaning that underlies all of lines 77–81.) to want
through lacking 81 bashful cunning coyness 84 maid handmaiden,
servant. fellow mate, equal 86 will desire it. My mistress i.e., the
woman I adore and serve (not an illicit sexual partner)

And I thus humble ever.

MIRANDA   My husband, then?

FERDINAND   Ay, with a heart as willing   89
As bondage e'er of freedom. Here's my hand.

MIRANDA [clasping his hand]
And mine, with my heart in 't. And now farewell
Till half an hour hence.

FERDINAND   A thousand thousand!   92

Exeunt [Ferdinand and Miranda, separately].

PROSPERO
So glad of this as they I cannot be,
Who are surprised with all; but my rejoicing   94
At nothing can be more. I'll to my book,
For yet ere suppertime must I perform
Much business appertaining.   *Exit.* 97

♣

3.2   *Enter Caliban, Stephano, and Trinculo.*

STEPHANO   Tell not me. When the butt is out, we will 1
drink water, not a drop before. Therefore bear up and 2
board 'em. Servant monster, drink to me.   3

TRINCULO   Servant monster? The folly of this island! 4
They say there's but five upon this isle. We are three
of them; if th' other two be brained like us, the state 6
totters.

STEPHANO   Drink, servant monster, when I bid thee.
Thy eyes are almost set in thy head. [*Giving a drink.*] 9

TRINCULO   Where should they be set else? He were a 10
brave monster indeed if they were set in his tail.   11

STEPHANO   My man-monster hath drowned his tongue
in sack. For my part, the sea cannot drown me. I
swam, ere I could recover the shore, five and thirty 14
leagues off and on. By this light, thou shalt be my 15
lieutenant, monster, or my standard.   16

TRINCULO   Your lieutenant, if you list; he's no standard. 17

STEPHANO   We'll not run, Monsieur Monster.   18

TRINCULO   Nor go neither, but you'll lie like dogs and 19
yet say nothing neither.

STEPHANO   Mooncalf, speak once in thy life, if thou
beest a good mooncalf.

CALIBAN
How does thy honor? Let me lick thy shoe.
I'll not serve him. He is not valiant.

TRINCULO   Thou liest, most ignorant monster, I am in 25
case to jostle a constable. Why, thou debauched fish, 26
thou, was there ever man a coward that hath drunk so
much sack as I today? Wilt thou tell a monstrous lie, 28
being but half a fish and half a monster?

CALIBAN
Lo, how he mocks me! Wilt thou let him, my lord?

TRINCULO   "Lord," quoth he? That a monster should be
such a natural!   32

CALIBAN
Lo, lo, again! Bite him to death, I prithee.

STEPHANO   Trinculo, keep a good tongue in your head.
If you prove a mutineer—the next tree! The poor mon- 35
ster's my subject, and he shall not suffer indignity.

CALIBAN
I thank my noble lord. Wilt thou be pleased
To hearken once again to the suit I made to thee?

STEPHANO   Marry, will I. Kneel and repeat it. I will 39
stand, and so shall Trinculo.   [*Caliban kneels.*] 40

Enter Ariel, invisible.

CALIBAN
As I told thee before, I am subject to a tyrant,
A sorcerer, that by his cunning hath
Cheated me of the island.

ARIEL [*mimicking Trinculo*]
Thou liest.

CALIBAN   Thou liest, thou jesting monkey, thou!
I would my valiant master would destroy thee.
I do not lie.

STEPHANO   Trinculo, if you trouble him any more in 's
tale, by this hand, I will supplant some of your teeth. 48

TRINCULO   Why, I said nothing.

STEPHANO   Mum, then, and no more.—Proceed.

CALIBAN
I say by sorcery he got this isle;
From me he got it. If thy greatness will
Revenge it on him—for I know thou dar'st,
But this thing dare not—   54

STEPHANO   That's most certain.

CALIBAN
Thou shalt be lord of it, and I'll serve thee.

STEPHANO   How now shall this be compassed? Canst 57
thou bring me to the party?

CALIBAN
Yea, yea, my lord. I'll yield him thee asleep,
Where thou mayst knock a nail into his head.

ARIEL   Thou liest; thou canst not.

CALIBAN
What a pied ninny's this! Thou scurvy patch!—   62
I do beseech thy greatness, give him blows
And take his bottle from him. When that's gone

89 willing desirous **92 A thousand thousand** i.e., a thousand thousand farewells **94 with all** by everything that has happened, or, *withal,* "with it" **97 appertaining** related to this
3.2. Location: Another part of the island.
1 out empty **2–3 bear . . . 'em** (Stephano uses the terminology of maneuvering at sea and boarding a vessel under attack as a way of urging an assault on the liquor supply.) **4 folly of** i.e., stupidity found on **6 be brained** are endowed with intelligence **9 set** fixed in a drunken stare, or, sunk, like the sun **10 set** placed **11 brave** fine, splendid **14 recover** gain, reach **15 leagues** units of distance, each equaling about three miles. **off and on** intermittently. **By this light** (An oath: by the light of the sun.) **16 standard** standard-bearer, ensign (as distinguished from *lieutenant,* lines 16–17) **17 list** prefer. **no standard** i.e., not able to stand up **18 run** (1) retreat (2) urinate (taking Trinculo's *standard,* line 17, in the old sense of "conduit") **19 go** walk. **lie** (1) tell lies (2) lie prostrate (3) excrete

25–26 in case . . . constable i.e., in fit condition, made valiant by drink, to taunt or challenge the police **26 debauched** (1) seduced away from proper service and allegiance (2) depraved **28 sack** Spanish white wine **32 natural** (1) idiot (2) natural as opposed to unnatural, monsterlike **35 the next tree** i.e., you'll hang **39 Marry** i.e., indeed. (Originally an oath, "by the Virgin Mary.") **40 s.d. invisible** i.e., wearing a garment to connote invisibility, as at 1.2.377 **48 supplant** uproot, displace **54 this thing** i.e., Trinculo **57 compassed** achieved **62 pied ninny** fool in motley. **patch** fool

He shall drink naught but brine, for I'll not show
  him
Where the quick freshes are.   66
STEPHANO   Trinculo, run into no further danger. Inter-
rupt the monster one word further and, by this hand,   68
I'll turn my mercy out o' doors and make a stockfish of 69
thee.
TRINCULO   Why, what did I? I did nothing. I'll go farther
off.   72
STEPHANO   Didst thou not say he lied?
ARIEL   Thou liest.
STEPHANO   Do I so? Take thou that. [*He beats Trinculo.*]
As you like this, give me the lie another time.   76
TRINCULO   I did not give the lie. Out o' your wits and
hearing too? A pox o' your bottle! This can sack and
drinking do. A murrain on your monster, and the   79
devil take your fingers!
CALIBAN   Ha, ha, ha!
STEPHANO   Now, forward with your tale. [*To Trinculo.*]
Prithee, stand further off.
CALIBAN
Beat him enough. After a little time
I'll beat him too.
STEPHANO   Stand farther.—Come, proceed.
CALIBAN
Why, as I told thee, 'tis a custom with him
I' th' afternoon to sleep. There thou mayst
  brain him,
Having first seized his books; or with a log
Batter his skull, or paunch him with a stake,   90
Or cut his weasand with thy knife. Remember   91
First to possess his books, for without them
He's but a sot, as I am, nor hath not   93
One spirit to command. They all do hate him
As rootedly as I. Burn but his books.
He has brave utensils—for so he calls them—   96
Which, when he has a house, he'll deck withal.   97
And that most deeply to consider is
The beauty of his daughter. He himself
Calls her a nonpareil. I never saw a woman
But only Sycorax my dam and she;
But she as far surpasseth Sycorax
As great'st does least.
STEPHANO   Is it so brave a lass?   104
CALIBAN
Ay, lord. She will become thy bed, I warrant,   105
And bring thee forth brave brood.
STEPHANO   Monster, I will kill this man. His daughter
and I will be king and queen—save Our Graces!—and
Trinculo and thyself shall be viceroys. Dost thou like
the plot, Trinculo?
TRINCULO   Excellent.
STEPHANO   Give me thy hand. I am sorry I beat thee;

but, while thou liv'st, keep a good tongue in thy head.
CALIBAN
Within this half hour will he be asleep.
Wilt thou destroy him then?
STEPHANO   Ay, on mine honor.
ARIEL [*aside*]   This will I tell my master.
CALIBAN
Thou mak'st me merry; I am full of pleasure.
Let us be jocund. Will you troll the catch   119
You taught me but whilere?   120
STEPHANO   At thy request, monster, I will do reason,   121
any reason.—Come on, Trinculo, let us sing.   *Sings.* 122
  "Flout 'em and scout 'em   123
  And scout 'em and flout 'em!
    Thought is free."
CALIBAN   That's not the tune.   126
            Ariel plays the tune on a tabor and pipe.
STEPHANO   What is this same?
TRINCULO   This is the tune of our catch, played by the
picture of Nobody.   129
STEPHANO   If thou beest a man, show thyself in thy
likeness. If thou beest a devil, take 't as thou list.   131
TRINCULO   O, forgive me my sins!
STEPHANO   He that dies pays all debts. I defy thee. 133
Mercy upon us!
CALIBAN   Art thou afeard?
STEPHANO   No, monster, not I.
CALIBAN
Be not afeard. The isle is full of noises,
Sounds, and sweet airs, that give delight and hurt not.
Sometimes a thousand twangling instruments
Will hum about mine ears, and sometimes voices
That, if I then had waked after long sleep,
Will make me sleep again; and then, in dreaming,
The clouds methought would open and show riches
Ready to drop upon me, that when I waked
I cried to dream again.   145
STEPHANO   This will prove a brave kingdom to me,
where I shall have my music for nothing.
CALIBAN   When Prospero is destroyed.
STEPHANO   That shall be by and by. I remember the 149
story.
TRINCULO   The sound is going away. Let's follow it,
and after do our work.
STEPHANO   Lead, monster; we'll follow. I would I could
see this taborer! He lays it on.   154
TRINCULO   Wilt come? I'll follow, Stephano.
            Exeunt [following Ariel's music].

66 **quick freshes** running springs 68 **one word further** i.e., one more time 69 **turn . . . doors** i.e., forget about being merciful. **stockfish** dried cod beaten before cooking 72 **off** away 76 **give me the lie** call me a liar to my face 79 **murrain** plague. (Literally, a cattle disease.) 90 **paunch** stab in the belly 91 **weasand** windpipe 93 **sot** fool 96 **brave utensils** fine furnishings 97 **deck withal** furnish it with 104 **brave** splendid, attractive 105 **become** suit (sexually)

119 **jocund** jovial, merry. **troll the catch** sing the round 120 **but whilere** only a short time ago 121–122 **reason, any reason** anything reasonable 123 **Flout** scoff at. **scout** deride 126 s.d. **tabor** small drum 129 **picture of Nobody** (Refers to a familiar figure with head, arms, and legs but no trunk.) 131 **take 't . . . list** i.e., take my defiance as you please, as best you can 133 **He . . . debts** i.e., if I have to die, at least that will be the end of all my woes and obligations 145 **to dream** desirous of dreaming 149 **by and by** very soon 154 **lays it on** i.e., plays the drum vigorously

3.3   *Enter Alonso, Sebastian, Antonio, Gonzalo,*
        Adrian, Francisco, etc.

GONZALO
  By 'r lakin, I can go no further, sir.   1
  My old bones aches. Here's a maze trod indeed
  Through forthrights and meanders! By your
      patience,   3
  I needs must rest me.
ALONSO   Old lord, I cannot blame thee,   4
  Who am myself attached with weariness,   5
  To th' dulling of my spirits. Sit down and rest.   6
  Even here I will put off my hope, and keep it
  No longer for my flatterer. He is drowned   8
  Whom thus we stray to find, and the sea mocks
  Our frustrate search on land. Well, let him go.   10
                          [*Alonso and Gonzalo sit.*]
ANTONIO [*aside to Sebastian*]
  I am right glad that he's so out of hope.   11
  Do not, for one repulse, forgo the purpose   12
  That you resolved t' effect.
SEBASTIAN [*to Antonio*]   The next advantage
  Will we take throughly.
ANTONIO [*to Sebastian*]   Let it be tonight,   14
  For, now they are oppressed with travel, they   15
  Will not, nor cannot, use such vigilance   16
  As when they are fresh.
SEBASTIAN [*to Antonio*]   I say tonight. No more.   17

      Solemn and strange music; and Prospero on
      the top, invisible.

ALONSO
  What harmony is this? My good friends, hark!
GONZALO   Marvelous sweet music!

      Enter several strange shapes, bringing in a
      banquet, and dance about it with gentle actions of
      salutations; and, inviting the King, etc., to eat,
      they depart.

ALONSO
  Give us kind keepers, heavens! What were these?   20
SEBASTIAN
  A living drollery. Now I will believe   21
  That there are unicorns; that in Arabia
  There is one tree, the phoenix' throne, one phoenix   23
  At this hour reigning there.
ANTONIO   I'll believe both;
  And what does else want credit, come to me   25

And I'll be sworn 'tis true. Travelers ne'er did lie,
Though fools at home condemn 'em.
GONZALO   If in Naples
  I should report this now, would they believe me
  If I should say I saw such islanders?
  For, certes, these are people of the island,   30
  Who, though they are of monstrous shape, yet note, 31
  Their manners are more gentle, kind, than of
  Our human generation you shall find
  Many, nay, almost any.
PROSPERO [*aside*]   Honest lord,
  Thou hast said well, for some of you there present
  Are worse than devils.
ALONSO   I cannot too much muse   36
  Such shapes, such gesture, and such sound,
      expressing—
  Although they want the use of tongue—a kind   38
  Of excellent dumb discourse.
PROSPERO [*aside*]   Praise in departing.   39
FRANCISCO
  They vanished strangely.
SEBASTIAN   No matter, since
  They have left their viands behind, for we have
      stomachs.   41
  Will 't please you taste of what is here?
ALONSO   Not I.
GONZALO
  Faith, sir, you need not fear. When we were boys,
  Who would believe that there were mountaineers   44
  Dewlapped like bulls, whose throats had hanging at
      'em   45
  Wallets of flesh? Or that there were such men   46
  Whose heads stood in their breasts? Which now we
      find   47
  Each putter-out of five for one will bring us   48
  Good warrant of.
ALONSO   I will stand to and feed,   49
  Although my last—no matter, since I feel   50
  The best is past. Brother, my lord the Duke,   51
  Stand to, and do as we.   [*They approach the table.*] 52

      Thunder and lightning. Enter Ariel, like a harpy,
      claps his wings upon the table, and with a quaint
      device the banquet vanishes.

3.3. Location: Another part of the island.
1 By 'r lakin by our Ladykin, by our Lady   **3 forthrights and mean-**
ders paths straight and crooked   **4 needs must** have to   **5 attached**
seized   **6 To . . . spirits** to the point of being dull-spirited   **8 for**
as   **10 frustrate** frustrated   **11 right** very   **12 for** because of
14 throughly thoroughly   **15 now** now that.   **travel** (Spelled *trauaile*
in the Folio and carrying the sense of labor as well as traveling.)
16 use apply   **17 s.d. on the top** at some high point of the tiring-
house or the theater, on a third level above the gallery   **20 kind**
keepers guardian angels   **21 living** with live actors.   **drollery** comic
entertainment, caricature, puppet show   **23 phoenix** mythical bird
consumed to ashes every five hundred to six hundred years, only to
be renewed into another cycle   **25 want credit** lack credence

30 certes certainly   **31 monstrous** unnatural   **36 muse** wonder at
38 want lack   **39 Praise in departing** i.e., save your praise until the
end of the performance. (Proverbial.)   **41 viands** provisions.   **stom-**
achs appetites   **44 mountaineers** mountain dwellers   **45 Dewlapped**
having a dewlap, or fold of skin hanging from the neck, like cattle
46 Wallets pendent folds of skin, wattles   **47 in their breasts** (i.e.,
like the Anthropophagi described in *Othello*, 1.3.146)   **48 putter-out**
. . . one one who invests money or gambles on the risks of travel on
the condition that the traveler who returns safely is to receive five
times the amount deposited; hence, any traveler   **49 Good warrant**
assurance.   **stand to** fall to; take the risk   **50 Although my last** even
if this were to be my last meal   **51 best** best part of life   **52 s.d.**
harpy a fabulous monster with a woman's face and breasts and a vulture's body, supposed to be a minister of divine vengeance.   **quaint**
device ingenious stage contrivance.   **the banquet vanishes** i.e., the
food vanishes; the table remains until line 82

ARIEL
You are three men of sin, whom Destiny—   53
That hath to instrument this lower world   54
And what is in 't—the never-surfeited sea   55
Hath caused to belch up you, and on this island   56
Where man doth not inhabit, you 'mongst men
Being most unfit to live. I have made you mad;
And even with suchlike valor men hang and drown   59
Their proper selves.   [Alonso, Sebastian, and Antonio
                                        draw their swords.]
                    You fools! I and my fellows   60
Are ministers of Fate. The elements
Of whom your swords are tempered may as well   62
Wound the loud winds, or with bemocked-at stabs   63
Kill the still-closing waters, as diminish   64
One dowl that's in my plume. My fellow ministers   65
Are like invulnerable. If you could hurt,   66
Your swords are now too massy for your strengths   67
And will not be uplifted. But remember—
For that's my business to you—that you three
From Milan did supplant good Prospero;
Exposed unto the sea, which hath requit it,   71
Him and his innocent child; for which foul deed
The powers, delaying, not forgetting, have
Incensed the seas and shores, yea, all the creatures,
Against your peace. Thee of thy son, Alonso,
They have bereft; and do pronounce by me
Ling'ring perdition, worse than any death   77
Can be at once, shall step by step attend
You and your ways; whose wraths to guard you
    from—   79
Which here, in this most desolate isle, else falls   80
Upon your heads—is nothing but heart's sorrow   81
And a clear life ensuing.   82

        He vanishes in thunder; then, to soft music, enter
        the shapes again, and dance, with mocks and
        mows, and carrying out the table.

PROSPERO
Bravely the figure of this harpy hast thou   83
Performed, my Ariel; a grace it had devouring.   84
Of my instruction hast thou nothing bated   85
In what thou hadst to say. So, with good life   86
And observation strange, my meaner ministers   87

Their several kinds have done. My high charms
    work,   88
And these mine enemies are all knit up
In their distractions. They now are in my power;   90
And in these fits I leave them, while I visit
Young Ferdinand, whom they suppose is drowned,
And his and mine loved darling.   [*Exit above.*]
GONZALO
I' the name of something holy, sir, why stand you   94
In this strange stare?
ALONSO   O, it is monstrous, monstrous!   95
Methought the billows spoke and told me of it;   96
The winds did sing it to me, and the thunder,
That deep and dreadful organ pipe, pronounced
The name of Prosper; it did bass my trespass.   99
Therefor my son i' th' ooze is bedded; and   100
I'll seek him deeper than e'er plummet sounded,   101
And with him there lie mudded.   *Exit.*
SEBASTIAN   But one fiend at a time,
I'll fight their legions o'er.
ANTONIO   I'll be thy second.   104
                    Exeunt [*Sebastian and Antonio*].
GONZALO
All three of them are desperate. Their great guilt,   105
Like poison given to work a great time after,
Now 'gins to bite the spirits. I do beseech you,   107
That are of suppler joints, follow them swiftly
And hinder them from what this ecstasy   109
May now provoke them to.
ADRIAN   Follow, I pray you.
                    Exeunt omnes.

                          ❖

4.1   *Enter Prospero, Ferdinand, and Miranda.*

PROSPERO
If I have too austerely punished you,
Your compensation makes amends, for I
Have given you here a third of mine own life,   3
Or that for which I live; who once again
I tender to thy hand. All thy vexations   5
Were but my trials of thy love, and thou
Hast strangely stood the test. Here, afore heaven,   7
I ratify this my rich gift. O Ferdinand,
Do not smile at me that I boast her off,   9

53–56 whom . . . up you you whom Destiny, controller of the sublunary world as its instrument, has caused the ever hungry sea to belch up   **59 suchlike valor** i.e., the reckless valor derived from madness   **60 proper** own   **62 whom** which.   **tempered** composed and hardened   **63 bemocked-at** scorned   **64 still-closing** always closing again when parted   **65 dowl** soft, fine feather   **66 like** likewise, similarly.   **If** even if   **67 massy** heavy   **71 requit** requited, avenged   **77 perdition** ruin, destruction   **79 whose** (Refers to the heavenly powers.)   **80 else** otherwise   **81 is nothing** there is no way   **82 clear** unspotted, innocent.   **s.d. mocks and mows** mocking gestures and grimaces   **83 Bravely** finely, dashingly   **84 a grace . . . devouring** i.e., you gracefully caused the banquet to disappear as if you had consumed it (with puns on *grace*, meaning "gracefulness" and "a blessing on the meal," and on *devouring*, meaning "a literal eating" and "an all-consuming or ravishing grace")   **85 bated** abated, omitted   **86 So** in the same fashion.   **good life** faithful reproduction   **87 observation strange** exceptional attention to detail.   **meaner** i.e., subordinate to Ariel

88 several kinds individual parts   **90 distractions** trancelike state   **94 why** (Gonzalo was not addressed in Ariel's speech to the *three men of sin*, line 53, and is not, as they are, in a maddened state; see lines 105–107.)   **95 it** i.e., my sin (also in line 96)   **96 billows** waves   **99 bass my trespass** proclaim my trespass like a bass note in music   **100 Therefor** in consequence of that   **101 plummet** a lead weight attached to a line for testing depth.   **sounded** probed, tested the depth of   **104 o'er** one after another   **105 desperate** despairing and reckless   **107 bite the spirits** sap their vital powers through anguish   **109 ecstasy** mad frenzy
4.1. Location: Before Prospero's cell.
3 a third i.e., Miranda, into whose education Prospero has put a third of his life (?) or who represents a large part of what he cares about, along with his dukedom and his learned study (?)   **5 tender** offer
7 strangely extraordinarily   **9 boast her off** i.e., praise her so, or, perhaps an error for "boast of her"; the Folio reads "boast her of"

For thou shalt find she will outstrip all praise
And make it halt behind her.

FERDINAND   I do believe it   11
Against an oracle.   12

PROSPERO
Then, as my gift and thine own acquisition
Worthily purchased, take my daughter. But
If thou dost break her virgin-knot before
All sanctimonious ceremonies may   16
With full and holy rite be ministered,
No sweet aspersion shall the heavens let fall   18
To make this contract grow; but barren hate,
Sour-eyed disdain, and discord shall bestrew
The union of your bed with weeds so loathly   21
That you shall hate it both. Therefore take heed,
As Hymen's lamps shall light you.

FERDINAND   As I hope   23
For quiet days, fair issue, and long life,   24
With such love as 'tis now, the murkiest den,
The most opportune place, the strong'st suggestion   26
Our worser genius can, shall never melt   27
Mine honor into lust, to take away   28
The edge of that day's celebration   29
When I shall think or Phoebus' steeds are foundered   30
Or Night kept chained below.

PROSPERO   Fairly spoke.
Sit then and talk with her. She is thine own.
        [Ferdinand and Miranda sit and talk together.]
What, Ariel! My industrious servant, Ariel!   33

        Enter Ariel.

ARIEL
What would my potent master? Here I am.

PROSPERO
Thou and thy meaner fellows your last service   35
Did worthily perform, and I must use you
In such another trick. Go bring the rabble,   37
O'er whom I give thee power, here to this place.
Incite them to quick motion, for I must
Bestow upon the eyes of this young couple
Some vanity of mine art. It is my promise,   41
And they expect it from me.

ARIEL   Presently?   42

PROSPERO   Ay, with a twink.   43

ARIEL
Before you can say "Come" and "Go,"
And breathe twice, and cry "So, so,"
Each one, tripping on his toe,
Will be here with mop and mow.   47
Do you love me, master? No?

PROSPERO
Dearly, my delicate Ariel. Do not approach
Till thou dost hear me call.

ARIEL   Well; I conceive.   Exit. 50

PROSPERO
Look thou be true; do not give dalliance   51
Too much the rein. The strongest oaths are straw
To the fire i' the blood. Be more abstemious,
Or else good night your vow!

FERDINAND   I warrant you, sir,   54
The white cold virgin snow upon my heart   55
Abates the ardor of my liver.

PROSPERO   Well.   56
Now come, my Ariel! Bring a corollary,   57
Rather than want a spirit. Appear, and pertly!—   58
No tongue! All eyes! Be silent.   Soft music.   59

        Enter Iris.

IRIS
Ceres, most bounteous lady, thy rich leas   60
Of wheat, rye, barley, vetches, oats, and peas;   61
Thy turfy mountains, where live nibbling sheep,
And flat meads thatched with stover, them to keep;   63
Thy banks with pionèd and twillèd brims,   64
Which spongy April at thy hest betrims   65
To make cold nymphs chaste crowns; and thy
    broom groves,   66
Whose shadow the dismissèd bachelor loves,   67
Being lass-lorn; thy poll-clipped vineyard;   68
And thy sea marge, sterile and rocky hard,   69
Where thou thyself dost air: the queen o' the sky,   70
Whose watery arch and messenger am I,   71
Bids thee leave these, and with her sovereign grace,   72
        Juno descends [slowly in her car].
Here on this grass plot, in this very place,
To come and sport. Her peacocks fly amain.   74

47 mop and mow gestures and grimaces   **50 conceive** understand
51 true true to your promise   **54 good night** i.e., say good-bye to.
warrant guarantee   **55 The white . . . heart** i.e., the ideal of chastity
and consciousness of Miranda's chaste innocence enshrined in my
heart   **56 liver** (as the presumed seat of the passions)   **57 corollary**
surplus, extra supply   **58 want** lack.   **pertly** briskly   **59 No tongue**
all the beholders are to be silent (lest the spirits vanish).   **s.d. Iris**
goddess of the rainbow and Juno's messenger   **60 Ceres** goddess of
the generative power of nature.   **leas** meadows   **61 vetches** plants
for forage, fodder   **63 meads** meadows.   **stover** winter fodder for cattle   **64 pionèd and twillèd** undercut by the swift current and protected by roots and branches that tangle to form a barricade
65 spongy wet.   **hest** command   **66 broom groves** clumps of broom,
gorse, yellow-flowered shrub   **67 dismissèd bachelor** rejected male
lover   **68 poll-clipped** pruned, lopped at the top, or *pole-clipped,*
"hedged in with poles"   **69 sea marge** shore   **70 thou . . . air** you
take the air, go for walks.   **queen o' the sky** i.e., Juno   **71 watery
arch** rainbow   **72 s.d. Juno descends** i.e., starts her descent from the
"heavens" above the stage (?)   **74 peacocks** birds sacred to Juno and
used to pull her chariot.   **amain** with full speed

11 halt limp   **12 Against an oracle** even if an oracle should declare
otherwise   **16 sanctimonious** sacred   **18 aspersion** dew, shower
21 weeds (in place of the flowers customarily strewn on the marriage
bed)   **23 As . . . you** i.e., as you long for happiness and concord in
your marriage. (Hymen was the Greek and Roman god of marriage;
his symbolic torches, the wedding torches, were supposed to burn
brightly for a happy marriage and smokily for a troubled one.)   **24 issue** offspring   **26 suggestion** temptation   **27 worser genius** evil genius, or, evil attendant spirit.   **can** is capable of   **28 to** so as to
29 edge keen enjoyment, sexual ardor   **30 or** either.   **foundered**
broken down, made lame. (Ferdinand will wait impatiently for the
bridal night.)   **33 What** now then   **35 meaner fellows** subordinates
37 trick device.   **rabble** band, i.e., the *meaner fellows* of line 35
41 vanity (1) illusion (2) trifle (3) desire for admiration, conceit
42 Presently immediately   **43 with a twink** in the twinkling of an eye

Approach, rich Ceres, her to entertain.   75

Enter Ceres.

CERES
Hail, many-colored messenger, that ne'er
Dost disobey the wife of Jupiter,
Who with thy saffron wings upon my flowers   78
Diffusest honeydrops, refreshing showers,
And with each end of thy blue bow dost crown   80
My bosky acres and my unshrubbed down,   81
Rich scarf to my proud earth. Why hath thy queen   82
Summoned me hither to this short-grassed green?

IRIS
A contract of true love to celebrate,
And some donation freely to estate   85
On the blest lovers.

CERES   Tell me, heavenly bow,
If Venus or her son, as thou dost know,   87
Do now attend the Queen? Since they did plot
The means that dusky Dis my daughter got,   89
Her and her blind boy's scandaled company   90
I have forsworn.

IRIS   Of her society   91
Be not afraid. I met her deity   92
Cutting the clouds towards Paphos, and her son   93
Dove-drawn with her. Here thought they to have
  done   94
Some wanton charm upon this man and maid,   95
Whose vows are that no bed-right shall be paid
Till Hymen's torch be lighted; but in vain.
Mars's hot minion is returned again;   98
Her waspish-headed son has broke his arrows,   99
Swears he will shoot no more, but play with
  sparrows   100
And be a boy right out.

[Juno alights.]

CERES   Highest Queen of state,   101
Great Juno, comes; I know her by her gait.   102

JUNO
How does my bounteous sister? Go with me   103
To bless this twain, that they may prosperous be,
And honored in their issue.   *They sing:* 105

JUNO
Honor, riches, marriage blessing,
Long continuance, and increasing,

Hourly joys be still upon you!   108
Juno sings her blessings on you.

CERES
Earth's increase, foison plenty,   110
Barns and garners never empty,   111
Vines with clustering bunches growing,
Plants with goodly burden bowing;

Spring come to you at the farthest
In the very end of harvest!   115
Scarcity and want shall shun you;
Ceres' blessing so is on you.

FERDINAND
This is a most majestic vision, and
Harmonious charmingly. May I be bold   119
To think these spirits?

PROSPERO   Spirits, which by mine art
I have from their confines called to enact
My present fancies.

FERDINAND   Let me live here ever!
So rare a wondered father and a wife   123
Makes this place Paradise.

*Juno and Ceres whisper, and send
Iris on employment.*

PROSPERO   Sweet now, silence!
Juno and Ceres whisper seriously;
There's something else to do. Hush and be mute,
Or else our spell is marred.

IRIS *[calling offstage]*
You nymphs, called naiads, of the windring brooks,   128
With your sedged crowns and ever-harmless looks,   129
Leave your crisp channels, and on this green land   130
Answer your summons; Juno does command.
Come, temperate nymphs, and help to celebrate   132
A contract of true love. Be not too late.

Enter certain nymphs.

You sunburned sicklemen, of August weary,   134
Come hither from the furrow and be merry.   135
Make holiday; your rye-straw hats put on,
And these fresh nymphs encounter every one   137
In country footing.   138

*Enter certain reapers, properly habited. They join
with the nymphs in a graceful dance, towards the
end whereof Prospero starts suddenly, and speaks;
after which, to a strange, hollow, and confused
noise, they heavily vanish.*

PROSPERO *[aside]*
I had forgot that foul conspiracy
Of the beast Caliban and his confederates

75 **entertain** receive   78 **saffron** yellow   80 **bow** i.e., rainbow   81 **bosky** wooded.   **unshrubbed down** open upland   82 **scarf** (The rainbow is like a colored silk band adorning the earth.)   85 **estate** bestow   87 **son** i.e., Cupid.   **as** as far as   89 **that** whereby.   **dusky** dark.   **Dis . . . got** (Pluto, or *Dis*, god of the infernal regions, carried off Proserpina, daughter of Ceres, to be his bride in Hades.)   90 **her** i.e., Venus'.   **scandaled** scandalous   91 **society** company   92 **her deity** i.e., Her Highness   93 **Paphos** place on the island of Cyprus, sacred to Venus   94 **Dove-drawn** (Venus' chariot was drawn by doves.)   **done** placed   95 **wanton charm** lustful spell   98 **Mars's hot minion** i.e., Venus, the beloved of Mars.   **returned** i.e., returned to Paphos   99 **waspish-headed** hotheaded, peevish   100 **sparrows** (Supposed lustful, and sacred to Venus.)   101 **right out** outright.   **Highest . . . state** most majestic Queen   102 **gait** i.e., majestic bearing   103 **sister** i.e., fellow goddess (?)   105 **issue** offspring

108 **still** always   110 **foison plenty** plentiful harvest   111 **garners** granaries   115 **In . . . harvest** i.e., with no winter in between   119 **charmingly** enchantingly   123 **wondered** wonder-performing, wondrous   128 **naiads** nymphs of springs, rivers, or lakes.   **windring** wandering, winding (?)   129 **sedged** made of reeds.   **ever-harmless** ever innocent   130 **crisp** curled, rippled   132 **temperate** chaste   134 **sicklemen** harvesters, field workers who cut down grain and grass.   **of August weary** i.e., weary of the hard work of the harvest   135 **furrow** i.e., plowed fields   137 **encounter** join   138 **country footing** country dancing.   **s.d. properly** suitably.   **heavily** slowly, dejectedly

Against my life. The minute of their plot
Is almost come. [*To the Spirits.*] Well done! Avoid; no
   more!   142

FERDINAND [*to Miranda*]
This is strange. Your father's in some passion
That works him strongly.

MIRANDA   Never till this day   144
Saw I him touched with anger so distempered.

PROSPERO
You do look, my son, in a moved sort,   146
As if you were dismayed. Be cheerful, sir.
Our revels now are ended. These our actors,   148
As I foretold you, were all spirits and
Are melted into air, into thin air;
And, like the baseless fabric of this vision,   151
The cloud-capped towers, the gorgeous palaces,
The solemn temples, the great globe itself,   153
Yea, all which it inherit, shall dissolve,   154
And, like this insubstantial pageant faded,
Leave not a rack behind. We are such stuff   156
As dreams are made on, and our little life   157
Is rounded with a sleep. Sir, I am vexed.   158
Bear with my weakness. My old brain is troubled.
Be not disturbed with my infirmity.   160
If you be pleased, retire into my cell   161
And there repose. A turn or two I'll walk
To still my beating mind.

FERDINAND, MIRANDA   We wish your peace.   163
             Exeunt [*Ferdinand and Miranda*].

PROSPERO
Come with a thought! I thank thee, Ariel. Come.   164

Enter Ariel.

ARIEL
Thy thoughts I cleave to. What's thy pleasure?   165

PROSPERO   Spirit,
We must prepare to meet with Caliban.

ARIEL
Ay, my commander. When I presented Ceres,   167
I thought to have told thee of it, but I feared
Lest I might anger thee.

PROSPERO
Say again, where didst thou leave these varlets?

ARIEL
I told you, sir, they were red-hot with drinking;
So full of valor that they smote the air
For breathing in their faces, beat the ground
For kissing of their feet; yet always bending   174
Towards their project. Then I beat my tabor,

At which, like unbacked colts, they pricked their
   ears,   176
Advanced their eyelids, lifted up their noses   177
As they smelt music. So I charmed their ears   178
That calflike they my lowing followed through   179
Toothed briers, sharp furzes, pricking gorse, and
   thorns,   180
Which entered their frail shins. At last I left them
I' the filthy-mantled pool beyond your cell,   182
There dancing up to the chins, that the foul lake
O'erstunk their feet.

PROSPERO   This was well done, my bird.   184
Thy shape invisible retain thou still.
The trumpery in my house, go bring it hither,   186
For stale to catch these thieves.

ARIEL   I go, I go.   *Exit.*   187

PROSPERO
A devil, a born devil, on whose nature
Nurture can never stick; on whom my pains,
Humanely taken, all, all lost, quite lost!
And as with age his body uglier grows,
So his mind cankers. I will plague them all,   192
Even to roaring.

    Enter Ariel, loaden with glistering apparel, etc.

      Come, hang them on this line.   193

[*Ariel hangs up the showy finery; Prospero and
Ariel remain, invisible.*] *Enter Caliban, Stephano,
and Trinculo, all wet.*

CALIBAN
Pray you, tread softly, that the blind mole may
Not hear a foot fall. We now are near his cell.

STEPHANO Monster, your fairy, which you say is a
harmless fairy, has done little better than played the
jack with us.   198

TRINCULO Monster, I do smell all horse piss, at which
my nose is in great indignation.

STEPHANO So is mine. Do you hear, monster? If I
should take a displeasure against you, look you—

TRINCULO Thou wert but a lost monster.

CALIBAN
Good my lord, give me thy favor still.
Be patient, for the prize I'll bring thee to
Shall hoodwink this mischance. Therefore speak
   softly.   206
All's hushed as midnight yet.

---

142 Avoid withdraw   **144 works** affects, agitates   **146 moved sort**
troubled state, condition   **148 revels** entertainment, pageant
151 baseless fabric unsubstantial theatrical edifice or contrivance
153 great globe (With a glance at the Globe Theatre.)   **154 which it
inherit** who subsequently occupy it   **156 rack** wisp of cloud   **157 on**
of   **158 rounded** surrounded (before birth and after death), or,
crowned, rounded off   **160 with** by   **161 retire** withdraw, go
163 beating agitated   **164 with a thought** i.e., on the instant, or,
summoned by my thought, no sooner thought of than here
165 cleave cling, adhere   **167 presented** acted the part of, or, introduced   **174 bending** aiming

176 unbacked unbroken, unridden   **177 Advanced** lifted up   **178 As**
as if   **179 lowing** mooing   **180 furzes, gorse** prickly shrubs
182 filthy-mantled covered with a slimy coating   **184 O'erstunk**
smelled worse than, or, caused to stink terribly   **186 trumpery** cheap
goods, the *glistering apparel* mentioned in the following stage direction   **187 stale** (1) decoy (2) out-of-fashion garments (with possible
further suggestions of "horse piss," as in line 199, and "steal," pronounced like *stale*. *For stale* could also mean "fit for a prostitute."
192 cankers festers, grows malignant   **193 line** lime tree or linden.
s.d. Prospero and Ariel remain (The staging is uncertain. They may
instead exit here and return with the spirits at line 256.)   **198 jack** (1)
knave (2) will-o'-the-wisp   **206 hoodwink this mischance** (Misfortune
is to be prevented from doing further harm by being hooded like a
hawk and also put out of remembrance.)

TRINCULO   Ay, but to lose our bottles in the pool—

STEPHANO   There is not only disgrace and dishonor in that, monster, but an infinite loss.

TRINCULO   That's more to me than my wetting. Yet this is your harmless fairy, monster!

STEPHANO   I will fetch off my bottle, though I be o'er 213 ears for my labor.   214

CALIBAN
Prithee, my king, be quiet. Seest thou here,
This is the mouth o' the cell. No noise, and enter.
Do that good mischief which may make this island
Thine own forever, and I thy Caliban
For aye thy footlicker.

STEPHANO   Give me thy hand. I do begin to have bloody thoughts.

TRINCULO [seeing the finery]   O King Stephano! O peer! 222 O worthy Stephano! Look what a wardrobe here is for thee!

CALIBAN
Let it alone, thou fool, it is but trash.

TRINCULO   Oho, monster! We know what belongs to a frippery. O King Stephano!   [He puts on a gown.] 227

STEPHANO   Put off that gown, Trinculo. By this hand, 228 I'll have that gown.

TRINCULO   Thy Grace shall have it.

CALIBAN
The dropsy drown this fool! What do you mean   231
To dote thus on such luggage? Let 't alone   232
And do the murder first. If he awake,
From toe to crown he'll fill our skins with pinches, 234
Make us strange stuff.

STEPHANO   Be you quiet, monster.—Mistress line, is 236 not this my jerkin? [He takes it down.] Now is the jerkin 237 under the line. Now, jerkin, you are like to lose your 238 hair and prove a bald jerkin.   239

TRINCULO   Do, do! We steal by line and level, an 't like 240 Your Grace.

STEPHANO   I thank thee for that jest. Here's a garment for 't. [He gives a garment.] Wit shall not go unrewarded while I am king of this country. "Steal by line and level" is an excellent pass of pate. There's another 245 garment for 't.

TRINCULO   Monster, come, put some lime upon your 247 fingers, and away with the rest.

CALIBAN
I will have none on 't. We shall lose our time,
And all be turned to barnacles, or to apes   250
With foreheads villainous low.   251

STEPHANO   Monster, lay to your fingers. Help to bear 252 this away where my hogshead of wine is, or I'll turn 253 you out of my kingdom. Go to, carry this.   254

TRINCULO   And this.

STEPHANO   Ay, and this.
[They load Caliban with more and more garments.]

A noise of hunters heard. Enter divers spirits, in
shape of dogs and hounds, hunting them about,
Prospero and Ariel setting them on.

PROSPERO   Hey, Mountain, hey!

ARIEL   Silver! There it goes, Silver!

PROSPERO   Fury, Fury! There, Tyrant, there! Hark! Hark!
[Caliban, Stephano, and Trinculo are driven out.]
Go, charge my goblins that they grind their joints
With dry convulsions, shorten up their sinews   261
With agèd cramps, and more pinch-spotted make
them   262
Than pard or cat o' mountain.

ARIEL   Hark, they roar!   263

PROSPERO
Let them be hunted soundly. At this hour   264
Lies at my mercy all mine enemies.
Shortly shall all my labors end, and thou
Shalt have the air at freedom. For a little   267
Follow, and do me service.   Exeunt.

❧

5.1   Enter Prospero in his magic robes, [with his staff,]
          and Ariel.

PROSPERO
Now does my project gather to a head.
My charms crack not, my spirits obey, and Time   2
Goes upright with his carriage. How's the day?   3

ARIEL
On the sixth hour, at which time, my lord,   4
You said our work should cease.

PROSPERO   I did say so,
When first I raised the tempest. Say, my spirit,

213–214 o'er ears i.e., totally submerged and perhaps drowned **222 King . . . peer** (Alludes to the old ballad beginning, "King Stephen was a worthy peer.") **227 frippery** place where cast-off clothes are sold **228 Put off** put down, or, take off **231 dropsy** disease characterized by the accumulation of fluid in the connective tissue of the body **232 luggage** cumbersome trash **234 crown** head **236 Mistress line** (Addressed to the linden or lime tree upon which, at line 193, Ariel hung the glistering apparel.) **237 jerkin** jacket made of leather **238 under the line** under the lime tree (with punning sense of being south of the equinoctial line or equator; sailors on long voyages to the southern regions were popularly supposed to lose their hair from scurvy or other diseases. Stephano also quibbles bawdily on losing hair through syphilis, and in Mistress and jerkin.) **like** likely **239 bald** (1) hairless, napless (2) meager **240 Do, do** i.e., bravo. (Said in response to the jesting or to the taking of the jerkin, or both.) **by line and level** i.e., by means of plumb line and carpenter's level, methodically (with pun on line, "lime tree," line 238, and steal, pronounced like stale, i.e., prostitute, continuing Stephano's bawdy quibble). **an 't like** if it please **245 pass of pate** sally of wit. (The metaphor is from fencing.)

247 lime birdlime, sticky substance (to give Caliban sticky fingers) **250 barnacles** barnacle geese, formerly supposed to be hatched from barnacles attached to trees or to rotting timber; here, evidently used, like apes, as types of simpletons **251 villainous** miserably **252 lay to** start using **253 this** i.e., the glistering apparel. **hogshead** large cask **254 Go to** (An expression of exhortation or remonstrance.) **261 dry** associated with age, arthritic (?) **convulsions** cramps **262 agèd** characteristic of old age **263 pard** panther or leopard. **cat o' mountain** wildcat **264 soundly** thoroughly (and suggesting the sounds of the hunt) **267 little** little while longer **5.1. Location:** Before Prospero's cell. **2 crack** collapse, fail. (The metaphor is probably alchemical, as in project and gather to a head, line 1.) **3 his carriage** its burden. (Time is no longer heavily burdened and so can go upright, "standing straight and unimpeded.") **4 On** approaching

How fares the King and 's followers?
ARIEL   Confined together
In the same fashion as you gave in charge,
Just as you left them; all prisoners, sir,
In the line grove which weather-fends your cell.   10
They cannot budge till your release. The King,   11
His brother, and yours abide all three distracted, 12
And the remainder mourning over them,
Brim full of sorrow and dismay; but chiefly
Him that you termed, sir, the good old lord,
     Gonzalo.
His tears runs down his beard like winter's drops
From eaves of reeds. Your charm so strongly works
     'em   17
That if you now beheld them your affections   18
Would become tender.
PROSPERO   Dost thou think so, spirit?
ARIEL
Mine would, sir, were I human.
PROSPERO   And mine shall.   20
Hast thou, which art but air, a touch, a feeling   21
Of their afflictions, and shall not myself,
One of their kind, that relish all as sharply   23
Passion as they, be kindlier moved than thou art?   24
Though with their high wrongs I am struck to the
     quick,
Yet with my nobler reason 'gainst my fury
Do I take part. The rarer action is   27
In virtue than in vengeance. They being penitent,
The sole drift of my purpose doth extend
Not a frown further. Go release them, Ariel.
My charms I'll break, their senses I'll restore,
And they shall be themselves.
ARIEL   I'll fetch them, sir.
                                            Exit.
[Prospero traces a charmed circle with his staff.]
PROSPERO
Ye elves of hills, brooks, standing lakes, and groves, 33
And ye that on the sands with printless foot
Do chase the ebbing Neptune, and do fly him
When he comes back; you demi-puppets that   36
By moonshine do the green sour ringlets make,   37
Whereof the ewe not bites; and you whose pastime
Is to make midnight mushrooms, that rejoice   39
To hear the solemn curfew; by whose aid,   40
Weak masters though ye be, I have bedimmed   41
The noontide sun, called forth the mutinous winds,

And twixt the green sea and the azured vault   43
Set roaring war; to the dread rattling thunder   44
Have I given fire, and rifted Jove's stout oak   45
With his own bolt; the strong-based promontory   46
Have I made shake, and by the spurs plucked up   47
The pine and cedar; graves at my command
Have waked their sleepers, oped, and let 'em forth
By my so potent art. But this rough magic   50
I here abjure, and when I have required   51
Some heavenly music—which even now I do—
To work mine end upon their senses that   53
This airy charm is for, I'll break my staff,   54
Bury it certain fathoms in the earth,
And deeper than did ever plummet sound
I'll drown my book.   Solemn music.

Here enters Ariel before; then Alonso, with a
frantic gesture, attended by Gonzalo; Sebastian and
Antonio in like manner, attended by Adrian and
Francisco. They all enter the circle which Prospero
had made, and there stand charmed; which
Prospero observing, speaks:

[*To Alonso.*] A solemn air, and the best comforter   58
To an unsettled fancy, cure thy brains,   59
Now useless, boiled within thy skull! [*To Sebastian*
     and Antonio.] There stand,   60
For you are spell-stopped.—
Holy Gonzalo, honorable man,
Mine eyes, e'en sociable to the show of thine,   63
Fall fellowly drops. [*Aside.*] The charm dissolves
     apace,   64
And as the morning steals upon the night,
Melting the darkness, so their rising senses
Begin to chase the ignorant fumes that mantle   67
Their clearer reason.—O good Gonzalo,   68
My true preserver, and a loyal sir
To him thou follow'st! I will pay thy graces   70
Home both in word and deed.—Most cruelly   71
Didst thou, Alonso, use me and my daughter.
Thy brother was a furtherer in the act.—   73
Thou art pinched for 't now, Sebastian. [*To Antonio.*]
     Flesh and blood,   74
You, brother mine, that entertained ambition,
Expelled remorse and nature, whom, with
     Sebastian,   76
Whose inward pinches therefore are most strong,
Would here have killed your king, I do forgive thee,
Unnatural though thou art.—Their understanding
Begins to swell, and the approaching tide

10 line grove grove of lime trees.   **weather-fends** protects from the weather   **11 your release** you release them   **12 distracted** out of their wits   **17 eaves of reeds** thatched roofs   **18 affections** disposition, feelings   **20 human** (Spelled *humane* in the Folio and encompassing both senses.)   **21 touch** sense, apprehension   **23–24 that . . . they** I who experience human passions as acutely as they   **24 kindlier** (1) more sympathetically (2) more naturally, humanly   **27 rarer** nobler   **33–50 Ye . . . art** (This famous passage is an embellished paraphrase of Golding's translation of Ovid's *Metamorphoses*, 7.197–219.)   **36 demi-puppets** puppets of half size, i.e., elves and fairies   **37 green sour ringlets** fairy rings, circles in grass (actually produced by mushrooms)   **39 midnight mushrooms** mushrooms appearing overnight   **40 curfew** evening bell, usually rung at nine o'clock, ushering in the time when spirits are abroad   **41 Weak masters** i.e., subordinate spirits, as in 4.1.35 (?)

43 the azured vault i.e., the sky   **44–45 to . . . fire** I have discharged the dread rattling thunderbolt   **45 rifted** riven, split.   **oak** a tree that was sacred to Jove   **46 bolt** lightning bolt   **47 spurs** roots   **50 rough** violent   **51 required** requested   **53 their senses that** the senses of those whom   **54 airy charm** i.e., music   **58 air** song.   **and** i.e., which is   **59 fancy** imagination   **60 boiled** i.e., extremely agitated   **63 sociable** sympathetic.   **show** appearance   **64 Fall** let fall   **67 ignorant fumes** fumes that render them incapable of comprehension.   **mantle** envelop   **68 clearer** growing clearer   **70 pay thy graces** requite your favors and virtues   **71 Home** fully   **73 furtherer** accomplice   **74 pinched** punished, afflicted   **76 remorse** pity.   **nature** natural feeling.   **whom** i.e., who

Will shortly fill the reasonable shore   81
That now lies foul and muddy. Not one of them
That yet looks on me, or would know me.—Ariel,
Fetch me the hat and rapier in my cell.
            [*Ariel goes to the cell and returns immediately.*]
I will discase me and myself present   85
As I was sometime Milan. Quickly, spirit!   86
Thou shalt ere long be free.
                        Ariel sings and helps to attire him.

ARIEL
            Where the bee sucks, there suck I.
            In a cowslip's bell I lie;
            There I couch when owls do cry.   90
            On the bat's back I do fly
            After summer merrily.   92
        Merrily, merrily shall I live now
        Under the blossom that hangs on the bough.

PROSPERO
Why, that's my dainty Ariel! I shall miss thee,
But yet thou shalt have freedom. So, so, so.
To the King's ship, invisible as thou art!
There shalt thou find the mariners asleep
Under the hatches. The Master and the Boatswain
Being awake, enforce them to this place,
And presently, I prithee.   101
ARIEL
I drink the air before me and return
Or ere your pulse twice beat.   *Exit.* 103
GONZALO
All torment, trouble, wonder, and amazement
Inhabits here. Some heavenly power guide us
Out of this fearful country!
PROSPERO   Behold, sir King,   106
The wrongèd Duke of Milan, Prospero.
For more assurance that a living prince
Does now speak to thee, I embrace thy body;
And to thee and thy company I bid
A hearty welcome.   [*Embracing him.*]
ALONSO   Whe'er thou be'st he or no,
Or some enchanted trifle to abuse me,   112
As late I have been, I not know. Thy pulse   113
Beats as of flesh and blood; and, since I saw thee,
Th' affliction of my mind amends, with which
I fear a madness held me. This must crave—   116
An if this be at all—a most strange story.   117
Thy dukedom I resign, and do entreat   118
Thou pardon me my wrongs. But how should
    Prospero   119
Be living, and be here?

PROSPERO [*to Gonzalo*]   First, noble friend,
Let me embrace thine age, whose honor cannot   121
Be measured or confined.   [*Embracing him.*]
GONZALO   Whether this be
Or be not, I'll not swear.
PROSPERO   You do yet taste
Some subtleties o' th' isle, that will not let you   124
Believe things certain. Welcome, my friends all!
[*Aside to Sebastian and Antonio.*] But you, my brace
    of lords, were I so minded,   126
I here could pluck His Highness' frown upon you
And justify you traitors. At this time   128
I will tell no tales.
SEBASTIAN   The devil speaks in him.
PROSPERO   No.
[*To Antonio.*] For you, most wicked sir, whom to call
    brother
Would even infect my mouth, I do forgive
Thy rankest fault—all of them; and require
My dukedom of thee, which perforce I know   133
Thou must restore.
ALONSO   If thou be'st Prospero,
Give us particulars of thy preservation,
How thou hast met us here, whom three hours
    since   136
Were wrecked upon this shore; where I have lost—
How sharp the point of this remembrance is!—
My dear son Ferdinand.
PROSPERO   I am woe for 't, sir.   139
ALONSO
Irreparable is the loss, and Patience
Says it is past her cure.
PROSPERO   I rather think
You have not sought her help, of whose soft grace   142
For the like loss I have her sovereign aid   143
And rest myself content.
ALONSO   You the like loss?
PROSPERO
As great to me as late, and supportable   145
To make the dear loss, have I means much weaker   146
Than you may call to comfort you; for I
Have lost my daughter.
ALONSO   A daughter?
O heavens, that they were living both in Naples,
The king and queen there! That they were, I wish   151
Myself were mudded in that oozy bed   152
Where my son lies. When did you lose your
    daughter?
PROSPERO
In this last tempest. I perceive these lords
At this encounter do so much admire   155
That they devour their reason and scarce think   156

[margin note: 96 Antonio's response]

81 reasonable shore shores of reason, i.e., minds. (Their reason returns, like the incoming tide.) **85 discase** disrobe **86 As . . . Milan** in my former appearance as Duke of Milan **90 couch** lie **92 After** i.e., pursuing **96 So, so, so** (Expresses approval of Ariel's help as valet.) **101 presently** immediately **103 Or ere** before **106 fearful** frightening **112 trifle** trick of magic. **abuse** deceive **113 late** lately **116 crave** require **117 An . . . all** if this is actually happening. **story** i.e., explanation **118 Thy . . . resign** (Alonso made arrangement with Antonio at the time of Prospero's banishment for Milan to pay tribute to Naples; see 1.2.113–127.) **119 wrongs** wrongdoings

121 thine age your venerable self **124 subtleties** illusions, magical powers (playing on the idea of "pastries, concoctions") **126 brace** pair **128 justify you** prove you to be **133 perforce** necessarily **136 whom** i.e., who **139 woe** sorry **142 of . . . grace** by whose mercy **143 sovereign** efficacious **145 late** recent **145–146 supportable . . . have I** to make the deeply felt loss bearable, I have **151 That** so that **152 mudded** buried in the mud **155 admire** wonder **156 devour their reason** i.e., are openmouthed, dumbfounded

Their eyes do offices of truth, their words 157
Are natural breath. But, howsoever you have 158
Been jostled from your senses, know for certain
That I am Prospero and that very duke
Which was thrust forth of Milan, who most
strangely 161
Upon this shore, where you were wrecked, was
landed
To be the lord on 't. No more yet of this,
For 'tis a chronicle of day by day, 164
Not a relation for a breakfast nor
Befitting this first meeting. Welcome, sir.
This cell's my court. Here have I few attendants,
And subjects none abroad. Pray you, look in. 168
My dukedom since you have given me again,
I will requite you with as good a thing, 170
At least bring forth a wonder to content ye
As much as me my dukedom. 172

Here Prospero discovers Ferdinand and Miranda,
playing at chess.

MIRANDA   Sweet lord, you play me false. 173
FERDINAND   No, my dearest love,
I would not for the world.
MIRANDA
Yes, for a score of kingdoms you should wrangle, 176
And I would call it fair play.
ALONSO   If this prove 177
A vision of the island, one dear son 178
Shall I twice lose.
SEBASTIAN   A most high miracle!
FERDINAND [*approaching his father*]
Though the seas threaten, they are merciful;
I have cursed them without cause. [*He kneels.*]
ALONSO   Now all the blessings
Of a glad father compass thee about! 182
Arise, and say how thou cam'st here.
[*Ferdinand rises.*]
MIRANDA   O, wonder!
How many goodly creatures are there here!
How beauteous mankind is! O brave new world 185
That has such people in 't!
PROSPERO   'Tis new to thee.
ALONSO
What is this maid with whom thou wast at play?
Your eld'st acquaintance cannot be three hours. 188
Is she the goddess that hath severed us,
And brought us thus together?

156–158 scarce . . . breath scarcely believe that their eyes inform them accurately as to what they see or that their words are naturally spoken **161 of** from **164 of day by day** requiring days to tell **168 abroad** away from here, anywhere else **170 requite** repay **172 s.d. discovers** i.e., by opening a curtain, presumably rearstage **173 play me false** i.e., press your advantage **176–177 Yes . . . play** i.e., yes, even if we were playing for twenty kingdoms, something less than the whole world, you would still press your advantage against me, and I would lovingly let you do it as though it were fair play, or, if you were to play not just for stakes but literally for kingdoms, my complaint would be out of order in that your "wrangling" would be proper **178 vision** illusion **182 compass** encompass, embrace **185 brave** splendid, gorgeously apparelled, handsome **188 eld'st** longest

FERDINAND   Sir, she is mortal;
But by immortal Providence she's mine.
I chose her when I could not ask my father
For his advice, nor thought I had one. She
Is daughter to this famous Duke of Milan,
Of whom so often I have heard renown,
But never saw before; of whom I have
Received a second life; and second father
This lady makes him to me.
ALONSO   I am hers.
But O, how oddly will it sound that I
Must ask my child forgiveness!
PROSPERO   There, sir, stop.
Let us not burden our remembrances with
A heaviness that's gone.
GONZALO   I have inly wept, 202
Or should have spoke ere this. Look down, you
gods,
And on this couple drop a blessèd crown!
For it is you that have chalked forth the way 205
Which brought us hither.
ALONSO   I say amen, Gonzalo!
GONZALO
Was Milan thrust from Milan, that his issue 207
Should become kings of Naples? O, rejoice
Beyond a common joy, and set it down
With gold on lasting pillars: In one voyage
Did Claribel her husband find at Tunis,
And Ferdinand, her brother, found a wife
Where he himself was lost; Prospero his dukedom
In a poor isle; and all of us ourselves 214
When no man was his own.
ALONSO [*to Ferdinand and Miranda*] Give me your hands. 215
Let grief and sorrow still embrace his heart 216
That doth not wish you joy!
GONZALO   Be it so! Amen! 217

Enter Ariel, with the Master and Boatswain
amazedly following.

O, look, sir, look, sir! Here is more of us.
I prophesied, if a gallows were on land,
This fellow could not drown.—Now, blasphemy, 220
That swear'st grace o'erboard, not an oath on shore? 221
Hast thou no mouth by land? What is the news?
BOATSWAIN
The best news is that we have safely found
Our King and company; the next, our ship—
Which, but three glasses since, we gave out split— 225
Is tight and yare and bravely rigged as when 226
We first put out to sea.
ARIEL [*aside to Prospero*]   Sir, all this service
Have I done since I went.

202 heaviness sadness. **inly** inwardly **205 chalked . . . way** marked as with a piece of chalk the pathway **207 Was Milan** was the Duke of Milan **214–215 all . . . own** all of us have found ourselves and our sanity when we all had lost our senses **216 still** always. **his** that person's **217 That** who **220 blasphemy** i.e., blasphemer **221 That swear'st grace o'erboard** i.e., you who banish heavenly grace from the ship by your blasphemies. **not an oath** aren't you going to swear an oath **225 glasses** i.e., hours. **gave out** reported, professed to be **226 yare** ready. **bravely** splendidly

PROSPERO [aside to Ariel]   My tricksy spirit!   228

ALONSO
These are not natural events; they strengthen   229
From strange to stranger. Say, how came you
    hither?

BOATSWAIN
If I did think, sir, I were well awake,
I'd strive to tell you. We were dead of sleep,   232
And—how we know not—all clapped under
    hatches,
Where but even now, with strange and several
    noises   234
Of roaring, shrieking, howling, jingling chains,
And more diversity of sounds, all horrible,
We were awaked; straightway at liberty;
Where we, in all her trim, freshly beheld
Our royal, good, and gallant ship, our Master
Cap'ring to eye her. On a trice, so please you,   240
Even in a dream, were we divided from them   241
And were brought moping hither.

ARIEL [aside to Prospero]   Was 't well done?   242

PROSPERO [aside to Ariel]
Bravely, my diligence. Thou shalt be free.

ALONSO
This is as strange a maze as e'er men trod,
And there is in this business more than nature
Was ever conduct of. Some oracle   246
Must rectify our knowledge.

PROSPERO   Sir, my liege,
Do not infest your mind with beating on   248
The strangeness of this business. At picked leisure,   249
Which shall be shortly, single I'll resolve you,   250
Which to you shall seem probable, of every   251
These happened accidents; till when, be cheerful   252
And think of each thing well. [Aside to Ariel.] Come
    hither, spirit.   253
Set Caliban and his companions free.
Untie the spell. [Exit Ariel.] How fares my gracious
    sir?
There are yet missing of your company
Some few odd lads that you remember not.   257

*Enter Ariel, driving in Caliban, Stephano, and
Trinculo, in their stolen apparel.*

STEPHANO   Every man shift for all the rest, and let no   258
man take care for himself; for all is but fortune. Cora-   259
gio, bully monster, coragio!   260

TRINCULO   If these be true spies which I wear in my   261
head, here's a goodly sight.

CALIBAN
O Setebos, these be brave spirits indeed!   263
How fine my master is! I am afraid   264
He will chastise me.

SEBASTIAN   Ha, ha!
What things are these, my lord Antonio?
Will money buy 'em?

ANTONIO   Very like. One of them
Is a plain fish, and no doubt marketable.

PROSPERO
Mark but the badges of these men, my lords,   270
Then say if they be true. This misshapen knave,   271
His mother was a witch, and one so strong
That could control the moon, make flows and ebbs,
And deal in her command without her power   274
These three have robbed me, and this demidevil—
For he's a bastard one—had plotted with them   276
To take my life. Two of these fellows you
Must know and own. This thing of darkness I   278
Acknowledge mine.

CALIBAN   I shall be pinched to death.

ALONSO
Is not this Stephano, my drunken butler?

SEBASTIAN   He is drunk now. Where had he wine?

ALONSO
And Trinculo is reeling ripe. Where should they   282
Find this grand liquor that hath gilded 'em?   283
[To Trinculo.] How cam'st thou in this pickle?   284

TRINCULO   I have been in such a pickle since I saw you
last that, I fear me, will never out of my bones. I shall
not fear flyblowing.   287

SEBASTIAN   Why, how now, Stephano?

STEPHANO   O, touch me not! I am not Stephano, but a
cramp.

PROSPERO   You'd be king o' the isle, sirrah?   291

STEPHANO   I should have been a sore one, then.   292

ALONSO [pointing to Caliban]
This is a strange thing as e'er I looked on.

PROSPERO
He is as disproportioned in his manners
As in his shape.—Go, sirrah, to my cell.
Take with you your companions. As you look
To have my pardon, trim it handsomely.   297

CALIBAN
Ay, that I will; and I'll be wise hereafter

228 **tricksy** ingenious, sportive   229 **strengthen** increase   232 **dead of sleep** deep in sleep   234 **several** diverse   240 **Cap'ring to eye** dancing for joy to see.   **On a trice** in an instant   241 **them** i.e., the other crew members   242 **moping** in a daze   246 **conduct** guide   248 **infest** harass, disturb.   **beating on** worrying about   249 **picked** chosen, convenient   250 **single** privately, by my own human powers.   **resolve** satisfy, explain to   251 **probable** plausible   251–252 **of every These** about every one of these   252 **accidents** occurrences   253 **well** favorably   257 **odd** unaccounted for   258 **shift** provide.   **for all the rest** (Stephano drunkenly gets wrong the saying "Every man for himself.")   259–260 **Coragio** courage   260 **bully monster** gallant monster. (Ironical.)

261 **true spies** accurate observers (i.e., sharp eyes)   263 **brave** handsome   264 **fine** splendidly attired   270 **badges** emblems of cloth or silver worn by retainers to indicate whom they serve. (Prospero refers here to the stolen clothes as emblems of their villainy.)   271 **true** honest   274 **deal . . . power** wield the moon's power, either without her authority or beyond her influence, or, even though to do so was beyond Sycorax's own power   276 **bastard** counterfeit   278 **own** recognize, admit as belonging to you   282 **reeling ripe** stumblingly drunk   283 **gilded** (1) flushed, made drunk (2) covered with gilt (suggesting the horse urine)   284 **pickle** (1) fix, predicament (2) pickling brine (in this case, horse urine)   287 **flyblowing** i.e., being fouled by fly eggs (from which he is saved by being pickled)   291 **sirrah** (Standard form of address to an inferior, here expressing reprimand.)   292 **sore** (1) tyrannical (2) sorry, inept (3) wracked by pain   297 **trim** prepare, decorate

And seek for grace. What a thrice-double ass   299
Was I to take this drunkard for a god
And worship this dull fool!

PROSPERO   Go to. Away!

ALONSO
Hence, and bestow your luggage where you found it.

SEBASTIAN   Or stole it, rather.

[*Exeunt Caliban, Stephano, and Trinculo.*]

PROSPERO
Sir, I invite Your Highness and your train
To my poor cell, where you shall take your rest
For this one night; which, part of it, I'll waste   306
With such discourse as, I not doubt, shall make it
Go quick away: the story of my life,
And the particular accidents gone by   309
Since I came to this isle. And in the morn
I'll bring you to your ship, and so to Naples,
Where I have hope to see the nuptial
Of these our dear-belovèd solemnized;
And thence retire me to my Milan, where   314
Every third thought shall be my grave.

ALONSO   I long
To hear the story of your life, which must
Take the ear strangely.

PROSPERO   I'll deliver all;   317
And promise you calm seas, auspicious gales,
And sail so expeditious that shall catch   319
Your royal fleet far off. [*Aside to Ariel.*] My Ariel,
chick,   320
That is thy charge. Then to the elements
Be free, and fare thou well!—Please you, draw near.   322

Exeunt omnes [*except Prospero*].

299 **grace** pardon, favor   306 **waste** spend   309 **accidents** occurrences   314 **retire me** return   317 **Take** take effect upon, enchant.
deliver declare, relate   319–320 **catch . . . far off** enable you to
catch up with the main part of your royal fleet, now afar off enroute
to Naples (see 1.2.235–236)   322 **draw near** i.e., enter my cell

Epilogue   *Spoken by* PROSPERO.

Now my charms are all o'erthrown,
And what strength I have 's mine own,
Which is most faint. Now, 'tis true,
I must be here confined by you
Or sent to Naples. Let me not,
Since I have my dukedom got
And pardoned the deceiver, dwell
In this bare island by your spell,
But release me from my bands   9
With the help of your good hands.   10
Gentle breath of yours my sails   11
Must fill, or else my project fails,
Which was to please. Now I want   13
Spirits to enforce, art to enchant,   14
And my ending is despair,
Unless I be relieved by prayer,   16
Which pierces so that it assaults   17
Mercy itself, and frees all faults.   18
As you from crimes would pardoned be,   19
Let your indulgence set me free.   *Exit.* 20

Epilogue.
9 bands bonds   **10 hands** i.e., applause (the noise of which would
break the spell of silence)   **11 Gentle breath** favorable breeze (produced by hands clapping or favorable comment)   **13 want** lack
14 enforce control   **16 prayer** i.e., Prospero's petition to the audience   **17 assaults** rightfully gains the attention of   **18 frees** obtains
forgiveness for   **19 crimes** sins   **20 indulgence** (1) humoring, lenient
approval (2) remission of punishment for sin

The Two Noble Kinsmen

The Two Noble Kinsmen was probably first performed in 1613 or 1614, and was revived for performance at court in 1619 and again seemingly in 1625–1626. Rights were subsequently assigned to the publisher of the so-called Beaumont and Fletcher Folio, 1646. The play actually appeared in print in a second edition, entitled *Fifty Comedies and Tragedies, Written by Francis Beaumont, and John Fletcher, Gentlemen,* 1679—of which, in fact, a good number were by Beaumont or by Fletcher alone, with many others by Fletcher in collaboration with other dramatists. The play did not appear in the First Folio of Shakespeare's plays in 1623 or in subsequent editions of that work. Perhaps for these reasons, *The Two Noble Kinsmen* was for centuries excluded from the Shakespeare canon and is still only occasionally studied or performed. Shakespeare was so famous that his name was often attached to plays in which he had no part; was *The Two Noble Kinsmen* one of these? Why would Shakespeare want to collaborate when his name was so well known?

Whatever his personal reasons, however, Shakespeare does seem to have done just that. Perhaps his own retirement, seemingly announced in *The Tempest,* turned out to be a semi-retirement. John Fletcher was his younger colleague and, in effect, successor as playwright for the King's Men. The two are often thought to have collaborated in writing *Henry VIII* at about the same time, although here the evidence is less certain and Shakespeare's role in any case more dominant. Earlier, in the 1590s, Shakespeare had agreed to help revise a controversial play by writing a new scene for *The Book of Sir Thomas More,* originally perhaps by Anthony Munday and others. Shakespeare's name was linked with that of Fletcher in the authorship of the seemingly lost play *Cardenio,* c. 1612–1613. Shakespeare was loyal to his acting company and may have helped them out with collaborations on other occasions.

On the basis of style, metrics, distinctive rhythms, vocabulary, linguistic preferences for forms like *ye* and *'em* (both of these characteristic of Fletcher), tone, characterization, and a kind of theatrical abruptness that Fletcher seems to have cultivated, many editors and critics come to a general consensus, not shared by all, that Shakespeare seems to have written all of Act 1, the first scene of Act 2, the first two scenes of Act 3, scene 3 of Act 4, and most of the final act except scene 2. This division would give to Shakespeare the scenes that dramatize Duke Theseus's resolve to defend the cause of three slain kings against Creon of Thebes, Palamon and Arcite's dilemma in serving the tyrant Creon and their brave defeat in battle by Theseus's Athenian army, Emilia's defense of friendship between women, Arcite and Palamon's quarrel in the forest after one has been released from captivity by Theseus and the other freed from prison by the Jailer's enamored daughter, the Jailer's Daughter's forlorn lament at Palamon's neglect of her, a touching scene in which the Jailer and a Doctor overhear manifestations of the Jailer's Daughter's mad affliction, and the long concluding action in which Palamon and Arcite's rival claims to Emilia are sorted out by divine will.

Fletcher is then left with the bulk of the play's middle action, including the startling scene in which the imprisoned Palamon and Arcite fall instantly from their unwavering friendship into bitter enmity once they have both seen Emilia, Arcite's encounter (after he has been released from prison) with some country rustics who tell him of public games in which Palamon resolves to compete, his success there in winning the right to be Emilia's "servant," several scenes of the Jailer's Daughter's increasing madness, some broadly comic subplot business in which a pedantic schoolmaster and his rustic companions prepare a Morris dance to be performed in Theseus's presence, Palamon and Arcite's determination to fight each other even at the certain cost of their being captured and sentenced to death by Theseus, Emilia's inability to choose between Palamon and Arcite even when it appears that her choice would save one of them from death, and still more.

Even a quick outline suggests how Fletcher seems to have preferred the scenes of unexpected reversals of the action in which plausibility of motivation yields precedence to self-conscious theatrical artifice. Some of the scenes assigned to Fletcher exploit sexuality in novel situations, as when the Doctor advises the Wooer of the Jailer's Daughter to disguise himself as Palamon, for whose love the Daughter has lost her wits. The Doctor insists that her whim is to be indulged in every detail, even if the Wooer must climb into bed with her. When the father protests that marriage should come before sexual fulfillment, the Doctor is curt with such a prudish idea: "Nev'r cast away your child for honesty [chastity]," he admonishes (5.2.22). This droll exploitation of a tittilating situation is characteristic of Fletcher. The Prologue and Epilogue are almost certainly by him.

Whatever their mode of collaboration in writing *The Two Noble Kinsmen,* Shakespeare and Fletcher chose to dramatize a tale from Chaucer's *Canterbury Tales,* the Knight's tale, which is about noble friendship. Palamon and Arcite are cousins and devoted friends, "dearer in love than blood" (1.2.1). When we first see them, they are considering what guidance their friendship can provide them in the corrupted world of Thebes. Under the rule of their uncle Creon, "a most unbounded tyrant" (1. 63), Thebes is a place of carnal temptation and political favoritism. Their virtuous behavior makes them aliens and the subjects of mockery. "Not to be ev'n jump / As they are here were to be strangers" (11. 40–41), Arcite insists, and yet the alternative of swimming along in "The common stream" would be enough to turn them both into "mere monsters" (11. 10, 42). They resolve not to ape the mannerisms and dress of their contemporaries, and long for war as a means of purging the enervating softness of peace. Yet war, when it comes, provides only another dilemma, for military action in support of a tyrant undermines the very purpose for which they wish to fight. Ultimately the calling of military duty prevails, and they are captured by Theseus's Athenian army after having surpassed all others in the battle.

The mutual fondness of these cousins is not the only study in this play of friendship under duress. Duke Theseus of Athens and his general, Pirithous, are friends in the tradition of Alexander and Hephaestion, Damon and Pythias, and other figures from classical legend and history. Pirithous is reputed to have descended into Hades with Theseus to help carry off Persephone. "How his longing / Follows his friend!" exclaims Theseus's sister-in-law Emilia as she sees Pirithous eagerly depart to join Theseus in the military campaign against Thebes (1.3.26–27). Delayed for a time by Theseus's command that he see to the ceremonies that the war has interrupted, Pirithous cannot devote his full energies to matters of peace; his heart is with Theseus on the field of battle. Theseus's bride, Hippolyta, quite agrees with her sister Emilia: Theseus and Pirithous have shared so many dangers, she says, that "Their knot of love, / Tied, weaved, entangled . . . May be outworn, never outdone" (11. 41–44). As is always the case in such conventional debates about friendship and love, or love and honor, rival claims test friendship to prove its durability. Pirithous's loyalty to Theseus overcomes all other considerations.

Emilia and Hippolyta, as sisters, discuss friendship between women, comparing it to friendship between men. "Theirs has more ground," concedes Emilia, "is more maturely seasoned, / More buckled with strong judgment." Yet Emilia's own love for the now-dead Flavina, whom she once enjoyed as a playfellow, had qualities of innocence, of mutual devotion to chastity, and of intermingling of souls that men seemingly cannot match. "Like the elements / That know not what nor why, yet do effect / Rare issues by their operance, our souls / Did so to one another," Emilia longingly recalls. Their tastes were instinctively identical; their mannerisms and garments were so alike that neither could discern who had begun the fashion. Emilia's conclusion is that "true love 'tween maid and maid may be / More than in sex dividual"—that is, between persons of the opposite sex (1.3.55–82). At first, then, both men and women in this play find bonding to a person of the same sex more perfect

and fulfilling than heterosexual love. The situation recalls that of A Midsummer Night's Dream, where that play's Duke Theseus also marries Hippolyta, Queen of the Amazons. The very image of the Amazonian maiden is of a woman armed to defend herself against men.

These familiar topics of love versus honor and the battle of the sexes, eloquently set up by Shakespeare in the first act, inevitably lead to complications and testings in the second and third acts. Even in the first act, choices must be faced in terms of a code of chivalric honor. Theseus, about to marry Hippolyta but petitioned by three widows to avenge the dishonor done to their royal husbands by Creon, postpones his marital happiness to march against Thebes. Pirithous must reconcile the claims of duty and of his longing to be with Theseus on the field of battle. Palamon and Arcite seek ways to justify their military service in support of a tyrant and a corrupt state. Emilia announces her resolution to live and die a virgin, while her sister Hippolyta determines to go ahead with her marriage to Theseus, in a sisterly debate that reminds us of Luciana and her married sister Adriana in The Comedy of Errors.

Fletcher's theatrical strategy in the middle acts of the play is to subject these conventional polarities of love and honor to surprising and disarmingly improbable turns of events. In the prison where Palamon and Arcite lie languishing after their capture by Theseus's army, the Jailer's Daughter falls immediately and disastrously in love with Palamon, even though she readily concedes that Arcite is as handsome (2.4.16) and that "To marry him [Palamon] is hopeless, / To be his whore is witless" (11. 4–5). For their part, the two young men, resolving in the best stoical fashion to embrace their imprisonment as a way to repudiate a bad world and rely instead on their own sustaining friendship, fall instantly to quarreling when Emilia appears in the courtyard below their window (2.2.1–284). Palamon claims precedence because he has seen Emilia first. Whereas they previously regarded women as "The poison of pure spirits" and worse than a distraction (1. 75), they now devote their loyalties to love alone and look upon each other as villains worthy only of sudden death. Neither has yet spoken a word with the lady in question.

The pattern of flamboyant theatrical artifice continues to unfold. Once Arcite is released from prison for some unexplained reason and banished from Athens (11. 251–252), his only wish is to return in some disguise so that he may be near Emilia; once Palamon in turn is freed by the lovesick Jailer's Daughter at considerable risk to herself and her poor father, Palamon's sole hope is to see Emilia again. When the two cousins encounter one another by chance in the forest near Athens (another recollection of A Midsummer Night's Dream), their fierce determination to undo each other is almost comically mediated by the solicitude of each warrior that the other be properly armed. The hyperbolic vaunting, the unexpected coincidences, the lack of plausible motivation are highly theatrical and self-conscious in a way that is characteristic not only of Fletcher's other plays but of Jacobean drama in the 1610s and indeed of some of Shakespeare's own final work.

Throughout, the major characters operate in response to a code of aristocratic behavior that is eminently suited to a play about heroic chivalry. Arcite, in disguise as one who is competing in the "pastimes" devised to entertain Theseus and his court (2.3.76), amply displays his "noble qualities" to all who see him, even though they suppose him a stranger. "His body / And fiery mind illustrate a brave father," says Hippolyta; that is, he is nobly descended (2.5.21–22). He speaks well: "All his words are worthy" (1. 29). With a modesty and *sprezzatura* aptly suited to his noble station, he allows that he knows well the aristocratic pursuits of hawking and hunting, and most of all horsemanship. "I dare not praise / My feat in horsemanship," he says, "yet they that know me / Would say it was my best piece" (11. 11–14). Elsewhere, as often is the case in Shakespeare, horsemanship is a sure sign of aristocratic bearing, as when Pirithous describes Arcite as able to hold his saddle "bravely" even on a vicious horse that eventually topples over backward on its rider and crushes him (5.4.48–84). Arcite is "as brave a knight as e'er / Did spur a noble steed" (5.3.115–116). Palamon and Arcite's insistence on duelling even at the risk of the law's judgment is another mark of their inherent nobleness, even if the play also dramatizes the conflict between that aristocratic code of duelling and Theseus's insistence (reflecting Elizabethan and Jacobean official policy) that quarrels must be submitted to the authority of the state (3.6.132 ff.). Palamon and Arcite's followers in the climactic trial by combat in Act 5 are elaborately described as worthy of their greatness, with "all the ornament of honor" in their outward appearance and behavior; they "are all the sons of honor" (4.2.75–141). Theseus too is governed by the code of aristocratic honor, and his final resolution to allow Palamon and Arcite to settle their differences in a state-sponsored public arena through trial by combat is presented as a suitable solution for chivalric strife.

Even the comedy of this play, chiefly by Fletcher, is well suited to the aristocratic presuppositions of the main plot. The countrymen who tell Arcite about the upcoming pastimes in which he can compete to win the favor of Theseus and Emilia are country rustics whose rude mannerisms are contrasted at every turn with those of Arcite. Their conversation is often about sexuality, about jealous wives who must be "boarded" and "stowed" in suitable fashion, about the "wenches" with whom they will dance before the Duke, and so on (2.3.25–66). Like the shipwrecked hero of *Pericles,* who similarly obtains from poor country folk a means of competing in courtly games as a stranger, Arcite is beholden to these good-natured bumpkins and immeasurably far above them in noble graces. "'Tis a pretty fellow," one of them allows (1. 77). The pedantic Schoolmaster Ger-

ald, who, with his tedious Latinisms, presents a Morris dance before the Duke, reminds us of the schoolmaster Holofernes in *Love's Labor's Lost* and Peter Quince in *A Midsummer Night's Dream;* indeed, the business of devising a play within the play, witnessed by an amused critical audience onstage, is a medley of motifs out of Shakespeare. The plot line of the distraught Jailer's Daughter, sometimes comic, sometimes touching, borrows elements of mad talk from Ophelia in *Hamlet* and of medical eavesdropping from Lady Macbeth's sleepwalking in *Macbeth.* The Jailer's Daughter's song of "Willow, willow, willow" (4.1.80) would appear to be an explicit allusion to Desdemona's song in *Othello.* At every point, the play's subplot material seems intended to reflect through parody and comic exaggeration the heroic themes of love versus honor and the display of chivalric nobility.

Staging is appropriately ceremonial and elaborate. The play opens with a procession headed by Hymen, god of marriage, and including a courtly entourage of Theseus, his bride-to-be, and others, all elaborately robed in costumes and garlands symbolic of their ceremonial roles. A boy sings a hymn to love and marriage. The interruption of this grand entrance by the three widowed petitioners signals the sorts of conflicts that will continue to challenge the courtly ideals of perfect love, friendship, and honor. The battle between Thebes and Athens and later athletic contests are decorously conducted offstage (1.4 s.d., 2.5 s.d.), but the entrances of Theseus and other dignitaries continue to be heralded by the blaze of cornets and other flourishes. Repeated kneelings underscore the hierarchical structure of the Athenian court and the obedience that Theseus expects to his authority. Music accompanies the ceremonials of interment devised for the three dead kings (1.5 s.d.). The theater building is used to its fullest extent, as when Palamon and Arcite appear in prison "*above*" (2.1.48 s.d.) and look down upon Emilia on the main stage, gathering flowers as though in a garden adjacent to the prison. The sounds of cornets and halooing are heard from various directions to signify the celebration of May Day (3.1 s.d.).

Doors are used to suggest locations: Palamon enters, presumably in the forest, "*as out of a bush*" (3.1.30), and Palamon and Arcite enter to their final trial at opposite doors (5.1.7 s.d.). A Morris dance provides opportunity for numerous quaint characters in costume, including a baboon, the Lord and Lady of May (i.e., Robin Hood and Maid Marian), the Chambermaid, the Servingman, mine Host and his fat Spouse, the rustic countryman called the Clown, and the Fool (3.5.128–135). The dance itself is an elaborate if lower-class entertainment that is hard to recapture through reading the play text, and it certainly required music, including a taborer or player on pipe and drum. Palamon and Arcite fight a duel in full armor; the dialogue makes much of the stage business of their dressing each other for the encounter (3.6.16–131).

The play's last act is especially ceremonial, as though calling upon ceremony as a visual language of closure. Palamon and Arcite are brought onstage from opposite doors at the beginning of Act 5 to "tender their holy prayers" before the gods, asking for divine judgment in their strife. First Arcite and then Palamon approach the altars of their respective immortal patrons, Mars and Venus. The staging is uncertain. Conceivably, one altar is to stand in turn for the altar of Mars and Venus, and then for Diana when Emilia in her turn implores the gods' assistance; the elaborate stage business requires a trapdoor, of which the theater where the play was performed might have provided only one. Still, it is quite possible that three altars were provided onstage at once, giving the balanced, antithetical, and symbolic sense of location that the last act visually demands. Mars's altar answers Arcite's entreaties with *"clanging of armor, with a short thunder"* (5.1.61 s.d.) in an auspicious sign that Mars will grant Arcite the desired ascendancy. Palamon and his followers hear *"music"* at Venus's altar and see doves (1. 129 s.d.) as a "fair token" of truth in love. Emilia's ceremonial at Diana's altar is the most elaborate, requiring as it does *"still music,"* garlands and flowers, and a *"silver hind, in which is conveyed incense and sweet odors."* The oblation being set afire on the altar, *"the hind vanishes under the altar, and in the place ascends a rose tree, having one rose upon it."* This rose subsequently falls from a tree to the accompaniment of *"a sudden twang of instruments"* (11. 136–168 s.d.). These symbolic actions, signifying that virginity will yield chastely to love's erotic fulfillment, demand the services of a trap door, but the first two ceremonies do not. Perhaps then Diana's altar is centrally placed and is flanked by the representations of war and love. Such a configuration would give visual confirmation to the last act's movement toward a reconciliation in which the seemingly competing demands of military prowess, eros, and chaste denial are finally given their respective places in the crowning ceremonial of marriage. Staging thus embodies the antitheses of this chivalric play by visually juxtaposing male and female, friendship and love, love and honor, and by seeking a way to bring these opposites together.

Whatever Shakespeare's exact share may have been, *The Two Noble Kinsmen* displays many of the characteristics of the late Shakespeare, not only in the freedom of the verse, with its run-on lines and hypermetric effects, but also in the play's fascination with romantic plotting. The play that Shakespeare and Fletcher fashioned out of an old Chaucerian tale is one that portrays chivalric ideals through the medium of theatrical artifice. Like *Pericles*, whose narrator is Chaucer's contemporary John Gower, *The Two Noble Kinsmen* goes back to a quaint and improbable fiction of medieval times where fancy and imagination can do their work of theatrical transformation. Staging is elaborate, especially at the close, as in *Cymbeline*. The gods intervene directly in the play's denouement, as in all the late romances (though the gods in *The Tempest* are of Prospero's devising).

As in the romances as a group, the audience is asked to approach, in a spirit of wonder combined perhaps with ironic detachment, a work that is self-consciously theatrical in its depiction of supernatural effects. The gods have their way in *The Two Noble Kinsmen*. The human protagonists stand in awe at their final deliverance from their own worst selves. Palamon and Arcite, in their perverse but noble attempts to destroy each other for love, fulfill the will of destiny that is revealed to them at the altars of Mars, Venus, and Diana: the brave Arcite is to die on horseback, the lover Palamon is to win the lady Emilia, and she is to find marital happiness even while preserving her ideal of chaste marriage. The ending is contrived to a striking degree, in that it depends on a physical accident; and yet it is no more arbitrary than the ending of *Cymbeline*. What seems accident to mere mortals is seen finally by the play's protagonists as part of a deeper heavenly design. "O you heavenly charmers," Theseus apostrophizes the gods in a choric close, "What things you make of us! For what we lack / We laugh, for what we have are sorry, still / Are children in some kind." Theseus's conclusion from this is one of pious acceptance: "Let us be thankful / For that which is" (5.4.131–135). The audience, even while it is openly encouraged to see the play's romantic structure as theatrical artifice, is also invited to ponder what deeper ideologies may be embodied in Shakespeare's and Fletcher's depiction of dramatic art as pattern, order, ornament, contrivance, and vision.

The Two Noble Kinsmen

[Dramatis Personae

PROLOGUE

THESEUS, *Duke of Athens*
HIPPOLYTA, *Queen of the Amazons, later married to Theseus*
EMILIA, *her sister*
PIRITHOUS, *friend of Theseus*

PALAMON ⎱ *the two noble kinsmen, cousins, nephews*
ARCITE ⎰ *of Creon, the King of Thebes*

HYMEN, *god of marriage*
A BOY
ARTESIUS, *an Athenian soldier*
Three QUEENS, *widows of three kings killed at the siege of Thebes*
VALERIUS, *a Theban*
A HERALD
A WOMAN *attending Emilia*
An Athenian GENTLEMAN
MESSENGERS
Six KNIGHTS, *three following Palamon and three Arcite*
A SERVANT
THE JAILER *in charge of Theseus' prison*
THE JAILER'S DAUGHTER
THE JAILER'S BROTHER
THE WOOER *of the Jailer's Daughter*
Two FRIENDS *of the Jailer*
A DOCTOR
Six COUNTRYMEN, *one dressed as a babion, or baboon*
A SCHOOLMASTER *named Gerald*
NELL, *a country wench*
Four other country wenches: Friz, Maudline, Luce, and Barbery
A TABORER *named Timothy*
Nymphs, attendants, maids, executioner, guard

EPILOGUE

SCENE: *Athens and Thebes.*]

Prologue

Flourish. [Enter Prologue.]

PROLOGUE
New plays and maidenheads are near akin:
Much followed both, for both much money gi'en, 2
If they stand sound and well. And a good play, 3
Whose modest scenes blush on his marriage day 4
And shake to lose his honor, is like her 5
That after holy tie and first night's stir 6
Yet still is modesty, and still retains 7
More of the maid to sight than husband's pains. 8
We pray our play may be so; for I am sure
It has a noble breeder and a pure, 10
A learnèd, and a poet never went 11
More famous yet 'twixt Po and silver Trent. 12
Chaucer, of all admired, the story gives; 13
There, constant to eternity, it lives. 14
If we let fall the nobleness of this, 15
And the first sound this child hear be a hiss,
How will it shake the bones of that good man,
And make him cry from under ground, "O, fan
From me the witless chaff of such a writer
That blasts my bays and my famed works makes lighter 20
Than Robin Hood!" This is the fear we bring; 21
For, to say truth, it were an endless thing,
And too ambitious, to aspire to him, 23
Weak as we are, and almost breathless swim
In this deep water. Do but you hold out
Your helping hands, and we shall tack about 26
And something do to save us. You shall hear
Scenes, though below his art, may yet appear 28
Worth two hours' travail. To his bones sweet sleep; 29
Content to you. If this play do not keep 30
A little dull time from us, we perceive 31
Our losses fall so thick we must needs leave.

Flourish. [Exit.]

❖

s.d. Flourish fanfare to announce the arrival or departure of a notable person   2 Much followed eagerly sought after   3 stand sound seem healthy   4 his marriage day i.e., its first day of performance   5 shake . . . honor (1) tremble at the thought of loss of virginity (2) fear disgrace at the hands of the audience   6 holy . . . stir marriage and sexual consummation that night   7 is modesty (1) remains chaste (2) is modest about the play's success   7–8 still . . . pains still appears more like a virgin than like a woman transformed into a wife by her husband's exertions. (The moral edge that is given to virginity over married chastity is characteristic of the play as a whole.)   10 breeder (1) sire (2) author   11–12 a poet . . . Trent there never was a more famous poet anywhere in Europe (literally, between the river Po in northern Italy and the Trent in England)   13 of by   14 There i.e., in "The Knight's Tale" of *The Canterbury Tales*   15 let fall allow to collapse   20 blasts my bays withers my poetic reputation   21 Than Robin Hood i.e., than popular ballad material   23 him Chaucer   26 tack about turn about in the water, as though sailing, in response to the wind generated by the audience's applause   28 his Chaucer's.   may which may   29 travail spelled 'travell' in the original quarto, suggesting (1) the actors' exertions (2) the audience's journey of imagination   30–31 If . . . from us i.e., unless this play manages to be entertaining and thereby protect us against declining audiences

1.1   [*Music.*] *Enter Hymen with a torch burning; a boy in a white robe before, singing and strewing flowers; after Hymen a nymph, encompassed in her tresses, bearing a wheaten garland; then Theseus between two other nymphs with wheaten chaplets on their heads; then Hippolyta, the bride, led by Pirithous, and another holding a garland over her head, her tresses likewise hanging; after her, Emilia, holding up her train; [Artesius and attendants.*]*

BOY [*singing as they enter*]
    Roses, their sharp spines being gone,
    Not royal in their smells alone,
        But in their hue;
    Maiden pinks, of odor faint,
    Daisies smell-less, yet most quaint,   5
        And sweet thyme true;
    Primrose, firstborn child of Ver,   7
    Merry springtime's harbinger,
        With her bells dim;   9
    Oxlips, in their cradles growing,   10
    Marigolds, on deathbeds blowing,   11
        Lark's-heels trim;   12
    (*Strew flowers*) All dear Nature's children sweet
    Lie 'fore bride and bridegroom's feet,
        Blessing their sense.   15
    Not an angel of the air,
    Bird melodious or bird fair,
        Is absent hence.
    The crow, the sland'rous cuckoo, nor   19
    The boding raven, nor chough hoar   20
        Nor chatt'ring pie,   21
    May on our bridehouse perch or sing,
    Or with them any discord bring,
        But from it fly.   24

    Enter three Queens in black, with veils stained, with imperial crowns. The first Queen falls down at the foot of Theseus; the second falls down at the foot of Hippolyta; the third before Emilia.

FIRST QUEEN [*to Theseus*]
    For pity's sake and true gentility's,   25
    Hear and respect me.   26

SECOND QUEEN [*to Hippolyta*]
    For your mother's sake,
    And as you wish your womb may thrive with fair ones,
    Hear and respect me.
THIRD QUEEN [*to Emilia*]
    Now for the love of him whom Jove hath marked   29
    The honor of your bed, and for the sake   30
    Of clear virginity, be advocate   31
    For us and our distresses. This good deed
    Shall raze you out o' th' book of trespasses   33
    All you are set down there.   34
THESEUS [*to First Queen*]
    Sad lady, rise.
HYPPOLYTA [*to Second Queen*]   Stand up.
EMILIA [*to Third Queen*]   No knees to me.
    What woman I may stead that is distressed   36
    Does bind me to her.   37
                [*The Second and Third Queens rise.*]
THESEUS [*to First Queen*]
    What's your request? Deliver you for all.   38
FIRST QUEEN [*kneeling still*]
    We are three queens whose sovereigns fell before
    The wrath of cruel Creon; who endured   40
    The beaks of ravens, talons of the kites,
    And pecks of crows in the foul fields of Thebes. 42
    He will not suffer us to burn their bones,
    To urn their ashes, nor to take th' offense
    Of mortal loathsomeness from the blest eye
    Of holy Phoebus, but infects the winds   46
    With stench of our slain lords. O pity, Duke!
    Thou purger of the earth, draw thy feared sword 48
    That does good turns to th' world; give us the bones
    Of our dead kings, that we may chapel them;   50
    And of thy boundless goodness take some note   51
    That for our crownèd heads we have no roof
    Save this, which is the lion's and the bear's,   53
    And vault to everything.
THESEUS   Pray you, kneel not;   54
    I was transported with your speech and suffered
    Your knees to wrong themselves. I have heard the fortunes
    Of your dead lords, which gives me such lamenting
    As wakes my vengeance and revenge for 'em.
    King Capaneus was your lord; the day
    That he should marry you, at such a season   60
    As now it is with me, I met your groom   61

1.1 Location: Athens. Enroute to the temple where the marriage is to take place.
s.d. **Hymen** god of marriage. **a nymph . . . tresses** a young woman with her hair unbound, as a token of virginity. **wheaten garland** symbol of fecundity. **chaplets** garlands **5 quaint** ingeniously contrived **7 Ver** spring personified **9 bells dim** pale bell-shaped flowers **10 Oxlips . . . growing** cowslip-like flowers with the bud cradled by surrounding petals and leaves **11 on deathbeds blowing** flowering on graves **12 Lark's-heels** larkspur **15 Blessing their sense** conferring well-being on their senses **19 sland'rous cuckoo** The cuckoo was despised for seeming to mock married men as potential cuckolds and for laying its eggs in other birds' nests. **20 boding** prophesying bad fortune. **chough hoar** gray-feathered jackdaw **21 pie** magpie **24 s.d. stained** dyed black to betoken mourning **25 gentility's** nobility's **26 respect** pay considerate attention to

29–30 **marked . . . bed** destined to be your honorable husband **31 clear** pure **33–34 raze . . . there** erase from the book of heaven's judgment all your sins set down there **36–37 What . . . to her** whatsoever woman in distress that I can assist will by her very situation obligate me to her (without further kneeling on her part) **37 s.d. rise** (The stage directions to rise and kneel again are conjectural in their placement.) **38 Deliver** speak **40 who** i.e., the queens' three husbands **42 fields** battlefields **46 Phoebus** i.e., the sun, Apollo **48 purger of the earth** i.e., champion against wrong (like the sun, that purges the earth of disease) **50 chapel** inter in a chapel **51 of** out of **53 this** the sky **54 vault** roof **60 should** was about to **61 groom** bridegroom

By Mars's altar. You were that time fair—
Not Juno's mantle fairer than your tresses,
Nor in more bounty spread her. Your wheaten
  wreath 64
Was then nor threshed nor blasted; Fortune at you 65
Dimpled her cheek with smiles. Hercules, our
  kinsman—
Then weaker than your eyes—laid by his club; 67
He tumbled down upon his Nemean hide 68
And swore his sinews thawed. O Grief and Time, 69
Fearful consumers, you will all devour! 70
FIRST QUEEN   O, I hope some god,
Some god hath put his mercy in your manhood,
Whereto he'll infuse power and press you forth 73
Our undertaker.
THESEUS   O, no knees, none, widow; 74
Unto the helmeted Bellona use them 75
And pray for me, your soldier.
         [The First Queen rises.]
Troubled I am.   *[He] turns away.*
SECOND QUEEN *[kneeling]*   Honored Hippolyta,
Most dreaded Amazonian, that hast slain 78
The scythe-tusked boar; that with thy arm, as strong 79
As it is white, wast near to make the male 80
To thy sex captive, but that this thy lord,
Born to uphold creation in that honor 82
First nature styled it in, shrunk thee into 83
The bound thou wast o'erflowing, at once subduing 84
Thy force and thy affection; soldieress
That equally canst poise sternness with pity, 86
Whom now I know hast much more power on him 87
Then ever he had on thee, who ow'st his strength 88
And his love too, who is a servant for 89
The tenor of thy speech: dear glass of ladies, 90
Bid him that we, whom flaming war doth scorch,
Under the shadow of his sword may cool us!
Require him he advance it o'er our heads. 93
Speak 't in a woman's key, like such a woman 94
As any of us three; weep ere you fail.
Lend us a knee;

But touch the ground for us no longer time 97
Than a dove's motion when the head's plucked off. 98
Tell him if he i' th' blood-sized field lay swoll'n, 99
Showing the sun his teeth, grinning at the moon, 100
What you would do.
HIPPOLYTA   Poor lady, say no more.
I had as lief trace this good action with you 102
As that whereto I am going, and never yet 103
Went I so willing way. My lord is taken 104
Heart-deep with your distress. Let him consider.
I'll speak anon.
         [The Second Queen rises.]
THIRD QUEEN *[kneel to Emilia]* O, my petition was 106
Set down in ice, which by hot grief uncandied 107
Melts into drops; so sorrow, wanting form, 108
Is pressed with deeper matter.
EMILIA   Pray stand up; 109
Your grief is written in your cheek.
THIRD QUEEN   O, woe!
You cannot read it there; there through my tears, 111
Like wrinkled pebbles in a glassy stream, 112
You may behold 'em. Lady, lady, alack! 113
He that will all the treasure know o' th' earth
Must know the center too; he that will fish 115
For my least minnow, let him lead his line 116
To catch one at my heart. O, pardon me!
Extremity, that sharpens sundry wits, 118
Makes me a fool.
         [The Third Queen rises.]
EMILIA   Pray you say nothing, pray you. 119
Who cannot feel nor see the rain, being in 't, 120
Knows neither wet nor dry. If that you were 121
The ground-piece of some painter, I would buy you 122
T' instruct me 'gainst a capital grief, indeed 123
Such heart-pierced demonstration; but alas, 124
Being a natural sister of our sex, 125

97–98 But . . . off The Second Queen seems to suggest that Hippolyta make her request deftly and gracefully, in a moment. A headless dove is soon motionless. **touch the ground** (1) kneel (2) maintain this position in argument **99 blood-sized field** battlefield smeared with blood, as with *size* or glutinous substance **100 Showing . . . moon** grinning as a skull does **102–104 had . . . way** i.e., would just as gladly speak on your behalf as go ahead with my impending marriage, which I look forward to more willingly than anything I've ever done **104 taken** struck, afflicted **106–109 my petition . . . matter** i.e., my petition, coldly formal when expressed in mere words, is melted by my hot grief into teardrops; thus my sorrow, lacking shape or power of expression, is pressed out in tears by the deep cause of my grief **111–113 You . . . 'em** i.e., you cannot read my grief truly on my cheek, in the external sign; look through my tears into my eyes, as you would look at pebbles distorted in their shape through the rippling water of a clear stream **115 Must . . . too** must mine deeply **116 lead** attach a lead weight to (so that the fishing gear may sink deeply) **118–119 Extremity . . . fool** extremity of grief, which produces clever speech from some minds, prompts me to speak distractedly **120 Who** anyone who. (Emilia's point is that the Third Queen's tears are eloquent enough to move any person of feeling.) **121–124 If that . . . demonstration** if you were merely depicted by some painter as an image intended to provide moral example, I would buy the painting to help me anticipate and thus ward off a deadly grief, indeed just such a heart-piercing instance as your sad case represents **125 Being . . . sex** i.e., since you are a living woman, not a painting

64 Nor . . . her nor enveloped her in more luxuriant tresses **64–65 Your . . . blasted** your garland woven of wheat (a token of fecundity, as at 1.1 s.d.) was neither threshed (punning on "thrashed," beaten) nor withered **67 weaker than your eyes** subdued by your gaze **68 Nemean hide** One of Hercules's twelve labors was to kill and skin the Nemean lion. **69 thawed** i.e., rendered powerless (by love) **70 all devour** devour all things **73–74 press . . . undertaker** press you into service as our champion **75 Bellona** goddess of war **78–79 that . . . boar** Atalanta, a huntress like Hippolyta, helped kill the fearful wild boar of Calydon (see Chaucer's "The Knight's Tale" and Ovid, *Metamorphoses*, Book 8). **80 wast near to make** was on the verge of making **82–83 Born . . . it in** i.e., destined to restore and maintain the natural hierarchy of the sexes, as ordained since the beginning of time **84 The bound . . . o'erflowing** the circumscribed limits that you were attempting to exceed, like a river overflowing its banks **86 poise** counterpoise, balance **87 on** over **88 who ow'st** you who now own or control **89–90 who . . . ladies** i.e., Theseus, who is obedient in love to your every command: you who are a mirror or model for all ladies **93 Require him** request of him that. **advance** lift, hold aloft **94 key** tone, style

Your sorrow beats so ardently upon me 126
That it shall make a counter-reflect 'gainst 127
My brother's heart and warm it to some pity,
Though it were made of stone. Pray have good
    comfort.

THESEUS
Forward to th' temple. Leave not out a jot
O' th' sacred ceremony.

FIRST QUEEN   O, this celebration 131
Will longer last and be more costly than 132
Your suppliants' war. Remember that your fame 133
Knolls in the ear o' th' world; what you do quickly 134
Is not done rashly; your first thought is more
Than others' labored meditance, your premeditating 136
More than their actions. But, O Jove, your actions,
Soon as they move, as ospreys do the fish, 138
Subdue before they touch. Think, dear Duke, think 139
What beds our slain kings have.

SECOND QUEEN   What griefs our beds, 140
That our dear lords have none.

THIRD QUEEN   None fit for th' dead. 141
Those that with cords, knives, drams, precipitance, 142
Weary of this world's light, have to themselves
Been death's most horrid agents, human grace
Affords them dust and shadow.

FIRST QUEEN   But our lords 145
Lie blist'ring 'fore the visiting sun, 146
And were good kings when living. 147

THESEUS
It is true, and I will give you comfort
To give your dead lords graves; 149
The which to do must make some work with Creon.

FIRST QUEEN
And that work presents itself to th' doing. 151
Now 'twill take form; the heats are gone tomorrow. 152
Then, bootless toil must recompense itself 153
With its own sweat. Now he's secure, 154
Not dreams we stand before your puissance, 155
Rinsing our holy begging in our eyes
To make petition clear.

SECOND QUEEN   Now you may take him, 157
Drunk with his victory.

THIRD QUEEN   And his army full
Of bread and sloth.

THESEUS [to Artesius] Artesius, that best knowest
How to draw out, fit to this enterprise, 160
The prim'st for this proceeding, and the number 161
To carry such a business: forth and levy 162
Our worthiest instruments, whilst we dispatch 163
This grand act of our life, this daring deed 164
Of fate in wedlock.

FIRST QUEEN [to the other Queens] Dowagers, take hands. 165
Let us be widows to our woes; delay 166
Commends us to a famishing hope. 167

ALL [THE QUEENS]   Farewell.

SECOND QUEEN
We come unseasonably; but when could grief
Cull forth, as unpanged judgment can, fitt'st time 169
For best solicitation?

THESEUS   Why, good ladies,
This is a service, whereto I am going,
Greater than any was; it more imports me 172
Than all the actions that I have foregone, 173
Or futurely can cope.

FIRST QUEEN   The more proclaiming 174
Our suit shall be neglected, when her arms, 175
Able to lock Jove from a synod, shall 176
By warranting moonlight corslet thee. O, when 177
Her twinning cherries shall their sweetness fall 178
Upon thy tasteful lips, what wilt thou think 179
Of rotten kings or blubbered queens? What care 180
For what thou feel'st not, what thou feel'st being
    able 181
To make Mars spurn his drum? O, if thou couch 182
But one night with her, every hour in 't will
Take hostage of thee for a hundred, and 184
Thou shalt remember nothing more than what
That banquet bids thee to.

HIPPOLYTA [to Theseus]   Though much unlike 186
You should be so transported, as much sorry 187
I should be such a suitor, yet I think, 188
Did I not, by th' abstaining of my joy— 189

---

126 **ardently** burningly, sun-like in intensity   127 **make a counter-reflect** reflect back from me as from a mirror   131–133 **O, this . . . war** The First Queen urges Theseus to consider that the wedding ceremony will consume precious time, during which the queens' supplications and their struggle with Creon will languish.   134 **Knolls** tolls   136 **labored meditance** laborious thought   138–139 **as ospreys . . . touch** osprey hawks, which dive spectacularly on fish in the water, were thought to subdue their prey with a powerful emanating influence even before they struck   140 **What griefs our beds** i.e., think in what beds of grief we lie, so to speak   141 **None . . . dead** i.e., the cold ground on which they lie is no fit bed for a dead warrior   142 **drams** poisons.   **precipitance** suicidal leaps. (The Third Queen's point is that even suicides are allowed some kind of burial.)   145 **dust and shadow** i.e., to lie in quiet darkness in the earth   146 **visiting** surveying, overseeing   147 **And** i.e., and yet, unlike suicides   149 **To give** by giving   151–154 **presents . . . sweat** calls for action immediately. It can be shaped, like heated metal, now, but will soon cool. Tomorrow, all effort will be fruitless and will have to be content with the effort itself.   154 **he** i.e., Creon   155 **your puissance** your mighty self   157 **To . . . clear** to purify our supplication and stress our point

160 **draw out** choose   161 **prim'st** best   162 **carry** carry out.   **forth** go forth   163 **instruments** agents, i.e., soldiers   164–165 **This . . . wedlock** Theseus' view here of his marriage as a heroic deed, a counter-adventure, is quite different from the view that the queens are presenting (e.g., ll. 174 ff.).   166–167 **delay . . . hope** the delay (occasioned by this marriage) commits us to a dying hope   169 **Cull forth** choose, select.   **unpanged** unafflicted by the pangs of sorrow   172 **more imports me** is more important to me   173 **foregone** previously achieved   174 **futurely can cope** can achieve in the future.   **The more proclaiming** making it all the more clear that   175 **shall** is bound to be   175–177 **when . . . thee** when the arms of her (Hippolyta) who is able to prevent even Jove from attending some other engagement shall, by the light of the sanctioning moon, encircle you in the grip of her body-armor   178 **twinning cherries** cherry lips.   **fall** let fall   179 **tasteful** capable of tasting   180 **rotten** with decaying flesh.   **blubbered** tear-stained   180–182 **Though . . . drum?** Why should you care for something that does not touch you personally, at a time when what you do feel is enough to make you set aside military duty?   182 **couch** lie   184 **Take . . . hundred** i.e., commit you to a hundred more such hours   186–188 **Though . . . suitor** even though it would be much unlike you to be lifted into transports thus, and as much as I regret being the one to request (that you postpone the wedding). Theseus would also dislike it if the queens were so transported.   189 **of** from

Which breeds a deeper longing—cure their surfeit,   190
That craves a present med'cine, I should pluck   191
All ladies' scandal on me. [*She kneels.*] Therefore,
sir,   192
As I shall here make trial of my prayers,
Either presuming them to have some force,
Or sentencing for aye their vigor dumb,   195
Prorogue this business we are going about, and
hang   196
Your shield afore your heart, about that neck
Which is my fee, and which I freely lend   198
To do these poor queens service.
ALL [THE] QUEENS [*to Emilia*]   O, help now!
Our cause cries for your knee.
EMILIA [*to Theseus, kneeling*]   If you grant not
My sister her petition in that force,   201
With that celerity and nature which   202
She makes it in, from henceforth I'll not dare   203
To ask you anything, nor be so hardy
Ever to take a husband.
THESEUS   Pray stand up.

[*Hippolyta and Emilia rise.*]

I am entreating of myself to do
That which you kneel to have me.—Pirithous,
Lead on the bride; get you and pray the gods   208
For success and return; omit not anything   209
In the pretended celebration.—Queens,   210
Follow your soldier. [*To Artesius*] As before, hence
you,   211
And at the banks of Aulis meet us with
The forces you can raise, where we shall find
The moiety of a number for a business   214
More bigger looked.   [*Exit Artesius.*]
[*To Hippolyta*]   Since that our theme is haste,   215
I stamp this kiss upon thy current lip;   216
Sweet, keep it as my token.—Set you forward,   217
For I will see you gone.
[*The marriage procession moves*] *towards the temple.*
[*To Emilia*] Farewell, my beauteous sister.—
Pirithous,   219
Keep the feast full; bate not an hour on 't.

PIRITHOUS   Sir,   220
I'll follow you at heels. The feast's solemnity   221
Shall want till your return.
THESEUS   Cousin, I charge you,   222
Budge not from Athens. We shall be returning
Ere you can end this feast, of which I pray you
Make no abatement.—Once more, farewell all.

Exeunt [*the procession*].

FIRST QUEEN
Thus dost thou still make good the tongue o' th'
world.   226
SECOND QUEEN
And earn'st a deity equal with Mars.
THIRD QUEEN   If not above him, for
Thou, being but mortal, makest affections bend   229
To godlike honors; they themselves, some say,   230
Groan under such a mast'ry.   231
THESEUS   As we are men,
Thus should we do; being sensually subdued,   232
We lose our human title. Good cheer, ladies!   233
Now turn we towards your comforts.

Flourish. Exeunt.

❧

1.2   *Enter Palamon and Arcite.*

ARCITE
Dear Palamon, dearer in love than blood,
And our prime cousin, yet unhardened in   2
The crimes of nature, let us leave the city   3
Thebes, and the temptings in 't, before we further
Sully our gloss of youth.   5
And here to keep in abstinence we shame   6
As in incontinence; for not to swim   7
I' th' aid o' th' current were almost to sink,
At least to frustrate striving; and to follow   9
The common stream, 'twould bring us to an eddy
Where we should turn or drown; if labor through,   11
Our gain but life and weakness.   12
PALAMON   Your advice
Is cried up with example. What strange ruins,   13
Since first we went to school, may we perceive

190 **Which . . . longing** Hippolyta's point is that by abstaining virtuously from the joys of marriage, she (and Theseus, too) can engender a deeper longing by making more precious and well-earned the reward. **surfeit** excess (of grief) **191 present** immediate **191–192 I should . . . on me** I should invite the scorn of all ladies for my scandalous behavior **195 Or . . . dumb** or condemning them forever as ineffectual (if they fail), as if they had never been spoken **196 Prorogue** postpone **198 my fee** due to me (in marriage) **201–203 in that force . . . it in** with the same intensity, speed, and natural feeling she uses in making her petition **208 get you** get you hence, depart **209 return** our victorious return **210 pretended** intended **211 your soldier** i.e., Theseus himself **214–215 The moiety . . . looked** a part of an armed force raised to deal with a larger enterprise. (An army, raised for some other campaign, is now to be turned against Thebes.) **215 Since that our theme** since our business **216 current** (1) legal and genuine, like a coin stamped with the royal image (2) currant-red. (The quarto spelling, *currant*, allows for both meanings.) **217 my token** a keepsake from me **219 sister** sister-in-law-to-be **220 full** fully. **bate . . . on 't** don't omit one hour of it

221 **solemnity** ceremonial dignity **222 want** be lacking. **Cousin** a term used by royal figures to address their courtiers **226 the tongue o' th' world** your reputation among all peoples **229–231 makest . . . mast'ry** subdue your passions to your godlike sense of honor; the gods themselves, some people say, suffer under passions that master them **232 being sensually subdued** if we allow ourselves to be subdued by our sensual natures **233 human title** claim to be called human

1.2 Location: Thebes.
2 prime chief, dearest **3 The crimes of nature** those vices to which the human race is prone, ever since the Fall from the Garden of Eden **5 Sully . . . youth** stain the luster of our youth **6–7 here . . . incontinence** even though we practice abstinence, our presence here in Thebes is so shameful that the fact itself makes abstinence seem no better than unrestrained sexual indulgence **9 to frustrate striving** to frustrate ourselves by our unappreciated efforts to love chastely **11 turn** eddy about aimlessly **11–12 if labor . . . weakness** even if we were to escape the eddy, we would gain only a strengthless survival **13 cried up with example** proclaimed by many instances. **ruins** persons ruined by extravagance

Walking in Thebes? Scars and bare weeds 15
The gain o' th' martialist, who did propound 16
To his bold ends honor and golden ingots, 17
Which though he won, he had not, and now flirted 18
By peace for whom he fought. Who then shall offer
To Mars's so scorned altar? I do bleed 20
When such I meet, and wish great Juno would 21
Resume her ancient fit of jealousy 22
To get the soldier work, that peace might purge 23
For her repletion, and retain anew 24
Her charitable heart, now hard and harsher 25
Than strife or war could be.
ARCITE   Are you not out? 26
Meet you no ruin but the soldier in
The cranks and turns of Thebes? You did begin 28
As if you met decays of many kinds.
Perceive you none that do arouse your pity
But th' unconsidered soldier?
PALAMON   Yes, I pity
Decays where'er I find them, but such most
That, sweating in an honorable toil,
Are paid with ice to cool 'em.
ARCITE   'Tis not this 34
I did begin to speak of; this is virtue 35
Of no respect in Thebes. I spake of Thebes, 36
How dangerous, if we will keep our honors, 37
It is for our residing, where every evil
Hath a good color; where every seeming good's 39
A certain evil; where not to be ev'n jump 40
As they are here were to be strangers, and 41
Such things to be, mere monsters.
PALAMON   'Tis in our power 42
(Unless we fear that apes can tutor 's) to 43
Be masters of our manners. What need I
Affect another's gait, which is not catching 45
Where there is faith? Or to be fond upon 46
Another's way of speech, when by mine own
I may be reasonably conceived—saved too, 48
Speaking it truly? Why am I bound 49

By any generous bond to follow him 50
Follows his tailor, haply so long until 51
The followed make pursuit? Or let me know 52
Why mine own barber is unblessed, with him 53
My poor chin too, for 'tis not scissored just 54
To such a favorite's glass? What canon is there 55
That does command my rapier from my hip 56
To dangle 't in my hand, or to go tip-toe 57
Before the street be foul? Either I am 58
The fore-horse in the team, or I am none
That draw i' th' sequent trace. These poor slight
    sores 60
Need not a plantain. That which rips my bosom 61
Almost to th' heart's—
ARCITE   Our uncle Creon.
PALAMON   He,
A most unbounded tyrant, whose successes
Makes heaven unfeared and villainy assured 64
Beyond its power there's nothing; almost puts 65
Faith in a fever, and deifies alone
Voluble chance; who only attributes 67
The faculties of other instruments 68
To his own nerves and act; commands men service, 69
And what they win in 't, boot and glory; one 70
That fears not to do harm; good, dares not. Let 71
The blood of mine that's sib to him be sucked 72
From me with leeches! Let them break and fall 73
Off me with that corruption.
ARCITE   Clear-spirited cousin, 74
Let's leave his court, that we may nothing share
Of his loud infamy; for our milk 76
Will relish of the pasture, and we must 77
Be vile or disobedient, not his kinsmen 78
In blood unless in quality.
PALAMON   Nothing truer. 79
I think the echoes of his shames have deafed 80
The ears of heav'nly justice: widows' cries

15 **bare weeds** threadbare garments 16–17 **The gain . . . ends** are the reward of the soldier, who had proposed as a reward for his martial deeds 18 **Which . . . had not** which though he earned, he never actually received. **flirted** jeered at 20 **I do bleed** i.e., my heart bleeds 21–26 **could be** Palamon wishes that war might break out again, renewing the conflict that came about when Juno vented her hatred on Thebes in retaliation for her husband Jupiter's affair with Alcmene in that city. War would put honorable soldiers to work. Peace, purging herself through war of her own excesses of decadent indolence, would paradoxically be more charitable than the harsh present reality of unchaste behavior. 26 **out** mistaken (in pitying only the soldier) 28 **cranks** winding streets 34 **Are . . . 'em** i.e., are fobbed off ungratefully 35–36 **this . . . respect** i.e., no one cares for military honor 37 **will** wish to 39 **Hath a good color** assumes a pleasant appearance 40–42 **where . . . monsters** where not to go along exactly with Theban customs will brand us as strangers; yet to be as the Thebans are would make us utter monsters 43 **Unless . . . tutor 's** unless we are so insecure as to copy the behavior of those who are themselves mere imitators of others 45–46 **Affect . . . faith** model myself on another person's bearing, which should have no attraction for me when I practice self-reliance 46 **fond upon** infatuated with 48 **conceived** understood 48–49 **saved . . . truly** i.e., I can reasonably hope to be saved from eternal damnation by own speech, if I speak the truth

50 **generous bond** honorable and gentlemanly obligation. **follow** imitate 51 **Follows** who follows, puts himself in the hands of 51–52 **haply . . . pursuit** perchance until he who was followed (the tailor) starts pursuing the follower (with a request for payment or a lawsuit) 53 **unblessed** not in favor 54 **for** because 54–55 **just . . . glass** precisely according to the latest fashion as reflected in the mirror of one who is much in favor 55 **canon** law 56–58 **That . . . foul** Carrying one's rapier in one's hand and tiptoeing even when the streets are not dirty are here seen as affectations of the dandy. 60 **That . . . trace** that pull in the traces among a team of horses following behind the leader. Palamon insists on being the leader or else no part of the team. 61 **plantain** a plant used in healing wounds 64–65 **Makes . . . nothing** seem to suggest that villains need not fear heaven's justice and that no superior divine authority exists beyond human power 67 **Voluble chance** mutable fortune 67–69 **who . . . act** who attributes the capabilities and achievements of those who serve him to his own sinews (*nerves*) and deeds alone 69–70 **comands . . . glory** forces men to follow him and then arrogates to himself both the glory and the spoils they have won in battle 71 **good, dares not** dares not do any good (lest it leave him vulnerable to those he might trust) 72 **sib** akin 73 **leeches . . . break** These bloodsucking worms, used by physicians to purge the blood, were allowed to fill to bursting and then fall off. 74 **Clear-spirited** noble-minded 76 **loud** notorious 76–77 **our . . . pasture** our milk (like that of cows) will acquire the flavor of what we have eaten; we will become vile like Creon 78–79 **not . . . quality** becoming bound to him in character no less than in blood 80 **deafed** deafened

Descend again into their throats, and have not
Due audience of the gods.   83

Enter Valerius.

                              Valerius.

VALERIUS
The King calls for you; yet be leaden-footed   84
Till his great rage be off him. Phoebus, when   85
He broke his whipstock and exclaimed against   86
The horses of the sun, but whispered to   87
The loudness of his fury.

PALAMON   Small winds shake him.   88
But what's the matter?

VALERIUS
Theseus, who where he threats appalls, hath sent   90
Deadly defiance to him and pronounces
Ruin to Thebes, who is at hand to seal   92
The promise of his wrath.

ARCITE   Let him approach.
But that we fear the gods in him, he brings not   94
A jot of terror to us. Yet what man   95
Thirds his own worth—the case is each of ours—   96
When that his action's dregged with mind assured   97
'Tis bad he goes about.

PALAMON   Leave that unreasoned.   98
Our services stand now for Thebes, not Creon.
Yet to be neutral to him were dishonor,   100
Rebellious to oppose; therefore we must
With him stand to the mercy of our fate,
Who hath bounded our last minute.

ARCITE   So we must.   103
Is 't said this war's afoot, or it shall be   104
On fail of some condition?

VALERIUS   'Tis in motion;   105
The intelligence of state came in the instant   106
With the defier.

PALAMON   Let's to the King, who, were he   107
A quarter carrier of that honor which   108
His enemy come in, the blood we venture   109
Should be as for our health, which were not spent,   110
Rather laid out for purchase. But alas,   111

Our hands advanced before our hearts, what will   112
The fall o' th' stroke do damage?

ARCITE   Let th' event,   113
That never-erring arbitrator, tell us
When we know all ourselves, and let us follow
The becking of our chance.   *Exeunt.* 116

                           ❧

1.3   *Enter Pirithous, Hippolyta, Emilia.*

PIRITHOUS
No further.

HIPPOLYTA   Sir, farewell. Repeat my wishes   1
To our great lord, of whose success I dare not
Make any timorous question; yet I wish him
Excess and overflow of power, an 't might be   4
To dure ill-dealing fortune. Speed to him!   5
Store never hurts good governors.

PIRITHOUS   Though I know   6
His ocean needs not my poor drops, yet they   7
Must yield their tribute there. [*To Emilia*] My
    precious maid,
Those best affections that the heaven infuse   9
In their best-tempered pieces keep enthroned   10
In your dear heart!

EMILIA   Thanks, sir. Remember me
To our all-royal brother, for whose speed
The great Bellona I'll solicit; and   13
Since in our terrene state petitions are not   14
Without gifts understood, I'll offer to her
What I shall be advised she likes. Our hearts
Are in his army, in his tent.

HIPPOLYTA   In 's bosom.
We have been soldiers, and we cannot weep
When our friends don their helms, or put to sea,
Or tell of babes broached on the lance, or women   20
That have sod their infants in—and after ate
    them—   21
The brine they wept at killing 'em; then if
You stay to see of us such spinsters, we   23
Should hold you here forever.

PIRITHOUS   Peace be to you
As I pursue this war, which shall be then   25
Beyond further requiring.   *Exit Pirithous.*

---

83 **Due audience of** proper attention from   84 **be leaden-footed** answer the summons slowly   85–88 **Phoebus . . . fury** the sun god, when he vented his fury on the horses that drew his chariot (after his son Phaethon had had to be destroyed for misgoverning his father's chariot), merely whispered compared to the loudness of Creon's present anger. (See Ovid, *Metamorphoses*, 2.398 ff.)   90 **appalls** makes pale, terrifies   92 **who** i.e., Theseus. **seal** ratify, carry out   94 **But** were it not that   95–96 **what . . . worth** any man whatever cuts down by one third his own physical valor and moral worth   97–98 **When . . . about** when what he is about to do is turned by his mind into mere dregs of evil. (Arcite is concerned that the dishonor of serving the tyrant Creon will severely hamper their fighting ability and morale.)   98 **Leave that unreasoned** consider it not so deeply   100 **Yet to be** to continue to be.   **were** would be   103 **bounded . . . minute** ordained our final moments on earth   104–105 **or . . . condition?** or is war contingent on Thebes's accepting or refusing certain conditions?   106–107 **The intelligence . . . defier** the tidings of Creon's decision to fight were virtually synchronous with the arrival of Theseus's challenge   108–109 **A quarter . . . come in** possessed of a mere fourth of the honor that his enemy (Theseus) brings to the battle   110–111 **Should . . . purchase** would be therapeutic, like a medical bloodletting, the blood being not wasted but put to profitable use (in defending an honorable cause)

112–113 **Our . . . damage?** but if we lift our hands in battle before we have any stomach for the fight, what damage may the fatal blow do?   116 **becking of our chance** beckoning of our destiny (which will reveal all to us in the fullness of time)
1.3 Location: Athens, at the edge of the city, toward Thebes.
1 **No further** Hippolyta and Emilia have escorted Pirithous to the city gates for his departure; here they must stay behind.   4–5 **an . . . dure** to endure, if need be   5–6 **Speed . . . governors** may he prosper! Abundance (the "overflow of power" in line 4) never hurts those who manage things well and know themselves (since such persons will not be corrupted by the power they have).   7 **drops** i.e., drops of blood   9 **affections** good dispositions   10 **their best-tempered pieces** those persons whom the heavens have made of best temper or quality   12 **speed** success   13 **Bellona** goddess of war   14 **terrene** earthly   20 **broached** spitted, impaled   21 **sod** boiled   23 **spinsters** women involved solely in domestic chores   25 **As** while, as long as   25–26 **which . . . requiring** which war, when I have triumphed, will no longer require your prayers

EMILIA   How his longing   26
  Follows his friend! Since his depart, his sports,   27
  Though craving seriousness and skill, passed
    slightly   28
  His careless execution, where nor gain   29
  Made him regard, or loss consider, but
  Playing one business in his hand, another
  Directing in his head, his mind nurse equal   32
  To these so diff'ring twins. Have you observed him   33
  Since our great lord departed?
HIPPOLYTA   With much labor;
  And I did love him for 't. They two have cabined   35
  In many as dangerous as poor a corner,   36
  Peril and want contending; they have skiffed   37
  Torrents whose roaring tyranny and power   38
  I' th' least of these was dreadful, and they have   39
  Fought out together where Death's self was lodged;   40
  Yet fate hath brought them off. Their knot of love,   41
  Tied, weaved, entangled, with so true, so long,
  And with a finger of so deep a cunning,   43
  May be outworn, never undone. I think   44
  Theseus cannot be umpire to himself,
  Cleaving his conscience into twain and doing
  Each side like justice, which he loves best.
EMILIA   Doubtless   47
  There is a best, and reason has no manners   48
  To say it is not you. I was acquainted
  Once with a time when I enjoyed a playfellow;
  You were at wars when she the grave enriched,
  Who made too proud the bed; took leave o' th'
    moon—   52
  Which then looked pale at parting—when our
    count   53
  Was each eleven.
HIPPOLYTA   'Twas Flavina.
EMILIA   Yes.
  You talk of Pirithous' and Theseus' love.
  Theirs has more ground, is more maturely seasoned,   56
  More buckled with strong judgment, and their
    needs   57
  The one of th' other may be said to water
  Their intertangled roots of love. But I,

And she I sigh and spoke of, were things innocent;   60
  Loved for we did, and, like the elements   61
  That know not what nor why, yet do effect
  Rare issues by their operance, our souls
  Did so to one another. What she liked
  Was then of me approved, what not, condemned—
  No more arraignment. The flower that I would
    pluck   66
  And put between my breasts—O, then but
    beginning
  To swell about the blossom—she would long   68
  Till she had such another, and commit it
  To the like innocent cradle, where, phoenix-like,   70
  They died in perfume. On my head no toy   71
  But was her pattern; her affections—pretty,   72
  Though happily her careless wear—I followed   73
  For my most serious decking. Had mine ear   74
  Stol'n some new air, or at adventure hummed one   75
  From musical coinage, why, it was a note   76
  Whereon her spirits would sojourn—rather dwell
    on—
  And sing it in her slumbers. This rehearsal—   78
  Which seely innocence wots well, comes in   79
  Like old importment's bastard—has this end: 80
  That the true love 'tween maid and maid may be   81
  More than in sex dividual.
HIPPOLYTA   You're out of breath,   82
  And this high-speeded pace is but to say
  That you shall never—like the maid Flavina—
  Love any that's called man.
EMILIA
  I am sure I shall not.
HIPPOLYTA   Now alack, weak sister,
  I must no more believe thee in this point—
  Though in 't I know thou dost believe thyself—
  Than I will trust a sickly appetite,
  That loathes even as it longs. But sure, my sister,
  If I were ripe for your persuasion, you   92
  Have said enough to shake me from the arm
  Of the all-noble Theseus, for whose fortunes
  I will now in and kneel, with great assurance

---

27 his depart Theseus's departure. **his sports** Pirithous's amusements, diversions **28–29 passed . . . execution** received only Pirithous's cursory attention **29 nor** neither **32–33 nurse . . . twins** i.e., evenly divided between his caring for his sports (such as hunting and martial practice) and his longing to be with Theseus **35–37 have . . . contending** have shared soldiers' quarters in many a place that was as dangerous as poorly furnished, the danger and the paucity of comfort contending as to which was more oppressive **37–38 skiffed Torrents** braved turbulent waters in light skiffs **39 I' th' least of these** at their least threatening **40 Fought . . . lodged** battled it out with Death itself in Death's own dominion. (According to legend, Theseus descended with Pirithous, King of the Lapithae, to Hades to help him carry off Persephone, for which crime he suffered imprisonment in Hades until rescued by Hercules.) **41 brought them off** rescued them **43 cunning** skill **44 outworn** worn out (by death) **47 like** equal. **which** i.e., Hippolyta or Pirithous **48 There is a best** Emilia responds to Hippolyta's modest disclaimer by insisting that of course Theseus loves his bride best. **52 Who . . . moon** who was too fine to grace the bed of death; who departed from this mortal sublunary sphere and from the service of the goddess of chastity **53 count** age **56 ground** firm foundation **57 buckled with** restrained by, held in by

60 things innocent innocent young beings **61 for** simply because. **elements** i.e. earth, water, air, and fire, out of which the entire universe was thought to be composed. By their *operance* or operation, the four elements *effect Rare issues* (11. 62–3), i.e., bring about wondrous results in the infinite variety of creation. **66 No more arraignment** without needing any formal accusation **68 To swell . . . blossom** The image applies to the flower and to Emilia's breasts. **70–71 phoenix-like . . . perfume** The phoenix was said to build a nest of "sweet-smelling sticks" that was then set on fire by the sun, consuming the mythical bird to ashes from which arose a new and unique phoenix. An emblem of immortality. **71–72 no toy . . . pattern** no bit of finery that was not emulated by her and imitated in turn from what she wore **72–73 her affections . . . wear** what she chose to wear—pretty even when perchance casual **74 serious decking** carefully thought out attire **75–76 Stol'n . . . coinage** caught some new tune, or randomly hummed an improvized one of my own **78–82 This . . . dividual** this narrative of mine, which blissful innocence recognizes as the imperfect representation (as if it were an illegitimate child) of some meaningful old tale, is meant to show that true love between two young women can be greater than the love between persons of the opposite sex. **92 ripe . . . persuasion** disposed to be won over by your argument

That we, more than his Pirithous, possess
The high throne in his heart.

EMILIA   I am not
Against your faith, yet I continue mine.   *Exeunt.*

❖

1.4   *Cornets. A battle struck within; then a retreat.*
Flourish. Then enter [from one door] Theseus,
victor. [A Herald follows with attendants bearing
Palamon and Arcite. From another door] the three
Queens meet him and fall on their faces before him.

FIRST QUEEN
To thee no star be dark!

SECOND QUEEN   Both heaven and earth   1
Friend thee forever!

THIRD QUEEN   All the good that may
Be wished upon thy head, I cry amen to 't!

THESEUS
Th' impartial gods, who, from the mounted
    heavens,   4
View us their mortal herd, behold who err
And in their time chastise. Go and find out
The bones of your dead lords, and honor them
With treble ceremony; rather than a gap
Should be in their dear rights, we would supply 't.
But those we will depute, which shall invest   10
You in your dignities, and even each thing   11
Our haste does leave imperfect. So adieu,
And heaven's good eyes look on you.
                              Exeunt Queens.
          [Theseus points to Palamon and Arcite.]
                              What are those?

HERALD
Men of great quality, as may be judged   14
By their appointment. Some of Thebes have told 's 15
They are sisters' children, nephews to the King.

THESEUS
By th' helm of Mars, I saw them in the war,
Like to a pair of lions, smeared with prey,
Make lanes in troops aghast. I fixed my note   19
Constantly on them, for they were a mark   20
Worth a god's view. What prisoner was 't that told
    me
When I inquired their names?

HERALD   Wi' leave, they're called   22
Arcite and Palamon.

THESEUS   'Tis right; those, those.
They are not dead?

HERALD
Nor in a state of life. Had they been taken
When their last hurts were given, 'twas possible
They might have been recovered. Yet they breathe
And have the name of men.

THESEUS   Then like men use 'em.   28
The very lees of such, millions of rates,   29
Exceed the wine of others. All our surgeons   30
Convent in their behoof; our richest balms,   31
Rather than niggard, waste; their lives concern us 32
Much more than Thebes is worth. Rather than have
    'em   33
Freed of this plight, and in their morning state, 34
Sound and at liberty, I would 'em dead;   35
But forty-thousandfold we had rather have 'em
Prisoners to us than death. Bear 'em speedily
From our kind air, to them unkind, and minister   38
What man to man may do—for our sake more,
Since I have known frights, fury, friends' behests, 40
Love's provocations, zeal, a mistress' task,   41
Desire of liberty, a fever, madness,   42
Hath set a mark which nature could not reach to   43
Without some imposition, sickness in will   44
O'er-wrestling strength in reason. For our love   45
And great Apollo's mercy, all our best   46
Their best skill tender.—Lead into the city,
Where, having bound things scattered, we will post 48
To Athens 'fore our army.   *Flourish. Exeunt.*

❖

1.5   *Music. Enter the Queens with [attendants bearing]*
the hearses of their knights in a funeral solemnity,
etc.

          [*Song*]

Urns and odors bring away;   1
Vapors, sighs darken the day;

1.4 Location: At the siege of Thebes.
s.d. Cornets trumpet calls signifying battle.   **within** offstage, behind
the stage façade.   **retreat** withdrawal after combat, not necessarily in
flight   **1 no star be dark** may no planet or heavenly body be obscure
and unfavorable   **4 mounted** high   **10–11 But . . . dignities** but I
will deputize others to perform these ceremonies which will clothe
you in the dignities that you and your dead husbands have deserved.
(Having performed his vow to guarantee the burial of the dead kings,
Theseus is eager to return to his marriage.)   **11 even** make even,
complete   **14 quality** rank   **15 appointment** accoutrement, armor
19 Make . . . aghast hew their way through troops that were aghast.
note attention   **20 mark** object of attention   **22 Wi' leave** by your
leave, if you'll allow me to say so

28 have . . . men are nominally still alive   **29 The very . . . rates**
the mere dregs or last physical remnants of such men, by millions of
times   **30–31 All . . . behoof** call together all our surgeons on their
behalf   **32 niggard** save in a niggardly fashion   **33–35 Rather . . .
dead** Theseus would rather these redoubtable warriors on the enemy
side were dead than at liberty and in sound health, as they presumably were this morning before the battle began.   **38 kind . . . unkind**
The air of Athens that Theseus cherishes is dangerous to her enemies,
especially since air was thought to be infectious to open wounds.
(The battle appears to have been fought near Athens, which is not far
from Thebes in any case.)   **40–45 Since . . . reason** Theseus has
known men like Palamon and Arcite to strive for something nearly impossible and quite unreasonable, when their natural common sense is
overwhelmed by some compelling desire to please friends, lovers, or
country, or in response to some equally impulsive emotion.   **44 imposition** compulsion   **46 Apollo** here invoked as god of healing.   **all
our best** let all our best surgeons   **48 post** hasten

1.5. Location: outside Thebes. A marginal note in the quarto specifies
at 1. 26 in the previous scene that the ''hearses'' are to be made
''ready'' for this present scene.
s.d. their knights their husband kings.   **etc.** This notation invites the
use of extras, conventional props, and blocking through which the
acting company is to stage a solemn procession suitable to the weight
of the occasion.   **Song** The song may be sung by the three queens,
but possibly by attendant singers.   **1 odors** incense.   **away** along

Our dole more deadly looks than dying;   3
Balms and gums and heavy cheers,   4
Sacred vials filled with tears,
  And clamors through the wild air flying.

Come all sad and solemn shows
That are quick-eyed Pleasure's foes;
We convent naught else but woes,   9
We convent naught else but woes.

THIRD QUEEN
This funeral path brings to your household's grave;   11
Joy seize on you again; peace sleep with him!

SECOND QUEEN
And this to yours.

FIRST QUEEN   Yours this way. Heavens lend   13
A thousand differing ways to one sure end.

THIRD QUEEN
This world's a city full of straying streets,
And death's the market-place where each one
  meets.   16
  Exeunt severally.

❖

2.1   *Enter Jailer and Wooer.*

JAILER   I may depart with little while I live; something I   1
may cast to you, not much. Alas, the prison I keep,   2
though it be for great ones, yet they seldom come;
before one salmon you shall take a number of minnows. I am given out to be better lined than it can   5
appear to me report is a true speaker. I would I were   6
really that I am delivered to be. Marry, what I   7
have—be it what it will—I will assure upon my   8
daughter at the day of my death.

WOOER   Sir, I demand no more than your own offer,
and I will estate your daughter in what I have   11
promised.

JAILER   Well, we will talk more of this when the   13
solemnity is past. But have you a full promise of her?   14
When that shall be seen, I tender my consent.   15

WOOER   I have, sir.

Enter [Jailer's] Daughter [with rushes].

Here she comes.

JAILER [*to Daughter*]   Your friend and I have chanced
to name you here, upon the old business; but no

more of that now. So soon as the court hurry is over
we will have an end of it. I' th' meantime look   21
tenderly to the two prisoners. I can tell you they are   22
princes.

JAILER'S DAUGHTER   These strewings are for their cham-   24
ber. 'Tis pity they are in prison, and 'twere pity they   25
should be out. I do think they have patience to make   26
any adversity ashamed. The prison itself is proud   27
of 'em, and they have all the world in their chamber.   28

JAILER   They are famed to be a pair of absolute men.   29

JAILER'S DAUGHTER   By my troth, I think fame but stam-   30
mers 'em; they stand a grece above the reach of report.   31

JAILER   I heard them reported in the battle to be the   32
only doers.   33

JAILER'S DAUGHTER   Nay, most likely, for they are
noble suff'rers. I marvel how they would have looked
had they been victors, that with such a constant
nobility enforce a freedom out of bondage, making
misery their mirth and affliction a toy to jest at.   38

JAILER   Do they so?

JAILER'S DAUGHTER   It seems to me they have no more
sense of their captivity than I of ruling Athens. They
eat well, look merrily, discourse of many things, but
nothing of their own restraint and disasters. Yet some
time a divided sigh, martyred as 'twere i' th' deliver-   44
ance, will break from one of them, when the other
presently gives it so sweet a rebuke that I could   46
wish myself a sigh to be so chid, or at least a sigher to
be comforted.

WOOER   I never saw 'em.

JAILER   The Duke himself came privately in the night,   50
and so did they; what the reason of it is, I know not.   51

Enter Palamon and Arcite above [in shackles].

Look, yonder they are. That's Arcite looks out.   52

JAILER'S DAUGHTER   No, sir, no, that's Palamon. Arcite
is the lower of the twain; you may perceive a part of   54
him.   55

JAILER   Go to, leave your pointing. They would not   56
make us their object. Out of their sight!   57

JAILER'S DAUGHTER   It is a holiday to look on them,
Lord, the diff'rence of men!   59
  Exeunt [Jailer, Wooer, and Daughter].

❖

3 Our . . . dying our mourning has a more grim appearance than
death itself   **4 gums** resins burned to produce incense.   **heavy cheers**
sad countenances   **9 convent** (1) assemble (2) suit   **11 brings** leads.
household's grave family monument and burial plot   **13 And this** and
this path   **16 s.d. severally** separately. The funeral procession divides
into three, each queen going through a stage door accompanied by
the hearse of her dead husband.
2.1. Location: Athens. A prison garden, on the main stage, with the
prison cell above in the theater gallery.
1 depart with part with, give away   **2 cast to** confer upon (in the way
of dowry)   **5 given out** reputed.   **lined** with purse crammed full of
wealth   **6 report** rumor   **7 that** that which.   **delivered** rumored,
said.   **Marry** an oath, originally "by the Virgin Mary"   **8 assure**
guarantee to settle   **11 estate** settle an estate upon   **13–14 the solemnity** i.e., the royal wedding of Theseus and Hippolyta; the "court
hurry" of 1. 20   **14 of** from   **15 seen** understood to have occurred.
tender offer

21–22 look tenderly to tend carefully   **24 strewings** rushes or reeds
strewn on the floor and changed from time to time   **25 pity . . . pity**
The Jailer's Daughter takes pity on them as prisoners, but would hate
to see them set free.   **26–27 to make . . . ashamed** to put to shame
any adversity by their noble resolution   **28 they have . . . chamber**
i.e., their friendship is a world unto itself   **29 absolute men** complete
gentlemen   **30–31 stammers** describes only haltingly   **31 grece** step.
They stand above anything reputation can say of them.   **32–33 the
only doers** the ones whose brave feats immeasurably outdid those of
any others   **38 toy** trifle   **44 divided** broken, incomplete   **46 presently** instantly   **50 privately** secretly.   **51 s.d. above** in the gallery over
the stage   **52 looks out** who looks out   **54 lower** less tall   **54–55
you . . . of him** i.e., you can partly see Arcite through the prison
window   **56 Go to** i.e., "Come, come, enough of that"
56–57 They . . . object they have no wish to see us   **59 the
diff'rence of men** how much finer some men are than others

2.2

PALAMON
 How do you, noble cousin?

ARCITE   How do you, sir?

PALAMON
 Why, strong enough to laugh at misery
 And bear the chance of war; yet we are prisoners
 I fear forever, cousin.

ARCITE   I believe it,
 And to that destiny have patiently
 Laid up my hour to come.

PALAMON   O cousin Arcite,   6
 Where is Thebes now? Where is our noble country?
 Where are our friends and kindreds? Never more
 Must we behold those comforts, never see
 The hardy youths strive for the games of honor,
 Hung with the painted favors of their ladies,   11
 Like tall ships under sail; then start amongst 'em
 And, as an east wind, leave 'em all behind us,
 Like lazy clouds, whilst Palamon and Arcite,
 Even in the wagging of a wanton leg,   15
 Outstripped the people's praises, won the garlands
 Ere they have time to wish 'em ours. O, never
 Shall we two exercise, like twins of honor,
 Our arms again, and feel our fiery horses   19
 Like proud seas under us. Our good swords, now—
 Better the red-eyed god of war nev'r wore—   21
 Ravished our sides, like age must run to rust   22
 And deck the temples of those gods that hate us;
 These hands shall never draw 'em out like lightning
 To blast whole armies more.

ARCITE   No, Palamon,   25
 Those hopes are prisoners with us. Here we are,
 And here the graces of our youths must wither
 Like a too-timely spring. Here age must find us,   28
 And—which is heaviest, Palamon—unmarried.   29
 The sweet embraces of a loving wife,
 Loaden with kisses, armed with thousand Cupids,   31
 Shall never clasp our necks; no issue know us;   32
 No figures of ourselves shall we ev'r see   33
 To glad our age, and, like young eagles, teach 'em   34
 Boldly to gaze against bright arms, and say   35
 "Remember what your fathers were, and conquer!"
 The fair-eyed maids shall weep our banishments
 And in their songs curse ever-blinded Fortune,
 Till she for shame see what a wrong she has done
 To youth and nature. This is all our world;

We shall know nothing here but one another;
Hear nothing but the clock that tells our woes.   42
The vine shall grow, but we shall never see it;
Summer shall come, and with her all delights,
But dead-cold winter must inhabit here still.

PALAMON
 'Tis too true, Arcite. To our Theban hounds
 That shook the agèd forest with their echoes
 No more now must we hollo; no more shake   48
 Our pointed javelins, whilst the angry swine   49
 Flies like a Parthian quiver from our rages,   50
 Struck with our well-steeled darts. All valiant uses— 51
 The food and nourishment of noble minds—
 In us two here shall perish; we shall die—
 Which is the curse of honor—lastly,   54
 Children of grief and ignorance.   55

ARCITE   Yet, cousin,
 Even from the bottom of these miseries,
 From all that fortune can inflict upon us,
 I see two comforts rising, two mere blessings,   58
 If the gods please, to hold here a brave patience,
 And the enjoying of our griefs together.
 Whilst Palamon is with me, let me perish
 If I think this our prison.

PALAMON   Certainly
 'Tis a main goodness, cousin, that our fortunes   63
 Were twinned together. 'Tis most true, two souls   64
 Put in two noble bodies, let 'em suffer   65
 The gall of hazard, so they grow together,   66
 Will never sink; they must not, say they could.   67
 A willing man dies sleeping and all's done.   68

ARCITE
 Shall we make worthy uses of this place
 That all men hate so much?

PALAMON   How, gentle cousin?   70

ARCITE
 Let's think this prison holy sanctuary,
 To keep us from corruption of worse men.
 We are young and yet desire the ways of honor
 That liberty and common conversation,   74
 The poison of pure spirits, might, like women,   75
 Woo us to wander from. What worthy blessing
 Can be but our imaginations   77
 May make it ours? And here being thus together,   78
 We are an endless mine to one another.   79
 We are one another's wife, ever begetting

2.2. Palamon and Arcite probably remain onstage in a continuation of scene 1, but since the quarto explicitly has them "*Exeunt*" and then "*Enter . . . in prison*," the Q scene division is retained.
6 Laid up . . . come devoted the rest of my life   **11 painted favors** brightly colored tokens of favor in love, such as a scarf or glove **15 Even . . . leg** i.e., with seemingly effortless motion, sportively **19 arms** armor, weapons   **21 red-eyed god of war** Mars, red-eyed with fury   **22 Ravished** seized violently from   **25 blast** blight, destroy **28 too-timely** prematurely blooming   **29 heaviest** most burdensome **31 Loaden** loaded   **32 issue** offspring   **33 figures** likenesses   **34 glad** gladden   **34–35 like . . . arms** we will never be able to teach our children to look fearlessly at the arms of opponents, much as eagles are reputed to be able to gaze directly at the sun

42 tells counts   **48 hollo** cry encouragement   **49 swine** wild boar **50 Parthian** The Parthians, fierce warriors, were famed for their ability to shoot while in real or feigned retreat.   **51 uses** pursuits (such as hunting)   **54 lastly** finally   **55 Children . . . ignorance** i.e., sadly and forgotten   **58 mere** unmixed   **63 main goodness** major blessing, piece of good luck   **64 twinned** The quarto spelling, *twyn'd*, suggests (1) paired inseparably (2) entwined.   **65–66 let . . . hazard** even if they should suffer the rubs of misfortune   **66 so** provided that   **67 say** even if   **68 A willing . . . sleeping** one who is stoically prepared for death dies as though going gently to sleep   **70 gentle** well-born, gracious   **74 common conversation** indiscriminate dealings with people **75 like women** as if they were women. (Liberty and common conversation are personified as temptresses wooing the young men away from honor.)   **77–78 Can . . . ours?** can there be that in our imaginations we cannot make ours? Are we not able to possess any blessing in our imaginations?   **79 mine** resource

New births of love; we are father, friends,
  acquaintance;
We are in one another, families;
I am your heir, and you are mine. This place
Is our inheritance; no hard oppressor
Dare take this from us. Here, with a little patience,
We shall live long and loving. No surfeits seek us;
The hand of war hurts none here, nor the seas
Swallow their youth. Were we at liberty,
A wife might part us lawfully, or business;
Quarrels consume us; envy of ill men   90
Crave our acquaintance. I might sicken, cousin,   91
Where you should never know it, and so perish
Without your noble hand to close mine eyes,
Or prayers to the gods. A thousand chances,
Were we from hence, would sever us.
PALAMON   You have made me—
I thank you, cousin Arcite—almost wanton   96
With my captivity. What a misery
It is to live abroad, and everywhere!   98
'Tis like a beast, methinks. I find the court here,   99
I am sure, a more content; and all those pleasures   100
That woo the wills of men to vanity
I see through now, and am sufficient
To tell the world 'tis but a gaudy shadow
That old Time, as he passes by, takes with him.
What had we been, old in the court of Creon,   105
Where sin is justice, lust and ignorance
The virtues of the great ones? Cousin Arcite,
Had not the loving gods found this place for us,
We had died as they do, ill old men, unwept,   109
And had their epitaphs, the people's curses.   110
Shall I say more?
ARCITE   I would hear you still.
PALAMON   Ye shall.
  Is there record of any two that loved
  Better than we do, Arcite?
ARCITE   Sure there cannot.
PALAMON
  I do not think it possible our friendship
  Should ever leave us.
ARCITE   Till our deaths it cannot.

Enter Emilia and her Woman [below].

And after death our spirits shall be led
To those that love eternally.

  [*Palamon sees Emilia and is speechless.*]

                              Speak on, sir. 117
EMILIA [*as they gather flowers*]
  This garden has a world of pleasures in 't.
  What flower is this?

WOMAN   'Tis called narcissus, madam.   119
EMILIA
  That was a fair boy, certain, but a fool   120
  To love himself. Were there not maids enough?   121
ARCITE [*to Palamon*]
  Pray, forward.
PALAMON   Yes.
EMILIA [*to her Woman*]   Or were they all hard-hearted? 122
WOMAN
  They could not be to one so fair.
EMILIA   Thou wouldst not.
WOMAN
  I think I should not, madam.
EMILIA   That's a good wench;
  But take heed to your kindness, though.
WOMAN   Why, madam?
EMILIA
  Men are mad things.
ARCITE [*to Palamon*]   Will ye go forward, cousin?   126
EMILIA [*to her Woman*]
  Canst not thou work such flowers in silk, wench?
WOMAN   Yes. 127
EMILIA
  I'll have a gown full of 'em, and of these.
  This is a pretty color; will 't not do
  Rarely upon a skirt, wench?
WOMAN   Dainty, madam.   130
ARCITE [*to Palamon*]
  Cousin, cousin, how do you, sir? Why, Palamon!
PALAMON
  Never tell now was I in prison, Arcite.
ARCITE
  Why, what's the matter, man?
PALAMON [*indicating Emilia*]   Behold and wonder!
  By heaven, she is a goddess.
ARCITE [*seeing Emilia*]   Ha!
PALAMON   Do reverence;
  She is a goddess, Arcite.
EMILIA [*to her Woman*]   Of all flowers
  Methinks a rose is best.
WOMAN   Why, gentle madam?
EMILIA
  It is the very emblem of a maid;
  For when the west wind courts her gently,
  How modestly she blows, and paints the sun   139
  With her chaste blushes! When the north comes
    near her,   140
  Rude and impatient, then, like chastity,
  She locks her beauties in her bud again,
  And leaves him to base briers.

90–91 envy . . . acquaintance evil men might enviously seek us out (and thus drive us apart)   96 wanton sportive   98 abroad at liberty   99 the court i.e., the court that we create for ourselves, as distinguished from the courts of Creon or Theseus   100 more greater   105 What . . . old what would we have been like, if we had grown old   109 they i.e., the "great ones" of l. 107.   ill evil   110 their epitaphs i.e., the same remembrance they got   117 To . . . eternally to those lovers whose spirits dwell in the Elysian Fields

119–121 narcissus . . . himself As punishment for his refusal to return the love of the nymph Echo, Narcissus fell fruitlessly in love with his own image in a fountain; eventually he was transformed into the flower that bears his name (Ovid, *Metamorphoses*, 3).   122 forward continue with what you were saying. (Also in l. 126.)   126 Men are mad things Emilia warns her Woman that a kindly disposition toward handsome young men, however indicative of goodness of heart, may get a young woman into trouble.   127 work embroider   130 Rarely excellently   139 she blows . . . sun the rose blooms, and adds color to the sun's rays   140 north north wind   143 And . . . briers and leaves the north wind with nothing but her briers

WOMAN   Yet, good madam,   143
  Sometimes her modesty will blow so far   144
  She falls for 't; a maid,   145
  If she have any honor, would be loath
  To take example by her.
EMILIA   Thou art wanton.   147
ARCITE [to Palamon]
  She is wondrous fair.
PALAMON   She is all the beauty extant.
EMILIA [to her Woman]
  The sun grows high; let's walk in. Keep these
    flowers;
  We'll see how near art can come near their colors.
  I am wondrous merry-hearted; I could laugh now.   151
WOMAN
  I could lie down, I am sure.
EMILIA   And take one with you?   152
WOMAN
  That's as we bargain, madam.
EMILIA   Well, agree then.

        Exeunt Emilia and [her] Woman.

PALAMON
  What think you of this beauty?
ARCITE   'Tis a rare one.
PALAMON
  Is 't but a rare one?
ARCITE   Yes, a matchless beauty.
PALAMON
  Might not a man well lose himself and love her?
ARCITE
  I cannot tell what you have done; I have,
  Beshrew mine eyes for 't! Now I feel my shackles.   158
PALAMON You love her, then?
ARCITE Who would not?
PALAMON And desire her?
ARCITE Before my liberty.
PALAMON I saw her first.
ARCITE That's nothing.
PALAMON But it shall be.
ARCITE I saw her too.
PALAMON Yes, but you must not love her.
ARCITE
  I will not, as you do, to worship her
  As she is heavenly and a blessèd goddess.
  I love her as a woman, to enjoy her;
  So both may love.
PALAMON You shall not love at all.
ARCITE Not love at all? Who shall deny me?
PALAMON
  I, that first saw her; I, that took possession
  First with mine eye of all those beauties
  In her revealed to mankind. If thou lov'st her,

  Or entertain'st a hope to blast my wishes,   177
  Thou art a traitor, Arcite, and a fellow
  False as thy title to her. Friendship, blood,
  And all the ties between us I disclaim
  If thou once think upon her.
ARCITE   Yes, I love her,
  And if the lives of all my name lay on it,   182
  I must do so. I love her with my soul;
  If that will lose ye, farewell, Palamon.
  I say again I love, and, in loving her, maintain
  I am as worthy and as free a lover,   186
  And have as just a title to her beauty,
  As any Palamon or any living
  That is a man's son.
PALAMON   Have I called thee friend?
ARCITE
  Yes, and have found me so. Why are you moved
    thus?   190
  Let me deal coldly with you. Am not I   191
  Part of your blood, part of your soul? You have told
    me
  That I was Palamon, and you were Arcite.
PALAMON   Yes.
ARCITE
  Am not I liable to those affections,   194
  Those joys, griefs, angers, fears, my friend shall
    suffer?
PALAMON
  Ye may be.
ARCITE   Why then would you deal so cunningly,
  So strangely, so unlike a noble kinsman,
  To love alone? Speak truly, do you think me
  Unworthy of her sight?
PALAMON   No, but unjust
  If thou pursue that sight.
ARCITE   Because another
  First sees the enemy, shall I stand still
  And let mine honor down, and never charge?
PALAMON
  Yes, if he be but one.
ARCITE   But say that one   203
  Had rather combat me?
PALAMON   Let that one say so,   204
  And use thy freedom; else, if thou pursuest her,   205
  Be as that cursèd man that hates his country,
  A branded villain.
ARCITE   You are mad.
PALAMON   I must be.
  Till thou art worthy, Arcite, it concerns me;   208
  And in this madness if I hazard thee   209
  And take thy life, I deal but truly.

144–145 **Sometimes . . . for 't** The Woman observes that the rose eventually blooms so openly, in despite of modesty, that it goes past its prime and decays. (*Blow* can suggest being puffed up with vanity.) A woman following such an example might well fall into temptation. 147 **Thou art wanton** you're being witty 151–152 **laugh . . . lie down** The Woman continues the sexual joking with her reference to a card game called "Laugh and lay (or lie) down." 152 **one** someone, a man 158 **Beshrew** i.e., may the devil take (a mild curse)

177 **blast** blight, destroy 182 **name** family. **lay** depended 186 **free** noble 190 **moved** angered 191 **coldly** calmly 194 **affections** feelings 203 **but one** The code of chivalry would forbid Arcite to join Palamon in engaging with a single opponent, two against one. 204–205 **Let . . . freedom** If that opponent were to indicate a preference for engaging with you, not me, you could go ahead and exercise your free choice by engaging with that person. (The "opponent" in this argument has become Emilia, not a hypothetical warrior.) 208 **Till . . . me** i.e., until you behave worthily to me once again, by forgoing your claim to Emilia, the issue engages my honor 209 **hazard thee** put your life at hazard

ARCITE   Fie, sir!
You play the child extremely. I will love her,
I must, I ought to do so, and I dare,
And all this justly.
PALAMON   O, that now, that now   213
Thy false self and thy friend had but this fortune   214
To be one hour at liberty, and grasp   215
Our good swords in our hands! I would quickly
    teach thee
What 'twere to filch affection from another.
Thou art baser in it than a cutpurse.
Put but thy head out of this window more,
And, as I have a soul, I'll nail thy life to 't.   220
ARCITE
Thou dar'st not, fool, thou canst not, thou art feeble.
Put my head out? I'll throw my body out
And leap the garden, when I see her next,   223

            Enter Jailer [above].

And pitch between her arms to anger thee.   224
PALAMON
No more; the keeper's coming. I shall live
To knock thy brains out with my shackles.
ARCITE   Do.
JAILER
By your leave, gentlemen.
PALAMON   Now, honest keeper?
JAILER
Lord Arcite, you must presently to th' Duke.
The cause I know not yet.
ARCITE   I am ready, keeper.
JAILER
Prince Palamon, I must awhile bereave you
Of your fair cousin's company.
                Exeunt Arcite and Jailer.
PALAMON   And me too,
Even when you please, of life. Why is he sent for?
It may be he shall marry her; he's goodly,   233
And like enough the Duke hath taken notice   234
Both of his blood and body. But his falsehood!   235
Why should a friend be treacherous? If that
Get him a wife so noble and so fair,
Let honest men ne'er love again. Once more
I would but see this fair one. Blessèd garden,
And fruit and flowers more blessèd, that still
    blossom
As her bright eyes shine on ye! Would I were,
For all the fortune of my life hereafter,
Yon little tree, yon blooming apricot.
How I would spread and fling my wanton arms
In at her window! I would bring her fruit
Fit for the gods to feed on; youth and pleasure
Still as she tasted should be doubled on her,   247
And, if she be not heavenly, I would make her   248

So near the gods in nature they should fear her;

            Enter Jailer [above].

And then I am sure she would love me.—How
    now, keeper?
Where's Arcite?
JAILER   Banished. Prince Pirithous
Obtained his liberty; but never more,
Upon his oath and life, must he set foot
Upon this kingdom.
PALAMON   He's a blessèd man.
He shall see Thebes again, and call to arms
The bold young men that, when he bids 'em charge,
Fall on like fire. Arcite shall have a fortune,   257
If he dare make himself a worthy lover,
Yet in the field to strike a battle for her;   259
And if he lose her then, he's a cold coward.
How bravely may he bear himself to win her
If he be noble Arcite—thousand ways!
Were I at liberty, I would do things
Of such a virtuous greatness that this lady,
This blushing virgin, should take manhood to her   265
And seek to ravish me.
JAILER   My lord, for you
I have this charge too.
PALAMON   To discharge my life.   267
JAILER
No, but from this place to remove your lordship;
The windows are too open.
PALAMON   Devils take 'em
That are so envious to me! Prithee kill me.
JAILER
And hang for 't afterward.
PALAMON   By this good light,
Had I a sword I would kill thee.
JAILER   Why, my lord?
PALAMON
Thou bring'st such pelting scurvy news continually, 273
Thou art not worthy life. I will not go.
JAILER
Indeed you must, my lord.
PALAMON   May I see the garden?
JAILER
No.
PALAMON   Then I am resolved, I will not go.
JAILER
I must constrain you then; and, for you are
    dangerous,   277
I'll clap more irons on you.
PALAMON   Do, good keeper.
I'll shake 'em so, ye shall not sleep;
I'll make ye a new morris. Must I go?   280

213–215 O . . . liberty would that you and I had but one hour of
freedom from this prison   220 to 't i.e., to the window frame. Palamon will not allow Arcite to gaze any more at Emilia in the garden
below their window.   223 leap leap down into   224 pitch thrust myself   233 goodly handsome   234 like likely   235 blood breeding,
lineage   247 Still as whenever   248 be not is not already

257 Fall on begin the battle.   fortune chance   259 strike a battle
fight a battle, engage the enemy force   265 take manhood to her go
on the offensive, like a male. (Palamon pictures himself here as the
raped object of desire.)   267 discharge my life release me from life
(playing sardonically on the Jailer's charge, ''order,'' and on the idea
of discharging a firearm)   273 pelting paltry, contemptible   277 for
since   280 morris a morris dance, in which the dancers wore bells
around their legs; the sound might be thought to resemble the clank-
ing of chains

JAILER
There is no remedy.

PALAMON   Farewell, kind window;
May rude wind never hurt thee.—O my lady,
If ever thou hast felt what sorrow was,
Dream how I suffer!—Come, now bury me.

Exeunt Palamon and Jailer.

❖

2.3   *Enter Arcite.*

ARCITE
Banished the kingdom? 'Tis a benefit,
A mercy I must thank 'em for; but banished
The free enjoying of that face I die for,   3
O, 'twas a studied punishment, a death   4
Beyond imagination—such a vengeance
That, were I old and wicked, all my sins
Could never pluck upon me. Palamon,
Thou hast the start now; thou shalt stay and see
Her bright eyes break each morning 'gainst thy
    window
And let in life into thee; thou shalt feed
Upon the sweetness of a noble beauty
That nature nev'r exceeded, nor nev'r shall.
Good gods, what happiness has Palamon!
Twenty to one, he'll come to speak to her,   14
And if she be as gentle as she's fair,
I know she's his; he has a tongue will tame
Tempests and make the wild rocks wanton.
Come what can come,
The worst is death. I will not leave the kingdom.
I know mine own is but a heap of ruins,   20
And no redress there; if I go, he has her.
I am resolved another shape shall make me   22
Or end my fortunes. Either way I am happy;
I'll see her, and be near her or no more.   24

*Enter four Country people and one with a garland
before them. [Arcite stands apart.]*

FIRST COUNTRYMAN   My masters, I'll be there, that's   25
certain.

SECOND COUNTRYMAN   And I'll be there.

THIRD COUNTRYMAN   And I.

FOURTH COUNTRYMAN   Why then, have with ye, boys!   29
'Tis but a chiding. Let the plough play today; I'll   30
tickle 't out of the jades' tails tomorrow.   31

FIRST COUNTRYMAN   I am sure to have my wife as
jealous as a turkey; but that's all one. I'll go through,   33
let her mumble.

SECOND COUNTRYMAN   Clap her aboard tomorrow   35
night, and stow her, and all's made up again.

THIRD COUNTRYMAN   Ay, do but put a fescue in her   37
fist, and you shall see her take a new lesson out and be   38
a good wench. Do we all hold against the maying?   39

FOURTH COUNTRYMAN   Hold? What should ail us?   40

THIRD COUNTRYMAN   Arcas will be there.

SECOND COUNTRYMAN   And Sennois and Rycas, and
three better lads nev'r danced under green tree; and
ye know what wenches, ha! But will the dainty   44
dominie, the schoolmaster, keep touch, do you think?   45
For he does all, ye know.   46

THIRD COUNTRYMAN   He'll eat a hornbook e'er he fail.   47
Go to, the matter's too far driven between him and the   48
tanner's daughter to let slip now; and she must see the
Duke, and she must dance too.

FOURTH COUNTRYMAN   Shall we be lusty?   51

SECOND COUNTRYMAN   All the boys in Athens blow   52
wind i' th' breech on 's! And here I'll be and there   53
I'll be, for our town, and here again and there again.
Ha, boys, hey for the weavers!

FIRST COUNTRYMAN   This must be done i' th' woods.

FOURTH COUNTRYMAN   O, pardon me.   57

SECOND COUNTRYMAN   By any means, our thing of   58
learning says so; where he himself will edify the Duke   59
most parlously in our behalfs. He's excellent i' th'   60
woods; bring him to th' plains, his learning makes no   61
cry.   62

THIRD COUNTRYMAN   We'll see the sports, then every
man to 's tackle. And, sweet companions, let's re-   64
hearse, by any means, before the ladies see us, and do
sweetly, and God knows what may come on 't.   66

FOURTH COUNTRYMAN   Content. The sports once
ended, we'll perform. Away, boys, and hold!   68

[They start to go.]

ARCITE *[coming forward]*   By your leaves, honest   69
friends; pray you, whither go you?

FOURTH COUNTRYMAN   Whither? Why, what a question's that?

ARCITE   Yes, 'tis a question to me that know not.

THIRD COUNTRYMAN   To the games, my friend.

---

35 Clap her aboard board her. The sexual wordplay continues in *stow
her,* "place your cargo belowdecks in her," and in *all's made up:* (1)
all's supplied for a journey (2) the quarrel is patched up (3) the hole is
stopped up.   **37 a fescue** a pointer used in pointing out letters for
children learning to read   **38 take . . . out** learn a new lesson
39 hold against the maying hold to our intention with respect to the
May Day celebration   **40 ail us** prevent us from taking part   **44–
45 dainty dominie** fastidious schoolmaster   **45 keep touch** keep faith,
keep his promise   **46 he does all** all depends on him   **47 hornbook**
an alphabet etc. protected by a layer of cowhorn or similar animal
horn cut thin enough to be virtually transparent, used in classrooms
48 the matter's . . . driven things have gone too far   **51 lusty** jolly,
lively   **52–53 All . . . on 's** i.e., may all the lads of Athens pant and
puff as they run behind us   **57 O, pardon me** i.e., I beg to differ
58 By any means i.e., in the woods, certainly   **58–59 thing of learning** i.e., schoolmaster   **60 parlously** cleverly   **61 plains** open country   **61–62 makes no cry** is awed into muteness (like dogs no longer
yelping after their prey). The Second Countryman suggests that the
schoolmaster is a yokel who would look out of place away from their
rustic location.   **64 tackle** i.e., bells and other gear for the morris
dance   **66 on 't** of it   **68 hold** hold to your promise   **69 honest**
worthy

2.3. Location: Outside Athens.
3 die would die   **4 studied** premeditated   **14 come** find occasion
20 mine own my own kingdom (Thebes)   **22 another shape** i.e., a
disguise   **24 no more** be no more, perish   **25 masters** sirs. (Used often among workmen and citizens.)   **29–30 have . . . chiding** I'll join
you, boys; the worst thing that can happen to me is a scolding (for
not ploughing).   **30–31 I'll . . . tomorrow** i.e., I'll make up for lost
time tomorrow by whipping the old horses into working faster.
33 that's all one no matter

SECOND COUNTRYMAN [*to Arcite*]
  Where were you bred, you know it not?
ARCITE   Not far, sir.
  Are there such games today?
FIRST COUNTRYMAN   Yes, marry, are there,
  And such as you never saw. The Duke himself
  Will be in person there.
ARCITE   What pastimes are they?
SECOND COUNTRYMAN
  Wrestling and running. [*To his companions*] 'Tis a
    pretty fellow.
THIRD COUNTRYMAN [*to Arcite*]
  Thou wilt not go along?
ARCITE   Not yet, sir.
FOURTH COUNTRYMAN   Well, sir,
  Take your own time.—Come, boys.
FIRST COUNTRYMAN   My mind misgives me,   81
  This fellow has a vengeance trick o' th' hip;   82
  Mark how his body's made for 't.
SECOND COUNTRYMAN   I'll be hanged, though,
  If he dare venture. Hang him, plum porridge!   84
  He wrestle? He roast eggs! Come, let's be gone,
    lads.   85
                        Exeunt four. [*Arcite remains.*]
ARCITE
  This is an offered opportunity
  I durst not wish for. Well I could have wrestled—   87
  The best men called it excellent—and run
  Swifter than wind upon a field of corn,   89
  Curling the wealthy ears, never flew. I'll venture, 90
  And in some poor disguise be there. Who knows
  Whether my brows may not be girt with garlands,
  And happiness prefer me to a place   93
  Where I may ever dwell in sight of her?
                                        Exit Arcite.

2.4   *Enter Jailer's Daughter, alone.*

JAILER'S DAUGHTER
  Why should I love this gentleman? 'Tis odds   1
  He never will affect me. I am base,   2
  My father the mean keeper of his prison,   3
  And he a prince. To marry him is hopeless,
  To be his whore is witless. Out upon 't,
  What pushes are we wenches driven to   6
  When fifteen once has found us! First I saw him;   7
  I, seeing, thought he was a goodly man;

He has as much to please a woman in him—
If he please to bestow it so—as ever
These eyes yet looked on. Next I pitied him,
And so would any young wench, o' my conscience,
That ever dreamed, or vowed her maidenhead   13
To a young handsome man. Then I loved him,
Extremely loved him, infinitely loved him,
And yet he had a cousin, fair as he too.
But in my heart was Palamon, and there,
Lord, what a coil he keeps! To hear him   18
Sing in an evening, what a heaven it is!
And yet his songs are sad ones. Fairer spoken
Was never gentleman. When I come in
To bring him water in a morning, first
He bows his noble body, then salutes me thus: 23
"Fair, gentle maid, good morrow; may thy goodness
Get thee a happy husband." Once he kissed me;
I loved my lips the better ten days after.
Would he would do so ev'ry day! He grieves much,
And me as much to see his misery.
What should I do to make him know I love him?
For I would fain enjoy him. Say I ventured   30
To set him free? What says the law then? [*She snaps
  her fingers*] Thus much
For law or kindred! I will do it,
And this night; ere tomorrow he shall love me.
                                        Exit.

❖

2.5   [*A*] *short flourish of cornets, and shouts within.
        Enter Theseus, Hippolyta, Pirithous, Emilia,
        Arcite* [*disguised*] *with a garland, etc.*

THESEUS [*to Arcite*]
  You have done worthily. I have not seen,
  Since Hercules, a man of tougher sinews.
  Whate'er you are, you run the best and wrestle   3
  That these times can allow.
ARCITE   I am proud to please you. 4
THESEUS
  What country bred you?
ARCITE   This; but far off, prince.
THESEUS
  Are you a gentleman?
ARCITE   My father said so,
  And to those gentle uses gave me life.   7
THESEUS
  Are you his heir?
ARCITE   His youngest, sir.
THESEUS   Your father
  Sure is a happy sire, then. What proves you?   9

81–82 **My mind . . . hip** I'm worried that this fellow may have a
fearsome ability to catch his opponent on the hip in wrestling
84 **plum porridge** i.e., weakling (literally, stewed fruit)   85 **He roast
eggs!** i.e., he might as soon turn cook as wrestler   87 **could have
wrestled** was expert in wrestling   89 **corn** grain   90 **wealthy** rich,
plentiful.   **never flew** Arcite seemed to fly as he raced across a grainfield, not touching the ground.   93 **happiness prefer** good fortune
advance
2.4. Location: Somewhere near the prison.
1 **'Tis odds** the likelihood is that   2 **affect** love.   **base** of low social
station   3 **mean** lowly   6 **pushes** exertions, extremes   7 **fifteen** the
age of fifteen

13 **vowed** dedicated   18 **coil he keeps** tumult he stirs up   23 **salutes**
greets   30 **fain** willingly
2.5. Location: The arena for wrestling, running etc., near Athens.
3 **run . . . wrestle** are the best runner and wrestler   4 **allow** boast of
7 **to . . . life** my father bred me to the accomplishments of a gentleman   9 **What proves you?** What accomplishments do you have to
demonstrate your gentlemanly breeding?

ARCITE
A little of all noble qualities.   10
I could have kept a hawk and well have hallooed   11
To a deep cry of dogs; I dare not praise   12
My feat in horsemanship, yet they that knew me   13
Would say it was my best piece; last, and greatest, 14
I would be thought a soldier.

THESEUS   You are perfect.   15

PIRITHOUS
Upon my soul, a proper man.

EMILIA   He is so.   16

PIRITHOUS [to Hippolyta]
How do you like him, lady?

HIPPOLYTA   I admire him.   17
I have not seen so young a man, so noble—
If he say true—of his sort.

EMILIA   Believe,   19
His mother was a wondrous handsome woman;
His face, methinks, goes that way.

HIPPOLYTA   But his body
And fiery mind illustrate a brave father.

PIRITHOUS
Mark how his virtue, like a hidden sun,   23
Breaks through his baser garments.

HIPPOLYTA   He's well got, sure.   24

THESEUS [to Arcite]
What made you seek this place, sir?

ARCITE   Noble Theseus,
To purchase name, and do my ablest service   26
To such a well-found wonder as thy worth;   27
For only in thy court, of all the world,
Dwells fair-eyed honor.

PIRITHOUS   All his words are worthy.

THESEUS [to Arcite]
Sir, we are much indebted to your travel,   30
Nor shall you lose your wish.—Pirithous,
Dispose of this fair gentleman.

PIRITHOUS   Thanks, Theseus.   32
[To Arcite] Whate'er you are, you're mine, and I shall
  give you
To a most noble service, to this lady,
This bright young virgin; pray observe her
  goodness.   35
You have honored her fair birthday with your
  virtues,
And as your due you're hers. Kiss her fair hand, sir.

ARCITE
Sir, you're a noble giver. [To Emilia] Dearest beauty,
Thus let me seal my vowed faith.
                                              [He kisses her hand.]

When your servant,
Your most unworthy creature, but offends you,   40
Command him die, he shall.

EMILIA   That were too cruel.
If you deserve well, sir, I shall soon see 't.
You're mine, and somewhat better than your rank
I'll use you.

PIRITHOUS [to Arcite]
I'll see you furnished, and because you say
You are a horseman, I must needs entreat you
This afternoon to ride—but 'tis a rough one.   47

ARCITE
I like him better, prince; I shall not then
Freeze in my saddle.

THESEUS [to Hippolyta]   Sweet, you must be ready—
And you, Emilia, and you, friend, and all—
Tomorrow by the sun, to do observance   51
To flow'ry May in Dian's wood.—Wait well, sir,
Upon your mistress.—Emily, I hope
He shall not go afoot.

EMILIA   That were a shame, sir,
While I have horses. [To Arcite] Take your choice;
  and what
You want at any time, let me but know it.   56
If you serve faithfully, I dare assure you
You'll find a loving mistress.

ARCITE   If I do not,
Let me find that my father ever hated: 59
Disgrace and blows.

THESEUS   Go lead the way; you have won it. 60
It shall be so: you shall receive all dues
Fit for the honor you have won; 'twere wrong
  else.—
Sister, beshrew my heart, you have a servant   63
That, if I were a woman, would be master;
But you are wise.

EMILIA   I hope too wise for that, sir.
                                    Flourish. Exeunt omnes.

❖

2.6   Enter Jailer's Daughter, alone.

JAILER'S DAUGHTER
Let all the dukes and all the devils roar;
He is at liberty. I have ventured for him,   2
And out I have brought him. To a little wood
A mile hence I have sent him, where a cedar,
Higher than all the rest, spreads like a plane,   5
Fast by a brook, and there he shall keep close   6
Till I provide him files and food, for yet
His iron bracelets are not off. O Love,
What a stout-hearted child thou art! My father
Durst better have endured cold iron than done it.   10

---

10 **qualities** accomplishments   11 **could have kept** was trained to
keep   12 **deep cry** deep-mouthed yelping (of hounds in pursuit of
game)   13 **feat** skill   14 **piece** example, accomplishment   15 **would
be thought** profess myself to be   16 **proper** excellent, handsome
17 **admire** marvel at   19 **sort** class, rank.   **Believe** you may rest assured that   23 **virtue** moral and personal excellence, strength
24 **got** begotten, born   26 **purchase name** gain reputation   27 **well-
found** well-approved   30 **travel** (1) coming to this court (2) endeavor-
ing so nobly (in the contests)   32 **Dispose of** make provision for, find
a place for   35 **observe** show respect for, honor

40 **but offends you** offends you in the smallest way   47 **a rough one**
i.e., a temperamental horse   51 **by the sun** at dawn   56 **want** lack
59 **that** that which   60 **it** i.e., the honor of leading the return to court
63 **Sister** sister-in-law
2.6. Location: Athens. Somewhere near the prison.
2 **He** Palamon.   **ventured** risked dangers   5 **plane** plane tree, sycamore   6 **Fast by** near by.   **close** concealed   10 **Durst . . . it**
would rather have encountered armed assailants than to have done
this deed

I love him beyond love and beyond reason,
Or wit, or safety. I have made him know it;   12
I care not, I am desperate. If the law
Find me and then condemn me for 't, some
  wenches,
Some honest-hearted maids, will sing my dirge,
And tell to memory my death was noble,
Dying almost a martyr. That way he takes   17
I purpose is my way too. Sure, he cannot
Be so unmanly as to leave me here.
If he do, maids will not so easily
Trust men again. And yet he has not thanked me
For what I have done; no, not so much as kissed
  me,
And that, methinks, is not so well; nor scarcely
Could I persuade him to become a free man,
He made such scruples of the wrong he did
To me and to my father. Yet I hope,
When he considers more, this love of mine
Will take more root within him. Let him do
What he will with me, so he use me kindly;   29
For use me so he shall, or I'll proclaim him,   30
And to his face, no man. I'll presently   31
Provide him necessaries and pack my clothes up,
And where there is a path of ground I'll venture,   33
So he be with me. By him, like a shadow   34
I'll ever dwell. Within this hour the hubbub
Will be all o'er the prison; I am then
Kissing the man they look for. Farewell, father!
Get many more such prisoners, and such daughters,   38
And shortly you may keep yourself. Now to him.   39

                                              [*Exit.*]

                            ❋

3.1   *Cornets in sundry places. Noise and hallooing as
          people a-maying. Enter Arcite, alone.*

ARCITE
  The Duke has lost Hippolyta; each took   1
  A several laund. This is a solemn rite   2
  They owe bloomed May, and the Athenians pay it   3
  To th' heart of ceremony. O Queen Emilia,   4
  Fresher than May, sweeter
  Than her gold buttons on the boughs, or all   6
  Th' enameled knacks o' th' mead or garden—yea,   7
  We challenge too the bank of any nymph   8
  That makes the stream seem flowers; thou, O jewel   9

12 **wit** human understanding   17 **way** direction, path   29 **so** provided.   **kindly** (1) benevolently (2) as my sexual nature requires   30 **so** thus   31 **no man** (1) no gentleman (2) impotent   33 **a path of ground** a path to be found anywhere (in the forest)   34 **So** provided that   38 **Get** (1) acquire (2) beget   39 **And . . . yourself** i.e., and soon you can keep guard over yourself, with neither prisoners nor daughter.   **him** Palamon

3.1. Location: A forest near Athens.
s.d. in sundry places i.e., from various locations offstage   **1–2 took . . . laund** headed for a different glade   **3 bloomed** in full blossom   **4 To . . . ceremony** with full ceremony   **6 buttons** buds   **7 enameled knacks** ornamental delicacies (i.e., flowers).   **mead** meadow   **8–9 We . . . flowers** i.e., I dare compare my mistress's beauty with any bank of a stream belonging to a guardian spirit (or nymph) and reflecting its flowered beauty in the water

O' th' wood, o' th' world, hast likewise blessed a
  pace   10
With thy sole presence; in thy rumination   11
That I, poor man, might eftsoons come between   12
And chop on some cold thought! Thrice blessèd
  chance   13
To drop on such a mistress, expectation   14
Most guiltless on 't! Tell me, O Lady Fortune,   15
Next after Emily my sovereign, how far
I may be proud. She takes strong note of me,   17
Hath made me near her, and this beauteous morn,
The prim'st of all the year, presents me with   19
A brace of horses; two such steeds might well
Be by a pair of kings backed, in a field   21
That their crowns' titles tried. Alas, alas,   22
Poor cousin Palamon, poor prisoner, thou
So little dream'st upon my fortune that
Thou think'st thyself the happier thing, to be
So near Emilia! Me thou deem'st at Thebes,
And therein wretched, although free; but if
Thou knew'st my mistress breathed on me, and that
I eared her language, lived in her eye, O coz,   29
What passion would enclose thee!

      *Enter Palamon as out of a bush, with his shackles;
      [he] bends his fist at Arcite.*

PALAMON   Traitor kinsman,   30
  Thou shouldst perceive my passion if these signs
  Of prisonment were off me, and this hand
  But owner of a sword. By all oaths in one,
  I and the justice of my love would make thee
  A confessed traitor, O thou most perfidious
  That ever gently looked, the void'st of honor   36
  That ev'r bore gentle token, falsest cousin   37
  That ever blood made kin! Call'st thou her thine?
  I'll prove it in my shackles, with these hands,   39
  Void of appointment, that thou liest, and art   40
  A very thief in love, a chaffy lord,   41
  Not worth the name of villain. Had I a sword,
  And these house-clogs away—
ARCITE   Dear cousin Palamon—   43
PALAMON
  Cozener Arcite, give me language such   44
  As thou hast showed me feat.

10 **pace** narrow passage (through the woods)   11–15 **in thy . . . on 't!** O, would that I, poor man, meditating on you, might enter into your thoughts from time to time and, by interrupting them, bring about an exchange of some cold thought for thoughts of love! What a thrice blessed fortune, to happen upon such a mistress, when least expecting to do so!   17 **She . . . me** Emily watches me solicitously   19 **prim'st** finest   21 **backed** mounted   21–22 **field . . . tried** battlefield on which their titles to their crowns were being contested   29 **eared . . . eye** took in her speech at my ear and lived under her gaze.   **coz** cousin   30 **passion** anger.   **enclose thee** enfold you in its grasp   **s.d. as out of a bush** i.e., either through a door understood to represent a hiding place in the forest, or possibly out of a stage structure provided for this act.   **bends** shakes, aims   36 **gently looked** had the appearance of a gentleman   37 **bore gentle token** wore signs of gentility   39 **in my shackles** even with these shackles on   40 **Void of appointment** lacking accouterments of arms   41 **chaffy** worthless as chaff   43 **house-clogs** shackles confining the prisoner to his cell   44 **Cozener** deceiver (with a familiar pun on *cousin* in 1. 43)   44–45 **give . . . feat** match your words to your deeds. *feat* = apt, apropos.

ARCITE   Not finding in   45
The circuit of my breast any gross stuff
To form me like your blazon holds me to   47
This gentleness of answer: 'tis your passion
That thus mistakes, the which, to you being enemy,
Cannot to me be kind. Honor and honesty
I cherish and depend on, howsoev'r
You skip them in me, and with them, fair coz,   52
I'll maintain my proceedings. Pray be pleased   53
To show in generous terms your griefs, since that 54
Your question's with your equal, who professes   55
To clear his own way with the mind and sword   56
Of a true gentleman.
PALAMON   That thou durst, Arcite!   57
ARCITE
My coz, my coz, you have been well advertised   58
How much I dare; you've seen me use my sword
Against th' advice of fear. Sure of another   60
You would not hear me doubted, but your silence   61
Should break out, though i' th' sanctuary.
PALAMON   Sir,   62
I have seen you move in such a place which well   63
Might justify your manhood; you were called
A good knight and a bold. But the whole week's not
  fair
If any day it rain; their valiant temper   66
Men lose when they incline to treachery,
And then they fight like compelled bears—would
  fly   68
Were they not tied.
ARCITE   Kinsman, you might as well
Speak this and act it in your glass as to   70
His ear which now disdains you.
PALAMON   Come up to me,
Quit me of these cold gyves, give me a sword,   72
Though it be rusty, and the charity
Of one meal lend me. Come before me then,
A good sword in thy hand, and do but say
That Emily is thine, I will forgive
The trespass thou hast done me—yea, my life,   77
If then thou carry 't; and brave souls in shades   78
That have died manly, which will seek of me
Some news from earth, they shall get none but this:
That thou art brave and noble.
ARCITE   Be content;
Again betake you to your hawthorn house.   82

With counsel of the night I will be here   83
With wholesome viands. These impediments   84
Will I file off. You shall have garments and
Perfumes to kill the smell o' th' prison. After,
When you shall stretch yourself and say but "Arcite, 87
I am in plight," there shall be at your choice   88
Both sword and armor.
PALAMON   O you heavens, dares any
So noble bear a guilty business? None   90
But only Arcite; therefore none but Arcite
In this kind is so bold.
ARCITE   Sweet Palamon—
PALAMON
I do embrace you and your offer; for   93
Your offer do 't I only; sir, your person   94
Without hypocrisy I may not wish   95
More than my sword's edge on 't.

Wind horns off. Cornets [sounded].

ARCITE   You hear the horns. 96
Enter your muset, lest this match between 's   97
Be crossed ere met. Give me your hand; farewell.   98
I'll bring you every needful thing; I pray you,
Take comfort and be strong.
PALAMON   Pray hold your promise,
And do the deed with a bent brow. Most certain   101
You love me not; be rough with me, and pour
This oil out of your language. By this air,   103
I could for each word give a cuff, my stomach   104
Not reconciled by reason.
ARCITE   Plainly spoken,   105
Yet pardon me hard language. When I spur   106
My horse, I chide him not; content and anger
In me have but one face.

Wind horns.
                        Hark, sir, they call   108
The scattered to the banquet. You must guess   109
I have an office there.
PALAMON   Sir, your attendance   110
Cannot please heaven, and I know your office
Unjustly is achieved.
ARCITE   'Tis a good title.   112
I am persuaded this question, sick between 's,   113
By bleeding must be cured. I am a suitor   114
That to your sword you will bequeath this plea,   115
And talk of it no more.

83 With . . . night under cover of darkness, witnessed only by the night 84 viands food 87 stretch rouse 88 in plight in readiness, engaged 90 bear . . . business undertake an ignoble enterprise 93–96 for . . . on 't Palamon accepts Arcite's offer, but without acknowledging any personal thanks to one whom he frankly wishes only to kill. 96 s.d. Wind horns off sound horns offstage (indicative of a hunt) 97 muset meuse or opening in a hedge used by hunted game for concealment 98 crossed ere met thwarted before it takes place 101 bent frowning 103 oil i.e., calming and reconciling words 104 stomach anger 105 reason i.e., your temperate speech 106 pardon . . . language pardon me if I refrain from using harsh speech 108 have but one face look outwardly alike 109 The scattered the hunters, who have separated during the hunt 110 office function (of waiting on Emilia) 112 'Tis . . . title it is a title I have justly earned 113–115 I am . . . plea I am convinced that the contention that sickens us both can be cured only by our swords, drawing blood as a doctor bleeds patients to affect a cure. I beg of you to refer this lawsuit to your sword.

47 blazon description or catalogue, as on a shield in heraldry 52 skip overlook 53–56 Pray . . . way please use courteous speech in setting forth your grievances, since your dispute is with one who is your equal, and who affirms his intention of vindicating his own behavior 57 That thou durst if only you would dare to do that 58 advertised informed, put on notice 60–62 Against . . . sanctuary when prudence would advise caution. Surely you would not permit my honor to be doubted by some other person; you would break silence to defend me even if you were in hiding. 63 place i.e., field of battle or lists for a tournament 66 temper temperament 68 compelled bears In bear-baiting, bears were tied to a stake and attacked by dogs. would who would 70 in your glass to yourself, in your mirror 72 Quit me of release me from. gyves shackles 77 trespass insult, wrong 78 carry 't win the day. shades the dark world of Hades, the abode of the dead 82 betake . . . house i.e., go to your place of hiding in the woods

PALAMON   But this one word:
　　You are going now to gaze upon my mistress—
　　For note you, mine she is—
ARCITE   Nay then—
PALAMON   Nay, pray you—
　　You talk of feeding me to breed me strength;
　　You are going now to look upon a sun
　　That strengthens what it looks on. There you have
　　A vantage o'er me, but enjoy 't till
　　I may enforce my remedy. Farewell.
　　　　　　Exeunt [separately, Palamon as into his hawthorn
　　　　　　house].

❖

3.2   Enter Jailer's Daughter alone [with a file].

JAILER'S DAUGHTER
　　He has mistook the brake I meant, is gone   1
　　After his fancy. 'Tis now well-nigh morning.   2
　　No matter; would it were perpetual night,
　　And darkness lord o' th' world. Hark, 'tis a wolf!
　　In me hath grief slain fear, and but for one thing,
　　I care for nothing, and that's Palamon.
　　I reck not if the wolves would jaw me, so   7
　　He had this file. What if I hallooed for him?
　　I cannot halloo. If I whooped, what then?
　　If he not answered, I should call a wolf,
　　And do him but that service. I have heard   11
　　Strange howls this livelong night; why may 't not be
　　They have made prey of him? He has no weapons;
　　He cannot run; the jingling of his gyves
　　Might call fell things to listen, who have in them   15
　　A sense to know a man unarmed, and can
　　Smell where resistance is. I'll set it down   17
　　He's torn to pieces; they howled many together,
　　And then they fed on him. So much for that.
　　Be bold to ring the bell. How stand I then?   20
　　All's chared when he is gone. No, no, I lie;   21
　　My father's to be hanged for his escape,   22
　　Myself to beg, if I prized life so much   23
　　As to deny my act, but that I would not,
　　Should I try death by dozens. I am moped;   25
　　Food took I none these two days,
　　Sipped some water. I have not closed mine eyes
　　Save when my lids scoured off their brine. Alas,   28
　　Dissolve, my life! Let not my sense unsettle,   29
　　Lest I should drown, or stab, or hang myself.

3.2. Location: The forest.
1 brake thicket   2 After his fancy as his wishes prompt him   7 reck
care. jaw gnaw. so provided   11 And . . . service i.e., and accomplish nothing more than to bring a wolf who would then threaten
Palamon's life as well as mine   15 fell things savage beasts   17 set it
down record it as for a fact that   20 the bell i.e., the bell rung by the
bellman to announce a person's death. How stand I what plight am
I in   21 chared done for. (To chare is to accomplish a turn of work, a
chore.)   22 his Palamon's   23 Myself to beg I would be forced to
beg for my living (as the daughter of an executed man)   25 Should
. . . dozens even if I had to suffer death many times or in many
forms. moped stupefied, melancholic   28 scoured . . . brine
skimmed off the briny tears from my eyes   29 sense sanity

O state of nature, fail together in me,   31
Since thy best props are warped! So which way
　　now?   32
The best way is the next way to a grave;   33
Each errant step beside is torment. Lo,   34
The moon is down, the crickets chirp, the screech
　　owl
Calls in the dawn. All offices are done   36
Save what I fail in; but the point is this—
An end, and that is all.   38
　　　　　　　　　　　　　　　　　　　Exit.

❖

3.3   Enter Arcite with meat, wine, and files.

ARCITE
　　I should be near the place.—Ho! Cousin Palamon!

　　　　Enter Palamon [as out of a bush].

PALAMON
　　Arcite?
ARCITE   The same. I have brought you food and files.
　　Come forth and fear not. Here's no Theseus.
PALAMON
　　Nor none so honest, Arcite.
ARCITE   That's no matter;
　　We'll argue that hereafter. Come, take courage;
　　You shall not die thus beastly. Here, sir, drink;
　　I know you are faint. Then I'll talk further with you.
PALAMON
　　Arcite, thou mightst now poison me.
ARCITE   I might;
　　But I must fear you first. Sit down and, good now,   9
　　No more of these vain parleys. Let us not,
　　Having our ancient reputation with us,   11
　　Make talk for fools and cowards. To your health, sir!
　　　　　　　　　　　　　　　　　　　　[He drinks.]
PALAMON
　　Do.
ARCITE   Pray sit down, then, and let me entreat you,
　　By all the honesty and honor in you,
　　No mention of this woman; 'twill disturb us.
　　We shall have time enough.
PALAMON   Well, sir, I'll pledge you.   16
　　　　　　　　　　　　　　　　　　　　[He drinks.]
ARCITE
　　Drink a good hearty draught; it breeds good blood,
　　　　man.   17
　　Do not you feel it thaw you?

31–32 state . . . warped may I die at once, since my natural
strength is failing and since I have lost Palamon   33 next nearest
34 beside not to that purpose   36 Calls in summons. offices
duties   38 An end i.e., death
3.3. Location: The forest, as before.
9 must should have to. good now i.e., please, for goodness' sake
11 ancient long-established   16 pledge drink a toast to   17 breeds
good blood Wine was thought to resupply the blood.

PALAMON
Stay, I'll tell you after a draught or two more.
ARCITE
Spare it not; the Duke has more, coz. Eat now.
PALAMON
Yes.   [*He eats.*]
ARCITE   I am glad you have so good a stomach.   21
PALAMON
I am gladder I have so good meat to 't.
ARCITE
Is 't not mad lodging here in the wild woods,
    cousin?
PALAMON
Yes, for them that have wild consciences.
ARCITE   How tastes your victuals?
Your hunger needs no sauce, I see.
PALAMON   Not much.
But if it did, yours is too tart, sweet cousin.
What is this?
ARCITE   Venison.
PALAMON   'Tis a lusty meat.   28
Give me more wine. Here, Arcite, to the wenches
We have known in our days!   [*He drinks.*]
            The Lord Steward's daughter—
Do you remember her?
ARCITE   After you, coz.   31
PALAMON
She loved a black-haired man.
ARCITE   She did so. Well, sir?
PALAMON
And I have heard some call him Arcite, and—
ARCITE
Out with 't, faith.
PALAMON   She met him in an arbor.
What did she there, coz? Play o' th' virginals?   35
ARCITE
Something she did, sir.
PALAMON   Made her groan a month for 't— 36
Or two, or three, or ten.
ARCITE   The marshal's sister   37
Had her share, too, as I remember, cousin,
Else there be tales abroad. You'll pledge her?
PALAMON   Yes.   39
                                [*They drink.*]
ARCITE
A pretty brown wench 'tis. There was a time   40
When young men went a-hunting—and a wood,
And a broad beech—and thereby hangs a tale.
Heigh ho!

PALAMON   For Emily, upon my life! Fool,
Away with this strained mirth. I say again,   44
That sigh was breathed for Emily. Base cousin,
Dar'st thou break first?
ARCITE   You are wide.
PALAMON   By heaven and earth, 46
There's nothing in thee honest.
ARCITE   Then I'll leave you;
You are a beast now.
PALAMON   As thou mak'st me, traitor.
ARCITE
There's all things needful: files, and shirts, and
    perfumes.
I'll come again some two hours hence and bring
That that shall quiet all.
PALAMON   A sword and armor.   51
ARCITE
Fear me not. You are now too foul. Farewell.   52
Get off your trinkets; you shall want naught.
PALAMON   Sirrah— 53
ARCITE
I'll hear no more.   *Exit.*
PALAMON   If he keep touch, he dies for 't.   54
                    Exit, [as into the bush].

❖

3.4   *Enter Jailer's Daughter.*

JAILER'S DAUGHTER
I am very cold, and all the stars are out too,
The little stars and all, that look like aglets.
The sun has seen my folly.—Palamon!—   2
Alas, no; he's in heaven. Where am I now?
Yonder's the sea, and there's a ship. How 't
    tumbles!
And there's a rock lies watching under water.
Now, now, it beats upon it; now, now, now,
There's a leak sprung, a sound one. How they cry! 8
Open her before the wind, you'll lose all else.   9
Up with a course or two, and tack about, boys.   10
Good night, good night, you're gone. I am very
    hungry;
Would I could find a fine frog! He would tell me
News from all parts o' th' world. Then would I
    make
A carrack of a cockleshell, and sail   14
By east and north-east to the king of pygmies,

44 **strained** artificial   46 **break** i.e., break our convenant not to speak of Emilia.   **wide** wide of the mark   51 **quiet** put an end to   52 **Fear me not** i.e., don't worry about my not doing all I promised. (Palamon has just reiterated his demands.)   **foul** filthy   53 **trinkets** i.e., the shackles, still to be filed off.   **want naught** lack nothing   54 **keep touch** keep his promise
3.4. Location: The forest, as before.
2 **aglets** spangles, ornamental studs peeping through eyelet-holes   8 **sound** robust   9 **Open her** unfurl her sails. (The talk of storms and sailing vessels is indicative of the Daughter's madness.)   10 **course** sails furled on the lower yard until they are hauled up and unfurled   14 **carrack** large merchant ship or fighting vessel

21 **stomach** appetite   28 **lusty** agreeable, fortifying   31 **After you** i.e., go ahead with your toast, and I'll reciprocate   35 **virginals** a spinet-like keyboard instrument (with sexual suggestion here)   36– 37 **groan . . . ten** i.e., suffer a pregnancy. (*Ten* is an approximation for nine.)   39 **tales** false rumors   40 **brown** dark-complexioned, brunette

For he tells fortunes rarely. Now my father,   16
Twenty to one, is trussed up in a trice   17
Tomorrow morning. I'll say never a word.
(*Sing*)
   For I'll cut my green coat a foot above my knee,
   And I'll clip my yellow locks an inch below
     mine e'e;
   Hey, nonny, nonny, nonny.
   He s' buy me a white cut, forth for to ride,   22
   And I'll go seek him through the world that is
     so wide;
   Hey, nonny, nonny, nonny.
O for a prick now, like a nightingale,   25
To put my breast against! I shall sleep like a top else.
                           Exit.

❧

3.5   *Enter a schoolmaster [Gerald], six Countrymen,*
      [one of whom is dressed as a] babion, five
      Wenches, with a taborer [Timothy]

SCHOOLMASTER   Fie, Fie,
What tediosity and disinsanity   2
Is here among ye? Have my rudiments   3
Been labored so long with ye, milked unto ye,
And, by a figure, even the very plum broth   5
And marrow of my understanding laid upon ye?   6
And do you still cry "Where?" and "How?" and
   "Wherefore?"
You most coarse frieze capacities, ye jean
   judgments,   8
Have I said, "Thus let be," and "There let be,"
And "Then let be," and no man understand me?
Proh deum, medius fidius, ye are all dunces!   11
Forwhy, here stand I. Here the Duke comes. There
   are you,   12
Close in the thicket. The Duke appears. I meet him,   13
And unto him I utter learnèd things
And many figures. He hears, and nods, and hums,   15
And then cries, "Rare!", and I go forward. At length   16
I fling my cap up; mark there! Then do you,
As once did Meleager and the boar,   18

16 **rarely** excellently   17 **is . . . trice** will be hanged quickly   22 **s' buy** shall buy.   **cut** common laboring horse (with cut tail or a gelding). Also a slang word suggesting the female sexual anatomy.
25 **prick** thorn (against which the nightingale was thought to lean in order to stay awake). Probably with bawdy suggestion.
3.5. Location: The forest still.
s.d. **babion** baboon.   **taborer** player on the tabor or small drum (and probably on the pipe as well)   2 **tediosity and disinsanity** pedantic Latinisms for *tediousness and complete folly*   3 **rudiments** basic teachings   5 **by a figure** to use a figure of speech   5–6 **plum . . . marrow** i.e., essence   8 **frieze capacities** persons with homespun mental capacities.   **jean** made of twilled cotton (named originally for Genoa)   11 **Proh . . . fidius** so help me the God of faith   12 **Forwhy** wherefore, because   13 **Close** hidden   15 **figures** figures of speech   16 **Rare** remarkable, excellent   18 **Meleager and the boar** Evidently the Schoolmaster instructs the rustics to present themselves before Duke Theseus as though acting out the story of the Greek warrior's slaying of the Calydonian boar; Hippolyta, at 1.1.78-79, is seemingly associated with the story. They are to come forward gracefully (*break comely out*), arrange themselves in order (*cast . . . decently*), and dance (*by a figure, trace and turn*). To trace is to step, "tread a measure," dance.

Break comely out before him. Like true lovers,
Cast yourselves in a body decently,
And sweetly, by a figure, trace and turn, boys.   21
FIRST COUNTRYMAN
And sweetly we will do it, Master Gerald.
SECOND COUNTRYMAN
Draw up the company. Where's the taborer?
THIRD COUNTRYMAN [*calling*]
Why, Timothy!
TABORER   Here, my mad boys. Have at ye!   24
SCHOOLMASTER
But I say, where's their women?
FOURTH COUNTRYMAN   Here's Friz and Maudline.
SECOND COUNTRYMAN
And little Luce with the white legs, and bouncing
   Barbery.   26
FIRST COUNTRYMAN
And freckled Nell, that never failed her master.
SCHOOLMASTER
Where be your ribbons, maids? Swim with your
   bodies,   28
And carry it sweetly and deliverly,   29
And now and then a favor and a frisk.   30
NELL
Let us alone, sir.
SCHOOLMASTER   Where's the rest o' th' music?   31
THIRD COUNTRYMAN
Dispersed, as you commanded.
SCHOOLMASTER   Couple then,   32
And see what's wanting. Where's the babion?—   33
My friend, carry your tail without offense
Or scandal to the ladies; and be sure
You tumble with audacity and manhood,
And when you bark, do it with judgment.
BABION   Yes, sir.
SCHOOLMASTER
Quousque tandem? Here is a woman wanting.   38
FOURTH COUNTRYMAN
We may go whistle; all the fat's i' th' fire.   39
SCHOOLMASTER   We have,
As learnèd authors utter, washed a tile;   40
We have been *fatuus* and labored vainly.   41
SECOND COUNTRYMAN
This is that scornful piece, that scurvy hilding   42
That gave her promise faithfully she would be
   here—
Cicely, the seamster's daughter.   44
The next gloves that I give her shall be dogskin.   45
Nay, an she fail me once—you can tell, Arcas,
She swore by wine and bread she would not break.   47

21 **trace** step, "tread a measure," dance   24 **Have at ye** i.e., here we go, have a go at it   26 **bouncing** strapping, plump   28 **Swim** move gracefully   29 **carry it** execute the dance movement. **deliverly** nimbly   30 **favor** gesture of friendly regard, such as bowing or blowing a kiss.   **frisk** caper, jig   31 **Let us alone** leave it to us. **music** musicians   32 **Couple** arrange yourself in pairs   33 **wanting** lacking   38 **Quousque tandem** how long, then (from the beginning of Cicero's Latin oration *Contra Catiline:* ''How long, then, Catiline, will you abuse our patience?'')   39 **We . . . fire** i.e., we are out of luck, all's come to nothing   40 **washed a tile** i.e., striven in vain   41 **fatuus** foolish   42 **This . . . hilding** that's a scornful wench, that wretched jade   44 **seamster's** tailor's   45 **dogskin** cheap leather   47 **by wine and bread** by the Mass.   **break** break her promise

SCHOOLMASTER   An eel and woman,
A learnèd poet says, unless by th' tail
And with thy teeth thou hold, will either fail.   50
In manners this was false position.   51

FIRST COUNTRYMAN
A fire ill take her! Does she flinch now?

THIRD COUNTRYMAN   What   52
Shall we determine, sir?

SCHOOLMASTER   Nothing;   53
Our business is become a nullity,
Yea, and a woeful and a piteous nullity.

FOURTH COUNTRYMAN
Now, when the credit of our town lay on it,
Now to be frampold, now to piss o' th' nettle!   57
Go thy ways, I'll remember thee, I'll fit thee!   58

Enter Jailer's Daughter.

JAILER'S DAUGHTER [*sings*]
The *George Alow* came from the south,   59
    From the coast of Barbary-a;
And there he met with brave gallants of war,   61
    By one, by two, by three-a.

"Well hailed, well hailed, you jolly gallants,
    And whither now are you bound-a?
O let me have your company
    Till I come to the sound-a."

There was three fools fell out about an owlet—

[*She sings*]
The one he said it was an owl,
    The other he said nay,   68
The third he said it was a hawk,
    And her bells were cut away.   71

THIRD COUNTRYMAN
There's a dainty madwoman, master,
Comes i' th' nick, as mad as March hare.   73
It we can get her dance, we are made again.   74
I warrant her, she'll do the rarest gambols.   75

FIRST COUNTRYMAN
A madwoman? We are made, boys.

SCHOOLMASTER [*to the Jailer's Daughter*]
And are you mad, good woman?

JAILER'S DAUGHTER
I would be sorry else. Give me your hand.

SCHOOLMASTER   Why?

JAILER'S DAUGHTER   I can tell your fortune.
You are a fool. Tell ten; I have posed him. Buzz!   81
Friend, you must eat no white bread; if you do,

Your teeth will bleed extremely. Shall we dance, ho?
I know you, you're a tinker. Sirrah tinker,   84
Stop no more holes but what you should.

SCHOOLMASTER   *Dii boni!*   85
A tinker, damsel?

JAILER'S DAUGHTER   Or a conjurer.
Raise me a devil now, and let him play   87
Qui passa o' th' bells and bones.

SCHOOLMASTER   Go take her,   88
And fluently persuade her to a peace.   89
Et opus exegi, quod nec Iovis ira, nec ignis.   90
Strike up, and lead her in.

SECOND COUNTRYMAN   Come, lass, let's trip it.   91

JAILER'S DAUGHTER   I'll lead.

THIRD COUNTRYMAN   Do, do.

SCHOOLMASTER
Persuasively and cunningly.

                                   Wind horns.
                          Away, boys!   94
I hear the horns. Give me some meditation,   95
And mark your cue.

                    Exeunt all but [the] Schoolmaster.
                    Pallas, inspire me!   96

Enter Theseus, Pirithous, Hippolyta, Emilia,
Arcite, and train.

THESEUS   This way the stag took.

SCHOOLMASTER   Stay and edify.   98

THESEUS   What have we here?

PIRITHOUS   Some country sport, upon my life, sir.

THESEUS [*To the Schoolmaster*]
Well, sir, go forward; we will edify.
                    [*Seats are brought for Theseus and the ladies.*]
Ladies, sit down; we'll stay it.   [*They sit.*] 102

SCHOOLMASTER
Thou doughty Duke, all hail! All hail, sweet ladies!   103

THESEUS [*to Pirithous and the ladies*]
This is a cold beginning.   104

SCHOOLMASTER
If you but favor, our country pastime made is.   105
We are a few of those collected here
That ruder tongues distinguish "villager";   107
And to say verity, and not to fable,
We are a merry rout, or else a rabble,   109
Or company, or, by a figure, chorus,   110
That 'fore thy dignity will dance a morris.   111

50 either fail both prove too slippery   **51 In . . . position** i.e., Cicely's failed promise was like a false assertion in logic   **52 A fire . . . her** (1) may a fire consume her (2) may venereal disease infect her   **53 determine** decide to do   **57 be frampold, piss o' th' nettle** be ill-tempered, recalcitrant   **58 Go . . . fit thee** Go right ahead, I'll be even with you (said to the absent Cicely)   **59 The George Alow** This ship was featured in a popular ballad, of which the Jailer's Daughter sings a fragment. *Alow* might suggest "low on the horizon."   **61 gallants of war** warships   **68–71 The one . . . away** a nursery rhyme   **71 bells** In falconry, the birds flew with bells hung from their legs.   **73 th' nick** the nick of time   **74 dance** to dance.   **we are made again** our fortunes are restored   **75 rarest gambols** most elegant leaps in dancing   **81 Tell . . . Buzz!** count to ten; he can't, I've stumped him. Pshaw!

84 tinker Itinerant peddlers who mended kitchenware and the like were thought of as rogues and vagabonds. The reference to stopping holes (1. 85) is given a sexual double meaning.   **85 Dii boni** good gods   **87–88 let . . . bones** let him play a popular dance tune, *Qui (Chi) passa per questa strada* ("Who passes through this street"), using bells and bones as musical and percussion instruments   **89–91 fluently . . . Strike up** with graceful speech, persuade her to dance peacefully with us. "And I have completed a work which neither the anger of Jove nor fire [shall undo]." Start the music. (The Latin quotation is from Ovid's *Metamorphoses*.)   **94 s.d. Wind** sound   **95 meditation** time to think   **96 Pallas** Pallas Athene   **98 edify** be instructed   **102 stay it** stay to attend the presentation   **103 doughty** valiant, worthy   **104 cold** Theseus puns on the meteorological meaning of "hail."   **105 favor** grant the favor of your attention   **107 ruder** country-bred.   **distinguish** classify or characterize as   **109 rout** assembly   **110 figure** figure of speech   **111 'fore thy dignity** in your royal presence

And I that am the rectifier of all,   112
By title *pedagogus*, that let fall   113
The birch upon the breeches of the small ones,
And humble with a ferula the tall ones,   115
Do here present this machine, or this frame;   116
And, dainty Duke, whose doughty dismal fame   117
From Dis to Daedalus, from post to pillar,   118
Is blown abroad, help me, thy poor well-willer,
And with thy twinkling eyes, look right and straight
Upon this mighty "Morr" of mickle weight.   121
"Is" now comes in, which, being glued together,   122
Makes "Morris," and the cause that we came hither.   123
The body of our sport, of no small study,   124
I first appear, though rude, and raw, and muddy,
To speak before thy noble grace this tenner,   126
At whose great feet I offer up my penner.   127
The next, the Lord of May and Lady bright;   128
The Chambermaid and Servingman, by night
That seek out silent hanging; then mine Host   130
And his fat Spouse, that welcomes to their cost   131
The gallèd traveller, and with a beck'ning   132
Informs the tapster to inflame the reck'ning;   133
Then the beest-eating Clown; and next the Fool;   134
The Babion with long tail and eke long tool,   135
Cum multis aliis that make a dance;   136
Say "ay," and all shall presently advance.   137

THESEUS
Ay, ay, by any means, dear dominie.

PIRITHOUS   Produce!   138

SCHOOLMASTER   (*knock for [the] school*)
Intrate, filii; come forth and foot it.   139

Music.

*Enter the [Countrymen, the Taborer, the Wenches,
and the Jailer's Daughter. They] dance [a morris].*

Ladies, if we have been merry,
And have pleased ye with a derry,   141
And a derry and a down,
Say the schoolmaster's no clown.
Duke, if we have pleased thee too,
And have done as good boys should do,
Give us but a tree or twain
For a maypole, and again,
Ere another year run out,
We'll make thee laugh, and all this rout.

THESEUS
Take twenty, dominie. [*To Hippolyta*] How does my
    sweetheart?

HIPPOLYTA
Never so pleased, sir.

EMILIA   'Twas an excellent dance,
And for a preface, I never heard a better.   152

THESEUS
Schoolmaster, I thank you.—One see 'em all
    rewarded.   153

PIRITHOUS
And here's something to paint your pole withal.
                    [*He gives them money.*]

THESEUS   Now to our sports again.   155

SCHOOLMASTER
May the stag thou hunt'st stand long,   156
And thy dogs be swift and strong;
May they kill him without lets,   158
And the ladies eat his dowsets.   159
            Wind horns [within. Exeunt Theseus and train.]
Come, we are all made. *Dii deaeque omnes!*   160
Ye have danced rarely, wenches.   *Exeunt.*

❖

3.6   *Enter Palamon from the bush.*

PALAMON
About this hour my cousin gave his faith
To visit me again, and with him bring
Two swords and two good armors. If he fail,   3
He's neither man nor soldier. When he left me,
I did not think a week could have restored
My lost strength to me, I was grown so low
And crest-fall'n with my wants. I thank thee, Arcite,
Thou art yet a fair foe; and I feel myself,
With this refreshing, able once again
To outdure danger. To delay it longer   10

112 rectifier one who corrects, the director, but also the one who
corrects and spanks students (in ll. 113-115)   **113 pedagogus**
schoolmaster   **115 ferula** cane used to punish older students
116 this machine . . . frame this device, this construction (the entertainment)   **117 dainty** gracious.   **dismal** unpropitious (to your enemies). (The words are chosen partly for their alliteration.)   **118 From
Dis to Daedalus** from the underworld to the labyrinth of Daedalus
(again with alliterative effect)   **121–123 "Morr" . . . "Is" . . .
"Morris"** To achieve this pedantry, the Schoolmaster has evidently
outfitted two of his dancers to depict "Morr" (perhaps signifying
"Moor") and "Is" (perhaps "ice"); when they stand together, the result is "Morris."   **121 mickle** much   **124 The body . . . study** (1) the
substance of our entertainment, mastered with no small amount of effort (2) I, as the structural centerpiece of our entertainment, a person
of considerable learning   **126 tenner** i.e., ten-syllable line (punning
also on *tenor*, purport)   **127 penner** leather sheath for pens
128 Lady i.e., Queen of May, Maid Marian   **130 silent hanging** wall
or bed curtains behind which to seek concealment   **131–132 to
their . . . traveller** chafed and weary travellers, who find their welcome a costly one   **133 inflame the reck'ning** inflate the bill
134 beest-eating eating the first milk to be drawn from a cow after it
gives birth. Such a diet characterizes the Clown as a country bumpkin.   **135 tool** penis   **136 Cum multis aliis** with many others
137 presently immediately   **138 dominie** schoolmaster.   **Produce**
bring them forth.   **s.d. knock for [the] school** The schoolmaster signals for those under his tutelage to enter.   **139 Intrate, filii** Come in,
my boys.   **foot it** dance

141 derry ballad, refrain. ("Derry down derry" is a common nonsense refrain.)   **152 for** as for   **153 One** someone   **155 sports**
hunting   **156 stand long** hold out a long time (thus providing good
sport)   **158 lets** hindrances   **159 dowsets** testicles—considered a
delicacy   **160 Dii deaeque omnes** all gods and goddesses
3.6. Location: The forest still. Palamon's entrance "from the bush"
suggests some sort of visual indication at a stage door or structure.
3 armors suits of armor   **10 outdure** endure, outlast

Would make the world think, when it comes to
   hearing,   11
That I lay fatting like a swine to fight,   12
And not a soldier. Therefore this blest morning
Shall be the last; and that sword he refuses,   14
If it but hold, I kill him with; 'tis justice.   15
So, love and fortune for me!

Enter Arcite with [suits of] armor and swords.

                O, good morrow.
ARCITE
Good morrow, noble kinsman.
PALAMON   I have put you
To too much pains, sir.
ARCITE   That too much, fair cousin,
Is but a debt to honor and my duty.
PALAMON
Would you were so in all, sir. I could wish ye   20
As kind a kinsman as you force me find   21
A beneficial foe, that my embraces   22
Might thank ye, not my blows.
ARCITE   I shall think either
Well done, a noble recompense.
PALAMON   Then I shall quit you.   24
ARCITE
Defy me in these fair terms, and you show   25
More than a mistress to me. No more anger,
As you love anything that's honorable!
We were not bred to talk, man; when we are armed,
And both upon our guards, then let our fury,
Like meeting of two tides, fly strongly from us,
And then to whom the birthright of this beauty   31
Truly pertains—without upbraidings, scorns,   32
Despisings of our persons, and such poutings,
Fitter for girls and schoolboys—will be seen,
And quickly, yours or mine. Will 't please you arm,
   sir?
Or if you feel yourself not fitting yet   36
And furnished with your old strength, I'll stay,
   cousin,
And ev'ry day discourse you into health,
As I am spared. Your person I am friends with,   39
And I could wish I had not said I loved her,
Though I had died; but loving such a lady,   41
And justifying my love, I must not fly from 't.

PALAMON
Arcite, thou art so brave an enemy
That no man but thy cousin's fit to kill thee.
I am well and lusty; choose your arms.
ARCITE   Choose you, sir.   45
PALAMON
Wilt thou exceed in all, or dost thou do it   46
To make me spare thee?
ARCITE   If you think so, cousin,
You are deceivèd, for, as I am a soldier,
I will not spare you.
PALAMON   That's well said.
ARCITE   You'll find it.   49
PALAMON
Then, as I am an honest man, and love
With all the justice of affection,
I'll pay thee soundly.
          [He chooses one suit of armor.]
          This I'll take.
ARCITE *[indicating the other suit]*   That's mine, then.   52
I'll arm you first.
PALAMON   Do. Pray thee tell me, cousin,
Where gott'st thou this good armor?
ARCITE *[arming Palamon]*   'Tis the Duke's,
And to say true, I stole it. Do I pinch you?
PALAMON
No.
ARCITE Is 't not to heavy?
PALAMON   I have worn a lighter,
But I shall make it serve.
ARCITE   I'll buckle 't close.
PALAMON
By any means.
ARCITE   You care not for a grand guard?   58
PALAMON
No, no, we'll use no horses. I perceive
You would fain be at that fight.
ARCITE   I am indifferent.   60
PALAMON
Faith, so am I. Good cousin, thrust the buckle
Through far enough.
ARCITE   I warrant you.
PALAMON   My casque now.   62
ARCITE
Will you fight bare-armed?
PALAMON   We shall be the nimbler.
ARCITE
But use your gauntlets, though. Those are o' th'
   least.   64
Prithee take mine, good cousin.

---

11 when . . . hearing when the matter is generally known **12 fatting . . . fight** lazing about in my preparations for fighting like a swine being fattened for the kill **14–15 that sword . . . hold** the sword he brings for me to use (having chosen the other one for himself), so long as it remains whole. (At 1. 45 Palamon offers Arcite his choice of weapons.) **20–22 Would . . . foe** I wish you were as honorable in all things as you are in providing these weapons and armor. I could wish you were as kind a kinsman as what you oblige me to find you are instead: an enemy who does me this benefit (of providing armor). **24 quit** repay **25 show** show yourself to be **31–32 to whom . . . pertains** the one who can claim the beautiful Emilia by right of birth **36 fitting** prepared **39 As I am spared** as far as I have time **41 Though I had died** even if my remaining silent had killed me

45 lusty healthy, strong **46 exceed in all** go beyond me in everything that is chivalrous **49 You'll find it** i.e., I mean to do what I've said I'll do **52 pay** reward, punish **58 grand guard** armor plate covering the breast and left shoulder, used in tournaments and hence appropriate for tilting on horseback (as Palamon implies in 1. 59) **60 would . . . fight** would prefer to fight that way, mounted **62 warrant** promise. **casque** helmet **64 gauntlets** plated gloves. **o' th' least** insufficient

PALAMON   Thank you, Arcite.
How do I look? Am I fall'n much away?   66
ARCITE
Faith, very little; love has used you kindly.
PALAMON
I'll warrant thee, I'll strike home.
ARCITE   Do, and spare not.
I'll give you cause, sweet cousin.
PALAMON   Now to you, sir.
[Arming Arcite] Methinks this armor's very like that,
    Arcite,
Thou wor'st that day the three kings fell, but lighter.
ARCITE
That was a very good one, and that day,
I well remember, you outdid me, cousin;
I never saw such valor. When you charged
Upon the left wing of the enemy,
I spurred hard to come up, and under me   76
I had a right good horse.
PALAMON   You had indeed;
A bright bay, I remember.
ARCITE   Yes, but all
Was vainly labored in me; you outwent me,
Nor could my wishes reach you. Yet a little
I did by imitation.
PALAMON   More by virtue.   81
You are modest, cousin.
ARCITE   When I saw you charge first,
Methought I heard a dreadful clap of thunder
Break from the troop.
PALAMON   But still before that flew
The lightning of your valor. Stay a little;
Is not this piece too strait?
ARCITE   No, no, 'tis well.   86
PALAMON
I would have nothing hurt thee but my sword;
A bruise would be dishonor.
ARCITE   Now I am perfect.   88
PALAMON
Stand off, then.
ARCITE   Take my sword; I hold it better.   89
PALAMON
I thank ye. No, keep it; your life lies on it.   90
Here's one; if it but hold, I ask no more
For all my hopes. My cause and honor guard me!
ARCITE
And me my love!

        They bow several ways, then advance and stand.

                    Is there aught else to say?   93
PALAMON
This only, and no more: thou art mine aunt's son,
And that blood we desire to shed is mutual—
In me, thine, and in thee, mine. My sword

66 **fall'n much away** much reduced in weight   76 **come up** come up
from the rear   81 **virtue** manliness   86 **strait** tight-fitting   88 **perfect**
i.e., correctly armed in every detail   89 **hold it better** regard it as the
better one   90 **lies** depends   93 **s.d. several ways** in various directions, as though to those witnessing a tournament

Is in my hand, and if thou kill'st me,
The gods and I forgive thee. If there be
A place prepared for those that sleep in honor,
I wish his weary soul that falls may win it.
Fight bravely, cousin. Give me thy noble hand.
ARCITE [*as they clasp hands*]
Here, Palamon. This hand shall never more
Come near thee with such friendship.
PALAMON   I commend thee. 103
ARCITE
If I fall, curse me, and say I was a coward,
For none but such dare die in these just trials.   105
Once more farewell, my cousin.
PALAMON   Farewell, Arcite.

            [*They*] fight. Horns within. They stand.

ARCITE
Lo, cousin, lo, our folly has undone us.
PALAMON   Why?
ARCITE
This is the Duke, a-hunting, as I told you.
If we be found, we are wretched. O, retire
For honor's sake, and safely, presently
Into your bush again. Sir, we shall find
Too many hours to die in. Gentle cousin,
If you be seen, you perish instantly
For breaking prison, and I, if you reveal me,
For my contempt. Then all the world will scorn us,   115
And say we had a noble difference,   116
But base disposers of it.
PALAMON   No, no, cousin,   117
I will no more be hidden, nor put off
This great adventure to a second trial.   119
I know your cunning, and I know your cause;
He that faints now, shame take him! Put thyself   121
Upon thy present guard.
ARCITE   You are not mad?   122
PALAMON
Or I will make th' advantage of this hour
Mine own, and what to come shall threaten me   124
I fear less than my fortune. Know, weak cousin,   125
I love Emilia, and in that I'll bury
Thee and all crosses else.
ARCITE   Then come what can come,   127
Thou shalt know, Palamon, I dare as well
Die as discourse or sleep. Only this fears me: 129
The law will have the honor of our ends.   130
Have at thy life!

103 **commend thee** commend you to the gods   105 **For none . . .
trials** i.e., only the unworthy are sure to lose in trial by combat, since
the gods will give victory to the just   115 **contempt** i.e., contempt toward the throne, in consorting with one who is royally banished
116–117 **we had . . . of it** we had a noble quarrel but were guilty of
conducting it in defiance of royal command   119 **adventure** venture
121 **faints** proves faint-hearted   122 **Upon . . . guard** on guard at
once   124–125 **what . . . fortune** I fear whatever the future may
threaten me with less than the outcome of this present fight
127 **crosses else** other thwartings or afflictions   129 **fears** frightens
130 **of our ends** of our deaths through dishonorable execution (rather
than permitting us to fight each other honorably)

PALAMON   Look to thine own well, Arcite!

[They] fight again.

Horns. Enter Theseus, Hippolyta, Emilia,
Pirithous, and train. [Palamon and Arcite are
separated.]

THESEUS
What ignorant and mad malicious traitors
Are you, that 'gainst the tenor of my laws
Are making battle, thus like knights appointed,   134
Without my leave and officers of arms?   135
By Castor, both shall die.
PALAMON   Hold thy word, Theseus.   136
We are certainly both traitors, both despisers
Of thee and of thy goodness. I am Palamon,
That cannot love thee, he that broke thy prison;
Think well what that deserves. And this is Arcite;
A bolder traitor never trod thy ground,
A falser nev'r seemed friend. This is the man
Was begged and banished, this is he contemns thee 143
And what thou dar'st do, and in this disguise,
Against thine own edict, follows thy sister,
That fortunate bright star, the fair Emilia,
Whose servant—if there be a right in seeing,   147
And first bequeathing of the soul to—justly
I am; and, which is more, dares think her his.
This treachery, like a most trusty lover,
I called him now to answer. If thou be'st
As thou art spoken, great and virtuous,
The true decider of all injuries,   153
Say "Fight again," and thou shalt see me, Theseus,
Do such a justice thou thyself wilt envy.
Then take my life; I'll woo thee to 't.
PIRITHOUS   O heaven,   156
What more than man is this!
THESEUS   I have sworn.
ARCITE   We seek not
Thy breath of mercy, Theseus. 'Tis to me   158
A thing as soon to die as thee to say it,   159
And no more moved. Where this man calls me
    traitor,   160
Let me say thus much: if in love be treason,
In service of so excellent a beauty,
As I love most, and in that faith will perish,
As I have brought my life here to confirm it,
As I have served her truest, worthiest,
As I dare kill this cousin that denies it,
So let me be most traitor, and ye please me.   167

For scorning thy edict, Duke, ask that lady   168
Why she is fair, and why her eyes command me
Stay here to love her; and if she say "traitor,"
I am a villain fit to lie unburied.
PALAMON
Thou shalt have pity of us both, O Theseus,
If unto neither thou show mercy. Stop,
As thou art just, thy noble ear against us;
As thou art valiant, for thy cousin's soul,   175
Whose twelve strong labors crown his memory,
Let's die together at one instant, Duke.   177
Only a little let him fall before me,
That I may tell my soul he shall not have her.
THESEUS
I grant your wish, for to say true, your cousin
Has ten times more offended, for I gave him
More mercy than you found, sir, your offenses   182
Being no more than his.—None here speak for 'em,
For ere the sun set both shall sleep for ever.
HIPPOLYTA [*to Emilia*]
Alas, the pity! Now or never, sister,
Speak not to be denied. That face of yours
Will bear the curses else of after ages
For these lost cousins.
EMILIA   In my face, dear sister,
I find no anger to 'em, nor no ruin;
The misadventure of their own eyes kill 'em.
Yet that I will be woman and have pity, [*kneeling*]
My knees shall grow to th' ground but I'll get
    mercy.   192
Help me, dear sister; in a deed so virtuous,
The powers of all women will be with us.
Most royal brother—
HIPPOLYTA [*kneeling*]   Sir, by our tie of marriage—
EMILIA
By your own spotless honor—
HIPPOLYTA   By that faith,
That fair hand, and that honest heart you gave
    me—
EMILIA
By that you would have pity in another,   198
By your own virtues infinite—
HIPPOLYTA   By valor,
By all the chaste nights I have ever pleased you—   200
THESEUS
These are strange conjurings.
PIRITHOUS [*kneeling*]   Nay then, I'll in too.
By all our friendship, sir, by all our dangers,
By all you love most, wars and this sweet lady—
EMILIA
By that you would have trembled to deny   204
A blushing maid—

---

134 **appointed** accoutered in arms   135 **and officers of arms** and the
permission of my officers charged with supervising such combat
136 **Castor** one of Jupiter's sons, twin brother of Pollux.   **Hold** keep
143 **Was begged** whose life was begged of you. (See 2.2.251–
254.)   **contemns** scorns   147 **servant** knight devoted to the service of
the lady he loves. Palamon claims a prior right to be Emilia's "servant" by virtue of having seen her first and having given his soul to
her (11. 147–148).   153 **injuries** wrongful acts   156 **Then** after that
158–160 **'Tis . . . moved** my death would mean no more to me than
it would to you in uttering the judgment   167 **So . . . me** if that is
what "traitor" means, you will gratify me by calling me such

168 **For** as for   175 **thy cousin's** Hercules's, who was famous for his
twelve labors (1. 176)   177 **Let's** let the two of us   182 **More . . .**
found Theseus released Arcite from prison, though banishing him,
while Palamon remained in prison.   192 **but** unless and until
198 **that** your hope that.   **in** from   200 **chaste nights** nights spent in
monogamous wedded happiness   204–205 **By . . . maid** by the
chivalrous obligations that you would not wish to deny to a maiden in
distress

HIPPOLYTA   By your own eyes, by strength,   205
In which you swore I went beyond all women,   206
Almost all men, and yet I yielded, Theseus—
PIRITHOUS
To crown all this, by your most noble soul,
Which cannot want due mercy, I beg first—   209
HIPPOLYTA
Next hear my prayers—
EMILIA   Last let me entreat, sir—
PIRITHOUS
For mercy.
HIPPOLYTA   Mercy.
EMILIA   Mercy on these princes.
THESEUS
Ye make my faith reel. [To Emilia] Say I felt   212
Compassion to 'em both, how would you place it?
                                        [They rise.]
EMILIA
Upon their lives—but with their banishments.
THESEUS
You are a right woman, sister; you have pity,   215
But want the understanding where to use it.
If you desire their lives, invent a way
Safer than banishment. Can these two live,
And have the agony of love about 'em,
And not kill one another? Every day
They'd fight about you, hourly bring your honor   221
In public question with their swords. Be wise, then,   222
And here forget 'em; it concerns your credit
And my oath equally. I have said they die;
Better they fall by th' law than one another.
Bow not my honor.
EMILIA   O my noble brother,   226
That oath was rashly made, and in your anger;
Your reason will not hold it. If such vows   228
Stand for express will, all the world must perish.   229
Beside, I have another oath 'gainst yours,
Of more authority, I am sure more love,
Not made in passion neither, but good heed.   232
THESEUS
What is it, sister?
PIRITHOUS   Urge it home, brave lady.   233
EMILIA
That you would nev'r deny me anything
Fit for my modest suit and your free granting.
I tie you to your word now; if ye fail in 't,
Think how you maim your honor—
For now I am set a-begging, sir, I am deaf
To all but your compassion—how their lives   239
Might breed the ruin of my name, opinion.   240
Shall anything that loves me perish for me?
That were a cruel wisdom. Do men prune

The straight young boughs that blush with thousand
    blossoms
Because they may be rotten? O Duke Theseus,   244
The goodly mothers that have groaned for these,   245
And all the longing maids that ever loved,
If your vow stand, shall curse me and my beauty,
And in their funeral songs for these two cousins
Despise my cruelty, and cry woe worth me,   249
Till I am nothing but the scorn of women.
For heaven's sake, save their lives and banish 'em.
THESEUS
On what conditions?
EMILIA   Swear 'em never more   252
To make me their contention, or to know me,   253
To tread upon thy dukedom, and to be,
Wherever they shall travel, ever strangers
To one another.
PALAMON   I'll be cut a-pieces
Before I take this oath. Forget I love her?
O all ye gods, despise me then. Thy banishment   258
I not mislike, so we may fairly carry   259
Our swords and cause along; else never trifle,
But take our lives, Duke. I must love and will,
And for that love must and dare kill this cousin
On any piece the earth has.
THESEUS   Will you, Arcite,   263
Take these conditions?
PALAMON   He's a villain, then.
PIRITHOUS   These are men!
ARCITE
No, never, Duke. 'Tis worse to me than begging
To take my life so basely. Though I think
I never shall enjoy her, yet I'll preserve
The honor of affection, and die for her,
Make death a devil.   269
THESEUS
What may be done? For now I feel compassion.
PIRITHOUS
Let it not fall again, sir.
THESEUS   Say, Emilia,   271
If one of them were dead, as one must, are you
Content to take th' other to your husband?   273
They cannot both enjoy you. They are princes
As goodly as your own eyes, and as noble
As ever fame yet spoke of. Look upon 'em,
And, if you can love, end this difference.
I give consent.—Are you content too, princes?
PALAMON AND ARCITE
With all our souls.
THESEUS   He that she refuses
Must die, then.
PALAMON AND ARCITE   Any death thou canst invent,
Duke.

206 went beyond excelled 209 want be lacking in 212 Ye . . .
reel you shake my hitherto unwavering oath 215 right veritable,
typical. sister sister-in-law 221–222 bring . . . question fight
publicly over the honor of being your servant 226 Bow . . . honor
do not oblige me to yield dishonorably 228 hold it keep to it
229 Stand . . . will take the place of fixed and self-aware decision
232 passion anger. good heed thoughtfully 233 home to the quick
239 their lives i.e., their deaths 240 name, opinion reputation

244 be become 245 groaned groaned in childbearing 249 worth
befall, betide 252 Swear 'em oblige them to swear 253 know acknowledge 258 Thy banishment the banishment you propose
259 so provided. fairly fitly, justly 263 piece piece of ground
269 Make . . . devil i.e., though you should make death as terrifying
as the devil himself; or, by making death a frightful monster, thus
shame death itself 271 fall diminish, fail 273 to for, as

PALAMON
If I fall from that mouth, I fall with favor,   281
And lovers yet unborn shall bless my ashes.

ARCITE
If she refuse me, yet my grave will wed me,
And soldiers sing my epitaph.

THESEUS [*to Emilia*]   Make choice, then.

EMILIA
I cannot, sir; they are both too excellent.
For me, a hair shall never fall of these men.   286

HIPPOLYTA
What will become of 'em?

THESEUS   Thus I ordain it,
And by mine honor, once again, it stands,
Or both shall die. [*To Palamon and Arcite*] You shall
    both to your country,
And each, within this month, accompanied
With three fair knights, appear again in this place,
In which I'll plant a pyramid; and whether,   292
Before us that are here, can force his cousin
By fair and knightly strength to touch the pillar,
He shall enjoy her; the other lose his head,
And all his friends; nor shall he grudge to fall,   296
Nor think he dies with interest in this lady.   297
Will this content ye?

PALAMON   Yes. Here, cousin Arcite,
I am friends again till that hour.

ARCITE   I embrace ye.
                                        [*They embrace.*]

THESEUS
Are you content, sister?

EMILIA   Yes, I must, sir,
Else both miscarry.

THESEUS [*to Palamon and Arcite*]
                    Come, shake hands again, then,
And take heed, as you are gentlemen, this quarrel
Sleep till the hour prefixed, and hold your course.

PALAMON
We dare not fail thee, Theseus.

THESEUS   Come, I'll give ye
Now usage like to princes and to friends.
When ye return, who wins I'll settle here;   306
Who loses yet I'll weep upon his bier.

                                        Exeunt.

❖

4.1   *Enter Jailer and his Friend.*

JAILER
Hear you no more? Was nothing said of me
Concerning the escape of Palamon?
Good sir, remember.

---

281 from that mouth condemned by her   **286 For me** on my account   **292 plant a pyramid** erect an obelisk or pillar.   **whether** whichever of you two   **296−297 And . . . lady** and all his followers shall die also; nor shall he protest that the sentence is unjust, or that he continues to have a claim upon Emilia   **306 who . . . here** whoever wins I'll make a member of my court here in Athens
4.1. Location: The prison.

FIRST FRIEND   Nothing that I heard,
For I came home before the business
Was fully ended. Yet I might perceive,
Ere I departed, a great likelihood
Of both their pardons; for Hippolyta
And fair-eyed Emily, upon their knees,
Begged with such handsome pity that the Duke,
Methought, stood staggering whether he should
    follow
His rash oath or the sweet compassion
Of those two ladies; and to second them
That truly noble prince, Pirithous—
Half his own heart—set in too, that I hope   14
All shall be well; neither heard I one question
Of your name or his 'scape.

                    Enter Second Friend.

JAILER   Pray heaven it hold so.

SECOND FRIEND
Be of good comfort, man! I bring you news,
Good news.

JAILER   They are welcome.

SECOND FRIEND   Palamon has cleared you,   18
And got your pardon, and discovered how   19
And by whose means he escaped, which was your
    daughter's,
Whose pardon is procured too, and the prisoner,
Not to be held ungrateful to her goodness,
Has given a sum of money to her marriage—
A large one, I'll assure you.

JAILER   Ye are a good man
And ever bring good news.

FIRST FRIEND   How was it ended?

SECOND FRIEND
Why, as it should be: they that nev'r begged
But they prevailed had their suits fairly granted;
The prisoners have their lives.

FIRST FRIEND   I knew 'twould be so.

SECOND FRIEND
But there be new conditions, which you'll hear of
At better time.

JAILER   I hope they are good.

SECOND FRIEND   They are honorable;
How good they'll prove I know not.

                    Enter Wooer.

FIRST FRIEND   'Twill be known.

WOOER
Alas, sir, where's your daughter?

JAILER   Why do you ask?

WOOER
O sir, when did you see her?

SECOND FRIEND [*aside*]   How he looks!

JAILER
This morning.

WOOER   Was she well? Was she in health?
Sir, when did she sleep?

---

14 that so that   **18 They** the news   **19 discovered** revealed

FIRST FRIEND   These are strange questions.

JAILER
I do not think she was very well, for now
You make me mind her, but this very day   37
I asked her questions, and she answered me
So far from what she was, so childishly,   39
So sillily, as if she were a fool,
An innocent, and I was very angry.   41
But what of her, sir?

WOOER   Nothing but my pity;
But you must know it, and as good by me
As by another that less loves her.

JAILER
Well, sir?

FIRST FRIEND   Not right?   Not well?

SECOND FRIEND   No, sir, not well.   45

WOOER
'Tis too true, she is mad.

FIRST FRIEND   It cannot be.

WOOER
Believe you'll find it so.

JAILER   I half suspected
What you told me. The gods comfort her!
Either this was her love to Palamon,
Or fear of my miscarrying on his 'scape,   50
Or both.

WOOER   'Tis likely.

JAILER   But why all this haste, sir?

WOOER
I'll tell you quickly. As I late was angling   52
In the great lake that lies behind the palace,
From the far shore, thick set with reeds and sedges,
As patiently I was attending sport,   55
I heard a voice—a shrill one; and attentive,
I gave my ear, when I might well perceive
'Twas one that sung, and by the smallness of it   58
A boy or woman. I then left my angle   59
To his own skill, came near, but yet perceived not 60
Who made the sound, the rushes and the reeds
Had so encompassed it. I laid me down
And listened to the words she sung, for then,
Through a small glade cut by the fishermen,   64
I saw it was your daughter.

JAILER   Pray go on, sir.

WOOER
She sung much, but no sense, only I heard her
Repeat this often: "Palamon is gone,
Is gone to th' wood to gather mulberries;
I'll find him out tomorrow."

FIRST FRIEND   Pretty soul!

WOOER
"His shackles will betray him; he'll be taken,
And what shall I do then? I'll bring a bevy,

A hundred black-eyed maids that love as I do,
With chaplets on their heads of daffadillies,   73
With cherry lips and cheeks of damask roses,   74
And all we'll dance an antic 'fore the Duke,   75
And beg his pardon." Then she talked of you, sir— 76
That you must lose your head tomorrow morning,
And she must gather flowers to bury you,
And see the house made handsome. Then she sung
Nothing but "Willow, willow, willow," and between
Ever was "Palamon, fair Palamon,"
And "Palamon was a tall young man." The place   82
Was knee-deep where she sat. Her careless tresses 83
A wreath of bulrush rounded; about her stuck   84
Thousand freshwater flowers of several colors,
That methought she appeared like the fair nymph
That feeds the lake with waters, or as Iris,   87
Newly dropped down from heaven. Rings she made
Of rushes that grew by, and to 'em spoke
The prettiest posies: "Thus our true love's tied," 90
"This you may lose, not me," and many a one;
And then she wept, and sung again, and sighed,
And with the same breath smiled and kissed her
  hand.

SECOND FRIEND
Alas, what pity it is!

WOOER   I made in to her.   94
She saw me, and straight sought the flood. I saved
  her   95
And set her safe to land, when presently
She slipped away, and to the city made
With such a cry and swiftness that, believe me,
She left me far behind her. Three or four
I saw from far off cross her—one of 'em   100
I knew to be your brother—where she stayed   101
And fell, scarce to be got away. I left them with her 102

*Enter [Jailer's] Brother, [Jailer's] Daughter, and
others.*

And hither came to tell you. Here they are.

JAILER'S DAUGHTER [*sings*]
May you never more enjoy the light . . . (etc.)
Is not this a fine song?

JAILER'S BROTHER   O, a very fine one.

JAILER'S DAUGHTER
I can sing twenty more.

JAILER'S BROTHER   I think you can.

JAILER'S DAUGHTER
Yes, truly can I; I can sing "The Broom,"
And "Bonny Robin." Are not you a tailor?

JAILER'S BROTHER
Yes.

---

37 **mind** think of.   **but** only   39 **So far . . . was** so differently from
her usual way   41 **innocent** simpleton   45 **right** in her right mind
50 **miscarrying on** suffering misfortune on account of   52 **late** recently.   **angling** fishing   55 **attending sport** i.e., waiting for a bite
58 **smallness** softness   59 **angle** fishing tackle   60 **To his own skill** to
manage itself   64 **glade** clearing

73 **chaplets** garlands of flowers   74 **of damask roses** rose-colored
75 **antic** quaint or grotesque pageant   76 **beg his pardon** beg the life
of Palamon   82 **tall** handsome, valiant   83–84 **Her . . . rounded** a
garland of bulrushes encircled her disheveled tresses   87 **Iris** goddess
of the rainbow and messenger of Hera   90 **posies** short mottoes, often
inscribed within rings   94 **made in to** advanced toward   95 **straight
. . . flood** immediately got in the water   100 **cross** intercept
101 **stayed** halted   102 **scarce . . . away** almost unremovable

JAILER'S DAUGHTER
Where's my wedding gown?

JAILER'S BROTHER   I'll bring it tomorrow.

JAILER'S DAUGHTER
Do, very rarely; I must be abroad else   110
To call the maids and pay the minstrels,
For I must lose my maidenhead by cocklight;   112
'Twill never thrive else.
(Sings)   O fair, O sweet . . . [etc.]

JAILER'S BROTHER [to the Jailer]
You must ev'n take it patiently.

JAILER   'Tis true.

JAILER'S DAUGHTER
Good ev'n, good men. Pray, did you ever hear
Of one young Palamon?

JAILER   Yes, wench, we know him.

JAILER'S DAUGHTER
Is 't not a fine young gentleman?

JAILER   'Tis, love.

JAILER'S BROTHER [to the others]
By no mean cross her; she is then distempered   119
Far worse than now she shows.

FIRST FRIEND [to the Jailer's Daughter]
                              Yes, he's a fine man.

JAILER'S DAUGHTER
O, is he so? You have a sister.

FIRST FRIEND   Yes.

JAILER'S DAUGHTER
But she shall never have him, tell her so,
For a trick that I know. You'd best look to her, 123
For if she see him once, she's gone—she's done
And undone in an hour. All the young maids
Of our town are in love with him, but I laugh at 'em
And let 'em all alone. Is 't not a wise course?

FIRST FRIEND   Yes.

JAILER'S DAUGHTER
There is at least two hundred now with child by
    him—
There must be four; yet I keep close for all this, 129
Close as a cockle; and all these must be boys—   130
He has the trick on 't—and at ten years old   131
They must be all gelt for musicians,   132
And sing the wars of Theseus.

SECOND FRIEND [to the others]   This is strange.

JAILER'S BROTHER [to the Second Friend]
As ever you heard, but say nothing.

FIRST FRIEND   No.

JAILER'S DAUGHTER
They come from all parts of the dukedom to him.
I'll warrant ye, he had not so few last night   136
As twenty to dispatch. He'll trickle 't up   137
In two hours, if his hand be in.

JAILER [to the others]   She's lost   138
Past all cure.

JAILER'S BROTHER   Heaven forbid, man!

JAILER'S DAUGHTER [to the Jailer]
Come hither; you are a wise man.

FIRST FRIEND [to the Second Friend]   Does she know
    him?

SECOND FRIEND [to the First Friend]
No; would she did.

JAILER'S DAUGHTER   You are master of a ship?

JAILER   Yes.

JAILER'S DAUGHTER   Where's your compass?

JAILER   Here.

JAILER'S DAUGHTER   Set it to th' north;   145
And now direct your course to th' wood, where
    Palamon
Lies longing for me. For the tackling,   147
Let me alone. Come, weigh, my hearts, cheerly all. 148
Owgh, owgh, owgh! 'Tis up.   149
The wind's fair. Top the bowline.   150
Out with the mainsail! Where's your whistle,
    master?

JAILER'S BROTHER   Let's get her in.

JAILER   Up to the top, boy!

JAILER'S BROTHER   Where's the pilot?

FIRST FRIEND   Here.

JAILER'S DAUGHTER   What kenn'st thou?   156

SECOND FRIEND   A fair wood.

JAILER'S DAUGHTER   Bear for it, master. Tack about. 158
(Sings)
When Cynthia with her borrowed light . . . (etc.)
                                        Exeunt.

❧

4.2   Enter Emilia alone with two pictures.

EMILIA
Yet I may bind those wounds up, that must open
And bleed to death for my sake else; I'll choose,
And end their strife. Two such young handsome
    men
Shall never fall for me; their weeping mothers,
Following the dead cold ashes of their sons,
Shall never curse my cruelty. Good heaven,
What a sweet face has Arcite! If wise Nature,
With all her best endowments, all those beauties
She sows into the births of noble bodies,
Were here a mortal woman, and had in her   10
The coy denials of young maids, yet doubtless   11
She would run mad for this man. What an eye,
Of what a fiery sparkle and quick sweetnes ,   13

110 **rarely** early; excellently.   **abroad else** away from home other-wise   112 **cocklight** dawn   119 **mean** means.   **cross** contradict.   **distempered** mentally disordered   123 **For** because of   129 **keep close** keep to myself, keep still   130 **cockle** clam-like mollusk   131 **on 't** i.e., of begetting sons   132 **gelt for musicians** castrated before puberty to preserve the soprano or contralto voice   136–137 **not so few . . . As** no fewer than   137 **tickle 't up** finish up. (With sexual suggestion.)   138 **if . . . in** if he's in good form. (With sexual suggestion.)

145 **Set** orient   147–148 **For . . . alone** as for the rigging, leave it to me   148 **weigh** weigh anchor or hoist the mast   149 **Owgh** a grunting sound of exertion   150 **Top the bowline** haul in on the line used to hold steady the edge of a square sail in sailing close to the wind   156 **kenn'st thou** do you discern   158 **Bear** head
4.2 Location: Theseus's palace, Athens.
10–11 **and had . . . maids** and possessed the modest inclination of virtuous young maids to resist male blandishments   13 **quick** lively

Has this young prince! Here Love himself sits
    smiling;   14
Just such another wanton Ganymede   15
Set Jove afire with, and enforced the god
Snatch up the goodly boy and set him by him,
A shining constellation. What a brow,   18
Of what a spacious majesty, he carries,
Arched like the great-eyed Juno's, but far sweeter,
Smoother than Pelops' shoulder! Fame and Honor,   21
Methinks, from hence, as from a promontory   22
Pointed in heaven, should clap their wings and sing   23
To all the under world the loves and fights   24
Of gods and such men near 'em. Palamon   25
Is but his foil, to him a mere dull shadow;
He's swart and meager, of an eye as heavy   27
As if he had lost his mother, a still temper,   28
No stirring in him, no alacrity,
Of all this sprightly sharpness not a smile.   30
Yet these that we count errors may become him;
Narcissus was a sad boy but a heavenly.   32
O, who can find the bent of woman's fancy?   33
I am a fool; my reason is lost in me;
I have no choice, and I have lied so lewdly   35
That women ought to beat me. On my knees
I ask thy pardon! Palamon, thou art alone
And only beautiful, and these the eyes,
These the bright lamps of beauty, that command
And threaten love, and what young maid dare cross
    'em?   40
What a bold gravity, and yet inviting,
Has this brown manly face! O Love, this only   42
From this hour is complexion. Lie there, Arcite;   43
Thou art a changeling to him, a mere gypsy,   44
And this the noble body. I am sotted,   45
Utterly lost; my virgin's faith has fled me.
For if my brother but even now had asked me
Whether I loved, I had run mad for Arcite;   48
Now if my sister, more for Palamon.
Stand both together. Now come ask me, brother;
Alas, I know not! Ask me now, sweet sister;

I may go look. What a mere child is Fancy,   52
That, having two fair gauds of equal sweetness,   53
Cannot distinguish, but must cry for both!

    Enter a Gentleman.

How now, sir?
GENTLEMAN   From the noble Duke, your brother,
    Madam, I bring you news: the knights are come.
EMILIA
    To end the quarrel?
GENTLEMAN   Yes.
EMILIA   Would I might end first!
    What sins have I committed, chaste Diana,   58
    That my unspotted youth must now be soiled
    With blood of princes, and my chastity
    Be made the altar where the lives of lovers—
    Two greater and two better never yet
    Made mothers joy—must be the sacrifice   63
    To my unhappy beauty?

        *Enter Theseus, Hippolyta, Pirithous, and
        attendants.*

THESEUS   Bring 'em in   64
    Quickly, by any means; I long to see 'em.
                                    [*Exit one or more.*]
    [*To Emilia*] Your two contending lovers are
        returned,
    And with them their fair knights. Now, my fair
        sister,
    You must love one of them.
EMILIA   I had rather both,
    So neither for my sake should fall untimely.
THESEUS
    Who saw 'em?
PIRITHOUS   I awhile.
GENTLEMAN   And I.   70

        Enter a Messenger.

THESEUS
    From whence come you, sir?
MESSENGER   From the knights.
THESEUS   Pray speak,
    You that have seen them, what they are.
MESSENGER   I will, sir,
    And truly what I think. Six braver spirits
    Than these they have brought, if we judge by the
        outside,
    I never saw nor read of. He that stands
    In the first place with Arcite, by his seeming   76
    Should be a stout man, by his face a prince;   77
    His very looks so say him, his complexion   78
    Nearer a brown than black—stern and yet noble—

---

14 Love himself Cupid. (Emilia is comparing the two portraits; see also ll. 43 and 50.) **15 Ganymede** the young man whom Jove, infatuated, took to be his cupbearer **18 constellation** The zodiacal sign Aquarius was often thought to have been Ganymede transported to the sky. **21 Pelops' shoulder** Pelops's father, Tantalus, served the child to the gods in a banquet to see if they could tell the flesh from that of some animal. He managed to fool Demeter into eating part of the shoulder. The gods restored Pelops to life with the missing shoulder replaced by ivory. **22 hence** Arcite's brow **23 Pointed** coming to a point **24 the under world** the earth as seen from the heavens **25 near 'em** close to the gods in achievement **27 He's . . . meager** Palamon is swarthy and of deficient build. **heavy** sad **28 still temper** lethargic temperament **30 Of . . . smile** with not even a smile to match Arcite's sprightly keenness **32 Narcissus . . . heavenly** i.e., Narcissus too had a sad look about him (owing to his being punished for repulsing the love of Echo by becoming enamored of his own image in a fountain), and yet he was immortalized. **33 bent** inclination **35 choice** ability to choose. **lewdly** basely, ignorantly **40 cross** encounter, contradict **42–43 this . . . complexion** from this day forth, Palamon's dark complexion is the only one for me **44 a changeling** a child (usually stupid or ugly) thought to have been left by fairies in exchange for one stolen **45 sotted** besotted **48 Whether** which of the two. **had** would have

52 I . . . look i.e., for all my looking, I find no answer. **Fancy** love **53 gauds** toys, baubles **58 Diana** goddess associated with the moon and with chastity **63 joy** rejoice **64 unhappy** causing misfortune **70 awhile** recently **76 seeming** appearance **77 stout** valiant **78 say** proclaim

Which shows him hardy, fearless, proud of dangers.
The circles of his eyes show fire within him,
And as a heated lion, so he looks.   82
His hair hangs long behind him, black and shining
Like ravens' wings; his shoulders broad and strong,
Armed long and round; and on his thigh a sword   85
Hung by a curious baldric, when he frowns   86
To seal his will with. Better, o' my conscience,   87
Was never soldier's friend.

THESEUS
Thou hast well described him.

PIRITHOUS   Yet a great deal short,
Methinks, of him that's first with Palamon.

THESEUS
Pray speak him, friend.

PIRITHOUS   I guess he is a prince too,   91
And, if it may be, greater, for his show   92
Has all the ornament of honor in 't.
He's somewhat bigger than the knight he spoke of, 94
But of a face far sweeter; his complexion
Is, as a ripe grape, ruddy. He has felt
Without doubt what he fights for, and so apter   97
To make this cause his own. In 's face appears
All the fair hopes of what he undertakes,
And when he's angry, then a settled valor,
Not tainted with extremes, runs through his body,
And guides his arm to brave things. Fear he
    cannot;
He shows no such soft temper. His head's yellow,
Hard-haired and curled, thick-twined like ivy-tods, 104
Not to undo with thunder. In his face   105
The livery of the warlike maid appears,   106
Pure red and white, for yet no beard has blessed
    him;
And in his rolling eyes sits Victory,
As if she ever meant to court his valor.   109
His nose stands high, a character of honor;   110
His red lips, after fights, are fit for ladies.

EMILIA
Must these men die too?

PIRITHOUS   When he speaks, his tongue
Sounds like a trumpet. All his lineaments
Are as a man would wish 'em—strong and clean.
He wears a well-steeled ax, the staff of gold;
His age some five-and-twenty.

MESSENGER   There's another—
A little man, but of a tough soul, seeming
As great as any. Fairer promises
In such a body yet I never looked on.

PIRITHOUS
O, he that's freckle-faced?

MESSENGER   The same, my lord.
Are they not sweet ones?

PIRITHOUS   Yes, they are well.

MESSENGER   Methinks,   121
Being so few, and well disposed, they show   122
Great and fine art in nature. He's white-haired— 123
Not wanton white, but such a manly color   124
Next to an auburn; tough and nimble-set,   125
Which shows an active soul. His arms are brawny,
Lined with strong sinews. To the shoulder-piece   127
Gently they swell, like women new-conceived,   128
Which speaks him prone to labor, never fainting   129
Under the weight of arms; stout-hearted still,   130
But when he stirs, a tiger. He's grey-eyed,   131
Which yields compassion where he conquers; sharp 132
To spy advantages, and where he finds 'em,
He's swift to make 'em his. He does no wrongs,
Nor takes none. He's round-faced, and when he
    smiles
He shows a lover, when he frowns, a soldier.   136
About his head he wears the winner's oak,   137
And in it stuck the favor of his lady;   138
His age some six-and-thirty. In his hand
He bears a charging-staff embossed with silver.   140

THESEUS
Are they all thus?

PIRITHOUS   They are all the sons of honor.

THESEUS
Now, as I have a soul, I long to see 'em.
[To Hippolyta] Lady, you shall see men fight, now.

HIPPOLYTA   I wish it,
But not the cause, my lord. They would show   144
Bravely about the titles of two kingdoms;   145
'Tis pity love should be so tyrannous.

                                  [Emilia weeps.]
O, my soft-hearted sister, what think you?
Weep not till they weep blood. Wench, it must be.

THESEUS [to Emilia]
You have steeled 'em with your beauty.
    [To Pirithous] Honored friend,   149
To you I give the field; pray order it   150
Fitting the persons that must use it.

PIRITHOUS   Yes, sir.

THESEUS
Come, I'll go visit 'em; I cannot stay,   152
Their fame has fired me so. Till they appear,
Good friend, be royal.

PIRITHOUS   There shall want no bravery.   154

---

82 **heated** angry   85 **Armed . . . round** with long, well-shaped arms
86 **curious baldric** intricately designed belt worn across one shoulder
86–87 **when . . . with** which he uses to execute his furious will
91 **speak** describe   92 **show** appearance   94 **he** the messenger
97 **what . . . for** i.e., love   104 **ivy-tods** ivy bushes   105 **undo** be
undone or destroyed   106 **the warlike maid** Athene, warlike goddess, protector of Athens   109 **court** pay courteous attention to
110 **His . . . honor** The prominent Roman nose was thought to indicate honorableness.

121 **they** the freckles   122 **disposed** placed, situated   123 **white-haired** blond   124 **wanton** effeminate   125 **nimble-set** nimble of
build   127 **Lined** fortified   128 **new-conceived** newly pregnant
129 **speaks . . . labor** bespeaks one willing to strive hard (with a pun
on the ''labor'' of pregnancy)   130 **still** (1) always, under any conditions (2) at rest   131 **grey-eyed** blue-eyed   132 **Which . . . conquers**
which indicates his inclination to be compassionate to those he conquers   136 **shows** looks like   137 **oak** garland of oak leaves   138 **favor** glove, scarf or other token   140 **charging-staff** tilting lance   144–
145 **They . . . kingdoms** their splendor would be well suited to a contention between two kingdoms   149 **steeled** hardened   150 **the field**
the management of the contest   152 **stay** wait   154 **be royal** arrange
matters with royal generosity.   **want no bravery** lack no splendor

EMILIA [*to herself*]
Poor wench, go weep, for whosoever wins
Loses a noble cousin for thy sins.

Exeunt.

❧

4.3   *Enter Jailer, Wooer, Doctor.*

DOCTOR   Her distraction is more at some time of the
moon than at other some, is it not?   2
JAILER   She is continually in a harmless distemper,
sleeps little; altogether without appetite, save often
drinking; dreaming of another world, and a better;
and what broken piece of matter soe'er she's about,
the name "Palamon" lards it, that she farces ev'ry 7
business withal, fits it to every question.

Enter [Jailer's] Daughter.

Look where she comes. You shall perceive her behavior.   [*They stand apart.*]
JAILER'S DAUGHTER   I have forgot it quite; the burden 11
on 't was "Down-a, down-a," and penned by no 12
worse man than Geraldo, Emilia's schoolmaster. He's
as fantastical, too, as ever he may go upon 's legs; for 14
in the next world will Dido see Palamon, and then will 15
she be out of love with Aeneas.
DOCTOR   What stuff's here! Poor soul!
JAILER   Ev'n thus all day long.
JAILER'S DAUGHTER   Now for this charm that I told you
of, you must bring a piece of silver on the tip of your
tongue, or no ferry; then if it be your chance to come 21
where the blessed spirits are—there's a sight now!
We maids that have our livers perished, cracked to 23
pieces with love, we shall come there, and do nothing
all day long but pick flowers with Proserpine. Then 25
will I make Palamon a nosegay, then let him mark me, 26
then—
DOCTOR   How prettily she's amiss! Note her a little
further.
JAILER'S DAUGHTER   Faith, I'll tell you: sometime we go
to barley-break, we of the blessèd. Alas, 'tis a sore 31
life they have i' th' other place. Such burning, frying, 32
boiling, hissing, howling, chatt'ring, cursing—O,
they have shrewd measure, take heed! If one be mad, 34

or hang or drown themselves, thither they go, Jupiter
bless us, and there shall we be put in a cauldron of
lead and usurers' grease, amongst a whole million of 37
cutpurses, and there boil like a gammon of bacon that 38
will never be enough.   39
DOCTOR   How her brain coins!   40
JAILER'S DAUGHTER   Lords and courtiers that have got
maids with child, they are in this place; they shall
stand in fire up to the navel and in ice up to th' heart,
and there th' offending part burns and the deceiving part freezes—in truth a very grievous punishment,
as one would think, for such a trifle. Believe me,
one would marry a leprous witch to be rid on 't, I'll
assure you.
DOCTOR   How she continues this fancy! 'Tis not an en- 49
grafted madness, but a most thick and profound 50
melancholy.
JAILER'S DAUGHTER   To hear there a proud lady and a
proud city wife howl together! I were a beast an I'd call 53
it good sport. One cries, "O, this smoke!," th' other,
"This fire!"; one cries, "O, that ever I did it behind
the arras!', and then howls; th' other curses a 56
suing fellow and her garden house.   57
(*Sings*)
    I will be true, my stars, my fate . . . (etc.)
                               Exit [Jailer's] Daughter.
JAILER   What think you of her, sir?
DOCTOR   I think she has a perturbed mind, which I
cannot minister to.
JAILER   Alas, what then?
DOCTOR   Understand you she ever affected any man 63
ere she beheld Palamon?
JAILER   I was once, sir, in great hope she had fixed her
liking on this gentleman, my friend.
WOOER   I did think so too, and would account I had a 67
great penn'orth on 't to give half my state that both she 68
and I, at this present, stood unfeignedly on the same
terms.
DOCTOR   That intemp'rate surfeit of her eye hath distempered the other senses. They may return and
settle again to execute their preordained faculties, but
they are now in a most extravagant vagary. This you 74
must do: confine her to a place where the light may
rather seem to steal in than be permitted. Take upon
you, young sir, her friend, the name of Palamon; say
you come to eat with her, and to commune of love.
This will catch her attention, for this her mind beats
upon; other objects that are inserted 'tween her mind
and eye become the pranks and friskins of her 81
madness. Sing to her such green songs of love as she 82
says Palamon hath sung in prison; come to her stuck 83

4.3. Location: The prison.
2 at other some at other times   **7 lards** is inserted into. **farces** stuffs
(cooking terms)   **11-12 burden on 't** refrain of it   **14 fantastical** filled
with lively imagination. **ever . . . legs** anyone who can walk, any
person   **15 Dido** Queen of Carthage, deserted by Aeneas in Virgil's
Aeneid   **21 or no ferry** A coin was placed on the tongue of a deceased person as fare for being ferried across the Styx to the underworld by Charon.   **23 livers** supposed seat of the passions   **25 Proserpine** As this beautiful goddess was picking flowers in Sicily, she was
carried off by Hades to be his queen in the lower world.   **26 nosegay**
small bunch of flowers   **31 barley-break** a game played by various
couples, one couple in the center (called "hell") trying to catch the
others   **32 th' other place** i.e., hell   **34 shrewd measure** dire punishment

37 grease i.e., sweat   **38 gammon** ham   **38-39 that . . . enough** i.e.,
the torment will never cease   **40 coins** fabricates   **49–50 engrafted**
implanted in the mind   **53 I . . . an** I would be a beast if   **56 arras**
hanging screen placed in front of walls, allowing space behind for
concealment and assignations   **57 suing fellow** suitor. **garden house**
a suitable place for a seduction   **63 affected** felt passion for   **67–
68 would . . . on 't** would consider it a great bargain   **68 state** estate   **74 in . . . vagary** wandering out of bounds   **81 friskins** playful
encounters   **82 green** youthful   **83 stuck** decked out

in as sweet flowers as the season is mistress of, and thereto make an addition of some other compounded odors which are grateful to the sense. All this shall become Palamon, for Palamon can sing, and Palamon 88 is sweet and ev'ry good thing. Desire to eat with her, carve her, drink to her, and still among intermingle 90 your petition of grace and acceptance into her favor. Learn what maids have been her companions and playferes, and let them repair to her with "Palamon" 93 in their mouths, and appear with tokens, as if they 94 suggested for him. It is a falsehood she is in, which is 95 with falsehoods to be combatted. This may bring her to eat, to sleep, and reduce what's now out of square 97 in her into their former law and regiment. I have seen 98 it approved, how many times I know not; but, to 99 make the number more, I have great hope in this. I will between the passages of this project come in 101 with my appliance. Let us put it in execution, and 102 hasten the success, which doubt not will bring forth 103 comfort.

Exeunt.

❖

5.1   *Flourish. Enter Theseus, Pirithous, Hippolyta, attendants. [Three altars are visible.]*

THESEUS
Now let 'em enter, and before the gods
Tender their holy prayers. Let the temples
Burn bright with sacred fires, and the altars
In hallowed clouds commend their swelling incense
To those above us. Let no due be wanting;
They have a noble work in hand, will honor   6
The very powers that love 'em.

    *Flourish of cornets. Enter Palamon and Arcite and
    their knights [at opposite doors].*

PIRITHOUS   Sir, they enter.
THESEUS
You valiant and strong-hearted enemies,
You royal german foes, that this day come   9
To blow that nearness out that flames between ye,   10
Lay by your anger for an hour, and, dove-like,
Before the holy altars of your helpers,
The all-feared gods, bow down your stubborn
    bodies.
Your ire is more than mortal; so your help be,   14
And as the gods regard ye, fight with justice.   15

I'll leave you to your prayers, and betwixt ye
I part my wishes.
PIRITHOUS   Honor crown the worthiest!
    *Exeunt Theseus and his train, [including Pirithous
    and Hippolyta].*
PALAMON [*to Arcite*]
The glass is running now that cannot finish   18
Till one of us expire. Think you but thus,
That were there aught in me which strove to show   20
Mine enemy in this business, were 't one eye
Against another, arm oppressed by arm,
I would destroy th' offender, coz—I would,
Though parcel of myself. Then from this gather   24
How I should tender you.
ARCITE   I am in labor   25
To push your name, your ancient love, our kindred,
Out of my memory, and i' th' selfsame place
To seat something I would confound. So hoist we   28
The sails that must these vessels port even where   29
The heavenly limiter pleases.
PALAMON   You speak well.   30
Before I turn, let me embrace thee, cousin.   31
    [*They embrace.*]
This I shall never do again.
ARCITE   One farewell.
PALAMON
Why, let it be so; farewell, coz.
ARCITE   Farewell, sir.
    Exeunt Palamon and his knights.
Knights, kinsmen, lovers, yea, my sacrifices,
True worshipers of Mars, whose spirit in you
Expels the seeds of fear and th' apprehension   36
Which still is father of it: go with me   37
Before the god of our profession. There   38
Require of him the hearts of lions and   39
The breath of tigers, yea, the fierceness too,   40
Yea, the speed also—to go on, I mean;
Else wish we to be snails. You know my prize
Must be dragged out of blood; force and great feat
Must put my garland on, where she sticks,   44
The queen of flowers. Our intercession, then,   45
Must be to him that makes the camp a cistern   46
Brimmed with the blood of men. Give me your aid,   47
And bend your spirits towards him.

    *They [advance to Mars's altar, fall prostrate, and
    kneel].*

Thou mighty one, that with thy power hast turned
Green Neptune into purple;   50

---

88 **become** suit your role as   90 **carve** carve meat for.   **still among** mingled with these activities   93 **playferes** playfellows.   **repair** come
94 **tokens** love tokens   95 **suggested** pleaded.   **falsehood** delusion
97 **reduce** lead back   98 **regiment** order   99 **it approved** this course of treatment confirmed in practice   101 **passages** transactions
102 **appliance** application, administering   103 **success** outcome
5.1. Location: The forest, where Palamon and Arcite fought (in 3.6) and where the tournament is now to be held. Visible onstage are temples to Mars, Venus, and Diana, each with an altar.
6 **will** that will   9 **german** cousin   10 **blow that nearness out** blow out or extinguish the friendship and nearness of blood   14 **be** must be
15 **regard** watch over

18 **glass** hourglass   20 **show** appear as   24 **parcel** part   25 **tender** feel tenderly toward, treat   28 **confound** destroy   29 **port** transport, convey to port   30 **The heavenly limiter** God, who controls all things. (Man proposes, God disposes.)   31 **turn** turn away
36–37 **th' apprehension . . . of it** the anticipation or perception of danger which is ever the cause of fear   38 **of our profession** to whom we offer our services and who is patron of our military calling
39 **Require** request   40 **breath** endurance, "wind"   44 **garland** victor's wreath   44–45 **where . . . flowers** Emily, the queen of flowers, dwells in Arcite's heart.   46 **him** Mars   47 **Brimmed** filled to the brim   50 **Green Neptune** i.e., the sea

Whose havoc in vast field comets prewarn,   51
Unearthèd skulls proclaim; whose breath blows
    down
The teeming Ceres' foison; who dost pluck   53
With hand armipotent from forth blue clouds   54
The masoned turrets, that both mak'st and break'st   55
The stony girths of cities: me thy pupil,   56
Youngest follower of thy drum, instruct this day
With military skill, that to thy laud   58
I may advance my streamer, and by thee   59
Be styled the lord o' th' day. Give me, great Mars,   60
Some token of thy pleasure.   61

> *Here they fall on their faces as formerly, and there
> is heard clanging of armor, with a short thunder,
> as the burst of a battle, whereupon they all rise and
> bow to the altar.*

O great corrector of enormous times,   62
Shaker of o'er-rank states, thou grand decider   63
Of dusty and old titles, that heal'st with blood   64
The earth when it is sick, and cur'st the world
O' th' plurisy of people, I do take   66
Thy signs auspiciously, and in thy name
To my design march boldly. [*To his knights*] Let us
    go.   *Exeunt.*   68

> *Enter Palamon and his knights, with the former
> observance.*

PALAMON
Our stars must glister with new fire, or be   69
Today extinct. Our argument is love,
Which, if the goddess of it grant, she gives
Victory too. Then blend your spirits with mine,
You whose free nobleness do make my cause
Your personal hazard. To the goddess Venus
Commend we our proceeding, and implore
Her power unto our party.

> *Here they [advance to Venus's altar, prostrate
> themselves, and] kneel as formerly.*

Hail, sovereign queen of secrets, who hast power
To call the fiercest tyrant from his rage
And weep unto a girl; that hast the might   79
Even with an eye-glance to choke Mars's drum
And turn th' alarm to whispers; that canst make   81
A cripple flourish with his crutch, and cure him   82

Before Apollo; that mayst force the king   83
To be his subject's vassal, and induce
Stale gravity to dance! The polled bachelor—   85
Whose youth, like wanton boys through bonfires,
Have skipped thy flame—at seventy thou canst
    catch,   87
And make him, to the scorn of his hoarse throat,
Abuse young lays of love. What godlike power   89
Hast thou not power upon? To Phoebus thou
Add'st flames hotter than his; the heavenly fires
Did scorch his mortal son, thine him. The huntress,   92
All moist and cold, some say, began to throw
Her bow away and sigh. Take to thy grace
Me, thy vowed soldier, who do bear thy yoke
As 'twere a wreath of roses, yet is heavier   96
Than lead itself, stings more than nettles.
I have never been foul-mouthed against thy law;
Nev'r revealed secret, for I knew none; would not,
Had I kenned all that were. I never practiced   100
Upon man's wife, nor would the libels read   101
Of liberal wits. I never at great feasts   102
Sought to betray a beauty, but have blushed   103
At simp'ring sirs that did. I have been harsh
To large confessors, and have hotly asked them   105
If they had mothers; I had one, a woman,
And women 'twere they wronged. I knew a man
Of eighty winters—this I told them—who
A lass of fourteen brided; 'twas thy power   109
To put life into dust. The agèd cramp
Had screwed his square foot round;   111
The gout had knit his fingers into knots;
Torturing convulsions from his globy eyes   113
Had almost drawn their spheres, that what was life   114
In him seemed torture. This anatomy   115
Had by his young fair fere a boy, and I   116
Believed it was his, for she swore it was,
And who would not believe her? Brief, I am   118
To those that prate and have done, no companion;   119
To those that boast and have not, a defier;
To those that would and cannot, a rejoicer.
Yea, him I do not love that tells close offices   122
The foulest way, nor names concealments in
The boldest language. Such a one I am,   124
And vow that lover never yet made sigh
Truer than I. O then, most soft sweet goddess,

---

51 field battlefield   **53 The . . . foison** teeming crops ready for harvesting, the gift of Ceres, goddess of agriculture   **53–55 pluck . . . turrets** pull down with your mighty arm, from out of the sky, the stone-built fortifications   **56 girths** walls   **58 to thy laud** in praise of thee   **59 streamer** banner   **60 styled** titled   **61 s.d. burst** eruption   **62 enormous** abnormal, monstrous   **63 o'er-rank** overripe, decadent   **64 with blood** In battle, the blood falls to earth and nourishes it; in the medical practice of bleeding, the patient is cured by being rid of unwanted humors.   **66 plurisy** diseased superabundance. (Pleurisy, an inflammation of the lung sacks or pleura, was wrongly thought to be derived from the Latin *plus, plur-*, "more.")   **68 s.d. the former observance.** Palamon and his knights fulfill ceremonies at Venus's altar like those performed by Arcite and his knights at Mars's altar.   **69 stars** fortunes   **79 weep unto** make him weep before, imploring the favor of   **81 alarm** alarum, call to arms   **82 flourish with** wave about vigorously

83 Before Apollo sooner than Apollo, the god of medicine   **85 polled** bald, shorn   **87 Have skipped** has skipped over, jumped through unsinged   **89 Abuse** butcher (with his hoarse singing)   **92 his mortal son** Phaethon, who drove the sun god Phoebus's chariot too near the sun.   **the huntress** Diana or Artemis, goddess of chastity and of the moon, who fell in love with a shepherd (Endymion)   **96 is** it is   **100 kenned** known   **100–101 practiced Upon** attempted to seduce   **102 liberal** licentious   **103 betray** (1) tattle about (2) seduce   **105 large confessors** men who boast unrestrainedly of their sexual prowess with many women   **109 brided** took as his bride   **111 Had . . . round** had twisted his well-proportioned foot into a gouty misshapen mass   **113 globy** protruding   **114 drawn their spheres** popped out the eyeballs.   **that** so that   **115 anatomy** mere skeleton   **116 fere** partner (in marriage)   **118 Brief** in brief   **119 and have done** and did what they boast about   **122 close offices** secret affairs   **124 Such a one** i.e., one who condemns male boastfulness

Give me the victory of this question, which 127
Is true love's merit, and bless me with a sign 128
Of thy great pleasure.

Here music is heard. Doves are seen to flutter.
They fall again upon their faces, then on their
knees.

O thou that from eleven to ninety reign'st
In mortal bosoms, whose chase is this world 131
And we in herds thy game, I give thee thanks 132
For this fair token, which, being laid unto
Mine innocent true heart, arms in assurance
My body to this business. [*To his knights*] Let us rise
And bow before the goddess.   *They* [*rise and*] *bow.*
            Time comes on.   *Exeunt.* 136

Still music of record[*er*]*s. Enter Emilia in white,*
her hair about her shoulders, [*wearing*] *a wheaten*
wreath; one in white holding up her train, her hair
stuck with flowers; one before her carrying a silver
hind, in which is conveyed incense and sweet
odors; which being set upon the altar [*of Diana*]*,*
her maids standing aloof, she sets fire to it. Then
they curtsy and kneel.

EMILIA
O sacred, shadowy, cold, and constant queen, 137
Abandoner of revels, mute contemplative,
Sweet, solitary, white as chaste, and pure
As wind-fanned snow, who to thy female knights
Allow'st no more blood than will make a blush,
Which is their order's robe: I here, thy priest, 142
Am humbled 'fore thine altar. O vouchsafe
With that thy rare green eye, which never yet 144
Beheld thing maculate, look on thy virgin! 145
And, sacred silver mistress, lend thine ear—
Which nev'r heard scurril term, into whose port 147
Ne'er entered wanton sound—to my petition,
Seasoned with holy fear. This is my last
Of vestal office; I am bride-habited,
But maiden-hearted. A husband I have 'pointed, 151
But do not know him. Out of two I should
Choose one, and pray for his success, but I
Am guiltless of election. Of mine eyes 154
Were I to lose one—they are equal precious—
I could doom neither; that which perished should 156
Go to 't unsentenced. Therefore, most modest
    queen, 157
He of the two pretenders that best loves me 158
And has the truest title in 't, let him

Take off my wheaten garland, or else grant
The file and quality I hold I may 161
Continue in thy band. 162

Here the hind vanishes under the altar, and in the
place ascends a rose tree, having one rose upon it.

See what our general of ebbs and flows 163
Out from the bowels of her holy altar
With sacred act advances—but one rose! 165
If well inspired, this battle shall confound 166
Both these brave knights, and I, a virgin flower,
Must grow alone, unplucked.

Here is heard a sudden twang of instruments, and
the rose falls from the tree.   [The tree descends.]

The flower is fall'n, the tree descends. O mistress,
Thou here dischargest me. I shall be gathered; 170
I think so, but I know not thine own will.
Unclasp thy mystery!—I hope she's pleased;
Her signs were gracious.
                    They curtsy and exeunt.

❧

5.2   *Enter Doctor, Jailer, and Wooer in* [*the*] *habit of*
    Palamon.

DOCTOR   Has this advice I told you done any good
upon her?
WOOER   O, very much. The maids that kept her com-
pany have half persuaded her that I am Palamon.
Within this half-hour she came smiling to me, and
asked me what I would eat, and when I would kiss
her. I told her presently, and kissed her twice.
DOCTOR
'Twas well done. Twenty times had been far better,
For there the cure lies mainly.
WOOER   Then she told me 9
She would watch with me tonight, for well she
    knew 10
What hour my fit would take me.
DOCTOR   Let her do so, 11
And when your fit comes, fit her home, 12
And presently.
WOOER   She would have me sing.
DOCTOR
You did so?
WOOER   No.
DOCTOR   'Twas very ill done, then;
You should observe her ev'ry way.
WOOER   Alas, 15

I have no voice, sir, to confirm her that way.   16

DOCTOR
That's all one, if ye make a noise.   17
If she entreat again, do anything;
Lie with her if she ask you.

JAILER   Ho there, doctor!

DOCTOR
Yes, in the way of cure.

JAILER   But first, by your leave,
I' th' way of honesty.

DOCTOR   That's but a niceness.   21
Nev'r cast your child away for honesty.   22
Cure her first this way; then if she will be honest,   23
She has the path before her.

JAILER
Thank ye, doctor.

DOCTOR   Pray bring her in,
And let's see how she is.

JAILER   I will, and tell her
Her Palamon stays for her. But, doctor,   27
Methinks you are i' th' wrong still.   *Exit Jailer.*

DOCTOR   Go, go;
You fathers are fine fools! Her honesty?
An we should give her physic till we find that—   30

WOOER
Why, do you think she is not honest, sir?

DOCTOR
How old is she?

WOOER   She's eighteen.

DOCTOR   She may be,
But that's all one; 'tis nothing to our purpose.
Whate'er her father says, if you perceive
Her mood inclining that way that I spoke of,
Videlicet, the way of flesh—you have me?   36

WOOER
Yes, very well, sir.

DOCTOR   Please her appetite,
And do it home; it cures her, *ipso facto,*   38
The melancholy humor that infects her.

WOOER
I am of your mind, doctor.

Enter Jailer [and his] Daughter, [mad].

DOCTOR
You'll find it so. She comes; pray humor her.
[Doctor and Wooer stand aside.]

JAILER
Come, your love Palamon stays for you, child,
And has done this long hour, to visit you.

JAILER'S DAUGHTER
I thank him for his gentle patience.

He's a kind gentleman, and I am much bound to
him.
Did you nev'r see the horse he gave me?

JAILER   Yes.

JAILER'S DAUGHTER
How do you like him?

JAILER   He's a very fair one.   47

JAILER'S DAUGHTER
You never saw him dance?

JAILER   No.

JAILER'S DAUGHTER   I have, often.
He dances very finely, very comely,
And for a jig, come cut and long tail to him,   50
He turns ye like a top.

JAILER   That's fine indeed.   51

JAILER'S DAUGHTER
He'll dance the morris twenty mile an hour,
And that will founder the best hobby-horse,   53
If I have any skill, in all the parish;   54
And gallops to the tune of "Light o' love."   55
What think you of this horse?

JAILER   Having these virtues,
I think he might be brought to play at tennis.

JAILER'S DAUGHTER
Alas, that's nothing.

JAILER   Can he write and read too?

JAILER'S DAUGHTER
A very fair hand, and casts himself th' accounts   59
Of all his hay and provender. That hostler   60
Must rise betime that cozens him. You know   61
The chestnut mare the Duke has?

JAILER   Very well.

JAILER'S DAUGHTER
She is horribly in love with him, poor beast,   63
But he is like his master, coy and scornful.   64

JAILER
What dowry has she?

JAILER'S DAUGHTER   Some two hundred bottles,   65
And twenty strike of oats, but he'll ne'er have her.   66
He lisps in 's neighing able to entice   67
A miller's mare. He'll be the death of her.   68

DOCTOR   What stuff she utters!
[The Wooer approaches her.]

JAILER
Make curtsy; here your love comes.

16 **confirm** fortify, encourage   17 **That's all one** it's all the same
21 **honesty** chaste marriage.   **niceness** fastidiousness   22 **Nev'r . . .
honesty** don't abandon her to her affliction merely out of regard for
her chastity   23 **will** wishes to be   27 **stays** waits   30 **An . . . that** if
we were to give her medical treatment until we were assured of her
chastity   36 **Videlicet** namely.   **have** understand   38 **home** thoroughly.   **cures her** cures her of.   **ipso facto** by that very act

47 **fair** good-looking   50 **come . . . to him** i.e., no matter what
other kinds of horse (with docked or long tails) there are to compete
with him   51 **ye** for you   53 **founder** lame, disable, cause to collapse.   **hobby-horse** a morris dancer with a figure of a horse fastened
around his waist, or a toy horse   54 **skill** judgment   55 **Light o' love**
a ballad on the subject of inconstancy in love   59 **fair hand** attractive
penmanship.   **casts . . . accounts** keeps personal tabs on the accounts   60–61 **That hostler . . . him** any caretaker of horses who
wants to cheat this horse will have to get up early to do so   63 **She
. . . him** the mare . . . the horse that can write etc.   64 **his master**
i.e., Palamon, who is imagined to have given the Jailer's Daughter
this horse.   **coy** disdainful   65 **bottles** bundles   66 **strike** bundles,
usually bushel or half-bushel   67 **able** i.e., so affectingly as to be
able   68 **A miller's mare** Miller's mares were proverbially sedate and
abstemious, presumably because they incessantly pulled to turn the
mill.

WOOER   Pretty soul,
How do ye? [*She curtsies*] That's a fine maid; there's
a curtsy!

JAILER'S DAUGHTER
Yours to command i' th' way of honesty.
How far is't now to th' end o' th' world, my
masters?

DOCTOR
Why, a day's journey, wench.

JAILER'S DAUGHTER [*to the Wooer*]
                              Will you go with me?

WOOER
What shall we do there, wench?

JAILER'S DAUGHTER   Why, play at stool-ball. 75
What is there else to do?

WOOER   I am content,
If we shall keep our wedding there.

JAILER'S DAUGHTER   'Tis true, 77
For there, I will assure you, we shall find
Some blind priest for the purpose, that will venture
To marry us; for here they are nice, and foolish. 80
Besides, my father must be hanged tomorrow,
And that would be a blot i' th' business.
Are not you Palamon?

WOOER   Do not you know me?

JAILER'S DAUGHTER
Yes, but you care not for me. I have nothing
But this poor petticoat and two coarse smocks. 85

WOOER
That's all one; I will have you.

JAILER'S DAUGHTER   Will you surely? 86

WOOER
Yes, by this fair hand, will I.

JAILER'S DAUGHTER   We'll to bed then.
WOOER Ev'n when you will.   [*He kisses her.*]

JAILER'S DAUGHTER [*wiping her mouth*]
                    O sir, you would fain be nibbling.

WOOER
Why do you rub my kiss off?

JAILER'S DAUGHTER   'Tis a sweet one,
And will perfume me finely against the wedding. 90
[*Pointing to the Doctor*] Is not this your cousin Arcite?

DOCTOR   Yes, sweetheart,
And I am glad my cousin Palamon
Has made so fair a choice.

JAILER'S DAUGHTER   Do you think he'll have me?
DOCTOR
Yes, without doubt.

JAILER'S DAUGHTER [*to the Jailer*] Do you think so too?
JAILER   Yes.

JAILER'S DAUGHTER
We shall have many children. [*To the Doctor*] Lord,
how you're grown!
My Palamon, I hope, will grow too, finely,
Now he's at liberty. Alas, poor chicken,
He was kept down with hard meat and ill lodging, 98
But I'll kiss him up again.

Enter a Messenger.

MESSENGER
What do you here? You'll lose the noblest sight
That ev'r was seen.

JAILER   Are they i' th' field?
MESSENGER   They are.
You bear a charge there too.

JAILER   I'll away straight. 102
[*To the others*] I must ev'n leave you here.

DOCTOR   Nay, we'll go with you.
I will not lose the fight.

JAILER   How did you like her? 104
DOCTOR
I'll warrant you, within these three or four days
I'll make her right again. [*To the Wooer*] You must
not from her,
But still preserve her in this way.

WOOER   I will.
DOCTOR
Let's get her in.

WOOER [*to the Jailer's Daughter*]
                    Come, sweet, we'll go to dinner,
And then we'll play at cards.

JAILER'S DAUGHTER   And shall we kiss too?
WOOER
A hundred times.

JAILER'S DAUGHTER And twenty.
WOOER   Ay, and twenty.

JAILER'S DAUGHTER
And then we'll sleep together.

DOCTOR [*to the Wooer*]   Take her offer.
WOOER [*to the Jailer's Daughter*]
Yes, marry, will we.

JAILER'S DAUGHTER But you shall not hurt me.
WOOER
I will not, sweet.

JAILER'S DAUGHTER If you do, love, I'll cry.   *Exeunt.*

❖

5.3   *Flourish. Enter Theseus, Hippolyta, Emilia,*
Pirithous, and some attendants.

EMILIA [*to Pirithous*]
I'll no step further.
PIRITHOUS   Will you lose this sight?

75 **stool-ball** a cricket-like game with a stool-like wicket 77 **keep** celebrate 80 **nice** fastidious 85 **smocks** petticoats, undergarments 86 **That's all one** it doesn't matter 90 **against** in preparation for
98 **kept . . . meat** kept from growing by harsh fare (and with sexual meaning that runs throughout this passage) 102 **bear a charge** have official responsibilities 104 **lose the fight** lose the chance to see this armed encounter. **like** find (medically)
5.3. Location: near the tournament field, as in 5.1.

EMILIA
I had rather see a wren hawk at a fly   2
Than this decision. Ev'ry blow that falls   3
Threats a brave life; each stroke laments
The place whereon it falls, and sounds more like
A bell than blade. I will stay here.   6
It is enough my hearing shall be punished
With what shall happen, 'gainst the which there is
No deafing, but to hear; not taint mine eye   9
With dread sights it may shun.
PIRITHOUS [to Theseus]   Sir, my good lord,
Your sister will no further.
THESEUS   O, she must.
She shall see deeds of honor in their kind,   12
Which sometime show well, pencilled. Nature now   13
Shall make and act the story, the belief   14
Both sealed with eye and ear. [To Emilia] You must
be present;   15
You are the victor's meed—the prize and garland   16
To crown the question's title.
EMILIA   Pardon me;
If I were there, I'd wink.
THESEUS   You must be there;   18
This trial is as 'twere i' th' night, and you
The only star to shine.
EMILIA   I am extinct.   20
There is but envy in that light which shows   21
The one the other. Darkness, which ever was   22
The dam of Horror, who does stand accurst   23
Of many mortal millions, may even now,   24
By casting her black mantle over both,
That neither could find other, get herself   26
Some part of a good name, and many a murder   27
Set off whereto she's guilty.
HIPPOLYTA   You must go.   28
EMILIA
In faith, I will not.
THESEUS   Why, the knights must kindle
Their valor at your eye. Know, of this war
You are the treasure, and must needs be by
To give the service pay.
EMILIA   Sir, pardon me;   32
The title of a kingdom may be tried   33
Out of itself.
THESEUS   Well, well, then; at your pleasure.   34

Those that remain with you could wish their office   35
To any of their enemies.
HIPPOLYTA [to Emilia]   Farewell, sister.   36
I am like to know your husband 'fore yourself   37
By some small start of time. He whom the gods
Do of the two know best, I pray them he   39
Be made your lot.
    Exeunt Theseus, Hippolyta, Pirithous, etc. [Emilia
    remains, comparing two pictures of Palamon and
    Arcite.]
EMILIA
Arcite is gently visaged, yet his eye
Is like an engine bent, or a sharp weapon   42
In a soft sheath; mercy and manly courage
Are bedfellows in his visage. Palamon
Has a most menacing aspect; his brow   45
Is graved, and seems to bury what it frowns on;   46
Yet sometime 'tis not so, but alters to   47
The quality of his thoughts. Long time his eye   48
Will dwell upon his object. Melancholy   49
Becomes him nobly; so does Arcite's mirth;   50
But Palamon's sadness is a kind of mirth,
So mingled as if mirth did make him sad
And sadness merry. Those darker humors that   53
Stick misbecomingly on others, on him   54
Live in fair dwelling.   55

    Cornets. Trumpets sound as to a charge.

Hark how yon spurs to spirit do incite   56
The princes to their proof! Arcite may win me,   57
And yet may Palamon wound Arcite to   58
The spoiling of his figure. O, what pity   59
Enough for such a chance? If I were by,   60
I might do hurt, for they would glance their eyes
Toward my seat, and in that motion might
Omit a ward or forfeit an offense   63
Which craved that very time. It is much better   64
I am not there. O, better never born
Than minister to such harm!

    Cornets. A great cry and noise within,
    crying "A Palamon!"

    Enter Servant.

    What is the chance?   66

2 hawk fly on the attack   3 decision contest through which the rivalry will be decided   6 bell bell toll announcing a death   9 No . . . hear no way of preventing one's hearing.   not I will not   12–15 deeds . . . ear those honorable deeds in real life which are often so well represented in art. Nature now will both create and enact the story, so that belief in it will be confirmed by eye and ear.   16 meed prize   18 wink close my eyes   20 extinct extinguished   21 envy malice   22 The one the other Palamon and Arcite to each other   23 dam mother   24 Of by   26 That so that   27 name reputation   27–28 and . . . whereto and thus make compensation for many a murder of which   32 give . . . pay reward the service of the knight who triumphs   33–34 The title . . . itself (Emilia's point is that she need not be present at a contest over herself, just as a contest over a kingdom can be conducted in some other land.)

35–36 Those . . . enemies (Theseus replies that any who are obliged to remain with Emilia, away from the tournament, might wish such an unwelcome obligation on their worst enemies.)   37 like likely   39 know know to be   42 an engine bent i.e., a bow bent and ready to be discharged   45 aspect (1) look (2) astrological influence   46 graved engraved, furrowed   47 to in accordance with   48 quality nature   49 his its   50 so . . . mirth Arcite's mirth becomes Arcite   53–55 Those . . . dwelling those darker moods that seem out of place in others seem well suited to him   56 spirit bravery   57 proof trial by combat   58–59 to . . . figure sufficiently to disfigure him   59–60 what . . . chance? what pity would suffice for such a misfortune?   63 ward defensive posture.   offense attack   64 craved . . . time needed to seize that very moment   66 s.d. A Palamon! a cry of support from Palamon's supporters. The "A"-prefix is customary in such a shout.   66 the chance the way things have fallen out

SERVANT   The cry's "A Palamon!"

EMILIA

Then he has won. 'Twas ever likely;
He looked all grace and success, and he is
Doubtless the prim'st of men. I prithee run   70
And tell me how it goes.

Shout and cornets, crying "A Palamon!"

SERVANT   Still "Palamon."

EMILIA

Run and inquire.   [*Exit Servant.*]
                    [*To the picture in her right hand*]
                    Poor servant, thou hast lost.
Upon my right side still I wore thy picture,   73
Palamon's on the left—why so I know not;
I had no end in 't else; chance would have it so.   75
On the sinister side the heart lies; Palamon   76
Had the best-boding chance.

Another cry and shout within, and cornets.

                    This burst of clamor   77
Is sure th' end o' th' combat.

Enter Servant.

SERVANT

They said that Palamon had Arcite's body
Within an inch o' th' pyramid, that the cry
Was general "A Palamon!" But anon
Th' assistants made a brave redemption, and   82
The two bold titlers at this instant are
Hand to hand at it.

EMILIA   Were they metamorphosed   84
Both into one!—Oh, why? There were no woman   85
Worth so composed a man; their single share,   86
Their nobleness peculiar to them, gives   87
The prejudice of disparity, value's shortness   88
To any lady breathing.   89

Cornets. Cry within, "Arcite, Arcite!"

                    More exulting?
"Palamon" still?

SERVANT   Nay, now the sound is "Arcite."

EMILIA

I prithee lay attention to the cry;   91
Set both thine ears to th' business.

Cornets. A great shout and cry, "Arcite! Victory!"

SERVANT   The cry is
"Arcite" and "Victory!" Hark, "Arcite, victory!"
The combat's consummation is proclaimed   94
By the wind instruments.

EMILIA   Half-sights saw   95
That Arcite was no babe. God's lid, his richness   96
And costliness of spirit looked through him; it could   97
No more be hid in him than fire in flax,
Than humble banks can go to law with waters   99
That drift-winds force to raging. I did think   100
Good Palamon would miscarry, yet I knew not
Why I did think so. Our reasons are not prophets
When oft our fancies are. They are coming off.   103
Alas, poor Palamon!

*Cornets. Enter Theseus, Hippolyta, Pirithous,
Arcite as victor, and attendants, etc.*

THESEUS

Lo, where our sister is in expectation,
Yet quaking and unsettled! Fairest Emily,
The gods by their divine arbitrament   107
Have given you this knight; he is a good one
As ever struck at head. [*To Emilia and Arcite*] Give
    me your hands.
[*To Arcite*] Receive you her, [*to Emilia*] you him; be
    plighted with
A love that grows as you decay.

ARCITE   Emily,
To buy you I have lost what's dearest to me
Save what is bought, and yet I purchase cheaply,
As I do rate your value.

THESEUS   O loved sister,
He speaks now of as brave a knight as e'er
Did spur a noble steed. Surely the gods
Would have him die a bachelor, lest his race
Should show i' th' world too godlike. His behavior
So charmed me that methought Alcides was   119
To him a sow of lead. If I could praise   120
Each part of him to th' all I have spoke, your Arcite   121
Did not lose by 't; for he that was thus good   122
Encountered yet his better. I have heard
Two emulous Philomels beat the ear o' th' night   124
With their contentious throats, now one the higher,
Anon the other, then again the first,
And by and by out-breasted, that the sense   127
Could not be judge between 'em. So it fared
Good space between these kinsmen, till heavens did   129
Make hardly one the winner. [*To Arcite*] Wear the
    garland   130
With joy that you have won.—For the subdued,   131
Give them our present justice, since I know   132
Their lives but pinch 'em. Let it here be done.   133

70 **prim'st of** first among, finest of   73 **still** unceasingly   75 **end** purpose   76 **sinister** left   77 **best-boding** best-portending   82 **assistants** knights seconding Arcite.   **redemption** rescue   84 **Were they** would that they   85 **were** would be, could be   86 **so composed a man** a man thus made of both their best qualities   86–89 **their . . . breathing** the worthiness of either and the nobleness unique to each puts any woman at a disadvantage by comparison   91 **lay** apply   94 **consummation** completion

95 **Half-sights** even a quick glance   96 **God's lid** by God's eyelid. (An oath.)   97 **looked through** shone out of   99 **humble** low.   **go to law** i.e., contend   100 **drift-winds** driving winds   103 **off** off the field   107 **arbitrament** decision, deciding of a dispute   119–120 **that . . . lead** that I imagined even Hercules would seem, compared with Arcite, as slow-moving as a solidified heavy mass of lead obtained from a furnace   121 **to . . . spoke** to the extent that I have praised all of him   122 **Did** would   124 **emulous Philomels** contending nightingales   127 **out-breasted** outsung.   **sense** sense of hearing   129 **Good space** for some length of time   130 **hardly** by a close judgment call; or, after hard fighting   131 **For** as for   132 **present** immediate   133 **but pinch** only torment

The scene's not for our seeing; go we hence
Right joyful, with some sorrow. [*To Arcite*] Arm your
   prize;   135
I know you will not lose her.
             [*Arcite takes Emilia's arm in his.*]
                    Hippolyta,   136
I see one eye of yours conceives a tear,
The which it will deliver.
EMILIA   Is this winning?
O all you heavenly powers, where is your mercy?
But that your wills have said it must be so,
And charge me live to comfort this unfriended,   141
This miserable prince, that cuts away
A life more worthy from him than all women,
I should and would die too.
HIPPOLYTA   Infinite pity
That four such eyes should be so fixed on one
That two must needs be blind for 't.
THESEUS   So it is.
                        Flourish. Exeunt.

❖

5.4   *Enter, [guarded,] Palamon and his knights
       pinioned; Jailer, Executioner, etc.*

PALAMON
There's many a man alive that hath outlived
The love o' th' people; yea, i' th' selfsame state
Stands many a father with his child. Some comfort
We have by so considering. We expire,
And not without men's pity; to live still,
Have their good wishes. We prevent   6
The loathsome misery of age, beguile
The gout and rheum that in lag hours attend   8
For grey approachers. We come towards the gods
Young and unwappered, not halting under crimes   10
Many and stale—that sure shall please the gods   11
Sooner than such, to give us nectar with 'em,   12
For we are more clear spirits. My dear kinsmen,   13
Whose lives for this poor comfort are laid down,
You have sold 'em too too cheap.
    FIRST KNIGHT   What ending could be
Of more content? O'er us the victors have
Fortune, whose title is as momentary
As to us death is certain. A grain of honor
They not o'erweigh us.

---

135 **Arm** give your arm to 136 **lose** (1) lose possession of (2) forget
(3) release (spelled *loose* in Q) 141 **this unfriended** Arcite, who has
lost his best friend
**5.4. Location: near the tournament field, as in 3.6, 5.1, and 5.3. A
scaffold is visible onstage.**
6 **prevent** forestall 8 **rheum . . . approachers** catarrh and rheumatic
pains that in the lag end of life await grey-haired old persons approaching their sickly end 10 **unwappered** unwearied. **halting**
limping 11 **stale** out of date. **that** i.e., we who; or, that circumstance 12 **such** i.e., those who are old and sin-ridden. **to . . . 'em**
i.e., the gods will invite us to sup on nectar with them 13 **For** because. **clear** unsullied

---

SECOND KNIGHT   Let us bid farewell,
And with our patience anger tott'ring Fortune,
Who at her certain'st reels.
THIRD KNIGHT   Come, who begins?   21
PALAMON
Ev'n he that led you to this banquet shall
Taste to you all. [*To the Jailer*] Aha, my friend, my
   friend,   23
Your gentle daughter gave me freedom once;
You'll see 't done now forever. Pray, how does she?
I heard she was not well; her kind of ill
Gave me some sorrow.
JAILER   Sir, she's well restored,
And to be married shortly.
PALAMON   By my short life,
I am most glad on 't; 'tis the latest thing   29
I shall be glad of. Prithee tell her so.
Commend me to her, and to piece her portion   31
Tender her this.   [*He gives the Jailer his purse.*]
FIRST KNIGHT   Nay, let's be offerers all.
SECOND KNIGHT
Is it a maid?
PALAMON   Verily, I think so—
A right good creature, more to me deserving
Than I can quit or speak of.
ALL THE KNIGHTS   Commend us to her.   35
                        They give their purses.
JAILER
The gods requite you all, and make her thankful!
PALAMON
Adieu, and let my life be now as short
As my leave-taking.

    [*He mounts the scaffold and*] lays [*his head*] on
                           the block.

FIRST KNIGHT   Lead, courageous cousin.
SECOND *AND* THIRD KNIGHTS
We'll follow cheerfully.

    *A great noise within, crying "Run!" "Save!"
    "Hold!" Enter in haste a Messenger.*

MESSENGER
Hold, hold! O hold, hold, hold!

    Enter Pirithous in haste.

PIRITHOUS
Hold, ho! It is a cursèd haste you made   41
If you have done so quickly. Noble Palamon,   42
The gods will show their glory in a life
That thou art yet to lead.

---

21 **Who . . . reels** who is unstable even when she seems most favoring 23 **Taste . . . all** i.e., go first, like the official taster whose assignment it was to taste food before distinguished persons ate to see if
the food was poisoned 29 **latest** last 31 **piece her portion** piece out
her dowry 35 **quit** requite, repay 41 **made** would have made
42 have done had completed the execution

PALAMON   Can that be,
  When Venus, I have said, is false? How do things
    fare?
PIRITHOUS
  Arise, great sir, and give the tidings ear
  That are most rarely sweet and bitter.
PALAMON [*rising and descending from the scaffold*]   What
  Hath waked us from our dream?
PIRITHOUS   List, then. Your cousin,
  Mounted upon a steed that Emily
  Did first bestow on him, a black one, owing   50
  Not a hair-worth of white—which some will say   51
  Weakens his price, and many will not buy   52
  His goodness with this note, which superstition   53
  Here finds allowance—on this horse is Arcite   54
  Trotting the stones of Athens, which the calkins   55
  Did rather tell than trample, for the horse   56
  Would make his length a mile, if 't pleased his rider 57
  To put pride in him. As he thus went counting   58
  The flinty pavement, dancing, as 'twere, to th'
    music
  His own hooves made—for, as they say, from iron   60
  Came music's origin—what envious flint,   61
  Cold as old Saturn, and like him possessed   62
  With fire malevolent, darted a spark,   63
  Or what fierce sulfur else, to this end made,   64
  I comment not—the hot horse, hot as fire,   65
  Took toy at this and fell to what disorder   66
  His power could give his will; bounds, comes on
    end,   67
  Forgets school-doing, being therein trained   68
  And of kind manège. Pig-like he whines
  At the sharp rowel, which he frets at rather   70
  Than any jot obeys; seeks all foul means   71
  Of boist'rous and rough jadery to disseat   72
  His lord, that kept it bravely. When naught served, 73

  When neither curb would crack, girth break, nor
    diff'ring plunges   74
  Disroot his rider whence he grew, but that
  He kept him 'tween his legs, on his hind hooves
  On end he stands,
  That Arcite's legs, being higher than his head,
  Seemed with strange art to hang. His victor's wreath
  Even then fell off his head; and presently
  Backward the jade comes o'er, and his full poise   81
  Becomes the rider's load. Yet is he living,   82
  But such a vessel 'tis that floats but for   83
  The surge that next approaches. He much desires   84
  To have some speech with you. Lo, he appears.

      Enter Theseus, Hippolyta, Emilia, [with] Arcite in
      a chair [carried by attendants. Palamon approaches
      Arcite.]

PALAMON
  O, miserable end of our alliance!
  The gods are mighty, Arcite. If thy heart,
  Thy worthy, manly heart, be yet unbroken,
  Give me thy last words. I am Palamon,
  One that yet loves thee dying.
ARCITE   Take Emilia,
  And with her all the world's joy. Reach thy hand;   91
  Farewell. I have told my last hour. I was false,   92
  Yet never treacherous. Forgive me, cousin.
  One kiss from fair Emilia. [*Kisses her.*] 'Tis done.
  Take her; I die.   [*He dies.*]
PALAMON   Thy brave soul seek Elysium!
EMILIA
  I'll close thine eyes, prince. Blessèd souls be with
    thee!
  Thou art a right good man, and while I live,
  This day I give to tears.
PALAMON   And I to honor.   98
THESEUS [*to Palamon*]
  In this place first you fought; ev'n very here
  I sundered you. Acknowledge to the gods   100
  Our thanks that you are living.
  His part is played, and, though it were too short,
  He did it well. Your day is lengthened, and
  The blissful dew of heaven does arrouse you.   104
  The powerful Venus well hath graced her altar,
  And given you your love. Our master, Mars,
  Hath vouched his oracle, and to Arcite gave   107
  The grace of the contention. So the deities   108
  Have showed due justice. [*To the attendants*] Bear this
    hence.   [*Exeunt attendants with Arcite's body.*]

PALAMON   O cousin,
That we should things desire which do cost us
The loss of our desire! That naught could buy
Dear love but loss of dear love!
THESEUS   Never Fortune
Did play a subtler game: the conquered triumphs,
The victor has the loss. Yet in the passage   114
The gods have been most equal. Palamon,   115
Your kinsman hath confessed the right o' th' lady
Did lie in you, for you first saw her and
Even then proclaimed your fancy. He restored her
As your stol'n jewel, and desired your spirit
To send him hence forgiven. The gods my justice
Take from my hand, and they themselves become
The executioners. Lead your lady off,
And call your lovers from the stage of death,   123
Whom I adopt my friends.

          [*The knights approach from the scaffold.*]

                    A day or two
Let us look sadly, and give grace unto
The funeral of Arcite, in whose end   126
The visages of bridegrooms we'll put on
And smile with Palamon, for whom an hour,
But one hour since, I was as dearly sorry
As glad of Arcite, and am now as glad
As for him sorry. O you heavenly charmers,   131
What things you make of us! For what we lack
We laugh, for what we have are sorry, still
Are children in some kind. Let us be thankful
For that which is, and with you leave dispute   135
That are above our question. Let's go off,   136
And bear us like the time.   *Flourish. Exeunt.*   137

Epilogue   [*Enter Epilogue.*]

EPILOGUE
I would now ask ye how ye like the play,
But, as it is with schoolboys, cannot say;   2
I am cruel fearful. Pray yet stay awhile,   3
And let me look upon ye. No man smile?
Then it goes hard, I see. He that has
Loved a young handsome wench, then, show his
          face—
'Tis strange if none be here—and if he will,
Against his conscience, let him hiss, and kill   8
Our market. 'Tis in vain, I see, to stay ye.   9

Have at the worst can come, then! Now, what say
          ye?   10
And yet mistake me not; I am not bold:
We have no such cause. If the tale we have told—
For 'tis no other—any way content ye,
For to that honest purpose it was meant ye,
We have our end; and ye shall have ere long,   15
I dare say, many a better to prolong
Your old loves to us. We and all our might
Rest at your service. Gentlemen, good night.
          Flourish. [Exit.]

10 **Have . . . come** go ahead, then, do your damnedst   15 **end** intent, wish

114 **passage** (1) occurrence (2) exchange of blows   115 **equal** impartial, fair and balanced   123 **lovers** devoted followers   126 **in whose end** after which   131 **charmers** i.e., gods, with their magical powers capable of enchanting us   135–136 **and . . . question** and leave off disputing with you, whose high will we must not question   137 **bear . . . time** bear ourselves in a matter suitable to the sad and yet joyful occasion

Epilogue   2 **schoolboys** (Probably it is a juvenile actor who speaks.) **say** speak   3 **cruel** extremely   8–9 **kill Our market** spoil the demand for this play   9 **stay** restrain

The Poems

Venus and Adonis

Like most of his contemporaries, Shakespeare apparently did not regard the writing of plays as an elegant literary pursuit. He must have known that he was good at it, and he certainly became famous in his day as a playwright, but he took no pains over the publication of his plays. We have no literary prefaces for them, no indication that Shakespeare saw them through the press. Writing for the theater was rather like writing for the movies today: a profitable and even glamorous venture but subliterary. When Ben Jonson brought out his collected *Works* (mostly plays) during his lifetime, he was jeered at for his pretensions.

The writing of sonnets and other "serious" poetry, on the other hand, was conventionally a bid for true literary fame. Shakespeare's prefatory epistle to his *Venus and Adonis* betrays an eagerness for recognition. Deferentially, he seeks the sponsorship of the Earl of Southampton, in hopes of literary prestige as well as financial support. He speaks of *Venus and Adonis* as "the first heir of my invention," as though he had written no plays earlier, and promises Southampton a "graver labor" to appear shortly. *Venus and Adonis* in 1593 and *The Rape of Lucrece* in 1594 were, in fact, Shakespeare's first publications. Both were carefully and correctly printed. They were probably composed between June of 1592 and May of 1594, a period when the theaters were closed because of the plague. Shakespeare's belief in their importance to his literary career is confirmed by the reports of his contemporaries. Richard Barnfield singled them out as the works most likely to assure a place for Shakespeare in "fame's immortal book." Francis Meres, in his *Palladis Tamia: Wit's Treasury,* exclaimed in 1598 that "the sweet witty soul of Ovid lives in mellifluous and honey-tongued Shakespeare: witness his *Venus and Adonis,* his *Lucrece,* his sugared sonnets among his private friends, etc." Gabriel Harvey, although preferring *Lucrece* and *Hamlet* as more pleasing to "the wiser sort," conceded that "the younger sort takes much delight in Shakespeare's *Venus and Adonis.*" John Weever and still others add further testimonials to the extraordinary reputation of Shakespeare's nondramatic poems.

As Gabriel Harvey's puritanical comment on *Venus and Adonis* suggests, this poem was regarded as amatory and even risqué. It mirrored a current vogue for Ovidian erotic poetry, as exemplified by Thomas Lodge's *Scilla's Metamorphosis,* 1589 (in which an amorous nymph courts a reluctant young man), and by Christopher Marlowe's *Hero and Leander.* This latter poem, left unfinished at Marlowe's death in 1593 and published in 1598 with a continuation by George Chapman, was evidently circulated in manuscript, as were so many poems of this sophisticated sort, including Shakespeare's sonnets. Shakespeare may well have been influenced by Marlowe's tone of wryly comic detachment and sensuous grace. He may also have read Michael Drayton's *Endymion and Phoebe* (published in 1595 but written earlier), in which the erotic tradition is somewhat idealized into moral allegory. Most important, however, Shakespeare knew his Ovid, both firsthand and in Golding's English translation (1567). He appears to have combined three mythical tales from the *Metamorphoses.* The narrative outline is to be found in Venus' pursuit of Adonis (Book 10), but the bashful reluctance of the young man is more reminiscent of Hermaphroditus (Book 4) and Narcissus (Book 3). Hermaphroditus pleads youth as his reason for wishing to escape the clutches of the water nymph Salmacis and so is transformed with her into a single body containing both sexes; Narcissus evades the nymph Echo out of self-infatuation. Shakespeare has thus drawn a composite portrait of male coyness, a subject he was to explore further in the sonnets. Such a theme was suited to a nobleman of Southampton's youth and prospects. In tone it was also well suited to the aristocratic and intellectual set who read such poetry. Shakespeare here aimed at a more refined audience than that for which he wrote plays, though his theatrical audience must also have been generally intelligent. The ornate qualities of *Venus and Adonis* should be judged in the fashionable context of a sophisticated audience.

The poem is, among other things, a tour de force of stylized poetic techniques. The story itself is relatively uneventful, and the characters are static. For two-thirds of the poem, very little happens other than a series of amorous claspings, from which Adonis feebly attempts to extricate himself. Even his subsequent fight with the boar and his violent death are occasions for rhetorical pathos rather than for vivid narrative description. The story is essentially a frame. Similarly, we must not expect psychological insight or meaningful self-discovery. The conventions of amatory verse do not encourage a serious interest in character. Venus and Adonis are mouthpieces for contrasting attitudes toward love. They debate a favorite courtly topic in the style of John Lyly. Both appeal to conventional wisdom and speak in *sententiae,* or aphoristic pronouncements. Venus, for example, warning Adonis of the need for caution in pursuing the boar, opines that "Danger deviseth shifts; wit waits on fear" (line 690). Adonis, pleading his unreadiness for love, cites commonplace analogies: "No fisher but the ungrown fry forbears. / The mellow plum doth fall, the green sticks fast" (lines 526–

527). In substance, their arguments are equally conventional. Venus urges a carpe diem philosophy of seizing the moment of pleasure. "Make use of time, let not advantage slip; / Beauty within itself should not be wasted" (lines 129–130). She bolsters her claim with an appeal to the "law of nature," according to which all living things are obliged to reproduce themselves; only by begetting can humans conquer time and death. Yet, however close this position may be to a major theme of the sonnets, it does not go unchallenged. Adonis charges plausibly that Venus is only rationalizing her lust: "O strange excuse, / When reason is the bawd to lust's abuse!" (lines 791–792). His plea for more time in which to mature and prove his manliness is commendable, however much we may smile at his inability to be aroused by Venus' blandishments. Thus, neither contestant wins the argument. Venus is proved right in her fear that Adonis will be killed by the boar he hunts, but Adonis' rejection of idle lust for manly activity affirms a conventional truth. The debate is, in a sense, an ingeniously elaborate literary exercise, yet it also allows for reflection on contrasting views of love as sensual and spiritual, absurd and magnificent, funny and serious.

The narrator's persona is central to the ambivalence in the debate. He, too, speaks in *sententiae,* and his aphorisms appear to sympathize with both contestants. At times, he affirms the irresistible force of love: "What though the rose have prickles, yet 'tis plucked" (line 574). At other times, he laughs at Venus for her vacillation of mood: "Thy weal and woe are both of them extremes. / Despair and hope makes thee ridiculous" (lines 987–988). Like Ovid's usual persona, the speaker here is both intrigued and amused by love, compelled to heed its power and yet aware of the absurdities. The result is a characteristic Ovidian blend of irony and pathos. The irony is especially evident in the delightful comic touches that undermine the potential seriousness of the action: Venus like an Amazon pulling Adonis off his mount and tucking him under one arm, pouting and blushing; Adonis' horse chasing away after a mare in heat, leaving Adonis to fend for himself; Venus fainting at the thought of the boar and pulling Adonis right on top of her, "in the very lists of love, / Her champion mounted for the hot encounter" (lines 595–596). These devices distance us from the action and create an atmosphere of elegant entertainment. Yet the poem is also suffused with the rich pathos of sensuous emotion. The sensuousness would cloy without the ironic humor, whereas the humor would seem frivolous without the pathos.

The poem hints at moral allegory, in the manner of Ovidian mythologizing. Venus represents herself as the goddess, not only of erotic passion, but also of eternal love conquering time and death. Because Adonis perversely spurns this ideal, Venus concludes that human beauty must perish and that human happiness must be subject to mischance. Yet this reading is only one part of the argument and is contradicted by an opposing suggestion that Adonis is the rational principle attempting unsuccessfully to govern human lust (the boar and Adonis' unbridled horse). These contradictions, which derive from the structure of the poem as a debate and also from Renaissance Neoplatonism, confirm our impression that the allegory is not the true "meaning" of the poem but is part of an ambiguous view of love as both exalted and earthly, a mystery that we will never comprehend in single terms. The allegory elevates the seriousness, adding poetic dignity to what might otherwise appear to be an unabashedly erotic poem. We should not minimize the sexual teasing or fail to acknowledge our own erotic pleasure in it. Venus' repeated encounters with Adonis take the form of ingeniously varied positions, ending in coital embrace, although without consummation. Adonis' passive role invites the male reader to fantasize himself in Adonis' place, being seduced by the goddess of beauty. The famous passage comparing Venus' body to a deer park with "pleasant fountains," "sweet bottom grass," and "round rising hillocks" (lines 229–240) is graphic through the use of double entendre without being pornographic. The poem is equally explicit in its "banquet" of the five senses (lines 433–450). This is the "naughty" Ovid of the *Ars Amatoria.*

Shakespeare's poem is an embroidery of poetic flourishes, of "conceits" or ingeniously wrought similes, of artfully constructed digressions, such as the narrative of Adonis' horse, and of color symbolism. Images usually are drawn from nature (eagles, birds caught in nets, wolves, berries) or connote burning, blazing, and shining (torches, jewels). The dominant colors are red and white, usually paired antithetically: the red of the rising sun or Adonis' blushing face or Mars' ensign, the white of an alabaster hand or fresh bed linen or "ashy-pale" anger. Ironically, too, the boar's frothy-white mouth is stained with red, and Adonis' red blood blemishes his "wonted lily white." Adonis' flower, the anemone, is reddish-purple and white. A similarly balanced antithesis pervades the poem's rhetorical figures, as in the symmetrical repetition of words in grammatically parallel phrases (*parison),* or in phrases of equal length (*isocolon),* or in inverted order (*antimetabole),* or at the beginning and ending of a line (*epanalepsis),* and so on. These pyrotechnics may at first seem mechanical, but they, too, have a place in a work of art that celebrates both the erotic and the spiritual in love. Decoration has its function and is not mere embellishment for its own sake.

Venus and Adonis

"Vilia miretur vulgus; mihi flavus Apollo
Pocula Castalia plena ministret aqua."

To the RIGHT HONORABLE HENRY WRIOTHESLEY,
Earl of Southampton, and Baron of Titchfield.

RIGHT HONORABLE,

I know not how I shall offend in dedicating
my unpolished lines to your lordship, nor how the
world will censure me for choosing so strong a
prop to support so weak a burden; only if your
honor seem but pleased, I account myself highly
praised, and vow to take advantage of all idle
hours, till I have honored you with some graver
labor. But if the first heir of my invention prove   8
deformed, I shall be sorry it had so noble a
godfather, and never after ear so barren a land, for   10
fear it yield me still so bad a harvest. I leave it to
your honorable survey, and your honor to your
heart's content, which I wish may always answer
your own wish and the world's hopeful expectation.

Your honor's in all duty,

William Shakespeare.

Even as the sun with purple-colored face
Had ta'en his last leave of the weeping morn,
Rose-cheeked Adonis hied him to the chase.   2
Hunting he loved, but love he laughed to scorn.   3

Sick-thoughted Venus makes amain unto him,   5
And like a boldfaced suitor 'gins to woo him.

"Thrice-fairer than myself," thus she began,
"The field's chief flower, sweet above compare,
Stain to all nymphs, more lovely than a man,   9
More white and red than doves or roses are:
    Nature that made thee, with herself at strife,   11
    Saith that the world hath ending with thy life.   12

"Vouchsafe, thou wonder, to alight thy steed,   13
And rein his proud head to the saddlebow.   14
If thou wilt deign this favor, for thy meed   15
A thousand honey secrets shalt thou know.   16
    Here come and sit, where never serpent hisses,
    And being set, I'll smother thee with kisses;

"And yet not cloy thy lips with loathed satiety,
But rather famish them amid their plenty,
Making them red and pale with fresh variety—
Ten kisses short as one, one long as twenty.
    A summer's day will seem an hour but short,
    Being wasted in such time-beguiling sport."   24

With this she seizeth on his sweating palm,   25
The precedent of pith and livelihood,   26
And, trembling in her passion, calls it balm,
Earth's sovereign salve, to do a goddess good.   28
    Being so enraged, desire doth lend her force   29
    Courageously to pluck him from his horse.   30

Over one arm the lusty courser's rein,   31
Under her other was the tender boy,
Who blushed and pouted in a dull disdain,   33
With leaden appetite, unapt to toy;   34
    She red and hot as coals of glowing fire,
    He red for shame, but frosty in desire.

The studded bridle on a ragged bough
Nimbly she fastens. O, how quick is love!
The steed is stallèd up, and even now   39
To tie the rider she begins to prove.   40
    Backward she pushed him, as she would be
        thrust,
    And governed him in strength, though not in
        lust.

Motto: Vilia miretur, etc. Let the base vulgar admire trash; may
golden-haired Apollo serve me goblets filled from the Castalian
spring. (Ovid, *Amores,* 1.15.35 – 36.)
Dedication: Henry Wriothesley, Earl of Southampton (A popular and
brilliant young gentleman of nineteen years, already prominent at
court. Subsequent dedications by Shakespeare and others indicate that
he was a genuinely devoted patron of literature throughout his life.)
8 the first . . . invention (This phrase has been variously interpreted
to mean Shakespeare's first written work, his first printed work, his
first "invented" work in the sense that the plots of his plays were usually not original with him, his first work independent of collaborators,
or his first "literary" work, since plays were unliterary in the Elizabethan sense. The second and last are the most probable.) **10 ear**
plow, cultivate
2 the weeping morn the goddess of the dawn, Aurora, weeping tears
(i.e., the dew of morning) at being left by the sun-god. (In the Greek
myth, she weeps for the death of her lover, Tithonus.) **3 hied him**
betook himself, hastened

5 Sick-thoughted lovesick. **makes amain** hastens **9 Stain to** eclips-
ing (in beauty). **nymphs** i.e., young and beautiful women
11 – 12 Nature . . . life Nature, having striven to surpass herself in
making you her masterpiece, says that if you die the world will cease.
(The story of Adonis' death, and of the anemone that springs from his
blood, is a vegetation myth.) **13 Vouchsafe** deign. **alight** alight
from **14 the saddlebow** the arch in, or the pieces forming, the front
of the saddle. (The image is of reining the horse's head sharply back.)
15 meed reward **16 honey** sweet **24 wasted** spent **25 sweating**
i.e., indicative of youth; not dried with age **26 precedent** sign,
promise. **pith and livelihood** sexual strength and vitality **28 sover-**
eign efficacious **29 enraged** ardent **30 Courageously** lustfully.
pluck drag **31 lusty courser's** vigorous horse's **33 dull** moody, listless **34 unapt to toy** undisposed to dally amorously **39 stallèd** fastened, secured (as in a stall) **40 prove** try

So soon was she along as he was down,   43
Each leaning on their elbows and their hips.
Now doth she stroke his cheek, now doth he frown,
And 'gins to chide, but soon she stops his lips
  And kissing speaks, with lustful language broken, 47
  "If thou wilt chide, thy lips shall never open."

He burns with bashful shame; she with her tears
Doth quench the maiden burning of his cheeks.
Then with her windy sighs and golden hairs
To fan and blow them dry again she seeks.
  He saith she is immodest, blames her miss;   53
  What follows more, she murders with a kiss.

Even as an empty eagle, sharp by fast,   55
Tires with her beak on feathers, flesh, and bone,   56
Shaking her wings, devouring all in haste,
Till either gorge be stuffed or prey be gone,   58
  Even so she kissed his brow, his cheek, his chin,
  And where she ends she doth anew begin.

Forced to content, but never to obey,   61
Panting he lies and breatheth in her face.
She feedeth on the steam as on a prey,
And calls it heavenly moisture, air of grace,
  Wishing her cheeks were gardens full of flowers,
  So they were dewed with such distilling showers. 66

Look how a bird lies tangled in a net,   67
So fastened in her arms Adonis lies;
Pure shame and awed resistance made him fret,   69
Which bred more beauty in his angry eyes.
  Rain added to a river that is rank   71
  Perforce will force it overflow the bank.

Still she entreats, and prettily entreats,
For to a pretty ear she tunes her tale.
Still is he sullen, still he lours and frets,
Twixt crimson shame and anger ashy-pale.
  Being red, she loves him best; and being white,   77
  Her best is bettered with a more delight.   78

Look how he can, she cannot choose but love;
And by her fair immortal hand she swears
From his soft bosom never to remove,   81
Till he take truce with her contending tears,   82
  Which long have rained, making her cheeks all
   wet;
  And one sweet kiss shall pay this countless debt. 84

Upon this promise did he raise his chin,
Like a divedapper peering through a wave,   86

Who, being looked on, ducks as quickly in.
So offers he to give what she did crave;
  But when her lips were ready for his pay,   89
  He winks and turns his lips another way.   90

Never did passenger in summer's heat   91
More thirst for drink than she for this good turn.
Her help she sees, but help she cannot get;
She bathes in water, yet her fire must burn.   94
  "O, pity," 'gan she cry, "flint-hearted boy!
  'Tis but a kiss I beg. Why art thou coy?

"I have been wooed, as I entreat thee now,
Even by the stern and direful god of war,   98
Whose sinewy neck in battle ne'er did bow,
Who conquers where he comes in every jar;   100
  Yet hath he been my captive and my slave,
  And begged for that which thou unasked shalt
   have.

"Over my altars hath he hung his lance,
His battered shield, his uncontrollèd crest,   104
And for my sake hath learned to sport and dance,
To toy, to wanton, dally, smile, and jest,   106
  Scorning his churlish drum and ensign red,
  Making my arms his field, his tent my bed.   108

"Thus he that overruled I overswayed,
Leading him prisoner in a red-rose chain.
Strong-tempered steel his stronger strength obeyed,
Yet was he servile to my coy disdain.   112
  O, be not proud, nor brag not of thy might,
  For mastering her that foiled the god of fight!   114

"Touch but my lips with those fair lips of thine—   115
Though mine be not so fair, yet are they red—
The kiss shall be thine own as well as mine.   117
What seest thou in the ground? Hold up thy head.
  Look in mine eyeballs, there thy beauty lies;   119
  Then why not lips on lips, since eyes in eyes?

"Art thou ashamed to kiss? Then wink again,   121
And I will wink; so shall the day seem night.
Love keeps his revels where there are but twain;
Be bold to play, our sport is not in sight.   124
  These blue-veined violets whereon we lean
  Never can blab, nor know not what we mean.   126

"The tender spring upon thy tempting lip   127
Shows thee unripe, yet mayst thou well be tasted.

43 **along** lying at his side   47 **broken** interrupted   53 **miss** offense, misconduct   55 **sharp by fast** hungry as a result of fasting   56 **Tires** tears, feeds ravenously.   **on** at   58 **gorge** bird's crop   61 **content** acquiesce.   **obey** i.e., answer her lust   66 **So** provided that.   **distilling** gently falling, in fine droplets   67 **Look how** just as   69 **awed** daunted, overborne   71 **rank** full to overflowing   77 **Being** i.e., he being   78 **more** greater   81 **remove** move, remove herself   82 **take truce** come to terms   84 **countless** beyond reckoning   86 **divedapper** dabchick, a common English water bird

89 **for his pay** to be paid by him (with a kiss)   90 **winks** shuts his eyes (and winces)   91 **passenger** wayfarer   94 **water** i.e., her tears.   **fire** (of passion)   98 **direful** inspiring dread.   **god of war** Mars   100 **where** wherever.   **jar** fight   104 **uncontrolled** unconquered, unbowed.   **crest** i.e., of helmet   106 **toy, wanton, dally** sport amorously   108 **arms** (With a pun on "weapons.")   112 **coy** aloof, teasing   114 **foiled** vanquished   115 **Touch** i.e., if you touch   117 **thine . . . mine** i.e., mutual, shared   119 **there . . . lies** i.e., (1) see your beauty reflected there (2) your beauty lies in my beholding   121 **wink** close the eyes   124 **not in sight** observed by no one   126 **mean** intend   127 **spring** growth (i.e., downy hair)

Make use of time, let not advantage slip; 129
Beauty within itself should not be wasted. 130
    Fair flowers that are not gathered in their prime
    Rot and consume themselves in little time.

"Were I hard-favored, foul, or wrinkled old, 133
Ill-nurtured, crooked, churlish, harsh in voice,
O'erworn, despised, rheumatic, and cold, 135
Thick-sighted, barren, lean, and lacking juice, 136
    Then mightst thou pause, for then I were not for
      thee;
    But having no defects, why dost abhor me?

"Thou canst not see one wrinkle in my brow;
Mine eyes are gray and bright and quick in turning; 140
My beauty as the spring doth yearly grow, 141
My flesh is soft and plump, my marrow burning; 142
    My smooth moist hand, were it with thy hand
      felt, 143
    Would in thy palm dissolve, or seem to melt.

"Bid me discourse, I will enchant thine ear,
Or like a fairy, trip upon the green, 146
Or like a nymph, with long disheveled hair,
Dance on the sands, and yet no footing seen. 148
    Love is a spirit all compact of fire, 149
    Not gross to sink, but light, and will aspire. 150

"Witness this primrose bank whereon I lie;
These forceless flowers like sturdy trees support me. 152
Two strengthless doves will draw me through the sky, 153
From morn till night, even where I list to sport me. 154
    Is love so light, sweet boy, and may it be 155
    That thou shouldst think it heavy unto thee? 156

"Is thine own heart to thine own face affected? 157
Can thy right hand seize love upon thy left? 158
Then woo thyself, be of thyself rejected; 159
Steal thine own freedom and complain on theft. 160
    Narcissus so himself himself forsook, 161
    And died to kiss his shadow in the brook. 162

"Torches are made to light, jewels to wear,
Dainties to taste, fresh beauty for the use,
Herbs for their smell, and sappy plants to bear. 165
Things growing to themselves are growth's abuse. 166
    Seeds spring from seeds, and beauty breedeth
      beauty.
    Thou wast begot; to get it is thy duty. 168

"Upon the earth's increase why shouldst thou feed,
Unless the earth with thy increase be fed?
By law of nature thou art bound to breed,
That thine may live when thou thyself art dead; 172
    And so, in spite of death, thou dost survive,
    In that thy likeness still is left alive."

By this the lovesick queen began to sweat, 175
For where they lay the shadow had forsook them,
And Titan, tirèd in the midday heat, 177
With burning eye did hotly overlook them, 178
    Wishing Adonis had his team to guide, 179
    So he were like him, and by Venus' side. 180

And now Adonis, with a lazy sprite, 181
And with a heavy, dark, disliking eye,
His louring brows o'erwhelming his fair sight, 183
Like misty vapors when they blot the sky,
    Souring his cheeks, cries, "Fie, no more of love! 185
    The sun doth burn my face; I must remove." 186

"Ay me," quoth Venus, "young, and so unkind? 187
What bare excuses mak'st thou to be gone!
I'll sigh celestial breath, whose gentle wind
Shall cool the heat of this descending sun. 190
    I'll make a shadow for thee of my hairs;
    If they burn too, I'll quench them with my tears.

"The sun that shines from heaven shines but warm, 193
And, lo, I lie between that sun and thee.
The heat I have from thence doth little harm;
Thine eye darts forth the fire that burneth me,
    And were I not immortal, life were done 197
    Between this heavenly and earthly sun.

"Art thou obdurate, flinty, hard as steel?
Nay, more than flint, for stone at rain relenteth. 200
Art thou a woman's son, and canst not feel
What 'tis to love, how want of love tormenteth? 202

129 advantage opportunity **130 Beauty . . . wasted** beauty should not be wasted by being kept to itself **133 hard-favored** ugly. **foul** ugly **135 O'erworn** worn by time **136 Thick-sighted** dim-eyed **140 gray** i.e., blue. **quick in turning** animated **141 as . . . grow** is perennially renewed, like spring. **142 marrow** vital animal spirit. **burning** sexually ardent **143 moist** (Indicative of youth and passion, as with *sweating* in line 25.) **146 trip** dance **148 footing** footprint **149 compact** composed **150 gross** heavy. (The heavy elements, earth and water, sink; fire and air rise.) **aspire** rise **152 forceless** frail **153 doves** (Venus' chariot was depicted as being drawn by doves.) **154 list** desire **155 light** (1) rising, weightless (2) wanton **156 heavy** (1) weighty (2) troublous **157 affected** drawn by affection **158 upon thy left** i.e., by clasping the left hand **159 of** by **160 Steal . . . freedom** i.e., take your own affections captive. **on** of **161 Narcissus** a beautiful youth in classical mythology who, leaning over a pool to drink, fell in love with his reflection and stayed there until he died. He was afterward changed into a flower. (Ovid, *Metamorphoses*, 3.339–510.) **himself himself forsook** i.e., abandoned himself to a hopeless passion for himself **162 to kiss** i.e., seeking fruitlessly to kiss

165 sappy plants sap-bearing fruit trees **166 Things . . . abuse** things that grow solely for their own use abuse the very purpose of growth **168 get** beget, procreate **172 thine** your progeny **175 By this** by this time **177 Titan** the sun-god. **tirèd** attired **178 overlook** look upon **179 his team** i.e., Titan's team of horses **180 So . . . him** i.e., so that he, Titan, might be in Adonis' place **181 lazy sprite** dull spirit **183 o'erwhelming** overhanging so as to cover. **sight** eyes **185 Souring his cheeks** scowling **186 remove** move **187 unkind** unrelenting; unnatural **190 descending** just beginning to descend from the zenith and thus at its hottest **193 shines but warm** merely makes me warm (whereas you burn me up) **197 were done** would be undone, finished **200 relenteth** wears slowly away **202 want of love** being denied reciprocal love

O, had thy mother borne so hard a mind,
She had not brought forth thee, but died unkind.   204

"What am I, that thou shouldst contemn me this?   205
Or what great danger dwells upon my suit?   206
What were thy lips the worse for one poor kiss?   207
Speak, fair, but speak fair words, or else be mute.   208
   Give me one kiss, I'll give it thee again,   209
   And one for interest, if thou wilt have twain.

"Fie, lifeless picture, cold and senseless stone,   211
Well painted idol, image dull and dead,
Statue contenting but the eye alone,
Thing like a man, but of no woman bred!
   Thou art no man, though of a man's complexion,   215
   For men will kiss even by their own direction."   216

This said, impatience chokes her pleading tongue,
And swelling passion doth provoke a pause.
Red cheeks and fiery eyes blaze forth her wrong;   219
Being judge in love, she cannot right her cause.   220
   And now she weeps, and now she fain would
      speak,   221
   And now her sobs do her intendments break.   222

Sometimes she shakes her head and then his hand,   223
Now gazeth she on him, now on the ground;
Sometimes her arms enfold him like a band.   225
She would, he will not in her arms be bound;   226
   And when from thence he struggles to be gone,
   She locks her lily fingers one in one.

"Fondling," she saith, "since I have hemmed thee here   229
Within the circuit of this ivory pale,   230
I'll be a park, and thou shalt be my deer.   231
Feed where thou wilt, on mountain or in dale;
   Graze on my lips; and if those hills be dry,
   Stray lower, where the pleasant fountains lie.   234

"Within this limit is relief enough,   235
Sweet bottom grass and high delightful plain,   236
Round rising hillocks, brakes obscure and rough,   237

To shelter thee from tempest and from rain.
   Then be my deer, since I am such a park;
   No dog shall rouse thee, though a thousand
      bark."   240

At this Adonis smiles as in disdain,
That in each cheek appears a pretty dimple.   242
Love made those hollows, if himself were slain,   243
He might be buried in a tomb so simple,   244
   Foreknowing well, if there he came to lie,
   Why, there Love lived; and there he could not die.   246

These lovely caves, these round enchanting pits,
Opened their mouths to swallow Venus' liking.   248
Being mad before, how doth she now for wits?   249
Struck dead at first, what needs a second striking?
   Poor queen of love, in thine own law forlorn,   251
   To love a cheek that smiles at thee in scorn!

Now which way shall she turn? What shall she say?
Her words are done, her woes the more increasing;
The time is spent; her object will away,
And from her twining arms doth urge releasing.
   "Pity," she cries, "some favor, some remorse!"   257
   Away he springs and hasteth to his horse.

But, lo, from forth a copse that neighbors by,   259
A breeding jennet, lusty, young, and proud,   260
Adonis' trampling courser doth espy,
And forth she rushes, snorts, and neighs aloud.
   The strong-necked steed, being tied unto a tree,
   Breaketh his rein, and to her straight goes he.   264

Imperiously he leaps, he neighs, he bounds,
And now his woven girths he breaks asunder.   266
The bearing earth with his hard hoof he wounds,   267
Whose hollow womb resounds like heaven's thunder.
   The iron bit he crusheth 'tween his teeth,
   Controlling what he was controllèd with.

His ears up-pricked, his braided hanging mane
Upon his compassed crest now stand on end;   272
His nostrils drink the air, and forth again,
As from a furnace, vapors doth he send.
   His eye, which scornfully glisters like fire,
   Shows his hot courage and his high desire.   276

204 unkind unnaturally unrelenting, not fulfilling her natural function
205 contemn me this scornfully refuse me this request, or, scorn me
thus   **206 dwells upon** attends   **207 What** in what way   **208 Speak,
fair** speak, handsome youth.   **fair words** kind words   **209 Give** if
you give   **211 senseless** insensible   **215 complexion** outward appearance   **216 direction** inclination   **219 blaze forth** proclaim (with a
metaphorical sense of "seem to burn," "show by their flaming")
220 Being . . . cause i.e., although goddess and hence arbiter of
love, Venus cannot prevail in her own case   **221 fain** gladly   **222 do
. . . break** interrupt what she intends to say   **223 his hand** (i.e., not
in a handshake but in a gesture of frustration)   **225 like a band** as in
a bond or fetter   **226 would** i.e., would bind him   **229 Fondling**
foolish one   **230 pale** fence (i.e., her arms; the sexual topography is
continued in *fountains, bottom grass, hillocks, brakes,* etc.)   **231 park**
deer preserve.   **deer** (With a pun on *dear*.)   **234 fountains** (1) springs
(2) breasts   **235 limit** boundary.   **relief** (1) pasture (2) sexual pleasure
(3) variety of landscape   **236 bottom grass** valley grass (with an allusion to pubic hair).   **plain** i.e., Mons Veneris or the stomach (?)
237 brakes patches of dense fern and bracken (again with sexual suggestion).   **obscure** dark.   **rough** shaggy, dense

240 rouse cause to start from cover   **242 That** so that   **243 Love** Cupid.   **if** so that if   **244 simple** unadorned   **246 Love** (1) the essence
of love, loveliness (2) Cupid himself   **248 Opened . . . liking** i.e.,
looked so winsome in their dimpling that Venus was engulfed, swallowed up, by love.   **liking** desire   **249 how . . . wits** how may she
keep her sanity now?   **251 in . . . forlorn** condemned to suffer under
your own rule of love   **257 remorse** compassion   **259 copse . . . by**
neighboring thicket   **260 breeding** in heat.   **jennet** small Spanish
mare.   **lusty** spirited   **264 straight** straightway   **266 girths** cloth
belts securing the saddle   **267 bearing** receiving   **272 compassed
crest** arched ridge of the neck.   **stand on end** (The hairs of the mane
stand on end.)   **276 courage** passion

Sometimes he trots, as if he told the steps, 277
With gentle majesty and modest pride;
Anon he rears upright, curvets, and leaps, 279
As who should say, "Lo, thus my strength is tried, 280
    And this I do to captivate the eye
    Of the fair breeder that is standing by."

What recketh he his rider's angry stir, 283
His flattering "Holla," or his "Stand, I say"? 284
What cares he now for curb or pricking spur?
For rich caparisons or trappings gay? 286
    He sees his love, and nothing else he sees,
    For nothing else with his proud sight agrees.

Look when a painter would surpass the life, 289
In limning out a well-proportioned steed, 290
His art with nature's workmanship at strife,
As if the dead the living should exceed, 292
    So did this horse excel a common one
    In shape, in courage, color, pace, and bone. 294

Round-hoofed, short-jointed, fetlocks shag and long, 295
Broad breast, full eye, small head, and nostril wide,
High crest, short ears, straight legs and passing strong, 297
Thin mane, thick tail, broad buttock, tender hide: 298
    Look what a horse should have he did not lack, 299
    Save a proud rider on so proud a back.

Sometimes he scuds far off, and there he stares;
Anon he starts at stirring of a feather;
To bid the wind a base he now prepares, 303
And whe'er he run or fly they know not whether; 304
    For through his mane and tail the high wind
      sings,
    Fanning the hairs, who wave like feathered
      wings.

He looks upon his love and neighs unto her;
She answers him as if she knew his mind.
Being proud, as females are, to see him woo her,
She puts on outward strangeness, seems unkind, 310
    Spurns at his love and scorns the heat he feels, 311
    Beating his kind embraces with her heels. 312

Then, like a melancholy malcontent,
He vails his tail that, like a falling plume, 314
Cool shadow to his melting buttock lent;
He stamps and bites the poor flies in his fume. 316
    His love, perceiving how he was enraged,
    Grew kinder, and his fury was assuaged.

His testy master goeth about to take him, 319
When, lo, the unbacked breeder, full of fear, 320
Jealous of catching, swiftly doth forsake him, 321
With her the horse, and left Adonis there. 322
    As they were mad, unto the wood they hie them, 323
    Outstripping crows that strive to overfly them. 324

All swoll'n with chafing, down Adonis sits, 325
Banning his boisterous and unruly beast; 326
And now the happy season once more fits 327
That lovesick Love by pleading may be blest; 328
    For lovers say the heart hath treble wrong
    When it is barred the aidance of the tongue. 330

An oven that is stopped, or river stayed, 331
Burneth more hotly, swelleth with more rage;
So of concealèd sorrow may be said. 333
Free vent of words love's fire doth assuage; 334
    But when the heart's attorney once is mute, 335
    The client breaks, as desperate in his suit. 336

He sees her coming and begins to glow,
Even as a dying coal revives with wind,
And with his bonnet hides his angry brow, 339
Looks on the dull earth with disturbèd mind,
    Taking no notice that she is so nigh, 341
    For all askance he holds her in his eye. 342

O, what a sight it was, wistly to view 343
How she came stealing to the wayward boy!
To note the fighting conflict of her hue,
How white and red each other did destroy!
    But now her cheek was pale, and by and by 347
    It flashed forth fire, as lightning from the sky.

Now was she just before him as he sat,
And like a lowly lover down she kneels;
With one fair hand she heaveth up his hat,

---

277 told numbered **279 curvets** raises his forelegs and then springs with his hind legs before the forelegs reach the ground **280 As who should** as one might. **tried** tested **283 recketh he** does he care about or pay attention to. **stir** bustle, agitation **284 flattering** cajoling. **Holla** stop **286 caparisons** gaily ornamental cloth coverings for the saddle and harness **289 Look when** just as when **290 limning out** portraying, drawing **292 dead** inanimate **294 bone** frame **295 short-jointed** with short pasterns, the part of the horse's foot between the hoof and the fetlock. **fetlocks** lower part of horses' legs where the tuft of hair grows behind, just above the hoof. **shag** shaggy **297 crest** ridge of the neck. **passing** surpassingly **298 tender hide** i.e., delicate of hide, not coarse **299 Look what** whatever **303 bid the wind a base** challenge the wind to a contest. (From the children's game of prisoner's base.) **304 whe'er** whether. **whether** which of the two **310 outward strangeness** seeming indifference. **unkind** unattracted sexually, not responding to natural feeling **311 Spurns at** (1) kicks at (2) repels **312 kind** (1) affectionate, passionate (2) prompted by nature

314 vails lowers **316 fume** anger **319 testy** irritated. **goeth about** makes an effort **320 unbacked breeder** unbroken and riderless female in heat **321 Jealous of catching** fearful of being caught **322 horse** i.e., stallion **323 As** as if. **hie them** hasten **324 overfly them** fly faster than they can run, or, keep pace above them in flight **325 swoll'n with chafing** puffed with anger **326 Banning** cursing **327 fits** is fitting, is suited **328 Love** i.e., Venus, the goddess of love, not Cupid, as in lines 243–246 **330 aidance** help **331 stopped** stopped up. **stayed** dammed **333 may** it may **334 love's . . . assuage** assuages love's fire **335 the heart's attorney** i.e., the tongue **336 breaks** (1) goes bankrupt (2) breaks asunder, as the heart is said to break in rejected love **339 bonnet** hat. **hides . . . brow** pulls his hat down over his frowning brows **341 Taking** i.e., pretending to take **342 all . . . eye** he watches her out of the corner of his eye **343 wistly** earnestly, attentively **347 But now** a short time ago

Her other tender hand his fair cheek feels.
   His tenderer cheek receives her soft hand's print,   353
   As apt as new-fall'n snow takes any dint.   354

O, what a war of looks was then between them!
Her eyes petitioners to his eyes suing,
His eyes saw her eyes as they had not seen them;   357
Her eyes wooed still, his eyes disdained the wooing;
   And all this dumb play had his acts made plain   359
   With tears which, choruslike, her eyes did rain.   360

Full gently now she takes him by the hand,
A lily prisoned in a jail of snow,
Or ivory in an alabaster band,   363
So white a friend engirts so white a foe.   364
   This beauteous combat, willful and unwilling,
   Showed like two silver doves that sit a-billing.   366

Once more the engine of her thoughts began: 367
"O fairest mover on this mortal round,   368
Would thou wert as I am, and I a man,
My heart all whole as thine, thy heart my wound!   370
   For one sweet look thy help I would assure thee,   371
   Though nothing but my body's bane would cure
   thee."   372

"Give me my hand," saith he. "Why dost thou feel it?"   373
"Give me my heart," saith she, "and thou shalt
   have it.   374
O, give it me, lest thy hard heart do steel it,   375
And being steeled, soft sighs can never grave it.   376
   Then love's deep groans I never shall regard,
   Because Adonis' heart hath made mine hard."

"For shame," he cries, "let go, and let me go!
My day's delight is past, my horse is gone,
And 'tis your fault I am bereft him so.   381
I pray you hence, and leave me here alone;   382
   For all my mind, my thought, my busy care,
   Is how to get my palfrey from the mare."   384

Thus she replies: "Thy palfrey, as he should,
Welcomes the warm approach of sweet desire.
Affection is a coal that must be cooled,   387

Else, suffered, it will set the heart on fire.   388
   The sea hath bounds, but deep desire hath none;
   Therefore no marvel though thy horse be gone.

"How like a jade he stood, tied to the tree,   391
Servilely mastered with a leathern rein!
But when he saw his love, his youth's fair fee,   393
He held such petty bondage in disdain,
   Throwing the base thong from his bending crest,   395
   Enfranchising his mouth, his back, his breast.   396

"Who sees his true love in her naked bed,   397
Teaching the sheets a whiter hue than white,
But when his glutton eye so full hath fed,   399
His other agents aim at like delight?   400
   Who is so faint that dares not be so bold
   To touch the fire, the weather being cold?

"Let me excuse thy courser, gentle boy;
And learn of him, I heartily beseech thee,
To take advantage on presented joy.   405
Though I were dumb, yet his proceedings teach thee.   406
   O, learn to love; the lesson is but plain,
   And once made perfect, never lost again."   408

"I know not love," quoth he, "nor will not know it,
Unless it be a boar, and then I chase it;
'Tis much to borrow, and I will not owe it;   411
My love to love is love but to disgrace it;   412
   For I have heard it is a life in death,
   That laughs and weeps, and all but with a breath.   414

"Who wears a garment shapeless and unfinished?
Who plucks the bud before one leaf put forth?
If springing things be any jot diminished,   417
They wither in their prime, prove nothing worth.
   The colt that's backed and burdened being young   419
   Loseth his pride and never waxeth strong.

"You hurt my hand with wringing. Let us part
And leave this idle theme, this bootless chat.   422
Remove your siege from my unyielding heart;
To love's alarms it will not ope the gate.   424
   Dismiss your vows, your feignèd tears, your
     flattery;
   For where a heart is hard they make no battery."   426

353 tenderer i.e., even more tender than her hand   **354 dint** impression   **357 as** as if   **359 dumb play** dumb show.   **his** its.   **made plain** explained   **360 With** by.   **choruslike** providing a choric interpretation to the dumb show   **363 band** bond, fetter   **364 So . . . foe** so white is her passionate hand thus enclosing his unwilling white hand   **366 Showed** looked   **367 the engine of her thoughts** her tongue   **368 mover** one who moves or walks; mortal.   **mortal round** earth   **370 thy heart my wound** would that your heart suffered my wound   **371 For** in return for.   **thy help . . . thee** I would promise to help you   **372 bane** ruin, death (with a suggestion of sexual surrender)   **373 Give me** let go   **374 it** your hand   **375 give . . . it** give me back my heart, lest your hardness of heart turn it to steel (with a suggestion of *steal*: don't steal my heart from me)   **376 grave** engrave, make an impression on   **381 bereft** deprived of   **382 hence** go away   **384 palfrey** saddle horse   **387 Affection** passion.   **coal** ember.   **cooled** quenched through satisfaction of desire

388 suffered permitted to continue   **391 jade** spiritless, worn-out nag   **393 fair fee** due reward   **395 base** worthless, paltry.   **bending crest** arching ridge of the neck   **396 Enfranchising** freeing   **397 in . . . bed** naked in her bed   **399 But when** but that when   **400 agents** organs, senses   **405 on presented joy** of joy that presents itself   **406 dumb** unable to speak   **408 made perfect** learned completely   **411 borrow** assume as an obligation.   **owe** obligate myself to repay   **412 My . . . disgrace it** my only inclination toward love is a desire to render it contemptible, discredit it   **414 all . . . breath** all in the same breath   **417 springing** sprouting, immature   **419 backed** broken in   **422 idle** useless.   **bootless** profitless   **424 alarms** signals of attack   **426 battery** breach in a fortified wall

"What, canst thou talk?" quoth she, "hast thou a
    tongue?
O, would thou hadst not, or I had no hearing!
Thy mermaid's voice hath done me double wrong; 429
I had my load before, now pressed with bearing: 430
    Melodious discord, heavenly tune harsh
      sounding,
    Ear's deep sweet music, and heart's deep sore
      wounding.

"Had I no eyes but ears, my ears would love
That inward beauty and invisible; 434
Or were I deaf, thy outward parts would move 435
Each part in me that were but sensible. 436
    Though neither eyes nor ears, to hear nor see,
    Yet should I be in love by touching thee.

"Say that the sense of feeling were bereft me,
And that I could not see, nor hear, nor touch,
And nothing but the very smell were left me,
Yet would my love to thee be still as much;
    For from the stillitory of thy face excelling 443
    Comes breath perfumed that breedeth love by
      smelling.

"But, O, what banquet wert thou to the taste,
Being nurse and feeder of the other four!
Would they not wish the feast might ever last,
And bid Suspicion double-lock the door, 448
    Lest Jealousy, that sour unwelcome guest,
    Should, by his stealing in, disturb the feast?"

Once more the ruby-colored portal opened, 451
Which to his speech did honey passage yield, 452
Like a red morn, that ever yet betokened
Wreck to the seaman, tempest to the field, 454
    Sorrow to shepherds, woe unto the birds,
    Gusts and foul flaws to herdmen and to herds. 456

This ill presage advisedly she marketh. 457
Even as the wind is hushed before it raineth,
Or as the wolf doth grin before he barketh, 459
Or as the berry breaks before it staineth,
    Or like the deadly bullet of a gun,
    His meaning struck her ere his words begun.

And at his look she flatly falleth down,
For looks kill love, and love by looks reviveth;
A smile recures the wounding of a frown. 465

But blessèd bankrupt, that by love so thriveth! 466
    The silly boy, believing she is dead, 467
    Claps her pale cheek, till clapping makes it red;

And all amazed brake off his late intent, 469
For sharply he did think to reprehend her,
Which cunning Love did wittily prevent.
Fair fall the wit that can so well defend her! 472
    For on the grass she lies as she were slain, 473
    Till his breath breatheth life in her again.

He wrings her nose, he strikes her on the cheeks, 475
He bends her fingers, holds her pulses hard, 476
He chafes her lips; a thousand ways he seeks
To mend the hurt that his unkindness marred. 478
    He kisses her, and she, by her good will, 479
    Will never rise, so he will kiss her still. 480

The night of sorrow now is turned to day.
Her two blue windows faintly she upheaveth,
Like the fair sun, when in his fresh array
He cheers the morn and all the earth relieveth;
    And as the bright sun glorifies the sky,
    So is her face illumined with her eye,

Whose beams upon his hairless face are fixed,
As if from thence they borrowed all their shine.
Were never four such lamps together mixed, 489
Had not his clouded with his brow's repine; 490
    But hers, which through the crystal tears gave
      light,
    Shone like the moon in water seen by night.

"O, where am I?" quoth she, "in earth or heaven,
Or in the ocean drenched, or in the fire? 494
What hour is this? Or morn or weary even? 495
Do I delight to die, or life desire?
    But now I lived, and life was death's annoy; 497
    But now I died, and death was lively joy. 498

"O, thou didst kill me; kill me once again!
Thy eyes' shrewd tutor, that hard heart of thine, 500
Hath taught them scornful tricks and such disdain
That they have murdered this poor heart of mine;
    And these mine eyes, true leaders to their queen, 503
    But for thy piteous lips no more had seen. 504

"Long may they kiss each other, for this cure!   505
O, never let their crimson liveries wear!   506
And as they last, their verdure still endure,   507
To drive infection from the dangerous year!
    That the stargazers, having writ on death,   509
    May say the plague is banished by thy breath.

"Pure lips, sweet seals in my soft lips imprinted,   511
What bargains may I make, still to be sealing?   512
To sell myself I can be well contented,
So thou wilt buy and pay and use good dealing,   514
    Which purchase if thou make, for fear of slips   515
    Set thy seal manual on my wax-red lips.   516

"A thousand kisses buys my heart from me;
And pay them at thy leisure, one by one.
What is ten hundred touches unto thee?   519
Are they not quickly told and quickly gone?   520
    Say for nonpayment that the debt should double,
    Is twenty hundred kisses such a trouble?"

"Fair queen," quoth he, "if any love you owe me,   523
Measure my strangeness with my unripe years.   524
Before I know myself, seek not to know me.   525
No fisher but the ungrown fry forbears.   526
    The mellow plum doth fall; the green sticks fast,
    Or being early plucked is sour to taste.

"Look the world's comforter, with weary gait,   529
His day's hot task hath ended in the west;
The owl, night's herald, shrieks; 'tis very late;
The sheep are gone to fold, birds to their nest,
    And coal-black clouds that shadow heaven's light
    Do summon us to part and bid good night.

"Now let me say 'Good night,' and so say you;
If you will say so, you shall have a kiss."
"Good night," quoth she, and, ere he says "Adieu,"
The honey fee of parting tendered is.   538
    Her arms do lend his neck a sweet embrace;
    Incorporate then they seem; face grows to face;   540

Till, breathless, he disjoined, and backward drew
The heavenly moisture, that sweet coral mouth,
Whose precious taste her thirsty lips well knew,

Whereon they surfeit, yet complain on drouth.   544
    He with her plenty pressed, she faint with dearth,   545
    Their lips together glued, fall to the earth.

Now quick desire hath caught the yielding prey,
And gluttonlike she feeds, yet never filleth;
Her lips are conquerors, his lips obey,
Paying what ransom the insulter willeth,   550
    Whose vulture thought doth pitch the price so
    high   551
    That she will draw his lips' rich treasure dry.

And having felt the sweetness of the spoil,   553
With blindfold fury she begins to forage;
Her face doth reek and smoke, her blood doth boil,   555
And careless lust stirs up a desperate courage,   556
    Planting oblivion, beating reason back,   557
    Forgetting shame's pure blush and honor's wrack.   558

Hot, faint, and weary with her hard embracing,
Like a wild bird being tamed with too much handling,
Or as the fleet-foot roe that's tired with chasing,   561
Or like the froward infant stilled with dandling,   562
    He now obeys, and now no more resisteth,
    While she takes all she can, not all she listeth.   564

What wax so frozen but dissolves with temp'ring   565
And yields at last to every light impression?
Things out of hope are compassed oft with vent'ring,   567
Chiefly in love, whose leave exceeds commission.   568
    Affection faints not like a pale-faced coward,   569
    But then woos best when most his choice is
    froward.   570

When he did frown, O, had she then gave over,
Such nectar from his lips she had not sucked.
Foul words and frowns must not repel a lover.   573
What though the rose have prickles, yet 'tis plucked.
    Were beauty under twenty locks kept fast,
    Yet love breaks through and picks them all at last.   576

For pity now she can no more detain him;   577
The poor fool prays her that he may depart.   578
She is resolved no longer to restrain him,
Bids him farewell, and look well to her heart,   580

---

505 **they** i.e., your lips. **for** in payment for, as a means of effecting
506 **crimson liveries** uniforms or costumes of crimson. **wear** wear
out 507 **their verdure** may their fresh fragrance. (Alludes to belief in
the efficacy of certain herbs to ward off contagion.) 509 **writ on
death** predicted (by means of astrology) an epidemic of deadly plague
511 **seals . . . imprinted** stamps that have left their impression on my
soft lips 512 **still to be sealing** (1) to continue kissing always (2) to
seal a bargain 514 **So** provided that 515 **slips** errors or fraudulent
payment (which Venus suggests they avoid by means of a *seal manual*
or seal placed on the contract of their love) 516 **wax-red** (since wax
would be used in sealing) 519 **touches** i.e., kisses 520 **told**
counted 523 **owe** bear 524 **Measure . . . with** i.e., explain my reserve by 525 **to know me** (With erotic suggestion of carnal knowledge.) 526 **No . . . forbears** there is no fisherman who does not
throw back immature fish 529 **Look** see how. **world's comforter**
i.e., sun 538 **honey** sweet. **tendered is** is given 540 **Incorporate**
united into one body

544 **on drouth** of drought, of not having enough 545 **with . . .
pressed** oppressed with the plenty she bestowed on him 550 **insulter**
boasting conqueror 551 **vulture** i.e., ravenous. **pitch** set at a certain level or point 553 **spoil** plunder, conquest 555 **reek** i.e.,
steam 556 **careless** heedless 557 **Planting oblivion** implanting or
causing forgetfulness of all that she ought to remember 558 **wrack**
ruin 561 **with chasing** with being chased 562 **froward** fretful
564 **listeth** desires 565 **temp'ring** heating and working with the fingers 567 **out of** beyond. **compassed** encompassed, accomplished
568 **whose . . . commission** which intemperately goes beyond its instructions 569 **Affection** passion. **faints not** does not relent or fall
back 570 **his choice is froward** its chosen object is obstinate
573 **Foul** hostile, disagreeable 576 **picks them all** (Picking a lock often has sexual meaning in Shakespeare.) 577 **For pity** appealing to
his sense of pity 578 **fool** (An affectionate term.) 580 **and look well
to** i.e., and bids him take good care of

The which, by Cupid's bow she doth protest, 581
He carries thence encagèd in his breast.

"Sweet boy," she says, "this night I'll waste in sorrow, 583
For my sick heart commands mine eyes to watch. 584
Tell me, Love's master, shall we meet tomorrow?
Say, shall we, shall we? Wilt thou make the match?"
    He tells her no, tomorrow he intends
    To hunt the boar with certain of his friends.

"The boar!" quoth she, whereat a sudden pale, 589
Like lawn being spread upon the blushing rose, 590
Usurps her cheek. She trembles at his tale,
And on his neck her yoking arms she throws.
    She sinketh down, still hanging by his neck;
    He on her belly falls, she on her back.

Now is she in the very lists of love, 595
Her champion mounted for the hot encounter.
All is imaginary she doth prove. 597
He will not manage her, although he mount her, 598
    That worse than Tantalus' is her annoy, 599
    To clip Elysium and to lack her joy. 600

Even so poor birds, deceived with painted grapes, 601
Do surfeit by the eye and pine the maw; 602
Even so she languisheth in her mishaps,
As those poor birds that helpless berries saw. 604
    The warm effects which she in him finds missing 605
    She seeks to kindle with continual kissing.

But all in vain; good queen, it will not be.
She hath assayed as much as may be proved. 608
Her pleading hath deserved a greater fee; 609
She's Love, she loves, and yet she is not loved.
    "Fie, fie," he says, "you crush me, let me go!
    You have no reason to withhold me so."

"Thou hadst been gone," quoth she, "sweet boy, ere
        this,
But that thou toldst me thou wouldst hunt the boar.
O, be advised! Thou know'st not what it is 615
With javelin's point a churlish swine to gore,
    Whose tushes, never sheathed, he whetteth still, 617
    Like to a mortal butcher bent to kill. 618

"On his bow-back he hath a battle set 619
Of bristly pikes, that ever threat his foes; 620
His eyes like glowworms shine when he doth fret; 621
His snout digs sepulchers where'er he goes;
    Being moved, he strikes whate'er is in his way, 623
    And whom he strikes his crooked tushes slay.

"His brawny sides, with hairy bristles armed,
Are better proof than thy spear's point can enter; 626
His short thick neck cannot be easily harmed;
Being ireful, on the lion he will venter. 628
    The thorny brambles and embracing bushes,
    As fearful of him, part, through whom he rushes. 630

"Alas, he naught esteems that face of thine,
To which Love's eyes pays tributary gazes,
Nor thy soft hands, sweet lips, and crystal eyne, 633
Whose full perfection all the world amazes;
    But having thee at vantage—wondrous dread!— 635
    Would root these beauties as he roots the mead. 636

"O, let him keep his loathsome cabin still! 637
Beauty hath naught to do with such foul fiends.
Come not within his danger by thy will; 639
They that thrive well take counsel of their friends.
    When thou didst name the boar, not to dissemble, 641
    I feared thy fortune, and my joints did tremble. 642

"Didst thou not mark my face? Was it not white?
Sawest thou not signs of fear lurk in mine eye?
Grew I not faint, and fell I not downright? 645
Within my bosom, whereon thou dost lie,
    My boding heart pants, beats, and takes no rest,
    But, like an earthquake, shakes thee on my breast.

"For where Love reigns, disturbing Jealousy 649
Doth call himself Affection's sentinel,
Gives false alarms, suggesteth mutiny, 651
And in a peaceful hour doth cry 'Kill, kill!' 652
    Distempering gentle Love in his desire, 653
    As air and water do abate the fire. 654

"This sour informer, this bate-breeding spy, 655
This canker that eats up Love's tender spring, 656
This carry-tale, dissentious Jealousy, 657
That sometimes true news, sometimes false doth bring,
    Knocks at my heart and whispers in mine ear
    That if I love thee, I thy death should fear;

581 protest vow, affirm   **583 waste** spend   **584 watch** stay awake
589 pale pallor   **590 lawn** fine linen   **595 lists** tournament field (here
a site of sexual encounter)   **597 All . . . prove** she finds out, however, that the hot encounter is merely in her imagination.   **doth
prove** that she experiences   **598 manage** control, ride (as one manages a horse)   **599 Tantalus** a son of Zeus who was punished by perpetual hunger and thirst with food and drink always in sight yet untouchable.   **annoy** vexation, torment   **600 clip** embrace.   **Elysium**
blissful afterlife in classical mythology.   **and** and yet   **601 birds . . .
grapes** (Allusion to Zeuxis, a Greek painter of the fifth century B.C., so
skillful an artist that birds were said to peck at his picture of a bunch
of grapes.)   **602 Do . . . maw** gorge themselves visually but starve
the stomach   **604 As** like.   **helpless** affording no sustenance
605 warm effects sexual response   **608 assayed** tried.   **proved** experienced, tried   **609 pleading . . . fee** (A legal metaphor; she is *pleading* her own case.)   **615 advised** warned   **617 tushes** tusks.   **still**
continually   **618 Like to** like.   **mortal** deadly.   **bent to kill** intent on
killing

619 bow-back arched back, but suggestive also of a bowman's
quiver.   **battle** i.e., martial array   **620 ever threat** continually
threaten   **621 fret** i.e., gnash his teeth   **623 moved** angered
626 proof armor   **628 ireful** wrathful.   **venter** venture   **630 As** as if
633 eyne eyes   **635 at vantage** at a disadvantage   **636 root** root up.
mead meadow   **637 keep** occupy.   **cabin** den   **639 within his danger** within reach of his power to do harm.   **by thy will** intentionally
641 not to dissemble to tell the truth   **642 feared** feared for
645 downright forthwith   **649 Jealousy** apprehension   **651 suggesteth mutiny** incites dissension   **652 in a** i.e., disturbing a   **653 Distempering** quenching   **654 abate** extinguish   **655 bate-breeding**
strife-breeding   **656 canker** cankerworm.   **spring** young shoot of a
plant   **657 carry-tale** rumormonger

"And more than so, presenteth to mine eye 661
The picture of an angry chafing boar,
Under whose sharp fangs on his back doth lie
An image like thyself, all stained with gore,
  Whose blood upon the fresh flowers being shed
  Doth make them droop with grief and hang the
    head.

"What should I do, seeing thee so indeed, 667
That tremble at th' imagination? 668
The thought of it doth make my faint heart bleed,
And fear doth teach it divination. 670
  I prophesy thy death, my living sorrow,
  If thou encounter with the boar tomorrow.

"But if thou needs wilt hunt, be ruled by me; 673
Uncouple at the timorous flying hare, 674
Or at the fox which lives by subtlety,
Or at the roe which no encounter dare.
  Pursue these fearful creatures o'er the downs, 677
  And on thy well-breathed horse keep with thy
    hounds. 678

"And when thou hast on foot the purblind hare, 679
Mark the poor wretch, to overshoot his troubles 680
How he outruns the wind and with what care 681
He cranks and crosses with a thousand doubles. 682
  The many musets through the which he goes 683
  Are like a labyrinth to amaze his foes. 684

"Sometimes he runs among a flock of sheep,
To make the cunning hounds mistake their smell,
And sometimes where earth-delving coneys keep, 687
To stop the loud pursuers in their yell, 688
  And sometimes sorteth with a herd of deer. 689
  Danger deviseth shifts; wit waits on fear. 690

"For there his smell with others being mingled,
The hot scent-snuffing hounds are driven to doubt,
Ceasing their clamorous cry till they have singled
With much ado the cold fault cleanly out. 694
  Then do they spend their mouths; echo replies, 695
  As if another chase were in the skies.

"By this, poor Wat, far off upon a hill, 697
Stands on his hinder legs with listening ear,
To hearken if his foes pursue him still.
Anon their loud alarums he doth hear,

And now his grief may be comparèd well
To one sore sick that hears the passing bell. 702

"Then shalt thou see the dew-bedabbled wretch
Turn, and return, indenting with the way; 704
Each envious brier his weary legs do scratch, 705
Each shadow makes him stop, each murmur stay;
  For misery is trodden on by many,
  And, being low, never relieved by any.

"Lie quietly, and hear a little more.
Nay, do not struggle, for thou shalt not rise.
To make thee hate the hunting of the boar,
Unlike myself thou hear'st me moralize, 712
  Applying this to that, and so to so;
  For love can comment upon every woe.

"Where did I leave?" "No matter where," quoth he, 715
"Leave me, and then the story aptly ends;
The night is spent." "Why, what of that?" quoth she.
"I am," quoth he, "expected of my friends, 718
  And now 'tis dark, and going I shall fall."
  "In night," quoth she, "desire sees best of all.

"But if thou fall, O, then imagine this,
The earth, in love with thee, thy footing trips,
And all is but to rob thee of a kiss.
Rich preys make true men thieves; so do thy lips 724
  Make modest Dian cloudy and forlorn, 725
  Lest she should steal a kiss and die forsworn. 726

"Now of this dark night I perceive the reason: 727
Cynthia for shame obscures her silver shine 728
Till forging Nature be condemned of treason 729
For stealing molds from heaven that were divine,
  Wherein she framed thee, in high heaven's
    despite, 731
  To shame the sun by day and her by night. 732

"And therefore hath she bribed the Destinies
To cross the curious workmanship of Nature, 734
To mingle beauty with infirmities,
And pure perfection with impure defeature, 736
  Making it subject to the tyranny
  Of mad mischances and much misery;

"As burning fevers, agues pale and faint, 739
Life-poisoning pestilence and frenzies wood, 740

661 more than so even more than that **667–668 seeing . . . imagination** if I should actually see you dead, when merely imagining it makes me tremble **670 divination** power to prophesy **673 needs wilt hunt** insist upon hunting **674 Uncouple** unleash the hounds. **flying** fleeing pursuit **677 fearful** full of fears. **downs** rolling hills **678 well-breathed** not easily winded, in good condition **679 on foot** in chase. **purblind** dim-sighted **680 overshoot** run beyond **681 outruns the wind** i.e., leaves his scent far behind **682 cranks** twists and turns **683 musets** gaps in hedge or fence **684 amaze** bewilder **687 coneys** rabbits. **keep** dwell **688 yell** cry **689 sorteth** consorts, mingles **690 shifts** tricks. **wit waits** intelligence attends **694 cold fault** cold or lost scent **695 spend their mouths** give tongue **697 Wat** (A common name applied to the hare.)

702 sore very. **passing bell** bell tolled for a person who has just died **704 indenting** zigzagging **705 envious** malicious **712 Unlike . . . moralize** contrary to the usual way of the goddess of love, you hear me point out a moral application **715 leave** leave off. (But Adonis answers with another sense, "go away from.") **718 of** by **724 Rich . . . thieves** the chance of rich spoils (*preys*) will make thieves even of honest (*true*) men **725 Dian** Diana, goddess of the moon, chastity, and the hunt. (Even Diana would fall in love with Adonis.) **cloudy** obscured with clouds; sorrowful **726 forsworn** having broken her vow as the goddess of chastity **727 of** for **728 Cynthia** Diana, the moon **729 forging** counterfeiting **731 she** i.e., Nature. **in . . . despite** in defiance of high heaven **732 her** i.e., the moon **734 cross** thwart. **curious** ingenious **736 defeature** disfigurement **739 As** such as **740 frenzies wood** mad seizures

The marrow-eating sickness, whose attaint   741
Disorder breeds by heating of the blood;
    Surfeits, impostumes, grief, and damned despair   743
    Swear Nature's death for framing thee so fair.   744

"And not the least of all these maladies
But in one minute's fight brings beauty under.   746
Both favor, savor, hue, and qualities,   747
Whereat th' impartial gazer late did wonder,   748
    Are on the sudden wasted, thawed, and done,   749
    As mountain snow melts with the midday sun.

"Therefore, despite of fruitless chastity,   751
Love-lacking vestals and self-loving nuns,
That on the earth would breed a scarcity
And barren dearth of daughters and of sons,
    Be prodigal. The lamp that burns by night
    Dries up his oil to lend the world his light.   756

"What is thy body but a swallowing grave,
Seeming to bury that posterity
Which by the rights of time thou needs must have,
If thou destroy them not in dark obscurity?
    If so, the world will hold thee in disdain,
    Sith in thy pride so fair a hope is slain.   762

"So in thyself thyself art made away,   763
A mischief worse than civil homebred strife,   764
Or theirs whose desperate hands themselves do slay,
Or butcher sire that reaves his son of life.   766
    Foul cankering rust the hidden treasure frets,   767
    But gold that's put to use more gold begets."

"Nay, then," quoth Adon, "you will fall again
Into your idle overhandled theme.   770
The kiss I gave you is bestowed in vain,
And all in vain you strive against the stream;   772
    For, by this black-faced night, desire's foul nurse, 773
    Your treatise makes me like you worse and worse.   774

"If love have lent you twenty thousand tongues,
And every tongue more moving than your own,
Bewitching like the wanton mermaids' songs,   777
Yet from mine ear the tempting tune is blown;
    For know, my heart stands armèd in mine ear
    And will not let a false sound enter there,

"Lest the deceiving harmony should run
Into the quiet closure of my breast;   782
And then my little heart were quite undone,
In his bedchamber to be barred of rest.
    No, lady, no. My heart longs not to groan,
    But soundly sleeps, while now it sleeps alone.

"What have you urged that I cannot reprove?   787
The path is smooth that leadeth on to danger.
I hate not love, but your device in love,   789
That lends embracements unto every stranger.
    You do it for increase. O strange excuse,
    When reason is the bawd to lust's abuse!   792

"Call it not love, for Love to heaven is fled,
Since sweating Lust on earth usurped his name,
Under whose simple semblance he hath fed   795
Upon fresh beauty, blotting it with blame;   796
    Which the hot tyrant stains and soon bereaves,   797
    As caterpillars do the tender leaves.

"Love comforteth like sunshine after rain,
But Lust's effect is tempest after sun.
Love's gentle spring doth always fresh remain;
Lust's winter comes ere summer half be done.
    Love surfeits not, Lust like a glutton dies;
    Love is all truth, Lust full of forgèd lies.

"More I could tell, but more I dare not say;
The text is old, the orator too green.   806
Therefore, in sadness, now I will away.   807
My face is full of shame, my heart of teen;   808
    Mine ears, that to your wanton talk attended,
    Do burn themselves for having so offended."   810

With this, he breaketh from the sweet embrace
Of those fair arms which bound him to her breast
And homeward through the dark laund runs apace,   813
Leaves Love upon her back deeply distressed.
    Look how a bright star shooteth from the sky,
    So glides he in the night from Venus' eye;

Which after him she darts, as one on shore
Gazing upon a late-embarkèd friend,   818
Till the wild waves will have him seen no more,   819
Whose ridges with the meeting clouds contend.
    So did the merciless and pitchy night
    Fold in the object that did feed her sight.   822

Whereat amazed, as one that unaware   823
Hath dropped a precious jewel in the flood,   824

---

741 The marrow-eating sickness (Probably venereal disease; love is said to burn or melt the marrow, as in line 142; hence the *heating of the blood* in line 742.)   **attaint** infection   **743 impostumes** abscesses   **744 Swear . . . fair** (all these diseases) swear to undo Nature because she formed you so beautiful   **746 brings beauty under** subdues beauty   **747 favor** beauty of feature.   **savor** sweetness of smell.   **hue** (1) color (2) shape   **748 impartial** i.e., uninfluenced by love.   **late** lately   **749 wasted** wasted away.   **done** destroyed   **751 despite of** in defiance of.   **fruitless** barren   **756 his** its   **762 Sith** since   **763 thyself art made away** i.e., your futurity is destroyed   **764 mischief** evil   **766 reaves** bereaves   **767 cankering** consuming (like the cankerworm).   **frets** eats away   **770 idle** profitless   **772 stream** current   **773 night . . . nurse** i.e., night, the foul nourisher of evil desire   **774 treatise** discourse   **777 mermaids'** i.e., sirens'

782 closure enclosure   **787 urged** argued for.   **reprove** refute   **789 device** cunning, deceitful conduct   **792 bawd** procuress   **795 whose** i.e., Love's.   **simple semblance** guileless appearance.   **he** i.e., Lust   **796 blotting** soiling   **797 bereaves** spoils   **806 The text** the point being explicated (like the *text* of a sermon).   **green** young, unpracticed   **807 in sadness** seriously, truly   **808 teen** grief, vexation   **810 burn themselves** blush   **813 laund** glade   **818 late-embarkèd** having recently taken ship   **819 have him seen** allow him to be seen   **822 Fold in** enfold, close in   **823 amazed** dazed, confused.   **unaware** inadvertently   **824 flood** body of flowing water

Or stonished as night wanderers often are,   825
Their light blown out in some mistrustful wood,   826
   Even so confounded in the dark she lay,   827
   Having lost the fair discovery of her way.   828

And now she beats her heart, whereat it groans,
That all the neighbor caves, as seeming troubled,
Make verbal repetition of her moans.
Passion on passion deeply is redoubled: 832
   "Ay me!" she cries, and twenty times "Woe,
     woe!"
   And twenty echoes twenty times cry so.

She marking them begins a wailing note
And sings extemporally a woeful ditty
How love makes young men thrall and old men dote,   837
How love is wise in folly, foolish witty.
   Her heavy anthem still concludes in woe,   839
   And still the choir of echoes answer so.

Her song was tedious and outwore the night,
For lovers' hours are long, though seeming short.
If pleased themselves, others, they think, delight
In suchlike circumstance, with suchlike sport.
   Their copious stories, oftentimes begun,
   End without audience and are never done.

For who hath she to spend the night withal   847
But idle sounds resembling parasits,   848
Like shrill-tongued tapsters answering every call,   849
Soothing the humor of fantastic wits?   850
   She says " 'Tis so," they answer all " 'Tis so,"
   And would say after her, if she said "No."

Lo here the gentle lark, weary of rest,
From his moist cabinet mounts up on high,   854
And wakes the morning, from whose silver breast   855
The sun ariseth in his majesty,
   Who doth the world so gloriously behold   857
   That cedar tops and hills seem burnished gold.

Venus salutes him with this fair good morrow:
"O thou clear god, and patron of all light,   860
From whom each lamp and shining star doth borrow
The beauteous influence that makes him bright,   862
   There lives a son that sucked an earthly mother   863
   May lend thee light, as thou dost lend to other."   864

This said, she hasteth to a myrtle grove,
Musing the morning is so much o'erworn,   866
And yet she hears no tidings of her love.
She hearkens for his hounds and for his horn.
   Anon she hears them chant it lustily,   869
   And all in haste she coasteth to the cry.   870

And as she runs, the bushes in the way
Some catch her by the neck, some kiss her face,
Some twine about her thigh to make her stay.
She wildly breaketh from their strict embrace,   874
   Like a milch doe, whose swelling dugs do ache,   875
   Hasting to feed her fawn hid in some brake.   876

By this, she hears the hounds are at a bay,   877
Whereat she starts, like one that spies an adder
Wreathed up in fatal folds just in his way,   879
The fear whereof doth make him shake and shudder;
   Even so the timorous yelping of the hounds
   Appalls her senses and her spirit confounds.

For now she knows it is no gentle chase,
But the blunt boar, rough bear, or lion proud,
Because the cry remaineth in one place,
Where fearfully the dogs exclaim aloud.
   Finding their enemy to be so curst,   887
   They all strain court'sy who shall cope him first.   888

This dismal cry rings sadly in her ear,   889
Through which it enters to surprise her heart,   890
Who, overcome by doubt and bloodless fear,   891
With cold-pale weakness numbs each feeling part.   892
   Like soldiers, when their captain once doth yield,   893
   They basely fly and dare not stay the field.   894

Thus stands she in a trembling ecstasy,   895
Till, cheering up her senses all dismayed,
She tells them 'tis a causeless fantasy   897
And childish error that they are afraid;
   Bids them leave quaking, bids them fear no
     more—
   And with that word she spied the hunted boar,

Whose frothy mouth, bepainted all with red,
Like milk and blood being mingled both together,
A second fear through all her sinews spread,   903
Which madly hurries her she knows not whither.

---

825 **stonished** bewildered   826 **mistrustful** causing apprehension   827 **confounded** bewildered   828 **the fair . . . way** i.e., the best way for her to go, or, him by whose light she could make her way   832 **Passion** lamentation   837 **thrall** captive   839 **heavy** melancholy.   **still** continually   847 **withal** with   848 **parasits** parasites, flattering attendants   849 **tapsters** waiters in taverns   850 **Soothing . . . wits** i.e., complying with the whim of capricious tavern customers   854 **moist cabinet** dewy dwelling, nest   855 **whose silver breast** (Aurora, the dawn, is personified as a goddess bidding farewell to her lover, the sun.)   857 **behold** i.e., shine upon   860 **clear** bright   862 **influence** a supposed flowing or streaming of an ethereal fluid from a celestial body. (An astrological term.)   863 **a son** i.e., Adonis.   **sucked** suckled from   864 **May** who may

866 **Musing** wondering (that).   **o'erworn** advanced   869 **chant** i.e., sound   870 **coasteth to** approaches   874 **strict** tight   875 **milch doe** female deer producing milk.   **dugs** udders   876 **brake** thicket   877 **By this** by this time.   **at a bay** i.e., faced by their quarry, which, being cornered, has turned to make its stand   879 **folds** coils   887 **curst** savage   888 **strain court'sy** are punctiliously polite, stand upon ceremony; i.e., they hold back.   **cope** cope with   889 **dismal** foreboding ill   890 **surprise** assail suddenly   891 **bloodless fear** i.e., fear that causes the blood to draw to the heart and desert the features, leaving one *cold, pale,* and *weak* (line 892)   892 **feeling part** bodily part and organ of sense   893 **when . . . yield** once their commanding officer has yielded   894 **stay the field** remain in the battlefield and stand against the onslaught   895 **ecstasy** agitated state   897 **them** i.e., her senses   903 **sinews** nerves

This way she runs, and now she will no further,
But back retires to rate the boar for murther.   906

A thousand spleens bear her a thousand ways;   907
She treads the path that she untreads again;   908
Her more than haste is mated with delays,   909
Like the proceedings of a drunken brain,
    Full of respects, yet naught at all respecting,   911
    In hand with all things, naught at all effecting.   912

Here kenneled in a brake she finds a hound,   913
And asks the weary caitiff for his master,   914
And there another licking of his wound,
'Gainst venomed sores the only sovereign plaster;   916
    And here she meets another sadly scowling,
    To whom she speaks, and he replies with
      howling.

When he hath ceased his ill-resounding noise,
Another flapmouthed mourner, black and grim,   920
Against the welkin volleys out his voice;   921
Another and another answer him,
    Clapping their proud tails to the ground below,
    Shaking their scratched ears, bleeding as they go.

Look how the world's poor people are amazed   925
At apparitions, signs, and prodigies,
Whereon with fearful eyes they long have gazed,
Infusing them with dreadful prophecies;   928
    So she at these sad signs draws up her breath
    And, sighing it again, exclaims on Death.   930

"Hard-favored tyrant, ugly, meager, lean,   931
Hateful divorce of love!"—thus chides she Death—   932
"Grim-grinning ghost, earth's worm, what dost thou
      mean   933
To stifle beauty and to steal his breath,
    Who, when he lived, his breath and beauty set
    Gloss on the rose, smell to the violet?

"If he be dead—O no, it cannot be,
Seeing his beauty, thou shouldst strike at it!   938
O yes, it may; thou hast no eyes to see,   939
But hatefully at random dost thou hit.
    Thy mark is feeble age, but thy false dart   941
    Mistakes that aim and cleaves an infant's heart.

"Hadst thou but bid beware, then he had spoke,   943
And, hearing him, thy power had lost his power.   944
The Destinies will curse thee for this stroke;
They bid thee crop a weed, thou pluck'st a flower.
    Love's golden arrow at him should have fled,
    And not Death's ebon dart, to strike him dead.   948

"Dost thou drink tears, that thou provok'st such
      weeping?
What may a heavy groan advantage thee?
Why hast thou cast into eternal sleeping
Those eyes that taught all other eyes to see?
    Now Nature cares not for thy mortal vigor,   953
    Since her best work is ruined with thy rigor."   954

Here overcome, as one full of despair,
She vailed her eyelids, who, like sluices, stopped   956
The crystal tide that from her two cheeks fair
In the sweet channel of her bosom dropped;   958
    But through the floodgates breaks the silver rain,
    And with his strong course opens them again.   960

O, how her eyes and tears did lend and borrow!   961
Her eye seen in the tears, tears in her eye,
Both crystals, where they viewed each other's sorrow,   963
Sorrow that friendly sighs sought still to dry;   964
    But like a stormy day, now wind, now rain,
    Sighs dry her cheeks, tears make them wet again.

Variable passions throng her constant woe,
As striving who should best become her grief.   968
All entertained, each passion labors so   969
That every present sorrow seemeth chief,
    But none is best; then join they all together,   971
    Like many clouds consulting for foul weather.   972

By this, far off she hears some huntsman hallow;   973
A nurse's song ne'er pleased her babe so well.
The dire imagination she did follow   975
This sound of hope doth labor to expel;
    For now reviving joy bids her rejoice
    And flatters her it is Adonis' voice.

Whereat her tears began to turn their tide,   979
Being prisoned in her eye like pearls in glass;
Yet sometimes falls an orient drop beside,   981

906 **rate** berate 907 **spleens** impulses 908 **untreads** retraces
909 **mated** confounded, checked 911 **respects** designs, considerations. **yet . . . respecting** yet really considering nothing 912 **In
hand with** busy about 913 **kenneled** hiding as if in its kennel
914 **caitiff** wretch 916 **only sovereign plaster** best all-curing application 920 **flapmouthed** having broad, hanging lips or jowls
921 **welkin** sky 925 **Look how** just as 928 **Infusing** imbuing.
prophecies prophetic qualities 930 **exclaims on** denounces
931 **Hard-favored** ugly-faced 932 **divorce** terminator 933 **Grim-
grinning** i.e., grinning like a skull. **worm** i.e., cankerworm, con-
sumer of flowers (with the suggestion also of worms that devour
corpses) 938 **Seeing** i.e., that, seeing 939 **no eyes** (The eye sockets
of the skull of Death are empty.) 941 **mark** target

943 **bid beware** i.e., issued a warning of your approach. **he** i.e.,
Adonis 944 **his** its 948 **ebon** ebony, black 953 **cares . . . vigor**
does not fear your deadly power 954 **with** by 956 **vailed** lowered.
who . . . stopped which, like floodgates, stopped up 958 **channel**
i.e., cleavage 960 **his** its 961 **lend and borrow** i.e., reflect each
other 963 **crystals** i.e., mirrors or magic crystals 964 **friendly** i.e.,
consoling 968 **As** as if. **who** which (passion). **become** suit
969 **entertained** having been admitted 971 **best** supreme 972 **consulting for** gathering and conspiring to produce 973 **By this** by this
time. **hallow** halloo 975 **dire imagination** tragic train of thought.
follow pursue in her thoughts 979 **turn their tide** ebb 981 **orient**
shining. **beside** to one side

Which her cheek melts, as scorning it should pass,   982
    To wash the foul face of the sluttish ground,   983
    Who is but drunken when she seemeth drowned.   984

O hard-believing love, how strange it seems   985
Not to believe, and yet too credulous!   986
Thy weal and woe are both of them extremes.
Despair and hope makes thee ridiculous: 988
    The one doth flatter thee in thoughts unlikely;   989
    In likely thoughts the other kills thee quickly.

Now she unweaves the web that she hath wrought;
Adonis lives, and Death is not to blame;
It was not she that called him all to naught.   993
Now she adds honors to his hateful name:
    She clepes him king of graves and grave for kings,   995
    Imperious supreme of all mortal things.   996

"No, no," quoth she, "sweet Death, I did but jest.
Yet pardon me, I felt a kind of fear
Whenas I met the boar, that bloody beast,   999
Which knows no pity, but is still severe.   1000
    Then, gentle shadow—truth I must confess—   1001
    I railed on thee, fearing my love's decease.   1002

" 'Tis not my fault; the boar provoked my tongue.
Be wreaked on him, invisible commander.   1004
'Tis he, foul creature, that hath done thee wrong;
I did but act, he's author of thy slander.   1006
    Grief hath two tongues, and never woman yet   1007
    Could rule them both without ten women's wit."

Thus hoping that Adonis is alive,
Her rash suspect she doth extenuate;   1010
And that his beauty may the better thrive,
With Death she humbly doth insinuate;   1012
    Tells him of trophies, statues, tombs, and stories   1013
    His victories, his triumphs, and his glories.

"O Jove," quoth she, "how much a fool was I
To be of such a weak and silly mind
To wail his death who lives and must not die
Till mutual overthrow of mortal kind!   1018
    For, he being dead, with him is beauty slain,
    And, beauty dead, black chaos comes again.

"Fie, fie, fond love, thou art as full of fear   1021
As one with treasure laden, hemmed with thieves;   1022
Trifles, unwitnessèd with eye or ear,   1023
Thy coward heart with false bethinking grieves."   1024
    Even at this word she hears a merry horn,
    Whereat she leaps that was but late forlorn.   1026

As falcon to the lure, away she flies—
The grass stoops not, she treads on it so light—
And in her haste unfortunately spies
The foul boar's conquest on her fair delight;
    Which seen, her eyes, as murdered with the view,   1031
    Like stars ashamed of day, themselves withdrew;   1032

Or, as the snail, whose tender horns being hit,
Shrinks backward in his shelly cave with pain,
And there, all smothered up, in shade doth sit,
Long after fearing to creep forth again;
    So, at his bloody view, her eyes are fled
    Into the deep dark cabins of her head,

Where they resign their office and their light
To the disposing of her troubled brain,   1040
Who bids them still consort with ugly night   1041
And never wound the heart with looks again—   1042
    Who, like a king perplexèd in his throne,   1043
    By their suggestion gives a deadly groan.   1044

Whereat each tributary subject quakes,   1045
As when the wind, imprisoned in the ground,   1046
Struggling for passage, earth's foundation shakes,
Which with cold terror doth men's minds confound.
    This mutiny each part doth so surprise   1049
    That from their dark beds once more leap her
        eyes;

And, being opened, threw unwilling light
Upon the wide wound that the boar had trenched
In his soft flank, whose wonted lily white   1053
With purple tears, that his wound wept, was drenched.
    No flower was nigh, no grass, herb, leaf, or weed,
    But stole his blood and seemed with him to bleed.   1056

This solemn sympathy poor Venus noteth.
Over one shoulder doth she hang her head.
Dumbly she passions, franticly she doteth;   1059
She thinks he could not die, he is not dead.

982 melts i.e., dries. **as** as if **983 foul** dirty **984 Who . . . drowned** i.e., the earth greedily drinks up her tears while she seems drowned in grief **985–986 O . . . credulous** O skeptical love, how wary of believing you are, too credulous **988 Despair and hope** i.e., the rapid oscillation between despair and hope **989 The one** i.e., hope **993 him all to naught** Death wholly evil **995 clepes** names, calls **996 Imperious supreme** imperial ruler **999 Whenas** when **1000 still severe** incessantly ruthless **1001 shadow** specter **1002 railed on** reviled. **decease** decease **1004 wreaked** revenged. **invisible commander** i.e., Death, a specter that orders our final destiny **1006 act** i.e., act as agent **1007 two tongues** i.e., a double tongue, twice as loud and hard to control as a usual tongue. (Women are conventionally unable to rule their tongues in any case.) **1010 rash suspect** too hasty suspicion (of Death). **extenuate** excuse **1012 insinuate** ingratiate herself **1013 trophies** memorial monuments. **stories** narrates **1018 mutual** i.e., universal

1021 fond foolish **1022 hemmed with** hemmed about by **1023–1024 Trifles . . . grieves** mere trifles, not actually seen by eye or heard by ear, grieve your cowardly heart with false imaginings **1026 leaps** i.e., leaps for joy. **late** lately **1031 as** as if **1032 ashamed of** put to shame by. **withdrew** i.e., closed **1040 disposing** direction, ordering **1041 still consort** always remain **1042 with looks** by looking **1043 Who** which, i.e., the heart **1044 By their suggestion** incited by the eyes **1045 tributary subject** i.e., subordinate part of the body **1046 wind . . . ground** (The common Elizabethan explanation of earthquakes; compare with *1 Henry IV*, 3.1.30.) **1049 surprise** attack suddenly **1053 wonted** customary **1056 But stole** that did not steal **1059 passions** shows grief

Her voice is stopped, her joints forget to bow;   1061
Her eyes are mad that they have wept till now.   1062

Upon his hurt she looks so steadfastly
That her sight, dazzling, makes the wound seem three;   1064
And then she reprehends her mangling eye,
That makes more gashes where no breach should be.
    His face seems twain, each several limb is
        doubled;
    For oft the eye mistakes, the brain being troubled.

"My tongue cannot express my grief for one,
And yet," quoth she, "behold two Adons dead!
My sighs are blown away, my salt tears gone;
Mine eyes are turned to fire, my heart to lead.
    Heavy heart's lead, melt at mine eyes' red fire!
    So shall I die by drops of hot desire.   1074

"Alas, poor world, what treasure hast thou lost!
What face remains alive that's worth the viewing?
Whose tongue is music now? What canst thou boast
Of things long since, or anything ensuing?   1078
    The flowers are sweet, their colors fresh and trim,
    But true sweet beauty lived and died with him.

"Bonnet nor veil henceforth no creature wear!   1081
Nor sun nor wind will ever strive to kiss you.
Having no fair to lose, you need not fear;   1083
The sun doth scorn you, and the wind doth hiss you.
    But when Adonis lived, sun and sharp air
    Lurked like two thieves, to rob him of his fair.

"And therefore would he put his bonnet on,
Under whose brim the gaudy sun would peep;   1088
The wind would blow it off and, being gone,   1089
Play with his locks. Then would Adonis weep;
    And straight, in pity of his tender years,   1091
    They both would strive who first should dry his
        tears.

"To see his face the lion walked along
Behind some hedge, because he would not fear him;   1094
To recreate himself when he hath song,   1095
The tiger would be tame and gently hear him;
    If he had spoke, the wolf would leave his prey
    And never fright the silly lamb that day.   1098

"When he beheld his shadow in the brook,   1099
The fishes spread on it their golden gills;
When he was by, the birds such pleasure took

That some would sing, some other in their bills   1102
    Would bring him mulberries and ripe-red cherries;
    He fed them with his sight, they him with berries.

"But this foul, grim, and urchin-snouted boar,   1105
Whose downward eye still looketh for a grave,   1106
Ne'er saw the beauteous livery that he wore—   1107
Witness the entertainment that he gave.   1108
    If he did see his face, why then I know
    He thought to kiss him, and hath killed him so.

" 'Tis true, 'tis true! Thus was Adonis slain:
He ran upon the boar with his sharp spear,
Who did not whet his teeth at him again,   1113
But by a kiss thought to persuade him there;   1114
    And, nuzzling in his flank, the loving swine
    Sheathed unaware the tusk in his soft groin.

"Had I been toothed like him, I must confess,   1117
With kissing him I should have killed him first;
But he is dead, and never did he bless
My youth with his—the more am I accurst."
    With this, she falleth in the place she stood,   1121
    And stains her face with his congealèd blood.

She looks upon his lips, and they are pale;
She takes him by the hand, and that is cold;
She whispers in his ears a heavy tale,   1125
As if they heard the woeful words she told;
    She lifts the coffer-lids that close his eyes,   1127
    Where, lo, two lamps, burnt out, in darkness lies;

Two glasses, where herself herself beheld   1129
A thousand times, and now no more reflect,
Their virtue lost, wherein they late excelled,   1131
And every beauty robbed of his effect.   1132
    "Wonder of time," quoth she, "this is my spite,   1133
    That, thou being dead, the day should yet be
        light.

"Since thou art dead, lo, here I prophesy:
Sorrow on love hereafter shall attend.
It shall be waited on with jealousy,   1137
Find sweet beginning but unsavory end,
    Ne'er settled equally, but high or low,   1139
    That all love's pleasure shall not match his woe.   1140

1061 **forget to bow** are paralyzed (with grief)   **1062 till now** before now (in a lesser cause)   **1064 dazzling** being dazzled   **1074 So shall I die** (Venus imagines a terrible death by melted lead.)   **1078 long . . . ensuing** past or to come   **1081 Bonnet nor veil** neither hat nor veil (worn to guard a fair complexion, regarded as particularly beautiful, against the sun)   **1083 fair** beauty. (Also in line 1086.)   **1088 gaudy** brilliantly shining   **1089 being gone** it (the hat) being gone   **1091 straight** at once   **1094 would not fear** did not wish to frighten   **1095 To recreate . . . song** whenever he sang for his own recreation   **1098 silly** innocent   **1099 shadow** reflected image

1102 other others   **1105 urchin-snouted** having a snout like a hedgehog   **1106 still** continually.   **for a grave** i.e., as if for a grave in which to bury victims. (Compare with line 622, where the boar's snout *digs sepulchers* as it roots in the earth.)   **1107 livery** i.e., outside appearance.   **he** Adonis   **1108 entertainment** treatment, reception   **1113 again** in return   **1114 persuade** win over, or, persuade to stay   **1117 toothed** tusked   **1121 place** place where   **1125 heavy** sad   **1127 coffer-lids** lids covering chests of treasure, i.e., eyelids   **1129 glasses** mirrors   **1131 virtue** power (to see and to reflect)   **1132 his** its   **1133 time** i.e., the ages, human existence.   **spite** torment, vexation   **1137 It** love.   **with** by   **1139 Ne'er . . . low** i.e., (love will be) never equal between the two lovers; they will be from high and low social stations, or like high and low musical pitches   **1140 his** its

"It shall be fickle, false, and full of fraud,
Bud and be blasted in a breathing while;
The bottom poison, and the top o'erstrawed   1142
With sweets that shall the truest sight beguile.   1143
    The strongest body shall it make most weak,
    Strike the wise dumb and teach the fool to
      speak.

"It shall be sparing and too full of riot,   1147
Teaching decrepit age to tread the measures;   1148
The staring ruffian shall it keep in quiet,   1149
Pluck down the rich, enrich the poor with treasures;
    It shall be raging mad and silly mild,   1151
    Make the young old, the old become a child.

"It shall suspect where is no cause of fear;   1153
It shall not fear where it should most mistrust;
It shall be merciful and too severe,
And most deceiving when it seems most just;   1156
    Perverse it shall be where it shows most toward,   1157
    Put fear to valor, courage to the coward.

"It shall be cause of war and dire events
And set dissension twixt the son and sire,
Subject and servile to all discontents,   1161
As dry combustious matter is to fire.
    Sith in his prime Death doth my love destroy,   1163
    They that love best their loves shall not enjoy."

By this, the boy that by her side lay killed   1165
Was melted like a vapor from her sight,
And in his blood that on the ground lay spilled
A purple flow'r sprung up, checkered with white,   1168
    Resembling well his pale cheeks and the blood
    Which in round drops upon their whiteness
      stood.

She bows her head, the new-sprung flower to smell,
Comparing it to her Adonis' breath,
And says within her bosom it shall dwell,
Since he himself is reft from her by death.   1174
    She crops the stalk, and in the breach appears
    Green dropping sap, which she compares to tears.

"Poor flower," quoth she, "this was thy father's guise—   1177
Sweet issue of a more sweet-smelling sire—   1178
For every little grief to wet his eyes;   1179
To grow unto himself was his desire,   1180
    And so 'tis thine; but know, it is as good
    To wither in my breast as in his blood.

"Here was thy father's bed, here in my breast;
Thou art the next of blood, and 'tis thy right.
Lo, in this hollow cradle take thy rest;
My throbbing heart shall rock thee day and night.
    There shall not be one minute in an hour
    Wherein I will not kiss my sweet love's flower."

Thus, weary of the world, away she hies
And yokes her silver doves, by whose swift aid
Their mistress mounted through the empty skies   1191
In her light chariot quickly is conveyed,   1192
    Holding their course to Paphos, where their
      queen   1193
    Means to immure herself and not be seen.

1177 guise manner, way **1178 Sweet issue** i.e., you, the anemone, who are the sweet offspring **1179 For . . . eyes** to weep compassionately at every little sorrow **1180 To grow unto himself** to mature self-made and independent **1191–1192 mounted . . . conveyed** is quickly conveyed, mounted in her light chariot, through the empty skies **1193 Paphos** Venus' dwelling in Cyprus

1142 blasted blighted by frost. **breathing while** i.e., short time **1143 The bottom** i.e., the substance, what is inside. **top** surface. **o'erstrawed** strewn over **1147 sparing . . . riot** i.e., both niggardly and excessive **1148 tread the measures** dance. (An inappropriate action for the old.) **1149 staring** looking savage, glaring **1151 silly** innocently, feebly, humbly, weak-mindedly **1153 is** there is **1156 just** trustworthy **1157 Perverse** stubborn, contrary. **shows** looks. **toward** tractable **1161 Subject . . . discontents** (love will be) both the cause and the unwilling slave of every kind of dissension **1163 Sith** since **1165 By this** by this time **1168 flow'r** i.e., anemone **1174 reft** bereft

The Rape of Lucrece

The Rape of Lucrece is closely related to Venus and Adonis. The two were published about a year apart, in 1594 and 1593, respectively, and both were printed by Richard Field. Both are dedicated to the young Earl of Southampton, Henry Wriothesley, whose confidence and friendship Shakespeare appears to have gained during the interim between the two poems; the dedicatory preface to The Rape of Lucrece expresses assurance that the poem will be accepted. Stylistically, the two poems are of a piece: both are reliant on Petrarchan ornament and rhetorical showmanship and are steeped in Ovidian pathos. Yet they are complementary rather than similar in attitude and subject. The Rape of Lucrece appears to be the "graver labor" promised to Southampton in the dedication of the earlier poem, a planned sequel in which love would be subjected to a darker treatment. Venus and Adonis is chiefly about sensual pleasure, whereas The Rape of Lucrece is about heroic chastity. The first poem is amatory, erotic, and amusing, despite its sad end; the second is moral, declamatory, and lugubrious. As Gabriel Harvey observed (c. 1598–1601), "The younger sort takes much delight in Shakespeare's Venus and Adonis, but his Lucrece and his Tragedy of Hamlet, Prince of Denmark, have it in them to please the wiser sort."

Harvey's pairing of this poem with Hamlet suggests that, to Harvey at least, Shakespeare aspires to sublime effects in Lucrece. For his verse pattern, Shakespeare chooses the seven-line rhyme royal stanza, traditionally used for tragic expression, as in Geoffrey Chaucer's Troilus and Criseyde and several of the more formal Canterbury Tales, in John Lydgate's The Fall of Princes (1430–1438) and its continuation in A Mirror for Magistrates (1559), in Samuel Daniel's The Complaint of Rosamond, and others. Although Shakespeare turns to Ovid once again as his chief source, he chooses a tale of ravishment, suicide, and vengeance rather than one of titillating amatory pursuit. The story of Lucrece had gained wide currency in the ancient and medieval worlds as an exemplum of chaste conduct in women. Shakespeare seems to have known Livy's History of Rome (Book 1, chaps. 57–59), though he relied primarily on Ovid's Fasti (2.721–852). Among later versions, he may have known Chaucer's The Legend of Good Women and a translation of Livy in William Painter's The Palace of Pleasure (1566, 1575). He encountered other "complaints" in A Mirror for Magistrates and in Daniel's The Complaint of Rosamond, and it is to this well-established genre that Lucrece belongs. The poem had the desired effect of enhancing Shakespeare's reputation for elegant poetry; it was reprinted five times during his lifetime and was frequently admired by his contemporaries. Venus and Adonis was, to be sure, more popular still (it was reprinted nine times during Shakespeare's lifetime), but no one in Shakespeare's day seems to have regarded Lucrece as anything other than a noble work.

To understand the poem in terms of its own generic sense of form, we must recognize its conventions and not expect it to be other than what it professes to be. As in Venus and Adonis, plot and character are secondary. Although the story outlined in "The Argument" is potentially sensational and swift-moving, Shakespeare deliberately cuts away most of the action. We do not see Lucius Tarquinius' murder of his father-in-law and tyrannical seizure of Rome, or Collatinus' rash boasting of his wife Lucrece's virtue in the presence of the King's lustful son Sextus Tarquinius, nor, at the conclusion of the story, do we learn much about the avenging of Lucrece's rape. Shakespeare's focus is on the attitudes of the two protagonists immediately before and after the ravishment. Even here, despite opportunities for psychological probing, Shakespeare's real interest is not in the characters themselves so much as in the social ramifications of their actions. As Coppélia Kahn has shown (in Shakespeare Studies 9), the rape serves as a means of examining the nature of marriage in a patriarchal society in which competition for ownership and struggles for power characterize men's attitudes toward politics and sex. Using Rome as a familiar mirror for English customs, Shakespeare presents Lucrece as a heroine acting to uphold the institution of marriage. However innocently, she is the one who acquires the stain through being violated and must pay the cost of wifely duty in marriage. Her husband accepts the decorousness of her suicide as necessary for the preservation of his honor, however much he may grieve over her wrong. Like a number of Shakespeare's later heroines, such as Imogen in Cymbeline, Lucrece is portrayed as beautiful but not alluring, restrained even in her marriage bed. She arranges her death so as to make the most of its social implications.

Along with his interest in patriarchy and violence, Shakespeare frames the story of The Rape of Lucrece in terms of the political events that lead to the founding of the Roman republic. The corruption of the Tarquin dynasty raises issues about Roman values generally, and the poem ends with a strong repudiation of the old order. The villain of the poem is at once rapist and tyrant; the resolution is both a vindication of women as victims and a movement toward republicanism. To be sure, the patriarchy that has dictated the conditions of Lucrece's life and honor will remain intact in the republic; the wife is still her husband's possession, and her greatest obligation to state and family must be to ensure that the husband's honor remains unbesmirched. Nonetheless, the assumptions of Roman hierarchy have been held up to scrutiny.

Shakespeare casts his narrative in the form of a series of rhetorical disputations, each a set piece presented as a debate or as a formal declamation. The debates are built around familiar antitheses: honor versus lust, rude will versus conscience, "affection" versus reason, nobility versus baseness, and so on. Many of the images are similarly arranged in contrasting pairs: dove and owl, daylight and darkness, clear and cloudy weather, white and red. Tarquin debates with himself the reasons for and against rape; Lucrece tries to persuade him of the depravity of his course; Lucrece ponders suicide. These debates generate, in turn, a number of rhetorical apostrophes to marital fidelity (lines 22–28), to the ideal of kingship as a moral example to others (lines 610–637), to Night (lines 764–812), to Opportunity (lines 876–924), and to Time (lines 925–1022). Another rhetorical formula, perhaps the most successful in the poem, is the use of structural digression. The most notable describes a painting or tapestry of Troy with obvious relevance to Lucrece's sad fate: Troy is a city destroyed by a rape, Paris achieves his selfish pleasure at the expense of the public good, and Sinon wins his sinister victory through deceitful appearance (lines 1366–1568).

Throughout, the poem's ornament strives after heightened and elaborate effects. The comparisons, or "conceits," as the Elizabethans called them, are intentionally contrived and reliant on ingenious wordplay. Shakespeare puns on the word *will*, for example, as he does in his sonnets, where he takes advantage of his own first name being Will (see sonnet 135), and in *Venus and Adonis* (see line 365). In *The Rape of Lucrece*, the word is central to Shakespeare's depiction of Tarquin, as we see the ravisher holding a disputation between "frozen conscience and hot-burning will" (line 247), forcing the locks "between her chamber and his will" (line 302), feeding ravenously "in his will his willful eye" (line 417), and the like. These and other passages often frame the word in a polarity of "will" and "heart," and range over numerous meanings that include inclination, desire, appetite, sexual lust, request or command, volition, pleasure, permission, good will, and spontaneity. The fact that the word rhymes with "kill" and "ill" adds to its usefulness. Another kind of "conceit" found throughout *The Rape of Lucrece*—one that arises integrally from the poem's deepest concerns—is the extended military metaphor of a city under siege. Tarquin's heart beats an alarum, Lucrece's breasts are "round turrets" made pale by the assault (lines 432–441), and, in her subsequent death, she is likened to a "late-sacked island" surrounded by rivers of her own blood (line 1740). Elsewhere she is a house that has been pillaged, "Her

mansion battered by the enemy" (lines 1170–1171). Classical allusions are, of course, common, notably to the story of the rape of Philomel or Philomela (lines 1079, 1128, etc.). Rhetorical devices of antithesis are displayed with the same ornate versatility as in *Venus and Adonis*. In a poem on a serious subject, these devices may seem overly contrived to us. We should nevertheless recognize them as conventional in the genre to which *The Rape of Lucrece* belongs. We find a similar blending of the sensuous and the moral in the sometimes grotesque conceits of the Catholic poet Robert Southwell (d. 1595) and in the later baroque paradoxes of Richard Crashaw (d. 1649). Among Shakespeare's dramatic works, *Titus Andronicus* seems closest to *The Rape of Lucrece* in its pathos, refined sensationalism, and use of classical allusion, and specifically in the character of Lavinia, whose misfortunes and chaste dignity so much resemble those of Lucrece.

Throughout *The Rape of Lucrece*, we find a consciousness of the poem's own artistry. In Lucrece's tragic plight, Shakespeare explores art's ability to communicate through its various means of expression. Especially in the long passage on the painting of the fall of Troy (lines 1366–1568), Lucrece shows an understandable anxiety about art's ability to deceive. The painting is in some ways more realistic than life itself; the figures in the painting seem to move and are so cunningly rendered that they "mock the mind" (line 1414). The imaginary work is "conceit deceitful" (line 1423), able through synecdoche (using the part to represent the whole) to suggest a series of general truths lying behind the particulars that are shown. This power of art to deceive is most troublesome in the case of Sinon, the betrayer of Troy—"In him the painter labored with his skill / To hide deceit" (lines 1506–1507)—and has succeeded with such devastating effect that the viewer cannot tell from Sinon's mild appearance that he is, in fact, capable of limitless evil. In his capacity for deception, Sinon is like Tarquin, the seemingly attractive courtier who has ravaged Lucrece. Art is thus capable of misrepresentation for purposes of evil; its persuasive power, its imaginative vision, can be perverted to wrong ends. Seen through such art, Rome, too, is at once a great source of civilization and a nation whose values are cast seriously in doubt. *The Rape of Lucrece* thus grapples with issues of serious consequences—ones that also concerned Shakespeare in his early plays (such as *Titus Andronicus*) and indeed throughout his career as a dramatist.

The Rape of Lucrece

To the RIGHT HONORABLE HENRY WRIOTHESLEY, *Earl of Southampton, and Baron of Titchfield.*

The love I dedicate to your lordship is without end; whereof this pamphlet without beginning is but a superfluous moiety. The warrant I have of your honorable disposition, not the worth of my untutored lines, makes it assured of acceptance. What I have done is yours; what I have to do is yours; being part in all I have, devoted yours. Were my worth greater, my duty would show greater; meantime, as it is, it is bound to your lordship, to whom I wish long life still lengthened with all happiness.

Your lordship's in all duty,

William Shakespeare.

The Argument

Lucius Tarquinius, for his excessive pride surnamed Superbus, after he had caused his own father-in-law Servius Tullius to be cruelly murdered and, contrary to the Roman laws and customs, not requiring or staying for the people's suffrages, had possessed himself of the kingdom, went, accompanied with his sons and other noblemen of Rome, to besiege Ardea. During which siege, the principal men of the army meeting one evening at the tent of Sextus Tarquinius, the King's son, in their discourses after supper everyone commended the virtues of his own wife; among whom Collatinus extolled the incomparable chastity of his wife Lucretia. In that pleasant humor they all posted to Rome; and intending, by their secret and sudden arrival, to make trial of that which everyone had before avouched, only Collatinus finds his wife, though it were late in the night, spinning amongst her maids; the other ladies were all found dancing and reveling, or in several disports. Whereupon the noblemen yielded Collat-

inus the victory and his wife the fame. At that time Sextus Tarquinius, being inflamed with Lucrece' beauty, yet smothering his passions for the present, departed with the rest back to the camp; from whence he shortly after privily withdrew himself and was, according to his estate, royally entertained and lodged by Lucrece at Collatium. The same night he treacherously stealeth into her chamber, violently ravished her, and early in the morning speedeth away. Lucrece, in this lamentable plight, hastily dispatcheth messengers, one to Rome for her father, another to the camp for Collatine. They came, the one accompanied with Junius Brutus, the other with Publius Valerius; and finding Lucrece attired in mourning habit, demanded the cause of her sorrow. She, first taking an oath of them for her revenge, revealed the actor and whole manner of his dealing, and withal suddenly stabbed herself. Which done, with one consent they all vowed to root out the whole hated family of the Tarquins; and, bearing the dead body to Rome, Brutus acquainted the people with the doer and manner of the vile deed, with a bitter invective against the tyranny of the King, wherewith the people were so moved that with one consent and a general acclamation the Tarquins were all exiled and the state government changed from kings to consuls.

From the besiegèd Ardea all in post,
Borne by the trustless wings of false desire,
Lust-breathèd Tarquin leaves the Roman host
And to Collatium bears the lightless fire
Which, in pale embers hid, lurks to aspire
    And girdle with embracing flames the waist
    Of Collatine's fair love, Lucrece the chaste.

Haply that name of "chaste" unhapp'ly set
This bateless edge on his keen appetite,
When Collatine unwisely did not let
To praise the clear unmatchèd red and white
Which triumphed in that sky of his delight,
    Where mortal stars, as bright as heaven's beauties,
    With pure aspects did him peculiar duties.

For he the night before, in Tarquin's tent,
Unlocked the treasure of his happy state,
What priceless wealth the heavens had him lent
In the possession of his beauteous mate,

Dedication.
2 without beginning i.e., beginning *in medias res*, in the middle of the action   **3 moiety** part.   **warrant** assurance   **7 being . . . have** since you are part of everything I have done and have to do   **10 still** continually
The Argument.
2 Superbus "the Proud"   **5 requiring** requesting   **6 suffrages** consent
15 pleasant merry.   **posted** hastened   **18 avouched** affirmed
21–22 several disports various pastimes

27 privily secretly   **29 estate** rank   **38 habit** attire   **40 actor** doer
1 Ardea a city twenty-four miles south of Rome.   **post** haste   **2 trustless** treacherous   **3 Lust-breathèd** excited by lust   **4 Collatium** a city about ten miles east of Rome.   **lightless** i.e., smoldering invisibly
5 aspire rise, i.e., break into flames   **8 Haply** perchance.   **unhapp'ly** (1) unhappily (2) by mischance   **9 bateless** not to be blunted   **10 let** forbear   **12 sky** i.e., Lucrece's face   **13 mortal stars** i.e., Lucrece's eyes   **14 aspects** (1) looks (2) astrologically favorable position.   **peculiar** exclusively for him   **16 Unlocked the treasure** i.e., opened and revealed (in conversation) the riches

Reck'ning his fortune at such high proud rate   19
   That kings might be espousèd to more fame,   20
   But king nor peer to such a peerless dame.   21

O happiness enjoyed but of a few!
And, if possessed, as soon decayed and done   23
As is the morning's silver melting dew
Against the golden splendor of the sun!
An expired date, canceled ere well begun.   26
   Honor and beauty in the owner's arms
   Are weakly fortressed from a world of harms.   28

Beauty itself doth of itself persuade   29
The eyes of men without an orator;
What needeth then apology be made
To set forth that which is so singular?
Or why is Collatine the publisher   33
   Of that rich jewel he should keep unknown
   From thievish ears, because it is his own?

Perchance his boast of Lucrece' sovereignty   36
Suggested this proud issue of a king,   37
For by our ears our hearts oft tainted be.
Perchance that envy of so rich a thing,   39
Braving compare, disdainfully did sting   40
   His high-pitched thoughts, that meaner men
     should vaunt   41
   That golden hap which their superiors want.   42

But some untimely thought did instigate
His all too timeless speed, if none of those.   44
His honor, his affairs, his friends, his state   45
Neglected all, with swift intent he goes
To quench the coal which in his liver glows.   47
   O rash false heat, wrapped in repentant cold,
   Thy hasty spring still blasts and ne'er grows old!   49

When at Collatium this false lord arrived,
Well was he welcomed by the Roman dame,
Within whose face beauty and virtue strived
Which of them both should underprop her fame.
When virtue bragged, beauty would blush for shame;
   When beauty boasted blushes, in despite
   Virtue would stain that o'er with silver white.   56

But beauty, in that white entitulèd   57
From Venus' doves, doth challenge that fair field.   58

Then virtue claims from beauty beauty's red,   59
Which virtue gave the golden age to gild   60
Their silver cheeks, and called it then their shield,
   Teaching them thus to use it in the fight:
   When shame assailed, the red should fence the
     white.   63

This heraldry in Lucrece' face was seen,
Argued by beauty's red and virtue's white.   65
Of either's color was the other queen,
Proving from world's minority their right.   67
Yet their ambition makes them still to fight,   68
   The sovereignty of either being so great
   That oft they interchange each other's seat.   70

This silent war of lilies and of roses,
Which Tarquin viewed in her fair face's field,
In their pure ranks his traitor eye encloses,   73
Where, lest between them both it should be killed,
The coward captive vanquishèd doth yield
   To those two armies that would let him go
   Rather than triumph in so false a foe.   77

Now thinks he that her husband's shallow tongue,
The niggard prodigal that praised her so,   79
In that high task hath done her beauty wrong,
Which far exceeds his barren skill to show.
Therefore that praise which Collatine doth owe   82
   Enchanted Tarquin answers with surmise,   83
   In silent wonder of still-gazing eyes.

This earthly saint, adorèd by this devil,
Little suspecteth the false worshiper,
For unstained thoughts do seldom dream on evil;
Birds never limed no secret bushes fear.   88
So, guiltless, she securely gives good cheer   89
   And reverend welcome to her princely guest,
   Whose inward ill no outward harm expressed.

For that he colored with his high estate,   92
Hiding base sin in pleats of majesty,   93
That nothing in him seemed inordinate   94
Save sometimes too much wonder of his eye,
Which, having all, all could not satisfy;

19 high proud making him highly proud 20 espousèd i.e., joined, linked 21 But king but neither king 23 done done with 26 date period of time 28 fortressed from defended against 29 of itself by its own nature 33 publisher publicizer 36 sovereignty supremacy 37 Suggested tempted. issue offspring, son (i.e., Tarquin) 39 Perchance that i.e., perhaps it was that 40 Braving compare defying comparison 41 meaner less nobly born 42 hap fortune. want lack 44 timeless unseemly, unseasonable 45 state position 47 liver (Regarded as the seat of the passions.) 49 blasts is nipped by frost 56 o'er (Perhaps with a pun on or, "gold.") 57 entitulèd entitled, having a claim 58 doves (Venus' chariot was drawn by white doves.) challenge claim. field (1) battlefield (2) the surface of the shield, where the armorial device is displayed

59 Then . . . red then modesty claims that the color red really belongs to it, not to beauty (since modesty blushes) 60 gave the golden age i.e., bestowed on those who live innocently and purely, as in ancient times before the world grew corrupt. gild i.e., cover with a blush of modesty. (Gold and red were often considered interchangeable as colors.) 63 fence defend 65 Argued disputed and demonstrated 67 world's minority the long-ago golden age, mentioned in line 60 (since their right is as old as the doves of Venus and the first blush) 68 still always 70 seat throne 73 his . . . encloses surrounds and overwhelms his eye that traitorously contemplates her overthrow 77 in over 79 niggard prodigal unwisely lavish yet coming too short in praise 82 doth owe i.e., must still render, having fallen short on previous occasions 83 answers renders. surmise imagination, visual contemplation 88 limed snared with birdlime, a sticky substance placed on branches 89 securely unsuspiciously 92 that he colored i.e., he disguised his harmful intent 93 pleats cunning folds, concealments 94 That so that

But, poorly rich, so wanteth in his store   97
That, cloyed with much, he pineth still for more.

But she, that never coped with stranger eyes,   99
Could pick no meaning from their parling looks,   100
Nor read the subtle shining secrecies
Writ in the glassy margins of such books.   102
She touched no unknown baits, nor feared no hooks,
      Nor could she moralize his wanton sight   104
      More than his eyes were opened to the light.   105

He stories to her ears her husband's fame,   106
Won in the fields of fruitful Italy,
And decks with praises Collatine's high name,
Made glorious by his manly chivalry
With bruisèd arms and wreaths of victory.   110
      Her joy with heaved-up hand she doth express
      And, wordless, so greets heaven for his success.

Far from the purpose of his coming thither
He makes excuses for his being there.
No cloudy show of stormy blustering weather
Doth yet in his fair welkin once appear,   116
Till sable Night, mother of dread and fear,   117
      Upon the world dim darkness doth display
      And in her vaulty prison stows the day.

For then is Tarquin brought unto his bed,
Intending weariness with heavy sprite;   121
For, after supper, long he questionèd   122
With modest Lucrece, and wore out the night.
Now leaden slumber with life's strength doth fight,
      And everyone to rest himself betakes,
      Save thieves and cares and troubled minds that
      wakes.

As one of which doth Tarquin lie revolving   127
The sundry dangers of his will's obtaining;   128
Yet ever to obtain his will resolving,
Though weak-built hopes persuade him to abstaining.   130
Despair to gain doth traffic oft for gaining;   131
      And when great treasure is the meed proposed,   132
      Though death be adjunct, there's no death
      supposed.   133

Those that much covet are with gain so fond   134
That what they have not, that which they possess   135
They scatter and unloose it from their bond,   136
And so, by hoping more, they have but less;
Or, gaining more, the profit of excess   138
      Is but to surfeit, and such griefs sustain   139
      That they prove bankrupt in this poor-rich gain.

The aim of all is but to nurse the life
With honor, wealth, and ease in waning age;
And in this aim there is such thwarting strife   143
That one for all or all for one we gage: 144
As life for honor in fell battle's rage,   145
      Honor for wealth; and oft that wealth doth cost
      The death of all, and all together lost.

So that in venturing ill we leave to be   148
The things we are for that which we expect;   149
And this ambitious foul infirmity,   150
In having much, torments us with defect   151
Of that we have. So then we do neglect
      The thing we have, and, all for want of wit,   153
      Make something nothing by augmenting it.

Such hazard now must doting Tarquin make,
Pawning his honor to obtain his lust,
And for himself himself he must forsake.   157
Then where is truth, if there be no self-trust?
When shall he think to find a stranger just,
      When he himself himself confounds, betrays
      To slanderous tongues and wretched hateful
      days?

Now stole upon the time the dead of night,
When heavy sleep had closed up mortal eyes.
No comfortable star did lend his light;   164
No noise but owls' and wolves' death-boding cries
Now serves the season, that they may surprise
      The silly lambs. Pure thoughts are dead and still,   167
      While lust and murder wakes to stain and kill.

And now this lustful lord leapt from his bed,
Throwing his mantle rudely o'er his arm;
Is madly tossed between desire and dread;
Th' one sweetly flatters, th' other feareth harm;
But honest fear, bewitched with lust's foul charm,
      Doth too too oft betake him to retire,   174
      Beaten away by brainsick rude desire.

His falchion on a flint he softly smiteth, 176
That from the cold stone sparks of fire do fly,
Whereat a waxen torch forthwith he lighteth,
Which must be lodestar to his lustful eye; 179
And to the flame thus speaks advisedly: 180
    "As from this cold flint I enforced this fire,
    So Lucrece must I force to my desire."

Here pale with fear he doth premeditate
The dangers of his loathsome enterprise,
And in his inward mind he doth debate
What following sorrow may on this arise.
Then, looking scornfully, he doth despise
    His naked armor of still-slaughtered lust, 188
    And justly thus controls his thoughts unjust: 189

"Fair torch, burn out thy light, and lend it not
To darken her whose light excelleth thine;
And die, unhallowed thoughts, before you blot
With your uncleanness that which is divine.
Offer pure incense to so pure a shrine.
    Let fair humanity abhor the deed
    That spots and stains love's modest snow-white
    weed. 196

"O shame to knighthood and to shining arms!
O foul dishonor to my household's grave! 198
O impious act, including all foul harms! 199
A martial man to be soft fancy's slave! 200
True valor still a true respect should have; 201
    Then my digression is so vile, so base, 202
    That it will live engraven in my face.

"Yea, though I die, the scandal will survive
And be an eyesore in my golden coat; 205
Some loathsome dash the herald will contrive 206
To cipher me how fondly I did dote; 207
That my posterity, shamed with the note, 208
    Shall curse my bones, and hold it for no sin
    To wish that I their father had not been.

"What win I, if I gain the thing I seek?
A dream, a breath, a froth of fleeting joy.
Who buys a minute's mirth to wail a week?
Or sells eternity to get a toy? 214
For one sweet grape who will the vine destroy?

Or what fond beggar, but to touch the crown,
Would with the scepter straight be strucken
    down? 217

"If Collatinus dream of my intent,
Will he not wake and in a desperate rage
Post hither, this vile purpose to prevent? 220
This siege that hath engirt his marriage, 221
This blur to youth, this sorrow to the sage,
    This dying virtue, this surviving shame,
    Whose crime will bear an ever-during blame? 224

"O, what excuse can my invention make
When thou shalt charge me with so black a deed?
Will not my tongue be mute, my frail joints shake,
Mine eyes forgo their light, my false heart bleed? 228
The guilt being great, the fear doth still exceed;
    And extreme fear can neither fight nor fly,
    But cowardlike with trembling terror die.

"Had Collatinus killed my son or sire,
Or lain in ambush to betray my life,
Or were he not my dear friend, this desire
Might have excuse to work upon his wife,
As in revenge or quittal of such strife; 236
    But as he is my kinsman, my dear friend,
    The shame and fault finds no excuse nor end.

"Shameful it is; ay, if the fact be known, 239
Hateful it is. There is no hate in loving.
I'll beg her love. But she is not her own. 241
The worst is but denial and reproving.
My will is strong, past reason's weak removing.
    Who fears a sentence or an old man's saw 244
    Shall by a painted cloth be kept in awe." 245

Thus, graceless, holds he disputation 246
'Tween frozen conscience and hot-burning will,
And with good thoughts makes dispensation, 248
Urging the worser sense for vantage still,
Which in a moment doth confound and kill
    All pure effects, and doth so far proceed 251
    That what is vile shows like a virtuous deed.

Quoth he, "She took me kindly by the hand
And gazed for tidings in my eager eyes,
Fearing some hard news from the warlike band
Where her belovèd Collatinus lies.

---

176 **falchion** curved sword   179 **lodestar** the guiding polestar
180 **advisedly** deliberately   188 **His . . . lust** his poor defense against
his own lust, which is continually being slaughtered, i.e., temporarily
satiated, but never killed, or, his insatiable and vulnerable lust, which
will be his only poor armor in this enterprise   189 **justly** accurately,
closely   196 **weed** garment (i.e., chastity)   198 **my household's
grave** memorial tomb of my forebears   199 **including** encompassing
200 **fancy's** love's, infatuation's   201 **true respect** i.e., proper consideration for virtue   202 **digression** deviation (from honor)   205 **coat**
coat of arms   206 **dash** bar, stroke (devised by the heralds to indicate
something dishonorable in the pedigree)   207 **cipher** express in characters, indicate. **fondly** foolishly   208 **note** stigma, the heraldic bar
(line 206)   214 **toy** trifle

217 **straight** at once   220 **Post** hasten   221 **engirt** engirdled, as in a
siege   224 **ever-during** everlasting   228 **forgo their light** lose their
power of vision   236 **quittal** requital   239 **fact** deed   241 **she . . .
own** i.e., she is not entirely independent, since she has duties to her
husband   244 **Who** whoever. **sentence** moral sentiment. **saw** saying, proverb   245 **painted cloth** wall hanging in which moral tales
and maxims were sometimes depicted. (Compare with lines
1366–1456, where such a painted cloth is described.)   246 **graceless**
lacking in social and divine grace   248 **makes dispensation** dispenses, sets aside   251 **effects** intents and consequences

O, how her fear did make her color rise!
    First red as roses that on lawn we lay,   258
    Then white as lawn, the roses took away.

"And how her hand, in my hand being locked,
Forced it to tremble with her loyal fear!
Which struck her sad, and then it faster rocked,
Until her husband's welfare she did hear;
Wherat she smilèd with so sweet a cheer
    That had Narcissus seen her as she stood   265
    Self-love had never drowned him in the flood.

"Why hunt I then for color or excuses?   267
All orators are dumb when beauty pleadeth;
Poor wretches have remorse in poor abuses;   269
Love thrives not in the heart that shadows dreadeth.   270
Affection is my captain, and he leadeth;   271
    And when his gaudy banner is displayed,
    The coward fights and will not be dismayed.   273

"Then, childish fear, avaunt! Debating, die!   274
Respect and reason, wait on wrinkled age!   275
My heart shall never countermand mine eye.   276
Sad pause and deep regard beseems the sage;   277
My part is youth, and beats these from the stage.
    Desire my pilot is, beauty my prize;
    Then who fears sinking where such treasure lies?"

As corn o'ergrown by weeds, so heedful fear   281
Is almost choked by unresisted lust.
Away he steals with open listening ear,
Full of foul hope and full of fond mistrust,   284
Both which, as servitors to the unjust,
    So cross him with their opposite persuasion   286
    That now he vows a league, and now invasion.   287

Within his thought her heavenly image sits,
And in the selfsame seat sits Collatine.
That eye which looks on her confounds his wits;   290
That eye which him beholds, as more divine,   291
Unto a view so false will not incline,
    But with a pure appeal seeks to the heart,   293
    Which once corrupted takes the worser part;

And therein heartens up his servile powers,   295
Who, flattered by their leader's jocund show,   296
Stuff up his lust, as minutes fill up hours;
And as their captain, so their pride doth grow,
Paying more slavish tribute than they owe.
    By reprobate desire thus madly led,
    The Roman lord marcheth to Lucrece' bed.

The locks between her chamber and his will,
Each one by him enforced, retires his ward;   303
But, as they open, they all rate his ill,   304
Which drives the creeping thief to some regard.   305
The threshold grates the door to have him heard;
    Night-wandering weasels shriek to see him there;   307
    They fright him, yet he still pursues his fear.   308

As each unwilling portal yields him way,
Through little vents and crannies of the place
The wind wars with his torch to make him stay
And blows the smoke of it into his face,
Extinguishing his conduct in this case;   313
    But his hot heart, which fond desire doth scorch,
    Puffs forth another wind that fires the torch.

And being lighted, by the light he spies
Lucretia's glove, wherein her needle sticks.
He takes it from the rushes where it lies,   318
And gripping it, the needle his finger pricks,
As who should say, 'This glove to wanton tricks   320
    Is not inured. Return again in haste;   321
    Thou seest our mistress' ornaments are chaste."

But all these poor forbiddings could not stay him;   323
He in the worst sense consters their denial.   324
The doors, the wind, the glove that did delay him
He takes for accidental things of trial,   326
Or as those bars which stop the hourly dial,   327
    Who with a lingering stay his course doth let   328
    Till every minute pays the hour his debt.

"So, so," quoth he, "these lets attend the time,   330
Like little frosts that sometimes threat the spring,
To add a more rejoicing to the prime,   332

258 lawn fine white linen   265 Narcissus youth who fell in love with his own reflection in the water (but who would have fallen in love with Lucrece if he had seen her)   267 color pretext   269 Poor . . . abuses only lowborn, cowardly men feel remorse for their paltry misdeeds   270 shadows i.e., the chimeras of conscience   271 Affection passion   273 The coward i.e., even the coward   274 avaunt begone   275 Respect circumspection. wait on attend, accompany   276 heart (Here, "moral sense"; compare with lines 293 ff., where the heart is corrupted.)   277 Sad serious, reflective   281 corn grain   284 fond foolish   286 cross thwart   287 league treaty (of peace)   290 eye eye of lust. confounds his wits overwhelms his reason with lust   291 That eye . . . divine the eye of divine reason, reflecting on Collatine   293 seeks to the heart applies to the moral sense

295 servile powers base passions, appetites. (The image is the common one of the faculties as an army: the heart as captain of the sensible soul commands all the affections to serve him. Compare with lines 433 ff., below.)   296 jocund sprightly   303 retires his ward draws back its guard, i.e., the locking mechanism   304 rate his ill chide his evil (by creaking)   305 regard caution   307 weasels (Weasels were sometimes kept in houses as rat catchers.)   308 his fear i.e., the cause of his fear   313 conduct conductor, i.e., his torch (with a play on "behavior")   318 rushes reeds used as floor covering   320 who should one might   320–321 to wanton . . . inured has not become habituated to lascivious stratagems   323 stay restrain   324 consters construes   326 accidental . . . trial i.e., accidents that test his resolve, not portents   327 bars . . . dial minute marks on a clock face at which the minute hand seems to pause slightly   328 Who which. his its. let hinder   330 these . . . time i.e., these hindrances (like the minute marks) are part of the passage of time   332 more greater. prime spring

And give the sneapèd birds more cause to sing.   333
Pain pays the income of each precious thing;   334
   Huge rocks, high winds, strong pirates, shelves,
    and sands   335
   The merchant fears, ere rich at home he lands."

Now is he come unto the chamber door
That shuts him from the heaven of his thought,
Which with a yielding latch, and with no more,
Hath barred him from the blessèd thing he sought.
So from himself impiety hath wrought   341
   That for his prey to pray he doth begin,
   As if the heavens should countenance his sin.

But in the midst of his unfruitful prayer,
Having solicited th' eternal power
That his foul thoughts might compass his fair fair,   346
And they would stand auspicious to the hour,   347
Even there he starts. Quoth he, "I must deflower.   348
   The powers to whom I pray abhor this fact;   349
   How can they then assist me in the act?

"Then Love and Fortune be my gods, my guide!
My will is backed with resolution.
Thoughts are but dreams till their effects be tried;
The blackest sin is cleared with absolution;
Against love's fire fear's frost hath dissolution.
   The eye of heaven is out, and misty night   356
   Covers the shame that follows sweet delight."

This said, his guilty hand plucked up the latch,
And with his knee the door he opens wide.
The dove sleeps fast that this night owl will catch.
Thus treason works ere traitors be espied.
Who sees the lurking serpent steps aside;   362
   But she, sound sleeping, fearing no such thing,
   Lies at the mercy of his mortal sting.   364

Into the chamber wickedly he stalks,   365
And gazeth on her yet unstainèd bed.
The curtains being close, about he walks,   367
Rolling his greedy eyeballs in his head.
By their high treason is his heart misled,
   Which gives the watchword to his hand full soon
   To draw the cloud that hides the silver moon.   371

Look as the fair and fiery-pointed sun,   372
Rushing from forth a cloud, bereaves our sight,   373

Even so, the curtain drawn, his eyes begun
To wink, being blinded with a greater light.   375
Whether it is that she reflects so bright   376
   That dazzleth them, or else some shame
    supposed;
   But blind they are, and keep themselves enclosed.

O, had they in that darksome prison died,
Then had they seen the period of their ill!   380
Then Collatine again by Lucrece' side
In his clear bed might have reposèd still.   382
But they must ope, this blessèd league to kill,   383
   And holy-thoughted Lucrece to their sight   384
   Must sell her joy, her life, her world's delight.

Her lily hand her rosy cheek lies under,
Cozening the pillow of a lawful kiss,   387
Who, therefore angry, seems to part in sunder,
Swelling on either side to want his bliss;   389
Between whose hills her head entombèd is;
   Where, like a virtuous monument, she lies,   391
   To be admired of lewd unhallowed eyes.

Without the bed her other fair hand was,   393
On the green coverlet, whose perfect white
Showed like an April daisy on the grass,
With pearly sweat resembling dew of night.
Her eyes, like marigolds, had sheathed their light,
   And canopied in darkness sweetly lay,
   Till they might open to adorn the day.

Her hair, like golden threads, played with her breath—
O modest wantons, wanton modesty!—
Showing life's triumph in the map of death   402
And death's dim look in life's mortality.   403
Each in her sleep themselves so beautify   404
   As if between them twain there were no strife,
   But that life lived in death and death in life.

Her breasts like ivory globes circled with blue,
A pair of maiden worlds unconquerèd,
Save of their lord no bearing yoke they knew,
And him by oath they truly honorèd.
These worlds in Tarquin new ambition bred,
   Who, like a foul usurper, went about
   From this fair throne to heave the owner out.

What could he see but mightily he noted?
What did he note but strongly he desired?
What he beheld, on that he firmly doted,

333 **sneapèd** nipped or pinched with cold   334 **pays . . . of** is the price of obtaining, or, pays court to, as though attending the arrival of   335 **shelves** sandbars   341 **So . . . wrought** impiety has so wrested him away from his true nature   346 **compass** encompass, possess. **fair fair** virtuous fair one   347 **they** i.e., that they, the eternal powers of heaven   348 **starts** i.e., is startled, taken aback   349 **fact** deed   356 **out** extinguished   362 **Who** whoever   364 **mortal** deadly. **sting** bite (suggesting also "lust" and "penis")   365 **stalks** creeps, as in stalking a prey   367 **close** (around a four-poster bed)   371 **draw the cloud** i.e., draw back the bedcurtains   372 **Look as** just as   373 **bereaves** takes away
375 **wink** shut   376 **reflects** shines   380 **period** end.   **ill** wrongdoing   382 **clear** pure, innocent   383 **league** i.e., marriage   384 **to their sight** for the sake of what they (his eyes) will see   387 **Cozening** cheating   389 **to want his** i.e., protesting the lack of its   391 **monument** effigy on a tomb   393 **Without** on the outside of.   **bed** bedclothes   402 **the map of death** i.e., sleep. (*Map* means "image, picture.")   403 **life's mortality** life's least-living aspect, i.e., sleep   404 **Each** i.e., life and death

And in his will his willful eye he tired. 417
With more than admiration he admired
    Her azure veins, her alabaster skin,
    Her coral lips, her snow-white dimpled chin.

As the grim lion fawneth o'er his prey, 421
Sharp hunger by the conquest satisfied,
So o'er this sleeping soul doth Tarquin stay,
His rage of lust by gazing qualified— 424
Slacked, not suppressed, for, standing by her side, 425
    His eye, which late this mutiny restrains, 426
    Unto a greater uproar tempts his veins.

And they, like straggling slaves for pillage fighting, 428
Obdurate vassals fell exploits effecting, 429
In bloody death and ravishment delighting,
Nor children's tears nor mothers' groans respecting,
Swell in their pride, the onset still expecting. 432
    Anon his beating heart, alarum striking,
    Gives the hot charge and bids them do their
      liking.

His drumming heart cheers up his burning eye,
His eye commends the leading to his hand; 436
His hand, as proud of such a dignity,
Smoking with pride, marched on to make his stand
On her bare breast, the heart of all her land;
    Whose ranks of blue veins, as his hand did scale, 440
    Left their round turrets destitute and pale.

They, mustering to the quiet cabinet 442
Where their dear governess and lady lies,
Do tell her she is dreadfully beset,
And fright her with confusion of their cries.
She, much amazed, breaks ope her locked-up eyes,
    Who, peeping forth this tumult to behold,
    Are by his flaming torch dimmed and controlled. 448

Imagine her as one in dead of night
From forth dull sleep by dreadful fancy waking,
That thinks she hath beheld some ghastly sprite,
Whose grim aspect sets every joint a-shaking.
What terror 'tis! But she, in worser taking, 453
    From sleep disturbèd, heedfully doth view
    The sight which makes supposèd terror true.

Wrapped and confounded in a thousand fears,
Like to a new-killed bird she trembling lies.
She dares not look; yet, winking, there appears 458
Quick-shifting antics, ugly in her eyes. 459

Such shadows are the weak brain's forgeries,
    Who, angry that the eyes fly from their lights, 461
    In darkness daunts them with more dreadful
      sights.

His hand, that yet remains upon her breast—
Rude ram, to batter such an ivory wall!— 464
May feel her heart—poor citizen!—distressed,
Wounding itself to death, rise up and fall,
Beating her bulk, that his hand shakes withal. 467
    This moves in him more rage and lesser pity
    To make the breach and enter this sweet city.

First, like a trumpet, doth his tongue begin
To sound a parley to his heartless foe, 471
Who o'er the white sheet peers her whiter chin, 472
The reason of this rash alarm to know,
Which he by dumb demeanor seeks to show; 474
    But she with vehement prayers urgeth still 475
    Under what color he commits this ill. 476

Thus he replies: "The color in thy face, 477
That even for anger makes the lily pale, 478
And the red rose blush at her own disgrace,
Shall plead for me and tell my loving tale.
Under that color am I come to scale 481
    Thy never-conquered fort; the fault is thine,
    For those thine eyes betray thee unto mine.

"Thus I forestall thee, if thou mean to chide:
Thy beauty hath ensnared thee to this night, 485
Where thou with patience must my will abide—
My will that marks thee for my earth's delight,
Which I to conquer sought with all my might.
    But as reproof and reason beat it dead, 489
    By thy bright beauty was it newly bred.

"I see what crosses my attempt will bring; 491
I know what thorns the growing rose defends;
I think the honey guarded with a sting; 493
All this beforehand counsel comprehends.
But will is deaf and hears no heedful friends;
    Only he hath an eye to gaze on beauty
    And dotes on what he looks, 'gainst law or duty. 497

"I have debated, even in my soul,
What wrong, what shame, what sorrow I shall breed,
But nothing can affection's course control 500

---

417 **will** lust. **tired** (1) exhausted (2) glutted, fed ravenously. (A term from falconry.) 421 **fawneth** shows delight 424 **qualified** softened, abated 425 **Slacked** moderated. (The Q reading, "Slakt," could be modernized as "Slaked," with the same meaning.) 426 **late** lately, a moment ago 428 **slaves** i.e., base-born soldiers 429 **fell** fierce. **effecting** carrying out 432 **pride** lust. **still** continually 436 **commends** entrusts, commissions 440 **scale** ascend (as in military attack) 442 **mustering** gathering. **cabinet** i.e., heart 448 **controlled** overpowered 453 **taking** state of agitation 458 **winking** closing the eyes 459 **antics** phantoms, fantastic appearances, shapes

461 **fly . . . lights** flee away from their own eyebeams 464 **ram** battering ram 467 **bulk** i.e., chest, breast. **that** so that 471 **a parley** a summoning of the defenders to a negotiation. **heartless** disheartened 472 **peers** causes to peep out (as a defender would peer out over the fortifications) 474 **dumb demeanor** dumb show 475 **urgeth** cries out to know 476 **color** pretext 477 **color** hue (punning on the previous line) 478 **That . . . pale** that makes even the lily turn pale in anger (at being surpassed in paleness) 481 **color** banner (punning on lines 476 and 477) 485 **ensnared thee to** led you into the trap of 489 **as** as soon as. **it** my will or passion 491 **crosses** vexations 493 **think the honey** know the honey to be 497 **looks** sees 500 **affection's** passion's

Or stop the headlong fury of his speed.
I know repentant tears ensue the deed,
    Reproach, disdain, and deadly enmity;
    Yet strive I to embrace mine infamy." 502

This said, he shakes aloft his Roman blade,
Which, like a falcon towering in the skies,
Coucheth the fowl below with his wings' shade, 507
Whose crooked beak threats if he mount he dies. 508
So under his insulting falchion lies 509
    Harmless Lucretia, marking what he tells
    With trembling fear, as fowl hear falcon's bells. 511

"Lucrece," quoth he, "this night I must enjoy thee.
If thou deny, then force must work my way,
For in thy bed I purpose to destroy thee.
That done, some worthless slave of thine I'll slay,
To kill thine honor with thy life's decay; 516
    And in thy dead arms do I mean to place him,
    Swearing I slew him, seeing thee embrace him.

"So thy surviving husband shall remain
The scornful mark of every open eye, 520
Thy kinsmen hang their heads at this disdain,
Thy issue blurred with nameless bastardy; 522
And thou, the author of their obloquy,
    Shalt have thy trespass cited up in rhymes
    And sung by children in succeeding times.

"But if thou yield, I rest thy secret friend. 526
The fault unknown is as a thought unacted;
A little harm done to a great good end
For lawful policy remains enacted. 529
The poisonous simple sometimes is compacted 530
    In a pure compound; being so applied, 531
    His venom in effect is purified.

"Then, for thy husband and thy children's sake,
Tender my suit. Bequeath not to their lot 534
The shame that from them no device can take, 535
The blemish that will never be forgot,
Worse than a slavish wipe or birth hour's blot. 537
    For marks descried in men's nativity
    Are nature's faults, not their own infamy."

Here with a cockatrice' dead-killing eye 540
He rouseth up himself and makes a pause,
While she, the picture of pure piety,
Like a white hind under the gripe's sharp claws, 543
Pleads, in a wilderness where are no laws, 544
    To the rough beast that knows no gentle right, 545
    Nor aught obeys but his foul appetite.

But when a black-faced cloud the world doth threat,
In his dim mist th' aspiring mountains hiding,
From earth's dark womb some gentle gust doth get, 549
Which blows these pitchy vapors from their biding, 550
Hind'ring their present fall by this dividing; 551
    So his unhallowed haste her words delays, 552
    And moody Pluto winks while Orpheus plays. 553

Yet, foul night-waking cat, he doth but dally,
While in his hold-fast foot the weak mouse panteth.
Her sad behavior feeds his vulture folly, 556
A swallowing gulf that even in plenty wanteth. 557
His ear her prayers admits, but his heart granteth
    No penetrable entrance to her plaining; 559
    Tears harden lust, though marble wear with
      raining.

Her pity-pleading eyes are sadly fixed
In the remorseless wrinkles of his face; 562
Her modest eloquence with sighs is mixed,
Which to her oratory adds more grace.
She puts the period often from his place, 565
    And midst the sentence so her accent breaks 566
    That twice she doth begin ere once she speaks.

She conjures him by high almighty Jove,
By knighthood, gentry, and sweet friendship's oath, 569
By her untimely tears, her husband's love,
By holy human law and common troth, 571
By heaven and earth, and all the power of both,
    That to his borrowed bed he make retire 573
    And stoop to honor, not to foul desire. 574

Quoth she, "Reward not hospitality
With such black payment as thou hast pretended. 576

540 **cockatrice** the basilisk, said to be hatched by a serpent from a cock's egg and to kill by its breath and the rays it emitted from its eyes 543 **hind** female deer. **gripe's** vulture's, or griffin's 544 **Pleads** (With play on legal meaning.) 545 **gentle right** the right that should be given to the weak and noble. (*Gentle* means both "weak" and "nobly born.") 549 **doth get** comes into being 550 **pitchy** black. **their biding** where they hang 551 **their present fall** i.e., the imminent onset of the storm 552 **So . . . delays** thus her words delay his unhallowed haste 553 **winks** closes his eyes. **Orpheus** husband of Eurydice, who went to the underworld for her and charmed Pluto, ruler of the underworld, with his playing the lyre 556 **vulture folly** ravenous lewdness and madness 557 **gulf** maw, belly. **wanteth** craves insatiably 559 **plaining** lamentation 562 **wrinkles** i.e., frowns 565 **his place** its place (in the sentence; i.e., she speaks in broken phrases) 566 **accent** speech 569 **gentry** nobleness of birth and breeding 571 **troth** good faith 573 **borrowed** lent him for the night 574 **stoop** (Plays on the meanings "subject oneself," "debase oneself," and "stoop to the lure or prey" like a falcon.) 576 **pretended** proposed

502 **ensue** follow upon 507 **Coucheth** causes to couch, i.e., remain concealed. **his** i.e., the falcon's (whose shadow frightens the fowl) 508 **Whose** i.e., the falcon's. **he** i.e., the fowl 509 **insulting** exulting in triumph 511 **bells** (Falcons had bells attached to their feet.) 516 **To kill . . . decay** i.e., to destroy your honor even while also taking your life 520 **open eye** i.e., observer 522 **issue blurred** offspring tarnished. **nameless** the father's name being unknown 526 **rest** remain. **friend** lover 529 **For . . . enacted** is accepted as a lawful expedient 530 **simple** ingredient, drug. **compacted** mixed 531 **pure** i.e., benign, medically efficacious 534 **Tender** regard 535 **device** (1) contrivance (2) heraldic motto 537 **slavish wipe** brand with which slaves were marked. **birth hour's blot** unsightly birthmark

Mud not the fountain that gave drink to thee;
Mar not the thing that cannot be amended. 578
End thy ill aim before thy shoot be ended; 579
   He is no woodman that doth bend his bow 580
     To strike a poor unseasonable doe. 581

"My husband is thy friend; for his sake spare me.
Thyself art mighty; for thine own sake leave me.
Myself a weakling; do not then ensnare me.
Thou look'st not like deceit; do not deceive me.
My sighs, like whirlwinds, labor hence to heave thee.
   If ever man were moved with woman's moans,
     Be movèd with my tears, my sighs, my groans;

"All which together, like a troubled ocean,
Beat at thy rocky and wreck-threatening heart,
To soften it with their continual motion;
For stones dissolved to water do convert. 592
O, if no harder than a stone thou art,
   Melt at my tears, and be compassionate!
     Soft pity enters at an iron gate.

"In Tarquin's likeness I did entertain thee.
Hast thou put on his shape to do him shame?
To all the host of heaven I complain me.
Thou wrong'st his honor, wound'st his princely name.
Thou art not what thou seem'st; and if the same, 600
   Thou seem'st not what thou art, a god, a king;
     For kings like gods should govern everything.

"How will thy shame be seeded in thine age, 603
When thus thy vices bud before thy spring?
If in thy hope thou dar'st do such outrage, 605
What dar'st thou not when once thou art a king?
O, be remembered, no outrageous thing 607
   From vassal actors can be wiped away; 608
     Then kings' misdeeds cannot be hid in clay. 609

"This deed will make thee only loved for fear, 610
But happy monarchs still are feared for love. 611
With foul offenders thou perforce must bear, 612
When they in thee the like offenses prove.
If but for fear of this, thy will remove; 614
   For princes are the glass, the school, the book, 615
     Where subjects' eyes do learn, do read, do look.

"And wilt thou be the school where Lust shall learn?
Must he in thee read lectures of such shame?
Wilt thou be glass wherein it shall discern

Authority for sin, warrant for blame,
To privilege dishonor in thy name? 621
   Thou back'st reproach against long-living laud 622
     And mak'st fair reputation but a bawd.

"Hast thou command? By Him that gave it thee, 624
From a pure heart command thy rebel will.
Draw not thy sword to guard iniquity,
For it was lent thee all that brood to kill. 627
Thy princely office how canst thou fulfill,
   When, patterned by thy fault, foul Sin may say 629
     He learned to sin, and thou didst teach the way?

"Think but how vile a spectacle it were
To view thy present trespass in another.
Men's faults do seldom to themselves appear;
Their own transgressions partially they smother. 634
This guilt would seem death-worthy in thy brother.
   O, how are they wrapped in with infamies
     That from their own misdeeds askance their eyes! 637

"To thee, to thee, my heaved-up hands appeal, 638
Not to seducing lust, thy rash relier. 639
I sue for exiled majesty's repeal; 640
Let him return, and flattering thoughts retire. 641
His true respect will prison false desire 642
   And wipe the dim mist from thy doting eyne, 643
     That thou shalt see thy state and pity mine."

"Have done," quoth he. "My uncontrollèd tide
Turns not, but swells the higher by this let. 646
Small lights are soon blown out; huge fires abide,
And with the wind in greater fury fret.
The petty streams that pay a daily debt
   To their salt sovereign, with their fresh falls' haste 650
     Add to his flow but alter not his taste."

"Thou art," quoth she, "a sea, a sovereign king;
And lo, there falls into thy boundless flood
Black lust, dishonor, shame, misgoverning,
Who seek to stain the ocean of thy blood.
If all these petty ills shall change thy good,
   Thy sea within a puddle's womb is hearsed, 657
     And not the puddle in thy sea dispersed.

"So shall these slaves be king, and thou their slave; 659
Thou nobly base, they basely dignified;
Thou their fair life, and they thy fouler grave;
Thou loathèd in their shame, they in thy pride.

---

578 **amended** returned to its former purity 579 **shoot** shooting, hunting 580 **woodman** huntsman 581 **unseasonable** in foal or not yet bearing, out of the hunting season 592 **stones . . . convert** i.e., stones are worn away in time by water. **convert** change 600 **if the same** i.e., if you are actually Tarquin 603 **be seeded** ripen 605 **in thy hope** i.e., while you are yet only heir to the kingdom 607 **be remembered** bear in mind 608 **vassal actors** vassals or ordinary subjects who commit crimes 609 **in clay** i.e., even in death
610 **loved for fear** obeyed out of fear 611 **still . . . love** always are regarded with reverential awe stemming from love 612 **With . . . bear** you will have to put up with others' foul offenses 614 **but** only. **thy will remove** dissuade your lust 615 **glass** mirror and paradigm

621 **privilege** license 622 **Thou back'st** you support. **laud** praise 624 **Him** i.e., God 627 **that brood** i.e., the progeny of evil 629 **patterned** shown a precedent 634 **partially** showing partiality toward themselves. **smother** conceal 637 **askance** avert 638 **heaved-up** raised 639 **thy rash relier** on which you rashly rely, or, which rashly relies on you in your present emotional state 640 **repeal** recall from exile 641 **and flattering thoughts retire** and let those thoughts that flatter and egg on lust go away 642 **His true respect** true respect for him, or, his true judgment and respectfulness. **prison** imprison 643 **eyne** eyes 646 **let** hindrance 650 **salt sovereign** i.e., the sea 657 **hearsed** buried, coffined 659 **these slaves** i.e., lust, dishonor, etc.; see line 654

The lesser thing should not the greater hide;
    The cedar stoops not to the base shrub's foot,
    But low shrubs wither at the cedar's root.

"So let thy thoughts, low vassals to thy state—"
"No more," quoth he, "by heaven, I will not hear thee.
Yield to my love; if not, enforcèd hate,   668
Instead of love's coy touch, shall rudely tear thee. 669
That done, despitefully I mean to bear thee
    Unto the base bed of some rascal groom,   671
    To be thy partner in this shameful doom."

This said, he sets his foot upon the light,
For light and lust are deadly enemies;
Shame folded up in blind concealing night,
When most unseen, then most doth tyrannize.
The wolf hath seized his prey, the poor lamb cries;
    Till with her own white fleece her voice controlled 678
    Entombs her outcry in her lips' sweet fold.   679

For with the nightly linen that she wears
He pens her piteous clamors in her head,
Cooling his hot face in the chastest tears
That ever modest eyes with sorrow shed.
O, that prone lust should stain so pure a bed!   684
    The spots whereof could weeping purify,   685
    Her tears should drop on them perpetually.

But she hath lost a dearer thing than life,
And he hath won what he would lose again.
This forcèd league doth force a further strife;
This momentary joy breeds months of pain;
This hot desire converts to cold disdain.   691
    Pure Chastity is rifled of her store,
    And Lust, the thief, far poorer than before.

Look as the full-fed hound or gorgèd hawk,   694
Unapt for tender smell or speedy flight,   695
Make slow pursuit, or altogether balk   696
The prey wherein by nature they delight,
So surfeit-taking Tarquin fares this night.
    His taste delicious, in digestion souring,
    Devours his will, that lived by foul devouring.

O, deeper sin than bottomless conceit   701
Can comprehend in still imagination!
Drunken Desire must vomit his receipt   703
Ere he can see his own abomination.
While Lust is in his pride, no exclamation   705
    Can curb his heat or rein his rash desire,
    Till like a jade Self-will himself doth tire. 707

And then with lank and lean discolored cheek,
With heavy eye, knit brow, and strengthless pace,
Feeble Desire, all recreant, poor, and meek,   710
Like to a bankrupt beggar wails his case.   711
The flesh being proud, Desire doth fight with Grace, 712
    For there it revels, and when that decays,   713
    The guilty rebel for remission prays.   714

So fares it with this faultful lord of Rome,
Who this accomplishment so hotly chased;
For now against himself he sounds this doom, 717
That through the length of times he stands disgraced.
Besides, his soul's fair temple is defaced,
    To whose weak ruins muster troops of cares
    To ask the spotted princess how she fares. 721

She says her subjects with foul insurrection   722
Have battered down her consecrated wall,
And by their mortal fault brought in subjection 724
Her immortality, and made her thrall
To living death and pain perpetual,
    Which in her prescience she controllèd still, 727
    But her foresight could not forestall their will. 728

Ev'n in this thought through the dark night he
    stealeth,
A captive victor that hath lost in gain,   730
Bearing away the wound that nothing healeth,
The scar that will, despite of cure, remain,
Leaving his spoil perplexed in greater pain.   733
    She bears the load of lust he left behind,
    And he the burden of a guilty mind.

He like a thievish dog creeps sadly thence;
She like a wearied lamb lies panting there.
He scowls and hates himself for his offense;
She, desperate, with her nails her flesh doth tear.
He faintly flies, sweating with guilty fear;   740
    She stays, exclaiming on the direful night;   741
    He runs, and chides his vanished, loathed delight.

He thence departs a heavy convertite;   743
She there remains a hopeless castaway.
He in his speed looks for the morning light;
She prays she never may behold the day.

668 **enforcèd hate** force impelled by hatred 669 **coy** gentle
671 **groom** servant 678–679 **Till . . . fold** until, overmastering her
voice with her own nightwear, he buries her outcry as though in the
fold of her sweet lips. (*Fold* refers to her folded or compressed lips
and to a sheepfold; hence *pens* in line 681.) 684 **prone** eager, headlong 685 **could weeping** if weeping could 691 **converts** changes
694 **Look as** just as 695 **tender smell** delicate scent 696 **balk** turn
away from, let slip 701 **bottomless conceit** limitless imagination
703 **his receipt** what it has swallowed 705 **exclamation** protest
707 **jade** untrained or unbroken horse

710 **recreant** craven, cowed 711 **Like to** like 712 **proud** stubborn,
willful 713 **there** i.e., in the flesh. **when that decays** when the
reveling in pleasure subsides 714 **The guilty . . . prays** the flesh
prays for forgiveness 717 **sounds this doom** pronounces this judgment 721 **spotted princess** i.e., his contaminated soul, of whom the
temple, line 719, is the body 722 **subjects** i.e., the senses or passions 724 **mortal** deadly 727–728 **Which . . . will** i.e., which
senses or passions she theoretically governed in anticipation of any
act but could not, despite her foresight, restrain in their state of sexual
arousal. (Or, *Which* may possibly refer to death and damnation,
which the soul can foresee but not prevent.) 730 **A captive . . . gain**
one who has gained the prize at the cost of perpetual durance in sin
733 **spoil** prey, i.e., Lucrece 740 **faintly** cowardly 741 **exclaiming
on** denouncing 743 **heavy convertite** sad penitent

"For day," quoth she, "night's scapes doth open lay,   747
    And my true eyes have never practiced how
    To cloak offenses with a cunning brow.

"They think not but that every eye can see
The same disgrace which they themselves behold;
And therefore would they still in darkness be,
To have their unseen sin remain untold.
For they their guilt with weeping will unfold,   754
    And grave, like water that doth eat in steel,   755
    Upon my cheeks what helpless shame I feel."

Here she exclaims against repose and rest   757
And bids her eyes hereafter still be blind.   758
She wakes her heart by beating on her breast,
And bids it leap from thence, where it may find
Some purer chest to close so pure a mind.   761
    Frantic with grief thus breathes she forth her spite   762
    Against the unseen secrecy of night:

"O comfort-killing Night, image of hell,
Dim register and notary of shame,   765
Black stage for tragedies and murders fell,   766
Vast sin-concealing chaos, nurse of blame!   767
Blind muffled bawd, dark harbor for defame,   768
    Grim cave of death, whisp'ring conspirator
    With close-tongued treason and the ravisher!   770

"O hateful, vaporous, and foggy Night,
Since thou art guilty of my cureless crime,
Muster thy mists to meet the eastern light,
Make war against proportioned course of time;   774
Or if thou wilt permit the sun to climb
    His wonted height, yet ere he go to bed
    Knit poisonous clouds about his golden head.

"With rotten damps ravish the morning air;
Let their exhaled unwholesome breaths make sick
The life of purity, the supreme fair,   780
Ere he arrive his weary noontide prick;   781
And let thy musty vapors march so thick
    That in their smoky ranks his smothered light
    May set at noon and make perpetual night.

"Were Tarquin Night, as he is but Night's child,
The silver-shining queen he would distain;   786
Her twinkling handmaids too, by him defiled,   787
Through Night's black bosom should not peep again.

So should I have copartners in my pain;
    And fellowship in woe doth woe assuage,
    As palmers' chat makes short their pilgrimage.   791

"Where now I have no one to blush with me,   792
To cross their arms and hang their heads with mine,   793
To mask their brows and hide their infamy;   794
But I alone alone must sit and pine,   795
Seasoning the earth with showers of silver brine,
    Mingling my talk with tears, my grief with groans,
    Poor wasting monuments of lasting moans.   798

"O Night, thou furnace of foul reeking smoke!
Let not the jealous Day behold that face
Which underneath thy black all-hiding cloak
Immodestly lies martyred with disgrace!   802
Keep still possession of thy gloomy place,
    That all the faults which in thy reign are made
    May likewise be sepulchered in thy shade.

"Make me not object to the telltale Day.   806
The light will show charactered in my brow   807
The story of sweet chastity's decay,   808
The impious breach of holy wedlock vow.
Yea, the illiterate, that know not how
    To cipher what is writ in learnèd books,   811
    Will quote my loathsome trespass in my looks.   812

"The nurse, to still her child, will tell my story,
And fright her crying babe with Tarquin's name;
The orator, to deck his oratory,   815
Will couple my reproach to Tarquin's shame;
Feast-finding minstrels, tuning my defame,   817
    Will tie the hearers to attend each line,
    How Tarquin wrongèd me, I Collatine.

"Let my good name, that senseless reputation,   820
For Collatine's dear love be kept unspotted.
If that be made a theme for disputation,   822
The branches of another root are rotted,   823
And undeserved reproach to him allotted
    That is as clear from this attaint of mine   825
    As I, ere this, was pure to Collatine.

"O unseen shame, invisible disgrace!
O unfelt sore, crest-wounding, private scar!   828
Reproach is stamped in Collatinus' face,

And Tarquin's eye may read the mot afar,   830
How he in peace is wounded, not in war.
    Alas, how many bear such shameful blows,
    Which not themselves but he that gives them
        knows!

"If, Collatine, thine honor lay in me,
From me by strong assault it is bereft;
My honey lost, and I, a dronelike bee,
Have no perfection of my summer left,   837
But robbed and ransacked by injurious theft.
    In thy weak hive a wandering wasp hath crept
    And sucked the honey which thy chaste bee kept.

"Yet am I guilty of thy honor's wrack;
Yet for thy honor did I entertain him.
Coming from thee, I could not put him back,
For it had been dishonor to disdain him.
Besides, of weariness he did complain him,
    And talked of virtue. O unlooked-for evil,
    When virtue is profaned in such a devil!

"Why should the worm intrude the maiden bud?
Or hateful cuckoos hatch in sparrows' nests?
Or toads infect fair founts with venom mud?
Or tyrant folly lurk in gentle breasts?   851
Or kings be breakers of their own behests?   852
    But no perfection is so absolute
    That some impurity doth not pollute.

"The agèd man that coffers up his gold
Is plagued with cramps and gouts and painful fits,
And scarce hath eyes his treasure to behold,
But like still-pining Tantalus he sits,   858
And useless barns the harvest of his wits,   859
    Having no other pleasure of his gain
    But torment that it cannot cure his pain.

"So then he hath it when he cannot use it,
And leaves it to be mastered by his young,
Who in their pride do presently abuse it.   864
Their father was too weak, and they too strong,
To hold their cursèd-blessèd fortune long.
    The sweets we wish for turn to loathèd sours
    Even in the moment that we call them ours.

"Unruly blasts wait on the tender spring;
Unwholesome weeds take root with precious flowers;
The adder hisses where the sweet birds sing;
What virtue breeds, iniquity devours.

We have no good that we can say is ours   830
    But ill-annexèd Opportunity   874
    Or kills his life or else his quality.   875

"O Opportunity, thy guilt is great!
'Tis thou that execut'st the traitor's treason;
Thou sets the wolf where he the lamb may get;
Whoever plots the sin, thou 'point'st the season.   879
'Tis thou that spurn'st at right, at law, at reason;
    And in thy shady cell, where none may spy him,
    Sits Sin, to seize the souls that wander by him.

"Thou makest the vestal violate her oath;
Thou blowest the fire when temperance is thawed;
Thou smother'st honesty, thou murderest troth.   885
Thou foul abettor, thou notorious bawd,
Thou plantest scandal and displacest laud.   887
    Thou ravisher, thou traitor, thou false thief,
    Thy honey turns to gall, thy joy to grief!

"Thy secret pleasure turns to open shame,
Thy private feasting to a public fast,
Thy smoothing titles to a ragged name,   892
Thy sugared tongue to bitter wormwood taste.
Thy violent vanities can never last.
    How comes it then, vile Opportunity,
    Being so bad, such numbers seek for thee?

"When wilt thou be the humble suppliant's friend,
And bring him where his suit may be obtained?
When wilt thou sort an hour great strifes to end?   899
Or free that soul which wretchedness hath chained?
Give physic to the sick, ease to the pained?
    The poor, lame, blind, halt, creep, cry out for thee,
    But they ne'er meet with Opportunity.

"The patient dies while the physician sleeps;
The orphan pines while the oppressor feeds;   905
Justice is feasting while the widow weeps;
Advice is sporting while infection breeds.   907
Thou grant'st no time for charitable deeds.
    Wrath, envy, treason, rape, and murder's rages,
    Thy heinous hours wait on them as their pages.

"When Truth and Virtue have to do with thee,
A thousand crosses keep them from thy aid.   912
They buy thy help; but Sin ne'er gives a fee,   913
He gratis comes; and thou art well apaid   914
As well to hear as grant what he hath said.   915
    My Collatine would else have come to me
    When Tarquin did, but he was stayed by thee.

---

830 mot motto **837 Have . . . left** have nothing left of the honey I perfected in the summer **851 folly** sensuality. **gentle** noble (in rank and temperament) **852 behests** biddings, injunctions **858 still-pining** continually starving. **Tantalus** a son of Zeus who was punished by perpetual hunger and thirst with unreachable food and drink always in sight. (Renaissance commentators on Ovid glossed Tantalus as a usurer; hence the image of lines 859 ff.) **859 barns** stores, as in a barn **864 presently** immediately

874 ill-annexèd joined to the good for an evil purpose. **Opportunity** chance or circumstance **875 Or . . . quality** either destroys that good thing or else destroys what makes it good **879 'point'st** appointest **885 honesty** chastity. **troth** honesty **887 laud** praise **892 smoothing** flattering. **ragged** faulty, irregular **899 sort** choose, appoint **905 pines** starves **907 Advice** i.e., medical advice. **sporting** taking idle pleasure **912 crosses** hindrances **913 buy** i.e., have to pay for **914 apaid** satisfied **915 As . . . as** both to hear and

"Guilty thou art of murder and of theft,
Guilty of perjury and subornation,
Guilty of treason, forgery, and shift,   920
Guilty of incest, that abomination—
An accessory by thine inclination   922
    To all sins past and all that are to come,
    From the creation to the general doom.   924

"Misshapen Time, copesmate of ugly Night,   925
Swift subtle post, carrier of grisly care,   926
Eater of youth, false slave to false delight,
Base watch of woes, sin's packhorse, virtue's snare!   928
Thou nursest all, and murderest all that are.
    O, hear me then, injurious, shifting Time!   930
    Be guilty of my death, since of my crime.   931

"Why hath thy servant Opportunity
Betrayed the hours thou gav'st me to repose,
Canceled my fortunes, and enchainèd me
To endless date of never-ending woes?   935
Time's office is to fine the hate of foes,   936
    To eat up errors by opinion bred,   937
    Not spend the dowry of a lawful bed.

"Time's glory is to calm contending kings,
To unmask falsehood and bring truth to light,
To stamp the seal of time in agèd things,
To wake the morn and sentinel the night,   942
To wrong the wronger till he render right,
    To ruinate proud buildings with thy hours,
    And smear with dust their glittering golden
      towers;

"To fill with wormholes stately monuments,
To feed oblivion with decay of things,
To blot old books and alter their contents,   948
To pluck the quills from ancient ravens' wings,   949
To dry the old oak's sap and cherish springs,   950
    To spoil antiquities of hammered steel,
    And turn the giddy round of Fortune's wheel;

"To show the beldam daughters of her daughter,   953
To make the child a man, the man a child,   954
To slay the tiger that doth live by slaughter,
To tame the unicorn and lion wild,
To mock the subtle in themselves beguiled,   957
    To cheer the plowman with increaseful crops, 958
    And waste huge stones with little waterdrops. 959

"Why work'st thou mischief in thy pilgrimage,
Unless thou couldst return to make amends?
One poor retiring minute in an age   962
Would purchase thee a thousand thousand friends,
Lending him wit that to bad debtors lends.   964
    O, this dread night, wouldst thou one hour come
      back,
    I could prevent this storm and shun thy wrack! 966

"Thou ceaseless lackey to Eternity,   967
With some mischance cross Tarquin in his flight!   968
Devise extremes beyond extremity
To make him curse this cursèd crimeful night.
Let ghastly shadows his lewd eyes affright,
    And the dire thought of his committed evil
    Shape every bush a hideous shapeless devil.

"Disturb his hours of rest with restless trances;   974
Afflict him in his bed with bedrid groans;   975
Let there bechance him pitiful mischances
To make him moan, but pity not his moans.
Stone him with hardened hearts harder than stones,
    And let mild women to him lose their mildness,
    Wilder to him than tigers in their wildness.

"Let him have time to tear his curlèd hair,
Let him have time against himself to rave,
Let him have time of Time's help to despair,
Let him have time to live a loathèd slave,
Let him have time a beggar's orts to crave,   985
    And time to see one that by alms doth live   986
    Disdain to him disdainèd scraps to give.   987

"Let him have time to see his friends his foes,
And merry fools to mock at him resort;   989
Let him have time to mark how slow time goes
In time of sorrow, and how swift and short
His time of folly and his time of sport;
    And ever let his unrecalling crime   993
    Have time to wail th' abusing of his time.

"O Time, thou tutor both to good and bad,
Teach me to curse him that thou taught'st this ill!   996
At his own shadow let the thief run mad,
Himself himself seek every hour to kill!
Such wretched hands such wretched blood should
    spill;
    For who so base would such an office have
    As slanderous deathsman to so base a slave?   1001

"The baser is he, coming from a king,
To shame his hope with deeds degenerate.
The mightier man, the mightier is the thing
That makes him honored or begets him hate;
For greatest scandal waits on greatest state. 1006
    The moon being clouded presently is missed, 1007
    But little stars may hide them when they list.

"The crow may bathe his coal-black wings in mire,
And unperceived fly with the filth away,
But if the like the snow-white swan desire,
The stain upon his silver down will stay.
Poor grooms are sightless night, kings glorious day. 1013
    Gnats are unnoted wheresoe'er they fly,
    But eagles gazed upon with every eye.

"Out, idle words, servants to shallow fools, 1016
Unprofitable sounds, weak arbitrators!
Busy yourselves in skill-contending schools; 1018
Debate where leisure serves with dull debaters;
To trembling clients be you mediators.
    For me, I force not argument a straw, 1021
    Since that my case is past the help of law.

"In vain I rail at Opportunity,
At Time, at Tarquin, and uncheerful Night;
In vain I cavil with mine infamy, 1025
In vain I spurn at my confirmed despite. 1026
This helpless smoke of words doth me no right. 1027
    The remedy indeed to do me good
    Is to let forth my foul-defilèd blood. 1029

"Poor hand, why quiver'st thou at this decree?
Honor thyself to rid me of this shame!
For if I die, my honor lives in thee,
But if I live, thou liv'st in my defame.
Since thou couldst not defend thy loyal dame,
    And wast afeard to scratch her wicked foe,
    Kill both thyself and her for yielding so."

This said, from her betumbled couch she starteth,
To find some desperate instrument of death;
But this, no slaughterhouse, no tool imparteth 1039
To make more vent for passage of her breath,
Which, thronging through her lips, so vanisheth
    As smoke from Etna, that in air consumes, 1042
    Or that which from dischargèd cannon fumes.

"In vain," quoth she, "I live, and seek in vain
Some happy means to end a hapless life. 1045
I feared by Tarquin's falchion to be slain, 1046
Yet for the selfsame purpose seek a knife;
But when I feared, I was a loyal wife.
    So am I now.—O no, that cannot be!
    Of that true type hath Tarquin rifled me. 1050

"O, that is gone for which I sought to live,
And therefore now I need not fear to die.
To clear this spot by death, at least I give 1053
A badge of fame to slander's livery, 1054
A dying life to living infamy.
    Poor helpless help, the treasure stol'n away,
    To burn the guiltless casket where it lay!

"Well, well, dear Collatine, thou shalt not know
The stainèd taste of violated troth;
I will not wrong thy true affection so
To flatter thee with an infringèd oath; 1061
This bastard graft shall never come to growth. 1062
    He shall not boast who did thy stock pollute
    That thou art doting father of his fruit.

"Nor shall he smile at thee in secret thought,
Nor laugh with his companions at thy state,
But thou shalt know thy interest was not bought 1067
Basely with gold, but stol'n from forth thy gate.
For me, I am the mistress of my fate,
    And with my trespass never will dispense 1070
    Till life to death acquit my forced offense. 1071

"I will not poison thee with my attaint, 1072
Nor fold my fault in cleanly coined excuses; 1073
My sable ground of sin I will not paint, 1074
To hide the truth of this false night's abuses.
My tongue shall utter all; mine eyes, like sluices,
    As from a mountain spring that feeds a dale,
    Shall gush pure streams to purge my impure tale."

By this, lamenting Philomel had ended 1079
The well-tuned warble of her nightly sorrow,
And solemn night with slow sad gait descended
To ugly hell, when, lo, the blushing morrow

1003 his hope the hope people had of him as heir to the crown 1006 waits . . . state potentially attends those of most exalted rank 1007 presently at once 1013 grooms i.e., lowborn persons. are are like. sightless making things invisible; pitch dark 1016 Out (An exclamation of disapproval.) 1018 in . . . schools i.e., among scholars who perennially debate with words 1021 force value. a straw i.e., a straw's worth 1025 cavil with raise objections to 1026 spurn at (Literally, kick against.) confirmed despite unrecoverable injury 1027 helpless . . . words unavailing rhetoric 1029 let . . . blood bleed (1) as a remedy (line 1028) for illness, a standard form of medical treatment (2) as a means of death 1039 no slaughterhouse being no slaughterhouse. imparteth provides 1042 consumes wastes, vanishes

1045 happy fit (with a play of antithesis on hapless) 1046 falchion curved sword 1050 type stamp; example 1053 To clear i.e., in clearing. spot stain 1054 fame good reputation. livery clothing or uniform worn by those in service, bearing a heraldic badge on the sleeve to indicate in whose service the livery is worn. (Lucrece says that the livery of shame will be partially redeemed by the badge of an honorable death.) 1061 To flatter . . . oath i.e., to deceive you by presenting you with a bastard child, born through an enforced violation of my vow of chastity, as though the child were your own 1062 graft scion 1067 interest claim, property 1070 with . . . dispense never will pardon my offense. (To dispense is to grant dispensation.) 1071 to death acquit atone to death for 1072 attaint infection 1073 fold wrap up, conceal. cleanly coined cleverly counterfeited 1074 sable ground dark surface on a heraldic device 1079 Philomel i.e., the nightingale. Philomela was raped by her brother-in-law, Tereus, who cut out her tongue so that she could not disclose his villainy; she was changed into a nightingale.

Lends light to all fair eyes that light will borrow. 1083
   But cloudy Lucrece shames herself to see, 1084
   And therefore still in night would cloistered be.

Revealing day through every cranny spies
And seems to point her out where she sits weeping,
To whom she sobbing speaks: "O eye of eyes,
Why pry'st thou through my window? Leave thy
   peeping.
Mock with thy tickling beams eyes that are sleeping.
   Brand not my forehead with thy piercing light,
   For day hath naught to do what's done by night." 1092

Thus cavils she with everything she sees.
True grief is fond and testy as a child, 1094
Who, wayward once, his mood with naught agrees. 1095
Old woes, not infant sorrows, bear them mild: 1096
Continuance tames the one; the other, wild,
   Like an unpracticed swimmer plunging still,
   With too much labor drowns for want of skill.

So she, deep-drenchèd in a sea of care,
Holds disputation with each thing she views,
And to herself all sorrow doth compare;
No object but her passion's strength renews, 1103
And as one shifts, another straight ensues. 1104
   Sometimes her grief is dumb and hath no words,
   Sometimes 'tis mad and too much talk affords.

The little birds that tune their morning's joy
Make her moans mad with their sweet melody,
For mirth doth search the bottom of annoy;
Sad souls are slain in merry company. 1109
Grief best is pleased with grief's society.
   True sorrow then is feelingly sufficed 1112
   When with like semblance it is sympathized. 1113

'Tis double death to drown in ken of shore; 1114
He ten times pines that pines beholding food; 1115
To see the salve doth make the wound ache more;
Great grief grieves most at that would do it good; 1117
Deep woes roll forward like a gentle flood,
   Who, being stopped, the bounding banks
     o'erflows; 1119
   Grief dallied with nor law nor limit knows. 1120

"You mocking birds," quoth she, "your tunes entomb
Within your hollow-swelling feathered breasts,
And in my hearing be you mute and dumb.

My restless discord loves no stops nor rests; 1124
A woeful hostess brooks not merry guests. 1125
   Relish your nimble notes to pleasing ears; 1126
   Distress likes dumps, when time is kept with
     tears. 1127

"Come, Philomel, that sing'st of ravishment,
Make thy sad grove in my disheveled hair.
As the dank earth weeps at thy languishment,
So I at each sad strain will strain a tear 1131
And with deep groans the diapason bear; 1132
   For burden-wise I'll hum on Tarquin still, 1133
   While thou on Tereus descants better skill. 1134

"And whiles against a thorn thou bear'st thy part 1135
To keep thy sharp woes waking, wretched I,
To imitate thee well, against my heart
Will fix a sharp knife to affright mine eye,
Who, if it wink, shall thereon fall and die. 1139
   These means, as frets upon an instrument, 1140
   Shall tune our heartstrings to true languishment.

"And for, poor bird, thou sing'st not in the day, 1142
As shaming any eye should thee behold, 1143
Some dark deep desert seated from the way, 1144
That knows not parching heat nor freezing cold,
Will we find out; and there we will unfold
   To creatures stern sad tunes, to change their
     kinds. 1147
   Since men prove beasts, let beasts bear gentle
     minds."

As the poor frighted deer, that stands at gaze, 1149
Wildly determining which way to fly,
Or one encompassed with a winding maze,
That cannot tread the way out readily,
So with herself is she in mutiny,
   To live or die which of the twain were better
   When life is shamed and death reproach's debtor. 1155

1083 **will** would 1084 **cloudy** sorrowful. **shames** is ashamed
1092 **to do** to do with 1094 **fond** foolish 1095 **wayward once** once
in a peevish mood 1096 **them** themselves. **mild** mildly, calmly
1103 **No . . . renews** everything she considers renews the strength of
her sorrows 1104 **shifts** moves, yields place. **straight** at once
1109 **search** probe. **annoy** grief, injury 1112 **sufficed** contented
1113 **sympathized** matched 1114 **ken** sight 1115 **He** anyone.
pines hungers 1117 **would** which would 1119 **Who** which.
stopped dammed up. **bounding** containing, confining 1120 **dallied**
trifled. **nor . . . nor** neither . . . nor

1124 **restless** agitated (with a pun on the musical sense of having no
stops or *rests*, i.e., being ceaseless, without pause) 1125 **brooks** enjoys 1126 **Relish** (1) warble, make attractive (2) elaborate with musical ornamentation. **pleasing** capable of being pleased 1127 **dumps**
mournful songs 1131 **strain . . . strain** melody . . . force, squeeze
1132 **diapason** bass accompaniment below the melody 1133 **burden-wise** in the manner of an undersong or bass (with a play on *burden*, meaning "sorrow") 1134 **descants better skill** i.e., sing a musical elaboration in the upper register with better skill (than my bass
accompaniment) 1135 **against a thorn** (According to popular belief,
the nightingale perched deliberately with a thorn against her breast to
keep herself awake.) 1139 **Who** which, i.e., my heart. **if it wink**
i.e., if my eye should close in sleep 1140 **frets** bars placed on the
fingerboards of stringed instruments to regulate the fingering (with a
pun on *frets*, meaning "vexations") 1142 **for** because. **sing'st not
in the day** (One of the common errors of the time; nightingales sing
both by day and by night.) 1143 **As shaming** as though being
ashamed that, or, since you are ashamed that 1144 **desert** deserted
place. **seated from** situated away from 1147 **kinds** natures
1149 **at gaze** transfixed, bewildered 1155 **death reproach's debtor**
i.e., death by suicide would incur reproach

"To kill myself," quoth she, "alack, what were it
But with my body my poor soul's pollution?   1157
They that lose half with greater patience bear it
Than they whose whole is swallowed in confusion.   1159
That mother tries a merciless conclusion   1160
    Who, having two sweet babes, when death takes
      one,
    Will slay the other and be nurse to none.

"My body or my soul, which was the dearer,
When the one pure, the other made divine?
Whose love of either to myself was nearer,   1165
When both were kept for heaven and Collatine?
Ay me! The bark pilled from the lofty pine,   1167
    His leaves will wither and his sap decay;
    So must my soul, her bark being pilled away.

"Her house is sacked, her quiet interrupted,
Her mansion battered by the enemy,
Her sacred temple spotted, spoiled, corrupted,
Grossly engirt with daring infamy.   1173
Then let it not be called impiety
    If in this blemished fort I make some hole   1175
    Through which I may convey this troubled soul.   1176

"Yet die I will not till my Collatine
Have heard the cause of my untimely death,
That he may vow, in that sad hour of mine,
Revenge on him that made me stop my breath.
My stainèd blood to Tarquin I'll bequeath,
    Which, by him tainted, shall for him be spent,
    And as his due writ in my testament.   1183

"My honor I'll bequeath unto the knife
That wounds my body so dishonorèd.
'Tis honor to deprive dishonored life;   1186
The one will live, the other being dead.
So of shame's ashes shall my fame be bred,
    For in my death I murder shameful scorn;
    My shame so dead, mine honor is new born.

"Dear lord of that dear jewel I have lost,   1191
What legacy shall I bequeath to thee?
My resolution, love, shall be thy boast,
By whose example thou revenged mayst be.
How Tarquin must be used, read it in me:
    Myself, thy friend, will kill myself, thy foe,
    And for my sake serve thou false Tarquin so.

"This brief abridgment of my will I make:
My soul and body to the skies and ground;
My resolution, husband, do thou take;

Mine honor be the knife's that makes my wound;
My shame be his that did my fame confound;
    And all my fame that lives disbursèd be   1203
    To those that live and think no shame of me.

"Thou, Collatine, shalt oversee this will.
How was I overseen that thou shalt see it!   1206
My blood shall wash the slander of mine ill;
My life's foul deed my life's fair end shall free it.   1208
Faint not, faint heart, but stoutly say 'So be it.'
    Yield to my hand; my hand shall conquer thee.
    Thou dead, both die, and both shall victors be."

This plot of death when sadly she had laid,
And wiped the brinish pearl from her bright eyes,
With untuned tongue she hoarsely calls her maid,   1214
Whose swift obedience to her mistress hies;   1215
For fleet-winged duty with thought's feathers flies.
    Poor Lucrece' cheeks unto her maid seem so
    As winter meads when sun doth melt their snow.

Her mistress she doth give demure good morrow   1219
With soft slow tongue, true mark of modesty,
And sorts a sad look to her lady's sorrow,   1221
Forwhy her face wore sorrow's livery;   1222
But durst not ask of her audaciously
    Why her two suns were cloud-eclipsèd so,
    Nor why her fair cheeks over-washed with woe.

But as the earth doth weep, the sun being set,
Each flower moistened like a melting eye,
Even so the maid with swelling drops 'gan wet
Her circled eyne, enforced by sympathy   1229
Of those fair suns set in her mistress' sky,
    Who in a salt-waved ocean quench their light,
    Which makes the maid weep like the dewy night.

A pretty while these pretty creatures stand,   1233
Like ivory conduits coral cisterns filling.   1234
One justly weeps; the other takes in hand   1235
No cause but company of her drops' spilling.   1236
Their gentle sex to weep are often willing,
    Grieving themselves to guess at others' smarts,   1238
    And then they drown their eyes or break their
      hearts.

1203 disbursèd i.e., paid out as legacies **1206 overseen** deluded, taken advantage of (with quibble on *oversee*, line 1205, i.e., attend to as an executor of an estate) **1208 My . . . free it** my life's virtuous end will free my reputation of my life's foul deed **1214 untuned** discordant **1215 Whose . . . hies** who in swift obedience hastens to her mistress **1219 Her** to her **1221 sorts** adapts **1222 Forwhy** because **1229 circled eyne** rounded eyes, or, circled with red. **enforced** compelled **1233 pretty while** considerable while **1234 conduits** (Alludes to conduit spouts and fountains shaped in the form of human figures; the women's eyes run like conduits.)
1235–1236 takes . . . spilling acknowledges no cause for the shedding of teardrops other than to keep her mistress company **1238 to guess at** merely when they conjecture

---

1157 But . . . pollution but to add my poor soul's pollution (through suicide) to that of my body (through the rape) **1159 confusion** ruin **1160 conclusion** experiment **1165 Whose . . . either** love of which of the two **1167 pilled** peeled, stripped off, rifled **1173 daring** audacious **1175 fort** i.e., body **1176 convey** spirit away **1183 testament** last will and testament **1186 deprive** take away **1191 that dear jewel** i.e., my chastity (which)

For men have marble, women waxen, minds,   1240
And therefore are they formed as marble will.   1241
The weak oppressed, th' impression of strange kinds   1242
Is formed in them by force, by fraud, or skill.   1243
Then call them not the authors of their ill,
        No more than wax shall be accounted evil
        Wherein is stamped the semblance of a devil.

Their smoothness, like a goodly champaign plain,   1247
Lays open all the little worms that creep;   1248
In men, as in a rough-grown grove, remain
Cave-keeping evils that obscurely sleep.   1250
Through crystal walls each little mote will peep.   1251
        Though men can cover crimes with bold stern
            looks,
        Poor women's faces are their own faults' books.

No man inveigh against the withered flower,   1254
But chide rough winter that the flower hath killed.
Not that devoured, but that which doth devour,
Is worthy blame. O, let it not be hild   1257
Poor women's faults, that they are so fulfilled   1258
        With men's abuses. Those proud lords, to blame,   1259
        Make weak-made women tenants to their shame.   1260

The precedent whereof in Lucrece view,   1261
Assailed by night with circumstances strong   1262
Of present death, and shame that might ensue   1263
By that her death, to do her husband wrong.   1264
Such danger to resistance did belong   1265
        That dying fear through all her body spread;   1266
        And who cannot abuse a body dead?

By this, mild patience bid fair Lucrece speak   1268
To the poor counterfeit of her complaining: 1269
"My girl," quoth she, "on what occasion break
Those tears from thee, that down thy cheeks are
        raining?
If thou dost weep for grief of my sustaining,   1272
        Know, gentle wench, it small avails my mood.
        If tears could help, mine own would do me good.

"But tell me, girl, when went"—and there she stayed
Till after a deep groan—"Tarquin from hence?"
"Madam, ere I was up," replied the maid,
"The more to blame my sluggard negligence.   1278

Yet with the fault I thus far can dispense: 1279
        Myself was stirring ere the break of day,
        And, ere I rose, was Tarquin gone away.

"But, lady, if your maid may be so bold,
She would request to know your heaviness."   1283
"O, peace!" quoth Lucrece. "If it should be told,
The repetition cannot make it less;   1285
For more it is than I can well express,
        And that deep torture may be called a hell
        When more is felt than one hath power to tell.

"Go, get me hither paper, ink, and pen.
Yet save that labor, for I have them here.
What should I say? One of my husband's men
Bid thou be ready by and by to bear
A letter to my lord, my love, my dear.
        Bid him with speed prepare to carry it;
        The cause craves haste, and it will soon be writ."

Her maid is gone, and she prepares to write,
First hovering o'er the paper with her quill.
Conceit and grief an eager combat fight;   1298
What wit sets down is blotted straight with will;   1299
This is too curious-good, this blunt and ill.   1300
        Much like a press of people at a door
        Throng her inventions, which shall go before.   1302

At last she thus begins: "Thou worthy lord
Of that unworthy wife that greeteth thee,
Health to thy person! Next vouchsafe t' afford—
If ever, love, thy Lucrece thou wilt see—
Some present speed to come and visit me.
        So, I commend me from our house in grief.   1308
        My woes are tedious, though my words are brief." 1309

Here folds she up the tenor of her woe,   1310
Her certain sorrow writ uncertainly.   1311
By this short schedule Collatine may know   1312
Her grief, but not her grief's true quality.
She dares not thereof make discovery,   1314
        Lest he should hold it her own gross abuse,   1315
        Ere she with blood had stained her stained excuse. 1316

Besides, the life and feeling of her passion
She hoards, to spend when he is by to hear her,
When sighs and groans and tears may grace the
        fashion   1319
Of her disgrace, the better so to clear her

1240 waxen i.e., soft, impressionable   **1241 will** wills, wishes
1242 The weak when the weak are.   **strange kinds** natures unlike
their own   **1243 skill** cunning   **1247 champaign** level, open
1248 Lays open reveals.   **worms** reptiles, i.e., blemishes
1250 Cave-keeping remaining concealed in caves   **1251 mote** speck
1254 No man let no one   **1257 worthy** deserving of.   **hild** held
1258 fulfilled filled to the brim   **1259 lords, to blame** lords, who are
blameworthy, or, who are too much to blame (*too blame*), or, owners
of blame (*lords to blame*)   **1260 tenants . . . shame** i.e., occupying
and sharing a shame that is properly men's   **1261 precedent** proof,
example   **1262–1263 circumstances . . . death** a situation strongly
threatening immediate death   **1264 By that her death** by her very
death   **1265 danger** i.e., the danger of being defamed by Tarquin
1266 dying i.e., paralyzing   **1268 By this** by this time   **1269 counterfeit of her complaining** i.e., the maid, weeping like her   **1272 of
my sustaining** borne by me   **1278 to blame** at fault

1279 dispense give dispensation, find excuse   **1283 know your
heaviness** know the reason for your sadness   **1285 repetition** recital
1298 Conceit thought (of what she will write).   **eager** fierce
1299 wit thought.   **blotted** canceled.   **will** passion, feeling
1300 curious-good fastidiously, studiedly phrased   **1302 which . . .
before** contending as to who is to enter first   **1308 commend me** ask
to be remembered   **1309 tedious** prolonged, painful   **1310 tenor**
gist, summary   **1311 uncertainly** i.e., not in precise detail, vaguely
1312 schedule document, summary   **1314 thereof make discovery**
reveal its true extent and nature   **1315 abuse** wrongdoing   **1316 Ere
. . . excuse** i.e., before she had had a chance to excuse her shame
by shedding her own blood   **1319 fashion** fashioning

From that suspicion which the world might bear her.
　To shun this blot, she would not blot the letter   1322
　With words, till action might become them better.

To see sad sights moves more than hear them told,
For then the eye interprets to the ear
The heavy motion that it doth behold,   1326
When every part a part of woe doth bear.   1327
'Tis but a part of sorrow that we hear.
　　Deep sounds make lesser noise than shallow
　　　fords,   1329
　　And sorrow ebbs, being blown with wind of
　　　words.

Her letter now is sealed, and on it writ,
"At Ardea to my lord with more than haste."
The post attends, and she delivers it,   1333
Charging the sour-faced groom to hie as fast
As lagging fowls before the northern blast.   1335
　　Speed more than speed but dull and slow she
　　　deems;   1336
　　Extremity still urgeth such extremes.   1337

The homely villain curtsies to her low;   1338
And, blushing on her, with a steadfast eye
Receives the scroll without or yea or no,
And forth with bashful innocence doth hie.
But they whose guilt within their bosoms lie
　　Imagine every eye beholds their blame;
　　For Lucrece thought he blushed to see her shame,

When, silly groom, God wot, it was defect   1345
Of spirit, life, and bold audacity.
Such harmless creatures have a true respect   1347
To talk in deeds, while others saucily   1348
Promise more speed, but do it leisurely.
　　Even so this pattern of the worn-out age   1350
　　Pawned honest looks but laid no words to gage.   1351

His kindled duty kindled her mistrust,   1352
That two red fires in both their faces blazed.
She thought he blushed as knowing Tarquin's lust,
And, blushing with him, wistly on him gazed.   1355
Her earnest eye did make him more amazed.   1356
　　The more she saw the blood his cheeks replenish,
　　The more she thought he spied in her some
　　　blemish.

But long she thinks till he return again,   1359
And yet the duteous vassal scarce is gone.
The weary time she cannot entertain,   1361
For now 'tis stale to sigh, to weep, and groan.
So woe hath wearied woe, moan tirèd moan,
　　That she her plaints a little while doth stay,   1364
　　Pausing for means to mourn some newer way.

At last she calls to mind where hangs a piece   1366
Of skillful painting, made for Priam's Troy,   1367
Before the which is drawn the power of Greece,   1368
For Helen's rape the city to destroy,
Threat'ning cloud-kissing Ilion with annoy,   1370
　　Which the conceited painter drew so proud   1371
　　As heaven, it seemed, to kiss the turrets bowed.

A thousand lamentable objects there,
In scorn of nature, art gave lifeless life.   1374
Many a dry drop seemed a weeping tear,   1375
Shed for the slaughtered husband by the wife.
The red blood reeked, to show the painter's strife,   1377
　　And dying eyes gleamed forth their ashy lights
　　Like dying coals burnt out in tedious nights.

There might you see the laboring pioneer   1380
Begrimed with sweat and smearèd all with dust;
And from the towers of Troy there would appear
The very eyes of men through loopholes thrust,
Gazing upon the Greeks with little lust.   1384
　　Such sweet observance in this work was had   1385
　　That one might see those far-off eyes look sad.

In great commanders grace and majesty
You might behold, triumphing in their faces;
In youth, quick bearing and dexterity;   1389
And here and there the painter interlaces
Pale cowards marching on with trembling paces,
　　Which heartless peasants did so well resemble   1392
　　That one would swear he saw them quake and
　　　tremble.

In Ajax and Ulysses, O, what art
Of physiognomy might one behold!
The face of either ciphered either's heart;   1396
Their face their manners most expressly told.
In Ajax' eyes blunt rage and rigor rolled,
　　But the mild glance that sly Ulysses lent
　　Showed deep regard and smiling government.   1400

1322 blot . . . blot stain . . . mar 1326 heavy motion sad action
1327 every part i.e., of the body 1329 Deep sounds deep waters
(with pun on sounds, i.e., inlets of the sea, and "noise") 1333 post
messenger 1335 lagging falling behind in migratory flight
1336 Speed . . . deems she considers even extraordinary speed too
tedious and slow 1337 still ever 1338 homely simple and unhandsome. villain servant. curtsies bows 1345 silly groom simple menial. wot knows 1347–1348 have . . . deeds eagerly express
their duty in their acts of service (rather than flowery speech)
1350–1351 Even . . . gage in just this fashion, this perfect model of
old-fashioned loyalty pledged his service in wordless, honest looks
1352 kindled duty i.e., blushing obeisance. mistrust i.e., fear of her
shame being known 1355 wistly intently 1356 amazed embarrassed

1359 long she thinks she thinks it long 1361 entertain occupy
1364 stay halt 1366 piece picture (evidently in a tapestry)
1367 made for depicting 1368 drawn drawn up, arrayed. power
army 1370 cloud-kissing Ilion i.e., lofty-towered Troy. annoy harm
1371 conceited ingenious 1374 In scorn of i.e., defiantly rivaling.
lifeless inanimate 1375 dry drop i.e., drop of paint depicting a tear
1377 strife rivalry, i.e., with Nature; also the strife depicted in the
painting 1380 pioneer digger of trenches and mines 1384 lust
pleasure, delight 1385 sweet observance i.e., verisimilitude created
with loving attention to detail 1389 quick lively 1392 heartless
cowardly 1396 ciphered showed, expressed 1400 deep . . . government profound wisdom and serene self-control

There pleading might you see grave Nestor stand,   1401
As 'twere encouraging the Greeks to fight,
Making such sober action with his hand
That it beguiled attention, charmed the sight.
In speech, it seemed, his beard, all silver white,
    Wagged up and down, and from his lips did fly
    Thin winding breath, which purled up to the sky.   1407

About him were a press of gaping faces,
Which seemed to swallow up his sound advice,
All jointly listening, but with several graces,   1410
As if some mermaid did their ears entice;
Some high, some low, the painter was so nice.   1412
    The scalps of many, almost hid behind,   1413
    To jump up higher seemed, to mock the mind.   1414

Here one man's hand leaned on another's head,
His nose being shadowed by his neighbor's ear;
Here one being thronged bears back, all boll'n and red;   1417
Another, smothered, seems to pelt and swear;   1418
And in their rage such signs of rage they bear
    As, but for loss of Nestor's golden words,   1420
    It seemed they would debate with angry swords.

For much imaginary work was there,   1422
Conceit deceitful, so compact, so kind,   1423
That for Achilles' image stood his spear
Gripped in an armèd hand; himself, behind,
Was left unseen, save to the eye of mind.
    A hand, a foot, a face, a leg, a head,
    Stood for the whole to be imaginèd.

And from the walls of strong-besiegèd Troy,
When their brave hope, bold Hector, marched to field,
Stood many Trojan mothers, sharing joy
To see their youthful sons bright weapons wield;
And to their hope they such odd action yield   1433
    That through their light joy seemèd to appear,
    Like bright things stained, a kind of heavy fear.

And from the strand of Dardan where they fought   1436
To Simois' reedy banks the red blood ran,   1437
Whose waves to imitate the battle sought
With swelling ridges; and their ranks began
To break upon the gallèd shore, and then   1440
    Retire again, till, meeting greater ranks,
    They join and shoot their foam at Simois' banks.

To this well-painted piece is Lucrece come,
To find a face where all distress is stelled.   1444
Many she sees where cares have carvèd some,
But none where all distress and dolor dwelled,
Till she despairing Hecuba beheld,   1447
    Staring on Priam's wounds with her old eyes,
    Which bleeding under Pyrrhus' proud foot lies.

In her the painter had anatomized   1450
Time's ruin, beauty's wrack, and grim care's reign.
Her cheeks with chaps and wrinkles were disguised;   1452
Of what she was no semblance did remain.
Her blue blood, changed to black in every vein,
    Wanting the spring that those shrunk pipes had
      fed,   1455
    Showed life imprisoned in a body dead.

On this sad shadow Lucrece spends her eyes,   1457
And shapes her sorrow to the beldam's woes,   1458
Who nothing wants to answer her but cries   1459
And bitter words to ban her cruel foes.   1460
The painter was no god to lend her those;
    And therefore Lucrece swears he did her wrong,
    To give her so much grief and not a tongue.

"Poor instrument," quoth she, "without a sound,
I'll tune thy woes with my lamenting tongue,   1465
And drop sweet balm in Priam's painted wound,
And rail on Pyrrhus that hath done him wrong,
And with my tears quench Troy that burns so long,
    And with my knife scratch out the angry eyes
    Of all the Greeks that are thine enemies.

"Show me the strumpet that began this stir,
That with my nails her beauty I may tear.
Thy heat of lust, fond Paris, did incur   1473
This load of wrath that burning Troy doth bear.
Thine eye kindled the fire that burneth here,
    And here in Troy, for trespass of thine eye,
    The sire, the son, the dame, and daughter die.

"Why should the private pleasure of some one
Become the public plague of many moe?   1479
Let sin, alone committed, light alone   1480
Upon his head that hath transgressèd so;
Let guiltless souls be freed from guilty woe.
    For one's offense why should so many fall,
    To plague a private sin in general?   1484

1401 **pleading** making a persuasive oration 1407 **purled** curled
1410 **with several graces** i.e., in differing attitudes 1412 **Some . . .
low** some tall, some short. **nice** accurate, particular 1413 **scalps**
heads of hair 1414 **To . . . mind** (The artistic illusion deceives the
mind of the viewer into thinking he sees the movement of those in the
back of the crowd who are jumping higher to catch Nestor's oration.)
1417 **thronged** crowded. **bears** pushes. **boll'n** swollen up
1418 **pelt** scold 1420 **but . . . words** were it not that they would
thereby miss Nestor's speech 1422 **imaginary work** work of the
imagination 1423 **Conceit . . . kind** a contrived artifice, so effi-
ciently composed, so seemingly natural 1433 **they . . . yield** they
add such actions and emotions at odds with the joy 1436 **strand**
shore 1437 **Simois** river near Troy 1440 **gallèd** eroded

1444 **stelled** portrayed, engraved 1447 **Hecuba** Queen of Troy, wife
of King Priam 1450 **anatomized** laid open, dissected 1452 **chaps**
cracks and lines in the skin. **disguised** disfigured 1455 **spring** i.e.,
source of blood and life. **pipes** i.e., veins 1457 **shadow** image,
likeness 1458 **shapes** likens; compares. **beldam's** old woman's
1459 **wants to answer her** i.e., lacks in order to be perfectly like Lucrece in her sorrow 1460 **ban** curse 1465 **tune** sing 1473 **fond**
doting 1479 **moe** more 1480 **alone committed** committed by one
person alone. **light** alight 1484 **in general** collectively, publicly.
(Lucrece wonders why it should be necessary to punish the general
public for an individual's sin.)

"Lo, here weeps Hecuba, here Priam dies,
Here manly Hector faints, here Troilus swounds,   1486
Here friend by friend in bloody channel lies,   1487
And friend to friend gives unadvisèd wounds,   1488
And one man's lust these many lives confounds.
    Had doting Priam checked his son's desire,
    Troy had been bright with fame and not with
      fire."

Here feelingly she weeps Troy's painted woes,
For sorrow, like a heavy-hanging bell
Once set on ringing, with his own weight goes;   1494
Then little strength rings out the doleful knell.
So Lucrece, set a-work, sad tales doth tell
    To penciled pensiveness and colored sorrow;   1497
    She lends them words, and she their looks doth
      borrow.

She throws her eyes about the painting round,
And who she finds forlorn she doth lament.   1500
At last she sees a wretched image bound,   1501
That piteous looks to Phrygian shepherds lent.   1502
His face, though full of cares, yet showed content;
    Onward to Troy with the blunt swains he goes,   1504
    So mild that patience seemed to scorn his woes.   1505

In him the painter labored with his skill
To hide deceit and give the harmless show   1507
An humble gait, calm looks, eyes wailing still,   1508
A brow unbent that seemed to welcome woe;
Cheeks neither red nor pale, but mingled so
    That blushing red no guilty instance gave,   1511
    Nor ashy pale the fear that false hearts have.

But, like a constant and confirmèd devil,
He entertained a show so seeming just,   1514
And therein so ensconced his secret evil,   1515
That jealousy itself could not mistrust   1516
False-creeping craft and perjury should thrust
    Into so bright a day such black-faced storms,
    Or blot with hell-born sin such saintlike forms.

The well-skilled workman this mild image drew
For perjured Sinon, whose enchanting story   1521
The credulous old Priam after slew;   1522
Whose words like wildfire burnt the shining glory   1523

Of rich-built Ilion, that the skies were sorry,
    And little stars shot from their fixèd places
    When their glass fell wherein they viewed their
      faces.   1526

This picture she advisedly perused,   1527
And chid the painter for his wondrous skill,
Saying, some shape in Sinon's was abused;   1529
So fair a form lodged not a mind so ill.
And still on him she gazed, and gazing still,
    Such signs of truth in his plain face she spied   1532
    That she concludes the picture was belied.   1533

"It cannot be," quoth she, "that so much guile—"
She would have said "can lurk in such a look";
But Tarquin's shape came in her mind the while,
And from her tongue "can lurk" from "cannot" took.
"It cannot be" she in that sense forsook,
    And turned it thus: "It cannot be, I find,
    But such a face should bear a wicked mind.

"For even as subtle Sinon here is painted,
So sober-sad, so weary, and so mild,
As if with grief or travail he had fainted,   1543
To me came Tarquin armèd, too beguiled   1544
With outward honesty, but yet defiled
    With inward vice. As Priam him did cherish,
    So did I Tarquin; so my Troy did perish.

"Look, look, how listening Priam wets his eyes,
To see those borrowed tears that Sinon sheds!   1549
Priam, why art thou old and yet not wise?
For every tear he falls, a Trojan bleeds.   1551
His eye drops fire, no water thence proceeds;
    Those round clear pearls of his, that move thy
     pity,
    Are balls of quenchless fire to burn thy city.

"Such devils steal effects from lightless hell,   1555
For Sinon in his fire doth quake with cold,
And in that cold hot-burning fire doth dwell.
These contraries such unity do hold   1558
Only to flatter fools and make them bold.   1559
    So Priam's trust false Sinon's tears doth flatter   1560
    That he finds means to burn his Troy with
     water."   1561

1486 **swounds** swoons   1487 **channel** gutter   1488 **unadvisèd wounds** wounds they never intended for each other   1494 **his** its 1497 **penciled** painted.   **colored** painted   1500 **who** whoever 1501 **image** i.e., of Sinon, betrayer of Troy.   **bound** onward bound 1502 **piteous . . . lent** i.e., drew pitying looks from Phrygian shepherds. (Sinon deceived humble Trojans into pitying him as a deserter from the Greeks, thereby persuading them to admit the wooden horse.)   1504 **blunt swains** rustic peasants   1505 **patience** his patience.   **scorn** make light of   1507 **harmless show** outwardly harmless appearance   1508 **still** continually   1511 **guilty instance** symptom of guilt   1514 **entertained a show** kept up an appearance 1515 **ensconced** hid   1516 **jealousy** suspicion.   **mistrust** suspect (that)   1521 **For** to represent.   **enchanting** bewitching   1522 **The . . . slew** subsequently brought about the slaughter of credulous old Priam   1523 **wildfire** a highly inflammable mixture of tar, sulfur, grease, etc., used in war

1526 **glass** mirror (i.e., rich-built Troy)   1527 **advisedly** studiously 1529 **some shape** i.e., the figure of some other person.   **abused** slanderously portrayed   1532 **plain** honest   1533 **belied** falsified 1543 **travail** (The Quarto's *trauaile* also contains the idea of "travel.") 1544 **armèd** equipped, accoutered.   **beguiled** concealed or disguised by guile   1549 **borrowed** counterfeited.   **sheeds** sheds   1551 **he** i.e., Sinon.   **falls** lets fall   1555 **Such devils** (The ability to weep without real tears—*effects*—was attributed to devils.) 1558–1561 **These . . . water** i.e., this illusory coinciding of contraries, hot and cold, is designed to encourage and embolden fools, just as Sinon hoodwinks Priam into a false sense of security; thus, false Sinon's tears lull Priam into misplaced trust, so that Sinon finds means to burn Priam's Troy by use of false tears. (*Fools*, line 1559, can perhaps refer to Priam or to Sinon, and much of the grammar is ingeniously reversible.)   1559, 1560 **flatter** encourage with false hopes

Here, all enraged, such passion her assails
That patience is quite beaten from her breast.
She tears the senseless Sinon with her nails,   1564
Comparing him to that unhappy guest   1565
Whose deed hath made herself herself detest.
        At last she smilingly with this gives o'er:
        "Fool, fool!" quoth she, "his wounds will not be
            sore."

Thus ebbs and flows the current of her sorrow,
And time doth weary time with her complaining.
She looks for night, and then she longs for morrow,
And both she thinks too long with her remaining.
Short time seems long in sorrow's sharp sustaining;   1573
        Though woe be heavy, yet it seldom sleeps,   1574
        And they that watch see time how slow it creeps.   1575

Which all this time hath overslipped her thought
That she with painted images hath spent,
Being from the feeling of her own grief brought
By deep surmise of others' detriment,   1579
Losing her woes in shows of discontent.   1580
        It easeth some, though none it ever cured,
        To think their dolor others have endured.

But now the mindful messenger, come back,   1583
Brings home his lord and other company,
Who finds his Lucrece clad in mourning black,
And round about her tear-distainèd eye   1586
Blue circles streamed, like rainbows in the sky.
        These water galls in her dim element   1588
        Foretell new storms to those already spent.   1589

Which when her sad-beholding husband saw,
Amazedly in her sad face he stares.
Her eyes, though sod in tears, looked red and raw,   1592
Her lively color killed with deadly cares.
He hath no power to ask her how she fares;
        Both stood like old acquaintance in a trance,
        Met far from home, wond'ring each other's
            chance.   1596

At last he takes her by the bloodless hand
And thus begins: "What uncouth ill event   1598
Hath thee befall'n, that thou dost trembling stand?
Sweet love, what spite hath thy fair color spent?   1600
Why art thou thus attired in discontent?   1601
        Unmask, dear dear, this moody heaviness,   1602
        And tell thy grief, that we may give redress."

Three times with sighs she gives her sorrow fire   1604
Ere once she can discharge one word of woe.   1605
At length addressed to answer his desire,   1606
She modestly prepares to let them know
Her honor is ta'en prisoner by the foe,
        While Collatine and his consorted lords   1609
        With sad attention long to hear her words.   1610

And now this pale swan in her watery nest   1611
Begins the sad dirge of her certain ending:
"Few words," quoth she, "shall fit the trespass best,
Where no excuse can give the fault amending.
In me more woes than words are now depending,   1615
        And my laments would be drawn out too long,
        To tell them all with one poor tirèd tongue.

"Then be this all the task it hath to say:
Dear husband, in the interest of thy bed   1619
A stranger came, and on that pillow lay
Where thou wast wont to rest thy weary head;
And what wrong else may be imaginèd
        By foul enforcement might be done to me,
        From that, alas, thy Lucrece is not free.

"For in the dreadful dead of dark midnight,
With shining falchion in my chamber came
A creeping creature with a flaming light,
And softly cried, 'Awake, thou Roman dame,
And entertain my love! Else lasting shame   1629
        On thee and thine this night I will inflict,
        If thou my love's desire do contradict.

" 'For some hard-favored groom of thine,' quoth he,   1632
'Unless thou yoke thy liking to my will,
I'll murder straight, and then I'll slaughter thee   1634
And swear I found you where you did fulfill
The loathsome act of lust, and so did kill
        The lechers in their deed. This act will be
        My fame and thy perpetual infamy.'

"With this, I did begin to start and cry;
And then against my heart he set his sword,
Swearing, unless I took all patiently,
I should not live to speak another word;
So should my shame still rest upon record,
        And never be forgot in mighty Rome
        Th' adulterate death of Lucrece and her groom.   1645

"Mine enemy was strong, my poor self weak,
And far the weaker with so strong a fear.
My bloody judge forbade my tongue to speak;

1564 **senseless** inanimate; unfeeling   1565 **unhappy** causing unhappiness and misfortune   1573 **in . . . sustaining** when it is sustained by sharp sorrow   1574 **heavy** exhausting; sorrowful   1575 **watch** stay awake   1579 **surmise** conjecture, contemplation   1580 **shows of discontent** representations of sorrow, i.e., the painted scene of Troy's woe   1583 **mindful** diligent   1586 **tear-distainèd** tear-stained   1588 **water galls** fragments of rainbow, secondary rainbows (foretelling stormy weather).   **dim** cloudy.   **element** sky, i.e., face or eye   1589 **to** besides   1592 **sod** sodden, steeped   1596 **wond'ring . . . chance** wondering at or about each other's fortune   1598 **uncouth** unknown, strange   1600 **spite** injury.   **spent** expended, taken away   1601 **attired in discontent** (1) wrapped up in melancholy (2) dressed in mourning black (line 1585)   1602 **Unmask** reveal

1604–1605 **Three . . . woe** (The metaphor is that of discharging firearms by means of a match.)   1606 **addressed** prepared   1609 **consorted** companion   1610 **sad** serious   1611 **swan** (Alludes to the belief that the swan, ordinarily without a song, sings beautifully at its own death.)   1615 **depending** belonging, impending (with Latin sense of "weighing heavier")   1619 **in the interest** claiming possession   1629 **entertain** receive   1632 **hard-favored** ugly   1634 **straight** at once   1645 **adulterate** adulterous

No rightful plea might plead for justice there.
His scarlet lust came evidence to swear   1650
    That my poor beauty had purloined his eyes;
    And when the judge is robbed the prisoner dies.

"O, teach me how to make mine own excuse!
Or at the least this refuge let me find:
Though my gross blood be stained with this abuse,
Immaculate and spotless is my mind.
That was not forced, that never was inclined
    To accessory yieldings, but still pure   1658
    Doth in her poisoned closet yet endure."   1659

Lo, here the hopeless merchant of this loss,   1660
With head declined and voice dammed up with woe,   1661
With sad set eyes and wreathèd arms across,
From lips new waxen pale begins to blow   1663
The grief away that stops his answer so.
    But, wretched as he is, he strives in vain;
    What he breathes out his breath drinks up again.

As through an arch the violent roaring tide   1667
Outruns the eye that doth behold his haste,
Yet in the eddy boundeth in his pride
Back to the strait that forced him on so fast—
In rage sent out, recalled in rage, being past—
    Even so his sighs, his sorrows, make a saw,   1672
    To push grief on and back the same grief draw.   1673

Which speechless woe of his poor she attendeth,   1674
And his untimely frenzy thus awaketh: 1675
"Dear lord, thy sorrow to my sorrow lendeth
Another power; no flood by raining slaketh.   1677
My woe too sensible thy passion maketh   1678
    More feeling-painful. Let it then suffice   1679
    To drown one woe, one pair of weeping eyes.

"And for my sake, when I might charm thee so,   1681
For she that was thy Lucrece, now attend me:
Be suddenly revengèd on my foe,   1683
Thine, mine, his own. Suppose thou dost defend me   1684
From what is past. The help that thou shalt lend me
    Comes all too late, yet let the traitor die;
    For sparing justice feeds iniquity.   1687

"But ere I name him, you fair lords," quoth she,
Speaking to those that came with Collatine,
"Shall plight your honorable faiths to me,   1690
With swift pursuit to venge this wrong of mine;
For 'tis a meritorious fair design
    To chase injustice with revengeful arms.
    Knights, by their oaths, should right poor ladies' harms."

At this request, with noble disposition
Each present lord began to promise aid,
As bound in knighthood to her imposition,   1697
Longing to hear the hateful foe bewrayed.   1698
But she, that yet her sad task hath not said,   1699
    The protestation stops. "O, speak," quoth she,   1700
    "How may this forcèd stain be wiped from me?

"What is the quality of my offense,   1702
Being constrained with dreadful circumstance?   1703
May my pure mind with the foul act dispense,   1704
My low-declinèd honor to advance?   1705
May any terms acquit me from this chance?   1706
    The poisoned fountain clears itself again,
    And why not I from this compellèd stain?"

With this they all at once began to say
Her body's stain her mind untainted clears,
While with a joyless smile she turns away
The face, that map which deep impression bears   1712
Of hard misfortune, carved in it with tears.
    "No, no," quoth she, "no dame hereafter living
    By my excuse shall claim excuse's giving."   1715

Here with a sigh, as if her heart would break,
She throws forth Tarquin's name: "He, he," she says,
But more than "he" her poor tongue could not speak;
Till after many accents and delays,   1719
Untimely breathings, sick and short assays,
    She utters this: "He, he, fair lords, 'tis he,
    That guides this hand to give this wound to me."

Even here she sheathèd in her harmless breast
A harmful knife, that thence her soul unsheathed.
That blow did bail it from the deep unrest   1725
Of that polluted prison where it breathed.
Her contrite sighs unto the clouds bequeathed
    Her wingèd sprite, and through her wounds doth fly
    Life's lasting date from canceled destiny.   1729

1650 came evidence supplied evidence   **1658 To accessory yieldings** to a yielding that would make me an accessory to crime   **1659 poisoned closet** i.e., violated body   **1660 merchant of this loss** i.e., owner who has sustained this loss, Collatine   **1661 declined** bent down   **1663 new waxen** newly turned   **1667 arch** i.e., of a bridge, such as London Bridge or Clopton Bridge   **1672 saw** i.e., sawlike back-and-forth motion   **1673 and . . . draw** and draw the same grief back. (Collatine breathes and sighs, in and out.)   **1674 Which . . . attendeth** to which speechless woe of Collatine poor Lucrece pays heed   **1675 And . . . awaketh** and awakens him from his ill-timed distraction   **1677 Another power** added strength.   **no . . . slaketh** no flood is lessened by more rain   **1678–1679 My . . . painful** your passionate grief makes my woe, already too keenly felt, even more painfully perceived   **1681 so** i.e., in the person of my former self, still unravished   **1683 suddenly** quickly   **1684 his own** i.e., his own worst enemy   **1687 sparing** too lenient.   **feeds iniquity** encourages wrongdoing

1690 plight pledge   **1697 imposition** injunction   **1698 bewrayed** revealed, named   **1699 her . . . said** had not yet finished her sad task of speaking   **1700 protestation** resolution   **1702 quality** nature   **1703 with dreadful circumstance** in a situation filled with dread   **1704 with . . . dispense** receive pardon for the foul deed   **1705 advance** raise up   **1706 terms** mitigating grounds   **1712 map** i.e., image   **1715 By . . . giving** will be able to claim the right to offer (give) an excuse using my excuse as her precedent   **1719 accents** sounds expressive of emotion   **1725 bail it** pay for its release   **1729 Life's . . . destiny** i.e., the life that now has a perpetual existence, its subjugation to corporeal existence having been canceled

Stone-still, astonished with this deadly deed,
Stood Collatine and all his lordly crew,
Till Lucrece' father, that beholds her bleed,
Himself on her self-slaughtered body threw,
And from the purple fountain Brutus drew   1734
     The murderous knife, and, as it left the place,
     Her blood, in poor revenge, held it in chase;

And bubbling from her breast, it doth divide
In two slow rivers, that the crimson blood
Circles her body in on every side,
Who, like a late-sacked island, vastly stood   1740
Bare and unpeopled in this fearful flood.
     Some of her blood still pure and red remained,
     And some looked black, and that false Tarquin
       stained.

About the mourning and congealèd face
Of that black blood a watery rigol goes,   1745
Which seems to weep upon the tainted place;
And ever since, as pitying Lucrece' woes,
Corrupted blood some watery token shows,
     And blood untainted still doth red abide,
     Blushing at that which is so putrified.

"Daughter, dear daughter," old Lucretius cries,
"That life was mine which thou hast here deprived.   1752
If in the child the father's image lies,
Where shall I live now Lucrece is unlived?   1754
Thou wast not to this end from me derived.
     If children predecease progenitors,
     We are their offspring, and they none of ours.

"Poor broken glass, I often did behold   1758
In thy sweet semblance my old age new born;
But now that fair fresh mirror dim and old
Shows me a bare-boned death by time outworn.   1761
O, from thy checks my image thou hast torn,
     And shivered all the beauty of my glass,
     That I no more can see what once I was!

"O Time, cease thou thy course and last no longer,
If they surcease to be that should survive!   1766
Shall rotten Death make conquest of the stronger
And leave the faltering feeble souls alive?
The old bees die, the young possess their hive.
     Then live, sweet Lucrece, live again and see
     Thy father die, and not thy father thee!"

By this, starts Collatine as from a dream,
And bids Lucretius give his sorrow place;   1773
And then in key-cold Lucrece' bleeding stream   1774

He falls, and bathes the pale fear in his face,   1775
And counterfeits to die with her a space,   1776
     Till manly shame bids him possess his breath
     And live to be revengèd on her death.

The deep vexation of his inward soul
Hath served a dumb arrest upon his tongue,   1780
Who, mad that sorrow should his use control
Or keep him from heart-easing words so long,
Begins to talk; but through his lips do throng
     Weak words, so thick come in his poor heart's aid   1784
     That no man could distinguish what he said.

Yet sometimes "Tarquin" was pronouncèd plain,
But through his teeth, as if the name he tore.
This windy tempest, till it blow up rain,
Held back his sorrow's tide, to make it more.
At last it rains, and busy winds give o'er;
     Then son and father weep with equal strife
     Who should weep most, for daughter or for wife.

The one doth call her his, the other his,
Yet neither may possess the claim they lay.   1794
The father says, "She's mine." "O, mine she is,"
Replies her husband. "Do not take away
My sorrow's interest. Let no mourner say   1797
     He weeps for her, for she was only mine,
     And only must be wailed by Collatine."

"O," quoth Lucretius, "I did give that life
Which she too early and too late hath spilled."   1801
"Woe, woe," quoth Collatine, "She was my wife;
I owed her, and 'tis mine that she hath killed."   1803
"My daughter" and "my wife" with clamors filled
     The dispersed air, who, holding Lucrece' life,
     Answered their cries, "my daughter" and "my
       wife."   1806

Brutus, who plucked the knife from Lucrece' side,
Seeing such emulation in their woe,
Began to clothe his wit in state and pride,   1809
Burying in Lucrece' wound his folly's show.   1810
He with the Romans was esteemèd so
     As silly jeering idiots are with kings,   1812
     For sportive words and uttering foolish things.

But now he throws that shallow habit by   1814
Wherein deep policy did him disguise,   1815
And armed his long-hid wits advisedly   1816

1734 **Brutus** Lucius Junius Brutus, whose brother had been put to death by the father of the Tarquin in this poem   1740 **Who** which. **late-sacked** recently pillaged.   **vastly** in desolation   1745 **rigol** rim of serum   1752 **deprived** taken away   1754 **unlived** bereft of life   1758 **glass** mirror (i.e., Lucrece, the image of her father)   1761 **death** death's-head, skull   1766 **surcease** cease   1773 **give . . . place** yield him precedence in sorrowing   1774 **key-cold** cold as steel

1775 **pale fear** fearful pallor   1776 **counterfeits to die** gives the appearance of dying.   **a space** for a period of time   1780 **dumb arrest** injunction to be silent   1784 **thick** thickly, fast   1794 **possess . . . lay** take possession of what they claim (since she is dead)   1797 **interest** claim to possession   1801 **late** recently   1803 **owed** owned   1806 **Answered** echoed   1809 **state** dignity   1810 **folly's show** pretense of folly. (Lucius Junius Brutus had feigned madness to escape the fate of his brother; see the note for line 1734.)   1812 **silly jeering idiots** i.e., innocent court jesters   1814 **habit** cloak and disposition   1815 **policy** cunning   1816 **advisedly** with deliberation

To check the tears in Collatinus' eyes.
"Thou wrongèd lord of Rome," quoth he, "arise!
    Let my unsounded self, supposed a fool,   1819
    Now set thy long-experienced wit to school.

"Why, Collatine, is woe the cure for woe?
Do wounds help wounds, or grief help grievous
    deeds?
Is it revenge to give thyself a blow
For his foul act by whom thy fair wife bleeds?
Such childish humor from weak minds proceeds.   1825
    Thy wretched wife mistook the matter so
    To slay herself, that should have slain her foe.

"Courageous Roman, do not steep thy heart
In such relenting dew of lamentations,
But kneel with me and help to bear thy part
To rouse our Roman gods with invocations
That they will suffer these abominations—   1832
    Since Rome herself in them doth stand disgraced—
    By our strong arms from forth her fair streets
       chased.   1834

"Now, by the Capitol that we adore,
And by this chaste blood so unjustly stained,
By heaven's fair sun that breeds the fat earth's store, 1837
By all our country rights in Rome maintained,   1838
And by chaste Lucrece' soul that late complained
    Her wrongs to us, and by this bloody knife,
    We will revenge the death of this true wife."

This said, he struck his hand upon his breast,
And kissed the fatal knife, to end his vow;
And to his protestation urged the rest,   1844
Who, wondering at him, did his words allow.   1845
Then jointly to the ground their knees they bow,
    And that deep vow which Brutus made before
    He doth again repeat, and that they swore.

When they had sworn to this advisèd doom,   1849
They did conclude to bear dead Lucrece thence,
To show her bleeding body thorough Rome,   1851
And so to publish Tarquin's foul offense;   1852
Which being done with speedy diligence,
    The Romans plausibly did give consent   1854
    To Tarquin's everlasting banishment.

1819 **unsounded** unplumbed, unexplored   **1825 humor** disposition
1832 suffer permit   **1834 chased** i.e., to be chased away   **1837 fat**
fertile.   **store** abundance   **1838 country rights** rights we have as a
people   **1844 protestation** resolution   **1845 wondering** marveling,
being astounded.   **allow** approve   **1849 advisèd doom** considered
judgment   **1851 thorough** throughout   **1852 publish** make public
1854 plausibly with applause

The Phoenix and Turtle

"The Phoenix and Turtle" first appeared in a collection of poems called *Love's Martyr: Or, Rosalins Complaint* by Robert Chester (1601). This quarto volume offered various poetic exercises about the phoenix and the turtle "by the best and chiefest of our modern writers." The poem assigned to Shakespeare has been universally accepted as his and is one of his most remarkable productions. With a deceptively simple diction, in gracefully pure tetrameter quatrains and triplets, the poem effortlessly evokes the transcendental ideal of a love existing eternally beyond death. The occasion is an assembly of birds to observe the funeral rites of the phoenix and the turtle. The phoenix, legendary bird of resurrection from its own ashes, once more finds life through death in the company of the turtledove, emblem of pure constancy in affection. Their spiritual union becomes a mystical oneness in whose presence Reason stands virtually speechless. Baffled human discourse must resort to paradox in order to explain how two beings become one essence, "Hearts remote yet not asunder." Mathematics and logic are "confounded" by this joining of two spirits into a "concordant one." This paradox of oneness echoes scholastic theology and its expounding of the doctrine of the Trinity, in terms of persons, substance, accident, triunity, and the like, although, somewhat in the manner of John Donne's poetry, this allusion is more a part of the poem's serious wit than its symbolic meaning. The poignant brevity of this vision is rendered all the more mysterious by our not knowing what, if any, human tragedy may have prompted this metaphysical affirmation.

The Phoenix and Turtle

Let the bird of loudest lay   1
On the sole Arabian tree   2
Herald sad and trumpet be,   3
To whose sound chaste wings obey.   4

But thou shrieking harbinger,   5
Foul precurrer of the fiend,   6
Augur of the fever's end,   7
To this troop come thou not near.

From this session interdict
Every fowl of tyrant wing,   10
Save the eagle, feathered king;
Keep the obsequy so strict.

Let the priest in surplice white,
That defunctive music can,   14
Be the death-divining swan,   15
Lest the requiem lack his right.   16

And thou treble-dated crow,   17
That thy sable gender mak'st   18
With the breath thou giv'st and tak'st,   19
'Mongst our mourners shalt thou go.

Here the anthem doth commence.
Love and constancy is dead;
Phoenix and the turtle fled
In a mutual flame from hence.

So they loved, as love in twain   25
Had the essence but in one,
Two distincts, division none;   27
Number there in love was slain.   28

Title: Phoenix mythical bird that was thought to be consumed in flame and reborn in its own ashes, symbol of immortality; here regarded as female, though traditionally of both sexes. **Turtle** turtledove, symbol of constancy in love; here regarded as male (see line 31)
1 bird . . . lay the bird (possibly the nightingale) of loudest song
2 sole Arabian tree (The phoenix was thought to build its nest in a unique tree in Arabia.) **3 sad** solemn. **trumpet** trumpeter **4 chaste wings** i.e., the wings of the good birds that are being summoned. **obey** are obedient **5 shrieking harbinger** i.e., screech owl **6 precurrer** forerunner **7 Augur . . . end** i.e., prognosticator of death
10 fowl . . . wing bird of prey **14 defunctive** funereal. **can** knows, has skill in **15 death-divining swan** (Alludes to the belief that the swan foresees its own death and sings when it is about to die.)
16 his right its proper ceremony, or, its proper due (referring either to the *requiem* or to the *swan*) **17 treble-dated** i.e., living thrice as long as the normal span of life **18–19 That . . . tak'st** (Compare with *Hortus Sanitatis*, Bk. 3, sec. 34, in Seager's *Natural History in Shakespeare's Time*: "They [ravens] are said to conceive and to lay eggs at the bill. The young become black on the seventh day.") **sable gender** black offspring **25 So . . . as** they so loved that **27 distincts** separate or individual persons or things **28 Number . . . slain** i.e., their love, being of one essence, paradoxically renders the very concept of number meaningless; "one is no number"

Hearts remote yet not asunder,
Distance and no space was seen
Twixt this turtle and his queen;
But in them it were a wonder. 32

So between them love did shine, 33
That the turtle saw his right 34
Flaming in the phoenix' sight; 35
Either was the other's mine. 36

Property was thus appalled 37
That the self was not the same; 38
Single nature's double name 39
Neither two nor one was called. 40

Reason, in itself confounded, 41
Saw division grow together, 42
To themselves yet either neither, 43
Simple were so well compounded, 44

That it cried, "How true a twain 45
Seemeth this concordant one!
Love hath reason, Reason none, 47
If what parts can so remain." 48

Whereupon it made this threne 49
To the phoenix and the dove,
Co-supremes and stars of love, 51
As chorus to their tragic scene.

THRENOS

Beauty, truth, and rarity, 53
Grace in all simplicity,
Here enclosed, in cinders lie. 55

Death is now the phoenix' nest,
And the turtle's loyal breast
To eternity doth rest, 58

Leaving no posterity;
'Twas not their infirmity, 60
It was married chastity. 61

Truth may seem, but cannot be; 62
Beauty brag, but 'tis not she; 63
Truth and beauty buried be. 64

To this urn let those repair
That are either true or fair;
For these dead birds sigh a prayer.

60–61 'Twas . . . chastity i.e., it was not a defect in them to leave no posterity but an emblem of their mystical eternal trothplight
62–64 Truth . . . be i.e., fidelity and beauty as known to mortal perception are only illusory, for their ideal incarnation now lies buried with the phoenix and the turtle

32 But . . . wonder this phenomenon, had it been seen anywhere but in them, would have seemed amazing **33 So** in such a way **34 his right** his true nature, what pertained uniquely and rightly to him, or, what was due to him **35 sight** eyes **36 mine** i.e., very own. (The phoenix and turtle are so merged in one another's identity that each contains the other's being.) *Mine* also suggests "source of each other's treasure." **37–38 Property . . . same** i.e., the very idea of a peculiar or essential quality was thus confounded by the paradoxical revelation here that each lover's identity was merged into the other's and was no longer itself **39–40 Single . . . called** i.e., their nature was at once so single and double that it could not properly be called either one or two **41–44 Reason . . . compounded** i.e., Reason, which proceeds by making discriminations between separate entities, is confounded when it beholds a paradoxical union of such entities, each at once discrete and fused into a single being, at once a simple (i.e., made of one substance) and a compound **45 it** i.e., Reason **47–48 Love . . . remain** i.e., Love, which ordinarily lacks reason, is reasonable, and Reason itself lacks reason, if two that can be disunited or parted nevertheless remain thus in union **49 threne** lamentation, funeral song (from Greek *threnos*) **51 Co-supremes** joint rulers **53 truth** constancy in love (also in line 62) **55 enclosed** i.e., enclosed in *this urn* (line 65) **58 To eternity** for all eternity

A Lover's Complaint

Thomas Thorpe published "A Lover's Complaint" in his 1609 Quarto of Shakespeare's *Sonnets,* ascribing the poem to "William Shake-speare" in its title heading (sig. K^y). The ascription must not be given too much weight, for Thorpe evidently did not have Shakespeare's authorization to publish the sonnets and may possibly have added the last two sonnets from some other source. Yet the attribution of "A Lover's Complaint" to Shakespeare is entirely plausible and is refuted by no other claim. The poem was never assigned to any other author during Shakespeare's lifetime, and no convincing alternative candidate has come forward since then. Although some critics used to wonder if the poem were worthy of Shakespeare's genius, its density of metaphor and energy of wordplay are stylistically and intellectually very much like that of Shakespeare's mature work around or before the date of publication.

The poem takes as its point of departure the conventions of a familiar Elizabethan poetic genre: the "complaint." Often choosing as their setting a stylized pastoral landscape inhabited by rustic shepherds and shepherdesses, poems in this genre generally depicted the plaintive laments of deserted or unrequited lovers. Typically, the poet might catalogue the fickle lover's features and bewail in moralistic terms the dangerous consequences of blind passion. Elizabethans often expected this sort of didacticism in the genre and might, indeed, have been tempted to read Shakespeare's poem as a useful and moving object lesson to young women about the honeyed tongues of young wooers.

Yet the value of Shakespeare's poem goes far beyond the conventional demands of the genre, as did the contributions of other exceptional writers. Much as *As You Like It* shows us a complex, ironic vision of the pastoral, this poem explores the genre of the pastoral "complaint" with subtlety and range. Its multiple point of view is noteworthy. Beginning with the sympathetic voice of the poet-narrator, "A Lover's Complaint" introduces us to the forlorn maiden and then the old shepherd who becomes an audience for her tale of woe. He is a good listener, partly because he has sowed his own wild oats in his day (11. 58–60). The story he hears incorporates also the voice of the young man who has seduced the maiden; the passage in which the young man speaks directly to her, as reported to the old man and thus to us as readers, takes up much of the poem (11. 177–280).

Framed successively and concentrically by the points of view of the sad maiden, the old man, the poet, and ourselves, the male wooer is given free rein of expression in pleading for sympathy. The old man provides his own sympathy of regret and male acknowledgment of a kind of complicity, while the poet hovers in the background not simply as narrator but also as one who understands. The moralism is evident and yet is less important for us than the multiplicity of voices expressing in rich metaphorical language the tense and ultimately bitter struggle over sexuality that is so much a key to the "Dark Lady" sonnets as well. Thorpe's inclusion of the poem in his volume of the *Sonnets* suggests an integrity in that publishing venture.

A Lover's Complaint

From off a hill whose concave womb reworded   1
A plaintful story from a sistering vale,   2
My spirits t' attend this double voice accorded,   3
And down I laid to list the sad-tuned tale;   4
Ere long espied a fickle maid full pale,   5
Tearing of papers, breaking rings a-twain,   6
Storming her world with sorrow's wind and rain.

Upon her head a platted hive of straw,   8
Which fortified her visage from the sun,   9
Whereon the thought might think sometimes it saw   10
The carcass of a beauty spent and done.   11
Time had not scythèd all that youth begun,   12
Nor youth all quit, but spite of heaven's fell rage   13
Some beauty peeped through lattice of seared age.   14

Oft did she heave her napkin to her eyne,   15
Which on it had conceited characters,   16
Laund'ring the silken figures in the brine
That seasoned woe had pelleted in tears,   18
And often reading what contents it bears;
As often shrieking undistinguished woe,   20
In clamors of all size, both high and low.

Sometimes her leveled eyes their carriage ride,   22
As they did battery to the spheres intend;   23
Sometimes diverted, their poor balls are tied   24
To th' orbèd earth; sometimes they do extend   25
Their view right on; anon their gazes lend   26
To every place at once, and, nowhere fixed,   27
The mind and sight distractedly commixed.   28

Her hair, nor loose nor tied in formal plat,   29
Proclaimed in her a careless hand of pride;   30
For some, untucked, descended her sheaved hat,   31

Hanging her pale and pinèd cheek beside;   32
Some in her threaden fillet still did bide,   33
And, true to bondage, would not break from thence,
Though slackly braided in loose negligence.

A thousand favors from a maund she drew   36
Of amber, crystal, and of beaded jet,   37
Which one by one she in a river threw,
Upon whose weeping margent she was set,   39
Like usury applying wet to wet,   40
Or monarch's hands that lets not bounty fall
Where want cries some, but where excess begs all.   42

Of folded schedules had she many a one,   43
Which she perused, sighed, tore, and gave the flood;   44
Cracked many a ring of posied gold and bone,   45
Bidding them find their sepulchers in mud;
Found yet more letters sadly penned in blood,
With sleided silk feat and affectedly   48
Enswathed and sealed to curious secrecy.   49

These often bathed she in her fluxive eyes,   50
And often kissed, and often 'gan to tear;
Cried, "O false blood, thou register of lies,   52
What unapprovèd witness dost thou bear!   53
Ink would have seemed more black and damnèd here!"
This said, in top of rage the lines she rents,   55
Big discontent so breaking their contents.   56

A reverend man that grazed his cattle nigh—   57
Sometime a blusterer, that the ruffle knew   58
Of court, of city, and had let go by
The swiftest hours, observèd as they flew—   60
Towards this afflicted fancy fastly drew,   61
And, privileged by age, desires to know
In brief the grounds and motives of her woe.

So slides he down upon his grainèd bat,   64
And comely-distant sits he by her side,   65
When he again desires her, being sat,   66

1 **concave womb** hollow-shaped hillside. **reworded** echoed
2 **plaintful story** i.e., mournful sound (which turns out to be the griev-ing of a maiden). **sistering** neighboring 3 **attend** listen to. **double** (because echoed) **accorded** inclined, consented 4 **list** listen to. **sad-tuned** i.e., sung in a minor key 5 **fickle** i.e., perturbed, moody 6 **papers** i.e., love letters 8 **platted hive** i.e., woven hat 9 **fortified** protected 10 **the thought** the mind; that which thinks 11 **carcass** decaying, lifeless remnant. **spent** consumed 12–13 **all . . . quit** all the beauty of her youth, nor had youth abandoned her entirely 13 **fell** deadly, cruel 14 **seared** dried up 15 **heave** lift. **napkin** handkerchief. **eyne** eyes 16 **conceited characters** fanciful or emblematic devices 18 **seasoned** (1) matured (2) salted. **pelleted** formed into small globules 20 **undistinguished woe** incoherent cries of grief 22 **her . . . ride** i.e., her eyes, directed and aimed like a cannon, swiveled about as on a gun carriage 23 **As . . . intend** as if they did intend to direct their fire against the heavens 24 **balls** eye-balls 24–25 **are . . . earth** seem fixed to the orb-shaped earth, to the ground 26 **right on** straight in front of her 26–27 **lend . . . once** i.e., roll distractedly everywhere 28 **The mind . . . commixed** her mind and sight wildly confused or mingled 29 **nor . . . nor** nei-ther . . . nor. **in formal plat** neatly braided 30 **careless . . . pride** hand careless of appearances 31 **descended** hung from. **sheaved** straw

32 **Hanging . . . beside** hanging beside her pale cheek wasted with pining 33 **threaden fillet** i.e., ribbon binding her hair 36 **favors** love tokens. **maund** woven basket with handles 37 **beaded jet** jet beads 39 **weeping margent** moist bank (though *weeping* also ap-plies to her) 40 **usury** i.e., adding money to money; she adds tears to the river's water 42 **Where . . . all** i.e., (not) where the needy cry out for some charity, but where the rich beg all the bounty there is 43 **schedules** papers containing writing, i.e., letters 44 **gave the flood** threw in the stream 45 **posied** inscribed with a motto 48 **sleid-ed** separated into threads. **feat** featly, adroitly. **affectedly** lovingly 49 **Enswathed . . . secrecy** wrapped about (with the silk) and sealed (with wax) into careful secrecy 50 **fluxive** flowing 52 **blood** i.e., the blood in which the letters were written (line 47), but with a sense also of the *blood* or passion that has played her *false*. **register** record 53 **unapprovèd** unconfirmed, false 55 **in top of** in the height of. **rents** rends, tears 56 **discontent . . . contents** (With a play of anti-thesis.) 57 **reverend** aged 58 **Sometime** at one time. **blusterer** swaggerer. **ruffle** commotion, bustle 60 **swiftest hours** i.e., time of youth. **observèd as they flew** (This man has let his youth go by and disappear, but not without observing and learning from the years as they flew.) 61 **fancy** i.e., amorous passion and the person expressing it. **fastly** (1) quickly (2) in close proximity 64 **So . . . bat** and so he lowers himself by means of his club or staff that is worn and showing the grain 65 **comely-distant** at a decorous distance 66 **being** he being

Her grievance with his hearing to divide.   67
If that from him there may be aught applied   68
Which may her suffering ecstasy assuage,   69
'Tis promised in the charity of age.   70

"Father," she says, "though in me you behold   71
The injury of many a blasting hour,   72
Let it not tell your judgment I am old;
Not age, but sorrow, over me hath power.
I might as yet have been a spreading flower,   75
Fresh to myself, if I had self-applied   76
Love to myself and to no love beside.

"But, woe is me! Too early I attended   78
A youthful suit—it was to gain my grace—   79
O, one by nature's outwards so commended   80
That maidens' eyes stuck over all his face.   81
Love lacked a dwelling and made him her place;   82
And when in his fair parts she did abide,
She was new lodged and newly deified.   84

"His browny locks did hang in crooked curls,
And every light occasion of the wind   86
Upon his lips their silken parcels hurls.   87
What's sweet to do, to do will aptly find;   88
Each eye that saw him did enchant the mind,
For on his visage was in little drawn   90
What largeness thinks in Paradise was sawn.   91

"Small show of man was yet upon his chin;
His phoenix down began but to appear   93
Like unshorn velvet on that termless skin   94
Whose bare outbragged the web it seemed to wear.   95
Yet showed his visage by that cost more dear;   96
And nice affections wavering stood in doubt   97
If best were as it was, or best without.   98

"His qualities were beauteous as his form,   99
For maiden-tongued he was, and thereof free;   100
Yet, if men moved him, was he such a storm   101
As oft twixt May and April is to see,   102
    When winds breathe sweet, unruly though they be.

His rudeness so with his authorized youth   104
Did livery falseness in a pride of truth.   105

"Well could he ride, and often men would say,
'That horse his mettle from his rider takes.   107
Proud of subjection, noble by the sway,   108
What rounds, what bounds, what course, what stop
    he makes!'   109
And controversy hence a question takes,   110
Whether the horse by him became his deed,   111
Or he his manage by th' well-doing steed.   112

"But quickly on this side the verdict went:
His real habitude gave life and grace   114
To appertainings and to ornament,
Accomplished in himself, not in his case.   116
All aids, themselves made fairer by their place,   117
Came for additions, yet their purposed trim   118
Pieced not his grace, but were all graced by him.   119

"So on the tip of his subduing tongue
All kind of arguments and question deep,
All replication prompt and reason strong,   122
For his advantage still did wake and sleep.   123
To make the weeper laugh, the laugher weep,
He had the dialect and different skill,   125
Catching all passions in his craft of will,   126

"That he did in the general bosom reign   127
Of young, of old, and sexes both enchanted,
To dwell with him in thoughts, or to remain
In personal duty, following where he haunted.   130
Consents bewitched, ere he desire, have granted,   131
And dialogued for him what he would say,   132
Asked their own wills, and made their wills obey.   133

"Many there were that did his picture get
To serve their eyes, and in it put their mind,   135
Like fools that in th' imagination set

104–105 His . . . truth his roughness, privileged by his youth, thereby did dress falseness in a magnificent garment or concealment of truth   107 mettle vigor and strength of spirit   108 noble by the sway made noble by the way he's controlled   109 stop sudden check in a horse's "career" or trial gallop at full speed. (All the terms here are terms of manage, line 112, the schooling or handling of a horse.)   110 takes takes up, considers   111–112 Whether . . . steed whether it was owing to his horsemanship that his horse acted so becomingly or whether he seemed such a good rider because he had so good a horse   114 habitude constitution, temperament   116 case conditions and circumstances, e.g., the possession of so good a horse   117 place i.e., place near to him or on his person   118 Came for additions came in for consideration as additional graces.   purposed trim intended function as adornment   119 Pieced mended, augmented   122 replication reply.   reason strong persuasive argument   123 still continually.   ·wake and sleep i.e., work in varying moods, now actively, now insinuatingly   125 dialect manner of expression.   different varied, readily adaptable   126 passions (1) passions of his hearers (2) passions incorporated into his moving speech.   craft of will skill in persuasion   127 That so that.   general bosom hearts of all   130 In personal duty i.e., like a personal servant.   haunted frequented   131–133 Consents . . . obey i.e., women have consented to his will before he even asked them, have made up his love speeches to them for him, and have made themselves obey as if obeying their own desires   135 in it . . . mind let their minds become engrossed with it

67 divide share   68 If that if   69 ecstasy frenzy (of grief)   70 in the charity of age in the loving-kindness that old people can offer   71 Father i.e., old man   72 blasting blighting, withering   75 spreading unfolding   76 Fresh to myself i.e., like a flower that lives and dies unseen and unplucked   78 attended heeded   79 grace favor   80 nature's outwards the physical appearance given him by nature   81 stuck over i.e., were glued to   82 Love Venus   84 She . . . deified Love, already a goddess, was made doubly so when she dwelt with him   86 occasion chance breath   87 Upon . . . hurls (the wind) tosses the silken parcels, the curls, against his lips   88 to do will aptly find i.e., will find a doer or an occasion   90 in little in miniature   91 What . . . sawn what one supposes was seen in full scale in Paradise   93 phoenix i.e., suggesting his unique perfection (since only one phoenix, a mythical bird, exists at one time)   94 termless indescribable; youthful   95 bare outbragged bareness surpassed.   web i.e., covering, the downy beard   96 cost (1) expense (2) rich covering; i.e., his face seemed lovelier because of its rich or silken covering.   dear (1) costly (2) lovely   97 nice affections carefully discriminating tastes, inclinations   98 without i.e., lacking the downy beard   99 qualities were manner was as   100 maiden-tongued modest of speech, soft-spoken.   free eloquent; innocent   101 moved i.e., to anger   102 to see to be seen

The goodly objects which abroad they find 137
Of lands and mansions, theirs in thought assigned, 138
And laboring in more pleasures to bestow them 139
Than the true gouty landlord which doth owe them; 140

"So many have, that never touched his hand, 141
Sweetly supposed them mistress of his heart. 142
My woeful self, that did in freedom stand,
And was my own fee simple, not in part, 144
What with his art in youth, and youth in art,
Threw my affections in his charmèd power, 146
Reserved the stalk and gave him all my flower.

"Yet did I not, as some my equals did, 148
Demand of him, nor being desirèd yielded; 149
Finding myself in honor so forbid, 150
With safest distance I mine honor shielded. 151
Experience for me many bulwarks builded 152
Of proofs new-bleeding, which remained the foil 153
Of this false jewel and his amorous spoil. 154

"But, ah, who ever shunned by precedent
The destined ill she must herself assay? 156
Or forced examples, 'gainst her own content 157
To put the by-past perils in her way? 158
Counsel may stop awhile what will not stay; 159
For when we rage, advice is often seen 160
By blunting us to make our wits more keen. 161

"Nor gives it satisfaction to our blood 162
That we must curb it upon others' proof, 163
To be forbade the sweets that seems so good 164
For fear of harms that preach in our behoof. 165
O appetite, from judgment stand aloof! 166
The one a palate hath that needs will taste, 167
Though Reason weep and cry, 'It is thy last.'

"For further I could say 'This man's untrue,' 169
And knew the patterns of his foul beguiling; 170

Heard where his plants in others' orchards grew, 171
Saw how deceits were gilded in his smiling; 172
Knew vows were ever brokers to defiling; 173
Thought characters and words merely but art, 174
And bastards of his foul adulterate heart.

"And long upon these terms I held my city, 176
Till thus he 'gan besiege me: 'Gentle maid,
Have of my suffering youth some feeling pity,
And be not of my holy vows afraid.
That's to ye sworn to none was ever said; 180
For feasts of love I have been called unto, 181
Till now did ne'er invite, nor never woo. 182

" 'All my offenses that abroad you see 183
Are errors of the blood, none of the mind.
Love made them not. With acture they may be, 185
Where neither party is nor true nor kind. 186
They sought their shame that so their shame did find;
And so much less of shame in me remains 188
By how much of me their reproach contains. 189

" 'Among the many that mine eyes have seen,
Not one whose flame my heart so much as warmed, 191
Or my affection put to th' smallest teen, 192
Or any of my leisures ever charmed. 193
Harm have I done to them, but ne'er was harmed;
Kept hearts in liveries, but mine own was free, 195
And reigned, commanding in his monarchy.

" 'Look here what tributes wounded fancies sent me, 197
Of pallid pearls and rubies red as blood,
Figuring that they their passions likewise lent me 199
Of grief and blushes, aptly understood
In bloodless white and the encrimsoned mood— 201
Effects of terror and dear modesty, 202
Encamped in hearts but fighting outwardly. 203

" 'And, lo, behold these talents of their hair, 204
With twisted metal amorously impleached, 205
I have received from many a several fair, 206

137 objects i.e., of sight.   **abroad** round about them, in the world
138 theirs . . . assigned imagining those possessions to be their own
139 laboring . . . them striving to derive more pleasure from them
140 owe own   **141 So many** thus many persons, many women
142 them themselves   **144 was . . . part** i.e., had total control of my own destiny, as of land held in perpetuity, not partial control
146 charmèd power power to charm or cast a spell   **148 my equals** i.e., of those equal to me in age and station   **149 Demand . . . yielded** i.e., ask him to take me, or, yield myself to him the moment he desired me to   **150 in honor so forbid** forbidden by (maidenly) honor to do so (i.e., to yield at once)   **151 With safest distance** by staying at a safe distance   **152–153 Experience . . . new-bleeding** i.e., the experience of those recently undone in love by him provided me with many defenses   **153 foil** dark background used to show off the brilliance of a jewel   **154 this false jewel** i.e., the young man. **spoil** plunder; that which is spoiled   **156 assay** learn by experience   **157–158 Or . . . way** or, in order to deter her own present inclination, urged the dangers experienced by others in the past?   **159 stay** stop forever   **160 rage** i.e., in passion   **161 By . . . keen** in attempting to stop us, merely making us all the more ingenious and eager   **162 blood** passion   **163 proof** experience   **164 seems** seem   **165 preach in our behoof** offer us good advice aimed at benefiting us   **166 O appetite . . . aloof** O desire, you will always remain distant from judgment   **167 The one** i.e., passion, *appetite*.   **needs will taste** insists upon gratification   **169 say . . . untrue** tell of this man's faithlessness   **170 knew . . . beguiling** had examples of his treachery before me

171 plants i.e., children illegitimately begotten.   **orchards** i.e., wombs   **172 gilded** given a gilded (false) surface   **173 brokers** panders   **174 characters and words** i.e., the written and spoken word. **art** artifice   **176 city** citadel (of chastity)   **180 That's** that which is   **181–182 For . . . woo** I have been invited to other feasts of love before now, but never until now did I do the inviting and the wooing   **183 abroad** in the world around us   **185–186 With . . . kind** they may be physically performed where neither partner is faithful or truly in love   **188–189 And . . . contains** and I am all the less to blame by how little their reproaches really accuse me (rather than themselves)   **191 Not one . . . warmed** i.e., there is not one whose flame of passion so much as warmed my heart   **192 Or . . . teen** or gave my affection the least sorrow (*teen*)   **193 Or . . . charmed** or put a spell on any of my times of leisure   **195 in liveries** in the uniform of a person in service, i.e., almost enslaved   **197 wounded fancies** i.e., doting young women   **199 Figuring** symbolizing   **201 mood** mode, form, emotional state (i.e., blushing)   **202 Effects** the signs or results. **dear** precious; deeply felt   **203 Encamped . . . outwardly** (White and red contend visually in the alternation of pallor and blushing cheeks, while fear and maidenly shame occupy the hearts of the women who have been seduced.)   **204 talents** i.e., treasures, riches. (Literally, coins or valuable metal plates.)   **205 impleached** intertwined   **206 a several fair** different beautiful young women

Their kind acceptance weepingly beseeched,   207
With th' annexions of fair gems enriched,   208
And deep-brained sonnets that did amplify   209
Each stone's dear nature, worth, and quality.

" 'The diamond? Why, 'twas beautiful and hard,
Whereto his invised properties did tend;   212
The deep-green emerald, in whose fresh regard   213
Weak sights their sickly radiance do amend;   214
The heaven-hued sapphire and the opal blend   215
With objects manifold—each several stone,   216
With wit well blazoned, smiled or made some moan.   217

" 'Lo, all these trophies of affections hot,   218
Of pensived and subdued desires the tender,   219
Nature hath charged me that I hoard them not,
But yield them up where I myself must render,
That is, to you, my origin and ender;   222
For these, of force, must your oblations be,   223
Since, I their altar, you enpatron me.   224

" 'O, then, advance of yours that phraseless hand,   225
Whose white weighs down the airy scale of praise!   226
Take all these similes to your own command,   227
Hallowed with sighs that burning lungs did raise;   228
What me, your minister for you, obeys,   229
Works under you; and to your audit comes   230
Their distract parcels in combinèd sums.   231

" 'Lo, this device was sent me from a nun,
Or sister sanctified, of holiest note,   233
Which late her noble suit in court did shun,   234
Whose rarest havings made the blossoms dote;   235
For she was sought by spirits of richest coat,   236

But kept cold distance, and did thence remove   237
To spend her living in eternal love.   238

" 'But O, my sweet, what labor is 't to leave   239
The thing we have not, mast'ring what not strives,   240
Paling the place which did no form receive,   241
Playing patient sports in unconstrainèd gyves?   242
She that her fame so to herself contrives   243
The scars of battle scapeth by the flight,
And makes her absence valiant, not her might.   245

" 'O, pardon me, in that my boast is true!   246
The accident which brought me to her eye
Upon the moment did her force subdue,   248
And now she would the cagèd cloister fly.   249
Religious love put out religion's eye.   250
Not to be tempted, would she be immured,   251
And now to tempt all liberty procured.   252

" 'How mighty then you are, O, hear me tell!
The broken bosoms that to me belong   254
Have emptied all their fountains in my well,   255
And mine I pour your ocean all among.   256
I strong o'er them, and you o'er me being strong,   257
Must for your victory us all congest,   258
As compound love to physic your cold breast.   259

" 'My parts had power to charm a sacred nun,   260
Who, disciplined, ay, dieted in grace,   261
Believed her eyes when they t' assail begun,   262
All vows and consecrations giving place.
O most potential love! Vow, bond, nor space,   264
In thee hath neither sting, knot, nor confine,   265
For thou art all, and all things else are thine.

---

207 Their kind . . . beseeched who have besought me with their tears to accept their gifts kindly **208 annexions** additions **209 deep-brained** intricate. **amplify** enlarge upon, go into detail about **212 Whereto . . . tend** toward which its invisible properties incline. (*Invised*, used nowhere else, may be an error for *incised*, "engraved.") The young man, too, is beautiful and hard. **213 regard** aspect, sight **214 radiance** power of vision. (The emerald helps repair weak vision in those who look at it, just as the young man refreshes the eyes by his beauty.) **215–216 blend . . . manifold** blended of many colors (?), or, blended with (or that blends with) many objects presented to the sight (?) **216 several** particular **217 blazoned** proclaimed, cataloged (in the accompanying sonnets). **smiled . . . moan** symbolized joy or grief in love **218 affections** passions **219 pensived** saddened. **tender** offering **222 ender** end, conclusion. (You are the source of my life and that without which I cannot live.) **223 of force** perforce. **your oblations** offerings made at the altar of love for you **224 Since . . . me** since I am the altar (on which these gifts are offered) and you are my patron saint (to whom the altar is dedicated) **225 phraseless** indescribable **226 weighs . . . praise** outweighs in the scales any praise that can be offered to it in airy words **227 similes** i.e., symbolic love tokens or gems accompanied by symbolic explanation in the sonnets **228 Hallowed** consecrated. **burning** i.e., hot with passion **229–230 What . . . you** whatever is at the command of me, your minister or agent acting on your authority, is thus yours also **230 audit** accounting **231 distract** separate **233 note** reputation **234 Which . . . shun** who recently (before she became nun) shunned those who sued for her attention at court **235 Whose . . . dote** whose rare gift of beauty made the young courtiers (in the blossom of their life) dote on her **236 spirits** spirited young men. **coat** coat of arms, i.e., descent

237 remove depart **238 living** lifetime. **eternal love** love of the eternal God (i.e., she became a nun) **239–242 what . . . gyves** how can it be called a difficult thing to give up something we haven't tried yet, mastering an emotion that offers no resistance, *paling* or fencing in the heart upon which no lover has yet made any impression, patiently pretending to endure restraints that, in fact, impose no restraint and that one is not obliged to endure? **243 her fame . . . contrives** devises for herself a reputation (for renouncing love) **245 makes . . . might** i.e., shows valor only in avoiding temptation, not in confronting it directly **246 my boast** i.e., that she could resist me only by fleeing, not when she saw me **248 Upon the moment** at once **249 would . . . fly** wished to flee the locked convent **250 Religious . . . eye** i.e., love of me put out love of the divine **251–252 Not . . . procured** before she wished to be shut up from temptation, but now she sought liberty to venture everything. (The Quarto reads *enur'd* for *immured* and perhaps should be *inured*, habituated.) **254 bosoms** hearts **255–256 Have . . . among** have emptied all their affections into me as into a spring, and I in turn, like a river, pour all these fountains of affection into your ocean **257 strong** victorious **258 for** in consequence of. **us all** i.e., my admirers and myself. **congest** gather together **259 compound love** i.e., love compounded of the various loves of myself and my former loves. (*Compound* also has the suggestion of a drug.) **physic** cure **260 parts** qualities **261 disciplined** subjected to religious discipline. **dieted** nourished, controlled **262 they t' assail begun** they (my qualities or *parts*) began to assail her heart **264 potential** powerful **264–265 Vow . . . confine** against you vows have no strength (*sting*), bonds have no binding force (*knot*), and space is no barrier or impediment (*confine*)

" 'When thou impressest, what are precepts worth 267
Of stale example? When thou wilt inflame, 268
How coldly those impediments stand forth
Of wealth, of filial fear, law, kindred, fame!
Love's arms are peace, 'gainst rule, 'gainst sense, 271
   'gainst shame,
And sweetens, in the suffering pangs it bears, 272
The aloes of all forces, shocks, and fears. 273

" 'Now all these hearts that do on mine depend,
Feeling it break, with bleeding groans they pine, 275
And supplicant their sighs to you extend 276
To leave the battery that you make 'gainst mine, 277
Lending soft audience to my sweet design, 278
And credent soul to that strong-bonded oath 279
That shall prefer and undertake my troth.' 280

"This said, his watery eyes he did dismount, 281
Whose sights till then were leveled on my face; 282
Each cheek a river running from a fount
With brinish current downward flowed apace.
O, how the channel to the stream gave grace! 285
Who glazed with crystal gate the glowing roses 286
That flame through water which their hue encloses.

"O father, what a hell of witchcraft lies 288
In the small orb of one particular tear! 289
But with the inundation of the eyes
What rocky heart to water will not wear?
What breast so cold that is not warmèd here?
O cleft effect! Cold modesty, hot wrath, 293
Both fire from hence and chill extincture hath. 294

"For, lo, his passion, but an art of craft, 295
Even there resolved my reason into tears; 296
There my white stole of chastity I daffed, 297
Shook off my sober guards and civil fears; 298
Appear to him as he to me appears, 299
All melting; though our drops this difference bore: 300
His poisoned me, and mine did him restore.

"In him a plenitude of subtle matter, 302
Applied to cautels, all strange forms receives, 303
Of burning blushes, or of weeping water,
Or swooning paleness; and he takes and leaves, 305
In either's aptness, as it best deceives, 306
To blush at speeches rank, to weep at woes, 307
Or to turn white and swoon at tragic shows;

"That not a heart which in his level came 309
Could scape the hail of his all-hurting aim, 310
Showing fair nature is both kind and tame; 311
And, veiled in them, did win whom he would maim. 312
Against the thing he sought he would exclaim;
When he most burnt in heart-wished luxury, 314
He preached pure maid and praised cold chastity. 315

"Thus merely with the garment of a grace 316
The naked and concealèd fiend he covered, 317
That th' unexperient gave the tempter place, 318
Which like a cherubin above them hovered. 319
Who, young and simple, would not be so lovered? 320
Ay me! I fell, and yet do question make 321
What I should do again for such a sake. 322

"O, that infected moisture of his eye, 323
O, that false fire which in his cheek so glowed,
O, that forced thunder from his heart did fly, 325
O, that sad breath his spongy lungs bestowed, 326
O, all that borrowed motion seeming owed, 327
Would yet again betray the fore-betrayed,
And new pervert a reconcilèd maid!" 329

302 **subtle matter** matter capable of being variously impressed or formed 303 **cautels** crafty devices 305 **takes and leaves** uses one and avoids the other 306 **In either's aptness** whichever is more appropriate 307 **rank** gross 309 **That** so that. **level** range and aim. (Continues the metaphor of siege.) 310 **hail** i.e., of artillery 311 **Showing . . . tame** i.e., his aim being to represent his true nature as loving and docile 312 **And . . . maim** and, disguised thus in kindness and docility, or in *blushes, weeping,* and *paleness* (lines 304–305), won the heart of the woman he intended to harm 314 **heart-wished luxury** deeply desired lechery 315 **pure maid** as if he were an untouched virgin 316 **with . . . grace** with a charming outward show or appearance (perhaps suggesting also one of the three Graces) 317 **The naked . . . covered** he covered his fiendish inner self 318 **unexperient** inexperienced. **place** entry 319 **Which . . . hovered** who, resembling a cherub, hovered over his victims as though offering them protection 320 **simple** naive. **be so lovered** surrender to a lover like him 321 **question make** i.e., ask myself 322 **for such a sake** for someone like him, or, for the sake of falling into such pleasure, however brief 323 **infected** infectious 325 **forced** feigned. **from** that from 326 **spongy lungs** lungs that are spongelike (as all lungs are; perhaps with the suggestion of "blown up with flattery and pretended grief") 327 **all . . . owed** all that passion he seemed to possess himself but had, in fact, borrowed 329 **reconcilèd** penitent

267 **thou impressest** you make an impression on a heart or conscript it into your service 267–268 **what . . . example** of what worth are moralistic warnings based on stale old instances? 271 **Love's . . . shame** i.e., love's might enforces its own peace in the teeth of reason, good sense, and decorum 272 **pangs it bears** pangs that it (love) brings, the pangs that lovers must suffer 273 **aloes** i.e., bitterness. **forces** acts of force. **shocks** clashes 275 **break** i.e., break in disappointment at the threat of your rejecting me. **bleeding groans** (Each groan was thought to cost the heart a drop of blood.) 276 **supplicant** as supplicants 277 **leave** leave off 278–280 **Lending . . . troth** lending their support to my suit to you and credibility to the inviolable oath that thereby guarantees the truth of what I say 281 **dismount** lower (as in dismounting an artillery piece) 282 **leveled on** aimed at 285 **channel . . . stream** i.e., cheek to the flow of tears 286 **Who** which, i.e., the stream of tears. **gate** barrier, layer 288 **father** i.e., the old man to whom she is talking 289 **particular** single 293 **cleft** twofold. **wrath** passion (the wrath of love) 294 **extincture** extinguishing 295 **passion** passionate wooing. **but an art** merely an artifice 296 **resolved** dissolved 297 **stole** vestment. **daffed** doffed, put off 298 **guards** defenses. **civil** decorous, grave 299 **Appear** I did appear 300 **drops** i.e., tears (which here have medicinal qualities)

Sonnets

Shakespeare seems to have cared more about his reputation as a lyric poet than as a dramatist. He contributed to the major nondramatic genres of his day: to amatory Ovidian narrative in *Venus and Adonis,* to the Complaint in *The Rape of Lucrece,* to philosophical poetry in "The Phoenix and Turtle." He cooperated in the publication of his first two important poems, dedicating them to the young Earl of Southampton with a plea to him for sponsorship. To write poetry in this vein was more fashionable than to write plays, which one did mainly for money.

A poet with ambitions of this sort simply had to write a sonnet sequence. Sonneteering was the rage in England in the early and mid 1590s. Based on the sonneteering tradition of Francesco Petrarch, Sir Thomas Wyatt, and others, and gaining new momentum in 1591 with the publication of Sir Philip Sidney's *Astrophel and Stella,* the vogue ended almost as suddenly as it began, in 1596 or 1597. The sonnet sequences of this brief period bear the names of most well-known and minor poets of the day: *Amoretti* by Edmund Spenser (1595), *Delia* by Samuel Daniel (1591 and 1592), *Caelica* by Fulke Greville (not published until 1633), *Idea's Mirror* by Michael Drayton (1594), *Diana* by Henry Constable (1592), *Phyllis* by Thomas Lodge (1593), and the more imitative sequences of Barnabe Barnes, Giles Fletcher, William Percy, Bartholomew Griffin, William Smith, and Robert Tofte.

Shakespeare wrote sonnets during the heyday of the genre, for in 1598 Francis Meres, in his *Palladis Tamia: Wit's Treasury,* praised Shakespeare's "sugared sonnets among his private friends." Even though they were not printed at the time, we know from Meres' remark that they were circulated in manuscript among the cognoscenti and commanded respect. Shakespeare may actually have preferred to delay the publication of his sonnets, not through indifference to their literary worth, but through a desire not to seem too professional. The "courtly makers" of the English Renaissance, those gentlemen whose chivalric accomplishments were supposed to include versifying, looked on the writing of poetry as an avocation designed to amuse one's peers or to court a lady. Publication was not quite genteel, and many such authors affected dismay when their verses were pirated into print. The young wits about London of the 1590s, whether aristocratic or not, sometimes imitated this fashion. Like young John Donne, they sought the favorable verdict of their fellow wits at the Inns of Court (where young men studied law) and professed not to care about wider recognition. Whether Shakespeare was motivated in this way we do not know, but, in any event, his much-sought-after sonnet sequence was not published until 1609, long after the vogue had passed. The publisher, Thomas Thorpe, seems not to have obtained Shakespeare's authorization. Two sonnets, numbers 138 and 144, had been pirated ten years earlier by William Jaggard in *The Passionate Pilgrim,* 1599, a little anthology with some poems by Shakespeare and some wrongly attributed to him. The sonnets were not reprinted until 1640, either because the sonnet vogue had passed or because Thorpe's edition had been suppressed.

The unexplained circumstances of publication have given rise to a host of vexing and apparently unanswerable questions. Probably no puzzle in all English literature has provoked so much speculation and produced so little agreement. To whom are the sonnets addressed? Do they tell a consistent story, and, if so, do they tell us anything about Shakespeare's life? The basic difficulty is that we cannot be sure that the order in which Thorpe published the sonnets represents Shakespeare's intention, nor can we assume that Thorpe spoke for Shakespeare when he dedicated the sonnets to "Mr. W. H." As they stand, most of the first 126 sonnets appear to be addressed in warm friendship to a handsome young aristocrat, whereas sonnets 127–152 speak of the poet's dark-haired mistress. Yet the last two sonnets, 153–154, seem unrelated to anything previous and cast some doubt on the reliability of the ordering. Within each large grouping of the sonnets, moreover, we find evident inconsistencies: jealousies disappear and suddenly reappear, the poet bewails his absolute rejection by the friend and then speaks a few sonnets later of harmonious affection as though nothing had happened, and so on. Some sonnets are closely linked to their predecessors; some are apparently disconnected (although even here we must allow for the real possibility that Shakespeare intends juxtaposition and contrast). We cannot be sure if the friend of sonnets 1–126 is really one person or several. We can only speculate that the unhappy love triangle described in sonnets 40–42, in which the friend has usurped the poet's mistress, can be identified with the love triangle of the "Dark Lady" sonnets, 127–152. Most readers sense a narrative continuity of the whole yet find blocks of sonnets stubbornly out of place. The temptation to rearrange the order has proved irresistible, but no alternative order has ever won acceptance. The consensus is that Thorpe's order is at times suspect but may have more rationale than at first appears. It is, in any case, the only authoritative order we have.

No less frustrating is Thorpe's dedication "To the Only Begetter of These Ensuing Sonnets, Mr. W. H." Given the late and unauthorized publication, we cannot assume that Thorpe speaks for Shakespeare. Quite possibly he is only thanking the person who obtained the sonnets for him, making publication possible. Mundanely enough, Mr. W. H. could be William Hall, an associate of Thorpe's in the publishing business. Yet Elizabethan usage affords few instances of "begetter" in this sense of "obtainer." Recently, Donald Foster has offered new and persuasive arguments for the idea that "Mr. W. H." is only a typographical error of a common sort and that Thorpe meant to say "Mr. W. S.," Master William Shakespeare. In this case, "begetter" would mean simply "creator." This solution has a wonderful neatness about it, but other readers have wondered if it answers the seeming contradiction when Thorpe speaks of "Mr. W. H." and "our ever-living poet" in the dedication as though they are two people. Thorpe offers to Mr. W. H. "that eternity promised by our ever-living poet," as though Mr. W. H. were the very subject of those sonnets whom Shakespeare vows to immortalize.

This interpretation of "begetter" as "inspirer" has prompted many enthusiasts to search for a Mr. W. H. in Shakespeare's life, a nobleman who befriended him. The chief candidates are two. First is the young Earl of Southampton, to whom Shakespeare had dedicated *Venus and Adonis* and *The Rape of Lucrece*. The dedication to the second of these poems bespeaks a warmth and gratitude that had been lacking in the first. The Earl's name, Henry Wriothesley, yields initials that are the reverse of W. H. If this correspondence seems unconvincing, W. H. could stand for Sir William Harvey, third husband of Mary, Lady Southampton, the young Earl's mother. Some researchers would have us believe that Shakespeare wrote the sonnets for Lady Southampton, especially those urging a young man (her son) to marry and procreate. This entire case is speculative, however, and we have no evidence that Shakespeare had any dealings with Southampton after *The Rape of Lucrece*. The plain ascription "Mr. W. H." seems an oddly uncivil way for Thorpe to have addressed an earl. If meant for Southampton, the sonnets must have been written fairly early in the 1590s, for they give no hint of Southampton's later career: his courtship of Elizabeth Vernon, her pregnancy and their secret marriage in 1598, and his later involvement in Essex's Irish campaign and abortive uprising against Queen Elizabeth. Those literary sleuths who stress similarities to the Southampton relationship are too willing to overlook dissimilarities.

The next chief candidate for Mr. W. H. is William Herbert, third Earl of Pembroke, to whom, along with his brother, Shakespeare's colleagues dedicated the First Folio of 1623. In 1595, Pembroke's parents were attempting to arrange his marriage with Lady Elizabeth Carey, granddaughter of the first Lord Hunsdon, who was Lord Chamberlain and patron of Shakespeare's company. In 1597, another alliance was attempted with Bridget Vere, granddaughter of Lord Burghley. In both negotiations, young Pembroke objected to the girl in question. This hypothesis requires, however, an uncomfortably late date for

the sonnets and postulates a gap in age between Shakespeare and Pembroke that would have afforded little opportunity for genuine friendship. Pembroke was only fifteen in 1595; Shakespeare was thirty-one. Besides, no evidence supports the claim other than historical coincidence. The common initials W. H. can be made to produce other candidates as well, such as the Lincolnshire lawyer named William Hatcliffe proposed (to no one's satisfaction) by Leslie Hotson. Hotson wants to date most of the sonnets before 1589, since Hatcliffe came to London in 1587–1588. When such speculations are constructed on the single enigmatic testimonial of the dedication by Thomas Thorpe, who may well have had no connection with Shakespeare, we are left with a case that would not be worth describing had it not captured the imagination of so many researchers.

Biographical identifications have also been proposed for the various personages in the sonnet sequence, predictably with no better success. The rival poet, with "the proud full sail of his great verse" (sonnet 86), has been linked to Christopher Marlowe (who died in 1593), George Chapman, and others. The sequence gives us little to go on, other than that the rival poet possesses a considerable enough talent to intimidate the author of the sonnets and to ingratiate himself with the author's aristocratic friend. No biographical circumstances resembling this rivalry have come to light. Various candidates have also been found for the "Dark Lady." One is Mary Fitton, a lady-in-waiting at court who bore a child by Pembroke in 1601. Again, we have no evidence that Shakespeare knew her, nor is he likely to have carried on an affair with one of such high rank. A. L. Rowse has proposed Emilia Lanier, wife of Alfonso Lanier and daughter of a court musician named Bassano, a woman of suitably dark complexion perhaps but whose presumed connection with Shakespeare rests only on the reported rumor that she was a mistress of Lord Hunsdon. We are left finally without knowing who any of these people were, or whether indeed Shakespeare was attempting to be biographical at all.

The same irresolution afflicts the dating of the sonnets. Do they give hints of a personal chronicle extending over some years, following Thorpe's arrangement of the sonnets or some alternative order? Sonnet 104 speaks of three years having elapsed since the poet met his friend. Are there other signposts that relate to contemporary events? A line in sonnet 107 ("The mortal moon hath her eclipse endured") is usually linked to the death of Queen Elizabeth (known as Diana or Cynthia) in 1603, though Leslie Hotson prefers to see in it an allusion to the Spanish Armada, shaped for sea battle in a moonlike crescent when it met defeat in 1588. The newly built pyramids in sonnet 123 remind Hotson of the obelisks built by Pope Sixtus V in Rome, 1586–1589; other researchers have discovered pyramids erected on London's streets in 1603 to celebrate the coronation of James I. As these illustrations suggest, speculative dating can be used to support a hypothesis of early or late composition.

The wary consensus of most scholars is that the sonnets were written over a number of years; a large number, certainly, before 1598, but some perhaps later and even up to the date of publication in 1609.

However fruitless this quest for nonexistent certainties, it does at least direct us to a meaningful critical question: should we expect sonnets of this "personal" nature to be at least partly autobiographical? Shakespeare's sonnets have struck many readers as cries from the heart, voicing at times fears of rejection, self-hatred, and humiliation, and at other times a serene gratitude for reciprocated affection. This power of expression may, however, be a tribute to Shakespeare's dramatic gift rather than evidence of personal involvement. Earlier sonnet sequences, both Elizabethan and pre-Elizabethan, had established a variety of artistic conventions that tended to displace biography. Petrarch's famous *Rime*, or sonnets, later collected in his *Canzoniere*, though addressed to Laura in two sequences (during her life and after her death), idealized her into the unapproachable lady worshiped by the self-abasing and miserable lover. Petrarch's imitators—Serafino Aquilano, Pietro Bembo, Ludovico Ariosto, and Torquato Tasso among the Italians, Clement Marot, Joachim du Bellay, Pierre de Ronsard, and Philippe Desportes among the French Pléiade—reworked these conventions in countless variations. In England, the fashion was taken up by Sir Thomas Wyatt, the Earl of Surrey, George Gascoigne, Thomas Watson, and others. Spenser's *Amoretti* and Sidney's *Astrophel and Stella*, though inspired at least in part by real women in the poets' lives, are also deeply concerned with theories of writing poetry. Rejection of the stereotyped attitudes and relationships that had come to dominate the typical Petrarchan sonnet sequence is evidence not of biographical literalism in art but of a new insistence on lifelike emotion in art; as Sidney's muse urges him, "look in thy heart and write." Thus, both the Petrarchan and the anti-Petrarchan schools avoid biographical writing for its own sake. This is essentially true of all Elizabethan sonneteering, from Drayton's serious pursuit of platonic abstraction in his *Idea's Mirror* to the facile chorusing of lesser sonnet writers about Diana, Phyllis, Zepheria, or Fidessa.

The "story" connecting the individual poems of an Elizabethan sonnet sequence is never very important or consistent, even when we can be sure of the order in which the sonnets were written. Dante had used prose links in his *La Vita Nuova* (c. 1282) to stress narrative continuity, and so had Petrarch, but this sturdy framework had been abandoned by the late sixteenth century. Rather than telling a chronological story, the typical Elizabethan sonnet sequence offers a thematically connected series of lyrical meditations, chiefly on love but also on poetic theory, the adversities of fortune, death, or what have you. The narrative events mentioned from time to time are not the substance of the sequence but the occasion for meditative reflection. Attitudes need not be consistent throughout, and the characters need not be consistently motivated like dramatis personae in a play.

Shakespeare's sonnet sequence retains these conventions of Elizabethan sonneteering and employs many archetypal situations and themes that had been explored by his predecessors and contemporaries. His emphasis on friendship seems new, for no other sequence addressed a majority of its sonnets to a friend rather than to a mistress, but even here the anti-Petrarchan quest for spontaneity and candor is in the best Elizabethan tradition of Sidney and Spenser. Besides, the exaltation of friendship over love was itself a widespread Neoplatonic commonplace recently popularized in the writings of John Lyly. Shakespeare's sequence makes use of the structural design found in contemporary models. Even though we cannot reconstruct a rigorously consistent chronological narrative from the sonnets, we can discern overall patterns out of which the poet's emotional crises arise and upon which he constructs his meditative lyrics. Certain groupings, such as the sonnets addressed to the "Dark Lady," 127–152, in which individually they comment on one another through reinforcement or antithetical design and are thus enhanced by their context, achieve a plausible cohesion; a case can be made, in other words, for the order of the poems as Thorpe printed them. Even the last two sonnets, 153 and 154, have their defenders (see Michael J. B. Allen's essay in *Shakespeare Survey*, 1978). Juxtaposition is a favorite technique in Shakespeare's plays, and we must remember that he alone among the major Elizabethan sonneteers wrote for the stage.

Taking note of such considerations, we can account for most of the situations portrayed in Shakespeare's sonnets by postulating four figures: the poet-speaker himself, his friend, his mistress, and a rival poet. The order of events in this tangled relationship is not what the poet wishes to describe; instead, he touches upon this situation from time to time as he explores his own reaction to love in its various aspects.

The poet's relationship to his friend is a vulnerable one. This friend to whom he writes is aristocratic, handsome, and younger than he is. The poet is beholden to this friend as a sponsor and must consider himself as subservient, no matter how deep their mutual affection. Even at its happiest, their relationship is hierarchical. The poet abases himself in order to extol his friend's beauty and virtues (sonnets 52–54, 105–106). He confesses that his love would be idolatry, except that the friend's goodness excels all poetic hyperbole. As the older of the two, the poet sententiously urges his young friend to marry and eternize his beauty through the engendering of children (sonnets 1–17). Such a course, he argues, is the surest way to conquer devouring Time, the enemy of all earthly beauty and love. Yet elsewhere the poet exalts his own art as the surest defense against Time (sonnets 55, 60, 63–65, etc.). These conclusions are nominally contradictory, offering procreation in one instance and poetry in another as the best hope for immortality, but thematically the two are obviously related. In even the happiest of the sonnets, such as those giving thanks for "the marriage of true minds" (116, 123), the consciousness of devouring Time is inescapable. If love and celebratory poetry can sometimes triumph over Time, the victory is all the more precious because it is achieved in the face of such odds.

Love and perfect friendship are a refuge for the poet faced with hostile fortune and an indifferent world. He is too often "in disgrace with fortune and men's eyes" (sonnet 29), oppressed by his own failings, saddened by the facile success of opportunists (sonnets 66–68), ashamed of having sold himself cheap in his own profession (sonnets 110–111). If taken biographically, this could mean that Shakespeare was not happy about his career as actor and playwright, but the motif makes complete sense in the sonnet sequence without resort to biography. A biographical reading also raises the question of homosexual attraction, as urged recently anew by Joseph Pequigney in his *Such Is My Love* (University of Chicago Press, 1985). The bawdy reference in sonnet 20.12 to the friend's possession of "one thing to my purpose nothing" would seem to militate against the idea of a consummated homosexual relationship, while conversely many sonnets (such as 138) do point to the poet's consummation with his mistress. Still, the bond between poet and friend is extraordinarily strong, and certainly there is a danger that traditional scholarship has minimized the erotic bond between the poet and his friend out of a distaste for the idea. Occasional absences torture the poet with the physical separation, even though he realizes that pure love of the spirit ought not to be hampered by distance or time (sonnets 43–51). The absence is especially painful when the poet must confess his own disloyalty (sonnets 117–118). The chronology of these absences cannot be worked out satisfactorily, but the haunting theme of separation is incessant and overwhelming. By extension, it includes the fear of separation through death (sonnets 71–73, 126). The concern with absence is closely related to the poet's obsession with devouring Time.

All the poet's misfortunes would be bearable if love were constant, but his dependency on the aristocratic friend leaves him at the mercy of that friend's changeable moods. The poet must not complain when his wellborn friend entertains a rival poet (sonnets 78–86) or forms other emotional attachments, even with the poet's own mistress (sonnets 40–42). These disloyalties evoke outbursts of jealousy. The poet vacillates between forgiveness and recrimination. Sometimes even his forgiveness is self-loathing, in which the poet confesses he would take back the friend on any terms (sonnets 93–95). At times the poet grovels, conceding that he deserves no better treatment (sonnets 57–58), but at other times his stored-up resentment bursts forth (sonnets 93–95). The poet's fears, though presented in no clear chronological order, run the gamut from a fatalistic sense that

rejection will come one day (sonnet 49) to an abject and bitter final farewell (sonnet 87). Sometimes he is tormented by jealousy (sonnet 61) and sometimes by self-hate (sonnets 88–89).

The sonnets addressed to the poet's mistress, the "Dark Lady," similarly convey fear, self-abasement, and a panicky awareness of loss of self-control. In rare moments of happiness, the poet praises her dark features as proof of her being a real woman, not a Petrarchan goddess (sonnet 130). Too often, however, her lack of ideal beauty reminds the poet of his irrational enchantment (sonnets 148–150). She is tyrannous, disdainful, spiteful, disloyal, a "female evil" (sonnet 144) who has tempted away from the poet his better self, his friend. The poet is distressed not so much by her perfidy as by his own self-betrayal; he sees bitterly that he offends his nobler reason by his attachment to the rebellious flesh. He worships what others abhor and perjures himself by swearing to what he knows to be false (sonnets 150–152). His only hope for escape is to punish his flesh and renounce the vanity of all worldly striving (sonnet 146), but this solution evades him as he plunges helplessly back into the perverse enslavement of a sickened appetite.

This sketch of only some themes of the sequence may suggest the range and yet the interconnection of Shakespeare's meditations on love, friendship, and poetry. Patterns are visible, even if the exact chronology (never important in the Elizabethan sonnet sequence) cannot be determined. The pattern suggests a pivotal role for the sonnets in Shakespeare's development, as Richard Wheeler has urged in his *Shakespeare's Development* (University of California Press, 1981): the early sonnets about love and marriage pursue relationships central to the comedies, whereas subsequent sonnets move with increasing intensity toward the portrayal of promiscuity and degradation in erotic love and toward new assaults upon the binding power of friendship in such a way as to anticipate the darker vision of the tragedies. The playful and unthreatening heroine of the comedies gives way to a dark lady who inspires in the poet a compulsive and humiliating self-hatred; mutuality in friendship finds itself threatened by a one-sided relationship in which the abasement of the poet is answered by the indifference and infidelity of the friend. It as though in the sonnets Shakespeare opened the Pandora's box of hazardous erotic entanglements he was to dramatize in his late plays.

Shakespeare's concern with patterning is equally evident in matters of versification and imagery. The sonnets are written throughout in the "Shakespearean" or English form, *abab cdcd efef gg*. (Sonnet 126, written entirely in couplets, is an exception, perhaps because it was intended as the envoi to the series addressed to the poet's friend.) This familiar sonnet form, introduced by Wyatt and developed by Sidney, differs markedly from the octave-sestet division of the Petrarchan, or Italian, sonnet. The English form of three quatrains and a concluding couplet lends itself to a step-by-step development of idea and image, culminating in an epigrammatic two-line conclusion that may summarize the thought of the preceding twelve lines or give a sententious interpretation of the images developed up to this point. Sonnet 7 pursues the image of the sun at morning, noon, and evening through three quatrains, one for each phase of the day, and then in the couplet "applies" the image to the friend's unwillingness to beget children. Sonnet 29 moves from resentment of misfortune to a rejoicing in the friend's love and rhetorically mirrors this sudden elevation of mood in the image of the lark "at break of day arising / From sullen earth." Shakespeare's rhetorical and imagistic devices exploit the sonnet structure he inherited and perfected, and remind us again of the strong element of convention and artifice in these supremely "personal" sonnets. The recurring images—the canker on the rose, the pleading of a case at law, the seasonal rhythms of summer and winter, the alternations of day and night, the harmonies and dissonances of music—also testify to the artistic unity of the whole and to the artist's extraordinary discipline in evoking a sense of helpless loss of self-control.

Sonnets

To the Only Begetter of These Ensuing Sonnets

Mr. W. H.

All Happiness and That Eternity Promised
by Our Ever-living Poet
Wisheth the Well-wishing Adventurer in
Setting Forth

T. T.

1

From fairest creatures we desire increase,
That thereby beauty's rose might never die,
But as the riper should by time decease,
His tender heir might bear his memory;   4
But thou, contracted to thine own bright eyes,
Feed'st thy light's flame with self-substantial fuel,
Making a famine where abundance lies,
Thyself thy foe, to thy sweet self too cruel.   8
Thou that art now the world's fresh ornament
And only herald to the gaudy spring,
Within thine own bud buriest thy content,
And, tender churl, mak'st waste in niggarding.   12
    Pity the world, or else this glutton be:
    To eat the world's due, by the grave and thee.

2

When forty winters shall besiege thy brow
And dig deep trenches in thy beauty's field,
Thy youth's proud livery, so gazed on now,
Will be a tattered weed, of small worth held.   4
Then being asked where all thy beauty lies,
Where all the treasure of thy lusty days,
To say within thine own deep-sunken eyes
Were an all-eating shame and thriftless praise.   8
How much more praise deserved thy beauty's use
If thou couldst answer, "This fair child of mine
Shall sum my count and make my old excuse,"

1.1 increase procreation   **3 as** just as, while   **4 His** its, the ripening creation (including the young man).   **bear his memory** i.e., immortalize it by bearing its features   **5 contracted** (1) engaged, espoused (2) shrunk   **6 self-substantial** of your own substance   **10 only herald to** principal or unique messenger of   **11 thy content** (1) that which is contained in you; potential fatherhood (2) contentment   **12 mak'st . . . niggarding** squander your substance by being miserly. (An oxymoron, like *tender churl*, "youthful old miser.")   **14 the world's due** i.e., the offspring you owe to posterity.   **by . . . thee** (consumed) by death and by your willfully remaining childless
2.2 trenches i.e., wrinkles.   **field** (1) meadow (2) battlefield (3) heraldic background   **4 weed** garment (with a play on a *weed* growing in *beauty's field,* line 2)   **6 lusty** (1) vigorous (2) lustful   **7 deep-sunken** i.e., with age   **8 all-eating shame** shameful gluttony and one that would consume you with shame.   **thriftless praise** (1) praise of extravagance (2) idle praise   **9 deserved . . . use** would the proper investment and employment of your beauty deserve   **11 sum . . . excuse** even my account and make amends (for growing old or for consuming beauty during my life) in my old age

Proving his beauty by succession thine.   12
    This were to be new made when thou art old,
    And see thy blood warm when thou feel'st it cold.

3

Look in thy glass, and tell the face thou viewest
Now is the time that face should form another,
Whose fresh repair if now thou not renewest
Thou dost beguile the world, unbless some mother.   4
For where is she so fair whose uneared womb
Disdains the tillage of thy husbandry?
Or who is he so fond will be the tomb
Of his self-love, to stop posterity?   8
Thou art thy mother's glass, and she in thee
Calls back the lovely April of her prime;
So thou through windows of thine age shalt see,
Despite of wrinkles, this thy golden time.   12
    But if thou live remembered not to be,
    Die single, and thine image dies with thee.

4

Unthrifty loveliness, why dost thou spend
Upon thyself thy beauty's legacy?
Nature's bequest gives nothing, but doth lend,
And being frank she lends to those are free.   4
Then, beauteous niggard, why dost thou abuse
The bounteous largess given thee to give?
Profitless usurer, why dost thou use
So great a sum of sums, yet canst not live?   8
For having traffic with thyself alone,
Thou of thyself thy sweet self dost deceive.
Then how, when Nature calls thee to be gone,
What acceptable audit canst thou leave?   12
    Thy unused beauty must be tombed with thee,
    Which, usèd, lives th' executor to be.

5

Those hours, that with gentle work did frame
The lovely gaze where every eye doth dwell,
Will play the tyrants to the very same
And that unfair which fairly doth excel;   4

For never-resting Time leads summer on
To hideous winter and confounds him there,
Sap checked with frost and lusty leaves quite gone,
Beauty o'ersnowed and bareness everywhere.   8
Then, were not summer's distillation left
A liquid prisoner pent in walls of glass,
Beauty's effect with beauty were bereft,
Nor it nor no remembrance what it was.   12
    But flowers distilled, though they with winter
      meet,
      Leese but their show; their substance still lives
      sweet.

6

Then let not winter's ragged hand deface
In thee thy summer ere thou be distilled.
Make sweet some vial; treasure thou some place
With beauty's treasure ere it be self-killed.   4
That use is not forbidden usury
Which happies those that pay the willing loan;
That's for thyself to breed another thee,
Or ten times happier, be it ten for one.   8
Ten times thyself were happier than thou art,
If ten of thine ten times refigured thee;
Then what could death do, if thou shouldst depart,
Leaving thee living in posterity?   12
    Be not self-willed, for thou art much too fair
    To be death's conquest and make worms thine
    heir.

7

Lo, in the orient when the gracious light
Lifts up his burning head, each under eye
Doth homage to his new-appearing sight,
Serving with looks his sacred majesty;   4
And having climbed the steep-up heavenly hill,
Resembling strong youth in his middle age,
Yet mortal looks adore his beauty still,
Attending on his golden pilgrimage;   8
But when from highmost pitch, with weary car,
Like feeble age, he reeleth from the day,

---

12 **thine** i.e., derived from you   13 **were** would be
3.1 glass mirror   3 **fresh repair** youthful condition   4 **beguile** cheat.
unbless some mother withhold the happiness of childbearing from
some woman   5 **uneared** untilled, uncultivated   6 **husbandry** cultivation (with obvious suggestion of "playing the husband")   7 **fond** foolish, (self-)loving.   **will be** i.e., that he is willing to be   9 **thy mother's glass** the image of your mother   11 **windows of thine age** i.e.,
eyes dimmed by advancing years   13 **remembered not to be** in such
a way as not to be remembered, without children
4.1 Unthrifty (1) prodigal (2) unavailing   2 **thy beauty's legacy** the
beauty you inherited (and should pass on to your children)   4 **frank**
liberal, bounteous.   **are free** who are generous   7 **use** (1) use up (2)
fail to invest for profit. (See sonnet 6.5 and note.)   8 **live** (1) have a
livelihood (2) live in your posterity   9 **traffic** commerce. (The commercial and financial metaphor hints at sexual self-fascination.)
10 deceive cheat   13 **unused** (1) unemployed (2) not invested for
profit   14 **lives** would live (in your son)
5.1 frame make   2 **gaze** object of gazes   3 **play . . . to** oppress
4 **unfair** make unlovely.   **fairly** (1) in beauty (2) truly, honestly

5 **leads summer on** (1) guides the steps of summer (2) lures summer
6 **confounds** destroys   7 **lusty** vigorous   9 **summer's distillation** distilled perfume of flowers   10 **walls of glass** glass containers   11 **with
. . . bereft** would be lost along with beauty itself   12 **Nor it nor no**
(leaving behind) neither it (beauty) nor any   14 **Leese** lose.   **still** (1)
notwithstanding (2) always
6.1 ragged rough   3 **vial** (With suggestion of a womb.)   **treasure** enrich   5 **use** lending money at interest   6 **happies** makes happy.   **pay
. . . loan** willingly borrow on these terms and repay the loan
7 **That's . . . thee** i.e., such would be the case if you were to sire a
child like you   8 **Or . . . one** i.e., or indeed the happy mother (of
line 6) would be ten times happier were she to bear you ten children
instead of one. (*Ten for one* alludes to the highest legal rate of interest, one for ten.)   9 **Ten . . . art** i.e., ten children of yours would be
a tenfold blessing and would make you happier   10 **refigured** dupli-
cated, copied (producing one hundred grandchildren)   13 **self-willed**
(1) obstinate (2) bequeathed to self
7.1 orient east.   **light** i.e., sun   2 **under** earthly   9 **pitch** highest
point (as of a falcon's flight before it attacks).   **car** chariot (of the
sun-god)

The eyes, 'fore duteous, now converted are
From his low tract and look another way.   12
    So thou, thyself outgoing in thy noon,
    Unlooked on diest, unless thou get a son.

8

Music to hear, why hear'st thou music sadly?
Sweets with sweets war not, joy delights in joy.
Why lov'st thou that which thou receiv'st not gladly,
Or else receiv'st with pleasure thine annoy?   4
If the true concord of well-tunèd sounds,
By unions married, do offend thine ear,
They do but sweetly chide thee, who confounds
In singleness the parts that thou shouldst bear.   8
Mark how one string, sweet husband to another,
Strikes each in each by mutual ordering,
Resembling sire and child and happy mother
Who, all in one, one pleasing note do sing;   12
    Whose speechless song, being many, seeming one,
    Sings this to thee: "Thou single wilt prove none."

9

Is it for fear to wet a widow's eye
That thou consum'st thyself in single life?
Ah, if thou issueless shalt hap to die,
The world will wail thee like a makeless wife.   4
The world will be thy widow and still weep
That thou no form of thee hast left behind,
When every private widow well may keep,
By children's eyes, her husband's shape in mind.   8
Look what an unthrift in the world doth spend
Shifts but his place, for still the world enjoys it;
But beauty's waste hath in the world an end,
And, kept unused, the user so destroys it.   12
    No love toward others in that bosom sits
    That on himself such murd'rous shame commits.

10

For shame, deny that thou bear'st love to any,
Who for thyself art so unprovident!
Grant, if thou wilt, thou art beloved of many,
But that thou none lov'st is most evident;   4

For thou art so possessed with murd'rous hate
That 'gainst thyself thou stick'st not to conspire,
Seeking that beauteous roof to ruinate
Which to repair should be thy chief desire.   8
O, change thy thought, that I may change my mind!
Shall hate be fairer lodged than gentle love?
Be, as thy presence is, gracious and kind,
Or to thyself at least kindhearted prove: 12
    Make thee another self, for love of me,
    That beauty still may live in thine or thee.

11

As fast as thou shalt wane, so fast thou grow'st
In one of thine from that which thou departest;
And that fresh blood which youngly thou bestow'st
Thou mayst call thine when thou from youth
    convertest.   4
Herein lives wisdom, beauty, and increase;
Without this, folly, age, and cold decay.
If all were minded so, the times should cease
And threescore year would make the world away.   8
Let those whom Nature hath not made for store,
Harsh, featureless, and rude, barrenly perish;
Look whom she best endowed she gave the more,
Which bounteous gift thou shouldst in bounty cherish.   12
    She carved thee for her seal, and meant thereby
    Thou shouldst print more, not let that copy die.

12

When I do count the clock that tells the time,
And see the brave day sunk in hideous night;
When I behold the violet past prime,
And sable curls all silvered o'er with white;   4
When lofty trees I see barren of leaves
Which erst from heat did canopy the herd,
And summer's green, all girded up in sheaves,
Borne on the bier with white and bristly beard,   8
Then of thy beauty do I question make
That thou among the wastes of time must go,
Since sweets and beauties do themselves forsake
And die as fast as they see others grow;   12
    And nothing 'gainst Time's scythe can make
      defense
    Save breed, to brave him when he takes thee
      hence.

11 converted turned away   **12 tract** course   **14 get** beget
8.1 Music to hear i.e., you whom it is music to hear.   **sadly** gravely;
without joy   **4 thine annoy** what is harmful to you   **6 married** i.e.,
harmonized   **7–8 who . . . bear** you who destroy, by playing a single part only, the harmony (i.e., marriage) that you should sustain
9 sweet husband i.e., paired, as on the double strings of the lute, one
string vibrating sympathetically to the other   **10 each in each** i.e.,
with double resonance, sounding mutually   **13 Whose** i.e., the
strings'.   **being . . . one** i.e., making harmony out of several voices
14 Thou . . . none (Alludes to the proverb, "One is no number." The
single person who dies without posterity leaves nothing of himself behind.)
9.3 issueless without offspring   **4 makeless** mateless, i.e., widowed
5 still constantly, always   **7 private** individual, as distinguished from
the whole world   **8 By** by means of   **9 Look what** whatever.   **unthrift** spendthrift   **10 his** its.   **enjoys** uses, keeps in circulation
12 user i.e., he who should use it (with a suggestion of a *usurer* who
is miserly)

10.6 thou stick'st you scruple   **9 thought** intention.   **my mind** my
opinion of you   **11 presence** appearance, bearing
11.1–2 thou grow'st . . . departest i.e., you survive in a child of
your own, though you leave the world behind   **3 youngly** in youth
4 thou . . . convertest you change from youth (to old age)   **7 minded
so** sharing your intention (to have no children).   **times** succeeding
generations   **8 year** years   **9 for store** as a source of supply
10 Harsh hard-favored.   **featureless** having no attractive features or
appearance.   **rude** rudely fashioned   **11 Look whom** whomever
13 seal stamp from which impressions are made
12.1 tells (1) announces (2) counts   **2 brave** splendid   **4 sable** black
6 erst formerly   **7 girded** bundled   **8 bier** i.e., harvest cart (but with
suggestion of funeral bier).   **beard** i.e., the tufted grain (but suggesting also a dead man laid out for burial)   **9 do . . . make** I discuss
with myself   **14 breed** begetting offspring.   **brave him** defy Time

13

O, that you were yourself! But, love, you are
No longer yours than you yourself here live.
Against this coming end you should prepare,
And your sweet semblance to some other give.   4
So should that beauty which you hold in lease
Find no determination; then you were
Yourself again after yourself's decease,
When your sweet issue your sweet form should bear.   8
Who lets so fair a house fall to decay,
Which husbandry in honor might uphold
Against the stormy gusts of winter's day
And barren rage of death's eternal cold?   12
       O, none but unthrifts! Dear my love, you know
       You had a father; let your son say so.

14

Not from the stars do I my judgment pluck,
And yet methinks I have astronomy—
But not to tell of good or evil luck,
Of plagues, of dearths, or seasons' quality;   4
Nor can I fortune to brief minutes tell,
'Pointing to each his thunder, rain, and wind,
Or say with princes if it shall go well
By oft predict that I in heaven find.   8
But from thine eyes my knowledge I derive,
And, constant stars, in them I read such art
As truth and beauty shall together thrive
If from thyself to store thou wouldst convert.   12
       Or else of thee this I prognosticate:
       Thy end is truth's and beauty's doom and date.

15

When I consider every thing that grows
Holds in perfection but a little moment,
That this huge stage presenteth naught but shows
Whereon the stars in secret influence comment;   4
When I perceive that men as plants increase,
Cheerèd and checked even by the selfsame sky,
Vaunt in their youthful sap, at height decrease,
And wear their brave state out of memory;   8

Then the conceit of this inconstant stay
Sets you most rich in youth before my sight,
Where wasteful Time debateth with Decay
To change your day of youth to sullied night;   12
       And, all in war with Time for love of you,
       As he takes from you I engraft you new.

16

But wherefore do not you a mightier way
Make war upon this bloody tyrant, Time,
And fortify yourself in your decay
With means more blessèd than my barren rhyme?   4
Now stand you on the top of happy hours,
And many maiden gardens yet unset
With virtuous wish would bear your living flowers,
Much liker than your painted counterfeit.   8
So should the lines of life that life repair
Which this time's pencil, or my pupil pen,
Neither in inward worth nor outward fair
Can make you live yourself in eyes of men.   12
       To give away yourself keeps yourself still,
       And you must live, drawn by your own sweet
       skill.

17

Who will believe my verse in time to come
If it were filled with your most high deserts?
Though yet, heaven knows, it is but as a tomb
Which hides your life and shows not half your parts.   4
If I could write the beauty of your eyes
And in fresh numbers number all your graces,
The age to come would say, "This poet lies;
Such heavenly touches ne'er touched earthly faces."   8
So should my papers, yellowed with their age,
Be scorned like old men of less truth than tongue,
And your true rights be termed a poet's rage
And stretchèd meter of an antique song.   12
       But were some child of yours alive that time,
       You should live twice, in it and in my rhyme.

13.1 **yourself** i.e., your eternal self, not vulnerable to Time's decay
2 **here** i.e., here on earth   3 **Against** in anticipation of   6 **determination** end   10 **husbandry** careful management (with a pun on "being a husband")
14.1 **my judgment pluck** derive my conclusions   2 **have astronomy** am skilled in astrology   4 **seasons' quality** what the weather of the seasons will be like   5 **fortune . . . tell** foretell events to the precise minute   6 **'Pointing** appointing, assigning.   **each** each minute.   **his** its   7 **Or . . . well** or say if things will go well for certain rulers
8 **oft predict** frequent predictions   10–11 **read . . . As** gather such learning as, in effect, that   12 **store** replenishment (through the begetting of children).   **convert** turn   14 **doom and date** limit of duration, destruction
15.2 **Holds in perfection** maintains its prime   3 **stage** i.e., the world
5 **as** like   6 **Cheerèd and checked** (1) urged on, nourished, and held back, starved (2) applauded and hissed   7 **Vaunt** boast, exult.   **sap** vigor.   **at height decrease** i.e., no sooner reach full maturity but they (humans) start to decline   8 **brave** splendid.   **out of memory** until forgotten

9 **conceit** notion.   **inconstant stay** mutable brief time (on earth)
11 **wasteful . . . Decay** i.e., Time and Decay contend to see who can ruin you fastest, or join forces to do so, debating between them the best procedure   13 **all in war** fighting with might and main   14 **engraft you new** renew you by grafting, infusing new life into you (by means of my verse)
16.4 **barren** (1) unable to produce offspring (2) poetically sterile
6 **unset** (1) unplanted (2) unimpregnated   7 **virtuous wish** desire that is still chaste   8 **liker** more resembling you.   **painted** rendered by art (including poetry), artificial.   **counterfeit** portrait   9 **lines of life** lineage, i.e., children (whose lineaments are more lifelike than lines of verse or of a portrait).   **10 this time's pencil** a portraiture done in this present age.   **pupil** apprenticed, inexpert   11 **fair** beauty   12 **live** survive as   13 **give away yourself** i.e., marry and beget children.
keeps preserves   14 **skill** i.e., artistry in reproducing yourself, mightier than the poet's pen
17.3 **yet** as yet   4 **parts** qualities   6 **numbers** verses   10 **of . . . tongue** more garrulous than truthful   11 **rage** exaggerated inspiration
12 **stretchèd meter** overstrained poetry, poetic license

18

Shall I compare thee to a summer's day?
Thou art more lovely and more temperate.
Rough winds do shake the darling buds of May,
And summer's lease hath all too short a date.   4
Sometimes too hot the eye of heaven shines,
And often is his gold complexion dimmed;
And every fair from fair sometimes declines,
By chance or nature's changing course untrimmed.   8
But thy eternal summer shall not fade
Nor lose possession of that fair thou ow'st;
Nor shall Death brag thou wanderest in his shade,
When in eternal lines to time thou grow'st.   12
        So long as men can breathe or eyes can see,
        So long lives this, and this gives life to thee.

19

Devouring Time, blunt thou the lion's paws,
And make the earth devour her own sweet brood;
Pluck the keen teeth from the fierce tiger's jaws,
And burn the long-lived phoenix in her blood;   4
Make glad and sorry seasons as thou fleet'st,
And do whate'er thou wilt, swift-footed Time,
To the wide world and all her fading sweets.
But I forbid thee one most heinous crime: 8
O, carve not with thy hours my love's fair brow,
Nor draw no lines there with thine antique pen;
Him in thy course untainted do allow
For beauty's pattern to succeeding men.   12
        Yet, do thy worst, old Time. Despite thy wrong,
        My love shall in my verse ever live young.

20

A woman's face with Nature's own hand painted
Hast thou, the master-mistress of my passion;
A woman's gentle heart, but not acquainted
With shifting change, as is false women's fashion;   4
An eye more bright than theirs, less false in rolling,
Gilding the object whereupon it gazeth;
A man in hue, all hues in his controlling,
Which steals men's eyes and women's souls amazeth.   8
And for a woman wert thou first created,

Till Nature, as she wrought thee, fell a-doting,
And by addition me of thee defeated,
By adding one thing to my purpose nothing.   12
        But since she pricked thee out for women's
        pleasure,
        Mine be thy love and thy love's use their treasure.

21

So is it not with me as with that muse,
Stirred by a painted beauty to his verse,
Who heaven itself for ornament doth use
And every fair with his fair doth rehearse,   4
Making a couplement of proud compare
With sun and moon, with earth and sea's rich gems,
With April's firstborn flowers, and all things rare
That heaven's air in this huge rondure hems.   8
O, let me, true in love, but truly write,
And then, believe me, my love is as fair
As any mother's child, though not so bright
As those gold candles fixed in heaven's air.   12
        Let them say more that like of hearsay well;
        I will not praise that purpose not to sell.

22

My glass shall not persuade me I am old
So long as youth and thou are of one date;
But when in thee Time's furrows I behold,
Then look I death my days should expiate.   4
For all that beauty that doth cover thee
Is but the seemly raiment of my heart,
Which in thy breast doth live, as thine in me.
How can I then be elder than thou art?   8
O, therefore, love, be of thyself so wary
As I, not for myself, but for thee will,
Bearing thy heart, which I will keep so chary
As tender nurse her babe from faring ill.   12
        Presume not on thy heart when mine is slain;
        Thou gav'st me thine, not to give back again.

10 **fell a-doting** fell infatuatedly in love with you and so went mildly crazy   11 **defeated** defrauded, deprived   12 **to my purpose nothing** out of line with my wishes   13 **pricked** designated (with bawdy suggestion; the *thing* in line 12 is a phallus).   **for women's pleasure** to give (sexual) pleasure to women   14 **and . . . treasure** and let women enjoy the profits of love's *use* ("usury") as their treasure (with bawdy suggestion that the lover is to use the *treasure* of their bodies)
21.1 **muse** i.e., poet   2 **Stirred** inspired.   **painted** artificial, created by cosmetics   3 **Who . . . use** who does not scruple to invoke heaven itself as an ornament of praise for his mistress   4 **every . . . rehearse** compares his lady fair with every lovely thing   5 **Making . . . compare** joining (her) in proud comparison   8 **rondure** sphere.   **hems** encloses, encircles   12 **gold candles** i.e., stars. (The trite and exaggerated metaphor is of the sort the poet hopes to eschew.)   13 **like . . . well** like to deal in secondhand or trite expressions   14 **I will . . . sell** I, who do not intend to sell as a merchant might, will accordingly not indulge in extravagant and empty praise
22.1 **glass** mirror   2 **of one date** of an age, i.e., young   4 **look I I** foresee that.   **expiate** end   6 **seemly** becoming   10 **will** i.e., will take wary care of myself for your sake   11 **Bearing** since I bear.   **chary** carefully   13 **Presume not on** do not expect to receive back

18.4 **lease** allotted time.   **date** duration   5 **eye** i.e., sun   7 **fair from fair** beautiful thing from beauty   8 **untrimmed** stripped of ornament and beauty   10 **fair thou ow'st** beauty you own   12 **lines** i.e., of poetry.   **to . . . grow'st** you become incorporated into time, engrafted upon it   14 **this** i.e., this sonnet
19.4 **phoenix** legendary bird reputed to live for hundreds of years and then to be consumed alive (*in her blood*) in its own ashes, from which it is then reborn   5 **sorry** i.e., miserable, uncomfortable.   **thou fleet'st** you fleet, hurry   10 **antique** (1) old (2) antic, capricious, fantastic   11 **untainted** (1) unhit in tilting (2) unsullied   14 **My love** (1) my beloved (2) my affection for him
20.1 **with . . . hand** i.e., naturally beautiful   2 **master-mistress** i.e., both master and mistress, male and female.   **passion** love   4 **as . . . fashion** as is the way with women, who are false by nature   5 **rolling** i.e., roving   6 **Gilding** causing to shine brightly   7 **A man . . . controlling** one who has a manly appearance surpassing all other forms (suggesting, too, that he captivates all beholders and that his *hue* is womanly as well as manly)

23

As an unperfect actor on the stage
Who with his fear is put beside his part,
Or some fierce thing replete with too much rage,
Whose strength's abundance weakens his own heart,   4
So I, for fear of trust, forget to say
The perfect ceremony of love's rite,
And in mine own love's strength seem to decay,
O'ercharged with burden of mine own love's might.   8
O, let my books be then the eloquence
And dumb presagers of my speaking breast,
Who plead for love and look for recompense
More than that tongue that more hath more expressed.   12
    O, learn to read what silent love hath writ.
    To hear with eyes belongs to love's fine wit.

24

Mine eye hath played the painter and hath stelled
Thy beauty's form in table of my heart;
My body is the frame wherein 'tis held,
And perspective it is best painter's art.   4
For through the painter must you see his skill
To find where your true image pictured lies,
Which in my bosom's shop is hanging still,
That hath his windows glazèd with thine eyes.   8
Now see what good turns eyes for eyes have done:
Mine eyes have drawn thy shape, and thine for me
Are windows to my breast, wherethrough the sun
Delights to peep, to gaze therein on thee.   12
    Yet eyes this cunning want to grace their art:
    They draw but what they see, know not the heart.

25

Let those who are in favor with their stars
Of public honor and proud titles boast,
Whilst I, whom fortune of such triumph bars,
Unlooked for joy in that I honor most.   4

Great princes' favorites their fair leaves spread
But as the marigold at the sun's eye,
And in themselves their pride lies burièd,
For at a frown they in their glory die.   8
The painful warrior famousèd for fight,
After a thousand victories once foiled,
Is from the book of honor rasèd quite,
And all the rest forgot for which he toiled.   12
    Then happy I, that love and am beloved
    Where I may not remove nor be removed.

26

Lord of my love, to whom in vassalage
Thy merit hath my duty strongly knit,
To thee I send this written embassage
To witness duty, not to show my wit—   4
Duty so great, which wit so poor as mine
May make seem bare, in wanting words to show it,
But that I hope some good conceit of thine
In thy soul's thought, all naked, will bestow it;   8
Till whatsoever star that guides my moving
Points on me graciously with fair aspect,
And puts apparel on my tattered loving
To show me worthy of thy sweet respect.   12
    Then may I dare to boast how I do love thee;
    Till then not show my head where thou mayst
        prove me.

27

Weary with toil, I haste me to my bed,
The dear repose for limbs with travel tirèd;
But then begins a journey in my head,
To work my mind when body's work's expirèd.   4
For then my thoughts, from far where I abide,
Intend a zealous pilgrimage to thee,
And keep my drooping eyelids open wide,
Looking on darkness which the blind do see;   8
Save that my soul's imaginary sight
Presents thy shadow to my sightless view,
Which, like a jewel hung in ghastly night,
Makes black night beauteous and her old face new.   12
    Lo, thus by day my limbs, by night my mind,
    For thee and for myself no quiet find.

23.1 unperfect one who has not learned his lines **2 beside** out of
3 Or . . . rage i.e., or some wild animal overfilled with ungovernable
rage **4 heart** courage **5 for . . . trust** mistrusting myself and fearful
of not being trusted. **forget** forget how\ **9 books** (Possibly refers to
the sonnets or to *Venus and Adonis* and *The Rape of Lucrece* or, more
generally, the works of the persona poet.) **10 dumb presagers** silent
messengers or presenters **12 that tongue** the tongue of some rival
speaker. **more hath more expressed** has more often or more fully
said more **14 fine wit** sharp intelligence
24.1 played acted the part of. **stelled** fixed, installed; or perhaps
steeled, i.e., engraved. (The Quarto reads *steeld*.) **2 table** tablet,
wooden panel used for painting **3 frame** (1) picture frame (2) bodily
frame **4 perspective** an artist's method of producing a distorted picture that looks right only from an oblique point of view, or, a painter's technique used to produce the illusion of reality, or, the science
of optics **5 For . . . skill** i.e., you must look through the eyes of me,
the skillful painter **7 bosom's shop** i.e., heart **8 his** its. **glazèd** fitted with glass, paned. (The friend, looking into the poet's eyes, where
his own eyes are reflected, sees into the poet's heart.) **13 this cunning want** lack this skill. **grace** enhance **14 know not** do not perceive the thoughts of. (The poet cannot see into the heart of the
friend.)
25.3 of from **4 Unlooked for** (1) unexpectedly (2) out of the public
eye. **that** that which

5 their . . . spread i.e., flourish, blossom, prosper **6 But** only
7 lies burièd i.e., will die with the ending of their brief glory **8 a
frown** (1) a prince's frown (2) a cloud obscuring the sun **9 painful**
enduring much, striving. **famousèd** renowned. **fight** (Reads *worth*
in the 1609 Quarto; some editors retain and emend *quite* in line 11 to
forth. Other editors prefer *might*.) **11 rasèd** erased (or *razèd*, scraped
out) **12 the rest** i.e., his *thousand victories* **14 remove** i.e., be unfaithful. **removed** i.e., removed from favor
26.1 vassalage allegiance **4 witness** bear witness to. **wit** skill, literary ingenuity **5 wit** intelligence and skill **6 wanting** lacking
7 good conceit good conception, or, favorable opinion **8 all naked**
i.e., poor verse though it is. **bestow** give lodging to **9 moving** life
and deeds **10 Points on** directs its rays at. **aspect** influence (as of a
star) **14 prove** test
27.2 travel (with connotation also of *travail*; spelled *trauaill* in the
Quarto) **5 from far** i.e., far away from you **6 Intend** (1) set out
upon (2) have purposefully in mind **9 Save** except **10 thy shadow**
the image of you **14 For** on account of

28

How can I then return in happy plight
That am debarred the benefit of rest?
When day's oppression is not eased by night,
But day by night, and night by day, oppressed?   4
And each, though enemies to either's reign,
Do in consent shake hands to torture me,
The one by toil, the other to complain
How far I toil, still farther off from thee.   8
I tell the day, to please him, thou art bright
And dost him grace when clouds do blot the heaven;
So flatter I the swart-complexioned night,
When sparkling stars twire not, thou gild'st the even.   12
        But day doth daily draw my sorrows longer,
        And night doth nightly make grief's strength
            seem stronger.

29

When, in disgrace with fortune and men's eyes,
I all alone beweep my outcast state,
And trouble deaf heaven with my bootless cries,
And look upon myself and curse my fate,   4
Wishing me like to one more rich in hope,
Featured like him, like him with friends possessed,
Desiring this man's art and that man's scope,
With what I most enjoy contented least;   8
Yet in these thoughts myself almost despising,
Haply I think on thee, and then my state,
Like to the lark at break of day arising
From sullen earth, sings hymns at heaven's gate;   12
        For thy sweet love remembered such wealth brings
        That then I scorn to change my state with kings.

30

When to the sessions of sweet silent thought
I summon up remembrance of things past,
I sigh the lack of many a thing I sought,
And with old woes new wail my dear time's waste.   4
Then can I drown an eye, unused to flow,
For precious friends hid in death's dateless night,
And weep afresh love's long since canceled woe,
And moan th' expense of many a vanished sight.   8

Then can I grieve at grievances foregone,
And heavily from woe to woe tell o'er
The sad account of fore-bemoanèd moan,
Which I new pay as if not paid before.   12
        But if the while I think on thee, dear friend,
        All losses are restored and sorrows end.

31

Thy bosom is endearèd with all hearts,
Which I by lacking have supposèd dead,
And there reigns love and all love's loving parts,
And all those friends which I thought burièd.   4
How many a holy and obsequious tear
Hath dear religious love stol'n from mine eye
As interest of the dead, which now appear
But things removed that hidden in thee lie!   8
Thou art the grave where buried love doth live,
Hung with the trophies of my lovers gone,
Who all their parts of me to thee did give;
That due of many now is thine alone.   12
        Their images I loved I view in thee,
        And thou, all they, hast all the all of me.

32

If thou survive my well-contented day
When that churl Death my bones with dust shall cover,
And shalt by fortune once more re-survey
These poor rude lines of thy deceasèd lover,   4
Compare them with the bettering of the time,
And though they be outstripped by every pen,
Reserve them for my love, not for their rhyme,
Exceeded by the height of happier men.   8
O, then vouchsafe me but this loving thought:
"Had my friend's Muse grown with this growing age,
A dearer birth than this his love had brought
To march in ranks of better equipage;   12
        But since he died and poets better prove,
        Theirs for their style I'll read, his for his love."

28.4 **But . . . oppressed** i.e., but experiencing sleeplessness at night and fatigue during the day   6 **in . . . hands** i.e., come to a mutual agreement   7 **the other to complain** i.e., the night by causing me to complain   10 **And . . . heaven** i.e., and that you shine in place of the sun when the sun is overclouded   11 **So flatter I** similarly I gratify.   **swart** dark   12 **When . . . even** i.e., by saying that, when sparkling stars do not twinkle or peep out, you make bright the evening
29.3 **bootless** useless   4 **look upon myself** consider my predicament   5 **more rich in hope** with better prospects of success   6 **Featured** formed, i.e., having good looks.   **like him, like him** like a second man, like a third   7 **art** literary skill, learning.   **scope** range of powers   8 **most enjoy** possess most securely and take greatest pleasure in   10 **state** state of mind   14 **change** exchange
30.1 **sessions** (The metaphor is that of a court of law, continued in *summon up*, line 2.)   3 **sigh** sigh for   4 **new . . . waste** lament anew the wasting of precious time or time's erosion of those things held precious   5 **unused to flow** not prone to weep   6 **dateless** endless   7 **canceled** paid in full (by grieving)   8 **expense** loss, expenditure.   **sight** (1) something previously seen (2) sigh

9 **grievances foregone** sorrows past   10 **heavily** sadly.   **tell** count   11 **The sad . . . moan** the distressing total of previously uttered laments
31.1 **endearèd with all hearts** (1) beloved by all (2) made dear to me by representing and including those I have loved   2 **lacking** not having   3 **parts** attributes   5 **obsequious** suitable to mourning   6 **religious** dutiful, reverent   7 **interest of** that which is rightfully due to.   **which** who   8 **But . . . lie** i.e., no more than absent persons (now dead), whose best qualities are to be found concealed in you   10 **lovers** loved ones, friends   11 **parts** shares   12 **That due of many** that which was the due of many   13 **I loved** which I loved   14 **all they** (you) who comprise all of them
32.1 **my . . . day** i.e., the day of my death, which will content me well   3 **fortune** chance   4 **rude** unpolished.   **lover** friend   5 **bettering** i.e., improved writing, greater cultural sophistication   7 **Reserve** preserve.   **for my love** (1) out of love for me (2) for the sake of my love for you.   **rhyme** i.e., poetic skill   8 **height** superiority, highest achievement.   **happier** more gifted or fortunate   9 **vouchsafe me but** deign to bestow on me just   11 **dearer birth** i.e., better poem, better artistic creation   12 **better equipage** i.e., more finely wrought verse   13 **better prove** turn out to be superior

33

Full many a glorious morning have I seen
Flatter the mountaintops with sovereign eye,
Kissing with golden face the meadows green,
Gilding pale streams with heavenly alchemy;   4
Anon permit the basest clouds to ride
With ugly rack on his celestial face,
And from the forlorn world his visage hide,
Stealing unseen to west with this disgrace.   8
Even so my sun one early morn did shine
With all-triumphant splendor on my brow.
But out, alack! He was but one hour mine;
The region cloud hath masked him from me now.   12
   Yet him for this my love no whit disdaineth;
   Suns of the world may stain when heaven's sun
    staineth.

34

Why didst thou promise such a beauteous day
And make me travel forth without my cloak,
To let base clouds o'ertake me in my way,
Hiding thy bravery in their rotten smoke?   4
'Tis not enough that through the cloud thou break,
To dry the rain on my storm-beaten face,
For no man well of such a salve can speak
That heals the wound and cures not the disgrace.   8
Nor can thy shame give physic to my grief;
Though thou repent, yet I have still the loss.
Th' offender's sorrow lends but weak relief
To him that bears the strong offense's cross.   12
   Ah, but those tears are pearl which thy love sheds,
   And they are rich, and ransom all ill deeds.

35

No more be grieved at that which thou hast done.
Roses have thorns, and silver fountains mud,
Clouds and eclipses stain both moon and sun,
And loathsome canker lives in sweetest bud.   4
All men make faults, and even I in this,
Authorizing thy trespass with compare,
Myself corrupting, salving thy amiss,
Excusing thy sins more than thy sins are.   8
For to thy sensual fault I bring in sense—

Thy adverse party is thy advocate—
And 'gainst myself a lawful plea commence.
Such civil war is in my love and hate   12
   That I an accessary needs must be
   To that sweet thief which sourly robs from me.

36

Let me confess that we two must be twain,
Although our undivided loves are one;
So shall those blots that do with me remain,
Without thy help, by me be borne alone.   4
In our two loves there is but one respect,
Though in our lives a separable spite,
Which, though it alter not love's sole effect,
Yet doth it steal sweet hours from love's delight.   8
I may not evermore acknowledge thee,
Lest my bewailèd guilt should do thee shame,
Nor thou with public kindness honor me
Unless thou take that honor from thy name.   12
   But do not so; I love thee in such sort
   As, thou being mine, mine is thy good report.

37

As a decrepit father takes delight
To see his active child do deeds of youth,
So I, made lame by Fortune's dearest spite,
Take all my comfort of thy worth and truth.   4
For whether beauty, birth, or wealth, or wit,
Or any of these all, or all, or more,
Entitled in thy parts do crownèd sit,
I make my love engrafted to this store.   8
So then I am not lame, poor, nor despised,
Whilst that this shadow doth such substance give
That I in thy abundance am sufficed
And by a part of all thy glory live.   12
   Look what is best, that best I wish in thee.
   This wish I have; then ten times happy me!

38

How can my Muse want subject to invent
While thou dost breathe, that pour'st into my verse
Thine own sweet argument, too excellent

33.1 Full very   **5 Anon** soon afterward.   **basest** darkest; also, far below the royal glory of the sun in dignity and in altitude   **6 rack** mass
of cloud scudding before the wind   **12 region** of the upper air
14 Suns i.e., great men (with a pun on *sons of the world*, "mortal
men").   **stain** grow dim, be obscured, soiled.   **staineth** is clouded
over
34.3 To only to   **4 bravery** finery.   **rotten smoke** foul vapors   **8 disgrace** i.e., the scar, the disfigurement caused by his friend's neglect or
harsh treatment; the *loss* mentioned in line 10   **9 shame** repentance
for the wrong done.   **physic** remedy   **12 cross** affliction
35.3 stain dim, obscure   **4 canker** cankerworm   **6 Authorizing** sanctioning, justifying.   **compare** comparisons (as in this sonnet)   **7 Myself . . . amiss** excusing your misdeed, thereby bringing blame on
myself   **8 Excusing . . . are** going further to excuse your sins than
they warrant   **9 For . . . sense** i.e., I reason away your fleshly offenses with sophistical justifications

10 Thy . . . advocate I who profess to be your accuser find myself,
instead, pleading your case   **13 That . . . be** that I am compelled (by
my love) to be a guilty accomplice
36.1 twain parted   **3 blots** defects, stains of dishonor   **5 but one respect** a mutual regard, singleness of attitude   **6 separable spite** spiteful separation   **7 sole** unique   **9 not evermore acknowledge** nevermore admit my acquaintance with   **12 Unless . . . from** without
consequent loss of honor   **13 in such sort** in such a way   **14 As
. . . report** that since you are mine, your good reputation sustains
me also
37.3 made lame handicapped in life.   **dearest** most bitter   **4 of** in,
from   **5 wit** intelligence   **7 Entitled . . . sit** sit enthroned in first
place among your qualities   **8 I make . . . store** I add my love to this
abundance (and thereby flourish by drawing on their strength)
10 shadow idea (in the platonic sense).   **substance** actuality
13 Look what whatever
38.1 want . . . invent lack something to write about   **2 that** you who
3 Thine . . . argument yourself as subject

For every vulgar paper to rehearse? 4
O, give thyself the thanks, if aught in me
Worthy perusal stand against thy sight,
For who's so dumb that cannot write to thee,
When thou thyself dost give invention light? 8
Be thou the tenth Muse, ten times more in worth
Than those old nine which rhymers invocate;
And he that calls on thee, let him bring forth
Eternal numbers to outlive long date. 12
　　If my slight Muse do please these curious days,
　　The pain be mine, but thine shall be the praise.

39

O, how thy worth with manners may I sing,
When thou art all the better part of me?
What can mine own praise to mine own self bring?
And what is 't but mine own when I praise thee? 4
Even for this let us divided live,
And our dear love lose name of single one,
That by this separation I may give
That due to thee which thou deserv'st alone. 8
O absence, what a torment wouldst thou prove,
Were it not thy sour leisure gave sweet leave
To entertain the time with thoughts of love,
Which time and thoughts so sweetly doth deceive, 12
　　And that thou teachest how to make one twain
　　By praising him here who doth hence remain!

40

Take all my loves, my love, yea, take them all;
What hast thou then more than thou hadst before?
No love, my love, that thou mayst true love call;
All mine was thine before thou hadst this more. 4
Then if for my love thou my love receivest,
I cannot blame thee for my love thou usest;
But yet be blamed if thou this self deceivest
By willful taste of what thyself refusest. 8
I do forgive thy robbery, gentle thief,
Although thou steal thee all my poverty;
And yet love knows it is a greater grief

To bear love's wrong than hate's known injury. 12
　　Lascivious grace, in whom all ill well shows,
　　Kill me with spites; yet we must not be foes.

41

Those pretty wrongs that liberty commits
When I am sometimes absent from thy heart,
Thy beauty and thy years full well befits,
For still temptation follows where thou art. 4
Gentle thou art, and therefore to be won;
Beauteous thou art, therefore to be assailed;
And when a woman woos, what woman's son
Will sourly leave her till he have prevailed? 8
Ay me, but yet thou mightst my seat forbear,
And chide thy beauty and thy straying youth,
Who lead thee in their riot even there
Where thou art forced to break a twofold truth: 12
　　Hers, by thy beauty tempting her to thee,
　　Thine, by thy beauty being false to me.

42

That thou hast her, it is not all my grief,
And yet it may be said I loved her dearly;
That she hath thee is of my wailing chief,
A loss in love that touches me more nearly. 4
Loving offenders, thus I will excuse ye:
Thou dost love her because thou know'st I love her,
And for my sake even so doth she abuse me,
Suff'ring my friend for my sake to approve her. 8
If I lose thee, my loss is my love's gain,
And, losing her, my friend hath found that loss;
Both find each other, and I lose both twain,
And both for my sake lay on me this cross. 12
　　But here's the joy: my friend and I are one.
　　Sweet flattery! Then she loves but me alone.

43

When most I wink, then do mine eyes best see,
For all the day they view things unrespected;
But when I sleep, in dreams they look on thee,
And, darkly bright, are bright in dark directed. 4
Then thou, whose shadow shadows doth make bright,

---

4 **vulgar paper** common piece of writing.　**rehearse** recite, repeat
5 in me of my writing　**6 stand against** meet　**7 dumb** silent, lacking
in subject　**12 numbers** verses.　**date** duration　**13 curious** critical
14 pain labor
39.1 with manners decently, becomingly　**3 mine own praise** praise
of myself　**5 Even for** precisely because of　**10 not** not that　**11 entertain** pass, occupy　**12 Which . . . deceive** (thoughts of love),
which sweetly beguile away time and (sad) thoughts　**13 that** were it
not that.　**make one twain** i.e., divide the beloved person into two,
one absent in reality and the other present in imagination　**14 praising him here** i.e., invoking his presence here through my praising of
him
40.1 all my loves (1) all those whom I love (2) all the love I have.
(The young man addressed has taken away the poet's mistress.)　**3 No
. . . call** i.e., any love more than you had already—my complete affection—cannot be called true love　**5 my love . . . my love** love of
me . . . her whom I love　**6 for** because.　**thou usest** you enjoy
(sexually)　**7 this self** i.e., me, your other self. (Often emended to
thyself.)　**8 By . . . refusest** i.e., by tasting sexual pleasures that your
best self would refuse (?)　**10 steal . . . poverty** take for your own the
poor little that I have

12 **known** undisguised　**13 Lascivious grace** i.e., you who are gracious even in your lasciviousness
41.1 pretty graciously committed, sportive.　**liberty** licentiousness
3 befits (The subject is *wrongs,* line 1.)　**4 still** constantly　**7–8 And
. . . prevailed** i.e., when a woman woos, what man can resist until
he has scored? (*He* is sometimes emended to "she.")　**9 seat** place,
that which belongs to me (i.e., my mistress)　**11 Who** which.　**riot**
debauchery　**12 twofold truth** i.e., her plighted love and your
plighted friendship
42.3 is . . . chief is chief cause of my lamentation　**7 abuse** betray,
wrong　**8 Suff'ring** allowing.　**approve** try, test (in a sexual sense)
9 my love's hers whom I love, my mistress's　**10 losing her** i.e., I losing her　**12 for my sake** as though out of love for me.　**cross** torment
14 flattery gratifying deception
43.1 wink close my eyes in sleep　**2 unrespected** unnoticed, unregarded; not deserving notice　**4 And . . . directed** and, able to see in
the darkness (though still shut), are directed toward your brightness in
the dark　**5 whose . . . bright** whose image makes darkness bright

How would thy shadow's form form happy show
To the clear day with thy much clearer light,
When to unseeing eyes thy shade shines so! 8
How would, I say, mine eyes be blessèd made
By looking on thee in the living day,
When in dead night thy fair imperfect shade
Through heavy sleep on sightless eyes doth stay! 12
    All days are nights to see till I see thee,
    And nights bright days when dreams do show
      thee me.

44

If the dull substance of my flesh were thought,
Injurious distance should not stop my way;
For then despite of space I would be brought,
From limits far remote, where thou dost stay. 4
No matter then although my foot did stand
Upon the farthest earth removed from thee;
For nimble thought can jump both sea and land
As soon as think the place where he would be. 8
But, ah, thought kills me that I am not thought,
To leap large lengths of miles when thou art gone,
But that, so much of earth and water wrought,
I must attend time's leisure with my moan, 12
    Receiving naught by elements so slow
    But heavy tears, badges of either's woe.

45

The other two, slight air and purging fire,
Are both with thee, wherever I abide;
The first my thought, the other my desire,
These present-absent with swift motion slide. 4
For when these quicker elements are gone
In tender embassy of love to thee,
My life, being made of four, with two alone
Sinks down to death, oppressed with melancholy; 8
Until life's composition be recured
By those swift messengers returned from thee,
Who even but now come back again, assured

Of thy fair health, recounting it to me. 12
    This told, I joy; but then no longer glad,
    I send them back again and straight grow sad.

46

Mine eye and heart are at a mortal war
How to divide the conquest of thy sight;
Mine eye my heart thy picture's sight would bar,
My heart mine eye the freedom of that right. 4
My heart doth plead that thou in him dost lie—
A closet never pierced with crystal eyes—
But the defendant doth that plea deny
And says in him thy fair appearance lies. 8
To 'cide this title is impanelèd
A quest of thoughts, all tenants to the heart,
And by their verdict is determinèd
The clear eye's moiety and the dear heart's part, 12
    As thus: mine eye's due is thy outward part,
    And my heart's right thy inward love of heart.

47

Betwixt mine eye and heart a league is took,
And each doth good turns now unto the other.
When that mine eye is famished for a look,
Or heart in love with sighs himself doth smother, 4
With my love's picture then my eye doth feast
And to the painted banquet bids my heart;
Another time mine eye is my heart's guest
And in his thoughts of love doth share a part. 8
So, either by thy picture or my love,
Thyself, away, are present still with me;
For thou no farther than my thoughts canst move,
And I am still with them and they with thee; 12
    Or, if they sleep, thy picture in my sight
    Awakes my heart to heart's and eye's delight.

48

How careful was I, when I took my way,
Each trifle under truest bars to thrust,
That to my use it might unusèd stay
From hands of falsehood, in sure wards of trust! 4
But thou, to whom my jewels trifles are,

6 thy shadow's . . . show the substance of the shadow, i.e., your presence, make a gladdening sight **8 unseeing eyes** i.e., closed eyes of the dreamer **11 imperfect** unsubstantial, indistinct as in a dream **12 stay** linger, dwell **13 All . . . to see** all days are gloomy to behold **14 thee me** you to me (but also suggesting "me to you")
44.1 dull heavy **4 limits** regions, bounds. **where** to the place where **6 farthest earth removed** that part of the earth farthest removed **8 he** i.e., thought **9 ah, thought** ah, the thought **11 so . . . wrought** i.e., I, compounded to such an extent of the heavier elements, earth and water. (The lighter elements are fire and air.) **12 attend time's leisure** i.e., wait until time has leisure to reunite us **13 by** from **14 badges** signs, tokens. **either's** i.e., both earth's and water's, because the earth is heavy and the sea is salt and wet, both like tears
45.1 other two i.e., of the four elements discussed in sonnet 44. **slight** insubstantial. **purging** purifying **4 present-absent** (1) now here and immediately gone (2) simultaneously both present and absent **7 life** living body. **two alone** i.e., earth and water **8 melancholy** a humor thought to be induced by an excess of earth and water **9 composition** proper balance among the four elements. **recured** restored **10 swift messengers** i.e., fire and air, thought and desire

14 straight straightway
46.1 mortal deadly **2 conquest** (1) spoils (2) goods acquired in a legal action. **thy sight** the sight of you **3–4 Mine . . . right** my eye would issue an order prohibiting my heart from enjoying the sight of your picture, while my heart would deny to my eye the privilege of seeing your true self **6 closet** (1) small private room (2) cabinet **9 'cide** decide **10 quest** inquest, jury **12 moiety** portion **13 mine . . . part** i.e., the eye gets the outward appearance of the young man. The jury, composed entirely of those who are loyal to the heart, being its *tenants*, awards true love to the heart.)
47.1 a league is took an agreement is reached **3 When that** when **4 Or heart** or when my heart. **himself** itself **5 With** i.e., on **6 painted banquet** i.e., visual feast, perhaps an actual picture of the friend **12 still** constantly
48.1 took my way set out on my journey **2 truest** most trusty **3 to my use** for my own use and profit **3–4 stay . . . falsehood** remain out of the hands of thieves **5 to** compared to

Most worthy comfort, now my greatest grief,
Thou best of dearest and mine only care,
Art left the prey of every vulgar thief.   8
Thee have I not locked up in any chest,
Save where thou art not—though I feel thou art—
Within the gentle closure of my breast,
From whence at pleasure thou mayst come and part;   12
    And even thence thou wilt be stol'n, I fear,
    For truth proves thievish for a prize so dear.

49

Against that time, if ever that time come,
When I shall see thee frown on my defects,
Whenas thy love hath cast his utmost sum,
Called to that audit by advised respects;   4
Against that time when thou shalt strangely pass
And scarcely greet me with that sun, thine eye,
When love, converted from the thing it was,
Shall reasons find of settled gravity—   8
Against that time do I ensconce me here
Within the knowledge of mine own desart,
And this my hand against myself uprear,
To guard the lawful reasons on thy part.   12
    To leave poor me thou hast the strength of laws,
    Since why to love I can allege no cause.

50

How heavy do I journey on the way,
When what I seek, my weary travel's end,
Doth teach that ease and that repose to say,
"Thus far the miles are measured from thy friend!"   4
The beast that bears me, tired with my woe,
Plods dully on, to bear that weight in me,
As if by some instinct the wretch did know
His rider loved not speed being made from thee.   8
The bloody spur cannot provoke him on
That sometimes anger thrusts into his hide,
Which heavily he answers with a groan,
More sharp to me than spurring to his side;   12
    For that same groan doth put this in my mind:
    My grief lies onward and my joy behind.

51

Thus can my love excuse the slow offense
Of my dull bearer when from thee I speed:
From where thou art why should I haste me thence?
Till I return, of posting is no need.   4
O, what excuse will my poor beast then find
When swift extremity can seem but slow?
Then should I spur, though mounted on the wind;
In wingèd speed no motion shall I know.   8
Then can no horse with my desire keep pace;
Therefore desire, of perfect'st love being made,
Shall neigh—no dull flesh—in his fiery race.
But love, for love, thus shall excuse my jade: 12
    Since from thee going he went willful slow,
    Towards thee I'll run, and give him leave to go.

52

So am I as the rich whose blessèd key
Can bring him to his sweet up-lockèd treasure,
The which he will not every hour survey,
For blunting the fine point of seldom pleasure.   4
Therefore are feasts so solemn and so rare,
Since, seldom coming, in the long year set,
Like stones of worth they thinly placèd are,
Or captain jewels in the carcanet.   8
So is the time that keeps you as my chest,
Or as the wardrobe which the robe doth hide,
To make some special instant special blest
By new unfolding his imprisoned pride.   12
    Blessèd are you whose worthiness gives scope,
    Being had, to triumph; being lacked, to hope.

53

What is your substance, whereof are you made,
That millions of strange shadows on you tend?
Since everyone hath, every one, one shade,
And you, but one, can every shadow lend.   4
Describe Adonis, and the counterfeit
Is poorly imitated after you;

---

6 **worthy** valuable. **grief** anxiety, cause of sorrow (i.e., because of your absence and likeliness of being stolen) 8 **vulgar** common 12 **part** depart 14 **truth** i.e., even honesty itself
49.1 Against in anticipation of 3 **Whenas** when. **cast . . . sum** added up the sum total. (The metaphor is from closing accounts on a dissolution of partnership.) 4 **advised respects** careful consideration 5 **strangely** as a stranger 8 **of settled gravity** (1) for a dignified reserve or continued coldness (2) of sufficient weight 9 **ensconce** fortify, shelter 10 **desart** i.e., deserving, such as it is. (This Quarto spelling of desert, *desart*, indicates the rhyme with *part*.) 11 **this . . . uprear** I raise my own hand (as a witness) against my own interest 12 **To . . . part** i.e., to testify in behalf of the lawful reasons on your side of the case 14 **Since . . . cause** since I can urge no lawful cause why you should love me
50.1 heavy sadly and slowly 2–4 **When . . . friend** when the ease and repose I seek at journey's end will merely remind me that I have gone so many miles from my friend 8 **speed being made** (1) the making of hasting away (2) speed when, and because, he is being carried

51.1 slow offense offense consisting in slowness 2 **my dull bearer** i.e., the horse 4 **posting** riding swiftly 6 **swift extremity** extreme swiftness (in returning to you) 8 **In . . . know** even at the speed of flight I won't perceive the motion at all, won't feel as though I'm moving 11 **Shall . . . race** i.e., shall neigh proudly in its fire-swift race, since it, composed like fire of a lighter element, is not held back by the heavy flesh. (See sonnet 45.) 12 **for love** for love's sake. **jade** nag 14 **go** walk, as contrasted with running
52.1 as the rich like the rich man 4 **For blunting** lest he blunt. **fine** delicate; splendid. **seldom pleasure** pleasure sparingly enjoyed 5 **feasts** feast days. **solemn** ceremonious, festive. **rare** excellent; uncommon 8 **captain** principal. **carcanet** necklace of jewels 9 **keeps you** (1) watches over you (2) keeps you from me. **as** like 12 **his** its. **pride** splendor, proud treasure 13–14 **gives . . . hope** gives me opportunity, when you are with me, to rejoice, and when you are away from me, to hope for reunion
53.2 strange (1) exotic (2) not belonging to you. **tend** attend 3 **shade** shadow (as cast by the sun) 4 **And . . . lend** and yet you, being only one person, can cast all sorts of shadowy images or reflections (such as Adonis, Helen, etc.) 5 **Adonis** beautiful youth beloved of Venus. **counterfeit** likeness, portrait

On Helen's cheek all art of beauty set,
And you in Grecian tires are painted new.   8
Speak of the spring and foison of the year;
The one doth shadow of your beauty show,
The other as your bounty doth appear,
And you in every blessèd shape we know.   12
    In all external grace you have some part,
    But you like none, none you, for constant heart.

54

O, how much more doth beauty beauteous seem
By that sweet ornament which truth doth give!
The rose looks fair, but fairer we it deem
For that sweet odor which doth in it live.   4
The canker blooms have full as deep a dye
As the perfumèd tincture of the roses,
Hang on such thorns, and play as wantonly
When summer's breath their maskèd buds discloses;   8
But, for their virtue only is their show,
They live unwooed and unrespected fade,
Die to themselves. Sweet roses do not so;
Of their sweet deaths are sweetest odors made.   12
    And so of you, beauteous and lovely youth,
    When that shall vade, by verse distills your truth.

55

Not marble nor the gilded monuments
Of princes shall outlive this powerful rhyme,
But you shall shine more bright in these contents
Than unswept stone besmeared with sluttish time.   4
When wasteful war shall statues overturn,
And broils root out the work of masonry,
Nor Mars his sword nor war's quick fire shall burn
The living record of your memory.   8
'Gainst death and all-oblivious enmity
Shall you pace forth; your praise shall still find room
Even in the eyes of all posterity
That wear this world out to the ending doom.   12

So, till the judgment that yourself arise,
You live in this, and dwell in lovers' eyes.

56

Sweet love, renew thy force! Be it not said
Thy edge should blunter be than appetite,
Which but today by feeding is allayed,
Tomorrow sharpened in his former might.   4
So, love, be thou; although today thou fill
Thy hungry eyes even till they wink with fullness,
Tomorrow see again, and do not kill
The spirit of love with a perpetual dullness.   8
Let this sad interim like the ocean be
Which parts the shore where two contracted new
Come daily to the banks, that, when they see
Return of love, more blest may be the view;   12
    As call it winter, which being full of care
    Makes summer's welcome thrice more wished,
      more rare.

57

Being your slave, what should I do but tend
Upon the hours and times of your desire?
I have no precious time at all to spend,
Nor services to do, till you require.   4
Nor dare I chide the world-without-end hour
Whilst I, my sovereign, watch the clock for you,
Nor think the bitterness of absence sour
When you have bid your servant once adieu.   8
Nor dare I question with my jealous thought
Where you may be, or your affairs suppose,
But, like a sad slave, stay and think of naught
Save where you are how happy you make those.   12
    So true a fool is love that in your will,
    Though you do anything, he thinks no ill.

58

That god forbid, that made me first your slave,
I should in thought control your times of pleasure,
Or at your hand th' account of hours to crave,
Being your vassal, bound to stay your leisure!   4
O, let me suffer, being at your beck,

7–8 On . . . new set forth the entire art used to beautify the cheek of Helen of Troy, and the result will be a portrait of you in Grecian attire or headdress 9 foison abundance, i.e., autumn 12 you . . . know we recognize you in every shape that is graced with blessings 14 But . . . heart but in the matter of constancy you resemble no one and no one can resemble you
54.2 By by means of. truth (1) constancy (2) substance, integrity 5 canker blooms dog roses (outwardly attractive but not as sweetly scented as the damask rose). dye tincture 7 wantonly sportively 8 discloses causes to open 9 for because. their show in their appearance 10 unrespected unregarded 11 to themselves i.e., without profit to others 12 Of . . . made i.e., perfumes are made from the crushed petals of these roses 13 of you (1) distilled from you (2) with regard to you. lovely (1) lovable (2) handsome 14 When . . . truth when your physical beauty fades, your true substance will be distilled and preserved by (my) verse. (See sonnet 5.) vade (1) fade (2) go away
55.3 these contents i.e., the contents of my poems written in praise of you 4 Than unswept stone than in a memorial stone that has been left unswept, unattended. with by. sluttish neglectful, slovenly, whorish 5 wasteful laying waste 6 broils uprisings, battles 7 Nor Mars his sword neither Mars' sword (shall destroy) 9 all-oblivious enmity oblivion, at enmity with everything 12 That . . . doom that will last from now till doomsday. (That may refer to eyes, praise, or posterity.)

13 till . . . arise until the Judgment Day, when you will arise from the dead
56.1 love i.e., the spirit of love. (The friend is not directly mentioned in this sonnet.) 2 edge . . . appetite keenness is blunter than lust, craving 3 but only for 4 his its 6 wink shut 9 sad interim the unfortunate period of love's abatement or absence 10 parts the shore separates the shores. contracted new newly betrothed 11 banks shores 12 love the loved one 13 As just as appropriately
57.1 tend attend 5 world-without-end interminable 6 my . . . you watch the clock for you, my sovereign 7 Nor think nor dare I think 9 question with (1) debate with (2) seek to know by means of 10 suppose make conjectures about 11 sad sober 13 true (1) constant (2) utter. will desire. (This word, which is capitalized in the 1609 Quarto, is regarded by some as a pun on Shakespeare's first name; see sonnet 135.)
58.3 th' account . . . crave should crave an accounting of how you spend your time 4 stay await

Th' imprisoned absence of your liberty,
And, patience-tame to sufferance, bide each check,
Without accusing you of injury.   8
Be where you list, your charter is so strong
That you yourself may privilege your time
To what you will; to you it doth belong
Yourself to pardon of self-doing crime.   12
        I am to wait, though waiting so be hell,
        Not blame your pleasure, be it ill or well.

59

If there be nothing new, but that which is
Hath been before, how are our brains beguiled,
Which, laboring for invention, bear amiss
The second burden of a former child!   4
O, that record could with a backward look,
Even of five hundred courses of the sun,
Show me your image in some antique book,
Since mind at first in character was done!   8
That I might see what the old world could say
To this composèd wonder of your frame;
Whether we are mended, or whe'er better they,
Or whether revolution be the same.   12
        O, sure I am the wits of former days
        To subjects worse have given admiring praise.

60

Like as the waves make towards the pebbled shore,
So do our minutes hasten to their end;
Each changing place with that which goes before,
In sequent toil all forwards do contend.   4
Nativity, once in the main of light,
Crawls to maturity, wherewith being crowned,
Crookèd eclipses 'gainst his glory fight,
And Time that gave doth now his gift confound.   8
Time doth transfix the flourish set on youth
And delves the parallels in beauty's brow,
Feeds on the rarities of nature's truth,

And nothing stands but for his scythe to mow.   12
        And yet to times in hope my verse shall stand,
        Praising thy worth despite his cruel hand.

61

Is it thy will thy image should keep open
My heavy eyelids to the weary night?
Dost thou desire my slumbers should be broken
While shadows like to thee do mock my sight?   4
Is it thy spirit that thou send'st from thee
So far from home into my deeds to pry,
To find out shames and idle hours in me,
The scope and tenor of thy jealousy?   8
O, no, thy love, though much, is not so great;
It is my love that keeps mine eye awake,
Mine own true love that doth my rest defeat,
To play the watchman ever for thy sake.   12
        For thee watch I whilst thou dost wake elsewhere,
        From me far off, with others all too near.

62

Sin of self-love possesseth all mine eye,
And all my soul, and all my every part;
And for this sin there is no remedy,
It is so grounded inward in my heart.   4
Methinks no face so gracious is as mine,
No shape so true, no truth of such account;
And for myself mine own worth do define,
As I all other in all worths surmount.   8
But when my glass shows me myself indeed,
Beated and chapped with tanned antiquity,
Mine own self-love quite contrary I read;
Self so self-loving were iniquity.   12
        'Tis thee, myself, that for myself I praise,
        Painting my age with beauty of thy days.

63

Against my love shall be, as I am now,
With Time's injurious hand crushed and o'erworn;
When hours have drained his blood and filled his brow
With lines and wrinkles; when his youthful morn   4
Hath traveled on to age's steepy night,
And all those beauties whereof now he's king
Are vanishing or vanished out of sight,

---

6 Th' imprisoned . . . liberty the lack of freedom I suffer in being absent from you, arising from (of) your freedom and free behavior
7 And . . . check and, trained to endure any suffering, let me put up
with each rebuke   9 list please.   charter privilege   10 privilege au-
thorize   12 self-doing committed by yourself   13 am to must
59.1 that everything   3–4 laboring . . . child striving to give birth to
a new creation, merely miscarry with the repetition of something created before   5 record memory, especially memory preserved in writing   6 courses . . . sun years   8 Since . . . done since thought was
first expressed in writing   10 composèd wonder wonderful composition   11 mended improved.   whe'er whether   12 revolution . . .
same the revolving of the ages brings only repetition   13 wits discerning persons; poets
60.1 Like . . . shore just as waves move up the shingle beach
3 changing place with replacing   4 In . . . contend one after another, all struggle onward   5 Nativity i.e., the newborn infant.   once
(1) no sooner (2) formerly.   main main body, expanse. (The child is
seen as dwelling in the main or ocean of light.)   7 Crookèd perverse,
malignant   8 confound destroy   9 transfix the flourish pierce
through and destroy the decoration or embellishment, i.e., physical
beauty   10 delves the parallels digs the wrinkles, furrows   11 Feeds
. . . truth consumes the most precious things created by the fidelity
of nature

12 but . . . mow that can escape the mowing of Time's scythe
13 times in hope times to come
61.4 shadows images (but also suggesting spirits)   8 The scope . . .
jealousy the aim and purport of your suspicion (probably in apposi-
tion to shames and idle hours)   13 watch stay awake.   wake revel
62.5 Methinks it seems to me   7 for myself (1) by my own reckoning
(2) for my own pleasure   8 As (1) inasmuch as (2) as if.   other others
9 indeed as I actually am   10 Beated battered, weather-beaten.
tanned antiquity i.e., leathery old age   12 Self . . . iniquity it would
be wicked for the self to love such an aged and unattractive self
13 thee, myself i.e., you, with whom I identify myself.   for as
14 days i.e., youth
63.1 Against anticipating the time when.   love beloved   2 crushed
and o'erworn creased and worn threadbare (like a long-used garment)
5 traveled (1) journeyed (2) labored.   steepy precipitous, i.e., descending swiftly toward death

Stealing away the treasure of his spring;　　　8
For such a time do I now fortify
Against confounding age's cruel knife,
That he shall never cut from memory
My sweet love's beauty, though my lover's life.　　12
　　His beauty shall in these black lines be seen,
　　And they shall live, and he in them still green.

64

When I have seen by Time's fell hand defaced
The rich proud cost of outworn buried age;
When sometime lofty towers I see down-razed
And brass eternal slave to mortal rage;　　　4
When I have seen the hungry ocean gain
Advantage on the kingdom of the shore,
And the firm soil win of the watery main,
Increasing store with loss and loss with store;　　8
When I have seen such interchange of state,
Or state itself confounded to decay,
Ruin hath taught me thus to ruminate
That Time will come and take my love away.　　12
　　This thought is as a death, which cannot choose
　　But weep to have that which it fears to lose.

65

Since brass, nor stone, nor earth, nor boundless sea,
But sad mortality o'ersways their power,
How with this rage shall beauty hold a plea,
Whose action is no stronger than a flower?　　　4
O, how shall summer's honey breath hold out
Against the wrackful siege of battering days,
When rocks impregnable are not so stout,
Nor gates of steel so strong, but Time decays?　　8
O fearful meditation! Where, alack,
Shall Time's best jewel from Time's chest lie hid?
Or what strong hand can hold his swift foot back?
Or who his spoil of beauty can forbid?　　12
　　O, none, unless this miracle have might,
　　That in black ink my love may still shine bright.

66

Tired with all these, for restful death I cry:
As, to behold desert a beggar born,
And needy nothing trimmed in jollity,
And purest faith unhappily forsworn,　　　4
And gilded honor shamefully misplaced,
And maiden virtue rudely strumpeted,
And right perfection wrongfully disgraced,
And strength by limping sway disablèd,　　　8
And art made tongue-tied by authority,
And folly doctorlike controlling skill,
And simple truth miscalled simplicity,
And captive good attending captain ill.　　12
　　Tired with all these, from these would I be gone,
　　Save that, to die, I leave my love alone.

67

Ah, wherefore with infection should he live,
And with his presence grace impiety,
That sin by him advantage should achieve
And lace itself with his society?　　　4
Why should false painting imitate his cheek
And steal dead seeming of his living hue?
Why should poor beauty indirectly seek
Roses of shadow, since his rose is true?　　8
Why should he live, now Nature bankrupt is,
Beggared of blood to blush through lively veins,
For she hath no exchequer now but his,
And, proud of many, lives upon his gains?　　12
　　O, him she stores, to show what wealth she had
　　In days long since, before these last so bad.

68

Thus is his cheek the map of days outworn,
When beauty lived and died as flowers do now,
Before these bastard signs of fair were born,

9 For such a time (Parallel in construction with *Against* in line 1.) **fortify** raise works of defense　**10 confounding** destroying　**11 That** so that　**12 though** i.e., though he cut　**13 black** (1) inscribed in ink (2) the opposite of fair or beautiful　**14 still** (1) even in death (2) forever.　**green** i.e., as in springtime and youth
64.1 fell cruel　**2 The rich . . . age** i.e., those monuments that were the product of proud wealth and magnificent outlay in times now past and forgotten　**3 sometime** formerly　**4 brass . . . rage** i.e., seemingly indestructible brass subdued by the destructive power of decay　**7 of** at the expense of　**8 Increasing . . . store** one gaining as the other loses, and losing as the other gains　**9 state** condition　**10 state** pomp, greatness; condition in the abstract.　**confounded to decay** destroyed to the point of being in ruins　**12 love** beloved　**13 which cannot choose** (Modifies *thought*.)　**14 to have** because it now has
65.1 Since i.e., since there is neither　**2 But** but that.　**sad** grievous, solemn.　**o'ersways** overrules　**3 with this rage** against this destructive force (the *mortal rage* of 64.4).　**hold** maintain (as in a legal action)　**4 action** (1) efficacy (2) case (in law)　**6 wrackful** destructive　**7 stout** sturdy, impregnable　**8 decays** brings about their decay　**10 from Time's chest** i.e., away from being deposited by Time in his repository of forgetfulness　**12 spoil** despoliation, ravaging　**14 my love** (1) my beloved (2) the love I feel for him

66.1 all these i.e., the following　**2 As** for instance, namely.　**desert** i.e., those who have merit, as contrasted with *needy nothing* in the next line, those insignificant persons who deserve nothing or those who in beggarly worthlessness squander what little they have on *jollity* or finery　**4 unhappily forsworn** wretchedly and evilly betrayed　**5 gilded** golden, splendid (not here suggesting mere appearance of splendor)　**7 right** true.　**disgraced** banished from favor　**8 limping sway** halting leadership　**9 art** literature, learning.　**made tongue-tied** i.e., censored, stifled　**10 doctorlike** assuming a learned bearing.　**controlling** dominating, curbing　**11 miscalled simplicity** slandered as foolishness, naiveté　**12 attending** waiting on, subordinated to　**14 to die** in dying
67.1 wherefore why.　**with infection** i.e., with the world's ills, as enumerated in the preceding sonnet.　**he** i.e., the poet's friend　**3 That . . . achieve** with the result that sin should flourish by being associated with him　**4 lace . . . society** (1) adorn itself with his company (2) weave its way into his company　**6 dead seeming of** lifeless appearance from　**7 poor** inferior.　**indirectly** imitatively, or, falsely　**8 Roses of shadow** i.e., painted roses, cosmetically applied.　**since** (1) just because (2) since after all　**9-10 now . . . veins** i.e., seeing as Nature is bankrupt through supplying him all her arts, and is therefore now dependent on cosmetics to redden the complexion　**11 For** since.　**exchequer** i.e., treasury of natural beauty　**12 proud** i.e., though proudly boasting.　**gains** endowments　**13 stores** preserves, keeps in store　**14 last** i.e., recent days, the present
68.1 map embodiment, image　**3 bastard . . . fair** i.e., cosmetics.　**born** (Suggesting also *borne*, "worn.")

Or durst inhabit on a living brow;   4
Before the golden tresses of the dead,
The right of sepulchers, were shorn away
To live a second life on second head;
Ere beauty's dead fleece made another gay.   8
In him those holy antique hours are seen
Without all ornament, itself and true,
Making no summer of another's green,
Robbing no old to dress his beauty new;   12
        And him as for a map doth Nature store,
        To show false Art what beauty was of yore.

69

Those parts of thee that the world's eye doth view
Want nothing that the thought of hearts can mend;
All tongues, the voice of souls, give thee that due,
Utt'ring bare truth, even so as foes commend.   4
Thy outward thus with outward praise is crowned,
But those same tongues that give thee so thine own
In other accents do this praise confound
By seeing farther than the eye hath shown.   8
They look into the beauty of thy mind,
And that, in guess, they measure by thy deeds;
Then, churls, their thoughts, although their eyes were
        kind,
To thy fair flower add the rank smell of weeds.   12
        But why thy odor matcheth not thy show,
        The soil is this, that thou dost common grow.

70

That thou are blamed shall not be thy defect,
For slander's mark was ever yet the fair;
The ornament of beauty is suspect,
A crow that flies in heaven's sweetest air.   4
So thou be good, slander doth but approve
Thy worth the greater, being wooed of time,
For canker vice the sweetest buds doth love,
And thou present'st a pure unstainèd prime.   8
Thou hast passed by the ambush of young days,

Either not assailed, or victor being charged;
Yet this thy praise cannot be so thy praise
To tie up envy, evermore enlarged.   12
        If some suspect of ill masked not thy show,
        Then thou alone kingdoms of hearts shouldst owe.

71

No longer mourn for me when I am dead
Than you shall hear the surly sullen bell
Give warning to the world that I am fled
From this vile world, with vilest worms to dwell.   4
Nay, if you read this line, remember not
The hand that writ it, for I love you so
That I in your sweet thoughts would be forgot
If thinking on me then should make you woe.   8
O, if, I say, you look upon this verse
When I perhaps compounded am with clay,
Do not so much as my poor name rehearse,
But let your love even with my life decay,   12
        Lest the wise world should look into your moan
        And mock you with me after I am gone.

72

O, lest the world should task you to recite
What merit lived in me that you should love,
After my death, dear love, forget me quite;
For you in me can nothing worthy prove—   4
Unless you would devise some virtuous lie
To do more for me than mine own desert,
And hang more praise upon deceasèd I
Than niggard truth would willingly impart.   8
O, lest your true love may seem false in this,
That you for love speak well of me untrue,
My name be buried where my body is,
And live no more to shame nor me nor you.   12
        For I am shamed by that which I bring forth,
        And so should you, to love things nothing worth.

73

That time of year thou mayst in me behold
When yellow leaves, or none, or few, do hang
Upon those boughs which shake against the cold,

---

4 **inhabit** dwell   6 **The right of** rightly belonging in. (Wigs were made of dead persons' hair.)   8 **gay** lovely, gaudy   9 **holy antique hours** blessed ancient times   10 **all** any   13 **store** stock (with beauty) and preserve
69.2 Want lack.   **mend** improve upon   3–4 **the voice . . . commend** i.e., uttering heartfelt conviction, allow that as your due, thus saying what even your enemies would concede to be the bare truth   5 **outward praise** the kind of praise suited to mere outward qualities   6 **thine own** your due   7 **In other accents** in other terms and with another emphasis.   **confound** confute, destroy   10 **in guess** at a guess   12 **To . . . weeds** i.e., to the flower of your outward beauty, they contrastingly suggest something putrid within   13 **odor** i.e., reputation   14 **soil** (1) blemish, fault (2) origin, source, ground.   **common** cheapened by being too familiar and available to all, inferior (like a weed)
70.1 defect fault   2 **mark** target   3 **The . . . suspect** i.e., beauty is always attended by suspicion (*suspect*), as though suspicion were a necessary ornament to beauty   5 **So** provided that.   **approve** prove   6 **being . . . time** i.e., since it shows you are courted by the world   7 **canker vice** i.e., slander, that is like the cankerworm   8 **unstainèd prime** unspotted youth (like the pure, unspoiled flower that attracts the cankerworm)   9 **ambush . . . days** temptations of youth

10 **being charged** when you were assailed   11 **this thy praise** i.e., your former reputation for virtue.   **so** sufficiently   12 **To . . . enlarged** as to silence malice, which is always at liberty   13 **If . . . show** if some suspicion (*suspect*) of ill doing did not partly obscure your outward attractiveness   14 **owe** own
71.2 bell a passing bell for one who has died, rung once for each year of that person's life   8 **on** of, about.   **make you woe** cause you woe or make you woeful   10 **compounded** mingled   11 **rehearse** repeat   12 **even with** at the same time as   14 **with** because of; for loving; along with
72.1 recite tell   7 **hang** (as in hanging trophies on a funeral monument)   10 **of me untrue** (1) about me untruly (2) about me, flawed and inconstant as I am   11 **My name be** let my name be   12 **nor . . . nor** neither . . . nor   13 **that . . . forth** (Perhaps a deprecatory reference to the author's acting and writing of plays, but more probably his verse or his written work generally.)   14 **should you** i.e., you ought to be ashamed

Bare ruined choirs where late the sweet birds sang.   4
In me thou seest the twilight of such day
As after sunset fadeth in the west,
Which by and by black night doth take away,
Death's second self, that seals up all in rest.   8
In me thou seest the glowing of such fire
That on the ashes of his youth doth lie
As the deathbed whereon it must expire,
Consumed with that which it was nourished by.   12
　　This thou perceiv'st, which makes thy love more
　　　　strong,
　　To love that well which thou must leave ere long.

74

But be contented when that fell arrest
Without all bail shall carry me away;
My life hath in this line some interest,
Which for memorial still with thee shall stay.   4
When thou reviewest this, thou dost review
The very part was consecrate to thee.
The earth can have but earth, which is his due;
My spirit is thine, the better part of me.   8
So then thou hast but lost the dregs of life,
The prey of worms, my body being dead,
The coward conquest of a wretch's knife,
Too base of thee to be rememberèd.   12
　　The worth of that is that which it contains,
　　And that is this, and this with thee remains.

75

So are you to my thoughts as food to life,
Or as sweet-seasoned showers are to the ground.
And for the peace of you I hold such strife
As twixt a miser and his wealth is found: 4
Now proud as an enjoyer, and anon
Doubting the filching age will steal his treasure;
Now counting best to be with you alone,
Then bettered that the world may see my pleasure;   8
Sometimes all full with feasting on your sight,

And by and by clean starvèd for a look;
Possessing or pursuing no delight
Save what is had or must from you be took.   12
　　Thus do I pine and surfeit day by day,
　　Or gluttoning on all, or all away.

76

Why is my verse so barren of new pride?
So far from variation or quick change?
Why with the time do I not glance aside
To newfound methods and to compounds strange?   4
Why write I still all one, ever the same,
And keep invention in a noted weed,
That every word doth almost tell my name,
Showing their birth and where they did proceed?   8
O, know, sweet love, I always write of you,
And you and love are still my argument;
So all my best is dressing old words new,
Spending again what is already spent.   12
　　For as the sun is daily new and old,
　　So is my love still telling what is told.

77

Thy glass will show thee how thy beauties wear,
Thy dial how thy precious minutes waste;
The vacant leaves thy mind's imprint will bear,
And of this book this learning mayst thou taste.   4
The wrinkles which thy glass will truly show
Of mouthèd graves will give thee memory;
Thou by thy dial's shady stealth mayst know
Time's thievish progress to eternity.   8
Look what thy memory cannot contain
Commit to these waste blanks, and thou shalt find
Those children nursed, delivered from thy brain,
To take a new acquaintance of thy mind.   12
　　These offices, so oft as thou wilt look,
　　Shall profit thee and much enrich thy book.

73.4 choirs those areas of churches where the service is sung, here viewed as in ruins and resembling the arched shape of bare trees (with a hint of *quires*, gatherings of *leaves* [see line 2] in a book or manuscript). **late** lately   **8 seals** closes   **10 That** as.   **his** its   **12 with** (1) by (2) along with   **14 that** (1) me, your beloved (2) youth and life itself.   **leave** i.e., lose by the speaker's death
74.1 be contented . . . arrest do not be distressed when that cruel arrest (carried out by Death)   **3 line** verse.   **interest** legal concern, right, or title   **4 still** (1) always (2) despite death   **5 reviewest this** see this again (and view it with a critical eye)   **6 part was consecrate** part (of me) that was dedicated solemnly (as in a religious service)   **7 his** its   **11 The coward . . . knife** i.e., the cowardly conquest that even such a poor wretch as Mortality, or Death, can make with his scythe   **12 of . . . rememberèd** to be remembered by you   **13–14 The worth . . . remains** the only worth of my body is the spirit it contains, i.e., this verse, which will remain with you and endure through you
75.1 as food to life what food is to life   **2 sweet-seasoned** of the sweet season, i.e., spring   **3 of you** to be found in loving you   **6 Doubting** suspecting, fearing that.   **filching** thieving   **7 counting** (1) thinking it (2) reckoning, like a miser   **8 bettered** made happier, better pleased.   **see my pleasure** i.e., see me with you, enjoying your company

10 clean completely, absolutely.   **a look** (1) a glimpse of you (2) an exchange of glances   **12 from you** (Modifies both verbs, *had* and *must be took.*)   **13 pine and surfeit** starve and overeat   **14 Or . . . or** either . . . or.   **all away** i.e., all food being taken away
76.1 pride ornament   **2 quick change** fashionable innovation   **3 time** way of the world, fashion   **4 compounds** strange literary inventions, or perhaps, compound words, neologisms   **5 still all one** continually one way   **6 invention** literary creation.   **noted weed** familiar garment   **8 where** whence   **10 still** always.   **argument** subject, theme   **14 telling** (1) retelling (2) counting over. (Continuing the financial wordplay of *Spending* and *spent* in line 12, and in 75.7.)
77.1 glass mirror.   **wear** wear away   **2 dial** sundial   **3 vacant leaves** blank pages. (Apparently these lines accompanied the gift of a book of blank pages, a memorandum book.)   **thy mind's imprint** i.e., your reflections and ideas, to be set down in the memorandum book   **4 this learning** i.e., mental profit derived from reflecting and keeping a journal, as explained in lines 9 ff.   **6 mouthèd** all-devouring, gaping.   **memory** reminder   **7 shady stealth** stealthy shadow   **9 Look what** whatever   **10 waste blanks** blank pages   **10–12 thou . . . mind** you will see those thoughts, the children of your brain, nursed to maturity and ready to be newly acquainted with your mind
13 offices duties (of meditation and reflection)   **14 thy book** i.e., the memorandum book, where these reflections are to be set down

78

So oft have I invoked thee for my Muse
And found such fair assistance in my verse
As every alien pen hath got my use
And under thee their poesy disperse.   4
Thine eyes, that taught the dumb on high to sing
And heavy ignorance aloft to fly,
Have added feathers to the learnèd's wing
And given grace a double majesty.   8
Yet be most proud of that which I compile,
Whose influence is thine and born of thee.
In others' works thou dost but mend the style,
And arts with thy sweet graces gracèd be;   12
    But thou art all my art, and dost advance
    As high as learning my rude ignorance.

79

Whilst I alone did call upon thy aid,
My verse alone had all thy gentle grace,
But now my gracious numbers are decayed,
And my sick Muse doth give another place.   4
I grant, sweet love, thy lovely argument
Deserves the travail of a worthier pen,
Yet what of thee thy poet doth invent
He robs thee of and pays it thee again.   8
He lends thee virtue, and he stole that word
From thy behavior; beauty doth he give,
And found it in thy cheek; he can afford
No praise to thee but what in thee doth live.   12
    Then thank him not for that which he doth say,
    Since what he owes thee thou thyself dost pay.

80

O, how I faint when I of you do write,
Knowing a better spirit doth use your name,
And in the praise thereof spends all his might
To make me tongue-tied, speaking of your fame!   4
But since your worth, wide as the ocean is,
The humble as the proudest sail doth bear,
My saucy bark, inferior far to his,
On your broad main doth willfully appear.   8

Your shallowest help will hold me up afloat,
Whilst he upon your soundless deep doth ride;
Or, being wrecked, I am a worthless boat,
He of tall building and of goodly pride.   12
    Then if he thrive and I be cast away,
    The worst was this: my love was my decay.

81

Or I shall live your epitaph to make,
Or you survive when I in earth am rotten,
From hence your memory death cannot take,
Although in me each part will be forgotten.   4
Your name from hence immortal life shall have,
Though I, once gone, to all the world must die;
The earth can yield me but a common grave,
When you entombèd in men's eyes shall lie.   8
Your momument shall be my gentle verse,
Which eyes not yet created shall o'erread,
And tongues to be your being shall rehearse
When all the breathers of this world are dead.   12
    You still shall live—such virtue hath my pen—
    Where breath most breathes, even in the mouths
        of men.

82

I grant thou wert not married to my Muse,
And therefore mayst without attaint o'erlook
The dedicated words which writers use
Of their fair subject, blessing every book.   4
Thou art as fair in knowledge as in hue,
Finding thy worth a limit past my praise,
And therefore art enforced to seek anew
Some fresher stamp of these time-bettering days.   8
And do so, love; yet when they have devised
What strainèd touches rhetoric can lend,
Thou, truly fair, wert truly sympathized
In true plain words by thy true-telling friend;   12
    And their gross painting might be better used
    Where cheeks need blood; in thee it is abused.

78.2 fair favorable **3 As** that. **alien** belonging to others. **got my use** adopted my practice **4 under thee** i.e., with you as their muse or patron; under your influence. **disperse** circulate **5 on high** aloud (also anticipating *aloft*) **6 aloft to fly** i.e., to get off the ground **7 added . . . wing** i.e., enabled learned poets to fly higher still. (A falconry metaphor; birds could be given extra wing feathers.) **8 And . . . majesty** and have added to the majesty of poets already capable of it **9 compile** compose, write **10 influence** inspiration (with suggestion of astrological meaning) **11 mend the style** correct or improve the style (but with a suggestion of repairing the point of a writing quill or stylus, continuing the metaphor of *pen* and *feathers*) **12 arts** learning, literary culture **13 advance** lift up
79.3 numbers verse **4 give another place** yield place to another **5 thy lovely argument** the theme of your lovable qualities **6 travail** labor **7–8 Yet . . . again** yet whatever a poet under your patronage discovers as a literary subject concerning you he merely robs from you and gives you back your own again **11 afford** offer to pay
80.1 faint grow weak, falter **2 better spirit** i.e., rival poet, whom the speaker admires **5 wide . . . is** as wide as is the ocean **6 as** as well as **8 main** ocean. **willfully** perversely, boldly, in spite of all

10 soundless unfathomable **11 wrecked** shipwrecked **12 tall building** i.e., sturdy construction. **pride** splendor **13 cast away** (1) shipwrecked (2) abandoned **14 my love** (1) my love for you, which led me to be so reckless in my inferior boat (2) you, my beloved. **decay** ruin
81.1 Or whether **3 hence** (1) this poetry (2) the earth **4 in . . . part** every quality of mine (as distinguished from the poetry) **5 from hence** (1) from this poetry (2) henceforth **11 to be** i.e., of persons yet unborn. **rehearse** recite **12 breathers** living people. **this world** this present time **13 virtue** power **14 even in the** in the very
82.2 attaint blame, discredit. **o'erlook** look at, peruse **3 dedicated** devoted (with suggestion of "dedicatory"). **writers** i.e., other writers **4 blessing every book** i.e., you bestowing favor thus on the writings presented to you, or, writers commending their own work **5 hue** complexion, appearance **6 Finding . . . praise** in deciding that your worth forms a region beyond the capacities of my praise **8 Some . . . days** some more recently issued imprint, i.e., more up-to-date literary product of this culturally advanced age **11 wert truly sympathized** would be faithfully matched and described **13 gross painting** flattery that is heavily laid on, like a cosmetic **14 abused** misused, misapplied

83

I never saw that you did painting need,
And therefore to your fair no painting set;
I found, or thought I found, you did exceed
The barren tender of a poet's debt; 4
And therefore have I slept in your report,
That you yourself, being extant, well might show
How far a modern quill doth come too short,
Speaking of worth, what worth in you doth grow. 8
This silence for my sin you did impute,
Which shall be most my glory, being dumb;
For I impair not beauty, being mute,
When others would give life and bring a tomb. 12
    There lives more life in one of your fair eyes
    Than both your poets can in praise devise.

84

Who is it that says most which can say more
Than this rich praise—that you alone are you,
In whose confine immurèd is the store
Which should example where your equal grew? 4
Lean penury within that pen doth dwell
That to his subject lends not some small glory;
But he that writes of you, if he can tell
That you are you, so dignifies his story. 8
Let him but copy what in you is writ,
Not making worse what nature made so clear,
And such a counterpart shall fame his wit,
Making his style admirèd everywhere. 12
    You to your beauteous blessings add a curse,
    Being fond on praise, which makes your praises
      worse.

85

My tongue-tied Muse in manners holds her still,
While comments of your praise, richly compiled,
Reserve thy character with golden quill
And precious phrase by all the Muses filed. 4
I think good thoughts whilst other write good words,
And like unlettered clerk still cry "Amen"
To every hymn that able spirit affords
In polished form of well-refinèd pen. 8
Hearing you praised, I say " 'Tis so, 'tis true,"
And to the most of praise add something more;
But that is in my thought, whose love to you,
Though words come hindmost, holds his rank before. 12
    Then others for the breath of words respect,
    Me for my dumb thoughts, speaking in effect.

86

Was it the proud full sail of his great verse,
Bound for the prize of all-too-precious you,
That did my ripe thoughts in my brain inhearse,
Making their tomb the womb wherein they grew? 4
Was it his spirit, by spirits taught to write
Above a mortal pitch, that struck me dead?
No, neither he, nor his compeers by night
Giving him aid, my verse astonishèd. 8
He, nor that affable familiar ghost
Which nightly gulls him with intelligence,
As victors of my silence cannot boast;
I was not sick of any fear from thence. 12
    But when your countenance filled up his line,
    Then lacked I matter; that enfeebled mine.

87

Farewell! Thou art too dear for my possessing,
And like enough thou know'st thy estimate.
The charter of thy worth gives thee releasing;
My bonds in thee are all determinate. 4
For how do I hold thee but by thy granting,
And for that riches where is my deserving?
The cause of this fair gift in me is wanting,

83.1 painting i.e., artificial enhancement of beauty   **2 fair** beauty. **set** applied   **4 barren . . . debt** worthless homage that a poet can offer you   **5 slept . . . report** been neglectful in writing praisingly of you   **6 That** because, so that.   **extant** still alive and much in the public eye   **7 modern** (1) commonplace (2) up-to-date   **7–8 doth come . . . grow** comes too short, in describing your worth, of the actual worth that flourishes in you   **9–10 This . . . dumb** you imputed my silence to willful failure when, in fact, it will prove most to my credit   **11 being mute** (Modifies *I*.)   **12 bring a tomb** i.e., instead, they bring an inadequate monument that conceals lifelessly rather than enhances   **14 both your poets** i.e., (probably,) I and the rival poet
84.1–2 Who . . . praise what extravagant writer of praise can say more than this in way of praise.   **which** who   **3–4 In . . . grew** in whose person are contained all those rich qualities that would be needed as a model to produce again your equal in beauty   **5–6 Lean . . . glory** it is a poor piece of writing indeed that does not confer at least some glory on its subject   **8 so** sufficiently, thus   **10 clear** glorious, shining   **11 counterpart** copy, likeness.   **fame** endow with fame   **13 curse** (1) defect in character (2) burden for those seeking to praise you   **14 Being fond** doting.   **which . . . worse** (1) which encourages false flattery (2) which makes all praise seem inadequate in comparison to you
85.1 in . . . still politely remains silent   **2 comments . . . compiled** eulogies of you composed in fine language

3 Reserve thy character i.e., store up praise of you in their writings. (The Quarto reading, *Reserne* [i.e., *Reserve*] *their Character*, might mean "preserve their own writing.")   **golden** aureate, affected   **4 precious** affected.   **filed** polished   **5 other** others   **6–7 like . . . affords** like an illiterate assistant to a priest continually give my approval to every praising verse that the rival poet (and others like him) provides   **10 most** utmost   **11 that . . . thought** that which I add is added silently   **12 holds . . . before** is second to none in love   **13 Then . . . respect** then take notice of others for what they say   **14 speaking in effect** conveying what speech would say   **86.1 his** i.e., an unidentified rival poet's   **2 prize** capture, booty (as in a seized cargo vessel)   **3 inhearse** coffin up   **5 spirits** i.e., literary ancestors or contemporaries (with a suggestion also of *daemons*, attendant spirits)   **6 pitch** height. (A term from falconry.)   **dead** i.e., dumb, silent   **7 compeers by night** spirits (see line 5) visiting and aiding the poet in his dreams or nighttime reading   **8 astonishèd** struck dumb   **9 ghost** spirit (as in lines 5 and 7)   **10 gulls** misleads, gorges. **intelligence** information, ideas   **12 of** with   **13 countenance filled up** (1) approval repaired any defect in (2) beauty served as subject for   **14 lacked I matter** I had nothing left to write about
87.1 dear precious   **2 like** likely, probably.   **estimate** value   **3 charter of** privilege derived from.   **releasing** i.e., release from obligations of love   **4 determinate** ended, expired. (A legal term, as throughout this sonnet.)

And so my patent back again is swerving.   8
Thyself thou gav'st, thy own worth then not knowing,
Or me, to whom thou gav'st it, else mistaking;
So thy great gift, upon misprision growing,
Comes home again, on better judgment making.   12
      Thus have I had thee as a dream doth flatter,
      In sleep a king, but waking no such matter.

88

When thou shalt be disposed to set me light
And place my merit in the eye of scorn,
Upon thy side against myself I'll fight
And prove thee virtuous, though thou art forsworn.   4
With mine own weakness being best acquainted,
Upon thy part I can set down a story
Of faults concealed, wherein I am attainted,
That thou in losing me shall win much glory.   8
And I by this will be a gainer too;
For, bending all my loving thoughts on thee,
The injuries that to myself I do,
Doing thee vantage, double-vantage me.   12
      Such is my love, to thee I so belong,
      That for thy right myself will bear all wrong.

89

Say that thou didst forsake me for some fault,
And I will comment upon that offense;
Speak of my lameness, and I straight will halt,
Against thy reasons making no defense.   4
Thou canst not, love, disgrace me half so ill,
To set a form upon desirèd change,
As I'll myself disgrace, knowing thy will.
I will acquaintance strangle and look strange,   8
Be absent from thy walks, and in my tongue
Thy sweet belovèd name no more shall dwell,
Lest I, too much profane, should do it wrong
And haply of our old acquaintance tell.   12
      For thee against myself I'll vow debate,
      For I must ne'er love him whom thou dost hate.

90

Then hate me when thou wilt; if ever, now;
Now, while the world is bent my deeds to cross,
Join with the spite of fortune, make me bow,
And do not drop in for an after-loss.   4
Ah, do not, when my heart hath scaped this sorrow,
Come in the rearward of a conquered woe;
Give not a windy night a rainy morrow,
To linger out a purposed overthrow.   8
If thou wilt leave me, do not leave me last,
When other petty griefs have done their spite,
But in the onset come; so shall I taste
At first the very worst of fortune's might,   12
      And other strains of woe, which now seem woe,
      Compared with loss of thee will not seem so.

91

Some glory in their birth, some in their skill,
Some in their wealth, some in their body's force,
Some in their garments, though newfangled ill,
Some in their hawks and hounds, some in their horse;   4
And every humor hath his adjunct pleasure,
Wherein it finds a joy above the rest.
But these particulars are not my measure;
All these I better in one general best.   8
Thy love is better than high birth to me,
Richer than wealth, prouder than garments' cost,
Of more delight than hawks or horses be;
And having thee, of all men's pride I boast—   12
      Wretched in this alone, that thou mayst take
      All this away and me most wretched make.

92

But do thy worst to steal thyself away,
For term of life thou art assurèd mine,
And life no longer than thy love will stay,
For it depends upon that love of thine.   4
Then need I not to fear the worst of wrongs,
When in the least of them my life hath end;
I see a better state to me belongs
Than that which on thy humor doth depend.   8

---

8 patent charter granting rights of monopoly; hence, privilege.
swerving returning (to you)   **10 mistaking** i.e., overvaluing   **11 upon
misprision growing** arising out of error   **12 on . . . making** on your
forming a more accurate judgment
88.1 set me light make light of me, value me slightingly   **3 Upon thy
side** supporting your case (also *Upon thy part* in line 6)   **7 concealed**
not publicly known.   **attainted** dishonored   **8 That** so that.   **losing**
i.e., separating from (with a suggestion of *loosing*, "setting free," the
Quarto spelling)   **12 vantage** advantage
89.1 Say assert, claim   **2 comment** enlarge   **3 Speak . . . halt** i.e., if
you ascribe to me any kind of handicap, I immediately will limp to
show that you are right. (*Halt* also has the suggestion of ceasing to
object, remaining silent.)   **4 reasons** charges, arguments   **5 disgrace**
discredit   **6 To . . . change** to provide a pretext for (in the interest of
justifying) your change of affection and to set it in proper order   **7 As
. . . disgrace** as I will disfigure and depreciate myself   **8 acquaintance strangle** put an end to familiarity (with you).   **strange** like a
stranger   **9 walks** haunts   **12 haply** perchance   **13 vow debate** declare hostility, quarrel

90.2 bent determined.   **cross** thwart   **4 drop . . . after-loss** crush-
ingly add to my sorrow at some future time   **5–6 when . . . woe**
i.e., follow with an attack after I have recovered from my present misfortune.   **in the rearward of** behind. (A military metaphor.)
7 windy, rainy (Suggestive of sighs and tears.)   **8 linger out** protract.
purposed intended, inevitable   **11 in the onset** at the outset
13 strains (1) kinds (2) stresses
91.3 newfangled ill fashionably unattractive   **4 horse** horses   **5 humor** disposition, temperament.   **his adjunct** its corresponding
7 measure standard (of happiness); lot in life   **8 better** surpass, improve upon   **10 prouder** more splendid   **12 of . . . boast** I boast of
having the equivalent of all that is a source of pride in other men
92.1 But do i.e., but even if you do   **2 term of life** i.e., my lifetime
5–6 Then . . . end I need not fear what most people would call the
worst of misfortunes, since the seemingly lesser misfortune—loss of
your friendship—would prove fatal to me   **7–8 I see . . . depend**
i.e., I see that I am happier than most people whose happiness ends
when they are cast from favor, since my very existence will cease
when I am cast from favor and thus will end my misery.   **humor**
whim, fancy

Thou canst not vex me with inconstant mind,
Since that my life on thy revolt doth lie.
O, what a happy title do I find,
Happy to have thy love, happy to die!   12
    But what's so blessèd-fair that fears no blot?
    Thou mayst be false, and yet I know it not.

93

So shall I live, supposing thou art true,
Like a deceivèd husband; so love's face
May still seem love to me, though altered new,
Thy looks with me, thy heart in other place.   4
For there can live no hatred in thine eye,
Therefore in that I cannot know thy change.
In many's looks the false heart's history
Is writ in moods and frowns and wrinkles strange,   8
But heaven in thy creation did decree
That in thy face sweet love should ever dwell;
Whate'er thy thoughts or thy heart's workings be,
Thy looks should nothing thence but sweetness tell.   12
    How like Eve's apple doth thy beauty grow,
    If thy sweet virtue answer not thy show!

94

They that have power to hurt and will do none,
That do not do the thing they most do show,
Who, moving others, are themselves as stone,
Unmovèd, cold, and to temptation slow,   4
They rightly do inherit heaven's graces
And husband nature's riches from expense;
They are the lords and owners of their faces,
Others but stewards of their excellence.   8
The summer's flower is to the summer sweet,
Though to itself it only live and die,
But if that flower with base infection meet,
The basest weed outbraves his dignity.   12
    For sweetest things turn sourest by their deeds;
    Lilies that fester smell far worse than weeds.

95

How sweet and lovely dost thou make the shame
Which, like a canker in the fragrant rose,
Doth spot the beauty of thy budding name!
O, in what sweets dost thou thy sins enclose!   4
That tongue that tells the story of thy days,
Making lascivious comments on thy sport,
Cannot dispraise, but, in a kind of praise;
Naming thy name, blesses an ill report.   8
O, what a mansion have those vices got
Which for their habitation chose out thee,
Where beauty's veil doth cover every blot,
And all things turns to fair that eyes can see!   12
    Take heed, dear heart, of this large privilege;
    The hardest knife ill used doth lose his edge.

96

Some say thy fault is youth, some wantonness;
Some say thy grace is youth and gentle sport;
Both grace and faults are loved of more and less;
Thou mak'st faults graces that to thee resort.   4
As on the finger of a thronèd queen
The basest jewel will be well esteemed,
So are those errors that in thee are seen
To truths translated and for true things deemed.   8
How many lambs might the stern wolf betray,
If like a lamb he could his looks translate!
How many gazers mightst thou lead away,
If thou wouldst use the strength of all thy state!   12
    But do not so; I love thee in such sort
    As, thou being mine, mine is thy good report.

97

How like a winter hath my absence been
From thee, the pleasure of the fleeting year!
What freezings have I felt, what dark days seen!
What old December's bareness everywhere!   4
And yet this time removed was summer's time,
The teeming autumn, big with rich increase,
Bearing the wanton burden of the prime,
Like widowed wombs after their lords' decease.   8
Yet this abundant issue seemed to me
But hope of orphans and unfathered fruit,
For summer and his pleasures wait on thee,

---

10 **Since . . . lie** since if you desert me it will cost me my life
11 **happy title** right to be thought happy; fortunate legal right of ownership   13 **that fears** as to fear   14 **Thou . . . not** i.e., my worst fate would be to lose your affection without knowing it and thereby live on in an unloved state, unreleased by the death that certainty of your desertion would bring
93.1 **So** (Continues the thought of sonnet 92.)   **supposing** I supposing (incorrectly)   2 **face** appearance   3 **new** to something new   5 **For** since   6 **in . . . change** I won't be able to detect your changed affection from your looks   8 **moods** moody looks.   **strange** unfriendly
14 **answer . . . show** does not conform with your outward appearance
94.1 **and . . . none** and do not willfully try to do hurt   2 **show** i.e., show themselves capable of, or, seem to do   4 **cold** dispassionate
5 **inherit** (1) receive through inheritance (2) enjoy, make use of
6 **husband** carefully manage, preserve.   **expense** waste, expenditure
7 **They . . . faces** they are completely masters of themselves and of the qualities that appear in them   8 **but stewards** merely custodians or dispensers   9–10 **The . . . die** i.e., such self-contained persons may seem like flowers that live and die unto themselves, but, in fact, they have much sweetness and beauty to bestow   10 **it only** alone it
12 **outbraves his dignity** surpasses in show its worth   14 **Lilies . . . weeds** (This line appears in the anonymous play *Edward III*, usually dated before 1595 and attributed in part by some editors to Shakespeare.)

95.2 **canker** cankerworm that destroys buds and leaves   3 **name** reputation   6 **sport** amours   8 **blesses** graces   12 **all . . . fair** either (1) beauty's veil makes all things beautiful, or (2) all things become beautiful   13 **large** unlimited, licentious   14 **his** its
96.1 **wantonness** (1) exuberance (2) lechery   2 **gentle sport** gentlemanlike amorousness   3 **of more and less** by high and low   4 **Thou . . . resort** you convert into graces the faults that attend you   8 **translated** transformed   9 **stern** cruel   10 **like** i.e., unto those of
11 **away** astray   12 **the strength . . . state** the full power at your command, i.e., your wealth, charm, and social rank   13–14 **But . . . report** (The same couplet ends sonnet 36.)
97.5 **time removed** time of separation   6 **big** pregnant   7 **the wanton . . . prime** the fruit or offspring of wanton spring, i.e., the crops planted in springtime   9 **issue** offspring   10 **hope of orphans** orphaned hope   11 **his** its.   **wait on thee** attend on you, are at your disposal

And, thou away, the very birds are mute;   12
    Or, if they sing, 'tis with so dull a cheer
    That leaves look pale, dreading the winter's near.

98

From you have I been absent in the spring,
When proud-pied April, dressed in all his trim,
Hath put a spirit of youth in everything,
That heavy Saturn laughed and leapt with him.   4
Yet nor the lays of birds nor the sweet smell
Of different flowers in odor and in hue
Could make me any summer's story tell,
Or from their proud lap pluck them where they grew.   8
Nor did I wonder at the lily's white,
Nor praise the deep vermilion in the rose;
They were but sweet, but figures of delight
Drawn after you, you pattern of all those.   12
    Yet seemed it winter still, and, you away,
    As with your shadow I with these did play.

99

The forward violet thus did I chide:
"Sweet thief, whence didst thou steal thy sweet that
    smells,
If not from my love's breath? The purple pride
Which on thy soft cheek for complexion dwells   4
In my love's veins thou hast too grossly dyed."
The lily I condemnèd for thy hand,
And buds of marjoram had stol'n thy hair;
The roses fearfully on thorns did stand,   8
One blushing shame, another white despair;
A third, nor red nor white, had stol'n of both
And to his robbery had annexed thy breath,
But, for his theft, in pride of all his growth   12
A vengeful canker ate him up to death.
    More flowers I noted, yet I none could see
    But sweet or color it had stol'n from thee.

100

Where art thou, Muse, that thou forgett'st so long
To speak of that which gives thee all thy might?
Spend'st thou thy fury on some worthless song,
Dark'ning thy pow'r to lend base subjects light?   4
Return, forgetful Muse, and straight redeem
In gentle numbers time so idly spent;
Sing to the ear that doth thy lays esteem
And gives thy pen both skill and argument.   8
Rise, resty Muse, my love's sweet face survey
If Time have any wrinkle graven there;
If any, be a satire to decay,
And make Time's spoils despisèd everywhere.   12
    Give my love fame faster than Time wastes life;
    So thou prevent'st his scythe and crooked knife.

101

O truant Muse, what shall be thy amends
For thy neglect of truth in beauty dyed?
Both truth and beauty on my love depends;
So dost thou too, and therein dignified.   4
Make answer, Muse. Wilt thou not haply say,
"Truth needs no color with his color fixed,
Beauty no pencil, beauty's truth to lay,
But best is best, if never intermixed"?   8
Because he needs no praise, wilt thou be dumb?
Excuse not silence so, for 't lies in thee
To make him much outlive a gilded tomb
And to be praised of ages yet to be.   12
    Then do thy office, Muse; I teach thee how
    To make him seem, long hence, as he shows now.

102

My love is strengthened, though more weak in
    seeming;
I love not less, though less the show appear.
That love is merchandized whose rich esteeming
The owner's tongue doth publish everywhere.   4
Our love was new and then but in the spring
When I was wont to greet it with my lays,

---

13 with . . . cheer in so melancholy a fashion
98.2 proud-pied gorgeously multicolored. trim finery   4 That so
that. Saturn (A planet associated with melancholy, heavy.)   5 nor
the lays neither the songs   6 different flowers flowers differing
7 any summer's story i.e., any pleasant story   8 proud lap i.e., the
earth   11 but sweet . . . delight mere sweetness, mere delightful
forms or emblems   12 after resembling   14 shadow image, portrait.
these i.e., the flowers
99.1 forward early and presumptuous. (This sonnet has fifteen lines,
the first being introductory.)   2 thy sweet your scent   3 pride splendor   5 grossly obviously and heavily   6 for thy hand i.e., because it
has stolen its whiteness from your hand   7 And . . . hair i.e., and I
condemned the buds of marjoram for having stolen your hair.   buds
of marjoram (These are dark purple-red or auburn, and it may be that
the reference is to color, although marjoram is noted for its sweet
scent.)   8 on thorns did stand grew on thorny stems (with a suggestion of being apprehensive)   9 shame i.e., red for shame   10 nor red
neither (purely) red   11 to . . . annexed to this robbery had added
the robbery of   12 But, for although, in punishment for.   in pride
. . . growth in his prime   13 canker cankerworm   15 But except.
sweet scent (as in line 2)
100.3 fury poetic inspiration   4 Dark'ning debasing   5 straight
straightway   6 gentle numbers noble verses.   idly foolishly   7 lays
songs   8 argument subject   9 resty inactive, inert   10 If to see if
11 If any if there are any.   satire to satirist of, here one composing a
satire on Time as a despoiler   12 spoils acts of destruction, ravages
13 faster (1) more quickly (2) more firmly   14 thou prevent'st you
forestall, thwart.   crooked knife curved blade
101.1 what . . . amends what reparation will you make   2 truth . . .
dyed moral perfection and faith enhanced by physical beauty
3–4 Both . . . dignified i.e., both faith and beauty depend on my
love for their proper appreciation and recognition, and you, my
Muse, depend for your very office and dignity on that same function
5 haply perhaps   6 no . . . fixed no artificial color (with suggestion
of pretense) added to its natural and permanent color or hue   7 pencil paintbrush.   lay apply color to, as with a brush   8 intermixed
adulterated   9 dumb silent   12 of by   13 office function   14 long
hence long in the future.   shows appears
102.1 seeming outward appearance   3 merchandized degraded by
being treated as a thing of sale.   esteeming valuation   4 publish announce, advertise   6 wont . . . lays accustomed to salute it (our love)
with my song

As Philomel in summer's front doth sing
And stops her pipe in growth of riper days— 8
Not that the summer is less pleasant now
Than when her mournful hymns did hush the night,
But that wild music burdens every bough
And sweets grown common lose their dear delight. 12
    Therefore like her I sometimes hold my tongue,
    Because I would not dull you with my song.

103

Alack, what poverty my Muse brings forth,
That, having such a scope to show her pride,
The argument all bare is of more worth
Than when it hath my added praise beside. 4
O, blame me not if I no more can write!
Look in your glass, and there appears a face
That overgoes my blunt invention quite,
Dulling my lines and doing me disgrace. 8
Were it not sinful then, striving to mend,
To mar the subject that before was well?
For to no other pass my verses tend
Than of your graces and your gifts to tell; 12
    And more, much more, than in my verse can sit
    Your own glass shows you when you look in it.

104

To me, fair friend, you never can be old,
For, as you were when first your eye I eyed,
Such seems your beauty still. Three winters cold
Have from the forests shook three summers' pride, 4
Three beauteous springs to yellow autumn turned
In process of the seasons have I seen,
Three April perfumes in three hot Junes burned,
Since first I saw you fresh, which yet are green. 8
Ah, yet doth beauty, like a dial hand,
Steal from his figure and no pace perceived.
So your sweet hue, which methinks still doth stand,
Hath motion, and mine eye may be deceived, 12
    For fear of which, hear this, thou age unbred:
    Ere you were born was beauty's summer dead.

105

Let not my love be called idolatry,
Nor my belovèd as an idol show,
Since all alike my songs and praises be
To one, of one, still such, and ever so. 4
Kind is my love today, tomorrow kind,
Still constant in a wondrous excellence;
Therefore my verse, to constancy confined,
One thing expressing, leaves out difference. 8
"Fair, kind, and true" is all my argument,
"Fair, kind, and true" varying to other words;
And in this change is my invention spent,
Three themes in one, which wondrous scope affords. 12
    Fair, kind, and true have often lived alone,
    Which three till now never kept seat in one.

106

When in the chronicle of wasted time
I see descriptions of the fairest wights,
And beauty making beautiful old rhyme
In praise of ladies dead and lovely knights, 4
Then, in the blazon of sweet beauty's best,
Of hand, of foot, of lip, of eye, of brow,
I see their antique pen would have expressed
Even such a beauty as you master now. 8
So all their praises are but prophecies
Of this our time, all you prefiguring;
And, for they looked but with divining eyes,
They had not skill enough your worth to sing. 12
    For we, which now behold these present days,
    Have eyes to wonder, but lack tongues to praise.

107

Not mine own fears nor the prophetic soul
Of the wide world dreaming on things to come
Can yet the lease of my true love control,
Supposed as forfeit to a confined doom. 4
The mortal moon hath her eclipse endured,
And the sad augurs mock their own presage;
Incertainties now crown themselves assured,

7 **Philomel** the nightingale. **front** forehead, beginning **8 stops her pipe** stops singing. **riper** i.e., those of late summer and autumn **11 But . . . music** i.e., but because a profusion of wild birds' singing. (Refers to other poets.) **burdens** weighs down (but with a musical sense as well; a *burden* is a chorus) **14 dull** surfeit
103.1 poverty poor stuff **2 pride** splendor **3 argument all bare** subject alone, unadorned **5 no more can write** i.e., (1) am silent (2) cannot go beyond what you yourself are, cannot excel my own poverty of invention **6 glass** mirror **7 overgoes** surpasses; overwhelms. **blunt invention** unpolished style, writing **8 Dulling** i.e., making dull by comparison **11 pass** purpose, issue **13 sit** reside
104.4 pride splendor **6 process** the progression **9 dial hand** watch hand **10 Steal from** steal away from (with a suggestion of "rob from"). **his figure** (1) the dial's numeral (2) the friend's shape. **and . . . perceived** i.e., imperceptibly **11 hue** appearance, complexion. **still doth stand** remains motionless, unaltered **13 of which** i.e., that my eye may be deceived. (The poet, though wishing to believe that his friend never can be old, concedes that this is a deception.) **unbred** not yet born

105.2 show appear **3 Since** (1) simply because, or, (2) since it can be said in my defense that **4 still** always **8 difference** variety of other literary subjects; any kind of diversity that detracts from the young man's constancy (including any suggestion of quarreling or fluctuation of mood) **11 this change** variations on this theme. **invention** inventiveness. **spent** expended **13 alone** separately (in different people) **14 kept seat** resided; sat enthroned
106.1 wasted past, used up **2 wights** persons **3 beauty** (1) beauty of style and language (2) beauty of the persons described **5 blazon** i.e., glorification, cataloguing of qualities. (A heraldic metaphor.) **7 see** perceive (that). **their** i.e., of antique poets. **would have expressed** wished to express **8 master** possess, control **11 for** because. **divining** guessing or predicting as to the future **13 For we** for even we **14 praise** i.e., praise you worthily, sufficiently
107.1–2 soul . . . world collective consciousness of humanity **3 yet** now. **lease** term, allotted time. **control** set a limit to **4 Supposed . . . doom** though imagined to be destined to expire after a limited term **5 mortal moon** (Probably a reference to Queen Elizabeth, ill or deceased, most probably to her death in 1603; she was known as Diana, Cynthia, etc.) **6 And . . . presage** and the solemn prophets of disaster now mock their earlier predictions **7 Incertainties . . . assured** uncertainties have triumphantly given way to certainties

And peace proclaims olives of endless age.   8
Now with the drops of this most balmy time
My love looks fresh, and Death to me subscribes,
Since, spite of him, I'll live in this poor rhyme,
While he insults o'er dull and speechless tribes;   12
    And thou in this shalt find thy monument,
    When tyrants' crests and tombs of brass are spent.

108

What's in the brain that ink may character
Which hath not figured to thee my true spirit?
What's new to speak, what now to register,
That may express my love or thy dear merit?   4
Nothing, sweet boy; but yet, like prayers divine,
I must each day say o'er the very same,
Counting no old thing old—thou mine, I thine—
Even as when first I hallowed thy fair name.   8
So that eternal love in love's fresh case
Weighs not the dust and injury of age,
Nor gives to necessary wrinkles place,
But makes antiquity for aye his page,   12
    Finding the first conceit of love there bred
    Where time and outward form would show it dead.

109

O, never say that I was false of heart,
Though absence seemed my flame to qualify.
As easy might I from myself depart
As from my soul, which in thy breast doth lie.   4
That is my home of love; if I have ranged,
Like him that travels I return again,
Just to the time, not with the time exchanged,
So that myself bring water for my stain.   8
Never believe, though in my nature reigned
All frailties that besiege all kinds of blood,
That it could so preposterously be stained
To leave for nothing all thy sum of good;   12
    For nothing this wide universe I call
    Save thou, my rose; in it thou art my all.

110

Alas, 'tis true, I have gone here and there
And made myself a motley to the view,
Gored mine own thoughts, sold cheap what is most
    dear,
Made old offenses of affections new;   4
Most true it is that I have looked on truth
Askance and strangely. But, by all above,
These blenches gave my heart another youth,
And worse essays proved thee my best of love.   8
Now all is done, have what shall have no end.
Mine appetite I never more will grind
On newer proof, to try an older friend,
A god in love, to whom I am confined.   12
    Then give me welcome, next my heaven the best,
    Even to thy pure and most most loving breast.

111

O, for my sake do you with Fortune chide,
The guilty goddess of my harmful deeds,
That did not better for my life provide
Than public means which public manners breeds.   4
Thence comes it that my name receives a brand,
And almost thence my nature is subdued
To what it works in, like the dyer's hand.
Pity me then, and wish I were renewed,   8
Whilst, like a willing patient, I will drink
Potions of eisel 'gainst my strong infection;
No bitterness that I will bitter think,
Nor double penance, to correct correction.   12
    Pity me then, dear friend, and I assure ye
    Even that your pity is enough to cure me.

112

Your love and pity doth th' impression fill
Which vulgar scandal stamped upon my brow;
For what care I who calls me well or ill,

110.2 **motley** jester, fool.   **to the view** in the eyes of the world
3 **Gored** wounded   4 **Made . . . new** i.e., repeated old offenses or
made offense against old friendships in forming new attachments
5 **truth** constancy   6 **Askance and strangely** disdainfully, obliquely
and at a distance.   **by all above** by heaven   7 **blenches** swervings
8 **essays** experiments (in friendship)   9 **Now all** now that all that.
have what . . . end take what is eternal (my friendship)   10 **grind**
whet, sharpen   11 **newer proof** further experiment, experience.   **try**
test   12 **A god** godlike   13 **next my heaven** you, who are to me second only to heaven itself
111.2 **guilty goddess of** goddess responsible for   3 **life** livelihood
4 **Than . . . breeds** than providing me a means of livelihood that depends on catering to the public. (A probable reference to
Shakespeare's career as an actor.)   5 **receives a brand** is disgraced
(through prejudice against my occupation)   7 **like the dyer's hand**
(The dyer's hand is stained by the dye it handles, just as the poet's nature is almost overpowered by the medium in which he works—the
language of poetry and, more particulary, the theater.)   8 **renewed**
restored to what I was by nature, cleansed   10 **eisel** vinegar, used as
an antiseptic against the plague and also as an agent for removing
stains   11 **No bitterness** there is no bitterness   12 **Nor . . . correction** nor will I think it bitter to undertake a twofold penance in order
to correct what must be doubly corrected   14 **Even that your pity**
that very pity of yours
112.1 **doth th' impression fill** effaces the scar   2 **vulgar scandal** notoriety (for being an actor?)

8 **olives** (Conventionally associated with peace and probably pointing
here to King James I's resolutions of war with Spain and strife in Ireland.)   **of endless age** without foreseen end   9 **with the drops** i.e.,
healed as though by a balmy dew. (Balm was employed in the coronation ceremony for James in 1603, as in all such coronations.)
10 **subscribes** yields   12 **insults** triumphs   14 **crests** trophies adorning
a tomb.   **spent** expended, wasted away
108.1 **character** write   2 **figured** revealed, represented.   **true** constant   3 **register** record   7 **Counting . . . thine** dismissing no old
truth as out of date or shopworn, such as the truth that you are mine
and I yours   8 **hallowed** (As in "hallowed be thy name" from the
Lord's Prayer.)   9 **fresh case** new exterior and circumstance
10 **Weighs not** is unconcerned about   11 **place** consideration, pri-
macy   12 **aye** ever.   **page** servant, subordinate   13 **the first . . .
love** the first conception of love, experienced as though for the first
time.   **there** (1) in you (2) in my verse.   **bred** generated   14 **would**
try to, wish to
109.2 **flame** passion.   **qualify** temper, moderate   5 **ranged** traveled,
wandered   7 **Just . . . exchanged** punctual to the minute, not
changed by the period of separation   8 **water for my stain** i.e., tears,
to wash away the stain of my offense   10 **blood** temperament, sensual nature   12 **for** in exchange for

So you o'ergreen my bad, my good allow?   4
You are my all the world, and I must strive
To know my shames and praises from your tongue;
None else to me, nor I to none alive,
That my steeled sense or changes, right or wrong.   8
In so profound abysm I throw all care
Of others' voices that my adder's sense
To critic and to flatterer stoppèd are.
Mark how with my neglect I do dispense: 12
    You are so strongly in my purpose bred
    That all the world besides, methinks, are dead.

113

Since I left you, mine eye is in my mind,
And that which governs me to go about
Doth part his function and is partly blind,
Seems seeing, but effectually is out;   4
For it no form delivers to the heart
Of bird, of flower, or shape, which it doth latch;
Of his quick objects hath the mind no part,
Nor his own vision holds what it doth catch;   8
For if it see the rud'st or gentlest sight,
The most sweet-favor or deformedst creature,
The mountain or the sea, the day or night,
The crow or dove, it shapes them to your feature.   12
    Incapable of more, replete with you,
    My most true mind thus maketh mine eye untrue.

114

Or whether doth my mind, being crowned with you,
Drink up the monarch's plague, this flattery?
Or whether shall I say mine eye saith true,
And that your love taught it this alchemy,   4
To make of monsters and things indigest
Such cherubins as your sweet self resemble,
Creating every bad a perfect best

As fast as objects to his beams assemble?   8
O, 'tis the first, 'tis flattery in my seeing,
And my great mind most kingly drinks it up;
Mine eye well knows what with his gust is greeing,
And to his palate doth prepare the cup.   12
    If it be poisoned, 'tis the lesser sin
    That mine eye loves it and doth first begin.

115

Those lines that I before have writ do lie,
Even those that said I could not love you dearer;
Yet then my judgment knew no reason why
My most full flame should afterwards burn clearer.   4
But reckoning Time, whose millioned accidents
Creep in twixt vows and change decrees of kings,
Tan sacred beauty, blunt the sharp'st intents,
Divert strong minds to th' course of altering things—   8
Alas, why, fearing of Time's tyranny,
Might I not then say, "Now I love you best,"
When I was certain o'er incertainty,
Crowning the present, doubting of the rest?   12
    Love is a babe; then might I not say so,
    To give full growth to that which still doth grow.

116

Let me not to the marriage of true minds
Admit impediments. Love is not love
Which alters when it alteration finds,
Or bends with the remover to remove.   4
O, no, it is an ever-fixèd mark
That looks on tempests and is never shaken;
It is the star to every wandering bark,
Whose worth's unknown, although his height be
    taken.   8
Love's not Time's fool, though rosy lips and cheeks
Within his bending sickle's compass come;

---

4 So you o'ergreen provided that you cover as with green growth. **allow** approve **5 my all the world** everything to me **7–8 None . . . wrong** no one else but you affects my fixed and hardened sensibilities, whether for better or for worse **9 In so profound** into such a deep **10 Of** about. **voices** i.e., criticism. **adder's sense** i.e., deaf ears **11 critic** faultfinder **12 Mark . . . dispense** see how I excuse my disregard of the opinion of others **13 You . . . bred** you are so nurtured in my thoughts and are such a powerful influence over my intentions
113.1 mine . . . mind i.e., I'm guided by my mind's eye **2 that . . . about** i.e., my physical sight **3 part** (1) divide (2) abandon. **his** its, i.e., the physical eye's (also in lines 7 and 8) **4 Seems seeing** seems to be seeing. **effectually** in reality. **out** out of commission, ineffectual **5 heart** (Here portrayed as capable of receiving sense impressions and of consciousness, as in sonnet 47.) **6 latch** catch or receive the sight of **7 Of . . . part** i.e., the mind, attuned to its inner eye, takes no part in the fleeting and lively (*quick*) things seen by the physical sight **8 Nor . . . holds** nor does the eye itself retain. **catch** see glimpsingly **9 For . . . sight** for whether it see the most uncouth or most gracious sight **10 sweet-favor** sweet-featured **12 shapes . . . feature** makes them resemble you
114.1, 3 Or whether (Indicates alternative possibilities.) **1 crowned with you** elevated by possession of you **2 the monarch's . . . flattery** this pleasing delusion to which all monarchs are prone **4 your love** my love of you. **alchemy** science of transmuting base metals **5 indigest** chaotic, formless **6 cherubins** angelic forms (suggesting the youth and beauty of the friend) **7 Creating** creating out of

8 his beams its (the eye's) gaze **9 'tis flattery . . . seeing** my eye is flattering my mind (see lines 1–2) **11 what . . . greeing** what agrees with the mind's taste **12 to** to suit **13–14 'tis . . . begin** it extenuates the eye's sinful deed (of misleading the mind) that it tastes of the poison first, like an official taster sampling food before it is given to the king
115.5 reckoning Time (1) Time, which we reckon up (2) Time, which makes a reckoning. **millioned** numbered in millions **6 twixt vows** i.e., between the making of vows and their fulfillment **7 Tan** darken, i.e., coarsen. **sacred** deserving worship **8 to . . . things** into the current that flows toward decay of all things **9 fearing of** fearing **10 Might . . . say** i.e., wasn't it understandable for me to say then, when I wrote *Those lines* (line 1) **11 certain o'er incertainty** i.e., certain of my love's perfection then, as contrasted with the uncertainty of the future **12 Crowning** glorifying. **doubting of** fearing **13 then might . . . so** i.e., therefore it was wrong of me to say, "Now I love you best" (line 10) **14 To give** thereby attributing
116.2 Admit concede that there might be, allow consideration of. (An echo of the marriage service.) **3 alteration** i.e., in age, beauty, affection, health, circumstance **4 Or . . . remove** or changes simply because there is change in the person loved, inclines to inconstancy simply because the person loved is inconstant **5 mark** seamark, conspicuous object distinguishable at sea as an aid to navigation **8 Whose . . . taken** whose value is beyond estimation, although its altitude above the horizon can be determined (for purposes of navigation) **9 fool** plaything, laughingstock **10 his** i.e., Time's (also in line 11). **bending** curved. **compass** range

Love alters not with his brief hours and weeks,
But bears it out even to the edge of doom. 12
    If this be error and upon me proved,
    I never writ, nor no man ever loved.

117

Accuse me thus: that I have scanted all
Wherein I should your great deserts repay,
Forgot upon your dearest love to call,
Whereto all bonds do tie me day by day; 4
That I have frequent been with unknown minds,
And given to time your own dear-purchased right;
That I have hoisted sail to all the winds
Which should transport me farthest from your sight. 8
Book both my willfulness and errors down,
And on just proof surmise accumulate;
Bring me within the level of your frown,
But shoot not at me in your wakened hate, 12
    Since my appeal says I did strive to prove
    The constancy and virtue of your love.

118

Like as to make our appetites more keen
With eager compounds we our palate urge,
As to prevent our maladies unseen
We sicken to shun sickness when we purge: 4
Even so, being full of your ne'er-cloying sweetness,
To bitter sauces did I frame my feeding
And, sick of welfare, found a kind of meetness
To be diseased ere that there was true needing. 8
Thus policy in love, t' anticipate
The ills that were not, grew to faults assured,
And brought to medicine a healthful state
Which, rank of goodness, would by ill be cured. 12
    But thence I learn, and find the lesson true:
    Drugs poison him that so fell sick of you.

119

What potions have I drunk of siren tears,
Distilled from limbecks foul as hell within,
Applying fears to hopes and hopes to fears,
Still losing when I saw myself to win! 4
What wretched errors hath my heart committed,
Whilst it hath thought itself so blessèd never!
How have mine eyes out of their spheres been fitted
In the distraction of this madding fever! 8
O, benefit of ill! Now I find true
That better is by evil still made better;
And ruined love, when it is built anew,
Grows fairer than at first, more strong, far greater. 12
    So I return rebuked to my content,
    And gain by ills thrice more than I have spent.

120

That you were once unkind befriends me now,
And for that sorrow which I then did feel
Needs must I under my transgression bow,
Unless my nerves were brass or hammered steel. 4
For if you were by my unkindness shaken
As I by yours, you've passed a hell of time,
And I, a tyrant, have no leisure taken
To weigh how once I suffered in your crime. 8
O, that our night of woe might have remembered
My deepest sense how hard true sorrow hits,
And soon to you, as you to me then, tendered
The humble salve which wounded bosoms fits! 12
    But that your trespass now becomes a fee;
    Mine ransoms yours, and yours must ransom me.

121

'Tis better to be vile than vile esteemed
When not to be receives reproach of being,

12 bears . . . doom endures or holds out to the very Day of Judgment **117.1 scanted** come short in **3 upon . . . call** to pay my respects to your love, or, to invoke your aid **5 frequent** familiar. **unknown minds** strangers of no consequence **6 given . . . right** squandered that part of me which is rightly yours (and hence precious) on temporary matters and alliances **8 should** would **9 Book . . . down** record both my willful faults and errors **10 on . . . accumulate** to sure proof add surmise, suspicion **11 level** point-blank range, aim **13 appeal** legal appealing of the case. **1 . . . prove** my intention was to test

118.1 Like as just as **2 eager compounds** pungent, bitter concoctions. **urge** stimulate, prompt **3 As** just as. **prevent** anticipate, forestall. **unseen** not yet physically manifested **4 sicken . . . purge** induce a kind of sickness through purging (i.e., evacuation of stomach or bowel), in order to ward off greater sickness **5 Even so** in just the same way **6 bitter sauces** i.e., other loves, undesirable in comparison with you. **frame** adapt, direct **7 sick of welfare** surfeited and made ill by health and happiness (in love). **meetness** suitability **8 ere . . . needing** before there was any real necessity for it **9 policy** shortsighted calculation. **anticipate** forestall **10 assured** actual **11 to medicine** into a state of needing medical care **12 rank of goodness** gorged and sickened by good health **14 Drugs . . . you** i.e., the cure is worse than the disease. **so** thus

119.1 siren i.e., deceitful. (The poet seems to speak of an affair.) **2 limbecks** vessels used in distillation. **foul as hell within** i.e., possessing an inner ugliness and evil contrasted with a beautiful and seductive appearance **3 Applying . . . fears** trying vainly to control my wild hopes with a sense of fear and to assuage my fears with hope **4 Still** always. **saw myself** vainly expected **6 so blessèd never** never before so fortunate **7 How . . . fitted** how my eyes have popped out in convulsive fit **8 distraction** frenzy. **madding** maddening

120.1 befriends benefits (by giving me perspective on what I now need to do) **2–3 for . . . bow** i.e., realizing the sorrow I felt from your unkindness, I must now acknowledge my own guilt in being unkind to you **4 nerves** sinews **6 hell of** hellish **7 have . . . taken** have not taken the opportunity **8 weigh** consider. **in your crime** i.e., from your unkindness, my unfaithfulness. (If I suffered so, I should realize you've suffered, too, from my unkindness.) **9 that our night of woe** would that the dark and woeful time of our earlier estrangement. **remembered** reminded **10 sense** consciousness, apprehension **11 And . . . tendered** i.e., and would that I had quickly offered to you, as you did to me **12 humble salve** i.e., apology and remorse. **which . . . fits** which is just what wounded hearts need **13 that your trespass** that unkindness of yours. **fee** payment, compensation **14 ransoms** redeems, excuses

121. vile esteemed (to be) considered vile **2 When . . . being** when not to be vile receives the reproach of vileness. (It's even worse to be unjustly accused of wickedness than to be reproved when one's conduct is truly vile.)

And the just pleasure lost which is so deemed
Not by our feeling but by others' seeing.   4
For why should others' false adulterate eyes
Give salutation to my sportive blood?
Or on my frailties why are frailer spies,
Which in their wills count bad what I think good?   8
No, I am that I am, and they that level
At my abuses reckon up their own.
I may be straight though they themselves be bevel.
By their rank thoughts my deeds must not be shown,   12
    Unless this general evil they maintain:
    All men are bad, and in their badness reign.

122

Thy gift, thy tables, are within my brain
Full charactered with lasting memory,
Which shall above that idle rank remain
Beyond all date, even to eternity—   4
Or at the least, so long as brain and heart
Have faculty by nature to subsist;
Till each to razed oblivion yield his part
Of thee, thy record never can be missed.   8
That poor retention could not so much hold,
Nor need I tallies thy dear love to score;
Therefore to give them from me was I bold,
To trust those tables that receive thee more.   12
    To keep an adjunct to remember thee
    Were to import forgetfulness in me.

123

No, Time, thou shalt not boast that I do change.
Thy pyramids built up with newer might
To me are nothing novel, nothing strange;

They are but dressings of a former sight.   4
Our dates are brief, and therefore we admire
What thou dost foist upon us that is old,
And rather make them born to our desire
Than think that we before have heard them told.   8
Thy registers and thee I both defy,
Not wondering at the present nor the past,
For thy records and what we see doth lie,
Made more or less by thy continual haste.   12
    This I do vow and this shall ever be:
    I will be true, despite thy scythe and thee.

124

If my dear love were but the child of state,
It might for Fortune's bastard be unfathered,
As subject to Time's love or to Time's hate,
Weeds among weeds, or flowers with flowers gathered.   4
No, it was builded far from accident;
It suffers not in smiling pomp, nor falls
Under the blow of thrallèd discontent,
Whereto th' inviting time our fashion calls.   8
It fears not Policy, that heretic,
Which works on leases of short-numbered hours,
But all alone stands hugely politic,
That it nor grows with heat nor drowns with showers.   12
    To this I witness call the fools of Time,
    Which die for goodness, who have lived for crime.

125

Were 't aught to me I bore the canopy,
With my extern the outward honoring,
Or laid great bases for eternity

3–4 **And . . . seeing** and to lose justifiable pleasure because its justification has to depend not on our feelings but on the censorious attitudes of others   5 **false adulterate eyes** i.e., the eyes of those whose
own wickedness prompts them to misconstrue my innocent love
6 **Give . . . blood** i.e., greet me, in my lusty merriment, with familiarity and with a knowing wink of the eye   7 **Or . . . spies** or why
should there be persons more faulty than I spying on my fleshly indulgences   8 **Which in their wills** who by the measure of their prurient,
licentious minds   9 **am that** am what.   **level** (1) aim (2) guess
10 **abuses** misdoings.   **reckon up their own** i.e., merely enumerate
their own misdeeds   11 **bevel** out of square, crooked   12 **rank** ugly,
foul.   **shown** viewed, interpreted   14 **reign** i.e., prosper. (Only a
cynic would interpret my success in love as a paradoxical proof of my
sharing in general human depravity.)
122.1 **tables** writing tablet, memorandum book   2 **charactered with**
written by   3 **that idle rank** i.e., the relative unimportance of that
memorandum book (as compared with the memory itself)   6 **faculty**
. . . subsist natural power to survive   7 **each** i.e., brain and heart.
razed oblivion obliterating forgetfulness. (*Razed,* "effaced, destroyed," and *rased,* "erased, scraped away," often mean much the
same thing.)   **his** its   8 **missed** lost. (The poet is apologizing for having given away or lost a memorandum book written by the friend.)
9 **retention** i.e., the book, an instrument for retaining memoranda.
so much i.e., as much as is in my memory   10 **tallies** sticks notched
to serve for reckoning. (The notebook is such a mere *tally.*)   **score**
reckon   11 **to . . . me** i.e., to give away the writing tablet.   **bold**
i.e., bold in taking the liberty   12 **those tables** i.e., those of memory.
receive thee more retain more of you   13 **adjunct** aid   14 **Were**
would be.   **import** imply, impute
123.2 **pyramids** (May refer to obelisks or other structures erected in
Rome in 1586 or in London in 1603.)   3 **nothing** not at all

4 **dressings . . . sight** reconstructions in new form of things from the
past   5 **dates** life spans   7 **make . . . desire** consider them newly
created to our liking and reinvented by us   8 **told** reckoned, told
about   9 **registers** visual records, monuments   10 **wondering** marveling   11 **doth lie** deceives us   12 **Made more or less** i.e., raised one
minute and ruined the next (by Time), and alternately overvalued and
undervalued by us
124.1 **love** i.e., love for you.   **but . . . state** merely the product of
circumstance   2 **for . . . unfathered** be disavowed as nothing but the
bastard child of Fortune   3 **As** i.e., and accordingly regarded as
4 **Weeds . . . gathered** i.e., either despised as worthless like a weed
or cherished like a flower, as Fortune dictates   5 **accident** chance,
fortune   6–7 **It . . . discontent** it does not grow complacent in circumstances of pomp and finery, nor does it weaken under the blows
of adversity, turning melancholy.   **thrallèd** enslaved, oppressed
8 **Whereto . . . calls** to which the temptations of our present age expose all of us, or, which the age invites us to regard as fashionable
9 **Policy, that heretic** cunning expediency, false to the spirit of love
10 **Which . . . hours** which thinks only shortsightedly of short-term
gain and makes only short-term commitments   11 **hugely politic** prudent in a long-term sense   12 **nor . . . heat** i.e., neither flourishes
only in good times.   **showers** i.e., adversity   13 **witness call** call to
witness.   **fools** playthings, laughingstocks. (See sonnet 116.)
14 **Which . . . crime** those who have lived evilly and then attempt to
repent at their deaths or to die in a good cause
125.1 **Were 't . . . canopy** i.e., would it be anything to me if I did
public homage as one honors great persons by carrying over their
heads a cloth of state as they go in procession   2 **With . . . honoring**
honoring the external by means of external action   3 **laid . . . eternity** laid foundations for supposedly lasting monuments

Which proves more short than waste or ruining?   4
Have I not seen dwellers on form and favor
Lose all, and more, by paying too much rent,
For compound sweet forgoing simple savor,
Pitiful thrivers, in their gazing spent?   8
No, let me be obsequious in thy heart,
And take thou my oblation, poor but free,
Which is not mixed with seconds, knows no art
But mutual render, only me for thee.   12
        Hence, thou suborned informer! A true soul
        When most impeached stands least in thy control.

126

O thou, my lovely boy, who in thy power
Dost hold Time's fickle glass, his sickle hour;
Who hast by waning grown, and therein show'st
Thy lovers withering as thy sweet self grow'st;   4
If Nature, sovereign mistress over wrack,
As thou goest onwards, still will pluck thee back,
She keeps thee to this purpose, that her skill
May Time disgrace and wretched minutes kill.   8
Yet fear her, O thou minion of her pleasure!
She may detain, but not still keep, her treasure.
Her audit, though delayed, answered must be,
And her quietus is to render thee.   12

127

In the old age black was not counted fair,
Or if it were, it bore not beauty's name;
But now is black beauty's successive heir,
And beauty slandered with a bastard shame.   4
For since each hand hath put on nature's power,

Fairing the foul with art's false borrowed face,
Sweet beauty hath no name, no holy bower,
But is profaned, if not lives in disgrace.   8
Therefore my mistress' eyes are raven black,
Her brows so suited, and they mourners seem
At such who, not born fair, no beauty lack,
Sland'ring creation with a false esteem.   12
        Yet so they mourn, becoming of their woe,
        That every tongue says beauty should look so.

128

How oft, when thou, my music, music play'st
Upon that blessèd wood whose motion sounds
With thy sweet fingers when thou gently sway'st
The wiry concord that mine ear confounds,   4
Do I envy those jacks that nimble leap
To kiss the tender inward of thy hand,
Whilst my poor lips, which should that harvest reap,
At the wood's boldness by thee blushing stand!   8
To be so tickled, they would change their state
And situation with those dancing chips
O'er whom thy fingers walk with gentle gait,
Making dead wood more blest than living lips.   12
        Since saucy jacks so happy are in this,
        Give them thy fingers, me thy lips to kiss.

129

Th' expense of spirit in a waste of shame
Is lust in action; and, till action, lust
Is perjured, murderous, bloody, full of blame,
Savage, extreme, rude, cruel, not to trust,   4
Enjoyed no sooner but despisèd straight,
Past reason hunted, and no sooner had
Past reason hated, as a swallowed bait
On purpose laid to make the taker mad;   8
Mad in pursuit, and in possession so;
Had, having, and in quest to have, extreme;

4 Which . . . ruining which foundations proved to be shorter lived than the forces of decay and ruin **5 dwellers on** those who insist fulsomely upon (with pun on the idea of "tenants"). **form and favor** (1) courtly etiquette and the achieving of status through influence (2) figure and face **6 Lose . . . rent** lose all their wealth and then go into debt by overdoing their obligations to mere ceremony **7 For . . . savor** i.e., foregoing wholesome sincerity for the sake of obsequious flattery **8 Pitiful . . . spent** those thriving only in pitiful or worthless gains consumed by ceremonial observance **9 obsequious** (1) courtly (2) devoted **10 oblation** offering. **free** freely offered **11 seconds** inferior matter, adulterants. **art** artifice **12 render** exchange **13 suborned informer** perjured witness, the envious one who has charged the poet with self-interested flattery **14 impeached** accused **126.1** (This sonnet is made up of six couplets.) **2 Time's . . . hour** i.e., Time's hourglass by which we are constantly betrayed and the hour of final reckoning when all is cut down by Time's sickle (? The line may be corrupt.) **3 by waning grown** grown more youthful as age increases. **show'st** i.e., show by way of contrast with yourself **5 wrack** ruin. (Nature is mistress over decay in that she decays and renews.) **6 onwards** i.e., in life's journey **7 to** for **8 and . . . kill** and render powerless the passing of the minutes **9 minion** (1) darling (2) slave **10 She . . . treasure** i.e., Nature may keep and restore you for a time, but Time will ultimately triumph. **still** always **11 Her audit** i.e., the proverbial paying of one's debt to Nature through death; also, Nature's account to Time. **answered** settled **12 quietus** discharge, quittance. **render** surrender **127.1 old age** olden times. **black** darkness of hair and eyes. **fair** (1) beautiful (2) light-complexioned **2 it bore . . . name** i.e., it was not called so **3 now . . . heir** nowadays black has been named lawful successor to the title of beauty **4 beauty . . . shame** i.e., blonde beauty is declared illegitimate, created artificially by cosmetics **5 put on** assumed

6 Fairing the foul making the ugly beautiful. **borrowed face** i.e., cosmetics **7 no name . . . bower** no reputation or pride of family, and no sacred abode **8 profaned** i.e., scorned and violated by those who use cosmetics. **if not** or even **10 so suited** decked out in the same color and for the same reason **11 At** for. **no beauty lack** i.e., nonetheless make themselves attractive **12 Sland'ring . . . esteem** i.e., dishonoring nature by blurring the distinction between real and false beauty **13 they** i.e., my mistress' eyes. **becoming of** gracing or being graced by **128.2 wood** keys of the spinet or virginal. **whose motion** the motion of which **3 thou gently sway'st** you gently control **4 wiry concord** harmony produced by strings. **confounds** i.e., pleasurably overwhelms **5 jacks** (Literally, upright pieces of wood fixed to the key lever and fitted with a quill that plucks the strings of the virginal; here used of the keys and with a pun on *jacks* in the sense of "common fellows," as in line 13.) **8 by** beside, or, with. (The poet stands beside the lady as she plays, blushing to his very lips; he blushes in vexation at the *jacks'* boldness with her hand.) **9 they** i.e., my lips **13 jacks** (With a pun on "knaves, fellows" as in line 5.) **129.1–2 Th' expense . . . action** lust being consummated is the expenditure or dissipation of vital energy in an orgy of shameful extravagance and guilt. (*Spirit* also suggests "sperm.") **2 till action** until it achieves consummation **3 blame** (1) guilt (2) recrimination **4 rude** brutal. **to trust** to be trusted **5 straight** immediately **6 Past reason** madly, intemperately

A bliss in proof, and proved, a very woe;
Before, a joy proposed; behind, a dream.   12
　　All this the world well knows; yet none knows
　　　well
　　To shun the heaven that leads men to this hell.

130

My mistress' eyes are nothing like the sun;
Coral is far more red than her lips' red;
If snow be white, why then her breasts are dun;
If hairs be wires, black wires grow on her head.   4
I have seen roses damasked, red and white,
But no such roses see I in her cheeks;
And in some perfumes is there more delight
Than in the breath that from my mistress reeks.   8
I love to hear her speak, yet well I know
That music hath a far more pleasing sound.
I grant I never saw a goddess go;
My mistress, when she walks, treads on the ground.   12
　　And yet, by heaven, I think my love as rare
　　As any she belied with false compare.

131

Thou art as tyrannous, so as thou art,
As those whose beauties proudly make them cruel;
For well thou know'st to my dear doting heart
Thou art the fairest and most precious jewel.   4
Yet, in good faith, some say that thee behold
Thy face hath not the power to make love groan;
To say they err I dare not be so bold,
Although I swear it to myself alone.   8
And, to be sure that is not false I swear,
A thousand groans, but thinking on thy face,
One on another's neck, do witness bear
Thy black is fairest in my judgment's place.   12
　　In nothing art thou black save in thy deeds,
　　And thence this slander, as I think, proceeds.

132

Thine eyes I love, and they, as pitying me,
Knowing thy heart torment me with disdain,
Have put on black, and loving mourners be,
Looking with pretty ruth upon my pain.   4
And truly not the morning sun of heaven
Better becomes the gray cheeks of the east,

Nor that full star that ushers in the even
Doth half that glory to the sober west   8
As those two mourning eyes become thy face.
O, let it then as well beseem thy heart
To mourn for me, since mourning doth thee grace,
And suit thy pity like in every part.   12
　　Then will I swear beauty herself is black,
　　And all they foul that thy complexion lack.

133

Beshrew that heart that makes my heart to groan
For that deep wound it gives my friend and me!
Is 't not enough to torture me alone,
But slave to slavery my sweet'st friend must be?   4
Me from myself thy cruel eye hath taken,
And my next self thou harder hast engrossed.
Of him, myself, and thee I am forsaken—
A torment thrice threefold thus to be crossed.   8
Prison my heart in thy steel bosom's ward,
But then my friend's heart let my poor heart bail;
Whoe'er keeps me, let my heart be his guard;
Thou canst not then use rigor in my jail.   12
　　And yet thou wilt; for I, being pent in thee,
　　Perforce am thine, and all that is in me.

134

So, now I have confessed that he is thine,
And I myself am mortgaged to thy will,
Myself I'll forfeit, so that other mine
Thou wilt restore to be my comfort still.   4
But thou wilt not, nor he will not be free,
For thou art covetous and he is kind;
He learned but surety-like to write for me
Under that bond that him as fast doth bind.   8
The statute of thy beauty thou wilt take,
Thou usurer, that putt'st forth all to use,

7 **that full star** the evening star, Hesperus, i.e., Venus.   **even** evening
8 **Doth** i.e., lends.   **sober** somber, subdued in color   9 **mourning**
(Spelled *morning* in the Quarto, suggesting a pun on line 5.)   10 **beseem** suit   12 **suit thy pity like** dress your pity alike, make it alike
and consistent.   **in every part** i.e., in the heart as well as the eyes
14 **And . . . that** and that all those are ugly who
133.1 Beshrew i.e., a plague upon   2 **it** i.e., *that heart* (line 1), the
cruel heart of the Dark Lady   4 **slave to slavery** enslaved to slavery itself, to a slavish infatuation   6 **And . . . engrossed** i.e., and you have
put my dearest friend, my other self, under even greater restraint.
engrossed (1) driven into obsession (2) bought up wholesale
8 **crossed** thwarted, afflicted   9 **Prison** imprison.   **thy . . . ward** the
prison cell of your hard heart   10 **bail** set free by taking its place
11 **keeps** has custody of.   **his guard** my friend's guardhouse   12 **rigor**
harshness.   **my jail** i.e., my heart, where my friend is kept (and
where I can protect him from your harsh authority)   13 **pent** shut up
14 **and all** along with everything (including my friend's heart)
134.2 will (1) wishes (2) fleshly desire   3 **so . . . mine** provided that
my other self, my friend   5 **will not** does not wish to, won't
7 **surety-like** as security, as guarantor.   **write** sign the bond, endorse
(suggesting that the friend has taken the poet's place with the mistress)
8 **that bond . . . bind** that mortgage or bond (of sexual enslavement)
that now binds him as securely as it does me   9 **statute** a usurer's security or amount of money secured under his bond.   **take** call in, invoke. (The lady will exact the full forfeiture specified in the mortgage
as the amount to which her beauty entitles her.)   10 **use** (1) usury (2)
sexual pleasure

11 **in proof** while experienced.   **proved** i.e., afterward   12 **before** in
prospect
130.1 nothing not at all   3 **dun** dull grayish brown, mouse-colored
5 **damasked** mingled red and white   8 **reeks** emanates   11 **go** walk
13 **rare** extraordinary and unique   14 **she** woman.   **belied** misrepresented.   **compare** comparison
131.1 tyrannous pitiless and domineering.   **so as thou art** just as you
are (dark, not considered handsome)   3 **dear** fond   9 **to be sure** as
proof.   **false I** false that I   10 **but thinking on** when I do no more
than think of   11 **One . . . neck** one rapidly after another   12 **black**
dark complexion.   **my judgment's place** i.e., my opinion   14 **this**
slander (See lines 5–6.)   **proceeds** originates
132.1 as as if   2 **Knowing . . . torment** knowing that your heart torments   4 **ruth** pity   6 **becomes** adorns.   **cheeks** i.e., clouds

And sue a friend came debtor for my sake;
So him I lose through my unkind abuse.   12
    Him have I lost, thou hast both him and me;
    He pays the whole, and yet am I not free.

135

Whoever hath her wish, thou hast thy Will,
And Will to boot, and Will in overplus;
More than enough am I that vex thee still,
To thy sweet will making addition thus.   4
Wilt thou, whose will is large and spacious,
Not once vouchsafe to hide my will in thine?
Shall will in others seem right gracious,
And in my will no fair acceptance shine?   8
The sea, all water, yet receives rain still
And in abundance addeth to his store;
So thou, being rich in Will, add to thy Will
One will of mine, to make thy large Will more.   12
    Let no unkind no fair beseechers kill;
    Think all but one, and me in that one Will.

136

If thy soul check thee that I come so near,
Swear to thy blind soul that I was thy Will,
And will, thy soul knows, is admitted there;
Thus far for love my love suit, sweet, fulfill.   4
Will will fulfill the treasure of thy love,
Ay, fill it full with wills, and my will one.
In things of great receipt with ease we prove
Among a number one is reckoned none.   8
Then in the number let me pass untold,
Though in thy store's account I one must be;
For nothing hold me, so it please thee hold
That nothing me, a something, sweet, to thee.   12
    Make but my name thy love, and love that still,
    And then thou lovest me for my name is Will.

137

Thou blind fool, Love, what dost thou to mine eyes
That they behold and see not what they see?
They know what beauty is, see where it lies,
Yet what the best is take the worst to be.   4
If eyes corrupt by overpartial looks
Be anchored in the bay where all men ride,
Why of eyes' falsehood hast thou forgèd hooks,
Whereto the judgment of my heart is tied?   8
Why should my heart think that a several plot
Which my heart knows the wide world's common
        place?
Or mine eyes seeing this, say this is not,
To put fair truth upon so foul a face?   12
    In things right true my heart and eyes have erred,
    And to this false plague are they now transferred.

138

When my love swears that she is made of truth
I do believe her, though I know she lies,
That she might think me some untutored youth,
Unlearnèd in the world's false subtleties.   4
Thus vainly thinking that she thinks me young,
Although she knows my days are past the best,
Simply I credit her false-speaking tongue;
On both sides thus is simple truth suppressed.   8
But wherefore says she not she is unjust?
And wherefore say not I that I am old?
O, love's best habit is in seeming trust,
And age in love loves not to have years told.   12
    Therefore I lie with her, and she with me,
    And in our faults by lies we flattered be.

139

O, call not me to justify the wrong
That thy unkindness lays upon my heart;
Wound me not with thine eye but with thy tongue;

---

11 sue (With suggestion also of "woo.") **came** i.e., who became
12 my unkind abuse your ill usage and unkind deceiving (of me)
14 pays (With sexual suggestion.)
135.1 Will (This and the following sonnet and sonnet 143 ring
changes on the word *will*—sexual desire, temper, passion, and the
poet's name; possibly also the friend's name. The word can also suggest the sexual organs, male and female.) **3 vex** (by unwelcome
wooing). **still** continually **6 hide . . . thine** (With sexual suggestion.) **7 will in others** others' wills **10 his** its **13 Let . . . kill** let no
unkind word kill any who seek your favors, or, *Let "no" unkind,* etc.,
do not kill your wooers with the word *no* **14 Think . . . Will** i.e.,
think all your wooers and their wills to be but one, all comprised in
me
136.1 check rebuke. **come so near** i.e., come so near the truth
about you (in my previous sonnet); with suggestion of physical nearness also **2 blind** unperceptive **4 fulfill** grant **5 fulfill the treasure**
fill full the treasury (with suggestion of sexual entry) **6 my will** (Suggesting "my penis.") **one** one of them **7 receipt** capacity (suggesting profligacy) **8 one . . . none** (A variant of the common saying
"one is no number.") **9 untold** uncounted **10 in . . . account** in
your (huge) inventory (of lovers) **11–12 For . . . thee** i.e., consider
me too insignificant to think of, provided that you deign to hold insignificant me to you, my sweet, thereby making me something of
worth. (*Something* is sexually suggestive of "some thing.") **13 my
name** i.e., "will," that is, desire. **still** continually **14 for** because

137.1 Love Cupid, portrayed as blind **2 see not** do not comprehend
3 lies resides (and deceives through false appearance) **4 Yet . . . be**
yet take the worst for the best **5 corrupt by overpartial looks** corrupted by doting and frankly prejudiced gazing **6 Be . . . ride** have
brought me to anchor in a bay used by everyone, i.e., in the sexual
embrace of a wanton woman **7 Why . . . hooks** why have you,
Love, fashioned snares out of my eyes' delusion **9 think . . . plot**
think that to be a private field, i.e., that woman to be the exclusive
property of one man **10 knows** knows to be. **common place** (1) a
commons, a common pasture (2) a woman's body that is open, promiscuous **11 Or** i.e., or why should. **not** not so **14 false plague**
(1) plague of judging falsely (2) false woman
138.1 (A version of this sonnet appears in *The Passionate Pilgrim*.)
truth fidelity, constancy **2 believe** i.e., pretend to believe **5 vainly
thinking** acting as though I thought **7 Simply** (1) pretending to be
foolish (2) unconditionally. **credit** give credence to **9 unjust** unfaithful, deceitful **11 habit** demeanor (with, however, a suggestion of
garb, i.e., "something put on"). **seeming trust** apparent fidelity
12 age in love an aging person in love, or, in matters of love. **told**
(1) counted (2) divulged **13 lie with** (1) deceive (2) have sex with
14 And . . . be and so by lies we flatteringly deceive ourselves about
our moral lapses
139.1 call ask. **justify the wrong** i.e., condone something actually
taking place under my eyes **2 unkindness** i.e., flagrant infidelity
3 with thine eye i.e., with a roving eye. (See lines 5–6.)

Use power with power, and slay me not by art.
Tell me thou lov'st elsewhere, but in my sight,
Dear heart, forbear to glance thine eye aside;
What need'st thou wound with cunning when thy
      might
Is more than my o'erpressed defense can bide? 8
Let me excuse thee: "Ah, my love well knows
Her pretty looks have been mine enemies,
And therefore from my face she turns my foes,
That they elsewhere might dart their injuries." 12
      Yet do not so; but since I am near slain,
      Kill me outright with looks and rid my pain.

140

Be wise as thou art cruel; do not press
My tongue-tied patience with too much disdain,
Lest sorrow lend me words, and words express
The manner of my pity-wanting pain. 4
If I might teach thee wit, better it were,
Though not to love, yet, love, to tell me so,
As testy sick men, when their deaths be near,
No news but health from their physicians know. 8
For if I should despair, I should grow mad,
And in my madness might speak ill of thee.
Now this ill-wresting world is grown so bad,
Mad slanderers by mad ears believèd be. 12
      That I may not be so, nor thou belied,
      Bear thine eyes straight, though thy proud heart
      go wide.

141

In faith, I do not love thee with mine eyes,
For they in thee a thousand errors note;
But 'tis my heart that loves what they despise,
Who in despite of view is pleased to dote. 4
Nor are mine ears with thy tongue's tune delighted,
Nor tender feeling to base touches prone,
Nor taste, nor smell, desire to be invited
To any sensual feast with thee alone. 8
But my five wits nor my five senses can
Dissuade one foolish heart from serving thee,
Who leaves unswayed the likeness of a man,

Thy proud heart's slave and vassal wretch to be. 12
      Only my plague thus far I count my gain,
      That she that makes me sin awards me pain.

142

Love is my sin, and thy dear virtue hate,
Hate of my sin, grounded on sinful loving.
O, but with mine compare thou thine own state,
And thou shalt find it merits not reproving; 4
Or, if it do, not from those lips of thine
That have profaned their scarlet ornaments
And sealed false bonds of love as oft as mine,
Robbed others' beds' revenues of their rents. 8
Be it lawful I love thee as thou lov'st those
Whom thine eyes woo as mine importune thee.
Root pity in thy heart, that when it grows
Thy pity may deserve to pitied be. 12
      If thou dost seek to have what thou dost hide,
      By self-example mayst thou be denied!

143

Lo, as a careful huswife runs to catch
One of her feathered creatures broke away,
Sets down her babe and makes all swift dispatch
In pursuit of the thing she would have stay, 4
Whilst her neglected child holds her in chase,
Cries to catch her whose busy care is bent
To follow that which flies before her face,
Not prizing her poor infant's discontent: 8
So runn'st thou after that which flies from thee,
Whilst I, thy babe, chase thee afar behind;
But if thou catch thy hope, turn back to me,
And play the mother's part: kiss me, be kind. 12
      So will I pray that thou mayst have thy Will,
      If thou turn back and my loud crying still.

13 **thus far** to the following extent   14 **That . . . pain** i.e., that the sin brings with it its own punishment and contrition, thus presumably shortening my torment in purgatory after death (with a suggestion in *pain* of "sexual pleasure"; see sonnet 139)
142.1–2 Love . . . loving i.e., my sin is to love you, and your best virtue is to hate—hate that sin in me, the sin of loving you. (The bitter paradox here is that hatred of sin must be virtue, and yet the lady is herself deeply implicated in this sin; her hatred is more a disdainful rejection of the poet's love than a noble virtue.)   4 **it** i.e., my state   6–7 **That . . . mine** i.e., that have forsworn themselves in love as often as my lips. (The *scarlet ornaments* are lips and also red wax used to seal documents; they *seal* with a kiss.)   8 **Robbed . . . rents** i.e., and committed adultery with other women's husbands. (The metaphor is of income-yielding estates, *revenues,* whose *rents* or payments made by tenants are not properly paid; the husband does not pay what is owed to the wife in terms of marital affection and the producing of children.)   9–10 **Be . . . thee** i.e., I am as justified in loving you and imploring you with my eyes as you are in pursuing other men. (*Be it lawful* is a legal phrase meaning "let it be considered lawful that.")   12 **deserve** make you deserving   13 **what . . . hide** what you withhold, i.e., pity
143.1 careful distressed, full of cares, busy.   **huswife** housewife
5 holds her in chase chases after her   **7 flies** flees   **8 Not prizing** disregarding   **13 Will** (See sonnets 135, 136.)   **14 still** hush, make quiet

4 **with power** i.e., candidly, directly.   **art** artifice, cunning   7 **What** why   8 **bide** abide, withstand   11 **foes** i.e., the *pretty looks,* the beauty and wanton glances of line 10   13 **near** nearly   14 **rid** end. (*Rid my pain* also suggests "satiate my craving.")
140.4 pity-wanting (1) unpitied by you (2) pity-craving   5 **wit** wisdom, prudence   5–6 **better . . . so** (I would teach you that) even though you don't love me, yet, dear friend, it would be better to tell me that you do   8 **know** i.e., hear   11 **ill-wresting** misinterpreting in an evil sense.   **bad** bad (that)   13 **so** i.e., a *mad slanderer* who is believèd.   **belied** slandered   14 **wide** astray. (The image is from archery.)
141.2 errors flaws in beauty   4 **Who . . . view** which (i.e., the heart), in spite of what the eyes see   6 **Nor . . . prone** nor (is) my delicate sense of touch inclined toward carnal contact (with you)
9 **my five wits** (neither) my five intellectual senses, i.e., the common sense, imagination, fancy, estimation (judgment), and memory
11 **Who . . . man** i.e., which heart abandons the proper government of my person, leaving me the mere likeness of a man

144

Two loves I have, of comfort and despair,
Which like two spirits do suggest me still:
The better angel is a man right fair,
The worser spirit a woman colored ill.   4
To win me soon to hell, my female evil
Tempteth my better angel from my side,
And would corrupt my saint to be a devil,
Wooing his purity with her foul pride.   8
And whether that my angel be turned fiend
Suspect I may, yet not directly tell;
But being both from me, both to each friend,
I guess one angel in another's hell.   12
    Yet this shall I ne'er know, but live in doubt
    Till my bad angel fire my good one out.

145

Those lips that Love's own hand did make
Breathed forth the sound that said "I hate"
To me that languished for her sake;
But when she saw my woeful state,   4
Straight in her heart did mercy come,
Chiding that tongue that ever sweet
Was used in giving gentle doom,
And taught it thus anew to greet: 8
"I hate" she altered with an end,
That followed it as gentle day
Doth follow night, who like a fiend
From heaven to hell is flown away.   12
    "I hate" from hate away she threw,
    And saved my life, saying "not you."

146

Poor soul, the center of my sinful earth,
Thrall to these rebel powers that thee array,
Why dost thou pine within and suffer dearth,
Painting thy outward walls so costly gay?   4
Why so large cost, having so short a lease,

Dost thou upon thy fading mansion spend?
Shall worms, inheritors of this excess,
Eat up thy charge? Is this thy body's end?   8
Then, soul, live thou upon thy servant's loss,
And let that pine to aggravate thy store;
Buy terms divine in selling hours of dross;
Within be fed, without be rich no more.   12
    So shalt thou feed on Death, that feeds on men,
    And Death once dead, there's no more dying then.

147

My love is as a fever, longing still
For that which longer nurseth the disease,
Feeding on that which doth preserve the ill,
Th' uncertain sickly appetite to please.   4
My reason, the physician to my love,
Angry that his prescriptions are not kept,
Hath left me, and I desperate now approve
Desire is death, which physic did except.   8
Past cure I am, now reason is past care,
And frantic-mad with evermore unrest;
My thoughts and my discourse as madmen's are,
At random from the truth vainly expressed;   12
    For I have sworn thee fair and thought thee bright,
    Who art as black as hell, as dark as night.

148

O me, what eyes hath love put in my head,
Which have no correspondence with true sight!
Or, if they have, where is my judgment fled,
That censures falsely what they see aright?   4
If that be fair whereon my false eyes dote,
What means the world to say it is not so?
If it be not, then love doth well denote
Love's eye is not so true as all men's "no."   8
How can it? O, how can love's eye be true,
That is so vexed with watching and with tears?
No marvel then though I mistake my view;
The sun itself sees not till heaven clears.   12
    O cunning love, with tears thou keep'st me blind,
    Lest eyes well-seeing thy foul faults should find.

144.1 (This sonnet appears, somewhat altered, in *The Passionate Pilgrim*.) **2 suggest** urge, offer counsel, tempt. **still** continually **3 right fair** very handsome and blond **4 ill** i.e., dark of complexion **11 from me** away from me. (The poet suspects they are together.) **both . . . friend** friends to each other **12 I . . . hell** I suspect that she (the evil angel) has him in her power (i.e., her sexual embracement; *hell* is slang for the pudenda) **14 fire . . . out** drive out my good angel, stop seeing him (with the suggestion of driving him out of the lady's sexual body as one would use fire and smoke to drive an animal out of its burrow, and with the further suggestion that the *fire* is venereal disease. *Bad angel* also hints at bad coinage driving out good money.)
145.1 (This sonnet is in eight-syllable meter.) **5 Straight** at once **7 used . . . doom** accustomed to passing a mild sentence **13 "I hate" . . . threw** i.e., she separated the phrase "I hate" from the hatred I feared it expressed, from hateful meaning **13–14 hate away . . . And** (Punning perhaps on the name of Shakespeare's wife, Anne Hathaway.)
146.1 sinful earth body **2 Thrall to** (One of several conjectures; the Quarto repeats *My sinfull earth* from line 1.) **rebel powers** i.e., rebellious flesh. **array** dress, clothe **4 outward walls** i.e., the body, decked out in finery, cosmetics, etc. **5 so short a lease** (because we are lent the *mansion* of our body for so short a time)

6 mansion dwelling, i.e., the body **8 thy charge** that on which you have expended so much and that was put in your *charge* or custody **9 thy servant's** i.e., the body's **10 let that . . . store** let the body starve to increase your stock of spiritual riches **11 Buy . . . dross** i.e., purchase eternal life in return for giving up (selling) mere hours of wasteful pleasure; secure *terms* that only God can provide
147.1 still always **3 preserve the ill** sustain the illness **4 uncertain** finicky **7–8 I . . . except** I, in despair, now demonstrate that desire, which the advice of medicine (i.e., reason) forbade, proves fatal **9 care** medical care. (The line is an inversion of the proverb, "things past cure are past care," i.e., don't worry about what can't be helped. Reason, the physician, has ceased to care for his patient.) **10 evermore** constant and increasing **12 vainly** to no sensible purpose
148.4 censures judges **7 love** i.e., the self-deceiving nature of my love. **denote** indicate, demonstrate (that) **8 eye** (With a pun on "ay," yes.) **10 vexed** troubled. **watching** remaining awake **11 I** (Punning on "eye.") **mistake my view** err in what I see

149

Canst thou, O cruel, say I love thee not,
When I against myself with thee partake?
Do I not think on thee when I forgot
Am of myself, all tyrant for thy sake?   4
Who hateth thee that I do call my friend?
On whom frown'st thou that I do fawn upon?
Nay, if thou lour'st on me, do I not spend
Revenge upon myself with present moan?   8
What merit do I in myself respect
That is so proud thy service to despise,
When all my best doth worship thy defect,
Commanded by the motion of thine eyes?   12
    But, love, hate on, for now I know thy mind:
    Those that can see thou lov'st, and I am blind.

150

O, from what power hast thou this powerful might
With insufficiency my heart to sway?
To make me give the lie to my true sight
And swear that brightness doth not grace the day?   4
Whence hast thou this becoming of things ill,
That in the very refuse of thy deeds
There is such strength and warrantise of skill
That, in my mind, thy worst all best exceeds?   8
Who taught thee how to make me love thee more,
The more I hear and see just cause of hate?
O, though I love what others do abhor,
With others thou shouldst not abhor my state.   12
    If thy unworthiness raised love in me,
    More worthy I to be beloved of thee.

151

Love is too young to know what conscience is;
Yet who knows not conscience is born of love?
Then, gentle cheater, urge not my amiss,
Lest guilty of my faults thy sweet self prove.   4
For, thou betraying me, I do betray
My nobler part to my gross body's treason;
My soul doth tell my body that he may

Triumph in love; flesh stays no farther reason,   8
But, rising at thy name, doth point out thee
As his triumphant prize. Proud of this pride,
He is contented thy poor drudge to be,
To stand in thy affairs, fall by thy side.   12
    No want of conscience hold it that I call
    Her "love" for whose dear love I rise and fall.

152

In loving thee thou know'st I am forsworn,
But thou art twice forsworn, to me love swearing:
In act thy bed-vow broke, and new faith torn
In vowing new hate after new love bearing.   4
But why of two oaths' breach do I accuse thee,
When I break twenty? I am perjured most,
For all my vows are oaths but to misuse thee,
And all my honest faith in thee is lost.   8
For I have sworn deep oaths of thy deep kindness,
Oaths of thy love, thy truth, thy constancy,
And, to enlighten thee, gave eyes to blindness,
Or made them swear against the thing they see;   12
    For I have sworn thee fair. More perjured eye,
    To swear against the truth so foul a lie!

153

Cupid laid by his brand and fell asleep.
A maid of Dian's this advantage found,
And his love-kindling fire did quickly steep
In a cold valley-fountain of that ground;   4
Which borrowed from this holy fire of Love
A dateless lively heat, still to endure,
And grew a seething bath, which yet men prove
Against strange maladies a sovereign cure.   8
But at my mistress' eye Love's brand new-fired,
The boy for trial needs would touch my breast;

8 stays awaits.   **reason** reasoning talk   **9 rising** (With bawdy suggestion of erection, continued in *point, Proud, stand, fall.* Metaphors of
conjuration and of the compass needle's point are also invoked.)
10 triumphant prize spoils to be enjoyed in victory.   **Proud of** swelling with.   **pride** splendor; erection   **12 stand** (1) serve, undertake
business (2) be erect.   **fall** (as in battle; with sexual suggestion of detumescence)   **13 want** lack
152.1 forsworn i.e., faithless to my vows of love (perhaps marriage
vows)   **3 act** sexual act.   **bed-vow** marriage vows to your husband
3–4 new . . . bearing i.e., a new contract of fidelity is torn up by
your swearing hatred toward me, to whom you have only recently
professed love. (Or the *new faith* that is torn up may be that which
the lady has sworn to the friend.)   **7 but to misuse** merely to misrep-
resent, or, deceive   **8 And . . . lost** i.e., all my professions of honesty are belied when I perjure myself by praising you for loving constancy   **11 And . . . blindness** i.e., and, to invest you with
brightness, I made my eyes testify to things they did not see
13 eye (With a pun on "I.")
153.1 (This sonnet and the following seemingly have no direct connection with those preceding. They are derived ultimately, through
Renaissance adaptations, from an epigram by the fifth-century Byzan-
tine poet Marianus Scholasticus in the Greek Anthology.)   **brand**
torch (with phallic suggestion)   **2 maid** attendant virgin, votaress.
Dian Diana, goddess of chastity   **4 of that ground** i.e., nearby. (*Valley-fountain* suggests the female sexual anatomy; compare with
154.9.)   **6 dateless** endless, eternal.   **still** always   **7 grew** became.
seething bath spring of hot medicinal waters.   **yet** even today.
prove discover to be   **8 sovereign** efficacious   **9 new-fired** having
been reignited   **10 for trial** by way of test

149.2 partake take part (against myself)   **3–4 think . . . sake** put
consideration of you foremost when I am tyrannously neglectful of, or
oblivious of, myself and my best interests on your behalf.   **forgot** forgotten   **7 spend** vent   **8 present moan** immediate suffering and lamentation   **9 respect** value   **10 thy . . . despise** as to think it demean-
ing to serve you   **11 all my best** all that is best in me.   **defect**
insufficiency   **14 Those . . . blind** i.e., you scorn one who loves you
in a blind passion, in defiance of reason, and are drawn instead to
those who look at you admiringly
150.2 With insufficiency by means of all your shortcomings.   **sway**
rule   **3 give the lie to** accuse flatly of lying   **4 And . . . day** i.e., and
swear that what is so is not so, that what is fair and beautiful is not
fair and beautiful, since you are dark   **5 becoming . . . ill** i.e., ability
to show ill things in a becoming light   **6 in . . . deeds** in the most
debased of your actions   **7 warrantise of skill** warrant or assurance of
expertise   **12 state** i.e., condition of being helplessly in love
151.1 too young (Love is personified as the young Cupid.)   **2 conscience** guilty knowing, carnal knowledge (playing on *conscience,*
"moral sense," in line 1)   **3 urge** stress, invoke.   **amiss** sin   **5 betraying** (1) exposing (2) leading into temptation   **6 nobler part** i.e.,
soul

I, sick withal, the help of bath desired,
And thither hied, a sad distempered guest,   12
    But found no cure. The bath for my help lies
    Where Cupid got new fire—my mistress' eyes.

154

The little love god lying once asleep
Laid by his side his heart-inflaming brand,
Whilst many nymphs that vowed chaste life to keep
Came tripping by; but in her maiden hand   4
The fairest votary took up that fire
Which many legions of true hearts had warmed,
And so the general of hot desire
Was, sleeping, by a virgin hand disarmed.   8
This brand she quenchèd in a cool well by,
Which from Love's fire took heat perpetual,
Growing a bath and healthful remedy
For men diseased; but I, my mistress' thrall,   12
    Came there for cure, and this by that I prove:
    Love's fire heats water, water cools not love.

11 withal from it   **12 hied** hastened.   **distempered** sick. (The bath is
suggestive of the sweating cure for venereal disease.)
154.7 general inspirer and commander, i.e., Cupid   **9 by** nearby
11 Growing becoming   **12 thrall** slave, bondman   **13 cure** (With
suggestion of treatment for venereal disease, as in 153.7–14.)   **this**
i.e., the following proposition.   **that** i.e., my coming, which failed to
cure me

A Funeral Elegy for Master William Peter

"A Funeral Elegy for Master William Peter" by "W.S.," published in 1612 and recently proposed by Donald Foster as a work of Shakespeare, commemorates the life and tragic death of its subject. We know from other sources that William Peter was a gentleman of modest income, educated at Oxford, married with two children. He was murdered at the age of twenty-nine in January 1612, in Exeter, by an irresponsible young man named Edward Drew, who had quarreled with him. Drew was brought to trial and convicted but escaped execution. There is no direct evidence that Shakespeare knew William Peter, but Foster's analysis of the poem (some of it through computer analysis), along with the work of Richard Abrams and others, makes an intriguing case for its inclusion in the Shakespeare canon.

The poem is a fairly conventional example of the genre of elegy; indeed, it may be modeled to some extent on Samuel Daniel's "Funeral Poem" for the Earl of Devonshire and on Daniel's "The Complaint of Rosamond." W.S.'s *Elegy* bewails the untimely death of William Peter and offers itself as a monument to his "never-blemished name" (6) that will outlast the ravages of time. This theme of immortality through verse, central to Shakespeare's Sonnets, is found in numerous other Renaissance and ancient classical texts as well. The poet offers assurance that "Oblivion," so ready always to "tread on Merit in the dust," will not be able to "raze out the lamentable tomb" of William Peter's "short-lived deserts"; his worthiness will live on in "the hearts and memories of men," and especially in this present poem (9-16).

Time and Death are thus enemies with whom William Peter's affectionate and mourning rememberers must do battle. As in the Sonnets, Time is an envious destroyer (490) whose "strict flinty hand" afflicts us with the "discomfort" of a severe doom (547-552). Yet, Time can also assist in eternizing virtue. As "the father of unblushing Truth," Time should be able, some day, to "lay ope" the malice that has dared to thwart its authority (145-147). Time will commend William Peter's honesty to Time itself (160), enabling generations of loving persons to pass on from one to the others the remembrance of his goodness.

The malice to which the poem repeatedly alludes (34, 146, 267, 404), presumably the murder, is never described in detail, but seems to have been the work of unnamed persons who were intent on destroying William Peter's innocence and goodness. Malice works its poisonous effects through wounding "Defamation" and the forgeries of "Close-lurking Whisper" (416-417). Most worldlings are mere "slaves" driven by "hope of gain" (46), drawn into appetite and into "the glad sleights of ensnaring vice" (73). "Eminent courts" and places of "popular concourse" are alike dens of iniquity (129-130). To be great is to be in danger of the spiritual blindness that comes with "dignity" and high social rank (451-452).

The poet is intent on reproving malice not only because one of poetry's mandates is to defend virtue against its denigrators but also because the poet himself has experienced the painful bite of Envy. He laments that he has been "rewarded with some sadder taste / Of knowing shame," and can bear sad testimonial to his region's "thankless misconstruction" thrown accusingly upon his "name and credit" (137-140). His enemies appear to be envious persons whose own misfortunes have motivated them "to win / Justice by wrong" and to poison the poet's reputation, causing him to lose credit "in the place I lost it" (142-148).

About William Peter we do not learn from the poem a great deal by way of biographical detail; what little there is confirms the information given above. From the poem, he appears to have been a gentleman who died young and was survived by his brother, John, to whom the elegy is dedicated. He was a man of "learning and wit," in whose mind these qualities reinforced each other (56). Having been both "an husband and a father" (526), he left behind him a virtuously grieving widow (511-522).

Mostly, we learn what a "truly good" man William Peter was, in the poet's loving estimation, what a "pattern" he was for all ages of virtuous behavior (16-17). His "taintless goodness" and "desertful merit" were manifested in everything he did (418). His true nobleness was a "beauty of the mind" (470). He knew how to rule himself like a "little ordered commonwealth" (294), insisting that reason govern appetite (65-66) and that reason in turn be subject to the sway of "religion" (60). He chastened the flesh and its "sick desires," lest he give way to the temptations that assail "the weaker man" (75-76). He knew how to practice "fit moderation" (77). He was never given to "the vain / Of boast, such as the common breath affords" (326-327). He was, in short, "a kind, true, perfect gentlman" (90).

The poet repeatedly honors William Peter for his deep Christian faith. Peter's life itself declared "That Christ was his" (320). "Piety and zeal" taught his frail physical senses how to conduct themselves (62, 124). His soul has now taken "her flight to a diviner coast," that is, to heaven (199). His was a faith built to "persever" (331). His great model was Christ, who, to atone for human sinfulness, "Gave sweet redemption, offering up his blood / To conquer Death by death, and loose the traps / Of hell" (367-370).

To the poet as well, Christian duty must stand uppermost while we endure the dark days of human existence and while our lives are "encompassed in a mortal frame" (38). The world in which we live is a "frailer stage" (127) from which Death mercifully releases us. The very world, in the poet's view, will be "wintered in the storms / Of fearful consummation," and is "Expecting ever to be overthrown," on the verge of its own apocalyptic dissolution (171-174). The poet characterizes himself as a devout Christian who accepts the divine necessity of William Peter's untimely death and believes deeply in the justice of God's "day of Judgment and of love" but forbears to presume that he can predict God's punishment of those who have wronged his dead friend (375-378).

As in Shakespeare's Sonnets, the relation of speaker to the person being eulogized is that of loving "unfeigned friendship" (357) between an older poet and a younger man. The jealousies and self-abasement of the Sonnets are lacking here, leaving instead a testimonial of constancy (235, 315), bonds of unity (309), and "perfect amity" (324). The dead man whom the poet eulogizes was "A rock of friendship" (321). Appropriately, then, the writing of this poem is for the poet a "last act of friendship" (206).

Yet the poem offers little concrete support in any attempt to read a deep biographical connection in this poet's life, one in which male friendship might take on the dimensions of a profound psychological need. The idealization of loving friendship as presented here is conventional and gracefully expressed. The poem represents an appropriate way in which to commemorate a person for whom the poet had agreed to write a eulogy. Hints of the poet's own experience with malice and resentment (his "reputation with a witless sin," [144]) may remind us of Sonnet 111, in which the speaker of that poem complains that his name "receives a brand" of shame because of his public occupation, or of Sonnet 112's reference to a "vulgar scandal stamped upon my brow," or of "my bewailèd guilt" in Sonnet 36, but once again we must be wary of supposing that these hints offer much in the way of evidence about the writer or any direct connection to Shakespeare.

Perhaps the most interesting question posed by the *Elegy* has to do with the possibility that it expresses a troubled view of religious faith. The claim should not be overstated. The death of a beloved person is inevitably a time for reflection and speculation, even of doubt that Christian ideas of resurrection can offer sustained assurance. The form of the elegy demands that such ideas be explored and, to a degree, answered. Given that project, and its accompanying theme of poetry's great role in eternizing the virtues of those who have died, we can perhaps see that this poem examines the commonplaces of Christian consolation with some uncertainty. The poet seems to characterize Christian hope as little more than "the weak comfort of the hapless" (568), even while he expresses a belief that some kind of hope must nonetheless prevail. Part of that better hope lies in the eter-

nizing power of poetry. Death has taken William Peter in order to defend Death's kingdom against one who stood out against sin and death, but Death cannot touch his deservings; Death can only have his "frail and mortal parts" (490-493). William Peter has died to this world, "but doubly lives, / Once in his proper self, then in his name" (495-496). At the same time, the poet does not arrogate to himself a humanistic power to bestow immortality but instead sees that great function as divinely sanctioned.

The case for Shakespeare's having written this funeral elegy rests on its use of the initials "W.S." in the title, on Donald Foster's statistical documentation of word patterns through computer analysis, and on the poem itself (as analyzed also by Richard Abrams). Its density of metaphor and its complexity of phrasing (such as its use of hendiadys), even in the expression of philosophical and religious commonplaces, is considerable. To those who support a place for this poem in the Shakespeare canon, its style seems consistent with that of the mature Jacobean Shakespeare. In some ways the poem seems like "A Lover's Complaint," in that both poems are relatively minor pieces and yet are intelligently crafted. To skeptics, on the other hand, *A Funeral Elegy* remains too piously conventional in its treatment of the great themes of slander, death, and immortality through poetry to be attributable to Shakespeare even as an occasional piece. Not all tests of vocabulary uniformly endorse his authorship. The attribution remains uncertain.

A Funeral Elegy in Memory of the Late Virtuous Master William Peter of Whipton near Exeter by W.S.

To MASTER JOHN PETER
of Bowhay in Devon, Esquire.

The love I bore to your brother, and will do to
his memory, hath craved from me this last duty of
a friend; I am herein but a second to the privilege   3
of Truth, who can warrant more in his behalf than   4
I undertook to deliver. Exercise in this kind I will   5
little affect, and am less addicted to, but there   6
must be miracle in that labor which, to witness my   7
remembrance to this departed gentleman, I would
not willingly undergo. Yet whatsoever is here
done is done to him and to him only, for whom   10
and whose sake I will not forget to remember any
friendly respects to you, or to any of those that
have loved him for himself and himself for his
deserts.

W.S.
A FUNERAL ELEGY

Since time and his predestinated end
Abridged the circuit of his hopeful days,   2
Whiles both his youth and virtue did intend   3
The good endeavors of deserving praise,
What memorable monument can last
Whereon to build his never-blemished name
But his own worth, wherein his life was graced,
Sith as that ever he maintained the same?   8
    Oblivion in the darkest day to come,
When Sin shall tread on Merit in the dust,
Cannot raze out the lamentable tomb   11
Of his short-lived deserts; but still they must,
Even in the hearts and memories of men,
Claim fit respect, that they, in every limb   14

Rememb'ring what he was, with comfort then
May pattern out one truly good, by him.   16
    For he was truly good, if honest care
Of harmless conversation may commend   18
A life free from such stains as follies are,   19
Ill recompensèd only in his end.   20
    Nor can the tongue of him who loved him least—   21
If there can be minority of love   22
To one superlative above the rest   23
Of many men in steady faith—reprove   24
His constant temper in the equal weight   25
Of thankfulness and kindness. Truth doth leave   26
Sufficient proof he was in every right   27
As kind to give as thankful to receive.
    The curious eye of a quick-brained survey   29
Could scantly find a mote amidst the sun   30
Of his too-shortened days, or make a prey   31
Of any faulty errors he had done.   32
Not that he was above the spleenful sense   33
And spite of malice, but for that he had   34
Warrant enough in his own innocence
Against the sting of some in nature bad.
    Yet who is he so absolutely blessed   37
That lives encompassed in a mortal frame,   38
Sometime in reputation not oppressed   39
By some in nothing famous but defame?   40
Such in the by-path and the ridgeway lurk   41
That leads to ruin, in smooth pretense   42
Of what they do to be a special work   43
Of singleness, not tending to offense;   44
Whose very virtues are not to detract   45
Whiles hope remains of gain (base fee of slaves),   46
Despising chiefly men in fortunes wracked.   47
But Death to such gives unremembered graves.
    Now therein lived he happy, if to be
    Free from detraction happiness it be.
His younger years gave comfortable hope
To hope for comfort in his riper youth,
Which, harvest-like, did yield again the crop

Dedication 3–5 I am herein . . . deliver I can only second what Truth can say, since Truth is able to bear witness in behalf of William Peter more than I could do   **5–6 Exercise . . . affect** I aspire little to literary exercises of this elegaic kind   **7 miracle** (The poet suggests that in composing this poem in a genre of poetry he practices so little, he will need miraculous help.)   **10 to him** for him (Peter)
A Funeral Elegy 2 Abridged . . . days cut short the span of years that William Peter might have hoped to live   **3 did intend** intended to achieve (but didn't because cut off by death)   **8 Sith . . . same?** since he always sustained his own worthiness?   **11 lamentable** expressing grief, mournful   **14 they** people

16 May . . . him may admire him as a pattern of true goodness   **18 harmless conversation** virtuous dealings with others   **19 free . . . are** free from the stain of follies   **20 Ill . . . end** unjustly rewarded for his virtue only in his untimely death   **21–26 Nor . . . kindness** nor can even a person who had least regard for him—if there can be such as have only little love for one who, in steady faith, was superior to all others—say anything against his constancy of temperament, both in giving and receiving   **27 he . . . right** that he was in every way and by any standard of judgment   **29 curious** attentive, inquisitive. **quick-brained** ingenious   **30 a mote . . . sun** i.e., a tiny imperfection in him   **31–32 make a prey Of** find fault with, accuse   **33–34 Not . . . had** not that he could entirely escape malicious insinuations, but rather that he had   **37–40 Yet . . . defame?** yet what person alive can claim to be so wholly lucky as not to be slandered by some persons whose only claim to fame is that of defaming others?   **41–47 Such . . . wracked** such defamers lurk along the pathways that lead to ruin of reputation, suavely pretending that their efforts are sincere, not offenseful; their only pretended virtue is not to defame the rich and powerful who might benefit them, while they heap insults on those who have suffered at the hands of fortune. (William Peter was killed on road outside Exeter known as "the Ridgeway." The poet may also refer to the Ridgeway family, staunchly anti-Catholic, whereas the Peter family had recusant sympathies.)

Of education, bettered in his truth. 54
    Those noble twins of heaven-infusèd races, 55
Learning and wit, refinèd in their kind, 56
Did jointly both, in their peculiar graces, 57
Enrich the curious temple of his mind— 58
Indeed a temple in whose precious white 59
Sat Reason by Religion overswayed, 60
Teaching his other senses, with delight,
How Piety and Zeal should be obeyed;
Not fruitlessly in prodigal expense
Wasting his best of time, but so content
With Reason's golden mean to make defense
Against the assault of youth's encouragement,
As not the tide of this surrounding age 67
(When now his father's death had freed his will) 68
Could make him subject to the drunken rage
Of such whose only glory is their ill. 70
    He from the happy knowledge of the wise
Draws virtue to reprove securèd fools, 72
And shuns the glad sleights of ensnaring vice
To spend his spring of days in sacred schools. 74
    Here gave he diet to the sick desires 75
That day by day assault the weaker man,
And with fit moderation still retires 77
From what doth batter virtue now and then.
    But that I not intend in full discourse 79
To progress out his life, I could display 80
A good man in each part exact, and force 81
The common voice to warrant what I say. 82
For if his fate and heaven had decreed
That full of days he might have lived to see 84
The grave in peace, the times that should succeed 85
Had been best-speaking witnesses with me, 86
Whose conversation so untouched did move 87
Respect most in itself as who would scan 88
His honesty and worth by them might prove 89
He was a kind, true, perfect gentleman— 90
Not in the outside of disgraceful folly, 91
Courting opinion with unfit disguise, 92
Affecting fashions, nor addicted wholly 93
To unbeseeming blushless vanities,
    But suiting so his habit and desire
    As that his virtue was his best attire.

Not in the waste of many idle words
Cared he to be heard talk, nor in the float 98
Of fond conceit, such as this age affords, 99
By vain discourse upon himself to dote; 100
For his becoming silence gave such grace
To his judicious parts, as what he spake 102
Seemed rather answers which the wise embrace
Than busy questions such as talkers make.
    And though his qualities might well deserve 105
Just commendation, yet his furnished mind
Such harmony of goodness did preserve
As Nature never built in better kind;
Knowing the best, and therefore not presuming 109
In knowing, but for that it was the best, 110
Ever within himself free choice resuming
Of true perfection in a perfect breast,
So that his mind and body made an inn,
The one to lodge the other, both like framed 114
For fair conditions, guests that soonest win
Applause, in generality well famed. 116
    If trim behavior, gestures mild, discreet 117
Endeavors, modest speech, beseeming mirth, 118
True friendship, active grace, persuasion sweet, 119
Delightful love innated from his birth, 120
Acquaintance unfamiliar, carriage just, 121
Offenseless resolution, wished sobriety, 122
Clean-tempered moderation, steady trust, 123
Unburdened conscience, unfeigned piety—
If these, or all of these knit fast in one
Can merit praise, then justly may we say,
Not any from this frailer stage is gone 127
Whose name is like to live a longer day; 128
Though not in eminent courts or places great 129
For popular concourse, yet in that soil 130
Where he enjoyed his birth, life, death, and seat 131
Which now sits mourning his untimely spoil. 132
    And as much glory is it to be good
For private persons, in their private home,
As those descended from illustrious blood
In public view of greatness, whence they come.
    Though I, rewarded with some sadder taste
Of knowing shame, by feeling it have proved 138
My country's thankless misconstruction cast

---

54 **truth** constancy and veracity 55 **of . . . races** of heavenly descent, graced with heavenly qualities 56 **wit** intelligence. **kind** natures 57 **peculiar** special, unique 58 **curious** eager to learn; beautifully wrought 59 **white** (signifying purity) 60 **overswayed** guided (not "overpowered") 67 **As not** in such a way that not even 68 **When . . . will** Will Peter's father Otho died June 1607. 70 **whose . . . ill** whose only proud boast is their sinful behavior 72 **securèd** insolent, confident in their own folly 74 **To . . . . schools** i.e., to spend his youth in study at Oxford 75 **gave he diet to** he strictly dieted and starved 77 **still** ceaselessly 79–82 **But . . . say** were it not that I do not intend to tell the full story of his life, I could reveal goodness in every part of his life and compel common assent to that appraisal 84–85 **see . . . peace** die peacefully 85–86 **the times . . . me** succeeding generations would have proven most eloquent witnesses with me (of his virtue) 87–90 **Whose . . . gentleman** he whose unbesmirched dealings with others commanded respect in other persons in and of themselves, inasmuch that anyone who might wish to look into his honesty and worth could prove by his upright dealings that he was a kind, true, and complete gentleman 91 **Not . . . folly** not wearing the outer garments of disgraceful folly 92 **opinion** favorable opinion, fame 93 **Affecting** putting on the affectation of

98–99 **the float . . . conceit** the flood of inane witticism 99 **affords** provides, flaunts 100 **By . . dote** did he care to talk vainly and self-infatuatedly about himself 102 **as** that 105 **qualities** social graces and accomplishments 109–110 **and . . . best** and therefore not being proud of knowing what is best, but cherishing goodness for its own sake 114 **The one . . . other** the body serving as an inn (and hence also as a provincial theater) for his mind. **framed** fashioned 116 **in . . . famed** known to one and all 117 **trim** proper, elegant 118 **beseeming** seemly 119 **persuasion sweet** sound belief; sweet persuasiveness in his speech 120 **innated** made innate, produced from within 121–123 **Acquaintance . . . trust** remarkable friendships not marred by unsuitable liberties, correct deportment toward others, firmness of purpose that offended no one, admirable steadiness, unsullied moderation, firm trustworthiness 127 **Not any** no one. **this frailer stage** i.e., this sinful world 128 **like to live** likely to live in human memory 129–130 **places . . . concourse** popular gathering places. (William Peter will not be celebrated in the notoriety of courtly or public opinion.) 131 **seat** country family estate 132 **spoil** injury (having been pillaged or plundered by Death) 138 **proved** experienced and demonstrated

Upon my name and credit, both unloved   140
By some whose fortunes, sunk into the wane   141
Of plenty and desert, have strove to win   142
Justice by wrong, and sifted to embane   143
My reputation with a witless sin,   144
Yet Time, the father of unblushing Truth,
May one day lay ope malice which hath crossed it,   146
And right the hopes of my endangered youth,
Purchasing credit in the place I lost it—   148
Even in which place the subject of the verse   149
(Unhappy matter of a mourning style   150
Which now that subject's merits doth rehearse)   151
Had education and new being, while   152
By fair demeanor he had won repute
Amongst the all of all that livèd there,   154
For that his actions did so wholly suit   155
With worthiness, still memorable here.   156
　　The many hours till the Day of Doom   157
Will not consume his life and hapless end;   158
For, should he lie obscured without a tomb,   159
Time would to Time his honesty commend,   160
Whiles parents to their children will make known,
And they to their posterity impart,
How such a man was sadly overthrown
By a hand guided by a cruel heart;
　　Whereof as many as shall hear that sadness
　　Will blame the one's hard fate, the other's madness;   166
Whiles such as do recount that tale of woe,
Told by remembrace of the wisest heads,
Will in the end conclude the matter so
As they will all go weeping to their beds.
　　For, when the world lies wintered in the storms
Of fearful consummation and lays down   172
Th' unsteady change of his fantastic forms,   173
Expecting ever to be overthrown;   174
When the proud height of much-affected sin   175
Shall ripen to a head, and in that pride
End in the miseries it did begin   177
And fall amidst the glory of his tide;   178

Then in a book where every work is writ   179
Shall this man's actions be revealed, to show
The gainful fruit of well-employèd wit,
Which paid to heaven the debt that it did owe.
Here shall be reckoned up the constant faith,
Never untrue, where once he love professed—   184
Which is a miracle in men, one saith,   185
Long sought though rarely found; and he is best
　　Who can make friendship, in those times of change,
　　Admirèd more for being firm than strange.   188
　　When those weak houses of our brittle flesh   189
Shall ruined be by death, our grace and strength,
Youth, memory, and shape that made us fresh
Cast down, and utterly decayed at length;
When all shall turn to dust from whence we came,
And we low-leveled in a narrow grave,
What can we leave behind us but a name,
Which, by a life well led, may honor have?
　　Such honor, O thou youth untimely lost,
Thou didst deserve and hast; for though thy soul
Hath took her flight to a diviner coast,   199
Yet here on earth thy fame lives ever whole,
In every heart sealed up, in every tongue
Fit matter to discourse; no day prevented   202
That pities not thy sad and sudden wrong,
Of all alike belovèd and lamented.
　　And I here to thy memorable worth,
In this last act of friendship, sacrifice   206
My love to thee, which I could not set forth
In any other habit of disguise.
Although I could not learn, whiles yet thou wert,   209
To speak the language of a servile breath,
My truth stole from my tongue into my heart,   211
Which shall not thence be sundered, but in death.
And I confess my love was too remiss
That had not made thee know how much I prized
　　thee,
But that mine error was, as yet it is,
To think love best in silence; for I sized thee   216
By what I would have been, not only ready   217
In telling I was thine, but being so,   218
By some effect to show it. He is steady   219
Who seems less than he is in open show.   220
　　Since then I still reserved to try the worst   221
Which hardest Fate and Time thus can lay on me.
T' enlarge my thoughts was hinderèd at first,   223

---

140 both i.e., my name and credit (reputation) **141–144 sunk . . .
sin** fallen into a deserved eclipse of prosperity, have striven to right
the wrongs done to them by wronging others (especially me), and
have endeavored to poison my reputation with accusation of a foolish
sin **146 lay ope** lay open, expose. **crossed it** thwarted Truth **148–
152 Purchasing . . . being** redeeming my reputation even there where
I had lost it, in that very place where William Peter, the subject of my
verse (sad matter for me to recite in elegiac style), gained his education and manhood **154 the all of all** the best of persons **155 For
that** because **156 here** i.e., on earth **157–158 The many . . . end**
even the years that extend to the Day of Judgment when Time will
end cannot eradicate his life and tragic death **159 should he** even if
he should **160 Time . . . commend** Time would praise and safeguard his integrity and virtue to the end of eternity **166 the one's
. . . madness** the hard fate of William Peter and the madness of the
"cruel heart" who overthrew him **172–173 and lays . . . forms** and
casts aside the fluctuations and vicissitudes of this mad world. (The
picture is of the Apocalypse that will come at the end of time.) **174
ever** constantly, at any moment **175 much-affected** sought out and
practiced by many sinful human beings **177 End . . . begin** end as it
began, at the Day of Judgment **178 his** its (sin's)

179 a book . . . writ the book of God's judgment; hinting also at the
poet's own writings **184 once . . . professed** during his life he professed love and friendship **185 one saith** as my biblical or patristic
source says **188 Admirèd . . . strange** more admired for constancy
than for any novelties of fashion or show of aloofness **189 those . . .
flesh** i.e., our bodies **199 took** taken. **diviner coast** i.e., heaven
202 no day prevented that day will never come **206 sacrifice** make
an offering of **209 wert** were alive **211 My . . . heart** i.e., I loved
you in my heart, silently **216–220 for . . . show** for I measured your
worth by comparing you with what I wished to be myself, not simply
telling you of my fondness but trying to manifest it in my own conduct. The most trustworthy friend is one who does not parade his affection. **221 I still reserved** I have constantly continued my resolve
223 T' enlarge . . . first I was hindered at first in any attempt to express myself fully

While thou hadst life; I took this task upon me,
To register with mine unhappy pen 225
Such duties as it owes to thy desert,
And set thee as a precedent to men,
And limn thee to the world but as thou wert— 228
Not hired, as heaven can witness in my soul,
By vain conceit, to please such ones as know it, 230
Nor servile to be liked, free from control, 231
Which, pain to many men, I do not owe it. 232

    But here I trust I have dischargèd now
(Fair lovely branch too soon cut off) to thee
My constant and irrefragable vow, 235
As, had it chanced, thou mightst have done to me,
But that no merit strong enough of mine
Had yielded store to thy well-abled quill 238
Whereby t' enroll my name, as this of thine,
Hows'ere enrichèd by thy plenteous skill. 240

    Here, then, I offer up to memory
The value of my talent, precious man,
Whereby, if thou live to posterity,
Though 't be not as I would, 'tis as I can. 244
    In minds from whence endeavor doth proceed, 245
    A ready will is taken for the deed.

        Yet ere I take my longest last farewell
From thee, fair mark of sorrow, let me frame 248
Some ampler work of thank, wherein to tell
What more thou didst deserve than in thy name,
And free thee from the scandal of such senses 251
As in the rancor of unhappy spleen 252
Measure thy course of life, with false pretenses
Comparing by thy death what thou hast been. 254
    So in his mischiefs is the world accurst;
    It picks out matter to inform the worst.
        The willful blindness that hoodwinks the eyes
Of men enwrappèd in an earthy veil 258
Makes them most ignorantly exercise
And yield to humor when it doth assail, 260
Whereby the candle and the body's light 261
Darkens the inward eyesight of the mind,
Presuming still it sees, even in the night 263
Of that same ignorance which makes them blind.

Hence conster they with corrupt commentaries, 265
Proceeding from a nature as corrupt, 266
The text of malice, which so often varies 267
As 'tis by seeming reason underpropped. 268
    O, whither tends the lamentable spite
Of this world's teenful apprehension, 270
Which understands all things amiss, whose light
Shines not amidst the dark of their dissension?
True 'tis, this man, whiles yet he was a man, 274
Soothed not the current of besotted fashion, 274
Nor could disgest, as some loose mimics can, 275
An empty sound of overweening passion, 276
So much to be made servant to the base 277
And sensual aptness of disunioned vices, 278
To purchase commendation by disgrace, 279
Whereto the world and heat of sin entices. 280
    But in a safer contemplation,
Secure in what he knew, he ever chose
The ready way to commendation, 283
By shunning all invitements strange, of those 284
Whose illness is, the necessary praise 285
Must wait upon their actions; only rare 286
In being rare in shame (which strives to raise 287
Their name by doing what they do not care), 288
As if the free commission of their ill 289
Were even as boundless as their prompt desires; 290
Only like lords, like subjects to their will, 291
Which their fond dotage ever more admires. 292
    He was not so, but in a serious awe, 293
Ruling the little ordered commonwealth
Of his own self, with honor to the law
That gave peace to his bread, bread to his health, 296
Which ever he maintained in sweet content
And pleasurable rest, wherein he joyed 298
A monarchy of comfort's government,
Never until his last to be destroyed.
    For in the vineyard of heaven-favored learning
Where he was double-honored in degree, 302

225 **unhappy** (1) saddened by the task of mourning; (2) unfortunate
228 **limn** delineate.   **but** simply   230 **as know it** as are familiar with
"vain conceit"   231–232 **Nor . . . owe it** nor toadying to the rich
and powerful in hopes of their favor, preferring instead to be free of
such control, free of distasteful obligation in a way that will prove
painful to many men (who do not want to hear the truth about themselves)   235 **irrefragable** inviolable   238 **Had yielded store** would
have yielded material   240 **Hows'ere enriched** howsoever much my
poor worth might have been enriched   244 **Though 't . . . can** even
though it will not be as worthy a poem as I could wish (or, even if
your fame with posterity will not be all that I would wish), yet it is all
that I am able to do   245 **In . . . proceed** in minds such as my own
that undertake virtuous endeavors   248 **mark of sorrow** subject of my
grief; target of misfortune.   **frame** fashion   251 **senses** opinions expressed by individuals   252 **unhappy spleen** hateful malice   254
Comparing judging. (William Peter's detractors unfairly use the unhappy circumstances of his death as evidence of his not having lived
virtuously.)   258 **enwrapped . . . veil** made spiritually blind by
earthly concerns   260 **humor** capricious mood   261 **Whereby . . .
light** i.e., whereby the defective illumination that the physical senses
afford   263 **Presuming . . . sees** leading the blinded mind to presume
that it understands

265–268 **Hence . . . underpropped** hence inwardly blind persons interpret malice to suit their own purposes, corrupting its meaning because they themselves are corrupt, twisting its meaning even while
they seem to underprop their reading with specious reasoning   270
teenful apprehension vexatious attempts at comprehension   274
Soothed not did not flatter   275–280 **Nor . . . entices** nor could William Peter swallow the inflated expressions of regard that some dissipated yes-men employ, seeking to win favor by becoming a slave to
those sensual appetites and flattering means of seeking promotion that
the world holds out as base enticements. (*Disgest*=digest;
disunioned=ruptured, disjunct.)   283 **commendation** praise for true
virtue   284 **invitements** inducements, allurements   285–292
Whose . . . admires whose spiritual weakness is to need praise to motivate the virtuous deeds they should do for their own sakes, and who
are noteworthy only in being almost without shame (an emotion that
would otherwise goad them into doing, for the sake of reputation,
deeds they otherwise have no desire to perform), as if their freedom to
choose evil were as unlimited as their alacritous desires for evil; and
who are like lords only in being subject to their appetites, which their
foolish infatuation with evil prompts them to admire ever increasingly.
(The passage may also berate those who will never offer up praise
without hope of reward.)   293 **but . . . awe** but maintained in himself
a deep reverence for goodness   296 **That . . . health** that enabled
him to live moderately in peace and good health   298 **joyed** enjoyed
302 **double-honored** awarded the B.A. (1603) and the M.A. (1607)

His observation and discreet discerning
Had taught him in both fortunes to be free;   304
Whence now retired home, to a home indeed,
The home of his condition and estate,   306
He well provided 'gainst the hand of need,
Whence young men sometime grow unfortunate;
His disposition by the bonds of unity
So fastened to his reason that it strove
With understanding's grave immunity   311
To purchase from all hearts a steady love,
Wherein not any one thing comprehends   313
Proportionable note of what he was,   314
Than that he was so constant to his friends
As he would no occasion overpass   316
Which might make known his unaffected care,   317
In all respects of trial, to unlock   318
His bosom and his store, which did declare
That Christ was his, and he was friendship's rock;
A rock of friendship figured in his name,   321
Foreshowing what he was, and what should be,   322
Most true presage; and he discharged the same   323
In every act of perfect amity.

  Though in the complimental phrase of words   325
He never was addicted to the vain   326
Of boast, such as the common breath affords,
He was in use most fast, in tongue most plain;   328
Nor amongst all those virtues that forever
Adorned his reputation will be found
One greater than his faith, which did persever,
Where once it was protested, alway sound.   332
  Hence sprung the deadly fuel that revived
The rage which wrought his end, for, had he been
Slacker in love, he had been longer lived,
And not oppressed by Wrath's unhappy sin—   336
By Wrath's unhappy sin, which unadvised   337
Gave death for free good will and wounds for love.
Pity it was that blood had not been prized   339
At higher rate, and reason set above
Most unjust choler, which untimely drew   341
Destruction on itself, and, most unjust,
Robbed virtue of a follower so true
As Time can boast of, both for love and trust.
  So henceforth all (great glory to his blood)
Shall be but seconds to him, being good.   346

The wicked end their honor with their sin   347
In death, which only then the good begin.   348
  Lo, here a lesson by experience taught
For men whose pure simplicity hath drawn   350
Their trust to be betrayed by being caught
Within the snares of making truth a pawn;   352
Whiles it, not doubting whereinto it enters,   353
Without true proof and knowledge of a friend,   354
Sincere in singleness of heart, adventers   355
To give fit cause ere love begin to end.   356
  His unfeigned friendship, where it least was sought,   357
Him to a fatal timeless ruin brought;   358
Whereby the life that purity adorned   359
With real merit, by this sudden end   360
Is in the mouth of some in manner scorned,   361
Made questionable, for they do intend,   362
According to the tenor of the saw   363
Mistook, if not observed, writ long ago   364
When men were only led by Reason's law,   365
That "Such as is the end, the life proves so."   366
Thus He who to the universal lapse   367
Gave sweet redemption, offering up his blood
To conquer Death by death, and loose the traps   369
Of hell even in the triumph that it stood,
He thus, for that his guiltless life was spilt   371
By death, which was made subject to the curse,   372
Might in like manner be reproved of guilt   373
In his pure life, for that his end was worse.   374
  But O far be it, our unholy lips   375
Should so profane the deity above   376
As thereby to ordain revenging whips   377
Against the Day of Judgment and of love.   378
The hand that lends us honor in our days   379
May shorten when it please, and justly take
Our honor from us many sundry ways,

304 in both fortunes in good and bad fortune   **306 condition** social rank   **311 immunity** i.e., immunity against unreasoning passion   **313–314 Wherein . . . was** in whose disposition no single factor can sum up the whole of what he was   **316 As** that   **317 unaffected** without affectation, sincere   **318 In . . . trial** even in the most trying of circumstances   **321 his name** his name of Peter—the name of Saint Peter (Latin *Petrus*, rock), on whom Christ announced that he would build his church, and who serves as a model of enduring friendship   **322–323 and what . . . presage** and truly figuring forth the greatness of his qualities   **325 complimental** ceremonial; expressing compliments   **326 vain** vanity, emptiness   **328 He . . . plain** he was steadfast in deeds and plain in speech   **332 Where . . . protested** when once it had been solemnly asserted   **336 by . . . sin** by the evil and foreboding sin of wrath   **337 unadvised** without warning, rashly   **339 blood** life itself. (An allusion to the murder of William Peter.)   **341 choler** wrath   **346 Shall . . . good** will only be his followers, no matter how virtuous they are themselves

347 their honor i.e., the base worldly honor that the wicked often enjoy   **348 which . . . begin** whereas good persons begin to enjoy their true honor and reward only in death   **350 drawn** led   **352 Within . . . pawn** within the snares of the world, where truth is often held hostage   **353–356 Whiles . . . end** while trusting friendship, not fearing into what danger it advances without insisting on proofs or credentials from the friend, loyally pure of heart, would undertake to end such friendship only on the most undeniable grounds. (*Adventers* = "adventures," undertakes.) The poet describes how William Peter trustingly befriended the person, Edward Drew, who then murdered him.   **357–358 His . . . brought** the unfeigned friendship he extended to one who did not reciprocate it brought about his fatal untimely ruin   **359–366 Whereby . . . so** for which reason, the life that gained genuine merit by its purity was, because of his sudden and violent death, scorned and questioned by some observers, who quoted out of context an old proverb written long ago (but perhaps not honored even then) when Reason governed the human race: "A person's death reveals the worth of that person's life."   **367 He** Christ.   **to the universal lapse** to atone for the fall of Man (brought about by Adam's and Eve's sin)   **369 Death by death** mortal sin and death by His crucifixion.   **loose the traps** i.e., break open the gates   **371–374 He thus . . . worse** thus Christ, because his guiltless life ended in death, to which all humanity is subject, might (like William Peter) be reproved for a sinful life on the evidence of his having died a shameful death. (Or perhaps the "He" of this sentence is William Peter. In either case, his death is compared with that of Christ.)   **375–378 But . . . love** but far be it from us to blaspheme by presuming to judge those whom God will judge on the final Day of Judgment   **379 The hand** i.e., God's guiding hand

As best becomes that wisdom did us make.   382
The second brother, who was next begot   383
Of all that ever were begotten yet,
Was by a hand in vengeance rude and hot   385
Sent innocent to be in heaven set,
Whose fame the angels in melodious choirs
Still witness to the world. Then why should he,   388
Well profited in excellent desires,   389
Be more rebuked, who had like destiny?   390
Those saints before the everlasting throne
Who sit with crowns of glory on their heads,
Washed white in blood, from earth hence have not
   gone   393
All to their joys in quiet on their beds,
But tasted of the sour-bitter scourge
Of torture and affliction ere they gained
Those blessings which their sufferance did urge,   397
Whereby the grace fore-promised they attained.
      Let then the false suggestions of the froward,   399
Building large castles in the empty air,
By suppositions fond and thoughts untoward   401
(Issues of discontent and sick despair)
Rebound gross arguments upon their heart,
That may disprove their malice and confound   404
Uncivil loose opinions which insert   405
Their souls into the roll that doth unsound   406
Betraying policies, and show their brains,   407
Unto their shame, ridiculous; whose scope   408
Is envy, whose endeavors fruitless pains,   409
In nothing surely prosperous but hope,   410
And that same hope so lame, so unprevailing,
It buries self-conceit in weak opinion,   412
Which, being crossed, gives matter of bewailing   413
Their vain designs on whom want hath dominion.   414
      Such, and of such condition, may devise   415
Which way to wound with Defamation's spirit
(Close-lurking Whisper's hidden forgeries)   417
His taintless goodness, his desertful merit.   418

But whiles the minds of men can judge sincerely,
Upon assurèd knowledge, his repute
And estimation shall be rumored clearly
In equal worth; Time shall to time renew 't.   422
The grave, that in his ever-empty womb
Forever closes up the unrespected,   424
Who, when they die, die all, shall not entomb   425
His pleading best perfections as neglected.   426
They to his notice in succeeding years
Shall speak for him when he shall lie below;
When nothing but his memory appears
Of what he was, then shall his virtues grow.
His being but a private man in rank
(And yet not ranked beneath a gentleman)
Shall not abridge the commendable thank
Which wise posterity shall give him then;
For Nature, and his therein happy fate,
Ordained that by his quality of mind   436
T' ennoble that best part, although his state   437
Were to a lower blessedness confined.
Blood, pomp, state, honor, glory, and command,
Without fit ornaments of disposition,
Are in themselves but heath'nish and profaned,
And much more peaceful is a mean condition   442
Which, underneath the roof of safe content,
Feeds on the bread of rest, and takes delight
To look upon the labors it hath spent
For its own sustenance, both day and night;
Whiles others, plotting which way to be great,
How to augment their portion and ambition,
Do toil their giddy brains, and ever sweat
For popular applause and power's commission.
But one in honors, like a seelèd dove   451
Whose inward eyes are dimmed with dignity,   452
Does think most safety doth remain above,   453
And seeks to be secure by mounting high;
      Whence, when he falls, who did erewhile aspire,
      Fall deeper down for that he climbèd higher.   456
      Now men who in a lower region live,
Exempt from danger of authority,   458
Have fittest times in Reason's rules to thrive,
Not vexed with envy of priority,
      And those are much more noble in the mind
      Than many that have nobleness by kind.   462

382 that . . . make the divinely wise God who created us   383 The
second brother Abel.   next after Adam and Eve   385 by . . . hot by
the vengeful and rough hand of Cain   388 he William Peter   389
Well . . . desires well advantaged by a virtuous will   390 like destiny
i.e., a hard fate similar to that of Abel, of being struck down by a
brother or friend   393 Washed white in blood made pure through
martyrdom and bleeding. (The saints who have suffered martyrdom
and who enjoy eternal glory have not died peaceably in their beds.)
397 which . . . urge which their suffering did hasten on   399 suggestions of the froward insinuations of the evil-disposed   401 fond idle,
foolish.   untoward perverse, improper   404–407 and confound . . .
policies and defeat the barbarous, dissolute opinions of those who
wrongfully proclaim themselves to be defenders against false and seductive cunning   408–409 whose . . . envy whose thoughts and intents are limited entirely to envy. (The poet is speaking of the evil-
disposed persons of ll. 399 ff. who have practiced their malice on
William Peter.)   409 endeavors endeavors are   410 but hope but in
hope   412–414 It . . . dominion that it disguises the fatuous self-regard of these carping critics under the appearance of a specious argument which, when it is logically refuted, affords ample occasion for
deploring their frivolous and improverished intents   415 Such . . .
condition malicious and envious persons like this   417 Close-lurking
. . . forgeries i.e., the forged lies that are whispered by the malicious;
hence, the very spirit of Defamation   418 His William Peter's

422 Time . . . renew 't Time will renew Peter's reputation throughout
eternity   424 unrespected unregarded, forgotten   425 all utterly (in
body and human memory)   426 pleading pleading for his deserved
remembrance   436–437 Ordained . . . part ordained that he should
be ennobled by his best attribute, the quality of his mind   437 state
social rank   442 mean socially inferior   451 one in honors i.e., one
like William Peter, contrasted with the others of l. 447 who are evilly
ambitious. (Alternatively, ll. 451-456 can be read as describing the
fall of a worldling whose spiritual vision is dimmed by worldly concerns and who seeks security in exalted rank only to fall into misfortune.)   seelèd with eyes stitched shut, hoodwinked   452 Whose . . .
dignity whose spiritual vision is shaded from worldly temptation. (See
also n. 451.)   453 above in heaven, or in exemplary behavior here
on earth   456 for that because. (Peter's being struck down was all
the more tragic because he had mounted so high spiritually; but see
n. 451.)   458 Exempt . . . authority free from the corrupt influence of
having too much power and wealth   462 by kind by birth

Birth, blood, and ancestors are none of ours,
Nor can we make a proper challenge to them;   464
But virtues and perfections in our powers
Proceed most truly from us, if we do them.   466
Respective titles or a gracious style,   467
With all what men in eminence possess,
Are, without ornaments to praise them, vile;   469
The beauty of the mind is nobleness.
And such as have that beauty well deserve
Eternal characters, that after death   472
Remembrance of their worth we may preserve,
So that their glory die not with their breath.

Else what avails it in a goodly strife
Upon this face of earth here to contend,
The good t'exceed the wicked in their life,   477
Should both be like obscurèd in their end?   478
Until which end, there is none rightly can
Be termèd happy, since the happiness
Depends upon the goodness of the man,
Which afterwards his praises will express.

Look hither, then, you that enjoy the youth
Of your best days, and see how unexpected
Death can betray your jollity to ruth,   485
When Death, you think, is least to be repected!   486
The person of this model here set out   487
Had all that youth and happy days could give him,
Yet could not all-encompass him about
Against th' assault of Death, who, to relieve him,   490
Struck home but to the frail and mortal parts
Of his humanity, but could not touch
His flourishing and fair long-lived deserts,
Above Fate's reach, his singleness was such.   494

So that he dies but once, but doubly lives,
Once in his proper self, then in his name;
Predestinated Time, who all deprives,
Could never yet deprive him of the same.
And had the Genius which attended on him
Been possibilited to keep him safe   500
Against the rigor that hath overgone him,
He had been to the public use a staff,
Leading by his example in the path
Which guides to doing well, wherein so few
The proneness of this age to error hath
Informèd rightly in the courses true.   506

As then the loss of one, whose inclination
Strove to win love in general, is sad,
So specially his friends, in soft compassion,

Do feel the greatest loss they could have had.
Amongst them all, she who those nine of years   511
Lived fellow to his counsels and his bed
Hath the most share in loss; for I in hers
Feel what distemperature this chance hath bred.   514
The chaste embracements of conjugal love,
Who in a mutual harmony consent,
Are so impatient of a strange remove   517
As meager Death itself seems to lament,   518
And weep upon those cheeks which Nature framed   519
To be delightful orbs in whom the force
Of lively sweetness plays, so that, ashamed,
Death often pities his unkind divorce.   522
Such was the separation here constrained
(Well worthy to be termed a rudeness, rather);
For in his life his love was so unfeigned
As he was both an husband and a father—
The one in firm affection and the other
In careful providence, which ever strove   528
With joint assistance to grace one another   529
With every helpful furtherance of love.
But since the sum of all that can be said
Can be but that "He was good," which wholly
Includes all excellence can be displayed   533
In praise of virtue and reproach of folly,
    His due deserts this sentence on him gives: 535
    "He died in life, yet in his death he lives."
        Now runs the method of this doleful song   537
In accents brief to thee, O thou deceased!   538
To whom those pains do only all belong   539
As witnesses I did not love thee least.
For, could my worthless brain find out but how
To raise thee from the sepulcher of dust,
Undoubtedly thou shouldst have partage now   543
Of life with me, and heaven be counted just
If to a supplicating soul it would
Give life anew, by giving life again
Where life is missed; whereby Discomfort should
Right his old griefs and former joys retain,
Which now with thee are leapt into thy tomb
And buried in that hollow vault of woe,
Expecting yet a more severer doom   551
Than Time's strict flinty hand will let 'em know.   552
And now, if I have leveled mine account   553

464 Nor . . . them nor can we rightly lay claim to true nobleness by virtue of birth and ancestry   466 do exercise   467 Respective titles titles of respect.   gracious style honorific title   469 ornaments . . . them gracious qualities (such as nobleness of mind) to make them truly worthy of praise   472 characters representations. (The moral beauty of persons deserves to be written in an eternal alphabet.)   477–478 The good . . . end? if the virtuous should outshine the wicked in their lives only to be forgotten in their deaths?   485 ruth calamity, ruin, sorrow   486 respected taken into account, regarded   487 The person . . . out William Peter, here set forth as a model   490 to relieve him to assist itself in difficulty. (Death is imagined as taking William Peter in order to remove a threatening obstacle to the triumph of death and sin among humans.)   494 his . . . such so great was William Peter's integrity   500 possibilited enabled   506 Informèd instructed

511 nine of years (A puzzle; William Peter was married to Margaret Brewton for only three years.)   514 distemperature disorder of the spirit and of the elements making up life.   chance accident   517 impatient . . . remove unwilling to endure such an unaccountable taking away by death   518 meager emaciated, skeletal   519 those cheeks the cheeks of the widow   522 his unkind divorce the unnatural and unpitying separation of husband and wife that he, Death, has affected. (For Death to pity his own unpitying action is an oxymoron.)   528 careful providence (William Peter was a caring husband to his wife and father to his children.)   528–529 which . . . another which two roles, that of husband and of father, lent grace and assistance to each other   533 excellence excellence that . . .   535 His due deserts (thought of here as a single concept; hence the singular verb form, "gives").   sentence sententious thought, epigram   537 method rules appropriate to elegaic poetry   538 accents language, speech (including tone and meaning)   539 To . . . belong in whose loving memory I have taken the pains of writing this poem   543 partage part, share   551–552 Expecting . . . know i.e., awaiting the Day of Judgment   553 leveled evened up, settled

And reckoned up in a true measured score
Those perfect graces which were ever wont
To wait on thee alive, I ask no more,
But shall hereafter in a poor content   557
Immure those imputations I sustain,   558
Learning my days of youth so to prevent   559
As not to be cast down by them again—
Only those hopes which Fate denies to grant   561
In full possession to a captive heart,   562
Who, if it were in plenty, still would want   563
Before it may enjoy his better part,   564
From which detained, and banished in th' exile   565
Of dim misfortune, has none other prop   566
Whereon to lean and rest itself the while   567
But the weak comfort of the hapless, Hope.   568
        And Hope must, in despite of fearful change,
Play in the strongest closet of my breast,
Although perhaps I ignorantly range   571
And court opinion in my deep'st unrest.   572
But whither doth the stream of my mischance   573
Drive me beyond myself, fast friend, soon lost,   574
Long may thy worthiness thy name advance
Amongst the virtuous and deserving most,
        Who herein hast forever happy proved:
        In life thou livedst, in death thou died'st, beloved.

557–558 in . . . sustain in sad contentment put out of mind (literally, bury) the accusations that are made against me. (The poet hopes to learn from William Peter's noble example how to rise above slander.) 559 prevent excel, surpass; disarm   561–568 Only . . . Hope i.e., I ask only that I may not be cast down again by the sorts of hopes that Fate denies to grant fully to the heart of one who is hostage to Fate by reason of his love—a heart that, even if it had a full measure of its joy, still would hunger for the loved person's better excellences, and which, deprived as I now am by sad misfortune, can only prop itself up with the weak comfort of some indefinable hope (of seeing William Peter again after death). (The poet suggests that even if this high hope were granted, it would be granted only eventually, leaving him now to yearn still for his friend.)   571–572 Although . . . unrest even if (in opting for hope in my unrest) I disconsolately and ignorantly court popular opinion (and thus go along with pieties that my heart cannot really subscribe to, papering over the terrible loss while I get on with my worldly affairs)   573–574 But . . . lost but even if my misfortune may drive me out of my true self, O my dear friend, too soon lost to me

APPENDIX 1

Canon, Dates, and Early Texts

By "canon" we mean a listing of plays that can be ascribed to Shakespeare on the basis of reliable evidence. Such evidence is either "internal," derived from matters of style or poetics in the plays themselves (see General Introduction), or "external," derived from outside the play. The latter includes any reference by Shakespeare's contemporaries to his plays, any allusions in the plays themselves to contemporary events, the entering of Shakespeare's plays for publication in the Stationers' Register (S. R.), actual publication of the plays, and records of early performances. These matters of external evidence are also essential in attempting to date the plays.

The greatest single source of information is the First Folio text of Shakespeare's plays, sponsored by Shakespeare's fellow actors John Heminges and Henry Condell and published in 1623. It contains all the plays included in this present edition of Shakespeare except *Pericles* and offers strong presumptive evidence of being a complete and accurate compilation of Shakespeare's work by men who knew him and cherished his memory. It provides the only texts we have for these eighteen plays: *The Comedy of Errors, The Two Gentlemen of Verona, The Taming of the Shrew, I Henry VI, King John, As You Like It, Twelfth Night, Julius Caesar, All's Well That Ends Well, Measure for Measure, Timon of Athens, Macbeth, Antony and Cleopatra, Coriolanus, Cymbeline, The Winter's Tale, The Tempest,* and *Henry VIII.* This includes nearly half the known canon of Shakespeare's plays. Our debt to the First Folio is incalculable and confirms our impression of its reliability.

The information of the First Folio is further confirmed by contemporary references. In 1598, a cleric and minor writer of the period named Francis Meres wrote in his *Palladis Tamia:*

As the soul of Euphorbus was thought to live in Pythagoras, so the sweet, witty soul of Ovid lives in mellifluous and honey-tongued Shakespeare: witness his *Venus and Adonis,* his *Lucrece,* his sugared sonnets among his private friends, etc.

As Plautus and Seneca are accounted the best for comedy and tragedy among the Latins, so Shakespeare among the English is the most excellent in both kinds for the stage; for comedy, witness his *Gentlemen of Verona,* his *Errors,* his *Love's Labor's Lost,* his *Love's Labor's Won,* his *Midsummer's Night Dream,* and his *Merchant of Venice;* for tragedy his *Richard the II, Richard the III, Henry the IV, King John, Titus Andronicus* and his *Romeo and Juliet.*

Though this list was meant to offer praise, not to be an exhaustive catalogue, it is remarkably full. If the tantalizing *Love's Labor's Won* refers to *The Taming of the Shrew,* Meres' list of comedies is entirely complete down to 1598. Naturally, the list does not include the great "festive" comedies, *Much Ado About Nothing, As You Like It,* and *Twelfth Night,* since these were written at, or slightly later than, the time of Meres' comment. Meres correctly names all of Shakespeare's history plays except the *Henry VI* trilogy and of course the later histories, *Henry V* (1599) and *Henry VIII* (1613). He names both of Shakespeare's early tragedies that are not based on English history: *Titus Andronicus* and *Romeo and Juliet.* He tells us about the important nondramatic poems, which did not appear in the First Folio, since that volume is devoted exclusively to plays. Not much can be made of the order in which Meres names the plays, however, for we learn from other sources that *Richard III* clearly precedes *Richard II* in date of composition and that *King John* precedes the *Henry IV* plays.

Other writers of the 1590s add further confirming evidence. John Weever, in an epigram "*Ad Gulielmum Shakespeare,*" published in 1599, refers to "Rose-cheeked Adonis" and "Fair fire-hot Venus," to "Chaste Lucretia" and "Proud lust-stung Tarquin," and to "*Romeo, Richard—* more whose names I know not." Richard Barnfield, in *Poems in Divers Humors* (1598), praises Shakespeare for "*Venus*" and "*Lucrece.*" Both Thomas Nashe and Robert Greene seemingly refer to the *Henry VI* plays, missing from Meres' list. Nashe, in his *Pierce Penniless* (1592), speculates how it would "have joyed brave Talbot (the terror of the French) to think that after he had lain two hundred years in his tomb, he should triumph again on the stage." Talbot is the hero of *1 Henry VI,* and we know of no other play on the subject. Greene, in his *Greene's Groats-worth of Wit* (1592), lashes out at an "upstart crow, beautified with our feathers, that with his '*Tiger's heart wrapped in a player's hide*' supposes he is as well able to bombast out a blank verse as the best of you, and, being an absolute *Johannes Factotum,* is in his own conceit the only Shake-scene in a country." The line about "Tiger's heart" is deliberately misquoted from *3 Henry VI,* 1.4.137. (It is possible that this famous attack on Shakespeare was actually written not by Greene himself but by Henry Chettle, his literary executor.)

The Comedy of Errors (c. 1589–1594)

The earliest known edition of *The Comedy of Errors* is in the First Folio of 1623. Its first-mentioned production, however, was on Innocents Day, December 28, 1594, when a "Comedy of Errors (like to *Plautus* his *Menechmus*)" was performed by professional actors as part of the Christmas Revels at Gray's Inn (one of the Inns of Court, where young men studied law) in London. The evening's festivities are set down in *Gesta Grayorum,* a contemporary account of the revels, though not published until 1688. According to this record, the evening was marred by such tumult and disorder that the invited guests from the Inner Temple (another of the Inns of Court) refused to stay; thereafter, the night became known as "The Night of Errors." References to sorcery and enchantment in the play leave little doubt that it was Shakespeare's.

Some scholars argue that the play was not newly written for this occasion. To them, the play seems early: slight in characterization, and full of punning wit reminiscent of *Love's Labor's Lost* and *The Two Gentlemen of Verona.* Topical clues are suggestive but not conclusive. Chief of these is the joke about France being "armed and reverted, making war against her heir" (3.2.123–124). Unquestionably, this refers to France's civil wars between Henry of Navarre and his Catholic opposition. Since Henry became a Catholic and the King of France in 1593, most scholars prefer a date before 1593. Peter Alexander (*Shakespeare's Life and Art,* 1961) has even argued for a date prior to 1589, since Henry III died in that year, leaving Henry of Navarre as nominal king rather than heir. The sad truth is that we probably cannot attach too much weight to either conclusion. Allusions to the French civil wars during the early 1590s were common but also imprecise; the joke would have seemed relevant at almost any time up to 1595. The same is probably true of the allusion to Spain's sending "whole armadas of carracks" (3.2.135–136). This is often taken to refer to the Spanish Armada, 1588, but may refer instead to the Portuguese *Madre de Dios,* captured and brought to England in 1592, or to a similar venture. In short, it is virtually impossible to prove that *The Comedy of Errors* precedes *Love's Labor's Lost, The Two Gentlemen of Verona,* or *The Taming of the Shrew.* Those scholars who think it unlikely that the young gentlemen of Gray's Inn would have bestowed their attention on a play already five years old prefer a date of 1594.

A lost play called *The History of Error* was acted before the Queen by the Children of Paul's (a company of boy actors from St. Paul's School) at Hampton Court on New Year's night, 1577. About this play we know nothing other than its suggestive title, and speculation that Shakespeare may have adapted it has been generally abandoned.

The Folio text, based probably on Shakespeare's own manuscript, is generally a good text, although, as is common in authorial manuscripts, the form of the characters' names frequently varies in the stage directions and speech prefixes. Perhaps a few performance-oriented annotations have been added to the authorial manuscript.

Love's Labor's Lost (c. 1588–1597)

Love's Labor's Lost first appeared in a Quarto dated 1598, without entry in the Stationers' Register, the official record book of the London Company of Stationers (booksellers and printers). Its title page reads:

A PLEASANT Conceited Comedie CALLED, Loues labors lost. As it vvas presented before her Highnes this last Christmas. Newly corrected and augmented By W. Shakespere. Imprinted at London by W. W. [William White] for *Cutbert Burby.*1598.

Because the phrase "newly corrected and augmented" also appears on the title page of the good Quarto of *Romeo and Juliet,* issued in 1599 to correct a pirated Quarto of 1597, many scholars suspect that *Love's Labor's Lost* may similarly have appeared in a bad Quarto that is now lost. Such a circumstance would explain why the existing Quarto of *Love's Labor's Lost* was not registered: if the play had already been published, even in a pirated version, relicensing would have been unnecessary. (The *Romeo and Juliet* good Quarto was not registered for this reason.) But it is also entirely possible that the 1598 Quarto is simply reprinting an earlier lost good Quarto and that Burby is exaggerating his claims of correcting and augmenting.

The text shows clear signs of revision. Two long passages (see textual notes at 4.3.291 and 5.2.812) give duplicate readings of the same speeches, suggesting the printer mistakenly copied both the canceled version in his copy and the revision. Speech headings are unusually confused, sometimes referring to characters by their personal names (Navarre, Armado, Holofernes) and at other times by their generic titles (King, Braggart, Pedant). Some of these errors, notably the long uncanceled passages, suggest that the printer of the 1598 Quarto or of an earlier lost Quarto, perhaps new and relatively inexperienced, was copying from Shakespeare's working draft. Whether Shakespeare wrote this draft on one occasion or whether he revised an earlier version is, however, a matter on which scholars disagree. The First Folio text was set from the Quarto and thus gives us little additional information as to when or in what stages the play was written, though it may also have had occasional reference to a playhouse manuscript.

Francis Meres refers to the play in October of 1598 in his *Palladis Tamia.* The performance before Queen Elizabeth "last Christmas" was probably in late 1597. Robert Tofte tells us in his *Alba* (1598) that *"Love's Labour Lost,* I once did see a play / ycleped so." His phrasing suggests a performance seen sometime in the past, although he could mean that he saw it only once. Apart from these allusions, dating of the play must rely on its presumed internal allusions to contemporary events. Unfortunately, the play has attracted a lot of highly speculative topical hypotheses. One such describes a "School of Night" to which Sir Walter

Ralegh, Matthew Roydon, George Chapman, and others are supposed to have belonged. No objective evidence exists to prove the existence of such a school. Ralegh was tried for atheism but was acquitted. Other topical hypotheses are discussed briefly in the Introduction to the play. Some allusions to the historical King of Navarre and to his supporters, the Duc de Biron and the Duc de Longueville, are undeniable. These allusions tend to argue either for an early date (c. 1588–1589), when these persons had not yet become the chief figures in a bloody religious civil war in France and hence inappropriate subjects for light comedy, or for a date after 1594, when a satire of Navarre's perjury might seem relevant to the historical Navarre's renunciation of Protestantism in 1593. The influence of John Lyly and the children's drama also argues for an early date. If, on the other hand, the Muscovite masque in 5.2 contains a reference to the Gray's Inn (one of the Inns of Court, where young men studied law) revels of 1594, as several scholars have urged, some portions of the play may be from after that date. The hypothesis that Shakespeare revived an old play of his shortly before publication in 1598, although not universally accepted, offers at least a plausible explanation of the phrase "newly corrected and augmented" on the title page.

The Two Gentlemen of Verona (c. 1590–1594)

The Two Gentlemen of Verona was not published until the First Folio of 1623. Other than Francis Meres' listing of it in 1598 in his *Palladis Tamia: Wit's Treasury* (a slender volume on contemporary literature and art, valuable because it lists most of the plays of Shakespeare that existed at that time), evidence as to dating is scarce. No convincing allusions to contemporary events have been found. From the internal evidence of style, such as the relative density and sophistication of the dialogue, most scholars prefer an early date. The influence of John Lyly's romantic comedies, such as *Campaspe* (1584) and *Endymion* (1588), is still perceptible in the play's overly ingenious wit-combat.

A notable feature of the text, its grouping of characters' names at the beginning of each scene and the absence of any other stage directions except exits, seems to indicate that the manuscript was copied at some point by the scrivener Ralph Crane, probably from an authorial manuscript still containing a number of inconsistencies. The speech prefixes are sufficiently regular, on the other hand, that the text may have been prepared for the theater or else tidied up by Crane.

The Taming of the Shrew (c. 1590–1593)

The Taming of the Shrew was not printed until the First Folio of 1623. Francis Meres does not mention the play in 1598 in his *Palladis Tamia*, unless it is the mysterious

"*Loue labours wonne*" on his list. (Meres is not totally accurate, for he omits *Henry VI* from the history plays.) The play must have existed prior to 1598, however, for its style is comparable with that of *The Two Gentlemen of Verona* and other early comedies. Moreover, a play called *The Taming of a Shrew* appeared in print in 1594 (Stationers' Register, 1594). Four theories can be adduced to explain the problematic relationship of *A Shrew* to Shakespeare's play. The two least plausible theories are that Shakespeare, for some reason, reworked someone else's play shortly after its first performance or else wrote *A Shrew* himself as an early version. The third theory is that *A Shrew* represents an imitation of Shakespeare's play by some rival dramatist, who relied chiefly on his memory and who changed characters' names and the location to make the play seem his. Fourth and most plausibly, *A Shrew* may be a somewhat uncharacteristic kind of reported or "bad" Quarto, reconstructed and "improved" upon by a writer who also borrowed admiringly from Christopher Marlowe and other Elizabethan dramatists. In either of the latter two scenarios, Shakespeare's play would have to be dated earlier than May 1594.

The title page of *A Shrew* proclaims that "it was sundry times acted by the *Right honorable the Earle of* Pembrook his seruants." Quite possibly this derivative version was merely trying to capitalize on the original's stage success and was, in fact, describing performances of Shakespeare's play. Theater owner and manager Philip Henslowe's record of a performance of "*the Tamynge of A Shrowe*" in 1594 at Newington Butts, a mile south of London Bridge, may also refer to Shakespeare's play; certainly, the minute distinction between "A Shrew" and "The Shrew" is one that the official records of the time would overlook. The Admiral's men and the Lord Chamberlain's men, acting companies, were playing at Newington Butts at the time, either jointly or alternatingly. Since Shakespeare's company, the Lord Chamberlain's, later owned *The Shrew*, they may well have owned and acted it on this occasion in 1594, having obtained it from the Earl of Pembroke's men when that company disbanded in 1593. Many of Pembroke's leading players joined the Lord Chamberlain's, Shakespeare being quite possibly among them. (The possibility that he came to the Lord Chamberlain's from Lord Strange's men seems less certain today than it once did.) Several echoes of Shakespeare's play in other plays of the early 1590s tend to confirm a date in or before 1593. It is entirely possible, then, that *The Shrew* was acted by Pembroke's men in 1592–1593 and subsequently passed along to the Lord Chamberlain's.

The Folio text of this play is now generally thought to have been printed from Shakespeare's working manuscript or possibly from a transcript of his papers, with perhaps some theatrical annotations as well. Some signs of revision are discernible.

A Midsummer Night's Dream (c. 1595)

A Midsummer Night's Dream was entered on the Stationers' Register, the official record book of the London Company of Stationers (booksellers and printers), by Thomas Fisher on October 8, 1600, and printed by him that same year in Quarto:

A Midsommer nights dreame. As it hath beene sundry times publickely acted, by the Right honourable, the Lord Chamberlaine his seruants. Written by William Shakespeare. Imprinted at London, for Thomas Fisher, and are to be soulde at his shoppe, at the Signe of the White Hart, in Fleetestreete. 1600.

This text appears to have been set from Shakespeare's working manuscript. Its inconsistencies in time scheme and other irregularities may reflect some revision, although the inconsistencies are not noticeable in performance. A Second Quarto appeared in 1619, though falsely dated 1600; it was a reprint of the First Quarto, with some minor corrections and many new errors. A copy of this Second Quarto, evidently with some added stage directions and other minor changes from a theatrical manuscript in the company's possession, served as the basis for the First Folio text of 1623. Changes of speech assignment in the Folio text, especially in Act 5, may reflect a late revival over which Shakespeare had no control. Essentially, the First Quarto remains the authoritative text.

Other than Francis Meres' listing of the play in 1598 in his Palladis Tamia: Wit's Treasury, external clues as to date are elusive. Possibly the worry that a lion in a play might frighten the ladies (3.1.24–31) echoes published accounts of a baptismal feast at court in August 1594, when a blackamoor was chosen to draw in a chariot in place of a lion for fear of alarming nearby spectators. The description of unruly weather (2.1.88–114) has been related to the bad summer of 1594, but complaints about the weather are perennial. On the assumption that the play celebrates some noble wedding of the period, scholars have come up with a number of suitable marriages. Chief are those of Sir Thomas Heneage to Mary, Countess of Southampton, in 1594; of William Stanley, Earl of Derby, to Elizabeth Vere, daughter of the Earl of Oxford, in 1595; and of Thomas, son of Lord Berkeley, to Elizabeth, daughter of Lord Carey, in 1596. The Countess of Southampton was the widowed mother of the young Earl of Southampton, to whom Shakespeare had dedicated his Venus and Adonis and The Rape of Lucrece. No one has ever proved convincingly, however, that the play was written for any occasion other than commercial public performance. The play makes sense for a general audience and does not need to depend on references to a private marriage. Shakespeare was, after all, in the business of writing plays for his fellow actors, who earned their livelihood chiefly by public acting before large paying audiences. In any event, the search for a court marriage is a circular argument in terms of dating; suitable court marriages can be found for any year of the decade. In the last analysis, the play has to be dated on the basis of its stylistic affinity to plays like Romeo and Juliet and Richard II, works of the "lyric" mid-1590s. The "Pyramus and Thisbe" performance in A Midsummer Night's Dream would seem to bear an obvious relation to Romeo and Juliet, although no one can say for sure which came first.

The Merchant of Venice (c. 1596–1597)

The Stationers' Register, the official record book of the London Company of Stationers (booksellers and printers), for July 22, 1598, contains an entry on behalf of the printer James Roberts for "a booke of the Marchaunt of Venyce, or otherwise called the Iewe of Venyce, Prouided, that yt bee not prynted by the said James Robertes or anye other whatsoeuer without lycence first had from the Right honorable the lord Chamberlen." Roberts evidently enjoyed a close connection with the Chamberlain's men (Shakespeare's acting company) and seemingly was granted the special favor of registering the play at this time, even though the company did not wish to see the play published until later (or until they were paid). In 1600, at any rate, Roberts transferred his rights as publisher to Thomas Heyes and printed the volume for him with the following title:

The most excellent Historie of the Merchant of Venice. VVith the extreame crueltie of Shylocke the Iewe towards the sayd Merchant, in cutting a iust pound of his flesh: and the obtayning of Portia by the choyse of three chests. As it hath beene diuers times acted by the Lord Chamberlaine his Seruants. Written by William Shakespeare. AT LONDON, Printed by I. R. [James Roberts] for Thomas Heyes, and are to be sold in Paules Church-yard, at the signe of the Greene Dragon. 1600.

The text of this 1600 Quarto is generally a good one, based seemingly on an accurate copy of Shakespeare's papers by the dramatist himself or some reliable transcriber. It served as copy for the Second Quarto of 1619 (printed by William Jaggard for Thomas Pavier and fraudulently dated 1600) and for the First Folio of 1623. Although some theatrical manuscript seems also to have been consulted in preparation for the Folio text, the Folio variations appear to have little authority.

Francis Meres mentions the play in 1598 in his Palladis Tamia. Establishing an earlier limit for dating has proven not so easy. Many scholars have urged a connection with the Roderigo Lopez affair of 1594 (see the Introduction to the play). The supposed allusion to Lopez in the lines about "a wolf, who, hanged for human slaughter" (4.1.134) may simply indicate, however, that wolves were actually hanged for attacking men in Shakespeare's day (as dogs were for killing sheep). Besides, the Lopez case remained so notorious throughout the 1590s that even a proven allusion to it in

The Merchant would not limit the play to 1594 or 1595. Christopher Marlowe's play, *The Jew of Malta*, was revived in 1594 to exploit anti-Lopez sentiment but was also revived in 1596. There may be, moreover, an allusion in 1.1.27 to the *St. Andrew*, a Spanish ship captured at Cadiz in 1596, and Shylock's allusion to Jacob and Laban (1.3.69–88) may well echo Miles Mosse's *The Arraignment and Conviction of Usury*, 1595. If so, the likeliest date is 1596–1597.

Much Ado About Nothing (1598–1599)

"The Commedie of muche A doo about nothing a booke" was entered in the Stationers' Register, the official record book of the London Company of Stationers (booksellers and printers), on August 4, 1600, along with *As You Like It, Henry V,* and Ben Jonson's *Every Man in His Humor,* all marked as plays of "My lord chamberlens men" (Shakespeare's acting company) and all "to be staied"—that is, not published without further permission. Earlier in the same memorandum, written on a spare page in the Register, occurs the name of the printer James Roberts, whose registration of *The Merchant of Venice* in 1598 was similarly stayed, pending further permission to publish. Evidently, the Chamberlain's men were attempting to ensure that they were paid for any plays printed or else to prevent unauthorized publication of these very popular plays. If the latter was their motive, they were too late to forestall the appearance of a bad Quarto of *Henry V* in August of 1600, but they did manage to control release of the others. *Much Ado About Nothing* appeared later that same year in a seemingly authorized version:

Much adoe about Nothing. *As it hath been sundrie times publikely* acted by the right honourable, the Lord Chamberlaine his seruants. *Written by William Shakespeare.* LONDON Printed by V. S. [Valentine Sims] for Andrew Wise, and William Aspley. 1600.

Once thought to have been set up from a theatrical playbook and then used itself in the theater as a playbook before serving as copy for the First Folio of 1623, this 1600 Quarto text is now generally regarded as having been set from Shakespeare's own manuscript. The names of the actors Will Kempe and Richard Cowley appear among the speech prefixes in 4.2, indicating that Shakespeare had them in mind as he wrote; other irregularities in speech prefixes and scene headings (including "ghost" characters, such as Leonato's wife Innogen) read more like a manuscript in the last stages of revision than a playbook for a finished production. The Folio text was based on this 1600 Quarto, lightly annotated with reference to the playbook but providing little in the way of new readings other than the correction of obvious error.

Francis Meres does not mention the play in September of 1598 in his *Palladis Tamia,* unless (and this seems unlikely)

it is his *"Loue labours wonne."* Will Kempe, who played Dogberry, left the Chamberlain's men early in 1599. The likeliest date, then, is the winter of 1598–1599, though publication was not until 1600.

The Merry Wives of Windsor (1597–1601)

The Stationers' Register, the official record book of the London Company of Stationers (booksellers and printers), for January 18, 1602, carries an entry for "A booke called an excellent and pleasant conceited commedie of Sir John Faulstof and the merry wyves of Windesor," by assignment from John Busby to Arthur Johnson. Later that year, Thomas Creed printed the following Quarto:

A Most pleasant and excellent conceited Comedie, of Syr *Iohn Falstaffe,* and the merrie Wiues of *Windsor.* Entermixed with sundrie variable and pleasing humors, of Syr *Hugh* the Welch Knight, Iustice *Shallow,* and his wise Cousin M. *Slender.* With the swaggering vaine of Auncient *Pistoll,* and Corporall *Nym.* By *William Shakespeare.* As it hath bene diuers times Acted by the right Honorable my Lord Chamberlaines seruants. Both before her Maiestie, and else-where. LONDON Printed by T. C. [Thomas Creed] for Arthur Iohnson, and are to be sold at his shop in Powles Church-yard, at the signe of the Flower de Leuse and the Crowne. 1602.

This text is now generally regarded as a bad Quarto, memorially reconstructed perhaps by the actors who played the Host and Falstaff and shortened for touring in the provinces. A Second Quarto in 1619, printed by William Jaggard for Thomas Pavier, was based on it. The First Folio text of 1623, however, was taken from a manuscript evidently transcribed by Ralph Crane (hence, the "massed entries" of characters' names at the beginnings of scenes) and based perhaps on a theatrical playbook. It is the most authoritative text. Several interesting variant readings occur in the bad Quarto, despite its unreliability, and seem to indicate original readings that were altered in the Folio version for reasons of prudence. We find "garmombles" in place of the Folio "germans" at 4.5.74, and "Brook" in place of the Folio "Broome" throughout as the disguise name for the jealous Ford. "Garmombles" is often interpreted as an unflattering allusion to Frederick, Count Mömpelgard (see the Introduction to the play). "Brook" is a seeming dig at the family name of the powerful Henry Brooke (a descendant of Sir John Oldcastle), eighth Lord Cobham, whose intervention probably led to the similar changing of "Oldcastle" to "Falstaff" in *Henry IV.* The Quarto can also be used sparingly to correct errors and omissions in the Folio text when, as seems likely in a small number of instances, the omission looks like eyeskip in the Folio text, rather than actors' or reporters' interpolations in the Quarto.

On dating, two irreconcilable choices are still possible: 1597, when the Lord Chamberlain was elected to the Order of the Garter, and 1600–1601, after *Henry V* (1599), in which Nym had been introduced. (There is more on the Order of the Garter in the Introduction.) The Stationer's Register entry in January of 1602 provides a forward limit in time. Recent scholarly work tends to argue for the earlier date of 1597, though Francis Meres does not mention it in 1598 in his *Palladis Tamia.*

As You Like It (1598–1600)

"As you like yt, a booke" was entered in the Stationers' Register, the official record book of the London Company of Stationers (booksellers and printers), on August 4, 1600, along with *Much Ado About Nothing, Henry V,* and Ben Jonson's *Every Man in His Humor,* all labeled as "My lord chamberlens mens plaies" and all ordered "to be staied" from publication until further notice. Evidently, the Chamberlain's men (Shakespeare's acting company) were anxious to ensure payment or otherwise protect their rights to these very popular plays. Despite their efforts, *Henry V* was pirated that same month. *As You Like It* did not appear in print, however, until the First Folio of 1623. The Folio text is a good one, based seemingly on the theatrical playbook that still retained certain authorial features (conceivably, because an autograph fair copy served as the basis for it) or on a literary transcript either of the playbook or of an authorial manuscript.

Francis Meres does not mention the play in September of 1598 in his *Palladis Tamia.* However, the play contains an unusually clear allusion to Christopher Marlowe's *Hero and Leander* ("Who ever loved that loved not at first sight?" 3.5.82), of which the first extant edition appeared in 1598, although Shakespeare may well have known it earlier in manuscript or in some lost edition. Even so, other possible allusions, to the burning of satirical books in June of 1599 (see 1.2.85–86) and to the new Globe theater ("All the world's a stage," 2.7.138), point to a date between late 1598 and the summer of 1600, probably after *Much Ado About Nothing.*

Twelfth Night (1600–1602)

Twelfth Night was registered with the London Company of Stationers (booksellers and printers) in 1623 and was first published in the First Folio of that year in a good text set up from what may have been a scribal transcript of Shakespeare's draft manuscript or possibly the playbook (assuming that the scribe might omit theatrical notations). There was a brief delay in printing *Twelfth Night* in the First Folio, possibly because a transcript was being prepared. The play was first mentioned, however, in the *Diary* of a Middle Temple law student or barrister named John Manningham, who describes the festivities for Candlemas Day, February 2, 1602, as follows:

At our feast wee had a play called "Twelue Night, or What you Will," much like the Commedy of Errores, or Menechmi in Plautus, but most like and neere to that in Italian called *Inganni.* A good practise in it to make the Steward beleeve his Lady widdowe was in love with him, by couterfeyting a letter as from his Lady in generall termes, telling him what shee liked best in him, and prescribing his gesture in smiling, his apparaile, & c., and then when he came to practise making him beleeue they tooke him to be mad.

This entry was once suspected to be a forgery perpetrated by John Payne Collier, who published the *Diary* in 1831, but its authenticity is now generally accepted. The date accords with several possible allusions in the play itself. When Fabian jokes about "a pension of thousands to be paid from the Sophy" (2.5.176–177), he seems to be recalling Sir Anthony Shirley's reception by the Shah of Persia (the Sophy) between the summer of 1598 and late 1601. An account of this visit was entered in the Stationers' Register in November of 1601. Viola's description of Feste as "wise enough to play the fool" (3.1.60) may recall a poem beginning "True it is, he plays the fool indeed," published in 1600–1601 by Robert Armin (who had played the role of Feste). Maria's comparison of Malvolio's smiling face to "the new map with the augmentation of the Indies" (3.2.77–78) refers to new maps published in 1599 in which America (the Indies) was increased in size. Fabian's reference to sailing north and to the icicle on a Dutchman's beard (3.2.25–26) sounds like an allusion to William Barentz's Arctic expedition, first described in English in an account entered in the Stationers' Register on June 13, 1598, though no edition survives before 1609. Leslie Hotson (*The First Night of Twelfth Night,* 1954) has argued for a first performance at court on Twelfth Night in January of 1601, when Queen Elizabeth entertained Don Virginio Orsino, Duke of Bracciano, but this hypothesis has not gained general acceptance, partly because the role of Orsino in the play would scarcely flatter such a noble visitor and partly because there is no proof that any of Shakespeare's plays were originally commissioned for private performance. Nevertheless, the episode may have suggested to Shakespeare the name Orsino. All in all, a date between 1600 and early 1602 seems most likely. Francis Meres does not mention the play in 1598 in his *Palladis Tamia.*

All's Well That Ends Well (c. 1601–1605)

All's Well That Ends Well was first registered in the Stationers' Register, the official record book of the London Company of Stationers (booksellers and printers), in November of 1623 and was published in the First Folio of that same year. The text contains numerous inconsistencies in speech headings, "ghost" characters, anomalies of punctuation, and vague or literary stage directions, indicating it was set from the author's working papers, but these errors are not as extensive as once thought and the text is basically sound.

Shakespeare's manuscript may have been sporadically annotated by the bookkeeper. Its printing in the First Folio is unusually laden with errors.

Information on the date of the play is sparse. Francis Meres does not mention it in 1598 in his *Palladis Tamia*, unless it is the intriguing "*Loue labours wonne*" on his list. Its themes and style are more suggestive of the period of *Hamlet* and *Troilus and Cressida*. The common assumption today is that the play was written sometime around 1601–1605. It may be later than *Measure for Measure*; the two plays are closely related, but the order of composition is hard to determine. The role of Lavatch is clearly designed for the actor Robert Armin, who did not join Shakespeare's acting company until 1599 or 1600. Scholars once argued that *All's Well* is an early play later revised, but this means of explaining the inconsistencies in the text no longer seems necessary.

Measure for Measure (1603–1604)

Measure for Measure first appeared in the First Folio of 1623. The text was evidently set from scrivener Ralph Crane's copy, possibly of Shakespeare's own draft; the usual inconsistencies of composition have not yet been smoothed away by use in the theater. On the other hand, spellings tend to suggest that Crane was copying a transcript. A recent and controversial hypothesis is that Crane based his copy on a playbook in use after Shakespeare's death, which incorporated some theatrical adaptation by Thomas Middleton and some other reviser, including a song (4.1.1–6) that could have originated in *Rollo, Duke of Normandy* (c. 1617) by John Fletcher and others.

The first recorded performance (according to a Revels account document that has been argued to be of dubious authenticity) was on December 26, 1604, St. Stephen's Night, when "a play Caled Mesur for Mesur" by "Shaxberd" was acted in the banqueting hall at Whitehall "by his Maiesties plaiers." Shakespeare's acting company, previously the Lord Chamberlain's men, had become the King's men after the accession to the throne of James I in 1603. Several allusions in the play seem to point to the summer of 1604, when the theaters, having been closed for a year because of the plague, were reopened. A reference to the King of Hungary (1.2.1–5) may reflect anxieties in England over James' negotiations for a settlement with Spain; censorship would forbid a direct mentioning of Spain. Mistress Overdone's complaint about the war, the "sweat" (plague), the "gallows" (public executions), and poverty (1.2.81–83) are all suggestive of events in 1603–1604, when war with Spain and the plague were still very much in evidence. Duke Vincentio's reticent habits have been seen as a flattering reference to James' well-known dislike of crowds. Stylistically, the play is clearly later than *Twelfth Night* (1600–1602), so that a date close to the first recorded performance in 1604 is a necessity, even if we cannot be positive about all the supposed allusions to King James.

Troilus and Cressida (c. 1601–1602)

The textual history of *Troilus and Cressida* is complicated. On February 7, 1603, James Roberts entered in the Stationers' Register, the official record book of the London Company of Stationers (booksellers and printers), "when he hath gotten sufficient aucthority for yt, The booke of Troilus and Cresseda as yt is acted by my lord Chamberlens Men." On January 28, 1609, however, a new entry appeared in the Register, as though the first had never been made: "Richard Bonion Henry Walleys. Entred for their Copy vnder thandes of Master Segar deputy to Sir George Bucke and master warden Lownes a booke called the history of Troylus and Cressida." Later that year appeared the First Quarto with the following title:

THE Historie of Troylus and Cresseida. *As it was acted by the Kings Maiesties* seruants at the Globe. *Written by* William Shakespeare. LONDON Imprinted by *G. Eld* for *R Bonian* and *H. Walley*, and are to be sold at the spred Eagle in Paules Church-yard, ouer against the great North doore. 1609.

Before the first printing had sold out, still in 1609, the original title leaf was replaced by two new leaves containing a new title and an epistle. The title reads:

THE Famous Historie of Troylus *and* Cresseid. *Excellently expressing the beginning* of their loues, with the conceited wooing of *Pandarus* Prince of *Licia*. *Written by* William Shakespeare.

The epistle is addressed "A neuer writer, to an euer reader. Newes," and begins, "Eternall reader, you haue heere a new play, neuer stal'd with the Stage, neuer clapper-clawd with the palmes of the vulger, and yet passing full of the palme comicall."

The First Folio editors originally intended *Troilus and Cressida* to follow *Romeo and Juliet*. After three pages and a title page had been set up in this position, however, the play was removed (perhaps owing to copyright difficulties) and *Timon of Athens* was inserted instead. Later, *Troilus* was placed between the Histories and the Tragedies, almost entirely without pagination. See the Introduction for some possible explanations of the unusual publishing history.

The Quarto text was evidently set from a transcript of Shakespeare's working draft, made either by Shakespeare or by a scribe, or more probably from the working draft itself. The first three pages of the Folio text, those originally intended to follow *Romeo and Juliet*, were set from this First Quarto. The remaining pages of the First Folio, however, seem to have been based on a copy of the Quarto that had been collated with a manuscript, either Shakespeare's draft or more probably the playbook, which could itself have been a transcript of Shakespeare's fair copy of his original papers. As a result, both the Quarto and Folio texts have independent textual authority. Recent editorial study has paid increasing attention to the Folio text on the theory that its readings, when not manifestly corrupt, may represent either Shakespeare's second throughts as he fair copied or at least what the Folio collator found in Shakespeare's draft or the playbook. Hence, this edition, though using the First Quarto as its control text, introduces more Folio readings than are usually found in some previous editions; the Folio readings have been rejected only when there is some textual evidence against them.

The possibility that the play may not have been publicly performed and the failure of Shakespeare's company to provide the sequel promised at the end of *Troilus* suggest that the play was written not long before the first Stationers' Register entry of February 1603. Certainly the play was not an old favorite in the company's repertoire. Failure as a stage play might have led to an attempt at quick publication, aimed at sophisticated readers. The current fad for satire would also have provided a motive for prompt publication. Stylistically, *Troilus* belongs to the period of *Hamlet* (c. 1599–1601). A seeming allusion in the Prologue of *Troilus* to the "armed" Prologue of Ben Jonson's *Poetaster* (1601) helps set a probable early limit for date of composition; although the Prologue first appears in the First Folio of 1623 and may be an addition to the original play, it probably is not much later in date of composition. George Chapman's *The Seaven Bookes of Homers Iliads,* a source of information about the Trojan war, had appeared in 1598. The play is not mentioned by Francis Meres in 1598.

The Henry the Sixth Plays (c. 1589–1592)

The date and textual situation for *1 Henry VI* needs to be discussed in the context of all three *Henry VI* plays. *1 Henry VI* was not the first to be published. Shortened versions of *2* and *3 Henry VI* appeared in 1594 and 1595. One was titled as follows:

THE First part of the Contention betwixt the two famous Houses of Yorke and Lancaster, with the death of the good Duke Humphrey: And the banishment and death of the Duke of *Suffolke,* and the Tragicall end of the proud Cardinall of VVinchester, vvith the notable Rebellion of *Iacke Cade: And the Duke of Yorkes first claime vnto the Crowne.* LONDON Printed by Thomas Creed, for Thomas Millington, and are to be sold at his shop vnder Saint Peters Church in Cornwall. 1594.

Its sequel was titled as follows:

The true Tragedie of Richard *Duke of Yorke, and the death of* good King Henrie the Sixt, *with the whole contention betweene* the two Houses Lancaster and Yorke, as it was sundrie times acted by the Right Honourable the Earle of Pembrooke his seruants. Printed at London by P. S. [Peter Short] for Thomas Millington, and *are to be sold at his shoppe vnder Saint Peters Church in Cornwall.* 1595.

Once thought to be source plays for Shakespeare's *2* and *3 Henry VI,* these texts, the first a Quarto and the second an Octavo, have been independently demonstrated by Peter Alexander and Madeleine Doran to be "bad Quartos" or memorial reconstructions of Shakespeare's texts, put together by actors for sale to a printer or for acting in the provinces. As such, their textual authority is questionable but may be of significance in those occasional passages where the Folio compositors seem to have had recourse to later reprints (the Third Quartos) of these texts. In 1619 they were combined in a reprint by the printer William Jaggard called *The Whole Contention betweene the two Famous Houses, Lancaster and Yorke.* These texts are considerably shorter than the First Folio versions of 1623, which appeared there under the titles "The second Part of Henry the Sixt, with the death of the Good Duke HVMFREY," and "The third Part of Henry the Sixt, with the death of the Duke of YORKE." Since, as memorially reconstructed texts, they are ultimately derived from the playbook, these texts may contain some materials that were revised as the plays were put into performance, but the likelihood of contamination through reporting, actors' interpolations, and transmission are so great that the textual authority here must be regarded with great caution. The Folio texts seem to have been based on authorial manuscripts, although there is evidence, too, that both plays or portions thereof were printed from pages of the Third Quartos of each play or at least with some consultation of the respective Third Quartos by the Folio compositors. The Third Quarto of *2 Henry VI* may embody some independent authority (perhaps a theatrical manuscript), although not necessarily the author's; Q3 of *3 Henry VI* seems to have no such independent authority.

The text of *1 Henry VI,* based seemingly on an authorial manuscript that may have been annotated in the theater and possibly recopied, was first published in the First Folio of 1623. It alone of the three parts was registered for publication at this time. The Stationers' Register entry refers to this play as "The thirde parte of Henry the sixt." These circumstances have prompted many scholars to suspect that *1 Henry VI* was written after the other two plays, especially since those two plays do not often recall events of *1 Henry VI*—for example, they make no mention of its hero, Lord Talbot. The seeming fact that the 1594 and 1595 Quartos were pirated editions would, however, explain their publication before *1 Henry VI* and the necessity of registering Part One later. In other ways, *1 Henry VI* has shown itself to be no hasty afterthought, but a play with thematic unity throughout and a sense of direction anticipating the remainder of the series. Hence, some scholars now support Dr. Johnson's commonsense hunch that the three plays in this historical tetralogy were written in order, though the issue remains in doubt.

Although scholars have long questioned Shakespeare's authorship, especially in parts of *1 Henry VI,* the series as a whole is best regarded as his own work or at the very least dominated by his artistic conception throughout. The once prevailing and recently reasserted hypotheses of multiple authorship rest on questionable internal evidence, such as vocabulary or versification. What sounds like Thomas Nashe, Robert Greene, or George Peele in these very early plays may simply be the result of those men's undoubted influence on Shakespeare during his apprenticeship. Greene's famous diatribe at Shakespeare (see below) suggests that he was keenly aware of Shakespeare's facility for learning quickly from his contemporaries. The inconsistencies in these early plays, especially in Part One—mislineation, defective verse, inaccuracy in speech prefixes, confusion about time, discrepancy in facts—may be the result not of multiple authorship but of reliance on various sources, hasty composition, and problems of transcription. Again, however, the issue has not been finally resolved.

Several contemporary allusions to the *Henry VI* plays help considerably with dating the series. Thomas Nashe wrote in his *Pierce Penniless* (registered August 1592) that it would "have joyed brave Talbot (the terror of the French) to think that after he had lain two hundred years in his tomb, he should triumph again on the stage." Probably he was referring to Shakespeare's play. The reference in Henslowe's diary to a "ne" (new?) performance of *Harey the vi* in March of 1592 may or may not refer to Shakespeare's work, however, for this performance was by Lord Strange's men, whereas Shakespeare's *Henry VI* series is associated elsewhere with Pembroke's men. In any event, *3 Henry VI* must have been completed by the time of Robert Greene's death in September of 1592, when Greene (or his literary executor, Chettle) alludes plainly to it (1.4.137) in his angry remark about "an upstart crow, beautified with our feathers, that with his '*Tiger's heart wrapped in a player's hide*' supposes he is as well able to bombast out a blank verse as the best of you." These contemporary references are confirmed by allusions in the texts themselves, for all the *Henry VI* plays seem to contain echoes of Books 1–3 of Edmund Spenser's *Faerie Queene* (printed 1590), whereas *3 Henry VI* seems to have influenced parts of *The Troublesome Reign of King John* (printed 1591). An inclusive date of 1589–1591 or 1592 ought to account for the entire series.

Richard the Third (c. 1592–1594)

A Quarto edition of *Richard III*, registered by Andrew Wise on October 20, 1597, appeared later that same year with the following title:

THE TRAGEDY OF King Richard the third. Containing, His treacherous Plots against his brother Clarence: the pittifull murther of his iunocent nephewes: his tyrannicall vsurpation: with the whole course of his detested life, and most deserued death. As it hath beene lately Acted by the Right honourable the Lord Chamberlaine his seruants. AT LONDON Printed by Valentine Sims, for Andrew Wise, dwelling in Paules Chu[r]ch-yard, at the Signe of the Angell. 1597.

This text, one of the most perplexing in all Shakespeare, is generally regarded as a memorial reconstruction of a peculiar kind, in which the acting company banded together to reconstruct a play of which the copy was missing. The reconstructed version may have been cut, perhaps for provincial performance. This defective text was the basis of the 1597 Quarto, which was reprinted in 1598, 1602, 1605, 1612, 1622, 1629, and 1634, each of which was successively more error-laden than the previous one. The First Folio text of 1623 seems to have been set mainly from copies of the Third and Sixth Quartos (1602 and 1622), which had been sporadically but heavily corrected against an independent manuscript—possibly Shakespeare's own working manuscript or a copy of it. This manuscript source, some of which may have been interleaved into the printers' copy, represents a generally superior authority to that of the First Quarto. Parts of the Folio text, however, were set from an uncorrected copy of the Third Quarto (1602), and for those passages (3.1.1–158 and 5.3.48 to end of play) the First Quarto, from which the Third Quarto was derived, must serve as copy text. Otherwise, the Folio text is the most authoritative, though it must be approached with caution.

The situation is indeed fraught with unusual uncertainty, since there are many opportunities for the Folio to have perpetuated errors of the earlier Quartos; moreover, its "improvements" over the readings of those Quartos could in some instances be editorial sophistications. The First Quarto offers some readings that demand serious attention. Especially when the Folio's reading differs from those of the First Quarto and is instead derived from Quartos Two through Six, the First Quarto should be preferred unless it is manifestly wrong. At the same time, however, since the First Quarto may reflect adaptation of the original acting text, its changes may not represent Shakespeare's artistic intention either. For these reasons, one must be wary of the First Quarto's assignment of speeches when they vary from the Folio's assignments and also of the First Quarto's cuts, some of which are substantial.

The play is mentioned by Francis Meres in 1598 in his *Palladis Tamia*. John Weever names a "Richard" in his *Epigrams*, published in 1599. Most scholars date *Richard III* as 1592–1594, on the basis of its style and its close affinity to the *Henry VI* series (completed probably in 1591). The play may have been influenced by the anonymous *The True Tragedy of Richard III*, registered in June 1594 but probably written in 1590–1592 or even earlier. Shakespeare's play may also have been influenced by Thomas Kyd's *The Spanish Tragedy* (c. 1587) and by Christopher Marlowe's dramas (he died in 1593).

King John (c. 1594–1596)

The Life and Death of King John, as it is called in the original text, first appeared in the First Folio of 1623. That text appears to have been set up from Shakespeare's working manuscript as copied by two scribes with a view to future theatrical use, although the manuscript does not show signs of having been actually employed as a playbook. Apart from Francis Meres' listing of the play (in his *Palladis Tamia,* 1598), dating clues are scarce. Editors have suggested dates ranging from 1590 to 1598 and have proposed topical allusions to bolster their various arguments. The consensus today is that *King John* was probably written shortly before or after *Richard II* in about 1594–1595, or 1596, and that it was based primarily on an anonymous two-part play, *The Troublesome Reign of King John,* published in 1591. Many editors assume that Shakespeare would have preferred to write this historically independent play in the interim between his two four-play series (*Henry VI* through *Richard III* and *Richard II* through *Henry V*), rather than interrupt the flow of composition on either of those series. This suggestion is scarcely provable, however. In any case, the link between *Richard II* and *1 Henry IV* is not so close as to preclude interruption.

A major critic of the consensus view is E. A. J. Honigmann, editor of the Arden *King John* (1954), who argues for a date in 1590 preceding the publication in 1591 of *The Troublesome Reign of King John* (which he regards as a bad Quarto). Honigmann is joined by William Matchett in his Signet edition of *King John* (1966) and, earlier, by Peter Alexander in 1939. Otherwise, this argument has aroused controversy but has received little acceptance.

Richard the Second (c. 1595–1596)

On August 29, 1597, "The Tragedye of Richard the Second" was entered in the Stationers' Register, the official record book of the London Company of Stationers (booksellers and printers), by Andrew Wise, and was published by him later that same year:

THE Tragedie of King Richard the second. *As it hath beene publikely acted by the right Honourable the Lorde Chamberlaine his Seruants.* LONDON Printed by Valentine Simmes for Androw Wise, and are to be sold at his shop in Paules church yard at the signe of the Angel. 1597.

This is a good text, printed evidently from the author's papers or a nontheatrical transcript of them. Wise issued two more quartos of this popular play in 1598, each set from the previous quarto, and then in 1603 transferred his rights to the play to Matthew Law. This publisher issued in 1608 a Fourth Quarto "With new additions of the Parliament Sceane, and the deposing of King Richard" (according to the title page in some copies). The deposition scene has indeed been omitted from the earlier quartos, probably through censorship. A Fifth Quarto appeared in 1615, based on the Fourth Quarto. All the quartos after the first attribute the play to Shakespeare. The added deposition scene in Quartos 4 and 5 seems to have been memorially reconstructed. The First Folio text of 1623 gives a better version of the deposition scene, seemingly because the printers of the Folio had access to the manuscript playbook for this portion of the text. (Some scholars maintain that the Folio text was derived from an earlier quarto or quartos that had been marked up and used as a playbook, but that case has been weakened by recent research.) Most of the Folio text was probably set from an annotated copy of the Third Quarto, and perhaps a leaf in Act 5 from the Fifth Quarto. The annotation was evidently quite uneven, and so the most authoritative text for all but the deposition scene remains the First Quarto; nevertheless, at certain points (especially the first 900 lines, part of 3.2, and much of Act 5), the annotation with reference to the playbook seems to have been more thorough. At such points, the Folio readings deserve serious attention, and the stage directions are often illuminating.

Francis Meres mentions the play in 1598 in his *Palladis Tamia.* Clearly it had been written and performed prior to the Stationers' Register entry in August of 1597. Its earliest probable date is 1595, since the play seemingly is indebted to Samuel Daniel's poem, *The First Four Books of the Civil Wars,* published in that year. Shakespeare follows Daniel, for example, in increasing the Queen's age from eleven (according to the chronicles) to maturity, and in other significant details. On December 7, 1595, Sir Edward Hoby invited Sir Robert Cecil to his house in Cannon Row, "where as late as it shall please you a gate for your supper shall be open, and King Richard present himself to your view." Although it is by no means certain that this passage refers to a private performance of Shakespeare's play, stylistic considerations favor a date around 1595 rather than 1597. If, as some scholars contend, Daniel's *Civil Wars* was written after Shakespeare's play rather than before it, the date of *Richard II* might be as early as 1594.

Henry the Fourth, Part I (1596–1597)

On February 25, 1598, "The historye of Henry the IIIJ^th with his battaile of Shrewsburye against Henry Hottspurre of the Northe with the conceipted mirthe of Sir John Ffalstoff" was entered in the Stationers' Register, the official record book of the London Company of Stationers (booksellers and printers), by Andrew Wise. Later that year appeared the following quarto:

THE HISTORY OF HENRIE THE FOVRTH; With the battell at Shrewsburie, *betweene the King and Lord* Henry Percy, surnamed Henrie Hotspur of the North. *With the humorous conceits of Sir* Iohn Falstalffe. AT LONDON Printed by *P. S.* [Peter Short] for *Andrew Wise,* dwelling in Paules Churchyard, at the signe of the Angell. 1598.

Actually this was not the first quarto, for an earlier fragment of eight pages has survived, part of a text that served as copy for the first complete extant Quarto. Together, these quartos make up an excellent authoritative text, based seemingly on the author's papers or, more probably, a scribal transcript of them. Four more quartos appeared before the First Folio of 1623, each based on the previous quarto. The Folio itself was based on the last of these, perhaps with reference also to some kind of manuscript, although the number of authoritative readings that can be claimed for the Folio is small.

1 Henry IV shows signs of revision in the use of characters' names, most notably that of Falstaff. Plainly, the original version of the play called him Sir John Oldcastle, after one of the prince's companions in the anonymous *Famous Victories of Henry the Fifth* (c. 1588). The name "Oldcastle" was originally intended for *2 Henry IV* as well. The speech prefix "Old." is left standing at 1.2.119 in the Quarto of *2 Henry IV*, one or two lines of verse in *1 Henry IV* are one syllable short, evidently because "Oldcastle" has been altered to "Falstaff," and Falstaff is jokingly referred to as "my old lad of the castle" (*1 Henry IV*, 1.2.41). Moreover, there are several contemporary allusions to a play about a fat knight named Oldcastle. Apparently, Henry Brooke, Lord Cobham, a living descendant of the Lollard martyr Oldcastle of Henry V's reign, took umbrage at the profane use Shakespeare had made of this revered name, whereupon Shakespeare's acting company shifted to another less controversial name from the chronicles, Sir John Fastolfe or Falstaff (called "Falstaffe" in the Folio text of Shakespeare's *1 Henry VI* and assigned a cowardly role in the French wars of that play). The revision also changed the names of Oldcastle's cronies from Harvey and Russell to Peto and Bardolph. This edition retains the name "Falstaff," since Shakespeare clearly accepted it as the new name of the character in all his "Falstaff" plays.

Cobham was Lord Chamberlain from July 1596 until his death in March 1597, during which interval Shakespeare's company bore the name of Lord Hunsdon's men. Quite possibly, the difficulty over the name "Oldcastle" erupted during that period, for *1 Henry IV* seems to have been written and performed in late 1596 and early 1597, not long after Shakespeare had finished *Richard II* (c. 1595–1596).

Francis Meres, in his *Palladis Tamia, 1598*, refers to "*Henry the IV*" without specifying one or two parts. Publication of *1 Henry IV* in 1598 confirmed to the Elizabethan public that the changes in names to Falstaff, Peto, and Bardolph had taken place.

Henry the Fourth, Part II (1597–1598)

"The second parte of the history of Kinge Henry the IIIJ^th with the humours of Sir John Fallstaff: Wrytten by master Shakespere" was entered in the Stationers' Register, the official record book of the London Company of Stationers (booksellers and printers), by Andrew Wise and William Aspley on August 23, 1600. (This is the first time Shakespeare's name appeared in the Stationers' Register.) The Quarto was published later that year as

THE Second part of Henrie the fourth, continuing to his death, and *coronation of Henrie* the fift. With the humours of sir Iohn Fal*staffe, and swaggering* Pistoll. *As it hath been sundrie times publikely* acted by the right honourable, the Lord Chamberlaine his seruants. *Written by William Shakespeare.* LONDON Printed by V. S. [Valentine Sims] for Andrew Wise, and William Aspley. 1600.

One scene, 3.1, was omitted from Sims' first printing [Qa] of this Quarto, whereupon Sims reset two leaves as four new leaves [Qb] including not only the omitted 3.1, but also 2.4.340–390 and 3.2.1–104. Qb is therefore the best copy text for 3.1 and Qa for those portions that were reset. In addition, still other passages were omitted from both versions of the 1600 Quarto; they were later restored in, or added to, the First Folio. No further quartos appeared prior to the First Folio of 1623—an odd fact in view of *1 Henry IV*'s continued popularity but perhaps the result of a large printing of *2 Henry IV* in anticipation of heavy sales. At any rate, this Quarto text seems to have been based on Shakespeare's papers and was a reliable one except for some substantial omissions and for some misreadings, owing to the compositors' difficulty in reading an authorial manuscript that may have been unfinished. Speech prefixes are at times quite irregular, indicative of author's papers before they have received the attentions of the prompter. Of the omitted passages, some may have been the result of shortening for performance, but some suggest political censorship. Others suggest authorial revision. The Folio text restores or adds the omitted readings.

The relationship of Folio to Quarto text is extraordinarily difficult to determine. Perhaps the Folio compositors were using a manuscript that had been transcribed either from an extensively annotated copy of the Quarto or from a Quarto and a manuscript source jointly compared. Another hypothesis is that the copy for the Folio was made up from actors' parts. The Folio copy was, in any case, a strange transcript, showing perhaps some stage influence and possibly used as a playbook but less adequately provided with stage directions than most playbooks; perhaps the scribe imposed certain literary features. It seems to have been a special case. George Walton Williams (*Shakespeare Studies* 9:173) speculates that it was an edited transcript of a playbook prepared for Lord Cobham. Whatever its identity, it embodied tendencies toward sophistication and regularization that frequently render the Folio readings less authoritative than those of the Quarto. The Folio text does restore the passages excised from the Quarto, however, and on other occasions as well it provides what appear to be authentic corrections of, and authorial additions to, the

Quarto. The Quarto text is generally the most authoritative when it is not manifestly in error or lacking material found in the Folio, but the Folio corrections and additions have to be regarded with close attention.

Like *Part One* of *Henry IV*, *Part Two* shows signs of revision in the use of characters' names, most notably that of Falstaff. Plainly, the original version of both plays called him Sir John Oldcastle, after one of the prince's companions in the anonymous *Famous Victories of Henry the Fifth* (c. 1588). The speech prefix "Old." is left standing at 1.2.119 in the Quarto of *2 Henry IV*, and in *1 Henry IV* Falstaff is jokingly referred to as "my old lad of the castle" (1.2.41). Moreover, there are several contemporary allusions to a play about a fat knight named Oldcastle. See above, *Henry IV, Part I*, for an account of how Shakespeare's company appears to have changed to the less controversial name of Falstaff (along with Peto and Bardolph in place of Harvey and Russell) in order to avoid offending the family of Henry Brooke, Lord Cobham, a living descendant of the Lollard martyr Oldcastle of Henry V's reign.

Cobham was Lord Chamberlain from July 1596 until his death in March 1597, during which interval Shakespeare's company bore the name of Lord Hunsdon's men. Quite possibly, the difficulty over the name Oldcastle erupted during that period, for *1 Henry IV* seems to have been written and performed in late 1596 and early 1597, not long after Shakespeare had finished *Richard II* (c. 1595–1596). *2 Henry IV* must have been written before the end of 1598, so that Shakespeare could then begin *Henry V* in early 1599. Since *2 Henry IV* was begun using the names Oldcastle, Harvey, and Russell, however, there is reason to date it somewhat earlier, in 1597, before the squabble over the names broke out. Scholars who prefer a date in 1597 for *The Merry Wives* also date *2 Henry IV* early in 1597, since it appears to have introduced Shallow and Pistol before they appeared in *The Merry Wives*. Francis Meres refers in 1598 to "Henry the 4" without specifying one or two parts. Publication of *1 Henry IV* in 1598 assured the Elizabethan public that the changes in names to Falstaff, Peto, and Bardolph had taken place; a revised epilogue to the 1600 Quarto of *2 Henry IV* protests that "Oldcastle died a martyr, and this [Falstaff] is not the man," as though by way of apology or disclaimer. A play defending the reputation of the Lollard Oldcastle and attacking Falstaff, called *The History of the Life of Sir John Oldcastle, Lord Cobham, with his Martyrdom*, had been performed by the rival Admiral's men in 1599.

Henry the Fifth (1599)

An entry in the Stationers' Register, the official record book of the London Company of Stationers (booksellers and printers), for August 4, 1600, provides that "Henry the ffift" and three other plays belonging to the Lord Chamberlain's men (Shakespeare's acting company) are "to be staied" from publication until further permission is granted. Evidently, the Chamberlain's men were anxious to ensure they were paid or to prevent unauthorized publication. They did not succeed, in any event, in preventing the appearance of a pirated text of *Henry V*. An entry in the Stationers' Register for August 14 assigns to Thomas Pavier an already published work entitled "The historye of Henry the Vth with the battell of Agencourt." The Quarto volume to which this entry refers is the following:

THE CHRONICLE History of Henry the fift, With his battell fought at *Agin Court* in France. Togither with *Auntient Pistoll. As it hath bene sundry times playd by the Right honorable the Lord Chamberlaine his seruants.* LONDON Printed by *Thomas Creede,* for Tho. Millington, and Iohn Busby. And are to be sold at his house in Carter Lane, next the Powle head. 1600.

The text of this play is manifestly corrupt. It is considerably shorter than the First Folio version and completely omits the choruses and three entire scenes (1.1, 3.1, and 4.2). The remainder seems to have been put together by memorial reconstruction. This bad Quarto served as the basis for a Second Quarto printed by Thomas Creed for Thomas Pavier in 1602 and a third printed by William Jaggard for Thomas Pavier in 1619 but fraudulently dated 1608. The Folio text was printed seemingly from an authorial manuscript, perhaps with occasional reference to the Third Quarto (which contains some potentially troublesome contamination). The Folio text is thus the most reliable version, though the First Quarto is also an interesting witness, especially for visual effects recorded in its stage directions, for a few readings in the text, and for verse lineation of Pistol's speeches.

Francis Meres does not mention the play in 1598 in his *Palladis Tamia*, though he does mention "Henry the IV." The epilogue to *2 Henry IV* (written probably in 1597) promises that "our humble author will continue the story, with Sir John in it, and make you merry with fair Katharine of France"; since the prediction is not really accurate regarding Falstaff, we can be reasonably certain that Shakespeare had not yet begun *Henry V* in 1597. An allusion in the Chorus of Act 5 to "the General of our gracious Empress," who may in good time come home from Ireland with "rebellion broachèd on his sword," has been taken by virtually all editors to refer to the Earl of Essex, who left in March of 1599 to quell the Irish rebellion headed by Tyrone. Although Essex returned on September 28 of that same year, having failed utterly in his assignment, the departure of such a charismatic figure could have inspired Shakespeare's praising remark. A minority view holds that the choruses (which do not appear in the bad Quarto of 1600) could have been written later in 1601 for Essex's far more victorious successor, Lord Mountjoy (see Warren D. Smith's article on *Henry V* in *JEGP*, 1954). Still, Essex was more center stage during those exciting years, more likely to have been the subject of adulation. In any case, the play itself must have been written before August of 1600, most probably in 1599. The reference to "this wooden O" in the Chorus of Act 1 is often thought to be Shakespeare's compliment to the company's new theater, the Globe, which was ready for their use probably in 1599; but the play may have been produced at the Curtain instead.

King Henry the Eighth (1613)

The Famous History of the Life of King Henry the Eighth was first printed in the First Folio of 1623. The text is a good one, set from a careful transcript of Shakespeare's own manuscript (assuming that he was sole author). The stage directions are unusually elaborate. The first recorded performance was on June 29, 1613. A letter of July 2 in that year from Sir Henry Wotton to Sir Edmund Bacon tells of a performance of "a new play, called *All Is True*, representing some principal pieces of the reign of Henry VIII." During this performance, as King Henry was arriving as a masker at the house of Cardinal Wolsey (1.4), "certain chambers [cannons] being shot off at his entry, some of the paper, or other stuff, wherewith one of them was stopped, did light on the thatch, where being thought at first but an idle smoke, and their eyes more attentive to the show, it kindled inwardly, and ran round like a train, consuming within less than an hour the whole house to the very grounds." The identification of this *All Is True* with Shakespeare's play is certain. Other accounts include a letter from Thomas Lorkin to Sir Thomas Puckering, June 1613, asserting the fire to have started "while Burbage his company were acting at the Globe the play of Henry 8," a letter of 4 July from Henry Bluett to Richard Weeks, another of 8 July from John Chamberlain to Sir Ralph Winwood, and an account in John Stow's *Annals* as continued by Edmund Howe (1618).

Wotton calls it a new play, and stylistic considerations confirm this characterization. The play may also have helped provide entertainment for the betrothal and marriage of James I's daughter Elizabeth to the Elector Palatine earlier in 1613, though *Henry VIII* is not listed among the many plays acted on this occasion.

On the controversy over John Fletcher's purported share in the authorship of *Henry VIII*, see the play's Introduction.

Titus Andronicus (c. 1589–1592)

On February 6, 1594, "a Noble Roman Historye of Tytus Andronicus" was entered in the Stationers' Register, the official record book of the London Company of Stationers (booksellers and printers), to John Danter, along with "the ballad thereof." The entry probably, though not certainly, refers to Shakespeare's play. Later in that same year, at any rate, Danter published a Quarto volume with the following title:

THE MOST LAMENTABLE Romaine Tragedie of Titus Andronicus: As it was Plaide by the Right Honourable the Earle of *Darbie,* Earle of *Pembrooke,* and Earle of *Sussex* their Seruants. LONDON, Printed by Iohn Danter, and are to be sold by *Edward White & Thomas Millington,* at the little North doore of Paules at the signe of the Gunne. 1594.

This text seems to have been set from Shakespeare's manuscript in an unpolished state. A Second Quarto appeared in 1600, adding the name of the Lord Chamberlain's company to those who had acted the play. It was set up from a slightly damaged copy of the First Quarto. Although the Second Quarto made some improvements, these were probably by the compositor and not the author, or may have been made in a press-corrected Q1 no longer extant (since we have only one copy today). A Third Quarto (1611), set up from the second, contributed new errors. The First Folio text of 1623 was derived from the Third Quarto, but with an authentic added scene (3.2) from a manuscript source and with additional stage directions that suggest a playhouse playbook. One theory is that the copy used by the Folio printers, the Third Quarto, had been corrected from an annotated copy of the Second Quarto that had been used as a playbook, or perhaps directly from the playbook. Despite these improvements, the First Quarto clearly remains the authoritative text.

The date of *Titus* must be prior to 1594. Philip Henslowe's *Diary* records a performance of a "Titus & Ondronicus" by the Earl of Sussex's men on January 24, 1594, and indicates it was "ne" or new. This could certainly mean a new play, but it could also mean it was newly revised or newly acquired. Since the players on this occasion, Sussex's men, were listed third on the 1594 title page after Derby's and Pembroke's men, they may just have acquired *Titus.* Two allusions may point to an earlier date: *A Knack to Know a Knave* (performed in 1592) and *The Troublesome Reign of King John* (published 1591) may contain echoes of *Titus,* though the text of the former is memorially reconstructed and could therefore contain a remembered reference up to the date of publication in 1594. Stylistic considerations favor a date around 1590–1592 or even earlier.

The authorship of *Titus* would appear at first glance to be beyond question. Although the 1594 Quarto does not mention Shakespeare's name (a common omission in such early texts, especially since the author was as yet relatively unknown), Francis Meres in his *Palladis Tamia,* 1598, assigns the play to Shakespeare, and the Folio editors include it in the 1623 edition. Doubts began to arise, however, when Edward Ravenscroft observed in 1687 that he had been "told by some anciently conversant with the stage that it was not originally his, but brought by a private author to be acted, and he only gave some master touches to one or two of the principal parts or characters." This remark touched off a controversy that continues today; for example, J. Dover Wilson in his New Cambridge

Shakespeare (1948), J. C. Maxwell in his Arden edition (1953), and the Oxford Shakespeare editors (1986) still argue for the presence of Peele or an imitator of Peele, in the first scene especially. Nevertheless, Ravenscroft's testimonial is suspect both because it came one hundred years after the fact and because Ravenscroft himself was embarked on an adaptation of *Titus* and so might have wished to denigrate the original. The efforts at assigning portions of the play to Shakespeare's contemporaries have sometimes been motivated by a wish to rescue Shakespeare's reputation from the violent and garish effects of this play. Most recent criticism prefers to regard the play as an interesting experiment in revenge tragedy by a young artist, with many shrewdly characteristic Shakespearean touches. The external evidence of the Elizabethan period, at any rate, is on the side of awarding the play wholly to Shakespeare.

Henslowe's *Diary* records the performance of a "Tittus & Vespacia" on April 11, 1592, a "ne" play by Strange's men. Despite the similarity of the title, this play was probably on an independent subject.

Romeo and Juliet (1594–1596)

A corrupt and unregistered Quarto of *Romeo and Juliet* appeared in 1597 with the following title:

AN EXCELLENT conceited Tragedie OF Romeo and Iuliet, As it hath been often (with great applause) plaid publiquely, by the right Honourable the L. of *Hunsdon* his Seruants. LONDON, Printed by Iohn Danter. 1597.

This was a pirated edition issued by an unscrupulous publisher, no doubt to capitalize on the play's great popularity. It seems to have been memorially reconstructed by two or more actors (probably those playing Romeo and Paris), and possibly thereafter to have been used as a playbook. Its appearance seems to have caused the issuance two years later of a clearly authoritative version:

THE MOST EXcellent and lamentable Tragedie, of Romeo and *Iuliet. Newly corrected, augmented, and amended:* As it hath bene sundry times publiquely acted, by the right Honourable the Lord Chamberlaine his Seruants. LONDON Printed by Thomas Creede, for Cuthbert Burby, and are to be sold at his shop neare the Exchange. 1599.

This text is some 800 lines longer than the first and corrects errors in that earlier version. It seems at one point, however, to have been contaminated by the First Quarto, as though the manuscript source for the Second Quarto (probably the author's rough draft) was defective at some point. A passage from 1.2.53 to 1.3.34 was apparently set directly from the First Quarto. (On this matter, see George W. Williams' old-spelling edition of the play, Duke Univ. Press, 1964.) Q1 may also have influenced Q2 in some other isolated instances. Despite this contamination, however, the Second Quarto is the authoritative text, except for the passage of

direct indebtedness to Q1. Q2 served as the basis for the Third Quarto (1609), which in turn served as copy for the Fourth Quarto (undated, but placed in 1622) and the First Folio of 1623. A Fifth Quarto appeared in 1637. The Folio text may embody a few authoritative readings of its own, perhaps by way of reference to a theatrical manuscript.

Francis Meres, in his *Palladis Tamia,* 1598, assigns the play to Shakespeare. So does John Weever in his *Epigrams* of 1599. Internal evidence on dating is not reliable. The Nurse observes that "'Tis since the earthquake now eleven years" (1.3.24); however, it has been discovered that suitable earthquakes occurred in 1580, 1583, 1584, and 1585, giving us a wide choice of dates even if we accept the dubious proposition that the Nurse is speaking accurately. Astronomical reckoning of the position of the moon at the time the play purportedly takes place ("a fortnight and odd days" before Lammastide, August 1,1.3.16) indicates the year 1596; again, however, we have no reason to assume Shakespeare cared about this sort of internal accuracy. More suggestive perhaps is the argument that Danter's unauthorized publication in 1597 was seeking to exploit a popular new play—one the acting company certainly did not yet wish to see published, since it was a money-maker. Danter assigns the play to Lord Hunsdon's servants, a name that Shakespeare's company could have used only from July 22, 1596 (when the old Lord Chamberlain, Henry Carey, first Lord Hunsdon, died) to March 17, 1597 (when George Carey, second Lord Hunsdon, was appointed to his father's erstwhile position as Lord Chamberlain). Danter could simply have been using the name of the company at the time he pirated the play, but he may also have indicated performance in late 1596. Danter printed only the first four sheets, but he must have done so by February–March of 1597, when his presses were seized. Stylistically, the play is clearly of the "lyric" period of *A Midsummer Night's Dream* and *Richard II.* There are also stylistic affinities to the sonnets and to the narrative poems of 1593–1594. A date between 1594 and 1596 is likely, especially toward the latter end of this period. Whether the play comes before or after *A Midsummer Night's Dream* is, however, a matter of conjecture.

Julius Caesar (1599)

Julius Caesar was first published in the First Folio of 1623. The text is an excellent one, based evidently on a theater playbook or a transcript of it; some theatrical features, such as a provision for the doubling of Cassius and Caius Ligarius, appear to represent a staging configuration that Shakespeare had not anticipated. On the other hand, some stage directions sound authorial, as though Shakespeare's own words had survived into the playbook. Some confusions have survived as well, notably in the handling of Lucilius, Lucius, Titinius, and Pindarus in 4.2. In the Folio, the play is included among the tragedies and entitled *The Tragedy of Julius Caesar*, although the table of contents lists it as *The Life and death of Julius Caesar*.

The play's first performance must have occurred in 1599 or slightly earlier. On September 21, 1599, a Swiss visitor named Thomas Platter crossed the River Thames after lunch with a company of spectators to see "the tragedy of the first Emperor Julius Caesar" performed in a thatched-roofed building. The description fits the Globe, the Rose, and the Swan theaters, but the last of these was not in regular use. The Admiral's men at the Rose are not known to have had a Caesar play, whereas the Chamberlain's men certainly had Shakespeare's play about this time. They had only recently moved from their Theatre in the northeast suburbs of London to the Globe south of the river, and *Julius Caesar* was probably a new play for the occasion.

John Weever, in *The Mirror of Martyrs* (1601), is surely referring to Shakespeare's play when he describes "the many-headed multitude" listening first to "Brutus' speech, that Caesar was ambitious" and then to "eloquent Mark Antony." (The dedication to Weever's book claims he wrote it "some two years ago," in 1599; however, since this book has been shown to be heavily indebted to a work that first appeared in 1600, Weever's allusion is not as helpful in limiting the date as was once thought.) Ben Jonson's *Every Man in His Humor*, acted in 1599, may also contain allusions to Shakespeare's play. Francis Meres does not mention it in 1598 in his *Palladis Tamia*.

Hamlet (c. 1599–1601)

Like everything else about *Hamlet*, the textual problem is complicated. On July 26, 1602, James Roberts entered in the Stationers' Register, the official record book of the London Company of Stationers (booksellers and printers), "A booke called the Revenge of Hamlett Prince Denmarke as yt was latelie Acted by the Lord Chamberleyne his servantes." For some reason, however, Roberts did not print his copy of *Hamlet* until 1604, by which time the following unauthorized edition had appeared:

THE Tragicall Historie of HAMLET *Prince of Denmarke*[.] By William Shake-speare. As it hath beene diuerse times acted by his Highnesse seruants in the Cittie of London: as also in the two Vniuersities of Cambridge and Oxford, and else-where. At London printed for N. L. [Nicholas Ling] and Iohn Trundell. 1603.

This edition, the bad Quarto of *Hamlet*, seems to have been memorially reconstructed by actors who toured the provinces (note the references to Cambridge, Oxford, and so on), with some recollection of an earlier *Hamlet* play (the *Ur-Hamlet*) written before 1589 and acted during the 1590s. The piratical actors had no recourse to an authoritative manuscript. One of these actors may have played Marcellus and possibly Lucianus and Voltimand. Their

version seems to have been based on an adaptation of the company's original playbook, which itself stood once removed from Shakespeare's working papers by way of an intermediate manuscript. The resulting text is very corrupt, and yet it seems to have affected the more authentic text, because the compositors of the Second Quarto made use of it, especially when they typeset the first act.

The authorized Quarto of *Hamlet* appeared in 1604. Roberts, the printer, seems to have reached some agreement with Ling, one of the publishers of the bad Quarto, for their initials are now paired on the title page:

THE Tragicall Historie of HAMLET, *Prince of Denmarke*. By William Shakespeare. Newly imprinted and enlarged to almost as much againe as it was, according to the true and perfect Coppie. AT LONDON , Printed by I. R. [James Roberts] for N. L. [Nicholas Ling] and are to be sold at his shoppe vnder Saint Dunstons Church in Fleetstreet. 1604.

Some copies of this edition are dated 1605. This text was based seemingly on Shakespeare's own papers, with the bookkeeper's annotations, but is marred by printing errors and is at times contaminated by the bad Quarto—presumably, when the printers found Shakespeare's manuscript unreadable. This Second Quarto served as copy for a Third Quarto in 1611, Ling having meanwhile transferred his rights in the play to John Smethwick. A Fourth Quarto, undated but before 1623, was based on the Third.

The First Folio text of 1623 omits more than two hundred lines found in the Second Quarto, yet it supplies some clearly authentic passages. It seems to derive from a transcript of Shakespeare's draft, in which cuts made by the author were observed—cuts made by Shakespeare quite possibly because he knew the draft to be too long for performance and which had either not been marked in the Second Quarto copy or had been ignored there by the compositors. The Folio also incorporates other alterations seemingly made for clarity or in anticipation of performance. To this theatrically motivated transcript, Shakespeare apparently contributed some revisions. Subsequently, this version evidently was copied again by a careless scribe who took many liberties with the text. Typesetting from this inferior manuscript, the Folio compositors occasionally consulted the Second Quarto, but not often enough. Thus, even though the Folio supplies some genuine readings, as does the First Quarto when both the Folio and the Second Quarto are wrong, the Second Quarto remains the most authentic version of the text.

Since the text of the Second Quarto is too long to be accommodated in the two hours' traffic of the stage and since it becomes even longer when the words found only in the Folio are added, Shakespeare must have known it would have to be cut for performance and probably marked at least some omissions himself. Since he may have consented to such cuts primarily because of the constraints of time, however, this present edition holds to the view that the passages in question should not be excised from the text we read. The *Hamlet* presented here is doubtless longer than any version ever acted in Shakespeare's day and thus does not represent a script for any actual performance, but it may well represent the play as Shakespeare wrote it and then expanded it somewhat while also including passages that he may reluctantly have consented to cut for performance. It is also possible that some cuts were artistically intended, but, in the face of real uncertainty in this matter, an editorial policy of inclusion gives to the reader those passages that would otherwise have to be excised or put in an appendix on questionable grounds of authorial "intent."

Hamlet must have been produced before the Stationers' Register entry of July 26, 1602. Francis Meres does not mention the play in 1598 in his *Palladis Tamia*. Gabriel Harvey attributes the "tragedy of Hamlet, Prince of Denmark" to Shakespeare in a marginal note in Harvey's copy of Speght's Chaucer; Harvey acquired the book in 1598, but he could have written the note any time between then and 1601, or even 1603. More helpful in dating is *Hamlet's* clear reference to the so-called War of the Theaters, the rivalry between the adult actors and the boy actors whose companies had newly revived in 1598–1599 after nearly a decade of inactivity (see 2.2.337–362). The Children of the Chapel Royal began acting at Blackfriars in 1598 and provided such keen competition in 1599–1601 that the adult actors were at times forced to tour the provinces (see *Hamlet*, 2.2.332–362). *Hamlet's* reference to the rivalry appears, however, only in the Folio text and could represent a late addition. The reference to an "inhibition" imposed on acting companies "by the means of the late innovation" (2.2.332–333), printed in the 1604 Quarto, may possibly refer to the abortive uprising of the Earl of Essex on February 8, 1601, or to a decree issued by the Privy Council on June 22, 1600, restricting London companies to two performances a week in each of two playhouses. Revenge tragedy was also in fashion during these years: John Marston's *Antonio's Revenge*, for example, dates from 1599–1601, and *The Malcontent* is from about the same time or slightly later, though it is hard to tell who influenced whom. *Hamlet's* apparent indebtedness to John Florio's translation of Montaigne suggests that Shakespeare had access to that work in manuscript before its publication in 1603; the Florio had been registered for publication in 1595 and 1600.

Othello (c. 1603–1604)

On October 6, 1621, Thomas Walkley entered in the Stationers' Register, the official record book of the London Company of Stationers (booksellers and printers), "The Tragedie of Othello, the moore of Venice," and published the play in the following year:

THE Tragoedy of Othello, The Moore of Venice. *As it hath beene diuerse times acted at the* Globe, *and at the* Black-Friers, *by his Maiesties Seruants. Written by* VVilliam Shakespeare. LONDON, Printed by N. O. [Nicholas Okes] for *Thomas Walkley, and are to be sold at his shop, at the Eagle and Child, in Brittans Bursse. 1622.*

This text of this Quarto is a good one, based probably on a scribal transcript of Shakespeare's working manuscript, although it is some one hundred and sixty lines shorter than the Folio text of 1623 and may have been cut in the printing house to meet the constraints of space when the printer's copy was allocated to a fixed number of pages. The Folio text may have been derived (via an intermediate transcript) from a revision of the original authorial manuscript, in which Shakespeare himself copied over his work and made a large number of synonymous or nearly synonymous changes as he did so. These papers, edited by someone else to remove profanity as required by law and introducing other stylistic changes in the process, seemingly became the basis of the playbook and also of the Folio text.

The textual situation is thus complex. The Folio text appears to contain a significant number of authorial changes, but it was also worked on by one or more sophisticating scribes and by compositors whose changes are sometimes hard to distinguish from those of Shakespeare. The Quarto text was printed by a printing establishment that was not known for careful work but does stand close in some ways to a Shakespearean original. Editorially, then, the Folio is the copy text, and its readings are to be preferred when the Quarto is not clearly correct and especially when the Folio gives us genuinely new words, but the Quarto's readings demand careful consideration when the Folio text may be suspected of mechanical error (e.g., the shortening of words in full lines) or compositorial substitution of alternative forms, normalizations, and easy adjustments of meter. There are times when the Folio's compositor may have been misled by nearby words or letters in his copy. And, because the Folio's stage directions are probably scribal, attention should be paid to those in the Quarto.

According to a Revels account that was suspected of being a forgery soon after its publication in 1842 and is once again in doubt today, the earliest mention of the play is on "Hallamas Day, being the first of Nouembar," 1604, when "the Kings Maiesties plaiers" performed "A Play in the Banketinge house att Whit Hall Called The Moor of Venis." The play is attributed to "Shaxberd." Possible echoes of *Othello* in *The Honest Whore, Part I,* by Thomas Dekker and Thomas Middleton (1604) and in Richard Knolles' *History of the Turks* (1603) help fix a forward date of composition. Francis Meres does not list the play in 1598. On stylistic grounds, the play is usually dated in 1603 or 1604, although arguments are sometimes presented for a date as early as 1601 or 1602.

King Lear (c. 1605–1606)

On November 26, 1607, Nathaniel Butter and John Busby entered in the Stationers' Register, the official record book of the London Company of Stationers (booksellers and printers), "A booke called. Master William Shakespeare his historye of Kinge Lear, as yt was played before the Kinges maiestie at Whitehall vppon Sainct Stephens night at Christmas Last, by his maiesties servantes playinge vsually at the Globe on the Banksyde." Next year appeared the following Quarto:

M. William Shak-speare: HIS True Chronicle Historie of the life and death of King LEAR and his three Daughters. With the vnfortunate life of Edgar, sonne and heire to the Earle of Gloster, and his sullen and assumed humor of TOM of Bedlam: As it was played before the Kings Maiestie at Whitehall vpon S. Stephans night in Christmas Hollidayes. By his Maiesties seruants playing vsually at the Gloabe on the Bancke-side. LONDON, Printed for Nathaniel Butter, and are to be sold at his shop in Pauls Church-yard at the signe of the Pide Bull neere St. Austins Gate. 1608.

This Quarto is often called the "Pied Bull" Quarto in reference to its place of sale. Twelve copies exist today, in ten different "states," because proofreading was being carried on while the sheets were being run off in the press; the copies variously combine corrected and uncorrected sheets. A Second Quarto, printed in 1619 by William Jaggard for Thomas Pavier with the fraudulent date of 1608, was based on a copy of the First Quarto, combining corrected and uncorrected sheets.

The First Folio text of 1623 may have been typeset from a playbook cut for performance or from a transcript of such a manuscript, and the playbook in its turn appears to have been based on Shakespeare's fair copy (with revisions) of his first draft. The Folio compositors also almost certainly consulted a copy of the Second Quarto from time to time or may have typeset directly from this Quarto as annotated with reference to Shakespeare's fair copy. In writing the fair copy, Shakespeare may have marked some three hundred lines for deletion, but it is possible that he did so chiefly to shorten the time of performance. He also seems to have added some one hundred lines, an apparent contradiction in view of the need for cutting, but possibly dictated by Shakespeare's developing sense of his play. It is also possible that the cuts were carried out by someone else in the preparation of the playbook.

The First Quarto, on the other hand, appears to have been printed from Shakespeare's unrevised and evidently untidy working papers. It is often corrupt, owing in part to type shortages, compositorial difficulties with the manuscript, and other difficulties in Nicholas Okes' shop. Still, in some matters—especially variants indifferent in meaning (such as an/if or thine/thy)—the First Quarto may be closer to

Shakespeare's preferences than the Folio, behind which are several stages of transmission.

This edition agrees with most recent students of the Lear text that the Folio represents a theatrical revision, in which the cuts were devised for performance by Shakespeare's company and quite possibly by Shakespeare himself as a member of that company. The case for artistic preference in the making of those cuts, on the other hand, is less certain and may have been overstated. Many of the cuts have the effect of shortening scenes, especially in the latter half of the play. Some scenes, like 3.6, show open gaps as a result of the cutting: Lear's "Then let them anatomize Regan" (line 75) implies the trial of Goneril as it is dramatized in the First Quarto but cut from the Folio. Other omissions also read like expedients, although they can also be explained by a hypothesis of literary and theatrical rewriting; if Shakespeare himself undertook the cutting, he would presumably do so as expertly as possible. The fact that the Folio text gives no rewritten speeches may suggest that the large cuts were motivated by the need for shortening. This edition holds to the principle that it is unwise to omit the material cut from the Folio text, since we cannot be sure that Shakespeare would have shortened the text had there been no external constraints. At the same time, the added material in the Folio is clearly his and belongs in his conception of the play. The resulting text is a conflation, but one that avoids cutting material that Shakespeare may well have regretted having to excise.

The Stationers' Register entry for November 26, 1607, describes a performance at court on the previous St. Stephen's night, December 26, 1606. The title page of the First Quarto confirms this performance on St. Stephen's night. Such a performance at court was not likely to have been the first, however. Shakespeare's repeated use of Samuel Harsnett's Declaration of Egregious Popish Impostures, registered on March 16, 1603, sets an early limit for composition of the play. Other circumstances point to composition of the Quarto text in 1605 or 1606. In May of 1605, an old play called The True Chronicle History of King Leir was entered in the Stationers' Register as a "Tragecall historie," a phrase possibly suggesting the influence of Shakespeare's play, since the old King Leir does not end tragically. Moreover, the title page of the old King Leir, issued in 1605, proclaims the text to be "as it hath bene diuers and sundry times lately acted." In view of the unlikelihood that such an old play (written before 1594) would be revived in 1605, scholars have suggested that the title page was the publisher's way of trying to capitalize on the recent popularity of Shakespeare's play. In this case, the likeliest date for the composition of Shakespeare's King Lear would be in the winter of 1604–1605. Shakespeare certainly used the old King Leir as a chief source, but he need not have waited for its publication in 1605 if, as seems perfectly plausible, his company owned the playbook. This hypothesis of the publication of the old *King Leir* after performances of Shakespeare's play must do battle, however, with indications that Shakespeare did not write *King Lear* until late 1605 or 1606. Gloucester's mentioning of "These late eclipses in the sun and moon" (1.2.106) seems to refer to an eclipse of the moon in September and of the sun in October of 1605.

There may be echoes in the First Quarto of *King Lear* of *Eastward Ho!* by George Chapman, Ben Jonson, and John Marston, written in early 1605, and *Miseries of Enforced Marriage*, written by mid-1605. *King Lear* may allude to concerns at court about the King's frequent absences for hunting, about monopolies, the giving away of knighthoods, the King's need of money, and the like, all of which would have seemed pertinent in 1605–1606. The Folio revisions may date from some time around 1610, according to the editors of the Oxford Shakespeare.

Macbeth (c. 1606–1607)

Macbeth was first printed in the First Folio of 1623. It was set up from a playbook or a transcript of one. The text is unusually short and seems to have been cut for reasons of censorship or for some special performance. Moreover, all of 3.5 and parts of 4.1 (39–43, 125–132) appear to be interpolations, containing songs from Thomas Middleton's *The Witch* (c.1609–1616). Middleton may have been responsible for other alterations and additions.

An astrologer named Simon Forman, in his manuscript *The Book of Plays and Notes thereof per Formans for Common Policy*, records the first known performance of *Macbeth* on April 20, 1611, at the Globe Theatre. The play must have been in existence by 1607, however, for allusions to it seemingly occur in *Lingua* and *The Puritan* (both published in 1607) and in *The Knight of the Burning Pestle* (probably acted in 1607). On the other hand, the play itself seemingly alludes to James I's royal succession in 1603, to his touching for "the king's evil" (see 4.3.147), and to the trial of the notorious Gunpowder Plot conspirators in March of 1606. The interpolations from Middleton's *The Witch* are probably from a later date, perhaps after 1613.

Timon of Athens (c. 1605–1608)

Timon of Athens first appeared in the First Folio of 1623. The text seems to have been based on an unusually early draft of the author's papers, with manifest inconsistencies still present that would have been straightened out in a final draft. Another hypothesis is that joint authorship (with Thomas Middleton) contributed to the discrepancies about the value of money and the like. The play seems to have been a last-minute substitution in the Folio, to replace *Troilus and Cressida* when, for some reason (probably copyright difficulties), that play had to be removed from its original position following *Romeo and Juliet*. The Folio editors possibly had not intended to use *Timon* at all. The manuscript used by the printers seems to have been copied over in places by a second hand, as though the manuscript was too illegible for the printer to use.

Dating of the play is unusually difficult. No records of performances exist from the early seventeenth century; nor is there any trace of the play until it was registered for publication on November 8, 1623. Stylistically, it seems close to the late tragedies. Its pessimism reminds us of *King Lear*, and its use of Plutarch suggests *Antony and Cleopatra*. Theories of multiple authorship, once common but then out of favor, have recently been revived, suggesting Thomas Middleton as the author of perhaps one-third of the play.

Antony and Cleopatra (1606–1607)

On May 20, 1608, Edward Blount entered in the Stationers' Register, the official record book of the London Company of Stationers (booksellers and printers), "A booke Called. Anthony. and Cleopatra," along with "A booke called. The booke of Pericles prynce of Tyre." Blount was friendly with Shakespeare's company, and his entry may have been a "staying entry" designed to prevent some unscrupulous publisher from pirating these texts. If so, the tactic did not succeed with *Pericles,* issued in 1609 by another publisher, but it did succeed with *Antony and Cleopatra*. The play was first printed in the First Folio of 1623. It is a good text, set evidently from Shakespeare's own draft in a more finished state than most of his working papers, or possibly from a transcript of those papers, though not yet prepared to be a playbook.

The year 1608 is thus the latest possible date for *Antony and Cleopatra*. Evidently, it was written in 1606–1607, however, for a "newly altered" edition in 1607 of Samuel Daniel's play *Cleopatra* seems to have been influenced by Shakespeare's play. Shakespeare himself had probably consulted the original edition of *Cleopatra*, published in 1594, or the slightly revised edition of 1599, but Daniel's more thorough revision in 1607 shows signs of his having seen Shakespeare's play in the interim. Also, a play by Barnabe Barnes called *The Devil's Charter* (1607) may contain a parody of Cleopatra's death by asps. Although the printed text of this play advertises corrections and augmentations that could postdate a court performance in February of 1607, recent scholarship favors the likelihood that Barnes saw *Antony and Cleopatra* before that—perhaps in late 1606.

Coriolanus (c. 1608)

Coriolanus was first printed in the First Folio of 1623. Its text was perhaps set from a transcript of the playbook that clarified Shakespeare's stage directions while also preserving some authorial flavor in them and some Shakespearean spellings. Although printing errors are numerous, they are, for the most part, easy to correct. Dating of the play is uncertain. No early performance is on record. The late style and some possible allusions point to sometime around 1608. Menenius' fable of the belly (1.1.94 ff.) is probably indebted to William Camden's *Remains*, published 1605. The demonstrations of the plebeians about distribution of grain may allude to the Midland riots of 1607–1608. Echoes of the play may appear in Robert Armin's *The Italian Taylor and His Boy* and in Ben Jonson's *Epicoene*, both from 1609. Thus, a date in 1608 is plausible but only approximate.

Pericles (1606–1608)

On May 20, 1608, Edward Blount entered in the Stationers' Register, the official record book of the London Company of Stationers (booksellers and printers), "A booke called. The booke of Pericles prynce of Tyre." He also entered *Antony and Cleopatra* at this time, possibly hoping to forestall illegal publishing of these two texts. If so, the plan succeeded with *Antony* but not with *Pericles*. A corrupt Quarto of this play was printed in 1609 by William White:

THE LATE, And much admired Play, Called Pericles, Prince of Tyre. With the true Relation of the whole Historie, aduentures, and fortunes of the said Prince: As also, The no lesse strange, and worthy accidents, in the Birth and Life, of his Daughter MARIANA. As it hath been diuers and sundry times acted by his Maiesties Seruants, at the Globe on the Banck-side. By William Shakespeare. Imprinted at London for *Henry Gosson*, and are to be sold at the signe of the Sunne in Pater-noster row, &c. 1609.

Blount was a friend of the players, and the text he registered is likely to have been the playbook. (This would explain why it is referred to as "A booke called the booke of Pericles" in the Stationers' Register, since playbooks were known technically as "books.") White's text, on the other hand, is a memorially constructed text and at times unintelligible. Two reporters may have been at work, and the printing was done by at least three compositors. See the play's Introduction, for some examples of inconsistency in the text. Unfortunately, this bad text is the best we have, though George Wilkins' *The Painful Adventures of Pericles* (see below) may have been influenced directly by the play and may well afford some clues as to the wording of the text; a recent and controversial hypothesis argues that *The Painful Adventures* is as much a "report" of the play as is the corrupt Quarto. Subsequent Quartos appeared in 1609, 1611, 1619, and 1630, but each was set up from the previous edition, and all attempts in them at improvement are editorial rather than authorial. *Pericles* did not appear at all in the First Folio of 1623, perhaps because the editors

suspected it to be partly non-Shakespearean or because they did not possess a reliable text. Arguments for multiple authorship, though based essentially on internal evidence of the play's manifest inconsistencies, are still taken seriously by scholars. George Wilkins especially has been proposed as collaborator in the first two acts. The defects of the first two acts are generally more extensive than those found even in such bad Quartos as *Hamlet* or *Romeo and Juliet*. Philip Edwards has argued, on the other hand (*Shakespeare Survey 5*, 1952), that the differences between the first two acts and the last three can be accounted for by memorial reporting and compositorial error. This matter is still in dispute.

Pericles (though probably differing textually from the play we have today) must have been in existence by the date of the Stationers' Register entry in May of 1608. A play of *Pericles* was seen by the Venetian Ambassador to England, Zorzi Giustinian, sometime during his official stay from January 5, 1606, to November 23, 1608. George Wilkins' *The Painful Adventures of Pericles, Prince of Tyre*, published in 1608, was certainly derived in part from a play about Pericles: its title page offers the work "as it was lately presented by the worthy and ancient poet John Gower," and the final sentence of the Argument urges the reader "to receive this history in the same manner as it was under the habit of ancient Gower, the famous English poet, by the Kings Majesty's players excellently presented." The play to which Wilkins refers may have been Shakespeare's or perhaps some earlier version—just how early, no one can say. As it stands, however, the play appears to represent the beginning of Shakespeare's fascination with the genre of romance. As such, its date is usually set between 1606 and 1608.

Cymbeline (c. 1608–1610)

Cymbeline was first printed in the First Folio of 1623, where it was included among the tragedies. The text, a good one, was evidently set from a careful transcript (perhaps by the scrivener Ralph Crane) of an earlier manuscript, one in which two copyists may have been involved, basing their work either on Shakespeare's own papers or on a theatrical playbook that had incorporated many authorial stage directions. The first recorded performance was in 1611. Dr. Simon Forman, a quack astrologer, jotted down a description of *Cymbeline* in his commonplace book for that year; although he did not record the actual date he saw the play, he must have done so sometime between April and his sudden death on September 8 of that year. Stylistically, the play appears to follow *Pericles* (c. 1606–1608) and to precede *The Winter's Tale* (c. 1610–1611). *Cymbeline* may also follow and imitate Beaumont and Fletcher's *Philaster*, produced with great success in 1609, although the relative order of these similar plays remains doubtful. If

Cymbeline is the later of the two, it may have been written as late as 1610.

The Winter's Tale (c. 1609–1611)

The Winter's Tale was first printed in the First Folio of 1623. Its text is a good one, taken evidently from Ralph Crane's transcript of Shakespeare's own well-finished draft or possibly the playbook. As in most other Crane transcriptions, the stage directions are sparse, and the characters' names are grouped at the beginning of each scene. The first recorded performance was on May 15, 1611, when the quack astrologer Simon Forman saw the play at the Globe Theatre and recorded a summary of it in his commonplace book. Another performance that year at court, on November 5, is recorded in the *Revels Account* and still another, during the winter of 1612–1613. Quite possibly, the play was new at the time Forman saw it. It apparently contains an allusion to the dance of ten or twelve satyrs in Ben Jonson's *Masque of Oberon,* performed at court on January 1, 1611, although the passage in question from *The Winter's Tale* (4.4.324 ff.) is sometimes regarded as an interpolation written after the play itself. A 1623 entry in the *Office book* of Sir Henry Herbert, Master of the Revels, refers to *The Winter's Tale* as "an old play . . . formerly allowed of by Sir George Bucke." Bucke (or Buc) was first appointed Master of the Revels in 1610 but had occasionally licensed plays before that date during his predecessor's illness, so that the backward limit of 1610 cannot be considered absolute. Still, matters of style confirm the likelihood that Forman was seeing a new play in 1611.

The Tempest (c. 1611)

The Tempest was first printed in the First Folio of 1623. It occupies first place in the volume and is a scrupulously prepared text from a transcript by Ralph Crane of a theater playbook or of Shakespeare's draft after it had been annotated for production; or, Crane may have provided some of the elaboration of stage directions. Shakespeare's colleagues may have placed *The Tempest* first in the Folio because they considered it his most recent complete play. The first recorded performance was at court on November 1, 1611: "Hallomas nyght was presented att Whithall before ye kinges Maiestie a play Called the Tempest." The actors were "the Kings players" (*Revels Account*). The play was again presented at court during the winter of 1612–1613, this time "before the Princes Highnes the Lady Elizabeth and the Prince Pallatyne Elector." The festivities for this important betrothal and wedding were sumptuous and included at least thirteen other plays. Various arguments have been put forward that Shakespeare composed parts of *The Tempest,* especially the masque, for this occasion, but there is absolutely no evidence that the play was singled out for special prominence among the many plays presented, and

the masque is integral to the play as it stands. Probably the 1611 production was of a fairly new play. Simon Forman, who saw *Cymbeline* and *The Winter's Tale* in 1611, does not mention *The Tempest.* He died in September of 1611. According to every stylistic test, such as run-on and hypermetric lines, the play is very late. Shakespeare probably knew Sylvester Jourdain's *A Discovery of the Bermudas,* published in 1610, and William Strachey's *A True Reportory of the Wreck and Redemption,* dated July 1610, although not published until 1625.

The Two Noble Kinsmen (1613–1614)

The Two Noble Kinsmen did not appear in the Shakespeare First Folio of 1623. Publishing rights were first assigned in the Stationers' Register to John Waterson on April 8, 1634, as "a TragiComedy called the two noble kinsmen by Jo: ffletcher & Wm. Shakespeare." It was first published in 1634 in quarto by John Waterson as:

THE TWO NOBLE KINSMEN: Presented at the Blackfriers by the Kings Maiesties servants, with great applause: Written by the memorable Worthies of their time; Mr. *John Fletcher,* and Mr. *William Shakespeare,* Gent. Printed at *London* by *Tho. Cotes,* for *Iohn Waterson:* and are to be sold at the signe of the *Crowne* in *Pauls* Church-yard. 1634.

Waterson transferred his rights in the play on October 31, 1646, to Humphrey Moseley, along with two other plays, as by "Mr fflesher." Moseley's first collection of plays by Beaumont and Fletcher in 1647 did not in fact include *The Two Noble Kinsmen.* It did appear finally in Moseley's 1679 edition of *Fifty Comedies and Tragedies, Written by Francis Beaumont, and John Fletcher, Gentlemen.* Despite the attribution to Fletcher and Shakespeare in 1634, the omission of the play from the Beaumont and Fletcher collected works led to its being excluded from the Shakespeare canon until well into the nineteenth century. Today nearly all editors view the play as a collaboration between Shakespeare, who was entering on his retirement, and the dramatist who succeeded him at the King's men.

The 1634 Quarto text is a good one, perhaps based on a scribal transcript and containing theatrical annotations by the "bookkeeper" or prompter in the form of marginal notes warning the acting company to get properties ready and naming minor actors.

The likely date of first performance is in 1613 or 1614. An expanded version of the morris dance in 3.5 had served as the antimasque (a kind of grotesque comic subplot) for Beaumont's *Masque of the Inner Temple and Gray's Inn* on February 20, 1613, presented at court during the marriage festivities for James I's daughter Elizabeth to Frederick, the Elector Palatine. It seems likely that this highly celebratory court occasion would have taken precedence over commercial public performance. Ben Jonson's *Bartholomew Fair,* first performed on October 31, 1614, alludes to a play called "Palamon." Shakespeare died in 1616 and may have been in failing health toward the very end; 1613 and 1614 seem to have been his last years of writing.

Venus and Adonis (1592–1593)

On April 18, 1593, "a booke intituled, Venus and Adonis" was entered by Richard Field in the Stationers' Register, the official record book of the London Company of Stationers (booksellers and printers), and was published by him the same year. The Quarto contains a dedication written by Shakespeare to the Earl of Southampton. The text seems to have been carefully supervised through the press and to have been based on the author's manuscript. The poem was very popular and was reprinted nine times before Shakespeare's death. The First Folio of 1623, being limited to plays, did not include it or any other nondramatic poems. Contemporary references are numerous: Francis Meres and Richard Barnfield in 1598, Gabriel Harvey in 1598–1601, and John Weever in 1599, among others. Shakespeare probably wrote this poem shortly before its publication, since his intention was to present it to Southampton. The theaters closed from June 1592 to May 1594, giving Shakespeare a period of enforced leisure in which to write poetry.

The Rape of Lucrece (1593–1594)

Shakespeare promised a "graver labour" to Southampton in his dedication of Venus and Adonis, 1593, and The Rape of Lucrece is almost surely that promised sequel. It was registered in the Stationers' Register, the official record book of the London Company of Stationers (booksellers and printers), by John Harrison on May 9, 1594, and issued that same year as "printed by Richard Field, for Iohn Harrison." The printed text was probably based on Shakespeare's manuscript. Although not quite as popular as Venus and Adonis, the poem was reprinted five times during Shakespeare's lifetime. Contemporaries of Shakespeare who allude favorably to the poem include W. Har and Michael Drayton in 1594, William Covell in 1595, Francis Meres in 1598, Gabriel Harvey in 1598–1601, John Weever in 1599, and others. The date of composition of the poem is well fixed between the publication of Venus and Adonis in 1593 and that of The Rape of Lucrece itself in 1594.

The Phoenix and Turtle (by 1601)

"The Phoenix and Turtle" first appeared in a volume with the following title:

LOVES MARTYR: OR, ROSALINS COMPLAINT. *Allegorically shadowing the truth of Loue,* in the constant Fate of the Phoenix *and* Turtle. . . . by ROBERT CHESTER. . . . *To these are added some new compositions, of seuerall moderne Writers whose names are subscribed to their seuerall workes, vpon the first subiect: viz.* the Phoenix *and* Turtle.

The date 1601 appears on a separate title page. One poem is signed "William Shake-speare"; others are assigned to John Marston, George Chapman, and Ben Jonson.

A Lover's Complaint (c. 1601–1605)

A Lover's Complaint first appeared in Thomas Thorpe's 1609 edition of the sonnets. It may have been printed from the same transcript as that used to print the sonnets. The poem is not mentioned on the title page of the volume but has its own head-title on sig. Kᵛ: "A Louers complaint. BY William Shake-speare." For the reliability of this attribution, see the Introduction to A Lover's Complaint. Stylistic tests suggest a date around the time of Hamlet and All's Well That Ends Well, though any such suggestion is approximate.

The Sonnets (c. 1593–1603)

On May 20, 1609, "Thomas Thorpe Entred for his copie vnder thandes of master Wilson and master Lownes Warden a Booke called Shakespeares sonnettes." In the same year appeared the following volume:

SHAKE-SPEARES SONNETS. Neuer before Imprinted. AT LONDON By G. Eld *for T. T. and are to be solde by Iohn Wright,* dwelling at Christ Church gate. 1609.

Some copies of this same edition are marked to be sold by William Aspley rather than John Wright; evidently, Thorpe had set up two sellers to distribute the volume. The sonnets were not reprinted until John Benson's rearranged edition of 1640, possibly because the first edition had been suppressed or because sonnets were no longer in vogue. The 1609 edition may rest on a transcript of Shakespeare's sonnets by someone other than the author, and the edition itself is marred by misprints, though Thorpe was a reputable printer. Clearly, the poem was not supervised through the press as were Venus and Adonis and The Rape of Lucrece. All the evidence suggests that it was obtained without Shakespeare's permission from a manuscript that had been in private circulation (as we know from Francis Meres' 1598 allusion, in his Palladis Tamia, to Shakespeare's "sugared sonnets among his private friends"). Two sonnets, 138 and 144, had appeared in 1599 in The Passionate Pilgrim. On questions of dating and order of the sonnets, see the Introduction to The Sonnets in this volume.

A Funeral Elegy for Master William Peter (1612)

This poem was published in London by G. Eld, 1612, as A FVNERALL Elegye In memory of the late Vertuous Maister William Peeter of Whipton neere Excester. By W.S., soon after Peter was murdered on January 25, 1612.

Sources

The Comedy of Errors

The Comedy of Errors is based chiefly on the *Menaechmi* of Plautus (c. 254–184 B.C.). Shakespeare appears to have used the Latin, which was available to him in numerous Renaissance texts. He may also have known in manuscript the translation into English by "W. W." (? William Warner), published in 1595.

A comparison of the *Menaechmi* with Shakespeare's play suggests how much he has retained and what he has changed. As in Plautus, the story concerns two separated twins, one of whom (Menaechmus the Traveler of Syracuse) has come by chance, accompanied by his servant, Messenio, to the city of Epidamnum, where his long-lost brother, Menaechmus the Citizen, lives. Menaechmus the Citizen, in the company of the parasite Peniculus, quarrels with his wife and arranges lunch with the courtesan Erotium. The confusion begins when Menaechmus the Traveler is mistaken for his twin by Erotium's cook, Cylindrus, and then by Erotium herself, who invites him to lunch and to her bed. She bids him take a cloak (which Menaechmus the Citizen had given her that morning) to the dyer's for alteration. A short time later, Peniculus, too, mistakes Menaechmus the Traveler for the Epidamnian twin, upbraids him for having dined while the parasite was absent, and threatens to tell Menaechmus' wife of his carryings-on. Erotium's maid brings Menaechmus the Traveler a chain or bracelet to be mended at the goldsmith's. Menaechmus the Citizen now returns home from a busy day to a furious wife and a vindictive Peniculus. Among other matters, the wife demands the return of her cloak, which, as she suspects, her husband stole from her and gave to Erotium. The husband, locked out of his own house by his angry wife, must now confront Erotium, who insists that she gave her chain and the cloak to him. The Citizen goes to seek the help of his friends. Menaechmus the Traveler shows up at this point and is angrily abused by the wife and by her father, both of whom consider the supposed husband to be mad. They

send for a doctor, who arrives after Menaechmus the Traveler has fled; they detain Menaechmus the Citizen instead as a madman. Messenio the servant now returns to his supposed master and fights manfully with his master's captors. Finally, the two twins confront one another and unravel the mystery.

Shakespeare creates the two Dromios in place of Messenio, plays down the role of the courtesan, dignifies the part of the wife, invents the sympathetic role of Luciana her sister, eliminates the parasite and the wife's father, and replaces the courtesan's maid and cook with comic servants such as Luce, or Nell, the kitchen-wench in the household of Antipholus of Ephesus. The conventional doctor, Medicus, becomes the zany Dr. Pinch. The setting is Ephesus rather than Epidamnum. Plautus' detached ironic tone and his matter-of-fact depiction of courtesans and parasites are replaced by a thematic emphasis on patience and loyalty in marriage. The name "Dromio" may have come from John Lyly's *Mother Bombie*.

The dual identity of the servants and the superb confusion in Act 3 when Antipholus of Ephesus is locked out of his own house are derived in good part from Plautus' *Amphitruo*. In the relevant portion of that play, Amphitryon's wife Alcmena is courted by Jupiter, disguised as her husband, while Mercury guards the door in the guise of Amphitryon's slave Sosia. The real Sosia approaches but is so bewildered by Mercury's inventive wit that he begins to doubt his own identity. Later, at Jupiter's behest, Mercury again poses as Sosia to dupe Amphitryon and to deny him entrance to his own house. Ultimately, after Alcmena has given birth to twins, one by Jupiter (Hercules) and one by Amphitryon (Iphiclus), Jupiter tells Amphitryon the truth.

The "framing" action of *The Comedy of Errors*, concerning old Egeon's painful separation from his wife and their eventual reunion, is derived not from Plautus but from the story of Apollonius of Tyre. Shakespeare later used this story for *Pericles*, and for that play his sources were chiefly two: the *Confessio Amantis* by John Gower, Book 8, and Laurence Twine's *The Pattern of Painful Adventures*, translated from a French version based in turn on a popular story in the *Gesta Romanorum*. Perhaps Shakespeare was acquainted with these same versions when he wrote *The Comedy of Errors*; in 1576, Twine's account was entered in the Stationers' Register, the official record book of the London Company of Stationers (booksellers and printers), although the earliest extant edition dates from around 1594–1595. Gower's account had been printed by William Caxton (England's first printer) in 1493 and reprinted in 1532 and 1554.

In Gower's *Confessio*, Apollonius' wife Lucina gives birth to a daughter on board ship and, having apparently died in childbirth, is put into a chest and committed to the sea. Washing ashore at Ephesus, she is restored by the physician Cerimon. She becomes a priestess in the Temple of Diana.

Years later, Apollonius comes to Ephesus, is first reunited with his daughter Thaisa, and then is told in a vision to go to the Temple. There he discovers the "Abbess" to be his long-lost wife. Shakespeare has added the threatened hanging from which Egeon is finally rescued.

Love's Labor's Lost

No main source exists for *Love's Labor's Lost*. For his conception of an "academy" of aristocratic scholars, Shakespeare may have drawn on Pierre de la Primaudaye's *L'Académie française* (1577), translated into English in 1586, in which the ideals of scholarly withdrawal are discussed. The notion was, however, commonplace. Certain historical facts about Henry of Navarre may well have provided Shakespeare with a model for the play's action, especially the visit of Catherine de Medici with her daughter and the famous *l'escadron volant* (flying squadron) to Henry's court in 1578, and a similar visit in 1586 (see the Introduction to the play above). Published accounts of these visits were not available when Shakespeare wrote his play, but he may well have heard the gossip. John Lyly's plays provided Shakespeare with a literary model for the saucy boyish wit of Mote, Boyet, and others, and Armado and Mote are often thought to resemble Sir Tophas and the page Epiton in Lyly's *Endymion*. Traditions of the *commedia dell' arte* provided Shakespeare with stock comic models, especially those of the *dottore* or pedant (Holofernes), his parasite (Nathaniel, the curate), the *capitano* or braggart soldier (Armado), and the rustic servant (Costard). All of these types are individualized and rendered in English terms, however. Many literary quarrels in England in the 1590s have been adduced as possible sources for Shakespeare's play, especially the controversy between Thomas Nashe and Gabriel Harvey, but the evidence remains inconclusive.

The Two Gentlemen of Verona

Shakespeare appears to have combined two kinds of stories in *The Two Gentlemen of Verona:* one of romantic love triumphing over inconstancy and one of perfect friendship triumphing over perfidy. For the story of the deserted heroine and her inconstant lover, Shakespeare's main source was evidently *Diana Enamorada*, a Spanish pastoral by Jorge de Montemayor (published c. 1559). This work was translated into French in 1578 and 1587, and was published in English in 1598 by Bartholomew Yonge. Yonge states that he began his translation some nineteen years earlier. Possibly, then, Shakespeare saw it in manuscript, or he may have relied on the Spanish original or the French translation. A play, now lost, was performed at court in 1585 called *The*

History of Felix & Philiomena (i.e., Felismena). It must surely have been based on Montemayor's prose pastoral and may have provided Shakespeare with a dramatic model.

The story of Felix and Felismena is only one of the many narratives in *Diana Enamorada* that are set in contrast to the central story of Diana the shepherdess. It is told by Felismena as her own narrative, beginning in Book. 2. The story contains no character corresponding to Valentine, but Proteus and Julia find their equivalents in Felix and Felismena. The latter is attended by a maid, Rosina, like Julia's Lucetta, who is hypocritically scolded by her mistress for delivering a letter from Felix that Felismena, in fact, longs to have. Like Proteus in Shakespeare's play, Don Felix is sent off to court (in this case, the court of Princess Augusta Caesarina) to prevent his marriage to the orphaned Felismena. She follows after, appareled as a young man named Valerius (as Julia travels under the name of Sebastian). Stopping at an inn, she is invited by the host of the inn to hear some music, whereupon she happens to overhear the faithless Felix courting a lady named Celia (Shakespeare's Sylvia). Disguised as Valerius, Felismena ingratiates herself with Felix's servant Fabius and takes service with Don Felix. She is sent on embassages to Celia, with whom she converses about Felix's first love. Celia falls in love with "Valerius," like Olivia in *Twelfth Night,* and subsequently dies of unrequited passion. Hereupon the distraught Felix disappears. Later, in Book 7, we hear how Felismena, disguised as an Amazonian shepherdess, rescues Felix from his attackers and is reconciled with him. Felix acknowledges her beauty to be superior to that of Celia. Shakespeare has changed some important matters, notably Celia's falling in love with "Valerius" and her dying of unrequited love; Sylvia's remaining faithful to Valentine and following him into banishment are essential parts of her character in Shakespeare's account. Shakespeare also adds several new characters: the Duke of Milan (Sylvia's father), Thurio, Eglamour, Lance, Speed, and the outlaws. Still, the debt to *Diana Enamorada* is considerable.

In Sir Philip Sidney's *Arcadia* (1590), Zelmane follows Felismena's example by disguising herself as a page (Daiphantus) in the service of her beloved Pyrocles. When she falls ill and is on the verge of death, Zelmane's identity is revealed to Pyrocles. *Arcadia* also offers a noble example of perfect friendship in the relation between Pyrocles and Musidorus. Shakespeare used the *Arcadia* as a source elsewhere, especially in the Gloucester plot of *King Lear*.

The story of perfect friendship has many antecedents, including the fourteenth-century *Amis and Amiloun* and Richard Edwards' play about *Damon and Pythias* (1565). The falling-out of sworn friends over a woman is the central theme of Geoffrey Chaucer's "The Knight's Tale" and of John Lyly's *Euphues* (1578). Perhaps the most suggestive example of perfect friendship is the story of Titus and

Gisippus as it appears in Book 2, Chapter 12, of Sir Thomas Elyot's *The Governor* (1531). Elyot derived his account from Day 10, Novel 8, of Giovanni Boccaccio's *Decameron*. Titus and Gisippus were proverbially famous friends, like Damon and Pythias, and other Renaissance versions of the story were available (including a Latin school play of 1546[?] and a children's play at court in 1577, both now lost). Perhaps Shakespeare knew the story as a commonplace rather than having to depend on one particular literary source.

Elyot's version tells of two look-alike friends dwelling in Athens, of whom one, Gisippus, is persuaded by his kindred and acquaintances to marry. Despite a preference for the study of philosophy, he finds his fiancée most attractive. When, however, his Roman-born friend Titus falls desperately in love with the same lady and confesses as much to Gisippus, the husband-to-be generously proposes that Titus take his place on the wedding night. Because the binding element of the marriage contract is the bestowing of the ring in bed and the undoing of the girdle of virginity, the lady is now Titus' legal wife and returns with him to Rome. Gisippus, accused by the Athenians of having mismanaged the affair, follows his friend to Rome and is there wrongly accused of a murder. Titus' turn has now arrived to be magnanimous, and he insists that he be punished for the murder. Eventually, the real culprit, touched by this selflessness, confesses the crime, allowing Titus to return with Gisippus to Athens and forcibly to restore him to his rightful possessions.

Valentine's sojourn in the forest and his leadership of a band of outlaws would seem to be indebted to the tradition of Robin Hood, although no single source has been found. An analogue to the outlaw episode does appear in Henry Wotton's *A Courtly Controversy of Cupid's Cautels* (1578), where it is linked to a story of perfidy in friendship. Valentine's unwelcome rival Thurio may owe something to the braggart soldier, Captain Spavento, of the *commedia dell' arte* tradition. Sylvia's father, the Duke, is a similarly conventional comic stage type.

One final analogue worthy of note is a German play, *Julio und Hyppolita*, from a collection called *Englische Comedien und Tragedien* (1620). It may have been derived from performances by English players around 1600. Although some of its lines are suggestively close to those of Shakespeare's play, we cannot determine which version is prior to the other.

The Taming of the Shrew

Most recent critics agree that the play called *The Taming of a Shrew*, published in 1594, is derived from a now-lost earlier version of Shakespeare's play, to which the compiler added original material and borrowed or even plagiarized from other literary sources as well. It does not, then, appear to be a source for Shakespeare's play, as Geoffrey Bullough has argued in his *Narrative and Dramatic Sources of Shakespeare*. Apart from this question, all critics agree that Shakespeare's play consists of three elements, each with its own source: the romantic love plot of Lucentio and Bianca, the wife-taming plot of Petruchio and Kate, and the framing plot, or induction, of Christopher Sly.

The romantic love plot is derived from George Gascoigne's *Supposes,* a neoclassical comedy performed at Gray's Inn (one of the Inns of Court, where young men studied law in London) in 1566. Gascoigne's play was a rather close translation of Ludovico Ariosto's *I Suppositi* (1509), which in turn was based on two classical plays, Terence's *Eunuchus* and Plautus' *Captivi*. The heroine of Gascoigne's version (as of Ariosto's) is Polynesta, the resourceful daughter of Damon, a widower of Ferrara. Two suitors vie for Polynesta's hand: Dr. Cleander, an aged and miserly lawyer, and Erostrato, a Sicilian gentleman who has purportedly come to Ferrara to study. In fact, however, this "Erostrato" is the servant Dulippo in disguise, having changed places with his master. (These disguisings are the "supposes" of the title.) As a servant in Damon's household, "Dulippo" has secretly become the lover of Polynesta and has made her pregnant. Balia, the nurse or duenna, is their go-between. Meanwhile, "Erostrato" takes great delight in outwitting Dr. Cleander and his unattractive parasite, Pasiphilo. The counterfeit Erostrato's ruse is to produce a rich father who will guarantee a handsome dowry and thereby outbid Cleander in the contest for Polynesta's hand. The "father" he produces, however, is actually an old Sienese stranger, who is persuaded that he is in danger in Ferrara unless he cloaks his identity. Complications arise when Damon learns of his daughter's affair and throws the lover, "Dulippo," into a dungeon. The crafty Pasiphilo overhears this compromising information and resolves to cause mischief for all the principals. Moreover, when Erostrato's real father, Philogano, arrives in Ferrara, he is barred from his son's house by the counterfeit Philogano and resolves to get help. His clever servant, Litio, suggests employing the famous lawyer, Cleander. All is happily resolved when the real Dulippo proves to be the son of Dr. Cleander and the real Erostrato is revealed to be rich and socially eligible for Polynesta's hand in marriage. Cleander is even reconciled to his parasite, Pasiphilo.

Shakespeare, in his play, has almost entirely eliminated the satire of the law that is in his source. Gremio is aged and wealthy, but no shyster. The lover is not imprisoned in a dungeon. The parasite is gone, as also in *The Comedy of Errors*. Bianca does not consummate her affair with Lucentio, as does Polynesta, and hence has no need for a go-between like Balia. Shakespeare adapts a sophisticated neoclassical comedy, racy and cosmopolitan, to the moral standards of his public theater. The witless Hortensio, the tutoring in Latin, and the music lesson are Shakespeare's inventions.

The wife-taming plot of Petruchio and Kate reflects an ancient comic misogynistic tradition, still extant today in the Scottish folksong "The Cooper of Fife" or "The Wife Wrapped in Wether's Skin" (Francis James Child, *The English and Scottish Popular Ballads* [1888–1898], 5:104). Richard Hosley has argued (in *Huntington Library Quarterly*, 27, 1964) that Shakespeare's likeliest source was *A Merry Jest of a Shrewd and Curst Wife Lapped in Morel's Skin, for her Good Behavior* (printed c. 1550). In this version, the husband beats his shrewish wife with birch rods until she bleeds and faints, whereupon he wraps her in the raw salted skin of an old plow-horse named Morel. Like Kate, this shrewish wife has a gentle younger sister who is their father's favorite. This father warns the man who proposes to marry his older daughter that she is shrewish, but the suitor goes ahead and subsequently tames his wife with Morel's skin. Thereafter, at a celebratory dinner, everyone is impressed by the thoroughness of the taming.

Shakespeare avoids the misogynistic extremes of this story, despite the similarity of the narrative. Instead, he seems to have had in mind the more humanistic spirit of Erasmus' *A Merry Dialogue Declaring the Properties of Shrewd Shrews and Honest Wives* (translated 1557) and Juan Luis Vives' *The Office and Duty of an Husband* (translated 1555). Specific elements of the wife-taming plot have been traced to other possible sources. The scolding of a tailor occurs in Gerard Legh's *Accidence of Armory* (1562); a wife agrees with her husband's assertion of a patent falsehood in Don Juan Manuel's *El Conde Lucanor* (1335); and three husbands wager on the obedience of their wives in *The Book of the Knight of La Tour-Landry* (printed 1484).

The induction story, of the beggar duped into believing himself a rich lord, is an old tale occurring in the *Arabian Nights*. An interesting analogue occurs in P. Heuterus' *De Rebus Burgundicis* (1584), translated into the French of S. Goulart (1606?) and thence into the English of Edward Grimeston (1607). According to Heuterus, in 1440 Philip the Good of Burgundy actually entertained a drunken beggar in his palace "to make trial of the vanity of our life," plying him with fine clothes, bed, a feast, and the performance of "a pleasant comedy."

A Midsummer Night's Dream

No single source has been discovered that unites the various elements that we find in *A Midsummer Night's Dream*, but the four main strands of action can be individually discussed in terms of sources. The four strands are: (1) the marriage of Theseus (Duke of Athens) and Queen Hippolyta, (2) the romantic tribulations and triumphs of the four young lovers, (3) the quarrel of King Oberon and Queen Titania, together with the fairies' manipulations of human affairs, and (4) the "rude mechanicals" and their play of "Pyramus and Thisbe."

For his conception of Theseus, Shakespeare went chiefly to Geoffrey Chaucer's "The Knight's Tale" and to Thomas North's 1579 translation of "The Life of Theseus" in Plutarch's *Lives of the Noble Grecians and Romans*. Chaucer's Theseus is a duke of "wisdom" and "chivalrye," renowned for his conquest of the Amazons and his marriage to Hippolyta. Plutarch provides information concerning Theseus' other conquests (to which Oberon alludes in 2.1.77 ff.), including that of Antiopa. Shakespeare could have learned more about Theseus from Chaucer's *The Legend of Good Women* and from Ovid's *Metamorphoses*. He seems to have blended all or some of these impressions together with his own notion of a noble yet popular Renaissance ruler.

The romantic narrative of the four lovers appears to be original with Shakespeare, although one can find many analogous situations of misunderstanding and rivalry in love. Chaucer's "The Knight's Tale" tells of two friends battling over one woman. Shakespeare's own *The Two Gentlemen of Verona* gives us four lovers, properly matched at first until one of the men shifts his attentions to his friend's ladylove; eventually, all is righted when the false lover recovers his senses. Parallel situations arise in Sir Philip Sidney's *Arcadia* (1590) and in Jorge de Montemayor's *Diana Enamorada* (c. 1559), a source for *The Two Gentlemen*. What Shakespeare adds in *A Midsummer* is the intervention of the fairies in human love affairs.

Shakespeare's knowledge of fairy lore must have been extensive and is hard to trace exactly. Doubtless, much of it was from oral traditions about leprechauns, gremlins, and elves, who were thought to cause such mischief as spoiling fermentation or preventing milk from churning into butter; Puck's tricks mentioned in 2.1.34 ff. are derived from such lore. Yet Shakespeare seems to have consulted literary sources as well. In Chaucer's "The Merchant's Tale," Pluto and Proserpina as king and queen of the fairies intervene in the affairs of old January, his young wife May, and her lover Damyan. Fairies appear on stage in John Lyly's *Endymion* (1588), protecting true lovers and tormenting those who are morally tainted. Shakespeare later reflects this tradition in *The Merry Wives of Windsor* (1597–1601). The name Oberon probably comes from the French romance *Huon of Bordeaux* (translated by Lord Berners by about 1540), where Oberon is a dwarfish fairy king from the mysterious East who practices enchantment in a haunted wood. In Edmund Spenser's *The Faerie Queene*, Oberon is the Elfin father of Queen Gloriana (2.10. 75–76). Robert Greene's

James IV (c. 1591) also features Oberon as the fairy king, and a lost play called *Huon of Bordeaux* was performed by Sussex's men, an acting company, at about this same time. The name "Titania" comes from Ovid's *Metamorphoses*, where it is used as a synonym for both the enchantress Circe and the chaste goddess Diana. The name "Titania" does not appear in Arthur Golding's translation (1567), suggesting that Shakespeare found it in the original. Puck, or Robin Goodfellow, is essentially the product of oral tradition, although Reginald Scot's *The Discovery of Witchcraft* (1584) discusses Robin in pejorative terms as an incubus or hobgoblin in whom intelligent people no longer believe.

Scot also reports the story of a man who finds an ass's head placed on his shoulders by enchantment. Similar legends of transformation occur in Apuleius' *The Golden Ass* (translated by William Adlington, 1566) and in the well-known story of the ass's ears bestowed by Phoebus Apollo on King Midas for his presumption. Perhaps the most suggestive possible source for Shakespeare's clownish actors, however, is Anthony Munday's play *John a Kent and John a Cumber* (c. 1587–1590). In it a group of rude artisans, led by the intrepid Turnop, stage a ludicrous interlude written by their churchwarden in praise of his millhorse. Turnop's prologue is a medley of lofty comparisons. The entertainment is presented before noble spectators, who are graciously amused. *John a Kent* also features a lot of magic trickery, a boy named Shrimp whose role is comparable to that of Puck, and a multiple love plot.

"Pyramus and Thisbe" itself is based on the *Metamorphoses* (4.55 ff.). Other versions that Shakespeare may have known include Chaucer's *The Legend of Good Women,* a poem by William Griffith in 1562, George Pettie's *A Petite Palace of Pettie His Pleasure* (1576), *A Gorgeous Gallery of Gallant Inventions* (1578), and "A New Sonnet of Pyramus and Thisbe" from Clement Robinson's *A Handful of Pleasant Delights* (1584). Several of these, especially the last three, are bad enough to have given Shakespeare materials to lampoon, though the sweep of his parody goes beyond the particular story of Pyramus and Thisbe. The occasionally stilted phraseology of Golding's translation of the *Metamorphoses* contributed to the fun. According to Kenneth Muir (*Shakespeare's Sources*, 1957), Shakespeare must also have known Thomas Mouffet's *Of the Silkworms and Their Flies* (published 1599, but possibly circulated earlier in manuscript), which contains perhaps the most ridiculous of all versions of the Pyramus and Thisbe story. Shakespeare also appears to have been spoofing the inept dramatic style and lame verse of English dramas of the 1560s, 1570s, and 1580s, especially in their treatment of tragic sentiment and high emotion; *Cambises, Damon and Pythias,* and *Appius and Virginia* are examples.

The Merchant of Venice

Shakespeare's probable chief source for *The Merchant of Venice* was the first story of the fourth day of *Il Pecorone* (*The Dunce*), by Ser Giovanni Fiorentino. This collection of tales dates from the late fourteenth century but was first published in 1558 at Milan and was not published in English translation in Shakespeare's time. If Shakespeare was unable to read it in Italian, he may conceivably have consulted a translation in some now-lost manuscript; such translations did sometimes circulate. Behind Ser Giovanni's story lies an old tradition of a bond given for human flesh, as found in Persia, India, and the Twelve Tables of Roman Law. This legend first appears in English in the thirteenth-century *Cursor Mundi,* with a Jew as the creditor. A thirteenth-century version of the *Gesta Romanorum* (a popular collection of stories in Latin) adds a romantic love plot; the evil moneylender in this story is not Jewish. The hero pawns his own flesh to a merchant in order to win a lady. He succeeds on his third attempt, having learned to avoid a magic spell that had previously put him to sleep and cost him a large number of florins. When he goes to pay his forfeit, the lady follows him disguised as a knight, and foils the evil merchant by pointing out a quibbling distinction between flesh and blood.

Il Pecorone provided Shakespeare with a number of essential elements, although not all that he has included. Ser Giovanni's story tells of Giannetto, the adventurous youngest son of a Florentine merchant, who goes to live with his father's dearest friend, Ansaldo, in Venice. This worthy merchant gives him money to seek his fortune at sea. Unbeknownst to Ansaldo, Giannetto twice risks everything to woo the lady of Belmont: if he can succeed in sleeping with her, he will win her and her country, but, if he fails, he loses all his wealth. Twice Giannetto is given a sleeping medicine and has to forfeit everything. Returning destitute to Venice twice, he is reunited each time with Ansaldo and given the means to seek his fortune again. For the third such voyage, however, Ansaldo is driven to borrow ten thousand florins from a Jew, using the forfeiture of a pound of flesh as a guarantee. This time, one of the lady's maids warns Giannetto not to drink his wine, and he finally possesses the lady as his wife. Sometime later, remembering that the day of Ansaldo's forfeiture has arrived, Giannetto explains the predicament to his wife and is sent by her to Venice with a hundred thousand florins, but he arrives after the forfeiture has fallen due. The lady, however, following after him in the disguise of a doctor of laws, decrees that the Jew may have no blood and must take no more or no less than one pound of flesh. The Jew is jeered at and receives no money. The "doctor of laws" refuses any payment other than the ring Giannetto was given by his lady. Giving it up unwillingly, he returns to Belmont, where his lady vexes him about the ring but finally relents and tells him all. Shakespeare could thus have found in one source the wooing, the borrowing from a Jewish moneylender, the pound of flesh, the trial, and the business of the rings. The story provides no casket episode, courtship of Nerissa by Gratiano, elopement of Jessica, or clowning of Lancelot Gobbo. The Jew's motive is not prompted by the way he has been treated.

Shakespeare may also have known "The Ballad of Gernutus," a popular English work that seems to be older than the play. It has no love plot but dwells on the unnatural cruelty of a Jewish Venetian usurer who takes a bond of flesh for "a merry jest." Anthony Munday's prose *Zelauto* (1580), though its villain is a Christian rather than a Jewish moneylender, also features a bond of this sort, taken purportedly as a mere sport but with hidden malice. Truculento, the villain, takes the bond of two young men, Rodolfo and his friend Strabino, as surety for a loan. If they forfeit the loan, the young men are to lose their lands and their right eyes as well. The villain has a daughter, Brisana, whom he permits to marry Rodolfo, since Truculento expects to marry Rodolfo's sister Cornelia himself. When Cornelia instead marries Strabino, Truculento angrily takes the young men to court to demand his bond. The two brides disguise themselves as scholars and go to court, where they appeal for mercy and then foil Truculento by means of the legal quibble about blood.

Another possible source for the courtroom scene is *The Orator*, translated into English in 1596 from the French of Alexandre Sylvain. An oration, entitled "Of a Jew, who would for his debt have a pound of the flesh of a Christian," uses many specious arguments also employed by Shylock, and is forthrightly confuted in "The Christian's Answer."

Shylock's relationship to his daughter finds obvious earlier parallels in *Zelauto* and in Christopher Marlowe's play, *The Jew of Malta* (c. 1589), in which Barabas' daughter Abigail loves a Christian and ultimately renounces her faith. The actual elopement, however, is closer to the fourteenth story in Masuccio of Salerno's fifteenth-century *Il Novellino* (not published in English translation in Shakespeare's day).

The casket-choosing episode, not found in *Il Pecorone*, was a widespread legend, occurring, for example, in the story of *Barlaam and Josophat* (ninth-century Greek, translated into Latin by the thirteenth century), in Vincent of Beauvais' *Speculum Historiale*, in the *Legenda Aurea*, in Giovanni Boccaccio's *Decameron* (Day 10, Story 1), in John Gower's *Confessio Amantis*, and—closest to Shakespeare—in the *Gesta Romanorum* (translated into English in 1577 by Richard Robinson and "bettered" by him in 1595). In this last account, the choice is between a gold, silver, and lead casket, each with its own inscription. The first two inscriptions are like Shakespeare's; the third reads, "Thei that chese me, shulle fynde [in] me that God hathe

disposid." The chooser, however, is a maiden, and she is not preceded by other contestants.

An old play called *The Jew* is referred to by Stephen Gosson in 1579 as containing "the greediness of worldly choosers, and bloody minds of usurers." Scholars have speculated that this was a source play for Shakespeare, but actually we have too little to go on to make a reliable judgment. Gosson was surely not referring to Robert Wilson's *The Three Ladies of London* (c. 1581) in any case, even though it is sometimes suggested as an analogue to *The Merchant of Venice*, for its Jewish figure, named Gerontus (compare Gernutus in the ballad), is an exemplary person. Besides, the probable date of this play is later than Gosson's remark.

Much Ado about Nothing

Shakespeare's probable chief source for the Hero-Claudio plot of *Much Ado* was the twenty-second story from the *Novelle* of Matteo Bandello (Lucca, 1554). A French translation by François de Belleforest, in his *Histoires Tragiques* (1569 edition), was available to Shakespeare, as was the Italian original. The story of the maiden falsely accused was, however, much older than the story by Bandello. Perhaps the earliest version that has been found is the Greek romance *Chaereas and Callirrhoe*, fourth or fifth century A.D., in which the hero Chaereas, warned by envious rivals of his wife's purported infidelity, watches at dusk while an elegantly attired stranger is admitted by the maid to the house where Callirrhoe lives. Chaereas rushes in and strikes mistakenly at his wife in the dark but is acquitted of murder when the maid confesses her part in a conspiracy to delude Chaereas. Callirrhoe is buried in a deathlike trance but awakens in time to be carried off by pirates. The story reappears in a fifteenth-century Spanish romance, *Tirante el Blanco*, in which the princess Blanche is courted seemingly by a repulsive black man. This Spanish version probably inspired the account in Canto 5 of Ludovico Ariosto's *Orlando Furioso* (1516), to which all subsequent Renaissance versions are ultimately indebted.

In Ariosto's account, as translated into English by Sir John Harington (1591), the narrator is Dalinda, maid to the virtuous Scottish princess Genevra. Dalinda tells how she has fallen guiltily in love with Polynesso, Duke of Albany, an evil man who often makes love to Dalinda in her mistress' rooms but who longs in fact to marry Genevra. Consequently, Polynesso arranges for Genevra's noble Italian suitor, Ariodante, and Ariodante's brother Lurcanio, to witness the Duke's ascent to Genevra's window by a rope ladder. The woman who admits the Duke is, of course, not Genevra but Dalinda disguised as her mistress, having been duped into believing that the Duke merely wishes to satisfy his craving for Genevra by making love to her image.

Lurcanio publicly accuses the innocent Genevra and offers to fight anyone who defends her cause (compare Claudio's quarrel with Leonato). The evil Duke tries to get rid of Dalinda, but all is finally put to rights by Rinaldo (the hero of *Orlando Furioso*) and Ariodante. This account gives an unusually vivid motivation for the maid and the villain—a clearer motivation than in Shakespeare's play. A lost dramatic version, *Ariodante and Genevora,* was performed at the English court in 1583.

Shakespeare probably consulted not only Ariosto but also Edmund Spenser's *The Faerie Queene* (2.4), based on Ariosto. Spenser's emphasis is on the blind rage of Phedon, a young squire in love with Claribell. Phedon is tricked by his erstwhile friend Philemon and by Claribell's maid Pryene into believing Claribell false. Pryene's motive in dressing up as Claribell is to prove she is as beautiful as her mistress. When, after having slain Claribell for her supposed perfidy, Phedon learns the truth, he poisons Philemon and furiously pursues Pryene until he is utterly possessed by a mad frenzy.

Shakespeare's greatest debt is, however, to Bandello's story. In a number of details, the story is closer to Shakespeare's play than are those already discussed. Several names are substantially the same as in Shakespeare: the location is Messina, the father of the slandered bride is Lionato di' Lionati (compare Shakespeare's Leonato), and her lover is in the service of King Piero of Aragon (compare Don Pedro of Aragon). As in Shakespeare, a young knight (named Sir Timbreo) seeks the hand in marriage of his beloved (Fenicia) through the matchmaking offices of a noble emissary. The complication of this wooing is somewhat different in that Timbreo's friend Girondo also falls in love with Fenicia, but Girondo does then plot with a mischief-loving courtier (resembling Shakespeare's Don John) to poison Timbreo's mind against Fenicia, and Girondo thereupon escorts Timbreo to a garden, where they see Girondo's servant, elegantly dressed, enter Fenicia's window. No maid takes part in the ruse, however, nor indeed is any woman seen at the window. When Fenicia is wrongly accused, she falls into a deathlike trance and is pronounced dead by a doctor, but she is revived. Her father, believing in her innocence, sends her off to a country retreat and circulates the report that she is, in fact, dead. Soon both Timbreo and Girondo are stricken with remorse, Timbreo magnanimously spares his friend's life, and both confess the truth to Fenicia's family. A year later, Timbreo marries a wife chosen for him by Lionato who turns out, of course, to be Fenicia. Girondo marries her sister Belfiore. This account does not provide any equivalent for Beatrice and Benedick. Shakespeare enhances the Friar's role and provides a brother for Leonato. Claudio and Leonato are of comparable social station in Shakespeare, whereas Bandello makes a point of Timbreo's superior social rank.

A lost play, *Panecia* (1574–1575), may have been based on Bandello's work. One other version Shakespeare may have known is George Whetstone's *The Rock of Regard* (1576), based on Ariosto and Bandello. It contains a suggestive parallel to Claudio's rejection of Hero in church. Various Italian plays in the tradition of Luigi Pasqualigo's *Il Fedele* (1579), and also a version perhaps by Anthony Munday, *Fedele and Fortunio* (published 1585), are analogous in situation, though Shakespeare need not have known any of them.

For the Beatrice-Benedick plot, no source has been discovered, apart from Shakespeare's own earlier fascination with wit-combat and candid wooing in *Love's Labor's Lost* and *The Taming of the Shrew*. Nor has a plausible source been found for Dogberry and the watch.

The Merry Wives of Windsor

The Merry Wives of Windsor is indebted to no single source that combines the various elements found in the play: the courtship of Anne Page, the hoodwinking of Falstaff by the merry wives, the horse-stealing business, and the various "humors" portraits. Nor does any one element derive from a single source. The entire play is brilliantly improvised.

Many analogues exist to the courtship of Anne Page, for it is essentially a plot in which parents and unwelcome wooers are outwitted by resourceful young people. The Bianca-Lucentio plot of Shakespeare's own *The Taming of the Shrew* is a good enough instance. Similarly, analogues have been found to the discomfiture of Falstaff. In Ser Giovanni Fiorentino's *Il Pecorone* (Day 1, Novella 2), for example, a student twice cuckolds the very professor who is instructing him in the art of love. Comically, the student reports back to the professor at every turn and is coached in his next move. He doesn't know that the lady is the professor's wife, but the professor begins to suspect and so follows after. On the first occasion, the student escapes detection by hiding under a pile of newly washed linen. The second time, he slips out the door, whereupon the neighbors arrive and, finding no intruder, berate the professor for his mad suspicions. The wife's brothers even search the linen pile at the professor's suggestion but find nothing. They thrash the professor and chain him up as a madman. Next day, intending once again to report to the professor what has happened, the student discovers the truth. This version differs markedly from Shakespeare's in that the husband is the chief comic butt. Nevertheless, Shakespeare may have known it. Although *Il Pecorone* (1558) is not known to have been translated into English in the sixteenth century, Shakespeare had already used it (or some now-lost manuscript translation) as his chief source for *The Merchant of Venice*.

Certainly available to Shakespeare was a similar story, "Two Lovers of Pisa," from *Tarlton's News Out of Purgatory* (1590). In this story, the husband is again the one who is duped. An old doctor, wedded to a beautiful young wife, becomes by chance the confidential adviser of a young man who has fallen in love with the wife. The young man reports to the husband his plans and successes in detail. The lover thrice escapes detection (when warned by the lady's maid of the husband's approach) by hiding in a vat of feathers, in a false ceiling, and in an old chest full of legal documents. When on the third occasion the jealous husband sets fire to his own house, the lover is saved by the husband's order to carry out the chest of documents. At last, the lover reveals his knowledge of the husband's identity, and everyone laughs at the old fool. Elsewhere, Tarlton's book has suggestive references to Robin Goodfellow and other prankish spirits that may have influenced the concluding scene of *The Merry Wives of Windsor.*

The story "Of Two Brethren and Their Wives" in *Riche His Farewell to Military Profession* (1581) features two wives: one of "light disposition" and much given to adultery, and the other a tedious scold. The first wife desires to rid herself of her two erstwhile lovers, a doctor and a lawyer, in order to enjoy a new liaison with a soldier. Accordingly, she pretends to encourage the lawyer's advances, but when the lawyer comes to her she feigns the approach of her husband and enjoins the lawyer to hide in a large mailbag. Meanwhile, the merry wife has arranged for the doctor to come and pick up the mailbag, on the assumption that she will be hiding in it. The doctor thus carries off the lawyer, nearly suffocating from his close confinement, into the country, where the doctor expects to enjoy his rendezvous. Instead, the soldier accosts them, cudgeling first the body in the bag and then the one who has done the laborious carrying. The lawyer is no less astonished to discover where he has arrived than is the doctor to discover what he has been carrying.

For the background of Shakespeare's horse-stealing episodes and "humors" portraits, see the Introduction to the play. The explicit comparison between Falstaff's ludicrous fate in Windsor Forest and the legend of Actaeon is ultimately indebted to Ovid's *Metamorphoses* (3, 150–304 in Arthur Golding's translation, 1567). In this account, Actaeon, grandson of Cadmus and a mighty hunter, happens to disturb Diana and her nymphs while they are bathing naked. Transformed by the vengeful Diana into a horned stag, he is hunted to death by his own hounds.

As You Like It

Shakespeare's chief source for *As You Like It* was Thomas Lodge's graceful pastoral romance, *Rosalynde: Euphues' Golden Legacy* (1590). Lodge was indebted in turn to *The Tale of Gamelyn*, a fourteenth-century poem wrongly included by some medieval scribes as "The Cook's Tale" in Chaucer's *Canterbury Tales. Gamelyn* was not printed until 1721, but Lodge clearly had access to a manuscript of

it. Although Shakespeare may not have known *Gamelyn* directly, his play still retains the hearty spirit of this Robin Hood legend. (In later Robin Hood ballads, Gamelyn or Gandelyn is identified with Will Scarlet, a member of Robin Hood's band.)

Even a brief account of *Gamelyn* suggests how greatly the original tale is inspired by Robin Hood legends of outlaws valiantly defying the corrupt social order presided over by the Sheriff and his henchmen. Gamelyn, the youngest of three brothers, is denied his inheritance by his churlish eldest brother John. When Gamelyn demands his rights, John orders his men to beat Gamelyn, but the young man arms himself with a pestle and proves to be a formidable fighter. After defeating the champion wrestler in a local wrestling match (a lower-class sport befitting the social milieu of this story), Gamelyn returns home to find himself locked out by his brother. He kills the porter, flings the man's body down a well, and feasts his companions day and night for a week. John feigns a reconciliation and slyly asks if he can bind Gamelyn hand and foot merely to satisfy an oath he has sworn over the death of the porter. Gamelyn trustingly agrees and is made prisoner. After his bonds have been secretly loosed by Adam the Spencer (the steward), Gamelyn pretends to remain bound until the propitious moment for revenge and escape. The moment arrives during a feast of monks who churlishly refuse to help Gamelyn. With Adam's help, he fells many of them, ties up his brother, and escapes to the woods, where he and Adam are rescued from hunger by a band of merry outlaws. As their chief, Gamelyn becomes a champion of the poor and an enemy of rich churchmen. His brother, now sheriff, brands Gamelyn an outlaw and manages to imprison him, but Gamelyn's second brother, Sir Ote, stands bail for him. On the day of the trial, Gamelyn frees Sir Ote and hangs the Sheriff and the jury. Gamelyn finally obtains his inheritance and becomes chief officer of the King's royal forests. This story is uninfluenced by the pastoral tradition and contains no love plot. Its Robin Hood traditions are very much present, nonetheless, in Shakespeare's contrasting portrayal of a tyrannical court and of a just society in banishment.

Lodge retains the primitive vigor of *Gamelyn* but adds generous infusions of pastoral sentiment in the manner of Sir Philip Sidney's *Arcadia* (1590) and sententious moralizing in the manner of John Lyly's *Euphues* (1578). The pastoralism is presented in conventional terms, with none of the genial self-reflexive satire we find in Shakespeare. Psychological motive is intricate, often more so than in Shakespeare's play. The style is also heavily influenced by Lyly's exquisitely balanced, antithetical, and ornamented prose. For his pastoralism, Lodge was indebted not only to Sidney but also to the ancient pastoral tradition that included the Greek Theocritus and the Roman Virgil, the Italian Sannazaro *(Arcadia),* and the Portuguese Jorge de Montemayor *(Diana).* Pastoralism by Lodge's time had become thoroughly imbued with artificial conventions: abject lovers writing sonnets to their disdainful mistresses, princes and princesses in shepherds' disguise, idealized landscapes, stylized debate as to the relative merits of love and friendship, youth and age, city life and country life, and so on. Some of these conventions were derived also from the vogue of sonneteering pioneered by Francesco Petrarch and can thus be described as the stereotypes of "Petrarchism." Lodge accepts these conventions and gives us typical pastoral lovers even in his hero and heroine, although the elements he derived from *Gamelyn* certainly add a contrasting note of violence and danger.

Lodge's account begins much like that of *Gamelyn*. Saladyne, the envious eldest brother, bribes the champion wrestler to do away with Rosader (Orlando) in the wrestling match. Rosader succeeds instead in killing the wrestler and in winning the heart of Rosalynde, daughter of the banished King Gerismond. When she sends him a jewel, Rosader is not at all at a loss for words; indeed, he composes a Petrarchan sonnet on the spot. The usurping King Torismond (no relation to Gerismond), despite his evil nature, is impressed by Rosader's grace and martial prowess. Rosader returns home with friends, breaks open the door, and feasts his company. The wily Saladyne overwhelms Rosader in his sleep and binds him to a post, but Rosader is untied by Adam and makes havoc among the eldest brother's guests, as in *Gamelyn*. In this case, however, the guests are Saladyne's kindred and allies, all of whom have refused to help Rosader. The Sheriff tries to arrest Rosader and Adam, but they make good their escape to the Forest of Arden in France. They are saved from starvation by the kindly King Gerismond and his exiled followers. Rosalynde and King Torismond's daughter Alinda meanwhile have been banished from court and have taken abode in the forest under the names of Ganymede and Aliena. They befriend old Corydon (Corin) and young Montanus (Silvius), who is hopelessly in love with the haughty Phoebe. "Ganymede" poses as a woman to test Rosader in his wooing, and they are joined in a mock marriage. Saladyne, now repenting of his evil deeds, comes to the forest, is saved by his brother from a lion, and falls in love with Alinda (whom he helps to rescue from ruffians). The denouement is as in Shakespeare, although the triumphant return to society is more complete: King Torismond is slain, Gerismond is restored to his throne, Rosader is named heir-apparent, and all the friends are appropriately rewarded.

Despite Shakespeare's extensive indebtedness to this charming romance, there is a crucial difference: Lodge's pastoral world is never subjected to a wry or satirical exploration. Lodge offers no equivalent for Touchstone, the fool who sees the absurdity of both country and city; Jaques, the malcontent traveler; William and Audrey, the clownishly simple peasants; or Sir Oliver Mar-text, the ridiculous hedge-priest. Nor does Lodge tell of Le Beau, the court butterfly. Hymen is a Shakespearean addition, and the conversion of Duke Frederick by a hermit instead of his being overthrown and killed is a characteristically Shakespearean softening touch. Shakespeare's added characters are virtually all foils to the conventional pastoral vision he found in his source.

Twelfth Night

John Manningham's description of a performance of *Twelfth Night* on February 2, 1602, at the Middle Temple (one of the Inns of Court, where young men studied law in London), compares the play to Plautus' *Menaechmi* and to an Italian play called *Inganni*. The comment offers a helpful hint on sources. The *Menaechmi* had been the chief source for Shakespeare's earlier play, *The Comedy of Errors,* and that farce of mistaken identity clearly resembles *Twelfth Night* in the hilarious mix-ups resulting from the confusion of two look-alike twins. Shakespeare clearly profited from his earlier experimenting with this sort of comedy. *Twelfth Night* is not necessarily directly indebted to the *Menaechmi,* however, for Renaissance Italian comedy offered many imitations of Plautus from which Shakespeare could have taken his *Twelfth Night* plot. These include *Gl'Inganni* (1562) by Nicolò Secchi, another *Gl'Inganni* (1592) by Curzio Gonzaga, and, most important, an anonymous *Gl'Ingannati* (published 1537). This last play was translated into French by Charles Estienne as *Les Abusés* (1543) and adapted into Spanish by Lope de Rueda in *Los Engaños* (1567). A Latin version, *Laelia,* based on the French, was performed at Cambridge in the 1590s but never printed. Obviously, *Gl'Ingannati* was widely known, and Manningham was probably referring to it in his diary. To trace Shakespeare's own reading in this matter is difficult, owing to the large number of versions available to him, but we can note the suggestive points of comparison in each.

Both *Inganni* plays feature a brother and a sister mistaken for one another. In the later play (by Gonzaga), the sister uses the disguise name of "Cesare." In Secchi's *Inganni,* the disguised sister is in love with her master, who is told that a woman the exact age of his supposed page is secretly in love with him. Another play by Secchi, *L'Interesse* (1581), has a comic duel involving a disguised heroine. Of the Italian plays considered here, however, *Gl'Ingannati* is closest to Shakespeare's play. A short prefatory entertainment included with it in most editions features the name Malevolti. In the play itself, the heroine, Lelia, disguises herself as a page in the service of Flaminio, whom she secretly loves, and is sent on embassies to Flaminio's disdainful mistress Isabella. This lady falls in love with "Fabio," as Lelia calls herself. Lelia's father, Virginio, learning of her disguise and resolving to marry her to old Gherardo (Isabella's father), seeks out Lelia but instead mistakenly arrests her long-lost twin brother, Fabrizio, who has just arrived in Modena. Fabrizio is locked up as a madman in Isabella's room, whereupon Isabella takes the opportunity to betroth herself to the person she mistakes for "Fabio." A recognition scene clears up everything and leads to the marriages of Fabrizio to Isabella and Flaminio to Lelia. This story lacks the subplot of Malvolio, Sir Toby, et al. Nor is there a shipwreck.

Matteo Bandello based one of the stories in his *Novelle* (1554) on *Gl'Ingannati,* and this prose version was then translated into French by François de Belleforest in his *Histoires Tragiques* (1579 edition). Shakespeare may well have read both, for he consulted these collections of stories in writing *Much Ado About Nothing.* His most direct source, however, seems to have been the story of "Apollonius and Silla" by Barnabe Riche (an English soldier and fiction writer), in *Riche His Farewell to Military Profession* (1581), which was derived from Belleforest. Riche involves his characters in more serious moral predicaments than Shakespeare allows in his festive comedy. The plot situation is much the same: Silla (the equivalent of Shakespeare's Viola) is washed ashore near Constantinople, where, disguised as "Silvio," she takes service with a duke, Apollonius (Shakespeare's Orsino), and goes on embassies to the wealthy widow Julina (Shakespeare's Olivia), who proceeds at once to fall in love with "Silvio." When Silla's twin brother, the real Silvio, arrives, he is mistaken by Julina for his twin and is invited to a rendezvous, like Shakespeare's Sebastian. The differences at this point are marked, however, for Silvio becomes Julina's lover and leaves her pregnant when he departs the next day on his quest for Silla. Apollonius is understandably furious to learn of "Silvio's" apparent success with Julina and throws his page into prison. Julina is no less distressed when she learns that the supposed father of her child is in actuality a woman. Only Silvio's eventual return to marry Julina resolves these complications. Shakespeare eschews the pregnancy, the desertion, the imprisonment, and all of Riche's stern moralizing about the bestiality of lust that accompanies this lurid tale. Moreover, he adds the plot of Malvolio, for which Riche provides little suggestion. Shakespeare changes the location to Illyria, with its hint of delirium and illusion, and provides an English flavor in the comic scenes that intensifies the festive character of the play.

Shakespeare's reading may also have included the anonymous play *Sir Clyomon and Sir Clamydes* (c. 1570–1583), Sir Philip Sidney's *Arcadia* (1590), and Emmanuel Forde's prose romance *Parismus* (1598), in which one "Violetta" borrows the disguise of a page. Scholars have suggested that the Malvolio plot may reflect an incident at Queen Elizabeth's court in which the Comptroller of the Household, Sir William Knollys, interrupted a noisy late-night party dressed in only his nightshirt and a pair of spectacles, with a copy of the Italian pornographic writer Aretino's work in his hand. A similar confrontation between revelry and sobriety occurred in 1598: Ambrose Willoughby quieted a disturbance after the Queen had gone to bed and was afterward thanked by her for doing his duty. Such incidents were no doubt common, however, and there is no compelling reason to suppose Shakespeare was sketching from current court gossip.

All's Well That Ends Well

Shakespeare's only known source for *All's Well That Ends Well* is the tale of Giglietta of Nerbone from Boccaccio's *Decameron* (c. 1348–1358), as translated into English by William Painter in *The Palace of Pleasure* (1566, 1575). Painter may have based his translation on a French intermediary by Antoine le Maçon, and Shakespeare possibly knew the Italian and French versions, although the English was the most available to him. All three are essentially the same, except for the forms of the proper names. The Helena story is also widely dispersed in folktales.

In Painter's account, Giletta is the daughter of Gerardo of Narbona, physician to the ailing Count of Rossiglione. Giletta falls in love with the Count's son, Beltramo. When the Count dies, Beltramo is "left under the royal custody of the King" and is sent to Paris. Giletta's father dies soon after, and she, refusing many favorable offers of marriage, journeys to Paris and cures the King of a fistula. The King has promised her any husband as her reward but is loath to give her Beltramo. The young man, no less reluctant, goes through with the marriage ceremony but then escapes into Italy before the marriage is consummated. In Italy he joins the Florentines in a military campaign against the Senois (Sienese). His deserted wife, now countess, returns home and governs the domain of Rossiglione with great skill. When she writes to Beltramo, offering to depart if her presence displeases him, Beltramo sets for her the "impossible" demand of obtaining his ring and begetting a son by him. Hereupon she calls together the leaders of her domain and announces her intention of going on a pilgrimage of renunciation. Despite her people's great lamentation, she departs for Florence where she inquires after Beltramo and discovers that he is paying court to a poor gentlewoman (unnamed) who dwells with her mother. Giletta offers to obtain a dowry for this daughter if she will demand the ring from Beltramo and arrange an assignation so that Giletta may secretly take her place in Beltramo's bed. Beltramo reluctantly agrees to give up the cherished ring, and Giletta becomes his lover on not one but numerous occasions. When she is pregnant, she rewards the daughter with a dowry and then remains living in Florence until she is delivered of two sons. Beltramo has meanwhile been called home by his people. Giletta arrives home in time for a great feast, at which she prostrates herself before Beltramo and proves that she has performed the terms of his "impossible" task. Beltramo is persuaded by her constancy and wit to be true to his promise and reclaim her as his wife.

Except for Helena, many of the characters' names in Shakespeare's play are derived from Painter's version. Helena is Giletta in Painter, but her father is Gerardo of Narbona (compare Shakespeare's Gerard de Narbon or Narbonne), and the young man she vainly loves is Beltramo, Count of Rossiglione (i.e., Bertram, Count of Rossillion), who is left after his father's death "under the royal custody of the King" of France. Giletta is no ward and helpless dependent, however, as in Shakespeare; she is well-to-do, is cared for by her kinsfolk after her father's death, and refuses many favorable offers of marriage before journeying to Paris to cure the King of a fistula and claim her reward. Shakespeare's Helena, on the other hand, is not rich and so can serve as an example of innate virtue or "gentleness," in contrast with Bertram's hereditary nobility. Shakespeare enhances the roles of the Countess and Lafew, and makes the King more sympathetic than in Painter to Helena's (or Giletta's) cause: in Painter, the King is reluctant to give Giletta to Beltramo, whereas in Shakespeare the King becomes a spokesman for faith in the miraculous. Other courtiers in Shakespeare's play join the King in approving of Helena, so that, however much Bertram's resistance to an enforced marriage might seem understandable in most circumstances, his refusal of Helena is made to appear willful. Lavatch, the Countess' fool, quizzically expounds questions of moral consequence that are absent in Painter. Conversely, the added character Parolles highlights the callowness and insensitivity of Bertram, and serves as a scapegoat when Bertram belatedly gains a better understanding of himself. At the same time, Shakespeare eschews Painter's easy romantic ending for one that is highly problematic: he does not offer Bertram much opportunity to show a real change of heart toward Helena, as Painter does, and thus places a greater strain on credibility in this comedy of forgiveness. Helena, because she is so far below Bertram in wealth and position, is obliged to be more aggressive than her counterpart in Painter, which raises troublesome issues of female assertiveness. She does not enjoy Giletta's prerogative of governing Rossiglione in her husband's absence and winning such love from her advisers and subjects that they all lament her public resolution to go on a pilgrimage; Helena is thrown more on her own resources and so is at once more self-reliant and self-asserting.

Shakespeare also gives his play a unity of construction and an economy of time not found in the sources. Characters such as the King and Diana are not discarded once their primary role has been discharged but are brought importantly into the denouement. As in his use of other Italianate fictional sources, Shakespeare compresses time: for example, Helena vows to cure the King in two days rather than eight (as in Painter), and Helena sleeps with Bertram once rather than often. No convincing source has been found for the comic exposure of Parolles.

Measure for Measure

Stories about corrupt magistrates are ancient and universal, but Shakespeare's particular story in *Measure for Measure* seems to go back to an actual incident in the sixteenth-century Italian court of Don Ferdinando de Gonzaga. A Hungarian student named Joseph Macarius, writing from Vienna, tells about an Italian citizen accused of murder whose wife submitted to the embraces of the magistrate in hopes of saving her husband. When the magistrate executed her husband despite her having fulfilled her bargain, she appealed to the Duke, who ordered the magistrate to give her a dowry and marry her. Thereafter, the Duke ordered the magistrate to be executed. This incident seems to have inspired a Senecan drama by Claude Rouillet called *Phila-nira* (1556), a French translation of this play (1563), a novella in the *Hecatommithi* of G. B. Giraldi Cinthio (1565), and a play by Cinthio called *Epitia* (posthumously published in 1583). Shakespeare may have known both the prose and the dramatic versions by Cinthio.

In Cinthio's story, the wise Emperor Maximian appoints his friend Juriste to govern Innsbruck, warning him to rule justly or expect no mercy from the Emperor. Juriste rules long and well, to the satisfaction of his master and the people of Innsbruck. When a young man named Vico is brought before him for ravishing a virgin, Juriste assigns the mandatory sentence of death. Vico's sister, Epitia, an extraordinarily beautiful virgin of eighteen, pleads for Vico's life, urging that his deed was one of passion and that he stands ready to marry the girl he forced. The judge, secretly inflamed with lust for Epitia, promises to consider the matter carefully. She reports this seemingly encouraging news to Vico, who urges her to persevere. When, however, the judge proposes to take her chastity in return for her brother's life, Epitia is mortified and refuses unless Juriste will marry her. During another interim in these negotiations, Vico begs his sister to save his life at any cost. She then submits to Juriste on the condition that he will both marry her and spare Vico. Next morning, however, the jailer brings her the body of her decapitated brother. She lays her complaint before the Emperor, who confronts Juriste with his guilt. Conscience-stricken, Juriste confesses and begs for mercy. At first, Epitia demands strict justice, but when the Emperor compels Juriste to marry her and then be beheaded, she reveals "her natural kindness" and begs successfully for the life of her wronger. There are several important differences between this account and Shakespeare's play: Vico is actually killed, unlike Claudio, and Epitia sleeps with Juriste and then is married to him. No equivalent to Mariana appears, or to Lucio, Pompey, Mistress Overdone, Elbow, and other characters in the comic scenes of Shakespeare's play. No duke oversees the career of Juriste and ensures that no fatal wrong will occur.

Shakespeare may also have consulted Cinthio's play *Epitia,* but his chief source was George Whetstone's two-part play *Promos and Cassandra* (1578) and a novella on the same subject. In the English play, the corrupt judge is Promos, administrator of the city of Julio under the King of Hungary. The law forbidding adultery has lain in abeyance for some years when a young gentleman named Andrugio is arrested and condemned for "incontinency." His sister Cassandra, like Epitia in Cinthio's play, lays down her precious chastity to Promos in response to her brother's piteous entreaties. Promos gives his assurance that he will marry her and save Andrugio's life. When Promos instead treacherously orders the execution of Andrugio, the jailer secretly substitutes the head of a felon, newly executed and so mutilated as to be unrecognizable even by Cassandra. (This rescue is seen as an intervention "by the providence of God.") The King sentences Promos, just as the Emperor sentences Juriste in Cinthio's play, but in Whetstone's play the King refuses Cassandra's pleas for the life of her new husband until Andrugio reveals himself to be still alive and offers to die for Promos. The King forgives Andrugio on condition that he marry Polina, whom he has wronged. The play also features a courtesan named Lamia and her man, Rosko, who ingratiate themselves with the corrupt officer (Phallax) in charge of investigating their case. Phallax is ultimately caught and dismissed from office while Lamia is publicly humiliated.

Whetstone wrote a prose novella of this same story in the *Heptameron of Civil Discourses* (1582). Shakespeare appears to have consulted it as well as the play, for the prose version mentions the names of Isabella (as the narrator of the story) and Crassus (compare *Measure for Measure,* 4.5.8), and the King's awarding of measure for measure in his sentencing of Promos—"You shall be measured with the grace you bestowed on Andrugio"—may have given Shakespeare an idea for the title of his play. Shakespeare was also indebted for a few details to a version in Thomas Lupton's *Too Good to Be True* (1581).

Even though Shakespeare's play is closely related to Whetstone's play and novella, Shakespeare has changed much. He adds the motif of the Duke's mysterious disguise. (A not very compelling analogue to this motif occurs in Sir Thomas Elyot's *The Image of Governance,* 1541.) Shakespeare introduces the use of the bed trick, found also in his presumably earlier play *All's Well That Ends Well.* Most important, Shakespeare stresses the moral and legal complexity of his story. Isabella is about to renounce the world by entering a convent. By contrast, Lucio, a Shakespearean addition, is an engaging cynic, hedonist,

and slanderer. Claudio, although guilty of fornication, is only technically in violation of the laws against sexual license. Isabella does not surrender her chastity. Her breakdown in the scene with Claudio intensifies her emotional crisis and renders all the more triumphant her final ability to forgive Angelo. Angelo himself is made puritanical in temperament and is spared the actual consequences of his worst intentions so that he can be worthy of being forgiven. Isabella need not marry Angelo, since he has not actually seduced her; she is thus free to marry the Duke. No felon need be executed in Claudio's stead, for Providence provides a natural death in the prison. In the subplot, going well beyond the merest hints in Whetstone, Pompey is a brilliantly original innovation, Elbow a characteristically Shakespearean clown modeled on the earlier Dogberry of *Much Ado About Nothing,* and Escalus a significant spokesman for a moderate and practical course of equity in the law.

Troilus and Cressida

Shakespeare had access to Homer for information about the Trojan War, since George Chapman's translation of *Seven Books of the Iliads of Homer* had appeared in 1598, and earlier English translations of the entire *Iliad* were also available. Shakespeare ends his play with the death of Hector, as do Homer and some post-Homeric historians of the war, and portrays Achilles as a figure in tragic conflict with his sense of pride, as did Homer. Thersites and Nestor are based ultimately on the *Iliad.* Ajax's ludicrous boastfulness may owe something to Homer's Ajax Telamon, as well as to Ovid's account of the quarrel between Ulysses and Ajax over Achilles' armor (*Metamorphoses,* 12–13). Yet, for Shakespeare, and for most Englishmen of his time, the chief sources of information about the Trojan War were medieval romances. These were all pro-Trojan in their bias, since Englishmen traced their own mythic history to the lineage of Aeneas and tended to look on Homer as suspiciously pro-Greek. Medieval European culture generally was far more oriented to Roman than to Greek civilization; Greek texts went almost unread. In these circumstances, a pro-Trojan account of the war emerged and grew to considerable proportions, in which non-Homeric material became increasingly important.

The central work dealing with this expanded account of the war was Benoît de Sainte-Maure's *Roman de Troie* (c. 1160), a romance freely based on earlier accounts of two supposed eyewitnesses named Dictys the Cretan and Dares the Phrygian. Benoît not only narrates the war from Troy's point of view but introduces the love story of Troilus, "Breseida," and Diomedes. Benoît found a hint for this story in the *Iliad,* in which two Trojan maidens named Chryseis and Briseis are captured and given to Agamemnon and Achilles, respectively. When Chryseis' father calls down a plague on the Greeks for refusing to return Chryseis, Agamemnon reluctantly gives her up but then seizes Briseis from Achilles, thereby precipitating Achilles' angry retirement to his tent and all that disastrously follows. Benoît freely transforms this situation into the rivalry of Troilus and Diomed, who appear in Homer but in entirely different roles.

Benoît's *Roman de Troie* became the inspiration for subsequent medieval accounts of the Trojan War. Guido delle Colonne translated Benoît in his *Historia Troiana* (completed 1287). Giovanni Boccaccio based his *Il Filostrato* (c. 1338) on Guido and Benoît but made significant alterations: the love story became the focus of attention, and Pandarus assumed the important role of go-between. (In Homer, Pandarus is a fierce warrior.) Geoffrey Chaucer based his *Troilus and Criseyde* (c. 1385–1386) on Boccaccio, giving still greater attention to the states of mind of the two lovers and endowing Pandarus with a humorous disposition. Shakespeare certainly knew Chaucer's masterpiece. He also consulted, however, at least two other medieval accounts of the war: John Lydgate's *The History, Siege, and Destruction of Troy* (first printed 1513), based on Guido and Chaucer and known also as the *Troy Book,* and William Caxton's *The Recuyell of the Histories of Troy* (printed 1474, the first book printed in English), a translation from the French of Raoul Lefevre, who had followed Guido rather closely. In Caxton, for example, Shakespeare found materials for the Trojan debate in 2.2 and for Hector's visit to the Greek camp (4.5). In addition, Shakespeare was certainly familiar with the degeneration of Cressida's character since the time of Chaucer, as reflected for example in Robert Henryson's *The Testament of Cresseid* (published 1532), in which Cressida is punished for her faithlessness by leprosy and poverty.

Shakespeare pays a good deal more attention to the war than does Chaucer and portrays the lovers as caught in a conflict beyond their control. Shakespeare's Cressida is more sardonic and experienced in the ways of the world than is Chaucer's heroine, even though Chaucer's Criseyde is a widow and Shakespeare's Cressida is unmarried. The subtle and elaborate code of courtly love evoked by Chaucer has almost completely disappeared in Shakespeare's work, leaving in its wake a more dispiriting and cynical impression. Shakespeare's Troilus is still a faithful and earnest lover, as in Chaucer, but betrayed by his own chauvinistic ideals about honor and patriotism in a way that Chaucer's Troilus is not. Pandarus is more leering, giddy, vapid, and coarse than his Chaucerian counterpart. Diomedes is also changed for the worse, being more hard and cynical.

Among the non-Chaucerian characters, Achilles is made to appear more guilty and brutal than in Shakespeare's sources: Achilles orders his Myrmidons (i.e., his soldiers) to murder the unarmed Hector, even though Hector had previously spared Achilles in battle. Lydgate and Caxton report that Achilles' Myrmidons kill Troilus, not Hector (in Caxton, Achilles cuts off Troilus' head and then drags Troilus' body behind his horse), whereas in Homer Achilles kills Hector in battle and only then do his Myrmidons desecrate the body. Shakespeare refuses to glamorize the war, just as he refuses to glamorize the love story. He also compresses time, as he did with so many of his sources. The play begins only a short time before Cressida surrenders to Troilus; she is transferred to the Greeks immediately after she and Troilus become lovers; her surrender to Diomedes follows quickly after her transfer. This telescoping provides not only dramatic unity but also a sense of sudden and violent change.

Other plays on Troilus and Cressida are known to have existed in Shakespeare's time, such as a "new" play acted by the Admiral's men, an acting company, in 1596 and another by Thomas Dekker and Henry Chettle in 1599. Shakespeare may have known and even written in response to such productions by rival theatrical companies, but today nothing is known about these lost plays.

The Henry the Sixth Plays

The chief source for Shakespeare's conception of the entire *Henry VI* trilogy is Edward Hall's *The Union of the Two Noble and Illustre Families of Lancaster and York* (1542), a work written to glorify the Tudor monarchs by demonstrating how their lineage reconciled the fatally warring factions of Lancaster and York. Shakespeare may actually have done much of his reading for historical particulars in the second edition of Raphael Holinshed's *The Chronicles of England, Scotland, and Ireland* (1587), which included much of Hall's material. He may also have used John Foxe's *Acts and Monuments of Martyrs* (1583 edition), and still other sources. Richard Grafton's *Chronicle* (1568) plagiarized so heavily from Hall that one cannot always be sure which of the two Shakespeare may have consulted. In any event, Hall's interpretation provided an overview, although Shakespeare carefully distances himself from the Tudor apologetics and providential view of history we find in Hall.

To intensify Hall's theme of the horrors of civil dissension, Shakespeare takes considerable liberties with the chronicles. He frequently disregards chronology, telescopes events of many years into a single sequence, invents scenes and characters, and transfers details from one historical scene to another. The artistic unity of each play is his overriding consideration, not historical accuracy.

In *1 Henry VI,* for example, Shakespeare shows the English losing Orleans to the French and then retaking the city (1.5–2.1). In fact, Orleans was never retaken once it had fallen. Shakespeare has transferred events from the recapture of Le Mans to his partly invented account of Orleans. Talbot's visit to the Countess of Auvergne (2.3) is fictitious. The scene in the Temple Garden when the leaders of Lancaster and York pluck red and white roses (2.4) is fictitious in a different sense: antagonisms between the two factions certainly did exist, but not in the allegorically schematized fashion here pictured. In 3.2 Shakespeare shows us Rouen lost and recaptured in a day, whereas, in fact, the city was (like Orleans) never recovered. Shakespeare's intention is to suggest that France is lost through England's political divisions at home, not through any failure on the part of Lord Talbot. Shakespeare exalts Talbot's might and chivalry (hence the scene with the Countess of Auvergne), and contrastingly overstates the cowardice of Falstaff (called Falstolfe in Holinshed and Fastolfe in some other historical sources). Joan la Pucelle is another exaggeratedly evil foil to Talbot; Shakespeare combines her worst traits from Hall and Holinshed. The play covers the events of about three decades. When Henry V died in 1422, his son was less than one year old; by the time of Talbot's fall in 1453, the King was over thirty.

In *2 Henry VI*, Shakespeare accentuates the threat of popular unrest in a number of ways. He conflates reports of the Jack Cade rebellion in 1450 with those of the Peasants' Revolt in 1381, using the most unattractive features of each. Shakespeare ridicules the peasants' utopian aims and omits a list of sympathetic demands. Similarly, the dispute between the Armorer and his apprentice (1.3) is put into a context of courtly politics that we do not find in the chronicles. Simpcox's name and his lameness (2.1) are added to stress the farcical nature of this "miracle." (Shakespeare could have found this account in Thomas More's *Dialogue . . . of the Veneration and Worship of Images*, 1529, or in Foxe's *Acts and Monuments*.) Although the indictment of Suffolk (3.2) was historically an act of the House of Commons, Shakespeare portrays it as a near riot in which the people hammer at the King's very door with their strident demands. In every way, *2 Henry VI* stresses the fickleness, inhumanity, and ignorance of men caught up in a mob. Despite all this, however, the play alters its sources less than does *1 Henry VI*. And, for all its disapproval of mob unrest, Shakespeare's play is considerably less hostile toward the populace than an anonymous contemporary play, *The Life and Death of Jack Straw* (1590–1593).

3 Henry VI similarly alters its sources less than does *1 Henry VI*. The alterations are chiefly those of telescoping and highlighting for emphasis. The ritual killings, which form an integral part of the spectacle in *3 Henry VI*, are cleverly adapted or rearranged from chronicle accounts. Concerning the death of the Duke of York (1.4), for example, Hall reports merely that York died fighting manfully, whereas Holinshed tells us that the remorseless Clifford caused the dead York's head to be struck off "and set on it a crown of paper, fixed it on a pole, and presented it to the Queen." Shakespeare's version goes still further:

Queen Margaret mocks York while he is still alive by putting a paper crown on his head. The ritual killing of the Lancastrian Prince Edward (5.5) is similarly enhanced. Throughout, Shakespeare's purpose is to intensify the scourgelike role of the Yorkist Edward IV and his brethren. Among the three, Richard of Gloucester is the most ominous. Shakespeare introduces crookbacked Richard into the fighting (2.1) when historically this man was abroad.

According to Andrew Cairncross' Arden edition, *3 Henry VI* contains occasional allusions to Edmund Spenser's *The Faerie Queene* (see 2.1.9 ff. and *The Faerie Queene*, 1.5.2), to *A Mirror for Magistrates* (especially in the sections "Richard, Duke of York" and "King Henry the Sixth"), and to Arthur Brooke's *The Tragical History of Romeus and Juliet* (see 5.4.1–33 and *Romeus* 2.1359–1377). David Riggs argues (*Shakespeare's Heroical Histories: "Henry VI" and Its Literary Tradition*, 1971) that Christopher Marlowe's *Tamburlaine* (1587–1588) was an important source for Shakespeare's *Henry VI* plays and that behind *Tamburlaine* lay a classical rhetorical tradition of praise for heroism. Shakespeare would have thoroughly absorbed this tradition through the Tudor grammar-school curriculum.

Richard the Third

Richard the Third, like the *Henry VI* series, is based on Edward Hall's *The Union of the Two Noble and Illustre Families of Lancaster and York* (1542) and on the 1587 edition of Raphael Holinshed's *The Chronicles of England, Scotland, and Ireland*. Both of these historical compilations were deeply indebted for their hostile view of Richard III to Polydore Vergil and Thomas More. Vergil, a papal tax collector who came to England in 1501, spent many years under the patronage of Henry VII writing in Latin his *Anglica Historia* (first published in Basel, 1534). This work portrayed Richard negatively in order to glorify the claim of the Tudor monarch who had deposed Richard in 1485. Vergil argued that England's suffering was a divinely sent scourge, intended to cleanse England of rebelliousness and to prepare the English people for the providential reward of Tudor rule.

Thomas More's *The History of King Richard III*, left unfinished in 1513, was published in two slightly different versions: one in English (1557) and one in Latin (1566). Thomas More obtained much information and possibly an early draft of his narrative from Cardinal Morton, in whose household More lived as a youth. Morton had figured in the struggles of Richard III's reign—he was the Bishop of Ely from whom Richard requested the strawberries (3.4.32–33)—and had become a bitter enemy of the Yorkist king. Thomas More's own purpose in writing the life of Richard III was surely not to glorify Henry VII, with whom More had a strained relationship, but to characterize the evil of political opportunism. His portrait of Richard becomes that of the generic tyrant, behaving as such tyrants behaved in the various literary models from Renaissance Italy with which More was doubtless familiar. The result was, in any case, one-sided. The historical Richard seems to have been no worse than many another late medieval ruler and had indeed some admirable ideas on efficiency in government. More's blackened portrait, because it served the purposes of the Tudor state, became part of the legend and was available to Shakespeare in many versions. Holinshed incorporated verbatim a good deal of More's account.

Apart from Hall's and Holinshed's chronicles, those of Robert Fabyan (first published in 1516) and the *Annals* of John Stow (1580, 1592) may have provided Shakespeare with further details. Another possible source is *A Mirror for Magistrates* (first published in 1559), in which, for example, in "The Complaint of George, Duke of Clarence," we find the riddling prophecy about the letter *G* (see 1.1.39). A second edition of the *Mirror* (1563) contains the Complaints of Edward IV, Anthony Woodville (Lord Rivers), Hastings, Buckingham, Shore's wife, and others. Shakespeare's particular indebtedness to the *Mirror* is not great, though he certainly was familiar with it. The same is probably true of the Latin tragedy *Richardus Tertius* by Thomas Legge (1579) at Cambridge, which contains an interesting scene of Richard's wooing of the Lady Anne not reported in the chronicles. The anonymous *The True Tragedy of Richard III* (published 1594, written c. 1590–1592) may have been useful in its fusing of Senecan revenge motifs with English history and in its focus on the single figure of Richard. The Richard of this anonymous play is an overreacher, a worshiper of Fortune who meets his nemesis in the devoutly Christian Earl of Richmond. Opinion is divided as to whether Shakespeare actually used the play, chiefly because by 1590 he could have found the legend of Richard III set forth in so many works.

King John

To understand Shakespeare's use of sources in *King John*, we must first understand the play's relationship to the anonymous play *The Troublesome Reign of King John*, published in 1591. According to E. A. J. Honigmann (in his Arden edition of *King John*, 1954), *Troublesome Reign* is a bad Quarto pirated from Shakespeare's text rather than a source for it. *Troublesome Reign* does indeed show features of a bad Quarto. Moreover, a 1611 reprint of this play is attributed to "W. Sh." and another in 1622 to "W. Shakespeare." The Folio editors did not register *King John* for publication in 1623, as though assuming it had already been published in some form. Nevertheless, most scholars still hold to the view that *Troublesome Reign* is a source. (See "Date and Text.") Its early date, by 1591, would mean a still earlier date for a play on which it was based.

Honigmann's argument for dating *King John* in 1590 has not won general acceptance.

If, on the other hand, we accept the argument that Shakespeare was substantially rewriting an earlier play on King John, the pattern of his indebtedness becomes clear on two points: (1) *Troublesome Reign* was his main, though not his only, source, and (2) Shakespeare consciously toned down the earlier play's anti-Catholic excesses and scurrilous humor. His characters are more thoughtful and complex; the paradoxes of kingship, more disturbing. Shakespeare's alteration of a crude and chauvinistic source play into a subtle exploration of political rule anticipates his similar transformation of the irrepressible *Famous Victories of Henry V* (c. 1586–1587) into the *Henry IV* plays and *Henry V*.

Briefly, some differences between *Troublesome Reign* and *King John* are as follows. In *Troublesome Reign*, John is a hero and a martyr for his defiance of Rome. His claim to the English throne is unquestioned. The barons who rise against him are loyal to Rome. Vice is rampant in monasteries and other ecclesiastical institutions. An abbot is discovered to be hiding a nun in his treasure chest. John is poisoned by a monk who is in league with the abbot and who receives absolution for his deed. The Bastard, John's loyal supporter, is an invincible foe of ecclesiastical corruption and treason against the state. In Shakespeare, on the other hand, John's claim to the throne is dynastically questionable, and his treatment of his nephew Arthur is reprehensible. The barons' opposition to him is prompted by a genuine moral revulsion. Although they learn belatedly that rebellion is more destructive than the evil it seeks to correct, since rebellion provides a fatal opportunity for foreign opportunists such as the French Dauphin, the barons are not simply tools of the Papacy. The Bastard struggles, too, with his conscience over John's treatment of Arthur. The Church is often guilty of political duplicity, as are virtually all the kings and political leaders in the play, but the Church shows no signs of moral decadence. John is poisoned by a monk, but without evidence of conspiracy.

These contrasting estimates of King John reflect the two views of him held concurrently in Tudor England. One, the older and more critical, is that of medieval historians generally and Polydore Vergil in particular. The other, a more favorable estimate, is essentially a Protestant defense of John, a rewriting of history in order to view him (despite his failures) as a martyr of Catholic oppression and hence a forerunner of the Reformation. William Tyndale began this revisionist view of John in his *The Obedience of a Christian Man* (1528). The case was vividly expounded by John Bale in his *King Johan*, a play begun before 1536 and rewritten in 1538 and 1561. Whether the author of *Troublesome Reign*, or Shakespeare, consulted Bale is uncertain, but the author of *Troublesome Reign* was certainly heir to the Protestant tradition. A major repository of the Protestant view, in any event, was John Foxe's *Acts and Monuments* (1583 edition), known as the *Book of Martyrs;* more copies of this work were to be found in English households than of any other book except the Bible, and its influence on Shakespeare must have been considerable. Richard Grafton and Raphael Holinshed took the Protestant line in their chronicles and thus passed on the tradition to *Troublesome Reign.*

Shakespeare's play, though based primarily for its materials on *Troublesome Reign,* allows the expression of the more critical attitude toward John of the older non-Protestant line. Honigmann argues that Shakespeare also consulted the *Historia Maior* of Matthew Paris (published 1571) and perhaps the Latin manuscript *Wakefield Chronicle,* but scholarly opinion on this point is divided.

Richard the Second

Shakespeare's primary source for *Richard the Second* was the 1587 edition of Raphael Holinshed's *Chronicles* covering the years 1398 to 1400. As in his earlier *Henry VI* plays and *Richard III,* Shakespeare departs from historical accuracy in the interests of artistic design. Queen Isabel's part is almost wholly invented, for historically she was a child of eleven at the time the events in this play occurred. Her "Garden Scene" (3.4) is a fine piece of invention, bringing together images of order and disorder that are found in the rest of the play. The Duchess of York's role is entirely original; Holinshed reports the scene in which York's son Aumerle (the Earl of Rutland) rides to the new King and begs for mercy while his father simultaneously denounces him as a traitor, but the Duchess is never mentioned. Shakespeare has added the poignant conflict between husband and wife. Northumberland's role as conspirator against Richard and as hatchet man for Bolingbroke is greatly enlarged; for example, Holinshed never names the persons who engage in the original plotting against Richard. Shakespeare's Bolingbroke returns to England on his own initiative, whereas in Holinshed he does so at the barons' invitation, a change that accentuates the puzzle of Bolingbroke's motive. Another invention is the meeting between John of Gaunt and the Duchess of Gloucester (1.2). In fact, most of Gaunt's character and behavior has no basis in Holinshed at all. Shakespeare creates him to fill the role of thoughtfully conservative statesman, agonized by his son's banishment but doggedly obedient to his monarch. Finally, and most important, Shakespeare has greatly enlarged the role and the poetic nature of King Richard, especially in the final two acts.

Many of these alterations are Shakespeare's own; others derive from his reading in other sources. Samuel Daniel's *The First Four Books of the Civil Wars* (1595) may have

had an important influence. Although we cannot discount the possibility that Shakespeare's play may have been written first, the consensus today is that he knew Daniel's poem. It gave him the idea of the Queen's maturity and grief (although not the Garden Scene), and the final meeting of King and Queen. Daniel's Hotspur is unhistorically a young man, as in 2.3 of Shakespeare's play. Like Shakespeare, Daniel sees York as a man of "a mild temperateness." Daniel's Richard and Bolingbroke ride together into London, not separately as in Holinshed. In Daniel's poem, Bolingbroke's indirect manner of insinuating his desire for Richard's death ("And wished that some would so his life esteem / As rid him of these fears wherein he stood") is verbally close to Shakespeare's depiction of this scene. Richard's final soliloquies in these two works show an unmistakable similarity to one another.

Richard II's reign was a controversial subject in the 1590s and produced other plays of varying political coloration that Shakespeare must have known. *The Life and Death of Jack Straw* (anonymous, 1590–1593) distorts history in its friendly portrayal of Richard's role in the Peasants' Revolt of 1381 and whitewashes government policy. In contrast, the anonymous play *Thomas of Woodstock,* sometimes known as *1 Richard II* (1591–1595), is almost a call for open rebellion against tyranny. Many verbal similarities link this latter play with Shakespeare's *Richard II,* and, although scholars have difficulty in determining which was written first, the wary consensus is that Shakespeare borrowed from *Woodstock.* Such a hypothesis would explain some of the mysterious references to Woodstock's death in the first act of *Richard II,* since the anonymous play deals with historical events preceding those of Shakespeare's play. Shakespeare's debt to *Jack Straw,* on the other hand, is slight, even though he probably knew the play. Christopher Marlowe's *Edward II* (c. 1592), although dealing with another reign, probably taught Shakespeare much about constructing a play in which a weak king gains sympathy in his suffering, while his successor becomes morally tainted by the act of deposition.

Other sources have been proposed—so many, in fact, that Shakespeare's task of writing the play has been compared to that of a historical researcher. More probably he assimilated his wide and varied reading without any formal program of study. He had certainly read Edward Hall's *Union of the Two Noble and Illustre Families of Lancaster and York* (1542), a chief source for his earlier history plays, but in *Richard II* he seems to have recalled little more than its overall thematic pattern. Shakespeare must have known the Complaints of Mowbray and Richard in *A Mirror for Magistrates,* but the verbal echoes are slight in this case. The same is essentially true of *The Chronicles of England* by Jean Froissart, translated by Lord Berners (1525), and two French eyewitness accounts available to Shakespeare only in manuscript: the anonymous

Chronique de la Traïson et Mort de Richard Deux Roi d'Angleterre and Jean Créton's *Histoire du Roi d'Angleterre Richard*. The Froissart *Chronicles* perhaps gave some hints for Gaunt's refusal to avenge Gloucester's death, for Richard's insensitivity at Gaunt's death, and for Northumberland's role as conspirator. The *Traïson* is notably sympathetic to Richard in his decline, although Shakespeare might also have found this sympathy in Daniel's *Civil Wars*.

Shakespeare's second series of English history plays (*Richard II, 1* and *2 Henry IV, Henry V*) is even freer of the Tudor providential view of history than his first. The second series does not lead forward by any direct link to the reign of the Tudors, as does the first. Henry A. Kelly has shown (*Divine Providence in the England of Shakespeare's Histories,* 1970) that Shakespeare does not follow a single "Tudor myth" but allows spokesmen for both Richard II and his opponents to repeat arguments found in the various chronicles. This practice is especially evident in *Richard II,* in which some spokesmen eloquently warn of the disasters that will follow Bolingbroke's assumption of the throne, while other spokesmen are sympathetic to Bolingbroke's takeover as a political necessity.

Henry the Fourth, Part I

Shakespeare's chief historical source for *1 Henry IV* was the 1587 edition of Raphael Holinshed's *Chronicles,* but he also took some important ideas from Samuel Daniel's *The First Four Books of the Civil Wars* (1595). Following Daniel, Shakespeare readjusts the age of Hotspur (who was historically older than Henry IV) to match that of Prince Hal. Daniel's Hotspur is, like Shakespeare's, dauntless and stubborn, a turbulent yet noble spirit. The theme of a nemesis of rebellion afflicting Henry IV for his usurpation, only touched upon in Shakespeare's play, owes something to Daniel's presentation, although the idea of nemesis is to be found also in Holinshed. Both Holinshed and Daniel err in confusing the Edmund Mortimer whom Glendower captured with his nephew Edmund Mortimer, claimant to the throne; Shakespeare perpetuates this error. Hal's killing of Hotspur is unhistorical, since both Holinshed and Daniel report only that Hal bravely helped rescue his father from attack and that Hotspur was killed in the melee. Daniel does give prominence to Prince Henry in the battle, however, and implies that he and Hotspur will meet face-to-face. Shakespeare invents the scenes in which we see Mortimer as a devoted husband and Hotspur as a fond combatant in wit with his wife Kate; Holinshed merely informs us that these two men were married. Shakespeare greatly expands Glendower's fascination with magic and poetry, changing him from a ruthless barbarian (in Holinshed) into a cranky but charismatic Welshman. Hotspur, despite hints from Daniel and Holinshed, is chiefly Shakespeare's creation.

The most impressive transformations are those of Hal and Falstaff. Shakespeare knew many legends of Hal's wild youth: some from John Stow's *The Chronicles of England* (1580) and *The Annals of England* (1592); others from oral tradition. Many of these stories were also available in Holinshed. Shakespeare's readiest source, however, was a rowdy and chauvinistic play called *The Famous Victories of Henry the Fifth,* registered 1594 but usually ascribed to Richard Tarlton or Samuel Rowley around 1587 or 1588. This play covers all the events of the *Henry IV* plays and *Henry V* in one chaotic sequence. Prince Hal has three companions, Sir John Oldcastle, Tom, and Ned (cf. Ned Poins), in whose company he robs the King's receivers of 1,000 pounds, visits the old tavern in Eastcheap, vexes his father, and strikes the Lord Chief Justice. A crucial difference is that this Hal is truly unregenerate. He not only chases after women and robs, but encourages his companions to look forward to unrestricted license when he is King. Hal seems consciously to desire his father's death. Yet he does reform and banishes his companions beyond a ten-mile limit with a promise to assist them if they amend their conduct. Although Hal's reform is crude and sudden, his popularity aids him when he goes to war against the French. He is followed by a comic crew of London artisans and thieves, who prove invincible against the effete enemy.

Shakespeare owes much to this unsophisticated, vibrant account of Hal's riotous youth, but he has transformed it to his own use. He limits himself in *1 Henry IV* to the action leading up to the Battle of Shrewsbury in order to focus on the coming of age of Prince Henry and the pairing and contrasting of Hotspur, Falstaff, and King Henry IV as alternative models for Hal's behavior. He invents unforgettable comic characters, such as Mistress Quickly, Francis, and Bardolph. Most of all, Shakespeare's portrayal of Falstaff is essentially his own. Sir John Oldcastle of the anonymous play is a minor character, not Hal's closest companion. Falstaff owes something to the tradition of the guileful and inventive Vice of the Tudor morality play (especially when Falstaff is called jestingly "that reverend Vice, that gray Iniquity," 2.4.448), but the influence of the morality play is general rather than specific. To label Falstaff a "Vice" is to reduce him to comic tempter and villain. Falstaff is in part an allowed fool, a parasite, and a *miles gloriosus* or braggart soldier, but he transcends all these conventionalized types with his own unique vitality.

1 Henry IV suggests some acquaintance with the anonymous play *Thomas of Woodstock* (c. 1591–1595), which Shakespeare may also have used for *Richard II,* and with the Complaints of Owen Glendower and Northumberland in *A Mirror for Magistrates* (1559). In neither case is the debt extensive. More suggestive as possible sources are events and social conditions in Shakespeare's England: the Northern Rebellion of 1569 against Queen Elizabeth's government, abuses of military authority by unscrupulous officers, the dangerous state of the highways, the raucous vitality of tavern life in Eastcheap, and the like.

Henry the Fourth, Part II

As in the case of *1 Henry IV,* Shakespeare's chief historical source for *2 Henry IV* is the 1587 edition of Raphael Holinshed's *Chronicles.* Samuel Daniel's *Civil Wars* provides less pertinent material here than for *1 Henry IV,* so that Shakespeare is particularly indebted to Holinshed for historical information about the rebels' grievances, negotiations with the rebel leaders, King Henry IV's illness and death, and the Prince's succession to the throne. Changes are nonetheless prominent and telling. Shakespeare condenses time, giving an impression of failing health on the part of King Henry IV almost immediately after Shrewsbury, whereas historically the King reigned vigorously for ten years after that battle. The Earl of Northumberland is presented as more "crafty-sick" than in Holinshed, and Prince John, too, is shown in a disagreeable light by his cold-blooded handling of negotiations that in Holinshed are the responsibility of the Earl of Westmorland; Shakespeare thus tarnishes the integrity of both sides, accentuating (as he does also in the Induction spoken by Rumor) a mood of cynicism and world-weariness. The theme of nemesis for Henry IV's usurpation is touched upon in *2 Henry IV,* as in Daniel, and Henry is accordingly plagued by sleeplessness and mournful reflection.

Like Shakespeare's first play about Prince Hal, *2 Henry IV* makes extensive use of legends of Hal's wild youth. Some are from John Stow's *Chronicles of England* (1588) and *Annals of England* (1592). Sir Thomas Elyot's *The Governor* (1531) is the ultimate source of an account of Hal's boxing the ear of the Lord Chief Justice. Shakespeare evidently knew *The Governor* firsthand, though he could also have found the story reproduced almost verbatim in Stow; by the 1590s, it was widely circulated. Shakespeare certainly used the anonymous play (usually attributed to Richard Tarlton or Samuel Rowley) called *The Famous Victories of Henry the Fifth,* usually dated around 1587–1588. He had already used parts of this play for *1 Henry IV.* In *Famous Victories,* Shakespeare found a dramatization of the famous blow to the Lord Chief Justice's ear, interpreted there as a blow for freedom and against authority. He found also a vivid account of Hal's entry into his father's death chamber and the final reconciliation of father and son, followed by the coronation and the young King's rejection of his disreputable companions, Sir John Oldcastle, Tom, and Ned; they are banished beyond a ten-mile limit, though the new King will assist them if they behave. The anonymous play then goes on to recount King Henry's successful campaign against the French, as dramatized in *Henry V.*

Shakespeare's changes are as significant as his extensive borrowings. He mutes the parricidal suggestions of Hal's interview with his dying father; in the anonymous play, Hal can hardly wait to see his father in the grave. Shakespeare greatly expands the tavern scenes, with an added emphasis on Falstaff's age and dissipation; new characters, such as Pistol and Doll Tearsheet, with their rowdiness and colorful vituperation, surround Falstaff with signs of his increasing isolation from Hal. The venal country justices, Shallow and Silence, have no counterparts in *Famous Victories,* though that play does show a scene of farcical recruitment. Most of all, Shakespeare has immeasurably added to the humor and pathos of his chief comic character. Sir John Oldcastle of the anonymous play is a minor figure whose banishment at King Henry V's coronation is simply an appropriate gesture of the new King's reform. The characterization of Falstaff owes something to many traditional stage types, including the Vice of the morality play and the cowardly braggart soldier of classical comedy, but the richness and complexity are Shakespeare's own.

Henry the Fifth

Shakespeare's principal historical source for *Henry V,* as for *Richard II* and the *Henry IV* plays, was the 1587 edition of Raphael Holinshed's *Chronicles.* Holinshed's account of Henry V, however, depended so heavily on Edward Hall's *The Union of the Two Noble and Illustre Families of Lancaster and York* (1542) that we sometimes have difficulty knowing whether Shakespeare consulted Holinshed or Hall. He was certainly familiar with both. Shakespeare's sources all acclaim Henry V a hero-king. Samuel Daniel's *The First Four Books of the Civil Wars* (1595), which Shakespeare may have used for his account of the treasonous plot against Henry (2.2), also praises the King in encomiastic terms.

Shakespeare follows the order of events laid down in Holinshed and Hall: the personal rivalry between Henry and the French Dauphin, Henry's request for reassurance from the clergy as to the legitimacy of the war, the maneuvering of the clergy to forestall a bill in Parliament threatening to seize Church land, the foiling of a plot against Henry's life, the siege of Harfleur, and the glorious victory at Agincourt. Both Holinshed and Hall offer Shakespeare many particulars about the English claim to France: in both accounts, the Archbishop quotes the law—*In terram Salicam mulieres ne succedant*—and goes on at length about King Pharamond, the rivers Elbe and Saale, King Pepin, Hugh Capet, the Book of Numbers, and the rest. On the other hand, Shakespeare omits a three-year campaign that historically intervened between Agincourt and the peace treaty of Troyes. He passes over the Lollard controversy in England, with the execution of Sir John Oldcastle.

And, of course, he adds unforgettable characters whom we do not find in the chronicles—Welshmen, Irishmen, Scots, common soldiers, thieves—who show the unity of the British nation under King Henry's charismatic leadership.

For many of his additions to the chronicles, Shakespeare was indebted to the anonymous *The Famous Victories of Henry the Fifth* (c. 1588), a work to which he had turned earlier in writing *1* and *2 Henry IV*. This old play, not registered until 1594 and not printed until 1598, exists today only in a corrupt text; quite possibly Shakespeare knew a fuller and more authentic version that would have given him still more material. Other plays may have existed on the subject, for the Admiral's men (a rival acting company) acted a ''harey the v'' in 1595 and 1596 that may or may not have been *The Famous Victories*. In any event, the relationship between *Henry V* and *Famous Victories* is at times close. *Famous Victories* omits Henry's long campaign between Agincourt and the final peace treaty, as does Shakespeare's play. The Archbishop of *Famous Victories* discusses the French claim just before the arrival of the French Ambassador with the tennis balls. (In Holinshed, the tennis-ball incident occurs first, at Kenilworth, whereas the Archbishop's lecture occurs sometime later at a meeting of Parliament in Leicester.) Henry assures the French Ambassador that he has ''free liberty and license to speak.'' To the Dauphin's insolent gift, taunting Henry about his wild youth, the King suavely replies that ''My lord prince Dauphin is very pleasant with me'' and promises to repay the insult with balls of brass and iron. (Holinshed mentions this apparently nonhistorical legend only briefly.) When the French noblemen assembled at the French court hear of Henry's arrival on their shores, they tremble with fear, even though the Dauphin recklessly scoffs at so young and prodigal a king. Henry is accompanied to France by a ludicrous assortment of London artisans and thieves, such as John Cobbler, who bids farewell to his wife in a comic scene similar to Pistol's parting from the Hostess, and Derick, who turns the tables on a French soldier much as Pistol deals with Monsieur le Fer. When King Henry woos Katharine of France, he protests to her that he cannot speak flatteringly because he is a plain soldier. She asks in return: ''How should I love him, that hath dealt so hardly / With my father?'' Despite these resemblances, however, Shakespeare's *Henry V* is incomparably superior to the old play and contains many original scenes and characters, such as King Henry's touring of his camp incognito, the quarrel between Henry and Williams, and above all the scenes involving Fluellen and his fellow captains.

Other possible sources include the *Henrici Quinti Angliae Regis Gesta*, written by a chaplain in Henry V's army; the *Vita et Gesta Henrici Quinti*, erroneously ascribed to Thomas Elmham; the *Vita Henrici Quinti* by ''Titus Livius,'' translated in 1513 (in which the French brag about their horses and armor); a ballad called ''The Battle of Agincourt'' (c. 1530); and *The Annals of Cornelius Tacitus*, translated in 1598 (in which Germanicus walks disguised through his camp at night ''to sound the soldiers' mind,'' and hears his leadership praised).

King Henry the Eighth

Shakespeare's chief source for the first four acts of *Henry VIII*, as for many of his earlier history plays, was Raphael Holinshed's *Chronicles* (1587 edition). Holinshed presented him with conflicting views of Cardinal Wolsey, however, and traces of the conflict remain in Shakespeare's play. Much of Holinshed's work is actually a compilation of the writings of earlier historiographers. In this case, some of Holinshed's material is from the bitterly anti-Wolseyan *Anglica Historia* (1534) of Polydore Vergil. Accordingly, Holinshed gives decidedly unfavorable interpretations of Wolsey's animosity toward the Duke of Buckingham and his unscrupulous meddling in the question of the King's marriage. Vergil was particularly distressed by the way in which Katharine had been shabbily treated; he (and Holinshed) report her speeches in her own behalf with manifest approval. Shakespeare preserves this alignment of sympathies in which Katharine is the wrongly accused wife and Wolsey the scheming Machiavellian.

Other portions of Holinshed, on the other hand, derive from George Cavendish's *The Life and Death of Thomas Wolsey*, written sometime around 1557 and extensively used by the chroniclers, though not separately printed until 1641. Cavendish was a gentleman usher in the household of Cardinal Wolsey from 1526 to 1530. Although he moralizes about the lesson to be learned from Wolsey's ambitious rise and sudden fall, Cavendish speaks admiringly of the Cardinal as an extraordinarily great man. He captures in minutely observed detail the magnificence of Wolsey's prosperous estate. He gives a moving portrait of Wolsey after his fall, on his sickbed and near the end, saying to a companion: ''If I had served God as diligently as I have done the King, he would not have given me over in my gray hairs.'' This passage, borrowed verbatim by Holinshed from Cavendish, produces in turn the famous lines from Shakespeare: ''Had I but served my God with half the zeal / I served my king, he would not in mine age / Have left me naked to mine enemies'' (3.2.456–458).

For his fifth act, Shakespeare turned to John Foxe's *Acts and Monuments of Martyrs* (1583 edition). Here he encountered a particularly rabid Protestant point of view, which has left its impression not only on the fifth act but on portrayals of Wolsey (whom Foxe naturally deplored) in earlier scenes. Foxe's hero, Thomas Cranmer, emerges as the victor of Shakespeare's play. Although the triumphantly Protestant ending contrasts oddly with Shakespeare's earlier manifest sympathy for Queen Katharine, the duality of attitudes is somehow plausible and perhaps even typically

Elizabethan: Katharine suffered lamentably, and Henry and Wolsey treated her shabbily, but these great events did, after all, lead to the English Reformation and the rule of Queen Elizabeth. The ambiguity so often noted in *Henry VIII,* then, is an essential part of Shakespeare's sources, not merely because he used conflicting accounts, but because many Elizabethan Englishmen necessarily felt mixed emotions toward this chapter of their past.

Shakespeare may also have made use of Edward Hall's *The Union of the Two Noble and Illustre Families of Lancaster and York* (1542) and John Speed's *History of Great Britain* (1611). In addition, he probably knew a dramatic version of the reign of Henry VIII that had appeared about eight years before, *When You See Me You Know Me,* by Samuel Rowley (1603–1605).

Titus Andronicus

Although we do not possess today any work that Shakespeare could have used for his immediate source in *Titus,* we have an eighteenth-century chapbook called *The History of Titus Andronicus* that may tell us substantially what that source was like. This chapbook is similar to Shakespeare's play. According to Ralph Sargent (*Studies in Philology,* 1949), a closely related prose version, now lost, served as Shakespeare's chief source. This hypothesis is now generally accepted. Some scholars even argue that the Stationers' Register entry in 1594 by the printer John Danter for his publication of "a Noble Roman Historye of Tytus Andronicus" with "the ballad thereof" refers to just such a prose account. Of this we cannot be certain, for Danter did, after all, publish Shakespeare's play in that same year, and the ballad appears to owe some of its details to the play (though based primarily, it would seem, on the lost prose version). Still, the existence of a prose *History of Titus* when Shakespeare wrote his play seems likely. (A ballad of "Titus Andronicus' Complaint," published in 1620 in Richard Johnson's *The Golden Garland of Princely Pleasures,* attests to the continued currency of the story in the early seventeenth century.)

The prose *History* is a fictitious medley of revenge stories inspired by Seneca and Ovid. It is set in the last days of the Roman Empire but contains no recognizable historical characters or events. Titus Andronicus is a Roman senator who defends Rome against the Goths in a protracted ten-year struggle, losing twenty-two of his own sons in the conflict. He slays the Gothic King Tottilius in battle and captures the Queen, Attava. When Tottilius' two sons Alaricus and Abonus continue the assault on Rome, the Roman Emperor wearies of the conflict and resolves to marry Attava against the advice of his general, Andronicus. The Queen, naturally regarding Titus as an enemy, proceeds to obtain powerful positions for her own kinsmen. She succeeds in having Titus banished, but he is recalled by popular insistence. Attava has an affair with her nameless Moorish servant and has a black child by him. Discovery of the child leads to the Moor's banishment, but he, too, is later recalled. Attava opposes the marriage of Titus' daughter Lavinia to the Emperor's only son (by a former marriage), since she desires the possession of the empire for her own sons. The remainder of the story proceeds much as in the play, except that we do not learn what happens to Rome after Titus' death. Shakespeare's chief additions include Titus' candidacy for, and rejection of, the throne, the struggle between Saturninus and Bassianus, the sacrifice of Tamora's son Alarbus, and a greatly magnified role for Aaron the Moor.

Although the prose version itself made use of Ovid and Seneca, Shakespeare evidently consulted these authors directly as well. The play contains many explicit references to classical authors, most notably when Lavinia turns the pages of Ovid's *Metamorphoses* to the story of Philomela's rape (4.1). In Ovid's famous account (Book 6, 526 ff.), King Tereus of Thrace rapes Philomela, cuts out her tongue (but not her hands) to prevent her from revealing the crime, and keeps her prisoner. She nevertheless manages to weave her story into a tapestry and send it to her sister, Procne, who liberates Philomela and plots with her to serve Tereus' and Procne's son Itys to him at a banquet.

A similar grisly feast takes place in Seneca's *Thyestes,* from which Shakespeare may well have drawn some particulars. Atreus, the wronged avenger, murders the two sons of Thyestes and serves them to him. As in Shakespeare's play, there are two sons rather than one. Of these two sons, one is guilty of ambition, whereas Ovid's Itys is an innocent victim. The slayer is a male avenger, not (as in Ovid's account) the mother of the slain victim. Senecan conventions of underworld spirits of revenge and the like are also present in the play, though they may have reached Shakespeare by way of Thomas Kyd's *The Spanish Tragedy* and other plays of the late 1580s. The works of both Ovid and Seneca were commonly taught in Elizabethan grammar schools, though they were also available in English translation: Ovid by Arthur Golding (1567) and Seneca by Jasper Heywood (1560). Christopher Marlowe's *Tamburlaine* and *The Jew of Malta* certainly had an influence, especially on Shakespeare's conception of Aaron the Moor.

Two continental plays about Titus, the German *Tragaedia von Tito Andronico* (1620) and the Dutch *Aran en Titus* by Jan Vos (1641), were once thought to have been derived from an English play before 1594, which might then have served as a source for Shakespeare. In the German play, the name of Titus' son Lucius is Vespasian, and this fact has caused scholars to wonder if the "Tittus & Vespasia" acted in April 1592 by the acting company known as Lord Strange's men (as mentioned in Philip Henslowe's *Diary*) was about Titus Andronicus. Lucius' part is small for such prominence in a title, however, and the prevailing opinion today is that Henslowe's play was on an independent subject.

Romeo and Juliet

Shakespeare's chief source for *Romeo and Juliet* was a long narrative poem by Arthur Brooke called *The Tragical History of Romeus and Juliet, written first in Italian by Bandell and now in English by Ar. Br.* (1562). Other English versions of this popular legend were available to Shakespeare, in particular William Painter's *The Palace of Pleasure* (1566), but Shakespeare shows only a passing indebtedness to it. Brooke mentions having seen (prior to 1562) a play about the two lovers, but such an old play is not likely to have been of much service to Shakespeare. Nor does he appear to have extensively consulted the various continental versions that lay behind Brooke's poem. Still, these versions help explain the genesis of the story.

The use of a sleeping potion to escape an unwelcome marriage goes back at least to the *Ephesiaca* of Xenophon of Ephesus (by the fifth century A.D.). Masuccio of Salerno, in his *Il Novellino* (1476), seems to have been the first to combine this sleeping potion story with an ironic aftermath of misunderstanding and suicide (as found in the Pyramus and Thisbe story of Ovid's *Metamorphoses*). In Masuccio's account, the lovers Mariotto and Giannozza of Siena are secretly married by a friar. When Mariotto kills a prominent citizen of Siena in a quarrel, he is banished to Alexandria. Giannozza, to avoid marriage with a suitor of her father's choosing, takes a sleeping potion given her by the friar and is buried as though dead. She is thereupon taken from the tomb by the friar and sent on her way to Alexandria. Mariotto, however, having failed to hear from her because the messenger is intercepted by pirates, returns in disguise to her tomb where he is discovered and executed. Giannozza, hearing this sad news, retires to a Sienese convent and dies of a broken heart.

In Luigi da Porto's *Historia novellamente ritrovata di due Nobili Amanti* (published c. 1530), based on Masuccio's account, the scene shifts to Verona. Despite the feuding of their two families, the Montecchi and the Cappelletti, Romeo and Guilietta meet and fall in love at a carnival ball. Romeo at once forgets his unrequited passion for a scornful lady. Friar Lorenzo, an experimenter in magic, secretly marries the lovers. Romeo tries to avoid brawling with the Cappelletti, but when some of his own kinsmen suffer defeat, he kills Theobaldo Cappelletti. After Romeo's departure for Mantua, Guilietta's family arranges a match for her with the Count of Lodrone. Friar Lorenzo gives Guilietta a sleeping potion and sends a letter to Romeo by a fellow friar, but this messenger is unable to find Romeo in Mantua. Romeo, hearing of Guilietta's supposed death from her servant Peter, returns to Verona with a poison he already possesses. Guilietta awakens in time to converse with Romeo before he dies. Then, refusing the Friar's advice to retire to a convent, she dies by stopping her own breath. This story provides no equivalents for Mercutio and the Nurse, although a young man named Marcuccio appears briefly at the Cappelletti's ball.

Da Porto's version inspired that of Matteo Bandello in his *Novelle* of 1554. Some details are added: Romeo goes to the ball in a vizard (mask), he has a servant named Pietro, a rope ladder is given to the Nurse enabling Romeo to visit Julietta's chamber before their marriage, Romeo obtains a poison from one Spolentino, and so on. The young man at the ball, Marcuccio, is now named Mercutio but is still a minor figure. This Bandello version was translated into French by Pierre Boaistuau in his *Histoires Tragiques* (1559); Boaistuau adds the Apothecary (who is racked and hanged for his part in the tragedy) and has Romeo die before Juliet awakens and slays herself with Romeo's dagger.

Despite Arthur Brooke's implication on the title page that his version is based on Bandello, the narrative poem *Romeus and Juliet* is taken from Boaistuau. Brooke's poem is a severely pious work written in "Poulter's Measure," couplets with alternating lines of six and seven feet. Brooke openly disapproves of the lovers' carnality and haste, although fortunately the story itself remains sympathetic to Romeus and Juliet. Brooke stresses star-crossed fortune and the antithesis of love and hate. He reduces Juliet's age from eighteen (as in Bandello) to sixteen. (Shakespeare further reduces her age to less than fourteen.) Brooke's narrative is generally close to Shakespeare's, though with important exceptions. Shakespeare compresses time from some nine months to a few days. In Brooke, for example, some two weeks elapse between the masked ball and Romeus' encounter with Juliet in her garden, and about two months elapse between the marriage and Tybalt's death. In Shakespeare, Capulet moves the wedding up from Thursday to Wednesday, thereby complicating the time schedule for the lovers. Shakespeare also unifies his play by such devices as introducing Tybalt and Paris early in the story; in Brooke's poem, Tybalt appears only at the time he is slain, and Juliet's proposed marriage to Count Paris emerges as a threat only after Romeus' banishment. Shakespeare's greatest transformation is of the characters. Brooke's Juliet is scheming. His Mercutio remains a shadowy figure, as in Bandello et al. Brooke's Nurse is unattractive, although she does occasionally hint at comic greatness: for example, she garrulously confides to Romeus the details of Juliet's infancy and then keeps Juliet on tenterhooks while she prates about Romeus' fine qualities (lines 631–714). Even if Shakespeare's play is incomparably superior to Brooke's drably versified poem, the indebtedness is extensive.

Julius Caesar

Julius Caesar represents Shakespeare's first extensive use of the work of the first-century Greek biographer Plutarch, in

Thomas North's translation (based on the French, of Jacques Amyot) of *The Lives of the Noble Grecians and Romans* (1579 and 1595). Plutarch was to become Shakespeare's most often used source in the 1600s; prior to 1599 he had consulted it briefly on a number of other occasions. In *Julius Caesar*, he borrows details from three lives: Caesar, Brutus, and Antonius. He uses particular traits of character, such as Caesar's belief that it is "better to die once than always to be afraid of death," Brutus' determination to "frame his manners of life by the rules of virtue and study of philosophy," Cassius' choleric disposition and his "hating Caesar privately more than he did the tyranny openly," and Antonius' inclination to "rioting and banqueting."

The events of the play are substantially present in Plutarch, especially in "The Life of Julius Caesar." Antonius runs the course on the Feast of Lupercal to cure barrenness and offers the diadem to Caesar. Flavius and Marullus despoil the images of Caesar. Caesar observes that he mistrusts pale and lean men such as Brutus and Cassius. Papers are thrown by the conspirators where Brutus can find them, proclaiming "Thou sleepest, Brutus, and art not Brutus indeed." Caesar's death is preceded by prodigies: a slave's hand burns but is unconsumed, a sacrificial beast is found to contain no heart. When Caesar encounters the soothsayer who previously had warned him of his fate and boasts that "the ides of March be come," the soothsayer has the last word: "So they be, but yet are they not past." Brutus' wife Portia complains to him of being treated "like a harlot," not like a partner. Brutus commits what Plutarch calls two serious errors when he forbids his fellow conspirators to kill Antonius and when he permits Antonius to speak at Caesar's funeral. Cinna the Poet is slain by an angry crowd mistaking him for Cinna the conspirator. A ghost appears to Brutus shortly before the last battle saying, "I am thy ill angel, Brutus, and thou shalt see me by the city of Phillippes," to which Brutus replies, "Well, I shall see thee then." Antonius says of the vanquished conspirators that "there was none but Brutus only that was moved to do it, as thinking the act commendable of itself: but that all the other conspirators did conspire his death for some private malice or envy." Shakespeare's debt to Plutarch is greater than these few examples can indicate.

Of course, Shakespeare reshapes and selects, as in his history plays. He compresses into one day Caesar's triumphant procession, the disrobing of the images, and the offer of the crown to Caesar on the Lupercal, when, in fact, these events were chronologically separate. Casca is by and large an invented character, and Octavius' role is considerably enlarged. Brutus' servant Lucius is a minor but effective addition, illustrating Brutus' capacity for warmth and humanity. Brutus' two speeches after the assassination (as mentioned by Plutarch) become one, and Antonius' speech is made to follow immediately after. (In Plutarch, Antonius speaks the following day, after the reading of the will.)

Shakespeare accentuates the irrationality and vacillation of the mob, for in Plutarch the people are never much swayed by Brutus' rhetoric, even though they respectfully allow him to speak. The unforgettable speeches of both Brutus and Antonius are not set down at all in Plutarch. More compression of time occurs after the assassination: in Plutarch, Octavius does not arrive in Rome until some six weeks afterward and does not agree to the formation of the Triumvirate until more than a year of quarreling has taken place. The inexorable buildup of tension in Shakespeare's play is the result of careful selection from a vast amount of material. Shakespeare's borrowing from "The Life of Marcus Brutus" is no less extensive and is at the same time reshaped and given new emphasis.

Although Shakespeare depended heavily on Plutarch, he was also aware of later and conflicting traditions about Caesar. On the one hand, Dante's *Divine Comedy* (c. 1310–1321) consigns Brutus and Cassius to the lowest circle of hell, along with Judas Iscariot and other betrayers of their masters. Geoffrey Chaucer's "The Monk's Tale," from the *Canterbury Tales*, similarly portrays Caesar as the manly and uncorruptible victim of envious attackers. On the other hand, Montaigne stresses the hubris of Caesar in aspiring to divinity. (Shakespeare could have read Montaigne in the French original or, if he had access to a manuscript, in John Florio's English translation, published in 1603.) A pro-Brutus view could also be found in the Latin *Julius Caesar* of Marc-Antoine Muret (1553) and the French *César* of Jacques Grévin (1561). That Shakespeare knew these works is unlikely, but they kept alive a tradition with which he was certainly familiar. Possibly he knew such Roman works as Lucan's account of Caesar in the *Pharsalia* and Cicero's letters and orations, which were republican in tenor. Other possible sources include the *Chronicle of the Romans' Wars* by Appian of Alexandria (translated 1578), the anonymous play *Caesar's Revenge* (published 1606–1607, performed in the early 1590s at Oxford), and Thomas Kyd's *Cornelia* (translated from the French Senecan tragedy by Garnier). *Il Cesare* by Orlando Pescetti (1594) is now almost universally rejected as a possible source. The result of Shakespeare's acquaintance with both pro- and anti-Caesar traditions is that he subordinates his own political vision to a balanced presentation of history, showing the significant strengths and disabling weaknesses in both Caesar and the conspirators.

Hamlet

The ultimate source of the *Hamlet* story is Saxo Grammaticus' *Historia Danica* (1180–1208), the saga of one Amlothi or (as Saxo calls him) Amlethus. The outline of the story is essentially that of Shakespeare's play, even though the emphasis of the Danish saga is overwhelmingly on cunning, brutality, and bloody revenge. Amlethus' father is Horwendil, a Governor of Jutland, who bravely kills the King of

Norway in single combat and thereby wins the hand in marriage of Gerutha, daughter of the King of Denmark. This good fortune goads the envious Feng into slaying his brother Horwendil and marrying Gerutha, "capping unnatural murder with incest." Though the deed is known to everyone, Feng invents excuses and soon wins the approbation of the fawning courtiers. Young Amlethus vows revenge but, perceiving his uncle's cunning, feigns madness. His mingled words of craft and candor awaken suspicions that he may be playing a game of deception.

Two attempts are made to lure Amlethus into revealing that he is actually sane. The first plan is to tempt him into lechery, on the theory that one who lusts for women cannot be truly insane. Feng causes an attractive woman to be placed in a forest where Amlethus will meet her as though by chance; but Amlethus, secretly warned of the trap by a kindly foster brother, spirits the young lady off to a hideaway where they can make love unobserved by Feng's agents. She confesses the plot to Amlethus. In a second stratagem, a courtier who is reported to be "gifted with more assurance than judgment" hides himself under some straw in the Queen's chamber in order to overhear her private conversations with Amlethus. The hero, suspecting just such a trap, feigns madness and begins crowing like a noisy rooster, bouncing up and down on the straw until he finds the eavesdropper. Amlethus stabs the man to death, drags him forth, cuts the body into morsels, boils them, and flings the bits "through the mouth of an open sewer for the swine to eat." Thereupon he returns to his mother to accuse her of being an infamous harlot. He wins her over to repentant virtue and even cooperation. When Feng, returning from a journey, looks around for his counselor, Amlethus jestingly (but in part truly) suggests that the man went to the sewer and fell in.

Feng now sends Amlethus to the King of Britain with secret orders for his execution. However, Amlethus finds the letter to the British King in the coffers of the two unnamed retainers accompanying him on the journey and substitutes a new letter ordering their execution instead. The new letter, purportedly written and signed by Feng, goes on to urge that the King of Britain marry his daughter to a young Dane being sent from the Danish court. By this means, Amlethus gains an English wife and rids himself of the escorts. A year later Amlethus returns to Jutland, gets the entire court drunk, flings a tapestry (knitted for him by his mother) over the prostrate courtiers, secures the tapestry with stakes, and then sets fire to the palace. Feng escapes this holocaust, but Amlethus cuts him down with the King's own sword. (Amlethus exchanges swords because his own has been nailed fast into its scabbard by his enemies.) Subsequently, Amlethus convinces the people of the justice of his cause and is chosen King of Jutland. After ruling for several years, he returns to Britain, bigamously marries a Scottish queen, fights a battle with his first father-in-law, is betrayed by his second wife, and is finally killed in battle.

In Saxo's account, we thus find the prototypes of Hamlet, Claudius, Gertrude, Polonius, Ophelia, Rosencrantz, and Guildenstern. Several episodes are close in narrative detail to Shakespeare's play: the original murder and incestuous marriage, the feigned madness, the woman used as a decoy, the eavesdropping counselor, and especially the trip to England. A translation of Saxo into French by François de Belleforest, in *Histoires Tragiques* (1576 edition), adds a few details, such as Gertrude's adultery before the murder and Hamlet's melancholy. Belleforest's version is longer than Saxo's, with more psychological and moral observation and more dialogue. Shakespeare probably consulted it.

Shakespeare need not have depended extensively on these older versions of his story, however. His main source was almost certainly an old play of *Hamlet*. Much evidence testifies to the existence of such a play. The *Diary* of Philip Henslowe, a theater owner and manager, records a performance, not marked as "new," of a *Hamlet* at Newington Butts on June 11, 1594, by "my Lord Admiral's men" or "my Lord Chamberlain's men," probably the latter. Thomas Lodge's pamphlet, *Wit's Misery, and the World's Madness* (1596), refers to "the visard of the ghost which cried so miserably at the theater, like an oyster wife, 'Hamlet, revenge!' " And Thomas Nashe, in his *Epistle* prefixed to Robert Greene's romance *Menaphon* (1589), offers the following observation:

It is a common practice nowadays amongst a sort of shifting companions, that run through every art and thrive by none, to leave the trade of noverint, whereto they were born, and busy themselves with the endeavors of art, that could scarcely Latinize their neck verse if they should have need; yet English Seneca read by candlelight yields many good sentences, as "Blood is a beggar," and so forth; and if you entreat him fair in a frosty morning, he will afford you whole *Hamlets,* I should say handfuls, of tragical speeches. But O grief! *Tempus edax rerum,* what's that will last always? The sea exhaled by drops will in continuance be dry, and Seneca, let blood line by line and page by page, at length must needs die to our stage; which makes his famished followers to imitate the Kid in Aesop, who, enamored with the Fox's newfangles, forsook all hopes of life to leap into a new occupation; and these men, renouncing all possibilities of credit or estimation, to intermeddle with Italian translations . . .

Nashe's testimonial describes a *Hamlet* play, written in the Senecan style by some person born to the trade of "noverint," or scrivener, who has turned to hack writing and translation. The description has often been fitted to Thomas Kyd, though this identification is not certain. (Nashe could be punning on Kyd's name when he refers to "the Kid in Aesop.") Certainly Thomas Kyd's *The Spanish Tragedy* (c. 1587) shows many affinities with Shakespeare's play and provides many Senecan ingredients missing from Saxo and Belleforest: the ghost, the difficulty in ascertaining whether the ghost's words are believable, the resulting need for delay and a feigning of madness, the moral perplexities afflicting a sensitive man called upon to revenge, the play within the play, the clever reversals and ironically caused deaths in the catastrophe, the rhetoric of tragic passion. Whether or not Kyd, in fact, wrote the *Ur-Hamlet,* his extant play enables us to see more clearly what that lost play must have contained. The pirated First Quarto of *Hamlet* (1603) also offers a few seemingly authentic details that are not found in the authoritative Second Quarto but are found in the earlier sources and may have been a part of the *Ur-Hamlet.* For example, after Hamlet has killed Corambis (corresponding to Polonius), the Queen vows to assist Hamlet in his strategies against the King; later, when Hamlet has returned to England, the Queen sends him a message by Horatio warning him to be careful.

One last document sheds light on the *Ur-Hamlet.* A German play, *Der bestrafte Brudermord (Fratricide Punished),* from a now-lost manuscript dated 1710, seems to have been based on a text used by English actors traveling in Germany in 1586 and afterward. Though changed by translation and manuscript transmission, and too entirely different from Shakespeare's play to have been based on it, this German version may well have been based on Shakespeare's source-play. Polonius' name in this text, Corambus, is the Corambis of the First Quarto of 1603. (The name may mean "cabbage cooked twice," from *coramblebis,* a proverbially dull dish.)

Der bestrafte Brudermord begins with a prologue in the Senecan manner, followed by the appearance of the ghost to Francisco, Horatio, and sentinels of the watch. Within the palace, meanwhile, the King carouses. Hamlet joins the watch, confiding to Horatio that he is "sick at heart" over his father's death and his mother's hasty remarriage. The ghost appears to Hamlet, tells him how the juice of hebona was poured into his ear, and urges revenge. When Hamlet swears Horatio and Francisco to silence, the ghost (now invisible) says several times "We swear," his voice following the men as they move from place to place. Hamlet reveals to Horatio the entire circumstance of the murder. Later, in a formal session of the court, the new King speaks hypocritically of his brother's death and explains the reasons for his marriage to the Queen. Hamlet is forbidden to return to Wittenberg, though Corambus' son Leonhardus has already set out for France.

Some time afterward, Corambus reports the news of Hamlet's madness to the King and Queen, and presumes on the basis of his own youthful passions to diagnose Hamlet's malady as lovesickness. Concealed, he and the King overhear Hamlet tell Ophelia to "go to a nunnery." When players arrive from Germany, Hamlet instructs them in the natural style of acting and then requests them to perform a play before the King about the murder of King Pyrrus by his brother. (Death is again inflicted by hebona poured in the ear.) After the King's guilty reaction to the play, Hamlet finds him alone at prayers but postpones the killing lest the King's soul be sent to heaven. Hamlet kills Corambus behind the tapestry in the Queen's chamber and is visited again by the ghost (who says nothing, however). Ophelia, her mind deranged, thinks herself in love with a court butterfly named Phantasmo. (This creature is also involved in a comic action to help the clown Jens with a tax problem.)

The King sends Hamlet to England with two unnamed courtiers who are instructed to kill Hamlet after their arrival. A contrary wind takes them instead to an island near Dover, where Hamlet foils his two enemies by kneeling between them and asking them to shoot him on signal; at the proper moment, he ducks and they shoot one another. He finishes them off with their own swords and discovers letters on their persons ordering Hamlet's execution by the English King if the original plot should fail. When Hamlet returns to Denmark, the King arranges a duel between him and Corambus' son Leonhardus. If Leonhardus' poisoned dagger misses its mark, a beaker of wine containing finely ground oriental diamond dust is to do the rest. Hamlet is informed of the impending duel by Phantasmo (compare Osric), whom Hamlet taunts condescendingly and calls "Signora Phantasmo." Shortly before the duel takes place, Ophelia is reported to have thrown herself off a hill to her death. The other deaths occur much as in Shakespeare's play. The dying Hamlet bids that the crown be conveyed to his cousin, Duke Fortempras of Norway, of whom we have not heard earlier.

From the extensive similarities between *Hamlet* and this German play, we can see that Shakespeare inherited his narrative material almost intact, though in a jumble and so pitifully mangled that the modern reader can only laugh at the contrast. No source study in Shakespeare reveals so clearly the extent of Shakespeare's wholesale borrowing of plot and the incredible transformation he achieved in reordering his materials.

Othello

Shakespeare's main source for *Othello* was the seventh story from the third decade of G. B. Giraldi Cinthio's *Hecatommithi* (1565). Cinthio was available in French but not in English translation during Shakespeare's lifetime. The verbal echoes in Shakespeare's play are usually closer to the Italian original than to Gabriel Chappuys' French version of 1584. Cinthio's account may have been based on an actual incident occurring in Venice around 1508.

Shakespeare is considerably indebted to Cinthio's story for the essentials of the narrative: the marriage of a Moorish captain to a Venetian lady, Disdemona, whose relatives wish her to marry someone else, the mutual attraction to noble qualities of mind in both husband and wife, their happiness together at first, the dispatching of the Moor to Cyprus to take charge of the garrison there, Disdemona's insistence on accompanying her husband through whatever dangers may occur (though the sea voyage, as it turns out, is a very calm one), the ensign's treachery and resolve to destroy the Moor's happiness with Disdemona, her begging her husband to reinstate the squadron leader whom the Moor has demoted for fighting on guard duty (although no mention is made of drunkenness or of the ensign's role in starting the trouble), the ensign's insinuations to the Moor that his wife is cuckolding him because she is becoming weary of her marriage with a black man, the ensign's difficulty in providing ocular proof, his planting of Disdemona's handkerchief in the squadron leader's quarters and his showing the Moor that the handkerchief is now in the squadron leader's possession, his arranging for the Moor to witness at a distance a conversation between the ensign and squadron leader that is, in fact, not about Disdemona, Disdemona's confusion when she is asked to produce the handkerchief, the attack on the squadron leader in the dark, the murder of Disdemona in her bed, the Moor's deep regret at the loss of his wife, the eventual punishment of both the Moor and and the ensign, and the telling of the story publicly by the ensign's wife, who has heretofore kept silent because of her fear of her husband.

Although these correspondences in the story are many, Shakespeare has changed a great deal. He provides Desdemona with a caring and saddened father, Brabantio, out of Cinthio's brief suggestion of family opposition to her marriage, and adds the entire opening scene in which Iago arouses the prejudices of Brabantio. Roderigo is a brilliantly invented character used to reveal Iago's skill in manipulation. Cinthio's ensign, though thoroughly wicked, never expresses a resentment for the squadron leader's promotion and favored treatment by the Moor; instead, the ensign lusts for Disdemona and turns against her and the Moor only when his passion is unrequited. In his complex portrayal of a consuming and irrational jealousy in Iago, Shakespeare goes far beyond his source, making use as well of the inventive villainy of the Vice in the English late medieval morality play. In Cinthio's account, the ensign filches the handkerchief from Disdemona while she is hugging the ensign's three-year-old daughter; the ensign's wife is uninvolved in this mischief, though she does unwillingly learn of her husband's villainy (since he has an idea of using her in his plot) and later feels constrained to hold her tongue when Disdemona asks her if she knows why the Moor is behaving so strangely. (As is usual in prose narrative, the passage of time is much more extended than in Shakespeare's play.)

In the later portions of the story, the changes are more marked. Cinthio relates an episode in which the squadron leader, finding the handkerchief in his room, takes it back to Disdemona while the Moor is out but is interrupted by the Moor's unexpected return home; Shakespeare instead has Cassio approach Desdemona (earlier in the story) to beg her assistance in persuading Othello to reinstate him. Cinthio tells of a woman in the squadron leader's household who copies the embroidery of the handkerchief before it is returned and is seen with it at a window by the Moor; here,

Shakespeare finds a suggestion for Bianca, but her role is considerably augmented, partly with the help of a passing remark in Cinthio's account that the squadron leader is attacked and wounded as he leaves the house of a courtesan with whom he occasionally takes his pleasure. In the absence of any character corresponding to Roderigo, the Cinthio narrative assigns to the ensign himself the role of wounding the squadron leader. The manner in which Disdemona is murdered is strikingly different. Cinthio has nothing equivalent to the tender scene between Desdemona and Emilia as Desdemona prepares to go to bed. Cinthio's Moor hides the ensign in a dressing room next to his bedroom and commissions the ensign to bludgeon her to death with a sand-filled stocking, after which the two murderers cause the ceiling of the room to collapse on her and create the impression that a rafter has smashed her skull.

Cinthio also treats the aftermath of the murder in a very different way. The Moor, distracted with grief, turns on the ensign and demotes him, whereupon the ensign persuades the squadron commander to take vengeance on the Moor as his attacker (according to the lying ensign) and killer of Disdemona. When the squadron commander accuses the Moor before the Seigniory, the Moor keeps silent but is banished and eventually killed by Disdemona's relatives. The ensign, returning to his own country, gets in trouble by making a false accusation and dies as the result of torture. Cinthio sees this as God's retribution. The ensign's wife lives to tell her story, unlike Shakespeare's Emilia.

The changed ending is essential to Shakespeare's play. Emilia becomes a more complex figure than the ensign's wife: Shakespeare implicates her in the stealing of the handkerchief but also accentuates her love for Desdemona and her brave denunciation of her husband when at last she knows the full truth. Othello's ritual slaying of Desdemona avoids the appalling butchery of the source story. Shakespeare's ending is more unified, and brings both Othello and Iago to account for the deeds they have committed in this play. Most important, Shakespeare transforms a sensational murder story into a moving tragedy of love.

King Lear

The story of Lear goes back into ancient legend. The motif of two wicked sisters and a virtuous youngest sister reminds us of Cinderella. Lear himself appears to come from Celtic mythology. Geoffrey of Monmouth, a Welshman in close contact with Celtic legend, included a Lear or Leir as one of the pseudo-historical kings in his *Historia Regum Britanniae* (c. 1136). This fanciful mixture of history and legend traces a supposed line of descent from Brut, great-grandson of Aeneas of Troy, through Locrine, Bladud, Leir, Gorboduc, Ferrex and Porrex, Lud, Cymbeline, Bonduca, Vortigern, Arthur, and so forth, to the historical kings of England.

The Tudor monarchs made much of their purported claim to such an ancient dynasty, and in Shakespeare's day this mythology had a quasi-official status demanding a certain reverential suspension of disbelief.

King Leir, according to Geoffrey, is the father of three daughters, Gonorilla, Regan, and Cordeilla, among whom he intends to divide his kingdom. To determine who deserves most, he asks them who loves him most. The two eldest sisters protest undying devotion, but Cordeilla, perceiving how the others flatter and deceive him, renounces hyperbole and promises only to love him as a daughter should love a father. Furious, the King denies Cordeilla her third of the kingdom but permits her to marry Aganippus, King of the Franks, without dowry. Thereafter, Leir bestows his two eldest daughters on the Dukes of Albania and Cornubia (Albany and Cornwall), together with half the island during his lifetime and the possession of the remainder after his death. In due course, his two sons-in-law rebel against Leir and seize his power. Thereafter Maglaunus, Duke of Albania, agrees to maintain Leir with sixty retainers, but, after two years of chafing at this arrangement, Gonorilla insists that the number be reduced to thirty. Angrily, the King goes to Henvin, Duke of Cornubia, where all goes well for a time; within a year, however, Regan demands that Leir reduce his retinue to five knights. When Gonorilla refuses to take him back with more than one retainer, Leir crosses into France and is generously received by Cordeilla and Aganippus. An invasion restores Leir to his throne. Three years later, he and Aganippus die, after which Cordeilla rules successfully for five years until overthrown by the sons of Maglaunus and Henvin. In prison she commits suicide.

This story, as part of England's mythic genealogy, was repeated in various Tudor versions, such as *The First Part of the Mirror for Magistrates* (1574), William Warner's *Albion's England* (1586), and Raphael Holinshed's *Chronicles* (second edition, 1587). Warner refers to the King's sons-in-law as "the Prince of Albany" and "the Cornish prince"; Holinshed refers to them as "the Duke of Albania" and "the Duke of Cornwall" but reports that it is Cornwall who marries the eldest daughter Gonorilla. *The Mirror*, closer to Shakespeare in these details, speaks of "Gonerell" as married to "Albany" and of "Cordila" as married to "the King of France." Edmund Spenser's *The Faerie Queene* (2.10.27–32) reports that "Cordeill" or "Cordelia" ends her life by hanging herself. Other retellings appear in Gerard Legh's *Accidence of Armory* and William Camden's *Remains*. All of these accounts leave the story virtually unchanged.

Shakespeare's immediate source for *King Lear* was an old play called *The True Chronicle History of King Leir*. It was published in 1605 but plainly is much earlier in style. The Stationers' Register, the official record of the London Company of Stationers (booksellers and printers), for May 14, 1594, lists "A booke called the Tragecall historie of kinge Leir and his Three Daughters &c.," and a short time earlier Philip Henslowe's *Diary* records the performance of a "Kinge Leare" at the Rose Theatre on April 6 and 8, 1594. The actors were either the Queen's or the Earl of Sussex's men (two acting companies), though probably the Queen's. The play may have been written as early as 1588. George Peele, Robert Greene, Thomas Lodge, and Thomas Kyd have all been suggested as possible authors. Shakespeare probably knew the play before its publication in 1605.

This play of *Leir* ends happily, with the restoration of Leir to his throne. Essentially, the play is a legendary history with a strong element of romance. The two wicked sisters are warned of the King's plans for dividing his kingdom by an obsequious courtier named Skalliger (compare Oswald). It is Skalliger, in fact, who proposes the idea of apportioning the kingdom in accord with the lovingness of the daughters' responses. Cordella receives the ineffectual support of an honest courtier, Perillus (compare Kent) but is disinherited by her angry father. Trusting herself to God's mercy and setting forth alone to live by her own labor, Cordella is found by the Gallian King and his bluff companion Mumford, who have come to England disguised as palmers to see if the English King's daughters are as beautiful as reported. The King hears Cordella's sad story, falls in love with her, and woos her (still wearing his disguise) in the name of the Gallian King. When she virtuously suggests the palmer woo for himself, he throws off his disguise and marries her forthwith.

Meanwhile the other sons-in-law, Cornwall and Cambria (compare Albany), draw lots for their shares of the kingdom. Leir announces that he will sojourn with Cornwall and Gonorill first. Cornwall treats the King with genuine solicitude, but Gonorill, abetted by Skalliger, tauntingly drives her father away. The King acknowledges to his loyal companion Perillus that he has wronged Cordella. Regan, who rules her mild husband as she pleases, receives the King with seeming tenderness but secretly hires an assassin to end his life. (Gonorill is partner in this plot.) The suborned agent, frightened into remorse by a providentially sent thunderstorm, shows his intended victim the letter ordering the assassination.

The Gallian King and Cordella, who have previously sent ambassadors to Leir urging him to come to France, now decide to journey with Mumford into Britain disguised as countryfolk. Before they can do so, however, Leir and Perillus arrive in France, in mariners' garb, where they encounter Cordella and her party dressed as countryfolk. Cordella recognizes Leir's voice, and father and daughter are tearfully reunited. The Gallian King invades England and restores Leir to his throne.

Shakespeare has changed much in the narrative of his source. He discards not only the happy ending but also the attempted assassination and the numerous romancelike uses of disguise (although Tom o' Bedlam, in an added plot, repeatedly uses disguise). Shakespeare eliminates the humorous Mumford and replaces Perillus with both Kent and the Fool. He turns Cornwall into a villain and Albany into a belated champion of justice. He creates the storm scene out of a mere suggestion of such an event, serving a very different purpose, in his source.

Most of all, he adds the parallel plot of Gloucester, Edgar, and Edmund. Here Shakespeare derived some of his material from Sir Philip Sidney's *Arcadia* (1590). In Book 2, chapter 10 of this greatest of Elizabethan prose romances, the two heroes, Pyrocles and Musidorus, encounter a son leading his blind old father. The old man tells his pitiful tale. He is the deposed King of Paphlagonia, father of a bastard son named Plexirtus who, he now bitterly realizes, turned the King against his true son Leonatus—the very son who is now his guide and guardian. The true son, having managed to escape his father's order of execution, has been forced to live poorly as a soldier, while the bastard son has proceeded to usurp his father's throne. In his wretchedness, the King has been succored by his forgiving true son and has been prevented from casting himself off the top of a hill. At the conclusion of this narrative, the villain Plexirtus arrives and attacks Leonatus; reinforcements arrive on both sides, but eventually Plexirtus is driven off, enabling the King to return to his court and bestow the crown on Leonatus. The old King thereupon dies, his heart having been stretched beyond the limits of endurance.

Other parts of the *Arcadia* may have given Shakespeare further suggestions; for example, the disguises adopted by Kent and Edgar are like those of Zelmane and Pyrocles in Sidney's prose work, and Albany's speeches about anarchy and the monstrosity that results from assaults on the rule of law recall one of Sidney's deepest concerns. Edmund is decidedly indebted to the allegorical Vice figure of the late medieval morality play tradition. For Tom o' Bedlam's mad language, Shakespeare consulted Samuel Harsnett's *Declaration of Egregious Popish Impostures,* 1603. (See Kenneth Muir's Arden edition of *King Lear,* pp. 253–256, for an extensive comparison.)

Macbeth

Shakespeare's chief source for *Macbeth* was Raphael Holinshed's *Chronicles* (1587 edition). Holinshed had gone for most of his material to Hector Boece, *Scotorum Historiae* (1526–1527), who in turn was indebted to a fourteenth-century priest named John of Fordun and to a fifteenth-century chronicler, Andrew of Wyntoun. By the time Holinshed found it, the story of Macbeth had become more fiction than fact. The historical Macbeth, who ruled from 1040 to 1057, did take the throne by killing Duncan, but in a civil conflict between two clans contending for the kingship. Contemporary observers credit him with having been a good ruler. Although he was defeated by the Earl of

Northumbria (the Siward of Shakespeare's play) at Birnam Wood in 1054, the Earl was forced by his own losses to retire, and Macbeth ruled three years longer before being slain by Duncan's son Malcolm. Banquo and Fleance are fictional characters apparently invented by Boece.

In Holinshed's telling of the story, Duncan is a king with a soft and gentle nature, negligent in punishing his enemies and thereby an unwitting encourager of sedition. It falls to his cousin, Macbeth, a critic of this soft line, and to Banquo, the Thane of Lochaber, to defend Scotland against her enemies: first against Macdowald (Macdonwald in Shakespeare), with his Irish kerns and gallowglasses, and then against Sueno, King of Norway. (Shakespeare fuses these battles into one.) Shortly thereafter, Macbeth and Banquo encounter "three women in strange and wild apparel, resembling creatures of elder world," who predict their futures as in the play. Although Macbeth and Banquo jest about the matter, common opinion later maintains that "these women were either the Weird Sisters, that is (as ye would say), the goddesses of destiny, or else some nymphs or fairies, endued with knowledge of prophecy." Certainly Macbeth soon becomes the Thane of Cawdor, whereupon, jestingly reminded of the three sisters' promise by Banquo, he resolves to seek the throne. His way is blocked, however, by Duncan's naming of his eldest but still underage son Malcolm to be Prince of Cumberland and heir to the throne. Macbeth's resentment at this is understandable, since Scottish law provides that, until the King's son is of age, the "next of blood unto him"—that is, Macbeth himself, as Duncan's cousin—should reign. Accordingly, Macbeth begins to plot with his associates how to usurp the kingdom by force. His "very ambitious" wife urges him on because of her "unquenchable desire" to be queen. Banquo is one among many trusted friends with whose support Macbeth slays the King at Inverness or at Bothgowanan. (No mention is made of a visit to Macbeth's castle.) Malcolm and Donald Bane, the dead King's sons, fly for their safety to Cumberland, where Malcolm is well received by Edward the Confessor of England; Donald Bane proceeds on to Ireland.

Holinshed's Macbeth is at first no brutal tyrant, as in Shakespeare. For some ten years he rules well, using great liberality and correcting the laxity of his predecessor's reign. (Holinshed does suggest, to be sure, that his justice is only contrived to court popularity among his subjects.) Inevitably, however, the Weird Sisters' promise of a posterity to Banquo goads Macbeth into ordering the murder of his onetime companion. Fleance escapes Macbeth's henchmen in the dark and afterward founds the lineage of the Stuart kings. (This genealogy is fictitious.) Macbeth's vain quest for absolute power further causes him to build Dunsinane fortress. When Macduff refuses to help, the King turns against him and would kill him except that "a certain witch, whom he had in great trust," tells the King he need never fear a man born of woman nor any vanquishment till Birnam

Wood come to Dunsinane. Macduff flees for his safety into England and joins Malcolm, whereupon Macbeth's agents slaughter Macduff's wife and children at Fife. Malcolm, fearing that Macduff may be an agent of Macbeth, dissemblingly professes to be a voluptuary, miser, and tyrant, but, when Macduff responds as he should in righteous sorrow at Scotland's evil condition, Malcolm reveals his steadfast commitment to the cause of right. These leaders return to Scotland and defeat Macbeth at Birnam Wood, with their soldiers carrying branches before them. Macduff, proclaiming that he is a man born of no woman since he was "ripped out" of his mother's womb, slays Macbeth.

Despite extensive similarities, Shakespeare has made some significant changes. Duncan is no longer an ineffectual king. Macbeth can no longer justify his claim to the throne. Most important, Banquo is no longer partner in a broadly based though secret conspiracy against Duncan. Banquo is, after all, ancestor of James I (at least according to this legendary history), and so his hands must be kept scrupulously clean; King James disapproved of all tyrannicides, whatever the circumstances. Macbeth is no longer a just lawgiver. The return of Banquo's ghost to Macbeth's banqueting table is an added scene. Macbeth hears the prophecy about Birnam Wood and Macduff from the Weird Sisters, not, as in Holinshed, from some witch. Lady Macbeth's role is considerably enhanced, and her sleep walking scene is original. Shakespeare compresses time, as he usually does.

In making some of these alterations, Shakespeare turned to another story in Holinshed's chronicle of Scotland: the murder of King Duff by Donwald. King Duff, never suspecting any treachery in Donwald, often spends time at the castle of Forres, where Donwald is captain of the castle. On one occasion, Donwald's wife, bearing great malice toward the King, shows Donwald (who already bears a grudge against Duff) "the means whereby he might soonest accomplish" the murder. The husband and wife ply Duff's few chamberlains with much to eat and drink. Donwald abhors the act "greatly in heart" but perseveres "through instigation of his wife." Four of Donwald's servants actually commit the murder under his instruction. Next morning, Donwald breaks into the King's chamber and slays the chamberlains, as though believing them guilty. Donwald is so overzealous in his investigation of the murder that many lords begin to suspect him of having done it. For six months afterward, the sun refuses to appear by day and the moon by night.

The chronicle accounts in Holinshed of Malcolm and Edward the Confessor supplied Shakespeare with further details. A more important supplementary source may have been George Buchanan's *Rerum Scoticarum Historia* (1582), a Latin history not translated in Shakespeare's lifetime, presenting a more complex psychological portrait of the protagonist than in Holinshed. Finally, Shakespeare

may have used King James I's *Daemonology* (1597), John Studley's early seventeenth-century version of Seneca's *Medea*, Samuel Harsnett's *Declaration of Egregious Popish Impostures* (1603), and accounts of the Scottish witch trials published around 1590.

Timon of Athens

Shakespeare certainly made use of a brief passage from "The Life of Marcus Antonius" in Thomas North's English translation (from the French of Jacques Amyot) of the first-century Greek biographer Plutarch's *Lives of the Noble Grecians and Romans* (1579). This passage is a digression used to illustrate Antonius' embittered withdrawal to an Egyptian island after his defeat at Actium, in which he compares himself to the famous misanthrope of Athens, Timon. As Plutarch reports Timon's story, citing Plato and Aristophanes as his sources, Timon is a hater of mankind because he has been victimized by deception and ingratitude. Timon shuns all company but that of young Alcibiades and occasionally that of Apemantus. When asked by Apemantus why he favors Alcibiades, Timon replies that he knows Alcibiades will some day do great mischief to the Athenians. On another occasion, Timon mounts a public rostrum and invites his Athenian listeners to come hang themselves on a fig tree growing in his yard before he cuts it down (see 5.1.204–211). When Timon dies, he is buried upon the seashore (5.1.213–217). Plutarch transcribes two epitaphs—one by the poet Callimachus and one by Timon himself—both of which appear virtually word for word in Shakespeare's play (5.4.70–73). (Shakespeare probably meant to cancel one, for dramatically they are inconsistent with each other.) Plutarch thus provides Shakespeare not only with several incidents in the life of Timon but also with the link connecting Timon, Alcibiades, and Apemantus. The twenty-eighth novel in William Painter's *The Palace of Pleasure* (1566) retells the events narrated by Plutarch but without adding any new information.

Oddly, Shakespeare seems to have absorbed little from Plutarch's "Life of Alcibiades," though that account does tell how the general leaves Athens in disgrace and sides with Athens' enemies but ultimately relents when he sees that the Athenians are sorry for the injury they have done him. Alcibiades is a handsome young man and is fond of women; his concubine Timandra buries him. Despite these scattered hints, however, Plutarch's "Life of Alcibiades" provides no basis for Shakespeare's plot.

The comedy of Timon by Aristophanes, to which Plutarch alludes, has not survived. Nor has Plato's description. Apparently, these accounts were based on a historical figure of fifth-century Athens, Timon the son of Echecratides. Allusions to him in classical literature are common enough to suggest that his name had become synonymous with misanthropy. The fullest surviving classical record of this tradition is a dialogue by Lucian of Samosata (c. A.D. 125–180) called *Timon, or The Misanthrope*. No English translation was available in Shakespeare's lifetime, but he could have read Lucian in Italian, Latin, or French translation.

The dialogue begins as Timon, impoverished and abandoned by his fair-weather friends, calls upon Zeus to punish such injustice. Zeus hears this diatribe and learns from Hermes the sad tale of Timon's victimization by his ungrateful fellow mortals. Aware that he has been neglectful of this case, Zeus orders Hermes to descend with Plutus (Riches) and restore Timon to prosperity. Although Plutus fears he will be treated improvidently as before, Zeus is insistent. Plutus (personifying Riches) confesses to Hermes, as they descend, how he (i.e., wealth) deceives people. Hermes and Plutus find Timon digging, accompanied by Poverty, Toil, Endurance, and other such allegorical companions. Poverty and his fellows are reluctant to leave Timon, for they know he has been happier with them than in his former days; Timon, too, protests that he wants nothing to do with prosperity. Still, the will of the gods must be obeyed, and Timon discovers treasure where he is digging.

Just as he mordantly predicts, opportunists now seek him out. One is Gnathonides the flatterer, a former recipient of Timon's hospitality who only recently has repaid that kindness by offering Timon a noose. Another, Philiades, once received from Timon a farm as a dowry for his daughters but has spurned Timon in his poverty; now he makes a pretense of offering money, knowing Timon not to be in need. A third petitioner is the orator Demea, whose debt Timon once paid to obtain his release from jail; now, having insulted Timon in his poverty, Demea comes with a fulsome and patently fictitious decree that he has composed in Timon's honor. Fourth is Thrasicles, a hypocritical philosopher who preaches self-denial but drinks to excess and who professes to come now, not for his own benefit, but for those to whom he will gladly distribute Timon's new wealth. Timon drives them off one by one and then resorts to throwing stones at the ever increasing crowd of flatterers. (This parade of villains, and their satirical discomfiture, bear an interesting resemblance to Aristophanes' *The Birds*.)

Many details here are suggestive of Shakespeare's play and are not in Plutarch: Timon's generosity to friends (including the payment of a debt and the providing of a marriage dowry), his friends' ungrateful response when he is in need, the finding of gold in the ground followed by the reappearance of his former friends, the insincere offer of money, the flattering composition in praise of Timon. The personified abstractions are parablelike, as in Shakespeare's play. Yet verbal parallels between Shakespeare and Lucian are tenuous at best. Probably, Shakespeare knew some later version based on Lucian. Renaissance works inspired by Lucian are not hard to find, but none seems to be the direct source for Shakespeare. He is not likely to have known an Italian play called *Timone* by Matteo Maria Boiardo (c. 1487).

More suggestive of Shakespeare's play is an English academic play written at Cambridge (c. 1581–1600, or perhaps c. 1609–1610?) and preserved in the Dyce manuscript. (The editor Alexander Dyce first published this Elizabethan manuscript in 1842.) In this version, Timon's servant Laches warns against the effects of prodigality. When one friend, Eutrapelus, experiences financial trouble, Timon gives him five talents. Laches is driven out by Timon but returns disguised as a soldier to serve his master. At a final banquet, Timon mocks his guests with stones painted to resemble artichokes. When he finds gold, Timon's false mistress shows her readiness to take it. Even a farcical comic subplot reminds us that Shakespeare's *Timon* contains an unrelated and perhaps vestigial Fool scene. Yet this academic play may have been written after Shakespeare's play, though surely not based on it (since *Timon* was not published until 1623 and apparently was never acted), and the likeliest explanation for the similarities is a common source. Perhaps Shakespeare knew and used a play that is now lost.

Apemantus does not have a prominent role in any of the versions here discussed, though he is mentioned in Plutarch. Apemantus bears a resemblance to many satirical railers and crabbed philosophers in Renaissance literature, such as Diogenes in John Lyly's play of *Campaspe* (1584) and Jaques in Shakespeare's *As You Like It*.

Antony and Cleopatra

In writing *Antony and Cleopatra,* Shakespeare relied to an unusual extent on his chief source, "The Life of Marcus Antonius" in the first-century Greek biographer Plutarch's *The Lives of the Noble Grecians and Romans* (in an English version by Sir Thomas North, 1579). Perhaps the best-known example in all Shakespeare of his skillful use of source material is in 2.2.201–236, when Enobarbus describes the first meeting of Antony and Cleopatra on the river Cydnus. Putarch reports the event as follows:

She disdained to set forward otherwise but to take her barge in the river of Cydnus, the poop whereof was of gold, the sails of purple, and the oars of silver, which kept stroke in rowing after the sound of the music of flutes, hautboys, citterns, viols, and such other instruments as they played upon in the barge. And now for the person of herself: she was laid under a pavilion of cloth of gold of tissue, appareled and attired like the goddess Venus, commonly drawn in picture; and hard by her, on either hand of her, pretty fair boys appareled as painters do set forth god Cupid, with little fans in their hands with the which they fanned wind upon her. Her ladies and gentlewomen also, the fairest of them, were appareled like the nymphs Nereides (which are the mermaids of the waters) and like the Graces, some steering the helm, others tending the tackle and ropes of the barge, out of the which there came a wonderful passing sweet savor of perfumes that perfumed the wharf's side, pestered with innumerable multitudes of people. Some of them followed the barge all alongst the river's side; others also ran out of the city to see her coming in. So that in the end, there ran such multitudes of people one after another to see her that Antonius was left post alone in the marketplace, in his imperial seat, to give audience.

Shakespeare retains virtually every detail describing Cleopatra's barge: the poop of gold, the sails of purple, the oars of silver, the flutes, the boys with fans, the gentlewomen like the Nereides, and so on. He borrows phrases and images virtually intact from North, as in the account of Cleopatra's own person. Yet Shakespeare also transforms this scene by putting the description in the mouth of Enobarbus, a largely invented character. Enobarbus' sardonic view derived from military experience, his wry but genuine admiration for Cleopatra, and the prurient curiosity of his Roman listeners—all combine to produce the paradox of cloying appetite and insatiable hunger that helps to define the unforgettable greatness of Cleopatra as a character.

Shakespeare turns to Plutarch for other fabulous stories as well: eight wild boars roasted whole for only twelve guests (2.2.189–190), Cleopatra teasing Antony by causing an old dried salt fish to be placed on his fishing line (2.5.15–18), Menas the pirate suggesting to Pompey that they cut the anchor cable with all their noble guests still aboard (2.7.62–85), Cleopatra's sudden changes from weeping to laughing, and her willingness to be flattered by those who tell her Antony has married Octavia solely out of necessity (3.3), Octavius' tenderness for his sister, the ill-omened nesting of swallows in Cleopatra's sails (4.12.3–4), Antony's disregarding the advice of a valiant captain not to fight at sea (3.7.62–71), Cleopatra's study of swift means of death (5.2.353–356), Antony's jealous reaction to the embassy of the young Thyreus, or Thidias (3.13.86–170), the suicide of Antony's servant Eros (4.14.85–97), Cleopatra's difficulty in lifting Antony up to her tomb or monument (4.15.30–38), his warning that she should trust none but Proculeius (4.15.50), Cleopatra's deception of Caesar through persuading him that she desires to live (5.2.110–190), the countryman with the basket of figs (5.2.233–235), Cleopatra's death "attired and arrayed in her royal robes" attended by Charmian and Iras, and much more.

Despite these extensive and detailed borrowings, Shakespeare partly turned elsewhere for his estimate of his main characters. To Plutarch, Antony is the tragic victim of infatuation. For all Cleopatra's cultivation and fascination—she knows several languages and rules her country with royal bearing—she is the source of Antony's downfall. Plutarch's attitude is, like Enobarbus', admiring but ironic. "In the end," he writes, "the horse of the mind, as Plato termeth it, that is so hard of rein (I mean the unreined lust of concupiscence) did put out of Antonius' head all honest and commendable thoughts." This "Roman" view is present in *Antony and Cleopatra*, to be sure, but is counterbalanced by the "Egyptian" view that finds greatness in Antony and Cleopatra's capacity for love. Shakespeare's play sets up a debate among conflicting traditions, as found in various medieval and Renaissance treatments of this famous story. The moralistic perspective condemning vice was popular in medieval texts, such as *De Casibus Virorum Illustrium* and its continuation, John Lydgate's *The Fall of Princes*. The interpretation of Cleopatra as love's martyr was to be found in Geoffrey Chaucer's *The Legend of Good Women*. And, finally, the view of Antony and Cleopatra as heroic protagonists rising above their guilt found expression in several neo-Senecan dramas of the later sixteenth century. Most important for Shakespeare were *The Tragedy of Antony*, translated from Robert Garnier's *Marc Antoine* by Mary Herbert, Countess of Pembroke, in about 1590 (published 1592 and 1595), and *The Tragedy of Cleopatra* by Samuel Daniel (1594), a companion play dealing mainly with the end of Cleopatra's life. Garnier's play had been based on Étienne Jodelle's *Cléopâtre Captive* (1552), the first regular French tragedy. Shakespeare certainly gained from such works as these a sense of tragic greatness in his protagonists. He seems also to have been aware of favorable and unfavorable historical appraisals of Octavius Caesar as both a great ruler and a ruthless and even treacherous politician. One influential work on the more critical side may have been the *Chronicle of the Romans' Wars* by Appian of Alexandria (translated 1578). Virgil's *Aeneid* gave Shakespeare a model for a drama of passion set in the context of Roman history.

Coriolanus

Coriolanus probably represents Shakespeare's last use of the first-century Greek biographer Plutarch's *The Lives of the Noble Grecians and Romans,* as translated by Sir Thomas North (1579) from a French version by Jacques Amyot. "The Life of Caius Marcius Coriolanus" provided most of the material for Shakespeare's play, just as "The Life of Marcus Antonius" had provided most of the material for *Antony and Cleopatra*. Plutarch's Coriolanus is a man of exceeding nobility but also of excessive impatience and churlish incivility. In war he practices *virtus,* or "valiantness" as North translates it. He wins his title of Coriolanus by storming the city of Corioles (Corioli) almost single-handed. He is the son of a widow whose good opinion he cherishes; as Plutarch reports, "he thought nothing made him so happy and honorable as that his mother might hear everybody praise and commend him, that she might always see him return with a crown upon his head, and that she might still embrace him with tears running down her cheeks for joy." Coriolanus vehemently disapproves of leniency toward the populace, believing it to be an invitation to anarchy. He is, naturally, an enemy of the people's first tribunes, Junius Brutus and Sicinius Velutus, who, in Plutarch's estimation, "had only been the causers and procurers of this sedition."

Plutarch informs us that, when Coriolanus stands for consul and follows the custom of appearing in the marketplace clad only in a poor gown, the people remember his martial prowess; on the day of the election itself, however, they recall their old hate of him and refuse his candidacy. Coriolanus, in his typically choleric and intemperate fashion, makes no attempt to conceal his outrage at this insult. (Plutarch comments editorially on his behavior as "the fruits of self-will and obstinacy.") When he is banished, Coriolanus goes in disguise to Antium, to the house of Tullus Aufidius, his great rival, knowing perfectly well that "Tullus did more malice and envy him than he did all the Romans besides." Coriolanus and Tullus have long been admiring rivals: "they were ever at the encounter one against another, like lusty courageous youths striving in all emulation of honor, and had encountered many times together." Returning vengefully to Rome, Coriolanus is "determined at the first to persist in his obstinate and inflexible rancor," but finally relents through "natural affection," and receives his wife and mother. Volumnia's oration to him, reported in full by Plutarch, causes Coriolanus to cry out: "you have won a happy victory for your country, but mortal and unhappy for your son."

Shakespeare's changes simultaneously enhance the haughtiness of Coriolanus and the volatility of the commoners, thereby increasing the distance between the two sides. Shakespeare's Coriolanus is revolted by the custom of wearing a robe and showing his wounds to the people, and shows his contempt more snarlingly than in Plutarch's *Lives*. He is, unlike Plutarch's protagonist, reluctant to seek office and has to be persuaded to it by his mother and friends. Shakespeare minimizes the legitimate griefs of the Roman people—Plutarch makes it plain that the Senate does favor the rich and that the people are oppressed by usurers—and accentuates their political instability. Shakespeare shows them as being manipulated against Coriolanus by the scheming tribunes, whereas in Plutarch the people make up their own minds to oppose Coriolanus for the consulship. Shakespeare also magnifies the roles of Volumnia and of Menenius. Volumnia, though she is mentioned by Plutarch, takes no active part in the story until Coriolanus attacks Rome; Menenius' chief function in Plutarch is to relate the fable of the belly. Shakespeare compresses and rearranges events as he usually does: for example, in Plutarch the people actually leave Rome to demonstrate their grievances and agree to return only when granted the election of tribunes to represent their interests, whereas in Shakespeare the tribunes have already been elected when the play begins. In Shakespeare, Coriolanus is banished as the result of a dispute over his consulship, not (as in Plutarch) as the result of an insurrection over scarcity of grain.

Shakespeare probably also knew the story of Coriolanus in another classical source, Livy's *Roman History,* Book 2, as translated by Philemon Holland (1600). Other versions of the story were available to him, including an outline of Roman history by L. Annaeus Florus (also called Publius Annius Florus), written in the second century A.D., based chiefly on Livy. Plutarch, however, seems to have provided Shakespeare with virtually everything he needed. Even Shakespeare's alterations of Plutarch tend to enhance rather than revise Plutarch's overall thesis and appraisal of the characters in his history.

Pericles

Shakespeare derived his *Pericles* from the ancient Greek romance of Apollonius of Tyre. He had used the story once before, in *The Comedy of Errors.* Medieval versions of this enduringly popular legend include the ninth-century Latin *Historia Apollonii Regis Tyri,* Godfrey of Viterbo's *Pantheon* (c. 1186), the *Gesta Romanorum* (a collection of ancient tales in Latin), John Gower's *Confessio Amantis* (c. 1383–1393), and an English chronicle of *Appolyn of Thyre* translated for the printer Wynkyn de Worde by Robert Copland from a French source (1510). Shakespeare, and possibly the author of a lost earlier dramatic version, were chiefly indebted to Gower's *Confessio* and to Laurence Twine's *The Pattern of Painful Adventures,* a prose version registered in 1576 but existing today only in two editions from about 1594–1595 and 1607.

The order of events in Twine is much the same as in Shakespeare: the hero Apollonius' difficulty with the incestuous King Antiochus, his relieving of the city of Tharsus, his shipwreck at Pentapolis, and his falling in love with the King's daughter Lucina (Thaisa in the play), her childbearing and apparent death at sea, the discovery of her floating casket at Ephesus, her revival by the physician Cerimon and her retirement to the temple of Diana in Ephesus, her daughter Tharsia's (i.e., Marina's) capture by pirates and enslavement in a brothel, her conversion of Athanagoras (Lysimachus), the Governor of Machilenta (Mytilene), and Apollonius' eventual reunion with his daughter and wife. Gower's account, too, is much the same, with slightly different forms of the proper names: Appolinus' (Apollonius') wife is referred to as the King's daughter, Appolinus' daughter is Thaise, the man she marries is Atenagoras (or Athanagoras) of Mytilene, and so on.

Other than changing some proper names, including that of the hero, Shakespeare did not introduce many significant alterations. To be sure, Shakespeare has given a more sordid impression of the brothel in which Marina must dwell, and has dignified the character of Lysimachus so as to render him worthy of marrying Marina. In Twine's prose account, Athanagoras actually tries to buy Tharsia from the pirates at an auction; when he is outbid by a bawd, he resolves to be the first to visit Tharsia in her new residence. Shakespeare has provided a more decorous action for Lysimachus, although traces of the older and more licentious character occasionally show through and create the impression of inconsistency. For the most part, however, Shakespeare's play stays unusually close to the episodic narrative structure of his sources.

The relationship of George Wilkins' *The Painful Adventures of Pericles, Prince of Tyre* (1608) to Shakespeare's play is complex and uncertain. Beyond doubt, Wilkins' prose account is based in part on a *Pericles* play; Wilkins acknowledges in his Argument that this same story has been recently presented "by the King's Majesty's Players." The play he used may, however, not have been the *Pericles* we know from the corrupt 1609 Quarto. Parts of Wilkins' narrative are very close to the earlier *Pattern of Painful Adventures* by Twine. Kenneth Muir suggests (*Shakespeare's Sources*, 1957) that because Wilkins' novel is closer to the first two acts of Shakespeare's play than to the last three acts, Wilkins may have been using an older play that Shakespeare then revised, substantially rewriting the last three acts but changing little in the first two. Whether the presumed *Ur-Pericles* might have been Wilkins' own play is a matter of conjecture. The very existence of an *Ur-Pericles* is by no means universally accepted but cannot be ruled out as a possibility.

Cymbeline

Cymbeline deals with legendary and romantic history, in which traces of historical events can still be dimly perceived. A Cunobelinus, or Cymbeline, was, in fact, leader of the Celtic chieftains in southeast England during the period of Roman hegemony there, following Julius Caesar's invasion of the island in 54 B.C. Cunobelinus ruled from about 5 to 40 A.D., with his capital at Camulodunum (Colchester). He was a friend and ally of Augustus Caesar and enjoyed a peaceful reign. When the kingdom had passed to his sons (one of whom apparently was Caractacus), the Romans under Claudius pursued once again their conquest of England and subdued much of the southeast, though Caractactus escaped to Wales and became a leader of the resistance.

Beginning with Geoffrey of Monmouth's *Historia Regum Britanniae* (c. 1136), King Kymbelinus becomes a quasi-legendary figure. Geoffrey adds him to the genealogy of kings (along with Leir, Locrine, etc.) descended from Aeneas' great-grandson Brut, the mythical founder of Britain. Kymbelinus' reign was peaceful, according to Geoffrey, since the King, having been raised in Augustus Caesar's household, willingly paid tribute to Rome without being asked. When Kymbelinus' elder son Guiderius succeeded to the throne, however, said Geoffrey, he defied the Emperor Claudius over the tribute. Guiderius fell in battle and was succeeded by his brother Arviragus, who more than held his own against Claudius, eventually settling matters by negotiation.

By the time of Raphael Holinshed's *Chronicles* (1587 edition), the facts are badly confused. Holinshed admits he cannot be sure whether Kymbeline or some other British leader fought against Augustus Caesar, or whether Kymbeline paid tribute; he does report that Guiderius fought Augustus Caesar (rather than Claudius) but is uncertain as to whether the Romans lost or won. Edmund Spenser's *The Faerie Queene* (2.10. 50–51) affirms that Kimbeline fought the Romans over tribute and was slain in battle, whereupon his brother Arviragus took his place and compelled the Roman Claudius to a peace. (In other words, Spenser has conflated Cymbeline and Guiderius.) Shakespeare, like Spenser, imagines the great struggle with Rome and subsequent peace settlement to have taken place during Cymbeline's reign; following Holinshed, he assumes that Rome was then governed by Augustus Caesar. Shakespeare also seems to have consulted a vivid account of the battle in Thomas Blenerhasset's contribution to *The Second Part of the Mirror for Magistrates* (1578) and another account of Cymbeline's reign by John Higgins in the 1587 *Mirror for Magistrates*. Finally, Shakespeare turned for his background material to quite a different story in Holinshed, concerning a Scottish farmer named Hay who with his two sons helped defend Scotland against the Danes in 976. Shakespeare presumably found this story when reading for *Macbeth*, since it stands between the two accounts—Donwald's murder of Duff and Macbeth's murder of Duncan—that Shakespeare used in writing *Macbeth*. The exploits of Hay and his two sons resemble those of Belarius and the two princes in the final battle of *Cymbeline*.

The quasi-historical setting accounts for only a small part of *Cymbeline*, and Shakespeare had no special reason to set the facts straight. Most of his material is, after all, romantic. The central plot of a wager over a wife's virtue may have come from Giovanni Boccaccio's *Decameron*, ninth tale of the second day, although as a type this ancient story was widespread and presumably available to Shakespeare in many forms. Earlier versions include the thirteenth-century French *Roi Flore et la belle Jeanne*, the *Roman de la Violette* by Gerbert de Montreuil, a miracle play by Gautier de Coincy, and others. Boccaccio was available to Shakespeare in French translation but not in English.

A summary of Boccaccio's story suggests a number of particulars to which Shakespeare was indebted. Boccaccio tells of an Italian merchant, Bernabò of Genoa, who, at a gathering in Paris of fellow merchants discussing the wantonness of their wives, dares to affirm the absolute chastity of his own wife, Zinevra. A young merchant, Ambrogiuolo, makes a wager that he can seduce Zinevra and return with proof in three months. Going at once to Genoa, Ambrogiuolo discovers that Zinevra is indeed incorruptible. He therefore bribes an elderly lady, whom Zinevra has be-friended, to convey him hidden in a chest to the lady's bedroom. When the lady is asleep, he steals forth from hiding, memorizes details of her room, notes particularly a mole upon her left breast, and takes with him a purse, gown, ring, and sash. Returning to Paris, he convinces his fellow merchants and Bernabò that he has succeeded. Bernabò hereupon travels to within a few miles of Genoa, summons his wife, and secretly orders his servant to kill her on the way. The servant is reluctant to do so, however, and gladly takes only her cloak as evidence of having finished the job. Zinevra now makes her way disguised as a man to Alexandria and enters the service of the Sultan. One day she happens to recognize her own purse and girdle in a Venetian clothes shop in Palestine, inquires as to their owner, meets Ambrogiuolo in this way (who has journeyed to Palestine selling merchandise), and hears from Am-brogiuolo's own boastful lips the story of his treachery. She cannily manages to bring Ambrogiuolo and Bernabò before the Sultan, throws off her male disguise, and reveals the whole story. She pardons Bernabò and is reunited with him, but Ambrogiuolo is sentenced by the Sultan to be tied to a stake, smeared with honey, and left to be devoured by insects.

Shakespeare has altered the setting and has surrounded the story with other matters, such as King Cymbeline's lost sons, his quarrel with Rome, his difficulties with his Queen and her son, Cloten, and the like. Shakespeare's ending is much more forgiving toward Iachimo than in the narrative source. The circumstances of the denouement are changed. Still, the plot of Posthumus, Imogen, and Iachimo is extensively indebted to Boccaccio.

Shakespeare seems also to have known an English version, *Frederyke of Jennen* (Antwerp, 1518; London, 1520 and 1560), translated from the Dutch. In some details, it is closer to Shakespeare's play than is Boccaccio's story. For example, the merchants who witness the wager include a Spaniard, a Frenchman, a Florentine, and a Genoese (compare 1.4). Three of these merchants are not present when the villain returns to prove his victory, just as in 2.4 of Shakespeare's play. Also, the husband repents even before learning of his wife's innocence, as does Posthumus. Shakespeare greatly accentuates this motif of penance and forgiveness. Another source is a romantic play called *The Rare Triumphs of Love and Fortune*, acted before Queen Elizabeth in 1582, in which the princess Fidelia is banished by her father for falling in love, is betrayed and pursued by her boorish brother Armenio (compare Cloten), and is hospitably received by a banished courtier named Bomelio who lives hermitlike in a cave. "Fidele" is the name used by Shakespeare's Imogen to disguise her identity. Folk motifs are apparent throughout *Cymbeline;* the cruel Queen inevitably reminds us of Snow White's stepmother. Al-though Shakespeare may not have been acquainted with

that particular story, he clearly was interested in folk legend when he wrote *Cymbeline*. One other anonymous roman-tic play, *Sir Clyomon and Sir Clamydes* (c. 1570–1583), may have given Shakespeare some suggestions for his Welsh scenes.

Francis Beaumont and John Fletcher's *Philaster* was written about the same time as *Cymbeline* and seems to bear a significant resemblance to Shakespeare's play. Philas-ter is, like Posthumus, in love with a princess whose father intends her for another suitor. Many of the similarities can be attributed to the conventions of the romance genre just then coming into vogue, and no one can be sure whether Shakespeare's play came after or before *Philaster*. If *Cym-beline* is the later of the two, however, *Philaster* must be considered as a source.

The Winter's Tale

Shakespeare based *The Winter's Tale* on Robert Greene's romantic novel called *Pandosto: The Triumph of Time* (1588), or *The History of Dorastus and Fawnia* in its running title. Shakespeare changes the names, reverses the two kingdoms of Sicilia and Bohemia, compresses the element of time, and alters the unhappy ending that afflicts King Pandosto and Queen Bellaria of Bohemia (Leontes and Hermione of Sicilia). Otherwise, the narrative outline re-mains intact. The story begins with the state visit of King Egistus of Sicilia (Polixenes of Bohemia) to his boyhood companion, King Pandosto of Bohemia. Queen Bellaria entertains their guest with such warmth, "oftentimes coming herself into his bedchamber to see that nothing should be amiss to mislike him," that Pandosto grows jealous. He commands his cupbearer Franion (Camillo) to murder Egistus, and the latter seems to agree but instead warns his victim to flee with him. Their hasty departure appears to confirm Pandosto's worst suspicions. He sends the guard to arrest Bellaria as she plays with her young son Garinter (Mamillius). When the Queen gives birth to a daughter in prison, the King orders the child destroyed, but he relents upon the insistence of his courtiers and causes the infant to be set adrift in a small boat. The Queen nobly defends herself at her trial (in language that Shakespeare has copied in some detail). She herself requests that the oracle at Delphos be consulted. The oracle replies in words that Shakespeare has altered only slightly: "Bellaria is chaste, Egistus blameless, Franion a true subject, Pandosto treach-erous, his babe an innocent; and the King shall live without an heir if that which is lost be not found." Pandosto is immediately stricken with remorse, and, when Queen Bellaria collapses at the news of her son Garinter's death, she is truly and irrecoverably dead.

A similarly close parallel in the narrative, along with telling changes in a number of details, characterizes the story's second half. The babe is conveyed by a tempest to the coast of Sicilia and is discovered by an impoverished shepherd named Porrus. He and his wife Mopsa adopt the child, naming her Fawnia. By the age of sixteen, Fawnia's natural beauty rivals that of the goddess Flora. At a meeting of the farmers' daughters of Sicilia, where she is chosen mistress of the feast, Fawnia is seen by the King's son Dorastus on his way home from hawking. She counters his importunate suit with the argument that she is too lowly a match for him, but he replies that the gods themselves sometimes take earthly lovers. Her foster father, distressed by the Prince's repeated visits (though he comes in shepherd's costume), resolves to carry the jewels he found with Fawnia to the King and reveal her story, thereby escaping blame for the goings-on. Dorastus escapes with Fawnia to a ship, aided by his servant Capnio (compare Camillo). Capnio also fulfills a role given by Shakespeare to Autolycus, for he manages to trick the shepherd Porrus into thinking he can see the King if he comes aboard Dorastus' ship. A storm drives these voyagers to Bohemia where, because of the ancient enmity between Egistus and Pandosto, they disguise themselves. Pandosto, happening to hear of Fawnia's beauty, orders her and the others to be arrested as spies and summoned to court, whereupon he falls incestuously in love with the disguised Fawnia. He promises to free the young man (who has taken the name of Meleagrus to conceal his identity) only if he will relinquish his claim to Fawnia. King Egistus meanwhile has discovered his son's whereabouts and sends ambassadors to Bohemia demanding the return of Dorastus and the execution of Fawnia, Capnio, and Porrus. Pandosto, his love for Fawnia having turned to hate, is about to comply when Porrus reveals the circumstances of Fawnia's infancy. Overjoyed to rediscover his daughter, Pandosto permits her to marry Dorastus but then falls into a melancholy fit and commits suicide.

Shakespeare has almost entirely created some characters, such as Paulina, Antigonus, the clownish shepherd's son, and Autolycus, though Capnio does perform one of Autolycus' functions by inveigling the old shepherd aboard ship. Antigonus' journey to the seacoast of Bohemia with the infant Perdita and his fatal exit "pursued by a bear" are Shakespearean additions. The character of Time is also added, and the shift in tone from tragedy to romance is more pronounced than in Greene. The shepherdesses at the sheepshearing are Shakespearean. The old shepherd has a more substantial and comic role; Camillo is a stronger person than Capnio. Greene's Mopsa, the shrewish wife of old Porrus, disappears from the play. Shakespeare omits the incestuous love of Pandosto for his daughter and brings Hermione back to life. (For this motif of a statue made to breathe, he may well have recalled Ovid's account of Pygmalion in Ovid's *Metamorphoses*, Book 10.) Shakespeare's Leontes is more irrationally jealous than in Greene's

account. Leontes' purgative sorrow is more intense and also more restorative than in the source; he is a truly noble and tragicomic figure, the center of a play about forgiveness and renewal.

Shakespeare may also have known Francis Sabie's *The Fisherman's Tale* (1595) and its continuation, *Flora's Fortune* (1595). From Greene's pamphlets, describing in vividly colloquial detail the life of London's underworld, Shakespeare probably derived many of Autolycus' tricks.

The Tempest

No direct literary source for the whole of *The Tempest* has been found. Shakespeare does seem to have drawn material from various accounts of the shipwreck of the *Sea Venture* in the Bermudas, in 1609, although the importance of these materials should not be overstated. Several of the survivors wrote narratives of the shipwreck itself and of their life on the islands for some nine months. Sylvester Jourdain, in *A Discovery of the Bermudas*, published 1610, speaks of miraculous preservation despite the island's reputation for being "a most prodigious and enchanted place." William Strachey's letter, written in July of 1610 and published much later (1625) as *A True Repertory of the Wreck and Redemption . . . from the Islands of the Bermudas*, describes the panic among the passengers and crew, the much feared reputation of the island as the habitation of devils and wicked spirits, the actual beauty and fertility of the place with its abundance of wild life (compare Caliban's descriptions), and the treachery of the Indians they later encounter in Virginia. Shakespeare seems to have read Strachey's letter in manuscript and may have been acquainted with him. The storm scene in Chapter 4 of Laurence Twine's *The Pattern of Painful Adventures*, a major source for *Pericles*, may also have given Shakespeare material for the first scene of *The Tempest*. Shakespeare also kept up with travel accounts of Sir Walter Ralegh and Thomas Harriot, and knew various classical evocations of a New World. The name "Setebos" came from Richard Eden's *History of Travel* (1577), translated from Peter Martyr's *De Novo Orbe* and from other travel accounts of the period. (See the Introduction to *The Tempest* for the potential relevance of various journals of the circumnavigation of the globe.) All these hints are indeed suggestive, but they are scattered and relate more to the setting and general circumstance of Shakespeare's play than to the plot.

Shakespeare certainly consulted Michel de Montaigne's essay "Of the Cannibals," as translated by John Florio in 1603. Gonzalo's reverie on an ideal commonwealth (2.1.150–171) contains many verbal echoes of the essay. Montaigne's point is that supposedly civilized men who condemn as barbarous any society not conforming with their own are simply refusing to examine their own shortcomings. A supposedly primitive society may well embody perfect religion, justice, and harmony; civilized art can never rival the achievements of nature. The ideal commonwealth has no need of magistrates, riches, poverty, and contracts, all of which breed dissimulation and covetousness. The significance of these ideas for *The Tempest* extends well beyond the particular passage in which they are found. And Caliban himself, whose name is an anagram of "cannibal," illustrates (even though he is not an eater of human flesh) the truth of Montaigne's observation apropos of the intense and wanton cruelty he finds so widespread in so-called Western civilization: "I think there is more barbarism in eating men alive than to feed upon them being dead."

Prospero's famous valedictory speech to "Ye elves of hills, brooks, standing lakes, and groves" (5.1.33–57) owes its origin to Medea's similar invocation in Ovid's *Metamorphoses* (Book 7), which Shakespeare knew both in the Latin original and in Golding's translation: "Ye airs and winds, ye elves of hills, of brooks, of woods alone, / Of standing lakes . . ." Medea also anticipates Shakespeare's Sycorax. Medea thus provides material for the representation of both black and white magic in *The Tempest,* so carefully differentiated by Shakespeare. Ariel is part English fairy, like Puck, and part daemon. The pastoral situation in *The Tempest* is perhaps derived from Edmund Spenser's *The Faerie Queene,* Book 6 (with its distinctions between savage lust and true courtesy, between nature and art). Italian pastoral drama as practiced by Guarini and (in England) by John Fletcher may also have been an influence. The masque element in *The Tempest,* prominent as in much late Shakespeare, bears the imprint of the courtly masque tradition of Ben Jonson, Francis Beaumont, and John Fletcher. Virgil's *Aeneid* may have provided Shakespeare with a more indirect source, with its story of wandering in the Mediterranean and storm at sea, love in Carthage, the intervention of the gods, and the fulfillment of destiny in Italy.

A German play, *Die Schöne Sidea* by Jacob Ayrer, written before 1605, was once thought to have been based on an earlier version of *The Tempest* as performed by English players traveling in Germany. Today, the similarities between the two plays are generally attributed to conventions found everywhere in romance.

The Two Noble Kinsmen

For their chief source, John Fletcher and William Shakespeare turned to "The Knight's Tale" in Chaucer's *Canterbury Tales.* "Chaucer, of all admired, the story gives," the Prologue tells us (1.13). In general, the dramatists follow their source for their main plot, especially in the middle acts.

"The Knight's Tale" relates how Duke Theseus, "lord and governour" of Athens, conquers the reign of "Femenye" and leads home Queen Ipolita to be his wife in "greet solempnitee," bringing with them Ipolita's younger sister Emelye. Their approach to Athens is interrupted by the petitions of widowed queens whose royal husbands have been slain at Thebes by the tyrant Creon. Complaining that their husbands' bodies have been desecrated, they implore Theseus to avenge the outrage. The Duke, filled with pity and anger, marches to battle forthwith and slays Creon, restoring to the widows the bones of their dead husbands.

On the field of battle are discovered two wounded cousins, Palamon and Arcite, nephews of the dead Creon. Taken back to Athens as prisoners for whom Theseus will accept no ransom, they languish in prison for some years, until it happens one May morning that they see Emelye from their prison tower as she gathers flowers. Palamon sees her first and is immediately stricken with love; Arcite, inquiring into his cousin's distress, soon follows his example. Despite their being sworn friends, they quarrel over her.

Arcite, it turns out, is a long-time acquaintance of Theseus's dearest friend, Perotheus, who many years ago made a dangerous journey to hell with Theseus. At Perotheus's behest, Arcite is freed but is also banished from Athens on pain of death. This condition of being separated from Emelye is a torment to him. The still-imprisoned Palamon is no less inconsolable, fearing that Arcite will assemble an army to attack Athens and thus gain his advantage with Emelye. The narrator asks: Which lover is in a worse plight?

After a year or two of this misery, Arcite, in Thebes, is visited by the god Mercury in a dream, bidding him return to Athens. He does so in disguise, and manages to obtain the office of chamberlain in Emelye's dwelling, where he remains "A yeer or two" as "Page of the chambre of Emelye the brighte." Theseus appoints the admirable young man as squire of his chamber as well. Three more years pass in this happy circumstance. Palamon meantime has been in his dark and horrible prison for seven years. At length, with the help of "a freend," he manages to break prison and flee Athens, hiding in a grove of trees until he can make his way to Thebes and obtain armed assistance in winning Emelye as his wife.

One May morning, out hunting with Theseus, Arcite happens upon Palamon's grove and encounters his furious cousin. Arcite agrees to bring arms and armor so that they can fight it out over Emelye. Their subsequent match is interrupted by Theseus, who objects that they may not fight thus "With-outen juge or other officere." Revealing their identities, the two cousins confess that they have incurred Theseus's just wrath. When the Duke condemns both to death, however, Ipolyta and Emelye intervene for mercy's sake until he relents. Theseus decrees that the cousins are to contend for Emelye, each with a hundred knights, in the lists, some fifty weeks hence. The cousins each repair to Thebes to prepare for the event.

The lists are set up in grand fashion, with three altars: for Venus, goddess of love, to the east; for Mars, god of war, to the west; and for Diana, goddess of chastity, to the north. Each altar is elaborately decorated with symbolic paintings, statuary, and the like. The contenders arrive with their supporting kings, who are presented to the reader in elaborate detail. The fateful day commences with prayers offered by the protagonists to their respective patron-gods: Palamon to Venus, Emelye to Diana, and Arcite to Mars. Each petitioner is answered with enigmatic but seemingly hopeful signs: Palamon is to have his love, Emelye is to have (though not the life of virginal purity she most wishes) the suitor who loves her most, and Arcite is to have the victory. Saturn will oversee the way in which these seemingly conflicting demands among mortals and gods alike can be amicably resolved.

All is fulfilled as destined. When Palamon falls in the lists, Theseus awards Emelye to Arcite—much to the distress of Venus, who complains to Saturn, only to be told to await the final end. Sure enough, an infernal fury, sent by Pluto at the behest of Saturn, causes Arcite's steed to shy and buck, throwing Arcite head-first to the ground. Dying, Arcite bestows Emelye on his dear cousin. Theseus orders an elaborate funeral for Arcite. After a decorous interval of some years, the Duke decrees an end to mourning so that the marriage of Palamon and Emelye can take place. They live happily ever afterward, with never a word of jealousy or other vexation.

The playwrights' alterations of this tale are revealing, especially in Shakespeare's contributions in the first and fifth act. Theseus's friend Pirithous plays a larger role at first than in Chaucer, giving Shakespeare opportunity for developing the motif of friendship in various guises. Emilia's loving remembrance of her dearest childhood friend is newly provided, for much the same thematic purpose. The extensive philosophical debate between Palamon and Arcite about the corruptions of Theban civic life and their need for stoical withdrawal is not even hinted at in Chaucer. In the play's last act, Shakespeare substitutes for Chaucer's rich description of the tournament a report of off-stage combat, so that the focus is on Emilia and her emotional response to the news of changing fortunes in the battle. Saturn's role is eliminated in the play; the one mention of his name (5.4.62) is an indirect reminder that he no longer controls the action. The fury that Saturn sends via Pluto to goad Arcite's horse becomes, in Shakespeare's account, a "fire malevolent" or "fierce sulfur," of hellish origin only in a metaphorical sense. Venus's direct intervention on behalf of Palamon forms no part of Shakespeare's dramatized account. The gods are still invoked as presiding deities over a destiny that humans cannot predict, but with a far less immediate role for the Olympians.

Time passes in Chaucer in narrative fashion over a succession of years. The playwrights are understandably more interested in a dramatic compression of events. Arcite's release from prison at Pirotheus's (Pirithous's) behest is more carefully explained in Chaucer as the result of an old friendship. The appearance to Arcite of Mercury in a dream, urging him to return to Athens, has no counterpart in the play; throughout, actions of this sort are apt to be motivated more by human feeling than by divine ordinance. Palamon's escape from prison is accomplished with the help of a friend; it is at this point that the playwrights, especially Fletcher, devise a subplot of the infatuated Jailer's Daughter to assist in the escape.

Chaucer's interest is in chivalric pageantry and in the soliloquies of his protagonists, as they ponder they seeming cruelties of their fates. Chaucer focuses a good deal on Duke Theseus, as we might expect from a tale told by a knight in defense of knightly ideals. Theseus is a mighty warrior, a defender of the innocent, and an equitable judge. Chaucer seemingly does not hold it against Theseus that he condemns Arcite and Palamon to death for their crimes of disobedience, and in any case he listens mercifully to his petitioners. As raisoneur of the tale, Theseus's repeated conclusion is that the god of love is mighty and that those who fall under love's spell, gods and humans alike, are likely to act with noble foolishness. The play's serious thematic treatment of friendship seems a conscious choice on the part of the dramatists, especially Shakespeare.

Occasional verbal echoes attest to the playwrights' direct acquaintance with "The Knight's Tale," perhaps in Thomas Speght's edition first published in 1598 and enlarged in 1602. They may also have known Chaucer's source, the Teseida of Boccaccio, in which that author undertook to acclimatize the Roman epic (especially Virgil's Aeneid and Statius's Thebiad) to Renaissance themes. Shakespeare made use of Sir Thomas North's translation of Plutarch's "Life of Theseus" for the friendship of Theseus and Pirithous. Shakespeare's own earlier A Midsummer Night's Dream afforded the playwrights a portrait of Duke Theseus as he sets about to marry Hippolyta and to adjudicate amorous conflicts among his courtiers.

The plot of the Jailer's Daughter is apparently an invention, albeit with generous infusions from earlier models in the depiction of the Daughter's madness, especially from the mad songs of Ophelia in Hamlet. The treatment of the Daughter's mental and emotional illness by a doctor in 4.3 (see especially ll. 59–61) has some affinities to Lady Macbeth's plight; see Macbeth, 5.1 and 5.3.47–48. The Daughter's pathetic situation also recalls some earlier work of Fletcher, as for example The Coxcomb (c. 1609); the story is similar, too, to that of Mopsa in Book 4 of Philip Sidney's Arcadia (first printed in 1593).

Other elements of comic subplot material in The Two Noble Kinsmen borrow freely from Shakespeare's earlier plays and other materials. When Palamon returns to Athens and is helped by some countrymen to learn about the games in which he can compete (2.3 and 2.5), the story is close to that of Pericles's being assisted by some fishermen when he is washed ashore at Pentapolis (2.1). Fletcher's pedantic schoolmaster in 3.5 reminds us of Holofernes in *Love's Labor's Lost*, who, like Fletcher's Gerald, helps put on a ridiculous entertainment for royalty. *A Midsummer Night's Dream* presents a similar pageant devised by clownish countrymen, with a burgomask dance not unlike the antimasque of twelve dancers in *The Two Noble Kinsmen*. Shakespeare and Fletcher took this antimasque, featuring a clown, a baboon, etc., and pedant as usher, from an antimasque devised for Francis Beaumont's *Masque of the Inner Temple*. Philip Sidney's entertainment, "The Lady of May," provides still another model for this buffoonish entertainment.

Two earlier plays on the subject of Palamon and Arcite have not survived. The first (in two parts) was written and staged in 1566 by Richard Edwards, whose surviving play about friendship, *Damon and Pythias* (c. 1560–1565), gives us some indication of the importance of friendship in Renaissance discourse. Castiglione's *The Courtier* and Sidney's *Arcadia* are but two of many models here. A second lost play about Palamon and Arcite was staged by the Admiral's men in 1594, and a lost play about Damon and Pythias by Henry Chettle was acted by the same company in 1600.

Venus and Adonis

Venus and Adonis was Shakespeare's contribution to the vogue of Ovidian and erotic poetry in the 1580s and '90s that included Thomas Lodge's *Scilla's Metamorphosis* (1589), Michael Drayton's *Endimion and Phoebe* (published 1595), Christopher Marlowe's *Hero and Leander* (registered 1593), and John Marston's *Metamorphosis of Pygmalion's Image* (1598). On Shakespeare's combining of three passages from Ovid's *Metamorphoses*, see the Introduction to *Venus and Adonis*. A disdainful Adonis had evidently become a commonplace in the 1590s, for it appears in *Hero and Leander*, lines 12–14, Edmund Spenser's *Faerie Queene*, 3.1.35, and elsewhere.

The Rape of Lucrece

Shakespeare's chief source for *The Rape of Lucrece* was Ovid's *Fasti* (2, 721–852), which had not yet been translated into English. He also seems to have known Livy's *History of Rome* (1, 57–59), which had been translated by William Painter in his *The Palace of Pleasure* (1566), and Chaucer's *The Legend of Good Women* (which is, like Shakespeare's poem, indebted to Ovid and Livy). Shakespeare's version is considerably longer than any of these sources. Ovid, Livy, and Chaucer give narrative, swift-moving accounts; Shakespeare follows, instead, the

literary tradition of the "Complaint," as in *A Mirror for Magistrates* and in Samuel Daniel's *The Complaint of Rosamond*.

The Phoenix and Turtle

"The Phoenix and Turtle" is sometimes related to Chaucer's *The Parlement of Fowles*, an allegorical treatment of an assembly of birds. No indebtedness can be proved, however. Instead, as F. T. Price has shown in his Arden edition of *The Poems*, Shakespeare's chief "source" was the very anthology to which he contributed this remarkable piece. Called *Love's Martyr*, assembled by one Robert Chester, it contains some execrable verse but was built around a single vivid and intriguing emblem: the union in death of two mythic birds expressing a love beyond human reason. The idea was sufficiently compelling to attract not only Shakespeare but Jonson, Chapman, and Marston. The cooperation of these highly sophisticated writers may have been prompted by some kind of private *jeu d'esprit*, but Shakespeare's venture into fantasy produced extraordinary results.

A Lover's Complaint

This poem resembles other complaints of forsaken women, as in Ovid's *Amores* and Chaucer's *Legend of Good Women*, but no specific source is known.

The Sonnets

See the Introduction to *The Sonnets* for a discussion of the sonnet vogue in England of the 1590s, and the previous history of the sonnet in England and on the Continent.

A Funeral Elegy for Master William Peter

Among the elegaic poems that may have provided a model for this poem, the most significant is Samuel Daniel's "A Funeral Poem upon The Death of the Late Noble Earl of Devonshire" (1606). Elements are also taken from Daniel's *Delia* and *The Complaint of Rosamond*. There are numerous echoes of Shakespeare's works, both dramatic and nondramatic.

APPENDIX 3

Shakespeare in Performance

Shakespeare belonged to the leading dramatic company of his time and wrote plays to be acted by men who were his close professional associates, the actor-sharers in the company. Unfortunately, we do not know as much as we would like about the assignment of roles in his plays. The leading actor of the company, Richard Burbage, played Richard III, Hamlet, Othello, and King Lear. Probably, he also played such roles as Macbeth, Antony, Coriolanus, and Prospero. In several roles, he was impressive enough to have received contemporary mention. Will Kempe, a comic actor, took the part of Dogberry in *Much Ado About Nothing*, Peter in *Romeo and Juliet*, and probably other such buffoonish clowns. His departure from the company in 1599 made room for Robert Armin, a comic actor whose "style" was that of the wise or courtly fool. Shakespeare seemingly wrote for him the parts of Touchstone, Feste, Lavatch (in *All's Well*), and the Fool in *King Lear*. Shakespeare wrote his women's parts generally for boy actors and was to an extent dependent on their quality and number. The boys, who served as apprentices to the actor-sharers, needed several years of experience before they could handle a demanding part like Juliet or Cleopatra. Yet some boys did manage to reach this remarkable level of proficiency before their voices started changing. The company needed a succession of boys so that they could be replaced in the women's roles when they became young men. (Some of them stayed on as young adult actors.)

Apart from specialized roles for the leading actor, the fool, and the boys, Shakespeare's company was versatile. The actor-sharers, men like John Heminges, Henry Condell, Augustine Phillips, Thomas Pope, Richard Cowley, William Sly, and Shakespeare himself, undertook both major and minor roles as occasion demanded. In about 1603, John Lowin and Alexander Cooke joined the roster of principal actors in the King's company. Phillips died in 1605, making room for Samuel Gilburne. Sly died in 1608, and at this time William Ostler and John Underwood joined the company. Later prominent actors included Joseph Taylor, who played Iago, and Nathan Field. These men were all accomplished actors. From our point of view today, their acting might

seem formal or stylized, although considerably less so than the acting seen during Shakespeare's youth. As Hamlet's instructions to the players suggest (*Hamlet*, 3.2.1–45), Shakespeare's company put great stress on "naturalness" in acting and clearly believed that they had reformed the ranting abuses of the earlier sixteenth century. Even so, Jacobean stage conditions militated against the kind of naturalistic informality we know today. Boys played women's parts; the language of the plays was often poetically quite formal; soliloquies and asides to the audience were common; little scenery existed to create a visual illusion; public performance in open daylight on a broad apron stage before large audiences required a declamatory style of elocution; and the absence of artificial lighting precluded the use of nighttime effects for ghosts or storms. Even when Shakespeare's company performed indoors at court or at one of the so-called private theaters, as they did increasingly in the 1600s, the indoor lighting could not readily be dimmed or increased or focused as with electrical equipment today. Torches might be brought onstage to signify a nighttime setting, but not primarily to illuminate the spectacle. Costuming ordinarily employed sumptuous Elizabethan dress, although sometimes with special costuming effects for Romans, Jews, sailors, and such.

Shakespeare's first known great success was *1 Henry VI*, in which the heroic role of Lord Talbot made a strong impression. *Richard III* had a spectacular popularity. Other enduringly popular successes in Shakespeare's own day included *Titus Andronicus, Romeo and Juliet, Richard II, Henry IV, Hamlet, Othello, Pericles*, and many others. On the other hand, *Troilus and Cressida* seems to have been a flop, and *Timon of Athens* probably was never even finished or performed. We know nothing about *All's Well That Ends Well* until the publishing of the 1623 Folio.

Little is known of Shakespeare's plays in performance from the time of his death until 1642. His reputation was assured, but even as a classic he could not compete with the successful playwrights who succeeded him, particularly John Fletcher. To be sure, in a commendatory verse to a collection of Shakespeare's poems in 1640, Leonard Digges asserted that Falstaff, Benedick and Beatrice, and Malvolio still drew fuller houses than Ben Jonson's dramatic creations. Nevertheless, the publication of the First Folio of Shakespeare's works in 1623, including several texts based on the playbooks that the company had used for its actual performances, suggests that the King's men were no longer interested in guarding the exclusive rights to Shakespeare's plays. In any event, the closing of the theaters in 1642 by a Puritan-dominated Parliament put an end to legitimate theater in England until the Restoration of 1660. During the interregnum period, Shakespeare lived on in the theater only through the occasional surreptitious performance of "drolls" or farcical skits derived from *1 Henry IV* ("The Bouncing Knight," or Falstaff), *Hamlet* ("The Grave Makers"), and *A*

Midsummer Night's Dream ("The Merry Conceited Humors of Bottom the Weaver").

From the Restoration to Garrick (1660–1741)

The theater of the Restoration and early eighteenth century differed greatly from Shakespeare's Globe Theatre. Audiences, who in Shakespeare's later years were already more oriented toward courtly and sophisticated taste than in the 1590s, were by Restoration times virtually limited to a select group who came to see plays in elegant indoor theaters. At the beginning of the Restoration, the acting companies were restricted in number by royal patent to two. That of Sir William Davenant, the Duke of York's players, began to play at the old theater in Salisbury Court in 1660 but moved to a new theater in Lincoln's Inn Fields the following year and to Dorset Garden in 1671. The company under Thomas Killigrew's management, the King's company, moved in 1660 from the Red Bull to a theater built on Gibbons' Tennis Court in Vere Street and thence to a theater on Bridges Street, Drury Lane, in 1663. When this first so-called Theatre Royal was destroyed by fire in 1672, Killigrew's company set up temporarily in Lincoln's Inn Fields but then moved to the magnificent second Drury Lane Theatre, designed by Christopher Wren, in 1674. Each successive move brought the two companies to more elegant quarters and to a more fashionable part of town. The two companies united in 1682, chiefly because audiences were too small to support both. Thereafter, they performed usually in the Drury Lane Theatre, the smaller of the two houses. This single company was the sole source of legitimate drama in London until 1695, when the restiveness of some underpaid actors led to the establishment of a newly patented acting company in Lincoln's Inn Fields. The new company enlisted some impressive talent, notably Thomas Betterton, Elizabeth Barry, and Anne Bracegirdle. Despite such a powerful beginning, and a new theater in the Haymarket in 1705 designed by Sir John Vanbrugh, the project dwindled and ultimately failed, leaving the field to Colley Cibber at Drury Lane. All the actors united again in one company, and Haymarket became an opera house.

Restoration theaters increasingly made use of the kind of elaborate scenic adornment that, in Shakespeare's time, had been restricted almost entirely to the presentation of courtly masques. The early Restoration also saw use of the proscenium arch with a curtained stage behind it, although a considerable amount of the action still took place on the apron or outer stage. Scenic effects were sometimes lavish, and the tendency toward such spectacle encouraged the production of operatic versions of Shakespeare. Artificial lighting was, of course, necessary for indoor performance, and actresses were used for women's parts in the plays. All these changes moved away from the fluidity and flexibility of the Elizabethan open-air apron stage, devoid of scenery.

Acting styles were affected by the changes in stage and theater management. Perhaps the most significant development was the emergence of the theater manager who was also leading actor. His prominence was unlike anything seen in Shakespeare's day, despite Shakespeare's reliance on Richard Burbage for leading roles. Shakespeare's company shared responsibility more or less equally among the actor-sharers, who were expected to be versatile in the doubling of roles and in the performing of important secondary parts; the new companies of the Restoration and eighteenth century devoted most prominence to the director-manager-leading actor. This structural shift in the acting company placed new demands on Shakespeare's scripts and motivated a search for ways of curtailing his secondary roles in favor of the major parts. Plays with large roles for a central protagonist, such as *Macbeth* and *Hamlet,* became repeated favorites, whereas others lacking such a focus, like *The Comedy of Errors* or *Love's Labor's Lost,* were seldom produced. Women's roles underwent a similar change of emphasis as the companies moved from boy actors to mature (and at times notorious) women. The new actresses, like the leading men, demanded plays and parts suited to their talents, and Shakespeare's scripts were accordingly selected and revised to meet this need.

The most famous actor-managers of the period from the Restoration in 1660 until the advent of David Garrick in 1741 were Thomas Betterton and Colley Cibber. Betterton was famous for his Macbeth, Bassanio (in *The Merchant of Venice*), Brutus, Othello, and Hamlet. As a director, he presided over some of the most extensive alterations of Shakespeare that the age witnessed, as we shall see. Cibber, too, was simultaneously a leading actor, theater manager, director, and author of many revisions of Shakespeare. Other prominent actors and actresses included Barton Booth and Robert Wilks (who were also joint managers of the Drury Lane Theatre), Anne Bracegirdle (who acted Portia, Desdemona, and other Shakespearean roles), and Elizabeth Barry (known for Calpurnia, Lady Macbeth, and Queen Gertrude). The famous Nell Gwyn seemingly did not undertake prominent Shakespearean roles. These roles give some indication of the Shakespearean plays most in demand by the actors and actresses of the age.

What, more specifically, were productions of Shakespeare like, and what happened to Shakespeare's scripts during this period? The influences at work were many and included not only the theatrical factors already discussed—actor-managers and actresses in search of large roles, scenery, indoor lighting, small select audiences—but also matters of literary taste. Classical decorum came into high repute. Ben Jonson was admired as a more learned and "correct" author than Shakespeare. The age tended to regard Shakespeare as an untutored "natural" genius who wrote for unrefined audiences in an ignorant time. Any "improvements" to his text would only serve to elevate

Shakespeare to the refinement and elegance he deserved. The result was that the Restoration period saw more adaptations of Shakespeare than performances of anything like the original. Theatrical practice and literary taste reinforced one another to encourage productions that were "unified" according to the classical unities, tightened by the elimination of minor characters, and at the same time rendered more symmetrical and spectacular by the incorporation of parallel plots and scenic effects. Moreover, some unhappy endings of Shakespearean plays were altered to provide resolutions in keeping with neoclassical ideas of "poetic justice"—that is, a just punishment for the villains and a deserved reward for the virtuous.

In Dryden's and Davenant's version of *The Tempest* (1670), elaborate symmetry of design is the overriding consideration. The adapters hit on the notion of what they called a "counter plot": since Shakespeare had told the story of a young lady who has never seen a young man, why not provide the play with a young man who has never seen a young lady? And so the authors invent Hippolito, young Duke of Mantua, whom Prospero has brought with him to the island at the time of his banishment and hid in a cave, safe from the fatal gaze of women. Inevitably, however, Hippolito discovers and falls in love with a woman his own age: not Miranda, but Miranda's sister Dorinda. Hippolito must also do battle for a time with Ferdinand, who is unsuccessfully confined to another cave. Eventually, each Jack obtains his Jill. Caliban likewise has a sister, Sycorax, and Ariel has a fellow spirit named Milcha. Milcha's role became much amplified in Thomas Shadwell's operatic version of 1674.

Davenant's *The Law Against Lovers,* based on *Measure for Measure* and staged in early 1662, stresses balance in structure along with the paring away of secondary roles and the accentuation of poetic justice. Davenant has eliminated virtually all the comic characters and has changed Angelo into a sentimentalized villain who truly loves Isabella, never intends to kill Claudio, and finally wins Isabella's hand in marriage. To this adapted plot, Davenant has added a subplot of Benedick and Beatrice from *Much Ado About Nothing,* with Benedick as Angelo's brother and Beatrice as Angelo's ward. In his *Macbeth* (1674), Davenant catered to the current vogue for opera and special effects by providing dancing witches and a ghost of Duncan that continues to haunt Lady Macbeth. This version held the stage until 1744. Thomas Killigrew's company did an adaptation of *The Taming of the Shrew* called *Sauny the Scot* (1667), written by the actor John Lacy. Sauny is a replacement for Grumio, Petruchio's comic servant. Samuel Pepys disliked the play generally but did admire the added part of Sauny with his Scottish humors. Thomas Shadwell's *Timon of Athens or the Man-hater* (1678) gave great prominence to two women: Melissa, whom Timon intends to marry, and Evandra, his mistress whom he intends to leave. Evandra proves, however, to be Timon's only true friend, and they die in one another's arms.

The Restoration impulse to tighten up the classical unities can be seen in Dryden's *Troilus and Cressida, or Truth Found Too Late* (1679) and in his *All for Love, or the World Well Lost* (1678). The latter is not really an adaptation of Shakespeare so much as a replacement. It tells the story of Antony and Cleopatra with obvious indebtedness to Shakespeare but confines the action to the very last phase, when the lovers are besieged in Alexandria. The cast is limited to about nine named characters, as compared with about thirty-one in Shakespeare's play.

Perhaps the best-known adaptation of Shakespeare in the Restoration period was Nahum Tate's *King Lear* (1681). This version ends happily, with Lear restored to his throne. The adaptation so satisfied eighteenth-century audiences in their craving for poetic justice that Shakespeare's version was banished from the stage until 1838. In Tate's defense, we might point out that all versions of the story before Shakespeare's play had ended with Lear's regaining of his throne; Shakespeare's is the great exception. Tate's version provided a love affair between Edgar and Cordelia. She remains in England rather than going to France, wanders about on the heath during the storm, and is nearly ravished by Edmund until Edgar providentially emerges from his cave and drives off the villain's henchmen. Tate also banished the Fool as offensive to classical ideas of "pure" tragedy unmixed with comedy.

Some Shakespearean adaptations were motivated in part by political considerations; the theater of the period was aimed at a select audience, knowledgeable in affairs of state and attuned to the sharp rivalries between Catholic and Protestant or court and Parliament. Tate's revision of *Richard II*, called *The Sicilian Usurper* (1681), ran into political trouble as soon as it was performed. Despite his changing of the scene to Sicily and his plaintive insistence afterward that he had intended no offense, his play was seen by the government as an attack on King Charles and was silenced on the third day. Equally controversial, for political reasons, were Tate's unsuccessful *Ingratitude of a Commonwealth* (1682) and John Dennis' *The Invader of His Country* (1719), both based on *Coriolanus*. John Crowne adapted the *Henry VI* plays in 1680–1681 in such a way as to comment on the horrors of civil war, the dangers of mob rule, and the threat of religious extremism.

Other Restoration and early eighteenth-century adaptations include Thomas Otway's *Caius Marius* (1680), which took the place of Shakespeare's *Romeo and Juliet* until 1744, Tom Durfey's *The Injured Princess, or the Fatal Wager* (1682), based on *Cymbeline,* George Granville's *The Jew of Venice* (1701), which substituted for *The Merchant of Venice* until 1741, and Charles Burnaby's *Love Betrayed* (1703), based on *Twelfth Night.* Perhaps the best-known adaptation of the early eighteenth century is the *Richard III* (1700) of Colley Cibber, manager of the Drury Lane Theatre and poet laureate. Some of Cibber's inclusions from *3 Henry VI*, and his added lines—"Off with his head, so much for Buckingham," or "Richard's himself again!"—are still used in modern productions. (See, for example, Laurence Olivier's film version of *Richard III*.)

The Age of Garrick (1741–1776)

The trend toward dominance of the London stage by a single man, who was manager, director, author, and his own star actor, reached its zenith in the career of David Garrick. His first dramatic season in 1741–1742, at an unlicensed and short-lived theater in Goodman's Fields, included a resounding success in the role of Richard III. Soon he was hired at an enormous salary to act at Drury Lane. With some fellow actors, he made attempts to secure a patent for a new company in 1743, and in 1746–1747 he performed memorably with the actor James Quin at Covent Garden. (The Covent Garden Theatre had been providing successful competition for the Drury Lane Theatre since its opening in 1732.) In 1747, however, Garrick returned to Drury Lane and became its joint manager and its chief moving spirit until his retirement in 1776.

During his glorious career, Garrick revived many Shakespearean plays that had been virtually forgotten. His predecessors had contented themselves with the repetition of a few predictable favorites, such as *Hamlet, Othello, King Lear* (in Tate's version, naturally), *Macbeth* (with dancing witches), *Julius Caesar, Richard III* (as transmuted by Cibber), and *1 Henry IV*. Only toward the end of the period had a few of the comedies been occasionally revived. Under Garrick, many long-neglected plays joined the repertory. Garrick revived *Much Ado About Nothing* in 1748–1749 and *Cymbeline* in 1761–1762, playing the leading roles (Benedick and Posthumus) himself. He also staged lesser-known history plays, such as *King John* and *Henry VIII*. His *Antony and Cleopatra* in 1759 was the first since Shakespeare's time. Garrick was his own most brilliant actor in *Hamlet, Much Ado About Nothing*, and many others; yet he shied away from certain roles in which other actors excelled. For example, he tended to defer to James Quin and Spranger Barry in *Othello* (at Covent Garden), Charles Macklin as Shylock, Quin as Falstaff, and still others. Garrick also grew too old for Romeo, and so ultimately he abandoned that play. Thus, the Drury Lane repertory grew and changed with Garrick's age and acting abilities.

Despite the enormous boost Garrick gave to Shakespeare in the theater, and despite his occasional fidelity to something approaching the texts of the plays as Shakespeare wrote them, Garrick was still the child of his time in his predilection for adapted Shakespeare. His *Macbeth* was closer in some ways to the original than had generally been the case in the preceding century, and yet he omitted the Porter scene as offensive to the decorum of tragedy. His production of *Hamlet* in 1772 rewrote the one great Shakespearean tragedy that had heretofore escaped major revision. His *Romeo and Juliet* (1748) followed Otway's lead in having Juliet awake in the tomb before Romeo dies, and *The Fairies* (1755) entirely omitted the tradesmen of Athens and their performance of "Pyramus and Thisbe." Garrick's version of *The Tempest* was operatic, like Dryden's. *Katharine and Petruchio*, Garrick's adaptation of *The Taming of the Shrew* that included only the wife-taming plot, supplanted the Shakespearean original from 1756 to 1844 and remained popular long afterward. Garrick's *King Lear* (1756) retained Nahum Tate's happy ending with the love affair of Cordelia and Edgar and omitted the Fool, as Tate had done, even though the actual poetry of some scenes was brought noticeably closer to that of Shakespeare.

A small man with lively features, Garrick possessed an ability to transform himself in performing a role that became legendary. He went to hospitals for the insane and studied the behavior of inmates in order to prepare himself for Lear's mad scenes. His passion for a natural style based on observation from life was highly innovative in an age generally devoted to a more formal and rhetorical manner of delivery. Garrick's range of characterization was also extraordinary. He performed low-comedy parts with such verisimilitude that some spectators came away from the theater convinced that Garrick could be nothing other than a mean-spirited and worthless fellow. Yet his most famous effects were the violent passions: Hamlet's fear and awe in the presence of his father's ghost, Lear's ungovernable fury at his older daughters' ingratitude, and the like.

One contribution of questionable worth made by Garrick to Shakespearean stage history was his great Shakespeare Jubilee, held at Stratford over a three-day period in the summer of 1769. In its own day, the event was both praised as a great honor to Shakespeare's memory and vilified as an ostentatious charade. Its elaborate ceremonies were, in fact, notably lacking in the performance of Shakespeare's own works. The high point seems, instead, to have been Garrick's recitation of his "Ode Upon Dedicating the Town Hall, and Erecting a Statue to Shakespeare." Nevertheless, the celebration raised money for the maintenance of various historical monuments in Shakespeare's home town. The whole event did much to establish the vogue of Shakespeare worship that became so much a part of nineteenth-century Shakespeare criticism.

Other leading actors from Garrick's time—Charles Macklin, James Quin, Spranger Barry—did not attain his success, whatever their individual achievements. Macklin, an older actor than Garrick, never got over his resentment of the younger man's success. Garrick's leading ladies included Hannah Pritchard as Rosalind, Beatrice, and Lady

Macbeth; Peg Woffington as Rosalind, Isabella, Viola, Portia, and Mistress Ford; her rival, Anne Bellamy, as Juliet; Mary Ann Yates as Rosalind, Isabella, Cleopatra, and Lady Macbeth; and Susanna Cibber as Juliet. Their rivalries, especially that of Anne Bellamy and Peg Woffington, sometimes took the form of competition in gorgeous attire, and the costume managers at Drury Lane were kept busy supplying Mrs. Bellamy with jewels and satin in which to appear as Volumnia or Juliet. (One dress, fashioned for Mrs. Bellamy in the part of Cleopatra in *All for Love,* c. 1746, had belonged to the Princess of Wales and had been worn on her birthday, but was walked off with by the rival actress who was to play Octavia.) The prominence of such actresses gave impetus to the repeated performances of such comedies as *As You Like It* and *Measure for Measure.*

The Romantic Age: Kemble, Edmund Kean, Macready (1776–1843)

The Romantic Age was generally not a flourishing time for the English theater. As we can see from a survey of Shakespeare criticism (see the General Introduction), Romantic critics such as Lamb and Hazlitt held condescending views of theatrical performances of Shakespeare and preferred to read Shakespeare's text in the quiet of their own studies. The greatest literary figures of the age did not write for the stage; the occasional dramas written by the Romantic poets are usually "closet" dramas, designed to be read rather than acted. Garrick's huge success in producing Shakespeare proved hard to emulate. One reason for the decline may have been that Shakespeare on the stage had been so thoroughly made over into a neoclassical dramatist by Tate, Cibber, and Garrick that he no longer appealed to the taste of the new age. Many Romantic critics and readers, intent now on the study of Shakespeare's philosophical idealism and his conceptions of personality or "character," preferred the sublimity of Shakespeare's own poetry to the theatrical spectacle and classical "decorum" they found on the London stage.

The acting manager at Drury Lane from 1788 to 1802 was John Philip Kemble. Strained relations with the playwright Richard Brinsley Sheridan forced Kemble to leave Drury Lane in 1802 to undertake the management of Covent Garden, where he achieved a notable success and remained active until his retirement in 1817. Both theater buildings burned during this period—Covent Garden in 1808 and Drury Lane in 1809—but both were splendidly rebuilt. The new Covent Garden Theatre featured an ample stage and proscenium arch with wing and groove flats, encouraging extravagant settings to match the resplendent costumes and pageantry. Here, Kemble was able to perform before a large audience of some three thousand spectators and to indulge in more lavish sets than had before been possible. Kemble came to be noted for his attention to realistic details in

costuming and scenery. His *Henry VIII* (1788–1789) abounded in colorful processions; his *Coriolanus* (1789) was strikingly Roman in costume; his *The Tempest* (produced at this same time) "gave a terrible dance of Furies in one place, and a masque of Neptune and Amphitrite in another." Sarah Siddons, his best-known leading lady, excelled as Rosalind, Queen Katharine, Isabella, Hermione, and Lady Macbeth. Despite Kemble's popularity, however, his productions did not provide a return to Shakespeare's texts; indeed, his desire for spectacle often took him in the other direction. He restored some of Tate's additions to *King Lear* that Garrick had eliminated and usually performed Shakespearean plays in the altered versions to which the previous age had grown accustomed.

During the years following Kemble's retirement in 1817, the English theater came to a particularly low ebb. Standing out among mediocrities, Edmund Kean succeeded Kemble as the leading actor of the day and managed to impress even such a Romantic critic as William Hazlitt. He was impressive as Othello and Richard III, among other roles. He did make significant restorations in the text of *King Lear* (1823), including the last act with the death of Cordelia, but he still retained the love of Cordelia and Edgar, omitted the Fool, and compromised his task of restoration to such an extent that a contemporary reviewer complained justifiably of too much "plastering." During this period between 1817 and 1837, in fact, the English theater seems to have been more timid and bound by convention than its public would have desired. Stage traditions are often remarkably persistent, and those established by Tate, Cibber, and Garrick lived well beyond the age that created them.

It fell to William Charles Macready, manager of Covent Garden (1837–1839) and then of Drury Lane (1841–1843), to make a first serious attempt at restoration of Shakespeare's acting texts. Although not an astute financier, Macready was an actor whose sensitive style won him admirers among audiences now grown too refined for Kean's explosions of passion. In 1838, Macready staged *King Lear,* "free from the interpolations which have disgraced it for nearly two centuries," as a contemporary reviewer put it. However much closer it was to Shakespeare's play, to be sure, Macready's *King Lear* still left out Gloucester's blinding and otherwise rearranged and curtailed the play. A significant step had nonetheless been taken, and Macready followed his own lead in "restoring" many of the other plays, leaving in his *Diaries* a still interesting record of his thoughts on acting Shakespeare. By 1843, of all Shakespeare's plays only *Richard III, Romeo and Juliet,* and *The Taming of the Shrew* still held the stage as eighteenth-century adaptations.

In a reform of equal significance, an act of 1843 abolished the monopoly on theatrical companies that had been in effect since 1660. The controlling of patents or licenses had resulted, as we have seen, in the licensing of only two

London companies at most. After 1843, any company could perform plays in a theater that met the requirements of public safety. Freed of manipulative control and nearly free of the eighteenth-century acting versions of Cibber and Garrick, the English stage enjoyed greater vitality than it had known for some time.

The Later Nineteenth Century: Phelps, Charles Kean, Irving (1843–1902)

With the abolition of patent control in 1843, Drury Lane and Covent Garden fell into an almost immediate and overdue senility. (Drury Lane alone recovered and eventually flourished again.) In their place sprang up new theaters and new actors: in particular, Samuel Phelps at the Sadler's Wells Theatre and Charles Kean at the Princess's Theatre. A third important theater, the Haymarket, featured at various times Macready, Charles Kean and his wife Helen Faucit, and others. The recently introduced gas lighting now illuminated all the theaters. The Haymarket featured extensive remodeling, including a curtailment of the apron stage in front of the proscenium arch and curtain, an advancing of the orchestra and lights nearer the actors and scenic effects, and an interior "decorated in the most costly and elegant style." Phelps managed Sadler's Wells until 1862 and presented there a repertory of unparalleled richness, including many Elizabethan plays—*The Maid's Tragedy, The Duchess of Malfi, A New Way to Pay Old Debts*—in addition to those of Shakespeare. His actresses included Isabel Glyn (as Gertrude and Cleopatra) and Laura Addison (as Juliet and Imogen). Some notable revivals were *Timon of Athens, 2 Henry IV,* and *Pericles.* Charles Kean, Edmund Kean's son, indulged a passion for elaborate historical accuracy in the use of costumes and scenery—a trend toward spectacular verisimilitude that John Kemble and William Charles Macready had already done much to further.

Under the guidance of Phelps and Kean, and also Ben Webster at the Haymarket, the English theater revived long neglected and heavily adapted plays in something like their Shakespearean form. *The Taming of the Shrew* appeared at the Haymarket in 1844, *Richard III* at Sadler's Wells in 1845, and *Romeo and Juliet* at the Haymarket in 1845. *King Lear* underwent even further restoration under Phelps' direction, in 1845, than it had received from Macready in 1838. Phelps' *Macbeth* (1847) put aside the musical and spectacular additions that had so long afflicted the witch scenes. A contrary force was at work, however, in the pursuit of spectacular visual effects, for new cuttings were needed to make room for scene changes, and the costs of productions were beginning to increase at an alarming rate. As the age of Phelps and Kean came to an end (Kean retired in 1859), Shakespearean production on the London stage seemed poised on the verge of a new difficulty. F. B. Chatterton at the Drury Lane Theatre offered his ominous opinion that "Shakespeare spells ruin." Shakespeare was about to become, in other words, a heavy financial risk for the producer rather than a surefire commercial success. The cost of cumbersome and ornate stagings of Shakespeare continued to mount during the late nineteenth century.

During this era, the standard for Shakespearean productions was set by Henry Irving, manager of the Lyceum Theatre from 1878 until 1902, and by Ellen Terry, his leading lady. Irving, a talented director and producer, enjoyed an enormous success and eventually was honored by knighthood and by burial in Westminster Abbey (like Garrick before him). Irving's Shakespearean sets were always sumptuous, richly decorated, and attentive to details. His stage set for *Henry VIII* in 1892, for example, featured magnificent Tudor interiors with paneled wood ceilings and carved wooden arches, or renditions of Westminster Abbey with tall perpendicular Gothic stained-glass windows. His elaborate visual effects extended and fulfilled a tradition of spectacle in Shakespearean production begun in the Restoration period, continued in the eighteenth century, and elaborated further in the nineteenth by Kemble, Macready, and Charles Kean. From 1660 to 1902, in fact, Shakespearean production seldom questioned the value of elaborate spectacle; however much the twentieth-century stage may seem to us closer to the Shakespearean original of a bare and flexible arena, the modern stage is a departure from a long and cumulative tradition of some 240 years. And Irving's productions were impressive, although at great cost to the script. Irving's sets were so massive, and his need for supernumeraries so great, that every Shakespearean production had to be special and costly. Shakespeare was no longer material for a stock repertory, and his plays were produced by Irving with relative infrequency. Because the changing of scenes involved so much time and expense, the texts of the plays had always to be cut and rearranged. Cibber's and Garrick's unreliable revisions were a thing of the past, to be sure, but no actor-producer of the nineteenth century would have thought seriously for a moment of doing Shakespeare uncut.

In America, conditions were much the same, and indeed most productions of Shakespeare seen by Americans were either imported from England or inspired by English acting. Macready toured the United States in the 1820s and 1840s, and became involved in a celebrated quarrel with the American actor Edwin Forrest. Charles Kean and Irving also acted in America; Kean played opposite Edwin Forrest, whereas Irving performed in 1880 with Edwin Booth, the first American actor to win fame abroad. American Shakespeare of the Victorian era was, like its English counterpart, ornate and verisimilar, set behind a proscenium arch as though the audience were watching through a "fourth wall." On the American frontier, to be sure, the elaborate Shakespeare of the New York–Boston circuit gave way to something more impromptu. Much of it doubtless deserved the kind of roasting it received in Mark Twain's portrait of two fraudulent strolling Shakespearean actors in *Huckleberry Finn,* though even here we can see evidence of the enormous impact of Shakespeare on the culture of a new nation.

The Twentieth Century: Revival and Adaptation

The early years of the twentieth century saw the continuation and even extension of the opulent style championed by Henry Irving. The foremost actor-manager of the turn-of-the-century era was Herbert Beerbohm Tree, presiding genius at Her (His) Majesty's Theatre from its opening in 1897 until his death in 1917. His productions of Shakespeare in this theater outdid Irving in his own metier and were indeed lavish on an unprecedented scale. Live rabbits scurried across the stage in his *A Midsummer Night's Dream* (1911). The opening scene of *The Tempest* (1904) revealed a ship magnificently battered by a full-dress storm at sea. Tree's version of *Antony and Cleopatra* (1907) actually staged the first meeting of Antony and Cleopatra, instead of relying on Enobarbus' description of this event: Cleopatra appeared robed in silver, leading a huge procession through the streets of Alexandria. Such interpretations naturally called for a good deal of rearranging and curtailing of Shakespeare's texts. The scene intervals in Tree's *Macbeth* (1911) ran to forty-five minutes, and the whole production, even with a third of the text cut away, lasted four hours. His *King John* (1899) gave its viewers a tableau of Runnymede (as Charles Kean had done earlier, in 1852), even though the play never mentions Magna Carta. Olivia's garden in *Twelfth Night* (1901) revealed to the audience real grass, box hedges, statues, and running fountains. This set was, needless to say, particularly hard to move; scenes located at Duke Orsino's palace had somehow to be worked around the decor of Olivia's garden. Tree was a great success, as Irving had usually been. So, too, was Johnston Forbes-Robertson, renowned actor of Hamlet and Othello, who expurgated his texts to conform with Victorian standards of decency.

Despite popular fondness for Beerbohm Tree's grand style, however, a movement toward greater stage flexibility and a fidelity to Shakespeare's texts was under way. Frank Benson, who brought his repertory company from the provinces to the Lyceum Theatre in 1900, offered relatively straightforward productions. Benson produced *Hamlet,* for example, in two sessions (afternoon and evening), from an uncut text of the First Folio. A performance of this sort could not possibly use the unwieldy sets of a Tree production. Benson never could match Tree in popularity, since the times demanded an ornamental style. Even so, his impact was significant. One ingredient of his method was simple economic common sense: he lacked the means to stage Shakespeare as expensively as Tree had done and needed

also to be able to take his flexible productions on tour.

William Poel was more of an idealist and visionary than Benson, and also something of an eccentric. His aim in establishing the Elizabethan Stage Society in 1894 was to discover more about Shakespeare's own stage and to use that knowledge as a means of combating what he viewed as the stifling conventionality of the late Victorian theater. He was a passionate crusader for swiftly paced acting, continuity of scenes, a fluid stage, and intimacy between actors and audience. His performances were Elizabethan revivals—usually meticulously so, with Elizabethan costuming, an inner stage and open platform, and other aspects of historical reconstruction. Although his audiences were never large, he did prove that Elizabethan staging could work as practical theater. He performed *The Comedy of Errors* (1895) in Gray's Inn, where it had been performed in 1594 by Shakespeare's company. For his *Romeo and Juliet* (1905), he cast a girl of fourteen as Juliet and a boy of seventeen as Romeo. George Bernard Shaw saw the production and was impressed.

Another believer in Poel's work was Harley Granville-Barker. His productions of Shakespeare at the Savoy Theatre in 1912–1914 converted what had been an experimental movement into successful commercial theater. In Granville-Barker's view, Poel had gone too far in stripping bare the overornamented stage of Beerbohm Tree. Granville-Barker hit, instead, upon a format that provided the essential elements of Poel's reform and yet avoided the cult of austerity for its own sake. His opening production in 1912, *The Winter's Tale,* employed three acting areas for the entire play and stressed above all rapidity of pace and intimacy. He abolished footlights and realistic backdrops. In his *Twelfth Night* of the same year, he did away with the tradition of burlesque foolery in which the comic characters had long been played. These innovations naturally caused an uproar, but they also found favor with influential critics. Beerbohm Tree's edifices were soon to become a thing of the past.

The Old Vic Theatre and its acting company moved toward the new style of acting in the 1910s, mainly under the impetus of the producer Philip Ben Greet and the theater's manager, Lilian Baylis. This theater on London's bankside had been built in 1818 and had been named the Royal Victoria in 1833. Since 1914, the company has specialized in Shakespearean performance under the direction of Tyrone Guthrie and others. Renamed the National Theatre Company in 1963, this organization has continued to be a leader in modern Shakespearean production, now broadening its repertory to include non-Shakespearean plays and in 1975 moving into a new theater complex on the South Bank of the Thames. The roster of actors and actresses who have brightened the Old Vic stage over the years reads like a who's who in theater: John Gielgud, Ralph Richardson, Laurence Olivier, Michael Redgrave, Edith

Evans, Margaret Webster, Charles Laughton, Emlyn Williams, Trevor Howard, Peggy Ashcroft, Maurice Evans, Flora Robson, Vivien Leigh, Cedric Hardwicke, Claire Bloom, Donald Wolfit, Richard Burton, Wendy Hiller, and many more.

At Stratford, another theater devoted its repertory primarily to "restored" Shakespeare. Founded in 1879, the Shakespeare Memorial Theatre grew from a regional festival into the preeminent theater for Shakespeare in the world today. It prospered early under the management of Frank Benson and then W. Bridges-Adams, later attracting directors from the first ranks in English theater including Peter Brook, Peter Hall, Trevor Nunn, Anthony Quayle, Douglas Seale, Glen Byam Shaw, and Terry Hands. Since 1961, when it was renamed the Royal Shakespeare Company, the organization has grown to include four permanent theaters (two in Stratford, two in London) and a company of excellent actors. Its productions tour the world, most memorably Peter Brook's *A Misummer Night's Dream* (on tour 1970–1973). Seemingly a permanent, world-class Shakespeare company, the Royal Shakespeare Company has found itself challenged in recent years by austere budgets and by such impressive upstart companies as Kenneth Branagh's English Shakespeare Company.

Such success in England has spawned a host of imitators. In North America, the list of Shakespeare festivals stretches to more than one hundred. Among the best: the Canadian Shakespeare Festival at Stratford, Ontario; the American Shakespeare Festival at Stratford, Connecticut; the Colorado Shakespeare Festival at Boulder, Colorado; the Great Lakes Festival at Cleveland, Ohio; the Ashland Festival at Ashland, Oregon; and Joseph Papp's Shakespeare Festival in New York's Central Park. In Europe, especially in Germany and Scandinavia, and in Asia, especially in Hong Kong, Japan, and Taiwan, Shakespeare enjoys a special place in the repertory. Nor should the contributions of Australian and Indian productions be slighted. Throughout the world, directors, actors, and designers participate in a fruitful interchange, adding to the world's store of Shakespearean performance and bringing in audiences numbering millions. With a few quirky exceptions, all of these Shakespearean repertory companies employ to some extent an open-platform stage, quick shifting of scenery, and the like. In this important sense, Shakespearean production throughout the later twentieth century has remained true to the spirit of Benson, Poel, and Granville-Barker in their rebellion against Victorian embroidery and the constricting proscenium arch.

In another important sense, however, twentieth-century Shakespearean productions have sometimes returned to the practice of adapting Shakespeare in order to render him more palatable to contemporary tastes. Shakespeare has been remade in the image of modernity, much as the Restoration period remade him in neoclassical terms and much as the Victorians molded him into a great defender of social institutions. The process is neither new nor surprising; it is a way of assimilating Shakespeare and pays him the high compliment of needing to see him as a part of us, whoever we may be. In the modern world, the need has been for a Shakespeare who speaks to the vision of alienation, the futility of the political process, the inhumanity of war, and the struggles for human freedom. The occasional stridency of tone and the ideological insistence on extreme political meaning in some recent Shakespeare productions seem characteristically modern, and yet several eighteenth-century productions of *Richard II* and *Coriolanus* were similarly accused of taking sides in the political controversies of that day. To perceive the continuity in this process of updating Shakespeare is to acknowledge its timeless purpose in the theater as a way of interpreting Shakespeare to audiences. The cuttings and distortions of emphasis employed to give us an alienated *Hamlet,* for example, or an existentialist *King Lear,* are, for all their apparent newness, much like the rearrangements applied to Shakespeare's scripts in the earlier adaptations of Tate, Cibber, and Garrick.

An early instance of modern adaptation is Orson Welles' famous production of *Julius Caesar* (1937), drawing an analogy between the Caesar of the play and Benito Mussolini. Welles' satire of dictatorship was galvanizing to audiences threatened with the prospect of a fascist-dominated Europe, but the interpretation of the play was of necessity one-sided; it allowed for no ironic perception of both good and evil in Caesar's one-man rule. Similarly, a production of *Coriolanus* in Paris in the early 1930s caused political rioting when the radical left interpreted the play in their terms as an attack on dictatorship, and the extreme right conversely interpreted the play as an indictment of the cowardice and political opportunism of the mob and its leaders. This kind of adaptation of Shakespeare to modern ideological controversy found expression also in a 1938 production of *Troilus and Cressida* at the Westminster Theatre, when Britain was on the verge of a second World War; the production's mocking of war seemed to capture a current mood of disillusionment. Ever since, directors have found many ways of staging Shakespeare as though he were a fervent opponent of war.

The most influential figures in this movement have included Bertolt Brecht, a leader in the German experimental theater, and Jan Kott, author of *Shakespeare Our Contemporary.* Kott's book sees Shakespeare as one who speaks to our existentialist world. This view served as the basis, for example, of a Royal Shakespeare Company production of *Macbeth* in the 1960s starring Alec Guinness and Simone Signoret, in which life was presented as a grotesque experience comparable to that of Auschwitz. A production in 1964 by the same group of the *Henry IV* plays and *Henry V,* under Peter Hall's direction, showed the influence of Brecht in its exaggeratedly squalid tavern scenes and in its terrifying rendition of the Battle of Agincourt. Other productions of *Henry V* have also made the hero out to be a frightful prig (as George Bernard Shaw interpreted him), by emphasizing the ironies of Henry's "imperialistic" war against France and by interpreting his famous speeches as so much cynical rhetoric. To be sure, Laurence Olivier's overtly patriotic film version of *Henry V*, produced in wartime England with the sponsorship of the British government, emphasized those parts of the play that best agreed with Britain's wartime mood. The result was a stirring film that asked its audience not to be afraid to love one's country, its people, and its institutions. Yet, more recently, Kenneth Branagh's equally moving film (1989) has returned to a more characteristically postmodern view by reinterpreting the play as a personal struggle to fulfill the often grisly demands placed on a young man striving to be the warrior-king.

Some twentieth-century adaptations of Shakespeare have succeeded in what they did by not pretending to be anything other than lighthearted transmutations of his work into different genres. The American musical comedy version of *The Taming of the Shrew* by Cole Porter, called *Kiss Me, Kate* (1948), featured some delightful songs and did not attempt to take itself too seriously. Equally successful and honest was the rock musical version of *The Two Gentlemen of Verona* in New York, in 1972. Leonard Bernstein's *West Side Story* (1957) translated the ancient feud of the Capulets and Montagues from *Romeo and Juliet* into gang warfare, New York style. The analogy was perhaps a facile and sentimentalized one, but the contemporary music and the frenetic dancing gave a compelling impression of violence and speed. Other musicals have included *The Boys from Syracuse* (1938), based on *The Comedy of Errors; Swingin' the Dream* (1939), taken from *A Midsummer Night's Dream;* and *Your Own Thing* (1968), a rock adaptation of *Twelfth Night.* Once again, we can see a historical similarity between such productions and an earlier adaptation like Dryden's and Davenant's operatic *The Tempest,* although modern musical comedy has fortunately been seen as an innocent variation on Shakespeare, rather than as a replacement for the original, as often happened in the Restoration and eighteenth century.

A distinguishing feature of modern production and adaptation has been the translation of Shakespeare into contemporary settings, into period settings of an era between Shakespeare's and our own, or into current theatrical styles, such as the theater of the absurd and the theater of cruelty. Modern-dress Shakespeare on the English stage began with Barry Jackson's *Hamlet,* directed by H. K. Ayliff at the Birmingham Repertory Theatre and then transferred to London at the Kingsway Theatre in 1925. In 1928, Jackson brought his Birmingham Repertory *Macbeth,* also directed by Ayliff in modern dress, to the Royal Court Theatre in London. The idea, a sound one, was to use contemporary costume, as Shakespeare himself had done, and thus free the audience to concentrate on the universal character of the play. Subsequently, however, modern dress too often became a fad. The use of period setting was expertly handled in, for example, Tyrone Guthrie's Edwardian version of *All's Well That Ends Well* (Stratford, Canada, 1953), where the analogy to a complacent aristocratic society gave a clarifying perspective to Shakespeare's original setting in Renaissance France. Like modern dress, however, period setting involves an inherent risk that elements of the Shakespearean original will seem out of place and will have to be sacrificed or muddled through. Social titles like "Your Majesty" and "His Grace" may seem anachronistically jarring. In the American Shakespeare Festival production of *Much Ado About Nothing* at Stratford, Connecticut (1957), the setting on a Texas ranch and the portrayal of Dogberry as a bumbling sheriff in the fashion of then current television and movie Westerns may well have enhanced Dogberry's appeal for some of the audience, but it did so at the expense of the aristocratic relationships and social customs on which Shakespeare's play depends. Joseph Papp's version of the same play, staged in New York and then shown on commercial television in America in 1977, chose as its setting small-town America of the era of Teddy Roosevelt, replete with gramophones, ragtime bands, and high-wing collars. Dogberry and his watchmen became Keystone Cops in a familiar movie idiom. The analogy enlivened the comedy and made it frantically farcical but, again, at a price, since social distinctions in democratic America cannot approximate those of sixteenth-century England. Jonathan Miller's choice of late nineteenth-century Europe for his *The Merchant of Venice* (National Theatre, 1970, with Laurence Olivier as Shylock, subsequently televised) illustrates a similar reward and difficulty; the complacent prejudices of an anti-Semitic social order lend impact to Shylock's tragedy, but at the expense of a Renaissance context, in which disapproval of usury is essential to a Christian view of salvation.

Other examples of anachronistic setting, at times extreme, might include Jack Landau's *Troilus and Cressida* (Stratford, Connecticut, 1961) in the context of America's Civil War; Franco Zeffirelli's *Much Ado About Nothing* (National Theatre, London, 1965), set in modern-day Sicily; Theodore Komisarjevsky's *Macbeth* (Memorial Theatre, Stratford-upon-Avon, 1933) in a modern idiom of "twisted aluminum"; Tyrone Guthrie's *The Taming of the Shrew* (Stratford, Canada, 1954) as a Western; Joseph Papp's *Hamlet* (Public Theatre, New York, 1968) beginning the play with Hamlet in a coffinlike cradle at the foot of Claudius' and Gertrude's bed; and Michael Bogdanov's *Measure for Measure* (Stratford, Ontario, 1985) done as cabaret theater, with a sleazy master of ceremonies, transvestite dancers, quantities of black leather, strobe lights, and the like. Productions such as these are not, of course, the only choice of modern directors, and for more balanced interpretations one looks to Glen Byam Shaw and to many others who have created Shakespeare on stage in ways that are at once recognizable and innovative.

The controversy about adaptation of Shakespeare is still very much alive today and will undoubtedly remain so. The forms of Shakespearean adaptation have altered, but the issues have remained virtually unchanged since 1660. When and to what extent ought the text to be rewritten to conform with yesterday or today? Many observers would maintain that the dialogue between purists and adapters is not only inevitable, but healthy. The purist reformer, like William Poel, is needed as a voice of conscience and integrity, even though he or she is perhaps doomed to play the role of lonely visionary. The adapter's goal is, on the other hand, to "interpret" Shakespeare, and, although directors from David Garrick to Peter Brook willingly arrange and distort in their search for contemporary meaning, a lively director can certainly generate new interest in a work that might otherwise remain classically "pure" but lifeless. In any case, twentieth-century production has brought us a long way from the Romantic doldrums, during which most intelligent readers of Shakespeare could not bear to have their author desecrated by a performance on stage.

Shakespeare on Film and in Television

Versions of Shakespeare on film and in television inevitably require some adaptation to the new media and thus bring into particularly clear focus the controversy between purists and adapters that we have seen in relation to the stage. Despite the claims of enthusiasts that Shakespeare anticipated many film techniques with his cutting from scene to scene, his juxtaposing soliloquy with crowded scenes of action, and so on, film and theater remain unlike in essential ways. The camera does well in closely revealing the expressions of speakers during soliloquy or intimate scenes and can cross-cut to good effect in larger scenes, but the camera is unable to do what a spectator does continually in the theater: see live actors in the total space of that enclosure, isolated in the midst of that space or grouped in such ways as to suggest tensions or alignments, the whole spectacle simultaneously visible and in motion while the spectator remains still. The camera, by controlling and selecting and thinking for us, is less able to take in many things at once, despite its excellence at what it can do. Because the camera can record things of great natural beauty, like the sunrise (compare Friar Laurence's verbal description in Romeo and Juliet, 2.3.1–6) or a gently flowing river (compare the account of Ophelia's death in Hamlet, 4.7.167–184), it renders extraneous Shakespeare's evocation in words of what he was unable to bring

physically into the theater. The audience is not ordinarily present in film or television, thereby removing the opportunity for improvisation and appeals to the audience by a character like Iago. This is not to deny the camera's manifest abilities but rather to insist on the need for recognition of important differences between film and stage. The best films have been bold in this assumption of difference, though boldness itself is no guarantee of success.

Despite numerous attempts at filming Shakespeare in the days of silent film and early sound film, no movie versions of Shakespeare prior to World War II yield much more than antiquarian interest, with the problematic exception of Max Reinhardt's A Midsummer Night's Dream (1935), starring Mickey Rooney as Puck and James Cagney miscast as Bottom the Weaver. Laurence Olivier's Henry V (1944), on the other hand, demonstrated the potential of the film to a remarkable degree. Choosing a play in which Shakespeare repeatedly stresses the limitation of the stage, Olivier began his version in a plausible mockup of an Elizabethan theater and proceeded to let the camera take the spectator to the battlefields of France. The journey itself and eventual return to the Elizabethan theater, showing us adult actresses at one moment and boy actors stuffing oranges in their bosoms for breasts the next, becomes the focus of the theatrical and film experience, realizing thereby on film what Shakespeare appeals to in his verse. Olivier's Hamlet (1948), though marred by a trendy Freudian reading of Hamlet's relationship to his mother, was well cast and made innovative use of a camera that relentlessly explores the corridors of Elsinore Castle, searching out the heart of Hamlet's mystery. Olivier's Richard III (1955), perhaps the least original of his Shakespearean films to that date because of its predictable sets, nevertheless discovers ways of centering interest on Olivier's magnetic interpretation of the villain hero. His Othello (1965) was, like his other films, based on a successful stage production. Kenneth Branagh's Henry V (1989) mounted a successful challenge to Olivier's now classic film of 1944, providing a rich opportunity to compare an unabashedly patriotic interpretation with one that is more aware of the complex ethical problems of war and political rule.

Bold translation into the medium of film is certainly to be found in Akira Kurosawa's Throne of Blood (1957), a version of Macbeth as told in terms of Japanese history and folklore. Making no attempt to reproduce Shakespeare's language verbally, it offers instead arresting images of mist-shrouded forests and mysteriously disappearing witches, or spare interior sets, intensifying the loneliness of the murdering protagonists. Kurosawa's Ran (1986) retells King Lear as the story of a Japanese feudal warlord with three sons and a murderously ambitious daughter-in-law. Orson Welles' Chimes at Midnight, or Falstaff (1965–1966), recklessly rearranges the texts of 1 and 2 Henry IV, and miscasts some important minor roles, but it does achieve sensitivity in Welles' own portrayal of Falstaff as a fat comic who is at heart insecure and pleading for affection. Grigori Kozintsev's *Hamlet* (1964), using a heavily cut text by Boris Pasternak, is probably the best *Hamlet* on film because of uniformly sound casting and because the camera so eloquently translates *Hamlet*'s language into the director's five chosen images of stone, iron, fire, sea, and earth. Kozintsev is unafraid to cut and allow the film to do what it can do so well, and, if one accepts these premises, one sees a film of remarkable energy. Kozintsev's *King Lear* (1971) is no less forthright in embracing its medium, and to similar effect. The most controversial *King Lear* on film, however, and perhaps the most controversial Shakespearean film ever made, is Peter Brook's version (1970) starring Paul Scofield and based on a stage production that toured widely in the early 1960s. Unswervingly pessimistic, based in part on Brook's reading of Jan Kott, this version insists that Lear is indeed a troublesome father to Goneril and Regan; his followers make a shambles of the Duke of Albany's dining hall. Brook's wintry sets show us human beings enduring under the bleakest of circumstances. Cordelia's role is curtailed. These emphases have distressed many viewers and have raised familiar cries of directorial arrogance. Yet, to others, Brook's film is an achievement in film paralleled only (and in a very different way) by Olivier's *Henry V*. The casting is uniformly fine, and the scenes between Lear and Gloucester at Dover beach are as deeply moving as the play deserves. For all its unrelenting darkness of vision, the film does show touching affection and thus captures an image of goodness doing battle, at whatever disadvantageous odds, with evil. Perhaps nowhere can we find more aptly expressed the potentials and difficulties involved in adapting Shakespeare to film.

Other Shakespearean films to which serious critical attention has been devoted include John Houseman's and Joseph Mankiewicz's *Julius Casear* (1953), Renato Castellani's *Romeo and Juliet* (1954), Sergei Yotkevitch's *Othello* (1955), Orson Welles' *Othello* (1965), Franco Zeffirelli's *The Taming of the Shrew* (1966) and *Romeo and Juliet* (1968), Peter Hall's *A Midsummer Night's Dream* (1969), Roman Polanski's *Macbeth* (1971), and, most recently, Zeffirelli's *Hamlet* (1990), with Mel Gibson in the title role. Of Shakespeare on television, several productions have been mentioned already. The most notable undertaking, but also the most disappointing, is the BBC's taping of all the plays over a six-year period, beginning with six plays shown on American television in early 1979. The attempt at "definitive" performance lacking directorial bias and the use of studio production involving many non-Shakespearean actors yield bland results with occasional flashes of insight and demonstrate all too well the need for recognition of the critical differences between the camera and the stage. When those differences are integrated with Shakespeare's theatrical artistry, the results can be wonderfully effective, as the

BBC's *Measure for Measure,* for example, demonstrates. Yet the best Shakespeare on television is likely to originate in small-scale theater productions rather than from studio filming. Trevor Nunn's ritualistic *Macbeth*, for example, using the television camera almost as an added presence onstage, brings the viewer inside a weird, incantatory celebration of evil. Produced by Thames Television and now widely available on videotape, this *Macbeth*, starring Ian McKellen and Judi Dench, stands out as the finest production of the play many viewers will ever see.

One happy consequence of Shakespeare productions in the twentieth century, and of their availability to larger audiences than ever before, is the movement of Shakespeare performance from the periphery of Shakespeare studies to the center. Shakespeare in performance is now generally acknowledged as an important source of critical interpretation for artists, literary critics, and the general public.

THE ROYAL GENEALOGY OF ENGLAND, 1154–1625

THE PLANTAGENET KINGS

THE LANCASTRIAN KINGS

In these diagrams, reigning dates are given in parentheses; other dates indicate life span. Abbreviations: P., Prince, D., Duke, E., Earl; b., born, d., died, m., married. English monarchs are printed in boldface type. The spatial arrangement of names in a family usually but not always indicates order of birth.

In *1 Henry IV*, Shakespeare confuses the Edmund Mortimer who married Glendower's daughter, and died in 1409, with his nephew Edmund, fifth Earl of March, who asserted a claim to the English throne (see "The Yorkist Kings"). Shakespeare also refers to Henry Percy's (Hotspur's) wife as "Kate," though historically she was named Elizabeth.

Catherine Swynford, third wife of John of Gaunt (see "The Tudor Kings"), bore him children before their eventual marriage. These Beauforts, although later legitimized, were specifically barred from any claim to the English throne.

THE YORKIST KINGS

Edward III   m.   Philippa of Hainault

Edward   William   Lionel D. of Clarence   m.   Elizabeth de Burgh   John of Gaunt   Edmund Langley 1st D. of York   m.   Isabel of Castile   Thomas

Philippa   m.   Edmund Mortimer 3rd E. of March 1351–1381   Edward D. of Aumerle, later D. of York 1373–1415

Roger Mortimer 4th E. of March 1374–1398   m.   Eleanor Holland   Edmund d. 1409   m.   Daughter of Owen Glendower   Elizabeth   m.   Henry Percy (Hotspur)

Edmund Mortimer 5th E. of March 1391–1425   Anne Mortimer   m.   Richard E. of Cambridge 1375–1415

Richard Plantagenet   m.   Cecily Neville E. of Cambridge, later D. of York 1411–1460

Edward, E. of March 1442–1483 **Edward IV** (1461–1483)   m.   Elizabeth Woodville Lady Grey   Edmund, E. of Rutland 1443–1460   George D. of Clarence 1449–1478   m.   Isabell Neville, daughter of Richard E. of Warwick   Richard D. of Gloucester 1452–1485 **Richard III** (1483–1485)

Elizabeth b. 1465   m.   Henry Tudor (**Henry VII**)   **Edward V** 1470–1483 (1483)   Richard k. 1483   Edward   Margaret

THE TUDOR KINGS

Edward III

Edward   William   Lionel   (1) Blanche of Lancaster   m.   John of Gaunt D. of Lancaster   m.   (3) Catherine Swynford d. 1403   Edmund D. of York

Henry IV

Henry V   m.   Katherine of Valois   m.   (2) Owen Tudor   John Beaufort E. and later 1st D. of Somerset 1375–1410   m.   Margaret Holland   Henry Beaufort Bishop of Winchester, later cardinal 1377–1447   Thomas Beaufort D. of Exeter d. 1427   Richard E. of Cambridge

Richard Plantagenet

Henry E. of Somerset d. 1418   John 3rd E. of Somerset d. 1444   Edmund 2nd D. of Somerset d. 1455   **Edward IV**   **Richard III**

Jasper Tudor   Edmund Tudor E. of Richmond 1430–1456   m.   Margaret Beaufort 1443–1509   m.   (2) Thomas E. of Derby

Henry Tudor E. of Richmond 1457–1509 **Henry VII** (1485–1509)   m.   Elizabeth of York

Arthur P. of Wales d. 1502   (1) Katherine of Aragon   m.   **Henry VIII** 1491–1547 (1509–1547)   m.   (2) Anne Boleyn   m.   (3) Jane Seymour   Margaret   m.   James IV of Scotland

Mary I 1516–1558 (1553–1558)   **Elizabeth I** 1533–1603 (1558–1603)   **Edward VI** 1537–1553 (1547–1553)   James V

Mary Queen of Scots   m.   Henry Stuart Lord Darnley

James VI of Scotland and I of England 1566–1625 (1603–1625)

Maps

A map of London (below) of Shakespeare's time shows the prominent landmarks, as well as the theaters and other places where plays were performed.
  A map of England and Western France (opposite) gives the locations for the scenes of Shakespeare's history plays.

ENGLAND AND
WESTERN FRANCE

BIBLIOGRAPHY

Suggestions for Reading and Research

Abbreviations Used

Shakespeare Quarterly	SQ
Shakespeare Studies	ShakS
Shakespeare Survey	ShS

Works of Reference

Abbott, E. A. *A Shakespearian Grammar.* New ed., London, 1870.

Allen, Michael J. B., and Kenneth Muir, eds. *Shakespeare's Plays in Quarto.* Berkeley, 1981.

Andrews, John, ed. *William Shakespeare: His World, His Work, His Influence.* 3 vols. New York, 1985.

Bergeron, David M. *Shakespeare: A Study and Research Guide.* New York, 1975; 2nd ed., rev. David Bergeron and Geraldo de Sousa. Lawrence, Kans., 1987.

Berman, Ronald. *A Reader's Guide to Shakespeare's Plays.* Rev. ed., Glenview, Ill., 1973.

Bevington, David, compiler. *Shakespeare.* Goldentree Bibliographies. Arlington Heights, Ill., 1978.

Bullough, Geoffrey, ed. *Narrative and Dramatic Sources of Shakespeare.* 8 vols. London, 1957–1975.

Campbell, Oscar James, and Edward G. Quinn, eds. *The Reader's Encyclopedia of Shakespeare.* New York, 1966.

Chambers, E. K. *William Shakespeare: A Study of Facts and Problems.* 2 vols. Oxford, 1930.

Dent, R. W. *Shakespeare's Proverbial Language: An Index.* Berkeley, 1981.

Ebisch, Walther, in collaboration with L. L. Schücking. *A Shakespeare Bibliography.* Oxford, 1931. *A Supplement for the Years 1930–1935.* Oxford, 1937.

Garland Shakespeare Bibliographies, gen. ed. William Godshalk. Published in separate volumes for various plays, at varying dates. Garland: New York.

Greg, W. W. *A Bibliography of the English Printed Drama to the Restoration.* 4 vols. London, 1939–1959.

———, ed. *Shakespeare Quarto Facsimiles.* London, 1939—. (An incomplete set; Greg's work has been supplemented by Charlton Hinman.)

Harbage, Alfred. *Annals of English Drama, 975–1700.* Rev. S. Schoenbaum. Philadelphia, 1964.

Hart, Alfred. *Shakespeare and the Homilies.* Melbourne, 1934.

Hinman, Charlton, ed. *The Norton Facsimile: The First Folio of Shakespeare.* New York, 1968.

Hosley, Richard, ed. *Shakespeare's Holinshed.* New York, 1968.

Kökeritz, Helge. *Shakespeare's Names.* New Haven, 1959.

———. *Shakespeare's Pronunciation.* New Haven, 1953.

Long, John. *Shakespeare's Use of Music: Comedies.* Gainesville, Fla., 1955. *Final Comedies,* 1961; *Histories and Tragedies,* 1971.

McManaway, James G., and Jeanne Addison Roberts, compilers. *A Selective Bibliography of Shakespeare.* Charlottesville, Va., 1975.

Muir, Kenneth. *Shakespeare's Sources.* 2 vols. London, 1957.

———, and S. Schoenbaum, eds. *A New Companion to Shakespeare Studies.* London and New York, 1971.

Munro, John, ed. *The Shakespeare Allusion Book.* 2 vols. London and New York, 1909; reissued 1932.

Naylor, Edward W. *Shakespeare and Music.* New ed., London, 1931.

Noble, Richmond. *Shakespeare's Biblical Knowledge.* London, 1935.

———. *Shakespeare's Use of Song.* London, 1923.

Onions, C. T. *A Shakespeare Glossary.* Rev. and enlgd. R. D. Eagleson. Oxford, 1986.

Publications of the Modern Language Association of America (PMLA). Annual Bibliography.

Schmidt, Alexander. *Shakespeare-Lexicon.* 5th ed. Berlin, 1962.

Seager, H. W. *Natural History in Shakespeare's Time.* London, 1896.

Seng, Peter J. *The Vocal Songs in the Plays of Shakespeare.* Cambridge, Mass., 1967.

Shakespeare Bulletin.

Shakespeare-Jahrbuch.

Shakespeare Newsletter.

Shakespeare Quarterly. Annual Bibliography.

Shakespeare Studies.

Shakespeare Survey.

Smith, Gordon Ross. *A Classified Shakespeare Bibliography, 1936–1958.* University Park, Pa., 1963.

Spencer, T. J. B., ed. *Shakespeare's Plutarch.* Harmondsworth, Eng., 1964.

Spevack, Marvin. *A Complete and Systematic Concordance to the Works of Shakespeare.* 8 vols. Hildesheim, Ger., 1968–1970.

———. *The Harvard Concordance to Shakespeare.* Cambridge, Mass., 1973.

Sternfeld, Frederick W. *Music in Shakespearean Tragedy.* London, 1963, 1967.

Studies in Philology. Annual Bibliography through 1969.

Thomson, J. A. K. *Shakespeare and the Classics.* London, 1952.

Wells, Stanley, ed. *Shakespeare: Select Bibliographical Guides.* London, 1973.

———, ed. *The Cambridge Companion to Shakespeare Studies.* Cambridge, Eng., 1986.

Zesmer, David. *Guide to Shakespeare.* New York, 1976.

Life in Shakespeare's England

Allen, Don Cameron. *The Star-Crossed Renaissance.* Durham, N.C., 1941.

Baker, Herschel. *The Image of Man: A Study of the Idea of Human Dignity in Classical Antiquity, the Middle Ages, and the Renaissance.* Cambridge, Mass., 1961. (First published in 1947 as *The Dignity of Man.*)

———. *The Wars of Truth: Studies in the Decay of Christian Humanism in the Earlier Seventeenth Century.* Cambridge, Mass., 1952.

Bakhtin, Mikhail M. *Rabelais and His World,* trans. H. Iswolsky. Cambridge, Mass., 1968.

Barkan, Leonard. *Nature's Work of Art: The Human Body as Image of the World.* New Haven, 1975.

———. *The Gods Made Flesh: Metamorphosis and the Pursuit of Paganism.* New Haven, 1986.

Barroll, Leeds. *Politics, Plague, and Shakespeare's Theater: The Stuart Years.* Ithaca, N.Y., 1991.

Bindoff, S. T., et al., eds. *Elizabethan Government and Society.* Essays presented to Sir John Neale. London, 1961.

Bush, Douglas. *The Renaissance and English Humanism.* Toronto, 1939.

Buxton, John. *Elizabethan Taste.* London, 1963.

Byrne, Muriel St. Clare. *Elizabethan Life in Town and Country.* 8th ed. London, 1970.

Camden, Carroll. *The Elizabethan Woman.* Houston, 1952.

Caspari, Fritz. *Humanism and the Social Order in Tudor England.* Chicago, 1954.

Cassirer, Ernst. *The Platonic Renaissance in England,* trans. J. E. Pettegrove. Austin, Tex., 1953.

Einstein, Lewis. *Tudor Ideals.* New York, 1921.

Elton, G. R. *The Tudor Revolution in Government.* Cambridge, Eng., 1959.

Ferguson, Arthur B. *The Articulate Citizen and the English Renaissance.* Durham, N.C., 1965.

Gallagher, Lowell. *Medusa's Gaze: Casuistry and Conscience in the Renaissance.* Stanford, 1991.

Harrison, G. B. *An Elizabethan Journal.* London, 1928; supplements.

———. *A Jacobean Journal . . . 1603–1606.* London, 1941.

———. *A Second Jacobean Journal . . . 1607 to 1610.* Ann Arbor, Mich., 1958.

Haydn, Hiram. *The Counter-Renaissance.* New York, 1950.

Heninger, S. K., Jr. *A Handbook of Renaissance Meteorology.* Durham, N.C., 1960.

Hibbert, Christopher. *London: The Biography of a City.* Rev. ed. London, 1977.

Hirst, Derek. *Authority and Conflict: England, 1603–1658.* Cambridge, Mass., 1986.

Huizinga, Johan. *The Waning of the Middle Ages.* London, 1924; Baltimore, 1955.

Hurstfield, Joel. *Elizabeth I and the Unity of England.* London, 1960.

Jordan, Constance. *Renaissance Feminism: Literary Texts and Political Models.* Ithaca, N.Y., 1990.

Judges, A. V., ed. *The Elizabethan Underworld.* London and New York, 1930. Rpt., London, 1965.

Kelso, Ruth. *Doctrine for the Lady of the Renaissance.* Urbana, Ill., 1956.

———. *The Doctrine of the English Gentleman in the Sixteenth Century.* Urbana, Ill., 1929.

Knappen, M. M. *Tudor Puritanism.* Chicago, 1939.

Knights, L. C. *Drama and Society in the Age of Jonson.* London, 1937.

Kocher, Paul. *Science and Religion in Elizabethan England.* San Marino, Calif., 1953.

Levin, Harry. *The Myth of the Golden Age in the Renaissance.* Bloomington, Ind., 1969.

Lovejoy, A. O. *The Great Chain of Being.* Cambridge, Mass., 1936.

MacCaffrey, Wallace T. *The Shaping of the Elizabethan Regime.* Princeton, 1968.

Mattingly, Garrett. *The Armada.* Boston, 1959.

Mazzeo, Joseph A. *Renaissance and Revolution.* New York, 1965.

McElwee, W. *The Wisest Fool in Christendom.* [About James VI and I.] New York, 1958.

McPeek, James A. S. *The Black Book of Knaves and Unthrifts in Shakespeare and Other Renaissance Authors.* Storrs, Conn., 1969.

Morris, Lee, Jr. *Great Britain's Solomon: James VI and I in His Three Kingdoms.* Urbana, Ill., 1990.

Neale, John E. *Elizabeth I and Her Parliaments.* 2 vols. London and New York, 1953–1958.

———. *The Elizabethan House of Commons.* London, 1949.

———. *Queen Elizabeth I.* London, 1934; New York, 1957.

Nichols, John, ed. *The Progresses and Public Processions of Queen Elizabeth.* 3 vols. London, 1823.

Nicoll, Allardyce, ed. *Shakespeare in His Own Age.* ShS 17 (1964).

Patterson, Annabel. *Reading Holinshed's Chronicles.* Chicago, 1994.

Pearson, Lu Emily. *Elizabethans at Home.* Stanford, Calif., 1957.

Peck, Linda Levy. *Court Patronage and Corruption in Early Stuart England.* Boston, 1990.

Penrose, Boies. *Travel and Discovery in the Renaissance, 1420–1620.* Cambridge, Mass., 1955.

Quinones, Ricardo J. *The Renaissance Discovery of Time.* Cambridge, Mass., 1972.

Ramsey, Peter. *Tudor Economic Problems.* London, 1963.

Rowse, A. L. *The England of Elizabeth: The Structure of Society.* London, 1951.

Stallybrass, Peter, and Allon White. *The Politics and Poetics of Transgression.* Ithaca, N.Y., and London, 1986.

Stone, Lawrence. *The Crisis of the Aristocracy, 1558–1641.* Oxford, 1965.

———. *The Family, Sex and Marriage in England, 1500–1800.* London, 1977.

Stow, John. *Survey of London,* ed. C. L. Kingsford. Oxford, 1971.

Tawney, R. H. *Religion and the Rise of Capitalism.* New York, 1926, 1962.

Tillyard, E. M. W. *The Elizabethan World Picture.* London, 1943, 1967.

Underdown, David. *Revel, Riot, and Rebellion: Popular Politics and Culture in England, 1603–1660.* Oxford, 1985.

Whigham, Frank. *Ambition and Privilege: The Social Tropes of Elizabethan Courtesy Theory.* Berkeley, 1984.

Willson, David Harris. *King James VI & I.* New York, 1956.
Wilson, F. P. *Elizabethan and Jacobean.* Oxford, 1945.
Wilson, J. Dover, ed. *Life in Shakespeare's England.* Cambridge, Eng., 1911. 2nd ed., 1926.
Woodbridge, Linda. *Women and the English Renaissance.* Urbana, Ill., 1984.
Wright, Louis B. *Middle-Class Culture in Elizabethan England.* Chapel Hill, N.C., 1935.
Wrightson, Keith. *English Society, 1580–1680.* New Brunswick, N.J., 1982.
Zeeveld, W. Gordon. *Foundations of Tudor Policy.* Cambridge, Mass., 1948.

Shakespeare's Predecessors and Contemporaries

See also, under *Works of Reference,* Greg and Harbage; under *Shakespeare Criticism of the 1980s and 1990s,* Dollimore, Garber (*Cannibals*), Goldberg, Greenblatt, Jardine, Loomba, Mullaney, Newman, and Skura; under *The Histories,* Ribner; and, under *The Tragedies,* Bushnell.
Altman, Joel B. *The Tudor Play of Mind: Rhetorical Inquiry and the Development of Elizabethan Drama.* Berkeley, 1978.
Baker, Howard. *Induction to Tragedy.* Baton Rouge, 1939.
Barber, C. L. *Creating Elizabethan Tragedy: The Theater of Kyd and Marlowe.* Chicago, 1988.
Bartels, Emily C. *Spectacles of Strangeness: Imperialism, Alienation, and Marlowe* (Philadelphia, 1993).
Belsey, Catherine. *The Subject of Tragedy: Identity and Difference in Renaissance Drama.* London, 1985.
Bentley, Gerald Eades. *The Jacobean and Caroline Stage.* 7 vols. Oxford, 1941–1968.
Bevington, David. *From "Mankind" to Marlowe: Growth of Structure in the Popular Drama of Tudor England.* Cambridge, Mass., 1962.
———. *Tudor Drama and Politics.* Cambridge, Mass., 1968.
Bowers, Fredson T. *Elizabethan Revenge Tragedy, 1587–1642.* Princeton, 1940.
Braden, Gordon. *Renaissance Tragedy and the Senecan Tradition.* New Haven, 1985.
Briggs, Julia. *This Stage-Play World: English Literature and Its Background.* Oxford, 1983.
Bristol, Michael D. *Carnival and Theater: Plebeian Culture and the Structure of Authority in Renaissance England.* London, 1985.
Brooke, C. F. Tucker, ed. *The Shakespeare Apocrypha.* Oxford, 1908.
Burt, Richard. *Licensed by Authority: Ben Jonson and the Discourses of Censorship.* Ithaca, N.Y., 1993.
Caputi, Anthony. *John Marston, Satirist.* Ithaca, N.Y., 1961.
Chambers, E. K. *The Elizabethan Stage.* 4 vols. Oxford, 1923.
———. *The Mediaeval Stage.* 2 vols. Oxford, 1903.
Clemen, Wolfgang. *English Tragedy Before Shakespeare: The Development of Dramatic Speech,* trans. T. S. Dorsch. London, 1961.
Clubb, Louise George. *Italian Drama in Shakespeare's Time.* New Haven, 1989.
Cohen, Walter. *Drama of a Nation: Public Theater in Renaissance England and Spain.* Ithaca, N.Y., 1985.
Craik, T. W. *The Tudor Interlude.* Leicester, 1958, 1962.
Dessen, Alan C. *Elizabethan Drama and the Viewer's Eye.* Chapel Hill, N.C., 1977.
Doran, Madeleine. *Endeavors of Art: A Study of Form in Elizabethan Drama.* Madison, Wis., 1954, 1972.
Evans, G. B. *Elizabethan and Jacobean Drama: The Theatre in Its Time.* New York, 1990.
Farley-Hills, David. *Shakespeare and the Rival Playwrights, 1600–1606.* London, 1990.
Farnham, Willard. *The Medieval Heritage of Elizabethan Tragedy.* Berkeley, 1936.
Findlay, Alison. *Illegitimate Power: Bastards in Renaissance Drama.* Manchester, Eng., 1994.
Finkelpearl, Philip. *John Marston of the Middle Temple.* Cambridge, Mass., 1969.
Freer, Coburn. *The Poetics of Jacobean Drama.* Baltimore, 1981.
Gardiner, H. C. *Mysteries' End.* New Haven, 1946.
Gibbons, Brian. *Jacobean City Comedy.* London, 1968.
Hardison, O. B., Jr. *Christian Rite and Christian Drama in the Middle Ages.* Baltimore, 1965.
Hassel, R. Chris. *Renaissance Drama and the English Church Year.* Lincoln, Nebr., 1979.
Hattaway, Michael. *Elizabethan Popular Theatre: Plays in Performance.* London, 1982.
Hawkins, Harriett. *Likenesses of Truth in Elizabethan and Restoration Drama.* Oxford, 1972.
Honigmann, E. A. J., ed. *Shakespeare and His Contemporaries: Essays in Comparison.* Manchester, Eng., 1986.
Hunter, G. K. *John Lyly: The Humanist as Courtier.* Cambridge, Mass., 1962.
Kastan, David Scott, and Peter Stallybrass, eds. *Staging the Renaissance: Reinterpretations of Elizabethan and Jacobean Drama* (New York and London, 1991).
Kernan, Alvin. *The Cankered Muse: Satire of the English Renaissance.* New Haven, 1959.
Kirsch, Arthur C. *Jacobean Dramatic Perspectives.* Charlottesville, Va., 1972.
Kolve, V. A. *The Play Called Corpus Christi.* Palo Alto and London, 1966.
Leech, Clifford. *Shakespeare's Tragedies and Other Studies in Seventeenth Century Drama.* London, 1950.
Leggatt, Alexander. *Citizen Comedy in the Age of Shakespeare.* Toronto, 1973.
———. *Jacobean Public Theatre.* London, 1992.
Leishman, J. B., ed. *The Three Parnassus Plays (1598–1601).* London, 1949.
Levin, Harry. *The Overreacher: A Study of Christopher Marlowe.* Cambridge, Mass., 1952, 1964.
Levin, Richard. *The Multiple Plot in English Renaissance Drama.* Chicago, 1971.
Margeson, J. M. R. *The Origins of English Tragedy.* Oxford, 1967.
Maus, Katharine Eisaman. *Inwardness and Theatre in the English Renaissance Drama.* Chicago, 1995.
McAlindon, T. *English Renaissance Tragedy.* London, 1986.
McLuskie, Kathleen. *Renaissance Dramatists.* (Feminist Readings.) Atlantic Highlands, N.J., 1989.

Mulryne, J. R., and Margaret Shewring, eds. *Theatre and Government Under the Early Stuarts* (Cambridge, Eng., 1993).

Nicoll, Allardyce. *Masks, Mimes, and Miracles*. London, 1931.

Orgel, Stephen. *The Illusion of Power: Political Theater in the English Renaissance*. Berkeley, 1975.

Ornstein, Robert. *The Moral Vision of Jacobean Tragedy*. Madison, Wis., 1960.

Rabkin, Norman, ed. *Reinterpretations of Elizabethan Drama*. New York, 1969.

Rose, Mary Beth. *The Expense of Spirit: Love and Sexuality in English Renaissance Drama*. Ithaca, N.Y., 1988.

———. ed. *Renaissance Drama as Cultural History*. Evanston, Ill., 1990.

Salter, F. M. *Medieval Drama in Chester*. Toronto, 1955.

Sanders, Wilbur. *The Dramatist and the Received Idea: Studies in the Plays of Marlowe and Shakespeare*. Cambridge, Eng., 1968.

Shapiro, James. *Rival Playwrights: Marlowe, Jonson, Shakespeare* (New York, 1991).

Smith, David L., Richard Strier, and David Bevington, eds. *The Theatrical City: Culture, Theatre and Politics in London 1567–1649* (Cambridge, Eng., 1995).

Southern, Richard. *The Medieval Theatre in the Round*. London, 1957.

Spivack, Bernard. *Shakespeare and the Allegory of Evil*. New York, 1958.

Taylor, Jerome, and Alan H. Nelson, eds. *Medieval English Drama*. Chicago, 1972.

Waith, Eugene M. *The Herculean Hero in Marlowe, Chapman, Shakespeare, and Dryden*. New York, 1962.

———. *The Pattern of Tragicomedy in Beaumont and Fletcher*. New Haven, 1952.

Welsford, Enid. *The Court Masque*. Cambridge, Eng., 1927.

Wickham, Glynne. *Early English Stages, 1300 to 1660*. 3 vols. London, 1959–1972.

Wilson, F. P. *Marlowe and the Early Shakespeare*. Oxford, 1953.

Wilson, F. P., and G. K. Hunter. *The English Drama, 1485–1585*. London and New York, 1969.

Woolf, Rosemary. *The English Mystery Plays*. Berkeley and Los Angeles, 1972.

London Theaters and Dramatic Companies

See also, under *Shakespeare's Predecessors and Contemporaries*, Bentley, and Chambers (*Elizabethan Stage*).

Armstrong, William A. *The Elizabethan Private Theatres: Facts and Problems*. London, 1958.

Astington, John H., ed. *The Development of Shakespeare's Theater*. New York, 1992.

Beckerman, Bernard. *Shakespeare at the Globe, 1599–1609*. New York, 1962, 1967.

Berry, Herbert. *Shakespeare's Playhouses*. New York, 1987.

Bradley, David. *From Text to Performance in the Elizabethan Theatre: Preparing the Play for the Stage* Cambridge, Eng., 1992.

Brown, John Russell. *Shakespeare's Plays in Performance*. London, 1966.

Campbell, Lily B. *Scenes and Machines on the English Stage During the Renaissance*. Cambridge, Eng., 1923.

Clare, Janet. *"Art Made Tongue-Tied by Authority": Elizabethan and Jacobean Dramatic Censorship*. Manchester, Eng., 1990.

Cook, Ann Jennalie. *The Privileged Playgoers of Shakespeare's London, 1576–1642*. Princeton, 1981.

Dutton, Richard. *Mastering the Revels: The Regulation and Censorship of English Renaissance Drama*. Iowa City, 1991.

Feuillerat, Albert, ed. *Documents Relating to the Office of the Revels in the Time of Queen Elizabeth*. Louvain (Louven), Belgium, 1908.

Foakes, R. A., ed. *The Henslowe Papers: The Diary, Theatre Papers, and Bear Garden Papers*. In full and in facsimile. 3 vols. in 2. London, 1976.

Foakes, R. A., and R. T. Rickert, eds. *Henslowe's Diary*. London, 1961.

Gair, W. Reavley. *The Children of Paul's*. Cambridge, Eng., 1982.

Gildersleeve, Virginia C. *Government Regulation of the Elizabethan Drama*. New York, 1908.

Greg, W. W., ed. *Dramatic Documents from the Elizabethan Playhouses; Stage Plots; Actors' Parts; Prompt Books*. 2 vols. Oxford, 1931.

Gurr, Andrew. *The Shakespearean Stage, 1574–1642*. Cambridge, Eng., 1970. 2nd ed., 1980.

Gurr, Andrew, and John Orrell. *Rebuilding Shakespeare's Globe*. London and New York, 1989.

Harbage, Alfred. *Shakespeare's Audience*. New York, 1941.

Hodges, C. Walter. *The Globe Restored*. London, 1953; 2nd ed., New York, 1968.

Hosley, Richard. "The Discovery-space in Shakespeare's Globe," *ShS* 12 (1959), 35–46.

———. "The Gallery over the Stage in the Public Playhouse of Shakespeare's Time," *SQ*, 8 (1957), 15–31.

———. "A Reconstruction of the Second Blackfriars," *The Elizabethan Theatre*, ed. David Galloway. Toronto, 1969.

———. "Shakespeare's Use of a Gallery over the Stage," *ShS* 10 (1957), 77–89.

———. "Was There a Music-room in Shakespeare's Globe?" *ShS* 13 (1960), 113–123.

Ingram, William. *The Business of Playing: The Beginnings of the Adult Professional Theater in Elizabethan London*. Ithaca, N.Y., 1992.

Joseph, Bertram L. *Acting Shakespeare*. London, 1960.

Kernodle, G. R. *From Art to Theatre: Form and Convention in the Renaissance*. Chicago, 1944.

King, T. J. *Casting Shakespeare's Plays: London Actors and Their Roles, 1590–1642*. Cambridge, Eng., 1992.

———. *Shakespearean Staging, 1599–1642*. Cambridge, Mass., 1971.

Linthicum, Marie C. *Costume in the Drama of Shakespeare and His Contemporaries*. Oxford, 1936.

Mann, David. *The Elizabethan Player: Contemporary Stage Representation*. London, 1991.

McMillin, Scott. *The Elizabethan Theatre and "The Book of Sir Thomas More."* Ithaca, N.Y., 1987.

Nungezer, Edwin. *A Dictionary of Actors.* London and New Haven, 1929.

Rowan, D. F. "The English Playhouse: 1595–1630," *Renaissance Drama,* n.s. 4 (1971), 37–51.

Seltzer, Daniel. "Elizabethan Acting in *Othello,*" *SQ,* 10 (1959), 201–210.

———. "The Staging of the Last Plays," *Later Shakespeare,* ed. John Russell Brown and Bernard Harris, pp. 127–165. Stratford-upon-Avon Studies 8. London, 1966.

Shapiro, I. A. "The Bankside Theatres: Early Engravings," *ShS 1* (1948), 25–37.

———. "Robert Fludd's Stage-Illustration," *ShakS 2* (1966), 192–209.

Shapiro, Michael. *Children of the Revels: The Boys' Companies of Shakespeare's Time and Their Plays.* New York, 1977.

Smith, Irwin. *Shakespeare's Blackfriars Playhouse.* New York, 1964.

———. *Shakespeare's Globe Playhouse.* New York, 1956.

Smith, Warren D. *Shakespeare's Playhouse Practice: A Handbook.* Hanover, N.H., 1975.

Thompson, Peter. *Shakespeare's Theatre.* London, 1983.

Wickham, Glynne. *Early English Stages, 1300 to 1660.* 3 vols. London, 1959–1972.

Shakespeare's Life and Work

Alexander, Peter. *Shakespeare's Life and Art.* New ed., New York, 1961.

Baldwin, T. W. *William Shakspere's Small Latine and Lesse Greeke.* 2 vols. Urbana, Ill., 1944.

Chambers, E. K. *William Shakespeare: A Study of Facts and Problems.* 2 vols. Oxford, 1930.

Eccles, Mark. *Shakespeare in Warwickshire.* Madison, Wis., 1961.

Fripp, Edgar I. *Shakespeare, Man and Artist.* 2 vols. London, 1938.

Halliday, F. E. *Shakespeare: A Pictorial Biography.* London, 1956, 1964.

Harbage, Alfred. *Conceptions of Shakespeare.* Cambridge, Mass., 1966.

Hotson, Leslie. *Shakespeare Versus Shallow.* London, 1931.

Kay, Dennis. *Shakespeare: His Life, Work, and Era.* New York, 1992.

Lee, Sidney. *A Life of William Shakespeare.* New ed., London, 1925.

Levi, Peter. *The Life and Times of William Shakespeare.* London, 1988.

Matus, Irvin Leigh. *Shakespeare, In Fact.* New York, 1994.

Quennell, Peter. *Shakespeare: A Biography.* New York, 1963.

Reese, M. M. *Shakespeare: His World and His Work.* London and New York, 1953.

Rowse, A. L. *William Shakespeare: A Biography.* New York, 1963.

Schoenbaum, S. *Shakespeare's Lives.* Oxford and New York, 1970.

———. *William Shakespeare: A Documentary Life.* Oxford, 1975. Also published with fewer illustrations and a slightly revised text as *A Compact Documentary Life,* 1977.

Wells, Stanley. *Shakespeare: A Life in Drama.* New York and London, 1995.

Shakespeare's Language: His Development as Poet and Dramatist

See also, under *Works of Reference,* Abbott, Onions, and Schmidt.

Baxter, John. *Shakespeare's Poetic Styles: Verse into Drama.* London, 1980.

Bayfield, Matthew. *A Study of Shakespeare's Versification.* Cambridge, Eng., 1920.

Berry, Francis. *The Shakespeare Inset: Word and Picture.* London, 1965.

Berry, Ralph. *The Shakespearean Metaphor: Studies in Language and Form.* Totowa, N.J., 1978.

Byrne, Muriel St. Clare. "The Foundations of Elizabethan Language," *ShS 17* (1964), 223–239.

Charney, Maurice. *Shakespeare's Roman Plays: The Function of Imagery in the Drama.* Cambridge, Mass., 1961.

———. *Style in Hamlet.* Princeton, 1969.

Clemen, Wolfgang H. *The Development of Shakespeare's Imagery.* Cambridge, Mass., 1951.

Crane, Milton. *Shakespeare's Prose.* Chicago, 1951.

Cruttwell, Patrick. *The Shakespearean Moment and Its Place in the Poetry of the Seventeenth Century.* London, 1954.

Dobson, E. J. *English Pronunciation, 1500–1700.* 2 vols. 2nd ed. Oxford, 1968.

Doebler, John. *Shakespeare's Speaking Pictures: Studies in Iconic Imagery.* Albuquerque, 1974.

Doran, Madeleine. *Shakespeare's Dramatic Language.* Madison, Wis., 1976.

Evans, B. Ifor. *The Language of Shakespeare's Plays.* 3rd ed. London, 1964.

Halliday, F. E. *The Poetry of Shakespeare's Plays.* London, 1954.

Henn, T. R. *The Living Image.* London, 1972.

Hulme, Hilda M. *Explorations in Shakespeare's Language.* London, 1962.

Hussey, S. S. *The Literary Language of Shakespeare.* London, 1982.

Kökeritz, Helge. *Shakespeare's Names.* New Haven, 1959.

———. *Shakespeare's Pronunciation.* New Haven, 1953.

Mahood, M. M. *Shakespeare's Wordplay.* London, 1957.

Miriam Joseph, Sister. *Shakespeare's Use of the Arts of Language.* New York, 1947. Rpt. in part as *Rhetoric in Shakespeare's Time,* 1962.

Muir, Kenneth. "Shakespeare's Imagery—Then and Now," *ShS 18* (1965), 46–57.

Nares, Robert. *A Glossary . . . of Shakespeare and His Contemporaries.* New ed. J. O. Halliwell and Thomas Wright. 2 vols. London, 1859, 1905. Rpt. Detroit, 1966.

Ness, Frederic W. *The Use of Rhyme in Shakespeare's Plays.* New Haven and London, 1941.

Partridge Eric. *Shakespeare's Bawdy.* London, 1947, 1955.

Rebhorn, Wayne. *The Emperor of Men's Minds: Literature and the Renaissance Discourse of Rhetoric*. Ithaca, N.Y., 1995.

Sacks, Elizabeth. *Shakespeare's Images of Pregnancy*. New York, 1980.

Sipe, Dorothy L. *Shakespeare's Metrics*. New Haven and London, 1968.

Spurgeon, Caroline. *Shakespeare's Imagery and What It Tells Us*. Cambridge, Eng., 1935.

Thompson, Ann and John O. *Shakespeare: Meaning and Metaphor*. Iowa City, 1987.

Trousdale, Marion. *Shakespeare and the Rhetoricians*. Chapel Hill, N.C., 1982.

Vickers, Brian. *The Artistry of Shakespeare's Prose*. London, 1968.

Willcock, Gladys D. "Shakespeare and Elizabethan English," *ShS* 7 (1954), 12–24.

Wright, George T. *Shakespeare's Metrical Art*. Berkeley, 1988.

Textual Criticism and Bibliography

See also, under *The Henry the Fourth Plays*, Prosser; and, under *King Lear*, Urkowitz.

Alexander, Peter. *Shakespeare's "Henry VI" and "Richard III."* Cambridge, Eng., 1929.

Blayney, Peter. *The Texts of "King Lear" and Their Origins*. Vol. I. Cambridge, Eng., 1982.

Bowers, Fredson. *Bibliography and Textual Criticism*. Oxford, 1964.

——. *On Editing Shakespeare*. Charlottesville, Va., 1966.

——. *Principles of Bibliographical Description*. Princeton, 1949.

——. *Textual and Literary Criticism*. Cambridge, Eng., 1959.

Chambers, E. K. *William Shakespeare: A Study of Facts and Problems*. 2 vols. Oxford, 1930.

de Grazia, Margreta. *Shakespeare Verbatim: The Reproduction of Authenticity and the 1790 Apparatus*. Oxford, 1991.

Doran, Madeleine. *"Henry VI," Parts II and III: Their Relation to "The Contention" and "The True Tragedy."* Iowa City, 1928.

Duthie, G. I. *Elizabethan Shorthand and the First Quarto of "King Lear."* Oxford, 1949.

Gaskell, Philip. *A New Introduction to Bibliography*. New York and Oxford, 1972.

Greg, W. W. *The Editorial Problem in Shakespeare*. 3rd ed. Oxford, 1954.

——. *Principles of Emendation in Shakespeare*. London, 1928.

——. *The Shakespeare First Folio: Its Bibliographical and Textual History*. Oxford, 1955.

Hart, Alfred. *Stolne and Surreptitious Copies: A Comparative Study of Shakespeare's Bad Quartos*. Melbourne and London, 1942.

Hinman, Charlton. *The Printing and Proof-Reading of the First Folio of Shakespeare*. 2 vols. Oxford, 1963.

Honigmann, E. A. J. *The Stability of Shakespeare's Text*. London and Lincoln, Nebr., 1965.

Ioppolo, Grace. *Revising Shakespeare*. Cambridge, Mass., 1991.

Long, William B. "'A bed for woodstock': A Warning for the Unwary," *Medieval and Renaissance Drama in England, 2* (1985), 91–118.

McKerrow, Ronald B. *An Introduction to Bibliography for Literary Students*. Oxford, 1927.

——. *Prolegomena for the Oxford Shakespeare*. Oxford, 1939.

Mowat, Barbara, and Paul Werstine, eds. *The New Folger Library Shakespeare*. New York, 1992—.

Nosworthy, J. M. *Shakespeare's Occasional Plays: Their Origin and Transmission*. London and New York, 1965.

Pollard, Alfred W. *Shakespeare Folios and Quartos: A Study in the Bibliography of Shakespeare's Plays, 1594–1685*. London, 1909.

——. *Shakespeare's Fight with the Pirates and the Problems of the Transmission of His Text*. Rev. ed. Cambridge, Eng., 1937.

Sisson, C. J. *New Readings in Shakespeare*. 2 vols. Cambridge, Eng., 1956.

Taylor, Gary, and Michael Warren, eds. *The Division of the Kingdoms: Shakespeare's Two Versions of "King Lear."* Oxford, 1983.

Walker, Alice. *Textual Problems of the First Folio*. Cambridge, Eng., 1953.

Walton, J. K. *The Quarto Copy for the First Folio of Shakespeare*. Dublin, 1971.

Wells, Stanley. *Re-editing Shakespeare for the Modern Reader*. Oxford, 1984.

Wells, Stanley, and Gary Taylor. *Modernizing Shakespeare's Spelling*. Oxford, 1979.

Werstine, Paul. " 'Foul Papers' and 'Prompt-books': Printer's Copy for Shakespeare's *Comedy of Errors*," *Studies in Bibliography*, 41 (1988), 232–246.

Wilson, J. Dover. *The Manuscript of Shakespeare's "Hamlet" and the Problems of Its Transmission*. 2 vols. Cambridge, Eng., 1934.

Shakespeare Criticism to the 1930s

Babcock, Robert W. *The Genesis of Shakespeare Idolatry, 1766–1799*. Chapel Hill, N.C., 1931, 1964.

Badawi, M. M. *Coleridge: Critic of Shakespeare*. Cambridge, Eng., 1973.

Bentley, Gerald Eades. *Shakespeare and Jonson: Their Reputations in the Seventeenth Century Compared*. 2 vols. Chicago, 1945.

Bradby, Anne, ed. *Shakespeare Criticism, 1919–35*. London, 1936.

Coleridge, S. T. *Coleridge on Shakespeare: The Text of the Lectures of 1811–12*, ed. R. A. Foakes. Charlottesville, Va., 1971.

——. *Coleridge's Writings on Shakespeare*, ed. Terence Hawkes. New York, 1959.

Eastman, Arthur M. *A Short History of Shakespearean Criticism.* Ann Arbor, Mich., 1968.

Eastman, Arthur M., and G. B. Harrison, eds. *Shakespeare's Critics; from Jonson to Auden.* Ann Arbor, Mich., 1964.

Evans, G. Blakemore, ed. *Shakespeare: Aspects of Influence.* Cambridge, Mass., 1976.

Halliday, F. E. *Shakespeare and His Critics.* Rev. ed., London and New York, 1958, 1963.

Hazlitt, William. *Characters of Shakespear's Plays.* London, 1817.

Johnson, Samuel. *Johnson on Shakespeare,* ed. Arthur Sherbo. Vol. 7 of *The Yale Edition of the Works of Samuel Johnson.* New Haven, 1968.

Kermode, Frank, ed. *Four Centuries of Shakespearean Criticism.* New York, 1965.

Knight, G. Wilson. *The Shakespearian Tempest.* London, 1932, 1953.

Muir, Kenneth. "Fifty Years of Shakespearian Criticism: 1900–1950," *ShS* 4 (1951), 1–25.

Rabkin, Norman, ed. *Approaches to Shakespeare.* New York, 1964.

Ralli, Augustus. *A History of Shakespearian Criticism.* 2 vols. London, 1932.

Raysor, T. M., ed. *Samuel Taylor Coleridge: Shakespearean Criticism.* 2 vols. 2nd ed. London, 1960.

Schlegel, August Wilhelm. *Lectures on Dramatic Art and Literature,* trans. John Black, 1846. Rpt., New York, 1965.

Schücking, Levin L. *Character Problems in Shakespeare's Plays.* London, 1917; trans., 1922.

Shaw, G. B. *Shaw on Shakespeare,* ed. Edwin Wilson. New York, 1961.

Sherbo, Arthur. *Samuel Johnson, Editor of Shakespeare.* Urbana, Ill., 1956.

Siegel, Paul N., ed. *His Infinite Variety: Major Shakespearean Criticism Since Johnson.* Philadelphia, 1964.

Smith, David Nichol, ed. *Shakespeare Criticism: A Selection.* World's Classics, Oxford, 1916.

———, ed. *Eighteenth Century Essays on Shakespeare.* 2nd ed. Oxford, 1963.

Spencer, Hazelton. *Shakespeare Improved.* Cambridge, Mass., 1927.

Spingarn, J. E., ed. *Critical Essays of the Seventeenth Century.* Vol. 1. Oxford, 1908–1909.

Stoll, E. E. *Art and Artifice in Shakespeare.* Cambridge, Eng., 1933, 1962.

Van Doren, Mark. *Shakespeare.* New York, 1939.

Vickers, Brian, ed. *Shakespeare: The Critical Heritage.* Several volumes. London and Boston, 1974–.

Westfall, A. V. *American Shakespearean Criticism, 1607–1865.* New York, 1939.

Shakespeare Criticism from the 1940s to the 1970s

Armstrong, Edward A. *Shakespeare's Imagination: A Study of the Psychology of Association and Inspiration.* London, 1946.

Bethell, S. L. *Shakespeare and the Popular Dramatic Tradition.* London and Durham, N.C., 1944.

Bloom, Allan, with Harry V. Jaffa. *Shakespeare's Politics.* New York and London, 1964.

Bloom, Edward A., ed. *Shakespeare 1564–1964: A Collection of Modern Essays by Various Hands.* Providence, 1964.

Brown, John Russell. *Shakespeare's Plays in Performance.* London, 1966.

Brown, John Russell, and Bernard Harris, eds. *Early Shakespeare.* Stratford-upon-Avon Studies 3. London, 1961.

Bryant, J. A., Jr. *Hippolyta's View: Some Christian Aspects of Shakespeare's Plays.* Lexington, Ky., 1961.

Burckhardt, Sigurd. *Shakespearean Meanings.* Princeton, 1968.

Burke, Kenneth. *Language as Symbolic Action.* Berkeley, 1966.

Calderwood, James L. *Shakespearean Metadrama.* Minneapolis, 1971.

Colie, Rosalie L. *Shakespeare's Living Art.* Princeton, 1974.

Council, Norman. *When Honour's at the Stake: Ideas of Honour in Shakespeare's Plays.* London, 1973.

Dean, Leonard F., ed. *Shakespeare: Modern Essays in Criticism.* New York, 1967.

Driver, Tom F. *The Sense of History in Greek and Shakespearean Drama.* New York, 1960.

Dusinberre, Juliet. *Shakespeare and the Nature of Women.* New York, 1975.

Eagleton, Terence. *Shakespeare and Society.* New York and London, 1967.

Edwards, Philip. *Shakespeare and the Confines of Art.* London and New York, 1968.

Egan, Robert. *Drama Within Drama: Shakespeare's Sense of His Art.* New York, 1975.

Empson, William. *The Structure of Complex Words.* London, 1951.

Farrell, Kirby. *Shakespeare's Creation: The Language of Magic and Play.* Amherst, Mass., 1975.

Fiedler, Leslie A. *The Stranger in Shakespeare.* New York, 1972.

Fly, Richard D. *Shakespeare's Mediated World.* Amherst, Mass., 1976.

Frye, Roland M. *Shakespeare and Christian Doctrine.* Princeton, 1963.

Garber, Marjorie B. *Dream in Shakespeare: From Metaphor to Metamorphosis.* New Haven and London, 1974.

Goddard, Harold C. *The Meaning of Shakespeare.* Chicago, 1951.

Goldman, Michael. *Shakespeare and the Energies of Drama.* Princeton, 1972.

Granville-Barker, Harley. *Prefaces to Shakespeare.* 2 vols. Princeton, 1946–1947.

Harbage, Alfred. *As They Liked It.* New York, 1947.

———. *Shakespeare and the Rival Traditions.* New York, 1952.

Hawkes, Terence. *Shakespeare's Talking Animals: Language and Drama in Society.* London, 1973.

Hawkins, Harriett. *Poetic Freedom and Poetic Truth: Chaucer, Shakespeare, Marlowe, Milton.* Oxford, 1976.

Holland, Norman. *Psychoanalysis and Shakespeare.* New York, 1966.

———. *The Shakespearean Imagination.* New York, 1964.

Jones, Emrys. *The Origins of Shakespeare.* Oxford, 1977.

Jorgensen, Paul A. *Shakespeare's Military World.* Berkeley and Los Angeles, 1956.

Kernan, Alvin B., ed. *Modern Shakespearean Criticism.* New York, 1970.

———. *The Playwright as Magician: Shakespeare's Image of the Poet in the English Public Theater.* New Haven, 1979.

Kettle, Arnold, ed. *Shakespeare in a Changing World.* London and New York, 1964.

Knights, L. C. *Some Shakespearean Themes.* London, 1959.

Kott, Jan. *Shakespeare Our Contemporary.* New York, 1964.

Leavis, F. R. *The Common Pursuit.* London, 1952.

Levin, Richard. *New Readings vs. Old Plays: Recent Trends in the Reinterpretation of English Renaissance Drama.* Chicago, 1979.

McAlindon, T. *Shakespeare and Decorum.* London and New York, 1973.

Rabkin, Norman. *Shakespeare and the Common Understanding.* New York, 1967.

Ridler, Anne Bradby, ed. *Shakespeare Criticism, 1935–60.* London, 1963.

Righter, Anne. *Shakespeare and the Idea of the Play.* London, 1962.

Rossiter, A. P. *Angel with Horns.* London, 1961.

Sanders, Wilbur. *The Dramatist and the Received Idea: Studies in the Plays of Marlowe and Shakespeare.* Cambridge, Eng., 1968.

Sewell, Arthur. *Character and Society in Shakespeare.* London, 1951.

Siegel, Paul N. *Shakespeare in His Time and Ours.* Notre Dame, Ind., 1968.

Smith, Marion Bodwell. *Dualities in Shakespeare.* Toronto, 1966.

Soellner, Rolf. *Shakespeare's Patterns of Self-Knowledge.* Columbus, Ohio, 1972.

Spencer, Theodore. *Shakespeare and the Nature of Man.* New York, 1942.

Spivack, Bernard. *Shakespeare and the Allegory of Evil.* New York, 1958.

Stauffer, Donald. *Shakespeare's World of Images.* New York, 1949.

Stewart, J. I. M. *Character and Motive in Shakespeare.* London, 1949.

Stirling, Brents. *The Populace in Shakespeare.* New York, 1949.

Traversi, Derek. *An Approach to Shakespeare.* 2 vols. Rev. ed. London, 1968.

Turner, Frederick. *Shakespeare and the Nature of Time.* Oxford, 1971.

Van Laan, Thomas F. *Role-Playing in Shakespeare.* Toronto, 1978.

Watson, Curtis Brown. *Shakespeare and the Renaissance Concept of Honor.* Princeton, 1960.

Weimann, Robert. *Shakespeare and the Popular Tradition in the Theater,* ed. Robert Schwartz. Baltimore, 1978.

Whitaker, Virgil K. *Shakespeare's Use of Learning.* San Marino, Calif., 1953.

Zeeveld, W. Gordon. *The Temper of Shakespeare's Thought.* New Haven and London, 1974.

Shakespeare Criticism of the 1980s and 1990s, including New Historiciam, Gender Studies, and Poststructuralism

See also, under *Shakespeare's Predecessors and Contemporaries,* Belsey, Braden, Bristol, Cohen, Farley-Hills, Freer, McLuskie, Orgel, and Rose.

Adelman, Janet. *Suffocating Mothers: Fantasies of Maternal Origin in Shakespeare's Plays, "Hamlet" to "The Tempest."* Chicago, 1992.

Bamber, Linda. *Comic Women, Tragic Men: A Study of Gender and Genre in Shakespeare.* Stanford, 1982.

Barber, C. L. *The Whole Journey: Shakespeare's Power of Development.* Berkeley, 1986.

Berry, Ralph. *Shakespeare and the Awareness of the Audience.* New York, 1985.

———. *Shakespeare and Social Class.* Atlantic Highlands, N.J., 1988.

———. *Shakespearean Structures.* Totowa, N. J., 1981.

Boose, Lynda E. "The Father and the Bride in Shakespeare," *PMLA,* 97 (1982), 325–347.

Bristol, Michael. *Shakespeare's America, America's Shakespeare.* London, 1990.

Calderwood, James. *Shakespeare and the Denial of Death.* Amherst, Mass., 1987.

Callaghan, Dympna, Lorraine Helms, and Jyotsna Singh. *The Weyward Sisters: Shakespeare and Feminist Politics.* Cambridge, Eng., 1994.

Carey, John, ed. *English Renaissance Studies Presented to Dame Helen Gardner in Honour of Her Seventieth Birthday.* Oxford, 1980.

Cavell, Stanley. *Disowning Knowledge in Six Plays of Shakespeare.* Cambridge, Eng., 1987.

Charnes, Linda. *Notorious Identity: Materializing the Subject in Shakespeare.* Cambridge, Mass., 1993.

Cook, Ann Jennalie. *Making a Match: Courtship in Shakespeare and His Society.* Princeton, 1991.

Cox, John D. *Shakespeare and the Dramaturgy of Power.* Princeton, 1989.

Dash, Irene. *Wooing, Wedding, and Power: Women in Shakespeare's Plays.* New York, 1981.

Desmet, Christy. *Reading Shakespeare's Characters: Rhetoric, Ethics, and Identity.* Amherst, Mass., 1992.

Dolan, Frances E. *Dangerous Familiars: Representations of Domestic Crime in England, 1550–1700.* Ithaca, N.Y., 1994.

Dollimore, Jonathan. *Radical Tragedy: Religion, Ideology and Power in the Drama of Shakespeare and His Contemporaries.* Chicago, 1984; New York, 1989.

Dollimore, Jonathan, and Alan Sinfield. *Political Shakespeare: New Essays in Cultural Materialism.* Manchester, Eng., 1985.

Drakakis, John, ed. *Alternative Shakespeares.* London, 1985.

Dubrow, Heather, and Richard Strier, eds., *The Historical Renaissance: New Essays on Tudor and Stuart Literature and Culture*. Chicago, 1988.

Eagleton, Terence. *William Shakespeare*. Oxford, 1986.

Edwards, Philip, et al., eds. *Shakespeare's Styles*. Cambridge, Eng., 1980.

Engle, Lars. *Shakespearean Pragmatism: Market of His Time*. Chicago, 1993.

Erickson, Peter. *Patriarchal Structures in Shakespeare's Drama*. Berkeley, 1985.

Erickson, Peter, and Coppélia Kahn, eds. *Shakespeare's Rough Magic: Essays in Honor of C. L. Barber*. Newark, Del., 1985.

Evans, Malcolm. *Signifying Nothing: Truth's True Contents in Shakespeare's Text*. Athens, Ga., 1986.

Faas, Ekbert. *Shakespeare's Poetics*. Cambridge, Eng., 1986.

Farrell, Kirby. *Play, Death, and Heroism in Shakespeare*. Chapel Hill, N.C., 1989.

French, Marilyn. *Shakespeare's Division of Experience*. New York, 1981.

Garber, Marjorie. *Coming of Age in Shakespeare*. London, 1981.

———. *Shakespeare's Ghost Writers: Literature as Uncanny Causality*. London and New York, 1987.

———, ed. *Cannibals, Witches, and Divorce: Estranging the Renaissance*. Selected Papers from the English Institute, no. 11. Baltimore, 1987.

Gibbons, Brian. *Shakespeare and Multiplicity*. Cambridge, Eng., 1993.

Goldberg, Jonathan. *James I and the Politics of Literature: Jonson, Shakespeare, Donne, and Their Contemporaries*. Baltimore, 1983.

———. *Sodometries: Renaissance Texts, Modern Sexualities*. Stanford, 1992.

Gray, T. C., ed. *Mirror up to Shakespeare: Essays in Honor of G. R. Hibbard*. Toronto, 1984.

Greenblatt, Stephen. *Learning to Curse: Essays in Early Modern Culture*. London and New York, 1990.

———. *Marvelous Possessions: The Wonder of the New World*. Chicago, 1991.

———. *Renaissance Self-Fashioning: From More to Shakespeare*. Chicago, 1980.

———, ed. *Representing the English Renaissance*. Berkeley, 1988.

———. *Shakespearean Negotiations: The Circulation of Social Energy in Renaissance England*. Berkeley, 1988.

Greer, Germaine. *Shakespeare*. Oxford, 1986.

Hall, Kim F. *Things of Darkness: Economies of Race and Gender in Early Modern England*. Ithaca, N.Y., 1994.

Hapgood, Robert. *Shakespeare: The Theatre-Poet*. Oxford, 1988.

Hibbard, G. R. *The Making of Shakespeare's Dramatic Poetry*. Toronto, 1981.

Holland, Norman, et al., eds. *Shakespeare's Personality*. Berkeley, 1989.

Howard, Jean E. *Shakespeare's Art of Orchestration: Stage Technique and Audience Response*. Urbana, Ill., 1984.

———. *The Stage and Social Struggle in Early Modern England*. London, 1994.

Howard, Jean E., and Marion F. O'Connor, eds. *Shakespeare Reproduced: The Text in History and Ideology*. London and New York, 1987.

Jardine, Lisa. *Still Harping on Daughters: Women and Drama in the Age of Shakespeare*. Sussex and Totowa, N.J., 1983; New York, 1989.

Kahn, Coppélia. *Man's Estate: Masculine Identity in Shakespeare*. Berkeley, 1981.

Kamps, Ivo, ed. *Shakespeare Left and Right*. New York and London, 1991.

Kastan, David. *Shakespeare and the Shapes of Time*. Hanover, N.H., 1982.

Kirsch, Arthur. *Shakespeare and the Experience of Love*. Cambridge, Eng., 1981.

Knapp, Robert S. *Shakespeare—The Theater and the Book*. Princeton, 1989.

Lenz, Carolyn, et al., eds. *The Woman's Part: Feminist Criticism of Shakespeare*. Urbana, Ill., 1980.

Levith, Murray J. *Shakespeare's Italian Settings and Plays*. New York, 1989.

Loomba, Ania. *Gender, Race, Renaissance Drama*. Manchester, Eng., 1989.

Mahon, John W., and Thomas A. Pendleton, eds. *"Fanned and Winnowed Opinion": Shakespearean Essays Presented to Harold Jenkins*. London, 1987.

Marcus, Leah. *Puzzling Shakespeare: Local Reading and Its Discontents*. Berkeley, 1988.

McDonald, Russ, ed. *Shakespeare Reread: The Texts in New Contexts*. Ithaca, N.Y., 1994.

Mullaney, Steven. *The Place of the Stage: License, Play, and Power in Renaissance England*. Chicago, 1988.

Neely, Carol Thomas. *Broken Nuptials in Shakespeare's Plays*. New Haven, 1985.

Newman, Karen. *Fashioning Femininity and the English Renaissance Drama*. Chicago, 1991.

Novy, Marianne. *Love's Argument: Gender Relations in Shakespeare*. Chapel Hill, N.C., 1984.

———, ed. *Women's Re-Visions of Shakespeare*. Urbana, Ill., 1990.

Parker, Barbara. *A Precious Seeing: Love and Reason in Shakespeare's Plays*. New York, 1987.

Parker, Patricia, and Geoffrey Hartman, eds. *Shakespeare and the Question of Theory*. London, 1985.

Paster, Gail Kern. *The Body Embarrassed: Drama and the Disciplines of Shame in Early Modern England*. Ithaca, N.Y., 1993.

———. *The Idea of the City in the Age of Shakespeare*. Athens, Ga., 1985.

Patterson, Annabel. *Shakespeare and the Popular Voice*. Oxford, 1989.

Pitt, Angela. *Shakespeare's Women*. Totowa, N.J., 1981.

Rabkin, Norman. *Shakespeare and the Problem of Meaning*. Chicago, 1981.

Ranald, Margaret Loftis. *Shakespeare and His Social Context: Essays in Osmotic Knowledge and Literary Interpretation*. New York, 1987.

Roberts, Jeanne Addison. *The Shakespearean Wild: Geography, Genus, and Gender*. Lincoln, Nebr., 1991.

Salingar, Leo. *Dramatic Form in Shakespeare and the Jacobeans.* Cambridge, Eng., 1986.

Schwartz, Murray, and Coppélia Kahn, eds. *Representing Shakespeare: New Psychoanalytic Essays.* Baltimore, 1980.

Siemon, James R. *Shakespearean Iconoclasm.* Berkeley, 1985.

Sinfield, Alan. *Faultlines: Cultural Materialism and the Politics of Dissident Reading.* Berkeley, 1992.

Skura, Meredith Anne. *The Literary Use of the Psychoanalytic Process.* New Haven, 1981.

———. *Shakespeare the Actor and the Purposes of Playing.* Chicago, 1993.

Smith, Bruce R. *Homosexual Desire in Shakespeare's England.* Chicago, 1991.

Stockholder, Kay. *Dream Works: Lovers and Families in Shakespeare's Plays.* Toronto, 1987.

Summers, Joseph H. *Dreams of Love and Power: On Shakespeare's Plays.* Oxford, 1984.

Tennenhouse, Leonard. *Power on Display: The Politics of Shakespeare's Genres.* London, 1986.

Traub, Valerie. *Desire and Anxiety: Circulations of Sexuality in Shakespearean Drama.* London, 1992.

Vickers, Brian. *Appropriating Shakespeare: Contemporary Critical Quarrels.* New Haven, Conn., 1993.

Watson, Robert N. *The Rest Is Silence: Death as Annihilation in the English Renaissance.* Berkeley, 1994.

———. *Shakespeare and the Hazards of Ambition.* Cambridge, Mass., 1984.

Wayne, Valerie, ed. *The Matter of Difference: Materialist Feminist Criticism of Shakespeare.* Ithaca, N.Y., 1991.

Wells, Robin Headlam. *Shakespeare, Politics, and the State.* London, 1986.

Wheeler, Richard P. *Shakespeare's Development and the Problem Comedies: Turn and Counter-Turn.* Berkeley, 1981.

Shakespeare in Performance; Dramaturgy

See also, under *Shakespeare Criticism from the 1940s to the 1970s,* Goldman and Granville-Barker.

Ball, Robert Hamilton. *Shakespeare on Silent Film.* London and New York, 1968.

Bartholomeusz, Dennis. *Macbeth and the Players.* Cambridge, Eng., 1969.

Barton, John. *Playing Shakespeare.* London, 1984.

Berry, Francis. *The Shakespeare Inset: Word and Picture.* London, 1965.

Berry, Ralph. *Changing Styles in Shakespeare.* London, 1981.

Bevington, David. *Action Is Eloquence: Shakespeare's Language of Gesture.* Cambridge, Mass., 1984.

Branam, George C. *Eighteenth-Century Adaptations of Shakespearean Tragedy.* Berkeley and Los Angeles, 1956.

Brennan, Anthony. *Shakespeare's Dramatic Structures.* London, 1986.

———. *Onstage and Offstage Worlds in Shakespeare's Plays.* London, 1989.

Brockbank, Philip, ed. *Players of Shakespeare.* Cambridge, Eng., 1985.

Brown, Ivor. *Shakespeare and the Actors.* London, 1970.

Brown, John Russell. *Shakespeare's Plays in Performance.* London, 1966.

———. *Shakespeare's Dramatic Style.* London, 1970.

Bulman, J. C., and H. R. Coursen, eds. *Shakespeare on Television.* Hanover, N.H., 1988.

Carlisle, Carol Jones. *Shakespeare from the Greenroom: Actors' Criticisms of Four Major Tragedies.* Chapel Hill, N.C., 1969.

Cohn, Ruby. *Modern Shakespeare Offshoots.* Princeton, 1976.

Cook, Judith. *Shakespeare's Players.* London, 1983.

Dawson, Anthony B. *Indirections: Shakespeare and the Art of Illusion.* Toronto, 1978.

Dean, Winton. "Shakespeare in the Opera House," *ShS 18* (1965), 75–93.

Donohue, Joseph W., Jr. *Dramatic Character in the English Romantic Age.* Princeton, 1970.

Downer, Alan S. *The Eminent Tragedian, William Charles Macready.* Cambridge, Mass., 1966.

Eckert, Charles W., ed. *Focus on Shakespearean Films.* Englewood Cliffs, N.J., 1972.

Hartwig, Joan. *Shakespeare's Analogical Scene: Parody as Structural Syntax.* Lincoln, Nebr., 1983.

Hirsch, James E. *The Structures of Shakespearean Scenes.* New Haven, 1981.

Hogan, Charles B. *Shakespeare in the Theatre, 1701–1800.* 2 vols. Oxford, 1952–1957.

Homan, Sidney, ed. *Shakespeare's "More Than Words Can Witness": Essays on Visual and Nonverbal Enactment in the Plays.* Lewisburg, Pa., 1980.

———. *When the Theater Turns to Itself: The Aesthetic Metaphor in Shakespeare.* Newark, Del., 1981.

Jones, Emrys. *Scenic Form in Shakespeare.* Oxford, 1971.

Jorgens, Jack L. *Shakespeare on Film.* Bloomington, Ind., 1977.

Manvell, Roger. *Shakespeare and the Film.* London and New York, 1971.

McGuire, Philip C. *Speechless Dialect: Shakespeare's Open Silences.* Berkeley, 1985.

McGuire, Philip C., and David A. Samuelson. *Shakespeare: The Theatrical Dimension.* New York, 1979.

Odell, George C. D. *Shakespeare from Betterton to Irving.* 2 vols. New York, 1920, 1966.

Poel, William. *Shakespeare in the Theatre.* London, 1913, 1968.

Rutter, Carol, et al. *Clamorous Voices: Shakespeare's Women Today.* New York, 1989.

Shattuck, Charles H. *The Shakespeare Promptbooks: A Descriptive Catalogue.* Urbana, Ill., 1965.

———. *Shakespeare on the American Stage from the Hallams to Edwin Booth.* Washington, D.C., 1976; *from Booth and Barrett to Sothern and Marlowe,* Washington, D.C., 1987.

Slater, Ann Pasternak. *Shakespeare the Director.* Brighton, Sussex, and Totowa, N.J., 1982.

Speaight, Robert. *Shakespeare on the Stage: An Illustrated History of Shakespearian Performance.* London, 1973.

———. *William Poel and the Elizabethan Revival.* London, 1954.

Spencer, Hazelton. *Shakespeare Improved: The Restoration Versions in Quarto and on the Stage.* Cambridge, Mass., 1927.

Sprague, Arthur Colby. *Shakespeare and the Actors.* Cambridge, Mass., 1944.

———. *Shakespearian Players and Performances.* Cambridge, Mass., 1953.

Styan, J. L. *Shakespeare's Stagecraft.* Cambridge, Eng., 1967.

———. "Sight and Space: The Perception of Shakespeare on Stage and Screen," *Shakespeare, Pattern of Excelling Nature,* ed. David Bevington and Jay L. Halio. Newark, Del., 1978.

Thaler, Alwin. *Shakespeare to Sheridan.* Cambridge, Mass., 1922.

Trewin, J. C. *Shakespeare on the English Stage, 1900–1964.* London, 1964.

Van den Berg, Kent. *Playhouse and Cosmos: Shakespearean Theater as Metaphor.* Newark, Del., 1985.

Wells, Stanley. *Royal Shakespeare: Four Major Productions at Stratford-upon-Avon.* Manchester, Eng., 1977.

The Comedies

See also, under *Shakespeare Criticism of the 1980s and 1990s,* Drakakis (essay by Belsey), Erickson and Kahn (essay by Adelman), and Paster (Chapter 7).

Anderson, Linda. *A Kind of Wild Justice: Revenge in Shakespeare's Comedies.* Newark, Del., 1987.

Barber, C. L. *Shakespeare's Festive Comedy.* Princeton, 1959.

Barton, Anne. *The Names of Comedy.* Toronto, 1990.

Berry, Edward. *Shakespeare's Comic Rites.* Cambridge, Eng., 1984.

Berry, Ralph. *Shakespeare's Comedies: Explorations in Form.* Princeton, 1972.

———. *The Shakespearean Metaphor: Studies in Language and Form.* Totowa, N.J., 1978.

Bradbury, Malcolm, and David Palmer, eds., *Shakespearian Comedy.* London, 1972.

Brown, John Russell. *Shakespeare and His Comedies.* London, 1957, 1968.

Brown, John Russell, and Bernard Harris, eds. *Early Shakespeare.* Stratford-upon-Avon Studies 3. London, 1961. (Including an essay by Frank Kermode on "The Mature Comedies.")

Bryant, J. A., Jr. *Shakespeare and the Uses of Comedy.* Lexington, Ky., 1986.

Carroll, William C. *The Metamorphoses of Shakespearean Comedy.* Princeton, 1985.

Champion, Larry S. *The Evolution of Shakespeare's Comedy.* Cambridge, Mass., 1970.

Charlton, H. B. *Shakespearian Comedy.* London, 1938.

Charney, Maurice, ed. *Shakespearean Comedy.* New York, 1980.

Cody, Richard. *The Landscape of the Mind: Pastoralism and Platonic Theory in Tasso's "Aminta" and Shakespeare's Early Comedies.* Oxford, 1969.

Cook, Ann Jennalie. *Making a Match: Courtship in Shakespeare and His Society.* Princeton, 1991.

Elam, Keir. *Shakespeare's Universe of Discourse: Language-Games in the Comedies.* Cambridge, Eng., 1984.

Evans, Bertrand. *Shakespeare's Comedies.* Oxford, 1960.

Frye, Northrop. "The Argument of Comedy," *English Institute Essays 1948.* New York, 1949.

———. *A Natural Perspective: The Development of Shakespearean Comedy and Romance.* New York, 1965.

Hamilton, A. C. *The Early Shakespeare.* San Marino, Calif., 1967.

Hassel, R. Chris. *Faith and Folly in Shakespeare's Romantic Comedies.* Athens, Ga., 1980.

Hawkins, Sherman H. "The Two Worlds of Shakespearean Comedy," *ShakS* 3 (1967), 62–80.

Hunter, Robert G. *Shakespeare and the Comedy of Forgiveness.* New York, 1965.

Huston, J. Dennis. *Shakespeare's Comedies of Play.* New York, 1981.

Leggatt, Alexander. *Shakespeare's Comedy of Love.* London and New York, 1974.

Lerner, Laurence, ed. *Shakespeare's Comedies: An Anthology of Modern Criticism.* Baltimore, 1967.

Levin, Richard A. *Love and Society in Shakespearean Comedy: A Study of Dramatic Form and Content.* Newark, Del., 1985.

MacCary, W. Thomas. *Friends and Lovers: The Phenomenology of Desire in Shakespearean Comedy.* New York, 1985.

Miola, Robert S. *Shakespeare and Classical Comedy: The Influence of Plautus and Terence.* Oxford, 1994.

Nevo, Ruth. *Comic Transformations in Shakespeare.* London, 1980.

Newman, Karen. *Shakespeare's Rhetoric of Comic Character.* New York and London, 1985.

Ornstein, Robert. *Shakespeare's Comedies: From Roman Farce to Romantic Mystery.* Newark, Del., 1986.

Palmer, John. *Comic Characters of Shakespeare.* London, 1946.

Pettet, E. C. *Shakespeare and the Romance Tradition.* London, 1949.

Phialas, Peter G. *Shakespeare's Romantic Comedies.* Chapel Hill, N.C., 1966.

Richmond, Hugh M. *Shakespeare's Sexual Comedy.* Indianapolis, 1971.

Riemer, A. P. *Antic Fables: Patterns of Evasion in Shakespeare's Comedies.* New York and Manchester, Eng., 1980.

Salingar, Leo. *Shakespeare and the Traditions of Comedy.* Cambridge, Eng., 1974.

Smidt, Kristian. *Unconformities in Shakespeare's Early Comedies.* London, 1986.

Stevenson, David L. *The Love-Game Comedy.* New York, 1946.

Tillyard, E. M. W. *Shakespeare's Early Comedies.* London and New York, 1965.

Traversi, Derek. *Shakespeare: The Early Comedies*. London, 1960.

Turner, Robert Y. *Shakespeare's Apprenticeship*. Chicago, 1974.

Westlund, Joseph. *Shakespeare's Reparative Comedies: A Psychoanalytic View of the Middle Plays*. Chicago, 1984.

Williamson, Marilyn. *The Patriarchy of Shakespeare's Comedies*. Detroit, 1986.

The Problem Plays

Campbell, Oscar James. *Shakespeare's Satire*. London and New York, 1943, 1963.

Foakes, R. A. *Shakespeare, The Dark Comedies to the Last Plays: From Satire to Celebration*. Charlottesville, Va., 1971.

Frye, Northrop. *The Myth of Deliverance: Reflections on Shakespeare's Problem Comedies*. Toronto, 1983.

Jamieson, Michael. "The Problem Plays, 1920–1970: A Retrospect," *ShS 25* (1972), 1–10.

Lawrence, W. W. *Shakespeare's Problem Comedies*. New York, 1931, 1960.

Muir, Kenneth, and Stanley Wells, eds. *Aspects of Shakespeare's "Problem Plays": Articles Reprinted from "Shakespeare Survey."* Cambridge, Eng., 1982.

Ornstein, Robert, ed. *Discussions of Shakespeare's Problem Comedies*. Boston, 1961.

Schanzer, Ernest. *The Problem Plays of Shakespeare*. New York, 1963.

Thomas, Vivian. *The Moral Universe of Shakespeare's Problem Plays*. New York, 1987.

Tillyard, E. M. W. *Shakespeare's Problem Plays*. Toronto, 1949.

Wheeler, Richard P. *Shakespeare's Development and the Problem Comedies: Turn and Counter-Turn*. Berkeley, 1981.

Ure, Peter. *William Shakespeare: The Problem Plays*. London, 1961.

The Comedy of Errors

See also, under *The Comedies*, R. Berry, Charlton, Charney (essays by Shaw and Freedman), Cody, Evans, Hamilton, Huston, Leggatt, Nevo, Pettet, Richmond, Salingar, Tillyard, Traversi, and Turner.

Barber, C. L. "Shakespearian Comedy in *The Comedy of Errors*," *College English*, 25 (1964), 493–497.

Brooks, Charles. "Shakespeare's Romantic Shrews," *SQ*, 11 (1960), 351–356.

Brooks, Harold. "Themes and Structure in *The Comedy of Errors*," *Early Shakespeare*, ed. John Russell Brown and Bernard Harris, pp. 55–71. Stratford-upon-Avon Studies 3. London, 1961.

Clubb, Louise G. "Italian Comedy and *The Comedy of Errors*," *Comparative Literature*, 19 (1967), 240–251.

Elliott, G. R. "Weirdness in *The Comedy of Errors*," *University of Toronto Quarterly*, 9 (1939), 95–106.

Fergusson, Francis. "Two Comedies: *The Comedy of Errors* and *Much Ado About Nothing*," *The Human Image in Dramatic Literature*, pp. 144–157. New York, 1957.

Freedman, Barbara. "Egeon's Debt: Self-Division and Self-Redemption in *The Comedy of Errors*," *English Literary Renaissance*, 10 (1980), 360–383.

Knight, G. Wilson. *The Shakespearian Tempest*. London, 1932, 1953.

Lea, Kathleen M. *Italian Popular Comedy: A Study in the Commedia dell' Arte, 1560–1620, with Special Reference to the English Stage*. Oxford, 1934.

Salgādo, Gāmini. " 'Time's Deformed Hand': Sequence, Consequence, and Inconsequence in *The Comedy of Errors*," *ShS 25* (1972), 81–91.

Love's Labor's Lost

See also, under *The Comedies*, Barber, R. Berry, Charlton, Cody, Elam (Chapter 5), Hunter, Huston, Leggatt, MacCary, Nevo, and Stevenson; under *Shakespeare's Language*, Mahood; under *Shakespeare Criticism from the 1940s to the 1970s*, Calderwood and Hawkes; and, under *Shakespeare Criticism of the 1980s and 1990s*, Edwards et al. (essay by Hunter), Erickson and Kahn (essay by Levin), and Hibbard.

Agnew, Gates K. "Berowne and the Progress of *Love's Labour's Lost*," *ShakS 4* (1968), 40–72.

Boughner, D. C. "Don Armado and the *Commedia dell' Arte*," *Studies in Philology*, 37 (1940), 201–224.

Campbell, Oscar J. "*Love's Labour's Lost* Re-studied," *Studies in Shakespeare, Milton and Donne*, by University of Michigan English Department. New York, 1925.

Carroll, William C. *The Great Feast of Language in "Love's Labour's Lost."* Princeton, 1976.

Evans, Malcolm. "Mercury Versus Apollo: A Reading of *Love's Labour's Lost*," *SQ*, 26 (1975), 113–127.

Frye, Northrop. "Shakespeare's Experimental Comedy," *Stratford Papers on Shakespeare 1961*, ed. B. A. W. Jackson. Toronto, 1962.

Goldstien, Neal L. "*Love's Labour's Lost* and the Renaissance Vision of Love," *SQ*, 25 (1974), 335–350.

Greene, Thomas M. "*Love's Labour's Lost*: The Grace of Society," *SQ*, 22 (1971), 315–328. Rpt. in *The Vulnerable Text: Essays on Renaissance Literature*. New York, 1986.

Harbage, Alfred. "*Love's Labour's Lost* and the Early Shakespeare," *Philological Quarterly*, 41 (1962), 18–36.

Heninger, S. K., Jr. "The Pattern of *Love's Labour's Lost*," *ShakS 7* (1974), 25–53.

Hoy, Cyrus. "*Love's Labour's Lost* and the Nature of Comedy," *SQ*, 13 (1962), 31–40.

Hunter, Robert G. "The Function of the Songs at the End of *Love's Labour's Lost*," *ShakS 7* (1974), 55–64.

Lamb, Mary Ellen. "The Nature of Topicality in *Love's Labour's Lost*," *ShS 38* (1985), 49–59.

Montrose, Louis A. " 'Sport by Sport O'erthrown': *Love's Labour's Lost* and the Politics of Play," *Texas Studies in Literature and Language,* 18 (1977), 528–552.

Roesen, Bobbyann [Anne Barton]. *"Love's Labour's Lost,"* *SQ,* 4 (1953), 411–426.

Westlund, Joseph. "Fancy and Achievement in *Love's Labour's Lost,"* *SQ,* 18 (1967), 37–46.

Wilders, John. "The Unresolved Conflict in *Love's Labour's Lost,"* *Essays in Criticism,* 27 (1977), 20–33.

Yates, Frances A. *A Study of "Love's Labour's Lost."* Cambridge, Eng., 1936.

The Two Gentlemen of Verona

See also, under *The Comedies,* R. Berry, Bradbury and Palmer (essay by Ewbank), Champion, Charlton, Evans, Hunter, Leggatt, Nevo, Pettet, and Salingar.

Brooks, Harold F. "Two Clowns in a Comedy (to Say Nothing of the Dog): Speed, Launce (and Crab) in *The Two Gentlemen of Verona,"* *English Association Essays and Studies,* n.s. 16 (1963), 91–100.

Danby, John F. "Shakespeare Criticism and *Two Gentlemen of Verona,"* *Critical Quarterly,* 2 (1960), 309–321.

Lindenbaum, Peter. "Education in *The Two Gentlemen of Verona,"* *Studies in English Literature,* 15 (1975), 229–244.

Morse, Ruth. *"Two Gentlemen* and the Cult of Friendship," *Neuphilologische Mitteilungen,* 84:2 (1983), 214–224.

Rossky, William. *"The Two Gentlemen of Verona* as Burlesque," *English Literary Renaissance,* 12 (1982), 210–219.

Slights, Camille Wells. *"The Two Gentlemen of Verona* and the Courtesy Book Tradition," *ShakS* 16 (1983), 13–31.

Stephenson, William E. "The Adolescent Dream-World of *The Two Gentlemen of Verona,"* *SQ,* 17:2 (1966), 165-168.

Weimann, Robert. "Laughing with the Audience: *The Two Gentlemen of Verona* and the Popular Tradition of Comedy," *ShS* 22 (1969), 35–42.

The Taming of the Shrew

See also, under *The Comedies,* R. Berry, Charlton, Evans, Huston, Hawkins, Leggatt, Nevo, and Stevenson; under *Shakespeare Criticism from the 1940s to the 1970s,* E. A. Bloom (essay by Tillyard) and Garber; and, under *Shakespeare Criticism of the 1980s and 1990s,* Kahn, Lenz et al. (essay by Bean), Novy (*Love's Argument*), and Parker and Hartman (essay by Fineman).

Daniell, David. "The Good Marriage of Katherine and Petruchio," *ShS* 37 (1984), 23–31.

Greenfield, Thelma N. "The Transformation of Christopher Sly," *Philological Quarterly,* 33 (1954), 34–42.

Heilman, Robert B. *"The Taming* Untamed, or, The Return of the Shrew," *Modern Language Quarterly,* 27 (1966), 147–161.

Hibbard, G. R. *"The Taming of the Shrew:* A Social Comedy," *Shakespearean Essays,* ed. Norman Sanders and Alwin Thaler. Knoxville, Tenn., 1964.

Hosley, Richard. "Was There a 'Dramatic Epilogue' to *The Taming of the Shrew?"* *Studies in English Literature,* 1:2 (1961), 17–34.

Jayne, Sears. "The Dreaming of *The Shrew,"* *SQ,* 17 (1966), 41–56.

Newman, Karen. "Renaissance Family Politics and Shakespeare's *The Taming of the Shrew,"* *English Literary Renaissance,* 16 (1986), 86–100.

Saccio, Peter. "Shrewd and Kindly Farce," *ShS 37* (1984), 33–40.

Thompson, Ann, ed., *The Taming of the Shrew.* Cambridge, Eng., 1984.

Thorne, W. B. "Folk Elements in *The Taming of the Shrew,"* *Queen's Quarterly,* 75 (1968), 482–496.

West, Michael. "The Folk Background of Petruchio's Wooing Dance: Male Supremacy in *The Taming of the Shrew,"* *ShakS 7* (1974), 65–73.

A Midsummer Night's Dream

See also, under *The Comedies,* Barber, Brown and Harris (essays by Kermode and Merchant), Carroll, Evans, Huston, Leggatt, and Lerner (including a reprint of the essay by Olson listed below); under *Shakespeare Criticism from the 1940s to the 1970s,* Calderwood, Garber, Granville-Barker, and Kott; and, under *Shakespeare Criticism of the 1980s and 1990s,* Patterson (Chapter 3) and Summers.

Bevington, David. " 'But We Are Spirits of Another Sort': The Dark Side of Love and Magic in *A Midsummer Night's Dream,"* *Medieval and Renaissance Studies,* ed. Siegfried Wenzel. Chapel Hill, N.C., 1978.

Dent, R. W. "Imagination in *A Midsummer Night's Dream,"* *SQ,* 15:2 (1964), 115–129.

Doran, Madeleine. "Pyramus and Thisbe Once More," *Essays . . . in Honor of Hardin Craig,* ed. Richard Hosley, pp. 149–162. Columbia, Mo., 1962.

Fender, Stephen. *Shakespeare: "A Midsummer Night's Dream,"* London, 1968.

Girard, René. "Myth and Ritual in Shakespeare's *A Midsummer Night's Dream,"* *Textual Strategies: Perspectives in Post-Structuralist Criticism,* ed. Josué V. Harari. Ithaca, N.Y., 1979.

Montrose, Louis Adrian. " 'Shaping Fantasies': Figurations of Gender and Power in Elizabethan Culture," *Representations,* 2 (1.2, Spring 1983), 61–94.

Muir, Kenneth. "Pyramus and Thisbe: A Study in Shakespeare's Method," *SQ,* 5 (1954), 141–153.

Nemerov, Howard. "The Marriage of Theseus and Hippolyta," *Kenyon Review,* 18 (1956), 633–641.

Olson, Paul A. "A Midsummer Night's Dream and the Meaning of Court Marriage," *ELH,* 24 (1957), 95–119.

Schanzer, Ernest. "The Central Theme of *A Midsummer Night's Dream,"* *University of Toronto Quarterly,* 20 (1951), 233–238.

———. "The Moon and the Fairies in *A Midsummer Night's Dream,*" *University of Toronto Quarterly,* 24 (1955), 234–246.

Selbourne, David. *The Making of "A Midsummer Night's Dream."* London, 1982.

Siegel, Paul N. *"A Midsummer Night's Dream* and the Wedding Guests," *SQ,* 4 (1953), 139–144.

Taylor, Michael. "The Darker Purpose of *A Midsummer Night's Dream,*" *Studies in English Literature,* 9 (1969), 259-273.

Young, David P. *Something of Great Constancy: The Art of "A Midsummer Night's Dream."* New Haven, 1966.

The Merchant of Venice

See also, under *The Comedies,* Barber, Bradbury and Palmer (essay by Palmer), Brown and Harris (essays by J. R. Brown and Kermode), Evans, Leggatt, Levin, and Nevo; under *Shakespeare's Predecessors and Contemporaries,* Rose (ed. *Renaissance Drama,* essay by Whigham); under *Shakespeare Criticism from the 1940s to the 1970s,* Burckhardt, Fiedler, and Granville-Barker; and, under *Shakespeare Criticism of the 1980s and 1990s,* Erickson and Kahn (essays by Kahn and Wheeler), Garber (*Cannibals,* essay by Mullaney), Howard and O'Connor (essay by Moisan), Novy (*Love's Argument,* Chapter 4), and Rabkin (Chapter 1).

Auden, W. H. "Brothers and Others," *"The Dyer's Hand" and Other Essays.* New York, 1948.

Barnet, Sylvan, ed. *Twentieth Century Interpretations of "The Merchant of Venice."* Englewood Cliffs, N.J., 1970.

Berger, Harry, Jr. "Marriage and Mercifixion in *The Merchant of Venice:* The Casket Scene Revisited," *SQ,* 32 (1981), 155–162.

Cohen, D. M. "The Jew and Shylock," *SQ,* 31 (1980), 53–63.

Danson, Lawrence. *The Harmonies of "The Merchant of Venice."* New Haven and London, 1978.

Engle, Lars. " 'Thrift Is Blessing': Exchange and Explanation in *The Merchant of Venice,*" *SQ,* 37 (1986), 20–37.

Freud, Sigmund. "The Theme of the Three Caskets," *Complete Psychological Works of Sigmund Freud,* 12 (1911–1913), pp. 291–301. London, 1958.

Girard, René. " 'To Entrap the Wisest': A Reading of *The Merchant of Venice,*" *Literature and Society.* Selected Papers from the English Institute, 1978, ed. Edward W. Said. Baltimore, 1980.

Lever, J. W. "Shylock, Portia, and the Values of Shakespearian Comedy," *SQ,* 3 (1952), 383–386.

Lewalski, Barbara K. "Biblical Allusion and Allegory in *The Merchant of Venice,*" *SQ,* 13 (1962), 327–343.

MacKay, Maxine. "*The Merchant of Venice:* A Reflection of the Early Conflict Between Courts of Law and Courts of Equity," *SQ,* 15:4 (1964), 371–375.

Moody, A. D. *Shakespeare: "The Merchant of Venice."* London, 1964.

Newman, Karen. "Portia's Ring: Unruly Women and Structures of Exchange in *The Merchant of Venice,*" *SQ,* 38 (1987), 19–33.

Pettet, E. C. "*The Merchant of Venice* and the Problem of Usury," *English Association Essays and Studies,* 31 (1945), 19–33.

Shell, Marc. "The Wether and the Ewe: Verbal Usury in *The Merchant of Venice,*" *Kenyon Review,* n.s. 1:4 (1979), 65–92.

Sinsheimer, Hermann. *Shylock, the History of a Character; or, The Myth of the Jew.* London, 1947.

Stoll, E. E. "Shylock," *Journal of English and Germanic Philology,* 10 (1911), 236–279. Rpt. in *Shakespeare Studies.* New York, 1927, 1942.

Much Ado About Nothing

See also, under *The Comedies,* R. Berry, Brown, Evans, Hunter, Huston, Leggatt, Levin, Nevo, Newman, Ornstein, Salingar, and Stevenson; under *Shakespeare Criticism from the 1940s to the 1970s,* Rossiter and Siegel; and, under *Shakespeare Criticism of the 1980s and 1990s,* Howard and O'Connor (essay by Howard), Kirsch, Lenz et al. (essay by Hays), Neely, and Ranald.

Barish, Jonas A. "Pattern and Purpose in the Prose of *Much Ado About Nothing,*" *Rice U. Studies,* 60:2 (1974), 19–30.

Berger, Harry, Jr. "Against the Sink-a-Pace: Sexual and Family Politics in *Much Ado About Nothing,*" *SQ,* 33 (1982), 302–313.

Cook, Carol. " 'The Sign and Semblance of Her Honor': Reading Gender Difference in *Much Ado About Nothing,*" *PMLA,* 101 (1986), 186–202.

Davis, Walter R., ed. *Twentieth Century Interpretations of "Much Ado About Nothing."* Englewood Cliffs, N.J., 1969.

Everett, Barbara. *"Much Ado About Nothing,"* *Critical Quarterly,* 3 (1961), 319–335.

Fergusson, Francis. "Two Comedies: *The Comedy of Errors* and *Much Ado About Nothing,*" *The Human Image in Dramatic Literature.* New York, 1957.

Jorgensen, Paul A. *"Much Ado About Nothing,"* *SQ,* 5 (1954), 287–295. Rpt. in *Redeeming Shakespeare's Words.* Berkeley, 1962.

Lewalski, Barbara K. "Love, Appearance, and Reality: Much Ado About Something," *Studies in English Literature,* 8 (1968), 235–251.

Mulryne, J. R. *Shakespeare: "Much Ado About Nothing."* London, 1965.

Ormerod, David. "Faith and Fashion in *Much Ado About Nothing,*" *ShS* 25 (1972), 93–105.

Page, Nadine. "The Public Repudiation of Hero," *PMLA,* 50 (1935), 739–744.

Prouty, Charles T. *The Sources of "Much Ado About Nothing."* New Haven, 1950.

Taylor, Michael. *"Much Ado About Nothing:* The Individual in Society," *Essays in Criticism,* 23 (1973), 146–153.

The Merry Wives of Windsor

See also, under *The Comedies*, R. Berry, Carroll, Charlton, Evans, and Nevo; and, under *Shakespeare Criticism of the 1980s and 1990s*, Erickson and Kahn (essay by Barton), Howard and O'Connor (essay by Erickson), and Kahn (Chapter 5).

Bennett, A. L. "The Sources of Shakespeare's *Merry Wives*," *Renaissance Quarterly*, 23 (1970), 429–433.

Bradley, A. C. "The Rejection of Falstaff," *Oxford Lectures on Poetry*. London, 1909, 1961.

Bryant, J. A., Jr. "Falstaff and the Renewal of Windsor," *PMLA*, 89 (1974), 296–301.

Carroll, William. " 'A Received Belief': Imagination in *The Merry Wives of Windsor*," *Studies in Philology*, 74 (1977), 186–215.

Fleissner, Robert F. "The Malleable Knight and the Unfettered Friar: *The Merry Wives of Windsor* and Boccaccio," *ShakS* 11 (1978), 71–93.

Gilbert, Allan H. "The Merry Wives," *The Principles and Practice of Criticism: Othello, The Merry Wives, Hamlet*. Detroit, 1959.

Green, William. *Shakespeare's "Merry Wives of Windsor."* Princeton, 1962.

Hinely, Jan Lawson. "Comic Scapegoats and the Falstaff of *The Merry Wives of Windsor*," *ShakS* 15 (1982), 37–54.

Leggatt, Alexander. *Citizen Comedy in the Age of Shakespeare*. Toronto, 1973.

Parten, Anne. "Falstaff's Horns: Masculine Inadequacy and Feminine Mirth in *The Merry Wives of Windsor*," *Studies in Philology*, 82 (1985), 184–199.

Roberts, Jeanne Addison. *Shakespeare's English Comedy: "The Merry Wives of Windsor" in Context*. Lincoln, Nebr., 1979.

Steadman, John M. "Falstaff as Actaeon: A Dramatic Emblem," *SQ*, 14 (1963), 231–244.

As You Like It

See also, under *The Comedies*, Barber, R. Berry, Bradbury and Palmer (essay by Anne Barton), Brown, Hunter, Leggatt, Nevo, and Salingar; and, under *Shakespeare Criticism of the 1980s and 1990s*, Erickson, Lenz et al. (essay by Park), and Mahon and Pendleton (essay by Gibbons).

Barnet, Sylvan. "Strange Events: Improbability in *As You Like It*," *ShakS* 4 (1968), 119–131.

Bennett, Robert B. "The Reform of a Malcontent: Jaques and the Meaning of *As You Like It*," *ShakS* 9 (1976), 183–204.

Berry, Edward I. "Rosalynde and Rosalind," *SQ*, 31 (1980), 42–52.

Bono, Barbara J. "Mixed Gender, Mixed Genre in Shakespeare's *As You Like It*," *Renaissance Genres: Essays on Theory, History, and Interpretation*, ed. Barbara Kiefer Lewalski. Cambridge, Mass., 1986.

Cirillo, Albert R. "*As You Like It*: Pastoralism Gone Awry," *ELH*, 38 (1971), 19–39.

Doebler, John. *Shakespeare's Speaking Pictures: Studies in Iconic Imagery*. Albuquerque, 1974.

Doran, Madeleine. " 'Yet Am I Inland Bred,' " *SQ*, 15:2 (1964), 99–114.

Fortin, René E. " 'Tongues in Trees': Symbolic Patterns in *As You Like It*," *Texas Studies in Literature and Language*, 14 (1973), 569–582.

Gardner, Helen. "*As You Like It*," *More Talking of Shakespeare*, ed. John Garrett. London and New York, 1959.

Halio, Jay L. " 'No Clock in the Forest': Time in *As You Like It*," *Studies in English Literature*, 2 (1962), 197–207.

Hayles, Nancy K. "Sexual Disguise in *As You Like It* and *Twelfth Night*," *ShS* 32 (1979), 63–72.

Howard, Jean E. "Crossdressing: The Theatre, and Gender Struggle in Early Modern England," *SQ*, 39 (1988), 418–440.

Jamieson, Michael. *Shakespeare: "As You Like It."* London, 1965.

Kernan, Alvin B. *The Cankered Muse*. New Haven, 1959.

Knowles, Richard. "Myth and Type in *As You Like It*," *ELH*, 33 (1966), 1–22.

Kuhn, Maura Slattery. "Much Virtue in If," *SQ*, 28 (1977), 40–50.

Montrose, Louis Adrian. " 'The Place of a Brother' in *As You Like It*: Social Process and Comic Form," *SQ*, 32 (1981), 28–54.

Shaw, John. "Fortune and Nature in *As You Like It*," *SQ*, 6 (1955), 45–50.

Van den Berg, Kent. "Theatrical Fiction and the Reality of Love in *As You Like It*," *PMLA*, 90 (1975), 885–893.

Wilson, Rawdon. "The Way to Arden: Attitudes Toward Time in *As You Like It*," *SQ*, 26 (1975), 16–24.

Young, David. *The Heart's Forest*. New Haven, 1972.

Twelfth Night

See also, under *The Comedies*, Barber, E. Berry, Bradbury and Palmer (essay by Anne Barton), Brown, Brown and Harris (essay by Kermode), Hunter, Leggatt, Levin, Nevo, and Salingar; under *Shakespeare in Performance*, Hartwig; and, under *Shakespeare Criticism of the 1980s and 1990s*, Erickson and Kahn (essay by Booth), Greenblatt (*Shakespearean Negotiations*, Chapter 3), Howard, and Parker and Hartman (essay by Hartman).

Auden, W. H. "Music in Shakespeare," *"The Dyer's Hand" and Other Essays*. New York, 1948.

Bloom, Harold, ed. *Modern Critical Interpretations of "Twelfth Night."* New York, 1987.

Brown, John Russell. "Directions for *Twelfth Night*, or What You Will," *Tulane Drama Review*, 5:4 (1961), 77–88.

Downer, Alan S. "Feste's Night," *College English*, 13 (1952), 258–265.

Eagleton, Terence. "Language and Reality in *Twelfth Night*," *Critical Quarterly*, 9 (1967), 217–228.

Hollander, John. "*Twelfth Night* and the Morality of Indulgence," *Sewanee Review*, 67 (1959), 220–238.

Jenkins, Harold. "Shakespeare's *Twelfth Night,*" *Rice Institute Pamphlets,* 45:4 (1959), 19–42.

King, Walter N., ed. *Twentieth Century Interpretations of "Twelfth Night."* Englewood Cliffs, N.J., 1968.

Leech, Clifford. *"Twelfth Night" and Shakespearian Comedy.* Toronto, 1965.

Lewalski, Barbara K. "Thematic Patterns in *Twelfth Night,*" *ShakS* 1 (1965), 168–181.

Palmer, D. J. *Shakespeare, "Twelfth Night": A Casebook.* London, 1972.

Potter, Lois. *"Twelfth Night": Text and Performance.* London, 1985.

Salingar, L. D. "The Design of *Twelfth Night,*" *SQ,* 9 (1958), 117–139.

Summers, Joseph H. "The Masks of *Twelfth Night,*" *University of Kansas City Review,* 22 (1955), 25–32. Rpt. in *Shakespeare: Modern Essays in Criticism,* ed. Leonard F. Dean. Rev. ed. London and New York, 1967, 1969.

Wells, Stanley. *Royal Shakespeare.* Manchester, Eng., 1977. (Includes an account of John Barton's production of *Twelfth Night.*)

———, ed. *"Twelfth Night: Critical Essays.* New York, 1986.

Welsford, Enid. *The Fool: His Social and Literary History.* London, 1935.

Williams, Porter, Jr. "Mistakes in *Twelfth Night* and Their Resolution," *PMLA,* 76 (1961), 193–199.

All's Well That Ends Well

See also, under *The Comedies,* Hunter and Salingar; under *The Problem Plays,* Foakes, Frye, Muir and Wells, and Wheeler; under *The Tragedies,* Honigmann (Chapter 8); under *Shakespeare Criticism from the 1940s to the 1970s,* Rossiter; and, under *Shakespeare Criticism of the 1980s and 1990s,* Holland et al. (essay by Adelman), Kirsch, Mahon and Pendleton (essay by Nevo), and Neely.

Adams, John F. "*All's Well That Ends Well:* The Paradox of Procreation," *SQ,* 12 (1961), 261–270.

Bergeron, David M. "The Structure of Healing in *All's Well That Ends Well,*" *South Atlantic Bulletin,* 37:4 (1972), 25–34.

Bradbrook, M. C. "Virtue Is the True Nobility," *Review of English Studies,* n.s. 1 (1950), 289–301.

Calderwood, James L. "Styles of Knowing in *All's Well,*" *Modern Language Quarterly,* 25 (1964), 272–294.

Cole, Howard C. *The "All's Well" Story from Boccaccio to Shakespeare.* Urbana, Ill., 1981.

Donaldson, Ian. "*All's Well That Ends Well:* Shakespeare's Play of Endings," *Essays in Criticism,* 27 (1977), 34–55.

Godshalk, William Leigh. "*All's Well That Ends Well* and the Morality Play," *SQ,* 25 (1974), 61–70.

Halio, Jay L. "*All's Well That Ends Well,*" *SQ,* 15:1 (1964), 33–43.

Kastan, David Scott. "*All's Well That Ends Well* and the Limits of Comedy," *ELH,* 52 (1985), 575–589.

King, Walter N. "Shakespeare's 'Mingled Yarn', " *Modern Language Quarterly,* 21 (1960), 33–44.

Knight, G. Wilson. *The Sovereign Flower: On Shakespeare as the Poet of Royalism.* London, 1958.

Leech, Clifford. "The Theme of Ambition in *All's Well That Ends Well,*" *ELH,* 21 (1954), 17–29.

Leggatt, Alexander. "*All's Well That Ends Well:* The Testing of Romance," *Modern Language Quarterly,* 32 (1971), 21–41.

Price, Joseph G. *The Unfortunate Comedy: A Study of "All's Well That Ends Well" and Its Critics.* Toronto, 1968.

Styan, J. L. *Shakespeare in Performance: "All's Well That Ends Well."* Manchester, Eng., 1984.

Turner, Robert Y. "Dramatic Conventions in *All's Well That Ends Well,*" *PMLA,* 75 (1960), 497–502.

Warren, Roger. "Why Does It End Well? Helena, Bertram, and the Sonnets," *ShS* 22 (1969), 79–92.

Welsh, Alexander. "The Loss of Men and Getting of Children: *All's Well That Ends Well* and *Measure for Measure,*" *Modern Language Review,* 73 (1978), 17–28.

Measure for Measure

See also, under *The Comedies,* Hunter and Newman; under *The Problem Plays,* Frye, Schanzer, and Wheeler; under *Shakespeare Criticism from the 1940s to the 1970s,* Empson, Fly, Holland, Levin (pp. 171–193), and Sewell; and, under *Shakespeare Criticism of the 1980s and 1990s,* Cox, Dollimore, Dollimore and Sinfield (essays by Dollimore and McLuskie), Drakakis (essay by Rose), Goldberg (Chapter 5), Holland et al. (essay by Adelman), Kirsch, Marcus, Mullaney (Chapter 4), Skura (pp. 243–270), Summers, and Tennenhouse.

Bennett, Josephine Waters. *"Measure for Measure" as Royal Entertainment.* New York, 1966.

Chambers, R. W. "The Jacobean Shakespeare and *Measure for Measure,*" *Proceedings of the British Academy,* 23 (1937), 135–192.

Coghill, Nevill. "Comic Form in *Measure for Measure,*" *ShS* 8 (1955), 14–27.

Fergusson, Francis. *The Human Image in Dramatic Literature.* Garden City, N.Y., 1957.

Geckle, George L., ed. *Twentieth Century Interpretations of "Measure for Measure."* Englewood Cliffs, N.J., 1970.

Gless, Darryl. *"Measure for Measure,"* the Law, and the Convent. Princeton, 1979.

Hawkins, Harriett. *Likenesses of Truth in Elizabethan and Restoration Drama.* Oxford, 1972.

Knight, G. Wilson. "*Measure for Measure* and the Gospels," *The Wheel of Fire.* London, 1930, 1965.

Lascelles, Mary. *Shakespeare's "Measure for Measure."* London, 1953.

Leavis, F. R. "The Greatness of *Measure for Measure,*" *Scrutiny,* 10 (1942), 234–247.

Leggatt, Alexander. "Substitution in *Measure for Measure,*" *SQ,* 39, (1988), 342–359.

Miles, Rosalind. *The Problem of "Measure for Measure."* New York, 1976.

Nagarajan, S. "*Measure for Measure* and Elizabethan Betrothals," *SQ*, 14 (1963), 115–119.

Pater, Walter. *Appreciations*. London, 1889.

Pope, Elizabeth M. "The Renaissance Background of *Measure for Measure*," *ShS 2* (1949), 66–82.

Shell, Marc. *The End of Kinship: "Measure for Measure," Incest, and the Ideal of Universal Siblinghood*. Stanford, Calif., 1988.

Stead, C. K., ed. *Shakespeare's "Measure for Measure": A Casebook*. London, 1971.

Stevenson, David L. *The Achievement of "Measure for Measure."* Ithaca, N.Y., 1966.

Welsh, Alexander. "The Loss of Men and Getting of Children: *All's Well That Ends Well* and *Measure for Measure*," *Modern Language Review*, 73 (1978), 17–28.

Wilson, Harold S. "Action and Symbol in *Measure for Measure* and *The Tempest*," *SQ*, 4 (1953), 375–384.

Troilus and Cressida

See also, under *The Problem Plays*, especially Foakes and Frye; under *Shakespeare's Predecessors and Contemporaries*, Kernan and Ornstein; under *Shakespeare Criticism from the 1940s to the 1970s*, Colie, Council, Fly, Knights, Rossiter, Spencer, and Weimann; under *Shakespeare Criticism of the 1980s and 1990s*, Dollimore, Eagleton (Chapter 3), Novy (*Love's Argument*), Parker and Hartman (essays by Freund and Girard), Schwartz and Kahn (essay by Fineman), and Wheeler; and, under *The Tragedies*, Honigmann and Long.

Adamson, Jane. *"Troilus and Cressida."* Brighton, Sussex, 1987.

Adelman, Janet. " 'This Is and Is Not Cressid': The Characterization of Cressida," *The (M)other Tongue: Essays in Feminist Psychoanalytic Interpretation*, ed. Shirley Nelson Garner, Claire Kehane, and Madelon Sprengnether. Ithaca, N.Y., 1985.

Bayley, John. "Time and the Trojans," *Essays in Criticism*, 25 (1975), 55–73.

Campbell, Oscar James. *Comicall Satyre and Shakespeare's "Troilus and Cressida."* San Marino, Calif., 1938.

Coghill, Nevill. *Shakespeare's Professional Skills*. Cambridge, Eng., 1964, Chapter 5.

Cox, John D. "The Error of Our Eye in *Troilus and Cressida*," *Comparative Drama*, 10 (1976), 147–171.

Helton, Tinsley. "Paradox and Hypothesis in *Troilus and Cressida*," *ShakS 10* (1977), 115–131.

Kaula, David. "Will and Reason in *Troilus and Cressida*," *SQ*, 12 (1961), 271–283.

Kermode, Frank. " 'Opinion' in *Troilus and Cressida*," *Teaching the Text*, ed. Susanne Kappeler and Norman Bryson. London, 1983.

Kimbrough, Robert. *Shakespeare's "Troilus and Cressida" and Its Setting*. Cambridge, Mass., 1964.

Knight, G. Wilson. *The Wheel of Fire*. London, 1930, 1965.

Loggins, Vernon P. *The Life of Our Design: Organization and Related Strategies in "Troilus and Cressida."* Lanham, Md., 1992.

Mallin, Eric. "Emulous Factions and the Collapse of Chivalry: *Troilus and Cressida*," *Representations*, 29 (1990), 145–179.

Martin, Priscilla, ed. *"Troilus and Cressida": A Casebook*. London, 1976.

Nowottny, Winifred M. T. " 'Opinion' and 'Value' in *Troilus and Cressida*," *Essays in Criticism*, 4 (1954), 282–296.

Presson, Robert K. *Shakespeare's "Troilus and Cressida" and the Legends of Troy*. Madison, Wis., 1953.

Rabkin, Norman. "*Troilus and Cressida*: The Uses of the Double Plot," *ShakS 1* (1965), 265–282.

Taylor, Gary, "*Troilus and Cressida*: Bibliography, Performance, and Interpretation," *ShakS 15* (1982), 99–136.

Yoder, R. A. " 'Sons and Daughters of the Game': An Essay on Shakespeare's *Troilus and Cressida*," *ShS 25* (1972), 11–25.

The Histories

Alexander, Peter. *Shakespeare's "Henry VI" and "Richard III."* Cambridge, Eng., 1929.

Berry, Edward I. *Patterns of Decay: Shakespeare's Early Histories*. Charlottesville, Va., 1975.

Blanpied, John W. *Time and the Artist in Shakespeare's English Histories*. Newark, Del., 1983.

Calderwood, James L. *Metadrama in Shakespeare's Henriad: "Richard II" to "Henry V."* Berkeley, 1979.

Campbell, Lily B. *Shakespeare's "Histories": Mirrors of Elizabethan Policy*. San Marino, Calif., 1947.

Champion, Larry S. *Perspective in Shakespeare's English Histories*. Athens, Ga., 1980.

Coursen, H. R. *The Leasing Out of England: Shakespeare's Second Henriad*. Washington, D.C., 1982.

Dorius, R. J., ed. *Discussions of Shakespeare's Histories*. Boston, 1964.

Edwards, Philip. "The Hidden King: Shakespeare's History Plays," *Threshold of a Nation: A Study in English and Irish Drama*. Cambridge, Eng., 1979.

Forker, Charles R. "Shakespeare's Chronicle Plays as Historical-Pastoral," *ShakS 1* (1965), 85–104.

Jenkins, Harold. "Shakespeare's History Plays: 1900–1951," *ShS 6* (1953), 1–15.

Jones, Robert C. *These Valiant Dead: Renewing the Past in Shakespeare's Histories*. Iowa City, 1991.

Jorgensen, Paul A. *Shakespeare's Military World*. Berkeley and Los Angeles, 1956.

Kastan, David Scott. *Shakespeare and the Shapes of Time*. Hanover, N.H., 1982.

Kelly, Henry A. *Divine Providence in the England of Shakespeare's Histories*. Cambridge, Mass., 1970.

Knights, L. C. "Shakespeare's Politics: With Some Reflections on the Nature of Tradition," *Proceedings of the British Academy*, 43 (1957), 115–132.

Leggatt, Alexander. *Shakespeare's Political Drama: The History Plays and the Roman Plays*. London, 1988.

Manheim, Michael. *The Weak King Dilemma in the Shakespearean History Play*. Syracuse, N.Y., 1973.

Ornstein, Robert. *A Kingdom for a Stage*. Cambridge, Mass., 1972.

Palmer, John. *Political Characters of Shakespeare*. London, 1945.

Pierce, Robert B. *Shakespeare's History Plays: The Family and the State*. Columbus, Ohio, 1971.

Porter, Joseph. *The Drama of Speech Acts: Shakespeare's Lancastrian Tetralogy*. Berkeley, 1979.

Prior, Moody E. *The Drama of Power: Studies in Shakespeare's History Plays*. Evanston, Ill., 1973.

Rackin, Phyllis. "Anti-Historians: Women's Roles in Shakespeare's Histories," *Theatre Journal*, 37 (1985), 329–344.

———. *Stages of History: Shakespeare's English Chronicles*. Ithaca, N.Y., 1990.

Reese, M. M. *The Cease of Majesty*. London and New York, 1961.

Ribner, Irving. *The English History Play in the Age of Shakespeare*. Rev. ed. London, 1965.

Richmond, H. M. *Shakespeare's Political Plays*. New York, 1967.

Rossiter, A. P. "Ambivalence: The Dialectic of the Histories," *Talking of Shakespeare*, ed. John Garrett. London, 1954.

Saccio, Peter. *Shakespeare's English Kings: History, Chronicle, and Drama*. New York, 1977.

Sanders, Norman. "American Criticism of Shakespeare's History Plays," *ShakS* 9 (1976), 11–23.

Shaheen, Naseeb. *Biblical References in Shakespeare's History Plays*. Newark, Del., 1989.

Sprague, Arthur Colby. *Shakespeare's Histories: Plays for the Stage*. London, 1964.

Thayer, C. G. *Shakespearean Politics: Government and Misgovernment in the Great Histories*. Athens, Ohio, 1983.

Tillyard, E. M. W. *Shakespeare's History Plays*. London, 1944, 1961.

Traversi, Derek. *Shakespeare from "Richard II" to "Henry V."* Palo Alto, Calif., 1957.

Waith, Eugene M., ed. *Shakespeare: The Histories*. Englewood Cliffs, N.J., 1965. (A collection of essays.)

Watson, Donald G. *Shakespeare's Early History Plays: Politics and Play on the Elizabethan Stage*. Athens, Ga., 1990.

Wikander, Matthew H. *The Plays of Truth and State: Historical Drama from Shakespeare to Brecht*. Baltimore, 1986.

The Henry the Sixth Plays

See also, under *The Histories*, Alexander, Berry, Blanpied, Kelly, Manheim, Ornstein, Prior, Ribner, Saccio, and Tillyard; under *Shakespeare Criticism from the 1940s to the 1970s*, Brown and Harris (essay by Brockbank), Burckhardt, and Jones; and, under *Shakespeare Criticism of the 1980s and 1990s*, Berry (*Shakespearean Structures*, pp. 1–11), Edwards et al. (essay by Clemen), Hibbard, Kahn (Chapter 3), Marcus (Chapter 2), and Patterson (Chapter 2).

Berman, Ronald S. "Fathers and Sons in the Henry VI Plays," *SQ*, 13 (1962), 487–497.

Bevington, David. "The Domineering Female in *1 Henry VI*," *ShakS* 2 (1966), 51–58.

Clemen, Wolfgang H. "Anticipation and Foreboding in Shakespeare's Early Histories," *ShS* 6 (1953), 23–35.

Cox, John D. "*3 Henry VI*: Dramatic Convention and the Shakespearean History Play," *Comparative Drama*, 12 (1978), 42–60.

Dean, Paul. "Shakespeare's *Henry VI* Trilogy and Elizabethan 'Romance' Histories: The Origins of a Genre," *SQ*, 33 (1982), 34–48.

French, A. L. "The Mills of God and Shakespeare's Early History Plays," *English Studies*, 55 (1974), 313–324.

Greenblatt, Stephen. "Murdering Peasants, Status, Genre, and the Representation of Rebellion," *Representations*, 1 (1983), 1–29.

Leech, Clifford. "The Two-Part Play: Marlowe and the Early Shakespeare," *Shakespeare Jahrbuch*, 94 (1958), 90–106.

Price, Hereward T. *Construction in Shakespeare*. Ann Arbor, Mich., 1951.

Riggs, David. *Shakespeare's Heroical Histories: "Henry VI" and Its Literary Tradition*. Cambridge, Mass., 1971.

Rossiter, A. P., ed. *Woodstock, a Moral History*. London, 1946.

Swander, Homer. "The Rediscovery of *Henry VI*," *SQ*, 29 (1978), 146–163.

Utterback, Raymond V. "Public Men, Private Wills, and Kingship in *Henry VI, Part III*," *Renaissance Papers 1978* (1979), 47–54.

Wilson, F. P. *Marlowe and the Early Shakespeare*. Oxford, 1953.

Richard the Third

See also, under *The Histories*, Alexander, Berry, Campbell, Kelly, Ornstein, Prior, Ribner, and Saccio; under *Shakespeare's Predecessors and Contemporaries*, Sanders; under *Shakespeare Criticism from the 1940s to the 1970s*, Jones, Rossiter, and Spivack; under *Shakespeare Criticism of the 1980s and 1990s*, Dubrow and Strier (essay by Garber), and Lenz et al. (essay by Miner); and, under *The Tragedies*, Brooke and Hunter.

Anderson, Judith H. "Shakespeare's *Richard III*: The Metamorphosis of Biographical Truth to Fiction," *Biographical Truth: The Representation of Historical Persons in Tudor-Stuart Writing*. New Haven, 1984.

Bevington, David. " 'Why Should Calamity Be Full of Words?' The Efficacy of Cursing in *Richard III*," *Iowa State Journal of Research*, 56:1 (1981), 9–21.

Clemen, Wolfgang H. *A Commentary on Richard III,* trans. Jean Bonheim. London, 1968.

Colley, Scott. *"Richard's Himself Again": A Stage History of "Richard III."* New York, 1992.

French, A. L. "The World of *Richard III,*" *ShakS 4* (1968), 25–39.

Hankey, Julie, ed. *Plays in Performance: "Richard III."* Bristol, 1981. 2nd ed., 1988.

Heilman, Robert B. "Satiety and Conscience: Aspects of *Richard III,*" *Antioch Review,* 24 (1964), 57–73.

Hunter, Robert G. *Shakespeare and the Mystery of God's Judgments.* Athens, Ga., 1976.

Kendall, Paul Murray. *Richard the Third.* New York and London, 1956.

Krieger, Murray. "The Dark Generations of *Richard III,*" *Criticism,* 1 (1959), 32–48.

Neill, Michael. "Shakespeare's Halle of Mirrors: Play, Politics, and Psychology in *Richard III,*" *ShakS 8* (1975), 99–129.

Sher, Antony. *Year of the King: An Actor's Diary and Sketchbook.* London, 1985.

Sheriff, William E. "The Grotesque Comedy of *Richard III,*" *Studies in the Literary Imagination,* 5:1 (1972), 51–64.

Wheeler, Richard P. "History, Character, and Conscience in *Richard III,*" *Comparative Drama,* 7 (1971–72), 301–321.

King John

See also, under *The Histories,* Blanpied, Campbell, Champion, Edwards, Ornstein, Pierce, Rackin (*Stages of History*), Reese, Ribner, Saccio, Sprague, and Tillyard; under *Shakespeare Criticism from the 1940s to the 1970s,* Burckhardt and Jones; and, under *Shakespeare Criticism of the 1980s and 1990s,* Hibbard.

Berman, Ronald. "Anarchy and Order in *Richard III* and *King John,*" *ShS 20* (1967), 51–59.

Bonjour, Adrien. "The Road to Swinstead Abbey: A Study of the Sense and Structure of *King John,*" *ELH,* 18 (1951), 253–274.

Calderwood, James L. "Commodity and Honour in *King John,*" *University of Toronto Quarterly,* 29 (1960), 341–356.

Elliott, John R., Jr., "Shakespeare and the Double Image of King John," *ShakS 1* (1965), 64–84.

Elson, John. "Studies in the *King John* Plays," *J. Q. Adams Memorial Studies,* ed. J. McManaway et al., pp. 183–198. Washington, D.C., 1948.

Jones, Robert C. "Truth in *King John,*" *Studies in English Literature,* 25 (1985), 397–417.

Levin, Carole. " 'I Trust I May Not Trust Thee': Women's Visions of the World in Shakespeare's *King John,*" *Ambiguous Realities: Women in the Middle Ages and Renaissance,* ed. Carole Levin and Jeanie Watson, pp. 219–234. Detroit, 1987.

Matchett, William H. "Richard's Divided Heritage in *King John,*" *Essays in Criticism,* 12 (1962), 231–253.

Pettet, E. C. "Hot Irons and Fever: A Note on Some of the Imagery of *King John,*" *Essays in Criticism,* 4 (1954), 128–144.

Salter, F. M. "The Problem of *King John,*" *Proceedings and Transactions of the Royal Society of Canada,* 3rd ser. 43:2 (1949), 115–136.

Shirley, Frances A., ed. *"King John" and "Henry VIII": Critical Essays.* New York, 1988.

Simmons, J. L. "Shakespeare's *King John* and Its Source: Coherence, Pattern, and Vision," *Tulane Studies in English,* 17 (1969), 53–72.

Van de Water, Julia C. "The Bastard in *King John,*" *SQ,* 11 (1960), 137–146.

Waith, Eugene M. "*King John* and the Drama of History," *SQ,* 29 (1978), 192–211.

Richard the Second

See also, under *The Histories,* Campbell, Forker, Ornstein, Palmer, Porter, Reese, Ribner, Saccio and Tillyard; under *Shakespeare's Predecessors and Contemporaries,* Sanders; under *Shakespeare's Language,* Mahood and Trousdale; under *Shakespeare Criticism to the 1930s,* Coleridge (*Coleridge's Writings*); under *Shakespeare Criticism from the 1940s to the 1970s,* Bryant, Calderwood, Hawkes, Kernan (essay on the "Major History Plays"), and Rabkin (pp. 81–98); under *Shakespeare Criticism of the 1980s and 1990s,* Parker and Hartman (essay by Berger); and, under *The Tragedies,* Brooke and Mack Jr.

Altick, Richard D. "Symphonic Imagery in *Richard II,*" *PMLA,* 62 (1947), 339–365.

Barkan, Leonard. "The Theatrical Consistency of *Richard II,*" *SQ,* 29 (1978), 5–19.

Berger, Harry, Jr. "Textual Dramaturgy: Representing the Limits of Theatre in *Richard II,*" *Theatre Journal,* 39 (1987), 135–155.

Black, Matthew W. "The Sources of Shakespeare's *Richard II,*" *J. Q. Adams Memorial Studies,* ed. J. McManaway et al., pp. 199–216. Washington, D.C., 1948.

Bogard, Travis. "Shakespeare's Second Richard," *PMLA,* 70 (1955), 192–209.

Bonnard, George A. "The Actor in *Richard II,*" *Shakespeare Jahrbuch,* 87 (1952), 87–101.

Brooke, Nicholas, ed. *Shakespeare, "Richard II": A Casebook.* London, 1973.

Dean, Leonard F. "*Richard II:* The State and the Image of the Theater," *PMLA,* 67 (1952), 211–218.

Doran, Madeleine. "Imagery in *Richard II* and in *Henry IV,*" *Modern Language Review,* 37 (1942), 113–122.

Dorius, R. J. "A Little More Than a Little," *SQ,* 11 (1960), 13–26.

Elliott, John R., Jr., "History and Tragedy in *Richard II,*" *Studies in English Literature,* 8 (1968), 253–271.

Humphreys, A. R. *Shakespeare: "Richard II."* London, 1967.

Kantorowicz, Ernst H. *The King's Two Bodies: A Study in Medieval Political Theology.* Princeton, 1957.

Page, Malcolm. *Text and Performance: "Richard II."* Atlantic Highlands, N.J., 1987.

Pater, Walter. *Appreciations.* London, 1889.

Phialas, Peter G. "The Medieval in *Richard II,*" *SQ,* 12 (1961), 305–310.

Schoenbaum, S. "*Richard II* and the Realities of Power," *ShS* 28 (1975), 1–13.

Stirling, Brents. "Bolingbroke's 'Decision'," *SQ*, 2 (1951), 27–34.

Yeats, W. B. "At Stratford-upon-Avon," *Ideas of Good and Evil,* collected in *Essays and Introductions.* New York, 1961.

Zitner, Sheldon P. "Aumerle's Conspiracy," *Studies in English Literature,* 14 (1974), 239–257.

The Henry the Fourth Plays

See also, under *The Histories,* Blanpied, Calderwood, Campbell, Kelly, Manheim, Ornstein, Palmer, Porter, Prior, Reese, Saccio, Sprague, and Tillyard; under *Shakespeare Criticism to the 1930s,* Johnson and Smith (*Eighteenth Century,* essay by Morgann); under *Shakespeare Criticism from the 1940s to the 1970s,* Bryant, Burckhardt, Council, Goldman, Kernan (essay on the "Major History Plays"), Spivack, and Stewart; and, under *Shakespeare Criticism of the 1980s and 1990s,* Dollimore and Sinfield (essay by Greenblatt, originally published in *Glyph* 8 and in *Shakespearean Negotiations*), and Watson.

Auden, W. H. "The Prince's Dog," *"The Dyer's Hand" and Other Essays.* New York, 1948.

Barber, C. L. "Rule and Misrule in *Henry IV,*" *Shakespeare's Festive Comedy.* Princeton, 1959.

Barish, Jonas A. "The Turning Away of Prince Hal," *ShakS* 1 (1965), 9–17.

Berger, Harry, Jr. "Sneak's Noise, or Rumor and Detextualization in *2 Henry IV,*" *Kenyon Review,* n.s. 6:4 (1984), 58–78.

Berry, Edward I. "The Rejection Scene in *2 Henry IV,*" *Studies in English Literature,* 17 (1977), 201–218.

Bevington, David, ed. *"Henry the Fourth, Parts I and II"*: *Critical Essays.* New York, 1986.

Bradley, A. C. "The Rejection of Falstaff," *Oxford Lectures on Poetry.* London, 1909, 1961.

Brooks, Cleanth, and Robert B. Heilman, "Shakespeare, *Henry IV, Part I,*" *Understanding Drama.* New York, 1945.

Bryant, J. A., Jr., "Prince Hal and the Ephesians," *Sewanee Review,* 67 (1959), 204–219.

Dessen, Alan. "Dual Protagonists in *1 Henry IV,*" *Shakespeare and the Late Moral Plays.* Lincoln, Nebr., 1986.

Doran, Madeleine. "Imagery in *Richard II* and in *Henry IV,*" *Modern Language Review,* 37 (1942), 113–122.

Dorius, R. J., ed. *Twentieth Century Interpretations of "Henry IV Part I."* Englewood Cliffs, N.J., 1970.

Empson, William. "Falstaff and Mr. Dover Wilson," *Kenyon Review,* 15 (1953), 213–262.

Hawkins, Sherman H. "Virtue and Kingship in Shakespeare's *Henry IV,*" *English Literary Renaissance,* 5 (1975), 313–343.

Hunter, G. K. "*Henry IV* and the Elizabethan Two-Part Play," *Review of English Studies,* n.s. 5 (1954), 236–248.

———. "Shakespeare's Politics and the Rejection of Falstaff," *Critical Quarterly,* 1 (1959), 229–236.

Jenkins, Harold. *The Structural Problem in Shakespeare's "Henry the Fourth."* London, 1956.

Jorgensen, Paul. "The 'Dastardly Treachery' of Prince John of Lancaster," *PMLA,* 76 (1961), 488–492.

Knowles, Richard. "Unquiet and the Double Plot of *2 Henry IV,*" *ShakS* 2 (1966), 133–140.

Manley, Frank. "The Unity of Betrayal in *2 Henry IV,*" *Studies in the Literary Imagination,* 5:1 (1972), 91–110.

McLuhan, Herbert Marshall. "*Henry IV,* A Mirror of Magistrates," *University of Toronto Quarterly,* 17 (1948), 152–160.

Prosser, Eleanor. *Shakespeare's Anonymous Editors: Scribe and Compositor in the Folio Text of "2 Henry IV."* Stanford, 1981.

Seng, Peter J. "Songs, Time, and the Rejection of Falstaff," *ShS* 15 (1962), 31–40.

Toliver, Harold E. "Falstaff, the Prince, and the History Play," *SQ,* 16 (1965), 63–80.

Wharton, T. F. *"Henry the Fourth, Parts 1 and 2": Text and Performance.* London, 1983.

Wilson, J. Dover. *The Fortunes of Falstaff.* Cambridge, Eng., 1943.

Young, David P., ed. *Twentieth Century Interpretations of "Henry IV, Part Two."* Englewood Cliffs, N.J., 1968.

Henry the Fifth

See also, under *The Histories,* Calderwood, Campbell, Jorgensen, Kastan, Ornstein, Porter, Prior, Reese, Ribner, Saccio, Thayer, and Traversi; under *Shakespeare Criticism to the 1930s,* Hazlitt and Schlegel; under *Shakespeare Criticism from the 1940s to the 1970s,* Burckhardt, Goddard, Goldman, and Kernan (essay on the "Major History Plays"); and, under *Shakespeare Criticism of the 1980s and 1990s,* Dollimore and Sinfield (essays by Greenblatt and Tennenhouse), Drakakis (essay by Dollimore and Sinfield), Erickson, Patterson (Chapter 4), and Rabkin (Chapter 2).

Beauman, Sally, ed. *"Henry V" for the Centenary Season at the Royal Shakespeare Theatre.* Oxford, 1976. (Includes information on Terry Hands' *Henry V.*)

Berman, Ronald S., ed. *Twentieth Century Interpretations of "Henry V."* Englewood Cliffs, N.J., 1968.

Granville-Barker, Harley. "From *Henry V* to *Hamlet,*" *Proceedings of the British Academy,* 11 (1925), 283–309.

Levin, Richard. "Hazlitt on *Henry V,* and the Appropriation of Shakespeare," *SQ,* 35 (1984), 134–141.

Quinn, Michael, ed. *Shakespeare, "Henry V": A Casebook.* London, 1969.

Henry the Eighth

See also, under *The Histories,* Saccio and Waith (essay by Kermode); under *Shakespeare Criticism of the 1980s and 1990s,* Dollimore and Sinfield (essay by Tennenhouse);

under *The Problem Plays,* Foakes; and, under *The Romances,* Brown and Harris (essay by Harris), Felperin, Knight *(Crown of Life),* and Leech.

Alexander, Peter. "Conjectural History, or Shakespeare's *Henry VIII,*" *English Association Essays and Studies,* 16 (1930), 85–120.

Anderson, Judith H. "Shakespeare's *Henry VIII:* The Changing Relation of Truth to Fiction," *Biographical Truth: The Representation of Historical Persons in Tudor-Stuart Writing.* New Haven, 1984.

Baillie, William M. "*Henry VIII:* A Jacobean History," *ShakS* 12 (1979), 247–266.

Berman, Ronald. "*King Henry the Eighth:* History and Romance," *English Studies,* 48 (1967), 112–121.

Berry, Edward I. "*Henry VIII* and the Dynamics of Spectacle," *ShakS* 12 (1979), 229–246.

Bertram, Paul. "*Henry VIII:* The Conscience of the King," *In Defense of Reading,* ed. Reuben A. Brower and Richard Poirier. New York, 1962.

Bliss, Lee. "The Wheel of Fortune and the Maiden Phoenix of Shakespeare's *King Henry the Eighth,*" *ELH,* 42 (1975), 1–25.

Cespedes, Frank V. " 'We are one in fortunes': The Sense of History in *Henry VIII,*" *English Literary Renaissance,* 10 (1980), 413–438.

Cox, John D. "*Henry VIII* and the Masque," *ELH,* 45 (1978), 390–409.

Leggatt, Alexander. "*Henry VIII* and the Ideal England," *ShS* 38 (1985), 131–143.

Mincoff, Marco. "*Henry VIII* and Fletcher," *SQ,* 12 (1961), 239–260.

Richmond, H. M. "Shakespeare's *Henry VIII:* Romance Redeemed by History," *ShakS* 4 (1968), 334–349.

Shirley, Frances A., ed. *"King John" and "Henry VIII": Critical Essays.* New York, 1988.

Waith, Eugene M. "*Henry VIII* and the More Historical Tragedies," *The Pattern of Tragicomedy in Beaumont and Fletcher.* New Haven and London, 1952.

Wasson, John. "In Defense of *King Henry VIII,*" *Research Studies,* Washington State University, 32 (1964), 261–276.

Wiley, Paul L. "Renaissance Exploitation of Cavendish's *Life of Wolsey,*" *Studies in Philology,* 43 (1946), 121–146.

The Tragedies

Barroll, J. Leeds. *Artificial Persons: The Formation of Character in the Tragedies of Shakespeare.* Columbia, S. C., 1974.

Battenhouse, Roy. *Shakespearean Tragedy: Its Art and Its Christian Premises.* Bloomington, Ind., 1969.

Bradley, A. C. *Shakespearean Tragedy.* London, 1904. *(Hamlet, Othello, King Lear, Macbeth.)*

Brooke, Nicholas. *Shakespeare's Early Tragedies.* London and New York, 1968.

Brown, John Russell, and Bernard Harris, eds. *Early Shakespeare.* Stratford-upon-Avon Studies 3. London, 1961.

Bulman, James C. *The Heroic Idiom of Shakespearean Tragedy.* Newark, Del., 1985.

Bushnell, Rebecca. *Tragedies of Tyrants: Political Thought and Theater in the English Renaissance.* Ithaca, N.Y., 1990.

Campbell, Lily B. *Shakespeare's Tragic Heroes: Slaves of Passion.* Cambridge, Eng., 1930.

Champion, Larry S. *Shakespeare's Tragic Perspective.* Athens, Ga., 1976.

Charlton, H. B. *Shakespearian Tragedy.* Cambridge, Eng., 1948.

Cunningham, J. V. *Woe or Wonder: The Emotional Effect of Shakespearean Tragedy.* Denver, 1951. Rpt. in *Tradition and Poetic Structure.* Denver, 1960.

Danson, Lawrence. *Tragic Alphabet: Shakespeare's Drama of Language.* New Haven and London, 1974.

Dickey, Franklin M. *Not Wisely But Too Well: Shakespeare's Love Tragedies.* San Marino, Calif., 1957.

Eliot, T. S. "Shakespeare and the Stoicism of Seneca," *Selected Essays, 1917–1932.* London, 1932.

Evans, Bertrand. *Shakespeare's Tragic Practice.* Oxford, 1979.

Everett, Barbara. *Young Hamlet: Essays on Shakespeare's Tragedies.* Oxford, 1989.

Farnham, Willard. *Shakespeare's Tragic Frontier.* Berkeley, 1950.

Felperin, Howard. *Shakespearean Representation.* Princeton, 1977.

Foreman, Walter C., Jr. *The Music of the Close: The Final Scenes of Shakespeare's Tragedies.* Lexington, Ky.. 1978.

Frye, Northrop. *Fools of Time: Studies in Shakespearean Tragedy.* Toronto, 1967.

Goldman, Michael. *Acting and Action in Shakespearean Tragedy.* Princeton, 1985.

Hall, Michael. *The Structure of Love: Representational Patterns and Shakespeare's Love Tragedies.* Charlottesville, Va., 1989.

Harbage, Alfred, ed. *Shakespeare: The Tragedies.* Englewood Cliffs, N.J., 1964.

Hawkes, Terence. *Shakespeare and the Reason: A Study of the Tragedies and the Problem Plays.* London, 1964.

Holloway, John. *The Story of the Night: Studies in Shakespeare's Major Tragedies.* London and Lincoln, Nebr., 1961.

Honigmann, E. A. J. *Myriad-Minded Shakespeare: Essays, Chiefly on the Tragedies and Problem Plays.* New York, 1989.

Hunter, Robert Grams. *Shakespeare and the Mystery of God's Judgments.* Athens, Ga., 1976.

Kirsch, Arthur. *The Passions of Shakespeare's Tragic Heroes.* Charlottesville, Va., 1990.

Knight, G. Wilson. *The Wheel of Fire.* London, 1930, 1965.

Lawlor, John. *The Tragic Sense in Shakespeare.* London, 1960.

Leech, Clifford. *Shakespeare's Tragedies and Other Studies in Seventeenth-Century Drama.* London, 1950.

———, ed. *Shakespeare: The Tragedies.* Chicago, 1965.

Long, Michael. *The Unnatural Scene: A Study in Shakespearean Tragedy.* London, 1976.

McElroy, Bernard. *Shakespeare's Mature Tragedies.* Princeton, 1973.

Mack, Maynard. *Everybody's Shakespeare: Reflections Chiefly on the Tragedies.* Lincoln, Nebr., 1993.

———. "The Jacobean Shakespeare: Some Observations on the Construction of the Tragedies," *Jacobean Theatre,* ed. John Russell Brown and Bernard Harris. Stratford-upon-Avon Studies 1. London, 1960.

Mack, Maynard, Jr. *Killing the King: Three Studies in Shakespeare's Tragic Structure.* New Haven and London, 1973.

McAlindon, T. *Shakespeare's Tragic Cosmos.* Cambridge, Eng., 1991.

Miola, Robert S. *Shakespeare and Classical Tragedy: The Influence of Seneca.* Oxford, 1992.

Nevo, Ruth. *Tragic Form in Shakespeare.* Princeton, 1972.

Proser, Matthew N. *The Heroic Image in Five Shakespearean Tragedies.* Princeton, 1965.

Rackin, Phyllis. *Shakespeare's Tragedies.* New York, 1978.

Ribner, Irving, *Patterns in Shakespearean Tragedy.* New York, 1960.

Rosen, William. *Shakespeare and the Craft of Tragedy.* Cambridge, Mass., 1960.

Sanders, Wilbur, and Howard Jacobson. *Shakespeare's Magnanimity: Four Tragic Heroes, Their Friends and Families.* Oxford, 1978.

Shaheen, Naseeb. *Biblical References in Shakespeare's Tragedies.* Newark, Del., 1987.

Sisson, C. J. *Shakespeare's Tragic Justice.* Scarborough, Ont., 1961.

Smidt, Kristian. *Unconformities in Shakespeare's Tragedies.* New York, 1990.

Snyder, Susan. *The Comic Matrix of Shakespeare's Tragedies.* Princeton, 1979.

Speaight, Robert. *Nature in Shakespearian Tragedy.* London, 1955.

Spivack, Bernard. *Shakespeare and the Allegory of Evil.* New York, 1958.

Sternfeld, F. W. *Music in Shakespearean Tragedy.* London and New York, 1963.

Stirling, Brents. *Unity in Shakespearian Tragedy.* New York, 1956.

Whitaker, Virgil. *The Mirror up to Nature.* San Marino, Calif., 1965.

White, R. S. *Innocent Victims: Poetic Injustice in Shakespearean Tragedy.* 2nd ed. London, 1986.

Wilson, Harold S. *On the Design of Shakespearian Tragedy.* Toronto, 1957.

Young, David. *The Action to the Word: Structure and Style in Shakespearean Tragedy.* New Haven, 1990.

———. ed. *Shakespeare's Middle Tragedies: A Collection of Critical Essays.* Englewood Cliffs., N.J., 1993.

The Greek and Roman Tragedies

See also, under *Shakespeare Criticism of the 1980s and 1990s,* Paster (Chapter 3).

Brower, Reuben A. *Hero and Saint: Shakespeare and the Graeco-Roman Heroic Tradition.* New York and Oxford, 1971.

Cantor, Paul A. *Shakespeare's Rome: Republic and Empire.* Ithaca, N.Y., 1976.

Charney, Maurice, ed. *Discussions of Shakespeare's Roman Plays.* Boston, 1964.

———. *Shakespeare's Roman Plays: The Function of Imagery in the Drama.* Cambridge, Mass., 1961.

Knight, G. Wilson. *The Imperial Theme: Further Interpretations of Shakespeare's Tragedies Including the Roman Plays.* London, 1931, 1953.

MacCallum, M. W. *Shakespeare's Roman Plays and Their Background.* London, 1910.

Maxwell, J. C. "Shakespeare's Roman Plays: 1900–1956," *ShS 10* (1957), 1–11.

Miola, Robert S. *Shakespeare's Rome.* Cambridge, Eng., 1983.

Nicoll, Allardyce, ed. *Shakespeare Survey 10* (1957).

Phillips, James E., Jr. *The State in Shakespeare's Greek and Roman Plays.* New York, 1940.

Simmons, J. L. *Shakespeare's Pagan World: The Roman Tragedies.* Charlottesville, Va., 1973.

Spencer, T. J. B. "Shakespeare and the Elizabethan Romans," *ShS 10* (1957), 27–38.

———. *William Shakespeare: The Roman Plays.* London, 1963.

Stampfer, Judah. *The Tragic Engagement: A Study of Shakespeare's Classical Tragedies.* New York, 1968.

Thomas, Vivian. *Shakespeare's Roman Worlds.* London, 1989.

Thomson, J. A. K. *Shakespeare and the Classics.* London, 1952.

Traversi, Derek. *Shakespeare: The Roman Plays.* Palo Alto, Calif., 1963.

Velz, John W. "The Ancient World in Shakespeare: Authenticity or Anachronism? A Retrospect," *ShS 31* (1978), 1–12.

———. *Shakespeare and the Classical Tradition: A Critical Guide to Commentary, 1660–1960.* Minneapolis, 1968.

Titus Andronicus

See also, under *The Tragedies,* Brooke, Brown and Harris, Danson, and Spivack; under *The Greek and Roman Tragedies,* Brower (Chapter 4), Maxwell, Miola, Spencer (both titles), and Thomson; under *Shakespeare's Predecessors and Contemporaries,* Baker, Bowers, and Hattaway (Chapter 8); under *Shakespeare Criticism from the 1940s to the 1970s,* Calderwood; and, under *Shakespeare Criticism of the 1980s and 1990s,* Gray (essays by Hunter and Waith).

Barroll, J. Leeds. "Shakespeare and Roman History," *Modern Language Review,* 53 (1958), 327–343.

Bartels, Emily C. "Making More of the Moor: Aaron, Othello, and Renaissance Refashionings of Race," *SQ,* 41 (1990), 433–454.

Bradbrook, M. C. "Moral Heraldry: *Titus Andronicus, Rape of Lucrece, Romeo and Juliet,*" in *Shakespeare and Elizabethan Poetry.* London, 1951.

Ettin, Andrew V. "Shakespeare's First Roman Tragedy," *ELH*, 37 (1970), 325–341.

Green, Douglas E. "Interpreting 'her martyr'd signs': Gender and Tragedy in *Titus Andronicus*," *SQ*, 40 (1989), 317–326.

Hamilton, A. C. "*Titus Andronicus*: The Form of Shakespearian Tragedy," *SQ*, 14 (1963), 201–213.

Harris, Bernard. "A Portrait of a Moor," *ShS 11* (1958), 89–97.

Hunter, G. K. "Shakespeare's Earliest Tragedies: *Titus Andronicus* and *Romeo and Juliet*," *ShS 27* (1974), 1–9.

Kolin, Philip C., ed. *Titus Andronicus: Critical Essays*. New York, 1995.

Metz, G. Harold. "Stage History of *Titus Andronicus*," *SQ*, 28 (1977), 154–169.

Sommers, Alan. " 'Wilderness of Tigers': Structure and Symbolism in *Titus Andronicus*," *Essays in Criticism*, 10 (1960), 275–289.

Tricomi, Albert H. "The Aesthetics of Mutilation in *Titus Andronicus*," *ShS 27* (1974), 11–19.

———. "The Mutilated Garden in *Titus Andronicus*," *ShakS* 9 (1976), 89–105.

Waith, Eugene. "The Metamorphosis of Violence in *Titus Andronicus*," *ShS 10* (1957), 39–49.

Wilson, J. Dover. "*Titus Andronicus* on the Stage in 1595," *ShS 1* (1948), 17–22.

Romeo and Juliet

See also, under *The Tragedies*, Brooke, Brown and Harris (essay by Lawlor), Charlton, Dickey, Evans, Nevo, Ribner, and Snyder; under *Shakespeare's Language*, Mahood; under *Shakespeare Criticism to the 1930s*, Hazlitt; under *Shakespeare Criticism from the 1940s to the 1970s*, Calderwood, Granville-Barker, and Rabkin (pp. 162–184); under *Shakespeare Criticism of the 1980s and 1990s*, Edwards et al. (essay by Wells), Erickson and Kahn (essay by Snow), Lenz et al. (essay by Kahn), and Novy (*Love's Argument*); and, under *Shakespeare in Performance*, Brockbank (essay by Brenda Bruce).

Adams, Barry B. "The Prudence of Prince Escalus," *ELH*, 35 (1968), 32–50.

Auden, W. H. "Commentary on the Poetry and Tragedy of *Romeo and Juliet*." The Laurel Shakespeare, gen. ed. Francis Fergusson. New York, 1958.

Black, James. "The Visual Artistry of *Romeo and Juliet*," *Studies in English Literature*, 15 (1975), 245–256.

Evans, Bertrand. "The Brevity of Friar Lawrence," *PMLA*, 65 (1950), 841–865.

Evans, Robert O. *The Osier Cage: Rhetorical Devices in "Romeo and Juliet."* Lexington, Ky., 1966.

Everett, Barbara. "*Romeo and Juliet*: The Nurse's Story," *Critical Quarterly*, 14 (1972), 129–139.

Harrison, Thomas P. "*Romeo and Juliet, A Midsummer Night's Dream*: Companion Plays," *Texas Studies in Literature and Language*, 13 (1971–72), 209–213.

Hill, R. F. "Shakespeare's Early Tragic Mode," *SQ*, 9 (1958), 455–469.

Hosley, Richard. "The Use of the Upper Stage in *Romeo and Juliet*," *SQ*, 5 (1954), 371–379.

Levenson, Jill L. *Shakespeare in Performance: "Romeo and Juliet."* Manchester, Eng., 1987.

Levin, Harry. "Form and Formality in *Romeo and Juliet*," *SQ*, 11 (1960), 1–11.

Melchiori, Giorgio. "Peter, Balthasar, and Shakespeare's Art of Doubling," *Modern Language Review*, 78 (1983), 777–792.

Newman, Paula, and George Walton Williams. "Paris: The Mirror of Romeo," *Renaissance Papers 1981* (1982), 13–19.

Nosworthy, J. M. "The Two Angry Families of Verona," *SQ*, 3 (1952), 219–226.

Peterson, Douglas L. "*Romeo and Juliet* and the Art of Moral Navigation," *Pacific Coast Studies in Shakespeare*, ed. Thelma N. Greenfield and Waldo F. McNeir. Eugene, Oreg., 1966.

Pettet, E. C. "The Imagery of *Romeo and Juliet*," *English*, 8 (1950), 121–126.

Porter, Joseph. "Mercutio's Brother," *South Atlantic Review*, 49:4 (November 1984), 31–41.

———. *Shakespeare's Mercutio: His History as Drama*. Chapel Hill, N.C., 1988.

Tanselle, G. Thomas. "Time in *Romeo and Juliet*," *SQ*, 15:4 (1964), 349–361.

Utterback, Raymond V. "The Death of Mercutio," *SQ*, 24 (1973), 105–116.

Williams, George W., ed. *The Most Excellent and Lamentable Tragedie of Romeo and Juliet*. Durham, N.C., 1964.

Julius Caesar

See also, under *The Tragedies*, Brooke and Stirling; under *The Greek and Roman Tragedies*, Brower, Charney (both titles), Knight, Miola, and Traversi; under *Shakespeare's Language*, Doran; under *Shakespeare Criticism to the 1930s*, Shaw; under *Shakespeare Criticism from the 1940s to the 1970s*, Burckhardt, Council, Goldman (Chapter 4), Granville-Barker, Kernan (essay by Mack), Rabkin (pp. 105–119), and Stirling; under *Shakespeare Criticism of the 1980s and 1990s*, Berry (*Awareness of the Audience*); under *The Problem Plays*, Schanzer; and, under *The Histories*, Palmer.

Bonjour, Adrien. *The Structure of "Julius Caesar."* Liverpool, 1958.

Burke, Kenneth. "Antony in Behalf of the Play," *Southern Review*, 1 (1935), 308–319. Rpt. in *The Philosophy of Literary Form*. Baton Rouge, La., 1941.

Daiches, David. *Shakespeare: "Julius Caesar."* London, 1976.

Foakes, R. A. "An Approach to *Julius Caesar*," *SQ*, 5 (1954), 259–270.

Hartsock, Mildred E. "The Complexity of *Julius Caesar*," *PMLA*, 81 (1966), 56–62.

Knights, L. C. "Shakespeare and Political Wisdom: A Note on the Personalism of *Julius Caesar* and *Coriolanus*," *Sewanee Review*, 61 (1953), 43–55.

Levitsky, Ruth M. "The Elements Were So Mix'd . . . " *PMLA*, 88 (1973), 240–245.

Ornstein, Robert. "Seneca and the Political Drama of *Julius Caesar*," *Journal of English and Germanic Philology*, 57 (1958), 51–56.

Paster, Gail Kern. " 'In the Spirit of Men There Is No Blood': Blood as Trope of Gender in *Julius Caesar*," *SQ*, 40 (1989), 284–298.

Prior, Moody E. "The Search for a Hero in *Julius Caesar*," *Renaissance Drama*, n.s. 2 (1969), 81–101.

Ribner, Irving. "Political Issues in *Julius Caesar*," *Journal of English and Germanic Philology*, 56 (1957), 10–22.

Ripley, John. *"Julius Caesar" on Stage in England and America, 1599–1973*. Cambridge, Eng., 1980.

Vawter, Marvin L. " 'After Their Fashion': Cicero and Brutus in *Julius Caesar*," *ShakS* 9 (1976), 205–219.

———. " 'Division 'tween Our Souls': Shakespeare's Stoic Brutus," *ShakS* 7 (1974), 173–195.

Velz, John W. "Clemency, Will, and Just Cause in *Julius Caesar*," *ShS* 22 (1969), 109–118.

———. " 'If I Were Brutus Now . . . ': Role-Playing in *Julius Caesar*," *ShakS* 4 (1968), 149–159.

———. "Undular Structure in *Julius Caesar*," *Modern Language Review*, 66 (1971), 21–30.

Yoder, R. A. "History and the Histories in *Julius Caesar*," *SQ*, 24 (1973), 309–327.

Hamlet

See also, under *The Tragedies*, Bradley, Felperin, Goldman, Holloway, Kirsch, Mack, Mack Jr., Rosen, and Whitaker; under *The Greek and Roman Tragedies*, Brower; under *Shakespeare's Predecessors and Contemporaries*, Bowers and Rabkin (essay by Booth); under *Shakespeare Criticism to the 1930s*, Coleridge (*Coleridge's Writings*); under *Shakespeare Criticism from the 1940s to the 1970s*, Granville-Barker, Hawkes, and Righter; under *Shakespeare Criticism of the 1980s and 1990s*, Cavell (Chapter 5), Drakakis (essay by Rose), Erickson, Garber (*Shakespeare's Ghost Writers*, Chapter 6), Parker and Hartman (essays by Weimann, Ferguson, and Hawkes), Patterson (Chapters 1 and 5), and Schwartz and Kahn (essays by Fineman and Leverenz); under *Shakespeare in Performance*, Bevington; and, under *The Problem Plays*, Tillyard.

Alexander, Nigel. *Poison, Play, and Duel: A Study in "Hamlet."* London, 1971.

Alexander, Peter. *Hamlet: Father and Son.* New York and London, 1955.

Bevington, David, ed. *Twentieth Century Interpretations of "Hamlet."* Englewood Cliffs, N.J., 1968.

Bohannan, Laura. "Shakespeare in the Bush," *Natural History*, 75 (1966), 28–33. Rpt. in *Every Man His Way: Readings in Cultural Anthropology*, ed. Alan Dundes. Englewood Cliffs, N.J., 1968.

Bowers, Fredson T. "Hamlet as Minister and Scourge," *PMLA*, 70 (1955), 740–749.

Brown, John Russell, and Bernard Harris, eds. *Hamlet.* Stratford-upon-Avon Studies 5. London, 1963.

Calderwood, James L. *To Be and Not to Be: Negation and Metadrama in "Hamlet."* New York, 1983.

Charney, Maurice. *Style in "Hamlet."* Princeton, 1969.

Eliot, T. S. "Hamlet and His Problems," *Selected Essays, 1917–1932.* London and New York, 1932.

Erlich, Avi. *Hamlet's Absent Father.* Princeton, 1977.

Fergusson, Francis. *The Idea of a Theater.* Princeton, 1949.

Forker, Charles R. "Shakespeare's Theatrical Symbolism and Its Function in *Hamlet*," *SQ*, 14 (1963), 215–229.

Frye, Roland Mushat. *The Renaissance "Hamlet": Issues and Responses in 1600.* Princeton, 1984.

James, D. G. *The Dream of Learning.* Oxford, 1951.

Jones, Ernest. *Hamlet and Oedipus.* Rev. ed. New York, 1949, 1954.

Joseph, Bertram. *Conscience and the King.* London, 1953.

Kitto, H. D. F. *Form and Meaning in Drama.* London, 1956.

Knights, L. C. *An Approach to Hamlet.* London, 1960.

Levin, Harry. *The Question of Hamlet.* New York and London, 1959.

Lewis, C. S. "Hamlet: The Prince or the Poem?" *Proceedings of the British Academy*, 28 (1942), 139–154.

Mack, Maynard. "The World of *Hamlet*," *Yale Review*, 41 (1952), 502–523.

McGee, Arthur. *The Elizabethan Hamlet.* New Haven, 1987.

Muir, Kenneth, and Stanley Wells, ed., *Aspects of "Hamlet": Articles Reprinted from "Shakespeare Survey."* Cambridge, Eng., 1979. (Especially essay by Inga-Stina Ewbank.)

Murray, Gilbert. *Hamlet and Orestes.* Annual Shakespeare Lecture for the British Academy, 1914. London, 1919.

Nicoll, Allardyce, ed. *Shakespeare Survey 9* (1956).

Nietzsche, Friedrich. "The Birth of Tragedy or: Hellenism and Pessimism" (1872), *The Birth of Tragedy and The Case of Wagner*, trans. Walter Kaufmann. New York, 1967.

Rose, Mark. "*Hamlet* and the Shape of Revenge," *English Literary Renaissance*, 1 (1971), 132–143.

Wilson, J. Dover. *What Happens in "Hamlet."* London and New York, 1935, 1951.

Young, David. "Hamlet, Son of Hamlet," *Perspectives on "Hamlet,"* ed. William G. Holzberger and Peter B. Waldock. Lewisburg, Pa., and London, 1975.

Othello

See also, under *The Tragedies*, Bradley, Dickey, Goldman, Hawkes, Holloway, Knight, Snyder, and Spivack; under *Shakespeare's Language*, Doran; under *Shakespeare Criticism to the 1930s*, Coleridge (*Coleridge's Writings*) and Johnson; under *Shakespeare Criticism from the 1940s to the 1970s*, Empson, Fiedler, Granville-Barker, Ridler (essay by Gardner), and Sewell; and, under *Shakespeare Criticism of the 1980s and 1990s*, Cavell (Chapter 3), Erickson, Erickson and Kahn (essay by Wheeler), Greenblatt (*Renaissance Self-Fashioning*, Chapter 6), Howard and O'Connor (essay by Newman), Kirsch, Lenz et al. (essay by Neely), Novy (*Love's Argument*, Chapter 7), and Parker and Hartman (essays by Parker and Showalter).

Adamson, Jane. *"Othello" as Tragedy: Some Problems of Judgment and Feeling.* Cambridge, Eng., 1980.

Altman, Joel B. " 'Preposterous Conclusions': Eros, *Enargeia*, and the Composition of *Othello*," *Representations*, 18 (1987), 129–157.

Bartels, Emily C. "Making More of the Moor: Aaron, Othello, and Renaissance Refashionings of Race," *SQ*, 41 (1990), 433–454.

Bayley, John. *The Characters of Love*. London, 1960.

Boose, Lynda E. "Othello's Handkerchief: 'The Recognizance and Pledge of Love', " *English Literary Renaissance*, 5 (1975), 360–374.

Calderwood, James L. *The Properties of "Othello."* Amherst, Mass., 1989.

Dean, Leonard F., ed. *A Casebook on "Othello."* New York, 1961.

Everett, Barbara. "Reflections on the Sentimentalist's *Othello*," *Critical Quarterly*, 3 (1961), 127–139. (A comment on Leavis article below.)

Garner, S. N. "Shakespeare's Desdemona," *ShakS* 9 (1976), 233–252.

Hankey, Julie, ed. *Plays in Performance: "Othello."* Bristol, 1987.

Heilman, Robert B. *Magic in the Web: Action and Language in "Othello."* Lexington, Ky., 1956.

Hyman, Stanley Edgar. *Iago: Some Approaches to the Illusion of His Motivation*. New York, 1970.

Jones, Eldred. *Othello's Countrymen: The African in English Renaissance Drama*. London, 1965.

Leavis, F. R. "Diabolic Intellect and the Noble Hero: Or The Sentimentalist's Othello," *The Common Pursuit*. London, 1952. (A criticism of items by Bradley and Stoll on this list.)

Muir, Kenneth, ed. *Shakespeare Survey 21* (1968).

Nowottny, Winifred M. T. "Justice and Love in *Othello*," *University of Toronto Quarterly*, 21 (1952), 330–344.

Orkin, Martin. "Othello and the 'plain face' of Racism," *SQ*, 38 (1987), 166–188.

Rosenberg, Marvin. *The Masks of "Othello."* Berkeley, 1961.

Seltzer, Daniel. "Elizabethan Acting in *Othello*," *SQ*, 10 (1959), 201–210.

Snyder, Susan, ed. *"Othello": Critical Essays*. New York, 1988.

Stoll, E. E. *"Othello": An Historical and Comparative Study*. Minneapolis, 1915. Rpt. New York, 1964.

Wine, Martin L. *"Othello": Text and Performance*. London, 1984.

King Lear

See also, under *The Tragedies*, Bradley, Cunningham, Frye, Goldman, Holloway, Hunter, Kirsch, Knight, and Rosen; under *The Greek and Roman Tragedies*, Brower; under *Textual Criticism and Bibliography*, Blayney, and Taylor and Warren; under *Shakespeare's Language*, Doran; under *Shakespeare Criticism to the 1930s*, Hazlitt, Johnson, and Stoll; under *Shakespeare Criticism from the 1940s to the 1970s*, Bloom (essay by Jaffa), Burckhardt, Empson, Fly, Granville-Barker, Knights, Kott, and Sewell; under *Shakespeare Criticism of the 1980s and 1990s*, Boose,

Cavell (Chapter 2, identical with the Cavell entry below), Dollimore, Dubrow and Strier (essay by Strier), Erickson, Erickson and Kahn (essay by Berger), Garber (*Shakespeare's Ghost Writers*, Chapter 5), Greenblatt (*Shakespearean Negotiations*, Chapter 4), Novy (*Love's Argument*), and Patterson (Chapter 5); and, under *The Romances*, Felperin and Young.

Adelman, Janet, ed. *Twentieth Century Interpretations of "King Lear."* Englewood Cliffs, N.J., 1978.

Alpers, Paul J. "*King Lear* and the Theory of the 'Sight Pattern', " *In Defense of Reading*, ed. Reuben A. Brower and Richard Poirier. New York, 1962.

Booth, Stephen. *"King Lear," "Macbeth," Indefinition, and Tragedy*. New Haven, 1983.

Bratton, J. S., ed. *Plays in Performance: "King Lear."* Bristol, 1987.

Brooke, Nicholas. *Shakespeare: "King Lear."* London, 1963.

Cavell, Stanley. "The Avoidance of Love: A Reading of *King Lear*," *Must We Mean What We Say?* New York, 1969. Rpt. in *Disowning Knowledge in Six Plays of Shakespeare*. Cambridge, Eng., 1987.

Colie, Rosalie L., and F. T. Flahiff, eds. *Some Facets of "King Lear."* Toronto, 1974.

Danby, John F. *Shakespeare's Doctrine of Nature: A Study of "King Lear."* London, 1949.

Elton, William R. *King Lear and the Gods*. San Marino, Calif., 1966. Rpt. Lexington, Ky., 1988.

Everett, Barbara. "The New *King Lear*," *Critical Quarterly*, 2 (1960), 325–339.

Fraser, Russell A. *Shakespeare's Poetics in Relation to "King Lear."* London, 1962.

Freud, Sigmund. "The Theme of the Three Caskets," *Complete Psychological Works of Sigmund Freud*, 12 (1911–1913), pp. 291–301. London, 1958.

Goldberg, S. L. *An Essay on "King Lear."* Cambridge, Eng., 1974.

Hardison, O. B., Jr. "Myth and History in *King Lear*," *SQ*, 26 (1975), 227–242.

Heilman, Robert B. *This Great Stage: Image and Structure in "King Lear."* Baton Rouge, La., 1948. Rpt. Seattle, 1963.

James, D. G. *The Dream of Learning*. Oxford, 1951.

Jorgensen, Paul A. *Lear's Self-Discovery*. Berkeley, 1967.

Kahn, Coppélia. "The Absent Mother in *King Lear*," *Rewriting the Renaissance: The Discourses of Sexual Difference in Early Modern Europe*, ed. Margaret W. Ferguson et al. Chicago, 1986.

Keast, W. "Imagery and Meaning in the Interpretation of *King Lear*," *Modern Philology*, 47 (1949), 45–64.

Kernan, Alvin. "Formalism and Realism in Elizabethan Drama: The Miracles in *King Lear*," *Renaissance Drama*, 9 (1966), 59–66.

Kirsch, Arthur. "The Emotional Landscape of *King Lear*," *SQ*, 39 (1988), 154–170.

Lothian, J. M. *"King Lear": A Tragic Reading of Life*. Toronto, 1949.

Mack, Maynard. *King Lear in Our Time*. Berkeley, 1965.

Maclean, Norman. "Episode, Scene, Speech, and Word: The Madness of Lear," *Critics and Criticism*, ed. R. S. Crane. Chicago, 1952.

Muir, Kenneth, ed. *King Lear: Critical Essays.* New York, 1984.

Nicoll, Allardyce, ed. *Shakespeare Survey 13* (1960).

Reibetanz, John. *The "Lear" World: A Study of "King Lear" in Its Dramatic Context.* Toronto, 1977.

Rosenberg, Marvin. *The Masks of "King Lear."* Berkeley, 1972.

Sewall, Richard B. *The Vision of Tragedy.* New Haven, 1959.

Snyder, Susan. "*King Lear* and the Psychology of Dying," *SQ,* 33 (1982), 449–460.

Tate, Nahum. *The History of King Lear* (1681), ed. James Black. Lincoln, Nebr., 1975.

Urkowitz, Steven. *Shakespeare's Revision of "King Lear."* Princeton, 1980.

Macbeth

See also, under *The Tragedies,* Bradley, Felperin, Goldman, Holloway, Hunter, Kirsch, McElroy, Mack, Mack Jr., and Rosen; under *Shakespeare Criticism to the 1930s,* Smith (essay by De Quincey); under *Shakespeare Criticism from* the 1940s to the 1970s, Sanders and Sewell; under *Shakespeare Criticism of the 1980s and 1990s,* Garber (*Cannibals,* essay by Adelman), Howard and O'Connor (essay by Goldberg), Mullaney (Chapter 5), Schwartz and Kahn (essay by Gohlke), and Watson.

Bartholomeusz, Dennis. *"Macbeth" and the Players.* Cambridge, Eng., 1969.

Berger, Harry, Jr. "The Early Scenes of *Macbeth:* Preface to a New Interpretation," *ELH,* 47 (1980), 1–31.

Blisset, William. " 'The Secret'st Man of Blood': A Study of Dramatic Irony in *Macbeth,*" *SQ,* 10 (1959), 397–408.

Booth, Stephen. *"King Lear," "Macbeth," Indefinition, and Tragedy.* New Haven, 1983.

Brooks, Cleanth. "The Naked Babe and the Cloak of Manliness," *The Well Wrought Urn.* New York, 1947.

Brown, John Russell, ed. *Focus on "Macbeth."* London, 1982. (Includes an essay by Stallybrass.)

Calderwood, James L. *If It Were Done: "Macbeth" and Tragic Action.* Amherst, 1986.

Driver, Tom. *The Sense of History in Greek and Shakespearean Drama.* New York, 1960.

Elliott, G. R. *Dramatic Providence in "Macbeth."* Princeton, 1958.

Fergusson, Francis. "*Macbeth* as the Imitation of an Action," *English Institute Essays 1951* (1952), 31–43.

Freud, Sigmund. "Some Character-Types Met with in Psycho-Analytic Work," trans. E. Cobern Mayne, *Collected Papers.* Vol. 4, pp. 326–332. London, 1925.

Gardner, Helen. "Milton's 'Satan' and the Theme of Damnation in Elizabethan Tragedy," *English Association Essays and Studies,* n.s. 1 (1948), 46–66.

Hawkes, Terence, ed. *Twentieth Century Interpretations of "Macbeth."* Englewood Cliffs, N.J., 1976.

Heilman, Robert B. "The Criminal as Tragic Hero: Dramatic Methods," *ShS 19* (1966), 12–24.

Jorgensen, Paul A. *Our Naked Frailties: Sensational Art and Meaning in "Macbeth."* Berkeley, 1971.

Knights, L. C. "How Many Children Had Lady Macbeth? An Essay in the Theory and Practice of Shakespeare Criticism," *Explorations.* London, 1946. Rpt. Westport, Conn., 1975.

Moretti, Franco. " 'A Huge Eclipse': Tragic Form and the Deconsecration of Sovereignty," *Genre,* 15 (1982), in an issue entitled *The Forms of Power and the Power of Forms in the Renaissance,* ed. Stephen Greenblatt), 7–40.

Muir, Kenneth, ed. *Shakespeare Survey 19* (1966).

Paul, Henry N. *The Royal Play of Macbeth.* New York, 1950.

Rosenberg, Marvin. *The Masks of "Macbeth."* Berkeley, 1978.

Spender, Stephen. "Time, Violence, and *Macbeth,*" *Penguin New Writing,* 3. London, 1940–1941.

Williams, Raymond. "Monologue in *Macbeth,*" *Teaching the Text,* ed. Susanne Kappeler and Norman Bryson. London, 1983.

Timon of Athens

See also, under *The Tragedies,* Knight; under *The Greek and Roman Tragedies,* generally; under *Shakespeare's Predecessors and Contemporaries,* Kernan; under *Shakespeare Criticism to the 1930s,* Hazlitt and Johnson; under *Shakespeare Criticism from the 1940s to the 1970s,* Bloom (essay by Foakes), Burke, Empson, and Fly; under *Shakespeare Criticism of the 1980s and 1990s,* Paster (Chapter 4); and, under *The Problem Plays,* Campbell.

Bayley, John. "The Big Idea: *Timon of Athens,*" *Shakespeare and Tragedy.* London, 1981.

Bergeron, David M. "Alchemy and *Timon of Athens,*" *College Language Association Journal,* 13 (1970), 364–373.

———. "*Timon of Athens* and Morality Drama," *College Language Association Journal,* 10 (1967), 181–188.

Bradbrook, Muriel C. *Shakespeare the Craftsman.* London and New York, 1969.

Butler, Francelia. *The Strange Critical Fortunes of Shakespeare's "Timon of Athens."* Ames, Iowa, 1966.

Cook, David. "*Timon of Athens,*" *ShS* 16 (1963), 83–94.

Ellis-Fermor, Una. "*Timon of Athens:* An Unfinished Play," *Review of English Studies,* 18 (1942), 270–283.

Handelman, Susan. "*Timon of Athens:* The Rage of Disillusion," *American Imago,* 36 (1979), 45–68.

Honigmann, E. A. J. "*Timon of Athens,*" *SQ,* 12 (1961), 3–20.

Kahn, Coppélia. " 'Magic of Bounty': *Timon of Athens,* Jacobean Patronage, and Maternal Power," *SQ,* 38 (1987), 34–57.

Knights, L. C. "*Timon of Athens,*" *The Morality of Art: Essays Presented to G. Wilson Knight,* ed. D. W. Jefferson. London, 1969.

Lancashire, Anne. "*Timon of Athens:* Shakespeare's Dr. Faustus," *SQ,* 21 (1970), 35–44.

Levin, Harry. "Shakespeare's Misanthrope," *ShS* 26 (1973), 89–94.

Maxwell, J. C. "*Timon of Athens,*" *Scrutiny,* 15 (1948), 195–208.

Merchant, W. Moelwyn. "*Timon of Athens* and the Visual Conceit," *Shakespeare and the Artist.* London, 1959.

Muir, Kenneth. "*Timon of Athens* and the Cash-Nexus," *The Singularity of Shakespeare, and Other Essays.* Liverpool, 1977.

Pettet, E. C. "*Timon of Athens:* The Disruption of Feudal Morality," *Review of English Studies,* 23 (1947), 321–336.

Soellner, Rolf. *Timon of Athens: Shakespeare's Pessimistic Tragedy.* With a Stage History by Gary Jay Williams. Columbus, Ohio, 1979.

Walker, Lewis. "Fortune and Friendship in *Timon of Athens,*" *Texas Studies in Literature and Language,* 18 (1977), 577–600.

Antony and Cleopatra

See also, under *The Tragedies,* Frye, Goldman, Holloway, Mack, and Rosen; under *The Greek and Roman Tragedies,* Brower, Cantor, Charney, Miola, and Traversi; under *Shakespeare's Predecessors and Contemporaries,* Waith (*Herculean Hero*); under *Shakespeare's Language,* Doran; under *Shakespeare Criticism to the 1930s,* Coleridge (*Coleridge's Writings*); under *Shakespeare Criticism from the 1940s to the 1970s,* Bethell, Burke, Colie, Granville-Barker, Kettle (essay by Nandy), McAlindon, and Van Laan; under *Shakespeare Criticism of the 1980s and 1990s,* Bamber, Cavell (pp. 18–37), Dollimore (*Radical Tragedy*), Edwards et al. (essay by Hibbard), Erickson (Chapter 4), Holland et al. (essay by Sprengnether), and Neely; under *The Problem Plays,* Schanzer; under *The Histories,* Palmer; and, under *The Romances,* Brown and Harris (essay by Ornstein), Danby, and Felperin.

Adelman, Janet. *The Common Liar: An Essay on "Antony and Cleopatra."* New Haven, 1973.

Barroll, J. Leeds. *Shakespearean Tragedy: Genre, Tradition, and Change in "Antony and Cleopatra."* Washington, D.C., 1984.

Bono, Barbara J. "The Shakespearean Synthesis: *Antony and Cleopatra,*" *Literary Transvaluation: From Vergilian Epic to Shakespearean Tragicomedy.* Berkeley, 1984.

Bradley, A. C. *Oxford Lectures on Poetry.* London, 1909, 1961.

Kaula, David. "The Time Sense of *Antony and Cleopatra,*" *SQ,* 15:3 (1964), 211–223.

Knights, L. C. *Some Shakespearean Themes.* London, 1959.

Krook, Dorothea. "Tragic and Heroic in Shakespeare's *Antony and Cleopatra,*" *Scripta Hierosolymitana,* ed. Ariel Sachs, 1967.

Kuriyama, Constance Brown. "The Mother of the World: A Psychoanalytic Interpretation of Shakespeare's *Antony and Cleopatra,*" *English Literary Renaissance,* 7 (1977), 324–351.

Leavis, F. R. "*Antony and Cleopatra* and *All for Love:* A Critical Exercise," *Scrutiny,* 5 (1936–1937), 158–169.

Lloyd, Michael. "Cleopatra as Isis," *ShS* 12 (1959), 88–94.

Macdonald, Ronald R. "Playing Till Doomsday: Interpreting *Antony and Cleopatra,*" *English Literary Renaissance,* 15 (1985), 78–99.

Mack, Maynard. "*Antony and Cleopatra:* The Stillness and the Dance," *Shakespeare's Art: Seven Essays,* ed. Milton Crane. Chicago, 1973.

Markels, Julian. *The Pillar of the World: "Antony and Cleopatra" in Shakespeare's Development.* Columbus, Ohio, 1968.

Rackin, Phyllis. "Shakespeare's Boy Cleopatra, the Decorum of Nature, and the Golden World of Poetry," *PMLA,* 87 (1972), 201–212.

Reimer, A. P. *A Reading of Shakespeare's "Antony and Cleopatra."* Sydney, 1968.

Rose, Mark, ed. *Twentieth Century Interpretations of "Antony and Cleopatra."* Englewood Cliffs, N.J., 1977.

Stein, Arnold. "The Image of Antony: Lyric and Tragic Imagination," *Kenyon Review,* 21 (1959), 586–606.

Coriolanus

See also, under *The Tragedies,* Brown and Harris (essays by Hunter and Wickham), Danson, Holloway, and Rosen; under *The Greek and Roman Tragedies,* Brower, Cantor, Charney, Miola, and Phillips; under *Shakespeare's Predecessors and Contemporaries,* Waith (*Herculean Hero*); under *Shakespeare Criticism to the 1930s,* Hazlitt; under *Shakespeare Criticism from the 1940s to the 1970s,* Burke, Granville-Barker, Knights, Kott, and Rossiter; and, under *Shakespeare Criticism of the 1980s and 1990s,* Cavell (Chapter 4), Dollimore, Goldberg (Chapter 4), Howard and O'Connor (essays by Bristol and Sorge), Marcus (Chapter 4), Parker and Hartman (essay by Cavell), Patterson (Chapter 6), and Watson.

Adelman, Janet. " 'Anger's My Meat': Feeding, Dependency, and Aggression in *Coriolanus,*" *Shakespeare, Pattern of Excelling Nature,* ed. David Bevington and Jay L. Halio. Newark, Del., 1978.

Barton, Anne. "Livy, Machiavelli, and Shakespeare's *Coriolanus,*" *ShS 38* (1985), 115–129.

Berry, Ralph. "The Metamorphoses of *Coriolanus,*" *SQ,* 26 (1975), 172–183.

———. "Sexual Imagery in *Coriolanus,*" *Studies in English Literature,* 13 (1973), 301–316.

Bradley, A. C. *A Miscellany.* London, 1929.

Brecht, Bertolt. *Coriolanus,* trans. Ralph Manheim. *Bertolt Brecht: Collected Plays,* vol. 9, ed. Ralph Manheim and John Willett. New York, 1972.

Brockman, B. A., ed. *Shakespeare's "Coriolanus": A Casebook.* London, 1977.

Browning, I. R. "*Coriolanus*—'Boy of Tears', " *Essays in Criticism,* 5 (1955), 18–31.

Calderwood, James L. "*Coriolanus:* Wordless Meanings and Meaningless Words," *Studies in English Literature,* 6 (1966), 211–224.

Daniell, David. *"Coriolanus" in Europe.* London, 1980.

Fish, Stanley. "How to Do Things with Austin and Searle: Speech-Act Theory and Literary Criticism," *Is There a Text in This Class?* Cambridge, Mass., 1980.

Huffman, Clifford Chalmers. *"Coriolanus" in Context.* Lewisburg, Pa., 1971.

Jagendorf, Zvi. "*Coriolanus:* Body Politic and Private Parts," *SQ,* 41 (1990), 455–469.

MacLure, Millar. "Shakespeare and the Lonely Dragon," *University of Toronto Quarterly,* 24 (1955), 109–120.

Maxwell, J. C. "Animal Imagery in *Coriolanus," Modern Language Review,* 42 (1947), 417–421.

McCanles, Michael. "The Dialectic of Transcendence in Shakespeare's *Coriolanus," PMLA,* 82 (1967), 44–53.

Nemoianu, Virgil. "Coriolanus, or the Secondary as Hero," *A Theory of the Secondary: Literature, Progress, and Reaction.* Baltimore, 1989.

Oliver, H. J. "Coriolanus as Tragic Hero," *SQ,* 10 (1959), 53–60.

Phillips, James E., Jr., ed. *Twentieth Century Interpretations of "Coriolanus."* Englewood Cliffs, N.J., 1970.

Rabkin, Norman. "*Coriolanus:* The Tragedy of Politics," *SQ,* 17 (1966), 195–212.

Stockholder, Katherine. "The Other Coriolanus," *PMLA,* 85 (1970), 228–236.

The Romances

Adams, Robert M. *Shakespeare: The Four Romances.* New York, 1989.

Bentley, Gerald Eades. "Shakespeare and the Blackfriars Theatre," *ShS* 1 (1948), 38–50.

Bergeron, David M. *Shakespeare's Romances and the Royal Family.* Lawrence, Kans., 1985.

Brown, John Russell, and Bernard Harris, eds. *Later Shakespeare.* Stratford-upon-Avon Studies 8. London, 1966.

Danby, John F. *Poets on Fortune's Hill.* London, 1952. Reprinted as *Elizabethan and Jacobean Poets.* London, 1964.

Edwards, Philip. "Shakespeare's Romances: 1900–1957," *ShS* 11 (1958), 1–18. See also other articles in this issue.

Felperin, Howard. *Shakespearean Romance.* Princeton, 1972.

Foakes, R. A. *Shakespeare: From the Dark Comedies to the Last Plays.* London and Charlottesville, Va., 1971.

Frye, Northrop. *Anatomy of Criticism.* Princeton, 1957.
———. *A Natural Perspective: The Development of Shakespearean Comedy and Romance.* New York, 1965.
———. *The Secular Scripture: A Study of the Structure of Romance.* Cambridge, Mass., 1976.

Gesner, Carol. *Shakespeare and the Greek Romance: A Study of Origins.* Lexington, Ky., 1970.

Hartwig, Joan. *Shakespeare's Tragicomic Vision.* Baton Rouge, La., 1972.

Hoeniger, F. David. "Shakespeare's Romances Since 1958: A Retrospect," *ShS* 29 (1976), 1–10.

Hunt, Maurice. *Shakespeare's Romance of the Word.* Lewisburg, Pa., 1990.

Hunter, Robert Grams. *Shakespeare and the Comedy of Forgiveness.* New York, 1965.

James, D. G. "The Failure of the Ballad-Makers," *Scepticism and Poetry.* London, 1937.

Kay, Carol McGinnis, and Henry E. Jacobs, eds. *Shakespeare's Romances Reconsidered.* Lincoln, Nebr., 1978.

Kermode, Frank. *William Shakespeare: The Final Plays.* London, 1963.

Knight, G. Wilson. *The Crown of Life.* London, 1947, 1966.
———. *The Shakespearian Tempest.* London, 1932, 1953.

Leavis, F. R. "A Criticism of Shakespeare's Last Plays," *Scrutiny,* 10 (1942), 339–345. Rpt. in *The Common Pursuit.* London, 1952.

Leech, Clifford. "The Structure of the Last Plays," *ShS* 11 (1958), 19–30.

Marsh, D. R. C. *The Recurring Miracle: A Study of "Cymbeline" and the Last Plays.* Pietermaritzburg, Natal, 1962, 1964.

Mowat, Barbara A. *The Dramaturgy of Shakespeare's Romances.* Athens, Ga., 1976.

Nevo, Ruth. *Shakespeare's Other Language.* New York and London, 1987.

Peterson, Douglas L. *Time, Tide, and Tempest: A Study of Shakespeare's Romances.* San Marino, Calif., 1973.

Pettet, E. C. *Shakespeare and the Romance Tradition.* London, 1949.

Smith, Hallett. *Shakespeare's Romances.* San Marino, Calif., 1972.

Spencer, Theodore. "Appearance and Reality in Shakespeare's Last Plays," *Modern Philology,* 39 (1942), 265–274.

Strachey, Lytton. "Shakespeare's Final Period," *Books and Characters.* London, 1922.

Tillyard, E. M. W. *Shakespeare's Last Plays.* London, 1938, 1964.

Tobias, Richard C., and Paul G. Zolbrod, eds. *Shakespeare's Late Plays.* Athens, Ohio, 1974.

Traversi, Derek. *Shakespeare: The Last Phase.* New York, 1954.

Uphaus, Robert W. *Beyond Tragedy.* Lexington, Ky., 1981.

White, R. S. *Let Wonder Seem Familiar: Endings in Shakespeare's Romance Vision.* Atlantic Highlands, N.J., 1985.

Yates, Frances A. *Shakespeare's Last Plays: A New Approach.* London, 1975.

Young, David. *The Heart's Forest: A Study of Shakespeare's Pastoral Plays.* New Haven and London, 1972.

Pericles

See also, under *The Romances,* Adams, Bergeron, Brown and Harris (essay by Francis Berry), Danby, Felperin, Frye *(Natural Perspective),* Kermode, Knight *(Crown of Life),* Nevo, Peterson, and White; and, under *Shakespeare Criticism of the 1980s and 1990s,* Edwards et al. (essay by Ewbank) and Mullaney (Chapter 6).

Barber, C. L. " 'Thou That Beget'st Him That Did Thee Beget': Transformation in *Pericles* and *The Winter's Tale*," *ShS* 22 (1969), 59–67.

Brockbank, J. Philip. "*Pericles* and the Dream of Immortality," *ShS* 24 (1971), 105–116.

Dunbar, Mary Judith. " 'To the Judgement of Your Eye': Iconography and the Theatrical Art of *Pericles*," *Shakespeare, Man of the Theatre*, ed. Kenneth Muir et al. Newark, Del., 1983, pp. 86–97.

Edwards, Philip. "An Approach to the Problem of *Pericles*," *ShS* 5 (1952), 25–49.

Eliot, T. S. "Marina," *The Complete Poems and Plays, 1909–1950*. New York, 1952.

Helms, Lorraine. "The Saint in the Brothel: Or, Eloquence Rewarded," *SQ*, 41 (1990), 319–332.

Hoeniger, F. David. "Gower and Shakespeare in *Pericles*," *SQ*, 33 (1982), 461–479.

Hunt, Maurice. " 'Opening the Book of Monarchs' Faults': *Pericles* and Redemptive Speech," *Essays in Literature* (Western Illinois University), 12 (Fall, 1985), 155–170.

Muir, Kenneth. "Shakespeare's Hand in *Pericles*," *Shakespeare as Collaborator*. London, 1960.

Pitcher, John. "The Poet and Taboo: The Riddle of Shakespeare's *Pericles*," *English Association Essays and Studies* (1982), 14–29.

Cymbeline

See also, under *The Romances*, Brown and Harris (essay by Harris), Felperin, Frye *(Natural Perspective)*, Hartwig, Hunter, Kermode, Marsh, and Mowat; under *Shakespeare Criticism to the 1930s*, Shaw; under *Shakespeare Criticism from the 1940s to the 1970s*, Granville-Barker; under *Shakespeare Criticism of the 1980s and 1990s*, Carey (essay by Wickham), Dubrow and Strier (essay by Marcus), Kastan, Kirsch, Marcus (Chapter 3), and Schwartz and Kahn (essay by Skura); and, under *The Greek and Roman Tragedies*, Miola.

Brockbank, J. Philip. "History and Histrionics in *Cymbeline*," *ShS* 11 (1958), 42–49.

Freer, Coburn, "*Cymbeline*," *The Poetics of Jacobean Drama*. Baltimore, 1981, Chapter 4.

Gibbons, Brian. "Fabled *Cymbeline*," *Jahrbuch 1987*, Deutsche Shakespeare-Gesellschaft West, 78–99.

Gillies, John. "The Problem of Style in *Cymbeline*," *Southern Review* (University of Adelaide and Macquarie University), 15:3 (1982), 269–290.

Hoeniger, F. D. "Irony and Romance in *Cymbeline*," *Studies in English Literature*, 2 (1962), 219–228.

Kirsch, Arthur C. "*Cymbeline* and Coterie Dramaturgy," *ELH*, 34 (1967), 285–306.

Leggatt, Alexander. "The Island of Miracles: An Approach to *Cymbeline*," *ShakS* 10 (1977), 191–209.

Moffet, Robin. "*Cymbeline* and the Nativity," *SQ*, 13 (1962), 207–218.

Swander, Homer D. "*Cymbeline* and the 'Blameless Hero', " *ELH*, 31 (1964), 259–270.

Warren, Roger. "Theatrical Virtuosity and Poetic Complexity in *Cymbeline*," *ShS* 29 (1976), 41–50.

Wilson, Harold S. "*Philaster* and *Cymbeline*," *English Institute Essays 1951*, ed. Alan Downer, pp. 146–167. New York, 1952.

The Winter's Tale

See also, under *The Romances*, Felperin, Foakes, Hartwig, Hunter, Knight (*Crown of Life*), Mowat, and Young; under *Shakespeare Criticism from the 1940s to the 1970s*, Egan; and, under *Shakespeare Criticism of the 1980s and 1990s*, Carey (essay by Martz), Cavell (Chapter 6), Erickson, Neely, and Parker and Hartman (essay by Felperin).

Barber, C. L. " 'Thou That Beget'st Him That Did Thee Beget': Transformation in *Pericles* and *The Winter's Tale*," *ShS* 22 (1969), 59–67.

Bartholomeusz, Dennis. "*The Winter's Tale*" in *Performance in England and America, 1611–1976*. Cambridge, Eng., 1982.

Bethell, S. L. *The Winter's Tale: A Study*. London, 1947.

Coghill, Nevill. "Six Points of Stage-Craft in *The Winter's Tale*," *ShS* 11 (1958), 31–41.

Draper, R. P. "*The Winter's Tale*": *Text and Performance*. London, 1985.

Ewbank, Inga-Stina. "The Triumph of Time in *The Winter's Tale*," *Review of English Literature*, 5:2 (1964), 83–100.

Frey, Charles. *Shakespeare's Vast Romance: A Study of "The Winter's Tale."* Columbia, Mo., 1980.

Frye, Northrop. "Recognition in *The Winter's Tale*," *Essays on Shakespeare and Elizabethan Drama in Honor of Hardin Craig*, ed. R. Hosley, pp. 235–246. Columbia, Mo., 1962.

Gourlay, Patricia Southard. " 'O My Most Sacred Lady': Female Metaphor in *The Winter's Tale*," *English Literary Renaissance*, 5 (1975), 375–395.

Hoeniger, F. D. "The Meaning of *The Winter's Tale*," *University of Toronto Quarterly*, 20 (1950), 11–26.

Lawlor, John. "*Pandosto* and the Nature of Dramatic Romance," *Philological Quarterly*, 41 (1962), 96–113.

Lindenbaum, Peter. "Time, Sexual Love, and the Uses of Pastoral in *The Winter's Tale*," *Modern Language Quarterly*, 33 (1972), 3–22.

Matchett, William H. "Some Dramatic Techniques in *The Winter's Tale*," *ShS* 2 (1969), 93–107.

McDonald, Russ. "Poetry and Plot in *The Winter's Tale*," *SQ*, 36 (1985), 315–329.

Muir, Kenneth, ed. *Shakespeare, "The Winter's Tale": A Casebook*. London, 1968.

Neely, Carol Thomas. "*The Winter's Tale*: The Triumph of Speech," *Studies in English Literature*, 15 (1975), 321–338.

Proudfoot, G. Richard. "Verbal Reminiscence and the Two-Part Structure of *The Winter's Tale*," *ShS* 29 (1976), 67–78.

Pyle, Fitzroy. "*The Winter's Tale*": *A Commentary on the Structure*. London, 1968.

Schanzer, Ernest. "The Structural Pattern of *The Winter's Tale*," *Review of English Literature*, 5:2 (1964), 72–82.

Siemon, James Edward. " 'But It Appears She Lives': Iteration in *The Winter's Tale*," *PMLA*, 89 (1974), 10–16.

Tayler, Edward W. *Nature and Art in Renaissance Literature*. New York, 1964.

Wickham, Glynne. "Romance and Emblem: A Study in the Dramatic Structure of *The Winter's Tale*," *The Elizabethan Theatre III*, ed. David Galloway. Hamden, Conn., 1973.

Williams, John Anthony. *The Natural Work of Art: The Experience of Romance in Shakespeare's "Winter's Tale."* Cambridge, Mass., 1967.

The Tempest

See also, under *The Romances*, Brown and Harris (essay by Brockbank), Felperin, Frye *(Natural Perspective)*, Hartwig, Kermode, Mowat, Peterson, and Young; under *Shakespeare Criticism to the 1930s*, Coleridge *(Coleridge's Writings)*; under *Shakespeare Criticism from the 1940s to the 1970s*, Fiedler, Kernan *(Playwright as Magician, Chapter 6)*, and Kott; and, under *Shakespeare Criticism of the 1980s and 1990s*, Dollimore and Sinfield (essay by Brown), Drakakis (essay by Barker and Hulme), Garber *(Cannibals,* essay by Orgel), Greenblatt *(Shakespearean Negotiations, Chapter 5)*, Howard and O'Connor (essay by Cartelli), Lenz et al. (essay by Leininger), Schwartz and Kahn (essay by Sundelson), and Summers.

Auden, W. H. "The Sea and the Mirror: A Commentary on Shakespeare's *The Tempest*," *The Collected Poetry*. New York, 1945.

Berger, Harry, Jr. "Miraculous Harp: A Reading of Shakespeare's *Tempest*," *ShakS* 5 (1969), 253–283.

Berger, Karol. "Prospero's Art," *ShakS* 10 (1977), 211–239.

Brower, Reuben. "The Mirror of Analogy," *The Fields of Light*. New York, 1951.

Daniell, David. *"The Tempest."* The Critics Debate. Atlantic Highlands, N.J., 1989.

Frey, Charles. *"The Tempest* and the New World," *SQ,* 30 (1979), 29–41.

Hamilton, Donna. *Virgil and "The Tempest": The Politics of Imitation*. Columbus, Ohio, 1990.

Hawkes, Terence. "Playhouse—Workhouse," *That Shakespeherian Rag: Essays on a Critical Process*. London, 1986.

Hoeniger, F. D. "Prospero's Storm and Miracle," *SQ,* 7 (1956), 33–38.

James, D. G. *The Dream of Prospero*. Oxford, 1967.

James, Henry. "Introduction to *The Tempest*." Rpt. in *Henry James: Selected Literary Criticism*, ed. Morris Shapiro. London, 1963.

Knox, Bernard. *"The Tempest* and the Ancient Comic Tradition," *English Stage Comedy*, ed. W. K. Wimsatt. *English Institute Essays 1954.* New York, 1955.

Kott, Jan. *"The Tempest,* or Repetition," *Mosaic*, 10:3 (1977), 9–36.

Marx, Leo. "Shakespeare's American Fable," *The Machine in the Garden: Technology and the Pastoral Ideal in America*. London and New York, 1964.

Orgel, Stephen. "New Uses of Adversity: Tragic Experience in *The Tempest*," *In Defense of Reading*, ed. Reuben A. Brower and Richard Poirier. New York, 1962.

———. "Prospero's Wife," *Representations*, 8 (1984), 1–13.

Palmer, D. J., ed. *Shakespeare, "The Tempest": A Casebook.* London, 1968.

Skura, Meredith. "Discourse and the Individual: The Case of Colonialism in *The Tempest*," *SQ,* 40 (1989), 42–69.

Smith, Hallett, ed. *Twentieth Century Interpretations of "The Tempest."* Englewood Cliffs, N.J., 1969.

Vaughan, Alden T. "Shakespeare's Indian: The Americanization of Caliban," *SQ,* 39:2 (1988), 137–153.

William, David. *"The Tempest* on the Stage," *Jacobean Theatre*, ed. John Russell Brown and Bernard Harris, pp. 133–157. Stratford-upon-Avon Studies 1. London, 1960.

The Two Noble Kinsmen

See also, under *The Romances*, Hartwig and Mowat.

Abrams, Richard. "Gender Confusion and Sexual Politics in *The Two Noble Kinsmen," Themes in Drama 7: Drama, Sex and Politics*, ed. J. Redmond. Cambridge, Eng., 1985.

Berggren, Paula. "'For what we lack, / We laugh': Incompletion and *The Two Noble Kinsmen," Modern Language Studies*, 14 (1984), 3–17.

Bertram, Paul. *Shakespeare and The Two Noble Kinsmen*. New Brunswick, N.J., 1965.

Bruster, Douglas. "The Jailer's Daughter and the Politics of Madwomen's Language," *SQ,* 46 (1995), 277–300.

Edwards, Philip. "On the Design of *The Two Noble Kinsmen," A Review of English Literature*, 5 (1964), 89–105.

Frey, Charles H., ed. *Shakespeare, Fletcher, and The Two Noble Kinsmen*. Columbia, Mo., 1989.

Hoy, Cyrus. "The Language of Fletcherian Tragicomedy," *Mirror up to Shakespeare*, ed. J. C. Gray. Toronto, 1984, pp. 99–113.

Lief, Madelon, and Nicholas F. Radel. "Linguistic Subversion and the Artifice of Rhetoric in *The Two Noble Kinsmen," SQ,* 38 (1987), 405–425.

Mincoff, Marco. "The Authorship of *The Two Noble Kinsmen," English Studies*, 33 (1952), 97–115.

Mulryne, J. R. "Shakespeare's Knight's Tale, *Two Noble Kinsmen* and the Tradition of Chivalry," *Le Roman de chevalerie au temps de la Renaissance*, ed. Marie-Thérèse Jones-Davies. Paris, 1987.

Potter, Lois. "Topicality or Politics? *The Two Noble Kinsmen, 1613–34," The Politics of Tragicomedy: Shakespeare and After*, ed. Gordon McMullan and Jonathan Hope. London, 1992.

Waith, Eugene. "Shakespeare and Fletcher on Love and Friendship," *ShakS* 18 (1986), 235–249.

———. ed. *The Two Noble Kinsmen*. The Oxford Shakespeare. Oxford, 1989.

The Poems

Dubrow, Heather. *Captive Victors: Shakespeare's Narrative Poems and Sonnets.* Ithaca, N.Y., 1987.
Hulse, Clarke. *Metamorphic Verse: The Elizabethan Minor Epic.* Princeton, 1981.
Shakespeare Survey 15 (1962). Devoted chiefly to the poems and music, including the Sonnets.

Venus and Adonis

See also, under *The Poems,* Dubrow and Hulse (pp. 143–175); under *Shakespeare Criticism from the 1940s to the 1970s,* Rabkin; and, under *Shakespeare Criticism of the 1980s and 1990s,* Kahn (Chapter 2).
Allen, Michael J. B. "The Chase: The Development of a Renaissance Theme," *Comparative Literature,* 20 (1968), 301–312. (Includes discussion of *Venus and Adonis.*)
Asals, Heather. "*Venus and Adonis:* The Education of a Goddess," *Studies in English Literature,* 13 (1973), 31–51.
Beauregard, David N. "*Venus and Adonis:* Shakespeare's Representation of the Passions," *ShakS* 8 (1975), 83–98.
Belsey, Catherine. "Love as Trompe-l'oeil: Taxonomies of Desire in *Venus and Adonis,*" *SQ,* 46 (1995), 257–300.
Hamilton, A. C. "*Venus and Adonis,*" *Studies in English Literature,* 1:1 (1961), 1–15.
Jahn, J. D. "The Lamb of Lust: The Role of Adonis in Shakespeare's *Venus and Adonis,*" *ShakS* 6 (1970), 11–25.
Keach, William. "*Venus and Adonis,*" *Elizabethan Erotic Narratives: Irony and Pathos in the Ovidian Poetry of Shakespeare, Marlowe, and Their Contemporaries.* New Brunswick, N.J., 1977.
Muir, Kenneth. "*Venus and Adonis:* Comedy or Tragedy?" *Shakespearean Essays,* ed. Alwin Thaler and Norman Sanders. Knoxville, Tenn., 1964.
Rebhorn, Wayne A. "Mother Venus: Temptation in Shakespeare's *Venus and Adonis,*" *ShakS* 11 (1978), 1–29.
Sheidley, William E. "'Unless It Be a Boar': Love and Wisdom in Shakespeare's *Venus and Adonis,*" *Modern Language Quarterly,* 35 (1974), 3–15.
Streitberger, W. R. "Ideal Conduct in *Venus and Adonis,*" *SQ,* 26 (1975), 285–291.

The Rape of Lucrece

See also, under *The Poems,* Dubrow and Hulse (pp. 174–194); under *The Greek and Roman Tragedies,* Miola; and, under *Shakespeare Criticism of the 1980s and 1990s,* Parker and Hartman (essay by Vickers), and Siemon (Chapter 2).
Allen, Don Cameron. "Some Observations on *The Rape of Lucrece,*" *ShS* 15 (1962), 89–98.
Donaldson, Ian. "'A Theme for Disputation': Shakespeare's Lucrece," *The Rapes of Lucretia: A Myth and Its Transformations.* Oxford, 1982.

Fineman, Joel. "Shakespeare's *Will:* The Temporality of Rape," *Representations,* 20 (1987), 25–76.
Kahn, Coppélia. "The Rape in Shakespeare's *Lucrece,*" *ShakS* 9 (1976), 45–72.
Majors, G. W. "Shakespeare's First Brutus: His Role in *Lucrece,*" *Modern Language Quarterly,* 35 (1974), 339–351.
Walley, Harold R. "*The Rape of Lucrece* and Shakespearean Tragedy," *PMLA,* 76 (1961), 480–487.

The Phoenix and Turtle

See also, under *Shakespeare Criticism of the 1980s and 1990s,* Carey (essay by Buxton, pp. 44–55).
Alvarez, A. "William Shakespeare: *The Phoenix and the Turtle,*" *Interpretations,* ed. John Wain. London, 1955.
Arthos, John. *Shakespeare's Use of Dream and Vision,* Chapter 1. London and Totowa, N.J., 1977.
Ellrodt, Robert. "An Anatomy of *The Phoenix and the Turtle,*" *ShS* 15 (1962), 99–110.
Empson, William. "The Phoenix and the Turtle," *Essays in Criticism,* 16 (1966), 147–153.
Erikson, Roy T. "'Un certo amoroso martire': Shakespeare's *The Phoenix and the Turtle* and Giordano Bruno's *De gli eroici furori,*" *Spenser Studies,* 2 (1981), 193–215.
Garber, Marjorie. "Two Birds with One Stone: Lapidary Re-inscription in *The Phoenix and Turtle,*" *The Upstart Crow,* 5 (1984), 5–19.
Honigmann, E. A. J. "The Phoenix and the Turtle," *Shakespeare: The "Lost" Years,* pp. 90–113. Totowa, N.J., 1985.
Knight, G. Wilson. *The Mutual Flame: On Shakespeare's Sonnets and "The Phoenix and the Turtle."* London, 1955.
Matchett, William H. "*The Phoenix and the Turtle*": *Shakespeare's Poem and Chester's "Loues Martyr."* The Hague, 1965.
Petronella, Vincent F. "Shakespeare's *The Phoenix and the Turtle* and the Defunctive Music of Ecstasy," *ShakS* 8 (1975), 311–331.
Underwood, Richard Allan. *Shakespeare's "The Phoenix and Turtle": A Survey of Scholarship.* Salzburg, 1974.

A Lover's Complaint

Jackson, MacD. P. *Shakespeare's "A Lover's Complaint": Its Date and Authenticity.* Auckland, N.Z., 1965.
Muir, Kenneth. "A Lover's Complaint: A Reconsideration," *Shakespeare 1564–1964,* ed. E. A. Bloom, pp. 154–166. Providence, 1964.
Underwood, Richard Allan. *Shakespeare on Love: The Poems and the Plays. Prolegomena to a Variorum Edition of "A Lover's Complaint."* Salzburg, 1985.
Warren, Roger. "'A Lover's Complaint,' *All's Well,* and the Sonnets," *Notes and Queries,* n.s. 17 (1970), 130–132.

Sonnets

See also, under *The Poems,* Dubrow; under *Shakespeare Criticism from the 1940s to the 1970s,* Colie and Kernan (*Playwright as Magician,* Chapter 2); and, under *Shakespeare Criticism of the 1980s and 1990s,* Parker and Hartman (essay by Greene), and Wheeler (pp. 179–190).

Allen, Michael J. B. "Shakespeare's Man Descending a Staircase: Sonnets 126 to 154," *ShS 31* (1978), 127–138.

Booth, Stephen. *An Essay on Shakespeare's Sonnets.* New Haven, 1969.

———. ed. *Shakespeare's Sonnets, Edited with Analytic Commentary.* New Haven, 1977.

Bradley, A. C. *Oxford Lectures on Poetry.* London, 1909, 1961.

Fineman, Joel. *Shakespeare's Perjured Eye: The Invention of Poetic Subjectivity in the Sonnets.* Berkeley, 1986.

Herrnstein, Barbara, ed. *Discussions of Shakespeare's Sonnets.* Boston, 1964.

Hobday, C. H. "Shakespeare's Venus and Adonis Sonnets," *ShS 26* (1973), 103–109.

Hubler, Edward, Northrop Frye, Leslie A. Fiedler, Stephen Spender, and R. P. Blackmur. *The Riddle of Shakespeare's Sonnets.* New York, 1962.

Ingram, W. G., and Theodore Redpath, eds. *Shakespeare's Sonnets.* London, 1964.

Knight, G. Wilson. *The Mutual Flame: On Shakespeare's Sonnets and "The Phoenix and the Turtle."* London, 1955.

Krieger, Murray. *A Window to Criticism: Shakespeare's Sonnets and Modern Poetics.* Princeton, 1964.

Landry, Hilton. *Interpretations in Shakespeare's Sonnets.* Berkeley, 1963.

———. ed. *New Essays on Shakespeare's Sonnets.* New York, 1976.

Leishman, J. B. *Themes and Variations in Shakespeare's Sonnets.* London, 1961.

Lever, J. W. *The Elizabethan Love Sonnet.* London, 1956.

Melchiori, Giorgio. *Shakespeare's Dramatic Meditations: An Experiment in Criticism.* Oxford, 1976.

Muir, Kenneth. *Shakespeare's Sonnets.* London, 1979.

Pequigney, Joseph. *Such Is My Love: A Study of Shakespeare's Sonnets.* Chicago, 1985.

Ransom, John Crowe. *The World's Body.* New York and London, 1938, 1968.

A Funeral Elegy for Master William Peter

Abrams, Richard. "Breaching the Canon: Elegy by W. S.: The State of the Argument," *Shakespeare Newsletter,* 45.3 (1995), 51-54.

Foster, Donald W. *Elegy by W. S.: A Study in Attribution.* Newark, Del., and London, 1989.

Textual Notes

These textual notes do not offer an historical collation, either of the early quartos and folios or of more recent editions; they are simply a record of departures in this edition from the copy text. For most plays the notes give the adopted reading of this edition in bold face, followed by the rejected reading in the relevant copy text. Where two substantive early texts are involved, or where a reading from some other earlier edition has been adopted, the notes provide information on the source of the reading in square brackets. In a few texts, adopted readings of editions more recent than the First Folio are indicated by [eds.] Alterations in lineation are not indicated, nor are some minor and obvious typographical errors; changes in punctuation are indicated when the resulting change in meaning is substantive.

Abbreviations used:
F   The First Folio
Q   Quarto
O   Octavo
s.d.   stage direction
s.p.   speech prefix

The Comedy of Errors

Copy text: the First Folio. Scene divisions not marked in the Folio are provided at 1.2, 2.2, 3.2, 4.2, 4.3, and 4.4.

1.1. 1 s.p. [and elsewhere] **Egeon** *Marchant* **41** [and throughout] **Epidamnum** *Epidamium* **42 the** he **102 upon** vp **116 bark** backe **123 thee** they **151 health** helpe

1.2. s.d. Antipholus [of Syracuse] *Antipholis Erotes* [First] **Merchant** *a Marchant* **1 s.p.** [and elsewhere] **First Merchant** *Mer.* [also called *E. Mar.*] **4 arrival** a riuall **32 s.d. Exit** *Exeunt* **40 unhappy** vnhappie a **66 clock** cooke **94 s.d. Exit** *Exeunt*

2.1. s.d. Antipholus of Ephesus *Antipholis Sereptus* **11 o'door** adore **12 ill** thus **45 two** too **60 thousand** hundred **63 come home** come **111 Wear** Where **115 s.d. Exeunt** *Exit*

2.2. s.d. Antipholus of Syracuse *Antipholus Errotis* **6 s.d. of Syracuse** *Siracusia* **12 didst** did didst **14 s.p. S. Antipholus** *E. Ant.* **79 men** them **97 tiring** trying **101 e'en** in **135 off** of **174 stronger** stranger **185 offered** free'd **189 elves** Owles **193 drone** *Dromio* **194 not I** I not

3.1. 71 cake cake here **75 you** your **89 her** your **91 her** your **116** [and throughout] **Porcupine** *Porpentine*

3.2. s.d. Luciana *Iuliana* **1 s.p. Luciana** *Iulia* **4 building** buildings **ruinous** ruinate **16 attaint** attaine **21 but** not **26 wife** wise **46 sister's** sister **49 bed** bud **them** they **57 where** when **109 and** is **126 chalky** chalkle **136 carracks** Carrects

4.1. 1 s.p. [and elsewhere] **Second Merchant** *Mar.* **7 s.p.** [and elsewhere] **Angelo** *Gold.* **13 s.d. Enter . . . Ephesus** *Enter Antipholus Ephes. Dromio* **17 her** their **28 carat** charect **87 then** then sir

4.2. 6 Of Oh **34 One** On **48 That** Thus **61 'a** I **66 s.d. Exeunt** *Exit*

4.3. 1 s.p. S. Antipholus [not in F] **58 if you** if **78 s.d. Exeunt** *Exit*

4.4. 42 to prophesy the prophesie **105 those** these **106 s.d. Enter . . . strives** [after line 105 in F] **113 his** this **130 s.d.** [after line 131 in F] **Manent** *Manet* **143 s.d. Enter . . . drawn** *Enter Antipholus Siracusia with his Rapier drawne, and Dromio Sirac.* **146 s.d. Run all out** [after "bound again" in line 146 in F]

5.1. 121 death depth **168 s.p. Servant** [not in F] **175 scissors** Cizers **180 s.p. Servant** *Mess.* **195 s.p. Egeon** *Mar. Fat.* **283 s.p. Egeon** *Fa.* [and elsewhere *Fath.* and *Father*] **330 s.d. Antipholus . . . Syracuse** *Antipholus Siracusa, and Dromio Sir.* **357–362** [these lines follow line 346 in F] **358 Antipholus'** *Antholus* **403 ne'er** are **406 joy** go **408 s.d. Manent** *Manet* **414 s.d. Exeunt** *Exit*

Love's Labor's Lost

Copy text: the Quarto of 1598. The act and scene divisions here provided are not in Q. Act divisions are from F; scene divisions are editorial.

1.1. s.p. [and elsewhere] **King** *Ferdinand* **18 schedule** sedule **24 three** thee **31 pomp** pome **62 feast** fast **70 quite** quit **104 an** any **123 losing** loosing **127 s.p. Berowne** [at line 132 (*Ber.*) in Q] **130 public** publibue **possibly** possible **165 One** On **168 umpire** vmpier **180 s.p.** [and elsewhere] **Dull** *Constab.* **188 s.p.** [and elsewhere, except for lines 219 and 221] **Costard** *Clowne* **188 contempts** Contempls **216 welkin's** *welkis* **226 besieged** besedged **245 s.p. King** [not in Q; also at lines 247, 249, 252] **254 with, with** Which with **264 s.p. Dull** *Antho.* **273 worst** wost **286 s.p. King** *Ber.*

1.2. 3 s.p. [and elsewhere] **Mote** *Boy* **4 Why,** Why? **13–14 epitheton** apethaton **97 blushing** blush-in **126 deywoman** Day womand **128 s.p. Jaquenetta** *Maide* [and elsewhere *Maid*, *Ma.*] **139 s.p. Dull** *Clo.* **172 duello** [F] *Duella*

2.1. 13 s.p. [and elsewhere] **Princess** *Queene* **32 Importunes** Importuous **34 visaged** visage **36 s.d. Exit Boyet** [at line 35 in Q] **39 s.p. A lord** *Lor.* [also at line 80] **Lord Longaville** *Longauill* **40 s.p. Maria** 1. *Lady* **42–43 solemnizèd . . . Longaville.** solemnized. In *Normandie saw I this Longauill*, **44 parts** peerelesse **53 s.p. Maria** *Lad.* **56 s.p. Katharine** 2. *Lad.* **61 Alencon's** *Alansoes* **64 s.p. Rosaline** 3. *Lad.* **88 unpeopled** vnpeeled **90 s.p.** [and elsewhere] **King** *Nauar.* **115–126 s.p. Rosaline** *Kather.* or *Kath.* **100 it—will** it will, **130 of** of, of **142 demand** pemaund **144 On** One **180 mine own** my none **190 Non** No **195 Katharine** *Rosalin* **210 Rosaline** Katherin **221 s.p. Katharine** *La.* [also at line 224] **246 quote** coate **254 s.p. Rosaline** *Lad.* **255 s.p. Maria** *Lad.* 2 **256 s.p. Katharine** *Lad.* 3 **257 s.p. Maria** *Lad.* **258 s.p. Katharine** *Lad.*

3.1. 1 s.p. [and elsewhere] **Armado** *Bra.* **14 as if** if **15 through the nose** through; nose **18 thin-belly** thinbellies **26 penny** penne **65 voluble** volable **69 s.p.** [and elsewhere] **Mote** *Pag.* **72 the mail** thee male **plain** pline **133 ounce** ouce **136 remuneration** remuration **138 carries it.** carries it **141 My** [preceded by "O" in Q; also lines 145, 147, 149, 153, 155, 172] **178 Junior** *Iunios* **188 clock** Cloake **202 sue** shue

4.1. 3 s.p. Boyet *Forr.* **6 On** Ore **49 mistress** [F] *Mistrs* **70–71 saw . . . saw** See . . . see **71 overcame** couercame **75 King's** King **87 Adriano** Adriana **Armado** Armatho **128 s.d. Exit** [at line 126 in Q] **130 hit it** hit **134 ne'er** neare **136 pin is in** 144 o' th' one ath toothen **148 is a** is **s.d. Shout** Shoot. [The s.d. follows line 149 in Q.] **149 s.d. Exit** *Exeunt*

4.2. 3 s.p. [and elsewhere] **Holofernes** *Ped.* **8 s.p.** [and elsewhere] **Nathaniel** *Curat. Nath.* **14–15 explication; facere,** explication *facere*; **29 of taste** taste **30 indiscreet** indistreell **36 Dictynna . . . Dictynna** *Dictisima . . . dictisima* **51 ignorant** ignorault **call I** cald **53 scurrility** squirilitie **65 s.p. Holofernes** *Nath.* [the subsequent speech prefixes in this scene of Holofernes and Nathaniel are reversed in Q through line 147, except that the speech at line 104 is correctly assigned to Nathaniel, at lines 118–120 to *Pedan.*, and at lines 135-142 to *Ped.*] **69 pia mater** primater **71 in whom** whom **72 s.p. Nathaniel** *Holo.* **76 ingenious** ingenous **78 sapit** *sapis* **81 s.p. Holofernes** *Nath.* [also at lines 85, 91] **pierce-one** Person **88 Person** Parson **91 Fauste** *Facile* **pecus** *pecas* **omne** *omnia* **94–95 Venezia . . . prezia** vemchie, vencha, que non te vnde, que non te perreche **101 s.p. Nathaniel** *Holo.* **102 s.p. Holofernes** *Nath.* **stanza** stauze **104 s.p. Nathaniel** [missing in Q] **118 apostrophus** apostraphas **119 canzonet** cangent **120 Here** [the rest of this speech is assigned to *Nath.* in Q] **130 s.p. Holofernes** *Nath.* **133 writing** written **135 Sir Nathaniel** *Ped.* Sir *Holofernes* **143 s.p. Jaquenetta** *Mayd* **146 s.p. Nathaniel** *Holo.* **148 s.p. Holofernes** *Ped.* **156 ben bien**

4.3. 11 melancholy mallicholie [also in line 12] **12 here my** heare my **35 wilt** will **45 s.p. King** *Long.* **69 lose** loose **71 idolatry** ydotarie **83 quoted** coted **89 And I** And **95 ode** Odo **104 Wished** Wish **108 thorn** throne **151 coaches; in your tears** couches in your teares. **157 mote . . . mote** Moth . . . Moth **172 to . . . by** by . . . to **176 like you** like **Joan** Ione [Qb];

Loue [Qa]   **192 Where** [Q repeats the s.p. *King*]   **179 me? When** mee when   **184 s.d.** [after "God bless the king" in line 185 in Q]   **255 and usurping** vsurping   **256 doters** dooters   **279 Nothing** O nothing   **291 And . . . maladies** [Q follows with the following twenty-three lines that appear to be a first draft of lines 292 ff.:

And where that you haue vowd to studie (Lordes)
In that each of you haue forsworne his Booke.
Can you still dreame and poare and thereon looke.
For when would you my Lord, or you, or you,
Haue found the ground of Studies excellence,
Without the beautie of a womans face?
From womens eyes this doctrine I deriue,
They are the Ground, the Bookes, the Achadems,
From whence doth spring the true *Promethean* fire.
Why vniuersall plodding poysons vp
The nimble sprites in the arteries,
As motion and long during action tyres
The sinnowy vigour of the trauayler.
Now for not looking on a womans face,
You haue in that forsworne the vse of eyes:
And studie too, the causer of your vow.
For where is any Authour in the worlde,
Teaches such beautie as a womas eye:
Learning is but an adiunct to our selfe,
And where we are, our Learning likewise is.
Then when our selues we see in Ladies eyes,
With our selues.
Do we not likewise see our learning there?]

313 dainty Bacchus . . . taste. daintie, *Bachus* . . . taste,   **316 Subtle** Subtit   **333 authors** authour   **335 Let** Lets   **lose** loose [also in line 336]   **341 standards** standars   **356 betime** be time   **357 Allons! Allons!** Alone alone   **359 forsworn** forsorne
5.1.1 quod quid   **9 hominem** hominum   **24 abominable** abbominable   **25 insanie** infamie   **37 bone** bene   **28 Bone . . . Priscian** *Bome boon* for boon prescian   **31 gaudeo** gaudio   **33 Quare** *Quari*   **38 lived** lyud   **56 wave** wane   **57 venue** vene we   **66 manu** vnum   **73 wert** wart   **74 dunghill** *dungil*   **76 Dunghill** *dunghel*   **90 choice** chose   **96 importunate** important   **101 mustachio** mustachie   **106 secrecy** secretie   **109 antic** antique [also at line 143]   **115 Nathaniel** *Holofernes*   **117 rendered** rended   **assistance** assistants   **148 Allons** Alone
5.2. 13 ne'er neare   **17 ha' been a** a bin   **22 You'll** Yole   **28 cure . . . care** care . . . cure   **43 pencils, ho!** pensalls, How?   **53 s.p.** [and at line 57] *Maria Marg.*   **53 pearls** Pearle   **65 hests** deuice   **67 pair-taunt-like** perttaunt like   **74 wantonness** wantons be   **80 stabbed** stable   **83 peace. Love** Peace Loue   **89 sycamore** Siccamone   **93 companions. Warily** companions warely,   **96 they** thy   **122 parle** parlee   **123 love suit** Loue-feat   **134 too** two   **148 her** his   **152 ne'er** ere   **160 s.d. The . . . him** [after line 161 in Q]   **164 ever** euen   **176 strangers** stranges   **179 Princess** Princes   **213 yet? No dance!** yet no dance: **217 The . . . it** [assigned in Q to *Rosa.*]   **223 measure! Be** measure be   **225 Price** Prise   **232 s.p.** [and elsewhere] **Princess** *Quee.*   **243 s.p. Katharine** *Maria* [also at lines 245, 248, 249, 250, 254, 256]   **260 sense, so sensible** sense so sensible,   **265 s.d. Exeunt** *Exe*   **269 have; gross** haue grosse   **278 Non** No   **280 perhaps** perhapt   **298 vailing** varling   **300 woo** woe   **310 run** runs   **342 Construe** Consture   **353 unsullied** vnsallied   **375–377 foolish. When . . . eye, . . . light.** foolish when . . . eie: . . . light,   **397 lady.** Dart Ladie dart   **406 song** songue   **408 affectation** affection   **464 zany** saine   **479 allowed** aloude   **483 manage** nuage   **485** [Q supplies a s.p. here, "*Ber.*"]   **501 they** thy   **514 least** best   **529 de la guerra** delaguar   **544 leopard's** Libbards   **554 s.p. Princess** *Lady*   **563 this** his   **582** [Q has "*Exit Curat.*"]   **591 Judas** *Pede.* ludas   **596 proved** proud   **643 gilt** gift   **669 The . . . gone** [Q prints as a s.d. or as part of Armado's speech]   **686 on, stir** or, stir   **699 lose** loose   **746 wholesome** holdsome   **759 strange** straying   **764 gravities,** grauities.   **770 both—fair** both faire   **774 the ambassadors** embassadours   **778 this in** this   **808 entitled** intiled   **812 hermit** herrite   **812 Hence . . . breast** [Q follows with the following six lines that appear to be a first draft of lines 813 ff.:

Berow. And what to me my Loue? and what to me?
Rosal. You must be purged to, your sinnes are rackt.
You are attaint with faultes and periurie:
Therefore if you my fauour meane to get,
A tweluemonth shall you spende and neuer rest,
But seeke the weery beddes of people sicke.]

814 A wife [assigned to *Kath.* in Q]   **881** [Q supplies a s.p. here, *Brag.*]   **883** [Q supplies a s.p. here, *B.*]   **884 s.p. Spring** [not in Q]   **885–886** [the second and third lines of the song are transposed in Q]   **906 foul** full   **918 s.p. Armado** [not in Q]   **918–919 The . . . Apollo** [printed in larger type in Q without s.p.; F adds s.p. "*Brag.*" and "You that way: we this way," thus incorporating the ending into the text]

The Two Gentlemen of Verona

Copy text: the First Folio. Characters' name are grouped at the head of each scene. Act and scene divisions follow the Folio text throughout.
1.1. 26 swam swom   **66 leave** loue   **78 I a I**   **141 testerned** cestern'd
1.2. 80–81 tune, . . . note. tune: . . . note,   **97 your** you
1.3. 24 [and elsewhere] **whither** whether   **50** [here F repeats speech prefix "*Pro.*"]   **88 father calls** Fathers call's   **91 s.d. Exeunt** *Exeunt. Finis.*
2.1. 109 stead steed   **137 What, are** What are
2.2. 18 s.d. [and elsewhere] **Panthino** *Panthion* [in F, grouped with characters' names at head of scene, as with entrance directions generally]
2.3. 27 wood would   **37 tied** tide [also at lines 38, 40, and 52]
2.4. 60 know knew   **106 mistress** a Mistresse   **114 s.p. Servant** *Thur.*   **161 braggartism** Bragadisme   **163 makes** make   **188 s.d.** [at line 187 in F]   **193 Is it mine eye** It is mine   **211 s.d. Exit** *Exeunt*
2.5. 1 Milan Padua   **37 that my** that that my
3.1. 280 master's ship Mastership   **318 kissed fasting** fasting   **375 s.d. Exit** *Exeunt*
4.1. 35 had often had   **49 An heir, and near** And heire and Neece,
4.2. 17 s.d. Musicians *Musitian* [grouped with characters' names at head of scene]   **38 s.p. Musician** [not in F]   **95 hast** has't   **110 his** her
4.3. 19 abhors abhor'd   **42 Recking** Wreaking
4.4. 54 hangman Hangmans   **68 thou** thee   **72 to not** woo woe   **148 is.** is,   **149 well,** well;   **204 s.d. Exit** *Exeunt*
5.2. 7 s.p. Julia *Pro.*   **13 s.p. Julia** *Thu.*   **18 your peace** you peace   **47 you, stand not** you stand, not   **59 s.d. Exit** *Exeunt*
5.4. 26 this . . . hear! this? I see, and heere: **33 seizèd** ceazed   **49 me.** me,   **121 s.p. Outlaws** *Out-l.*

The Taming of The Shrew

Copy Text: The First Folio. The act and scene divisions are missing in the Folio except for Act 3, Act 4 (at 4.3), and Act 5 (at 5.2).
Ind.1. s.d. Christopher Sly [printed at the end of the s.d. in F as "*Christophero Sly*"]   **1 s.p.** [and elsewhere] **Sly** *Begger*   **10–11 thirdborough** Headborough   **16 Breathe** Brach   **21 s.p.** [and elsewhere] **First Huntsman** *Hunts.*   **81 s.p. First Player** *2. Player*   **87 s.p. Second Player** *Sincklo*   **99 s.p. First Player** *Plai.*   **134 peasant.** peasant,
Ind. 2. 2 lordship *Lord*   **18 Sly's** Sies   **26 s.p.** [and elsewhere] **Third Servingman** *3 Man*   **27 s.p.** [and elsewhere] **Second Servingman** *2 Man*   **47 s.p.** [and elsewhere] **First Servingman** *1 Man*   **53 wi' th'** with   **93 Greet** Greece   **99 s.p.** [and elsewhere] **Page** *Lady*   **125 s.p. Servingman** *Mes.*   **133 it. Is** it is
1.1. 3 fore for   **13 Vincentio** *Vincentio's*   **14 brought** brough   **24 satiety** sacietie   **25 Mi perdonate** *Me Pardonato*   **33 Ovid be** *Ouid;* be   **47 s.d. Manent** *Manet*   **163 captum** captam   **208 colored** Conlord   **227 time.** time,   **244 your** you   **248 s.d. speak** *speakes*

1.2. 17 s.d. wrings *rings*   **18 masters** mistris   **24 Con . . . trovato**
Contutti le core bene trobatto   **25 ben** *bene*   **26 Molto** *multo*
onorato *honorata*   **33 pip** peepe   **45 this's** this   **51 gross. But**
growes but   **few,** few.   **72 me, were she** me. Were she is   **120**
me and other more, me. Other more   **171 help me** helpe one
189 Antonio's *Butonios*   **190 his** my   **212 ours** yours   **265 feat**
seeke   **280 ben** *Been*
2.1. 8 thee, tell tel   **75—76 wooing.— Neighbors,** wooing neighbors:
79 unto you vnto   **104 Pisa. By report** Pisa by report,   **153**
struck stroke   **157 rascal fiddler** Rascall, Fidler   **168 s.d. Exeunt**
Exit   **186 bonny** bony   **244 askance** a sconce   **322 s.d. Exeunt**
Exit **328 in me**   **352 Valance** Vallens   **355 pail** pale   **373**
Marseilles Marcellus
3.1. 28 Sigeia *sigeria* [also at lines 33 and 42]   **43 steterat** *staterat*
47 [Aside] *Luc.*   **50 s.p. Bianca** [not in F]   **51 s.p. Lucentio** *Bian.*
53 s.p. Bianca *Hort.*   **76 clef** Cliffe   **80 change** charge   **odd** old
81 s.p. Servant *Nicke*
3.2. 13 behavior. behauiour,   **14 man,** man;   **29 of thy** of   **30 old**
news newes   **33 hear** heard   **54 swayed** Waid   **56 cheeked** chekt
128 to love Loue   **130 As I** As   **150 e'er** ere   **182 s.d. Music**
plays [after line 183 in F]   **199 s.p. Gremio** *Gra.*
4.1. 23 s.p. Curtis *Gru.*   **81 sleekly** slickely   **106 s.p. Grumio** *Gre.*
136 off of   **168 s.d. Curtis** *Curtis a Seruant* [after line 169 in F]
4.2. 4 s.p. Hortensio *Luc.*   **6 s.p. Lucentio** *Hor.* [and at line 8]   **7**
you? First resolve you first, resolue   **8 read that I profess, The**
reade, that I professe the   **13 none** me   **31 her** them   **72 Take**
. . . alone [assigned to "*Par.*" in F]   **in** me
4.3. [F has "*Actus Quartus. Scena Prima*" here]   **62 s.d. Enter Haber-**
dasher [after "gown" in F]   **63 s.p. Haberdahser** *Fel.*   **81 is a** is
88 like a like   **146 where,** where   **177 account'st** accountedst
4.4. s.d. [booted] [appears at line 18 in F]   **1 Sir** Sirs   **68 s.d. Exit** [af-
ter line 67 in F; F also adds a s.d., "*Enter Peter*," after line 68]
78 he's has   **91 except** expect
4.5. 14 An And   **18 is** in   **35 make a** make the   **37 where** whether
77 she be she
5.1. 4. [F has "*Exit*" here]   **6 master's** mistris   **42 brought** brough
50 master's Mistris   **62 copintank** copataine   **104 s.d. Exeunt** *Exit*
139 No Mo   **143 than never** then ueuer
5.2. [F has "*Actus Quintus*" here]   **2 done** come   **37 thee, lad** the
lad   **40 butt! An** but an   **45 bitter** better   **two** too   **52 s.p. Tranio**
Tri.   **57 ho** oh   **62 two** too   **65 for** sir   **132 a** fiue   **136 you're**
your   **152 maintenance commits** maintenance. Commits

A Midsummer Night's Dream

Copy text: the First Quarto of 1600. The act and scene divisions are
absent from the Quarto; the Folio provides act divisions only.
1.1. 4 wanes waues   **10 New** Now   **19 s.d. Lysander** Lysander *and*
Helena   **24 Stand forth, Demetrius** [printed as s.d. in Q]   **26**
Stand forth, Lysander [printed as s.d. in Q]   **74 their** there   **132**
Ay Eigh   **136 low** loue   **187 Yours would** Your words   **191 I'd**
ile**216 sweet** sweld   **219 stranger companies** strange companions
224 s.d. Exit Hermia [after line 223 in Q]
2.1. 1 s.p. [and elsewhere] Puck *Robin*   **61 s.p. [and elsewhere] Tita-**
nia *Qu.*   **61 Fairies** Fairy   **79 Aegles** Eagles   **109 thin** chinne
158 the west west   **183 off** of   **190 slay** stay   **slayeth** stayeth
194 thee the   **201 not nor** not, not   **206 lose** loose   **246 s.d.** [at
line 247 in Q]
2.2. 4 leathern lethten   **9 s.p. First Fairy** [not in Q; also at line 20]
13 s.p. Chorus [not in Q; also at line 24]   **44 comfort** comfor
45 Be Bet   **49 good** god   **53 is** it   **155 ate** eate
3.1. 52 s.p. Bottom *Cet.*   **72 s.p. Puck** *Ro.*   **77 s.p. bottom** *Pyra.*
[also at lines 79 and 98]   **78 Odors, odors** Odours, odorous   **83**
s.p. Puck *Quin.*   **84 s.p. Flute** *Thys.* [also at lines 88 and 97]
144 own owe   **157—158 Ready . . . go** [assigned to **Fairies** in Q]
170 s.p. Peaseblossom *1. Fai.*   **171 s.p. Cobweb** *1. Fai.*   **172 s.p.**
Mote *2. Fair.*   **173 s.p. Mustardseed** *3 Fai.*   **190 you of** you
196 s.d. Exeunt *Exit*

3.2. s.d. [Q: *Enter King of* Fairies*, and* Robin goodfellow]   **3 s.d.** [See
previous note.]   **6—7 love. / Near . . . bower,** loue, / Neere . . .
bower.   **15—16 brake. / When . . . take,** brake, / When . . . take:
19 mimic Minnick   **38 s.p. [and elsewhere] Puck** *Rob.*   **80 I so I**
85 sleep slippe   **213 like** life   **215 rend** rent   **220 passionate**
words words   **250 prayers** praise   **260 off** of   **299 gentlemen**
gentleman   **326 but** hut   **344 s.d. Exit** Exeunt   **406 Speak! In**
some bush? Speake in some bush.   **426 shalt** shat   **451 To your**
your
4.1. 5 s.p. [and elsewhere] Bottom *Clown*   **20 courtesy** curtsie   **24**
marvelous maruailes   **54 flowerets' flouriets**   **64 off** of   **72 o'er**
or   **81 five** fine   **82 ho** how   **116 Seemed** Seeme   **127 this is**
this   **137 s.d. Wind . . . up** *they all start vp.* Winde hornes
171 saw see   **190 found** fonnd   **198 let us** lets   **205 to expound**
expound   **208 a patched** patcht a   **213 ballad** Ballet
4.2. s.d. [Snout, and Starveling] Thisby *and the rabble*   **3 s.p. Starvel-**
ing *Flut.*   **5 s.p. Flute** *Thys.* [and at lines 9, 13, 19]   **29 no** not
5.1. 34 our Or   **107 s.p. [and elsewhere] Theseus** *Duke*   **122 his** this
150 s.d. Exeunt *Exit* [and at lines 153 in Q]   **155 Snout** *Flute*
190 up in thee now againe   **193 love! Thou art my** loue thou art,
my   **205 mural down** Moon vsed   **209 s.p. [and elsewhere] Hip-**
polyta *Dutch.*   **216 beasts in, a** beasts, in a   **270 gleams** beames
309 before before?   **315 mote** moth   **317 warrant** warnd
347 s.p. Bottom *Lyon*   **366 lion** Lyons   **367 behowls** beholds
414—415 And . . . rest [these lines are transposed in Q]

The Merchant of Venice

Copy text: the First Quarto of 1600 [Q]. The act and scene divisions
are absent from the Quarto; the Folio provides act divisions only.
1.1. s.d. [and elsewhere] Salerio, and Solanio *Salaryno,* and *Salanio*
7 s.p. [and elsewhere] Salerio *Salarino*   **19 Peering** Piring   **27**
docked docks   **85 jaundice** *laundies*   **112 tongue** togue   **113 Is It**
is   **128 off** of   **151 back** bake
1.2. 44 Palatine Palentine [and at line 57]   **53 Bone** *Boune*   **58**
throstle Trassell   **119 s.d. enter a Servingman** [after line 120
in Q]
1.3. 28 s.p. [and elsewhere] Shylock *Iew*   **76 compromised** compre-
myzd   **82 peeled** pyld   **110 spit** spet [also at lines 124 and 129]
125 day, another time day another time,
2.1. s.d. Morocco *Morochus*   **25 Sophy . . . prince,** Sophy, and a
Persian Prince   **31 thee** the   **35 page** rage
2.2. 1 s.p. [and elsewhere] Launcelot *Clowne*   **3 [and elsewhere in**
this scene] Gobbo *Iobbe*   **42 By** Be   **76 murder** muder   **94 last**
lost   **165 s.d. Exit Leonardo** [after line 164 in Q]   **168 a suit** sute
2.3. 11 did doe
2.4. 8 o'clock of clocke   **9 s.d.** [after line 9 in Q]   **14 Love news,**
Loue, newes   **20 s.d. Exit clown** [after line 23 in Q]   **39 s.d.**
Exeunt *Exit*
2.5. 44 Jewess' Iewes
2.6. 26 Who's whose [also at line 61]   **35 night, you** night you   **59**
gentlemen gentleman
2.7. 18 threatens. Men threatens men   **45 Spits** Spets   **69 tombs**
timber
2.8. 8 gondola Gondylo   **39 Slubber** slumber
2.9. 48 chaff chaft   **49 varnished** varnist   **judgment** *iudement*   **73**
[Q provides a s.p.: *Arrag.*]
3.1. 21 s.d. Enter Shylock [after line 22 in Q]   **46 courtesy** cursie
70 s.p. Man [not in Q]   **74 s.d.** [Q repeats the s.d. "*Enter Tuball*"]
100 Heard heere   **114 turquoise** Turkies
3.2. 23 eke ech   **61 live. With** liue with   **67 eyes** eye   **81 vice**
voyce   **84 stairs** stayers   **101 Therefore** Therefore then   **110**
shuddering shyddring   **199 loved; for intermission** lou'd for intermission,   **204 roof** rough   **217 s.d.** [after line 219 in Q]   **315**
s.p. Bassanio [not in Q]
3.3 s.d. Solanio *Salerio*   **24 s.p. Solanio** *Sal.*
3.4. 23 Hear other things: heere other things   **49 Padua** Mantua   **50**
cousin's cosin   **53 traject** Tranect   **80 near** nere   **81 my** my my
3.5. 20 e'en in   **26 comes** come   **74 merit it,** meane it, it   **81 a wife**
wife   **87 s.d. Exeunt** *Exit*

4.1. 30 his state this states **31 flint** flints **35 s.p.** [and elsewhere in this scene] Shylock *Iewe* **50 urine; for affection,** vrine for affection. **51 Mistress** Maisters **73 You may as well** well **74 Why he hath made the** the **bleat** bleake **75 pines** of Pines **100 is** as **113 lose** loose **136 whilst** whilest **228 No, not** Not not **233 tenor** tenure **270 off** of **322 off** of **396 s.p. Gratiano** Shy. **405 s.d. Exeunt** Exit

5.1. 26 s.p. Stephano Messen. [also at lines 28 and 33] **41 Lorenzo** Lorenzo, & **49 Sweet soul** [assigned in Q to Lancelot] **51 Stephano** Stephen **87 Erebus** Terebus **109 ho!** how **152 give it** giue **233 my** mine

Much Ado About Nothing

Copy text: the Quarto of 1600. The act and scene divisions are missing from the Quarto; the Folio provides act divisions only.

1.1. s.d. Messina Messina, Innogen, his wife **2 Pedro** Peter [also in line 9] **40 bird-bolt** Burbolt **141 all, Leonato. Signor** all: Leonato, signior **194 s.d. Pedro** Pedro, Iohn the bastard
1.2. 3 s.p. [and elsewhere] **Antonio** Old **6 event** euents **25 skill** shill
1.3. 46 brother's brothers **70 s.d. Exeunt** exit
2.1 s.d. Hero his wife, Hero **Ursula** [Q adds "and a kinsman"] **2 s.p.** [and elsewhere] **Antonio** brother **37 bearward** Berrord **44 Peter, for the heavens;** Peter: for the heauens, **67 hear** here **79 s.d. and Don** or dumb **80 a bout** about **94 s.p. Balthasar** Bene. [also at lines 97 and 99] **187 drover** Drouier **201 s.d. Leonato** Leonato, Iohn and Borachio, and Conrade **311 s.p.** [and elsewhere] **Don Pedro** Prince **369 s.d. Exeunt** exit
2.3. 7 s.d. [at line 5 in Q] **24 an** and **35 s.d. Claudio** Claudio, Musicke **61 s.p. Balthasar** [not in Q] **73–76 but . . . nonny** & c. **91 s.d.** [after line 90 in Q] **139 us of** of vs
3.1. s.d. Ursula Vrsley **23 s.d.** [after line 25 in Q] **111 on; I** on I
3.2. 27 can cannot **51 s.p. Don Pedro** Bene. **74 s.p.** [and elsewhere] **Don John** Bastard **91–92 manifest. For my brother, I . . . heart hath** manifest, for my brother (I . . . heart) hath **108 her then, tomorrow** her, then to morrow **118 her tomorrow** her to morrow
3.3. 17 s.p. Seacoal Watch 2 [also at line 27] **87 s.p. Seacoal** Watch [also at lines 95, 105, 125] **161 s.p. Seacoal** Watch 1 [also at line 165] **162 s.p. First Watch** Watch 2 [also at line 168] **171 s.p. Seacoal** [missing in Q]
3.4. 17 in it
3.5. 2 s.p. [and elsewhere] **Dogberry** Const. Dog. **7 s.p.** [and elsewhere] **Verges** Headb. **9 off** of **32 talking. As** talking as **50** [Q provides an "exit" at this point]
4.1. 4 s.p. Friar Fran. **167 tenure** tenure **202 princes** princesse
4.2. s.d. [Q reads "Enter the Constables, Borachio, and the Towne clearke in gownes."] **1 s.p. Dogberry** Keeper **2 s.p.** [and elsewhere in this scene] **Verges** Cowley **4 s.p. Dogberry** Andrew **9 s.p.** [and elsewhere in this scene] **Dogberry** Kemp **35 s.p. Conrade, Borachio** Both **39 Seacoal** Watch 1 [also at line 53] **47 First Watch** Watch 2 **51 s.p. Verges** Const. **67 s.p.** [and elsewhere] **Dogberry** Constable **69 s.p. Conrade** [missing in Q] **69 Off** of **73 s.p. Conrade** Couley **86 s.d. Exeunt** exit
5.1. 16 Bid And **97 anticly** antiquely, and **98 off** of **116 like** likt **179 on** one **189 Lackbeard there, he** Lack-beard, there hee **201 s.d.** [after line 197 in Q] **251 s.p. Verges** Con. 2
5.2. 41 s.d. [after line 42 in Q] **81 myself. So** my self so **97 s.d. Exeunt** exit
5.3. 2 s.p. A Lord Lord **3 s.p. Claudio** [missing in Q] **10 dumb** dead **11** [Q provides a s.p. "Claudio" here] **12 s.p. Balthasar** [missing in Q] **22 s.p. Claudio** Lo. **32 speed's** speeds
5.4. 53 s.p. Antonio Leo. **96 s.p. Benedick** Leon.

The Merry Wives of Windsor

Copy text: the First Folio. Act and scene divisions follow the Folio text throughout.

1.1. s.d. [Entering characters are grouped at the heads of scenes throughout the play.] **30 compromises** compremises **41 George Thomas** **56 s.p. Shallow** Slen. **84 Cotswold** Cotsall **131 Garter** Gater **164 careers** Car-eires **235 faul** fall **236 the 'ort** the 'ord [and in a few other instances dialect has been similarly regularized]
1.3. 14 lime [Q] liue **47 well** [Q] will **51 legion** [Q: legians] legend **59 oeillades** illiads **81 o' the ith'** **82 humor** [Q] honor **93, 98 Page** [Q] Ford **94 Ford** [Q] Page
1.4. 21 whey face wee-face **41 un boîtier vert** vnboyteene verd **46 Ma** mai **fort chaud** for ehando **m'en vais** man voi **47 la cour** le Court **affaire** affaires **49 mets-le à ma** mette le au mon **53 and** [Q] aad **57–58 qu'ai-j'oublié** que ay ie oublie **63 Larron** La-roone **82 baille** ballow **99 that, . . . mind:** that I know Ans mind, **115 goodyear** good-ier **149 that I will** that wee will
2.1. I have I haue **23 i' the** with The **48 What? Thou liest!** What thou liest? **55 praised** praise **59–60 Hundredth Psalm** hundred Psalms **130 and . . . of it** [Q; not in F] **137 Cathayan** Cataian **141 Whither** Whether [at 3.3.139, 141] **182 gentleman.** Gentleman **199 s.p. Ford** [Q] Shal. **201 Brook** [Q] Broome [and at line 203 and elsewhere] **204 mynheers** An-heires **216 s.d. Exeunt** [at line 223 in F]
2.2. 4 I will . . . equipage [Q; not in F] **21 honor** honoror **23, 50** [and elsewhere] **honor** honoror **25 you, you** you you **196 jewel. That** Iewell, that **224–225 exchange** enchange
2.3. 26 Galen Galien **30 Castilian** Castalion **34 Doctor. He** Docto)rhe **51 A word** [Q] a **56 mush** much **73 s.p. Page, Shallow, and Slender** All **77 But first** [Q; not in F]
3.1. 5 Petty-ward pittie-ward **29 God** Heauen **39 God save** [Q] 'Saue **40 God pless** [Q] 'Plesse **76–77 patience. In** patience in **83 urinals** [Q] Vrinal **84–85 for . . . appointments** [Q; not in F] **99–100 Give me . . . terrestrial; so** [Q; not in F] **105 lads** Lad
3.2. 7 s.p. [and elsewhere] **Mrs. Page** M. Pa. [used previously for Page]
3.3. 3 Robert Robin **12 Datchet** Dotchet **35 pumpkin** Pumpion **54 By the Lord** [Q; not in F] **58 not, Nature** not Nature **62 thee there's** thee. Ther's **68 Mistress** M. **72 limekiln** Lime-kill [also at 4.2.51] **176 foolish** foolishon **194 By** Be **208 heartily** hartly
3.4. 12 s.p. Fenton [not in F] **67 Fenton** Fenter **109 s.d. Exit** Exeunt
3.5. 30 sperm Spersme **56 he** be **82 By the Lord** [Q] Yes **141 s.d. Exit** Exeunt
4.1. 44 hung hing **56 Genitivo** Genitiue **57 Jenny's** Ginyes **64 lunatics** Lunaties **73 quae's** Ques
4.2. 51 s.p. Mrs. Page [not in F] **59 s.p. Mrs. Page** [Q] Mist. Ford **68** [and elsewhere] **Brentford** Brainford **91 direct** direct direct **95 misuse him** misuse **106 as lief** lief as **111 ging** gin **118 this** thi **167 not strike** strike **180 Jeshu** yea and no
4.3. 1 Germans desire Germane desires **7 them** [Q] him **9 house** [Q] houses
4.4. 7 cold gold **30 ragg'd horns** rag'd-hornes **32 makes** make **42** [Q, reading "Horne" for "Herne"; not in F] **60 s.p. Mrs. Ford** Ford **65 ne'er** neu'r **72 tire** time
4.5. 41 s.p. Simple Fal. **54 Thou art** [Q] Thou are **74–75 Reading . . . Colnbrook** Readins, of Maidenhead; of Cole-brooke **86 Hue** Huy [also in line 87] **97 to say my prayers** [Q; not in F]
4.6. 39 denote deuote
5.2. 3 my daughter my
5.3. 12 Hugh Herne
5.5. 2 hot-blooded hot-bloodied **3 Jove** Ioue **20 hail kissing-comfits** haile-kissing Comfits **48 Bead** Bede **65 ring.** ring, **66 bears,** beares: **67 More** Mote **70 sapphire, pearl** Saphire-pearle **93 s.p. Fairies** [not in F] **179 what, son** what sonne **193 white** greene **197 green** white **201 un garçon** oon Garsoon **un paysan** oon pesant **203 green** white **204 by** bee **By** be

As You Like It

Copy text: The First Folio. Act and scene divisions follow the Folio text throughout.

1.1. 105 she hee **154 s.p. Oliver** [not in F] **154 s.d. Exit** [at line 153 in F]

1.2. 3 I were were   **51 goddesses and** goddesses   **55 s.p. [and else-where] Touchstone** *Clow.*   **56 father** farher   **80 s.p. Celia** *Ros.*   **88 Le** the   **233–234 love / But** loue; / But   **251 s.d.** [at line 249 in F]   **280 [and occasionally elsewhere] Rosalind** *Rosaline*
1.3. 55 likelihood likelihoods   **76 her** per   **87 s.d. with Lords** &c   **124 be** by   **125 we in** in we
2.1. 49 much must   **50 friends** friend   **59 of the** of
2.3. 10 some seeme   **16 s.p. Orlando** [not in F]   **29 s.p. Orlando** *Ad.*   **50 woo** woe,   **71 seventeen** seauentie
2.4. 1 weary merry   **42 thy wound** they would   **65 you** your
2.5. 1 s.p. Amiens [not in F; also at line 35]   **38 s.d. All together here** [before line 35 in F]   **41–42 No . . . weather** &c   **46 s.p. Jaques** *Amy.*
2.7. s.d. Lords *Lord*   **10 [and elsewhere] woo** woe   **38 brain** braiue   **55 Not to seem** Seeme   **87 comes** come   **161 treble, pipes** treble pipes,   **173 s.p. Amiens** [not in F]   **182 Then** *The*   **190–193 heigh-ho . . . jolly** &c.   **201 master** masters
3.2. 26 good pood   **123 a desert** *Desert*   **143 her** his   **234 such fruit** fruite   **241 thy** the   **340 lectures** Lectors   **354 deifying** defying   **362 are** art
3.3. 52–53 so, Poor men alone? No so poore men alone: No   **88 s.p. Touchstone** *Ol.*   **99 s.d. Exit** *Exeunt*
3.4. 29 a lover Louer   **41 puny** puisny
3.5. 11 pretty, sure pretty sure   **105 erewhile** yerewhile   **128 I have** Haue
4.1. 1 me be me   **18 my** by   **36 gondola** Gundello   **44 thousandth** thousand   **72 warrant** warne   **148 hyena** Hyen   **202 it** in
4.2. 2 s.p. First Lord *Lord*   **7 s.p. Second Lord** *Lord*   **10 s.p. Second Lord** [not in F]
4.3. 5 s.d. [after line 3 in F]   **8 bid** did bid   **79–80 bottom; / The** bottom / The   **104–105 itself: / Under** it selfe / Vnder   **143 In** I   **156 his** this
5.1. 14 gi' ye   **36 sir** wit   **55 policy** police
5.2. 7 nor her nor   **31 overcame** ouercome
5.3. 15 s.p. Both Pages [not in F]   **18 In** *In the*   **ring** rang   **24–26 In . . . spring** *In spring time,* &c [also at lines 30–32 and 36–38]   **33–38** [this stanza comes after line 20 in F]
5.4. 25 s.d. Exeunt *Exit*   **34 s.d.** [at line 33 in F]   **80 so to the** so ro   **113 her** *his*   **150 s.p. Jaques de Boys** *2 Bro.* [also at line 182]   **163 them** him   **170 were** vvete   **197 trust they'll end, in** trust, they'l end in.   **s.d. Exeunt** *Exit*

Twelfth Night

Copy text: The First Folio. Act and scene divisions follow the Folio text throughout.

1.1. 1 s.p. [and throughout] Orsino *Duke*   **10–11 capacity / Receiveth** capacitie, / Receiueth   **11 sea, naught** sea. Nought
1.2. 15 Arion Orion
1.3. 51 s.p. Sir Andrew *Ma.*   **54 Mary Accost** Mary, accost   **96 curl by** coole my   **98 me** we   **132 dun** dam'd   **set** sit   **136 That's** That
1.5. 5 s.p. [and throughout] Feste *Clo.*   **85 gagged** gag'd [also at 5.1. 376]   **144 He's** Ha's   **163 s.d. Viola** *Uiolenta*   **296 County's** Countes   **306 s.d.** [F adds "*Finis, Actus primus*"]
2.2. 20 That sure That   **31 our** O   **32 made of, such** made, if such
2.3. 25 leman Lemon
2.4. 51 s.p. Feste [not in F]   **53 Fly . . . fly** Fye . . . fie   **55 yew** Ew   **88 I** It
2.5. 112 staniel stallion   **118 portend?** portend,   **142 born** become   **achieve** atcheeues   **156–157 Unhappy." Daylight** vnhappy daylight   **173 dear** deero   **203 s.d.** [F adds "*Finis Actus secundus*"]
3.1. 8 king Kings   **68 wise men** wisemens   **91 all ready** already   **124 grece** grize
3.2. 7 thee the the   **64 nine** mine
3.4. 15 s.d. [at line 14 in F, after "hither"]   **25 s.p. Olivia** *Mal.*   **65 s.d. Exeunt** *exit*   **72 tang** langer   **175 You** Yon   **222 thee** the   **228 sir. I am sure no** sir I am sure, no   **249 competent** computent   **397 s.d. Exeunt** *Exit*
4.2. 6 in in in   **38 clerestories** cleere stores   **71 sport to** sport
4.3. 1 s.p. Sebastian [not in F]   **35 s.d.** [F adds "*Finis Actus Quartus*"]

5.1. 173 He's H'as   **190 s.d.** [after line 187 in F]   **195 He's** has   **200 pavane** panyn   **205 help?** An helpe an   **285 He's** has   **389 tiny** tine   **406 With hey** hey

All's Well That Ends Well

Copy text: The First Folio. Act divisions are from the Folio; scene divisions are editorially provided.

1.1. 1 s.p. [and elsewhere] Countess *Mother*   **3 s.p. [and elsewhere] Bertram** *Ros.*   **70 Farewell. My** Farewell my   **130 got** goe   **148 th' one** ten   **159 wear** were
1.2. 3 s.p. [and elsewhere] First Lord *1. Lo. G.*   **15 s.p. [and else-where] Second Lord** *2. Lo. E.*   **18 Rossillion** Rosignoll   **52 him! He** him he   **76 s.d. Exeunt** *Exit*
1.3. 3 s.p. [and elsewhere] Rinaldo *Ste.*   **13 s.p. [and elsewhere] Lavatch** *Clo.*   **19 I** w   **75 With . . . stood** *bis*   **112 Dian no queen** Queene   **124 s.d. [and elsewhere] Helena** *Hellen*   **125** [F has s.p. here, *Old. Cou.*, used subsequently in other s.p.]   **127 rightly belong;** righlie belong   **168 loneliness** louelinesse   **174 th' one to th' other** 'ton tooth to th'other   **180 forswear 't. Howe'er,** forswear't how ere   **199 intenible** intemible   **233 Haply** Happily   **247 day and** day, an
2.1. 3–4 gain all, / The gaine, all / The   **5 s.p. First Lord** *Lord.* G   **15–16 it. When . . . shrinks, find** it, when . . . shrinkes: finde   **18 s.p. Second Lord** *L.G*   **25 s.p. Second Lord** *2 Lo. E*   **44 with his cicatrice** his sicatrice, with   **63 fee** see   **111 two, more dear. I** two: more deare I   **146 fits** shifts   **157 impostor** Impostrue   **175 nay** ne   **194 heaven** helpe   **212 meed** deed   **s.d. Exeunt** *Exit*
2.2. 1 s.p. [and elsewhere in scene] Countess *Lady*   **60 An end, sir! To** An end sir to
2.3. 1 s.p. [and elsewhere] Lafew *Ol. Laf.*   **21 indeed. If** indeede if   **34 minister; great** minister great   **44 Mort du vinaigre** *Mor du vinager*   **51 s.d. four** *3 or 4*   **70–71 choose; but, be refused, / Let** choose, but be refused; / Let   **76 s.d.** [at line 62 in F]   **94 her** heere   **96 s.p. Helena** *La.*   **99 s.p. Lafew** *Ol. Lord*   **125 when** whence   **129 name;** vileness: name! Vilenesse   **130 it is** is   **137–138 word's a slave / Debauched** words, a slaue / Debosh'd   **138–139 grave / A** graue: / A   **140–141 tomb / Of** Tombe. / Of   **168 eyes. When** eies, when   **170 it, I** it: I   **213 lattice** Lettice   **266 s.d.** [at line 264 in F]   **292 War** Warres   **293 detested** detected   **301 s.d. Exeunt** *Exit*
2.4. 16 fortunes fortune   **35 me?** [F adds a s.d., *Clo.*]   **56 You.—Come** you come
2.5. 27 End And   **29 one** on   **31 heard** hard   **89 s.p. Bertram** [at line 90 in F]   **89 men, mousieur?** men? Monsieur,
3.1. 9 s.p. Second Lord *French E*   **17 s.p. First Lord** *Fren. G*   **23 to the** to'th the
3.2. 9 sold hold   **18 E'en** In   **19 s.p. Countess** [not in F]   **45 s.p. [and throughout scene] Second Lord** *French E*   **47 s.p. [and throughout scene] First Lord** *French G*   **64 s.p. Countess** *Old La.*   **65 engrossest all** engrossest, all   **111 still-piercing** still-peering
3.4. 4 s.p. Rinaldo [not in F]   **9–10 hie. / Bless** hie, / Blesse   **10 peace, whilst** peace. Whilst   **18 s.p. Countess** [not in F]
3.5. s.d. daughter daughter, *Violenta*   **10 s.p. [and elsewhere] Mariana** *Maria*   **33 le** la   **66 warrant** write   **93 s.d. Exeunt** *Exit*
3.6. 1 s.p. [and throughout scene until line 109] First Lord *Cap. E*   **3 s.p. [and throughout scene until line 109] Second Lord** *Cap. G*   **36 his** this   **37 ore** ours   **109 s.p. First Lord** *Cap. G*   **111, 117 s.p. Second Lord** *Cap. E*
3.7. 19 Resolved Resolue   **41 steads** steeds   **46 wicked** lawfull
4.1. 1 s.p. [and throughout scene] First Lord *1. Lord E*   **69 s.p. [and throughout scene] First Soldier** *Inter.*   **90 art** are   **93 s.p. Second Soldier** *Sol.* [and at line 96]   **97 s.d. Exeunt** *Exit*
4.2. 6 monument. monument   **38 may** make   **snare** scarre
4.3. 1 s.p. [and throughout scene] First Lord *1. Lord E*   **2 s.p. [and throughout scene] Second Lord** *Cap.* E   **24 nobility, . . . stream** Nobility . . . streame,   **81 s.p. First Lord** *Ber.*   **89 effected** affected   **98 he's** ha s [also at line 268]   **118 Hush, hush** [assigned in F to Bertram]   **125 s.p. First Lord** *Cap.*   **138 All's one to him** [assigned in F to Parolles]   **199 lordship** Lord   **242 our** your   **316 s.p. Bertram** *Count*
4.4. 16 you your

4.5. 21 grass grace   **39 name** maine   **46 of** off   **70 home, I** home. I
5.1. 6 s.d. a Gentleman a *gentle Astringer* [after line 6 in F]
5.2. 1 Monsieur Mr.   **25 similes** smiles   **33 under her** vnder
5.3. 50 warped warpe   **59–60 carried, / To** carried / To   **60 sender turns** sender, turns   **72 s.p. Countess** [not in F]   **102 Plutus** *Platus*   **115 conjectural** connecturall   **123 tax** taze   **140 s.p. King** [not in F]   **154 s.d.** [at line 152 in F]   **155 since** sir   **157 s.d. Diana** *Diana, and Parrolles* [after line 157 in F]   **183 them. Fairer prove** them fairer: Proue   **208 sickens but** sickens: but   **217 infinite cunning** insuite comming   **314 are** is
Epilogue 4 strife *strift*

Measure for Measure

Copy text: the First Folio. Act and scene divisions are from the Folio except as indicated below.
1.1. 76 s.d. [at line 75 in F]
1.2. 58 s.p. [and elsewhere] Mistress Overdone *Bawd*   **83 s.d.** [after line 84 in F]   **85 s.p. [and elsewhere] Pompey** *Clo.*   **115** [F begins "*Scena Tertia*" here]   **134 morality** mortality
1.3. [F labels as "*Scena Quarta*"]   **20 steeds** weedes   **27 Becomes more** More   **54 s.d. Exeunt** *Exit*
1.4. [F labels as "*Scena Quinta*"]   **s.d. [and elsewhere] Isabella** *Isabell*   **2 s.p. [and throughout] Francisca** *Nun*   **5 sisterhood** Sisterstood   **17 stead** steed [also at 3.2. 252]   **54 givings-out** giuing-out   **61–62 mind, study, and fast. / He** minde: Studie, and fast / He   **72 He's** Has
2.1. 12 your our   **39 breaks** brakes   **139 s.d.** [at line 138 in F]
2.2. 63 back again againe   **104 ere** here
2.3. 41 law Loue
2.4. 9 sere feard   **17 s.d. Enter Servant** [after line 17 in F]   **30 s.d. Enter Isabella** [after line 30 in F]   **53 or** and   **75 craftily** crafty   **76 me be** be   **94 all-binding** all-building
3.1. 29 thee sire, thee, fire   **31 serpigo** Sapego   **52 me to hear them** them to heare me   **68 Though** Through   **91 enew** emmew   **96 damned'st** damnest   **131 penury** periury   **200 advisings. To . . . good a** aduisings, to . . . good; a   **216 by oath** oath
3.2. 0 [not marked as a new scene in F]   **8 law a** Law; a   **9 on** and   **26 eat, array** eate away   **48 it clutched** clutch'd   **74–75 bondage. If . . . patiently, why** bondage if . . . patiently: Why   **109 ungenerative** generatiue   **147 dearer** deare   **214 See** Sea
4.1. 1 s.p. Boy [not in F]   **20 s.d. Isabella** *Isabell*   **49 s.d.** [after line 48 in F]   **61 quests** Quest   **64 s.d. Enter . . . Isabella** [after line 64 in F]
4.2. 43–47 If . . . thief [assigned in F to *Clo.*]   **58 yare** y'are   **60 s.d.** [at line 59 in F]   **72 s.d. Enter Duke** [after line 72 in F]   **100 This . . . man** [assigned in F to *Duke*]   **lordship's** Lords   **101 s.p. Duke** *Pro.*   **120 s.d. Provost** [not in F]
4.3. 92 s.d. [at line 91 in F]   **93 Varrius** *Angelo*   **100 well** weale
4.4. 6 redeliver reliuer   **15–16 proclaimed. Betimes** proclaim'd betimes   **19 s.d.** [at line 18 in F]
4.5. 6 Flavius' *Flauia's*
5.1. 14 me we   **34 hear!** heere   **173 s.d. Enter Mariana** [after line 173 in F]   **174 her face** your face   **268 s.d.** [at line 267 in F]   **288 s.d.** [at line 286 in F]   **407 s.d. Mariana** *Maria*   **431 confiscation** confutation   **488 s.d. Juliet** *Iulietta*   **550 that's** that

Troilus and Cressida

Copy text: the Quarto of 1609. As a text seemingly based on Shakespeare's own manuscript, with many unsupplied or imprecise stage directions, mislineation, authorial punctuation, and the like, Q is a suitable copy text, even though the work of the Q compositors (three in number) reduces the reliability of that text's authority even in incidental matters. Substantively, the First Folio text (F) often gives what may perhaps be Shakespeare's later decisions in a manuscript that may also have been put to use in the theater. Some such manuscript

was used to annotate a copy of Q for the Folio printers. At the same time one needs to be careful not to include in an edited text those changes in F that appear likely to have been sophistications or compositorial errors. For these limited reasons only, Q serves as copy text for these collation notes, even though many readings that substantively vary between Q and F are decided in favor of F. All adopted readings are from [F] unless otherwise indicated; [eds.] means that the reading is that of some editor since the First Folio. [Fa] refers to the first setting of the Folio text, [Fb] to the second setting. Act and scene divisions are not provided in the Quarto or the Folio.
Prologue [F; not in Q]   **8 immures** emures [F]   **12 barks** [eds.] Barke [F]   **17 Antenorides** *Antenonidus*   **19 Spar** [eds.] Stirre [F]
1.1. 26 the [Q,Fa] of the [Fb]   **33 When she** [eds.] then she   **is she** she is   **55–57 heart / Her . . . voice; / Handlest . . . discourse—o!—** [eds.] heart: / Her . . . voice, / Handlest . . . discourse: O   **73 on of you** of you   **78 not kin** [Fb] kin [Q,Fa]   **79–80 what care** what   **85 her. For** her for   **99 woo** [eds.] woe   **100 stubborn-chaste** stubborne, chast   **104 resides** reides
1.2. 1 s.p. [and throughout] Alexander *Man*   **17 they** the   **34 struck** stroke   **36 s.d.** [F; not in Q]   **48 ye** [eds.] yea   **71 just . . . them; he** [eds.] just, . . . them he   **85 come** eome   **87 wit** [eds.] will   **117 lift** liste   **125 valiantly** valianty   **130 the** [eds.] thee   **148 pot** por   **177 s.d.** [at line 175 in Q]   **180 Ilium** Ilion   **189 s.d.** [after line 190 in Q]   **192 a man** man   **205 man's** man   **224–225 indifferent well** [eds.] indifferent, well [Q,F]   **236 ne'er** neuer   **241 s.d. Enter common soldiers** [F; not in Q]   **244–245 i' th' eyes** in the eyes   **249 among** amongst   **256 so forth** suchlike   **260 another** a   One a man   **269 too** two   **280 I'll** I wil   **281 bring, uncle?** [eds.] bring vncle: [Q] bring Vnkle. [F]   **283 s.d.** [F; not in Q]   **291 prize** price   **296 contents** content
1.3. 0 s.d. Sennet [F; not in Q]   **2 the jaundice on** these laundies ore   **13 every** euer   **19 think** call   **29 loud** broad   **31 thy godly the** godlike   **36 patient** ancient   **48 breese** Bryze   **61 thy** the   **67 On which the heavens ride, knit all the Greeks' ears** (On which heauen rides) knit all the Greekish eares   **70–74** [F; not in Q]   **75 basis** bases   **92 ill . . . evil** influence of euill Planets   **110 meets** melts   **119 includes** include   **128 in** with   **137 lives stands** liues stand   **143 sinew** sinow   **149 awkward** sillie   **159 unsquared** vnsquare   **164 just** right   **188 willed** wild   **195 and** our   **209 fineness** finesse   **214 s.d. Enter Aeneas** [F, not in Q]   **219 ears** eyes   **221 host** [eds.] heads   **236 fame** same   **238 Jove's** great *Ioues*   **247 affair** affaires   **250 him** with him   **252 sense** seat   **the** that   **256 loud** alowd   **262 this** his   **267 That seeks** And feeds   **276 compass** couple   **289 or means** a meanes   **294 One . . . one** A . . . no   **297 this withered brawn** my withered braunes   **298 will tell** tell   **302 forbid** forfend   **youth** men   **304 s.p. Agamemnon** [F; not in Q]   **305 first** sir   **309 s.d.** [F; not in Q]   **315 This 'tis** [F; not in Q]   **324 The True** the   **even as** as   **327 were** weare   **333 Yes** Why   **334 his honor** those honours   **336 this** the   **340 wild** vilde   **343 indices** [eds.] indexes [Q,F]   **352 from hence receives** the receiues from hence   a   **354–356** [F; not in Q]   **354 his** [eds.] in his [F]   **359 show our foulest wares** First shew foule wares   **361–2 yet . . . better** shall exceed, / By shewing the worst first   **368 wear** share   **369 we** it   **373 did** do   **377 as the worthier** for the better   **388 of it** there of   **391 tar** arre   **their** a
2.1. 8 there would would   **11 s.d.** [F; not in Q]   **14 vinewed'st** [eds.] vnsalted [Q] whinid'st [F]   **17 oration** oration without booke   **18 learn a** learne   **19 o' thy** [eds.] ath thy [Q]   **24 a fool** foole   **26–27 foot. An** foot, and   **27 thee** the   **38, 40, 41 s.p. Thersites, Ajax, Thersites** [F; not in Q]   **45 Thou scurvy** you scuruy   **55 s.d.** [F; not in Q]   **63 I do so** so do I   **71 I will** It will   **75 I'll** I   **88 for a** the   **101 an 'a** [Q] if he [F]   **out** at   **105 your** [eds.] their   **nails on their toes** nailes   **107 war** wars   **111 wit** as   as   **114 brach** [eds.] brooch   **122 fifth** first   **130 s.d.** [F; not in Q]
2.2. 3 damage domage   **14,15 surety** surely   **27 father** fathers   **33 at of** 34 them. Should . . . father** them should . . . father;   **47 Let's** Sets   **52 holding** keeping   **58 inclinable** attributiue   **64 shores** shore   **66 chose** choose   **69 spoiled** soild   **71 sieve** siue   **74 of** with   **79 stale** pale   **82 launched** lansh't   **86 noble** worthy   **100 s.d. Enter . . . ears** Enter Cassandra raving [Q, at line 96]   **104 old** elders   **106 clamor** clamours   **120 th' event** [eds.] euent   **149 off** of   **210 strike** shrike

2.3. 1 s.p. Thersites [not in Q] **19 dependent** depending **21 s.d. Enter Patroclus** [F; not in Q] **24 ha'** a **25 wouldst** couldst **31 art** art not **46 thyself** Thersites **49 mayst** must **54–59** [F; not in Q] **62–63 commanded of Agamemnon** commanded **66 to the creator** of the Prouer **68 Patroclus** Come Patroclus **69 s.d.** [F; not in Q] **73–74 Now . . . all** [F; not in Q] **73 serpigo** [eds.] Suppeago [F] **78 shent** [eds.] sent [F] sate [Q] **79 appertainments** appertainings **82 so say** say so **87 the** a **88 A word, my lord** [F; not in Q] **98 council that** composure **101 s.d. Enter Patroclus** [F; not in Q] **110 digestion's** digestion **111 Hear** Heere **129 pettish lunes** course, and time [Q] pettish lines [F] **his flows** and flowes **as** and **130 carriage of this action** streame of his commencement **135 Bring** [Q,Fb] ring [Fa] **140 enter you** entertaine **140 s.d. Exit Ulysses** [F; not in Q] **151 it** pride **152 clearer, Ajax** cleerer **157 I hate** I do hate **166 Why, will** Why will **167 the air** th'air **186 do** doth **190 Must** Shall **192 titled** liked **200 this** his **202 pash** push **204 'a** he **211 let** tell**humors** humorous **214 o'** of **218 'twould** two'od **219 'A . . . shares** [assigned in Q to Ajax] **221 He's . . . warm** [assigned in Q to Ajax] **Farce** Force **222 praises** praiers **in; his** his **225 You** Yon **231 thus with us** with us thus **241 beyond all** all thy **247 bourn** boord **248 Thy** This **255 s.p. Ulysses** Nest. **262 cull** call

3.1. 0 s.d. Music . . . Servant Enter Pandarus **1 not you** you not **3. s.p.** [and elsewhere] Servant Man **25 mean, friend** mean **31 who's** who is **33 visible** [eds.] invisible [Q,F] **37 that thou** thou **38 Cressida** Cressid **41 There's** theirs **52 Nell, he** Nel. he **76 supper you** super. You **90 poor disposer's** disposer's **106 lord** lad **107 hast** haste **113** [F; not in Q] **117 shaft confounds** shafts confound **120 O! O!** oh ho [and similarly in 122–125] **148 They're** Their **field** the field **149 woo** woe **151 these** this **159 thee** her

3.2. 3 he stays stays **3 s.d.** [F; not in Q] **8 a** to a **10 those** these **16 s.d.** [F; not in Q] **22 Swooning** [eds.] Sounding [Q,F] **23 subtle-potent** [eds.] subtill, potent [Q,F] **28 s.d.** [F; not in Q] **33 s.d.** [F; not in Q] **36 lose** [eds.] loose [Q,F] **37 unawares** vnwares **38 s.d. Pandarus and Cressida** pandar and Cressid **45 thills** filles **61 Cressida** Cressid **67 fears** [eds.] teares **80 This is** This **91 crown it. No perfection** louer part no affection **98 s.d.** [F, not in Q] **109 are** be **117 glance that ever—pardon** [eds.] glance; that euer pardon [Q,F] **121 grown** [eds.] grone [Q] grow [F] **131 Cunning** Comming **in** [eds.] from [Q,F] **132 My . . . from me** My very soule of councell **149–150 Where . . . what** I would be gone. / Where is my wit? I know not what I speake **156 might; that** might that **159 aye** age **175 similes, truth** simile's truth **179 Yet, after** After **184 and** or **197 witness. Here** [eds.] witness here [Q,F] **199 pains** paine **207 with a bed** [eds.; not in Q]

3.3. s.d. Calchas Chalcas **1 done you** done **3 to your** to **4 come** [eds.] loue **29 off** of **43 unplausive** vnpaulsiue **55 What, comes** What comes [Q,F] **69 s.d. Exit** [eds.] Exeunt [Q,F] **73 use** [eds.] us'd **101 shining** ayming **111 mirrored** [eds.] married **128 are.** [eds.] are [Q,F] **129 abject** obiect **141 on** one **142 shrinking** shriking **153 mail** [eds.] male [Q,F] **156 one** on **159 hedge** turn **161 hindmost** him, most **162–164 Or . . . on** [F; not in Q] **163 rear** neere [F] **165 past** passe **169 O, let** Let **179 give** [eds.] goe **185 Than** That **not stirs** stirs not **198 grain . . . gold** thing **199 th'uncomprehensive deeps** the vncomprehensiue depth **225 like a** like **234 we** they **242 s.d. Enter Thersites** [after line 242 in Q] **267 ambassador to him** Ambassador **275 the most** the **279 Grecian** [not in Q] **et cetera. Do** Do **295–296 o'clock** of the clock **301 but he's** but **o'** of **306 carry** beare

4.1. s.d. with a torch [F; not in Q] **4.1. s.d.** [and elsewhere] **Diomedes** [eds.] Diomed [Q,F] **5 you** your **18 But** Lul'd **22–23 backward. In humane gentleness,** back-ward, in humane gentlenesse: **39 Calchas'** Calcho's **42 do think** beleeue **46 whereof** wherefore **52 s.d.** [F; not in Q] **54 the soul** soule **55 merits** deserues **most** best **58 soilure** soyle **78 you** they

4.2. 18 off of **21 s.d.** [F; not in Q] **32–33 Ah, poor capoccia** [eds] a poore chipochia, **35 s.d. One knocks** [after line 36 in Q, after 33 in F] **36 Hoo!** [eds.] Who **59 s.d.** [F; not in Q] **65 us; and for him** him, and **74 nature** neighbor Pandar **79 s.p. Cressida** [not in Q] **87 wouldst** wouldest **89–90 knees I beseech you** knees **103 extremity** extreames **110 s.d.** [F; not in Q]

4.3.0 s.d. and [F; not in Q]

4.4. 6 affection affections **50 genius so** Genius **51 "Come"** so **54 the root** my throate **58 my love** loue **64 there's** there is **70 Wear** were **77** [F; not in Q] **gifts** guift [F] **78 flowing** swelling **79 person** portion **106 wear** were **122 zeal** [eds.] seale **135 I'll** l **139 s.d. Sound trumpet** [F; not in Q] **144–148** [F; not in Q] **144 s.p. Deiphobus** [eds.] Dio. [F] **148 s.d.** [after line 143 in Q,F]

4.5. s.d. Nestor [eds.] Nester, Calcas [Q,F] **2 time . . . courage.** [eds.] time. With starting courage, [Q,F] **16 toe** too **38 s.p. Menelaus** [eds.] Patr. **44 not** nor **49 too.** [eds.] then. [Q] **then?** [F] **60 accosting** [eds.] a coasting [Q,F] **64 s.d. Exeunt** [F; not in Q] **66 you** the **74 s.p. Achilles** [eds.; not in Q,F] **75 disprising** misprising **95** [F; not in Q] **96 s.p. Agamemnon** Vlises **99 in deeds** deeds **133 Of our rank feud** [F; not in Q] **134 drop** day **162 mine** my **164 of all **166–171** [F; not in Q] **179 Mock . . . oath** (Mock not thy affect, the vntraded earth) **188 And seen thee scorning** Despising many **189 thy** th' **191 unto** to some **194 hemmed** shrupd **200 Let** O let **207** [F; not in Q] **253 the** an **256 stithied** stichied **273 you** we **276 Beat . . . taborins** To taste your bounties **282 on heaven nor** on vpon the heauen nor **288 As** But **293 she loved** my Lord

5.1. 4 core curre **5 botch** [eds.] batch [Q,F] **12 need these** needs this **14 boy** box **15 thought** said **19 catarrhs** [F; not in Q] **i'** in **20 wheezing** whissing **26 mean'st** means **31 sarcenet** sacenet **32 tassel** toslell **51 Here's** her's **54 brother** be **56 hanging . . . leg** at his bare legge **54 farced** [eds.] forced [F] **59 he is** her's **60 dog** day **mule** Moyle **60–61 fitchew** Fichooke **63 not** [F; not in Q] **66 s.d. Enter . . . lights** Enter Agam: Vlysses, Nest: and Diomed with lights **68 light** lights **68 s.d.** [F; not in Q] **71 good** God **77 sewer** [eds.] sure **78 both at once** both **98 Calchas his** Calcas

5.2. 4 s.d. Enter . . . Ulysses [F; not in Q] **5 s.d. Enter Cressida** [after "to him" in line 6 in Q] **11 clef** Cliff **13 s.p. Cressida** [eds.] Cal. **16 should** shall **35 one** a **37 pray you** pray **41 Nay** Now **42 distraction** distruction **48 Why, how now, lord?** How now my lord? **49 Adieu, you** you **57 tickles these** tickles **59 But will** Will **60 la** [eds.] lo **63 sweet** my **69** [F; not in Q] **70 s.p. Cressida** Troy. **83 As I kiss thee** [eds.; continued as Cressida's speech in Q,F] **Nay . . . me** [eds.; assigned to Diomedes in Q,F] **87 s.p. Cressida** [F; not in Q] **92 one's** [eds.] on's [Q] one [F] **94 By** And by **109 s.d. Exit** [F; not in Q] **121 coact** Court **126 had deceptions** were deceptions **137 soil** spoile **139 'a** he **146 is** was **156 Ariachne's** Ariachna's [Qb] Ariathna's [Qa] **161 five** finde **164 bound** giuen **171 much as** [eds.] much

5.3. 14 s.p. Cassandra Cres. **20–22** [F; not in Q] **21 give** [eds.] count giue [Q] **use** [eds.] as [F] **23 s.p. Cassandra** [F; not in Q] **29 mean'st** meanest **45 mothers** Mother **58** [F; not in Q] **85 distraction** distruction **90 s.d.** [F; not in Q] **93 of worth** [eds.; not in Q] **96 s.d. Pandarus** [eds.] Pandar [Q,F] **104 o' these** [eds.] ath's [Q] o'th's [F] **112** [F follows with an alternate version, slightly varied, of 5.10.32-4]

5.4. 0 s.d. Alarum [F, at 5.2.112; not in Q] **4 young knave's** knaues **17 s.d. Enter . . . Troilus** [F; not in Q] **26 art thou** art

5.5. 5 s.p. Servant Man **s.d. Enter Agamemnon** [after "proof" in line 5 in Q] **7 Margareton** [eds.] Margaleron [Q,F] **11 Epistrophus** [eds.] Epostropus **Cedius** [eds.] Cedus **12 Thoas** [eds.] Thous **22 scalèd** scaling **schools** [eds.] sculls [Q] sculs [F] **25 the** a **41 luck** lust **43 s.p. Ajax** [F; not in Q]

5.6. 1 s.p. Ajax [F; not in Q] **2 s.p. Diomedes** [F; not in Q] **7 the** [eds.] thy [Q,F] **11 s.d. Exit Troilus** [F; not in Q] **Enter Hector** [F; not in Q] **13 s.p. Achilles** [F; not in Q] **21 s.d. Enter Troilus** [eds.; after line 21 in Q] **26 reck** [eds.] wreake **thou end** I end

5.7. 1 s.p. Achilles [F; not in Q] **8 s.d. Exeunt** [eds.] Exit **and** [F; not in Q] **10 'Loo** [eds.] lowe **10–11 double-horned Spartan** [eds.] double hen'd spartan [Q] double hen'd sparrow [F] **12 s.d. Exeunt** [eds.] Exit **13 s.p.** [and throughout scene] **Margareton** [eds.] Bast.

5.8. 3 good my **4 s.d. his** [F; not in Q] **11 Now** come **15 part** prat **16 s.p. Myrmidon** [eds.] One. [Q] Gree. [F] **Trojan trumpets** Troyans trumpet

5.9. 0 s.d. Sound retreat [F; not in Q] **Shout** [F, at the end of scene 8; not in Q] **1 shout is that** is this **3 slain! Achilles!** [F subst.] slaine Achilles, **6 a man as good** as good a man

5.10. 0 s.d. and [F; not in Q] **2 Never** *Troy*. Neuer **2 s.d.** [placement as in F; before line 2 in Q] **3 s.p. Troilus** [F; not in Q] **7 smite** [eds.] smile [Q,F] **20 Cold** Could [Q] Coole [F] **21 scare** [eds.] Scarre [Q,F] **21–22 But . . . dead** [F; not in Q] **23 yet. You vile abominable tents,** [F, subst.] yet you proud abhominable tents: [Q] **33 Ignomy and** ignomyny **36 world, world, world** world, world **39 desired** lou'd **50 your** my **51 hold-door** hold-ore **56 s.d. [Exit]** Exeunt [F; not in Q]

I Henry VI

Copy text: the First Folio. Act divisions are marked in F, except that Act 5 appears at 5.5; scene divisions, marked in Act 3, are otherwise editorially supplied except as indicated below.

1.1. 57 s.p. First Messenger *Mess.* [also at line 69] **60 Rouen** [not in F] **65** [and elsewhere] *Rouen* Roan **89 s.p. Second Messenger** *Mess.* **94 Reignier** *Reynold* **103 s.p. Third Messenger** *Mes.* **141 slain? Then I** slaine then? I **176 steal** send
1.2. 30 bred breed **47 s.p.** [and elsewhere] **Charles** *Dolph.* **63 s.d.** [and elsewhere] **Pucelle** *Puzel* **76 whilst** whilest **99 five** fine **103 s.d.** [and elsewhere] **la** *de* **113 rites** rights **131 halcyon** *Halcyons*
1.3. 6 s.p. First Servingman *Glost. 1. Man* [at line 8, 1. Man] **29 Humphrey** *Vmpheir* **30 Peeled** Piel'd **74 s.p. Officer** [not in F]
1.4. 10 Wont Went **25 gott'st** got's **27 Duke** Earle **63 Glasdale** *Glansdale* [also at line 66] **69 s.d. shoot** *shot* **89 Bear . . . bury it** [before line 87 in F] **95 Nero-like** like thee **107** [and elsewhere] **Dauphin** Dolphin
1.5. 16 hungry starvèd hungry-starued
1.6. 21 pyramid Pyramis **22 of** or
2.1. 5 s.p. A Sentinel *Sent.* **7 s.d. ladders** [F adds "Their Drummes beating a Dead March"; see textual note at 2.2. 6 s.d.] **28 all together** altogether **38 s.p. Sentinels** *Sent.* **54 s.p. Pucelle** *Ioane* [also at line 72] **77 s.d.** [F has *Exeunt* preceding this s.d.]
2.2. 6 s.d. their . . . march [appears at 2.1.7 in F] **20 Arc** Acre **38 Auvergne** Ouergne
2.4. 1 s.p. Plantagenet *Yorke* [and thus through Act 3] **57 law** you **117 wiped** whipt **132 gentlemen** gentle
2.5. 18 s.p. First Keeper *Keeper* [and at line 33] **35 s.p.** [and elsewhere] **Plantagenet** *Rich.* **71 King Richard** *Richard* **84 Cambridge then,** Cambridge, then **121 s.d. Exeunt** Exit **129 mine ill** my will
3.1. 52 s.p. Somerset [not in F] **53 s.p. Warwick** *Som.* **54 s.p. Somerset** [not in F] **74** [F provides an s.p. here, "*King*"] **164 that** that all
3.2. 10 s.p. First Soldier *Souldier* **13 Qui là** Che la **21–22 specify . . . in?** specifie? . . . in. **40 s.d. Burgundy** *Burgonie* [also at lines 42 and 75, etc.] **41 Good God** [Q] God **103 s.d. Exeunt** *Exit* **123 gleeks** glikes
3.3. 46–48 foe. . . . eyes, Foe, . . . Eyes.
3.4. 27 s.d. Manent *Manet*
4.1. s.d. Exeter, Governor and *Gouernor Exeter* **14 thee** the **48 my Lord** Lord **151 umpire** *Vmper* **173 s.d. Flourish** [at line 181 in F] **Manent** *Manet* **180 wist** wish
4.2. 3 calls call **15 s.p. General** *Cap.*
4.3. 5 Talbot . . . along, Talbot as he march'd along. **17 s.p.** [and throughout scene] **Lucy** 2 *Mes.* [or *Mes.*] **20 waist** waste **36 travel** trauaile **53 lands** Lauds
4.4. 13 Whither Whether **16 legions** Regions **27 Reignier** *Reignard* **31 horse** hoast
4.5. 55 s.d. Exeunt *Exit*
4.6. 57 s.d. Exeunt *Exit*
4.7. 18 antic antique **25 whether** whither **63 Wexford** Washford **64 Goodrich** *Goodrig* **89 have them** haue him **94 with them** with him **96 s.d. Exeunt** Exit
5.1. 0 [F here reads "*Scena secunda*"]
5.2. 0 [F here reads "*Scoena Tertia*"]
5.3. 57 her his **65** [and elsewhere in scene] **woo** woe **85 random** randon **106 in** iu **179 modestly** modestie **192 And** Mad

5.4. 28 suckedst suck'st **49 Arc** *Aire* **74 Machiavel** Macheuile **102 travail** trauell **123 s.p. Cardinal** *Win.* **127 breathe** breath **149 compromise** comprimize
5.5. 0 [F here reads "*Actus Quintus*"] **60 That most** Most **82 love** loue

2 Henry VI

Copy text: the First Folio. Act and scene divisions, missing in F except for "*Actus Primus. Scoena Prima*" at 1.1.0, are editorially provided.

1.1. 4 Princess Princes **37 s.d. kneeling** *Kneel* **56 s.p. Cardinal** [Q] *Win*. **57 duchies** Dutchesse **72 s.d. Exeunt** *Exit* **Manent** *Manet* **91 had** hath **99 Razing** Racing **107 roast** rost **130 s.p.** [and elsewhere] **Gloucester** *Hum.* **166 all together** altogether **167 hoist** hoyse **176 Protector** [Q] Protectors **177 s.d. Exeunt** *Exit* **190 thee** the **206 let's away** lets make hast away **211 s.d. Exeunt** *Exit* **254 in** [Q] in in
1.2. 1 s.p. [and elsewhere] **Duchess** *Elia.* **19 hour** thought **22 dream** dreames **38 are** [Q] wer **60 s.d. Exit Humphrey** [at line 59 in F]
1.3. 6 s.p. First Petitioner *Peter* **32 master** Mistresse **41 s.d. Exeunt** *Exit* **100** [F has "*Exit*" here] **104 denied** denay'd **142 I'd** [Q] I could **187 s.p.** [and throughout scene] **Horner** *Armorer* **212–213** [Q; not in F]
1.4. 25 s.p. Margery Jordan *Witch* **25 Asnath** *Asmath* **62 Aio te** *Aio* **63 posse** *posso*
2.1. 30 Lord-Protectorship Lords Protectorship **48 Cardinal** [aside to Gloucester] **I am with you** Cardinall, I am with you [as part of Gloucester's speech] **59 s.p. Townsman** *One* [also at line 61] **112 Alban** *Albones* **135 his** [Q] it
2.2. 45 was son was **46 son** Sonnes Sonne
2.3. 3 sins sinne **19 grave** ground **74 apron** Aporne
2.4. 88 too to
3.1. 211 strains strayes **218–219 eyes . . . good,** eyes; . . . good: **222 s.d. Exeunt** *Exit* **333–334 art . . . death; it** art; . . . death, it
3.2. 14 s.p. Somerset *Suffolke, Somerset* **26 Meg** *Nell* **75 leper** Leaper **79 Margaret** *Elianor* [also at lines 100 and 120] **113 losing** loosing **116 witch** watch **278 s.p. Commons** [not in F] **308 enemies** [Q] enemy **310 Could** [Q] Would **318 My** [Q] Mine **on** on **332 turn** turnes **391 breathe** breath
3.3. 8 s.p Cardinal [Q] *Beau.* **10 whe'er** where
4.1. 6 Clip Cleape **7 Breathe** Breath **48 Jove . . . I** [Q; not in F] **50 s.p. Suffolk** [Q; at line 51 in F] **70 Lieutenant. Yes, Pole. Suffolk. Pole?** [Q; not in F] **77 shalt** [Q] shall **85 mother's bleeding** Mother-bleeding **93 are** and **115–116 Lieutenant. Walter— / Whitmore** *Lieu.* Water: W. **117 Paene** Pine **119 s.p. Whitmore** *Wal.* [also at line 143] **133 s.p. Suffolk** [at line 134 in F] **142 s.d. Exeunt** *Exit*
4.2. 33 s.p. [and elsewhere] **Dick** [Q] *But.* [or "*Butch.*"] **34 fall** faile **46 s.p.** [and elsewhere] **Smith** *Weauer* [or "*Wea.*"] **99 an** a **131 this:** this **176 s.d. Exeunt** *Exit*
4.4. 19 have huae **27 s.p. First Messenger** *Mes.* **49 s.p. Second Messenger** *Mess.* **58 you be** you
4.5. s.d. enter enters
4.6. 9 s.p. Smith *But.* **13 Zounds** [Q] Come
4.7. 7 s.p. Holland *Iohn* [also at line 15] **44 on** [Q] in **63 lose** loose **66 hands** hands' **67 But Kent you?** you, **79 s.p. Bevis** *Geo.* **86 caudle** Candle **132 s.d. Exeunt** Exit
4.8. 12 rebel rabble
4.9. 0 s.d. terrace *Tarras* **33 calmed** calme
4.10. 6 o'er on **20 waning** warning **24 Zounds** [Q; not in F] **28 I'll** He **46 fare** farre **57 God** loue
5.1. 109 these thee **111 sons** [Q] sonne **113 for** of **149 bearherd** Berard [also at line 210] **194 or** and **195 s.p. Clifford** *Old Clif.* [and at lines 198 and 208] **201 household** [Q] housed **207 to** [Q] io
5.2. 8 [F repeats s.p. "*War.*"] **28 oeuvres** *eumenes* **31 s.p. Young Clifford** *Clif.* [also at line 84] **46 lose** loose
5.3. 29 faith [Q] hand

3 Henry VI

Copy text: the First Folio. Act and scene divisions, missing in F except for "Actus Primus. Scoena Prima" at 1.1.0, are editorially provided.
1.1. **2 s.p. York** *Pl.* [and elsewhere referred to in the s.p. as *Plan.* and *Plant.* as well as *Yorke*]   **6–7 himself, . . . abreast,** himselfe. . . . a-brest   **19 hap** hope   **21 I. Victorious . . . York,** I, victorious . . . *Yorke.*   **43 lords. Be** Lords be   **69 s.p. Exeter** [O] *Westm.*   **105 Thy** [O] My   **120 s.p. Northumberland** [O] *Henry*   **259 with me** [O] me   **261 from** [O] to   **273 s.d. Flourish** [at beginning of 1.2 in F]   **Exeunt** *Exit*
1.2. **47 s.d. a Messenger** [O] *Gabriel*   **49 s.p. Messenger** [O] *Gabriel*   **75 s.d. Exeunt** *Exit*
1.4. **180 s.d. Exeunt** [O] *Exit*
2.1. **94 s.d. Montague** *Mountacute*   **113 And . . . thought** [O; not in F]   **124 spleen,** Spleene.   **131 an idle** [O] a lazie   **144 his** [O] the
2.2. **89 Since** *Cla.*   **130 puts** put's   **133 s.p. Richard** [O] *War.*   **163 s.p.** [and elsewhere until 3.2] **George** [O] *Cla.*
2.5. **54 s.d.** [followed in F by "*and a Father that hath kill'd his Sonne at another doore*"]   **78 s.d.** [F reads: "*Enter Father, bearing of his Sonne*"]   **89 stratagems** Stragems   **119 E'en** Men   **139 Whither** Whether [also at 2.6.9]
2.6. **6 fall, thy** fall. Thy   **commixture** [O] Commixtures   **8 The common . . . flies** [O; not in F]   **19 Had** [O] Hed   **60 his** [O] is
3.1.s.d. two Keepers [O] *Sinklo, and Humfrey* [and throughout scene, in s.p.]   **7 scare** scarre   **12 s.p. Second Keeper** *Sink.*   **17 wast** was   **24 thee, sour adversity** the sower Aduersaries   **30 Is** I: **55 thou that** [O] thou
3.2. **1 s.p.** [and elsewhere] **King Edward** *King*   **8 s.p.** [and throughout] **Gloucester** *Rich.*   **18 s.p.** [and throughout] **Lady Grey** *Wid.*   **28 whip me, then** [O] then whip me   **123 honorably** [O] honourable   **175 rends** rents
3.3. **11 state** Seat   **78 s.p. Prince** *Edw.*   **124 eternal** [O] externall   **161 s.d.** [after line 160 in F]   **228 I'll** [O] I
4.1. **67 s.p. Queen Elizabeth** [O: *Queen*] *Lady Grey*   **93 thy** [O] the
4.2. **15 towns** Towne
4.3. **27 s.d. Hastings fly** *Hastings flyes*   **64 s.d. Exeunt** *Exit*
4.4. **2 s.p.** [and throughout scene] **Queen Elizabeth** [O: *Queen*] *Gray*   **4 What? Loss** What losse   **17 wean** waine
4.5. **4 stands** stand   **8 Comes** Come
4.6. **55 goods be** Goods   **88 s.d. Manent** *Manet*
4.8. **0 s.d. Exeter** Somerset   **50 s.d. A Lancaster! A York!** *A Lancaster, A Lancaster*
5.1. **78 an** in
5.3. **22–23 augmented . . . along.** augmented: . . . along,
5.4. **27 ragged** raged   **46 Lest** Least
5.5. **38 thou** the   **50 The Tower** [O] Tower   **77 butcher** [O] butcher *Richard*   **90 s.d. Exeunt** [O] *Exit*
5.6. **7 reckless** wreaklesse   **43 wast** was't   **84 keep'st** keept'st
5.7. **5 renowned** [O] Renowne   **25 thou shalt** [O] that shalt   **30 s.p. Queen Elizabeth** [O] *Cla.*   **Thanks** [O] Thanke   **38 Reignier** *Reynard*

Richard III

Copy text: the First Folio, except for two passages, 3.1.1–158 and 5.3.48 to end of play, for which Q1 is copy text. Unless otherwise indicated, the adopted readings are from the First Quarto of 1597 [Q1]. Act and scene divisions are marked in the copy text except as indicated below.
1.1. **1 s.p. Richard** [not in F]   **41 s.d. Enter . . . Brackenbury** [eds.] *Enter Clarence, and Brackenbury, guarded*   **45 the** th'   **52 for** but   **65 tempers him to this** tempts him to this harsh   **75 to her for his** for her   **88 An 't** and   **103 I** I do   **124 the** this   **133 prey** play
1.2. **27 life** [eds.] death   **38 s.p. Halberdier** [eds.] *Gen.*   **39 stand** Stand'st   **78 of a** of   **80 t' accuse** [eds.] to curse   **94 hand** hands   **141 thee** the   **171 words** word   **204 s.p. Richard** [not in F]   **205** [not in F]   **227 s.d. Exeunt** [eds.] *Exit* [also at line 229]   **228 Richard Sirs . . . corpse** [not in F]   **229 s.d. Exeunt** *Exit*

1.3. **17 come** comes   **lords** Lord   **19 s.p.** [and elsewhere] **Stanley** *Der.*   **54 whom** who   **63 of** on   **69** [not in F]   **109 s.d.** [after line 110 in F]   **114** [not in F]   **155 Ah, little** A little   **160 of** off   **309 s.p. Queen Elizabeth** *Mar.*   **342 s.p. First Murderer** *Vil.* [also at lines 350 and 355]   **351 doers. Be** assured dooers, be assur'd:
1.4. **9 Methought** [Q4] Me thoughts [also in line 24]   **13 Thence** There   **22 waters** water   **22, 23 my** mine   **25 Ten** A   **39 seek** find   **41 Which** Who   **64 my lord** Lord   **86 s.p. First Murderer** [eds.] 2. *Mur.*   **89 s.p. Second Murderer** [eds.] 1.   **99 s.d. Exit** [at line 97 in F]   **100 I** we   **122 Faith** [not in F]   **126 Zounds** come   **147 Zounds** [not in F]   **152 Tut** [not in F]   **192 to have redemption** for any goodnesse   **193** [not in F]   **240** [not in F]   **242 of** on   **269** [in F, printed after line 263]   **272 s.d. Stabs him** [after line 272 in F]
2.1. **s.d. Buckingham** [eds.] *Buckingham, Wooduill*   **5 in** to   **7 Rivers and Hastings** *Dorset* and *Riuers*   **39 God** heauen   **57 unwittingly** vnwillingly   **59 By** To   **68** [F follows with a line: "*Of you Lord Wooduill, and Lord Scales of you*"]   **93 but** and   **108 at** and
2.2. **1 s.p. Boy** *Edw.*   **3 s.p.** [and throughout scene] **Girl** [eds.] *Daugh.*   **3 do you** do   **26 his** a   **47 have I** haue   **83 weep** weepes   **84–85 Clarence . . . they** *Clarence* weep, so do not they   **87 Pour** Power   **142 Ludlow** London [also at line 154]   **145** [not in F]   **145 s.d. Manent** [eds.] *Manet*
2.3. **44 Ensuing** Pursuing [but the catchword on page 184 in F is "Ensuing"]
2.4. **1 hear** heard   **9 young** good   **21 s.p. Archbishop** *Car.* [Q1] *Yor.* [F]   **65 death** earth
3.1. **1–158** [based on Q1 as copy text]   **2 s.p.** [and elsewhere] **Richard** *Glo.*   **60** [bracketed s.d. from F]   **111 With all** withall [Q]   **150 s.d.** [A sennet] [from F]   **Hastings** *Hast. Dors.*   **Manent** [F2] manet
3.2. **20 councils** Councell   **78 as you do** as
3.3. **1** [not in F]
3.4. **9 methinks** we thinke   **58** [not in F]   **79 s.d. Exeunt** [after line 78 in F]   **Manent** *manet*   **82 raze** rowse
3.5. **4 wert** were   **20 innocence** Innocencie   **34 Look . . . Mayor** [not in F; after line 26 in Q1]   **66 cause** case   **74 meet'st advantage** meetest vantage   **104 Penker** [eds.] *Peuker*   **105 s.d. Exeunt** [eds.] *Exit Exeunt*   **109 s.d. Exit** *Exeunt*
3.6. **12 who's** who
3.7. **7 insatiate** vnsatiate   **20 mine** my   **33 spake** spoke   **40 wisdoms** wisdome   **43** [not in F]   **44 s.p. Richard** [not in F]   **54 we'll** we   **83 My lord** [not in F]   **125 her** his [also in lines 126 and 127]   **219 Zounds! I'll** we will   **220** [not in F]   **224 stone** Stones   **240 Richard** King *Richard*   **241 s.p. Mayor and Citizens** *All*   **247 cousin** Cousins
4.1. **s.d.** [F: *Enter the Queene, Anne Duchesse of Gloucester, the Duchesse of Yorke, and Marquesse Dorset*]   **15 s.p. Brackenbury** *Lieu.* [and at lines 18 and 26]
4.2. **36 My Lord** [not in F]   **72 there** then   **87 to** vnto   **90 Hereford** Hertford   **98–118 perhaps . . . today** [not in F]
4.3. **0** [scene division not in F]   **4 whom** who   **5 ruthless** ruthfull   **13 Which** And   **15 once** one   **20 gone; with . . . remorse** gone with . . . Remorse,   **31 at** and   **33 thee** the   **40 Breton** Britaine   **53 leads** leds
4.4. **0** [*Scena Tertia* in F]   **10 unblown** vnblowed   **39** [not in F]   **o'er** over [Q1]   **41 Harry** [eds.] Husband   **45 holp'st** hop'st   **52–53** [lines reversed in F]   **64 Thy** The   **112 weary** wearied   **118 nights . . . days** night . . . day   **128 intestate** intestine   **141 Where** Where't   **225 lanced** [eds.] lanch'd   **239 or** and   **268 would I** I would   **284 This is** this   **324 Of ten** [eds.] Often   **364–365** [lines reversed in F, and the s.p. *Queen Elizabeth* is missing]   **366 s.p. King Richard** [not in F]   **377 God** Heauen   **God's** Heauens   **392 in** with   **396 o'erpast** repast   **417 fond** found   **430 s.d. Exit Queen** [at line 429 in F]   **431 s.d. Enter Ratcliffe** [at line 432 in F]   **444 Ratcliffe** [eds.] *Catesby*   **459 Heyday** Hoyday   **498 s.p. First Messenger** *Mess.*   **503 s.p. Second Messenger** *Mess.*   **506 s.p. Third Messenger** *Mess.* [also at lines 509 and 517]   **518 s.p. Fourth Messenger** *Mess.*   **534 tidings** Newes, but
4.5. **0** [*Scena Quarta in F*]
5.1. **11 is, my lord** is
5.2. **11 center** Centry   **12 Near** Ne're   **17 swords** men

5.3. 0 [scene not marked in F]   **20 track** Tract   **28 you** [eds.] your   **48 ff.** [to the end of the play] [copy text is Q1]   **54 sentinels** [F] centinell [Q1]   **59 s.p. Catesby** [eds.] *Rat.*   **79 sit** [F] set [Q1; also at line 131]   **85 that. The** that the [Q1]   **100 sundered** sundried [Q1]   **107 s.d.** [**Richmond remains**] [substantially from F]   **139 s.p. Ghost of Rivers** *King* [Q1]   **141 s.p. Ghost of Grey** *Gray* [Q1]   **142 s.p. Ghost of Vaughan** *Vaugh.*   **145 Will** Wel [Q1]   **145 s.d.–150** [after line 158 in Q1]   **151 s.p. Ghosts** [F] *Ghost* [Q1]   **159 s.p. Ghost** [not in Q1]   **167 s.p. Ghost** [not in Q1]   **176 fall** [F] fals [Q1]   **183 am** and [Q1]   **209 My** Ratcliffe, my   **223 s.p. Lords** *Lo.* [Q1]   **226, 235 s.p. A Lord** *Lo.* [Q1]   **243 Richard except,** Richard, except   **270 s.d. Ratcliffe** *Rat. & c.*   **299 main** [F] matne [Q1]   **301 boot** bootes [Q1]   **304 s.p. King Richard** [at line 306 ("*King*") in Q1]   **324 Brittany** Brittaine   **351 them! Victory** them victorie [Q1]
5.5. 13 s.p. Stanley [not in Q1]   **13 Ferrers** *Ferri* [Q1]   **15 becomes** become [Q1]   **41 s.d. Exeunt** [F; not in Q1]

King John

Copy text: the First Folio. Act and scene markings are in F except as indicated below.
1.1. 30 s.d. Exeunt *Exit*   **49 s.d.** [after line 49 in F]   **50 s.p.** [and elsewhere] **Bastard** *Philip*   **75 whe'er** where [also at 2.1.167]   **79 yourself.** your selfe   **147 I** It   **188 'Tis too** 'Tis two   **189 conversion. Now** conuersion, now   **208 smack** smoake   **219 s.d.** [after line 221 in F]   **237 he get get** me! Sir me sir   **257 Thou** That
2.1. 0 [here F reads "*Scaena Secunda*"]   **1 s.p. King Philip** *Lewis* [also at line 18]   **37 work. Our** worke our   **63 Ate** Ace   **75 s.d. Drum beats** [after line 77 in F]   **89 s.p.** [and elsewhere] **King Philip** *Fran.*   **106 Geoffrey's.** In *Geffreyes* in   **113 breast** beast   **120 s.p.** [and elsewhere] **Eleanor** *Queen*   **127 John in manners—** *Iohn,* in manners   **144 shows** shooes   **149 Philip** *Lewis*   **150 s.p. King Philip** *Lew.*   **152 Anjou** *Angiers*   **166 s.p. Eleanor** *Qu. Mo.*   **187 plague; her sin** plague her sinne: **200 s.d. citizens** *a Citizen*   **215 Confronts your** Comfort yours   **232 in, your** in. Your   **252 invulnerable** involuerable   **259 roundure** rounder   **325 s.d.** [and throughout remainder of scene] **Citizen** *Hubert* (or *Hub.*)   **335 run** rome   **362 Who's** whose [also at 5.6.1]   **368 s.p. Hubert** *Fra.*   **371 Kinged** Kings   **463 cannon: fire** Cannon fire,   **469 s.p. Eleanor** *Old Qu.*   **488 Anjou** *Angiers*   **497 s.p.** [and elsewhere] **Lewis** *Dol.*   **534 well. Young** well young   **540 rites** rights   **572 lose** loose
3.1. 0 [here F reads "*Actus Secundus*"]   **74** [following this line, F reads "*Actus Tertius, Scaena prima*"]   **s.d. Austria** *Austria, Constance*   **110 day** daies   **148 task** tast   **155 God** heauen   **185 too. When . . . right,** too, when . . . right.   **196 it** that   **259 chafèd** cased   **283 oath. The** oath the   **317 s.p.** [and elsewhere] **Lewis** *Dolph.*   **323 s.p. King John** *Eng.*
3.2. 0. [F reads "*Scaena Secunda*"]   **4 s.d. Enter . . . Hubert** [after line 3 in F]   **10 s.d. Exeunt** *Exit*
3.3. 0 [scene not marked in F]
3.4. 0 [here F reads "*Scaena Tertia*"]   **s.d. Pandulph** *Pandulpho*   **2 armada** Armado   **44 not holy** holy   **64 friends** fiends   **110 world's** words   **182 make** makes
4.1. 6 s.p. First Executioner *Exec.* [also at line 85]   **7 scruples! Fear** scruples feare   **50 lain** lyen   **63 his** this   **80 wince** winch   **91 mote** moth   **120 mercy-lacking** mercy, lacking
4.2. 1 again crowned against crown'd   **42 when** then   **60–62 exercise. . . . occasions, let** exercise, . . . occasions: let   **73 Doth Do** 105 **s.d. Enter Messenger** [at line 103 in F]   **143 traveled** trauail'd   **247 blood and breath,** blood, and breathe   **261 haste** hast [also at line 269]
4.3. 33 man mans   **142–143 up! . . . royalty,** vp, . . . Royaltie!   **155 cincture** center   **159 s.d. Exeunt** *Exit*
5.1. 0 [here F reads "*Actus Quartus, Scaena prima*"]
5.2. 16 metal mettle   **26 Were** Was   **36 grapple** cripple   **43 hast thou** hast   **63 s.d. Pandulph** *Pandulpho*   **153 unhaired** vn-heard   **135 these** this   **145 his** this
5.3. 8 [and elsewhere] **Swinestead** *Swinsted*
5.4. 27 lose loose
5.5. 7 wound woon'd

5.6. 13 eyeless endles
5.7. 17 mind winde   **21 cygnet** Symet   **60 God** heauen   **108 give you** giue

Richard II

Copy text: the First Quarto of 1597 as press-corrected in all four extant copies [Q1]; and, for the deposition scene, 4.1.155–321, the First Folio. Act and scene divisions, absent in Q1, are from F except that F provides no scene marking at 5.4 and labels 5.5 and 5.6 as "*Scaena Quarta*" and "*Scaena Quinta*" respectively.
1.1. 15 presence. Face presence face   **118 by my** [F] by   **139 But** Ah but   **152 gentlemen** [F] gentleman   **162–163 Harry, when? / Obedience bids** Harry? when obedience bids. / Obedience bids   **176 gage. My** gage, my   **178 reputation; that** Reputation that   **192 parle** parlee   **205 s.d. Exeunt** *Exit*
1.2. 25 him. Thou him, thou   **42 alas** [not in Q1]   **47 sit** [F] set   **48 butcher** [Qb, F] butchers [Qa]   **58 it** [Q2–5, F] is   **59 empty** [Qb, F] emptines, [Qa]   **60 begun** begone   **70 hear** [F] cheere
1.3. 15 thee the   **33 comest** [Q5] comes   **58 thee** the   **104 s.p. First Herald** Herald   **108 his God** [F] God   **128 civil** [Qb, F] cruel [Qa]   **133 Draws** [Qb] Draw [Qa]   **136 wrathful iron** [Qb, F] harsh resounding [Qa]   **172 then but** [F] but   **180 you owe** [F] y'owe   **193 far** fare   **222 night** [Q4–5, F] nightes   **239 had it** had't   **241 sought** ought   **269 world** world:
1.4. 8 Bagot [F] *Bushie*   **20 our cousin,** [F] our Coosens   **23 Bagot here, and Green** [Q6; not in Q1]   **27 What** [Qb, F] With [Qa]   **47 hand. If** hand if   **52 s.d. Enter Bushy** [F] *Enter Bushie with newes*   **53 Bushy, what news** [F; not in Q1]   **65 s.p. All** [not in Q1]
2.1. 15 life's liues   **18 fond** found   **48 as a** [Q4–5, F] as   **68 s.d.** [after line 70 in Q1]   **70 reined** ragde   **102 encagèd** [F] inraged   **113 not** not, not   **124 brother** brothers   **156 kerns** [Qb, F] kerne   **161 coin** [Qb, F] coines [Qa]   **168 my** [Qb, F] mine   **177 the** [F] a   **209 seize** cease   **257 King's** [Q3–5, F] King   **277 Blanc** Blan   **278 Brittany** Brittaine   **284 Coint** Coines
2.2. 19 Show [Q6, F] Shows [Qa]   **31 though** [Q2–5, F] thought   **53 Harry** H.   **81 lose** loose
2.3. 30 lordship *Lo:*   **36 Hereford** [Q3–5, F] Herefords   **99 the lord** [F] Lord
2.4. 1 s.p. Welsh Captain *Welsh* (also at line 7)
3.2. 32 succor succors   **40 boldly** bouldy   **72 O'erthrows** [F] Ouerthrowes   **86 name! A** name a   **170 through** [Q2–5, F] thorough
3.3. 13 brief with you [F] briefe   **31 lord** [F] Lords   **59 rain** raigne.   **60 waters—on** water's on   **100 pastures'** pastors   **119 a prince and** princesse   **127 ourself** our selues
3.4. 11 joy griefe   **26 pins** [F] pines   **27 state, for** state for   **28 change; woe** change woe   **34 too** [F] two   **55 seized** ceasde   **57 We at** at   **80 Cam'st** [Q2–5, F] Canst
4.1. 23 him [Q3–5, F] them   **44 Fitzwater** [F] Fitzwaters   **55 As** As it   **56 sun to sun** sinne to sinne   **63 true. You** true you   **77 my bond** [Q3–5, F] bond   **110 thee** [Q2–5, F] the   **146 you** yon   **155–321** [This deposition scene is based on the First Folio text; Q1 has only: "Let it be so, and loe on wednesday next, / We solemnly proclaime our Coronation, / Lords be ready all." Unless otherwise indicated all the departures in F from lines 155–321 are taken from Q4.]   **184 and on** on   **252 and a** a   **256 Nor** No, nor   **297 manners** manner
5.1. 41 thee [Q2–5, F] the   **84 s.p. Northumberland** [F] *King*
5.2. 2 off [F] of   **11 thee** [F] the [also at lines 17 and 94]   **78 my troth** by my troth   **116 And** An
5.3. s.d. King *the King*   **10 While** Which   **31 the** my   **36 I may** [Q2–5, F] May   **68 And** An   **75 shrill-voiced** shril voice   **111 s.p. King Henry** *yorke*   **135–136 With . . . him** I pardon him with al my heart
5.4. s.d. Enter [F] *Manet*   **Exton, etc.** Exton, etc.
5.5. 20 through [F] thorow   **22 cannot, die** cannot die   **27 sit** [Q3–5, F] set   **33 treason makes** treasons make   **55 sounds that tell** sound that tells   **56 that** which   **58 hours, and times** times, and houres   **94 Spur-galled** Spurrde, galld

5.6. 8 Salisbury, Spencer [F] Oxford, Salisbury   **12 s.d. Fitzwater** *Fitzwaters*   **43 through the** [F] through

1 Henry IV

Copy text: the first complete Quarto of 1598 [Q1]; and, for 1.3.201 through 2.2.110, the fragment of an earlier Quarto (Q0). The act and scene divisions, missing in Q0 and Q1, are based on F except that F provides no break at 5.3.

1.1. 22 levy leauy   **39 Herdfordshire** Herdforshire   **62 a dear** deere   **69 blood, did** bloud. Did   **70 plains. Of** plains, of   **76 In faith, it is** [assigned in Q1 to King]
1.2. 16 king a king   **33 proof, now:** proofe. Now   **78 similes** smiles   **154 thou** the   **158 Peto, Bardolph** Haruey, Rossill
1.3. 194 good night god-night   **201 s.p. Hotspur** [missing in Q0–Q4]   **238 whipped** [Q1] whip [Q0]
2.1. 34 s.p. First Carrier *Car.*   **48 s.d.** [at line 47 in Q0]   **56 Weald** wild
2.2. s.d. Poins, Peto *Poines, and Peto &c*   **12 square** squire   **20 Bardolph** Bardol [and thus, or "Bardoll," throughout the play]   **34 mine** [Q1] my [Q0]   **42 Go hang** [F] Hang [Q0]   **51 s.p. and text BARDOLPH What news** [all assigned as continuation of Poins's speech in line 50]   **52 s.p. Gadshill** *Bar.*   **78 s.p. First Traveler** *Trauel.*   **82 s.p. Travelers** *Trauel.*   **86 s.p. Travelers** *Tra.*
2.3. 1 s.p. Hotspur [not in Q1]   **4 in the** the   **48 thee** the   **69 A roan** Roane
2.4. 33 precedent present   **36 s.p. Poins** *Prin.*   **171 s.p. Prince** *Gad*   **172 s.p. Gadshill** *Ross.* [also at lines 174 and 178]   **226 keech** catch   **242 eel-skin** ellskin   **322 s.d.** [after line 321 in Q1]   **337 Owen** O   **390 tristful** trustfull   **398 yet** so   **468 lean** lane   **518 Good** God [also at line 519]   **526 s.d. pockets** *pocket*   **530 s.p. Peto** [not in Q1]   **535 s.p. Prince** [not in Q1]
3.1. 55 coz coose [also at line 75]   **97 cantle** scantle   **126 meter** miter   **129 on** an   **261 hot Lord** Hot. Lord
3.2. 59 won wan   **84 gorged** gordge   **96 then** than   **145 northern** Northren   **161 s.d.** [after line 162 in Q1]
3.3. 35 that's that   **57 tithe** tight   **119 no thing** nothing   **135 owed** ought   **173 guests** ghesse   **200 o'clock** of clocke
4.1. 1 s.p. [and elsewhere] Hotspur *Per.*   **20 lord** mind   **55 is** tis   **96 doffed** daft   **105 cuisses** cushes   **108 dropped** drop   **116 altar** altars   **123 ne'er** neare   **126 cannot** can   **127 yet** it   **134 merrily** merely
4.2. 3 Coldfield cophill   **15 yeomen's** Yeomans   **31 feazed** fazd   **33–34 tattered** tottered   **80 s.d. Exit** *Exeunt*
4.3. 23 horse horses   **74 heirs . . . followed** heires, as Pages followed   **84 country's** Countrey
4.4. 0. s.d. Michael *Mighell* [and throughout]   **18 o'erruled** ouerrulde   **36 not, ere** not ere   **37 power he** power, he
5.1. s.d. Lancaster *Lancaster, Earle of Westmerland*   **2 bosky** bulky   **3 southern** Southren   **88 off** of   **114 s.d. Exeunt** *Exit*   **138 will it** wil
5.2. 3 undone vnder one   **8 Suspicion** Supposition   **12 merrily** merely   **25 s.d. Hotspur** Percy   **79 s.p. First Messenger** *Mes.*   **89 s.p. Second Messenger** *Mes.*   **94–95 withal / . . . day.** withall. / . . . day,
5.3. 1 in the in   **22 A** Ah   **35–36 ragamuffins** rag of Muffins
5.4. 4 s.p. [and elsewhere] Lancaster *P. Iohn*   **68 Nor** Now   **76 s.d. who** he   **92 enough. This** inough, this   **thee** the
5.5. 36 bend you bend, you

2 Henry IV

Copy text: the Quarto of 1600, of which 2.4.340 through 3.2.104 exists in two states: the original printing by Valentine Sims [Qa], and a second version with six reset pages [Qb] that had been expanded to include 3.1, inadvertently omitted from Qa. Qa is the copy text for those portions that were reset, Qb for 3.1 itself. In addition, the First Folio is copy text for certain passages excised from Q, as indicated

below. The act and scene divisions, missing in Q, are based on F, except that F labels 1.1 as "Scena Secunda," and so throughout Act I; omits scene markings at 4.2, 4.3, and 4.5; and labels 4.4 as "Scena Secunda."
The Actors' Names [taken from F, at the end of the play]
Induction.1. s.p. Rumor [not in Q]   **35 hold** hole   **36 Where** [F] When   **40 s.d. Rumor** *Rumours*
1.1. 7 s.d. [and elsewhere] Northumberland *Earle*   **27 s.d.** [at line 25 in Q]   **41 ill** [F] bad   **96 slain, say so** [F] slaine   **126 Too** [F] So   **161 s.p. Lord Bardolph** *Vmfr.*   **162** [assigned to *Bard.* in Q and Q0]   **164 Lean on your** [F] Leaue on you   **o'er** ore,   **165 passion,** passion   **166–179; 189–209** [F; not in Q]   **178 brought** bring [F]   **183 ventured, for . . . proposed** venturd for . . . proposde,   **201–202 religion,** Religion, . . . Thoughts:
1.2. 1 s.p. [and elsewhere] Falstaff *Iohn* [or *sir Iohn*]   **8 tends** [F] intends   **22 one of** [F] one off   **31 s.p. [and elsewhere] Page** *Boy*   **36 rascally** [F] rascall: **48 Where's Bardolph** [F; in Q, follows "through it" in line 47]   **49 into** [F] in   **86 me so?** me, so   **87 me? If** me, if   **96 age** [F] an ague   **119 s.p. Falstaff** [F] *Old.*   **142 slenderer** [F] slender   **159 on** [F] in   **168–169 bearward Berod** [F] the one   **171 this** [F] his   **171–172 them, are** [F] the one   **177 s.p. [and elsewhere] Chief Justice** *Lo.*   **192 him! For** him for   **ear** yeere   **201–202 you and Prince Harry** [F] you
1.3. s.d. Hastings *Hastings, Fauconbridge*   **1 s.p. [and elsewhere] Archbishop** *Bishop*   **5 s.p. Mowbray** *Marsh.*   **21–24, 36–55, 85–108** [F; not in Q]   **26 case** [F] cause   **28 on** [F] and   **29 with** [F] in   **58 one** [F] on   **59 through** [F] thorough   **66 a** [F] so   **71 Are** [F] And   **78 not** [F] not to   **79 To French** French   **84 'gainst** [F] against   **109 s.p. Mowbray** [F] *Bish.*
2.1. 0. s.d. two officers [F] *an Officer or two*   **2 vice** [F] view   **25 continuantly** [F] continually   **43 Sir John, I** [F] I   **71–72 all, all** [F] al   **78 Fie, what** [F] what   **102 mad** [F] made   **117 done** [F] done with   **143 German** Iarman   **145 tapestries** [F] tapestrie   **163 s.d. Exeunt** *exit* [after line 160 in Q]   **167, 171 s.p. Gower** *Mess.*   **167 Basingstoke** [F] Billingsgate
2.2. s.d. Poins *Poynes, sir Iohn Russel, with other*   **15 viz.** [F] with   **16 ones** [F] once   **22 made a shift to eat** [F] eate   **75 e'en now** enow   **81 rabbit** [F] rabble   **90 him be** [F] him   **109 conceive. The** conceiue the   **110 borrower's** borrowed   **118 Sure he** [F] He sure   **119 s.p. Prince [reads]** [not in Q or F]   **126 familiars** family   **149 heifers** Heicfors   **165 declension** descension   **166 prince** pince
2.3. 5 s.p. [and elsewhere] Lady Northumberland *Wife*   **9 s.p. [and elsewhere] Lady Percy** *Kate*   **11 endeared** [F] endeere   **23–45 He . . . grave** [F; not in Q]
2.4. 0. s.d. Drawer *Drawer or two*   **4 s.p. Second Drawer** *Draw.*   **12 s.d.** [at line 18 in Q]   **13 s.p. Third Drawer** *Dra.* [also at line 19]   **21 s.p. Second Drawer** [F] *Francis*   **22 s.p. [and elsewhere] Hostess** *Quickly*   **30 s.p. [and elsewhere] Doll** *Tere.*   **42–43 them; I** [F] I   **49 know; to** know to   **62 s.p. Doll** *Dorothy*   **82 Your** & your   **105 s.p. Doll** *Teresh.*   **107 s.d. Boy** *Bardolfes boy*   **173 Die men** [F] Men   **189 Quoit** Quaite   **196 Untwine** vntwinde   **215 Ah, rogue** a rogue   **219 A rascally** Ah rascally   **252 the scales** [F] scales   **253 avoirdupois** haber de poiz   **257 poll** poule   **265 master's** [F] master   **275 It** [F] a   **278 so** [F] to   **294 light flesh** light, flesh   **300 even now** [F] now   **313 Not? To** Not to   **340–389** [copy text for this passage is Qa]   **381 s.d. Exit** [Qb; not in Qa]
3.1 [this scene appears in Qb, not in Qa]   **18 mast** [F] masse   **22 billows** [F] pillowes   **26 thy** [F] them   **27 sea-boy** [F] season   **36 letters** letter   **59 years** [F] yeare   **81 nature of** [F] natures or   **85 beginnings** [F] beginning   **87 of** [F] or
3.2. 1–104 [copy text for this passage is Qa]   **23 bona-robas** [F] bona robes   **39 Stamford** Samforth   **45 fine** [Qb, F] fiue   **56 s.p. Shallow** [F] Bardolfe [Qa uncorr.; not in Qa corr. or Qb]   **67–68 accommodated** [F] accommodate   **82 s.p. Shallow** *Iust.* [Qa]   **87 Surecard** [F] Soccard   **111** [Q prints as s.d.: "Iohn prickes him"]   **144 for his** [F] pricke   **175 prick me** [F] pricke   **195–196 good . . . that** [F] master shallow   **209 Clement's Inn** [F] Clemham   **229–230 old dame's** [F] dames   **250 Shadow** Sadow   **271 traverse** trauers   **272 Thus, thus, thus** thas, thas, thas   **287 will** wooll   **298 s.d. Exeunt** *exit*   **299–331 On . . . end** [this speech assigned in Q to Shallow]   **312 invisible** inuincible   **genius** gemies   **314 ever** [F] ouer   **324 eelskin** [F, Q corr.] eele-shin [Q uncorr.]   **326 be** [F] he

4.1. 1 s.p. [and elsewhere] **Archbishop** Bish.   **9 tenor** tenure   **12 could** [F, Q corr.] would [Q uncorr.]   **30 Then, my lord** [F, Q corr.; not in Q uncorr.]   **34 rags** rage   **36 appeared** appeare   **45 figure** [F, Q corr.] figures [Q uncorr.]   **54 Briefly to this end: we** Briefly, to this end we   **55–79** [F; not in Q]   **93, 95 And . . . edge, To . . . cruelty** [Q uncorr.; not in Q corr. or F]   **103–139 O my . . . King** [F; not in Q]   **116 force** forc'd [F]   **139 indeed** and did [F]   **169–170 grievances. . . . redressed,** grieuances, . . . redrest.   **175 to our** [F] our   **180 And** At   **182 s.d.** [after "Which . . . it" in Q]   **185 not that.** not, that

4.2. s.d. [appears at 4.1.226 in Q]   **8 Than** [F] That   **man** [F] man talking   **19 imagined** imagine   **24 Employ** [F] Imply   **25–26 name, / In deeds dishonorable? you** name: / In deeds dishonorable you   **48 this** [F] his   **67 s.p. Prince John** [not in Q]   **69 s.p. Hastings** [F] Prince   **97 s.d.** [at line 96 in Q]   **117 and such acts as yours** [F; not in Q]   **122 these traitors** [F] this traitour

4.3. s.d. [Q: "Alarum. Enter Falstaffe. excursions"]   **25 s.d. retreat** [at line 23 in Q]   **41 I came** [F] there cosin, I came   **85 had** but had

4.4. s.d. Warwick Warwike, Kent   **32 melting** [F] meeting   **51 s.p.** [and elsewhere] **Clarence** Tho.   **52 Canst thou tell that** [F; not in Q]   **80 s.d. Enter Westmorland** [after line 80 in Q]   **93 s.d.** [after line 93 in Q]   **93 heaven** [F] heauens   **104 write** [F] wit   **letters** [F] termes   **112 s.p.** [and elsewhere] **Gloucester** Hum.   **120 and will break out** [F; not in Q]   **132 Softly, pray** [F; not in Q]

4.5. 1 s.p. King [not in Q]   **13 altered** [F, Q corr.] vttred [Q uncorr.]   **48 s.d.** [after line 47 in Q]   **75 The virtuous sweets** [F; not in Q]   **76 thighs** [F] thigh   **79 s.d.** [at line 81 in Q]   **81 have** hands [Q] hath [F]   **88 s.d.** [at line 87 in Q]   **91 s.p. Prince Harry**   **107 Which** [F] Whom   **148–149 bending. . . . me, when** bending, . . . me. When   **160 worst of** [F] worse then   **161 carat, is** [F] karrat   **177 O my son** [F; not in Q]   **178 it in** [F] in   **204 my** thy   **220 My gracious liege** [F; not in Q]   **226 s.p.** [and elsewhere] **Prince John** Lanc.

5.1. 13 headland hade land   **23 lost the other day** [F] lost   **Hinckley** [F] Hunkly   **56 all my** [F] my   **65 of him** [F] him

5.2. s.d. [Q: "Enter Warwike, duke Humphrey, L. chiefe Iustice, Thomas Clarence, Prince, Iohn Westmerland"]   **13 s.d. Westmorland** [at o.s.d. in Q]   **21 s.p. Gloucester, Clarence** Prin. ambo   **38–39 remission. . . . me,** remission, . . . me.   **44 s.p.** [and elsewhere] **King** Prince   **46 mix** mixt   **63 s.p. Princes** Bro.   **112 justice." You** Iustice you   **127 raze** race   **145 s.d. Exeunt** exit

5.3. 5–6 a goodly . . . a rich goodly . . . rich   **47 thee** the   **66 that. 'A** that a   **70 s.d.** [after line 82 in Q]   **83 s.d.** [after line 82 in Q]   **93 i' thy** ith thy   **103 Cophetua** Couetua   **128 knighthood** [F] Knight   **144 s.d. Exeunt** exit

5.4. s.d. Beadle Sincklo   **4 s.p.** [and throughout scene] **Beadle** Sincklo   **6 lately killed** [F] kild   **7 s.p.** [and throughout scene] **Doll** [F] Whoore   **11 He** [F] I

5.5. 1 s.p. First Groom 1 [and similarly in lines 2 and 3]   **15 s.p. Shallow** [F] Pist.   **17, 19 s.p. Shallow** Pist.   **24 s.p. Falstaff** [F; not in Q]   **71 our** [F] my   **97 me** [F; not in Q]   **97 s.d.** [after line 96 in Q]

Epilogue 23 before [F; not in Q]   **30 died a** [F] died   **32–33 and so . . . queen** [F; placed after line 15 in Q]

Henry V

Copy text: the First Folio. Act and scene divisions are for the most part editorially supplied; F marks "Actus Secundus" at Act 3, "Actus Tertius" at Act 4, "Actus Quartus" at 4.7, and "Actus Quintus" at Act 5.

Prologue. 1 s.p. Chorus [not in F; also in prologues to other acts]

1.2. 38 succedant succedaul   **45 Elbe** Elue [also at line 52]   **82 Ermengard** Ermengare   **90–91 day, / Howbeit** day. / Howbeit,   **115 s.p. Ely** Bish.   **131 blood** Bloods   **163 her** their   **166 s.p. A Lord** Bish. Ely   **197 majesty** Maiesties   **212 End** [Q; not in F]   **237 s.p. First Ambassador** Amb. [also at line 245]   **310 s.d. Flourish** [at the beginning of 2.0 in F]

2.1. 23 mare [Q] name   **28 s.p. Nym** [Q; not in F]   **42, 43 Iceland** Island   **73 thee defy** [Q] defie thee   **80 enough** enough to   **83 you** your   **105–106** [Q; not in F]   **betting** beating [Q]   **116 that's** that

2.2. 29 s.p. Grey Kni.   **87 furnish him** [Q] furnish   **107 a** an   **108 whoop** hoope   **114 All** And   **139 mark the** make thee   **140 sus-**

picion. . . . thee; suspition, . . . thee.   **147 Henry** [Q] Thomas   **148 Masham** [Q] Marsham   **159 Which I** Which   **176 have sought** [Q] sought   **181 s.d. Exeunt** Exit

2.3. 16–17 'a babbled a Table   **24 upward** vp-peer'd   **32 s.p. Hostess** Woman   **48 word** world

2.4. 0 s.d. Brittany Britaine   **1 s.p.** [and elsewhere] **French King** King   **132 Louvre** Louer   **146 s.d. Flourish** [at the beginning of 3.0 in F]

3.0. 6 fanning fayning   **17** [and elsewhere] **Harfleur** Harflew   **35 eke** eech

3.1. 7 conjure commune   **17 noblest** Noblish   **24 men** me   **32 Straining** Straying

3.2. 25 runs wins   **67 s.p.** [and elsewhere in scene] **Fluellen** Welch   **82 s.p.** [and elsewhere in scene] **Jamy** Scot   **87 s.p.** [and elsewhere in scene] **Macmorris** Irish   **102 quite** quit   **112 Chrish** Christ

3.3. 32 heady headly   **35 Defile** Desire   **43** [here F has s.d. "Enter Gouernour"]   **54 all. For** all for

3.4. 2 parles parlas [throughout the play, the French has been somewhat modernized, besides the emendations listed here]   **7 Elle** il   **8 Et les doigts** [assigned to Alice in F]   **9 s.p. Alice** Kat.   **les doigts** e doyt   **10 souviendrai** souemeray   **12 s.p. Katharine** Alice   **13 j'ai** Kath. l'ay   **14 les** le   **16 Nous** [not in F]   **40 pas déjà** y desia   **42 Non** Nome   **46 Sauf** Sans   **51 les** le [also in line 52]

3.5. 11 de du   **26 "Poor"** may Poore   **43 Vaudemont** Vandemont   **45 Foix . . . Boucicault** Loys, Lestrale, Bouciquall   **46 knights** Kings

3.6. 31 her [Q] his   **37 is make** [Q] makes   **111–112 lenity** Leuitie

3.7. 12 pasterns postures   **14 qui a** ches   **59 lief** liue   **65 et** est   **truie** truye leuye

4.0. 16 name nam'd   **20 cripple** creeple   **27 Presenteth** Presented

4.1. 3 Good God   **95 Thomas** Iohn   **158 deaths** [Q] death   **propose** purpose   **227 s.d. Exeunt** Exit [at line 222 in F].   **243 What is What?** is   **adoration** Odoration   **289 reckoning, ere . . . numbers** reckning of . . . numbers: . . .   **307 friends** friend

4.2. 4 eaux ewes   **6 Cieux** Cein   **11 dout** doubt   **47 drooping** drooping   **49 gimmaled** Iymold   **52 all impatient** all, impatient

4.3. 12 [placed after line 14 in F]   **48** [Q; not in F]   **124 'em** vm

4.4. 15 Or for   **36 à cette heure** asture   **37 couper** couppes   **54 l'avez** layt a   **57 remerciments** remercious   **58 j'ai tombé** Ie intombe   **59 très-distingué** tres distinie   **68 Sulvez-vous** Saaue vous

4.5. 2 perdu . . . perdu perdia . . . perdie   **3 Mort de** Mor Dieu   **16 by a** base   **24 s.d. Exeunt** Exit

4.6. 34 mistful mixtfull   **38 s.d. Exeunt** Exit

4.7. 22 e'en in   **69 s.p.** [and elsewhere in this scene] **Montjoy** Her.   **77 the** with   **109 countryman** Countrymen   **114 God** Good   **123 'a live** aliue   **126 'a lived** aliue   **161–162** [and elsewhere] **an't** and

4.8. 77 Boucicault Bouchiquald   **100 Vaudemont** Vandemont   **Lestralles** Lestrale   **104 Keighley** Ketly   **110–111 loss / On . . . other?** losse? / On . . . other,   **113 we** me   **121 in my** [Q] my

5.0. 29 but by

5.1. 39 By Jesu [Q] I say   **69 begun** began   **88 swear** swore

5.2. 1 s.p. [and throughout scene] **King Henry** King   **12 s.p.** [and throughout scene] **Queen Isabel** Quee.   **12 England** Ireland   **21 s.p.** [also elsewhere] **King Henry** Eng.   **45 fumitory** Femetary   **50 all** withall   **61 diffused** defus'd   **77 cursitory** curselarie   **93 Haply** Happily   **98 s.d. Manent** Manet   **114 s.p.** [and elsewhere] **Alice** Lady   **190 meilleur** melieus   **264 les** le   **265 baiser** buisse   **267 entend** entendre   **323 hath never** hath   **332 then in** in   **364 paction** Pation

Epilogue s.p. Chorus [not in F]

Henry VIII

Copy text: the First Folio. Act and scene divisions are marked in the Folio except as indicated below.

1.1. 42–45 All . . . function [assigned in F to Buckingham]   **47 as you guess** [assigned in F to Norfolk]   **63 web, 'a** Web. O   **64 way—** way   **69–70 that? . . . hell, the** that, . . . Hell? The   **79 council out,** Councell, out   **115 s.p.** [and elsewhere] **Wolsey** Car.   **120 venom** venom'd   **200 Hereford** Hertford   **219 Perk** Pecke   **chancellor** Councellour   **221 Nicholas** Michaell   **226 lord** Lords

1.2. 8 s.d. [F: *A noyse within crying roome for the Queene, vsher'd by the Duke of Norfolke. Enter the Queene, Norfolke and Suffolke: she kneels.*] [etc.]   **9 s.p.** [**and elsewhere**] **Katharine** *Queen*   **36 to** too   **67 business** *basenesse*   **156 feared** feare   **164 confession's** Commissions   **170 To gain** To   **180 To** For this to   **190 Bulmer** *Blumer*
1.3. s.d. Sands *Sandys* [elsewhere both *Sands* and *Sandys*]   **13 Or** A   **15 s.d.** [after "*Lovell*" in line 16 in F]   **34 oui** wee   **59 wherewithal: in him** wherewithall in him;   **66** [**and at 1.4. s.d. and elsewhere**] **Guildford** *Guilford*
1.4. 50 s.d. [after line 49 in F]   **68–69 assembly . . . here, they** assembly, heere they
2.1. 18 have him   **20 Perk** *Pecke*   **41 attainder** Attendure   **86 mark** make
2.2. 1 s.p. Chamberlain [not in F]   **104 commanding, you** commanding. You
2.3. 61 of you of you, to you   **81 s.d.** [after line 80 in F]
2.4. 7 come into the court & c [also in line 10]   **11 s.p. Katharine** [not in F]   **125 s.p. Griffith** *Gent. Ush.*   **131 s.d. Exeunt** *Exit*   **172 A** And   **217 summons. Unsolicited** Summons vnsolicited.   **237 return. With my approach,** returne, with my approch:
3.1. 3 s.p. Gentlewoman [not in F]   **23 s.d. Campeius** *Campian*   **61 your** our   **83 profit. Can** profit can   **119 he's** ha's
3.2. 143 glad gald   **172 filed** fill'd   **234 commission, lords?** Commission? Lords,   **293 Who** Whom   **344 Chattels** Castles
4.1. 20 s.p. Second Gentleman 1   **34 Kimbolton** Kymmalton   **55 s.p. First Gentleman** [not in F]   **101 Stokesley** *Stokeley*
4.2. 7 think thanke
5.1. 37 time Lime   **42 you, I think—I** you) I thinke I   **55 s.d. Exeunt** *Exit* [after line 54 in F]   **78 s.d. Enter . . . Denny** [after line 79 in F]   **139 precipice** Precepit   **140 woo** woe   **157 s.p. Lovell** *Gent.*
5.2. 4 s.d. Enter Keeper [after "*Sure you know me?*" in F]   **8 piece** Peere
5.3.0 [scene not marked in F]   **86, 87 s.p. Chancellor** *Cham.*   **133 this** his   **171 brother-love** Brother; loue   **173 heart** hearts
5.4.0 [labeled "*Scena Tertia*" in F]   **2 Paris** Parish   **4, 27 s.p. One** [not in F]   **83 a way** away
5.5. 0 [labeled "*Scena Quarta*" in F]   **38 ways** way

Titus Andronicus

Copy text: the First Quarto of 1594, except for 3.2, based on F. Act and scene divisions are missing from the Quarto; act divisions alone are marked in the Folio.

1.1. 14 seat, to virtue consecrate, seate to vertue, consecrate. [The punctuation variations from the edited text are considerable in this play and are generally not recorded in these notes.]   **18 s.p. Marcus** [not in Q]   **35 the field** [Q follows with a half line and three more lines: "and at this day, / To the Monument of that *Andronici* / Done sacrifice of expiation, / And slaine the Noblest prisoner of the *Gothes.*"]   **55 s.d. Exeunt** *Exit*   **64 s.p. Captain** [not in Q]   **69 s.d. three sons** *two sonnes*   **78 rites** rights [also at line 143]   **98 manes** *manus*   **129 s.d. Exeunt** *Exit*   **157 s.p. Lavinia** [not in Q]   **193 Rome** Roome   **227 Titan's** [F] Tytus   **243 Pantheon** Pathan   **265 chance** [F] change   **281 cuique** *cuicum*   **300 s.p.** [**and elsewhere**] **Saturninus** *Emperour*   **317 Phoebe** Thebe   **318 gallant'st** [F] gallanst   **334 Queen, Pantheon. Lords,** Queene: Panthean Lords   **359 s.p. Martius** *Titus two sonnes speakes*   **s.p. Quintus** [not in Q]   **361 s.p. Martius** *Titus sonne speakes*   **369 s.p. Quintus** 3. Sonne   **370 s.p. Martius** 2. Sonne [also at line 372]   **389 s.d. They all kneel** *they all kneele and say*   **390 s.p. All** [not in Q]   **391 s.d. Exeunt** *Exit*   **392 dreary** dririe [Q] sudden [F]   **399** [F; not in Q]   **475 s.p. Lucius** [F; not in Q]   **476 mildly** mi'd ie
2.1. 37 s.p. [**and elsewhere**] **Aaron** *Moore*   **110 than** this
2.2. 1 morn [F] Moone   **11** [Q provides a s.p.: *Titus*]   **24 run** runnes
2.3. 13 snake [F] snakes   **33 and** ann   **43 lose** loose   **69 try** [F] trie   **thy**   **72 swart** F (swarth) swartie [Q]   **85 note** notice   **88 s.p.** [**and elsewhere**] **Tamora** *Queene*   **131 ye desire** we desire   **150 heard** hard   **153 Some** *So me*   **158 thee! For** thee for   **160 ears** [F] yeares   **175 their** there   **180 satisfy** satisfice (?)   **192 s.p. Aaron**

[not in Q]   **208 s.d. Exit** [at line 207 in Q]   **210 unhallowèd** [F] vnhollow   **222 berayed in blood** bereaud in blood [Q, with marginal correction in contemporary handwriting: "heere reau'd of lyfe"]   **231 Pyramus** [F] Priamus   **236 Cocytus'** *Ocitus*   **260 s.p.** [**and elsewhere**] **Saturninus** *King*   **260 gripped** griude   **276** [Q provides a s.p.: *King*]   **291 fault** faults
2.4. 5 scrawl scrowle   **11 s.p. Marcus** [not in Q]   **27 him** them   **30 three** their
3.1. 0 s.d. over on   **17 urns** ruines   **21 on they** [F] out hy   **67 handless** handles   **146 his** her   **225 blow** flow   **281 employed:** imployde in these Armes [Q] employd in these things [F]
3.2 [the entire scene is missing in Q; copy text is F]   **s.d. banquet.** *Bnaket* [F]   **1 s.p.** [**and throughout scene**] **Titus** *An.*   **13 with outrageous** without ragious   **38 mashed** mesh'd   **39 complainer** complaynet   **52 thy knife** knife   **53 fly** Flys   **54 thee, murderer!** the murderour: **55 are cloyed** cloi'd   **72 myself** my selfes
4.1. 1 s.p. [**and throughout**] **Boy** [F] *Puer*   **10 s.p. Marcus** [not in Q]   **19 griefs** greeues   **42 Metamorphoses** Metamorphosis   **52 quotes** coats   **55 Forced** Frocd   **80 s.p. Titus** [not in Q]   **90 hope** hop (?) I op (?)
4.2. 15 lordships, that Lordships   **51 Good** God   **96 Alcides** *Alciades*   **125 that** [F] your
4.3. 56 Saturn *Saturnine*, to   **77 News . . . come** [assigned in Q to Clown]   **96 from you** [Q follows with four lines: *Titus.* Tell mee, can you deliuer an Oration to the Em- / perour with a grace. / *Clowne.* Nay truelie sir, I could neuer say grace in all / my life.]
4.4. 5 know, as know know   **48 By 'r** be   **93 feed** seede   **98 ears** [F] yeares   **105 on** [F] in
5.1. 9 s.p. A Goth *Goth* [also at lines 121, 153, and 162]   **17 s.p. All the Goths** [not in Q]   **20 s.p. Another Goth** *Goth*   **23 building, suddenly** building suddainely,   **43 here's** [F] her's   **53 Get me a ladder** [assigned in Q to Aaron]   **113 extreme** extreanie   **133 haystacks** haystalks
5.2. 18 it action [F] that accord   **38 them out** the mout   **49 globe** Globes   **52 murderers** murder   **caves** cares   **56 Hyperion's** *Epeons*   **61 they** them   **65 worldly** wordlie   **121 s.d. Enter Marcus** [after line 120 in Q]   **196 s.d.** [after line 203 in Q]
5.3. 3 s.p. A Goth *Got.*   **15 s.d. Sound trumpets** [after line 16 in Q]   **26 gracious lord** [F] Lord   **36 Virginius** *Viginius*   **124 witness, this is true.** witnes this is true,   **125 cause** course   **141 s.p. All** *Marcus*   **142 s.p. Marcus** [no s.p. here in Q; see previous note]   **144 adjudged** [F] adiudge   **146 s.p. All** [not in Q]   **154 bloodstained** blood slaine   **163 Sung** Song   **172 s.p. Boy** [F] *Puer*

Romeo and Juliet

Copy text: the Second Quarto of 1599, except for 1.2.53–1.3.34, for which Q1 (the First Quarto) is the prior authority. Act and scene divisions are absent from the Second Quarto and the Folio.

1.1. 27 it in [Q1] it   **38 side** sides   **73 s.p. Citizens** *Offi.*   **76 s.p. Capulet's Wife** *Wife*   **92 Verona's** *Neronas*   **120 drave** drive   **122 city's** Citie   **147 his** is   **153 sun** same   **177 create** [Q1] created   **179 well-seeming** welseeing   **189 grief to** [Q1] grief, too   **192 lovers'** loving   **202 Bid a** [Q1] A   **make** [Q1] makes   **206 markman** mark man   **211 unharmed** [Q1] vncharmd   **218 makes** make
1.2. 14 The earth Earth   **32 on** one   **38–39 written here.** written. Here   **46 One** [Q1] on   **70 and Livia** [Q1] Liuia [Q2]   **79 thee** [Q1] you [Q2]   **91 fires** fire [Q1]
1.3. 12 an [Q2] a [Q1]   **18 shall** [Q1] stal [Q2]   **33 wi' th'** [Q1: with] with the [Q2]   **50 s.p.** [**and elsewhere**] **Wife** *Old La.*   **66 disposition** [F] dispositions   **67, 68 honor** [Q1] houre   **100 it fly** [Q1] flie   **105 s.p.** [**and elsewhere**] **Wife** *Mo.*
1.4. 7–8 [Q1; not in Q2]   **23 s.p. Mercutio** *Horatio*   **31 quote** cote   **39 done** [Q1] dum   **42 of** Or   **45 like lamps** [Q1] lights lights   **47 five** fine   **57 atomi** [Q1] ottamie   **59–61** [these lines follow line 69 in Q2]   **66 film** Philome   **69 maid** [Q1] man   **72 O'er** [Q1] On   **74 on** one   **76 breaths** [Q1] breath   **80 parson's** Persons   **81 dreams he** [Q1] he dreams   **90 elflocks** Elklocks   **111 forfeit** [Q1] fofreit

1.5. s.d. [Q2 adds: "*Enter Romeo*"]   **1 s.p. First Servingman** *Ser.* [also at lines 6 and 12]   **3 s.p. Second Servingman** 1   **11 s.p. Third Servingman** 2   **14 s.p. Fourth Servingman** 3   **15 longest** longer   **17 s.p. Capulet** 1. *Capu.* [also at lines 35 and 40]   **18 a bout** about   **57 antic** antiicque   **96 ready** [Q1] did readie
2.0. Chorus **1 s.p. Chorus** [not in Q2]   **4 matched** match
2.1. 7 **Nay . . . too** [assigned in Q2 to Benvolio]   **10 one** [Q1] on   **11 Pronounce** [Q1] prouaunt   **dove** [Q1] day   **13 heir** [Q1] her   **14 trim** [Q1] true   **39 open-arse, and** open, or   **poppering** Poprin
2.2. 16 **do** [Q1] to   **20 eyes** [Q1] eye   **41–42 nor any . . . name** ô be some other name / Belonging to a man   **45 were** [Q1] wene   **82 pilot** Pylat   **83 washed** [Q1] washeth   **92–93 false . . . They** false at louers periuries. / They   **99 havior** behauiour   **101 more cunning** coying   **110 circled** [Q1] circle   **149, 151 s.p. Nurse** [not in Q2]   **150, 151 s.p. Juliet** [not in Q2]   **163 than mine** then   **168 nyas** Neece   **170 years** [Q1] yeare   **180 gyves** giues   **187 Sleep . . . breast** [Q1; assigned in Q2 to Juliet]   **189–190** [preceded in Q2 by an earlier version of lines 1–4 of the next scene, in which "fleckled darkness" reads "darknesse fleckted" and "and Titan's fiery wheels" reads "made by *Tytans* wheels"]
2.3. 2 **Check'ring** [Q1] Checking   **4 fiery** [Q1] burning   **22 sometime's** sometime   **50 me** me: **51 wounded. Both our** wounded both, our   **85 not. She whom** [Q1] me not, her
2.4. 18 **s.p. Benvolio** [Q1] *Ro.*   **28–29 phantasimes** phantacies   **33 pardon-me's** pardons mees   **40 but a** a   **68 Switch . . . switch** Swits . . . swits   **113–114 for himself** [Q1] himself   **205 dog's** dog   **212 s.d. Exeunt** *Exit*
2.5. 11 **three** there   **15 And** *M.* And   **26 I had** [Q1] I
2.6. 18 **gossamour** gossamours   **27 music's** musicke
3.1. 2 **Capels are** *Capels*   **67 injured** iniuried   **73 stoccado** stucatho   **90 your houses** houses   **107 soundly too. Your** soundly, to your   **121 Alive** He gan   **123 fire-eyed** [Q1] fier end   **136 s.p. First Citizen** *Citti.*   **138 s.p. First Citizen** *Citi.*   **141 all all:** all: **165 agile** [Q1] aged   **183 s.p. Montague** *Capu.*   **187 hate's** heart's   **191 I** [Q1] It   **196 s.d. Exeunt** *Exit*
3.2. 1 **s.p. Juliet** [not in Q2]   **9 By** And by   **15 grown** grow   **47 darting** arting   **49 shut** shot   **51 Brief sounds** Briefe, sounds,   **of my** my   **60 one** on   **72 It . . . did** [assigned in Q2 to Juliet]   **73 O . . . face** [assigned in Q2 to Nurse]   **76 Dove-feathered** Rauenous douefeatherd   **79 damnèd** dimme   **143 s.d. Exeunt** *Exit*
3.3. s.d. [Q2 has "*Enter Friar and Romeo*"]   **39** [Q2 follows with a line: "This may flyes do, when I from this must flie"]   **43** [printed in Q2 before line 40]   **52 Thou** [Q1] Then   **61 madmen** [Q1] mad man   **70 s.d. Knock** *Enter Nurse, and knocke*   **73 s.d. Knock** *They knocke*   **75 s.d. Knock** *Slud knock*   **80 s.d. Enter Nurse** [at line 78 in Q2]   **110 denote** [Q1] deuote   **117 lives** [Q1] lies   **121 lose** loose   **144 pout'st upon** puts vp   **168 disguised** disguise
3.4. 10 **s.d. [and elsewhere] Wife** *La.*   **13 be** [Q1] me   **23 We'll keep** Well, keepe
3.5. 13 **exhaled** exhale   **19 the** the the   **31 changed** change   **36 s.d. Enter Nurse** *Enter Madame and Nurse*   **54 s.p. Juliet** *Ro.*   **67 s.d.** [bracketed s.d. from Q1]   **82 pardon him** padon   **130–131 body . . . a bark** body? / Thou counterfeits. A barke   **133–134 is, . . . flood;** is: . . . floud,   **139 gives** giue   **142 How? Will** How wil   **151–152 proud . . . Thank** proud mistresse minion you? / Thanke   **160 s.p. [and elsewhere] Capulet** *Fa.*   **172 s.p. and text Capulet** O, God-i'-good-e'en Father, ô Godigeden   **173 s.p. Nurse** [not in Q2]   **182 liened** liand
4.1. 7 **talked** [Q1] talke   **45 cure** [Q1] care   **46 Ah** [Q1] O   **72 slay** [Q1] stay   **78 off** [Q1] of   **83 chopless** [Q1] chapels   **85 his tomb** his   **98 breath** [Q1] breast   **100 wanny** many   **110 In** Is [Q2 follows with a line: "Be borne to buriall in thy kindreds graue"]   **111 shalt** shall   **115 and he** an he   **116 waking** walking   **126 s.d. Exeunt** *Exit*
4.2. 3, 6 **s.p. Servingman** *Ser.*   **14 willed** wield   **38 s.p. [and elsewhere] Wife** *Mo.*   **47 s.d. Exeunt** *Exit*
4.3. 49 **wake** walke
4.4. 1 **s.p. [and elsewhere] Wife** *La.*   **12 s.d. Exeunt** *Exit*   **13 s.d.** [after line 14 in Q2]   **15 s.p. First Servingman** *Fel.*   **18 s.p. Second Servingman** *Fel.*   **21 Thou** Twou   **faith** father   **23 s.d.** [after line 21 in Q2]
4.5. 40 **all; life** all life   **41 long** [Q1] loue   **51 behold** bedold   **65 cure** care   **65–66 not . . . Heaven** not, / In these confusions heauen   **82 fond** some   **96 s.p. First Musician** *Musi.*   **99, 103 s.p. First Musician** *Fid.*   **99 by** [Q1] my. [Q2 has s.d. here:

"*Exit omnes*"]   **s.d. Enter Peter** *Enter Will Kemp*   **107 s.p. First Musician** *Minstrels* [and subsequently in this scene indicated by *Minst.* or *Minstrel*]   **123 Then . . . wit** [assigned in Q2 to 2 M]   **127 And . . . oppress** [Q1; not in Q2]   **133, 136 Pretty** [Q1] Prates   **145 s.d. Exeunt** *Exit*
5.1. 15 **fares my** [Q1[doth my Lady   **17, 27, 32 s.p. Balthaser** *Man*   **24 e'en** in   **defy** [Q1] denie   **33 s.d.** [at line 32, after "good lord," in Q2]   **76 pay** [Q1] pray   **86 Exit** *Exeunt*
5.3. 3 **yew** [Q1] young   **21 s.d. [Balthasar]** [Q1] *Peter*   **25 light. Upon** light vpon   **40, 43 s.p. Balthasar** *Pet.*   **68 conjuration** commiration   **71 s.p. Page** *Boy* [Q1; s.p. missing in Q2 and line treated as a s.d.]   **102 fair** faire? I will beleeue   **107 palace** pallat   **108** [Q2 has four undeleted lines here: "Depart againe, come lye thou in my arme, / Heer's to thy health, where ere thou tumblest in. / O true Appothecarie! / Thy drugs are quicke. Thus with a kisse I die."]   **123 s.p. [and elsewhere] Balthasar** *Man*   **137 yew** yong   **168 s.p. First Watch** *Watch* [also at lines 172, 195, 199]   **171 s.p. Page** *Watch boy*   **182 s.p. Second Watch** *Watch*   **183, 187 s.p. First Watch** *Chief. watch*   **187 too** too too   **190 shrieked** shrike   **194 our** your   **199 slaughtered** Slaughter   **201** [Q2 has a s.d. here: "*Enter Capulet and his wife*"]   **209 more early** [Q1] now earling   **232 that** thats   **274-275 place . . . This** place. To this same monument / This   **281 s.p. Page** *Boy*   **299 raise** raie

Julius Caesar

Copy text: the First Folio. Act divisions are marked in the Folio; scene divisions are editorially supplied.
1.1. s.d. [and elsewhere] **Marullus** *Murellus*   **37 Pompey . . . oft** Pompey many a time and oft?
1.2. s.d. [and elsewhere] **Calpurnia** *Calphurnia*   **24 s.d. Manent** *Manet*   **254 like. He** like he
1.3. 129 **In favor's like** Is fauors, like
2.1. 40 **ides** first   **67 of** of a   **83 put** path   **122 women, then,** women. Then   **136 oath, when** Oath. When   **214 eighth** eight   **268 his** hit   **281 the** tho   **310 s.d. Enter Lucuis and Ligarius** [after "with haste" in line 310 in F]   **314 s.p. [and through line 322] Ligarius** *Cai.*
2.2. 23 **did neigh** do neigh   **46 are** heare   **81 Of** And
2.3. 1 **s.p. Artemidorus** [not in F]
3.1. 40 **law** lane   **114 states** State   **116 lies** lye   **256 s.p. Antony** [not in F]   **277 s.d. Octavius'** *Octauio's* [also at 5.2.4]   **285 for** from
3.2. 106 **art** are   **205 s.p. All** [not in F]   **222 wit** writ   **260 s.d. Exeunt** *Exit*   **262 s.d. Enter Servant** [after "fellow" in F]
4.2. 34-36 **s.p. First, Second, Third Soldier** [not in F]   **50 Lucius** *Lucilius*   **52 Lucilius** *Luc.*   **s.d. Manent** *Manet*
4.3. 209–210 **off / If** off. / If   **230 s.d. Enter Lucius** [before line 230 in F]   **244, 246 [and throughout] Claudius** *Claudio*   **246 [and throughout] Varro** *Varrus*   **252 will** will it   **303, 307 s.p. Varro, Claudius** *Both*
5.1. 42 **teeth** teethes   **67 s.d. Exeunt** *Exit*   **70** [F has s.d.: "*Lucillius and Messala stand forth*"]   **71 s.p. Lucilius (stands forth)** *Luc.*   **73 s.p. Messala (stands forth)** *Messa.*   **99 rest** rests
5.3. 104 **Thasos** *Tharsus*   **108 Flavius** *Flauio*
5.4. 7 **s.p. Lucilius** [not in F]   **9 O** *Luc.* O   **12, 15 s.p. First Soldier** *Sold.*   **16 s.d. Enter Antony** [before line 16 in F]   **17 the news** thee newes
5.5 77 **With all** Withall

Hamlet

Copy text: the Second Quarto of 1604-1605 [Q2]. The First Folio text also represents an independently authoritative text; although seemingly not the correct choice for copy text, the Folio text is considerably less marred by typographical errors than is Q2. The adopted readings in these notes are from F unless otherwise indicated; [eds.] means that the adopted reading was first proposed by some editor since the time of F. Some readings are also supplied from the First Quarto of 1603 [Q1]. Act and scene divisions are missing in Q_q1-2; the Folio provides such markings only through 1.3 and at Act 2.

1.1. **1 Who's** Whose   **19 soldier** [F, Q1] souldiers   **44 off** [Q1] of   **48 harrows** harrowes   **67 sledded Polacks** [eds.] sleaded pollax   **77 why** [F, Q1] with   **cast** cost   **91 heraldry** [F, Q1] heraldy   **92 those** [F, Q1] these   **95 returned** returne   **97 cov'nant** comart   **98 designed** [eds.] desseigne   **112 e'en so** [eds.] enso   **119 tenantless** tennatlesse   **125 feared** [eds.] feare   **142 you** [F, Q1] your   **144 at it** it   **181 coveniently** [F, Q1] conuenient
1.2. s.d. Gertrude Gertradt (and elsewhere; also Gertrad)   **1 s.p. King** Claud.   **67 so** so much   **77 good** coold   **82 shapes** [Q3] chapes   **83 denote** deuote   **96 a** or   **105 corpse** [eds.] course   **112 you.** For you for   **129 sullied** [eds.] sallied [Q2] solid [F]   **132 self** seale   **133 weary** wary   **137 to this** thus   **140 satyr** [F4] satire   **143 would** [F, Q1] should   **149 even she** [F; not in Q2]   **175 to drink deep** [F, Q1] for to drinke   **178 to see** [F, Q1] to   **199 waste** [F2] wast [Q2, F]   **206 jelly with . . . fear,** gelly, with . . . feare   **210 Where, as** [Q5] Whereas   **225 Indeed, indeed** [F, Q1] Indeede   **241 Very Like, very like** [F, Q1] Very like   **242 hundred** hundreth   **243 s.p. Marcellus, Bernardo** [eds.] Both   **247 tonight** to nigh   **256 fare** farre   **257 eleven** a leaven   **259 Exeunt** [at line 258 in Q2]   **262 Foul** [F, Q1] fonde
1.3. 3 convoy is conuay, in   **12 bulk** bulkes   **18** [F; not in Q2]   **29 weigh** way   **49 like a** a   **74 Are** Or   **75 be** boy   **76 loan** loue   **110 Running** [eds.] Wrong [Q2] Roaming [F]   **116 springes** springs   **126 tether** tider   **130 implorators** imploratotors   **131 bawds** [eds.] bonds   **132 beguile** beguide
1.4. 2 is a is   **6 s.d. go off** [eds.] goes of   **17 revel** [Q3] reueale   **36 evil** [eds.] eale [Q2] ease [Q3]   **37 often dout** [eds.] of a doubt   **49 inurned** interr'd [Q2, Q1]   **61, 79 wafts** waues   **80 off** of   **82 artery** arture   **86 s.d. Exeunt** Exit   **87 imagination** [F, Q1] imagion
1.5. 1 Whither [eds.] Whether   **21 fretful porcupine** [F, Q1] fearfull Porpentine   **44 wit** [eds.] wits   **48 what a** what   **56 lust** [F, Q1] but   **angel** Angle   **57 sate** [F] sort   **59 scent** [eds.] sent   **68 alleys** [eds.] allies   **69 posset** possesse   **96 stiffly** swiftly   **119 bird** and   **128 s.d. Horatio, Marcellus** Booth [also at line 151]   **heaven, my lord** heauen   **138 Look you, I'll** I will   **157 s.d. cries** Ghost cries   **179 soe'er** so mere   **185 Well** well, well [Q1, Q2]
2.1. s.d. man [eds.] man or two   **3 marvelous** meruiles   **29 Faith, no** Fayth   **41 warrant** wit   **42 sullies** sallies   **43 wi' the** with   **60 o'ertook** or tooke   **64 takes** take   **76 s.d. Exit Reynaldo. Enter Ophelia** [after line 75 in Q2]   **107 passion** passions
2.2. 57 o'erhasty hastie   **73 three** [F, Q1] threescore   **90 since brevity** breuitie   **125 This** [Q2 has a speech prefix: Pol. This]   **126 above** about   **137 winking** working   **143 his** her   **148 watch** wath   **149 to a** to   **151 'tis** [F, Q1; not in Q2]   **170 s.d. Exeunt** [eds.] Exit   **210 sanity** sanctity   **212–213 and suddenly . . . him** [F; not in Q2]   **213 honorable lord** Lord   **214 most humbly take** take   **215 cannot, sir** cannot   **216 more** not more   **224 excellent** extent   **228–229 overhappy. On** euer happy on   **229 cap** lap   **240–270 Let . . . attended** [F; not in Q2]   **267 s.p. Rosencrantz, Guildenstern** Both [F]   **273 even** euer   **288 could** can   **292 off** of   **304 What a** What   **306–307 admirable, in action how . . . angel, in** [F, subst.] admirable in action, how . . . Angell in   **310 no, nor** nor   **314 you** yee   **321 of** on   **324–325 the clown . . . sear** [F; not in Q2]   **tickle** [eds.] tickled [F]   **326 blank** black   **337-362 How . . . too** [F; not in Q2]   **342 berattle** [eds.] be-ratled [F]   **349 most like** [eds.] like most [F]   **373 lest my** let me   **381 too** to   **398–399 tragical-historical, tragical-comical-historical-pastoral** [F; not in Q2]   **401 light . . . these** [eds.] light for the lawe of writ, and the liberty: these.   **425 By 'r** by   **429 e'en to 't** ento't   **French falconers** friendly Fankners   **433 s.p.** [and elsewhere] **First Player** Player   **436-437 caviare** cauiary   **443 affectation** affection   **446 tale** [F, Q1] talke   **454 the** 'th   **456 heraldry** [F, Q1] heraldy   **dismal. Head** dismall head   **474 Then senseless Ilium** [F; not in Q2]   **481 And, like** Like   **495 fellies** [F4] follies [Q2] Fallies [F]   **504 "Mobled queen" is good** [F; not in Q2; F reads "Inobled"]   **506 bisson** Bison   **514 husband's** [F, Q1] husband   **540 a** [F; not in Q2]   **541 or** [F, Q1] lines, or   **546 s.d. Exeunt players** [see textual note at line 548]   **547 till** tell   **548 s.d. Exeunt** [F; Q2 has "Exeunt Pol. and Players" after line 547]   **554 his** the   **556 and an** 559 to Hecuba** [F, Q1] to her   **561 the cue** that   **582 O, vengeance** [F; not in Q2]   **584 father** [Q1, Q3, Q4; not in Q2, F]   **588 scullion** [F] stallyon [Q2] scalion [Q1]   **600 the devil** a deale   **the devil** the deale

3.1. 1 And An   **28 too** two   **32 lawful espials** [F; not in Q2]   **33 Will** Wee'le   **46 loneliness** lowlines   **56 Let's withdraw** withdraw   **56 s.d. Enter Hamlet** [after line 55 in Q2]   **65 wished. To** wishto to   **73 disprized** despiz'd   **84 of us all** [F, Q1; not in Q2]   **86 sicklied** sickled   **93 well, well, well** well   **100 the** these   **108 your honesty** you   **119 inoculate** euocutat   **122 to a** a   **130 knaves all** knaues   **144 paintings too** [Q1] paintings   **146 jig, you amble** gig & amble   **147 lisp** list   **148 your ignorance** [F, Q1] ignorance   **155 Th' expectancy** Th' expectation   **159 music** musickt   **160 that** what   **161 tune** time   **162 feature** stature   **164** [Q2 has "Exit" at the end of this line]   **191 unwatched** vnmatcht
3.2. 10 tatters totters   **split** [F, Q1] spleet   **27 of the** of   **29 praise** praysd   **37 sir** [F; not in Q2]   **45 s.d. Enter . . . Rosencrantz** [after line 47 in Q2]   **88 detecting** detected   **96 now. My lord,** now my Lord.   **107 s.p. [and elsewhere] Queen** Ger.   **112–113** [F; not in Q2]   **127 devil** deule [Q2] Diuel [F]   **133 s.d. sound** [eds.] sounds   **Anon comes** Anon come   **135 miching** [F, Q1] munching   **140 keep counsel** [F, Q1] keepe   **153 s.p. [and throughout scene] Player King** King   **154 orbèd** orb'd the   **159 s.p. [and throughout scene] Player Queen** Quee.   **162 your** our   **164** [Q2 follows here with an extraneous unrhymed line: "For women feare too much, euen as they loue"]   **165 For** And   **166 In** Eyther   **none, in** 167 love** Lord   **179 Wormwood, wormwood** That's wormwood   **180 s.p. Player Queen** [not in Q2]   **188 like** [F, Q1] I be a widow be** [F] be a   **226 s.d. Exit** [F, Q1] Exeunt   **240 wince** [Q1] winch [Q2, F]   **241 s.d.** [after line 242 in Q2]   **254 Confederate** [F, Q1] Considerat   **256 infected** [F, Q1, Q4] inuected   **258 usurp** vsurps   **264** [F; not in Q2]   **274 with two** with   **288 s.d.** [F; after line 293 in Q2]   **308 start** stare   **317 of my** of   **343 s.d.** [after line 341 in Q2]   **357 thumb** the vmber   **366 to the top of** to   **370 can fret me** [F] fret me not [Q2] can fret me, yet [Q1]   **371 s.d.** [after line 372 in Q2]   **385 s.p. Polonius** [F; not in Q2]   **386 Leave me, friends** [so F; Q2 places before "I will say so," and assigns both to Hamlet]   **388 breathes** breakes   **390 bitter . . . day** business as the bitter day   **395 daggers** [F, Q1] dagger
3.3. 19 huge hough   **22 ruin** raine   **23 but with** but   **35 s.d. Exit** [after "I know" in F]   **50 pardoned** pardon   **58 Offense's** [eds.] Offences   **shove** showe   **73 pat . . . a-praying** but now a is a-praying   **75 revenged** reuendge   **79 hire and salary** base and silly   **81 With all** Withall
3.4. 4 shroud [Q1] [eds.] silence [Q2, F]   **5-6 with him . . . Mother, Mother, Mother** [F; not in Q2]   **7 warrant** wait   **8 s.d. Enter Hamlet** [at line 5 in Q2]   **21 inmost** most   **43 off** of   **51 tristful** heated   **53** [assigned in Q2 to Hamlet]   **60 heaven-kissing** heaue, a kissing   **89 panders** pardons   **91 mine . . . soul** my very eyes into my soule   **92 grainèd** greeued   **93 not leave** leaue there   **100 tithe** kyth   **146 Ecstasy** [F; not in Q2]   **150 I the** the   **165 live** leaue   **172 Refrain tonight** to refraine night   **193 ravel** rouell   **205 to breathe** [eds.] to breath   **222 a** [F, Q1] a most   **224 s.d. Exeunt** [eds.] Exit
4.2. 1 s.d. [Q2: "Enter Hamlet, Rosencraus, and others."]   **2-3** [F; not in Q2; the s.p. is "Gentlemen"]   **4 s.p. Hamlet** [not in Q2]   **5 s.d.** [F; not in Q2]   **7 Compounded** Compound   **19 ape** apple   **31–32 Hide . . . after** [F; not in Q2]
4.3. 44 With fiery quickness [F; not in Q2]   **56 and so** so   **72 were** will   **begun** begin
4.4. 20–21 name. To name To
4.5. 16 Let . . . in [assigned in Q2 to Horatio]   **20 s.d.** [after line 16 in Q2]   **38 with** all with   **52 clothes** close   **57 Indeed, la** Indeede   **83 in their** in   **98** [F; not in Q2]   **100 s.d.** [at line 97 in Q2]   **102 impetuous** [Q3, F2] impitious [Q2] impittious [F]   **109 They** The   **146 swoopstake** [eds.] soopstake [Q1 reads "Swoop-stake-like"]   **158 Let her come in** [assigned in Q2 to Laertes and placed before "How now, what noyse is that?"]   **s.d. Enter Ophelia** [after line 157 in Q2]   **162 Till** Tell   **165 an old** [F, Q1] a poore   **166–168, 170** [F; not in Q2]   **186 must** [F, Q1] may   **191 affliction** [F, Q1] afflictions   **199 All flaxen** Flaxen   **203 Christian** [F] Christians   **souls, I pray God** [F,Q1] soules   **204 you see** you   **217 trophy, sword** trophie sword
4.6. 7, 9 s.p. First Sailor Say.   **9 an 't** and   **22 good turn** turne   **26 bore** bord   **30 He** So   **31 will give** will

4.7. 6 proceeded proceede   **7 crimeful** criminall   **15 conjunctive** concliue   **22 gyves** Giues   **23 loud a wind** loued Arm'd   **25 had** haue   **37 How . . . Hamlet** [F; not in Q2]   **38 This** These   **46–47 your pardon** you pardon   **48 and more strange** [F; not in Q2]   **Hamlet** [F; not in Q2]   **56 shall live** [F, Q1] liue   **62 checking** the King   **78 ribbon** [eds.] ribaud   **89 my** me   **101 escrimers** [eds.] Scrimures   **116 wick** [eds.] weeke   **123 spendthrift** [Q5] spend thirfts   **135 on** ore   **139 pass** pace   **141 for that** for   **151 shape. If** shape if   **157 ha 't** hate   **160 prepared** prefard   **168 hoar** horry   **172 cold** cull-cold   **192 douts** [F "doubts"] drownes

5.1. 1 s.p. [and throughout] **First Clown** Clowne   **3 s.p.** [and throughout] **Second Clown** Other   **9 se offendendo** so offended   **12 and to** to   **Argal** or all   **34–37 SECOND CLOWN: Why . . . arms** [F; not in Q2]   **43 that frame** that   **55 s.d.** [before line 65 in Q2]   **60 stoup** soope   **70 daintier** dintier   **85 meant** [F, Q1, Q3] went   **89 mazard** messene   **106–107 Is . . . recoveries** [F; not in Q2]   **107–108 Will his** will   **109 double ones too** doubles   **120 O** or   **121** [F; not in Q2]   **143 Of all** Of   **165 nowadays** [F; not in Q]   **192 chamber** [F, Q1] table   **208–209 As thus** [F; not in Q2]   **216 winter's** waters   **226, 235 s.p. Priest** Doct.   **231 Shards, flints** Flints   **246 t' have** haue   **247 trebel** double   **262 and rash** rash   **288 thus** this   **296 s.d.** [Exit] **Horatio** and Horatio   **301 shortly** thereby   **302 Till** Tell

5.2. 5 Methought my thought   **6 bilboes** bilbo   **9 pall** fall   **17 unseal** vnfold   **19 Ah,** [eds.] A   **29 villainies** villaines   **30 Ere** Or   **43 "as"es** as sir   **52 Subscribed** Subscribe   **57, 68–80** [F; not in Q2]   **73 interim** [eds.] interim's [F]   **78 court** [eds.] count [F]   **81 s.p.** [and throughout] **Osric** Cour.   **82 humbly** humble   **93 Put your** you   **98 sultry** sully for or   **107 gentleman** [eds.] gentlemen   **109 feelingly** [Q4] fellingly   **114 dozy** [eds.] dazzie yaw** [eds.] raw   **141 his** [eds.] this   **142 him by them,** him, by them   **149 hangers** hanger   **156 carriages** carriage   **159 might be** be might   **162 impawned, as** [eds.] all [Q2] impon'd, as [F]   **174 purpose, I** purpose; I   **181 Yours, yours. 'A does** Yours doo's   **186 comply** so sir   **190 yeasty** histy   **191 fanned** [eds.] prophane [Q2] fond [F]   **winnowed** trennowed   **210 But thou** thou   **218 be now** be   **220 will come** well come   **238** [F; not in Q2]   **248 To keep** To   **till** all   **252 foils Come on** foils   **255 off** of   **261 bettered** better   **270 union** Vnice ["Onixe" in some copies]   **288 A touch, a touch, I** I   **302 afeard** sure   **316 Hamlet. Hamlet** Hamlet   **319 thy** [F, Q1] my   **327 murderous** [F; not in Q2]   **328 off** of   **thy union** [F, Q1] the Onixe   **345 ha 't** [eds.] hate [Q2] have 't [F]   **366 proud** prou'd   **369 s.p. First Ambassador** Embas.   **373** [and some other places] **Rosencrantz** Rosencraus   **381 th' yet** yet   **385 forced** for no   **394 on** no

Passages contained only in F and omitted from Q2 are noted in the textual notes above. It might be useful here to list the more important instances in which Q2 contains words, lines, and passages omitted in F.

1.1. 112–129 BERNARDO I think . . . countrymen
1.2. 58–60 wrung . . . consent
1.3. 9 perfume and
1.4. 17–38 This heavy-headed . . . scandal   **75–78** The very . . . beneath
2.1. 122 Come
2.2. 17 Whether . . . thus   **217** except my life   **363** very   **366** 'Sblood (and some other profanity passim)   **371** then   **444–445** as wholesome . . . fine   **521–522** of this   **589** Hum
3.2. 169–170 Where . . . there   **216–217** To . . . scope
3.4. 72–77 Sense . . . difference   **79–82** Eyes . . . mope   **168–172** That monster . . . put on   **174–177** the next . . . potency   **187** One word . . . lady   **209–217** There's . . . meet
4.1. 4 Bestow . . . while   **41–44** Whose . . . air
4.2. 4 But soft
4.3. 26–29 KING Alas . . . worm
4.4. 9–67 Enter Hamlet . . . worth
4.5. 33 Oho
4.7. 68–82 LAERTES My lord . . . graveness   **101–103** Th' escrimers . . . them   **115–124** There . . . ulcer
5.1. 154 There

5.2. 106–142 here is . . . unfellowed (replaced in F by "you are not ignorant of what excellence Laertes is at his weapon")   **154–155** HORATIO [to Hamlet] I knew . . . done   **193–207** Enter a Lord . . . lose, my lord (replaced in F by "You will lose this wager, my lord")   **222** Let be

Othello

Copy text: the First Folio. The adopted readings are from the Quarto of 1622 [Q1], unless otherwise indicated; [eds.] means that the adopted reading was first proposed by some editor subsequent to the First Folio. Act and scene divisions are marked in the Folio with the exception of 2.3.

1.1. 1 Tush, never Neuer   **4 'Sblood, but** But   **16 And, in conclusion** [Q1; not in F]   **26 togaed** Tongued   **30 other** others   **34 God bless** blesse   **68 full** fall   **thick-lips** Thicks-lips   **74 changes** chances   **75** [and elsewhere] **lose** [eds.] loose   **81 Thieves, thieves, thieves** Theeues, Theeues   **83 s.d. Brabantio above** [in F, printed as a speech prefix to line 84]   **88 Zounds, sir** Sir [also at line 111]   **103 bravery** knauerie   **119 are now** are   **158 pains** apines   **161 sign. That** [eds.] signe) that   **186 night** might
1.2. 34 Duke Dukes   **50 carrack** Carract   **64 her!** [eds.] her   **69 darlings** Deareling   **89 I do** do
1.3.1 There is There's   **these** this   **61 s.p. Duke and Senators** [All Q1] Sen.   **101 maimed** main'd   **108 upon** vp on   **s.p. Duke** [Q1; not in F]   **109 overt** ouer   **112 s.p.** [and elsewhere] **First Senator** Sen.   **124 till** tell   **132 battles** Battaile   **fortunes** Fortune   **141 travels'** Trauellours   **143 rocks, and** Rocks   **heads** head   **145 other** others   **147 Do grow** Grew   **149 thence** hence   **157 intentively** instinctiuely   **161 sighs** kisses   **204 Into your favor** [Q1; not in F]   **222 ear** eares   **227 sovereign** more soueraigne   **230 appetite, loveliness** appetite. Louelinesse   **233 couch** [eds.] Coach [F] Cooch [Q1]   **237 These** [eds.] This   **244 Nor I. I would** Nor would I   **251 did love** loue   **267 me** [eds.] my   **273 instruments** Instrument   **281 Desdemona. Tonight, my lord? Duke. This night** [Q1; not in F]   **285 With** And   **294 s.p. First Senator** Sen.   **296 s.d. Exeunt** Exit   **302 matters** matter   **303 the** the the   **329 beam** [eds.] braine [F] ballance [Q1]   **333–334 our unbitted** or vnbitted   **335 scion** [eds.] Seyen [F] syen [Q1]   **353 error** errors   **354 She . . . she must** [Q1; not in F]   **358 a super-subtle** super-subtle   **378–382 Roderigo. What . . . purse** [Q1; not in F]   **386 a snipe** Snpe   **389 He's** [Ha's Q1] She ha's   **396 ear** eares
2.1. 35 prays praye   **36 heaven** Heauens   **42 s.p. Third Gentleman** Gent.   **44 arrivance** Arriuancie   **45 this** the   **58 s.p. Second Gentleman** Gent. [also at lines 61, 68, and 95]   **72 clog** enclogge   **84 And . . . comfort** [Q1; not in F]   **90 tell me** tell   **94 the sea** Sea   **96 their** this   **107 list** leaue   **111 doors** doore   **156** [and elsewhere] **ne'er** neu'r   **158 such wight** such wightes   **170 gyve** [eds.] giue   **174 An** and   **175 courtesy** Curtsie   **176 clyster pipes** Cluster-pipes   **214 s.d. Exeunt** [eds.] Exit   **216 hither** thither   **229 again** a game   **239 fortune** Forune   **241–242 compassing** compasse   **243–244 finder out** finder   **244 occasions** occasion   **has** he's   **263 mutualities** mutabilities   **300 for wife** for wift   **307 rank** right   **308 nightcap** Night-Cape
2.2. 6 addiction [eds.] addition   **10 Heaven bless** Blesse
2.3. 27 stoup [eds.] stope   **38 unfortunate** infortunate   **52 lads** else   **57 to put** put to   **61, 71 God** heauen   **76 Englishman** Englishmen   **91 Then . . . auld** [Then . . . owd Q1] And take thy awl'd   **93 'Fore God** Why   **97 God's** heau'ns   **106 God forgive** Forgiue   **110 speak** I speake   **123 the** his   **138 s.d. Cry within: Help! Help** [from Q1: "Helpe, helpe, within"]   **139 Zounds, you** You   **152 God's will** Alas   **153 Montano—sir** Montano   **156 God's will, Lieutenant, hold** Fie, fie Lieutenant   **158 Zounds, I** I   **161 sense of place** [eds.] place of sense   **177 breast** breastes   **184 wont be** wont to be   **201 Zounds, if I** If I once   **212 leagued** [eds.] league   **218 Thus** This   **227 the** then   **246 well now** well   **250 vile** vil'd   **255 God** Heauen   **260 thought** had thought   **283 O God** Oh   **308 I'll** I   **311 denotement** [eds.] deuotement   **325–326 me here** me   **337 were 't** were   **356 s.d. Enter Roderigo** [after line 356 in F]   **369 hast** hath   **372 By the Mass** Introth   **378 on;** [on Q1] on   **379 the while** [eds.] a while

3.1. s.d. Musicians [eds.] *Musicians, and Clowne*   **5 s.d.** [and at lines 7, 9, and 15] **A Musician** *Mus.*   **21 s.d. Exeunt** [eds.] *Exit*   **22 hear** heare me   **26 General's wife** Generall   **31 Cassio. Do, good my friend** [Q1; not in F]   **42 s.d. Exit** at line 41 in F]   **52 To . . . front** [Q1; not in F]
3.3. 16 circumstance Circumstances   **41 you** your   **55 Yes, faith I** sooth   **66 or** on   **80 By' r Lady** Trust me   **103 you** he   **118 By heaven** Alas   **124 In** Of   **148 that all** that: All   **free to** free   **152 But some** Wherein   **160 oft** of   **161 wisdom then** wisdome [Q1]   **188 God** Heauen   **194 Is once** Is   **196 blown** blow'd   **199 dances well** Dances   **216 God** Heauen   **218 keep 't** [eds.] keepe [Q1] kept [F]   **230 I' faith** Trust me   **232 my** your   **249 disproportion** disproportions   **264 to hold** to   **275 qualities** Quantities   **289 of** to   **294 O, then heaven mocks** Heauen mock'd   **301 Faith** Why   **305 s.d. Exit** [at line 304 in F]   **328 faith** but   **345 s.d. Enter Othello** [after "I did say so" in F]   **354 of her** in her   **385 remorse;** [remorce. Q1] remorse [F]   **407 see, sir** see   **411 supervisor** super-vision   **439 then laid** laid   **440 Over** ore   **sighed** sigh   **kissed** kisse   **441 Cried** cry   **455 any that was** [eds.] any, it was   **468 mind perhaps** minde   **471 Ne'er feels** [eds.] Neu'r keepes
3.4. 23 that the   **37 It yet** It   **56 faith** indeed   **77 I' faith** Indeed   **79 God** Heauen   **83 Heaven bless** Blesse   **88 can, sir** can   **94–95 Desdemona. I pray . . . Cassio. Othello. The handkerchief!** [Q1; not in F]   **99 I' faith** Insooth   **100 Zounds** Away   **164 that** the   **172 I' faith** Indeed   **182 friend.** [eds.] friend,   **183 absence** [eds.] absence, [Q1] Absence: [F]   **188 by my faith** in good troth
4.1. 32 Faith Why   **36 Zounds, that's** that's   **45 work** workes   **52 No, forbear** [Q1; not in F]   **72 couch** [Coach Q1] Cowch;   **79 unsuiting** [Q1 corrected] vnfitting [Q1 uncorrected] resulting [F]   **81 'scuse** scuses   **97 clothes** Cloath   **103 conster** conserue   **105 you now** you   **109 power** dowre   **113 a woman** woman   **114 i' faith** indeed   **121 Do you** Do ye   **122 marry her** marry   **125 win** [eds.] winnes   **126 Faith** Why   **shall marry** marry   **133 beckons** becomes   **137 by this hand, she** [Q1; not in F]   **163 Faith, I I**   **165 Faith** Yes   **212 s.d.** [after line 210 in F]   **215 God save** Saue   **238 By my troth** Trust me   **251 Truly, an** Truely   **284 denote** deonte [F uncorrected] deuote [F corrected]
4.2. 32 Nay May   **33 knees** knee   **35 But not the words** [Q1; not in F]   **51 kinds** kind   **56 A** The   **66 Ay, there** [eds.] I heere   **71 ne'er** neuer   **83 Impudent strumpet** [Q1; not in F]   **96 keep** [eds.] keepes   **s.d. Enter Emilia** [after line 94 in F]   **162 then in** [eds.] them: or   **174 And . . . you** [Q1; not in F]   **177 you to** to   **190 Faith, I I**   **for** and   **201 By this hand** Nay   **232 takes** taketh   **236 of** [Q1; not in F]
4.3. 10 s.d. Exit [after line 9 in F]   **22 favor in them** fauour   **25 faith** Father   **26 before thee** before   **43 sighing** [eds.] *singing* [F corrected] *sining* [F uncorrected]   **73 Good troth** Introth   **74 By my troth** Introth   **78 Uds pity** why   **107 God** Heauen
5.1. 1 bulk Barke   **22 Be 't** But   **hear** heard   **36 Forth** For   **50 Did Do** Do   **91 O heaven** Yes, 'tis   **106 out o'** o'   **113 'Las, what's . . . What's** Alas, what is . . . What is   **116 dead** quite dead   **126 Faugh! Fie** Fie
5.2. 34 heaven Heauens   **37 say so** say   **56 Yes, presently** Presently   **61 Then Lord** O Heauen   **96 here** high   **104 Should** Did   **108 s.d. Enter Emilia** [after line 108 in F]   **121 O Lord** Alas   **131 heard** heare   **148 Nay, had** had   **225 O God! O heavenly God** Oh Heauen! oh heauenly Powres   **226 Zounds** Come   **248 have here** haue   **317 not. Here** [not: here Q1] not) heere   **357 Indian** Iudean

King Lear

Copy text: the First Folio, except for those 300 or so lines found only in the First Quarto of 1608 [Q1]. Unless otherwise indicated, adopted readings are from the corrected state of Q1. A few readings are supplied from the Second Quarto of 1619 [Q2]. All readings subsequent to 1619 are marked as supplied by "eds." Act and scene divisions are as marked in F, except that F does not mark 2.3 and 2.4, and omits 4.3 entirely, so that 4.4 is marked "*Scena Tertia*" and similarly with 4.5 and 4.6 (though 4.7 is marked "*Scena Septima*").

1.1. 5 equalities qualities   **20–22 account . . . yet** [eds.] account, though . . . for: yet   **35 liege** Lord   **55 words** word   **66 issue** issues   **68 Speak** [Q1; not in F]   **74 possesses** professes   **85 interessed** [eds.] interest   **104** [Q1; not in F]   **110 mysteries** [eds.] miseries [F] mistresse [Q1]   **135 turns** turne   **156 as a** as   **157 nor** nere   **161 s.d. Lear** Kear   **162 s.p. Kent** Lent   **165 s.p. Cornwall** [eds.] *Cor.*   **166 the** thy   **173 sentence** sentences   **191 s.p. Gloucester** *Cor.*   **217 best object** obiect   **229 well** will   **252 respects of fortune** respect and Fortunes   **272 Ye** [eds.] The   **285 shame them** with shame   **286 s.d. Exeunt** [eds.] *Exit*   **293 hath not** hath   **306 hit** sit
1.2. 1 s.p. [and elsewhere] **Edmund** *Bast.*   **21 top** [eds.] to'   **56 waked** wake   **97–99 Edmund. Nor . . . earth** [Q1; not in F]   **134 Fut, I I**   **136 Edgar** [Q1; not in F]   **137 and pat** [eds.] Pat [F] and out [Q1]   **147–155 as . . . come,** [Q1; not in F]   **182 s.d.** [at line 181 in F]
1.3. 3 s.p. [and elsewhere] **Oswald** [eds.] *Ste.*   **17–21** [Q1; not in F]   **26–27 I would . . . speak** [Q1; not in F]   **28 very** [Q1; not in F]
1.4. 1 well will   **32 canst** canst thou   **43 s.d. Enter steward** [eds.; after line 44 in F]   **50 daughter** Daughters   **76 s.d. Enter steward** [eds.; after line 77 in F]   **96 s.p. Kent** *Lear*   **Fool** my boy   **135 Dost** Do'st thou   **138–153 That . . . snatching** [Q1; not in F]   **158 crown** Crownes   **175 fools** Foole   **195 nor crumb** not crum   **214 it had** it's had   **229–232** [Q1; not in F]   **255 O . . . come** [Q1; not in F]   **303 Yea . . . this** [Q1; not in F]   **343 You're** Your are   **attasked** at task
1.5. s.d. Kent *Kent, Gentleman*   **51 s.d. Exit** *Exeunt*
2.1. 2 you your   **19 s.d.** [after line 18 in F]   **39 stand 's** stand   **69 I should** should I   **70 ay, though** though   **I never got him** [Q1; not in F]   **78 s.d.** [at line 76 in F, after "seeke it"]   **79 why** wher   **87 strange news** strangenesse   **100 spoil** wast   **122 poise** prize   **125 least thought** best though   **132 Flourish. Exeunt** [eds.] *Exeunt. Flourish.*
2.2. 22 clamorous clamours   **45 an** if   **52 What's** What is   **66 you'll** you will   **78 Bring . . . their** Being . . . the   **79 Renege** Reuenge   **80 gale** gall   **84 an** if   **101 take 't** take it   **109 flickering** flicking   **124 dread** dead   **127 their** there   **132 respect** respects   **142 s.d.** [at line 140 in F]   **144–148 His . . . with** [Q1; not in F]   **146 contemned'st** [eds.] temnest [Q1]   **148 King** King his Master, needs   **153** [Q1; not in F]   **154 Come . . . away** [assigned in F to Cornwall]   **good** [Q1; not in F]   **s.d. Exeunt** [eds.] *Exit*
155 Duke's Duke
2.3. 18 sheepcotes Sheeps-Coates
2.4. 2 messenger Messengers   **9 man's** man   **18–19** [Q1; not in F]   **30 panting** painting   **33 whose** those   **56 Hysterica** [eds.] *Historica*   **62 the** the   **74 have** hause   **128 you** your   **130 mother's** Mother   **183 s.d.** [after line 182 in F]   **185 s.d.** [at line 183 in F, after "stocks"]   **187 fickle** fickly   **190 s.d.** [after line 188 in F]   **213 hot-blooded** hot-bloodied   **297 s.d.** [after line 296 in F]   **302 bleak** high
3.1. 7–15 tears . . . all [Q1; not in F]   **10 outstorm** [eds.] out-scorne [Q1]   **30–42** [Q1; not in F]
3.2. 3 drowned drown   **38 s.d.** [after line 36 in F]   **85–86** [these lines follow line 92 in F]
3.3. 17 for 't for it
3.4. 7 skin. So 'tis skinso: 'tis   **10 thy** they   **12 This** the   **27 s.d.** [at line 26 in F]   **31 looped** lop'd   **38 s.d. Enter Fool** [F, after line 36: "*Enter Edgar, and Foole*"]   **44 s.d.** [after line 36 in F]   **46 blows the cold wind** blow the windes   **51 through fire** though Fire   **52 ford** Sword   **57, 58 Bless** Blisse   **90 deeply** deerely   **99 sessa** [eds.] *Sesey*   **112 s.d.** [after line 108 in F]   **114 fiend** [Q1; not in F]   **115 till the** at   **116 squinnies** [eds.] squints [F] squemes [Q1]   **134 stock-punished** stockt, punish'd   **hath had** hath   **173 in th'** into th'
3.5. 11 he which hee   **26 dearer** deere
3.6. 5 s.d. Exit [at line 3 in F]   **17–55** [Q1; not in F]   **21 justicer** [eds.] Iustice [Q1]   **22 Now** [Q2] no [Q1]   **24 eyes at trial, madam?** eyes, at tral madam   **25 burn** [eds.] broome [Q1]   **34 cushions** [eds.] cushings [Q1]   **36 robèd** robbed   **51 joint** [eds.] ioyne [Q1]   **53 on** [eds.] an [Q1]   **67 mongrel grim** Mongrill, Grim   **lym** [eds.] Hym   **69 Bobtail tike or trundle-tail** Or Bobtaile tight, or Troudle taile   **73 Sessa** sese   **76 makes** make   **85 s.d.** [after line 80 in F]   **97–101 Kent. Oppressèd . . . behind** [Q1; not in F]   **101 s.p. Gloucester** [not in F]   **102–105** [Q1; not in F]

3.7. 10 festinate [eds.] festiuate   **18 lord's dependents** Lords, dependants   **23 s.d. Exeunt** [eds.] Exit [after line 22 in F]   **61 rash** sticke   **66 dern** sterne   **75 s.p. First Servant** Seru. [also at lines 79, 82, 84]   **83** [F provides a stage direction: "Killes him"]   **102–110** [Q1; not in F]   **102 s.p. Second Servant** Seruant [and called "1 Ser" at line 106 in Q1]   **103 s.p. Third Servant** 2 Seruant [Q1]   **107 Roguish** [Qa; not in Qb]   **109 s.p. Third Servant** 2 Ser.   **110 s.d. Exeunt** Exit

4.1. 2 flattered. To be worst flatter'd, to be worst: **41 Then . . . gone** Get thee away   **57–62 Five . . . master** [Q1; not in F]   **60 Flibbertigibbet** [eds.] Stiberdigebit [Q1]   **60–61 mopping and mowing** [eds.] Mobing, & Mohing [Q1]

4.2. s.d. Bastard Bastard, and Steward   **2 s.d. steward** [Q1; placed at beginning in F]   **30 whistling** whistle   **32–51 I fear . . . deep** [Q1; not in F]   **33 its** [eds.] ith [Q1]   **48 these** [eds.] this [Q1]   **54–60 that . . . so** [Q1; not in F]   **58 to threat** threat [Q1 corrected]   **61 shows** seemes   **63–69, 70** [Q1; not in F]   **76 thereat enraged** threat-enrag'd   **80 justicers** [Q1 corrected] Iustices

4.3. 1–57 [scene omitted in F]   **11 sir** [eds.] say [Q1]   **16 strove** [eds.] streme [Q1]   **20 seemed** [eds.] seeme [Q1]   **22 dropped. In** dropt in   **32 then** her, then   **44 benediction, turned her** benediction turnd her,   **57 s.d. Exeunt** [eds.] Exit [Q1]

4.4. [F reads "Scena Tertia"]   **s.d. Doctor** Gentlemen   **3 fumiter** [eds.] femiter [Q1] Fenitar [F]   **6 century** Centery   **11 s.p. Doctor** Gent.   **18 distress** desires   **28 right** Rite

4.5. [F reads "Scena Quarta"];   **8 letters** Letter   **23 Somthing** Some things   **27 oeillades** [eds.] Eliads   **41 meet him** meet

4.6. [F reads "Scena Quinta"]   **17 walk** walk'd   **57 summit** Somnet   **66–67 strangeness. / Upon . . . cliff** What [eds.] strangeness. / Vpon . . . Cliffe. What   **71 enridgèd** enraged   **83 coining** crying   **97 white** the white   **124 they're** they are   **161 thine** thy   **164 Through** Thorough   **small** great   **165 Plate sin** [eds.] Place sinnes   **197 Ay . . . dust** [Q1; not in F]   **218 s.d. Exit** [after "moved on" in line 218 in F]   **235 Durst** Dar'st   **238 'cagion** 'casion   **263–264 not. / To** not / To   **269 done if . . . conqueror. Then** [eds.] done. If . . . Conqueror then   **274 and . . . venture** [Q1; not in F]   **275 indistinguished** indinguish'd   **288 s.d. Drum afar off** [after line 286 in F]

4.7. 0 s.d. Kent Kent, and Gentleman   **13 s.p. Doctor** Gent. [also at lines 18, 44, 52, 82]   **24 s.p. Doctor** [not in F; Q1 assigns to "Gent."]   **25 doubt not** doubt   **25–26 Cordelia. Very . . . there** [Q1; not in F]   **33 warring** iarring   **34–37 To stand . . . helm** [Q1; not in F]   **59 hands** hand   **60 No, sir** [Q1; not in F]   **83–84 and . . . lost** [Q1; not in F]   **91–103** [Q1; not in F]

5.1. 12–14 [Q1; not in F]   **18 me not** not   **19–20** [Q1; not in F]   **24–29 Where . . . nobly** [Q1; not in F]   **35** [Q1; not in F]   **41 s.d. Exeunt . . . armies** [after line 39 in F]   **48 love** loues

5.3. 13 and hear poor rogues and heare (poore Rogues)   **39–40** [Q1; not in F]   **49 and appointed guard** [Q1 corrected; not in F]   **56–61 At . . . place** [Q1; not in F]   **57 We** [Q1 corrected] mee [Q1 uncorrected]   **59 sharpness** [Q1 corrected] sharpes [Q1 uncorrected]   **72 s.p. Goneril** Alb.   **85 attaint** arrest   **86 sister** Sisters   **87 bar** [eds.] bare   **100 he is** hes   **105 Edmund. A herald, ho, a herald** [Q1; not in F]   **s.d. Enter a Herald** [after line 104 in F]   **106 s.p. Albany** [not in F]   **112 Captain. Sound, trumpet** [Q1; not in F]   **118 Edmund. Sound** [Q1; not in F]   **124–125 lost, / By . . . canker-bit.** lost / By Treasons tooth: bare-gnawne, and Canker-bit,   **132 the** my priuiledge, The   **135 Despite** Despise   **146 tongue some say of** tongue (some say) of   **149 those** these   **151 scarcely** scarely   **153 s.d. Fight** [eds.] Fights. ["Alarums. Fights" is opposite "Saue him, save him," in line 154 in F.]   **155 arms** Warre   **158 stopple** stop   **163 s.p. Goneril** Bast.   **163 s.d. Exit** [at line 162 after "for 't" in F]   **208–225 This . . . slave** [Q1; not in F]   **217 him** [eds.] me [Q1]   **241 s.d.** [after line 234 in F; F reads "Gonerill"]   **255 The captain** [Q1; not in F]   **262 you** your   **280 s.p. Captain** Gent.   **282 them** him   **294 You are** [eds.] Your'e [F] You'r [Q1]   **299 s.d.** [after "to him" in line 299 in F]

The above textual notes list all instances in which material not in F is included from Q1. To enable the reader to compare further the F and Q1 texts, a list is here provided of material not in Q1 that is to be found in F. There are some 100 lines in all.

1.1. 40–45 while . . . now   **49–50** Since . . . state   **64–65** and . . . rivers   **83–85** to whose . . . interested   **88–89** LEAR Nothing? CORDELIA Nothing   **165** ALBANY, CORNWALL Dear sir, forbear.

1.2. 112–117 This . . . graves   **169–175** I pray . . . brother

1.4. 260 ALBANY Pray . . . patient   **273** Of . . . you   **321–333** This . . . unfitness

2.4. 6 KENT No, my lord   **21** KENT By Juno . . . ay   **45–54** FOOL Winter's . . . year   **96–97** GLOUCESTER Well . . . man   **101–102** Are they . . . Fiery? The   **139–144** LEAR Say . . . blame   **298–299** CORNWALL Whither . . . horse

3.1. 22–29 Who . . . furnishings

3.2. 79–96 FOOL This . . . time. Exit

3.4. 17–18 In . . . endure   **26–27** In . . . sleep   **37–38** Fathom . . . Tom

3.6. 12–14 FOOL No . . . him   **85** Fool And . . . noon

4.1. 6–9 Welcome . . . blasts

4.2. 26 O, the . . . man

4.6. 165–170 Plate . . . lips

5.2. 11 GLOUCESTER And . . . too

5.3. 78 Dispose . . . thine   **91** GONERIL. An interlude   **147** What . . . delay   **226** ALBANY Speak, man   **316–317** Do you . . . look there

Macbeth

Copy text: the First Folio. Act and scene divisions follow the Folio text, except that 5.8 is not marked in the Folio.

1.1. 9 s.p. Second Witch All   **10 s.p. Third Witch** [not in F]   **11 s.p. All** [at line 9 in F]

1.2. 1 s.p. [and elsewhere] Duncan King   **13 gallowglasses** Gallowgrosses   **14 quarrel** Quarry   **21 ne'er** neu'r   **26 thunders break** Thunders

1.3. 32 Weird weyward [elsewhere in F spelled "weyward" or "weyard"]   **39 Forres** Soris   **97 death. As** death, as   **98 Came** Can   **111 lose** loose

1.4. 1 Are Or

1.5. 1 s.p. [and elsewhere] Lady Macbeth Lady   **12 lose** loose   **47 it** hit

1.6. 4 martlet Barlet   **9 most** must

1.7. 6 shoal Schoole   **48 do** no

2.1. 56 strides sides   **57 sure** sowre   **58 way they** they may

2.2. 13 s.d. [at line 8 in F, after "die"]

2.3. 41 s.d. [after line 40 in F]   **142 nea'er** neere

3.1. 76 s.p Murderers Murth.   **116 Both Murderers** Murth. [also at line 141]   **142 s.d. Exeunt** [at line 144 in F]

3.3. 7 and end

3.4. 79 time times   **122 s.d. Exeunt** Exit

3.6. 24 son Sonnes   **38 the** their

4.1. 34 cauldron Cawdron   **38 s.d. to** and   **59 germens** Germaine   **93 Dunsinane** Dunsmane   **94 s.d. Descends** Descend   **98 Birnam** Byrnan [also spelled "Byrnam" at line 93 and "Birnan," "Byrnane," and "Birnane" in Act 5]   **119 eighth** eight

4.2. 1 s.p. [and throughout] Lady Macduff Wife   **22 none** moue   **70–71 ones . . . methinks,** ones / To fright you thus. Me thinks   **80 s.d. Enter Murderers** [after "What are these faces" in F]   **81 s.p. [and throughout scene] First Murderer** Mur.   **84 shag-haired** shagge-ear'd

4.3. 4 downfall'n downfall   **15 deserve** discerne   **35 Fare** Far   **108 accurst** accust   **124 detraction, here** detraction. Heere   **134 thy** they   **144 essay** assay   **146 s.d.** [after "amend" in F]   **161 not** nor   **237 tune** time

5.1. 37 fear who feare? who

5.3. 41 Cure her Cure   **54 pristine** pristiue   **57 senna** Cyme   **62 s.d.** [at line 64 in F]

5.4. 16 s.p. Siward Sey.

Timon of Athens

Copy text: the First Folio. Act and scene divisions missing in the Folio, are editorially supplied.

The Actor's Names [F lists also Varro and Lucius as "Seruants to Vsurers," and the order of names has been changed for Apemantus and Ventidius]

1.1. s.d. and Merchant *Merchant, and Mercer*   **23 gum** Gowne
oozes vses   **27 chafes** chases   **43 man** men   **50 tax** wax   **77
conceived to scope.** conceyu'd, to scope   **92 hands** hand   **slip** sit
116 s.p. [and subsequently] *Old Athenian* Oldm.   **160 s.d. Exeunt**
Exit **184 s.d. Enter Apemantus** *Enter Apermantus* [after line 182 in
F]   **222 cost** cast   **227 s.p. Apemantus** pe.   **234 feigned** fegin'd
259 there! their   **286 Come** Comes   **287 taste** raste   **296 s.p.
First Lord** [not in F]
1.2. s.d. [and elsewhere] *Ventidius* Ventigius   **30 ever** verie   **41 their**
there   **91 thousands, did** thousands? Did   **98 'em. and** 'em? And
105 O, joy's e'en Oh ioyes, e'ne   **107 To forget their faults,** to
forget their Faults.   **113 s.d. Sound tucket** [F continues: *"Enter
the Maskers of Amazons with Lutes in their hands, dauncing and
playing"*]   **114 s.d. Enter Servant** [after "How now?" in F]
120 s.d. Enter Cupid [F continues: *"with the Maske of Ladies"*]
124 Th' ear There   **125 and smell** all   **129 s.p. First Lord** Luc.
s.d. [see notes at lines 113 an 120 above]   **144 s.d. singles**
single   **151 s.p. First Lady** 1 Lord   **167 s.d. Enter Flavius** [at line
176, after "welcome," in F]   **181 s.p. Second Servant** Ser.
211 rode rod   **213 s.p. Third Lord.** 1. L.
2.1. 34 Ay, go, sir. I go sir?   **35 in compt** in. Come
2.2. 1 s.p. [and elsewhere] *Flavius* Stew.   **4 resumes** resume   **11 s.p.**
[and elsewhere] *Varro's Servant* Var.   **13 s.p.** [and elsewhere] *Isidore's Servant* Isid.   **41 broken** debt, broken   **64 s.p.** [and else-
where] *All the Servants* Al.   [or All]   **75, 104 mistress'** Masters
81 s.p. Page Boy   **96 Ay. Would** I would   **132 proposed** propose
139 found sound   **160 of** or   **191 Flaminius** Flauius   **211 treasure, cannot** Treature cannot
3.1. s.d. Enter enters   **1 s.p.** [and elsewhere] *Lucullus' Servant* Ser.
3.2. 27 s.p. [and elsewhere] *Lucius* Lucil.   **61 s.d.** [at line 60 in F]
3.3. 5 Owes Owes   **15** [and elsewhere] *He's* Has   **23 I 'mongst**
'mong'st   **25 He'd** Had
3.4. s.d. Men man   **1 s.p.** [and elsewhere] *Varro's First Servant* Var.
man   **2 s.p.** [and elsewhere] *Titus' Servant* Tit.   [and elsewhere]
Hortensius' Servant Hort.   **3 s.p.** [and elsewhere] *Lucius' Servant*
Luci.   **6 s.p.** [and elsewhere] *Philotus' Servant* Phil.   **14 recoverable. I** recouerable, I feare: **15–16 purse,** / That is, purse,
that is: **45 s.p.** [and elsewhere] *Varro's Second Servant* 2. Varro
59 If If't   **78 an answer** answer   **88 s.p. Hortensius' Servant** 1.
Var.   **89 s.p. Both Varro's Servants** 2 Var.   **112 Sempronius** Sempronius Vllorxa
3.5. 18 An And   **23 behave** behooue   **51 lion,** Lyon?   **felon** fellow
52 judge, Iudge?   **53 suffering.** suffering,   **66 Why, I** Why
70 'em him   **85 honors** Honour
3.6. 1 s.p. [and so throughout scene]   **19 here's** heares
54 s.p. First and Second Lords Both   **80 tag** legge   **87 s.p. Others**
other   **91 with your** you with   **115 s.p. Third Lord** 2   **116 s.p.
Second Lord** 3
4.1. 6 steads! To generall filths steeds, to generall Filthes.   **8 fast;** fast
9 back, backe;   **13 Son** Some
4.3. 10 senator Senators   **12 pasture** Pastour   **13 lean** leaue   **16
grece** grize   **41 at, this** at. This   **88 tub-fast** Fubfast   **119 bars**
Barne   **124 thy** the   **135 s.p.** [and throughout scene] *Phrynia and
Timandra* Both   **158 scolds** scold'st   **187 thy human** the humane
206 fortune future   **225 mossed** moyst   **246 Outlives** Out:liues:
254 clasped claspt: **255 swathe, proceeded** swath proceeded,
257 drudges drugges   **258 command,** command'st: **287 my** thy
314 meddlers Medlars   **368–369 thee.** I'd beat thee, but thee, Ile
beate thee; But   **387 son and sire** Sunne and fire   **401 s.d.** [after
line 402 in F]   **402 them** then   **414 s.p.** [and throughout scene]
Banditti All   **439 villainy** Villaine   **439–440 do 't, Like workmen.**
doo't. Like Workemen,   **458 us, not** vs not   **462 s.d. Exeunt** *Exit*
479 grant'st grunt'st   **man, I** man. I   **482 I; all** I all   **497 mild**
wilde   **514 A** If not a
5.1. 5–6 Phrynia and Timandra *Phrinica* and *Timandylo*   **50 worship**
worshipt   **66 go naked; men** go, / Naked men   **70 men** man
115 in vain vaine   **125 chance** chanc'd   **132 cauterizing** Canther-
izing   **146 sense** since   **147 its own fail** it owne fall   **181 reverend'st** reuerends   **194 through** thorow
5.2. 1 s.p. [and throughout scene] *Third Senator* 1   **5 s.p.** [and
throughout scene] **Fourth Senator** 2   **14 s.p. First Senator** 3
5.3.2 Who's Whose
5.4. 27 out. out,   **28 Shame . . . excess** (Shame that they wanted,
cunning in excess)   **55 Descend** Defend   **65 s.p. Soldier** Mes.

Antony and Cleopatra

Copy text: the First Folio. Act and scene divisions, missing in the Folio, are editorially supplied.
1.1. 41 On One   **52 whose** who
1.2. 4 charge change   **41 fertile** foretell   **64-65 Alexas** [printed in F
as s.p.]   **83 Saw** Saue   **90 Alexas** Alexias   **93 s.p.** [and through
line 118] **First Messenger** Messen. (or Mess.)   **116 minds** windes
119 ho how   **120 s.p. Second Messenger** 1. Mes.   **121 s.p. Third
Messenger** 2. Mes.   **124 s.p. Fourth Messenger** 3. Mes.   **126 s.p.
Fourth Messenger** Mes.   **137 s.d. Enter Enobarbus** [after "hatch,"
line 137, in F]   **144 occasion** an occasion   **186 leave** loue   **191
Hath** Haue   **200 hair** heire   **202 place is** places   **requires** require
1.3. 2 who's Whose   **20 What, says** What sayes   **43 services**
Seruicles   **63 vials** Violles   **80 blood. No more.** blood no more?
82 by my by
1.4. 3 Our One   **8 Vouchsafed** vouchsafe   **9 abstract** abstracts   **34
s.p. First Messenger** Mes.   **44 deared** fear'd   **46 lackeying** lacking
48 s.p. Second Messenger Mes.   **57 wassails** Vassailes   **58
Modena** Medena   **59 Pansa** Pausa   **77 we** me
1.5. 3 mandragora Mandragoru   **5 time** time: **35 s.d. Alexas** Alexas
from Caesar   **52 dumbed** dumbe   **53 What, was** What was   **64
man** mans
2.1. 2 s.p. [and throughout scene] *Menas* Mene.   **22 joined** ioyne
39 ne'er neere   **42 warred** wan'd   **44-45 greater. . . . all,**
greater, . . . all:
2.2. 77 Alexandria; you Alexandria you   **113 soldier only. Speak**
Souldier, onely speake   **128 so** say   **129 reproof** proofe   **180 s.d.
Exeunt** *Exit omnes*   **Manent** Manet   **204 lovesick . . . The** Loue-
sicke. / With them the   **214 glow** gloue   **216 gentlewomen** Gentlewoman   **233 heard** hard
2.3. 23 afeard a feare   **225 thee; . . . to thee.** thee no more but:
when to thee,   **31 away** alway   **32** [and elsewhere] *Ventidius*
Ventigius   **41 s.d. Enter Ventidius** [after "Ventigius," line 41, in F]
2.4. 6 the Mount Mount   **9 s.p. Maecenas, Agrippa** Both
2.5. 2 s.p. All Omnes   **10 river. There** Riuer there   **11 off,** I off. I
12 finned fine   **23 s.d. Enter a Messenger** [after "Italy," line 23,
in F]   **28 him, there** him. / There   **44 is** 'tis   **85 s.d. Enter
. . . again** [after "sir" line 85, in F]
2.6. s.d. Agrippa Agrippa, Menas   **16 th' all-honored** all honor'd
19 is his   **39 s.p. Caesar, Antony, Lepidus** Omnes   **42–43 impatience. Though . . . telling,** impatience: though . . . telling.
58 compostion composition   **67 meanings** meaning   **71 more of**
more   **83 s.p. Caesar, Antony, Lepidus** All   **89 s.d. Manent** Manet
2.7. 1 their th' their   **4 colored** Conlord   **39 s.d. whispers in 's ear**
[at line 41 in F]   **93 is he** is   **101 grows** grow   **113 bear** beate
115 s.p. Boy [not in F]   **119 s.p. All** [not in F]   **122 off. Our** of
our   **126 Splits** Spleet's   **130 father's** Father   **132 s.p. Menas**
[not in F]
3.1. 5 s.p. [and throughout scene] *Silius* Romaine   **8 whither** whether
3.2. 10 s.p. Agrippa Ant.   **16 figures** Figure   **49 full** the full   **60
wept** weepe
3.3. 2 s.d. Enter . . . before [after "sir," line 2, in F]   **19 lookedst**
look'st
3.4. 8 them, then   **9 took 't** look't   **24 yours** your   **20 Your** You
38 has he's
3.5. 13 world would   **hast** hadst   **15 grind the one** grind
3.6. 13 he there hither   **the kings** the King   **30 being, that** being
that,   **73 Adallas** Adullas   **74 Manchus** Mauchus   **76 Comagene**
Comageat   **Polemon** Polemen   **77 Lycaonia** Licoania
3.7. 4 it is it it   **14 Photinus, an** Photinus an   **19 s.d. Canidius** Cam-
idias [also spelled "Camidius" in this scene and elsewhere]
21 Brundusium Brandusium   **23 Toryne** Troine   **29 s.p.** [and else-
where] *Canidius* Cam.   **36 muleteers** Militers   **52 Actium** Action
57 impossible; impossible   **67 s.d. Exeunt** *exit*   **70 leader's** led
Leaders leade   **73 s.p. Canidius** Ven.   **80 Well I** Well, I   **82 in**
with
3.8.6 s.d. Exeunt *exit*
3.9.4 s.d. Exeunt *exit*
3.10 s.d. Enobarbus Enobarbus and Scarus   **14 June** Inne   **28 he** his
3.11. 6 s.p. All Omnes   **19 that** them   **46 seize** cease   **50 led** lead
57 tow stowe.   **58 Thy** The
3.12. 0 s.d. Dolabella Dollabello   **13 lessens** Lessons

3.13. 26 caparisons Comparisons   **34 alike. That** alike, that   **55 Caesar** *Caesars*   **74 deputation** disputation   **76 kneel / Till** kneele. / Tell him,   **94 s.d. Enter a Servant** [after "him," in line 94, in F]   **104 This** the   **114–115 eyes,** / In . . . **filth** eyes / In . . . filth,   **133 s.d. Enter . . . Thidias** [after "whipped," in line 133, in F]   **140 whipped . . . Henceforth** whipt. For following him, henceforth   **165 smite** smile   **168 discandying** discandering   **171 sits** sets   **202 on** in   **204 s.d. Exit** *Exeunt*
4.2. 1 Domitius *Domitian*   **10 s.d. Enter . . . servitors** [after line 10 in F]   **20 s.p. All** *Omnes*
4.3. 8 s.p. Third 1   **25, 31 s.p. All** *Omnes*
4.4. 5 too too, *Anthony*   **6 s.p. Antony** [not in F, or mistakenly placed in line 5 as part of Cleopatra's speech]   **8 s.p. Cleopatra** [not in F]   **24 s.p. Captain** *Alex.*   **32–33 compliment . . . Now** Complement, Ile leaue thee. / Now
4.5. 1, 3, 6 s.p. Soldier *Eros*   **17 Dispatch.—Enobarbus** Dispatch *Enobarbus.* **s.d. Exeunt** *Exit*
4.6. 37-38 do 't . . . I doo't. I feele I
4.7 3 s.d. Exeunt *exit*   **8 s.d.** [after "heads," line 6, in F]
4.8. 2 gests guests   **18 My** Mine   **23 favoring** sauouring
4.12. 3 s.d. Alarum . . . fight [at 0. s.d. in F]   **4 augurer** Auguries   **21 spanieled** pannelled
4.13. 10 death. To death to'
4.14. 4 towered toward   **10 dislimns** dislimes   **19 Caesar** *Caesars*   **104 ho** how   **119 s.p. Dercetus** *Decre.*   **145 s.d. Exeunt** *Exit*
4.15. 26–27 me. If . . . operation. me, if . . . operation.   **56 lived the** liued. The   **78 e'en** in   **96 s.d. off** *of*
5.1. s.d. Maecenas *Menas*   **3 s.d. Dercetus** *Decretas*   **5, 13, 19 s.p. Dercetus** *Dec.*   **26 you sad, friends?** you sad Friends,   **28, 31 s.p. Agrippa** *Dol.*   **48 s.d.** [after "says," line 51, in F]   **54 intents** desires intents, desires,   **59 live** leaue
5.2. 26 dependency dependacie   **35** [F repeats s.p. *Pro.*]   **55 varletry** Varlotarie   **80 O,** the o' th'   **86 autumn 'twas** Anthony it was   **102 success but** successe: But   **103 smites** suites   **144 seal** seele   **156 soulless villain** Soule-lesse, Villain   **178 merits in our name,** merits, in our name   **207 s.d. Exit** [at line 206 in F]   **216 Ballad** Ballads   **223 my** mine   **228 Cydnus** *Cidrus*   **318 awry** away   **319 s.d. in** *in, and Dolabella*   **342–343 diadem . . . mistress;** Diadem; . . . Mistris

Coriolanus

Copy text: the First Folio. Act divisions are from the Folio; scene divisions are from subsequent editorial tradition.

1.1. 7 [and throughout play] **Marcius** *Martius*   **15 on** one   **33 s.p. Second Citizen** *All*   **42-43 accusations. He** Accusations he   **55 s.p. First Citizen** 2 *Cit.* [and so throughout scene]   **64 you. For your wants,** you for your wants.   **90 stale 't** scale't   **105 you. With** you with   **108 tauntingly** taintingly   **123 you.** you,   **125 awhile,** awhile;   **171 geese. You are no** Geese you are: No   **214 Shouting** Shooting   **218 unroofed** vnroo'st   **237 s.d. Junius** *Annius*   **240 Lartius** *Lucius*   **242 s.p.** [and at 1.1.246 and 1.5.21] *Lartius Tit.*   **245, 249** [and elsewhere] **First Senator** *Sen.*   **252 s.d. Manent** *Manet*
1.2. s.d. Corioles *Coriolus*   **4 on** one   **16 Whither** Whether   **27-28 Coriole. . . . before 's** Coriole / If . . . before's:
1.3. 37 that's that   **44 sword, contemning.—Tell** sword. Contenning, tell   **82 s.p. Virgilia** *Vlug.*   **84 yarn** yearne   **85 Ithaca** *Athica*   **105 lady. . . . now,** Ladie, as she is now:
1.4. 13 s.d. Corioles *Coriolus*   **18 up. Our** vp our   **20 s.d. Alarum far off** [after line 20 in F]   **32 herd of—Boils** Heard of Byles   **43 trenches. Follow 's** Trenches followes   **46 s.d. gates** *Gati* **and is shut in** [in F, this is part of the s.d. at line 43]   **57 left, Marcius.** left *Marcius,*   **58 entire,** intire;   **59 Were** Weare   **60 Cato's** *Calues*
1.5. 7 them, *them.*   **8 up.** vp,   **9 him!** him
1.6. 9 s.d. [after line 9 in F]   **21 Who's** Whose   **22 flayed** Flead   **30 wooed, in heart** woo'd in heart;   **53 Antiates** Antients   **70 Lesser** Lessen   **73 alone, or** alone: Or   **84 I** foure
1.7. 4 lose loose [and sometimes elsewhere]   **7 s.d. Exeunt** *Exit*
1.8. 11 masked. For maskt, for   **12 Wert** Wer't

1.9. 32 good . . . all good, and good store of all,   **41 may** [F provides a s.p., "*Mar.*"]   **49 shout** shoot   **64, 66** [and elsewhere] **Caius Marcius** *Marcus Caius*   **66 s.p. All** *Omnes*   **67, 78, 81, 89 s.p. Coriolanus** *Martius*   **93 s.d. A flourish. Cornets.** [at the beginning of line 10 in F]
1.10. 19 itself. Nor it selfe, nor
2.1. 18 with all withall   **24 how are** ho ware   **51 upon too** vppon, to   **57 cannot** can   **61 you** you you   **62 faces. If** faces, if   **64 bisson** beesome   **70-71 faucet-seller** Forcet-seller   **85 are. When . . . purpose,** are, when . . . purpose.   **106 s.p. Valeria, Virgilia** 2. *Ladies*   **122 pocket, the** Pocket? the   **123 brows, Menenius.** Browes: *Menenius.*   **155 s.d.** [after line 155 in F]   **160** [and elsewhere] **Lartius** *Latius*   **164 Coriolanus** *Martius Caius Coriolanus*   **177 wear** were   **179 s.p. Coriolanus** *Com.*   **185 You** Yon   **203 s.d. Brutus** *Enter Brutus*   **Sicinius** *Scicinius* [and sometimes elsewhere]   **233 napless** Naples   **254 touch** teach
2.2. 25 ascent assent   **67 s.p.** [and elsewhere] **First Senator** *Senat.*   **81 one on 's** on ones   **91 chin** Shinne   **92 bristled** brizled   **108 took; from face to foot** tooke from face to foote: **155 s.d. Manent** *Manet*   **160 here. On the marketplace** heere on th' Market place,
2.3. 28 wedg'd wadg'd   **38–39 it. I say, if** it, I say. If   **39 all together** altogether   **52 tongue** tougne   **67 but not** but   **88, 91, 106 s.p. Fourth Citizen** 1   **104 s.p. Fifth Citizen** 2   **11 s.p. Both Citizens** *Both*   **114 higher** higher   **115 toge** tongue   **118 do 't,** doo't?   **132 s.p. Sixth Citizen** 1. *Cit.*   **134 s.p. Seventh Citizen** 2. *Cit.*
3.1. 46 suppliants for Suppliants: for   **60 abused, set on. This** abus'd: set on, this   **94 good God!** There   **129 Their** There   **137 poll** pole   **146 Where one** Whereon   **164 He's** Has [also at line 165]   **169 bench? In a rebellion.** Bench, in a rebellion: **176 s.d. Enter an Aedile** [after line 175 in F]   **181 s.p. All Patricians** *All*   **187 s.p.** [and elsewhere] **All Plebeians** *All*   **189 s.p. All** [at line 191 in F]   **219 s.p. All Plebeians** *All Ple.*   **233 s.d.** [preceded in F by "*Exeunt*"]   **234 your** our   **235 s.p. Coriolanus** *Com.*   **242 s.p. Cominius** *Corio.*   **243 s.p. Coriolanus** *Mene.*   **245 s.p. Menenius** [not in F]   **283 comes't** com'st   **315 s.p. Sicinius** *Menen.*   **334 bring him** bring him in peace
3.2. 7 s.p. A Patrician *Noble*   **14 s.d. Enter Volumnia** [after line 6 in F]   **23 thwartings** things   **34 herd** heart   **67 son, these . . . nobles;** Sonne: These . . . Nobles,   **103 bear? Well, I** beare well? I   **104 plot to lose,** Plot, to loose   **115 drum, into a pipe** Drumme into a Pipe,   **117 lulls** lull
3.3 5 s.d. [after line 5 in F]   **34 for th'** fourth   **38 Throng** Through   **59 accents** Actions   **73 hell fold** hell. Fould   **76 clutched** clutcht: **77 numbers,** numbers   **107 it;** in it. In   **118 for** from   **143-144 blows! Despising . . . city, thus** blowes, despising . . . City. Thus   **145 s.d. Cominius** *Cominius, with Cumalijs*   **147 Hoo! Hoo!** Hoo, oo   **147 s.d.** [after line 145 in F]
4.1. 5 chances chances.   **24 thee** the   **34 wilt** will   **37 s.p. Virgilia** *Corio.*
4.2. 23 words, words.   **46 s.d. Exeunt** *Exit*   **55** [F has s.d., "*Exeunt*"]   **56 s.d. Exeunt** Exit
4.3. 9 approved appear'd   **32 will** well
4.4. 6 s.d. [after line 6 in F]   **23 hate** haue
4.5. 75 requited requitted: **83 Whooped** Hoop'd   **136 o'erbear 't** o're-beate   **152 s.d. Two** *Enter two*   **169 on** one   **181, 185 s.p. First and Second Servingmen** *Both*   **194 him, directly** him directly,   **195 Corioles;** Corioles   **209 sowl** sole   **211 polled** poul'd   **233 sleepy** sleepe
4.6. 10 s.d. [after line 9 in F]   **21 s.p.** [and elsewhere] **All citizens** *All*   **36 lamentation** Lamention   **61 come** comming   **78 s.p. Second Messenger** *Mes.*   **127 s.p. Both Tribunes** *Tri.*   **144 one** oue   **146 s.p. All citizens** *Omnes*   **151 us. That** vs, that   **165 s.d. Exeunt** *Exit*
4.7. 19 him. Although him, although   **21 fairly** fairely: **34 osprey** Aspray   **37 'twas** 'was   **39 defect** detect   **49 virtues** Vertue,   **55 falter** fouler
5.2. 65 by my my   **76 our** your   **88 pity note how much.** pitty: Note how much,   **95 s.d. Manent** *Manet*
5.3. 15 accept. To accept, to   **16 more, a** more: A   **48 prate** pray   **63 holp** hope   **66 curded** curdied   **127 s.p. Young Marcius** *Boy*   **149 fine** fiue   **152 charge** change   **163 clucked** clock'd   **169 with our** with him with our   **192 stead** steed

5.4. 40 s.p. [and throughout scene] Second Messenger *Mess.*   **49 s.d. all together** *altogether*   **51 cymbals** Symboles
5.5. 4 Unshout Vnshoot
5.6. 33 projects to accomplish, proiects, to accomplish   **43-44 it / For . . . him.** it: / For . . . him,   **46 lies, he** Lies; he   **56 second. When** second, when   **57 way his** way. His   **63 s.p. All Lords** *All*   **104 other** others   **117 pieces, Volsces. Men** peeces Volces men   **121 Fluttered** Flatter'd   **136 s.d. Draw** *Draw both* **kill** kils

Pericles

Copy text: the First Quarto of 1609. Act and scene divisions, missing in the Quarto, are derived from subsequent editorial tradition.

1.0. 1 s.p. Gower [not in Q; also in subsequent choruses throughout, except at 4.4, 5.2, and epilogue]   **6 holy-ales** Holydayes   **11 these** those   **39 a** of
1.1. 8 For th' For   **18 razed** racte   **23 the** th'   **25 boundless** bondlesse   **57 s.p. Antiochus** [not in Q; also at line 170]   **63 advice** advise   **100-101 clear . . . them. The** cleare: . . . them, the   **106 know;** . . . fit, know, . . . fit;   **112 our** your   **114 cancel** counsell   **128 you're** you   **137 'schew** shew   **160 s.d. Enter a Messenger** [after "done" in line 160 in Q]
1.2. 3 Be my By me   **5 quiet?** quiet,   **16 me: the** me the   **20 honor him** honour   **25 th' ostent** the stint   **30 am** once   **41 blast** sparke   **69-70 me . . . thyself.** me: . . . thy selfe,   **72 Where,** as Whereas   **80 seem** seemes   **84 Bethought me** Bethought   **85 fears** feare   **87 doubt—as . . . he doth** doo't, as no doubt he doth   **93 call 't** call   **122 word for faith,** word, for faith   **123 will sure** will   **124 we'll** will   **126 s.d. Exeunt** *Exit*
1.3. 1 s.p. Thaliard [not in Q]   **27 ears it** seas   **please** please: **28 seas** Sea   **30 s.p. Helicanus** [not in Q]   **34 betaken** betake   **39 s.d. Exeunt** *Exit*
1.4. 5 aspire aspire?   **13, 14 do** to   **13 deep** deepe: **14 lungs** toungs   **17 helps** helpers   **36 they** thy   **39 two summers** too sauers   **44 loved.** lou'de,   **58 thou** thee   **67 Hath** That   **these** the   **69 men** mee   **74 him's** himnes   **77 fear** leaue   **78 lowest,** lowest?   **97 s.p. All** *Omnes*   **196 ne'er** neuer
2.0. 11 Tarsus *Tharstill*   **12 speken** spoken   **22 Sends word** Sau'd one   **24 intent** in Tent   **murder** murdred [some corrected copies of Q have "had . . . murder"]
2.1. 6 left me left my   **12 ho** to   **Pilch** pelch   **31-32 devours** deuowre   **39 s.p. Third Fisherman** 1   **48 finny** fenny   **53 that?** that,   **55 it.** it?   **78 quotha** ke-tha   **82 holidays** all day   **83 more o'er** more; or   **91 your** you   **100 is** I   **122 pray** pary   **123 yet** yeat   **all thy** all   **130 it.** it   **131 thee from !—may** 't thee, Fame may   **148 d' ye** di'e [Q uncorr.] do'e [Q corr.]   **157 rapture** rupture   **160 delightful** delight   **167 equal** a Goale
2.2. 1 s.p. [and elsewhere] Simonides *King*   **4 daughter** daughter heere   **27 Piùe . . . forza** Pue Per doleera kee per forsa   **28 what's** with   **29 chivalry** Chiually   **30 pompae** Pompey   **33 Quod** Qui
2.3. 3 To I   **123 yours** your   **27 Envied** Enuies   **39 Yon** You   **40 tells me** tels   **45 son's** sonne   **52 stored** stur'd   **53 you do** do you   **109 s.d. They dance** [after "unclasp" in Q]   **113 to be** be   **115 s.p. Simonides** [not in Q]
2.4. 22 welcome. Happy welcome happy.   **34 death's** death   **40 s.p. All** *Omnes*
2.5. 74 s.d. Aside [after line 75 in Q]   **76, you, not** you not,   **78 s.d. Aside** [after line 79 in Q]   **92 s.p. Both** *Ambo*
3.0. 2 the house about about the house   **6 'fore** from   **7 crickets** Cricket   **13 eche** each   **17 coigns** Crignes   **21 stead** steed   **quest. At last from Tyre,** quest at last from *Tyre:*   **29 appease** oppresse   **35 Yravishèd** Iranyshed   **46 Fortune's mood** fortune mou'd   **57 not . . . told.** not? . . . told,   **58 hold** hold:
3.1. 1 Thou The   **7 Thou stormest** then storme   **8 spit** speat   **11 midwife** my wife   **14 s.d. Enter Lychorida** [after "Lychorida" in Q]   **34 Poor . . . nature** [Wilkins; not in Q]   **38 s.p. Master** 1. *Sayl* [also in lines 43 and 47]   **45 s.p. Sailor** 2. *Sayl*   **51 s.p. Master** 1   **52 custom** esterne   **53 for . . . straight** [printed in Q as part of the next line, after "As you think meet," the line assigned to Pericles]   **60 in the ooze** in oare   **62 And aye-** The ayre

65 paper Taper   **70 s.p. Sailor** 2   **73 s.p. Master** 2 [also in line 76]   **81 s.d. Exeunt** *Exit*
3.2. 6 ne'er neare   **19 quit** quite   **51 s.p. [and elsewhere] First Servant** *Seru.*   **58 bitumed** bottomed   **61-62 open. / Soft!** open soft; **68-69 too!** too'l   **Apollo** to Apollo,   **79 even** euer   **87 lain** lien   **95 breathes** breath
3.3. s.d. at Tarsus *Artharsus*   **6 haunt** hant   **31 Unscissored** vnsisterd   **hair** heyre   **32 ill** will   **37 s.p. Cleon** *Cler.*   **41 [and elsewhere] Lychorida** Lycherida
3.4. s.d. Thaisa *Tharsa*   **4 s.p. Thaisa** *Thar.*   **5 eaning** learning   **9 vestal** vastall   **11 s.p. Cerimon** *Cler.*   **17 s.d. Exeunt** Exit
4.0. 8 music, letters Musicks letters   **10 her** hie   **heart** art   **14 Seeks** Seeke   **15 hath our Cleon** our *Cleon* hath   **16 wench full grown** full growne wench   **17 ripe** right   **rite** sight   **21 she** they   **25 to the** too'th   **26 bird** bed   **29 Dian; still** *Dian* still,   **32 With** [after "might" in Q]   **35 given. This** giuen, this   **38 murder** murderer   **47 carry** carried   **48 on** one
4.1. 5 inflaming love i' thy in flaming, thy loue   **11 nurse's** Mistresse   **25 me.** me?   **27 On . . . margent** ere the sea marre it   **36 here. When** here, when   **40 courses. Go** courses, go   **66 stem** sterne   **76-77 killed? / Now** kild now?   **99 s.d. Exeunt** *Exit*   **105 aboard. If** aboard, if
4.2. 4 much much much   **42 s.p. First Pirate** *Sayler*   **73 was like** was   **88-89 men must stir** must stir   **103 i' the** ethe   **117-118 lovers; seldom but** Louers seldome, but   **124 s.p. Bawd** *Mari.*   **150 s.d. Exeunt** *Exit*
4.3. 1 are ere   **6 A** 0   **12 fact** face   **14-15 Fates; / To foster is** fates to foster it,   **27 prime** prince   **33 Marina's** *Marianas*   **35 through** thorow
4.4. 3 your our   **7 seem** seemes   **8 i' the** with   **9 story.** storie   **10 the** thy   **13 along. Behind** along behind,   **14 govern, if** gouerne it,   **mind,** mind.   **18 his** this   **19 grow on** grone   **20 gone.** gone   **23 See** [Q adds an s.p. here: *Gowr.*]   **24 true-owed** true olde   **26 o'ershowered,** ore-show'rd   **27 embarks. He** imbarques, hee   **29 puts** put   **to sea. He bears** to Sea he beares,   **48 scene** Steare
4.5. 9 s.d. Exeunt. *Exit*
4.6. s.d. three bawds *Bawdes* 3   **17 loon** Lowne   **22 may so;** may, so   **37 dignifies** dignities   **69 name 't** name   **88 aloof** aloft   **130 ways** way   **132 s.d. Bawd** *Bawdes*   **137 She** He   **154 ways** way   **167 Coistrel** custerell   **195 women** woman
5.0. 7 roses: Roses   **8 twin** Twine   **13 lost** left   **20 fervor** [Q corr.] former [Q uncorr.]
5.1. 1 s.p. Tyrian Sailor 1. *Say*   **7 s.p. Tyrian Sailor** 2. *Say*   **12 s.p. Tyrian Sailor** 1. *Say* [Q corr.] Hell [Q uncorr.]   **36 s.p. Lysimachus** [not in Q]   **37 Behold . . . person** [assigned to Lysimachus in Q]   **38 Till** Hell. Till   **night** wight   **43 s.p. First Lord** *Lord*   **48 deafened ports** defend parts   **51 with her** her is   **now** now   **60 gods** God   **68 presence** present   **72 I'd** I do   **wed** to wed   **73 one** on   **bounty** beautie   **75 feat** fate   **83 Marked** Marke   **91 weighed.** wayde,   **105 You're** your   **countrywoman** Countrey women   **106 Here** heare   **shores . . . shores** shewes . . . shewes   **114 cased** caste   **124 palace** *Pallas*   **126 make my** make   **129 say** stay   **134 thought'st** thoughts   **143 thou them?** thou   **166 dull** duld   **182 imposter** imposture   **185 s.p. Pericles** Hell.   **205 me but that,** me, but that   **212 life** like   **228-229 music? / Tell** Musicke tell,   **230 doubt** doat   **249 life** like   **264 suit** sleight
5.2. 8 Mytilin *Metalin*   **9 King. So** King, so   **14 interim, pray you, all** *Interim* pray, you all   **15 filled** fild   **16 willed** wild
5.3. 6 who whom   **15 nun** mum   **22 one** in   **29-30 look! / If** looke if   **38 Immortal** I,mortall   **51 s.p. Pericles** Hell.   **71 I bless** blesse   **79 credit, sir,** credit. Sir,   **91 preserved** preferd   **92 Led** Lead   **98 deed to** deede,   **79 credit, sir,** credit. Sir

Cymbeline

Copy text: the First Folio. Act and scene divisions are as in the Folio except as indicated below.

1.1. 2 courtiers' Courtiers: **30 [and elsewhere] Cassibelan** Cassibulan   **59 swaddling-clothes the other,** swathing cloathes, the other   **70** [F begins "*Scena Secunda*" here]   **98 Philario's** *Filorio's*   **118 cere** seare   **160 s.d. Enter Pisanio** [after *Exit*, line 160, in F]

1.2. [F labels *"Scena Tertia"*]
1.3. [F labels *"Scena Quarta"*]   **9 this** his
1.4 [F labels *"Scena Quinta"*]   **28 Briton** Britaine   **47 offend not** offend   **72 Britain.** Brittanie;   **others** others.   **74 but believe**
beleeue   **84 purchase** purchases   **128 thousand** thousands   **137
preserve** preseure
1.5 [F labels *"Scena Sexta"*]   **3 s.d. Exeunt** *Exit*   **77 s.d. Exit Pisanio**
[at line 76 in F]   **87 s.d. Exeunt** Exit
1.6 [F labels *"Scena Septima"*]   **7 desire** desires   **28 takes** take
36 th' unnumbered the number'd   **67 Briton** Britaine [and so
elsewhere for nominative form]   **72 be, will . . . languish** be:
will . . . languish: **104 Fixing** Fiering   **109 illustrous** illustrious
169 men's men   **170 descended** defended
2.1. 27 your you   **34 tonight** night   **51 s.d. Exeunt** *Exit*   **61 husband,
than** Husband. Then   **62 divorce he'd make!** diuorce, heel'd
make   **63 honor, keep** Honour. Keepe   **65 s.d. Exit** *Exeunt*
2.2 1 s.p. Helen *La.* [also at line 2]   **49 bare** beare   **51 s.d. Exeunt**
Exit
2.3. 20 s.p. Musician [not in F]   **29 s.p. Cloten** [not in F]   **30 vice**
voyce   **32 amend** amed   **48 solicits** solicity   **130 envy, if** Enuie.
If   **139 garment** Garments   **147 am** am.   **156 you** your
2.4. 6 hopes hope   **18 legions** Legion   **24 mingled** wing-led   **34
through** thorough   **37 s.p. Philario** *Post.*   **48 not** note   **58 you**
yon   **60 loses** looses   **61 leaves** leaue   **63 near** nere   **127 lose**
loose   **138 the** her
2.5. [scene not marked in F]   **16 German one** Iarmen on   **27 have a
name** name
3.1. 20 rocks Oakes   **53 be. We do say** be, we do. Say
3.2. 2 monster's her accuser Monsters her accuse   **67 score** store
ride rid   **78 here, not** heere, not
3.3. 2 Stoop Sleepe   **23 bauble** Babe   **28 know** knowes   **31 known,
well** knowne. Well   **34 for** or   **83 wherein they bow,** whereon
the Bowe   **86 Polydore** *Paladour*   **106 Morgan** Morgan
3.4. 79 afore 't a-foot   **90 make** makes   **102 blind first** first
3.5. 17 s.d. Exeunt *Exit*   **32 looks** looke   **40 strokes** stroke;,   **42 s.p.
Attendant** *Mes.*   **44 loud'st** lowd   **55 s.d. Exit** [after "days" in F]
141–142 insultment insulment
3.6. 27 [F begins *"Scena Septima"* here]
3.7. [F labels *"Scena Octaua"*]   **9 commends** commands
4.1. 18 her face thy face
4.2. 50–52 He . . . dieter [assigned in F to Arviragus]   **58 him** them
59 Grow, patience Grow patient   **124 thanks, ye** thanks the   **134
humor** Honor   **172 how** thou   **188 ingenious** ingenuous   **207
crare** care   **208 Might** Might'st   **226 ruddock** Raddocke   **293 is**
are   **294 s.p. Imogen awakes** [as stage direction in F]   **339 are** are
heere   **393 wild-wood leaves** wild wood-leaves
4.3. 40 betid betide
4.4 2 find we we finde   **17 the** their   **27 hard** heard
5.1. 1 wished am wisht   **32-33 begin / The fashion:** begin, / The fashion
5.3. 24 harts hearts   **42 stooped** stopt   **43 they** the   **47 before, some**
before some
5.4. 1 s.p. [and throughout scene] **First Jailer** *Gao.*   **15 constrained.
To** constrain'd, to   **50 deserved** d seru'd   **81 look** looke, looke
165 Oh, Oh, of   **169 sir** Sis   **197 s.d. Exeunt** [at line 206 in F]
5.5. 54 fine time   **62 s.p. Ladies** *La.*   **65 heard** heare   **128 saw** see
136 On, One   **207 got it** got   **264 from** fro   **315 on 's** one's
319 leave. leaue   **338 mere** neere   **339 treason;** Treason   **382 ye**
we   **390 brothers** Brother   **391 whither? These,** whether these?
392 battle, Battaile?   **395 chance;** chance?   **409 so** no   **439 s.p.
Soothsayer** [not in F]   **473 this yet** yet this

The Winter's Tale

Copy text: the First Folio. Characters' names are groups at the heads
of scenes throughout the play. Act and scene divisions are as marked
in the Folio.
The Names of the Actors [printed in F at the end of the play]
    Archidamus [after Autoclycus in F]
1.1. 9 us, we vs: we
1.2. 104 And A   **137–138 be?— / Affection, thy** be / Affection? thy
    148 What . . . brother [assigned in F to Leontes]   **151–153**

folly, . . . tenderness, . . . bosoms! folly? . . . tendernesse?
. . . bosomes?   **158 do** do's   **202–203 powerful, think it,**
. . . south. Be powrefull: thinke it: . . . South, be   **208 you,**
they you   **253 forth. In . . .** lord, forth in . . . (my Lord.)   **275
hobbyhorse** Holy-Horse   **386 How? Caught** How caught   **461
off. Hence!** off, hence:
2.1. 2 s.p. [and throughout scene] **First Lady** *Lady*   **91 fedarie** Feder-
arie
2.2. 32-33 me. / If . . . blister me, / If . . . blister.
2.3. 2 thus, mere weakness. If thus: meere weaknesse, if   **39 What**
Who   **61 good, so** good so,
3.2. 10 Silence [printed in F as a s.d.]   **s.d. Hermione, as to her trial
. . . Ladies** [at start of scene in F, as generally with the s.d. in this
play]   **33 Who** Whom   **99 Starred** Star'd   **156 woo** woe
3.3. 64 scar'd scarr'd   **116 made** mad
4.2. 13 thee. Thou thee, thou
4.3. 1 s.p. Autolycus [not in F]   **7 on** an   **10 With heigh, with heigh**
With heigh   **38 currants** Currence
4.4. 12 Digest it Digest   **13 swoon** sworne   **60 a fire** o'fire   **83 bastards. Of** bastards) of   **98 you** you   **160 out** on't   **218 s.p. Autolycus** [not in F]   **244 kilnhole** kill-hole   **297 s.p. Autolycus** [in
F, appears at line 298]   **299 Whither** Whether [and similarly
throughout song]   **310 gentleman** Gent.   **316 cape** *Crpe*   **339
square** squire   **355 reply, at least** reply at least,   **361 who** whom
421 acknowledged acknowledge   **425 who** whom   **430 see** neuer
see   **441 hoop** hope   **470 your** my   **473 sight as yet, I fear.** sight,
as yet I fear;   **485-486 fancy. If . . . obedient, I** fancie,
if . . . obedient: I   **503 our** her   **614 could** would   **filed** fill'd
off of   **644 flayed** fled   **708 know not** know   **738 to** at   **833 s.d.
Exeunt** [at 845 in F]
5.1. 6 Whilst Whilest [also at line 169]   **59 Where . . . appear**
(Where we Offendors now appeare)   **61 just** just such   **75 I have
done** [assigned in F to Cleomenes]   **84 s.d.Gentleman** *Seruant*
85 s.p. [and through line 110] **Gentleman** *Ser.*   **114 s.d. Exit** [after
"us" in line 115 in F]   **160 his, parting** his parting
5.2. 113 s.d. Exeunt *Exit*
5.3. 18 Lonely Louely   **67 fixture** fixure

The Tempest

Copy text: the First Folio. Characters' names are groups at the heads
of scenes throughout. Act and scene divisions are as marked in the
Folio.
Names of the Actors [printed in F at the end of the play]
1.1. 8 s.d. Ferdinand *Ferdinando*   **34 s.d. Exeunt** *Exit*   **36** [and else-
where] **wi' the** with   **38 s.d.** [at line 37 in F]
1.2. 99 exact, like exact. Like   **166 steaded much.** steeded much,
201 bowsprit Bore-spritt   **213 me. The** me the   **230 Bermudas**
Bermoothes   **263, 267 Algiers** Argier   **284 she** he   **288 service.
Thou** service, thou   **330 forth at** for that   **377, 399, s.d. Ariel's**
Ariel (or Ariell)   **385 s.d. Burden, dispersedly** [before "Hark,
hark!" in line 384 in F]   **387** [F provides a speech prefix, *Ar.*]
400 s.p. Ariel [not in F]
2.1. 38 s.p. Antonio *Seb.*   **39 s.p. Sebastian** *Ant.*   **232 throes** throwes
2.2. 9 mow moe   **116 spirits** sprights
3.1. 2 sets set
3.2. 26 debauched debosh'd   **51–52 isle; From me he** Isle / From
me, he   **123 scout** cout
3.3. 15 travel trauaile   **17 s.d. Solemn . . . invisible** [after "they are
fresh" in F, and followed by the s.d. at line 19, *Enter . . . depart*]
28 me me?   **29 islanders?** Islands;   **33 human** humaine
65 plume plumbe
4.1. 9 off of   **13 gift** guest   **25 love as 'tis now, the** loue, as 'tis now
the   **61 vetches** Fetches   **68 poll-clipped** pole-clipt   **74 Her** here
110 s.p. Ceres [not in F]   **123 wife** wise   **124 s.d.** [after line 127
in F]   **163 s.d. Exeunt** *Exit*   **193 s.d. Enter Ariel . . . etc.** [after
"on this line" in F, and followed by *Enter Caliban . . . all wet*]
193 them on on them   **232 Let 't** let's
5.1. 60 boiled boile   **72 Didst** Did   **75 entertained** entertaine   **82
lies ly** **88 s.p. Ariel** [not in F]   **236 Horrible,** horrible.   **238 her**
our   **249 business.** at businesse, at   **250 Which . . . single**
(Which shall be shortly single)   **259–260 Coragio** Corasio

The Two Noble Kinsmen

Copy text: the Quarto of 1634. Act and scene divisions follow Q except at 2.1.48, where Q indicates "Scaena 2." Subsequently, "Scaena 3" and the first "Scaena 4" in the Q text of Act 2 are renumbered in this edition as scenes 2 and 3; the second "Scaena 4" in Q corresponds to scene 4 in this edition, perhaps suggesting that the earlier Q markings at "Scaena 3" and the first "Scaena 4" are in error. Act 3 scenes 5 and 6 are misnumbered "6" and "7" in Q, skipping "5" in error.

Prologue. 26 tack *take*   **29 travail** *travell*

1.1 s.d. Music [after the s.d. in Q, together with indication of "The Song"]   **Pirithous** Theseus   **1 s.p. Boy** [not in Q]   **6 thyme** *Time*   **7 firstborn child** *firstborne, child*   **13–14 children sweet / Lie** *children:sweete- / Ly*   **16 angel** *angle*   **20 chough hoar** *Clough hee*   **41 talons** Tallents   **59 Capaneus was your lord; the** *Capaneus, was your Lord*   **68 Nemean** Nenuan   **90 thy** the   **104 willing way** willing, way   **112 pebbles** peobles   **glassy** glasse   **113 'em. Lady, lady, alack!** 'em (Lady, Lady, alacke)   **123 grief, indeed** greefe indeed   **132 longer** long   **138 move** mooves   ospreys Asprayes   **142 drams, precipitance** drams precipitance   **156 Rinsing** Wrinching   **159 Artesius** Artesuis   **178 twinning** twyning   **211 soldier. [To Artesius] As before, hence** Soldier (as before) hence   **212 Aulis** Anly   **218 s.d. [The marriage . . . temple** *Exeunt towards the Temple*   **225 Exeunt [the procession]** [no s.d. in Q; see textual note at 218 s.d.]

1.2. 41 are here were are, here were   **42 be, mere** be meere   **55 canon** Cannon   **65 power there's nothing; almost** power: there's nothing, almost   **70 glory; one** glory on; [Q corr.], glory on [Q uncorr.]

1.3. 31 one ore   **54 eleven** a eleven   **Flavina** *Flauia*   **58–64** [Q, in left margin, prints: "2. Hearses rea- / dy with Pala- / mon: and Arci- / te: the 3. / Queenes. / Theseus: and / his Lordes / ready."]   **65 not, condemned—** not condemd   **73 happily her careless wear—I** happely, her careles, were, I   **75 one** on   **76 musical** misicall   **79 seely innocence** fury-innocent   **82 dividual** iudiuidu-all   **out** ont

1.4. 18 smeared [Q corr.; succard, Q uncorr.]   **22 Wi'** We   **26** [Q prints s.d. in margin: "3.Hearses rea- / dy."]   **39 do—for** doe for   **40 friends' behests** friends, beheastes   **41 Love's provocations** Loves, provocations   **45 O'er-wrestling** Or wrastling   **49 'fore** for

1.5. 10 We convent . . . woes We convent, &C.

2.1. 16 s.d. Enter . . . Daughter [after "her?" in l. 14 in Q]   **20 that now. So** that. / Now, so   **32 grece** greise   **51 s.d. Enter . . . above** [after "the night" in l. 50 in Q]

2.2. 0 [Q reads: "Scaena 2. *Enter Palamon, and Arcite in prison.*"]   **3 war; yet we** warre yet, we   **20 us. Our** us, our   **21 wore** were   **22 Ravished** Bravishd   **64 twinned** twyn'd   **118 This . . . in 't** [printed as the continuation of Arcite's speech in Q]   **132 was I** I was   **192 your blood** yood blood   **223 s.d. Jailer** *Keeper* [also in s.p. and s.d. at ll. 227, 228, 230, 231 s.d., 249 s.d., and 251 to end of scene]   **243 apricot** Apricocke   **275 you** yon

2.3. 6 sins [Q corr.; fins, Q uncorr.]   **25 s.p. First Countryman** 1 [and so throughout scene]   **44 ye** yet   **59 says** sees   **87 Well I** Well, I

2.4. 34 night; ere night, or

2.5 [Q marks as "Scaena 4"]   **s.d. [A]** This [s.d. is in margin in Q]   **28 For** Fo

2.6. 3 him. To him to   **12–13 it; / I** it / I   **15–16 dirge, / And** Dirge. / And

3.1. 2 laund land   **11 presence; in** presence, in   **13 thought! Thrice** thought, thrice   **36 looked, the** lookd the   **void'st** voydes   **36–37 honor / That** honour. That   **38 kin! Call'st** kin, call'st   **42 Not** Nor   **96 s.d. off. Cornets** of Cornets [s.d. is placed after l. 95 in Q]   **97 muset** Musicke   **107 not** nor   **108 s.d. Wind horns** [after l. 106 in Q]   **112 'Tis** If

3.2. 1 mistook the brake mistooke; the Beake   **7 reck** wreake   **19 fed** feed   **25 dozens** dussons   **28 brine** bine

3.3. 12 sir! &c.   **24 them** then   **53 Sirrah—** Sir ha:

3.4. 9 Open Vpon   **10 tack** take   **19 a foot** afoote   **20 e'e** eie   **22 He s' buy** *He's buy*

3.5 [Q marks as "Scaena 6"]   **s.d. six** 4   **babion** *and Baum*   **Five** 2 or 3   **8 jean** jave   **21 figure, trace and** figure trace, and   **33 babion** *Bavian*   **60 From** [on previous line in Q; Q prints *"Daughter"* in margin]   **64–65** [Q prints "Chaire and / stooles out" in margin]   **65–66** [printed on one line in Q; also ll. 70–71]   **66 I come** *come* he said *sed*   **94 s.d. Wind horns** [opposite l. 92 in Q]   **96 s.d. Exeunt . . . Schoolmaster** [after "Away, boys!" in l. 94 in Q]   **101 s.p. Theseus** Per.   **134 beest-eating** beast eating   **135 Babion** *Bavian*   **139 s.p. Schoolmaster** [not in Q]   **139 s.d. Music** [Q prints *"Musicke Dance"* after l. 138]   **Enter . . . a morris** [Q prints "Knocke for / Schoole.Enter / The Dance." in margin at ll. 139–141]   **141 ye** *thee*   **144 thee** *three*   **153 you** yon   **159 s.d. Wind horns** [after "made" in l. 160 in Q]   **160 deaeque** *Deaeq;*

3.6 Scaena 7.   16 s.d. Enter . . . swords [after "morrow" in l. 16 in Q]   **armor** *Armors*   **39 spared. Your** spard, your   **86 strait** streight   **93 s.d. They . . . stand** [printed in margin at ll. 93–95 in Q, keyed to an asterisk after "love" in l. 93 in Q]   **112 die in. Gentle cousin,** dye in, gentle Cosen: **145 thine** this   **174–175 us; / As . . . valiant, for** us, / As . . . valiant; for   **228 it. If** it, if   **236 fail fall** 240 **name, opinion.** name; Opinion,   **242 prune** proyne   **272 must** muff   **279 s.p. Palamon and Arcite** *Both* [also in l. 280]   **285–286 excellent. For** excellent / For

4.1. 11 oath o'th   **46 'Tis** [Q repeats s.p. here, *"Woo."*]   **63 sung song** *Woo.*]   **84 wreath** wreake   **120 Far** For   **134 s.p. Jailer's Brother** *Daugh.*   **141 s.p. Second Friend** *1. Fr.*   **148 cheerly all** cheerely. / All. [as s.p.]   **150 bowline** Bowling   **158 Tack** take

4.2. 16 Jove afire Love a fire   **25 such** sueh   **27 swart** swarth   **40 'em?** 'em   **49–50 Palamon. / Stand** *Palamon, / Stand*   **54 s.d. Enter a Gentleman** *Enter Emil. and Gent:*   **55 How** *Emil.* How   **70 s.d. Enter a Messenger** *Enter Messengers. Curtis* [after l. 69 in Q]   **76 first** fitst   **81 fire** faire   **104 ivy-tods** Ivy tops   **109 court corect** 152 stay, stay.

4.3. 1–39 [lined as verse in Q]   **8 s.d. Enter . . . Daughter** [placed in Q after "business" in l. 8]   **22 spirits are—there's** spirits, as the'rs   **32 i' th' other** i'th / Thother   **39 enough.** enough. *Exit*   **45 truth** troth   **punishment** [Q corr.; punishuent, Q uncorr.]   **49–50 engrafted** engraffed   **53 were** [Q corr.; weare, Q uncorr.]   **54 th' other** another   **55 behind** [Q corr.; behold, Q uncorr.]   **69 same** [Q corr.; Sawe, Q uncorr.]   **85 sweet flowers** [Q corr.; sweet, flowers, Q uncorr.]   **90 carve** crave   **96 falsehoods** fasehoods

5.1 s.d. Flourish [before *"Exeunt"* at 4.3.104 in Q]   **7 s.d. Flourish of cornets** [after l. 5 in Q]   **17 s.d. Exeunt** *Exit*   **33 s.d. Exeunt . . . knights** [after "coz." in l. 33 in Q]   **37 father of** farther off   **46 cistern** Cestron   **51 Whose . . . prewarn** Comets prewarne, whose havocke in vaste Feild   **54 armipotent** armenypotent   **68 design march** designe; march   **boldly,** boldly, [Q corr.]; boldly [Q uncorr.]   **76 Her** [Q corr.; His, Q corr.]   **91 than his; the** then his the   **118 Brief, I** briefe I   **119 done, no companion** done; no Companion   **120 not, a defier;** not; a defyer   **121 cannot, a rejoicer.** cannot; a Rejoycer,   **130 O thou** *Pal.* O thou   **136 s.d. They . . . bow** [at l. 134 in Q]   **is** his   **151 maiden-hearted. A** mayden harted, a   **154 election. Of** election of

5.2. 3 kept hept   **37 Yes** Yet   **40 s.d. [mad]** *Maide*   **41 humor honour** honour   **55 tune** turne   **85 two coarse** too corse

5.3 s.d. Flourish [placed before *Exeunt* at 5.2.113 in Q]   **attendants** *Attendants, T. Tucke: Curtis*   **3 decision. Ev'ry blow** decision ev'ry; blow   **16 prize** price   **54 him** them   **66 s.d. Cornets . . . Palamon!** [after l. 64 in Q]   **Enter Servant** [after l. 66 in Q]   **75 in 't else; chance** in't; else chance   **77 s.d. Another . . . cornets** [after l. 75 in Q]   **89 s.d. Cornets. . . . Arcite!"** [after l. 88 in Q]   **92 s.d. Cornets. . . . Victory!"** [after l. 91 in Q]   **121 all I** all; I   **136 lose** loose   **139 your** you   **146 s.d. Flourish** [after "deliver" in l. 138 in Q]

5.4 s.d. etc. &c. *Gard.*   **1 s.p. Palamon** [not in Q]   **10 unwappered, not halting** unwapper'd not, halting   **35 quit** quight   **38 s.d. lays** *Lies*   **39 s.p. Second and Third Knights** *1.2.K.*   **47 rarely** early   **69 manège** mannadge   **79 victor's** [victors, Q corr.; victoros, Q uncorr.]   **87 mighty, Arcite. If** mightie *Arcite*, if   **104 arrouse** arowze   **107 Hath** Hast   **133–134 sorry, still / Are** sorry still, / Are

Epilogue 1 s.p. Epilogue [not in Q]

Venus and Adonis

Copy text: the Quarto of 1593.
185 Souring So wring **208 Speak, fair,** Speake fair **304 whe'er** where **457 marketh.** marketh, **458 raineth,** raineth: **570 woos** woes **621 shine when . . . fret;** shine, when . . . fret **680 overshoot** ouer-shut **748 th'** the th' **873 twine** twin'd **1013 stories** stories, **1027 falcon** Faulcons **1031 as** are **1054 was** had

The Rape of Lucrece

Copy text: the corrected Quarto of 1594 [Q corr.] A number of corrected readings are however rejected as sophistications; see text notes below at lines 31, 50, 125, 126.
24 morning's [Q corr., mornings] morning [Q uncorr.] **31 apology** [Q uncorr.] Apologies [Q corr.] **50 Collatium** [Q uncorr., Colatium] Colatia [Q corr.] **57 beauty, in . . . entituled** Beautie in . . . entituled, **58 doves, doth . . . field.** doues doth . . . field, **125 himself betakes** [Q uncorr.] themselues betake [Q corr.] **126 wakes** [Q uncorr.] wake [Q corr.] **555 panteth** pateth **560 wear** were **650 sovereign, with . . . haste** soueraigne with . . . hast, **688 lose** loose [also at lines 979 and 1158] **922 inclination** inclination. **1126 Relish** Ralish **1129 hair** heare **1229 eyne, enforced** eien inforst, **1249 remain** remaine. **1251 peep** peepe, **1263-1264 ensue / By . . . wrong.** insue. / By . . . wrong, **1312 schedule** Cedule **1350 this pattern of the** the pattern of this [in four copies of Q; it is uncertain which is the corrected state] **1386 far-off** farre of **1475 Thine** Thy **1543 travail** trauaile **1544 too** to **1580 Losing** Loosing **1648 forbade** forbod **1652 robbed** rob'd **1660 here** heare **1662 wreathèd** wretched **1680 one woe** on woe **1713 in it** it in **1768 faltering** foultring

A Lover's Complaint

Copy text: the Sonnet Quarto of 1609 [Q].
7 sorrow's sorrowes, **14 lattice** lettice **37 beaded** bedded **51 'gan** gaue **95 wear** were **103 breathe** breath **112 manage** mannad'g **118 Came** Can **131 Consents** Consent's **164 forbade** forbod **182 woo** vovv **198 pallid** palyd **204 hair** heir **205 metal** mettle **228 Hallowed** Hollowed **251 immured** enur'd **252 procured** procure **260 nun** Sunne **293 O** Or **303 strange** straing

The Sonnets

Copy text: the Quarto of 1609 [Q].
2.14 tattered totter'd [also at 26.11] **cold** could **6.4 beauty's** beautits **8.10 Strikes** Strike **12.4 all** or **13.7 Yourself** You selfe **15.8 wear** were **17.12 meter** miter **twice, in it and** twice in it, and **18.10 [and elsewhere] lose** loose **19.3 jaws** yawes **20.2 Hast** Haste **22.3 furrows** forrwes **23.6 rite** right **23.14 with** wit **wit** wiht **24.1 stelled** steeld **25.9 fight** worth **26.12 thy** their [also at 27.10, 35.8 (twice), 37.7, 43.11, 45.12, 46.3, 46.8, 46.13, 46.14, 69.5, 70.6, 85.3, 128.11, 128.14] **27.2 travel** trauaill **28.12 gild'st the** guil'st th' **28.14 strength** length **31.8 thee** there **34.2 travel** trauaile **34.12 cross** losse **34.13 sheds** sheeds **38.2 pour'st** poor'st **38.3 too** to **39.12 doth** dost **41.7 woos** woes **42.10 losing** loosing **44.12 attend time's** attend, times **44.13 naught** naughts **45.9 life's** liues **46.9 'cide** side **46.12 the** he **47.2 other.** other, **47.4 smother,** smother; **47.11 no** nor **50.6 dully** duly **51.10 perfect'st** perfects **55.1 monuments** monument **56.3 [and elsewhere] today** too daie **58.7 patience-tame to suffrance,** patience tame, to sufferance **59.6 hundred** hundreth **59.11 whe'er** where **61.14 off** of **too** to **62.10 chapped** chopt **63 traveled**

trauaild **65.12 of** or **67.6 seeming** seeing **69.3 due** end **69.14 soil** solye **71.13 Lest** Least [also at 72.1, 72.9, and elsewhere] **73.4 ruined** rn'wd **choirs** quiers **76.7 tell** fel **77.1 wear** were **77.10 blanks** blacks **82.8 these** the **83.7 too to** **85.3 Reserve** Reserne **88.8 losing** loosing **90.11 shall** stall **91.9 better** bitter **93.5 there** their **98.11 were** weare **99.4 dwells** dwells? **99.9 One** Our **99.13 ate** eate **102.8 her** his **106.12 skill** still **111.1 with** wish **112.14 are** y'are **113.6 latch** lack **113.13 more, replete with** more repleat, with **113.14 mine eye** mine **117.10 surmise accumulate;** surmise, accumilate **118.5 ne'er-cloying** nere cloying **118.10 were not, grew** were, not grew **119.4 losing** loosing **121.11 bevel.** beuel. **125.6 rent,** rent **125.7 sweet forgoing** sweet: Forgoing **126.2 sickle hour;** sickle, hower: **126.8 minutes** mynuit **127.2 were** weare' **127.10 brows** eyes **129.9 Mad** Made **129.10 quest to have,** quest, to haue **129.11 proved, a** proud and **132.6 the east** th' East **132.9 mourning** morning **138.12 to have t'** haue **140.5 were** weare **144.6 side** [adopted from *The Passionate Pilgrim*] sight **144.9 fiend** adopted from *The Passionate Pilgrim*] finde **146.2 Thrall to** My sinfull earth **147.7 approve** approoue. **153.14 eyes** eye

A Funeral Elegy for Master William Peter

Copy text: the Quarto of 1612 [Q].
8 that it **116 famed.** fam'd, **148 lost it—** lost it. **150–151 Unhappy . . . style / Which . . . rehearse)** Vnhappy . . . stile) / Which . . . rehearse, **328 fast, in** fast in **364 Mistook . . . ago** (Mistooke . . . agoe) **441 profane** prophaned **532 but that** but said that **544 just** iust: **548 retain,** retaine, **550 woe,** woe: **568 hapless, Hope** haplesse *Hope*

Glossary

*Shakespearean Words
and Meanings
of Frequent Occurrence*

A

'A: he (unaccented form).

Abate: lessen, diminish; blunt, reduce; deprive; bar, leave out of account, except; depreciate; humble.

Abuse (N): insult, error, misdeed, offense, crime; imposture, deception; also the modern sense.

Abuse (v): deceive, misapply, put to a bad use; maltreat; frequently the modern sense.

Addition: something added to one's name to denote rank; mark of distinction; title.

Admiration: wonder; object of wonder.

Admire: wonder at.

Advantage (N): profit, convenience, benefit; opportunity, favorable opportunity; pecuniary profit; often shades toward the modern sense.

Advantage (v): profit, be of benefit to, benefit; augment.

Advice: reflection, consideration, deliberation, consultation.

Affect: aim at, aspire to, incline toward; be fond of, be inclined; love; act upon contagiously (as a disease). (PAST PART.) **Affected:** disposed, inclined, in love, loved.

Affection: passion, love; emotion, feeling, mental tendency, disposition; wish, inclination; affectation.

Alarum: signal calling soldiers to arms (in stage directions).

An: if; but; **an if:** if, though, even if.

Anon: at once, soon; presently, by and by.

Answer: return, requite; atone for; render an account of, account for; obey, agree with; also the modern sense.

Apparent: evident, plain; seeming.

Argument: subject, theme, reason, cause; story; excuse.

As: according as; as far as; namely; as if; in the capacity of; that; so that; that is, that they.

Assay: try, attempt; accost, address; challenge.

Atone: reconcile; set at one.

Attach: arrest, seize.

Awful, awful: commanding reverential fear or respect; profoundly respectful or reverential.

B

Band: bond, fetters, manacle (leash for a dog). **Band** and **bond** are etymologically the same word; **band** was formerly used in both senses.

Basilisk: fabulous reptile said to kill by its look. The basilisk of popular superstition was a creature with legs, wings, a serpentine and winding tail, and a crest or comb somewhat like a cock. It was the offspring of a cock's egg hatched under a toad or serpent.

Bate: blunt, abate, reduce; deduct, except.

Battle: army; division of an army.

Beshrew: curse, blame; used as a mild curse, "Bad or ill luck to."

Bias: tendency, bent, inclination, swaying influence; term in bowling applied to the form of the bowl, the oblique line in which it runs, and the kind of impetus given to cause it to run obliquely.

Blood: nature, vigor; supposed source of emotion; passion; spirit, animation; one of the four humors (see **humor**).

Boot (N): advantage, profit; something given in addition to the bargain; booty, plunder.

Boot (v): profit, avail.

Brave (ADJ.): fine, gallant; splendid, finely arrayed, showy; ostentatiously defiant.

Brave (v): challenge, defy; make splendid.

Brook: tolerate, endure.

C

Can: can do; know; be skilled; sometimes used for *did.*

Capable: comprehensive; sensible, impressible, susceptible; capable of; gifted, intelligent.

Careful: anxious, full of care; provident; attentive.

Carry: manage, execute; be successful, win; conquer; sustain; endure.

Censure (N): judgment, opinion; critical opinion, unfavorable opinion.

Censure (v): judge, estimate; pass sentence or judgment.

Character (N): writing, printing, record; handwriting; cipher; face, features (bespeaking inward qualities).

Character (v): write, engrave, inscribe.

Check (N): reproof; restraint.

Check (v): reprove, restrain, keep from; control.

Circumstance: condition, state of affairs, particulars; adjunct details; detailed narration, argument, or discourse; formality, ceremony.

Clip: embrace; surround.

Close: secret, private; concealed; uncommunicative; enclosed.

Cog: cheat.

Coil: noise, disturbance, turmoil; fuss, to-do, bustle.

Color: appearance; pretext, pretense; excuse.

Companion: fellow (used contemptuously).

Complete: accomplished, fully endowed; perfect, perfect in quality; also frequently the modern sense.

Complexion: external appearance; temperament, disposition; the four complexions—sanguine, choleric, phlegmatic, and melancholy—corresponding to the four humors (see **humor**); also the modern sense.

Composition: compact, agreement, constitution.

Compound: settle, agree.

Conceit: conception, idea, thought; mental faculty, wit; fancy, imagination; opinion, estimate; device, invention, design.

Condition: temperament, disposition; characteristic, property, quality; social or official position, rank or status; covenant, treaty, contract.

Confound: waste, spend, invalidate, destroy; undo, ruin; mingle indistinguishably, mix, blend.

Confusion: destruction, overthrow, ruin; mental agitation.

Continent: that which contains or encloses; earth, globe; sum, summary.

Contrive: plot; plan; spend or pass (time).

Conversation: conduct, deportment; social intercourse, association.

Converse: hold intercourse; associate with, have to do with.

Cope: encounter, meet; have to do with.

Copy: model, pattern; example; minutes or memoranda.

Cousin: any relative not belonging to one's immediate family.

Cry you mercy: beg your pardon.

Cuckold: husband whose wife is unfaithful.

Curious: careful, fastidious; anxious, concerned; made with care, skillfully, intricately, or daintily wrought; particular.

Cursed, curst: shrewish, perverse, spiteful.

D

Dainty: minute; scrupulous, particular; particular about (with **of**); refined, elegant; also the modern sense.

Date: duration, termination, term of existence; limit or end of a term or period, term.

Dear: precious; best; costly; important; affectionate; hearty; grievous, dire; also the modern sense.

Debate: discuss; fight.

Decay (N): downfall, ruin; cause of ruin.

Decay (v): perish, be destroyed; destroy.

Defeat (N): destruction, ruin.

Defeat (v): destroy, disfigure, ruin.

Defy: challenge, challenge to a fight; reject; despise.

Demand (N): inquiry; request.

Demand (v): inquire, question; request.

Deny: refuse (to do something); refuse permission; refuse to accept; refuse admittance; disown.

Depart (N): departure.

Depart (v): part; go away from, leave, quit; take leave (of one another); **depart with, withal:** part with, give up.

Derive: gain, obtain; draw upon, direct (to); descend; pass by descent, be descended or inherited; trace the origin of.

Difference: diversity of opinion, disagreement, dissension, dispute; characteristic or distinguishing feature; alteration or addition to a coat of arms to distinguish a younger or lateral branch of a family.

Digest: arrange, perfect; assimilate, amalgamate; disperse, dissipate; comprehend, understand; put up with (FIG. from the physical sense of digesting food).

Discourse (N): reasoning, reflection; talk, act of conversing, conversation; faculty of conversing; familiar intercourse; relating (as by speech).

Discourse (v): speak, talk, converse; pass (the time) in talk; say, utter, tell, give forth; narrate, relate.

Discover: uncover, expose to view; divulge, reveal, make known; spy out, reconnoiter; betray; distinguish, discern; also the modern sense.

Dispose (N): disposal; temperament, bent of mind, disposition; external manner.

Dispose (v): distribute, manage, make use of; deposit, put or stow away; regulate, order, direct; come to terms. (PAST PART.) **Disposed:** in a good frame of mind; inclined to be merry.

Dispute: discuss, reason; strive against, resist.

Distemper (v): disturb; (N): disorder, ill humor; illness.

Doit: old Dutch coin, one-half an English farthing.

Doubt (N): suspicion, apprehension; fear, danger, risk; also the modern sense.

Doubt (v): suspect, apprehend; fear; also the modern sense.

Doubtful: inclined to suspect, suspicious, apprehensive; not to be relied on; almost certain.

Duty: reverence, respect, expression of respect; submission to authority, obedience; due.

E

Earnest: money paid as an installment to secure a bargain; partial payment; often used with *quibble* in the modern sense.

Ease: comfort, assistance, leisure; idleness, sloth, inactivity; also the modern sense.

Ecstasy: frenzy, madness, state of being beside oneself, excitement, bewilderment; swoon; rapture.

Element: used to refer to the simple substances of which all material bodies were thought to be composed; specifically earth, air, fire, and water, corresponding to the four humors (see **humor**); atmosphere, sky; atmospheric agencies or powers; that one of the four elements which is the natural abode of a creature; hence, natural surroundings, sphere.

Engage: pledge, pawn, mortgage; bind by a promise, swear to; entangle, involve; enlist; embark on an enterprise.

Engine: mechanical contrivance; artifice, device, plot.

Enlarge: give free scope to; set at liberty, release.

Entertain: keep up, maintain, accept; take into one's service; treat; engage (someone's) attention or thoughts; occupy, while or pass away pleasurably; engage (as an enemy); receive.

Envious: malicious, spiteful, malignant.

Envy: ill-will, malice; hate; also the modern sense.

Even: uniform; direct, straightforward; exact, precise; equable, smooth, comfortable; equal, equally balanced.

Event: outcome; affair, business; also frequently the modern sense.

Exclaim: protest, rail; accuse, blame (with **on**), reproach.

Excursion: stage battle or skirmish (in stage directions).

Excuse: seek to extenuate (a fault); maintain the innocence of; clear oneself, justify or vindicate oneself; decline.

F

Fact: deed, act; crime.

Faction: party, class, group, set (of persons); party strife, dissension; factious quarrel, intrigue.

Fail: die, die out; err, be at fault; omit, leave undone.

Fair (N): fair thing; one of the fair sex; someone beloved; beauty (the abstract concept).

Fair (ADJ.): just; clear, distinct; beautiful; of light complexion or color of hair.

Fair (ADV): fairly.

Fairly: beautifully, handsomely; courteously, civilly; properly, honorably, honestly; becomingly, appropriately; favorably, fortunately; softly, gently, kindly.

Fall: let fall, drop; happen, come to pass; befall; shades frequently toward the modern senses.

Falsely: wrongly; treacherously; improperly.

Fame: report; rumor; reputation.

Familiar (N): intimate friend; familiar or attendant spirit, demon associated with, and obedient to, a person.

Familiar (ADJ.): intimate, friendly; belonging to household or family, domestic; well-known; habitual, ordinary, trivial; plain, easily understood.

Fancy: fantasticalness; imaginative conception, flight of imagination; amorous inclination or passion, love; liking, taste.

Fantasy: fancy, imagination; caprice, whim.

Favor: countenance, face; complexion; aspect, appearance; leave, permission, pardon; attraction, charm, good will; **in favor:** benevolently.

Fear (N): dread, apprehension; dreadfulness; object of dread or fear.

Fear (V): be apprehensive or concerned about, mistrust, doubt; frighten, make afraid.

Fearful: exciting or inspiring fear, terrible, dreadful; timorous, apprehensive, full of fear.

Feature: shape or form of body, figure; shapeliness, comeliness.

Fellow: companion; partaker, sharer (of); equal, match; customary form of address to a servant or an inferior (sometimes used contemptuously or condescendingly).

Fine (N): end, conclusion; **in fine:** finally.

Fine (ADJ.): highly accomplished or skillful; exquisitely fashioned, delicate; refined, subtle; frequently the modern sense.

Flaw: fragment; crack, fissure; tempest, squall, gust of wind; outburst of passion.

Flesh: reward a hawk or hound with a piece of flesh of the game killed to excite its eagerness of the chase; hence, to inflame by a foretaste of success; initiate or inure to bloodshed (used for a first time in battle); harden, train.

Flourish: fanfare of trumpets (in stage directions).

Fond: foolish, doting; **fond of:** eager for; also the modern sense.

Fool: term of endearment and pity; frequently the modern sense.

For that, for why: because.

Forfend: forbid, avert.

Free: generous, magnanimous; candid, open; guiltless, innocent.

Front: forehead, face; foremost line of battle; beginning.

Furnish: equip, fit out (furnish forth); endow; dress, decorate, embellish.

G

Gear: apparel, dress; stuff, substance, thing, article; discourse, talk; matter, business, affair.

Get: beget.

Gloss: specious fair appearance; lustrous surface.

Go to: expression of remonstrance, impatience, disapprobation, or derision.

Grace (N): kindness, favor, charm, divine favor; fortune, luck; beneficent virtue; sense of duty or propriety; mercy, pardon; embellish; **do grace:** reflect credit on, do honor to, do a favor for.

Grace (V): gratify, delight; honor, favor.

Groat: coin equal to four pence.

H

Habit: dress, garb, costume; bearing, demeanor, manner; occasionally in the modern sense.

Happily: haply, perchance, perhaps; fortunately.

Hardly: with difficulty.

Have at: I shall come at (you) (i.e., listen to me), I shall attack (a person or thing); let me at.

Have with: I shall go along with; let me go along with; come along.

Having: possession, property, wealth, estate; endowments, accomplishments.

Head: armed force.

Hind: servant, slave; rustic, boor, clown.

His: its. **His** was historically the possessive form of both the masculine and neuter pronouns. **Its,** although not common in Shakespeare's time, occurs in the plays occasionally.

Holp: helped (archaic past tense).

Home: fully, satisfactorily, thoroughly, plainly, effectually; to the quick.

Honest: holding an honorable position, honorable, respectable; decent, kind, seemly, befitting, proper; chaste; genuine; loosely used as an epithet of approbation.

Humor: mood, temper, cast of mind, temperament, disposition; vagary, fancy, whim; moisture (the literal sense); a physiological and, by transference, a psychological term applied to the four chief fluids of the human body—phlegm, blood, bile or choler, and black bile or melancholy. A person's disposition and temporary state of mind were determined according to the relative proportions of these fluids in the body; consequently, a person was said to be phlegmatic, sanguine, choleric, or melancholy.

I

Image: likeness; visible form; representation; embodiment, type; mental picture, creation of the imagination.

Influence: supposed flowing from the stars or heavens of an ethereal fluid, acting upon the characters and destinies of men (used metaphorically).

Inform: take shape, give form to, imbue, inspire; instruct, teach; charge (against).

Instance: evidence, proof, sign, confirmation; motive, cause.

Invention: power of mental creation, the creative faculty; work of the imagination, artistic creation, premeditated design; device, plan, scheme.

J

Jar (N): discord in music; quarrel, discord.
Jar (V): be out of tune; be discordant, quarrel.
Jump: agree, tally, coincide, fit exactly; risk, hazard.

K

Keep: continue, carry on; dwell, lodge, guard, defend, care for, employ, be with; restrain, control; confine in prison.
Kind (N): nature, established order of things; manner, fashion, respect; race, class, kindred, family; **by kind:** naturally.
Kind (ADJ.): natural; favorable; affectionate.
Kindly (ADJ.): natural, appropriate; agreeable; innate; benign.
Kindly (ADV): naturally; gently, courteously.

L

Large: liberal, bounteous, lavish; free, unrestrained; **at large:** at length, in full; in full detail, as a whole, in general.
Late: lately.
Learn: teach; inform (someone of something); also the modern sense.
Let: hinder.
Level: aim; also shades toward the modern sense.
Liberal: possessed of the characteristics and qualities of wellborn persons, genteel, becoming, refined; free in speech; unrestrained by prudence or decorum; licentious.
Lie: be in bed; be still; be confined, be kept in prison; dwell, sojourn, reside, lodge.
Like: please, feel affection; liken, compare.
List (N): strip of cloth, selvedge; limit, boundary; desire.
List (V): choose, desire, please; listen to.
Liver: the seat of love and of violent passions generally (see also **spleen**).
'Long of: owing to, on account of.
Look: power to see; take care, see to it; expect; seek, search for.

M

Make: do; have to do (with); consider; go; be effective, make up, complete; also the modern sense.
Manage: management, conduct, administration; action and paces to which a horse is trained; short gallop at full speed.
Marry: mild interjection equivalent to "Indeed!" Originally, an oath by the Virgin Mary.
May: can; also frequently the modern sense to denote probability; **might** has corresponding meanings and uses.
Mean, means (N): instrument, agency, method; effort; opportunity (for doing something); something interposed or intervening; money, wealth (frequently in the plural form); middle position, medium; tenor or alto part in singing (usually in the singular form).
Mean (ADJ.): average, moderate, middle; of low degree, station, or position; undignified, base.

Measure (N): grave or stately dance, graceful motion; tune, melody, musical accompaniment; treatment meted out; moderation, proportion; limit; distance, reach.
Measure (V): judge, estimate; traverse.
Mere: absolute, sheer; pure, unmixed; downright, sincere.
Mew (up): coop up (as used of a hawk), shut up, imprison, confine.
Mind (N): thoughts, judgment, opinion, message; purpose, intention, desire; disposition; also the modern sense of the mental faculty.
Mind (V): remind; perceive, notice, attend; intend.
Minion: saucy woman, hussy; follower; favorite, favored person, darling (often used contemptuously).
Misdoubt (N): suspicion.
Misdoubt (V): mistrust, suspect.
Model: pattern, replica, likeness.
Modern: ordinary, commonplace, everyday.
Modest: moderate, marked by moderation, becoming; characterized by decency and propriety; chaste.
Moiety: half; share; small part, lesser share; portion, part of.
Mortal: fatal; deadly, of or for death; belonging to mankind; human, pertaining to human affairs.
Motion: power of movement; suggestion, proposal; movement of the soul; impulse, prompting; also the modern sense.
Move: make angry; urge, incite, instigate, arouse, prompt; propose, make a proposal to, apply to, appeal to, suggest; also the modern sense.
Muse: wonder, marvel; grumble, complain.

N

Napkin: handkerchief.
Natural: related by blood; having natural or kindly feeling; also the modern sense.
Naught: useless, worthless; wicked, naughty.
Naughty: wicked; good for nothing, worthless.
Nerves: sinews.
Nice: delicate; fastidious, dainty, particular, scrupulous; minute, subtle; shy, coy; reluctant, unwilling; unimportant, insignificant, trivial; accurate, precise; wanton, lascivious.
Nothing: not at all.

O

Of: from, away from; during; on; by; as regards; instead of; **out of:** compelled by; made from.
Offer: make an attack; menace; venture, dare, presume.
Opinion: censure; reputation or credit; favorable estimate of oneself; self-conceit, arrogance; self-confidence; public opinion, reputation; also the modern sense.
Or: before; also used conjunctively where no alternative is implied; **or . . . or:** either . . . or; whether . . . or.
Out (ADV.): without, outside; abroad; fully, quite; at an end, finished; at variance, aligned the wrong way.
Out (INTERJ.): an expression of reproach, impatience, indignation, or anger.
Owe: own; also the modern sense.

P

Pack (v): load; depart, begone; conspire.

Pageant: show, spectacle, spectacular entertainment; device on a moving carriage.

Pain: punishment, penalty; labor, trouble, effort; also frequently the modern sense.

Painted: specious, unreal, counterfeit.

Parle: parley, conference, talk; bugle call for parley.

Part (v): depart, part from; divide.

Particular (N): detail; personal interest or concern; details of a private nature; single person.

Party: faction, side, part, cause; partner, ally.

Pass (v): pass through, traverse; exceed; surpass; pledge.

Passing (ADJ. and ADV.): surpassing, surpassingly, exceedingly.

Passion (N): powerful or violent feeling, violent sorrow or grief; painful affection or disorder of the body; sorrow; feelings or desires of love; passionate speech or outburst.

Passion (v): sorrow, grieve.

Peevish: silly, senseless, childish; perverse, obstinate, stubborn; sullen.

Perforce: by violence or compulsion; forcibly; necessarily.

Phoenix: mythical Arabian bird believed to be the only one of its kind; it lived five or six hundred years, after which it burned itself to ashes and reemerged to live through another cycle.

Physic: medical faculty; healing art, medical treatment; remedy, medicine, healing property.

Pitch: height; specifically, the height to which a falcon soars before swooping on its prey (often used figuratively); tarlike substance.

Policy: conduct of affairs (especially public affairs); prudent management; stratagem, trick; contrivance; craft, cunning.

Port: bearing, demeanor; state, style of living, social station; gate.

Possess: have or give possession or command (of something); inform, acquaint; also the modern sense.

Post (N): courier, messenger; post-horse; haste.

Post (v): convey swiftly; hasten, ignore through haste (with **over** or **off**).

Practice (N): execution; exercise (especially for instruction); stratagem, intrigue; conspiracy, plot, treachery.

Practice (v): perform, take part in; use stratagem, craft, or artifice; scheme, plot; play a joke on.

Pregnant: resourceful; disposed, inclined; clear, obvious.

Present (ADJ.): ready, immediate, prompt, instant.

Present (v): represent.

Presently: immediately, at once.

Prevent: forestall, anticipate, foresee; also the modern sense.

Process: drift, tenor, gist; narrative, story; formal command, mandate.

Proof: test, trial, experiment; experience; issue, result; proved or tested strength of armor or arms; also the modern sense.

Proper: (one's or its) own; peculiar, exclusive; excellent; honest, respectable; handsome, elegant, fine, good-looking.

Proportion: symmetry; size; form, carriage, appearance, shape; portion, allotment; rhythm.

Prove: make trial of; put to test; show or find out by experience.

Purchase (N): acquisition; spoil, booty.

Purchase (v): acquire, gain, obtain; strive, exert oneself; redeem, exempt.

Q

Quaint: skilled, clever; pretty, fine, dainty; handsome, elegant; carefully or ingeniously wrought or elaborated.

Quality: that which constitutes (something); essential being; good natural gifts; accomplishment, attainment, property; art, skill; rank, position; profession, occupation, business; party, side; cause; manner, style; cause, occasion.

Quick: living (used substantively to mean "living flesh"); alive, lively, sharp, piercing; hasty, impatient; with child.

Quillets: verbal niceties, subtle distinctions.

Quit: requite, reward; set at liberty; acquit, remit; pay for, clear off.

R

Rack (v): stretch or strain beyond normal extent or capacity to endure; strain oneself; distort.

Rage (N): madness, insanity; vehement pain; angry disposition; violent passion or appetite; poetic enthusiasm; warlike ardor or fury.

Rage (v): behave wantonly or riotously; act with fury or violence; enrage; pursue furiously.

Range: extend or lie in the same plane (with); occupy a position; rove, roam; be inconstant; traverse.

Rank (ADJ.): coarsely luxuriant; puffed up, swollen, fat, abundant; full, copious; rancid; lustful; corrupt, foul.

Rate (N): estimate; value or worth; estimation, consideration; standard, style.

Rate (v): allot; calculate, estimate, compute; reckon, consider; be of equal value (with); chide, scold, berate; drive away by chiding or scolding.

Recreant (N): traitor, coward, cowardly wretch (also as ADJ.).

Remorse: pity, compassion; also the modern sense.

Remove: removal, absence; period of absence; change.

Require: ask, inquire of, request.

Resolve: dissolve, melt, dissipate; answer; free from doubt or uncertainty, convince; inform; decide; also the modern sense.

Respect (N): consideration, reflection, act of seeing, view; attention, notice; decency, modest deportment; also the modern sense.

Respect (v): esteem, value, prize; regard, consider; heed, pay attention to; also the modern sense.

Round: spherical; plain, direct, brusque; fair; honest.

Roundly: plainly, unceremoniously.

Rub: obstacle (a term in the game of bowls); unevenness; inequality.

S

Sack: generic term for Spanish and Canary wines; sweet white wine.

Sad: grave, serious; also the modern sense.

Sadness: seriousness; also the modern sense.
Sans: without (French preposition).
Scope: object, aim, limit; freedom, license; free play.
Seal: bring to completion or conclusion, conclude, confirm, ratify, stamp; also the modern sense.
Sennet: a series of notes sounded on a trumpet to herald the approach or departure of a procession (used in stage directions).
Sense: mental faculty, mind; mental perception, import, rational meaning; physical perception; sensual nature; **common sense:** ordinary or untutored perception, observation or knowledge.
Sensible: capable of physical feeling or perception, sensitive; capable of or exhibiting emotion; rational; capable of being perceived.
Serve: be sufficient; be favorable; succeed; satisfy the need for; serve a turn; answer the purpose.
Several: separate, distinct, different; particular, private; various.
Shadow: shade, shelter; reflection; likeness, image; ghost; representation, picture of the imagination, phantom; also the modern sense.
Shift: change; stratagem, strategy, trick, contrivance, device to serve a purpose; **make shift:** manage.
Shrewd: malicious, mischievous, ill-natured; shrewish; bad, of evil import, grievous; severe.
Sirrah: ordinary or customary form of address to inferiors or servants; disrespectful form of address.
Sith: since.
Smock: woman's undergarment; used typically for "a woman."
Something: somewhat.
Sometime: sometimes, from time to time; once, formerly; at times, at one time.
Speed (N): fortune, success; protecting and assisting power; also the modern sense.
Speed (v): fare (well or ill); succeed; be successful; assist, guard, favor.
Spleen: the seat of emotions and passions; violent passion; fiery temper; malice; anger, rage; impulse, fit of passion; caprice; impetuosity (see also **liver**).
Spoil: destruction, ruin; plunder; slaughter, massacre.
Starve: die of cold or hunger; be benumbed with cold; paralyze, disable; allow or cause to die.
State: degree, rank; social position, station; pomp, splendor, outward display, clothes; court, household of a great person; shades into the modern sense.
Stay: wait, wait for; sustain; stand; withhold, withstand; stop.
Stead: assist; be of use to, benefit, help.
Still: always, ever, continuously or continually, constant or constantly; silent, mute; also modern senses.
Stomach: appetite, inclination, disposition; resentment; angry temper, resentful feeling; proud spirit, courage.
Straight: immediately.
Strange: belonging to another country or person, foreign, unfriendly; new, fresh; ignorant; estranged.
Success: issue, outcome (good or bad); sequel, succession, descent (as from father to son).

Suggest: tempt; prompt; seduce.
Suggestion: temptation.

T

Table: memorandum, tablet; surface on which something is written or drawn.
Take: strike; bewitch; charm; infect; destroy; repair to for refuge; modern senses.
Tall: goodly, fine; strong in fight, valiant.
Target: shield.
Tax: censure, blame, accuse.
Tell: count; relate.
Thorough: through.
Throughly: thoroughly.
Toward: in preparation; forthcoming, about to take place; modern senses.
Toy: trifle, idle fancy; folly.
Train: lure, entice, allure, attract.
Trencher: wooden dish or plate.
Trow: think, suppose, believe; know.

U

Undergo: undertake, perform; modern sense.
Undo: ruin.
Unfold: disclose, tell, make known, reveal; communicate.
Unhappy: evil, mischievous; fatal, ill-fated; miserable.
Unjust: untrue, dishonest; unjustified, groundless; faithless, false.
Unkind: unnatural, cruel, faulty; compare **kind.**
Use (N): custom, habit; interest paid.
Use (v): make practice of; be accustomed; put out at interest.

V

Vail: lower, let fall.
Vantage: advantage; opportunity; benefit, profit; superiority.
Virtue: general excellence; valor, bravery; merit, goodness, honor; good accomplishment, excellence in culture; power; essence, essential part.

W

Want: lack; be in need of; be without.
Watch: be awake, lie awake, sit up at night, lose sleep; keep from sleep (TRANS.).
Weed: garment, clothes.
Welkin: sky, heavens.
Wink: close the eyes; close the eyes in sleep; have the eyes closed; seem not to see.
Withal: with; with it, this, or these; together with this; at the same time.
Wot: know.

Index

The letter n. following a reference indicates a footnote